Irregular Serials & Annuals

An International Directory

1987-88

Irregular Serials & Annuals
is compiled by
R.R. Bowker Company
a division of Reed Publishing (USA) Inc.
Serials Bibliography Department

Leigh Carol Yuster, Executive Editor
Jacqueline Mullikin, Editor
Richard Oosterom, Editor
Edvika Popilskis, Editor, Data Sources

Amine Babaali and Maria Christina, Associate Editors
Maria Christopher, Ewa Kowalska, Frank McDermott, and
Geoffrey Welchman, Assistant Editors

Dorothy Hodges and Lisa Pabarue, Editorial Assistants

Michael Brown, Susan Cupo, Theressa Carey, Terence Carlson,
Karl Dusza, Marilyn Herrmann, Margareta Leon,
Anne Seppala-Holtzman, and Eline van de Poel, Contributing Editors

Programming and processing were done by the
Bowker Systems & Operations Departments
Michael Gold, Director, Systems Development
Lisa Medvin-Ludwig, Systems Analyst
Jack Murphy, Manager, Computer Operations

Peter Simon, Vice President, Database Publishing Group

Irregular Serials & Annuals 1987-88

An International Directory

Thirteenth Edition

The Bowker International Serials Database

R. R. BOWKER COMPANY
Division of Reed Publishing USA
New York and London

Published by R.R. Bowker Company
Division of Reed Publishing (USA) Inc.
245 W. 17th St., New York, NY 10011

Copyright © 1987 by Reed Publishing (USA) Inc.
All rights reserved.

Except as permitted under the Copyright Act of 1976, no part of this publication may be reproduced or transmitted in any form or by any means, stored in any information storage and retrieval system, without prior written permission of R.R. Bowker Company, 245 West 17th Street, New York, New York 10011.

International Standard Book Number 0-8352-2382-5
International Standard Serial Number 0000-0043
Library of Congress Catalog Card Number 67-25026

Printed and bound in the United States of America.

No payment is either solicited or accepted for the inclusion of entries in this publication. R.R. Bowker Company has used its best efforts in collecting and preparing material for inclusion in this publication, but does not warrant that the information herein is complete or accurate, and does not assume, and hereby disclaims, any liability to any person for any loss or damage caused by errors or omissions in this publication, whether such errors or omissions result from negligence, accident or any other cause.

Contents

INTERNATIONAL SERIALS DATABASE	vi
PREFACE	vii
USER'S GUIDE	ix
ABBREVIATIONS	
General Abbreviations	xiv
Money Symbols	xv
Micropublishers	xvi
Country of Publication Codes	xviii
Abstracting and Indexing Services	xxi
SUBJECT GUIDE TO ABSTRACTING AND INDEXING	xxxi
INTERNATIONAL STANDARD SERIAL NUMBER (ISSN)	xxxiii
SUBJECTS	xxxv
CROSS-INDEX TO SUBJECTS	xxxix
CLASSIFIED LIST OF SERIALS	1
SERIALS AVAILABLE ONLINE	1131
VENDOR LISTING/SERIALS ONLINE	1141
CESSATIONS	1145
INDEX TO PUBLICATIONS OF INTERNATIONAL ORGANIZATIONS	
International Organizations	1169
International Congress Proceedings	1178
European Communities	1182
United Nations	1183
ISSN INDEX	1189
TITLE INDEX	1617

International Serials Database

The *Ulrich's* family of directories is maintained, updated and generated from the Bowker International Serials Database. The database includes some 139,700 entries of 59,000 publishers and corporate authors from 197 countries around the world. From this database, the following publications and services are generated:

ULRICH'S INTERNATIONAL PERIODICALS DIRECTORY

The current edition of *Ulrich's International Periodicals Directory* lists some 70,800 periodicals in 542 subject areas. Each entry provides title, frequency of publication, publisher name and address, country of publication code, and Dewey Decimal Classification number. Additional bibliographic and buying information provided when available includes: ISSN, subscription price, year first published, language of text, if advertising and book reviews are included, where abstracted or indexed, corporate author, variant forms of title, whether or not available from a subscription agency, whether available online, and more. Additional sections include Periodicals Available Online, Vendors of Online Periodicals, Cessations, an Index to Publications of International Organizations, and a Title Index.

IRREGULAR SERIALS & ANNUALS
An International Directory

Irregular Serials and Annuals provides data on some 35,900 serials, annuals, continuations, conference proceedings, and other publications issued irregularly or less frequently than twice a year. Entries are alphabetical by title under 490 subject headings, and data includes all features that are also provided in *Ulrich's*, its companion directory. In addition to containing all the special sections provided in *Ulrich's, Irregular Serials & Annuals* includes an ISSN index. All titles included in the Bowker International Serials Database with ISSNs are listed in this index.

THE BOWKER INTERNATIONAL SERIALS DATABASE UPDATE
A Supplement to *Ulrich's International Periodicals Directory* and *Irregular Serials & Annuals*

This quarterly provides continuous worldwide, up-to-date information on new serial titles, title changes, and cessations. It contains all the data you need to keep current between editions of *Ulrich's International Periodicals Directory* and *Irregular Serials & Annuals*.

Each issue lists some 1,500 periodicals, irregular serials or annuals which are new or newly added to our database. It utilizes the same subject arrangement as the base volumes and provides the same full bibliographic annotation for each item. Approximately 1,000 title changes and cessations are also included in each issue.

The arrrangement of the *Bowker International Serials Database Update* follows the format of the base volumes. Pagination is continuous throughout each volume, and indexes for title changes and titles are cumulated in each issue.

THE BOWKER INTERNATIONAL SERIALS DATABASE ONLINE

The entire Bowker International Serials Database is available online through Dialog, BRS and the European Space Agency, and is updated monthly. In addition to title and subject access, The Bowker International Serials Database Online provides access to serials and periodicals by frequency of publication, country of publication, ISSN, Dewey Decimal Number, circulation, special features such as book reviews or illustrations, and more. Users can also employ "key word" techniques and combine access points to instantly locate those publications that meet their precise needs. These additional access points provide enhanced capabilities for effective core-list and collection development and other uses. Also maintained in the database and available online are all titles which were listed as ceased in prior and current hardcopy editions of *Ulrich's* and *Irregular Serials and Annuals* dating back to 1974.

ULRICH'S PLUS (CD-ROM)

Ulrich's Plus provides the entire Bowker International Serials Database on CD-ROM, on a quarterly basis, each a complete cumulative update. *Ulrich's Plus* offers all the search capabilities of online, and more. There are 10 primary and 13 secondary search choices, which set up the basic search. In addition, the combined set choice permits searches based upon several criteria. Citations can be brief, with only title, country of origin, price, circulation and ISSN, to permit users to quickly review the information before calling up the more detailed information given in the full citation.

ULRICH'S AND IRREGULAR SERIALS AND ANNUALS ON MICROFICHE

The entire Bowker International Serials Database is also available on microfiche on a quarterly subscription, with each set a complete cumulative update. The microfiche provides access through the following indexes: Subject Index, Cessation Index, Online Availability Index, Vendor Listings of Serials & Periodicals Available Online, ISSN Index and Title Index. A unique feature is that *full* entries are listed in *both* the Subject Index *and* the Title Index.

Preface

This 13th edition of *Irregular Serials and Annuals* continues our commitment to supplying complete and up-to-date information which is often difficult to locate for serials and continuations such as proceedings, transactions, advances, progresses, reports, yearbooks, handbooks, annual reviews, and monographic series, which constitute the "twilight" area between books and serials. First published in 1967, *Irregular Serials and Annuals* is part of a prodigious international database, now available in a variety of formats—from hardcopy, to online, to microfiche and finally to CD-ROM. *Irregular Serials and Annuals* and its companion products insure that our users are informed on the vast information resources available. Today librarians, researchers, and students have this comprehensive serials database available in any format desired—and with the multitude of search methods, the data is even easier to locate.

Technological advances continue unabated... 371 serials and abstracting and indexing services are also available as online databases. Users who need information in an online format will find notations on serials that are also available online, or in an online format only, included in the main entries found in the "Classified List of Serials."

In addition, these serials are brought together in two indexes, "Serials Available Online," an alphabetical listing of serials available online in addition to hardcopy (or only available online); and a "Vendor Listing/Serials Online" which gives full names and addresses for indentified vendors and an alphabetical listing of all serials each has available online.

In this time of the information explosion, serials, journals and periodicals continue to be the primary source of current, topical news in all fields of endeavor. The very nature of serials and periodicals is broad coverage, even within a specific subject. It is our intention to provide subject headings that allow for both broad coverage and some specificity. Evaluating our subject heading file is a continuous process; new subject areas are studied extensively before new subjects are added to our file. Interest in numismatics, philately, needlework, handicrafts and antiques has grown steadily in past years, and warranted listing as independent subjects. "Antiques", "Needlework", "Numismatics" and "Philately" are no longer tied to "Hobbies" as subheadings. In addition, a new independent subject heading has been added, "Arts and Handicrafts." Since hobbies continue to consume much of our leisure time, "Hobbies" remains an independent subject heading. Magazines of particular interest to men were formerly listed under "General Interest Periodicals." They can now be found under the new independent subject "Men's Interests."

This 13th edition of *Irregular Serials & Annuals* contains information on more than 35,900 serials published throughout the world. More than 22,000 entries from the 11th edition have been updated to reflect the most current information available. More than 1,700 periodical titles have been added, reflecting serials listed in *The Bowker International Serials Database Update* through Volume 2, Number 3.

Irregular Serials & Annuals includes titles issued annually or less frequently than once a year, or irregularly; serials published at least twice under the same title, and those first publications which plan to have subsequent issues. Due to the great number of serials, we have established certain criteria for inclusion, while maintaining our aim of maximum title coverage that will satisfy the widest range of use. We include all publications except those which are essentially administrative in content, such as membership directories, annual reports, house organs, or local interest publications. Also not included are government publications below the state level that can be easily found elsewhere, comic books, puzzle and game books, and "custom search" publications, byproducts of electronic databases.

Periodicals published at regular intervals, issued more frequently than once a year are contained in *Irregular Serials*' companion volume *Ulrich's International Periodicals Directory*, which lists some 70,730 titles. Both of these volumes contain complete bibliographic information for research and ordering. The importance of both of these bibliographic tools and their interrelationship is reflected in their being published simultaneously.

The *Bowker International Serials Database* is a sophisticated and unique machine-readable file which allows for continuous maintenance in a number of ways. The database is maintained by country, publisher and/or corporate author, and title, enabling the editors to eliminate confusing duplicate entries which occur in a database maintained solely in title sequence. This also allows us to maintain publisher profiles by country.

Mailings are accomplished annually to the more than 59,000 publishers from 197 countries in the database. This insures accurate and up-to-date information directly from publishers on current titles, as well as new titles, title changes, and cessations. In addition, updating of the database is done daily from information received from publishers throughout the year. All post-office returns are researched, and entries from publishers whose address cannot be located are suspended from the file. Information about title changes, cessations and new titles not received by the deadline for this edition will appear in *The Bowker International Serials Database Update*, and can always be found in the online database through three major vendors, DIALOG, BRS and the European Space Agency.

This edition of *Irregular Serials & Annuals* continues to see the extensive addition of abstracting and indexing information, important for fast retrieval of the large stores of information available today. We continue to input and update U.S. and Canadian telephone numbers; in addition, foreign telephone numbers have been input when supplied by the publisher.

This edition of *Irregular Serials & Annuals* is arranged in seven sections: the "Classified List of Serials," "Serials Available Online," "Vendor Listing/Serials Online," "Cessations," "Index to Publications of International Organizations," "ISSN Index" and the "Title Index." Unique to *Irregular Serials & Annuals* is the "ISSN Index," which lists more than 82,300 current ISSNs with title, and over 14,400 former and ceased title ISSNs, for all entries in *The Bowker International Serials Database*. This index is valuable both as an aid to online database searchers and as a tool for title verification. A full description and explanation of each of these sections can be found in the "User's Guide," which begins on page ix. In addition, a "Cross-Index to Subjects," giving 1475 key words leading to 490 subject headings used in the "Classified List of Serials," is provided beginning on page xxxix.

I extend my appreciation and thanks to Jackie Mullikin, Editor, and the staff of serials editors for their dedication and hard work in maintaining the serials database. My thanks also to Peter Simon, Vice President of the Database Publishing Group, for his continued support in the management of the serials database. And finally, many thanks to all members of the Operations, Systems and Production Departments for their roles in the completion of this edition of *Irregular Serials & Annuals*.

The entire serials staff and myself extend our thanks and appreciation to all our users for the continued support of *The Bowker International Serials Database*. We continue to strive for excellence in serials information; comments and suggestions are welcome in order to keep our database and its bibliographic products of the highest quality.

Leigh Carol Yuster
Executive Editor
International Serials Database

User's Guide

This directory offers two major access methods for locating periodicals: by subject in the CLASSIFIED LIST OF SERIALS, and alphabetically in the TITLE INDEX. Ceased serials are listed in a separate CESSATIONS section. Other indexes provide listings of selected periodicals in specific categories. These indexes are SERIALS AVAILABLE ONLINE, VENDOR LISTING/SERIALS ONLINE, PUBLICATIONS OF INTERNATIONAL ORGANIZATIONS, and ISSN INDEX.

In addition, separate subheadings for "Abstracting, Bibliographies and Statistics" under major subject headings provide convenient access to these types of publications. Page references for these subheadings are given in the "Subject Guide to Abstracting and Indexing" on p. xxxi. This Subject Guide provides an overview of subjects for which abstracting and indexing publications have been identified.

This "User's Guide" is separated into three divisions for ease of use: (I) Section Descriptions, (II) Full Entry Content Description, and (III) Cataloging Rules for Main Entry Title.

I Section Descriptions

CLASSIFIED LIST OF SERIALS

This is the main section of the book, containing bibliographic information for currently published serials classified by subject. Entries are arranged alphabetically by title within each subject heading. Subject cross-references in the text direct the user to the location of subheadings.

A complete listing of the "Subjects" used in the CLASSIFIED LIST OF SERIALS appears on p. xxxv. To aid international users, this list is translated into four languages. For additional guidance on the subject classification scheme, the user should also consult the "Cross-Index to Subjects" on p. xxxix, which contains additional key word references.

Each serial is listed with full bibliographic information only once. If a serial covers several subjects, title cross-references appear under the related headings, directing the user to the heading where the full entry is listed.

The "Cataloging Rules for Main Entry Title" section of this "User's Guide" explains the title cataloging rules followed in compiling the Bowker International Serials Database.

TITLE INDEX

The TITLE INDEX is the second major access point for serials. To locate a serial by its title, the user should be familiar with title cataloging rules as described in the "Cataloging Rules for Main Entry Title" paragraphs of this "User's Guide."

The TITLE INDEX lists all current and ceased serials included in this directory. *Italic* type indicates the page number where the complete entry will be found; page numbers in roman type refer to related subject categories.

For serials with identical titles published within a country, the city of publication is added in parentheses, and sometimes the year of first publication is given to further distinguish the titles.

If a serial title consists of or contains an acronym, a cross-reference is provided from the full name to the acronym form of the title.

Cross-references are provided from former titles and variant titles, and from the alternate language titles of multiple-language publications. The TITLE INDEX also lists the country code for all serials, along with the ISSN, if known.

SERIALS AVAILABLE ONLINE

This section is an alphabetical listing of all serials known to be available online, either in addition to hard-copy, or online only. It includes publisher name and address and names of online vendors, if known. The number in parentheses at the end of each entry is the page number where the full entry appears in the CLASSIFIED LIST OF SERIALS.

VENDOR LISTING/SERIALS ONLINE

This section is an alphabetical listing of identified vendors of online periodicals. The entry includes addresses and telephone numbers for the vendor and an alphabetical listing of all titles known to be available. All periodicals listed in this index also have full bibliographic entries in the CLASSIFIED LIST OF SERIALS. Consult the TITLE INDEX or the SERIALS AVAILABLE ONLINE listing for page number.

CESSATIONS

In this section, entries for serials which have ceased since the last edition are listed alphabetically by title. The cessation entry includes: title, Dewey Decimal Classification number, former frequency of publication, publisher name and address, country-of-publication code, and, if available, other information such as ISSN, subtitle, corporate author, year of first issue and year ceased. Titles which were originally planned as continuing series but which have closed are included in the CESSATIONS section although back issues may still be available.

If a title has "ceased" because a new title is being used, there will not be an entry in the CESSATIONS section. Instead, the entry is maintained in the CLASSIFIED LIST OF SERIALS under the new title, with a "Formerly" or "Former title" indication.

INDEX TO PUBLICATIONS OF INTERNATIONAL ORGANIZATIONS

Complexity of corporate author structure, as well as title page variations in multilingual texts, compound the problems in cataloging international publications. This special index is provided so that the user may have one reference point for these titles. This index consists of four sections:

   International Organizations
   International Congress Proceedings
   European Communities
   United Nations

The index contains all current titles listed in the Bowker International Serials Database, including periodicals. The user must consult the CLASSIFIED LIST OF SERIALS for the full bibliographic information pertaining to these titles. Page references are provided for titles which appear in this directory. Titles without page numbers will be found in the 26th Edition of the companion volume, *Ulrich's International Periodicals Directory.*

ISSN INDEX

The ISSN INDEX lists serials in order by ISSN number. It includes all serials contained in the Bowker International Serials Database, whether current or ceased, to which an ISSN has been assigned in our file. A dagger symbol (†) indicates that the title is ceased. If an ISSN appears twice, it usually indicates that the serial has split into two or more parts. Titles which have changed, and for which new ISSNs have been assigned, will show cross-references from one ISSN to the new ISSN. If no new ISSN has been assigned, the cross-reference is from ISSN to new title.

A full description of the ISSN and its use is provided on p. xxxiii.

II Full Entry Content Description

CONTENTS OF MAIN ENTRY IN THE CLASSIFIED LIST OF SERIALS

Basic Information
The following items are mandatory for listing and appear in all entries: main entry title, frequency of publication, publisher address, country code, and Dewey Decimal Classification number.

Dewey Decimal Classification Number
The Dewey Decimal number is printed at the top of each entry. More than one Dewey number may have been assigned if a serial covers several subjects.

Country Code
The Country Code is printed at the top of each entry following the Dewey Decimal number. A complete list of country codes used will be found on p. xviii.

ISSN
The ISSN for the main entry title is printed immediately following the country code. Not all publications have been assigned ISSN, and lack of a number does not render a publication ineligible for listing.

Title Information
The main title is printed in upper case as the first item in the entry. Titles are cataloged according to rules described below in the "Cataloging Rules for Main Entry Title" section. For multiple-language publications, the parallel language title is also printed in upper-case, immediately following the main entry title, and is separated from it by a slash.

An asterisk printed after the title indicates that the information in the entry was not verified by the publisher for this edition.

The subtitle is printed in lower case after the title.

Variant titles or translated edition titles are given within the entry and are labeled as such.

Former titles are given at the end of the entry, along with publication dates if known. If a former title also had an ISSN, the ISSN is listed in parentheses after the former title. Many entries contain extensive former title information, providing a history of changes which may be useful for bibliographic record-keeping.

The Key Title, which is assigned at the time of ISSN assignment by the responsible center of the International Serials Data System, is given only if it is different from the main entry title.

Year First Published
The year first published is given if provided by the publisher. If information is lacking, a volume number and specific year may be provided to indicate the approximate age of the publication.

Frequency
The frequency of publication is given in abbreviated form, such as "a." for annual, "irreg." for irregular. All abbreviations used are listed in the "General Abbreviations" on p. xiv.

Price
Unless otherwise indicated, the price given is the annual price for an individual subscription in the currency of the country of origin. The price in U.S. dollars may also be given in parentheses if it is provided by the publisher. No attempt is made to convert foreign currency to U.S. dollars. Separate postage information is not given, since postal rates vary widely.

Publisher Information
Many serials are editorially controlled by a sponsoring organization or corporate author and published by a commercial publisher. In these instances, the commercial publisher's name and address are given, and the name of the corporate author is given in parentheses immediately preceding. In other instances, either a sponsoring organization or a commercial publisher has sole responsibility, and only one name is given. We avoid listing printers as publishers, preferring the name and address of someone with editorial responsibility. For the same reason, we avoid listing distributors as publishers.

If no publisher name is given, it is assumed that the publisher name is the same as the title.

If the publisher is also the editor, the person's name is given with the notation "Ed. & Pub."

Subscription or Distribution Address
A second address is given only if the address for ordering subscriptions is different from the publisher's address. Distributors are listed only if we have been informed that a particular organization is the exclusive distributor.

Telephone
Telephone numbers are given when provided by the publisher. U.S. and Canadian numbers are given in standard North American format. Numbers in other countries are provided in the same format as supplied by the publisher, resulting in some inconsistencies. Users are advised to consult an international operator before placing calls.

Editor
Usually only one name is given, preceded by the notation "Ed." Advanced degrees and titles are omitted, except

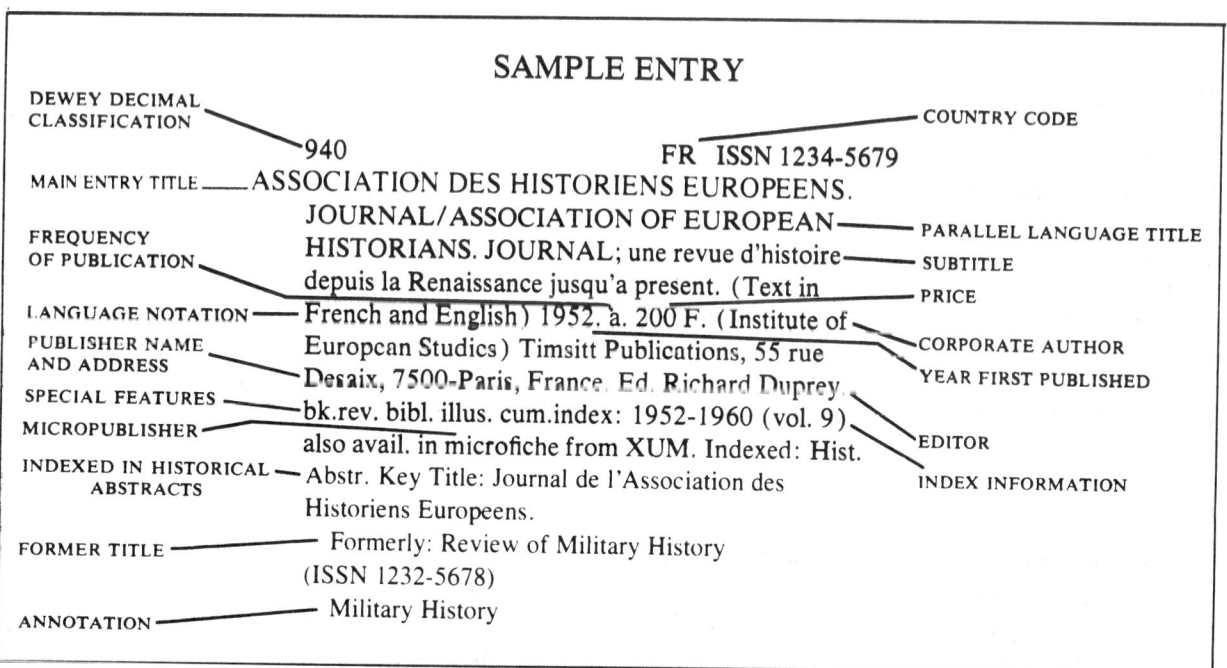

Special Features
A listing of special features may include such items as book or other types of reviews, advertising (usually meaning commercial, not classified advertising), charts, illustrations, bibliography section, article abstracts, and an annual index to the periodical's contents.

Circulation
All circulation figures used are approximate. Circulation is given only if provided by the publisher. The notation "controlled" indicates that the publication is available only to qualified persons, usually members of a particular trade or profession.

Format
Formats other than standard magazine format are noted in parentheses. If a publication is available in microform, a notation is made which includes a three-letter code for the vendor, if known. A list of names, addresses, and telephone numbers of the micropublishers is provided on p. xvi.

Abstracting and Indexing
The notation "Indexed:" precedes a list of abbreviations for all abstracting and indexing services known to cover the serial on a regular basis. The complete names of the abstracting and indexing services are listed with their abbreviations on p. xxi. All currently published abstracting and indexing services are also listed as entries in the CLASSIFIED LIST OF SERIALS.

Online Availability
If a serial is known to be available in a full-text online format, a bullet symbol (●) precedes the information. Online availability is noted whether it is in addition to hardcopy or in this format exclusively. Vendors are also listed if known. For a complete overview of serials available online, consult the separate SERIALS AVAILABLE ONLINE index on p. 1131. Complete names and addresses of vendors, with a listing of serials known to be available through them, are in the separate VENDOR LISTING/SERIALS ONLINE on p. 1141.

Annotation
To aid users in locating serials for selected sub-classifications under a heading, a one- or two-word *annotation* may be provided, printed in italic type as the last line in the entry, for ease in scanning.

Text before this section: for medical, military and religious titles; absence of a title does not mean that the editor has none. The abbreviation "Ed.Bd." indicates editorship by three or more persons.

III Cataloging Rules For Main Entry Title

The majority of titles in the Bowker International Serials Database were cataloged according to *Anglo-American Cataloging Rules* prior to 1978, the date of the new edition of *Anglo-American Cataloging Rules*. The new *AACR II* reflects a trend toward the Key Title concept of cataloging as used by the International Serials Data System (ISDS) and published in its *International Standard Bibliographic Description for Serials* (1974).

Because recataloging a database the size of Bowker's was not feasible, our cataloging rules were modified but not radically changed. Cross-references are provided in the TITLE INDEX from variant forms of title, such as Key Title, to aid users searching by other methods.

Whenever possible, main entry title cataloging is done from a sample of the title page of the most recent issue, according to the following rules:

Articles at the beginning of titles are omitted, or are bypassed in filing.

Serials with distinctive titles are usually entered under title. For example:

Milton Studies
Annual Bulletin of Historical Literature

If a title consists only of a generic term followed by the name of the issuing body, or if the name of the issuing cody clarifies the content of the publication, entry is under the name of the issuing body. For example:

Proceedings of the Association of American Law Schools
is entered as
Association of American Law Schools. Proceedings

Compendium of Approved Projects, issued by the United Nations Development Programme
is entered as
United Nations. Development Programme. Compendium of Approved Projects

A title which consists of a subject modified generic term followed by the name of the issuing body is considered nondistinctive and is entered under the name of the issuing body. For example:

Annual Meeting Scientific Proceedings of the American Animal Hospital Association
is entered as
American Animal Hospital Association. Annual Meeting Scientific Proceedings

Government publications with nondistinctive titles are entered under the name of the government jurisdiction of the issuing body, although distinctive titles of government organizations may be entered directly under title. For example:

Great Britain. Economic and Social Research Council. Report
but
Statistical Abstract of Iceland

Titles which begin with the initials of the issuing body are entered under the initials. Cross-references from the full name are provided in the TITLE INDEX.

If a geographic name is part of the name of the issuing body, entry will be under the common form of the name of the body. For example:

University of Chicago. Graduate School of Business. Selected Papers
not
Chicago. University. Graduate School of Business. Selected Papers

Note, however, that government publications retain similar cataloging as government jurisdiction.

Canada. Statistics Canada. Field Crop Reporting Series

Multilingual titles are entered under the first title given on the title page, or the first title reported by the publisher if the title page is not available. Titles in other languages are entered directly after the main entry title. Cross-references are provided in the TITLE INDEX for each language title.

FILING RULES

Due to the restrictions imposed by computer filing of titles, the following special filing rules should be noted.

Articles and prepositions within titles are alphabetized as words:

Journal of Surveying Engineering
precedes
Journal of the Alleghenies

Hyphenated words are treated as separate words:

Electri-Onics Desk Manual
precedes
Electrical Blue Book

However, words indicating compass points (northeast, southwest, etc.) are filed as one word regardless of how printed:

South East Asia Library Group Newsletter
Southeast Asia Papers
South-East Asia Stamp Catalog

Titles entered under corporate author or government jurisdiction are sequenced before distinctive titles that begin with the same words:

British Columbia. Ministry of Energy, Mines and Petroleum Resources. Annual Report
precedes
British Columbia Government News

Acronyms and initials are treated as such and are listed at the beginning of each letter of the alphabet. Exceptions are the abbreviations U.N. (United Nations), U.S. (United States), Gt. Britain (Great Britain), and St. (Saint), which are filled as words:

U.T.S.A. Annual
United Society of Artists. Publication
U.S. Air Force Academy Library. Special Bibliography Series

Titles in excess of 36 characters which are identical may not sort sequentially. The editors suggest that users scan the entire sequence of identical titles to locate specific entries.

Diacritical marks have been omitted. The German and Scandinavian umlaut has been replaced by the letter "e" following the vowels a, e, and u. In Danish, Norwegian and Swedish, the letter å is sequenced as "aa" and the letter ø as "oe."

Abbreviations
General Abbreviations

a.	annual
abstr.	abstracts
adv.	advertising
approx.	approximately
B.R.D.	Federal Republic of Germany
bi-m.	every two months
bibl.	bibliographies
bk.rev.	book reviews
c/o	care of
charts	charts (diagrams, graphs, tables)
circ.	circulation
contr.	controlled
cum.ind.	cumulative index
Cy.	county
d.	daily
D.D.R.	German Democratic Republic
dance rev.	dance reviews
Dir.	Director
Ed., Eds.	Editor, Editors
Ed.Bd.	Editorial Board
film rev.	film reviews
fortn.	fortnightly
ISSN	International Standard Serial Number
illus.	illustrations
irreg.	irregular
m.	monthly
mkt.	market prices
music rev.	music reviews
N.S.	New Series
pat.	patents
play rev.	play reviews (theatre reviews)
Prof.	Professor
q.	quarterly
record rev.	record reviews
s-a.	twice annually
s-m.	twice monthly
s-w.	twice weekly
stat.	statistics
subscr.	subscription
tele.rev.	television reviews
3/m.	3 times a month
3/yr.	3 times a year
tr.lit.	trade literature (manufacturers' catalogues, etc.)
tr.mk.	trade marks
w.	weekly
‡	not available from a subscription agency
*	not updated

Money Symbols

SYMBOL	UNIT	COUNTRY
Arg.$	peso	Argentina
Aus.$	dollar	Australia
B.	baht	Thailand
B.$	dollar	Brunei Darussalam, Belize
Bl.	balboa	Panama
Bol.$	peso	Bolivia
Br.	birr	Ethiopia
Bs.	bolivar	Venezuela
C.$	cordoba; dollar	Nicaragua, Cayman Islands
Can.$	dollar	Canada
CFPF	franc	New Caledonia
Col.	colon	Costa Rica, El Salvador
Col.$	peso	Colombia
Cr.$	cruzeiro	Brazil
D.	dalasi	Gambia
DH., Dh.	dirham	Morocco, United Arab Emirates
DM.	mark	West Germany
din.	dinar	Algeria, Jordan, Kuwait, Libya, Tunisia, Yugoslavia
$	dollar; peso	various
Dr.	drachma	Greece
E.	emalangeni	Swaziland
EAs.	shilling	East Africa, Somalia, Tanzania, Uganda
EC$.	dollar	Dominica, St. Lucia
Esc.	escudo	Angola, Portugal, Mozambique
F.	franc	Djibouti, France, Guadeloupe, Mali, Martinique, Monaco, Rwanda
F$	dollar	Fiji
fl.	guilder; florin	Netherlands, Netherlands Antilles, Surinam
FMG.	franc	Malagasy Republic
Fmk.	mark; markka	Finland
Fr.	franc	Belgium, Liechtenstein, Luxembourg, Switzerland
Fr.CFA	franc	African Financial Community, Benin, Burkina Faso, Burundi, Cameroon, Central African Republic, Chad, Congo, Gabon, Ivory Coast, Niger, Reunion, Senegal, Togo
Ft.	forint	Hungary
g.	guarani	Paraguay
Gde.	gourde	Haiti
G.$	dollar	Guyana
HK$	dollar	Hong Kong
I.D.	dinar	Iran, Iraq
IS	shekel	Israel
Jam.$	dollar	Jamaica
K.	kina; kwacha	Malawi, Papua New Guinea, Zambia
Kcs.	koruny	Czechoslovakia
Kr.	krona; krone	Scandinavian countries
KShs.	shilling	Kenya
L.	lempira; lira	Honduras, Italy
Le.	leone	Sierra Leone
lei	lei	Rumania
lv.	lev	Bulgaria
M.	mark	East Germany
M.$	dollar; ringgit	Malaysia
Mex.$	peso	Mexico
$m.n.	moneda nacional	various
NC.	cedi	Ghana
NT.$	dollar	Republic of China (Taiwan)
N.Z.$	dollar	New Zealand
P.	pula; peso	Botswana, Philippines, various
£	pound	Ireland, Gt. Britain, Malta
£C	pound	Cyprus
£E	pound	Egypt
£L	pound; dinar	Lebanon
£N	pound; naira	Nigeria
£S	pound	Syria
ptas.	peseta	Spain
Q.	quetzal	Guatemala
R.	rand	South Africa, Lesotho, Namibia
RD.$	peso	Dominican Republic
Rps.	rupiah	Indonesia
Rs.	riel; rial; rupee	Cambodia, India, Iran, Mauritius, Nepal, Pakistan, Seychelles, Sri Lanka
Rub.	ruble	U.S.S.R.
S/	sucre; sole	Ecuador, Peru
S.	schilling	Austria
S.$	dollar	Singapore
SRl.	riyal	Saudia Arabia
SL.	pound	Sudan
TK.	taka	Bangladesh
TL.	pound; lira	Turkey
T.T.$	dollar	Trinidad and Tobago
UM	ouguiya	Mauritania
Urg.$	peso	Uruguay
VN.$	dollar	Vietnam
Won	won (hwan)	Korea
Y	yuan	Peoples Republic of China
Yen	yen	Japan
YRl.	rial	Yemen
Z	zaire	Zaire
Z.$	dollar	Zimbabwe
Zl.	zloty	Poland

Micropublishers

AMS	AMS Press, Inc. 56 E. 13th St. New York, NY 10003 212-777-4700	JOH	Johnson Reprint Microeditions (Microeditions phased out) 111 Fifth Ave. New York, NY 10003 212-614-3200
BLH	Bell & Howell Micro Photo Division Old Mansfield Rd. Wooster, OH 44691 216-264-6666	JSC	J. S. Canner & Co. 49-65 Lansdowne St. Boston, MA 02115 617-437-1923
BLI	Balch Institute 18 S. 7th St. Philadelphia, PA 19106 215-925-8090	KTO	Kraus Reprints & Periodicals Division of Kraus-Thomson Organization, Ltd. One Water St. White Plains, NY 10601 914-761-9600
CLA	Canadian Library Association Microfilm Project 200 Elgin St. Ottawa, Ont. K2P 1L5, Canada 613-232-9625	LCP	The Library of Congress Photoduplication Service 20 First St., S.E. Washington, DC 20540 202-287-5650
EDR	Eric Document Reproduction Service Box 190 Arlington, VA 22210 703-823-0500; 800-227-3742	LIB	Library Microfilms 737 Loma Verde Ave. Palo Alto, CA 94303 415-494-1812
FCM	Fairchild Microfilms Fairchild Publications, Inc. 7 E. 12th St. New York, NY 10003 212-741-4000	MCA	Microfilming Corporation of America (Operation phased out) 130 Fifth Ave. New York NY 10011 212-645-3000
GMC	General Microfilm Co. 70 Coolidge Hill Rd. Watertown, MA 02172 617-926-5557	MCE	Professional Data Services (formerly Microcard Editions) c/o Congressional Information Services 4520 East-West Hwy, Ste. 800 Bethesda, MD 20814 301-365-1550
HPL	Harvester Press Microfilm Publications Ltd. 16 Ship St. Brighton, Sussex BN1 1AD England (0273) 28320	MIM	Microforms International Marketing Co. (Subsidiary of Pergamon Press, Inc.) Maxwell House Fairview Park Elmsford, NY 10523 914-592-7700
IDC	Inter Documentation Co., AG. Poststrasse 14 6300 Zug Switzerland	MML	Micromedia Limited 158 Pearl St. Toronto, Ontario M5H 1L3 Canada 416-593-5211
ISI	Institute for Scientific Information 3501 Market St. Philadelphia, PA 19104 215-386-0100	MMP	McLaren Micropublishing P.O. Box 972, Station F Toronto, Ontario M4Y 2N9 Canada
JAI	JAI Press Inc. 36 Sherwood Pl. P.O. Box 1678 Greenwich, CT 06836 203-661-7602		

MICROPUBLISHERS

NBI	Newsbank, Inc. 58 Pine St. New Canaan, CT 06840 203-966-1100; 800-243-7694	UMI	University Microfilms International 300 N. Zeeb Rd. Ann Arbor, MI 48106 313-761-4700
NTI	National Technical Information Service 5285 Port Royal Rd. Springfield, VA 22161 703-487-4600	UNM	University of Michigan Library Interlibrary Lending Circulation Department Harlan Hatcher Graduate Library Ann Arbor, MI 48104
NYT	New York Times Information Bank 229 W. 43rd St. New York, NY 10036 212-556-1234	UNW	University of Wisconsin Library Interlibrary Loan Department 728 State St. Madison, WI 53706
OMP	Oxford Microform Publications Ltd. (Subsidiary of Pergamon Press, Ltd.) Headington Hill Hall Oxford 0X3 OBW, England	WDS	Dawson Microfiche Cannon House Parkfarm Road Folkestone, Kent CT19 5EE England
PMC	Princeton Microfilm Corp. P.O. Box 2073 Princeton, NJ 08543 609-452-2066; 800-257-9502	WMP	World Microfilm Publications Ltd. 62 Queen's Grove London NW8 6ER England (01) 586-3092
RRI	Fred B. Rothman & Co. 10368 W. Centennial Rd. Littleton, CO 80127 303-979-5657	WSH	William S. Hein & Co., Inc. 1285 Main St. Buffalo, NY 14209 716-882-2600; 800-828-7581
TMI	Tennessee Microfilms P.O. Box 1096 Nashville, TN 37202		

Country of Publication Codes

This list of countries and their codes has been taken from the list used by the Library of Congress in the MARC II format, 1972. The list used here is not the complete list of the MARC II format and is limited to presently existing national entities. The states of the United States, provinces and territories of Canada, divisions of the United Kingdom, and republics of the USSR are not listed separately.

The codes are mnemonic in most cases. The first letter of the two-letter code is the same as the first letter of the place name. Special codes not in the MARC format are used for publications of two international organizations: EI for European Communities and UN for United Nations and related organizations.

Country Code Sequence

AA -ALBANIA	GL -GREENLAND	PG -GUINEA-BISSAU
AE -ALGERIA	GM -GAMBIA	PH -PHILIPPINES
AF -AFGHANISTAN	GO -GABON	PK -PAKISTAN
AG -ARGENTINA	GP -GUADELOUPE	PL -POLAND
AN -ANDORRA	GR -GREECE	PN -PANAMA
AO -ANGOLA	GT -GUATEMALA	PO -PORTUGAL
AQ -ANTIGUA	GU -GUAM	PP -PAPUA NEW GUINEA
AS -AMERICAN SAMOA	GV -GUINEA	PR -PUERTO RICO
AT -AUSTRALIA	GW -GERMANY, WEST (BRD)	PY -PARAGUAY
AU -AUSTRIA	GY -GUYANA (BRITISH GUIANA)	QA -QATAR
AY -ANTARCTICA	HK -HONG KONG	RE -REUNION
BA -BAHRAIN	HO -HONDURAS	RH -ZIMBABWE
BB -BARBADOS	HT -HAITI	RM -RUMANIA
BD -BURUNDI	HU -HUNGARY	RW -RWANDA
BE -BELGIUM	IC -ICELAND	RY -RYUKYU ISLANDS, SOUTHERN
BF -BAHAMAS	IE -IRELAND	SA -SOUTH AFRICA
BG -BANGLADESH	II -INDIA	SE -SEYCHELLES
BH -BELIZE	IO -INDONESIA	SF -SAO TOME E PRINCIPE
BL -BRAZIL	IQ -IRAQ	SG -SENEGAL
BM -BERMUDA	IR -IRAN	SI -SINGAPORE
BO -BOLIVIA	IS -ISRAEL	SJ -SUDAN
BP -BRITISH SOLOMON ISLANDS	IT -ITALY	SK -SIKKIM
BR -BURMA	IV -IVORY COAST	SL -SIERRA LEONE
BS -BOTSWANA	JA -JAPAN	SM -SAN MARINO
BT -BHUTAN	JM -JAMAICA	SO -SOMALIA
BU -BULGARIA	JO -JORDAN	SP -SPAIN
BX -BRUNEI DARUSSALAM	KE -KENYA	SQ -SWAZILAND
CB -CAMBODIA	KN -KOREA, NORTH	SR -SURINAM
CC -CHINA, MAINLAND	KO -KOREA, SOUTH	SU -SAUDI ARABIA
CD -CHAD	KU -KUWAIT	SW -SWEDEN
CE -SRI LANKA	LB -LIBERIA	SX -NAMIBIA (SOUTH-WEST AFRICA)
CF -CONGO (BRAZZAVILLE)	LE -LEBANON	SY -SYRIA
CH -CHINA, REPUBLIC OF	LH -LIECHTENSTEIN	SZ -SWITZERLAND
CJ -CAYMAN ISLANDS	LO -LESOTHO	TG -TOGO
CK -COLOMBIA	LS -LAOS	TH -THAILAND
CL -CHILE	LU -LUXEMBOURG	TI -TUNISIA
CM -CAMEROON	LY -LIBYA	TO -TONGA
CN -CANADA	MC -MONACO	TR -TRINIDAD & TOBAGO
CR -COSTA RICA	MF -MAURITIUS	TS -UNITED ARAB EMIRATES
CS -CZECHOSLOVAKIA	MG -MALAGASY REPUBLIC (MADAGASCAR)	TT -TRUST TERRITORY, PACIFIC ISLDS
CU -CUBA	MH -MACAO	TU -TURKEY
CV -CAPE VERDE	MJ -MONTSERRAT	TZ -TANZANIA
CX -CENTRAL AFRICAN REPUBLIC	MK -SULTANATE OF OMAN	UA -EGYPT (ARAB REPUBLIC OF EGYPT)
CY -CYPRUS	ML -MALI	UG -UGANDA
CZ -CANAL ZONE	MM -MALTA	UI -UNITED KINGDOM MISC. ISLANDS
DK -DENMARK	MP -MONGOLIA	UK -UNITED KINGDOM
DM -BENIN	MQ -MARTINIQUE	UN -UNITED NATIONS
DQ -DOMINICA	MR -MOROCCO	UR -U S S R
DR -DOMINICAN REPUBLIC	MU -MAURITANIA	US -UNITED NATIONS
EC -ECUADOR	MW -MALAWI	UV -BURKINA FASO
EG -EQUATORIAL GUINEA	MX -MEXICO	UY -URUGUAY
EI -EUROPEAN COMMUNITIES	MY -MALAYSIA	VB -VIRGIN ISLANDS (BRITISH)
ES -EL SALVADOR	MZ -MOZAMBIQUE	VC -VATICAN CITY
ET -ETHIOPIA	NA -NETHERLANDS ANTILLES	VE -VENEZUELA
FA -FAEROE ISLANDS	NE -NETHERLANDS	VI -VIRGIN ISLANDS (U.S.)
FG -FRENCH GUIANA	NG -NIGER	VN -VIETNAM
FI -FINLAND	NL -NEW CALEDONIA	WS -WESTERN SAMOA
FJ -FIJI	NN -VANUATU (NEW HEBRIDES)	XC -MALDIVE ISLANDS
FK -FALKLAND ISLANDS	NO -NORWAY	XI -ST. KITTS-NEVIS
FP -FRENCH POLYNESIA	NP -NEPAL	XK -SAINT LUCIA
FR -FRANCE	NQ -NICARAGUA	XM -SAINT VINCENT
FT -DJIBOUTI	NR -NIGERIA	YE -YEMEN
GD -GRENADA	NU -NAURU	YS -YEMEN, SOUTHERN
GE -GERMANY, EAST (DDR)	NZ -NEW ZEALAND	YU -YUGOSLAVIA
GH -GHANA	PE -PERU	ZA -ZAMBIA
GI -GIBRALTAR		ZR -ZAIRE

Country Sequence

AFGHANISTAN - AF
ALBANIA - AA
ALGERIA - AE
AMERICAN SAMOA - AS
ANDORRA - AN
ANGOLA - AO
ANTARCTICA - AY
ANTIGUA - AQ
ARGENTINA - AG
AUSTRALIA - AT
AUSTRIA - AU
BAHAMAS - BF
BAHRAIN - BA
BANGLADESH - BG
BARBADOS - BB
BELGIUM - BE
BELIZE - BH
BENIN - DM
BERMUDA - BM
BHUTAN - BT
BOLIVIA - BO
BOTSWANA - BS
BRAZIL - BL
BRITISH SOLOMON ISLANDS - BP
BRUNEI DARUSSALAM - BX
BULGARIA - BU
BURKINA FASO - UV
BURMA - BR
BURUNDI - BD
CAMBODIA - CB
CAMEROON - CM
CANADA - CN
CANAL ZONE - CZ
CAPE VERDE - CV
CAYMAN ISLANDS - CJ
CENTRAL AFRICAN REPUBLIC - CX
CHAD - CD
CHILE - CL
CHINA, MAINLAND - CC
CHINA, REPUBLIC OF - CH
COLOMBIA - CK
CONGO (BRAZZAVILLE) - CF
COSTA RICA - CR
CUBA - CU
CYPRUS - CY
CZECHOSLOVAKIA - CS
DENMARK - DK
DJIBOUTI - FT
DOMINICA - DQ
DOMINICAN REPUBLIC - DR
ECUADOR - EC
EGYPT (ARAB REPUBLIC OF EGYPT) - UA
EL SALVADOR - ES
EQUATORIAL GUINEA - FG
ETHIOPIA - ET
EUROPEAN COMMUNITIES - EI
FAEROE ISLANDS - FA
FALKLAND ISLANDS - FK
FIJI - FJ
FINLAND - FI
FRANCE - FR
FRENCH GUIANA - FG
FRENCH POLYNESIA - FP
GABON - GO
GAMBIA - GM
GERMANY, EAST (DDR) - GE

GERMANY, WEST (BRD) - GW
GHANA - GH
GIBRALTAR - GI
GREECE - GR
GREENLAND - GL
GRENADA - GD
GUADELOUPE - GP
GUAM - GU
GUATEMALA - GT
GUINEA - GV
GUINEA-BISSAU - PG
GUYANA (BRITISH GUIANA) - GY
HAITI - HT
HONDURAS - HO
HONG KONG - HK
HUNGARY - HU
ICELAND - IC
INDIA - II
INDONESIA - IO
IRAN - IR
IRAQ - IQ
IRELAND - IE
ISRAEL - IS
ITALY - IT
IVORY COAST - IV
JAMAICA - JM
JAPAN - JA
JORDAN - JO
KENYA - KE
KOREA, NORTH - KN
KOREA, SOUTH - KO
KUWAIT - KU
LAOS - LS
LEBANON - LE
LESOTHO - LO
LIBERIA - LB
LIBYA - LY
LIECHTENSTEIN - LH
LUXEMBOURG - LU
MACAO - MH
MALAGASY REPUBLIC (MADAGASCAR) - MG
MALAWI - MW
MALAYSIA - MY
MALDIVE ISLANDS - XC
MALI - ML
MALTA - MM
MARTINIQUE - MQ
MAURITANIA - MU
MAURITIUS - MF
MEXICO - MX
MONACO - MC
MONGOLIA - MP
MONTSERRAT - MJ
MOROCCO - MR
MOZAMBIQUE - MZ
NAMIBIA (SOUTH-WEST AFRICA) - SX
NAURU - NU
NEPAL - NP
NETHERLANDS - NE
NETHERLANDS ANTILLES - NA
NEW CALEDONIA - NL
NEW ZEALAND - NZ
NICARAGUA - NQ
NIGER - NG
NIGERIA - NR

NORWAY - NO
PAKISTAN - PK
PANAMA - PN
PAPUA NEW GUINEA - PP
PARAGUAY - PY
PERU - PE
PHILIPPINES - PH
POLAND - PL
PORTUGAL - PO
PUERTO RICO - PR
QATAR - QA
REUNION - RE
RUMANIA - RM
RWANDA - RW
RYUKYU ISLANDS, SOUTHERN - RY
SAINT KITTS-NEVIS-XI
SAINT LUCIA - XK
SAINT VINCENT - XM
SAN MARINO - SM
SAO TOME E PRINCIPE - SF
SAUDI ARABIA - SU
SENEGAL - SG
SEYCHELLES - SE
SIERRA LEONE - SL
SIKKIM - SK
SINGAPORE - SI
SOMALIA - SO
SOUTH AFRICA - SA
SPAIN - SP
SRI LANKA - CE
SUDAN - SJ
SULTANATE OF OMAN - MK
SURINAM - SR
SWAZILAND - SQ
SWEDEN - SW
SWITZERLAND - SZ
SYRIA - SY
TANZANIA - TZ
THAILAND - TH
TOGO - TG
TONGA - TO
TRINIDAD & TOBAGO - TR
TRUST TERRITORY, PACIFIC ISLDS - TT
TUNISIA - TI
TURKEY - TU
UGANDA - UG
UNITED ARAB EMIRATES - TS
UNITED KINGDOM - UK
UNITED KINGDOM MISC. ISLANDS - UI
UNITED NATIONS - UN
UNITED STATES - US
URUGUAY - UY
U S S R - UR
VANUATU (NEW HEBRIDES) - NN
VATICAN CITY - VC
VENEZUELA - VE
VIETNAM - VN
VIRGIN ISLANDS (BRITISH) - VB
VIRGIN ISLANDS (U.S.) - VI
WESTERN SAMOA - WS
YEMEN - YE
YEMEN, SOUTHERN - YS
YUGOSLAVIA - YU
ZAIRE - ZR
ZAMBIA - ZA
ZIMBABWE - RH

Abstracting and Indexing Services

This list contains the full names of all abstracting and indexing services whose abbreviations are used in entries in the Classified List of Periodicals. For all currently published abstracting and indexing services, entries containing full bibliographic information will be found in the Classified List of Periodicals. Consult the Title Index for page numbers. (Bibliographic information for ceased titles can be found in the Bowker International Serials Database online.)

A

A.A.P.P.Abstr.	Amino Acids, Peptides & Proteins Abstracts (Now: Biochemistry Abstracts, Part 3: Amino Acids, Peptides & Proteins)
AAR	Accounting Articles
ABC	Abstracts in BioCommerce
A.B.C.Pol.Sci.	ABC Pol. Sci: A Bibliography of Contents: Political Science and Government
ABTICS	Abstracts and Book Title Index Card Service (Ceased)
A.D.&D.	Alcohol, Drugs and Driving: Abstracts and Reviews
AESIS	A E S I S Quarterly (Australian Earth Sciences Information System)
A.I.C.P.	Anthropological Index to Current Periodicals in the Library of the Museum of Mankind
A.I.D.Res.Dev. Abstr.	A.I.D. Research & Development Abstracts (Agency for International Development)
A.I.P.P.	Annual Index to Poetry in Periodicals
AIT Reports	A I T Reports and Publications on Renewable Energy Resources. Abstracts (Asian Institute of Technology)
API Abstr.	A P I Abstracts/Literature (American Petroleum Institute)
A.S.&T.Ind.	Applied Science & Technology Index
ASCA	Automatic Subject Citation Alert
ASEAN Manage. Abstr.	A S E A N Management Abstracts (Association of South East Asian Nations)
ASTIS	A S T I S Bibliography (Arctic Science & Technology Information System)
Abr.R.G.	Abridged Reader's Guide to Periodical Literature
Abstr.Anthropol.	Abstracts in Anthropology
Abstr.Bk.Rev. Curr.Leg.Per.	Abstracts of Book Reviews in Current Legal Periodicals
Abstr.Bulg.Sci. Med.Lit.	Abstracts of Bulgarian Scientific Medical Literature
Abstr.Bull.Inst. Pap.Chem.	Institute of Paper Chemistry. Abstract Bulletin
Abstr.Comput. Lit.	Abstracts of Computer Literature (Ceased)
Abstr.Crim.& Pen.	Abstracts on Criminology and Penology (Now: Criminology and Penology Abstracts)
Abstr.Engl.Stud.	Abstracts of English Studies
Abstr.Folk.Stud.	Abstracts of Folklore Studies (Ceased)
Abstr.Health Care Manage. Stud.	Abstracts of Health Care Management Studies
Abstr.Health Eff.Environ. Pollut.	Abstracts on Health Effects of Environmental Pollutants
Abstr.Hosp. Manage.Stud.	Abstracts of Hospital Management Studies (Now: Abstracts of Health Care Management Studies)
Abstr.Hyg.	Abstracts on Hygiene and Communicable Diseases
Abstr.J.Earthq. Eng.	Abstract Journal in Earthquake Engineering
Abstr.Mil.Bibl.	Abstracts of Military Bibliography
Abstr.Musl.Rel.	European Muslims and Christian-Muslim Relations. Abstracts. (Ceased)
Abstr.N.Amer. Geol.	Abstracts on North American Geology
Abstr.Pop.Cult.	Abstracts of Popular Culture (Ceased)
Abstr.Soc.Work.	Abstracts for Social Workers (Now: Social Work Research & Abstracts)
Abstr.Trop.Agri.	Abstracts on Tropical Agriculture
Abstrax	Abstrax
Access	Access: the Supplementary Index to Periodicals
Account.& Data Proc.Abstr.	Accounting & Data Processing Abstracts (see Anbar)
Account.Ind.	Accountant's Index
Acid Pre.Dig.	Acid Precipitation Digest
Acid Rain Abstr.	Acid Rain Abstracts
Acoust.Abstr.	Acoustics Abstracts
Adol.Ment. Hlth. Abstr.	Adolescent Mental Health Abstracts
Agri.Eng.Abstr.	Agricultural Engineering Abstracts
Agri.Ind.	Agriculture Index (Now: Biological & Agricultural Index)

Agrindex	Agrindex		**B**
Air Un.Lib.Ind.	Air University Library Index to Military Periodicals	B.C.I.R.A.	B.C.I.R.A. Abstracts of International Foundry Literature (British Cast Iron Research Association)
Alloys Ind.	Alloys Index		
Alt.Press Ind.	Alternative Press Index	BIM	Bibliography and Index of Micropaleontology
Amer.Bibl.Slavic. & E.Eur.Stud.	American Bibliography of Slavic and East European Studies	BIZ	Internationale Bibliographie der Zeitschriftenliteratur aus Allen Gebieten des Wissens
Amer.Hist.& Life	America: History & Life (Parts A,B,C)		
Amer.Hum.Ind.	American Humanities Index	BMT	B M T Abstracts (British Maritime Technology)
Amer.Stat.Ind.	American Statistics Index		
Anal.Abstr.	Analytical Abstracts	B.P.I.	Business Periodicals Index
Anbar	Anbar Publications Ltd.	BPIA	Business Publications Index and Abstracts (Ceased)
	Accounting & Data Processing Abstracts		
	Marketing & Distribution Abstracts	B.R.I.	BioResearch Index (Now: Biological Abstracts/ R R M (Reports, Reviews, Meetings))
	Personnel & Training Abstracts		
	Top Management Abstracts		
	Work Study & O and M Abstracts	BSL Indus.	Abstracts of Bulgarian Scientific Literature. Industry, Building and Transport
Anim.Behav. Abstr.	Animal Behavior Abstracts		
Anim.Breed. Abstr.	Animal Breeding Abstracts	Bangladesh Agr. Sci.Abstr.	Bangladesh Agricultural Sciences Abstracts
Ap.Ind.	Apple Index	Bank.Lit.Ind.	Banking Literature Index
Apic.Abstr.	Apicultural Abstracts	Behav.Abstr.	Behavioural Abstracts
Appl.Ecol.Abstr.	Applied Ecology Abstracts (Now: Ecology Abstracts)	Ber.Biochem. Biol.	Berichte Biochemie und Biologie (Ceased)
Appl.Mech.Rev.	Applied Mechanics Review	Bibl.Agri.	Bibliography of Agriculture
Aqua.Sci.& Fish.Abstr.	Aquatic Sciences & Fisheries Abstracts	Bibl.& Ind.Geol.	Bibliography & Index of Geology
		Bibl.Books Child.	Bibliography of Books for Children
Aquacult.Abstr.	ASFA Aquaculture Abstracts	Bibl.Cart.	Bibliographia Cartographica
Archit.Per.Ind.	Architectural Periodicals Index	Bibl.Dev.Med.& Child Neur.	Bibliography of Developmental Medicine & Child Neurology
Arct.Bibl.	Arctic Bibliography (Ceased)		
Art & Archaeol. Tech.Abstr.	Art and Archaeology Technical Abstracts	Bibl.Engl.Lang. & Lit.	Bibliography of English Language and Literature (Now: Annual Bibliography of English Language and Literature)
Art Ind.	Art Index		
Artbibl.	Artbibliographies Current Titles		
Artbibl.Mod.	Artbibliographies Modern	Bibl.Hist.Med.	Bibliography of the History of Medicine
Arts & Hum. Cit.Ind.	Arts & Humanities Citation Index		
		Bibl.Ind.	Bibliographic Index
Ash.G.Bot.Per.	Asher's Guide to Botanical Periodicals (Now: Guide to Botanical Periodicals) (Ceased)	Bibl.IULA	Bibliographia I U L A (International Union of Local Authorities)
		Bibl.Pflanz.	Bibliographie der Pflanzenschutzliteratur
Astron.& Astrophys. Abstr.	Astronomy and Astrophysics Abstracts	Bibl.Repro.	Bibliography of Reproduction
		Bibliogr.Bras. Odontol.	Bibliografia Brasileira Odontologia
Astron. Jahresber.	Astronomischer Jahresbericht (Now: Astronomy and Astrophysics Abstracts)	Bioeng.Abstr.	Bioengineering Abstracts
		Biog.& Gen.Master File Ind.	Biography and Genealogy Master File Index
Aus.Educ.Ind.	Australian Education Index	Biog.Ind.	Biography Index
Aus.Leg.Mon. Dig.	Australian Legal Monthly Digest	Biol.Abstr.	Biological Abstracts
		Biol.& Agr.Ind.	Biological & Agricultural Index
Aus.P.A.I.S.	Australian Public Affairs Information Service (Now: APAIS: Australian Public Affairs Information Service)	Biol.Dig.	Biology Digest
		Biotech.Abstr.	Biotechnology Research Abstracts
		Biul.Inst.Hod. Aklim.Rosl.	Instytut Hodowli i Aklimatyzacji Roslin. Biuletyn
Aus.Rd.Ind.	Australian Road Index		
Aus.Sci.Ind.	Australian Science Index (Ceased)		
Aus.Speleo Abstr.	Australian Speleo Abstracts	Biwk.Pap.Rad. Chem.& Photochem.	Biweekly List of Papers on Radiation Chemistry and Photochemistry
Avery Ind. Archit.Per.	Avery Index to Architectural Periodicals		

Bk.Rev.Dig.	Book Review Digest	CJPI	Criminal Justice Periodical Index
Bk.Rev.Ind.	Book Review Index	C.L.I.	Current Law Index
Bk.Rev.Mo.	Book Reviews of the Month	CLOA	Current Literature on Aging
Br.Archaeol.Abstr.	British Archaeological Abstracts	CMI	Canadian Magazine Index
		C.P.I.	Current Physics Index
Br.Ceram.Abstr.	British Ceramic Abstracts	C.R.E.J.	Contents of Recent Economics Journals
Br.Educ.Ind.	British Education Index		
Br.Geol.Lit.	British Geological Literature	C.R.I. Abstr.	C R I Abstracts (Cement Research Institute of India)
Br.Hum.Ind.	British Humanities Index		
Br.Rail.Bd.	British Railways Board. Monthly Review of Technical Literature	CS Ind.	Canadian Statistics Index
		CSI Fed.Ind.	C S I Federal Index (Capitol Services, Inc.)
Br.Tech.Ind.	British Technology Index (Now: Current Technology Index)		
		CWHM	Current Work in the History of Medicine
Build.Manage.Abstr.	Building Management Abstracts (Now: Technical Information Service-TIS)		
		Cab.Vid.Ind.	Cable-Video Index
Bull.Anal.Ent.Med.Vet.	Bulletin Analytique d'Entomologie Medicale et Veterinaire (Ceased)	Cadscan	Cadscan
		Cal.Tiss.Abstr.	Calcified Tissue Abstracts
Bull.Hyg.	Bulletin of Hygiene (Now: Abstracts on Hygiene and Communicable Diseases)	Can.B.P.I.	Canadian Business Periodicals Index (Now: Canadian Business Index)
		Can.Educ.Ind.	Canadian Education Index
Bull.Inst. Pasteur	Institut Pasteur. Bulletin	Can.Ind.	Canadian Periodical Index
		Can.Rev.Comp.Lit.	Canadian Review of Comparative Literature
Bull.Signal.	Bulletin Signaletique (Now: P A S C A L Explore, P A S C A L Folio, P A S C A L Thema) (Programme Applique a la Selection et la Compilation Automatique de la Literature)	Canadiana	Canadiana
		Canon Law Abstr.	Canon Law Abstracts
		Carcinog.Abstr.	Carcinogenesis Abstracts
		Cath.Ind.	Catholic Periodical & Literature Index (Formerly: Catholic Periodical Index)
Bull.Thermodyn.& Thermochem.	Bulletin of Thermodynamics & Thermochemistry (Now: Bulletin of Chemical Thermodynamics)	Ceram.Abstr.	Ceramic Abstracts
		Chem.Abstr.	Chemical Abstracts
Bus.Comput.Ind.	Business Computer Index	Chem.Eng.Abstr.	Chemical Engineering Abstracts
Bus.Educ.Ind.	Business Education Index	Chem.Indus.Notes	Chemical Industry Notes
Bus.Ind.	Business Index	Chem.Infd.	Chemischer Informationsdienst
		Chem.Titles	Chemical Titles
		Chemorec.Abstr.	Chemoreception Abstracts
		Chicago Psychoanal.Lit.Ind.	Chicago Psychoanalytic Literature Index

C

CALL	C A L L (Current Awareness—Library Literature)	Child.Auth.& Illus.	Children's Authors and Illustrators
		Child.Bk.Rev.Ind.	Children's Book Review Index
C.C.L.P.	Contents of Current Legal Periodicals (Now: Legal Contents)	Child Devel. Abstr.	Child Development Abstracts and Bibliography
C.C.M.J.	Contents of Contemporary Mathematical Journals (Now: Current Mathematical Publications)	Child.Lit.Abstr.	Children's Literature Abstracts
		Chr.Per.Ind.	Christian Periodical Index
CCR	Current Christian Abstracts	Clin-Alert	Clin-Alert
CERDIC	Bulletin du CERDIC (Centre des Recherche et de Documentation des Institutions Chretiennes) (Ceased)	Coll.Stud.Pers.Abstr.	College Student Personnel Abstracts (Now: Higher Education Abstracts)
		Commun.Abstr.	Communication Abstracts
CHNI	Consumer Health & Nutrition Index	Community Ment.Health Rev.	Community Mental Health Review (Now: Prevention in Human Services)
C.I.J.E.	Current Index to Journals in Education		
CINAHL (also C.I.N.L.)	Cumulative Index to Nursing and Allied Health Literature	Compumath	Compumath Citation Index
		Comput.& Info.Sys.	Computer and Information Systems Abstract Journal
CIRF Abstr.	C I R F Abstracts (Now: T&D Abstracts) (Ceased)	Comput.Abstr.	Computer Abstracts
		Comput.& Contr.Abstr.	Computer & Control Abstracts (See Science Abstracts)
C.I.S. Abstr.	C I S Abstracts (Centre International d'Information de Securite et Hygiene du Travail)		
		Comput.Bus.	Computer Business
C.I.S. Ind.	C I S Index (Congressional Information Service)	Comput.Cont.	Computer Contents

Comput.Indus.Up.	Computer Industry Update
Comput.Lit.Ind.	Computer Literature Index (Formerly: Quarterly Bibliography of Computers and Data Processing)
Comput.Rev.	Computing Reviews
Concr.Abstr.	Concrete Abstracts
Consum.Ind.	Consumers Index
Cont.Pg.Educ.	Contents Pages in Education
Cont.Pg.Manage.	Contents Pages in Management (Formerly: Current Contents in Management)
Copper Abstr.	Copper Abstracts (Now: International Copper Information Bulletin
Corros.Abstr.	Corrosion Abstracts (Ceased)
Crim.Just.Abstr.	Criminal Justice Abstracts
Crime Delinq. Abstr.	Crime and Delinquency Abstracts (Ceased)
Crime Delinq.Lit.	Crime & Delinquency Literature (Now: Criminal Justice Abstracts)
Cub.Stud.	Cuban Studies
Cum.Comput. Abstr.	Cumulative Computer Abstracts (Ceased)
Curr.Adv.Ecol.Sci.	Current Advances in Ecological Sciences
Curr.Adv.Plant Sci.	Current Advances in Plant Science
Curr.Aus.N.Z. Leg. Lit.Ind.	Current Australian and New Zealand Legal Literature Index
Curr.Bibl. Aquatic Sci.& Fish	Current Bibliography for Aquatic Sciences & Fisheries (Now: Aquatic Sciences and Fisheries Abstracts
Curr.Biotech.Abstr.	Current Biotechnology Abstracts
Curr.Bk.Rev.Cit.	Current Book Review Citations (Ceased)
Curr.Chem.React.	Current Chemical Reactions
Curr.Cont.	Current Contents
Curr.Cont.Africa	Current Contents Africa (Ceased)
Curr.Dig.Sov. Press	Current Digest of Soviet Press
Curr.Ind. Commonw. Leg.Per.	Current Index to Commonwealth Legal Periodicals (Ceased)
Curr.Ind.Stat.	Current Index to Statistics
Curr.Leather Lit.	Current Leather Literature
Curr.Lit.Blood	Current Literature of Blood (Ceased)
Curr.Lit.Fam.Plan.	Current Literature in Family Planning
Curr.Pack.Abstr.	Current Packaging Abstracts
Curr.Pap.Phys.	Current Papers in Physics
Curr.Tech.Ind.	Current Technology Index
Curr.Tit. Electrochem.	Current Titles in Electrochemistry
Curr.Tit.Ocean	Current Titles in Ocean, Coastal, Lake & Waterway Sciences
Cyb.Abstr.	Cybernetics Abstracts

D

D.A.	Dissertation Abstracts (Now: Dissertation Abstracts International)
DM&T	Defense Markets and Technology (Now: Aerospace Defense Markets and Technology)
DNP	Digest of Neurology & Psychiatry
DSH Abstr.	D S H Abstracts (Deafness, Speech and Hearing)
Dairy Sci.Abstr.	Dairy Science Abstracts
Data Process.Dig.	Data Processing Digest
Deep Sea Res.& Oceanogr.Abstr.	Deep Sea Research & Oceanographic Abstracts (Now: Deep-Sea Research with Oceanographic Literature Review)
Dent.Abstr.	Dental Abstracts
Dent.Ind.	Index to Dental Literature
Devindex	Devindex (Ceased)
Diab.Lit.Ind.	Diabetes Literature Index (Ceased)
Dir.Pub.Proc.SSH	Directory of Published Proceedings, Series S S H - Social Sciences/Humanities
Doc.Abstr.	Documentation Abstracts (Now: Information Science Abstracts)
Doc.Geogr.	Documentatio Geographica (Now: Dokumentation zur Raumentwicklung) (Ceased)
Dok.Arbeitsmed.	Dokumentation Arbeitsmedizin (Now: Beruf und Gesundheit)
Dok.Raum.	Dokumentation zur Raumentwicklung (Ceased)
Dok.Str.	Dokumentation Strasse

E

EC Ind.	E C Index (European Communities)
E.I.	E I (Excerpta Indonesica)
ERIC	Eric Clearinghouse (See: C.I.J.E.)
Ecol.Abstr.	Ecological Abstracts
Econ.Abstr.	Economic Abstracts (Now: Key to Economic Science)
Educ.Admin.Abstr.	Educational Administration Abstracts
Educ.Ind.	Education Index
Educ.Tech.Abstr.	Educational Technology Abstracts
Ekist.Ind.	Ekistic Index
Elec.& Electron. Abstr.	Electrical & Electronics Abstracts
Electroanal.Abstr.	Electroanalytical Abstracts (Ceased)
Electron.Abstr.J.	Electronics Abstracts Journal (Now: Electronics and Communications Abstracts Journal)
Electron.& Communic. Abstr.J.	Electronics and Communications Abstracts Journal
Endocrin.Abstr.	Endocrinology Abstracts
Endocrin.Ind.	Endocrinology Index (Ceased)
Energy Abstr.	Energy Abstracts
Energy Ind.	Energy Index
Energy Info.Abstr.	Energy Information Abstracts
Energy Res.Abstr.	Energy Research Abstracts
Eng.Ind.	Engineering Index (Now: Engineering Index Monthly and Author Index)
Eng.Ind.India	Engineering Index of India
Eng.Mat.Abstr.	Engineering Materials Abstracts
Entomol.Abstr.	Entomology Abstracts
Environ.Abstr.	Environment Abstracts

ABSTRACTING AND INDEXING

Environ.Ind.	Environment Index
Environ.Per.Bibl.	Environmental Periodicals Bibliography
Environ.Qual. Abstr.	Environmental Quality Abstracts (Ceased)
Ergon.Abstr.	Ergonomics Abstracts
Except.Child Educ. Abstr.	Exceptional Child Education Abstracts (Now: Exceptional Child Education Resources)
Excerp.Bot.	Excerpta Botanica
Excerp.Criminol.	Excerpta Criminologica (Now: Criminology and Penology Abstracts)
Excerp.Med.	Excerpta Medica

F

F.A.C.T.	Fuel Abstracts and Current Titles (Now: Fuel and Energy Abstracts)
FAMLI	FAMLI (Family Medicine Literature Index)
F.R.	Fanatic Reader
Fababean Abstr.	Fababean Abstracts
Farm & Garden Ind.	Farm & Garden Index
Fed Print	Fed in Print
Fert.Abstr.	Fertilizer Abstracts (Ceased)
Field Crop Abstr.	Field Crop Abstracts
Film Lit.Ind.	Film Literature Index
Fluidex	Fluidex
	Consists of:
	Civil Engineering Hydraulic Abstracts
	Current Fluid Engineering Titles (Ceased)
	Fluid Flow Measurement Abstracts
	Fluid Power Abstracts
	Fluid Sealing Abstracts
	Industrial Aerodynamics Abstracts
	Industrial Jetting Report
	Pipelines Abstracts
	Pumps and Other Fluids Machinery Abstracts
	Pumps and Turbines (Ceased)
	River and Flood Control Abstracts
	Solid Liquid Flow Abstracts
	Tribos-Tribology Abstracts
	World Ports and Harbours Abstracts
	World Ports and Harbours News (Ceased)
Food Sci.&Tech. Abstr.	Food Science and Technology Abstracts
Foreign Leg.Per.	Index to Foreign Legal Periodicals
Forest.Abstr.	Forestry Abstracts
Forest Prod.Abstr.	Forest Products Abstracts
Foul.Prev.Res.Dig.	Fouling Prevention Research Digest
Fr.Bibl.	French 20 Bibliography
Fuel & Energy Abstr.	Fuel & Energy Abstracts
Fut.Abstr.	Future - Abstracts
Fut.Surv.	Future Survey

G

G.Indian Per.Lit.	Guide to Indian Periodical Literature
G.Perf.Arts	Guide to the Performing Arts (Ceased)
G.Soc.Sci.& Rel. Per.Lit.	Guide to Social Science and Religion in Periodical Literature
Gas Abstr.	Gas Abstracts
Gastroenterol: Abstr.& Cit.	Gastroenterology: Abstracts & Citations (Ceased)
Gdlns.	Guidelines
Gen.Phys.Adv. Abstr.	General Physics Advance Abstracts
Gen.Sci.Ind.	General Science Index
Geneal.Per.Ind.	Genealogical Periodical Annual Index
Genet.Abstr.	Genetics Abstracts
Geo.Abstr.	Geographical Abstracts (Parts A, B, C, D, E, F, G)
Geophys.Abstr.	Geophysical Abstracts (Ceased)
GeoRef	See: Bibliography and Index of Geology
Geosci.Doc.	Geoscience Documentation
Geotech.Abstr.	Geotechnical Abstracts
Geotimes	Geotimes
Ger.J.Psych.	German Journal of Psychology
Gleanings	Gleanings
Graph.Arts Abstr.	Graphic Arts Abstracts
Graph.Arts Lit. Abstr.	Graphic Arts Literature Abstracts

H

HR Rep.	Human Rights Internet Reporter
HRIS	H R I S Abstracts (Highway Research Information Service)
Helminthol.Abstr.	Helminthological Abstracts
Hlth.Dev.Alerts	Health Devices Alerts
Hlth.Phys.Educ.& Rec.	Health, Physical Education and Recreation Microform Publication Bulletin
Herb.Abstr.	Herbage Abstracts
High.Educ.Abstr.	Higher Education Abstracts
High.Educ.Curr. Aware.Bull.	Higher Education Current Awareness Bulletin
Hisp.Amer.Per.Ind.	Hispanic American Periodicals Index
Hist.Abstr.	Historical Abstracts
Hort.Abstr.	Horticultural Abstracts
Hosp.Abstr.	Hospital Abstracts (Now: Health Service Abstracts)
Hosp.Abstr.Serv.	Hospital Abstracts Service (Ceased)
Hosp.Lit.Ind.	Hospital Literature Index
Hum.Ind.	Humanities Index
Human Resour. Abstr.	Human Resources Abstracts
Hung.Build.Bull.	Hungarian Building Bulletin
Hung.Lib.& Info. Sci.Abstr.	Hungarian Library and Information Science Abstracts
Hwy.Res.Abstr.	Highway Research Abstracts (Ceased)

I

IBM PC Ind.	I B M PC Index (Personal Computer)
I.C.U.I.S.Abstr.	I C U I S Abstracts Service (Institute on the Church in Urban Industrial Society) (Now: I C U I S Justice Ministries)
I D A	International Development Abstracts
I.M.M.Abstr.	I M M Abstracts (Institute of Mining & Metallurgy)
I.N.E.P.	Index to New England Periodicals
INIS Atomind.	I N I S Atomindex (International Nuclear Information System)
INSPEC	See: Sci.Abstr.
I.P.A.	International Pharmaceutical Abstracts
I.R.A.	Information Resources Annual
I.R.E.B.I.	Indices de Revista de Bibliotecologia
ISIS	I S I S Guide to Psi Periodicals (Inner-Space Interpreters Service)
ISMEC	I S M E C Bulletin (Information Service in Mechanical Engineering)
Immun.Abstr.	Immunology Abstracts
Ind.Agri.Am.Lat. Caribe	Indice Agricole de America Latina y el Caribe
Ind.Amer.Per. Verse	Index of American Periodical Verse
Ind.Artic.Jew.Stud.	Index of Articles on Jewish Studies
Ind.Bk.Rev.Hum.	Index to Book Reviews in the Humanities
Ind.Bus.Rep.	Index to Business Reports
Ind.Chem.	Index Chemicus (Now: Current Abstracts of Chemistry & Index Chemicus)
Ind.Child.Mag.	Subject Index to Children's Magazines (Now: Children's Magazines Guide)
Ind.Curr.Urb.Doc.	Index to Current Urban Documents
Ind.Develop.Abstr.	Industrial Development Abstracts
Ind.Econ.J.	Index of Economic Journals (Now: Index of Economic Articles in Journal and Collective Volumes)
Ind.Free Per.	Index to Free Periodicals
Ind.Heb.Per.	Index to Hebrew Periodicals
Ind.How To Do It	Index to How to Do It Information
Ind.Hyg.Dig.	Industrial Hygiene Digest
Ind.India	Index India
Ind.Islam.	Index Islamicus
Ind.Jew.Per.	Index to Jewish Periodicals
Ind.Lit.Amer. Indian	Index to Literature on the American Indian (Ceased)
Ind.Lit.Dent.	Indice de la Literatura Dental Periodica en Castellano
Ind.Little Mag.	Index to Little Magazines
Ind.Med.	Index Medicus
Ind.Med.Esp.	Indice Medico Espanol
Ind.N.Z.Per.	Index to New Zealand Periodicals
Ind.Per.Art.Relat. Law	Index to Periodical Articles Related to Law
Ind.Per.Blacks	Index to Periodical Articles by and about Blacks
Ind.Per.Lit.	Index to Indian Periodical Literature (Ceased)
Ind.Per.Negroes	Index to Periodical Articles by & about Negroes (Now: Index to Periodical Articles by & about Blacks)
Ind.Phil.Per.	Index to Philippine Periodicals
Ind.Rheum.	Annual Index of Rheumatology
Ind.S.A.Per.	Index to South African Periodicals
Ind.Sci.Rev.	Index to Scientific Reviews
Ind.Sel.Per.	Index to Selected Periodicals (Now: Index to Periodical Articles by & about Blacks)
Ind.SST.	Index to Spanish Science and Technology
Ind.U.S.Gov.Per.	Index to U.S. Government Periodicals
Ind.Vet.	Index Veterinarius
Indian Educ.Abstr.	Indian Education Abstracts
Indian Lib.Sci. Abstr.	Indian Library Science Abstracts
Indian Psychol. Abstr.	Indian Psychological Abstracts
Indian Sci.Abstr.	Indian Science Abstracts
Indian Sci.Ind.	Indian Science Index (Ceased)
Info.Media & Tech.	Information Media and Technology
Inform.Sources	Information Sources
Inpharma	InPharma
Instrum.Abstr.	Instrument Abstracts (Now: Metron) (Ceased)
Int.Abstr.Biol.Sci.	International Abstracts of Biological Sciences (Now: Current Awareness in Biological Sciences)
Int.Abstr.Oper.Res.	International Abstracts in Operations Research
Int.Aerosp.Abstr.	International Aerospace Abstracts
Int.Bibl.Soc.Sci.	International Bibliography of the Social Sciences: Anthropology, Political Science, Economics, Sociology (Ceased)
Int.Build.Serv. Abstr.	International Building Services Abstracts
Int.Dredg.Abstr.	International Dredging Abstracts (Now: World Ports and Harbours; see Fluidex)
Int.G.Class.Stud.	International Guide to Classical Studies (Ceased)
Int.Ind.	International Index (Now: Social Sciences Index and Humanities Index)
Int.Ind.Film Per.	International Index to Film Periodicals
Int.Nurs.Ind.	International Nursing Index (Now: International Nursing Index, Including Nursing Citation Index)
Int.Packag.Abstr.	International Packaging Abstracts
Int.Polit.Sci.Abstr.	International Political Science Abstracts
Int.Z.Bibelwiss.	Internationale Zietschriften fuer Bibelwissenschaft und Grenzgebiete
Intl.Bibl.Burns	International Bibliography on Burns
Intl.Bibl.S.S.Econ.	International Bibliography of the Social Sciences: Economic Science
Intl.Bibl.S.S.Pol. Sci.	International Bibliography of the Social Sciences: Political Science
Intl.Bibl.S.S. Soc.Cult.Anthro.	International Bibliography of the Social Sciences: Social and Cultural Anthropology

ABSTRACTING AND INDEXING   xxvii

Intl.Civil Eng. Abstr.	International Civil Engineering Abstracts
Intl.Ind.TV.	International Index to Television Periodicals
Intl.Mgmt.Info.	International Management Information Business Digest (Ceased)
Intl.Polym.Sci.& Tech.	International Polymer Science and Technology
Iron & Steel Indus. Pr.	Iron and Steel Industry Profile

J

JAMA	JAMA: The Journal of the American Medical Association
JCT	Japan Computer Technology and Applications Abstracts
J.Cont.Quant.Meth.	Journal Contents of Quantitative Methods
J.Curr.Laser Abstr.	Journal of Current Laser Abstracts
J.of Abstr.Int.Educ.	Journal of Abstracts in International Education
J.of Diss.& Soc.Ch.	Journals of Dissent and Social Change
J.of Doc.	Journal of Documentation
J.of Econ.Abstr.	Journal of Economic Abstracts (Now: Journal of Economic Literature)
J.of Econ.Lit.	Journal of Economic Literature
J.of Ferroc.	Journal of Ferrocement
Jap.Per.Ind.	Japanese Periodicals Index
Jazz Ind.	Jazz Index

K

Key to Econ.Sci.	Key to Economic Science
Key Word Ind.Ser.Titl.	Keyword Index to Serial Titles
Key Word Ind. Wildl.Res.	Key Word Index to Wildlife Research

L

LAMP	L A M P (Literature Analysis of Microcomputer Publications)
LCR	Literary Criticism Register
LHTN	Library Hi Tech News
L.I.I.	Life Insurance Index (Ceased)
LISA	Library & Information Science Abstracts
L.R.I.	Legal Resource Index
Lab.Haz.Bull	Laboratory Hazards Bulletin
Landwirt. Zentralbl.	Landwirtschaftliches Zentralblatt (Now: Agroselekt)
Lang.& Lang. Behav.Abstr.	Language and Language Behaviour Abstracts (Now: LLBA Linguistics and Language Behavior Abstracts)
Lang.Teach.& Ling.Abstr.	Language Teaching and Linguistics Abstracts (Now: Language Teaching)
Lat.Lit.Fam.Plan.	Latest Literature in Family Planning
Law Ofc.Info.Svc.	Law Office Information Service
Lead Abstr.	Lead Abstracts (Now: Leadscan)
Left Ind.	Left Index
Leg.Cont.	Legal Contents
Leg.Info.Manage.Ind.	Legal Information Management Index
Leg.Per.	Index to Legal Periodicals
Lib.Lit.	Library Literature
Lib.Sci.Abstr.	Library Science Abstracts (Now: Library & Information Science Abstracts)
Lit.Automat.	Literature on Automation (Now: New Literature on Automation)

M

MEDOC	MEDOC: Index to U.S. Government Publications in the Medical and Health Sciences
MEDSOC	Medical Socioeconomic Research Sources (Ceased)
MELSA	MELSA Messenger (Metropolitan Library Service) (Ceased)
M.L.A.	MLA Abstracts of Articles in Scholarly Journals (Ceased)
M.M.R.I.	Multi-Media Reviews Index (Now: Media Review Digest)
Mag.Ind.	Magazine Index
Maize Abstr.	Maize Abstracts
Man-Environ.Sys.	Man-Environment Systems
Manage.Abstr.	Management Abstracts (India)
Manage.& Market. Abstr.	Management and Marketing Abstracts
Manage.Cont.	Management Contents
Mar.Aff.Bibl.	Marine Affairs Bibliography
Mar.Sci.Cont.Tab.	Marine Science Contents Tables
Mark.Res.Abstr.	Market Research Abstracts
Mass Spectr.Bull.	Mass Spectrometry Bulletin
Math.R.	Mathematical Reviews
Med.Abstr.	Medical Abstract Service (Ceased)
Med.Care.Rev.	Medical Care Review
Med.Res.Ind.	Medical Research Index (Now: Medical Research Centres)
Media Rev.Dig.	Media Review Digest
Ment.Retard.Abstr.	Mental Retardation Abstracts (Now: Developmental Disabilities Abstracts) (Ceased)
Met.Abstr.	Metallurgical Abstracts (Now: Metals Abstracts) see also: Cleaning/Finishing/Coating Digest Corrosion Prevention/Inhibition Digest Heat Processing Abstracts
Met.Finish.Abstr.	Metal Finishing Abstracts (Now: Surface Treatment Technology Abstracts)
Meteoro.& Geo-astrophys. Abstr.	Meteorological & Geoastrophysical Abstracts
Meth.Per.Ind.	Methodist Periodical Index (Now: United Methodist Periodical Index) (Ceased)

Mgmt.Abstr.	Management Abstracts (Trinidad)
Mich.Doc.	Michigan Documents
Mich.Mag.Ind.	Michigan Magazine Index
Microbiol.Abstr.	Microbiological Abstracts
Microcomp.Ind.	Microcomputer Index
Microcomp.Indus.Up.	Microcomputer Industry Update
Mid.East: Abstr. & Ind.	Middle East: Abstracts and Index
Mineral.Abstr.	Mineralogical Abstracts
Mkt.Inform.Guide	Marketing Information Guide (Ceased)
Multi.Scler.Abstr.	Multiple Sclerosis Indicative Abstracts (Ceased)
Music Artic. Guide	Music Article Guide
Music Ind.	Music Index
Mycol.Abstr.	Abstracts of Mycology

N

NAA	N A A (Nordic Archaeological Abstracts)
NASA	N A S A Patent Abstracts Bibliography (National Aeronautics and Space Administration)
Nav.Abstr.	Naval Abstracts (Ceased)
Neurosci.Abstr.	Neurosciences Abstracts
New Per.Ind.	New Periodicals Index (Ceased)
New Sil.Tech	New Silver Technology
New Test.Abstr.	New Testament Abstracts
Noise Pollut. Publ.Abstr.	Noise Pollution Publications Abstracts
Nucl.Sci.Abstr.	Nuclear Science Abstracts (Superseded by: I N I S Atomindex & E R D A Research Abstracts)
Numis.Lit.	Numismatic Literature
Nurs.Abstr.	Nursing Abstracts
Nurs.Res.Abstr.	Nursing Research Abstracts
Nutr.Abstr.	Nutrition Abstracts & Reviews (Now: Nutrition Abstracts and Reviews Series A: Human and Experimental; Nutrition Abstracts and Reviews Series B: Livestock Feeds and Feeding)
Nutr.Plan.	Nutrition Planning

O

Occup.Saf.& Health Abstr.	Occupational Safety & Health Abstracts
Ocean.Abstr.	Oceanic Abstracts
Ocean.Abstr.Bibl.	Oceanic Abstracts and Bibliography (Now: Deep Sea Research with Oceanographic Literature Review)
Ocean.Ind.	Oceanic Index (Now: Oceanic Abstracts)
Old Test.Abstr.	Old Testament Abstracts
Oncol.Abstr.	Oncology Abstracts
Oper.Res.Manage.Sci.	Operations Research/Management Science
Ophthal.Lit.	Ophthalmic Literature
Oral Res.Abstr.	Oral Research Abstracts (Ceased)

P

P.A.I.S.	P A I S Bulletin (Public Affairs Information Service)
P.A.I.S.For.Lang.Ind.	Public Affairs Information Service Foreign Language Index
PC Abstr.	P C Abstracts (Personal Computing)
PHRA	Poverty & Human Resources Abstracts (Now: Human Resources Abstracts)
P.I.R.A.	P.I.R.A. Marketing Abstracts (Packaging Industry Research Association) (Now: Management and Marketing Abstracts)
P.L.I.I.	Property & Liability Insurance Index (Ceased)
P.M.I.	Photography Magazine Index
PMR	Popular Magazine Review
P.N.I.	Pharmaceutical News Index
PROMT	Predicasts Overview of Markets and Technologies
PSA	Police Science Abstracts
Packag.Abstr.	Packaging Abstracts (Now: International Packaging Abstracts)
Packag.Sci.Tech.	Packaging Science and Technology Abstracts
Paper.& Bd.Abstr.	Paper and Board Abstracts
Past.Care & Couns. Abstr.	Pastoral Care & Counseling Abstracts (Now: Abstracts of Research in Pastoral Care and Counseling)
Peace Res.Abstr.	Peace Research Abstracts Journal
Peace Res.Rev.	Peace Research Reviews
Peat Abstr.	Peat Abstracts
Perf.Arts Biog. Master Ind.	Performing Arts Biography Master Index
Periodex	Periodex (Now: Point de Repere)
Pers.Lit.	Personnel Literature
Pers.Manage.Abstr.	Personnel Management Abstracts
Petrol.Abstr.	Petroleum Abstracts
Petrol.Energy B.N.I.	Petroleum/Energy Business News Index
Pharmacog.Tit.	Pharmacognosy Titles (Ceased)
Phil.Ind.	Philosopher's Index
Philip.Abstr.	Philippine Abstracts (Now: Philippine Science & Technology Abstracts Bibliography)
Photo.Abstr.	Photographic Abstracts
Photo.Ind.	Photography Index
Photosyn.Bibl.	Photosynthesis Bibliography
Phys.Abstr.	Physics Abstracts (See: Science Abstracts)
Phys.Ber.	Physikalische Berichte (Now: Physics Briefs)
Phys.Ed.Ind.	Physical Education Index
Pinpointer	Pinpointer
Plant Breed.Abstr.	Plant Breeding Abstracts
Plant Grow.Reg.Abstr.	Plant Growth Regulator Abstracts

Plast.Abstr.	Plastic Abstracts (Ceased)
Pol.Tech.Abstr.	Polish Technical Abstracts (Now: Polish Technical and Economic Abstracts)
Polit.Sci.Abstr.	Political Science Abstracts
Pollut.Abstr.	Pollution Abstracts
Pop.Mus.Per.Ind.	Popular Music Periodicals Index (Ceased)
Pop.Per.Ind.	Popular Periodical Index
Popul.Ind.	Population Index
Potato Abstr.	Potato Abstracts
Poult.Abstr.	Poultry Abstracts
Pr.Briefs	Predi-Briefs
Predi.F & S Ind. Eur.	Predicasts F & S Index Europe
Predi.F & S Ind. Intl.	Predicasts F & S Index International
Predi.F & S Ind. U.S.	Predicasts F & S Index United States
Psychoanal.Abstr.	Psychoanalytic Abstracts
Psychol.Abstr.	Psychological Abstracts
Psychol.R.G.	Psychological Reader's Guide (Ceased)
Psychopharmacol. Abstr.	Psychopharmacology Abstracts (Ceased)
Psycscan	Psycscan: Applied Psychology
Psycscan C.P.	Psycscan: Clinical Psychology
Pt.de Rep.	Point de Repere (Formed by the merger of: Periodex and RADAR)
Pub.Admin.Abstr.	Public Administration Abstracts and Index of Articles (Now: Documentation in Public Administration)

Q

Qual.Contr. Appl.Stat.	Quality Control and Applied Statistics

R

RADAR	Repertoire Analytique d'Articles des Revues du Quebec (Now: Point de Repere)
RAPRA	RAPRA Abstracts (Rubber and Plastics Research Association of Great Britain)
R.G.	Readers' Guide to Periodical Literature
RICS	R I C S Abstracts and Reviews (Now: R I C S Library Information Service Abstracts and Reviews) (Royal Institute of Chartered Surveyors)
RILA	R I L A (International Repertory of the Literature of Art)
RILM	R I L M Abstracts of Music Literature (International Repertory of Music Literature)
Reac.	Reactions
Ref.Pt.Food Indus.Abstr.	Reference Point: Food Industry Abstracts
Ref.Sour.	Reference Sources
Ref.Zh.	Referativnyi Zhurnal
Refug.Abstr.	Refugee Abstracts
Rehabil.Lit.	Rehabilitation Literature (Ceased)
Rel.& Theol.Abstr.	Religious & Theological Abstracts
Rel.Ind.One	Religion Index One: Periodicals
Rel.Ind.Two	Religion Index Two: Multi-Author Works
Rel.Per.	Index to Religious Periodical Literature (Now: Religion Index One: Periodicals & Religion Index Two: Multi-Author Works)
Res.Educ.	Research in Education (Now: Resources in Education)
Res.High.Educ. Abstr.	Research into Higher Educaton Abstracts
Resour.Ctr.Ind.	Resource Center Index
Rev.Appl.Entomol.	Review of Applied Entomology (Series A, B)
Rev.Appl.Mycol.	Review of Applied Mycology (Now: Review of Plant Pathology)
Rev.Plant Path.	Review of Plant Pathology
Rheol.Abstr.	Rheology Abstracts
Rice Abstr.	Rice Abstracts
Risk Abstr.	Risk Abstracts
Robomat.	Robomatix Reporter
Rom.Sci.Abstr.	Romanian Scientific Abstracts
Rural Recreat. Tour.Abstr.	Rural Recreation and Tourism Abstracts (Now: Leisure, Recreation and Tourism Abstracts)

S

S.A.Waterabstr.	S.A. Waterabstracts (South Africa) (Ceased)
SCIMP	S C I M P: European Index of Management Periodicals (Selective Cooperative Index of Management Periodicals)
SOPODA	Social Planning, Policy and Development Abstracts
SSCI	Social Science Citation Index
Saf.Sci.Abstr.	Safety Science Abstracts Journal
Sage Fam.Stud. Abstr.	Sage Family Studies Abstracts
Sage Pub.Admin. Abstr.	Sage Public Administration Abstracts
Sage Urb.Stud. Abstr.	Sage Urban Studies Abstracts
Sci.Abstr.	Science Abstracts A. Physics Abstracts B. Electrical Engineering Abstracts C. Computer & Control Abstracts
Sci.Cit.Ind.	Science Citation Index
Sci.Res.Abstr.	Science Research Abstracts
Seed Abstr.	Seed Abstracts
Sel.Bibl.Homosex.	Selected Bibliography of Homosexuality
Sel.J.Water	Selected Journals on Water
Sel.Water Res.	Selected Water Resource Abstracts (Now: Hydro-Abstracts)

Sh.& Vib.Dig.	Shock and Vibration Digest		**U**
Sinop.Odontol.	Sinopse de Odontologia (Ceased)		
So.Pac.Per.Ind.	South Pacific Periodicals Index	Urb.Aff.Abstr.	Urban Affairs Abstracts
Soc.Sci.Ind.	Social Sciences Index		
Soc.Work Res.& Abstr.	Social Work Research & Abstracts		**V**
Sociol.Abstr.	Sociological Abstracts	Va.Hist.Abstr.	Virginia Historical Abstracts
Sociol.Educ.Abstr.	Sociology of Education Abstracts	Vert.File Ind.	Vertical File Index
Soft.Abstr.Eng.	Software Abstracts for Engineers	Vet.Bull.	Veterinary Bulletin
Soil & Fert.	Soils & Fertilizers	Virol.Abstr.	Virology Abstracts
Solid St.Abstr.	Solid State Abstracts (Now: Solid State Abstracts Journal)	Vis.Ind.	Vision Index (Ceased)
		VITIS	Vitis – Viticulture and Enology Abstracts
South.Bap.Per.Ind.	Southern Baptist Periodical Index (Ceased)		
Speleol.Abstr.	Speleological Abstracts		**W**
Sports Per.Ind.	Sports Periodicals Index		
Sportsearch	Sportsearch	W.R.C.Inf.	W.R.C. Information (Water Research Centre) (Now: Aqualine Abstracts)
Sri Lanka Sci.Ind.	Sri Lanka Science Index		
St.Educ.J.Ind.	State Education Journal Index	Water Pollut.Abstr.	Water Pollution Abstracts (Now: Aqualine Abstracts)
Stamp J.Ind.	Stamp Journals Index		
Stat.Theor. Meth.Abstr.	Statistical Theory and Method Abstracts	Water Resour.Abstr.	Water Resources Abstracts (Now: Hydro-Abstracts)
Steel Cas.Abstr.	Steel Castings Abstracts	Weed Abstr.	Weed Abstracts
Stud.Wom.Abstr.	Studies on Women Abstracts	Wild Life Rev.	Wildlife Review (Ceased)
Sugar Ind.Abstr.	Sugar Industry Abstracts (Now: Tate & Lyle's Sugar Industry Abstracts)	Wom.Stud.Abstr.	Women's Studies Abstracts
		Work Rel.Abstr.	Work Related Abstracts
		World Agri.Econ.& Rural Sociol. Abstr.	World Agricultural Economics & Rural Sociology Abstracts
	T		
TBRI	Technical Book Review Index	World Alum.Abstr.	World Aluminum Abstracts
T.C.E.A.	Theoretical Chemical Engineering Abstracts	World Bibl.Soc.Sec.	World Bibliography of Social Security
		World Fish.Abstr.	World Fisheries Abstracts (Ceased)
Tech.Educ.Abstr.	Technical Education Abstracts	World Surf.Coat.	World Surface Coatings Abstracts
Tech.Zentralbl.	Technisches Zentralblatt	World Text.Abstr.	World Textile Abstracts
Tel.Alert	Telecommunications Alert		
Telegen	Telegen Reporter		
Text.Digest.	Textile Digest		
Text.Tech.Dig.	Textile Technology Digest		**Y**
Therm.Abstr.	Thermal Abstracts (Now: International Building Services Abstracts)	Yrbk.Assoc.Educ.& Rehab.Blind	Association for Education and Rehabilitation of the Blind and Visually Handicapped. Yearbook
Tob.Abstr.	Tobacco Abstracts		
Tob.Bibl.	Tobacco Bibliography		
Top Manage.Abstr.	Top Management Abstracts (See: Anbar)		
Tox.Abstr.	Toxicology Abstracts		**Z**
Tr.& Indus.Ind.	Trade & Industry Index		
Trans.Res.Abstr.	Transportation Research Abstracts (Ceased)	Zent.Math.	Zentralblatt fuer Mathematik und ihre Grenzgebiete
Trop.Abstr.	Tropical Abstracts (Now: Abstracts on Tropical Agriculture)	Zion.Lit.	Zionist Literature
		Zoo.Rec.	Zoological Record
Trop.Dis.Bull.	Tropical Diseases Bulletin		

Subject Guide to Abstracting and Indexing

The 121 subject headings listed below are major subjects which contain a sub-category headed "Abstracting, Bibliographies, Statistics." This sub-category, which follows the major subject headings in the Classified List of Periodicals, identifies publications which abstract and/or index publications in the relevant subject. Bibliographies and statistical publications pertaining to the subject are also included in this sub-category. This guide will enable users to quickly locate subject areas of interest for which abstracting and indexing publications have been identified and to build profiles by combination of relevant subject areas. Page numbers refer to the first page on which the sub-category appears.

SUBJECT CATEGORY	PAGE
A	
Adventure and Romance	14
Advertising and Public Relations	16
Aeronautics and Space Flight	22
Agriculture	38
Anthropology	78
Archaeology	96
Architecture	100
Art	113
Astronomy	118
B	
Beverages	120
Biography	136
Biology	149
Birth Control	179
Blind	180
Building and Construction	188
Business and Economics	202
C	
Ceramics, Glass and Pottery	320
Chemistry	325
Children and Youth	334
Classical Studies	339
Clothing Trade	340
College and Alumni	342
Communications	345
Computers	353

SUBJECT CATEGORY	PAGE
Conservation	368
Consumer Education and Protection	369
Criminology and Law Enforcement	373
D	
Dance	375
Drug Abuse and Alcoholism	378
E	
Earth Sciences	381
Education	422
Electricity and Electrical Engineering	461
Encyclopedias and General Almanacs	463
Energy	468
Engineering	475
Environmental Studies	500
Ethnic Interests	506
F	
Fire Prevention	507
Fish and Fisheries	514
Folklore	517
Food and Food Industries	521
Forests and Forestry	529
G	
Gardening and Horticulture	534
Genealogy and Heraldry	537

Geography 551
Gerontology and Geriatrics 552

H

Heating, Plumbing and Refrigeration 554
History 562
Hobbies 614
Home Economics 615
Homosexuality 616
Hospitals 618
Hotels and Restaurants 621
Housing and Urban Planning 627
Humanities: Comprehensive Works 634

I

Industrial Health and Safety 636
Instruments 637
Insurance 642
Interior Design and Decoration 643

J

Jewelry, Clocks and Watches 645
Journalism 647

L

Labor Unions 649
Law 668
Leather and Fur Industries 672
Library and Information Sciences 687
Linguistics 709
Literary and Political Reviews 712
Literature 738

M

Machinery 746
Mathematics 755
Medical Sciences 768
Meetings and Congresses 796
Metallurgy 801
Meteorology 808
Metrology and Standardization 810
Military 813
Mines and Mining Industry 821
Motion Pictures 825
Museums and Art Galleries 831
Music 843

N

Nutrition and Dietetics 847

O

Occupations and Careers 849
Oriental Studies 854

P

Packaging 855
Paints and Protective Coatings 856
Paleontology 858
Paper and Pulp 859
Patents, Trademarks and Copyrights 861
Petroleum and Gas 867
Pharmacy and Pharmacology 873
Philosophy 883
Photography 885
Physical Fitness and Hygiene 886
Physics 892
Plastics 901
Political Science 911
Population Studies 925
Printing 931
Psychology 938
Public Administration 947
Public Health and Safety 958
Publishing and Book Trade 963

R

Real Estate 966
Religions and Theology 974
Rubber 986

S

Sciences: Comprehensive Works 1003
Shoes and Boots 1005
Social Sciences: Comprehensive Works 1014
Social Services and Welfare 1022
Sociology 1031
Sound Recording and Reproduction 1032
Sports and Games 1036

T

Technology: Comprehensive Works 1072
Textile Industries and Fabrics 1075
Theater 1079
Tobacco 1080
Transportation 1084
Travel and Tourism 1119

V

Veterinary Science 1123

W

Water Resources 1127
Women's Interests 1130

International Standard Serial Number (ISSN)

1. What is the ISSN?

An internationally accepted, concise, unique and unambiguous code for the identification of serial publications. One ISSN represents one serial.

The ISSN consists of seven numbers with an eighth check digit calculated according to Modulus 11 and used to verify the number in computer processing. A hyphen is printed after the fourth digit, as a visual aid, and the abbreviation ISSN precedes the number.

A code indicating country of publication may be printed preceding the ISSN as an additional identifer; for example, UK ISSN 1234-5679.

2. How did the ISSN evolve as an international system?

The International Organization for Standardization Technical Committee 46 (ISO/TC 46) is the agency responsible for the development of the ISSN as an international standard. The organization responsible for the administration and assignment of ISSN is the International Center (IC) of the International Serials Data System (ISDS). The IC/ISDS, supported by the French government and Unesco, is located in Paris.

The implementation of the ISSN system started with the numbering of the 70,000 titles in the serials database of the R.R. Bowker Company (*Ulrich's International Periodicals Directory* and *Irregular Serials and Annuals*). The next serials database numbered was the *New Serial Titles 1950/70* cumulation listing 220,000 titles, cumulated, converted to magnetic tape and published by the R.R. Bowker Company in collaboration with the Serials Record Division of the Library of Congress. These two databases were used as the starting base for the implementation of the ISSN.

3. What types of publications are assigned ISSN?

For assignment of ISSN, a serial is defined by the International Serials Data System as: "a publication in print or in non-print form, issued in successive parts, usually having numerical or chronological designations, and intended to be continued indefinitely."

4. How is ISSN used?

ISSN, the tool for communication of basic information about a serial title with a minimum of error, is used for such processes as ordering, billing, inventory control, abstracting, and indexing. Authors use ISSN for copyright. In library processes, ISSN is used in operations such as acquisitions, claiming, binding, accessioning, shelving, cooperative cataloging, circulation, interlibrary loans, and retrieval of requests.

5. May a publication have an International Standard Book Number (ISBN) and an ISSN?

Yes! Monographic series (separate works issued indefinitely under a common title, generally in a uniform format with numeric designation) and annuals or titles planned to be issued indefinitely under the same title may be defined as serials. The ISSN is assigned to the serial title, while an ISBN is assigned to each individual title or monograph in the series.

A new ISBN is assigned to each volume or edition by the publisher, while the ISSN, which is assigned by the International Center, national or regional center, remains the same for each issue. Both numbers should be printed on the copyright page of each volume, with initials or words preceding each number for immediate identification. With the availability of both ISSN and ISBN, the problem of defining the overlap of serials and monographs has been resolved.

SAMPLE TITLE

ADVANCES IN THE BIOSCIENCES
ISSN 0065-3446
Vol. 1 Proceedings: Berlin. Schering Symposium of Endocrinology, Berlin. Ed. by Gerhard Raspe. 1969. 40.00 (ISBN 0-08-013395-9). Pergamon.
Vol. 2 Proceedings. Schering Symposium on Biodynamics & Mechanisms of Action of Steroid Hormones, Berlin. Ed. by Gerhard Raspe. 1969. 41.25 (ISBN 0-08-006942-8). Pergamon.
Vol. 3 Proceedings. Schering Workshop on Steroid Metabolism "in Vitro Versus in Vivo," Berlin. Ed. by Gerhard Raspe. 1969. 41.25 (ISBN 0-08-017544-9). Pergamon.
Vol. 4 Proceedings. Schering Symposium on Mechanisms Involved in Conception. Berlin. Ed. by Gerhard Raspe. 1970. text ed. 41.25 (ISBN 0-08-017546-5) Pergamon.
Vol. 25 Development of Responsiveness to Steroid Hormones. Alvin M. Kaye & Myra Kaye et al. LC 79-42938. 1980. 66.00 (ISBN 0-08-024940-X). Pergamon Press.

6. *Where should the ISSN appear on the serial?*

In a prominent position on or in each issue of the serial, such as front cover, back cover, title or copyright pages. ISDS recommends that the ISSN of a periodical be printed, whenever possible, in the upper right corner of the front cover.

Promotional and descriptive materials about the serial should include the ISSN.

7. *When a title changes is a new ISSN assigned?*

In most instances, a new ISSN is assigned when a title changes. However, the determination is made by the International Center or the national or regional center of ISDS. Publishers should report all title changes to their respective centers.

8. *How does a publisher apply for an ISSN?*

The publisher should maintain contact with the national, regional or International Center of ISDS. They require bibliographic evidence of the serial, including a copy of the title page and cover. There is no charge to the publisher for the assignment of ISSN.

For full information, publishers should contact the national library or bibliographic center in the country where they are publishing. The address for the International Center is:

> International Serials Data System (ISDS)
> International Center (for the Registration of
>   Serial Publications)
> 20 rue Bachaumont
> 75002 Paris, France

The address for the National Center in the United States is:

> National Serials Data Program
> Library of Congress
> Washington, DC 20540
> (202) 426-6451

Subjects

ENGLISH	FRENCH	GERMAN	SPANISH
Abstracting and Indexing Services	Services d'Analyse et Indexage	Referate-und Indexdienste	Servicios de Extractos e Indices
Adventure and Romance	Aventure et Romance	Abenteuer und Liebesgeschichte	Aventura y Romance
Advertising and Public Relations	Publicité et Relations Publiques	Reklamewesen und Public Relations	Publicidad y Relaciones Públicas
Aeronautics and Space Flight	Aéronautique et Astronautique	Luft- und Raumfahrt	Aeronáutica y Vuelo Espacial
Computer Applications	Applications des Ordinateurs	Computer Anwendung	Aplicaciónes de los Ordenadores
Agriculture	Agriculture	Landwirtschaft	Agricultura
Agricultural Economics	Agriculture Economique	Agrarökonomie	Economía Agrícola
Agricultural Equipment	Outillage Agricole	Gerate	Aparatos Agrícolas
Computer Applications	Applications des Ordinateurs	Computer Anwendung	Aplicaciónes de los Ordenadores
Crop Production and Soil	Récolte et Terre	Produkte und Boden	Producción de Cosecha, Tierra
Dairying and Dairy Products	Production Laitière	Milchwirtschaft	Lechería y Productos Lácteos
Feed, Flour and Grain	Pature, Farine et Grain	Futter, Mehl und Getreide	Forraje, Granos y Harina
Poultry and Livestock	Elevage	Geflügel-und Viehwirtschaft	Ganadería
Anthropology	Anthropologie	Anthropologie	Antropología
Antiques	Antiquités	Antiquitäten	Antiguedades
Archaeology	Archeologie	Archaeologie	Arqueología
Computer Applications	Applications des Ordinateurs	Computer Anwendung	Aplicaciónes de los Ordenadores
Architecture	Architecture	Architektur	Arquitectura
Art	Art	Kunst	Arte
Computer Applications	Applications des Ordinateurs	Computer Anwendung	Aplicaciónes de los Ordenadores
Arts and Handicrafts	Arts et Metiers	Kunst und Handwerk	Artes y Manos de Obra
Astrology	Astrologie	Astrologie	Astrología
Astronomy	Astronomie	Astronomie	Astronomía
Beauty Culture	Soins de Beauté	Schönheitspflege	Belleza Personal
Perfumes and Cosmetics	Parfums et Cosmétiques	Kosmetik und Parfüme	Perfumes y Cosméticos
Beverages	Boissons	Getränke	Bebidas
Bibliographies	Bibliographies	Bibliographien	Bibliografías
Biography	Biographie	Biographie	Biografía
Biology	Biologie	Biologie	Biología
Biological Chemistry	Chimie Biologique	Biochemie	Química Biológica
Biophysics	Biophysique	Biophysik	Biofísica
Botany	Botanique	Botanik	Botánica
Cytology and Histology	Cytologie et Histologie	Zytologie und Histologie	Citología e Histología
Entomology	Entomologie	Entomologie	Entomología
Genetics	Génétique	Genetik	Genética
Microbiology	Microbiologie	Mikrobiologie	Microbiología
Microscopy	Microscopie	Mikroskopie	Microscopia
Ornithology	Ornithologie	Ornithologie	Ornitología
Physiology	Physiologie	Physiologie	Fisiología
Zoology	Zoologie	Zoologie	Zoología
Birth Control	Réglementation de la Natalité	Geburtenregelung	Reglamentación del Nacimiento
Blind	Aveugles	Blinde	Ciegos
Building and Construction	Batiment et Construction	Bauwesen	Edificios y Construcción
Carpentry and Woodwork	Charpenterie et Menuiserie	Zimmerhandwerk und Holzbau	Carpintería y Ebanistería
Hardware	Quincaillerie	Metallbaustoffe	Quincalla
Business and Economics	Affaires et Economie	Wirtschaft und Handel	Negocios y Economía
Accounting	Comptabilité	Rechnungswesen	Contabilidad
Banking and Finance	Banque et Finance	Bank-und Finanzwesen	Bancos y Finanzas
Banking and Finance-Computer Applications	Banque et Finance-Applications des Ordinateurs	Bank-und Finanzwesen-Computer Anwendung	Bancos y Finanzas-Aplicaciónes de los Ordenadores
Chamber of Commerce Publications	Publications des Chambres de Commerce	Veröffentlichungen von Handelkammern	Publicaciones de las Cámaras de Comercio
Computer Applications	Applications des Ordinateurs	Computer Anwendung	Aplicaciónes de los Ordenadores
Cooperatives	Coopératives	Genossenschaften	Cooperativos
Domestic Commerce	Commerce Interieur	Binnenhandel	Comercio Interior
Economic Situation and Conditions	Situations et Conditions Economiques	Wirtschaftliche Situation und Verhältnisse	Situaciones y Condiciones Económicas
Economic Systems and Theories, Economic History	Systémes et Theories Economiques, Histoire Economique	Ökonomische Systeme und Theorien, Wirtschaftsgeschichte	Sistemas y Teorías Económicos, Historia Ecónomica
International Commerce	Commerce International	Aussenhandel	Comercio Internacional
International Development and Assistance	Développement et Assistance Internationaux	Internationale Entwicklungshilfe	Desarrollo y Asistencia Internacionales
Investments	Investissements	Investitionen	Inversiones
Labor and Industrial Relations	Travail et Relations Industrielles	Arbeits- und Industrielle Beziehungen	Trabajo y Realciones Industriales
Macroeconomics	Macroeconomique	Makroökonomie	Macroeconomía
Management	Gestion	Betriebsführung	Gerencia
Marketing and Purchasing	Cours et Achats	Marketing und Kauf	Compra y Venta
Office Equipment and Services	Matériel et Entretien de Bureaux	Büroeinrichtung und Service	Equipo y Servicios de Oficinas
Personnel Management	Direction de Personnel	Personal Führung	Dirección de Empleados
Production of Goods and Services	Production	Produktion	Producción
Public Finance, Taxation	Finance Publique, Impots	Staatsfinanzen, Steuerwesen	Finanza Publica, Impuestos
Small Business	Petites et Moyennes Affaires	Kleinbetrieb	Negocios Pequeños
Trade and Industrial Directories	Directoires de Commerce et Industrie	Firmenverzeichnisse	Directorios de Comercio y Industria
Ceramics, Glass and Pottery	Céramique, Verrerie et Poterie	Keramik, Glas und Töpferei	Cerámica, Vidrio y Porcelana
Chemistry	Chimie	Chemie	Química

SUBJECTS

Analytical Chemistry	Chimie Analytique	Analytische Chemie	Química Analítica
Crystallography	Cristallographie	Kristallographie	Cristalografía
Electrochemistry	Electrochemie	Elektrochemie	Electroquímica
Inorganic Chemistry	Chimie Inorganique	Anorganische Chemie	Química Inorgánica
Organic Chemistry	Chimie Organique	Organische Chemie	Química Orgánica
Physical Chemistry	Chimie Physique	Physikalische Chemie	Fisicoquímica
Children and Youth	Enfance et Adolescence	Kinder und Jugendliche	Niños y Jóvenes
About	Au Sujet de	Über	Acerca
For	Pour	Für	Para
Civil Defense	Defense Civile	Ziviler Bevölkerungsschutz	Defensa Civil
Classical Studies	Etudes Classiques	Klassische Studien	Estudios Clásicos
Cleaning and Dyeing	Nettoyage et Teinturerie	Reinigen und Farben	Limpieza y Tintura
Clothing Trade	Vêtement	Bekleidungsgewerbe	Industria de Vestidos
Fashions	Mode	Moden	Modas
Clubs	Clubs	Klubs	Clubes
College and Alumni	Université et Diplomés	Universitäten und Hochschul-Absolventen	Universidades y Exalumnos
Communications	Communications	Nachrichtentechnik	Comunicaciones
Computer Applications	Applications des Ordinateurs	Computer Anwendung	Aplicaciónes de los Ordenadores
Postal Affairs	Postes	Postwesen	Correo
Radio and Television	Radio et Télévision	Rundfunk und Fernsehen	Radio y Televisión
Telephone and Telegraph	Téléphone et Télégraphe	Telephon und Telegraph	Teléfono y Telégrafo
Computers	Ordinateurs	Computer	Ordenadores
Artificial Intelligence	Intelligence Artificielle	Künstliche-Intelligenz	Inteligencia Artificial
Automation	Automation	Automatishe	Automación
Calculating Machines	Calculateurs	Rechenmaschine	Calculadoras
Circuits	Circuits	Kreisbewegung	Circuitos
Computer Architecture	Architecture de la Machine	Computer Architektur	Arquitectura de los Ordenadores
Computer-Assisted Instruction	Enseignement Assisté par Ordinateur	Computer Beistande Anweisung	Instrucción con la Ayuda de Ordenador
Computer Engineering	Technique d'Ordinateur	Computer Bewerkstellingen	Ingeniería de Ordenador
Computer Games	Jeux des Ordinateurs	Computer Spiele	Juegos de Ordenadores
Computer Graphics	Conception Assistée par Ordinateur	Computer Graphische	Diseño con la Ayuda de Ordenador
Computer Industry	Industrie d'Ordinateur	Computer Fleiss	Industrias de los Ordenadores
Computer Industry Directories	Annuaire de la Industrie Ordinateur	Computer Fleiss Fernsprechbuch	Directorios de los Ordenadores
Computer Industry, Vocational Guidance	Industrie d'Ordinateur, Orientation Professionnelle	Computer Fleiss Berufsberatung Ratschlag	Industria de los Ordenadores Gobierno Práctico
Computer Music	Musique d'Ordinateur	Computer Musik	Música de Ordenadores
Computer Networks	Reseaux des Ordinateurs	Computer Netzwerk	Red para Transmición de Datos
Computer Programming	Programme Machine	Computer Programm	Programa de Ordenador
Computer Sales	Ventes des Ordinateurs	Computer Verkaufen	Ventas de Ordenadores
Computer Security	Protection des Ordinateurs	Computer Sicherheit	Protección de los Ordenadores
Computer Simulation	Simulation des Ordinateurs	Computer Verstellung	Simulation de los Ordenadores
Computer Systems	Systemes des Ordinateurs	Computer Systemen	Sistemas de los Ordenadores
Cybernetics	Cybernetiques		Cibernéticas
Data Communications, Data Transmission Systems	Données de Communication	Daten Bekanntmachung, Daten Verschickung Systems	Datos de Comunicación
Data Base Management	Gestion de Base de Données		Gestión de Banco de Datos
Electronic Data Processing	Traitement de l'Information Electronique	Elektrisiert- Daten Aufbereitung	Proceso de Datos Electronico
Hardware	Materiel	Eisenwaren	Equipo Físico
Information Science, Information Theory	Théorie de l'Information	Nachrichtenswissenschaft, Nachrichtenstheorie	Teoría de la Información
Machine Theory	Theorie de Machine	Maschinetheorie	Teoría de la Maquina
Microcomputers	Micro-Ordinateurs	Mikrocomputer	Microordenadores
Minicomputers	Mini-Ordinateurs	Minicomputer	Miniordenadores
Personal Computers	Ordinateurs Privé	Persoenlichecomputer	Ordenador Personal
Software	Ligiciel	Weichwaren	Soporte Lógico
Theory of Computing	Théorie de Traitement	Computertheorie	Theoria de Cálculo
Word Processing	Traitement de Textes	Wortbehandlung	Proceso de la Palabras
Conservation	Conservation	Landschaftsschutz	Conservación
Consumer Education and Protection	Protection de Consommateur	Verbraucherswirtschaftsschutz	Protección del Consumidor
Criminology and Law Enforcement	Criminologie et Police	Kriminologie und Strafvollzug	Criminología y Acción Policial
Criminology and Law Enforcement Security	Criminologie et Police Securité	Kriminologie und Strafvollzug Sicherheit	Criminología y Accion Policial Seguridad
Dance	Danse	Tanz	Baile
Deaf	Sourds	Gehörlose	Sordos
Drug Abuse and Alcoholism	Toxicomanie et Alcoolisme	Rauschgiftsucht und Alkoholismus	Drogadismo y Alcoholismo
Earth Sciences	Sciences Géologiques	Wissenschaften der Erde	Ciencias Geológicas
Geology	Géologie	Geologie	Geología
Geophysics	Géophysique	Geophysik	Geofísica
Hydrology	Hydrologie	Hydrologie	Hidrología
Oceanography	Océanographie	Ozeanographie	Oceanografía
Education	Education	Bildungswesen	Educación
Adult Education	Enseignement des Adultes	Erwachsenenbildung	Enseñanza de Adultos
Computer Applications	Applications des Ordinateurs	Computer Anwendung	Aplicaciónes de los Ordenadores
Guides to Schools and Colleges	Guides d'Ecoles et Colleges	Führer zur Schulen und Universitaten	Guías de Escuelas y Colegios
Higher Education	Enseignement Supérieur	Hochschulwesen	Enseñanza Superior
International Education Programs	Programmes d'Education Internationale	Internazionale Erziehungs-Programme	Programas de Enseñanza Internacional
School Organization and Administration	Organisation et Administration de l'Ecole	Organisation und Verwaultung von dem Schule	Administración y Dirección de la Escuela
Special Education and Rehabilitation	Enseignement Special et Réhabilitation	Fachunterricht und Rehabilitierung	Enseñanza Especial y Rehabilitación
Teaching Methods and Curriculum	Méthodes Pédagogiques et Programmes Scolaires	Lehrmethoden und Lehrplan	Métodos de Enseñanza y Plan de Estudios
Electricity and Electrical Engineering	Electicité et Technique Electrique	Elektrizität und Elektrotechnik	Electricidad y Electrotécnica
Encyclopedias and General Almanacs	Encyclopédies et Almanachs Générales	Enzyklopädien und Allgemeine Nachschlagewerke	Enciclopedias y Almanaques Generales
Energy	Energie	Energie	Energía
Engineering	Génie	Ingenieurwesen	Ingeniería
Chemical Engineering	Génie Chimique	Chemieingenieurwesen	Ingeniería Química
Civil Engineering	Génie Civil	Bauingenieurwesen	Ingeniería Civil
Computer Applications	Applications des Ordinateurs	Computer Anwendung	Aplicaciónes de los Ordenadores
Engineering Mechanics and Materials	Mechanique de Génie et Materiels	Ingenieurwesen Mechanik und Materialien	Mecanica de Ingeniería y Materiales

SUBJECTS

Hydraulic Engineering	Génie Hydraulique	Wasserbau	Ingeniería Hidráulica
Mechanical Engineering	Génie Mécanique	Maschinenbau	Ingeniería Mecánica
Environmental Studies	Science de l'Environnement	Umweltschutz	Ciencias Ecológicas
Computer Applications	Applications des Ordinateurs	Computer Anwendung	Aplicaciónes de los Ordenadores
Ethnic Interests	Publications de l'Orientation Ethnïque	Veröffentlichungen von Minoritäten	Publicaciones de Temas Etnicos
Fire Prevention	Précaution contre l'Incendie	Brandbekaempfung	Prevención del Fuego
Fish and Fisheries	Poisson et Peche	Fische und Fischerei	Pesca y Pescados
Folklore	Folklore	Volkskunde	Folklore
Food and Food Industries	Alimentation et Industries Alimentaires	Nahrungsmittel und Lebensmittelindustrie	Alimentos e Industrias Alimenticias
Bakers and Confectioners	Boulangerie et Confiserie	Bäcker- und Konditorgewerbe	Panaderías y Dulcerías
Grocery Trade	Epicerie	Kolonialwarenhandel	Abacerías
Forest and Forestry	Forêts et Exploitation Forestière	Forstwesen und Waldwirtschaft	Bosques y Selvicultura
Lumber and Wood	Bois	Holz	Maderas
Funerals	Funérailles	Beerdigungen	Funerales
Gardening and Horticulture	Jardinage et Horticulture	Gartenpflege und Gartenbau	Jardinería y Horticultura
Florist Trade	Commerce des Fleurs	Blumenhandel	Floristas
Genealogy and Heraldry	Généalogie et Science Héraldique	Genealogie und Wappenkunde	Genealogía y Heráldica
Computer Applications	Applications des Ordinateurs	Computer Anwendung	Aplicaciónes de los Ordenadores
General Interest Periodicals (Subdivided by country)	Publications d'Intérêt Général (Selon pays)	Allgemeine Zeitschriften (nach Land)	Periódicos de Interés General (por país)
Geography	Géographie	Geographie	Geografia
Gerontology and Geriatrics	Gérontologie	Gerontologie	Gerontologiá y Geriátrica
Giftware and Toys	Cadeaux et Jouets	Geschenkartikel und Spielwaren	Regalos y Juguetes
Heating, Plumbing, and Refrigeration	Chauffage, Plomberie et Réfrigeration	Heizung, Kühlung und Installation	Calefaccion, Plomería y Refrigeración
History	Histoire	Geschichte	Historia
Computer Applications	Applications des Ordinateurs	Computer Anwendung	Aplicaciónes de los Ordenadores
History of Africa	Histoire de l'Afrique	Geschichte-Afrika	Historia de Af.ica
History of Asia	Histoire de l'Asie	Geschichte-Asien	Historia de Asia
History of Australasia	Histoire de l'Australasie	Geschichte-Australasien	Historia de Australasia
History of Europe	Histoire de l'Europe	Geschichte-Europa	Historia de la Europa
History of North and South America	Histoire de l'Amérique du Nord et du Sud	Geschichte-Nord- und Südamerika	Historia de la América del Norte y de la del Sur
History of Near East	Histoire du Proche-Orient	Geschichte-Nahe Osten	Historia del Cercano Oriente
Hobbies	Passe-Temps	Hobbies	Pasatiempos
Home Economics	Economie Domestique	Hauswirtschaft	Economía Doméstica
Homosexuality	Homosexualisme	Homosexualität	Homosexualismo
Hospitals	Hôpitaux	Krankenhäuser	Hospitales
Hotels and Restaurants	Hôtels et Restaurants	Hotels und Restaurants	Hoteles y Restaurantes
Housing and Urban Planning	Lógement et Urbanisme	Wohnungswesen und Stadteplanung	Viviendas y Urbanismo
Humanities: Comprehensive Works	Humanités: Oeuvres Comprehensives	Geisteswissenschaften	Humanidades: Obras Comprensivas
Computer Applications	Applications des Ordinateurs	Computer Anwendung	Aplicaciónes de los Ordenadores
Industrial Health and Safety	Médicine du Travail et Prevention	Arbeitsmedizin und Arbeitsschutz	Sanidad y Seguridad del Trabajo
Instruments	Instruments	Instrumente	Instrumentos
Insurance	Assurances	Versicherungswesen	Seguros
Interior Design and Decoration	Agencements Intérieurs et Décoration	Innenarchitektur und Innenausstattung	Diseño del Interior y Ornamentación
Furniture and House Furnishing	Meubles et Articles pour la Maison	Möbel und Wohnungseinrichtung	Muebles y Artículos para el Hogar
Jewelry, Clocks and Watches	Bijouterie et Horlogerie	Schmuck and Uhren	Joyería y Relojería
Journalism	Journalisme	Journalismus	Periodismo
Labor Unions	Syndicalisme	Gewerkschaften	Sindicatos
Law	Droit	Recht	Derecho
Computer Applications	Applications des Ordinateurs	Computer Anwendung	Aplicaciónes de los Ordenadores
International Law	Droit International	Völkerrecht	Derecho Internacional
Leather and Fur Industries	Maroquinerie et Pelleterie	Leder und Pelz	Pieles y Cuero
Library and Information Science	Bibliothéconomie et Informatique	Bibliothek-und Informationswissenschaft	Bibliotecología y Ciencia de la Información
Computer Applications	Applications des Ordinateurs	Computer Anwendung	Aplicaciónes de los Ordenadores
Linguistics	Linguistique	Sprachwissenschaft	Linguistica
Computer Applications	Applications des Ordinateurs	Computer Anwendung	Aplicaciónes de los Ordenadores
Literary and Political Reviews	Revues Littéraires et Politiques	Literarische und Politische Zeitschriften	Revistas Literarias y Políticas
Literature	Litterature	Literatur	Literatura
Poetry	Poésie	Poesie	Poesía
Machinery	Machines	Maschinenwesen	Maquinaria
Mathematics	Mathématiques	Mathematik	Matemática
Computer Applications	Applications des Ordinateurs	Computer Anwendung	Aplicaciónes de los Ordenadores
Medical Sciences	Sciences Médicales	Medizinische Wissenschaften	Ciencias Médicas
Allergology and Immunology	Allergologie et Immunologie	Allergie und Immunologie	Alergología e Imunología
Anaesthesiology	Anesthésiologie	Anaesthesiologie	Anestesiología
Cancer	Cancer	Krebs	Cancer
Cardiovascular Diseases	Maladies Cardiovasculaires	Kreislauferkrankungen	Enfermedades Cardiovasculares
Chiropractics, Homeopathy, Osteopathy	Chiropraxie, Homépathie, Ostéopathie	Chiropraktik, Homöopathie, Osteopathie	Quiropractica, Homeopatía Osteopatía
Communicable Diseases	Maladies Contagieuses	Infektiöse Krankheiten	Enfermedades Contagiosas
Computer Applications	Applications des Ordinateurs	Computer Anwendung	Aplicaciónes de los Ordenadores
Dentistry	Dentisterie	Zahnmedizin	Dentisteria
Dermatology and Venereology	Dermatologie et Maladies Vénériennes	Dermatologie und Geschlechtskrankheiten	Dermatología y Venereologia
Endocrinology	Endocrinologie	Endokrinologie	Endocrinología
Experimental Medicine Laboratory Technique	Médicine Expérimentale, Techniques de Laboratoire	Versuchsmedizin, Laboratoriumstechnik	Medicina Experimental, Tecnicas del Laboratorio
Forensic Sciences	Médecine Légale	Gerichtliche Medizin	Ciencias Forenses
Gastroenterology	Gastroentérologie	Gastroenterologie	Gastroenterología
Hematology	Hématologie	Hämatologie	Hematología
Hypnosis	Hypnose	Hypnose	Hipnotismo
Nurses and Nursing	Personnel et Soins Infirmiers	Krankenpflege	Enfermeras y Enfermería
Obstetrics and Gynecology	Obstétrique et Gynécologie	Gynäkologie und Geburtshilfe	Obstetricia y Ginecología
Ophthalmology and Optometry	Ophtalmologie et Optométrie	Opthalmologie und Optometrie	Oftalmología y Optometría
Orthopedics and Traumatology	Orthopédie et Traumatologie	Orthopädie und Traumatologie	Ortopedia y Traumatologia
Otorhinolaryngology	Otorhinolaryngologie	Otorhinolaryngologie	Otorinolaringología
Pediatrics	Pédiatrie	Pädiatrie	Pediatría
Psychiatry and Neurology	Psychiatrie et Neurologie	Psychiatrie und Neurologie	Psiquiatría y Neurología
Radiology and Nuclear Medicine	Radiologie et Médecine Nucléaire	Radiologie und Nuklearmedizin	Radiología y Medicina Nuclear
Respiratory Diseases	Maladies Respiratoires	Atmungskrankheiten	Enfermedades Respiratorios

xxxviii SUBJECTS

Rheumatology	Rhumatologie	Rheumatologie	Reumatología
Sports Medicine	Médecine du Sport	Sportmedizin	Medicina de Deportes
Surgery	Chirurgie	Chirurgie	Cirugía
Urology and Nephrology	Urologie et Néphrologie	Urologie und Nephrologie	Urología y Nefrología
Men's Interests	Interêts Masculins	Männer Interessen	Intereses masculinas
Meetings and Congresses	Réunions et Congrès	Tagungen und Kongresse	Conferencias y Congresos
Metallurgy	Métallurgie	Metallurgie	Metalurgia
Welding	Soudure	Schweissen	Soldadura
Meteorology	Météorologie	Meteorologie	Meteorología
Metrology and Standardization	Métrologie et Standardisation	Mass-und Gewichtskunde, Normung	Metrología y Normalización
Military	Militaires	Militärwesen	Militares
Mines and Mining Industry	Mines et Resources Minières	Bergbau und Hüttenwesen	Mines y Minerales
Motion Pictures	Cinéma	Film und Kino	Películas
Museums and Art Galleries	Musées et Galleries	Museen und Kunstgalerien	Museos y Galerías del Arte
Music	Musique	Musik	Música
Computer Applications	Applications des Ordinateurs	Computer Anwendung	Aplicaciónes de los Ordenadores
Needlework	Travaux à l'Aiguille	Nedelarbeiten	Bordados
Numismatics	Numismatique	Numismatik	Numismática
Nutrition and Dietetics	Nutrition et Diététique	Ernährung und Diätetik	Nutrición y Dieta
Occupations and Careers	Occupations et Carrières	Berufe	Empleos y Ocupaciones
Oriental Studies	Etudes Orientales	Orientalistik	Estudios Orientales
Packaging	Emballage	Verpackung	Empaque
Paints and Protective Coatings	Couleurs et Peintures	Farben	Pinturas y Manos Protectores
Paleontology	Paléontologie	Paleontologie	Paleontología
Paper and Pulp	Papier et Pulpe	Papier und Papierstoff	Papel y Pasta
Parapsychology and Occultism	Parapsychologie et Occultisme	Parapsychologie und Okkultismus	Parapsicología y Ocultismo
Patents, Trademarks and Copyrights	Brevets, Marques de Fabrique et Droits d'Auteur	Patente, Schutzmarken und Urheberrechte	Patentes, Marcas de Fabrica y Derechos de Autor
Petroleum and Gas	Pétrole et Gas Naturel	Petroleum und Gas	Petróleo y Gas Natural
Pets	Animaux Familiers	Haustiere	Animales Domésticos
Pharmacy and Pharmacology	Pharmacie et Pharmacologie	Pharmazie und Pharmakologie	Farmacia y Farmacología
Philately	Philatelie	Philatélie	Filatelia
Philosophy	Philosophie	Philosophie	Filosofía
Photography	Photographie	Photographie	Fotografía
Physical Fitness and Hygiene	Santé Physique et Hygiène	Gesundheitszustand und Hygiene	Salud Física e Higiene
Physics	Physique	Physik	Física
Heat	Chaleur	Wärme	Calor
Mechanics	Mécanique	Mechanik	Mecánica
Nuclear Energy	Energie Nucléaire	Kernphysik	Energía Nuclear
Optics	Optique	Optik	Optica
Sound	Son	Schall	Sonido
Plastics	Plastiques	Kunststoffe	Plásticos
Political Sciences	Sciences Politiques	Politische Wissenschaften	Ciencias Políticas
Civil Rights	Droits Civiques	Bürgerrechte	Derechos Civiles
International Relations	Relations Internationales	Internationale Beziehungen	Relaciones Internacionales
Population Studies	Démographie	Bevölkerungswissenschaft	Demografía
Printing	Imprimerie	Druck	Imprenta
Computer Applications	Applications des Ordinateurs	Computer Anwendung	Aplicaciónes de los Ordenadores
Psychology	Psychologie	Psychologie	Psicología
Public Administration	Administration Publique	Öffentliche Verwaltung	Administración Pública
Computer Applications	Applications des Ordinateurs	Computer Anwendung	Aplicaciónes de los Ordenadores
Municipal Government	Gouvernement Municipal	Kommunalverwaltung	Gobierno Municipal
Public Health and Safety	Santé Publique et Prevention	Öffentliche Gesundheitspflege	Salud Pública y Seguridad
Publishing and Book Trade	Edition et Commerce du Livre	Verlagswesen und Buchhandel	Editoriales y Librería
Computer Applications	Applications des Ordinateurs	Computer Anwendung	Aplicaciónes de los Ordenadores
Real Estate	Immobilières	Grundbesitz und Immobilien	Bienes Raices
Religions and Theology	Religions et Théologie	Religion und Theologie	Religión y Teología
Islamic	Islamique	Islamische	Islámico
Judaic	Judaique	Jüdäistische	Judaísmo
Oriental	Oriental	Orientalische	Oriental
Protestant	Protestant	Evangelische	Protestante
Roman Catholic	Catholique romain	Römisch-katholische	Católico romano
Other Sects	Autres sectes	Andere Sekte	Otras sectas
Rubber	Caoutchouc	Gummi	Caucho
Sciences: Comprehensive Works	Sciences: Oeuvres Comprehensives	Wissenschaften: Umfassende Werke	Ciencias: Obras Comprensivas
Computer Applications	Applications des Ordinateurs	Computer Anwendung	Aplicaciónes de los Ordenadores
Shoes and Boots	Chaussures et Bottes	Schuhe und Stiefel	Zapatos y Botas
Social Sciences: Comprehensive Works	Sciences Sociales: Oeuvres Comprehensives	Sozialwissenschaften: Umfassende Werke	Ciencias Sociales: Obras Comprensivas
Social Services and Welfare	Service Social et Protection Sociale	Sozialpflege und Fürsorge	Asistencia Social
Sociology	Sociologie	Soziologie	Sociología
Computer Applications	Applications des Ordinateurs	Computer Anwendung	Aplicaciónes de los Ordenadores
Sound Recording and Reproduction	Enregistrement et Reproduction du Son	Tonaufnahme und Tonwiedergabe	Grabaciones y Reproducciones Sonoras
Sports and Games	Sports et Jeux	Sport und Spiele	Deportes y Juegos
Ball Games	Jeux de Balle	Ballspiele	Juegos de Pelota
Bicycles and Motorcycles	Bicyclettes et Motocyclettes	Fahrräder und Motorräder	Bicicletas y Motocicletas
Boats and Boating	Bateaux et Canotage	Boote und Bootssport	Botes
Horses and Horsemanship	Equitation	Pferde und Reitsport	Caballos y Equitación
Outdoor Life	Vie en Plein Air	Im Freien	Vida de Campo
Statistics	Statistique	Statistik	Estadísticas
Technology: Comprehensive Works	Technologie: Oeuvres Comprehensives	Technologie: Umfassende Werke	Tecnologia: Obras Comprensivas
Textile Industries and Fabrics	Textiles	Textil	Textiles y Telas
Theater	Théâtre	Theater	Teatro
Tobacco	Tabac	Tabak	Tabaco
Transportation	Transports	Transport	Transporte
Air Transport	Transport Aérien	Luftverkehr	Transporte Aéreo
Automobiles	Automobiles	Kraftfahrzeugen	Automóviles
Computer Applications	Applications des Ordinateurs	Computer Anwendung	Aplicaciónes de los Ordenadores
Railroads	Chemins de Fer	Eisenbahnen	Ferrocarriles
Roads and Traffic	Routes et Circulation	Strassen und Strassenverkehr	Caminos y Circulación
Ships and Shipping	Navires et Transport Maritimes	Schiffe und Schiffahrt	Barcos y Embarques
Trucks and Trucking	Transports Routiers	Lastkraftwagen	Camiones
Travel and Tourism	Voyages et Tourisme	Reisen und Tourismus	Viajes y Turismo
Veterinary Sciences	Science Vétérinaire	Tierheilkunde	Veterinaria
Water Resources	Ressources de l'Eau	Wasserwirtschaft	Recursos de Aqua
Women's Interests	Publications d'Intérêt Feminin	Veröffentliche für Frauen	Publicaciones de Temas Femininas

Cross-Index to Subjects

Abortions see BIRTH CONTROL 179
Abrasives see MACHINERY 745, see also METALLURGY 796
ABSTRACTING AND INDEXING 1
ABSTRACTING AND INDEXING SERVICES 1
Accident Prevention see INDUSTRIAL HEALTH AND SAFETY 635, see also TRANSPORTATION - Roads and Traffic 1095
ACCOUNTING 220
Acoustics see PHYSICS - Sound 899
Activation Analysis see PHYSICS - Nuclear Energy 895
Actuarial Science see INSURANCE 637, see also MATHEMATICS 746
Acupuncture see MEDICAL SCIENCES 756
Addictions see DRUG ABUSE AND ALCOHOLISM 376
Adhesives see ENGINEERING - Chemical Engineering 477
ADULT EDUCATION 426
ADVENTURE AND ROMANCE 13
ADVENTURE AND ROMANCE — Abstracting, Bibliographies, Statistics 14
ADVERTISING AND PUBLIC RELATIONS 14
ADVERTISING AND PUBLIC RELATIONS — Abstracting, Bibliographies, Statistics 16
Advertising Art see ADVERTISING AND PUBLIC RELATIONS 14
Aerodynamics see PHYSICS - Mechanics 894
AERONAUTICS AND SPACE FLIGHT 17, see also ENGINEERING - Mechanical Engineering 491, TRANSPORTATION - Air Transport 1087
AERONAUTICS AND SPACE FLIGHT — Abstracting, Bibliographies, Statistics 22
AERONAUTICS AND SPACE FLIGHT — Computer Applications 22
Aerophysics see PHYSICS - Mechanics 894
Aerospace Medicine see MEDICAL SCIENCES 756
Aesthetics see ART 100, see also PHILOSOPHY 875
African History see HISTORY - History of Africa 564
African Studies see HISTORY - History of Africa 564
Agricultural Aviation see AERONAUTICS AND SPACE FLIGHT 17
Agricultural Chemistry see AGRICULTURE 22, see also CHEMISTRY 321
AGRICULTURAL ECONOMICS 44
Agricultural Engineering see AGRICULTURE 22, see also ENGINEERING 469
AGRICULTURAL EQUIPMENT 51
Agricultural Marketing see AGRICULTURE - Agricultural Economics 44, see also FOOD AND FOOD INDUSTRIES - Grocery Trade 522
AGRICULTURE 22, see also FOOD AND FOOD INDUSTRIES 517, FORESTS AND FORESTRY 523, GARDENING AND HORTICULTURE 531
AGRICULTURE — Abstracting, Bibliographies, Statistics 38
AGRICULTURE — Agricultural Economics 44
AGRICULTURE — Agricultural Equipment 51
AGRICULTURE — Computer Applications 51
AGRICULTURE — Crop Production And Soil 51
AGRICULTURE — Dairying And Dairy Products 61
AGRICULTURE — Feed, Flour And Grain 63
AGRICULTURE — Poultry And Livestock 64
Agronomy see AGRICULTURE 22
Air Conditioning see HEATING, PLUMBING AND REFRIGERATION 553
Air Defense see MILITARY 810
Air Force see MILITARY 810
Air Law see AERONAUTICS AND SPACE FLIGHT 17, see also LAW 649, TRANSPORTATION - Air Transport 1087
Air Navigation see AERONAUTICS AND SPACE FLIGHT 17
Air Pollution see ENVIRONMENTAL STUDIES 493
AIR TRANSPORT 1087
Airline In-Flight Magazines see TRANSPORTATION - AIR TRANSPORT 1087

Airplanes see AERONAUTICS AND SPACE FLIGHT 17, see also TRANSPORTATION - Air Transport 1087
Airports see AERONAUTICS AND SPACE FLIGHT 17, see also TRANSPORTATION - Air Transport 1087
Alcoholic Beverages see BEVERAGES 119
Alcoholism see DRUG ABUSE AND ALCOHOLISM 376
Algae see BIOLOGY - Botany 153
ALLERGOLOGY AND IMMUNOLOGY 773
Almanacs, General see ENCYCLOPEDIAS AND GENERAL ALMANACS 121
Alumni see COLLEGE AND ALUMNI 341
Amateur Radio see COMMUNICATIONS - Radio and Television 347
Amusement Guides see COMMUNICATIONS - Radio and Television 347, see also MUSIC 832, THEATER 1076, TRAVEL AND TOURISM 1105
ANAESTHESIOLOGY 774
Analogue Computation see COMPUTERS - Hardware 361, see also COMPUTERS - Theory of Computing 363
ANALYTICAL CHEMISTRY 326
Anatomy see BIOLOGY 137, see also MEDICAL SCIENCES 756
Ancient History see ARCHAEOLOGY 79, see also HISTORY 554
Angiology see MEDICAL SCIENCES - Cardiovascular Diseases 776
Animals see AGRICULTURE - Poultry and Livestock 64, see also BIOLOGY - Zoology 172, LEATHER AND FUR INDUSTRIES 672, PETS 868, SPORTS AND GAMES - Horses and Horsemanship 1042, VETERINARY SCIENCE 1120
ANTHROPOLOGY 68, see also ARCHAEOLOGY 79
ANTHROPOLOGY — Abstracting, Bibliographies, Statistics 78
Antibiotics see PHARMACY AND PHARMACOLOGY 869
ANTIQUES 79
Antiquities see CLASSICAL STUDIES 336
Apparel see CLOTHING TRADE 339
Appliances see ELECTRICITY AND ELECTRICAL ENGINEERING 450, see also HEATING, PLUMBING AND REFRIGERATION 553, INTERIOR DESIGN AND DECORATION - Furniture and House Furnishings 643
Applied Mechanics see ENGINEERING - Engineering Mechanics and Materials 485
Apprenticeship see OCCUPATIONS AND CAREERS 847
Aquariums see BIOLOGY - Zoology 172, see also FISH AND FISHERIES 507, PETS 868
ARCHAEOLOGY 79, see also ANTHROPOLOGY 68, ART 100, HISTORY 554
ARCHAEOLOGY — Abstracting, Bibliographies, Statistics 96
ARCHAEOLOGY — Computer Applications 96
Archery see SPORTS AND GAMES 1032
ARCHITECTURE 96, see also BUILDING AND CONSTRUCTION 181, ENGINEERING - Civil Engineering 480, HOUSING AND URBAN PLANNING 621
ARCHITECTURE — Abstracting, Bibliographies, Statistics 100
Archives see HISTORY 554, see also LIBRARY AND INFORMATION SCIENCES 672
Area Planning see HOUSING AND URBAN PLANNING 621
Armed Forces see MILITARY 810
ART 100
ART — Abstracting, Bibliographies, Statistics 113
ART — Computer Applications 113
Art Exhibitions see MUSEUMS AND ART GALLERIES 826
Art History see ART 100
Arteriosclerosis see MEDICAL SCIENCES - Cardiovascular Diseases 776
Arthritis see MEDICAL SCIENCES - Rheumatology 793
ARTIFICIAL INTELLIGENCE see COMPUTERS - ARTIFICIAL INTELLIGENCE 354

Arts see ART 100, see also DANCE 374, LITERATURE 713, MOTION PICTURES 822, MUSIC 832, THEATER 1076
ARTS AND HANDICRAFTS 113
Asbestos see BUILDING AND CONSTRUCTION 181
Asian History see HISTORY - History of Asia 568
Asphalt see BUILDING AND CONSTRUCTION 181, see also ENGINEERING - Civil Engineering 480, TRANSPORTATION - Roads and Traffic 1095
Asthma see MEDICAL SCIENCES - Respiratory Diseases 792
ASTROLOGY 114
Astronautics see AERONAUTICS AND SPACE FLIGHT 17
ASTRONOMY 114
ASTRONOMY — Abstracting, Bibliographies, Statistics 118
Astrophysics see ASTRONOMY 114
Athletics see MEDICAL SCIENCES - Sports Medicine 793, see also SPORTS AND GAMES 1032
Atmospheric Sciences see METEOROLOGY 802
Atomic Energy see ENERGY 463, see also PHYSICS - Nuclear Energy 895
Audio Equipment see ELECTRICITY AND ELECTRICAL ENGINEERING 450, see also SOUND RECORDING AND REPRODUCTION 1031
Audio-Visual Education see EDUCATION - Teaching Methods and Curriculum 446, see also MOTION PICTURES 822
Audiology see MEDICAL SCIENCES - Otorhinolaryngology 786
Auditing see BUSINESS AND ECONOMICS - Accounting 220
AUTOMATION see COMPUTERS - Automation 355
Automobile Racing see SPORTS AND GAMES 1032
AUTOMOBILES 1090
Aviation see AERONAUTICS AND SPACE FLIGHT 17, see also TRANSPORTATION - Air Transport 1087
Aviculture see BIOLOGY - Ornithology 169
Bacteriology see BIOLOGY - Microbiology 167, see also MEDICAL SCIENCES - Communicable Diseases 777
Badminton see SPORTS AND GAMES 1032
BAKERS AND CONFECTIONERS 522
BALL GAMES 1037
Ballet see DANCE 374
BANKING AND FINANCE 222
Banking Law see BUSINESS AND ECONOMICS - Banking and Finance 222, see also LAW 649
Barbering see BEAUTY CULTURE 118
Baseball see SPORTS AND GAMES - Ball Games 1037
Batteries see ELECTRICITY AND ELECTRICAL ENGINEERING 450, see also TRANSPORTATION - Automobiles 1090
BEAUTY CULTURE 118
BEAUTY CULTURE — Perfumes And Cosmetics 118
Beekeeping see AGRICULTURE 22
Beer see BEVERAGES 119
Behavioral Sciences see PSYCHOLOGY 932, see also SOCIOLOGY 1023
BEVERAGES 119, see also FOOD AND FOOD INDUSTRIES 517
BEVERAGES — Abstracting, Bibliographies, Statistics 120
Biblical Studies see RELIGIONS AND THEOLOGY 966
BIBLIOGRAPHIES 121, see also ABSTRACTING AND INDEXING SERVICES 1, LIBRARY AND INFORMATION SCIENCES 672, PUBLISHING AND BOOK TRADE 959
BICYCLES AND MOTORCYCLES 1041
Billiards see SPORTS AND GAMES - Ball Games 1037
Biochemistry see BIOLOGY - Biological Chemistry 150
Biocybernetics see MEDICAL SCIENCES 756
Bioenergetics see BIOLOGY 137, see also PHYSICAL FITNESS AND HYGIENE 885
BIOGRAPHY 133
BIOGRAPHY — Abstracting, Bibliographies, Statistics 136
BIOLOGICAL CHEMISTRY 150
BIOLOGY 137, see also MEDICAL SCIENCES 756
BIOLOGY — Abstracting, Bibliographies, Statistics 149
BIOLOGY — Biological Chemistry 150
BIOLOGY — Biophysics 152
BIOLOGY — Botany 153
BIOLOGY — Cytology And Histology 162
BIOLOGY — Entomology 163
BIOLOGY — Genetics 166
BIOLOGY — Microbiology 167
BIOLOGY — Microscopy 169
BIOLOGY — Ornithology 169
BIOLOGY — Physiology 171
BIOLOGY — Zoology 172
Biometeorology see METEOROLOGY 802
Biometry see BIOLOGY 137, see also STATISTICS 1047
Bionics see COMPUTERS - Cybernetics 359
BIOPHYSICS 152
Birds see BIOLOGY - Ornithology 169, see also CONSERVATION 363, PETS 868
BIRTH CONTROL 179
BIRTH CONTROL — Abstracting, Bibliographies, Statistics 179
Black Studies see ETHNIC INTERESTS 501
BLIND 179, see also EDUCATION - Special Education and Rehabilitation 444, MEDICAL SCIENCES - Ophthalmology and Optometry 785, SOCIAL SERVICES AND WELFARE 1015
BLIND — Abstracting, Bibliographies, Statistics 180
Blood Transfusion see MEDICAL SCIENCES - Cardiovascular Diseases 776
BOATS AND BOATING 1041
Bobsleighing see SPORTS AND GAMES - Outdoor Life 1043
Bond Market see BUSINESS AND ECONOMICS - Investments 265
Book Collecting see PUBLISHING AND BOOK TRADE 959
Book Illustrating see PUBLISHING AND BOOK TRADE 959
Book Reviews see LITERATURE 713, see also PUBLISHING AND BOOK TRADE 959
Book Trade see BIBLIOGRAPHIES 121, see also PRINTING 930, PUBLISHING AND BOOK TRADE 959
Bookbinding see PUBLISHING AND BOOK TRADE 959

Bookkeeping see BUSINESS AND ECONOMICS - Accounting 220
Booksellers see PUBLISHING AND BOOK TRADE 959
Boots see SHOES AND BOOTS 1005
BOTANY 153, see also AGRICULTURE - Crop Production and Soil 51, GARDENING AND HORTICULTURE 531
Bottling see BEVERAGES 119, see also PACKAGING 854
Bowling see SPORTS AND GAMES - Ball Games 1037
Boxes see PACKAGING 854
Boxing see SPORTS AND GAMES 1032
Braille see BLIND 179
Brass Instruments see MUSIC 832
Brewing see BEVERAGES 119
Bricks see BUILDING AND CONSTRUCTION 181, see also CERAMICS, GLASS AND POTTERY 319
Bridge see SPORTS AND GAMES 1032
Bridge Construction see ENGINEERING - Civil Engineering 480
Broadcasting see COMMUNICATIONS - Radio and Television 347
Bryology see BIOLOGY - Botany 153
Buddhism see RELIGIONS AND THEOLOGY 966
BUILDING AND CONSTRUCTION 181, see also ARCHITECTURE 96, ENGINEERING - Civil engineering 480, HOUSING AND URBAN PLANNING 621
BUILDING AND CONSTRUCTION — Abstracting, Bibliographies, Statistics 188
BUILDING AND CONSTRUCTION — Carpentry And Woodwork 189
BUILDING AND CONSTRUCTION — Hardware 189
Bullfighting see SPORTS AND GAMES 1032
Burns see MEDICAL SCIENCES - Orthopedics and Traumatology 786
Buses see TRANSPORTATION - Automobiles 1090
Business Administration see BUSINESS AND ECONOMICS - Management 278
BUSINESS AND ECONOMICS 190
BUSINESS AND ECONOMICS — Abstracting, Bibliographies, Statistics 202
BUSINESS AND ECONOMICS — Accounting 220
BUSINESS AND ECONOMICS — Banking And Finance 222
BUSINESS AND ECONOMICS - Banking and Finance - Computer Applications see also COMPUTERS - Electronic Data Processing 360
BUSINESS AND ECONOMICS — Banking And Finance - Computer Applications 234
BUSINESS AND ECONOMICS — Chamber Of Commerce Publications 234
BUSINESS AND ECONOMICS — Computer Applications 238
BUSINESS AND ECONOMICS — Cooperatives 238
BUSINESS AND ECONOMICS — Domestic Commerce 239
BUSINESS AND ECONOMICS — Economic Situation And Conditions 240
BUSINESS AND ECONOMICS — Economic Systems And Theories, Economic History 250
BUSINESS AND ECONOMICS — International Commerce 252
BUSINESS AND ECONOMICS — International Development And Assistance 261
BUSINESS AND ECONOMICS — Investments 265
BUSINESS AND ECONOMICS — Labor And Industrial Relations 269
BUSINESS AND ECONOMICS — Macroeconomics 277
BUSINESS AND ECONOMICS — Management 278
BUSINESS AND ECONOMICS — Marketing And Purchasing 282
BUSINESS AND ECONOMICS — Office Equipment And Services 286
BUSINESS AND ECONOMICS — Personnel Management 286
BUSINESS AND ECONOMICS — Production Of Goods And Services 287
BUSINESS AND ECONOMICS — Public Finance, Taxation 292
BUSINESS AND ECONOMICS — Small Business 301
BUSINESS AND ECONOMICS — Trade And Industrial Directories 301
Business Law see BUSINESS AND ECONOMICS 190, see also LAW 649
Butane see PETROLEUM AND GAS 862
Cable Television see COMMUNICATIONS - Radio and Television 347
Cables see COMMUNICATIONS - Telephone and Telegraph 350, see also ELECTRICITY AND ELECTRICAL ENGINEERING 450
Cafeterias see HOTELS AND RESTAURANTS 619
Calculating Machines see BUSINESS AND ECONOMICS - Accounting 220, see also ELECTRICITY AND ELECTRICAL ENGINEERING 450, MATHEMATICS 746
Calendars of Events see MEETINGS AND CONGRESSES 795, see also TRAVEL AND TOURISM 1105
Calligraphy see ART 100
Camping see SPORTS AND GAMES - Outdoor Life 1043, see also TRAVEL AND TOURISM 1105
Canals see TRANSPORTATION - Ships and Shipping 1098
CANCER 774
Candy see FOOD AND FOOD INDUSTRIES - Bakers and Confectioners 522
Canning and Preserving see FOOD AND FOOD INDUSTRIES 517, see also HOME ECONOMICS 614
Canoeing see SPORTS AND GAMES - Boats and Boating 1041
Canon Law see RELIGIONS AND THEOLOGY 966
Canvas see TEXTILE INDUSTRIES AND FABRICS 1073
Carboniferous Geology see EARTH SCIENCES - Geophysics 398
Cardiology see MEDICAL SCIENCES - Cardiovascular Diseases 776
CARDIOVASCULAR DISEASES 776
Cardiovascular Surgery see MEDICAL SCIENCES - Surgery 793
Careers see OCCUPATIONS AND CAREERS 847
Cargo Handling see TRANSPORTATION - Ships and Shipping 1098
Caribbean History see HISTORY - History of North and South America 602
CARPENTRY AND WOODWORK 189
Carpets and Rugs see INTERIOR DESIGN AND DECORATION - Furniture and House Furnishings 643
Cartography see GEOGRAPHY 540
Cartoons see ART 100
Catering see HOTELS AND RESTAURANTS 619
Cattle see AGRICULTURE - Poultry and Livestock 64
Caves see EARTH SCIENCES - Geology 382
Cement see BUILDING AND CONSTRUCTION 181
Cemeteries see FUNERALS 531
CERAMICS, GLASS AND POTTERY 319, see also ART 100, ARTS AND HANDICRAFTS 113

CERAMICS, GLASS AND POTTERY — Abstracting, Bibliographies, Statistics 320
Cereals see AGRICULTURE - Feed, Flour and Grain 63, see also FOOD AND FOOD INDUSTRIES 517
Cerebral Palsy see MEDICAL SCIENCES - Psychiatry and Neurology 788
CHAMBER OF COMMERCE PUBLICATIONS 234
Chambers of Commerce see BUSINESS AND ECONOMICS - Chamber of Commerce Publications 234
Chaplains see MILITARY 810, see also RELIGIONS AND THEOLOGY 966
Charities see SOCIAL SERVICES AND WELFARE 1015
CHEMICAL ENGINEERING 477
CHEMISTRY 321
CHEMISTRY — Abstracting, Bibliographies, Statistics 325
CHEMISTRY — Analytical Chemistry 326
CHEMISTRY — Crystallography 327
CHEMISTRY — Electrochemistry 328
CHEMISTRY — Inorganic Chemistry 328
CHEMISTRY — Organic Chemistry 329
CHEMISTRY — Physical Chemistry 331
Chemotherapy see BIOLOGY - Biological Chemistry 150, see also MEDICAL SCIENCES 756, PHARMACY AND PHARMACOLOGY 869
Chess see SPORTS AND GAMES 1032
Chest Diseases see MEDICAL SCIENCES - Respiratory Diseases 792
Child Psychology see PSYCHOLOGY 932
Child Welfare see CHILDREN AND YOUTH - About 333, see also SOCIAL SERVICES AND WELFARE 1015
CHILDREN AND YOUTH — About 333
CHILDREN AND YOUTH — Abstracting, Bibliographies, Statistics 334
CHILDREN AND YOUTH — For 335
CHIROPRACTICS, HOMEOPATHY, OSTEOPATHY 777
Chromatography see CHEMISTRY - Analytical Chemistry 326
Church History see RELIGIONS AND THEOLOGY 966
Cigarettes and Cigars see TOBACCO 1079
CIRCUITS see COMPUTERS - Circuits 355
Circulatory System see MEDICAL SCIENCES - Cardiovascular Diseases 776
Circus see THEATER 1076
Cities and Towns see HOUSING AND URBAN PLANNING 621, see also PUBLIC ADMINISTRATION - Municipal Government 950
Citizenship see POLITICAL SCIENCE 901
Citrus Fruits see AGRICULTURE - Crop Production and Soil 51, see also FOOD AND FOOD INDUSTRIES 517, GARDENING AND HORTICULTURE 531
City Planning see HOUSING AND URBAN PLANNING 621
Civil Aeronautics see TRANSPORTATION - Air Transport 1087
CIVIL DEFENSE 336, see also MILITARY 810
CIVIL ENGINEERING 480
CIVIL RIGHTS 912
Civil Service see OCCUPATIONS AND CAREERS 847, see also PUBLIC ADMINISTRATION 938
CLASSICAL STUDIES 336, see also ARCHAEOLOGY 79, HISTORY 554, LINGUISTICS 689, LITERATURE 713
CLASSICAL STUDIES — Abstracting, Bibliographies, Statistics 339
CLEANING AND DYEING 339
Climatology see METEOROLOGY 802
Clinical Medicine see MEDICAL SCIENCES 756
CLOTHING TRADE 339
CLOTHING TRADE — Abstracting, Bibliographies, Statistics 340
CLOTHING TRADE — Fashions 340
CLUBS 340
Coaching see SPORTS AND GAMES 1032
Coastal Engineering see ENGINEERING - Hydraulic Engineering 490
Coffee and Tea see FOOD AND FOOD INDUSTRIES 517
Cognitive Studies see PSYCHOLOGY 932
Coins see NUMISMATICS 844
Collectibles see ANTIQUES 79
Collectors and Collecting see HOBBIES 614
COLLEGE AND ALUMNI 341, see also CLUBS 340, EDUCATION - Higher Education 431
COLLEGE AND ALUMNI — Abstracting, Bibliographies, Statistics 342
College Management see EDUCATION - Higher Education 431, see also EDUCATION - School Organization and Administration 442
Colloids see CHEMISTRY - Physical Chemistry 331, see also PHYSICS 886
Combustion see CHEMISTRY - Physical Chemistry 331, see also PHYSICS - Heat 894
Commerce see BUSINESS AND ECONOMICS - Domestic Commerce 239, see also BUSINESS AND ECONOMICS - International Commerce 252
Commercial Art see ADVERTISING AND PUBLIC RELATIONS 14, see also ART 100
Commercial Education see EDUCATION - Teaching Methods and Curriculum 446
Commercial Law see BUSINESS AND ECONOMICS 190, see also LAW 649
COMMUNICABLE DISEASES 777
COMMUNICATIONS 342, see also JOURNALISM 645
COMMUNICATIONS — Abstracting, Bibliographies, Statistics 345
COMMUNICATIONS — Computer Applications 346
COMMUNICATIONS — Postal Affairs 346
COMMUNICATIONS — Radio And Television 347
COMMUNICATIONS — Telephone And Telegraph 350
Communism see BUSINESS AND ECONOMICS - Economic Systems and Theories, Economic History 250, see also POLITICAL SCIENCE 901
Community Affairs see PUBLIC ADMINISTRATION - Municipal Government 950
Comparative Psychology see PSYCHOLOGY 932
Compressed Air see ENGINEERING - Mechanical Engineering 491

COMPUTERS 351, see also COMPUTERS - Information Science and Information Theory 361
COMPUTERS — Abstracting, Bibliographies, Statistics 353
COMPUTERS — Artificial Intelligence 354, see also COMPUTERS - Cybernetics 359
COMPUTERS — Automation 355

COMPUTERS — Circuits 355, see also COMPUTERS - Computer Engineering 356
COMPUTERS — Computer Architecture 356, see also COMPUTERS - Computer Engineering 356
COMPUTERS — Computer Assisted Instruction 356, see also EDUCATION - Computer Applications 427
COMPUTERS — Computer Engineering 356, see also COMPUTERS - Computer Architecture 356
COMPUTERS — Computer Graphics 356, see also PRINTING - Computer Applications 932
COMPUTERS — Computer Industry 357
COMPUTERS — Computer Industry Directories 357
COMPUTERS — Computer Industry, Vocational Guidance 357, see also EDUCATION 409, OCCUPATIONS AND CAREERS 847
COMPUTERS — Computer Music 357, see also MUSIC - Computer Applications 844
COMPUTERS — Computer Networks 357
COMPUTERS — Computer Programming 357, see also COMPUTERS - Software 362
COMPUTERS — Computer Sales 358, see also BUSINESS AND ECONOMICS - Marketing and Purchasing 282
COMPUTERS — Computer Security 358
COMPUTERS — Computer Simulation 358
COMPUTERS — Computer Systems 358, see also COMPUTERS - Computer Architecture 356
COMPUTERS — Cybernetics 359, see also COMPUTERS - Artificial Intelligence 354
COMPUTERS — Data Base Management 360
COMPUTERS — Data Communications And Data Transmission Systems 360
COMPUTERS — Electronic Data Processing 360, see also BUSINESS AND ECONOMICS - Banking and Finance - Computer Applications 234
COMPUTERS — Hardware 361
COMPUTERS — Information Science And Information Theory 361, see also COMPUTERS 351
COMPUTERS — Microcomputers 361, see also COMPUTERS - Personal Computers 362
COMPUTERS — Minicomputers 362
COMPUTERS — Personal Computers 362, see also COMPUTERS - Microcomputers 361
COMPUTERS — Software 362, see also COMPUTERS - Computer Programming 357
COMPUTERS — Theory Of Computing 363
COMPUTERS — Word Processing 363
Conchology see BIOLOGY - Zoology 172
Confectioners see FOOD AND FOOD INDUSTRIES - Bakers and Confectioners 522
Congenital Abnormalities see BIOLOGY - Genetics 166, see also MEDICAL SCIENCES 756
Congresses see MEETINGS AND CONGRESSES 795
CONSERVATION 363, see also ENVIRONMENTAL STUDIES 493, FISH AND FISHERIES 507, FORESTS AND FORESTRY 523, WATER RESOURCES 1123
CONSERVATION — Abstracting, Bibliographies, Statistics 368
Constitutional Law see LAW 649, see also POLITICAL SCIENCE 901
Construction see BUILDING AND CONSTRUCTION 181, see also ENGINEERING - Civil Engineering 480
Consumer Credit see BUSINESS AND ECONOMICS - Banking and Finance 222
CONSUMER EDUCATION AND PROTECTION 368
CONSUMER EDUCATION AND PROTECTION — Abstracting, Bibliographies, Statistics 369
Consumer Electronics see ELECTRICITY AND ELECTRICAL ENGINEERING 450
Contact Lenses see MEDICAL SCIENCES - Ophthalmology and Optometry 785
Containers see PACKAGING 854
Contraception see BIRTH CONTROL 179
Contractors see BUILDING AND CONSTRUCTION 181
Convention Dates see MEETINGS AND CONGRESSES 795
Cookery see HOME ECONOMICS 614, see also HOTELS AND RESTAURANTS 619
COOPERATIVES 238
Copying and Duplicating see PHOTOGRAPHY 884, see also PRINTING 930
Copyrights see PATENTS, TRADEMARKS AND COPYRIGHTS 860
Corporation Law see BUSINESS AND ECONOMICS - Management 278, see also LAW 649
Correspondence Education see EDUCATION - Adult Education 426
Corrosion see METALLURGY 796, see also PAINTS AND PROTECTIVE COATINGS 855
Cosmetics see BEAUTY CULTURE - Perfumes and Cosmetics 118
Counseling see EDUCATION 409, see also PSYCHOLOGY 932, SOCIAL SERVICES AND WELFARE 1015
Crafts see ARTS AND HANDICRAFTS 113
Credit and Collections see BUSINESS AND ECONOMICS - Banking and Finance 222
Credit Unions see BUSINESS AND ECONOMICS - Banking and Finance 222
Cricket see SPORTS AND GAMES 1032
Criminal Law see CRIMINOLOGY AND LAW ENFORCEMENT 369, see also LAW 649
CRIMINOLOGY AND LAW ENFORCEMENT 369
CRIMINOLOGY AND LAW ENFORCEMENT — Abstracting, Bibliographies, Statistics 373
CRIMINOLOGY AND LAW ENFORCEMENT — Security 374
CROP PRODUCTION AND SOIL 51
Croquet see SPORTS AND GAMES - Ball Games 1037
Cryogenic Engineering see ENGINEERING - Mechanical Engineering 491
Cryogenics see PHYSICS - Heat 894
CRYSTALLOGRAPHY 327
Currency see BUSINESS AND ECONOMICS - Banking and Finance 222
Curriculum and Methods see EDUCATION - Teaching Methods and Curriculum 446

Customs and Excise see BUSINESS AND ECONOMICS - Public Finance, Taxation 292
Cybernetic Medicine see MEDICAL SCIENCES 756
CYBERNETICS see COMPUTERS - Cybernetics 359
Cystic Fibrosis see MEDICAL SCIENCES 756
CYTOLOGY AND HISTOLOGY 162
DAIRYING AND DAIRY PRODUCTS 61
DANCE 374, see also MUSIC 832, THEATER 1076
DANCE — Abstracting, Bibliographies, Statistics 375
DATA BASE MANAGEMENT see COMPUTERS - Data Base Management 360
DATA COMMUNICATIONS AND DATA TRANSMISSION SYSTEMS see COMPUTERS - Data Communications and Data Transmission Systems 360
Data Processing see COMPUTERS - Electronic Data Processing 360
DEAF 375, see also EDUCATION - Special Education and Rehabilitation 444, MEDICAL SCIENCES - Otorhinolaryngology 786, SOCIAL SERVICES AND WELFARE 1015
Decoration see INTERIOR DESIGN AND DECORATION 643
Defense see CIVIL DEFENSE 336, see also MILITARY 810
Delinquency see CHILDREN AND YOUTH - About 333, see also CRIMINOLOGY AND LAW ENFORCEMENT 369, SOCIAL SERVICES AND WELFARE 1015
Demography see POPULATION STUDIES 920
DENTISTRY 778
Department Stores see BUSINESS AND ECONOMICS - Marketing and Purchasing 282
DERMATOLOGY AND VENEREOLOGY 780
Desalination see ENVIRONMENTAL STUDIES 493, see also WATER RESOURCES 1123
Design see ART 100
Detective Magazines see ADVENTURE AND ROMANCE 13
Detectives see CRIMINOLOGY AND LAW ENFORCEMENT 369
Diabetes see MEDICAL SCIENCES - Endocrinology 780
Dialysis see MEDICAL SCIENCES - Urology and Nephrology 795
Diecasting see ENGINEERING 469
Diesel Engines see ENGINEERING - Mechanical Engineering 491
Dietetics see NUTRITION AND DIETETICS 845
Digestive System see MEDICAL SCIENCES - Gastroenterology 782
Digital Computers see COMPUTERS - Hardware 361
Diplomatic Service see POLITICAL SCIENCE - International Relations 914
Disarmament see MILITARY 810, see also POLITICAL SCIENCE 901
Disk Drives see COMPUTERS - Hardware 361
Distilling see BEVERAGES 119
Documentation see COMPUTERS - Computer Programming 357, see also COMPUTERS - Software 362
Domestic Animals and Birds see PETS 868, see also VETERINARY SCIENCE 1120
DOMESTIC COMMERCE 239
Drafting see ENGINEERING 469, see also TECHNOLOGY: COMPREHENSIVE WORKS 1067
Drama see LITERATURE 713, see also THEATER 1076
Drawing and Sketching see ART 100
DRUG ABUSE AND ALCOHOLISM 376
DRUG ABUSE AND ALCOHOLISM — Abstracting, Bibliographies, Statistics 378
Drugs see PHARMACY AND PHARMACOLOGY 869
Dry Goods see CLOTHING TRADE 339, see also TEXTILE INDUSTRIES AND FABRICS 1073
Dyes and Dyeing see CLEANING AND DYEING 339, see also TEXTILE INDUSTRIES AND FABRICS 1073
E C G see MEDICAL SCIENCES - Cardiovascular Diseases 776
E E G see MEDICAL SCIENCES - Psychiatry and Neurology 788
EARTH SCIENCES 378
EARTH SCIENCES — Abstracting, Bibliographies, Statistics 381
EARTH SCIENCES — Geology 382
EARTH SCIENCES — Geophysics 398
EARTH SCIENCES — Hydrology 402
EARTH SCIENCES — Oceanography 404
Ecclesiastical Art see ART 100, see also RELIGIONS AND THEOLOGY 966
Ecclesiastical Law see RELIGIONS AND THEOLOGY 966
Ecology see BIOLOGY 137, see also CONSERVATION 363, ENVIRONMENTAL STUDIES 493
Economic Geology see EARTH SCIENCES - Geology 382
ECONOMIC SITUATION AND CONDITIONS 240
ECONOMIC SYSTEMS AND THEORIES, ECONOMIC HISTORY 250
ECONOMICS 409, see also BUSINESS AND ECONOMICS 190
Editing see JOURNALISM 645, see also PUBLISHING AND BOOK TRADE 959
EDUCATION 409, see also CHILDREN AND YOUTH - About 333
EDUCATION — Abstracting, Bibliographies, Statistics 422
EDUCATION — Adult Education 426
EDUCATION — Computer Applications 427, see also COMPUTERS - Computer Assisted Instruction 356
EDUCATION — Guides To Schools And Colleges 428
EDUCATION — Higher Education 431
EDUCATION — International Education Programs 441
EDUCATION — School Organization And Administration 442
EDUCATION — Special Education And Rehabilitation 444
EDUCATION — Teaching Methods And Curriculum 446
Educational Films see EDUCATION - Teaching Methods and Curriculum 446, see also MOTION PICTURES 822
Educational Psychology see PSYCHOLOGY 932
Egyptology see ARCHAEOLOGY 79, see also ART 100, HISTORY - History of Africa 564
ELECTRICITY AND ELECTRICAL ENGINEERING 450, see also COMMUNICATIONS 342, PHYSICS 886
ELECTRICITY AND ELECTRICAL ENGINEERING — Abstracting, Bibliographies, Statistics 461
ELECTROCHEMISTRY 328
ELECTRONIC DATA PROCESSING see COMPUTERS - Electronic Data Processing 360
Electronics see ELECTRICITY AND ELECTRICAL ENGINEERING 450
Electroplating see ELECTRICITY AND ELECTRICAL ENGINEERING 450, see also METALLURGY 796
Electrotherapy see MEDICAL SCIENCES - Psychiatry and Neurology 788, see also MEDICAL SCIENCES - Radiology and Nuclear Medicine 792
Embroidery and Needlework see NEEDLEWORK 844
Embryology see BIOLOGY 137, see also MEDICAL SCIENCES 756
Emigration see POPULATION STUDIES 920
Emotionally Disturbed Children see EDUCATION - Special Education and Rehabilitation 444
Employment see BUSINESS AND ECONOMICS - Labor and Industrial Relations 269, see also OCCUPATIONS AND CAREERS 847
Encephalitis see MEDICAL SCIENCES - Psychiatry and Neurology 788
ENCYCLOPEDIAS AND GENERAL ALMANACS 462
ENCYCLOPEDIAS AND GENERAL ALMANACS — Abstracting, Bibliographies, Statistics 463
ENDOCRINOLOGY 780
ENERGY 463
ENERGY — Abstracting, Bibliographies, Statistics 468
ENGINEERING 469
ENGINEERING — Abstracting, Bibliographies, Statistics 475
ENGINEERING — Chemical Engineering 477
ENGINEERING — Civil Engineering 480
ENGINEERING — Computer Applications 484
ENGINEERING — Engineering Mechanics and Materials 485
ENGINEERING — Hydraulic Engineering 490
ENGINEERING — Mechanical Engineering 491
Engines see ENGINEERING - Mechanical Engineering 491, see also TRANSPORTATION 1080
English Language - Study and Teaching see LINGUISTICS 689
Engraving see ART 100, see also PRINTING 930
Entertainment see COMMUNICATIONS - Radio and Television 342, see also DANCE 374, MOTION PICTURES 822, MUSIC 832, SPORTS AND GAMES 1032, THEATER 1076, TRAVEL AND TOURISM 1105
ENTOMOLOGY 163
Environmental Health see ENVIRONMENTAL STUDIES 493, see also PUBLIC HEALTH AND SAFETY 952
ENVIRONMENTAL STUDIES 493, see also CONSERVATION 363
ENVIRONMENTAL STUDIES — Abstracting, Bibliographies, Statistics 500
Enzymes see BIOLOGY - Biological Chemistry 150, see also MEDICAL SCIENCES 756
Ephemerides see ASTRONOMY 114
Epidemiology see PUBLIC HEALTH AND SAFETY 952
Epilepsy see MEDICAL SCIENCES - Psychiatry and Neurology 788
Ergonomics see BUSINESS AND ECONOMICS - Labor and Industrial Relations 269, see also PSYCHOLOGY 932
Erosion see AGRICULTURE - Crop Production and Soil 51, see also CONSERVATION 363
Esperanto see LINGUISTICS 689
ETHNIC INTERESTS 501
ETHNIC INTERESTS — Abstracting, Bibliographies, Statistics 506
Ethnography see ANTHROPOLOGY 68, see also SOCIOLOGY 1023
Eugenics see BIOLOGY - Genetics 166
European History see HISTORY - History of Europe 573
Exceptional Children, Education see EDUCATION - Special Education and Rehabilitation 444
EXPERIMENTAL MEDICINE, LABORATORY TECHNIQUE 781
Exports and Imports see BUSINESS AND ECONOMICS - International Commerce 252
Extrasensory Perception see PARAPSYCHOLOGY AND OCCULTISM 860
Fabrics see TEXTILE INDUSTRIES AND FABRICS 1073
Family Planning see BIRTH CONTROL 179
Farm Equipment see AGRICULTURE - Agricultural Equipment 51, see also MACHINERY 745
Farm Management see AGRICULTURE 22
FASHIONS 340
FEED, FLOUR AND GRAIN 63
Fellowships see EDUCATION - Higher Education 431
Feminist Movement see POLITICAL SCIENCE - Civil Rights 912, see also WOMEN'S INTERESTS 1128
Fencing see SPORTS AND GAMES 1032
Fertilizers see AGRICULTURE - Crop Production and Soil 51
Fiction see ADVENTURE AND ROMANCE 13, see also LITERATURE 713, PUBLISHING AND BOOK TRADE 959
Filmmaking see MOTION PICTURES 822
Finance see BUSINESS AND ECONOMICS - Banking and Finance 222, see also BUSINESS AND ECONOMICS - Investments 265
Finishing see PAINTS AND PROTECTIVE COATINGS 855
Fire Insurance see INSURANCE 637
FIRE PREVENTION 506
FIRE PREVENTION — Abstracting, Bibliographies, Statistics 507
Firearms see HOBBIES 614, see also SPORTS AND GAMES 1032
First Aid see MEDICAL SCIENCES 756, see also PUBLIC HEALTH AND SAFETY 952
FISH AND FISHERIES 507, see also BIOLOGY - Zoology 172
FISH AND FISHERIES — Abstracting, Bibliographies, Statistics 514
Fishing, Sport see SPORTS AND GAMES - Outdoor Life 1043
Flax see AGRICULTURE - Crop Production and Soil 51, see also TEXTILE INDUSTRIES AND FABRICS 1073
Floor Coverings see INTERIOR DESIGN AND DECORATION - Furniture and House Furnishings 643
Floral Decorations see ART 100, see also GARDENING AND HORTICULTURE 531
FLORIST TRADE 534
Flowers see BIOLOGY - Botany 153, see also GARDENING AND HORTICULTURE 531

Fluid Power see ENGINEERING - Mechanical Engineering 491
Flying see AERONAUTICS AND SPACE FLIGHT 17, see also TRANSPORTATION - Air Transport 1087
Flying Saucers see AERONAUTICS AND SPACE FLIGHT 17
FOLKLORE 514
FOLKLORE — Abstracting, Bibliographies, Statistics 517
FOOD AND FOOD INDUSTRIES 517
FOOD AND FOOD INDUSTRIES — Abstracting, Bibliographies, Statistics 521
FOOD AND FOOD INDUSTRIES — Bakers And Confectioners 522
FOOD AND FOOD INDUSTRIES — Grocery Trade 522
Football see SPORTS AND GAMES - Ball Games 1037
Footwear see LEATHER AND FUR INDUSTRIES 672, see also SHOES AND BOOTS 1005
Foreign Affairs see POLITICAL SCIENCE - International Relations 914
Foreign Aid see BUSINESS AND ECONOMICS - International Development and Assistance 261
Foreign Commerce see BUSINESS AND ECONOMICS - International Commerce 252
Foreign Legion see MILITARY 810
FORENSIC SCIENCES 782
Forest Fires see FORESTS AND FORESTRY 523
FORESTS AND FORESTRY 523
FORESTS AND FORESTRY — Abstracting, Bibliographies, Statistics 529
FORESTS AND FORESTRY — Lumber And Wood 529
Foundry Practices see METALLURGY 796
Fraternal Organizations see CLUBS 340
Freight see TRANSPORTATION 1080
French Language - Study and Teaching see LINGUISTICS 689
Frequency Modulation see COMMUNICATIONS - Radio and Television 347, see also SOUND RECORDING AND REPRODUCTION 1031
Fretted Instruments see MUSIC 832
Frozen Food see FOOD AND FOOD INDUSTRIES 517
Fruit see AGRICULTURE - Crop Production and Soil 51, see also FOOD AND FOOD INDUSTRIES 517, GARDENING AND HORTICULTURE 531
Fuel see ENERGY 463, see also HEATING, PLUMBING AND REFRIGERATION 553, MINES AND MINING INDUSTRY 813, PETROLEUM AND GAS 862
Fundraising see SOCIAL SERVICES AND WELFARE 1015
FUNERALS 531
Fur see LEATHER AND FUR INDUSTRIES 672
Furnaces see HEATING, PLUMBING AND REFRIGERATION 553, see also METALLURGY 796
FURNITURE AND HOUSE FURNISHINGS 643, see also HOME ECONOMICS 614
Galleries see MUSEUMS AND ART GALLERIES 826
Gambling see SPORTS AND GAMES 1032
Game Breeding see AGRICULTURE - Poultry and Livestock 64
Games see SPORTS AND GAMES 1032
Garages see TRANSPORTATION - Automobiles 1090
GARDENING AND HORTICULTURE 531, see also AGRICULTURE 22, BIOLOGY - Botany 153
GARDENING AND HORTICULTURE — Abstracting, Bibliographies, Statistics 534
GARDENING AND HORTICULTURE — Florist Trade 534
Gas Chromatography see CHEMISTRY - Analytical Chemistry 326
Gas Dynamics see PHYSICS - Mechanics 894
Gas Turbines see ENGINEERING - Mechanical Engineering 491
GASTROENTEROLOGY 782
Gastronomy see HOME ECONOMICS 614
Gemstones see JEWELRY, CLOCKS AND WATCHES 644
GENEALOGY AND HERALDRY 534
GENEALOGY AND HERALDRY — Abstracting, Bibliographies, Statistics 537
GENERAL INTEREST PERIODICALS — Africa 537
GENERAL INTEREST PERIODICALS — Argentina 537
GENERAL INTEREST PERIODICALS — Australasia 537
GENERAL INTEREST PERIODICALS — Australia 538
GENERAL INTEREST PERIODICALS — Bangladesh 538
GENERAL INTEREST PERIODICALS — Brazil 538
GENERAL INTEREST PERIODICALS — Bulgaria 538
GENERAL INTEREST PERIODICALS — Canada 538
GENERAL INTEREST PERIODICALS — Central America 538
GENERAL INTEREST PERIODICALS — Cuba 538
GENERAL INTEREST PERIODICALS — Denmark 538
GENERAL INTEREST PERIODICALS — Germany, West 538
GENERAL INTEREST PERIODICALS — Great Britain 538
GENERAL INTEREST PERIODICALS — Greenland 538
GENERAL INTEREST PERIODICALS — Guatemala 538
GENERAL INTEREST PERIODICALS — India 539
GENERAL INTEREST PERIODICALS — Indonesia 539
GENERAL INTEREST PERIODICALS — Israel 539
GENERAL INTEREST PERIODICALS — Italy 539
GENERAL INTEREST PERIODICALS — Japan 539
GENERAL INTEREST PERIODICALS — Libya 539
GENERAL INTEREST PERIODICALS — Pakistan 539
GENERAL INTEREST PERIODICALS — Peru 539
GENERAL INTEREST PERIODICALS — Poland 539
GENERAL INTEREST PERIODICALS — Puerto Rico 539
GENERAL INTEREST PERIODICALS — Scandinavia 539
GENERAL INTEREST PERIODICALS — Singapore 539
GENERAL INTEREST PERIODICALS — South America 539
GENERAL INTEREST PERIODICALS — Sudan 539
GENERAL INTEREST PERIODICALS — Sweden 540
GENERAL INTEREST PERIODICALS — Tanzania 540
GENERAL INTEREST PERIODICALS — U S S R 540
GENERAL INTEREST PERIODICALS — United States 540
GENERAL INTEREST PERIODICALS — Uruguay 540
GENERAL INTEREST PERIODICALS — Venezuela 540
GENERAL INTEREST PERIODICALS — Vietnam 540
GENERAL INTEREST PERIODICALS — West Indies 540
GENERAL INTEREST PERIODICALS — Yugoslavia 540
GENERAL INTEREST PERIODICALS — Zambia 540
Generators see ELECTRICITY AND ELECTRICAL ENGINEERING 450
GENETICS 166
Geochemistry see EARTH SCIENCES - Geology 382
Geodesy see EARTH SCIENCES - Geophysics 398, see also GEOGRAPHY 540
GEOGRAPHY 540, see also TRAVEL AND TOURISM 1105
GEOGRAPHY — Abstracting, Bibliographies, Statistics 551
GEOLOGY 382
Geomagnetism see EARTH SCIENCES - Geophysics 398
GEOPHYSICS 398
German Language - Study and Teaching see LINGUISTICS 689
GERONTOLOGY AND GERIATRICS 551
GERONTOLOGY AND GERIATRICS — Abstracting, Bibliographies, Statistics 552
GIFTWARE AND TOYS 552
Glaciology see EARTH SCIENCES - Geology 382
Glass see CERAMICS, GLASS AND POTTERY 319
Glaucoma see MEDICAL SCIENCES - Ophthalmology and Optometry 785
Gliders see AERONAUTICS AND SPACE FLIGHT 17
Golf see SPORTS AND GAMES - Ball Games 1032
Government see POLITICAL SCIENCE 901, see also PUBLIC ADMINISTRATION 938
Graphic Arts see ART 100, see also PRINTING 930
Graphology see PSYCHOLOGY 932
Greenhouses see GARDENING AND HORTICULTURE 531
Greeting Cards see GIFTWARE AND TOYS 552
GROCERY TRADE 522
GUIDES TO SCHOOLS AND COLLEGES 428
Guns see SPORTS AND GAMES 1032
Gymnastics see SPORTS AND GAMES 1032
Gynecology see MEDICAL SCIENCES - Obstetrics and Gynecology 784
Hair Removal see BEAUTY CULTURE 118
Hairdressing see BEAUTY CULTURE 118
Handbags see CLOTHING TRADE 339, see also LEATHER AND FUR INDUSTRIES 672
Handicrafts see ARTS AND HANDICRAFTS 113
Harbors see TRANSPORTATION - Ships and Shipping 1098
HARDWARE 189
HARDWARE (COMPUTER) see COMPUTERS - Hardware 361
Harnesses see LEATHER AND FUR INDUSTRIES 672
Health Foods see FOOD AND FOOD INDUSTRIES 517, see also NUTRITION AND DIETETICS 845, PHYSICAL FITNESS AND HYGIENE 885
Health Insurance see INSURANCE 637
Hearing see DEAF 375, see also MEDICAL SCIENCES - Otorhinolaryngology 786
Heart Diseases see MEDICAL SCIENCES - Cardiovascular Diseases 776
HEAT 894
HEATING, PLUMBING AND REFRIGERATION 553, see also BUILDING AND CONSTRUCTION 181, ENGINEERING - Mechanical Engineering 491
HEATING, PLUMBING AND REFRIGERATION — Abstracting, Bibliographies, Statistics 554
Helicopters see AERONAUTICS AND SPACE FLIGHT 17
HEMATOLOGY 783
Heraldry see GENEALOGY AND HERALDRY 534
Herbs see AGRICULTURE 22, see also GARDENING AND HORTICULTURE 531
Heredity see BIOLOGY - Genetics 166
Hides see LEATHER AND FUR INDUSTRIES 672
HIGHER EDUCATION 431
Highways see ENGINEERING - Civil Engineering 480, see also TRANSPORTATION - Roads and Traffic 1095
Histochemistry see BIOLOGY - Cytology and Histology 162
Histology see BIOLOGY - Cytology and Histology 162
Historic Sites see HISTORY 554, see also TRAVEL AND TOURISM 1105
HISTORY 554, see also ARCHAEOLOGY 79, BIOGRAPHY 133, CLASSICAL STUDIES 336
HISTORY — Abstracting, Bibliographies, Statistics 562
HISTORY — History Of Africa 564
HISTORY — History Of Asia 568
HISTORY — History Of Australasia And Other Areas 572
HISTORY — History Of Europe 573
HISTORY — History Of North And South America 602
HISTORY — History Of The Near East 611
HOBBIES 614, see also SPORTS AND GAMES 1032
HOBBIES — Abstracting, Bibliographies, Statistics 614
Hockey see SPORTS AND GAMES 1032
HOME ECONOMICS 614
HOME ECONOMICS — Abstracting, Bibliographies, Statistics 615
Homeopathy see MEDICAL SCIENCES - Chiropractics, Homeopathy, Osteopathy 777
HOMOSEXUALITY 615
HOMOSEXUALITY — Abstracting, Bibliographies, Statistics 616
Hormones see MEDICAL SCIENCES - Endocrinology 780
Horology see JEWELRY, CLOCKS AND WATCHES 644
HORSES AND HORSEMANSHIP 1042
Horticulture see GARDENING AND HORTICULTURE 531
Hosiery see CLOTHING TRADE 339
Hospital Supplies see HOSPITALS 616, see also PHARMACY AND PHARMACOLOGY 869
HOSPITALS 616, see also MEDICAL SCIENCES 756
HOSPITALS — Abstracting, Bibliographies, Statistics 618
HOTELS AND RESTAURANTS 619
HOTELS AND RESTAURANTS — Abstracting, Bibliographies, Statistics 621
House Furnishings see INTERIOR DESIGN AND DECORATION - Furniture and House Furnishings 643
Household Management see HOME ECONOMICS 614

HOUSING AND URBAN PLANNING 621, see also BUILDING AND CONSTRUCTION 181, PUBLIC ADMINISTRATION 938, REAL ESTATE 964
HOUSING AND URBAN PLANNING — Abstracting, Bibliographies, Statistics 627
Human Ecology see SOCIOLOGY 1023
Human Geography see GEOGRAPHY 540, see also POPULATION STUDIES 920
Humanism see PHILOSOPHY 875
HUMANITIES: COMPREHENSIVE WORKS 628
HUMANITIES: COMPREHENSIVE WORKS — Abstracting, Bibliographies, Statistics 634
HUMANITIES: COMPREHENSIVE WORKS — Computer Applications 634
Hunting see SPORTS AND GAMES - Outdoor Life 1043
HYDRAULIC ENGINEERING 490
Hydroelectric Engineering see ELECTRICITY AND ELECTRICAL ENGINEERING 450
Hydrography see WATER RESOURCES 1123
HYDROLOGY 402
Hygiene see INDUSTRIAL HEALTH AND SAFETY 635, see also PHYSICAL FITNESS AND HYGIENE 885, PUBLIC HEALTH AND SAFETY 952
Hypertension see MEDICAL SCIENCES - Cardiovascular Diseases 776
Illumination see ELECTRICITY AND ELECTRICAL ENGINEERING 450
Immigration see POPULATION STUDIES 920
Immunology see MEDICAL SCIENCES - Allergology and Immunology 773
Imports see BUSINESS AND ECONOMICS - International Commerce 252
Indexing Services see ABSTRACTING AND INDEXING SERVICES 1
Indoor Games and Amusements see HOBBIES 614, see also SPORTS AND GAMES 1032
Industrial Arts see TECHNOLOGY 1067
Industrial Chemistry see ENGINEERING - Chemical Engineering 477
Industrial Design see ENGINEERING 469, see also TECHNOLOGY: COMPREHENSIVE WORKS 1067
Industrial Engineering see BUSINESS AND ECONOMICS - Production of Goods and Services 287, see also ENGINEERING 469, TECHNOLOGY: COMPREHENSIVE WORKS 1067
INDUSTRIAL HEALTH AND SAFETY 635
INDUSTRIAL HEALTH AND SAFETY — Abstracting, Bibliographies, Statistics 636
Industrial Relations see BUSINESS AND ECONOMICS - Labor and Industrial Relations 269, see also BUSINESS AND ECONOMICS - Personnel Management 286
Industry see BUSINESS AND ECONOMICS - Production of Goods and Services 287
Infectious Diseases see MEDICAL SCIENCES - Communicable Diseases 777, see also PUBLIC HEALTH AND SAFETY 952
Information Science see COMPUTERS - Information Science and Information Theory 361, see also LIBRARY AND INFORMATION SCIENCES 672, LIBRARY AND INFORMATION SCIENCES - Computer Applications 688
Information Theory see COMPUTERS - Information Science and Information Theory 361
INORGANIC CHEMISTRY 328
Input-Output Systems see COMPUTERS - Hardware 361
Insects see BIOLOGY - Entomology 163
INSTRUMENTS 636
INSTRUMENTS — Abstracting, Bibliographies, Statistics 637
Insulation see BUILDING AND CONSTRUCTION 181, see also HEATING, PLUMBING AND REFRIGERATION 553
INSURANCE 637
INSURANCE — Abstracting, Bibliographies, Statistics 642
Intensive Care Medicine see MEDICAL SCIENCES 756
INTERIOR DESIGN AND DECORATION 643, see also HOME ECONOMICS 614
INTERIOR DESIGN AND DECORATION — Abstracting, Bibliographies, Statistics 643
INTERIOR DESIGN AND DECORATION — Furniture And House Furnishings 643
Internal Medicine see MEDICAL SCIENCES 756
International Affairs see BUSINESS AND ECONOMICS - International Development and Assistance 261, see also LITERARY AND POLITICAL REVIEWS 709, POLITICAL SCIENCE - International relations 914
INTERNATIONAL COMMERCE 252
INTERNATIONAL DEVELOPMENT AND ASSISTANCE 261
INTERNATIONAL EDUCATION PROGRAMS 441
INTERNATIONAL LAW 669
INTERNATIONAL RELATIONS 914
Interplanetary Flight see AERONAUTICS AND SPACE FLIGHT 17
INVESTMENTS 265
Ionization see CHEMISTRY - Electrochemistry 328
Irrigation see AGRICULTURE 22, see also CONSERVATION 363, ENGINEERING 469, WATER RESOURCES 1123
ISLAM 975
Italian Language - Study and Teaching see LINGUISTICS 689
JEWELRY, CLOCKS AND WATCHES 644
JEWELRY, CLOCKS AND WATCHES — Abstracting, Bibliographies, Statistics 645
Job Opportunities see BUSINESS AND ECONOMICS - Labor and Industrial Relations 269, see also OCCUPATIONS AND CAREERS 847
Jogging see PHYSICAL FITNESS AND HYGIENE 885
JOURNALISM 645
JOURNALISM — Abstracting, Bibliographies, Statistics 647
JUDAISM 976
Judo see SPORTS AND GAMES 1032
Jute see TEXTILE INDUSTRIES AND FABRICS 1073
Juvenile Delinquency see CHILDREN AND YOUTH - About 333, see also CRIMINOLOGY AND LAW ENFORCEMENT 369
Juvenile Literature see CHILDREN AND YOUTH - For 335, see also PUBLISHING AND BOOK TRADE 959
Karate see SPORTS AND GAMES 1032

Kinetics see CHEMISTRY - Organic Chemistry 329, see also CHEMISTRY - Physical Chemistry 331, PHYSICS 886
Knit Goods see CLOTHING TRADE 339, see also TEXTILE INDUSTRIES AND FABRICS 1073
Knitting see NEEDLEWORK 844
LABOR AND INDUSTRIAL RELATIONS 269
Labor Law see BUSINESS AND ECONOMICS - Labor and IndustrialRelations 269, see also LAW 649
LABOR UNIONS 647
LABOR UNIONS — Abstracting, Bibliographies, Statistics 649
Laboratory Animals see MEDICAL SCIENCES - Experimental Medicine, Laboratory Technique 781
LABORATORY TECHNIQUE 649
Laboratory Techniques see INSTRUMENTS 636, see also MEDICAL SCIENCES - Experimental Medicine, Laboratory Technique 781
Land Management see CONSERVATION 363
Land Reclamation see AGRICULTURE - Crop Production and Soil 51
Landscaping see ARCHITECTURE 96, see also GARDENING AND HORTICULTURE 531
Language, Study and Teaching see LINGUISTICS 689
Laryngology see MEDICAL SCIENCES - Otorhinolaryngology 786
Lasers see ELECTRICITY AND ELECTRICAL ENGINEERING 450, see also PHYSICS - Optics 899
Lathes see MACHINERY 745
Latin American History see HISTORY - History of North and South America 602
Latin Language and Literature see CLASSICAL STUDIES 336, see also LINGUISTICS 689
Laundries see CLEANING AND DYEING 339
LAW 649
LAW — Abstracting, Bibliographies, Statistics 668
LAW — Computer Applications 669
Law Enforcement see CRIMINOLOGY AND LAW ENFORCEMENT 369
LAW — International Law 669
Lawns see GARDENING AND HORTICULTURE 531
LEATHER AND FUR INDUSTRIES 672, see also SHOES AND BOOTS 1005
LEATHER AND FUR INDUSTRIES — Abstracting, Bibliographies, Statistics 672
Legal Aid see LAW 649
Legislation see LAW 649, see also POLITICAL SCIENCE 901, PUBLIC ADMINISTRATION 938
Leprosy see MEDICAL SCIENCES - Communicable Diseases 777
Leukemia see MEDICAL SCIENCES - Hematology 783
Lexicography see LINGUISTICS 689
LIBRARY AND INFORMATION SCIENCES 672, see also BIBLIOGRAPHIES 121, COMPUTERS - Information Science and Information Theory 361, PUBLISHING AND BOOK TRADE 959
LIBRARY AND INFORMATION SCIENCES — Abstracting, Bibliographies, Statistics 687
LIBRARY AND INFORMATION SCIENCES — Computer Applications 688
Library Bookbinding see LIBRARY AND INFORMATION SCIENCES 672, see also PUBLISHING AND BOOK TRADE 959
Lighting see ELECTRICITY AND ELECTRICAL ENGINEERING 450, see also INTERIOR DESIGN AND DECORATION - Furniture and House Furnishings 643
Limnology see EARTH SCIENCES - Hydrology 402
LINGUISTICS 689
LINGUISTICS — Abstracting, Bibliographies, Statistics 709
LINGUISTICS — Computer Applications 709
Liquor see BEVERAGES 119
LITERARY AND POLITICAL REVIEWS 709, see also LITERATURE 713
LITERARY AND POLITICAL REVIEWS — Abstracting, Bibliographies, Statistics 712
Literary Criticism see LITERARY AND POLITICAL REVIEWS 709, see also LITERATURE 713
LITERATURE 713, see also LINGUISTICS 689, LITERARY AND POLITICAL REVIEWS 709
LITERATURE — Abstracting, Bibliographies, Statistics 738
LITERATURE — Poetry 739, see also LITERARY AND POLITICAL REVIEWS 709
Lithography see PRINTING 930
Little Magazines see LITERARY AND POLITICAL REVIEWS 709
Livestock see AGRICULTURE - Poultry and Livestock 64, see also VETERINARY SCIENCE 1120
Locks see BUILDING AND CONSTRUCTION -Hardware 189
Lubrication and Lubricants see ENGINEERING - Mechanical Engineering 491, see also PETROLEUM AND GAS 862
Luggage see LEATHER AND FUR INDUSTRIES 672
LUMBER AND WOOD 529, see also BUILDING AND CONSTRUCTION - Carpentry and Woodwork 189
Machine Translating see COMPUTERS - Computer Programming 357, see also LINGUISTICS 689
MACHINERY 745, see also AGRICULTURE - Agricultural Equipment 51, ENGINEERING - Mechanical Engineering 491, TECHNOLOGY: COMPREHENSIVE WORKS 1067
MACHINERY — Abstracting, Bibliographies, Statistics 746
MACROECONOMICS 277
Macromolecules see CHEMISTRY - Organic Chemistry 329
Magazine Business see PUBLISHING AND BOOK TRADE 959
Magic see HOBBIES 614
Magnetism see ELECTRICITY AND ELECTRICAL ENGINEERING 450
Mail Order Business see BUSINESS AND ECONOMICS - Marketing and Purchasing 282
Malacology see BIOLOGY - Zoology 172
MANAGEMENT 278
Manufacturing see BUSINESS AND ECONOMICS - Production of Goods and Services 287
Marijuana see DRUG ABUSE AND ALCOHOLISM 376
Marine Biology see BIOLOGY 137, see also EARTH SCIENCES - Oceanography 404

Marine Engineering see ENGINEERING 469, see also TRANSPORTATION - Ships and Shipping 1098
Maritime Law see LAW 649
MARKETING AND PURCHASING 282
Marxism see BUSINESS AND ECONOMICS - Economic Systems and Theories, Economic History 250, see also POLITICAL SCIENCE 901
Masonry see BUILDING AND CONSTRUCTION 181
Mass Transit see TRANSPORTATION 1080
Mathematical Geography see GEOGRAPHY 540
Mathematical Physics see PHYSICS 886
MATHEMATICS 746
MATHEMATICS — Abstracting, Bibliographies, Statistics 755
MATHEMATICS — Computer Applications 755
Mechanical Drawing see ENGINEERING 469, see also TECHNOLOGY: COMPREHENSIVE WORKS 1067
MECHANICAL ENGINEERING 491, see also MACHINERY 745, TECHNOLOGY 1067
Mechanical Handling see MACHINERY 745, see also TECHNOLOGY: COMPREHENSIVE WORKS 1067, TRANSPORTATION 1080
Mechanical Translating see COMPUTERS - Computer Programming 357, see also LINGUISTICS 689
MECHANICS 894
Medical Bacteriology see MEDICAL SCIENCES - Communicable Diseases 777
Medical Engineering see MEDICAL SCIENCES 756
Medical Jurisprudence see MEDICAL SCIENCES - Forensic Sciences 782
Medical Parasitology see MEDICAL SCIENCES - Communicable Diseases 777
MEDICAL SCIENCES 756, see also BIOLOGY 137, DRUG ABUSE AND ALCOHOLISM 376, GERONTOLOGY AND GERIATRICS 551, HOSPITALS 616, INDUSTRIAL HEALTH AND SAFETY 635, NUTRITION AND DIETETICS 845, PHARMACY AND PHARMACOLOGY 869, PHYSICAL FITNESS AND HYGIENE 885, PUBLIC HEALTH AND SAFETY 952
MEDICAL SCIENCES — Abstracting, Bibliographies, Statistics 768
MEDICAL SCIENCES — Allergology And Immunology 773
MEDICAL SCIENCES — Anaesthesiology 774
MEDICAL SCIENCES — Cancer 774
MEDICAL SCIENCES — Cardiovascular Diseases 776
MEDICAL SCIENCES — Chiropractics, Homeopathy, Osteopathy 777
MEDICAL SCIENCES — Communicable Diseases 777
MEDICAL SCIENCES — Computer Applications 778
MEDICAL SCIENCES — Dentistry 778
MEDICAL SCIENCES — Dermatology And Venereology 780
MEDICAL SCIENCES — Endocrinology 780
MEDICAL SCIENCES — Experimental Medicine, Laboratory Technique 781
MEDICAL SCIENCES — Forensic Sciences 782
MEDICAL SCIENCES — Gastroenterology 782
MEDICAL SCIENCES — Hematology 783
MEDICAL SCIENCES — Nurses And Nursing 783
MEDICAL SCIENCES — Obstetrics And Gynecology 784
MEDICAL SCIENCES — Ophthalmology And Optometry 785
MEDICAL SCIENCES — Orthopedics And Traumatology 786
MEDICAL SCIENCES — Otorhinolaryngology 786
MEDICAL SCIENCES — Pediatrics 787
MEDICAL SCIENCES — Psychiatry And Neurology 788
MEDICAL SCIENCES — Radiology And Nuclear Medicine 792
MEDICAL SCIENCES — Respiratory Diseases 792
MEDICAL SCIENCES — Rheumatology 793
MEDICAL SCIENCES — Sports Medicine 793
MEDICAL SCIENCES — Surgery 793
MEDICAL SCIENCES — Urology And Nephrology 795
Medieval Studies see HISTORY - History of Europe 573, see also LITERATURE 713, PHILOSOPHY 875
MEETINGS AND CONGRESSES 795
MEETINGS AND CONGRESSES — Abstracting, Bibliographies, Statistics 796
Memory Structures see COMPUTERS - Hardware 361
Menswear see CLOTHING TRADE 339
Mental health see PSYCHOLOGY 932
Mental Hygiene see PUBLIC HEALTH AND SAFETY 952
Mental Retardation see EDUCATION - Special Education and Rehabilitation 444, see also MEDICAL SCIENCES - Psychiatry and Neurology 788, PSYCHOLOGY 932
Merchandising see BUSINESS AND ECONOMICS - Marketing and Purchasing 282
Metabolism see BIOLOGY - Physiology 171, see also MEDICAL SCIENCES 756
Metal Industries see METALLURGY 796
METALLURGY 796, see also MINES AND MINING INDUSTRY 813
METALLURGY — Abstracting, Bibliographies, Statistics 801
METALLURGY — Welding 802
Metaphysics see PHILOSOPHY 875
METEOROLOGY 802
METEOROLOGY — Abstracting, Bibliographies, Statistics 808
METROLOGY AND STANDARDIZATION 808
METROLOGY AND STANDARDIZATION — Abstracting, Bibliographies, Statistics 810
MICROBIOLOGY 167
MICROCOMPUTERS see COMPUTERS - Microcomputers 361
Microfilming see PHOTOGRAPHY 884
Microphotography see PHOTOGRAPHY 884
MICROSCOPY 169
Microwaves see ELECTRICITY AND ELECTRICAL ENGINEERING 450
Midwifery see MEDICAL SCIENCES - Obstetrics and Gynecology 784
Migration see POPULATION STUDIES 920
MILITARY 810
MILITARY — Abstracting, Bibliographies, Statistics 813
Military Engineering see ENGINEERING 469
Military Law see LAW 649, see also MILITARY 810
Military Medicine see MEDICAL SCIENCES 756
Millinery see CLOTHING TRADE 339
Milling see AGRICULTURE - Feed, Flour and Grain 63

Mineral Resources see EARTH SCIENCES - Geology 382, see also MINES AND MINING INDUSTRY 813
Mineralogy see MINES AND MINING INDUSTRY 382
MINES AND MINING INDUSTRY 813
MINES AND MINING INDUSTRY — Abstracting, Bibliographies, Statistics 821
MINICOMPUTERS see COMPUTERS - Minicomputers 362
Missiles see AERONAUTICS AND SPACE FLIGHT 17
Mobile Homes see HOUSING AND URBAN PLANNING 621, see also TRANSPORTATION 1080
Models and Model Building see HOBBIES 614
Modems see COMPUTERS - Hardware 361
Mollusca see BIOLOGY - Zoology 172
Monitors see COMPUTERS - Hardware 361
Morphology see BIOLOGY 137, see also MEDICAL SCIENCES 756
Mosses see BIOLOGY - Botany 153
Motels see HOTELS AND RESTAURANTS 619
MOTION PICTURES 822
MOTION PICTURES — Abstracting, Bibliographies, Statistics 825
Motor Scooters see SPORTS AND GAMES - Bicycles and Motorcycles 1041
Motorcycles see SPORTS AND GAMES - Bicycles and Motorcycles 1041
Mountaineering see SPORTS AND GAMES - Outdoor Life 1043
Movies see MOTION PICTURES 822
Multiple Sclerosis see MEDICAL SCIENCES - Psychiatry and Neurology 788
MUNICIPAL GOVERNMENT 950
Municipal Law see LAW 649, see also PUBLIC ADMINISTRATION - Municipal Government 950
Municipal Transportation see TRANSPORTATION 1080
MUSEUMS AND ART GALLERIES 826
MUSEUMS AND ART GALLERIES — Abstracting, Bibliographies, Statistics 831
MUSIC 832
MUSIC — Abstracting, Bibliographies, Statistics 843
MUSIC — Computer Applications 844, see also COMPUTERS - Computer Music 357
Music Therapy see EDUCATION - Special Education and Rehabilitation 444, see also MUSIC 832
Mutual Funds see BUSINESS AND ECONOMICS - Investments 265
Mycology see BIOLOGY - Botany 153
Mysteries see ADVENTURE AND ROMANCE 13, see also LITERATURE 713
Mythology see FOLKLORE 514
Narcotics see DRUG ABUSE AND ALCOHOLISM 376, see also PHARMACY AND PHARMACOLOGY 869
Natural Food see NUTRITION AND DIETETICS 845
Natural Resources see CONSERVATION 363, see also ENVIRONMENTAL STUDIES 493
Naturalization see POLITICAL SCIENCE 901
Nautical Arts and Sciences see TRANSPORTATION - Ships and Shipping 1098
Naval Architecture see TRANSPORTATION - Ships and Shipping 1098
Naval Engineering see TRANSPORTATION - Ships and Shipping 1098
Naval Medicine see MEDICAL SCIENCES 756
NEEDLEWORK 844
Nephrology see MEDICAL SCIENCES - Urology and Nephrology 795
Neurology see MEDICAL SCIENCES - Psychiatry and Neurology 788
Neurophysiology see MEDICAL SCIENCES - Psychiatry and Neurology 788
Neuroradiology see MEDICAL SCIENCES - Radiology and Nuclear Medicine 792
Neurosurgery see MEDICAL SCIENCES - Psychiatry and Neurology 788, see also MEDICAL SCIENCES - Surgery 793
Newspaper Business see JOURNALISM 645
Noise Control see ENGINEERING - Mechanical Engineering 491
North American History see HISTORY - History of North and South America 602
Notions see GIFTWARE AND TOYS 552
NUCLEAR ENERGY 895
Nuclear Medicine see MEDICAL SCIENCES - Radiology and Nuclear Medicine 792
Nudism see PHYSICAL FITNESS AND HYGIENE 885
NUMISMATICS 844
Nurseries see GARDENING AND HORTICULTURE - Florist Trade 534
NURSES AND NURSING 783
Nursing Homes see HOSPITALS 616, see also SOCIAL SERVICES AND WELFARE 1015
NUTRITION AND DIETETICS 845, see also FOOD AND FOOD INDUSTRIES 517, HOSPITALS 616, PHARMACY AND PHARMACOLOGY 869, PHYSICAL FITNESS AND HYGIENE 885
NUTRITION AND DIETETICS — Abstracting, Bibliographies, Statistics 847
OBSTETRICS AND GYNECOLOGY 784
Occultism see PARAPSYCHOLOGY AND OCCULTISM 860
Occupational Therapy see EDUCATION - Special Education and Rehabilitation 444, see also MEDICAL SCIENCES 756
OCCUPATIONS AND CAREERS 847, see also BUSINESS AND ECONOMICS - Labor and Industrial Relations 269
OCCUPATIONS AND CAREERS — Abstracting, Bibliographies, Statistics 849
OCEANOGRAPHY 404
OFFICE EQUIPMENT AND SERVICES 286
Oils and Fats see CHEMISTRY - Organic Chemistry 329
Old Age see GERONTOLOGY AND GERIATRICS 551
Old Age Insurance see INSURANCE 637
OPHTHALMOLOGY AND OPTOMETRY 785
OPTICS 899
Optometry see MEDICAL SCIENCES - Ophthalmology and Optometry 785
ORGANIC CHEMISTRY 329
ORIENTAL RELIGIONS 977
ORIENTAL STUDIES 849, see also HISTORY - History of Asia 568, LINGUISTICS 689, LITERATURE 713, PHILOSOPHY 875
ORIENTAL STUDIES — Abstracting, Bibliographies, Statistics 854
ORNITHOLOGY 169
Orthodontics see MEDICAL SCIENCES - Dentistry 778
ORTHOPEDICS AND TRAUMATOLOGY 786
Osteopathy see MEDICAL SCIENCES - Chiropractics, Homeopathy, Osteopathy 777

Otology see MEDICAL SCIENCES - Otorhinolaryngology 786
OTORHINOLARYNGOLOGY 786
OUTDOOR LIFE 1043
PACKAGING 854
PACKAGING — Abstracting, Bibliographies, Statistics 855
PAINTS AND PROTECTIVE COATINGS 855
PAINTS AND PROTECTIVE COATINGS — Abstracting, Bibliographies, Statistics 856
Paleobotany see BIOLOGY - Botany 153
PALEONTOLOGY 856
PALEONTOLOGY — Abstracting, Bibliographies, Statistics 858
PAPER AND PULP 858, see also FORESTS AND FORESTRY - Lumber and Wood 529
PAPER AND PULP — Abstracting, Bibliographies, Statistics 859
Papyrus see PAPER AND PULP 858
Parachuting see SPORTS AND GAMES 1032
Paraplegia see MEDICAL SCIENCES - Psychiatry and Neurology 788
PARAPSYCHOLOGY AND OCCULTISM 860
Parasitology see BIOLOGY 137
Parent Teacher Associations see EDUCATION - School Organization and Administration 442
Parenting see CHILDREN AND YOUTH - About 333
Parks and Recreation Areas see CONSERVATION 363, see also SPORTS AND GAMES - Outdoor Life 1043, TRAVEL AND TOURISM 1105
PATENTS, TRADEMARKS AND COPYRIGHTS 860
PATENTS, TRADEMARKS AND COPYRIGHTS — Abstracting, Bibliographies, Statistics 861
Paving see BUILDING AND CONSTRUCTION 181, see also TRANSPORTATION - Roads and Traffic 1095
Peat see HEATING, PLUMBING AND REFRIGERATION 553
PEDIATRICS 787
Penology see CRIMINOLOGY AND LAW ENFORCEMENT 369
Pensions see BUSINESS AND ECONOMICS - Labor and Industrial Relations 269, see also INSURANCE 637, SOCIAL SERVICES AND WELFARE 1015
Performing Arts see DANCE 374, see also MOTION PICTURES 822, MUSIC 832, THEATER 1076
PERFUMES AND COSMETICS 118
Peripherals see COMPUTERS - Hardware 361
PERSONAL COMPUTERS see COMPUTERS - Personal Computers 362
PERSONNEL MANAGEMENT 286
Pest Control see AGRICULTURE 22, see also BIOLOGY - Entomology 163, PUBLIC HEALTH AND SAFETY 952
PETROLEUM AND GAS 862
PETROLEUM AND GAS — Abstracting, Bibliographies, Statistics 867
Petrology see EARTH SCIENCES - Geology 382
PETS 868
PHARMACY AND PHARMACOLOGY 869, see also MEDICAL SCIENCES 756
PHARMACY AND PHARMACOLOGY — Abstracting, Bibliographies, Statistics 873
Philanthropy see SOCIAL SERVICES AND WELFARE 1015
PHILATELY 874
Philology see LINGUISTICS 689
PHILOSOPHY 875
PHILOSOPHY — Abstracting, Bibliographies, Statistics 883
Phonetics see LINGUISTICS 689
Phonographs see MUSIC 832, see also SOUND RECORDING AND REPRODUCTION 1031
Photogrammetry see GEOGRAPHY 540, see also PHOTOGRAPHY 884
Photographic Surveying see ENGINEERING - Civil Engineering 480
PHOTOGRAPHY 884, see also MOTION PICTURES 822
PHOTOGRAPHY — Abstracting, Bibliographies, Statistics 885
Photomechanical Processing see PRINTING 930
PHYSICAL CHEMISTRY 331
Physical Education see EDUCATION - Teaching Methods and Curriculum 446, see also SPORTS AND GAMES 1032
PHYSICAL FITNESS AND HYGIENE 885
PHYSICAL FITNESS AND HYGIENE — Abstracting, Bibliographies, Statistics 886
Physical Therapy see MEDICAL SCIENCES 756
PHYSICS 886
PHYSICS — Abstracting, Bibliographies, Statistics 892
PHYSICS — Heat 894
PHYSICS — Mechanics 894
PHYSICS — Nuclear Energy 895
PHYSICS — Optics 899
PHYSICS — Sound 899
PHYSIOLOGY 171
Planned Parenthood see BIRTH CONTROL 179
Plant Breeding see AGRICULTURE - Crop Production and Soil 51, see also BIOLOGY - Botany 153, GARDENING AND HORTICULTURE 531
Plasma Physics see PHYSICS 886
Plastic Surgery see MEDICAL SCIENCES - Surgery 793
PLASTICS 900, see also CHEMISTRY - Physical chemistry 331, ENGINEERING - Chemical Engineering 477
PLASTICS — Abstracting, Bibliographies, Statistics 901
Plays see LITERATURE 713, see also THEATER 1076
Plumbing see HEATING, PLUMBING AND REFRIGERATION 553
POETRY 739
Police see CRIMINOLOGY AND LAW ENFORCEMENT 369
Poliomyelitis see MEDICAL SCIENCES - Psychiatry and Neurology 788
Political Reviews see LITERARY AND POLITICAL REVIEWS 709
POLITICAL SCIENCE 901, see also LITERARY AND POLITICAL REVIEWS 709, PUBLIC ADMINISTRATION 938
POLITICAL SCIENCE — Abstracting, Bibliographies, Statistics 911
POLITICAL SCIENCE — Civil Rights 912
POLITICAL SCIENCE — International Relations 914
Pollution see ENVIRONMENTAL STUDIES 493, see also PUBLIC HEALTH AND SAFETY 952

Polymers see CHEMISTRY 321, see also ENGINEERING - Chemical Engineering 477
POPULATION STUDIES 920
POPULATION STUDIES — Abstracting, Bibliographies, Statistics 925
Ports see TRANSPORTATION - Ships and Shipping 1098
Portuguese LANGUAGE - Study and Teaching see LINGUISTICS 689
POSTAL AFFAIRS 346
Pottery see CERAMICS, GLASS AND POTTERY 319
POULTRY AND LIVESTOCK 64
Power Plants see ELECTRICITY AND ELECTRICAL ENGINEERING 450, see also ENERGY 463
Pre-school Education see EDUCATION 409
Precision Mechanics see INSTRUMENTS 636
Prefabricated Houses see BUILDING AND CONSTRUCTION 181
Preventive Medicine see PUBLIC HEALTH AND SAFETY 952
PRINTING 930
PRINTING — Abstracting, Bibliographies, Statistics 931
PRINTING — Computer Applications 932, see also COMPUTERS - Computer Graphics 356
Prisons see CRIMINOLOGY AND LAW ENFORCEMENT 369
Private Schools see EDUCATION - Guides to Schools and Colleges 428, see also EDUCATION - School Organization and Administration 442
Produce see FOOD AND FOOD INDUSTRIES 517
PRODUCTION OF GOODS AND SERVICES 287
Programmed Instruction see EDUCATION - Teaching Methods and Curriculum 446
Programming, Automatic see COMPUTERS - Computer Programming 357
Proofreading see JOURNALISM 645, see also PRINTING 930
Prosthetics see MEDICAL SCIENCES - Orthopedics and Traumatology 786
Protective Coatings see PAINTS AND PROTECTIVE COATINGS 855
PROTESTANTISM 978
Protozoology see BIOLOGY - Zoology 172
PSYCHIATRY AND NEUROLOGY 788
Psychic Phenomena see PARAPSYCHOLOGY AND OCCULTISM 860
Psychical Research see PARAPSYCHOLOGY AND OCCULTISM 860
Psychoanalysis see PSYCHOLOGY 932
Psychological Testing see PSYCHOLOGY 932
PSYCHOLOGY 932
PSYCHOLOGY — Abstracting, Bibliographies, Statistics 938
Psychosomatic Medicine see MEDICAL SCIENCES 756
Psychotherapy see MEDICAL SCIENCES - Psychiatry and Neurology 788
PUBLIC ADMINISTRATION 938, see also POLITICAL SCIENCE 901
PUBLIC ADMINISTRATION — Abstracting, Bibliographies, Statistics 947
PUBLIC ADMINISTRATION — Municipal Government 950
Public Affairs see POLITICAL SCIENCE 901, see also PUBLIC ADMINISTRATION 938, SOCIAL SCIENCES 1005
PUBLIC FINANCE, TAXATION 292
PUBLIC HEALTH AND SAFETY 952, see also DRUG ABUSE AND ALCOHOLISM 376, ENVIRONMENTAL STUDIES 493, FIRE PREVENTION 506, FUNERALS 531, HOSPITALS 616, INDUSTRIAL HEALTH AND SAFETY 635, MEDICAL SCIENCES 756
PUBLIC HEALTH AND SAFETY — Abstracting, Bibliographies, Statistics 958
Public Relations see ADVERTISING AND PUBLIC RELATIONS 14
Public Transportation see TRANSPORTATION 1080
Public Utilities see ELECTRICITY AND ELECTRICAL ENGINEERING 450, see also PETROLEUM AND GAS 862, PUBLIC ADMINISTRATION 938
Public Welfare see SOCIAL SERVICES AND WELFARE 1015
Public Works see BUILDING AND CONSTRUCTION 181, see also ENGINEERING - Civil Engineering 480, HOUSING AND URBAN PLANNING 621, PUBLIC ADMINISTRATION 938
Publicity see ADVERTISING AND PUBLIC RELATIONS 14
PUBLISHING AND BOOK TRADE 959, see also BIBLIOGRAPHIES 121, LIBRARY AND INFORMATION SCIENCES 672, PATENTS, TRADEMARKS AND COPYRIGHTS 860, PRINTING 930
PUBLISHING AND BOOK TRADE — Abstracting, Bibliographies, Statistics 963
PUBLISHING AND BOOK TRADE — Computer Applications 964
Pulp see PAPER AND PULP 858
Puppets see HOBBIES 614, see also THEATER 1076
Puzzles see SPORTS AND GAMES 1032
Quality Control see BUSINESS AND ECONOMICS - Management 278, see also METROLOGY AND STANDARDIZATION 808
Quantum Chemistry see CHEMISTRY - Physical Chemistry 331
Quarries see MINES AND MINING INDUSTRY 813
Race Relations see POLITICAL SCIENCE - Civil Rights 912, see also SOCIOLOGY 1023
Racing see SPORTS AND GAMES - Horses and Horsemanship 1042, see also TRANSPORTATION - Automobiles 1090
Radar see COMMUNICATIONS 342
Radiation see ASTRONOMY 114, see also BIOLOGY - Biophysics 152, CHEMISTRY - Physical Chemistry 331, MEDICAL SCIENCES - Radiology and Nuclear Medicine 792, PHYSICS - Nuclear Energy 895
Radio Advertising see ADVERTISING AND PUBLIC RELATIONS 14, see also COMMUNICATIONS - Radio and Television 347
RADIO AND TELEVISION 347
Radiobiology see BIOLOGY 137
Radiocarbon see PHYSICS - Nuclear Energy 895
RADIOLOGY AND NUCLEAR MEDICINE 792
Railroad Engineering see TRANSPORTATION - Railroads 1094
RAILROADS 1094
Railway Ties see FORESTS AND FORESTRY - Lumber and Wood 529, see also TRANSPORTATION - Railroads 1094
Rare Earths see CHEMISTRY - Inorganic Chemistry 328
Reading Guides and Aids see ABSTRACTING AND INDEXING SERVICES 1, see also BIBLIOGRAPHIES 121, EDUCATION - Teaching Methods and Curriculum 446, LIBRARY AND INFORMATION SCIENCES 672
REAL ESTATE 964, see also BUILDING AND CONSTRUCTION 181, HOUSING AND URBAN PLANNING 621
REAL ESTATE — Abstracting, Bibliographies, Statistics 966

Recorded Music see MUSIC 832, see also SOUND RECORDING AND REPRODUCTION 1031
Recreation see DANCE 374, see also HOBBIES 614, SPORTS AND GAMES 1032
Recreation Areas see CONSERVATION 363, see also TRAVEL AND TOURISM 1105
Recreational Vehicles see TRANSPORTATION - Automobiles 1090
Red Cross see SOCIAL SERVICES AND WELFARE 1015
Refrigeration see HEATING, PLUMBING AND REFRIGERATION 553, see also PHYSICS - Heat 894
Regional Planning see HOUSING AND URBAN PLANNING 621
Rehabilitation see EDUCATION - Special Education and Rehabilitation 444, see also MEDICAL SCIENCES 756, SOCIAL SERVICES AND WELFARE 1015
RELIGIONS AND THEOLOGY 966
RELIGIONS AND THEOLOGY — Abstracting, Bibliographies, Statistics 974
RELIGIONS AND THEOLOGY — Islamic 975
RELIGIONS AND THEOLOGY — Judaic 976
RELIGIONS AND THEOLOGY — Oriental 977
RELIGIONS AND THEOLOGY — Other Denominations And Sects 983
RELIGIONS AND THEOLOGY — Protestant 978
RELIGIONS AND THEOLOGY — Roman Catholic 980
Religious History see RELIGIONS AND THEOLOGY 966
Reproduction and Fertility see BIOLOGY 137, see also MEDICAL SCIENCES 756
Research and Development see TECHNOLOGY: COMPREHENSIVE WORKS 1067
Resins see PLASTICS 900
Resorts see HOTELS AND RESTAURANTS 619, see also TRAVEL AND TOURISM 1105
RESPIRATORY DISEASES 792
Restaurants see HOTELS AND RESTAURANTS 619
Retailing see BUSINESS AND ECONOMICS - Marketing and Purchasing 282
Rheology see PHYSICS - Mechanics 894
RHEUMATOLOGY 793
Rhinology see MEDICAL SCIENCES - Otorhinolaryngology 786
ROADS AND TRAFFIC 1095
Robotics see COMPUTERS - Artificial Intelligence 354
Rockets see AERONAUTICS AND SPACE FLIGHT 17
Rodeo see SPORTS AND GAMES - Horses and Horsemanship 1042
Roller Skating see SPORTS AND GAMES 1032
ROMAN CATHOLICISM 980
RUBBER 985, see also ENGINEERING - Chemical Engineering 477, PLASTICS 900
RUBBER — Abstracting, Bibliographies, Statistics 986
Rugby see SPORTS AND GAMES - Ball Games 1037
Safety Education see BUSINESS AND ECONOMICS - Labor and Industrial Relations 269, see also INDUSTRIAL HEALTH AND SAFETY 635, PUBLIC HEALTH AND SAFETY 952, TRANSPORTATION - Roads and Traffic 1095
Sailing see SPORTS AND GAMES - Boats and Boating 1041
Salesmanship see BUSINESS AND ECONOMICS - Marketing and Purchasing 282
Sanitary Engineering see PUBLIC HEALTH AND SAFETY 952
Sanitation see ENGINEERING - Civil Engineering 480, see also PHYSICAL FITNESS AND HYGIENE 885, PUBLIC HEALTH AND SAFETY 952
Savings and Loan see BUSINESS AND ECONOMICS - Banking and Finance 222
Scholarships see EDUCATION - Higher Education 431
SCHOOL ORGANIZATION AND ADMINISTRATION 442
Science Fiction see ADVENTURE AND ROMANCE 13, see also LITERATURE 713
SCIENCES: COMPREHENSIVE WORKS 986
SCIENCES: COMPREHENSIVE WORKS — Abstracting, Bibliographies, Statistics 1003
SCIENCES: COMPREHENSIVE WORKS — Computer Applications 1005
Scooters see SPORTS AND GAMES - Bicycles and Motorcycles 1041
Sculpture see ART 100
Seaweed see BIOLOGY - Botany 153, see also EARTH SCIENCES - Oceanography 404
Securities see BUSINESS AND ECONOMICS - Investments 265
SECURITY 374
Sediment Data see ENGINEERING - Hydraulic Engineering 490
Sedimentology see EARTH SCIENCES - Geophysics 398
Seeds see AGRICULTURE - Crop Production and Soil 51
Seismology see EARTH SCIENCES - Geophysics 398
Selling see ADVERTISING AND PUBLIC RELATIONS 14, see also BUSINESS AND ECONOMICS - Marketing and Purchasing 282
Semantics see LINGUISTICS 689
Semiconductors see ELECTRICITY AND ELECTRICAL ENGINEERING 450
Senior Citizens see GERONTOLOGY AND GERIATRICS 551
Service Stations see PETROLEUM AND GAS 862, see also TRANSPORTATION - Automobiles 1090
Sewage and Waste Treatment see PUBLIC ADMINISTRATION 938, see also PUBLIC HEALTH AND SAFETY 952
Sewing see CLOTHING TRADE - Fashions 340, see also NEEDLEWORK 844
Sex Education see PHYSICAL FITNESS AND HYGIENE 885
Sheet Metal see METALLURGY 796
Shipbuilding see TRANSPORTATION - Ships and Shipping 1098
SHIPS AND SHIPPING 1098
SHOES AND BOOTS 1005, see also LEATHER AND FUR INDUSTRIES 672
SHOES AND BOOTS — Abstracting, Bibliographies, Statistics 1005
Shooting see SPORTS AND GAMES - Outdoor Life 1043
Short Wave see COMMUNICATIONS - Radio and Television 347
Shorthand see BUSINESS AND ECONOMICS - Office Equipment and Services 286
Sign Manufacturing see ADVERTISING AND PUBLIC RELATIONS 14
Silicosis see MEDICAL SCIENCES 756
Site Selection see HOUSING AND URBAN PLANNING 621, see also REAL ESTATE 964
Skating see SPORTS AND GAMES 1032
Skeet Shooting see SPORTS AND GAMES - Outdoor Life 1043
Skiing see SPORTS AND GAMES - Outdoor Life 1043

Slavonic Languages - Study and Teaching see LINGUISTICS 689
SMALL BUSINESS 301
Smoking see DRUG ABUSE AND ALCOHOLISM 376, see also PHYSICAL FITNESS AND HYGIENE 885, PUBLIC HEALTH AND SAFETY 952, TOBACCO 1079
Snack Foods see FOOD AND FOOD INDUSTRIES - Bakers and Confectioners 522
Soap see BEAUTY CULTURE - Perfumes and Cosmetics 118
Soccer see SPORTS AND GAMES - Ball Games 1037
Social Insurance see INSURANCE 637, see also SOCIAL SERVICES AND WELFARE 1015
Social Psychology see PSYCHOLOGY 932, see also SOCIOLOGY 1023
SOCIAL SCIENCES: COMPREHENSIVE WORKS 1005
SOCIAL SCIENCES: COMPREHENSIVE WORKS — Abstracting, Bibliographies, Statistics 1014
Social Security see INSURANCE 637, see also SOCIAL SERVICES AND WELFARE 1015
SOCIAL SERVICES AND WELFARE 1015
SOCIAL SERVICES AND WELFARE — Abstracting, Bibliographies, Statistics 1022
Socialism see BUSINESS AND ECONOMICS - Economic Systems and Theories, Economic History 250, see also POLITICAL SCIENCE 901
SOCIOLOGY 1023, see also POPULATION STUDIES 920
SOCIOLOGY — Abstracting, Bibliographies, Statistics 1031
Soft Drinks see BEVERAGES 119
SOFTWARE see COMPUTERS - Software 362
Soil see AGRICULTURE - Crop Production and Soil 51, see also CONSERVATION 363, ENGINEERING - Civil Engineering 480
Solar Energy see ASTRONOMY 114, see also ENERGY 463, PHYSICS 886
Solar Energy Engineering see ENGINEERING - Mechanical Engineering 491
Solid Waste see ENVIRONMENTAL STUDIES 493
SOUND 899
SOUND RECORDING AND REPRODUCTION 1031
SOUND RECORDING AND REPRODUCTION — Abstracting, Bibliographies, Statistics 1032
South American History see HISTORY - History of North and South America 602
Space Flight see AERONAUTICS AND SPACE FLIGHT 17
Spanish Language - Study and Teaching see LINGUISTICS 689
Spearfishing see SPORTS AND GAMES - Outdoor Life 1043
SPECIAL EDUCATION AND REHABILITATION 444
Spectroscopy see PHYSICS - Optics 899
Speech and Hearing Disorders see DEAF 375, see also EDUCATION - Special Education and Rehabilitation 444, MEDICAL SCIENCES - Psychiatry and Neurology 788
Speech - Study and Teaching see EDUCATION - Special Education and Rehabilitation 444, see also LINGUISTICS 689
Speleology see EARTH SCIENCES - Geophysics 398
Spices see FOOD AND FOOD INDUSTRIES 517
Spinning see NEEDLEWORK 844
Spiritualism see PARAPSYCHOLOGY AND OCCULTISM 860
Sporting Goods see SPORTS AND GAMES 1032
SPORTS AND GAMES 1032
SPORTS AND GAMES — Abstracting, Bibliographies, Statistics 1036
SPORTS AND GAMES — Ball Games 1037
SPORTS AND GAMES — Bicycles And Motorcycles 1041
SPORTS AND GAMES — Boats And Boating 1041
SPORTS AND GAMES — Horses And Horsemanship 1042
SPORTS AND GAMES — Outdoor Life 1043
Sports Cars see TRANSPORTATION - Automobiles 1090
Sports Medicine see MEDICAL SCIENCES - Surgery 793
Sportswear see CLOTHING Trade 339
Stained Glass see ART 100, see also CERAMICS, GLASS AND POTTERY 319
Standards see METROLOGY AND STANDARDIZATION 808
Stationery and Office Equipment see BUSINESS AND ECONOMICS -Office Equipment and Services 286
STATISTICS 1047, see also POPULATION STUDIES 920
Stenography see BUSINESS AND ECONOMICS - Office Equipment and Services 286
Sterilization see BIRTH CONTROL 179
Stock and Stock-Breeding see AGRICULTURE - Poultry and Livestock 64
Stocks and Bonds see BUSINESS AND ECONOMICS - Investments 265
Storage Batteries see ELECTRICITY AND ELECTRICAL ENGINEERING 450
Store Display and Promotion see ADVERTISING AND PUBLIC RELATIONS 14
Street Lighting see ELECTRICITY AND ELECTRICAL ENGINEERING 450, see also PUBLIC ADMINISTRATION - Municipal Government 950
Stress see PSYCHOLOGY 932
Student Aid see EDUCATION 409
Supermarkets see FOOD AND FOOD INDUSTRIES - Grocery Trade 522
Surfing see SPORTS AND GAMES - Outdoor Life 1043
SURGERY 793
Surgical Instruments see MEDICAL SCIENCES - Surgery 793
Surveying see ENGINEERING - Civil Engineering 480, see also GEOGRAPHY 540
Swimming see SPORTS AND GAMES 1032
Synthetic Fabrics see TEXTILE INDUSTRIES AND FABRICS 1073
Table Tennis see SPORTS AND GAMES - Ball Games 1037
Tailoring see CLOTHING TRADE 339
Talking Books see BLIND 179
Tape Drives see COMPUTERS - Hardware 361
Tape Recording see SOUND RECORDING AND REPRODUCTION 1031
Tariffs see BUSINESS AND ECONOMICS - International Commerce 252, see also BUSINESS AND ECONOMICS - Public Finance, Taxation 292
TAXATION 1067, see also BUSINESS AND ECONOMICS - Public Finance, Taxation 292
Taxicabs see TRANSPORTATION - Automobiles 1090
Tea see FOOD AND FOOD INDUSTRIES 517
TEACHING METHODS AND CURRICULUM 446
TECHNOLOGY: COMPREHENSIVE WORKS 1067

TECHNOLOGY: COMPREHENSIVE WORKS — Abstracting, Bibliographies, Statistics 1072
Telecommunications see COMMUNICATIONS 342, see also ELECTRICITY AND ELECTRICAL ENGINEERING 450
Telegraph see COMMUNICATIONS - Telephone and Telegraph 350
TELEPHONE AND TELEGRAPH 350
Television see COMMUNICATIONS - Radio and Television 347, see also MOTION PICTURES 822
Tennis see SPORTS AND GAMES - Ball Games 1037
Terminals see COMPUTERS - Hardware 361
Textbooks see EDUCATION - Teaching Methods and Curriculum 446, see also PUBLISHING AND BOOK TRADE 959
TEXTILE INDUSTRIES AND FABRICS 1073
TEXTILE INDUSTRIES AND FABRICS — Abstracting, Bibliographies, Statistics 1075
Thanatology see MEDICAL SCIENCES 756
THEATER 1076
THEATER — Abstracting, Bibliographies, Statistics 1079
Theology see RELIGIONS AND THEOLOGY 966
THEORY OF COMPUTING see COMPUTERS - Theory of Computing 363
Theosophy see PHILOSOPHY 875, see also RELIGIONS AND THEOLOGY 966
Thermodynamics see CHEMISTRY - Physical Chemistry 331, see also PHYSICS - Heat 894
Thoracic Surgery see MEDICAL SCIENCES - Surgery 793
Thrombosis see MEDICAL SCIENCES - Cardiovascular Diseases 776
Timber see FORESTS AND FORESTRY - Lumber and Wood 529
Timetables see TRANSPORTATION 1080
Tires see RUBBER 985, see also TRANSPORTATION - Automobiles 1090
TOBACCO 1079
TOBACCO — Abstracting, Bibliographies, Statistics 1080
Toiletries see BEAUTY CULTURE 118
Tools see MACHINERY 745
Touring see TRAVEL AND TOURISM 1105
Tourist Camps see HOTELS AND RESTAURANTS 619, see also TRAVEL AND TOURISM 1105
Town Planning see HOUSING AND URBAN PLANNING 621
Toxicology see MEDICAL SCIENCES 756, see also PHARMACY AND PHARMACOLOGY 869
Toys see GIFTWARE AND TOYS 552
Track and Field see SPORTS AND GAMES 1032
Tractors see AGRICULTURE - Agricultural Equipment 51
Trade see BUSINESS AND ECONOMICS - Domestic Commerce 239, see also BUSINESS AND ECONOMICS - International Commerce 252
TRADE AND INDUSTRIAL DIRECTORIES 301
Trade Shows see MEETINGS AND CONGRESSES 795
Trade Unions see LABOR UNIONS 647
Trademarks see PATENTS, TRADEMARKS AND COPYRIGHTS 860
Traffic see TRANSPORTATION - Roads and Traffic 1095
Trailers see TRANSPORTATION 1080
Transistors see ELECTRICITY AND ELECTRICAL ENGINEERING 450
Translation Services see LINGUISTICS 689
TRANSPORTATION 1080
TRANSPORTATION — Abstracting, Bibliographies, Statistics 1084
TRANSPORTATION — Air Transport 1087
TRANSPORTATION — Automobiles 1090
TRANSPORTATION — Computer Applications 1093
Transportation Law see LAW 649
TRANSPORTATION — Railroads 1094
TRANSPORTATION — Roads And Traffic 1095
TRANSPORTATION — Ships And Shipping 1098
TRANSPORTATION — Trucks And Trucking 1104
Trapping see LEATHER AND FUR INDUSTRIES 672
Trapshooting see SPORTS AND GAMES - Outdoor Life 1043
Traumatology see MEDICAL SCIENCES - Orthopedics and Traumatology 786
TRAVEL AND TOURISM 1105, see also GEOGRAPHY 540, HOTELS AND RESTAURANTS 619
TRAVEL AND TOURISM — Abstracting, Bibliographies, Statistics 1119
Treaties see LAW - International Law 669
Trees see FORESTS AND FORESTRY 523, see also GARDENING AND HORTICULTURE 531
Tropical Diseases see MEDICAL SCIENCES - Communicable Diseases 777
Tuberculosis see MEDICAL SCIENCES - Respiratory Diseases 792
Typewriters see BUSINESS AND ECONOMICS - Office Equipment and Services 286
Typography see PRINTING 930
Ultrasonics see PHYSICS - Sound 899
Underground Periodicals see LITERARY AND POLITICAL REVIEWS 709, see also POLITICAL SCIENCE 901
Underwear see CLOTHING TRADE 339
Unemployment see BUSINESS AND ECONOMICS - Labor and Industrial Relations 269
Unidentified Flying Objects see AERONAUTICS AND SPACE FLIGHT 17
Unions see LABOR UNIONS 647
U. S. Armed Forces see MILITARY 810
Universities and Colleges see EDUCATION - Higher Education 431
Upholstery see INTERIOR DESIGN AND DECORATION - Furniture and House Furnishings 643
Urban Renewal see HOUSING AND URBAN PLANNING 621
UROLOGY AND NEPHROLOGY 795
Utilities see ELECTRICITY AND ELECTRICAL ENGINEERING 450, see also PUBLIC ADMINISTRATION 938
Vaccines see PHARMACY AND PHARMACOLOGY 869
Vacuum Sciences see ENGINEERING - Mechanical Engineering 491, see also PHYSICS - Mechanics 894
Vegetarianism see NUTRITION AND DIETETICS 845
Vending Machines see BUSINESS AND ECONOMICS - Marketing and Purchasing 282
Venereology see MEDICAL SCIENCES - Dermatology and Venereology 780
Ventilation see HEATING, PLUMBING AND REFRIGERATION 553
Veterans see MILITARY 810
VETERINARY SCIENCE 1120
VETERINARY SCIENCE — Abstracting, Bibliographies, Statistics 1123
Video see COMMUNICATIONS - Radio and Television 347, see also MOTION PICTURES 822
Virology see BIOLOGY - Microbiology 167
Vital Statistics see POPULATION STUDIES 920
Vitamins see PHARMACY AND PHARMACOLOGY 869
Viticulture see AGRICULTURE - Crop Production and Soil 51
Vocational Education see EDUCATION - Teaching Methods and Curriculum 409, see also OCCUPATIONS AND CAREERS 847
Volume Feeding see HOTELS AND RESTAURANTS 619
Wages see BUSINESS AND ECONOMICS - Labor and Industrial Relations 269
Waste Reclamation see ENVIRONMENTAL STUDIES 493
Watchmaking see JEWELRY, CLOCKS AND WATCHES 644
Water Pollution see ENVIRONMENTAL STUDIES 493
WATER RESOURCES 1123, see also AGRICULTURE 22, CONSERVATION 363, ENVIRONMENTAL STUDIES 493, PUBLIC HEALTH AND SAFETY 952
WATER RESOURCES — Abstracting, Bibliographies, Statistics 1127
Water Sports see SPORTS AND GAMES 1032
Weather see METEOROLOGY 802
Weaving see NEEDLEWORK 844, see also TEXTILE INDUSTRIES AND FABRICS 1073
Weights and Measures see METROLOGY AND STANDARDIZATION 808
WELDING 802
Welfare see SOCIAL SERVICES AND WELFARE 1015
Wildlife see BIOLOGY 137, see also CONSERVATION 363
Window Covering see INTERIOR DESIGN AND DECORATION - Furniture and House Furnishings 643
Windows see BUILDING AND CONSTRUCTION 181, see also CERAMICS, GLASS AND POTTERY 319
Wine see BEVERAGES 119
Wire see MACHINERY 745, see also METALLURGY 745
Wit and Humor see LITERARY AND POLITICAL REVIEWS 709
WOMEN'S INTERESTS 1128
WOMEN'S INTERESTS — Abstracting, Bibliographies, Statistics 1130
Women's Liberation Movement see POLITICAL SCIENCE - Civil Rights 912, see also WOMEN'S INTERESTS 1128
Women's Wear see CLOTHING TRADE 339
Wood see BUILDING AND CONSTRUCTION - Carpentry and Woodwork 189, see also FORESTS AND FORESTRY - Lumber and Wood 529
Wood Pulp see PAPER AND PULP 858
Woodwork see BUILDING AND CONSTRUCTION - Carpentry and Woodwork 189
WORD PROCESSING see COMPUTERS - Word Processing 363
Wrestling see SPORTS AND GAMES 1032
Writers and Writing see JOURNALISM 645, see also LITERATURE 713, PUBLISHING AND BOOK TRADE 959
Yachting see SPORTS AND GAMES - Boats and Boating 1041
Yoga see PHILOSOPHY 875, see also PHYSICAL FITNESS AND HYGIENE 885
Youth see CHILDREN AND YOUTH - About 333
Zoning see HOUSING AND URBAN PLANNING 621
ZOOLOGY 172
Zootechniques see AGRICULTURE - Poultry and Livestock 64, see also VETERINARY SCIENCE 1120

Classified List of Serials

ABSTRACTING AND INDEXING

UNIVERSITY MICROFILMS INTERNATIONAL NEWSLETTER. see *LIBRARY AND INFORMATION SCIENCES* — *Abstracting, Bibliographies, Statistics*

ABSTRACTING AND INDEXING SERVICES

see also Bibliographies

A B C POL SCI; a bibliography of contents: political science and government. see *POLITICAL SCIENCE* — *Abstracting, Bibliographies, Statistics*

A.E.T.F.A.T. INDEX; releve des travaux de phanerogamie systematique et des taxons nouveaux concernant l'Afrique au sud du Sahara et Madagascar. (Association pour l'Etude Taxonomique de la Flore d'Afrique Tropicale) see *BIOLOGY* — *Abstracting, Bibliographies, Statistics*

A P A I S: AUSTRALIAN PUBLIC AFFAIRS INFORMATION SERVICE; subject index to current literature. see *PUBLIC ADMINISTRATION* — *Abstracting, Bibliographies, Statistics*

A P I ABSTRACTS/LITERATURE. (American Petroleum Institute) see *PETROLEUM AND GAS* — *Abstracting, Bibliographies, Statistics*

A P I ABSTRACTS/OILFIELD CHEMICALS. (American Petroleum Institute) see *PETROLEUM AND GAS* — *Abstracting, Bibliographies, Statistics*

A P I ABSTRACTS/PATENTS. (American Petroleum Institute) see *PETROLEUM AND GAS* — *Abstracting, Bibliographies, Statistics*

A S M BIBLIOGRAPHY SERIES. (American Society for Metals) see *METALLURGY* — *Abstracting, Bibliographies, Statistics*

011   CN ISSN 0226-1685
A S T I S BIBLIOGRAPHY. 1979. a. Can.$75. Arctic Science & Technology Information System, Arctic Institute of North America, University of Calgary, 2500 University Dr. N.W., Calgary, Alta. T2N 1N4, Canada. TEL 403-220-4036. Ed. C. Ross Goodwin. circ. 150. (microfiche)

050 011   US ISSN 0001-334X
ABRIDGED READERS' GUIDE TO PERIODICAL LITERATURE. 1935. m. (Sep.-May) (annual cumulations) $50. H.W. Wilson Co., 950 University Ave., Bronx, NY 10452. TEL 212-588-8400. Ed. Jean Marra.

ABSTRACT JOURNAL IN EARTHQUAKE ENGINEERING. see *ENGINEERING* — *Abstracting, Bibliographies, Statistics*

ABSTRACT NEWSLETTER: ADMINISTRATION AND MANAGEMENT. see *PUBLIC ADMINISTRATION* — *Abstracting, Bibliographies, Statistics*

ABSTRACT NEWSLETTER: AGRICULTURE & FOOD. see *AGRICULTURE* — *Abstracting, Bibliographies, Statistics*

ABSTRACT NEWSLETTER: CIVIL ENGINEERING. see *ENGINEERING* — *Abstracting, Bibliographies, Statistics*

ABSTRACT NEWSLETTER: COMPUTERS, CONTROL & INFORMATION THEORY. see *COMPUTERS* — *Abstracting, Bibliographies, Statistics*

ABSTRACT NEWSLETTER: ELECTROTECHNOLOGY. see *ELECTRICITY AND ELECTRICAL ENGINEERING* — *Abstracting, Bibliographies, Statistics*

ABSTRACT NEWSLETTER: ENERGY. see *ENERGY* — *Abstracting, Bibliographies, Statistics*

ABSTRACT NEWSLETTER: GOVERNMENT INVENTIONS FOR LICENSING. see *TECHNOLOGY: COMPREHENSIVE WORKS* — *Abstracting, Bibliographies, Statistics*

ABSTRACT NEWSLETTER: HEALTH PLANNING & HEALTH SERVICES RESEARCH. see *PHYSICAL FITNESS AND HYGIENE* — *Abstracting, Bibliographies, Statistics*

ABSTRACT NEWSLETTER: MANUFACTURING TECHNOLOGY. see *TECHNOLOGY: COMPREHENSIVE WORKS* — *Abstracting, Bibliographies, Statistics*

ABSTRACT NEWSLETTER: MATERIALS SCIENCES. see *ENGINEERING* — *Abstracting, Bibliographies, Statistics*

ABSTRACT NEWSLETTER: NATURAL RESOURCES & EARTH SCIENCES. see *CONSERVATION* — *Abstracting, Bibliographies, Statistics*

ABSTRACT NEWSLETTER: OCEAN TECHNOLOGY & ENGINEERING. see *EARTH SCIENCES* — *Abstracting, Bibliographies, Statistics*

ABSTRACT NEWSLETTER: PHYSICS. see *PHYSICS* — *Abstracting, Bibliographies, Statistics*

ABSTRACT NEWSLETTER: PROBLEM-SOLVING INFORMATION FOR STATE AND LOCAL GOVERNMENTS. see *PUBLIC ADMINISTRATION* — *Abstracting, Bibliographies, Statistics*

ABSTRACT NEWSLETTER: URBAN AND REGIONAL TECHNOLOGY AND DEVELOPMENT. see *HOUSING AND URBAN PLANNING* — *Abstracting, Bibliographies, Statistics*

011   US
ABSTRACTING AND INDEXING SERVICES DIRECTORY. 1982. irreg. $90. Gale Research Company, Book Tower, Detroit, MI 48226. TEL 313-961-2242. Ed. John Schmittroth.

ABSTRACTS FROM CURRENT SCIENTIFIC AND TECHNICAL LITERATURE. see *FOOD AND FOOD INDUSTRIES* — *Abstracting, Bibliographies, Statistics*

ABSTRACTS IN ANTHROPOLOGY. see *ANTHROPOLOGY* — *Abstracting, Bibliographies, Statistics*

ABSTRACTS IN MARYLAND ARCHEOLOGY. see *ARCHAEOLOGY* — *Abstracting, Bibliographies, Statistics*

ABSTRACTS OF BULGARIAN SCIENTIFIC LITERATURE. AGRICULTURE AND FORESTRY. VETERINARY MEDICINE. see *AGRICULTURE* — *Abstracting, Bibliographies, Statistics*

ABSTRACTS OF BULGARIAN SCIENTIFIC LITERATURE. ECONOMICS AND LAW. see *BUSINESS AND ECONOMICS* — *Abstracting, Bibliographies, Statistics*

ABSTRACTS OF BULGARIAN SCIENTIFIC LITERATURE. INDUSTRY, BUILDING AND TRANSPORT. see *BUSINESS AND ECONOMICS — Abstracting, Bibliographies, Statistics*

ABSTRACTS OF BULGARIAN SCIENTIFIC LITERATURE. MATHEMATICAL AND PHYSICAL SCIENCES. see *MATHEMATICS — Abstracting, Bibliographies, Statistics*

ABSTRACTS OF BULGARIAN SCIENTIFIC LITERATURE. NAUKI ZA ZEMIATA. see *EARTH SCIENCES — Abstracting, Bibliographies, Statistics*

ABSTRACTS OF BULGARIAN SCIENTIFIC LITERATURE. PHILOSOPHY, SOCIOLOGY, SCIENCE OF SCIENCES, PSYCHOLOGY AND PEDAGOGICS. see *EDUCATION — Abstracting, Bibliographies, Statistics*

ABSTRACTS OF BULGARIAN SCIENTIFIC MEDICAL LITERATURE. see *MEDICAL SCIENCES — Abstracting, Bibliographies, Statistics*

ABSTRACTS OF HEALTH CARE MANAGEMENT STUDIES. see *HOSPITALS — Abstracting, Bibliographies, Statistics*

ABSTRACTS OF MILITARY BIBLIOGRAPHY. see *MILITARY — Abstracting, Bibliographies, Statistics*

ABSTRACTS OF RESEARCH IN PASTORAL CARE AND COUNSELING. see *RELIGIONS AND THEOLOGY — Abstracting, Bibliographies, Statistics*

ABSTRACTS OF UPPSALA DISSERTATIONS IN SCIENCE. see *SCIENCES: COMPREHENSIVE WORKS — Abstracting, Bibliographies, Statistics*

ABSTRACTS ON CASSAVA. see *AGRICULTURE — Abstracting, Bibliographies, Statistics*

ABSTRACTS ON FIELD BEANS. see *AGRICULTURE — Abstracting, Bibliographies, Statistics*

ABSTRACTS ON TROPICAL AGRICULTURE. see *AGRICULTURE — Abstracting, Bibliographies, Statistics*

011　　　　　　　　　US　ISSN 0095-5698
ACCESS: THE SUPPLEMENTARY INDEX TO PERIODICALS. 1975. 3/yr. $112.50. John Gordon Burke Publishers, Inc., Box 1492, Evanston, IL 60204-1492.
●Also available online.
Incorporating: Monthly Periodical Index.

ACCOUNTANTS' INDEX. see *BUSINESS AND ECONOMICS — Abstracting, Bibliographies, Statistics*

ACCOUNTING & DATA PROCESSING ABSTRACTS. see *COMPUTERS — Abstracting, Bibliographies, Statistics*

ACOUSTICS ABSTRACTS. see *PHYSICS — Abstracting, Bibliographies, Statistics*

AEROSPACE DEFENSE MARKETS AND TECHNOLOGY. see *MILITARY — Abstracting, Bibliographies, Statistics*

016　309　　　　　　UK
AFRICA INDEX TO CONTINENTAL PERIODICAL LITERATURE. 1977. a. price varies. Hans Zell Publishers (Subsidiary of: K.G. Saur Ltd.) P.O. Box 56, 52 St. Giles, Oxford OX1 3EL, England. Ed. Colin Darch. (back issues avail.)
Continues: Africa Index (ISSN 0378-4797)

AGRARIRODALMI SZEMLE. see *AGRICULTURE — Abstracting, Bibliographies, Statistics*

AGRICULTURAL ABSTRACTS FOR TANZANIA. see *AGRICULTURE — Abstracting, Bibliographies, Statistics*

AGRICULTURAL ENGINEERING ABSTRACTS. see *AGRICULTURE — Abstracting, Bibliographies, Statistics*

AGRONOMY ABSTRACTS. see *AGRICULTURE — Abstracting, Bibliographies, Statistics*

AGROSELEKT. REIHE 1: LANDTECHNIK; an agricultural abstracting journal. see *AGRICULTURE — Abstracting, Bibliographies, Statistics*

AGROSELEKT. REIHE 2: PFLANZENPRODUKTION; an agricultural abstracting journal. see *AGRICULTURE — Abstracting, Bibliographies, Statistics*

AGROSELEKT. REIHE 3: TIERPRODUKTION; an agricultural abstracting journal. see *AGRICULTURE — Abstracting, Bibliographies, Statistics*

011　　　　　　UA　ISSN 0303-2728
AHRAM INDEX. 1974. m. $60. Al-Ahram Newspaper, Al-Ahram Organization and Microfilming Centre, Al-Galaa St., Cairo, Egypt. adv. circ. 300. (also avail. in microfilm)
Index to Asiatic journals

AIR UNIVERSITY LIBRARY INDEX TO MILITARY PERIODICALS. see *MILITARY — Abstracting, Bibliographies, Statistics*

ALLOYS INDEX. see *METALLURGY — Abstracting, Bibliographies, Statistics*

ALTERNATIVE PRESS INDEX; an index to alternative and radical publications. see *LITERARY AND POLITICAL REVIEWS — Abstracting, Bibliographies, Statistics*

AMERICA: HISTORY AND LIFE. PART A: ARTICLE ABSTRACTS AND CITATION. see *HISTORY — Abstracting, Bibliographies, Statistics*

AMERICA: HISTORY AND LIFE. PART B: INDEX TO BOOK REVIEWS. see *HISTORY — Abstracting, Bibliographies, Statistics*

AMERICA: HISTORY AND LIFE. PART D: ANNUAL INDEX. see *HISTORY — Abstracting, Bibliographies, Statistics*

AMERICAN ASSOCIATION OF STRATIGRAPHIC PALYNOLOGISTS. ABSTRACTS OF PAPERS PRESENTED AT THE ANNUAL MEETINGS. see *EARTH SCIENCES — Abstracting, Bibliographies, Statistics*

AMERICAN HERITAGE CUMULATIVE INDEX. see *HISTORY — Abstracting, Bibliographies, Statistics*

AMERICAN HUMANITIES INDEX. see *HUMANITIES: COMPREHENSIVE WORKS — Abstracting, Bibliographies, Statistics*

AMERICAN PUBLIC OPINION INDEX. see *SOCIOLOGY — Abstracting, Bibliographies, Statistics*

ANIMAL BREEDING ABSTRACTS; a monthly abstract of world literature. see *BIOLOGY — Abstracting, Bibliographies, Statistics*

ANTHROPOLOGICAL INDEX TO CURRENT PERIODICALS IN THE LIBRARY OF THE MUSEUM OF MANKIND. see *ANTHROPOLOGY — Abstracting, Bibliographies, Statistics*

ANTHROPOLOGISCHER ANZEIGER. see *ANTHROPOLOGY — Abstracting, Bibliographies, Statistics*

APICULTURAL ABSTRACTS. see *AGRICULTURE — Abstracting, Bibliographies, Statistics*

APPLIED HEALTH PHYSICS ABSTRACTS AND NOTES. see *PHYSICS — Abstracting, Bibliographies, Statistics*

APPLIED SCIENCE AND TECHNOLOGY INDEX; a cumulative subject index to English language periodicals in the fields of aeronautics and space science, automation, chemistry, construction, earth sciences, electricity and electronics, etc. see *ENGINEERING — Abstracting, Bibliographies, Statistics*

AQUATIC SCIENCES & FISHERIES ABSTRACTS. PART 1: BIOLOGICAL SCIENCES & LIVING RESOURCES. see *WATER RESOURCES — Abstracting, Bibliographies, Statistics*

AQUATIC SCIENCES & FISHERIES ABSTRACTS. PART 2: OCEAN TECHNOLOGY, POLICY AND NON-LIVING RESOURCES. see *WATER RESOURCES — Abstracting, Bibliographies, Statistics*

ART AND ARCHAEOLOGY TECHNICAL ABSTRACTS; abstracts of the technical literature on archaeology and the fine arts. see *ART — Abstracting, Bibliographies, Statistics*

ARTBIBLIOGRAPHIES CURRENT TITLES. see *ART — Abstracting, Bibliographies, Statistics*

ARTBIBLIOGRAPHIES MODERN. see *ART — Abstracting, Bibliographies, Statistics*

ASIAN GEOTECHNICAL ENGINEERING ABSTRACTS. see *EARTH SCIENCES — Abstracting, Bibliographies, Statistics*

ASTRONOMY AND ASTROPHYSICS ABSTRACTS. see *ASTRONOMY — Abstracting, Bibliographies, Statistics*

ATOMIC ABSORPTION & EMISSION SPECTROMETRY ABSTRACTS. see *PHYSICS — Abstracting, Bibliographies, Statistics*

AUDIOCASSETTE FINDER. (National Information Center for Educational Media) see *EDUCATION — Abstracting, Bibliographies, Statistics*

AUSTRALIAN ROAD INDEX. see *TRANSPORTATION — Abstracting, Bibliographies, Statistics*

AUSTRALIAN ROAD RESEARCH IN PROGRESS. see *ENGINEERING — Abstracting, Bibliographies, Statistics*

AVERY INDEX TO ARCHITECTURAL PERIODICALS. see *ARCHITECTURE — Abstracting, Bibliographies, Statistics*

B C I R A ABSTRACTS OF INTERNATIONAL LITERATURE ON METAL CASTINGS PRODUCTION. (British Cast Iron Research Association (BCIRA)) see *METALLURGY — Abstracting, Bibliographies, Statistics*

B I C E R I ABSTRACTS FROM TECHNICAL AND PATENT PUBLICATIONS. (British Internal Combustion Engine Research Institute Ltd.) see *ENGINEERING — Abstracting, Bibliographies, Statistics*

B I H E P. (Bibliographic Index of Health Education Periodicals) see *PHYSICAL FITNESS AND HYGIENE — Abstracting, Bibliographies, Statistics*

BANGLADESH AGRICULTURAL SCIENCES ABSTRACTS. see *AGRICULTURE — Abstracting, Bibliographies, Statistics*

BANYASZATI SZAKIRODALMI TAJEKOZTATO/ MINING ABSTRACTS. see *MINES AND MINING INDUSTRY — Abstracting, Bibliographies, Statistics*

BARBADOS. STATISTICAL SERVICE. OVERSEAS TRADE REPORT. see *BUSINESS AND ECONOMICS — Abstracting, Bibliographies, Statistics*

BARRON'S INDEX. see *BUSINESS AND ECONOMICS — Abstracting, Bibliographies, Statistics*

BELGIAN ENVIRONMENTAL RESEARCH INDEX. see *ENVIRONMENTAL STUDIES — Abstracting, Bibliographies, Statistics*

BELGIAN PATENTS ABSTRACTS. see *PATENTS, TRADEMARKS AND COPYRIGHTS — Abstracting, Bibliographies, Statistics*

BERUF UND GESUNDHEIT/OCCUPATIONAL HEALTH. see *INDUSTRIAL HEALTH AND SAFETY — Abstracting, Bibliographies, Statistics*

ABSTRACTING AND INDEXING SERVICES

BIBLIOGRAPHY AND INDEX OF GEOLOGY. see *EARTH SCIENCES* — *Abstracting, Bibliographies, Statistics*

BIOENGINEERING ABSTRACTS. see *ENGINEERING* — *Abstracting, Bibliographies, Statistics*

BIOGRAPHY AND GENEALOGY MASTER INDEX. see *BIOGRAPHY* — *Abstracting, Bibliographies, Statistics*

BIOGRAPHY INDEX; a quarterly index to biographical material in books and magazines. see *BIOGRAPHY* — *Abstracting, Bibliographies, Statistics*

BIOLOGICAL AND AGRICULTURAL INDEX; a subject index to periodicals in the fields of biology and agriculture and related sciences. see *BIOLOGY* — *Abstracting, Bibliographies, Statistics*

BIOSIS/CAS SELECTS: BIOCHEMISTRY OF FERMENTED FOODS. see *FOOD AND FOOD INDUSTRIES* — *Abstracting, Bibliographies, Statistics*

BIOSIS SEARCH GUIDE; BIOSIS previews edition. see *BIOLOGY* — *Abstracting, Bibliographies, Statistics*

BOOK REVIEW DIGEST; an index to reviews of current books. see *PUBLISHING AND BOOK TRADE* — *Abstracting, Bibliographies, Statistics*

BOOK REVIEW INDEX: ANNUAL CLOTHBOUND CUMULATIONS. see *LITERATURE* — *Abstracting, Bibliographies, Statistics*

BREASTFEEDING ABSTRACTS. see *CHILDREN AND YOUTH* — *Abstracting, Bibliographies, Statistics*

BRITISH CERAMIC ABSTRACTS. see *CERAMICS, GLASS AND POTTERY* — *Abstracting, Bibliographies, Statistics*

BRITISH EDUCATION INDEX. see *EDUCATION* — *Abstracting, Bibliographies, Statistics*

BRITISH HUMANITIES INDEX. see *HUMANITIES: COMPREHENSIVE WORKS* — *Abstracting, Bibliographies, Statistics*

BRITISH LIBRARY. DOCUMENT SUPPLY CENTRE. INDEX OF CONFERENCE PROCEEDINGS RECEIVED. see *MEETINGS AND CONGRESSES* — *Abstracting, Bibliographies, Statistics*

BRITISH LIBRARY. PRECIS VOCABULARY FICHE. see *LIBRARY AND INFORMATION SCIENCES* — *Abstracting, Bibliographies, Statistics*

BRITISH LIBRARY. SUBJECT AUTHORITY FICHE. see *LIBRARY AND INFORMATION SCIENCES* — *Abstracting, Bibliographies, Statistics*

BRITISH PATENTS ABSTRACTS. see *PATENTS, TRADEMARKS AND COPYRIGHTS* — *Abstracting, Bibliographies, Statistics*

BUILDING ABSTRACTS SERVICE C I B. see *BUILDING AND CONSTRUCTION* — *Abstracting, Bibliographies, Statistics*

BULLETIN BIBLIOGRAPHIQUE INTERNATIONAL DU MACHINISME AGRICOLE/INTERNATIONAL FARM MACHINERY ABSTRACTS. see *AGRICULTURE* — *Abstracting, Bibliographies, Statistics*

BULLETIN OF CHEMICAL THERMODYNAMICS (1977) see *CHEMISTRY* — *Abstracting, Bibliographies, Statistics*

BULLETIN SIGNALETIQUE. PART 521: SOCIOLOGIE - ETHNOLOGIE. see *SOCIOLOGY* — *Abstracting, Bibliographies, Statistics*

BULLETIN SIGNALETIQUE. PART 524: SCIENCES DU LANGAGE. see *LINGUISTICS* — *Abstracting, Bibliographies, Statistics*

BUSINESS PERIODICALS INDEX; a cumulative subject index to English language periodicals in the fields of accounting, advertising and public relations, automation, banking, communications, economics, finance and investments, insurance, labor, management, etc. see *BUSINESS AND ECONOMICS* — *Abstracting, Bibliographies, Statistics*

C I N D A; an index to the literature on microscopic neutron data. see *PHYSICS* — *Abstracting, Bibliographies, Statistics*

C I S ABSTRACTS. (International Labour Office) see *INDUSTRIAL HEALTH AND SAFETY* — *Abstracting, Bibliographies, Statistics*

011   350   US   ISSN 0741-2878
C I S FEDERAL REGISTER INDEX. 1984. a. $595. Congressional Information Service, Inc., 4520 East-West Hwy., Ste. 800, Bethesda, MD 20814. TEL 301-654-1550. Ed. Mel Keebaugh. cum.index. (back issues avail.; reprint service avail.)

C I S INDEX. (Congressional Information Service, Inc.) see *PUBLIC ADMINISTRATION* — *Abstracting, Bibliographies, Statistics*

C R R E R I S RENEWABLE ENERGY INDEX. see *ENERGY* — *Abstracting, Bibliographies, Statistics*

C R R I ROAD ABSTRACTS. (Central Road Research Institute) see *ENGINEERING* — *Abstracting, Bibliographies, Statistics*

C S I CONGRESSIONAL RECORD ABSTRACTS: ENERGY EDITION. see *PUBLIC ADMINISTRATION* — *Abstracting, Bibliographies, Statistics*

CALCIFIED TISSUE ABSTRACTS. see *BIOLOGY* — *Abstracting, Bibliographies, Statistics*

011   US   ISSN 0730-1367
CALIFORNIA PERIODICALS INDEX. 1977. a. $95. Gabriel Micrographics (Subsidiary of: Minnesota Scholarly Press, Inc.) Box 224, Mankato, MN 56001. TEL 507-387-4964. Ed. Opal Kissinger. bk. rev. (also avail. in microfilm)

CANADA. GEOLOGICAL SURVEY. INDEX OF PUBLICATIONS OF THE GEOLOGICAL SURVEY OF CANADA. see *EARTH SCIENCES* — *Abstracting, Bibliographies, Statistics*

CANADIAN BUILDING ABSTRACTS. see *BUILDING AND CONSTRUCTION* — *Abstracting, Bibliographies, Statistics*

CANADIAN BUSINESS INDEX. see *BUSINESS AND ECONOMICS* — *Abstracting, Bibliographies, Statistics*

016   370   CN   ISSN 0008-3453
CANADIAN EDUCATION INDEX/REPERTOIRE CANADIEN SUR L'EDUCATION. (Text in English or French) 1965. 3/yr. (3rd issue - annual cumulation) Can.$184. Canadian Education Association, 252 Bloor St. W., Ste. 8-200, Toronto, Ont. M5S 1V5, Canada. TEL 416-924-7721. Ed. Maureen Davis. circ. 350.

CANADIAN GOVERNMENT BUYER. see *BUSINESS AND ECONOMICS* — *Marketing And Purchasing*

CANADIAN JEWISH CONGRESS. NATIONAL ARCHIVES NEWSLETTER. see *ETHNIC INTERESTS*

CANADIAN LOCATIONS OF JOURNALS INDEXED FOR MEDICINE/DEPOTS CANADIENS DES REVUES INDEXEES POUR MEDECINE. see *MEDICAL SCIENCES* — *Abstracting, Bibliographies, Statistics*

011   051   CN   ISSN 0829-8777
CANADIAN MAGAZINE INDEX. 1985. m. (plus a. cum.) price varies. Micromedia Ltd., 158 Pearl St., Toronto, Ont. M5H 1L3, Canada. TEL 416-593-5211. Ed. Luci Lemieux. (back issues avail.)

CANADIAN NEWS INDEX. see *JOURNALISM* — *Abstracting, Bibliographies, Statistics*

011   CN   ISSN 0008-4719
CANADIAN PERIODICAL INDEX. (Text in English and French) 1938. m. (annual cumulation) subscription rates on request. ‡ Globe Mail Ltd., 444 Front St. W., Toronto, Ont. M5V 2S9, Canada. Ed. Sylvia Morrison. index. cum.index: 1948-1959. circ. 1,725.
   Formerly: Canadian Index to Periodicals and Documentary Films.

CARCINOGENESIS ABSTRACTS. see *MEDICAL SCIENCES* — *Abstracting, Bibliographies, Statistics*

CATALOG OF MUSEUM PUBLICATIONS AND MEDIA; a directory and index of publications and audiovisuals available from U.S. and Canadian institutions. see *MUSEUMS AND ART GALLERIES* — *Abstracting, Bibliographies, Statistics*

CATHOLIC PERIODICAL AND LITERATURE INDEX. see *RELIGIONS AND THEOLOGY* — *Abstracting, Bibliographies, Statistics*

CENTRE INTERNATIONAL DE DOCUMENTATION ARACHNOLOGIQUES. LISTE DES TRAVAUX ARACHNOLOGIQUES. see *BIOLOGY* — *Abstracting, Bibliographies, Statistics*

CERAMIC ABSTRACTS. see *CERAMICS, GLASS AND POTTERY* — *Abstracting, Bibliographies, Statistics*

CHEMICAL ABSTRACTS SERVICE SOURCE INDEX. see *CHEMISTRY* — *Abstracting, Bibliographies, Statistics*

CHEMISCHER INFORMATIONSDIENST. see *CHEMISTRY* — *Abstracting, Bibliographies, Statistics*

CHEMORECEPTION ABSTRACTS; chemical senses & applied techniques. see *CHEMISTRY* — *Abstracting, Bibliographies, Statistics*

CHILD DEVELOPMENT ABSTRACTS AND BIBLIOGRAPHY. see *CHILDREN AND YOUTH* — *Abstracting, Bibliographies, Statistics*

CHILDREN'S BOOK REVIEW INDEX. see *CHILDREN AND YOUTH* — *Abstracting, Bibliographies, Statistics*

CHILDREN'S LITERATURE ABSTRACTS. see *PUBLISHING AND BOOK TRADE* — *Abstracting, Bibliographies, Statistics*

CHINESE SCIENCE ABSTRACTS. see *SCIENCES: COMPREHENSIVE WORKS* — *Abstracting, Bibliographies, Statistics*

CHRISTIAN PERIODICAL INDEX; an index to subjects, authors and book reviews. see *RELIGIONS AND THEOLOGY* — *Abstracting, Bibliographies, Statistics*

CIVIL ENGINEERING HYDRAULICS ABSTRACTS. see *ENGINEERING* — *Abstracting, Bibliographies, Statistics*

CLIN-ALERT. see *PHARMACY AND PHARMACOLOGY* — *Abstracting, Bibliographies, Statistics*

COMBINED CUMULATIVE INDEX TO PEDIATRICS. see *MEDICAL SCIENCES* — *Abstracting, Bibliographies, Statistics*

COMMODITY YEARBOOK STATISTICAL ABSTRACT SERVICE. see *AGRICULTURE* — *Abstracting, Bibliographies, Statistics*

COMMUNICATION ABSTRACTS. see *COMMUNICATIONS* — *Abstracting, Bibliographies, Statistics*

COMPUMATH CITATION INDEX. see *MATHEMATICS* — *Abstracting, Bibliographies, Statistics*

COMPUTER ABSTRACTS. see *COMPUTERS* — *Abstracting, Bibliographies, Statistics*

COMPUTER & CONTROL ABSTRACTS. see *COMPUTERS — Abstracting, Bibliographies, Statistics*

COMPUTER AND INFORMATION SYSTEMS ABSTRACT JOURNAL; an abstract journal pertaining to the theory, design, fabrication and application of computer and information systems. see *COMPUTERS — Abstracting, Bibliographies, Statistics*

COMPUTER CONTENTS; semi-monthly compilation of tables of contents from more than 250 of the latest computer periodicals. see *COMPUTERS — Abstracting, Bibliographies, Statistics*

COMPUTER INDUSTRY UPDATE. see *COMPUTERS — Abstracting, Bibliographies, Statistics*

COMPUTER LITERATURE INDEX. see *COMPUTERS — Abstracting, Bibliographies, Statistics*

COMPUTING JOURNAL ABSTRACTS. see *COMPUTERS — Abstracting, Bibliographies, Statistics*

CONCRETE ABSTRACTS. see *BUILDING AND CONSTRUCTION — Abstracting, Bibliographies, Statistics*

011   US   ISSN 0194-0546
CONFERENCE PAPERS ANNUAL INDEX. a. $303. Cambridge Scientific Abstracts, 5161 River Rd., Bethesda, MD 20816. TEL 301-951-1400. Ed. P. Eilers.
• Also available online. Vendors: DIALOG.
Formerly: Current Programs Annual Index.

CONSUMERS INDEX; product evaluations and information sources. see *CONSUMER EDUCATION AND PROTECTION — Abstracting, Bibliographies, Statistics*

CONTENTS OF RECENT ECONOMICS JOURNALS. see *BUSINESS AND ECONOMICS — Abstracting, Bibliographies, Statistics*

COPPER IN AGRICULTURE; a quarterly bulletin of abstracts. see *AGRICULTURE — Abstracting, Bibliographies, Statistics*

CORROSION ABSTRACTS; abstracts of the world's literature on corrosion and corrosion mitigation. see *METALLURGY — Abstracting, Bibliographies, Statistics*

CORROSION CONTROL ABSTRACTS. see *METALLURGY — Abstracting, Bibliographies, Statistics*

COTTON AND TROPICAL FIBRES ABSTRACTS. see *AGRICULTURE — Abstracting, Bibliographies, Statistics*

CRIMINAL JUSTICE ABSTRACTS. see *CRIMINOLOGY AND LAW ENFORCEMENT — Abstracting, Bibliographies, Statistics*

CRIMINAL JUSTICE PERIODICAL INDEX. see *CRIMINOLOGY AND LAW ENFORCEMENT — Abstracting, Bibliographies, Statistics*

CRIMINOLOGY & PENOLOGY ABSTRACTS. see *CRIMINOLOGY AND LAW ENFORCEMENT — Abstracting, Bibliographies, Statistics*

CROP PHYSIOLOGY ABSTRACTS. see *AGRICULTURE — Abstracting, Bibliographies, Statistics*

CUMULATED ABRIDGED INDEX MEDICUS. see *MEDICAL SCIENCES — Abstracting, Bibliographies, Statistics*

CUMULATED INDEX MEDICUS. see *MEDICAL SCIENCES — Abstracting, Bibliographies, Statistics*

CUMULATIVE INDEX TO NURSING & ALLIED HEALTH LITERATURE (C I N A H L) see *MEDICAL SCIENCES — Abstracting, Bibliographies, Statistics*

CURRENT AUSTRALIAN AND NEW ZEALAND LEGAL LITERATURE INDEX. see *LAW — Abstracting, Bibliographies, Statistics*

CURRENT AWARENESS IN BIOLOGICAL SCIENCES. see *BIOLOGY — Abstracting, Bibliographies, Statistics*

CURRENT BIBLIOGRAPHIES ON SCIENCE & TECHNOLOGY: BIOLOGY, PHARMACY & FOOD SCIENCE. see *BIOLOGY — Abstracting, Bibliographies, Statistics*

CURRENT BIBLIOGRAPHIES ON SCIENCE AND TECHNOLOGY: MECHANICAL ENGINEERING & CONSTRUCTION ENGINEERING. see *METALLURGY — Abstracting, Bibliographies, Statistics*

CURRENT CAREER AND OCCUPATIONAL LITERATURE. see *OCCUPATIONS AND CAREERS — Abstracting, Bibliographies, Statistics*

CURRENT CHEMICAL REACTIONS. see *CHEMISTRY — Abstracting, Bibliographies, Statistics*

CURRENT CONTENTS/CLINICAL MEDICINE. see *MEDICAL SCIENCES — Abstracting, Bibliographies, Statistics*

CURRENT CONTENTS/SOCIAL & BEHAVIORAL SCIENCES. see *SOCIOLOGY — Abstracting, Bibliographies, Statistics*

CURRENT DIGEST OF THE SOVIET PRESS. see *POLITICAL SCIENCE — Abstracting, Bibliographies, Statistics*

CURRENT INDEX TO JOURNALS IN EDUCATION. see *EDUCATION — Abstracting, Bibliographies, Statistics*

016 311   US   ISSN 0364-1228
CURRENT INDEX TO STATISTICS; applications-methods-theory. 1976. a. $40. American Statistical Association, 806 15th St., N.W., Washington, DC 20005. TEL 202-393-3253. (Co-sponsor: Institute of Mathematical Statistics) index. circ. 2,000.
• Also available online. Vendors: BRS, DIALOG, European Space Agency.

CURRENT LAW INDEX. see *LAW — Abstracting, Bibliographies, Statistics*

CURRENT LEATHER LITERATURE. see *LEATHER AND FUR INDUSTRIES — Abstracting, Bibliographies, Statistics*

CURRENT PACKAGING ABSTRACTS. see *PACKAGING — Abstracting, Bibliographies, Statistics*

CURRENT PAPERS IN PHYSICS; containing about 78,000 titles of research articles from the world's physics journals. see *PHYSICS — Abstracting, Bibliographies, Statistics*

CURRENT PHYSICS INDEX. see *PHYSICS — Abstracting, Bibliographies, Statistics*

CURRENT RESEARCH IN BRITAIN. BIOLOGICAL SCIENCES. see *BIOLOGY — Abstracting, Bibliographies, Statistics*

CURRENT RESEARCH IN BRITAIN. PHYSICAL SCIENCES. see *SCIENCES: COMPREHENSIVE WORKS — Abstracting, Bibliographies, Statistics*

CURRENT RESEARCH IN BRITAIN. SOCIAL SCIENCES. see *SOCIAL SCIENCES: COMPREHENSIVE WORKS — Abstracting, Bibliographies, Statistics*

CURRENT TECHNOLOGY INDEX. see *TECHNOLOGY: COMPREHENSIVE WORKS — Abstracting, Bibliographies, Statistics*

CURRENT TITLES IN ELECTROCHEMISTRY. see *CHEMISTRY — Abstracting, Bibliographies, Statistics*

CURRENT TITLES IN OCEAN, COASTAL, LAKE & WATERWAY SCIENCES; reader's information bulletin and service. see *EARTH SCIENCES — Abstracting, Bibliographies, Statistics*

CYBERNETICS ABSTRACTS. see *COMPUTERS — Abstracting, Bibliographies, Statistics*

CYSTIC FIBROSIS CLUB ABSTRACTS. see *MEDICAL SCIENCES — Abstracting, Bibliographies, Statistics*

DANSK ARTIKELINDEKS: AVISER OG TIDSSKRIFTER/DANISH INDEX OF ARTICLES: NEWSPAPERS AND PERIODICALS. see *JOURNALISM — Abstracting, Bibliographies, Statistics*

DENTAL ABSTRACTS. see *MEDICAL SCIENCES — Abstracting, Bibliographies, Statistics*

DEVELOPMENT INFORMATION ABSTRACTS. see *BUSINESS AND ECONOMICS — Abstracting, Bibliographies, Statistics*

DIGEST OF NEUROLOGY & PSYCHIATRY. see *MEDICAL SCIENCES — Abstracting, Bibliographies, Statistics*

011   AT   ISSN 0110-666X
DIRECTORY OF AUSTRALIAN ASSOCIATIONS. (Supplement published between editions) 1978. every 30 mos. Aus.$120 (supplement Aus.$25) Margaret Gee Media Group, 45 Flinders Ln., Melbourne, Vic. 3000, Australia. adv.

DIRECTORY OF SCIENTIFIC PERIODICALS OF PAKISTAN. see *SCIENCES: COMPREHENSIVE WORKS — Abstracting, Bibliographies, Statistics*

DIRECTORY OF THE CULTURAL ORGANIZATIONS OF THE REPUBLIC OF CHINA. see *EDUCATION — Abstracting, Bibliographies, Statistics*

DISSERTATION ABSTRACTS INTERNATIONAL. SECTION B: PHYSICAL SCIENCES AND ENGINEERING. see *TECHNOLOGY: COMPREHENSIVE WORKS — Abstracting, Bibliographies, Statistics*

DOCUMENTATION LIST: AFRICA. see *HISTORY — Abstracting, Bibliographies, Statistics*

DOKUMENTATION RHEOLOGIE/ DOCUMENTATION RHEOLOGY. see *PHYSICS — Abstracting, Bibliographies, Statistics*

DOKUMENTATION TRIBOLOGIE/ DOCUMENTATION TRIBOLOGY. see *ENGINEERING — Abstracting, Bibliographies, Statistics*

E C INDEX; publications and documents of the European Communities. see *BUSINESS AND ECONOMICS — Abstracting, Bibliographies, Statistics*

E F I NYTT/E F I NEWS. (Ekonomiska Forskningsinstitutet) see *BUSINESS AND ECONOMICS — Abstracting, Bibliographies, Statistics*

ECOLOGY ABSTRACTS. see *WATER RESOURCES — Abstracting, Bibliographies, Statistics*

ECONOMIC TITLES/ABSTRACTS; semi-monthly providing concise information of interest to business, trade, industry, economic libraries and research institutes. see *BUSINESS AND ECONOMICS — Abstracting, Bibliographies, Statistics*

EDUCATION GUIDELINES. see *EDUCATION*

EDUCATION INDEX; an author-subject index to educational publications in the English language. see *EDUCATION — Abstracting, Bibliographies, Statistics*

EDUCATIONAL ADMINISTRATION ABSTRACTS. see *EDUCATION — Abstracting, Bibliographies, Statistics*

EDUCATIONAL TECHNOLOGY ABSTRACTS. see *EDUCATION — Abstracting, Bibliographies, Statistics*

EIGHT PEAK INDEX OF MASS SPECTRA. see *CHEMISTRY — Abstracting, Bibliographies, Statistics*

EKISTIC INDEX. see *SOCIOLOGY — Abstracting, Bibliographies, Statistics*

ELECTRICAL & ELECTRONICS ABSTRACTS. see *ELECTRICITY AND ELECTRICAL ENGINEERING — Abstracting, Bibliographies, Statistics*

ELECTRON SPIN RESONANCE SPECTROSCOPY ABSTRACTS. see *PHYSICS — Abstracting, Bibliographies, Statistics*

ELECTRONIC PUBLISHING ABSTRACTS. see *COMPUTERS — Abstracting, Bibliographies, Statistics*

ELECTRONICS AND COMMUNICATIONS ABSTRACTS. see *COMMUNICATIONS — Abstracting, Bibliographies, Statistics*

ELECTRONICS AND COMMUNICATIONS ABSTRACTS JOURNAL; an abstract journal involving the theory, design and application of electronic devices and systems. see *COMMUNICATIONS — Abstracting, Bibliographies, Statistics*

ELEKTROTECHNIKAI SZAKIRODALMI TAJEKOZTATO/ELECTRICAL ENGINEERING ABSTRACTS. see *ELECTRICITY AND ELECTRICAL ENGINEERING — Abstracting, Bibliographies, Statistics*

ENDOCRINOLOGY ABSTRACTS. see *MEDICAL SCIENCES — Abstracting, Bibliographies, Statistics*

ENERGY ABSTRACTS. see *ENERGY — Abstracting, Bibliographies, Statistics*

ENERGY ABSTRACTS FOR POLICY ANALYSIS. see *ENERGY — Abstracting, Bibliographies, Statistics*

ENERGY INDEX. see *ENERGY — Abstracting, Bibliographies, Statistics*

ENERGY INFORMATION ABSTRACTS. see *ENERGY — Abstracting, Bibliographies, Statistics*

ENERGY INFORMATION INDEX/ABSTRACTS ANNUAL. see *ENERGY — Abstracting, Bibliographies, Statistics*

ENERGY RESEARCH ABSTRACTS. see *ENERGY — Abstracting, Bibliographies, Statistics*

ENGINEERED MATERIALS ABSTRACTS. see *ENGINEERING — Abstracting, Bibliographies, Statistics*

ENGINEERING INDEX CUMULATIVE INDEX. see *ENGINEERING — Abstracting, Bibliographies, Statistics*

ENGINEERING INDEX MONTHLY AND AUTHOR INDEX; abstracting and indexing services covering sources of the world's engineering literature. see *ENGINEERING — Abstracting, Bibliographics, Statistics*

ENGINEERING SCIENCES DATA UNIT INDEX. see *ENGINEERING — Abstracting, Bibliographies, Statistics*

ENTOMOLOGY ABSTRACTS. see *BIOLOGY — Abstracting, Bibliographies, Statistics*

ERGONOMICS ABSTRACTS. scc *ENGINEERING — Abstracting, Bibliographies, Statistics*

800 011   US   ISSN 0014-083X
ESSAY AND GENERAL LITERATURE INDEX; an index to collections of essays and works of a composite nature that have reference value. 1900. s-a. (annual and 5 year cumulations) $70. ‡ H. W. Wilson Co., 950 University Ave., Bronx, NY 10452. TEL 212-588-8400. Ed. John Greenfieldt. cum. index: 1900-1969.

EURO ABSTRACTS SECTION I. EURATOM AND EEC RESEARCH. see *PHYSICS — Abstracting, Bibliographies, Statistics*

EURO ABSTRACTS SECTION II. COAL AND STEEL. see *MINES AND MINING INDUSTRY — Abstracting, Bibliographies, Statistics*

EXCERPTA MEDICA. SECTION 1: ANATOMY, ANTHROPOLOGY, EMBRYOLOGY & HISTOLOGY. see *MEDICAL SCIENCES — Abstracting, Bibliographies, Statistics*

EXCERPTA MEDICA. SECTION 2: PHYSIOLOGY. see *MEDICAL SCIENCES — Abstracting, Bibliographies, Statistics*

EXCERPTA MEDICA. SECTION 3: ENDOCRINOLOGY. see *MEDICAL SCIENCES — Abstracting, Bibliographies, Statistics*

EXCERPTA MEDICA. SECTION 4: MICROBIOLOGY: BACTERIOLOGY, MYCOLOGY AND PARASITOLOGY. see *MEDICAL SCIENCES — Abstracting, Bibliographies, Statistics*

EXCERPTA MEDICA. SECTION 5: GENERAL PATHOLOGY AND PATHOLOGICAL ANATOMY. see *MEDICAL SCIENCES — Abstracting, Bibliographies, Statistics*

EXCERPTA MEDICA. SECTION 6: INTERNAL MEDICINE. see *MEDICAL SCIENCES — Abstracting, Bibliographies, Statistics*

EXCERPTA MEDICA. SECTION 7: PEDIATRICS AND PEDIATRIC SURGERY. see *MEDICAL SCIENCES — Abstracting, Bibliographies, Statistics*

EXCERPTA MEDICA. SECTION 8: NEUROLOGY AND NEUROSURGERY. see *MEDICAL SCIENCES — Abstracting, Bibliographies, Statistics*

EXCERPTA MEDICA. SECTION 9: SURGERY. see *MEDICAL SCIENCES — Abstracting, Bibliographies, Statistics*

EXCERPTA MEDICA. SECTION 10: OBSTETRICS AND GYNECOLOGY. see *MEDICAL SCIENCES — Abstracting, Bibliographies, Statistics*

EXCERPTA MEDICA. SECTION 11: OTORHINOLARYNGOLOGY. see *MEDICAL SCIENCES — Abstracting, Bibliographies, Statistics*

EXCERPTA MEDICA. SECTION 12: OPHTHALMOLOGY. see *MEDICAL SCIENCES — Abstracting, Bibliographies, Statistics*

EXCERPTA MEDICA. SECTION 13: DERMATOLOGY AND VENEREOLOGY. see *MEDICAL SCIENCES — Abstracting, Bibliographies, Statistics*

EXCERPTA MEDICA. SECTION 14: RADIOLOGY. see *MEDICAL SCIENCES — Abstracting, Bibliographies, Statistics*

EXCERPTA MEDICA. SECTION 15: CHEST DISEASES, THORACIC SURGERY AND TUBERCULOSIS. see *MEDICAL SCIENCES — Abstracting, Bibliographies, Statistics*

EXCERPTA MEDICA. SECTION 16: CANCER. see *MEDICAL SCIENCES — Abstracting, Bibliographies, Statistics*

EXCERPTA MEDICA. SECTION 17: PUBLIC HEALTH, SOCIAL MEDICINE & HYGIENE. see *PUBLIC HEALTH AND SAFETY — Abstracting, Bibliographies, Statistics*

EXCERPTA MEDICA. SECTION 19: REHABILITATION AND PHYSICAL MEDICINE. see *MEDICAL SCIENCES — Abstracting, Bibliographies, Statistics*

EXCERPTA MEDICA. SECTION 20: GERONTOLOGY AND GERIATRICS. see *GERONTOLOGY AND GERIATRICS — Abstracting, Bibliographies, Statistics*

EXCERPTA MEDICA. SECTION 23: NUCLEAR MEDICINE. see *MEDICAL SCIENCES — Abstracting, Bibliographies, Statistics*

EXCERPTA MEDICA. SECTION 24: ANESTHESIOLOGY. see *MEDICAL SCIENCES — Abstracting, Bibliographies, Statistics*

EXCERPTA MEDICA. SECTION 25: HEMATOLOGY. see *MEDICAL SCIENCES — Abstracting, Bibliographies, Statistics*

EXCERPTA MEDICA. SECTION 26: IMMUNOLOGY, SEROLOGY AND TRANSPLANTATION. see *MEDICAL SCIENCES — Abstracting, Bibliographies, Statistics*

EXCERPTA MEDICA. SECTION 27: BIOPHYSICS, BIO-ENGINEERING AND MEDICAL INSTRUMENTATION. see *MEDICAL SCIENCES — Abstracting, Bibliographies, Statistics*

EXCERPTA MEDICA. SECTION 28: UROLOGY AND NEPHROLOGY. see *MEDICAL SCIENCES — Abstracting, Bibliographies, Statistics*

EXCERPTA MEDICA. SECTION 29: CLINICAL BIOCHEMISTRY. see *MEDICAL SCIENCES — Abstracting, Bibliographies, Statistics*

EXCERPTA MEDICA. SECTION 31: ARTHRITIS AND RHEUMATISM. see *MEDICAL SCIENCES — Abstracting, Bibliographies, Statistics*

EXCERPTA MEDICA. SECTION 32: PSYCHIATRY. see *MEDICAL SCIENCES — Abstracting, Bibliographies, Statistics*

EXCERPTA MEDICA. SECTION 33: ORTHOPEDIC SURGERY. see *MEDICAL SCIENCES — Abstracting, Bibliographies, Statistics*

EXCERPTA MEDICA. SECTION 34: PLASTIC SURGERY. see *MEDICAL SCIENCES — Abstracting, Bibliographies, Statistics*

EXCERPTA MEDICA. SECTION 35: OCCUPATIONAL HEALTH AND INDUSTRIAL MEDICINE. see *MEDICAL SCIENCES — Abstracting, Bibliographies, Statistics*

EXCERPTA MEDICA. SECTION 36: HEALTH ECONOMICS AND HOSPITAL MANAGEMENT. see *HOSPITALS — Abstracting, Bibliographies, Statistics*

EXCERPTA MEDICA. SECTION 38: ADVERSE REACTIONS TITLES. see *MEDICAL SCIENCES — Abstracting, Bibliographies, Statistics*

EXCERPTA MEDICA. SECTION 46: ENVIRONMENTAL HEALTH AND POLLUTION CONTROL. see *ENVIRONMENTAL STUDIES — Abstracting, Bibliographies, Statistics*

EXCERPTA MEDICA. SECTION 47: VIROLOGY. see *MEDICAL SCIENCES — Abstracting, Bibliographies, Statistics*

EXCERPTA MEDICA. SECTION 48: GASTROENTEROLOGY. see *MEDICAL SCIENCES — Abstracting, Bibliographies, Statistics*

EXCERPTA MEDICA. SECTION 49: FORENSIC SCIENCE. see *MEDICAL SCIENCES — Abstracting, Bibliographies, Statistics*

EXCERPTA MEDICA. SECTION 50: EPILEPSY. see *MEDICAL SCIENCES — Abstracting, Bibliographies, Statistics*

EXCERPTA MEDICA. SECTION 51: LEPROSY AND RELATED SUBJECTS. see *MEDICAL SCIENCES — Abstracting, Bibliographies, Statistics*

F.A.I. ABSTRACT SERVICE. (Fertiliser Association of India) see *AGRICULTURE — Abstracting, Bibliographies, Statistics*

FABA BEAN ABSTRACTS. see *AGRICULTURE — Abstracting, Bibliographies, Statistics*

FANATIC READER. see *GENERAL INTEREST PERIODICALS — United States*

FARM AND GARDEN INDEX. see *AGRICULTURE — Abstracting, Bibliographies, Statistics*

FIELD CROP ABSTRACTS; monthly abstract journal on world annual cereal, legume, root, oilseed and fibre crops. see *AGRICULTURE — Abstracting, Bibliographies, Statistics*

FIHRIST; index to Arabic periodical literature. see *BIBLIOGRAPHIES*

FILM & VIDEO FINDER. see *EDUCATION — Abstracting, Bibliographies, Statistics*

FILM LITERATURE INDEX. see *MOTION PICTURES — Abstracting, Bibliographies, Statistics*

FLOUR MILLING AND BAKING RESEARCH ASSOCIATION ABSTRACTS. see *FOOD AND FOOD INDUSTRIES — Abstracting, Bibliographies, Statistics*

FLUID FLOW MEASUREMENT ABSTRACTS. see *ENGINEERING — Abstracting, Bibliographies, Statistics*

FLUID POWER ABSTRACTS. see *ENGINEERING — Abstracting, Bibliographies, Statistics*

FLUID SEALING ABSTRACTS. see *ENGINEERING — Abstracting, Bibliographies, Statistics*

FOOD SCIENCE AND TECHNOLOGY ABSTRACTS. see *FOOD AND FOOD INDUSTRIES — Abstracting, Bibliographies, Statistics*

FOREST PRODUCTS ABSTRACTS. see *FORESTS AND FORESTRY — Abstracting, Bibliographies, Statistics*

FORESTRY ABSTRACTS; compiled from world literature. see *FORESTS AND FORESTRY — Abstracting, Bibliographies, Statistics*

FORESTRY ABSTRACTS. LEADING ARTICLE REPRINT SERIES. see *FORESTS AND FORESTRY — Abstracting, Bibliographies, Statistics*

FRANCEXPORT. see *BUSINESS AND ECONOMICS — Trade And Industrial Directories*

FRENCH PATENTS ABSTRACTS. see *PATENTS, TRADEMARKS AND COPYRIGHTS — Abstracting, Bibliographies, Statistics*

FUEL AND ENERGY ABSTRACTS; a summary of world literature on all technical and scientific aspects of fuel and power. see *PETROLEUM AND GAS — Abstracting, Bibliographies, Statistics*

FUTURE - ABSTRACTS. see *SOCIAL SCIENCES: COMPREHENSIVE WORKS — Abstracting, Bibliographies, Statistics*

FUTURE SURVEY; a monthly abstract of books, articles and reports concerning trends, forecasts and ideas about the future. see *SCIENCES: COMPREHENSIVE WORKS — Abstracting, Bibliographies, Statistics*

GAS ABSTRACTS. see *PETROLEUM AND GAS — Abstracting, Bibliographies, Statistics*

GENERAL SCIENCE INDEX. see *SCIENCES: COMPREHENSIVE WORKS — Abstracting, Bibliographies, Statistics*

GENETICS ABSTRACTS. see *BIOLOGY — Abstracting, Bibliographies, Statistics*

GEOGRAPHICAL ABSTRACTS A (LANDFORMS AND THE QUATERNARY) see *GEOGRAPHY — Abstracting, Bibliographies, Statistics*

GEOGRAPHICAL ABSTRACTS B (CLIMATOLOGY AND HYDROLOGY) see *GEOGRAPHY — Abstracting, Bibliographies, Statistics*

GEOGRAPHICAL ABSTRACTS C (ECONOMIC GEOGRAPHY) see *GEOGRAPHY — Abstracting, Bibliographies, Statistics*

GEOGRAPHICAL ABSTRACTS D (SOCIAL & HISTORICAL GEOGRAPHY) see *GEOGRAPHY — Abstracting, Bibliographies, Statistics*

GEOGRAPHICAL ABSTRACTS E (SEDIMENTOLOGY) see *EARTH SCIENCES — Abstracting, Bibliographies, Statistics*

GEOGRAPHICAL ABSTRACTS F (REGIONAL AND COMMUNITY PLANNING) see *HOUSING AND URBAN PLANNING — Abstracting, Bibliographies, Statistics*

GEOGRAPHICAL ABSTRACTS G (REMOTE SENSING PHOTOGRAMMETRY AND CARTOGRAPHY) see *GEOGRAPHY — Abstracting, Bibliographies, Statistics*

GEOLOGICAL ABSTRACTS: ECONOMIC GEOLOGY. see *EARTH SCIENCES — Abstracting, Bibliographies, Statistics*

GEOLOGICAL ABSTRACTS: GEOPHYSICS AND TECTONICS. see *EARTH SCIENCES — Abstracting, Bibliographies, Statistics*

GEOLOGICAL ABSTRACTS: PALAEONTOLOGY AND STRATIGRAPHY. see *EARTH SCIENCES — Abstracting, Bibliographies, Statistics*

GEOLOGICAL ABSTRACTS: SEDIMENTARY GEOLOGY. see *EARTH SCIENCES — Abstracting, Bibliographies, Statistics*

GEOLOGICAL SOCIETY OF AMERICA. ABSTRACTS WITH PROGRAMS. see *EARTH SCIENCES — Abstracting, Bibliographies, Statistics*

GEOSCIENCE DOCUMENTATION; a bi-monthly journal for the study of geoscience literature. see *EARTH SCIENCES — Abstracting, Bibliographies, Statistics*

GEOTECHNICAL ABSTRACTS. see *ENGINEERING — Abstracting, Bibliographies, Statistics*

GERMAN JOURNAL OF PSYCHOLOGY; a quarterly of abstracts and review articles. see *PSYCHOLOGY — Abstracting, Bibliographies, Statistics*

GERMAN PATENTS ABSTRACTS. see *PATENTS, TRADEMARKS AND COPYRIGHTS — Abstracting, Bibliographies, Statistics*

GERONTOLOGICAL ABSTRACTS. see *GERONTOLOGY AND GERIATRICS — Abstracting, Bibliographies, Statistics*

GESELLSCHAFT FUER BIBLIOTHEKSWESEN UND DOKUMENTATION DES LANDBAUES. MITTEILUNGEN. see *AGRICULTURE — Abstracting, Bibliographies, Statistics*

GEZINSWETENSCHAPPELIJKE DOCUMENTATIE; Jaarboek. see *POPULATION STUDIES — Abstracting, Bibliographies, Statistics*

GHANA SCIENCE ABSTRACTS. see *SCIENCES: COMPREHENSIVE WORKS — Abstracting, Bibliographies, Statistics*

GRAPHIC ARTS ABSTRACTS. see *PRINTING — Abstracting, Bibliographies, Statistics*

011 US
GUIDE TO SPECIAL ISSUES AND INDEXES OF PERIODICALS. 1962. irreg., latest 1985. $35. Special Libraries Association, 1700 18th St., N.W., Washington, DC 20009. TEL 202-234-4700. Ed. Miriam Uhlan.

011 011 US
GUIDE TO U S GOVERNMENT PUBLICATIONS. a. $275. Documents Index, Inc., Box 195, McLean, VA 22101. TEL 703-356-2434. Ed. John L. Andriot.

GUIDELINES; a subject guide for Australian libraries. see *LIBRARY AND INFORMATION SCIENCES — Abstracting, Bibliographies, Statistics*

H R I S ABSTRACTS. (Highway Research Information Service) see *TRANSPORTATION — Abstracting, Bibliographies, Statistics*

HEALTH EDUCATION INDEX; and guide to voluntary social welfare organizations. see *PHYSICAL FITNESS AND HYGIENE — Abstracting, Bibliographies, Statistics*

HEALTH PHYSICS RESEARCH ABSTRACTS. see *PUBLIC HEALTH AND SAFETY — Abstracting, Bibliographies, Statistics*

HELMINTHOLOGICAL ABSTRACTS. SERIES A: ANIMAL AND HUMAN HELMINTHOLOGY. see *AGRICULTURE — Abstracting, Bibliographies, Statistics*

HELMINTHOLOGICAL ABSTRACTS. SERIES B: PLANT NEMATOLOGY. see *AGRICULTURE — Abstracting, Bibliographies, Statistics*

HERBAGE ABSTRACTS; monthly abstract journal on grassland husbandry and fodder crop production. see *AGRICULTURE — Abstracting, Bibliographies, Statistics*

HIGH ENERGY PHYSICS INDEX/ HOCHENERGIEPHYSIK-INDEX. see *PHYSICS — Abstracting, Bibliographies, Statistics*

HIGHER EDUCATION ABSTRACTS; abstracts of periodical literature, monographs and conference papers on college students, faculty and administration. see *EDUCATION — Higher Education*

HISTORICAL ABSTRACTS. PART A: MODERN HISTORY ABSTRACTS, 1450-1914. see *HISTORY — Abstracting, Bibliographies, Statistics*

HISTORICAL ABSTRACTS. PART B: TWENTIETH CENTURY ABSTRACTS, 1914 TO THE PRESENT. see *HISTORY — Abstracting, Bibliographies, Statistics*

HOBBYINDEKS FOR BOERNEBIBLIOTEKER. see *HOBBIES*

011 HK ISSN 0379-5853
HONGKONGIANA; an index to selected Hong Kong Periodicals. (Text in Chinese and English) 1978. a. HK.$200($30) Hong Kong Polytechnic Library, Hung Hom, Kowloon, Hong Kong. Ed. John Chor-shing Lam. circ. 500. (back issues avail.)

HORTICULTURAL ABSTRACTS; compiled from world literature and temperate and tropical fruits, vegetables, ornaments, plantation crops. see *GARDENING AND HORTICULTURE — Abstracting, Bibliographies, Statistics*

HOSPITAL LITERATURE INDEX. see *HOSPITALS — Abstracting, Bibliographies, Statistics*

301 016 US ISSN 0099-2453
HUMAN RESOURCES ABSTRACTS; an international information service. 1966. q. $55 to individuals; institutions $110. Sage Publications, Inc., 2111 W. Hillcrest Dr., Newbury Park, CA 91320 TEL 805-499-0721. (And Sage Publications, Ltd., 28 Banner St., London EC1Y 8QE, England) Ed.Bd. adv. index. (also avail. in microfilm from UMI; back issues avail.; reprint service avail. from UMI) Indexed: Curr.Lit.Fam.Plan.
Formerly: Poverty and Human Resources Abstracts (ISSN 0032-5864)

ABSTRACTING AND INDEXING SERVICES

HUMANITIES INDEX; an author and subject index to periodicals in the fields of archaeology and classical studies, area studies, folklore, history, language and literature, literary and political criticism, performing arts, philosophy, religion and theology, and related subjects. see *HUMANITIES: COMPREHENSIVE WORKS — Abstracting, Bibliographies, Statistics*

HUNGARIAN R AND D ABSTRACTS. SCIENCE AND TECHNOLOGY. see *SCIENCES: COMPREHENSIVE WORKS — Abstracting, Bibliographies, Statistics*

HYDRO-ABSTRACTS. see *WATER RESOURCES — Abstracting, Bibliographies, Statistics*

I B M - P C INDEX. see *COMPUTERS — Abstracting, Bibliographies, Statistics*

I C S S R JOURNAL OF ABSTRACTS AND REVIEWS: SOCIOLOGY & SOCIAL ANTHROPOLOGY. (Indian Council of Social Science Research) see *ANTHROPOLOGY — Abstracting, Bibliographies, Statistics*

I C U I S JUSTICE MINISTRIES. (Institute on the Church in Urban Industrial Society) see *RELIGIONS AND THEOLOGY — Abstracting, Bibliographies, Statistics*

I M M ABSTRACTS; a survey of world literature on the economic geology and mining of all minerals (except coal), mineral processing and non-ferrous extraction metallurgy. (Institution of Mining and Metallurgy) see *MINES AND MINING INDUSTRY — Abstracting, Bibliographies, Statistics*

I N I S ATOMINDEX. see *PHYSICS — Abstracting, Bibliographies, Statistics*

IMMUNOLOGY ABSTRACTS. see *MEDICAL SCIENCES — Abstracting, Bibliographies, Statistics*

011   MY   ISSN 0126-9062
INDEKS SURATKHABAR MALAYSIA/ MALAYSIAN NEWSPAPER INDEX. English edition: Malaysian Newspaper Index (ISSN 0127-7448) (In two parts) (Editions in Bahasa and English) 1979. q. M.$30 english edition M.$40. National Library of Malaysia, Bibliography and Indexing Division - Perpustakan Negara Malaysia, 3rd Fl., Wisma, Sachdev, Jalan Raja Laut, 50572 Kuala Lumpur, Malaysia (Orders to: University of Malaya Cooperative Bookshop Ltd, Library Building, University of Malaya, 59700 Kuala Lumpur, Malaysia) Ed. Noraini Omar. circ. 200.

INDEX ASIA SERIES IN HUMANITIES. see *HUMANITIES: COMPREHENSIVE WORKS — Abstracting, Bibliographies, Statistics*

INDEX CHEMICUS. see *CHEMISTRY — Abstracting, Bibliographies, Statistics*

INDEX DOCUMENTATION-ECONOMIE-SCIENCE-TECHNIQUE. see *BUSINESS AND ECONOMICS — Abstracting, Bibliographies, Statistics*

954 015   II   ISSN 0019-3844
INDEX INDIA; a quarterly documentation list of selected articles, editorials, notes, and letters, etc., from periodicals and newspapers published in the English language all over the world. (Text in English) 1967. q. Rs.600. Rajasthan University Library, Gandhi Nagar, Jaipur 302004, India. Ed. S.N. Mathur. adv. bk. rev. bibl. index.

INDEX MEDICUS. see *MEDICAL SCIENCES — Abstracting, Bibliographies, Statistics*

016 610   BL   ISSN 0100-4743
INDEX MEDICUS LATINOAMERICANO. (Text in English, Portuguese and Spanish) 1979. q. Cr.$276.80($80) (Panamerican Health Organization-World Health Organization) Latin American Health Sciences Inform Center, Rua Botucatu, 862, Caixa Postal 20.381, V. Clementino, 04023 Sao Paulo, Brazil. circ. 500. (back issues avail.)

INDEX OF AMERICAN PERIODICAL VERSE. see *LITERATURE — Abstracting, Bibliographies, Statistics*

INDEX OF ARTICLES ON JEWISH STUDIES/ RESHIMAT MA'AMARIM BE-MADA'E HA-YAHADUT. see *RELIGIONS AND THEOLOGY — Abstracting, Bibliographies, Statistics*

INDEX OF CURRENT RESEARCH ON PIGS. see *AGRICULTURE — Abstracting, Bibliographies, Statistics*

INDEX OF ECONOMIC ARTICLES IN JOURNALS AND COLLECTIVE VOLUMES. see *BUSINESS AND ECONOMICS — Abstracting, Bibliographies, Statistics*

INDEX OF INDUSTRIAL RELATIONS LITERATURE. see *BUSINESS AND ECONOMICS — Abstracting, Bibliographies, Statistics*

INDEX OF MATHEMATICAL PAPERS. see *MATHEMATICS — Abstracting, Bibliographies, Statistics*

INDEX OF REVIEWS IN ORGANIC CHEMISTRY. see *CHEMISTRY — Abstracting, Bibliographies, Statistics*

INDEX TO CHINESE LEGAL PERIODICALS. see *LAW — Abstracting, Bibliographies, Statistics*

011   CH   ISSN 0378-0112
INDEX TO CHINESE PERIODICALS. (Text mainly in Chinese; occasionally in English) 1970. q., from 1984. $37. National Central Library, 20 Chung Shan S. Rd., Taipei, Taiwan, Republic of China.
Combines: Index to Chinese Periodicals-Humanities and Social Sciences (ISSN 0046-8886) & Index to Chinese Periodicals-Science and Technology (ISSN 0046-8894)

INDEX TO CURRENT URBAN DOCUMENTS. see *HOUSING AND URBAN PLANNING — Abstracting, Bibliographies, Statistics*

INDEX TO DENTAL LITERATURE; an alphabetical author and subject index to dental literature. see *MEDICAL SCIENCES — Abstracting, Bibliographies, Statistics*

INDEX TO FOREIGN LEGAL PERIODICALS. see *LAW — Abstracting, Bibliographies, Statistics*

011   US   ISSN 0147-5630
INDEX TO FREE PERIODICALS. 1976. s-a. $25. Pierian Press, Box 1808, Ann Arbor, MI 48106. TEL 313-434-5530. Ed. Arnold N. Rzepecki.

029   US   ISSN 0073-5930
INDEX TO HOW TO DO IT INFORMATION; a periodical index. 1963. a. $20. ‡ Norman Lathrop Enterprises, 2342 Star Dr., Box 198, Wooster, OH 44691. TEL 216-262-5587. Ed. Norman Lathrop. cum.index every 5 yrs.
Formerly: Aids Index to How to do It Information.

INDEX TO INDIAN MEDICAL PERIODICALS. see *MEDICAL SCIENCES — Abstracting, Bibliographies, Statistics*

INDEX TO LEGAL PERIODICALS. see *LAW — Abstracting, Bibliographies, Statistics*

011   MY   ISSN 0127-4880
INDEX TO MALAYSIAN CONFERENCES/ INDEKS PERSIDANGAN MALAYSIA. (Text in English and Malay) 1976. a. M.50. National Library, Bibliography and Indexing Division, Third Floor, Wisma Sachdev, Jalan Raja Laut, 50572 Kuala Lumpur, Malaysia (Orders to: University of Malaya Co-operative Bookshop Ltd., Library Building, University of Malaya, 59700 Kuala Lumpur, Malaysia) Ed. Wan Hajrah Wan Aris. circ. 200.

011   US   ISSN 0163-0466
INDEX TO NEW ENGLAND PERIODICALS; an index to selected regional publications. 1977-19??; suspended; resumed 1985. q. (with annual cumulation) $65 paperbound; hardbound $90. (Atlantic Indexing Co.) Diana Witt Associates, 201 Sheridan Ave., No. 5, Minneapolis, MN 55405. Ed. Diana Witt. circ. 185. (back issues avail.)

INDEX TO PERIODICAL ARTICLES BY AND ABOUT BLACKS. see *ETHNIC INTERESTS — Abstracting, Bibliographies, Statistics*

INDEX TO PERIODICAL ARTICLES RELATED TO LAW; selected journals not included in the Index to Legal Periodicals. see *LAW — Abstracting, Bibliographies, Statistics*

011 700   US   ISSN 0893-0139
INDEX TO REPRODUCTIONS IN ART PERIODICALS. 1987. q. $44. Data Arts, Box 15453, Seattle, WA 98115. TEL 206-783-9580. Ed. Eugene C. Burt.

INDEX TO SCIENTIFIC REVIEWS. see *SCIENCES: COMPREHENSIVE WORKS — Abstracting, Bibliographies, Statistics*

INDEX TO SOUTH AFRICAN PERIODICALS/ REPERTORIUM VAN SUID-AFRIKAANSE TYDSKRIFARTIKELS. see *PUBLISHING AND BOOK TRADE — Abstracting, Bibliographies, Statistics*

INDEX TO THAI PERIODICAL LITERATURE. see *SOCIAL SCIENCES: COMPREHENSIVE WORKS — Abstracting, Bibliographies, Statistics*

INDEX TO THE BOSTON GLOBE. see *JOURNALISM — Abstracting, Bibliographies, Statistics*

011 350   US   ISSN 0198-9014
INDEX TO THE CODE OF FEDERAL REGULATIONS. 1977. a. $745. Congressional Information Service, Inc., 4520 East-West Hwy., Ste. 800, Bethesda, MD 20814. TEL 301-654-1550. Ed. Carolyn Cohen. index. cum.index: 1977-1984. (reprint service avail.)

INDEX TO THE NATIONAL ASSEMBLY RECORDS/KUK HOE HOE EU ROK SAEGIN. see *LIBRARY AND INFORMATION SCIENCES — Abstracting, Bibliographies, Statistics*

INDEX TO THE NATIONAL OBSERVER. see *JOURNALISM — Abstracting, Bibliographies, Statistics*

INDEX TO THE ST. LOUIS POST-DISPATCH (WOOSTER) see *JOURNALISM — Abstracting, Bibliographies, Statistics*

INDEX TO THE ST. PAUL PIONEER PRESS AND DISPATCH. see *JOURNALISM — Abstracting, Bibliographies, Statistics*

INDEX TO THE SAN FRANCISCO CHRONICLE. see *JOURNALISM — Abstracting, Bibliographies, Statistics*

051 011   US   ISSN 0098-4604
INDEX TO U.S. GOVERNMENT PERIODICALS. Microfiche edt.: Current U.S. Government Periodicals on Microfiche. 1974. q. plus a. cum. $375. Infordata International Inc., Ste. 4602, 175 E. Delaware Place, Chicago, IL 60611. TEL 312-266-0260. Ed. Ivan A. Watters, Jr. bk. rev. abstr. bibl. cum.index. circ. 1,000. (also avail. in microfiche; reprint service avail.)

INDEX TO USA TODAY. see *JOURNALISM — Abstracting, Bibliographies, Statistics*

INDEX VETERINARIUS; a classified subject and author index produced by computer processes of current literature on veterinary science with approximately 23,000 titles. see *VETERINARY SCIENCE — Abstracting, Bibliographies, Statistics*

INDIA. MINISTRY OF EDUCATION AND SOCIAL WELFARE. DEPARTMENT OF SOCIAL WELFARE. DOCUMENTATION SERVICE BULLETIN. see *SOCIAL SCIENCES: COMPREHENSIVE WORKS — Abstracting, Bibliographies, Statistics*

INDIAN EDUCATION ABSTRACTS. see *EDUCATION — Abstracting, Bibliographies, Statistics*

INDIAN GEOLOGICAL INDEX. see *EARTH SCIENCES — Abstracting, Bibliographies, Statistics*

INDIAN INSTITUTE OF TECHNOLOGY, MADRAS. PH.D. DISSERTATION ABSTRACTS. see *TECHNOLOGY: COMPREHENSIVE WORKS — Abstracting, Bibliographies, Statistics*

INDIAN LIBRARY SCIENCE ABSTRACTS. see *LIBRARY AND INFORMATION SCIENCES — Abstracting, Bibliographies, Statistics*

INDIAN PSYCHOLOGICAL ABSTRACTS. see *PSYCHOLOGY — Abstracting, Bibliographies, Statistics*

INDIAN SCIENCE ABSTRACTS. see *SCIENCES: COMPREHENSIVE WORKS — Abstracting, Bibliographies, Statistics*

011   CU
INDICE GENERAL DE PUBLICACIONES PERIODICAS CUBANAS. 1970. a. $23. (Biblioteca Nacional Jose Marti, Departmento de Hemeroteca e Informacion de Humanidades) Ediciones Cubanas, Sub-Direccion de Exportacion, Apd. 605, Havana, Cuba. index. circ. 2,000.

INDICE MEDICO ESPANOL. see *MEDICAL SCIENCES — Abstracting, Bibliographies, Statistics*

INDUSTRIAL ABSTRACTS FOR TANZANIA. see *TECHNOLOGY: COMPREHENSIVE WORKS — Abstracting, Bibliographies, Statistics*

INDUSTRIAL AERODYNAMICS ABSTRACTS. see *ENGINEERING — Abstracting, Bibliographies, Statistics*

INDUSTRIAL DEVELOPMENT ABSTRACTS; U N I D O industrial information system (I N D I S) (United Nations Industrial Development Organization) see *BUSINESS AND ECONOMICS — Abstracting, Bibliographies, Statistics*

011   BE   ISSN 0252-1105
INFORMATION RESOURCES ANNUAL; an abstracting and indexing service. 1983. a. $100. Herman-Karel de Jaeger Information Resources Research, c/o Bibliotheque Royale Albert 1er, Centre National de Documentation Scientifique et Technique, 4 bd. de l'Empereur, B-1000 Brussels, Belgium. Ed. H-K. de Jaeger. adv. bk. rev. circ. 1, 000.
Formerly (until 1982): Information Resources Quarterly.

INFORMATION SCIENCE ABSTRACTS. see *LIBRARY AND INFORMATION SCIENCES — Abstracting, Bibliographies, Statistics*

INSTITUTE OF MARINE ENGINEERS TECHNICAL REPORTS. see *TRANSPORTATION — Abstracting, Bibliographies, Statistics*

INSTITUTE OF PAPER CHEMISTRY. ABSTRACT BULLETIN. see *PAPER AND PULP — Abstracting, Bibliographies, Statistics*

INSURANCE INDEX. see *INSURANCE — Abstracting, Bibliographies, Statistics*

INSURANCE PERIODICALS INDEX. see *INSURANCE — Abstracting, Bibliographies, Statistics*

INTERNATIONAL ABSTRACTS IN OPERATIONS RESEARCH. see *COMPUTERS — Abstracting, Bibliographies, Statistics*

INTERNATIONAL AEROSPACE ABSTRACTS. see *AERONAUTICS AND SPACE FLIGHT — Abstracting, Bibliographies, Statistics*

INTERNATIONAL BIOPHYSICS CONGRESS. ABSTRACTS. see *BIOLOGY — Abstracting, Bibliographies, Statistics*

INTERNATIONAL BUILDING SERVICES ABSTRACTS. see *HEATING, PLUMBING AND REFRIGERATION — Abstracting, Bibliographies, Statistics*

INTERNATIONAL CIVIL ENGINEERING ABSTRACTS. see *ENGINEERING — Abstracting, Bibliographies, Statistics*

INTERNATIONAL DEVELOPMENT ABSTRACTS. see *GEOGRAPHY — Abstracting, Bibliographies, Statistics*

INTERNATIONAL INDEX TO FILM PERIODICALS. see *MOTION PICTURES — Abstracting, Bibliographies, Statistics*

INTERNATIONAL JOURNAL OF ROCK MECHANICS AND MINING SCIENCES & GEOMECHANICS ABSTRACTS. see *MINES AND MINING INDUSTRY — Abstracting, Bibliographies, Statistics*

INTERNATIONAL NURSING INDEX INCLUDING NURSING CITATION INDEX. see *MEDICAL SCIENCES — Abstracting, Bibliographies, Statistics*

INTERNATIONAL PACKAGING ABSTRACTS. see *PACKAGING — Abstracting, Bibliographies, Statistics*

INTERNATIONAL PETROLEUM ABSTRACTS. see *PETROLEUM AND GAS — Abstracting, Bibliographies, Statistics*

INTERNATIONAL PHARMACEUTICAL ABSTRACTS; key to the world's literature of pharmacy. see *PHARMACY AND PHARMACOLOGY — Abstracting, Bibliographies, Statistics*

INTERNATIONAL POLITICAL SCIENCE ABSTRACTS/DOCUMENTATION POLITIQUE INTERNATIONALE. see *POLITICAL SCIENCE — Abstracting, Bibliographies, Statistics*

INTERNATIONAL RAYON AND SYNTHETIC FIBRES COMMITTEE. STATISTICAL YEARBOOK. see *TEXTILE INDUSTRIES AND FABRICS — Abstracting, Bibliographies, Statistics*

IRRIGATION AND POWER ABSTRACTS. see *WATER RESOURCES — Abstracting, Bibliographies, Statistics*

JAHRESVERZEICHNIS DER HOCHSCHULSCHRIFTEN DER DDR, DER BRD UND WESTBERLINS. see *EDUCATION — Abstracting, Bibliographies, Statistics*

JAPANESE PERIODICALS INDEX. HUMANITIES AND SOCIAL SCIENCE SECTION/ZASSHI KIJI SAKUIN. JIMBUN SHAKAI-HEN. see *HUMANITIES: COMPREHENSIVE WORKS — Abstracting, Bibliographies, Statistics*

JOURNAL OF ABSTRACTS IN INTERNATIONAL EDUCATION. see *EDUCATION — Abstracting, Bibliographies, Statistics*

JOURNAL OF CURRENT LASER ABSTRACTS. see *PHYSICS — Abstracting, Bibliographies, Statistics*

KEY ABSTRACTS - ARTIFICIAL INTELLIGENCE. see *ELECTRICITY AND ELECTRICAL ENGINEERING — Abstracting, Bibliographies, Statistics*

KEY ABSTRACTS - ELECTRONIC CIRCUITS. see *ELECTRICITY AND ELECTRICAL ENGINEERING — Abstracting, Bibliographies, Statistics*

KEY ABSTRACTS - ELECTRONIC INSTRUMENTATION. see *METROLOGY AND STANDARDIZATION — Abstracting, Bibliographies, Statistics*

KEY ABSTRACTS - MEASUREMENTS IN PHYSICS. see *METROLOGY AND STANDARDIZATION — Abstracting, Bibliographies, Statistics*

KEY ABSTRACTS - POWER SYSTEMS & APPLICATIONS. see *ELECTRICITY AND ELECTRICAL ENGINEERING — Abstracting, Bibliographies, Statistics*

KEY ABSTRACTS - ROBOTICS & CONTROL. see *ELECTRICITY AND ELECTRICAL ENGINEERING — Abstracting, Bibliographies, Statistics*

KEY ABSTRACTS - SEMICONDUCTOR DEVICES. see *ELECTRICITY AND ELECTRICAL ENGINEERING — Abstracting, Bibliographies, Statistics*

KEY TO ECONOMIC SCIENCE; semi-monthly review of abstracts on economics, finance, trade, industry, foreign aid, management, marketing, labour. see *BUSINESS AND ECONOMICS — Abstracting, Bibliographies, Statistics*

KEY WORD INDEX OF WILDLIFE RESEARCH. see *SCIENCES: COMPREHENSIVE WORKS — Abstracting, Bibliographies, Statistics*

KEYWORD INDEX TO SERIAL TITLES. see *LIBRARY AND INFORMATION SCIENCES — Abstracting, Bibliographies, Statistics*

KOREA (REPUBLIC). NATIONAL BUREAU OF STATISTICS. REPORT ON MINING AND MANUFACTURING SURVEY/ KWANGGONGUP TONGGYE ZO SA BOGO SEO. see *MINES AND MINING INDUSTRY — Abstracting, Bibliographies, Statistics*

016   KO
KOREAN PERIODICALS INDEX/JEONG-GI KANHAENGMUL KISA SAEGIN. (Text in Korean) 1945. bi-m. (plus annual cum.) free. National Assembly, Library, Processing & Reference Bureau, Yoido-Dong 1, Yeongdeungpo-Gu, Seoul, S. Korea. bibl. circ. 1,000. (also avail. in microform)

KOREAN SCIENTIFIC ABSTRACTS. see *SCIENCES: COMPREHENSIVE WORKS — Abstracting, Bibliographies, Statistics*

LANGUAGE TEACHING. see *EDUCATION — Abstracting, Bibliographies, Statistics*

LASER RAMAN & INFRARED SPECTROSCOPY ABSTRACTS. see *PHYSICS — Abstracting, Bibliographies, Statistics*

LATHROP REPORT ON NEWSPAPER INDEXES. see *JOURNALISM — Abstracting, Bibliographies, Statistics*

LEADSCAN; a review of recent technical literature on the uses of lead and its products. see *METALLURGY — Abstracting, Bibliographies, Statistics*

LEFT INDEX; a quarterly index to periodicals of the left. see *POLITICAL SCIENCE*

LEGAL CONTENTS; semi-monthly compilation of tables of contents from more than 320 business magazines and journals. see *LAW — Abstracting, Bibliographies, Statistics*

LEGAL INFORMATION MANAGEMENT INDEX. see *LAW*

LEGAL RESOURCE INDEX. see *LAW — Abstracting, Bibliographies, Statistics*

LEISURE, RECREATION AND TOURISM ABSTRACTS. see *TRAVEL AND TOURISM — Abstracting, Bibliographies, Statistics*

LEITUNG UND PLANUNG VON WISSENSCHAFT UND TECHNIK. see *BUSINESS AND ECONOMICS — Abstracting, Bibliographies, Statistics*

LIBRARY & INFORMATION SCIENCE ABSTRACTS. see *LIBRARY AND INFORMATION SCIENCES — Abstracting, Bibliographies, Statistics*

LIBRARY LIT. see *LIBRARY AND INFORMATION SCIENCES — Abstracting, Bibliographies, Statistics*

LIBRARY LITERATURE; an index to library and information science. see *LIBRARY AND INFORMATION SCIENCES — Abstracting, Bibliographies, Statistics*

LINGUISTICS AND LANGUAGE BEHAVIOR ABSTRACTS. see *LINGUISTICS — Abstracting, Bibliographies, Statistics*

LITERARY CRITICISM REGISTER; a monthly listing of studies in English and American literature. see *LITERATURE — Abstracting, Bibliographies, Statistics*

M L A INTERNATIONAL BIBLIOGRAPHY OF BOOKS AND ARTICLES ON THE MODERN LANGUAGES AND LITERATURES. (Modern Language Association of America) see *BIBLIOGRAPHIES*

070.5 011 US
MAGAZINE INDEX. m. $1890. Information Access Company, 11 Davis Dr., Belmont, CA 94002. TEL 800-227-8431. (microform; also avail. on CD-ROM)
●Also available online. Vendors: BRS, DIALOG, Mead Data Central.

MAIZE ABSTRACTS. see *AGRICULTURE — Abstracting, Bibliographies, Statistics*

029.4 015 MY ISSN 0126-5040
MALAYSIAN PERIODICALS INDEX/INDEKS MAJALAH MALAYSIA. (Text in Bahasa, Chinese, English and Tamil) 1973. s-a. M.$75. National Library of Malaysia, Bibliography and Indexing Division - Perpustakaan Negara Malaysia, 3rd Fl., Wisma Sachdev, Jalan Raja Laut, Kuala Lumpur 10-06, Malaysia (Orders to: University of Malaya Co-operative Bookshop Ltd, Library Building, University of Malaya, 59700 Kuala Lumpur, Malaysia) Ed. Siti Rodziah Othman. circ. 200.

MANAGEMENT ABSTRACTS. see *BUSINESS AND ECONOMICS — Abstracting, Bibliographies, Statistics*

MANAGEMENT ABSTRACTS. see *BUSINESS AND ECONOMICS — Abstracting, Bibliographies, Statistics*

MANAGEMENT AND MARKETING ABSTRACTS. see *BUSINESS AND ECONOMICS — Abstracting, Bibliographies, Statistics*

MANAGEMENT CONTENTS; semi-monthly compilation of tables of contents from more than 320 business magazines and journals. see *BUSINESS AND ECONOMICS — Abstracting, Bibliographies, Statistics*

MARKET RESEARCH ABSTRACTS. see *BUSINESS AND ECONOMICS — Abstracting, Bibliographies, Statistics*

MARKETING & DISTRIBUTION ABSTRACTS. see *BUSINESS AND ECONOMICS — Abstracting, Bibliographies, Statistics*

MASS SPECTROMETRY BULLETIN. see *CHEMISTRY — Abstracting, Bibliographies, Statistics*

MATHEMATICAL REVIEWS; a reviewing journal covering the world literature of mathematical research. see *MATHEMATICS — Abstracting, Bibliographies, Statistics*

MEDIA REVIEW DIGEST; the only complete guide to reviews of non-book media. see *MOTION PICTURES — Abstracting, Bibliographies, Statistics*

MEDICAL CARE REVIEW. see *PUBLIC HEALTH AND SAFETY — Abstracting, Bibliographies, Statistics*

METALS ABSTRACTS. (American Society for Metals) see *METALLURGY — Abstracting, Bibliographies, Statistics*

METALS ABSTRACTS INDEX. (American Society for Metals) see *METALLURGY — Abstracting, Bibliographies, Statistics*

METEOROLOGICAL AND GEOASTROPHYSICAL ABSTRACTS. see *METEOROLOGY — Abstracting, Bibliographies, Statistics*

051 015 US ISSN 0026-2250
MICHIGAN MAGAZINE INDEX. 1967. q. free. ‡ Library of Michigan, Box 30007, Lansing, MI 48909. TEL 517-373-1593. Ed. Leelyn Johnson. index. circ. 400. (microfiche)

MICROBIOLOGY ABSTRACTS. SECTION B. BACTERIOLOGY. see *BIOLOGY — Microbiology*

MICROCOMPUTER INDEX. see *COMPUTERS — Abstracting, Bibliographies, Statistics*

011 CN ISSN 0707-3135
MICROLOG INDEX. (Text in English and French) 1979. m.(with annual cumulation) Can.$450. Micromedia Ltd., 158 Pearl St., Toronto, Ont. M5H 1L3, Canada. TEL 416-593-5211. Ed. Rosemary McClelland. circ. 500.
●Also available online. Vendors: CISTI.
Supersedes: Publicat Index to Canadian Federal Publications (ISSN 0384-9813) & Urban Canada (ISSN 0384-9821) & Canadian Urban Sources (ISSN 0317-2775) & Profile Index to Canadian and Municipal Government Publications (ISSN 0316-4608)

915.6 016 US ISSN 0162-766X
MIDDLE EAST: ABSTRACTS AND INDEX. 1978. a. $200. Northumberland Press, 1717 Boulevard of the Allies, Pittsburgh, PA 15219. TEL 412-281-6179. Ed. Amy C. Lowenstein. adv. bk. rev.
●Also available online. Vendors: DIALOG.

MISSISSIPPI STATE UNIVERSITY ABSTRACTS OF THESES AND DISSERTATIONS. see *EDUCATION — Abstracting, Bibliographies, Statistics*

MOESSBAUER SPECTROSCOPY ABSTRACTS. see *PHYSICS — Abstracting, Bibliographies, Statistics*

MONATSSCHRIFT FUER BRAUWISSENSCHAFT. see *BEVERAGES — Abstracting, Bibliographies, Statistics*

MULTICULTURAL EDUCATION ABSTRACTS. see *EDUCATION — Abstracting, Bibliographies, Statistics*

MUSIC ARTICLE GUIDE. see *MUSIC — Abstracting, Bibliographies, Statistics*

MUSIC-IN-PRINT SERIES. see *MUSIC — Abstracting, Bibliographies, Statistics*

MUSIC INDEX; a subject-author guide to over 300 current international periodicals. see *MUSIC — Abstracting, Bibliographies, Statistics*

N A A. (Nordic Archaeological Abstracts) see *ARCHAEOLOGY — Abstracting, Bibliographies, Statistics*

N A S A PATENT ABSTRACTS BIBLIOGRAPHY: A CONTINUING BIBLIOGRAPHY. SECTION 1. ABSTRACTS. (U.S. National Aeronautics and Space Administration) see *PATENTS, TRADEMARKS AND COPYRIGHTS — Abstracting, Bibliographies, Statistics*

N B O ABSTRACTS. (National Buildings Organisation) see *ENGINEERING — Abstracting, Bibliographies, Statistics*

N.E.S.F.A. INDEX: SCIENCE FICTION MAGAZINES AND ANTHOLOGIES. (New England Science Fiction Association Inc.) see *ADVENTURE AND ROMANCE — Abstracting, Bibliographies, Statistics*

N I C E M INDEX TO PRODUCERS AND DISTRIBUTORS. (National Information Center for Educational Media) see *MOTION PICTURES — Abstracting, Bibliographies, Statistics*

N I C E M INDEX TO 35MM EDUCATIONAL FILMSTRIPS. (National Information Center for Educational Media) see *EDUCATION — Abstracting, Bibliographies, Statistics*

NATIONAL AERONAUTICAL LABORATORY. SELECTED ABSTRACTS FROM RUSSIAN AND OTHER FOREIGN SCIENTIFIC LITERATURE. see *AERONAUTICS AND SPACE FLIGHT*

NEPAL DOCUMENTATION; occasional bibliography. see *BUSINESS AND ECONOMICS — Abstracting, Bibliographies, Statistics*

NEUROSCIENCES ABSTRACTS. see *MEDICAL SCIENCES — Abstracting, Bibliographies, Statistics*

NEUTRON ACTIVATION ANALYSIS ABSTRACTS. see *PHYSICS — Abstracting, Bibliographies, Statistics*

NEW LITERATURE ON AUTOMATION. see *COMPUTERS — Abstracting, Bibliographies, Statistics*

NEW TESTAMENT ABSTRACTS; a record of current literature. see *RELIGIONS AND THEOLOGY — Abstracting, Bibliographies, Statistics*

NEW ZEALAND SCIENCE ABSTRACTS. see *SCIENCES: COMPREHENSIVE WORKS — Abstracting, Bibliographies, Statistics*

011 US
NORTHERN REGIONAL RESEARCH CENTER PUBLICATIONS AND PATENTS. 1940. a. free. U.S. Department of Agriculture, Agricultural Research Service, Northern Regional Research Center, 1815 N. University, Peoria, IL 61604. TEL 309-685-4011. bibl. pat. circ. 700. (back issues avail.)

NOTES AND ABSTRACTS IN AMERICAN AND INTERNATIONAL EDUCATION. see *EDUCATION — Abstracting, Bibliographies, Statistics*

NUCLEAR MAGNETIC RESONANCE SPECTROMETRY ABSTRACTS. see *PHYSICS — Abstracting, Bibliographies, Statistics*

NURSING ABSTRACTS. see *MEDICAL SCIENCES — Abstracting, Bibliographies, Statistics*

NUTRITION ABSTRACTS AND REVIEWS. SERIES A: HUMAN AND EXPERIMENTAL. see *NUTRITION AND DIETETICS — Abstracting, Bibliographies, Statistics*

NUTRITION ABSTRACTS AND REVIEWS. SERIES B: LIVESTOCK FEEDS AND FEEDING. see *AGRICULTURE — Abstracting, Bibliographies, Statistics*

O A P E C ENERGY BIBLIOGRAPHY. (Organization of Arab Petroleum Exporting Countries) see *PETROLEUM AND GAS*

O A P E C LIBRARY INDEX. (Organization of Arab Petroleum Exporting Countries) see *PETROLEUM AND GAS*

OCEANIC ABSTRACTS. see *EARTH SCIENCES — Abstracting, Bibliographies, Statistics*

OFFSHORE ABSTRACTS. see *PETROLEUM AND GAS — Abstracting, Bibliographies, Statistics*

OLD TESTAMENT ABSTRACTS. see *RELIGIONS AND THEOLOGY — Abstracting, Bibliographies, Statistics*

ONCOLOGY ABSTRACTS. see *MEDICAL SCIENCES — Abstracting, Bibliographies, Statistics*

016 658 US ISSN 0030-3658
OPERATIONS RESEARCH/MANAGEMENT SCIENCE; international literature digest service. 1961. m. $138. Executive Sciences Institute, Inc., Drawer M, Whippany, NJ 07981. TEL 201-887-1233. Ed. Arnold J. Rosenthal. abstr. charts. illus. stat. index.

016 362.7 NE
OVERZICHT TIJDSCHRIFTARTIKELEN. 6/yr. fl.23. Werkverband Integratie Jeugdwelzijnswerk, Postbus 3101, 3502 GC Utrecht, Netherlands. circ. 300.

P A I S BULLETIN. (Public Affairs Information Service, Inc.) see *BUSINESS AND ECONOMICS — Abstracting, Bibliographies, Statistics*

P A I S FOREIGN LANGUAGE INDEX. see *BUSINESS AND ECONOMICS — Abstracting, Bibliographies, Statistics*

P A S C A L EXPLORE. PART 11: PHYSIQUE ATOMIQUE ET MOLECULAIRE. PLASMAS. see *PHYSICS — Abstracting, Bibliographies, Statistics*

P A S C A L EXPLORE. PART 12: ETAT CONDENSE. see PHYSICS — *Abstracting, Bibliographies, Statistics*

P A S C A L EXPLORE. PART 20: ELECTRONIQUE ET TELECOMMUNICATIONS. see *ELECTRICITY AND ELECTRICAL ENGINEERING — Abstracting, Bibliographies, Statistics*

P A S C A L EXPLORE. PART 27: METHODES DE FORMATION ET TRAITEMENT DES IMAGES. see *PHYSICS — Abstracting, Bibliographies, Statistics*

P A S C A L EXPLORE. PART 32: METROLOGIE ET APPAREILLAGE EN PHYSIQUE ET PHYSICOCHIMIE. see *METROLOGY AND STANDARDIZATION — Abstracting, Bibliographies, Statistics*

P A S C A L EXPLORE. PART 49: METEOROLOGIE. see *METEOROLOGY — Abstracting, Bibliographies, Statistics*

P A S C A L EXPLORE. PART 64: ENDOCRINOLOGIE HUMAINE ET EXPERIMENTALE. ENDOCRINOPATHIES. see *MEDICAL SCIENCES — Abstracting, Bibliographies, Statistics*

P A S C A L EXPLORE. PART 65: PSYCHOLOGIE. PSYCHOPATHOLOGIE. PSYCHIATRIE. see *MEDICAL SCIENCES — Abstracting, Bibliographies, Statistics*

P A S C A L EXPLORE. PART 71: OPHTALMOLOGIE. see *MEDICAL SCIENCES — Abstracting, Bibliographies, Statistics*

P A S C A L EXPLORE. PART 72: OTORHINOLARYNGOLOGIE. STOMATOLOGIE. PATHOLOGIE CERVICOFACIALE. see *MEDICAL SCIENCES — Abstracting, Bibliographies, Statistics*

P A S C A L EXPLORE. PART 73: DERMATOLOGIE. MALADIES SEXUELLEMENT TRANSMISSIBLES. see *MEDICAL SCIENCES — Abstracting, Bibliographies, Statistics*

P A S C A L EXPLORE. PART 74: PNEUMOLOGIE. see *MEDICAL SCIENCES — Abstracting, Bibliographies, Statistics*

P A S C A L EXPLORE. PART 75: CARDIOLOGIE ET APPAREIL CIRCULATOIRE. see *MEDICAL SCIENCES — Abstracting, Bibliographies, Statistics*

P A S C A L EXPLORE. PART 76: GASTROENTEROLOGIE, FOIE, PANCREAS, ABDOMEN. see *MEDICAL SCIENCES — Abstracting, Bibliographies, Statistics*

P A S C A L EXPLORE. PART 77: NEPHROLOGIE. VOIES URINAIRES. see *MEDICAL SCIENCES — Abstracting, Bibliographies, Statistics*

P A S C A L EXPLORE. PART 78: NEUROLOGIE. see *MEDICAL SCIENCES — Abstracting, Bibliographies, Statistics*

P A S C A L EXPLORE. PART 79: PATHOLOGIE ET PHYSIOLOGIE OSTEOARTICULAIRES. see *MEDICAL SCIENCES — Abstracting, Bibliographies, Statistics*

P A S C A L EXPLORE. PART 80: HEMATOLOGIE. see *MEDICAL SCIENCES — Abstracting, Bibliographies, Statistics*

P A S C A L EXPLORE. PART 81: MALADIES METABOLIQUES. see *MEDICAL SCIENCES — Abstracting, Bibliographies, Statistics*

P A S C A L EXPLORE. PART 82: GYNECOLOGIE. OBSTETRIQUE. ANDROLOGIE. see *MEDICAL SCIENCES — Abstracting, Bibliographies, Statistics*

P A S C A L EXPLORE. PART 83: ANESTHESIE ET REANIMATION. see *MEDICAL SCIENCES — Abstracting, Bibliographies, Statistics*

P A S C A L EXPLORE. PART 84: GENIE BIOMEDICAL. INFORMATIQUE BIOMEDICALE. see *MEDICAL SCIENCES — Abstracting, Bibliographies, Statistics*

P A S C A L FOLIO. PART 21: ELECTROTECHNIQUE. see *ELECTRICITY AND ELECTRICAL ENGINEERING — Abstracting, Bibliographies, Statistics*

P A S C A L FOLIO. PART 41: GISEMENTS METALLIQUES ET NON-METALLIQUES. ECONOMIE MINIERE. see *MINES AND MINING INDUSTRY — Abstracting, Bibliographies, Statistics*

P A S C A L FOLIO. PART 54: REPRODUCTION DES VERTEBRES. EMBRYOLOGIE DES VERTEBRES ET DES INVERTEBRES. see *MEDICAL SCIENCES — Abstracting, Bibliographies, Statistics*

P A S C A L THEMA. PART 230: ENERGIE. see *PHYSICS — Abstracting, Bibliographies, Statistics*

P A S C A L THEMA. PART 240: METAUX. METALLURGIE. see *METALLURGY — Abstracting, Bibliographies, Statistics*

P A S C A L THEMA. PART 245: SOUDAGE, BRASAGE ET TECHNIQUES CONNEXES. see *METALLURGY — Abstracting, Bibliographies, Statistics*

P A S C A L THEMA. PART 251: CANCEROLOGIE (CANCERNET) see *MEDICAL SCIENCES — Abstracting, Bibliographies, Statistics*

PACKAGING SCIENCE AND TECHNOLOGY ABSTRACTS/REFERATEDIENST VERPACKUNG. see *PACKAGING — Abstracting, Bibliographies, Statistics*

PAKISTAN SCIENCE ABSTRACTS. see *SCIENCES: COMPREHENSIVE WORKS — Abstracting, Bibliographies, Statistics*

PAPER AND BOARD ABSTRACTS. see *PAPER AND PULP — Abstracting, Bibliographies, Statistics*

PEACE RESEARCH ABSTRACTS JOURNAL. see *POLITICAL SCIENCE — Abstracting, Bibliographies, Statistics*

PEAT ABSTRACTS. see *MINES AND MINING INDUSTRY — Abstracting, Bibliographies, Statistics*

PERSONNEL & TRAINING ABSTRACTS. see *BUSINESS AND ECONOMICS — Abstracting, Bibliographies, Statistics*

PERSONNEL MANAGEMENT ABSTRACTS. see *BUSINESS AND ECONOMICS — Abstracting, Bibliographies, Statistics*

PETROLEUM ABSTRACTS. see *PETROLEUM AND GAS — Abstracting, Bibliographies, Statistics*

PETROLEUM/ENERGY BUSINESS NEWS INDEX. see *PETROLEUM AND GAS — Abstracting, Bibliographies, Statistics*

PHARMACEUTICAL NEWS INDEX. see *PHARMACY AND PHARMACOLOGY — Abstracting, Bibliographies, Statistics*

PHARMINDEX. see *PHARMACY AND PHARMACOLOGY — Abstracting, Bibliographies, Statistics*

PHILIPPINE SCIENCE AND TECHNOLOGY ABSTRACTS BIBLIOGRAPHY. see *SCIENCES: COMPREHENSIVE WORKS — Abstracting, Bibliographies, Statistics*

PHOTOGRAPHIC ABSTRACTS. see *PHOTOGRAPHY — Abstracting, Bibliographies, Statistics*

PHOTOGRAPHY MAGAZINE INDEX. see *PHOTOGRAPHY — Abstracting, Bibliographies, Statistics*

PHYSICAL EDUCATION INDEX. see *PHYSICAL FITNESS AND HYGIENE — Abstracting, Bibliographies, Statistics*

PHYSICAL REVIEW ABSTRACTS. see *PHYSICS — Abstracting, Bibliographies, Statistics*

PHYSICAL REVIEW/INDEX. see *PHYSICS — Abstracting, Bibliographies, Statistics*

PHYSICS ABSTRACTS. see *PHYSICS — Abstracting, Bibliographies, Statistics*

PHYSICS BRIEFS/PHYSIKALISCHE BERICHTE; an abstracting journal covering all fields of physics. see *PHYSICS — Abstracting, Bibliographies, Statistics*

011   AT ISSN 0031-9910
PINPOINTER; a subject guide to popular periodicals. 1963. bi-m. Aus.$45. Libraries Board of South Australia, Box 419, G.P.O., Adelaide, S.A. 5001, Australia (Subscr. to: National Library of Australia, Canberra, A.C.T. 2600, Australia) cum.index. circ. 350. (processed; also avail. in microfiche)

PIPELINES ABSTRACTS. see *PETROLEUM AND GAS — Abstracting, Bibliographies, Statistics*

PLANT BREEDING ABSTRACTS. see *GARDENING AND HORTICULTURE — Abstracting, Bibliographies, Statistics*

PLANT GROWTH REGULATOR ABSTRACTS. see *AGRICULTURE — Abstracting, Bibliographies, Statistics*

PLANT PROTECTION ABSTRACTS. see *AGRICULTURE — Abstracting, Bibliographies, Statistics*

PLAY INDEX. see *LITERATURE — Abstracting, Bibliographies, Statistics*

016   CN
POINT DE REPERE; index analytique de periodiques de langue Francaise. 1984. q. Can.$170($184) (includes annual cumulation) Centrale des Bibliotheques, 1685 Est rue Fleury, Montreal, Que. H2C 1T1, Canada. TEL 418-643-4408. Ed. Nicole Gilbert. index. circ. 650. (also avail. in microfiche)
 Formed by the merger of: Periodex (ISSN 0300-3663) & R A D A R (ISSN 0315-2316)

POLAROGRAPHY ABSTRACTS. see *PHYSICS — Abstracting, Bibliographies, Statistics*

POLICE SCIENCE ABSTRACTS. see *CRIMINOLOGY AND LAW ENFORCEMENT — Abstracting, Bibliographies, Statistics*

POLISH ARCHAEOLOGICAL ABSTRACTS. see *ARCHAEOLOGY — Abstracting, Bibliographies, Statistics*

POLISH TECHNICAL AND ECONOMIC ABSTRACTS. see *TECHNOLOGY: COMPREHENSIVE WORKS — Abstracting, Bibliographies, Statistics*

016   PL
POLITECHNIKA WROCLAWSKA. BIBLIOTEKA GLOWNA I OSRODEK INFORMACJI NAUKOWO-TECHNICZNEJ. PRACE NAUKOWE. PRACE BIBLIOGRAFICZNE. 1975. irreg., no.14, 1985. price varies. Politechnika Wroclawska, Wybrzeze Wyspianskiego 27, 50-370 Wroclaw, Poland (Dist. by: Ars Polona-Ruch, Krakowskie Przedmiescie 7, Warsaw, Poland) Ed. J. Ciekot. circ. 500.

POLSKA BIBLIOGRAFIA ANALITYCZNA MECHANIKI/POLISH SCIENTIFIC ABSTRACTS ON MECHANICS. see *MACHINERY — Abstracting, Bibliographies, Statistics*

051 011   US   ISSN 0740-3763
POPULAR MAGAZINE REVIEW. 1984. w. $245.
Data Base Communications Corp., Box 325,
Topsfield, MA 01983. TEL 617-887-6667. Ed.
Gerald M. Seaman. bk. rev. index. circ. 3,000.
(looseleaf format; back issues avail.)
●Also available online. Vendors: BRS.

011   US   ISSN 0092-9727
POPULAR PERIODICAL INDEX. 1973. s-a. $20.
Robert M. Bottorff, Ed. & Pub., Box 2157, Wayne,
NJ 07470. TEL 201-595-0714.

POPULATION INDEX. see *POPULATION STUDIES* — *Abstracting, Bibliographies, Statistics*

POTATO ABSTRACTS. see *AGRICULTURE* — *Abstracting, Bibliographies, Statistics*

POULTRY ABSTRACTS. see *AGRICULTURE* — *Abstracting, Bibliographies, Statistics*

PREDI-BRIEFS. see *BUSINESS AND ECONOMICS* — *Abstracting, Bibliographies, Statistics*

PREDICASTS F & S INDEX EUROPE. see *BUSINESS AND ECONOMICS* — *Abstracting, Bibliographies, Statistics*

PREDICASTS F & S INDEX INTERNATIONAL. see *BUSINESS AND ECONOMICS* — *Abstracting, Bibliographies, Statistics*

PREDICASTS F & S INDEX OF CORPORATE CHANGE. see *BUSINESS AND ECONOMICS* — *Abstracting, Bibliographies, Statistics*

PREDICASTS F & S INDEX UNITED STATES. see *BUSINESS AND ECONOMICS* — *Abstracting, Bibliographies, Statistics*

PREDICASTS FORECASTS. see *BUSINESS AND ECONOMICS* — *Abstracting, Bibliographies, Statistics*

PREDICASTS OVERVIEW OF MARKETS AND TECHNOLOGIES. see *ENGINEERING* — *Abstracting, Bibliographies, Statistics*

PRODUCTIVITY INSIGHTS. see *TECHNOLOGY: COMPREHENSIVE WORKS* — *Abstracting, Bibliographies, Statistics*

PSYCHOLOGICAL ABSTRACTS. see *PSYCHOLOGY* — *Abstracting, Bibliographies, Statistics*

PSYCSCAN: APPLIED PSYCHOLOGY. see *PSYCHOLOGY* — *Abstracting, Bibliographies, Statistics*

PSYCSCAN: CLINICAL PSYCHOLOGY. see *PSYCHOLOGY* — *Abstracting, Bibliographies, Statistics*

PSYCSCAN: DEVELOPMENTAL PSYCHOLOGY. see *PSYCHOLOGY* — *Abstracting, Bibliographies, Statistics*

PSYCSCAN: LEARNING AND COMMUNICATION DISORDERS AND MENTAL RETARDATION. see *PSYCHOLOGY* — *Abstracting, Bibliographies, Statistics*

PUBLIZISTIKWISSENSCHAFTLICHER REFERATEDIENST. see *JOURNALISM* — *Abstracting, Bibliographies, Statistics*

PUMPS AND OTHER FLUIDS MACHINERY ABSTRACTS. see *MACHINERY* — *Abstracting, Bibliographies, Statistics*

658.5 016 311   US   ISSN 0033-5207
QUALITY CONTROL AND APPLIED
STATISTICS; abstract service. 1956. m. $148.
Executive Sciences Institute, Inc., Drawer M,
Whippany, NJ 07981. TEL 201-887-1233. Eds.
Arnold J. Rosenthal, Dorothy S. Rosenthal. abstr.
bibl. charts. illus. stat. index.

R A P R A ABSTRACTS. see *RUBBER* — *Abstracting, Bibliographies, Statistics*

R I C S LIBRARY INFORMATION SERVICE ABSTRACTS AND REVIEWS. (Royal Institution of Chartered Surveyors) see *ENGINEERING* — *Abstracting, Bibliographies, Statistics*

R I L M ABSTRACTS OF MUSIC LITERATURE. (International Repertory of Music Literature) see *MUSIC* — *Abstracting, Bibliographies, Statistics*

REFERATE ORGAN: SCHWEISSEN UND VERWANDTE VERFAHREN/BULLETIN OF ABSTRACTS: WELDING AND ALLIED PROCESSES. see *METALLURGY* — *Abstracting, Bibliographies, Statistics*

REFERATIVNYI ZHURNAL. ASTRONOMIYA. see *ASTRONOMY* — *Abstracting, Bibliographies, Statistics*

REFERATIVNYI ZHURNAL. EKONOMIKA, ORGANIZATSIYA, TEKHNOLOGIYA I OBORUDOVANIE POLIGRAFICHESKOGO PROIZVODSTVA. see *PRINTING* — *Abstracting, Bibliographies, Statistics*

REFERATIVNYI ZHURNAL. ELEKTRONIKA. see *ELECTRICITY AND ELECTRICAL ENGINEERING* — *Abstracting, Bibliographies, Statistics*

REFERATIVNYI ZHURNAL. ELEKTROSVYAZ'. see *ELECTRICITY AND ELECTRICAL ENGINEERING* — *Abstracting, Bibliographies, Statistics*

REFERATIVNYI ZHURNAL. ELEKTROTEKHNIKA. see *ELECTRICITY AND ELECTRICAL ENGINEERING* — *Abstracting, Bibliographies, Statistics*

REFERATIVNYI ZHURNAL. FIZIKA. see *PHYSICS* — *Abstracting, Bibliographies, Statistics*

REFERATIVNYI ZHURNAL. FOTOKINOTEKHNIKA. see *PHOTOGRAPHY* — *Abstracting, Bibliographies, Statistics*

REFERATIVNYI ZHURNAL. GORNOE DELO. see *MINES AND MINING INDUSTRY* — *Abstracting, Bibliographies, Statistics*

REFERATIVNYI ZHURNAL. IMMUNOLOGIYA - ALLERGOLOGIYA. see *MEDICAL SCIENCES* — *Abstracting, Bibliographies, Statistics*

REFERATIVNYI ZHURNAL. ISSLEDOVANIE KOSMICHESKOGO PROSTRANSTVA. see *ASTRONOMY* — *Abstracting, Bibliographies, Statistics*

REFERATIVNYI ZHURNAL. KHIMICHESKOE, NEFTEPERERABATYVAYUSCHCHEE I POLIMERNOE MASHINOSTROENIE. see *HEATING, PLUMBING AND REFRIGERATION* — *Abstracting, Bibliographies, Statistics*

REFERATIVNYI ZHURNAL. KORROZIYA I ZASHCHITA OT KORROZII. see *METALLURGY* — *Abstracting, Bibliographies, Statistics*

REFERATIVNYI ZHURNAL. MATEMATIKA. see *MATHEMATICS* — *Abstracting, Bibliographies, Statistics*

REFERATIVNYI ZHURNAL. MEDITSINSKAYA GEOGRAFIYA. see *MEDICAL SCIENCES* — *Abstracting, Bibliographies, Statistics*

REFERATIVNYI ZHURNAL. METALLURGIYA. see *METALLURGY* — *Abstracting, Bibliographies, Statistics*

REFERATIVNYI ZHURNAL. METROLOGIYA I IZMERITEL'NAYA TEKHNIKA. see *METROLOGY AND STANDARDIZATION* — *Abstracting, Bibliographies, Statistics*

REFERATIVNYI ZHURNAL. OBORUDOVANIE PISHCHEVOI PROMYSHLENNOSTI. see *FOOD AND FOOD INDUSTRIES* — *Abstracting, Bibliographies, Statistics*

REFERATIVNYI ZHURNAL. ONKOLOGIYA. see *MEDICAL SCIENCES* — *Abstracting, Bibliographies, Statistics*

REFERATIVNYI ZHURNAL. POZHARNAYA OKHRANA. see *PUBLIC HEALTH AND SAFETY* — *Abstracting, Bibliographies, Statistics*

REFERATIVNYI ZHURNAL. PROMYSHLENNYI TRANSPORT. see *MACHINERY* — *Abstracting, Bibliographies, Statistics*

REFERATIVNYI ZHURNAL. RADIATSIONNAYA BIOLOGIYA. see *MEDICAL SCIENCES* — *Abstracting, Bibliographies, Statistics*

REFERATIVNYI ZHURNAL. SVARKA. see *METALLURGY* — *Abstracting, Bibliographies, Statistics*

REFERATIVNYI ZHURNAL. TEKHNOLOGIYA MASHINOSTROENIYA. see *MACHINERY* — *Abstracting, Bibliographies, Statistics*

REFERATIVNYI ZHURNAL. TEPLO I MASSOBMEN. see *ENERGY* — *Abstracting, Bibliographies, Statistics*

REFERATIVNYI ZHURNAL. YADERNYE REAKTORY. see *PHYSICS* — *Abstracting, Bibliographies, Statistics*

REFERENCE POINT: FOOD INDUSTRY ABSTRACTS. see *FOOD AND FOOD INDUSTRIES* — *Abstracting, Bibliographies, Statistics*

REFERENCE SOURCES. see *PUBLISHING AND BOOK TRADE* — *Abstracting, Bibliographies, Statistics*

REGISTER OF INDEXERS. see *LIBRARY AND INFORMATION SCIENCES*

RELIGION INDEX ONE: PERIODICALS. see *RELIGIONS AND THEOLOGY* — *Abstracting, Bibliographies, Statistics*

RELIGIOUS & THEOLOGICAL ABSTRACTS. see *RELIGIONS AND THEOLOGY* — *Abstracting, Bibliographies, Statistics*

011   US   ISSN 0362-7535
RESEARCH ABSTRACTS (ANN ARBOR) 1976. q.
$15. University Microfilms International, 300 N.
Zeeb Rd., Ann Arbor, MI 48106. TEL 313-761-4700.
   Supersedes (1973-1976, vol.1, nos. 1-2):
Monograph Abstracts (Ann Arbor) (ISSN 0092-1149)

RESEARCH INDEX. see *BUSINESS AND ECONOMICS* — *Abstracting, Bibliographies, Statistics*

RESEARCH INTO HIGHER EDUCATION ABSTRACTS. see *EDUCATION* — *Abstracting, Bibliographies, Statistics*

RESOURCES IN EDUCATION. see *EDUCATION* — *Abstracting, Bibliographies, Statistics*

REVIEW OF APPLIED ENTOMOLOGY. SERIES A: AGRICULTURAL; consisting of abstracts of reviews of current literature on applied entomology throughout the world. see *AGRICULTURE* — *Abstracting, Bibliographies, Statistics*

REVIEW OF APPLIED ENTOMOLOGY. SERIES B: MEDICAL AND VETERINARY. see *VETERINARY SCIENCE* — *Abstracting, Bibliographies, Statistics*

REVIEW OF PLANT PATHOLOGY; consisting of abstracts and reviews of current literature on plant pathology. see *BIOLOGY* — *Abstracting, Bibliographies, Statistics*

RHEOLOGY ABSTRACTS; a survey of world literature. see *PHYSICS* — *Abstracting, Bibliographies, Statistics*

RICE ABSTRACTS. see *AGRICULTURE* — *Abstracting, Bibliographies, Statistics*

RISK ABSTRACTS; a quarterly journal of abstracts, reviews and references. see *ENVIRONMENTAL STUDIES — Abstracting, Bibliographies, Statistics*

ROBOMATIX ANNUAL INDEX. see *COMPUTERS — Abstracting, Bibliographies, Statistics*

ROBOMATIX REPORTER. see *COMPUTERS — Abstracting, Bibliographies, Statistics*

011 RM
ROMANIAN SCIENTIFIC ABSTRACTS. s-a. Academy of Social and Political Sciences of the S.R.R., Office of Information and Documentation in Social and Political Sciences, Bd. Republicii 17, sector 3, 70431 Bucharest, Rumania (Subscr. to: ILEXIM - P.O. Box 136-137, 13 Decembrie St., no.3, 11226 Bucharest, Rumania) Ed. Mircea Ioanid.

RUMANIAN SCIENTIFIC ABSTRACTS. see *SCIENCES: COMPREHENSIVE WORKS — Abstracting, Bibliographies, Statistics*

RURAL DEVELOPMENT ABSTRACTS. see *PUBLIC ADMINISTRATION — Abstracting, Bibliographies, Statistics*

RURAL EXTENSION, EDUCATION AND TRAINING ABSTRACTS. see *EDUCATION*

S A E TECHNICAL LITERATURE ABSTRACTS. (Society of Automotive Engineers) see *TRANSPORTATION — Abstracting, Bibliographies, Statistics*

S C I M P; European index of management periodicals. (Selective Cooperative Index of Management Periodicals) see *BUSINESS AND ECONOMICS — Abstracting, Bibliographies, Statistics*

S.D.C. BULLETIN. (Scientific Documentation Centre Ltd.) see *PHYSICS — Abstracting, Bibliographies, Statistics*

S E C I N ABSTRACTS. JOURNAL. (Socio-Economic Information Network) see *SOCIOLOGY — Abstracting, Bibliographies, Statistics*

614.8 016 US ISSN 0160-1342
SAFETY SCIENCE ABSTRACTS JOURNAL. 1973. 4/yr. $365. Cambridge Scientific Abstracts, 5161 River Rd., Bethesda, MD 20816. TEL 301-951-1400. bk. rev. film rev. abstr. bibl. pat. stat. tr.lit. index. cum.index. circ. 472. (also avail. in microfilm) Indexed: Oncol.Abstr.
●Also available online. Vendors: DIALOG, Pergamon Infoline.
Formerly: Safety Science Abstracts (ISSN 0092-542X)

SAGE FAMILY STUDIES ABSTRACTS. see *SOCIOLOGY — Abstracting, Bibliographies, Statistics*

SAGE PUBLIC ADMINISTRATION ABSTRACTS. see *PUBLIC ADMINISTRATION — Abstracting, Bibliographies, Statistics*

SAGE RACE RELATIONS ABSTRACTS. see *POLITICAL SCIENCE — Abstracting, Bibliographies, Statistics*

SAGE URBAN STUDIES ABSTRACTS. see *HOUSING AND URBAN PLANNING — Abstracting, Bibliographies, Statistics*

SCANP. (Scandinavian Periodicals Index in Economics and Business) see *BUSINESS AND ECONOMICS — Abstracting, Bibliographies, Statistics*

SCHOOL ORGANISATION & MANAGEMENT ABSTRACTS. see *EDUCATION — Abstracting, Bibliographies, Statistics*

SCIENCE CITATION INDEX. see *SCIENCES: COMPREHENSIVE WORKS — Abstracting, Bibliographies, Statistics*

SCOTTISH ABSTRACT OF STATISTICS. see *STATISTICS*

SEED ABSTRACTS. see *AGRICULTURE — Abstracting, Bibliographies, Statistics*

SELECTED JOURNALS ON WATER. see *WATER RESOURCES — Abstracting, Bibliographies, Statistics*

SELECTED RAND ABSTRACTS; a quarterly guide to publications of the Rand Corporation. see *SCIENCES: COMPREHENSIVE WORKS — Abstracting, Bibliographies, Statistics*

SELECTED WATER RESOURCES ABSTRACTS. see *WATER RESOURCES — Abstracting, Bibliographies, Statistics*

SERIAL SOURCES FOR THE BIOSIS DATA BASE. see *BIOLOGY — Abstracting, Bibliographies, Statistics*

SEXUALLY TRANSMITTED DISEASES. ABSTRACTS & BIBLIOGRAPHY. see *MEDICAL SCIENCES — Abstracting, Bibliographies, Statistics*

SHIP ABSTRACTS; information service on ship technology, ship operation and ocean engineering. see *TRANSPORTATION — Abstracting, Bibliographies, Statistics*

SHORT STORY INDEX; an index to stories in collections and periodicals. see *LITERATURE — Abstracting, Bibliographies, Statistics*

011 SI ISSN 0377-7928
SINGAPORE PERIODICALS INDEX. (Text in Malay, Chinese and English) 1969/70. a. price varies. National Library, Stamford Rd, Singapore 0617, Singapore. Ed. R. Chandran. circ. 400.

SMALL ANIMAL ABSTRACTS. see *AGRICULTURE — Abstracting, Bibliographies, Statistics*

SOCIAL SCIENCES CITATION INDEX. see *SOCIAL SCIENCES: COMPREHENSIVE WORKS — Abstracting, Bibliographies, Statistics*

SOCIAL SCIENCES INDEX; an author and subject index to periodicals in the fields of anthropology, area studies, economics, environmental science, geography, law and criminology, medical sciences, political science, psychology, public administration, sociology and related subjects. see *SOCIAL SCIENCES: COMPREHENSIVE WORKS — Abstracting, Bibliographies, Statistics*

SOCIAL WORK RESEARCH AND ABSTRACTS. see *SOCIAL SERVICES AND WELFARE — Abstracting, Bibliographies, Statistics*

SOCIOLOGICAL ABSTRACTS. see *SOCIOLOGY — Abstracting, Bibliographies, Statistics*

SOCIOLOGY OF EDUCATION ABSTRACTS. see *EDUCATION — Abstracting, Bibliographies, Statistics*

SOILS AND FERTILIZERS; abstracts of world literature. see *AGRICULTURE — Abstracting, Bibliographies, Statistics*

SOLID-LIQUID FLOW ABSTRACTS. see *ENGINEERING — Abstracting, Bibliographies, Statistics*

SOLID STATE ABSTRACTS JOURNAL; an abstract journal involving the physics, metallurgy, crystallography, chemistry and device technology of solids. see *PHYSICS — Abstracting, Bibliographies, Statistics*

SORGHUM AND MILLETS ABSTRACTS. see *AGRICULTURE — Abstracting, Bibliographies, Statistics*

SOUTH AFRICA. GOVERNMENT GAZETTE INDEX. see *PUBLIC ADMINISTRATION — Abstracting, Bibliographies, Statistics*

SOUTHEAST/EAST ASIAN ENGLISH PUBLICATIONS IN PRINT. see *BUSINESS AND ECONOMICS — Trade And Industrial Directories*

SOYABEAN ABSTRACTS. see *AGRICULTURE — Abstracting, Bibliographies, Statistics*

SPAIN. INSTITUTO GEOLOGICO Y MINERO. CATALOGO DE EDICIONES. see *EARTH SCIENCES — Abstracting, Bibliographies, Statistics*

SPEECH INDEX; an index to 259 collections of orations and speeches for various occasions. see *LINGUISTICS — Abstracting, Bibliographies, Statistics*

SPELEOLOGICAL ABSTRACTS/BULLETIN BIBLIOGRAPHIQUE SPELEOLOGIQUE. see *EARTH SCIENCES — Abstracting, Bibliographies, Statistics*

SPORT FISHERY ABSTRACTS; an abstracting service for fishery research and management. see *FISH AND FISHERIES — Abstracting, Bibliographies, Statistics*

SPORTS DOCUMENTATION CENTRE. SERIAL. see *EDUCATION — Abstracting, Bibliographies, Statistics*

SPORTS PERIODICALS INDEX. see *SPORTS AND GAMES — Abstracting, Bibliographies, Statistics*

015 CE
SRI LANKA PERIODICALS INDEX. (Text in English and Sinhala) 1969. s-a. free on exchange to libraries and research institutes. ‡ Department of National Museums, National Museum Library, Box 854, Sir Marcus Fernando Mawatha, Colombo 7, Sri Lanka. bibl. index.
Formerly (through vol.5): Ceylon Periodical Index.

SRI LANKA SCIENCE INDEX. see *SCIENCES: COMPREHENSIVE WORKS — Abstracting, Bibliographies, Statistics*

STATE EDUCATION JOURNAL INDEX; an annotated index to materials in the field of education. see *EDUCATION — Abstracting, Bibliographies, Statistics*

310 016 NE ISSN 0039-0518
STATISTICAL THEORY AND METHOD ABSTRACTS. 1959. q. $85. International Statistical Institute, 428 Prinses Beatrixlaan, Postbus 950, NL-2270 AZ Voorburg, Netherlands. Ed. J.W.E. Vos. adv. abstr. index. circ. 1,400. Indexed: Math.R. Hort.Abstr.
Formerly: International Journal of Abstracts.

STUDIES ON WOMEN ABSTRACTS. see *WOMEN'S INTERESTS — Abstracting, Bibliographies, Statistics*

011 MF
SUBJECT INDEX TO ARTICLES IN NEWSPAPERS IN MAURITIUS. Cover title: Newspapers Index: Mauritius. (Text in English) publication began and suspended 1978; resumed 1983. s-a. City Library, City Hall, Port Louis, Mauritius.

016 310 UK
SUBJECT INDEX TO SOURCES OF COMPARATIVE INTERNATIONAL STATISTICS. 1978. irreg. £60($170) C.B.D. Research Ltd., 15 Wickham Rd., Beckenham, Kent BR3 2JS, England.

948 011 FI ISSN 0355-4074
SUOMEN SANOMALEHTIEN MIKROFILMIT/ MICROFILMED NEWSPAPERS OF FINLAND. (Text in Finnish, Swedish, and English) 1971. quintennial. free. Helsinki University Library, Box 312, 00171 Helsinki, Finland. circ. 300.

SURFACE TREATMENT TECHNOLOGY ABSTRACTS. see *METALLURGY — Abstracting, Bibliographies, Statistics*

SURFACE WAVE ABSTRACTS. see *PHYSICS — Abstracting, Bibliographies, Statistics*

TATE AND LYLE'S SUGAR INDUSTRY ABSTRACTS. see *FOOD AND FOOD INDUSTRIES — Abstracting, Bibliographies, Statistics*

TECHNICAL BOOK REVIEW INDEX. see *SCIENCES: COMPREHENSIVE WORKS — Abstracting, Bibliographies, Statistics*

TECHNICAL EDUCATION ABSTRACTS. see
EDUCATION — *Abstracting, Bibliographies,
Statistics*

TELECOMMUNICATIONS ALERT; a unique
monthly reporting and highlighting service covering
all current developments in telecommunications. see
COMMUNICATIONS — *Abstracting,
Bibliographies, Statistics*

TEXTILE DIGEST. see *TEXTILE INDUSTRIES
AND FABRICS* — *Abstracting, Bibliographies,
Statistics*

TEXTILE TECHNOLOGY DIGEST. see *TEXTILE
INDUSTRIES AND FABRICS* — *Abstracting,
Bibliographies, Statistics*

THANATOLOGY ABSTRACTS. see
PSYCHOLOGY — *Abstracting, Bibliographies,
Statistics*

THEATRE/DRAMA ABSTRACTS. see
THEATER — *Abstracting, Bibliographies, Statistics*

THEOLOGICAL AND RELIGIOUS
BIBLIOGRAPHIES. see *RELIGIONS AND
THEOLOGY* — *Abstracting, Bibliographies,
Statistics*

THEORETICAL CHEMICAL ENGINEERING
ABSTRACTS. see *ENGINEERING* —
Abstracting, Bibliographies, Statistics

THESIS ABSTRACTS. see *AGRICULTURE* —
Abstracting, Bibliographies, Statistics

TOBACCO ABSTRACTS; world literature on
Nicotiana. see *TOBACCO* — *Abstracting,
Bibliographies, Statistics*

TOP MANAGEMENT ABSTRACTS. see *BUSINESS
AND ECONOMICS* — *Abstracting, Bibliographies,
Statistics*

TOXICOLOGY ABSTRACTS. see *PHARMACY
AND PHARMACOLOGY* — *Abstracting,
Bibliographies, Statistics*

TRADESCOPE. see *BUSINESS AND
ECONOMICS* — *Trade And Industrial Directories*

TRANSKEI GOVERNMENT GAZETTE INDEX.
see *PUBLIC ADMINISTRATION* — *Abstracting,
Bibliographies, Statistics*

TRIBOS - TRIBOLOGY ABSTRACTS. see
ENGINEERING — *Abstracting, Bibliographies,
Statistics*

TURKISH DISSERTATION INDEX. see
SCIENCES: COMPREHENSIVE WORKS —
Abstracting, Bibliographies, Statistics

U S S R REPORT: CHEMISTRY. see
CHEMISTRY — *Abstracting, Bibliographies,
Statistics*

U S S R REPORT: CYBERNETICS, COMPUTERS,
AND AUTOMATION TECHNOLOGY. see
COMPUTERS — *Abstracting, Bibliographies,
Statistics*

U S S R REPORT: ELECTRONICS AND
ELECTRICAL ENGINEERING. see
*ELECTRICITY AND ELECTRICAL
ENGINEERING* — *Abstracting, Bibliographies,
Statistics*

U S S R REPORT: ENGINEERING AND
EQUIPMENT. see *ENGINEERING* —
Abstracting, Bibliographies, Statistics

U S S R REPORT: MATERIALS SCIENCE AND
METALLURGY. see *ENGINEERING* —
Abstracting, Bibliographies, Statistics

U S S R REPORT: PHYSICS AND
MATHEMATICS. see *MATHEMATICS* —
Abstracting, Bibliographies, Statistics

U S S R REPORT: SPACE. see *EARTH
SCIENCES* — *Abstracting, Bibliographies,
Statistics*

U.S. NATIONAL CENTER FOR HEALTH
STATISTICS. CATALOG OF PUBLICATIONS.
see *PUBLIC HEALTH AND SAFETY* —
Abstracting, Bibliographies, Statistics

UNIVERSIDAD DE BUENOS AIRES. INSTITUTO
DE ECONOMIA. BIBLIOGRAFIA SOBRE
ECONOMIA NACIONAL. see *BUSINESS AND
ECONOMICS* — *Abstracting, Bibliographies,
Statistics*

URBAN ABSTRACTS. see *PUBLIC
ADMINISTRATION* — *Abstracting,
Bibliographies, Statistics*

URBAN AFFAIRS ABSTRACTS. see *PUBLIC
ADMINISTRATION* — *Abstracting,
Bibliographies, Statistics*

VACUUM; the international journal and abstracting
service for vacuum science and technology. see
PHYSICS — *Abstracting, Bibliographies, Statistics*

VANDERBILT UNIVERSITY. ABSTRACTS OF
THESES. see *EDUCATION* — *Abstracting,
Bibliographies, Statistics*

VEGYIPARI SZAKIRODALMI TAJEKOZTATO/
CHEMICAL ENGINEERING ABSTRACTS. see
CHEMISTRY — *Abstracting, Bibliographies,
Statistics*

VEREIN DEUTSCHER INGENIEURE.
INFORMATIONSDIENST.
INSTANDHALTUNG. see *ENGINEERING* —
Abstracting, Bibliographies, Statistics

020 011   US   ISSN 0042-4439
VERTICAL FILE INDEX; a subject and title index to
selected pamphlet material. 1932. m.(Sep.-July) $30.
‡ H. W. Wilson Co., 950 University Ave., Bronx,
NY 10452. TEL 212-588-8400. Ed. Trina King.
●Also available online. Vendors: Wilsonline.

VETERINARY BULLETIN; a monthly abstract
journal on veterinary science. see *VETERINARY
SCIENCE* — *Abstracting, Bibliographies, Statistics*

VIROLOGY ABSTRACTS. see *MEDICAL
SCIENCES* — *Abstracting, Bibliographies,
Statistics*

VITIS; Berichte ueber Rebenforschung mit
Dokumentation der Weinbauforschung. see
BEVERAGES — *Abstracting, Bibliographies,
Statistics*

VITIS - VITICULTURE AND ENOLOGY
ABSTRACTS. see *AGRICULTURE* —
Abstracting, Bibliographies, Statistics

WATER POLLUTION CONTROL FEDERATION
CONFERENCE. ABSTRACTS OF TECHNICAL
PAPERS. see *ENVIRONMENTAL STUDIES* —
Abstracting, Bibliographies, Statistics

WEED ABSTRACTS; compiled from world literature.
see *AGRICULTURE* — *Abstracting,
Bibliographies, Statistics*

WEED SCIENCE SOCIETY OF AMERICA.
ABSTRACTS. see *AGRICULTURE* —
Abstracting, Bibliographies, Statistics

WELLNESS MEDIA: AN AUDIOVISUAL
SOURCEBOOK. (National Information Center for
Educational Media) see *PHYSICAL FITNESS
AND HYGIENE* — *Abstracting, Bibliographies,
Statistics*

011 051   US   ISSN 0884-3279
WESTERN NEW YORK INDEX. 1983. m. $150.
Buffalo & Erie County Public Library, Lafayette Sq.,
Buffalo, NY 14203. TEL 716-846-7181. index.
(back issues avail.)

WILDLIFE REVIEW (FORT COLLINS); an
abstracting service for wildlife management. see
CONSERVATION — *Abstracting, Bibliographies,
Statistics*

WIND ENGINEERING ABSTRACTS. see
ENERGY — *Abstracting, Bibliographies, Statistics*

WOMEN STUDIES ABSTRACTS. see *WOMEN'S
INTERESTS* — *Abstracting, Bibliographies,
Statistics*

WORK RELATED ABSTRACTS. see *BUSINESS
AND ECONOMICS* — *Abstracting, Bibliographies,
Statistics*

WORK STUDY & O AND M ABSTRACTS. see
BUSINESS AND ECONOMICS — *Abstracting,
Bibliographies, Statistics*

WORLD AGRICULTURAL ECONOMICS AND
RURAL SOCIOLOGY ABSTRACTS; abstracts of
world literature. see *AGRICULTURE* —
Abstracting, Bibliographies, Statistics

WORLD ALUMINUM ABSTRACTS; a monthly
review of the world's technical literature on
aluminum. see *METALLURGY* — *Abstracting,
Bibliographies, Statistics*

WORLD DIRECTORY OF SOCIAL SCIENCE
INSTITUTIONS. see *SOCIAL SCIENCES:
COMPREHENSIVE WORKS* — *Abstracting,
Bibliographies, Statistics*

WORLD PORTS AND HARBOURS ABSTRACTS.
see *TRANSPORTATION* — *Abstracting,
Bibliographies, Statistics*

WORLD SURFACE COATING ABSTRACTS. see
PAINTS AND PROTECTIVE COATINGS —
Abstracting, Bibliographies, Statistics

WORLD TEXTILE ABSTRACTS. see *TEXTILE
INDUSTRIES AND FABRICS* — *Abstracting,
Bibliographies, Statistics*

YONSEI UNIVERSITY. GRADUATE SCHOOL.
ABSTRACTS OF FACULTY RESEARCH
REPORTS. see *EDUCATION* — *Abstracting,
Bibliographies, Statistics*

YUKON BIBLIOGRAPHY UPDATE. see
BIBLIOGRAPHIES

ZAMBIA SCIENCE ABSTRACTS. see *SCIENCES:
COMPREHENSIVE WORKS* — *Abstracting,
Bibliographies, Statistics*

ZENTRALBLATT FUER MATHEMATIK UND
IHRE GRENZGEBIETE/MATHEMATICS
ABSTRACTS. see *MATHEMATICS* —
Abstracting, Bibliographies, Statistics

ZIMBABWE RESEARCH INDEX; register of current
research in Zimbabwe. see *SCIENCES:
COMPREHENSIVE WORKS* — *Abstracting,
Bibliographies, Statistics*

ZINCSCAN; a review of recent technical literature on
the uses of zinc and its products. see
METALLURGY — *Abstracting, Bibliographies,
Statistics*

ACCOUNTING

see Business and Economics—Accounting

ADULT EDUCATION

see Education—Adult Education

ADVENTURE AND ROMANCE

813   US
ANNUAL WORLD'S BEST S F. 1965. a. $2.95. D A
W Books, Inc., 1633 Broadway, New York, NY
10019. TEL 212-397-8017. Ed. Donald A.
Wollheim. circ. 100,000. (back issues avail.)
Science fiction

808.838　　　　　　US　　ISSN 0275-3715
AURORA (MADISON); S F science fiction/
speculative feminism. Variant title: Aurora S F.
1975. irreg. (approx. 2/yr.) $10 for 3 nos. Society
for the Furtherance and Study of Fantasy and
Science Fiction, Inc. (SF3), Box 1624, Madison, WI
53701-1624. Ed. Diane Martin. adv. bk. rev. film
rev. circ. 500. (back issues avail.)
　　Formerly: Janus.

813　　　　　　US　　ISSN 0095-7119
BEST SCIENCE FICTION OF THE YEAR. 1972. a.
$2.50. Ballantine Books., 201 East 50th St., New
York, NY 10022. TEL 212-751-2600.

808.838　　　　　　GW
BEYOND S F ANTHOLOGY. 1983. irreg. $2.50.
Fabula Press Agency, Bezgenrieter Str. 85, 7326
Heiningen, W. Germany (B.R.D.) illus. circ. 500.
(back issues avail.)

800　　　　　　US　　ISSN 0193-6875
CONTRIBUTIONS TO THE STUDY OF SCIENCE
FICTION AND FANTASY. 1982. irreg. price
varies. Greenwood Press, 88 Post Rd. W., Box
5077, Westport, CT 06881. TEL 203-226-3571. Ed.
Marshall Tymn.

808.838　　　　　　UK
CYPHER. irreg., (approx. s-a) £1.50 for 5 issues; in
U.S. $3 for 4. Plovers Barrow, School Road
Nomansland, Salisbury, Wilts, England (Avail. in
U.S. from Cy Giauvin, 17829 Peters, Roseville, MI
48066) Ed. James Goddard. adv. bk. rev. film rev.
illus. circ. 500.
　　Science fiction reviews

808.838　　　　　　UK
FANTASY TALES; a magazine of the weird and
unusual. 1977. irreg., no.14, 1985. £3($11) for 3
nos. 194 Station Rd., Kings Heath, Birmingham B14
7TE, England. Eds. Stephen Jones, David Sutton.
adv. illus. circ. 1,500.

GOTHIC. see LITERATURE

808　　　　　　US　　ISSN 0190-3314
GREEN FEATHER. 1979. a. $5. Green Feather
Magazine, Box 2633, Lakewood, OH 44107. Ed.
Gary S. Skeens. adv. bk. rev. illus. tr.lit. circ. 175.
(back issues avail.)

830　　　　　　DK　　ISSN 0108-0830
H S G'S AARBOG. Variant titles: Hvad Skovsoeen
Gemte's Science Fiction-Aarbog. H S G's Science
Fiction & Fantasy Aarbog. 1982. a. Kr.15. Hvad
Skovsoeen Gemte, Hjallesevej 20, 5000 Odense,
Denmark. illus.

808.838　　　　　　US
IT GOES ON THE SHELF. 1980. irreg. free. Purple
Mouth Press, 713 Paul St., Newport News, VA
23605. TEL 804-380-6595. Ed. Ned Brooks. adv.
bk. rev. circ. 350.
　　Former titles: Skiffy Thyme & Skiffy Bag.

800　　　　　　UK
JULES VERNE VOYAGES. 1978. a. £5($15) (Jules
Verne Circle) High Orchard Press, High Orchard,
125 Markyate Rd., Dagenham, Essex RM8 2LB,
England. Ed. F. James. circ. 100.
　　Works of Jules Verne

MASIFORM D. see LITERATURE

813　　　　　　US　　ISSN 0000-0302
MYSTERY & DETECTION ANNUAL.* 1972. a. 152
S. Clark Dr., Beverly Hills, CA 90211. bk. rev. circ.
1,200. Indexed: M.L.A.

808.838　　　　　　US
MYSTERY TIME. 1983. a. $5. Hutton Publieations,
Box 2377, Coeur d'Alene, ID 83814. TEL 208-667-
7511. Ed. Linda Hutton. circ. 50.

808.838　　　　　　US
NEBULOUSFAN. 1977. irreg., no.9, 1979. (Wing
Nuts Wing Club) David Thayer, Ed. & Pub., 7209
DeVille Dr., Ft. Worth, TX 76118. TEL 817-498-
4003. bk. rev. illus. circ. 500.

808.838　　　　　　CN　　ISSN 0229-1932
NEW CANADIAN FANDOM. (Text in English and
French) 1981. irreg. (approx. 2/yr) Can.$2 per no.
Negative Entropy Press, Box 4655, P.S.S.E.,
Edmonton, Alta T6E 5G5, Canada. Ed. Robert
Runte. adv. bk. rev. film rev. circ. 500.
　　Science fiction

810　　　　　　US　　ISSN 0474-3326
ORBIT (NEW YORK); a science fiction anthology.
1966. irreg., no.18, 1976. Harper and Row
Publishers, Inc., 10 E. 53rd St., New York, NY
10022. TEL 212-593-7000. Ed. Damon Knight.

808.838　　　　　　US
OWLFLIGHT; alternative science fiction and fantasy.
1981. irreg. $10 for 3. Unique Graphics, 1025 55th
St., Oakland, CA 94608. TEL 415-655-3024. Ed.
Millea Kenin. adv. bk. rev. circ. 1,000. (back issues
avail.)

808　　　　　　UK
PHOTO LOVE ANNUAL. a. Fleetway Annuals,
Kings Reach Tower, Stamford St., London SE1 9LS,
England. Ed. F. Lister.

808.838　　　　　　US
PONTINE DOSSIER. 1946. a. $50. Box 261, Culver
City, CA 90230. Ed. C.J. Gustafson. bk. rev. circ. 5,
100.
　　Sherlockiana

052　　　　　　UK
SHERLOCK HOLMES MYSTERY BOOK. 1981.
irreg. World Distributors (Manchester) Ltd., P.O.
Box 111, 12 Lever St., Manchester M60 1TS,
England.

810　　　　　　US
TRUMPET. 1965. irreg., nos.12/14, latest. $3 per no.
Trumpet Publications, 1131 White, Kansas City,
MO 64126. TEL 816-483-5610. Ed. Ken Keller.
adv. circ. 3,000.
　　Former titles: Nickelodeon; Trumpet.
　　Science fiction

800　　　　　　UK
WELLSIANA; world of H. G. Wells. 1908. a. £5($15)
High Orchard Press, High Orchard, 125 Markyate
Rd., Dagenham, Essex RM8 2LB, England. Eds.
Royston King, E. Ford. adv. bk. rev. circ. 100.
(looseleaf format)

810　　　　　　US
WHISPERS. 1973. irreg. $12.95. Whispers Press, 70
Highland Ave., Binghamton, NY 13905. Ed. Stuart
David Schiff. adv. bk. rev. illus. circ. 3,000.

808.838　　　　　　US
YEAR'S BEST FANTASY STORIES. 1975. a. D A
W Books, Inc., 1633 Broadway, New York, NY
10019. TEL 212-397-8017. Ed. Arthur W. Saha.

808.838　　　　　　US
YEAR'S BEST HORROR STORIES. 1972. a. D A W
Books, Inc., 1633 Broadway, New York, NY 10019.
TEL 212-397-8017. Ed. Karl Edward Wagner.

808.838　　　　　　US
YEAR'S BEST SCIENCE FICTION;* annual
collection. 1984. a. $10.95 paperback; hardcover
$19.95. Bluejay Books Inc., 26 Douglas Rd.,
Chappaqua, NY 10514-3105. Ed. Gardner Dozois.
bibl. circ. 10,000. (back issues avail.)

ADVENTURE AND ROMANCE —
Abstracting, Bibliographies, Statistics

808.838　　　　　　US　　ISSN 0361-3038
N.E.S.F.A. INDEX: SCIENCE FICTION
MAGAZINES AND ANTHOLOGIES. 1966. a.
price varies. New England Science Fiction
Association Inc., Box G., MIT Branch P.O.,
Cambridge, MA 02139. Ed. Ann A. Broomhead.
circ. 1,000.
　　Formerly (1966-1970): Index to the Science
Fiction Magazines (ISSN 0579-6059)

808.838　　　　　　US
SCIENCE FICTION AND FANTASY RESEARCH
INDEX. 1981. a. price varies. S F B R I, 3608
Meadow Oaks Lane, Bryan, TX 77802. Ed. H.W.
Hall. circ. 500.
　　Formerly: Science Fiction Research Index.

ADVERTISING AND PUBLIC
RELATIONS

see also Business and
Economics—Marketing and Purchasing

659.1　　　　　　US　　ISSN 0065-3586
AD GUIDE: AN ADVERTISER'S GUIDE TO
SCHOLARLY PERIODICALS. 1958-1979/80;
resumed 1986. biennial. $150. American University
Press Services, Inc., 1 Park Ave., Ste. 1102, New
York, NY 10016 TEL 212-889-3510. Ed. Constance
B. Levinson. adv. bk. rev. index. circ. (controlled)

659.1　　　　　　UK　　ISSN 0065-3578
ADVERTISER'S ANNUAL. 1925. a. £38. Thomas
Skinner Directories, Windsor Court, East Grinstead
House, East Grinstead, West Sussex RH19 1XB,
England. adv. circ. 4,000.

659.1　　　　　　US　　ISSN 0276-9751
ADVERTISING AGE YEARBOOK. 1981. a. price
varies. Crain Books (Subsidiary of: Crain
Communications, Inc.) 740 Rush St., Chicago, IL
60611. TEL 312-649-5250. Eds. K. Sederberg, D.
Morris. index.

ADVERTISING LAW ANTHOLOGY. see LAW

659.13　　　　　　US
ADVERTISING SPECIALTY REGISTER:
PRODUCT RESEARCH AND SOURCE DATA.
a. membership. Advertising Specialty Institute, 1120
Wheeler Way, Langhorne, PA 19047. circ. 5,900.

659.1　　　　　　UK　　ISSN 0065-3659
ADVERTISING STANDARDS AUTHORITY,
LONDON. ANNUAL REPORT. 1962/63. a.
£1.75. Advertising Standards Authority Ltd., Brook
House, 2-16 Torrington Place, London WC1E 7HN,
England. Ed. D.B. Williamson. circ. 4,000.

909　　　　　　US　　ISSN 0740-5111
AMERICAN UNIVERSITY STUDIES. SERIES 15.
COMMUNICATIONS. 1984. irreg. Peter Lang
Publishing, Inc., 62 W. 45th St., New York, NY
10036. TEL 212-302-6740. Ed. Jay Wilson.

741.67　　　　　　US　　ISSN 0270-2525
ANDY AWARDS.* a. price varies. Advertising Club
of New York, 45 E. 45th St., New York, NY
10017. TEL 202-697-0877. circ. 2,000.

659.1　　　　　　FR
ANNUAIRE GENERAL DE LA PUBLICITE. 1938.
a. 500 F. Nouvelles Editions de la Publicite, 9 rue
Leo-Delibes, 75116 Paris, France. Ed. Marco Eilfa.
adv. circ. 2,500.
　　Former titles: Annuaire General des Publicitaires
de France; Groupement des Directeurs Publicitaires
de France. Annuaire (ISSN 0072-7792)

741.67 659　　　　　　JA　　ISSN 0548-1643
ANNUAL OF ADVERTISING ART IN JAPAN/
NENKAN KOKOKU BIJUTSU. (Text in English
and Japanese) 1957. a. $120. (Art Directors Club of
Tokyo - Tokyo Ato Direkutazu Kurabu) Bijutsu
Shuppan-sha, Inaoka Bld., 2-36, Kanda Jinbo-cho,
Chiyoda-ku, Tokyo 101, Japan. adv. circ. 4,000.
(back issues avail.)
　　Advertising art

659.1　　　　　　IT
ANNUARIO ITALIANO PUBBLICITA
MARKETING RELAZIONI PUBBLICHE. 1982.
a. L.60000. Ediemme srl, Via della Scrofa, 14, I-
00186 Rome, Italy. Ed. Francesco Marraro. adv.
circ. 2,000.

659.1　　　　　　BL　　ISSN 0570-3956
ANUARIO BRASILEIRO DE PROPAGANDA.
1968. a. Editora Meio e Mensagem Ltda, Rua
Caetes 139, 05016 Sao Paulo, Brazil. Ed. J.C. Salles
Neto. adv. circ. 10,000.

070　　　　　　HK
ASIAN PRESS AND MEDIA DIRECTORY. (Text
in English) 1974. a. Syme Media Enterprises Ltd.,
16/F, Shing Lee Comm'l Bldg., 6-12 Wing Kut St.,
Central, Hong Kong. adv.

659.1　　　　　　US　　ISSN 0067-0537
AUDARENA STADIUM GUIDE AND
INTERNATIONAL DIRECTORY. Variant title:
Amusement Business's AudArena Stadium Guide.
1959. a. $40. Billboard Publications Inc.,
Amusement Business Division, Box 24970,
Nashville, TN 37202. TEL 615-748-8100. Ed. Steve
Rogers. adv. circ. 10,000.
　　Formerly: Arena, Auditorium, Stadium Guide
(ISSN 0518-3979)

ADVERTISING AND PUBLIC RELATIONS

659.1 301.16 US
B/P A A MEMBERSHIP DIRECTORY AND YELLOW PAGES. 1986. biennial. $25 to non-members. Business Professional Advertising Association, 205 E. 42nd St., New York, NY 10017. TEL 212-661-0222. Ed. Lee Rosen. circ. 5,000.

659.2 UK
B T A STUDYCARDS. (British Trade Alphabet); publication of educational projects. 1953. a. free; avail. only in U.K. Shaw's Price Guides Ltd., Station Rd., Abingdon, Oxon OX14 3LE, England. Ed. A. Rothery. adv. circ. 30,000. (cards)
Formerly: British Trades Alphabet (ISSN 0068-2632)

659.2 US ISSN 0161-4363
BACON'S INTERNATIONAL PUBLICITY CHECKER. 1974. a. $155. Bacon's Information International Ltd., 332 S. Michigan Ave., Chicago, IL 60604. TEL 312-922-2400. circ. 500.

659.1 US
BEST IN ADVERTISING. (Subseries of: Print Casebooks) 1975. a. $19.50. R C Publications, Inc., 104 Fifth Ave., 9th Fl., New York, NY 10011 TEL 301-229-9040. (Subscr. to: 6400 Goldsboro Rd., Bethesda, MD 20817) illus.
Formerly: Best in Advertising Campaigns (ISSN 0360-8263)
Advertising art

741.67 UK
BRITISH DESIGN & ART DIRECTION ANNUAL. 1962. a. £45. (Designers & Art Directors Association) Polygon Editions S.A.R.L., 12 Carlton House Terrace, London SW1Y 5AH, England. Ed. Edward Booth-Clibborn. Indexed: Mgmt.& Market.Abstr.
Formerly: Design and Art Direction Annual.

659.1 US ISSN 0883-9999
BURRELLE'S NEW ENGLAND MEDIA DIRECTORY. 1975. biennial. $95. Burrelle's Media Directories, Information Services, 75 E. Northfield Rd., Livingston, NJ 07039. TEL 201-992-6600. Ed. Donna Horvath. adv. circ. 3,000.
Incorporating (1979-1986): Maine Media Directory; Former titles: New England Media Directory; Directory of New England Newspapers, College Publications, Periodicals, and Radio and Television Stations (ISSN 0195-7619)

659.1 US ISSN 0883-9778
BURRELLE'S NEW JERSEY MEDIA DIRECTORY. biennial. $70. Burrelle's Media Directories, 75 E. Northfield Ave., Livingston, NJ 07039. TEL 201-992-7070. (Affiliate: New England Newsclip Agency, Inc.) Ed. Donna Horvath. adv.
Formerly: New Jersey Media Directory (ISSN 0195-6817)

659.1 US
BURRELLE'S NEW YORK STATE MEDIA DIRECTORY. a. $85. Burrelle's Media Directories, 75 E. Northfield Ave., Livingston, NJ 07039. TEL 201-992-7070. (Affiliate: New England Newsclip Agency, Inc)
Formerly: New York State Media Directory.

659.1 US ISSN 0276-7872
BURRELLE'S PENNSYLVANIA MEDIA DIRECTORY. 1981. a. $38. Burrelle's Media Directories, 75 E. Northfield Ave., Livingston, NJ 07039. TEL 201-992-7070.

658.5 659 FR
CADEAU ET L'ENTREPRISE; les techniques de stimulation des ventes. a. 420 F. Agence de Diffusion et de Publicite, 24 Place du General Catroux, 75017-Paris, France.

659.1 200 US
CHRISTIAN CHAMBER OF COMMERCE. CLASSIFIED MEMBERSHIP DIRECTORY. Short title: C C C Yellow Pages. (Each directory is published annually for a city) free. Christian Chamber of Commerce, Box 430, Hockley, TX 77447. Ed. John P. Hansen. circ. 5,000. (back issues avail.)
Formerly: Christian Chamber of Commerce. Membership Directory and Buyers Guide.

659 US ISSN 0738-9000
CREATIVE BLACK BOOK. 1970. a. $100. Creative Black Book, 401 Park Ave. S., New York, NY 10016. TEL 212-684-4255. Ed. S. Waldman. adv. circ. 35,000.

659.1 776 US ISSN 0740-283X
CREATIVE BLACK BOOK. PORTFOLIO EDITION. 1984. a. $65. Creative Black Book, 401 Park Ave. So., New York, NY 10016. TEL 212-684-4255. (back issues avail.)

740 US ISSN 0097-6075
CREATIVITY. 1971. a. $34.50. (Art Direction Magazine) Advertising Trade Publications, Inc., 10 E. 39th St., New York, NY 10016. Ed. Don Barron. circ. 6,500.
Supersedes (1960-1965): Advertising Directions.
Advertising art

659.1 658 JA ISSN 0911-5625
CROSS AND TALK; for communications between you and the world. (Text in Japanese) a. A L C Press Inc., Eifuku 2-Chome, Suginami-Ku, Tokyo 168, Japan. Ed.Bd.

659.1 US ISSN 0163-3392
CURRENT ISSUES AND RESEARCH IN ADVERTISING. 1978. a. price varies. University of Michigan, Graduate School of Business Administration, Division of Research, Monroe and Tappan St., Ann Arbor, MI 48109. TEL 313-764-1316. Eds. James H. Leigh, Claude R. Martin, Jr. circ. 850. (back issues avail.)

659.1 770 DK ISSN 0108-0814
DANSKE REKLAMEFOTOGRAFER. 1982. a. Kr.135. Dansk Cerebration-International Marketing Management A-S, Oerbaekvej 739, 5220 Odense SOE, Denmark. Ed. Helen Ramsdahl. adv. illus.

659.1 GW
DEUTSCHER WERBEKALENDER; Taschenbuch fuer Marketing und Werbung. 1964. a. DM.48. Info-Verlag H. G. Thal, Norfer Weg 78, 4040 Neuss, W. Germany (B.R.D.) Ed. H.G. Thal. adv. circ. 6,000.
Formerly: Taschenbuch der Werbung (ISSN 0082-1802)

659 GW ISSN 0419-0637
DIALOG DER GESELLSCHAFT; Schriftenreihe fuer Publizistik und Kommunikationswissenschaft. 1966. irreg., vol. 10, 1979. price varies. Verlag Regensburg, Daimlerweg 58, Postfach 6748/6749, 4400 Muenster, W. Germany (B.R.D.) Ed. Henk Prakke.

DIRECT MAIL DATABOOK. see *BUSINESS AND ECONOMICS — Marketing And Purchasing*

DIRECT MARKETING MARKET PLACE; the directory of the direct marketing industry. see *BUSINESS AND ECONOMICS — Marketing And Purchasing*

659.1 US ISSN 0070-5365
DIRECTORY OF CORPORATE AFFILIATIONS; who owns whom. 1967. a. $349. National Register Publishing Co. (Subsidiary of: Standard Rate & Data Service) 3004 Glenview Rd., Wilmette, IL 60091. TEL 312-256-6067. Ed. Margaret Deuson. circ. 12,000.
●Also available online.

659.1 070 070.5 US
DIRECTORY OF FLORIDA WRITERS. 1982. a. $9.45. Cassell Communications Inc., 3600 N.W. 34th St., Box 9844, Ft. Lauderdale, FL 33310. TEL 305-485-0795. Ed. Dana K. Cassell. circ. 1,240.

DIRECTORY OF MAILING LIST HOUSES. see *BUSINESS AND ECONOMICS — Trade And Industrial Directories*

DIRECTORY OF MAILING LIST HOUSES (NEW YORK) see *BUSINESS AND ECONOMICS — Trade And Industrial Directories*

606 659.152 US ISSN 0361-4255
DIRECTORY OF NORTH AMERICAN FAIRS AND EXPOSITIONS. Variant title: Amusement Business's Directory North American Fairs. 1888. a. $29.95. Billboard Publications, Inc., Amusement Business Division, Box 24970, Nashville, TN 37202. TEL 615-748-8100. Ed. Tom Powell. circ. 2,200.
Formerly (until 1972): Cavalcade and Directory of Fairs (ISSN 0069-1291)

659.2 US ISSN 0163-6537
DIRECTORY OF PERSONAL IMAGE CONSULTANTS. 1978. biennial. $25. Image Industry Publications, 10 Bay St. Landing, No. 7K, Staten Island, NY 10301. TEL 718-273-3229. Ed. Jacqueline Thompson. adv. circ. 3,000.

659 GW ISSN 0085-0349
EUROPA HANDBUCH DER WERBEGESELLSCHAFTEN. 1962. a. DM.96. Team Verlag GmbH und Fachzeitschriften KG, Auwanne 19, 8757 Karlstein 1, W. Germany (B.R.D.) Ed. Horst P. Czerner. adv. circ. 2,500.

FREELANCERS OF NORTH AMERICA. see *PUBLISHING AND BOOK TRADE*

GRAPHIS ANNUAL; international annual of advertising and editorial graphics. see *ART*

659.1 VE
GUIA VENEZOLANA DE PUBLICIDAD Y MERCADEO. 1967. a. Bs.400($60) M.G. Ediciones Especializadas, Avenida Maturin, No. 15, Urb. Los Cedros, El Bosque, Caracas 1050, Venezuela. Ed. Montserrat Giol. adv. circ. 2,000.

659.1 UK
GUIDE TO PREMIUM USERS. 1965. a. £85. M.S. Surveys & Promotional Services Ltd., Hesketh House, Portman Sq., London W1H 0JH, England. Ed. Judith Watson.

GUIDE TO PUBLISHERS AND RELATED INDUSTRIES IN JAPAN. see *PUBLISHING AND BOOK TRADE*

659 US
HANDBOOK OF ADVERTISING AND MARKETING SERVICES. 1975. a. $50. Executive Communications, Inc., 919 Third Ave. 9th Fl., New York, NY 10022. TEL 212-421-3713. Ed. Sue Fulton. circ. 1,200.
Former titles: Directory of Advertising and Marketing Services; Handbook of Independent Advertising and Marketing Services.

HEALTHCARE MARKETING ABSTRACTS. see *HOSPITALS*

659.2 UK ISSN 0073-3059
HOLLIS PRESS AND PUBLIC RELATIONS ANNUAL; classified guide to press contacts, public relations departments, news and information sources, public relations consultancies UK and worldwide and services to communications and the media. 1967. a. (with quarterly supplements) £36.50. Hollis Directories Ltd., Contact House, Lower Hampton Rd., Sunbury-On-Thames, Middlesex TW16 5HG, England. Ed. Nesta Hollis. adv. bk. rev. bibl. index. circ. 5,500. (back issues avail.)
Incorporating: Contact. The UK News Contact Directory.

659.1 US
IDEASWORTH. 1965. a. free. ‡ Specialty Advertising Association International, 1404 Walnut Hill Ln., Irving, TX 75038. TEL 214-258-0404. Ed. Richard G. Ebel. illus. tr.lit. circ. 22,000.
Formerly: Specialty Advertising Report (ISSN 0038-6871)

ILLUSTRATED BUYERS GUIDE TO EXHIBITS; directory of portable and modular displays. see *BUSINESS AND ECONOMICS — Marketing And Purchasing*

659.1 UK ISSN 0538-4168
INTERNATIONAL ADVERTISING ASSOCIATION. UNITED KINGDOM CHAPTER. CONCISE GUIDE TO INTERNATIONAL MARKETS. (In 4 vols.) 1966. irreg. £15 per vol.; £50 for all 4 vols. ‡ Leslie Stinton & Partners, 39A London Rd., Kingston-Upon-Thames, Surrey KT2 6ND, England. Ed. Leslie Stinton. adv. circ. 1,000.

659.1 KE
KENYA MEDIA ADVERTISING REVIEW. 1973. a. EAs.1000($100) Corcoran & Tyrrell Ltd., Box 44365, Nairobi, Kenya. Ed. Tony Corcoran. stat. circ. 60.

659.1 KU
KUWAIT ADVERTSING AGE. a. (Concept Creative Consultants Ltd.) Kuwait Advertising Agency, P.O. Box 44247, Hawalli, Kuwait. adv.

ADVERTISING AND PUBLIC RELATIONS — ABSTRACTING, BIBLIOGRAPHIES, STATISTICS

659.1   GE
LEIPZIGER MESSEJOURNAL. (Text in English) a. Leipziger Messeamt, Markt 11/15, 701 Leipzig, E. Germany (D.D.R.) Ed. Ines Schymura. Indexed: Key to Econ.Sci.

659.1   US   ISSN 0076-2148
MADISON AVENUE HANDBOOK. 1958. a. $30. Peter Glenn Publications, Inc., 17 E. 48th St., New York, NY 10017. TEL 212-688-7940. Ed. Peter Glenn. adv. circ. 21,000.

MADRIKH PIRSUM. see *BUSINESS AND ECONOMICS — Trade And Industrial Directories*

659   GW   ISSN 0085-3119
MARKEN-HANDBUCH DER WERBUNG UND ETATBETREUUNG. 1960. a. DM.83. Team Verlag GmbH und Fachzeitschriften KG, Auwanne 19, 8757 Karlstein 1, W. Germany (B.R.D.) Ed. Horst P. Czerner. adv. circ. 2,500.

741.67   US
MARKET RESEARCH REPORT. 1982. irreg. $7.50 to non-members; members $3.75. Graphic Arts Technical Foundation, 4615 Forbes Ave., Pittsburgh, PA 15213. Ed. Michael G. Coulson.

659.2   CN   ISSN 0228-5215
MEDIA EDITORIAL PROFILE EDITION. 1981. a. Can.$28. Maclean-Hunter Ltd., Business Publication Division, 777 Bay St., Toronto, Ont. M5W 1A7, Canada. Ed. Irvine Brace. circ. 5,500.

659.1   DK   ISSN 0076-5821
MEDIA SCANDINAVIA; a Scandinavian advertising media directory. (Text in Danish and English) 1952. a. Kr.415. Danske Reklamebureauers Brancheforening - Danish Association of Advertising Agencies, Gl. Strand 44, DK-1202 Copenhagen K, Denmark. adv. circ. 2,100.

659.1   BL
MIDIA. 1977. a. free. Editora Rural, Rua Gabriela 333, Porto Alegre, Brazil.

MORGAN REPORT ON DIRECTORY PUBLISHING. see *TRAVEL AND TOURISM*

659.1   US
N A D CASE REPORT. 1973. m. Council of Better Business Bureaus, Inc., National Advertising Division, 845 Third Ave., New York, NY 10022. TEL 212-754-1358. Ed. Ronald H. Smithies. circ. 5,700.

659.1   CN   ISSN 0077-5177
NATIONAL LIST OF ADVERTISERS. 1939. a. Can.$43. Maclean-Hunter Ltd., Business Publication Division, Maclean-Hunter Bldg., 777 Bay St., Toronto, Ont. M5W 1A7, Canada. TEL 416-596-5891. Ed. Irvine Brace.

381   US
NEW DETROIT PROGRESS REPORT. 1968. a. New Detroit Inc., 719 Griswold, One Kennedy Sq., Detroit, MI 48226. TEL 313-496-2000. Ed. Maureen C. McDonald.
Formerly: New Detroit Incorporated.

015   US
NEWSPAPER CIRCULATION ANALYSIS; part 2 newspaper rates & data. 1957. a. $93. Standard Rate & Data Service, Inc., 3004 Glenview Rd., Wilmette, IL 60091. TEL 312-256-6067. Ed. Otis Kirchhoefer. adv. circ. 6,779.

659.1   US
NEWSPAPER PROMOTION YEARBOOK. 1950. a. membership. International Newspaper Promotion Association, 11600 Sunrise Valley Dr., Reston, VA 22090. TEL 703-648-1094. circ. 1,500.

659.1   US
NO DEADLINE. 1965. irreg. $18. Robert Eastman, Inc., Box 368, Ithaca, NY 14851. TEL 607-273-4241. Ed. Robert Eastman. adv. bk. rev. illus. circ. 8,970.

070   659.1   UK
O P M A OVERSEAS MEDIA GUIDE. 1965. a. £7.50. Overseas Press and Media Association, 122 Shaftesbury Ave., London W1V 8HA, England. Ed. Barbara Cruttenden. adv. circ. 5,000(controlled)
Formerly (until 1987): Overseas Media Guide (ISSN 0078-7132)

O'DWYER'S DIRECTORY OF PUBLIC RELATIONS EXECUTIVES. see *BIOGRAPHY*

659   US   ISSN 0078-3374
O'DWYER'S DIRECTORY OF PUBLIC RELATIONS FIRMS. 1969. a. $90. J.R. O'Dwyer Co., Inc., 271 Madison Ave., New York, NY 10016. TEL 212-679-2471. adv. circ. 2,000.

659.1   DK   ISSN 0070-2854
OPLAGSTAL OG MARKEDSTAL/CIRCULATION DATA AND MARKETING DATA. 1959. a. Kr.335. Dansk Oplagskontrol - Danish Audit Bureau of Circulations, 5 Frederiksberggade, DK-1459 Copenhagen K, Denmark. circ. 450.

P R PLANNER - EUROPE. see *BUSINESS AND ECONOMICS — Trade And Industrial Directories*

P R PLANNER - U.K. see *BUSINESS AND ECONOMICS — Trade And Industrial Directories*

PRODUCER'S MASTERGUIDE; the international production manual for motion pictures, television, commercials, cable and videotape industries in the United States, Canada, the United Kingdom, Ireland, Bermuda and the Caribbean Islands. see *MOTION PICTURES*

PRODUKTIONSHAANDBOGEN; grafisk produktion - reklamevirksomhed. see *PRINTING*

659.2   US
PROFESSIONAL'S GUIDE TO PUBLIC RELATIONS SERVICES. 1968. a. $90. Public Relations Publishing Co., 888 Seventh Ave., New York, NY 10106. TEL 212-315-8000. Ed. Richard Weiner. circ. 1,000.

659.1   UK
PROMOTION. a. £40. M.S. Surveys & Promotional Services Ltd., Hesketh House, Portman Sq., London W1 0JH, England. Ed. Judith Watson.

PUBLIC RELATIONS SOCIETY OF AMERICA DIRECTORY. see *BUSINESS AND ECONOMICS — Trade And Industrial Directories*

659.1   UK
PUBLIC RELATIONS YEARBOOK. a. (Public Relations Consultants Association) Financial Times Business Information, 102 Clerkenwell Road, London EC1M 5SA, England.

PUBLICITY REVIEW. see *ART*

R S V P: DIRECTORY OF CREATIVE TALENT. (Repondez S'il Vous Plait) see *ART*

659.13   CN   ISSN 0706-8085
REACHING THE MANITOBA MARKET. 1977. a. free. Manitoba Community Newspapers Association, 204-254 Edmonton St., Winnipeg, Man. R3C 3Y4, Canada. TEL 204-947-1691. Ed. B.G. McCallum. adv. circ. 1,500.

659.2   FR   ISSN 0080-1194
REPERTOIRE PRATIQUE DE LA PUBLICITE. 1968/69. a. 141 F. Editions Jacquemart, 19 rue des Pretres-Saint-Germain-l'Auxerrois, Paris 1, France.

659.15   UK
S D E A CATALOGUE OF SHOPFITTINGS AND DISPLAY. 1980. a. £5. Shop and Display Equipment Association, 24 Croydon Rd., Caterham, Surrey CR3 6YR, England. Ed. Lawrence Cutler. adv. circ. 3,000.
Formerly: S D E A Members Catalogue of Shopfittings and Display.

659.1   UK
SIGN DIRECTORY AND YEARBOOK. 1970. a. £4.10. A.E. Morgan Publications Ltd., Stanley House, 9 West St., Epsom, Surrey, England. Ed. D. Young. adv.

659.102   US   ISSN 0081-4229
STANDARD DIRECTORY OF ADVERTISERS. (In 2 editions: Classified and Geographical) 1915. a. $235. National Register Publishing Co., Inc., (Subsidiary of: Standard Rate & Data Service) 3004 Glenview Rd., Wilmette, IL 60091. TEL 312-256-6067. Ed. Robert Weicherding. adv. circ. 11,000(classified edt.); 2,800(geographical edt.)

STANDARD DIRECTORY OF INTERNATIONAL ADVERTISERS AND ADVERTISING AGENCIES. see *BUSINESS AND ECONOMICS — Trade And Industrial Directories*

659.1   TH
TELEPHONE ORGANIZATION OF THAILAND. ANNUAL REPORT. (Text in English and Thai) 1954. a. Telephone Organization of Thailand, Thanon Phloen Chit, Bangkok Metropolis 10500, Thailand. Ed. Kamphonwut Sukhsong.

TRADESHOW & EXHIBIT MANAGER BUYERS GUIDE. see *BUSINESS AND ECONOMICS — Trade And Industrial Directories*

659.1   333.33   070.5   US
U S REAL ESTATE REGISTER. 1967. a. $49. Barry Inc., Box 551, Wilmington, MA 01887. TEL 617-658-0441. circ. 8,000.
Formerly: Industrial/Commercial Real Estate Managers' Directory.

659.2   FR   ISSN 0066-9253
UNION DES ASSOCIATION FRANCAISES DE RELATIONS PUBLIQUES. ANNUAIRE. 1963. a. membership. Union des Association Francaises de Relations Publiques, B.P. 8, Douvrin, 62138 Haisnes, France. adv. circ. 1,500.

659.1   US   ISSN 0073-2893
UNITED STATES & CANADIAN MAILING LISTS. Title varies: Catalog of Mailing Lists. 1950. biennial. free. ‡ Fritz S. Hofheimer, Inc., 88 Third Avenue, Mineola, NY 11501. TEL 516-248-4600. Ed. Irene Hofheimer. stat. circ. 175,000 (controlled)

V.I.P. DU MARKETING ET DE LA PUBLICITE. see *BUSINESS AND ECONOMICS — Marketing And Purchasing*

070   SZ
VERBREITUNGSDATEN DER SCHWEIZER PRESSE. (Text in German) 1968. triennial. 75 Fr.($40) Verband Schweizerischer Werbegesellschaften, Seestrasse 5, CH-8002 Zurich, Switzerland. Ed.Bd. circ. 250. (also avail. in magnetic tape)
Formerly: Streudaten der Schwizer Presse.

659.1   AU
WERBEALMANACH. 1978. a. S.300. Manstein Verlag, Am Modenapark 6, 1030 Vienna, Austria. Ed. H.J. Jost-Manstein. circ. 2,000.

WHERE SHALL I GO TO COLLEGE TO STUDY ADVERTISING? see *EDUCATION — Guides To Schools And Colleges*

WHO'S WHO IN PUBLIC RELATIONS (INTERNATIONAL) see *BIOGRAPHY*

659   US   ISSN 0568-0301
WORLD ADVERTISING EXPENDITURES. 1953. annual. $125 non-members. ‡ (International Advertising Association) Starch INRA Hooper Inc., 566 E. Boston Post, Mamaroneck, NY 10543. TEL 914-698-0800. adv.
Formerly: Biennial Survey of Advertising Expenditures Around the World (ISSN 0074-1272)

659.2   UK
WORLD ADVERTISING REVIEW. 1924. a. £29.95. Cassell Ltd., 1 St. Anne's Rd., Eastbourne, E. Sussex BN21 3UN, England. circ. 5,000.
Formerly: Modern Publicity (ISSN 0077-0108)

100 BOOKS ON ADVERTISING. see *ADVERTISING AND PUBLIC RELATIONS — Abstracting, Bibliographies, Statistics*

ADVERTISING AND PUBLIC RELATIONS — Abstracting, Bibliographies, Statistics

659.1   US   ISSN 0162-3125
BACON'S PUBLICITY CHECKER. (In 2 vols.: Magazines & Newspapers) 1952. a. (plus 3 suppl.) $140. Bacon's Publishing Company, Inc., 332 S. Michigan Ave., Chicago, IL 60604. TEL 312-922-2400. Ed. Wilfrid Budd.

659.1   US
INTERNATIONAL MEDIA GUIDE. CONSUMER MAGAZINES WORLDWIDE. 1976. a. $75. Directories International, Inc. (Subsidiary of: Hanson Publishing Group) 150 Fifth Ave., New York, NY 10011. TEL 212-807-1660. Ed. Diane Lieberwitz.
Former titles: International Media Guide. Consumer Magazines Edition; Media Guide International. Consumer Magazines Edition; Media Guide International. Airline Inflight/Travel Magazines Edition; Media Guide International. Airline Inflight Magazines Edition.

659   US   ISSN 0093-9447
INTERNATIONAL MEDIA GUIDE. NEWSPAPERS: WORLDWIDE. 1972. a. $97.50. Directories International, Inc. (Subsidiary of: Hanson Publishing Group) 150 Fifth Ave., New York, NY 10011. TEL 212-807-1660. Ed. Diane Lieberwitz. adv. circ. 1,300.
Former titles: Media Guide International. Newspapers/Newsmagazines Edition; Newsmedia Guide International; Newspapers and Newsmagazines Worldwide.

070   US
INTERNATIONAL MEDIA GUIDES. BUSINESS/PROFESSIONAL PUBLICATIONS EDITION. (Published in 4 regional vols.: Europe; Asia/Pacific; Latin America; Middle East/Africa) 1971. a. $360 for all four vols. Directories International, Inc., (Subsidiary of: Hanson Publishing Group) 150 Fifth Ave., New York, NY 10011. TEL 212-807-1660. Ed. Diane Lieberwitz. adv. circ. 1,000.
Former titles: Media Guide International. Business/Professional Publications Edition (ISSN 0164-1743); Media Guide International. Business Publications Edition (ISSN 0098-9398); Newsmedia Guide International.

659 314   IE
IRELAND (EIRE) CENTRAL STATISTICS OFFICE. BUSINESS OF ADVERTISING AGENCIES. a. Central Statistics Office, Ardee Rd., Dublin 6, Ireland.
Formerly (until 1984): Ireland (Eire) Central Statistics Office. Inquiry into Advertising Agencies Activities. (ISSN 0075-0581)
Stencilled releases

659.2   AT
100 BOOKS ON ADVERTISING. 1939. biennial. $1. University of Missouri, School of Journalism, c/o Robert Haverfield, Ed., 17 Gears Ave., Drummoyne N.S.W. 2047, Australia. adv. bk. rev. bibl. circ. 6, 000.

AERONAUTICS AND SPACE FLIGHT

see also Transportation—Air Transport

629.4   US
A A S GODDARD MEMORIAL SYMPOSIUM. PROCEEDINGS. (Subseries of Advances in the Astronautical Sciences and Science and Technology Series) 1961. a. price varies. (American Astronautical Society, Inc.) Univelt, Inc., Box 28130, San Diego, CA 92128. TEL 619-746-4005.

629.1   US   ISSN 0730-3564
A A S HISTORY SERIES. (Supplement to: Advances in the Astronautical Sciences) 1977. irreg., vol.5, 1982. price varies. (American Astronautical Society) Univelt, Inc., Box 28130, San Diego, CA 92128. TEL 619-746-4005. Ed. Frederick C. Durant III. bibl. charts. illus. circ. 1,250. (back issues avail.) Indexed: Biol.Abstr. Eng.Ind. Curr.Cont. Sci.Abstr. Int.Aerosp.Abstr. INSPEC.

629.4   US   ISSN 0065-7417
A A S MICROFICHE SERIES. (Supplement to: Advances in the Astronautical Sciences (0065-7417)) 1968. irreg. (approx. 5 vols. yrly.); vol.50, 1984. price varies. (American Astronautical Society, Inc.) Univelt, Inc., Box 28130, San Diego, CA 92128. TEL 619-746-4005. Ed. H. Jacobs. bibl. charts. illus. cum.index: 1968-1978. circ. 100. (microfiche) Indexed: Chem.Abstr. Eng.Ind. Sci.Abstr. Int.Aerosp.Abstr.

629.1   US
A I A A/A S M E/S A E STRUCTURES, STRUCTURAL DYNAMICS, AND MATERIALS CONFERENCE. PROCEEDINGS. 1976. a. $150 to non-members; members $120. American Institute of Aeronautics & Astronautics, 1633 Broadway, New York, NY 10019. TEL 212-581-4300. Indexed: Int.Aerosp.Abstr.

629.1   US
A I A A ATMOSPHERIC FLIGHT MECHANICS CONFERENCE PROCEEDINGS. a. $80 to non-members; members $60. American Institute of Aeronautics and Astronautics, 1633 Broadway, New York, NY 10104. TEL 212-581-4300. Indexed: Int.Aerosp.Abstr.

629.1 621.384   US
A I A A COMMUNICATIONS SATELLITE SYSTEMS CONFERENCE. TECHNICAL PAPERS. 1972. biennial. $100 to non-members; members $65. American Institute of Aeronautics and Astronautics, 1633 Broadway, New York, NY 10019. TEL 212-581-4300. Indexed: Int.Aerosp.Abstr. VITIS.
Telecommunication

629.13 629.4   US   ISSN 0065-8693
A I A A ROSTER. 1964. biennial. $79.95 to non-members; members $39.95. American Institute of Aeronautics and Astronautics, 1633 Broadway, New York, NY 10019. TEL 212-581-4300.

629.13   CS
A R T I REPORTS. (Aeronautical Research and Test Institute) (Text in English; summaries in Czech, French, German, Russian) 1962. irreg., (4-6/yr.) exchange basis. Vyzkumny a Zkusebni Letecky Ustav, Beranovych 130, Prague 9-Letnany, 19905 Czechoslovakia. Ed. Jiri Kucera. (also avail. in microfilm; microfiche; back issues avail.)

629.4   US   ISSN 0065-3373
ADVANCES IN SPACE SCIENCE AND TECHNOLOGY. 1959. irreg., vol.11, 1972. Academic Press, Inc., Orlando, FL 32887. TEL 305-345-2000.
Formerly: Advances in Space Science and Technology. Supplement.

629.4   US   ISSN 0065-3438
ADVANCES IN THE ASTRONAUTICAL SCIENCES. (Contains several sub-series: Guidance and Control; Joint AAS/DGLR Conference Proceedings; Space Manufacturing; AAS Anniversary Conference Proceedings) 1957. irreg., vol.58, 1985. price varies per vol. (American Astronautical Society) Univelt, Inc., Box 28130, San Diego, CA 92128. TEL 619-746-4005. Ed. H. Jacobs. adv. bibl. charts. illus. index: 1957-1978/79. circ. 600. (back issues avail.) Indexed: Biol.Abstr. Chem.Abstr. Eng.Ind. Sci.Abstr. Int.Aerosp.Abstr. INSPEC.

629.13   BL
AERO. irreg. Cr.$150. J. Ribeiro de Mendonca, Av. Alfonso de Taunay, 143, Barra de Tijuca, Rio de Janeiro, Brazil. illus.

629.1   SA   ISSN 0257-8573
AERONAUTICA MERIDIANA. (Text in English; summaries in Afrikaans and English) 1980. biennial. R.5.00($6.50) Aeronautical Society of South Africa, c/o School of Mechanical Engineering, Witwatersrand University, 1 Jan Smith Ave., Johannesburg 2001, South Africa. Ed. A Nurik. circ. 1,000. (back issues avail.) Indexed: Ind.S.A.Per.
Formerly: Aeronautical Society of South Africa. Journal (ISSN 0250-3786)

629   AG   ISSN 0325-9293
AERONAVEGACION COMERCIAL ARGENTINA. irreg., latest edt. 1979/80. price varies. Instituto Nacional de Estadistica y Censos, Hipolito Yrigoyen 250, Buenos Aires, Argentina. charts. stat.

629.13   BE   ISSN 0065-3713
AERONOMICA ACTA. (Text in Dutch, English or French, with preliminary material also in other languages) 1959. irreg., latest 1985. price varies. Institut d'Aéronomie Spatiale de Belgique, Ave. Circulaire 3, 1180 Brussels, Belgium.

629.1   US
AEROSPACE INDUSTRIES ANNUAL REPORT. 1983. a. free. Aerospace Industries Association, 1725 DeSales St., N.W., Washington, DC 20036. TEL 202-429-4600. Ed. John F. Loosbrock. circ. 2, 000. (back issues avail.)

629.1   JA
AEROSPACE INDUSTRY YEARBOOK. (Text in Japanese) 1974. a. 7000 Yen. Society of Japanese Aerospace Companies, Inc. - Nihon Koku Uchu Kogyokai, Hibiya Park Bldg, 8-1 Yurakucho 1-chome, Chiyoda-ku, Tokyo 100, Japan. circ. 1,000.

629.1 600   US
AEROSPACE TESTING SEMINAR. PROCEEDINGS. 1975. $25. Institute of Environmental Sciences, 940 E. Northwest Hwy., Mt. Prospect, IL 60056. TEL 312-255-1561. (Co-sponsor: Aerospace Corporation)

629.1   BL
AEROSPACO.* 1972. irreg. Editora Imagem Nova, Rua da Graca, 201, Conj. 41, C.E.P. 01125, Sao Paulo, Brazil. illus.

387.7   CN   ISSN 0568-3424
AIR CANADA. ANNUAL REPORT. (Text in English and French) a. Air Canada, Place Air Canada, Montreal, Que. H2Z 1X5, Canada. TEL 514-879-7766.

629.1   US   ISSN 0192-8740
AIR TRAFFIC CONTROL ASSOCIATION. FALL CONFERENCE PROCEEDINGS. 1977. a. $20. Air Traffic Control Association, Inc., 2020 N. 14th St., Ste. 410, Arlington, VA 22201. TEL 703-522-5717. Ed. Lawrence G. Culhane. circ. 1,200. (back issues avail.)

629.1   UN   ISSN 0065-4876
AIRCRAFT ACCIDENT DIGEST. (Issued as a subseries of: Air Navigation. Series F: Circulars) (Editions in English, French, Spanish) 1951. irreg., latest issue, no.29, 1984. price varies. International Civil Aviation Organization, 1000 Sherbrooke St. W., Montreal, Que. H3A 2R2, Canada.

629.1   UK
AIRCRAFT ILLUSTRATED ANNUAL. a. price varies. Ian Allan Ltd., Coombelands House, Addlestone, Weybridge, Surrey KT15 0HY, England. Ed. Peter R. March. circ. 9,500. (reprint service avail. from UMI)

387.732   UK   ISSN 0002-2683
AIRCRAFT INDUSTRY RECORD. irreg. $130. Aviation Studies International, Sussex House, Parkside, Wimbledon, London SW19 5NB, England.

629.1 387.7   US
AIRMAN'S INFORMATION MANUAL. 1947. a. $6.70. Tab Books, Inc., Box 40, Blue Ridge Summit, PA 17214. illus. index.

629.4   US   ISSN 0516-9593
AMERICAN ASTRONAUTICAL SOCIETY. PROCEEDINGS OF THE ANNUAL MEETING. (Subseries of Advances in the Astronautical Sciences) a. price varies. (American Astronautical Society, Inc.) Univelt, Inc., Box 28130, San Diego, CA 92128. TEL 619-746-4005.

629.133   US
AMERICAN HELICOPTER SOCIETY. ANNUAL FORUM. PROCEEDINGS. 1943. a. price varies. American Helicopter Society, Inc., 217 N. Washington St., Alexandria, VA 22314. circ. 500.
Formerly: American Helicopter Society. National Forum. Proceedings (ISSN 0065-8510)
Helicopters

340 387.7   CN   ISSN 0701-158X
ANNALS OF AIR AND SPACE LAW/ANNALES DE DROIT AERIEN ET SPATIAL. 1976. a. Can.$50. McGill University, Centre for Research of Air and Space Law, 3690 Peel St., Montreal H3A 1W9, Canada. TEL 514-392-6721. Ed. Nicolas M. Matte. bk. rev. cum.index: 1976-1985. circ. 700. (back issues avail.) Indexed: Leg.Per. C.L.I. L.R.I.

AERONAUTICS AND SPACE FLIGHT

629.13   FR
ASSOCIATION AERONAUTIQUE ET ASTRONAUTIQUE DE FRANCE. ANNUAIRE. 1961. a. 100 F. Association Aeronautique et Astronautique de France, 80 rue Lauriston, 75116 Paris, France. adv. circ. 1,200.
    Formerly (1964-1974): Association Francaise des Ingenieurs et Techniciens de l'Aeronautique et de l'Espace. Annuaire (ISSN 0066-9245)

ASSOCIATION TECHNIQUE MARITIME ET AERONAUTIQUE, PARIS. BULLETIN. see TRANSPORTATION — Ships And Shipping

629.1   US
ASTRODYNAMICS. (Subseries of Advances in the Astronautical Sciences) 1965. biennial. price varies. (American Astronautical Society) Univelt, Inc., Box 28130, San Diego, CA 92128. TEL 619-746-4005. Indexed: Eng.Ind. Int.Aerosp.Abstr.

629.13   AT   ISSN 0084-7364
AUSTRALIAN GLIDING YEARBOOK. 1969. a. Aus.$2.50. Gliding Federation of Australia, Box 1650, Adelaide, S.A. 5001, Australia. Ed. Allan Ash. adv. bk. rev. circ. 4,600.
    Gliding

629.132   JA
AVIATION ANNUAL OF JAPAN.* (Text in Japanese) 1976. a. 5000 Yen. Nihon Koku Kyokai, Kokukaikan Bunkan, 1-18-2 Shinbashi, Minato-ku, Tokyo 105, Japan.

629.13   UK   ISSN 0143-1145
AVIATION EUROPE. 1947. a. £40. Sell's Publications Ltd., 55 High St., Epsom, Surrey KT19 8DW, England. adv. bk. rev. circ. 5,000.
    Incorporating: Sell's British Aviation (ISSN 0080-8695)

616.98   US   ISSN 0067-2661
AVIATION MEDICAL EDUCATION SERIES. 1965. irreg. U.S. Federal Aviation Administration, Aviation Medicine Office, 800 Independence Ave., S.W., Washington, DC 20590. TEL 202-655-4000.
    Aerospace medicine

629.1   US
AVIATION/SPACE WRITERS ASSOCIATION. YEARBOOK AND DIRECTORY;* including roster of membership. 1938. a. $25. Aviation Space Writers Association, 21 E. State St., Ste. 730, Columbus, OH 43215-4210. Ed. D.B. Priest. circ. 500.
    Formerly: Aviation/Space Writers Association Manual.

629.13   629.4   US
AVIATION WEEK & SPACE TECHNOLOGY. MARKETING DIRECTORY. 1955. a. $9. McGraw-Hill Publications Co., 1221 Avenue of the Americas, New York, NY 10020. Ed. William H. Gregory. adv. index. circ. 125,421. (also avail. in microform from UMI) Indexed: Mag.Ind.

629.132   UK
B W P A MAGAZINE. 1955. a. membership. British Women Pilots Association, Rochester Airport, Chatham, Kent ME5 9SD, England. Ed. Lola Mcrobert. adv. bk. rev. circ. 500. (processed)

629.13   UY
C I D A. 1976. irreg. free. Direccion General de Aviacion Civil, Centro de Investigacion y Difusion Aeronautico Espacial, Yi 1182, Montevideo, Uruguay. bk. rev. circ. 2,000.

629.13   II   ISSN 0077-2968
CATALOGUE OF N A L TECHNICAL TRANSLATIONS. (Text in English) 1972. a. exchange basis. National Aeronautical Laboratory, Box 1779, Kodihalli, Bangalore 560017, India. (Affiliate: Council of Scientific and Industrial Research) Ed. C. V. Suryanara Yanan. (processed)

629.4   FR   ISSN 0069-2034
CENTRE NATIONAL D'ETUDES SPATIALES. RAPPORT D'ACTIVITE. (Text in French; summaries in English) 1962. a. free. Centre National d'Etudes Spatiales, 18 Ave. E. Belin, 31055 Toulouse Cedex, France. Ed. J.P. Bordet. circ. 2,000.

629.4   341   US   ISSN 0069-5831
COLLOQUIUM ON THE LAW OF OUTER SPACE. PROCEEDINGS. 1958. a. $59.50 to non-members; members $29.50. (International Space Institute) American Institute of Aeronautics and Astronautics, 1633 Broadway, New York, NY 10019. (back issues avail.) Indexed: Int.Aerosp.Abstr.

COMMERCIAL AIR TRANSPORT INDUSTRY. see MILITARY

629.1   JA
COMMITTEE FOR AEROSPACE STRUCTURES. RESEARCH REPORT. (Text in Japanese) 1957. a. 3000 Yen($20) Committee for Aerospace Structures, c/o Department of Aeronautics, University of Tokyo, 7-3-1 Hongo, Bunkyo-ku, Tokyo 113, Japan. Ed. Kyohei Kondo. circ. 200. (back issues avail.)

629.1   US
COMMONWEALTH OF PENNSYLVANIA. AIRPORT DIRECTORY. a. free. Department of Transportation, Bureau of Aviation, Transportation & Safety Bldg., Rm. 716, Harrisburg, PA 17120.
    Supersedes: Pennsylvania. Bureau of Aviation. Aviation Newsletter.

629.13   US
COMMONWEALTH OF PENNSYLVANIA AERONAUTICAL CHART. a. free. Department of Transportation, Bureau of Aviation, Transportation & Safety Bldg., Rm. 716, Harrisburg, PA 17120.

629.1   600   US
CONFERENCE ON SPACE SIMULATION. PROCEEDINGS. irreg., 14th, 1986. price varies. Institute of Environmental Sciences, 940 E. Northwest Hwy., Mt. Prospect, IL 60056. TEL 312-255-1561. (Co-sponsors: American Institute of Aeronautics and Astronautics; American Society for Testing and Materials; National Aeronautics and Space Administration)

629.8   US   ISSN 0090-5267
CONTROL AND DYNAMIC SYSTEMS: ADVANCES IN THEORY AND APPLICATIONS. a., vol.24, 1986. $55. Academic Press, Inc., Orlando, FL 32887. TEL 305-345-2000. Ed. Cornelius T. Leondes. illus. Indexed: Appl.Mech.Rev. Chem.Abstr. Key Title: Control and Dynamic Systems.
    Continues: Advances in Control Systems (ISSN 0065-2466)

629.1   SZ
CURRENT AIRCRAFT PRICES. a. 300 Fr.($150) Interavia S.A., 86 Av. Louis Casai, Case Postale 162, CH-1216 Cointrin-Geneva, Switzerland.

629.13   GW
D F V L R-FORSCHUNGSBERICHTE UND D F V L R-MITTEILUNGEN. (Text in English or German) 1964. irreg. price varies. Deutsche Forschungs- und Versuchsanstalt fuer Luft- und Raumfahrt e.V., Linder Hoehe, Postfach 906058, D-5000 Cologne 90, W. Germany (B.R.D.) index. Indexed: Appl.Mech.Rev. Chem.Abstr. Int.Aerosp.Abstr.
    Formerly (until 1978): Deutsche Luft-und Raumfahrt Forschungsberichte (ISSN 0070-4245)

629.13   GW   ISSN 0070-3966
D F V L R JAHRESBERICHT. 1969. a. free. Deutsche Forschungs- und Versuchsanstalt fuer Luft- und Raumfahrt e.V., Linder Hoehe, Postfach 906058, D-5000 Cologne 90, W. Germany (B.R.D.)

629.13   629.4   GW   ISSN 0070-4083
D.G.L.R. JAHRBUECHER. 1952. a. price varies. Deutsche Gesellschaft fuer Luft und Raumfahrt e.V., Godesberger Allee 70, 5300 Bonn 2, W. Germany (B.R.D.) index.
    Formerly: Wissenschaftliche Gesellschaft fuer Luft- und Raumfahrt. Jahrbuecher.

629.132   DK   ISSN 0107-0886
D I F FLYAARBOG. a. membership. Dansk Ingenioerforening, Flyveteknisk Sektion, Vester Farimagsgade 31, DK-1606 Copenhagen V, Denmark.
    Formerly: Dansk Ingenioerforening. Flyveteknisk Sektion. Aarbog.

629.1   DK   ISSN 0109-6605
DANSK RUMFORSKNINGINSTITUT. PUBLIKATIONER. irreg. (Dansk Rumforskninginstitut - Danish Space Research Institut) Bibliotekscentralen, Telegrafvej 5, DK-2750 Ballerup, Denmark.

DEVELOPMENTS IN SOLAR SYSTEM AND SPACE SCIENCE. see ASTRONOMY

629.13   UK
DIRECTED ENERGY AND AVIONICS DATA SHEETS. irreg. $280. Aviation Studies International, Sussex House, Parkside, Wimbledon, London SW19 5NB, England.
    Formerly: Avionics Data Sheets.

629.13   US
DIRECTORY OF AVIATION AND SPACE EDUCATION.* 1975. biennial. $10. American Society for Aerospace Education, 1810 Michael Faraday Dr., No. 101, Reston, VA 22090-5391. Ed. Wayne R. Matson. circ. 200,000. (also avail. in microfilm)
    Formerly: Directory of Aerospace Education.

629.1   DK   ISSN 0109-1115
E S A FOELGEFORSKNING. (European Space Agency); bevillinger til stoette af internationale samarbejdsprojekter inden for rumforskningen, beretning. 1979. a. Forskningssekretaraitet, Holmens Kanal 7, 1060 Copenhagen K, Denmark. illus.

629.13   FR
E S A SCIENTIFIC-TECHNICAL REPORTS, NOTES AND MEMORANDA. 1964. irreg. European Space Agency, 8-10 rue Mario Nikis, 75738 Paris Cedex 15, France.
    Formerly (1964-1975): E S R O Scientific-Technical Reports, Notes and Memoranda.

629.1   621.38   FR   ISSN 0531-7444
EUROPEAN ORGANISATION FOR CIVIL AVIATION ELECTRONICS. GENERAL ASSEMBLY. ANNUAL REPORT. (Text in English and French) 1964. a. free. European Organization for Civil Aviation Electronics, 11 rue Hamelin, 75783 Paris Cedex 16, France. circ. 200.

629.13   UK   ISSN 0071-402X
FARNBOROUGH AIR SHOW (PUBLIC PROGRAMME) biennial. ‡ Society of British Aerospace Companies Ltd., 29 King St. St. James's, London, SW1Y 6RD, England.

341.46   US   ISSN 0533-0963
FEDERAL AVIATION REGULATIONS FOR PILOTS. 1947. a. $5.70. Tab Books, Inc., Box 40, Blue Ridge Summit, PA 17214. index.

629.1   GW
FLIEGERKALENDER. 1979. a. DM.19.80. Verlag E.S. Mittler und Sohn GmbH, Steintorwall 17, Postfach 2352, 4900 Herford, W. Germany (B.R.D.) Ed. Hans M. Namislo. adv. abstr. charts. illus. stat. circ. 6,000.

629.13   SW   ISSN 0081-5640
FLYGTEKNISKA FOERSOEKSANSTALTEN. MEDDELANDE/REPORT. (Text in English) 1944. irreg. price varies. (Aeronautical Research Institute of Sweden) Almqvist & Wiksell International, Box 62, S-101 20 Stockholm, Sweden. Ed. Brit Berg.

629.13   US   ISSN 0163-1144
FLYING ANNUAL & BUYERS' GUIDE. 1965. a. $2.95. C B S Magazines, Flying, 1515 Broadway, New York, NY 10036. TEL 212-719-6000. Ed. Richard Collins. adv. circ. 165,000.
    Former titles: Flying Buyers Guide; Flying Annual and Pilots' Buying Guide; Flying Annual and Pilots' Guide (ISSN 0071-6286)

629.13   FR   ISSN 0078-3773
FRANCE. OFFICE NATIONAL D'ETUDES ET DE RECHERCHES AEROSPATIALES. ACTIVITIES. (Editions in English & French) 1965. a. free. ‡ Office National d'Etudes et de Recherches Aerospatiales, 29, Avenue de la Division-Leclerc, 92320 Chatillon, France. circ. 750 (English edt.) 2, 250 (French edt.)
    Formerly (until 1968): France. Office National d'Etudes et de Recherches Aerospatiales. Recueil de Notes sur l'Activite de ONERA.

AERONAUTICS AND SPACE FLIGHT

629.13   FR   ISSN 0078-3781
FRANCE. OFFICE NATIONAL D'ETUDES ET DE RECHERCHES AEROSPATIALES. NOTES TECHNIQUES. (Text in French; abstract in English) 1946. irreg.(about 20 per year) price varies. Office National d'Etudes et de Recherches Aerospatiales, 29 Ave. de la Division-Leclerc, 92320 Chatillon, France. Ed. Claude Sevestre. index. cum.index: 1950-1976. circ. 250. Indexed: Appl.Mech.Rev.

629.13   FR   ISSN 0078-379X
FRANCE. OFFICE NATIONAL D'ETUDES ET DE RECHERCHES AEROSPATIALES. PUBLICATIONS. (Text in French; abstract in English) 1946. irreg. (approx. 5 per year) price varies. Office National d'Etudes et de Recherches Aerospatiales, 29 Avenue de la Division-Leclerc, 92320 Chatillon, France. Ed. Claude Sevestre. index. cum.index: 1947-1976. circ. 250. Indexed: Appl.Mech.Rev.

629.1   US   ISSN 0317-056X
FROM THE GROUND UP. 1946. irreg. $15.95 per no. Aviation Publishers Co. Ltd., Box 1361, Sta. B, Ottawa, Ont. K1P 5R4, Canada. TEL 613-745-2943.

629.135   US   ISSN 0094-3975
FUNDAMENTALS OF AEROSPACE INSTRUMENTATION. Represents: Instrument Society of America. International I S A Aerospace Instrumentation Symposium. Tutorial Proceedings. a. price varies. Instrument Society of America, 67 Alexander Dr., Box 12277, Research Triangle Park, NC 27709. TEL 919-549-8411. (reprint service avail. from, UMI, ISI and publisher)

629.13   UK   ISSN 0072-5595
GREAT BRITAIN. AERONAUTICAL RESEARCH COUNCIL. CURRENT PAPER SERIES. 1950. irreg. price varies. H.M.S.O., P.O. Box 569, London SE1 9NH, England. (reprint service avail. from UMI)

629.13   UK   ISSN 0072-5609
GREAT BRITAIN. AERONAUTICAL RESEARCH COUNCIL. REPORTS AND MEMORANDA SERIES. irreg. price varies. H.M.S.O., P.O. Box 569, London SE1 9NH, England. (reprint service avail. from UMI)

629.1   US
GUIDANCE AND CONTROL. (Subseries of Advances in the Astronautical Sciences) 1979. a. price varies. (American Astronautical Society) Univelt, Inc., Box 28130, San Diego, CA 92128. TEL 619-746-4005. Indexed: Eng.Ind. Int.Aerosp.Abstr.

001.94   US
HILBERG-EASLEY REPORT. irreg. 377 Race St., Berea, OH 44017. Ed. Rick Hilberg.
Unidentified flying objects

387.7   US   ISSN 0018-2443
HISTORICAL AVIATION ALBUM. 1965. a. $12 per no. ‡ Paul R. Matt, Box 33, Temple City, CA 91780. TEL 818-286-7655. Eds. Kenn C. Rust, Thomas G. Foxworth. charts. illus. stat. tr.mk. circ. 3,500. (tabloid format, also avail. in microform from UMI)

629.1   US
I E E E/A E S S DAYTON CHAPTER SYMPOSIUM. 1979. a. price varies. (I E E E, Aerospace and Electronic Systems Society, Dayton Section) Institute of Electrical and Electronics Engineers, Inc., 345 E. 47th St., New York, NY 10017 TEL 212-705-7900. (Subscr. addr: 445 Hoes Lane, Piscataway, NJ 08854)
Former titles (1980-1984): I E E E/A E S S Symposium (Proceedings); Until 1979· I E E E/A E S-S Seminar.

629.1   US
I E E E/A I A A DIGITAL AVIONICS SYSTEMS CONFERENCE. PROCEEDINGS. Variant title in alternate years: A I A A/I E E E Digital Avionics Systems Conference. Proceedings. (Publication alternates between IEEE and AIAA) 1975. biennial. price varies. (I E E E, Aerospace and Electronic Systems Society) Institute of Electrical and Electronics Engineers, Inc., 345 E. 47th St., New York, NY 10017 TEL 212-705-7900. (Subscr. to: 445 Hoes Lane, Piscataway, NJ 08854) (Co-sponsor: American Institute of Aeronautics and Astronautics)
Former titles (1981): A I A A/I E E E Digital Avionics Systems Conference. Technical Papers; (1979): Digital Avionics Systems Conference (Publication); (1975-1977): A I A A Digital Avionics Systems Conference (Preprints)

629.13   US
I E E E AEROSPACE APPLICATIONS CONFERENCE. DIGEST. 1980? a. price varies. (I E E E, Los Angeles South Bay Harbor Section) Institute of Electrical and Electronics Engineers, Inc., 345 E. 47th St., New York, NY 10017 TEL 212-705-7900. (Subscr. addr.: 445 Hoes Lane, Piscataway, NJ 08854)

I E E E/E A S C O N. ELECTRONICS AND AEROSPACE CONFERENCE. (RECORD) see *ELECTRICITY AND ELECTRICAL ENGINEERING*

629.4   US   ISSN 0547-3578
I E E E NATIONAL AEROSPACE AND ELECTRONICS CONFERENCE. PROCEEDINGS. Abbreviated title: N A E C O N. a. (I E E E, Aerospace and Electronic Systems Society) Institute of Electrical and Electronics Engineers, Inc., 345 E. 47th St., New York, NY 10017 TEL 212-705-7900. (Subscr. address: 445 Hoes Lane, Piscataway, NJ 08854)
Former titles: National Aerospace Electronics Conference. Proceedings; National Aerospace and Electronics Conference. Record (ISSN 0065-373X)

629.47   US   ISSN 0275-9306
I E E E POWER ELECTRONICS SPECIALISTS CONFERENCE. RECORD. Short title: P E S C Record. 1970. a. price varies. (I E E E, Aerospace and Electronics Systems Society) Institute of Electrical and Electronics Engineers, Inc., 345 E. 47th St., New York, NY 10017 TEL 212-705-7900. (Subscr. address: 445 Hoes Lane, Piscataway, NJ 08854) illus.
Former titles, 1972: I E E E Power Processing and Electronics Specialists Conference. Record (ISSN 0090-2381); (1970-1971): Power Conditioning Specialists Conference. Record (ISSN 0079-4414)

629.1   II   ISSN 0376-5466
INDIA. DEPARTMENT OF SPACE. ANNUAL REPORT. (Editions in English & Hindi) 1973. a. controlled free circ. Department of Space, Cauvery Bhavan, F-Block, Kempegowda Rd., Bangalore 560009, India. Ed. P. Nanda Kumar. circ. 4,000.

629.13   US
INSTITUTE OF NAVIGATION. NATIONAL TECHNICAL MEETING PROCEEDINGS. a. $50. Institute of Navigation, Ste. 832, 815 15th St. N.W., Washington, DC 20005. TEL 202-783-4121.
Supersedes (after 1984): National Aerospace Meeting. Proceedings.

629.1   US   ISSN 0096-7238
INSTRUMENTATION IN THE AEROSPACE INDUSTRY. (Subseries of International Instrumentation Symposium (0277-7576)) a. Instrument Society of America, 67 Alexander Dr., Research Triangle Park, NC 27709. TEL 919-549-8411. (also avail. in microform from UMI; reprint service avail. from ISI, UMI and publisher)
Supersedes in part: I S A Aerospace Instrumentation Symposium. Proceedings (ISSN 0536-2008)

629.1   SZ   ISSN 0074-1116
INTERAVIA A B C; aerospace directory. (Text in English) 1936. a. 325 Fr. Interavia S.A., 86 Av. Louis Casai, Case Postale 162, 1216 Cointrin-Geneva, Switzerland. Ed. J. Didelot. adv. index. Indexed: Bus.Ind. Tr.& Indus.Ind.

629.13   FR
INTERNATIONAL AERONAUTIC FEDERATION. ANNUAL INFORMATION BULLETIN. a. 50 F. International Aeronautic Federation, 6 rue Galilee, 75782 Paris Cedex 16, France.
Formerly: International Aeronautic Federation. General Conference Minutes (of the) Business Meetings (ISSN 0534-6509)

387.7   US
INTERNATIONAL AIR SAFETY AND CORPORATE AVIATION SAFETY SEMINAR PROCEEDINGS. a., 26th, Lisbon, 1973. price varies. Flight Safety Foundation, Inc., 5510 Columbia Pike, Arlington, VA 22204-3194. TEL 703-820-2777. (also avail. in microform from UMI)
Formerly: International Air Safety Seminar Proceedings (ISSN 0270-5176)

629.4   US
INTERNATIONAL ASTRONAUTICAL FEDERATION (I A F). INTERNATIONAL CONGRESS. INVITED PAPERS. irreg., 35th, 1984, Lausanne. $94.50 to non-members; members $64.50. American Institute of Aeronautics and Astronautics, 1633 Broadway, New York, NY 10019. TEL 212-581-4300. Ed. Luigi G. Napolitano.

629.1   UN   ISSN 0074-2244
INTERNATIONAL CIVIL AVIATION ORGANIZATION. AIRWORTHINESS COMMITTEE. REPORT OF MEETING. (Editions in English, French, Spanish, Russian) irreg., 13th, Montreal, 1979. price varies. International Civil Aviation Organization, 1000 Sherbrooke St. W., Montreal, Que. H3A 2R2, Canada.

629.1   UN   ISSN 0074-2333
INTERNATIONAL CIVIL AVIATION ORGANIZATION. ALL-WEATHER OPERATIONS PANEL. REPORT OF MEETING. (Editions in English, French, Russian, Spanish) irreg., 10th, Montreal, 1984. price varies. International Civil Aviation Organization, 1000 Sherbrooke St. W., Montreal, Que. H3A 2R2, Canada.

629.1   UN   ISSN 0074-2384
INTERNATIONAL CIVIL AVIATION ORGANIZATION. ASSEMBLY. REPORT OF THE TECHNICAL COMMISSION. (Editions in Arabic, English) irreg., 24th, 1983. price varies. International Civil Aviation Organization, 1000 Sherbrooke St. W., Montreal, Que. H3A 2R2, Canada.

629.1   UN   ISSN 0074-2252
INTERNATIONAL CIVIL AVIATION ORGANIZATION. AUTOMATED DATA INTERCHANGE SYSTEMS PANEL. REPORT OF MEETING. (Editions in English, French, Russian, Spanish) irreg., 10th, Montreal, 1982. price varies. International Civil Aviation Organization, 1000 Sherbrooke St. W., Montreal, Que. H3A 2R2, Canada.

629.1   UN   ISSN 0074-252X
INTERNATIONAL CIVIL AVIATION ORGANIZATION. OBSTACLE CLEARANCE PANEL. REPORT OF MEETING. (Editions in English, French, Spanish) irreg., 3rd, Montreal, 1971. price varies. International Civil Aviation Organization, 1000 Sherbrooke St. W., Montreal, Que. H3A 2R2, Canada.

629.1   UN   ISSN 0074-2228
INTERNATIONAL CIVIL AVIATION ORGANIZATION. (PANEL ON) APPLICATION OF SPACE TECHNIQUES RELATING TO AVIATION. REPORT OF MEETING. (Editions in English, French, Spanish) irreg., 4th, Montreal, 1971. price varies. International Civil Aviation Organization, 1000 Sherbrooke St. W., Montreal, Que. H3A 2R2, Canada.

629.1   UN   ISSN 0074-2562
INTERNATIONAL CIVIL AVIATION ORGANIZATION. SONIC BOOM PANEL. REPORT OF THE MEETING. (Editions in English, French, Spanish) irreg., 2nd, Montreal, 1973. price varies. International Civil Aviation Organization, 1000 Sherbrooke St. W., Montral, Que. H3A 2R2, Canada.

AERONAUTICS AND SPACE FLIGHT

629.1   UN   ISSN 0074-2570
INTERNATIONAL CIVIL AVIATION ORGANIZATION. TECHNICAL PANEL ON SUPERSONIC TRANSPORT. REPORT OF MEETING. (Editions in English, French, Spanish, Russian) irreg., 4th, Montreal, 1973. price varies. International Civil Aviation Organization, 1000 Sherbrooke St. W., Montreal, Que. H3A 2R2, Canada.

629.1   UN   ISSN 0074-2589
INTERNATIONAL CIVIL AVIATION ORGANIZATION. VISUAL AIDS PANEL. REPORT OF MEETING. (Editions in English, French, Spanish) irreg., 9th, Montreal, 1980. price varies. International Civil Aviation Organization, 1000 Sherbrooke St. W., Montreal, Que. H3A 2R2, Canada.

INTERNATIONAL CONFERENCE ON AEROSPACE COMPUTERS IN ROCKETS AND SPACECRAFT. PROCEEDINGS. see *AERONAUTICS AND SPACE FLIGHT — Computer Applications*

INTERNATIONAL CONFERENCE ON THE ENVIRONMENTAL IMPACT OF AEROSPACE OPERATIONS IN THE HIGH ATMOSPHERE. (PROCEEDINGS) see *ENVIRONMENTAL STUDIES*

629.1   US   ISSN 0730-2010
INTERNATIONAL CONGRESS ON INSTRUMENTATION IN AEROSPACE SIMULATION FACILITIES. RECORD. 1964. biennial. price varies. (I E E E, Aerospace and Electronic Systems Society) Institute of Electrical and Electronics Engineers, Inc., 345 E. 47th St., New York, NY 10017 TEL 212-705-7900. (Subscr. address: 445 Hoes Lane, Piscataway, NJ 08854) Key Title: I C I A S F Record.
    Formerly (1964-1966): International Congress on Instrumentation in Aerospace Simulation Facilities. Proceedings (ISSN 0730-1790)

629.1   US
INTERNATIONAL FLIGHT INFORMATION MANUAL. a. with q. supplements. $27. U.S. Federal Aviation Administration, 800 Independence Ave., S.W., Washington, DC 20591 TEL 202-655-4000. (Orders to: Supt. of Documents, Washington, DC 20402)

INTERNATIONAL RADAR CONFERENCE. RECORD. see *COMMUNICATIONS*

629.13   GW   ISSN 0579-6938
INTERNATIONALER WELTKONGRESS DER U F O-FORSCHER. DOKUMENTARBERICHT.* a. Ventla-Verlag, Postfach 17185, 62 Wiesbaden, West Germany (B.R.D.)

629.13   IS   ISSN 0075-0972
ISRAEL ANNUAL CONFERENCE ON AVIATION AND ASTRONAUTICS. PROCEEDINGS. 1958. a. $45. Technion - Israel Institute of Technology, Department of Aeronautical Engineering, Liryat Hatechnion, Haifa 32 000, Israel. TEL 04-292260. Indexed: Appl.Mech.Rev.

JANE'S AIRPORT EQUIPMENT. see *TRANSPORTATION — Air Transport*

629.133   UK   ISSN 0075-3017
JANE'S ALL THE WORLD AIRCRAFT. 1909. a. £60($141.50) Jane's Publishing Co., 238 City Rd., London E.C.1, England (U.S. subscr. to: 20 Park Plaza, Boston, MA 02116) Ed. John W.R. Taylor. adv. index.

629.1   UK
JANE'S AVIATION REVIEW. 1981. a. Jane's Publishing Co., 238 City Rd., London E.C.1., England. Ed. Michael J.H. Taylor. charts. illus.
    Formerly: Jane's Aviation Annual.

629.1   UK
JANE'S AVIONICS. 1982. a. $100. Jane's Publishing Co., 238 City Rd., London E.C.1, England (Subscr.to: Jane's Publishing Inc., 20 Park Plaza, Boston, MA 02116) Ed. Michael Wilson. adv. index.

629.1   UK
JANE'S SPACEFLIGHT DIRECTORY. a. $120. Jane's Publishing Co. Ltd., 238 City Rd., London EC1V 2PU, England (Subscr. to: 20 Park Plaza, Boston, MA 02116) Ed. Reginald Turnill.

JAPAN AVIATION DIRECTORY. see *BUSINESS AND ECONOMICS — Trade And Industrial Directories*

JORNADAS NACIONALES DE DERECHO AERONAUTICO Y ESPACIAL. TRABAJOS. see *TRANSPORTATION — Air Transport*

001.94   US
JOURNAL OF U F O STUDIES. irreg. $7.50. Center for U F O Studies, 1955 John's Drive, Glenview, IL 60025. TEL 312-724-2480. bibl. illus.

629.13   SW   ISSN 0280-1078
KUNGLIGA TEKNISKA HOEGSKOLAN. FLYGTEKNISK INSTITUTIONEN. K T H AERO MEMO F I. (Text in English, Swedish) 1948. irreg. Kungliga Tekniska Hoegskolan, Institutionen foer Flygteknik - Royal Institute of Technology, Division of Aeronautics, S-100 44 Stockholm, Sweden. circ. 35.

629.13   US   ISSN 0024-5704
LOCKHEED ORION SERVICE DIGEST. 1962. irreg., no.40, 1982. free. ‡ Lockheed-California Co., Burbank, CA 91510. TEL 818-847-6121. Ed. Wayne Cradduck. charts. illus. circ. 6,000(controlled)

629.1   DK   ISSN 0108-4550
LUFT OG RUMFARTSAARBOGEN. 1982. a. Kr.164. Luft og Rumfartsforlaget, Aeblevadsvej 5, 5883 Oure, Denmark (Orders to: Danske Boghendleres Kommissionsanstalt, Siljaugade 6, 2300 Copenhagen S, Denmark) Ed. B. Aalbaek-Nielsen. illus. circ. 3,000.

629.1   GW
M B B INTERNATIONAL; a paper for Messerschmitt-Boelkow-Blohm GmbH staff and friends. (Text in English) a. free to qualified personnel. Messerschmitt-Boelkow-Blohm GmbH, Postfach 801109, 8000 Munich 80, W. Germany (B.R.D.) Ed. Alfred Beck. illus.

MANAGEMENT (BALTIMORE); a bibliography for N A S A managers. see *BUSINESS AND ECONOMICS — Management*

629.1   US
MASSACHUSETTS INSTITUTE OF TECHNOLOGY. FLIGHT TRANSPORTATION LABORATORY. F T L REPORTS AND MEMORANDA. 1966. irreg. price varies. Massachusetts Institute of Technology, Department of Aeronautics & Astronautics, Rm. 33-412, Flight Transportation Lab, Cambridge, MA 02139. Dir. Robert W. Simpson. charts. illus.
    Formerly: Massachusetts Institute of Technology. Flight Transportation Laboratory. F T L Reports.

MILITARY AIRCRAFT MARKINGS. see *MILITARY*

001.94   US
MUFON U F O SYMPOSIUM PROCEEDINGS. 1971. a. $10. Mutual U F O Network, Inc., 103 Oldtowne Rd., Seguin, TX 78155-4099. TEL 512-379-9216. Eds. Walter H. Andrus, Jr., Richard H. Hall. circ. 1,000.
    Unidentified flying objects

629.13   US   ISSN 0077-3093
N A S A FACTS. irreg. U.S. National Aeronautics and Space Administration, Washington, DC 20546 TEL 202-755-2320. (Orders to: Supt. of Documents, Washington, DC 20402)

629.13   US   ISSN 0077-2623
N A S A - UNIVERSITY CONFERENCE ON MANUAL CONTROL (PAPERS) 1965. a. $3. U.S. National Aeronautics and Space Administration, 600 Maryland Ave. S.W., Washington, DC 20546 TEL 202-755-2320. (Order from: National Technical Information Service, Springfield, VA 22161)

629.13   II   ISSN 0077-2976
NATIONAL AERONAUTICAL LABORATORY. ANNUAL REPORT. (Text in English) 1960/61. a. exchange basis. National Aeronautical Laboratory, Box 1779 Kodihalli, Bangalore 560017, India. (Affiliate: Council of Scientific and Industrial Research) circ. 500.

629.1   II
NATIONAL AERONAUTICAL LABORATORY. CASE STUDIES. 1980. irreg. exchange basis. National Aeronautical Laboratory, Box 1779, Kodihalli, Bangalore 560017, India. circ. 100.

629.1 011   II
NATIONAL AERONAUTICAL LABORATORY. SELECTED ABSTRACTS FROM RUSSIAN AND OTHER FOREIGN SCIENTIFIC LITERATURE. 1978. q. exchange basis. National Aeronautical Laboratory, Box 1779, Kodihalli, Bangalore 560017, India.

629.13   II   ISSN 0077-300X
NATIONAL AERONAUTICAL LABORATORY. TECHNICAL NOTE. (Text in English) 1960. irreg., latest issue 1978. exchange basis. National Aeronautical Laboratory, Box 1779, Kodihalli, Bangalore 560017, India. (Affiliate: Council of Scientific and Industrial Research) circ. 500. Indexed: Appl.Mech.Rev.

629.13   US   ISSN 0499-9320
NATIONAL AERONAUTICS AND SPACE ADMINISTRATION. TECHNICAL MEMORANDUM. irreg. U.S. National Aeronautics and Space Administration, Scientific and Technical Information Facility, Box 8757, Baltimore/Washington International Airport, MD 21240 TEL 301-621-0153. (Order from: N T I S, Springfield, VA 22161) (also avail. in microfiche) Indexed: Biol.Abstr. GeoRef. Key Title: N A S A Technical Memorandum.

629.13   US   ISSN 0077-3131
NATIONAL AERONAUTICS AND SPACE ADMINISTRATION. TECHNICAL NOTES. irreg. U.S. National Aeronautics and Space Administration, Scientific and Technical Information Facility, Box 8757, Baltimore-Washington International Airport, MD 21240 TEL 301-621-0153. (Order from: National Technical Information Service, Springfield, VA 22161) Indexed: Appl.Mech.Rev. Biol.Abstr.

629.13   US   ISSN 0077-314X
NATIONAL AERONAUTICS AND SPACE ADMINISTRATION. TECHNICAL REPORTS. irreg. U.S. National Aeronautics and Space Administration, Scientific and Technical Information Facility, Box 8757, Baltimore-Washington International Airport, MD 21240 TEL 301-621-0153. (Orders to: Supt. of Documents, Washington, DC 20402) Indexed: Appl.Mech.Rev. Biol.Abstr.

629.13   US   ISSN 0077-3158
NATIONAL AERONAUTICS AND SPACE ADMINISTRATION. TECHNICAL TRANSLATIONS. irreg. U.S. National Aeronautics and Space Administration, Scientific and Technical Information Facility, Box 8757, Baltimore-Washington International Airport, MD 21240 TEL 301-621-0153. (Order from: National Technical Information Service, 5285 Port Royal Rd., Springfield, VA 22151) (also avail. in microfiche) Indexed: Appl.Mech.Rev. Biol.Abstr.

629.13   CN   ISSN 0077-5541
NATIONAL RESEARCH COUNCIL, CANADA. NATIONAL AERONAUTICAL ESTABLISHMENT. AERONAUTICAL REPORT (L R SERIES) 1951. irreg. free. National Research Council of Canada, N A E Publications Section, Ottawa K1A 0R6, Canada. TEL 613-993-2413. circ. 750. Indexed: Appl.Mech.Rev. Eng.Ind.

NATIONAL RESEARCH COUNCIL, CANADA. NATIONAL AERONAUTICAL ESTABLISHMENT. MECHANICAL ENGINEERING REPORTS. see *ENGINEERING — Mechanical Engineering*

629.13   FR   ISSN 0550-8452
NORTH ATLANTIC TREATY ORGANIZATION. ADVISORY GROUP FOR AEROSPACE RESEARCH AND DEVELOPMENT. A G A R D ANNUAL MEETING.* a. Advisory Group for Aerospace Research and Development, 7, rue Ancelle, 92 Neuilly-sur-Seine, France.

AERONAUTICS AND SPACE FLIGHT

629.13   FR   ISSN 0549-7191
NORTH ATLANTIC TREATY ORGANIZATION. ADVISORY GROUP FOR AEROSPACE RESEARCH AND DEVELOPMENT. A G A R D CONFERENCE PROCEEDINGS.* (Issued by the avionics panel) irreg. Advisory Group for Aerospace Research and Development, 7, rue Ancelle, 92 Neuilly-sur-Seine, France.

629.13   614.7   US   ISSN 0887-4301
NORTHROP UNIVERSITY LAW JOURNAL OF AEROSPACE, BUSINESS AND TAXATION. 1979. a. $6. Northrop University, School of Law, 5800 W. Arbor Vitae St., Los Angeles, CA 90045. adv. bk. rev. circ. 250. Indexed: Leg.Per. C.L.I. L.R.I.
     Formerly (until vol.5 1985): Northrop University Law Journal of Aerospace, Energy and the Enviornment (ISSN 0196-1489)

001.94   UK   ISSN 0262-7795
O S E A P CENTRE UPDATE. 1982. irreg. £5 (joint subscr. with O S E A P Journal) Organisation for Scientific Evaluation of Aerial Phenomena, 2 Acer Ave., Crewe, Cheshire, England. Ed. David L. Rees. bk. rev. circ. 135.
     Unidentified flying objects

001.94   UK   ISSN 0262-5954
O S E A P JOURNAL. 1982. irreg. £5 (joint subscr. with O S E A P Centre Update) Organisation for Scientific Evaluation of Aerial Phenomena, 2 Acer Ave., Crewe, Cheshire, England. Ed. Mark A. Tyrrell. circ. 135.
     Unidentified flying objects

629.13   US   ISSN 0092-3591
OVERVIEW OF THE F A A ENGINEERING & DEVELOPMENT PROGRAMS. (Subseries of its Report no. FAA-EM) 1974. irreg., latest 1975. free to qualified personnel. U.S. Federal Aviation Administration, 800 Independence Ave., S.W., Washington, DC 20591. TEL 202-655-4000. Ed. Eugene Rehrig. illus.

629.1   AT   ISSN 0156-3726
PACIFIC AVIATION YEARBOOK. 1979. a. Aus.$75. Peter Isaacson Publications, 45-50 Porter St., Prahran, Vic. 3181, Australia. adv.

629.4   US
PROCEEDINGS ON NONDESTRUCTIVE EVALUATION. 1974. biennial. price varies. Nondestructive Testing Information Analysis Center, Box 28510, San Antonio, TX 78284. TEL 512-522-2362. (Co-sponsor: South Texas Section, ASNT) Ed. D.W. Moore, G.A. Matzkanin. circ. 500.
     Former titles (before 15th): Symposium on Nondestructive Evaluation of Components and Materials in Aerospace, Weapons Systems and Nuclear Applications (ISSN 0082-0857); (1st through 4th): Symposium on Nondestructive Testing of Aircraft and Missile Components (ISSN 0082-0865)

629.1   US   ISSN 0376-0421
PROGRESS IN AEROSPACE SCIENCES. (Text in English, French and German) 1961. 4/yr. $135 (annual bound volume $132) Pergamon Press, Inc., Journals Division, Maxwell House, Fairview Park, Elmsford, NY 10523 TEL 914-592-7700. (And Headington Hill Hall, Oxford OX3 0BW, England) Ed. J.P. Finley. (also avail. in microform from MIM,UMI) Indexed: Sci.Abstr. Int.Aerosp.Abstr.
     Formerly: Progress in Aeronautical Sciences (ISSN 0079-6026)

629.13   629.4   US   ISSN 0079-6050
PROGRESS IN ASTRONAUTICS AND AERONAUTICS SERIES. (Vols. 1-8 published as Progress in Astronautics and Rocketry. Vols. 1-23 published by Academic Press) 1968. irreg., latest issue vol.108. American Institute of Aeronautics and Astronautics, 1633 Broadway, New York, NY 10019. TEL 212-581-4300. Indexed: Chem.Abstr. Int.Aerosp.Abstr.

R E M E JOURNAL. (Royal Electrical & Mechanical Engineers) see *ENGINEERING — Mechanical Engineering*

RADIO TECHNICAL COMMISSION FOR AERONAUTICS. PROCEEDINGS OF THE ANNUAL ASSEMBLY MEETING. see *COMMUNICATIONS — Radio And Television*

629   GW
REUSS JAHRBUCH DER LUFT- UND RAUMFAHRT. 1951. a. DM.59.50. Suedwestdeutsche Verlagsanstalt GmbH, Am Marktplatz, Postfach 5760, 6800 Mannheim 1, W. Germany (B.R.D.) Ed. Tilman Reuss. adv. bk. rev. index.
     Formerly: Jahrbuch der Luftfahrt und Raumfahrt (ISSN 0075-269X)

ROYAL AUSTRALIAN AIR FORCE ACADEMY JOURNAL. see *MILITARY*

629.1   SW   ISSN 0080-5149
SAAB TECHNICAL NOTES. (Text in English) 1950. irreg. available on exchange. Saab-Scania, Aerospace Division, S-581 88 Linkoeping, Sweden. Ed. O. Holme. circ. 600. Indexed: Appl.Mech.Rev.
     Formerly: Saab-Scania Technical Notes.

629.13   US   ISSN 0278-4017
SCIENCE AND TECHNOLOGY SERIES. Issued also as: Advances in the Astronautical Sciences. Supplement. (Contains several sub-series: European Space Symposium; Space Safety and Rescue; Goddard Memorial Symposia) 1964. irreg., vol.62, 1985. price varies per vol. (American Astronautical Society, Inc.) Univelt, Inc., Box 28130, San Diego, CA 92128. TEL 619-746-4005. Ed. Horace Jacobs. bibl. charts. illus. circ. 1,250. (back issues avail.) Indexed: Biol.Abstr. Chem.Abstr. Curr.Cont. Eng.Ind. Sci.Abstr. Int.Aerosp.Abstr. INSPEC.
     Formerly: Science and Technology (San Diego) (ISSN 0080-7451)

001.94   DK
SKANDINAVISK U F O INFORMATION. NEWSLETTER. (Text in English) irreg. Skandinavisk U F O Information, Box 6, 2820 Gentofte, Denmark.
     Unidentified flying objects

629.13   US
SMITHSONIAN STUDIES IN AIR AND SPACE. 1977. irreg., no.6, 1985. Smithsonian Institution Press, 955 L'Enfant Plaza, Rm. 2100, Washington, DC 20560. TEL 202-287-3738. Ed. Barbara T. Spann. circ. 1,600. (reprint service avail. from UMI) Indexed: GeoRef.

629.1   US
SOCIETY OF FLIGHT TEST ENGINEERS. ANNUAL SYMPOSIUM PROCEEDINGS. vol.4, 1973. a. $35. Society of Flight Test Engineers, Box 4047, Lancaster, CA 93539. TEL 805-948-3067. illus.

629.1   US
SPACE BENEFITS: SECONDARY APPLICATION OF AEROSPACE TECHNOLOGY IN OTHER SECTORS OF THE ECONOMY. a. U.S. National Aeronautics and Space Administration, Washington, DC 20546. TEL 202-755-2320.

629.4   JA
SPACE IN JAPAN. biennial. 1500 Yen. Science and Technology Agency - Nihon Kagaku Gijutsucho, 2-2-1 Kasumigaseki, Chiyoda-ku, Tokyo 100, Japan (Subscr. to: Keidanren (Federation of Economic Organizations), 1-9-4 Otemachi, Chiyoda-ku , Tokyo 100, Japan) illus.

629.1   NO
SPACE RESEARCH IN NORWAY. (Text in English) 1963. a. free. Norwegian Space Center, P.O. Box 85, Smestad, N-0309 Oslo 3, Norway. Ed. Arne Gundersen. bk. rev. illus. circ. 1,100.
     Former titles: Space Activity in Norway; Norway. Komite for Romforskning. N.S.R.C. Report (ISSN 0452-3687)

SURINAM. CENTRAAL BUREAU LUCHTKARTERING. JAARVERSLAG. see *GEOGRAPHY*

001.94   CN   ISSN 0707-7106
SWAMP GAS JOURNAL. 1978. irreg. free contr. circ. Ufology Research of Manitoba, Box 1918, Winnipeg General Post Office, Winnipeg, Man. R3C 3R2, Canada. Ed. C. Rutkowski. bk. rev. circ. 250.
     Unidentified flying objects

629.13   IS   ISSN 0072-9302
T.A.E. REPORT. (Text in English) 1959. irreg. $10. Technion - Israel Institute of Technology, Department of Aeronautical Engineering, Haifa, Israel. TEL 04-292260. Indexed: Appl.Mech.Rev.

629.132   CN   ISSN 0316-2494
TAILSPINNER. 1972. irreg. Waterloo-Wellington Flying Club, Breslau, Ont., Canada.
     Formerly: Talespinner (ISSN 0316-2540)

629.132   CN
TOWLINE. irreg. (approx. 10/yr.) membership. Edmonton Soaring Club, Box 472, Edmonton, Alta. T5J 2K3, Canada. Ed. Paul Ravelle. circ. 100.

001.94   DK   ISSN 0109-2596
U F O FORSKNING. (Unidentified Flying Objects) 1983. irreg., 2-3/yr. Kr.28 per no. Skandinavisk UFO Information, Postbox 6, 2820 Gentofte, Denmark. Ed. Lars K. Lassen. adv. bk. rev. illus. circ. 200.

U S S R REPORT: SPACE BIOLOGY AND AEROSPACE MEDICINE. see *MEDICAL SCIENCES*

629.1   US
U.S. AERONAUTICAL INFORMATION PUBLICATION. Short title: U.S. A I P. biennial with q. amendments. $70. U.S. Federal Aviation Administration, 800 Independence Ave., S.W., Washington, DC 20591 TEL 202-655-4000. (Orders to: Supt. of Documents, Washington, DC 20402) (also avail. in looseleaf format)

U.S. NATIONAL AERONAUTICS AND SPACE ADMINISTRATION. EARTH RESOURCES LABORATORY. RESEARCH AND TECHNOLOGY. ANNUAL REPORT. see *EARTH SCIENCES*

629.13   600   US
U.S. NATIONAL AERONAUTICS AND SPACE ADMINISTRATION. RESEARCH AND TECHNOLOGY OPERATING PLAN (RTOP) SUMMARY. 1970. a. U.S. National Aeronautics and Space Administration, Scientific and Technical Information Facility, Box 8757, Baltimore-Washington International Airport, MD 21240. TEL 301-621-0153. circ. 600(controlled)
     Supersedes: U.S. National Aeronautics and Space Administration. Research and Technology Program Digest. Flash Index (ISSN 0077-3115)

629.4   629.13   JA   ISSN 0082-4828
UNIVERSITY OF TOKYO. INSTITUTE OF SPACE AND AERONAUTICAL SCIENCE. REPORT. (Text and summaries in English) 1964. irreg., vol.35, 1970. University of Tokyo, Institute of Space and Aeronautical Science - Tokyo Daigaku Uchu Koku Kenkyusho, 4-6-1 Komaba, Meguro-ku, Tokyo 153, Japan. Ed. Eiji Niki. index. Indexed: Sci.Abstr.

629.1388   CN   ISSN 0082-5239
UNIVERSITY OF TORONTO. INSTITUTE FOR AEROSPACE STUDIES. PROGRESS REPORT. 1952. a. available on exchange. University of Toronto, Institute for Aerospace Studies, 4925 Dufferin St., Downsview, Ont. M3H 5T6, Canada. TEL 416-667-7723. circ. 450.

629.1   CN   ISSN 0082-5255
UNIVERSITY OF TORONTO. INSTITUTE FOR AEROSPACE STUDIES. REPORT. Variant title: U T I A S Report. 1948. irreg. exchange basis. University of Toronto, Institute for Aerospace Studies, 4925 Dufferin St., Downsview, Ont. M3H 5T6, Canada. TEL 416-667-7723. circ. 450.

629.1388   CN   ISSN 0082-5247
UNIVERSITY OF TORONTO. INSTITUTE FOR AEROSPACE STUDIES. REVIEW. 1950. irreg. available on exchange. University of Toronto, Institute for Aerospace Studies, 4925 Dufferin St., Downsview, Ont. M3H 5T6 Canada. TEL 416-667-7723. circ. 450. (back issues avail.)

629.1   CN   ISSN 0082-5263
UNIVERSITY OF TORONTO. INSTITUTE FOR AEROSPACE STUDIES. TECHNICAL NOTE. Variant title: U T I A S Technical Note. 1954. irreg. available on exchange. University of Toronto, Institute for Aerospace Studies, 4925 Dufferin St., Downsview, Ontario M3H 5T6, Canada. TEL 416-667-7723. circ. 450. (back issues avail.)

629.1   627   BE
VON KARMAN INSTITUTE FOR FLUID DYNAMICS. LECTURE SERIES. 1968. irreg. 6.200 Fr. Von Karman Institute for Fluid Dynamics - Institut von Karman de Dynamique des Fluides, Chaussee de Waterloo 72, B-1640 Rhode Saint Genese, Belgium. Ed. N.V. Toubeau.

AERONAUTICS AND SPACE FLIGHT — ABSTRACTING, BIBLIOGRAPHIES, STATISTICS

629.1 NZ
WHITES AIR DIRECTORY & WHO'S WHO IN NEW ZEALAND AVIATION. (Including the South Pacific) 1947. a. NZ.$25. Modern Productions Ltd., P.O. Box 2040, Auckland 1, New Zealand. Ed. S.C. Niblock. adv. circ. 950.

629.1 FR
WORLD AERONAUTICAL RECORDS. (Text in English and French) 1920. a. 500 F. (for 5 years) International Aeronautic Federation, 6 rue Galilee, 75782 Paris, France. circ. 1,000.
Formerly: International Aeronautic Federation. Latest World Records.

629.13 GW ISSN 0065-2024
ZUERL'S ADRESSBUCH DER DEUTSCHEN LUFT- UND RAUMFAHRT. 1950. a. DM.64. Luftfahrt-Verlag Walter Zuerl, Amselweg 6, 8031 Woerthsee-Steinebach, W. Germany (B.R.D.) Ed. Walter Zuerl. adv. bk. rev. circ. 3,000.

AERONAUTICS AND SPACE FLIGHT — Abstracting, Bibliographies, Statistics

629.13 US
AEROSPACE FACTS AND FIGURES. 1945. a. $10.95. (Aerospace Industries Association) McGraw-Hill Publishing Co., 1221 Ave. of the Americas, New York, NY 10020. Ed. Janet Ferguson. charts. stat.

629.1 FJ
FIJI. BUREAU OF STATISTICS. AIRCRAFT STATISTICS. a. $1. Bureau of Statistics, Box 2221, Suva, Fiji.

629.13 016 JA ISSN 0454-191X
FOREIGN AERO-SPACE LITERATURE/ GAIKOKU KOKU UCHU BUNKEN MOKUROKU. (Text in Japanese and English) 1962. a. 5200 Yen. National Diet Library - Kokuritsu Kokkai Toshokan, 1-10-1 Nagata-cho, Chiyoda-ku, Tokyo 100, Japan.

387.7 FR
FRANCE. DIRECTION GENERALE DE L'AVIATION CIVILE. BULLETIN STATISTIQUE. 1960. a. free. Direction Generale de l'Aviation Civile, Service des Transports Aeriens, 39 rue Washington, 75008 Paris, France. circ. 600.

629.13 016 US ISSN 0020-5842
INTERNATIONAL AEROSPACE ABSTRACTS. 1961. s-m. $950 contr. circ. American Institute of Aeronautics and Astronautics, Technical Information Service, 555 W. 57th St., Ste. 1200, New York, NY 10019. TEL 212-247-6500. Ed. Irene W. Bogolubsky. abstr. index. circ. 875. (also avail. in magnetic tape; back issues avail.)
●Also available online. Vendors: DIALOG, European Space Agency, Mead Data Central.

INTERNATIONAL CIVIL AVIATION ORGANIZATION. INDEXES TO I C A O PUBLICATIONS. ANNUAL CUMULATION. see TRANSPORTATION — Abstracting, Bibliographies, Statistics

629.1 016 CN ISSN 0077-5568
NATIONAL RESEARCH COUNCIL, CANADA. NATIONAL AERONAUTICAL ESTABLISHMENT. PUBLICATIONS LIST AND SUPPLEMENTS. 1965. irreg. free. National Research Council of Canada, N A E - Publications Section, Ottawa, Ont. K1A 0R6, Canada. TEL 613-993-2413. circ. 1,800. Indexed: Excerp.Med. GeoRef.

387.7 NZ ISSN 0467-8966
NEW ZEALAND CIVIL AVIATION STATISTICS. 1958. a. free. (Ministry of Transport, Civil Aviation Division) New Zealand Government Printer, Private Bag, Wellington, New Zealand. Ed.Bd. stat. circ. 2,000.

REFERATIVNYI ZHURNAL. ISSLEDOVANIE KOSMICHESKOGO PROSTRANSTVA. see ASTRONOMY — Abstracting, Bibliographies, Statistics

AERONAUTICS AND SPACE FLIGHT — Computer Applications

621.381 FR
INTERNATIONAL CONFERENCE ON AEROSPACE COMPUTERS IN ROCKETS AND SPACECRAFT. PROCEEDINGS.* 1969. irreg., 1st, Paris, 1968. $15. Imprimerie des Grandchamps, 161 boulevard Brune, 75 Paris 14, France.

AGRICULTURAL ECONOMICS

see Agriculture—Agricultural Economics

AGRICULTURAL EQUIPMENT

see Agriculture—Agricultural Equipment

AGRICULTURE

see also Agriculture—Agricultural Economics; Agriculture—Agricultural Equipment; Agriculture—Computer Applications; Agriculture—Crop Production and Soil; Agriculture—Dairying and Dairy Products; Agriculture—Feed, Flour and Grain; Agriculture—Poultry and Livestock; Food and Food Industries; Forests and Forestry; Gardening and Horticulture

A A G BIJDRAGEN. (Afdeling Agrarische Geschiedenis) see HISTORY — History Of Europe

630 580 US
A L P R NEWS. a. free. (Association for Arid Lands Studies) International Center for Arid and Semi-Arid Land Studies, Texas Tech University, Box 4620 Tech Sta., Lubbock, TX 79409-4620. Eds. Nancy Hood, J.R. Goodin.

630 ET
A R D U PUBLICATION. 1966. irreg. price varies. Arussi Rural Development Unit, Box 3376, Addis Ababa, Ethiopia. charts. cum.index.
Supersedes: C A D U Publications (ISSN 0069-3405)

630 US ISSN 0066-0566
A S A SPECIAL PUBLICATION. 1963. irreg., no.43, 1982. American Society of Agronomy, Inc., 677 S. Segoe Rd., Madison, WI 53711. TEL 608-274-1212. Indexed: Biol.Abstr. GeoRef. Soils & Fert.

630 DK ISSN 0107-0304
AARSSKRIFT FOR TOENDER LANDBRUGSSKOLE. 1979. a. Kr.50. Toender Landbrugsskole, Vestre Omfartsvej, 6270 Toender, Denmark. illus.

630 634 RM
ACADEMIA DE STIINTE AGRICOLE SI SILVICE. BULLETIN. (Text in French) 1970. a. exchange basis. Academia de Stiinte Agricole si Silvice, Bd. Marasti Nr.61, Bucharest 71331, Rumania. Ed. Ileana Muresan.

ACCADEMIA DELLE SCIENZE DI SIENA DETTA DE FISIOCRITICI. ATTI. see MEDICAL SCIENCES

630 PL ISSN 0860-2832
ACTA ACADEMIAE AGRICULTURAE AC TECHNICAE OLSTENENSIS. AGRICULTURA/ AGRICULTURE. 1956. irreg. price varies. Akademia Rolniczo-Techniczna, Blok 21, 10-718 Olsztyn-Kortowo, Poland (Dist. by: Ars Polona-Ruch, Krakowskie Przedmiescie 7, Warsaw, Poland) Ed.Bd. Indexed: Geo.Abstr.
Former titles: Akademia Rolniczo-Techniczna. Agriculture; Aademia Rolniczo-Techniczna. Zeszyty Naukowe (ISSN 0324-9204); Wyzsza Szkola Rolnicza, Olsztyn. Zeszyty Naukowe (ISSN 0078-4583)

630 PL ISSN 0860-262X
ACTA ACADEMIAE AGRICULTURAE AC TECHNICAE OLSTENENSIS. GEODAESIA ET RURIS REGULATIO/GEODESY AND AGRICULTURAL ARRANGEMENT. (Subseries of Its: Zeszyty Naukowe) (Text in Polish; summaries in English and Russian) 1968. irreg. price varies. Akademia Rolniczo-Techniczna, Blok 21, 10-718 Olsztyn-Kortowo, Poland (Dist. by: Ars Polona-Ruch, Krakowskie Przedmiescie 7, 00-901 Warsaw, Poland) Ed.Bd. illus.
Formerly: Geodezja i Urzadzenia Rolne (ISSN 0324-9174)

ACTA AGROBOTANICA. see BIOLOGY — Botany

630 CS
ACTA MUSEORUM AGRICULTURAE. (Text in English, German, French, Russian) irreg. Ustav Vedeckotechnickych Informaci, Ceskoslovenska Akademie Zemedelska, Slezska 7, 120 56 Prague 1, Czechoslovakia. (Co-sponsor: International Association of Museums of Agriculture)

630 US ISSN 0172-4207
ADVANCED SERIES IN AGRICULTURAL SCIENCES. 1975. irreg., vol.16, 1987. price varies. Springer-Verlag, 175 Fifth Ave., New York, NY 10010 TEL 212-460-1500. (Also Berlin, Heidelberg, Tokyo and Vienna) Ed.Bd. (reprint service avail. from ISI) Indexed: Biol.Abstr.

630 US ISSN 0065-2113
ADVANCES IN AGRONOMY. 1949. irreg., vol.38, 1986. (American Society for Agronomy, Inc.) Academic Press, Inc., Orlando, FL 32887. TEL 305-345-2000. Ed. N.C. Brady. Indexed: Biol.Abstr. Biol.& Agr.Ind. Chem.Abstr. Sci.Cit.Ind. Field Crop.Abstr. GeoRef. Herb.Abstr. Hort.Abstr. Ind.Sci.Rev. Plant Breed.Abstr. Rev.Plant Path. Soils & Fert. Weed Abstr.

630 572 JA ISSN 0285-1601
AFRICAN STUDY MONOGRAPHS. (Text and summaries in English) 1981. a. Kyoto University, Center for African Area, 46 Shimoadachi-Cho, Yoshida, Sakyo, Kyoto 606, Japan. Ed.Bd. circ. 1,200. (back issues avail.)

630 572 JA ISSN 0286-9667
AFRICAN STUDY MONOGRAPHS. SUPPLEMENTARY ISSUE. irreg. Kyoto University, Center for African Area, 46 Shimoadachi-Cho, Yoshida, Sakyo, Kyoto 606, Japan.

636.2 BL
AGENDA DOS CRIADORES E AGRICULTORES. 1976. a. $25. Editora dos Criadores Ltda., Rua Venancio Aires, 31, 05024 Sao Paulo, SP, Brazil. Ed. Luiz de Almeida Penna. adv. charts. illus. stat. mkt. circ. 10,000.
Cattle

AGLINK INDEX AND CATALOGUE. see AGRICULTURE — Abstracting, Bibliographies, Statistics

630 581 NZ
AGLINK LEAFLETS. 1974. irreg. NZ.$25 per no. Ministry of Agriculture and Fisheries, Information Services, Private Bag, Wellington, New Zealand. Ed. B. Greenfield. Indexed: Sel.Water Res.Abstr.
Formed by the merger of: New Zealand Agriculture & Agricultural Science and Technology & Farm Production and Practice & Horticultural Produce and Practice.

AGRARSOZIALE GESELLSCHAFT. GESCHAEFTS- UND ARBEITSBERICHT. see SOCIOLOGY

AGRARSOZIALE GESELLSCHAFT. KLEINE REIHE. see SOCIOLOGY

AGRARSOZIALE GESELLSCHAFT.
MATERIALSAMMLUNG. see *SOCIOLOGY*

630   CN
AGRI-BOOK MAGAZINE. CORN IN CANADA.
1975. a. Can.$5. A I S Communications Ltd., Box
1060, 145 Thames Rd. W., Exeter, Ont. N0M 1S0,
Canada. TEL 519-235-2400. Ed. Peter Lewington.
adv. circ. 30,680. (back issues avail.)

630   CN
AGRI-BOOK MAGAZINE. POTATOES IN
CANADA. 1981. a. Can.$5. A I S Communications
Ltd., Box 1060, 145 Thames Rd. W., Exeter, Ont.
N0M 1S0, Canada. TEL 519-235-0400. Ed. Elinor
Humphries. adv. circ. 4,324. (back issues avail.)

630   CN
AGRI-BOOK MAGAZINE. SEED IN CANADA.
1984. a. Can.$5. A I S Communications Ltd., Box
1060, 145 Thames Rd. W., Exeter, Ont. N0M 1S0.
TEL 519-235-2400. Ed. Peter Darbishire. adv. circ.
7,684. (back issues avail.)

630   IT
AGRICOLTORE VERONESE. a. Unione Provinciale
Agricoltori di Verona, Via Locatelli 3, 37100
Verona, Italy.

630   SP
AGRICULTURA ESPANOLA EN (YEAR)
(Supplement to - Panorama de Agricultura en (year))
a. Ministerio de Agricultura, Secretaria General
Tecnica, Paseo Infante 1, Madrid 7, Spain. illus.
charts. stat.
    Formerly: Agricultura Espanola (ISSN 0065-
440X)

630 639.2   SP
AGRICULTURA, LA PESCA Y LA
ALIMENTACION ESPANOLAS. 1982. a. 1500
ptas. Ministerio de Agricultura, Pesca y
Alimentacion, Secretaria General Tecnica, Paseo de
Infanta Isabel, 1, 28014 Madrid, Spain.

AGRICULTURA Y LA PESCA ESPANOLAS. see
FISH AND FISHERIES

630   KE
AGRICULTURAL DEVELOPMENT
CORPORATION. ANNUAL REPORT. (Text in
English) 1966. a., latest 1981/82. free. Agricultural
Development Corporation, Box 47101,
Development House, Nairobi, Kenya. circ. 500.

630   PK
AGRICULTURAL DEVELOPMENT IN
PAKISTAN. (Text in English) 1967. a. $15. Press
Corporation of Pakistan, 1/6-e, Block 6, P.E.
C.H.S., Karachi 2906, Pakistan. Ed. Saeed Hafeez.
circ. 10,000.

354   MY
AGRICULTURAL DIRECTORY OF MALAYSIA.
(Text in English) 1972. a. M.$10. University of
Malaya, Agricultural Graduates Alumni, c/o Faculty
of Agriculture, Lembah Pantai, Kuala Lumpur 22-
11, Malaysia. illus.

630   AT
AGRICULTURAL LAND BULLETIN. 1983. irreg.
price varies. Department of Agriculture, P.O. Box
K220, Haymarket, N.S.W. 2000, Australia. circ.
500.

630   II
AGRICULTURAL PRICES IN INDIA. (Text in
English) 1957. irreg. Rs.183.70($66.14) Ministry of
Agriculture, Department of Agriculture and
Cooperation, Directorate of Economics and
Statistics, A-2E-3 Kasturba Gandhi Marg Barracks,
New Delhi 110001, India (Order from: Controller
of Publications, Civil Lines, Delhi 110054, India)
Ed. Shandar Dhar Sharma. circ. 550.
    Formerly: All India Report on Agricultural
Census.

630   CY
AGRICULTURAL REGIONS OF CYPRUS. (Text in
English) 1982. irreg. EC$2. Ministry of Finance,
Department of Statistics and Research, Nicosia,
Cyprus.

630   US
AGRICULTURAL RESEARCH CENTER.
PROCEEDINGS OF THE ANNUAL MEETING.
no.37, 1976. a. Agricultural Research Center, Inc.,
1305 E. Main St., Lakeland, FL 33801. TEL 813-
686-1017.

630   UK
AGRICULTURAL RESEARCH CENTRES; a world
directory of organizations and programmes.
triennial. £175. Longman Group Ltd., Fourth Ave.,
Harlow, Essex CM19 5AA, England (Dist. in U.S.
and Canada by: Gale Research Co. Ltd., Book
Tower, Detroit, MI 48226)
    Formerly: Agricultural Research Index (ISSN
0065-4531)

630   GY   ISSN 0065-4523
AGRICULTURAL RESEARCH GUYANA. 1967.
irreg. free. Central Agricultural Station, Research
Division, Mon Repos, E.C. Demerara, Guyana. bk.
rev.

630   IS
AGRICULTURAL RESEARCH ORGANIZATION.
SPECIAL PUBLICATIONS. (Text in English and
Hebrew) 1971. irreg. price varies. (Agricultural
Research Organization) Agricultural Research
Organization (Subsidiary of: Scientific Publications)
Volcani Center, P.O. Box 6, Bet Dagan, Israel.
Indexed: Biol.Abstr.

631   CN   ISSN 0707-7793
AGRICULTURAL SCIENCE BULLETIN. 1964.
irreg. free. University of Saskatchewan, Extension
Division, Saskatoon, Sask. S7N 0W0, Canada. TEL
306-343-2100. Ed. Bert Wolfe Writer. circ. 4,000.
    Former titles: Agricultural Science (ISSN 0381-
5927); Information (ISSN 0381-5919); Supersedes:
Saskatchewan Farm Science (ISSN 0048-9174)

630   NE   ISSN 0169-4901
AGRICULTURAL SCIENCE IN THE
NETHERLANDS. (Text in English) 1953. triennial.
$10. International Agricultural Centre, P.O. Box 88,
6700 A B Wageningen, Netherlands. circ. 5,000.
(tabloid format)

631   AT
AGRICULTURAL SHOWS ANNUAL. 1972. a. free.
Agricultural Societies Council of New South Wales,
Agriculture House, 195 Macquarie St., Sydney,
N.S.W. 2000, Australia. Ed. M. Knowles. adv. circ.
2,000.
    Former titles: Country Shows Annual (ISSN
0311-1946); Country Shows Bulletin.

630   NR   ISSN 0065-454X
AGRICULTURAL SOCIETY OF NIGERIA.
PROCEEDINGS. 1962. a. free. Agricultural Society
of Nigeria, c/o Dr. T. I. Ashaye, P. M. B. 5029,
Ibadan, Nigeria. Ed. Q.B. Anthonio. adv. bk. rev.
circ. 1,000.

630   UK   ISSN 0262-2394
AGRICULTURAL STATISTICS, ENGLAND. 1972.
a. £16.50. H.M.S.O., P.O. Box 569, London SE1
9NH, England. (Co-sponsors: Ministry of
Agriculture, Fisheries and Food; Department of
Agriculture for Scotland; Ministry of Agriculture, N.
Ireland) (reprint service avail. from UMI)
    Supersedes in part: Agricultural Statistics,
England and Wales (ISSN 0065-4558)

630   UK   ISSN 0065-4590
AGRICULTURAL STATISTICS, UNITED
KINGDOM. 1972. a. price varies. H.M.S.O., P.O.
Box 569, London SE1 9NH, England. (Co-sponsor:
Ministry of Agriculture, Fisheries and Food)
(reprint service avail. from UMI)

630   JA   ISSN 0515-8672
AGRICULTURE ASIA/AJIA NOGYO. (Text in
English) 1963. a. 3000 Yen($10) Association of
Agricultural Relations in Asia - Ajia Nogyo Koryu
Konwakai, 5-27-11 Sendagaya, Shibuya-ku, Tokyo
151, Japan. Ed. Shoken Yokoyama. Indexed: Field
Crop Abstr. Herb.Abstr.

630   UK
AGRICULTURE IN SCOTLAND. 1912. a. price
varies. Department of Agriculture and Fisheries,
Chesser House, 500 Gorgie Rd., Edinburgh EH11
3AW, Scotland (Avail. from H.M.S.O., 13a Castle
St., Edinburgh EH2 3AR, Scotland)

630 943.7   CS
AGRIKULTURA. a. (Slovenske Pol'nohospodarske
Muzeum) Priroda, Krizkova 9, 815 34 Bratislava,
Czechoslovakia. cum.index: vol.1-10 (1962-1971)

630   CN   ISSN 0065-4655
AGRO-NOUVELLES. (Text in French) 1965. irreg.
Order of Agrologists of Quebec, 262 Ouest Blvd.
Henri-Bourassa, Montreal, Que. H3L 1N6, Canada.
TEL 514-884-9510.

630   US   ISSN 0002-1822
AGROBOREALIS. 1969. irreg. (1-2/yr.) free.
University of Alaska, Fairbanks, Agricultural and
Forestry Experiment Station, Fairbanks, AK 99701.
TEL 907-474-7188. Ed. Mayo Murray. charts. illus.
stat. circ. 7,500. (also avail. in microfiche) Indexed:
Biol.Abstr. Curr.Cont. Excerp.Med. Nutr.Abstr.
Field Crop Abstr. Forest.Abstr. Forest Prod.Abstr.
Herb.Abstr. Ind.Vet. Vet.Bull.

630 540   UK
AGROCHEMICALS HANDBOOK. 1983. irreg.
(every 3-4 yrs.) £145($275) Royal Society of
Chemistry, The University, Nottingham NG7 2RD,
England. Eds. D. Hartley, H. Kidd. circ. 2,500.
(looseleaf format; also avail. in magnetic tape)

630 580   MZ   ISSN 0044-6858
AGRONOMIA MOCAMBICANA. Represents:
Instituto de Investigacao Agronomica de
Mocambique. Comunicacoes. (Text in Portuguese;
summaries in English and Portuguese) 1967. irreg.
price varies. Instituto de Investigacao Agronomica
de Mocambique, Centro de Documentacao Agraria,
C.P. 3658, Maputo 11, Mozambique. charts. illus.
stat. index. circ. 400-500. Indexed: Biol.Abstr.
Chem.Abstr. GeoRef.

630   US   ISSN 0065-4663
AGRONOMY: A SERIES OF MONOGRAPHS.
1949. irreg., no.23, 1983. price varies. American
Society of Agronomy, Inc., 677 South Segoe Rd.,
Madison, WI 53711. Indexed: Biol.Abstr.
Chem.Abstr.

630   RH
AGRONOMY INSTITUTE. ANNUAL REPORT. a.
free. Ministry of Lands, Agriculture and Rural
Resettlement, Research and Specialist Services,
Information Services, Box 8108, Causeway, Harare,
Zimbabwe. circ. 250. (back issues avail.)

630   NR   ISSN 0065-471X
AHMADU BELLO UNIVERSITY. INSTITUTE FOR
AGRICULTURAL RESEARCH. ANNUAL
REPORT. 1962-1969; Resumed 1980. a. £N3.
Ahmadu Bello University, Institute for Agricultural
Research, P.M.B. 1044, Zaria, Nigeria. Indexed:
Field Crop Abstr. Herb.Abstr. Rev.Plant Path.

630   PL
AKADEMIA ROLNICZA, KRAKOW.
ROLNICTWO. irreg., no. 15, 1975. price varies.
Akademia Rolnicza, Krakow, Al. Mickiewicza 21,
30-120 Krakow, Poland. Indexed: Chem.Abstr.

630   PL   ISSN 0137-1754
AKADEMIA ROLNICZA, POZNAN. ROCZNIKI.
ROLNICTWO. (Text in Polish; summaries in
English and Russian) 1959. irreg. price varies.
Akademia Rolnicza, Poznan, Ul. Wojska Polskiego
28, 60-637 Poznan, Poland. Indexed: Bibl.Agri.

630   PL   ISSN 0208-8436
AKADEMIA ROLNICZA, POZNAN. ROCZNIKI.
ROZPRAWY NAUKOWE. (Text in Polish;
summaries in English and Russian) 1959. irreg. price
varies. Akademia Rolnicza, Poznan, Ul. Wojska
Polskiego 28, 60-637 Poznan, Poland. Indexed:
Bibl.Agri.

630   PL
AKADEMIA ROLNICZA W SZCZECINIE.
INFORMATORY. 1968. irreg., latest 1984. price
varies. Akademia Rolnicza, Janosika 8, 71-424
Szczecin, Poland. Ed. Prof. Mieczyslaw Jasnowski.
bk. rev. Indexed: Chem.Abstr. Nutr.Abstr. Field
Crop Abstr.

630   PL
AKADEMIA ROLNICZA W SZCZECINIE.
ROZPRAWY. 1966. irreg., no.108, 1986. price
varies. Akademia Rolnicza, Janosika 8, 71-424
Szczecin, Poland. Ed. Prof. Mieczyslaw Jasnowski.
bk. rev. Indexed: Chem.Abstr. Nutr.Abstr. Field
Crop Abstr.

AGRICULTURE

630   PL
AKADEMIA ROLNICZA W SZCZECINIE. ZESZYTY NAUKOWE. ROLNICTWO. 1958. irreg., no. 92, 1982. price varies. Akademia Rolnicza, Janosika 8, 71-424 Szczecin, Poland. Ed. Prof. Mieczyslaw Jasnowski. bk. rev. Indexed: Chem.Abstr. Nutr.Abstr. Field Crop Abstr.

630 581   PL
AKADEMIA ROLNICZA W SZCZECINIE. ZESZYTY NAUKOWE. ROLNICTWO. SERIA PRZYRODNICZA. 1977. irreg., no.107, 1984. price varies. Akademia Rolnicza, Janosika 8, 71-424 Szczecin, Poland. Ed. Prof. Mieczyslaw Jasnowski. bk. rev. Indexed: Chem.Abstr. Nutr.Abstr. Field Crop Abstr.

630   PL
AKADEMIA ROLNICZA, WROCLAW. ROLNICTWO. 1955. a. price varies. Akademia Rolnicza, Wroclaw - Section of Publishing and Printing of the Agricultural University, Norwida 25, 50-375 Wroclaw, Poland (Subscr. to: Ars Polona, Krakowskie Przedmiescie 7, 00-068 Warsaw, Poland) circ. 400.
    Formerly: Wyzsza Szkola Rolnicza, Wroclaw. Rolnictwo.

630 634.9 635   US
ALABAMA AGRICULTURAL EXPERIMENT STATION. RESEARCH REPORT SERIES. 1983. irreg., no.4, 1986. Alabama Agricultural Experiment Station, 103 Comer Hall, Auburn University, AL 36849. TEL 205-826-4877. Ed. R.E. Stevenson. circ. 4,000. (back issues avail.)

630   CN
ALBERTA AGRICULTURE. ANNUAL REPORT. 1905. a. free. Department of Agriculture, Printmedia Branch, 7000 113th St., Edmonton, Alta. T6H 5T6, Canada. TEL 403-427-2121. circ. controlled.
    Former titles: Alberta. Department of Agriculture. Annual Report (ISSN 0065-597X); Alberta. Water Resources Division. Annual Report.

630 338.1   US
AMERICAN ASSOCIATION OF NURSERYMEN DIRECTORY FOR THE NURSERY INDUSTRY AND RELATED ASSOCIATIONS. a. $15 to non-members. American Association of Nurserymen, 1250 I St., N.W., Ste. 500, Washington, DC 20005. TEL 202-789-2900. adv. circ. 3,500.
    Former titles: American Association of Nurserymen Membership Directory & Allied Landscape Industry Member Directory (ISSN 0098-793X)

630   PL   ISSN 0365-1118
ANNALES UNIVERSITATIS MARIAE CURIE-SKLODOWSKA. SECTIO E. AGRICULTURA. (Text in English or Polish; summaries in English, French, German and Russian) 1946. a. price varies. Uniwersytet Marii Curie-Sklodowskiej, Plac Marii Curie-Sklodowskiej 5, 20-031 Lublin, Poland. Ed. A. Szember. circ. 650. Indexed: Biol.Abstr. Chem.Abstr. Excerp.Med. Nutr.Abstr. Anim.Breed.Abstr. Field Crop Abstr. Forest.Abstr. Herb.Abstr. Hort.Abstr. Plant Breed.Abstr. Rev.Appl.Entomol. Soils & Fert. Weed Abstr.

630   FR   ISSN 0066-2534
ANNUAIRE DE LA FRANCE RURALE DANS LE MARCHE COMMUN. a., 21st ed., 1985. (Ministere de l'Agriculture) Euro-Publi Marcel Puget, 9 Bd. des Italiens, 75002 Paris, France.

630 915.2   JA
ANNUAL REVIEW OF AGRICULTURE, KINKEI DISTRICT/KINKI NOGYO JOSEI HOKOKU. (Text in Japanese) 1964. a. Kinki Agricultural Administration Bureau - Kinki Nosei-kyoku, 102 Shimochoja-machi Saguru, Nishinotoin-dori, Kamigyo-ku, Kyoto 602, Japan.

630   IT   ISSN 0066-4502
ANNUARIO DELL'AGRICOLTURA ITALIANA. (Summaries in English) 1946. a. L.60000. Istituto Nazionale di Economia Agraria, Via Berberini 36, 00187 Rome, Italy. bk. rev. circ. 1,500.

636.2 658   BL   ISSN 0518-0937
ANUARIO DOS CRIADORES. 1960. a. $25. Editora dos Criadores Ltda., Rua Venancio Aires, 31, 05024 Sao Paulo, SP, Brazil. circ. 10,000.

630 634.9   PH   ISSN 0115-0820
ARANETA RESEARCH JOURNAL. (Text in English; summaries in English and Filipino) 1953. a. P.10($5) G. Araneta University Foundation, Victoneta Park, Malabon, Metro Manila 3104, Philippines. Ed. Tomas G. Brual. abstr. bibl. charts. stat. circ. 8,000. Indexed: Biol.Abstr. Field Crop Abstr. Herb.Abstr. Hort.Abstr. Plant Breed.Abstr. Rev.Plant Path. Soils & Fert.

630   AG
ARGENTINA. SECRETARIA DE ESTADO DE AGRICULTURA Y GANADERIA. COMUNICADO DE PRENSA. no. 107, 1979. irreg. Secretaria de Estado de Agricultura y Ganaderia, Paseo Colon 922, 1063 Buenos Aires, Argentina. stat. (processed)

630   AG
ARGENTINA. SERVICIO NACIONAL DE ECONOMIA Y SOCIOLOGIA RURAL. PUBLICACION E S R. irreg. Servicio Nacional de Economia y Sociologia Rural, Paseo Colon 974, Buenos Aires, Argentina.

630   UK
ASIAN AGRIBUSINESS BUYERS GUIDE. 1984. a. $80. International Trade Publications Ltd., Queensway House, 2 Queensway, Redhill, Surrey RH1 1QS, England. Ed. Geoff Napier.
    Formerly: Asian Agriculture Buyers Guide (ISSN 0265-833X)

630 020   CR   ISSN 0074-0748
ASOCIACION INTERAMERICANA DE BIBLIOTECARIOS Y DOCUMENTALISTAS AGRICOLAS. BOLETIN ESPECIAL. 1966. irreg., no.23, 1985. membership. Asociacion Interamericana de Bibliotecarios y Documentalistas Agricolas, Codigo Postal 7170, Turrialba, Costa Rica. Ed. Ana Maria Paz de Erickson. circ. 800.

630 070.48   FR
ASSOCIATION DES JOURNALISTES AGRICOLES. ANNUAIRE. a. Association des Journalistes Agricoles, 9 rue Papillon, 75009 Paris, France. circ. 2,000.

630 664   NE   ISSN 0066-9040
ASSOCIATION EURATOM-ITAL. ANNUAL REPORT. 1961. a. free. Research Institute ITAL, Keyenbergseweg 6, Postbus 48, 6700 AA Wageningen, Netherlands. circ. 500.

350 630   AT   ISSN 0812-1729
AUSTRALIA. DEPARTMENT OF PRIMARY INDUSTRY. RURAL INDUSTRY DIRECTORY. 1958. a. Aus.$7.80. (Department of Primary Industry) Australian Government Publishing Service, G.P.O. Box 84, Canberra, A.C.T. 2601, Australia. Ed. G.B. MacAffee.

630   AU   ISSN 0067-2262
AUSTRIA. BUNDESMINISTERIUM FUER LAND- UND FORSTWIRTSCHAFT. TAETIGKEITSBERICHT. 1959. a. S.180. Stubenring 1, 1010 Vienna, Austria. circ. 1,600.

630   BL   ISSN 0101-0697
BANCO DE BIBLIOGRAFIAS. 1978. irreg. free. Empresa Brasileira de Pesquisa Agropecuaria, Departamento de Infromacao e Documentacao, Edificio Venancio 2000, Caixa Postal 04-0315, 70312 Brasilia, Brazil. circ. 600.

633.72   BG
BANGLADESH TEA RESEARCH INSTITUTE. ANNUAL REPORT.* (Text in English) 1973. irreg. Tk.20. Bangladesh Tea Research Institute, Srimangal, Sylhet, Bangladesh.
    Tea

630 338.1   NE
BEDRIJFSUITKOMSTEN TOT FINANCIELE POSITIE; samenvattend overzicht van landbouwbedrijven tot en met boekjaar. 1977. a. price varies. Landbouw-Economisch Instituut, Conradkade 175, 2517 CL The Hague, Netherlands. Ed. M.N. de Groot.

630   GW   ISSN 0522-604X
BEHOERDEN UND ORGANISATIONEN DER LAND- FORST- UND ERNAEHRUNGSWIRTSCHAFT. approx. a. DM.109. B. Behr's Verlag GmbH, Averhoffstr. 10, 2000 Hamburg 76, W. Germany (B.R.D.)

630   BE   ISSN 0303-9056
BELGIUM. RIJKSSTATION VOOR LANDBOUWTECHNIEK. MEDEDELINGEN. (Text mainly in Dutch; summaries in English, French and German) 1964. irreg. price varies. Rijksstation voor Landbouwtechniek, Van Gansberghelaan 115, B-9220 Merelbeke, Belgium. Ed. A. Maton. circ. (controlled) (back issues avail.) Indexed: Biol.& Agr.Ind.

630   BH
BELIZE. DEPARTMENT OF AGRICULTURE. ANNUAL REPORT AND SUMMMARY OF STATISTICS. 1937. a. $2. Ministry of Natural Resources, Department of Agriculture, Belmopan, Belize. stat. circ. 350. Indexed: Field Crop Abstr. Herb.Abstr. Rev.Plant Path.

630   GW   ISSN 0301-2689
BERICHTE UEBER LANDWIRTSCHAFT. SONDERHEFTE. (Text in German; summaries in English and German) irreg., no. 198, 1985. price varies. Verlag Paul Parey (Hamburg), Spitalerstr. 12, 2000 Hamburg 1, W. Germany (B.R.D.) circ. 2,000. (reprint service avail. from ISI) Indexed: Biol.Abstr. Curr.Cont.

630 639.2   BM
BERMUDA. DEPARTMENT OF AGRICULTURE AND FISHERIES. REPORT FOR THE YEAR. 1905. a. free (subject to availability) Department of Agriculture and Fisheries, P.O. Box HM 834, Hamilton HM CX, Bermuda. Dir. E.A. Manuel. circ. 222. (back issues avail.) Indexed: Biol.Abstr. Field Crop Abstr. Herb.Abstr. Hort.Abstr. Rev.Plant Path.

630   GW   ISSN 0405-6485
BETRIEBS- UND ARBEITSWIRTSCHAFT IN DER PRAXIS; eine Schriftenreihe fuer die Landwirtschaft. 1955. irreg., no.21, 1976. price varies. Verlag Paul Parey (Hamburg), Spitalerstr. 12, 2000 Hamburg 1, W. Germany (B.R.D.) bibl. illus. index. (reprint service avail. from ISI)

630   II   ISSN 0067-6454
BHARAT KRISHAK SAMAJ. YEAR BOOK. (Text in English) 1964. a. Rs.25($5) Bharat Krishak Samaj - Farmer's Forum, India, A-1 Nizamuddin West, New Delhi 110003, India.

630   BL
BIBLIOGRAFIA BRASILEIRA DE AGRICULTURA (YEAR) 1978. irreg. Cr.$300($21) Instituto Brasileiro de Informacao em Ciencia e Tecnologia, SCRN 708/709 Bloco B Loja 18E 30, 70740 Brasilia DF, Brazil. bk. rev. circ. 300.
    Supersedes (1969-1975): Bibliografia Brasileira de Ciencias Agricolas (ISSN 0067-6594); Bibliografia Brasileira de Agricultura (ISSN 0100-6800)

BIBLIOGRAPHIES AND LITERATURE OF AGRICULTURE. see *AGRICULTURE — Abstracting, Bibliographies, Statistics*

BIBLIOGRAPHY OF AGRICULTURE. see *AGRICULTURE — Abstracting, Bibliographies, Statistics*

630 634.9   GW   ISSN 0067-5849
BIOLOGISCHE BUNDESANSTALT FUER LAND- UND FORSTWIRTSCHAFT, BERLIN-DAHLEM. MITTEILUNGEN. (Text and summaries in English and German) 1906. irreg. price varies. (Biologische Bundesanstalt fuer Land- und Forstwirtschaft in Berlin-Dahlem) Verlag Paul Parey (Berlin), Lindenstr. 44-47, 1000 Berlin 61, W. Germany (B.R.D.) illus. Indexed: Biol.Abstr. Biotech.Abstr. Field Crop Abstr. Forest.Abstr. Forest Prod.Abstr. Herb.Abstr. Hort.Abstr. Plant Breed.Abstr. Rev.Appl.Entomol. Rev.Plant Path. Soils & Fert. Weed Abstr.

BIOTECHNOLOGY AND GENETIC ENGINEERING REVIEWS. see *BIOLOGY*

630 634.9 634.9   US
BIOTECHNOLOGY IN AGRICULTURE AND FORESTRY. 1986. irreg. price varies. Springer-Verlag, 175 Fifth Ave., New York, NY 10160 TEL 212-460-1500. (Also Berlin, Heidelberg, Tokyo, Vienna) (reprint servie avail. from ISI)

AGRICULTURE

631　　　　　　　　SA
BLOEMFONTEIN AGRICULTURAL SHOW
CATALOGUE. (Text in Afrikaans and English) a.
Dryer Advertising, 21-25 Kruase St., P.O. Box 286,
Bloemfontein, South Africa. Ed. F. de Jaeger. adv.

630　　　　　　BL　ISSN 0101-5117
BOLETIM DE PESQUISA. 1981. irreg. price varies.
Centro Nacional de Pesquisa de Mandioca e
Fruticultura, Rua Embrapa s/n, Caixa Postal 007,
44380 Cruz das Almas, Bahia, Brazil. Indexed:
Chem.Abst.

630　　　　　　AG　ISSN 0084-7968
BOLSA DE CEREALES. REVISTA
INSTITUCIONAL. NUMERO ESTADISTICO. a.
Bolsa de Cereales, Avda. Corrientes 127, 1043
Buenos Aires, Argentina.

630　　　　　　BS　ISSN 0068-0478
BOTSWANA. MINISTRY OF AGRICULTURE.
ANNUAL REPORT. (Reports available for various
divisions of the Ministry of Agriculture) a. free.
Ministry of Agriculture, Private Bag 0033,
Gaborone, Botswana. Indexed: Field Crop Abstr.
Herb.Abstr.

630　574　　　BL　ISSN 0006-8705
BRAGANTIA. (Text in Portuguese; summaries in
English) 1941. irreg. (approx. 1-2/yr.)
Cr.$5000($30) Instituto Agronomico, Servicio de
Divulgacao Tecnico-Cientifica, Caixa Postal 28,
13001 Campinas, Sao Paulo, Brazil. Ed. Celso
Valdevino Pommer. bibl. charts. illus. index. circ.
1,500. Indexed: Biol.Abstr. Chem.Abstr. Bibl.Agri.
Herb.Abstr. Plant Breed.Abstr. Field Crop Abstr.
Trop.Abstr. Geo.Abstr. Helminthol.Abstr.
Hort.Abstr. Rev.Appl.Entomol. Rev.Plant Pathol.
Soils & Fert. VITIS. Weed Abstr.

630　636.2　　　GW
BRAUNVIEHZUCHTER. 1921. a. Wurttembergischer
Braunviehzuchtverband e.V., Waldseer Str. 13, 7950
Biberach, W. Germany (B.R.D.)

639.2　630　　　BL　ISSN 0100-8064
BRAZIL. CENTRO NACIONAL DE PESQUISA
DE MANDIOCA E FRUTICULTURA.
CIRCULAR TECNICA. 1980. irreg. price varies.
Centro Nacional de Pesquisa de Mandioca e
Fruticultura, Rua Embrapa s/n, Caixa Postal 007,
44380 Cruz das Almas, Bahia, Brazil.

630　　　　　　BL　ISSN 0100-8854
BRAZIL. CENTRO NACIONAL DE PESQUISA
DE MANDIOCA E FRUTICULTURA.
COMUNICADO TECNICO. 1975. irreg. price
varies. Centro Nacional de Pesquisa de Mandioca e
Fruticultura, Rua Embrapa s/n, Caixa Postal 007,
44380 Cruz das Almas, Bahia, Brazil. Indexed:
Chem.Abstr.

630　338.4　　　BL
BRAZIL. MINISTERIO DA AGRICULTURA.
ESCRITORIO DE ESTATISTICA. OLEOS E
GORDURAS VEGETAIS. 1971. a. Ministerio da
Agricultura, Escritorio de Estatistica, Espanada dos
Ministerios, Bloco 8, 6 Andar, Brasilia 70000,
Brazil. stat. circ. 800. (processed)

630　　　　　　BL
BRAZIL. MINISTERIO DA AGRICULTURA.
SUBSECRETARIA DE PLANEJAMENTO E
ORCAMENTO. PRODUCAO E
ABASTECIMENTO, PERSPECTIVAS E
PROPOSICOES: SINTESE. irreg. Ministerio da
Agricultura, Subsecretaria de Planejamento e
Orcamento, Brasilia, Brazil. stat.

630　338.91　　CN　ISSN 0227-3802
BRITISH COLUMBIA. MINISTRY OF
AGRICULTURE AND FOOD. AGRICULTURAL
AID TO DEVELOPING COUNTRIES. 1972. a.
Ministry of Agriculture and Food, Parliament
Bldgs., Victoria, B.C. V8V 1X4, Canada. Ed. P.H.
Pettyfer.

630　　　　　　CN
BRITISH COLUMBIA. MINISTRY OF
AGRICULTURE AND FOOD D.A.T.E.
PROGRAM REPORT. 1974. a. Ministry of
Agriculture and Food, Victoria, B.C., Canada. TEL
604-387-5121. Ed. Reg Miller. circ. 1,500.
　　Formerly: British Columbia. Ministry of
Agriculture D.A.T.E. Program Report.

BULLETIN OF AGRI-HORTICULTURE. see
GARDENING AND HORTICULTURE

630　　　　　　IC　ISSN 0251-2661
BUNADARRIT. 1887. a. $10 to non-members.
Bunadarfelag Islands - Agricultural Society of
Iceland, Box 7080, Reykjavik, Iceland. Ed. Jonas
Jonsson. circ. 3,600. Indexed: Nutr.Abstr.
Anim.Breed.Abstr.

630　　　　　　MW
BUNDA COLLEGE OF AGRICULTURE.
RESEARCH BULLETIN. (Text in English) 1970.
a. exchange basis. Bunda College of Agriculture,
Research and Publications Committee, Box 219,
Lilongwe, Malawi. Ed. V.W. Saka. circ. 500.
(processed) Indexed: Chem.Abstr. Bibl.Agri. Field
Crop Abstr. Geo.Abstr.

630　　　　　　AU
BUNDESVERSUCHSANSTALT FUER
ALPENLAENDISCHE LANDWIRTSCHAFT
GUMPENSTEIN. VERSUCHSERGEBNISSE.
1950. irreg. S.60. Bundesanstalt fuer
Alpenlaendische Landwirtschaft Gumpenstein,
Gumpenstein, Austria. circ. 300.
　　Continues: Bundesanstalt fuer Alpine
Landwirtschaft. Versuchsergebnisse.

338.1　　　　　UV
BURKINA FASO. SERVICE DES STATISTIQUES
AGRICOLES. ANNUAIRE. 1970. a. Service des
Statistiques Agricoles, Ministere de l'Agriculture et
de l'Elevage, B.P. 7010, Ouagadougou, Burkina
Faso. circ. 500.
　　Formerly: Upper Volta. Service des Statistiques
Agricoles. Annuaire.

630　　　　　　US
C A A P DIRECTORY: WHOLESALERS OF
ORGANIC PRODUCE & PRODUCTS. 1983. a.
$18. California Agrarian Action Project, Box 464,
Davis, CA 95617. TEL 916-756-8518. Ed. Edie
Stanley. adv. circ. 1,000.

630　　　　　　US　ISSN 0271-7190
C A R D REPORT. 1971. irreg. Iowa State
University, Center for Agricultural and Rural
Development, Ames, IA 50010. TEL 515-294-5980.
Ed. Brian Holding. circ. 500. Indexed: Rural
Recreat.Tour.Abstr. Soils & Fert. World
Agri.Econ.& Rural Sociol.Abstr.

630　　　　　　CK　ISSN 0120-3169
C I A T REPORT. (Editions in English and Spanish)
1980. a. Centro Internacional de Agricultura
Tropical, Communication and Information Support
Unit - International Center for Tropical Agriculture,
Apdo. Aereo 67-13, Cali, Colombia. Indexed:
Biol.Abstr. Anim.Breed.Abstr. Herbage Abstr.
Plant Breeding Abstr.
　　Supersedes: Centro Internacional de Agricultura
Tropical. Annual Report; Centro Internacional de
Agricultura Tropical. CIAT Highlights.

630　　　　　　CN
CANADA. AGRICULTURE CANADA.
RESEARCH STATION, MELFORT,
SASKATCHEWAN. RESEARCH STATION
REPORT. 1953. a. free. Agriculture Canada,
Research Station, Melfort, Saskatchewan, Box 1240,
Melfort, Sask., Canada. TEL 306-752-2776. Ed. Dr.
S.F. Beacom. circ. 1,000.
　　Formerly (until 1986): Canada. Agriculture
Canada. Research Station, Melfort, Saskatchewan.
Research Highlights. Annual Publications (ISSN
0068-7472)

CANADIAN PAPERS IN RURAL HISTORY. see
HISTORY — History Of North And South
America

631　　　　　　SA
CAPE SHOW PROGRAMME & CATALOGUE.
(Text in Afrikaans and English) a. Western Province
Agricultural Society, P.O. Box 107, Eppindust 7475,
Cape Town, South Africa. adv. circ. 22,000.

630　　　　　　BL
CENTRAL NACIONAL DE PESQUISA DE
MANDIOCA E FRUTICULTURA. RELATORIO
TECNICO ANUAL. 1977. a. (Empresa Brasileira
de Pesquisa Agropecuaria, Vinculada ao Ministerio
da Agricultura) Central Nacional de Pesquisa de
Mandioca e Fruticultura, Rua EMBRAPA, Caixa
Postal 007, Cruz das Almas, 44.380 Cruz das
Almas, Bahia, Brasil. abstr. bibl. charts. circ. 1,000.
Indexed: Chem.Abstr.

630　338.1　581　　II　ISSN 0374-7115
CENTRAL PLANTATION CROPS RESEARCH
INSTITUTE. ANNUAL REPORT. (Text in
English) 1970. a. free. Central Plantation Crops
Research Institute, Kasaragod 670 124, Cannanore
District, Kerala, India. Ed. K.V. Ahamed Bavappa.
circ. 600. Indexed: Biol.Abstr.

638.2　　　　　II　ISSN 0304-6818
CENTRAL SERICULTURAL RESEARCH AND
TRAINING INSTITUTE. ANNUAL REPORT.
(Text in English) 1964. a. Central Sericultural
Research and Training Institute, Manandavadi Rd.,
Srirampura, Mysore 570008, India. circ.
200(controlled) Key Title: Annual Report - Central
Sericultural Research and Training Institute.

354.69　　　　　MG
CENTRE NATIONAL DE RECHERCHES
APPLIQUES AU DEVELOPPEMENT RURAL.
DEPARTEMENT DE RECHERCHES
AGRONOMIQUES. RAPPORT ANNUEL. a.
Centre National de la Recherche Appliquee au
Developpement Rural, Departement de Recherches
Agronomiques, B. P. 1690, Antananarivo, Malagasy
Republic.

630　　　　　　MG
CENTRE NATIONAL DE RECHERCHES
APPLIQUES AU DEVELOPPEMENT RURAL.
DEPARTEMENT DE RECHERCHES
AGRONOMIQUES. RAPPORT D'ACTIVITE.
irreg. Centre National de la Recherche Appliquee
au Developpement Rural, Departement de
Recherches Agronomiques, B.P.1690, Antananarivo,
Malagasy Republic.

630　　　　　　MX　ISSN 0084-8697
CENTRO DE INVESTIGACIONES AGRICOLAS
DE TAMAULIPAS. INFORME ANUAL DE
LABORES. 1968. a. free. Centro de Investigaciones
Agricolas de Tamaulipas, A.P. 172, Rio Bravo,
Tamaulipas, Mexico.

631.091　　　　BL　ISSN 0100-8102
CENTRO DE PESQUISA AGROPECUARIA DO
TROPICO UMIDO. BOLETIM DE PESQUISA.
(Text in Portuguese; summaries in English,
Portuguese) 1976. irreg. (Centro de Pesquisa
Agropecuaria do Tropico Umido) Empresa Brasileira
de Pesquisa Agropecuaria, Caixa Postal 48, 66000
Belem-Para, Brazil. bibl. charts. stat. circ. 1,000.
Indexed: Agrindex. Bibl.Agri. Abstr.Trop.Agri.
　　Formerly (until 1980): Instituto de Pesquisa
Agropecuaria do Norte. Boletim Tecnico.

630　　　　　　BL　ISSN 0100-0845
CENTRO DE PESQUISAS DO CACAU. BOLETIN
TECNICO. 1970. irreg. Cr.$2500($60) to
institutions. (Comissao Executiva do Plano da
Lavoura Cacaueira) Centro de Pesquisas do Cacau,
Caixa Postal 7, 45600 Itabuna-Bahia, Brazil. Ed.
Jorge Octavio Alves Moreno. Indexed: Biol.Abstr.

630　　　　　　BL　ISSN 0100-5065
CENTRO DE PESQUISAS DO CACAU. INFORME
TECNICO. 1963. a. Cr.$3000($15) to institutions.
(Comissao Executiva do Plano da Lavoura
Cacaueira) Centro de Pesquisas do Cacau, Caixa
Postal 7, 45600 Itabuna-Bahia, Brazil. Ed. Jorge
Octavio Alves Moreno. Indexed: Biol.Abstr.

630　　　　　　AT　ISSN 0084-8735
CHIASMA. 1963. a. Aus.$3. University of New
England, Rural Science Undergraduates' Society,
Armidale, N.S.W. 2331, Australia. Ed. Brian
Warren. adv. bk. rev. circ. 1,500.

630　　　　　　CL
CHILE. INSTITUTO DE INVESTIGACIONES
AGROPECUARIAS. MEMORIA ANUAL. 1965.
a. exchange basis. Instituto de Investigaciones
Agropecuarias, Casilla 439-3, Santiago, Chile.
Indexed: Anim.Breed.Abstr.

630　　　　　　PN
CIENCIA AGROPECUARIA. (Text in Spanish;
summaries in English) 1978. a. $3.50 (or exchange)
Instituto de Investigacion Agropecuaria de Panama,
Centro de Informacion y Documentacion
Agropecuaria, Apartado 58, Santiago de Veraguas,
Panama. abstr. bibl. charts.

AGRICULTURE

630   CU
CIENCIA Y TECNICA EN LA AGRICULTURA. SERIE: APICULTURA. (Table of contents and abstracts in English) 1985. a. exchange basis. Centro de Informacion y Documentacion Agropecuario, Gaveta Postal 4149, Havana 4, Cuba (Dist. by: Ediciones Cubanas, Obispo No. 461, Aptdo. 605, Havana, Cuba) Indexed: Agrindex.

630   MX   ISSN 0084-8689
CIRCULAR C I A T. 1968. a. free. Centro de Investigaciones Agricolas de Tamaulipas, Apartado Postal 172, Rio Bravo, Tamaulipas, Mexico.

634   CE
COCOS. (Text in English) 1950. a. Rs.20($5) Coconut Research Institute, Bandirippuwa Estate, Lunuwila, Sri Lanka. Ed. D.T. Wettasinghe. adv. bibl. charts. illus. cum.index every 10 yrs. circ. 800. (back issues avail.) Indexed: Biol.Abstr. Chem.Abstr. Field Crop.Abstr. Indian Sci.Abstr. Trop.Abstr. Hort.Abstr. Plant Breed.Abstr. Sri Lanka Sci.Ind. Soils & Fert.
    Formerly: Ceylon Coconut Quarterly (ISSN 0009-0824)
    Coconut products

630   BL
COLECAO C E D E S. GRANDES TEMAS.* 1982. irreg. Camara de Estudos e Debates Economicos e Sociais, c/o Paulo Robello de Castro, Av. 13 de Maio, 23-12-5/1218, Rio de Janeiro, RJ, Brazil.

630   SA
COLIMPEX AGRICULTURAL EXECUPAD. (Text in Afrikaans and English) a. Colimpex Africa (Pty) Ltd., P.O. Box 889, Wendywood 2144, South Africa. adv.

630   JA   ISSN 0388-0028
COLLEGE OF DAIRYING. JOURNAL; CULTURAL AND SOCIAL SCIENCES/ RAKUNO GAKUEN DAIGAKU KIYO, JINBUN SHAKAIKAGAKU HEN. (Text mainly in Japanese; occasionally in English and German; summaries mainly in English) 1961. a. on exchange basis. Rakuno Gakuen University, 582 Bunkyodai-Midorimachi, Ebetsu, Hokkaido 069, Japan. Ed.Bd. circ. 1,000.
    Supersedes in part: College of Dairy Agriculture, Hokkaido. Journal (ISSN 0069-570X)

630 664 635 613.26   US   ISSN 0194-4096
COMMENTS FROM C A S T. 1976. irreg. Council for Agricultural Sciences and Technology, Box 1550, Iowa State University Sta., Ames, IA 50010-1550. TEL 515-292-2125. Eds. William W. Marion, Charles A. Black. (back issues avail.)

631   RH   ISSN 0259-3238
COMMERCIAL AGRICULTURE IN ZIMBABWE. (Text in English) 1984. a. Z.$10. (Commercial Farmer's Union) Modern Farming Publications Trust, Agriculture House, Moffat St., Box 1622, Harare, Zimbabwe. Ed. Michael Rook. adv. circ. 10,000.

630   AT   ISSN 0156-2444
COMMONWEALTH SCIENTIFIC AND INDUSTRIAL RESEARCH ORGANIZATION. DIVISION OF TROPICAL CROPS AND PASTURES. RESEARCH REPORT. 1977. irreg. free. C.S.I.R.O., Division of Tropical Crops and Pastures, St. Lucia, Brisbane, Qld. 4067, Australia.

630   AT   ISSN 0157-9711
COMMONWEALTH SCIENTIFIC AND INDUSTRIAL RESEARCH ORGANIZATION. DIVISION OF TROPICAL CROPS AND PASTURES. TROPICAL AGRONOMY TECHNICAL MEMORANDUM. 1976. irreg. free. C.S.I.R.O., Division of Tropical Crops and Pastures, St. Lucia, Brisbane, Qld. 4067, Australia. Indexed: Biol.Abstr.

630   AT   ISSN 0158-7390
COMMONWEALTH SCIENTIFIC AND INDUSTRIAL RESEARCH ORGANIZATION. INSTITUTE OF ANIMAL AND FOOD SCIENCES. ANNUAL REPORT. 1980. a. Aus.$2. C.S.I.R.O., Institute of Animal and Food Sciences, P.O. Box 225, Dickson, A.C.T. 2602, Australia. Ed. A.T. Healy. circ. 2,600. Indexed: Biol.Abstr. Aus.Sci.Ind.

630   US
CORNELL INTERNATIONAL AGRICULTURE MIMEOGRAPHS. 1963. irreg., 3-4/yr. single copies free; $0.25 for each additional copy. Cornell University, Program in International Agriculture, 384 Caldwell Hall, Ithaca, NY 14853 (Orders to: Mailing Room, 7 Research Park, Ithaca, NY 14853) Ed. L.W. Zuidema. circ. 900. Indexed: Rural Recreat.Tour.Abstr. World Agri.Econ.& Rural Sociol.Abstr.
    Formerly: Cornell International Agricultural Development Mimeographs (ISSN 0070-0010)

630   US   ISSN 0739-4330
COUNTY AGENTS DIRECTORY; the reference book for agricultural extension workers. 1915. a. $18.95. Century Communications, Inc., 5520-G Touhy Ave., Skokie, IL 60077-3234. adv. circ. 6,000.

CRITICAL REPORTS ON APPLIED CHEMISTRY. see *CHEMISTRY*

630 635   UK   ISSN 0263-9459
CRUCIFERAE NEWSLETTER. 1976. a. free. Eucarpia, c/o A.B. Wills, Ed., Scottish Crop Research Institute, Invergowrie, Dundee DD2 5DA, Scotland. TEL 08267731. bk. rev. circ. 500. Indexed: Chem.Abstr. Plant Breed.Abstr.

631.091   CU   ISSN 0138-838X
CUBA. CENTRO DE INFORMACION Y DOCUMENTACION AGROPECUARIO. BOLETIN DE RESENAS. SERIE: ARROZ. (Abstracts in English) 1974. irreg. exchange basis. Centro de Informacion y Documentacion Agropecuario, Gaveta Postal 4149, Havana 4, Cuba (Dist. by: Ediciones Cubanas, Obispo No. 461, Aptdo. 605, Havana, Cuba) Indexed: Agrindex.
    Formerly: Cuba. Centro de Informacion y Divulgacion Agropecuario. Boletin de Resenas. Serie: Arroz.

CUBA. CENTRO DE INFORMACION Y DOCUMENTACION AGROPECUARIO. BOLETIN DE RESENAS. SERIE: MEJORAMIENTO ANIMAL. see *BIOLOGY — Zoology*

630   UK
CUMBRIA AND NORTH LANCASHIRE FARMING YEAR BOOK. a. Border Press Agency Ltd., 12 Lonsdale St., Carlisle CA1 1DD, England.

630 631   PK
CURRENT AGRO-TECHNOLOGY FOR POTATO PRODUCTION. 1981. every 2-3 yrs. Pakistan Agricultural Research Council, Agricultural Documentation Wing, Box 1031, F-7/2, Islamabad, Pakistan. Ed. Mahfooz Ali Shah. circ. 1,000.

630   CY   ISSN 0070-2307
CYPRUS. AGRICULTURAL RESEARCH INSTITUTE. ANNUAL REPORT. 1962/63. a. free. ‡ Ministry of Agriculture and Natural Resources, Agricultural Research Institute, Nicosia, Cyprus. Ed.Bd. bk. rev. circ. 1,000. Indexed: Biol.Abstr. Anim.Breed.Abstr. Hort.Abstr. Rev.Appl.Entomol. Rev.Plant Path.

630   CY   ISSN 0253-6749
CYPRUS. AGRICULTURAL RESEARCH INSTITUTE. MISCELLANEOUS REPORTS. (Text in English or Greek) 1980. irreg. free. Agricultural Research Institute, Nicosia, Cyprus. Ed. P.I. Orphanos. circ. 600.

630   CY   ISSN 0070-2315
CYPRUS. AGRICULTURAL RESEARCH INSTITUTE. TECHNICAL BULLETIN. 1966. irreg., no.62, 1984. free. Ministry of Agriculture and Natural Resources, Agricultural Research Institute, Nicosia, Cyprus. Ed.Bd. circ. 1,000. Indexed: Biol.Abstr. Nutr.Abstr.

630   CY
CYPRUS. DEPARTMENT OF AGRICULTURE. ANNUAL REPORT. (Text in English) 1895/96. a. free. Department of Agriculture, Nicosia, Cyprus. circ. 750.

630   CY   ISSN 0379-0924
CYPRUS. DEPARTMENT OF STATISTICS AND RESEARCH. AGRICULTURAL STATISTICS. (Text in English) a. EC$2. Department of Statistics and Research, Ministry of Finance, Nicosia, Cyprus.
    Formerly: Cyprus. Department of Statistics and Research. Agricultural Survey.

D S I R DISCUSSION PAPER. (Department of Scientific and Industrial Research) see *SCIENCES: COMPREHENSIVE WORKS*

630   DK   ISSN 0107-1815
DENMARK. MILJOESTYRELSEN. OVERSIGT OVER GODKENDTE BEKAEMPELSESMIDLER. Spine title: Bekaempelsesmidler. 1965. irreg. Kr.41. Miljoestyrelsen - Ministry of Environment, Strandgade 29, 1401 Copenhagen K, Denmark (Orders to: Danske Boghendleres Kommissionsanstalt, Siljangade 6, 2300 Copenhagen S, Denmark) circ. 5,000.
    Formerly: Oversigt over Klassificerede Bekaempelsesmidler.

630   DK   ISSN 0589-6665
DENMARK. STATENS BYGGEFORSKNINGSINSTITUT. LANDBRUGSBYGGERI. 1985. irreg. Kr.91.50. (Statens Byggeforskninginstitut) Bibliotekscentralen, Telegrafvej 5, DK-2750 Ballerup, Denmark.

DEVELOPMENTS IN AGRICULTURAL AND MANAGED FOREST ECOLOGY. see *FORESTS AND FORESTRY*

630.24 668.6   MX
DICCIONARIO AGROQUIMICO. 1985. a. San Bernardino 17, Col. de Valle, 03100 Mexico, D.F., Mexico. circ. 30,000.

630   FR   ISSN 0759-3686
DICTIONNAIRE-ANNUAIRE DE L'AGRICULTURE; organismes-dirigeants-fournisseurs. Short title: DIC-AGRI. 1966. a. 390 F. Agri-Editions, 92 rue du Dessous des Berges, 75013 Paris, France. Ed. Robert Faure. adv. index. circ. 15,000.

630   CK
DIRECTORIO AGROPECUARIO DE COLOMBIA. biennial. Col.3000($10) (Sociedad de Agricultores de Colombia) Corporacion Editorial Interamericana, Avda. Jimenez 403 (of 907), Apdo. 14965, Bogota 1, Colombia.

630   UK   ISSN 0265-8275
DIRECTORY OF BRITISH BIOTECHNOLOGY. 1984. biennial. £70. Longman Group Ltd., Fourth Ave., Harlow, Essex CM20 1AA, England. Ed. M.G. Burdon. adv. (back issues avail.)

630   EI   ISSN 0537-6297
DOCUMENTATION EUROPEENNE - SERIE AGRICOLE. Italian ed.: Documentazione Europea - Serie Agricola (ISSN 0537-6300); German ed.: Europaeische Dokumentation - Schriftenreihe Landwirtschaft (ISSN 0537-6327) (Edition also in Dutch) 1968. irreg. Commission of the European Communities, Direction Generale de la Presse et Information, Rue de la Loi 200, 1049 Brussels, Belgium (Dist. in U.S. by European Community Information Service, 2100 M St. N.W., Ste. 707, Washington D.C. 20037) circ. controlled.

334   DQ
DOMINICA. REGISTRAR OF CO-OPERATIVE SOCIETIES. REPORT.* irreg. Ministry of Agriculture, Trade and Natural Resources, Roseau, Dominica, West Indies. charts.

630   AG
E A G PUBLICACIONES. Secretaria de Estado de Agricultura y Ganaderia, Servicio Nacional de Economia y Sociologia Rural, Paseo Colon 922, 1063 Buenos Aires, Argentina. charts. stat. (processed)
    Formed by the merger of: S E A G Boletin del Maiz (ISSN 0036-1232); (1968-19??): S E A G Boletin del Trigo (ISSN 0036-1240) & S E A G Boletin del Algodon (ISSN 0036-1224)

630 301.4157   US
EARTH CIRCLES. irreg., approx. 3-4 yr. Northwest Lesbian Women's Agricultural Network, Route 1, Box 1406, Lopez, WA 98261. Ed. Bobbie Sumburg.

630   UK
EAST OF ENGLAND SHOW CATALOGUE. 1968. a. £2. ‡ East of England Agricultural Society, East of England Showground, Peterborough PE2 0XE, England. Ed. Roy W. Bird. adv. circ. 6,000.

AGRICULTURE

630   IS
EKARAI ISRAEL. irreg. free. Farmers in Israel Association, P.O. Box 209, Tel Aviv 61 001, Israel. TEL 03-252227.

310   ES
EL SALVADOR. DIRECCION GENERAL DE ECONOMIA AGROPCUARIA. ANUARIO DE ESTADISTICAS AGROPCUARIAS. a. Direccion General de Economia Agropecuaria, Boulevard de los Heroes, Edificio Latinoamericano, San Salvador, El Salvador.

630   BL   ISSN 0071-1276
ESCOLA SUPERIOR DE AGRICULTURA "LUIZ DE QUEIROZ". ANAIS. (Summaries in English and Portuguese) 1944. a. $13 or exchange. Universidade de Sao Paulo, Escola Superior de Agricultura "Luiz de Queiroz", Caixa Postal 9, 13400 Piracicaba, Sao Paulo, Brazil. Ed.Bd. bibl. circ. 1,000. Indexed: Biol.Abstr. Bull.Signal. Chem.Abstr. Agrindex. Bibl.Agri. Hort.Abstr. Helminthol.Abstr. Soils & Fert.

630   BL   ISSN 0071-1292
ESCOLA SUPERIOR DE AGRICULTURA "LUIZ DE QUEIROZ". BOLETIM DE DIVULGACAO. 1962. irreg., no.28, 1981. $10 or on exchange. Universidade de Sao Paulo, Escola Superior de Agricultura "Luiz de Queiroz", Box 9, 13400 Piracicaba, Sao Paulo, Brazil. circ. 500. Indexed: Biol.Abstr. Bull.Signal. Chem.Abstr. Bibl.Agri. Agri.Ind. Hort.Abstr. Soils & Fert.

630   AG   ISSN 0325-1799
ESTACION EXPERIMENTAL REGION AGROPECUARIA PERGAMINO. INFORME TECNICO. (Summaries in English) 1960. irreg. exchange basis. ‡ Instituto Nacional de Tecnologia Agropecuaria, Estacion Experimental Regional Agropecuaria Pergamino, C.C.31, 2700 Pergamino, Argentina. circ. 2,000(controlled) (also avail. in microfilm) Indexed: Nutr.Abstr. Bibl.Agri. Field Crop Abstr. Herb.Abstr. Plant Breed.Abstr. Rev.Plant Path.
    Formerly: Estacion Experimental Agropecuaria Pergamino. Informe Tecnico (ISSN 0020-0832)

630   540   UK
EUROPEAN DIRECTORY OF AGROCHEMICAL PRODUCTS. 1984. biennial. £235($456) Royal Society of Chemistry, The University, Nottingham NG7 2RD, England (Subsc. to: Distribution Centre, Blackhorse Road, Letchworth, Herts, SG6 1HN, England) Ed.Bd. circ. 500. (also avail. in magnetic tape)

630   UN   ISSN 0071-6960
F A O AGRICULTURAL DEVELOPMENT PAPER. (Text in English, French and Spanish) irreg., no.99, 1975. price varies. Food and Agriculture Organization of the United Nations, Distribution and Sales Section, Via delle Terme di Caracalla, 00100 Rome, Italy (Dist. in U.S. by: Bernan Associates-Unipub, 4611-F Assembly Drive, Lanham, MD 20706-4391) Indexed: Biol.Abstr.

350   630   UN   ISSN 0071-7045
F A O LEGISLATIVE SERIES. (Text in English and French) 1957. irreg., no.38, 1986. price varies. Food and Agriculture Organization of the United Nations, Distribution and Sales Section, Via delle Terme di Caracalla, 00100 Rome, Italy (Dist. in U.S. by: Bernan Associates-Unipub, 4611-F Assembly Drive, Lanham, MD 20706-4391)

630   UN   ISSN 0429-9353
F A O REGIONAL CONFERENCE FOR AFRICA. 1960. biennial, 13th 1984, Harare, Zimbabwe. price varies. Food and Agriculture Organization of the United Nations, Distribution and Sales Section, Via delle Terme di Caracalla, I-00100 Rome, Italy (Dist. in U.S. by: Bernan Associates-Unipub, 4611-F Assembly Drive, Lanham, MD 20706-4391)

630   UN
F A O REGIONAL CONFERENCE FOR ASIA AND THE PACIFIC. REPORT. (Included in FAO. Agriculture in Asia and the Far East) (Issued also in French as its Rapport) 1949. irreg., 17th 1984, Islamabad. price varies. Food and Agriculture Organization of the United Nations, Distribution and Sales Section, Via delle Terme di Caracalla, I-00100 Rome, Italy (Dist. in U.S. by: Bernan Associates-Unipub, 4611-F Assembly Drive, Lanham, MD 20706-4391)
    Formerly: F A O Regional Conference for Asia and the Far East. Report (ISSN 0427-8070)

630   UN
F A O REGIONAL CONFERENCE FOR EUROPE. REPORT OF THE CONFERENCE. (In cooperation with the UN Economic Commission for Europe) irreg., 14th 1984, Reykjavik, Iceland. price varies. Food and Agriculture Organization of the United Nations, Distribution and Sales Section, Via delle Terme di Caracalla, I-00100 Rome, Italy (Dist. in U.S. by: Bernan Associates-Unipub, 4611-F Assembly Drive, Lanham, MD 20706-4391)

630   UN
F A O REGIONAL CONFERENCE FOR LATIN AMERICA AND THE CARIBBEAN. REPORT. irreg., 18th 1984, Buenos Aires, Argentina. price varies. Food and Agriculture Organization of the United Nations, Distribution and Sales Section, Via delle Terme di Caracalla, I-00100 Rome, Italy (Dist. in U.S. by: Bernan Associates-Unipub, 4611-F Assembly Drive, Lanham, MD 20706-4391)
    Formerly: F A O Regional Conference for Latin America. Report.

630   UN   ISSN 0427-8089
F A O REGIONAL CONFERENCE FOR THE NEAR EAST. REPORT. 1962. irreg., 17th 1984, Aden. price varies. Food and Agriculture Organization of the United Nations, Distribution and Sales Section, Via delle Terme di Caracalla, I-00100 Rome, Italy (Dist. in U.S. by: Bernan Associates-Unipub, 4611-F Assembly Drive, Lanham, MD 20706-4391)

630   UN   ISSN 0532-0313
F A O TERMINOLOGY BULLETIN. price varies. Food and Agriculture Organization of the United Nations, Distribution and Sales Section, Via delle Terme di Caracalla, I-00100 Rome, Italy (Dist. in U.S. by: Bernan Associates-Unipub, 4611-F Assembly Drive, Lanham, MD 20706-4391) Indexed: Food Sci.& Tech.Abstr.

630   574   CK   ISSN 0304-2847
FACULTAD NACIONAL DE AGRONOMIA MEDELLIN. (Text in Spanish; summaries in English and Spanish) 1939. a. Col.$90($15) Facultad Nacional de Agronomia Medellin, Biblioteca Facultad de Agronomia, Universidad Nacional de Colombia, Apartado 568, Medellin, Colombia. cum.index: 1939-1981. circ. 1,000. (back issues avail.) Indexed: Biol.Abstr. Field Crop Abstr. Forest.Abstr. Herb.Abstr. Plant Breed.Abstr. Rev.Appl.Entomol. Rev.Plant Path. Soils & Fert.

338.1   UK
FARM INCOMES IN ENGLAND. 1950. a. price varies. H.M.S.O., P.O. Box 569, London SE1 9NH, England. (Co-sponsor: Ministry of Agriculture, Fisheries and Food) (reprint service avail. from UMI)
    Formerly: Farm Incomes in England and Wales (ISSN 0071-3910)

630   CN   ISSN 0014-8024
FARM LETTER/LETTRE AU CULTIVATEUR. (Text in English & French) irreg. free. Agriculture Canada, Communications Branch, Ottawa, Ont., K1A 0C7, Canada. TEL 613-995-5222.

630   AT
FARMERS HANDBOOK & BUDGETING GUIDE. 1973. biennial. Aus.$20. Agribusiness Counsellors Pty. Ltd., Box 7099, Cloisters Square, Perth, W.A. 6000, Australia.

630   US   ISSN 0272-3417
FARMING UNCLE; periodical for natural people and mother nature lovers. 1977. irreg. $4. Farming Uncle, Inc., Box 91, Liberty, NY 12754. Ed. Louis Toro. adv. bk. rev. illus. stat. circ. 1,000. (back issues avail.) Indexed: Alt.Press Ind.

630   US
FERTILIZER INDUSTRY ROUND TABLE. PROCEEDINGS. 1955. a. $35 per copy. Fertilizer Industry Round Table, Box 5036, Glen Arm, MD 21057. Ed. Albert Spillman. circ. 500.

630   FJ   ISSN 0071-4844
FIJI. MINISTRY OF AGRICULTURE & FISHERIES. ANNUAL REPORT. (Text in English) 1906. a. F.$1. Ministry of Agriculture & Fisheries, Box 358, Suva, Fiji. Indexed: Nutr.Abstr. Field Crop Abstr. Herb.Abstr. Rev.Appl.Entomol. Rev.Plant Path.
    Formerly: Fiji. Department of Agriculture. Annual Report.

630   FJ
FIJI. MINISTRY OF AGRICULTURE & FISHERIES. ANNUAL RESEARCH REPORT. (Text in English) N.S. 1969. a. F.$2($3.75) per no. Ministry of Agriculture & Fisheries, Box 358, Suva, Fiji.
    Formerly: Fiji Department of Agriculture. Annual Research Report.

630   338.1   NE
FINANCIELE POSITIE VAN DE LANDBOUW; boekjaar en vergelijkingen met voorgaande jaren. 1975. a. price varies. Landbouw-Economisch Instituut, Conradkade 175, 2517 CL The Hague, Netherlands. Ed. M.N. de Groot.

FLORIDA. DIVISION OF PLANT INDUSTRY. BIENNIAL REPORT. see *BIOLOGY — Botany*

630   UN   ISSN 0532-0208
FOOD AND AGRICULTURE ORGANIZATION OF THE UNITED NATIONS. BASIC TEXTS. (Text in English, French and Spanish) 1960. a. Food and Agriculture Organization of the United Nations, Distribution and Sales Section, Via delle Terme di Caracalla, I-00100 Rome, Italy (Dist. in U.S. by: Bernan Associates-Unipub, 4611-F Assembly Drive, Lanham, MD 20706-4391)

630   UN   ISSN 0071-6944
FOOD AND AGRICULTURE ORGANIZATION OF THE UNITED NATIONS CONFERENCE. REPORT. biennial, 1985, 23rd session. price varies. Food and Agriculture Organization of the United Nations, Distribution and Sales Section, Via delle Terme di Caracalla, Rome, Italy (Dist. in U.S. by: Bernan Associates-Unipub, 4611-F Assembly Drive, Lanham, MD 20706-4391) Indexed: Chem.Abstr. Nutr.Abstr.

630   AT
FORAGE. 1958. a. University of Melbourne, School of Agriculture, Parkville, N.S.W. 3052, Australia. (Co-sponsor: La Trobe University, School of Forestry) Ed.Bd. adv. circ. 1,500.

FORD ALMANAC; for farm and home. see *ENCYCLOPEDIAS AND GENERAL ALMANACS*

630   330   US
FRUIT AND VEGETABLE TRUCK RATE AND COST SUMMARY. 1975. a. $8. Federal-State Market News Service (San Francisco), 630 Sansome St., Rm. 727, San Francisco, CA 94111.

630   JA
FUKUI UNIVERSITY. FACULTY OF EDUCATION. MEMOIRS. SERIES 3: APPLIED SCIENCE AND AGRICULTURAL SCIENCE. (Text in Japanese; summaries in English & Japanese) a. Fukui University, Faculty of Education, 9-1, 3-chome, Bunkyo, Fukui 910, Japan.

630   575.1   JA   ISSN 0435-1096
GAMMA FIELD SYMPOSIA. (Text in English; summaries in Japanese) 1962. a. exchange basis. Institute of Radiation Breeding - Norin-sho Nogyo Seibutsu Shigen Kenkyusho, Omiya-machi, Naka-gun, Ibaraki 319-22, Japan. Indexed: Chem.Abstr.

630   GW   ISSN 0343-7477
GERMANY (FEDERAL REPUBLIC, 1949-). BUNDESMINISTERIUM FUER ERNAEHRUNG, LANDWIRTSCHAFT UND FORSTEN. JAHRESBERICHT. FORSCHUNG IM GESCHAEFTSBEREICH DES BUNDESMINISTERS FUER ERNAERUNGLAND, WIRTSCHAFT UND FORSTEN. 1962. a. DM.130. Bundesministerium fuer Ernaehrung, Landwirtschaft und Forsten, 5300 Bonn 1, W. Germany (B.R.D.) circ. 370.
    Formerly: Germany (Federal Republic, 1949-). Bundesministerium fuer Ernaehrung, Landwirtschaft und Forsten. Jahresbericht. Forschung im Bereich des Bundesministers. (ISSN 0072-1573)

AGRICULTURE

630   JA   ISSN 0072-4513
GIFU UNIVERSITY. FACULTY OF AGRICULTURE. RESEARCH BULLETIN/GIFU DAIGAKU NOGAKUBU KENKYU HOKOKU. (Text and summaries in English or Japanese) 1951. irreg., no. 28, 1969. free. Gifu University, Faculty of Agriculture - Gifu Daigaku Nogakuba, 3-1 Naka Monzen-cho, Kagamihara, Gifu 504, Japan (Subscr. to: 1-1 Yanagito, Gifu 501-11, Japan) Ed. Shosaku Senda. circ. 750. Indexed: Biol.Abstr. Chem.Abstr. Nutr.Abstr. Dairy Sci.Abstr. Field Crop Abstr. Forest.Abstr. Herb.Abstr. Hort.Abstr. Ind.Vet. Plant Breed.Abstr. Rural Recreat.Tour.Abstr. Rev.Plant Path. Vet.Bull.

GRAINLIST (YEAR) see *BUSINESS AND ECONOMICS — Trade And Industrial Directories*

630   UK   ISSN 0072-6729
GREAT BRITAIN. MINISTRY OF AGRICULTURE, FISHERIES AND FOOD. TECHNICAL BULLETIN. irreg. price varies. H.M.S.O., P.O. Box 569, London SE1 9NH, England. (Co-sponsor: Ministry of Agriculture, Fisheries and Food) (reprint service avail. from UMI) Indexed: Biol.Abstr. Chem.Abstr. Nutr.Abstr. Anim.Breed.Abstr. Field Crop Abstr. Herb.Abstr. Plant Breed.Abstr. Rev.Appl.Entomol. Rev.Plant Path. Soils & Fert.

630   UK   ISSN 0017-4092
GREENSWARD. 1962. a. £2($6) to non-members. ‡ South West Scotland Grassland Society, Auchincruive, Ayr, Scotland. Ed. R.D. Harkess. adv. bk. rev. abstr. charts. circ. 800. Indexed: Field Crop Abstr. Herb.Abstr.

630   MW
GUIDE TO AGRICULTURAL PRODUCTION IN MALAWI. (Text in English) 1968. a. K.3. Ministry of Agriculture, Extension Aids Branch, Box 30134, Lilongwe 3, Malawi. circ. 5,000.

630 070   UK
GUILD OF AGRICULTURAL JOURNALISTS YEAR BOOK.* 1958. a. £5. Graham Cherry Organization, c/o P. Bell, Goldfield Mill House, Miswell Lane, Tring, Herts HP23 4EU, England.

630   DK   ISSN 0107-122X
HAANDBOG FOR D J V K: AGRONOMER, FORSTKANDIDATER, HORTONOMER, LICENTIATER. 1980. irreg. Kr.200. Danmarks Jordbrugsvidenskabelige Kandidatforbund, Gammeltorv 22, 1017 Copenhagen K, Denmark. Ed. Kjeld Suhr. illus. circ. 5,000.
    Formerly: Danmarks Jordbrugsvidenskabelige Kandidatforbund. Medlemsfortegnelse.

HESSE. MINISTER FUER LANDESENTWICKLUNG, UMWELT, LANDWIRTSCHAFT UND FORSTEN. MITTEILUNGEN. LAND UND UMWELT. see *FOOD AND FOOD INDUSTRIES — Grocery Trade*

630   US   ISSN 0073-2230
HILGARDIA; a journal of agricultural science. 1925. irreg. exchange basis only. University of California, Berkeley, Division of Agriculture and Natural Resources, 2120 University Ave., Berkeley, CA 94720. Ed. Richard Venne. circ. 1,800. Indexed: Biol.Abstr. Biol. & Agr.Ind. Chem.Abstr. Curr.Cont. Sci.Cit.Ind. Forest.Abstr. Forest Prod.Abstr. Geo.Abstr. Helminthol.Abstr. Ind.Sci.Rev. Rev.Appl.Entomol. VITIS.

630   GW   ISSN 0340-9783
HOHENHEIMER ARBEITEN. 1961. irreg., no. 77, 1975. (Universitaet Hohenheim) Verlag Eugen Ulmer, Wollgrasweg 41, Postfach 700561, 7000 Stuttgart 70, W. Germany (B.R.D.) bk. rev. Indexed: Chem.Abstr. Anim.Breed.Abstr.

630   JA   ISSN 0018-344X
HOKKAIDO UNIVERSITY. FACULTY OF AGRICULTURE. JOURNAL. (Text in English) 1902. irreg. exchange basis. ‡ Hokkaido University, Faculty of Agriculture - Hokkaido Dagaiku Nogakubu, Nishi-9-chome, Kita 9-jo, Kita-ku, Sapporo 060, Japan. Ed. Hideo Okajima. charts. illus. (also avail. in microfilm) Indexed: Biol.Abstr. Chem.Abstr. Abstr.Bull.Inst.Pap.Chem. Field Crop Abstr. Herb.Abstr. Plant Breed.Abstr. Rev.Appl.Entomol. Rev.Plant Path. Soils & Fert.

HUNGARIAN BUILDING BULLETIN. see *BUILDING AND CONSTRUCTION*

630   CL   ISSN 0073-4675
IDESIA. (Text in Spanish; summaries in English) 1970. irreg. price varies. Universidad del Norte, Departamento de Agricultura, Arica, Chile. Ed. Raul Cortes. bk. rev. charts. bibl. illus. stat. Indexed: Biol.Abstr. Chem.Abstr.

630   NR
IFE JOURNAL OF AGRICULTURE. 1967. a. £N1.50. (University of Ife, Faculty of Agriculture) University of Ife Press, Ile-Ife, Nigeria. Ed. A.E. Akingbohungbe. bk. rev. circ. 500.
    Formerly (until 1979): University of Ife. Faculty of Agriculture. Annual Research Report (ISSN 0579-7195)

630   US   ISSN 0749-1573
IMPACT (YEAR) 1890. a. free. (Georgia Agricultural Experiment Stations) University of Georgia, College of Agriculture, Division of Agricultural Communications, Athens, GA 30602. TEL 404-542-3621. Ed. Kathleen Sheridan. illus. circ. 10,000. (back issues avail.)
    Formerly: University of Georgia. Agricultural Experiment Stations. Annual Report.

630   II   ISSN 0084-781X
INDIAN AGRICULTURE IN BRIEF. (Text in in English) 1958. a. Rs.60($21.60) Ministry of Agriculture, Department of Agriculture and Cooperation, Directorate of Economics and Statistics, A-2E-3 Kasturba Gandhi Marg Barracks, New Delhi 110001, India. Ed. Chandar Dhar Sharma. circ. 2,200.

INDIAN JOURNAL OF HEREDITY. see *BIOLOGY — Genetics*

630   II   ISSN 0252-9920
INDIAN REVIEW OF LIFE SCIENCES. (Text in English) 1981. a. $40. University of Jodhpur, Botany Department, Box 14, Jodhpur 342 001, Rajasthan, India. Ed. David N. Sen. Indexed: Chem.Abstr. Weed Abstr.

630   US   ISSN 0073-6783
INDIANA. AGRICULTURAL EXPERIMENT STATION. INSPECTION REPORT. 1956. irreg. price varies. Purdue University, Agricultural Experiment Station, c/o Dallas Dinger, West Lafayette, IN 47907. TEL 317-494-5600.

630   US   ISSN 0073-6791
INDIANA. AGRICULTURAL EXPERIMENT STATION. RESEARCH BULLETIN. 1957. irreg. (12-15/yr.) single copy free. Purdue University, Agricultural Experiment Station, c/o Dallas Dinger, West Lafayette, IN 47907. TEL 317-494-5600. Ed. Eldon E. Fredericks. circ. 2,500. Indexed: Helminthol.Abstr.

631.091   CK   ISSN 0120-2391
INFORME ANUAL DEL PROGRAMA DE PASTOS TROPICALES. English edition: Tropical Pasture Program Annual Report (ISSN 0120-2383) 1975. a. limited distribution. Centro Internacional de Agricultura Tropical, Communication and Information Support Unit - International Center for Tropical Agriculture, Apartado Aereo 67-13, Cali, Colombia.
    Tropical

630   RW
INSTITUT DES SCIENCES AGRONOMIQUES DU RWANDA. DEPARTEMENT DES PRODUCTIONS VEGETALES. COMPTE RENDU DES TRAVAUX. a. Institut des Sciences Agronomiques, Departement des Productions Vegetales, B.P. 138, Butare, Rwanda.

630   TI   ISSN 0020-238X
INSTITUT NATIONAL DE LA RECHERCHE AGRONOMIQUE DE TUNISIE. DOCUMENTS TECHNIQUES. (Text in French; summaries in English) 1963. irreg., no.85, 1981. price varies per no. Institut National de la Recherche Agronomique de Tunisie, Bibliotheque, Avenue de l'Independance, 2049 Ariana, Tunis, Tunisia. Indexed: Biol.Abstr.

630   ZR
INSTITUT NATIONAL POUR L'ETUDE ET LA RECHERCHE AGRONOMIQUE. RAPPORT ANNUEL. a. Institut National pour l'Etude et la Recherche Agronomique, B.P. 1513, Kisangani, Zaire. illus.

631   GR   ISSN 0365-5814
INSTITUT PHYTOPATHOLOGIQUE BENAKI. ANNALES. (Text in Greek; English and French edition) 1935. irreg. $40. Institut Phytopathologique Benaki, 8 Delta St., Kiphissia, 14561 Athens, Greece. Ed.Bd. charts. illus. index. circ. 700. (back issues avail.) Indexed: Biol.Abstr. Chem.Abstr. Biotech.Abstr. Helminthol.Abstr. Hort.Abstr. Plant Breed.Abstr. Rev.Appl.Entomol. Rev.Plant Path. Soils & Fert. Weed Abstr.

630   BG
INSTITUTE OF NUCLEAR AGRICULTURE. ANNUAL REPORT. (Text in English) irreg. Tk.40. Institute of Nuclear Agriculture, c/o Bangladesh Agricultural University, Mymensingh, Bangladesh.

630   BL
INSTITUTO BRASILEIRO DE ECONOMIA. CENTRO DE ESTUDOS AGRICOLAS. AGROPECUARIA. irreg. free. Fundacao Getulio Vargas, C.P. 9052, 22250 Rio de Janeiro, R.J., Brazil.

630   CK   ISSN 0538-0391
INSTITUTO COLOMBIANO AGROPECUARIO. BOLETIN TECNICO. no. 45, 1977. irreg. Instituto Colombiano Agropecuario, Apdo. Aereo 151123, El Dorado, Bogota, Colombia. illus. circ. 2,500. Indexed: Biol.Abstr.

630   SP   ISSN 0374-8189
INSTITUTO DE ECONOMIA Y PRODUCCIONES GANADERAS DEL EBRO. COMUNICACIONES. 1970. irreg., no.11, 1980. free. Instituto de Economia y Producciones Ganaderas del Ebro, Miguel Servet, 177, Zaragoza, Spain. circ. 500. Indexed: Biol.Abstr. Bull.Signal. Anim.Breed.Abstr. World Agri.Econ.& Rural Sociol.Abstr.

630   SP   ISSN 0375-3417
INSTITUTO DE ECONOMIA Y PRODUCCIONES GANADERAS DEL EBRO. TRABAJOS. (Text in Spanish) 1970. irreg., no.61, 1983. free. Instituto de Economia y Producciones Ganaderas del Ebro, Miguel Servet, 177, Zaragoza-13, Spain. circ. 500. Indexed: Biol.Abstr. Bull.Signal. Anim.Breed.Abstr. World Agri.Econ.& Rural Sociol.Abstr.

INSTITUTO DE INVESTIGACAO AGRONOMICA DE ANGOLA. DIVISAO DE METEOROLOGIA AGRICOLA. ANUARIO. see *METEOROLOGY*

630   AO   ISSN 0078-2254
INSTITUTO DE INVESTIGACAO AGRONOMICA DE ANGOLA. RELATORIO. 1962. a. available on exchange. Instituto de Investigacao Agronomica de Angola, C.P. 406, Nova Lisboa, Angola. Indexed: Trop.Abstr.

630   AO   ISSN 0078-2262
INSTITUTO DE INVESTIGACAO AGRONOMICA DE ANGOLA. SERIE CIENTIFICA. 1968. irreg., no.37, 1974. price varies. Instituto de Investigacao Agronomica de Angola, C.P. 406, Nova Lisboa, Angola. Indexed: Biol.Abstr. Trop.Abstr.

630   AO   ISSN 0078-2270
INSTITUTO DE INVESTIGACAO AGRONOMICA DE ANGOLA. SERIE TECNICA. 1968. irreg., no. 44, 1970. price varies. Instituto de Investigacao Agronomica de Angola, C.P. 406, Nova Lisboa, Angola. Indexed: Biol.Abstr. Trop.Abstr.

630   MZ   ISSN 0077-1791
INSTITUTO DE INVESTIGACAO AGRONOMICA DE MOCAMBIQUE. CENTRO DE DOCUMENTACAS AGRARIA. MEMORIAS. (Summaries in English, French and Portuguese) 1966. irreg. price varies. ‡ Instituto de Investigacao Agronomica de Mocambique, Centro de Documentacao Agraria, C.P. 3658, Maputo 11, Mozambique. illus. index. circ. 500. Indexed: Biol.Abstr.

630   CR
INSTITUTO INTERAMERICANO DE COOPERACION PARA LA AGRICULTURA - O E A. DOCUMENTOS OFICIALES. (Text in English, Spanish) 1971. biennial. free. Instituto Interamericano de Cooperacion para la Agricultura - O E A, Apdo. 55, 2200 Coronado, San Jose, Costa Rica. Ed. Andre Quellette. circ. 1,500.
    Formerly: Instituto Interamericano de Ciencias Agricolas de la O E A. Documentos Oficiales (ISSN 0301-4355)

630   AG   ISSN 0325-1772
INSTITUTO NACIONAL DE TECNOLOGIA AGROPECUARIA. ESTACION EXPERIMENTAL REGIONAL AGROPECUARIA. BOLETIN DE DIVULGACION TECNICA. 1970. irreg. Instituto Nacional de Tecnologia Agropecuaria, Estacion Experimental Regional Agropecuaria, Casilla de Correo No. 31, 2700 Pergamino, Argentina. circ. 1,500. Indexed: Biol.Abstr.
  Formerly: Instituto Nacional de Tecnologia Agropecuaria. Estacion Experimental Regional Agropecuaria. Publicacion Tecnica.

630 340   PE
INSTITUTO PERUANO DE DERECHO AGRARIO. CUADERNOS AGRARIOS. 1977. irreg. Instituto Peruano de Derecho Agrario, Apartado 11549, Jesus Maria, Lima, Peru.

630 664   PO
INSTITUTO SUPERIOR DE AGRONOMIA. ANAIS. (Text in English, French and Portuguese; summaries in English and French) 1920. a. price varies. Instituto Superior de Agronomia, Tapada da Ajuda, 1399 Lisbon Codex, Portugal. circ. 900. (back issues avail.)

630 635   RM   ISSN 0557-465X
INSTITUTUL AGRONOMIC CLUJ-NAPOCA. BULETINUL. SERIA AGRICULTURA. (Text in Romanian; summaries in English) 1975. a. 35 lei($10) Institutul Agronomic "Dr. Petru Groza", Str. Manastur No. 3, 3400 Cluj-Napoca, Rumania. Ed. Ioan Puia. circ. 500. (back issues avail.) Indexed: Biol.Abstr. Field Crop Abstr. Landwirt.Zentralbl.
  Former titles: Institutul Agronomic Cluj-Napoca. Buletinul. Seria Agricultura se Horticultura & Institutul Agronomic Cluj-Napoca. Buletinul.

630   RM   ISSN 0379-8364
INSTITUTUL AGRONOMIC ION IONESCU DE LA BRAD. LUCRARI STIINTIFICE. SERIA AGRONOMIE. 1957. a. Institutul Agronomic "Ion Ionescu de la Brad", Aleea M. Sadoveanu, Nr. 3, Jassy, Rumania. Indexed: Biol.Abstr. Chem.Abstr. Field Crop Abstr. Herb.Abstr. Hort.Abstr. Plant Breed.Abstr. Soils & Fert.
  Supersedes in part: Institutul Agronomic Ion Ionescu de la Brad. Lucrari Stiintifice. Seria Agronomie-Horticultura (ISSN 0075-3505)

630 595.7 576 591   RM
INSTITUTUL DE CERCETARI PENTRU PROTECTIA PLANTELOR. ANALELE/ RESEARCH INSTITUTE FOR PLANT PROTECTION. ANNALS. (Text in Rumanian; summaries in English and Russian) 1965. a. 150 lei. (Academy of Agricultural and Forestry Sciences) Centrul de Material Didactic si Propag. Agricola, Cal.Serban Voda 34, Bucharest, Rumania (Subscr. to: Research Institute for Plant Protection, bd. Ion Ionescu de la Brad no.8, 71592 Bucharest, Rumania) circ. 500. (back issues avail.) Indexed: Biol.Abstr. Rev.Appl.Entomol. Rev.Plant Path.

630 574   PL   ISSN 0208-5933
INSTYTUT SADOWNICTWA I KWIACIARSTWA W SKIERNIEWICACH. SERIA A: PRACE DOSWIADCZALNE Z ZAKRESU SADOWNICTWA. (Text in Polish; summaries in English) 1955. Irreg. 450 Zl.($10) Research Institute of Pomology and Floriculture - Instytut Sadownictwa i Kwiaciarstwa, Ul. Pomologiczna 18, 96-100 Skierniewice, Poland. circ. 1,000. Indexed: Biol.Abstr. Ref.Zh.

632   PL   ISSN 0020-448X
INSTYTUTU OCHRONY ROSLIN. BIULETYN. (Summaries in English and Russian) 1960. irreg. free. Instytut Ochrony Roslin, Miczurina 20, 60-318 Poznan, Poland. Eds. W. Wegorek, J.J. Lipa. illus. index. circ. 1,000. Indexed: Biol.Abstr. Helminthol.Abstr. Plant Breed.Abstr. Rev.Appl.Entomol. Rev.Plant Path. Soils & Fert.
  Plant protection

630   CR
INTER-AMERICAN INSTITUTE FOR COOPERATION ON AGRICULTURE. EXECUTIVE COMMITTEE. YEARLY MEETING REPORT. 1955. a. Instituto Interamericano de Cooperacion para la Agricultura - O E A, Executive Committee, Apartado 55-2200, San Jose, Costa Rica. Ed. Rodolfo Chena Gonzalez. circ. 1,500. (also avail. in microfilm)
  Former titles: Inter-American Institute of Agricultural Sciences. Technical Advisory Council. Junta Directiva. Reunion Anual. Resoluciones y Documentos; Inter-American Institute of Agricultural Sciences. Technical Advisory Council. Report of the Meeting.

630   CR
INTER-AMERICAN INSTITUTE FOR COOPERATION ON AGRICULTURE. INFORME ANUAL. (Editions in English and Spanish) 1942/43. a. free. Instituto Interamericano de Cooperacion para la Agricultura - O E A, Apdo. 55, 2200 Coronado, San Jose, Costa Rica. Ed. Andre Quellette. circ. 2,300. (also avail. in microform)
  Formerly: Inter-American Institute of Agricultural Sciences. Informe Anual (ISSN 0538-3277)

338.1   UK   ISSN 0074-1736
INTERNATIONAL ASSOCIATION OF SEED CRUSHERS. PROCEEDINGS OF THE ANNUAL CONGRESS. 1910. a. £12. International Association of Seed Crushers, 8 Salisbury Square, London EC4P 4AN, England.

638.1   RM   ISSN 0074-2007
INTERNATIONAL BEEKEEPING CONGRESS. REPORTS. biennial since 1963; 24th, Buenos Aires, Argentina, 1973. $15. International Federation of Beekeepers' Associations "Apimondia", Str. Pitar Mos Nr. 20, Bucharest, Romania.

630   CK   ISSN 0120-2235
INTERNATIONAL CENTER FOR TROPICAL AGRICULTURE. BEAN PROGRAM ANNUAL REPORT. Cover title: Beans. a. limited distribution. Centro Internacional de Agricultura Tropical, Communication and Information Support Unit - International Center for Tropical Agriculture, Apdo. Aereo 67-13, Cali, Colombia.

INTERNATIONAL COMMISSION ON IRRIGATION AND DRAINAGE. REPORT. see *WATER RESOURCES*

338.1   FR   ISSN 0074-5863
INTERNATIONAL FEDERATION OF AGRICULTURAL PRODUCERS. GENERAL CONFERENCE PROCEEDINGS. (Editions in English and French) 1946. biennial, 27th, Bonn , W. Germany, 1986. International Federation of Agricultural Producers, 21 rue Chaptal, 75009 Paris, France.

631.091   NR
INTERNATIONAL INSTITUTE OF TROPICAL AGRICULTURE. ANNUAL REPORT. (Text in English and French) 1971. a. International Institute of Tropical Agriculture, Oyo Rd., P.M.B. 5320, Ibadan, Nigeria. Indexed: Chem.Abstr. Helminthol.Abstr.
  Formerly (until 1974): International Institute of Tropical Agriculture. Report.
  Tropical

630   NR   ISSN 0331-4340
INTERNATIONAL INSTITUTE OF TROPICAL AGRICULTURE. RESEARCH HIGHLIGHTS. (Text in English and French) 1976. a. International Institute of Tropical Agriculture, P.M.B. 5320, Ibadan, Nigeria.

630 011   US
INTERNATIONAL SOCIETY OF CITRICULTURE. PROCEEDINGS. 1973. irreg. price varies. International Society of Citriculture, c/o Prof. C.W. Coggins Jr, Department of Botany and Plant Sciences, University of California, Riverside, CA 92521. circ. 1,000. Indexed: Biol.Abstr. Hort.Abstr.

338.1   UK
INTERNATIONAL WHEAT COUNCIL. ANNUAL REPORT. (Editions in English, French, Russian and Spanish) 1949/50. a. free. International Wheat Council, Haymarket House, 28 Haymarket, London SW1Y 4SS, England. stat.
  Formerly: International Wheat Council. Report for Crop Year (ISSN 0539-1296)

338.1   UK   ISSN 0539-130X
INTERNATIONAL WHEAT COUNCIL. RECORD OF OPERATIONS OF MEMBER COUNTRIES. 1959/60. a. International Wheat Council, Haymarket House, 28 Haymarket, London SW1Y 4SS, England. stat. circ. controlled. (processed)

338.1   UK   ISSN 0539-1326
INTERNATIONAL WHEAT COUNCIL. SECRETARIAT PAPERS. 1961. irreg. International Wheat Council, Haymarket House, 28 Haymarket, London SW1Y 4SS, England. stat.

630   US   ISSN 0097-3416
IOWA AGRICULTURE AND HOME ECONOMICS EXPERIMENT STATION. RESEARCH BULLETIN. 1911. irreg. exchange basis. ‡ (Iowa Agriculture and Home Economics Experiment Station) Iowa State University of Science and Technology, 205 Morrill Hall, Ames, IA 50011. TEL 515-294-5616. Ed. John F. Heer. charts. illus. stat. cum.index. circ. controlled. (back issues avail.) Indexed: Biol.Abstr. Chem.Abstr. Curr.Cont. Ref.Zh. Bibl.Agri.

630   US   ISSN 0097-5125
IOWA AGRICULTURE AND HOME ECONOMICS EXPERIMENT STATION. SPECIAL REPORT. 1936. irreg. exchange basis. ‡ Iowa State University of Science and Technology, 205 Morrill Hall, Ames, IA 50011. TEL 515-294-5616. (Co-sponsor: Iowa Cooperative Extension Service in Agriculture and Home Economics) Ed. John F. Heer. charts. illus. stat. cum.index. (back issues avail.) Indexed: Biol.Abstr. Curr.Cont. Nutr.Abstr. Ref.Zh. Sci.Cit.Ind. Bibl.Agri.

630   IE
IRELAND. DEPARTMENT OF AGRICULTURE. ANNUAL REPORT. a. £4.40. Government Publications Sales Office, Sun Alliance House, Molesworth St., Dublin 2, Ireland. Indexed: Anim.Breed.Abstr.
  Formerly: Ireland. Department of Agriculture and Fisheries. Annual Report (ISSN 0075-0646)

630   IE
IRELAND (EIRE) CENTRAL STATISTICS OFFICE. ESTIMATED OUTPUT, INPUT AND INCOME ARISING IN AGRICULTURE. a. Central Statistics Office, Earlsfort Terrace, Dublin 2, Ireland.
  Former titles: Ireland (Eire) Central Statistics Office. Agricultural Output; Ireland (Eire) Central Statistics Office. Estimated Gross and Net Agricultural Output; Ireland (Eire) Central Statistics Office. Estimates of the Quantity and Value of Agricultural Output (ISSN 0075-0557)
  Stencilled releases

630   IE   ISSN 0790-4568
IRISH COOPERATIVE ORGANIZATION SOCIETY. ANNUAL REPORT. 1895. a. £3. Irish Cooperative Organization Society Ltd., Plunkett House, 84 Merrion Square, Dublin 2, Ireland. Ed. J. Smith. circ. controlled.
  Formerly: Irish Agricultural Organization Society. Annual Report (ISSN 0075-0719)

630 600   IS
ISRAEL. INSTITUTE FOR TECHNOLOGY AND STORAGE OF AGRICULTURAL PRODUCTS. SCIENTIFIC ACTIVITIES. (Text in English or Hebrew) triennial. $4. Agricultural Research Organization, Israel Institute for Technology and Storage of Agricultural Products, Volcani Center, Box 6, Bet Dagan, Israel. Ed. Y. Russo Aro. circ. 2,500.

AGRICULTURE

630　　　　　　IS
ISRAEL. RURAL PLANNING AND DEVELOPMENT AUTHORITY. AGRICULTURAL AND RURAL ECONOMIC REPORT. (Text in Hebrew) a. free. Ministry of Agriculture, Rural Planning and Economic Development, P.O. Box 7011, Hakirya, Tel-Aviv, Israel. circ. 500.
　　Former titles: Israel. Rural Planning and Development Authority. Agricultural and Rural Development Report; Israel. Agriculture and Settlement Planning and Development Center. Agricultural and Rural Development Report; Israel. Agricultural and Settlement Planning and Development Center. Statistical Series for the Agricultural Year (ISSN 0075-0964); Israel. Agricultural and Settlement Planning and Development Center. Statistical Series of the Budgetary Year (ISSN 0075-1294)

630　　　　　　IT　　ISSN 0075-1669
ITALY. ISTITUTO CENTRALE DI STATISTICA. ANNUARIO DI STATISTICA AGRARIA. 1965. a. L.10000. Istituto Centrale di Statistica, Via Cesare Balbo 16, Rome, Italy. circ. 1,500.

630　634.9　　JA　　ISSN 0446-5458
JAPAN. MINISTRY OF AGRICULTURE AND FORESTRY. ANNUAL REPORT/NORIN-SHO NENPO. (Text in Japanese) 1953. a. 6000 Yen. (Association of Agriculture and Forestry Statistics - Norin-sho Daijin Kanbo) Government Publications Service Center, 1-2-1 Kasumigaseki, Chiyoda-ku, Tokyo 100, Japan. bk. rev. illus. stat.
　　Continues: Norin Suisan Nenkan.

JAPAN METEOROLOGICAL AGENCY. AGRICULTURAL METEOROLOGY. ANNUAL REPORT. see METEOROLOGY

630　　　　　　JO
JORDAN. DEPARTMENT OF STATISTICS. AGRICULTURAL STATISTICAL YEARBOOK AND AGRICULTURAL SAMPLE SURVEY. (Text in Arabic and English) 1966. a. $10. Department of Statistics, Amman, Jordan.

630　　　　　　DK　　ISSN 0108-884X
JORDBRUG; den aarlige rapport om jordbrugets erhvervmaessige forhold. (Includes supplement) (Text in Danish; summaries in English) 1982. a. Kr.10. Landbrugsministeriet, Slotsholmsgade 10, 1216 Copenhagen K, Denmark (Orders to: Danske Boghendleres Kommissionsanstalt, Siljangade 6, 2300 Copenhagen S, Denmark) circ. 1,500.

630　　　　　　FI　　ISSN 0782-4386
JOURNAL OF AGRICULTURAL SCIENCE IN FINLAND. (Text in English with some Finnish, Swedish and German; summaries in English) 1929. irreg. (4-6/yr.) Fmk.150. Suomen Maataloustieteellinen Seura - Scientific Agricultural Society of Finland, SF-05950 Hyvinkaa 95, Finland. Ed. Ulla Lallukka. charts. illus. index. circ. 750. (reprint service avail. from ISI) Indexed: Agrindex. Anim.Breed.Abstr. Biol.Abstr. Curr.Cont. Excerp.Med. Chem.Abstr. Dairy Sci.Abstr. Field Crop Abstr. Food Sci.& Tech.Abstr. Nutr.Abstr. Herb.Abstr. Hort.Abstr. Plant Breed.Abstr. Soils & Fert. Helminthol.Abstr. Ind.Vet. Weed Abstr. Rural Recreat.Tour.Abstr. Vet.Bull.
　　Former titles: Scientific Agricultural Society of Finland. Journal (ISSN 0024-8835); Maataloustieteelinen Aikakauskirja.

630　　　　　　US　　ISSN 0146-3071
JOURNAL OF SEED TECHNOLOGY. 1908. a. Association of Official Seed Analysts, Illinois Department of Agriculture Laboratory, Springfield, IL 62706. TEL 217-785-8487. Ed. Robert Yaklich. cum.index: 1908-1937; 1938-1959. circ. 400. (back issues avail) Indexed: Biol.Abstr. Chem.Abstr. Field Crop Abstr. Herb.Abstr. Hort.Abstr. Rev.Plant Path. Weed Abstr.
　　Supersedes (as of 1976): Association of Official Seed Analysts. Proceedings (ISSN 0097-1324)

JOURNAL OF SOIL AND WATER CONSERVATION IN INDIA. see CONSERVATION

630　　　　　　PO
JUNTA NACIONAL DOS PRODUTOS PECUARIOS. PUBLICACOES. (Text in Portuguese; summaries in English) irreg. Junta Nacional dos Produtos Pecuarios, R. Padre Antonio Vieira No. 1, 1000 Lisbon, Portugal. Indexed: Biol.Abstr.

630　334.683　　MY
K S M REVIEW. (Kerjasama Serbaguna Malaysia) (Text in Chinese, English and Malay) 1970. q. free. Malaysian Multi-Purpose Cooperative Society, Wisma MCA, Jalan Ampang, Kuala Lumpur, Malaysia. Ed. Tan Ken Sin. adv. illus. circ. 100,000.
　　Formerly: Malaysian Multi-Purpose Cooperative Society. Review.

630　　　　　　GW
K T B L - SCHRIFTEN. 1947. irreg, no.312, 1986. price varies. (Bundesminesterium fuer Ernaehrung, Landwirtschaft und Forsten) Kuratorium fuer Technik und Bauwesen in der Landwirtschaft e.V., Bartningsstr. 49, 6100 Darmstadt 12, W. Germany (B.R.D.) charts. illus. Indexed: Excerp.Med. Agri.Eng.Abstr. Dairy Sci.Abstr. Geo.Abstr. Rural Recreat.Tour.Abstr. Soils & Fert. World Agri.Econ.& Rural Sociol.Abstr.

574　574　　JA　　ISSN 0374-8804
KAGAWA PREFECTIVE AGRICULTURAL EXPERIMENT STATION. BULLETIN. (Text in Japanese; summaries in English and Japanese) 1949. a. Kagawa Prefecture Agricultural Experiment Station, Kagawa-ken Nogyo Shikenjo, Busshozan-cho, Takamatsu-shi, Kagawa, Japan. Ed. Kozo Morioka. circ. 500. Indexed: Biol.Abstr.

338.1　　　　　US
KANSAS. STATE BOARD OF AGRICULTURE. ANNUAL REPORT WITH FARM FACTS. 1872. a. $5. State Board of Agriculture, 109 S.W. 9th St., Topeka, KS 66612. TEL 913-296-3556. Ed. Carole A. Jordan. illus. stat. circ. 8,000.
　　Continues: Kansas. State Board of Agriculture. Report; Formed by the merger of: Kansas. State Board of Agriculture. Annual Report & Farm Facts; Formerly: Kansas Agriculture Report (ISSN 0091-6900); Supersedes: Kansas. State Board of Agriculture. Biennial Report to the Governor.

630　　　　　　TH　　ISSN 0075-5192
KASETSART JOURNAL. (Text in English or Thai) 1961. s-a. B.125($20) Kasetsart University, Bangkok 9, Thailand. Ed. Phaitoon Ingkasuwan. Indexed: Chem.Abstr. Field Crop Abstr. Herb.Abstr. Plant Breed.Abstr. Rev.Plant Path.

630　　　　　　KE
KENYA. MINISTRY OF AGRICULTURE. SCIENTIFIC RESEARCH DIVISION. ANNUAL REPORT. 1964? a. Ministry of Agriculture, Scientific Research Division, Nairobi, Kenya (Orders to: Government Printing and Stationery Department, Box 30128, Nairobi, Kenya) Indexed: Field Crop Abstr. Herb.Abstr. Rev.Plant Path.
　　Formerly: Kenya. Ministry of Agriculture. Research Division. Annual Report.

630　574　　JA　　ISSN 0452-2370
KOBE UNIVERSITY. FACULTY OF AGRICULTURE. SCIENCE REPORTS. (Text in English and Japanese; summaries in English) 1953. a. exchange basis. Kobe University, Faculty of Agriculture, 1 Rokkodai-cho, Nada-ku, Kobe 657, Japan. circ. 800. Indexed: Biol.Abstr.

630　574　　JA　　ISSN 0389-0473
KOCHI UNIVERSITY. AGRICULTURAL SCIENCE. RESEARCH REPORTS. (Text in English and Japanese; summaries in English) 1968. a. Kochi University, Akebonocho, Kochi-shi, Kochi-ken, Japan. Indexed: Biol.Abstr. Helminthol.Abstr. Hort.Abstr. Rev.Plant Path.

630　620　　JA　　ISSN 0450-6219
KOCHI UNIVERSITY. FACULTY OF AGRICULTURE. MEMOIRS. (Text in English and Japanese; summaries in English) 1956. a. Kochi University, Faculty of Agriculture, Monobe, Nankokushi, Kochi-ken, Japan. Indexed: Biol.Abstr.

630　636.089　　DK　　ISSN 0109-4998
KONGELIGE VETERINAER OG LANDBOHOEJSKOLE. HAANDBOG. 1982. a. Kr.30. Kongelige Veterinaer og Landbohoejskole, Sturendes Raad, Copenhagen, Denmark.
　　Formerly: Haandbog for Studerende ved Landbohoejskolen.

690　　　　　　DK　　ISSN 0106-8237
KONGELIGE VETERINAER- OG LANDBOHOEJSKOLE. JORDBRUGSTEKNISK INSTITUT. MEDDELELSE. irreg. price varies. D S R Boghandel, Thorvaldsensvej 40, 1871 Copenhagen V, Denmark.

KONGELIGE VETERINAER OG LANDBOHOEJSKOLE. SKOVBRUGINSTITUTET. MEDDELELSER. see VETERINARY SCIENCE

630　　　　　　NE
KONINKLIJK INSTITUUT VOOR DE TROPEN. AFDELING AGRARISCH ONDERZOEK. BULLETIN/ROYAL TROPICAL INSTITUTE. INFORMATION AND DOCUMENTATION. BULLETIN. 1914. irreg. Koninklijk Instituut voor de Tropen, Mauritskade 63, 1092 AD Amsterdam, Netherlands. illus. circ. 500. (back issues avail.) Indexed: Key to Econ.Sci.

630　　　　　　NE
KONINKLIJK INSTITUUT VOOR DE TROPEN. AFDELING PLATTELANDSONTWIKKELING. COMMUNICATIONS AND BULLETINS. irreg. Koninklijk Instituut voor de Tropen, Mauritskade 63, 1092 AD Amsterdam, Netherlands. illus.
　　Formerly: Koninklijk Instituut voor de Tropen. Afdeling Agrarisch Onderzoek. Communication.

630　　　　　　KO
KOREA (REPUBLIC). OFFICE OF RURAL DEVELOPMENT. RESEARCH REPORT. (Text in Korean; summaries in English) 1958. a. free. Ministry of Agriculture & Fishery, Office of Rural Development, Seodun-Dong, Suweon, S. Korea. Ed. Kun Hwan Yun. circ. 1,230. (also avail. in microfiche) Indexed: Excerp.Med. Nutr.Abstr. Hort.Abstr. Vet.Bull.
　　Formerly: Korea (Republic). Office of Rural Development. Agricultural Research Report (ISSN 0075-6865)

630　　　　　　JA　　ISSN 0075-7373
KYOTO PREFECTURAL UNIVERSITY. SCIENTIFIC REPORTS: AGRICULTURE/ KYOTO-FURITSU DAIGAKU GAKUJUTSU HOKOKU NAGAKU. (Text in Japanese; summaries in English) 1951. irreg., no. 28, 1976. available only on exchange. Kyoto Prefectural University - Kyoto-furitsu Daigaku, Shimogamo Hangi-cho, Sakyo-ku, Kyoto 606, Japan. Ed. Z. Hayashino. Indexed: Biol.Abstr. Nutr.Abstr. Dairy Sci.Abstr. Field Crop Abstr. Herb.Abstr. Plant Breed.Abstr. Rev.Appl.Entomol. Soils & Fert.

630　　　　　　JA　　ISSN 0451-1476
KYOTO UNIVERSITY. RESEARCH INSTITUTE FOR FOOD SCIENCE. BULLETIN. (Text in English and Japanese; summaries in English) 1949. a. free. Kyoto University, Research Institute for Food Science, Uji, Kyoto 611, Japan. Ed. Yukei Morita. (back issues avail.) Indexed: Chem.Abstr.

630　　　　　　JA
KYUSHU UNIVERSITY. INSTITUTE OF TROPICAL AGRICULTURE. BULLETIN. (Text in English) 1975. a. on exchange basis. Kyushu University, Institute of Tropical Agriculture, 13 Hakazaki, Higashiku, Fukuoka 812, Japan. Ed.Bd. circ. 100. (back issues avail.) Indexed: Rev.Plant Path. Soils & Fert.

630　　　　　　GW　　ISSN 0455-2342
LANDARBEIT UND TECHNIK. irreg., no. 35, 1968. price varies. (Max-Planck-Institut fuer Landarbeit und Landtechnik) Verlag Paul Parey (Hamburg), Spitalerstr. 12, 2000 Hamburg 1, W. Germany (B.R.D.) Ed. Gerhardt Preuschen. bibl. illus. index. (reprint service avail. from ISI)

LANDBOHISTORISK TIDSSKRIFT; bol og by. see HISTORY — History Of Europe

630　　　　　　NE
LANDBOUWCIJFERS. 1954. a. Landbouw-Economisch Instituut, Conradkade 175, 2517 CL The Hague, Netherlands. Ed. M.N. de Groot.

630　　　　　　NE　　ISSN 0083-6990
LANDBOUWHOGESCHOOL, WAGENINGEN. MISCELLANEOUS PAPERS. 1968. irreg. price varies. (State Agricultural University) H. Veenman en Zonen, Box 7, Wageningen, Netherlands. (back issues avail.) Indexed: Biol.Abstr. Nutr.Abstr. Dairy Sci.Abstr. Field Crop Abstr. Forest.Abstr. Geo.Abstr. GeoRef. Herb.Abstr. Hort.Abstr. Plant Breed.Abstr. Rev.Appl.Entomol. Rural Recreat.Tour.Abstr. Rev.Plant Path. Soils & Fert. World Agri.Econ.& Rural Sociol.Abstr.

AGRICULTURE

630　　　　　SR
LANDBOUWPROEFSTATION SURINAME.
JAARVERSLAG/AGRICULTURAL
EXPERIMENT STATION SURINAME.
ANNUAL REPORT. (Text in Dutch; summaries in English) 1903. a. fl.15. Department of Agriculture and Fisheries, Landbouwproefstation, Box 160, Paramaribo, Surinam. charts. illus. stat. circ. 500. Indexed: Field Crop Abstr. Herb.Abstr. Hort.Abstr.

630　　　　　DK　ISSN 0108-4003
LANDBRUGETS ORGANISATIONSHAANDBOG. 1967. irreg., vol. 6, 1983. Kr.20. Landbrugets Oplysnings- og Konferencevirksomhed, Vesterbrogade 6D, 1620 Copenhagen V, Denmark. Ed.Bd. illus.

630　　　　　DK　ISSN 0105-4244
LANDBRUGETS SAMRAAD FOR FORSKNING OG FORSOEG. KORTLAEGNING. 1976. a. Landbrugets Samraad for Forskning og Forsoeg, Axelborg /4 vaer. 19, Vesterbrogade 4A, 1620 Copenhagen V, Denmark.

630　　　　　DK　ISSN 0108-4518
LANDBRUGETS SAMRAAD FOR FORSKNING OG FORSOEG. RAMMEPLANER. 1977. a. Landbrugets Samraad for Forskning og Forsoeg, Axelborg /4 vaer. 19, Vesterbrogade 4A, 1620 Copenhagen V, Denmark.

630　　　　　DK　ISSN 0302-4946
LANDBRUGSAARBOG. 1899. a. Kr.125. Kongelige Danske Landhusholdningsselskab, Rolighedsvej 26, 1958 Frederiksberg C, Denmark.
　Formerly: Landoekonomisk Aarbog.

LANDBRUKETS AARBOK. JORDBRUK, HAGEBRUK, SKOGBRUK. see *FORESTS AND FORESTRY*

LANDSCAPE HISTORY. see *HISTORY — History Of Europe*

LENTIL ABSTRACTS. see *AGRICULTURE — Abstracting, Bibliographies, Statistics*

630　　　　　NZ　ISSN 0069-3839
LINCOLN COLLEGE. FARMERS' CONFERENCE. PROCEEDINGS. 1951. a. price varies. Lincoln College, Canterbury, New Zealand. Indexed: Nutr.Abstr. Field Crop Abstr. Herb.Abstr.

630　　　　　UK　ISSN 0368-7708
LONG ASHTON RESEARCH STATION. REPORT. 1903. a. £4.50. Long Ashton Research Station, Long Ashton, Bristol BS18 9AF, England. Ed. R.K. Atkin. index. circ. 2,500. Indexed: Biol.Abstr. Field Crop Abstr. Herb.Abstr. Hort.Abstr. Rev.Appl.Entomol. Rev.Plant Path. VITIS. Weed Abstr.

394.6　　　　　US　ISSN 0093-0687
LOUISIANA FAIRS AND FESTIVALS. a. Department of Agriculture, Baton Rouge, LA 70804. TEL 504-342-7011.

630　　　　　RH
LOWVELD RESEARCH STATIONS. ANNUAL REPORT. a. free. Ministry of Lands, Agriculture and Rural Resettlement, Research and Specialist Services, Information Services, Box 8108, Causeway, Harare, Zimbabwe. circ. 250. (back issues avail.) Indexed: Biol.Abstr.

630　　　　　IO　ISSN 0024-9556
MADJALAH PERTANIAN.* 1949. irreg., (4-12/yr.) free. Directorate of Agriculture Extension - Dircktorat Penyaluhan Pertanian, Jalan Ragunan, Pasarminggu, Djakarta, Indonesia. Ed. Soekandar Wiriaatmadja. charts. stat. circ. 6,000.

630　　　　　LE　ISSN 0076-2369
MAGON. SERIE SCIENTIFIQUE.* (Text and summaries in English and French) 1965. irreg., no.33, 1970. free. Institut de Recherches Agronomiques, Laboratoire Regional Veterinaire, Fanar, Lebanon.

630　　　　　LE　ISSN 0076-2377
MAGON. SERIE TECHNIQUE.* (Text in Arabic, English and French; summaries in English and French) 1965. irreg., no.11, 1970. free. Institut de Recherches Agronomiques, Laboratoire Regional Veterinaire, Fanar, Lebanon. Indexed: Biol.Abstr.

630　　　　　HU　ISSN 0076-2423
MAGYAR TUDOMANYOS AKADEMIA. AGRARTUDOMANYOK OSZTALYA. MONOGRAFIASOROZAT. (Text in Hungarian; occasional summaries in English, German, Italian or Russian) 1955. irreg. price varies. Akademiai Kiado, Publishing House of the Hungarian Academy of Sciences, P.O. Box 24, H-1363 Budapest, Hungary.

630　574　　　　US
MAINE AGRICULTURAL EXPERIMENT STATION. ANNUAL REPORT. 1886. a. free. (Maine Agricultural Experiment Station) University of Maine Press, Winslow Hall, Orono, ME 04469-0163. Ed. G.W. Simpson. circ. 1,500. (also avail. in microfilm; back issues avail.)

630　　　　　US　ISSN 0734-9564
MAINE AGRICULTURAL EXPERIMENT STATION. MISCELLANEOUS REPORT. 1948. irreg., no.309, 1985. free. Maine Agricultural Experiment Station, University of Maine, 1 Winslow Hall, Orono, ME 04469-0163. (also avail. in microfilm)

630　　　　　US　ISSN 0734-9556
MAINE AGRICULTURAL EXPERIMENT STATION. TECHNICAL BULLETIN. 1962. irreg., vol.124, 1986. free. Maine Agriculture Experiment Station, University of Maine, 1 Winslow Hall, Orono, ME 04469-0163. TEL 207-581-3211. (also avail. in microfilm) Indexed: Biol.Abstr.

630　　　　　UG　ISSN 0075-4730
MAKERERE UNIVERSITY. FACULTY OF AGRICULTURE. HANDBOOK.* 1963. irreg. Makerere University, Faculty of Agriculture, Box 7062, Kampala, Uganda.

630　　　　　UG　ISSN 0075-4773
MAKERERE UNIVERSITY. FACULTY OF AGRICULTURE. TECHNICAL BULLETIN. 1962. irreg. ‡ Makerere University, Faculty of Agriculture, Box 7062, Kampala, Uganda.

630　　　　　MW
MALAWI. DEPARTMENT OF AGRICULTURAL RESEARCH. ANNUAL REPORT. a. K.10 price varies. Government Printer, P.O. Box 37, Zomba, Malawi. Indexed: Biol.Abstr. Anim.Breed.Abstr. Dairy Sci.Abstr. Field Crop Abstr. Herb.Abstr. Rev.Appl.Entomol. Rev.Plant Path.
　Incorporating (as of 1975): Agricultural Research Council of Malawi. Annual Report (ISSN 0065-4515); Formerly (1963/64-1969/70): Malawi. Department of Agriculture. Annual Report (ISSN 0076-3047)

630　639.2　　　MY
MALAYSIA. MINISTRY OF AGRICULTURE. TECHNICAL AND GENERAL BULLETINS. 1957, N.S. 1973. irreg. Ministry of Agriculture, Publications Officer, Swettenham Rd., Kuala Lumpur, Malaysia. Indexed: Anim.Breed.Abstr. Rev.Appl.Entomol. Soils & Fert.
　Former titles: Malaysia. Ministry of Agriculture. Technical Bulletins; Malaysia. Ministry of Agriculture & Rural Development. Technical Bulletins.

634　　　　　MY
MALAYSIAN PINEAPPLE. (Text and summaries in English) 1971. irreg, latest vol. 2, 1972. Malayan Pineapple Industry Board, Pineapple Research Station, Box 101, Pekan Nenas, Johor, Malaysia. illus. circ. 1,500.

630　　　　　CN　ISSN 0084-3865
MANITOBA AGRICULTURE YEARBOOK. 1963. a. Manitoba Agriculture, Economic Analysis Branch, 903-401 York Ave., Winnipeg, Man. R3C 0P8, Canada. Ed. Bob Ward. circ. 4,000.

630　　　　　US　ISSN 0190-7492
MARKETING CALIFORNIA ORNAMENTAL CROPS. 1968. a. $8. Federal-State Market News Service (San Francisco), 630 Sansome St., Rm. 727, San Francisco, CA 94111.

630　658.8　　　US
MARKETING CALIFORNIA STRAWBERRIES. 1950. a. $8. Federal-State Market News Service (San Francisco), 630 Sansome St., Rm. 727, San Francisco, CA 94111.

630　　　　　MF
MAURITIUS. MINISTRY OF AGRICULTURE, FISHERIES AND NATURAL RESOURCES. ANNUAL REPORT. 1913. a. R.50. Ministry of Agriculture, Fisheries and Natural Resources, Agricultural Services, Reduit, Mauritius. Indexed: Biol.Abstr.
　Formerly: Mauritius. Ministry of Agriculture and Natural Resources and the Environment. Annual Report.

630　　　　　MF
MAURITIUS. MINISTRY OF AGRICULTURE, FISHERIES AND NATURAL RESOURCES. TECHNICAL BULLETIN. 1979. a. free. Ministry of Agriculture, Fisheries and Natural Resources, Agricultural Services, Reduit, Mauritius.
　Formerly: Mauritius. Ministry of Agriculture and Natural Resources and the Environment. Technical Bulletin.

630　　　　　MF
MAURITIUS CHAMBER OF AGRICULTURE. PRESIDENT'S REPORT. (Text in English) 1853. a. Mauritius Chamber of Agriculture, Box 312, Port Louis, Mauritius. circ. 900.

630　330.9　　　MX
MEXICO. INSTITUTO NACIONAL DE INVESTIGACIONES FORESTALES, AGRICOLAS Y PECUARIAS. FOLLETOS DE INVESTIGACION. (Text in Spanish; summaries in English and Spanish) 1979. irreg. free. Instituto Nacional de Investigaciones Forestales, Agricolas y Pecuarias, Departamento de Difusion Tecnica, Apdo. Postal 6-882, 06600 Mexico, D.F., Mexico. Ed.Bd. charts. circ. 3,000. Indexed: Biol.Abstr.
　Formerly: Mexico. Instituto Nacional de Investigaciones Agricolas. Folletos de Investigacion.

630　　　　　MX
MEXICO. INSTITUTO NACIONAL DE INVESTIGACIONES FORESTALES, AGRICOLAS Y PECUARIAS. TEMAS DIDACTICAS. 1976. irreg. free. Instituto Nacional de Investigaciones Forestales, Agricolas y Pecuarias, Departamento de Difusion Tecnica, Apdo. Postal 6-882, 06600 Mexico, D.F., Mexico. Ed.Bd. charts. circ. 3,000.
　Formerly: Mexico. Instituto Nacional de Investigaciones Agricolas. Temas Didacticas.

630　　　　　UK　ISSN 0264-5408
MIDDLE EAST AGRIBUSINESS BUYERS GUIDE. a. $80. International Trade Publications Ltd., Queensway House, 2 Queensway, Redhill, Surrey RH1 1QS, England. Ed. Geoff Napier.

630　　　　　US
MINNESOTA AGRICULTURAL EXPERIMENT STATION. STATION BULLETIN. irreg., approx. 10/yr. price varies. (Minnesota Agricultural Experiment Station) University of Minnesota, Department of Communication Resources, 433 Coffey Hall, 1420 Eckles Ave., St. Paul, MN 55108. circ. 1,000. Indexed: Biol.Abstr.

630　636　　　US
MISSOURI. DEPARTMENT OF AGRICULTURE. WEEKLY MARKET SUMMARY. 1981. w. $6. Department of Agriculture, Box 630, 1616 Missouri Blvd., Jefferson City, MO 65102. TEL 314-751-4211. Ed. Sam Shelton. circ. 1,900.

631　　　　　HU　ISSN 0077-2658
NAGYUZEMI GAZDALKODAS KERDESEI. 1961. irreg. price varies. (Magyar Tudomanyos Akademia) Akademiai Kiado, Publishing House of the Hungarian Academy of Sciences, P.O. Box 24, H-1363 Budapest, Hungary.

NATIONAL AGRICULTURAL PLASTICS ASSOCIATION. PROCEEDINGS. see *PLASTICS*

630　　　　　CE
NATIONAL AGRICULTURAL SOCIETY OF SRI LANKA. JOURNAL. (Text in English) 1964. a. Rs.5.50($2) ‡ National Agricultural Society of Sri Lanka, Faculty of Agriculture, University of Sri Lanka, Peradeniya, Sri Lanka. Ed. Dr. Y.D.A. Senanayake. adv. illus. circ. 250. Indexed: Biol.Abstr. Chem.Abstr. Trop.Abstr. Dairy Sci.Abstr. Field Crop Abstr. Herb.Abstr. Hort.Abstr. Plant Breed.Abstr. Sri Lanka Sci.Ind. Rural Recreat.Tour.Abstr. Rev.Plant Path. World Agri.Econ.& Rural Sociol.Abstr.
　Formerly: National Agricultural Society of Ceylon. Journal (ISSN 0547-3616)

AGRICULTURE

630   UK
NATIONAL FARMERS' UNION HANDBOOK. a. £2.25. National Farmers' Union, Agriculture House, Knightsbridge, London SW1X 7NJ, England.

630   UK
NATIONAL FEDERATION OF FRUIT AND POTATO TRADES. ANNUAL HANDBOOK AND LIST OF MEMBERS. a. £4 to members; non-members £10. National Federation of Fruit and Potato Trades Ltd., 103/107 Market Towers, 1 Nine Elms Lange, London SW8 5NQ, England. Ed. Ann M. Stirling.

NATIONAL FOOD RESEARCH INSTITUTE. REPORT. see *FOOD AND FOOD INDUSTRIES*

631   JA   ISSN 0077-4863
NATIONAL INSTITUTE OF AGRICULTURAL SCIENCES, TOKYO. BULLETIN. SERIES H (FARM MANAGEMENT, LAND UTILIZATION, RURAL LIFE) (Text in English or Japanese with English summaries) 1951. irreg., no. 49, 1977. avail. on exchange basis only. Department of Agricultural Development, Agricultural Research Center, 3-1-1 Kannondai, Yatabe-machi, Ibaraki-ken 305, Japan. Ed. F. Suzuki. Indexed: Field Crop Abstr. Herb.Abstr. VITIS.

630   JA
NATIONAL RESEARCH INSTITUTE OF AGRICULTURAL ECONOMICS. ANNUAL REPORT/NOGYO SOGO KENKYUSHO NENPO. (Text in Japanese) 1949. a. National Research Institute of Agricultural Economics - Norinsuisan-Sho Nogyo Sogo Kenkyusho, 2-2-1 Nishigahara, Kita-ku, Tokyo 114, Japan.
Formerly: National Research Institute of Agriculture. Annual Report.

630   JA
NATIONAL RESEARCH INSTITUTE OF VEGETABLES, ORNAMENTAL PLANTS AND TEA. BULLETIN. (Summaries in English) 1962. a. exchange basis. National Research Institute of Vegetables, Ornamentals Plants and Tea, 2769 Kanaya, Haibara, Shizuoka, Japan. Ed.Bd. Indexed: Biol.Abstr. Chem.Abstr. Food Sci.& Tech.Abstr. Hort.Abstr. Plant Breed.Abstr.
Former titles: National Research Institute of Tea. Bulletin (ISSN 0528-7820); (until 1973): Tea Research Station. Bulletin.

630   CH   ISSN 0077-5819
NATIONAL TAIWAN UNIVERSITY. COLLEGE OF AGRICULTURE. MEMOIRS. (Text in Chinese and English; summaries in English) 1936. irreg. National Taiwan University, College of Agriculture, Taipei, Taiwan, Republic of China. Ed.Bd. circ. 500. Indexed: Biol.Abstr. Excerp.Med. Field Crop Abstr. Geo.Abstr. Herb.Abstr. Hort.Abstr. Ind.Vet. Rev.Plant Path. Soils & Fert. VITIS. Vet.Bull. Weed Abstr.

630   NP
NEPAL. DEPARTMENT OF AGRICULTURAL EDUCATION AND RESEARCH. ANNUAL REPORT.* (Text in English) a. Department of Agricultural Education and Research, Lalitpur, Nepal.

630   US   ISSN 0077-832X
NEW HAMPSHIRE. AGRICULTURAL EXPERIMENT STATION, DURHAM. RESEARCH REPORTS. 1961. irreg., latest issue, 1985. free. University of New Hampshire, Agricultural Experiment Station, Durham, NH 03824. TEL 603-862-1234. Indexed: Curr.Cont.

630   US   ISSN 0077-8338
NEW HAMPSHIRE. AGRICULTURAL EXPERIMENT STATION, DURHAM. STATION BULLETINS. 1888. irreg. free. University of New Hampshire, Agricultural Experiment Station, Durham, NH 03824. TEL 603-862-1234. circ. 100. Indexed: Curr.Cont.

630   US
NEW JERSEY AGRICULTURE. 1961. a. free. Department of Agriculture, CN 330, Trenton, NJ 08625. TEL 609-292-6931. Ed. Amanda Q. Zich. stat.
Incorporates (1961-1984): New Jersey. Department of Agriculture. Highlights of the Annual Report (ISSN 0077-846X)

630   US   ISSN 0548-5967
NEW MEXICO. AGRICULTURAL EXPERIMENT STATION. RESEARCH REPORT. no.348, 1977. irreg., latest 575. New Mexico State University, Agricultural Experiment Station, Drawer 3AI, Las Cruces, NM 88003. TEL 505-646-2701. Ed. Norman L. Newcomer. Indexed: Biol.Abstr. Curr.Cont. Nutr.Abstr. ASCA.

630   639.2   350   AT
NEW SOUTH WALES. DEPARTMENT OF AGRICULTURE. ANNUAL REPORT. 1890. a. McKell Building, Rawson Place, P.O. Box K220, Haymarket, N.S.W. 2000, Australia. Ed. A.S. Mitchell. circ. 1,500. (back issues avail.) Indexed: Biol.Abstr.

630   AT   ISSN 0725-6361
NEW SOUTH WALES. DEPARTMENT OF AGRICULTURE. PLANT DISEASE SURVEY. 1930. a. free. Department of Agriculture, Biological and Chemical Research Institute, P.O. Box K220, Haymarket 2000, New South Wales, Australia. Ed. R.W. McLeod. circ. 234. (back issues avail.) Indexed: Biol.Abstr. Helminthol.Abstr. Rev.Plant Path.

630   AT   ISSN 0369-5867
NEW SOUTH WALES. DEPARTMENT OF AGRICULTURE. SCIENCE BULLETIN. 1912. irreg. price varies. Department of Agriculture, P.O. Box K220, Haymarket, N.S.W. 2000, Australia. Ed. A.S. Mitchell. circ. 750.

630   AT   ISSN 0311-8576
NEW SOUTH WALES. DEPARTMENT OF AGRICULTURE. TECHNICAL BULLETIN. 1974. irreg. price varies. Department of Agriculture, P.O. Box K220, Haymarket, N.S.W. 2000, Australia. Ed. A.S. Mitchell. circ. 750.

NEW YORK'S FOOD AND LIFE SCIENCES BULLETIN. see *NUTRITION AND DIETETICS*

630   JA   ISSN 0385-8634
NIIGATA UNIVERSITY. FACULTY OF AGRICULTURE. BULLETIN/NIIGATA DAIGAKU NOGAKUBU KENKYU HOKOKU. (Text in Japanese) 1951. a. exchange basis. Niigata University, Faculty of Agriculture - Niigata Daigaku Nogakubu, 8050 Igarashi 2, Niigata-Shi, 950-21, Japan. Indexed: Excerp.Med. Field Crop Abstr. Herb.Abstr. Plant Breed.Abstr. Rev.Plant Path. Weed Abstr.
Formerly (until 1977): Niigata Agricultural Science.

630   JA   ISSN 0549-4826
NIIGATA UNIVERSITY. FACULTY OF AGRICULTURE. MEMOIRS/NIIGATA DAIGAKU NOGAKUBU KIYO. (Text in Japanese and English) 1961. a. exchange basis. Niigata University, Faculty of Agriculture - Niigata Daigaku Nogakubu, 8050 Igarashi 2, Niigata-Shi, 950-21, Japan. circ. 500. Indexed: Biol.Abstr. Chem.Abstr. Helminthol.Abstr. Plant Breed.Abstr. Rev.Plant Path. VITIS.

630   NR   ISSN 0331-6742
NOMA. 1978. a. 3 n. per issue. Ahmadu Bello University, Institute for Agricultural Research, P.M.B. 1044, Zaria, Nigeria. Ed. B.O. Uchegbu. bk. rev. charts. (processed) Indexed: Biol.Abstr. Anim.Breed.Abstr. Dairy Sci.Abstr. Hort.Abstr. Rev.Appl.Entomol. Rural Recreat.Tour.Abstr. Soils & Fert. World Agri.Econ.& Rural Sociol.Abstr.
Formerly (until 1978): Samaru Agricultural Newsletter (ISSN 0036-3731)

631.2   NO   ISSN 0065-0218
NORGES LANDBRUKSHOEGSKOLE. INSTITUTT FOR BYGNINGSTEKNIKK. BYGGEKOSTNADSINDEKS FOR DRIFTSBYGNINGER I JORDBRUKET. PRISUTVIKLINGEN. 1958. a. free. Norges Landbrukshoegskole, Institutt for Bygningsteknikk, Box 15, N-1432 Aas-NLH, Norway.

630   US
NORTH CAROLINA. DEPARTMENT OF AGRICULTURE. AGRICULTURAL REVIEW. 1925. a. free. Department of Agriculture, Raleigh, NC 27611. TEL 919-733-4216. Ed. James F. Devine. adv. circ. 61,984. (tabloid format)

630   US
NORTH CAROLINA SEED LAW. 1971. irreg. free. Department of Agriculture, Box 27647, Raleigh, NC 27611. TEL 919-733-7125. circ. controlled. (tabloid format)

353.9   US
NORTH DAKOTA. DEPARTMENT OF AGRICULTURE. BIENNIAL REPORT. 1890. biennial. free. Department of Agriculture, Bismarck, ND 58505. TEL 701-224-2231. Ed. DiAnne Olson. illus. stat. circ. 600.
Formerly: North Dakota. Department of Agriculture. Annual Report (ISSN 0093-8203)

630   UK   ISSN 0078-1746
NORTHERN IRELAND. DEPARTMENT OF AGRICULTURE. ANNUAL REPORT ON RESEARCH AND TECHNICAL WORK. 1963. a. £24. ‡ Department of Agriculture, Dundonald House, Upper Newtownards Rd., Belfast BT4 3SB, N. Ireland. Ed. C.E. Wright. circ. 375. (back issues avail.) Indexed: Biol.Abstr. Anim.Breed.Abstr. Field Crop.Abstr. Herb.Abstr. Hort.Abstr. Rev.Appl.Entomol. Rev.Plant.Path.

630   UK   ISSN 0078-1754
NORTHERN IRELAND. DEPARTMENT OF AGRICULTURE. RECORD OF AGRICULTURAL RESEARCH. 1963. irreg., vol.33, 1985. £8.50. ‡ Department of Agriculture, Dundonald House, Upper Newtownards Rd., Belfast BT4 3SB, N. Ireland. Ed. C.E. Wright. circ. 360. Indexed: Biol.Abstr. Nutr.Abstr. Anim.Breed.Abstr. Field Crop Abstr. Helminthol.Abstr. Herb.Abstr. Ind.Vet. Plant Breed.Abstr. Rev.Appl.Entomol. Rev.Plant Path. Soils & Fert. Vet.Bull. Weed Abstr.

NUCLEUS. see *PHYSICS — Nuclear Energy*

NUTRITION SOCIETY OF INDIA. PROCEEDINGS. see *NUTRITION AND DIETETICS*

630   US   ISSN 0078-3951
OHIO AGRICULTURAL RESEARCH AND DEVELOPMENT CENTER, WOOSTER. RESEARCH BULLETIN. 1888. irreg., no.1175, 1985. single copies free. Ohio State University, Ohio Agricultural Research and Development Center, Wooster, OH 44691. TEL 216-263-3777. Ed. Edward H. Roche. bibl. charts. illus. circ. 1,100. Indexed: Biol.Abstr. Curr.Cont. Excerp.Med. Nutr.Abstr. Field Crop Abstr. Helminthol.Abstr. Herb.Abstr. Plant Breed.Abstr. Rev.Appl.Entomol. Rural Recreat.Tour.Abstr. Soils & Fert. World Agri.Econ.& Rural Sociol.Abstr.

630   US   ISSN 0078-396X
OHIO AGRICULTURAL RESEARCH AND DEVELOPMENT CENTER, WOOSTER. RESEARCH CIRCULAR. 1888. irreg., no.292, 1984. single copies free. Ohio State University, Ohio Agricultural Research and Development Center, Wooster, OH 44691. TEL 216-263-3777. Ed. Edward H. Roche. bibl. charts. illus. circ. 1,100. (back issues avail.) Indexed: Biol.Abstr. Curr.Cont. Nutr.Abstr. Field Crop Abstr. Forest.Abstr. Forest Prod.Abstr. Herb.Abstr. Hort.Abstr. Ind.Vet. Plant Breed.Abstr. Rev.Appl.Entomol. Rural Recreat.Tour.Abstr. Soils & Fert. Vet.Bull. World Agri.Econ.& Rural Sociol.Abstr.

630   634.9   US   ISSN 0736-8003
OHIO STATE UNIVERSITY. AGRICULTURAL RESEARCH AND DEVELOPMENT CENTER. SPECIAL CIRCULAR. 1925. irreg., no.111, 1985. free. Ohio State University, Agricultural Research and Development Center, U.S. 250 & Ohio 83 S., Wooster, OH 44691. TEL 216-263-3777. Ed. Edward H. Roche. bibl. charts. illus. circ. 2,500. (back issues avail.)

630   CN   ISSN 0078-4664
ONTARIO. AGRICULTURAL RESEARCH INSTITUTE. REPORT. 1962/63. a. free. Agriculture Research Institute of Ontario, Legislative Bldg., Queen's Park, Toronto, Ont. M7A 1A3, Canada. TEL 416-965-6695. Dir. J.C. Rennie. circ. 2,000. Indexed: Hort.Abstr.

AGRICULTURE 33

630 PN
PANAMA. INSTITUTO DE INVESTIGACION AGROPECUARIA. INFORME ANUAL. 1976. a. Instituto de Investigacion Agropecuaria de Panama, Centro de Informacion y Documentacion Agropecuaria, Apartado 58, Santiago, Veraguas, Panama. Dir. Rodrigo Tarte.

630 PN
PANAMA. INSTITUTO DE INVESTIGACION AGROPECUARIA. MEMORIA. REUNION PANAMENA DE INFORMACION AGRICOLA. 1980. a. Instituto de Investigacion Agropecuaria de Panama, Centro de Informacion y Documentacion Agropecuaria, Apartado 6-4391, El Dorado Panama, Panama. (Co-sponsor: Grupo Panameno de Informacion Agricola) Ed. Vielka Chang-Yau. circ. 300.

630 SP
PANORAMA DE AGRICULTURA EN (YEAR) a. 300 ptas. Ministerio de Agricultura, Secretaria General Tecnica, Paseo de Infanta Isabel 1, Madrid 7, Spain. charts. stat.

630 BL
PARANA, BRAZIL. SECRETARIA DE ESTADO DA AGRICULTURA. PLANO DE ACAO. 1976. a. free. Secretaria de Estado da Agricultura, Caixa Postal 464, 8000 Curitiba, Parana, Brazil. circ. 5,000.

630 BL ISSN 0100-8161
PESQUISA EM ANDAMENTO. 1980. irreg. price varies. Centro Nacional de Pesquisa de Mandioca e Fruticultura, Rua Embrapa s/n, Caixa Postal 007, 44380 Cruz das Almas, Bahia, Brazil.

PHILIPPINE AGRICULTURAL METEOROLOGY BULLETIN. see *METEOROLOGY*

630.7 PH
PHILIPPINES. BUREAU OF VOCATIONAL EDUCATION. AGRICULTURAL EDUCATION PROGRAM; INFORMATION AND STATISTICAL GUIDE. (Text in English) irreg. Bureau of Vocational Education, Manila, Philippines. stat.

630 MY ISSN 0126-575X
PLANTER. 1920. a. M.$120. Incorporated Society of Planters, P.O. Box 10262, 50708 Kuala Lumpur, Malaysia. Ed. M. Rajadurai. adv. bk. rev. circ. 3500. Indexed: Excerp.Med. Abst.Trop.Agri. Field Crop Abstr. Geo.Abstr. Herb.Abstr. Hort.Abstr. Rural Recreat.Tour.Abstr. Rev.Plant Path. Soils & Fert. World Agri.Econ. & Rural Sociol.Abstr.

630 PL ISSN 0079-4708
POZNANSKIE TOWARZYSTWO PRZYJACIOL NAUK. KOMISJA NAUK ROLNICZYCH I KOMISJA NAUK LESNYCH. PRACE. (Text in Polish; summaries in English or German) 1950. irreg., vol. 50, 1980. price varies. (Poznanskie Towarzystwo Przyjaciol Nauk) Panstwowe Wydawnictwo Naukowe, Ul.Miodowa 10, Warsaw, Poland (Dist. by Ars Polona-Ruch, Krakowskie Przedmiescie 7, Warsaw, Poland) (Co-sponsor: Komisja Nauk Lesnych) Ed. Eugeniusz Matusiewicz. bibl. charts. illus. Indexed: Chem.Abstr.

630 CS
PRAMENY A STUDIE. Ustav Vedeckotechnickych Informaci, Ceskoslovenska Akademie Zemedelska, Slezska 7, 120 56 Prague 1, Czechoslovakia.

630 338 SP ISSN 0079-5895
PRODUCTO NETO DE LA AGRICULTURA ESPANOLA. a. Ministerio de Agricultura, Secretaria General Tecnica, Paseo Infante Isabel 1, Madrid 7, Spain.

630 PR ISSN 0163-8238
PUERTO RICO. AGRICULTURAL EXPERIMENT STATION. BULLETIN. (Text and summaries in English and Spanish) 1911. irreg. price varies. University of Puerto Rico, Agricultural Experiment Station, Publications Section, Venezuela Contract Station, Rio Piedras, PR 00927. Ed. Samuel O. Velez-Delgado. circ. 2,000. (back issues avail.) Indexed: Biol.Abstr. Helminthol.Abstr. Rev.Plant Path.

630 CN ISSN 0701-6557
QUEBEC (PROVINCE) MINISTERE DE L'AGRICULTURE. RAPPORT ANNUEL: MERITE AGRICOLE. 1972. a. Ministere de l'Agricultre, Quebec, P.Q., Canada. TEL 418-643-4991. illus.
Formerly: Quebec (Province) Ministere de l'Agriculture. Rapport du Merite Agriculture.

QUEENSLAND. LAND ADMINISTRATION COMMISSION. ANNUAL REPORT. see *PUBLIC ADMINISTRATION*

630 YU ISSN 0033-8583
RADOVI POLJOPRIVREDNOG FAKULTETA UNIVERZITETA U SARAJEVU. (Text in Yugoslavian; summaries in Dutch, English, German) 1953. a. $11.50. Univerzitet u Sarajevu, Poljoprivredni Fakultet, Zagrebacka 18, Sarajevo, Yugoslavia. Ed. Taib Saric. circ. 520. Indexed: Chem.Abstr. Nutr.Abstr. Anim.Breed.Abstr. Dairy Sci.Abstr. Field Crop Abstr. Herb.Abstr. Hort.Abstr. Plant Breed.Abstr. Rural Recreat.Tour.Abstr. Soils & Fert. Weed Abstr. World Agri.Econ.& Rural Sociol.Abstr.

630 SA
RAND SHOW LIVESTOCK & PRODUCE CATALOGUE. (Text in Afrikaans and English) a. R.0.50. Witwatersrand Agricultural Society, Box 31777, Braamfontein, Johannesburg 2000, South Africa. Ed. J.H. Kleynhans. adv.

338.1 630 US
REPORT ON VIRGINIA'S INDUSTRY OF AGRICULTURE. Cover title: Virginia's Industry of Agriculture. Report to the Governor. (Former name of issuing body: Virginia. Board of Agriculture and Commerce) a. Department of Agriculture and Consumer Services, Box 1163, Richmond, VA 23209. TEL 804-786-3978. charts. illus. stat.

630 PH
RESEARCH AT LOS BANOS. (Text in English) 1961. q. P.60($20) University of the Philippines at Los Banos, Office of the Director of Research, College, Laguna 3720, Philippines. Ed. Rosario G. Gabatin. circ. 1,000. (back issues avail.)
Formerly: Agriculture at Los Banos.

630.8 US ISSN 0731-9649
RESEARCH: VIRGINIA TECH. 1981. a. free. Virginia Polytechnic Institute and State University, Research Division, 340 Burruss Hall, Blacksburg, VA 24061. TEL 703-961-5281. Ed. Mary C. Holliman. circ. 2,000. Indexed: Biol.Abstr. Curr.Cont. Nutr.abstr. Ocean.Abstr. Plant Breed Abstr.
Supersedes: Virginia Polytechnic Institute and State University. Research Division. Bulletin; Virginia Polytechnic Institute and State University. Research Division. Report (ISSN 0097-1510)

338.1 UK
REVIEW OF THE WORLD WHEAT SITUATION. (Text in English, French, Russian and Spanish) 1960. a. International Wheat Council, Haymarket House, 28 Haymarket, London SW1Y 4SS, England. charts. stat.
Formerly: International Wheat Council. Review of the World Grains Situation (ISSN 0539-1318)

630 AG ISSN 0080-2069
REVISTA AGRONOMICA DEL NOROESTE ARGENTINO. 1953. irreg. $3. Universidad Nacional de Tucuman, Facultad de Agronomia y Zootecnia, Casilla de Correos 32, 4000 San Miguel de Tucuman, Argentina. Indexed: Biol.Abstr. Trop.Abstr. Dairy Sci.Abstr. Field Crop Abstr. Herb.Abstr. Hort.Abstr. Rural Recreat.Tour.Abstr. Rev.Plant Path. VITIS. World Agri.Econ.& Rural Sociol.Abstr.

REVISTA DE DERECHO Y REFORMA AGRARIA. see *LAW*

581 630 CU ISSN 0138-6492
REVISTA PLANTAS MEDICINALES. (Table of contents and abstracts in English) 1981. a. exchange basis. Centro de Informacion y Divulgacion Agropecuario, Gaveta Postal 4149, Havana 4, Cuba (Dist. by: Ediciones Cubanas, Obispo No. 461, Apdo. 605, Havana, Cuba) abstr. Indexed: Agrindex.

630 PL ISSN 0080-3685
ROCZNIKI NAUK ROLNICZYCH. SERIA D. MONOGRAFIE. (Text in Polish, English and Russian; summaries in English and Russian) 1903. irreg., vol.203, 1984. price varies. (Polska Akademia Nauk, Wydzial Nauk Rolniczych i Lesnych) Panstwowe Wydawnictwo Naukowe, Ul. Miodowa 10, 00-251 Warsaw, Poland (Dist. by: Ars Polona, Krakowskie Przedmiescie 7, 00-068 Warsaw, Poland) Ed. Bohdan Dobrzanski. bibl. circ. 360. Indexed: Anim.Bread.Abstr. Field Crop Abstr. Herb.Abstr. Hort.Abstr. Rev.Appl.Entomol.

ROCZNIKI NAUK ROLNICZYCH. SERIA H. RYBACTWO. see *FISH AND FISHERIES*

630 UK ISSN 0080-4134
ROYAL AGRICULTURAL SOCIETY OF ENGLAND. JOURNAL. 1839. a. £6 to non-members. Royal Agricultural Society of England, National Agricultural Centre, Kenilworth, Warwickshire, England. adv. index. circ. 17,000. Indexed: Biol.Abstr. Nutr.Abstr. Agri.Eng.Abstr. Anim.Breed.Abstr. Dairy Sci.Abstr. Field Crop Abstr. Geo.Abstr. Herb.Abstr. Hort.Abstr. Ind.Vet. Plant Breed.Abstr. RICS. Soils & Fert. Vet.Bull. Weed Abstr. World Agri.Econ.& Rural Sociol.Abstr.

630 SA
ROYAL AGRICULTURAL SOCIETY OF NATAL. ROYAL SHOW CATALOGUE. a. R.2. Royal Agricultural Society of Natal, Box 524, Pietermaritzburg 3200, South Africa. adv.

630 UK
ROYAL BATH & WEST SHOW CATALOGUE. 1852. a. £1. Royal Bath and West and Southern Counties Society, The Showground, Shepton Mallet, Somerset BA4 6QN, England. Ed. Derek I. Jarman. adv. circ. 3,000.
Formerly: Bath and West Show Catalogue.

630 UK
ROYAL HIGHLAND AND AGRICULTURAL SOCIETY OF SCOTLAND. REVIEW. 1969. a. 60p. Royal Highland and Agricultural Society of Scotland, Ingliston, Newbridge, Midlothian, Scotland. Ed. J.D.G. Davidson. adv. circ. 23,000. (tabloid format)
Formerly: Royal Highland and Agricultural Society of Scotland. Show Guide and Review.

338.01 AT ISSN 0067-2106
RURAL INDUSTRY DIRECTORY. 1958. a. free. Department of Primary Industry, Canberra, A.C.T. 2600, Australia.
Former titles: Australian Agriculture, Fisheries and Forestry Directory; Australian Primary Industry Organizations.

630 UK ISSN 0141-898X
RURAL TECHNOLOGY GUIDE. 1977. irreg. price varies (free to official bodies in developing countries) Tropical Development and Research Institute, Publications Section, College House, Wrights Lane, London W8 5SJ, England. Indexed: Field Crop Abstr. Forest.Abstr. Herb.Abstr. Rural Recreat.Tour.Abstr. World Agri.Econ.& Rural Sociol.Abstr.

630 AT ISSN 0814-4990
RUTHERGLEN RESEARCH INSTITUTE. RESEARCH REPORT. 1982. biennial. free. Rutherglen Research Institute, Department of Agriculture and Rural Affairs, 166 Wellington Parade, Melbourne, Victoria 3685, Australia. Ed. T.G. Reeves. circ. 1,000.
Formerly: Rutherglen, Australia. Research Station. Digest of Recent Research (ISSN 0080-5009)

630 636 RW
RWANDA. MINISTERE DE L'AGRICULTURE ET DE L'ELEVAGE. RAPPORT ANNUEL. a. Ministere de l'Agriculture et de l'Elevage, B.P. 621, Kigali, Rwanda.

SAINT MARY'S UNIVERSITY. ATLANTIC REGION GEOGRAPHICAL STUDIES. see *GEOGRAPHY*

630 NR ISSN 0080-5769
SAMARU MISCELLANEOUS PAPER. 1963. irreg. price varies. Ahmadu Bello University, Institute for Agricultural Research, P.M.B. 1044, Zaria, Nigeria. Indexed: Biol.Abstr. Rural Recreat.Tour.Abstr. World Agri.Econ.& Rural Sociol.Abstr.

AGRICULTURE

630 NR ISSN 0080-5777
SAMARU RESEARCH BULLETIN. 1960. price varies. Ahmadu Bello University, Institute for Agricultural Research, P.M.B. 1044, Zaria, Nigeria. Indexed: Biol.Abstr.

630 658.8 US
SAN FRANCISCO FRESH FRUIT AND VEGETABLE WHOLESALE MARKET PRICES. 1932. a. $8. Federal-State Market News Service (San Francisco), 630 Sansome St., Rm. 727, San Francisco, CA 94111.

630 MY ISSN 0080-6420
SARAWAK. DEPARTMENT OF AGRICULTURE. RESEARCH BRANCH. ANNUAL REPORT. (Text in English) 1962/63. a., latest 1977. M.20. ‡ Department of Agriculture, State Complex, Kuching, Sarawak, Malaysia. Indexed: Field Crop Abstr. Herb.Abstr. Hort.Abstr. Rev.Appl.Entomol. Rev.Plant Path.

630 CN ISSN 0319-3578
SASKATCHEWAN. DEPARTMENT OF AGRICULTURE. ANNUAL REPORT. 1905. a. Department of Agriculture, Walter Scott Bldg., Regina, Sask. S4S 0B1, Canada. TEL 306-565-5160. charts. illus. circ. 1,500. (also avail. in microfiche)

630 CN ISSN 0080-648X
SASKATCHEWAN. DEPARTMENT OF AGRICULTURE. FAMILY FARM IMPROVEMENT BRANCH. TECHNICAL BULLETIN. 1961. irreg. free. Department of Agriculture, Family Farm Improvement Branch, 1318 Winnipeg St., Regina, Sask. S4R 1J6, Canada. TEL 306-565-6281.

630 UK
SAUDI ARABIAN AGRICULTURE GUIDE. a. $65. Beacon Publications PLC., York House, Newton Close, Park Farm, Wellingborough, Northamptonshire NN8 3UW, England.

630 UK ISSN 0143-8654
SCHOOL OF AGRICULTURE, ABERDEEN. ANNUAL REPORT. a. North of Scotland College of Agriculture, 581 King St., Aberdeen AB9 1UD, Scotland. Indexed: Anim.Breed.Abstr. Helminthol.Abstr. Rural Recreat.Tour.Abstr. Rev.Plant Path. Soils & Fert. Weed Abstr. World Agri.Econ. & Rural Sociol.Abstr.
 Formerly: North of Scotland College of Agriculture, Aberdeen. Annual Report (ISSN 0550-8525)

630 340 AU
SCHRIFTENREIHE FUER AGRARWIRTSCHAFT. 1973. irreg. price varies. Oesterreichische Gesellschaft Agrarrecht, Peter Jordan Strasse 82, A-1190 Vienna, Austria. circ. 200 (approx.)

SEOUL NATIONAL UNIVERSITY. FACULTY PAPERS. BIOLOGY AND AGRICULTURE SERIES. see *BIOLOGY*

638 JA ISSN 0581-5908
SERICULTURAL EXPERIMENT STATION. ANNUAL REPORT/SANSHI SHIKENJO, NEMPO.* (Text in Japanese) 1960. a. Sericultural Experiment Station, 1-2 Owashi Yatabe-machi, Tsukuba-gun, Ibaraki 305, Japan.
 Silk

630 JA ISSN 0037-3702
SHIKOKU NATIONAL AGRICULTURAL EXPERIMENT STATION. BULLETIN. (Text in Japanese; summaries in English) 1953. a. exchange basis. Shikoku National Agricultural Experiment Station - Norin Suisan-sho Shikoku Nogyo Shikenjo, 3 Zentsuji-cho, Zentsuji-city, Kagawa-ken 765, Japan. Ed. Shigeo Oba. circ. 1,000. Indexed: Biol.Abstr. Chem.Abstr. Excerp.Med. Field Crop.Abstr. Helminthol.Abstr. Herb.Abstr. Hort.Abstr. Plant Breed.Abstr. Rural Recreat.Tour.Abstr. Rev.Plant Path. Soils & Fert. Weed Abstr. World Agri.Econ.& Rural Sociol.Abstr.

SHINSHU UNIVERSITY. FACULTY OF TEXTILE SCIENCE AND TECHNOLOGY. JOURNAL. SERIES A: BIOLOGY. see *BIOLOGY*

638.2 JA
SHINSHU UNIVERSITY. FACULTY OF TEXTILE SCIENCE AND TECHNOLOGY. JOURNAL. SERIES E: AGRICULTURE AND SERICULTURE. (Text in English and Japanese) 1955. irreg. exchange basis. Shinshu University, Faculty of Textile Science and Technology - Shinshu Daigaku Sen'i Gakubu, 3-15-1 Tokida, Ueda, Nagano 386, Japan. Indexed: Biol.Abstr.

630 370 DK ISSN 0108-2671
SKOLE & LANDBRUG. 1978. irreg. (1-2/yr.) free. Landbrugsraadet, Sektion for Samfundskontakt, Axelborg, Axeltorv 3, 1609 Copenhagen V, Denmark. illus.

630 SA
SOUTH AFRICA. DEPARTMENT OF AGRICULTURE. AGRICULTURAL BULLETINS. (Editions in Afrikaans and English) 1925. irreg. (10-12/yr.) price varies. ‡ Department of Agriculture and Water Supply, Private Bag X144, Pretoria 0001, South Africa. charts. illus. stat. circ. 1,100. Indexed: Biol.Abstr. Plant Breed.Abstr.
 Former titles: South Africa. Department of Agriculture and Fisheries. Agricultural Bulletins; South Africa. Department of Agricultural Technical Services. Agricultural Bulletins (ISSN 0002-1393)

630 SA
SOUTH AFRICA. DEPARTMENT OF AGRICULTURE. AGRICULTURAL RESEARCH. (Each yr. consists of 5 sections) 1961. a. free. Department of Agriculture and Water Supply, Private Bag X144, Pretoria 0001, South Africa. Ed. P.J.J. Steyn. circ. 100. Indexed: Anim.Breed.Abstr. Hort.Abstr.
 Former titles: South Africa. Department of Agriculture and Fisheries. Agricultural Research; South Africa: Department of Agricultural Technical Services. Agricultural Research (ISSN 0081-2145)

630 SA
SOUTH AFRICA. DEPARTMENT OF AGRICULTURE. OFFICIAL LIST OF PROFESSIONAL RESEARCH WORKERS, LECTURING STAFF AND EXTENSION WORKERS IN THE AGRICULTURAL FIELD. 1965. a. free. ‡ Department of Agriculture and Water Supply, Private Bag X144, Pretoria 0001, South Africa. circ. controlled.
 Former titles: South Africa. Department of Agriculture and Fisheries. Offical List of Professional Research Workers, Lecturing Staff and Extension Workers in the Agricultural Field; South Africa. Department of Agricultural Technical Services. Official List of Professional Research Workers, Lecturing Staff and Extension Workers in the Agricultural Field.

630 SA
SOUTH AFRICA. DEPARTMENT OF AGRICULTURE. REPORT OF THE CHIEF FOR AGRICULTURE AND WATER SUPPLY. 1960/61. a. price varies. ‡ Department of Agriculture and Water Supply, Private Bag X144, Pretoria 0001, South Africa. circ. 1,000. Indexed: Helminthol.Abstr. Rev.Plant Path. Weed Abstr.
 Formerly: South Africa. Department of Agriculture. Report of the Secretary for Agricultural Technical Services & South Africa. Department of Agriculture and Fisheries. Report of the Secretary for Agricultural Technical Services; South Africa. Department of Agricultural Technical Services. Report of the Secretary for Agricultural Technical Services (ISSN 0081-2153)

630 SA
SOUTH AFRICA. DEPARTMENT OF AGRICULTURE. SCIENCE BULLETINS. (Text in Afrikaans & English) 1911. irreg. price varies. Department of Agriculture and Water Supply, Private Bag X144, Pretoria 0001, South Africa. Ed. P.J.J. Steyn. charts. illus. stat. circ. 1,500. Indexed: Biol.Abstr. Chem.Abstr.
 Former titles: South Africa. Department of Agriculture and Fisheries. Science Bulletins; South Africa. Department of Agricultural Technical Services. Science Bulletins (ISSN 0038-1934)

630 SA
SOUTH AFRICA. DEPARTMENT OF AGRICULTURE. SPECIAL PUBLICATIONS. irreg. Department of Agriculture and Water Supply, Private Bag X144, Pretoria 0001, South Africa.
 Former titles: South Africa. Department of Agriculture and Fisheries. Special Publications; South Africa. Department of Agricultural Technical Services. Special Publication (ISSN 0081-2161)

630 SA
SOUTH AFRICA. DEPARTMENT OF AGRICULTURE. TECHNICAL COMMUNICATION. 1960. irreg., no.118, 1974. free. ‡ Department of Agriculture and Water Supply, Private Bag X144, Pretoria 0001, South Africa. Ed. P.J.J. Steyn. circ. 1,100. Indexed: Biol.Abstr. GeoRef. Rev.Plant Path.
 Formerly: South Africa. Department of Agriculture and Fisheries. Technical Communication; South Africa. Department of Agricultural Technical Services. Technical Communication (ISSN 0081-217X)

630 SP ISSN 0210-3311
SPAIN. INSTITUTO NACIONAL DE INVESTIGACIONES AGRARIAS. COMUNICACIONES. SERIE: GENERAL. (Text in Spanish; summaries in English) 1976. irreg. Instituto Nacional de Investigaciones Agrarias, Jose Abascal 56, Madrid 3, Spain. bibl. charts. illus. circ. 2,000. Indexed: Biol.Abstr.

630 SP ISSN 0210-329X
SPAIN. INSTITUTO NACIONAL DE INVESTIGACIONES AGRARIAS. COMUNICACIONES. SERIE: PRODUCCION VEGETAL. 1973. irreg. 175 ptas. Instituto Nacional de Investigaciones Agrarias, Jose Abascal 56, Madrid 3, Spain. bibl. charts. circ. 2,000. Indexed: Biol.Abstr. Plant Breed.Abstr. Soils & Fert. Weed.Abstr.

630 SP ISSN 0302-8755
SPAIN. INSTITUTO NACIONAL DE INVESTIGACIONES AGRARIAS. COMUNICACIONES. SERIE: PROTECCION VEGETAL. 1974. irreg. (Instituto Nacional de Investigaciones Agrarias) Ministerio de Agricultura, Pesca y Alimentacion, Jose Abascal, 56, Madrid 3, Spain. charts. illus. circ. 2,000. Indexed: Biol.Abstr. Field Crop Abstr. Herb.Abstr. Rev.Plant Path.

630 SP ISSN 0210-2560
SPAIN. INSTITUTO NACIONAL DE INVESTIGACIONES AGRARIAS. COMUNICACIONES. SERIE: TECNOLOGIA AGRARIA. 1974. Instituto Nacional de Investigaciones Agrarias, Jose Abascal 56, Madrid 3, Spain. bibl. charts. circ. 2,000. Indexed: Biol.Abstr. Soils & Fert.

630 SP
SPAIN. INSTITUTO NACIONAL DE INVESTIGACIONES AGRARIAS. INVESTIGACION AGRARIA: PRODUCCION Y PROTECCION VEGETALES. 1986. irreg. Instituto Nacional de Investigaciones Agrarias, Jose Abascal, 56, 28003 Madrid, Spain.

630 SP ISSN 0213-0602
SPAIN. MINISTERIO DE AGRICULTURA, PESCA Y ALIMENTACION. INFORMACION EXTRANJERO. BOLETIN. biennial. 2000 ptas. to individuals; students 1500 ptas.; foreign 2500 ptas. Ministerio de Agricultura, Pesca y Alimentacion, Secretaria General Tecnica, Paseo de Infanta Isabel, 1, 28014 Madrid, Spain.

630 UN ISSN 0081-4539
STATE OF FOOD AND AGRICULTURE. (Text in English, French and Spanish) 1947. a. $16. Food and Agriculture Organization of the United Nations, Distribution and Sales Section, Via delle Terme di Caracalla, Rome, Italy (Dist. in U.S. by: Bernan Associates-Unipub, 4611-F Assembly Drive, Lanham, MD 20706-4391)

630 DK ISSN 0106-8857
STATENS HUSDYRBRUGSFORSOEG. MEDDELELSE. (Text in Danish) irreg. Kr.175. Statens Husdyrbrugsforsoeg, Administration, P.O. Box 39, DK-8833 Oerum SDRL, Denmark. (back issues avail.)

STATISTICAL YEAR BOOK OF INDONESIA. see *POPULATION STUDIES*

AGRICULTURE

630   US
STORRS AGRICULTURAL EXPERIMENT STATION. BULLETIN. 1888. irreg., no.471, 1985. price varies, usually free. Storrs Agricultural Experiment Station, Agricultural Publications, U-35, University of Agriculture, Storrs, CT 06268. TEL 203-486-3334. circ. 300. Indexed: Biol.Abstr. GeoRef.

630   US   ISSN 0069-8997
STORRS AGRICULTURAL EXPERIMENT STATION. RESEARCH REPORT. 1964. irreg., no.79, 1984. price varies, usually free. ‡ Storrs Agricultural Experiment Station, Agricultural Publications, U-35, University of Connecticut, Storrs, CT 06268. TEL 203-486-3334. circ. 300(approx.) Indexed: Biol.Abstr. Excerp.Med.

630   US   ISSN 0730-6490
SUGAR PROCESSING RESEARCH CONFERENCE. PROCEEDINGS. 1982. irreg. U.S. Department of Agriculture, Agricultural Research Service (New Orleans), Box 53326, New Orleans, LA 70153. Indexed: Chem.Abstr.
   Formerly: Technical Session on Cane Sugar Refining Research. Proceedings.

630   US   ISSN 0160-0680
SULPHUR IN AGRICULTURE. 1977. a. free to qualified personnel. Sulphur Institute, 1725 K St., N.W., Washington, DC 20006. TEL 202-331-9660. Ed. Judith A. Jacobs. circ. 3,000. (back issues avail.) Indexed: Biol.Abstr. Chem.Abstr. Field Crop Abstr. Herb.Abstr. Soils & Fert.
   Supersedes: Sulphur Institute Journal (ISSN 0039-4904)

630   SW
SVERIGES LANTBRUKSUNIVERSITET. INSTITUTIONEN FOER VAEXTODLING. RAPPORTER OCH AVHANDLINGAR. 1973. irreg. Sveriges Lantbruksuniversitet, Institutionen foer Vaextodling - Swedish University of Agricultural Sciences, Department of Plant Husbandry, Box 7043, S-750 07 Uppsala, Sweden. Indexed: Biol.Abstr. Hort.Abstr. Plant Breed.Abstr.
   Formerly (until 1977): Lantbrukshoegskolan Institutionen foer Vaextodling. Rapporter och Arhandlingar (ISSN 0346-7236)

338.1   SQ
SWAZILAND. CENTRAL STATISTICAL OFFICE. CENSUS OF INDIVIDUAL TENURE FARMS. 1968/69. a., latest 1980/81. free. Central Statistical Office, P.O. Box 456, Mbabane, Swaziland. stat. circ. 600. (processed)

354.68   SQ
SWAZILAND. MINISTRY OF AGRICULTURE. ANNUAL REPORT. 1967. a. Ministry of Agriculture, Mbabane, Swaziland. stat. Indexed: Anim.Breed.Abstr. Field Crop Abstr. Herb.Abstr. Hort.Abstr. Rev.Appl.Entomol.

630   PL
SZKOLA GLOWNA GOSPODARSTWA WIEJSKIEGO - AKADEMIA ROLNICZA. ROZPRAWY NAUKOWE I MONOGRAFIE/ WARSAW AGRICULTURAL UNIVERSITY. TREATISES AND MONOGRAPHS. (Until 1980, part of Zeszyty Naukowe series) (Text in Polish or English) 1957. irreg. $5 per no. Warsaw Agricultural University Press, Ul. Nowoursynowska 166, 02-766 Warsaw, Poland (Dist. by: Ars Polona-Ruch, Krakowskie Przedmiescie 7, 00-068 Warsaw, Poland) Ed. H. Sandner.

630   CH
TAIWAN AGRICULTURAL RESEARCH INSTITUTE. ANNUAL REPORT. (Text in Chinese) 1946. a. Taiwan Agricultural Research Institute, Taichung, Taiwan, Republic of China. charts. illus. stat.

630 581   CH
TAIWAN AGRICULTURAL RESEARCH INSTITUTE. RESEARCH SUMMARY. irreg., latest June 1975. Taiwan Agricultural Research Institute, Taichung, Taiwan, Republic of China.

630   JA   ISSN 0082-156X
TAMAGAWA UNIVERSITY. FACULTY OF AGRICULTURE. BULLETIN. (Text in English, German and Japanese; summaries in English and German) 1960. a. available on exchange. Tamagawa University, Faculty of Agriculture - Tamagawa Daigaku Nogakubu, 6-1-1 Tamagawagakuen, Machida, Tokyo 194, Japan. Indexed: Biol.Abstr. Excerp.Med. Field Crop Abstr. Herb.Abstr. Hort.Abstr. Plant Breed.Abstr. Rev.Plant Path. VITIS. Weed Abstr.

630 070   GW   ISSN 0082-1845
TASCHENBUCH FUER AGRARJOURNALISTEN. 1957. a. DM.29.50. (Verband der Agrarjournalisten) B. Behr's Verlag GmbH, Averhoffstr. 10, 2000 Hamburg 76, W. Germany (B.R.D.)

630   AT   ISSN 0082-1993
TASMANIA. DEPARTMENT OF AGRICULTURE. ANNUAL REPORT. 1928. a. free. ‡ Department of Agriculture, Box 192 B, G.P.O., Hobart, Tasmania, Australia. Ed. J.M. Glover. circ. 350. Indexed: Biol.Abstr. Anim.Breed.Abstr. Field Crop Abstr. Herb.Abstr. Weed Abstr.

630   IS   ISSN 0333-5879
TECHNION - ISRAEL INSTITUTE OF TECHNOLOGY. FACULTY OF AGRICULTURAL ENGINEERING. PUBLICATIONS. (Text in English & Hebrew) 1964. irreg. free. Technion - Israel Institute of Technology, Lowdermilk Department of Agricultural Engineering, Technion City, Haifa 32000, Israel. circ. controlled.

THOMAS SAY FOUNDATION MONOGRAPHS. see *BIOLOGY — Entomology*

630   PE
TIERRA Y SOCIEDAD. 1978. irreg. Archivo del Fuero Agrario, Paita 429, Lima, Peru.

630   JA   ISSN 0387-172X
TOHOKU NATIONAL AGRICULTURAL EXPERIMENT STATION. MISCELLANEOUS PUBLICATION. (Text in Japanese or English; summaries in English) 1978. irreg. Tohoku National Agricultural Experiment Station, Shimo-Kuriyagawa Morioka, Iwate 020-01, Japan.

630   JA
TOHOKU UNIVERSITY. INSTITUTE FOR AGRICULTURAL RESEARCH. REPORTS. (Text in English) 1950. a. free. Tohoku University, Institute for Agricultural Research - Tohoku Daigaku Nogaku Kenkyusho, 2-1-1 Katahira, Sendai 980, Japan. Ed. Norindo Takahashi. Indexed: Biol.Abstr. Chem.Abstr.
   Formerly: Tohoku University. Research Institutes. Science Reports. Series D: Agriculture (ISSN 0082-4666)

631.3   DK   ISSN 0563-8887
TOOLS AND TILLAGE; a journal on the history of the implements of cultivation and other agricultural processes. (Text in English; summaries in German) 1968. a. Nationalmuseet, Oplysningsafdelingen, Ny Vestergade 10, DK-1471 Copenhagen K, Denmark. Ed.Bd. bk. rev. charts. illus. Indexed: M.L.A. Br.Archaeol.Abstr.

630.7   JA   ISSN 0082-5360
TOTTORI UNIVERSITY. FACULTY OF AGRICULTURE. JOURNAL. (Text in European languages) 1951. a. exchange basis only. Tottori University, Faculty of Agriculture - Tottori Daigaku Nogakubu, 1-1 Koyama-cho, Tottori 680, Japan. Ed.Bd. Indexed: Biol.Abstr. Field Crop Abstr. Forest.Abstr. Forest Prod.Abstr. Herb.Abstr. Ind.Vet. Plant Breed.Abstr. Vet.Bull. Weed Abstr.

TRAINING FOR AGRICULTURE AND RURAL DEVELOPMENT. see *EDUCATION — Adult Education*

630   TU   ISSN 0082-6928
TURKEY. DEVLET ISTATISTIK ENSTITUSU. TARIM ISTATISTIKLERI OZETI/SUMMARY OF AGRICULTURAL STATISTICS. (Text in Turkish and English) 1963. a. free or on exchange basis. State Institute of Statistics, Necatibey Caddesi 114, Ankara, Turkey.

630   TU   ISSN 0082-6936
TURKEY. DEVLET ISTATISTIK ENSTITUSU. TARIMSAL YAPI VE URETIM/ AGRICULTURAL STRUCTURE AND PRODUCTION. (Text in English and Turkish) 1951. a. free. State Institute of Statistics, Necatibey Caddesi 114, Ankara, Turkey.

630   II   ISSN 0067-3471
U A S EXTENSION SERIES. 1967. irreg., no. 13, 1983. University of Agricultural Sciences, Bangalore, Communication Centre, Hebbal, Bangalore 560024, Karnataka, India. Ed. K.M. Jayaramaiah. circ. 500. (also avail. in microform from UMI; reprint service avail. from ISI and UMI)

630   II   ISSN 0067-348X
U A S MISCELLANEOUS SERIES. 1965. irreg., no. 33, 1984. price varies. University of Agricultural Sciences, Bangalore, Communication Centre, Hebbal, Bangalore 560024, Karnataka, India. Ed. K.M. Jayaramaiah. circ. 500. (also avail. in microform from UMI; reprint service avail. from ISI and UMI)

U S - CANADIAN RANGE MANAGEMENT; a selected bibliography on ranges, pastures, wildlife, livestock, and ranching. see *BIBLIOGRAPHIES*

630   GW
UEBERSICHTEN ZUR TIERERNAEHRUNG. 1973. irreg. (2-4/yr.) DM.7.60 per issue. Deutsche Landwirtschafts-Gesellschaft Verlags GmbH, Ruesterstr. 13, 6000 Frankfurt/Main, W. Germany (B.R.D.) Ed.Bd. Indexed: Chem.Abstr. Nutr.Abstr. Anim.Breed.Abstr. Field Crop Abstr. Herb.Abstr. Ind.Vet. Vet.Bull.

630 370   FR   ISSN 0082-7711
UNION NATIONALE DE L'ENSEIGNEMENT AGRICOLE PRIVE. ANNUAIRE. 1968. a. 120 Fr. Union Nationale de l'Enseignement Agricole Prive, 14 rue Drouot, 75009 Paris, France. adv. bk. rev.

UNITED FARMERS TRADING AGENCY YEAR BOOK AND DIARY. see *BUSINESS AND ECONOMICS — Domestic Commerce*

630.8   US   ISSN 0092-1785
U.S. AGRICULTURAL RESEARCH SERVICE. A R S - N C. 1972. irreg., no. 20, 1975. ‡ U.S. Department of Agriculture, Agricultural Research Service, North Central Region, 1815 N. University St., Peoria, IL 61604-3999. illus. Indexed: Biol.Abstr. Key Title: A.R.S. N.C. Agricultural Research Service. North Central Region.

630   US   ISSN 0082-9315
U.S. BUREAU OF THE CENSUS. CENSUS OF AGRICULTURE. 1840. quinquennial. price varies. U.S. Bureau of the Census., Customer Services, Washington, DC 20233 TEL 301-763-4100. (Orders to: Supt. of Documents, Washington, DC 20402) (also avail. in microfiche)

630   US
U.S. DEPARTMENT OF AGRICULTURE. AGRICULTURAL COOPERATIVE SERVICE. COOPERATIVE INFORMATION REPORT. 1977. irreg. free. U.S. Department of Agriculture, Agricultural Cooperative Service, 14th St., & Independence Ave, S.W., Washington, DC 20250. TEL 202-655-4000.
   Supersedes: U.S. Department of Agriculture. Farmer Cooperative Service. Information (Series) (ISSN 0082-9765)

630   US   ISSN 0065-4612
U.S. DEPARTMENT OF AGRICULTURE. AGRICULTURE HANDBOOK. 1949. irreg. U.S. Department of Agriculture, Washington, DC 20250. TEL 202-655-4000. Indexed: Biol.Abstr. Forest.Abstr. Forest Prod.Abstr.

630.82   US   ISSN 0065-4639
U.S. DEPARTMENT OF AGRICULTURE. AGRICULTURE INFORMATION BULLETIN. 1949. irreg. U.S. Department of Agriculture, Washington, DC 20250. TEL 202-655-4000. Indexed: Biol.Abstr. Forest.Abstr. Forest Prod.Abstr. GeoRef. Rural Recreat.Tour.Abstr. Soils & Fert. World Agri.Econ.& Rural Sociol.Abstr.

630 US ISSN 0082-9803
U.S. DEPARTMENT OF AGRICULTURE.
REPORT OF THE SECRETARY OF
AGRICULTURE. 1862. a. free. U.S. Department of
Agriculture, Office of Information, OGPA,
Washington, DC 20250. TEL 202-655-4000.

630 US ISSN 0082-9811
U.S. DEPARTMENT OF AGRICULTURE.
TECHNICAL BULLETIN. 1927. irreg. U.S.
Department of Agriculture., Washington, DC 20250.
TEL 202-655-4000. Indexed: Biol.Abstr. Field Crop
Abstr. Forest.Abstr. Forest Prod.Abstr.
Herb.Abstr. Hort.Abstr. Rev.Appl.Entomol.
Rev.Plant Path. Soils & Fert.

630.58 US ISSN 0084-3628
U.S. DEPARTMENT OF AGRICULTURE.
YEARBOOK OF AGRICULTURE. 1894. a. price
varies. U.S. Department of Agriculture, 14th St. &
Independence Ave. S.W., Washington, DC 20250
TEL 202-655-4000. (Orders to: Supt. to Documents,
Washington, DC 20402) Indexed: Biol.Abstr.
Nutr.Abstr. Plant Breed.Abstr.

630 VE ISSN 0041-8285
UNIVERSIDAD CENTRAL DE VENEZUELA.
FACULTAD DE AGRONOMIA. REVISTA. (Text
mainly in Spanish; summaries in English and
Spanish.) 1952. irreg., vol.12, 1982. Bs.172 or on
exchange. Universidad Central de Venezuela,
Facultad de Agronomia, Apdo. 4579, Maracay-
Edo. Aragua 2101, Venezuela. Ed. Francisco
Fernandez Yepez. bibl. charts. illus. stat. circ. 1,
500. Indexed: Biol.Abstr. Chem.Abstr. Nutr.Abstr.
Agrindex. Field Crop Abstr. Herb.Abstr.
Hort.Abstr. Ind.Agr.Am.Lat.Caribe. Plant
Breed.Abstr. Rev.Appl.Entomol. Rev.Plant Path.
Soils & Fert. Weed Abstr.

630 VE
UNIVERSIDAD CENTRAL DE VENEZUELA.
FACULTAD DE AGRONOMIA. REVISTA
ALCANCE. (Text in Spanish; summaries in
English) 1956. irreg. price varies. Universidad
Central de Venezuela, Facultad de Agronomia,
Apdo. 4579, Maracay, Edo. Aragua, Venezuela.
abstr. bibl. illus. circ. 1,500. Indexed: Biol.Abstr.
Bibl.Agri.

630 UY
UNIVERSIDAD DE LA REPUBLICA. FACULTAD
DE AGRONOMIA. BOLETIN. 1953. irreg.
Universidad de la Republica, Facultad de
Agronomia, Avda. Garzon, Casilla de Correo 1238,
Montevideo, Uruguay. circ. 500. Indexed:
Biol.Abstr.

630 UY ISSN 0077-1260
UNIVERSIDAD DE URUGUAY. FACULTAD DE
AGRONOMIA. BOLETIN. 1953. irreg. free on
exchange. ‡ Universidad de Uruguay, Facultad de
Agronomia, Avda. Garzon 780, Montevideo,
Uruguay. circ. 1,000. Indexed: Biol.Abstr.
Chem.Abstr.

UNIVERSIDADE DE SAO PAULO. INSTITUTO
DE PESQUISAS ECONOMICAS.
ESTATISTICAS BASICAS DO SETOR
AGRICOLA NO BRASIL. see
AGRICULTURE — Abstracting, Bibliographies,
Statistics

630 BL ISSN 0084-8646
UNIVERSIDADE FEDERAL DO CEARA.
ESCOLA DE AGRONOMIA. DEPARTAMENTO
DE FITOTECNIA. RELATORIA TECNICO.*
irreg. free. Universidade Federal do Ceara, Escola
de Agronomia, Departamento de Filotecnia, Caixa
Postal 354, Fortaleza, Ceara 60000, Brazil.

630 BL
UNIVERSIDADE FEDERAL DO RIO GRANDE
DO SUL. FACULDADE DE AGRONOMIA.
BOLETIM TECNICO. (Text in Portuguese;
summaries in English) 1985. irreg. Cr.$30.
Universidade Federal do Rio Grande do Sul,
Faculdade de Agronomia, Departamento de Solos,
Bento Goncalves 7712, Caixa Postal 776, 90000
Porto Alegre, R.S., Brazil (Dist. by: Instituto Rio
Grandense do Arroz, Dpto. de Obras e Assistencia
Tecnica, Av. Julio de Castilhos, 585- 1 andar,
90.000 Porto Alegre, Brazil) bibl. charts. illus. circ.
300. Indexed: Biol.Abstr. Chem.Abstr. Field Crop
Abstr.

630 IT ISSN 0365-0502
UNIVERSITA DEGLI STUDI DI BARI. FACOLTA
DI AGRARIA. ANNALI. 1939. a. exchange.
Universita degli Studi di Bari, Facolta di Agraria,
Via G. Amendola 165/a, 70126 Bari, Italy. Ed.Bd.
index. circ. 500. (back issues avail.)

630 IT ISSN 0082-6871
UNIVERSITA DI TORINO. FACOLTA DI
AGRARIA. ANNALI. (Text in Italian; summaries
in English) 1962. a. available on exchange.
Universita di Torino, Facolta di Agraria, Via P.
Giuria 15, 10126 Turin, Italy. Ed. Italo Currado.
index. circ. 600. (back issues avail.) Indexed:
Biol.Abstr.

630 634.9 AU ISSN 0256-4246
UNIVERSITAET FUER BODENKULTUR IN
WIEN. DISSERTATIONEN. 1972. irreg., no.29,
1986. price varies. (Universitaet fuer Bodenkultur in
Wien) Verband der Wissenschaftlichen
Gesellschaften Oesterreichs, Lindengasse 37, A-
1070 Vienna, Austria.
Formerly: Hochschule fuer Bodenkultur in Wien.
Dissertationen.

630 GW ISSN 0075-4609
UNIVERSITAET GIESSEN. ERGEBNISSE
LANDWIRTSCHAFTLICHER FORSCHUNG.
1956. irreg. DM.25 per no. FB 17
Agrarwissenschaften, Bismarkstr. 24, 6300 Giessen,
W. Germany (B.R.D.) Ed. H. Boland. circ. 250.
Indexed: Geo.Abstr.

630 GW
UNIVERSITAET KIEL.
AGRARWISSENSCHAFTLICHE FAKULTAET.
SCHRIFTENREIHE. 1950. irreg., no.66, 1984.
price varies. Verlag Paul Parey (Hamburg),
Spitalerstr. 12, 2000 Hamburg 1, W. Germany
(B.R.D.) bibl. illus. index. (reprint service avail.
from ISI) Indexed: Biol.Abstr. Agri.Eng.Abstr.

UNIVERSITATEA DIN CRAIOVA. ANALE.
SERIA: BIOLOGIE, AGRONOMIE,
HORTICULTURA. see BIOLOGY

630 SQ
UNIVERSITY COLLEGE OF SWAZILAND.
AGRICULTURAL RESEARCH DIVISION.
ANNUAL REPORT. 1970. a. University College of
Swaziland, Agricultural Research Division,
Swaziland Campus, P.O. Luyengo, Swaziland.
Indexed: Biol.Abstr. Field Crop Abstr. Herb.Abstr.
Hort.Abstr.
Former titles: University of Botswana, Lesotho
and Swaziland. Agricultural Research Division.
Annual Report; University of Botswana, Lesotho
and Swaziland. Faculty of Agriculture. Research
Division. Annual Report; Swaziland. Department of
Agriculture. Research Division. Report.

630 II ISSN 0067-3455
UNIVERSITY OF AGRICULTURAL SCIENCES,
BANGALORE. ANNUAL REPORT. 1964-65. a.
Rs.15. University of Agricultural Sciences,
Bangalore, Communication Centre, Hebbal,
Bangalore 560024, Karnataka, India. Ed. K.M.
Jayaramaiah. circ. 1,000. (also avail. in microform
from UMI; reprint service avail. ISI and UMI)
Indexed: Biol.Abstr. Field Crop Abstr. Herb.Abstr.
Hort.Abstr.

630 II
UNIVERSITY OF AGRICULTURAL SCIENCES,
BANGALORE. COLLABORATIVE SERIES.
(Text in English) 1968. irreg., no. 3, 1976. price
varies. University of Agricultural Sciences,
Bangalore, Communication Centre, Hebbal,
Bangalore 560024, Karnataka, India. (reprint service
avail. from ISI and UMI)

630 II
UNIVERSITY OF AGRICULTURAL SCIENCES,
BANGALORE. EDUCATIONAL SERIES. (Text
in English) 1969. irreg., no. 7, 1981. price varies.
University of Agricultural Sciences, Bangalore,
Communication Centre, Hebbal, Bangalore 560024,
Karnataka, India. (reprint service avail. from ISI and
UMI)

630 II
UNIVERSITY OF AGRICULTURAL SCIENCES,
BANGALORE. INFORMATION SERIES. (Text
in English) irreg., no.8, 1979. price varies.
University of Agricultural Sciences, Bangalore,
Communication Centre, Hebbal, Bangalore 560024,
Karnataka, India. (reprint service avail. from ISI and
UMI)

630 II
UNIVERSITY OF AGRICULTURAL SCIENCES,
BANGALORE. RESEARCH MONOGRAPH
SERIES. irreg., no. 4, 1978. price varies. University
of Agricultural Sciences, Bangalore, Communication
Centre, Hebbal, Bangalore 560024, Karnataka,
India. (reprint service avail. from ISI and UMI)

630 II
UNIVERSITY OF AGRICULTURAL SCIENCES,
BANGALORE. RESEARCH REVIEW SERIES.
(Text in English) 1977. irreg., latest issue no. 5.
University of Agriculture Sciences, Bangalore,
Communication Center, Hebbal, Bangalore 560024,
Karnataka, India. (reprint service avail. from ISI,
UMI)

630 II
UNIVERSITY OF AGRICULTURAL SCIENCES,
BANGALORE. TECHNICAL INFORMATION
SERIES. (Text in Kannada) 1975. irreg., no.4, 1980.
price varies. University of Agricultural Sciences,
Bangalore, Communication Centre, Hebbal,
Bangalore 560024, Karnataka, India. (reprint service
avail. from ISI and UMI)

630 II
UNIVERSITY OF AGRICULTURAL SCIENCES,
BANGALORE. TECHNICAL SERIES. (Text in
English) 1973. irreg., latest issue no. 45, 1984. price
varies. University of Agricultural Sciences,
Bangalore, Communication Centre, Hebbal,
Bangalore 560024, Karnataka, India. (reprint service
avail. from ISI and UMI) Indexed: Biol.Abstr.

630 II
UNIVERSITY OF AGRICULTURAL SCIENCES,
BANGALORE. U A S TEXTBOOK SERIES.
(Text in English) 1979. irreg. University of
Agricultural Sciences, Bangalore, Communication
Center, Hebbal, Bangalore 560024, Karnataka,
India. (reprint service avail. from ISI, UMI)

630 636.089 TZ
UNIVERSITY OF DAR ES SALAAM. FACULTY
OF AGRICULTURE, FORESTRY AND
VETERINARY SCIENCE. ANNUAL RECORD
OF RESEARCH. (Text in English) 1979. a. $6.
Sokoine University of Agriculture, Box 3022,
Morogoro, Tanzania. Ed. M. Mgheni. circ. 1,000.

630 US ISSN 0072-1271
UNIVERSITY OF GEORGIA. COLLEGE OF
AGRICULTURE EXPERIMENT STATIONS.
BULLETIN. irreg. free controlled circ. ‡ University
of Georgia, College of Agriculture Experiment
Stations, Connor Hall, Athens, GA 30602. TEL
404-542-3621. Ed. Kathleen Sheridan. Indexed:
Excerp.Med.

630 US ISSN 0072-128X
UNIVERSITY OF GEORGIA. COLLEGE OF
AGRICULTURE EXPERIMENT STATIONS.
RESEARCH REPORTS. 1967. irreg., no. 43, 1969.
controlled free circ. ‡ University of Georgia, College
of Agriculture Experiment Stations, Connor Hall,
Athens, GA 30602. TEL 404-542-3621. Ed.
Kathleen Sheridan. circ. 1,500. Indexed: Nutr.Abstr.
Field Crop Abstr. Herb.Abstr. Hort.Abstr. Plant
Breed.Abstr. Rural Recreat.Tour.Abstr. Soils &
Fert. World Agri.Econ.& Rural Sociol.Abstr.

630 US
UNIVERSITY OF ILLINOIS AT URBANA-
CHAMPAIGN. AGRICULTURAL
EXPERIMENT STATION. RESEARCH
PROGRESS. 1888. biennial. free. University of
Illinois at Urbana-Champaign, Agricultural
Experiment Station, 47 Mumford Hall, 1301 W.
Gregory Dr., Urbana, IL 61801. TEL 217-333-0240.
Ed. L. McCarthy. circ. 1,700.

AGRICULTURE

630   CN
UNIVERSITY OF MANITOBA. FACULTY OF AGRICULTURE. ANNUAL PROGRESS REVIEW: AGRICULTURAL RESEARCH, TEACHING AND EXTENSION. 1954. a. University of Manitoba, Faculty of Agriculture, Winnipeg, Man., Canada. TEL 204-474-9423. circ. 1,000.
    Formerly: University of Manitoba. Faculty of Agriculture. Progress Report on Agricultural Research and Experimentation (ISSN 0076-4051)

630   574   JA   ISSN 0474-7852
UNIVERSITY OF OSAKA PREFECTURE. BULLETIN. SERIES B: AGRICULTURE AND BIOLOGY/OSAKA-FURITSU DAIGAKU KIYO, B NOGAKU, SEIBUTSUGAKU. (Text in Japanese and European languages) 1951. a. exchange basis. University of Osaka Prefecture - Osaka-furitsu Daigaku, 4-804 Mozuume-machi, Sakai-shi, Osaka 591, Japan. Indexed: Biol.Abstr. Chem.Abstr. Field Crop Abstr. Herb.Abstr. Hort.Abstr. Ind.Vet. Plant Breed.Abstr. Soils & Fert. Vet.Bull.

630   PH
UNIVERSITY OF THE PHILIPPINES AT LOS BANOS. AGRARIAN REFORM INSTITUTE. OCCASIONAL PAPERS. 1975. irreg. free. University of the Philippines at Los Banos, Agrarian Reform Institute, Laguna 3720, Philippines. Ed. Honorio C. Batangantang. circ. 500.

630   JA   ISSN 0370-4246
UNIVERSITY OF THE RYUKYUS. COLLEGE OF AGRICULTURE. SCIENCE BULLETIN/ RYUKYU DAIGAKU NOGAKUBU GAKUJUTSU HOKOKU. (Text in English or Japanese) 1954. a. free. University of the Ryukyus, College of Agriculture - Ryukyu Daigaku Nogakubu, 59 Senbaru, Nishihara-cho, Okinawa 90301, Japan. circ. 400. Indexed: Biol.Abstr. Nutr.Abstr. Forest.Abstr. Hort.Abstr. Ind.Vet. Plant Breed.Abstr. Vet.Bull. Weed Abstr.

630   JA   ISSN 0386-250X
VEGETABLE AND ORNAMENTAL CROPS RESEARCH STATION. BULLETIN. SERIES B. (Text in Japanese; summaries in English) 1977. irreg. 92 Nabeyashiki, Shimokuriyagawa, Morioka, Iwata, Japan (Subscr. to: Morioka Branch, Vegetable and Ornamental Crops Research Station, Shimokuriyagawa, Morioka, Iwate 020-01, Japan) Ed. Katsuya Takada. circ. 800.

338.1   VE   ISSN 0083-5366
VENEZUELA. MINISTERIO DE AGRICULTURA Y CRIA. DIRECCION DE ECONOMICA Y ESTADISTICA AGROPECUARIA. ANUARIO ESTADISTICO AGROPECUARIO. 1961. a. free. Ministerio de Agricultura y Cria, Direccion de Planificacion y Estadistica, Division de Estadistica, Torre Norte, Torre Norte-Caracas, Venezuela.

630   398   GW
VEREIN OBERPFAELZISCHES BAUERNMUSEUM. MITTEILUNGEN. 1964. a. Verein Oberpfaelzisches Bauernmuseum e.V., Regensburgerstr. 51, 8470 Nabburg, W. Germany (B.R.D.) circ. 500.

630   US   ISSN 0083-5706
VERMONT. AGRICULTURAL EXPERIMENT STATION, BURLINGTON. RESEARCH REPORT. 1951. irreg., no.45, 1985. free. Vermont Agricultural Experiment Station, University of Vermont, Burlington, VT 05405. Ed. LaRae M. Donnellan.
    Before 1968: Vermont. Agricultural Experiment Station, Burlington. Miscellaneous Publications Series.

630   US   ISSN 0083-5714
VERMONT. AGRICULTURAL EXPERIMENT STATION, BURLINGTON. STATION BULLETIN SERIES. 1887. irreg., no.692, 1984. free. Vermont Agricultural Experiment Station, University of Vermont, Morrill Hall, Burlington, VT 05405. Ed. LaRae M. Donnellan.

630   US   ISSN 0083-5722
VERMONT. AGRICULTURAL EXPERIMENT STATION, BURLINGTON. PAMPHLET SERIES. 1943. irreg., no.41, 1978. free. Vermont Agricultural Experiment Station, University of Vermont, Burlington, VT 05405. Ed. LaRae M. Donnellan.

630   US
VERMONT. AGRICULTURAL EXPERIMENT STATION, BURLINGTON. TECHNICAL NOTES. 1981. irreg., no.2, 1982. free. Vermont Agricultural Experiment Station, University of Vermont, Burlington, VT 05405. Ed. LaRae M. Donnellan. circ. 500.

630   US   ISSN 0742-7425
VIRGINIA POLYTECHNIC INSTITUTE AND STATE UNIVERSITY. COLLEGE OF AGRICULTURE AND LIFE SCIENCES. INFORMATION SERIES. 1982. irreg. Virginia Polytechnic Institute and State University, College of Agriculture and Life Sciences, Blacksburg, VA 24061. TEL 703-961-6986. Ed. Mary C. Holliman. circ. 1,000.

630   US
VIRGINIA POLYTECHNIC INSTITUTE AND STATE UNIVERSITY. VIRGINIA AGRICULTURAL EXPERIMENT STATION. AGRICULTURAL RESEARCH DIGEST. 1984. irreg. Virginia Polytechnic Institute and State University, Virginia Agricultural Experiment Station, Blacksburg, VA 24061. TEL 703-961-6986. Ed. Mary C. Holliman. circ. 1,000.
    Formerly: Virginia Polytechnic Institute and State University. College of Agriculture and Life Sciences. Virginia Agricultural Station. Agricultural Research Digest.

630   US
VIRGINIA POLYTECHNIC INSTITUTE AND STATE UNIVERSITY. VIRGINIA AGRICULTURAL EXPERIMENT STATION. BULLETIN. 1981. irreg. Blacksburg, VA 24061. TEL 703-961-6986. Ed. Mary C. Holliman. circ. 1,000.

631   630   CS
VYSKUMNY USTAV LUK A PASIENKOV V BANSKEJ BYSTRICI. VEDECKE PRACE. (Text in Czech and Slovak; summaries in English and Russian) vol.17, 1983. biennial. (Vyskumny Ustav Luk a Pasienkov) Priroda, Krizkova 9, 815 34 Bratislava, Czechoslovakia. Ed. Alena Capkova. Indexed: Biol.Abstr.

630   574   CS
VYSKUMNY USTAV RASTINNEJ VYROBY V PIESTANOCH. VEDECKE PRACE. (Text in Slovak; summaries in English, Russian) 1961. a. (Vyskumny Ustav Rastlinnej Vyroby v Pestanoch) Priroda, Krizkova 9, 815 34 Bratislava, Czechoslovakia. circ. 400. Indexed: Biol.Abstr. Nutr.Abstr.

630   PL   ISSN 0208-5712
WARSAW AGRICULTURAL UNIVERSITY. S G G W - A R. ANNALS. AGRICULTURE. (Szkola Glowna Gospodarstwa Wiejskiego - Akademia Rolnicza) (Until 1980, part of Zeszyty Naukowe series of Akademia Rolnicza, Warsaw) (Text mainly in English; occasionally in French, German or Russian; summaries in Polish) 1957. irreg. $6. Warsaw Agricultural University Press, Ul. Nowoursynowska 166, 02-766 Warsaw, Poland. Ed. B. Gej.

630   664   LB
WEST AFRICA RICE DEVELOPMENT ASSOCIATION. OCCASIONAL PAPER. (Text in English and French) 1980. irreg. free. West Africa Rice Development Association, Box 1019, Monrovia, Liberia. Ed. Dunstan S.C. Spencer. circ. 1,200 (both edts.) (also avail. in microfiche; back issues avail.)

630   US
WEST VIRGINIA. AGRICULTURAL AND FORESTRY EXPERIMENT STATION. ANNUAL REPORT. 1980. a. West Virginia University, Agricultural and Forestry Experiment Station, College of Agriculture and Forestry, Morgantown, WV 26506-6108. Ed. John Luchok. circ. 2,500.

630   634.9   US
WEST VIRGINIA. AGRICULTURAL AND FORESTRY EXPERIMENT STATION. BULLETIN. 1888. free. West Virginia University, Agricultural and Forestry Experiment Station, College of Agriculture and Forestry, Morgantown, WV 26506-6108. TEL 304-293-6368. Indexed: Biol.Abstr. Curr.Cont. Nutr.Abstr.

634.9   US
WEST VIRGINIA. AGRICULTURAL AND FORESTRY EXPERIMENT STATION. CIRCULAR. no. 119, 1981. irreg. West Virginia University, Agricultural and Forestry Experiment Station, Morgantown, WV 26506. Ed.Bd. charts. Indexed: Biol.Abstr.

630   US
WEST VIRGINIA. AGRICULTURAL AND FORESTRY EXPERIMENT STATION. CURRENT REPORT. 1952. irreg., no. 75, 1981. free. West Virginia University, Agricultural and Forestry Experiment Station, College of Agriculture and Forestry, Morgantown, WV 26506. TEL 304-293-6368. Ed. John Luchok. circ. 5,000. Indexed: Biol.Abstr. Curr.Cont. Plant Breed.Abstr.
    Formerly: West Virginia. Agricultural Experiment Station, Morgantown. Current Report (ISSN 0083-8381)

630   AT   ISSN 0726-9366
WESTERN AUSTRALIA. DEPARTMENT OF AGRICULTURE. ANNUAL REPORT. a. Department of Agriculture, Jarrah Rd., South Perth, W.A. 6151, Australia. Indexed: Biol.Abstr.

630   AT   ISSN 0729-0012
WESTERN AUSTRALIA. DEPARTMENT OF AGRICULTURE. BULLETIN. 1905? irreg. Department of Agriculture, Jarrah Rd., South Perth, W.A. 6151, Australia.

630   AT   ISSN 0083-8675
WESTERN AUSTRALIA. DEPARTMENT OF AGRICULTURE. TECHNICAL BULLETIN. 1969. irreg. free. ‡ Department of Agriculture, Jarrah Rd., South Perth W.A. 6151, Australia. Ed. D.A. Johnston. circ. 475. (back issues avail.) Indexed: Aus.Sci.Ind.

630   US
WHAT'S DEVELOPING IN ALASKA. irreg. University of Alaska, Cooperative Extension Service, Fairbanks, AK 99701. TEL 907-474-2746. Ed. Helen L. McNicholas.

630   CN
WHO'S WHO IN BRITISH COLUMBIA AGRICULTURE. 1978. a. Can.$5. Country Life Ltd., 1345 Johnston Rd., White Rock, B.C. V4B 3Z3, Canada. TEL 604-536-7622. Ed. D.M. Young.

630   UK
WHO'S WHO IN WORLD AGRICULTURE. (2 Vols.) 1979. irreg., 2nd edt. 1985. £215. Longman Group Ltd., Fourth Ave., Harlow, Essex CM19 5AA, England (Dist. in U.S. and Canada by: Gale Research Co. Ltd., Book Tower, Detroit, MI 48226)

WORKING PAPERS ON WOMEN IN INTERNATIONAL DEVELOPMENT. see BUSINESS AND ECONOMICS — International Development And Assistance

630   JA   ISSN 0513-1715
YAMAGUCHI UNIVERSITY. FACULTY OF AGRICULTURE. BULLETIN. 1980. a. Yamaguchi University, Faculty of Agriculture, 1677-1 Yoshida, Yamaguchi, Japan. Indexed: Biol.Abstr. Field Crop Abstr. Herb.Abstr. Ind.Vet. Plant Breed.Abstr. Rev.Plant Path. Soils & Fert. Vet.Bull.

630   BG
YEARBOOK OF AGRICULTURAL STATISTICS OF BANGLADESH. (Text in English) 1973/1975. a. Tk.150($35) Bangladesh Bureau of Statistics, Secretariat, Dacca 2, Bangladesh. circ. 500.
    Former titles: Agricultural Statistics of Bangladesh (ISSN 0065-4566); Agricultural Yearbook of Bangladesh.

ZAMBIA. DEPARTMENT OF AGRICULTURE. RESEARCH AND SPECIALIST SERVICES. ANNUAL REPORT. see AGRICULTURE — Crop Production And Soil

630   ZA   ISSN 0084-4853
ZAMBIA. MINISTRY OF AGRICULTURE. ANNUAL REPORT. 1964. a. Government Printer, P.O. Box 136, Lusaka, Zambia.

AGRICULTURE — ABSTRACTING, BIBLIOGRAPHIES, STATISTICS

630 940   CS
ZEMEDELSKE MUZEUM. VEDECKE PRACE/ MUSEUM OF AGRICULTURE. SCIENTIFIC WORKS. (Text in Czech; summaries in English, German, Russian) 1959. a. price varies. Zemedelske Muzeum, Ustav Vedeckotechnickych Informaci Pro Zemedelstvi (UVTIZ FMZVZ), Slezska 7, 120 56 Prague 2, Czechoslovakia (Subscr. to: Artia, Ve Smeckach 30, 111 27 Prague 1, Czechoslovakia) Ed. Zdenek Tempir. bk. rev. circ. 700.
Formerly: Ceskoslovenske Akademie Zemedlskych Ved z Dejin Zemedlstvi a Lesnictve.

630   PL   ISSN 0084-5477
ZESZYTY PROBLEMOWE POSTEPOW NAUK ROLNICZYCH. (Text and summaries in English, French, German, Polish and Russian) 1956. irreg., vol.309, 1984. price varies. (Polska Akademia Nauk, Wydzial Nauk Rolniczych i Lesnych) Panstwowe Wydawnictwo Naukowe, Miodowa 10, 00-251 Warsaw, Poland (Dist. by: Ars Polona, Krakowskie Przedmiescie 7, 00-068 Warsaw, Poland) Ed. S. Zawadzki. Indexed: Chem.Abstr. Vet.Bull.

630   RH
ZIMBABWE. AGRICULTURAL AND RURAL DEVELOPMENT AUTHORITY. ANNUAL REPORT AND ACCOUNTS. a. Agricultural and Rural Development Authority, Salisbury, Zimbabwe.

630   RH
ZIMBABWE. CENTRAL STATISTICAL OFFICE. AGRICULTURAL PRODUCTION IN TRIBAL TRUST LAND IRRIGATION SCHEMES AND TILCOR ESTATES. 1970. a. Rhod.$0.75. Central Statistical Office, Box 8063, Causeway, Salisbury, Zimbabwe. circ. 130.
Formerly: Rhodesia. Central Statistical Office. Agricultural Production in Tribal Trust Land Irrigation Schemes.

AGRICULTURE — Abstracting, Bibliographies, Statistics

630 664 016 011   US   ISSN 0364-7994
ABSTRACT NEWSLETTER: AGRICULTURE & FOOD. w. $89. U.S. National Technical Information Service, 5285 Port Royal Rd., Springfield, VA 22161. TEL 703-487-4630. Ed. Linda J. LaGarde. index. (back issues avail.)
Former titles: Weekly Abstract Newsletter: Agriculture and Food; Weekly Government Abstracts. Agriculture and Food.

630 016 011   BU   ISSN 0001-3463
ABSTRACTS OF BULGARIAN SCIENTIFIC LITERATURE. AGRICULTURE AND FORESTRY. VETERINARY MEDICINE. Variant title: Veterinarno-Medicinski Nauki. 1956. q. 1.30 lv. per no. (Akademiia na Selskostopanskite Nauki) Publishing House of the Bulgarian Academy of Sciences, Acad. G. Bonchev St., Bldg. 6, 1113 Sofia, Bulgaria (Dist. by: Hemus, 6, Rouski Blvd., 1000 Sofia, Bulgaria) bibl. index. circ. 1,280. Indexed: Chem.Abstr. Ind.Med. Forest.Abstr. Field Crop Abstr. Forest Prod.Abstr. Herb.Abstr. Helminthol.Abstr. Plant Breed.Abstr. Rev.Plant Path. Weed Abstr. VITIS. Vet.Bull.

631 016   CK   ISSN 0120-2898
ABSTRACTS ON CASSAVA. (Editions in English and Spanish) 1975. 3/yr. Cr.$2000($35) Centro Internacional de Agricultura Tropical, Centro de Informacion sobre Yuca - International Center for Tropical Agriculture, Communication and Information Support Unit, Apdo. Aereo 67-13, Cali, Colombia. circ. 650.

631 016   CK   ISSN 0120-2928
ABSTRACTS ON FIELD BEANS. (Editions in English and Spanish) 1978. 3/yr. $35. Centro Internacional de Agricultura Tropical, Centro de Informacion sobre Frijol - International Center for Tropical Agriculture, Communication and Information Support Unit, Apdo. Aereo 67-13, Cali, Colombia. bk. rev. circ. 950.

631.091 016   NE   ISSN 0304-5951
ABSTRACTS ON TROPICAL AGRICULTURE. (Text and summaries in English) 1975. m. fl.400($120) Royal Tropical Institute, Information and Documentation, Mauritskade 63, 1092 AD Amsterdam, Netherlands. Ed. Carla Pesch. adv. bk. rev. abstr. circ. 900. (back issues avail.) Indexed: Agri.Eng.Abstr. E.I. Key to Econ.Sci.
●Also available online. Vendors: Orbit Information Technologies.
Formerly: Tropical Abstracts (ISSN 0041-3208)

630   NZ   ISSN 0112-2320
AGLINK INDEX AND CATALOGUE. 1982. a. NZ.$35. Ministry of Agriculture and Fisheries, Information Services, Private Bag, Wellington, New Zealand. Ed. B. Greenfield. circ. 4,000.
Formerly: AgLink Index.

630 016   HU   ISSN 0002-1067
AGRARIRODALMI SZEMLE. 1951. m. 6400 Ft.($142) Mezogazdasagi es Elelmezesugyi Miniszterium, Informacios Kozpontja, Attila ut. 93, 1253 Budapest 13, Hungary (Subscr. to: Kultura, Box 149, H-1389 Budapest, Hungary) Ed. Joseph Vago. bk. rev. abstr. charts. illus. index. circ. 300.

630 016   TZ   ISSN 0251-2440
AGRICULTURAL ABSTRACTS FOR TANZANIA. 1978. q. Library Services Board, National Documentation Centre, P.O. Box 9283, Dar es Salaam, Tanzania.
Formerly: Abstracting and Indexing Bulletin for Agricultural and Animal Husbandry.

630 620 016   UK   ISSN 0308-8863
AGRICULTURAL ENGINEERING ABSTRACTS. (Former name of issuing body: Commonwealth Agricultural Bureaux) 1976. m. £127($224) to non-members. C.A.B. International, Farnham House, Farnham Royal, Slough SL2 3BN, England (U.S. subscr. to: C.A.B. International, North American Office, 845 North Park Ave., Tucson, AR 85719) circ. 450. (also avail. in microfiche; back issues avail.) Indexed: Dairy Sci.Abstr. Field Crop Abstr. Herb.Abstr. Weed Abstr.
●Also available online. Vendors: BRS, CISTI, DIMDI, DIALOG, European Space Agency.

630 338.1   GR   ISSN 0065-4574
AGRICULTURAL STATISTICS OF GREECE. (Text in English and Greek) 1961. a., latest 1982. $4. National Statistical Service, Publications and Information Division, 14-16 Lycourgou St., 10166 Athens, Greece.

630 338.1   MY
AGRICULTURAL STATISTICS OF SABAH. (Text in English) 1971. a. contr. free circ. Department of Agriculture, Information Division, Kota Kinabalu, Sabah, Malaysia. charts. stat. circ. 500.

630 338.1   MY
AGRICULTURAL STATISTICS OF SARAWAK. 1971. a, latest 1983. M.$5. Department of Agriculture, State Complex, Kuching, Sarawak, Malaysia, Kuching, Sarawak, Malaysia. Indexed: Field Crop Abstr. Herb.Abstr.

630 016   US   ISSN 0065-4671
AGRONOMY ABSTRACTS. 1950. a. $6 to non-members. American Society of Agronomy, Inc., 677 South Segoe Rd., Madison, WI 53711. TEL 608-274-1212. circ. 12,500. Indexed: GeoRef. Plant Breed.Abstr.

630 016   GE   ISSN 0233-2655
AGROSELEKT. REIHE 1: LANDTECHNIK; an agricultural abstracting journal. 1955. m. M.300. (Akademie der Landwirtschaftswissenschaften der DDR, Institut fuer Landwirtschaftliche Information und Dokumentation) Akademie-Verlag, Leipziger Str. 3-4, 1086 Berlin, E. Germany (D.D.R.) Ed. W. Kleeberg. bk. rev. abstr. index. circ. 520.
Formerly: Landwirtschaftliches Zentralblatt. Abteilung 1: Landtechnik (ISSN 0023-818X)
Engineering

630 016   GE   ISSN 0233-2701
AGROSELEKT. REIHE 2: PFLANZENPRODUKTION; an agricultural abstracting journal. 1956. m. M.420. (Akademie der Landwirtschaftswissenschaften der DDR, Institut fuer Landwirtschaftliche Information und Dokumentation) Akademie-Verlag, Leipziger Str. 3-4, 1086 Berlin, E. Germany (D.D.R.) Ed. W. Kleeberg. adv. bk. rev. index; cum.index. circ. 650. Indexed: Plant Breed.Abstr.
Formerly: Landwirtschaftliches Zentralblatt. Abteilung 2: Pflanzliche Produktion (ISSN 0023-8198)

636.082 016   GE   ISSN 0233-2752
AGROSELEKT. REIHE 3: TIERPRODUKTION; an agricultural abstracting journal. 1956. m. M.420. (Akademie der Landwirtschaftswissenschaften der DDR, Institut fuer Landwirtschaftliche Information und Dokumentation) Akademie-Verlag, Leipziger Str. 3-4, 1086 Berlin, E. Germany (D.D.R.) Ed. W. Kleeberg. bk. rev. abstr. index. cum.index. circ. 650.
Formerly: Landwirtschaftliches Zentralblatt. Abteilung 3: Tierzucht, Tierernaehrung, Fischerei (ISSN 0023-8201)

338.1   US   ISSN 0065-5694
ALASKA AGRICULTURAL STATISTICS. 1960. a. $10. Crop and Livestock Reporting Service, Box 799, Palmer, AK 99645 (Order from: Crop Reporting Board Publications, Rm. 5829, South Bldg., U.S. Department of Agriculture, Washington, DC 20250) Ed. DeLon A. Brown.
Formerly (1960-62): Alaska Farm Production (ISSN 0516-4850)

630   RE   ISSN 0336-5697
ANNUAIRE DE STATISTIQUE AGRICOLE DU DEPARTEMENT DE LA REUNION. 1973. a. Service de Statistique Agricole, 97489 Saint-Denis, Reunion.

638.1 016   UK   ISSN 0003-648X
APICULTURAL ABSTRACTS. 1950. 4/yr. £87($150) International Bee Research Association, Hill House, Gerrards Cross, Bucks SL9 ONR, England. Ed. David Lowe. adv. bk. rev. pat. tr.lit. index. cum.index: 1950-1972; 1973-1983 (microfiche) circ. 1,000. Indexed: Biol.& Agri.Ind. Chem.Abstr. Apic.Abstr. Forest.Abstr. Forest Prod.Abstr. Plant Breed.Abstr. Rev.Appl.Entomol.
●Also available online. Vendors: DIALOG, European Space Agency.

338.1 318   AG   ISSN 0066-7269
ARGENTINA. JUNTA NACIONAL DE CARNES. SINTESIS ESTADISTICA. Title varies; issued 1956-59, 1961-69 as: Argentine Republic. Junta Nacional de Carnes. Resena. 1934. a. Arg.$9600. Junta Nacional de Carnes, Biblioteca, San Martin 459 1 Piso, Buenos Aires, Argentina. index. circ. 2,000.

338.1 318   AG
ARGENTINA. SECRETARIA DE ESTADO DE AGRICULTURA Y GANADERIA. AREA DE TRABAJO DE LECHERIA. RESENA ESTADISTICA. 1964. irreg. free. Secretaria de Estado de Agricultura y Ganaderia, Area de Trabajo de Lecheria, Paseo Colon 922, 1063 Buenos Aires, Argentina. stat. circ. 1,000. (processed; also avail. in cards)

631   US   ISSN 0099-5010
ARKANSAS AGRICULTURAL EXPERIMENT STATION. RESEARCH SERIES. 1949. 10/yr. University of Arkansas, Agricultural Experiment Station, Agricultural Publications A-110, Fayetteville, AR 72701. TEL 501-575-5647. Ed. Raymond Barclay, Jr. circ. 1,000. Indexed: Biol.Abstr.
Formerly (until 1985): Arkansas Agricultural Experiment Station. Mimeograph Series.

636 319.4   AT
AUSTRALIA. BUREAU OF STATISTICS. LIVESTOCK AND LIVESTOCK PRODUCTS, AUSTRALIA. a. Aus.$2.30. Australian Bureau of Statistics, Box 10, Belconnen, A.C.T. 2616, Australia. stat. circ. 2,000.

AGRICULTURE — ABSTRACTING, BIBLIOGRAPHIES, STATISTICS 39

634 319.4 AT ISSN 0810-9176
AUSTRALIA. BUREAU OF STATISTICS. TASMANIAN OFFICE. FRUIT. a. Australian Bureau of Statistics, Tasmanian Office, Box 66A, Hobart, Tasmania 7001, Australia. illus. circ. 620.
Formerly: Australia. Bureau of Statistics. Tasmanian Office. Fruit Production (ISSN 0314-1667)

338.1 AT
AUSTRALIA. BUREAU OF STATISTICS. VALUE OF AGRICULTURAL COMMODITIES PRODUCED, AUSTRALIA. a. Aus.$2.30. Australian Bureau of Statistics, P.O. Box 10, Belconnen, A.C.T. 2616, Australia. circ. 1,500.
Formerly: Australia. Bureau of Statistics. Value of Primary Production, Excluding Mining, and Indexes of Quantum and Unit Gross Value of Agricultural Production (ISSN 0312-6242)

338.1 319 AT
AUSTRALIA. BUREAU OF STATISTICS. VICTORIAN OFFICE. VALUE OF AGRICULTURAL COMMODITIES PRODUCED. 1967. a. free. Australian Bureau of Statistics, Victorian Office, Box 2796Y, G.P.O., Melbourne, Vic. 3001, Australia. circ. 750.
Former titles: Australia. Bureau of Statistics. Victorian Office. Value of Primary Commodities Produced (Excluding Mining); Australia. Bureau of Statistics. Victorian Office. Value of Primary Production.

630 AU
AUSTRIA. STATISTISCHES ZENTRALAMT. ERGEBNISSE DER LANDWIRTSCHAFTLICHEN MASCHINENZAEHLUNG. (Subseries of: Beitraege zur Oesterreichischen Statistik) 1953. irreg. S.130. Hintere Zollamtsstr. 2b, 1033 Vienna, Vienna. circ. 500.

630 314 AU ISSN 0067-2327
AUSTRIA. STATISTISCHES ZENTRALAMT. ERGEBNISSE DER LANDWIRTSCHAFTLICHEN STATISTIK. (Subseries of: Beitraege zur Oesterreichischen Statistik) 1946. a. S.120. Hintere Zollamtsstr. 2b, 1033 Wien, Austria. circ. 500.

630 016 BG
BANGLADESH AGRICULTURAL SCIENCES ABSTRACTS. Short title: B A S A. (Text in English) 1974. biennial. Tk.50($20) Bangladesh Agricultural University Old Boys' Association, c/o Dept. of Soil Science, Bangladesh Agricultural University, Mymensingh, Bangladesh. (Co-sponsor: Bangladesh Agricultural Research Council) Ed. M. Eaqub. abstr. circ. 500.

630 CL
BIBLIOGRAFIA AGRICOLA CHILENA. 1977. a. $15. Instituto de Investigaciones Agropecuarias, Programa de Informacion y Documentacion, Casilla 439-3, Santiago, Chile. Eds. Sonia Elso, Veronica Bravo. (back issues avail.)

BIBLIOGRAFIA AGROMETEOROLOGII/ BIBLIOGRAPHY OF AGROMETEOROLOGY. see METEOROLOGY — Abstracting, Bibliographies, Statistics

630 PL ISSN 0208-4252
BIBLIOGRAFIA PRAC MAGISTERKICH, DOKTOSKICH I HABILITACYJNYCH PRZYJETYCH W S G G W - A R W WARSZAWIE. (Szkola Glowna Gospodarstwa Wiejskiego-Akademia Rolnicza) a. (Warsaw Agricultural University-S G G W-A R) Warsaw Agricultural University Press, Ul. Nowoursynowska 166, 02-766 Warsaw, Poland (Dist. by: Ars Polona-Ruch, Krakowkie Przedmiescie 7, 00-068 Warsaw, Poland) Ed. J. Lewandowski.

630 PL ISSN 0208-4260
BIBLIOGRAFIA PUBLIKACJI PRACOWNIKOW S G G W - A R W WARSZAWIE. (Szkola Glowna Gospodarstwa Wiejskiego-Akademia Rolnicza) a. (Warsaw Agricultural University-S G G W-A R) Warsaw Agricultural University Press, Ul. Nowoursynowska 166, 02-766 Warsaw, Poland (Dist. by: Ars Polona-Ruch, Krakowkie Przedmiescie 7, 00-068 Warsaw, Poland) Ed. J. Lewandowski.

630 US
BIBLIOGRAPHIES AND LITERATURE OF AGRICULTURE. 1978. irreg., no.19, 1981. price varies. U.S. Department of Agriculture, Office of Governmental and Public Affairs, National Agricultural Library, 14th and Independence Ave., S. W., Washington, DC 20250. TEL 301-344-3778. Ed. Eugene M. Farkas. circ. 1,000.

630 016 US ISSN 0006-1530
BIBLIOGRAPHY OF AGRICULTURE. 1942. m. plus a. cum. $565 (annual cum. $505) (U.S. National Agricultural Library, Technical Information Systems) Oryx Press, 2214 N. Central Ave., Phoenix, AZ 85004-1483. TEL 602-254-6156. (also avail. in microform from UMI; back issues avail.; reprint service avail. from UMI)
●Also available online. Vendors: CISTI

BIOLOGICAL AND AGRICULTURAL INDEX; a subject index to periodicals in the fields of biology and agriculture and related sciences. see BIOLOGY — Abstracting, Bibliographies, Statistics

338.1 318 BL
BRAZIL. MINISTERIO DA AGRICULTURA. ESCRITORIO DE ESTATISTICA. CADASTRO DAS EMPRESAS PRODUTORAS DE OLEOS, GORDURAS VEGETAIS E SABPRODUTOS. 1970. triennial. free. Ministerio da Agricultura, Escritorio de Estatistica, Esplanada dos Ministerios, Bloco 8, 6 Andar, Brasilia 7000, Brazil. circ. 800. (processed)

338.1 318 BL
BRAZIL. MINISTERIO DA AGRICULTURA. ESCRITORIO DE ESTATISTICA. PECUARIA, AVICULTURA, APICULTURA, SERICICULTURA. a. free. Ministerio da Agricultura, Escritorio de Estatistica, Esplanada dos Ministerios, Bloco 8-6 Andar, Rio de Janeiro, Brazil. stat.

631.3 016 FR ISSN 0007-4160
BULLETIN BIBLIOGRAPHIQUE INTERNATIONAL DU MACHINISME AGRICOLE/INTERNATIONAL FARM MACHINERY ABSTRACTS. (Includes: Quarterly Supplement - ISSN 0150-6544) (Text in English, French, German and Spanish) 1966. 10/yr. 330 F. (International Commission of Agricultural Engineering) Centre National de Machinisme Agricole du Genie Rural, des Eaux et des Forets(CEMAGREF), Parc de Tourvoie, 92160 Antony, France. Ed. R. Carillon. bk. rev. circ. 900. Indexed: Agri.Eng.Abstr.

338.1 016 UK
C.A.B. INTERNATIONAL BUREAU OF AGRICULTURAL ECONOMICS. ANNOTATED BIBLIOGRAPHIES SERIES A. (Former name of issuing body: Commonwealth Agricultural Bureaux) 1971. irreg. price varies. C.A.B. International, Bureau of Agricultural Economics, Farnham House, Farnham Royal, Slough SL2 3BN, England. abstr. bibl. index. Indexed: Sociol.Abstr. Geo.Abstr.
●Also available online. Vendors: BRS, CISTI, DIMDI, DIALOG, European Space Agency.
Formerly: Commonwealth Bureau of Agricultural Economics. Annotated Bibliographies Series A.

338.1 016 UK
C.A.B. INTERNATIONAL BUREAU OF AGRICULTURAL ECONOMICS. ANNOTATED BIBLIOGRAPHIES. SERIES B: AGRICULTURAL POLICY AND RURAL DEVELOPMENT IN AFRICA. (Former name of issuing body: Commonwealth Agricultural Bureaux) 1971. irreg. price varies. C.A.B. International, Bureau of Agricultural Economics, Farnham House, Farnham Royal, Slough SL2 3BN, England. Ed. M.A. Bellamy. abstr. bibl. index. Indexed: Sociol.Abstr. Geo.Abstr.
●Also available online. Vendors: BRS, CISTI, DIMDI, DIALOG, European Space Agency.
Formerly: Commonwealth Bureau of Agricultural Economics. Annotated Bibliographies. Series B: Agricultural Policy and Rural Development in Africa.

631.4 016 UK
C.A.B. INTERNATIONAL BUREAU OF SOILS. ANNOTATED BIBLIOGRAPHIES. (Former name of issuing body: Commonwealth Agricultural Bureaux) 1965. irreg. price varies. C.A.B. International, Bureau of Soils, Farnham House, Farnham Royal, Slough SL2 3BN, England. (also avail. in microfiche) Indexed: Pollut.Abstr. Geo.Abstr.
●Also available online. Vendors: BRS, CISTI, DIMDI, DIALOG, European Space Agency.
Formerly: Commonwealth Bureau of Soils. Annotated Bibliographies (ISSN 0305-2524)

338.1 US ISSN 0527-2181
CALIFORNIA FRUIT AND NUT ACREAGE. a. California Crop and Livestock Reporting Service, Box 1258, Sacramento, CA 95814. TEL 916-445-6076. stat.
Formerly: Production and Marketing California Grapes, Raisins and Wine (ISSN 0095-411X)

338.1 US ISSN 0361-9095
CALIFORNIA LIVESTOCK STATISTICS. a. California Crop and Livestock Reporting Service, Box 1258, Sacramento, CA 95806. TEL 916-445-6076.

338.1 317 CN ISSN 0068-712X
CANADA. STATISTICS CANADA. FARM NET INCOME/REVENU NET AGRICOLE. (Catalog 21-202) (Text in English and French) 1940. a. Can.$32($33) Statistics Canada, Communications Division, 3rd Floor, R.H. Coats Bldg., Ottawa, Ont. K1A 06T, Canada TEL 613-993-7276. (Subscr. to: Publications Sales and Services, Ottawa, Ont. K1A 0T6, Canada) (also avail. in microform from MML)

338.17 CN ISSN 0383-008X
CANADA. STATISTICS CANADA. FRUIT AND VEGETABLE PRODUCTION/PRODUCTION DE FRUITS ET DE LEGUMES. (Catalogue 22-003) (Text in English and French) 1932. irreg.(seasonal) Can.$60($68) Statistics Canada, Communications Division, 3rd Floor, R.H. Coats Bldg., Ottawa, Ont. K1A 0T6, Canada TEL 613-993-7276. (Subscr. to: Publications Sales and Services, Ottawa, Ont. K1A 0T6, Canada) (also avail. in microform from MML)

638.16 CN ISSN 0829-3163
CANADA. STATISTICS CANADA. HONEY PRODUCTION AND VALUE, PRODUCTION FORECAST/PRODUCTION ET VALEUR DU MIEL, PROVISION DE LA PRODUCTION. (Catalogue 23-210) (Text in English and French) 1938. a. Can.$10($11) Statistics Canada, Communications Division, 3rd Floor, R.H. Coats Bldg., Ottawa, Ont. K1A 0T6, Canada TEL 613-993-7276. (Subscr. to: Publicatons Sales and Services, Ottawa, Ont. K1A 0T6, Canada) (also avail. in microform from MML)
Former titles: Canada. Statistics Canada. Honey Production/Production de Miel (ISSN 0319-3799); Canada. Statistics Canada. Crops Section. Production and Value Estimate of Honey.

630 CN ISSN 0068-7146
CANADA. STATISTICS CANADA. INDEX OF FARM PRODUCTION/INDICE DE LA PRODUCTION AGRICOLE. (Catalog 21-203) (Text in English and French) 1948. a. Can.$17($18) Statistics Canada, Communications Division, 3rd Floor, R.H. Coats Bldg., Ottawa, Ont. K1A 0T6, Canada TEL 613 993 7276. (Subscr. to: Publications Sales and Services, Ottawa, Ont. K1A 0T6, Canada) (also avail. in microform from MML)

636 CN ISSN 0068-7154
CANADA. STATISTICS CANADA. LIVESTOCK AND ANIMAL PRODUCTS STATISTICS/ STATISTIQUE DU BETAIL ET DES PRODUITS ANIMAUX. (Catalog 23-203) (Text in English and French) 1909. a. Can.$30($31) Statistics Canada, Communications Division, 3rd Floor, R.H. Coats Bldg., Ottawa, Ont. K1a 0T6, Canada TEL 613-993-7276. (Subscr. to: Publications Sales and Services, Ottawa, Ont. K1A 0T6, Canada) (also avail. in microform from MML)

AGRICULTURE — ABSTRACTING, BIBLIOGRAPHIES, STATISTICS

338.1 317 633.6   CN   ISSN 0317-9672
CANADA. STATISTICS CANADA. PRODUCTION AND VALUE OF MAPLE PRODUCTS/PRODUCTION ET VALEUR DES PRODUITS DE L'ERABLE. (Catalogue 22-204) (Text in English and French) 1938. a. Can.$10($11) Statistics Canada, Communications Division, 3rd Floor, R.H. Coats Bldg., Ottawa, Ont. K1A 0T6, Canada TEL 613-993-7276. (Subscr. to: Publications Sales and Services, Ottawa, Ont. K1A 0T6, Canada) (also avail. in microform from MML)

636.5   CN   ISSN 0068-7189
CANADA. STATISTICS CANADA. PRODUCTION OF POULTRY AND EGGS/PRODUCTION DE VOLAILLE ET OEUFS. (Catalog 23-202) (Text in English and French) 1936. a. Can.$30($31) Statistics Canada, Communications Division, 3rd Floor, R.H. Coats Bldg., Ottawa, Ont. K1A 0T6, Canada TEL 613-993-7276. (Subscr. to: Publications Sales and Services, Ottawa, Ont. K1A 0T6, Canada) (also avail. in microform from MML)

338.1   CN   ISSN 0527-6179
CANADA. STATISTICS CANADA. SHORN WOOL PRODUCTION/PRODUCTION DE LAINE TONDUE. (Catalog 23-204) (Text in English and French) 1931. a. Can.$10($11) Statistics Canada, Communications Division, 3rd Floor, R.H. Coats Bldg., Ottawa, Ont. K1A 0T6, Canada TEL 613-993-7276. (Subscr. to: Publications Sales and Services, Ottawa, Ont. K1A 0T6, Canada) (also avail. in microform from MML)

338 633.83   II
CARDAMOM STATISTICS. (Text in English) irreg. Cardamom Board, Chittoor Rd., Cochin 682018, India.

011   IS
CENTRAL LIBRARY OF AGRICULTURAL SCIENCES. ACQUISITION LIST. irreg. free. Central Library of Agricultural Sciences, P.O. Box 12, Rehovot 76 100, Israel. TEL 054-71751.

338.1 016   US   ISSN 0010-3241
COMMODITY YEARBOOK STATISTICAL ABSTRACT SERVICE. 3/yr. $65. ‡ Commodity Research Bureau (Subsidiary of: Knight-Ridder) 100 Church St., Ste. 1850, New York, NY 10007. TEL 212-406-4545. Ed. Seymour Gaylinn. charts. mkt. stat.

630 319   NZ
COMPENDIUM OF NEW ZEALAND FARM PRODUCTION STATISTICS. biennial. Meat & Wool Boards' Economic Service, P.O. Box 5179, Wellington, New Zealand. circ. 4,000.

630 016   UK   ISSN 0261-5436
COPPER IN AGRICULTURE; a quarterly bulletin of abstracts. 1980. 4/yr. £28. Micronutrient Bureau, M.B. House, Wigginton, Tring, Herts. HP23 6ED, England.

633 016   UK   ISSN 0308-6577
COTTON AND TROPICAL FIBRES ABSTRACTS. 1976. m. £56($96) to non-members. C.A.B. International, Farnham House, Farnham Royal, Slough SL2 3BN, England (U.S. subscr. to: C.A.B. International, North American Office, 845 North Park Ave., Tucson, AR 85719) circ. 200. (also avail. in microfiche; back issues avail.) Indexed: Field Crop Abstr. Herb.Abstr.
●Also available online. Vendors: BRS, CISTI, DIMDI, DIALOG, European Space Agency.

631 016   UK   ISSN 0306-7556
CROP PHYSIOLOGY ABSTRACTS. (Former name of issuing body: Commonwealth Agricultural Bureaux) 1975. m. £138($244) C.A.B. International, Farnham House, Farnham Royal, Slough SL2 3BN, England (U.S. subscr. to: C.A.B. International, North American Office, 845 N. Park Ave., Tucson, AR 85719) circ. 250. (also avail. in microfiche; back issues avail.)
●Also available online. Vendors: BRS, CISTI, DIMDI, DIALOG, European Space Agency.

CURRENT BIBLIOGRAPHIES ON SCIENCE & TECHNOLOGY: BIOLOGY, PHARMACY & FOOD SCIENCE. see *BIOLOGY — Abstracting, Bibliographies, Statistics*

310   CY
CYPRUS. DEPARTMENT OF STATISTICS AND RESEARCH. CENSUS OF POULTRY. (Text in English) 1982. irreg. cyprus pounds 0.75. Ministry of Finance, Department of Statistics and Research, Nicosia, Cyprus.

338.1 314   DK
DENMARK. DANMARKS STATISTIK. LANDBRUGSSTATISTIK/AGRICULTURAL STATISTICS. (Text in Danish; notes in English) 1936. a. Kr.60.66. Danmarks Statistik, Sejroegade 11, 2100 Copenhagen OE, Denmark. index.
Formerly: Denmark. Danmarks Statistik. Landbrugsstatistik Herunder Gartneri og Skovbrug (ISSN 0070-3559)

338.1 314   NE
E E G VADEMECUM/SELECTED AGRI-FIGURES OF THE E.E.C. (Text in Dutch, English, French, and German) 1960. biennial. free. Ministerie van Landbouw en Visserij, Directie Voorlichting en Externe Betrekkingen - Ministry of Agriculture and Fisheries, Postbus 20401, 2500 EK 's-Gravenhage, Netherlands. Ed. M.N. de Groot. circ. 5,000.
Formerly: Geselecteerde Agrarische Cijfers van de E E C (ISSN 0072-4211)

318 338.1   ES
EL SALVADOR. DIRECCION GENERAL DE ECONOMIA AGROPECUARIA. PROGNOSTICO DE ALGODON. irreg. Direccion General de Economia Agropecuaria, Departamento de Estadisticas Agropecuarias, Boulevard de los Heroes, Edificio Latinoamericano, San Salvador, El Salvador. charts. stat.

633 310   ES
EL SALVADOR. DIRECCION GENERAL DE ECONOMIA AGROPECUARIA. PROGNOSTICO DE ZAFRA. irreg. Direccion General de Economia Agropecuaria, Boulevard de los Heroes, Edificio Lationamericano, San Salvador, El Salvador. stat.

630 310   PN   ISSN 0378-2581
ESTADISTICA PANAMENA. SITUACION ECONOMICA. SECCION 312. PRODUCCION PECUARIA. 1954. a. Bl.0.75. Direccion de Estadistica y Censo, Contraloria General, Apartado 5213, Panama 5, Panama. circ. 1,400.

338.1   PN   ISSN 0378-2565
ESTADISTICA PANAMENA. SITUACION ECONOMICA. SECCION 312. SUPERFICIE SEMBRADA Y COSECHA DE ARROZ, MAIZ Y FRIJOL DE BEJUCO. 1954. a. Bl.0.75. Direccion de Estadistica y Censo, Contraloria General, Apartado 5213, Panama 5, Panama. circ. 1,400.
Formerly: Estadistica Panamena. Situacion Economica. Seccion 312. Superficie Sembrada y Cosecha de Arroz y Maiz.

630 310   PN   ISSN 0378-2573
ESTADISTICA PANAMENA. SITUACION ECONOMICA. SECCION 312. SUPERFICIE SEMBRADA Y COSECHA DE CAFE, TABACO Y CANA DE AZUCAR. 1954. a. Bl.0.75. Direccion de Estadistica y Censo, Contraloria General, Apartado 5213, Panama 5, Panama. circ. 1, 400.

630 310   PN   ISSN 0378-2530
ESTADISTICA PANAMENA. SITUACION ECONOMICA. SECCION 351. PRECIOS PAGADOS POR EL PRODUCTOR AGROPECUARIO. 1973. a. Bl.0.75. Direccion de Estadistica y Censo, Contraloria General, Apartado 5213, Panama 5, Panama. circ. 1,100.

631.8 016   II   ISSN 0014-5564
F.A.I. ABSTRACT SERVICE. (Text in English) 1962. m. Rs.20. Fertiliser Association of India, Near Jawaharlal Nehru University, New Delhi 110067, India. Ed. V. Sarangan. abstr. circ. 1,000.
Fertilizers

631 016   UK   ISSN 0260-8456
FABA BEAN ABSTRACTS. (Former name of issuing body: Commonwealth Agricultural Bureaux) 1981. q. £55($96) C.A.B. International, Farnham House, Farnham Royal, Slough SL2 3BN, England (U.S. Subscr. to: Bernan Associates-Unipub, 4611-F Assembly Dr., Lanham, MD 20706-4391)
●Also available online. Vendors: BRS, CISTI, DIMDI, DIALOG, European Space Agency.

016 630   US   ISSN 0193-8487
FARM AND GARDEN INDEX. 1978. q. $170. Bell & Howell Microphoto, Old Mansfield Rd., Wooster, OH 44691. Ed.Bd. bk. rev. index.

338.1 314   UK
FARM BUSINESS STATISTICS FOR SOUTH EAST ENGLAND. 1969. a. price varies. Wye College (University of London), Department of Agricultural Economics, Ashford, Kent, England. Ed.Bd. charts. stat. circ. 800.

338.1   NZ   ISSN 0110-084X
FARMING STATISTICS. 1969. a. free. Department of Lands and Survey, Wellington, New Zealand. Ed. B.J. Takhar. circ. 150.

631.8   II   ISSN 0430-327X
FERTILISER ASSOCIATION OF INDIA. FERTILISER STATISTICS. (Text in English) 1956. a. Rs.50. Fertiliser Association of India, Near Jawaharlal Nehru University, New Delhi 110067, India. Ed.Bd. charts. stat.

633 016   UK   ISSN 0015-069X
FIELD CROP ABSTRACTS; monthly abstract journal on world annual cereal, legume, root, oilseed and fibre crops. 1948. m. £250($445) to non-members. C.A.B. International, Farnham Royal, Slough SL2 3BN, England (U.S. subscr. to: C.A.B. International, North American Office, 845 N. Park Ave., Tucson, AR 85719) bk. rev. abstr. bibl. index. circ. 1,300. (also avail. in microfiche; back issues avail.) Indexed: Anim.Breed.Abstr. Apic.Abstr. Dairy Sci.Abstr. Forest.Abstr. Helminthol.Abstr. Plant Breed.Abstr. Rev.Appl.Entomol. Rural Recreat.Tour.Abstr. Weed Abstr. World Agri.Econ. & Rural Sociol.Abstr.
●Also available online. Vendors: BRS, CISTI, DIMDI, DIALOG, European Space Agency.

338.1   FI   ISSN 0356-2913
FINLAND. TILASTOKESKUS. MAATILATALOUS/FINLAND. STATISTIKCENTRALEN. GAARDSBRUK/FINLAND. CENTRAL STATISTICAL OFFICE. FARM ECONOMY. (Section 39 of Official Statistics of Finland) (Text in English, Finnish, and Swedish) 1977. a. Fmk.65. Tilastokeskus, Annankatu 44, SF-00100 Helsinki 10, Finland (Subscr. to: Government Printing Centre, Box 516, SF-00101 Helsinki 10, Finland)

FLOUR MILLING AND BAKING RESEARCH ASSOCIATION ABSTRACTS. see *FOOD AND FOOD INDUSTRIES — Abstracting, Bibliographies, Statistics*

630   UN
FOOD AND AGRICULTURE ORGANIZATION OF THE UNITED NATIONS. ASIA AND THE PACIFIC COMMISSION ON AGRICULTURAL STATISTICS. PERIODIC REPORT. irreg. free. Food and Agriculture Organization of the United Nations, Regional Office for Asia and the Far East, Milawan Mansion, Phra Atit Rd., Bangkok 2, Thailand.
Formerly: Asia and the Far East Commision on Agricultural Statistics. Periodic Report.

630 338.1   FR   ISSN 0243-6167
FRANCE. MINISTERE DE L'AGRICULTURE. INFORMATIONS RAPIDES. STATISTIQUES DES ENTREPRISES. 1978. irreg. 60 F. Ministere de l'Agriculture, Service Central des Enquetes et Etudes Statistiques, 4 av. de Saint Mande, 75570 Paris Cedex 12, France.
Formerly: France. Ministere de l'Agriculture. Informations Rapides Agro-Alimentaires.

338.1   FR   ISSN 0244-5271
FRANCE. MINISTERE DE L'AGRICULTURE. SERIES "S". SYNTHESE STATISTIQUE COMPTES ET REVENUS. (Text in French) 1974. irreg. 50 F. per no. Ministere de l'Agriculture, Service Central des Enquetes et Etudes Statistiques, 4 av. de Saint Mande, 75570 Paris Cedex 12, France.

AGRICULTURE — ABSTRACTING, BIBLIOGRAPHIES, STATISTICS

314 338.1   GW   ISSN 0072-3681
GERMANY (FEDERAL REPUBLIC, 1949-).
STATISTISCHES BUNDESAMT. FACHSERIE 3,
LAND- UND FORTSTWIRTSCHAFT,
FISCHEREI; REIHE 2: BETRIEBS-, ARBEITS-
UND EINKOMMENSVERHAELTNISSE.
(Consists of several subseries) irreg. price varies. W.
Kohlhammer-Verlag GmbH, Abt.
Veroeffentlichungen des Statistischen Bundesamtes,
Philipp-Reis-Str. 3, Postfach 421120, 6500 Mainz
42, W. Germany (B.R.D.)

633 338.1 314   GW
GERMANY (FEDERAL REPUBLIC, 1949-).
STATISTISCHES BUNDESAMT. FACHSERIE 3,
LAND- UND FORTWIRTSCHAFT, FISCHEREI;
REIHE 3: BODENNUETZUENG UND
PFLANZLICHE ERZEUGUNG. 1961. a.
DM.11.80. W. Kohlhammer-Verlag GmbH, Abt.
Veroeffentlichungen des Statistischen Bundesamtes,
Philipp-Reis-Str. 3, Postfach 421120, 6500 Mainz
42, W. Germany (B.R.D.)
Former titles: Germany (Federal Republic, 1949-)
Statistisches Bundesamt. Fachserie 3, Reihe 3:
Pflanzliche Erzeugung; Germany (Federal Republic,
1949-) Statistisches Bundesamt. Fachserie 3, Reihe
3: Gartenbau und Weinwirtschaft.

636 338.1   GW
GERMANY (FEDERAL REPUBLIC, 1949-).
STATISTISCHES BUNDESAMT. FACHSERIE 3,
LAND- UND FORSTWIRTSCHAFT,
FISCHEREI; REIHE 4: VIEHBESTAND UND
TIERISCHE ERZEUGUNG. m. DM.11.80. W.
Kohlhammer-Verlag GmbH, Abt.
Veroeffentlichungen des Statistischen Bundesamtes,
Philipp-Reis-Str. 3, Postfach 421120, 6500 Mainz
42, W. Germany (B.R.D.)
Formerly: Germany (Federal Republic, 1949-).
Statistisches Bundesamt. Fachserie 3, Reihe 4:
Tierische Erzeugung.

338.1 314   GW   ISSN 0072-3894
GERMANY (FEDERAL REPUBLIC, 1949-).
STATISTISCHES BUNDESAMT. FACHSERIE
17, PREISE, REIHE 1: PREISE UND
PREISINDIZES FUER DIE LAND- UND
FORSTWIRTSCHAFT. m. DM.57.60. W.
Kohlhammer-Verlag GmbH, Abt.
Veroeffentlichungen des Statistischen Bundesamtes,
Philipp-Reis-Str. 3, Postfach 421120, 6500 Mainz
42, W. Germany (B.R.D.)

GERMANY (FEDERAL REPUBLIC, 1949-).
STATISTISCHES BUNDESAMT. FACHSERIE
16, REIHE 1: ARBEITERVERDIENSTE IN DER
LANDWIRTSCHAFT. see *BUSINESS AND
ECONOMICS — Abstracting, Bibliographies,
Statistics*

630   GW   ISSN 0433-860X
GESELLSCHAFT FUER BIBLIOTHEKSWESEN
UND DOKUMENTATION DES LANDBAUES.
MITTEILUNGEN. (Text in German; summaries
occasionally in English) 1959. irreg. (2-3/yr.)
DM.15($5.50) per number. Gesellschaft fuer
Bibliothekswesen und Dokumentation des
Landbaues, Paracelsusstrasse 2, 7000 Stuttgart 70,
W. Germany (B.R.D.) Ed.Bd. adv. bk. rev. bibl.
cum.index: 1958-1973. circ. 150(controlled) (back
issues avail.)

595.1 016   UK   ISSN 0300-8339
HELMINTHOLOGICAL ABSTRACTS. SERIES A:
ANIMAL AND HUMAN HELMINTHOLOGY.
1932. m. £166($291) to non-members. C.A.B.
International, Institute of Parasitology, Farnham
House, Farnham Royal, Slough SL2 3BN, England.
adv. bk. rev. abstr. index. cum.index. circ. 1,200.
(also avail. in microfiche; back issues avail.)
Indexed: Abstr.Hyg. Rev.Appl.Entomol.
Trop.Dis.Bull. Vet.Bull.
●Also available online. Vendors: BRS, CISTI,
DIMDI, DIALOG, European Space Agency.

595.1 016   UK   ISSN 0300-8320
HELMINTHOLOGICAL ABSTRACTS. SERIES B:
PLANT NEMATOLOGY. 1970. q. £73($127) to
non-members. C.A.B. International, Institute of
Parasitology, Farnham House, Farnham Royal,
Slough SL2 3BN, England. adv. bk. rev. abstr.
index. circ. 1,000. (also avail. in microfiche; back
issues avail.) Indexed: Forest.Abstr. Forest
Prod.Abstr. Rev.Appl.Entomol. Vet.Bull.
●Also available online. Vendors: BRS, CISTI,
DIMDI, DIALOG, European Space Agency.

633 016   UK   ISSN 0018-0602
HERBAGE ABSTRACTS; monthly abstract journal
on grassland husbandry and fodder crop production.
1931. m. £144($255) to non-members. C.A.B.
International, Farnham House, Farnham Royal,
Slough SL2 3BN, England (U.S. subscr. to: Bernan
Associates-Unipub, 4611-F Assembly Dr., Lanham,
MD 20706-4391) adv. bk. rev. abstr. index. circ. 1,
400. (also avail. in microfiche; back issues avail.)
Indexed: Nutr.Abstr. Apic.Abstr.
●Also available online. Vendors: BRS, CISTI,
DIMDI, DIALOG, European Space Agency.

630 314   HU   ISSN 0441-4683
HUNGARY. KOZPONTI STATISZTIKAI
HIVATAL. MEZOGAZDASAGI STATISZTIKAI
ZSEBKONYU. a. 50 Ft. Statisztikai Kiado Vallalat,
Kaszasdulo u. 2, P.O.B.99, 1300 Budapest 3,
Hungary (Subscr. to: Kultura, Box 149, H-1389
Budapest, Hungary)

630   HU   ISSN 0230-4066
HUNGARY. KOZPONTI STATISZTIKAI
HIVATAL. MEZOGAZDASAGI STATISZTIKAI
EVKONYV/YEARBOOK OF AGRICULTURAL
STATISTICS. 1981. a. Statisztikai Kiado Vallalat,
Kaszasdulo u.2, H-1033 Budapest, Hungary (Subscr.
to: Kultura, P.O. Box 149, H-1389 Budapest,
Hungary) circ. 2,000.

338.1   US   ISSN 0094-1271
IDAHO AGRICULTURAL STATISTICS. 1972. a.
$5. Department of Agriculture, Idaho Agricultural
Statistics Service, Box 1699, Boise, ID 83701. Ed.
R.C. Max. circ. 2,500.

636.4 016   UK   ISSN 0568-2800
INDEX OF CURRENT RESEARCH ON PIGS.
1954. a. £13($23) C.A.B. International, Farnham
House, Farnham Royal, Slough SL2 3BN, England.
Ed. Dr. R. Braude. circ. 1,300. Indexed: Nutr.Abstr.
Anim.Breed.Abstr. Helminthol.Abstr.
●Also available online. Vendors: BRS, CISTI,
DIMDI, DIALOG, European Space Agency.

631.8   II
INDIAN FERTILIZER STATISTICS. (Text in
English) 1967. a. free. Ministry of Chemicals and
Fertilizers, Economics and Statistics Division, New
Delhi, India. stat. circ. controlled. Indexed: Soils &
Fert.

630 016   CK   ISSN 0073-7151
INDICE AGRICOLA COLOMBIANO. 1961-62. a.
Col.250($30.) Instituto Colombiano Agropecuario,
Apdo. Aereo 151123, El Dorado, Bogota, Colombia.

630 016   CK
INSTITUTO COLOMBIANO AGROPECUARIO.
CATALOGO DE PUBLICACIONES
PERIODICAS. 1975. a. (with irreg. supplements)
free. Instituto Colombiano Agropecuario, Biblioteca
Agropecuaria, Division de Comunicacion Rural,
Apdo. Aereo 151123, Bogota, D.E., Colombia. Ed.
Francisco Salazar. circ. 1,000.

630 016   CR   ISSN 0301-438X
INTER-AMERICAN CENTRE FOR
AGRICULTURAL DOCUMENTATION AND
INFORMATION. DOCUMENTACION E
INFORMACION AGRICOLA. (Text in various
languages) 1973. irreg. Instituto Interamericano de
Cooperacion para la Agricultura - O E A, Apdo. 55,
2200 Coronado, San Jose, Costa Rica. bk. rev. circ.
800. (also avail. in microform)
Formed by the merger of: Inter-American
Institute of Agricultural Sciences. Center for
Training and Research. Bibliotecologia y
Documentacion (ISSN 0074-0926) & Inter-
American Institute of Agricultural Sciences.
Bibliografias (ISSN 0085-1949)

631   PH
INTERNATIONAL BIBLIOGRAPHY OF
CROPPING SYSTEMS.* 1976-1979. a. $25.50.
International Rice Research Institute, Library and
Documentation Center, Box 933, Manila,
Philippines. Indexed: Field Crop Abstr. Herb.Abstr.

633 016   PH   ISSN 0074-2031
INTERNATIONAL BIBLIOGRAPHY OF RICE
RESEARCH.* 1963. a. $60 price varies.
International Rice Research Institute, Library and
Documentation Center, Box 933, Manila,
Philippines. cum.index every 5 years. Indexed: Field
Crop Abstr. Herb.Abstr.

637 016   BE   ISSN 0538-7086
INTERNATIONAL DAIRY FEDERATION.
CATALOGUE OF I D F PUBLICATIONS.
CATALOGUE DES PUBLICATIONS DE LA F I
L. (Text in English and French) 1973. a. free.
International Dairy Federation, Square Vergote, 41,
1040 Brussels, Belgium. bk. rev. circ. 3,000.
(processed)

631.6 016   NE   ISSN 0074-6436
INTERNATIONAL INSTITUTE FOR LAND
RECLAMATION AND IMPROVEMENT.
BIBLIOGRAPHY. (Text in English) 1960. irreg.
price varies. International Institute for Land
Reclamation and Improvement, P.O. Box 45, 6700
AA Wageningen, Netherlands. Indexed: Field Crop
Abstr. Herb.Abstr. Rural Recreat.Tour.Abstr.
Soils & Fert. World Agri.Econ.& Rural
Sociol.Abstr.

633   US
IOWA AGRICULTURAL STATISTICS. 1964. a. $1.
c/o Agricultural Statistician, Federal Bldg., Rm.
833, 210 Walnut St., Des Moines, IA 50309. TEL
515-284-4340. (Co-sponsors: Iowa Department of
Agriculture; United States Department of
Agriculture) illus. stat. circ. 3,500.
Supersedes: Iowa. Crop and Livestock Reporting
Service. Planting to Harvest. Weather and Field
Crops (ISSN 0163-4976)

636 314   IE
IRELAND. CENTRAL STATISTICS OFFICE.
DISTRIBUTION OF CATTLE AND PIGS BY
SIZE OF HERD. biennial. Central Statistics Office,
Earlsfort Terrace, Dublin 2, Ireland. charts. stat.
Stencilled releases

630   IE
IRELAND. CENTRAL STATISTICS OFFICE.
ESTIMATED AREA, YIELD AND PRODUCE
OF CROPS. a. Central Statistics Office, Earlsfort
Terrace, Dublin 2, Ireland. (processed)

636.4 314   IE
IRELAND. CENTRAL STATISTICS OFFICE. PIG
ENUMERATION. s-a. Central Statistics Office,
Earlsfort Terrace, Dublin 2, Ireland. charts. stat.

631.5 636   IE
IRELAND (EIRE) CENTRAL STATISTICS
OFFICE. CROPS AND LIVESTOCK
ENUMERATION. a. Central Statistics Office,
Earlsfort Terrace, Dublin 2, Ireland.
Former titles (until 1984): Ireland (Eire) Central
Statistics Office. Crops and Pasture and Numbers of
Livestock; Ireland (Eire) Central Statistics Office.
Crops and Livestock Numbers. (ISSN 0075-0549)
Stencilled releases

IRRIGATION AND POWER ABSTRACTS. see
*WATER RESOURCES — Abstracting,
Bibliographies, Statistics*

636 314   IT   ISSN 0390-6426
ITALY. ISTITUTO CENTRALE DI STATISTICA.
ANNUARIO STATISTICO DELLA
ZOOTECNIA, DELLA PESCA E DELLA
CACCIA. 1963. a. L.5500. Istituto Centrale di
Statistica, Via Cesare Balbo 16, 00100 Rome, Italy.
circ. 1,200.
Formerly: Italy. Istituto Centrale di Statistica.
Annuario Statistiche Zootecniche (ISSN 0075-1774)

630 310   IV
IVORY COAST. MINISTERE DE
L'AGRICULTURE. STATISTIQUES
AGRICOLES. 1970. a. Ministere de l'Agriculture,
Abidjan, Ivory Coast.

338.1   US
KENTUCKY AGRICULTURAL STATISTICS. 1948.
a. free. Department of Agriculture, Crop and
Livestock Reporting Service, Box 1120, Louisville,
KY 40201. Ed. David D. Williamson. illus. circ. 5,
000.

316 630   KE   ISSN 0300-2373
KENYA. CENTRAL BUREAU OF STATISTICS.
AGRICULTURAL CENSUS (LARGE FARM
AREAS) irreg. price varies. Central Bureau of
Statistics, Ministry of Finance & Planning, Box
30266, Nairobi, Kenya (Orders to: Government
Printing and Stationery Office, Box 30128, Nairobi,
Kenya)

AGRICULTURE — ABSTRACTING, BIBLIOGRAPHIES, STATISTICS

630   UK   ISSN 0260-8464
LENTIL ABSTRACTS. 1981. a. £17($27) C.A.B. International, Farnham House, Farnham Royal, Slough SL2 3BN, England. Ed. N.J. Pryor. abstr. index. circ. 200. (back issues avail.)
● Also available online. Vendors: BRS, CISTI, DIMDI, DIALOG, European Space Agency.

338.1   LB
LIBERIA. MINISTRY OF AGRICULTURE. PRODUCTION ESTIMATES OF MAJOR CROPS. a. Ministry of Agriculture, Monrovia, Liberia. (Co-sponsor: Ministry of Planning and Economic Affairs)
Formerly: Liberia. Ministry of Agriculture. National Rice Production Estimates.

630   338.1   LB
LIBERIA. MINISTRY OF AGRICULTURE. STATISTICAL HANDBOOK. triennial. Ministry of Agriculture, Monrovia, Liberia.

338.1   630   II   ISSN 0304-6184
MADHYA PRADESH. DIRECTORATE OF AGRICULTURE. AGRICULTURAL STATISTICS. (Text in English) a. Directorate of Agriculture, Bhopal, India. Key Title: Agricultural Statistics, Madhya Pradesh.

633.1   016   UK   ISSN 0267-2987
MAIZE ABSTRACTS. 1975. q. £122($212) C.A.B. International, Farnham House, Farnham Royal, Slough SL2 3BN, England (U.S. subscr. to: C.A.B. International, North American Office, 845 N. Park Ave., Tucson, AR 85719) circ. 850. (also avail. in microfiche; back issues avail.)
● Also available online. Vendors: BRS, CISTI, DIMDI, DIALOG, European Space Agency.
Formerly: Maize Quality Protein Abstracts (ISSN 0305-9162)

630   MG
MALAGASY REPUBLIC. MINISTERE DE LA PRODUCTION AGRICOLE ET LA REFORME AGRAIRE. STATISTIQUES AGRICOLES. ANNUAIRE. (Text in French) 1969. a. FMG.5185. Ministere de la Production Agricole et de la Reforme Agraire, Service de la Statistique Agricole, B.P. 49, Antananarivo, Malagasy Republic. circ. 100.

630   MW   ISSN 0076-3292
MALAWI. NATIONAL STATISTICAL OFFICE. NATIONAL SAMPLE SURVEY OF AGRICULTURE. 1970. irreg. (approx. every 5 yrs.) K.6.50 per no. ‡ National Statistical Office, Box 333, Zomba, Malawi. stat. (processed)
Incorporating: Malawi. National Statistical Office. Compendium of Agricultural Statistics (ISSN 0085-3011)

630   338.1   MM
MALTA. CENTRAL OFFICE OF STATISTICS. CENSUS OF AGRICULTURE AND FISHERIES. a. £0.65. Central Office of Statistics, Auberge d'Italie, Valletta, Malta (Subscr. to: Information Division, Auberge de Castille, Valletta, Malta)
Formerly: Malta. Office of Statistics. Census of Agriculture (ISSN 0076-3454)

338.1   US   ISSN 0092-9794
MASSACHUSETTS AGRICULTURAL STATISTICS.* Cover title, 1973: Agricultural Statistics, Massachusetts. 1972. a. free. New England Crop and Livestock Reporting Service, 105 Loudon Rd., Bldg. 3, Concord, NH 03301-5605. (Co-sponsors: Massachusetts Department of Food & Agriculture; U.S. Department of Agriculture) illus. stat.

NETHERLANDS. CENTRAAL BUREAU VOOR DE STATISTIEK. STATISTIEK DER LONEN IN DE LANDBOUW. STATISTICS OF WAGES IN AGRICULTURE. see BUSINESS AND ECONOMICS — Abstracting, Bibliographies, Statistics

630   NE   ISSN 0168-3918
NETHERLANDS. CENTRAAL BUREAU VOOR DE STATISTIEK. STATISTIEK VAN DE LAND- EN TUINBOUW. STATISTICS OF AGRICULTURE. (Text in Dutch and English) 1949. a. fl.26. Centraal Bureau voor de Statistiek, Prinses Beatrixlaan 428, Voorburg, Netherlands (Orders to: Staatsuitgeverij, Christoffel Plantijnstraat, The Hague, Netherlands)

338.1   US   ISSN 0077-8540
NEW MEXICO AGRICULTURAL STATISTICS. 1962. a. free. Department of Agriculture, Agricultural Statistical Service, P.O. Box 3189, Las Cruces, NM 88001. (Co-sponsor: U.S. Department of Agriculture)

630   NZ   ISSN 0110-4624
NEW ZEALAND. DEPARTMENT OF STATISTICS. AGRICULTURAL STATISTICS. a. NZ.$15.40. Department of Statistics, Private Bag, Wellington, New Zealand (Subscr. to: Government Printing Office, Publications, Private Bag, Wellington, New Zealand)
Formerly: New Zealand. Department of Statistics. Statistical Report of Farm Production (ISSN 0077-9822)

631.4   016   NZ   ISSN 0110-165X
NEW ZEALAND. SOIL BUREAU. BIBLIOGRAPHIC REPORT. 1971. irreg. price varies. Soil Bureau, Private Bag, Lower Hutt, New Zealand. Indexed: Geo.Abstr. GeoRef.

630   627   NZ   ISSN 0111-0829
NEW ZEALAND AGRICULTURAL ENGINEERING INSTITUTE. CURRENT PUBLICATIONS. a. free. New Zealand Agricultural Engineering Institute, Lincoln College, Canterbury, New Zealand.

338.1   317   US
NORTH DAKOTA AGRICULTURAL STATISTICS. 1956. a. $15. North Dakota Agricultural Statistics Service, Box 3166, Fargo, ND 58108. TEL 701-237-5771. Ed. R.F. Carver. circ. 4,000.
Formerly: North Dakota Crop and Livestock Statistics (ISSN 0078-1541)

664.7   US
NORTH DAKOTA GRAIN AND OILSEED TRANSPORTATION STATISTICS. 1975. a. free. North Dakota State University, Upper Great Plains Transportation Institute, Fargo, ND 58105.

630   NO   ISSN 0078-1894
NORWAY. STATISTISK SENTRALBYRAA. JORDBRUKSSTATISTIKK/AGRICULTURAL STATISTICS. (Subseries of its Norges Offisielle Statistikk) (Text in Norwegian and English) 1937. a. Kr.45. Statistisk Sentralbyraa, Box 8131 Dep., 033 Oslo 1, Norway. circ. 1,750.

633.1   016   UK   ISSN 0309-135X
NUTRITION ABSTRACTS AND REVIEWS. SERIES B: LIVESTOCK FEEDS AND FEEDING. 1977. m. £166($291) to non-members. C.A.B. International, Farnham House, Farnham Royal, Slough SL2 3BN, England (U.S. subscr. to: C.A.B. International, North American Office, 845 N. Park Ave., Tucson, AR 85719) circ. 1,700. (also avail. in microfiche; back issues avail.) Indexed: Biol.Abstr. Anim.Breed.Abstr. Anal.Abstr. Dairy Sci.Abstr. Field Crop Abstr. Forest.Abstr. Herb.Abstr. Ind.Vet. Rural Recreat.Tour.Abstr. Vet.Bull. World Agri.Econ.& Rural Sociol.Abstr.
● Also available online. Vendors: BRS, CISTI, DIMDI, DIALOG, European Space Agency.
Supersedes in part: Nutrition Abstracts and Reviews (ISSN 0029-6619)

016   632   US
OHIO AGRICULTURAL RESEARCH AND DEVELOPMENT CENTER, WOOSTER. LIST OF REFERENCES: MAIZE VIRUS AND MYCOPLASMA DISEASES. 1971. irreg. free. Ohio State University, Ohio Agricultural Research and Development Center, Wooster, OH 44691. TEL 216-263-3700. Ed. R.M. Ritter. circ. controlled.
Formerly: Ohio Agricultural Research and Development Center, Wooster. Library. List of References: Maize Virus Diseases and Corn Stunt.

631.4   016   CX   ISSN 0538-2769
ORGANIZATION OF AFRICAN UNITY. INTER-AFRICAN BUREAU FOR SOILS. BIBLIOGRAPHIE. 1951. irreg. $20. Organization of African Unity, Inter-African Bureau for Soils, B.P. 1352, Bangui, Central African Republic. Ed. M.A. Rasheed.

630   PK
PAKISTAN. FOOD AND AGRICULTURE DIVISION. AGRICULTURAL STATISTICS OF PAKISTAN. (Text in English) 1952. a. free. Ministry of Food, Agriculture and Rural Development, Food and Agriculture Division, Planning Unit, 210-H-G-6/3, Islamabad, Pakistan.
Formerly: Pakistan. Food and Agricultural Division. Yearbook of Agricultural Statistics (ISSN 0078-8139)

630   011   PN
PANAMA. INSTITUTO DE INVESTIGACION AGROPECUARIA. BIBLIOGRAFIA. 1980. a. Instituto de Investigacion Agropecuaria de Panama, Centro de Informacion y Documentacion Agropecuaria, Apartado 6-4391, El Dorado Panama, Panama. Eds. Osvaldo Cerrud, Vielka Chang-Yau. circ. 700.

338.1   PH
PHILIPPINES. BUREAU OF AGRICULTURAL ECONOMICS. CROP AND LIVESTOCK STATISTICS. (Text in English) 1954. a. Bureau of Agricultural Economics, Ben-Lor Bldg., 1184 Quezon Ave., Quezon City, Philippines. Ed. J.C. Alix. circ. 500.
Formerly: Philippines. Bureau of Agricultural Economics. Crop, Livestock and Natural Resources Statistics (ISSN 0079-1512)

631   016   UK   ISSN 0305-9154
PLANT GROWTH REGULATOR ABSTRACTS. 1975. m. £83($149) C.A.B. International, Farnham House, Farnham Royal, Slough SL2 3BN, England (U.S. subscr. to: C.A.B. International, North American Office, 845 N. Park Ave., Tucson, AR 85719) circ. 550. (also avail. in microfiche; back issues avail.)
● Also available online. Vendors: BRS, CISTI, DIMDI, DIALOG, European Space Agency.

630   016   IS   ISSN 0032-0897
PLANT PROTECTION ABSTRACTS. (Text in English) 1965. q. free. Makhteshim Agan, P.O. Box 60, Beersheva, Israel. Ed. J.Y. Rein. index. circ. 1,700.

630   314   PL
POLAND. GLOWNY URZAD STATYSTYCZNY. ROCZNIK STATYSTYCZNY ROLNICTWA I GOSPODARKI ZYWNOSCIOWEJ. YEARBOOK OF AGRICULTURAL STATISTICS. (Issued in its Seria Roczniki Branzowe. Branch Yearbooks) irreg., latest 1982. Glowny Urzad Statystyczny, Al. Niepodleglosci 208, 00-925 Warsaw, Poland.
Formerly: Poland. Glowny Urzad Statystyczny. Rolniczy Rocznik Statystyczny. Yearbook of Agricultural Statistics (ISSN 0079-2810)

631   314   PL
POLAND. GLOWNY URZAD STATYSTYCZNY. WYNIKI SPISU ROLNICZEGO. UZYTKOWANIE GRUNTOW I POWIERZCHNIA ZASIEWOW, ORAZ ZWIERZETA GOSPODARSKIE. (Subseries of its: Statystyka Polski) 1966. a. 23 Zl. Glowny Urzad Statystyczny, Al. Niepodleglosci 208, 00-925 Warsaw, Poland.
Formerly: Poland. Glowny Urzad Statystyczny. Uzytkowanie Gruntow i Powierzchnia Zasiewow Oraz Zwierzeta Gospodarskie (ISSN 0079-2861)

630   PO   ISSN 0079-4139
PORTUGAL. INSTITUTO NACIONAL DE ESTATISTICA. ESTATISTICAS AGRICOLAS. CONTINENTE, ACORES E MADEIRA. (Text in Portuguese and French) 1943. a. Esc.375. Instituto Nacional de Estatistica, Av. Antonio Jose de Almeida, 1078 Lisbon Codex, Portugal (Orders to: Imprensa Nacional, Casa da Moeda, Direccao Comercial, rua D. Francisco Manuel de Melo 5, 1000 Lisbon, Portugal)
Formerly: Portugal. Instituto Nacional de Estatistica. Estatisticas Agricolas (ISSN 0377-225X)

633.491   016   UK   ISSN 0308-7344
POTATO ABSTRACTS. 1976. m. £73($128) C.A.B. International, Farnham House, Farnham Royal, Slough SL2 3BN, England (U.S. subscr. to: C.A.B. International, North American Office, 845 N. Park Ave., Tucson, AR 85719) circ. 350. (also avail. in microfiche; back issues avail.)
● Also available online. Vendors: BRS, CISTI, DIMDI, DIALOG, European Space Agency.
Potatoes

AGRICULTURE — ABSTRACTING, BIBLIOGRAPHIES, STATISTICS

636.5 016   UK   ISSN 0306-1582
POULTRY ABSTRACTS. 1975. m. £110($197)
C.A.B. International, Farnham House, Farnham
Royal, Slough SL2 3BN, England (U.S. subscr. to:
C.A.B. International, North American Office, 845
N. Park Ave., Tucson, AR 85719) circ. 500. (also
avail. in microfiche; back issues avail.) Indexed:
Rev.Appl.Entomol.
●Also available online. Vendors: BRS, CISTI,
DIMDI, DIALOG, European Space Agency.
Poultry

636.5 310   US   ISSN 0565-1980
POULTRY MARKET STATISTICS. a. $4. U.S.
Agricultural Marketing Service, Washington, DC
20250. TEL 202-447-6911.
   Formerly: U.S. Agricultural Marketing Service.
Dairy and Poultry Market Statistics.
Poultry

338.1   CN
PRINCE EDWARD ISLAND. ECONOMICS,
MARKETING & STATISTICS BRANCH.
AGRICULTURAL STATISTICS. 1966. a. ‡
Department of Agriculture, P.O. Box 2000,
Charlottetown, P.E.I. C1A 7N8, Canada. TEL 902-
892-4101. (Co-sponsor: Statistics Canada) illus.
stat. circ. 750.

318 338.1   VE
PRODUCCION AGRICOLA - PERIODO DE
INVIERNO. 1965. irreg., latest issue 1976. free.
Ministerio de Agricultura y Cria, Direccion de
Planificacion y Estadistica, Division de Estadistica,
Torre Norte, Centro Simon Bolivar, Caracas,
Venezuela.

318 630   VE
PRODUCCION AGRICOLA - PERIODO DE
VERANO. 1965. irreg., latest issue 1976. free.
Ministerio de Agricultura y Cria, Direccion de
Planificacion y Estadistica, Division de Estadistica,
Torre Norte, Centro Simon Bolivar, Caracas,
Venezuela.

011 630   CN
QUEBEC. BUREAU DE STATISTIQUE.
STATISTIQUES DE L'AGRICULTURE, DES
PECHES ET DE L'ALIMENTATION, EDITION
(YEAR) a. Bureau de Statistique, 117, Rue Saint-
Andre, Quebec, PQ G1K 3Y3, Canada. TEL 416-
643-5116.

632.9 016   UK   ISSN 0305-0076
REVIEW OF APPLIED ENTOMOLOGY. SERIES
A: AGRICULTURAL; consisting of abstracts of
reviews of current literature on applied entomology
throughout the world. 1913. m. £172($308) to non-
members. C.A.B. International, Institute of
Entomology, Farnham House, Farnham Royal,
Slough SL2 3BN, England. Ed.Bd. adv. bk. rev.
abstr. index. circ. 1,850. (also avail. in microfilm;
back issues avail.) Indexed: Chem.Abstr.
Abstr.Hyg. Apic.Abstr. Field Crop Abstr.
Forest.Abstr. Forest Prod.Abstr. Helminthol.Abstr.
Herb.Abstr. Plant Breed.Abstr. Rev.Appl.Entomol.
Rev.Plant Path.
●Also available online. Vendors: BRS, CISTI,
DIMDI, DIALOG, European Space Agency.
Pest control

631 016   UK   ISSN 0141-0164
RICE ABSTRACTS. 1978. m. £83($149) C.A.B.
International, Farnham House, Farnham Royal,
Slough SL2 3BN, England (U.S. subscr. to: C.A.B.
International, North American Office, 845 N. Park
Ave., Tucson, AR 85719) circ. 300. (also avail. in
microfiche; back issues avail.)
●Also available online. Vendors: BRS, CISTI,
DIMDI, DIALOG, European Space Agency.

318 338.1   AG
SANTIAGO DEL ESTERO. DIRECCION
GENERAL DE INVESTIGACIONES
ESTADISTICA Y CENSOS. ESTADISTICA
AGRICOLA-GANADERA. irreg. free. Direccion
General de Investigaciones Estadistica y Censos,
Palacio de los Tribunales, Santiago del Estero,
Argentina. Dir. Jose H. Alegre.

631 016   UK   ISSN 0141-0180
SEED ABSTRACTS. 1978. m. £83($149) C.A.B.
International, Farnham House, Farnham Royal,
Slough SL2 3BN, England (U.S. subscr. to: C.A.B.
International, North American Office, 845 N. Park
Ave., Tucson, AR 85719) circ. 450. (also avail. in
microfiche; back issues avail.) Indexed: Weed Abstr.
●Also available online. Vendors: BRS, CISTI,
DIMDI, DIALOG, European Space Agency.

630   SE
SEYCHELLES. PRESIDENT'S OFFICE.
STATISTICS DIVISION. AGRICULTURE
SURVEY. irreg. Rs.60. President's Office,
Department of Finance, Statistic Division, Box 206,
Mahe, Seychelles. stat.

636 016   UK   ISSN 0306-7580
SMALL ANIMAL ABSTRACTS. 1975. q. £55($96)
C.A.B. International, Farnham House, Farnham
Royal, Slough SL2 3BN, England (U.S. subscr. to:
C.A.B. International, North American Office, 845
N. Park Ave., Tucson, AR 85719) circ. 250. (also
avail. in microfiche; back issues avail.) Indexed:
Rev.Appl.Entomol.
●Also available online. Vendors: BRS, CISTI,
DIMDI, DIALOG, European Space Agency.

631.8 016   UK   ISSN 0038-0792
SOILS AND FERTILIZERS; abstracts of world
literature. 1937. m. £250($445) to non-members.
C.A.B. International, Bureau of Soils, Farnham
House, Farnham Royal, Slough SL2 3BN, England
(U.S. subscr. to: C.A.B. International, North
American Office, 845 N. Park Ave., Tucson, AR
85719) adv. bk. rev. abstr. index. circ. 1,900.
Indexed: Biol.Abstr. Chem.Abstr. Nutr.Abstr.
Dairy Sci.Abstr. Field Crop Abstr. Forest.Abstr.
Forest Prod.Abstr. Helminthol.Abstr. Herb.Abstr.
Rural Recreat.Tour.Abstr. Rev.Plant Path. Weed
Abstr. World Agri.Econ.& Rural Sociol.Abstr.
●Also available online. Vendors: BRS, CISTI,
DIMDI, DIALOG, European Space Agency.

633.1 016   UK   ISSN 0308-2970
SORGHUM AND MILLETS ABSTRACTS. 1976. m.
£56($96) C.A.B. International, Farnham House,
Farnham Royal, Slough SL2 3BN, England (U.S.
subscr. to: C.A.B. International, North American
Office, 845 N. Park Ave., Tucson, AR 85719) circ.
250. (also avail. in microfiche; back issues avail.)
Indexed: Field Crop Abstr. Herb.Abstr.
●Also available online. Vendors: BRS, CISTI,
DIMDI, DIALOG, European Space Agency.

338.1 316   SA
SOUTH AFRICA. DEPARTMENT OF
AGRICULTURE AND FISHERIES. DIVISION
OF ECONOMIC SERVICES. ABSTRACT OF
AGRICULTURAL STATISTICS. (Text in
Afrikaans and English) 1958. a., latest 1984. free. ‡
Department of Agriculture and Fisheries, Division
of Economic Services, Private Bag X246, Pretoria
0001, South Africa. circ. controlled.
   Formerly: South Africa. Department of
Agricultural Economics and Marketing. Division of
Agricultural Marketing Research. Abstract of
Agricultural Statistics.

631 016   UK   ISSN 0141-0172
SOYABEAN ABSTRACTS. 1978. m. £67($116)
C.A.B. International, Farnham House, Farnham
Royal, Slough SL2 3BN, England (U.S. subscr. to:
C.A.B. International, North American Office, 845
N. Park Ave., Tucson, AR 85719) circ. 250. (also
avail. in microfiche; back issues avail.)
●Also available online. Vendors: BRS, CISTI,
DIMDI, DIALOG, European Space Agency.

630 310   SP
SPAIN. MINISTERIO DE AGRICULTURA.
SECRETARIA GENERAL TECNICA.
ANUARIO DE ESTADISTICA AGRARIA. 1972.
a. Ministerio de Agricultura, Secretaria General
Tecnica, Servicio de Publicaciones Agrarias, Paseo
de Infante Isabel, 1, Madrid-7, Spain. charts.

630 338.1   SP
SPAIN. MINISTERIO DE AGRICULTURA.
SECRETARIA GENERAL TECNICA. CUENTAS
DEL SECTOR AGRARIO. no.4, 1979. irreg.
Ministerio de Agricultura, Secretaria General
Tecnica, Paseo Infante 1, Madrid 7, Spain. charts.
stat.

630   EI   ISSN 0081-4946
STATISTICAL OFFICE OF THE EUROPEAN
COMMUNITIES. STATISTIQUE AGRICOLE.
1961. irreg., 6-8 issues per yr. 15000 Fr.($36.20)
includes yearbook. Rue Alcide de Gasperi, B.P.
1907, Luxembourg, Luxembourg (Dist. in the U.S.
by: European Community Information Service, 2100
M St., NW, Suite 707, Washington, DC 20037)

630 332 380.5 312   TH
STATISTICAL SUMMARY OF THAILAND. (Text
in English) 1973. a. price varies. National Statistical
Office, Statistical Reports Division, Larn Luangm
Road, Bangkok 10100, Thailand. circ. 700.

631   US   ISSN 0081-5128
STATISTICS OF FARMER COOPERATIVES. a.
free. U.S. Department of Agriculture, Agricultural
Cooperative Service, 14th St. & Independence Ave.,
S.W., Washington, DC 20250. TEL 202-655-4000.

338.1 630   GW   ISSN 0072-1581
STATISTISCHES JAHRBUCH UEBER
ERNAEHRUNG, LANDWIRTSCHAFT UND
FORSTEN DER BUNDESREPUBLIK
DEUTSCHLAND. 1956. a. DM.118.
Bundesministerium fuer Ernaehrung, Landwirtschaft
und Forsten, Abteilung 2, 5300 Bonn, W. Germany
(B.R.D.)

630   SW   ISSN 0082-0199
SWEDEN. STATISTISKA CENTRALBYRAAN.
JORDBRUKSSTATISTISK AARSBOK. (Text in
Swedish; summaries in English) 1965. a. Kr.150.
Statistiska Centralbyraan, Distribution, S-701 89
Oerebro, Sweden. circ. 1,500.

630 314   SW   ISSN 0082-0288
SWEDEN. STATISTISKA CENTRALBYRAAN.
STATISTISKA MEDDELANDEN. SUBGROUP J
(AGRICULTURE) (Text in Swedish; table heads
and summaries in English) 1963 N.S. irreg. Kr.900.
Statistiska Centralbyraan, Distribution, S-701 89
Oerebro, Sweden. circ. 1,175.

631 636   TZ
TANZANIA. MINISTRY OF AGRICULTURE AND
LIVESTOCK DEVELOPMENT. BULLETIN OF
CROP STATISTICS. (Text in English) 1975. a.
Ministry of Agriculture and Livestock Development,
Planning and Marketing Division, Statistics Section,
Box 9192, Dar es Salaam, Tanzania. Ed. M.S.
Ravivarma. circ. 200.
   Former titles: Tanzania. Ministry of Agriculture.
Bulletin of Crop Statistics; Bulletin of Crop and
Livestock Statistics.

338.1   US   ISSN 0091-1550
TEXAS LIVESTOCK STATISTICS. (Subseries of:
Texas Department of Agriculture. Bulletin) 1968. a.
free. Crop and Livestock Reporting Service, Box 70,
Austin, TX 78767. TEL 512-482-5581. Dir. Dennis
Findley. charts. illus. mkt. stats. circ. 2,800.

633 317   US   ISSN 0091-4673
TEXAS SMALL GRAINS STATISTICS. (Subseries of:
Texas. Department of Agriculture. Bulletin) 1968. a.
free. Crop and Livestock Reporting Service, Box 70,
Austin, TX 78767. TEL 512-482-5581. Dir. Dennis
Findley. charts. illus. mkt. stats. circ. 2,500.

630 001.3 016   II   ISSN 0379-3990
THESIS ABSTRACTS. (Text in English) 1975. q.
Rps.100($20) Haryana Agricultural University,
Hisar 125004, Haryana, India. Ed. R.P. Bansal. adv.
circ. 500.

338.109   US   ISSN 0082-9714
U.S. DEPARTMENT OF AGRICULTURE.
AGRICULTURAL STATISTICS. 1936. a. price
varies. U.S. Department of Agriculture., 14th St. &
Independence Ave. S.W., Washington, DC 20250
TEL 202-655-4000. (Orders to: Supt. of Documents,
Washington, DC 20402)

636 317   US
U.S. DEPARTMENT OF AGRICULTURE.
ANIMAL AND PLANT HEALTH INSPECTION
SERVICE. COOPERATIVE STATE-FEDERAL
BRUCELLOSIS ERADICATION PROGRAM:
STATISTICAL TABLES. a. free. U.S. Animal and
Plant Health Inspection Service, 6505 Belcrest Rd.,
Federal Center Bldg., Hyattsville, MD 20782. TEL
301-436-8645. stat.

AGRICULTURE — AGRICULTURAL ECONOMICS

636 317   US
U.S. DEPARTMENT OF AGRICULTURE. ANIMAL AND PLANT HEALTH INSPECTION SERVICE. COOPERATIVE STATE-FEDERAL BOVINE TUBERCULOSIS ERADICATION PROGRAM: STATISTICAL TABLES. a. free. U.S. Animal and Plant Health Inspection Service, 6505 Belcrest Rd., Federal Center Bldg., Hyattsville, MD 20782. TEL 301-436-8645. stat.

338.1 382 317   US
U.S. FOREIGN AGRICULTURAL TRADE STATISTICAL REPORT, CALENDAR YEAR. (Supplement to the bi-m.: Foreign Agricultural Trade of the United States) 1971. a. U.S. Department of Agriculture, Economics Management Staff, Information Division, 1301 New York Ave., Washington, DC 20005 TEL 202-783-3238. (Subscr. to: Supt. of Documents, Washington, DC 20402)

338.1 382 317   US
U.S. FOREIGN AGRICULTURAL TRADE STATISTICAL REPORT, FISCAL YEAR. (Supplement to the bi-m.: Foreign Agricultural Trade of the United States) a. free. U.S. Department of Agriculture, Economics Management Staff, Information Division, 1301 New York Ave., Washington, DC 20005 TEL 202-783-3238. (Subscr. to: Supt. of Documents, Washington, DC 20402)

630   BL
UNIVERSIDADE DE SAO PAULO. INSTITUTO DE PESQUISAS ECONOMICAS. ESTATISTICAS BASICAS DO SETOR AGRICOLA NO BRASIL. 1983. irreg. Universidade de Sao Paulo, Instituto de Pesquisas Economicos, Faculdade de Economia e Administracao, Caixa Postal 11474, 01000-Sao Paulo, Brazil.

630 317   US
UTAH AGRICULTURAL STATISTICS. 1971. a. free. Department of Agriculture, 350 N. Redwood Rd., Salt Lake City, UT 84116. TEL 801-533-5421. (Co-sponsor: U.S. Department of Agriculture, Statistical Reporting Service)

338.1 318   VE   ISSN 0085-7653
VENEZUELA. MINISTERIO DE AGRICULTURA Y CRIA. DIRECCION DE ECONOMIA Y ESTADISTICA AGROPECUARIA. DIVISION DE ESTADISTICA. PLAN DE TRABAJO.* a. Ministerio de Agricultura y Cria, Direccion de Economia y Estadistica Agropecuaria, Division de Estadistica, Caracas, Venezuela.

634.3 011   UK   ISSN 0175-8292
VITIS - VITICULTURE AND ENOLOGY ABSTRACTS. Variant title: Vitis - V E S. 4/yr. DM.50. International Food Information Service (IFIS), Lane End House, Shinfield, Reading RG2 9BB, England. (Co-sponsor: Bundesforschungsanstalt fuer Rebenzuchtung Geilweilerhof) index.

338.1   US   ISSN 0095-4330
WASHINGTON AGRICULTURAL STATISTICS. 1973. a. Crop and Livestock Reporting Service, Department of Agriculture, Box 609, Olympia, WA 98507. TEL 206-754-8919. circ. 3,000.

632.58 016   UK   ISSN 0043-1729
WEED ABSTRACTS; compiled from world literature. 1954. m. £122($218) to non-members. C.A.B. International, Farnham House, Farnham Royal, Slough SL2 3BN, England (U.S. subscr. to: C.A.B. International, North American Office, 845 N. Park Ave., Tucson, AR 85719) bk. rev. abstr. index. circ. 2,250. (also avail. in microfiche; back issues avail.) Indexed: Biol.Abstr. Chem.Abstr. Field Crop Abstr. Forest.Abstr. Forest Prod.Abstr. Herb.Abstr. Ind.Vet. Rev.Appl.Entomol. Rural Recreat.Tour.Abstr. Vet.Bull. World Agri.Econ.& Rural Sociol.Abstr.
●Also available online. Vendors: BRS, CISTI, DIMDI, DIALOG, European Space Agency.

632.58 632   US
WEED SCIENCE SOCIETY OF AMERICA. ABSTRACTS. 1956. a. Weed Science Society of America, 309 W. Clark St., Champaign, IL 61820. TEL 217-356-3182. (reprint service avail. from UMI,ISI) Indexed: Biotech.Abstr. Weed Abstr.
Formerly (until 1967): Weed Society of America. Abstracts (ISSN 0511-4144)

633.18 016   LB
WEST AFRICA RICE DEVELOPMENT ASSOCIATION. CURRENT BIBLIOGRAPHY. (Text in English and French) 1974. irreg. West Africa Rice Development Association, Box 1019, Monrovia, Liberia.

338.1 016 301   UK   ISSN 0043-8219
WORLD AGRICULTURAL ECONOMICS AND RURAL SOCIOLOGY ABSTRACTS; abstracts of world literature. 1959. m. £191($345) to non-members. C.A.B. International, Farnham House, Farnham Royal, Slough SL2 3BN, England (U.S. subscr. to: C.A.B. International, North American Office, 845 N. Park Ave., Tucson, AR 85719) adv. bk. rev. abstr. index; cum.index. circ. 1,250. (also avail. in microfiche; back issues avail.) Indexed: Nutr.Abstr. Anim.Breed.Abstr. Dairy Sci.Abstr. Field Crop Abstr. Forest.Abstr. Herb.Abstr. Key to Econ.SCi.
●Also available online. Vendors: BRS, CISTI, DIMDI, DIALOG, European Space Agency.
Supersedes: Digest of Agricultural Economics and Marketing.

338.1   UK   ISSN 0512-3844
WORLD WHEAT STATISTICS. (Text in English, French, Russian and Spanish) 1955. a. ‡ International Wheat Council, Haymarket House, 28 Haymarket, London SW1Y 4SS, England.

316 630   ZA
ZAMBIA. CENTRAL STATISTICAL OFFICE. AGRICULTURAL AND PASTORAL PRODUCTION (COMMERCIAL AND NON-COMMERCIAL) 1965/66. a., latest 1977/78. K.3. Central Statistical Office, P.O. Box 31908, Lusaka, Zambia.
Supersedes in part: Zambia. Central Statistical Office. Agricultural and Pastoral Production (ISSN 0080-1305)

338.1   ZA
ZAMBIA. CENTRAL STATISTICAL OFFICE. AGRICULTURAL AND PASTORAL PRODUCTION (COMMERCIAL FARMS) a. Central Statistical Office, P.O. Box 31908, Lusaka, Zambia.
Supersedes in part: Zambia. Central Statistical Office. Agricultural and Pastoral Production (ISSN 0080-1305)

630   ZA
ZAMBIA. CENTRAL STATISTICAL OFFICE. AGRICULTURAL AND PASTORAL PRODUCTION (NON-COMMERCIAL) 1972. a., latest 1977-78. K.3. Central Statistical Office, P.O. Box 31908, Lusaka, Zambia.
Supersedes in part: Zambia. Central Statistical Office. Agricultural and Pastoral Production (ISSN 0080-1305)

AGRICULTURE — Agricultural Economics

338.1   US
A C S RESEARCH REPORT. irreg. Agricultural Cooperative Service, 14th St. and Independence Ave., S.W., Washington, DC 20250. TEL 202-447-9172.

338.1   UK   ISSN 0065-4337
AGRARIAN DEVELOPMENT STUDIES. 1965. irreg. price varies. Wye College (University of London), Department of Agricultural Economics, Kent, England. Ed. I. Carruthers. bk. rev. index.

338.1   GW   ISSN 0065-4345
AGRARMARKT-STUDIEN. 1966. irreg., no.30, 1985. price varies. (Universitaet Kiel, Institut fuer Agrarpolitik und Marktlehre) Verlag Paul Parey (Hamburg), Spitalerstr. 12, 2000 Hamburg 1, W. Germany (B.R.D.) Ed. Hans Stamer. illus. bibl. index. (reprint service avail. from ISI)

630 338.1   UK
AGRICULTURAL CO-OPERATIVES IN THE UNITED KINGDOM. STATISTICS. 1970. a. £5. Plunkett Foundation for Co-Operative Studies, 31 St. Giles, Oxford OX1 3LF, England. (Co-sponsors: Food from Britain; Federation of Agricultural Co-Operatives (U.K.)) circ. 1,100.
Formerly: Agricultural Co-Operation in the United Kingdom: Summary of Statistics (ISSN 0142-4998)

338.1   CN
AGRICULTURAL CREDIT CORPORATION OF SASKATCHEWAN. ANNUAL REPORT. 1973. a. Agricultural Credit Corporation of Saskatchewan, Regina, Sask. S4s 0B1, Canada. TEL 306-787-6464. Ed. Morley L. Machin.
Formerly: Saskatchewan FarmStart Corporation. Annual Report (ISSN 0709-325X)

338.1   MW
AGRICULTURAL DEVELOPMENT AND MARKETING CORPORATION. ANNUAL REPORT AND STATEMENT OF ACCOUNTS. a. free. Agricultural Development and Marketing Corporation, Box 5052, Limbe, Malawi. stat.
Supersedes: Agricultural Development and Marketing Corporation. Annual Report & Agricultural Development Corporation. Balance Sheet and Accounts; Which was formerly: Farmers Marketing Board. Balance Sheet and Accounts.

338.1 332   PK   ISSN 0065-4426
AGRICULTURAL DEVELOPMENT BANK OF PAKISTAN. ANNUAL REPORT AND STATEMENT OF ACCOUNTS. a. Agricultural Development Bank of Pakistan, Shafi Court, Merewether Rd., Karachi, Pakistan.

338.1   CN   ISSN 0708-5206
AGRICULTURAL DEVELOPMENT CORPORATION OF SASKATCHEWAN. ANNUAL REPORT. a. Agricultural Development Corporation of Saskatchewan, Regina, Sask., Canada. TEL 306-565-5035.

338.1   UK
AGRICULTURAL ENTERPRISE STUDIES IN ENGLAND AND WALES. 1970. irreg., latest no.94, 1985. University of Reading, Department of Agricultural Economics & Management, 4 Earley Gate, Whiteknights Rd., P.O. Box 237, Reading RG6 2AR, England.

338.1   US
AGRICULTURAL FINANCE OUTLOOK AND SITUATION. 1961. a. $4.50. U.S. Department of Agriculture, Economics Management Staff, Information Division, 1301 New York Ave., N.W., Washington, DC 20005 TEL 202-783-3238. (Subscr. to: Supt. of Documents, 1301 N.Y. Ave., N.W., Rm. 228, Washington, DC 20005-4789)
●Also available online. Vendors: DIALOG.
Formerly (until 1980): Agricultural Finance Outlook (ISSN 0501-9117)

338.1   US   ISSN 0002-1466
AGRICULTURAL FINANCE REVIEW. 1938. a. free. Cornell University, Department of Agricultural Economics, Ithaca, NY 14853. Ed. John Brake. bk. rev. charts. mkt. stat. index. circ. 2,000. Indexed: P.A.I.S. J.of Econ.Abstr. Geo.Abstr. Ind.U.S.Gov.Per. Rural Recreat.Tour.Abstr. World Agri.Econ.& Rural Sociol.Abstr.

338.1   BG
AGRICULTURAL PRODUCTION LEVELS IN BANGLADESH. (Text in English) 1976. a. free. Bangladesh Bureau of Statistics, Secretariat, Dacca 2, Bangladesh. Ed. A.K.M. Ghulam Rabbani. charts. stat.

338.1   UK   ISSN 0065-4493
AGRICULTURAL PROGRESS. 1924. a. £12.50. Agricultural Education Association, c/o A.R. Staniforth, Ed., 5 Capel Close, Oxford OX2 7LA, England. adv. bk. rev. circ. 1,000. Indexed: Biol.Abstr. Nutr.Abstr. Anim.Breed.Abstr. Dairy Sci.Abstr. Field Crop Abstr. Geo.Abstr. Herb.Abstr. Ind.Vet. Plant Breed Abstr. RICS. Soils & Fert. Vet.Bull. World Agri.Econ.& Rural Sociol.Abstr.

630 330.8   UN
AGRICULTURAL REVIEW FOR EUROPE. 1958. irreg., latest no.28, vol.6, 1985. price varies. (Economic Commission for Europe (ECE)) United Nations Publications, Room DC2-0853, New York, NY 10017 (Or Distribution and Sales Section, Palais des Nations, 1211 Geneva 10, Switzerland)
Former titles: Review of the Agricultural Situation in Europe at the End of (Year) & Agricultural Market Review.

AGRICULTURE — AGRICULTURAL ECONOMICS

338.1 330.8   UN
AGRICULTURAL TRADE IN EUROPE. 1960. a. $11. (Economic Commission for Europe (ECE)) United Nations Publications, Room DC2-0853, New York, NY 10017 (Or Distribution and Sales Section, Palais des Nations, 1211 Geneva 10, Switzerland)

338.1 331   II   ISSN 0084-6066
AGRICULTURAL WAGES IN INDIA. (Text and summaries in English) 1950. a. Rs.166($59.76) Ministry of Agriculture, Department of Agriculture and Cooperation, Directorate of Economics and Statistics, A-2E-3 Kasturba Gandhi Marg Barracks, New Delhi 110001, India. Ed. Chandar Dhar Sharma. circ. 250.

338.1   FR
AGRICULTURE AFRICAINE.* 1979. a. 635 F. Ediafric-la Documentation Africaine, 57 ave. d'Iena, 75016 Paris, France.

338   US
AGROINDUSTRY: LATIN AMERICAN INDUSTRIAL REPORT. (Avail. for each of 22 Latin American countries) 1985. a. $435 per country report per industry covered. Aurora International, Box 9099, Bridgeport, CT 06601-2099. TEL 203-368-0579. Ed. Andres C. Aquino.

338.1   PL   ISSN 0137-1711
AKADEMIA ROLNICZA, POZNAN. ROCZNIKI. EKONOMIKA I ORGANIZACJA ROLNICTWA. (Text in Polish; summaries in English and Russian) 1974. irreg. price varies. Akademia Rolnicza, Poznan, Ul. Wojska Polskiego 28, 60-637 Poznan, Poland. Indexed: Bibl.Agri.

338.1   NE
AKKERBOUW. irreg. Landbouw-Economisch Instituut, Afdeling Landbouw, Conradkade 175, 2517 CL The Hague, Netherlands.

338.1   CN   ISSN 0708-3017
ALBERTA. AGRICULTURAL PROCESSING BRANCH. PROCESSING & MANUFACTURING GUIDE. 1975. biennial. free. Agricultural Processing Branch, 7000-113 St., Edmonton, Alta. T6H 5T6, Canada. TEL 403-427-4010. Ed. A. Drohomirecki. charts. illus. circ. 2,000.
    Former titles: Directory of Alberta's Agricultural Processing Industry & Agricultural Processing and Manufacturing Guide (ISSN 0708-3025)

338.1   US
AMERICAN AGRICULTURAL ECONOMICS ASSOCIATION. HANDBOOK-DIRECTORY. irreg. $15. American Agricultural Economics Association, c/o Secretary-Treasurer, 80 Heady Hall, Iowa State University, Ames, IA 50011-1070. TEL 515-294-8700.
    Formerly: American Agricultural Economics Association. Handbook.

338.1   SP   ISSN 0210-637X
ANUARIO HORTOFRUTICOLA ESPANOL. (Text in English, French, German, Spanish) 1968. a. 4000 ptas. Sucro S.A., Hernan Cortes, 5, 46004 Valencia, Spain. adv. circ. 5,000.

338.1   BL
ASPECTOS GERAIS E PRINCIPAIS TENDENCIAS DA AGROPECUARIA PARAIBANA. a. Comissao Estadual de Planajamento Agricola, Paraiba, Brazil. illus.

338.1   AT   ISSN 0815-1458
AUSTRALIA. BUREAU OF AGRICULTURAL ECONOMICS. OCCASIONAL PAPERS. no.4, 1971. irreg. price varies. Bureau of Agricultural Economics, Department of Primary Industry, G.P.O. Box 1563, Canberra, A.C.T. 2601, Australia (Subscr.to: Australian Government Publishing Service, G.P.O. Box 84, Canberra, A.C.T. 2601, Australia) Indexed: Nutr.Abstr. Rural Recreat.Tour.Abstr. World Agri.Econ.& Rural Sociol.Abstr.

350   AT   ISSN 0313-2781
AUSTRALIA. DEPARTMENT OF PRIMARY INDUSTRY. AUSTRALIAN PLAGUE AND LOCUST COMMISSION. ANNUAL REPORT. 1976. a. free. (Department of Primary Industry) Australian Government Publishing Service, G.P.O. Box 1563, Canberra, A.C.T. 2601, Australia.

338.1 331   PH
AVERAGE WAGE RATES OF FARM WORKERS IN THE PHILIPPINES. irreg. free. Bureau of Agricultural Economics, Ben-Lor Building, 1184 Quezon Ave., Quezon City, Philippines. Ed. Rebecca Rola-Gabutero. circ. 500.

338.1   PE
BANCO AGRARIO DEL PERU. MEMORIA. no.45, 1976. a. Banco Agrario del Peru, c/o Axel Pflucker Otoya, Augusto Wiese 543-547, Lima, Peru.

338.1   BG   ISSN 0070-8143
BANGLADESH. DIRECTORATE OF AGRICULTURAL MARKETING. AGRICULTURAL MARKETING SERIES.* (Text in English) irreg. Directorate of Agricultural Marketing, Dacca, Bangladesh.

BEDRIJFSUITKOMSTEN TOT FINANCIELE POSITIE; samenvattend overzicht van landbouwbedrijven tot en met boekjaar. see *AGRICULTURE*

338.1   AU
BERICHT UEBER DIE LAGE DER OESTERREICHISCHEN LANDWIRTSCHAFT. 1959. a. S.250($12) Bundesministerium fuer Land- und Forstwirtschaft, Stubenring 1, A-1010 Vienna, Austria. circ. 2,700. Indexed: Nutr.Abstr.

338.1 631   BS
BOTSWANA. MINISTRY OF AGRICULTURE. FARM MANAGEMENT SURVEY RESULTS. 1980. a. free. Ministry of Agriculture, Division of Planning and Statistics, Private Bag 003, Gaborone, Botswana. bibl. stat. circ. 400. (back issues avail.)
    Formerly: Botswana. Ministry of Commerce and Industry. Farm Management Survey Results.

338.1   BL
BRAZIL. COMPANHIA DE FINANCIAMENTO DA PRODUCAO. RELATORIO ANUAL DA C F P. a. Ministerio da Agricultura, Comissao de Financiamento da Producao, W3 Norte, Quadra 514, Bloco B, 70760 Brasilia, Brazil.
    Formerly: Brazil. Ministerio da Agricultura. Commissao de Financiamento da Producao. Relatorio Anual da C F P.

338.1   BL
BRAZIL. SUPERINTENDENCIA DO DESENVOLVIMENTO DO NORDESTE. DEPARTAMENTO DE AGRICULTURA E ABASTECIMENTO. PROGRAMA DE TRABALHO PARA A AGRICULTURA NORDESTINA. irreg. Superintendencia do Desenvolvimento do Nordeste, Departamento de Agricultura e Abastecimento, Recife, Brazil.

338.1   DK   ISSN 0106-0805
C D R PROJECT PAPER. 1969. irreg. Centre for Development Research, Ny Kongensgade 9, 1472 Copenhagen K, Denmark. circ. 200.

338.1   DK   ISSN 0108-6596
C D R RESEARCH REPORTS. 1982. irreg, approx. 4/yr. Kr.120. Centre for Development Research, Ny Kongensgade 9, DK-1472 Copenhagen K, Denmark. circ. 500.

630 338.1   VE
CALENDARIO AGRICOLA. 1970. irreg. free. Ministerio de Agricultura y Cria, Direccion de Planificacion y Estadistica, Division de Estadistica, Torre Norte, Centro Simon Bolivar, Caracas, Venezuela. stat.

338.1   US
CALIFORNIA AGRICULTURAL EXPORT DIRECTORY. 1982. a. $16. Department of Food and Agriculture, 1220 N St., Sacramento, CA 95814. TEL 916-445-6076. Ed. Mark Woerner. circ. 1,600.

338.1   CN   ISSN 0068-7286
CANADA. AGRICULTURE CANADA. ECONOMICS BRANCH. TRADE IN AGRICULTURAL PRODUCTS. (Issued as subseries of Dept's Economic Branch Bulletin) a. free. Agriculture Canada, Economics Branch, Ottawa, Ont. K1A 0C5, Canada. TEL 613-995-5222.

CANADA. GRAIN COMMISSION. ECONOMICS AND STATISTICS DIVISION. VISIBLE GRAIN SUPPLIES AND DISPOSITION. see *AGRICULTURE — Feed, Flour And Grain*

338.1 636   CN
CANADA. MARKETING AND TRADE DIVISION. ANIMAL AND ANIMAL PRODUCTS: OUTLOOK. irreg. free. Agriculture Canada, Marketing and Trade Division, Ottawa, Ont. K1A 0C5, Canada. TEL 613-995-5222. illus.

330   CN   ISSN 0383-414X
CANADA. NATIONAL FARM PRODUCTS MARKETING COUNCIL. ANNUAL REPORT. (Text in French) 1972/73. a. free. National Farm Products Marketing Council, P.O. Box 3430, Sta. D, Ottawa, Ont. K1P 6L4, Canada. Ed. Susan Leah. circ. 2,000.

338.1   CN
CANADIAN AGRICULTURAL ECONOMICS AND FARM MANAGEMENT SOCIETY. PROCEEDINGS OF THE WORKSHOP. 1968. a. Can.$50 (included in subscr. to Canadian Journal of Agricultural Economics) Canadian Agricultural Economics and Farm Management Society, 151 Slater St., Ottawa, Ont. K1P 5H4, Canada. circ. 850. (also avail. in microfilm from UMI)
    Formerly: Canadian Agricultural Economics Society. Proceedings of the Workshop (ISSN 0707-4808)

338.1   IS
CENTER FOR AGRICULTURAL ECONOMIC RESEARCH, REHOVOT. WORKING PAPERS. 1969. irreg. Center for Agricultural Economic Research, Box 12, Rehovot, Israel.

CENTRAL PLANTATION CROPS RESEARCH INSTITUTE. ANNUAL REPORT. see *AGRICULTURE*

338.1 551   SP   ISSN 0210-8623
CENTRO DE EDAFOLOGIA Y BIOLOGIA APLICADA. ANUARIO. (Text in Spanish; summaries in English and Spanish) 1975. a. 2000 ptas. avail. on exchange basis. Centro de Edafologia y Biologia Aplicada, Cordel de Merinas, No.40, Apdo. 257, Salamanca, Spain (Subscr. to: Servicio de Publicaciones, Universidad de Salamanca, Patio de Escuelas s/n, Salamanca, Spain) Ed. L. Garcia Criado. bibl. charts. stats. circ. 1,000. (back issues avail.) Indexed: Chem.Abstr. Helminthol.Abstr. Hort.Abstr. Plant Breed.Abstr. Soils & Fert. Rural Recreat.Tour.Abstr. World Agri.Econ.& Rural Sociol.Abstr.

630 338.1   CR
CIFRAS SOBRE PRODUCCION AGROPECUARIA. 1975. a. free. Banco Central de Costa Rica, Departamento de Investigaciones y Estadistica, Apdo. 10058, San Jose, Costa Rica. charts. circ. 400.

COLLEGE OF DAIRYING. JOURNAL; CULTURAL AND SOCIAL SCIENCES/ RAKUNO GAKUEN DAIGAKU KIYO, JINBUN SHAKAIKAGAKU HEN. see *AGRICULTURE*

338.1   EI
COMMISSION OF THE EUROPEAN COMMUNITIES. MARCHES AGRICOLES: SERIE "PRIX". NOTES EXPLICATIF. (Text in Dutch, English, French, German, Italian) a. Commission of the European Communities, Services de Renseignement et de Diffusion de Documents, Rue de Loi 200, 1049 Brussels, Belgium (Dist. in the U.S. by: European Community Information Service, 2100 M St., N.W., Ste. 707, Washington, DC 20037)

338.1 636   EI
COMMISSION OF THE EUROPEAN COMMUNITIES. MARCHES AGRICOLES: SERIE "PRIX". PRODUITS ANIMAUX. 1970. irreg., 6-9/yr. free. Commission of the European Communities, Services de Renseignement et de Diffusion des Documents, Rue de la Loi 200, 1049 Brussels, Belgium (Dist. in the U.S. by: European Community Information Service, 2100 M St., N.W., Ste. 707, Washington, DC 20037) circ. controlled.
    Supersedes a publication issued under the same title from 1965, no. 4-1969. Numbered alternately with its Marches Agricoles: Serie "Prix" Produits Vegetaux (ISSN 0423-7323)

AGRICULTURE — AGRICULTURAL ECONOMICS

338.1 633 EI
COMMISSION OF THE EUROPEAN COMMUNITIES. MARCHES AGRICOLES: SERIE "PRIX". PRODUITS VEGETAUX. 1970. irreg., 6-9/yr. free. Commission of the European Communities, Rue de la Loi 200, 1049 Brussels, Belgium (Dist. in the U.S. by: European Community Information Service, 2100 M St., N.W., Ste. 707, Washington, DC 20037) circ. controlled.
Supersedes a publication issued under the same title from 1965 no. 4-1969, numbered alternately with its Marches Agricoles: Serie "Prix" Produits Animaux. (ISSN 0531-366X) Issued 1962-1965, no. 3 in a single edition with Produits Animaux as its Marches Agricoles: Series "Prix" (ISSN 0423-7323)

333 AT ISSN 0810-4387
COMMONWEALTH SCIENTIFIC AND INDUSTRIAL RESEARCH ORGANIZATION. DIVISION OF WATER AND LAND RESOURCES. 1959. irreg. (approx. 2/yr.) Aus.$0.80 per issue. C.S.I.R.O., Division of Water and Land Resources, P.O. Box 1666, Canberra City, ACT 2601, Australia. Ed. Margaret Lowe. circ. 800. Indexed: Biol.Abstr. Aus.Sci.Ind. Field Crop Abstr. Geo.Abstr. Herb.Abstr. Hort.Abstr.
Formerly: Commonwealth Scientific and Industrial Research Organization. Division of Land Use Research. Technical Paper (ISSN 0069-746X)

338.1 BL ISSN 0102-2253
CONGRESSO BRASILEIRO DE ECONOMIA E SOCIOLOGIA RURAL. ANAIS. 1962. a. $60. Sociedade Brasileira de Economia Rural, Edificio Brasilia Radio Center, Av. W/3 Norte-Quadra 702, Salas 1049/50, Brazil, 70710 Brasilia, D.F. (Subscr. addr.: L. Eduardo Acosta H., Shis Qi Conj. 12, Casa 03, 71.600 Brasilia, Brazil) bk. rev. circ. 1,000.
Formerly: Sociedade Brasileira de Economistas Rurais. Anais da Reuniao.

630.1 338.1 UK
CO-OPERATIVE COMMUNICATIONS. 1979. irreg. (2-3/yr.) 30p. Plunkett Foundation for Co-Operative Studies, 31 St. Giles St., Oxford OX1 3LF, England. Ed. T.F. Riordan. circ. 800.

338.1 US ISSN 0093-6553
COST OF PICKING AND HAULING FLORIDA CITRUS FRUITS. (Subseries of Agricultural Economics Report) a. University of Florida, Institute of Food and Agricultural Sciences, Food and Resource Economics Department, Gainesville, FL 32601. TEL 904-392-1733. stat.

338.7 II ISSN 0304-6907
COTTON CORPORATION OF INDIA. ANNUAL REPORT. (Text in English) a. Cotton Corporation of India, Air India Building, 12th Floor, Nariman Point, Bombay 400 021, India. Key Title: Annual Report--Cotton Corporation of India.

338.1 CU
CUBA. CENTRO DE INFORMACION Y DOCUMENTACION AGROPECUARIO. BOLETIN DE RESENAS. SERIE: ECONOMIA AGROPECUARIA. (Abstracts in English) 1986. irreg. exchange basis. Centro de Informacion y Documentacion Agropecuario, Gaveta Postal 4149, Havana 4, Cuba (Dist. by: Ediciones Cubanas, Obispo No. 461, Aptdo. 605, Havana, Cuba) Indexed: Agrindex.

338.1 CY ISSN 0379-0827
CYPRUS. AGRICULTURAL RESEARCH INSTITUTE. AGRICULTURAL ECONOMICS REPORT. 1973. irreg., no.14, 1983. free. Ministry of Agriculture and Natural Resources, Agricultural Research Institute, Nicosia, Cyprus. circ. 1,000.

338.1 BL
DADOS SOBRE A SITUACAO DA AGROPECUARIA MUNICIPAL NO ESTADO DO PARANA. a. Associacao de Credito e Assistencia Rural, Caixa Postal 900, Belo Horizonte 30000, Minas Gerais, Brazil.

338.1 DK ISSN 0107-5357
DENMARK. JORDBRUGSOEKONOMISK INSTITUT. RAPPORT.* irreg., 5-7/yr. price varies. Jordbrugsoekonomisk Institut, Valby Langgade 19, DK-2500 Valby, Denmark.

338.1 DK ISSN 0107-5675
DENMARK. JORDBRUGSOEKONOMISK INSTITUT. SERIE A: LANDBRUGETS REGNSKABSSTATISTIK;* economic results in Danish Agriculture. Short title: Landbrugsregnskabsstatistik. (Text in Danish; summaries in English) 1917. a. $35. Jordbrugsoekonomisk Institut, Valby Langgade 19, DK-2500 Valby, Denmark.

338.1 DK ISSN 0107-5683
DENMARK. JORDBRUGSOEKONOMISK INSTITUT. SERIE B: OEKONOMIEN I LANDBRUGETS DRIFTSGRENE/ECONOMICS OF AGRICULTURAL ENTERPRISES.* 1982. a. Kr.25. Jordbrugsoekonomisk Institut, Valby Langgade 19, DK-2500 Valby, Denmark.
Formerly: Regnkabsresultater.

338.1 DK ISSN 0107-5691
DENMARK. JORDBRUGSOEKONOMISK INSTITUT. SERIE C: LANDBRUGETS PRISFORHOLD.* 1967. a. Kr.12. Jordbrugsoekonomisk Institut, Rolighedsvej 25, DK-1958 Frederiksberg C, Denmark. Ed. Arne Larsen.

338.1 DK ISSN 0107-5705
DENMARK. JORDBRUGSOEKONOMISK INSTITUT. SERIE D: GARTNERI-REGNSKABSSTATISTIK;* economic results in Danish horticulture. Short title: Gartneriregnskabsstatistik. (Text in Danish; summaries in English) a. Kr.40. Jordbrugsoekonomisk Institut, Valby Langgade 19, DK-2500 Valby, Denmark.

630 338.1 UK ISSN 0307-689X
DIRECTORY OF AGRICULTURAL CO-OPERATIVES IN THE UNITED KINGDOM. 1970. a. £9. Plunkett Foundation for Co-Operative Studies, 31 St. Giles, Oxford OX1 3LF, England. (Co-sponsors: Food from Britain; Federation of Agricultural Co-Operatives (U.K.)) circ. 900.

338.1 631 FR ISSN 0374-6003
ECOLE NATIONALE SUPERIEURE D'AGRONOMIE ET DES INDUSTRIES ALIMENTAIRES. BULLETIN. (Text in French; summaries in English) 1959. a. 140 F.($20) (Institut National Polytechniques de Nancy, Ecole National Superieure d'Agronomie et des Industries Alimentaires) Bibliotheque Agronomique, 2 Av. de la Foret de Haye, 54500 Vandoeuvre, France. charts. Indexed: Biol.Abstr. Chem.Abstr. Food Sci.& Tech.Abstr. VITIS.

338.1 UK
ECONOMIC REPORT ON SCOTTISH AGRICULTURE. 1981. a. price varies. Department of Agriculture and Fisheries, Chesser House, 500 Gorgie Rd., Edinburgh EH11 3AW, Scotland (Avail. from: Scottish Office Library, Rm. 2/65 New St., Andrews House, Edinburgh EH1 3TG, Scotland) Indexed: Nutr.Abstr. Anim.Breed.Abstr. Dairy Sci.Abstr. Geo.Abstr.
Incorporating: Scottish Agricultural Economics; Some Studies of Current Economic Conditions in Scottish Farming (ISSN 0080-7966) & Agricultural Statistics, Scotland (ISSN 0065-4582)

634 338.1 UK ISSN 0070-8763
ECONOMICS OF FRUIT FARMING. 1949. irreg. price varies. ‡ Wye College (University of London), Department of Agricultural Economics, Ashford, Kent, England.

338.1 FR ISSN 0068-4899
ECONOMIES ET SOCIETES. SERIE AG. PROGRES ET AGRICULTURE. 1962. irreg. 300 F. Presses Universitaires de Grenoble, B.P. 47 X, 38040 Grenoble, France. Ed.Bd. circ. 1,600.

630 338.1 VE
ENCUESTA AGROPECUARIA. 1969. a. free. Ministerio de Agricultura y Cria, Direccion de Planificacion y Estadistica, Division de Estadistica, Caracas, Venezuela. stat.

338.1 PN ISSN 0250-4324
ESTADISTICA PANAMENA. SITUACION ECONOMICA. SECCION 312. SIEMBRA Y COSECHA DE HORTILIZAS. 1972. a. Bl.0.75. Direccion de Estadistica y Censo, Contraloria General, Apdo. 5213, Panama 5, Panama. circ. 800.

338.1 UN
F A O AGRICULTURAL SERVICES BULLETIN. (Editions in English, French and Spanish) 1968. irreg. price varies. Food and Agriculture Organization of the United Nations (FAO), Distribution and Sales Section, Via delle Terme di Caracalla, 00100 Rome, Italy (Dist. in U.S. by: Bernan Associates-Unipub, 4611-F Assembly Dr., Lanham, MD 20706-4391) Ed. K. Richmond. Indexed: Nutr.Abstr. Food Sci.& Tech.Abstr. Rural Recreat.Tour.Abstr. World Agri.Econ.& Rural Sociol.Abstr.

338.1 UN ISSN 0071-7002
F A O COMMODITY REVIEW AND OUTLOOK. (Text in English, French and Spanish) 1961. a. price varies. Food and Agriculture Organization of the United Nations, Distribution and Sales Section, Via delle Terme di Caracalla, 00100 Rome, Italy (Dist. in U.S. by: Bernan Associates-Unipub, 4611-F Assembly Drive, Lanham, MD 20706-4391) Indexed: Nutr.Abstr.

338.1 UN
F A O FERTILIZER AND PLANT NUTRITION BULLETIN. (Editions in English, French and Spanish) irreg., no.11, 1986. price varies. Food and Agriculture Organization of the United Nations, Distribution and Sales Section, Via delle Terme di Caracalla, 00100 Rome, Italy (Dist. in U.S. by: Bernan Associates-Unipub, 4611-F Assembly Drive, Lanham, MD 20706-4391) Indexed: Geo.Abstr. Soils & Fert.

338.1 US
FARM BUSINESS MANAGEMENT; annual report for North East and East Central Minnesota. 1955. a. $5. Staples Technical Institute, Staples, MN 56479. TEL 218-894-1053. Ed. DelRay D. Lecy. charts. index. circ. 1,200.

338.1 UK ISSN 0071-3848
FARM CLASSIFICATION IN ENGLAND AND WALES. 1963. a. price varies. H.M.S.O., P.O. Box 569, London SE1 9NH, England. (Co-sponsor: Ministry of Agriculture, Fisheries and Food) (reprint service avail. from UMI)

332.71 338.1 334 US
FARM CREDIT ADMINISTRATION. ANNUAL REPORT. 1933. a. free. Farm Credit Administration, 1501 Farm Credit Dr., McLean, VA 22102-5090. TEL 703-883-4000. Ed. Christine D. Quinn. circ. 1,000.
Former titles (until 1984): U.S. Farm Credit Administration. Annual Report of the Farm Credit Administration and the Cooperative Farm Credit System & U.S. Farm Credit Administration. Annual Report of the Farm Credit Administration on the Work of the Cooperative Farm Credit System (ISSN 0083-0542)

338.1 US
FARM INCOME. a. free. North Carolina Crop & Livestock Reporting Service, Box 27767, 1 W. Edenton St., Raleigh, NC 27611. TEL 919-755-4394. Ed. Doris D. Watson. circ. 4,000.

338.1 UN ISSN 0430-084X
FARM MANAGEMENT NOTES FOR ASIA AND THE FAR EAST. 1965. biennial. free. Food and Agriculture Organization of the United Nations, Regional Office for Asia and the Pacific, FAO Regional Commission on Farm Management for Asia and the Far East, Maliwan Mansion, Phra Atit Rd., Bangkok 2, Thailand. circ. 300.

338.1 UK
FARM MANAGEMENT POCKETBOOK. a. price varies. Wye College (University of London), Department of Agricultural Economics, Ashford, Kent, England.

338.1 UK
FARMING IN THE EAST MIDLANDS. FINANCIAL RESULTS. 1947/48. a. £3 (approx.) ‡ University of Nottingham, School of Agriculture, University Park, Nottingham NG7 2RD, England. Eds. H.W.T. Kerr, R.J. Babington. circ. 1,000.

FINANCIELE POSITIE VAN DE LANDBOUW; boekjaar en vergelijkingen met voorgaande jaren. see *AGRICULTURE*

AGRICULTURE — AGRICULTURAL ECONOMICS

630 338.1 UN ISSN 0532-0194
FOOD AND AGRICULTURE ORGANIZATION OF THE UNITED NATIONS. AGRICULTURAL PLANNING STUDIES. 1963. irreg., no.20, 1985. Food and Agriculture Organization of the United Nations, Distribution and Sales Section, Via delle Terme di Caracalla, I-00100 Rome, Italy (Dist. in U.S. by: Bernan Associates-Unipub, 4611-F Assembly Drive, Lanham, MD 20706-4391) Indexed: Nutr.Abstr.& Rev. Rural Recreat.Tour.Abstr. World Agri.Econ.& Rural Sociol.Abstr.

338.1 UN ISSN 0071-7118
FOOD AND AGRICULTURE ORGANIZATION OF THE UNITED NATIONS. PRODUCTION YEARBOOK. (Text in English, French and Spanish) 1947. a. price varies. Food and Agriculture Organization of the United Nations, Distribution and Sales Section, Via delle Terme di Caracalla, Rome, Italy (Dist. in U.S. by: Bernan Associates-Unipub, 4611-F Assembly Drive, Lanham, MD 20706-4391) Indexed: Nutr.Abstr. Dairy Sci.Abstr. Hort.Abstr. Soils & Fert.

338.1 382 UN ISSN 0071-7126
FOOD AND AGRICULTURE ORGANIZATION OF THE UNITED NATIONS. TRADE YEARBOOK. (Text in English, French and Spanish) 1947. a. price varies. Food and Agriculture Organization of the United Nations, Distribution and Sales Section, Via delle Terme di Caracalla, Rome, Italy (Dist. in U.S. by: Bernan Associates-Unipub, 4611-F Assembly Drive, Lanham, MD 20706-4391) Indexed: Anim.Breed.Abstr. Dairy Sci.Abstr. Hort.Abstr.

630 338.1 US ISSN 0193-9025
FOOD RESEARCH INSTITUTE STUDIES. 1960. irreg. $20. Food Research Institute, Stanford University, Stanford, CA 94305. TEL 415-723-4160. Ed. Walter P. Falcon. bibl. charts. stat. circ. 1,200. (also avail. in microfilm from UMI; reprint service avail. from UMI) Indexed: Biol.Abstr. Biol.& Agri.Ind. Curr.Cont. Nutr.Abstr. P.A.I.S. Abstr.Trop.Agri. Agrindex. Bibl.Agri. C.R.E.J. Field Crop Abstr. Ind.Econ.J. J.of Econ.Lit. Rural Recreat.Tour.Abstr. World Agri.Econ.& Rural Sociol.Abstr.
  Formerly (1968-1974): Food Research Institute Studies in Agricultural Economics, Trade, and Development (ISSN 0015-6566)

FRANCE. CAISSE NATIONALE DE CREDIT AGRICOLE. RAPPORT SUR LE CREDIT AGRICOLE MUTUEL. see *BUSINESS AND ECONOMICS — Banking And Finance*

338.1 FR ISSN 0243-6108
FRANCE. MINISTERE DE L'AGRICULTURE. INFORMATIONS RAPIDES. FRUITS. (Text in French) 1977. irreg. 100 F. Ministere de l'Agriculture, Service Central des Enquetes et Etudes Statistiques, 4 av. de Saint Mande, 75570 Paris Cedex 12, France.

338.1 FR ISSN 0243-6140
FRANCE. MINISTERE DE L'AGRICULTURE. INFORMATIONS RAPIDES. LEGUMES. (Text in French) 1977. irreg. 240 F. Ministere de l'Agriculture, Service Central des Enquetes et Etudes Statistiques, 4 av. de Saint Mande, 75570 Paris Cedex 12, France.

FRANCE. MINISTERE DE L'AGRICULTURE. INFORMATIONS RAPIDES. STATISTIQUES DES ENTREPRISES. see *AGRICULTURE — Abstracting, Bibliographies, Statistics*

338.1 FR
FRANCE. MINISTERE DE L'AGRICULTURE. INFORMATIONS RAPIDES. VITICULTURE. (Text in French) 1978. irreg. 40 F. Ministere de l'Agriculture, Service Central des Enquetes et Etudes Statistiques, 4 av. de Saint Mande, 75570 Paris Cedex 12, France.

338.1 FR ISSN 0243-6574
FRANCE. MINISTERE DE L'AGRICULTURE. SERIES "S". DEPARTEMENTS D'OUTRE-MER. (Text in French) 1975. irreg. 50 F. per no. Ministere de l'Agriculture, Service Central des Enquetes et Etudes Statistiques, 4 av. de Saint Mande, 75570 Paris Cedex 12, France.

338.1 FR ISSN 0243-6647
FRANCE. MINISTERE DE L'AGRICULTURE. SERIES "S". INDUSTRIES AGRICOLES ET ALIMENTAIRES. (Text in French) 1974. irreg. 50 F. per no. Ministere de l'Agriculture, Service Central des Enquetes et Etudes Statistiques, 4 av. de Saint Mande, 75570 Paris Cedex 12, France.

338.1 FR ISSN 0243-8585
FRANCE. MINISTERE DE L'AGRICULTURE. SERIES "S". METHODES ET APPLICATIONS SCIENTIFIQUES. (Text in French) 1980. irreg. 50 F. per no. Ministere de l'Agriculture, Service Central des Enquetes et Etudes Statistiques, 4 av. de Saint Mande, 75570 Paris Cedex 12, France.

338.1 FR ISSN 0243-6566
FRANCE. MINISTERE DE L'AGRICULTURE. SERIES "S". PRODUCTION ANIMALE. (Text in French) 1975. irreg. 50 F. per no. Ministere de l'Agriculture, Service Central des Enquetes et Etudes Statistiques, 4 av. de Saint Mande, 75570 Paris, France.

338.1 FR ISSN 0755-3218
FRANCE. MINISTERE DE L'AGRICULTURE. SERIES "S". PRODUCTION VEGETALE ET FORESTIERES. (Text in French) 1975. irreg. 50 F. per no. Ministere de l'Agriculture, Service Central des Enquetes et Etudes Statistiques, 4 av. de Saint Mande, 75570 Paris Cedex 12, France.
  Incorporating: France. Ministere de l'Agriculture. Series "S". Statistique Forestiere (ISSN 0243-6655); Formerly: France. Ministere de l'Agriculture. Series "S". Production Vegetale (ISSN 0243-6558)

338.1 FR ISSN 0291-8102
FRANCE. MINISTERE DE L'AGRICULTURE. SERIES "S". RESEAU D'INFORMATION COMPTABLE AGRICOLE. (Text in French) 1980. irreg. 50 F. per no. Ministere de l'Agriculture, Service Central des Enquetes et Etudes Statistiques, 4 av. de Saint Mande, 75570 Paris Cedex 12, France.

338.1 FR ISSN 0243-6639
FRANCE. MINISTERE DE L'AGRICULTURE. SERIES "S". STRUCTURES ET ENVIRONNEMENT DES EXPLOITATIONS. (Text in French) 1975. irreg. 50 F. per no. Ministere de l'Agriculture, Service Central des Enquetes et Etudes Statistiques, 4 av. de Saint Mande, 75570 Paris Cedex 12, France.

FRANCE. MINISTERE DE L'AGRICULTURE. SERIES "S". SYNTHESE STATISTIQUE COMPTES ET REVENUS. see *AGRICULTURE — Abstracting, Bibliographies, Statistics*

338.1 GM ISSN 0301-8423
GAMBIA. PRODUCE MARKETING BOARD. ANNUAL REPORT. 1971. a. free. Produce Marketing Board, Box 284, Marina Foreshore, Banjul, Gambia. illus.
  Continues: Gambia. Oilseeds Marketing Board. Report.

338.1 US
GIANNINI FOUNDATION OF AGRICULTURAL ECONOMICS. INFORMATION SERIES. 1964. irreg. University of California, Berkeley, Giannini Foundation of Agricultural Economics, 207 Giannini Hall, Berkeley, CA 94720 TEL 415-642-6000. (Subscr. to: University of California, Publications, Agriculture and Natural Resources, 6701 San Pablo Ave., Oakland CA 94608)
  Formerly: Information Series on Agricultural Economics (ISSN 0073-7887)

338.1 US ISSN 0575-4208
GIANNINI FOUNDATION OF AGRICULTURAL ECONOMICS. MONOGRAPH. no.10, 1961. irreg., no.36, 1978. University of California, Berkeley, Giannini Foundation of Agricultural Economics, 207 Giannini Hall, Berkeley, CA 94720 TEL 415-642-6000. (Subscr. to: University of California, Publications, Agriculture and Natural Resources, 6701 San Pablo Ave., Oakland, CA 94608)

338.1 US ISSN 0072-4459
GIANNINI FOUNDATION OF AGRICULTURAL ECONOMICS. RESEARCH REPORT. 1930. irreg., no.325, 1978. free. ‡ University of California, Berkeley, Giannini Foundation of Agricultural Economics, 207 Giannini Hall, Berkeley, CA 94720 TEL 415-642-6000. (Subscr. to: University of California, Publications, Agriculture and Natural Resources, 6701 San Pablo Ave., Oakland CA 94608) Indexed: Amer.Bibl.Agri.Econ. World Agri.Econ.& Rural Sociol.Abstr.

338.1 FR ISSN 0242-2085
GRAPH-AGRI; annuaire de graphiques agricoles. 1979. a. 95 F. Ministere de l'Agriculture, Service Central des Enquetes et Etudes Statistiques, 4 av. de Saint Mande, 75570 Paris Cedex 12, France.

630 658.8 DK
GROVVARELEDEREN.* 20-21/yr. Skolegade 5, 3. sal. 8000 Arhus C, Denmark. adv. circ. 2,200.

338.1 GT
GUATEMALA. BANCO NACIONAL DE DESARROLLO AGRICOLA. MEMORIA. 1971. a. Banco Nacional de Desarrollo Agricola, 9 Calle No. 9-47, Zona 1, Guatemala, Guatemala. stat.

338.1 US
I F P R I RESEARCH REPORT. 1976. irreg. (approx. 7/yr.) free. International Food Policy Research Institute, 1776 Massachusetts Ave., N.W., Washington, DC 20036. TEL 202-862-5600. Ed. Barbara Rose. bibl. charts. illus. stat. circ. 8,000. (also avail. in microfiche from NTI; back issues avail.)

338.1 310 II
INDIA. DEPARTMENT OF RURAL DEVELOPMENT. ADMINISTRATIVE INTELLIGENCE DIVISION. PROGRESS REPORT ON SMALL FARMERS DEVELOPMENT AGENCY PROGRAMME. a. Ministry of Agriculture and Irrigation, Directorate of Economics and Statistics, A-2E/3 Kasturba Gandhi Marg Barracks, New Delhi 110001, India. stat.

338.1 310 II
INDIA. DEPARTMENT OF RURAL DEVELOPMENT. ADMINISTRATIVE INTELLIGENCE DIVISION. SOME SPECIAL PROGRAMMES OF RURAL DEVELOPMENT; STATISTICS. a. Ministry of Agriculture and Irrigation, Directorate of Economics and Statistics, A-2E/3 Kasturba Gandhi Marg Barracks, New Delhi 110001, India. stat.

338.1 II
INDIA. MINISTRY OF AGRICULTURE. BULLETIN ON COMMERCIAL CROPS STATISTICS. (Text in English) 1961. irreg. Rs.67.85($24.43) Ministry of Agriculture, Department of Agriculture and Cooperation, Directorate of Economics and Statistics, A-2E-3 Kasturba Gandhi Marg Barracks, New Delhi 110001, India (Order from: Controller of Publications, Civil Lines, Delhi 110054, India) Ed. Chandar Dhar Sharma. circ. 350.
  Formerly: Economic Survey of Indian Agriculture (ISSN 0085-0160)

338.1 636.5 II
INDIA. MINISTRY OF AGRICULTURE. BULLETIN ON FOOD STATISTICS. (Text in English) 1972. a. Rs.71.50($25.74) Ministry of Agriculture, Department of Agriculture and Cooperation, Directorate of Economics and Statistics, A-2E-3 Kasturba Gandhi Marg Barracks, New Delhi 110001, India. Ed. Chandar Dhar Sharma. charts. illus. stat. circ. 600.
  Formerly: Studies in the Economics of Poultry Farming in Punjab.

338.1 BL
INDUSTRIAS DO ARROZ NO RIO GRANDE DO SUL. 1968. biennial. free. Instituto Rio Grandense do Arroz, Av. Julio de Castilhos 585-1, C.P. 1927, 90000 Porto Alegre RS, Brazil. Ed. Magno Soares da Rocha. circ. 500.

AGRICULTURE — AGRICULTURAL ECONOMICS

338.1 US
INFORMATION SERIES IN AGRICULTURAL ECONOMICS. (University of California. Division of Agricultural Sciences. Bulletin Series) 1963. irreg., 1-5/yr. free. University of California, Berkeley, Giannini Foundation of Agricultural Economics, 207 Giannini Hall, Berkeley, CA 94720. TEL 415-642-6000. Ed. Gordon King. circ. 7,500. Indexed: Amer.Bibl.Agri.Econ. World Agri.Econ.& Rural Sociol.Abstr.

338.1 EI ISSN 0073-7895
INFORMATION SERVICE OF THE EUROPEAN COMMUNITIES. NEWSLETTER ON THE COMMON AGRICULTURAL POLICY.* irreg. (approx. 20 nos./yr.) Press and Information Service of the European Communities, 224 rue de la Loi, 1004 Brussels, Belgium.

338.1 338.9 CM
INSTITUT PANAFRICAIN POUR LE DEVELOPPEMENT. TRAVAUX MANUSCRITS. 1972. irreg. price varies. ‡ Institut Panafricain pour le Developpement, Centre de Documentation, B.P. 4078, Douala, Cameroon. circ. 200.

338.1 SZ ISSN 0074-2856
INTERNATIONAL CONFEDERATION FOR AGRICULTURAL CREDIT. ASSEMBLY AND CONGRESS REPORTS. 1951. irreg., 1973, 7th Congress, St. Louis, U.S.A. International Confederation for Agricultural Credit, 24 Beethovenstr., 8002 Zurich, Switzerland. circ. 500.

338.13 UK ISSN 0074-2902
INTERNATIONAL CONFERENCE OF AGRICULTURAL ECONOMISTS. PROCEEDINGS. 1929. triennial, 18th, 1982, Jakarta, Indonesia. ‡ (International Association of Agricultural Economists) Gower Publishing Co. Ltd., Gower House, Croft Rd., Aldershot, Hamps GU11 3HR, England. Eds. Kazushi Ohkawa, A.H. Maunder. circ. 2,000 (approx.) Indexed: World Agri.Econ.& Rural Sociol.Abstr.

331.88 SZ ISSN 0538-7477
INTERNATIONAL FEDERATION OF PLANTATION, AGRICULTURAL AND ALLIED WORKERS. REPORT OF THE SECRETARIAT TO THE I F P A A W WORLD CONGRESS. irreg., 5th, 1982, Geneva. International Federation of Plantation, Agricultural and Allied Workers, 17 rue Necker, CH-1201 Geneva, Switzerland.

301 338.1 IE ISSN 0021-1249
IRISH JOURNAL OF AGRICULTURAL ECONOMICS AND RURAL SOCIOLOGY. (Text in English) 1967. a. £2.50 per no. An Foras Taluntais, 19 Sandymount Ave., Dublin 4, Ireland. Ed. Fergus O'Neill. adv. bk. rev. charts. illus. stat. index. circ. 900. Indexed: P.A.I.S. Dairy Sci.Abstr. Field Crop Abstr. Herb.Abstr. Rural Recreat.Tour.Abstr. World Agri.Econ.& Rural Sociol.Abstr.

333 JA
IWATE UNIVERSITY. MOUNTAINS LAND USE RESEARCH LABORATORY. BULLETIN. (Text in Japanese and English) 1968. irreg. exchange basis. Iwate University, Mountains Land Use Research Station - Iwate Daigaku Nogakubu Fuzoku Sanchi Riyo, 3-18-8 Ueda, Morioka 020, Iwate, Japan.

338.1 KE
KENYA. MINISTRY OF AGRICULTURE. CENTRAL DEVELOPMENT AND MARKETING UNIT. YIELDS, COSTS, PRICES. a. Ministry of Agriculture, Central Development and Marketing Unit, Box 30028, Nairobi, Kenya.

333 US ISSN 0075-7837
LAND ECONOMICS MONOGRAPHS. 1966. irreg. ‡ (University of Wisconsin-Madison, Land Tenure Center) University of Wisconsin Press, 114 N. Murray St., Madison, WI 53715. TEL 608-262-4952. (reprint service avail. from UMI)

333 630 US ISSN 0084-0793
LAND TENURE CENTER. PAPER. Short title: L T C Paper. (Some texts in Spanish and Portuguese) 1965. irreg., no.128, 1986. $4 in North America (excluding Mexico) and Western Europe; free elsewhere. University of Wisconsin-Madison, Land Tenure Center, 1300 University Ave., Madison, WI 53706. TEL 608-262-3657. Ed. Jane B. Knowles.

333 US ISSN 0084-0815
LAND TENURE CENTER. RESEARCH PAPER. (Some texts in Spanish and Portuguese) 1964. irreg., no.90, 1986. $4 in North America (excluding Mexico) and Western Europe; free elsewhere. University of Wisconsin-Madison, Land Tenure Center, 1300 University Ave., Madison, WI 53706. TEL 608-262-3657. Ed. Jane B. Knowles.

338.1 DK ISSN 0107-1300
LANDBOFORENINGERNES DRIFTSOEKONOMISKE VIRKSOMHED, REGNSKABRESULTATER, KALENDERAAR. 1979. a. free. Samvirkende Danske Landboforeningers Landsudvalg for Driftsoekonomi, Kongsgaardsvej 28, 8260 Viby J., Denmark. illus. circ. 12,000.

338.1 NE
LANDBOUW-ECONOMISCH INSTITUUT. BEDRIJFSUITKOMSTEN IN DE LANDBOUW. 1970. a. price varies. Landbouw-Economisch Instituut, Afdeling Landbouw, Conradkade 175, 2517 CL The Hague, Netherlands. stat.

338.1 NE
LANDBOUW-ECONOMISCH INSTITUUT. LANDBOUW-ECONOMISCH BERICHT. (Summary in English) 1972. a. price varies. Landbouw-Economisch Instituut, Stafafdeling, Conradkade 175, 2517 CL The Hague, Netherlands.

338.1 NZ ISSN 0110-7720
LINCOLN COLLEGE. AGRICULTURAL ECONOMICS RESEARCH UNIT. DISCUSSION PAPER. 1968. irreg. $8.50 per no; also avail. on exchange. Lincoln College, Canterbury, New Zealand.

338.1 NZ ISSN 0069-3790
LINCOLN COLLEGE. AGRICULTURAL ECONOMICS RESEARCH UNIT. RESEARCH REPORT. 1964. irreg. $12 per no; also avail. on exchange. Lincoln College, Canterbury, New Zealand. Indexed: Bibl.Agri. Rural Recreat.Tour.Abstr. World Agri.Econ.& Rural Sociol.Abstr.

338.7 II ISSN 0304-7245
MADHYA PRADESH STATE AGRO-INDUSTRIES DEVELOPMENT CORPORATION LTD. ANNUAL REPORT. (Text in English) a. Madhya Pradesh State Agro-Industries Development Corporation Ltd., New Market, T. T. Nagar, Bhopal, India. Key Title: Annual Report - Madhya Pradesh State Agro-Industries Development Corporation Ltd.

381.41 CN ISSN 0527-6624
MARKETING BOARDS IN CANADA/OFFICES DE COMMERCIALISATION AU CANADA. (Text in English and French) 1973. a. Agriculture Canada, Economics Branch, Sir John Carling Building, Carling Ave., Ottawa K1A 0C5, Canada. TEL 613-995-5222.

381.45 US ISSN 0094-2510
MARKETING CALIFORNIA DRIED FRUITS: PRUNES, RAISINS, DRIED APRICOTS & PEACHES. a. $4. Federal-State Market News Service, 1220 N St., Sacramento, CA 95814. stat. Key Title: Marketing California Dried Fruits.

338.1 US ISSN 0098-8928
MARKETING CALIFORNIA PEARS FOR FRESH MARKET. a. $4. Federal-State Market News Service, 1220 N St., Sacramento, CA 95814.

338.1 US ISSN 0065-4442
MICHIGAN STATE UNIVERSITY. AGRICULTURAL ECONOMICS REPORT. 1965. irreg. (approx. 5/yr.) Michigan State University, Department of Agricultural Economics, 202 Agriculture Hall, E. Lansing, MI 48824-1039. TEL 517-355-5560. circ. controlled. (processed) Indexed: GeoRef. Rural Recreat.Tour.Abstr. World Agri.Econ.& Rural Sociol.Abstr.

338.1 US
MINNESOTA AGRICULTURAL ECONOMIST. 1914. irreg. free. University of Minnesota, Department of Agricultural & Applied Economics, 1994 Buford Ave., St. Paul, MN 55108. TEL 612-625-7723. Ed. Kent Olson. charts. illus. circ. 3,650. (back issues avail.) Indexed: P.A.I.S.

338.1 BE
MUSEE ROYAL DE L'AFRIQUE CENTRALE. ANNALES. SERIE IN 8. SCIENCES ECONOMIQUES/KONINKLIJK MUSEUM VOOR MIDDEN-AFRIKA. ANNALEN. REEKS IN 8. ECONOMISCHE WETENSCHAPPEN. 1947. irreg., no.15, 1985. price varies. Musee Royal de l'Afrique Centrale, 13 Steenweg op Leuven, B-1980 Tervuren, Belgium. charts. illus. Indexed: Forest.Abstr. Forest Prod.Abstr.

338.1 SA
NATIONAL FRESH PRODUCE MARKET, JOHANNESBURG. ANNUAL TRADING RESULTS/JAARLISKE HANDELSYFERS. 1935. a. free. National Fresh Produce Market, Box 577, Johannesburg 2000, South Africa. stat. circ. 750.

338.1 US
NEW MEXICO STATE UNIVERSITY. AGRICULTURAL EXPERIMENT STATION. BULLETIN. irreg., latest no. 717. New Mexico State University, Agricultural Experiment Station, Drawer 3AI, Las Cruces, NM 88003. TEL 505-646-2701. Ed. Norman L. Newcomer. Indexed: Anim.Breed.Abstr. Field Crop Abstr. Herb.Abstr. Rural Recreat.Tour.Abstr. Soils & Fert. World Agri.Econ.& Rural Sociol.Abstr.

338.1 636 NZ ISSN 0078-0197
NEW ZEALAND POULTRY BOARD. REPORT; AND NEW ZEALAND MARKETING AUTHORITY REPORT AND STATEMENT OF ACCOUNTS. 1953. a. free. ‡ New Zealand Poultry Board, 56 Victoria St., P.O. Box 379, Wellington, New Zealand. circ. 1,000.

333 NO ISSN 0801-2334
NORGES LANDBRUKSHOEGSKOLE. INSTITUTT FOR JORDSKIFTE OG AREALPLANLEGGING. MELDING/AGRICULTURAL UNIVERSITY OF NORWAY. DEPARTMENT OF LAND USE PLANNING. SERIE. 1956. irreg. (2-4/yr.); no.45, 1985. price varies. Norges Landbrukshoegskole, Institutt for Jordskifte og Arealplanlegging - Agricultural University of Norway, Box 29, N-1432 Aas-NLH, Norway. Indexed: Biol.Abstr. Nutr.Abstr.
 Formerly: Norges Landbrukshoejskole. Institutt for Jordskifte og Eiendomsutforming. Melding (ISSN 0065-0242)

338.1 NO ISSN 0333-2500
NORGES LANDBRUKSOEKONOMISKE INSTITUTT. DRIFTSGRANSKINGER I JORD- OG SKOGBRUK. 1912. a. Kr.20. Norsk Institutt for Landbruksoekonomisk Forskning, Postboks 8024 Dep., 0030 Oslo 1, Norway. Ed. Sveinung Soelverud. circ. 4,000.
 Formerly: Norges Landbruksoekonomiske Institutt. Driftsgranskinger i Jordbruket (ISSN 0078-1223)

630 570 JA ISSN 0365-9860
OKAYAMA UNIVERSITY. BERICHTE DES OHARA INSTITUTS FUER LANDWIRTSCHAFTLICHE BIOLOGIE. (Text in English) 1916. a. exchange basis. Okayama University, Institute for Agricultural and Biological Sciences, 2-20-1 Chuo, Kurashiki 710, Japan. Ed. Isao Aoyama. circ. 875. Indexed: Biol.Abstr. Chem.Abstr. GeoRef. Plant Breed.Abstr. Rev.Plant Path.

338.1 US
OUTLOOK (YEAR) PROCEEDINGS. Variant title: Annual Agricultural Outlook Conference. Proceedings. 1982. a. $15 per no. U.S. Department of Agriculture, World Agricultural Outlook Board, Rm. 5143 S. Bldg., Washington, DC 20250-3800. TEL 202-447-5447. Ed. Raymond L. Bridge. index. circ. 1,000. Indexed: Bibl.Agri.
●Also available online. Vendors: BRS, DIALOG.

338.1 UK
OXFORD AGRARIAN STUDIES. 1933. a. £6. Agricultural Economics Institute, Dartington House, Little Clarendon St., Oxford, England. Ed. G.T. Jones. bibl. charts. stat. index. circ. 450. Indexed: Nutr.Abstr. Curr.Cont. World Agri.Econ. & Rural. Sociol.Abstr. Agri.Eng.Abstr. Dairy Sci.Abstr. Forest.Abstr. Forest Prod.Abstr. Geo.Abstr. Hort.Abstr. Int.Abstr.Oper.Res. Rural Recreat.Tour.Abstr. World Agri.Econ.& Rural Sociol.Abstr.
 Formerly: Farm Economist (ISSN 0014-7931)
Economics

AGRICULTURE — AGRICULTURAL ECONOMICS

PAKISTAN. EXPORT PROMOTION BUREAU. FRESH FRUITS. see *BUSINESS AND ECONOMICS — International Commerce*

338.1   BL
PERNAMBUCO, BRAZIL. SECRETARIA DA AGRICULTURA. PLANO ANUAL DE TRABALHO. a. Secretaria da Agricultura, Recife, Brazil.
    Formerly: Brazil. Departamento de Agricultura e Abastecimento. Plano Anual de Trabalho do D A A.

338.1   PH   ISSN 0079-1520
PHILIPPINES. BUREAU OF AGRICULTURAL ECONOMICS. REPORT. (Text in English) 1953. a. Bureau of Agricultural Economics, Ben-Lor Bldg., 1184 Quezon Ave., Quezon City, Philippines. Ed. J.C. Alix. circ. 500.

630   338.1   PH
PHILIPPINES. DEPARTMENT OF AGRARIAN REFORM. PLANNING SERVICE. ANNUAL REPORT. (Text in English) 1973. a. Department of Agrarian Reform, Planning Service, Manila, Philippines.

338.1   PH
PHILIPPINES. NATIONAL ECONOMIC AND DEVELOPMENT AUTHORITY. FOOD BALANCE SERIES. irreg., no.7, 1976. National Economic and Development Authority, Box 1116, Manila, Philippines.

PLUNKETT DEVELOPMENT SERIES. see *BUSINESS AND ECONOMICS — Cooperatives*

338.1   633   UK   ISSN 0079-4309
POTATO MARKETING BOARD, LONDON. ANNUAL REPORT AND ACCOUNTS. a. Potato Marketing Board, 50 Hans Crescent, Knightsbridge, London SW1X 0NB, England. Indexed: Field Crop Abstr. Herb.Abstr.

338.1   BL   ISSN 0302-5195
PRECOS PAGOS PELOS AGRICULTORES. 1969. a. (Instituto Brasileiro de Economia, Centro de Estudos Agricolas) Fundacao Getulio Vargas, C.P. 9052, 22250 Rio de Janeiro, R.J., Brazil. stat.

338.1   BL   ISSN 0100-5219
PRECOS RECEBIDOS PELOS AGRICULTORES. 1970. a. (Instituto Brasileiro de Economia, Centro de Estudos Agricolas) Fundacao Getulio Vargas, C.P. 9052, 22250 Rio de Janeiro, R.J., Brazil.

338.1   330.8   UN
PRICES OF AGRICULTURAL PRODUCTS AND SELECTED INPUTS IN EUROPE AND NORTH AMERICA. 1950. biennial. price varies. (Economic Commission for Europe (ECE)) United Nations Publications, New York, NY 10017 (Or Distribution and Sales Section, Palais des Nations, 1211 Geneva 10, Switzerland)

338.1   AT
PROFESSIONAL FARM MANAGEMENT GUIDEBOOK. 1967. irreg. (approx. 1/yr.) Aus.$3. University of New England, Agricultural Business Research Institute, Armidale, N.S.W. 2351, Australia. circ. 4,000.

338.1   II
RAJASTHAN AGRICULTURALIST. (Text in English) 1961. a. S.K.N. College of Agriculture, University of Udaipur, Jobner 303 329, Rajasthan, India. Ed. K.K. Vyas. Indexed: Biol.Abstr.

338.1   SP
RED CONTABLE AGRARIA NACIONAL. irreg. Ministerio de Agricultura, Secretaria General Tecnica, Paseo de Infanta Isabel 1, Madrid 7, Spain. charts. stat.

630   658.8   II
REPORT ON THE MARKETING OF TOBACCO IN ANDHRA PRADESH. a. Rs.9.90. Directorate of Marketing, Hyderabad, Andhra Pradesh, India. charts. stat.

338.1   US   ISSN 0276-1653
RESEARCH IN DOMESTIC AND INTERNATIONAL AGRIBUSINESS MANAGEMENT; a research annual. 1980. a. $23.75 to individuals; institutions $47.50. J A I Press Inc., Box 1678, 36 Sherwood Pl., Greenwich, CT 06836-1678. TEL 203-661-7602. Ed. Ray A. Goldberg.

338.1   HU   ISSN 0541-9417
RESEARCH INSTITUTE FOR AGRICULTURAL ECONOMICS. BULLETIN. (Text in English) 1962. irreg. exchange basis. Agrargazdasagi Kutato Intezet - Research Institute for Agricultural Economics, Zsil u. 3-5, P.O. Box 5, 1355 Budapest 55, Hungary. Ed. Adam Bisztray. Indexed: Rural Recreat.Tour.Abstr. World Agri.Econ.& Rural Sociol.Abstr.
    Formerly: Hungarian Academy of Sciences. Research Institute for Agricultural Economics. Bulletin.

338.1   BL
RETROSPECTIVA DA AGROPECUARIA. 1976. 2/yr. (Instituto Brasileiro de Economia, Centro de Estudos Agricolas) Fundacao Getulio Vargas, C.P. 9052, 22250 Rio de Janeiro, R.J., Brazil. Ed.Bd. charts. stat.
    Supersedes (as of 1980): Agropecuaria.

338.1   PL   ISSN 0080-3715
ROCZNIKI NAUK ROLNICZYCH. SERIA G. EKONOMIKA ROLNICTWA. (Text in Polish; summaries in English, Polish or Russian) 1903. irreg., vol.83, 1983. price varies. (Polska Akademia Nauk, Komitet Organizacii Produkcji Rolnej i Wyzywienia Kraju) Panstwowe Wydawnictwo Naukowe, Miodowa 10, 00-251 Warsaw, Poland (Dist. by: Ars Polona, Krakowskie Przedmiescie 7, 00-068 Warsaw, Poland) Ed. Z. Wojtaszek. bibl. charts. circ. 430.

630   UG   ISSN 0080-4851
RURAL DEVELOPMENT RESEARCH PAPER. 1965. irreg. price varies. Department of Rural Economy, P.O. Box 7062, Kampala, Uganda.

SCANDINAVIAN INSTITUTE OF AFRICAN STUDIES. RURAL DEVELOPMENT. see *ANTHROPOLOGY*

SOUTH PACIFIC COMMISSION. HANDBOOK. see *FISH AND FISHERIES*

SOUTH PACIFIC COMMISSION. INFORMATION CIRCULAR. see *FISH AND FISHERIES*

SOUTH PACIFIC COMMISSION. INFORMATION DOCUMENT. see *FISH AND FISHERIES*

SOUTH PACIFIC COMMISSION. OCCASIONAL PAPER. see *FISH AND FISHERIES*

SOUTH PACIFIC COMMISSION. REPORT OF S P C FISHERIES TECHNICAL MEETINGS. see *FISH AND FISHERIES*

630   301.35   SP   ISSN 0373-5796
SPAIN. INSTITUTO NACIONAL DE INVESTIGACIONES AGRARIAS. ANALES. SERIE: ECONOMIA Y SOCIOLOGIA AGRARIAS. (Text in Spanish; summaries in English, French, German) 1971. irreg. (approx 1/yr.) 800 ptas. per issue. (Instituto Nacional de Investigaciones Agrarias) Ministerio de Agricultura Pesca y Alimentacion, Jose Abascal 56, Madrid 3, Spain. Ed. J.L. Fernandez-Cavada. bk. rev. charts. circ. 1,500.
    Supersedes in part: Spain. Instituto Nacional de Investigaciones Agronomica, Anales.

338.1   SP   ISSN 0210-332X
SPAIN. INSTITUTO NACIONAL DE INVESTIGACIONES AGRARIAS. COMUNICACIONES. SERIE: ECONOMIA Y SOCIOLOGIA AGRARIAS. no.9, 1981. irreg., no.18, 1985. Instituto Nacional de Investigaciones Agrarias, Jose Abascal 56, 28003 Madrid, Spain. charts. bibl.

338.1   SP   ISSN 0213-635X
SPAIN. INSTITUTO NACIONAL DE INVESTIGACIONES AGRARIAS. INVESTIGACION AGRARIA: ECONOMIA. 1986. irreg. Ministerio de Agricultura, Pesca y Alimentacion, Instituto Nacional de Investigaciones Agrarias, Jose Abascal, 56, 28003 Madrid, Spain. TEL 442 31 99.

338.1   GW   ISSN 0081-7198
STUDIEN ZUR AGRARWIRTSCHAFT. 1967. irreg., no.23, 1983. price varies. I F O Institut fuer Wirtschaftsforschung, Poschingerstr. 5, 8000 Munich 80, W. Germany (B.R.D.) circ. 500. Indexed: Rural Recreat.Tour.Abstr. World Agri.Econ.& Rural Sociol.Abstr.

333   338.1   UK   ISSN 0081-8453
STUDIES IN RURAL LAND USE. 1954. irreg., no.11, 1972. price varies. Wye College (University of London), Department of Environmental Studies and Countryside Planning, Ashford, Kent, England. circ. 1,000. Indexed: Geo.Abstr. World Agri.Econ.& Rural Sociol.Abstr.

338.1   630   SJ
SUDAN YEARBOOK OF AGRICULTURAL STATISTICS. (Text in English) 1974. a. Department of Agricultural Economics, Statistics Division, P.O. Box 1246, Khartoum, Sudan.
    Supersedes: Bulletin of Agricultural Statistics of the Sudan.

338.1   GW   ISSN 0170-8309
TECHNISCHE UNIVERSITAET BERLIN. INSTITUT FUER SOZIALOEKONOMIE DER AGRARENTWICKLUNG. ANNUAL REPORT (ABRIDGED VERSION) 1965. a. Technische Universitaet Berlin, Fachbereich Internationale Agrarentwicklung, Hellriegelstr. 6, 1000 Berlin 33 (Dahlem), W. Germany (B.R.D.) circ. 100. (processed)

338.1   GW   ISSN 0170-8376
TECHNISCHE UNIVERSITAET BERLIN. INSTITUT FUER SOZIALOEKONOMIE DER AGRARENTWICKLUNG. JAHRESBERICHT. 1960. a. free. Technische Universitaet Berlin, Fachbereich Internationale Agrarentwicklung, Hellriegelstr. 6, 1000 Berlin 33 (Dahlem), W. Germany (B.R.D.) circ. 150. (processed)
    Formerly (until 1976): Technische Universitaet Berlin. Institut fuer Sozialoekonomie der Agrarentwicklung. Taetigkeitsbericht (ISSN 0067-6039)

338.1   MY   ISSN 0304-8349
UNITED PLANTING ASSOCIATION OF MALAYSIA. ANNUAL REPORT. (Text in English) 1968. a. M.$2.50. United Planting Association of Malaysia, Box 10272, Kuala Lumpur 01-02, Malaysia. circ. 1,100.

338.1   US   ISSN 0083-0445
U.S. DEPARTMENT OF AGRICULTURE. AGRICULTURAL ECONOMICS REPORT. 1961. irreg. U.S. Department of Agriculture, Washington, DC 20250. TEL 202-655-4000. Indexed: Geo.Abstr. Rural Recreat.Tour.Abstr. World Agri.Econ.& Rural Sociol.Abstr.
    Reports 1-233 (1916-1972) issued as: U.S. Department of Agriculture. Economic Research Service. Agricultural Economics Report.

338.14   US   ISSN 0082-9781
U.S. DEPARTMENT OF AGRICULTURE. MARKETING RESEARCH REPORT. 1952. irreg. U.S. Department of Agriculture, Washington, DC 20250. Indexed: Rural Recreat.Tour.Abstr. World Agri.Econ.& Rural Sociol.Abstr.

338.1   US   ISSN 0082-979X
U.S. DEPARTMENT OF AGRICULTURE. PRODUCTION RESEARCH REPORTS. 1956. irreg. U.S. Department of Agriculture, Washington, DC 20250. TEL 202-655-4000. Indexed: Biol.Abstr. Pollut.Abstr.

338.1   382   US   ISSN 0083-0976
U.S. FOREIGN AGRICULTURAL SERVICE. FOOD AND AGRICULTURAL EXPORT DIRECTORY. 1972. biennial. free controlled circ. U.S. Department of Agriculture, Foreign Agricultural Service, Export Programs Division, Rm. 4944-S, Washington, DC 20250. TEL 202-447-3031. adv. bk. rev. circ. 5,000.

338.1   IT
UNIVERSITA DEGLI STUDI DI TRIESTE. ISTITUTO DI RICERCHE ECONOMICO AGRARIE. PUBBLICAZIONE. 1971. irreg. Universita degli Studi di Trieste, Istituto di Ricerche Economico-Agrarie, Trieste, Italy. Indexed: Geo.Abstr.

AGRICULTURE — AGRICULTURAL ECONOMICS

338.1 301   CN
UNIVERSITY OF ALBERTA. DEPARTMENT OF RURAL ECONOMY. BULLETIN. 1976. irreg. free. University of Alberta, Department of Rural Economy, Edmonton, Alta. T6G 2H1, Canada. TEL 403-432-4225. circ. 7,500. (back issues avail.) Indexed: Nutr.Abstr.
    Formed by the merger of: University of Alberta. Department of Agricultural Economics and Rural Sociology. Research Bulletin (ISSN 0065-6046) & University of Alberta. Department of Agricultural and Rural Sociology. Technical Bulletin & University of Alberta. Department of Agricultural Economics and Rural Sociology. Bulletin.

338.1   US
UNIVERSITY OF FLORIDA. FOOD AND RESOURCE ECONOMICS DEPARTMENT. ECONOMIC INFORMATION REPORT. 1969. irreg., no.123, 1979. free. ‡ University of Florida, Institute of Food and Agricultural Sciences, c/o Dr. Leo Polopolus, Chairman, Food and Resource Economics Department, Gainesville, FL 32611. TEL 904-392-1733. Ed. Cecil N. Smith. circ. 2,500.
    Former titles: University of Florida. Food and Resource Economics Department. Economics Report; University of Florida. Institute of Food and Agricultural Sciences. Agricultural Economics Series.

338.1   US   ISSN 0073-5213
UNIVERSITY OF ILLINOIS AT URBANA-CHAMPAIGN. DEPARTMENT OF AGRICULTURAL ECONOMICS. AGRICULTURAL FINANCE PROGRAM REPORT. 1970. irreg., latest 1970. price varies. ‡ University of Illinois at Urbana-Champaign, Department of Agricultural Economics, Urbana, IL 61801. TEL 217-333-7425.

338.1   US   ISSN 0160-3027
UNIVERSITY OF ILLINOIS AT URBANA-CHAMPAIGN. DEPARTMENT OF AGRICULTURAL ECONOMICS. LANDLORD AND TENANT SHARES. 1961. a. free. University of Illinois at Urbana-Champaign, Department of Agricultural Economics, Urbana, IL 61801. TEL 217-333-2638. Ed. John T. Scott. stat. circ. controlled.

338.1   US   ISSN 0073-523X
UNIVERSITY OF ILLINOIS AT URBANA-CHAMPAIGN. DEPARTMENT OF AGRICULTURAL ECONOMICS. RESEARCH REPORT. 1954. irreg. ‡ University of Illinois at Urbana-Champaign, Department of Agricultural Economics, Urbana, IL 61801. TEL 217-333-1811. Indexed: Rural Recreat.Tour.Abstr. World Agri.Econ.& Rural Sociol.Abstr.

338.1   UK
UNIVERSITY OF READING. DEPARTMENT OF AGRICULTURAL ECONOMICS & MANAGEMENT. DEVELOPMENT STUDIES. 1971. irreg., latest no.27. £2.50. ‡ University of Reading, Department of Agricultural Economics & Management, Reading, England. illus. stat.

338.1   UK   ISSN 0557-6911
UNIVERSITY OF READING. DEPARTMENT OF AGRICULTURAL ECONOMICS AND MANAGEMENT. FARM BUSINESS DATA. 1974. a. £3. ‡ University of Reading, Department of Agricultural Economics & Management, 4 Earley Gate, Whiteknights Rd., Reading RG6 2AR, England. Ed. A.K. Giles. bibl. charts. stat.

338.1 664   UK
UNIVERSITY OF READING. DEPARTMENT OF AGRICULTURAL ECONOMICS & MANAGEMENT. FOOD ECONOMICS STUDIES. 1984. irreg. University of Reading, Department of Agricultural Economics & Management, 4 Earley Gate, Whiteknights Rd., P.O. Box 237, Reading RG6 2AR, England. Eds. Alan Swinbank, Jim Burns.

338.1   UK   ISSN 0486-0845
UNIVERSITY OF READING. DEPARTMENT OF AGRICULTURAL ECONOMICS AND MANAGEMENT. MISCELLANEOUS STUDIES. 1957. irreg., latest no.74, 1985. price varies. ‡ University of Reading, Department of Agricultural Economics & Management, 4 Earley Gate, Whiteknights Rd., Reading RG6 2AR, England. charts. Indexed: Geo.Abstr. Rural Recreat.Tour.Abstr. World Agri.Econ.& Rural Sociol.Abstr.

338.1   AT   ISSN 0817-8771
UNIVERSITY OF SYDNEY. DEPARTMENT OF AGRICULTURAL ECONOMICS. RESEARCH REPORT. 1957. irreg., no.10, 1986. price varies. ‡ University of Sydney, Department of Agricultural Economics, Sydney, N.S.W. 2006, Australia. circ. 400. (processed)
    Formerly: University of Sydney. Department of Agriculture Economics. Mimeographed Report. (ISSN 0082-0555)

630 338.1   VE
VENEZUELA. MINISTERIO DE AGRICULTURA Y CRIA. DIRECCION DE PLANIFICACION Y ESTADISTICA. ESTADISTICAS AGROPECUARIAS DE LAS ENTIDADES FEDERALES. 1962. biennial. free. Ministerio de Agricultura y Cria, Direccion de Planificacion y Estadistica, Division de Estadistica, Torre Norte, Caracas, Venezuela.

338.1   UR
VOPROSY EKONOMIKI SEL'SKOGO KHOZYAISTVA DAL'NEGO VOSTOKA. irreg. 0.57 Rub. Akademiya Nauk S.S.S.R., Dal'nevostochnyi Nauchnyi Tsentr, Ul. Leninskaya 50, Vladivostok, Russian S.F.S.R., U.S.S.R.

338.1 301.35   PL   ISSN 0208-5720
WARSAW AGRICULTURAL UNIVERSITY. S G G W - A R. ANNALS. AGRICULTURAL ECONOMICS AND RURAL SOCIOLOGY. (Szkola Glowna Gospodarstwa Wiejskiego - Akademia Rolnicza) (Text mainly in English; occasionally in French, German or Russian; summaries in Polish) 1957. irreg. $6 per no. Warsaw Agricultural University Press, Ul. Nowoursynowska 166, 02-766 Warsaw, Poland (Dist. by: Ars Polona-Ruch, Krakowskie Przedmiescie 7, 00-068 Warsaw, Poland) Ed. J. Okuniewski.

630   AT
WESTERN AUSTRALIA. DEPARTMENT OF AGRICULTURE. RURAL ECONOMICS AND MARKETING SECTION. REPORT ON THE MARKET MILK INDUSTRY IN WESTERN AUSTRALIA. irreg. Department of Agriculture, Rural Economics and Marketing Section, Perth, W.A., Australia.

630 338.1   US
WORLD AGRICULTURE REGIONAL SUPPLEMENT: CHINA. a. U.S. Department of Agriculture, Economics Management Staff, Information Division, 1301 New York Ave., N.W., Washington, DC 20005 TEL 202-783-3238. (Subscr. to: Supt. of Documents, Washington, DC 20402)
    Formerly: Agricultural Situation in the People's Republic of China.

338.1   US
WORLD AGRICULTURE REGIONAL SUPPLEMENT: EAST ASIA AND OCEANIA. a. U.S. Department of Agriculture, Economics Management Staff, Information Division, 1301 New York Ave., N.W., Washington, DC 20005 TEL 202-783-3238. (Subscr. to: Supt. of Documents, Washington, DC 20402)
    Formerly: World Agriculture Regional Supplement: East Asia.

630 338.1   US
WORLD AGRICULTURE REGIONAL SUPPLEMENT: EASTERN EUROPE. a. U.S. Department of Agriculture, Economics Management Staff, Information Division, 1301 New York Ave., N.W., Washington, DC 20005 TEL 202-783-3238. (Subscr. to: Supt. of Documents, Washington, DC 20402)
    Former titles: Agricultural Situation in Eastern Europe (ISSN 0098-4000); Eastern Europe Agricultural Situation (ISSN 0422-1494)

630 338.1   US
WORLD AGRICULTURE REGIONAL SUPPLEMENT: MIDDLE EAST AND NORTH AFRICA. a. U.S. Department of Agriculture, Economics Management Staff, Information Division, 1301 New York Ave., N.W., Washington, DC 20005 TEL 202-783-3238. (Subscr. to: Supt. of Documents, Washington, DC 20402)
    Former titles: World Agriculture Regional Supplement: Africa and the Middle East (ISSN 0278-8063); Africa and West Asia Agricultural Situation (ISSN 0148-7094); Agricultural Situation in Africa and West Asia (ISSN 0094-5528)

338.1   US
WORLD AGRICULTURE REGIONAL SUPPLEMENT: SOUTH ASIA. a. U.S. Department of Agriculture, Economics Management Staff, Information Division, 1301 New York Ave., N.W., Washington, DC 20005 TEL 202-783-3238. (Subscr. to: Supt. of Documents, Washington, DC 20402)

338.1   US
WORLD AGRICULTURE REGIONAL SUPPLEMENT: SOUTHEAST ASIA. a. U.S. Department of Agriculture, Economics Management Staff, Information Division, 1301 New York Ave., N.W., Washington, DC 20005 TEL 202-783-3238. (Subscr. to: Supt. of Documents, Washington, DC 20402)

338.1   US
WORLD AGRICULTURE REGIONAL SUPPLEMENT: SUBSAHARAN AFRICA. a. U.S. Department of Agriculture, Economics Management Staff, Information Division, 1301 New York Ave., N.W., Washington, DC 20005 TEL 202-783-3238. (Subscr. to: Supt. of Documents, Washington, DC 20402)

630 338.1   US
WORLD AGRICULTURE REGIONAL SUPPLEMENT: U S S R. a. U.S. Department of Agriculture, Economics Management Staff, Information Division, 1301 New York Ave., N.W., Washington, DC 20005 TEL 202-783-3238. (Subscr. to: Supt. of Documents, Washington, DC 20402)
    Former titles: World Agriculture Regional Supplement: Soviet Union; Agricultural Situation in the Soviet Union (ISSN 0360-4098)

630 338.1   US
WORLD AGRICULTURE REGIONAL SUPPLEMENT: WESTERN EUROPE. a. U.S. Department of Agriculture, Economics Management Staff, Information Division, 1301 New York Ave., N.W., Washington, DC 20005 TEL 202-783-3238. (Subscr. to: Supt. of Documents, Washington, DC 20402)
    Formerly: Agricultural Situation in Western Europe.

630 338.1   US
WORLD AGRICULTURE REGIONAL SUPPLEMENT: WESTERN HEMISPHERE. a. U.S. Department of Agriculture, Economics Management Staff, Information Division, 1301 New York Ave., N.W., Washington, DC 20005 TEL 202-783-3238. (Subscr. to: Supt. of Documents, Washington, DC 20402)
    Former titles: World Agriculture Regional Supplement: Latin America; Agricultural Situation in the Western Hemisphere (ISSN 0501-9257)

338.1   US   ISSN 0733-2378
WORLD FOOD TRADE AND U.S. AGRICULTURE. 1981. a. Iowa State University, World Food Institute, 102 E.O. Bldg., Ames, IA 50011. TEL 515-294-7699. Ed. Joy C. Banyas. circ. 5,500. (also avail. in microfiche)

338.1   UK
WYE COLLEGE (UNIVERSITY OF LONDON). AGRARIAN DEVELOPMENT UNIT. OCCASIONAL PAPER. 1974. irreg. price varies. Wye College (University of London), Department of Agricultural Economic, Ashford, Kent, England. Indexed: Geo.Abstr. Rural Recreat.Tour.Abstr. World Agri.Econ.& Rural Sociol.Abstr.

338.1 631   UK
WYE COLLEGE (UNIVERSITY OF LONDON). DEPARTMENT OF AGRICULTURAL ECONOMICS. FARM BUSINESS UNIT. OCCASIONAL PAPER. 1978. irreg. price varies. Wye College (University of London), Department of Agricultural Economics, Farm Business Unit, Ashford, Kent, England. Indexed: Rural Recreat.Tour.Abstr. World Agri.Econ.& Rural Sociol.Abstr.
    Formerly: Wye College (University of London). School of Rural Economics and Related Studies. Farm Business Unit. Occasional Paper.

630 338.1   UK   ISSN 0142-498X
YEAR BOOK OF AGRICULTURAL CO-OPERATION. 1927. a. £8.90. Plunkett Foundation for Co-Operative Studies, 31 St. Giles St., Oxford OX1 3LF, England. (Co-sponsor: International Co-Operative Alliance) circ. 500. Indexed: World Agri.Econ.& Rural Sociol.Abstr.

AGRICULTURE — CROP PRODUCTION AND SOIL

AGRICULTURE — Agricultural Equipment

631.3   CU
ACTUALIDADES DE LA INGENIERIA AGRONOMICA.* irreg. exchange. Universidad de la Habana, Institute de Ciencias Agropecuarias, Dirreccion de Informacion Cientifico-Tecnica, Apdo. 18-19, San Jose de las Lajas, Provincia la Habana, Cuba. Ed.Bd. charts. stat.

631.3   SA
AGRICULTURAL ENGINEERING IN SOUTH AFRICA. (Text and summaries in Afrikaans and English) 1967. a. R.2.50($2.50) South African Institute of Agricultural Engineers, P.O. Box 719, Silverton 0127, South Africa. circ. 400. (back issues avail.) Indexed: Ind.S.A.Per.

631.3 636   AT   ISSN 0812-955X
AUSTRALIAN SMALL FARMS DIRECTORY; services, supplies, equipment. 1984. a. Aus.$12.95. Second Back Row Press, P.O. Box 43t., Leura, N.S.W. 2781, Australia. Ed. Mark Pearson. circ. 5,000.

AUTO NYTS LEVERANDOERREGISTER. see *TRANSPORTATION* — *Automobiles*

BOTSWANA. MINISTRY OF AGRICULTURE. DIVISION OF ARABLE CROPS RESEARCH. ANNUAL REPORT. see *AGRICULTURE — Crop Production And Soil*

631.3   CU
CUBA. CENTRO DE INFORMACION Y DOCUMENTACION AGROPECUARIO. BOLETIN DE RESENAS. SERIE: MECANIZACION DE LA AGRICULTURA. (Abstracts in English) 1974. irreg. exchange basis. Centro de Informacion y Documentacion Agropecuario, Gaveta Postal 4149, Havana 4, Cuba (Dist. by: Ediciones Cubanas, Obispo No. 461, Aptdo. 605, Havana, Cuba) Indexed: Agrindex.
Formerly: Cuba. Centro de Informacion y Divulgacion Agropecuario. Boletin de Resenas. Serie: Mecanizacion.

631.3   DK   ISSN 0302-5349
DANSK MASKINHANDLERFORENING. HANDBOG. 1966. irreg. Kr.180. Dansk Maskinhandlerforening, Noerrebrogade 7, 2200 Copenhagen V, Denmark.

631.3   JA   ISSN 0071-3937
FARM MACHINERY YEARBOOK/NOGYO KIKAI NENKAN. (Text in Japanese; summary, contents and statistical section in English) 1943. a. 10300 Yen. Shin-Norinsha Co., Ltd., 2-7 Kanda Nishikicho, Chiyoda-ku, Tokyo 101, Japan. Ed. Yoshisuke Kishida. adv. circ. 10,000.

631.3   FR
FICHES TECHNIQUES R.T.D. APPLICATIONS AGRICOLES. (Revue Technique Diesel) irreg. price varies. Editions Techniques pour l'Automobile et l'Industrie, 20-22 rue de la Saussiere, 92100 Boulogne-Billancourt, France. charts. illus. (looseleaf format)

631.3   UK   ISSN 0017-3932
GREEN BOOK; the authority on tractors and farm equipment. 1951. a. £40. Industrial Newspapers Ltd., Queensway House, Queensway, Redhill, Surrey RH1 1QS, England (Distr. by: Guardian Communications Ltd., Albany House, Hurst St., Birmingham B5 1BD, England) Ed. H. Catling. adv. illus. circ. 4,000. (reprint service avail. from UMI)

631.3   FR
GUIDE-ANNUAIRE DE L'EQUIPEMENT AGRICOLE; catalogue officiel du Salon International de la Machine Agricole. (Text in French; summaries in English, German, Italian and Spanish) 1922. a. 7 F. ‡ Salon International de la Machine Agricole, 24 rue du Pont, 92522 Neuilly-sur-Seine Cedex, France. adv. index.

631.3   IS
INSTITUTE OF AGRICULTURAL ENGINEERING, BET DAGAN. SCIENTIFIC ACTIVITIES. (Text in English) irreg. Institute of Agricultural Engineering, Bet Dagan, Israel. illus. circ. 300. Indexed: Biol.Abstr.

631.3   NG   ISSN 0534-4794
INTER-AFRICAN CONFERENCE OF THE MECHANISATION OF AGRICULTURE MEETING.* 1955. irreg. (Commission for Technical Co-Operation in Africa South of the Sahara) Maison de l'Afrique, B.P. 878, Niamey, Republic of Niger.

631.3   DK   ISSN 0107-461X
LANDBRUGETS MASKINOVERSIGT. 1972. irreg. Kr.250. Landsudvalget for Bygninger og Maskiner, Kongsgaardsvej 28, DK-8260 Viby J, Denmark. Ed. Poul Casper. circ. 1,000.

631.3   US
NEAL'S CATALOG FILE. 1981. a. A C I Advertising, Inc., Box 31579, St. Louis, MO 63131. TEL 314-966-2580. adv. circ. 5,400.

631.3 643   NR
NIGERIAN STORED PRODUCTS RESEARCH INSTITUTE. ANNUAL REPORT. 1956. a., latest no.17, 1980. Nigerian Stored Products Research Institute, P.M.B. 12543, Lagos, Nigeria. Ed. J.O. Oyeniran. charts. illus. stat. index. circ. 3,000. (back issues avail.)

621 631   PL   ISSN 0137-6918
POLITECHNIKA POZNANSKA. ZESZYTY NAUKOWE. MASZYNY ROBOCZE I POJAZDY. (Text in Polish; Summaries in English and Russian) 1956. irreg., no.12, 1972. price varies. Politechnika Poznanska, Pl. Curie-Sklodowskiej 5, Poznan, Poland. Ed. Henryk Kozlowiecki. circ. 150.
Formerly: Politechnika Poznanska. Zeszyty Naukowe. Mechanizacja i Elektryfikacja Rolnictwa (ISSN 0076-5805)

631.3   AT   ISSN 0079-4422
POWER FARMING TECHNICAL ANNUAL. 1937. a. Aus.$9.50. Pacific Publications (Australia) Pty. Ltd., G.P.O. Box 3408, Sydney, N.S.W. 2001, Australia. Ed. John Fearn. adv.

631.3   CN   ISSN 0831-2338
PRAIRIE FARMERS CATALOGUE. 1979. a. free. Prairie Publishing Co., P.O. Box 100, Oakville, Manitoba R0H 0Y0, Canada. TEL 204-267-2102. Ed. Dale H. Crampton. circ. 150,000.

631.3   JA
PRODUCT FILE FOR AGRICULTURAL MACHINERY AND RELATED MATERIAL. (Text in Japanese) 1972. a. 7000 Yen. Farm Machinery Industrial Research Corp, Shin-Norin Bldg., 2-7 Kanda Nishikicho, Chiyoda-ku, Tokyo 101, Japan. Ed. Y. Kishida. adv. circ. 10,000.

631.3   PL   ISSN 0080-3677
ROCZNIKI NAUK ROLNICZYCH. SERIA C. TECHNIKA ROLNICZA. (Text in Polish; summaries in English, Polish, Russian) 1903. irreg., vol.75, 1983. price varies. (Polska Akademia Nauk, Komitet Techniki Rolniczej) Panstwowe Wydawnictwo Naukowe, Miodowa 10, 00-251 Warsaw, Poland (Dist. by: Ars Polona, Krakowskie Przedmiescie 7, 00-068 Warsaw, Poland) Ed. S. Pabis. bibl. charts. illus. circ. 300. Indexed: Biol.Abstr. Dairy Sci.Abstr. Field Crop Abstr. Herb.Abstr.
Title Varies: Roczniki Nauk Rolniczych. Seria C. Mechanizacja Rolnictwa.

631.3   FR   ISSN 0082-5662
TRACTOCATALOGUE;* guide technique de mecanique agricole. 1955. a. 100 F. Editions Gozlan, 57 Rue Ordener, 75018 Paris, France.

631.3   UK   ISSN 0084-2184
WORLD PLOUGHING CONTEST. OFFICIAL HANDBOOK. (Text in English and in language of country in which the contest is held) 1954. a. price varies. World Ploughing Organization, Whiteclose, Longtown, Carlisle, Cumbria CA6 5TY, England. TEL (0228) 791153. Ed. Alfred Hall. adv. index. circ. 10,000.

AGRICULTURE — Computer Applications

630   CN
SIMULATION MONOGRAPHS; a series on computer simulation in agriculture and its supporting sciences. 1972. irreg. price varies. Pudoc, Postbus 4, 6700 AA Wageningen, Netherlands. TEL 8370-84440.

AGRICULTURE — Crop Production And Soil

see also *Agriculture—Feed, Flour and Grain; Gardening and Horticulture; Rubber; Tobacco*

631   UK
A F R C INSTITUTE OF ENGINEERING RESEARCH. DIVISIONAL NOTES. 1984. irreg. £3. Agricultural & Food Research Council, Institute of Engineering Research, Wrest Park, Silsoe, Bedford MK45 4HS, England.
Formerly (until 1986): National Institute of Agricultural Engineering. Divisional Notes (ISSN 0267-5471)

631   UK
A F R C INSTITUTE OF ENGINEERING RESEARCH. REPORTS. 1971. irreg. price varies. Agricultural & Food Research Council, Institute of Engineering Research, Wrest Park, Silsoe, Bedford MK45 4HS, England.
Formerly (until 1986): National Institute of Agricultural Engineering. Reports (ISSN 0077-4804)

631   UK
A F R C INSTITUTE OF ENGINEERING RESEARCH. TRANSLATIONS. 1956. irreg. price varies. ‡ Agricultural & Food Research Council, Institute of Engineering Research, Wrest Park, Silsoe, Bedford MK45 4HS, England. Ed. E. Harris.
Supersedes (as of 1987): National Institute of Agricultural Engineering. Translations (ISSN 0077-4812)
Agricultural engineering

631   US   ISSN 0197-8748
A P R E S PROCEEDINGS. a. $5. American Peanut Research and Education Society, c/o Dr. James R. Sholar, Oklahoma State University, 376 Ag Hall, Stillwater, OK 74078. TEL 405-624-6423. circ. 750. Indexed: Biol.Abstr. Chem.Abstr.
Former titles: American Peanut Research and Education Association. Proceedings (ISSN 0160-6719); American Peanut Research and Education Association. Journal (ISSN 0587-503X)

631   US
A S A E STANDARDS. 1954. a. $59 to non-members; members $27. American Society of Agricultural Engineers, 2950 Niles Rd., St. Joseph, MI 49085. TEL 616-429-0300. Ed. Russell Hahn. (also avail. in microfilm)
Supersedes: Agricultural Engineers Yearbook of Standards (ISSN 0065-4477)
Agricultural engineering

630   PL   ISSN 0065-0919
ACTA AGRARIA ET SILVESTRIA. SERIES AGRARIA. (Text in Polish; summaries in English and Russian) 1961. irreg. (1-2/yr.) price varies. (Polska Akademia Nauk, Oddzial w Krakowie, Komisja Nauk Rolniczych i Lesnych) Ossolineum, Publishing House of the Polish Academy of Sciences, Rynek 9, Wroclaw, Poland (Dist. by Ars Polona-Ruch, Krakowskie Przedmiescie 7, Warsaw, Poland) Ed. Jan Filipek. Indexed: Biol.Abstr. Chem.Abstr. Excerp.Med. Field Crop Abstr. Herb.Abstr. Plant Breed.Abstr. Soils & Fert. Weed Abstr.

630   GW   ISSN 0301-2735
ADVANCES IN AGRONOMY AND CROP SCIENCE/FORTSCHRITTE IM ACKER- UND PFLANZENBAU. (Supplement to: Journal of Agronmy and Crop Science/Zeitschrift fuer Acker- und Pflanzenbau) (Text and summaries in English or German) 1973. irreg. price varies. Verlag Paul Parey (Berlin), Lindenstrasse 44-47, 1000 Berlin 61, W. Germany (B.R.D.) Ed. G. Geisler. Indexed: Biol.Abstr. Curr.Cont. Field Crop Abstr. Herb.Abstr. Plant Breed.Abstr. Soils & Fert.

AGRICULTURE — CROP PRODUCTION AND SOIL

631.7 US ISSN 0275-7915
ADVANCES IN IRRIGATION. 1982. a., vol.3, 1985. $65. Academic Press, Inc., Orlando, FL 32887. TEL 305-345-2000. Ed. Daniel Hillel.

630 GW ISSN 0301-2727
ADVANCES IN PLANT BREEDING/ FORTSCRITTE DER PFLANZENZUECHTUNG. (Supplement to: Zeitschrift fuer Pflanzenzuechtung) (Text in English or German; summaries in English, French, German) 1971. irreg., no.10, 1979. price varies. Verlag Paul Parey (Berlin), Lindenstr. 44-47, 1000 Berlin 61, W. Germany (B.R.D.) Indexed: Biol.Abstr. Curr.Cont. Plant Breed.Abstr.

631 FR
AG'CHEM BUSINESS. 1985. a. $6.50.
Documentation Agricole, 28 rue Basse, B.P. 629, 59024 Lille, France. circ. 8,000.

630.24 CN
AGRI-BOOK MAGAZINE. ELEVATOR MANAGER, FARM CHEMICAL & FERTILIZER DEALER. 1976. a. Can.$5. A I S Communications Ltd, Box 1060, 145 Thames Rd. W., Exeter, Ont. N0M 1S0, Canada. TEL 519-235-2400. Ed. Peter Darbishire. adv. circ. 4,870. (back issues avail.)
Agricultural chemistry

AGRI HORTIQUE GENETICA. see *BIOLOGY — Botany*

630 IS
AGRICULTURAL ENGINEERING. SCIENTIFIC ACTIVITIES. (Text in English) triennial. price varies. Agricultural Research Organization (Subsidiary of: Scientific Publications) Volcani Center, Box 6, Bet Dagan, Israel.

AGRICULTURAL ENGINEERING IN SOUTH AFRICA. see *AGRICULTURE — Agricultural Equipment*

630.24 668.6 NE
AGRO CHEMIE-KOERIER. Dutch edition of: Pflanzenschutz-Kurier. 1959. 3/yr. free. Bayer Nederland B.V., Postbus 105, 6800 AC Arnhem, Netherlands (Main office: Bayer Pflanzenschutz, Leverkusen, W. Germany (B.R.D.)) charts. illus. circ. 30,900 (controlled)
Agricultural chemistry

630.24 668.6 DK ISSN 0900-5285
AGRO-KEMI. 1978. a. free. Bibliotekscentralen, Telegrafvej 5, DK-2750 Ballerup, Denmark.

631 NZ ISSN 0110-6589
AGRONOMY SOCIETY OF NEW ZEALAND. PROCEEDINGS. (Text in English) 1971. a. NZ.$20($11) Agronomy Society of New Zealand, Crop Research Division, D.S.I.R. Private Bag, Christchurch, New Zealand. Ed. N.J. Withers. circ. 400. (back issues avail.) Indexed: Biol.Abstr. Nutr.Abstr. Field Crop Abstr. Herb.Abstr. Hort.Abstr. Soils & Fert.

631.4 NR ISSN 0065-4728
AHMADU BELLO UNIVERSITY. INSTITUTE FOR AGRICULTURAL RESEARCH. SOIL SURVEY BULLETIN. 1956. irreg, no.39, 1969. price varies. Ahmadu Bello University, Institute for Agricultural Research, P.M.B. 1044, Zaria, Nigeria.

631.7 PL
AKADEMIA ROLNICZA, POZNAN. ROCZNIKI. MELIORACJE. (Summaries in English and Russian) 1972. irreg. price varies. Akademia Rolnicza, Poznan, Ul. Wojska Polskiego 28, 60-637 Poznan, Poland. Indexed: Bibl.Agri. Forest.Abstr.
Formerly: Akademia Rolnicza, Poznan. Rocznik. Melioracje Wodne (ISSN 0208-8932)

630 PL
AKADEMIA ROLNICZA W SZCZECINIE. ZESZYTY NAUKOWE. ROLNICTWO. SERIA AGROTECHNICZNA. 1977. irreg., no. 110, 1984. price varies. Akademia Rolnicza, Janosika 8, 71-424 Szczecin, Poland. Ed. Prof. Mieczyslaw Jasnowski. bk. rev. Indexed: Chem.Abstr. Nutr.Abstr. Field Crop Abstr.

630 PL
AKADEMIA ROLNICZA W SZCZECINIE. ZESZYTY NAUKOWE. ROLNICTWO. SERIA TECHNICZNA. 1978. irreg., no.73, 1978. price varies. Akademia Rolnicza, Janosika 8, 71-424 Szczecin, Poland. Ed. Prof. Miczyslaw Jasnowski. bk. rev. Indexed: Chem.Abstr. Nutr.Abstr. Field Crop Abstr.

AKTUELLE LITERATURINFORMATIONEN AUS DEM OBSTBAU. see *GARDENING AND HORTICULTURE — Abstracting, Bibliographies, Statistics*

631.5 368 CN ISSN 0319-3535
ALBERTA HAIL AND CROP INSURANCE CORPORATION. ANNUAL REPORT.* 1970. a. Alberta Hail and Crop Insurance Corporation, Bag Service 16, 5718 56th St., Lacombe, Alta. T0C 1S0, Canada.

633 UK
ANIMAL AND GRASSLAND RESEARCH INSTITUTE, HURLEY, ENGLAND (BERKSHIRE) TECHNICAL REPORTS. 1965. irreg. price varies. Animal and Grassland Research Institute, Hurley, Maidenhead, Berks SL6 5LR, England. (Co-sponsor: Agricultural and Food Research Council) Ed. W.A.D. Donaldson. circ. 600. Indexed: Biol.Abstr. Anim.Breed.Abstr. Field Crop Abstr. Herb.Abstr. Soils & Fert. Weed Abstr.
Formerly: Grassland Research Institute, Hurley, England (Berkshire) Technical Reports (ISSN 0072-5552)

634 338.1 FR ISSN 0066-3131
ANNUAIRE FRUCTIDOR; annuaire international des fruits, legumes, primeurs, derives et industries annexes. 1935. a. 600 F. Editions Fructidor, 20 bis Avenue des Deux-Routes, Avignon (Vaucluse), France.

ANNUAL BOOK OF A S T M STANDARDS. VOLUME 04.08. SOIL AND ROCK; BUILDING STONES. see *ENGINEERING — Engineering Mechanics And Materials*

464.8 AG ISSN 0066-5207
ANUARIO F.H.I. ARGENTINA: FRUTAS Y HORTALIZAS INDUSTRIARIZADAS Y FRESCAS/F.H.I. ANNUAL: FRESH AND INDUSTRIALIZED FRUITS AND VEGETABLES. (Text in Spanish; summaries in English) 1965. irreg. $10. Riccardo Luchini, Ed. & Pub., 2455 Canning, 1425 Buenos Aires, Argentina. adv. bk. rev. circ. 1,500.

631.5 II
AREA AND PRODUCTION OF PRINCIPAL CROPS IN INDIA. SUMMARY TABLES. (Text and summaries in English) 1951-52. a. Rs.169($60.84) Ministry of Agriculture, Department of Agriculture and Cooperation, Directorate of Economics and Statistics, A-2E-3 Kasturba Gandhi Marg Barracks, New Delhi 110001, India. Ed. Chandar Dhar Sharma. circ. 700.
Formerly: Estimates of Area and Production of Principal Crops in India. Summary Tables (ISSN 0085-0314)

ARKANSAS AGRICULTURAL EXPERIMENT STATION. RESEARCH SERIES. see *AGRICULTURE — Abstracting, Bibliographies, Statistics*

631.5 BL
ARMAZENAGEM. irreg. Companhia Brasileira de Armazenamento, Palacio do Desenvolvimento, Brasilia, Brazil. illus.

632 US ISSN 0066-9431
ASSOCIATION OF AMERICAN PESTICIDE CONTROL OFFICIALS. OFFICIAL PUBLICATION. 1964/65. a. $10. Department of Agriculture, c/o Michael K. Fresvik, Treas., 90 W. Plato Blvd., St. Paul, MN 55107. TEL 612-296-8547. (Co-Sponsor: Association of American Pesticide Control Officials, Inc.)

631.8 US ISSN 0094-8764
ASSOCIATION OF AMERICAN PLANT FOOD CONTROL OFFICIALS. OFFICIAL PUBLICATION. 1947. a. $10. Association of American Plant Food Control Officials, Inc., Division of Regulatory Services, University of Kentucky, Lexington, KY 40546. TEL 606-257-2668. Ed. D.L. Terry. circ. 400.
Formerly: Association of American Fertilizer Control Officials. Official Publication.

631.5 US
ASSOCIATION OF OFFICIAL SEED CERTIFYING AGENCIES. PRODUCTION PUBLICATION. 1959. a. $10. Association of Official Seed Certifying Agencies, 3709 Hillsborough St., Raleigh, NC 27607. TEL 919-737-2851. Ed. Foil W. McLaughlin. circ. 500.
Formerly: International Crop Improvement Association. Production Publication (ISSN 0538-7043)

350 631 AT
AUSTRALIA. DEPARTMENT OF PRIMARY INDUSTRY. RAW COTTON MARKETING ADVISORY COMMITTEE. ANNUAL REPORT. 1968. a. free. Department of Primary Industry, Field Crops Division, Edmund Barton Bldg., Broughton St., Barton, A.C.T. 2600, Australia.

350 631 AT ISSN 0572-0451
AUSTRALIA. DEPARTMENT OF PRIMARY INDUSTRY. WHEAT INDUSTRY RESEARCH, A.C.T. ANNUAL REPORT. 1958. a. free. Department of Primary Industry, Field Crops Division, Edmund Barton Bldg., Broughton St., Barton, A.C.T. 2600, Australia.

350 631 AT
AUSTRALIAN OILSEEDS INDUSTRY STATISTICS. 1978. a. free. Department of Primary Industry, Field Crops Division, Edmund Barton Bldg., Broughton St., Barton, A.C.T. 2600, Australia.

632 AT ISSN 0310-0405
AUSTRALIAN WEED CONTROL HANDBOOK. 1973. biennial, latest 1984. price varies. Plant Press, 3A Ipswich St., Toowoomba, Qld 4350, Australia. Ed. J.T. Swarbrick. adv. circ. 3,000.

631.5 BG ISSN 0070-8151
BANGLADESH. DIRECTORATE OF AGRICULTURE. SEASON AND CROP REPORT.* (Text in English) a. Directorate of Agriculture, Dacca, Bangladesh.

633.18 BG
BANGLADESH RICE RESEARCH INSTITUTE. ANNUAL REPORT. (Text in English) 1976. a. Tk.30. Bangladesh Rice Research Institute, Publications and Public Relations Division, Joydebpur, Dacca, Bangladesh. Ed. Mohammad H.R. Talukdar. stat. circ. 1,000.

630.24 GW
BAYER AGROCHEM COURIER. 1956. irreg. (3-4/yr.) Bayer AG, Agrochemicals Sector, D-5090 Leverkusen, W. Germany (B.R.D.) Ed. Conrad Ritter. circ. 1,200,000.

630 US ISSN 0084-7747
BEAN IMPROVEMENT COOPERATIVE. ANNUAL REPORT. 1959. a. $10 for 2 yrs. (Bean Improvement Cooperative) New York State Agricultural Experiment Station, Department of Seed and Vegetable Sciences, Geneva, NY 14456. TEL 315-787-2011. Ed. Dr. M.H. Dickson. circ. 350. Indexed: Plant Breed.Abstr.

631.4 US
BENCHMARK SOILS PROJECT. TECHNICAL REPORT SERIES. 1979. irreg. free. (U.S. Agency for International Development, Bureau of Science and Technology) University of Hawaii, College of Tropical Agriculture and Human Resources, 2500 Dole St., Honolulu, HI 96822. TEL 808-948-8858.

631 676 JA
BENIBANA. 1974. irreg. free. Tsutomu Yamaguchi Ed. & Pub., 32, Koyama-minami, Kamifusa-Cho, Kita-Ku, Kyoto 603, Japan. index. circ. 300.

AGRICULTURE — CROP PRODUCTION AND SOIL

631   NE
BESCHRIJVENDE RASSENLIJST VOOR LANDBOUWGEWASSEN. vol.58, 1983. a. fl.9.25. (Rijksinstituut voor het Rassenonderzoek van Cultuurgewassen) B.V. Drukkerij en Uitgeverij Leiter-Nypels, Postbus 831, 6200 AV Maasticht, Netherlands. TEL 043-211055. Ed.Bd.

630   CE   ISSN 0379-1564
BIBLIOGRAPHICAL SERIES ON COCONUT. (Text in English) 1967. a. $10. Coconut Research Institute, Coconut Information Centre, Bandirippuwa Estate, Lunuwila, Sri Lanka. circ. 100.

631.4   US   ISSN 0081-1890
BOOKS IN SOILS AND THE ENVIRONMENT SERIES. 1967. irreg., vol.12, 1985. price varies. Marcel Dekker, Inc., 270 Madison Ave., New York, NY 10016. TEL 212-696-9000. Ed. A.D. McLaren.
Formerly: Soil Science Library.

631   631.3   BS
BOTSWANA. MINISTRY OF AGRICULTURE. DIVISION OF ARABLE CROPS RESEARCH. ANNUAL REPORT. 1947-1959. a. free. (Ministry of Agriculture, Department of Agricultural Research, Division of Arable Crop Research) Government Printer, Agricultural Research Station, Private Bag 0033, Gaborone, Botswana. circ. 250. (tabloid format; back issues avail.) Indexed: Biol.Abstr.

BOTSWANA. MINISTRY OF AGRICULTURE. FARM MANAGEMENT SURVEY RESULTS. see *AGRICULTURE — Agricultural Economics*

631   663   340   BL
BRAZIL. INSTITUTO DO ACUCAR E DO ALCOOL. CONSELHO DELIBERATIVO. COLETANEA DE RESOLUCOES (E) PRESIDENCIA. COLETANEA DE ATOS. 1972. irreg. Instituto do Acucar e do Alcool, Divisao de Estudo e Planejamento, Divisao Administrativa, Servico de Documentacao, Caixa Postal 420, Rio de Janeiro, Brazil. (Affiliate: Brazil. Ministerio da Industria e do Comercio)
Formed by the merger of: Brazil. Instituto do Acucar e do Alcool. Conselho Deliberativo. Coletanea de Resolucoes & Brazil. Instituto do Acucar e do Alcool. Presidencia. Coletanea de Actas.
Laws and regulations governing sugar and alcohol

631.7   BL   ISSN 0100-123X
BRAZIL. SERVICO NACIONAL DE LEVANTAMENTO E CONSERVACAO DE SOLOS. BOLETIM TECNICO. 1966. irreg. free to qualified personnel. Servico Nacional de Levantamento e Conservacao de Solos, Rua Jardim Botanico 1024, 22460 Rio de Janeiro RJ, Brazil. illus.
Formerly: Brazil. Departamento Nacional de Pesquisa Agropecuaria. Divisao de Pesquisa Pedologica. Boletim Tecnico.

630   CN
BRITISH COLUMBIA. MINISTRY OF AGRICULTURE AND FOOD. FIELD CROP PRODUCTION GUIDE. 1978. a. Can.$3. Ministry of Agriculture and Food, Publications Office, Parliament Bldg., Victoria, B.C. V8W 2Z7, Canada.
Formerly: Ministry of Agriculture. Field Crop Production Guide (ISSN 0228-8117)

631.5   CN
BRITISH COLUMBIA. MINISTRY OF AGRICULTURE AND FOOD. GRAPE PRODUCTION GUIDE. a. Can.$3. Ministry of Agriculture and Food, Publications Office, Parliament Bldg., Victoria, B.C. V8W 2Z7, Canada. TEL 604-387-5121.
Formerly: Ministry of Agriculture. Grape Production Guide (ISSN 0701-9858)

631.5   CN
BRITISH COLUMBIA. MINISTRY OF AGRICULTURE AND FOOD. GREENHOUSE-CUCUMBER AND TOMATO PRODUCTION GUIDE. a. Can.$3. Ministry of Agriculture and Food, Publications Office, Parliament Bldg., Victoria, B.C. V8W 2Z7, Canada.
Formerly: Ministry of Agriculture. Greenhouse-Cucumber and Tomato Production Guide (ISSN 0711-8309)

631.5   CN
BRITISH COLUMBIA. MINISTRY OF AGRICULTURE AND FOOD. GREENHOUSE-ORNAMENTAL PRODUCTION GUIDE. a. Can.$3. Ministry of Agriculture and Food, Publications Office, Parliament Bldg., Victoria, B.C. V8W 2Z7, Canada. TEL 604-387-5121.
Formerly: Ministry of Agriculture. Greenhouse-Ornamental Production Guide (ISSN 0824-8206)

631.5   CN
BRITISH COLUMBIA. MINISTRY OF AGRICULTURE AND FOOD. NURSERY PRODUCTION GUIDE. a. Can.$3. Ministry of Agriculture and Food, Publications Office, Parliament Bldg., Victoria, B.C. V8W 2Z7, Canada. TEL 604-387-5121. Indexed: Geo.Abstr.
Formerly: Ministry of Agriculture. Nursery Production Guide (ISSN 0705-5757)

631.5   CN
BRITISH COLUMBIA. MINISTRY OF AGRICULTURE AND FOOD. TREE FRUIT. 1978. a. Can.$3. Ministry of Agriculture and Food, Publications Office, Parliament Bldg., Victoria, B.C. V8W 2Z7, Canada.
Formerly: Ministry of Agriculture. Tree Fruit Production Guide (ISSN 0705-470X)

631.5   CN
BRITISH COLUMBIA. MINISTRY OF AGRICULTURE AND FOOD. VEGETABLE PRODUCTION GUIDE. a. Can.$3. Ministry of Agriculture and Food, Publications Office, Parliament Bldg., Victoria, B.C. V8W 2Z7, Canada. TEL 604-387-5121.
Formerly: Ministry of Agriculture. Vegetable Production Guide (ISSN 0318-3661)

633   AG   ISSN 0068-3418
BUENOS AIRES. INSTITUTO DE FITOTECNIA. BOLETIN INFORMATIVO. (Text in Spanish; summaries in English) 1954. irreg., no.43, 1984. avail. on exchange basis. Instituto Nacional de Tecnologia Agropecuaria, Centro de Investigaciones en Ciencias Agronomicas, Departamento de Genetica, Casilla de Correo No. 25, 1712 Castelar, Argentina. Indexed: Plant Breed.Abstr. Ref.Zh.

633   JA   ISSN 0068-4090
BULLETIN OF SUGAR BEET RESEARCH. SUPPLEMENT/TENSAI KENKYU HOKOKU HOKAN. Also known as: Proceedings of Sugar Beet Research. (Text in Japanese; summaries in English) 1963. a. free. Sugar Beet Institute, Japan Sugar Beet Improvement Foundation, Hitsujigaoka 1, Sapporo, Hokkaido 062, Japan.

BUNDESANSTALT FUER PFLANZENBAU, VIENNA. JAHRBUCH. see *BIOLOGY — Botany*

BURKINA FASO. DIRECTION DE L'HYDRAULIQUE ET DE L'EQUIPEMENT RURAL. SERVICE I.R.H. RAPPORT D'ACTIVITES. see *WATER RESOURCES*

633   US   ISSN 0735-2689
C R C CRITICAL REVIEWS IN PLANT SCIENCES. 1983. irreg. $104. C R C Press, Inc., 2000 Corporate Blvd., N.W., Boca Raton, FL 33431. Ed. B.V. Conger. Indexed: Chem.Abstr. Sci.Cit.Ind. Ind.Sci.Rev.

634   US   ISSN 0068-5720
CALIFORNIA MACADAMIA SOCIETY. YEARBOOK. 1955. a. $17.50 membership. California Macadamia Society, Box 1290, Fallbrook, CA 92028. Ed. Jim Russell. cum.index: 1955-62; 1963-68. circ. 600.

631.4   627   628.44
614.7   CN
CANADA. AGRICULTURE CANADA. ANNUAL REPORT OF PRAIRIE FARM REHABILITATION ADMINISTRATION/RAPPORT ANNUAL: RETABLISSEMENT AGRICOLE DES PRAIRIES. 1937. a. free. Agriculture Canada, Communications Unit, 1901 Victoria Ave., Regina, Sask. S4P 0R5, Canada. stat. circ. 3,000.
Former titles: Canada. Agriculture Canada. Annual Report on Prairie Farm Rehabilitation and Related Activities/Rapport Annual: Retablissement Agricole des Prairies et Travaux Connexes; Canada. Department of Regional Economic Expansion. Annual Report on Prairie Farm Rehabilitation and Related Activities/Rapport Annuel: Retablissement Agricole des Prairies et Travaux Connexes.

Soil and water conservation

630   CN
CANADA. AGRICULTURE CANADA. ENGINEERING & STATISTICAL RESEARCH INSTITUTE, OTTAWA. RESEARCH REPORT. 1960/66. irreg. contr.free circ. Agriculture Canada, Engineering & Statistical Research Institute, Ottawa, Ont. K1A 0C6, Canada. TEL 613-995-5222. circ. 300.
Formerly: Canada. Department of Agriculture. Engineering Research Service, Ottawa. Research Report (ISSN 0068-7294)

Agricultural engineering

632   CN   ISSN 0068-8185
CANADIAN AGRICULTURAL INSECT PEST REVIEW. 1923. a. free. Agriculture Canada, Research Program Services, c/o J. S. Kelleher, Neatby Bldg., Rm. 1133, Ottawa K1A 0C6, Canada. TEL 613-995-9073. Ed. J.S. Kellcher. index. cum.index every 10 years. circ. 350. Indexed: Biol.Abstr. Rev.Appl.Entomol.
Formerly: Canadian Insect Pest Review.

632   CN   ISSN 0227-7980
CANADIAN PEST MANAGEMENT SOCIETY PROCEEDINGS. 1954. a. Can.$10. Canadian Pest Management Society, c/o J.A. Scott, Pesticides Directorate, Agriculture Canada, Ottawa, Ont. K1A 0C6, Canada. TEL 613-993-4544. circ. 200. Indexed: Chem.Abstr. Pollut.Abstr. Rev.Appl.Entomol. Weed Abstr.
Continues: Agricultural Pesticide Society. Annual Meeting. Proceedings (ISSN 0065-4485)

631.5   CN   ISSN 0068-9610
CANADIAN SEED GROWERS ASSOCIATION. ANNUAL REPORT. 1903/04. a. Canadian Seed Growers Association, P.O. Box 8455, Ottawa, Ont. K1G 3T1, Canada. TEL 613-236-0497. circ. 6,000.

632.9   US
CEREAL RUST BULLETIN. 1963. irreg. free. University of Minnesota, Cereal Rust Laboratory, St. Paul, MN 55108. TEL 612-373-2851. Ed. Alan P. Roelfs. circ. 500. (looseleaf format) Indexed: Field Crop Abstr. Herb.Abstr. Plant Breed.Abstr. Rev.Plant Path.

631   RH
CHEMISTRY AND SOIL RESEARCH INSTITUTE. ANNUAL REPORT. (Text in English) 1964. a. free. Ministry of Agriculture, Department of Research and Specialist Services, Chemistry and Soil Research Institute, P.O. Box 8100, Causeway, Harare, Zimbabwe. Ed. T.J.J. Madziva. circ. 300. (back issues avail.)

634   US   ISSN 0412-6300
CITRUS ENGINEERING CONFERENCE. TRANSACTIONS. 1955. a. $15. Citrus Engineering Conference, Florida Section, Box 3386, Orlando, FL 32802. TEL 305-422-8134. circ. 350. (back issues avail.)

COMMISSION OF THE EUROPEAN COMMUNITIES. MARCHES AGRICOLES: SERIE "PRIX". PRODUITS VEGETAUX. see *AGRICULTURE — Agricultural Economics*

631.5   AT
COMMONWEALTH SCIENTIFIC AND INDUSTRIAL RESEARCH ORGANIZATION. DIVISION OF PLANT INDUSTRY. REPORT. 1980. biennial. free. ‡ C.S.I.R.O., Division of Plant Industry, G.P.O. Box 1600, Canberra, A.C.T. 2601, Australia. Ed. M. Paine. Indexed: Biol.Abstr. Field Crop Abstr. Herb.Abstr.
Supersedes: Commonwealth Scientific and Industrial Research Organization. Division of Plant Industry. Annual Report (ISSN 0069-7540)

631.4   AT   ISSN 0725-8526
COMMONWEALTH SCIENTIFIC AND INDUSTRIAL RESEARCH ORGANIZATION. DIVISION OF SOILS. DIVISIONAL REPORT. 1975. irreg. free. C.S.I.R.O., Division of Soils, Private Bag 2, Glen Osmond, S.A. 5064, Australia. Indexed: Field Crop Abstr. Herb.Abstr. Soils & Fert.

AGRICULTURE — CROP PRODUCTION AND SOIL

631.4   AT   ISSN 0729-4336
COMMONWEALTH SCIENTIFIC AND INDUSTRIAL RESEARCH ORGANIZATION. DIVISION OF SOILS. RESEARCH REPORT. 1949. a. free. C.S.I.R.O., Division of Soils, Private Bag No. 2, Glen Osmond, S.A. 5064, Australia (Subscr. to: CSIRO, Editorial & Publications Service, Box 89, East Melbourne, Vic. 3002, Australia) circ. 1,500. Indexed: Biol.Abstr. Soils & Fert.
 Formerly (until 1975): Commonwealth Scientific and Industrial Research Organization. Division of Soils. Biennial Report (ISSN 0069-7583)

631.4   AT   ISSN 0365-723X
COMMONWEALTH SCIENTIFIC AND INDUSTRIAL RESEARCH ORGANIZATION. DIVISION OF SOILS. TECHNICAL PAPERS. 1971. irreg. Aus.$2 per issue. C.S.I.R.O., Division of Soils, Private Bag 2, Glen Osmond, S. A. 5064, Australia (Subscr. to: CSIRO, Editorial & Publications Service, Box 89, East Melbourne, Vic. 3002, Australia) Indexed: Biol.Abstr. Excerp.Med. GeoRef. Soils & Fert.

631.5 581   AT   ISSN 0158-538X
COMMONWEALTH SCIENTIFIC AND INDUSTRIAL RESEARCH ORGANIZATION. DIVISION OF TROPICAL CROPS AND PASTURES. ANNUAL REPORT. 1959. a. free. C.S.I.R.O., Division of Tropical Crops and Pastures, St. Lucia, Brisbane, Qld. 4067, Australia. Ed. G.T. Adams. Indexed: Biol.Abstr.

631 636   AT   ISSN 0159-6071
COMMONWEALTH SCIENTIFIC AND INDUSTRIAL RESEARCH ORGANIZATION. DIVISION OF TROPICAL CROPS AND PASTURES. GENETIC RESOURCES COMMUNICATION. 1980. irreg. free. C.S.I.R.O., Division of Tropical Crops and Pastures, St. Lucia, Brisbane, Qld. 4067, Australia.

631.5 581   AT
COMMONWEALTH SCIENTIFIC AND INDUSTRIAL RESEARCH ORGANIZATION. DIVISION OF TROPICAL CROPS AND PASTURES. TECHNICAL PAPER. 1961. irreg. Aus.$1 per issue. C.S.I.R.O., Division of Tropical Crops and Pastures, 306 Carmody Rd., St. Lucia, Qld. 4067, Australia. circ. 900. Indexed: Biol.Abstr. Aus.Sci.Ind.
 Formerly: Commonwealth Scientific and Industrial Research Organization. Division of Tropical Pastures. Technical Paper (ISSN 0069-7613)

633   US   ISSN 0069-9993
CORN ANNUAL. 1970. a. free. Corn Refiners Association, Inc., 1001 Connecticut Ave. N.W., Washington, DC 20036. TEL 202-331-1634. Ed. Kyd D. Brenner. circ. 12,000.

631   US
CORNELL RECOMMENDATIONS FOR COMMERCIAL VEGETABLE PRODUCTION. 1969. a. $3 per no. ‡ New York State College of Agriculture and Life Sciences, Cornell University, Ithaca, NY 14853.
 Formerly: Vegetable Production Recommendations.

630.24   PO
CORREIO AGRICOLA (PORTUGAL) Portuguese edition of: Pflanzenschutz-Kurier. 1964. irreg. free. Bayer Portugal S A R L, Apdo. 2365, Lisbon, Portugal (Main Office: Bayer Pflanzenschutz, Leverkusen, W. Germany (B.R.D.)) Ed. J.C. Silva Dias. charts. illus. circ. controlled.

633   KE
COTTON LINT AND SEED MARKETING BOARD. ANNUAL REPORT AND ACCOUNTS. (Text in English) a. Cotton Lint and Seed Marketing Board, Box 30477, Nairobi, Kenya.

631   RH
CROP BREEDING INSTITUTE. ANNUAL REPORT. 1975. a. free. Ministry of Lands, Agriculture and Rural Settlement, Department of Research Information Services, P.O. Box 8108, Causeway, Harare, Zimbabwe. circ. 250. (back issues avail.)

631   CN
CROPS GUIDE. (Supplement to Country Guide) 1972. a. Public Press Ltd., 1760 Ellice Ave., Winnipeg, Man. R3H OB6, Canada. TEL 204-774-1861. circ. 138,019. (microform; also avail. in microfilm from UMI)

634   CU   ISSN 0138-8339
CUBA. CENTRO DE INFORMACION Y DIVULGACION AGROPECUARIO. BOLETIN DE RESENAS. SERIE: CITRICOS. (Abstracts in English) 1974. irreg. exchange basis. Centro de Informacion y Documentacion Agropecuario, Gaveta Postal 4149, Havana 4, Cuba (Dist. by: Ediciones Cubanas, Obispo No. 461, Aptdo. 605, Havana, Cuba) Indexed: Agrindex.
 Formerly: Cuba. Centro de Informacion y Documentacion Agropecuario. Boletin de Resenas. Serie: Citricos y Otras Frutales.

631   CU   ISSN 0138-8436
CUBA. CENTRO DE INFORMACION Y DOCUMENTACION AGROPECUARIO. BOLETIN DE RESENAS. SERIE: CAFE Y CACAO. (Abstracts in English) 1980. irreg. exchange basis. Centro de Informacion y Documentacion Agropecuario, Gaveta Postal 4149, Havana 4, Cuba (Dist. by: Ediciones Cubanas, Obispo No. 461, Aptdo. 605, Havana, Cuba) Indexed: Agrindex.
 Formerly: Cuba. Centro de Informacion y Divulgacion Agropecuario. Boletin de Resenas. Serie: Cafe y Cacao.

631   CU   ISSN 0138-8231
CUBA. CENTRO DE INFORMACION Y DOCUMENTACION AGROPECUARIO. BOLETIN DE RESENAS. SERIE: HORTALIZAS, PAPAS, GRANOS Y FIBRAS. (Abstracts in English) 1984. irreg. exchange basis. Centro de Informacion y Documentacion Agropecuario, Gaveta Postal 4149, Havana 4, Cuba (Dist. by: Ediciones Cubanas, Obispo No. 461, Aptdo. 605, Havana, Cuba) Indexed: Agrindex.
 Supersedes in part: Cuba. Centro de Informacion y Divulgacion Agropecuario. Boletin de Resenas. Serie: Viandas, Hortalizas y Granos.

631   CU   ISSN 0138-8088
CUBA. CENTRO DE INFORMACION Y DOCUMENTACION AGROPECUARIO. BOLETIN DE RESENAS. SERIE: PROTECCION DE PLANTAS. (Abstracts in English) 1974. irreg. exchange basis. Centro de Informacion y Documentacion Agropecurario, Gaveta Postal 4149, Havana 4, Cuba (Dist. by: Ediciones Cubanas, Obispo No. 461, Aptdo. 605, Havana, Cuba) Indexed: Agrindex.
 Formerly: Cuba. Centro de Informacion y Divulgacion Agropecuario. Boletin de Resenas. Serie: Proteccion de Plantas.

631.7   CU   ISSN 0138-788X
CUBA. CENTRO DE INFORMACION Y DOCUMENTACION AGROPECUARIO. BOLETIN DE RESENAS. SERIE: RIEGO Y DRENAJE. (Abstracts in English) 1974. irreg. exchange basis. Centro de Informacion y Documentacion Agropecuario, Gaveta Postal 4149, Havana 4, Cuba (Dist. by: Ediciones Cubanas, Obispo No. 461, Aptdo. 605, Havana, Cuba) Indexed: Agrindex.
 Formerly: Cuba. Centro de Informacion y Divulgacion Agropecuario. Boletin de Resenas. Serie: Riego y Drenaje.

631.7   CU   ISSN 0138-7936
CUBA. CENTRO DE INFORMACION Y DOCUMENTACION AGROPECUARIO. BOLETIN DE RESENAS. SERIE: SUELOS Y AGROQUIMICA. (Abstracts in English) 1974. irreg. exchange basis. Centro de Informacion y Documentacion Agropecuario, Gaveta Postal 4149, Havana 4, Cuba (Dist. by: Ediciones Cubanas, Obispo No. 461, Aptdo. 605, Havana, Cuba) Indexed: Agrindex.
 Formerly: Cuba. Centro de Informacion y Divulgacion Agropecuario. Boletin de Resenas. Serie: Suelos y Agroquimica.

631   CU
CUBA. CENTRO DE INFORMACION Y DOCUMENTACION AGROPECUARIO. BOLETIN DE RESENAS. SERIE: VIANDAS TROPICALES. 1974. irreg exchange basis. Centro de Informacion y Documentacion Agropecuario, Gaveta Postal 4149, Havana 4, Cuba (Dist. by: Ediciones Cubanas, Obispo No. 461, Aptdo. 605, Havana, Cuba)
 Supersedes in part: Cuba. Centro de Informacion y Divulgacion Agropecuario. Boletin de Resenas. Serie: Viandas, Hortalizas y Granos; Formerly: Cuba. Centro de Informacion y Documentacion Agropecuario. Boletin de Resenas. Serie: Viandas, Hortalizas y Granos.

CURRENT AGRO-TECHNOLOGY FOR POTATO PRODUCTION. see *AGRICULTURE*

631   CY   ISSN 0070-234X
CYPRUS. DEPARTMENT OF AGRICULTURE. SOILS AND PLANT NUTRITION SECTION. REPORT. (Text in English) 1959. biennial. free. ‡ Ministry of Agriculture and Natural Resources, Soils and Plant Nutrition Section, Nicosia, Cyprus. circ. 150.

631.7 627   BL
D N O C S - FINS E ATIVIDADES. irreg. Departamento Nacional de Obras Contra as Secas, Fortaleza, Ceara, Brazil. illus.

632   UK   ISSN 0305-2680
DESCRIPTIONS OF PLANT VIRUSES. 1970. a. £7.50($14) Association of Applied Biologists, National Vegetable Research Station, Wellesbourne, Warwick CV35 9EF, England (U.S. subscr. to: Bernan Associates-Unipub, 4611-F Assembly Dr., Lanham, MD 20706-4391) Eds. A.F. Murant, B.D. Harrison. circ. 1,300. (back issues avail.)

632.9   ET   ISSN 0418-761X
DESERT LOCUST CONTROL ORGANIZATION FOR EASTERN AFRICA. ANNUAL REPORT. 1962/1963. a, Desert Locust Control Organization for Eastern Africa, P.O. Box 4255, Addis Ababa, Ethiopia. Indexed: Rev.Appl.Entomol.
 Supersedes: East Africa High Commissions Desert Locust Survey. Report.

631   NE
DEVELOPMENTS IN CROP SCIENCE. 1975. irreg., vol.7, 1984. price varies. Elsevier Science Publishers B.V., Box 211, 1000 AE Amsterdam, Netherlands.

631   NE
DEVELOPMENTS IN PLANT AND SOIL SCIENCES. 1981. irreg. Martinus Nijhoff Publishers, Postbus 163, Spuiboulevard 50, 3317 JA Dordrecht, Netherlands. Indexed: Chem.Abstr.

631.4   NE
DEVELOPMENTS IN SOIL SCIENCE. 1972. irreg., vol.14, 1986. price varies. Elsevier Science Publishers B.V., Box 211, 1000 AE Amsterdam, Netherlands. Indexed: Biol.Abstr. GeoRef.

631   VE
DIRECTORIO INDUSTRIAL AZUCARERO. 1972. a. Bs.50. Distribuidora Venezolana de Azucares, Departamento de Promocion Industrial, Edificio Torre Europa, Av. de Miranda, Caracas 106, Venezuela. adv. charts. stat.

633.83   II
DIRECTORY OF CARDAMOM PLANTERS. (Text in English) 1974. irreg. Rs.50. Cardamom Board, Chittoor Rd., Cochin 682018, India.

DIRECTORY OF INTERNATIONAL TRADE. see *BUSINESS AND ECONOMICS — International Commerce*

631.4   FR   ISSN 0180-9555
DOCUMENTS PEDOZOOLOGIQUES. (Text in French; summaries in English) 1979. irreg. free to qualified personnel. Institut National de la Recherche Agronomique, Laboratoire de Zooecologie du Sol, CEPE, B.P. 5051, F-34044 Montpellier Cedex, France. Ed. M.B. Bouche. circ. 300. Indexed: Biol.Abstr. Chem.Abstr. PASCAL. Zoo.Rec.

AGRICULTURE — CROP PRODUCTION AND SOIL

631.8   GW
DUENGUNGSRATSCHLAEGE FUER DEN BAUERNHOF. 1938. irreg. DM.2. Fachverband Stickstoffindustrie, Sternstr. 9-11, 4000 Duesseldorf 1, W. Germany (B.R.D.) Ed. Helmut Nieder. circ. 50,000.

633.491   NE
E A P R ABSTRACTS OF CONFERENCE PAPERS. (Text in English, French, German) 1961 (1st Conference in 1960) triennial. $15. European Association for Potato Research, Box 20, 6700 AA Wageningen, Netherlands. circ. 1,200. Indexed: Field Crop Abstr. Herb.Abstr.
    Formerly (until 1975): European Association for Potato Research. Proceedings of the Triennial Conference (ISSN 0071-2507)

631 635   UK   ISSN 0306-6398
EAST MALLING RESEARCH STATION. ANNUAL REPORT. 1914. a. £6($12) East Malling Research Station, East Malling, Maidstone, Kent, England. circ. 3,000. Indexed: Biol.Abstr. Apic.Abstr. Field Crop Abstr. Helminthol.Abstr. Herb.Abstr. Hort.Abstr. Rev.Appl.Entomol. Rev.Plant Path. Weed Abstr.

ECOLE NATIONALE SUPERIEURE D'AGRONOMIE ET DES INDUSTRIES ALIMENTAIRES. BULLETIN. see AGRICULTURE — Agricultural Economics

ECONOMICS OF FRUIT FARMING. see AGRICULTURE — Agricultural Economics

630.24 668.6   EC
ECUADOR. INSTITUTO NACIONAL DE INVESTIGACIONES AGROPECUARIAS. INFORME TECNICO. irreg. Instituto Nacional de Investigaciones Agropecuarias, Departamento de Comunicacion, Casilla 2600, Quito, Ecuador.

631 581   SP   ISSN 0365-1800
ESTACION EXPERIMENTAL DE AULA DEI. ANALES. (Text and summaries in English and Spanish) 1948. irreg. Estacion Experimental de Aula Dei, Apdo. de Correos 202, C/Montanana 177, Zaragoza, Spain. (Co-sponsor: Consejo Superior de Investigaciones Cientificas) circ. 1,000. (back issues avail.) Indexed: Biol.Abstr. Bull.Signal. Chem.Abstr. Hort.Abstr. Plant Breed.Abstr. Soils & Fert. VITIS. Zoo.Rec.

632   FR   ISSN 0071-2396
EUROPEAN AND MEDITERRANEAN PLANT PROTECTION ORGANIZATION. PUBLICATIONS. SERIES B: PLANT HEALTH NEWSLETTER. (Editions in English and French) 1950. irreg. free contr. circ. ‡ European and Mediterranean Plant Protection Organization, 1 rue le Notre, 75016 Paris, France. Ed. I.M. Smith. (processed) Indexed: Biol.Abstr.
    Formerly: Surveys of the Position of Various Pests and Diseases in Europe and the Mediterranean Area.

633   BE   ISSN 0071-2825
EUROPEAN GRASSLAND FEDERATION. PROCEEDINGS OF THE GENERAL MEETING. 1965. irreg., 7th, 1978, Belgium. 48 Fr. European Grassland Federation, c/o Rijksstation voor Plantenveredeling, Burg. Van Gansberghelaan 109, 9220 Merelbeke, Belgium (Inquiries to: J.W. Minderhoud, Department of Field Crops and Grassland Husbandry, State Agricultural University, Haarweg 33, Wageningen, Netherlands) circ. 340.

631.8   UN
F A O FERTILIZER YEARBOOK. (Tables in English and French with Spanish glossary; text in English, French and Spanish) 1951. a. price varies. Food and Agriculture Organization of the United Nations, Distribution and Sales Section, Via delle Terme di Caracalla, 00100 Rome, Italy (Dist. in U.S. by: Bernan Associates-Unipub, 4611-F Assembly Drive, Lanham, MD 20706-4391)
    Former titles: Annual Fertilizer Review (ISSN 0084-6546); Fertilizers: An Annual Review of World Production, Consumption and Trade (ISSN 0071-464X); Annual Review of World Production, Consumption and Trade of Fertilizers.

630.24 668.6   US   ISSN 0430-0750
FARM CHEMICALS HANDBOOK. 1914. a. $50. Meister Publishing Co., 37841 Euclid Ave., Willoughby, OH 44094. TEL 216-942-2000. Ed. Charlotte Sine. adv. circ. 11,708.
    Supersedes: American Fertilizer Handbook.

631   UK   ISSN 0071-3961
FARMING IN THE EAST MIDLANDS. a. £3. University of Nottingham, School of Agriculture, University Park, Nottingham NG7 2RD, England.
    Formerly: Farm Management Notes.

FEDERACION NACIONAL DE CAFETEROS DE COLOMBIA. INFORME DE LABORES DE LOS COMITES DEPARTAMENTALES DE CAFETEROS. see FOOD AND FOOD INDUSTRIES

631.8   US   ISSN 0071-4623
FERTILIZER SCIENCE AND TECHNOLOGY SERIES. 1968. irreg., vol.5, 1986. price varies. Marcel Dekker, Inc., 270 Madison Ave., New York, NY 10016. TEL 212-696-9000. Ed. A.V. Slack. (also avail. in microform from RPI) Indexed: Chem.Abstr.
Fertilizers

631.8   US   ISSN 0071-4631
FERTILIZER TRENDS. 1956. biennial. $6. Tennessee Valley Authority, National Fertilizer Development Center, Muscle Shoals, AL 35660. TEL 205-386-2915. circ. 5,000.
Fertilizers

FIJI SUGAR YEAR BOOK. see FOOD AND FOOD INDUSTRIES

632.3   UN
FOOD AND AGRICULTURE ORGANIZATION OF THE UNITED NATIONS. ASIA AND PACIFIC PLANT PROTECTION COMMISSION. INFORMATION LETTER. 1958. irreg. free. Food and Agriculture Organization of the United Nations, Regional Office for Asia and the Pacific, Maliwan Mansion, Phra Atit Rd., Bangkok 10200, Thailand. circ. 500.
    Formerly: Food and Agriculture Organization of the United Nations. Plant Protection Committee for Southeast Asia and Pacific Region. Information Letter.

631   UN
FOOD AND AGRICULTURE ORGANIZATION OF THE UNITED NATIONS. ASIA AND PACIFIC PLANT PROTECTION COMMISSION. TECHNICAL DOCUMENT. (Text and summaries in English) 1958. irreg. (6-8/yr.) free. Food and Agriculture Organization of the United Nations, Regional Office for Asia and the Pacific, Maliwan Mansion, Phra Atit Rd., Bangkok 10200, Thailand. circ. 500(controlled) Indexed: Rev.Appl.Entomol. Rev.Plant Path. Weed Abstr.
    Formerly: Food and Agricultural Organization of the United Nations. Plant Protection Committee for Southeast Asia and Pacific Region. Technical Document (ISSN 0428-9765)

631.4   UN   ISSN 0532-0437
FOOD AND AGRICULTURE ORGANIZATION OF THE UNITED NATIONS. SOILS BULLETINS. (Editions in English, French, Spanish) 1965. irreg., no.55, 1986. Food and Agriculture Organization of the United Nations, Distribution and Sales Section, Via delle Terme di Caracalla, I-00100 Rome, Italy (Dist. in U.S. by: Bernan Associates-Unipub, 4611-F Assembly Drive, Lanham, MD 20706-4391) bibl.

631.4   UN   ISSN 0532-0488
FOOD AND AGRICULTURE ORGANIZATION OF THE UNITED NATIONS. WORLD SOIL RESOURCES REPORTS. irreg., no.57, 1985. Food and Agriculture Organization of the United Nations, Distribution and Sales Section, Via delle Terme di Caracalla, I-00100 Rome, Italy. Indexed: Rural Recreat.Tour.Abstr. Soils & Fert. World Agri.Econ.& Rural Sociol.Abstr.

631.7   DK   ISSN 0109-5498
FORTEGNELSE OVER FABRIKANTER OG IMPORTOERER AF GOEDNINGER OG GRUNDFORBEDRINGSMIDLER. 1964. a. free. Landbrugministeriets Goedningstilsyn, Lottenborgvej 24, 2800 Lynby, Denmark. Ed. M. Brink.
    Formerly: Fortegnelse over Fabrikanter og Importoerer af Goedningsstoffer og Grundforbedringsmidler.

380.1   FR
FRUCTIDOR INTERNATIONAL. 1935. a. 600 F. Editions Fructidor, 14 bd. Montmartre, Paris, France. adv. circ. 6,000.

FUNGI CANADENSES. see BIOLOGY — Botany

632.9   US   ISSN 0148-9038
FUNGICIDE AND NEMATICIDE TESTS. (Text in English and Spanish) a. $7. American Phytopathological Society, 3340 Pilot Knob Rd., St. Paul, MN 55121. TEL 612-454-7250. index. circ. 1, 000. (back issues avail.) Indexed: Helminthol.Abstr. Rev.Plant Path. Soils & Fert.
Pest control

630.24 668.6   DK   ISSN 0901-1943
GOEDSKINGRAPPORT. irreg. (Skovstyrelsen) Bibliotekscentralen, Telegrafvej 5, DK-2750 Ballerup, Denmark.

633   SA   ISSN 0256-6702
GRASSLAND SOCIETY OF SOUTHERN AFRICA. JOURNAL. (Text and summaries in Afrikaans or English) 1984. a. $25. ‡ Grassland Society of Southern Africa, c/o A. Smith, P.O. Box 750, 3290 Howick, South Africa. Ed. M.M. Wolfson. adv. cum.index. circ. 600. Indexed: Biol.& Agr.Ind. Chem.Abstr. Bibl.Agri. Field Crop Abstr. Geo.Abstr. Herb.Abstr. Soils & Fert.
    Supersedes (1966-1983): Grassland Society of Southern Africa. Proceedings of the Annual Congresses (ISSN 0072-5560)

632.9   UK   ISSN 0261-6963
GREAT BRITAIN. AGRICULTURAL SCIENCE SERVICE. RESEARCH AND DEVELOPMENT REPORTS: CROP AND PEST DISEASES. 1981. a. £4.50. H.M.S.O., P.O. Box 569, London SE1 9NH, England. (Co-sponsor: Ministry of Agriculture, Fisheries and Food)
    Supersedes in part: Great Britain. Pest Infestation Control Laboratory. Report (ISSN 0072-6486)

631   UK   ISSN 0261-717X
GREAT BRITAIN. AGRICULTURAL SCIENCE SERVICE. RESEARCH AND DEVELOPMENT REPORTS: CROP NUTRITION AND SOIL SCIENCE. 1981. a. £3.50. H.M.S.O., P.O. Box 569, London SE1 9NH, England. (Co-sponsor: Ministry of Agriculture, Fisheries and Food)
    Supersedes in part: Great Britain. Pest Infestation Control Laboratory. Report (ISSN 0072-6486)

632.9   UK   ISSN 0261-7161
GREAT BRITAIN. AGRICULTURAL SCIENCE SERVICE. RESEARCH AND DEVELOPMENT REPORTS: MAMMAL AND BIRD PESTS. 1981. a. £2.95. H.M.S.O., P.O. Box 569, London NE1 9NH, England. (Co-sponsor: Ministry of Agriculture, Fisheries and Food)
    Supersedes in part: Great Britain. Pest Infestation Control Laboratory. Report (ISSN 0072-6486)

632.9   UK
GREAT BRITAIN. AGRICULTURAL SCIENCE SERVICE. RESEARCH AND DEVELOPMENT REPORTS: PESTICIDE SCIENCE. 1981. a. £3.50. H.M.S.O., P.O. Box 569, London SE1 9NH, England. (Co-sponsor: Ministry of Agriculture, Fisheries and Food)
    Supersedes in part: Great Britain. Pest Infestation Control Laboratory. Report (ISSN 0072-6486)

632.9   UK
GREAT BRITAIN. AGRICULTURAL SCIENCE SERVICE. RESEARCH AND DEVELOPMENT REPORTS: STORAGE PEST. 1981. a. £2.95. H.M.S.O., P.O. Box 569, London SE1 9NH, England. (Co-sponsor: Ministry of Agriculture, Fisheries and Food)
    Supersedes in part: Great Britain. Pest Infestation Control Laboratory. Report (ISSN 0072-6486)

631.4   UK   ISSN 0072-7180
GREAT BRITAIN. SOIL SURVEY OF ENGLAND AND WALES. RECORDS. 1970. irreg., no.105, 1987. price varies. Soil Survey of England and Wales, Rothamsted Experimental Station, Harpenden, Herts AL5 2JQ, England. Indexed: Geo.Abstr. Soils & Fert.

631.4   UK   ISSN 0072-7199
GREAT BRITAIN. SOIL SURVEY OF ENGLAND AND WALES. REPORT. 1967. a. price varies. Soil Survey of England and Wales, Rothamsted Experimental Station, Harpenden, Herts AL5 2JQ, England.

AGRICULTURE — CROP PRODUCTION AND SOIL

631.4   UK   ISSN 0072-7202
GREAT BRITAIN. SOIL SURVEY OF ENGLAND AND WALES. SPECIAL SURVEYS. 1969. irreg., no.14, 1986. price varies. Soil Survey of England and Wales, Rothamsted Experimental Station, Harpenden, Herts AL5 2JQ, England. Indexed: Geo.Abstr. Soils & Fert.

631.4   UK   ISSN 0072-7210
GREAT BRITAIN. SOIL SURVEY OF ENGLAND AND WALES. TECHNICAL MONOGRAPHS. 1969. irreg., no.17, 1985. price varies. Soil Survey of England and Wales, Rothamsted Experimental Station, Harpenden, Herts AL5 2JQ, England. Indexed: Geo.Abstr. Soils & Fert.

631   SA
GUIDE TO THE USE OF PESTICIDES AND FUNGICIDES IN THE REPUBLIC OF SOUTH AFRICA. (Editions in English and Afrikaans) 1961. a. R.5. Department of Agriculture and Water Supply, Private Bag X116, Pretoria 0001, South Africa (Orders to: Division of Agricultural Information, Private Bag X144, Pretoria 0001, South Africa) Ed.Bd. circ. 5,000.
Formerly: Guide to the Use of Insecticides and Fungicides in South Africa.

633.6   GY
GUYANA SUGAR CORPORATION. ANNUAL REPORTS AND ACCOUNTS. 1976. a. Guyana Sugar Corporation, 22 Church St., Georgetown, Guyana. illus. circ. 2,000.

633.6   US   ISSN 0073-1358
HAWAIIAN PLANTERS' RECORD. 1909. irreg. (q. until 1956) exchange basis only. Hawaiian Sugar Planters' Association, Experiment Station, Box 1057, Aiea, HI 96701. TEL 808-487-5561. index. Indexed: Biol.Abstr. Chem.Abstr. Rev.Appl.Entomol.

633.6   US   ISSN 0073-1366
HAWAIIAN SUGAR PLANTERS' ASSOCIATION EXPERIMENT STATION. ANNUAL REPORT. 1947. a. exchange basis only. Hawaiian Sugar Planters' Association, Experiment Station, Box 1057, Aiea, HI 96701. TEL 808-487-5561. Indexed: Biol.Abstr. Rev.Appl.Entomol. Weed Abstr.

633.491   US   ISSN 0018-1986
HINTS TO POTATO GROWERS. 1920. irreg. (2-4/yr.) $10 to non-members. New Jersey State Potato Association, Box 231 Blake Hall, Cook College, Rutgers University, New Brunswick, NJ 08903. Ed. Dr. Melvin Henninger. charts. stat. circ. 150. (processed)
Potatoes

631.4   JA   ISSN 0073-2923
HOKKAIDO NATIONAL AGRICULTURAL EXPERIMENT STATION. SOIL SURVEY REPORT/HOKKAIDO NOGYO SHIKENJO DOJO CHOSA HOKOKU. (Text and summaries in Japanese or English) 1951. a. available on exchange. Hokkaido National Agricultural Experiment Station, 1 Hitsujigaoka, Toyohira-ku, Sapporo 004, Japan (Dist. in U.S. by: New York Agricultural Experiment Station, Geneva, NY 14456) circ. 800. (also avail. in microform) Indexed: Biol.Abstr.

631   RH
HORTICULTURE AND COFFEE RESEARCH INSTITUTE. ANNUAL REPORT. PART 1. HORTICULTURAL RESEARCH CENTRE. (Text in English) 1976. a. free. Ministry of Agriculture, Horticulture and Coffee Research Institute, P.O. Box 3748, Marondera, Zimbabwe (Orders to: P.O. Box 8108, Causeway, Zimbabwe) Ed. M.L. Vogel. circ. 300.

631   RH
HORTICULTURE AND COFFEE RESEARCH INSTITUTE. ANNUAL REPORT. PART 2. COFFEE RESEARCH STATION. 1976. a. free. Ministry of Agriculture, Horticulture and Coffee Research Institute, P.O. Box 3748, Marondera, Zimbabwe (Orders to: P.O. Box 8108, Causeway, Zimbabwe) Ed. D. Kumah. circ. 300.

631   RH
HORTICULTURE AND COFFEE RESEARCH INSTITUTE. ANNUAL REPORT. PART 3. RHODES EXPERIMENTAL STATION. 1976. a. free. Ministry of Agriculture, Horticulture and Coffee Research Institute, B.P. 3748, Marondera, Zimbabwe (Orders to: P.O. Box 8108, Causeway, Zimbabwe) circ. 300.

631   SZ
I P I BULLETIN. 1974. irreg., no.9, 1986. price varies. International Potash Institute, Postfach, CH-3048 Worblaufen-Bern, Switzerland. Indexed: Biol.Abstr. Field Crop Abstr. Herb.Abstr. Soils & Fert.

631   SZ
I P I RESEARCH TOPICS. 1976. irreg., no.13, 1986. price varies. International Potash Institute, Postfach, CH-3048 Worblaufen-Bern, Switzerland. Indexed: Biol.Abstr. Field Crop Abstr. Herb.Abstr. Soils & Fert.

631.8   FR
I S M A TECHNICAL CONFERENCE. PROCEEDINGS. (Published by host country; 1976, Netherlands) biennial. 250 Fr. per no. International Superphosphate Manufacturers Association, Ltd., 28 rue Marbeuf, 75008 Paris, France. Ed. L.J. Carpentier.
Fertilizers

354   II
INDIA. CARDAMOM BOARD. ANNUAL REPORT. (Text in English) a. Cardamom Board, Chittoor Rd., Cochin 682018, India.

633   II   ISSN 0073-649X
INDIAN INSTITUTE OF SUGARCANE RESEARCH, LUCKNOW. ANNUAL REPORT. (Text in English) 1954. a. exchange basis. Indian Institute of Sugarcane Research, Indian Council of Agricultural Research, Lucknow 2, Uttar Pradesh, India. Indexed: Rev.Plant Path.

631   PL   ISSN 0373-7837
INSTYTUT HODOWLI I AKLMATYZACJI ROSLIN. BIULETYN/INSTITUTE OF PLANT BREEDING AND ACCLIMATIZATION BULLETIN. (Text in Polish; summaries in English and Russian) 1951. irreg., (approx. 4/yr.) 2000 Zl.($21) Instytut Hodowli i Aklimatyzacji Roslin - Plant Breeding and Acclimatization Institute, Radzikow, 05-870 Blonie, Poland. adv. bk. rev. Indexed: Biol.Abstr. Field Crop Abstr. Herb.Abstr. Plant Breed.Abstr. Rev.Plant Path.

INSTITUT PHYTOPATHOLOGIQUE BENAKI. ANNALES. see *AGRICULTURE*

633   IS
INSTITUTE OF FIELD AND GARDEN CROPS. SCIENTIFIC ACTIVITIES. (Text in English) triennial. $7. Agricultural Research Organization (Subsidiary of: Scientific Publications) Volcani Centre, P.O. Box 6, Bet-Dagan, Israel. Ed. Vivian Priel. Indexed: Biol.Abstr.

630   IS
INSTITUTE OF PLANT PROTECTION. SCIENTIFIC ACTIVITIES. (Text in English) triennial. $5. Agricultural Research Organization, Institute of Plant Protection, Volcani Center, Box 6, Bet Dagan, Israel. Ed. V. Priel.
Plant protection

631.4   IS
INSTITUTE OF SOILS & WATER. SCIENTIFIC ACTIVITIES. (Text in English) triennial. Agricultural Research Organization, Institute of Soils & Water, Division of Scientific Publications, Volcani Center, Box 6, Bet Dagan, Israel.

633.41   RM
INSTITUTUL DE CERCETARI PENTRU CEREALE SI PLANTE TEHNICE. LABORATOR SFECLA DE ZAHAR. ANALE. LUCRARI STIINTIFICE. (Text in Romanian; summaries in English, German and Russian) 1968. a. 80 lei. Institutul de Cercetari Pentru Cereale si Plante Tehnice, Laborator Sfecla de Zahar, Str. Fundaturii, Nr. 2, Brasov, Romania. Indexed: Biol.Abstr. Weed Abstr.
Formerly: Institutul de Cercetari Pentru Cultura Cartofului si Sfeclei de Zahar, Brasov. Anale. Sflecla de Zahar (ISSN 0074-0381)

633.491   RM
INSTITUTUL DE CERCETARI SI PRODUCTIE A CARTOFULUI, BRASOV. ANALE. LUCRARI STIINTIFICE. (Text in Romanian; summaries in English, German and Russian) 1969. a. 280 lei. Institutul de Cercetare si Productie a Cartofului, Str. Fundaturii, Nr. 2, Brasov, Romania. Indexed: Biol.Abstr. Field Crop Abstr. Herb.Abstr. Plant Breed.Abstr.
Formerly: Institutul de Cercetari Pentru Cultura Cartofului si Sfeclei de Zahar, Brasov. Anale. Cartoful (ISSN 0074-0373)

631   NE   ISSN 0434-6785
INSTITUUT VOOR BODEMVRUCHTBAARHEID. JAARVERSLAG. (Text in Dutch; summaries in English) 1916. a. free. Instituut voor Bodemvruchtbaarheid, Department of Agriculture and Fisheries - Institute for Soil Fertility, Postbus 30003, 9750 RA Haren, Netherlands. Ed. C.H.E. Werkhoven. circ. 1,000. (back issues avail.) Indexed: Biol.Abstr. Field Crop Abstr. Herb.Abstr. Hort.Abstr. Soils & Fert.

631.6 333.91 614.7   NE   ISSN 0165-0610
INSTITUUT VOOR CULTUURTECHNIEK EN WATERHUISHOUDING. JAARVERSLAG. a. Instituut voor Cultuurtechniek en Waterhuishouding - Institute for Land and Water Management Research, Box 35, 6700 AA Wageningen, Netherlands. Eds. A.F.M. Schoots, B. ten Cate. circ. 600.

631.6   NE
INSTITUUT VOOR CULTUURTECHNIEK EN WATERHUISHOUDING. MEDEDELING. NIEUWE SERIE. (Text in Dutch) 1958. irreg., no.43, 1986. free. ‡ Instituut voor Cultuurtechniek en Waterhuishouding - Institute for Land and Water Management Research, P.O. Box 35, 6700 AA Wageningen, Netherlands. Eds. A.F.M. Schoots, B. ten Cate. circ. 600. (back issues avail.) Indexed: Bull.Signal. Field Crop Abstr. Geo.Abstr. Herb.Abstr. Meteor.& Geoastrophys.Abstr. Soils & Fert. Water Resour.Abstr. World Agri.Econ.& Rural Sociol.Abstr.
Formed by the merger of: Instituut voor Cultuurtechniek en Waterhuishouding. Mededeling (ISSN 0074-0411) & Instituut voor Cultuurtechniek en Waterhuishouding. Verspreide Overdrukken (ISSN 0074-0438)

631 333.91   NE
INSTITUUT VOOR CULTUURTECHNIEK EN WATERHUISHOUDING. RAPPORTEN. NIEUWE SERIE. 1982. irreg., no.19, 1986. Instituut voor Cultuurtechniek en Waterhuishouding - Institute for Land and Water Research, P.O. Box 35, 6700 AA Wageningen, Netherlands. Eds. A.F.M Schoots, B. ten Cate. circ. 200. (back issues avail.)

631 333.91   NE
INSTITUUT VOOR CULTUURTECHNIEK EN WATERHUISHOUDING. REPORTS. (Text in English) 1981. irreg., no.16, 1986. Insituut voor Cultuurtechniek en Waterhuishouding - Institute for Land and Water Management Research, P.O. Box 35, 6700 AA Wageningen, Netherlands. Ed. A.F.M Schoots. circ. 200. (back issues avail.)

631.6 614.7 333.91   NE
INSTITUUT VOOR CULTUURTECHNIEK EN WATERHUISHOUDING. TECHNICAL BULLETINS. NEW SERIES. (Text in English) 1958. irreg., no.52, 1986. free. ‡ Instituut voor Cultuurtechniek en Waterhuishouding - Institute for Land and Water Management Research, P.O. Box 35, 6700 AA Wageningen, Netherlands. Ed. A.F.M. Schoots. circ. 1,500. (back issues avail.) Indexed: Bull.Signal. Field Crop Abstr. GeoRef. Herb.Abstr. Hort.Abstr. Meteor.& Geoastrophys.Abstr. Water Resour.Abstr. World Agri.Econ.& Rural Sociol.Abstr.
Formed by the merger of: Instituut voor Cultuurtechniek en Waterhuishouding. Technical Bulletin (ISSN 0074-042X) & Instituut voor Cultuurtechniek en Waterhuishouding. Miscellaneous Reprints.

632 581   NE   ISSN 0074-0446
INSTITUUT VOOR PLANTENZIEKTENKUNDIG ONDERZOEK. JAARVERSLAG. Dutch edition: Institute of Phytopathological Research. Annual Report. (Editions in Dutch and English) 1950. a. price varies. Instituut voor Plantenziektenkundig Onderzoek, P.O. Box 9060, 6700 GW Wageningen, Netherlands. Ed. G.S. Roosje.

632 581　　　　　NE　ISSN 0019-0349
INSTITUUT VOOR PLANTENZIEKTENKUNDIG
ONDERZOEK. MEDEDELING/INSTITUTE OF
PHYTOPATHOLOGICAL RESEARCH.
COMMUNICATIONS. (Text in Dutch, English or
German; summaries in English) 1950. irreg., no.907,
1984. price varies. Instituut voor
Plantenziektenkundig Onderzoek, P.O. Box 9060,
6700 GW Wageningen, Netherlands. Ed. G.S.
Roosje. Indexed: Bull.Signal. Plant Breed.Abstr.
Rev.Appl.Mycol.

630　　　　　FR　ISSN 0074-2694
INTERNATIONAL COMMISSION OF
AGRICULTURAL ENGINEERING. REPORTS
OF CONGRESS. (Proceedings published by
organizing committee) 1930. irreg., 9th, 1979, East
Lansing, Michigan. International Commission of
Agricultural Engineering, c/o Secretary General, 17
rue de Javel, 75015 Paris, France.
Agricultural engineering

631.8　　　　　UK
INTERNATIONAL CONFERENCE ON
FERTILIZERS. PROCEEDINGS. 8th, 1985. irreg.,
latest 10th, 1986. £80($120) British Sulphur Corp.
Ltd., Parnell House, 25 Wilton Rd., London SW1V
1NH, England.

633　　　　　US
INTERNATIONAL COTTON ADVISORY
COMMITTEE. COUNTRY STATEMENTS
PRESENTED IN CONNECTION WITH THE
PLENARY MEETINGS. 35th, 1976. a. $15.
International Cotton Advisory Committee, 1225
19th St., N.W. Ste. 650, Washington, DC 20036.
TEL 202-463-6660. stat.

633　　　　　UR　ISSN 0074-6185
INTERNATIONAL GRASSLAND CONGRESS.
PROCEEDINGS. 1927. irreg., 12th, 1974, Moscow.
International Grassland Congress, All-Union
Research Forage Institute, c/o Dr. V. Igloviv,
Moscow Region, Lugovaya, Russian S.F.S.R.,
U.S.S.R. Indexed: Field Crop Abstr. Herb.Abstr.
Weed Abstr.

631.6　　　　　NE　ISSN 0074-6428
INTERNATIONAL INSTITUTE FOR LAND
RECLAMATION AND IMPROVEMENT.
ANNUAL REPORT. (Text in English) 1960. a. free
on exchange. International Institute for Land
Reclamation and Improvement, P.O. Box 45, 6700
AA Wageningen, Netherlands. Indexed: Field Crop
Abstr. Herb.Abstr. Soils & Fert. Weed Abstr.

631.6　　　　　NE　ISSN 0074-6452
INTERNATIONAL INSTITUTE FOR LAND
RECLAMATION AND IMPROVEMENT.
PUBLICATION. (Text in English) 1958. irreg. price
varies. International Institute for Land Reclamation
and Improvement, P.O. Box 45, 6700 AA
Wageningen, Netherlands. Indexed: Forest.Abstr.
Forest Prod.Abstr.

633.6　　　　　BE　ISSN 0074-6460
INTERNATIONAL INSTITUTE FOR SUGAR
BEET RESEARCH. REPORTS OF THE WINTER
CONGRESS. Variant title: I I R B Winter Congress
Proceedings. (Text and summaries in English,
French or German) 1958. a. 1500 Fr. International
Institute for Sugar Beet Research, 47 rue Montoyer,
B-1040 Brussels, Belgium. Ed.Bd. adv. circ. 700.
(back issues avail.) Indexed: Weed Abstr.

632　　　　　US　ISSN 0145-6288
INTERNATIONAL PLANT PROTECTION
CENTER. INFOLETTER. (Text in English &
Spanish) 1970. irreg. free. International Plant
Protection Center, Oregon State Univ., Corvallis,
OR 97331. TEL 503-754-3541. (Co-sponsors: U.S.
Agency for International Development; Consortium
for International Crop Protection) Ed. Allan
Deutsch. bk. rev. bibl. circ. 8,000.

631.8　　　　　SZ　ISSN 0074-7491
INTERNATIONAL POTASH INSTITUTE.
COLLOQUIUM. PROCEEDINGS. 1963. irreg.,
19th, 1985. International Potash Institute, Postfach,
CH-3048 Worblaufen-Bern, Switzerland. Indexed:
Biol.Abstr. Chem.Abstr.
Fertalization

631.8　　　　　SZ
INTERNATIONAL POTASH INSTITUTE.
CONGRESS PROCEEDINGS. irreg., 13th, 1986,
Bern. International Potash Institute, Postfach, CH-
3048 Worblaufen-Bern, Switzerland.
　　Formerly: International Potash Institute. Congress
Report (ISSN 0074-7505)
Fertilization

338.1　　　　　UK　ISSN 0074-8706
INTERNATIONAL SUGAR ORGANIZATION.
ANNUAL REPORT. a. free. International Sugar
Organization, 28 Haymarket, London SW1Y 4SP,
England.

668.62 631.85　　　UK　ISSN 0074-8714
INTERNATIONAL SUPERPHOSPHATE AND
COMPOUND MANUFACTURERS
ASSOCIATION LIMITED. TECHNICAL
MEETING. PROCEEDINGS.* (Text in English
and French) 1947. biennial. membership (non-
members £ 25) International Superphosphate and
Compound Manufacturers Association Ltd., 121
Gloucester Pl, London W1, England.
　　Issued formerly under previous name of
organization: International Superphosphate
Manufacturers Association. Technical Meeting.
Proceedings.

631.5　　　　　BE　ISSN 0368-9697
INTERNATIONAL SYMPOSIUM ON CROP
PROTECTION. PROCEEDINGS. (Published in
Rijksuniversiteit te Gent. Faculteit
Landbouwwetenschappen. Mededelingen) (Text and
summaries in Dutch, English, French and German)
1948. a., 33th, 1985, Ghent. 2000 Fr.
Rijksuniversiteit te Gent, Faculteit
Landbouwwetenschappen, Coupure Links 536, B-
9000 Ghent, Belgium. circ. 250. Indexed:
Chem.Abstr. Agri.Ind. Helminthol.Abstr.
　　Formerly: International Symposium on Crop
Protection. Communications (ISSN 0074-8803)

631.5　　　　　US　ISSN 0160-7499
IRRIGATION ASSOCIATION. TECHNICAL
CONFERENCE PROCEEDINGS.* 1977. a. $12.
Irrigation Association, 1911 N. Ft. Myer Dr.,
Arlington, VA 22209. Ed. W.D. Anderson. circ. 2,
000. Indexed: Biol.Abstr. Key Title: Technical
Conference Proceedings-Irrigation Association.
　　Formerly: Sprinkler Irrigation Association.
Technical Conference Proceedings.

631　　　　　IT　ISSN 0304-0550
ISTITUTO SPERIMENTALE PER LA
FLORICOLTURA. ANNALI. (Text and summaries
in English and Italian) 1968. a. Istituto Sperimentale
per la Floricoltura, Corso degli Inglesi 508, 18038
Sanremo, Italy. circ. 400. Indexed: Biol.Abstr.

633.61　　　　　JM
JAMAICAN ASSOCIATION OF SUGAR
TECHNOLOGISTS. PROCEEDINGS. 1937. a.
membership. Jamaican Association of Sugar
Technologists, c/o Sugar Industry Research
Institute, Agricultural Division, Mandeville,
Jamaica. Ed. Trevor Falloon. circ. 500.

631　　　　　US　ISSN 0094-2391
JOURNAL OF AGRONOMIC EDUCATION. 1972.
a. $10 non-members; members $8. American
Society of Agronomy, Inc., 677 S. Segoe Rd.,
Madison, WI 53711. TEL 608-274-1212. Ed. W.A.
Anderson. adv. bk. rev. cum.index: vols.1-5 in vol.6.

631　　　　　DK　ISSN 0106-9276
KARTOFFEL-NYT. 1979. irreg. free to libraries.
Kartoffelafgiftsfonden, Tvaerkajen 4, 6700 Esbjerg,
Denmark. TEL 45-5-129-944. circ. 6,000.

631　　　　　KE
KENYA. NATIONAL CEREALS AND PRODUCE
BOARD. ANNUAL REPORT. a. National Cereals
and Produce Board, Nairobi, Kenya.
　　Supersedes: Kenya. Maize and Produce Board.
Report & Kenya. Wheat Board. Report.

631.7　　　　　KE　ISSN 0075-5915
KENYA. NATIONAL IRRIGATION BOARD.
REPORTS AND ACCOUNTS. 1967. irreg; latest
issue, 1973/74. free to recognized institutions.
National Irrigation Board, Lenana Rd., P.O. Box
30372, Nairobi, Kenya.

631　　　　　NE
LISSE. LABORATORIUM VOOR
BLOEMBOLLENONDERZOEK.
JAARVERSLAG. (Text in Dutch; summaries in
English) 1953. a. fl.13. Laboratorium voor
Bloembollenonderzoek, Vennestraat 22, Postbus 85,
2160 AB Lisse, Netherlands. circ. 500. (back issues
avail.) Indexed: Biol.Abstr.

632.9　　　　　UN
LOCUST NEWSLETTER. (Editions in English and
French) 1961. a. free. Food and Agriculture
Organization of the United Nations, Locust Control
and Emergency Operations Group, Distribution and
Sales Section, Via delle Terme di Caracalla, 00100
Rome, Italy.

632.9　　　　　ML　ISSN 0459-6803
LOCUSTA. (Text in English or French) 1954. irreg.
Organisation Internationale Contre le Criquet
Migrateur Africain - International African Migratory
Locust Organization, B.P. 136, Bamako, Mali.

668.65　　　　　US　ISSN 0099-1929
LOUISIANA. DEPARTMENT OF AGRICULTURE.
ANALYSIS OF OFFICIAL PESTICIDE
SAMPLES; ANNUAL REPORT. a. Department of
Agriculture, Box 44345, Capitol Sta., Baton Rouge,
LA 70804. TEL 504-342-7011. Key Title: Analysis
of Official Pesticide Samples.
Agricultural chemistry

631　　　　　FR
MACHINERY - BUSINESS. (Text in English and
French) 1985. a. $6.50. Documentation Agricole, 28
rue Basse, B.P. 629, 59024 Lille, France. circ. 8,000.

MANITOBA CROP INSURANCE
CORPORATION. ANNUAL REPORT. see
INSURANCE

MEGADRILOGICA. see *BIOLOGY — Zoology*

631.7　　　　　CN
MERITE DU DEFRICHEUR. RAPPORT DE
L'ORDRE DU MERITE AGRICOLE.* 1950. a.
free contr. circ. Editeur Officiel du Quebec, 1283
Bd. Charest ouest, Quebec G1N 2C9, Canada. TEL
413-643-3895. Ed. Benoit Roy. circ. 5,000.
　　Formerly: Merite du Defricheur. Rapport de
l'Ordre du Merite du Defricheur (ISSN 0076-6577)

631.4　　　　　US
MONOGRAPHS ON SOIL AND RESOURCES
SURVEY. irreg. price varies. Oxford University
Press, 200 Madison Ave., New York, NY 10016
TEL 212-679-7300. (And Ely House, 37 Dover St.,
London W1X 4AH, England) Ed.Bd.
　　Supersedes: Monographs on Soil Survey.

631　　　　　UN
MUTATION BREEDING NEWSLETTER. (Text in
English) 1972. irreg. free. International Atomic
Energy Agency, Wagramer Strasse 5, Box 100, A-
1400 Vienna, Austria. (Co-sponsor: Food and
Agriculture Organization) circ. 750. Indexed: Plant
Breed.Abstr.

632.9　　　　　PH
N C P C ANNUAL REPORT. 1969. a. free. National
Crop Protection Center, College, Laguna 3720,
Philippines. circ. 2,000. Indexed: Biol.Abstr.
　　Formerly: University of the Phillipines at Los
Banos. Rodent Research Center. Annual Report.

NABOR CARRILLO LECTURE SERIES.
PROCEEDINGS. see *ENGINEERING — Civil
Engineering*

631　　　　　TZ
NATIONAL AGRICULTURAL RESEARCH
PROGRAMME. PROJECT REPORT. (Text in
English) a. Ministry of Agriculture, Crop
Development Division, Box 9071, Dar es Salaam,
Tanzania.
　　Formerly: National Agricultural Research
Programme. Summary of Programmes.

AGRICULTURE — CROP PRODUCTION AND SOIL

638   UK
NATIONAL INSTITUTE OF AGRICULTURAL BOTANY, CAMBRIDGE, ENGLAND. ANNUAL REPORT AND ACCOUNTS. 1919. a. £2.50. National Institute of Agricultural Botany, Huntingdon Rd., Cambridge CB3 0LE, England. circ. 7,000. Indexed: Biol.Abstr. Field Crop Abstr. Herb.Abstr. Weed Abstr.
    Formerly: National Institute of Agricultural Botany, Cambridge, England. Annual Report of the Council and Accounts (ISSN 0077-4782)

631   UK   ISSN 0305-1277
NATIONAL INSTITUTE OF AGRICULTURAL BOTANY, CAMBRIDGE, ENGLAND. FARMERS LEAFLETS. a. price varies. National Institute of Agricultural Botany, Huntington Rd., Cambridge CB3 0LE, England. Indexed: Field Crop Abstr. Herb.Abstr. Plant Breed.Abstr.

630   UK   ISSN 0077-4790
NATIONAL INSTITUTE OF AGRICULTURAL BOTANY, CAMBRIDGE, ENGLAND. JOURNAL. 1922. a. £10. National Institute of Agricultural Botany, Huntingdon Rd., Cambridge CB3 0LE, England. index. circ. 5,000. Indexed: Chem.Abstr. Agri.Eng.Abstr. Field Crop Abstr. Herb.Abstr. Hort.Abstr. Plant Breed.Abstr. Rev.Plant Path. Soils & Fert. Weed Abstr.

631   UK   ISSN 0140-4199
NATIONAL INSTITUTE OF AGRICULTURAL BOTANY, CAMBRIDGE, ENGLAND. TECHNICAL LEAFLETS. 1977. a. price varies. National Institute of Agricultural Botany, Huntingdon Rd., Cambridge CB3 0LE, England.

631   UK   ISSN 0470-1321
NATIONAL INSTITUTE OF AGRICULTURAL BOTANY, CAMBRIDGE, ENGLAND. VEGETABLE GROWERS LEAFLETS. a. price varies. National Institute of Agricultural Botany, Huntingdon Rd., Cambridge CB3 0LE, England.

634   US   ISSN 0092-2633
NATIONAL PEACH COUNCIL. PROCEEDINGS. a. $10. National Peach Council, Box 1085, Martinsburg, WV 25401. TEL 304-267-6024. adv. illus.

631.8   NE   ISSN 0169-2313
NETHERLANDS FERTILIZER TECHNICAL BULLETIN. (Text in English) 1966. irreg., no.16, 1986. free. Nederlandse Meststoffen Instituut, Landbouwkundig Bureau - Netherlands Fertilizer Institute, Zoutmanstraat 44, 2518 GS The Hague, Netherlands. Ed. P.F.J. van Burg. bk. rev. circ. 1,000. Indexed: Biol.Abstr.
    Formerly: Netherlands Nitrogen Technical Bulletin (ISSN 0077-7595)

338.1   US   ISSN 0098-9541
NEW JERSEY ORCHARD AND VINEYARD SURVEY. irreg., approx. quinquennial. Crop Reporting Service, Rm. 204, Health and Agriculture Bldg., Trenton, NJ 08625. TEL 609-292-6385. illus.

631   AT   ISSN 0705-470X
NEW SOUTH WALES. DEPARTMENT OF AGRICULTURE. SOIL SURVEY BULLETIN. 1954. irreg. price varies. Department of Agriculture, PMB 10, Rydalmere, N.S.W. 2116, Australia. circ. 500.

633   US   ISSN 0276-8798
NEW YORK AGRICULTURAL STATISTICS. a. free. ‡ New York Crop Reporting Service, c/o Department of Agriculture and Markets, Albany, NY 12235. circ. 2,800.

631.4   NZ   ISSN 0304-1735
NEW ZEALAND. SOIL BUREAU. SCIENTIFIC REPORT. 1971. irreg. price varies. Soil Bureau, Private Bag, Lower Hutt, New Zealand. bibl. Indexed: Biol.Abstr. GeoRef.

630 627   NZ   ISSN 0077-9520
NEW ZEALAND AGRICULTURAL ENGINEERING INSTITUTE. ANNUAL REPORT. 1965/66. a. free. New Zealand Agricultural Engineering Institute, Lincoln College, Canterbury, New Zealand.
    Agricultural engineering

NOGAKU KENKYU. see BIOLOGY

631.4   US   ISSN 0078-1320
NORTH AMERICAN FOREST SOILS CONFERENCE. PROCEEDINGS. 1958. quinquennial. $23. Society of American Foresters, 5400 Grosvenor Ln., Bethesda, MD 20814. TEL 301-897-8720. (Co-sponsors: Soil Science Society of Canada; Canadian Institute of Forestry) (also avail. in microform from UMI) Indexed: Forest.Abstr. Forest Prod.Abstr.

630.24 668.6   US   ISSN 0065-4418
NORTH CAROLINA AGRICULTURAL CHEMICALS MANUAL. 1948. a. $7.50. North Carolina State University, School of Agriculture-Life Sciences, Box 7603, Raleigh, NC 27695. TEL 919-737-3173. index. circ. 5,000.
    Agricultural chemistry

631   US   ISSN 0078-1703
NORTHEASTERN WEED SCIENCE SOCIETY. PROCEEDINGS. 1946. a. $20 ($4 for supplement) Northeastern Weed Science Society, c/o R.A. Ashley, Sec.-Treas., Plant Science Dept.,U-67, University of Connecticut, Storrs, CT 06268. TEL 203-486-3435. Ed. B. Morose. index. circ. 700. Indexed: Biol.Abstr. Chem.Abstr.
    Formerly: Northeastern Weed Control Conference.

634   CN   ISSN 0078-2386
NOVA SCOTIA FRUIT GROWERS ASSOCIATION. ANNUAL REPORT AND PROCEEDINGS. 1874. a. Can.$12. Nova Scotia Fruit Growers Association, Kentville, N.S., Canada. adv. circ. 500. Indexed: Chem.Abstr. Hort.Abstr.

631 551   CN
ONTARIO INSTITUTE OF PEDOLOGY. DEPARTMENT OF LAND RESOURCE SCIENCE. PROGRESS REPORT. 1955. irreg. Ontario Institute of Pedology, Department of Land Resource Science, Blackwood Hall, University of Guelph, Guelph, Ont. N1G 2W1, Canada. TEL 519-824-4120. circ. 2,000.

OSSERVATORIO REGIONALE PER LE MALATTIE DELLA VITE. OSSERVAZIONI DI METEOROLOGIA, FENOLOGIA E PATOLOGIA DELLA VITE. see BIOLOGY — Botany

631.5   PK   ISSN 0078-7930
PAKISTAN CENTRAL COTTON COMMITTEE. AGRICULTURAL SURVEY REPORT.* (Text in English) no.2, 1960. irreg. Pakistan Central Cotton Committee, Secretary, Moulvi Tamizuddin Khan Rd., Karachi 1, Pakistan.

631.5   PK   ISSN 0078-7949
PAKISTAN CENTRAL COTTON COMMITTEE. TECHNOLOGICAL BULLETIN. SERIES A.* (Head of title: Pakistan Institute of Cotton Research and Technology) (Text in English) 1960. irreg. Pakistan Central Cotton Committee, Secretary, Moulvi Tamizuddin Khan Rd., Karachi 1, Pakistan.

631.5   PK   ISSN 0078-7957
PAKISTAN CENTRAL COTTON COMMITTEE. TECHNOLOGICAL BULLETIN. SERIES B.* (Head of Title: Pakistan Institute of Cotton Research and Technology) (Text in English) 1959. irreg. Pakistan Central Cotton Committee, Secretary, Moulvi Tamizuddin Khan Rd., Karachi 1, Pakistan.

631.4   GE   ISSN 0031-4056
PEDOBIOLOGIA. (Text in English, French, German and Russian; summaries in English) 1961. irreg.(6-12/yr) M.180 per vol. VEB Gustav Fischer Verlag, Villengang 2, Postfach 176, 6900 Jena, E. Germany (D.D.R.) Ed. E. von Toerne. bk. rev. bibl. charts. illus. tr.lit. index. (reprint service avail. from ISI) Indexed: Biol.Abstr. Chem.Abstr. Curr.Cont. Excerp.Med. Forest.Abstr. Forest Prod.Abstr. Geo.Abstr. Helminthol.Abstr. Soils & Fert.

631.4   FR   ISSN 0378-181X
PEDOFAUNA. (Text in English, French, and German) 1964 N.S. irreg. 200 Fr. for 3 years. International Society of Soil Science, Sub-Commission D, Centre National de Recherche Scientifique, 4 Av. du Petit Chateau, F-91800 Brunoy, France, Belgium. Ed. George Wauthy. bk. rev. circ. 500. Indexed: Soils & Fert.
    Formerly (until vol.23, 1976): Biologie du Sol (ISSN 0067-8805)

338.1   US   ISSN 0079-046X
PENNSYLVANIA CROP AND LIVESTOCK ANNUAL SUMMARY. a. free. Crop Reporting Service, 2301 N. Cameron St., Harrisburg, PA 17120. TEL 717-787-3904. circ. 5,000.
    Formerly: Pennsylvania Crop Reporting Service. C.R.S. (ISSN 0079-0478); Incorporates: Pennsylvania's Machinery Custom Rates.

631   US
PEOPLE, FOOD & LAND. 1974. a. $15 (includes monthly bulletin) People, Food & Land Foundation, 35751 Oak Spring Dr., Tollhouse, CA 93677. TEL 209-855-3710. Ed. George Ballis. bk. rev. circ. 1, 150.

632.9   US   ISSN 0092-6752
PESTICIDES (SACRAMENTO) 1921. a. Department of Food and Agriculture, Pesticides Enforcement, 1220 N St., Sacramento, CA 95814. TEL 916-445-9280. circ. 1,200. Indexed: PROMT. Rev.Appl.Entomol.
    Formerly: Economic Poisons.

632.9   II
PESTICIDES ANNUAL. (Text in English) a. Rs.60. Colour Publications Pvt. Ltd., 126-A Dhuruwadi, Off Dr. Nariman Rd., Bombay 400025, India. illus.

632.9 664   DK   ISSN 0108-2086
PESTICIDRESTER I DANSKE LEVNEDSMIDLER/PESTICIDE RESIDUES IN DANISH FOOD. (Text in English and Danish) 1983. biennial. Kr.70. Miljoeministeriet, Levnedsmiddelstyrelsen, Moerkhoej Bygade 19, DK-2860 Soeborg, Denmark (Orders to: Danske Boghandleres Kommissionsanstalt, Siljangade 6, 2300 Copenhagen S, Denmark) circ. 600. Indexed: Chem.Abstr.
    Formerly: Rapport over Pesticidrester i Danske Levnedsmidler.

354.599   PH
PHILIPPINE COCONUT AUTHORITY. AGRICULTURAL RESEARCH DEPARTMENT. ANNUAL REPORT. (Text in English) 1974. a. Philippine Coconut Authority, Agricultural Research Department, Box 295, Davao, Philippines. illus. stat. circ. 500.

631   IS   ISSN 0334-2123
PHYTOPARASITICA: ISRAEL JOURNAL OF PLANT PROTECTION SCIENCES. 1973. irreg. (3-4/yr.) $65. (Phytopathological Society of Israel) Agricultural Research Foundation (Subsidiary of: Scientific Publications) Volcani Centre, P.O. Box 6, Bet Dagan, Israel. (Co-sponsor: Weed Science Society of Israel) Ed. Vivian R. Priel. index. circ. 500. Indexed: Biol.Abstr. Chem.Abstr. Curr.Cont. Excerp.Med. Biotech.Abstr. Field Crop Abstr. Helminthol.Abstr. Herb.Abstr. Hort.Abstr. Rev.Appl.Entomol. Rev.Plant Path. Soils & Fert. VITIS. Weed Abstr.

632   IT
PHYTOPHAGA. (Text in Italian; summaries in English, French and Italian) 1955. biennial. Universita degli Studi di Palermo, Istituto di Entomologia Agraria, Viale delle Scienze, 90128 Palermo, Italy.
    Formerly (until 1983): Universita degli Studi di Palermo. Istituto di Entomologia Agraria. Bollettino (ISSN 0078-8619)

631 663 340   BL
PLANO DA SAFRA ACUCAR E ALCOOL. irreg. Instituto do Acucar e do Alcool, Praca Quinze de Novembro 42, Rio de Janeiro, Brazil. (Affiliate: Brazil. Ministerio da Industria e do Comercio)
    Laws and regulations governing sugar and alcohol

631.5   UK   ISSN 0079-2225
PLANT BREEDING INSTITUTE, CAMBRIDGE. ANNUAL REPORT. 1959. a. £5. Plant Breeding Institute, Trumpington, Cambridge, England. Ed.Bd. circ. 1,000. (also avail. in microfiche) Indexed: Plant Breed.Abstr. Weed Abstr.

631 595.7   RH
PLANT PROTECTION RESEARCH INSTITUTE. ANNUAL REPORT. a. free. Ministry of Lands, Agriculture and Rural Resettlement, Research and Specialist Services, Information Services, Box 8108, Causeway, Harare, Zimbabwe. circ. 250. (back issues avail.) Indexed: Biol.Abstr.

AGRICULTURE — CROP PRODUCTION AND SOIL

630 635   CH
PLANT PROTECTION SOCIETY OF THE REPUBLIC OF CHINA. ANNUAL REPORT. (Text in English) 1973. a. Plant Protection Society of the Republic of China, Plant Protection Center, 189 Chung Cheng Rd., Wufeng, Taichung Hsien, Taiwan 431, Republic of China.

631   DK   ISSN 0106-8113
PLANTEAVLSARBEJDET I DE LANDOEKONOMISKE FORENINGER. (Text in Danish) 1979. a. Kr.75. Landssekontoret for Planteavl, Kongsgaardsvej 28, 8260 Viby J., Denmark.
    Formerly: Planteavlsarbejdet i Landbo- og Husmandsforeningerne.

632.9   DK   ISSN 0108-4887
PLANTEBESKYTTELSEMIDLER; anerkendt til bekaempelse af plantesygdomme og skadedyr. 1977. a. Kr.15 to individuals; free to institutions. Statens Planteavlsforsoeg, Kongevejen 83, 2800 Lyngby, Denmark (Subscr. to: Statens Plantevaernscenter, Institut for Pesticider, Lottenborgvej 2, 2800 Lyngby, Denmark)

631   DK   ISSN 0109-3312
PLANTEVAERN I LANDBRUGET. 1984. a. Kr.30.50. Landbrugets Informationskontor, Greve Strand, Denmark. circ. 8,000.
    Formerly: Gule Oversigt.

631   US   ISSN 0730-2207
PLANTING BREEDING REVIEWS. 1983. a. $54. (American Society for Horticultural Science) A V I Publishing Company, 250 Post Rd. East, Box 831, Westport, CT 06881. TEL 203-226-0738. (Co-sponsors: Crop Science Society of America; Society of American Foresters; National Council of Plant Breeders) Ed. Jules Janick. cum.index 1982-1986. circ. 1,200.

631.4   PL   ISSN 0079-2985
POLISH JOURNAL OF SOIL SCIENCE. (Text in English; summaries in Polish and Russian) 1968. irreg., vol.14, 1983. price varies. (Polska Akademia Nauk, Komitet Gleboznawstwa i Chemii Rolnej) Panstwowe Wydawnictwo Naukowe, Ul. Miodowa 10, 00-251 Warsaw, Poland (Dist. by: Ars Polona, Krakowskie Przedmiescie 7, 00-068 Warsaw, Poland) Ed. B. Dobrzanski. bibl. charts. illus. Indexed: Biol.Abstr. Chem.Abstr. Excerp.Med. Field Crop Abstr. Herb.Abstr. Soils & Fert. Weed Abstr.

631 581   JA   ISSN 0386-6688
POLLEN SCIENCE. (Text in Japanese; summaries in English) 1971. a. 3.000 Yen. Pollen Science Group Kyoto, c/o Sanji Ichikawa, 83, Iwakura Ohosagi-Chyo, Sakyo-Ku, Kyoto City 606, Japan. circ. 200.

POTATO MARKETING BOARD, LONDON. ANNUAL REPORT AND ACCOUNTS. see AGRICULTURE — Agricultural Economics

631.5   IS
PROFITABILITY OF CITRUS GROWING IN ISRAEL/HA-RIVHIYUT SHEL GIDUL HADARIM. (Issued as the Institute's Publications. Series F) (Text in Hebrew) 1968/69. irreg. IS.45($3) Institute of Farm Income Research, 6 Hachashmonaim Blvd., Tel-Aviv 67018, Israel.

631.5   IS   ISSN 0079-595X
PROFITABILITY OF COTTON GROWING IN ISRAEL/HA-RIVHIYUT SHEL GIDUL HA-KUTNAH. (Issued as the Institute's Publications. Series C) (Text in Hebrew) 1964/65. irreg. IS.45($3) per issue. Institute of Farm Income Research, 6 Hachashmonaim Blvd., Tel-Aviv 67018, Israel.

631   BL   ISSN 0100-526X
PROGNOSTICO. (Text in Portuguese) 1972. a. Instituto de Economia Agricola, Av. Miguel Stefano, CEP 04301, Sao Paulo S.P., Brazil. stat. circ. controlled.
    Formerly: Prognostico da Agricultura Paulista.

631.5   BL   ISSN 0100-5316
PROGNOSTICO REGIAO CENTRO-SUL. (Text in Portuguese) 1974. a. exchange basis. Instituto de Economia Agricola, Av. Miguel Estefano 3900, CEP 04301, Sao Paulo SP, Brazil. stat. circ. controlled.

631.8   US   ISSN 0730-7322
PROGRESS (MUSCLE SHOALS) 1966. a. free. Tennessee Valley Authority, National Fertilizer Development Center, Muscle Shoals, AL 35660. TEL 205-386-2915. circ. 8,000. Indexed: Amer.Stat.Ind. Rural Recreat.Tour.Abstr. Soils & Fert. World Agri.Econ.& Rural Sociol.Abstr.
    Former titles: National Fertilizer Development Center. Annual Report (ISSN 0077-4510) & Tennessee Valley Authority. Agricultural and Chemical Development Annual Report.

630   PL   ISSN 0079-7154
PRZEGLAD NAUKOWEJ LITERATURY ROLNICZEJ I LESNEJ; gleboznawstwo, chemia rolna, ogolna uprawa roli i roslin i siedliska lesne. 1955. a. price varies. (Polskie Towarzystwo Gleboznawcze) Panstwowe Wydawnictwo Naukowe, Miodowa 10, 00-251 Warsaw, Poland (Dist. by: Ars Polona, Krakowskie Przedmiescie 7, 00-068 Warsaw, Poland) Ed. W. Trzcinski. circ. 1,210.

631   NE
RASSENLIJST VOOR FRUITGEWASSEN. quinquennial. fl.12.50. (Rijksinstituut voor het Rassenonderzoek van Cultuurgewassen) B.V. Drukkerijen Uitgeverij Leiter-Nypels, Postbus 831, 6200 AV Maasticht, Netherlands. TEL 043-11055. Ed.Bd.

631   NE
RASSENLIJST VOOR GROENTEGEWASSEN: GLASGROENTEN. vol.32, 1983. a. fl.13.75. (Rijksinstituut voor het Ressenonderzoek van Cultuurgewassen) B.V. Drukkerij en Uitgeverij Leiter-Nypels, Postbus 831, 6200 AV Maasticht, Netherlands. Ed.Bd.

631   NE
RASSENLIJST VOOR GROENTEGEWASSEN: VOLLEGRONDSGROENTEN. vol.32, 1983. a. fl.14. (Rijksinstituut voor het Rassenonderzoek van Cultuurgewassen) B.V. Drukkerijen Uitgeverij Leiter-Nypels, Postbus 831, 6200 AV Maasticht, Netherlands. Ed.Bd.

631   IO
RESEARCH INSTITUTE FOR ESTATE CROPS, BOGOR. COCOA STATISTICS/BALAI PENELITIAN PERKEBUNAN, BOGOR. STATISTIK COKLAT. (Text in Indonesian and English) 1969. a. Rps.2000. Research Institute for Estate Crops - Balai Penelitian Perkebunan Bogor, Jl. Taman Kencana 1, Box 81, Bogor, Indonesia. (Co-sponsor: Central Bureau for Statistics) circ. 1, 000. Indexed: Hort.Abstr. RAPRA. Trop.Abstr.

631 315   IO
RESEARCH INSTITUTE FOR ESTATE CROPS, BOGOR. COFFEE STATISTICS/BALAI PENELITIAN PERKEBUNAN, BOGOR. STATISTIK KOPI. (Text in Indonesian and English) 1968. a. Rps.2000. Research Institute for Estate Crops - Balai Penelitian Perkebunan Bogor, Jl. Taman Kencana 1, Box 81, Bogor, Indonesia. (Co-sponsor: Central Bureau for Statistics) circ. 1, 000. Indexed: Hort.Abstr. RAPRA. Trop.Abstr.

631   IO
RESEARCH INSTITUTE FOR ESTATE CROPS, BOGOR. COMMUNICATIONS. (Text in English) 1971. irreg. Research Institute for Estate Crops - Balai Penelitian Perkebunan Bogor, Jl. Taman Kencana 1, Box 81, Bogor, Indonesia. Indexed: Hort.Abstr. RAPRA. Trop.Abstr.

631 315   IO
RESEARCH INSTITUTE FOR ESTATE CROPS, BOGOR. RUBBER STATISTICS/BALAI PENELITIAN PERKEBUNAN, BOGOR. STATISTIK KARET. (Text in Indonesian and English) 1968. a. Rps.2000. Research Institute for Estate Crops - Balai Penelitian Perkebunan Bogor, Jl. Taman Kencana 1, Box 81, Bogor, Indonesia. (Co-sponsor: Central Bureau for Statistics) circ. 1, 000. Indexed: Hort.Abstr. RAPRA. Trop.Abstr.

633   NE
RIJKSINSTITUUT VOOR HET RASSENONDERZOEK VAN CULTUURGEWASSEN. JAARVERSLAG. 1955. a. free. Rijksinstituut voor het Rassenonderzoek van Cultuurgewassen - Government Institute for Research on Varieties of Cultivated Plants, Postbus 32, 6700 AA Wageningen, Netherlands. circ. 230.
    Formerly: Instituut voor Rassenonderzoek van Landbouwgewassen. Jaarverslag (ISSN 0168-9843)

633   NE
RIJKSINSTITUUT VOOR HET RASSENONDERZOEK VAN CULTUURGEWASSEN. MEDEDELINGEN. (Text and summaries in Dutch, English, French or German) 1949. irreg., no.85, 1985. free. Rijksinstituut voor het Rassenonderzoek van Cultuurgewassen - Government Institute for Research on Varieties of Cultivated Plants, Postbus 32, 6700 AA Wageningen, Netherlands. circ. 2,500.
    Formerly: Instituut voor Rassenonderzoek van Landbouwgewassen. Mededelingen (ISSN 0080-3065)

633 635   PL   ISSN 0080-3650
ROCZNIKI NAUK ROLNICZYCH. SERIA A. PRODUKCJA ROSLINNA. (Text in Polish; summaries in English, Polish, Russian) 1903. irreg., vol.106, 1984. price varies. (Polska Akademia Nauk, Komitet Uprawy Roslin) Panstwowe Wydawnictwo Naukowe, Miodowa 10, 00-251 Warsaw, Poland (Dist. by: Ars Polona, Krakowskie Przedmiescie 7, 00-068 Warsaw, Poland) Ed. L. Smierzchalski. bibl. charts. circ. 750. Indexed: Biol.Abstr. Chem.Abstr. Excerp.Med. Nutr.Abstr. Field Crop Abstr. Helminthol.Abstr. Herb.Abstr. Hort.Abstr. Rev.Appl.Entomol. Rev.Plant Path. Soils & Fert.

632.9   PL   ISSN 0080-3693
ROCZNIKI NAUK ROLNICZYCH. SERIA E. OCHRONA ROSLIN. (Text mainly in Polish, occasionally in English; summaries in English and Russian) 1970. irreg., vol.10, 1983. price varies. (Polska Akademia Nauk, Komitet Ochrony Roslin) Panstwowe Wydawnictwo Naukowe, Ul. Miodowa 10, 00-251 Warsaw, Poland (Dist. by: Ars Polona, Krakowskie Przedmiescie 7, 00-068 Warsaw, Poland) Ed. Wladyslaw Wegorek. bibl. charts. illus. circ. 610. Indexed: Helminthol.Abstr. Plant Breed.Abstr. Rev.Appl.Entomol. Soils & Fert.

631.4   PL   ISSN 0080-3707
ROCZNIKI NAUK ROLNICZYCH. SERIA F. MELIORACJI I VZYTKOW ZIELONYCH. (Text in Polish; summaries in English and Russian) 1903. irreg., vol.80, 1980. price varies. (Polska Akademia Nauk, Komitet Melioracji) Panstwowe Wydawnictwo Naukowe, Miodowa 10, 00-251 Warsaw, Poland (Dist. by: Ars Polona, Krakowskie Przedmiescie 7, 00-068 Warsaw, Poland) Ed. Jerzy Ostromecki. bibl. Indexed: Nutr.Abstr. Field Crop Abstr. Herb.Abstr. Plant Breed.Abstr. Rev.Plant Path. Soils & Fert.

631 574.192   UK   ISSN 0262-1215
ROTHAMSTED EXPERIMENTAL STATION. REPORT. 1908. a. £10. Rothamsted Experimental Station, Harpenden, Herts AL5 2JQ, England. Ed. Judith Palmer. circ. 2,000. (back issues avail.) Indexed: Biol.Abstr. Helminthol.Abstr.

631.4   US   ISSN 0081-1904
S S S A SPECIAL PUBLICATION SERIES. 1967. irreg., no.14, 1984. price varies. Soil Science Society of America, 677 S. Segoe Rd., Madison, WI 53711. TEL 608-273-8080. (Affiliate: American Society of Agronomy) Indexed: Biol.Abstr. GeoRef.

631   FR
SEED - BUSINESS. (Text in English and French) 1984. a. $6.50. Documentation Agricole, 28 rue Basse, B.P. 629, 59024 Lille, France. circ. 8,000.

631.5   US   ISSN 0080-8504
SEED TRADE BUYER'S GUIDE. 1917. a. $10. Scranton Gillette Communications, Inc., 380 Northwest Highway, Des Plaines, IL 60016. TEL 312-298-6622. Ed. Laura L. King. adv. circ. 3,900. (also avail. in microform from UMI)

633.6   CU
SERIE CANA DE AZUCAR.* (Text in Spanish; summaries in English) 1967. irreg. exchange. Academia de Ciencias de Cuba, Instituto de Investigaciones de la Cana de Azucar, Avda. Van Troi No. 17203, Rancho Boyeros, Cuba. illus. circ. 5,000. (back issues avail.)

SITUATION DE LA VITICULTURE DANS LE MONDE. see BEVERAGES

631   MW
SMALLHOLDER TEA AUTHORITY. ANNUAL REPORT. 1968. a. Smallholder Tea Authority, Box 80, Thyolo, Malawi. circ. controlled.

AGRICULTURE — CROP PRODUCTION AND SOIL

632   JA   ISSN 0081-170X
SOCIETY OF PLANT PROTECTION OF NORTH JAPAN. ANNUAL REPORT/KITANIHON BYOGAICHU KENKYUKAI KAIHO. (Summaries in English) 1950. a. 2000 Yen($1.50) Society of Plant Protection of North Japan - Kita Nihon Byogaichu Kenkyukai, c/o Tohoku National Agricultural Experiment Station, 3 Shimofurumichi, Yotsuya, Omagari 014-01, Japan. Ed. Hiroshi Kagawa. adv. cum.index 1950-1959, 1960-1969. Indexed: Chem.Abstr. Helminthol.Abstr. Rev.Plant Path.

631.4   US
SOIL AND CROP SOCIETY OF FLORIDA. ANNUAL PROCEEDINGS. a. University of Florida, Institute of Food and Agricultural Sciences, Soil and Crop Science Society of Florida, 304 Newell Hall, Gainesville, FL 32611. Ed. E.S. Horner. Indexed: Biol.Abstr. Chem.Abstr. Excerp.Med. ASCA. Geo.Abstr. GeoRef. Helminthol.Abstr.

631.4   CE
SOIL SCIENCE SOCIETY OF SRI LANKA. JOURNAL. (Text in English) 1970. a. Rs.40($2) Soil Science Society of Sri Lanka, Faculty of Agriculture, University of Sri Lanka, Peradeniya, Sri Lanka. Ed. R.B. Mapa. adv. bk. rev. circ. 150. Indexed: Sri Lanka Sci.Ind.
Formerly: Soil Science Society of Ceylon. Journal.

631.4   AT   ISSN 0081-1912
SOILS AND LAND USE SERIES. 1949. irreg. Aus.$5 per issue. C.S.I.R.O., Division of Soils, Private Bag No. 2, Glen Osmond, S.A. 5064, Australia (Subscr. to: CSIRO, Editorial & Publications Service, Box 89, East Melbourne, Vic. 3002, Australia) circ. 700. Indexed: Biol.Abstr. Soils & Fert.

631.4   AT
SOILS NEWS. 1957? irreg. Australian Society of Soil Science, c/o G. J. Hamilton, Ed., Soil Conservation Service, P.O. Box 249, Cowra, N.S.W. 2794, Australia. bk. rev. circ. 700.

631   UN
SOILS NEWSLETTER. (Text in English) 1978. irreg. free. International Atomic Energy Agency, Wagramer Strasse 5, Box 100, A-1400 Vienna, Austria. (Co-sponsor: Food and Agriculture Organization) circ. 450.

631   SA   ISSN 0375-2682
SOUTH AFRICAN SUGAR ASSOCIATION EXPERIMENT STATION. ANNUAL REPORT. (Text in Afrikaans and English) a. free. South African Sugar Association Experiment Station, Mount Edgecombe, Natal 4300, South Africa. illus. circ. 3,000. (back issues avail.)

631   SA
SOUTH AFRICAN SUGAR ASSOCIATION EXPERIMENT STATION. BULLETIN. (Text in English) irreg. free. South African Sugar Association Experiment Station, Mount Edgecombe, Natal 4300, South Africa. charts. illus. circ. 3,000. (back issues avail.)

630.24   US   ISSN 0362-4463
SOUTHERN WEED SCIENCE SOCIETY. PROCEEDINGS. a. $15. Southern Weed Science Society, c/o Claude J. Cruse, 309 W. Clark St., Champaign, IL 61820. TEL 217-356-3182. Indexed: Biol.Abstr. Hort.Abstr. Soils & Fert. Weed Abstr.

633   US   ISSN 0275-4509
SOYA BLUEBOOK. 1947. a. $25. ‡ American Soybean Association, Box 27300, St. Louis, MO 63141. TEL 314-432-1600. Ed. Carole Clow. adv. charts. stat. circ. 2,500. (also avail. in microfilm; back issues avail.)
Formerly (until 1980): Soybean Digest Blue Book (ISSN 0081-3222)

633   SP
SPAIN. DIRECCION GENERAL DE LA PRODUCCION AGRARIA. CAMPANA ALGODONERA. irreg. Ministerio de Agricultura, Direccion General de la Produccion Agraria, Madrid, Spain.

631 614.7   UK   ISSN 0561-6832
SPORTS TURF RESEARCH INSTITUTE. JOURNAL. 1929. a. £14. Sports Turf Research Institute, Bingley, West Yorkshire BD16 1AU, England. adv. bk. rev. index. circ. 4,500. (back issues avail.) Indexed: Biol.Abstr.

SPRENGER INSTITUUT. COMMUNICATIONS. see FOOD AND FOOD INDUSTRIES

SPRENGER INSTITUUT. JAARVERSLAG/ ANNUAL REPORT. see FOOD AND FOOD INDUSTRIES

631   DK   ISSN 0105-6514
STATENS PLANTEAVLSFORSOEG. MEDDELELSE. (Text in Danish) 1898. irreg., no.87, 1985. Kr.105. Ministry of Agriculture, Danish Research Service on Plant and Soil Science, Information Service, Lottenborgvej 2, DK-2800 Lynby, Denmark. Ed. O. Wagn. circ. 8,000.

631   DK   ISSN 0106-8598
STATSFROEKONTROLLEN. BERETNING. (Text in Danish, summaries in English) 1886. a. free. (Ministry of Agriculture) EF Direktoratet, Frederiksborgade 18, 1360 Copenhagen, Denmark. TEL 02 88 33 66. Ed. Erik Madsen. stat. (Back issues avail.)

631.8   GW   ISSN 0081-5535
DER STICKSTOFF. 1963. irreg. free. Fachverband Stickstoffindustrie, Sternstr. 9-11, 4000 Duesseldorf 1, W. Germany (B.R.D.) Ed. Helmut Nieder. circ. 10,000.
Fertilizers

631   BE
SUCRERIE BELGE. (Text in French) 1872. a. Societe Generale des Fabricants de Sucre de Belgique, 182 av. Tervuren, 1150 Brussels, Belgium. (Co-sponsor: Societe Technique et Chimique de Sucrerie de Belgique) Ed. R. Hulpiau. adv. circ. 1, 200. Indexed: Chem.Abstr. Excerp.Med. Nutr.Abstr. Field Crop Abstr. Herb.Abstr.

631   SJ   ISSN 0562-5068
SUDAN COTTON REVIEW. (Text in English) 1958. a. Cotton Public Corporation, Box 1672, Khartoum, Sudan.

630   PL   ISSN 0082-1276
SZCZECINSKIE TOWARZYSTWO NAUKOWE. WYDZIAL NAUK PRZYRODNICZO- ROLNICZYCH. PRACE. (Text in Polish; summaries in English, German and Russian) 1959. irreg. price varies. Szczecinskie Towarzystwo Naukowe, Wydzial Nauk Przyrodniczo-Rolniczych, Rycerska 3, 70-537 Szczecin, Poland (Dist. by: Ars Polona-Ruch, Krakowskie Przedmiescie 7, Warsaw, Poland) Indexed: Biol.Abstr.

631   DK
TABELBILAG TIL LANDSFORSOEGENE; forsoeg og undersoegelser i de landoekonomiske foreninger. 1979. a. Kr.35. Landsudvalget for Planteavl, Kongaardsvej 28, 8260 Viby J., Denmark.

633   CH
TAIWAN SUGAR RESEARCH INSTITUTE. ANNUAL REPORT. (Text in English) a. Taiwan Sugar Research Institute, Tai-Wan Tang Yeh Yen Chiu So, Tainan, Taiwan, Republic of China. illus. Indexed: Biol.Abstr. Excerp.Med. Field Crop Abstr. Herb.Abstr. Hort.Abstr. Plant Breed Abstr. Rev.Plant Path.

631   II   ISSN 0082-1586
TAMIL NADU. DEPARTMENT OF STATISTICS. SEASON AND CROP REPORT. (Text in English) 1902/03. a. Rs.5. Director of Statistics, Madras 600006, India (Subscription to: Government Publication Depot, 166 Anna Road, Madras 600006, India)

631.5   GW   ISSN 0082-1799
TASCHENBUCH DER PFLANZENARZTES. 1951. a. DM.32. Landwirtschaftsverlag GmbH, Huelsebrockstr. 2, Postfach 480249, 4400 Muenster-Hiltrup, W. Germany (B.R.D.)

632.9 595.7   AT
TASMANIA. DEPARTMENT OF AGRICULTURE. INSECT PEST SURVEY. 1969. a. free to institutions. Tasmanian Department of Agriculture, Entomology Section, G.P.O. Box 192B, Hobart 7001, Tasmania, Australia. Ed. A. Terauds. circ. 150. Indexed: Biol.Abstr.

TEA RESEARCH ASSOCIATION. MEMORANDUM. see *BEVERAGES*

TEA RESEARCH ASSOCIATION. OCCASIONAL SCIENTIFIC PAPERS. see *BEVERAGES*

TEA RESEARCH ASSOCIATION. TOCKLAI EXPERIMENTAL STATION. SCIENTIFIC ANNUAL REPORT. see *BEVERAGES*

631   MG   ISSN 0563-1637
TERRE MALGACHE/TANY MALAGASY. (Text in French) 1967. irreg., no.20, 1980. FMG.2000. Universite de Madagascar, Etablissement d'Enseignement Superieur des Sciences Agronomiques, B.P. 175, Antananarivo, Malagasy Republic. charts. illus. stat. circ. 1,500. Indexed: Curr.Cont.Africa.

633   US   ISSN 0092-153X
TEXAS FIELD CROP STATISTICS. (Subseries of Texas. Dept. of Agriculture. Bulletin) 1968. a. free. Department of Agriculture, P.O. Box 12847, Austin, TX 78711. TEL 512-475-6346. charts. illus. mkt. stats. circ. 3,600.

631.8   TH   ISSN 0085-7246
THAILAND. DIVISION OF AGRICULTURAL CHEMISTRY. REPORT ON FERTILIZER EXPERIMENTS AND SOIL FERTILITY RESEARCH.* (Text in English) 1966. irreg. Ministry of Agriculture, Division of Agricultural Chemistry, Bangkok 9, Thailand.

354.54   II
TOBACCO EXPORT PROMOTION COUNCIL. ANNUAL REPORT AND ACCOUNTS. (Text in English) a. Tobacco Export Promotion Council, World Trade Centre, 123-C Mount Rd., Madras 600006, India. stat.

620.24 668.6   JA   ISSN 0563-8313
TOKYO UNIVERSITY OF AGRICULTURE & TECHNOLOGY. ANNUAL REPORT. (Text in English and Japanese) 1949. biennial. on exchange. Tokyo University of Agriculture and Technology, Fuchu-shi, Tokyo, Japan.

631   MW
TREE NUT AUTHORITY. REPORT. (Text in English) 1970. a. Tree Nut Authority, Box 950, Blantyre, Malawi. stat.
Supersedes: Tung Board. Annual Report.

631 581 664   UK
TROPICAL DEVELOPMENT & RESEARCH INSTITUTE. CROP AND PRODUCT SERIES. 1971. irreg. price varies. Tropical Development & Research Institute, c/o Mrs. Sue Black, College House, Wrights Lane, London W8 5SJ, England. Indexed: Biol.Abstr.

632   TZ   ISSN 0082-6642
TROPICAL PESTICIDES RESEARCH INSTITUTE. ANNUAL REPORT. 1957. a. available on exchange basis. Tropical Pesticides Research Institute, P.O. Box 3024, Arusha, Tanzania. Indexed: Biol.Abstr. Hort.Abstr. Rev.Appl.Entomol. Rev.Plant Path.

633   US   ISSN 0363-8561
U.S. CROP REPORTING BOARD. CROP PRODUCTION. m. with annual summary. $30 for 16 nos. U.S. Crop Reporting Board, Washington, DC 20250 TEL 202-655-4000. (Subscr. to: Supt. of Documents, Washington, DC 20540) Key Title: Crop Production.
●Also available online. Vendors: DIALOG.

632   US   ISSN 0083-0518
U.S. ENVIRONMENTAL PROTECTION AGENCY. PESTICIDES ENFORCEMENT DIVISION. NOTICES OF JUDGEMENT UNDER FEDERAL INSECTICIDE, FUNGICIDE, AND RODENTICIDE ACT. (Publication EN-342) irreg. free. U.S. Environmental Protection Agency, M St. N.W., Washington, DC 20460.

631.4   US   ISSN 0083-3304
U.S. SOIL CONSERVATION SERVICE. NATIONAL ENGINEERING HANDBOOK. irreg. U.S. Soil Conservation Service, c/o Dept. of Agriculture, Box 2890, Washington, DC 20013. TEL 202-447-4543. (also avail. in microfiche)

AGRICULTURE — DAIRYING AND DAIRY PRODUCTS

631.4 US ISSN 0083-3320
U.S. SOIL CONSERVATION SERVICE. SOIL SURVEY INVESTIGATION REPORTS. 1967. irreg. U.S. Soil Conservation Service, Department of Agriculture, Box 2890, Washington, DC 20013. TEL 202-447-4543. Indexed: GeoRef.

631.4 US ISSN 0083-3339
U.S. SOIL CONSERVATION SERVICE. TECHNICAL PUBLICATIONS. irreg. U.S. Soil Conservation Service, U.S. Dept. of Agriculture, Washington, DC 20250. TEL 202-447-4543. Indexed: GeoRef.

631.7 PE
UNIVERSIDAD NACIONAL AGRARIA. TALLER DE ESTUDIOS ANDINOS. SERIE ANDES CENTRALES. no.4, 1977. irreg. Universidad Nacional Agraria, Taller de Estudios Andinos, Apdo. 456, La Molin, Lima, Peru.

631 PE
UNIVERSIDAD NACIONAL DE AGRARIA. TALLER DE ESTUDIOS ANDINOS. SERIE COSTA CENTRAL. 1978. irreg. Universidad Nacional Agraria, Taller de Estudios Andinos, Departamento de Ciencias Humanas, Apdo. 456, La Molina, Lima, Peru.

631 US
UNIVERSITY OF GEORGIA. AGRICULTURAL EXPERIMENT STATIONS. SOUTHERN COOPERATIVE SERIES BULLETIN. irreg., latest 1983. University of Georgia, Agricultural Experiment Stations, Athens, GA 30602. Ed. Kathleen Sheridan.

631.4 CN ISSN 0085-1329
UNIVERSITY OF GUELPH. DEPARTMENT OF LAND RESOURCE SCIENCE. PROGRESS REPORT. 1954. a. free. University of Guelph, Department of Land Resource Science, Guelph, Ont. N1G 2W1, Canada. TEL 519-824-4120. Ed.Bd. bibl. charts. illus. circ. 1,000. (processed)

633 TR
UNIVERSITY OF THE WEST INDIES. ANNUAL REPORT ON COCOA RESEARCH. 1930. a. University of the West Indies, St. Augustine, Trinidad. Ed. A.J. Kennedy. bibl. illus. circ. 200. Indexed: Biol.Abstr.

630.24 SW ISSN 0346-4997
VAEXTSKYDDS - KURIREN. Swedish edition of: Pflanzenschutz - Kurier. 1960. irreg. free. Bayer (Sverige) AB, Agro-Kemi, Hemsoegatan 10 A, S-211 24 Malmoe, Sweden. Ed. Gunnar Holma. charts. illus. circ. 40,000(controlled)

632 US ISSN 0507-6773
VERTEBRATE PEST CONFERENCE. PROCEEDINGS. 1962. biennial. $15. Vertebrate Pest Council, c/o Wildlife Extension, University of California, Davis, CA 95616. TEL 916-752-6409. Ed. T.P. Salmon. circ. 1,000. Indexed: Biol.Abstr. Biotech.Abstr.

630 UR
VSESOYUZNYI NAUCHNO-ISSLEDOVATEL'SKII INSTITUT ZERNOVOGO KHOZYAISTVA. TRUDY. 1964. irreg. price varies. (Vsesoyuznaya Akademiya Sel'skokhozyaistvennykh Nauk im. V.I. Lenina) Agropromizdat Union, Sadovaya-Spasskaya, 18, 107807 Moscow B-53, Russian S.F.S.R., U.S.S.R. bibl. illus. circ. 3,500. Indexed: Chem.Abstr.

VYSKUMNY USTAV LUK A PASIENKOV V BANSKEJ BYSTRICI. VEDECKE PRACE. see AGRICULTURE

631.7 PL ISSN 0208-5771
WARSAW AGRICULTURAL UNIVERSITY. S G G W - A R. ANNALS. LAND RECLAMATION. (Szkola Glowna Gospodarstwa Wiejskiego - Akademia Rolnicza) (Until 1980, part of Zeszyty Naukowe series of Akademia Rolnicza, Warsaw) (Text mainly in English; occasionally in French, German or Russian; summaries in Polish) 1957. irreg. $6 per no. Warsaw Agricultural University Press, Ul. Nowoursynowska 166, 02-766 Warsaw, Poland (Dist. by: Ars Polona-Ruch, Krakowskie Przedmiescie 7, 00-680 Warsaw, Poland) Ed. S. Lojewski. Indexed: Chem.Abstr.

632 US ISSN 0511-411X
WEED CONTROL MANUAL AND HERBICIDE GUIDE. a. $30. Meister Publishing Co., 37841 Euclid Ave., Willoughby, OH 44094. TEL 216-942-2000. Ed. Maud Boettger. circ. 10,000.

631 581 UK
WELSH PLANT BREEDING STATION. ANNUAL REPORT. 1958. a. £2. Welsh Plant Breeding Station, Plas Gogerddan, Aberystwyth, Dyfed SY23 3EB, Wales. (Co-sponsor: University College of Wales) circ. 1,500. Indexed: Biol.Abstr.

631.4 UK ISSN 0083-7938
WELSH SOILS DISCUSSION GROUP. REPORT. 1960. a. price varies. Welsh Soils Discussion Group, c/o Dr. D.A. Jenkins, Dept. of Biochemistry & Soil Science, University College of North Wales, Bangor, Gwynedd LL57 2UW, Wales. circ. 250. Indexed: Chem.Abstr. Soils & Fert.

633.18 LB
WEST AFRICA RICE DEVELOPMENT ASSOCIATION. ANNUAL REPORT. a. West Africa Rice Development Association, Box 1019, Monrovia, Liberia.

WEST AUSTRALIAN NUT AND TREE CROP ASSOCIATION YEARBOOK. see FOOD AND FOOD INDUSTRIES

631 636.3 AT
WESTERN AUSTRALIA. DEPARTMENT OF AGRICULTURE. DIVISION OF PLANT PRODUCTION. ANNUAL REPORT. a. Department of Agriculture, Division of Plant Production., Perth, W.A., Australia. circ. 150.
Formerly: Western Australia. Department of Agriculture. Wheat and Sheep Division. Annual Report.

630 US
WILEY SERIES IN GEOTECHNICAL ENGINEERING. 1951. irreg., unnumbered, latest 1985. price varies. John Wiley & Sons, Inc., 605 Third Ave., New York, NY 10016. TEL 212-850-6000. Eds. T. William Lambe, Robert V. Whitman.
Former titles: Series in Geotechnical Engineering; Soil Engineering Series.

661 UK
WORLD DIRECTORY OF FERTILIZER MANUFACTURERS. irreg., 6th edt., 1986. £130($200) British Sulphur Corp. Ltd., Parnell House, 25 Wilton Rd., London SW1V 1NH, England. (reprint service avail. from UMI)

661 UK
WORLD DIRECTORY OF FERTILIZER PRODUCTS. irreg., 6th edt., 1986. £95($150) British Sulphur Corp. Ltd., Parnell House, 25 Wilton Rd., London SW1V 1NH, England. (reprint service avail. from UMI)

631.8 UK ISSN 0512-2953
WORLD FERTILIZER ATLAS. 1964. irreg., 7th edt., 1983. £99($125) British Sulphur Corp. Ltd., Parnell House, 25 Wilton Rd., London, SW1V 1NH, England. (reprint service avail. from UMI)

661 UK
WORLD GUIDE TO FERTILIZER PLANT AND EQUIPMENT. irreg. £20($40) British Sulphur Corp. Ltd., Parnell House, 25 Wilton Rd., London SW1V 1NH, England. (reprint service avail. from UMI)

631.8 UK
WORLD GUIDE TO FERTILIZER PROCESSES AND PLANT SUPPLIERS. irreg. £30($60) British Sulphur Corp. Ltd., Parnell House, 25 Wilton Rd., London SW1V 1NH, England. (reprint service avail. from UMI)
Formerly: World Guide to Fertilizer Processes and Constructors.

631.8 UK
WORLD SURVEY OF PHOSPHATE DEPOSITS. irreg., latest 5th, 1987. £160($250) British Sulphur Corp. Ltd., Parnell House, 25 Wilton Rd., London SW1V 1NH, England. (reprint service avail. from UMI)

631.8 UK
WORLD SURVEY OF SULPHUR RESOURCES. irreg., latest 1985. £275($450) British Sulphur Corp. Ltd., Parnell House, 25 Wilton Rd., London SW1V 1NH, England. (reprint service aval. from UMI)

WYE COLLEGE (UNIVERSITY OF LONDON). DEPARTMENT OF AGRICULTURAL ECONOMICS. FARM BUSINESS UNIT. OCCASIONAL PAPER. see AGRICULTURE — Agricultural Economics

631 630 ZA
ZAMBIA. DEPARTMENT OF AGRICULTURE. RESEARCH AND SPECIALIST SERVICES. ANNUAL REPORT. a. free. Department of Agriculture, Research Branch, Principal Research Officer, Mountmakulu Research Station, Private Bag 7, Chilanga, Zambia.

631.4 ZA
ZAMBIA. MINISTRY OF AGRICULTURE AND WATER DEVELOPMENT. LAND USE BRANCH. SOIL SURVEY REPORT. (Text in English) 1967. irreg. exchange basis. Ministry of Agriculture and Water Development, Land Use Branch, c/o Soil Survey Unit, Mount Makulu Research Station, Bag 7, Chilanga, Zambia. (Co-sponsor: Norwegian Agency for International Development) Ed. W.J. Veldkamp. circ. controlled.
Formerly: Zambia. Ministry of Lands and Agriculture. Land Use Branch. Soil Survey Report.

338.1 RH
ZIMBABWE. CENTRAL STATISTICAL OFFICE. AGRICULTURAL PRODUCTION IN PURCHASE LANDS: NATIONAL AND PROVINCIAL TOTALS. (Text in English) 1969. a. Rhod.$0.75. Central Statistical Office, P.O. Box 8063, Causeway, Salisbury, Zimbabwe. circ. 180.
Formerly: Rhodesia. Central Statistical Office. Agricultural Production in African Purchase Lands. Part 1: National and Provincial Totals.

ZIMBABWE. CENTRAL STATISTICAL OFFICE. CENSUS OF REGISTERED DECIDUOUS FRUIT GROWERS. see GARDENING AND HORTICULTURE

630 RH
ZIMBABWE. CENTRAL STATISTICAL OFFICE. CROP PRODUCTION OF LARGE-SCALE COMMERCIAL AGRICULTURAL UNITS. a. Z.$100($1.36) Central Statistical Office, Box 8063, Causeway, Zimbabwe. circ. 500. (tabloid format; back issues avail.)

633.51 RH
ZIMBABWE. COTTON RESEARCH INSTITUTE. ANNUAL REPORT. (Text in English) 1969. a. contr.free circ. Ministry of Lands, Agriculture and Rural Settlement, Department of Research Information Services, Information Services, P.O. Box 8108, Causeway, Zimbabwe. circ. 300. (back issues avail.) Indexed: Field Crop Abstr. Herb.Abstr.

631 RH
ZIMBABWE. MINISTRY OF AGRICULTURE. SEED SERVICES. ANNUAL REPORT. a. free. Ministry of Lands, Agriculture and Rural Resettlement, Research and Specialist Services, Information Services, Box 8108, Causeway, Harare, Zimbabwe. circ. 250. (back issues avail.) Indexed: Biol.Abstr.

AGRICULTURE — Dairying And Dairy Products

see also Agriculture—Poultry and Livestock

637 UK
A F R C INSTITUTE OF FOOD RESEARCH TECHNICAL BULLETINS. (Former name of issuing body: National Institute for Research in Dairying) 1979. irreg. price varies. Agriculture and Food Research Council, Institute of Food Research Technical Bulletins, Church Lane, Shinfield, Reading RG2 9AT, England. Ed. F.H. Dodd. circ. 1,150. Indexed: Chem.Abstr. Dairy Sci.Abstr.
Former titles: N I R D Technical Bulletins & N I R D - H R I Technical Bulletins.

AGRICULTURE — DAIRYING AND DAIRY PRODUCTS

637　　　　　　　　　　CN
ALBERTA. DEPARTMENT OF AGRICULTURE. PRODUCTION ECONOMICS BRANCH. ECONOMICS OF MILK PRODUCTION IN ALBERTA. a. Alberta Agriculture, Production & Resource Economics Branch, 3rd Floor, 7000-113 Street, Edmonton, Alb. T6H 5T6, Canada. TEL 403-427-2727.

637.1　　　　　US　　ISSN 0065-7263
AMERICAN ASSOCIATION OF MEDICAL MILK COMMISSIONS. METHODS AND STANDARDS FOR THE PRODUCTION OF CERTIFIED MILK.* 1909. a. free. American Association of Medical Milk Commissions, Inc., c/o Hopping, Box 1063, Roswell, GA 30077.

637　　　　　　FR　　ISSN 0084-6538
ANNUAIRE NATIONAL DU LAIT. 1950. a. 670 F. Editions Comindus, 1 rue Descombes, 75017 Paris, France.

637　　　　　　UK　　ISSN 0069-4932
COATES'S HERD BOOK (DAIRY) 1822. a. £10($20) Shorthorn Society of the United Kingdom of Great Britain and Ireland, 4th St. National Agricultural Centre, Kenilworth, Warwickshire CV8 2LG, England. Ed. J. Wood Roberts. circ. 700.

637　　　　　　JA　　ISSN 0388-001X
COLLEGE OF DAIRYING. JOURNAL; NATURAL SCIENCE/RAKUNO GAKUEN DAIGAKU KIYO, SHIZEN KAGAKU HEN. (Text mainly in Japanese; occasionally in English and German; summaries mainly in English) 1961. a. exchange basis. Rakuno Gakuen University, 582 Bunkyodai-Midorimachi, Ebetsu, Hokkaido 069, Japan. Ed.Bd. circ. 1,000. Indexed: Biol.Abstr. Chem.Abstr. Curr.Cont. Dairy Sci.Abstr. Vet.Bull.
　　Supersedes in part: College of Dairy Agriculture, Hokkaido. Journal (ISSN 0069-570X)

637　　　　　　IE
DAIRY EXECUTIVE. DIRECTORY AND DIARY. 1906. a. £50 per issue. Dairy Executives' Association, 33 Kildare St., Dublin, 2, Ireland. Ed. Kyran Lynch. adv. bk. rev. circ. 2,000.
　　Former titles: Irish Creamery Managers' Association. Creamery Directory and Diary; Irish Creamery Managers' Association. Creamery Yearbook and Diary (ISSN 0075-0751)

637　　　　　　CN　　ISSN 0707-7904
DAIRY INDUSTRY RESEARCH REPORT. 1974. a. Can.$8. University of Guelph, Department of Animals Poultry Science, Guelph, Ont. N1G 2W1, Canada. TEL 519-824-4120. Ed. Dr. J.F. Hurnik. circ. 250. Indexed: Anim.Breed.Abstr.

637　　　　　　US
DAIRY: LATIN AMERICAN INDUSTRIAL REPORT. (Avail. for each of 22 Latin American countries) 1985. a. $435 per country report per industry covered. Aurora International, Box 9099, Bridgeport, CT 06601-2099. TEL 203-368-0579. Ed. Andres C. Aquino.

637　　　　　　US
DAIRY PRODUCER HIGHLIGHTS. 1950. a. free. ‡ National Milk Producers Federation, 1840 Wilson Blvd., Arlington, VA 22201. TEL 704-243-6111. Ed. Barbara Rodier. charts. stat. circ. 5,000.

637　　　　　　US
DAIRY ROUNDUP. 1973. a. free. ‡ Kent Feeds, Inc., 1600 Oregon St., Muscatine, IA 52761. TEL 319-264-4211. (tabloid format)

637　　　　　　NZ
DAIRYFARMING ANNUAL. 1948. a. NZ.$2.50. Massey University, Animal Science Department, Palmerston North, New Zealand. Ed. G.F. Wilson. circ. 800. (back issues avail.) Indexed: Biol.Abstr. Dairy Sci.Abstr. Anim.Breed.Abstr. Field Crop Abstr. Herb.Abstr.

637　　　　　　US
DAIRYMAN BUYERS GUIDE & DIRECTORY. 1984. a. $20. Robert M. McCune, Pub., 14970 Chandler, Box 819, Corona, CA 91718. TEL 714-735-2730. Ed. Dennis J. Halladay. adv. tr.lit. circ. 28,241. (reprint service avail.)

637　　　　　　DK　　ISSN 0024-9645
DANISH DAIRY INDUSTRY. (Text in English) 1976. biennial. Association of Dairy Engineers, Hestehaven 3, 5260 Odense 3, Denmark. (Co-sponsor: Association of Danish Dairy Managers) Ed. K. Mark Christensen. adv. charts. illus. mkt.stat. index. circ. 20,000. Indexed: Chem.Abstr. Dairy Sci.Abstr. Rural Recreat.Tour.Abstr. World Agri.Econ.& Rural Sociol.Abstr.

637　　　　　　DK　　ISSN 0366-3221
DENMARK. STATENS MEJERIFROSOEG. BERETNING. irreg. Kr.35. Statens Mejeriforsoeg - Danish Research Institute for Dairy Industry, Hilleroed, Denmark.

338.1　　　　　UK
E E C DAIRY FACTS AND FIGURES. a. Milk Marketing Board, Thames Ditton, Surrey, England. Indexed: Dairy Sci.Abstr.

637　　　　　　FR
EUROPE LAITIERE; annuaire international des produits laitiers - producteurs, negociants, fournisseurs. a. S.E.P.T, 2 Villa Carman, Boite Postale 95, 92164 Antony Cedex, France.

637　　　　　　DK
FAELLESUDVALGET FOR STATENS MEJERI-OG HUSDYRBRUGSFORSOG. BERETNING. (Text in Danish; summaries in English) 1974. irreg. Statens Husdyrbrugsforsorg Administration - National Institute of Animal Science, Rolighedsvej 25, DK 1958 Frederiksberg C, Denmark. (back issues avail.) Indexed: Nutr.Abstr.

637　636　　　　GW
FLEISCHLEISTUNGSPRUEFUNG FUER RINDER, LEGELEISTUNGSPRUEFUNG FUER HUEHNER, FLEISCHLEISTUNGSPRUEFUNG FUER SCHAFE. 1966. a. DM.3. Anstalt fuer Leistungspruefungen in der Tierzucht fuer das Land Nordrhein-Westfalen, Im Woeholz 1, 4780 Lippstadt-Eickelborn, W. Germany (B.R.D.) Ed. F. Luke.

637　　　　　　UK　　ISSN 0266-9021
HANNAH RESEARCH. 1930. a. free. Hannah Research Institute, Ayr KA6 5HL, Scotland. TEL (0292) 76013/7. Ed. Dr. P.D. Wilson. bibl. charts. illus. circ. 650. (also avail. in microfiche) Indexed: Biol.Abstr. Anim.Breed.Abstr. Dairy Sci.Abstr. Field Crop Abstr. Herb.Abstr.
　　Formerly (until 1983): Hannah Research Institute. Report (ISSN 0301-6315)

637　664　　　　JA　　ISSN 0285-1806
HOKKAIDO EIYO SYOKURYO GAKKAISHI/HOKKAIDO SOCIETY OF FOOD AND NUTRITION. JOURNAL. (Text and summaries in Japanese) 1954. a. 1.300 Yen($6.50) Hokkaido Society of Food and Nutrition, c/o Department of Biochemistry, Hokkaido University School of Medicine, N-15-W-7, Kita-ku, Sapporo 060, Japan. Ed. Yoh Imai. adv. circ. 1,000.

637.1　　　　　US　　ISSN 0074-1671
INTERNATIONAL ASSOCIATION OF MILK CONTROL AGENCIES. PROCEEDINGS OF ANNUAL MEETINGS. 1937. a. $8. International Association of Milk Control Agencies, c/o R.C. Pearce, New York Dept. of Agriculture and Markets, Albany, NY 12226. TEL 518-474-2121. circ. controlled.

637　　　　　　BE　　ISSN 0074-4484
INTERNATIONAL DAIRY FEDERATION. ANNUAL BULLETIN/FEDERATION INTERNATIONALE DE LAITERIE. BULLETIN ANNUEL. (Text in English and French) 1960. a., no.200, 1986. 6000 Fr. International Dairy Federation, Square Vergote 41, 1040 Brussels, Belgium. index. cum.index. circ. 1,500. Indexed: Biol.Abstr. Chem.Abstr. Nutr.Abstr. Curr.Pack.Abstr. Dairy Sci.Abstr. Food Sci.& Tech.Abstr. Rural Recreat.Tour.Abstr. World Agri.Econ.& Rural Sociol.Abstr.

637　　　　　　BE　　ISSN 0538-7078
INTERNATIONAL DAIRY FEDERATION. ANNUAL MEMENTO/FEDERATION INTERNATIONALE DE LAITERIE. MEMENTO ANNUEL. 1968. a. free. International Dairy Federation, Square Vergote 41, 1040 Brussels, Belgium. circ. 1,500. Indexed: Dairy Sci.Abstr.

637　　　　　　BE　　ISSN 0538-7094
INTERNATIONAL DAIRY FEDERATION. INTERNATIONAL STANDARD/FEDERATION INTERNATIONALE DE LAITERIE. NORME INTERNATIONALE. 1955. irreg., no.122, 1985. price varies. International Dairy Federation, Square Vergote 41, 1040 Brussels, Belgium. circ. 3,000. Indexed: Biol.Abstr.

636.234　　　　　UI　　ISSN 0446-7310
JERSEY AT HOME. 1951. a. £4 to non-members. Royal Jersey Agricultural & Horticultural Society, Springfield, St. Helier, Jersey, Channel Islands. Ed. D.I. Frigot. adv. bk. rev. stat. tr.lit. circ. controlled.

354　　　　　　KE　　ISSN 0453-5944
KENYA. DAIRY BOARD. ANNUAL REPORT. a. Dairy Board, Nairobi, Kenya. illus.

637　540　　　　FI　　ISSN 0367-2387
MEIJERITIETEELLINEN AIKAKAUSKIRJA/FINNISH JOURNAL OF DAIRY SCIENCE. (Text in English, Finnish and German; summaries in English) 1939. a. Fmk.40. Finnish Society of Dairy Science - Meijeritieteellinen Seura r.y., HY Maitolaitos, Viikki, 00710 Helsinki 71, Finland. Eds. Matti Antila, Sade Mantere-Alhonen. adv. circ. 600. (back issues avail.) Indexed: Biol.Abstr. Chem.Abstr. Dairy Sci.Abstr.

637　　　　　　DK　　ISSN 0302-833X
MEJERIBRUGETS UGE-NYT. 1973. w. $40. Danske Mejeriers Faellesorganisation, Frederiks Alle 22, 8000 Aarhus C, Denmark. Ed. Henning Mortensen. circ. 4,000.

637.1　　　　　US
MILK FACTS.* a. free. Milk Industry Foundation, 888 16th St., N.W., Washington, DC 20006.

338.4　　　　　US
MINNESOTA DAIRY PLANTS. 1910. a. free. Agricultural Department, 90 W. Plato Blvd., St. Paul, MN 55107. TEL 612-296-3647. Ed.Bd. circ. 400.

637　　　　　　II　　ISSN 0301-8407
NATIONAL DAIRY RESEARCH INSTITUTE. ANNUAL REPORT. (Text in English) 1923. a. free. National Dairy Research Institute, Karnal 132001, Haryana, India. Ed. A.V. Pusalkar. circ. 2,500. Indexed: Biol.Abstr. Anim.Breed.Abstr. Dairy Sci. Abstr. Field Crop Abstr. Food Sci.& Tech. Abstr. Herb.Abstr.

637　　　　　　NE　　ISSN 0168-518X
NETHERLANDS. CENTRAAL BUREAU VOOR DE STATISTIEK. PRODUCTIE STATISTIEK VAN DE ZUIVELINDUSTRIE/PRODUCTION STATISTICS OF THE DAIRY INDUSTRY. (Text in Dutch and English) 1952. a. Centraal Bureau voor de Statistiek, Prinses Beatrixlaan 428, Voorburg, Netherlands (Orders to: Staatsuitgeverij, Christoffel Plantijnstraat, The Hague, Netherlands)
　　Formerly: Netherlands. Centraal Bureau voor de Statistiek. Zuivelstatistiek/Dairy Statistics (ISSN 0077-7528)

637　　　　　　US　　ISSN 0732-9121
NEW YORK STATE DAIRY STATISTICS. a. free. ‡ New York Crop Reporting Service, c/o Department of Agriculture and Markets, Albany, NY 12235. circ. 1,800.
　　Former titles: New York Dairy Statistics; New York Crop Reporting Service. Statistics Relative to the Dairy Industry in New York State (ISSN 0077-8974)

354　　　　　　NZ
NEW ZEALAND. DAIRY BOARD. ANNUAL REPORT AND STATEMENT OF ACCOUNTS. (Includes Statistical Supplements) 1962. a. NZ.$5. New Zealand Dairy Board, P.O. Box 417, Wellington, New Zealand. Ed. N.H. Martin. illus. stat. circ. 25,000.
　　Supersedes: New Zealand. Dairy Production and Marketing Board. Annual Report and Statement of Accounts (ISSN 0545-7041)

637　　　　　　NZ
NEW ZEALAND DAIRY RESEARCH INSTITUTE BIENNIAL REVIEW. biennial. New Zealand Dairy Research Institute, Private Bag, Palmerston North, New Zealand.
　　Formerly: New Zealand Dairy Research Institute Annual Report (ISSN 0112-4048)

353.9 US ISSN 0091-9446
NORTH DAKOTA. MILK STABILIZATION BOARD. ANNUAL REPORT OF ADMINISTRATIVE ACTIVITIES. (Report year ends June 30) 1968. a. North Dakota Milk Stabilization Board, 2061/2 North 6th St., Rm. 5, Bismarck, ND 58501. TEL 701-224-2988. circ. 300.

637 IS
PROFITABILITY OF DAIRY IN ISRAEL/HA-RIVHIYUT SHEL 'ANAF HA-REFET. (Issued as the Institute's Publications. Series D) (Text in Hebrew) 1964/65. irreg. IS.45($3) Institute of Farm Income Research, 6 Hachashmonaim Blvd., Tel-Aviv 67018, Israel.

637 636 CS
RESEARCH INSTITUTE OF ANIMAL PRODUCTION AT NITRA. SCIENTIFIC WORKS. 1961. biennial. 20 Kcs. (Research Institute of Animal Production, Nitra) Priroda, Krizkova 9, Bratislava, Czechoslovakia. circ. 500. Indexed: Biol.Abstr.

637 JA ISSN 0082-4763
SNOW BRAND MILK PRODUCTS COMPANY. RESEARCH LABORATORY. REPORTS/ YUKIJIRUSHI NYUGYO GIJUTSU KENKYUSHO HOKOKU. (Text in Japanese; summaries in English and Japanese) 1950. irreg., approx. 1 per year. free. ‡ Snow Brand Milk Products Co. Ltd. - Yukijirushi Nyugyo K. K., Research Laboratory, 1-1-2 Minamidai, Kawagoe, Saitama 350, Japan. Ed. Hiromichi Hayashi. circ. 400. Indexed: Chem.Abstr. Dairy Sci.Abstr.

354.68 SA
SOUTH AFRICA. DAIRY BOARD. ANNUAL REPORT. (Text in Afrikaans and English) 1946. a. free. Dairy Board - Suiwelraad, Box 1284, Pretoria 0001, South Africa. Ed. J.C. Erasmus. circ. 1,000.
Former titles: South Africa. Dairy Control Board. Annual Report; South Africa. Milk Board. Annual Report.

637 636 SW ISSN 0347-9706
UNIVERSITY OF AGRICULTURAL SCIENCES. REPORT. (Text in English and Swedish; summaries in English) 1973. irreg., no.62 1984. University of Agricultural Sciences, Department of Animal Breeding and Genetics, Box 7023, S-75007 Uppsala, Sweden.

WESTERN AUSTRALIA. DEPARTMENT OF AGRICULTURE. RURAL ECONOMICS AND MARKETING SECTION. REPORT ON THE MARKET MILK INDUSTRY IN WESTERN AUSTRALIA. see *AGRICULTURE — Agricultural Economics*

AGRICULTURE — Feed, Flour And Grain

633.2 US
AMERICAN FORAGE AND GRASSLAND COUNCIL. PROCEEDINGS OF THE RESEARCH INDUSTRY CONFERENCE. 1968. a. price varies. American Forage and Grassland Council, 2021 Rebel Rd., Lexington, KY 40503.

633.2 US
ASSOCIATION OF AMERICAN FEED CONTROL OFFICIALS. OFFICIAL PUBLICATION. a. $15. (Association of American Feed Control Officials) American Feed Control Officials, c/o West Virginia Department of Agriculture, State Capitol Bldg., Charleston, WV 25305. TEL 304-348-2226. Ed. Clyde Jones. circ. 2,000. (back issues avail.)

BAKING DIRECTORY/BUYERS GUIDE. see *BUSINESS AND ECONOMICS — Trade And Industrial Directories*

633 AT
BULK WHEAT. 1967. a. free. Grain Handling Authority of New South Wales, 25 Commonwealth St., Sydney, N.S.W. 2000, Australia. Ed. John V. Hoban. adv. circ. 30,000.

382 633.1 CN
CANADA. GRAIN COMMISSION. ECONOMICS AND STATISTICS DIVISION. CANADIAN GRAIN EXPORTS. a. Grain Commission, Economics and Statistics Division, 747-303 Main St., Winnipeg, Man. R3C 3H5, Canada. TEL 204-949-2759.
Continues: Canada. Board of Grain Commissioners. Canadian Grain Exports.

633.1 338.14 CN ISSN 0380-8718
CANADA. GRAIN COMMISSION. ECONOMICS AND STATISTICS DIVISION. VISIBLE GRAIN SUPPLIES AND DISPOSITION. 1952/53. a. free. Grain Commission, Economics and Statistics Division, 747-303 Main St., Winnipeg, Man. R3C 3H5, Canada. TEL 204-949-2759. circ. 1,500.
Continues: Canada. Grain Commission. Marketings, Distribution and Visible Carry-over of Canadian Grain in and Through Licensed Elevators (ISSN 0068-7065)

633 CN ISSN 0700-2866
CANADA. GRAINS COUNCIL. ANNUAL REPORT. (Text in English and French) 1970. a. free. Grains Council, 760-360 Main St., Winnipeg, Man. R3C 3Z3, Canada. TEL 204-942-2254. circ. controlled. (tabloid format)

633.1 CN
CANADA. GRAINS COUNCIL. STATISTICAL HANDBOOK. 1974. a. Can.$15. Grains Council, 760-360 Main St., Winnipeg, Man. R3C 2Z3, Canada. TEL 204-942-2254. circ. 2,000.

633.1 CN ISSN 0317-1892
CANADIAN GRAIN COMMISSION GRAIN RESEARCH LABORATORY. ANNUAL REPORT. (Editions in English, French) 58th report, 1984. a. free. Canadian Grain Commission, Grain Research Laboratory, 1404-303 Main St., Winnipeg, Man. R3C 3G8, Canada. TEL 204-949-4626. Ed. P.R. March. circ. 1,150.

633 AT ISSN 0069-7680
COMMONWEALTH SCIENTIFIC AND INDUSTRIAL RESEARCH ORGANISATION. WHEAT RESEARCH UNIT. REPORT. 1960/61. a. Aus.$2. C.S.I.R.O., Editorial & Publications Service, 314 Albert St., E. Melbourne, Vic. 3002, Australia. Indexed: Biol.Abstr.

633.2 CU ISSN 0138-7839
CUBA. CENTRO DE INFORMACION Y DOCUMENTACION AGROPECUARIO. BOLETIN DE RESENAS. SERIE: PASTOS Y FORRAJES. (Abstracts in English) 1974. irreg. exchange basis. Centro de Informacion y Documentacion Agropecuario, Gaveta Postal 4149, Havana 4, Cuba (Dist. by: Ediciones Cubanas, Obispo No. 461, Aptdo. 605, Havana, Cuba) Indexed: Agrindex.
Formerly: Cuba. Centro de Informacion y Divulgacion Agropecuario. Boletin de Resenas. Serie: Pastos.

633.2 664.7 US
DISTILLERS FEED CONFERENCE. PROCEEDINGS.* 1945. a. $2. Distillers Feed Research Council, Box 23097, Des Moines, IA 50322-9407. Indexed: Chem.Abstr.

633.1 US ISSN 0071-450X
FEED ADDITIVE COMPENDIUM. 1963. a. (with 11 supplements) $140. Miller Publishing Co., 12400 Whitewater Dr., Ste. 160, Box 2400, Minnetonka, MN 55343. TEL 612-931-0211. Ed. Roy Leidahl. adv. circ. 2,700. (reprint service avail. from UMI)

633.1 US ISSN 0071-4518
FEED INDUSTRY RED BOOK; reference book and buyers' guide for the feed manufacturing industry. 1938. a. $22. Communications Marketing, Inc., 7535 Office Ridge Circle, Eden Prairie, MN 55344. TEL 612-941-5820. Ed. Bruce W. Smith.
Formerly: Feed Bag Red Book.

GRAIN GUIDE/NORTH AMERICAN GRAIN YEARBOOK. see *BUSINESS AND ECONOMICS — Trade And Industrial Directories*

633 PH ISSN 0115-1142
I R R I. RESEARCH HIGHLIGHTS. 1974. a. $17.50 price varies. International Rice Research Institute, Box 933, Manila, Philippines. Indexed: Field Crop Abstr. Herb.Abstr. Rev.Appl.Entomol. Rev.Plant Path.

633 PH ISSN 0074-7793
I R R I ANNUAL REPORT. (Text in English) 1963. a. price varies. International Rice Research Institute, Box 933, Manila, Philippines. index. circ. 5,000. (also avail. in microfiche) Indexed: Biol.Abstr. Bibl.Agri. B.R.I. Field Crop Abstr. Herb.Abstr. Plant Breed.Abstr. Rev.Appl.Entomol. Rev.Plant Path. Trop.Abstr. Weed Abstr. World Agri.Econ.& Rural Sociol.Abstr.

633 PH ISSN 0115-3862
I R R I RESEARCH PAPER SERIES. 1976. irreg. (approx. 15/yr.) $1.25 per no. International Rice Research Institute, Box 933, Manila, Philippines. Indexed: Biol.Abstr. Field Crop Abstr. Herb.Abstr. Plant Breed.Abstr. Rev.Appl.Entomol. Rural Recreat.Tour.Abstr. Soils & Fert. World Agri.Econ.& Rural Sociol.Abstr.

INSTITUTO DE PESQUISAS ZOOTECNICAS "FRANCISCO OSORIO". ANUARIO TECNICO. see *AGRICULTURE — Poultry And Livestock*

633.8 YU ISSN 0074-6223
INTERNATIONAL HOP GROWERS CONVENTION. REPORT OF CONGRESS.* (Supplement to: Hopfenrundschau) a. International Hop Growers Convention, Titova 19, Ljubljana, Yugoslavia.

633.1 IT
ISTITUTO SPERIMENTALE PER LA CEREALICOLTURA. ANNALI. (Text and summaries in English and Italian) 1970. a. free. Istituto Sperimentale per la Cerealicoltura, Via Cassia 176, 00191 Rome, Italy. Ed. Prof. Angelo Bianchi. Indexed: Biol.Abstr. Field Crop.Abstr. Herb.Abstr. Soils & Fert.

633 US
KANSAS CORN PERFORMANCE TESTS. (Subseries of its: Report of Progress) 1939. a. free. ‡ Kansas State University, Agricultural Experiment Station, Manhattan, KS 66506. TEL 913-532-7251. Ed. Ted L. Walter. stat. circ. 10,000.

633 US
KANSAS SORGHUM PERFORMANCE TESTS. GRAIN & FORAGE. (Subseries of its: Report of Progress) 1958. a. free. ‡ Kansas State University, Agricultural Experiment Station, Manhattan, KS 66506. TEL 913-532-7251. Ed. Ted L. Walter. stat. circ. 12,000.
Formerly: Kansas Grain Sorghum Performance Tests.

633 US
KANSAS STATE UNIVERSITY. FOOD AND FEED GRAIN INSTITUTE. TECHNICAL ASSISTANCE IN GRAIN STORAGE, PROCESSING AND MARKETING, AND AGRIBUSINESS DEVELOPMENT. (In 4 subseries: Technical Assistance Reports (US ISSN 0453-2481); Manuals; Special Reports; Research Reports) 1968. irreg. Kansas State University, Food and Feed Grain Institute, Shellenberger Hall, Manhattan, KS 66506. TEL 913-532-6161. (Co-sponsor: U.S. Agency for International Development) circ. 150. (also avail. in microform)
Formerly (1968-1974): Kansas State University. Food and Feed Grain Institute. Technical Assistance in Food Grain Drying, Storage, Handling and Transportation (ISSN 0071-7150)

MILLING DIRECTORY/BUYERS GUIDE. see *BUSINESS AND ECONOMICS — Trade And Industrial Directories*

633 US ISSN 0077-5789
NATIONAL SOYBEAN PROCESSORS ASSOCIATION. YEARBOOK. 1936. a. $25. ‡ National Soybean Processors Association, 1255 Twenty Third St. N.W., Washington, DC 20037. TEL 202-452-8040. circ. 2,500.

633.7 NE ISSN 0168-5333
NETHERLANDS. CENTRAAL BUREAU VOOR DE STATISTIEK. PRODUKTIESTATISTIEKEN: VEEVOEDERINDUSTRIE. a. fl.9. Centraal Bureau voor de Statistiek, Prinses Beatrixlaan 428, Voorburg, Netherlands (Orders to: Staatsuitgeverij, Christoffel Plantijnstraat, The Hague, Netherlands)

AGRICULTURE — POULTRY AND LIVESTOCK

633.11　　　　　NZ　ISSN 0078-0219
NEW ZEALAND WHEAT REVIEW. 1945. triennial. free. Department of Scientific and Industrial Research, Crop Research Division, Private Bag, Christchurch, New Zealand. Eds. H.J. Bezar, D.S.C. Wright. bk. rev. circ. 3,200. Indexed: Field Crop Abstr. Herb.Abstr. Plant Breed.Abstr. Soils & Fert.

633.1　636.5　　　　　CN
OUTLOOK. 1976. a. Can.$5. Grains Council, 760-360 Main St., Winnipeg, Man. R3C 3Z3, Canada. TEL 204-942-2254.

633　　　　　US
PENNSYLVANIA. DEPARTMENT OF AGRICULTURE. SEED REPORT. 1927. a. free. Department of Agriculture, Bureau of Plant Industry, 2301 N. Cameron St., Harrisburg, PA 17110-9408. TEL 717-787-4843. Ed. R. Deppen.

633.1　　　　　BL
REUNIAO GERAL DE CULTURA DO ARROZ. ANAIS. 1976. a. Instituto Rio Grandese do Arroz, Biblioteca, Caixa Postal 1927, Porto Alegre, Brazil. Indexed: Field Crop Abstr. Herb.Abstr. Weed Abstr.

338.1　　　　　SA
SOUTH AFRICA. MAIZE BOARD. REPORT ON MAIZE FOR THE FINANCIAL YEAR. (Report year ends April 30) (Editions in English and Afrikaans) a. free. ‡ Maize Board - Mielieraad, P.O. Box 669, Pretoria 0001, South Africa. illus. circ. 4,000.
　　Formerly: South Africa. Maize Board. Review of the Maize Position.

633.11　　　　　SA
SOUTH AFRICA. WHEAT BOARD. ANNUAL REPORT. (Report year ends Sept. 30th) 1939. a. R.2. ‡ Wheat Board - Koringraad, P.O. Box 908, Pretoria 0001, South Africa. illus. stat. circ. 510 (combined)

633.2　　　　　GW　ISSN 0170-7809
Z M P BILANZ GETREIDE-FUTTERMITTEL. 1975. a. DM.18. Zentrale Markt und Preisberichtstelle fuer Erzeugnisse der Land-, Forst- und Ernaehrungswirtschaft, Godesberger Allee 142-148, 5300 Bonn-2, W. Germany (B.R.D.)

AGRICULTURE — Poultry And Livestock

see also Agriculture—Dairying and Dairy Products; Leather and Fur Industries; Veterinary Science

636.2　　　　　UK
ABERDEEN - ANGUS HERD BOOK. 1884. a. £15. Aberdeen-Angus Cattle Society, Pedigree House, 6 King's Place, Perth, Scotland. circ. 350. (back issues avail.)
　Cattle

636.2　　　　　UK　ISSN 0001-317X
ABERDEEN - ANGUS REVIEW. 1919. a. £3. Aberdeen-Angus Cattle Society, Pedigree House, 6 Kings Place, Perth, Scotland. Ed. E.J. Gillanders. adv. illus. mkt. circ. 2,600.
　Cattle

636　　　　　PL　ISSN 0065-0935
ACTA AGRARIA ET SILVESTRIA. SERIES ZOOTECHNICA. (Text in Polish; summaries in English and Russian) 1961. irreg. (1-2/yr.) price varies. (Polska Akademia Nauk, Oddzial w Krakowie, Komisja Nauk Rolniczych i Lesnych) Ossolineum, Publishing House of the Polish Academy of Sciences, Rynek 9, Wroclaw, Poland (Dist. by Ars Polona-Ruch, Krakowskie Przedmiescie 7, Warsaw, Poland) Ed. Thomas M. Janowski. bibl. charts. Indexed: Biol.Abstr. Chem.Abstr. Excerp.Med. Nutr.Abstr.& Rev. Anim.Breed.Abstr. Field Crop Abstr. Herb.Abstr. Ind.Vet. Soils & Fert. Vet.Bull.

636　　　　　US
ADVANCES IN MEAT RESEARCH SERIES. 1985. a. $57.50. A V I Publishing Company, Box 831, 250 Post Rd., East, Westport, CT 06881. TEL 203-226-0738. Eds. A.M. Pearson, T.R. Dutson.

AKADEMIA ROLNICZA, POZNAN. ROCZNIKI. ZOOTECHNIKA. see *BIOLOGY — Zoology*

636　　　　　PL
AKADEMIA ROLNICZA W SZCZECINIE. ZESZYTY NAUKOWE. ZOOTECHNIKA. 1966. irreg., no.111, 1984. price varies. Akademia Rolnicza, Janosika 8, 71-424 Szczecin, Poland. Ed. Prof. Mieczyslaw Jasnowski. bk. rev. Indexed: Chem.Abstr. Nutr.Abstr. Field Crop Abstr.

636　　　　　PL
AKADEMIA ROLNICZA W SZCZECINIE. ZESZYTY NAUKOWE. ZOOTECHNIKA. TERATOLOGICA SCRIPTA. 1975. irreg., no. 81, 1979. price varies. Akademia Rolnicza, Janosika 8, 71-424 Szczecin, Poland. Ed. Prof. Mieczyslaw Jasnowski. bk. rev. Indexed: Chem.Abstr. Nutr.Abstr. Field Crop Abstr.

636.4　　　　　CN　ISSN 0044-7145
ALBERTA LANDRACE ASSOCIATION. NEWSLETTER. 1959. irreg. Alberta Landrace Swine Association, c/o N. Helfrich, Box 250, Rockford, Alberta, Canada.
　Hogs

636.587　　　　　US　ISSN 0065-745X
AMERICAN BANTAM ASSOCIATION. YEARBOOK. 1917. a. membership. American Bantam Association, Box 127, Augusta, NJ 07822. Ed. Fred P. Jeffrey. adv. circ. 3,000.

636.2　　　　　US　ISSN 0065-8081
AMERICAN DEXTER CATTLE ASSOCIATION. HERD BOOK. 1920. a. $5. American Dexter Cattle Association, 707 W. Water St., Box 56, Decorah, IA 52101. Ed. Kay Moore Baker. cum.index 1960-1981.
　Cattle

636　　　　　US
AMERICAN FEED INDUSTRY ASSOCIATION. ANNUAL MEETING OF THE NUTRITION COUNCIL. PROCEEDINGS. 1944. a. $5. American Feed Industry Association, Inc., Nutrition Council, 1701 N. Ft. Myer Dr., Arlington, VA 22209. Ed.Bd. circ. 1,500. (back issues avail.) Indexed: Biol.Abstr.
　　Formerly: American Feed Manufacturers Association. Annual Meeting of the Nutrition Council. Proceedings.

636.39　　　　　US　ISSN 0065-8456
AMERICAN GOAT SOCIETY. YEAR BOOK.*
　Includes: A G S Dairy Goat Yearbook. 1935. a. $2. American Goat Society, Inc., 122 Cypress St., Santa Ana, CA 92701. Ed. Melinda Overton. adv. index. circ. 400.

AMERICAN MEAT SCIENCE ASSOCIATION. RECIPROCAL MEAT CONFERENCE. PROCEEDINGS. see *FOOD AND FOOD INDUSTRIES*

636　　　　　AT　ISSN 0728-5965
ANIMAL PRODUCTION IN AUSTRALIA. 1956. biennial. Aus.$30($18.40) Pergamon Press Australia Ltd., c/o C.S.I.R.O., P.O. Box 1600, Canberra, A.C.T., 2601, Australia. Ed. H. Dove. circ. 2,485. (back issues avail.) Indexed: Biol.Abstr. Chem.Abstr. Nutr.Abstr. Anim.Breed.Abstr. Dairy Sci.Abstr. Field Crop Abstr. Helminthol.Abstr. Herb.Abstr. Ind.Vet. Rural Recreat.Tour.Abstr. Vet.Bull. World Agri.Econ.& Rural Sociol.Abstr.
　　Former titles: Australian Society of Animal Production. Proceedings (ISSN 0067-2149); Animal Production in Australia.

636　　　　　FR　ISSN 0066-3328
ANNUAIRE NATIONAL DE L'AVICULTURE. 1956. a. 410 F. Editions Comindus, 1 rue Descombes, 75017 Paris, France.

636　　　　　FR　ISSN 0293-9967
ANNUAIRE OFFICIEL DE LA CHARCUTERIE. (Text in French) a. 580 F. Editions Comindus, 1 rue Descombes, 75017 Paris, France.

636.5　　　　　BL
ANUARIO AGRICOLA E AVICOLA. 1912. a. Editora C Q Ltda., Av. Fagundes Filho 343, Caixa Postal 8034, Sao Paulo, SP, Brazil. Ed. Oswaldo Gessulli. adv. circ. 15,000.

636.5　　　　　BL
ANUARIO AVICOLA. 1912. a. Gessulli Editores Ltda., Av. Fagundes Filho 343, Caixa Postal 9034, Sao Paulo, SP, Brazil. Ed. Elisabeta Puccia. adv. circ. 15,000.

338.1　　　　　AG
ARGENTINA. MERCADO NACIONAL DE HACIENDA. ANUARIO. a. Mercado Nacional de Hacienda, Tellier 2406, Buenos Aires 1440, Argentina. illus. stat.
　　Continues: Argentine Republic. Mercado Nacional de Hacienda. Memoria (ISSN 0570-8621)

636　　　　　VE
ASOCIACION LATINOAMERICANA DE PRODUCCION ANIMAL. MEMORIA. (Text in Spanish; summaries in English, Spanish, Portuguese) 1966. a. $15. Asociacion Latinoamericana de Produccion Animal, Apartado Postal 4653, Maracay 2101-A, Venezuela. Ed. Claudio F. Chicco. abstr. cum.index: vols. 1-10. circ. 1,500. (back issues avail.) Indexed: Biol.Abstr. Nutr.Abstr. Anim.Breed.Abstr. Dairy Sci.Abstr. Rural Recreat.Tour.Abstr. World Agri.Econ.& Rural Sociol.Abstr.

350　636　　　　　AT　ISSN 0728-6929
AUSTRALIA. DEPARTMENT OF PRIMARY INDUSTRY. POULTRY INDUSTRY ASSISTANCE. ANNUAL REPORT. 1966. a. free. Department of Primary Industry, Livestock and Pastoral Division, Edmund Barton Bldg., Broughton St., Barton, A.C.T. 2600, Australia.

636.2　664.9　　　　　AT
AUSTRALIAN MEAT RESEARCH COMMITTEE. ANNUAL REPORT. 1966/67. a. free. (Department of Agriculture) Australian Meat and Livestock Corporation, G.P.O. Box 4129, Sydney 2001, Australia. Indexed: Anim.Breed.Abstr. Field Crop Abstr. Herb.Abstr.

AUSTRALIAN SMALL FARMS DIRECTORY; services, supplies, equipment. see *AGRICULTURE — Agricultural Equipment*

636.4　　　　　AT
AUSTRALIAN STUD PIG HERD BOOK. 1911. a. Aus.$5. (Australian Pig Breeders' Society) Westons Publishing Company, P.O. Box 189, Kiama, N.S.W. 2533, Australia. Ed. C.W. Foley. adv. circ. 1,000.
　Hogs

636.2　　　　　US
BEEF ROUNDUP. 1973. a. free. Kent Feeds, Inc., 1600 Oregon St., Muscatine, IA 52761. TEL 319-264-4211. (tabloid format)
　Cattle

636.3　　　　　UK
BLACKFACE SHEEP BREEDERS' ASSOCIATION JOURNAL. 1948. a. free. Blackface Sheep Breeders' Association, c/o A.M. Fenton, 26 York Place, Perth PH2 8EN, Scotland. adv. bk. rev. circ. 1,700(controlled) (processed)

636　　　　　UK　ISSN 0067-9224
BLOODSTOCK BREEDERS' REVIEW. 1912. a. £65. Sagittarius Bloodstock Associates Ltd., 26 Charing Cross Road, London WC2H 0DJ, England. Ed. Susan Cameron. bk. rev. circ. 1,400.

636.587　　　　　US　ISSN 0068-0117
BOOK OF BANTAMS. 1963. irreg.(quadrennial or quinquennial) $3.50. American Bantam Association, Box 127, Augusta, NJ 07822. Ed. George Fitterer. circ. 10,000.
　Poultry

636　　　　　SA
BORDER AGRICULTURAL SHOW PRIZE LIST. (Text in Afrikaans and English) a. Border Agricultural Society, Komani St., P.O. Box 159, Queenstown, South Africa. adv. circ. 7,000.

636.3　　　　　UK
BORDER LEICESTER FLOCK BOOK. 1890. a. £10 to non-members. Society of Border Leicester Sheep Breeders, 15 Chesser Loan, Edinburgh EH14 1SY, Scotland. Ed. Colin E. Douglas. circ. 500.
　Sheep

AGRICULTURE — POULTRY AND LIVESTOCK

636   BS
BOTSWANA. MINISTRY OF AGRICULTURE. LIVESTOCK MANAGEMENT SURVEY RESULTS. 1983. a. free. Ministry of Agriculture, Division of Planning and Statistics, Private Bag 003, Gaborone, Botswana.

BRAUNVIEHZUCHTER. see *AGRICULTURE*

636.2   UK   ISSN 0068-2012
BRITISH FRIESIAN HERD BOOK. (Supplementary Register avail.) 1909. a. £30. British Friesian Cattle Society of Great Britain & Ireland, Scotsbridge House, Rickmansworth, Herts, WD3 3BB, England.
Cattle

636.39   UK   ISSN 0068-2039
BRITISH GOAT SOCIETY. HERD BOOK. 1886. a. £5. British Goat Society, Moreton House, Moretonhampstead, Devon, England.

636.39   UK   ISSN 0068-2047
BRITISH GOAT SOCIETY. YEAR BOOK. 1921. a. £3.50. British Goat Society, Moreton House, Moretonhampstead, Devon, England. Indexed: Anim.Breed.Abstr.

636.932   UK
BRITISH RABBIT COUNCIL YEAR BOOK. a. £0.50. British Rabbit Council, 7 Kirkgate, Newark, Notts., England. circ. 9,000.

BUNADARRIT. see *AGRICULTURE*

636   UV
C E B V. no.7, 1974. irreg. Communaute Economique du Betail et de la Viande, Secretariat, Ouagadougou, Burkina Faso.

619   CN
CANADA. AGRICULTURE CANADA. ANIMAL RESEARCH CENTRE. RESEARCH REPORT. 1964. a. free. Agriculture Canada, Animal Research Centre, Ottawa, Ont. K1A OC6, Canada. TEL 613-993-6002. circ. 325.
Formerly: Canada. Agriculture Canada. Animal Research Institute. Research Report (ISSN 0066-1899)

636   CN   ISSN 0068-7324
CANADA. AGRICULTURE CANADA. LIVESTOCK MARKET REVIEW. a. free. Agriculture Canada, Ottawa, Canada. TEL 613-995-5880.

CANADA. MARKETING AND TRADE DIVISION. ANIMAL AND ANIMAL PRODUCTS: OUTLOOK. see *AGRICULTURE — Agricultural Economics*

636.5   CN   ISSN 0068-8134
CANADA WHO'S WHO OF THE POULTRY INDUSTRY. 1955. a. Can.$10. Farm Papers Ltd., 105A, 9547-152nd St., Surrey, B.C. V3R 5Y5, Canada. TEL 604-585-3131. Ed. Anthony Greaves. adv. illus. stat. index. circ. 6,422.

636.3   CN   ISSN 0319-7387
CANADIAN CO-OPERATIVE WOOL GROWERS MAGAZINE. 1958. a. membership. Canadian Cooperative Wool Growers Ltd., Box 130, Carleton Place, Ont. K7C 3P3, Canada. Ed. Eric Bjergso. adv. circ. 12,000.
Former titles: Canadian Wool Grower; Canadian Wool Grower and Sheep Breeder (ISSN 0045-5598)
Sheep

636   CN   ISSN 0382-6406
CANADIAN JERSEY HERD RECORD. vol.38, 1978. irreg. Canadian Jersey Cattle Club, 343 Waterloo Ave., Guelph, Ont. N1H 3K1, Canada. TEL 519-821-1020.
Continues: Canadian Jersey Cattle Club. Record (ISSN 0382-6414)

636   CN   ISSN 0008-4344
CANADIAN LACOMBE BREEDERS ASSOCIATION. NEWSLETTER. 1958. irreg. (3-4/yr.) Dr. H.T. Fredeen, Ed. & Pub., 2320-41 Ave. N.E., Calgary, Alberta T2E 6W8, Canada. mkt. circ. 300. (processed)
Formerly: Lacombe News.

636.5   NE
CENTRUM VOOR ONDERZOEK EN VOORLICHTING VOOR DE PLUIMVEEHOUDERIJ. HET SPELDERHOLT. JAARVERLAG. (Text in Dutch; summaries in Dutch and English) 1962. a. fl.10. Spelderholt Centre for Poultry Research and Extension, Spelderholt 9, 7361 DA Beekbergen, Netherlands. Ed. G.P. Teunis. bk. rev. circ. 500. Indexed: Biol.Abstr.
Formerly: Instituut voor Pluimveeonderzoek Het Spelderholt. Jaarverslag.

636.2   UK   ISSN 0069-4924
COATES'S HERD BOOK (BEEF) 1882. a. £10 to members. Beef Shorthorn Cattle Society, Pedigree House, 6 King's Place, Perth PH2 8AD, Scotland. Ed. Mrs. Barbara M. McDonald. adv. circ. 800.
Cattle

636   CK
COLEGA AGROPECUARIO. 1976. irreg. Sociedad de Ingenieros Agronomos de Antioquia, Calle 54 no. 45-36, Apdo. Aereos 51185, Medellin, Colombia. (Co-sponsors: Colegio de Medicos Veterinarios y Zootecnistas de Antioqua; Association Nacional de Tecnologos Agropecuarios)

COMMISSION OF THE EUROPEAN COMMUNITIES. MARCHES AGRICOLES: SERIE "PRIX". PRODUITS ANIMAUX. see *AGRICULTURE — Agricultural Economics*

COMMONWEALTH SCIENTIFIC AND INDUSTRIAL RESEARCH ORGANIZATION. DIVISION OF ANIMAL PRODUCTION TECHNICAL REPORT. see *BIOLOGY — Physiology*

COMMONWEALTH SCIENTIFIC AND INDUSTRIAL RESEARCH ORGANIZATION. DIVISION OF TROPICAL CROPS AND PASTURES. GENETIC RESOURCES COMMUNICATION. see *AGRICULTURE — Crop Production And Soil*

636.5   CU
CUBA. CENTRO DE INFORMACION Y DIVULGACION AGROPECUARIO. BOLETIN DE RESENAS. SERIE: AVICULTURA. 1974. irreg. $5 or exchange basis. Centro de Informacion y Divulgacion Agropecuario, Calle 11 no. 1057, Gaveta Postal 4149, Havana 4, Cuba.
Formerly: Cuba. Centro de Informacion y Documentacion Agropecuario. Boletin de Resenas. Serie: Avicultura.

636.4   CU
CUBA. CENTRO DE INFORMACION Y DOCUMENTACION AGROPECUARIO. BOLETIN DE RESENAS. SERIE: GANADO PORCINO. (Abstracts in English) 1974. irreg. exchange basis. Centro de Informacion y Documentacion Agropecuario, Gaveta Postal 4149, Havana 4, Cuba (Dist. by: Ediciones Cubanas, Obispo No. 461, Aptdo. 605, Havana, Cuba) Indexed: Agrindex.
Formerly: Cuba. Centro de Informacion y Divulgacion Agropecuario. Boletin de Resenas. Serie: Ganado Porcino.

636   BL
D N P A. irreg. Ministerio da Agricultura, Departamento Nacional de Producao Animal, Brasilia, Brazil. stat.

636.2   UK   ISSN 0070-2986
DAVY'S DEVON HERD BOOK. 1884. a. £10. Devon Cattle Breeders' Society, Court House, The Square, Wiveliscombe, Somerset, England. circ. 250.
Cattle

636   DK   ISSN 0105-9807
DENMARK. STATENS HUSDYRBRUGSFORSOEG. INDEKS; indeks for beretninger og meddelelser. 1978. triennial. Kr.15. Statens Husdyrbrugsforsoeg - National Institute of Animal Science, Rolighedsvej 25, 1958 Frederiksberg C, Denmark.

636   DK   ISSN 0105-6883
DENMARK. STATENS HUSDYRBRUGSFORSOG. BERETNING. (Text in Danish; summaries in English) 1883. irreg. price varies. Statens Husdyrbrugs Forsoeg - National Institute of Animal Science, Rolighedsvej 25, 1958 Frederiksberg C, Denmark. circ. 1,300. Indexed: Nutr.Abstr. Anim.Breed.Abstr. Dairy Sci.Abstr. Field Crop Abstr. Herb.Abstr. Rural Recreat.Tour.Abstr. World Agri.Econ.& Rural Sociol.Abstr.
Supersedes: Denmark. Forsoegslaboratoriet. Beretning (ISSN 0005-8904)

636.3   UK
DORSET DOWN FLOCK BOOK. 1906. a. $3 to non-members. Dorset Down Sheep Breeders' Association, c/o The Secretary, Brierley House, Summer Lane, Combe Down, Bath, England. Ed. D.V. Child. adv. circ. 150.
Sheep

637.5   US
EGG PRODUCTION TESTS: UNITED STATES AND CANADA. 1959. a. free. U.S. Animal and Plant Health Inspection Service, Bldg 265, BARC-E, Beltsville, MD 20705. TEL 301-344-2527. Ed. R.D. Schar. circ. 15,000.

636.5   ES
ENCUESTA AVICOLA. irreg. exchange. Direccion General de Economia Agropecuaria, Boulevad de los Heroes, Edificio Latinoamericano, San Salvador, El Salvador. Dir. Rene Aguilar Giron. stat.

636.2   UK   ISSN 0071 0571
ENGLISH GUERNSEY HERD BOOK. 1885. a. £8. English Guernsey Cattle Society, The Bury Farm, Pednor Rd., Chesham, Bucks. HP5 2LA, England. index.
Cattle

ESTACION EXPERIMENTAL REGION AGROPECUARIA PERGAMINO. INFORME TECNICO. see *AGRICULTURE*

636   IT   ISSN 0071-2477
EUROPEAN ASSOCIATION FOR ANIMAL PRODUCTION. PUBLICATIONS. (Each no. available from a different source) (Text in English, French and German) 1950. irreg., no.33, 1986. price varies. European Association for Animal Production, Corso Trieste 67, 00198 Rome, Italy. Indexed: Biol.Abstr. Chem.Abstr.

636   IT   ISSN 0071-2485
EUROPEAN ASSOCIATION FOR ANIMAL PRODUCTION. SYMPOSIA ON ENERGY METABOLISM. (Subseries of: European Association for Animal Production. Publications) 1958. quadriennial; 9th, Norway, 1982. European Association for Animal Production, c/o Dr. J. Boyazoglu, Sec.-Gen., Corso Trieste 67, 00198 Rome, Italy.

636   UN
F A O ANIMAL PRODUCTION AND HEALTH SERIES. (Editions in English, French and Spanish) irreg. price varies. Food and Agriculture Organization of the United Nations, Distribution and Sales Section, Via delle Terme di Caracalla, 00100 Rome, Italy (Dist. in U.S. by: Bernan Associates-Unipub, 4611-F Assembly Drive, Lanham, MD 20706-4391) Indexed: Nutr.Abstr. Rev.Appl.Entomol.
Incorporating: F A O Agricultural Studies (ISSN 0071-6987)

636.932   DK   ISSN 0900-288X
FAELLESUDVALGET TIL KANINAVLENS FREMME BERETNING. 1965. biennial. Kr.45. Faellesudvalget til Kaninavlens Fremme, Birkevaenget 74, 6600 Vejen, Denmark. illus.

636   UK   ISSN 0144-6169
FARM ANIMAL WELFARE CO-ORDINATING EXECUTIVE. NEWSLETTER. 1979. a. free. Farm Animal Welfare Co-ordinating Executive, c/o Miss D. Hayman, Springhill House, 280 London Rd., Cheltenham GL52 6HS, England. Ed. Robin Corbett. circ. 3,000.

FLEISCHLEISTUNGSPRUEFUNG FUER RINDER, LEGELEISTUNGSPRUEFUNG FUER HUEHNER, FLEISCHLEISTUNGSPRUEFUNG FUER SCHAFE. see *AGRICULTURE — Dairying And Dairy Products*

AGRICULTURE — POULTRY AND LIVESTOCK

636.3   UK
FLOCK BOOK OF DEVON CORNWALL LONGWOOL SHEEP. 1977. a. £5. Devon and Cornwall Longwool Flockbook Association, Sudridge, Beaford, Winkleigh, Devon, England. circ. 100.

636.3   UK
FLOCK BOOK OF OXFORD DOWN SHEEP. 1889. a. £1.50. Oxford Down Sheep Breeder's Association, Woodhouse Farm, Woodhouses Auckland Co., Durham DL1 40LL, England. Ed. Julie A. Sedgewick. circ. 100.

636.4   DK   ISSN 0107-6922
FORTEGNELSE OVER ANERKENDTE AVLSCENTRE, ASPIRANTBESAETNINGER, OPFORMERINGSBESAETNINGER. 1980. a. Landsudvalget for Svineavl og Produktion, Axelborg, Axeltorv 3, 1609 Copenhagen V, Denmark.
    Formerly: Fortegnelse over Anerkendte Avlscentre, Fremavlssteder, Aspirantbesaetninger, Opformeringsbesaetninger.

636   591   GW   ISSN 0301-2743
FORTSCHRITTE IN DER TIERPHYSIOLOGIE UND TIERERNAEHRUNG/ADVANCES IN ANIMAL PHYSIOLOGY AND ANIMAL NUTRITION. (Supplement to: Zeitschrift fuer Tierphysiologie, Tierernaehrung und Futtermittelkunde) (Text and summaries in English and German) 1972. irreg., no.16, 1985. price varies. Verlag Paul Parey (Hamburg), Spitalerstr. 12, 2000 Hamburg 1, W. Germany (B.R.D.) Ed. Walter Lenkeit. bibl. illus. index. (reprint service avail. from ISI) Indexed: Biol.Abstr. Chem.Abstr. Ind.Med. Nutr.Abstr. Biotech.Abstr. Food Sci.& Tech.Abstr.

636   UK
GALLOWAY HERD BOOK. 1878. a. £6. Galloway Cattle Society, 131 King St., Castle Douglas, Kirkcudbrightshire DG7 1LZ, Scotland. Ed. Chris Graves.
    Cattle

636.2   UK   ISSN 0430-9928
GALLOWAY JOURNAL. a. free. Galloway Cattle Society, 131 King St., Castle Douglas, Kirkcudbrightshire DG7 1LZ, Scotland. Ed. Chris Graves. adv. circ. 2,000.
    Cattle

636   GW   ISSN 0434-0035
GIESSENER SCHRIFTENREIHE TIERZUCHT UND HAUSTIERGENETIK. 1961. irreg., no.49, 1985. price varies. Verlag Paul Parey (Hamburg), Spitalerstr. 12, 2000 Hamburg 1, W. Germany (B.R.D.) bibl. illus. index. (reprint service avail. from ISI) Indexed: Biol.Abstr.

636   UK   ISSN 0261-698X
GREAT BRITAIN. AGRICULTURAL SCIENCE SERVICE. RESEARCH AND DEVELOPMENT REPORTS: ANIMAL SCIENCE. 1958. irreg. £3.50. H.M.S.O., P.O. Box 569, London SE1 9NH, England. (Co-sponsor: Ministry of Agriculture, Fisheries and Food)
    Supersedes in part: Great Britain. Pest Infestation Control Laboratory. Report (ISSN 0072-6486)

636.2   DK   ISSN 0900-8012
HANDBOG FOR KAVEGHOLD. 1985. a. Landbrugets Informationskontor, Greve Strand, Denmark.

636.5   US   ISSN 0082-9722
HATCHERIES AND DEALERS PARTICIPATING IN THE NATIONAL POULTRY IMPROVEMENT PLAN. 1937. a. free. U.S. Animal and Plant Health Inspection Service, Animal Physiology and Genetics Institute, Building 265, BARC-E, Beltsville, MD 20705. TEL 301-344-2527. Ed. R.D. Schar. circ. 6,500.
    Formerly: U.S. Department of Agriculture. Animal Science Research Branch. Hatcheries and Dealers Participating in the National Improvement Plan.

636.39   UK
HERD BOOK. 1886. a. £5. British Goat Society, MoretonHouse, Moretonhampstead, Devon, England.

636.39   AT   ISSN 0310-2971
HERD BOOK FOR ANGORA GOATS IN AUSTRALIA. 1972. a. Aus.$20 free to members. Angora Mohair Breeders of Australia, 2/65 Dundas Court, Phillip, A.C.T. 2606, Australia. Ed. J. Hall. adv. circ. 3,000.

636.2   UK   ISSN 0073-1943
HERD BOOK OF HEREFORD CATTLE. 1846. a. £15. ‡ Hereford Herd Book Society, Hereford House, 3 Offa Street, Hereford HR1 2LL, England.

636.2   UK   ISSN 0073-1951
HEREFORD BREED JOURNAL. 1932. a. £2. ‡ Hereford Herd Book Society, Hereford House, 3 Offa Street, Hereford HR1 2LL, England.
    Cattle

636.006   UN   ISSN 0255-0040
I L C A ANNUAL REPORT. French edition (ISSN 0255-3473) (Editions in English and French) a. International Livestock Centre for Africa, Box 5689, Addis Ababa, Ethiopia. charts. illus.

636   UN
I L C A PROCEEDINGS. 1980. irreg. International Livestock Centre for Africa, Box 5689, Addis Ababa, Ethiopia.

636.006   UN
I L C A PROGRAMME AND BUDGET. 1974. a. International Livestock Centre for Africa, Box 5689, Addis Ababa, Ethiopia. circ. controlled.
    Former titles: International Livestock Centre for Africa. Programme and Budget; International Livestock Centre for Africa. Report on Activities.

636   UN
I L C A RESEARCH REPORT. (Editions in English and French) 1982. irreg., latest no.13, 1986. International Livestock Centre for Africa, Box 5689, Addis Ababa, Ethiopia.
    Formerly: International Livestock Centre for Africa. Research Report.

INDIA. MINISTRY OF AGRICULTURE. BULLETIN ON FOOD STATISTICS. see *AGRICULTURE — Agricultural Economics*

636.5   II
INDIAN POULTRY INDUSTRY YEARBOOK. 1974. a. $50. S.P. Gupta, Ed. & Pub., A-25 Priyadarshini Vihar, Patparganj Rd., Delhi 110092, India. adv. bk. rev. circ. 2,000. Indexed: Nutr.Abstr. Anim.Breed.Abstr.

636   CU   ISSN 0138-7537
INFORMACION EXPRESS. SERIE: GANADO EQUINO. 1977. a. exchange basis. Centro de Informacion y Documentacion Agropecuario, Gaveta Postal 4149, Havana 4, Cuba (Dist. by: Ediciones Cubanas, Obispo No. 461, Aptdo. 605, Havana, Cuba) Indexed: Agrindex.

636.2   BL
INSEMINACAO ARTIFICIAL. irreg. Ministerio da Agricultura, Departamento Nacional de Producao Animal, Divisao de Fisiopatologia da Inseminacao Artificial, Brasilia, Brazil.

636   RW
INSTITUT DES SCIENCES AGRONOMIQUES DU RWANDA. DEPARTEMENT DES PRODUCTIONS ANIMALES. COMPTE RENDU DES TRAVAUX. a. Institut des Sciences Agronomiques, Departement des Productions Animales, B.P. 138, Butare, Rwanda.

636   633.11   BL
INSTITUTO DE PESQUISAS ZOOTECNICAS "FRANCISCO OSORIO". ANUARIO TECNICO. 1973. a. Instituto de Pesquisas Zootecnicas "Francisco Osorio", Rua Goncalves Dias, 661, 90, 000 Porto Alegre RS, Brazil. circ. 800. Indexed: Nutr.Abstr.

591   636.089   SP
INSTITUTO DE ZOOTECNIA. FACULTAD DE VETERINARIA. CATALOGO DE PUBLICACIONES. 1961. a. exchange basis. Instituto de Zootecnia, Facultad de Veterinaria, Publicaciones, Av. Medina Azahara 9, 14005 Cordoba, Spain. (Affiliate: Consejo Superior de Investigaciones Cientificas) bibl. circ. 700.

636   636.089   RM   ISSN 0557-4668
INSTITUTUL AGRONOMIC CLUJ-NAPOCA. BULETINUL. SERIA ZOOTEHNIE SI MEDICINA VETERINARA. (Text in Rumanian; summaries in English) 1975. a. 35 lei($10) Institutul Agronomic "Dr. Petru Groza", Str. Manastur No. 3, 3400 Cluj-Napoca, Rumania. Ed. Ioan Puia. circ. 500. (back issues avail.) Indexed: Biol.Abstr. Ind.Vet. Landwirt.Zentralbl. Vet.Bull.

636   RM   ISSN 0075-3513
INSTITUTUL AGRONOMIC ION IONESCU DE LA BRAD. LUCRARI STIINTIFICE, SERIA ZOOTECHNIE - MEDICINA VETERINARIA. 1957. a. Institutul Agronomic "Ion Ionescu de la Brad", Aleea M. Sadoveanu, Nr. 3, Jassy, Rumania. Indexed: Biol.Abstr. Nutr.Abstr. Anim.Breed.Abstr. Ind.Vet. Vet.Bull.

636   NE
INSTITUUT VOOR VEEVOEDINGSONDERZOEK. JAARVERSLAG. (Text in Dutch; summaries in English) 1900. a. price varies. Instituut voor Veevoedingsonderzoek - Institute for Livestock Feeding and Nutrition Research, Runderweg 2, Postbus 160, 8200 AD Lelystad, Netherlands. Indexed: Excerp.Med. Field Crop Abstr. Herb.Abstr.
    Formerly: Instituut voor Veevoedingsonderzoek "Hoorn". Jaarverslag (ISSN 0074-0489)

636.2   636.5   US
INTERNATIONAL CONFERENCE ON LIVESTOCK AND POULTRY IN THE TROPICS (PROCEEDINGS) (Text in Spanish and English) 1967. a. $5. ‡ University of Florida, Center for Tropical Agriculture, 3028 McCarty Hall, Gainesville, FL 32611. TEL 904-392-1965. (Co-sponsors: Institute of Food and Agricultural Sciences, Florida Cooperative Extension Service) Ed. Hugh Popenoe. circ. 500.
    Formerly: Livestock and Poultry in Latin America. Annual Conference (ISSN 0085-2805)
    Cattle and poultry

338.1   AT   ISSN 0534-9869
INTERNATIONAL EGG MARKETING CONFERENCE. PROCEEDINGS.* 1962. irreg. Australian Egg Board, 263 Castlereagh St., Sydney, Australia.

636   UN
INTERNATIONAL MARKETS FOR MEAT. (Editions in English, French, German) 1981. a. 12 Fr. General Agreement on Tariffs and Trade, Centre William Rappard, 154 rue de Lausanne, CH-1211 Geneve 21, Switzerland.
    Formerly: World Market for Bovine Meat.

636   SP   ISSN 0074-6959
INTERNATIONAL MEETING OF ANIMAL NUTRITION EXPERTS. PROCEEDINGS. (Text in English, French, Italian and Spanish) 1958. irreg. $8. Ritena, P.O.B. 466, Barcelona, Spain. Ed. J. Amich-Gali. bk. rev. cum.index every 6 years. circ. 1,200.

INTERNATIONAL MEETING ON CATTLE DISEASES. REPORTS. see *VETERINARY SCIENCE*

IRELAND (EIRE) CENTRAL STATISTICS OFFICE. CROPS AND LIVESTOCK ENUMERATION. see *AGRICULTURE — Abstracting, Bibliographies, Statistics*

636   IE
IRELAND (EIRE) CENTRAL STATISTICS OFFICE. LIVESTOCK ENUMERATION. a. Central Statistics Office, Earlsfort Terrace, Dublin 2, Ireland. (processed)
    Formerly (until 1984): Ireland (Eire) Central Statistics Office. Livestock Numbers (ISSN 0075-059X)

636.5   GW   ISSN 0447-2713
JAHRBUCH FUER DIE GEFLUEGELWIRTSCHAFT. a. DM.6. (Zentralverband der Deutschen Gefluegelwirtschaft) Verlag Eugen Ulmer, Wollgrasweg 41, Postfach 700561, 7000 Stuttgart 70, W. Germany (B.R.D.) Ed. Dr. Hermann Vogt, Celle. circ. 4,500.
    Poultry

AGRICULTURE — POULTRY AND LIVESTOCK

636 UK
JERSEY HERD BOOK AND MEMBERS DIRECTORY. 1958. a. £16.50. ‡ Jersey Cattle Society of the U.K., Jersey House, 154 Castle Hill, Reading, Berks. RG1 7RP, England.
Former titles: Combined Jersey Herd Book, Directory and Elite Register of the U.K; Jersey Herd Book and Directory of the U.K. (ISSN 0075-3629); Jersey Herd Book of the U.K.

JOURNAL OF ANIMAL SCIENCE. SUPPLEMENT. see *VETERINARY SCIENCE*

636 SX
KARAKUL. 1958. a. Board of Karakul Breeders Society of South Africa, Head Office, P.O. Box 128, Windoek 9100, Namibia. Ed. B. Von Kunow. adv. circ. 2,000.

636.5 DK ISSN 0105-9882
LANDSUDVALGET FOR FJERKRAE. MEDDELELSE. irreg. Landsudvalget for Fjerkrae, Vester Farimagsgade 1, 1606 Copenhagen V, Denmark.

636.2 DK ISSN 0900-050X
LIMOUSINE NYT. 1979. irreg. (3-4/yr.) membership. Dansk Limousine Forening, Kongsgaardsvej 28, 8260 Viby J, Denmark. Ed. Susanne Lykke-Hansen.

636 US
LIVESTOCK: LATIN AMERICAN INDUSTRIAL REPORT. (Avail. for each of 22 Latin American countries) 1985. a. $435 per country report per industry covered. Aurora International, Box 9099, Bridgeport, CT 06601-2099. TEL 203-368-0579. Ed. Andres C. Aquino.

636 US ISSN 0076-1052
LOUISIANA STATE UNIVERSITY. ANIMAL SCIENCE DEPARTMENT. LIVESTOCK PRODUCERS' DAY REPORT. 1961. a. free. ‡ Louisiana State University, Animal Science Department, Baton Rouge, LA 70803. (Co-sponsors: Louisiana Agricultural Experiment Station; Louisiana Cooperative Extention Service) circ. 2,000.

636 UK ISSN 0076-5716
MEAT AND LIVESTOCK COMMISSION, BUCKS., ENGLAND. INDEX OF RESEARCH. 1961. a. £5. Meat and Livestock Commission, Queensway House, Bletchley, Milton Keynes MK2 2EF, England. Ed. Dr. D.R. Melrose. Indexed: Anim.Breed.Abstr.
Formerly: Index of Pig Research.

MEAT TRADE YEARBOOK & DIARY. see *FOOD AND FOOD INDUSTRIES*

636.2 US ISSN 0076-7824
MICHIGAN BEEF CATTLE DAY REPORT. 1965. a. free. Michigan State University, Agricultural Experiment Station, Agriculture Hall, East Lansing, MI 48824. TEL 517-655-1722. Eds. Dan Fox, Harlan Ritchie. circ. 4,000. (reprint service avail. from UMI,ISI)
Cattle

MISSOURI. DEPARTMENT OF AGRICULTURE. WEEKLY MARKET SUMMARY. see *AGRICULTURE*

636 US ISSN 0077-3255
NATIONAL ASSOCIATION OF ANIMAL BREEDERS. ANNUAL PROCEEDINGS. 1952. a. price varies. National Association of Animal Breeders, 401 Bernadette St., Box 1033, Columbia, MO 65205. TEL 314-445-4406. Ed. William M. Durfey.

636 US
NATIONAL HEREFORD HOG RECORD ASSOCIATION. ANNUAL NEWSLETTER. 1942. a. National Hereford Hog Record Association, Rte. 1, Box 37, Flandreau, SD 57028. TEL 605-997-2116. Ed. Ruby Schrecengost. circ. 300. (looseleaf format; back issues avail.)

636 JA ISSN 0289-4238
NATIONAL INSTITUTE OF ANIMAL INDUSTRY, IBARAKI, JAPAN. ANNUAL REPORT. (Text in Japanese) a. National Institute of Animal Industry - Chikusan Shikenjo, Tsukuba Norindanchi P.O. Box 5, Ibaraki 305, Japan.
Formerly: National Institute of Animal Industry, Chiba, Japan. Annual Report.

636 JA
NATIONAL INSTITUTE OF ANIMAL INDUSTRY, IBARAKI, JAPAN. BULLETIN/ CHIKUSAN SHIKENJO, IBARAKI, JAPAN. CHIKUSAN SHIKENJO KENKYU HOKOKU. (Text in Japanese; summaries in English) 1963. irreg. National Institute of Animal Industry - Chikusan Shikenjo, Tsukuba Norindanci P.O. Box 5, Ibaraki 305, Japan. Ed.Bd. abstr. charts. illus. circ. 1,100. Indexed: Biol.Abstr. Chem.Abstr. Nutr.Abstr. Dairy Sci.Abstr. Anim.Breed.Abstr. Bibl.Agri. Dairy Sci.Abstr. Field Crop Abstr. Food Sci.& Tech.Abstr. Herb.Abstr. Plant Breed.Abstr.
Formerly: National Institute of Animal Industry, Chiba, Japan. Bulletin. (ISSN 0077-488X)

636 JA
NATIONAL INSTITUTE OF ANIMAL INDUSTRY, IBARAKI, JAPAN. BULLETIN SUMMARIES. (Summaries in English) 1963. irreg. National Institute of Animal Industry - Chikusan Shikenjo, Tsukuba Norindanchi P.O. Box 5, Ibaraki 305, Japan. Ed.Bd. circ. 300. Indexed: Biol.Abstr. Chem.Abstr. Nutr.Abstr. Anim.Breed.Abstr. Bibl.Agri. Dairy Sci.Abstr. Bibl.Repro. Ind.Vet. Vet.Bull.
Formerly: National Institute of Animal Industry, Chiba, Japan. (ISSN 0077-4898)

636.4 UK ISSN 0077-5312
NATIONAL PIG BREEDERS' ASSOCIATION HERD BOOK. 1885. irreg. £5 to non-members. National Pig Breeders' Association, 7 Rickmansworth Rd., Watford, Herts., WD1 7HE, England. Ed. G.E. Welsh.
Hogs

636 338.1 NZ ISSN 0078-0138
NEW ZEALAND. MEAT AND WOOL BOARDS' ECONOMIC SERVICE. ANNUAL REVIEW OF THE SHEEP INDUSTRY; review of physical and economic conditions in sheepfarming in New Zealand. 1952. a. free, limited distribution; also avail. on exchange. Meat and Wool Boards' Economic Service, P.O. Box 5179, Wellington, New Zealand. circ. 2,500. Indexed: Anim.Breed.Abstr.

NEW ZEALAND POULTRY BOARD. REPORT; AND NEW ZEALAND MARKETING AUTHORITY REPORT AND STATEMENT OF ACCOUNTS. see *AGRICULTURE — Agricultural Economics*

636 NZ ISSN 0370-2731
NEW ZEALAND SOCIETY OF ANIMAL PRODUCTION. PROCEEDINGS. 1941. a. NZ.$28. New Zealand Society of Animal Production, Ruakura Agricultural Research Centre, Private Bag, Hamilton, New Zealand. Ed. T. Reardon. circ. 1,200. Indexed: Anim.Breed.Abstr. Biol.Abstr. Nutr.Abstr.

OUTLOOK. see *AGRICULTURE — Feed, Flour And Grain*

636 PK ISSN 0083-8292
PAKISTAN. DIRECTORATE OF LIVESTOCK FARMS. REPORT. (Text in English) 1962/63. a. Directorate of Livestock Farms, 16 Cooper Rd., Lahore, Pakistan. circ. 100.

636.4 US
PORK ROUNDUP. 1973. a. free. ‡ Kent Feeds Inc., 1600 Oregon St., Muscatine, IA 52761. TEL 319-264-4211. (tabloid format)
Hogs

636.5 338.1 CN ISSN 0032-5775
POULTRY MARKET REVIEW. 1950. a. free. Agriculture Canada, Livestock Development Division, Ottawa, Ont., Canada. TEL 613-995-5880. circ. 2,000.

POULTRY MARKET STATISTICS. see *AGRICULTURE — Abstracting, Bibliographies, Statistics*

636.2 US
POULTRY ROUNDUP. 1973. a. free. Kent Feeds, Inc., 1600 Oregon St., Muscatine, IA 52761. TEL 319-264-4211.

636.5 IS ISSN 0079-5968
PROFITABILITY OF POULTRY FARMING IN ISRAEL/HA-RIVHIYUT SHEL 'ANAF HA-LUL. (Issued as the Institute's Publications, Series B) (Text in Hebrew) 1964/65. irreg. IS.45($3) per issue. Institute of Farm Income Research, 6 Hachashmonaim Blvd., Tel-Aviv 67018, Israel.

636 NE
RAPPORT I V V O. (Text in Dutch and English) 1965. irreg. price varies. Instituut voor Veevoedingsonderzoek - Institute for Livestock Feeding and Nutrition Research, Runderweg 2, Postbus 160, 8200 AD Lelystad, Netherlands.
Formerly: Instituut voor Veevoedingsonderzoek "Hoorn." Report.

636.2 UK
RED POLL HERD BOOK. 1874. a. £10. Red Poll Cattle Society, 6 Church St., Woodbridge, Suffolk, England. Ed. Philip Ryder-Davies. adv. circ. 200.

RESEARCH INSTITUTE OF ANIMAL PRODUCTION AT NITRA. SCIENTIFIC WORKS. see *AGRICULTURE — Dairying And Dairy Products*

636 PL ISSN 0080-3669
ROCZNIKI NAUK ROLNICZYCH. SERIA B. ZOOTECHNICZNA. (Text in Polish; summaries in English, Polish or Russian) 1903. irreg., vol.101, 1983. price varies. (Polska Akademia Nauk, Komitet Nauk Zootechnicznych) Panstwowe Wydawnictwo Naukowe, Miodowa 10, 00-251 Warsaw, Poland (Dist. by: Ars Polona, Krakowskie Przedmiescie 7, 00-068 Warsaw, Poland) Ed. F. Wilczak. bibl. charts. circ. 550. Indexed: Biol.Abstr. Chem.Abstr. Nutr.Abstr.& Rev. Anim.Bread.Abstr. Dairy Sci.Abstr. Field Crop Abstr. Herb.Abstr. Ind.Vet. Vet.Bull.

636.3 UK
ROMNEY SHEEP BREEDERS' SOCIETY. FLOCK BOOK. 1895. a. £3. Romney Sheep Breeders' Society, Geneva, School Road, St. Mary in the Marsh, Romney Marsh, Kent, England. Ed. David Roberts. adv. circ. 1,000.

636.085 US ISSN 0036-0104
RURAL ROUNDUP. 1950. a. free. ‡ Kent Feeds Inc., Muscatine, IA 52761. TEL 319-264-4211. charts. illus. (tabloid format)

RWANDA. MINISTERE DE L'AGRICULTURE ET DE L'ELEVAGE. RAPPORT ANNUEL. see *AGRICULTURE*

636.3 ET
SHEEP AND GOATS IN HUMID WEST AFRICA. irreg. International Livestock Centre for Africa, P.O. Box 5689, Addis Ababa, Ethiopia.

636 UN
SMALL RUMINANT AND CAMEL GROUP DOCUMENT. 1985. irreg. International Livestock Centre for Africa, Box 5689, Addis Ababa, Ethiopia.

636 UN
SMALL RUMINANT AND CAMEL GROUP NEWSLETTER. 1984. irreg. International Livestock Center for Africa, P.O. Box 5689, Addis Ababa, Ethiopia.

338.1 AG ISSN 0081-0630
SOCIEDAD RURAL ARGENTINA. MEMORIA. (Supplements its Annales) 1887. a. free. ‡ Sociedad Rural Argentina, Florida 460, Buenos Aires, Argentina. circ. 15,000.

636 NL
SOUTH PACIFIC COMMISSION. REGIONAL CONFERENCE OF DIRECTORS OF AGRICULTURE, LIVESTOCK PRODUCTION AND FISHERIES. REPORT. irreg. South Pacific Commission, B.P. D5, Naumea Cedex, New Caledonia.
Formerly: Regional Conference of Directors of Agriculture, Livestock Production and Fisheries. Report.

636 636.089   SP   ISSN 0211-1314
SPAIN. INSTITUTO NACIONAL DE
INVESTIGACIONES AGRARIAS.
COMUNICACIONES. SERIE: HIGIENE Y
SANIDAD. Variant title: Higiene y Sanidad
Animal. no.4, 1980. irreg. Instituto Nacional de
Investigaciones Agrarias, Jose Abascal 56, Madrid 3,
Spain. charts. bibl. Indexed: Ind.Vet. Vet.Bull.

636   SP   ISSN 0210-3303
SPAIN. INSTITUTO NACIONAL DE
INVESTIGACIONES AGRARIAS.
COMUNICACIONES. SERIE: PRODUCCION
ANIMAL. no.7, 1981. irreg. Instituto Nacional de
Investigaciones Agrarias, Jose Abascal 56, Madrid 3,
Spain. bibl. charts. stat. Indexed: Biol.Abstr.
Anim.Breed.Abstr. Rev.Appl.Entomol.

636   SP
SPAIN. INSTITUTO NACIONAL DE
INVESTIGACIONES AGRARIAS.
INVESTIGACION AGRARIA: PRODUCCION Y
SANIDAD ANIMALES. 1986. irreg. Ministerio de
Agricultura, Pesca y Alimentacion, Instituto
Nacional de Investigaciones Agrarias, Jose Abaseal
56, 28003 Madrid, Spain.

636.2   DK   ISSN 0108-0903
STAMBOG OVER KOEER AF ROED DANSK
MALKERACE. 1981. a. Kr.40. Landsudvalget for
Kvaeg, Stambogsfoereningen for RDM,
Kongsgaardsvej 28, 8260 Viby, Denmark.

636.2   DK   ISSN 0105-0281
STAMBOG OVER KVAEG AF ROED DANSK
MALKERACE. 1972. a. Kr.40. Stambogsudvalget
for Kvaeg af Roed Dansk Malkerace, Eksp.
Landsudvalget for Kvaeg, Landskontoret,
Kongsgaardsvej 28, 8260 Viby J, Denmark.
  Former titles: Stambog og Elitestambog over Tyre
af Roed Dansk Malkerace; Elitestambog over Koeer
af Roed Dansk Malkerace.

636.2   NE
STIERENBOEK. a. fl.269.75. C. Misset B.V.,
Hanzestr. 1, 7006 RH Doetinchem, Netherlands
(Subscr. to: Postbus 4, 7000 BA Doetinchem,
Netherlands) circ. 1,500.

636.3   UK
SUFFOLK SHEEP SOCIETY FLOCK BOOK. 1887.
a. £12.50. Suffolk Sheep Society, Bucklesham Rd.,
Ipswich, England. Ed. Jean M. Mallett. circ. 1,900.

SUFFOLK STUD BOOK. see *SPORTS AND
GAMES — Horses And Horsemanship*

636.2   SA   ISSN 0081-9220
SUID-AFRIKAANSE GUERNSEY. Short title: S.A.
Guernsey. (Text in Afrikaans and English) 1960. a.
free. South African Guernsey Cattle Breeders
Society - Suid-Afrikaanse Guernsey
Beestelersgenootskap, P.O. Box 248, Humansdorp
6300, South Africa. Ed. K.E. Cadle. adv. circ. 2,
000.
  Cattle

636.4   DK   ISSN 0106-7338
SVINEAVL OG -PRODUKTION I DANMARK.
1973. a. free. Landsudvalget for Svin - National
Committee of Pig Breeding and Production,
Axelborg, Axeltorv 3, 1609 Copenhagen V,
Denmark. illus. circ. 30,000.

636.5   US   ISSN 0082-8661
TABLES ON HATCHERY AND FLOCK
PARTICIPATION IN THE NATIONAL
POULTRY IMPROVEMENT PLAN. 1937. a. free.
‡ U.S. Animal and Plant Health Inspection Service,
Bldg. 265, BARC-E, Beltsville, MD 20705. TEL
301-344-2527. Ed. R.D. Scher. circ. 4,000.
  Incorporating: U.S. Agricultural Research Service.
Animal Science Research Division. Tables on
Hatchery and Flock Participation in the National
Turkey Improvement Plan (ISSN 0082-867X)

636.4   US   ISSN 0082-1608
TAMWORTH ANNUAL. 1965. irreg. single copy
free; additional copies $0.25 ea. Tamworth Swine
Association, 414 Van Deman St., Washington Court
House, OH 43160. Ed. Robert Highfield. bk. rev.
circ. 1,500.
  Hogs

636   US
TECHNICAL CONFERENCE ON ARTIFICAL
INSEMINATION AND REPRODUCTION. 1966.
biennial. price varies. National Association of
Animal Breeders, 401 Bernadette St., Box 1033,
Columbia, MO 65205. TEL 314-445-4406. Ed.
William M. Durfey. Indexed: Anim.Breed.Abstr.

UNIVERSITY OF AGRICULTURAL SCIENCES.
REPORT. see *AGRICULTURE — Dairying And
Dairy Products*

636   CN   ISSN 0084-618X
UNIVERSITY OF ALBERTA. DEPARTMENT OF
ANIMAL SCIENCE. ANNUAL FEEDERS' DAY
REPORT. 1921. a. free. ‡ University of Alberta,
Department of Animal Science, Faculty of
Extension, Edmonton, Alta. T6G 2GA, Canada.
TEL 403-432-5050. Ed. Dr. J.P. Bowland. circ. 6,
000. (tabloid format; also avail. in microfilm from
UMI) Indexed: Biol.Abstr.

636 382   UY
URUGUAY. INSTITUTO NACIONAL DE
CARNES. ANUARIO ESTADISTICO DE
FAENA Y EXPORTACION. 1970. a. free.
Instituto Nacional de Carnes, Montevideo, Uruguay.
circ. 1,500.
  Formed by the merger of: Uruguay. Instituto
Nacional de Carnes. Departamento de
Exportaciones. Exportacion de Carnes, Estadisticas
& Uruguay. Instituto Nacional de Carnes.
Departamento de Exportaciones. Anuario.

639   VE
VENEZUELA. MINISTERIO DE AGRICULTURA
Y CRIA. DIVISION DE ESTADISTICA.
ENCUESTA AVICOLA NACIONAL. 1962. a.
free. Ministerio de Agricultura y Cria, Direccion de
Planificacion y Estadistica, Division de Estadistica,
Centro Simon Bolivar, Caracas, Venezuela. illus.

639   VE
VENEZUELA. MINISTERIO DE AGRICULTURA
Y CRIA. DIVISION DE ESTADISTICA.
ENCUESTA DE GANADO PORCINO. a.
Ministerio de Agricultura y Cria, Direccion de
Planificacion y Estadistica, Division de Estadistica,
Torre Norte, Centro Simon Bolivar, Caracas,
Venezuela.

636   PL   ISSN 0208-5739
WARSAW AGRICULTURAL UNIVERSITY. S G G
W A R. ANNALS. ANIMAL SCIENCE. (Szkola
Glowna Gospodarstwa Wiejskiego - Akademia
Rolnicza) (Until 1980, part of Zeszyty Naukowe
series of Akademia Rolnicza, Warsaw) (Text mainly
in English; occasionally in French, German or
Russian; summaries in Polish) 1957. irreg. $6 per
no. Warsaw Agricultural University Press, Ul.
Nowoursynowska 166, 02-766 Warsaw, Poland
(Dist. by: Ars Polona-Ruch, Krakowskie
Przedmiescie 7, 00-608 Warsaw, Poland) Ed. A.
Lysak.
  Continues: Akademia Rolnicza, Warsaw. Zeszyty
Naukowe. Zootechnika; Which was formerly:
Szkolna Glowna Gospodarstwa Wiejskiego. Zeszyty
Naukowe. Zootechnika (ISSN 0509-7134)

636 639.2   GW   ISSN 0170-7353
WER UND WAS IN DER DEUTSCHEN FLEISCH-
FISCH- UND FEINKOST-INDUSTRIE. 1976.
biennial. DM.108. B. Behr's GmbH & Co.,
Averhoffstr. 10, 2000 Hamburg 76, W. Germany
(B.R.D.)

636   AT
WESTERN AUSTRALIA. DEPARTMENT OF
AGRICULTURE. ANIMAL DIVISION.
ANNUAL REPORT. a. Department of Agriculture,
Animal Division, Perth, W.A., Australia.

636   AT
WESTERN AUSTRALIA. DIVISION OF ANIMAL
PRODUCTION. ANNUAL REPORT. a.
Department of Agriculture, Animal Division, Perth,
W.A., Australia.

WHO'S WHO IN THE EGG AND POULTRY
INDUSTRIES. see *BIOGRAPHY*

636   NZ
WOOL. vol.6, 1976. a. exchange basis. Massey Wool
Association (Inc.), P.O. Box 12342, Wellington
North, New Zealand. Ed. Warwick Massey. adv.
circ. 2,000. Indexed: Biol.Abstr. Rural
Recreat.Tour.Abstr. Text.Tech.Dig. World
Agri.Econ.& Rural Sociol.Abstr. World Text.Abstr.
  Sheep

636   UY   ISSN 0084-1552
WORLD CONFERENCE ON ANIMAL
PRODUCTION. PROCEEDINGS. (Proceedings
published by organizing committee) (Text in
English, French, German or Spanish) 1963. irreg.,
1973, 3rd, Melbourne. World Association for
Animal Production, c/o Dr. Hernan Caballero,
Secretary General, Casilla de Correos 1217,
Montevideo, Uruguay.

636.5   US   ISSN 0084-2532
WORLD'S POULTRY SCIENCE ASSOCIATION.
REPORT OF THE PROCEEDINGS OF
INTERNATIONAL CONGRESS. quadrennial.
$20. World's Poultry Science Association, c/o I.L.
Peterson, Sec., USA Branch - World's Poultry
Science Association, NPIP, VS, APHIS, USDA,
Federal Center Bldg., Hyattsville, MD 20782 (For
16th, Inquire: Lauriston von Schmidt, Rua Aurora,
291-1 Andar-Sala 16, 01209 Sao Paulo, SP, Brazil)
14th, 1974, New Orleans; 15th, 1978, Sao Paulo.
  Proceedings published in host country

636   RH
ZIMBABWE. CENTRAL STATISTICAL OFFICE.
LARGE SCALE AGRICULTURAL UNITS. 1969.
a. Rhod.$1($1.36) Central Statistical Office, P.O.
Box 8063, Causeway, Salisbury, Zimbabwe. circ.
300.
  Former titles: Zimbabwe. Central Statistical
Office. Agricultural Production in European Areas:
Livestock. National and Provincial Totals; Rhodesia.
Central Statistical Office. Agricultural Production in
European Areas. Part 1. Livestock. National and
Provincial Totals.

636   RH
ZIMBABWE. MINISTRY OF AGRICULTURE.
DIVISION OF LIVESTOCK AND PASTURES.
ANNUAL REPORT. 9173. a. free. Ministry of
Lands, Agriculture and Rural Resettlement,
Research and Specialist Services, Information
Services, Box 8108, Causeway, Harare, Zimbabwe.
circ. 800. (back issues avail.)

AIR TRANSPORT

see *Transportation — Air Transport*

ALLERGOLOGY AND IMMUNOLOGY

see *Medical Sciences — Allergology and
Immunology*

ANAESTHESIOLOGY

see *Medical Sciences — Anaesthesiology*

ANALYTICAL CHEMISTRY

see *Chemistry — Analytical Chemistry*

ANTHROPOLOGY

see also *Folklore*

ANTHROPOLOGY

572 US ISSN 0738-064X
A M S STUDIES IN ANTHROPOLOGY. 1983. irreg. price varies. A M S Press, Inc., 56 E. 13th St., New York, NY 10003. TEL 212-777-4700. (back issues avail.)

A P U PRESS ALASKANA BOOK SERIES. (Alaska Pacific University Press) see *HISTORY — History Of North And South America*

572 US
A S A RESEARCH METHODS IN SOCIAL ANTHROPOLOGY. 1976. irreg., vol.2, 1984. price varies. (Association of Social Anthropologists of the Commonwealth) Academic Press Inc., Orlando, FL 32887. index.
Formerly: A S A Monographs (ISSN 0066-9679)

572 990 AT ISSN 0314-8769
ABORIGINAL HISTORY. 1977. a. Aus.$8.50. (Australian National University, Department of Pacific and S.E. Asian History) Aboriginal History Inc., G.P.O. Box 4, Canberra, A.C.T.2601, Australia. Ed.Bd. bk. rev. circ. 800. (back issues avail.)

ACTA ETHNOLOGICA SLOVACA. see *FOLKLORE*

572 GW ISSN 0400-4043
ACTA HUMBOLDTIANA. irreg., vol.11, 1987. price varies. (Deutsche Ibero-Amerika-Stiftung) Franz Steiner Verlag Wiesbaden GmbH, Birkenwaldstr. 44, Postfach 347, D-7000 Stuttgart 1, W. Germany (B.R.D.) Ed. Wolfgang Haberland.

572 370 PL
ACTA UNIVERSITATIS LODZIENSIS: FOLIA ETHNOGRAPHICA. (Text in Polish; summaries in various languages) irreg. Uniwersytet Lodzki, Drukarnia Wojskowa, Ul. Gdanska 130, Lodz, Poland (Dist. by: Ars Polona-Ruch, Krakowskie Przedmiescie 7, Warsaw, Poland)

ACTA UNIVERSITATIS LODZIENSIS: FOLIA ZOOLOGICA ET ANTHROPOLOGICA. see *BIOLOGY — Zoology*

572 US ISSN 0065-1850
ADAN E. TREGANZA ANTHROPOLOGY MUSEUM. PAPERS. 1960. irreg., no.16, 1980. price varies. San Francisco State University, Adan E. Treganza Anthropology Museum, 1600 Holloway Ave., San Francisco, CA 94132. TEL 415-469-1642. Ed. James Dotta. circ. 450.
Formerly: California. State College, San Francisco. Department of Anthropology. Occasional Papers in Anthropology.

AFRICAN STUDY MONOGRAPHS. see *AGRICULTURE*

AFRICAN STUDY MONOGRAPHS. SUPPLEMENTARY ISSUE. see *AGRICULTURE*

572 BE
AFRICANA GANDENSIA. 1976. irreg. Rijksuniversiteit te Gent, Seminarie voor Afrikaanse Cultuurgeschiedenis, St. Pietersplein 4, B-9000 Ghent, Belgium. Indexed: Curr.Cont.Africa.

572 UR
AKADEMIYA NAUK S.S.S.R. INSTITUT ETNOGRAFII. POLEVYE ISSLEDOVANIYA. 1975. irreg. price varies. Izdatel'stvo Nauka, Podsosenskii per., 21, Moscow K-62, Russian S.F.S.R., U.S.S.R. (Subscr. to: Mezhdunarodnaya Kniga, Moscow, G-200, Russian S.F.S.R., U.S.S.R.) illus.

ALASKA NATIVE LANGUAGE CENTER RESEARCH PAPERS. see *LINGUISTICS*

572 913 CN ISSN 0831-5671
ALGONQUIAN CONFERENCE PAPERS. (Text in English and French) 1976. a. price varies. Carleton University, Department of Linguistics, Ottawa, Ont. K1S 5B6, Canada. TEL 613-564-5573. Ed. William Cowan. circ. 300.

ALT-THUERINGEN. see *HISTORY — History Of Europe*

ALTERNATE ROUTES; a critical review. see *SOCIAL SCIENCES: COMPREHENSIVE WORKS*

301.2 US
AMERICAN ANTHROPOLOGICAL ASSOCIATION. ABSTRACTS OF MEETINGS. a. price varies. American Anthropological Association, 1703 New Hampshire Ave., N.W., Washington, DC 20009. TEL 202-232-8800. adv.

572 US ISSN 0065-8200
AMERICAN ETHNOLOGICAL SOCIETY. PROCEEDINGS OF SPRING MEETING. 1957. a. price varies. West Publishing Co., Box 3526, St. Paul, MN 55165. TEL 612-228-2500. Ed. Robert F. Spenser. Indexed: Lang.& Lang.Behav.Abstr.

060 301.2 US ISSN 0569-4833
AMERICAN FOUNDATION FOR THE STUDY OF MAN. PUBLICATIONS.* irreg. price varies. Allen Press, Inc., 1041 New Hampshire St., Box 368, Lawrence, KS 66044. TEL 301-338-6987. (reprint service avail. from UMI)

572 US ISSN 0065-9452
AMERICAN MUSEUM OF NATURAL HISTORY. ANTHROPOLOGICAL PAPERS. 1907. irreg. price varies. American Museum of Natural History, Central Park W. at 79th St., New York, NY 10024. TEL 212-873-1300. Ed. Brenda Jones. circ. 1,500. Indexed: Biol.Abstr. Bull.Signal. Hist.Abstr. SSCI. Amer.Hist.& Life. Zoo.Rec.

572 UY
AMERINDIA; revista de prehistoria y etnologia de America. 1962. biennial. Centro de Estudios Arqueologicos y Antropologicos Americanos, Zubillaga 1117, Montevideo, Uruguay. bk. rev. Indexed: M.L.A.

ANALES DE ARQUEOLOGIA Y ETNOLOGIA. see *ARCHAEOLOGY*

572 410 ZR ISSN 0254-4296
ANNALES AEQUATORIA. 1980. a. $15. Missionnaires du Sacre Coeur, B.P. 1064, Mbandaka, Zaire (Subscr. to: M.S.C. Aequatoria, Te Boelaerlei, 11, B-2200 Borgerhout, Belgium) Ed. Honore Vinck. adv. bk. rev. circ. 450. Indexed: Bull.Signal.
Supersedes (1938-1962): Aequatoria.

572 RM
ANNUAIRE ROUMAIN D'ANTHROPOLOGIE. vol.17, 1980. a. 40 lei($42) (Academia Republicii Socialista Rumania) Editura Academiei Republicii Socialiste Rumania, Calea Victoriei 125, 79717 Bucharest, Rumania (Subscr. to: ROMPRESFILATELIA, Export-Import Presa, Calea Grivitei 64-66, P.O. Box 12-201, 78104 Bucharest, Rumania) Ed. Olga Necrasov. Indexed: Biol.Abstr. Excerp.Med.

301.2 US
ANNUAL EDITIONS: ANTHROPOLOGY. 1974. a. $9.50. Dushkin Publishing Group, Inc., Sluice Dock, Guilford, CT 06437. TEL 203-453-4351. Ed. Ian Nielsen. illus.
Formerly: Annual Editions: Readings in Anthropology (ISSN 0095-5582)

572 US ISSN 0084-6570
ANNUAL REVIEW OF ANTHROPOLOGY. 1972. a. $31. Annual Reviews Inc., 4139 El Camino Way, Palo Alto, CA 94306. TEL 415-493-4400. Ed. Bernard J. Siegel. bibl. charts. index. cum.index. (back issues avail.; reprint service avail. from ISI) Indexed: Biol.Abstr. Chem.Abstr. Curr.Cont. Psychol.Abstr. SSCI. Br.Archaeol.Abstr. Curr.Cont.Africa. Geo.Abstr. Lang.& Lang.Behav.Abstr. M.M.R.I.

572 PE ISSN 0254-9212
ANTHROPOLOGICA (LIMA) 1983. a. $6.50. Pontificia Universidad Catolica del Peru, Departamento de Ciencias Sociales, Fondo Editorial, Apdo. 1761, Lima 100, Peru. Ed. Alejandro Ortiz Rescaniere.
Incorporating: Revista de Debates: Debates en Antropologia; Which supersedes in part: Debates en Antropologia.

572 914 DK ISSN 0106-0880
ANTHROPOLOGICAL ANALYSES. irreg. Kr.122. (Archeology of Svendborg) Bibliotekscentralen, Telegrafvej 5, DK-2750 Ballerup, Denmark.

572 AT ISSN 0066-4677
ANTHROPOLOGICAL FORUM; an international journal of social and cultural anthropology and comparative sociology. 1963. irreg. Aus.$6 per no. University of Western Australia Press, Department of Anthropology, Nedlands, W.A. 6009, Australia. Ed. Ronald M. Berndt. adv. bk. rev. circ. 500. Indexed: E.I.

ANTHROPOLOGICAL LITERATURE; an index to periodical articles and essays. see *ANTHROPOLOGY — Abstracting, Bibliographies, Statistics*

572 301.2 GW ISSN 0066-4685
ANTHROPOLOGIE. (Text in German and Czech) 1962/63. irreg., vol.23, 1985. DM.36. (Moravske Museum, Brno, CS) Dr. Rudolf Habelt GmbH, Am Buchenhang 1, 5300 Bonn 1, W. Germany (B.R.D.) Ed. J. Jelinek.

301.2 AU ISSN 0066-4693
ANTHROPOLOGISCHE GESELLSCHAFT, VIENNA. MITTEILUNGEN. 1870. a. price varies. Verlag Ferdinand Berger and Soehne OHG, Wienerstr. 21-23, A-3580 Horn, Austria. Indexed: Biol.Abstr. Hist.Abstr. Amer.Hist.& Life. Br.Archaeol.Abstr.

572 II ISSN 0003-5556
ANTHROPOLOGIST.* (Text in English) 1954. irreg. $5. University of Delhi, Department of Anthropology, Delhi 110007, India. Ed. P.C. Biswas.

570 US ISSN 0003-5564
ANTHROPOLOGY U C L A. 1969. a. $10 to individuals; institutions $15. University of California, Los Angeles, Department of Anthropology, 405 Hilgard Ave., Los Angeles, CA 90024. TEL 213-825-2055. Ed.Bd. adv. bk. rev. charts. circ. 250. (reprint service avail. from ISI) Indexed: Curr.Cont. SSCI. Abstr.Anthropol.

ANTHROPOS; studie z oboru anthropologie, paleoethnologie, paleontologie a kvarterni geologie. see *PALEONTOLOGY*

572 IT ISSN 0391-3163
ANTHROPOS. 1979. irreg., no.11, 1986. price varies. Liguori Editore s.r.l., Via Mezzocannone 19, 80134 Naples, Italy. TEL 081/20 6077. Ed. Vittorio Lanternari.

573 GR
ANTHROPOS: YEARBOOK IN ANTHROPOLOGY. 1974. a. $12. Anthropological Association of Greece, Daphnomili 5, 114 71 Athens, Greece. Ed. Aris N. Poulianos. bk. rev. circ. 1,000. Indexed: GeoRef.

301.2 PL ISSN 0137-1460
ANTROPOLOGIA. (Text in Polish; summaries in English) 1971. irreg., no.4, 1976. irreg. Uniwersytet im. Adama Mickiewicza w Poznaniu, Wieniawskiego 1, 61-712 Poznan, Poland (Dist. by: Ars Polona, Krakowskie Przedmiescie 7, 00-068 Warsaw, Poland)
Formerly: Uniwersytet im. Adama Mickiewicza w Poznaniu. Wydzial Biologii i Nauk o Ziemi. Seria Antropologia.

572 PE
ANTROPOLOGIA ANDINA. 1976. a. $10. Centro de Estudios Andinos Cuzco, Apartado 582, Cuzco, Peru. Ed. J. Flores Ochoa. adv. bk. rev. circ. 1,000.

301.2 EC
ANTROPOLOGIA ECUATORIANA. 1978. irreg. S/50 per no. Casa de la Cultura Ecuatoriana, Seccion Academica de Antropologia y Arqueologia, Casilla 67, Quito, Ecuador.

573 PE
ANTROPOLOGIA FISICA. 1976. irreg. S/200($4) Museo Nacional de Antropologia y Arqueologia, Plaza Bolivar s/n Pueblo Libre, Lima, Peru.

572 PO ISSN 0870-0990
ANTROPOLOGIA PORTUGUESA. (Summaries in English or French.) 1983. a. exchange basis. Universidade de Coimbra, Museu e Laboratorio Antropologico, 3000 Coimbra, Portugal. bk. rev. circ. 1,000.

572 BL
ANUARIO ANTROPOLOGICO. 1976. a. $20.
Edicoes Tempo Brasileiro Ltda, Rua Gago Coutinho
61, C.P. 16099, ZC-01 Laranjeiras, Rio de Janeiro,
Brazil. Dir. Roberto Cardosa de Oliveira.

572 SP ISSN 0210-5810
ANUARIO DE ESTUDIOS AMERICANOS. a. 1500
ptas. Consejo Superior de Investigaciones
Cientificas, Serrano 117, Madrid, Spain. Ed. Jose
Julio Perlado. Indexed: Hist.Abstr. Amer.Hist.&
Life. Hisp.Amer.Per.Ind.

301.2 398 SP ISSN 0210-7732
ANUARIO DE EUSKO-FOLKLORE; etnografia y
paletnografia. 1921. a. Sociedad de Estudios Vascos,
Churruca, 7-2, 20004 San Sebastian, Spain. circ.
500. (back issues avail.)

572 MX
ANUARIO INDIGENISTA/INDIANIST
YEARBOOK. (Text in Spanish; summaries in
English) 1962. a. Instituto Indigenista
Interamericano, Insurgentes Sur 1690, Colonia
Florida, Mexico 01030, D.F., Mexico. Ed.
Alejandro Camino. bk. rev. circ. controlled.
(processed) Indexed: Hist.Abstr. Amer.Hist.& Life.
Hisp.Amer.Per.Ind.

APPLICATIONS ET TRANSFERTS. (Societe
d'Etudes Linguistiques et Anthropologiques de
France (SELAF)) see LINGUISTICS

ARCHAEOLOGIA AUSTRIACA; Beitraege zur
Palaeanthropologie, Ur- und Fruehgeschichte
Oesterreichs. see ARCHAEOLOGY

301.2 AU ISSN 0066-6513
ARCHIV FUER VOELKERKUNDE. 1946. a. price
varies. (Museum fuer Voelkerkunde) Wilhelm
Braumueller, Universitaets-Verlagsbuchhandlung
GmbH, Servitengasse 5, A-1092 Vienna, Austria.
bk. rev. circ. 800. Indexed: Curr.Cont.Abstr. E.I.

572 IT
ARCHIVIO PER L'ANTROPOLOGIA E LA
ETNOLOGIA. (Text in English, French and
Italian) 1871. a. L.140000. Societa Italiana di
Antropologia e Etnologia, Palazzo Nonfinito, Via
del Proconsolo, 12, 50129 Florence, Italy.

572 MX
ARCHIVO HISTORICO DIOCESANO DE SAN
CRISTOBAL DE LAS CASAS. BOLETIN. 1981.
irreg., vol.3, no.1-2, 1986. $23. Instituto de Asesoria
Antropologica para la Region Maya, Archivo
Historico Diocesano, Apdo. 6, San Cristobal de las
Casas, Chiapas-C.P. 29200, Mexico. Ed. Angelica
Inda. circ. 500.

913 US ISSN 0271-0641
ARIZONA STATE UNIVERSITY
ANTHROPOLOGICAL RESEARCH PAPERS.
1969. irreg. (2-5/yr.) price varies per no. Arizona
State University, Department of Anthropology,
Tempe, AZ 85287. TEL 602-965-6213. Ed. G.A.
Clark. circ. 750.

ASCLEPIO; archivo Iberoamericano de historia de la
medicina. see MEDICAL SCIENCES

ASIE DU SUD-EST ET MONDE INSULINDIEN.
see LINGUISTICS

570 US ISSN 0066-9172
ASSOCIATION FOR SOCIAL ANTHROPOLOGY
IN OCEANIA. MONOGRAPH SERIES. 1970.
irreg. price varies. University Press of America,
4720 Boston Way, Lanham, MD 20706 TEL 301-
459-3366. (Also avail. from: UMI, 300 N. Zeeb Rd.,
Ann Arbor, MI 48106) Ed. Vern Carroll. Indexed:
Sociol.Abstr.

301.2 390 PL ISSN 0067-0316
ATLAS POLSKICH STROJOW LUDOWYCH. (Text
in Polish; summaries in Czech, English and
German) 1949. irreg. price varies. Polskie
Towarzystwo Ludoznawcze, Ul. Szewska 36, 50-139
Wroclaw, Poland (Dist. by Ars Polona, Krakowskie
Przedmiescie 7, Warsaw, Poland) Ed. Barbar
Bazielich. circ. 1,800.

572 301.2 US
BALLENA PRESS ANTHROPOLOGICAL
PAPERS. 1973. irreg., no.29, 1985. price varies.
Ballena Press, 823 Valparaiso Ave., Menlo Park, CA
94025. TEL 415-323-9261. Ed. Thomas C.
Blackburn.

BAUERNHAEUSER AUS MITTELEUROPA;
Aufmasse und Publikationen von Gerhard Eitzen.
see ARCHITECTURE

BEITRAEGE ZUR AFRIKAKUNDE. see
HISTORY — History Of Africa

301.2 GW ISSN 0408-8514
BEITRAEGE ZUR MITTELAMERIKANISCHEN
VOELKERKUNDE. 1953. irreg., no.14, 1977. price
varies. (Hamburgisches Museum fuer Voelkerkunde)
Klaus Renner Verlag, Am Sonnenhang 8, 8021
Hohenschaeftlarn, W. Germany (B.R.D.)

BERNICE PAUAHI BISHOP MUSEUM,
HONOLULU. OCCASIONAL PAPERS. see
SCIENCES: COMPREHENSIVE WORKS

BERNICE PAUAHI BISHOP MUSEUM,
HONOLULU. SPECIAL PUBLICATIONS. see
SCIENCES: COMPREHENSIVE WORKS

BIBLIOGRAFICA FOLCLORICA. see FOLKLORE

301.2 PE
BIBLIOTECA DE CULTURA ANDINA.
EDICIONES. 1978. irreg. price varies. G. Herrera
Editores, Plaza San Martin 957-601, Lima, Peru.

301.2 PY
BIBLIOTECA PARAGUAYA DE
ANTROPOLOGIA. 1980. irreg. price varies.
Universidad Catolica Nuestra Senora de la
Asuncion, Centro de Estudios Antropologicos,
Casilla de Correo 1718, Asuncion, Paraguay. circ. 1,
000. (back issues avail.)

572 NE ISSN 0067-8023
BIBLIOTHECA INDONESICA. (Text in English)
1968. irreg. price varies. (Koninklijk Instituut voor
Taal-, Land- en Volkenkunde) Foris Publications,
Box 509, 3300 AM Dordrecht, Netherlands.

572 PY ISSN 0560-4168
BOLETIN DE LA SOCIEDAD CIENTIFICA DEL
PARAGUAY Y DEL MUSEO ETNOGRAFICO.
1957. irreg. Museo Etnografico, Espana 395,
Asuncion, Paraguay. (Co-sponsor: Sociedad
Cientifica del Paraguay) bibl.

572 BL
BRAZIL. MUSEU DO INDIO. BOLETIM.
ANTROPOLOGIA. (Text in Portuguese; summaries
in English & Portuguese) 1974. irreg. Museu do
Indio, Biblioteca Marechal Rondon, Rua das
Palmeiras 55, Botafogo, CEP. 22270 Rio de Janeiro,
Brazil. bibl. charts.

BULLETIN OF TIBETOLOGY. see HISTORY —
History Of Asia

BY OG BYGD; Norsk Folkemuseums aarbok. see
HISTORY — History Of Europe

CAESARAUGUSTA. see ARCHAEOLOGY

951.7 FR
CAHIERS D'ETUDES MONGOLES ET
SIBERIENNES. 1970. a. price varies. Universite de
Paris X (Paris-Nanterre), Laboratoire d'Ethnologie
et de Sociologie Comparative, Laboratoire
d'Ethnologie et de Sociologie Comparative, 200
Ave. de la Republic, 92001 Nanterre, France. Ed.
Robert Hamyon. bk. rev. bibl. circ. 500. (back issues
avail.) Indexed: Hist.Abstr. M.L.A. Amer.Hist.&
Life.
Formerly: Etudes Mongoles.

CAHIERS DES EXPLORATEURS. see
GEOGRAPHY

CALGARY ARCHAEOLOGIST. see
ARCHAEOLOGY

572 301 UK ISSN 0068-6719
CAMBRIDGE PAPERS IN SOCIAL
ANTHROPOLOGY. 1958. irreg., no.11, 1983.
$37.50. Cambridge University Press, Edinburgh
Bldg., Shaftesbury Rd., Cambridge CB2 2RU,
England (And 32 E. 57 St., New York NY 10022)
Ed.Bd.

572 UK
CAMBRIDGE STUDIES IN CULTURAL
SYSTEMS. 1977. irreg. price varies. Cambridge
University Press, Edinburgh Bldg., Shaftesbury Rd.,
Cambridge CB2 2RU, England (And 32 E. 57th St.,
New York, NY 10022) Ed. Clifford Geertz.

572 UK
CAMBRIDGE STUDIES IN ORAL AND
LITERATE CULTURE. 1981. irreg. price varies.
Cambridge University Press, Edinburgh Bldg.,
Shaftesbury Rd., Cambridge CB2 2RU, England
(And 32 E. 57th St., New York, NY 10022)

572 UK ISSN 0068-6794
CAMBRIDGE STUDIES IN SOCIAL
ANTHROPOLOGY. 1967. irreg. price varies.
Cambridge University Press, Edinburgh Bldg.,
Shaftesbury Rd., Cambridge CB2 2RU, England
(and 32 E. 57 St., New York, NY 10022) Ed. Jack
Goody. Indexed: Math.R.

301 CN ISSN 0316-1897
CANADA. NATIONAL MUSEUM OF MAN.
MERCURY SERIES. CANADIAN CENTRE
FOR FOLK CULTURE STUDIES. PAPERS/
CANADA. MUSEE NATIONAL DE L'HOMME.
COLLECTION MERCURE. CENTRE
CANADIEN D'ETUDES SUR LA CULTURE
TRADITIONNELLE. DOSSIERS. (Text in English
or French) 1972. irreg., no.43, 1982. free. (National
Museum of Man) National Museums of Canada,
Ottawa, Ontario K1A 0M8, Canada. TEL 613-992-
4397.

572 CN ISSN 0316-1862
CANADA. NATIONAL MUSEUM OF MAN.
MERCURY SERIES. CANADIAN ETHNOLOGY
SERVICE. PAPERS/CANADA. MUSEE
NATIONAL DE L'HOMME. COLLECTION
MERCURE. SERVICE CANADIEN
D'ETHNOLOGIE. DOSSIERS. (Text in English or
French) 1972. irreg., no.85, 1982. free. (National
Museum of Man) National Museums of Canada,
Ottawa, Ontario K1A 0M8, Canada. TEL 613-992-
3497.

572 CN ISSN 0225-9958
CANADIAN REVIEW OF PHYSICAL
ANTHROPOLOGY/REVIEW CANADIENNE
D'ANTHROPOLOGIE PHYSIQUE. (Text in
English, French) 1979. a. Can.$25($20) University
of Calgary, Department of Anthropology, 2500
University Drive N.W., Calgary, Alta. T2N 1N4,
Canada. Ed. James D. Paterson. bk. rev. film rev.
charts. illus. stat. circ. 150. Indexed:
Abstr.Anthropol.

CARNEGIE MUSEUM OF NATURAL HISTORY.
ANNALS OF (THE) CARNEGIE MUSEUM. see
SCIENCES: COMPREHENSIVE WORKS

CARNEGIE MUSEUM OF NATURAL HISTORY.
BULLETIN. see SCIENCES: COMPREHENSIVE
WORKS

301.2 US
CASE STUDIES IN CULTURAL
ANTHROPOLOGY. irreg. price varies. Holt,
Rinehart and Winston, Inc., 383 Madison Ave.,
New York, NY 10017. TEL 212-688-9100.

572 UK ISSN 0069-0880
CASS LIBRARY OF AFRICAN STUDIES.
AFRICANA MODERN LIBRARY. 1967. irreg.,
no.18, 1972. price varies. Frank Cass & Co. Ltd.,
Gainsborough House, 11 Gainsborough Rd., London
E11 1RS, England (Dist. in U.S. by: Biblio
Distribution Center, 81 Adams Drive, Totowa, N.J.
07512)

572 US
CENTER FOR ANTHROPOLOGICAL STUDIES.
ETHNOHISTORICAL REPORT SERIES. 1980.
irreg. price varies. Center for Anthropological
Studies, Box 14576, Albuquerque, NM 87191. Dir.
Albert E. Ward. circ. 1,000.

572 301 ZR
CENTRE D'ETUDES ETHNOLOGIQUES.
PUBLICATIONS. SERIE 2: MEMOIRES ET
MONOGRAPHIES. 1970. irreg., no.93, 1984. C E
E B A Publications, B.P. 246, Zaire (Foreign
subscriptions to: Steyler-Presse-Vetrieb, Box 2460,
D-4060 Nettetal 2, W. Germany (B.R.D.)) bibl.
charts. illus.

572 960 ZR
CENTRE D'ETUDES ETHNOLOGIQUES
BANDUNDU. PUBLICATIONS. 1966. irreg.,
latest no.94, 1986. price varies. C E E B A, B.P.
246, Bandundu, Zaire. Ed. Hermann Hochegger.
bibl. charts. circ. 700.
Formerly: Centre d'Etudes Ethnologiques.
Publications (ISSN 0577-1331)

ANTHROPOLOGY

301.2 913   PO
CENTRO DE ESTUDOS REGIONAIS. BOLETIM CULTURAL. 1984. a. $5. Centro de Estudos Regionais, Largo 9 de Abril, 4900 Viana do Castelo, Portugal. circ. 1,000.

CERAMICA DE CULTURA MAYA. see *ARCHAEOLOGY*

572 913   SX
CIMBEBASIA. (Text mainly in English) 1962. irreg. price varies. Department of National Education, State Museum, P.O. Box 1203, 9000 Windhoek, Namibia. Ed. C.C. Coetzee. circ. 400. (back issues avail.) Indexed: Biol.Abstr. Nutr.Abstr. Ind.S.A.Per. Zoo.Rec.
     Formerly: Namibia. State Museum. Memoir.

572   FR   ISSN 0578-3917
CIVILISATION MALGACHE. 1964. irreg. (Universite de Madagascar, Faculte des Lettres et Sciences Humaines, MG) Editions Cujas, 4,6,8, rue de la Maison Blanche, 75013 Paris, France.

572   US   ISSN 0069-4487
CLASSICS IN ANTHROPOLOGY. 1964. irreg., latest 1979. price varies. University of Chicago Press, 5801 S. Ellis Ave., Chicago, IL 60637. TEL 312-962-7600. Ed. Rodney Needham. (reprint service avail. from UMI,ISI)

301.2   ES
COLECCION ANTROPOLOGIA E HISTORIA. irreg. Ministerio de Educacion, Administracion del Patrimonio Cultural, Biblioteca del Museo Nacional, Avda. Revolucion, Colonia San Benito, San Salvador, El Salvador. bibl. charts. illus.

572 913.031   IT
COLLANA DI STUDI PALETNOLOGICI. 1977. irreg. (Universita degli Studi di Pisa, Istituto di Antropologia e Paleontologia Umana) Giardini Editori e Stampatori, Via Santa Bibbiana 28, 56100 Pisa, Italy.

572   GW
COLLECTANEA INSTITUTI ANTHROPOS. 1967. irreg., no.31, 1985. price varies. Anthropos Institut, Arnold-Janssen-Str. 20, D-5205 Sankt Augustin, W. Germany (B.R.D.) Ed.Bd. illus.

572   US   ISSN 0146-4167
COLLOQUIA IN ANTHROPOLOGY. 1977. irreg., latest vol. 2, no.12, 1978. $6 per vol. Fort Burgwin Research Center, Inc., Southern Methodist University, Dallas, TX 72575. Ed. Ronald K. Wetherington.

301.2   PE
COMUNIDADES Y CULTURAS PERUANAS. 1973. irreg., no.20, 1986. price varies. Instituto Linguistico de Verano, Departamento de Estudios Etno-Linguisticos, Lima 100, Lima 100, Peru. Ed. Mary Ruth Wise. (also avail. in microfiche; back issues avail.)

301.2   PE
CONGRESO INTERNACIONAL DE AMERICANISTAS. ACTAS. (Text in Castellano and English) 1971. irreg., no.6, 1972. (Instituto de Estudios Peruanos) I E P Ediciones, Horacio Urteaga 694 (Campe de Marte), Lima 11, Peru. (back issues avail.)

572 301   MX   ISSN 0074-0810
CONGRESOS INDIGENISTAS INTERAMERICANOS. ACTAS. every 4 yrs., 9th, 1985, Santa Fe, New Mexico. Instituto Indigenista Interamericano, Insurgentes Sur 1690, Colonia Florida, Mexico 01030, D.F., Mexico. circ. controlled.
     Formerly: Inter-American Conference on Indian Life. Acta/Congresos Indigenistas Interamericanos. Acta.

572   SI   ISSN 0217-2992
CONTRIBUTIONS TO SOUTHEAST ASIAN ETHNOGRAPHY. irreg. price varies. National University of Singapore, Department of Sociology, Kent Ridge, Singapore 0511, Singapore. Indexed: E.I.

572 301.2   US   ISSN 0198-9871
CONTRIBUTIONS TO THE STUDY OF POPULAR CULTURE. 1981. irreg. price varies. Greenwood Press, Box 5007, 88 Post Rd. W., Westport, CT 06881. TEL 203-226-3571.

572   NE
CULTURE, ILLNESS AND HEALING; studies in comparative cross-cultural research. (Text in English) 1980. irreg. price varies. D. Reidel Publishing Company, P.O. Box 17, 3300 AA Dordrecht, Netherlands. Eds. Allan Young, Margaret Lock.

DAGESTANSKII ETNOGRAFICHESKII SBORNIK. see *SOCIOLOGY*

DATOS ETNO-LINGUISTICOS. see *LINGUISTICS*

572   DK
DENMARK. NATIONALMUSEET. PUBLICATIONS: ETHNOGRAPHICAL SERIES. irreg., latest vol.15, 1975. price varies. Nationalmuseet, Oplysningsafdelingen, Ny Vestergade 10, DK-1471 Copenhagen K, Denmark (Dist. in the U.S. by: Humanities Press, 171 First Ave., Atlantic City, NJ 07716)

301.2   US   ISSN 0077-7951
DESERT RESEARCH INSTITUTE PUBLICATIONS IN THE SOCIAL SCIENCES. 1962. irreg. price varies. University of Nevada, Desert Research Institute, Social Sciences Center, Box 60220, Reno, NV 89506. TEL 702-673-7303. circ. 750-800. Indexed: Abstr.Anthropol. GeoRef.

301.2 572   UK
DYN; the journal of the Durham University Anthropological Society. 1970. irreg., (a. or biennial) £2. University of Durham, Anthropological Society, 43 Old Elvet, Durham City DH1 3HN, England. Ed. R.H. Layton. bk. rev. circ. 200. (processed)

572 913   US   ISSN 0070-8232
EASTERN NEW MEXICO UNIVERSITY. CONTRIBUTIONS IN ANTHROPOLOGY. 1968. irreg., vol.11, 1984. price varies. Eastern New Mexico University, Department of Behavioral and Social Sciences, Station No.3, Portales, NM 88130. Ed. Dan Joyce. circ. 750. Indexed: Abstr.Anthropol.

572   US
ECONOMIC ANTHROPOLOGY. 1983. irreg. (Society for Economic Anthropology) University Press of America, Inc., 4720 Boston Way, Lanham, MD 20706. Ed. Sutti Ortiz.
     Formerly: Monographs in Economic Anthropology.

ESTUDIOS ETNOHISTORICOS DEL ECUADOR. see *HISTORY — History Of North And South America*

301.2   PO   ISSN 0870-6891
ESTUDOS DE ANTROPOLOGIA CULTURAL. 1965. irreg. Esc.210. Instituto de Investigacao Cientifica Tropical, Centro de Antropologia Cultural e Social, Rua Jau 47, 1300 Lisbon, Portugal (Subscr. to: Centro de Documentacao e Informacao, Rua Jau 46, 1300 Lisbon, Portugal) circ. 2,000.

301.2   GW   ISSN 0071-1837
ETHNOGRAPHICA. (Text in German and Czech) 1959. irreg., no.5/6, 1966. price varies. (Moravske Museum, Brno, CS) Dr. Rudolf Habelt GmbH, Am Buchenhang 1, 5300 Bonn 1, W. Germany (B.R.D.) Ed. L. Kunz.

301.2   SW   ISSN 0081-5632
ETHNOGRAPHICAL MUSEUM OF SWEDEN. MONOGRAPH SERIES. 1953. irreg., no.15, 1981. price varies. Etnografiska Museet - Ethnographical Museum of Sweden, S-115 27 Stockholm, Sweden. Ed. Ulla Wagner. circ. 2,000.

572   DK   ISSN 0425-4597
ETHNOLOGIA EUROPAEA; internationale Zeitschrift der europaeischen Ethnologie. irreg. DM.48. Ai O, Hestehaven 3, DK-5260 Odeuse, Denmark. Indexed: M.L.A.

572   SW   ISSN 0348-9698
ETHNOLOGIA SCANDINAVICA; a journal for Nordic ethnology. (Text in English) 1971. a. Kr.110. Royal Gustav Adolf Academy, Nordic Humanistic Research Councils, Finngatan 8, S-223 62 Lund, Sweden (Subscr. to: Ethnologia Scandinavica Nya Distribution, Box 65, S-237 00 Bjaerred, Sweden) Ed. Nils-Arvid Bringeus. bk. rev. circ. 25. Indexed: M.L.A.
     Supersedes (1937-1971): Folkl-Liv.

572   SW
ETHNOLOGICA SCANDINAVICA; a journal for nordic ethnology. (Text in English) 1971. a. Kr.110. Royal Gustav Adolf Academy, Nordic Humanistic Research Councils, Finngatan 8, S-223 62 Lund, Sweden. Ed. Nils-Arvid Bringeus. bk. rev. cum.index: 1971-1980.

572   YU
ETNOGRAFSKI MUZEJ NA CETINJU. GLASNIK. 1961. irreg. Etnografski Muzej na Cetinju, Trg Revolucije, Cetinje, Yugoslavia.

572   YU
ETNOGRAFSKI MUZEJ U BEOGRADU. GLASNIK. 1926. a. Etnografski Muzej u Beogradu, Studentski trg 13, Belgrade, Yugoslavia.

572   IT
ETNOLOGIA-ANTROPOLOGIA CULTURALE. 1974. a. L.35000. R.E.A.C., Corso Vitt. Emanuele 110, 80121 Naples, Italy. Ed.Bd. adv. bk. rev. circ. 2,000.

572   SW
ETNOLOGISKA STUDIER. 1935. irreg. price varies. Goeteborgs Etnografiska Museum, N. Hamngatan 12, S-411 14 Goeteborg, Sweden. Ed. Kjell Zetterstroem. circ. 1,600.

572 410   ZR
ETUDES AEQUATORIA. 1982. irreg. Missionnaires du Sacre Coeur, B.P. 1064, Mbandaka, Zaire. Ed. Honore Vinck. circ. 500.

572   IV   ISSN 0423-5673
ETUDES EBURNEENNES. 1951. a. Institut Fondamental d'Afrique Noire, Centre de Cote-d'Ivoire, Direction de la Recherche Scientifique, Ministere de l'Education Nationale, Abidjan, Ivory Coast. bibl. illus.

ETUDES ETHNO-LINGUISTIQUES MAGHREB-SAHARA. see *LINGUISTICS*

572   NG
ETUDES NIGERIENNES. 1953. irreg. Institut de Recherches en Sciences Humaines (IRSH), Service de Documentation, B.P. 318, Niamey, Niger. illus.

EUROPE DE TRADITION ORALE. see *LINGUISTICS*

EVOLUTIONARY MONOGRAPHS. see *BIOLOGY*

EVOLUTIONARY THEORY; an international journal of fact and interpretation. see *BIOLOGY*

572   SW   ISSN 0348-971X
FATABUREN; Nordiska Museets och Skansen aarsbok. (Text in Swedish; summaries in English) 1906. a. Kr.150. Nordiska Museet, 115 21 Stockholm, Sweden. circ. 10,000. (back issues avail.) Indexed: M.L.A.

572   US   ISSN 0071-4739
FIELDIANA: ANTHROPOLOGY. 1895. irreg. price varies. Field Museum of Natural History, Division of Publications, Roosevelt Rd. at Lake Shore Dr., Chicago, IL 60605-2496. TEL 312-922-9410. Ed. Dr. Timothy Plowman. bibl. charts. illus. index. circ. 500. (back issues avail.; reprint service avail. from UMI) Indexed: Biol.Abstr. E.I.

FILM AUSTRALIA CATALOGUE. see *MOTION PICTURES*

FINSKT MUSEUM. see *ARCHAEOLOGY*

574 970   US
FLORIDA STATE MUSEUM. CONTRIBUTIONS. ANTHROPOLOGY AND HISTORY. 1956. irreg., no.18, 1973. price varies. ‡ Florida State Museum, University of Florida, Gainesville, FL 32611. TEL 904-392-1721. Ed. Jerald T. Milanich. bibl. charts. illus. circ. 450. (processed)
     Formerly (until 1971): Florida State Museum. Contributions. Social Sciences (ISSN 0071-6162)

572   DK   ISSN 0900-1131
FOEROYAR. irreg. Kr.98. Bibliotekscentralen, Telegrafvej 5, DK-2750 Ballerup, Denmark.

572   VE   ISSN 0428-8254
FOLIA ANTROPOLOGICA.* 1962. irreg. Museo de Ciencias Naturales, Plaza Morelos, Los Caobos, Caracas 101, Venezuela. abstr.

ANTHROPOLOGY

572 301.2 DK ISSN 0085-0756
FOLK; DANSK ETNOGRAFISK TIDSSKRIFT.
(Text in English and German) 1959. a. price varies.
Dansk Etnografisk Forening - Danish
Ethnographical Association, Nationalmuseet, DK-
1471 Copenhagen K, Denmark. Ed.Bd. bk. rev. bibl.
illus. circ. 1,000.

572 UK ISSN 0430-8778
FOLK LIFE; a journal of ethnological studies. 1963. a.
$15. Society for Folk Life Studies, Welsh Folk
Museum, St. Fagans, Cardiff CF5 6XB, Wales. Ed.
W. Linnard. adv. bk. rev. illus. index. circ. 500.
Indexed: Curr.Cont. M.L.A. Arts & Hum.Cit.Ind.
Br.Archaeol.Abstr. RILA.

572 FI ISSN 0085-0764
FOLKLIVSSTUDIER. (Subseries of Svenska
Litteratursaellsteapet i Finland. Skrifter) (Text in
Swedish; summaries in English and German) 1945.
irreg., no.17, 1986. Fmk.100. ‡ Svenska
Litteratursaellskapet i Finland, Snellmansg. 9-11,
00170 Helsinki 17, Finland. circ. (controlled)

301.21 GW
FORSCHUNGEN ZUR VOLKSKUNDE. irreg.,
no.49, 1983. price varies. Verlag Regensberg,
Daimlerweg 58, Postfach 6748/6749, 4400
Muenster, W. Germany (B.R.D.) Eds. B.Koetting,
A. Schroeer.

572 301.2 MX
FUENTES PARA EL ESTUDIO DE LA CULTURA
MAYA. 1983. irreg. Universidad Nacional
Autonoma de Mexico, Centro de Estudios Mayas,
Torre 2 de Humanidades, Piso 11, Ciudad
Universitaria, 04510 Mexico-DF, Mexico (Orders
to: Distribuidora de Libros-UNAM, Porto Alegre
260 Col. San Andres, Tetepilco, Mexico 09440-
D.F. Mexico) Ed. Mercedes de la Garza. circ. 3,
000.

572 BL
FUENTES PRIMARIAS. 1983. irreg. $20. Museo
Nacional de Etnografia y Folklore, Calle Ingavi 916,
Casilla 5817, La Paz, Bolivia. circ. 1,000.

572 AT ISSN 0072-1190
GEORGE ERNEST MORRISON LECTURES IN
ETHNOLOGY. irreg. Australian National
University, Research School of Pacific Studies, P.O.
Box 4, Canberra, A.C.T. 2600, Australia.

GERMANIA. see ARCHAEOLOGY

572 SW ISSN 0436-2020
GOETEBORGS ETNOGRAFISKA MUSEUM.
AARSTRYCK. (Text in English, Spanish and
Swedish) 1906. biennial. Goeteborgs Etnografiska
Museum, N. Hamngatan 12, 411 14 Goeteborg,
Sweden.

301.2 SW ISSN 0348-4076
GOTHENBURG STUDIES IN SOCIAL
ANTHROPOLOGY. (Subseries of Acta
Universitatis Gothoburgensis) 1978. irreg., no.9,
1986. price varies; also exchange basis. Acta
Universitatis Gothoburgensis, Box 5096, S-402 22
Goeteborg, Sweden (Dist. in U.S., Canada, and
Mexico by: Humanities Press, Inc., 171 First Ave.,
Atlantic Highlands, NJ 07716) Ed. Goeran Aijmer.

572 US
GUIDE TO DEPARTMENTS OF
ANTHROPOLOGY (YEAR) 1968. a., 25th ed. $20
non-members; members $12. American
Anthropological Association, 1703 New Hampshire
Ave., N.W., Washington, DC 20009. TEL 202-232-
8800. Ed. Susan Birch. index. circ. 500.

301.2 398 900 410 US ISSN 8756-7245
GYPSY LORE SOCIETY. NORTH AMERICAN
CHAPTER. PUBLICATIONS. (Text in English,
Romani) 1981. irreg., no.3, 1986. $12.50. Gypsy
Lore Society, North American Chapter, 2104
Dexter Ave., No. 203, Silver Spring, MD 20902.
TEL 301-681-3123. Ed. Joanne Grumet. circ. 200.

301.2 GW ISSN 0072-9469
HAMBURGISCHES MUSEUM FUER
VOELKERKUNDE. MITTEILUNGEN. (Text in
German, occasionally in English or French) 1971,
N.S. a. price varies. ‡ Hamburgisches Museum fuer
Voelkerkunde, Binderstr. 14, 2000 Hamburg 13, W.
Germany (B.R.D.) Ed. J. Zwernemann. circ. 500.

572 US
HISTORY OF ANTHROPOLOGY. 1983. a. $19.95.
University of Wisconsin Press, 114 N. Murrary St.,
Madison, WI 53715. TEL 608-262-8782. Ed.
George W. Stocking. bibl. index. circ. 1,000. (reprint
service avail from UMI)

572 NZ
HOCKEN LECTURE. 1969. irreg. price varies. ‡
University of Otago, Hocken Library, P.O. Box 56,
Dunedin, New Zealand. Ed. S.R. Strachan. circ.
500.

572 575.1 US
I C H E INTERNATIONAL COMMISSION ON
HUMAN ECOLOGY. 1965. irreg. price varies.
Institute for Human Evolution, Box 3495, Grand
Central Sta., New York, NY 10163.
Former titles: Institute for Human Evolution.
Monographs & I A A E E (International
Association for the Advancement of Ethnology and
Eugenics). Monographs (ISSN 0074-1523)
Ethnography

572 SA ISSN 0073-893X
I S M A OCCASIONAL PAPERS. (Text in English)
1964. irreg., latest no.6, 1969. price varies. ‡
Institute for the Study of Man in Africa, University
of the Witwatersrand Medical School, Rm. 2B10,
York Road, Parktown, 2193, Johannesburg, South
Africa. Ed. Noam J. Pines. circ. 800.

572 SA ISSN 0073-8921
I S M A PAPERS. (Text in English) 1961. irreg.,
latest no.39, 1983. $1 per no. for non-members. ‡
Institute for the Study of Man in Africa, University
of the Witwatersrand Medical School, Rm. 2B10,
York Road, Parktown, 2193, Johannesburg, South
Africa. Ed. Noam J. Pines. circ. 800.

572 AU
I U A E S COMMISSION ON URGENT
ANTHROPOLOGICAL RESEARCH.
NEWSLETTER. (Text in English) 1976. irreg.,
latest no.6, 1984. (International Committee on
Urgent Anthropological and Ethnological Research)
Verlag Stiglmayr, Wienerstr. 141, 2822 Foehrenau,
Austria. Ed. Anna Hohenwart-Gerlachstein. index.
circ. 800.

572 DK ISSN 0107-556X
I W G I A BOLETIN. (Text in Spanish) 1979. irreg.
$18 to individuals; $32 to institutions. International
Work Group for Indigenous Affairs, Fiolstraede 10,
DK-1171 Copenhagen K, Denmark. cum.index.
Indexed: HR Rep.

572 323.4 DK ISSN 0105-4503
I W G I A DOCUMENTS; documentation of
oppression of ethnic groups in various countries.
Spanish edition: I W G I A Documento (ISSN
0108-9927) (Editions in English and Spanish) 1971.
irreg. (approx. 4/yr.), no.51, 1984. $18 to
individuals; institutions $32. International Work
Group for Indigenous Affairs, Fiolstraede 10, DK-
1171 Copenhagen K, Denmark. cum.index. Indexed:
HR Rep.

572 323.4 DK ISSN 0105-6387
I W G I A NEWSLETTER. irreg., (approx. 4/yr.)
no.44, 1985. International Work Group for
Indigenous Affairs, Fiolstraede 10, DK-1171
Copenhagen K, Denmark. Indexed: HR Rep.

572 NR
IGBO PHILOSOPHY.* 1971. a. £N0.2 per no. Igbo
Philosophical Association, Bigard Memorial
Seminary, P.M.B. 921, Enugu, East Central State,
Nigeria. Ed. Rev. Fr. C. E. Ohaeri.

570 BL ISSN 0073-4691
IHERINGIA. SERIE ANTROPOLIGIA. (Text in
English, French, German, Latin, Portuguese and
Spanish) 1969. irreg. price varies. Fundacao
Zoobotanica do Rio Grande do Sul, Museu de
Ciencias Naturais, Caixa Postal 1188, 90.000 Porto
Alegre, Rio Grande do Sul, Brazil. Ed. Jose
Willibaldo Thome. bibl. illus. circ. 1,000. Indexed:
Biol.Abstr. Zoo.Rec.

572 US ISSN 0095-2915
ILLINOIS. STATE MUSEUM. RESEARCH SERIES.
PAPERS IN ANTHROPOLOGY. 1972. irreg.,
no.4, 1979. price varies. Illinois State Museum,
Springfield, IL 62706. TEL 217-782-7386. Key
Title: Papers in Anthropology (Springfield)

572 US ISSN 0073-5167
ILLINOIS STUDIES IN ANTHROPOLOGY. 1961.
irreg. University of Illinois Press, 54 E. Gregory
Dr., Champaign, IL 61820. TEL 217-333-0950.
(reprint service avail. from UMI) Indexed:
Biol.Abstr.

INDIAN REVIEW OF LIFE SCIENCES. see
AGRICULTURE

301.2 974 573 GW ISSN 0341-8642
INDIANA; contributions to ethnology and linguistics,
archaeology and physical anthropology of Indian
America. (Text in English, German or Spanish)
1973. irreg. price varies. (Ibero-Amerikanisches
Institut Preussischer Kulturbesitz Berlin) Gebr.
Mann Verlag, Lindenstr. 76, Postfach 110303, 1000
Berlin 61, W. Germany (B.R.D.)

570 US ISSN 0073-6899
INDIANA HISTORICAL SOCIETY. PREHISTORY
RESEARCH SERIES. 1937. irreg. $15. Indiana
Historical Society, 315 W. Ohio St., Indianapolis,
IN 46202. TEL 317-232-1882. circ. 1,000.

572 FR
INSTITUT D'ETHNOLOGIE. ARCHIVES ET
DOCUMENTS, MICRO EDITION. SCIENCES
HUMAINES. a. Musee de l'Homme, Institut
d'Ethnologie, Palais de Chaillot, Place du
Tracadero, 75116 Paris, France.

572 551 PE
INSTITUT FRANCAIS D'ETUDES ANDINES.
TRAVAUX. (Text in French and Spanish;
summaries in English) 1949. irreg. $8. Institut
Francais d'Etudes Andines, Casilla 278, Lima 18,
Peru.

INSTITUT FUER DEN WISSENSCHAFTLICHEN
FILM. PUBLIKATIONEN ZU
WISSENSCHAFTLICHEN FILMEN. SEKTION
ETHNOLOGIE. see MOTION PICTURES

572 PE
INSTITUTO DE ESTUDIOS ANDINOS. TRABAJO
DE CAMPO. 1976. irreg. Instituto de Estudios
Andinos, Apartado 289, Huancayo, Peru.

572 PE
INSTITUTO DE ESTUDIOS PERUANOS.
PROYECTO DE ESTUDIOS ETNOLOGICOS
DEL VALLE DE CHANCAY. MONOGRAFIA.
no.5, 1968. irreg., latest no.7. I E P Ediciones,
Horacio Urteaga 694 (Campo de Marte), Lima 11,
Peru. Indexed: Geo.Abstr.

572 MX
INSTITUTO INDIGENISTA INTERAMERICANO
SERIE DE EDICIONES ESPECIALES. 1967.
irreg. Instituto Indigenista Interamericano,
Insurgentes Sur 1690, Colonia Florida, Mexico
01030, D.F., Mexico. illus. circ. controlled.

570 MX ISSN 0076-7611
INSTITUTO NACIONAL DE ANTROPOLOGIA E
HISTORIA. COLECCION CIENTIFICA. 1967.
irreg., latest no.148. Instituto Nacional de
Antropologia e Historia, Cordoba 47, Mexico 7,
D.F., Mexico.
Formerly: Instituto Nacional de Antropologia e
Historia. Series Cientifica.

INSTITUTUM CANARIUM YEARBOOK.
ALMOGAREN. see ARCHAEOLOGY

572 AU ISSN 0538-5865
INTERNATIONAL COMMITTEE ON URGENT
ANTHROPOLOGICAL AND ETHNOLOGICAL
RESEARCH. BULLETIN. (Text in English,
French, German) 1958. a. As.140. (International
Committee on Urgent Anthropological and
Ethnological Research) Verlag Stiglmayr, Wienerstr.
141, 2822 Foehrenau, Austria (Subscr. to:
International Commission on Urgent
Anthropological and Ethnological Research, c/o
Institut fuer Voelkerkunde, Universitaet Wien,
Universitaetsstr. 7, A-1010 Vienna, Austria) Ed. Dr.
Anna Hohenwart-Gerlachstein. charts. illus. stat.
circ. 600. (back issues avail.) Indexed:
Curr.Cont.Africa. E.I.

572 972.9   CN   ISSN 0538-6381
INTERNATIONAL CONGRESS FOR THE STUDY OF PRE-COLUMBIAN CULTURES OF THE LESSER ANTILLES. PROCEEDINGS. 1963. irreg., vol.9, 1982. price varies. International Congress for the Study of Pre-Columbian Cultures of the Lesser Antilles, University of Manitoba, Department of Anthropology, Winnipeg, Manitoba. Ed. Louis Allaire.

572   UK   ISSN 0074-3496
INTERNATIONAL CONGRESS OF ANTHROPOLOGICAL AND ETHNOLOGICAL SCIENCES. PROCEEDINGS. irreg., 10th, Delhi; 11th, 1983, Quebec/Vancouver, 12th Zagreb. International Union of Anthropological and Ethnological Sciences, c/o Prof. Eric Sunderland, University College of N. Wales, Bangor, Gwynedd LL57 2DG, Wales.
Proceedings published by organizing committee

572 591   US   ISSN 0074-3895
INTERNATIONAL CONGRESS OF PRIMATOLOGY. PROCEEDINGS. 1967. biennial. no subscriptions avail. International Primatological Society, Inquiries only to: Dr. Gisela Epple, Sec.-Gen., Monell Chemical Senses Center, 3500 Market St., Philadelphia, PA 19104. TEL 215-898-5150. Ed.Bd. Indexed: Biol.Abstr.
Published in host country: Japan, 1974; 6th, London; 7th, 1979, Bangalore; 8th, 1980, Florence.

410 572   US   ISSN 0197-3746
INTERNATIONAL MUSEUM OF CULTURES. PUBLICATION. (Text in English; some vols. avail. in Spanish or Portuguese) 1976. irreg. price varies. (International Museum of Cultures) Summer Institute of Linguistics Inc., 7500 W. Camp Wisdom Rd., Dallas, TX 75236. TEL 214-298-3331. Ed. William R. Merrifield. (also avail. in microfiche; back issues avail.)
Formerly: Summer Institute of Linguistics. Museum of Anthropology Publication.

572   PE
INVESTIGACIONES DE CAMPO. 1976. irreg. S/200($4) Museo Nacional de Antropologia y Arqueologia, Plaza Bolivar s/n Pueblo Libre, Lima, Peru.

572 796   US   ISSN 0021-0331
IO. 1964. a. $32. (Society for the Study of Native Arts and Sciences) North Atlantic Books, 2320 Blake St., Berkeley, CA 94704. TEL 415-540-7934. Ed. Richard Grossinger. illus. circ. 3,000. (tabloid format; back issues avail.)

JAHRBUCH FUER OSTDEUTSCHE VOLKSKUNDE. see FOLKLORE

JERNAL ANTROPOLOJI DAN SOSIOLOJI. see SOCIOLOGY

800   BO
JISUNU. 1974. irreg. Bol.$40($2) (Academia de la Culturas Nativas de Oriente Boliviano) Editorial los Huerfanos, Casilla 2225, Santa Cruz de la Sierra, Bolivia. Ed.Bd. adv. bibl. tr.lit. circ. 1,000.

301.2 614.7 338.91   II   ISSN 0250-8346
JOURNAL OF HIMALAYAN STUDIES AND REGIONAL DEVELOPMENT. (Text in English) 1977. a. Rs.100($15) Garhwal University, Institute of Himalayan Studies and Regional Development, Box 12, Srinagar, Garhwal 246174, India. Ed. Tej Vir Singh. adv. bk. rev. circ. 1,000. Indexed: Geo.Abstr.
Formerly: Himalaya.

JUDAICA IBEROAMERICANA. see ETHNIC INTERESTS

KALULU; bulletin of Malawian oral literature and cultural studies. see LITERATURE

572   FI   ISSN 0355-1830
KANSATIETEELLINEN ARKISTO. (Text in English, Finnish, German and Swedish) 1934. irreg. Suomen Muinaismuistoyhdistys, Nervanderinkatu 13, 00100 Helsinki 10, Finland. Indexed: M.L.A.

572   US
KATUNOB: OCCASIONAL PUBLICATIONS IN MESOAMERICAN ANTHROPOLOGY. 1967. irreg., no.18, 1981. price varies per no. University of Northern Colorado, Museum of Anthropology, Attn. George E. Fay, Ed., Greeley, CO 80639. TEL 303-351-1890.

572   NE   ISSN 0074-0470
KONINKLIJK INSTITUUT VOOR TAAL-, LAND-EN VOLKENKUNDE. TRANSLATION SERIES. (Text in English) 1956. irreg. price varies. Foris Publications, Box 509, 3300 AM Dordrecht, Netherlands.

572   NE
KONINKLIJK INSTITUUT VOOR TAAL-, LAND-EN VOLKENKUNDE. VERHANDELINGEN. (Text in Dutch and English) 1938. irreg. price varies. Foris Publications, Box 509, 3300 AM Dordrecht, Netherlands.

572   US   ISSN 0023-4869
KROEBER ANTHROPOLOGICAL SOCIETY. PAPERS. 1950. irreg., approx. 2/yr. membership. Kroeber Anthropological Society, Dept. of Anthropology, Univ. of California, Berkeley, CA 94720. TEL 415-642-6932. Ed.Bd. bk. rev. charts. illus. cum.index. circ. 500. Indexed: Hist.Abstr. Amer.Hist.& Life. Art & Archaeol.Tech.Abstr.

LACITO DOCUMENTS AFRIQUE. see LINGUISTICS

LACITO DOCUMENTS ASIE-AUSTRONESIE. see LINGUISTICS

LACITO DOCUMENTS EURASIE. see LINGUISTICS

LACTATION REVIEW. see MEDICAL SCIENCES — Pediatrics

LANGUES ET CIVILISATIONS A TRADITION ORALE. see LINGUISTICS

LANGUES ET CULTURES AFRICAINES. see LINGUISTICS

LANGUES ET CULTURES DU PACIFIQUE. see LINGUISTICS

LAW & ANTHROPOLOGY; internationales Jahrbuch fuer Rechtsanthropologie. see LAW

301.2   GH
LEGON FAMILY RESEARCH PAPERS. 1974. irreg., no.2, 1975. price varies. University of Ghana, Institute of African Studies, Box 73, Legon, Ghana.

572   US
LIBRARY OF ANTHROPOLOGY. 1971. a. price varies. Gordon and Breach Science Publishers, 50 West 23rd St., New York, NY 10010. TEL 212-206-8900. Ed. Anthony LaRuffa.

LODZKIE STUDIA ETNOGRAFICZNE. see FOLKLORE

572 301   UK   ISSN 0077-1074
LONDON SCHOOL OF ECONOMICS MONOGRAPHS ON SOCIAL ANTHROPOLOGY. 1940. irreg., no.56, 1982. price varies. Athlone Press Ltd., 44 Bedford Row, London WC1R 4LY, England (Dist. in U.S. by: Athlone Press, Atlantic Highlands, NJ 07716) (reprint service avail. from UMI)

LOUISIANA STATE UNIVERSITY. DEPARTMENT OF GEOGRAPHY & ANTHROPOLOGY. MISCELLANEOUS PUBLICATIONS. see EARTH SCIENCES

LUD. see SOCIOLOGY

572 560 913.031   II   ISSN 0258-0446
MAN & ENVIRONMENT. (Text in English) 1977. a. Rs.80($10) Indian Society for Prehistoric and Quaternary Studies, c/o Department of Archaeology, Deccan College, Pune - 411 006, India. Ed. D.P. Agrawal. bk. rev. circ. 500. Indexed: Biol.Abstr.

301.29   MY   ISSN 0303-3171
MAN AND SOCIETY/MANUSIA DAN MASYARAKAT. (Text in English or Malay) 1972. a. $4. (University of Malaya, Anthropology and Sociology Department - Universiti Malaya, Jabatan Antropologi dan Sosiologi) University of Malaya Press, c/o University Library, Pantai Valley, Kuala Lumpur, Selangor, Malaysia. Ed. A. Kahar Bador. adv. bk. rev. circ. 1,000.

572 300   AT
MAN IN SOUTHEAST ASIA. 1968. irreg. (2-4/yr.) Aus.$3. University of Queensland, Department of Anthropology, Sociology and Geography, Brisbane, Qld. 4067, Australia. Eds. Drs. Donald & Elise Tugby. bibl. circ. 600. Indexed: E.I.

572   US   ISSN 0076-4116
MANKIND QUARTERLY MONOGRAPH SERIES. 1961. irreg. Institute for the Study of Man, Inc., 1133 13 St., N.W., Ste. Comm. 2, Washington, DC 20005. TEL 202-789-0231. Indexed: Biol.Abstr.

572 301.2   PL   ISSN 0076-521X
MATERIALY I PRACE ANTROPOLOGICZNE. (Text in English or Polish; summaries in English or German) 1938. irreg., no.104, 1983. price varies. (Polska Akademia Nauk, Zaklad Antropologii) Panstwowe Wydawnictwo Naukowe, Miodowa 10, 00-251 Warsaw, Poland (Dist. by: Ars Polona, Krakowskie Przedmiescie 7, 00-068 Warsaw, Poland) Ed. E. Piasecki. bibl. illus. Indexed: Biol.Abstr.

301.2   DK   ISSN 0106-1062
MEDDELELSER OM GROENLAND, MAN & SOCIETY. 1979. irreg. (Kommissionen for Videnskabelige Undersoegelser i Groenland, GL - Commission for Scientific Research in Greenland) Nyt Nordisk Forlag - Arnold Busck A-S, Koebmagergade 49, DK-1150 Copenhagen K, Denmark. Ed. Torben Segersnap. charts.illus. Indexed: Biol.Abstr.
Formerly: Greenland, Man and Society; Supersedes in part (1878-1979): Meddelelser om Groenland (ISSN 0025-6676)

572   US   ISSN 0564-8602
MEMPHIS STATE UNIVERSITY. ANTHROPOLOGICAL RESEARCH CENTER. OCCASIONAL PAPERS. 1967. irreg., no.13, 1985. $3.50 price varies. Memphis State University, Anthropological Research Center, Memphis, TN 38152. TEL 901-454-2080. Ed. Charles H. McNutt. circ. 200.

301.2 660   PE
METALURGIA. 1976. irreg. S/200($4) Museo Nacional de Antropologia y Arqueologia, Plaza Bolivar s/n Pueblo Libre, Lima, Peru. Indexed: Fuel & Energy Abstr.

301.2 398   MX
MEXICO. DEPARTAMENTO DE INVESTIGACION DE LAS TRADICIONES POPULARES. BOLETIN. 1975. irreg. Departamento de Investigacion de las Tradiciones Populares, Direccion General de Arte Popular, Apdo. Postal 1856, Mexico, D.F., Mexico.

572   US
MICHIGAN STATE UNIVERSITY. MUSEUM PUBLICATIONS. ANTHROPOLOGICAL SERIES. 1971. irreg. price varies. Michigan State University, Museum, East Lansing, MI 48824. TEL 517-355-2370. Ed.Bd. charts. illus. circ. 1,500.

572   GW
MICRO-BIBLIOTHECA ANTHROPOS. 1953. irreg. price varies. Anthropos Institut, D-5205 St. Augustin (bei Bonn), W. Germany (B.R.D.) (microfilm)

572   PN
MONOGRAFIAS ANTROPOLOGICAS. 1980. irreg. Asociacion Panamena de Antropologia, Panama, Panama.

MONOGRAPHS AND THEORETICAL STUDIES IN SOCIOLOGY AND ANTHROPOLOGY IN HONOUR OF NELS ANDERSON. see SOCIOLOGY

MONTALBAN. see HUMANITIES: COMPREHENSIVE WORKS

572   SZ   ISSN 0072-0828
MUSEE D'ETHNOGRAPHIE DE LA VILLE DE GENEVE. BULLETIN ANNUEL. 1958. a. 20 Fr. Musee d'Ethnographie de la Ville de Geneve, 65-67 Bd. Carl-Vogt, 1205 Geneva, Switzerland. Ed. L. Necker. circ. 1,000.

572 BE
MUSEE ROYAL DE L'AFRIQUE CENTRALE. ARCHIVES D'ANTHROPOLOGIE. Short title: Archives d'Anthropologie. 1960. irreg., no.29, 1986. price varies. Musee Royal de l'Afrique Centrale, 13 Steenweg op Leuven, B-1980 Tervuren, Belgium. Indexed: Lang.& Lang.Behav.Abstr.
 Continues: Archives d'Ethnographie (ISSN 0563-1742)

572 301.2 DR
MUSEO DEL HOMBRE DOMINICANO. PAPELES OCASIONALES. 1973. irreg. price varies. Museo del Hombre Dominicano, Calle Pedro Henriquez Urena, Santo Domingo, Dominican Republic.

MUSEO DEL HOMBRE DOMINICANO. SERIE CATALOGOS Y MEMORIAS. see *MUSEUMS AND ART GALLERIES*

572 301.2 DR
MUSEO DEL HOMBRE DOMINICANO. SERIE CONFERENCIAS. 1974. irreg. price varies. Museo del Hombre Dominicano, Calle Pedro Henriquez Urena, Santo Domingo, Dominican Republic.

301.2 DR
MUSEO DEL HOMBRE DOMINICANO. SERIE ESTUDIO Y ARTE. 1977. irreg. price varies. Museo del Hombre Dominicano, Calle Pedro Henriquez Urena, Plaza de la Cultura, Santo Domingo, Dominican Republic. illus.

301.2 DR
MUSEO DEL HOMBRE DOMINICANO. SERIE INVESTIGACIONES ANTROPOLOGICAS. 1975. irreg. no.20, 1982. price varies. Museo del Hombre Dominicano, Calle Pedro Henriquez Urena, Plaza de la Cultura, Santo Domingo, Dominican Republic. charts. illus.

MUSEO DEL HOMBRE DOMINICANO. SERIE MESA REDONDA. see *MUSEUMS AND ART GALLERIES*

573 PE
MUSEO NACIONAL DE ANTROPOLOGIA Y ARQUEOLOGIA. SERIE: ANTROPOLOGIA FISICA. 1976. irreg. Museo Nacional de Antropologia y Arqueologia, Plaza Bolivar, Pueblo Libre, Lima 21, Peru.

572 913 PE
MUSEO NACIONAL DE ANTROPOLOGIA Y ARQUEOLOGIA. SERIE: INVESTIGACIONES DE CAMPO. 1976. irreg. Museo Nacional de Antropologia y Arqueologia, Plaza Bolivar, Pueblo Libre, Lima 21, Peru.

MUSEO NACIONAL DE ANTROPOLOGIA Y ARQUEOLOGIA. SERIE: METALURGIA. see *ARCHAEOLOGY*

572 UY ISSN 0077-1244
MUSEO NACIONAL DE HISTORIA NATURAL. COMMUNICACIONES ANTROPOLOGICAS. 1956. irreg. free on exchange. Museo Nacional de Historia Natural, Montevideo, Uruguay.

572 MX ISSN 0076-7158
MUSEU NACIONAL DE ANTROPOLOGIA. CUADERNOS. 1963. irreg., no.4, 1967. price on request. Museu Nacional de Antropologia, Calz. de la Milla y Reforma, Mexico 7, D.F., Mexico.

572 BL ISSN 0080-3189
MUSEU NACIONAL, RIO DE JANEIRO. BOLETIM. NOVA SERIE. ANTROPOLOGIA. 1942. irreg, no.31, 1979. exchange only. Museu Nacional, Quinta da Boa Vista, Rio de Janiero, GB 08, Brazil. bibl. Indexed: Biol.Abstr.

301.2 960 GW ISSN 0067-5962
MUSEUM FUER VOELKERKUNDE, BERLIN. VEROEFFENTLICHUNGEN. NEUE FOLGE. ABTEILUNG: AFRIKA. 1960. irreg., vol. 8, 1972. price varies. Staatliche Museen Preussischer Kulturbesitz, Berlin, Arnimallee 23/27, 1000 Berlin 33, W. Germany (B.R.D.)

301.2 970 980 GW
MUSEUM FUER VOELKERKUNDE, BERLIN. VEROEFFENTLICHUNGEN. NEUE FOLGE. ABTEILUNG: AMERIKANISCHE NATURVOELKER. 1967. irreg., vol.7, 1986. price varies. Staatliche Museen Preussischer Kulturbesitz, Berlin, Arnimallee 23/27, 1000 Berlin 33, W. Germany (B.R.D.)

301.2 990 GW ISSN 0067-5989
MUSEUM FUER VOELKERKUNDE, BERLIN. VEROEFFENTLICHUNGEN. NEUE FOLGE. ABTEILUNG: SUEDSEE. 1961. irreg., vol.11, 1982. price varies. Staatliche Museen Preussischer Kulturbesitz, Berlin, Arnimallee 23/27, 1000 Berlin 33, W. Germany (B.R.D.)

572 HU ISSN 0580-3594
MUVELTSEG ES HAGYOMANY. (Summaries in English, French, German and Russian) 1961. irreg., vol.25, 1983. Kossuth Lajos Tudomanyegyetem, Neprajzi Intezet, Egyetem Ter 1, 4010 Debrecen, Hungary. bibl. illus.

301.2 PL ISSN 0076-0315
MUZEUM ARCHEOLOGICZNE I ETNOGRAFICZNE, LODZ. PRACE I MATERIALY. SERIA ETNOGRAFICZNA. (Text in Polish; summaries in French) 1957. irreg., no.23, 1984. price varies. ‡ Panstwowe Wydawnictwo Naukowe, Miodowa 10, 00-251 Warsaw, Poland (Dist. by: Ars Polona, Krakowskie Przedmiescie 7, 00-068 Warsaw, Poland) Ed. Irena Lechowa. circ. 520.

572 PL ISSN 0084-2796
MUZEUM ETNOGRAFICZNE, WROCLAW. ZESZYTY ETNOGRAFICZNE. (Issued as part of: Rocznik Etnografii Slaskiej) 1963. a. price varies. Muzeum Etnograficzne, Wroclaw, Kazimierza Wielkiego 33, 50-077 Wroclaw, Poland.

301.2 PL ISSN 0068-4643
MUZEUM GORNOSLASKIE W BYTOMIU. ROCZNIK. SERIA ETNOGRAFIA. (Text in Polish; summaries in English or German and Russian) 1966. irreg. price varies. Muzeum Gornoslaskie, Pl. Thaelmanna 2, 41-902 Bytom, Poland (Dist. by: Ars Polona-Ruch, Krakowskie Przedmiescie 7, Warsaw, Poland)

301.2 398 CS ISSN 0554-9256
NAPRSTKOVO MUZEUM ASIJSKYCH, AFRICKYCH A AMERICKYCH KULTUR. ANNALS. (Text in English, French, German, Spanish) 1962. a. exchange basis. (Narodni Muzeum v Praze) Naprstkovo Muzeum Asijskych, Africkych a Americkych Kultur, Betlemske nam. 1, 110 00 Prague 1, Czechoslovakia. Ed. Libuse Bohackova. bk. rev. circ. 500.

570 PH ISSN 0076-3772
NATIONAL MUSEUM OF THE PHILIPPINES. MONOGRAPH SERIES. (Text in English) 1970. irreg. price varies. National Museum of the Philippines, Rizal Park, Manila, Philippines. Ed. Rosario B. Tantoco. circ. controlled.

572 JA ISSN 0385-3039
NATIONAL SCIENCE MUSEUM. BULLETIN. SERIES D: ANTHROPOLOGY/KOKURITSU KAGAKU HAKUBUTSUKANN KENKYU HOKU. D - RUI: JINRUIGAKU. (Text in English) 1957. a. exchange basis. National Science Museum - Kokuritsu Kagaku Hakubutsukan, 7-20 Ueno Park, Daito-ku, Tokyo 110, Japan. Indexed: Biol.Abstr.

913 CH
NATIONAL TAIWAN UNIVERSITY. DEPARTMENT OF ANTHROPOLOGY. BULLETIN. (Text in Chinese and English) 1953. irreg. $6 per no. ‡ National Taiwan University, Department of Anthropology, Taipei, Taiwan, Republic of China. Ed.Bd. bk. rev. circ. 1,000.
 Formerly (until 1981): National Taiwan University. Department of Archaeology and Anthropology. Bulletin (ISSN 0077-5843)

572 551 560 SZ
NATURHISTORISCHES MUSEUM BASEL. VEROEFFENTLICHUNGEN. 1960. irreg. Naturhistorisches Museum Basel, Augustinergasse 2, 4001 Basel, Switzerland. Ed.Bd. circ. 7,500. (back issues avail.) Indexed: Biol.Abstr.

570 HU ISSN 0077-6599
NEPRAJZI ERTESITO/ETHNOGRAPHIC REVIEW. (Text in Hungarian; summaries in English, French, German, Russian) 1900. a. exchange basis. Neprajzi Muzeum, Kossuth Lajos ter 12, 1055 Budapest, Hungary.

390 HU ISSN 0028-2774
NEPRAJZI KOZLEMENYEK. (Text in Hungarian; summaries in English & Russian) 1956. a. exchange basis. Neprajzi Muzeum, Kossuth Lajos ter 12, 1055 Budapest, Hungary. bk. rev.

570 301.2 HU ISSN 0077-6602
NEPRAJZI TANULMANYOK. 1968. irreg. price varies. (Magyar Tudomanyos Akademia, Neprajzi Kutato Csoport) Akademiai Kiado, Publishing House of the Hungarian Academy of Sciences, P.O. Box 24, H-1363 Budapest, Hungary.

572 US ISSN 0077-7897
NEVADA. STATE MUSEUM, CARSON CITY. ANTHROPOLOGICAL PAPERS. 1959. irreg., no.19, 1984. price varies. ‡ Nevada State Museum, Department of Anthropology, Capitol Complex, Carson City, NV 89710. TEL 702-885-4217. Indexed: Abstr.Anthropol.

572 CN ISSN 0711-5342
NEXUS; the Canadian student journal of anthropology. 1980. a. Can.$7.50 to individuals; Can. $15 to institutions. c/o Department of Anthropology, McMaster University, Hamilton, Ont. L8S 4L9, Canada. TEL 416-525-9140. Ed. Nancy Arbuthnot. adv. bk. rev. circ. 65. (also avail. in microfilm from UMI; reprint service avail. from UMI)
 Formerly (from 1975-1980): Journal of Anthropology at McMaster.

500.9 CN ISSN 0078-1053
NORDICANA. (Text and summaries in English and French) 1964. irreg. (approx. 3-5 nos. per year) price varies. Universite Laval, Centre d'Etudes Nordiques, Quebec C1K 7P4, Canada. TEL 418-656-3340. Ed. I. Grenier.
 Until no.49 (1986) issued as: Quebec (City) Universite Laval. Centre d'Etudes Nordiques. Travaux Divers.

572 NO ISSN 0029-3601
NORVEG; journal of Nordic ethnology. (Text in English, German and Norwegian) a. $29. Norwegian University Press, Kolstadgt. 1, Box 2959-Toeyen, 0608 Oslo 6, Norway (U.S. address: Publications Expediting Inc., 200 Meacham Ave., Elmont, NY 11003) Eds. Knut Kolsrud, Bjarne Hodne. circ. 650.

572 US ISSN 0078-3005
OCCASIONAL PAPERS IN ANTHROPOLOGY. 1968. irreg., no.11, 1979. Pennsylvania State University, Department of Anthropology, 409 Social Sciences Bldg., University Park, PA 16802. TEL 814-865-2509. circ. 500. Indexed: SSCI.

572 AT
OCCASIONAL PAPERS IN ANTHROPOLOGY. 1973. irreg., no.9, 1980. Aus.$4. University of Queensland, Anthropology Museum, St. Lucia, Qld. 4067, Australia. Ed. Dr. Peter K. Lauer. circ. 300.

301.2 US
OCCASIONAL PUBLICATIONS IN NORTHEASTERN ANTHROPOLOGY. 1976. irreg., latest, no.9. price varies. Fund for Anthropology, Franklin Pierce College, Rindge, NH 03461. TEL 603-899-5111. Ed. Howard R. Sargent. bibl. illus. circ. 400.

301.2 GH
ODAWURU IN SERIES. 1968. irreg. price varies. University of Ghana, Institute of African Studies, Box 73, Legon, Ghana.

OESTERREICHISCHE VOLKSKUNDLICHE BIBLIOGRAPHIE. see *FOLKLORE*

OESTERREICHISCHES MUSEUM FUER VOLKSKUNDE: VEROEFFENTLICHUNGEN. see *FOLKLORE*

572 US ISSN 0078-432X
OKLAHOMA ANTHROPOLOGICAL SOCIETY. BULLETIN. 1952. a. membership. Oklahoma Anthropological Society, c/o Rose King, Corres. Sec., 1000 Horn St., Muskogee, OK 74403. TEL 918-682-5091. Ed. Don G. Wyckoff. circ. 500. Indexed: Abstr.Anthropol.

ANTHROPOLOGY

572 US ISSN 0474-0696
OKLAHOMA ANTHROPOLOGICAL SOCIETY. MEMOIR. 1964. irreg. price varies. Oklahoma Anthropological Society, c/o Rose King, Corres. Sec., 1000 Horn St., Muskogee, OK 74403. TEL 918-682-5091. circ. 500. Indexed: Abstr.Anthropol.

572 US ISSN 0742-1184
OTHER REALITIES;* descriptive, methodological and theoretical texts. 1979. irreg., latest no.6. price varies. (University of California, Los Angeles, Department of Anthropology) Undena Publications, 6355 Green Valley Circle, No. 213, Culver City, CA 90230-7064. Ed. J. Maquet. (back issues avail.)

301.2 US
OXFORD MONOGRAPHS ON SOCIAL ANTHROPOLOGY. irreg. price varies. Oxford University Press, 200 Madison Ave., New York, NY 10016 TEL 212-679-7300. (And Ely House, 37 Dover St., London W1X 4AH, England) Ed. Bd.

P.E.I. COMMUNITY STUDIES. (Prince Edward Island) see SOCIOLOGY

572 US ISSN 0078-740X
PACIFIC ANTHROPOLOGICAL RECORDS. 1968. irreg. price varies. (Bishop Museum, Department of Anthropology) Bishop Museum Press, Box 19000-A, Honolulu, HI 96817.

572 GW ISSN 0078-7809
PAIDEUMA; Mitteilungen zur Kulturkunde. (Text in English, French, German) 1938. a. DM.60. (Universitaet Frankfurt, Frobenius Institut) Franz Steiner Verlag Wiesbaden GmbH, Birkenwaldstr. 44, Postfach 347, D-7000 Stuttgart 1, W. Germany (B.R.D.) Ed. Eike Haberland. adv. illus. circ. 860. (back issues avail.) Indexed: Curr.Cont. Amer.Hum.Ind. Curr.Cont.Africa. E.I.

573 PE
PALEOBIOLOGIA. 1976. irreg. S/200($4) Museo Nacional de Antropologia y Arqueologia, Plaza Bolivar s/n Pueblo Libre, Lima, Peru.

572 301 NE ISSN 0317-8382
PAPERS ON EUROPEAN AND MEDITERRANEAN SOCIETIES. 1974. irreg. price varies. Universiteit van Amsterdam, Antropologisch-Sociologisch Centrum, Euromed, Sarphatistraat 106A, 1018 GV Amsterdam, Netherlands. Eds. J.F. Boissevain, J. Verrips. circ. 200.

570 US
PENNSYLVANIA. HISTORICAL AND MUSEUM COMMISSION. ANTHROPOLOGICAL SERIES. 1971. irreg., latest issue no.6. Historical and Museum Commission, Box 1026, Harrisburg, PA 17108-1026. TEL 717-783-2618. Eds. Barry Kent, Harold Myers.

PEOPLES OF EAST AFRICA. see HISTORY — History Of Africa

572 II
PERSPECTIVES IN PRIMATE BIOLOGY. 1983. irreg., vol.2, 1987. $69. Today & Tomorrow's Printers and Publishers, 24B/5 Original Road, Karol Bagh, New Delhi 110 005, India. Ed. P.K. Seth.

572 PE
PERU INDIGENA. 1948-1961; resumed 1967. irreg. (aprox. 2/yr.) Instituto Indigenista Peruano, Avda. Salaverry, Lima, Peru.

572 BL ISSN 0553-8467
PESQUISAS: PUBLICACOES DE ANTROPOLOGIA. (Numbering is in continuation of articles published in Pesquisas) no.6, 1960. irreg. price varies or exchange basis. (Universidade do Vale do Rio dos Sinos, Instituto Anchietano de Pesquisas) Unisinos, Av. Unisinos, 950, 93000 Sao Leopoldo RS, Brazil.
Supersedes in part: Pesquisas.

PILIPINAS; an interdisciplinary scholarly journal of Philippine studies. see HISTORY — History Of Asia

572 VC
PONTIFICO MUSEO MISSIONARIO ETNOLOGICO. ANNALI. 1937. a. Pontificio Museo Missionario Etnologico, Citta del Vaticano, Rome, Italy. bibl.
Formerly: Annali Lateranensi (1937-1962)

573 GW ISSN 0343-3528
PRIMATE REPORT. irreg. price varies. Verlag Erich Goltze GmbH und Co. KG, Stresemannstr. 28, 3400 Goettingen, W. Germany (B.R.D.) Ed. A. Spiegel.

572 949.7 YU
PROBLEMI SJEVERNOG JADRANA. (Text in Croatian; summaries in Italian) 1963. irreg. Jugoslovenska Akademija Znanosti i Umjetnosti, Zrinski trg. 11, 41000 Zagreb, Yugoslavia (Subscr. to: Zavod za Povijesne i Drustvene Znanosti J.A.Z.U., Brace Supak 5, 51000 Rijeka, Yugoslavia) circ. 700. (back issues avail.)

PURUSHARTHA. see SOCIAL SCIENCES: COMPREHENSIVE WORKS

572 US
QUEENS COLLEGE PUBLICATIONS IN ANTHROPOLOGY. 1975. a. price varies. Queens College Press, c/o Dyanne Maue, Academic 1302, Flushing, NY 11367. TEL 718-520-7599. Ed. Gloria Levitas. circ. 500. (back issues avail.)

572 SA ISSN 0079-9815
RAYMOND DART LECTURES. 1964. irreg., no.24, 1987. price varies. (Institute for the Study of Man in Africa) Witwatersrand University Press, Jan Smuts Ave., Johannesburg 2001, South Africa. Ed. N.J. Pines. circ. 750.

READINGS IN LONG ISLAND ARCHAEOLOGY AND ETHNOHISTORY. see HISTORY — History Of North And South America

RECHERCHES PHILOSOPHIQUES AFRICAINES. see PHILOSOPHY

572 574 JA ISSN 0286-4568
REICHORUI KENKYUJO NENPO/KYOTO UNIVERSITY. PRIMATE RESEARCH INSTITUTE. ANNUAL REPORT. (Text in Japanese) 1971. a. free. Kyoto University, Primate Research Institute, Kanrin, Inuyama-Shi, Aichi-Ken 484, Japan. circ. 1,000. (back issues avail.)

572 FR
REPERTOIRE DE L'ETHNOLOGIE DE LA FRANCE. irreg., latest 1982. 60 F. Documentation Francaise, 29-31 Quai Voltaire, 75340 Paris Cedex 07, France.

572 301 900 910 GW ISSN 0722-6349
RESEARCH; contributions to interdisciplinary anthropology. (Text in English) 1982. a. DM.25($15) (Association for International Scientific Communication) Edition Herodot im Rader Verlag, Kongress Str.5, D-5100 Aachen, W. Germany (B.R.D.) Ed. Mohan Krischke Ramaswamy. circ. 750.

301.51 572 US ISSN 0190-1281
RESEARCH IN ECONOMIC ANTHROPOLOGY; an annual compilation of research. (Supplement avail.: Forms and Essays in Economic History in Honor of William N. Parker) 1978. a. $23.75 to individuals; institutions $47.50. J A I Press Inc., Box 1678, 36 Sherwood Pl., Greenwich, CT 06836. TEL 203-661-7602. Ed. Barry Isaac.

301.2 US
RESOURCES FOR THE STUDY OF ANTHROPOLOGY. irreg. price varies. Houghton Mifflin Co., One Beacon St., Boston, MA 02107. TEL 617-725-5000.

572 CK
REVISTA COLOMBIANA DE ANTROPOLOGIA. 1944. a. exchange basis. (Instituto Colombiano de Cultura) Instituto Colombiano de Antropologia, Apdo. Nacional 407, Bogota, Colombia. Ed. Roberta Pineoa. bk. rev. circ. 2,000.

570 BL ISSN 0034-7701
REVISTA DE ANTROPOLOGIA. 1953. a. $3. (Associacao Brasileira de Antropologia) Universidade de Sao Paulo, Faculdade de Filosofia, Letras e Ciencias Humanas, Caixa Postal 5459, Sao Paulo, Brazil. Ed. Egon Schaden. bk. rev. circ. 800. Indexed: Biol.Abstr. Hisp.Amer.Per.Ind.

RHEINISCH-WESTFAELISCHE ZEITSCHRIFT FUER VOLKSKUNDE. see HISTORY — History Of Europe

573 UK
RIDGE DETAIL IN NATURE. 1979. a. $5. Fingerprint Society, 4 Kingfisher Close, Biggleswade, Bedfordshire SG18 8EA, England. Ed. J. Berry. circ. 100.

301.2 NE
RIJKSUNIVERSITEIT TE LEIDEN. INSTITUUT VOOR CULTURELE ANTROPOLOGIE EN SOCIOLOGIE DER NIET-WESTERSE VOLKEN. PUBLICATIE. vol.11, 1975. irreg. price varies. Rijksuniversiteit te Leiden, Instituut voor Culturele Antropologie en Sociologie der Niet-Westerse Volken, Stationsplein 10, P.O. Box 9507, 2300 RA Leiden, Netherlands.

572 IT ISSN 0085-5723
RIVISTA DI ANTROPOLOGIA.* (Text in Italian; summaries in English and French) 1893. a. $15. Istituto Italiano di Antropologia, Citta Universitaria, Rome, Italy. Ed. Venerando Correnti. (back issues avail.)

572 CN ISSN 0316-1277
ROYAL ONTARIO MUSEUM. ETHNOGRAPHY MONOGRAPH. 1973. irreg. price varies. Royal Ontario Museum, Publication Services, 100 Queen's Park, Toronto, Ont. M5S 2C6, Canada. TEL 416-586-5586.

SAGE SERIES IN CROSS CULTURAL RESEARCH AND METHODOLOGY. see PSYCHOLOGY

929 948 NO ISSN 0581-4480
SAMISKE SAMLINGER. (Numbers not issued in consecutive order) 1952. irreg., latest 1976. price varies. Norsk Folkemuseum, Bygdoey, Oslo 2, Norway.

572 US ISSN 0080-5890
SAN DIEGO MUSEUM OF MAN. ETHNIC TECHNOLOGY NOTES. 1967. irreg., no.19, 1984. price varies. San Diego Museum of Man, Balboa Park, San Diego, CA 92101. TEL 619-239-2001.

572 US ISSN 0080-5904
SAN DIEGO MUSEUM OF MAN. PAPERS. 1929. irreg., vo.2, no.18, 1985. price varies. San Diego Museum of Man, Balboa Park, San Diego, CA 92101. TEL 619-239-2001. Ed. Dr. Spencer L. Rogers. index.

301.2 338.1 SW
SCANDINAVIAN INSTITUTE OF AFRICAN STUDIES. RURAL DEVELOPMENT. Short title: Rural Development Series. irreg. (Nordiska Afrikainstitutet - Scandinavian Institute of African Studies) Almqvist and Wiksell International, Box 62, S-101 20 Stockholm, Sweden (Dist. in U.S. by: Africana Publishing Company, 101 Fifth Ave., New York, NY 10003)

SCOTTISH STUDIES. see HISTORY — History Of Europe

SCRIPTA MEDITERRANEA. see HISTORY — History Of The Near East

572 914.606 SP
SEMANA INTERNACIONAL DE ANTROPOLOGIA VASCA. ACTAS. irreg. Gran Enciclopedia Vasca, Apdo. 1510, Calzadas de Mallona 8, Bilbao 6, Spain.
Basque

SERIE DE VOCABULARIOS Y DICCIONARIOS INDIGENAS "MARIANO SILVA Y ACEVES". see LINGUISTICS

572 JA
SHAKAI-JINRUIGAKU NENPO. (Text in Japanese) 1975. a. 2500 Yen($10) (Tokyo Metropolitan University, Society for Social Anthropology) Kobundo, 1-7-13 Kanda Surugadai, Chiyoda-ku, Tokyo, Japan. Eds. Toichi Mabuchi, Jiro Suzuki. adv. circ. 2,000.

SLOVACI V ZAHRANICI. see HISTORY — History Of Europe

572 CS
SLOVENSKEHO NARODNEHO MUZEA. FONTES ETNOGRAFICKEHO. 1962. irreg. price varies. (Slovenske Narodne Muzeum) Osveta, Ul. Osloboditelov 21, 036 54 Martin, Czechoslovakia. Ed. Alojz Habovstiak. charts. illus. maps. circ. 800.
Supersedes in part: Fontes.

ANTHROPOLOGY

572   YU
SLOVENSKI ETNOGRAF. (Text in Slovenian; summaries in English, French, German) 1948. a. $15. Slovenski Etnografski Muzej, Presernova cesta 20, Ljubljana, Yugoslavia. bk. rev. circ. 1,000. Indexed: M.L.A.

572   US   ISSN 0081-0223
SMITHSONIAN CONTRIBUTIONS TO ANTHROPOLOGY. 1965. irreg., no.32, 1986. Smithsonian Institution Press, 955 L'Enfant Plaza, Rm. 2100, Washington, DC 20560. TEL 202-287-3738. Ed. Barbara T. Spann. circ. 2,100. (reprint service avail. from UMI) Indexed: Biol.Abstr. GeoRef.

572   914.6   SP   ISSN 0213-0297
SOCIEDAD DE ESTUDIOS VASCOS. CUADERNOS DE SECCION. ANTROPOLOGIA-ETNOGRAFIA. 1982. irreg. (Sociedad de Estudios Vascos) Eusko Ikaskuntza, S.A., Churruca, 7 - 2, 20004 Donostia, Spain.

SOCIETE D'ETUDES LINGUISTIQUES ET ANTHROPOLOGIQUES DE FRANCE. NUMEROS SPECIAUX. see *LINGUISTICS*

SOCIETE DES EXPLORATEURS ET DES VOYAGEURS FRANCAIS. ANNUAIRE GENERAL. see *GEOGRAPHY*

301.2   BE
SOCIETE ROYALE BELGE D'ANTHROPOLOGIE ET DE PREHISTOIRE. BULLETIN. (Text in English, Flemish & French; summaries in English and French) 1882. a. 1200 Fr. Societe Royale Belge d'Anthropologie et de Prehistoire, 29 rue Vautier, 1040 Brussels, Belgium. bk. rev. illus. circ. 350. Indexed: Excerp.Med. A.I.C.P. Br.Archaeol.Abstr. GeoRef.

SOCIETE SUISSE DES AMERICANISTES. BULLETIN/SCHWEIZERISCHE AMERIKANISTEN-GESELLSCHAFT. BULLETIN. see *HISTORY — History Of North And South America*

SOCIOLINGUISTIQUE; systemes de langues et interactions sociales et culturelles. see *LINGUISTICS*

SOCIOLOGICAL OBSERVATIONS. see *SOCIOLOGY*

SOLOMON ISLANDS MUSEUM ASSOCIATION. JOURNAL. see *MUSEUMS AND ART GALLERIES*

SOUTH AFRICAN MUSEUM. ANNALS/SUID-AFRIKAANSE MUSEUM. ANNALE. see *PALEONTOLOGY*

SOUTH ASIA: JOURNAL OF SOUTH ASIAN STUDIES. see *HISTORY — History Of Asia*

572   US   ISSN 0081-2994
SOUTHERN ANTHROPOLOGICAL SOCIETY. PROCEEDINGS. 1968. a. price varies. University of Georgia Press, Athens, GA 30602. TEL 404-542-2830.

572   II
SPECTRA OF ANTHROPOLOGICAL PROGRESS. (Text in English) 1978. irreg. Rs.25($6) University of Delhi, Department of Anthropology, Delhi 110007, India.

572   YU
SRPSKA AKADEMIJA NAUKA I UMETNOSTI. ETNOGRAFSKI INSTITUT. GLASNIK. (Text in Serbo-Croatian; summaries in English, French, German, Russian) 1894. irreg. Srpska Akademija Nauka i Umetnosti, Etnografski Institut, Knez-Mihailova 35, Belgrade, Yugoslavia. bk. rev. bibl.

572   YU
SRPSKA AKADEMIJA NAUKA I UMETNOSTI. ETNOGRAFSKI INSTITUT. ZBORNIK RADOVA. vol.6, 1973. irreg. Srpska Akademija Nauka i Umetnosti, Etnografski Institut, Knez-Mihailova 35, Belgrade, Yugoslavia.

572   301.2   YU   ISSN 0081-4067
SRPSKI ETNOGRAFSKI ZBORNIK. NASELJA I POREKLO STANOVNISTVA. (Text in Serbo-Croatian; summaries in English, French, German or Russian) 1902. irreg. price varies. Srpska Akademija Nauka i Umetnosti, Knez Mihailova 35, 11001 Belgrade, Yugoslavia (Dist. by: Prosveta, Terazije 16, Belgrade, Yugoslavia) circ. 1,000.

572   301.2   390   YU   ISSN 0081-4075
SRPSKI ETNOGRAFSKI ZBORNIK. RASPRAVE I GRADJA. (Text in Serbo-Croatian; summaries in English, French, German or Russian) 1934. irreg. price varies. Srpska Akademija Nauka i Umetnosti, Knez Mihailova 35, 11001 Belgrade, Yugoslavia (Dist. by: Prosveta, Terazije 16, Belgrade, Yugoslavia) circ. 1,000.

572   301.2   390   YU   ISSN 0081-4083
SRPSKI ETNOGRAFSKI ZBORNIK. SRPSKE NARODNE UMOTVORINE. (Text in Serbo-Croatian; summaries in English, French, German or Russian) 1927. irreg. price varies. Srpska Akademija Nauka i Umetnosti, Knez Mihailova 35, 11001 Belgrade, Yugoslavia (Dist. by: Prosveta, Terazije 16, Belgrade, Yugoslavia) circ. 1,000.

572   390   YU   ISSN 0081-4091
SRPSKI ETNOGRAFSKI ZBORNIK. ZIVOT I OBICAJI NARODNI. (Text in Serbo-Croatian; summaries in English, French, German or Russian) 1894. irreg. price varies. Srpska Akademija Nauka i Umetnosti, Knez Mihailova 35, 11001 Belgrade, Yugoslavia (Dist. by: Prosveta, Terazije 16, Belgrade, Yugoslavia) circ. 1,000.

STAATLICHES MUSEUM FUER VOELKERKUNDE DRESDEN. ABHANDLUNGEN UND BERICHTE. see *MUSEUMS AND ART GALLERIES*

572   DK   ISSN 0108-1012
STOFSKIFTE. 1977. irreg. (2-4/yr.) membership. Antropologforeningen i Danmark, Koebenhavns Universitet, Institut for Etnologi og Antropologi, Frederiksholms Kanal 4, 1220 Copenhagen K, Denmark. Ed. Poul Pedersen. adv. illus. circ. 750.

572   301.2   IT
STUDI ETNO-ANTROPOLOGICI. 1974. irreg. L.40000. Consiglio Nazionale delle Ricerche, Corso Vittorio Emanuele 110, Naples, Italy. adv. bk. rev.
Former titles: Etnologia; Rivista di Etnografia.

572   560   IT   ISSN 0392-6788
STUDI PER L'ECOLOGIA DEL QUATERNARIO. 1979. a. L.35000. Laboratorio di Ecologia del Quaternario, Via del Proconsolo, 12, Firenze, Italy. Ed. E. Borzatti von Loewenstern. circ. 800.

572   SW   ISSN 0491-2705
STUDIA ETHNOGRAPHICA UPSALIENSIA. 1956. a. (Uppsala Universitet, Institutionen foer Allmaem och Jaemfoerande Etnografi) Almqvist & Wiksell International, Box 62, S-101 20 Stockholm, Sweden.

572   SW
STUDIA ETHNOLOGICA UPSALIENSIA. 1976. irreg. price varies. (Universitet i Uppsala) Almqvist and Wiksell International, Box 62, S-101 20 Stockholm, Sweden.

572   FI   ISSN 0085-6835
STUDIA FENNICA; review of finnish linguistics and ethnology. (Text in English or German) 1933. a. Fmk.120. Suomalaisen Kirjallisuuden Seura - Finnish Literature Society, Hallituskatu 1, P.O. Box 259, 00170 Helsinki 17, Finland. Ed. Lauri Honko. adv. bibl. circ. 1,000. Indexed: M.L.A.

572   GW
STUDIA INSTITUTI ANTHROPOS. 1950. irreg., no. 39, 1981. price varies. Anthropos Institut, D-5205 St. Augustin (bei Bonn), W. Germany (B.R.D.) illus.

572   US   ISSN 0585-5578
STUDIA SUMIRO-HUNGARICA. (Text in English and Hungarian) 1968. irreg., vol.3, 1974. Gilgamesh Publishing Co., 6050 Boulevard East, 20-A, West New York, NJ 07093. Ed. Miklos Erdy. bibl. charts. illus. circ. 2,000.

572   GW   ISSN 0170-3544
STUDIEN ZUR KULTURKUNDE. (Text in English, French and German) irreg., vol.84, 1987. price varies. (Universitaet Frankfurt, Frobenius-Institut) Franz Steiner Verlag Wiesbaden GmbH, Birkenwaldstr. 44, Postfach 347, D-7000 Stuttgart 1, W. Germany (B.R.D.) Ed. Eike Haberland.

301.2   US   ISSN 0585-6523
STUDIES IN ANTHROPOLOGICAL METHOD. irreg. price varies. Holt, Rinehart and Winston, Inc., 383 Madison Ave., New York, NY 10017. TEL 212-688-9100.

301.2   GW
STUDIES IN ANTHROPOLOGY. 1974. irreg. price varies. Walter de Gruyter & Co., Mouton Publishers, Postfach 110240, D-1000 Berlin 11, W. Germany (B.R.D.) (U.S. addr.: Mouton Publishers, division of Walter de Gruyter, Inc., 200 Saw Mill River Road, Hawthorne, NY 10532)

301.2   US
STUDIES IN ANTHROPOLOGY. 1974. irreg., vol.41, 1985. Academic Press, Inc., Orlando, FL 32887. TEL 305-345-2000. Ed. Eugene A. Hammel.

572   US
STUDIES IN CULTURAL ANTHROPOLOGY. irreg., vol.10, 1986. U M I Research Press, 300 N. Zeeb Rd., Ann Arbor, MI 48106. Ed. Conrad Kottak.

572   GW
STUDIES IN EUROPEAN SOCIETY. 1973. irreg. price varies. Walter de Gruyter & Co., Mouton Publishers, Postfach 110240, D-1000 Berlin 11, W. Germany (B.R.D.) (U.S. addr.: Mouton Publishers, division of Walter de Gruyter, Inc., 200 Saw Mill River Rd., Hawthorne, NY 10532) Ed. John Friedl.

572   GW   ISSN 0081-7953
STUDIES IN GENERAL ANTHROPOLOGY. 1963. irreg. price varies. Walter de Gruyter & Co., Mouton Publishers, Postfach 110240, D-1000 Berlin 11, W. Germany (B.R.D.) (U.S. addr.: Mouton Publishers, division of Walter de Gruyter, Inc., 200 Saw Mill River Road, Hawthorne, NY 10532)

572   US   ISSN 0733-5776
STUDIES IN MAYAN LINGUISTICS. (Sub-series of: University of Missouri at Columbia. Museum of Anthropology. Miscellaneous Publications in Anthropology) 1975. irreg., no.4, 1981. price varies. University of Missouri-Columbia, Department of Anthropology, Columbia, MO 65201. TEL 314-882-2121.

572   301   GW   ISSN 0081-8496
STUDIES IN SOCIAL ANTHROPOLOGY. 1966. irreg. price varies. Walter de Gruyter & Co., Mouton Publishers, Postfach 110240, D-1000 Berlin 11, W. Germany (B.R.D.) (U.S. addr.: Mouton Publishers, division of Walter de Gruyter, Inc., 200 Saw Mill River Rd., Hawthorne, NY 10532)

301.2   NE
STUDIES IN SOUTH ASIAN CULTURE. 1969. irreg., vol.12, 1985. E.J. Brill, P.O. Box 9000, 2300 PA Leiden, Netherlands.

STUDIES ON RELIGION IN AFRICA. see *RELIGIONS AND THEOLOGY*

570   RM   ISSN 0039-3886
STUDII SI CERCETARI DE ANTROPOLOGIE. (Summaries in English and French) 1964. a. 40 lei($42) (Academia Republicii Socialiste Romania, Editura Academiei Republicii Socialiste Rumania, Calea Victoriei 125, 79717 Bucharest, Rumania (Subscr. to: ROMPRESFILATELIA, Calea Grivitei 64-66, P.O. Box 12-201, 78104 Bucharest, Rumania) Ed. Olga Necrasov. bk. rev. charts. illus. index. Indexed: Biol.Abstr.
Formerly: Probleme de Antropologie.

301.2   572   SJ   ISSN 0562-5130
SUDAN SOCIETY/AL-MUJTAMA. (Text in Arabic and English) 1962. a. University of Khartoum, Social Studies Society, Faculty of Economic and Social Studies, Box 321, Khartoum, Sudan.

SUID-AFRIKAANSE KULTUURHISTORIESE MUSEUM. BULLETIN/SOUTH AFRICAN CULTURAL HISTORY MUSEUM. BULLETIN. see *HISTORY — History Of Africa*

ANTHROPOLOGY

SUOMALAIS-UGRILAISEN SEURAN. AIKAKAUSKIRJA/SOCIETE FINNO-OUGRIENNE. JOURNAL. see *LINGUISTICS*

SUOMEN MUSEO. see *ARCHAEOLOGY*

572 323.4 UK ISSN 0308-2857
SURVIVAL INTERNATIONAL REVIEW. 1976. a. £15($30) Survival International, 29 Craven St., London WC2N 5NT, England. Ed. Marcus Colchester. adv. bk. rev. circ. 2,000. (also avail. in microfiche) Indexed: HR Rep.

572 UK ISSN 0307-823X
SUSSEX ANTHROPOLOGY. 1976. irreg. £1.20 for 3 nos. c/o Dr. Brian V. Street, University of Sussex, School of Social Studies, Falmer, Brighton, England. Ed.Bd. circ. 500.
Formerly: Sussex Essays in Anthropology.

572 US
TEBIWA. 1958. a. $8. Idaho Museum of Natural History, Idaho State University, Box 8096, Pocatello, ID 83209. TEL 208-236-0211. Ed. Barry L. Keller. abstr. 10-yr. cum.index in vol. 11. circ. 500. (also avail. in microform from UMI; reprint service avail. from UMI) Indexed: Biol.Abstr. Abstr.Anthropol. Geo.Abstr. GeoRef.
Former titles: Tebiwa Miscellaneous Papers; until vol.18: Tebiwa (ISSN 0040-0823)
Natural history

572 US
TENNESSEE ANTHROPOLOGICAL ASSOCIATION. MISCELLANEOUS PAPER. 1976. irreg. membership. Tennessee Anthropological Association, Dept. of Anthropology, University of Tennessee, Knoxville, TN 37996-0720. TEL 615-974-4408. Charles H. Faulkner. circ. 300.

572 US
THEATA. 1973. irreg. $5. University of Alaska, Cross Cultural Communications, Gruening Bldg., 5th Fl., Fairbanks, AK 99701. TEL 907-474-7694. Ed. P. Kwachka. circ. 750.

301.2 UK
THEMES IN SOCIAL ANTHROPOLOGY. 1983. irreg. price varies. Manchester University Press, Oxford Rd., Manchester M13 9PL, England. Eds. D. Turton, M. Strathern.

572 RM
TIBISCUS. SERIA ETNOGRAFIE. (Text in Rumanian; summaries in German) a. Muzeul Banatului, Piata Huniade Nr. 1, Timisoara, Rumania.

390 970.1 MX ISSN 0040-8239
TLALOCAN; revista de fuentes para el conocimiento de las culturas indigenas de Mexico. (Text in English, Spanish & Indian languages of Mexico) 1942. irreg. $8 (for 4 nos.) Universidad Nacional Autonoma de Mexico, Instituto de Esteticas, Ciudad Universitaria, Mexico 20, D.F., Mexico. Eds. I. Bernal, F. Horcasitas. illus. circ. 600. Indexed: M.L.A.

572 PO ISSN 0304-243X
TRABALHOS DE ANTROPOLOGIA E ETNOLOGIA. (Text occasionally in English, French, German and Portuguese) 1918. irreg., approx. a. price varies. Sociedade Portugucsa de Antropologia e Etnologia, Faculdade de Ciencias, Universidade do Porto, 4000 Porto, Portugal. Ed. Vitor Manuel de Oliveira Jorge. adv. bk. rev. illus. circ. 1,000.
Formerly: Sociedade Portuguesa de Antropologia e Etnologia. Trabalhos.

572 NO ISSN 0332-5997
TRADISJON; tidsskrift for folkeminnevitenskap. 1971. a. $21. Norwegian University Press, Kolstadgt. 1, Box 2959-Toeyen, 0608 Oslo 6, Norway (U. S. address: Box 258, Irvington-on-Hudson, NY 10533) Ed. Reimund Kvideland. circ. 800. Indexed: M.L.A.

572 US
TRANSWORLD IDENTITY SERIES. 1982. irreg. Eurolingua, Box 101, Bloomington, IN 47402-0101.

911 GW ISSN 0082-6413
TRIBUS; Jarhbuch des Linden-Museums Stuttgart. (Text in German; occasionally in English) 1951. a. DM.39. Linden-Museum Stuttgart-Staatliches Museum fuer Voelkerkunde, Hegelplatz 1, 7000 Stuttgart 1, W. Germany (B.R.D.) Eds. Klaus J. Brandt, Ingrid Heermann. adv. bk. rev. circ. 600(controlled)

UEBERSEE-MUSEUM, BREMEN. VEROEFFENTLICHUNGEN. REIHE B: VOELKERKUNDE. see *FOLKLORE*

572 GW ISSN 0341-9274
UEBERSEE-MUSEUM, BREMEN. VEROEFFENTLICHUNGEN. REIHE D: VOELKERKUNDLICHE MONOGRAPHIEN. 1976. irreg., vol.14, 1985. price varies. Uebersee-Museum, Bremen, Bahnhofsplatz 13, 2800 Bremen, W. Germany(B.R.D.) Ed. Herbert Ganslmayr.

572 UY ISSN 0250-6564
UNIVERSIDAD DE LA REPUBLICA. FACULTAD DE HUMANIDADES Y CIENCIAS. REVISTA. SERIE CIENCIAS ANTROPOLOGICAS. N.S. 1979. irreg. exchange basis. Universidad de la Republica, Facultad de Humanidades y Ciencias, Seccion Revista, Tristan Narvaja 1674, Montevideo, Uruguay. Dir. Beatriz Martinez Osorio.
Supersedes in part: Universidad de la Republica. Facultad de Humanidades. Revista.

572 SP ISSN 0080-9101
UNIVERSIDAD DE SEVILLA. SEMINARIO DE ANTROPOLOGIA AMERICANA. PUBLICACIONES. 1960. irreg. price varies. Universidad de Sevilla, San Fernando 4, Seville, Spain. Ed. Alfredo Jimenez-Nunez.

572 MX ISSN 0076-7298
UNIVERSIDAD NACIONAL AUTONOMA DE MEXICO. INSTITUTO DE INVESTIGACIONES ANTROPOLIGICAS. SERIE ANTROPOLOGICA. 1944. irreg., no.11, 1969. price varies. Universidad Nacional Autonoma de Mexico, Instituto de Investigaciones Antropologicas, Departamento de Distribucion de Libros Universitarias, Porto Alegre 260, Colonia San Andres Tetepilco, Mexico, D.F. 09440, Mexico.
Incorporates: Universidad Nacional Autonoma de Mexico. Instituto de Investigaciones Antropologicas. Cuadernos Serie Antropologica (ISSN 0076-7263)

301.2 PE
UNIVERSIDAD NACIONAL DEL CENTRO DEL PERU. CUADERNOS UNIVERSITARIOS. SERIE: ESTUDIOS ANDINOS DEL CENTRO. (Numbers not issued consecutively) no.4, 1978. irreg. Universidad Nacional del Centro del Peru, Departamento de Publicaciones, Calle Puno 635, Huancayo, Peru.

UNIVERSIDADE DE SAO PAULO. INSTITUTO DE ESTUDOS BRASILEIROS. PUBLICACOES. see *GEOGRAPHY*

UNIVERSIDADE DE SAO PAULO. INSTITUTO DE ESTUDOS BRASILEIROS. REVISTA. see *GEOGRAPHY*

572 BL
UNIVERSIDADE DE SAO PAULO. MUSEU PAULISTA. COLECAO. SERIE DE ETNOLOGIA. 1975. a. Universidade de Sao Paulo, Museu Paulista, Caixa Postal 42.503, Parque da Independencia, 04263 Sao Paulo, Brazil. Ed. Setembrino Petri.
Supersedes in part (since 1975): Museu Paulista. Colecao (ISSN 0080-6382)

572 BL ISSN 0080-6390
UNIVERSIDADE DE SAO PAULO. MUSEU PAULISTA. REVISTA. (Text in Portuguese; summaries in English) 1895; N.S. 1947. a. Universidade de Sao Paulo, Museu Paulista, C.P. 42503, 04263 Sao Paulo-SP, Brazil. Indexed: Hisp.Amer.Per.Ind.

572 BL ISSN 0581-6076
UNIVERSIDADE FEDERAL DE SANTA CATARINA. MUSEU DE ANTROPOLOGIA. ANAIS. 1968. irreg. free or exchange basis. ‡ Universidade Federal de Santa Catarina, Museu de Antropologia, Cx. Postal 476, Campus Universitario, Trindade, 88000 Florianopolis, S.C., Brazil. Ed. Neusa Maria Bloemer. bk. rev. bibl. charts. illus.

572 GW ISSN 0170-3099
UNIVERSITAET FRANKFURT. SEMINAR FUER VOELKERKUNDE. ARBEITEN. irreg., vol.17, 1985. price varies. Franz Steiner Verlag Wiesbaden GmbH, Birkenwaldstr. 44, Postfach 347, D-7000 Stuttgart 1, W. Germany (B.R.D.) Ed.Bd.

301 IV
UNIVERSITE NATIONALE DE COTE D'IVOIRE. ANNALES. SERIE F: ETHNOSOCIOLOGIE. 1969. irreg., vol.8, 1979. price varies. Universite Nationale de Cote d'Ivoire, Institut d'Ethnosociologie, B.P. 859, Abidjan 08, Ivory Coast. bk. rev. bibl. charts. illus. circ. 1,000. Indexed: P.A.I.S.For.Lang.Ind.
Formerly: Universite d'Abidjan. Annales. Serie F: Ethnosociologie.

UNIVERSITY OF CALIFORNIA, BERKELEY. LANGUAGE BEHAVIOR RESEARCH LABORATORY. WORKING PAPER SERIES. see *LINGUISTICS*

572 US ISSN 0068-6336
UNIVERSITY OF CALIFORNIA PUBLICATIONS. ANTHROPOLOGICAL RECORDS. 1937. irreg. price varies. University of California Press, 2120 Berkeley Way, Berkeley, CA 94720. TEL 415-642-4247. Indexed: Biol.Abstr.

572 US ISSN 0068-6379
UNIVERSITY OF CALIFORNIA PUBLICATIONS IN ANTHROPOLOGY. 1937. irreg., vol.15, 1983. price varies. University of California Press, 2120 Berkeley Way, Berkeley, CA 94720. TEL 415-642-4247. Ed.Bd.

572 US
UNIVERSITY OF CHICAGO STUDIES IN ANTHROPOLOGY. SERIES IN SOCIAL, CULTURAL, AND LINGUISTIC ANTHROPOLOGY. 1975. irreg. $6. University of Chicago, Department of Anthropology, 1126 E. 59th St., Chicago, IL 60637. TEL 312-947-1000.

301.2 GH ISSN 0533-8646
UNIVERSITY OF GHANA. INSTITUTE OF AFRICAN STUDIES. LOCAL STUDIES SERIES. irreg. price varies. University of Ghana, Institute of African Studies, Box 73, Legon, Ghana.

572 US
UNIVERSITY OF IDAHO ANTHROPOLOGICAL MONOGRAPHS. 1970. irreg., latest no. 4. price varies. (University of Idaho, Alfred W. Bowers Laboratory of Anthropology) University Press of Idaho, Moscow, ID 83843. TEL 208-885-6123. Indexed: Abstr.Anthropol.

572 US ISSN 0085-2457
UNIVERSITY OF KANSAS. DEPARTMENT OF ANTHROPOLOGY. PUBLICATIONS IN ANTHROPOLOGY. 1969. irreg., no.11, 1979. price varies. ‡ University of Kansas, Department of Anthropology, c/o Exchange and Gifts Dept., Lawrence, KS 66045. TEL 913-864-2700. Ed. Robert Jerome Smith. circ. 1,000. Key Title: University of Kansas Publications in Anthropology.

572 913.031 410 CN ISSN 0227-0072
UNIVERSITY OF MANITOBA ANTHROPOLOGY PAPERS. 1973. irreg. price varies. University of Manitoba, Department of Anthropology, U M A P Committee, Winnipeg, Manitoba R3T 2N2, Canada. TEL 204-474-9423. Ed.Bd. circ. 100.

572 US ISSN 0076-5066
UNIVERSITY OF MASSACHUSETTS. DEPARTMENT OF ANTHROPOLOGY. RESEARCH REPORTS. 1968. irreg., no.24, 1985. $10. ‡ University of Massachusetts, Department of Anthropology, Amherst, MA 01003. TEL 413-545-2221. Ed. Sylvia H. Forman. adv. circ. 1,000.

572 US ISSN 0076-8367
UNIVERSITY OF MICHIGAN. MUSEUM OF ANTHROPOLOGY. ANTHROPOLOGICAL PAPERS. 1949. irreg., no.76, 1986. price varies. University of Michigan, Museum of Anthropology, University Museums Building, Ann Arbor, MI 48109. TEL 313-764-0485. (also avail. in microform from UMI) Indexed: Biol.Abstr.

572   US   ISSN 0076-8375
UNIVERSITY OF MICHIGAN. MUSEUM OF ANTHROPOLOGY. MEMOIRS. 1969. irreg., no.18, 1985. price varies. University of Michigan, Museum of Anthropology, University Museums Building, Ann Arbor, MI 48109. TEL 313-764-0485.

572   US
UNIVERSITY OF MICHIGAN. MUSEUM OF ANTHROPOLOGY. TECHNICAL REPORTS. 1971. irreg., no.17, 1985. price varies. University of Michigan, Museum of Anthropology, University Museums Bldg., Rm. 4009, Ann Arbor, MI 48109. TEL 313-764-0485. Indexed: Biol.Abstr.

572   US
UNIVERSITY OF MISSOURI, COLUMBIA. MUSEUM OF ANTHROPOLOGY. ANNUAL REPORTS. 1975. a. price varies. University of Missouri-Columbia, Museum of Anthropology, 104 Swallow Hall, Columbia, MO 65211. TEL 314-882-2121.

572   US
UNIVERSITY OF MISSOURI, COLUMBIA. MUSEUM OF ANTHROPOLOGY. MISCELLANEOUS PUBLICATIONS IN ANTHROPOLOGY. 1972. irreg., no.16, 1980. price varies. University of Missouri-Columbia, Museum of Anthropology, 104 Swallow Hall, Columbia, MO 65211. TEL 314-882-2121.

572   US   ISSN 0362-1235
UNIVERSITY OF MISSOURI, COLUMBIA. MUSEUM OF ANTHROPOLOGY. MUSEUM BRIEFS. 1969. irreg., no.26, 1982. price varies. ‡ University of Missouri-Columbia, Museum of Anthropology, 104 Swallow Hall, Columbia, MO 65211. TEL 314-882-2121. Ed. Lawrence H. Feldman. Key Title: Museum Briefs.

572 917   US
UNIVERSITY OF MISSOURI MONOGRAPHS IN ANTHROPOLOGY. 1974. irreg., no.7, 1984. price varies. University of Missouri-Columbia, Museum of Anthropology, 104 Swallow Hall, Columbia, MO 65211. TEL 314-882-2121. Ed.Bd.

572   US   ISSN 0085-1205
UNIVERSITY OF NORTHERN COLORADO. MUSEUM OF ANTHROPOLOGY. OCCASIONAL PUBLICATIONS IN ANTHROPOLOGY. ETHNOLOGY SERIES. 1967. irreg. price varies. University of Northern Colorado, Museum of Anthropology, Attn. George E. Fay, Ed., Greeley, CO 80639. TEL 303-351-1890. circ. 800. (processed)

572   US   ISSN 0085-1213
UNIVERSITY OF NORTHERN COLORADO. MUSEUM OF ANTHROPOLOGY. OCCASIONAL PUBLICATIONS IN ANTHROPOLOGY. MISCELLANEOUS SERIES. 1967. irreg. price varies. University of Northern Colorado, Museum of Anthropology, Attn. George E. Fay, Ed., Greeley, CO 80639. TEL 303-352-1890. circ. 500. (processed)

572   US   ISSN 0078-6071
UNIVERSITY OF OREGON ANTHROPOLOGICAL PAPERS. 1971. irreg., vol. 31, 1984. price varies. University of Oregon, Department of Anthropology, Eugene, OR 97403. TEL 503-686-5102. Ed. C. Melvin Aikens. circ. 500.

UNIVERSITY OF SOUTH CAROLINA. INSTITUTE OF ARCHEOLOGY AND ANTHROPOLOGY. ANNUAL REPORT. see *ARCHAEOLOGY*

UNIVERSITY OF TENNESSEE. DEPARTMENT OF ANTHROPOLOGY. REPORT OF INVESTIGATIONS. see *ARCHAEOLOGY*

572   US   ISSN 0083-4947
UNIVERSITY OF UTAH ANTHROPOLOGICAL PAPERS. 1950. irreg., no.111, 1986. price varies. University of Utah Press, Salt Lake City, UT 84112. TEL 801-581-6771. Ed. C. Melvin Aikens. Indexed: Biol.Abstr.

572 390 301.2   CS   ISSN 0083-4106
UNIVERZITA KOMENSKEHO. FILOZOFICKA FAKULTA. ZBORNIK: ETHNOLOGIA SLAVICA; an international review of Slavic ethnology. (Text and summaries in various languages) 1969. a. exchange basis. Univerzita Komenskeho, Filozoficka Fakulta, Gondova 2, 806 01 Bratislava, Czechoslovakia. Ed. Jan Podolak. bk. rev. circ. 1,075.

572 301.2   PL   ISSN 0083-4327
UNIWERSYTET JAGIELLONSKI. ZESZYTY NAUKOWE. PRACE ETNOGRAFICZNE. 1963. irreg., no.697, 1983. price varies. ‡ Panstwowe Wydawnictwo Naukowe, Miodowa 10, 00-251 Warsaw, Poland (Dist. by: Ars Polona, Krakowskie Przedmiescie 7, 00-068 Warsaw, Poland) Ed. Jadwiga Klimaszewska. index. circ. 600.

572   IT
UOMO & CULTURA; rivista di studi antropologici. biennial. Universita di Palermo, 37 via Ruggero Settimo, 30139 Palermo, Italy.

301.2   SW   ISSN 0348-5099
UPPSALA STUDIES IN CULTURAL ANTHROPOLOGY. (Subseries of Acta Universitatis Upsaliensis) irreg. (Uppsala Universitet) Almqvist & Wiksell International, Box 62, S-101 20 Stockholm, Sweden. Ed. Anita Jacobson-Widding.

301.2 301   PE
URBANIZACION, MIGRACIONES Y CAMBIOS EN LA SOCIEDAD PERUANA. (Text in Castellano) 1968. irreg., latest no.8. price varies. (Instituto de Estudios Peruanos) I E P Ediciones, Horacio Urteaga 694 (Campe de Marte), Lima 11, Peru. (back issues avail.)

VEREIN FUER VOLKSKUNDE IN WIEN. SONDERSCHRIFTEN. see *FOLKLORE*

572   CR   ISSN 0304-3703
VINCULOS. (Text in English, Spanish) 1975. irreg. $6 or exchange basis. Museo Nacional de Costa Rica, Departamento de Antropologia e Historia, Apdo. 749, San Jose, Costa Rica. Ed.Bd. charts. illus. Indexed: Hisp.Amer.Per.Ind.

301.2   GW   ISSN 0073-0270
VOELKERKUNDLICHE ABHANDLUNGEN. 1964. irreg. price varies. (Niedersaechsisches Landesmuseum, Hannover) Dietrich Reimer Verlag, Unter den Eichen 57, 1000 Berlin 45, W. Germany (B.R.D.) Ed. Hans Becher. circ. 500.

572   AU
VOELKERKUNDLICHE VEROEFFENTLICHUNGEN. irreg. price varies. (Anthropologische Gesellschaft in Wien) Verlag Ferdinand Berger und Soehne OHG, Wienerstr. 21-23, A-3580 Horn, Austria. Ed. Paul Spindler.

WEIMARER MONOGRAPHIEN ZUR UR- UND FRUEHGESCHICHTE. see *ARCHAEOLOGY*

572   US
WENNER - GREN FOUNDATION FOR ANTHROPOLOGICAL RESEARCH. ANNUAL REPORT. 1942. irreg. free. ‡ Wenner - Gren Foundation for Anthropological Research, Inc., 1865 Broadway, New York, NY 10023. TEL 212-957-8750. circ. 4,000.
    Formerly: Wenner - Gren Foundation for Anthropological Research. Report (ISSN 0083-7997)

572   CN   ISSN 0829-0547
WESTERN CANADIAN ANTHROPOLOGIST. 1968. a. Can.$6 to individuals; institutions Can.$10. University of Saskatchewan, Department of Anthropology and Archaeology, Saskatoon. Sask., S7N 0W0, Canada. TEL 306-966-4175. bk. rev. circ. 500. (back issues avail.)
    Formerly (until 1984): Napao: A Saskatchewan Anthropology Journal (ISSN 0077-2755)

572 575.1   US
WHITE PAPER ON HUMAN ECOLOGY. irreg. price varies. International Commission on Human Ecology, Box 3495, Grand Central Sta., New York, NY 10163.
    Former titles: Institute for Human Evolution. Reprint & I A A E E (International Association for the Advancement of Ethnology and Eugenics). Reprint (ISSN 0074-1515)
    Ethnography

WIENER VOELKERKUNDLICHE MITTEILUNGEN. see *FOLKLORE*

572   US
YALE UNIVERSITY. DEPARTMENT OF ANTHROPOLOGY. PUBLICATIONS IN ANTHROPOLOGY. 1936. irreg. Yale University, Department of Anthropology, 2114 Yale Station, New Haven, CT 06520. TEL 203-432-3670. Ed. Leopold Pospisil.

573   US   ISSN 0096-848X
YEARBOOK OF PHYSICAL ANTHROPOLOGY (WASHINGTON) (Published as a supplement to the American Journal of Physical Anthropology) 1945. a. (American Association of Physical Anthropologists) Alan R. Liss, Inc., 41 E. 11th St., New York, NY 10003. TEL 202-232-8800. Ed. Francis E. Johnston. Indexed: Biol.Abstr. SSCI.

301.2 572   CN
YEARBOOK OF SYMBOLIC ANTHROPOLOGY. 1975. a. 8p. Universite Laval, Department de l'Anthropologie, Quebec, P.Q. G1K 7P4, Canada TEL 418-656-2131. (Subscr. to: C. Hurst & Co., Seager Bldg., Brookmill Rd., London S.E. 8, England) Ed. Erik Schulmmer.

ZEMALJSKI MUZEJ BOSNE I HERCEGOVINE. GLASNIK. ETNOLOGIJA. see *FOLKLORE*

ANTHROPOLOGY — Abstracting, Bibliographies, Statistics

572 016   US   ISSN 0001-3455
ABSTRACTS IN ANTHROPOLOGY. 1970. 8/yr. (in 2 vols., 4 nos./vol.) $190. Baywood Publishing Co., Inc., 120 Marine St., Box D, Farmingdale, NY 11753. TEL 516-249-2464. Eds. Linda Smith, Roger Moeller. abstr. index. Indexed: Br.Archaeol.Abstr. E.I.

572   GW   ISSN 0173-2986
ABSTRACTS IN GERMAN ANTHROPOLOGY. (Text in English) 1980. s-a. DM.48($29) to individuals, institutions DM.63($38) (Association for International Scientific Communication) Edition Herodot in Rader Verlag, Kongress Str.5, D-5100 Aachen, W. Germany (B.R.D.) Ed. Rolf Husmann. adv. bk. rev. circ. 750. (back issues avail.) Indexed: Br.Archaeol.Abstr. E.I.

572 016   UK
ANTHROPOLOGICAL INDEX TO CURRENT PERIODICALS IN THE LIBRARY OF THE MUSEUM OF MANKIND. 1963. q. £43($64) Royal Anthropological Institute of Great Britain and Ireland, 56 Queen Anne St., London W1M 9LA, England. Ed. David Jones. bibl. Indexed: E.I.
    Former titles: Royal Anthropological Institute of Great Britain and Ireland. Library. Anthropological Index (ISSN 0003-5467); Royal Anthropological Institute of Great Britain and Ireland. Library. Index to Current Periodicals Received in the Library.

572   US   ISSN 0190-3373
ANTHROPOLOGICAL LITERATURE; an index to periodical articles and essays. 1979. q. $80 to individuals; institutions $100. Harvard University, Tozzer Library, 21 Divinity Ave., Cambridge, MA 02138. Ed. G. Edward Evans. bibl. circ. 500. (microfiche; back issues avail.)

572 016   GW   ISSN 0003-5548
ANTHROPOLOGISCHER ANZEIGER. (Text in English and German, occasionally in French and Italian) 1924. q. E. Schweizerbart'sche Verlagsbuchhandlung, Johannesstr. 3A, 7000 Stuttgart 1, W. Germany (B.R.D.) Eds. G. Hauser, H. Walter. adv. bk. rev. charts. illus. Indexed: Biol.Abstr. Excerp.Med. Ind.Med. Dent.Ind.

291 301.2   GW   ISSN 0067-706X
BIBLIOGRAPHIE ZUR SYMBOLIK, IKONOGRAPHIE UND MYTHOLOGIE. 1968. a. DM.40. Verlag Valentin Koerner, H.-Sielcken-Str. 36, Postfach 304, D-7570 Baden-Baden 1, W. Germany (B.R.D.) Eds. Werner Bies, Hermann Jung. adv. bk. rev. circ. 1,000.

572   US   ISSN 0742-6844
BIBLIOGRAPHIES AND INDEXES IN
ANTHROPOLOGY. 1984. irreg. price varies.
Greenwood Press (Subsidiary of: Congressional
Information Service, Inc.) 88 Post Rd. W., Box
5007, Westport, CT 06881. TEL 203-226-3571.

BULLETIN SIGNALETIQUE. PART 521:
SOCIOLOGIE - ETHNOLOGIE. see
SOCIOLOGY — Abstracting, Bibliographies,
Statistics

301.2 890 410 959   NE   ISSN 0046-0885
E I. (Excerpta Indonesica) (Text in English) 1970. s-a.
fl.29($12) (Documentation Centre for Modern
Indonesia) Koninklijk Instituut voor Taal-, Land- en
Volkenkunde, Reuvensplaats 2, P.O. Box 9515,
2300 RA Leiden, Netherlands. TEL (071) 14 83 33.
Ed. R.S. Karni. adv. bk. rev. abstr. bibl. cum.index
every 10 nos. circ. 1,000. (also avail. in microfiche
from IDC) Indexed: Key to Econ.Sci.

EXCERPTA MEDICA. SECTION 1: ANATOMY,
ANTHROPOLOGY, EMBRYOLOGY &
HISTOLOGY. see MEDICAL SCIENCES —
Abstracting, Bibliographies, Statistics

573   US
FILMS: THE VISUALIZATION OF
ANTHROPOLOGY. 1972. every 2-3 years, latest
1985. Pennsylvania State University, Audio-Visual
Services, University Park, PA 16802. TEL 814-865-
6314.

016 300.7   II
I C S S R JOURNAL OF ABSTRACTS AND
REVIEWS: SOCIOLOGY & SOCIAL
ANTHROPOLOGY. (Text in English) 1972. s-a.
Rs.15($4) to individuals; institutions Rs. 20. Indian
Council of Social Science Research, 35, Ferozshah
Rd., New Delhi 110001, India (Subscr. address:
Behavioural Sciences Centre, 32, Netaji Subhash
Marg, New Delhi 110002, India) Ed.Bd. index. circ.
450. (back issues avail.)
    Formerly: I C S S R Journal of Abstracts and
Reviews (ISSN 0302-7546)

572 016   US   ISSN 0085-2074
INTERNATIONAL BIBLIOGRAPHY OF THE
SOCIAL SCIENCES. SOCIAL AND CULTURAL
ANTHROPOLOGY. Title page also reads:
International Bibliography of Social and Cultural
Anthropology. 1955. a. $110. Methuen Inc., 29 W.
35th St., New York, NY 10001-2291. circ. 2,000.

572 016   NE   ISSN 0074-0462
KONINKLIJK INSTITUUT VOOR TAAL-, LAND-
EN VOLKENKUNDE. BIBLIOGRAPHICAL
SERIES. (Text in English) 1965. irreg. price varies.
Foris Publications, Box 509, 3300 AM Dordrecht,
Netherlands.

ANTIQUES

see also Art

ANTIKE KUNST. BEIHEFTE. see ART

745.1   DK   ISSN 0109-2499
ANTIKVITETSUDSTILLING, ODD-FELLOW
PALAEET. 1955. a. Kr.25. (Danske
Antikvitetshandleres Udstilling) Dansk Kunst- og
Antikvitetshandler Union, Larsbjoernsstraede 6,
1454 Copenhagen K, Denmark. illus.

700   US
ANTIQUARIAN. a. $2.50. Clinton County Historical
Association, Box 332, Plattsburgh, NY 12901. Ed.
Allan Everest.

745.1   US
ANTIQUES DIRECTORY. 1985. a. $4.95.
Abbotsford Press, Box 2097, Southbury, CT 06488.
TEL 203-262-6642. Ed. Jeanne Gardner. adv. circ.
8,250.

745.1   UK
ANTIQUES FOLIO. 1963. a. £2.50($5) Antiques &
General Advertising, Old Rectory, Hopton Castle,
Craven Arms, Salop SY7 0QJ, England. Ed. Tony
Keniston. adv. bk. rev. illus. index. circ. 15,000.
    Incorporating: Antiques in Britain (ISSN 0003-
5955)

745.1   GW
ANTIQUITTAETEN UND KUNST ADRESSEN
LEXIKON. 1985. a. F.Ch. Heel Verlag,
Koenigswinterer Strasse, 5300 Bonn 3 (Oberkassel),
W. Germany (B.R.D.) Ed. G. Demarest. circ. 10,
000.

ARCHAEOLOGIA. see ARCHAEOLOGY

745.1   US   ISSN 0084-6783
ART AT AUCTION; THE YEAR AT SOTHEBY'S
AND PARKE-BERNET. 1967. a. $45. (Sotheby
Publications) Philip Wilson Publishers Ltd., c/o
Harper & Row, 10 E. 53 St., New York, NY 10022.
Ed. Joan A. Speers. illus. index.

745.1   UK
BRITISH ANTIQUE DEALERS' ASSOCIATION
HANDBOOK. 1986. a. £5. British Antique Dealers'
Association (B.A.D.A.), 20 Rutland Gate, London
SW7 1BD, England. Ed. Helen Wilks. adv. circ. 8,
000.

745.1   UK
BRITISH ART & ANTIQUES DIRECTORY. 1949. a.
£9.50. Antique Collector, 72 Broadwick St., London
W1V 2BP, England. Ed. David Coombs. adv. bk.
rev. circ. 3,500.
    Formerly: British Art and Antiques Yearbook
(ISSN 0140-8763)

745 355   US   ISSN 0094-1182
CIVIL WAR COLLECTORS' DEALER
DIRECTORY. 1974. irreg., latest 1987/88. $4.95.
Essential Press, 5512 Buggy Whip Dr., Centreville,
VA 22020. Ed. C.L. Batson. adv. circ. 1,000.

745.1   US
FLEA MARKET ALMANAC; official U.S. flea
market directory. 1973. a. $7.95. Maverick
Publications, Box 243, Bend, OR 97709. TEL 503-
382-6978. Ed. Kenneth Asher. adv. bk. rev. illus.
circ. 15,000.
    Formerly: Flea Market Quarterly.

381   US   ISSN 0364-023X
FLEA MARKET TRADER. 1977. biennial. $8.95.
Schroeder Publishing Co. Inc., Box 3009, Paducah,
KY 42001. TEL 502-898-6211. Eds. Sharon & Bob
Huxford. illus.

739.7 355   SP   ISSN 0436-029X
GLADIUS; etudes sur les armes anciennes,
l'armement, l'art militaire et la vie culturelle en
Orient et Occident. (Text in English, French,
German and Spanish) 1961. a. price varies. Consejo
Superior de Investigaciones Cientificas, Instituto de
Estudios Sobre Armas Antiguas, Apdo. 4, Jarandilla
(Caceres), Spain. Ed. Ada Bruhn Dehoffmeyer. bk.
rev. bibl. illus. index. cum.index. circ. 625.
Indexed: Br.Archaeol.Abstr. Numis.Lit.

745.1   UK
GUIDE TO THE ANTIQUE SHOPS OF BRITAIN.
a. $16. Antique Collectors' Club, 5 Church St.,
Woodbridge, Suffolk, England.

GUILD OF MASTER CRAFTSMEN DIRECTORY
OF MEMBERS. see BUILDING AND
CONSTRUCTION

629.222   US   ISSN 0363-4639
HEMMING'S VINTAGE AUTO ALMANAC. 1976.
a. $9.95. Watering, Inc., Box 256, Bennington, VT
05201 TEL 802-442-3101. (Subscr. address: Box
945, Bennington, VT 05201) Ed. David Brownell.
illus. circ. 25,000.
    Formerly: Vintage Auto Almanac.

739.7   CN   ISSN 0440-9221
HISTORICAL ARMS SERIES. 1963. irreg. price
varies. Museum Restoration Service, Box 390,
Bloomfield, Ont. K0K 1G0, Canada. TEL 613-393-
2980. Ed. S. James Gooding. adv. bk. rev. circ. 1,
500.

INTERNATIONAL WHO'S WHO IN ART AND
ANTIQUES. see ART

650   US
JAPANESE SWORD SOCIETY OF THE U.S.
BULLETIN. 1959. a. $15. Japanese Sword Society
of the U.S., Inc., Box 4387, Grasso Plaza Branch,
St. Louis, MO 63123. Ed. Ronald C. Hartmann.
adv. bk. rev. circ. 900.

745.1   US
KOVEL'S ANTIQUES AND COLLECTIBLES
PRICE LIST. a. $9.95. Crown Publishers, Inc., One
Park Ave., New York, NY 10016. TEL 212-532-
9200. Eds. Ralph Kovel, Terry Kovel.
    Formerly: Kovel's Antiques Price List.

KUNSTPREIS-JAHRBUCH. see ART

745.1   US
LYLE OFFICIAL ANTIQUES REVIEW. 1971/72. a.
$24.95. Apollo Book (Distributor), 5 Schoolhouse
Ln., Poughkeepsie, NY 12603. TEL 914-462-0040.
Ed. Tony Curtis. adv. illus. index. circ. 30,000.

739.7 355   US
MILITARY DEALERS AND COLLECTORS
DIRECTORY. 1981. a? $7.75. Haas Publications,
Box 775, Worthington, OH 43085. Ed. David L.
Hartline.

745.1 700   US
MILLER'S ANTIQUE PRICE GUIDE (YEAR) a.
$18.95. Apollo Book (Distributor), 5 Schoolhouse
Ln., Poughkeepsie, NY 12603. TEL 914-462-0040.

745.1   UK
MILLERS ANTIQUES PRICE GUIDE. 1980. a.
£12.95. Millers Publications Ltd., Sissinghurst
Court, Sissinghurst, Cranbrook, Kent, England
(Distr. in U.S. by: Viking-Penguin Inc., 40 West
23rd St., New York, N.Y. 10010) Eds. Martin and
Judith Miller. adv. illus. circ. 100,000.

737   PO   ISSN 0085-364X
N U M U S NUMISMATICA, MEDALHISTICA,
ARGUEOLOGIA. (Text in English, French and
Portuguese; summaries in English and French) 1952.
a. Esc.250. Sociedade Portuguesa de Numismatica,
Rua de Costa Cabral, 664, 4200 Porto, Portugal.
Ed.Bd. bk. rev. bibl. charts. illus. cum.index 1968-
72. circ. 2,000.

NATIONAL CAROUSEL ASSOCIATION.
CAROUSEL ARCHIVES. see ART

POSTCARD ART/POSTCARD FICTION. see ART

709   US   ISSN 0583-9181
SOCIETY FOR THE PRESERVATION OF LONG
ISLAND ANTIQUITIES. NEWSLETTER. 1967. a.
Society for the Preservation of Long Island
Antiquities, 93 North Country Rd., Setauket, NY
11733. TEL 516-941-9444. Key Title: Newsletter-
Society for the Preservation of Long Island
Antiquities.

745.1 700   US
SOTHEBY'S INTERNATIONAL PRICE GUIDE:
ANTIQUES AND COLLECTIBLES. irreg. $35.
Apollo Book (Distributor), 5 Schoolhouse Ln.,
Poughkeepsie, NY 12603. TEL 914-462-0040.

739.7   DK
VAABENHISTORISKE AARBOEGER. (Text in
Danish; summaries in English and German) 1934. a.
Kr.225. Vaabenhistorisk Selskab, Danish Arms and
Armour Society, "Brobyvang", Freerslev, DK-3400
Hilleroed, Denmark. Ed. Arne Orloff. bk. rev. cum.
index (vols. 1-10 in vol. 10; vols. 11-20 in vol. 20)

ARCHAEOLOGY

see also Paleontology

913   NO   ISSN 0800-0816
A M S - SKRIFTER. (Text in Norwegian; summaries
in English or German) 1976. irreg. Arkeologisk
Museum i Stavanger, Box 478, 4001 Stavanger,
Norway. Ed.Bd.
    Formerly: Arkeologisk Museum i Stavanger.
Skrifter.

913   NO   ISSN 0332-6411
A M S - SMAATRYKK. 1978. irreg. Arkeologisk
Museum i Stavanger, Box 478, 4001 Stavanger,
Norway.

913   NO   ISSN 0332-6306
A M S - VARIA. (Summaries in English) 1978. irreg.
Arkeologisk Museum i Stavanger, Box 478, 4001
Stavanger, Norway. Ed.Bd.

ARCHAEOLOGY

ACADEMIE DES INSCRIPTIONS ET BELLES-LETTRES. ETUDES ET COMMENTAIRES. see *LINGUISTICS*

913   PL   ISSN 0079-3566
ACADEMIE POLONAISE DES SCIENCES. CENTRE D'ARCHEOLOGIE MEDITERRANEENNE. ETUDES ET TRAVAUX. (Text in English and French) 1959. irreg. price varies. Panstwowe Wydawnictwo Naukowe, Ul. Miodowa 10, 00-251 Warsaw, Poland (Dist. by: Ars Polona, Krakowskie Przedmiescie 7, 00-068 Warsaw, Poland) Ed. Kazimierz Michalowski. illus.

913   IT   ISSN 0333-1512
ACTA AD ARCHAEOLOGIAM ET ARTIUM HISTORIAM PERTINENTIA (MISCELLANEOUS) (Text in language of contributor) 1981. irreg. price varies. (Istituto di Norvegia in Roma) Giorgio Bretschneider, Via Crescenzo 43, 00193 Rome, Italy. Indexed: Art & Archaeol.Tech.Abstr. RILA.

913   IT   ISSN 0065-0900
ACTA AD ARCHAEOLOGIAM ET ARTIUM HISTORIAM PERTINENTIA (MONOGRAPH) (Text in language of contributor) 1962. irreg., vol.9, 1981. price varies. (Istituto di Norvegia in Roma) Giorgio Bretschneider, Via Crescenzio 43, 00193 Rome, Italy. circ. 700. Indexed: Art & Archaeol.Tech.Abstr. RILA.

913   SW   ISSN 0065-1001
ACTA ARCHAELOGICA LUNDENSIA: MONOGRAPHS OF LUNDS UNIVERSITETS HISTORISKA MUSEUM. SERIES IN 4. (Text in English and German) 1954. irreg., no.18, 1984. price varies. Liber Forlag, S-205 10 Malmo, Sweden. bk. rev.

571   SW   ISSN 0065-0994
ACTA ARCHAELOGICA LUNDENSIA: MONOGRAPHS OF LUNDS UNIVERSITETS HISTORISKA MUSEUM. SERIES IN 8. (Text in English, German and Swedish) 1957. irreg., No.14, 1985. price varies. Liber Forlag, S-205 10 Malmo, Sweden. Ed. Berta Stjernquist. bk. rev.

913   DK   ISSN 0065-101X
ACTA ARCHAEOLOGICA. (Text in English and German) a. Kr.408. Munksgaard, 35 Noerre Soegade, DK-1370 Copenhagen K, Denmark. Ed. C.F. Becker. adv. bk. rev. circ. 800. (reprint service avail. from ISI) Indexed: Curr.Cont. SSCI. Arts.& Hum.Ind. Br.Archaeol.Abstr. Numis.Lit.

913   PL   ISSN 0001-5229
ACTA ARCHAEOLOGICA CARPATHICA. (Text in English, German, Polish and Russian; summaries in English,French, German and Polish) 1958. a. price varies. (Polska Akademia Nauk, Oddzial w Krakowie, Komisja Archeologiczna) Ossolineum, Publishing House of the Polish Academy of Sciences, Rynek 9, Wroclaw, Poland (Dist. by: Ars Polona-Ruch, Krakowskie Przedmiescie 7, Warsaw, Poland) Ed. Zenon Wozniak. bk. rev. Indexed: Br.Archaeol.Abstr. GeoRef. Numis.Lit.

913   PL   ISSN 0065-0986
ACTA ARCHAEOLOGICA LODZIENSIA. (Text in Polish, summaries in English and French) 1954. a. price varies. (Lodzkie Towarzystwo Naukowe) Ossolineum, Publishing House of the Polish Academy of Sciences, Rynek 9, Wroclaw, Poland (Dist. by: Ars Polona - Ruch, Krakowskie Przedmiescie 7, Warsaw, Poland) Ed. Konrad Jazdzewski. bk. rev. Indexed: Numis.Lit.

913   BE
ACTA ARCHAEOLOGICA LOVANIENSIA. 1962. a. price varies. Katholieke Universiteit Leuven, Departement Archeologie en Kunstwetenschap, Blijde Inkomstraat 21, B-3000 Louvain, Belgium. Ed. J. Mertens. circ. 450. Indexed: Br.Archaeol.Abstr. Numis.Lit.

913   SZ   ISSN 0065-1052
ACTA BERNENSIA: BEITRAEGE ZUR PRAEHISTORISCHEN, KLASSISCHEN UND JUENGEREN ARCHAEOLOGIE. 1963. irreg. price varies. Staempfli und Cie AG, Postfach 2728, 3001 Berne, Switzerland. Eds. H. G. Bandi, H. Mueller-Beck. Indexed: Br.Archaeol.Abstr.

913   SP
ACTA HISTORICA ET ARCHAEOLOGICA MEDIAEVALIA. 1980. a. 1800 ptas. Universidad de Barcelona, Departamento de Historia Medieval, Palesgrafia y Diplomatica, Torre B, Planta 6a, 08028 Barcelona, Spain. Eds. Manuel Riu, Salvador Claramunt. adv. circ. 1,000.

913 943   GW   ISSN 0341-1184
ACTA PRAEHISTORICA ET ARCHAEOLOGICA. 1970. a. Wissenschaftsverlag Volker Spiess GmbH, Potsdamer Str. 199, 1000 Berlin 30, W. Germany (B.R.D.) Indexed: Br.Archaeol.Abstr. Numis.Lit.

913 900 400   SW
ACTA REGIAE SOCIETATITIS HUMANIORUM LITTERATUM LUNDENSIS. (Text in English, French, German and Swedish) 1960. irreg., no.77, 1983. price varies. Liber Forlag, S-205 10, Malmo, Sweden. Ed. Berta Stjernquist.

913   GW
ACTA REI CRETARIAE ROMANAE FAUTORUM. SUPPLEMENTA. 1974. irreg. price varies. Dr. Rudolf Habelt GmbH, Auf der Wacht 435, CH 4303 Kaiseraugst, W. Germany (B.R.D.)

ACTA UNIVERSITATIS DE ATTILA JOZSEF NOMINATAE. ACTA ANTIQUA ET ARCHAEOLOGICA. see *CLASSICAL STUDIES*

913   PL
ACTA UNIVERSITATIS LODZIENSIS: FOLIA ARCHAEOLOGICA. (Text in Polish; summaries in various languages) irreg. Uniwersytet Lodzki, Drukarnia Wojskowa, Ul. Gdanska 130, Lodz, Poland (Dist. by: Ars Polona-Ruch, Krakowskie Przedmiescie 7, Warsaw, Poland)

913   PL   ISSN 0137-6616
ACTA UNIVERSITATIS NICOLAI COPERNICI. ARCHEOLOGIA. 1968. irreg. price varies. Uniwersytet Mikolaja Kopernika, Fosa Staromiejska 3, Torun, Poland (Dist. by Osrodek Rozpowszechniania Wydanictw Naukowych PAN, Palac Kultury i Nauki, 00-901 Warsaw, Poland) Formerly: Uniwersytet Mikolaja Kopernika, Torun. Nauki Humanistyczno-Spoleczne. Archeologia (ISSN 0083-4467)

913   US   ISSN 0162-8003
ADVANCES IN ARCHAEOLOGICAL METHOD AND THEORY. 1978. irreg., vol.9, 1986. $49.50. Academic Press, Inc., Orlando, FL 32887. TEL 305-345-2000. Ed. Michael B. Schiffer. Indexed: Chem.Abstr. Br.Archaeol.Abstr. Numis.Lit.

913   US   ISSN 0733-5121
ADVANCES IN WORLD ARCHAEOLOGY. 1982. irreg., vol.5, 1986. Academic Press, Inc., Orlando, FL 32887. TEL 305-345-2000. Eds. Fred Wendorf, Angela Close. Indexed: Br.Archaeol.Abstr.

913   SZ
AEGYPTICA HELVETICA. 1974. irreg., latest no.10. price varies. (Universite Geneva, Faculte des Lettres) Editions Belles-Lettres, Case Postale 32, 1211 Geneva 20, Switzerland. (Co-sponsor: Universitaet Basel) Ed. Robert Hari. circ. 600.

AEGYPTOLOGISCHE FORSCHUNGEN. see *HISTORY — History Of The Near East*

930.1 770   UK   ISSN 0140-9220
AERIAL ARCHAEOLOGY. (Summaries in English, French and German) 1977. a. £4.50. Aerial Archaeology Publications, 15 Colin McLean Rd., East Dereham, Norfolk NR19 2RY, England. Ed. Derek A. Edwards. Indexed: Br.Archaeol.Abstr. Geo.Abstr.

913   UK   ISSN 0263-0338
AFRICAN ARCHAEOLOGICAL REVIEW. 1983. a. $32 to individuals; institutions $54. Cambridge University Press, Edinburgh Bldg., Shaftesbury Rd., Cambridge CB2 2RU, England (And 32 E. 57th St., New York, NY 10022) Ed. Nicholas David. adv. bk. rev.

913   UR
AKADEMIYA NAUK S.S.S.R. INSTITUT ARKHEOLOGII. KRATKIE SOOBSHCHENIYA. vol.147, 1976. irreg. price varies. (Akademiya Nauk S.S.S.R., Institut Arkheologii) Izdatel'stvo Nauka, Podsosenskii Per., 21, Moscow K-62, Russian S.F.S.R., U.S.S.R. (Subscr. to: Mezhdunarodnaya Kniga, Moscow, G-200, Russian S.F.S.R., U.S.S.R.) Ed. I.I. Kruglikova. circ. 2,150. Indexed: Numis.Lit.

914   SP
AKAL UNIVERSITARIA. SERIE: ARQUEOLOGIA. irreg., no.49, 1983. Akal Editor, Paseo de Sta. Maria de la Cabeza, 132, Madrid 26, Spain. Ed. Ramon Akal Gonzalez.

917   US
ALABAMA ARCHAEOLOGICAL SOCIETY. SPECIAL PUBLICATION. 1974. irreg. Alabama Archaeological Society, 7608 Teal Dr. S.W., Huntsville, AL 35802. TEL 205-881-9389. Ed. B Bart Henson. circ. 500. (also avail. in microform from UMI; reprint service avail. from UMI)

ALGONQUIAN CONFERENCE PAPERS. see *ANTHROPOLOGY*

ALLE TIDERS ODSHERREDS. see *HISTORY — History Of Europe*

970.1   US
AMERICAN INDIAN ARCHAEOLOGICAL INSTITUTE. OCCASIONAL PAPER. 1974. irreg., latest issue no.3, 1982. American Indian Archaeological Institute, Inc., Box 260, Rt. 199, Washington, CT 06793. TEL 203-868-0518. circ. 2,000.

AMERICAN RESEARCH CENTER IN EGYPT. JOURNAL. see *ART*

913 572   US   ISSN 0066-0027
AMERICAN SCHOOL OF PREHISTORIC RESEARCH. BULLETINS. (Vols. not issued consecutively) 1936. irreg., no.38, 1986. price varies. Peabody Museum of Archaeology and Ethnology, Harvard University, 11 Divinity Ave., Cambridge, MA 02138. TEL 617-495-3938. Ed. Mary Strother. Indexed: Biol.Abstr.

AMERICAN SCHOOLS OF ORIENTAL RESEARCH. ANNUAL. see *HISTORY — History Of The Near East*

917   US
AMERICAN SOCIETY FOR CONSERVATION ARCHAEOLOGY. PROCEEDINGS. 1976. a. $10. American Society for Conservation Archaeology, c/o Editor, 465 Westminster Rd., Brooklyn, NY 11218. Ed. Joel I. Klein. bk. rev. circ. 450.

341   SP
AMPURIAS; revista de prehistoria, arqueologia y etnologia. 1939. a. 2000 ptas. (or exchange) Diputacion Provincial de Barcelona, Instituto de Prehistoria y Arqueologia, Palacio del Museo Arqueologico, Parque de Montjuich, Barcelona 4, Spain. bibl. illus. circ. controlled. Indexed: Hist.Abstr. Amer.Hist.& Life. Br.Archaeol.Abstr. Numis.Lit.

913.031   NE   ISSN 0569-9843
ANALECTA PRAEHISTORICA LEIDENSIA. 1964. irreg. price varies. (Rijksuniversiteit te Leiden, Institute for Prehistory) Leiden University Press, c/o E.J. Brill Publishers, P.O. Box 9000, 2300 PA Leiden, Netherlands. Indexed: Art & Archaeol.Tech.Abstr. Br.Archaeol.Abstr. GeoRef.

918 572   AG   ISSN 0325-0288
ANALES DE ARQUEOLOGIA Y ETNOLOGIA. 1940. a. exchange basis. Universidad Nacional de Cuyo, Instituto de Arqueologia y Etnologia, Casilla Correo 345, Mendoza, Argentina. Ed. Dr. Juan Schobinger. bk. rev. circ. 800. Indexed: Hist.Abstr. Amer.Hist.& Life.
Former titles (1945-1946): Anales del Instituto de Etnologia Americana; (1940-1944): Anales del Instituto de Etnografica Americana.

913   UK   ISSN 0066-1546
ANATOLIAN STUDIES. 1951. a. £7($25.50) British Institute of Archaeology at Ankara, c/o British Academy, 20-21 Cornwall Terrace, London NW1 4QP, England (Subscr. addr.: 69 Arlington Rd., London NW1 7ES, England) Ed. Prof. O.R. Gurney. index. circ. 800. Indexed: Br.Hum.Ind. Art & Archaeol.Tech.Abstr. Numis.Lit.

ANATOLICA. see *HISTORY — History Of Asia*

915.49   CE
ANCIENT CEYLON. (Text in English) 1971. irreg. $10. Department of Archaeology, Sir Marcus Fernando Rd., Colombo 7, Sri Lanka. bk. rev. illus.

ANCIENT MONUMENTS SOCIETY TRANSACTIONS. see *ARCHITECTURE*

ARCHAEOLOGY

913   II
ANDHRA PRADESH, INDIA. DEPARTMENT OF ARCHAEOLOGY AND MUSEUMS. ANNUAL REPORT. (Text in English) irreg. price varies. Department of Archaeology and Museums, Hyderabad, 500 001, Andhra Pradesh, India.

ANDHRA PRADESH, INDIA. DEPARTMENT OF ARCHAEOLOGY AND MUSEUMS. ARCHAEOLOGICAL SERIES. see *ART*

913   II
ANDHRA PRADESH, INDIA. DEPARTMENT OF ARCHAEOLOGY AND MUSEUMS. ARCHAEOLOGICAL SERIES: A.P. JOURNAL OF ARCHAEOLGY. (Text in English) 1978. irreg. price varies. Department of Archaeology and Museums, Gunfoundry, Hyderabad 500 001, Andhra Pradesh, India. circ. 500.

571 954   II
ANDHRA PRADESH, INDIA. DEPARTMENT OF ARCHAEOLOGY AND MUSEUMS. EPIGRAPHY SERIES. (Text in English) 1967. irreg., no.11, 1975-76. price varies. Department of Archaeology and Museums, Hyderabad 500001, Andhra Pradesh, India (Or: Publication Bureau, Directorate of Government Printing, Chanchalguda, Hyderabad, Andhra Pradesh, India)
  Formerly: Andhra Pradesh, India. Department of Archaeology. Epigraphy Series (ISSN 0066-1651)

914   SP   ISSN 0561-3663
ANEJOS DE ARCHIVO ESPANOL DE ARQUEOLOGIA. 1951. irreg. price varies. Consejo Superior de Investigaciones Cientificas, Instituto Espanol de Arqueologia, Medinaceli 4, Madrid 14, Spain. illus.

914.2   UK   ISSN 0306-5790
ANGLESEY ANTIQUARIAN SOCIETY TRANSACTIONS. (Text in English and Welsh) 1913. a. £4. Anglesey Antiquarian Society and Field Club, c/o Hon. Secretary, 1 Fronheulog, Tregarth, Bangor, Gwynedd, Wales. Ed. A.D. Carr. bk. rev. charts. illus. circ. 1,000. (tabloid format) Indexed: Br.Archaeol.Abstr.

913   HU   ISSN 0133-6924
ANTAEUS. (Text in German) 1970. a. exchange basis. Magyar Tudomanyos Akademia, Regeszeti Intezet - Archaeological Institute of the Hungarian Academy of Sciences, Uri utca 49, 1250 Budapest, Hungary. Ed. Laszlo Torok.
  Formerly (until 1986): Ungarische Akademie der Wissenschaften. Archaelogisches Institut. Mitteilungen.

ANTHROPOLOGICAL ANALYSES. see *ANTHROPOLOGY*

ANTICHITA, ARCHEOLOGIA, STORIA DELL'ARTE. see *ART*

914   IT
ANTICHITA PISANE; rivista di Archeologia e di Topografia Storica. vol.2, 1975. irreg. (Universita degli Studi di Pisa, Scuola Speciale per Archeologi Preistorici) Pacini Editore, Via della Faggiola 17, 56100 Pisa, Italy.

ANTIKE KUNST. BEIHEFTE. see *ART*

ANTIQUITAS. REIHE 3. ABHANDLUNGEN ZUR VOR- UND FRUEHGESCHICHTE, ZUR KLASSISCHEN UND PROVINZIAL-ROEMISCHEN ARCHAEOLOGIE UND ZUR GESCHICHTE DES ALTERTUMS. see *HISTORY*

ANTIQUITES AFRICAINES. see *HISTORY — History Of Africa*

913   IT
AQUILEIA NOSTRA. 1930. a. Associazione Nazionale per Aquileia, Casa Bertoli, Via Popone 6, 33051 Aquileia, Italy. TEL 0431 91113. circ. 750. (back issues avail.)

913   BE   ISSN 0772-7488
ARCHAELOGIA BELGICA. 1950. irreg. price varies. Service National des Fouilles - Nationale Dienst voor Opgravingen, Parc de Cinquantenaire 1, B-1040 Brussels, Belgium.

913   GW
ARCHAELOGISCHE FORSCHUNGEN. 1975. irreg. (Deutsches Archaeologisches Institut Berlin) Mann Verlag, Lindenstr. 76, 1000 Berlin 61, W. Germany (B.R.D.) (back issues avail.)

913   GW   ISSN 0066-5886
ARCHAEO-PHYSIKA. 1965. irreg., vol.11, 1981. price varies. Rheinland Verlag, Kennedy-Ufer 2, 5000 Cologne 2, W. Germany (B.R.D.) (Distr. by: Rudolf Habelt GmbH, Am Buchenhang 1, 5300 Bonn 1, W. Germany(B.R.D.)) Indexed: Br.Archaeol.Abstr. Geo.Abstr.

913 709 929 745.1   UK   ISSN 0261-3409
ARCHAEOLOGIA. 1770. irreg., vol.107, 1982. £30. Society of Antiquaries of London, Burlington House, London W1V OHS, England. Ed. Sarah Macready. circ. 2,000. (also avail. in microfilm from UMI; reprint service avail. from UMI) Indexed: Br.Hum.Ind.   Art & Archaeol.Tech.Abstr. Br.Archaeol.Abstr.   Numis.Lit.   RILA.

913 943.6 571   AU   ISSN 0003-8008
ARCHAEOLOGIA AUSTRIACA; Beitraege zur Palaeanthropologie, Ur- und Fruehgeschichte Oesterreichs. (Supplements avail.) 1948. a. price varies. (Universitaet Wien, Institut fuer Ur- und Fruehgeschichte) Franz Deuticke, Helferstorfer Str. 4, A-1010 Vienna, Austria. TEL 636429. Ed. Herwig Friesinger. bk. rev. bibl. charts. illus. cum.index. circ. 400. (back issues avail.) Indexed: Chem.Abstr.   Br.Archaeol.Abstr.

571   UK   ISSN 0066-5894
ARCHAEOLOGIA CANTIANA. 1858. a. £7 to individuals; £10 to institutions. Kent Archaeological Society, c/o Mrs. M. Lawrence, The Museum, St. Faith's St., Maidstone, Kent, England. Ed. A.P. Detsicas. adv. bk. rev. index; cum.index. circ. 1,750. Indexed: Br.Hum.Ind.   Br.Archaeol.Abstr. Numis.Lit.

913   CS   ISSN 0231-5823
ARCHAEOLOGIA HISTORICA. 1976. a. price varies. Muzejni a Vlastivedna Solecnost, Gagarinova 1, 659 37 Brno, Czechoslovakia. Ed. Vladimir Nekuda. bk. rev. illus. circ. 1,500.

560   JA   ISSN 0402-852X
ARCHAEOLOGIA JAPONICA. (Text in Japanese; summaries in English) 1948. irreg. 2000 Yen. Japanese Archaeologists Association - Nippon Kokogaku Kyokai, c/o Waseda Daigaku Kokogaku Kenkyushitsu, 647 Totsukamachi 1-chome, Shinjuku-ku, Tokyo 160, Japan.

913 943.8   PL   ISSN 0066-5924
ARCHAEOLOGIA POLONA. (Text in English, French, German and Spanish) 1958. a. $20. (Polska Akademia Nauk, Instytut Historii Kultury Materialnej) Ossolineum, Publishing House of the Polish Academy of Sciences, Rynek 9, 50-106 Wroclaw, Poland (Dist. by Ars Polona-Ruch, Krakowskie Przedmiescie 7, Warsaw, Poland) Ed. Witold Hensel.

913   BE
ARCHAEOLOGIA TRANSATLANTICA. 1981. irreg., latest no.7, 1985. price varies. Universite Catholique de Louvain, Institut Superieur d'Archeologie et d'Histoire de l'Art, 31 place Blaise Pascal, 1348 Louvain-la-Neuve, Belgium. (Co-sponsor: Brown University, Center for Old World Archaeology and Art)

913   ZA   ISSN 0570-6068
ARCHAEOLOGIA ZAMBIANA. (Text in English) no.4, 1971. irreg., (1-2/yr.) Commission for the Preservation of Natural and Historical Monuments and Relics, P.O. Box 60124, Livingstone, Zambia.

913   GW   ISSN 0066-5932
ARCHAEOLOGICA SLOVACA. CATALOGI. 1968. irreg. price varies. (Instituti Archaeologici Nitriensis Academiae Scientiarum Slovacae, CS) Dr. Rudolf Habelt GmbH, Am Buchenhang 1, 5300 Bonn 1, W. Germany (B.R.D.) Ed. A. Tocik.

913   GW   ISSN 0066-5940
ARCHAEOLOGICA SLOVACA. FONTES. (Text in Czech and German) 1957. irreg. price varies. (Instituti Archaeologici Nitriensis Academiae Scientiarum Slovacae, CS) Dr. Rudolf Habelt GmbH, Am Buchenhang 1, 5300 Bonn 1, W. Germany (B.R.D.) Ed. A. Tocik.

ARCHAEOLOGICAL COMPLETION REPORT SERIES. see *HISTORY — History Of North And South America*

913   UK
ARCHAEOLOGICAL EXCAVATIONS. 1978. a. price varies. H.M.S.O., Box 569, London S.E.1., England.

913   IS
ARCHAEOLOGICAL EXCAVATIONS. (Text in English) 1982. a. Israel Department of Antiquities and Culture, P.O. Box 586, Jerusalem, Israel.

913   US   ISSN 0066-5975
ARCHAEOLOGICAL EXPLORATION OF SARDIS. MONOGRAPHS. 1971. irreg., vol.8, 1983. Harvard University Press, 79 Garden St., Cambridge, MA 02138. TEL 617-495-2600.

571 913   UK   ISSN 0066-5983
ARCHAEOLOGICAL JOURNAL. 1844. a. membership. Royal Archaeological Institute, 96 New Walk, Leicester LE1 6TD, London NW8 9EL, England. Ed. R.T. Schadla-Hall. bk. rev. index. cum.index every 25 years. circ. 2,500. (also avail. in microform from UMI) Indexed: Br.Hum.Ind. Br.Tech.Ind.   Br.Archaeol.Abstr.   Numis.Lit.   RILA.

913   UK   ISSN 0141-8971
ARCHAEOLOGICAL REPORTS. 1977. a. £1.50. University of Durham, Old Shire Hall, Durham, England. (Co-sponsor: University of Newcastle-upon-Tyne) Ed. A.F. Harding. Indexed: Br.Hum.Ind.

913   US
ARCHAEOLOGICAL RESEARCH TOOLS. 1981. irreg., vol.2, 1982. price varies. University of California, Los Angeles, Institute of Archaeology, 405 Hilgard Ave., Los Angeles, CA 90024. TEL 213-825-7411.

913   US   ISSN 0739-5612
ARCHAEOLOGICAL SOCIETY OF CONNECTICUT. BULLETIN. 1936. a. $12.50. Archaeological Society of Connecticut, Archaeological Services, Box 386, 68 Sunny Ridge, Bethlehem, CT 06751. TEL 203-266-7741. Ed. Roger Moeller. bk. rev. film rev. bibl. charts. illus. index. circ. 350. (back issues avail.) Indexed: Abstr.Anthropol.

913   US   ISSN 0003-8067
ARCHAEOLOGICAL SOCIETY OF DELAWARE. BULLETIN. 1933. irreg. membership. Archaeological Society of Delaware, Box 301, Wilmington, DE 19899. TEL 302-571-4011. Ed. Elwood Wilkins. charts. illus. (also avail. in microform from UMI) Indexed: Abstr.Anthropol.

917   US
ARCHAEOLOGICAL SOCIETY OF DELAWARE. MONOGRAPH. 1976. irreg. Archaeological Society of Delaware, Box 301, Wilmington, DE 19899. TEL 302-571-4011.

917   US
ARCHAEOLOGICAL SOCIETY OF NEW MEXICO. PAPERS. 1968. a. $20 to individuals; institutions $15.00 (includes newsletter) Archaeological Society of New Mexico, Box 3485, Albuquerque, NM 87190-3485. Ed. Anne Poore. circ. 300.

913   US
ARCHAEOLOGICAL SOCIETY OF NORTH CAROLINA. NEWSLETTER. 1949. irreg. latest no.87, 1986. $25 to institutions. (Archaeological Society of North Carolina) University of North Carolina, Research Laboratories of Anthropology, Box 2 Alumni Bldg., 004A, Chapel Hill, NC 27514. TEL 919-962-6574. Ed. David Moore. circ. 350.

913   BE
ARCHAEOLOGICUM BELGII SPECULUM. (Text in Dutch and French) 1968. irreg., no.11, 1979. price varies. Service National des Fouilles - Nationale Dienst voor Opgravingen, Parc du Cinquantenaire 1, B-1040 Brussels, Belgium.

913.031   GW   ISSN 0066-6009
ARCHAEOLOGISCHE FUNDE UND DENKMAELER DES RHEINLANDES. 1960. irreg., vol.4, 1979. price varies. Rheinland-Verlag, Kennedy-Ufer 2, 5000 Cologne 21, W. Germany (B.R.D.) (Distr. by: Rudolf Habelt Verlag, Am Buchenhang 1, 5300 Bonn 1, W. Germany (B.R.D))

ARCHAEOLOGY

913   GW
ARCHAEOLOGISCHE INFORMATIONEN. MITTEILUNGEN ZUR UR- UND FRUEHGESCHICHTE. 1972. irreg. price varies. (Deutsche Gesellschaft fuer Ur- und Fruehgeschichte) Dr. Rudolf Habelt GmbH, Am Buchenhang 1, 5300 Bonn 1, W. Germany (B.R.D.) Indexed: Br.Archaeol.Abstr.

913.5   GW   ISSN 0066-6033
ARCHAEOLOGISCHE MITTEILUNGEN AUS IRAN. NEUE FOLGE. 1968. a. DM.145. (Deutsches Archaeologisches Institut, Abt. Teheran) Dietrich Reimer Verlag, Unter den Eichen 57, 1000 Berlin 45, W. Germany (B.R.D.) Indexed: Art & Archaeol.Tech.Abstr.

913   UK   ISSN 0308-8456
ARCHAEOLOGY IN BRITAIN (YEAR) 1976. a. Council for British Archaeology, 112 Kennington Rd., London SE11 6RE, England. circ. 1,000. (back issues avail.) Indexed: Br.Archaeol.Abstr.
    Supersedes in part: C B A Annual Report.

913   KO
ARCHAEOLOGY IN KOREA. (Text in Korean; summaries in English) 1973. a. exchange. Seoul National University, University Museum, Seoul Taehakkyo Pangmulgwan, S. Korea. Ed. Kim Won-Yong. bk. rev. circ. 500.

917   US   ISSN 0360-1021
ARCHAEOLOGY OF EASTERN NORTH AMERICA. 1973. a. $12.50. Eastern States Archeological Federation, Archaeological Services, Box 386, 68 Sunny Ridge, Bethlehem, CT 06751. TEL 203-266-7741. Ed. Dennis Curry. illus. circ. 500.

913 551.46   FR
ARCHAEONAUTICA. 1977. irreg. Editions du C N R S, 295 rue St. Jacques, 75005 Paris, France. Ed. Bernard Liou. Indexed: Br.Archaeol.Abstr.

913   GR
ARCHAILOGIKE HETAIREIA EN ATHENAIS. PRAKTIKA. 1837. a. Archailogike Hetaireia en Athenais, Odos el Venizelou 22, Athens, Greece. illus. circ. 500.

913   GR
ARCHAIOLOGIKE EPHEMERIS. (Text in English, French, German and Greek) 1837. irreg. Athenais Archaiologike Hetaireia, Odos Venizelou 22, Athens, Greece. bibl. cum.index vols.1-21 (1837-1874); vols.22-62 (1883-1923) circ. 600. Indexed: Numis.Lit.

ARCHEION EUVOIKON MELETON. see HISTORY — History Of Europe

ARCHEION PONTOU. see HISTORY — History Of Europe

ARCHEION THESSALIKON MELETON. see HISTORY — History Of Europe

913   IT   ISSN 0392-0038
ARCHEOGRAFO TRIESTINO; raccolta di opusculi e notizie per Trieste e perl'Istria. 1828. a. L.20000. Societa di Minerva, Piazza Hortis n.4, Trieste, Italy. circ. 300.

913   PL   ISSN 0554-8195
ARCHEOLOGIA (POZNAN) (Text in Polish; summaries in German or English) 1966. irreg., no. 26, 1976. price varies. Adam Mickiewicz University Press, Marchlewskiego 128, 61-874 Poznan, Poland.
    Formerly: Uniwersytet im. Adama Mickiewicza w Poznaniu. Wydzial Filozoficzno-Historyczny. Prace. Seria Archeologia.

913   PL   ISSN 0066-605X
ARCHEOLOGIA (WROCLAW) (Text in English, French, German and Polish; summaries in French and Russian) 1950. a. $28. (Polska Akademia Nauk, Instytut Historii Kultury Materialnej) Ossolineum, Publishing House of the Polish Academy of Sciences, Rynek 9, 50-106 Wroclaw, Poland (Dist. by Ars Polona-Ruch, Krakowskie Przedmiescie 7, Warsaw, Poland) Ed. Z. Nowicka. Indexed: Numis.Lit.

913   IT   ISSN 0003-8172
ARCHEOLOGIA CLASSICA. 1949. a. L.170000. (Universita degli Studi di Roma, Istituti di Archeologia e Storia dell'Arte Greca e Romana e di Etruscologia e Antichita Italiche) Erma di "Bretschneider", Via Cassiodoro 19, 00193 Rome, Italy. bk. rev. charts. illus. index. Indexed: M.L.A. Br.Archaeol.Abstr.

913   US
ARCHEOLOGICAL SOCIETY OF SOUTH CAROLINA. OCCASIONAL PAPERS. 1979. irreg. price varies. Archeological Society of South Carolina, Inc., Institute of Archeology and Anthropology, University of South Carolina, Columbia, SC 29208. TEL 803-777-8170. Ed. Chester B. DePratter. bk. rev. circ. 500.

914 943.7   CS
ARCHEOLOGICKE VYSKUMY A NALEZY NA SLOVENSKU. 1974. irreg. Archeologicky Ustav Slovenskej Akademie Vied, 949 21 Nitra-hrad, Czechoslovakia. Ed. Bohuslav Chropovsky. circ. 500.

913   FR   ISSN 0335-5233
ARCHEOLOGIE EN BRETAGNE. 1974. irreg. 100 F.($9.35) Association Privee Archeologie en Bretagne, Faculte des Lettres, 20 av. Le Gorgeu, B.P. 813, 29285 Brest, France. Ed. Rene Sanquer. bk. rev. circ. 400. (also avail. in microfiche; back issues avail.) Indexed: Br.Archaeol.Abstr.

571 913   FR   ISSN 0066-6084
ARCHEOLOGIE MEDITERRANEENNE. 1965. irreg. price varies. Editions Klincksieck, 11 rue de Lille, 75005 Paris, France.

913   BE   ISSN 0066-6025
ARCHEOLOGISCHE KAARTEN VAN BELGIE. (Text in Dutch and French) 1968. irreg. price varies. Service National des Fouilles - Nationale Dienst voor Opgravingen, Parc du Cinquantenaire 1, B-1040 Brussels, Belgium.

ARCHIV FUER PAPYRUSFORSCHUNG UND VERWANDTE GEBIETE. see HISTORY

ARHEOLOGIA MOLDOVEI/ARCHEOLOGIE DE LA MOLDAVIE. see HISTORY — History Of Europe

913   YU   ISSN 0350-7165
ARHEOLOSKI MUZEJ U ZAGREBU. VJESNIK. (Text in Croatian; summaries in English, French, German) 1879. a. Arheoloski Muzej u Zagrebu, Trg. N. Zrinskog 19, 41000 Zagreb, Yugoslavia. bk. rev. illus. circ. 600.

913   YU   ISSN 0570-8966
ARHEOLOSKI VESTNIK/ACTA ARCHAEOLOGICA. (Text in English, French, German, Italian, Serbo-Croatian, Slovenian) 1950. a. $15. Slovenska Akademija Znanosti in Umetnosti, Institut za Arheologijo, Novi trg 3, 61000 Ljubljana, Yugoslavia. (Co-sponsor: Znanstvenoraziskovalni Center S A Z U) Ed. Bogo Grafenauer. bk. rev. circ. 1,100. Indexed: Curr.Cont. Numis.Lit.

913   US
ARIZONA ARCHAEOLOGIST. 1965. a. price varies. Arizona Archaeological Society, Inc., Box 9665, Phoenix, AZ 85068. TEL 602-488-3981. (back issues avail.)

917   US   ISSN 0587-3533
ARKANSAS ARCHEOLOGICAL SURVEY. PUBLICATIONS ON ARCHEOLOGY. POPULAR SERIES. 1969. irreg. price varies. Arkansas Archeological Survey Publications, Box 1249, Fayetteville, AR 72702-1249. TEL 501-575-3556. charts. illus.

917   US   ISSN 0277-6308
ARKANSAS ARCHEOLOGICAL SURVEY. PUBLICATIONS ON ARCHEOLOGY. RESEARCH REPORTS. 1975. irreg., no.24, 1985. price varies. Arkansas Archeological Survey Publications, Box 1249, Fayetteville, AR 72702-1249. TEL 501-575-3556.

917   US   ISSN 0882-5491
ARKANSAS ARCHEOLOGICAL SURVEY. PUBLICATIONS ON ARCHEOLOGY. RESEARCH SERIES. 1967. irreg., no.25, 1985. price varies. Arkansas Archeological Survey Publications, Box 1249, Fayetteville, AR 72701. TEL 501-575-3556. charts. illus. Indexed: GeoRef.

913   US
ARKANSAS ARCHEOLOGICAL SURVEY. PUBLICATIONS ON ARCHEOLOGY. TECHNICAL PAPERS. 1981. irreg., no.2, 1984. price varies. Arkansas Archeological Survey Publications, Box 1249, Fayettevelle, AR 72702-1249. TEL 501-575-3556. Ed. W. Fredrick Limp.

913   US   ISSN 0004-1718
ARKANSAS ARCHEOLOGIST. 1960. a. $10 (includes Field Notes) Arkansas Archeological Society, Box 1222, Fayetteville, AR 72702-1222. TEL 501-575-3556. Ed. Hester A. Davis. illus. maps. circ. 750. Indexed: Hist.Abstr. Amer.Hist.& Life.

914   DK   ISSN 0901-0815
ARKEOLOGISKE UDGRAVNINGER I DANMARK. 1985. a. free. (Danmark National Museet) Bibliotekscentralen, Telegrafvej 5, DK-2750 Ballerup, Denmark (Subscr. to: Frederiksholm Kanal 12, DK-1220 Copenhagen K, Denmark)

ARKHEOGRAFICHESKII EZHEGODNIK. see HISTORY

913   UR
ARKHEOLOGICHESKIE RABOTY V TADZHIKISTANE. vol.11, 1971. irreg. 1.45 Rub. (Akademiya Nauk Tadzhikskoi S.S.R., Institut Istorii) Izdatel'stvo Donish, Ul. Aini 121, Korp. 2, Dushanbe, Tadzhik S.S.R., U.S.S.R. Ed. B. Litvinskii.

913   UR
ARKHEOLOGIYA I ETNOGRAFIYA UDMURTII. 1975. irreg. 1 Rub. per issue. Udmurdskii Institut Istorii, Ekonomiki, Literatury, Sovetskaya, 14, 426020 Izhevsk, Udmurt A.S.S.R., U.S.S.R. circ. 500.

571 913   PE   ISSN 0066-7803
ARQUEOLOGICAS. (Text in Spanish; occasionally in language of author) 1957. irreg. latest, no.15, 1974. price varies. Museo Nacional de Antropologia y Arqueologia, Casilla 3640, Lima, Peru. Ed. Ruth Shady Solis. circ. 1,750.

913 398   SW   ISSN 0432-1251
ARSTRYCK. 1953. biennial. Kr.130. Goeteborgs Historiska Museet, N. Hamngaten 12, Goteborg, Sweden. circ. 1,500. (back issues avail.)

ART ROMANIC. see ART

ARTE E ARCHEOLOGIA; studi e documenti. see ART

ARTE Y ARQUEOLOGIA. see ART

913   AT   ISSN 0044-9075
ARTEFACT. 1965. a. Aus.$17. Archaeological and Anthropological Society of Victoria, G.P.O. 328C, Melbourne, Vic. 3001, Australia. Ed. G. Presland. bk. rev. circ. 280. Indexed: Abstr.Anthropol. Aus.P.A.I.S.

ARTIBUS ASIAE SUPPLEMENTA. see ART

913   US   ISSN 0066-829X
ASIAN AND PACIFIC ARCHAEOLOGY SERIES. 1967. irreg., no.9, 1981. price varies. (University of Hawaii, Social Science Research Institute) University of Hawaii Press, 2840 Kolowalu St., Honolulu, HI 96822. TEL 808-948-8697. (reprint service avail. from UMI,ISI)

ATLAS POLSKICH STROJOW LUDOWYCH. see ANTHROPOLOGY

AUSTRALIAN FILMS; a catalogue of scientific, educational and cultural films. see MOTION PICTURES

913   AT   ISSN 0810-1868
AUSTRALIAN JOURNAL OF HISTORICAL ARCHAEOLOGY. 1983, Vol.1. a. Aus.$25. Australian Society for Historical Archaeology, Box 220 Home Building, University of Sydney, N.S.W., 2006, Australia. Ed. G. Connah. bk. rev. circ. 400. (also avail. in microform; back issues avail.)
    Supersedes (from 1973-19??): Australian Society for Historical Archeology. (Annual Publication); Studies in Historical Archeology.

AZANIA. see HISTORY — History Of Africa

ARCHAEOLOGY

913 930   FR
B E F A R. PUBLICATION. 1877. irreg., (1-2/yr.)
price varies. (Bibliotheque des Ecoles Francaises
d'Athenes et de Rome) Diffusion de Boccard, 11
rue de Medicis, 75006 Paris, France. Ed.Bd. bibl.

913   GW   ISSN 0418-9698
BAGHDADER MITTEILUNGEN. 1960. a.
(Deutsches Archaeologisches Institut) Gebr. Mann
Verlag, Lindenstr. 76, D-1000 Berlin 61, W.
Germany (B.R.D.)

914   GW   ISSN 0341-910X
BEITRAEGE ARCHAEOLOGIE DES
ROMISCHEN RHEINLANDS. 1968. irreg.
Rheinland Verlag, Kennedy-Ulfer 2, 5000 Cologne,
W. Germany (B.R.D.) (Subscr. to: Rudolf Habelt
Verlag, Am Buchenhang 1, 5300 Bonn, W.
Germany (B.R.D.))

914   GW   ISSN 0341-9185
BEITRAEGE ZUR ARCHAEOLOGIE DES
    MITTELALTERS. 1968. irreg. Rheinland Verlag,
Kennedy-Ufer 2, 5000 Cologne, W. Germany
(B.R.D.) (Subscr. to: Rudolf Habelt Verlag, Am
Buchenhang 1, 5300 Bonn, W. Germany (B.R.D.))
Indexed: Br.Archaeol.Abstr.

913   GW   ISSN 0067-5245
BEITRAEGE ZUR UR- UND
FRUEHGESCHICHTLICHEN ARCHAEOLOGIE
DES MITTELMEERKULTURRAUMES. 1965.
irreg., no. 25/26 1981. price varies. Dr. Rudolf
Habelt GmbH, Am Buchenhang 1, 5300 Bonn 1, W.
Germany (B.R.D.) Ed. H. Hauptmann.

914   GW   ISSN 0341-9193
BEITRAEGE ZUR URGESCHICHTE DES
RHEINLANDES. 1974. irreg. Rheinland Verlag,
Kennedy-Ufer 2, 5000 Cologne, W. Germany
(B.R.D.) (Subscr. to: Rudolf Habelt Verlag, Am
Buchenhang 1, 5300 Bonn, W. Germany (B.R.D.))
Indexed: Br.Archaeol.Abstr.

BELGIUM. COMMISSION ROYALE DES
MONUMENTS ET DES SITES. BULLETIN. see
ARCHITECTURE

913   UK
BERKSHIRE ARCHAEOLOGICAL COMMITTEE.
PUBLICATION. 1975. irreg. Berkshire
Archaeological Committee, c/o Trust for Wessex
Archaeology, 65 the Close, Salisbury, Wilts SP1
2EN, England.

914   UK   ISSN 0309-3093
BERKSHIRE ARCHAEOLOGICAL JOURNAL.
1871. a. £2. Berkshire Archaeological Society, 9
Warwick Rd., Reading RG2 7AX, England. Ed. R.J.
Taylor. bk. rev. bibl. illus. index. Indexed:
Br.Archaeol.Abstr. Numis.Lit.

913   GW   ISSN 0344-5089
BERLINER BEITRAEGE ZUR
ARCHAEOMETRIE. (Text in English and
German) 1976. a. DM.50. Staatliche Museen,
Preussischer Kulturbesitz, Schlossstr. 1a, 1000 Berlin
19, W. Germany (B.R.D.) Ed. J. Riederer. bk. rev.
circ. 800.

914   SZ
BERN. UNIVERSITAET. ARCHAEOLOGISCHES
SEMINAR. HEFTE. (Text in French and German)
1975. a. price varies. Archaeologisches Seminar der
Universiaet Bern, Schwanengasse 7, 3011 Bern,
Switzerland. Ed. D. Willers. illus. circ. 200.

913   LE   ISSN 0067-6195
BERYTUS ARCHEOLOGICAL STUDIES. (Text in
English, French and German) 1934. a. $15.
American University of Beirut, Faculty of Arts and
Sciences, Box 1786, Beirut, Lebanon. Eds. William
A. Ward, Helga Seiden. bk. rev. circ. 500. (back
issues avail.) Indexed: Numis.Lit.

BIBLIOGRAPHIE ZUR ARCHAEO-ZOOLOGIE
UND GESCHICHTE DER HAUSTIERE. see
BIBLIOGRAPHIES

913   RM   ISSN 0067-7388
BIBLIOTECA DE ARHEOLOGIE. (Text in
Rumanian; summaries in French) 1957. irreg.,
vol.46, 1984. (Academia de Stiinte Sociale si
Politice, Institutul de Arheologie) Editura
Academiei Republicii Socialiste Rumania, Calea
Victoriei 125, 79717 Bucharest, Rumania (Subscr.
to: ARTEXIM, Export-Import Presa, Str. Piata
Scinteii nr.1, P.O. Box 33-16, 70055 Bucharest,
Rumania)

913   SP   ISSN 0067-7507
BIBLIOTECA PRAEHISTORICA HISPANA. 1958.
irreg. price varies. Centro de Estudios Historia,
Departamento de Prehistoria, Palacio del Museo
Arqueologico Nacional, Serrano, 13, 28001 Madrid,
Spain.

913   PL   ISSN 0067-7639
BIBLIOTEKA ARCHEOLOGICZNA. (Text in
Polish; summaries in English or French) 1948.
irreg., vol.30, 1985. price varies. (Polskie
Towarzystwo Archeologiczne i Numizmatyczne)
Ossolineum, Publishing House of the Polish
Academy of Sciences, Rynek 9, Wroclaw, Poland
(Dist. by Ars Polona-Ruch, Krakowskie
Przedmiescie 7, Warsaw, Poland)

913 400   US   ISSN 0732-6467
BIBLIOTHECA AEGYPTIA;* the philology and
archaeology of ancient Egypt. 1980. irreg. price
varies. Undena Publications, 6355 Green Valley
Circle, No. 213, Culver City, CA 90230-7064.
Ed.Bd. bibl. charts. illus. circ. 500.

960 090   BE   ISSN 0067-7817
BIBLIOTHECA AEGYPTIACA. 1932. irreg., no.16,
1975. price varies. Fondation Egyptologique Reine
Elisabeth, Parc du Cinquantenaire 10, B-1040
Brussels, Belgium.

914   SP   ISSN 0519-9603
BIBLIOTHECA ARCHAEOLOGICA. 1960. irreg.
price varies. Consejo Superior de Investigaciones
Cientificas, Instituto Espanol de Arqueologia,
Medinaceli 4, Madrid 14, Spain. illus.

BIBLIOTHECA LATINA MEDII ET RECENTIORI
AEVI. see HISTORY — History Of Europe

913   FR   ISSN 0067-8309
BIBLIOTHEQUE DES CAHIERS
ARCHEOLOGIQUES. 1966. a. price varies.
Editions A. et J. Picard, 82 rue Bonaparte, 75006
Paris, France. Ed. Andre Grabar.

913   UK   ISSN 0140-4202
BIRMINGHAM & WARWICKSHIRE
ARCHAEOLOGICAL SOCIETY.
TRANSACTIONS. 1871. a. £8. Birmingham &
Warwickshire Archaeological Society, Birmingham &
Midland Institute, Margaret Street, Birmingham B3
3BS, England. Eds. Mrs. R. Taylor, D. Hooke. bk.
rev. charts. illus. circ. 450. Indexed: Br.Hum.Ind.
Br.Archaeol.Abstr. Numis.Lit.

913   GW
BOREAS; Muensterske Beitraege zur Archaeologie.
1978. a. Verlag Ernst Wasmuth, Fuerststr. 133,
Postfach 2728, 7400 Tuebingen, W. Germany
(B.R.D.) Indexed: Sci.Cit.Ind. Numis.Lit.

BRACARA AUGUSTA; revista cultural de
Regionalismo e historia. see HISTORY — History
Of Europe

914   BE
BRAIVES. 1981. irreg., latest no.3, 1985. 1400 Fr.
Universite Catholique de Louvain, Institut Superieur
d'Archeologie et d'Histoire de l'Art, 1 place Blaise
Pascal, 1348 Louvain-la-Neuve, Belgium.

913   CS
BRATISLAVA-STUDIA. 1975. irreg. price varies.
(Archiv) Obzor, Ceskoslovenskej Armady 35, 815
85 Bratislava, Czechoslovakia.

BREIFNE; journal of Cumann Seanchais Bhreifne. see
HISTORY — History Of Europe

913   GW   ISSN 0068-0907
BREMER ARCHAEOLOGISCHE BLAETTER.
1960. irreg., no.7, 1976. price varies. (Bremer
Gesellschaft fuer Vorgeschichte) Dr. Rudolf Habelt
GmbH, Am Buchenhang 1, 5300 Bonn 1, W.
Germany (B.R.D.) (Co-sponsor: Focke-Musuem;
Vaeterkunde-Museum) Ed. K.H. Brandt.

914.2   UK   ISSN 0263-1091
BRISTOL AND AVON ARCHAEOLOGY. 1982. a.
£2. Bristol and Avon Archaeological Research
Group, Bristol City Museum, Queens Rd., Bristol
BS8 1RL, England. Ed. R. Iles. bk. rev. charts.
illus. index. circ. 300. Indexed: Br.Archaeol.Abstr.
    Supersedes: B A R G Review (ISSN 0144-6576);
Formerly (until 1980): B A R G Bulletin.

913   UK   ISSN 0068-1032
BRISTOL AND GLOUCESTERSHIRE
ARCHAEOLOGICAL SOCIETY, BRISTOL,
ENGLAND. TRANSACTIONS. 1876. a.
membership; institutions £6. Bristol and
Gloucestershire Archaeological Society, 22
Beaumont Rd., Gloucester GL2 0EJ, England. Eds.
S. Blake, A. Saville. bk. rev. cum.index every 10
years (vol. 79-90 in 1974) circ. 800. Indexed:
Br.Hum.Ind. Br.Archaeol.Abstr. Numis.Lit. RILA.

913 709 723   UK
BRITISH ARCHAEOLOGICAL ASSOCIATION.
CONFERENCE TRANSACTIONS. irreg. British
Archaeological Association, c/o 61 Old Park
Ridings, Winchmore Hill, London N21 2ET,
England. Indexed: Br.Archaeol.Abstr.

571 913   UK   ISSN 0068-1288
BRITISH ARCHAEOLOGICAL ASSOCIATION.
JOURNAL. 1843. a. individuals £5; libraries £7.
British Archaeological Association, c/o 61 Old Park
Ridings, Winchmore Hill, London, N21 2ET,
England. Ed. P. Everson. bk. rev. cum.index every 5
years. circ. 1,000. Indexed: Br.Hum.Ind.
Br.Archaeol.Abstr. Numis.Lit. RILA.

913   UK   ISSN 0068-2454
BRITISH SCHOOL AT ATHENS. ANNUAL. 1894.
a. £45. British School at Athens, 31-34 Gordon Sq.,
London WC1H 0PY, England. Ed. Prof. R.A.
Tomlinson. index. circ. 600. Indexed: Br.Hum.Ind.
Br.Tech.Ind. Art & Archaeol.Tech.Abstr.
Br.Archaeol.Abstr. Numis.Lit.

913   UK   ISSN 0068-2462
BRITISH SCHOOL AT ROME. PAPERS.
ARCHAEOLOGY. 1902. a. £19. British School at
Rome, Tuke Bldg., Regent's College, Inner Circle,
Regent's Park, London NW1 4NS, England. Ed. N.
Purcell. index. circ. 1,000. Indexed: Br.Hum.Ind.
Br.Archaeol.Abstr. RILA.

571   BU   ISSN 0068-3620
BULGARSKA AKADEMIIA NA NAUKITE.
ARKHEOLOGICHESKI INSTITUT IZVESTIIA.
(Summaries in various languages) 1910. irreg. price
varies. Publishing House of the Bulgarian Academy
of Sciences, Acad. G. Bonchev St., Bldg. 6, 1113
Sofia, Bulgaria (Dist. by: Hemus, 6, Rouski Blvd.,
1000 Sofia, Bulgaria) Ed. D. Angelov. circ. 970.

913   MR   ISSN 0068-4015
BULLETIN D'ARCHEOLOGIE MAROCAINE.
1956. a. Insititut National des Sciences, de
l'Archeologie et du Patrimoine, Ave. John Kennedy,
Rabat-Souissi, Morocco. Indexed: Numis.Lit.

914   RM
BULLETIN D'ARCHEOLOGIE SUD-EST
EUROPEENNE.* irreg. Association Internationale
d'Etudes du Sud-Est Europeen, Str. I.C. Frimu Nr.
9, Bucharest, Rumania. bibl. illus.

BULLETIN DE CORRESPONDANCE
HELLENIQUE. see CLASSICAL STUDIES

913   UK
BULLETIN OF EXPERIMENTAL
ARCHAEOLOGY. 1980. a. £2. University of
Southampton, Department of Adult Education,
University Rd., Highfield, Southampton S09 NH,
England. Ed. D.E. Johnston. bk. rev. index. circ. 75.
Indexed: Br.Archaeol.Abstr.

914 949.7   YU
BUZETSKI ZBORNIK. 1976. a. 400 din. Opcinska
Konferencija S.S.R.N. Buzet, 51 420 Buzet,
Yugoslavia. circ. 1,000.

BYHORNET; nyt fra Egnsmuseet i Pederstrup. see
HISTORY — History Of Europe

913   UK   ISSN 0589-9028
C B A ANNUAL REPORT. a. Council for British
Archaeology, 112 Kennington Rd., London SE11
6RE, England. (back issues avail.)

ARCHAEOLOGY

913 737 SP ISSN 0007-9502
CAESARAUGUSTA. vol.10, no.18, 1951. a. 400 ptas. (Seminario de Argueologia y Numismatica Aragonesas) Institucion Fernando el Catolico, Pl. de Espana 2, Zaragoza, Spain. bk. rev. bibl. charts. illus. index. cum.index. Indexed: Hist.Abstr. Amer.Hist.& Life. Br.Archaeol.Abstr. Numis.Lit.

914 FR
CAHIERS ALSACIENS D'ARCHEOLOGIE D'ART ET D'HISTOIRE. (Text in French) 1909. a. 150 F. Societe pour la Conservation des Monuments Historiques d'Alsace, 2 place du Chateau, 67000 Strasbourg, France. bk. rev. circ. 1,000.
Incorporating (1857-1956): Societe pour la Conservation des Monuments Historiques d'Alsace. Bulletin.

913 BE
CAHIERS BINCHOIS; revue de la Societe d'Archeologie et des Amis du Musee de Binche. 1978. a. 300 Fr. Societe d'Archeologie et des Amis du Musee de Binche, 7130 Binche, Belgium.

913.38 CN ISSN 0317-5065
CAHIERS DES ETUDES ANCIENNES. 1972. irreg. price varies. Universite du Quebec a Trois Rivieres, C.P. 500, Trois-Rivieres. Que. G9A 5H7, Canada TEL 418-657-3551. (Dist. by: Exportlivre, C.P. 305, Saint Lambert, Quebec J4P 3P8, Canada) Ed. Pierre Senay. illus. circ. 700.

913 FR ISSN 0180-9261
CAHIERS DU MEMONTOIS. (Text in French) 1978. irreg. price varies. Groupe Archeologique de Memontois, Malain, 21410 Pont-de-Pany, France. Ed.Bd. charts. illus. circ. 1,000. (back issues avail.)

571 IT
CAHIERS LIGURES DE PREHISTOIRE ET DE PROTOHISTOIRE. (Text in French) 1952. a. L.20000 per no. Istituto Internazionale di Studi Liguri - International Institute of Ligurian Studies, Museo Bicknell, 39 bis via Romana, 18012 Bordighera, Italy. circ. 1,000.
Formerly: Cahiers Ligures de Prehistoire et d'Archeologie (ISSN 0575-108X); Supersedes (1931-1949): Cahiers d'Histoire et d'Archeologie.

913 572 CN ISSN 0384-191X
CALGARY ARCHAEOLOGIST. 1973. a. Can.$6. (University of Calgary, Department of Archaeology) Western Publishers, Box 30193, Sta. "B", 526 16th Ave. N.W., Calgary, Alta. T2M 4P1, Canada. TEL 403-284-7578. Ed. Dr. V. Markotic. bk. rev. circ. 400. (looseleaf format; back issues avail.)

913 979.4 US
CALIFORNIA ARCHAEOLOGICAL REPORTS. 1961. irreg., latest no. 24. price varies. Department of Parks and Recreation, P.O. Box 2390, Sacramento, CA 95811. TEL 916-445-6477. Ed. Peter D. Schulz. circ. 800.
Formerly: California. Department of Parks and Recreation. Archaeological Report (ISSN 0068-5550)

942 UK ISSN 0068-659X
CAMBRIDGE AIR SURVEYS. 1952. irreg. price varies. Cambridge University Press, Edinburgh Bldg., Shaftesbury Rd., Cambridge CB2 2RU, England (and 32 E. 57 St., New York NY 10022)

CAMBRIDGE ANTIQUARIAN SOCIETY. PROCEEDINGS. see *HISTORY — History Of Europe*

917 CN ISSN 0317-2244
CANADA. NATIONAL MUSEUM OF MAN. MERCURY SERIES. ARCHAEOLOGICAL SURVEY OF CANADA. PAPERS/CANADA. MUSEE NATIONAL DE L'HOMME. COLLECTION MERCURE. COMMISSION ARCHAEOLOGIQUE DU CANADA. DOSSIERS. (Text in English or French) 1972. irreg., no.111, 1982. free. (National Museum of Man) National Museums of Canada, Ottawa, Ont. K1A 0M8, Canada. TEL 613-992-4397. charts. illus. cum.index.

971.01 CN ISSN 0705-2006
CANADIAN JOURNAL OF ARCHAEOLOGY. (Text in English and French) 1977. a. Can.$25 to individuals; students Can.$20, institutions Can.$30. Canadian Archaeological Association, c/o Donald Mitchell, Ed., University of Victoria, Dept. of Anthropology, Victoria, British Columbia V8W 2Y2, Canada TEL 613-746-7693. (Subscr. addr.: c/o Secretary-Treasurer, Canadian Archaeological Association, 101 Knutsen Ave., Yellowknife, N.W.T. X1A 2Y3, Canada) bk. rev. illus. circ. 500. Indexed: Br.Archaeol.Abstr.
Formerly: Canadian Archaeological Association. Bulletin (ISSN 0315-761X)

913 942 UK ISSN 0069-0198
CANTERBURY ARCHAEOLOGICAL SOCIETY. OCCASIONAL PAPERS. 1956. irreg., no.7, 1974. price varies. Canterbury Archaeological Society, c/o L. D. Lyle, 3 Queen's Ave., Canterbury, Kent CT2 8AY, England.

914 AU ISSN 0411-129X
CARNUNTUM JAHRBUCH. 1955. a. Verlag Hermann Boehlaus Nachf., Schmalzhofgasse 4, Postfach 167, 1061 Vienna, Austria.
Formerly: Roemische Forschungen in Niederoesterreich. Beiheft.

CASA DE VELASQUEZ, MADRID. MELANGES/ CASA DE VELASQUEZ, MADRID. MISCELLANIES. see *ART*

913 US ISSN 0890-5592
CATASTROPHISM AND ANCIENT HISTORY. PROCCEDINGS. 1983. a. $15. Catastrophism and Ancient History Press, 3431 Club Dr., Los Angeles, CA 90064. TEL 213-559-1076. Ed. Marvin Arnold Luckerman. circ. 1,000. (also avail. in microfiche) Indexed: Old Test.Abstr.

913 FR
CENTRE DE RECHERCHES ARCHEOLOGIQUES. CAHIER. 1980. irreg. 133 F. Centre National de la Recherche Scientifique, Centre de Recherches Archeologiques, 15, Quai Anatole-France, 75700 Paris, France. Ed. B.P. Groslier.

913 016 BE ISSN 0069-1992
CENTRE NATIONAL DE RECHERCHES ARCHEOLOGIQUES EN BELGIQUE. REPERTOIRES ARCHEOLOGIQUES. SERIE A: REPERTOIRES BIBLIOGRAPHIQUES/ NATIONAAL CENTRUM VOOR OUDHEIDKUNDIGE NAVORSINGEN IN BELGIE. OUDHEIDKUNDIGE REPERTORIA. REEKS A: BIBLIOGRAFISCHE REPERTORIA. (Text in Dutch and French) 1960. irreg. (approx. a.) price varies. Centre National de Recherches Archeologiques en Belgique, 1 Parc du Cinquantenaire, 1040 Brussels, Belgium.

913 BE ISSN 0069-200X
CENTRE NATIONAL DE RECHERCHES ARCHEOLOGIQUES EN BELGIQUE. REPERTOIRES ARCHEOLOGIQUES. SERIE B: REPERTOIRES DES COLLECTIONS. (Text in Dutch and French) 1965. irreg. price varies. Centre National de Recherches Archeologiques en Belgique, 1 Parc du Cinquantenaire, 1040 Brussels, Belgium.

913 BE ISSN 0069-2018
CENTRE NATIONAL DE RECHERCHES ARCHEOLOGIQUES EN BELGIQUE. REPERTOIRES ARCHEOLOGIQUES. SERIE C: REPERTOIRES DIVERS. (Text in Dutch and French) 1964. irreg. price varies. Centre National de Recherches Archeologiques en Belgique, 1 Parc du Cinquantenaire, 1040 Brussels, Belgium.

913.031 709 IT
CENTRO CAMUNO DI STUDI PREISTORICI. ARCHIVI. 1968. irreg., vol.8, 1982. $32. Centro Camuno di Studi Preistorici, 25044 Capo di Ponte, Brescia, Italy. charts. illus.

913 709 IT ISSN 0577-2168
CENTRO CAMUNO DI STUDI PREISTORICI. BOLLETTINO. (Text in various languages) 1967. a. $40. Centro Camuno di Studi Preistorici, 25044 Capo di Ponte, Brescia, Italy. Ed. Emmanuel Anati. bk. rev. bibl. charts. illus. Indexed: Br.Archaeol.Abstr.

913.031 709 IT
CENTRO CAMUNO DI STUDI PREISTORICI. STUDI CAMUNI. irreg., vol.8, 1980. $9. Centro Camuno di Studi Preistorici, 25044 Capo di Ponte, Brescia, Italy. illus.

CENTRO CAMUNO DI STUDI PREISTORICI. SYMPOSIA. see *ART*

CENTRO DE ESTUDOS REGIONAIS. BOLETIM CULTURAL. see *ANTHROPOLOGY*

913 IT ISSN 0069-2204
CENTRO STUDI PER LA MAGNA GRECIA, NAPLES. PUBBLICAZIONI PROPRIE.* 1959. irreg., no.6, 1969. price varies. Centro Studi per la Magna Grecia, Istituto di Archeologia, Via Porta di Massa 1, 80133 Naples, Italy.

913 572 US ISSN 0577-3334
CERAMICA DE CULTURA MAYA. 1961. irreg., no.14, 1984. $5. ‡ Ceramica De Cultura Maya, c/o Muriel Kirkpatrick, Coordinator, Laboratory of Anthropology, Temple University, Philadelphia, PA 19122. TEL 215-787-1418. Eds. Carol A. Gifford, Muriel Kirkpatrick. charts. illus. circ. 175. (back issues avail.)

CERCLE D'HISTOIRE ET D'ARCHEOLOGIE DE SAINT-GHISLAIN ET DE LA REGION. ANALES. see *HISTORY — History Of Europe*

CERCLE HISTORIQUE ET FOLKLORIQUE DE BRAINE-LE-CHATEAU DE TUBIZE ET DES REGIONS VOISINES. ANNALES. see *HISTORY — History Of Europe*

914 BE
CERCLE ROYAL D'HISTOIRE ET D'ARCHEOLOGIE D'ATH ET DE LA REGION ET MUSEES ATHOIS. ANNALES. 1913. biennial. 500 Fr. includes Bulletin. Cercle Royal d'Histoire et d'Archeologie d'Ath et de la Region et Musees Athois, 38 rue du Chapelain, 7800 Ath, Belgium.

914 BE ISSN 0771-5692
CERCLE ROYAL D'HISTOIRE ET D'ARCHEOLOGIE D'ATH ET DE LA REGION ET MUSEES ATHOIS. ETUDES ET DOCUMENTS. 1969. a. Cercle Royal d'Histoire et d'Archeologie d'Ath et de la Region et Musees Athois, 38 rue du Chapelain, 7800 Ath, Belgium.

913 UK ISSN 0307-6628
CHESHIRE ARCHAEOLOGICAL BULLETIN. 1973. a. £2.50. 11 Wold Court, Hawarden, Clwyd CH5 3LN, Wales. Ed. Janet A. Rutter. adv. bk. rev. circ. 250. Indexed: Br.Archaeol.Abstr.

CHIAKA CHRONIKA. see *HISTORY — History Of Europe*

913 US ISSN 0882-2042
CHICORA FOUNDATION RESEARCH SERIES. 1984. irreg. Chicora Foundation, Inc., Box 8664, Columbia, SC 29202. TEL 803-783-4645. Ed. Michael Trinkley. circ. 50.

913 GW ISSN 0069-3715
CHIRON. 1971. a. DM.98. (Deutsches Archaeologisches Institut, Kommission fuer Alte Geschichte und Epigraphik) C.H. Beck'sche Verlagsbuchhandlung, Wilhelmstr. 9, 8000 Munich 40, W. Germany (B.R.D.) circ. 600. Indexed: Numis.Lit.

CIMBEBASIA. see *ANTHROPOLOGY*

CIRCOLO CULTURALE B.G. DUNS SCOTO DI ROCCARAINOLA. ATTI. see *GENERAL INTEREST PERIODICALS — Italy*

913 940 UK
CIRENCESTER EXCAVATIONS. 1981. irreg., latest vol.3. price varies. Cirencester Excavation Committee, Corinium Museum, Park St., Cirencester, Gloucestershire GL7 2BX, England. circ. 1,000. Indexed: Br.Archaeol.Abstr.

918 IT
COLLANA CORPUS ANTIQUITATUM AMERICANENSIUM ITALIA. 1981. irreg. (Unione Accademica Nazionale) Multigrafica Editrice, Viale Quattro Venti 52/A, 00152 Rome, Italy.

914 IT
COLLANA CORPUS VASORUM ANTIQUORUM ITALIA. 1950. irreg. (Unione Accademica Nazionale) Multigrafica Editrice, Viale Quattro Venti 52/A, 00152 Rome, Italy. (back issues avail.)

COLLANA DI STUDI PALETNOLOGICI. see *ANTHROPOLOGY*

913 IT ISSN 0392-0879
COLLEZIONI E MUSEI ARCHEOLOGICI DEL VENETO. 1973. irreg., vol.17, 1981. price varies. Giorgio Bretschneider, Via Crescenzo 43, 00193 Rome, Italy. Ed. Gustavo Traversari. (back issues avail.)

975 917.55 US ISSN 0069-5971
COLONIAL WILLIAMSBURG ARCHAEOLOGICAL SERIES. 1960. irreg., no.10, 1983. price varies. ‡ Colonial Williamsburg Foundation, Box C, Williamsburg, VA 23187. TEL 804-229-1000. Ed. Ivor Noel Hume.

917 US
COLONIAL WILLIAMSBURG OCCASIONAL PAPERS IN ARCHAEOLOGY. 1973. irreg. price varies. Colonial Williamsburg Foundation, Box C, Williamsburg, VA 23187. TEL 804-229-1000.

913 720 FR ISSN 0758-2722
COMMISSION DEPARTEMENTALE D'HISTOIRE ET D'ARCHEOLOGIE. BULLETIN. 1849; N.S. 1889. a. 85 F. Commission Departementale d'Histoire et d'Archeologie, Archives Departementales, Prefecture, 62020 Arras Cedex, France. Indexed: Br.Archaeol.Abstr.
Former titles: Commission Departementale des Monuments Historiques du Pas-de-Calais. Bulletin (ISSN 0750-1331); Commission Departementale d'Histoire et d'Archeologie du Pas-de-Calais; Commission Departementale des Monuments Historiques du Pas-de-Calais. Bulletin.

913 IT
COMMISSIONE ARCHEOLOGICA COMUNALE DI ROMA. BULLETTINO. 1872. a. price varies. L'Erma di Bretschneider, Via Cassiodoro 19, 00193 Rome, Italy. TEL 06 687 41 27. circ. 1,500.

913 FR ISSN 0069-8881
CONGRES ARCHEOLOGIQUE DE FRANCE (PUBLICATION.) 1834. a. 285 F.($50) Societe Francaise d'Archeologie, Musee National des Monuments Francais, Palais de Chaillot, Aile de Paris, 75116 Paris, France. cum.index: 1834-1925; 1926-1954; 1955-1975. circ. 2,500.

918 UY
CONGRESO NACIONAL DE ARQUEOLOGIA. ACTAS. Centro de Estudios Arqueologicos, Casilla de Correos 6436, Montevideo, Uruguay. Ed. Jorge Baeza.

913 PO ISSN 0084-9189
CONIMBRIGA. (Text in English, French, Portuguese, Spanish) 1959. a. Esc.600. Universidade de Coimbra, Instituto de Arqueologia - University of Coimbra, Institute of Archaeology, 3049 Coimbra, Portugal (Subscr. to: Casa do Castelo, Rua da Sofia, 3000-Coimbra, Portugal) Ed. Jorge de Alarcao. bk. rev. circ. 450.

915.4 II ISSN 0376-7965
CONSERVATION OF CULTURAL PROPERTY IN INDIA. (Text in English) 1966. a. Rs.15($3) Indian Association for the Study of Conservation of Cultural Property, c/o National Archives of India, Janpath, New Delhi 110001, India. Ed. O. P. Agrawal. adv. bibl. circ. 500. Indexed: Art & Archaeol.Tech.Abstr.

913 UK ISSN 0307-5087
CONTREBIS. 1974. a. £2 per copy. Lancaster Archaeological Society, c/o Lancaster City Museum, Market Square, Lancaster LA1 1HT, England. Ed. A.J. White. bk. rev. bibl. illus. circ. 200. Indexed: Br.Archaeol.Abstr. Numis.Lit.

CORK HISTORICAL AND ARCHAEOLOGICAL SOCIETY. JOURNAL. see *HISTORY — History Of Europe*

913 UK ISSN 0070-024X
CORNISH ARCHAEOLOGY. 1962. a. £8. Cornwall Archaeological Society, c/o Royal Institution of Cornwall, River St., Truro, Cornwall, England (Subscr. to: Miss D. G. Harris, 25 Park View, Truro, Cornwall, England) Indexed: Br.Archaeol.Abstr. Numis.Lit.

913 SP
CORPUS DE MOSAICOS ROMANOS DE ESPANA. 1978. irreg. price varies. Consejo Superior de Investigaciones Cientificas, Instituto Espanol de Arqueologia, Medinaceli 4, Madrid 14, Spain. illus.

CORSI INTERNAZIONALI DI CULTURA SULL'ARTE RAVENNATE E BIZANTINA. ATTI. see *ART*

913 IE
COUNTY KILDARE ARCHAEOLOGICAL SOCIETY. JOURNAL. 1891. a. £3 to non-members. County Kildare Archaeological Society, Tullig, Dublin Road Naas, County Kildare, Ireland. Ed. C. Costello. bk. rev. charts. illus. circ. 400. (back issues avail.) Indexed: Br.Hum.Ind. Br.Archaeol.Abstr. RILA.

571 913 IE ISSN 0070-1327
COUNTY LOUTH ARCHAEOLOGICAL AND HISTORICAL JOURNAL. 1904. a. £5. County Louth Archaeological and Historical Society, 5, Oliver Plunkett Park, Dundalk, Ireland. Ed. Noel Ross. bk. rev. circ. 650. Indexed: Br.Archaeol.Abstr. RILA.
Formerly: County Louth Archaeological Journal.

913 IT ISSN 0391-1527
CRONACHE POMPEIANE. (Text in English, French, German and Italian) 1975. a. L.30000. (Associazione Internazionale "Amici di Pompei") Gaetano Macchiaroli Editore, Via Carducci 55, Naples 80121, Italy.

913.031 SP
CUADERNOS DE PREHISTORIA. 1976. irreg. price varies. Universidad de Granada, Secretariado de Publicaciones, Antiguo Colegio Maximo de Cartjuo, Granada, Spain. Ed. Fernanado Molina Gonzalez.

913 UK
CUMBERLAND AND WESTMORLAND ANTIQUARIAN AND ARCHAEOLOGICAL SOCIETY. RESEARCH SERIES. 1979. irreg. price varies. Cumberland and Westmorland Antiquarian and Archaeological Society, Per Titus Wilson, Kendal, England. Eds. B. Jones, W. Wiseman.

913 UK ISSN 0309-7986
CUMBERLAND AND WESTMORLAND ANTIQUARIAN AND ARCHAEOLOGICAL SOCIETY. TRANSACTIONS. 1866. a. price varies. Cumberland and Westmorland Antiquarian and Archaeological Society, Per Titus Wilson, Kendal, England. Eds. B.C. Jones, W.G. Wiseman.

913 560 US ISSN 8755-898X
CURRENT RESEARCH IN THE PLEISTOCENE. (Text occasionally in Chinese, Portuguese or Spanish) 1984. a. $12 to individuals; institutions $15. University of Maine at Orono, Center for the Study of Early Man, 495 College Ave., Orono, ME 04473. TEL 207-581-2197. Ed. Jim I. Mead. circ. 400. Indexed: Geo.Abstr.
Formerly: Center for the Study of Early Man. Current Research.

913 571 CY ISSN 0070-2374
CYPRUS. DEPARTMENT OF ANTIQUITIES. ANNUAL REPORT. 1934. a. Mils.28. Department of Antiquities, Nicosia, Cyprus.

913 571 CY ISSN 0070-2366
CYPRUS. DEPARTMENT OF ANTIQUITIES. MONOGRAPHS. 1953. irreg., no.15, 1977. price varies. Department of Antiquities, Nicosia, Cyprus.

913 FR
DELEGATION ARCHEOLOGIQUE FRANCAISE EN IRAN. CAHIERS. 1971. a. price varies. Association Paleorient, Delegation Archeologique Francaise en Iran, B.P. 5005, 75222 Paris Cedex 05, France. Ed. G. Dollfus. illus. circ. 500.

914 DK
DENMARK. NATIONALMUSEET. PUBLICATIONS: ARCHAEOLOGICAL HISTORICAL SERIES. (Text in Danish, English, French and German) irreg. price varies. Nationalmuseet, Oplysningsafdelingen, Ny Vestergade 10, DK-1471 Copenhagen K, Denmark (Dist. in the U.S. by: Humanities Press, 171 First Ave., Atlantic City, NJ 07716)

571 913 UK ISSN 0070-3788
DERBYSHIRE ARCHAEOLOGICAL JOURNAL. 1879. a. £4. Derbyshire Archaeological Society, 12 Longbow Close, Stretton, Burton-on-Trent DE13 0XY, England. Ed. D.V. Fowkes. circ. 650. Indexed: Br.Hum.Ind. Br.Archaeol.Abstr. Numis.Lit.

913 GW
DEUTSCHE ORIENT-GESELLSCHAFT. ABHANDLUNG. 1913. irreg., vol.21, 1985. price varies. Gebr. Mann Verlag, Lindenstr. 76, Postfach 110303, 1000 Berlin 61, W. Germany (B.R.D.) (Co-sponsor: Deutsches Archaeologisches Institut) Formerly: Uruk-Warka: Abhandlungen der Deutschen Orient-Gesellschaft (ISSN 0083-4793)

913 UK ISSN 0305-5795
DEVON ARCHAEOLOGICAL SOCIETY. PROCEEDINGS. 1929. a. £6 to individuals; institutions £8; students £3. Devon Archaeological Society, R.A.M. Museum, Queen St., Exeter EX4 3RX, England. circ. 600. Indexed: Br.Hum.Ind. Br.Archaeol.Abstr. Numis.Lit.

913 UK ISSN 0264-7540
DEVON ARCHAEOLOGY. 1983. a. £1. Devon Archaeological Society, Royal Albert Museum, Queen St., Exeter EX4 3RX, England. circ. 1,250.

DIRECTORY OF HISTORIANS OF LATIN AMERICAN ART. see *ART*

913 571 US ISSN 0070-668X
DISCOVERIES IN THE JUDAEAN DESERT OF JORDAN. irreg., vol.7, 1982. price varies. Oxford University Press, 200 Madison Ave., New York, NY 10016 TEL 212-679-7300. (and Ely House, 37 Dover St., London W1X 4AH, England)

914 BE ISSN 0419-4241
DISSERTATIONES ARCHAEOLOGICAE GANDENSES. 1953. irreg., no.23, 1986. price varies. Uitgeverij de Tempel, 41 Tempelhof, Bruges, Belgium.

913 UK
DORSET NATURAL HISTORY & ARCHAEOLOGICAL SOCIETY. MONOGRAPH SERIES. 1980. irreg. Dorset County Museum, Dorchester, Dorset, England. Ed. J.C. Chaplin.

DORSET NATURAL HISTORY AND ARCHAEOLOGICAL SOCIETY. PROCEEDINGS. see *SCIENCES: COMPREHENSIVE WORKS*

914 947 UR
DREVNEISHIE GOSUDARSTVA NA TERRITORII S.S.S.R/ANCIENT STATES IN THE TERRITORY OF THE U.S.S.R; materialy i issledovaniya. (Text in Russian; summaries in English) 1976. irreg., (approx. a.) price varies. (Akademiya Nauk S.S.S.R., Institut Istorii S.S.S.R.) Izdatel'stvo Nauka, Profsoyuznaya 94a, 117485 Moscow, Russian S.F.S.R., U.S.S.R. (Subscr. to: Akademkniga, Michurinskii pr. 12, 117485 Moscow, Russian S.F.S.R., U.S.S.R.) Ed. A.P. Novosel'tsev. bk. rev. circ. 4,250.

913 US
DUMBARTON OAKS CONFERENCE PROCEEDINGS. 1968. irreg., latest 1985. price varies. Dumbarton Oaks, Publications Office, 1703 32nd St., N.W., Washington, DC 20007. TEL 202-342-3259. Ed. Elizabeth P. Boone. bibl. charts. illus. circ. 1,500. (back issues avail.)

709 US ISSN 0070-7546
DUMBARTON OAKS PAPERS. 1940. irreg., no.34, 1980. price varies. (Dumbarton Oaks Center for Byzantine Studies) J. J. Augustin, Inc., Locust Valley, NY 11560. TEL 516-676-1510. Indexed: Amer.Bibl.Slavic & E.Eur.Stud. Art & Archaeol.Tech.Abstr. Numis.Lit. RILA.

ARCHAEOLOGY

940   US   ISSN 0070-7554
DUMBARTON OAKS STUDIES. 1950. irreg. price varies. (Dumbarton Oaks Center for Byzantine Studies) J. J. Augustin, Inc., Locust Valley, NY 11560. TEL 516-676-1510.

942.8   UK
DURHAM ARCHAEOLOGICAL JOURNAL. 1862. biennial. £6 to institutions; individuals £10. ‡ Architectural and Archaeological Society of Durham and Northumberland, c/o Department of Archaeology, 46 Saddler St., Durham DH1 3NU, England. Ed. Anthony Harding. bk. rev. circ. 300. (back issues avail.) Indexed: Br.Hum.Ind. Br.Archaeol.Abstr.
    Former titles: Durham Archaeological Record (ISSN 0265-8038); (until 1984): Architectural and Archaeological Society of Durham and Northumberland. Transactions. New Series (ISSN 0066-6203)

913 940   NE   ISSN 0420-1078
DUTCH ARCHAEOLOGICAL AND HISTORICAL SOCIETY. STUDIES. 1969. irreg., vol.11, 1985. price varies. E. J. Brill, P.O. Box 9000, 2300 PA Leiden, Netherlands.

913   UK   ISSN 0307-2460
EAST ANGLIAN ARCHAEOLOGY. REPORT. 1975. irreg. price varies. Norfolk Archaeological Unit, Union House, Gressenhall, Dereham, Norfolk NR20 4DR, England. Ed. Peter Wade-Martins. Indexed: Br.Archaeol.Abstr.

942.5   UK
EAST MIDLANDS ARCHAEOLOGY. a. £2. East Midland Committee of Field Archaeologists, Trent Valley Archaeological Research Committee, Archaeology Dept., University of Nottingham, University Park, Nottingham, England. Ed. John Samuels. adv. bk. rev. circ. 500. Indexed: Geo.Abstr.
    Formerly: East Midland Archaeological Bulletin (ISSN 0424-1088)

913   UK   ISSN 0012-852X
EAST RIDING ARCHAEOLOGIST. 1968. irreg. £2.50 to institutions. East Riding Archaeological Society, 26 Redland Drive, Kirk Ella, Hull HU10 7UZ, England. Ed.Bd. charts. illus. circ. 400.

EASTERN NEW MEXICO UNIVERSITY. CONTRIBUTIONS IN ANTHROPOLOGY. see *ANTHROPOLOGY*

913   US
EASTERN STATES ARCHAEOLOGICAL FEDERATION. BULLETIN. 1941. a. $12.50. Eastern States Archeological Federation, c/o William Jack Hranicky, Ed., Box 4190m, Arlington, VA 22204. circ. 500. (back issues avail.)

913   FR
ECOLE FRANCAISE DE ROME. COLLECTION. irreg., (4-5/yr.) price varies. Diffusion de Boccard, 11 rue de Medicis, 75006 Paris, France.
    Supersedes: Ecole Francaise de Rome. Melanges: Supplement.

913   FR
ECOLE FRANCAISE DE ROME. MELANGES: ANTIQUITE. (In two vols.) a. Diffusion de Boccard, 11 rue de Medicis, 75006 Paris, France. Indexed: Br.Archaeol.Abstr. Numis.Lit.

962 932   UA   ISSN 0082-7835
EGYPT. SERVICE DES ANTIQUITES. ANNALES. (Text in language of author) 1900. irreg. price varies. ‡ c/o Centre of Egyptian documentation, El Malek el Adel Abou Bakr, Cairo, Egypt. Ed. Alia sherif. bk. rev. cum. index: vols. 1-30; 31-40.

EIRENE. see *HISTORY — History Of Europe*

571   US   ISSN 0070-9573
EL PASO ARCHAEOLOGICAL SOCIETY. SPECIAL REPORTS. 1963. a. price varies. El Paso Archaeological Society, Inc., Box 4345, El Paso, TX 79914. TEL 915-751-3295. Ed. H. Davis. bk. rev. circ. 300. (also avail. in microform)

913   BE
ELKAB. 1971. irreg., no.2, 1979. price varies. Fondation Egyptologique Reine Elisabeth, Comite des Fouilles Belges en Egypte, Parc du Cinquantenaire 10, B-1040 Brussels, Belgium.

913   II   ISSN 0013-9564
EPIGRAPHIA INDICA. (Text in English) 1888. irreg. Rs.64 per vol.(8 nos. per vol) Archaeological Survey of India, Old University Office Bldg., Mysore 570005, India (Order from: Controller of Publications, Government of India, Civil Lines, Delhi 110054, India) Ed. K.G. Krishnan. bk. rev. charts. illus. index every 2 years. circ. 740. Indexed: E.I.

913 410   US   ISSN 0192-5148
EPIGRAPHIC SOCIETY. OCCASIONAL PUBLICATIONS. Short title: E S O P. 1974. a. membership. Epigraphic Society, Inc., 6625 Bamburgh Dr., San Diego, CA 92117. TEL 619-571-1344. Ed. H. Barraclough Fell. adv. bk. rev. cum.index: vols.1-10, 1984. circ. 800. (back issues avail) Indexed: Lang.& Lang.Behav.Abstr.

913   GW
ERDSTALL. 1975. a. DM.15. Arbeitskreis fuer Erdstallforschung, Schorndorferstr. 31, D-8495 Roding, W. Germany (B.R.D.)

913 933   IS   ISSN 0071-108X
ERETZ-ISRAEL. ARCHAEOLOGICAL, HISTORICAL AND GEOGRAPHICAL STUDIES. (Text in English and Hebrew) 1951. biennial, vol.18, 1985. $60. Israel Exploration Society, P.O. Box 7041, Jerusalem, Israel. Eds. Y. Yadin, B. Mazar. circ. 2,000. Indexed: Ind.Heb.Per.

918   CL
ESTUDIO ATACAMENOS. 1973. irreg. exchange basis. Universidad del Norte, Museo de Arqueologia, San Pedro de Atacama, Chile.

913   MR   ISSN 0071-2027
ETUDES ET TRAVAUX D'ARCHEOLOGIE MAROCAINE. 1965. irreg. Institut National des Sciences, de l'Archeologie et du Patrimoine, Ave. John Kenedy, Rabat-Souissi, Morocco.

913.031   FR
ETUDES PREHISTORIQUES; revue du Sud-Est Rhodanien et Mediterraneen. 1971. irreg. 40 F. Societe d'Etudes Prehistoriques, c/o Secretariat: Jean Combier, 71570 Romaneche-Thorins, France. Ed. Jean Combier. bk. rev. bibl. illus. circ. 1,000. Indexed: Br.Archaeol.Abstr.

913   SP   ISSN 0071-3279
EXCAVACIONES ARQUEOLOGICAS EN ESPANA. 1962. irreg. Subdireccion General de Arqueologia, Serrano 13, Madrid 28001, Spain.

914   UK   ISSN 0141-2264
EXCAVATION OF THE ROMAN FORTS OF THE CLASSIS BRITANNICA AT DOVER 1970-1977. 1981. irreg. £9.80. Kent Archaeological Rescue Unit, Dover Castle, Kent C1B HQ, England.

913   US   ISSN 0071-3287
EXCAVATIONS AT DURA-EUROPOS. irreg. price varies. (Yale University) J. J. Augustin, Inc., Locust Valley, NY 11560. TEL 516-676-1510. (Co-sponsor: French Academy of Inscriptions and Letters)

FEDERATION ARCHEOLOGIQUE ET HISTORIQUE DE BELGIQUE. ANNALES/ FEDERATIE VAN NEDERLANDSTALIGE VERENIDENIS VOOR OUDHEIDKUNDE EN GESCHIEDENIS VAN BELGISCHE. JAARBOEKEN. see *HISTORY — History Of Europe*

FELIX RAVENNA; RIVISTA DI ANTICHITA RAVENNATI, CRISTIANE E BIZANTINE. see *ART*

914 573   FI   ISSN 0355-1814
FINSKT MUSEUM. (Text in English, German and Swedish) 1894. a. Suomen Muinaismuistoyhdistys, Nervanderinkatu 13, 00100 Helsinki 10, Finland. cum.index 1894-1943. Indexed: Hist.Abstr. Amer.Hist.& Life. Br.Archaeol.Abstr. Numis.Lit.

943.8 913   PL   ISSN 0071-6863
FONTES ARCHAEOLOGICI POSNANIENSES/ ANNALES MUSEI ARCHAEOLOGICI POSNANIENSIS. (Text in Polish; summaries in English, French and German) 1951. a. price varies. Muzeum Archeologiczne, Ul. Wodna 27, Palac Gorkow, 61-781 Poznan, Poland (Dist. by Ars Polona-Ruch, Krakowskie Przedmiescie 7, Warsaw, Poland) Ed. Lech Krzyzaniak. bk. rev. circ. 600. Indexed: Br.Archaeol.Abstr.
    Formerly: Fontes Praehistorici.

913   CS   ISSN 0015-6183
FONTES ARCHAEOLOGICI PRAGENSES. (Text in English, French, German, Russian) 1958. irreg. price varies. Narodni Muzeum, Historicke Muzeum, Vitezneho Unora 74, 115 79 Prague 1, Czechoslovakia. Ed. Jiri Bren. charts. illus. stat. cum.index. circ. 700. (tabloid format)

914   IT
FORMA ITALIAE. SERIE I. 1977. irreg., no.10, 1984. price varies. Casa Editrice Leo S. Olschki, Casella Postale 66, 50100 Florence, Italy.

914   IT
FORMA ITALIAE. SERIE II. DOCUMENTI. 1972. irreg., no.2, 1981. price varies. Casa Editrice Leo S. Olschki, Casella Postale 66, 50100 Florence, Italy. circ. 1,000. Indexed: Int.Nurs.Ind.

FORSCHUNGEN ZUR KUNSTGESCHICHTE UND CHRISTLICHEN ARCHAEOLOGIE. see *ART*

FORSCHUNGEN ZUR RECHTSARCHAEOLOGIE UND RECHTLICHEN VOLKSKUNDE. see *LAW*

913   FR
FOUILLES DE DELPHES: COLLECTION. irreg. Diffusion de Boccard, 11 rue de Medicis, 75006 Paris, France.

913   FR   ISSN 0071-8394
FRANCE. COMITE DES TRAVAUX HISTORIQUES ET SCIENTIFIQUES. BULLETIN ARCHEOLOGIQUE. (In two fascicules: Antiquites Nationales; Afrique du Nord) 1883. a. price varies. Ministere de l'Education Nationale, Comite des Travaux Historiques et Scientifiques, 3-5 bd. Pasteur, 75015 Paris, France. cum.index: 1883-1940. circ. 750. Indexed: GeoRef.

913   FR   ISSN 0071-8416
FRANCE. COMITE DES TRAVAUX HISTORIQUES ET SCIENTIFIQUES. SECTION D'ARCHEOLOGIE. ACTES DU CONGRES NATIONAL DES SOCIETES SAVANTES. 1957 (congress of 1954) a. price varies. Ministere de l'Education Nationale, Comite des Travaux Historiques et Scientifiques, 3-5 bd. Pasteur, 75015 Paris, France. index. circ. 650.

709   GW   ISSN 0071-9757
FUEHRER ZU ARCHAEOLOGISCHEN DENKMAELERN IN DEUTSCHLAND. 1983. irreg., vol.15 1987. DM.14.80. (Nordwestdeutscher und West- und Sueddeutscher Verband fuer Altertumsforschung) Konrad Theiss Verlag Gmbh, Villastr. 11, 7000 Stuttgart, W. Germany (B.R.D.) index.

913   GW
FUNDBERICHTE AUS BADEN-WUERTTEMBERG. 1974. a. price varies. (Landesdenkmalamt Baden-Wuerttemberg) E. Schweizerbart'sche Verlagsbuchhandlung, Johannesstr. 3A, 7000 Stuttgart 1, W. Germany (B.R.D.) Ed. Helga Schach-Doerges. bk. rev. Indexed: Br.Archaeol.Abstr. Numis.Lit.
    Formerly (1922-1971): Fundberichte aus Schwaben, Neue Folge (ISSN 0071-9897)

913   GW   ISSN 0071-9889
FUNDBERICHTE AUS HESSEN. 1961. irreg., no.21, 1981. price varies. Dr. Rudolf Habelt GmbH, Am Buchenhang 1, 5300 Bonn 1, W. Germany (B.R.D.) Indexed: Br.Archaeol.Abstr.

914 709   GW   ISSN 0723-8630
FUNDE UND AUSGRABUNGEN IM BEZIRK TRIER. 1969. a. DM.10. Rheinisches Landesmuseum Trier, Ostallee 44, D-5500 Trier, W. Germany (B.R.D.) Ed.Bd. circ. 2,000. (back issues avail.)

914.8   DK   ISSN 0109-1441
FYNBOER OG ARKAEOLOGI. 1979. irreg. (2-4/yr.) free. Fyns Stiftsmuseum, Hollufgaard, Hestehaven 201, 5220 Odense SOE, Denmark. Ed. Eigil Nikolajsen. bk. rev. illus. circ. 800.

FYNSKE MINDER. see *HISTORY — History Of Europe*

913   FR   ISSN 0072-0119
GALLIA. SUPPLEMENT. 1943. irreg., no.27, 1974. price varies. Editions du C N R S, 295 rue St. Jacques, 75005 Paris, France.

ARCHAEOLOGY

913   FR   ISSN 0072-0100
GALLIA PREHISTOIRE. SUPPLEMENT. 1958. irreg., no.7, 1973. price varies. Editions du C N R S, 295 rue St. Jacques, 75005 Paris, France. Indexed: GeoRef.

GAYA. see *HISTORY — History Of Europe*

GDANSKIE TOWARZYSTWO NAUKOWE. WYDZIAL 1. NAUK SPOLECZNYCH I HUMANISTYCZNYCH. KOMISJA ARCHEOLOGICZNA. PRACE. see *HISTORY — History Of Europe*

913 709   SZ   ISSN 0072-0585
GENAVA; revue d'archeologie et d'histoire de l'art. 1923. a. 55 Fr. Musee d'Art et d'Histoire, Geneva, Rue Charles Galland, 1211 Geneva 3, Switzerland. Ed.Bd. Indexed: Numis.Lit. RILA.

913   GW   ISSN 0016-8874
GERMANIA. 1917. a. DM.60. (Deutsches Archaeologisches Institut, Roemisch-Germanische Kommission) Verlag Phillip von Zabern, Welschnonnengasse 11-13, D-6500 Mainz, W. Germany (B.R.D.) Ed.Bd. bk. rev. abstr. bibl. charts. illus. index. cum.ind. 1917-1958. Indexed: SSCI. Br.Archaeol.Abstr. Numis.Lit.

913   GW   ISSN 0418-9779
GERMANISCHE DENKMAELER DER VOELKERWANDERUNGSZEIT. irreg., vol.12, 1986. price varies. Franz Steiner Verlag Wiesbaden GmbH, Birkenwaldstr. 44, Postfach 347, 7000 Stuttgart 1, W. Germany (B.R.D.) Ed. Kurt Bohner.

913   SZ   ISSN 0072-4270
GESELLSCHAFT PRO VINDONISSA. JAHRESBERICHT. 1907. a. price varies. Gesellschaft pro Vindonissa, Vindonissa Museum, 5200 Brugg, Switzerland. Indexed: Br.Archaeol.Abstr.

708   SZ   ISSN 0072-4289
GESELLSCHAFT PRO VINDONISSA. VEROEFFENTLICHUNGEN. 1942. irreg. price varies. Gesellschaft pro Vindonissa, Vindonissa Museum, 5200 Brugg, Switzerland.

913   UK   ISSN 0305-8980
GLASGOW ARCHAEOLOGICAL JOURNAL. 1969. a. £3. Glasgow Archaeological Society, c/o Department of Archaeology, University of Glasgow, Glasgow G12 8QQ, Scotland. Ed. Dr. Alex Morrison. bk. rev. circ. 350. (back issues avail.) Indexed: Br.Archaeol.Abstr. Numis.Lit.

916   SA   ISSN 0304-3460
GOODWIN SERIES. OCCASIONAL PAPERS. (Text in English and Afrikaans) 1972. irreg., no.5, 1986. R.30 (free to subscribers to South African Archaeological Society) South African Archaeological Society, P.O. Box 15700, 8018 Vlaeberg, South Africa. Ed. Janette Deacon. circ. 1, 100.

GORTANIA; atti del Museo Friulano di Storia Naturale. see *EARTH SCIENCES*

571 942   UK   ISSN 0072-6842
GREAT BRITAIN. DEPARTMENT OF THE ENVIRONMENT. ARCHAEOLOGICAL REPORTS. 1956. irreg. price varies. H.M.S.O., Box 569, London SE1 9NH, England. Indexed: Br.Archaeol.Abstr.

GREAT BRITAIN. ROYAL COMMISSION ON ANCIENT AND HISTORICAL MONUMENTS IN WALES. INTERIM REPORT. see *HISTORY — History Of Europe*

GREAT BRITAIN. ROYAL COMMISSION ON THE HISTORICAL MONUMENTS OF ENGLAND. INTERIM REPORT. see *HISTORY — History Of Europe*

913   UK
GREATER MANCHESTER ARCHAELOGICAL JOURNAL. a. Greater Manchester Archaeological Unit, University of Manchester, Oxford Rd., Manchester M13 9PL, England.

913   PO
GRUPO DE INVESTIGACAO ARQUEOLOGICA DO NORTE. TRABALHOS. 1982. irreg. Grupo de Investigacao Arqueologica do Norte, Rua de Santiago 237-4450, S. da Hora (Matosinhos), Porto, Portugal. circ. 1,000.

914   IT
GUIDE AI MUSEI E AGLI SCAVI ARCHEOLOGICI DELLA CALABRIA. 1975. irreg. L.2000. Edizioni Parallelo 38, Via 3 Settembre 7, 89100 Reggio Calabria, Italy.

913 580 590   NO   ISSN 0332-8554
GUNNERIA. (Text and summaries in English, German and Norwegian) 1971. irreg., no. 38, 1981. Universitetet i Trondheim, Vitenskapmuseet - University of Trondheim, Museum, Erling Skakkes Gt. 47 B, 7000 Trondheim, Norway. Ed.Bd. circ. controlled. Indexed: Biol.Abstr. Chem.Abstr. Formerly (until no. 26, 1977): Kongelige Norske Videnskabers Selskab. Museet. Miscellanea.

GWECHALL. see *HISTORY — History Of Europe*

913   GW   ISSN 0072-9183
HABELTS DISSERTATIONSDRUCKE. REIHE KLASSISCHE ARCHAEOLOGIE. 1969. irreg., no. 23, 1985. price varies. Dr. Rudolf Habelt GmbH, Am Buchenhang 1, 5300 Bonn 1, W. Germany (B.R.D.)

913   GW   ISSN 0341-3152
HAMBURGER BEITRAEGE ZUR ARCHAEOLOGIE. 1971. irreg., vol.11, 1986. price varies. Verlag Helmut Buske, Schlueterstr. 14, 2000 Hamburg 13, W. Germany (B.R.D.) Ed.Bd. Indexed: Br.Archaeol.Abstr.

940   UK   ISSN 0142-8950
HAMPSHIRE FIELD CLUB AND ARCHAEOLOGICAL SOCIETY PROCEEDINGS. 1885. a. £8. Hampshire Field Club, c/o M. Hicks, King Alfred's College, Winchester, England. Ed. K. Qualmann. bk. rev. charts. illus. circ. 900. (back issues avail.) Indexed: Br.Geol.Lit. Br.Archaeol.Abstr. Geo.Abstr. Numis.Lit. RILA. Formerly: Hampshire Field. Proceedings.

914   DK   ISSN 0105-1660
HARJA. 1976. irreg. (approx. a.) Kr.25. Harja-Arkaeologisk Forening, c/o A. Jaeger, Adelgade 139, 5400 Bogense, Denmark. illus.

HIKUIN. see *HISTORY — History Of Europe*

913 940   YU
HISTORIA ARCHAEOLOGICA. (Text in Serbo-Croatian; summaries in English) 1976. a. Arheoloski Muzej Istre u Puli, M. Balote 3, Pula, Yugoslavia. Ed. Branko Marusic. bibl. charts. illus.

HISTORISCHER VEREIN FUER DAS FUERSTENTUM LIECHTENSTEIN. JAHRBUCH. see *HISTORY — History Of Europe*

913   US   ISSN 0160-1040
I A. (Industrial Archeology) 1976. a. $6. Society for Industrial Archeology, Room 5020, National Museum of American History, Smithsonian Institution, Washington, DC 20560. TEL 202-357-2058. Ed. David R. Starbuck. adv. bk. rev. illus. circ. 1,200. (back issues avail.) Indexed: Avery Ind.Archit.Per.

913   UK   ISSN 0261-068X
I A M S NEWSLETTER. (Institute of Archaeo-Metallurgical Studies) 1980. irreg. University of London, Institute of Archaeology, London WC1H 0PY, England. illus. Indexed: CERDIC.

570   US   ISSN 0360-0270
ILLINOIS. STATE MUSEUM. REPORTS OF INVESTIGATIONS. 1948. irreg., no.41, 1986. price varies. Illinois State Museum, Springfield, IL 62706. TEL 217-782-7386. bibl. charts. illus. Indexed: Biol.Abstr. Key Title: Reports of Investigations - Illinois State Museum.

ILLINOIS. STATE MUSEUM. SCIENTIFIC PAPERS SERIES. see *SCIENCES: COMPREHENSIVE WORKS*

INDIANA; contributions to ethnology and linguistics, archaeology and physical anthropology of Indian America. see *ANTHROPOLOGY*

913   GW
INFORMATIONSBLAETTER ZU NACHBARWISSENSCHAFTEN DER UR- UND FRUEHGESCHICHTE. 1970. a. price varies. Dr. Rudolf Habelt GmbH, Am Buchenhang 1, 5300 Bonn 1, W. Germany (B.R.D.)

913   PL   ISSN 0085-1876
INFORMATOR ARCHEOLOGICZNY. 1968. a. free. Osrodek Dokumentacji Zabytkow, Ul. Brzozowa 35, 00-258 Warsaw, Poland. (Co-sponsor: Polskie Towarzystwo Archeologiczne i Numizmatyczne) Ed. Marek Konopka.

913   GW
INSCHRIFTEN GRIECHISCHER STAEDTE AUS KLEINASIEN. 1972. irreg., no.31, 1986. price varies. (Oesterreichische Akademie der Wissenschaften, Kommission fuer die Archaeologische Erforschung, AU) Dr. Rudolf Habelt GmbH, Am Buchenhang 1, 5300 Bonn 1, W. Germany (B.R.D.)

913   BE
INSTITUT ARCHEOLOGIQUE DU LUXEMBOURG. ANNALES. 1847. a. 650 Fr. (combined price with Bulletin) Institut Archeologique du Luxembourg, Bibliotheque, 13 rue des Martyrs, 6700 Arlon, Belgium.

913   BE
INSTITUT ARCHEOLOGIQUE LIEGEOIS. BULLETIN. 1850. a. 850 Fr. Ministere de l'Education Nationale et de la Culture Francaise, Insitut Archeologique Liegeois, Quai de Maastricht 13, 4000 Liege, Belgium. Indexed: Numis.Lit.

913   UA   ISSN 0255-0962
INSTITUT FRANCAIS D'ARCHEOLOGIE ORIENTALE DU CAIRE. BULLETIN. (Text in English, French and German) 1901. a. £E25($35) Institut Francais d'Archeologie Orientale du Caire, 37 Sharia Sheikh Aly Youssef, Mounira, Cairo, Egypt. circ. 800. (back issues avail.)

INSTITUT HISTORIQUE ET ARCHEOLOGIQUE NEERLANDAIS DE ISTAMBOUL. PUBLICATIONS. see *HISTORY — History Of Asia*

913 949.8   RM   ISSN 0074-039X
INSTITUTUL DE ISTORIE SI ARHEOLOGIE "A.D. XENOPOL" - IASI. ANUARUL. 1963. a. $38. Editura Academiei Republicii Socialiste Rumania, Calea Victoriei 125, 79717 Bucharest, Rumania (Subscr. to: ARTEXIM, Str. Piata Scinteii 1, P.O. Box 33-16, 70055 Bucharest, Rumania) Ed. M. Petrescu-Dimbovita. Indexed: Hist.Abstr. Amer.Hist.& Life.

914 949.8   RM   ISSN 0065-048X
INSTITUTUL DE ISTORIE SI ARHEOLOGIE - CLUJ-NAPOCA. ANUARUL. vol.23, 1980. a. $38. Editura Academiei Republicii Socialiste Rumania, Calea Victoriei 125, 79717 Bucharest, Rumania (Subscr. to: ARTEXIM, Str. Piata Scinteii 1, P.O. Box 33-16, 70055 Bucharest, Rumania) Ed. Stefan Pascu.

913 400   AU
INSTITUTUM CANARIUM YEARBOOK. ALMOGAREN. (Text in English, French, German, Spanish; summaries in English, German, Spanish) 1970. a. S.350($25) ‡ Burgfried Verlag, P.O. Box 48, A 5400 Hallein, Austria. Ed. Herbert F. Nowak. bk. rev. circ. 500. Indexed: Curr.Cont.Africa. Formerly: Almogaren.

571 930   IT   ISSN 0074-1469
INTERNATIONAL ASSOCIATION FOR CLASSICAL ARCHAEOLOGY. PROCEEDINGS OF CONGRESS. (Proceedings published by host country) irreg., 1978, 11th, London. International Association for Classical Archaeology, 49 Piazza San Marco, 00186 Rome, Italy.

571   UK   ISSN 0074-3429
INTERNATIONAL CONGRESS FOR PAPYROLOGY. PROCEEDINGS. triennial, 15th Congress 1977, Brussels. DM.120. International Association of Papyrologists, c/o Dr. R.A. Coles, Papyrology Rooms, Ashmolean Museum, Oxford, England.
Proceedings published by organizing committee

913   GE
INVENTARIA ARCHAEOLOGICA. 1982. irreg. M.20. (Union Internationale des Sciences pre- et Protohistoriques) VEB Deutscher Verlag der Wissenschaften, Postfach 1216, 1080 Berlin, E. Germany (D.D.R.) Ed. Joachim Herrmann.

913　　　　　　　GW ISSN 0075-0034
INVENTARIA ARCHAEOLOGICA BELGIQUE. (Text in French) 1956. irreg. price varies. (International Congress of Prehistoric and Protohistoric Sciences) Dr. Rudolf Habelt GmbH, Am Buchenhang 1, 5300 Bonn 1, W. Germany (B.R.D.)

913 943.7　　　　GW ISSN 0075-0042
INVENTARIA ARCHAEOLOGICA CESKOSLOVENSKO. (Text in French) 1961. irreg., no.4, 1967. DM.20. (International Congress of Prehistoric and Protohistoric Sciences) Dr. Rudolf Habelt GmbH, Am Buchenhang 1, 5300 Bonn 1, W. Germany (B.R.D.)

913　　　　　　　GW ISSN 0075-0050
INVENTARIA ARCHAEOLOGICA DENMARK. (Text in English) 1965. irreg., no.11, 1983. DM.20. (International Congress of Prehistoric and Protohistoric Sciences) Dr. Rudolf Habelt GmbH, Am Buchenhang 1, 5300 Bonn 1, W. Germany (B.R.D.)

913　　　　　　　GW ISSN 0075-0069
INVENTARIA ARCHAEOLOGICA DEUTSCHLAND. 1954. irreg., no.18, 1979. DM.20. (International Congress of Prehistoric and Protohistoric Sciences) Dr. Rudolf Habelt GmbH, Am Buchenhang 1, 5300 Bonn 1, W. Germany (B.R.D.)

913　　　　　　　GW ISSN 0075-0077
INVENTARIA ARCHAEOLOGICA ESPANA. (Text in Spanish) 1958. irreg., no.7, 1967. price varies. (International Congress of Prehistoric and Protohistoric Sciences) Dr. Rudolf Habelt GmbH, Am Buchenhang 1, 5300 Bonn 1, W. Germany (B.R.D.)

913　　　　　　　GW ISSN 0075-0085
INVENTARIA ARCHAEOLOGICA FRANCE. (Text in French) 1956. irreg., no.4, 1976. price varies. (International Congress of Prehistoric and Protohistoric Sciences) Dr. Rudolf Habelt GmbH, Am Buchenhang 1, 5300 Bonn 1, W. Germany (B.R.D.)

913　　　　　　　GW ISSN 0075-0093
INVENTARIA ARCHAEOLOGICA GREAT BRITAIN. (Text in English) 1955. irreg. DM.20. (International Congress of Prehistoric and Protohistoric Sciences) Rudolf Habelt Gmbh, Am Buchenhang 1, 5300 Bonn 1, W. Germany (B.R.D.)

913　　　　　　　GW ISSN 0075-0107
INVENTARIA ARCHAEOLOGICA ITALIA. (Text in Italian) 1961. irreg., 1967, no.4. price varies. (International Congress of Prehistoric and Protohistoric Sciences) Dr. Rudolf Habelt GmbH, Am Buchenhang 1, 5300 Bonn 1, W. Germany (B.R.D.)

913　　　　　　　GW ISSN 0075-0115
INVENTARIA ARCHAEOLOGICA JUGOSLAVIJA. (Text in French) 1957. irreg., no.28, 1983. DM.20. (International Congress of Prehistoric and Protohistoric Sciences) Dr. Rudolf Habelt GmbH, Am Buchenhang 1, 5300 Bonn 1, W. Germany (B.R.D.)

913　　　　　　　GW ISSN 0075-0123
INVENTARIA ARCHAEOLOGICA NORWAY. (Text in English) 1966. irreg. DM.20. (International Congress of Prehistoric and Protohistoric Sciences) Dr. Rudolf Habelt GmbH, Am Buchenhang 1, 5300 Bonn 1, W. Germany (B.R.D.)

913　　　　　　　GW ISSN 0075-0131
INVENTARIA ARCHAEOLOGICA OESTERREICH. 1956. irreg. DM.20. (International Congress of Prehistoric and Protohistoric Sciences) Dr. Rudolf Habelt GmbH, Am Buchenhang 1, 5300 Bonn 1, W. Germany (B.R.D.)

913　　　　　　　GW ISSN 0075-014X
INVENTARIA ARCHAEOLOGICA POLOGNE. (Text in French) 1958. irreg., no.54, 1985. DM.20. (International Congress of Prehistoric and Protohistoric Sciences) Dr. Rudolf Habelt GmbH, Am Buchenhang 1, 5300 Bonn 1, W. Germany (B.R.D.)

913　　　　　　　GW
INVENTARIA ARCHAEOLOGICA THE NETHERLANDS. 1971. irreg. DM.20. Dr. Rudolf Habelt GmbH, Am Buchenhang 1, 5300 Bonn 1, W. Germany (B.R.D.)

913　　　　　　　GW ISSN 0075-0158
INVENTARIA ARCHAEOLOGICA UNGARN. 1962. irreg., no.3, 1971. price varies. (International Congress of Prehistoric and Protohistoric Sciences) Dr. Rudolf Habelt GmbH, Am Buchenhang 1, 5300 Bonn 1, W. Germany (B.R.D.)

917　　　　　　　US ISSN 0535-5729
IOWA ARCHEOLOGICAL SOCIETY. JOURNAL. 1951. a. membership. Iowa Archeological Society, c/o Office of the State Archaeologist, University of Iowa, Iowa, IA 52242. TEL 319-335-2389. Ed. Stephen C. Lensink. bk. rev. circ. 450.

571　　　　　　　US ISSN 0085-2252
IOWA STATE ARCHAEOLOGIST. REPORT. 1970. irreg., no.16, 1983. price varies. Office of State Archeologist, Eastlawn Bldg., University of Iowa, Iowa City, IA 52242. TEL 319-353-2121. Ed. Duane Anderson. bibl. charts. illus. circ. 750. (reprints avail. from UMI)

913 390　　　　NE ISSN 0021-0870
IRANICA ANTIQUA; dealing with archaeology, history, religion, art and literature of ancient Persia. (Text in English, French or German) 1961. irreg., vol.20, 1986. price varies. E. J. Brill, P.O. Box 9000, 2300 PA Leiden, Netherlands. Eds. R. Ghirsman, L. Vanden Berghe. Indexed: Numis.Lit.

913　　　　　　　UK ISSN 0021-0889
IRAQ. 1934. a. $25. British School of Archaeology in Iraq, Gertrude Bell Memorial, 31-34 Gordon Square, London WC1H 0PY, England. Eds. J.D. Hawkins, D. Collon. charts. illus. index. cum.index: vols. 1-30. circ. 650. Indexed: Br.Hum.Ind. Old Test.Abstr. Rel.Ind.One.

913　　　　　　　FI ISSN 0355-3108
ISKOS. (Text in English, Finnish and Swedish) 1976. irreg. Suomen Muinaismuistoyhdistys, Nervanderinkatu 13, 00100 Helsinki 10, Finland.

ISLENZKA FORNLEIFAFELAGS. ARBOK. see HISTORY — History Of Europe

571　　　　　　　IS ISSN 0066-488X
ISRAEL. MINISTRY OF EDUCATION AND CULTURE. DEPARTMENT OF ANTIQUITIES AND MUSEUMS. ATIQOT (ENGLISH SERIES) Title varies: Archaeological Excavation Reports. (Text in English) 1955. irreg., vol.14, 1980. price varies. Ministry of Education and Culture, Department of Antiquities and Museums, P.O.B. 586, Jerusalem, Israel. Ed. Ayala Sussmann. circ. 1, 500.

913　　　　　　　IS ISSN 0067-0138
ISRAEL. MINISTRY OF EDUCATION AND CULTURE. DEPARTMENT OF ANTIQUITIES AND MUSEUMS. ATIQOT (HEBREW SERIES) (Text in Hebrew; summaries in English) 1955. irreg., vol. 7, 1974. price varies. Ministry of Education and Culture, Department of Antiquities and Museums, P.O.B. 586, Jerusalem, Israel. Ed. Ayala Sussmann. circ. 1,500.

913 950　　　　GW ISSN 0341-9142
ISTANBULER MITTEILUNGEN. a. Verlag Ernst Wasmuth, Fuerstr. 133, 7400 Tuebingen, W. Germany (B.R.D.) circ. 500.

571　　　　　　　IT ISSN 0530-9867
ISTITUTO INTERNAZIONALE DI STUDI LIGURI. COLLEZIONE DI MONOGRAFIE PREISTORICHE ED ARCHEOLOGICHE. (Text in Italian, French and Spanish) 1946. irreg. price varies. Istituto Internazionale di Studi Liguri, Via Romana, 39 bis, 18012 - Bordighera, Italy. circ. 1, 000.

930.1 709　　　IT
ISTITUTO NAZIONALE DI ARCHEOLOGIA E STORIA DELL'ARTE. RIVISTA. 1929. a. L.100000. Istituto Nazionale di Archeologia e Storia dell'Arte, Piazza S. Marco 49, Rome, Italy. Eds. Licia Magnante Torti, Paolo Pellegrino. circ. 800. (back issues avail.) Indexed: RILA.

913　　　　　　　IT
ISTITUTO UNIVERSITARIO DI BERGAMO. STUDI ARCHEOLOGICI. 1981. a. L.300000. Istituto Universitario di Bergamo, Via Salvecchio 19, 24100 Bergamo, Italy. TEL 035-217195. Ed. Marco Tizzoni. circ. 275.

930.1　　　　　　IT
ISTITUTO UNIVERSITARIO ORIENTALE DI NAPOLI. SEMINARIO DI STUDI DEL MONDO CLASSICO. SEZIONE ARCHEOLOGIA E STORIA ANTICA. ANNALI. (Text in English, French and Italian) 1979. a. L.60,000. Herder Editrice e Libreria s.r.l., Piazza Montecitorio 120, 00186 Rome, Italy. Ed. Bruno D'Agostino. bk. rev. index. (back issues avail.)

913 947　　　　BU ISSN 0204-403X
IZVESTIYA NA MUZEITE OT IUGOIZTOCHNA BULGARIYA. 1976. a. Darzharno Izdatelstov Kristo G. Danov, Ul. Petko Karavelov 17, 4000 Plodiv, Bulgaria (Subscr. to: Hemus Foreign Trade Co., 6 Ruski Blvd., 1000 Sofia, Bulgaria)

913 947　　　　BU ISSN 0204-4072
IZVESTIYA NA MUZEITE OT IUZHNA BULGARIYA. 1975. a. Darzharno Izdatelstov Kristo G. Danov, Ul. Petko Karavelov 17, 4000 Plodiv, Bulgaria (Subscr. to: Hemus Foreign Trade Co., 6 Ruski Blvd., 1000 Sofia, Bulgaria)

IZVESTIYA NA MUZEITE V SEVEROZAPADNA BULGARIYA. see HISTORY — History Of Europe

JESCHEIDENIS VAN WORTEL. (Hoogstratens Oudheidkundige Kring) see HISTORY — History Of Europe

913　　　　　　　II
JOURNAL OF ARCHAEOLOGY IN ANDHRA PRADESH. (Text in English) 1979. irreg. price varies. Department of Archaeology and Museums, Hyderabad 500001, Andhra Pradesh, India. Ed. V.V. Krishna Sastry. bk. rev. circ. 500.

914　　　　　　　DK ISSN 0108-464X
JOURNAL OF DANISH ARCHAEOLOGY. 1982. a. Kr.140. Odense University Press, 136 Pjentedamsgade, DK-5000 Odense, Denmark. illus. Indexed: Br.Archaeol.Abstr.

913　　　　　　　UK ISSN 0307-5133
JOURNAL OF EGYPTIAN ARCHAEOLOGY. (Text in English; occasionally in French and German) 1914. a. £30 to non-members; members £15. Egypt Exploration Society, 3 Doughty News, London WC1N 2PG, England. Ed. M.A. Leahy. bk. rev. cum.index every 5 years. circ. 3,500. (back issues avail.) Indexed: Br.Hum.Ind. Old Test.Abstr.

JOURNAL OF JURISTIC PAPYROLOGY. see LAW

913　　　　　　　US ISSN 0883-9697
JOURNAL OF MIDDLE ATLANTIC ARCHAEOLOGY. 1985. a. $12.50. Archaeological Services, 68 Sunny Ridge Rd., Box 386, Bethlehem, CT 06751. TEL 203-266-7741. Ed. Roger W. Moeller. illus. circ. 200. Indexed: Abstr.Anthropol.

913　　　　　　　US ISSN 0147-9024
JOURNAL OF NEW WORLD ARCHAEOLOGY. 1975. irreg., vol.7, 984. $20 per vol. University of California, Los Angeles, Institute of Archaeology, 405 Hilgard Ave., Los Angeles, CA 90024. TEL 213-825-7411. Ed. Brian D. Dillon. bibl. charts. illus. index. circ. 200. (back issues avail.)

913　　　　　　　IS ISSN 0075-4501
JUDEAN DESERT STUDIES. (Text in English) 1963. irreg. price varies. Israel Exploration Society, P.O. Box 7041, Jerusalem, Israel.

JYSK ARKAEOLOGISK SELSKABS. SKRIFTER/ JUTLAND ARCHAEOLOGICAL SOCIETY. PUBLICATIONS. see HISTORY — History Of Europe

917　　　　　　　US
K A C RESEARCH SERIES. irreg. (Center for American Archeology, Kampsville Archaeological Center) Center for American Archeology Press, Kampsville, IL 62053. TEL 618-653-4316.
　Formerly: C A A Research Series; Superseded (1982-1984): Northwestern University. Center for American Archeology. Research Series.

917　　　　　　　US
KAMPSVILLE SEMINARS IN ARCHEOLOGY.* 1982. irreg. (Northwestern University, Center for American Archeology) Center for American Archeology, Box 22, Kampsville, IL 62053-0022. Ed. David L. Asch.

913 FR ISSN 0453-3429
KARTHAGO. no.16, 1971/72. biennial. 250 F. for vol.20. (Universite de Paris I (Pantheon-Sorbonne), Centre d'Etudes Archeologiques de la Mediterranee Occidentale) Editions Klincksieck, 11 rue de Lille, 75005 Paris, France. Ed. M.G. Picard. bibl. illus. circ. 750.

913 FR ISSN 0075-5184
KARTHAGO. COLLECTION EPIGRAPHIQUE. 1968. irreg. price varies. (Universite de Paris I (Paris-Sorbonne), Centre d'Etudes Archeologiques de la Mediterranee Occidentale) C.E.A.M.O., 3 rue Michelet, 75006 Paris, France. Ed. Peeters France. adv. bk. rev. circ. 750.

956 IS
KEDEM; excavations at the City of David - Yigal Shiloh. (Text in English) 1975. irreg. price varies. Hebrew University of Jerusalem, Institute of Archaeology, Jerusalem, Israel (Subscr. to: Israel Exploration Society, P.O. Box 7041, Jerusalem, Israel) Ed.Bd. circ. 1,550.

913 GW
KEILSCHRIFTTEXTE AUS BOGHAZKOI. 1939. irreg., vol.30, 1984. price varies. (Academie der Wissenschaften und der Literatur Mainz) Gebr. Mann Verlag, Lindenstr. 76, Postfach 110303, 1000 Berlin 61, W. Germany (B.R.D.) Ed. Heinrich Otten.

KEILSCHRIFTURKUNDEN AUS BOGHAZKOEI. see HISTORY — History Of Asia

913 US
KENT STATE RESEARCH PAPERS IN ARCHAEOLOGY. 1981. irreg. Kent State University Press, Kent, OH 44242. TEL 216-672-7913. Ed. Mark F. Seeman.

941.5 IE ISSN 0085-2503
KERRY ARCHAEOLOGICAL AND HISTORICAL SOCIETY. JOURNAL. 1968. a. £4 free to members. Kerry Archaeological and Historical Society, County Library, Tralee, Co Kerry, Ireland. Ed. Rev. Kieran O'Shea. circ. 450. Indexed: Br.Archaeol.Abstr.

913 GW ISSN 0075-6512
KOELNER JAHRBUCH FUER VOR- UND FRUEHGESCHICHTE. 1955. irreg., vol.17, 1980. price varies. (Roemisch-Germanisches Museum) Gebr. Mann Verlag, Lindenstr. 76, Postfach 110303, 1000 Berlin 61, W. Germany (B.R.D.) (Co-sponsor: Archaeologische Gesellschaft, Cologne) Indexed: Numis.Lit.

913 930 IT ISSN 0392-0887
KOKALOS. (Text in various languages) 1964. irreg., vol.25, 1979. price varies. (Universita degli Studi di Palermo, Istituto di Storia Antica) Giorgio Bretschneider, Via Crescenzo 43, 00193 Rome, Italy. Indexed: Numis.Lit.

KONINKLIJKE KRING VOOR OUDHEIDKUNDE LETTEREN EN KUNST VAN MECHELEN. HANDELINGEN. see HISTORY — History Of Europe

913 BE
KONINKLIJKE OUDHEIDKUNDIGE KRING VAN ANTWERPEN. JAARBOEK. (Text in Dutch) 1910. a. Koninklijke Oudheidkundige Kring van Antwerpen, Leopoldstr. 57, 2000 Antwerp, Belgium.
Formerly: Antwerpens Oudheidkundige Kring. Jaarboek.

914 GW ISSN 0342-0736
KUNDE; Zeitschrift fuer Ur- und Fruehgeschichte. 1933. a. DM.48. Niedersaechsischer Landesverein fuer Urgeschichte, Am Maschpark 5, D-3000 Hannover 1, W. Germany (B.R.D.) Ed. Heinz Schirnig. bk. rev. circ. 800. (back issues avail.)

KUNGLIGA VITTERHETS-, HISTORIE- OCH ANTIKVITETS AKADEMIEN. ANTIKVARISKT ARKIV. see ART

913 GW ISSN 0075-725X
KUNST UND ALTERTUM AM RHEIN. 1956. irreg., vol.106, 1981. price varies. Rheinland- Verlag, Kennedy-Ufer 2, 5000 Cologne 21, W. Germany (B.R.D.) (Distr. by: Rudolf Habelt Verlag GmbH, Am Buchenhang 1, 5300 Bonn, W. Germany (B.R.D.))

914 069 DK ISSN 0900-8047
LAEGAEST: ARKEOLOGI I NORDLESVIG. a. Kr.25. (Haderslevmuseum) Bibliotekscentralen, Telegrafvej 5, DK-2750 Ballerup, Denmark.

913 PO
LEBA; estudos de quaternario, pre-historia e arqueologia. 1978. a. $170. Instituto de Investigacao Cientifica Tropical, Centro de Pre-historia e Arqueologia, Travessa Conde de Ribeira, 9, 1300 Lisbon, Portugal. Ed. Miguel Ramos. bk. rev. circ. 2,000.
Formerly: Leba Revista.

913 940 UK ISSN 0140-3990
LEICESTERSHIRE ARCHAEOLOGICAL AND HISTORICAL SOCIETY. TRANSACTIONS. 1866. a. £6. Leicestershire Archaeological and Historical Society, The Guildhall, Guildhall Lane, Leicester LE1 5FQ, England. Ed. Dr. D.T. Williams. adv. bk. rev. circ. 600. Indexed: Br.Hum.Ind. Br.Archaeol.Abstr. Geo.Abstr.

913 UK ISSN 0075-8914
LEVANT; Journal of the British School of Archaeology in Jerusalem and the British Institute at Amman for Archaeology and History. 1969. a. $25. British School of Archaeology in Jerusalem, c/o British Academy, 20-21 Cornwall Terrace, London NW1 4QP, England. (Co-sponsor: British Institute at Amman) Ed. P. Bienkowski. circ. 700. (back issues avail.) Indexed: Old Test.Abstr. Abstr.Anthropol. New Test.Abstr. Rel.Ind.One. Rel.& Theol.Abstr.

913 UK ISSN 0459-4487
LINCOLNSHIRE HISTORY AND ARCHAEOLOGY. 1966. a. Society for Lincolnshire History & Archaeology, Exchequergate Arch, Lincoln LN2 1PZ, England. Ed.Bd. bk. rev. circ. 865. Indexed: Br.Hum.Ind. Br.Archaeol.Abstr. Numis.Lit.

571 913 UK
LONDON AND MIDDLESEX ARCHAEOLOGICAL SOCIETY. SPECIAL PAPERS. 1976. irreg. membership. London and Middlesex Archaeological Society, c/o A. Wilmott, Ed., 34 Almshouse Lane, Newmillerdam, Wakefield, Yorks. WF2 7ST, England. circ. 900. Indexed: Br.Archaeol.Abstr.

571 913 UK ISSN 0076-0501
LONDON AND MIDDLESEX ARCHAEOLOGICAL SOCIETY. TRANSACTIONS. 1855. a. membership. London and Middlesex Archaeological Society, c/o A. Wilmott, Ed., 34 Almshouse Lane, Newmillerdam, Wakefield, Yorks. WF2 7ST, England. circ. 900. Indexed: Br.Hum.Ind. Br.Archaeol.Abstr. Numis.Lit.

913 UK
LONDON AND MIDDLESEX ARCHAEOLOGICAL SOCIETY & SURREY ARCHAEOLOGICAL SOCIETY. JOINT PUBLICATION. 1978. irreg. membership. Surrey Archaeological Society, Castle Arch, Guildford, Surrey GU1 3SZ, England. (Co-sponsor: London and Middlesex Archaeological Society) Ed. Joanna Bird. (back issues avail.)

913 SW ISSN 0458-4767
LUND UNIVERSITET. HISTORISKA MUSEUM. MEDDELANDEN. 1930. biennial. (Historiska Museet) Liber Forlag, S-205 10, Malmo, Sweden. Indexed: Br.Archaeol.Abstr.
Formerly (1930-1975): Lund Universitet. Historiska Museet Samt Mynt-och Medaljkabinettet. Meddelanden.

913 GW
MADRIDER MITTEILUNGEN. 1960. a. price varies. Deutsches Archaeologisches Institut, Abteilung Madrid, Welschnonnengasse 12A, Postfach 4065, 6500 Mainz, W. Germany (B.R.D.) Indexed: Hist.Abstr. Amer.Hist.& Life.

913 HU ISSN 0076-2504
MAGYARORSZAG REGESZETI TOPOGRAFIAJA. 1967. irreg., vol.7, 1986. price varies. (Magyar Tudomanyos Akademia) Akademiai Kiado, Publishing House of the Hungarian Academy of Sciences, P.O. Box 24, H-1363 Budapest, Hungary.

571 II ISSN 0076-2520
MAHARAJA SAYAJIRAO UNIVERSITY OF BARODA. DEPARTMENT OF ARCHAEOLOGY AND ANCIENT HISTORY. ARCHAEOLOGY SERIES. (Text in English) 1953. irreg., (approx. 1/yr.) price varies. Maharaja Sayajirao University of Baroda, Department of Archaeology and Ancient History, Baroda 390002, Gujarat, India. Ed. K.T.M. Hegde. circ. 500.

913 948 NO
MAIHAUGEN. 1931. irreg. Kr.120. (Maihaugen) Sandvigske Samlinger, 2600 Lillehammer, Norway.
Formerly (1931-1949): Sandvigske Samlinger. Aarbok.

MAINZER ZEITSCHRIFT; Mittelrheinisches Jahrbuch fuer Archaeologie, Geschichte und Kunst. see ART

MAKEDONIKA. see HISTORY — History Of Europe

MAN & ENVIRONMENT. see ANTHROPOLOGY

913 440 FR
MARI ANNALES DE RECHERCHES INTERDISCIPLINAIRES. 1982. a. price varies. Editions Recherches sur les Civilisations, 9 rue Anatole de la Forge, 75017 Paris, France.

917 US
MARYLAND. GEOLOGICAL SURVEY. ARCHEOLOGICAL STUDIES. 1973. irreg., no.3, 1985. price varies. Maryland Geological Survey, 2300 St. Paul St., Baltimore, MD 21218. TEL 301-554-5500. charts. illus. circ. 1,000. (back issues avail.)

918 PE
MATERIALES PARA LA ARQUEOLOGIA DEL PERU. 1981. irreg. Instituto Nacional de Cultura, Proyecto Especial de Irrigacion Jequetepeque-Zana, Lima, Peru.

MATERIALIEN ZUR ROEMISCH-GERMANISCHEN KERAMIK. see CERAMICS, GLASS AND POTTERY

MATERIALY ZACHODNIO-POMORSKIE. see HISTORY — History Of Europe

913 UK ISSN 0076-6097
MEDIEVAL ARCHAEOLOGY. 1957. a. £8. Society for Medieval Archaeology, University College, Gower St., London WC1E 6BT, England. Ed. D. Hinton. bk. rev. circ. 1,500. Indexed: Br.Hum.Ind. Art & Archaeol.Tech.Abstr. Br.Archaeol.Abstr. Numis.Lit. RILA.

913 IT ISSN 0076-6615
MESOPOTAMIA; rivista di archeologia. (Text in English and Italian) 1966. a. price varies. (Universita degli Studi di Torino) Licosa SpA, Via Lamarmora, 45, 50121 Florence, Italy. (Co-sponsor: Centro Ricerche Archeologiche e Scavi di Torino per Il Medio Oriente e l'Asia) circ. 1,000. Indexed: Numis.LIt.

917 US ISSN 0735-5467
MISSOURI ARCHAEOLOGICAL SOCIETY. SPECIAL PUBLICATIONS. 1957. irreg. $15. Missouri Archaeological Society, 329 Noyes Hall, University of Missouri, MO 65211 TEL 314-882-3544. (Subscr. to: Box 958, Columbia, MO 65205) Ed. M. Raymond Wood. bibl. charts. illus. index. circ. 1,500 (controlled) (back issues avail.)

913 US ISSN 0076-9576
MISSOURI ARCHAEOLOGIST. 1935. irreg. membership. Missouri Archaeological Society, Inc., 15 Switzler Hall, Columbia, MO 65211 TEL 314-882-3544. (Subscr. to: Box 958, Columbia, MO 65205) Ed. Robert T. Bray. charts. illus. circ. 1,500. (back issues avail.) Indexed: Abstr.Anthropol.

913 IT ISSN 0067-009X
MONGRAFIE DELLA SCUOLA ARCHEOLOGICA DI ATENE E DELLE MISSIONI ITALIANE IN ORIENTE.* 1964. irreg. price varies. (Scuola Archeologica di Atene) L'Erma di Bretschneider, Via Cassiodoro 19, 00193 Rome, Italy. TEL 687 41 27. circ. 750.

ARCHAEOLOGY

913   SP
MONOGRAFIAS ARQUEOLOGICAS. 1982. irreg. Universidad Autonoma de Madrid, Departamento de Prehistoria y Arqueologia, M. Huerta-Ibiza 52, Madrid 9, Spain.

913   IT   ISSN 0077-0493
MONOGRAFIE DI ARCHEOLOGIA LIBICA. 1948. irreg., no.19, 1984. price varies. Erma di "Bretschneider", Via Cassiodoro 19, 00193 Rome, Italy.

913   BE
MONOGRAPHIES REINE ELISABETH. 1971. irreg., latest vol.4, 1978. price varies. Fondation Egyptologique Reine Elisabeth, Parc du Cinquantenaire 10, B-1040 Brussels, Belgium.

960 090   BE   ISSN 0077-1376
MONUMENTA AEGYPTIACA. 1968. irreg., latest no.4, 1979. price varies. Fondation Egyptologique Reine Elisabeth, Parc du Cinquantenaire 10, B-1040 Brussels, Belgium.

913   GW   ISSN 0077-1384
MONUMENTA AMERICANA. (Text in German; occasionally also in English or Spanish) 1965. irreg., vol.9, 1973. price varies. (Ibero-Amerikanisches Institut Preussischer Kulturbesitz Berlin) Gebr. Mann Verlag, Lindenstr. 76, Postfach 110303, 1000 Berlin 61, W. Germany (B.R.D.) Ed. Gerdt Kutscher.

913   US   ISSN 0363-7565
MONUMENTA ARCHAEOLOGICA (LOS ANGELES) 1976. irreg., vol.12, 1986. University of California, Los Angeles, Institute of Archaeology, 405 Hilgard Ave., Los Angeles, CA 90024. TEL 213-825-7411. Ed. Ernestine S. Elster.

913 709   GW   ISSN 0077-1406
MONUMENTA ARTIS ROMANAE. 1959. irreg., vol.16, 1986. price varies. Gebr. Mann Verlag, Lindenstr. 76, Postfach 110303, 1000 Berlin 61, W. Germany (B.R.D.) Ed. Heinz Kaehler.

MONUMENTA HISTORICA BUDAPESTINENSIA. see *HISTORY — History Of Europe*

MORAVSKE MUZEUM BRNO. CASOPIS. see *HISTORY — History Of Europe*

MUSE. see *ART*

MUSEE GUIMET, PARIS. BIBLIOTHEQUE D'ETUDES. see *ART*

MUSEE GUIMET, PARIS. ETUDE DES COLLECTIONS DU MUSEE. see *ART*

MUSEO ARCHEOLOGICO DI TARQUINIA. MATERIALI. see *MUSEUMS AND ART GALLERIES*

914   SP
MUSEO ARQUEOLOGICO DE VALLADOLID. MONOGRAFIAS. 1974. irreg. Museo Arqueologico de Valladolid, Palacio de Fabio Nelli, Valladolid, Spain. illus.

913   SP
MUSEO ARQUEOLOGICO NACIONAL. CATALOGOS CIENTIFICOS. irreg. Museo Arqueologico Nacional, Serrano 13, Madrid 1, Spain.

913   SP
MUSEO ARQUEOLOGICO NACIONAL. MONOGRAFIAS ARQUEOLOGICAS. no.5, 1979. irreg. Museo Arqueologico Nacional, Serrano 13, Madrid 1, Spain.

MUSEO NACIONAL DE ANTROPOLOGIA Y ARQUEOLOGIA. SERIE: INVESTIGACIONES DE CAMPO. see *ANTHROPOLOGY*

913 572   PE
MUSEO NACIONAL DE ANTROPOLOGIA Y ARQUEOLOGIA. SERIE: METALURGIA. 1976. irreg. Museo Nacional de Antropologia y Arqueologia, Plaza Bolivar, Pueblo Libre, Lima 21, Peru. Ed. Ruth Shady Solis.

913   IS   ISSN 0082-2620
MUSEUM OF ANTIQUITIES OF TEL-AVIV-YAFO. PUBLICATIONS. 1964. irreg. $1. Museum of Antiquities of Tel-Aviv-Yafo, Box 8406, Tel Aviv-Jaffa, Israel.

914 069   YU   ISSN 0350-9370
MUZEJSKI VJESNIK/MUSEUM NEWS MAGAZINE. (Text in Croatian; summaries in German) 1978. a. free. North-West Croatian Museums, Muzejsko Drustvo Sjeverozapadne Hrvatske, 42000 Varazdin, Yugoslavia. Ed. Darko Sacic. bk. rev. circ. 800. (back issues avail.)

914   RM
MUZEUL DE ISTORIE AL REPUBLICII SOCIALISTE ROMANIA. CERCETARI ARHEOLOGICE. 1975. a. Muzeul de Istorie al Republicii Socialiste Romania, Calea Victoriei 12, Bucharest, Rumania. Ed.Bd.

913 943.8   PL   ISSN 0458-1520
MUZEUM ARCHEOLOGICZNE I ETNOGRAFICZNE, LODZ. PRACE I MATERIALY. SERIA ARCHEOLOGICZNA. (Summaries in English, French or German) 1956. irreg., no.28, 1981. price varies. ‡ Panstwowe Wydawnictwo Naukowe, Miodowa 10, 00-251 Warsaw, Poland (Dist. by: Ars Polona, Krakowskie Przedmiescie 7, 00-068 Warsaw, Poland) Ed. Konrad Jazdzewski. circ. 500.

943.8   PL   ISSN 0075-7039
MUZEUM ARCHEOLOGICZNE, KRAKOW. MATERIALY ARCHEOLOGICZNE. 1959. irreg., 1972, no. 13. Muzeum Archeologiczne, Krakow, Poselska 3, 31-002 Krakow, Poland.

913   PL   ISSN 0068-4635
MUZEUM GORNOSLASKIE W BYTOMIU. ROCZNIK. SERIA ARCHEOLOGIA. (Text in Polish; summaries in German and Russian) 1962. irreg. price varies. Muzeum Gornoslaskie, Pl. Thaelmanna 2, 41-902 Bytom, Poland (Dist. by Ars Polona-Ruch, Krakowskie Przedmiescie 7, Warsaw, Poland)

913   GW   ISSN 0342-1406
NACHRICHTEN AUS NIEDERSACHSENS URGESCHICHTE. 1967. a. DM.60. (Arcaeologische Kommission fuer Niedersachsen) Verlag August Lax, Kreuzstr. 21, Postfach 10 08 65, 3200 Hildesheim, W. Germany (B.R.D.) Indexed: Br.Archaeol.Abstr. Numis.Lit.

913 560   SA   ISSN 0374-9665
NATIONAL MUSEUM. MEMOIRS. (Text and summaries in Afrikaans and English) 1952. irreg. price varies. National Museum, Box 266, Bloemfontein 9300, South Africa. Ed. S. Louw. abstr. bibl. charts. illus. stat. circ. 850. (back issues avail.)

NATIONAL TAIWAN UNIVERSITY. DEPARTMENT OF ANTHROPOLOGY. BULLETIN. see *ANTHROPOLOGY*

NATUR UND MENSCH: JAHRESMITTEILUNGEN DER NATURHISTORISCHEN GESELLSCHAFT NUERNBERG. see *BIOLOGY*

913 574 550   GW   ISSN 0077-6149
NATURHISTORISCHE GESELLSCHAFT NUERNBERG. ABHANDLUNGEN. 1851. irreg. price varies. Naturhistorische Gesellschaft Nuernberg e.V., Gewerbemuseumsplatz 4, Luitpoldhaus, 8500 Nuernberg 1, W. Germany (B.R.D.) circ. 2,500. Indexed: Biol.Abstr.

913 980   US   ISSN 0077-6297
NAWPA PACHA. (Text in English, French, Inca and Spanish; contributions in other languages accepted) 1963. a. $15 to individuals; institutions $18. Institute of Andean Studies, Box 9307, Berkeley, CA 94709. Eds. John H. Rowe, Patricia J. Lyon. circ. 550.
International series for Andean archaeology

913   PL
NEA PAPHOS. (Text in French and Polish) 1976. irreg., vol.2, 1977. (Polska Akademia Nauk, Zaklad Archeologii Srodziemnomorskiej) Panstwowe Wydawnictwo Naukowe, Miodowa 10, 00-251 Warsaw, Poland (Dist. by: Ars Polona, Krakowskie Przedmiescie 7, 00-068 Warsaw, Poland) Ed. Kazimierz Michalowski. bibl. illus.

NEDERLANDS INSTITUUT TE ROME. MEDEDELINGEN. see *HISTORY — History Of Europe*

913 953   NE
NETHERLANDS INSTITUTE OF ARCHAEOLOGY AND ARABIC STUDIES IN CAIRO. PUBLICATIONS. 1973. irreg., vol.4, 1981. price varies. E. J. Brill, P.O. Box 9000, 2300 PA Leiden, Netherlands.

913   GW   ISSN 0548-2682
NEUE AUSGRABUNGEN UND FORSCHUNGEN AUS NIEDERSACHSENS URGESCHICHTE. 1963. a. price varies. (Arcaeologische Kommission fuer Niedersachsen) Verlag August Lax, Postfach 10 08 65, 3200 Hildesheim, W. Germany (B.R.D.)

NEVADA. STATE MUSEUM, CARSON CITY. ANTHROPOLOGICAL PAPERS. see *ANTHROPOLOGY*

917   US   ISSN 0077-8346
NEW HAMPSHIRE ARCHEOLOGIST. 1950. a. $10. New Hampshire Archeological Society, c/o Phillips Exeter Academy, Dept. of Anthropology, Exeter, NH 03833. TEL 603-772-4311. Ed. D. Starbuck. illus. circ. 250.

913   UK
NEW STUDIES IN ARCHAEOLOGY. 1976. irreg. price varies. Cambridge University Press, Edinburgh Bldg., Shaftesbury Rd., Cambridge CB2 2RU, England (And 32 E. 57th St., New York, NY 10022) Ed.Bd.

913   US
NEW WORLD ARCHAEOLOGICAL FOUNDATION. PAPERS. 1959. irreg. price varies. Brigham Young University, New World Archaeological Foundation, Provo, UT 84602. Ed. Susanna M. Ekholm. circ. 1,000.

913   NZ   ISSN 0110-540X
NEW ZEALAND JOURNAL OF ARCHAEOLOGY. 1979. a. 17.50. New Zealand Archaeological Association, P.O. Box 6337, Dunedin, New Zealand (Orders to: Dr. F. Leach, Anthropology Department, Otago University, P.O. Box 56, Dunedin, New Zealand) (Co-sponsor: University of Otago) Ed. J. Davidson. charts. illus. circ. 350.

NORSK SJOEFARTSMUSEUM. AARSBERETNING. see *HISTORY — History Of Europe*

913   UK   ISSN 0305-4659
NORTHAMPTONSHIRE ARCHAEOLOGY. 1966. a. £15 to non-members. Northamptonshire Archaeological Society, c/o Brian Dix, Ed., 32 Wordsworth Rd., Kettering, Northants NN16 9LB, England (Subscr. addr.: c/o Mrs. W. Parry, 59 Gordon St., Northampton NN2 6BY, England) bk. rev. illus. circ. 200. Indexed: Br.Archaeol.Abstr. Geo.Abstr.
Formerly (until 1973): Northamptonshire Federation of Archaeological Societies. Bulletin.

NORTHUMBRIANA; true Northumberland's own magazine. see *LITERATURE*

914   SP   ISSN 0211-1748
NOTICIARIO ARQUEOLOGICO HISPANICO: ARQUEOLOGIA. 1953. irreg. Subdireccion General de Arqueologia, Palacio del Museo Arquelogico Nacional, Serrano, 13 (1), Madrid 28001, Spain. bibl. illus. circ. 1,200. Indexed: Br.Archaeol.Abstr.

913 700   DK   ISSN 0085-3208
NY CARLSBERG GLYPTOTEK. MEDDELELSER. (Text in Danish; summaries in English, French, and German) 1944. a. Kr.90. Ny Carlsberg Glyptotek, Dantes Plads 1556, Copenhagen V, Denmark. Ed. Flemming Johansen. circ. 1,000. Indexed: RILA.

OBEROESTERREICHISCHER MUSEALVEREIN. JAHRBUCH. see *HISTORY — History Of Europe*

ODENSE UNIVERSITY CLASSICAL STUDIES. see *CLASSICAL STUDIES*

913   AU
OESTERREICHISCHES ARCHAEOLOGISCHES INSTITUT. JAHRESHEFTE. 1965. a. S.700. Oesterreichisches Archaeologisches Institut, Universitaet, Dr. Karl Lueger-Ring 1, A-1010 Vienna, Austria. circ. 450.
Supersedes: Oesterreichisches Archaeologisches Institut. Jahreshefte: Grabungen (ISSN 0078-3579)

OKRESNI ARCHIV OLOMOUC. VYROCNI ZPRAVA. see *HISTORY — History Of Europe*

OKRESNI MUZEUM V BLANSKU. SBORNIK. see *HISTORY — History Of Europe*

913   SW   ISSN 0078-5520
OPUSCULA ATHENIENSIA. (Issued in Svenska Institutet i Athen. Skrifter) (Text in English, French, German) 1951. irreg., no.16, 1986. price varies. Paul Aastroems Forlag, Vaestra Hamngatan 3, S-41117 Goeteborg, Sweden. Ed. B. Ahlrot. bk. rev. circ. 1,000. Indexed: Numis.Lit.

913   US
OXFORD MONOGRAPHS ON CLASSICAL ARCHAEOLOGY. irreg. price varies. Oxford University Press, 200 Madison Ave., New York, NY 10016 TEL 212-679-7300. (And Ely House, 37 Dover St., London W1X 4AH, England) Ed.Bd.

913 940   UK   ISSN 0308-5562
OXONIENSIA. 1936. a. £8. Oxfordshire Architectural and Historical Society, Ashmolean Museum, Oxford, England. Ed. John Blair. bk. rev. bibl. charts. illus. index. circ. 500. Indexed: Br.Hum.Ind. Br.Archaeol.Abstr. Geo.Abstr. Numis.Lit.

913 500   BE
PACT. 1977. a. price varies. European Study Group on Physical, Chemical and Mathematical Techniques Applied to Archaeology, c/o T. Hackens, ed., 28 Av. Leopold, B-1330 Rixensart, Belgium. Ed. Tony Hackens. circ. 1,000. Indexed: Chem.Abstr. Art & Archaeol.Tech.Abstr. GeoRef.

571   PK   ISSN 0078-7868
PAKISTAN ARCHAEOLOGY. (Text in English) 1964. a. price varies. Department of Archaeology and Museums, 27-A Central Union Commercial Area, Shaheed-e-Millat Rd., Karachi 8, Pakistan.

913   CS
PAMATKY ARCHEOLOGICKE. BIBLIOGRAPHICAL REGISTER. irreg., latest issue, 1974. fl.60 per no. (Ceskoslovenska Akademie Ved, Archeologicky Ustav) Academia Publishing House of the Czechoslovak Academy of Sciences, Vodickova 40, 112 29 Prague 1, Czechoslovakia (Distributor in Western countries: John Benjamins B.V., Amsteldijk 44, Amsterdam (Z.), Netherlands) Ed. Jan Rataj.

PAMYATNIKI KUL'TURY. NOVYE OTKRYTIYA/ MONUMENTS OF CULTURE. NEW DISCOVERIES. see *ART*

PAN AMERICAN INSTITUTE OF GEOGRAPHY AND HISTORY. COMMISSION ON HISTORY. BIBLIOGRAFIAS. see *HISTORY — History Of North And South America*

960   BE   ISSN 0078-9402
PAPYROLOGICA BRUXELLENSIA. 1962. irreg., no.19, 1979. Fondation Egyptologique Reine Elisabeth, Parc du Cinquantenaire 10, B-1040 Brussels, Belgium.

917   US
PEABODY MUSEUM BULLETINS. 1976. irreg., no.3, 1978. price varies. Peabody Museum of Archaeology and Ethnology, Harvard University, 11 Divinity Ave., Cambridge, MA 02138. TEL 617-495-3938.

913 572   US   ISSN 0079-029X
PEABODY MUSEUM OF ARCHAEOLOGY AND ETHNOLOGY. MEMOIRS. (Vols. not issued consecutively) 1896. irreg., vol.15, 1983. price varies. Peabody Museum of Archaeology and Ethnology, Harvard University, 11 Divinity Ave., Cambridge, MA 02138. TEL 617-495-3938. Ed. Mary Strother.

913   US
PEABODY MUSEUM OF ARCHAEOLOGY AND ETHNOLOGY. MONOGRAPHS. 1974. irreg., vol. 7, 1983. price varies. Peabody Museum of Archaeology and Ethnology, Harvard University, 11 Divinity Ave., Cambridge, MA 02138. TEL 617-495-3938. Ed. Mary Strother.

913 572   US   ISSN 0079-0303
PEABODY MUSEUM OF ARCHAEOLOGY AND ETHNOLOGY. PAPERS. (Vols. not issued consecutively) 1891. irreg., vol.77, 1986. price varies. Peabody Museum of Archaeology and Ethnology, Harvard University, 11 Divinity Ave., Cambridge, MA 02138. TEL 617-495-3938. Ed. Mary Strother. Indexed: Biol.Abstr. GeoRef.

PERITIA. see *HISTORY — History Of Europe*

PERSICA. see *HISTORY — History Of Asia*

943.8 913   PL   ISSN 0079-3256
POLSKA AKADEMIA NAUK. ODDZIAL W KRAKOWIE. KOMISJA ARCHEOLOGICZNA. PRACE. (Text in English, German and Polish; summaries in English, German and Russian) 1960. irreg., no. 24, 1985. price varies. Ossolineum, Publishing House of the Polish Academy of Sciences, Rynek 9, 50-106 Wroclaw, Poland (Dist. by: Ars Polona-Ruch, Krakowskie Przedmiescie 7, Warsaw, Poland)

913   UK   ISSN 0079-4236
POST-MEDIEVAL ARCHAEOLOGY. 1967. a. £8. Society for Post-Medieval Archaeology, c/o P. Davey, Hon, Treas., P.O. Box 147, Liverpool LG9 3BX, England. Ed. D.W. Crossley. bk. rev. cum. index: vols. 1-5, 6-10. circ. 850. (back issues avail.) Indexed: Br.Archaeol.Abstr. Abstr.Anthropol. Numis.Lit. RILA.

913   PL   ISSN 0137-3250
POZNANSKIE TOWARZYSTWO PRZYJACIOL NAUK. KOMISJA ARCHEOLOGICZNA. PRACE. (Text in Polish; summaries in German) 1922. irreg., vol.10, 1979. (Poznanskie Towarzystwo Przyjaciol Nauk, Komisja Archeologiczna) Panstwowe Wydawnictwo Naukowe, Miodowa 10, 00-251 Warsaw, Poland (Dist. by Ars Polona, Krakowskie Przedmiescie 7, 00-068 Warsaw, Poland) Ed.Bd. circ. 420. Indexed: Chem.Abstr.

PRAZSKY SBORNIK HISTORICKY. see *HISTORY — History Of Europe*

913 574.5   US
PREHISTORIC ARCHAEOLOGY AND ECOLOGY. 1973. irreg., latest 1984. price varies. University of Chicago Press, 5801 S. Ellis Ave., Chicago, IL 60637. TEL 312-962-7700. Eds. Karl W. Butzer, Leslie F. Freeman. adv. bk. rev. (reprint service avail. from UMI,ISI)

913   UK   ISSN 0079-497X
PREHISTORIC SOCIETY, LONDON. PROCEEDINGS. 1911. a. £10. Prehistoric Society, Museum Bookshop, 36 Great Russell St., London WC18 3PP, England. Ed. T. Champion. bk. rev. circ. 2,000. Indexed: Br.Hum.Ind. SSCI. Art & Archaeol.Tech.Abstr. Br.Archaeol.Abstr. Geo.Abstr. Numis.Lit.

PRINCETON MONOGRAPHS IN ART AND ARCHAEOLOGY. see *ART*

913   UR
PROBLEMY ARKHEOLOGII I ETNOGRAFII. 1977. irreg. 0.73 Rub. per no. Leningradskii Universitet, Universitetskaya Nab. 7/9, Leningrad B-164, Russian S.F.S.R., U.S.S.R. circ. 1,185.

913   PL   ISSN 0079-7138
PRZEGLAD ARCHEOLOGICZNY. (Text in English and Polish; summaries in English and German) 1919. a. price varies. (Polska Akademia Nauk, Instytut Historii Kultury Materialnej) Ossolineum, Publishing House of the Polish Academy of Sciences, Rynek 9, Wroclaw, Poland (Dist. by: Ars Polona-Ruch, Krakowskie Przedmiescie 7, Warsaw, Poland) Ed. Tadeusz Wislanski. bk. rev. circ. 500. Indexed: Br.Archaeol.Abstr.

PUTEOLI; studi di storia antica. see *HISTORY — History Of Europe*

571   SP   ISSN 0079-8215
PYRENAE: CRONICA ARQUEOLOGICA; annual scientific journal. 1965. a. 300 ptas.($6) Universidad de Barcelona, Facultad de Filosofia y Letras, Instituto de Arqueologia, Avenido de Jose Antonio 585, Barcelona 7, Spain. Ed. Juan Maluquer de Motes. bk. rev. circ. 600. Indexed: Numis.Lit.

913   IT   ISSN 0079-8258
QUADERNI DI ARCHEOLOGIA DELLA LIBIA. 1950. irreg., no.13, 1983. price varies. Erma di "Bretschneider", Via Cassiodoro, 19, 00193 Rome, Italy.

913   SP   ISSN 0210-8291
QUADERNS DE TREBALL. no.4, 1981. irreg. (Universidad Autonoma de Barcelona, Departament de Prehistoria i Arqueologia) Institut de Prehistoria i Arqueologia de la Diputacio de Barcelona, Barcelona, Spain.

913.031   GW   ISSN 0375-7471
QUARTAER; Jahrbuch fuer Erforschung des Eiszeitalters und der Steinzeit. (Text in English, French and German) 1946. a. price varies. (Hugo-Obermaier-Gesellschaft) Verlag Ludwig Roehrscheid, Fuerstenstr. 3, Postfach 1268, D-5300 Bonn 1, W. Germany (B.R.D.) Eds. Dr. Gisela Freund, Dr. E.W. Guenther. bk. rev. circ. 2,000. (reprint service avail. from UMI) Indexed: Br.Archaeol.Abstr. GeoRef.

913 930   GW   ISSN 0079-9149
QUELLENSCHRIFTEN ZUR WESTDEUTSCHEN VOR- UND FRUEHGESCHICHTE. 1939. irreg., no.10, 1982. price varies. Dr. Rudolf Habelt GmbH, Am Buchenhang 1, 5300 Bonn 1, W. Germany (B.R.D.) Ed. R. Stampfuss.

913   SP   ISSN 0034-0863
REAL SOCIEDAD ARQUEOLOGICA. BOLETIN ARQUEOLOGICO. (Text mainly in Spanish) 1901. a. $10. Real Sociedad Arqueologica Tarraconense, Museo Nacional Arqueologic, Tarragona, Spain (Subscr. to: Apartado 573, Tarragona, Spain) Ed. Rodolfo Cortes. bk. rev. abstr. illus. circ. 1,000 (controlled)

914   BE
RECHERCHES ARCHEOLOGIQUES EN HAINAUT OCCIDENTAL. BILAN. (Text in French) 1972. irreg. Cercle Royal d'Histoire et d'Archeologie d'Ath et de la Region et Musees Athois, 38 rue du Chapelain, 7800 Ath, Belgium.

RECHERCHES ET DOCUMENTS D'ART ET D'ARCHEOLOGIE. see *ART*

913   US
REDISCOVERY; journal of Archaeology. 1968. a. $4.95. Illinois Association for Advancement of Archaeology, c/o E. Neiburger, Ed., 1000 North Ave., Waukejan, IL 60085. adv. bk. rev. circ. 750.

REPORTS IN MACKINAC HISTORY AND ARCHAEOLOGY. see *HISTORY — History Of North And South America*

913   GE   ISSN 0232-2609
RESTAURIERUNG UND MUSEUMSTECHNIK. 1976. irreg. price varies. Museum fuer Ur- und Fruehgeschichte Thueringens, Humboldtstr. 11, 5300 Weimar, E. Germany (D.D.R.) Ed. R. Feustel.

REVIEW OF SCOTTISH CULTURE. see *ETHNIC INTERESTS*

914   FR   ISSN 0767-709X
REVUE ARCHEOLOGIQUE DE L'OUEST. 1984. a. 160 Fr. Association R.A.O., c/o Laboratoire d'Archeometrie, Universite de Rennes, 35042 Rennes, France. (back issues avail.)

913   FR   ISSN 0557-7705
REVUE ARCHEOLOGIQUE NARBONNAISE. 1968. a. price varies. Diffusion de Boccard, 11, rue de Medicis, 75006 Paris, France. Indexed: Numis.Lit.

913   BE   ISSN 0035-077X
REVUE BELGE D'ARCHEOLOGIE ET D'HISTOIRE DE L'ART. 1931. a. 1200 Fr. Academie Royale d'Archeologie de Belgique, c/o Musee Bellevue, 7 Place de Palais, 1000 Brussels, Belgium. bk. rev. illus. circ. 400. Indexed: Art Ind. Art & Archaeol.Tech.Abstr. RILA.

REVUE BELGE DE NUMISMATIQUE ET DE SIGILLOGRAPHIE. see *NUMISMATICS*

REVUE DES ARCHEOLOGUES ET HISTORIENS D'ART DE LOUVAIN. see *ART*

REVUE DES ETUDES GRECQUES. see *CLASSICAL STUDIES*

ARCHAEOLOGY

913 940   FR
REVUE HISTORIQUE ET ARCHEOLOGIQUE DU MAINE. vol.52, 1972. irreg. 40. Societe Historique et Archeologique du Maine, 7 rue de la Reine Berengere 1, Le Mans, France. Ed. Denis Bealet. bibl. circ. 450.

913 943   SZ
REVUE HISTORIQUE VAUDOISE.* vol.73, 1975. a. 35 Fr. Societe Vaudoise d'Histoire et d'Archeologie, Rue du Maupas 47, CH-1004 Lausanne, Switzerland. Ed. Laurette Wettstein. charts. illus.

913   GW   ISSN 0557-7853
RHEINISCHE AUSGRABUNGEN. 1968. irreg., no. 21, 1981. price varies. (Landschaftsverband Rheinland) Rheinland-Verlag, Kennedy-Ufer 2, 5000 Cologne 21, W. Germany (B.R.D.) (Distr. by: Rudolf Habelt Verlag, Am Buchenhang 1, 5300 Bonn, W. Germany (B.R.D.)) Indexed: Br.Archaeol.Abstr.

913   GW   ISSN 0067-9968
RHEINISCHES LANDESMUSEUM, BONN. SCHRIFTEN. 1965. irreg. price varies. Rheinland-Verlag, Kennedy-Ufer 2, 5000 Cologne 21, W. Germany (B.R.D.) (Distr. by: Rudolf Habelt Verlag, Am Buchenhang 1, 5300 Bonn 1, W. Germany (B.R.D.))

914   NE   ISSN 0467-006X
RIJKSDIENST VOOR HET OUDHEIDKUNDIG BODEMONDERZOEK TE AMERSFOORT. BERICHTEN. (Text in Dutch, English and German) 1950. a. Rijksdienst voor het Oudheidkundig Bodemonderzoek te Amersfoort, Staatsuitgeverij, 2500 The Hague, Netherlands.

913   NE
RIJKSMUSEUM VAN OUDHEDEN, LEIDEN. OUDHEIDKUNDIGE MEDEDELINGEN. (Text in English, French, German) 1907. a. price varies. Rijksmuseum van Oudheden, Postbus 11114, 2301 EC Leiden, Netherlands. Eds. H.D. Schneider, G.J. Verwers. circ. 400.

913 975   US   ISSN 0271-6925
RIPLEY P. BULLEN MONOGRAPHS IN ANTHROPOLOGY AND HISTORY. 1978. irreg. price varies. (Florida State Museum) University Presses of Florida, 15 N.W. 15th St., Gainesville, FL 32603. TEL 904-392-1351. Ed. Jerald T. Milanich. (back issues avail.)

913 709   IT   ISSN 0080-3235
RIVISTA ARCHEOLOGICA DELL'ANTICA PROVINCIA E DIOCESI DI COMO; periodico di antichita ed arte. 1872. a. price varies. Societa Archeologica Comense, Piazza Medaglie d'Oro 1, 22100 Como, Italy. bk. rev. circ. 1,200. (back issues avail.) Indexed: Numis.Lit.
Formerly: Rivista Archeologica della Provincia di Como.

913   IT   ISSN 0392-0895
RIVISTA DI ARCHEOLOGIA. (Text in various languages) 1977. a. Giorgio Bretschneider, Via Crescenzo 43, 00193 Rome, Italy. Ed. Gustavo Traversari. (back issues avail.)

913 709   GW   ISSN 0080-3782
ROEMISCHE BRONZEN AUS DEUTSCHLAND. 1960. irreg. price varies. Philipp Von Zabern, Welschnonnengasse 11, Postfach 4065, 6500 Mainz, W. Germany (B.R.D.) Ed. Heinz Menzel. index.

913   DK   ISSN 0107-2366
ROMANSKE STENARBEJDER. 1981. irreg. Kr.140. Hikuin, Moesgaard, 8270 Hoejbjerg, Denmark. Ed. Jens Vellev. illus.

914   GW   ISSN 0341-9312
ROMISCH-GERMANISCHEN KOMMISSION. BERICHTE. a., vol.65, 1984. DM.50. Verlag Philipp Von Zabern, Welschnonnengasse 11-13, D-6500 Mainz, W. Germany (B.R.D.)

914.2 820   IE   ISSN 0035-8991
ROYAL IRISH ACADEMY. PROCEEDINGS. SECTION C: ARCHAEOLOGY, CELTIC STUDIES, HISTORY, LINGUISTICS AND LITERATURE. 1836. irreg. price varies. Royal Irish Academy, 19 Dawson St., Dublin 2, Ireland. Ed. B. Young. charts. illus. index; cum.index. Indexed: Curr.Cont. Arts & Hum.Cit.Ind. Br.Archaeol.Abstr. Br.Archaeol.Abstr. Hist.Abstr. Numis.Lit.

913   CN   ISSN 0316-1285
ROYAL ONTARIO MUSEUM. ARCHAEOLOGY MONOGRAPHS. 1973. irreg. price varies. Royal Ontario Museum, Publication Services, 100 Queen's Park, Toronto, Ont. M5S 2C6, Canada. TEL 416-586-5586. Ed.Bd. bibl. illus.

913   CN
ROYAL ONTARIO MUSEUM. ARCHAEOLOGY OCCASIONAL PAPERS. 1959. irreg. Royal Ontario Museum, Publication Services, 100 Queen's Park, Toronto, Ont. M5S 2C6, Canada. TEL 416-586-5586. illus.
Formerly: Royal Ontario Museum. Art and Archaeology. Occasional Papers (ISSN 0082-5077)

SAGA OCH SED. see FOLKLORE

913   GW   ISSN 0080-5866
SAMOS. 1961. irreg. price varies. (Deutsches Archaeologisches Institut) Dr. Rudolf Habelt GmbH, Am Buchenhang 1, 5300 Bonn 1, W. Germany (B.R.D.)

SASKATCHEWAN. DEPARTMENT OF CULTURE AND RECREATION. ANNUAL REPORT. see ART

917   CN
SASKATCHEWAN ARCHAEOLOGY. 1980. a. Can.$10 to individuals; institutions Can.$16. Saskatchewan Archaeological Society, Box 1012, Regina, Saskatchewan S4P 3B2, Canada. Ed. Gerald Conaty. circ. 400. (back issues avail.)

SCHRIFTEN DES OESTERREICHISCHEN KULTURINSTITUTS KAIRO. ARCHAEOLOGISCH-HISTORISCHE ABTEILUNG. see HISTORY — History Of The Near East

913 930   GE   ISSN 0080-696X
SCHRIFTEN UND QUELLEN DER ALTEN WELT. (Text in German, Greek or Latin) 1959. irreg., vol. 35, 1982. price varies. (Akademie der Wissenschaften der DDR, Zentralinstitut fuer Alte Geschichte und Archaeologie) Akademie-Verlag, Leipziger Str. 3-4, 1086 Berlin, E. Germany (D.D.R.)

914   SZ
SCHWEIZER BEITRAEGE ZUR KULTURGESCHICHTE UND ARCHAEOLOGIE DES MITTELALTERS. 1974. irreg. Walter Verlag AG, Amthausquai 21, CH-4600 Olten, Switzerland. illus. circ. 1,000.

913   UK   ISSN 0262-4389
SCOTTISH ARCHAEOLOGICAL REVIEW. 1982. biennial. $20. Archaeological Review, c/o Department of Archaeology, Glasgow G12 8QQ, Scotland (Subscr. to: Martinus Nijhoff, P.O.B. 269, 2501 AX, The Hague, Netherlands) Eds. J.B. Stevenson, J.C. Barrett. bk. rev. Indexed: Br.Archaeol.Abstr.

SCRIPTA MEDITERRANEA. see HISTORY — History Of The Near East

913   SW
SCRIPTA MINORE. REGIAE SOCIETATIS HUMANIORUM LITTERARUM LUNDENSIS. (Text in English) 1957. a. price varies. Liber Forlag, S-205 10, Malmo, Sweden. Ed. Berta Stjernquist.

913   IT
SCUOLA ARCHEOLOGICA DI ATENE E DELLE MISSIONI ITALIANE IN ORIENTE. ANNUARIO. 1914; N.S. 1983. irreg. latest 1986. L.330000. L'Erma di Bretschneider, Via Cassiodoro 19, 00193 Rome, Italy. TEL 06 687 41 27. circ. 750. (back issues avail.)

387   IS   ISSN 0077-5193
SEFUNIM. (Text in English, French, Hebrew) 1966. irreg., latest no. 1981. $10. National Maritime Museum Foundation, P.O. Box 44855, Haifa 31447, Israel. Ed. Joseph Ringel. adv. bk. rev. circ. 2,000.

913 930   IT   ISSN 0392-0909
SIKELIKA. SERIE ARCHEOLOGICA. 1979. irreg., vol. 2, 1980. price varies. (Centro Siciliano di Studi Storico-Archeologici "Biagio Pace") Giorgio Bretschneider, Via Crescenzo 43, 00193 Rome, Italy. (back issues avail.)

SIKELIKA. SERIE STORICA. see HISTORY

913   PL   ISSN 0080-9594
SILESIA ANTIQUA. (Summaries in English, French and German) 1959. a. price varies. (Muzeum Archeologiczne, Wroclaw) Ossolineum, Publishing House of the Polish Academy of Sciences, Rynek 9, 50-106 Wroclaw, Poland (Dist. by: Ars Polona-Ruch, Krakowskie Przedmiescie 7, Warsaw, Poland) Ed. J. Lodowski. Indexed: Br.Archaeol.Abstr.

913   PL   ISSN 0080-9993
SLAVIA ANTIQUA; rocznik poswiecony starozytnosciom slowianskim. (Text in German, Polish, Russian; summaries in English and French) 1948. a. price varies. (Uniwersytet im. Adama Mickiewicza, Instytut Archeologii) Panstwowe Wydawnictwo Naukowe, Miodowa 10, 00-251 Warsaw, Poland (Dist. by: Ars Polona, Krakowskie Przedmiescie 7, 00-068 Warsaw, Poland) Ed. Witold Hensel. adv. bk. rev. charts. circ. 500. Indexed: Numis.Lit.

913   CS
SLOVENSKE NARODNE MUZEUM. ARCHEOLOGICKY USTAV. FONTES ARCHEOLOGICKEHO. 1972. irreg., no.5, 1981. price varies. (Slovenske Narodne Muzeum) Osveta, Ul. Oslobodoitelov 21, 036 54 Martin, Czechoslovakia. Ed. Alojz Habovstiak. charts. illus. maps. circ. 800.
Supersedes in part: Slovenske Narodne Muzeum. Archeologicky Ustav. Fontes.

SLOVENSKE NARODNE MUZEUM. ZBORNIK. see HISTORY — History Of Europe

913   SP   ISSN 0213-3024
SOCIEDAD DE ESTUDIOS VASCOS. CUADERNOS DE SECCION. PREHISTORIA Y ARQUEOLOGIA. 1984. irreg. (Sociedad de Estudios Vascos) Eusko Ikaskuntza, S.A., Churruca, 7 - 2, 20004 Donostia, Spain.

913   IT
SOCIETA TIBURTINA DI STORIA E D'ARTE. ATTI E MEMORIE. 1921. a. Societa Tiburtina di Storia e d'Arte, Villa d'Este, 00019 Tivoli, Italy.

914   FR
SOCIETE ARCHEOLOGIQUE DE TARN ET GARONNE. BULLETIN ARCHEOLOGIQUE, HISTORIQUE ET ARTISTIQUE. 1869. a. 70 F. Societe Archeologique de Tarn et Garonne, Rue des Soubirous-Bas, Tarn et Garonne, Montauban, France. (Co-sponsors: Conseil General du Tarn et Garonne; Caisse d'Epargne de Montauban) Ed.Bd. bk. rev.

914   FR
SOCIETE ARCHEOLOGIQUE DE TOURAINE. BULLETIN. 1868. a. Musee de l'Hotel Gouin, 25 rue du Commerce, 37000 Tours, France.

913   FR
SOCIETE ARCHEOLOGIQUE DE TOURAINE. MEMOIRES. 1842. irreg. Musee de l'Hotel Gouin, 25 rue du Commerce, 3700 Tours, France. Ed.Bd. charts. illus.

913   UA   ISSN 0068-5283
SOCIETE D'ARCHEOLOGIE COPTE. BIBLIOTHEQUE DE MANUSCRITS. 1934; N.S. 1967. irreg., latest issue in print: no.3, no.4 in preparation. £E3 per no. Society for Coptic Archaeology, 222 rue Ramses, Cairo, Egypt. bk. rev.

913   UA   ISSN 0068-5291
SOCIETE D'ARCHEOLOGIE COPTE. BULLETIN. (Text in French, English, German, Italian) 1935. irreg. £E10 per no. Society for Coptic Archaeology, 222 rue Ramses, Cairo, Egypt. bk. rev. cum.index: vols. 1-20 in vol. 20.

913   UA   ISSN 0068-5305
SOCIETE D'ARCHEOLOGIE COPTE. TEXTES ET DOCUMENTS. 1942. irreg., latest no.15; nos.16 & 17 in prep. £E5 per no. Society for Coptic Archaeology, 222 rue Ramses, Cairo, Egypt. bk. rev.

949.33   BE
SOCIETE D'ARCHEOLOGIE, D'HISTOIRE ET DE FOLKLORE DE NIVELLES ET DU BRABANT WALLON. ANNALES. 1879. irreg. 300 Fr. Societe d'Archeologie d'Histoire et de Folklore de Nivelles et du Brabant Wallon, Musee de Nivelles, 27 rue de Bruxelles, Nivelles, Belgium. Ed. J.L. Delattre. illus. circ. 500.

914	FR
SOCIETE D'ARCHEOLOGIE ET D'HISTOIRE DE LA CHARENTE MARITIME. BULLETIN DE LIAISON. 1974. a. 10 F. Societe d'Archeologie et d'Histoire de la Charente Maritime, Musee Archeologique, Esplanade A. Malraux, 17100 Saintes, France.

913 940 900	SZ	ISSN 0081-0959
SOCIETE D'HISTOIRE ET D'ARCHAEOLOGIE DE GENEVE. BULLETIN. 1892. a. 5 Fr. Societe d'Histoire et d'Archeologie de Geneve, c/o Bibliotheque Publique et Universitaire de Geneve, Promenade des Bastions, Geneva, Switzerland. index.

913	FR	ISSN 0081-0967
SOCIETE D'HISTOIRE ET D'ARCHEOLOGIE DE LA GOELE. BULLETIN D'INFORMATION. 1968. a. 20 F. Societe d'Histoire et d'Archeologie de la Goele, Mairie, Dammartin-en-Goele 77230, France. adv. circ. 1,000.

913	FR	ISSN 0081-1181
SOCIETE NATIONALE DES ANTIQUAIRES DE FRANCE. BULLETIN. 1857. a. 250 F. Societe Nationale des Antiquaires de France., Pavillon Mollien, Palais du Louvre, Paris 75001, France (Orders to: Diffusion de Boccard, 11 rue de Medicis, 75006 Paris, France) circ. 800. Indexed: Numis.Lit. RILA.

SOCIETE SUISSE DES AMERICANISTES. BULLETIN/SCHWEIZERISCHE AMERIKANISTEN-GESELLSCHAFT. BULLETIN. see *HISTORY — History Of North And South America*

917	US
SOCIETY FOR AMERICAN ARCHAEOLOGY. MEMOIR SERIES. irreg. price varies. 1511 K St., N.W., Washington, DC 20005. TEL 202-638-6079.

917	US
SOCIETY FOR AMERICAN ARCHAEOLOGY. SPECIAL PUBLICATIONS SERIES. irreg. 1511 K St., N.W., Washington, DC 20005. TEL 202-638-6079.

913	US	ISSN 0735-1399
SOCIETY FOR COMMERCIAL ARCHAEOLOGY. NEWS JOURNAL. 1977. irreg. (2-4/yr.) $15. Society for Commercial Archaeology, c/o National Museum of American History, Rm. 5010, Washington, DC 20560. Eds. E. James Peters, Carol J. Dyson. bk. rev. circ. 300. (looseleaf format; back issues avail.)

913	US
SOCIETY FOR HISTORICAL ARCHAEOLOGY. SPECIAL PUBLICATION SERIES. 1976. a. included in subscr. to Historical Archaeology. Society for Historical Archaeology, Box 231033, Pleasant Hill, CA 94523-1033. Ed. Ronald L. Michael. illus.

913	UK	ISSN 0306-4859
SOCIETY FOR LINCOLNSHIRE HISTORY AND ARCHAEOLOGY. ANNUAL REPORT AND STATEMENT OF ACCOUNTS. a. Society for Lincolnshire History & Archaeology, Exchequergate Arch, Lincoln LN2 1PZ, England.

SOCIETY OF ANTIQUARIES OF SCOTLAND. MONOGRAPH SERIES. see *HISTORY — History Of Europe*

913 500.9	UK	ISSN 0081-2056
SOMERSET ARCHAEOLOGY AND NATURAL HISTORY. 1849. a. membership. Somerset Archaeological & Natural History Society, Taunton Castle, Taunton, England. Eds. John C. Pentney, Josephine P.M. Pentney. bk. rev. index; cum.index: vols. 81-115 (1935-1971) circ. 1,000. Indexed: Br.Hum.Ind. Br.Archeol.Abstr. Numis.Lit. Formerly: Somersetshire Archaeological and Natural History Society. Proceedings.

SOUTH AFRICAN MUSEUM. ANNALS/SUID-AFRIKAANSE MUSEUM. ANNALE. see *PALEONTOLOGY*

SOUTH INDIAN ART AND ARCHAEOLOGICAL SERIES. see *ART*

913	UK	ISSN 0457-7817
SOUTH STAFFORDSHIRE ARCHAEOLOGICAL AND HISTORICAL SOCIETY. TRANSACTIONS. 1960. a. £14. South Staffordshire Archaeological and Historical Society, William Salt Library, Eastgate St., Stafford ST16 2LZ, England. Ed. Dr. N. Tringham. illus. circ. 330. (also avail. in microfilm from UMI; reprint service avail. from UMI) Indexed: Br.Hum.Ind. Br.Archaeol.Abstr. RILA.

913	US
SOUTHERN ILLINOIS UNIVERSITY, CARBONDALE. CENTER FOR ARCHAEOLOGICAL INVESTIGATIONS. OCCASIONAL PAPER. irreg. price varies. Southern Illinois University, Carbondale, Center For Archaeological Investigations, Carbondale, IL 62901. TEL 618-536-5529.

913	US
SOUTHERN ILLINOIS UNIVERSITY, CARBONDALE. CENTER FOR ARCHAEOLOGICAL INVESTIGATIONS. RESEARCH PAPER. 1978. irreg. price varies. Southern Illinois University, Carbondale, Center for Archaeological Investigations, Carbondale, IL 62901. TEL 618-536-5529. Ed. Susan H. Wilson. circ. 500.

913	US	ISSN 0085-6525
SOUTHERN INDIAN STUDIES. 1949. a. $10 to individuals; $25 to institutions. (Archaeological Society of North Carolina) University of North Carolina, Research Laboratories of Anthropology, Box 2 Alumni Bldg., Chapel Hill, NC 27514. TEL 919-962-6574. Ed. David Moore. bk. rev. bibl. illus. circ. 350. (also avail. in microfilm from MCA) Indexed: Hist.Abstr.

913	PL	ISSN 0081-3834
SPRAWOZDANIA ARCHEOLOGICZNE. (Text mainly in Polish, sometimes in English; summaries in English) 1955. a. price varies. (Polska Akademia Nauk, Instytut Historii Kultury Materialnej) Ossolineum, Publishing House of the Polish Academy of Sciences, Rynek 9, 50-106 Wroclaw, Poland (Dist. by: Ars Polona-Ruch, Krakowskie Przedmiescie 7, Warsaw, Poland) Ed. J. Machnik. Indexed: Br.Archaeol.Abstr.

SRPSKA AKADEMIJA NAUKA I UMETNOSTI. ODELJENJE DRUSTVENIH NAUKA. SPOMENIK. see *SOCIAL SCIENCES: COMPREHENSIVE WORKS*

913.031	YU	ISSN 0350-0241
STARINAR. (Text in Serbo-Croatian; summaries mostly in French) 1884; N.S. 1950. a. Arheoloski Institut - Institiute of Archaeology, Knez Mihailova 35, 11001 Belgrade, Yugoslavia (Subscr. to: Jugoslovenska Knjiga, Agencija za Uvoz-Izvoz, trg. Republike 5, 1100 Belgrade, Yugoslavia) Eds. Djurdje Boskovic, Borislav Jovanovic. bk. rev. bibl. illus. circ. 800. (back issues avail.)

913	IT
STUDI EBLAITI. (Text in English, French, German, Italian) 1979. irreg. $35. Universita di Roma "La Sapienza", Piazza Montecitorio 120, 00186 Rome, Italy. circ. 1,000. (back issues avail.)

913 900	IT	ISSN 0585-4911
STUDI GENUENSI. (Text in Italian) 1970. a. L.20000($12.50) Istituto Internazionale di Studi Liguri, Via Romana 39 Bis, 18020 Bordighera, Italy. circ. 1,000. Indexed: M.L.A.

913	HU	ISSN 0081-6280
STUDIA ARCHAEOLOGICA. (Text in German) 1963. irreg., latest vol.8, 1984. price varies. (Magyar Tudomanyos Akademia, Regeszeti Intezet) Akademiai Kiado, Publishing House of the Hungarian Academy of Sciences, P.O. Box 24, H-1363 Budapest, Hungary.

913	IT	ISSN 0081-6299
STUDIA ARCHAEOLOGICA. 1961. irreg., no.40, 1984. price varies. Erma di "Bretschneider", Via Cassiodoro, 19, 00193 Rome, Italy.

913	GW
STUDIA ARCHAEOLOGICA. 1969. irreg., no.64, 1980. price varies. (Universidad, Santiago de Compostela, Seminario de Arqueologia, SP) Dr. Rudolf Habelt GmbH, Am Buchenhang 1, 5300 Bonn 1, W. Germany (B.R.D.) (Co-sponsor: Universidad de Valladolid. Departamento de Prehistoria y Arqueologia)

913	PL	ISSN 0081-6302
STUDIA ARCHEOLOGICZNE. (Issued as a Subseries of the Acta Universitatis Wratislaviensis) (Text in Polish; summaries in German) 1965. irreg. price varies. (Uniwersytet Wroclawski) Panstwowe Wydawnictwo Naukowe, Miodowa 10, 00-251 Warsaw, Poland (Dist. by: Ars Polona, Krakowskie Przedmiescie 7, 00-068 Warsaw, Poland) Ed. Jozef Kazmierczyk. charts. illus. circ. 545.

913 220	NE	ISSN 0081-6396
STUDIA FRANCISCI SCHOLTEN MEMORIAE DICATA. 1952. irreg., vol. 5, 1982. Nederlands Instituut voor Het Nabije Oosten - Netherlands Institute for the Near East, Witte Singel 24, Box 9515, 2300 RA Leiden, Netherlands.

913 551	PL	ISSN 0137-530X
STUDIA I MATERIALY DO DZIEJOW ZUP SOLNYCH W POLSCE. (Text in Polish; summaries in English) 1965. a. 250 Zl.($2) Muzeum Zup Krakowskich, Park Kingi, 32-020 Wieliczka, Poland. (Co-sponsor: Ministerstwo Kultury i Sztuki) Ed. M.A. Roman Kedra. bk. rev. circ. 400. (back issues avail.)

913	PL	ISSN 0081-6787
STUDIA PALMYRENSKIE. (Text in Polish; summaries in French) 1966. irreg., no.8, 1985. price varies. (Uniwersytet Warszawski, Zaklad Archeologii Srodziemnomorskiej) Wydawnictwa Uniwersytetu Warszawskiego, Ul. Obozna 8, 00-927 Warsaw, Poland (Dist. by: CHZ ARS Polona, Krakowskie Przedmiescie 7, Warsaw, Poland) circ. 500.

913	SW	ISSN 0081-7414
STUDIER I NORDISK ARKEOLOGI/STUDIES IN NORTH EUROPEAN ARCHAEOLOGY. (Text in Swedish; some numbers have English summaries) 1953. irreg., no.14/15, 1981. price varies. Fornminnesfoereningen i Goeteborg, Norra Hamngatan 14, S-41114 Goeteborg, Sweden. (Co-sponsor: Goetebrgs Arkeologiska Museum)

STUDIES IN ANCIENT ART AND ARCHAEOLOGY. see *ART*

913	US
STUDIES IN ARCHAEOLOGICAL SCIENCE. 1971. irreg., vol.14, 1985. Academic Press Inc., Orlando, FL 32887. TEL 305-345-2000. Ed. G. W. Dimbleby.

913	SW	ISSN 0081-8232
STUDIES IN MEDITERRANEAN ARCHAEOLOGY. MONOGRAPH SERIES. (Text in English, French and German) 1962. irreg., no.75, 1986. price varies. Paul Aastroems Foerlag, Vaestra Hamngatan 3, S-41117 Goeteborg, Sweden. circ. 1, 000. Indexed: Art & Archaeol.Tech.Abstr.

913	SW
STUDIES IN MEDITERRANEAN ARCHAEOLOGY. POCKET-BOOK SERIES. (Text in English, French and German) 1974. irreg., no.46, 1986. Paul Aastroems Foerlag, Vaestra Hamngatan 3, S-41117 Goeteborg, Sweden. circ. 3, 000.

913	US	ISSN 0585-7023
STUDIES IN PRE-COLUMBIAN ART AND ARCHAEOLOGY. 1966. irreg., no.28, 1986. price varies. Dumbarton Oaks, Publications Office, 1703 32nd St., N.W., Washington, DC 20007. TEL 202-342-3259. Ed. Elizabeth P. Boone. bibl. charts. illus. circ. 1,500. (back issues avail.)

913	IS
STUDIUM BIBLICUM FRANCISCANUM. MUSEUM. 1976. irreg., no. 7, 1984. price varies. Franciscan Printing Press, Box 14064, 91140 Jerusalem, Israel. circ. 1,000.

ARCHAEOLOGY

914.2 942   UK   ISSN 0262-6004
SUFFOLK INSTITUTE OF ARCHAEOLOGY AND HISTORY. PROCEEDINGS. 1849. a. £8. Suffolk Institute of Archaeology and History, c/o E.A. Martin, Hon. Secy., Oak Tree Farm, Finborough Rd., Hitcham, Ipswich, Suffolk IP7 7LS, England. Ed. D. Allen. circ. 700.

913   IQ   ISSN 0081-9271
SUMER; journal of archaeology in Iraq. (Text in Arabic and other languages) 1945. a. ID.10.000. State Antiquities Organization, Jamal Abdul Nasr St., Baghdad, Iraq. Indexed: GeoRef. Numis.Lit.

913 700   FI   ISSN 0355-1822
SUOMEN MUINAISMUISTOYHDISTYKSEN AIKAKAUSKIRJA. (Text in English, Finnish, German and Swedish) 1874. irreg. Suomen Muinaismuistoyhdistys, Nervanderinkatu 13, 00100 Helsinki 10, Finland.

913 572   FI   ISSN 0355-1806
SUOMEN MUSEO. (Text in English, Finnish and German) 1894. a. Suomen Muinaismuistoyhdistys, Nervanderinkatu 13, 00100 Helsinki, Finland. Indexed: Br.Archaeol.Abstr. Numis.Lit.

913   UK   ISSN 0309-7803
SURREY ARCHAEOLOGICAL COLLECTIONS. 1858. a. membership. Surrey Archaeological Society, Castle Arch, Guildford, Surrey GU1 3SX, England. Ed. Viscountess Hanworth. bk. rev. cum.index: vols. 1-71. (back issues avail.) Indexed: Br.Hum.Ind. Br.Archaeol.Abstr. Br.Archaeol.Abstr. Numis.Lit.

913   UK   ISSN 0308-342X
SURREY ARCHAEOLOGICAL SOCIETY. RESEARCH VOLUMES. 1974. irreg. membership. Surrey Archaeological Society, Castle Arch, Guildford, Surrey GU1 3SX, England. Indexed: Br.Archaeol.Abstr.

913   SW   ISSN 0081-9921
SVENSKA INSTITUTET I ATHEN. SKRIFTER. (Latin title: Acta Instituti Atheniensis Regni Sueciae. Includes Opuscula Atheniensia) 1951. irreg., no.34, 1986. price varies. (Swedish Institute in Athens) Paul Aastroems Forlag, Vaestra Hamngatan 3, S-41117 Gothenberg, Sweden. Ed. B. Ahlrot. bk. rev. circ. 1,000.

913   IT   ISSN 0081-993X
SVENSKA INSTITUTET I ROM. SKRIFTER. ACTA SERIES PRIMA. (Latin title: Acta Instituti Romani Regni Sueciae. Includes Opuscula Archaeologica and Opuscula Romana) 1932. irreg., no.42, 1985. price varies. Svenska Institutet i Rom - Swedish Institute in Rome, c/o Paul Aastroem, V. Hamng. 3, S-41117 Goeteborg, Sweden (Dist. by: Paul Aastroems Foerlag, Vaestra Hamngatan 3, S-41117, Gothenburg, Sweden) Ed. Brita Ahlrot. bk. rev. circ. 1,000.

913   PL   ISSN 0082-044X
SWIATOWIT. (Text in Polish; summaries in English and French) 1899. irreg., vol.35, 1982. price varies. (Uniwersytet Warszawski, Instytut Archeologii) Wydawnictwa Uniwersytetu Warszawskiego, Ul. Obozna 8, 00-927 Warsaw, Poland (Distr. by: CHZ ARS Polona, Krakowskie Przedmiescie 7, 00-068 Warsaw, Poland) circ. 500.

913 737   GW
SYLLOGE NUMMORUM GRAECORUM DEUTSCHLAND. STAATLICHE MUENZSAMMLUNG MUENCHEN. (1957-1968 (Vol. 1-18) Sammlung v. Aulock; from 1968 issued under new numbering with Staatliche Muenzsammlung Muenchen) 1957, N.S. 1968. irreg., no. 7, 1985. price varies. (Deutsches Archaeologisches Institut) Gebr. Mann Verlag, Lindenstr. 76, Postfach 110303, 1000 Berlin 61, W. Germany (B.R.D.) cum.index (1957-1968 in vol. 19) Formerly: Sylloge Nummorum Graecorum Deutschland (ISSN 0082-061X)

TALOHA. see *MUSEUMS AND ART GALLERIES*

571   GW   ISSN 0067-4974
TECHNISCHE BEITRAEGE ZUR ARCHAEOLOGIE. Title varies: Beitraege zur Archaeologie. 1959. irreg. price varies. (Roemisch-Germanisches Zentralmuseum, Mainz) Dr. Rudolf Habelt GmbH, Am Buchenhang 1, 5300 Bonn 1, W. Germany (B.R.D.) Ed. H. Menzel.

917   US   ISSN 0040-3180
TENNESSEE ARCHAEOLOGIST. 1944. a. $3. Tennessee Archaeological Society, University of Tennessee, Knoxville, TN 37916. Ed. Alfred K. Guthe.

913 930   IT   ISSN 0452-2907
TESTIMONIA SICILIAE ANTIQUA. 1981. irreg. price varies. (Istituto Siciliano per la Storia Antica) Giorgio Bretschneider, Via Crescenzo 43, 00193 Rome, Italy.

913 976.4   US   ISSN 0082-2930
TEXAS ARCHEOLOGICAL SOCIETY. BULLETIN. 1929. a. $15 includes newsletter. Texas Archeological Society, Center for Archaeological Research, Univ. of Texas at San Antonio, San Antonio, TX 78285. TEL 512-691-4462. bk. rev. circ. 950. Indexed: GeoRef.

917   US   ISSN 0495-2944
TEXAS ARCHEOLOGICAL SOCIETY. SPECIAL PUBLICATION. 1962. irreg., no.3, 1976. price varies. Texas Archeological Society, Center for Archaeological Research, Univ. of Texas at San Antonio, San Antonio, TX 78285. TEL 512-691-4462.

913 976.4   US   ISSN 0082-2949
TEXAS ARCHEOLOGY. 1957. irreg. free with Texas Archaeological Society Bulletin. Texas Archeological Society, Center for Archaeological Research, Univ. of Texas at San Antonio, San Antonio, TX 78285. TEL 512-691-4462. bk. rev. circ. 1,000.

942   UK   ISSN 0309-9210
THOROTON SOCIETY OF NOTTINGHAMSHIRE. TRANSACTIONS. 1897. a. membership. Thoroton Society of Nottinghamshire, Nottinghamshire Record Office, County House, High Pavement, Nottingham NG1 1HR, England. Eds. A. Henstock, H. Wheeler. bk. rev. cum.index: vols. 1-80. circ. 500. Indexed: Br.Hum.Ind. Br.Archaeol.Abstr. Numis.Lit.

913   GW   ISSN 0082-450X
TIRYNS. (Text in German) 1912. irreg., vol. 9, 1980. price varies. (Deutsches Archaeologisches Institut, Athens, GR) Philipp Von Zabern, Welschnonnengasse 11, Postfach 4065, 6500 Mainz, W. Germany (B.R.D.)

913 700   SW   ISSN 0349-764X
TJUSTBYGDEN. 1926. a. Kr.50. Tjustbydens Kulturhistoiska Forening, Kulbackens Museum, Box 257, S-593 01 Vastervik, Sweden. Ed.Bd. adv.

913   PL
TOWARZYSTWO NAUKOWE W TORUNIU. PRACE ARCHEOLOGICZNE. (Text in Polish; summaries in German) irreg., 1982, vol. 8. price varies. Towarzystwo Naukowe w Toruniu, Ul. Wysoka 16, 87-100 Torun, Poland (Dist. by: Ars Polona-Ruch, Krakowskie Przedmiescie 7, P.O. Box 1001, 00-068 Warsaw, Poland) circ. 750.

913   SP   ISSN 0082-5638
TRABAJOS DE PREHISTORIA. NUEVA SERIE. 1960-68; N.S. 1969. a. 6000 ptas. Centro de Estudios Historica, Departamento de Prehistoria, Palacio del Museo Arqueologico Nacional, Serrano, 13, 28001 Madrid, Spain.

913 669   UK   ISSN 0143-1250
TRANSACTIONS OF THE MONUMENTAL BRASS SOCIETY. 1887. a. £8. Guildhall Library, Manuscripts Department, Aldermanbury, London RC2P 2EJ, England. Ed. S.G.H. Freeth. bk. rev. cum.index. circ. 800. (back issues avail.) Indexed: RILA.

913   GW   ISSN 0082-643X
TRIERER GRABUNGEN UND FORSCHUNGEN. (Text in German) 1929. irreg., vol.15, 1985. price varies. (Rheinisches Landesmuseum, Trier) Philipp Von Zabern, Welschnonnengasse 11, Postfach 4065, 6500 Mainz, W. Germany (B.R.D.) index. Indexed: Br.Archaeol.Abstr.

914 709 737   GW   ISSN 0041-2953
TRIERER ZEITSCHRIFT FUER GESCHICHTE UND KUNST DES TRIERER LANDES UND SEINER NACHBARGEBIETE. 1926. a. DM.65. Rheinisches Landsmuseum Trier, Ostallee 44, D-5500 Trier, W. Germany (B.R.D.) Ed.Bd. bk. rev. circ. 750. (back issues avail.)

913   UK   ISSN 0082-7355
ULSTER JOURNAL OF ARCHAEOLOGY. 1938. a. membership. Ulster Archaeological Society, Archaeology Dept., Queens University, 17 University Square, Belfast BT7 1NN, N. Ireland. Ed. J.P Mallory. bk. rev. index. circ. 550. Indexed: Br.Archaeol.Abstr. Numis.Lit.

913 350   US
U.S. NATIONAL PARK SERVICE. ANNUAL REPORT TO CONGRESS ON THE FEDERAL ARCHEOLOGICAL PROGRAM. 1974. a. free. U.S. Department of the Interior, National Park Service, Archeological Assistance Division, Box 37127, Washington, DC 20013-7127. TEL 202-343-4101. circ. 2,000. (back issues avail.)

913   SP   ISSN 0067-4184
UNIVERSIDAD DE BARCELONA. INSTITUTO DE ARQUEOLOGIA Y PREHISTORIA. PUBLICACIONES EVENTUALES. 1960. irreg., 1975, no. 26. price varies. Universidad de Barcelona, Instituto de Arqueologia y Prehistoria, Barcelona 7, Spain.

UNIVERSIDAD DE MURCIA. ANALES DE PREHISTORIA Y ARQUEOLOGIA. see *HISTORY — History Of Europe*

913.031   SP
UNIVERSIDAD DE OVIEDO. DEPARTAMENTO DE PREHISTORIA Y ARQUEOLOGIA. PUBLICACIONES. irreg. Universidad de Oviedo, Departamento de Prehistoria y Arqueologia, Oviedo, Spain.

918   CL
UNIVERSIDAD DEL NORTE. MUSEO DE ARQUEOLOGIA. DOCUMENTOS PARA LA INVESTIGACION. 1974. irreg. exchange. Universidad del Norte, Museo de Arqueologia, San Pedro de Atacama, Chile.

918   PE
UNIVERSIDAD NACIONAL MAYOR DE SAN MARCOS. SEMINARIO DE HISTORIA RURAL ANDINA. SEMINARIO ARQUEOLOGICO. 1977. irreg. Universidad Nacional Mayor de San Marcos, Seminario de Historia Rural, Lima, Peru.

572   BL
UNIVERSIDADE CATOLICA DE GOIAS. GABINETE DE ARQUEOLOGIA. ANUARIO DE DIVULGACAO CIENTIFICA. 1974. a. Universidade Catolica de Goias, Gabinete de Arqueologia, Caixa Postal, 86, Goiania 74000, Brazil. illus.

918   BL
UNIVERSIDADE DE SAO PAULO. MUSEU PAULISTA. COLECAO. SERIE DE ARQUEOLOGIA. 1975. irreg. Universidade de Sao Paulo, Museu Paulista, Caixa Postal 42.503, Parque da Independencia, 04263 Sao Paulo, Brazil. Ed. Setembrino Petri.
     Supersedes in part (since 1975): Museu Paulista. Colecao (ISSN 0080-6382)

913 800 930 400   IT   ISSN 0076-1818
UNIVERSITA DEGLI STUDI DI MACERATA. FACOLTA DI LETTERE E FILOSOFIA. ANNALI. 1968. a. L.60000. (Universita degli Studi di Macerata, Facolta di Lettere e Filosofia) Editrice Antenore, Via Don Minzoni, I-62100 Macerata, Italy. Ed. Giovanni Ferretti. bk. rev. circ. 500. (back issues avail.) Indexed: M.L.A.

913   GW
UNIVERSITAET BONN. SEMINAR FUER ORIENTALISCHE KUNSTGESCHICHTE. VEROEFFENTLICHUNGEN. REIHE A. NIMRUZ. 1974. irreg. price varies. Dr. Rudolf Habelt GmbH, Am Buchenhang 1, 5300 Bonn 1, W. Germany (B.R.D.) Ed. Klaus Fischer.

UNIVERSITE CATHOLIQUE DE LOUVAIN. INSTITUT SUPERIEUR D'ARCHEOLOGIE ET D'HISTOIRE DE L'ART. DOCUMENTS DE TRAVAIL. see *ART*

913 709 BE
UNIVERSITE CATHOLIQUE DE LOUVAIN.
INSTITUT SUPERIEUR D'ARCHEOLOGIE ET
D'HISTOIRE DE L'ART. PUBLICATIONS.
(Includes two subseries: Aurifex Archaeologica
Transatlantica and Numismatica Lovaniensia) (Text
in English and French) 1972. irreg., no.52, 1986.
price varies. Universite Catholique de Louvain,
Institut Superieur d'Archeologie et d'Histoire de
l'Art, 1 place Blaise Pascal, 1348 Louvain-La-
Neuve, Belgium. Ed. T. Hackens. charts. illus. circ.
1,000.

UNIVERSITE DE MADAGASCAR. MUSEE
D'ART ET D'ARCHEOLOGIE. TRAVAUX ET
DOCUMENTS. see ART

UNIVERSITE DE TOULOUSE II (LE MIRAIL).
INSTITUT D'ART PREHISTORIQUE.
TRAVAUX. see ART

914 948 NO
UNIVERSITETS OLDSAKSAMLING. AARBOK.
(Text in English, French and Norwegian) 1927. a.
Kr.100. Universitetets Oldsaksamling, Frederiksgt. 2,
Oslo, Norway. Ed. Egil Mikkelsen. circ. 1,000.
Indexed: Br.Archaeol.Abstr.

560 CN
UNIVERSITY OF CALGARY.
ARCHAEOLOGICAL ASSOCIATION.
ARCHAEOLOGICAL CONFERENCE.
PROCEEDINGS. 1969. a. price varies. ‡ University
of Calgary, Archaeological Association, Department
of Archaeology, 2920-24th Ave. N.W., Calgary,
Alta. T2N 1N4, Canada. TEL 403-220-7578. circ.
250.
Formerly: University of Calgary. Archaeological
Association. Paleo-Environmental Workshop.
Proceedings (ISSN 0068-5437)

571 US ISSN 0068-5933
UNIVERSITY OF CALIFORNIA, BERKELEY.
ARCHAEOLOGICAL RESEARCH FACILITY.
CONTRIBUTIONS. 1965. irreg., no.45, 1984. price
varies. University of California, Berkeley,
Archaeological Research Facility, Berkeley, CA
94720. TEL 415-642-6000. Ed. John A. Graham.
circ. 400. (also avail. in microform from UMI)

913 US
UNIVERSITY OF CALIFORNIA, LOS ANGELES.
INSTITUTE OF ARCHAEOLOGY.
MONOGRAPH SERIES. 1970. irreg., no.27, 1986.
University of California, Los Angeles, Institute of
Archaeology, 405 Hilgard Ave., Los Angeles, CA
90024. TEL 213-825-7411. Ed. Ernestine S. Elster.
Formerly: University of California, Los Angeles.
Institute of Archaeology. Archaeological Survey.
Special Monograph Series (ISSN 0068-6204)

913 US
UNIVERSITY OF CALIFORNIA, LOS ANGELES.
INSTITUTE OF ARCHAEOLOGY.
OCCASIONAL PAPERS. 1974. irreg., no.15, 1985.
price varies. University of California, Los Angeles,
Institute of Archaeology, 405 Hilgard Ave., Los
Angeles, CA 90024. TEL 213-825-7411.

913 UK ISSN 0144-3313
UNIVERSITY OF EDINBURGH. DEPARTMENT
OF ARCHAEOLOGY. OCCASIONAL PAPERS.
1978. irreg., (1-2/yr.) University of Edinburgh,
Department of Archaeology, 19 George Sq.,
Edinburgh EH8 9JZ, Scotland.

913 UK ISSN 0076-0722
UNIVERSITY OF LONDON. INSTITUTE OF
ARCHAEOLOGY. BULLETIN. 1958. a. price
varies. ‡ University of London, Institute of
Archaeology, 31-34 Gordon Square, London WC1H
OPY, England. Ed. J.D. Evans. bk. rev. circ. 800.
(also avail. in microfilm from UMI) Indexed:
Br.Archaeol.Abstr. Geo.Abstr. Numis.Lit.

913 UK ISSN 0141-8505
UNIVERSITY OF LONDON. INSTITUTE OF
ARCHAEOLOGY. OCCASIONAL
PUBLICATION. 1977. irreg., no.11, 1985.
University of London, Institute of Archaeology, 31-
34 Gordon Square, London WC1H OPY, England.
Indexed: Br.Archaeol.Abstr.

913 SW
UNIVERSITY OF LUND. ARCHAEOLOGICAL
INSTITUTE. PAPERS. YEARBOOK/
MEDDELANDE FRAAN LUNDS
UNIVERSITET HISTORISKA MUSEUM. (Text in
English) a. Almqvist & Wiksell International, Box
1034, S-171 21 Solna, Sweden.

915 II ISSN 0076-2202
UNIVERSITY OF MADRAS. ARCHAEOLOGICAL
SERIES.* 1967. irreg. University of Madras,
Chepauk, Triplicane, Madras 600005, Tamil Nadu,
India.

UNIVERSITY OF MANITOBA ANTHROPOLOGY
PAPERS. see ANTHROPOLOGY

UNIVERSITY OF MISSOURI MONOGRAPHS IN
ANTHROPOLOGY. see ANTHROPOLOGY

913 US ISSN 0085-1221
UNIVERSITY OF NORTHERN COLORADO.
MUSEUM OF ANTHROPOLOGY.
OCCASIONAL PUBLICATIONS IN
ANTHROPOLOGY. ARCHAEOLOGY SERIES.
1967. irreg. price varies. University of Northern
Colorado, Museum of Anthropology, George E.
Fay, Ed., Greeley, CO 80639. TEL 303-351-1890.
circ. 300. (processed)

913 US ISSN 0160-3078
UNIVERSITY OF OKLAHOMA.
ARCHAEOLOGICAL RESEARCH AND
MANAGEMENT CENTER. PROJECT REPORT
SERIES. 1978. irreg. price varies. University of
Oklahoma, Archaeological Research and
Management Center, 1808 Newton Dr., Rm 44,
Norman, OK 73019. TEL 405-325-7211. Ed. Rain
Vehik.

913 US ISSN 0160-3086
UNIVERSITY OF OKLAHOMA.
ARCHAEOLOGICAL RESEARCH AND
MANAGEMENT CENTER. RESEARCH
SERIES. 1978. irreg. price varies. University of
Oklahoma, Archaeological Research and
Management Center, 1808 Newton Dr., Rm. 44,
Norman, OK 73019. TEL 405-325-7211. Ed. Rain
Vehik.

913 572 US
UNIVERSITY OF SOUTH CAROLINA.
INSTITUTE OF ARCHEOLOGY AND
ANTHROPOLOGY. ANNUAL REPORT. 1976. a.
University of South Carolina, Institute of
Archeology and Anthropology, Columbia, SC
29208. TEL 803-777-8170. Ed. Kenneth A. Pinson.
circ. 1,750.

917 572 US
UNIVERSITY OF TENNESSEE. DEPARTMENT
OF ANTHROPOLOGY. REPORT OF
INVESTIGATIONS. 1964. irreg., vol.42, 1985.
price varies. (University of Tennessee, Department
of Anthropology) University of Tennessee Press,
252 S. Stadium Hall, Knoxville, TN 37996. TEL
615-974-4408. circ. 750.

913 US
UNIVERSITY OF WASHINGTON. OFFICE OF
PUBLIC ARCHAEOLOGY. RECONNAISSANCE
REPORTS. 1975. irreg., no.46, 1985. University of
Washington, Office of Public Archaeology,
Publication Series, 305 Engineering Annex,
University of Washington, Seattle, WA 98195. TEL
206-543-8359.

913 947 870 CS ISSN 0231-7915
UNIVERZITA J. E. PURKYNE. FILOZOFICKA
FAKULTA. SBORNIK PRACI. E: RADA
ARCHEOLOGICKO-KLASICKA. irreg. (approx.
a.) Univerzita J. E. Purkyne, Filozoficka Fakulta, A.
Novaka 1, 602 00 Brno, Czechoslovakia.

UNIVERZITA KOMENSKEHO. FILOZOFICKA
FAKULTA. ZBORNIK: MUSAICA. see ART

913 PL ISSN 0083-4300
UNIWERSYTET JAGIELLONSKI. ZESZYTY
NAUKOWE. PRACE ARCHEOLOGICZNE.
1960. irreg. price varies. ‡ Panstwowe Wydawnictwo
Naukowe, Miodowa 10, 00-251 Warsaw, Poland
(Dist. by: Ars Polona, Krakowskie Przedmiescie 7,
00-068 Warsaw, Poland) Ed. Janusz K. Kozlowski.
circ. 700.

914 NO
VIKING; tidsskrift for Norron arkeologi/journal of
Norse archaeology. (Text in Norwegian; summaries
in English) 1937. a. Kr.100. Norsk Arkeologisk
Selskap, Frederiksgt. 2-3, Oslo 1, Norway. Ed.Bd.
adv. charts. illus. Indexed: Br.Archaeol.Abstr.

913.031 666 YU
VJESNIK ZA ARHEOLOGIJU I HISTORIJU
DALMATINSKU/BULLETIN D'ARCHEOLOGIE
ET D'HISTOIRE DALMATES. (Text in Croatian,
Italian; summaries in English, French, German)
1878. irreg. price varies. Arheoloski Muzej, Zrinsko-
Frankopanska 25, P.O. Box 15, 58000 Split,
Yugoslavia. circ. 750. (back issues avail.)

VLASTIVEDNY ZBORNIK POVAZIA. see
HISTORY — History Of Europe

914 943.7 CS
VYZKUMY V CECHACH. 1969. irreg., last 1984.
Archeologicky Ustav C S A V, Letenska 4, 118-01
Prague 1, Czechoslovakia. Ed. E. Cujanova. illus.
Supersedes: Ceskoslovenska Akademie Ved
Archeologicky Ustav. Zachranne Oddeleni. Bulletin.

913 GW
WEGE VOR- UND FRUEHGESCHICHTLICHER
FORSCHUNG. 1972. irreg. price varies. Dr. Rudolf
Habelt GmbH, Am Buchenhang 1, 5300 Bonn 1, W.
Germany (B.R.D.) Eds. Rolf Hachmann, Frauke
Stein.

913 GE ISSN 0232-265X
WEIMARER MONOGRAPHIEN ZUR UR- UND
FRUEHGESCHICHTE. 1978. irreg. price varies.
Museum fuer Ur- und Fruehgeschichte Thueringens,
Humboldtstr. 11, 5300 Weimar, E. Germany
(D.D.R.) Ed. R. Feustel.

913 NR ISSN 0083-8160
WEST AFRICAN JOURNAL OF ARCHAEOLOGY.
(Text in English or French) 1971. a. £N6.25.
(University of Ibadan, Department of Archaeology)
Ibadan University Press, University of Ibadan,
Ibadan, Nigeria. adv. bk. rev. Indexed: SSCI.
Br.Archaeol.Abstr. Curr.Cont.Africa.
Before 1970: West African Archaeological
Newsletter.

WHO'S WHO IN INDIAN RELICS. see HOBBIES

WILBOUR MONOGRAPHS. see HISTORY

500.2 574.9 UK
WILTSHIRE ARCHAEOLOGICAL AND
NATURAL HISTORY MAGAZINE (1982) 1853.
a. membership. ‡ Wiltshire Archaeological and
Natural History Society, 41 Long St., Devizes,
Wiltshire SN10 1NS, England. adv. bk. rev. circ. 1,
000. Indexed: Br.Hum.Ind. Br.Archaeol.Abstr.
Numis.Lit.
Formed by the 1982 merger of: Wiltshire
Archaeological Magazine (ISSN 0309-3476) &
Wiltshire Natural History Magazine (ISSN 0309-
3468); Previously known as: Wiltshire
Archaeological and Natural History Magazine
(ISSN 0084-0335)

913 500.2 UK
WILTSHIRE ARCHAEOLOGICAL AND
NATURAL HISTORY SOCIETY. ANNUAL
REPORT (1983) 1978. a. Wiltshire Archaeological
and Natural History Society, 41 Long St., Devizes,
Wiltshire SN10 1NS, England.
Formerly: Wiltshire Archaeological and Natural
History Society Annual Bulletin.

930 YU
WISSENSCHAFTLICHE MITTEILUNGEN DES
BOSNISCH-HERZEGOWINISCHEN
LANDESMUSEUMS. ARCHAEOLOGIE. (Text in
German) 1976. irreg. Zemaljski Muzej Bosne i
Hercegovine, Vojvode Putnika 7, Sarajevo,
Yugoslavia. Ed. Vlajko Palavestra.

914.03 UK ISSN 0084-1226
WOOLHOPE NATURALISTS' FIELD CLUB,
HEREFORDSHIRE. TRANSACTIONS. 1851. a.
membership. Woolhope Club, Hereford Library,
Hereford, England. Ed. J.W. Tonkin. circ. 650.
Indexed: Br.Hum.Ind. Br.Archaeol.Abstr.
Numis.Lit.

913   UK   ISSN 0143-2389
WORCESTERSHIRE ARCHAEOLOGICAL SOCIETY. TRANSACTIONS. 1923. biennial. £5. Worcestershire Archaeological Society, c/o Robin Whittaker, Ed., 14 Scobell Close, Pershore, Worcs. WR10 1QJ, England (Subscr. addr.: c/o Mrs. E.I. Leatherbarrow, Overdale, 34 Highfield Rd., Malvern Link, Worcestershire, England) circ. 350. (also avail. in microform from UMI)

913   US
WORLD ARCHAELOGICAL SOCIETY. SPECIAL PUBLICATION. 1971. irreg. price varies. ‡ World Archaeological Society, c/o Ron Miller, Ed., Lake Rd. 65-48, HCR-1-Box 445, MO 65672. bibl. illus.

571 913   UK   ISSN 0084-4276
YORKSHIRE ARCHAEOLOGICAL JOURNAL. 1869. a. £12.50 to individuals; institutions £15. Yorkshire Archaeological Society, Claremont, 23 Clarendon Rd., Leeds LS2 9NZ, England. Ed. R.M. Butler. circ. 1,400. Indexed: Br.Hum.Ind. Br.Archaeol.Abstr. Numis.Lit. RILA.

913   GW   ISSN 0340-0824
ZEITSCHRIFT FUER ARCHAEOLOGIE DES MITTELALTERS. 1973. a. DM.75. Rheinland-Verlag, Kennedy-Ufer 2, 5000 Cologne 21, W. Germany (B.R.D.) (Distr. by: Rudolf Habelt Verlag, Am Buchenhang 1, 5300 Bonn, W. Germany (B.R.D.)) Eds. Walter Janssen, Heiko Steuer. Indexed: Br.Archaeol.Abstr. RILA.

913   GW   ISSN 0084-5388
ZEITSCHRIFT FUER PAPYROLOGIE UND EPIGRAPHIK. 1967. irreg., no.66, 1986. DM.130. Dr. Rudolf Habelt GmbH, Am Buchenhang 1, 5300 Bonn 1, W. Germany (B.R.D.) Indexed: Numis.Lit.

913   YU   ISSN 0581-7501
ZEMALJSKI MUZEJ BOSNE I HERCEGOVINE. GLASNIK. ARHEOLOGIJA. (Text mainly in Serbo-Croatian; summaries in German or Serbo-Croatian) vol.29, 1974. a. Zemaljski Muzej Bosne i Hercegovine, Vojvode Putnika 7, Sarajevo, Yugoslavia. Ed. Borivoj Covic. bk. rev. bibl. illus. Indexed: Chem.Abstr.
Continues: Glasnik Zemaljskog Muzeja u Sarajevu.

ZENTRALINSTITUTS FUER ALTE GESCHICHTE UND ARCHAEOLOGIE. VEROEFFENTLICHEN. see HISTORY

ZESZYTY GLIWICKIE. see HISTORY — History Of Europe

913   SZ
ZUERCHER ARCHAEOLOGISCHE HEFTE. 1976. irreg., no.5, 1987. 12 Fr. per no. Universitaet Zuerich, Archaeologische Sammlung, Raemistr. 73, 8006 Zurich, Switzerland.

ZYGOS (1982); annual edition on the Hellenic fine arts. see ART

ARCHAEOLOGY — Abstracting, Bibliographies, Statistics

913 011   US   ISSN 0743-4251
ABSTRACTS IN MARYLAND ARCHEOLOGY. 1983. s-a. $3. Council for Maryland Archeology, c/o Louis Berger and Associates, 100 Halsted St., Orange, NJ 07019 (Subscr. to: Beth Acuff, Secy.-Treas., NPS Applied Archeology Center, 11710 Hunters Ln., Rockville, MD 20852) Ed. R. Michael Stewart. (back issues avail.)

913 700   US
ARCHAEOLOGICAL INSTITUTE OF AMERICA. ABSTRACTS OF THE GENERAL MEETING. 1975. a. $5. Archaeological Institute of America (Boston), Box 1901, Kenmore Sta., Boston, MA 02215. TEL 617-353-9361. Ed. Fred S. Kleiner. abstr. circ. 1,000. (back issues avail)

016 930   GW
ARCHAEOLOGISCHE BIBLIOGRAPHIE. (Supplement to Deutsches Archaeologisches Institut. Jahrbuch) 1914. a. price varies. Walter de Gruyter und Co., Genthiner Str. 13, 1000 Berlin 30, W. Germany (B.R.D.) (U.S. adress: Walter de Gruyter, Inc., 200 Saw Mill Rd., Hawthorne, N.Y. 10532) bibl. circ. 800. Indexed: Br.Archaeol.Abstr.

ART AND ARCHAEOLOGY TECHNICAL ABSTRACTS; abstracts of the technical literature on archaeology and the fine arts. see ART — Abstracting, Bibliographies, Statistics

BULLETIN SIGNALETIQUE. PART 521: SOCIOLOGIE - ETHNOLOGIE. see SOCIOLOGY — Abstracting, Bibliographies, Statistics

962 932   UA
EGYPTIAN MUSEUM. LIBRARY. CATALOGUE. 1966. irreg. price varies. (Organisation des Antiquites Egyptiennes, Museums Service) Egyptian Museum, Library, Midan-el-Tahrir, Kasr el-Nil, Cairo, Egypt. Eds. Dia Abou-Ghazi, Abdel-Mohsen El-Khachab. adv. bk. rev. index in preparation.
Formerly: Egyptian National Museum. Library. Catalogue (ISSN 0068-5275)

948 010   DK   ISSN 0105-6492
N A A. (Nordic Archaeological Abstracts) (Text in English) 1975. a. Kr.125. Viborg Stiftsmuseum, DK-8800 Viborg, Denmark (Subscr. to: Museumstjenesten, Sjorupvej, Lysgaard, DK-8800 Viborg, Denmark) Eds. Mette Iversen, Ulf Naesman. Indexed: Br.Archaeol.Abstr.

913 016   PL   ISSN 0137-4885
POLISH ARCHAEOLOGICAL ABSTRACTS. (Text in English) 1972. a. price varies. (Polska Akademia Nauk, Instytut Historii Kultury Materialnej, Zaklad Archeologii Wielkopolski) Ossolineum, Publishing House of the Polish Academy of Sciences, Rynek 9, 50-106 Wroclaw, Poland (Dist. by: Ars Polona - Ruch, Krakowskie Przedmeiscie 7, Warsaw, Poland) Ed. W. Dzieduszycki. abstr. bibl. circ. 630. Indexed: Br.Archaeol.Abstr.

914 016   SW
SWEDISH ARCHAEOLOGY. Issued with: Nordic Archaeological Abstracts. 1949. every 5 yrs., latest no.7, 1983. Kr.120. Svenska Arkeologiska Samfundet - Swedish Archaeological Society, Box 5405, S-114 84 Stockholm, Sweden. Eds. Ake Hyenstrand, Pontus Helstrom. circ. 500. Indexed: Br.Archaeol.Abstr.
Formerly: Swedish Archaeological Bibliography (ISSN 0586-2000)

ARCHAEOLOGY — Computer Applications

001.6 930.1   UK
COMPUTER APPLICATIONS IN ARCHAEOLOGY. 1974. biennial. price varies. University of Birmingham, Computer Centre, Birmingham, England. Ed. S. Laflin. Indexed: Art & Archaeol.Tech.Abstr. Br.Archaeol.Abstr.

SCIENCE AND ARCHAEOLOGY. see SCIENCES: COMPREHENSIVE WORKS — Computer Applications

ARCHITECTURE

see also Building and Construction; Engineering—Civil Engineering; Housing and Urban Planning; Real Estate

A R I S. (Art Research in Scandinavia) see ART

720   UK
A S C MINI-FILE. 1911. a. £17. Standard Catalogue Information Services Ltd., Medway Wharf Rd., Tonbridge, Kent TN9 1QR, England. circ. 15,000.
Formerly: Architects Standard Catalogues (ISSN 0066-6181)

720   US   ISSN 0192-5067
A S L A MEMBERS HANDBOOK. a. $40 to non-members. American Society of Landscape Architects, 1733 Connecticut Ave., N.W., Washington, DC 20009. TEL 202-466-7730. adv. circ. 10,000.

720   FR   ISSN 0001-3994
ACADEMIE D'ARCHITECTURE. 1840. irreg. 80 F. Hotel de Chaulnes, 9 Place des Vosges, 75004 Paris, France. bk. rev. illus. stat. index. circ. 2,000.

720   FR   ISSN 0084-5876
ACADEMIE D'ARCHITECTURE, PARIS. ANNUAIRE.* irreg. free to members. Academie d'Architecture, 70 rue Amelot, 75005 Paris, France.

720 370.58   US
ACCREDITED PROGRAMS IN ARCHITECTURE; and first professional degrees conferred on completion of their curricula in architecture. 1940. a. free. National Architectural Accrediting Board, Inc., 1735 New York Ave. N. W., Washington, DC 20006. TEL 202-783-2007. Dir. John M. Wilson-Jeronimo. circ. 20,000.
Former titles (1972-74): Accredited Schools of Architecture; Until 1972: List of Accredited Schools of Architecture (ISSN 0077-3166)

720   IS   ISSN 0334-794X
ADRICHALUT. (Text in English and Hebrew) irreg. Association of Engineers and Architects in Israel, P.O. Box 3082, Tel Aviv, Israel. TEL 03-240274.

AMACADMY. see ART

AMERICAN ACADEMY IN ROME. MEMOIRS. see ART

720   US   ISSN 0272-0906
AMERICAN INSTITUTE OF ARCHITECTS. INTERNATIONAL DIRECTORY. 1981. irreg. Archimedia, Box 4403, Topeka, KS 66604.

720   SP
ANALES DE LA UNIVERSIDAD HISPALENSE. SERIE: ARQUITECTURA. irreg. price varies. Universidad de Sevilla, San Fernando 4, Seville, Spain.

720 913 690   UK
ANCIENT MONUMENTS SOCIETY TRANSACTIONS. 1924. a. £5. Ancient Monuments Society, St. Andrew-by-the-Wardrobe, Queen Victoria St., London EC4V 5DE, England. bk. rev. bibl. circ. 2,000. Indexed: Br.Hum.Ind. Br.Tech.Ind. Curr.Cont. Br.Archaeol.Abstr. Geo.Abstr.

720   IT
ANNALI DELL'ARCHITETTURA ITALIANA CONTEMPORANEA. 1985. a. Officina Edizioni, Passeggiata di Ripetta 25, 00186 Rome, Italy. Eds. Maristella Casciato, Giorgio Muratori.

720   MX
ANUARIO DE ARQUITECTURA MEXICANA. 1977. a. Instituto Nacional de Bellas Artes, Museo de Arte Moderno, Paseo de la Reforma y Gandhi, Chalpultepec, Mexico 5, D.F., Mexico.

720   UK   ISSN 0066-6092
ARCHIGRAM.* 1961. irreg., 1970, no.9. price varies. Archigram Group, 59, Aberdare Gardens, London N.W.6, England. Ed. Peter Cook. adv. bk. rev. circ. 6,000. Indexed: Avery Ind.Archit.Per.

720   UK
ARCHITECTS. a. £35. (Royal Institute of British Architects) R I B A Publications Ltd., Finsbury Mission, Moreland St., London EC1V 8VB, England.
Formerly: R I B A Directory of Practices.

720   SA
ARCHITECTS DIRECTORY. 1981. a. R.40. Institute of South African Architects, Professional Promotion Directorate, Box 3952, Cape Town 8000, South Africa. adv. circ. 6,000.

666.1
ARCHITECTS' GUIDE TO GLASS, METAL & GLAZING. 1972. a. $3. U S Glass Publications, Inc., 2701 Union Ave. Extended, Suite 410, Memphis, TN 38112-4479. TEL 901-452-6802. Ed. Felicia T. Stott. adv. bk. rev. charts. illus. stat. circ. 12,000. (back issues avail.)

720   US   ISSN 0066-6173
ARCHITECT'S HANDBOOK OF PROFESSIONAL PRACTICE. 1917. irreg., with supplements. $80 to non-members; members 55. American Institute of Architects, 1735 New York Avenue N.W., Washington, DC 20006. TEL 202-626-7300. circ. 7,800.

ARCHITECTURE

720   HU   ISSN 0066-6270
ARCHITECTURA. 1966. irreg. price varies. (Magyar Tudomanyos Akademia) Akademiai Kiado, Publishing House of the Hungarian Academy of Sciences, Box 24, H-1363 Budapest, Hungary. (Co-sponsor: Magyar Epitomuveszek Szovetsege) Indexed: Arts & Hum.Cit.Ind.

720   DK   ISSN 0106-3030
ARCHITECTURA; arkitekturhistorisk aarsskrift. 1979. a. Kr.128. Selskabet for Arkitekturhistorie, Soholm Park 1, DK-2900 Hellerup, Denmark. Ed. Esbjorn Hiort. Indexed: Br.Tech.Ind. Arts & Hum.Cit.Ind. RILA.

ARCHITECTURAL & BUILDING DIRECTORY OF INDIA. see *BUSINESS AND ECONOMICS — Trade And Industrial Directories*

720   UK
ARCHITECTURAL ANNUAL REVIEW. 1977. a. £14.95. Diplomatic & Consular Year Book International Ltd., 11/13 Cricklewood Lane, London NW2 1EJ, England. Ed. Kimberly O'Brien. adv. bk. rev. circ. 5,000.
     Formerly (until 1982): Architectural Association Annual Review (ISSN 0143-2796)

720   UK
ARCHITECTURAL HERITAGE SOCIETY OF SCOTLAND. JOURNAL AND ANNUAL REPORT. 1972. a. £2. Architectural Heritage Society of Scotland, 43b Manor Place, Edinburgh EH3 7EB, Scotland. Ed. Deborah Howard. adv. bk. rev. circ. 1,000. Indexed: RILA.
     Former titles: Scottish Georgian Society. Annual Report and Bulletin; (until 1981): Scottish Georgian Society. Annual Report; Which incorporated: Scottish Georgian Society. Bulletin.

720   UK   ISSN 0066-622X
ARCHITECTURAL HISTORY; journal of the Society of Architectural Historians of Great Britain. 1958. a. £12. Society of Architectural Historians of Great Britain, Rm. 208, Chesham House, 30 Warwick St., London W1R 6AB, England. Ed. Peter Draper. circ. 1,100. Indexed: Br.Hum.Ind. Br.Tech.Ind. Curr.Cont. Archit.Per.Ind. Arts & Hum.Cit.Ind. Avery Ind.Archit.Per. Br.Archaeol.Abstr. Ind.Bk.Rev.Hum. RILA.

720   US   ISSN 0570-6483
ARCHITECTURAL INDEX. 1949. a. price varies. Box 1168, Boulder, CO 80306. TEL 303-449-3748. Eds. Ervin J. Bell, Mary Ellen Brennan. circ. 4,000. (back issues avail.)

720   UK
ARCHITECTURAL MONOGRAPHS. (Text in English; summaries in French, German, Italian and Spanish) 1978. irreg. £45($85) to individuals; students £39.50 ($65) (for four issues) A.D. Editions Ltd., 42 Leinster Gardens, London W2 3AN, England. Ed. Dr. Andreas C. Papadakis. adv. circ. 12,000. (back issues avail.) Indexed: Curr.Cont. Arts & Hum.Cit.Ind.

720   UK
ARCHITECTURAL SERVICES BOOKS OF PLANS. 1969. a. £4. Plan Magazines Ltd., 45 Station Rd., Redhill, Surrey, England. Ed. John Bailey. circ. 40,000.

720   US
ARCHITECTURE AND URBAN DESIGN. irreg., vol.16, 1986. U M I Research Press, 300 N. Zeeb Rd., Ann Arbor, MI 48106. Ed. Stephen Foster.

720   GR   ISSN 0066-6262
ARCHITECTURE IN GREECE/ ARCHITECTONIKA THEMATA. (Text in English and Greek) 1967. a. $25. Orestis B. Doumanis, Ed. & Pub., P.O. Box 3545, GR-102 10 Athens, Greece. adv. bk. rev. index. circ. 5,000. (back issues avail.)

720.7   US   ISSN 0092-7856
ARCHITECTURE SCHOOLS IN NORTH AMERICA. 1947. irreg. (approx. biennial) $12.95. Association of Collegiate Schools of Architecture, 1735 New York Ave., N.W., Washington, DC 20006 TEL 202-785-2324. (And Peterson's Guides, Inc., 228 Alexander St., Princeton, NJ 08540) Ed. Richard E. McCommons. (reprint service avail. from UMI)
     Incorporating: A C S A Faculty Directory.

720   GW
ARCHITEKTENHANDBUCH SCHLESWIG-HOLSTEIN. 1977. a. DM.95. Christians & Reim Verlag GmbH, Dammtorstr. 30, Postfach 302824, D-2000 Hamburg 36, W. Germany (B.R.D.) index. (back issues avail.)

720   GW
ARCHITEKTENKAMMER NIEDERSACHSEN. 1977. a. DM.95. Christians & Reim Verlag GmbH, Dammtorstr. 30, Postfach 302824, D-2000 Hamburg 36, W. Germany (B.R.D.) index. (back issues avail.)

720   IT
ARCHITETTURA URBANISTICA: METODI DI PROGRAMMAZIONE E PROGETTI. 1975. irreg., no.5, 1978. price varies. Giardini Editori e Stampatori, Via Santa Bibbiana 28, 56100 Pisa, Italy. Ed. Giacomo Donato.

ARTS ASIATIQUES. see *ART*

720   US   ISSN 0194-410X
ASSOCIATION OF COLLEGIATE SCHOOLS OF ARCHITECTURE. PROCEEDINGS OF THE ANNUAL MEETING. 1979. a. $20 softcover. Association of Collegiate Schools of Architecture, 1735 New York Ave., N.W., Washington, DC 20006. TEL 202-785-2324. (also avail. in microform from UMI) Key Title: Proceedings of the A C S A Annual Meeting.

720   IT
ASSOCIAZIONE PER L'ARCHEOLOGIA INDUSTRIALE. BOLLETINO. 1980. irreg. free. Associazione per l'Archeologia Industriale, Centro Documentaz. per il Mezzogiorno, Via Generale Parisi, 24, 80132 Naples, Italy. (back issues avail.)

720 900 572   GW
BAUERNHAEUSER AUS MITTELEUROPA; Aufmasse und Publikationen von Gerhard Eitzen. 1984. irreg. DM.25. Arbeitskreis fuer Hausforschung e.V., Nachtigallental, 6553 Sobernheim/Nahe, W. Germany (B.R.D.)

BEFORE YOU BUILD. see *BUILDING AND CONSTRUCTION*

722   BE   ISSN 0522-7496
BELGIUM. COMMISSION ROYALE DES MONUMENTS ET DES SITES. BULLETIN. 1950. N.S. 1970/71. a., vol.7, 1978. price varies. Commission Royale des Monuments et des Sites, Rue Joseph II, 30, B-1040 Brussels, Belgium.
     Formerly: Commissions Royales d'Art et d'Archeologie. Bulletin.

BIBLIOTECA MARSILIO: ARCHITETTURA E URBANISTICA. see *HOUSING AND URBAN PLANNING*

BRITISH ARCHAEOLOGICAL ASSOCIATION. CONFERENCE TRANSACTIONS. see *ARCHAEOLOGY*

721   FI
BYGDESERIEN. (Text in Swedish) 1979. a. Aalands Folkminnesfoerbund, Aalands Museum, Obbergsvaegen 1, SF-22101 Mariehamn, Finland.

720   US
CALIFORNIA ARCHITECTURE AND ARCHITECTS. 1980. irreg., no.6, 1986. price varies. Hennessey & Ingalls, Inc., 8321 Campion Dr., Los Angeles, CA 90045. TEL 213-458-9074. Ed. David Gebhard.

CAMBRIDGE URBAN AND ARCHITECTURAL STUDIES. see *HOUSING AND URBAN PLANNING*

720   IT
CENTRO INTERNAZIONALE DI STUDI DI ARCHITETTURA ANDREA PALLADIO. 1959. a. price varies. Basilica Palladiana, Domus Comestabilis, C.P. 593, 36100 Vicenza, Italy. Ed.Bd. Indexed: RILA.

CERCLE HUTOIS DES SCIENCES ET BEAUX-ARTS. ANNALES. see *HISTORY — History Of Europe*

724   US
CHICAGO ARCHITECTURAL JOURNAL. 1981. a. $15. (Chicago Architectural Club) Rizzoli International Publications Inc., 597 5th Ave., New York, NY 10017. illus. circ. 3,000. Indexed: Br.Tech.Ind.

720   UK   ISSN 0268-7518
CHURCH MONUMENTS. 1979. a. £5 to individuals; institutions £6.50. Church Monuments Society, 15 Charlbury Rd., Oxford OX2 6UT, England (Subscr. to: Ms. M. Coghlan, Hon. Membership Secy., 4 Cherrey St., Pinner, Middx. HA5 2TE, England) Ed.Bd. adv. bk. rev. circ. 400.
     Supersedes: International Society for the Study of Church Monuments. Bulletin (ISSN 0143-4128)

726 704.948   UK   ISSN 0262-4966
CHURCHSCAPE. 1981. a. £1.95. Council for the Care of Churches, 83 London Wall, London EC2M 5NA, England. Ed. David Williams. adv. bk. rev. bibl. illus. circ. 1,100.

690 712   UK
CIVIC TRUST AWARDS. 1959. a. £3. Civic Trust, 17 Carlton House Terrace, London SW1Y 5AW, England. Ed.Bd. (back issues avail.)

720 700   US   ISSN 0009-871X
CLEMSON UNIVERSITY. COLLEGE OF ARCHITECTURE. SEMESTER REVIEW; a journal of educational thought. 1967. a. $6. Clemson University, Clemson Architectural Foundation, Clemson, SC 29631. TEL 803-656-3081. Ed. D.L. Collins. charts. illus. stat. circ. 1,200.

720   SP
COLECCION ARQUITECTURA/PERSPECTIVAS. irreg. Editorial Gustavo Gili, S.A., Rosellon 87-89, Apdo. de Correos 35.149, Barcelona 29, Spain.

720   SP
COLECCION ARQUITECTURA Y CRITICA. irreg. Editorial Gustavo Gili, S.A., Rosellon 87-89, Apdo. de Correos 35.149, Barcelona 29, Spain.

COLECCION CIENCIA URBANISTICA. see *HOUSING AND URBAN PLANNING*

720   SP   ISSN 0071-1632
COLECCION ESTRUCTURAS Y FORMAS. irreg. Editorial Gustavo Gili, S.A., Rosellon 87-89, Barcelona 15, Spain.
     Formerly: Estructuras y Formas.

720   SP   ISSN 0082-2701
COLECCION TEMAS DE ARQUITECTURA ACTUAL. irreg. Editorial Gustavo Gili, S.A., Rosellon 87-89, Barcelona 15, Spain.

720   SA
COLIMPEX ARCHITECT'S EXECUPAD. (Text in Afrikaans and English) a. Colimpex Africa (Pty) Ltd., P.O. Box 889, Wendywood 2144, South Africa. adv.

712   US
COLLOQUIUM ON THE HISTORY OF LANDSCAPE ARCHITECTURE. PAPERS. 1972. irreg., vol.9, 1986. price varies. (Studies in Landscape Architecture) Dumbarton Oaks, Research Library and Collection, 1703 32nd St. N.W., Washington, DC 20007. TEL 202-342-3259. Ed. Elisabeth MacDougall. circ. 1,150.

COMMISSION DEPARTEMENTALE D'HISTOIRE ET D'ARCHEOLOGIE. BULLETIN. see *ARCHAEOLOGY*

720 690   UK
CONSTRUCTION HISTORY. 1985. biennial. £6 to non-members. Chartered Institute of Building, Englemere, King's Ride, Ascot, Berks. SL5 8BJ, England. Ed. Mark Swenarton. abstr. (back issues avail.)

720   US
CONTEMPORARY ARCHITECTS. 1980. quinquennial. St. Martin's Press, Scholarly and Reference Division, 175 Fifth Ave., New York, NY 10010. TEL 212-674-5151. Ed. Muriel Emanuel.

CORDELL'S WHO'S WHO IN DESIGN SPECIFYING. see *BUILDING AND CONSTRUCTION*

ARCHITECTURE

720　　　　　　　US　ISSN 0070-038X
CORPUS PALLADIANUM. 1968. irreg. $56. Pennsylvania State University Press, 215 Wagner Bldg., University Park, PA 16802. TEL 814-865-1327. (reprint service avail. from UMI)

COURTAULD INSTITUTE ILLUSTRATION ARCHIVES. ARCHIVE 1. see *ART*

720　　　　　　　SI　ISSN 0217-7706
CREATIVE HOMES. 1985. a. S.8 per no. Times Periodicals Private Ltd., 1 New Industrial Road, Singapore 1953, Singapore. adv. illus. circ. 20,000.

720　　　　　　　UK
DAILY MAIL BOOK OF HOME PLANS. 1954. a. £2.95. Plan Magazines, 45 Station Rd., Redhill, Surrey, England. Ed. John M. Bailey. adv. circ. 60,000.

DEHIO: HANDBUCH DER DEUTSCHEN KUNSTDENKMAELER. see *ART*

720　745　　　　　GR
DESIGN AND ART IN GREECE/THEMATA CHOROU & TECHNON. (Text in English and Greek) 1970. a. $25. Orestis B. Doumanis, Ed.& Pub., P.O. Box 3545, GR-102 10 Athens, Greece. adv. index. circ. 5,000. (back issues avail.)
　　Formerly: Design in Greece (ISSN 0074-1191)

DESIGNERS WEST RESOURCE DIRECTORY. see *INTERIOR DESIGN AND DECORATION*

725　658　　　　　US　ISSN 0192-2297
DIRECTORY OF ARCHITECTS FOR HEALTH FACILITIES. 1975. irreg. $30 to non-members; members $24. American Hospital Association, 840 North Lake Shore Dr., Chicago, IL 60611. TEL 312-280-6000.

720　　　　　　　UK
DIRECTORY OF OFFICIAL ARCHITECTURE AND PLANNING. 1956. biennial. £30. Longman Group Ltd., Fourth Ave., Harlow, Essex CM19 5AA, England.
　　Formerly: Directory of Official Architects and Planners (ISSN 0070-5977)

DISCOVERY (RICHMOND) see *HISTORY*

720　　　　　　　UK　ISSN 0307-1634
E A A REVIEW. 1957. a. £10 to non-members. ‡ (Edinburgh Architectural Association) Edinburgh Pictorial Ltd., Smith's Place House, Edinburgh 6, Scotland. Ed. Roger Taylor. adv. circ. 1,200.
　　Formerly: Edinburgh Architectural Association E A A Yearbook.

720　　　　　　　UK　ISSN 0140-5039
E A R. (Edinburgh Architecture Research) 1973. a. £3. University of Edinburgh, Department of Architecture, c/o Prof. C.B. Wilson, 20 Chambers St., Edinburgh EH1 1JZ, Scotland. circ. 250. Indexed: Br.Tech.Ind.

720　155　　　　　US
ENVIRONMENTAL DESIGN RESEARCH ASSOCIATION. ANNUAL CONFERENCE PROCEEDINGS. Short title: E D R A. Annual Conference Proceedings. (Each issue has a distinctive title) 1969. a. $35 to non-members; members $30. Environmental Design Research Association, L'Enfant Plaza Sta., Box 23129, Washington, DC 20024. TEL 301-657-2651. Ed.Bd. circ. 900. (back issues avail.; reprint service avail.) Indexed: Psychol.Abstr. Psychol.Abstr. Soc.Sci.Ind.

720　　　　　　　UK
FACULTY OF ARCHITECTS & SURVEYORS DIARY. a. (Faculty of Architects & Surveyors) Welbecson Ltd., Strawberry Street, Hull, Humberside, HU9 1EX, England.

943　　　　　　　AU
FUNDBERICHTE AUS OESTERREICH. vol.12, 1973. a. price varies. Bundesdenkmalamt, Abteilung fuer Bodendenkmalpflege, Saeulenstiege, Hofburg, A-1010 Vienna, Austria. Ed. Horst Adler. charts. illus. Indexed: Br.Archaeol.Abstr. Numis.Lit.

720　　　　　　　JA
G A DOCUMENT. (Global Architecture) irreg. 2900 Yen. A.D.A. Edita Tokyo Co. Ltd., 3-12-14 Sendagaya, Shibuya-ku, Tokyo, Japan. Ed. Yukio Futagawa. (back issues avail.) Indexed: Br.Tech.Ind.

724　　　　　　　JA
G A/GLOBAL ARCHITECTURE. irreg. $14.95. A.D.A. Edita Tokyo Co., Ltd, 3-12-14 Sendagaya, Shibuya-ku, Tokyo, Japan. illus. (back issues avail.)

728　352.7　　　　JA
G A HOUSES. (Global Architecture) irreg. $22.50. A.D.A. Edita Tokyo Co., Ltd., 3-12-14 Sendagaya, Shibuya-Ku, Tokyo, Japan. Ed. Yukio Futagawa. illus. Indexed: Br.Tech.Ind.

GENTSE BIJDRAGEN TOT DE KUNSTGESCHIEDENIS. see *ART*

GOTHENBURG STUDIES IN ART AND ARCHITECTURE. see *ART*

720　　　　　　　US　ISSN 0194-3650
HARVARD ARCHITECTURE REVIEW. 1980. a. $25. Rizzoli International Publications, Inc., 597 Fifth Ave., New York, NY 10017. TEL 212-223-0100. illus. (also avail. in microform from UMI; reprint service avail. from UMI) Indexed: Br.Tech.Ind.

HISTORIC GUELPH; the royal city. see *HISTORY* — *History Of North And South America*

720　　　　　　　US
HISTORY OF WORLD ARCHITECTURE. irreg. $45. Harry N. Abrams, Inc., 100 Fifth Ave., New York, NY 10011. TEL 212-206-7715.

720　690　　　　　HK
HONG KONG ARCHITECTS & DESIGNERS CATALOGUE. 1976. a. HK.$100. Far East Trade Press Ltd., 15/F Lockhart Centre, 301 Lockhart Road, Hong Kong, Hong Kong. adv. circ. 5,700.

720　　　　　　　US　ISSN 0073-3571
HOUSE BEAUTIFUL'S HOUSES AND PLANS. 1957. a. $2.95. Hearst Magazines, House Beautiful Home Interest Group (Subsidiary of: Hearst Corporation) 1700 Broadway, New York, NY 10019. TEL 212-903-5100. Ed. Gordon Firth. circ. 175,000.

920　　　　　　　II　ISSN 0256-4017
INDIAN ARCHITECTS DIRECTORY. 1969. biennial. Rs.150. Architects Publishing Corp. of India, 51 Sujata, Rani Sati Marg, Malad East, Bombay 400097, India. Ed. A.K. Gupta. adv. circ. 3,000.
　　Formerly: All India Architects Directory (ISSN 0587-4793)

721　　　　　　　YU
INSTITUT ZA ARHITEKTURU I URBANIZAM SRBIJE. ZBORNIK RADOVA. vol.7, 1975. a. Institut za Arhitekturu i Urbanizam Srbije, Bulevar Revolucije 73/II, Belgrade, Yugoslavia. Ed. N. Pejovic. charts. illus. tr.lit.

720　　　　　　　FR　ISSN 0075-0018
INVENTAIRE GENERAL DES MONUMENTS ET DES RICHESSES ARTISTIQUES DE LA FRANCE. 1969. irreg. price varies. (Ministere des Affaires Culturelles) Imprimerie Nationale, Service es Ventes, 59128 Flers en Escrebieux, France.

720　　　　　　　IE　ISSN 0021-1206
IRISH GEORGIAN SOCIETY. BULLETIN. 1958. a. $15. Irish Georgian Society, Leixlip Castle, Leixlip, Co. Kildare, Ireland. Ed. Desmond Guinness. adv. bk. rev. illus. index. circ. 5,000. (also avail. in microform from UMI; reprint service avail. from UMI) Indexed: Br.Tech.Ind. RILA.

ISLAMIC ART AND ARCHITECTURE. see *ART*

720　　　　　　　IT
ISTITUTO DI STORIA DELL'ARCHITETTURA. QUADERNI. 1953. a. (Universita di Roma, Istituto di Storia dell'Architettura) Multigrafica Editrice, Viale Quattro Venti 52/A, 00152 Rome, Italy. (back issues avail.)

720　　　　　　　FR　ISSN 0183-5742
L'IVRE DE PIERRES. 1977. irreg. Presses Universitaires de France, Champ Vallon, 01420 Seyssel, France.

720　700　　　　　YU
IZ STAROG I NOVOG ZAGREBA. (Text in Serbo-Croatian; summaries in German) 1957. quadrennial. 800 din.($3) per issue. Muzej Grada Zagreba, Opaticka 20, 41000 Zagreb, Yugoslavia. charts. illus. circ. 1,000.

720　700　690　352.7　GW
KUNST AM BAU. 1979. irreg. (3-4/yr.) DM.9. Berufsverband Bildender Kunstler Berlins, Koethener Str. 44, D-1000 Berlin 61, W. Germany (B.R.D.) Ed.Bd. adv. bk. rev.

720　　　　　　　GW
LANDESKONSERVATOR RHEINLAND. ARBEITSHEFT. 1971. irreg., no.36, 1982. price varies. (Kultusministerium, Landeskonservator Rheinland) Rheinland-Verlag, Kennedy-Ufer 2, 5000 Cologne 21, W. Germany (B.R.D.) (Distr. by: Rudolf Habelt Verlag GmbH, Am Buchenhang 1, 5300 Bonn, W. Germany (B.R.D.))

720　　　　　　　US　ISSN 0195-5764
LANDSCAPE ARCHITECTURE TECHNICAL INFORMATION SERIES. Short title: L A T I S. 1978. irreg. $15 to non-members. American Society of Landscape Architects, 1733 Connecticut Ave., N.W., Washington, DC 20009. TEL 202-466-7730. circ. 10,000.

LANDSCAPE HISTORY. see *HISTORY* — *History Of Europe*

720　690　　　　　CN　ISSN 0315-8756
LOG HOUSE. 1974. a. Can.$6. Log House Publishing Co. Ltd., P.O. Box 1205, Prince George, B. C. V2L 4V3, Canada. Ed. Mary Mackie. bk. rev. circ. 15,000. (back issues avail.)
　　Formerly: Canadian Log House.

725　　　　　　　US
MANHATTAN OFFICE BUILDINGS: DOWNTOWN. a. Yale Robbins, Inc., 31 E. 28 St., New York, NY 10016. TEL 212-683-5700. Ed. Yale Robbins.

725　　　　　　　US
MANHATTAN OFFICE BUILDINGS: MIDTOWN. a. Yale Robbins, Inc., 31 E. 28 St., New York, NY 10016. TEL 212-683-5700. Ed. Yale Robbins.

725　　　　　　　US
MANHATTAN OFFICE BUILDINGS: MIDTOWN SOUTH. a. Yale Robbins, Inc., 31 E. 28th St., New York, NY 10016. TEL 212-683-5700.

MARQUEE. see *THEATER*

725　　　　　　　US
MASTERGUIDE. 1985. a. PacTel Publishing, 1600 S. Main St., Ste.290, Walnut Creek, CA 94704. TEL 415-932-6300. adv. circ. 113,000.

720　700　　　　　BE
MELANGES D'HISTOIRE DE L'ARCHITECTURE. 1973. irreg. price varies. Universite Catholique de Louvain, Institut Superieur d'Archeologie et d'Histoire de l'Art, 1 place Blaise Pascal, 1348 Louvain-la-Neuve, Belgium.

720　　　　　　　US
MISSISSIPPI. STATE BOARD OF ARCHITECTURE. ANNUAL REPORT. a. Board of Architecture, Box 16273, Jackson, MS 39206. TEL 601-981-2961.

720　　　　　　　AU　ISSN 0026-8607
DAS MODERNE HEIM; mit der "Internationalen Bauchronik". (Text in English, French and German) 1950. a. S.100. Oskar Riedel, Ed.& Pub., Schottenring 28, A-1010 Vienna, Austria. adv. illus. index. circ. 10,000.

712　　　　　　　US　ISSN 0272-247X
NATIONAL DIRECTORY OF LANDSCAPE ARCHITECTURE FIRMS. biennial. $10 to non-members. American Society of Landscape Architects, 1733 Connecticut Ave., NW, Washington, DC 20009. TEL 202-466-7730.

720.9　　　　　　US　ISSN 0077-474X
NATIONAL INSTITUTE FOR ARCHITECTURAL EDUCATION. YEARBOOK.* 1964. a. $15. National Institute for Architectural Education, 30 W. 22nd St., New York, NY 10010. TEL 212-924-7000. circ. 200.
　　Formerly: National Institute for Architectural Education. Bulletin.

ARCHITECTURE

720 US
NATIONAL TRUST FOR HISTORIC PRESERVATION. INFORMATION. 1976. irreg., no.36, 1984. National Trust for Historic Preservation, 1785 Massachusetts Ave., N.W., Washington, DC 20036. TEL 202-673-4000. (back issues avail.)

725 NE
NETHERLANDS. RIJKSDIENST VOOR DE MONUMENTENZORG. JAARVERSLAG. 1974. a. fl.12.50. Rijksdienst voor de Monumentenzorg, Broederplein 41, Zeist, Netherlands. Ed. A.P. Smaal. illus. circ. 3,000.

720 NO ISSN 0332-6578
NORSKE ARKITEKTKONKURRANSER. Enclosed in: Arkitektnytt (ISSN 0004-1998) 1953. irreg. Kr.175 includes Arkitektnytt. Norske Arkitekters Landsforbund - Norwegian Architects' League, Josefinesgt. 34, Oslo 3, Norway. Ed. Annemor Meinstad. illus. index.
Competition results.

720 US ISSN 0078-1444
NORTH CAROLINA STATE UNIVERSITY. SCHOOL OF DESIGN. (STUDENT PUBLICATION MAGAZINE) 1951. irreg; vol.29, 1986. price varies. North Carolina State University, School of Design, Raleigh, NC 27695-7701. TEL 919-737-2202. adv. bk. rev. circ. 1,000. Indexed: Br.Tech.Ind.

720 690 SZ
OEFFENTLICHE BAUMAPPE DER OSTSCHWEIZ. a. 12 Fr. Fachpresse Goldach, Hudson & Co., CH-9403 Goldach, Switzerland. Ed. Willi Muller. adv. charts.

OLD-HOUSE JOURNAL CATALOG. see *BUILDING AND CONSTRUCTION*

720 HU ISSN 0073-4063
ORSZAGOS MUEMLEKI FELUGYELOSEG. KIADVANYOK. (Text in Hungarian; summaries in German) 1960. irreg., no.8, 1977. price varies. (Orszagos Muemlekvedelmi Bizottsag) Akademiai Kiado, Publishing House of the Hungarian Academy of Sciences, P.O. Box 24, H-1363 Budapest, Hungary.

OXONIENSIA. see *ARCHAEOLOGY*

P & T. (Produtos e Tecnicas) see *BUILDING AND CONSTRUCTION*

720 AT ISSN 0158-7374
PERIOD BUILDING RESTORATION TRADES & SUPPLIERS DIRECTORY. 1980. a. Aus.$4.50. Mount Eagle Publications, P.O. Box 84, Heidelberg, Vic. 3084, Australia. Ed. Kennith Lloyd Jones. adv. circ. 10,000.

720 US ISSN 0079-0958
PERSPECTA; THE YALE ARCHITECTURAL JOURNAL.* 1951. a. $30 to individuals; institutions $40. Rizzoli International Publications, 597 Fifth Ave., New York, NY 10017. (also avail. in microfilm from UMI; reprint service avail. from ISI,UMI) Indexed: Curr.Cont. Arts & Hum.Cit.Ind.

720 UK
PLANAHOME BOOK OF HOME PLANS. a. £5. Plan Magazines Ltd., 45 Station Road, Redhill Surrey, England. Ed. John Bailey.

720 PL
POLITECHNIKA GDANSKA. RAPORT. WYDZIAL ARCHITEKTURY. 1982. a. price varies. Politechnika Gdanska, Ul. Majakowskiego 11/12, 80-952 Gdansk 6, Poland.

720 PL ISSN 0518-3138
POLITECHNIKA GDANSKA. ZESZYTY NAUKOWE. ARCHITEKTURA. (Text in Polish; summaries in English and Russian) 1958. irreg. price varies. Politechnika Gdanska, Majakowskiego 11/12, 81-952 Gdansk 6, Poland (Dist. by: Osrodek Rozpowszechniania Wydawnictw Naukowych Pan, Palac Kultury i Nauki, 00-901 Warsaw, Poland)

720 PL ISSN 0137-1371
POLITECHNIKA KRAKOWSKA. ZESZYTY NAUKOWE. ARCHITEKTURA. (Text in Polish; summaries in English, French, German, Russian) 1956. irreg. price varies. Politechnika Krakowska, Ul. Warszawska 24, 31-155 Krakow, Poland (Dist. by: Ars Polona-Ruch, Krakowskie Przedmiescie 7, 00-068 Warsaw, Poland) bibl. charts. illus. circ. 200.

720 700 PL ISSN 0137-6233
POLITECHNIKA WROCLAWSKA. INSTYTUT ARCHITEKTURY I URBANISTYKI. PRACE NAUKOWE. KONFERENCJE. 1977. irreg., no.4, 1984. price varies. Politechnika Wroclawska, Wybrzeze Wyspianskiego 27, 50-370 Wroclaw, Poland (Dist. by: Ars Polona-Ruch, Krakowskie Przedmiescie 7, Warsaw, Poland) Ed. Jerzy Ciekot.

720 700 PL ISSN 0324-9905
POLITECHNIKA WROCLAWSKA. INSTYTUT ARCHITEKTURY I URBANISTYKI. PRACE NAUKOWE. MONOGRAFIE. (Text in Polish; summaries in English and Russian) 1969. irreg., no.11, 1985. price varies. Politechnika Wroclawska, Wybrzeze Wyspianskiego 27, 50-370 Wroclaw, Poland (Dist. by: Ars Polona-Ruch, Krakowskie Przedmiescie 7, Warsaw, Poland) Ed. Jerzy Ciekot.

720 700 PL ISSN 0324-9891
POLITECHNIKA WROCLAWSKA. INSTYTUT ARCHITEKTURY I URBANISTYKI. PRACE NAUKOWE. STUDIA I MATERIALY. (Text in Polish; summaries in English and Russian) 1971. irreg., no.5, 1979. price varies. Politechnika Wroclawska, Wybrzeze Wyspianskiego 27, 50-370 Wroclaw, Poland (Dist. by: Ars Polona-Ruch, Krakowskie Przedmiescie 7, Warsaw, Poland) Ed. Marian Kloza.

POLITECHNIKA WROCLAWSKA. INSTYTUT HISTORII ARCHITEKTURY, SZTUKI I TECHNIKI. PRACE NAUKOWE. KONFERENCJE. see *ART*

POLITECHNIKA WROCLAWSKA. INSTYTUT HISTORII ARCHITEKTURY, SZTUKI I TECHNIKI. PRACE NAUKOWE. MONOGRAFIE. see *ART*

POLITECHNIKA WROCLAWSKA. INSTYTUT HISTORII ARCHITEKTURY, SZTUKI I TECHNIKI. PRACE NAUKOWE. STUDIA I MATERIALY. see *ART*

711 720 PL ISSN 0079-3450
POLSKA AKADEMIA NAUK. ODDZIAL W KRAKOWIE. KOMISJA URBANISTYKI I ARCHITEKTURY. TEKA. (Text in Polish; summaries in English and Russian) 1967. a. price varies. Ossolineum, Publishing House of the Polish Academy of Sciences, Rynek 9, 50-106 Wroclaw, Poland (Dist. by Ars Polona-Ruch, Krakowskie Przedmiescie 7, Warsaw, Poland) Ed. Janusz Bogdanowski.

720 US
PRINCETON JOURNAL: STUDIES IN THEMATIC ARCHITECTURE.* 1983. biennial. $18. (Princeton University, School of Architecture) Princeton Architectural Press, 2 Research Way, Princeton, NJ 08540-6628. Ed. Taisto Makela. circ. 2,000. (back issues avail.)

720 US ISSN 0190-8766
PROFILE; official directory of the American Institute of Architects. 1978. biennial. $110 hardcover to non-members, members $99. (American Institute of Architects) Archimedia, Box 4403, Topeka, KS 66614. TEL 913-267-5433. Ed. Henry W. Schirmer. circ. 4,000.

720 AT ISSN 0818-1233
R A I A MEMO. 1984. irreg. membership. Royal Australian Institute of Architects, National Headquarters, 2A Mugga Way, Red Hill, A.C.T. 2603, Australia. Ed. Simon Johnstone. circ. 6,500.
Formerly: R A I A News.

720 IE
R I A I ARCHITECTS YEARBOOK. 1909. a. £5. (Royal Institute of the Architects of Ireland) Clavis Press, 33 Priory Drive, Stillorgan, Co. Dublin, Ireland. Ed. Brendan Millar. adv. bk. rev. index. circ. 1,100.
Formerly: Royal Institute of the Architects of Ireland. Yearbook (ISSN 0080-4444)

720 UK
REGISTER OF ARCHITECTS. 1932. a. Architects' Registration Council, 73 Hallam St., London W1N 6EE, England.

720.5 CN ISSN 0705-1913
REVIEW OF ARCHITECTURE AND LANDSCAPE ARCHITECTURE. 1977. irreg. c/o Irving Grossman, Alumni Association, Faculty of Architecture and Landscape Architecture, 9 Sultan St., Toronto, Ont. M5S 1L6, Canada. TEL 416-978-2011. circ. 2,000.

720 US
REVISIONS: PAPERS IN ARCHITECTURAL THEORY. 1985. biennial. $15. Princeton Architectural Press, 40 Witherspoon St., Princeton, NJ 08540. TEL 609-924-7911. Ed. Beatriz Colomina. circ. 3,000.

720 LU
REVUE FORMES NOUVELLES/NEUE FORMEN/ NEW FORMS. (Text in English, French and German) 1952. irreg. 20 rue des Trevires, Luxembourg, Luxembourg. Ed. J.A. Schmit. adv. circ. 4,500.

720 IT ISSN 0080-2964
RICERCHE SULLE DIMORE RURALI IN ITALIA. 1938. irreg., no.30, 1973. price varies. (Consiglio Nazionale delle Ricerche) Casa Editrice Leo S. Olschki, Casella Postale 66, 50100 Florence, Italy. Eds. Lucio Gambi, Giuseppe Barbieri. circ. 1,000.

720 IE ISSN 0080-472X
ROYAL SOCIETY OF ULSTER ARCHITECTS. YEAR BOOK. 1928. a. free to members. Nicholson and Bass Ltd, 3 Clarence St. W., Belfast BT2 7GP, Ireland. Ed.Bd. adv. circ. 1,000.

720 SI ISSN 0217-7668
S I A YEARBOOK. 1967. a. S.35. Singapore Institute of Architects, Publications Board, Block 23, Outram Park 02-393/397, Singapore 0316, Singapore. adv. circ. 1,700.

SASKATCHEWAN. DEPARTMENT OF CULTURE AND RECREATION. ANNUAL REPORT. see *ART*

SOUTH INDIAN ART AND ARCHAEOLOGICAL SERIES. see *ART*

SPON'S ARCHITECTS' & BUILDERS' PRICE BOOK. see *BUILDING AND CONSTRUCTION*

720 CE
SRI LANKA INSTITUTE OF ARCHITECTS. JOURNAL. a. Sri Lanka Institute of Architects, 50 Rosmead Pl., Colombo 7, Sri Lanka.

SRPSKA AKADEMIJA NAUKA I UMETNOSTI. ODELJENJE DRUSTVENIH NAUKA. SPOMENIK. see *SOCIAL SCIENCES: COMPREHENSIVE WORKS*

720 IT
STORIA ARCHITETTURA; rivista di architettura e restauro. 1974. a. (Universita di Roma, Istituto di Storia dell'Architettura) Multigrafica Editrice, Viale Quattro Venti 52/A, 00152 Rome, Italy. Indexed: RILA. RILA.

720 IT ISSN 0081-6140
STUDI D'ARCHITETTURA ANTICA. 1966. irreg., no.5, 1971. price varies. Erma di "Bretschneider", Via Cassiodoro, 19, 00193 Rome, Italy.

711 720 PL ISSN 0081-6566
STUDIA I MATERIALY DO TEORII I HISTORII ARCHITEKTURY I URBANISTYKI. (Text in Polish; summaries in English and Russian) 1959. irreg., no.9, 1971. price varies. (Polska Akademia Nauk) Panstwowe Wydawnictwo Naukowe, Miodowa 10, 00-251 Warsaw, Poland (Dist. by: Ars Polona, Krakowskie Przedmiescie 7, 00-068 Warsaw, Poland)

STUDIES IN CISTERCIAN ART AND ARCHITECTURE. see *ART*

ARCHITECTURE — ABSTRACTING, BIBLIOGRAPHIES, STATISTICS

720   CN
TECHNICAL UNIVERSITY OF NOVA SCOTIA. SCHOOL OF ARCHITECTURE. REPORT SERIES. 1970. irreg., no.45, 1981. price varies. ‡ Technical University of Nova Scotia, Faculty of Architecture, Box 1000, Halifax, N.S. B3J 2X4, Canada. TEL 902-429-8300. Ed. Peter Manning. circ. 1,000.
    Formerly: Nova Scotia Technical College. School of Architecture. Report Series (ISSN 0078-2491)

720   700   US
THRESHOLD. a. $15. University of Illinois at Chicago, School of Architecture, Office of Publication Services (M-C 291), Box 4348, Chicago, IL 60680. illus.

724   UK   ISSN 0260-4116
TRADITIONAL KENT BUILDINGS; studies by students at the School of Architecture, Canterbury College of Art. 1980. irreg. £1.50. Kent County Council Education Committee, School of Architecture, Canterbury College of Art, New Dover Rd., Canterbury, England. Ed. Jane Wade. illus. circ. 1,500. Indexed: Br.Tech.Ind.

720   IT   ISSN 0082-6006
TRATTATI DI ARCHITETTURA. 1966. irreg., latest 1985. price varies. Edizioni Il Polifilo, Via Borgonuovo 2, 20121 Milan, Italy.

720   IS   ISSN 0041-4549
TVAI; periodical for architecture, town planning, industrial design & the plastic arts. (Text in Hebrew; summaries in English) 1966. a. $5 per no. T V A I, 27, Shlomo Hamelech St., Tel-Aviv, Israel. Ed. Aba Elhanani. adv. bk. rev. illus. circ. 1,500.

720   SP   ISSN 0580-6712
UNIVERSIDAD DE MURCIA. MONTEAGUDO. 1953. irreg., vol.2, 1986. ($350) Universidad de Murcia, Secretariado de Publicaciones e Intercambio Cientifico, Santo Cristo, 1, 30001 Murcia, Spain. TEL 968 24 92 00.

720   SP   ISSN 0078-8732
UNIVERSIDAD DE NAVARRA. ESCUELA DE ARQUITECTURA. COLECCION DE ARQUITECTURA. 1971. irreg., no.13, 1986. price varies. Ediciones Universidad de Navarra, S.A., Apdo. 396, 31080 Pamplona, Spain.
    Formerly: Universidad de Navarra. Escuela de Arquitectura. Manuales: Arquitectura.

720   IT
UNIVERSITA DEGLI STUDI DI GENOVA. ISTITUTO DI PROGETTAZIONE ARCHITETTONICA. QUADERNO.* 1968. irreg. L.10500 per issue. Universita degli Studi di Genova, Istituto di Progettazione Architettonica, Via Opera Pia Cousa 11, Genoa 16145, Italy. illus.

720   UK   ISSN 0070-8992
UNIVERSITY OF EDINBURGH. ARCHITECTURE RESEARCH UNIT. REPORT. 1966. irreg. price varies. University of Edinburgh, Architecture Research Unit, 55 George Sq., Edinburgh EH8 9JU, Scotland.

720   690   UK   ISSN 0143-7283
UNIVERSITY OF STRATHCLYDE. DEPARTMENT OF ARCHITECTURE & BUILDING SCIENCE. RESEARCH BULLETIN. 1970. biennial. £5.00. University of Strathclyde, Department of Architecture & Building Science, 131 Rottenrow, Glasgow G4 0NG, Scotland. Ed. Michael Munday. circ. 400.

UNIVERSITY OF TORONTO. DEPARTMENT OF GEOGRAPHY. PAPERS ON PLANNING & DESIGN. see HOUSING AND URBAN PLANNING

720   UK   ISSN 0306-0624
UNIVERSITY OF YORK. INSTITUTE OF ADVANCED ARCHITECTURAL STUDIES. RESEARCH PAPERS. 1971. irreg., no.23, 1985. price varies. University of York, Institute of Advanced Architectural Studies, Kings Manor, York YO1 2EP, England. illus. circ. 500.

940   UK   ISSN 0083-6079
VICTORIAN SOCIETY. ANNUAL. 1958. a. price varies. ‡ Victorian Society, 1 Priory Gardens, Bedford Park, London W4 1TT, England. Ed. Ian Sutton. adv. circ. 3,500. Indexed: RILA.

728   GW   ISSN 0083-8047
WERKEN UND WOHNEN. 1957. irreg., vol.16, 1982. price varies. Rheinland-Verlag, Kennedy-Ufer 2, 5000 Cologne 21, W. Germany (B.R.D.) (Distr. by: Rudolf Habelt Verlag, Am Buchenhang 1, 5300 Bonn, W. Germany (B.R.D.)) Ed. Matthias Zender.

WORLD CULTURAL GUIDES. see TRAVEL AND TOURISM

YALE PUBLICATIONS IN THE HISTORY OF ART. see ART

720   CN
YARDSTICKS FOR COSTING. Variant title: Canadian Architect's Yardsticks for Costing. 1971. a. Can.$85. Southam Communications Ltd., 1450 Don Mills Rd., Don Mills, Ont. M3B 2X7, Canada. TEL 416-445-6641. Ed. Jas. A. Murray. adv. circ. 2, 195.

720.6   UK
YORK GEORGIAN SOCIETY. ANNUAL REPORT. 1943. a. membership. York Georgian Society, Kings, Manor, York YO1 2EW, England. Ed. Nancy Sumner. bk. rev. illus. circ. 600. Indexed: RILA.

720   UR
ZODCHESTVO. 1975. irreg. 2.96 Rub. (Soyuz Arkhitektorov S.S.S.R.) Stroiizdat, Shchousseva, rm. 60, Moscow, Russian S.F.S.R., U.S.S.R.
    Formerly: Sovetskaya Arkhitektura.

ARCHITECTURE — Abstracting, Bibliographies, Statistics

850   016   US   ISSN 0194-1356
ARCHITECTURE SERIES: BIBLIOGRAPHY. 1978. m. (approx. 20/m.) $900. Vance Bibliographies, 112 N. Charter St., Box 229, Monticello, IL 61856. TEL 217-762-3831. Ed. Judith Vance. bibl. index. circ. 100. (back issues avail.) Indexed: GeoRef.

ART AND ARCHITECTURE BIBLIOGRAPHIES. see ART — Abstracting, Bibliographies, Statistics

ART AND ARCHITECTURE INFORMATION GUIDE SERIES. see ART — Abstracting, Bibliographies, Statistics

720   016   US
AVERY INDEX TO ARCHITECTURAL PERIODICALS. (Hardcopy ceased in 1974) 1963. irreg. (Columbia University, Avery Architectural Library) G. K. Hall & Co., 70 Lincoln St., Boston, MA 02111. TEL 617-423-3990.
    ●Available only online. Vendors: Research Libraries Information Network.

016.7   US   ISSN 0360-2699
BIBLIOGRAPHIC GUIDE TO ART AND ARCHITECTURE. a. G. K. Hall & Co., 70 Lincoln St., Boston, MA 02111. TEL 617-423-3990.
    Formerly: Art and Architecture Book Guide (ISSN 0098-2822)

BIBLIOGRAPHIE ZUR KUNSTGESCHICHTLICHEN LITERATUR IN OST- UND SUEDOSTEUROPAEISCHEN ZEITSCHRIFTEN. see ART — Abstracting, Bibliographies, Statistics

N B O ABSTRACTS. (National Buildings Organisation) see ENGINEERING — Abstracting, Bibliographies, Statistics

ART

see also Advertising and Public Relations; Hobbies; Museums and Art Galleries

700   SW   ISSN 0044-5711
A R I S. (Art Research in Scandinavia) (Text in English and Swedish) 1969. irreg. price varies. Institute of Art History, Kyrkogatan 19, S-222 22 Lund, Sweden. Ed. Prof. Sven Sandstroem. bk. rev. illus. circ. 700.

700   US   ISSN 0065-0129
A. W. MELLON LECTURES IN THE FINE ARTS. 1956. irreg., no.27, 1981. price varies. Princeton University Press, 3175 Princeton Pike, Lawrenceville, NJ 08648. TEL 609-896-1344. (reprint service avail. from UMI)

700   800   780   GW   ISSN 0567-4999
ABHANDLUNGEN ZUR KUNST-, MUSIK- UND LITERATURWISSENSCHAFT. no.3, 1958. irreg., vol.370, 1986. price varies. Bouvier Verlag Herbert Grundmann, Am Hof 32, Postfach 1268, 5300 Bonn 1, W. Germany (B.R.D.) Indexed: M.L.A.

700   AG
ACADEMIA NACIONAL DE BELLAS ARTES. ANUARIO. 1973. a. $120. Emece Editores S.A., Apdo. Especial Numero 84, 1000 Buenos Aires, Argentina. Ed.Bd. illus. circ. 700.

700   BE
ACADEMIAE ANALECTA. MEDEDELINGEN VAN DE KONINKLIJKE ACADEMIE VOOR WETENSCHAPPEN, LETTEREN EN SCHONE KUNSTEN VAN BELGIE. SERIES 3: KLASSE DER SCHONE KUNSTEN. (Text in Dutch and English; summaries in English) 1938. irreg. price varies. Koninklijke Academie voor Wetenschappen, Letteren en Schone Kunsten van Belgie, 1 Hertogsstraat, B-1000 Brussels, Belgium (Subscr. to: Brepols Publishers, Baron Frans du Fourstraat, B-2300 Turnhout, Belgium) Ed. G. Verbeke. circ. 1, 000. (back issues avail.)

700   BE
ACADEMIE ROYALE DES SCIENCES, DES LETTRES ET DES BEAUX-ARTS DE BELGIQUE. CLASSE DES BEAUX-ARTS. MEMOIRES. irreg. price varies. Academie Royale des Sciences, des Lettres et des Beaux-Arts de Belgique., Classe des Beaux-Arts, Palais des Academies, 1 rue Ducale, 1000 Brussels, Belgium (Subscr. to: Office International des Periodiques, 114 Ave. Brand Withloch, 1040 Brussels, Belgium)

ADVANCEMENT 2: LITERATURE, MEDIA ARTS, OPERA-MUSICAL THEATRE, VISUAL ARTS. see LITERATURE

AEGYPTOLOGISCHE FORSCHUNGEN. see HISTORY — History Of The Near East

700   640   JA   ISSN 0388-7367
AICHI KYOIKU DAIGAKU KENKYU HOKOKU. 1975. a. exchange basis. Aichi University of Education, 1, Hirosawa, Igaya-Cho, Kariya-shi, Aichi-Ken 448, Japan. circ. 600.

AILERON; a literary journal. see LITERATURE

AISTHESIS; revista chilena de investigaciones esteticas. see PHILOSOPHY

700   CN   ISSN 0704-9056
ALBERTA ART FOUNDATION. ANNUAL REPORT. 1972. a. free. Alberta Art Foundation, 4th floor, Beaver House, 10158 103 St., Edmonton, Alba. T5J 0X6. TEL 403-427-9968. Ed. W. Tin Ng. circ. 300.

ALEA. see LITERATURE

ALPHA. see LITERATURE

700   US
AMACADMY. a. American Academy in Rome, 41 E. 65th St., New York, NY 10021. TEL 212-535-4250. Ed. Calvin G. Rand.

700   720   IT   ISSN 0065-6801
AMERICAN ACADEMY IN ROME. MEMOIRS. 1917. irreg. price varies. American Academy in Rome, Library, Via Angelo Masina, 5, Rome, 00153, Italy. Indexed: Numis.Lit.

700   708   US   ISSN 0065-6968
AMERICAN ART DIRECTORY. 1898. biennial. $94.50. (Jaques Cattell Press) R. R. Bowker Company, Database Publishing Group, 245 W. 17th St., New York, NY 10011. TEL 800-521-8110. index.

707 US ISSN 0146-9606
AMERICAN ARTIST DIRECTORY OF ART
SCHOOLS & WORKSHOPS. 1964. a. $2.50.
American Artist Magazine, (Subsidiary of: Billboard
Publications Inc.) 1515 Broadway, New York, NY
10036. TEL 212-764-7300. Ed. M. Stephen
Doherty. adv. circ. 163,000. (also avail. in
microform)
  Former titles: American Artist Art School
Directory; Art School Directory.

751.6 US ISSN 0272-3727
AMERICAN INSTITUTE FOR CONSERVATION
OF HISTORIC AND ARTISTIC WORKS.
PREPRINTS OF PAPERS PRESENTED AT THE
ANNUAL MEETING. a. $15. American Institute
for Conservation of Historic and Artistic Works,
3545 Williamsburg Ln., N.W., Washington, DC
20008. TEL 202-364-1036. Indexed: Art &
Archaeol.Tech.Abstr. Key Title: Preprints of Papers
Presented at the Annual Meeting- American
Institute for Conservation of Historic and Artistic
Works.

709 US ISSN 0065-9991
AMERICAN RESEARCH CENTER IN EGYPT.
JOURNAL. 1962. a. $20. J. J. Augustin, Inc.,
Locust Valley, NY 11560. TEL 516-676-1510. Ed.
Gerald E. Kadish. bk. rev. circ. 800. Indexed: Art &
Archaeol.Tech.Abstr.

709 US ISSN 0732-6432
AMERICAN RESEARCH CENTER IN EGYPT.
REPORTS. 1980. irreg., no.8, 1985. price varies.
(American Research Center in Egypt,Inc.) Undena
Publications, 17042 Devonshire St., Northridge, CA
91365. TEL 818-366-1744. Ed. Paul Walker. bibl.
illus. charts. (back issues avail.) Indexed: Math.R.

AMERICAN SOCIETY FOR ARMENIAN
STUDIES. JOURNAL. see ETHNIC INTERESTS

AMERICAN SOCIETY OF BOOKPLATE
COLLECTORS AND DESIGNERS. YEAR
BOOK. see HOBBIES

709 TU ISSN 0066-1333
ANADOLU SANATI ARASTIRMALARI/
RESEARCHES ON ANATOLIAN ART. (Text in
English and Turkish; summaries in English) 1968.
irreg. TL.35. Technical University of Istanbul,
Department of the History of Architecture and
Preservation - Istanbul Teknik Universitesi,
Gumussuyu Caddesi 87, Beyoglu, Istanbul, Turkey.
Ed. Dogan Kuban. circ. 1,000.

700 913 II
ANDHRA PRADESH, INDIA. DEPARTMENT OF
ARCHAEOLOGY AND MUSEUMS.
ARCHAEOLOGICAL SERIES. (Text in English)
irreg. price varies. Department of Archaeology and
Museums, Hyderabad 500001, Andhra Pradesh,
India (Or: Publications Bureau, Directorate of
Government Printing, Chanchalguda, Hyderabad,
Andhra Pradesh, India)
  Formerly: Andhra Pradesh, India. Department of
Archaeology and Museums. Art and Architectural
Series.

ANGELTREAD. see LITERATURE

700 GR ISSN 0066-2119
ANNALES D'ESTHETIQUE/CHRONIKA
AISTHETIKES. (Text in English, French and
Greek) 1962. a. $15. Societe Hellenique
d'Esthetique - Hellenic Society for Aesthetics,
Vassilissis Sophias 79, Athens 115 21, Greece.
Ed.Bd. bk. rev. circ. 1,000. Indexed: Phil.Ind.

700 FR
ANNUAIRE DE L'ART INTERNATIONAL. 1961.
biennial. 230 F. Patrick Sermadiras Ed.& Pub., 11
rue Arsene Houssaye, 75008 Paris, France. adv. bk.
rev. illus. circ. 20,000.

700 FR ISSN 0066-3263
ANNUAIRE INTERNATIONAL DES VENTES.
(Editions in French and English) 1963. a. 630 F.
Librairie Fischbacher, 33 rue de Seine, 75006 Paris,
France. Ed. E. Mayer.

700 FR ISSN 0066-3352
ANNUAIRE NATIONAL DES BEAUX-ARTS.
1960. biennial. Editions Dany Thibaud, 52 rue
Labrouste, 75015 Paris, France.

338.4 US ISSN 0096-1388
ANNUAL REPORT OF THE ARTS ACTIVITIES
IN ALABAMA. Cover title: Arts in Alabama.
1967. a. free. Alabama State Council on the Arts
and Humanities, 323 Adams Ave., Montgomery, AL
36130. TEL 205-832-6011. Ed. Sharon Heflin. illus.
circ. 1,500.
  Formerly: Biennial Report of the Arts Activities
in Alabama (ISSN 0094-0402)

709 913 IT
ANTICHITA, ARCHEOLOGIA, STORIA
DELL'ARTE. (Text in French and Italian) irreg.
Angelo Longo Editore, Via Paolo Costa 33, P.O.
Box 431, 48100 Ravenna, Italy.

700 SZ ISSN 0066-4782
ANTIKE KUNST. BEIHEFTE. (Text in English,
French or German) 1963. irreg., vol.13, 1984. price
varies. Vereinigung der Freunde Antiker Kunst, c/o
Archaeologisches Seminar der Universitaet,
Schoenbeinstr. 20, CH-4056 Basel, Switzerland.
Ed.Bd. circ. 550.

ANTIQUARIAN. see ANTIQUES

ANTIQUES FOLIO. see ANTIQUES

700 SP ISSN 0302-6965
ANUARIO DEL ARTE ESPANOL. 1973. a. Iberico
Europea de Ediciones, S.A., Serrano 44, Madrid 1,
Spain. illus.

ANZEIGER DES GERMANISCHEN
NATIONALMUSEUMS. see HISTORY — History
Of Europe

ARCHAEOLOGIA. see ARCHAEOLOGY

ARCHAEOLOGICAL INSTITUTE OF AMERICA.
ABSTRACTS OF THE GENERAL MEETING.
see ARCHAEOLOGY — Abstracting,
Bibliographies, Statistics

706 US ISSN 0066-6637
ARCHIVES OF ASIAN ART. 1945. a. $25
prepayment. (Friends of Asia Society Galleries)
Asia Society, 725 Park Ave., New York, NY 10021.
TEL 212-288-6400. Ed. Ricahrd Barnhart.
cum.index: 1945-65. circ. 600(approx.) (back issues
avail.)
  Until 1966 Issued As: Chinese Art Society of
America. Archives.

ARCHIVIO PER L'ALTO ADIGE; rivista di studi
alpini. see LINGUISTICS

ARET FORTALT I BILLEDER. see HISTORY —
History Of Europe

353.9 700 US ISSN 0098-7387
ARIZONA COMMISSION ON THE ARTS.
REPORT TO THE GOVERNOR. a. free.
Commission on the Arts, 417 W. Roosevelt St.,
Phoenix, AZ 85003. TEL 602-255-5882. illus. Key
Title: Report to the Governor - Arizona
Commission on the Arts.
  Formerly: Arizona Commission on the Arts and
Humanities. Report to the Governor.

ARMAS E TROFEUS; revista de historia, heraldica,
genealogia e arte. see HISTORY — History Of
Europe

ARS ORIENTALIS; the arts of Islam and the East.
see ORIENTAL STUDIES

700 AG
ARS, REVISTA DE ARTE. a. Rodriguez Pena 339,
Buenos Aires, Argentina. Ed. I.I. Schlagman.

709 SW ISSN 0066-7919
ARS SUECICA. (Subseries of Acta Universitatis
Upsaliensis) (Text in Swedish; summaries in English
or German) 1966. irreg., vol.4, 1977. price varies.
(Uppsala Universitet, Institute of Art History)
Almqvist & Wiksell International, Box 62, S-101 20
Stockholm, Sweden. Ed. Rudolf Zeitler.

700 US
ARSENAL; surrealist subversion. 1970. irreg., latest
1983. $6.95. Black Swan Press-Surrealist Editions,
1726 W. Jarvis Ave., Chicago, IL 60626. Ed.
Franklin Rosemont. bk. rev. bibl. circ. 3,000.

730 UN ISSN 0004-5535
ART; journal of the professional artist/le porte-
parole de l'artiste professionnel. (Text in English
and French; occasionally in Spanish) 1953. a. free.
Unesco, International Association of Art -
Association Internationale des Arts Plastiques, 1 rue
Miollis, 75015 Paris, France. Ed. Dunbar Marshall-
Malagola. circ. 2,000.

ART AND DESIGN IN THE REGION. see
EDUCATION — Higher Education

704 II ISSN 0004-3044
ART AND LIFE. (Text mainly in English;
occasionally in English & Bengali) 1967. a. Rs.8($1)
Art Study Centre, B 20-185 Bhelupura, Varanasi 1,
India. Ed. R.N. Mukerji. adv. bk. rev. charts. illus.
circ. 100.

701 US
ART AND PHILOSOPHY. 1983. irreg. Haven
Publishing Corporation, Box 2046, New York, NY
10001. Eds. Hugh Curtler, Doug Bolling.

700 II
ART AND THE ARTIST. 1962. irreg. Rs.3 per no.
Academy of Fine Arts, 14/2 Old China Bazar St.,
Calcutta 1, India. Ed.Bd. illus. Indexed: Art Ind.

700 659.106 US
ART DIRECTORS ANNUAL. 1922. a. $49.95. (Art
Directors Club Inc.) A D C Publications, 250 Park
Ave. S., New York, NY 10003. TEL 212-674-0500.
Ed. Paula Radding. adv. circ. 40,000.
  Former titles: Annual of Advertising, Editorial
and Television Art and Design with the Annual
Copy Awards; until 1973: Annual of Advertising,
Editorial and Television Art and Design (ISSN
0066-4014)

704 FR ISSN 0066-7951
ART ET LES GRANDES CIVILISATIONS. 1965. a.
Editions Mazenod, 33 rue de Naples, Paris 8,
France.

700 AT
ART GALLERY NEWS. 1969? irreg. Aus.$0.05 per
no. Benalla Art Gallery Society, Kitson Court,
Benalla, Vic. 3672, Australia.

709 US
ART HISTORY SERIES. 1977. irreg. price varies.
Decatur House Press, Ltd., 2122 Decatur Pl., N.W.,
Washington, DC 20008. TEL 203-673-4030. Ed.
Frank DiFederico. index.

702.8 US
ART MATERIAL TRADE NEWS DIRECTORY.
1952. a. $24.95. Communication Channels, Inc.,
6255 Barfield Rd., Atlanta, GA 30328. TEL 404-
256-9800. Ed. Barbara Katinsky. adv. circ. 10,000.
  Former titles: Art Material Directory and
Product Information Guide; Art Material Trade
News Directory of Craft Materials.

700 069.5 US
ART NEWS DIRECTORY OF CORPORATE ART
COLLECTIONS. 1982. a. $69.95. International Art
Alliance, Inc., Box 1608, Largo, FL 34294. TEL
813-581-7328. Ed. Shirley Reiff Howarth. circ. 2,
000.
  Formerly: Directory of Corporate Art
Collections.

700 US ISSN 0193-6867
ART REFERENCE COLLECTION. 1980. irreg.,
no.5, 1984. price varies. Greenwood Press, 88 Post
Rd. W., Box 5007, Westport, CT 06881. TEL 203-
226-3571. Ed. Pamela J. Parry.

700 914 SP
ART ROMANIC. (Contains 2 series, Monografies and
Tematica) (Text in Catalan) irreg., no.10, 1979.
1000 ptas. Artestudi Edicions, Provenca 552,
Barcelona 26, Spain. adv. bk. rev. illus.

700   US
ART SALES INDEX: OIL PAINTINGS, DRAWINGS, WATER COLOURS AND SCULPTURE. (Text in English and French; summaries in English) 1968/69. a. $160. Apollo Book (Distributor), 5 Schoolhouse Ln., Poughkeepsie, NY 12603. TEL 914-462-0040. Ed. Richard Hislop. adv. index. circ. 3,000.
 Former titles: Annual Art Sales Index: Oil Paintings, Drawings, Water Colours and Sculptures; Annual Art Sales Index: Oil Paintings, Drawings and Watercolours (ISSN 0308-5910); Annual Art Sales Index (1979) (ISSN 0143-0688); Formed by the merger of: Annual Art Sales Index: Watercolours and Drawings; Annual Art Sales Index: Oil Paintings.

700   UK
ART WORKERS GUILD. ANNUAL REPORT. 1885. a. membership. Art Workers Guild, 6 Queen Sq., London WC1N 3AR, England. Ed. D.G. Pullen. bibl. illus. circ. 400(controlled)

709 SA ISSN 0004-3389
DE ARTE. (Text in Afrikaans and English) 1967. a. R.6.50. University of South Africa, Department of History of Art and Fine Arts, Box 392, Pretoria 0001, South Africa. Ed. M. Arnold. adv. bk. rev. play rev. bibl. illus. circ. 1,220. (back issues avail.) Indexed: Ind.S.A.Per.
 History

709 913 IT
ARTE E ARCHEOLOGIA; studi e documenti. 1971. irreg., no.24, 1985. price varies. Casa Editrice Leo S. Olschki, Casella Postale 66, 50100 Florence, Italy.

709 IT
ARTE VENETA; rivista di storia dell'arte. 1947. a. L.140000. Gruppo Editoriale Electa, Via Trantacoste, 7, Milan, Italy. Ed. Rodolfo Pallucchini. adv. circ. 2,500. Indexed: Art & Archaeol.Tech.Abstr. RILA.

700 913 BO ISSN 0587-5447
ARTE Y ARQUEOLOGIA. 1969-1983 (vol.8 and 9); to resume publication in 1986. biennial. $10. (Universidad Mayor de San Andres, Instituto de Estudios Bolivianos) Museo Nacional de Arte, Casilla Postal 609, La Paz, Bolivia. Ed. Teresa Gisbert. adv. circ. 500. Indexed: Hist.Abstr. Amer.Hist.& Life.

709.5 SZ
ARTIBUS ASIAE SUPPLEMENTA. 1937. a. price varies. (Arthur M. Sackler Foundation, US) Artibus Asiae Publishers, 6612 Ascona, Switzerland. Ed. Alexander C. Soper. bibl. illus.

700 EC
ARTISTAS ECUATORIANOS. (Text in English and Spanish) 1976. irreg. $30. Ediciones Paralelo Cero, Box 1135, Av. 12 de Octubre 186, Quito, Ecuador. Dir. Hector Merino Valencia. illus.

708.11 CN
ARTISTS IN CANADA: UNION LIST OF ARTISTS FILES/ARTISTES DU CANADA. LISTE COLLECTIVE DES DOSSIERS D'ARTISTES. (Text in English and French) 1970. irreg. Can.$10. National Museums of Canada, Ottawa, Ont. K1A 0M8, Canada TEL 613-990-0587. (Order from: Friends of the National Gallery of Canada, 75 Albert St., R-1103-1, Ottawa K1A 0M8, Canada)
 Former titles: Artists in Canada; National Gallery of Canada. Library. Checklist of Canadian Artists Files (ISSN 0078-6993)

700 US ISSN 0161-0546
ARTIST'S MARKET; where to sell your commercial art. 1979. a. $16.95. F & W Publications, Inc., 9933 Alliance Rd., Cincinnati, OH 45242. TEL 513-984-0717. Ed. Susan Conner.
 Supersedes in part: Art and Crafts Market (ISSN 0147-2461); Former titles: Artist's and Photographer's Market (ISSN 0146-8294); Artist's Market (ISSN 0361-607X); (Until 1973): Cartoonists' Market.

730 US ISSN 0164-1298
ARTPARK. a. Artpark, Inc., Public Relations Department, Box 371, Lewiston, NY 14092.

705 706 AT ISSN 0066-8095
ARTS. 1958. irreg. Aus.$5 to individuals; Aus. $3 to institutions. University of Sydney, Arts Association, University of Sydney, Sydney, N.S.W., Australia. TEL 02-692-2656. Ed. Geoffrey Little. bk. rev. circ. 500.

070.5 UK
ARTS ADDRESS BOOK; a classified guide to national (U.K. & Ireland) and international arts organizations with details of their activities and publications. 1983. triennial. £9.95. Peter Marcan Publications, 31 Rowliff Rd., High Wycombe, Bucks, England. circ. 1,000.

700 US
ARTS & BUSINESS COUNCIL. ANNUAL REPORT. a. Arts & Business Council, 130 E. 40th St., New York, NY 10016. TEL 212-683-5555.

709.5 FR ISSN 0004-3958
ARTS ASIATIQUES. (Text in French, occasionally in English) 1954. irreg., (1-2/yr.) price varies. (Ecole Francaise d'Extreme Orient, Jean Maisonneuve Librarie d'Amerique et d'Orient) Editions d'Amerique et d'Orient, 11 rue Saint Sulpice, 75006 Paris, France. Eds. Jean Filliozat, Jeannine Auboyer. adv. bk. rev. charts. illus. circ. 1,500.

700 AT
ARTS COUNCIL OF AUSTRALIA. ANNUAL REPORT. 1948. a. Arts Council of Australia, Ste. 605, 6th Fl., Phoenix House, 32-34 Bridge St., Sydney, N.S.W. 2000, Australia. Ed. Jennifer Bott. circ. 1,500.

700 UK ISSN 0066-8133
ARTS COUNCIL OF GREAT BRITAIN. ANNUAL REPORT AND ACCOUNTS. 1945. a. £2. Arts Council of Great Britain, 105 Piccadilly, London W1V 0AU, England (Dist. by: H.M.S.O., P.O.B. 569, London S.E.1, England)

746 730 FR
ARTS ET OBJETS DU MAROC. Cover title: Maroc. no.2, 1974. irreg. 50 F. 8 rue Saint-Marc, 75002 Paris, France. Ed. G.J. Malgras. illus.

700 II
ARTS OF HIMACHAL. 1975. irreg. price varies. State Museum, Simla, Department of Languages and Cultural Affairs, Simla, Himachal Pradesh, India. Ed. Vishwa Chander Ohri. circ. 1,000.

707.2 US ISSN 0066-8168
ARTS PATRONAGE SERIES. 1970. irreg., no.12, 1983. price varies. Washington International Arts Letter, Box 15240, Washington, DC 20003. TEL 202-328-1900. Ed. Daniel Millsaps.

700 UK
ARTS REVIEW YEARBOOK. 1973. a. £12.45. Starcity Ltd., 69 Faroe Rd., London W14 0EL, England. Ed. Graham Hughes. adv.

700 AT ISSN 0311-0095
ARTVIEWS. 1972? irreg. Aus.$0.40 each. Artists' Guild of Australia, 156 Banksia St., Pagewood, N.S.W. 2035, Australia.

700 330 US
AUCTION PRICES OF AMERICAN ARTISTS-VOLUME 5. irreg. $40. Apollo Book (Distributor), 5 Schoolhouse Ln., Poughkeepsie, NY 12603. TEL 914-462-0040.

700 US
AUDIOZINE. 1977. irreg. $15 per no. (Mamelle Inc.) Contemporary Arts Press, Box 3123, San Francisco, CA 94119. TEL 415-431-7672. (audio cassette)

AURORA; Jahrbuch der Eichendorff-Gesellschaft. see LITERATURE

AURORA-BUCHREIHE. see LITERATURE

700 GW ISSN 0067-0642
AUS FORSCHUNG UND KUNST. 1968. irreg., no.23, 1982. price varies. (Geschichtsverein fuer Kaernten, AU) Dr. Rudolf Habelt GmbH, Am Buchenhang 1, 5300 Bonn 1, W. Germany (B.R.D.) Ed. Gotbert Moro.

AUSGABE; ein Literatur- und Kunstmagazin. see LITERATURE

AUSTRIA. BUNDESMINISTERIUM FUER UNTERRICHT UND KUNST. SCHRIFTENREIHE. see EDUCATION — Teaching Methods And Curriculum

700 069 708 US
AWARDS IN THE VISUAL ARTS. 1982. a. price varies. Southeastern Center for Contemporary Arts, 750 Marguerite Dr., Box 11927, Winston-Salem, NC 27116-1927. TEL 919-725-1904. circ. 3,000. (back issues avail.)

B L A C. (Black Literature and Arts Congress) see ETHNIC INTERESTS

700 910 SP
BAETICA; estudios de arte, geografia e historia. 1978. a. Universidad de Malaga, Facultad de Filosofia y Letras, Avda. Generalisimo, 23, Malaga, Spain.

BAMPTON LECTURES IN AMERICA. see RELIGIONS AND THEOLOGY

BARBACANE; revue des pierres et des hommes. see LITERATURE

BARBADOS MUSEUM AND HISTORICAL SOCIETY. JOURNAL. see HISTORY — History Of North And South America

700 GW ISSN 0341-9150
BAYERISCHE DENKMALPFLEGE. JAHRBUCH. 1947. a. DM.48. (Bayerisches Landesamt fuer Denkmalpflege) Deutsche Kunstverlag GmbH, Vohburger Str. 1, 8000 Munich 21, W. Germany (B.R.D.)

700 GW
BAYERISCHE STAATSGEMAELDESAMMLUNGEN. JAHRESBERICHT. 1972. a. membership. Bayerische Staatsgemaeldesammlungen, Barer Str. 29, 8000 Munich 40, W. Germany (B.R.D.) TEL (089)23 80 50. Ed.Bd. circ. 1,500.

700 CN ISSN 0315-2359
BEAUX-ARTS. 1972. irreg. price varies. 3625 St. Laurent, Montreal, P.Q. H2X 2V5, Canada. Ed. Tom Dean. circ. 1,000. (back issues avail.)

740 810 US
BEBOP DRAWING CLUB BOOK. 1974. irreg. Artman's Press, 1511 McGee Ave., Berkeley, CA 94703. Ed. Glenn Myles. illus.

700 GW ISSN 0067-4893
BEIHEFTE DER BONNER JAHRBUECHER. 1950. irreg., no.41, 1981. price varies. Rheinland-Verlag, Kennedy-Ufer 2, 5000 Cologne 21, W. Germany (B.R.D.) (Distr. by: Rudolf Habelt Verlag, Am Buchenhang 1, 5300 Bonn, W. Germany (B.R.D.)) Indexed: RILA.

700 GW ISSN 0067-5121
BEITRAEGE ZUR KUNST DES CHRISTLICHEN OSTENS. 1964. irreg. price varies. Verlag Aurel Bongers, Dortmunder str. 67, Postfach 100 264, 4350 Recklinghausen, W. Germany (B.R.D.) illus.

709 GW
BEITRAEGE ZUR KUNSTGESCHICHTE. irreg., vol.18, 1982. price varies. Walter de Gruyter und Co., Genthiner Str. 13, 1000 Berlin 30, W. Germany (B.R.D.) (U.S. addr.: Walter de Gruyter, Inc., 200 Saw Mill Rd., Hawthorne, N.Y. 10532) Ed. Wolfgang Schultz.

BEST EDITORIAL CARTOONS OF THE YEAR. see LITERARY AND POLITICAL REVIEWS

BEST IN COVERS AND POSTERS. see PUBLISHING AND BOOK TRADE

745.4 US ISSN 0360-8271
BEST IN ENVIRONMENTAL GRAPHICS. (Subseries of: Print Casebooks) 1975. a. $19.50. R C Publications, Inc., 104 Fifth Ave., 9th Fl., New York, NY 10011 TEL 301-229-9040. (Subscr. to: 6400 Goldsboro Rd., Bethesda, MD 20817) illus.

BIBLIOGRAPHY OF APPRAISAL LITERATURE. see REAL ESTATE — Abstracting, Bibliographies, Statistics

BIBLIOTECA NAPOLETANA DI STORIA E ARTE. see HISTORY — History Of Europe

700   PL   ISSN 0067-7698
BIBLIOTEKA KRAKOWSKA. 1897. irreg., vol.122, 1981. price varies. Towarzystwo Milosnikow Historii i Zabytkow Krakowa, Ul. Sw. Jana 12, 31-018 Krakow, Poland (Dist. by: Ars Polona-Ruch, Krakowskie Przedmiescie 7, Warsaw, Poland) Ed. Janina Bieniarzowna.

700   US
BIRTHSTONE. 1975. irreg. $6.50 for 4 nos. Birthstone Magazine, c/o Dan Brady, Ed., 1319 6th Ave., San Francisco, CA 94122. Ed.Bd. bk. rev. circ. 700.

700   GW   ISSN 0068-0036
BONNER BEITRAEGE ZUR KUNSTWISSENSCHAFT. 1950. irreg., no.11, 1971. price varies. Rheinland-Verlag, Kennedy-Ufer 2, 5000 Cologne 21, W. Germany (B.R.D.) (Distr. by: Rudolf Habelt Verlag, Am Buchenhang 1, 5300 Bonn, W. Germany (B.R.D.)) Eds. Herbert Von Einem, Heinrich Luetzler.

BOOKS AND ARTICLES ON ORIENTAL SUBJECTS PUBLISHED IN JAPAN. see HISTORY — History Of Asia

BOSS. see LITERATURE

BREATHLESS MAGAZINE. see LITERATURE

BRITISH ARCHAEOLOGICAL ASSOCIATION. CONFERENCE TRANSACTIONS. see ARCHAEOLOGY

BRITISH COLUMBIA ART TEACHERS' ASSOCIATION. JOURNAL. see EDUCATION — Teaching Methods And Curriculum

700   GW   ISSN 0720-0056
BRUCKMANNS PANTHEON; internationale Jahres Zeitschrift fuer Kunst. (Text and summaries in English, French, and German) 1928. a. DM.98. F. Bruckmann Munich, Verlag und Druck GmbH, Nymphenburger Str. 86, 8000 Munich 20, W. Germany (B.R.D.) TEL (089)1257340. Ed. Erhardt D. Stiebner. adv. bk. rev. abstr. bibl. illus. index. circ. 2,000. Indexed: Art Ind. Curr.Cont. Arts & Hum.Cit.Ind. Artbibl. Ind.Bk.Rev.Hum. RILA.
Formerly: Pantheon (ISSN 0031-0999)

708   GW   ISSN 0572-7146
BRUECKE-ARCHIV. 1967. irreg., no. 9/10, 1977/78. price varies. Bruecke-Museum, Bussardsteig 9, 1000 Berlin 33, W. Germany (B.R.D.) Ed. Leopold Reidemeister. illus. Indexed: RILA.

709   NZ
BULLETIN OF NEW ZEALAND ART HISTORY. 1972. a. NZ.$7.50. University of Auckland, Department of Art History, Private Bag C. 1, Auckland, New Zealand. Eds. Tony Green, Michael Dunn. bk. rev. circ. 400.

700   US   ISSN 0068-4295
BURT FRANKLIN ART HISTORY AND ART REFERENCE SERIES. (Text in various languages) 1968. irreg., no.44, 1973. price varies. Lenox Hill Publishing and Distributing Corporation, 235 E. 44th St., New York, NY 10017. (back issues avail.)

700   PL   ISSN 0067-947X
BYDGOSKIE TOWARZYSTWO NAUKOWE. WYDZIAL NAUK HUMANISTYCZNYCH. PRACE. SERIA D: (SZTUKA) irreg., no.3, 1965. price varies. Bydgoskie Towarzystwo Naukowe, Jezuicka 4, Bydgoszcz, Poland (Dist. by: Ars Polona-Ruch, Krakowskie Przedmiescie 7, Warsaw, Poland)

700   UK   ISSN 0260-5821
C T O. (Call to Order); counterreactionary journal of contemporary art. 1980. irreg. £3 per no. 149 Kathleen Rd., Sholing, Southampton, Hants. SO2 8LP, England. Ed. Alex Tsander.

709   US   ISSN 0068-5909
CALIFORNIA STUDIES IN THE HISTORY OF ART. 1962. irreg. price varies. University of California Press, 2120 Berkeley Way, Berkeley, CA 94720. TEL 415-642-4247.

700 780 792   CN   ISSN 0576-4300
CANADA COUNCIL ANNUAL REPORT AND SUPPLEMENT/RAPPORT ANNUEL DU CONSEIL DES ARTS DU CANADA ET SON SUPPLEMENT. (Text in English and French) 1958. a. free. Canada Council, Communications Service, Box 1047, 99 Metcalfe St., Ottawa, Ont. K1P 5V8, Canada. TEL 613-598-4365. charts. stat. circ. 5,000.

706.5   CN
CANADIAN ART SALES INDEX. 1980. a. Can.$24.95. Westbridge Fine Art Marketing Services, 2245 Granville St., Vancouver, B.C. V6H 3G1, Canada. TEL 604-734-4944. Ed. Anthony R. Westbridge. adv. circ. 2,000.

700   CN   ISSN 0383-5405
CANADIAN ARTISTS SERIES/COLLECTION: ARTISTES CANADIENS. (Editions in English & French) 1973. irreg., no.10, 1986. price varies. National Museums of Canada, Ottawa, Ont. K1A 0M8, Canada. TEL 613-990-1969. illus. circ. 5,000.

700   CN   ISSN 0068-8487
CANADIAN CONFERENCE OF THE ARTS. MISCELLANEOUS REPORTS. (Text in English and French) 1969. irreg. prices on request. Canadian Conference of the Arts, 126 York St., ste. 400, Ottawa, Ont. K1N 5T5, Canada.

CANADIAN REVIEW OF ART EDUCATION RESEARCH. see EDUCATION

CANADIAN SOCIETY FOR EDUCATION THROUGH ART. ANNUAL JOURNAL. see EDUCATION

709 913   FR   ISSN 0076-230X
CASA DE VELASQUEZ, MADRID. MELANGES/ CASA DE VELASQUEZ, MADRID. MISCELLANIES. (Text in French and Spanish) 1965. a. price varies. Diffusion de Boccard, 11 rue de Medicis, 75006 Paris, France. Indexed: Hist.Abstr. Amer.Hist.& Life.

750   IT
CATALOGO DELL'ARTE ITALIANA DELL'OTTOCENTO. 1964. a. L.140000. Giorgio Mondadori e Associati S.p.A., Centro Direzionale, Palazzo Canova, 20090 Milan 2 - Segrate, Italy. Ed. Paolo Levi. adv. illus.
Former titles (until 1983): Catalogo della Pittura Italiana dell' Ottocento; Catalogo Bolaffi della Pittura Italiana dell'Ottocento.

700   IT
CATALOGO DELL'ARTE MODERNA ITALIANA. 1962. a. L.140000. Giorgio Mondadori e Associati S.p.A., Centro Direzionale, Palazzo Canova, 20090 Milan 2 - Segrate, Italy. Ed. Paolo Levi. adv. illus.
Former titles: Catalogo Nazionale Bolaffi d'Arte Moderna; (1964-1970): Catalogo Bolaffi d'Arte Moderna (ISSN 0576-8861); (1962-1963): Collezionista d'Arte Moderna.

760   IT
CATALOGO DELLA GRAFICA ITALIANA. 1970. a. L.120000. Giorgio Mondadori e Associati S.p.A., Centro Direzionale, Palazzo Canova, 20090 Milan 2 - Segrate, Italy. Ed. Paolo Levi. adv. illus.
Former titles: Catalogo Nazionale Bolaffi della Grafica; Catalogo Bolaffi della Grafica Italiana.

709   IT
CATALOGO DELLA SCULTURA ITALIANA. 1976. a. L.110000. Giorgio Mondadori e Associati S.p.A., Centro Direzionale, Palazzo Canova, Milan 2 - Segrate, Italian. Ed. Paolo Levi.

700 746   SZ
CATALOGUE BIENNALE INTERNATIONALE DE LAUSANNE. (Text in English and French) 1962. biennial. 15 Fr. International Centre of Ancient and Modern Tapestry - Centre International de la Tapisserie Ancienne et Moderne, 4 Av. Villamont, 1005 Lausanne, Switzerland. adv. circ. 7,700.
Formerly: Biennale Internationale de la Tapisserie (ISSN 0067-849X)

750   UN   ISSN 0069-1135
CATALOGUE OF REPRODUCTIONS OF PAINTINGS PRIOR TO 1860. (Text in English, French and Spanish) 1950. irreg., 1972, 9th ed. Unesco, 7-9 Place de Fontenoy, 75700 Paris, France (Dist. in U.S. by: Bernan Associates-Unipub, 4611-F Assembly Dr., Lanham, MD 20706-4391)

750   UN   ISSN 0069-1143
CATALOGUE OF REPRODUCTIONS OF PAINTINGS, 1860-1973. (Text in English, French and Spanish) 1950. irreg., no.9, 1973. Unesco, 7-9 Place de Fontenoy, Paris, France (Dist. in U.S. by: Bernan Associates-Unipub, 4611-F Assembly Dr., Lanham, MD 20706-4391)

CENACOLO; arte e letteratura. see LITERATURE

700 780   CM
CENTRE CULTUREL FRANCAIS DE YAOUNDE. PROGRAMME SAISON. (Text in French) a. Centre Culturel Francais de Yaounde, B.P. 513, Yaounde, Cameroon.

CENTRE D'HISTOIRE ET D'ART DE LA THUDINIE. PUBLICATIONS. see HISTORY — History Of Europe

740 745.2   FR
CENTRE NATIONAL D'ART ET DE CULTURE GEORGES POMPIDOU. ANNUAIRE DES CONCEPTEURS. a. Centre National d'Art et de Culture Georges Pompidou, Centre de Creation Industrielle, Centre Beaubourg, 75004 Paris, France.

CENTRO CAMUNO DI STUDI PREISTORICI. ARCHIVI. see ARCHAEOLOGY

CENTRO CAMUNO DI STUDI PREISTORICI. BOLLETTINO. see ARCHAEOLOGY

CENTRO CAMUNO DI STUDI PREISTORICI. STUDI CAMUNI. see ARCHAEOLOGY

709 913   IT
CENTRO CAMUNO DI STUDI PREISTORICI. SYMPOSIA. irreg., vol.3, 1983. $90. Centro Camuno di Studi Preistorici, 25044 Capo di Ponte, Brescia, Italy.

700   DK   ISSN 0109-3479
CHARLOTTENBORG FORAARSUDSTILLINGEN. 1984. a. Bibliotekscentralen, Telegrafvej 5, DK-2750 Ballerup, Denmark.

CHOICE (BINGHAMTON); a magazine of poetry and graphics. see LITERATURE — Poetry

CHURCHSCAPE. see ARCHITECTURE

CIBA COLLECTION OF MEDICAL ILLUSTRATIONS. see MEDICAL SCIENCES

CINMAY SMRTI PATHAGARA. see LITERATURE

700   IT
CIVETTA. no.2, 1974. irreg.; no.6, 1977. price varies. Giardini Editori e Stampatori, Via Santa Bibbiana 28, 56100 Pisa, Italy. Ed. Nicola Micieli.

700 945   IT   ISSN 0069-4355
CIVILTA VENEZIANA. FONTI E TESTI. SERIE PRIMA: FONTI E TESTI PER LA STORIA DELL'ARTE VENETA. 1959. irreg., no.8, 1972. price varies. (Fondazione Giorgio Cini) Casa Editrice Leo S. Olschki, Casella Postale 66, 50100 Florence, Italy. circ. 1,000.

940   NE
CLAVIS KLEINE KUNSTHISTORISCHE MONOGRAFIEEN. 1984. a. price varies. Walburg Pers, Zaadmarkt 84a-86, Box 222, 7200 AE Zutphen, Netherlands. TEL 05750-10522. (Co-sponsor: Clavis Stichting Publicaties Middeleeuwse Kunst)

940   NE
CLAVIS KUNSTHISTORISCHE MONOGRAFIEEN. 1984. a. price varies. Walburg Pers, Zaadmarkt 84a-86, Box 222, 7200 AE Zutphen, Netherlands. TEL 05750-10522. (Co-sponsor: Clavis Stichting Publicaties Middeleeuwse Kunst)

CLEMSON UNIVERSITY. COLLEGE OF ARCHITECTURE. SEMESTER REVIEW; a journal of educational thought. see ARCHITECTURE

COLECCION ETHOS-ARTE. see MUSIC

700   SP
COLLECCIO DE MATERIALS. (Text in Catalan) 1977. irreg. Artestudi Edicions, Provenca 552, Barcelona 26, Spain.

COMITATUS; A JOURNAL OF MEDIEVAL AND RENAISSANCE STUDIES. see *LITERATURE*

CONFERENCE ON EDITORIAL PROBLEMS: UNIVERSITY OF TORONTO. see *LITERATURE*

700   US
CONTEMPORARY AMERICAN ART CRITICS. irreg., vol.7, 1985. U M I Research Press, 300 N. Zeeb Rd., Ann Arbor, MI 48106. Ed. Donald Kuspit.

700   US
CONTEMPORARY ARTISTS. irreg. $65. Harry N. Abrams, Inc., 100 Fifth Ave., New York, NY 10011. TEL 212-206-7715. Indexed: Child.Auth.& Illus.

150   UK   ISSN 0069-973X
CONTROL MAGAZINE. 1965. a. £20. 5 London Mews, London W.2, England. Ed. S. Willats. circ. 700. (also avail. in microform) Indexed: Artbibl.

700   DK   ISSN 0107-9794
CORNER. 1986. a. Kr.25. Klampenborgvej 248, DK-2800 Lyngby, Denmark. Ed. Uffe Thorlacius.

700   US   ISSN 0363-4574
CORNFIELD REVIEW; an annual of the creative arts. 1976. a. $1. Ohio State University Marion Campus, 1465 Mt. Vernon Ave., Marion, OH 43302-5695. TEL 614-389-2361. Ed. David Citino. illus. circ. 750.

700 943   GE   ISSN 0232-1459
CORPUS VITREARUM MEDII AEVI. 1976. irreg. (latest 1981) (Institut fuer Denkmalpflege in der DDR) Akademie-Verlag Berlin, Leipziger Str. 3-4, 1086 Berlin, E. Germany (D.D.R.)

700 913   IT
CORSI INTERNAZIONALI DI CULTURA SULL'ARTE RAVENNATE E BIZANTINA. ATTI. (Text in English, French, German and Italian) 1953. a. Angelo Longo Editore, Via Paolo Costa 33, P.O. Box 431, 48100 Ravenna, Italy.

709   UK   ISSN 0307-8051
COURTAULD INSTITUTE ILLUSTRATION ARCHIVES. ARCHIVE 1. irreg. £25 per no. (Courtauld Institute, University of London) Harvey Miller Publishers, 20 Marryat Rd., London SW19 5BD, England.

709   UK   ISSN 0307-806X
COURTAULD INSTITUTE ILLUSTRATION ARCHIVES. ARCHIVE 2. irreg. £25 per no. (Courtauld Institute, University of London) Harvey Miller Publishers, 20 Marryat Rd., London SW19 5BD, England.
    Formerly: 15th and 16th Century Sculpture in Italy.

720 709   UK   ISSN 0307-8078
COURTAULD INSTITUTE ILLUSTRATION ARCHIVES. ARCHIVE 3. irreg. £25 per no. (Courtauld Institute, University of London) Harvey Miller Publishers, 20 Marryat Rd., London SW19 5BD, England.

709   UK   ISSN 0307-8086
COURTAULD INSTITUTE ILLUSTRATION ARCHIVES. ARCHIVE 4. irreg. £25 per no. (Courtauld Institute, University of London) Harvey Miller Publishers, 20 Marryat Rd., London SW19 5BD, England.

CREATIVE HANDBOOK. see *ARTS AND HANDICRAFTS*

CREATIVE HANDBOOK DIARY. see *ARTS AND HANDICRAFTS*

CREATIVE SOURCE AUSTRALIA; the wizards of Oz. see *ARTS AND HANDICRAFTS*

CREATIVITY. see *ADVERTISING AND PUBLIC RELATIONS*

700   US
CRISS-CROSS ART COMMUNICATIONS. no.5, 1977. irreg. $15 for four issues. Criss-Cross Foundation, Box 2022, Boulder, CO 80306. Ed.Bd. adv. circ. 2,000. (also avail. in microform from UMI; reprint service avail. from UMI; back issues avail.)

CROTON REVIEW. see *LITERATURE*

700   AG   ISSN 0070-1688
CUADERNOS DE HISTORIA DEL ARTE. 1961. a. Arg.$28.50. Instituto de Historia del Arte, Universidad Nacional de Cuyo, Faculdad de Filosofia y Letras, Centro Universitario, Parque Gral San Martin, Mendoza, Argentina. Ed.Bd. bk. rev.

700   SP   ISSN 0211-0768
D'ART. (Text in Catalan and Spanish) 1972. a. 700 ptas.($12.50) Universitat de Barcelona, Departamento D'Historia de L'Art, Facultat de Geografia i Historia, Baldirl Reixach S/N, 85028 Barcelona, Spain. TEL 333 12 08. Ed. Dr. Pere Salabert. bk. rev. circ. 1,000. (back issues avail.)

DADA/SURREALISM. see *LITERATURE*

700   DK   ISSN 0109-8411
DANSK ARTIST FORBUND. SHOW GUIDE. 1982. biennial. free to Institutions. Dansk Artist Forbund, Vendersgade 24, 1363 Copenhagen K, Denmark. illus. circ. 2,000.

700   DK   ISSN 0108-8572
DANSK KUNSTNERRAAD. 1983. irreg. free. Strandgade 6, 1401 Copenhagen K, Denmark. illus.

740   DK   ISSN 0109-3339
DANSKE ILLUSTRATORER. 1983. a. Kr.135. Dansk Cerebration-International Marketing Management A-S, Oerbekvej 739, 5220 Odense SOE, Denmark. Ed. Helen Ramsdahl. adv.
    Formerly: Tegnebogen Danske Illustratorer.

700 720   GE
DEHIO: HANDBUCH DER DEUTSCHEN KUNSTDENKMAELER. 1965. irreg., vol.5, 1983. (Institut fuer Denkmalpflege in der DDR) Akademie-Verlag Berlin, Leipziger Str. 3-4, 1086 Berlin, E. Germany (D.D.R.)

700 830 069 780   GW
DEINE STADT; Kunst, Kultur und Leben in Braunschweig. 1979. a. DM.6. Stadt Braunschweig, Kulturamt, Steintorwall 14, 3300 Braunschweig, W. Germany (B.R.D.)

706   US
DELAWARE ART MUSEUM. ANNUAL REPORT. 1912. a. free. ‡ Delaware Art Museum, 2301 Kentmere Parkway, Wilmington, DE 19806. TEL 302-571-9590. Ed. Melissa H. Mulrooney. circ. 2, 500.
    Formerly: Wilmington Society of the Fine Arts. Report (ISSN 0084-0327)

686.3 095   GW   ISSN 0341-2474
DENKMAELER DER BUCHKUNST. 1976. irreg., vol.7, 1987. price varies. Anton Hiersemann Verlag, Rosenbergstr. 113, Postfach 723, 7000 Stuttgart 1, W. Germany (B.R.D.)

700   DK   ISSN 0107-2951
DENMARK. STATENS KUNSTFOND. BERETNING. 1965. a. free. Statens Kunstfond - Danish State Art Foundation, Sankt Annae Plads 10B, 1250 Copenhagen K, Denmark. circ. 2,500.

DESIGN AND ART IN GREECE/THEMATA CHOROU & TECHNON. see *ARCHITECTURE*

700 800   UK   ISSN 0309-7994
DEVONSHIRE ASSOCIATION FOR THE ADVANCEMENT OF SCIENCE, LITERATURE AND ART. REPORT AND TRANSACTIONS. a. Devonshire Press, Torquay 7, England. Indexed: RILA.

920 830   GW   ISSN 0070-4695
DICHTER UND ZEICHNER. 1963. irreg. price varies. Graphikum, Muehlenbergring 1, D-3406 Bovenden 1, W. Germany (B.R.D.) Eds. H. Mock, J.M. Kurz. circ. 1,500.

700 920   US
DICTIONARY OF CONTEMPORARY AMERICAN ARTISTS. 1971. irreg., latest 1982. St. Martin's Press, Scholarly and Reference Division, 175 Fifth Ave., New York, NY 10010. TEL 212-674-5151. Ed. Paul Cummings.

700   FR   ISSN 0070-4776
DICTIONNAIRE DES VALEURS DES MEUBLES ET OBJETS D'ART. 1965. irreg. 400 F. (vol. 1); 117F.(vol. 2) Librairie Fischbacher, 33 rue de Seine, 75006 Paris, France. Ed. E. Mayer.

700   UK   ISSN 0144-7459
DIRECTORY OF ARTS CENTRES. 1981. irreg. £6.50. (Arts Council of Great Britain) J. Offord (Publicatons) Ltd., 12 The Avenue, Eastbourne, E. Sussex BN21 3YA, England. Ed. Sheena Barbour. adv. illus.

700 913   US
DIRECTORY OF HISTORIANS OF LATIN AMERICAN ART. 1979. irreg., 2nd edt., 1981. $8. University of Texas at San Antonio, Research Center for the Visual Arts, San Antonio, TX 78285. TEL 512-691-4358. Ed. Jacinto Quirarte. circ. 1, 000.

700   CN   ISSN 0832-865X
DIRECTORY OF THE ARTS. (Text in English and French) a. Can.$18.95 to members; non-members Can.$19.95. Canadian Conference of the Arts, 126 York St., Ste. 400, Ottawa, Ont. K1N 5T5, Canada. TEL 613-238-3561.
    Incorporates: Who's Who: A Guide to Federal and Provincial Departments and Agencies, Their Funding Programs and the People Who Head Them (ISSN 0384-2355); Who Does What: A Guide to National Associations, Service Organizations and Unions Operating in the Arts (ISSN 0700-2661)

709   CN   ISSN 0383-4514
DOCUMENTS IN THE HISTORY OF CANADIAN ART/DOCUMENTS D'HISTOIRE DE L'ART CANADIEN. (Text in French or English) 1974. irreg., no.2, 1976. Can.$10. National Museums of Canada, Ottawa, Ont., K1A 0M8, Canada. TEL 613-990-1969. illus. circ. 5,000.

705   DR
DOMINICAN REPUBLIC. DIRECCION GENERAL DE BELLAS ARTES. CATALOGO DE LA BIENAL DE ARTES PLASTICAS. irreg. Direccion General de Bellas Artes, Santo Domingo, Dominican Republic. illus.

DRAGON. see *LITERATURE*

DUMBARTON OAKS CONFERENCE PROCEEDINGS. see *ARCHAEOLOGY*

EDITOR'S CHOICE; poetry, fiction and art. see *LITERATURE*

700   DK   ISSN 0109-3304
EFTERSYN. 1973. irreg. (approx. a.) Kr.345. Arne Bruun Rasmussen Kunstauktioner, Bredgade 33, 1260 Copenhagen K, Denmark. illus.

ENCYCLIA. see *SCIENCES: COMPREHENSIVE WORKS*

700   FR
ENNEMI. 1980. a. Christian Bourgois Editeur, 8 rue Garanciere, 75006 Paris, France. Ed. G.G. Lemaire. illus. circ. 2,000.

709   MX   ISSN 0071-1659
ESTUDIOS DE ARTE Y ESTETICA. 1958. irreg., latest issue, 1972. price varies. ‡ Universidad Nacional Autonoma de Mexico, Instituto de Investigaciones Esteticas, Torre de Humanidades, Ciudad Universitaria, Mexico 20, D.F., Mexico.

709   MX   ISSN 0071-1748
ESTUDIOS Y FUENTES DEL ARTE EN MEXICO. 1955. irreg., no.36, 1978. price varies. ‡ Universidad Nacional Autonoma de Mexico, Instituto de Investigaciones Esteticas, Torre de Humanidades, Ciudad Universitaria, Mexico 20, D.F., Mexico.

700 800   PO
ESTUDOS ITALIANOS EM PORTUGAL. (Text in Italian and Portuguese) 1939. irreg., 1968-69, no. 31-32. Esc.150($5.50) (Istituto Italiano di Cultura in Portogallo) Papelaria Fernandes, Largo do Rato 13, Lisbon 2, Portugal. bk. rev. bibl. illus. stat. tr.lit. cum.index. circ. 500. (tabloid format; also avail. in cards)

709   BE   ISSN 0071-1969
ETUDES D'HISTOIRE DE L'ART.* 1964. irreg. price varies. Institut Historique Belge de Rome, c/o Archives Generales du Royaume, 2-6 rue de Ruysbroeck, B-1000 Brussels, Belgium. circ. controlled.

700 FR ISSN 0071-2426
EUROPEAN ART EXHIBITIONS. CATALOG.
1954. irreg. Council of Europe, Publications Section, F-67006 Strasbourg, France (Dist. in U.S. by: Worldwide Books, 37-39 Antwerp St., Boston, MA 02135)

741.5 UK
EUROPEAN ILLUSTRATION. (Text in English, French and German) 1975. a. £1. Polygon Editions S.A.R.L., 12 Carlton House Terrace, London S.W.1, England. Ed. Edward Booth-Clibborn. illus. circ. 10,000.

700 800 IT
EVENTI E INTERVENTI. irreg. Angelo Longo Editore, Via Paolo Costa 33, P.O. Box 431, 48100 Ravenna, Italy.

EXETER'S STUDIES IN AMERICAN & COMMONWEALTH ARTS. see *LITERATURE*

760 GW ISSN 0172-2859
EXLIBRISKUNST UND GRAPHIK. JAHRBUCH. 1979. a. DM.110. Deutsche Exlibris-Gesellschaft e.V., Am Fallersleber Tore 5, D-3300 Braunschweig, W. Germany (B.R.D.) Ed. Norbert H. Ott. adv.
Formerly: Exlibriskunst und Graphik (ISSN 0075-2630)

EXPLORATIONS IN RENAISSANCE CULTURE. see *HISTORY — History Of Europe*

EXPRESSION; revue culturelle feminine internationale. see *WOMEN'S INTERESTS*

700 913 IT ISSN 0085-0500
FELIX RAVENNA; RIVISTA DI ANTICHITA RAVENNATI, CRISTIANE E BIZANTINE. 1970. a. L.35000($34) (Universita degli Studi di Bologna, Istituto di Antichita Ravennati e Bizantine) Edizioni del Girasole Ravenna, Via Baccarini 80, 48100 Ravenna, Italy. Ed. Raffaella Farioli Campanati. bk. rev. circ. 500. Indexed: RILA.

709 SW ISSN 0071-481X
FIGURA. NOVA SERIES; Uppsala studies in the history of art. (Subseries of Acta Universitatis Upsaliensis) (Text in English or German) 1951-59 (no. 1-12); N.S. 1959. irreg., no.17, 1978. price varies. (Uppsala Universitet, Institute of Art History) Almqvist & Wiksell International, Box 62, S-101 20 Stockholm, Sweden. Ed. Rudolf Zeitler.

700 CN ISSN 0315-2456
FILE. 1972. irreg. Can.$5 per no. Art Metropole, 217 Richmond St. W., Toronto, Ont. M5V 1W2, Canada. Ed.Bd. adv. bk. rev. circ. 3,000. (also avail. in microfilm; reprint service avail. from MML)

FILM AUSTRALIA CATALOGUE. see *MOTION PICTURES*

707 CN ISSN 0318-7489
FINE. (Supplement avail.: F A C T A Newsletter) 1965. a. Can.$15. Alberta Teachers' Association, Fine Arts Council, 11010 142nd St., Edmonton, Alta. T5N 2R1, Canada. TEL 403-453-2411. Ed. Jim Simpson. bk. rev. circ. 617. (tabloid format) Indexed: Can.Educ.Ind.

700 US
FINE ARTS WORK CENTER IN PROVINCETOWN. VISUAL CATALOGUE. a. free. Fine Arts Work Center in Provincetown, Inc., 24 Pearl St., Box 565, Provincetown, MA 02657. TEL 617-487-9960. illus.
Formerly: Fine Arts Work Center in Provincetown. Newsletter.

745.5 US
FLORIDA FOLKLIFE RESOURCE DIRECTORY. 1977. a. $2. Department of State, Bureau of Florida Folklife Programs, Box 265, White Springs, FL 32096. TEL 904-397-2192. circ. 1,000.
Former titles: Florida Festival Arts Directory; (until 1980): Florida Folk Arts Directory (ISSN 0162-5616)

709 PL ISSN 0071-6723
FOLIA HISTORIAE ARTIUM. (Text in Polish; summaries in French) 1964. a. price varies. (Polska Akademia Nauk, Oddzial w Krakowie, Komisja Teorii i Historii Sztuki) Ossolineum, Publishing House of the Polish Academy of Sciences, Rynek 9, Wroclaw, Poland (Dist. by: Ars Polona-Ruch, Krakowskie Przedmiescie 7, Warsaw, Poland) Ed. L. Kalinowski. Indexed: Artbibl. RILA.

709 900 IT
FONTI E STUDI PER LA STORIA DI BOLOGNA E DELLE PROVINCE EMILIANE E ROMAGNOLE. 1969. irreg., vol.7, 1981. price varies. ALFA Edizioni, Via Santo Stefano 13, I-40125 Bologna, Italy. circ. 4,000.

709 913 GW ISSN 0532-2189
FORSCHUNGEN ZUR KUNSTGESCHICHTE UND CHRISTLICHEN ARCHAEOLOGIE. irreg., vol.15, 1986. price varies. Franz Steiner Verlag Wiesbaden GmbH, Birkenwaldstr. 44, Postfach 347, D-7000 Stuttgart 1, W. Germany (B.R.D.) Eds. Richard Hamann-MacLean, Otto Feld.

700 US ISSN 0071-9382
FREER GALLERY OF ART, WASHINGTON, D.C. OCCASIONAL PAPERS. 1947. irreg., vol.4, 1971. Smithsonian Institution, Jefferson Dr., S.W. at 12th St., Washington, DC 20560. TEL 202-357-1432.

FUEHRER ZU ARCHAEOLOGISCHEN DENKMAELERN IN DEUTSCHLAND. see *ARCHAEOLOGY*

FUNDE UND AUSGRABUNGEN IM BEZIRK TRIER. see *ARCHAEOLOGY*

FYNSKE MINDER. see *HISTORY — History Of Europe*

700 AT
GALLERY. 1968. a. Aus.$20($13) (National Gallery Society of Victoria) Mount Eagle Publications, P.O. Box 84, Heidelberg, Vic. 3084, Australia. Ed. Paton Forster. adv. index. circ. 16,000. (back issues avail.)

GENAVA; revue d'archeologie et d'histoire de l'art. see *ARCHAEOLOGY*

700 720 BE ISSN 0772-7151
GENTSE BIJDRAGEN TOT DE KUNSTGESCHIEDENIS. (Text and summaries in Dutch, English, French and German) 1934. biennial. price varies. Rijksuniversiteit Gent, Sectie Kunstgeschiedenis en Oudheidkunde van de Faculteit Letteren en Wijsbegeerte, Blandijnberg 2, B-9000 Gent, Belgium. illus. circ. 120. (back issues avail.)

700 US
GORDON'S PRINT PRICE ANNUAL (YEAR) a. $285. Apollo Book (Distributor), 5 Schoolhouse Ln., Poughkeepsie, NY 12603. TEL 914-462-0040.

709 720 SW ISSN 0348-4114
GOTHENBURG STUDIES IN ART AND ARCHITECTURE. (Subseries of Acta Universitatis Gothoburgensis) 1978. irreg., no.3, 1985. price varies; also exchange basis. Acta Universitatis Gothoburgensis, Box 5096, S-402 22 Goeteborg, Sweden (Dist. in U.S., Canada, and Mexico by: Humanities Press, Inc., 171 First Ave., Atlantic Highlands, NJ 07716) Ed. Maj-Brit Wadell.

760 JA ISSN 0072-548X
GRAPHIC ARTS JAPAN. (Text in English) 1959. a. $25. Japan Printers' Association, Publicity Bureau, 16-8, 1-chome, Shintomi, Chuo-ku, Tokyo, Japan. Ed. Seizo Kimura. adv. bk. rev. circ. 5,000. (back issues avail.) Indexed: Graph.Arts Lit.Abstr.

659.1 760 SZ ISSN 0072-5528
GRAPHIS ANNUAL; international annual of advertising and editorial graphics. (Text in English, French, German) 1952. a. 112 Fr.($59.50) B. Martin Pedersen Graphis Press Corp, 107 Dufourstrasse, CH-8008 Zurich, Switzerland (Dist. by: Watson-Guptill Publications, P.O. Box 2014, Lakewood, NJ 08701) Ed. B. Martin Pedersen. index. circ. 16,000.

769.5 SZ
GRAPHIS POSTERS; international annual of poster art. (Text in English, French and German) 1973. a. 105 Fr.($59.50) B. Martin Pedersen Graphis Press Corp, 107 Dufourstrasse, 8008 Zurich, Switzerland (Dist. by: Watson-Guptill Publications, P.O. Box 2014, Lakewood, NJ 08701) Ed. B. Martin Pedersen. illus. circ. 7,500.

700 382 UK ISSN 0072-5668
GREAT BRITAIN. DEPARTMENT OF TRADE. EXPORT OF WORKS OF ART. a. H.M.S.O., P.O. Box 569, London SE1 9NH, England. (reprint service avail. from UMI)

700 FR ISSN 0066-3069
GUIDE EUROPEEN DE L'AMATEUR D'ART, DE L'ANTIQUAIRE ET DU BIBLIOPHILE. Short title: Guide Emer. (Text in English, French, German, Italian) 1947. biennial. 215 F. Editions Emer, 50 rue Quai de l'Hotel-de-Ville, 75004 Paris, France. Ed. Charles de Talhouet. adv. circ. 16,000.

700 US
GUIDE TO NATIONAL ENDOWMENT FOR THE ARTS. 1972. a. limited free distribution. National Endowment for the Arts, Public Information Office, Washington, DC 20506. TEL 202-682-5400. circ. 20,000.
Formerly: National Endowment for the Arts. Guide to Programs (ISSN 0547-6658)

700 600 JA ISSN 0533-6627
GUNMA UNIVERSITY, FACULTY OF EDUCATION. ANNUAL REPORT: ART, TECHNOLOGY, HEALTH & PHYSICAL EDUCATION, AND SCIENCE OF HUMAN LIVING SERIES. (Text in Japanese; summaries in English) 1966. a. exchange basis. Gunma University, Faculty of Education, Gunma University Library, 4-2. Aramaki, Maebashi, Gunma 371, Japan. Ed.Bd. Indexed: Biol.Abstr.

745 DK ISSN 0107-9611
HAANDARBEJDETS FREMME. AARETS KORSSTING. (Text in Danish, English and German) 1960. a. Kr.65($14) Haandarbejdets Fremme, Copenhagen, Denmark.
Formerly: Haandarbejdets Fremme. Kalender.

709.4 GW ISSN 0072-9205
HABELTS DISSERTATIONSDRUCKE. REIHE KUNSTGESCHICHTE. 1953. irreg., no.8, 1985. price varies. Dr. Rudolf Habelt GmbH, Am Buchenhang 1, 5300 Bonn 1, W. Germany (B.R.D.)

700 DK ISSN 0085-1361
HAFNIA; COPENHAGEN PAPERS IN THE HISTORY OF ART. (Text in English, French, and German) 1970. a. Kr.175. Koebenhavns Universitet, Institute of Art History, Esplanaden 34 B, 1263 Copenhagen K, Denmark (Dist. by: Rosenkilde og Bagger Forlag, 3 Kron-Prinsens-Gade, Copenhagen K, Denmark) Eds. Oystein Hjort, Marianne Marcussen. circ. 600. Indexed: RILA.

HARVESTER. see *LITERATURE*

701.18 US
HIGHLIGHTS OF PERSIAN ART. 1979. a. $55.25. Bibliotheca Persica, 450 Riverside Dr., No. 4, New York, NY 10027. TEL 212-280-4366. Eds. Richard Ettinghausen, Ehsan Yarshater. circ. 2,000.
Formerly: Persian Art Series.

700 UY
HISPANIC AMERICAN ARTS; all you want or must know, about everything, in all the fields of Hispanic American arts. (Text in Spanish; summaries in English and Spanish) 1974. irreg., (approx. 2-4 yr.) $20. Eduardo Darino, Ed. & Pub., Casilla de Correo 1677, Montevideo, Uruguay (U.S. Subscr. to: Darino, Box 1496-GCS, New York, NY 10163) bk. rev. film rev. play rev. bibl. illus. index.
Formerly: Latinamerican Arts; Incorporating: C B A Boletin Informativo.

700 PL ISSN 0083-4270
HISTORIA SZTUKI. (Text in Polish; summaries in German or English) 1959. irreg. price varies. Adam Mickiewicz University Press, Marchlewskiego 128, 61-874 Poznan, Poland.
Formerly: Uniwersytet im. Adama Mickiewicza w Poznaniu. Zeszyty Naukowe. Historia Sztuki.

700 301.412 US ISSN 0739-0718
HUE POINTS. 1982. irreg., (2-3/yr.) $30. Women's Caucus for Art, National Office, Moore College of Art, 20th & Parkway, Philadelphia, PA 19103. TEL 215-854-0922. Ed.Bd. adv. bk. rev. circ. 3,000.

IDAHO (MOSCOW) see *LITERATURE*

700 GW
IKONENKALENDER. (Calendar in English and German) a. DM.32. Verlag Aurel Bongers, Dortmunder str.67, Postfach 100 264, 4350 Recklinghausen, W. Germany (B.R.D.) illus.

700 US ISSN 0445-3387
ILLINOIS. STATE MUSEUM. HANDBOOK OF COLLECTIONS. 1963. irreg., no.4, 1983. Illinois State Museum, Springfield, IL 62706. TEL 217-782-7386.

760 JA
ILLUSTRATION IN JAPAN. (Text in Japanese and English) 1972. a. (Daiichi Shuppan Center) Kodansha Ltd., 12-21, Otowa 2-chome, Bunkyo-ku, Tokyo 112, Japan.

700 US ISSN 0085-1760
INDEX OF ART IN THE PACIFIC NORTHWEST. 1970. irreg., no.12, 1977. price varies. (University of Washington, Henry Art Gallery) University of Washington Press, Seattle, WA 98105. TEL 206-543-4050.

INDEX TO REPRODUCTIONS IN ART PERIODICALS. see ABSTRACTING AND INDEXING SERVICES

INDUSTRIAL SABOTAGE. see LITERATURE — Poetry

700 BE ISSN 0085-1892
INSTITUT ROYAL DE PATRIMOINE ARTISTIQUE. BULLETIN/KONINKLIJK INSTITUUT VOOR HET KUNSTPATRIMONIUM. BULLETIN. (Text and summaries in Dutch, French) 1958. a. 625 Fr.($6) ‡ Institut Royal du Patrimoine Artistique, 1 Parc du Cinquantenaire, 1040 Brussels, Belgium. Ed. Jacqueline Folie, (back issues avail.) Indexed: Art & Archeol.Tech.Abstr. RILA.

INTERFERENCES, ARTS, LETTRES. see LITERATURE

702.8 US
INTERNATIONAL ART MATERIAL DIRECTORY AND BUYERS GUIDE. 1952. a. Syndicate Magazines, Inc., 390 Fifth Ave., New York, NY 10018. TEL 212-613-9700. adv.

700 FR
INTERNATIONAL ASSOCIATION OF PERFORMING ARTS LIBRARIES AND MUSEUMS. CONGRESS PROCEEDINGS. (Publisher of proceedings varies) 1957. irreg. International Association of Performing Arts Libraries and Museums, 1 rue de Sully, 75004 Paris, France.
    Formerly: International Society for Performing Arts Libraries and Museums. Congress Proceedings (ISSN 0074-7882)

700 US ISSN 0074-1922
INTERNATIONAL AUCTION RECORDS. 1967. a. $184. Editions Publisol, Box 339, Gracie Sta., New York, NY 10028. TEL 212-289-3981. Ed. E. Mayer. adv. circ. 5,000.

700 382 US
INTERNATIONAL AUCTION RECORDS. a. $185. Apollo Book (Distributor), 5 Schoolhouse Ln., Poughkeepsie, NY 12603. TEL 914-462-0040.

709 FR ISSN 0074-4190
INTERNATIONAL CONGRESS ON THE HISTORY OF ART. PROCEEDINGS. 1873. quinquennial, 1968, 22nd, Budapest. (International Committee on the History of Art, SP) Institut d'Art et d'Archeologie, 3 rue Michelet, 75006 Paris, France.
    Proceedings published in host country

700 GW ISSN 0074-4565
INTERNATIONAL DIRECTORY OF ARTS. (Text in English, French, German, Italian, Spanish) 1949. biennial. DM.245($130) Art Address Verlag Mueller GmbH & Co. KG, Grosse Eschenheimer Str. 16, Postfach 100152, 6000 Frankfurt 1, W. Germany (B.R.D.) Ed. Michael Zils. adv. index. circ. 10,000.

700 382 US
INTERNATIONAL DIRECTORY OF ARTS (YEAR) a. Apollo Book (Distributor), 5 Schoolhouse Ln., Poughkeepsie, NY 12503. TEL 914-462-0040.

700 920 UK
INTERNATIONAL WHO'S WHO IN ART AND ANTIQUES. 1972. irreg. price varies. Melrose Press Ltd., 3 Regal Ln., Soham, Ely, Cambridgeshire CB7 5BA, England.

INTERPLAY (MALIBU); proceedings of symposia in comparative literature and the arts. see LITERATURE

INTERVENTI CLASSENSI. see LITERATURE

INVENTAIRE GENERAL DES MONUMENTS ET DES RICHESSES ARTISTIQUES DE LA FRANCE. see ARCHITECTURE

709 956 US ISSN 0742-1125
ISLAMIC ART AND ARCHITECTURE.* 1981. irreg. price varies. Undena Publications, 6355 Green Valley Circle, No. 213, Culver City, CA 90230-7064. Ed. A. Daneshvari.

ISTITUTO NAZIONALE DI ARCHEOLOGIA E STORIA DELL'ARTE. RIVISTA. see ARCHAEOLOGY

L'IVRE DE PIERRES. see ARCHITECTURE

IZ STAROG I NOVOG ZAGREBA. see ARCHITECTURE

708 US ISSN 0362-1979
J. PAUL GETTY MUSEUM JOURNAL. 1975. a. price varies. J. Paul Getty Museum, 17985 Pacific Coast Highway, Malibu, CA 90265. TEL 213-459-7611. Ed. Andrea P.A. Belloli. illus. circ. 500. (back issues avail.) Indexed: Art Ind. RILA.

700 BE ISSN 0066-3174
JAARBOEK DER SCHONE KUNSTEN/ ALGEMEEN JAARBOEK DER SCHONE KUNSTEN. (Text in Dutch, French) 1928. a. 450 Fr.($15) Editions ARTO, 85 Avenue Winston Churchill, 1180 Brussels, Belgium. adv. bk. rev. circ. 4,000.
    Formerly: Dessinateurs, Peintres et Sculpteurs de Belgique (ISSN 0070-3869)

700 616.89 JA
JAPANESE BULLETIN OF ART THERAPY. (Text in Japanese and other languages) 1969. a. 4000 Yen($20) Societe Japonaise de Psychopathologie de l'Expression, c/o Neuropsychiatric Research Institute, 91 Bentencho, Shinjuku-ku, Tokyo 162, Japan. Ed. Dr. Yoshihito Tokuda. adv. bk. rev. bibl. charts. illus. stat. circ. 4,500(controlled) (back issues avail.)

JAPANESE SWORD SOCIETY OF THE U.S. BULLETIN. see ANTIQUES

JEOPARDY. see LITERATURE

700 NE ISSN 0160-208X
JOURNAL OF JEWISH ART. (Text in English, French) 1974. a. $25. (Hebrew University of Jerusalem) E.J. Brill, P.O. Box 9000, 2300 PA Leiden, Netherlands. Ed. Bezalel Narkiss. bk. rev. bibl. illus. circ. 2,000. (also avail. in microform from UMI; back issues avail.; reprint service avail. from UMI) Indexed: Curr.Cont. Ind.Jew.Per. RILA.

701.18 US
JOURNAL OF THE THEORY AND CRITICISM OF THE VISUAL ARTS. 1981. a. $8. Arizona State University, School of Art, Tempe, AZ 85287. Eds. Joseph E. Young, Robert E. Barela. illus. circ. 1,200. (back issues avail.)

JUNIOR AUTHORS AND ILLUSTRATORS SERIES. see JOURNALISM

700 FI ISSN 0075-4633
JYVASKYLA STUDIES IN THE ARTS. 1967. irreg. price varies; available on exchange. Jyvaskylan Yliopisto - University of Jyvaskyla, Seminaarinkatu 15, 40100 Jyvaskyla 10, Finland. Ed. Lauri Routila. circ. 450.

708 AU ISSN 0022-7587
KAERNTNER MUSEUMSSCHRIFTEN. 1954. irreg. price varies. Landesmuseum fuer Kaernten, Museumgasse 2, A-9010 Klagenfurt, Austria. circ. 200.

KALAVA HA SAHITYAYA. see LITERATURE

KALDRON. see LITERATURE — Poetry

769.5 CS
KATALOG SLOVENSKYCH PLAGATOV. 1975. irreg. price varies. Matica Slovenska, Mudronova 35, 036 52 Martin, Czechoslovakia.

700 PL ISSN 0075-5257
KATALOG ZABYTKOW SZTUKI W POLSCE. 1953. irreg. price varies. (Polska Akademia Nauk, Instytut Sztuki) Wydawnictwa Artystyczne i Filmowe, Pulawska 61, Warsaw, Poland TEL 048-22-45-53-01. (Dist. by: Ars Polona-Ruch, Krakowskie Przedmiescie 7, Warsaw, Poland) Ed. Jerzy Zygmunt Lozinski. circ. 3,250.

KENYA NATIONAL ACADEMY OF SCIENCES. ANNUAL REPORT. see SCIENCES: COMPREHENSIVE WORKS

709 GW ISSN 0075-6563
KOLLOQUIUM UEBER SPAETANTIKE UND FRUEHMITTELALTERLICHE SKULPTUR. (Text in German) 1968. irreg. price varies. Philipp Von Zabern, Welschnonnengasse 13A, Postfach 4065, 6500 Mainz, W. Germany (B.R.D.) Ed. Vladimir Milojcic.

709 913 SW ISSN 0083-6737
KUNGLIGA VITTERHETS-, HISTORIE- OCH ANTIKVITETS AKADEMIEN. ANTIKVARISKT ARKIV. (Text in English, German and Swedish) 1954. irreg., no.72, 1986. price varies. Kungliga Vitterhets-, Historie- och Antikvitets Akademien - Royal Academy of Letters, History and Antiquities, Villagatan 3, 114 32 Stockholm, Sweden (Dist. by: Almqvist & Wiksell International, P.O. Box 45150, S104-30 Stockholm, Sweden) index.

KUNST AM BAU. see ARCHITECTURE

709.5 GW ISSN 0023-5393
KUNST DES ORIENTS/ART OF THE ORIENT. (Text in English and German) 1950. a. DM.96. Franz Steiner Verlag Wiesbaden GmbH, Birkenwaldstr. 44, Postfach 347, D-7000 Stuttgart 1, W. Germany (B.R.D.) Ed. Klaus Brisch. adv. bk. rev. illus. index. circ. 600. (back issues avail.) Indexed: Artbibl.

705 AU ISSN 0075-7241
KUNST-KATALOG: AUKTIONEN. 1947. irreg. S.900. Dorotheum, Dorotheergasse 11, A 1011 Vienna, Austria. adv. bk. rev. circ. 6,000.

700 DK ISSN 0454-6520
KUNST OG MUSEUM. 1966. a. Kr.60. (Foreningen af Danske Kunstmuseer) Museumstjenesten, Sjoerupvej 1, Lysgaard, 8800 Viborg, Denmark. illus.

709 AU ISSN 0075-2312
KUNSTHISTORISCHE SAMMLUNGEN IN WIEN. JAHRBUCH. 1926. a. price varies. (Kunsthistorisches Museum in Wien) Verlag Anton Schroll und Co., Spengergasse 39, A-1051 Vienna, Austria. Indexed: Numis.Lit. RILA.

700 900 IT
KUNSTHISTORISCHES INSTITUT IN FLORENZ. MITTEILUNGEN. (Text in English, German, Italian) 1908. a. DM.140. Kunsthistorisches Institut in Florenz, Via Giusti 44, I-50121 Florence, Italy. Eds. Gerhard Ewald, Guenter Passavant. bibl. illus. index. circ. 1,000(controlled) Indexed: Curr.Cont. Art Ind. RILA.

705 AU
KUNSTJAHRBUCH DER STADT LINZ. 1961. a. S.250. (Stadtmuseum Linz) Anton Schroll und Co., Spengergasse 39, A-1051 Vienna, Austria. Ed. Georg Wacha. bk. rev. circ. 450. Indexed: RILA.
    Formerly: Linzer Jahrbuch fuer Kunstgeschichte (ISSN 0075-9732)

700 DK ISSN 0107-8933
KUNSTMUSEETS AARSSKRIFT.* (Summaries in English, French, German and Italian) 1913. irreg. Kr.85. Statens Museum for Kunst, Solvgade 48-50, DK-1307 Copenhagen K, Denmark. illus. Indexed: RILA.

706.5 GW ISSN 0174-352X
KUNSTPREIS-JAHRBUCH. a. DM.152. Weltkunst Verlag GmbH, Nymphenburgerstr. 84, 8000 Munich 19, W. Germany(B.R.D.) Ed. Josef Koenig. adv. illus. circ. 9,000.
    Formerly: Art-Price Annual.

701 GW ISSN 0723-6638
KURT-SCHWITTERS-ALMANACH. 1982. a. DM.19.80 per no. Postscriptum-Verlag GmbH, Annenstr. 8, D-3000 Hannover 1, W. Germany (B.R.D.) Ed. Michael Erlhoff. circ. 1,500. (back issues avail.)

ART 107

L C A QUARTERLY. (Lawyers for the Creative Arts) see *LAW*

709   II   ISSN 0458-6506
LALIT KALA. vol.20, 1981. a. National Academy of Art - Lalit Kala Akademi, Rabindra Bhavan, New Delhi 110001, India.

709   AU   ISSN 0007-280X
LANDESMUSEUM FUER KAERNTEN. BUCHREIHE. 1954. irreg. price varies. Landesmuseum fuer Kaernten, Museumgasse 2, A-9010 Klagenfurt, Austria. circ. 400. Indexed: GeoRef.

700   US   ISSN 0362-7047
LATVJU MAKSLA. (Text in Latvian) 1975. irreg. $9 per no. American Latvian Association in the United States, Inc., Latvian Institute, Box 4578, Rockville, MD 20850-0071. TEL 301-340-1914. Ed. Arnolds Sildegs. adv. bk. rev. illus. circ. 1,500.

700   NE   ISSN 0460-2048
LEIDSE KUNSTHISTORISCHE REEKS. 1966. irreg., vol.2, 1969. price varies. Leiden University Press, c/o E.J. Brill Publishers, Postbus 9000, 2300 PA Leiden, Netherlands.

700 330   US
LEONARD'S ANNUAL INDEX OF ART AUCTIONS (YEAR) a. $175. Apollo Book (Distributor), 5 Schoolhouse Ln., Poughkeepsie, NY 12603. TEL 914-462-0040.

745   US
LETTERHEADS; the international annual of letterhead design. 1977. a. $30. Art Direction Book Co., 10 E. 39th St., New York, NY 10016. Ed. David E. Carter. adv. circ. 5,000.

700   US
LIBRARY OF GREAT PAINTERS. irreg. $40. Harry N. Abrams, Inc., 100 Fifth Ave., New York, NY 10011. TEL 212-206-7715.

700   US   ISSN 0161-4223
LIGHTWORKS. 1975. irreg., no.18, 1986/87. $15 to individuals; institutions $20. Lightworks Magazine, Inc., Box 1202, Birmingham, MI 48012. TEL 313-626-8026. Ed. Charlton Burch. bk. rev. film rev. illus. circ. 2,000. (back issues avail.)

700   UR
LITUANISTIKA V S.S.S.R. ISKUSSTVOVEDENIE; nauchno-informatsionnyi sbornik. (Text in Russian) 1978. a. 0.30 Rub. Akademiya Nauk Litovskoi S.S.R., Nauchno-Informatsionnyi Tsentr, Michurino g-ve 1/46, Vilnius, Lithuanian S.S.R., U.S.S.R. Ed. A. Balsys. circ. 350.

700 708   US
LOCUS (NEW YORK) 1975. irreg., latest 1985. $39. Filsinger & Company Ltd., 288 W. 12 St., New York, NY 10014. TEL 212-243-7421. Ed. Cheryl Filsinger.
Formerly: Locus Select.

700   US
LYLES OFFICIAL ARTS REVIEW. a. $24.95. Apollo Book (Distributor), 5 Schoolhouse Ln., Poughkeepsie, NY 12603. TEL 914-462-0040.

MAGIC CHANGES; the annual for independent artists. see *LITERATURE*

MAGIRA. see *LITERATURE*

709 943   HU   ISSN 0076-2490
MAGYARORSZAG MUEMLEKI TOPOGRAFIAJA. (Text in Hungarian; summaries in English, German, Russian) 1956. irreg., vol.9, 1978. price varies. (Magyar Tudomanyos Akademia) Akademiai Kiado, Publishing House of the Hungarian Academy of Sciences, P.O. Box 24, H-1363 Budapest, Hungary.

MAINFRAENKISCHES JAHRBUCH FUER GESCHICHTE UND KUNST. see *HISTORY — History Of Europe*

943 913 709   GW   ISSN 0076-2792
MAINZER ZEITSCHRIFT; Mittelrheinisches Jahrbuch fuer Archaeologie, Geschichte und Kunst. 1906. a. price varies. Mainzer Altertumsverein e.V., Rheinallee 3b, 6500 Mainz, W. Germany (B.R.D.) Ed. Friedrich Schuetz. circ. 770. Indexed: Br.Archaeol.Abstr. RILA.

393   US   ISSN 0277-8726
MARKERS. 1979/80. a. price varies. Association for Gravestone Studies, c/o Rosalee F. Oakley, Exec. Director, 46 Plymouth Rd., Needham, MA 02192. TEL 617-455-8180. Ed. Theodore Chase.

705   US   ISSN 0076-4701
MARSYAS. 1941. biennial. $8. New York University, Institute of Fine Arts, 14 E. 78th St., New York, NY 10021 (Dist. by: J.J. Augustin, Inc., Locust Valley, N.Y. 11560) circ. 500. (also avail. in microform from UMI) Indexed: Art Ind. RILA.

MASSSTAEBE. see *HUMANITIES: COMPREHENSIVE WORKS*

708   CN   ISSN 0383-5391
MASTERPIECES IN THE NATIONAL GALLERY OF CANADA/CHEFS-D'OEUVRE DE LA GALERIE NATIONALE DU CANADA. (Text in English and French) 1971. irreg., no.12, 1978. price varies. National Museums of Canada, Ottawa, Ont. K1A 0M8, Canada. TEL 613-990-1969. Eds. Charles Hill, Michael Pantazzi. illus. circ. 5,000.

700 300   US   ISSN 0160-8797
MASTER'S THESES IN THE ARTS AND SOCIAL SCIENCES. 1976. a. $30 to libraries. Research Publications, Box 92, Cedar Falls, IA 50613. TEL 319-273-6412. Ed. H.M. Silvey.

500 808   US   ISSN 0272-5657
ME. Variant title: Dirigo: Me. 1980. irreg., approx. q. $20. Pittore Euforico, Box 1132, Peter Stuyvesant Sta., New York, NY 10009. TEL 212-673-2705. Ed. Carlo Pittore. adv. bk. rev. illus. circ. 1,000. (tabloid format; back issues avail.)
Formerly: Me, Too.

MEDIAEVALIA. see *HISTORY — History Of Europe*

MEDIEVAL ACADEMY BOOKS. see *HISTORY — History Of Europe*

MEDIEVAL ACADEMY REPRINTS FOR TEACHING. see *HISTORY — History Of Europe*

MELANGES D'HISTOIRE DE L'ARCHITECTURE. see *ARCHITECTURE*

708.147   US   ISSN 0192-6950
METROPOLITAN MUSEUM OF ART. NOTABLE ACQUISITIONS. a. Metropolitan Museum of Art, Fifth Ave. and 82nd St., New York, NY 10028.

MEUSE. see *LITERATURE*

709   US
MICHIGAN STATE UNIVERSITY. MUSEUM PUBLICATIONS. FOLK ART SERIES. irreg. price varies. Michigan State University, Museum, East Lansing, MI 48824. TEL 517-355-2370.

MILLER'S ANTIQUE PRICE GUIDE (YEAR) see *ANTIQUES*

700   IT
MINIATURA E ARTI MINORI IN CAMPANIA. no.10, 1975. irreg., no.13, 1978. price varies. (Banca Sannitica) Societa Editrice Napoletana s.r.l., Corso Umberto I 34, 80138 Naples, Italy. Ed. Mario Rotili.

700   US   ISSN 0076-9096
MINNEAPOLIS INSTITUTE OF ARTS. ANNUAL REPORT. 1961. a. Minneapolis Society of Fine Arts, 2400 Third Ave. S., Minneapolis, MN 55404. TEL 612-870-3046. circ. 8,000.

708 700   US   ISSN 0076-910X
MINNEAPOLIS INSTITUTE OF ARTS. BULLETIN. 1914. biennial. $7.50. Minneapolis Society of Fine Arts, 2400 Third Ave. S., Minneapolis, MN 55404. TEL 612-870-3046. Ed. Louise Lincoln. circ. 15,000. (also avail. in microform from UMI) Indexed: RILA.

700   US
MODERN ARTISTS. irreg. $12.50. Harry N. Abrams, Inc., 100 Fifth Ave., New York, NY 10011. TEL 212-206-7715.

700 800   US   ISSN 0161-5866
MONEY BUSINESS: GRANTS AND AWARDS FOR CREATIVE ARTISTS. 1978. irreg., 2nd edt., 1982. $6. Artists Foundation, Inc., c/o Dorothea Boniello, 110 Broad St., Boston, MA 02110. TEL 617-482-8100. Ed.Bd. circ. 1,000.

700   US   ISSN 0544-845X
MONOGRAPHS ON AMERICAN ART. 1968. irreg., no.4, 1975. price varies. Sheldon Memorial Art Gallery, 12th & R St., University of Nebraska, Lincoln, NE 68588. TEL 402-472-2461. illus.

700   US
MONOGRAPHS ON THE FINE ARTS. irreg. price varies. (College Art Association of America) Pennsylvania State University Press, 215 Wagner Bldg., University Park, PA 16802. Ed. Carol F. Lewine.
Formerly: College Art Association Monographs.

MONUMENTA ARTIS ROMANAE. see *ARCHAEOLOGY*

700 950   NE
MONUMENTA GRAECA ET ROMANA. 1977. irreg., vol.6, 1986. E. J. Brill, P.O. Box 9000, 2300 PA Leiden, Netherlands. Ed. H. F. Mussche.

700   SP
MONUMENTS DE LA CATALUNYA ROMANICA. (Contains 2 series: Comarques and Museus) (Text in Catalan) 1978. irreg. Artestudi Edicions, Provenca 552, Barcelona 26, Spain. illus.

700   IT
MOSTRE E MUSEI. 1975. irreg., no.8, 1983. price varies. Societa Editrice Napoletana s.r.l., Corso Umberto I 34, 80138 Naples, Italy. Ed. Raffaello Causa.

700 800 780   US   ISSN 8756-890X
MOVEMENTS IN THE ARTS. 1985. irreg. price varies. Greenwood Press, Box 5007, 88 Post Rd. W., Westport, CT 06881. TEL 203-226-3571.

709   GW   ISSN 0077-1899
MUENCHENER JAHRBUCH DER BILDENDEN KUNST. 1950. a. price varies. (Staatliche Kunstsammlungen Bayerns) Prestel-Verlag, Mandlstr. 26, 8000 Munich 40, W. Germany (B.R.D.) Indexed: RILA.

700 959   US
MUQARNAS; an annual on Islamic art and architecture. a. Yale University Press, 92-A Yale St., New Haven, CT 06520.

700   JA
MUSASHINO ART UNIVERSITY. BULLETIN. (Text in Japanese; summaries in English) 1963. irreg., no.16, 1981. free. Musashino Art University, 1-736 Ogawa-machi, Kodaira-shi, Tokyo 187, Japan. illus.

913 708   US   ISSN 0077-2194
MUSE. 1967. a. $5. University of Missouri-Columbia, Museum of Art and Archaeology, One Pickard Hall, Columbia, MO 65211. TEL 314-882-3591. Ed. Forrest McGill. circ. 2,500. Indexed: Numis.Lit. RILA.

700   FR   ISSN 0078-9704
MUSEE GUIMET, PARIS. BIBLIOTHEQUE D'ETUDES. 1892. irreg. price varies. Presses Universitaires de France, 108 bd. Saint Germain, 75279 Paris Cedex 6, France (Service des Periodiques, 12 rue Jean de Beauvais, 75005 Paris) (reprint service avail. from KTO)

700   FR   ISSN 0078-9712
MUSEE GUIMET, PARIS. ETUDE DES COLLECTIONS DU MUSEE. irreg. Presses Universitaires de France, 108 bd. Saint Germain, 75279 Paris Cedex 6, France (Service des Periodiques, 12 rue Jean de Beauvais, 75005 Paris) (reprint service avail. from KTO)

709.4   FR   ISSN 0027-3783
MUSEE INGRES. BULLETIN. (Special nos. avail.) 1956. a. 120 F. Societe des Amis du Musee d'Ingres, 19 rue de l'Hotel de Ville, 82000 Montauban, France. Ed. Evelyne Dayrens. bk. rev. illus. circ. 800. Indexed: RILA.
History

MUSEUM FUER VOELKERKUNDE, BERLIN. VEROEFFENTLICHUNGEN. NEUE FOLGE. ABTEILUNG: AMERIKANISCHE NATURVOELKER. see *ANTHROPOLOGY*

MUSEUM OF FAR EASTERN ANTIQUITIES. BULLETIN. see *MUSEUMS AND ART GALLERIES*

MUSEUM YEAR. see *MUSEUMS AND ART GALLERIES*

MUSICA, IMMAGINE, TEATRO. see *MUSIC*

700   PL   ISSN 0068-4678
MUZEUM GORNOSLASKIE W BYTOMIU. ROCZNIK. SERIA SZTUKA. (Text in Polish; summaries in German and Russian) 1964. irreg. price varies. Muzeum Gornoslaskie, Pl. Thaelmanna 2, 41-902 Bytom, Poland (Dist. by: Ars Polona-Ruch, Krakowskie Przedmiescie 7, Warsaw, Poland)

NATIONAL ART EDUCATION ASSOCIATION. RESEARCH MONOGRAPH. see *EDUCATION — Teaching Methods And Curriculum*

NATIONAL ASSOCIATION OF SCHOOLS OF ART AND DESIGN. DIRECTORY. see *EDUCATION — Guides To Schools And Colleges*

707.4   US
NATIONAL ASSOCIATION OF WOMEN ARTISTS. ANNUAL EXHIBITION CATALOG. 1889. a. $5. National Association of Women Artists, 41 Union Sq., W., Rm. 906, New York, NY 10003. TEL 212-675-1616. adv. circ. 1,000 (controlled)

745.1   US
NATIONAL CAROUSEL ASSOCIATION. CAROUSEL ARCHIVES. 1977. a. $15. National Carousel Association, c/o Anne Hinds, 10511 S.E. Crystal Lake Ln., Milwaukee, OR 97222. TEL 503-653-2482. Ed. Penny Wilkes. circ. 450.
    Formerly: National Carousel Association. Carousel Census.

700   US
NATIONAL DIRECTORY OF ARTS AND EDUCATION SUPPORT BY BUSINESS CORPORATIONS. (Subseries of: Arts Patronage Series) 1979. biennial or triennial, $75. Washington International Arts Letter, Box 15240, Washington, DC 20003. TEL 202-328-1900. Ed. Daniel Millsaps.
    Formerly: National Directory of Arts Support by Business Corporations; Supersedes in part: Arts Support by Private Foundations and Business Corporations.

700   US
NATIONAL DIRECTORY OF ARTS SUPPORT BY PRIVATE FOUNDATIONS. (Subseries of: Arts Patronage Series) 1972. biennial or triennial; latest 5th edt., 1987. $79.95. Washington International Arts Letter, Box 15240, Washington, DC 20003. TEL 202-328-1900. Ed. Daniel Millsaps.
    Formerly: Arts Support by Private Foundations; Supersedes in part: Arts Support by Private Foundations and Business Corporations.

700   US
NATIONAL DIRECTORY OF GRANTS AND AID TO INDIVIDUALS IN THE ARTS, INTERNATIONAL. 1970. triennial or quadrennial, latest 6th edt., 1987. $19.95. Washington International Arts Letter, Box 15240, Washington, DC 20003. TEL 202-328-1900. Ed. Nancy A. Fandel. (reprint service avail. from UMI)
    Formerly: Grants and Aid to Individuals in the Arts.

700 792.8   US
NATIONAL FOUNDATION FOR ADVANCEMENT IN THE ARTS. ANNUAL REPORT. 1981. a. National Foundation for Advancement in the Arts, 100 N. Biscayne Blvd., Ste. 1801, Miami, FL 33132. Ed. Cornelia Pereira. circ. 10,000.

708.1 069   UK   ISSN 0140-7430
NATIONAL GALLERY, LONDON. TECHNICAL BULLETIN. 1977. a. £7.50. National Gallery Publications, Trafalgar Sq., London WC2N 5DN, England. Ed. Dr. Ashok R. Roy. illus. circ. 2,000. (back issues avail.) Indexed: Art & Archeol.Tech.Abstr. RILA.

700   US   ISSN 0091-7222
NATIONAL GALLERY OF ART. ANNUAL REPORT. 1970. a. $1.25. ‡ National Gallery of Art, Washington, DC 20565. TEL 202-737-4215. illus. circ. 8,500.

709 951   CH
NATIONAL INSTITUTE OF COMPILATION AND TRANSLATION. COLLECTED PAPERS ON HISTORY AND ART OF CHINA. irreg. National Institute of Compilation and Translation, Committee for Compilation and Examination of the Series of Chinese Classics, Taipei, Taiwan, Republic of China.

730   US   ISSN 0363-5937
NATIONAL/INTERNATIONAL SCULPTURE CONFERENCE. PROCEEDINGS. 1960. biennial. International Sculpture Center, 1050 Potomac St., N.W., Washington, DC 20007. TEL 202-965-6066. illus. circ. 1,000. Key Title: Proceedings of the National/International Sculpture Conference.

709   NE   ISSN 0169-6726
NEDERLANDS KUNSTHISTORISCH JAARBOEK. (Text in Dutch; summaries in English) 1950. a. fl.145. Free University of Amsterdam, De Boelelaan 1105, 1081 HV Amsterdam, Netherlands. Ed. E. de Jong. circ. 550. (back issues avail.) Indexed: RILA.

NEW DEPARTURES; international review of literature & the lively arts. see *LITERATURE*

701.18   UK
NEW ENGLISH ART CLUB. a. 17 Carlton House Terrace, London SW1Y 5BD, England.

700   US   ISSN 0149-791X
NEW MEXICO STUDIES IN THE FINE ARTS. 1976. a. price varies. University of New Mexico, Alburquerque, Department of Art and Art History, Alburquerque, NM 87131. TEL 505-277-0111. Ed. P. Walch. circ. 800. Indexed: RILA.

NEW TOY. see *LITERARY AND POLITICAL REVIEWS*

700   US   ISSN 0085-4174
NEWSLETTER ON CONTEMPORARY JAPANESE PRINTS. 1971. irreg. free. Helen & Felix Juda Collection, 644 S. June St., Los Angeles, CA 90005. Ed. Irene Drori. illus.

709   GW   ISSN 0078-0537
NIEDERDEUTSCHE BEITRAEGE ZUR KUNSTGESCHICHTE. 1961. a. DM.60. (Niedersaechsisches Landesmuseum, Hannover) Deutscher Kunstverlag GmbH, Vohburger Str. 1, 8000 Munich 21, W. Germany (B.R.D.) Ed. Hans Werner Grohn. circ. 800. Indexed: RILA.

700 808   US   ISSN 0739-2974
NORTHERN LIGHTS STUDIES IN CREATIVITY. 1984. biennial. $6. University of Maine at Presque Isle, 181 Main St., Presque Isle, ME 04769. TEL 207-762-7761. Ed. Stanley Scott. adv. bk. rev. circ. 500. (back issues avail.)

700   DK   ISSN 0109-5544
NY ABSTRAKTION. 1981. a. (Satens Museums for Kunst) Biblioteksceltralen, Telegrafvej 5, DK-2750 Ballerup, Denmark.

NY CARLSBERG GLYPTOTEK. MEDDELELSER. see *ARCHAEOLOGY*

700   DK   ISSN 0078-3285
ODENSE UNIVERSITY STUDIES IN ART HISTORY. (Text in German and Italian) 1970. irreg., no.4, 1986. price varies. Odense University Press, 36, Pjentedamsgade, DK-5000 Odense, Denmark. (back issues avail.)

OESTERREICHISCHE VOLKSKUNDLICHE BIBLIOGRAPHIE. see *FOLKLORE*

OESTERREICHISCHES MUSEUM FUER VOLKSKUNDE: VEROEFFENTLICHUNGEN. see *FOLKLORE*

OFFICIAL SOUVENIR GUIDE TO THE EDINBURGH FESTIVAL. see *TRAVEL AND TOURISM*

709   US   ISSN 0731-3284
OHIO ARTS COUNCIL. BIENNIAL REPORT. 1965. biennial. free. Ohio Arts Council, 727 E. Main St., Columbus, OH 43205. TEL 614-466-2613. Ed.Bd. illus. stat. circ. 500.
    Formerly: Ohio Arts Council. Annual Report.

700   DK   ISSN 0108-3511
OMKRING ET KUNSTVAERK. 1980. irreg. Kr.2 per no. Randers Kunstmuseum, Stemannsgade 2, 8900 Randers, Denmark. Ed. Nina Hobolth. illus.

700   CN
ONTARIO ARTS COUNCIL. ANNUAL REPORT. (Text in English and French) 1963. a. Ontario Arts Council, Ste. 500, 151 Bloor St. W., Toronto, Ont. M5S 1T6, Canada. TEL 416-961-1660. Ed. Adrian Mann. circ. 3,500. (back issues avail.)

700   US   ISSN 0078-6551
ORIENTAL STUDIES. no.8, 1970. irreg. price varies. Freer Gallery of Art, Smithsonian Institution, Jefferson Dr., S.W. at 12th St., Washington, DC 20560. TEL 202-357-1432.

700   US   ISSN 0030-5529
THE ORIGINAL ART REPORT; committed to the preservation, comprehension, and progress of artists, art, and the people. Short title: TOAR. 1967. irreg. $14.50. ‡ Frank Salantrie, Ed. & Pub., Box 1641, Chicago, IL 60690. TEL 312-588-6897. bk. rev. (back issues avail.)

700 913   UR
PAMYATNIKI KUL'TURY. NOVYE OTKRYTIYA/ MONUMENTS OF CULTURE. NEW DISCOVERIES. (Text in Russian; summaries in English) 1974. irreg. price varies. (Akademiya Nauk S.S.S.R., Nauchnyi Sovet po Istorii Mirovoi Kul'tury) Izdatel'stvo Nauka, Podsosenskii Per. 21, Moscow K-62, Russian S.F.S.R., U.S.S.R. (Subscr. to: Mezhdunarodnaya Kniga, Moscow, G-200, Russian S.F.S.R., U.S.S.R.) Ed.Bd. illus.

700 800   US
PAN-EROTIC REVIEW. 1987. a. $30. Red Alder Books, Box 2992, Santa Cruz, CA 95063. TEL 408-426-7082. Ed. David Steinberg. bk. rev. bibl. film rev. illus. play rev.

709   US   ISSN 0193-8061
PHOEBUS; a journal of art history. 1978. a. $12. Arizona State University, School of Art, Tempe, AZ 85281. TEL 602-965-3468. bk. rev. illus. circ. 1,200. Indexed: RILA.

740   IT   ISSN 0079-2055
PIANETA FRESCO. 1967. a. L.2200. ‡ Ettore Sottsass, Ed. & Pub., 14 via Manzoni, Milan 20121, Italy. Ed. Fernanda Pivano Sottsass. circ. 500.

700   IT   ISSN 0079-242X
POCKET LIBRARY OF STUDIES IN ART. 1948. irreg., vol.25, 1985. price varies. Casa Editrice Leo S. Olschki, Casella Postale 66, 50100 Florence, Italy. circ. 1,200.

POLITECHNIKA WROCLAWSKA. INSTYTUT ARCHITEKTURY I URBANISTYKI. PRACE NAUKOWE. KONFERENCJE. see *ARCHITECTURE*

POLITECHNIKA WROCLAWSKA. INSTYTUT ARCHITEKTURY I URBANISTYKI. PRACE NAUKOWE. MONOGRAFIE. see *ARCHITECTURE*

POLITECHNIKA WROCLAWSKA. INSTYTUT ARCHITEKTURY I URBANISTYKI. PRACE NAUKOWE. STUDIA I MATERIALY. see *ARCHITECTURE*

709 720   PL   ISSN 0860-1194
POLITECHNIKA WROCLAWSKA. INSTYTUT HISTORII ARCHITEKTURY, SZTUKI I TECHNIKI. PRACE NAUKOWE. KONFERENCJE. 1985. irreg. price varies. Politechnika Wroclawska, Wybrzeze Wyspianskiego 27, 50-370 Wroclaw, Poland (Dist. by: Ars Polona-Ruch, Krakowskie Przedmiescie 7, Warsaw, Poland) Ed. Jerzy Ciekot.

709 720   PL   ISSN 0324-9662
POLITECHNIKA WROCLAWSKA. INSTYTUT HISTORII ARCHITEKTURY, SZTUKI I TECHNIKI. PRACE NAUKOWE. MONOGRAFIE. (Text in Polish; summaries in English and Russian) 1971. irreg., no.10, 1987. price varies. Politechnika Wroclawska, Wybrzeze Wyspianskiego 27, 50-370 Wroclaw, Poland (Dist. by: Ars Polona-Ruch, Krakowskie Przedmiescie 7, Warsaw, Poland) Ed. Jery Ciekot. circ. 530.

709 720   PL   ISSN 0324-9654
POLITECHNIKA WROCLAWSKA. INSTYTUT HISTORII ARCHITEKTURY, SZTUKI I TECHNIKI. PRACE NAUKOWE. STUDIA I MATERIALY. (Text in Polish; summaries in English and Russian) 1972. irreg., no.9, 1987. price varies. Politechnika Wroclawska, Wybrzeze Wyspianskiego 27, 50-370 Wroclaw, Poland (Dist. by: Ars Polona-Ruch, Krakowskie Przedmiescie 7, Warsaw, Poland) Ed. Jery Ciekot. circ. 390.

700 686   PL   ISSN 0079-3132
POLONIA TYPOGRAPHICA SAECULI SEDECIMI. (Text in Polish; summaries in French and Russian) 1936. irreg., no.12, 1981. price varies. (Polska Akademia Nauk, Instytut Badan Literackich) Ossolineum, Publishing House of the Polish Academy of Sciences, Rynek 9, Wroclaw, Poland (Dist. by: Ars Polona-Ruch, Krakowskie Przedmiescie 7, Warsaw, Poland) Ed. Alodia Kawecka-Gryczowa. circ. 400.

POLYMERS PAINT AND COLOUR YEAR BOOK. see *PAINTS AND PROTECTIVE COATINGS*

800 700   US
POSTCARD ART/POSTCARD FICTION. 1974. irreg. (1-2/yr.) $1.75. Martha Rosler, Ed. & Pub., 143 McGuinness Blvd., Brooklyn, NY 11222. TEL 718-834-1466. Ed. Martha Rosler. circ. 600.

709   PL   ISSN 0079-466X
POZNANSKIE TOWARZYSTWO PRZYJACIOL NAUK. KOMISJA HISTORII SZTUKI. PRACE. (Text in Polish; summaries in French) 1923. irreg., vol.11, 1979. price varies. (Poznanskie Towarzystwo Przyjaciol Nauk, Wydzial Nauk o Sztuce) Panstwowe Wydawnictwo Naukowe, Ul. Miodowa 10, 00-251 Warsaw, Poland (Dist. by: Ars Polona, Krakowskie Przedmiescie 7, 00-068 Warsaw, Poland) charts. illus.

060 709   PL
PRACE POPULARNONAUKOWE. ZABYTKI POLSKI POLNOCNEJ. (Subseries of: Polski Polnocnej. ISSN 0138-0516) 1961. irreg., vol.41, 1983. price varies. (Towarzystwo Naukowe w Toruniu) Panstwowe Wydawnictwo Naukowe, Miodowa 10, 00-251 Warsaw, Poland (Dist. by: Ars Polona-Ruch, Krakowskie Przedmiescie 7, 00-068 Warsaw, Poland) Ed. S. Salmonowicz.
Supersedes in part (as from 1975): Prace Popularnonaukowe (ISSN 0079-4805)

PRENT 190; new circle of collectors of modern graphic art. see *PRINTING*

PRINCETON ESSAYS ON THE ARTS. see *HUMANITIES: COMPREHENSIVE WORKS*

700 913   US   ISSN 0079-5208
PRINCETON MONOGRAPHS IN ART AND ARCHAEOLOGY. 1932. irreg., latest, no. 44. price varies. Princeton University Press, 3175 Princeton Pike, Lawrenceville, NJ 08648. TEL 609-896-1344. (reprint service avail. from UMI)

700 380.1   US
PRINTWORLD DIRECTORY OF CONTEMPORARY PRINTS (YEAR) a. $59.95. Apollo Book (Distributor), 5 Schoolhouse Ln., Poughkeepsie, NY 12603. TEL 914-462-0040.

700   US
PUBLIC ILLUMINATION MAGAZINE. 1979. irreg., no.34, 1986. 257 Lafayette St., New York, NY 10012. TEL 212-226-2529. Ed. Zagreus Bowery. circ. 1,000.

700 900 400   SW
PUBLICATIONS OF THE NEW SOCIETY OF LETTERS AT LUND. (Text in English, German or Swedish; summaries in English or German) 1921. irreg., no.77, 1983. Liber Forlag, S-205 10, Malmo, Sweden. Ed. Bo Westerhult.

745.5 659.2   UK   ISSN 0033-3921
PUBLICITY REVIEW. 1965. irreg. 25p. per no. Aubrey Bush Publications, 17 Balmoral Rd., Forest Rd., Nottingham NG1 4HX, England. adv. bk. rev.
Handicrafts

700 659.1   US
R S V P: DIRECTORY OF CREATIVE TALENT. (Repondez S'il Vous Plait) 1975. a. $16.95. 253 Washington Ave., Box 314, Brooklyn, NY 11205. Eds. Richard Lebenson, Kathleen Creighton. adv. circ. 12,000. (back issues avail.)

700 800   US
REAL LIFE MAGAZINE. 1979. irreg. $8. Box 1564, Madison Sq. Sta., New York, NY 10159. TEL 718-852-8085. Ed. Thomas Lawson. adv. bk. rev. circ. 1, 500.

700   FR   ISSN 0080-0074
RECHERCHES ET DOCUMENTS D'ART ET D'ARCHEOLOGIE. 1937. irreg. price varies. (Musee Guimet. Paris) Presses Universitaires de France, 108 bd. Saint Germain, 75279 Paris Cedex 6, France (Service des Periodiques, 12 rue Jean de Beauvais, 75005 Paris) (reprint service avail. from KTO)

704.943   AU   ISSN 0034-3935
RELIGIOESE GRAPHIK; Blaetter fuer Freunde Christlicher Gebrauchsgraphik. 1946. irreg. (2-3/yr.) S.10($0.50) per no. Stephanus-Verlag, Box 303, A-1071 Vienna, Austria. Ed. Josef Franz Aumann. bk. rev. illus. circ. 2,500.

700   FR
REPERES; cahiers d'art contemporain. 1947. irreg. 520 Fr. Galerie Maeght Lelong, 13 rue de Teheran, 75008 Paris, France. Ed. Daniel Lelong. illus.
Formerly (until 1982): Derriere le Miroir (ISSN 0011-9113)

700   AG
REVISTA DE ESTETICA/AESTHETICS MAGAZINE. (Text in English and Spanish) 1983. irreg., no.4, 1985. Centro de Arte y Comunicacion, Escuela de Altos Estudios/School of High Studies, Elpidio Gonzalez 4070, 1407 Buenos Aires, Argentina.

REVUE BELGE D'ARCHEOLOGIE ET D'HISTOIRE DE L'ART. see *ARCHAEOLOGY*

700 913 780.01   BE   ISSN 0080-2530
REVUE DES ARCHEOLOGUES ET HISTORIENS D'ART DE LOUVAIN. 1968. a. 1800 Fr. Universite Catholique de Louvain, Association des Diplomes en Archeologie et Histoire de l'Art, College Erasme, 1 place Blaise Pascal, B-1348 Louvain-la-Neuve, Belgium. Ed. Tony Hackens. bk. rev. circ. 850. Indexed: Art & Archaeol.Tech.Abstr. Numis.Lit. RILA.

709   RM   ISSN 0080-262X
REVUE ROUMAINE D'HISTOIRE DE L'ART. SERIE BEAUX-ARTS. 1963. a. $45. (Academia de Stiinte Sociale si Politice) Editura Academiei Republicii Socialiste Rumania, Calea Victoriei 125, 79717 Bucharest, Rumania (Subscr. to: ROMPRESFILATELIA, Calea Grivitei 64-66, P.O. Box 12-201, 78104 Bucharest, Rumania) Ed. V. Dragut. Indexed: Numis.Lit. RILA.
Formerly: Revue Roumaine de l'Histoire de l'Art. Serie Arts Plastiques.

709   RM   ISSN 0080-2638
REVUE ROUMAINE D'HISTOIRE DE L'ART. SERIE THEATRE, MUSIQUE, CINEMATOGRAPHIE. 1963. a. $45. (Academia de Stiinte Sociale si Politice) Editura Academiei Republicii Socialiste Rumania, Calea Victoriei 125, 79717 Bucharest, Rumania (Subscr. to: ROMPRESFILATELIA, Calea Grivitei 64-66, P.O. Box 12-201, 78104 Bucharest, Rumania) Ed. Mihnea Gheorghiu.

700   IT
RIPARTIZIONE CULTURA E SPETTACOLO. RASSEGNA DI STUDI E DI NOTIZIE. 1973. irreg. (Ripartizione Cultura e Spettacolo) Civiche Raccolte d'Arte Applicata ed Incisioni, Castello Sforzesco, 20121 Milan, Italy. illus.

700   IT
RIVISTA D'ARTE; studi documentari sulla storia delle arte in Toscana. 1903; N.S. 1984. a. L.65000. (Fondazione Horne) Casa Editrice Leo S. Olschki, Casella Postale 66, 50100 Florence, Italy. Dir. Ugo Procacci. adv. circ. 1,000. Indexed: RILA.

709   PL   ISSN 0080-3472
ROCZNIK HISTORII SZTUKI. (Text in Polish; summaries in English, French and German) 1956. a. price varies. (Polska Akademia Nauk, Instytut Sztuki) Ossolineum, Publishing House of the Polish Academy of Sciences, Rynek 9, Wroclaw, Poland (Dist. by: Ars Polona-Ruch, Krakowskie Przedmiescie 7, Warsaw, Poland) circ. 500. Indexed: RILA.

ROEMISCHE BRONZEN AUS DEUTSCHLAND. see *ARCHAEOLOGY*

750   UK
ROYAL INSTITUTE OF OIL PAINTERS. PUBLICATION. a. £1. Royal Institute of Oil Painters, 17 Carlton House Terrace, London SW1Y 5BD, England. (Co-sponsor: Federation of British Artists)

750   UK
ROYAL INSTITUTE OF PAINTERS IN WATER COLOURS. PUBLICATION. a. £1. Royal Institute of Painters in Water Colours, 17 Carlton House Terrace, London SW1Y 5BD, England. (Co-sponsor: Federation of British Artists)

ROYAL ONTARIO MUSEUM. HISTORY, TECHNOLOGY AND ART MONOGRAPHS. see *HISTORY*

706   UK
ROYAL SOCIETY OF BRITISH ARTISTS. PUBLICATION. 1890. a. £1. Royal Society of British Artists, 17 Carlton House Terrace, London SW1Y 5BD, England. circ. 5,000.

706   UK
ROYAL SOCIETY OF MARINE ARTISTS. PUBLICATION. 1946. a. £1. Royal Society of Marine Artists, 17 Carlton House Terrace, London SW1Y 5BD, England.

700   UK
ROYAL SOCIETY OF MINIATURE PAINTERS, SCULPTORS AND GRAVERS. a. £1. Royal Society of Miniature Painters, Sculptors and Gravers, 17 Carlton House Terrace, London SW1Y 5BD, England. (Co-sponsor: Federation of British Artists)

757   UK
ROYAL SOCIETY OF PORTRAIT PAINTERS. PUBLICATION. 1981. a. £1. Royal Society of Portrait Painters, 17 Carlton House Terrace, London SW1Y 5BD, England.

RUSSIAN POETICS IN TRANSLATION. see *LITERATURE*

709   US   ISSN 0194-049X
RUTGERS ART REVIEW. 1980. a. $9. Rutgers University, New Brunswick, NJ 08903. TEL 201-932-7041. Ed. Nicholas J. Capasso. Indexed: RILA.

709   IT   ISSN 0080-5394
SAGGI E MEMORIE DI STORIA DELL'ARTE. 1957. irreg., no.14, 1984. price varies. (Fondazione Giorgio Cini) Casa Editrice Leo S. Olschki, Casella Postale 66, 50100 Florence, Italy. circ. 500. Indexed: RILA.

730   UY
SALON NACIONAL DE ARTES PLASTICAS Y VISUALES. a. Comision Nacional de Artes Plasticas y Visuales, Buenos Aires 668, Montevideo, Uruguay. illus.

700   US   ISSN 0581-4766
SAMUEL H. KRESS FOUNDATION. ANNUAL REPORT. 1963. a. Samuel H. Kress Foundation, 174 E. 80th St., New York, NY 10021. TEL 212-861-4993. circ. 1,200.

SANDS; a literary magazine. see *LITERATURE*

700 CN
SASKATCHEWAN. DEPARTMENT OF CULTURE AND RECREATION. ANNUAL REPORT. 1972. a. free. Department of Culture and Recreation, Regina, Sask., Canada. TEL 306-787-5759. Ed. Rick Folk. illus. circ. 800.
Formerly: Saskatchewan. Department of Culture and Youth. Annual Report (ISSN 0317-4344)

354 CN
SASKATCHEWAN CENTRE OF THE ARTS. ANNUAL REPORT. a. Saskatchewan Centre of the Arts, c/o George C. Haynes, 200 Lakeshore Drive, Regina, Sask. S4S 0B3, Canada. TEL 306-584-5050.

709.9 JM ISSN 0036-5068
SAVACOU; a journal of the Caribbean artists movement. 1970. irreg; 1-2/yr. $15. (Caribbean Artists Movement) Savacou Publications, Box 170, Mona, Kingston 7, Jamaica, W. Indies. Ed. Edward Kamau Brathwaite. adv. bk. rev. bibl. circ. 2,000. Indexed: M.L.A.

700 GW ISSN 0723-0788
SCHRIFTENREIHE DER HOCHSCHULE DER KUENSTE BERLIN. 1980. irreg. price varies. (Hochschule der Kuenste Berlin) Colloquium Verlag, Unter den Eichen 93, 1000 Berlin 45, W. Germany (B.R.D.) circ. 1,000.

700 GW ISSN 0080-7176
SCHRIFTTUM ZUR DEUTSCHEN KUNST. 1934; N.S. 1962. irreg., vol.45, 1985. price varies. (Deutscher Verein fuer Kunstwissenschaft) Deutscher Verlag fuer Kunstwissenschaft, Lindenstr. 76, 1000 Berlin 61, W. Germany (B.R.D.)

700 UK ISSN 0036-911X
SCOTTISH ART REVIEW. 1946. irreg. membership. (Glasgow Museums and Art Galleries Department) Glasgow Art Gallery and Museums Association, Kelvingrove, Glasgow G3 8AG, Scotland. Ed. Patricia L.G. Bascom. adv. bk. rev. illus. circ. 5,000. (also avail. in microform from UMI; reprint service avail. from UMI) Indexed: Br.Hum.Ind. Art Ind. RILA.

700 NE ISSN 0080-8350
SCRIPTA ARTIS MONOGRAPHIA. (Text in English, French and German) 1968. irreg. price varies (approx. $25) A P A-Hissink & Co., Postbus 122, 3600 AC Maarssen, Netherlands.

746 JA ISSN 0583-0664
SHINSHU UNIVERSITY. FACULTY OF TEXTILE SCIENCE AND TECHNOLOGY. JOURNAL. SERIES D: ARTS. (Text in Japanese and European languages; summaries in English) 1956. irreg. exchange basis. Shinshu University, Faculty of Textile Science and Technology - Shinshu Daigaku Sen'i Gakubu, 3-15-1 Tokida, Ueda, Nagano 386, Japan.

SIBYL-CHILD. see *WOMEN'S INTERESTS*

700 US
SKETCH BOOK. 1937. a. $5. Kappa Pi International Honorary Art Fraternity, 9321 Paul Adrian Dr., Crestwood, MO 63126. Ed. Arthur Kennon. circ. 1,000 (controlled)

730 DK ISSN 0107-4911
SKULPTUR VEKSOELUND. 1978. a. Kr.25. Veksoelund, c/o Poul Hansen, Kirkestraede 6, 3670 Veksoe, Denmark. illus.

700 US
SMITHSONIAN INSTITUTION. ARCHIVES OF AMERICAN ART. NEWSLETTER. 1971. 1-2/yr. membership. Smithsonian Institution, Archives of American Art, Washington, DC 20560. TEL 202-357-2781. circ. 1,700.

700 SP ISSN 0212-3215
SOCIEDAD DE ESTUDIOS VASCOS. CUADERNOS DE SECCION. ARTES PLASTICAS Y MONUMENTALES. 1982. irreg. (Sociedad de Estudios Vascos) Eusko Ikaskuntza, S.A., Churruca, 7 - 2, 20004 Donostia, Spain.

SOCIETE DES SCIENCES, LETTRES ET ARTS DE BAYONNE. BULLETIN. see *LITERATURE*

SOCIETY FOR RENAISSANCE STUDIES. OCCASIONAL PAPERS. see *LITERATURE*

SOCIETY FOR THE PRESERVATION OF LONG ISLAND ANTIQUITIES. NEWSLETTER. see *ANTIQUES*

740 UK
SOCIETY OF GRAPHIC ARTISTS. PUBLICATION. a. Society of Graphic Artists, 17 Carlton House Terrace, London SW1Y 5BD, England.

730 UK
SOCIETY OF PORTRAIT SCULPTORS. PUBLICATION. a. £1. Society of Portrait Sculptors, 17 Carlton House Terrace, London SW1Y 5BD, England.

706 UK
SOCIETY OF WILDLIFE ARTISTS. PUBLICATION. a. £1. Society of Wildlife Artists, 17 Carlton House Terrace, London SW1Y 5BD, England.

706 UK
SOCIETY OF WOMEN ARTISTS. PUBLICATION. a. £1. Society of Women Artists, 17 Carlton House Terrace, London SW1Y 5BD, England.

700 CH
SOOCHOW UNIVERSITY JOURNAL OF CHINESE ART HISTORY. (Text in Chinese or English) 1973. a. $15 per no. Soochow University, Wai Shuang Hsi, Shih Lin, Taipei, Taiwan, Republic of China. Ed.Bd. illus. circ. 800.

SOTHEBY'S INTERNATIONAL PRICE GUIDE: ANTIQUES AND COLLECTIBLES. see *ANTIQUES*

700 US ISSN 0081-2684
SOUTH CAROLINA ARTS COMMISSION. ANNUAL REPORT. 1968. a. ‡ Arts Commission, 1800 Gervais St., Columbia, SC 29201. TEL 803-758-3442. Ed. Jayne Darke. circ. 250.

954 913 II
SOUTH INDIAN ART AND ARCHAEOLOGICAL SERIES. (Text in English) 1976. irreg. Equator and Meridian, 8 Selvamnagar, Thanjavur 613001, Tamilnadu, India.

700 US
SOUTHEASTERN COLLEGE ART CONFERENCE REVIEW. Short title: S E C A C Review. 1967. a. $10. Georgia Institute of Technology, College of Agriculture, Atlanta, GA 30332. TEL 404-894-4887. Ed. Robert M. Craig. bk. rev. illus. circ. 500. Indexed: RILA.
Formerly (until 1976): S E C A C Review and Newsletter (ISSN 0584-4118)

730 UR
SOVETSKAYA SKUL'PTURA. vol.74, 1976. irreg. 2.344 Rub. per no. Izdatel'stvo Sovetskii Khudozhnik, Ul.Chernyakhovskogo, 4a, Moscow a-319, Russian S.F.S.R., U.S.S.R. Ed. V. Tikhanova. bibl. illus. circ. 10,000.

SPANNER (LONDON, 1974) see *LITERARY AND POLITICAL REVIEWS*

SPECULUM ANNIVERSARY MONOGRAPHS. see *HISTORY — History Of Europe*

708.1 US
SPENCER MUSEUM OF ART. REGISTER. 1951. a. price varies. University of Kansas, Spencer Museum of Art, Lawrence, KS 66045. TEL 913-864-4710. Ed. Carol Shankel. illus. index. circ. 1,000. Indexed: RILA.
Formerly: University of Kansas. Museum of Art. Register (ISSN 0041-9672)

709 US
SPONSORED RESEARCH IN THE HISTORY OF ART. 1982. a. price varies. National Gallery of Art, Center for Advanced Study in the Visual Arts, Washington, DC 20565. Ed. Claire Richter Sherman. circ. 4,500.
Formerly: History of Art Research Reports.

700 780 YU ISSN 0081-4008
SRPSKA AKADEMIJA NAUKA I UMETNOSTI. ODELJENJE LIKOVNE I MUZICKE UMETNOSTI. POSEBNA IZDANJA. (Text in Serbo-Croatian; summaries in English, French, German or Russian) 1954. irreg. price varies. Srpska Akademija Nauka i Umetnosti, Knez Mihailova 35, 11001 Belgrade, Yugoslavia (Dist. by: Prosveta, Terazije 16, Belgrade, Yugoslavia) circ. 1,000.

069 700 GE ISSN 0067-6004
STAATLICHE MUSEEN ZU BERLIN. JAHRBUCH. FORSCHUNGEN UND BERICHTE. 1957. a. price varies. Akademie-Verlag, Leipziger Str. 3-4, 1086 Berlin, E. Germany (D.D.R.) Indexed: Numis.Lit. RILA.

700 GW
STAEDEL JAHRBUCH. 1967. biennial. price varies. (Staedelsches Museum-Verein and Stadt Frankfurt Am Main) Prestel-Verlag, Mandlstr. 26, 8000 Munich 40, W. Germany (B.R.D.) Indexed: RILA.

STAFFRIDER MAGAZINE. see *LITERATURE*

069 DK ISSN 0108-2833
STEMMER FRA OLDTIDEN. irreg. Kr.73.20. (Museum Tusculanum) Bibliotekscentralen, Telegrafvej 5, DK-2750 Ballerup, Denmark.

700 IT ISSN 0081-5845
STORIA DELLA MINIATURA. STUDI E DOCUMENTI. 1962. irreg., no.6, 1985. price varies. Casa Editrice Leo S. Olschki, Casella Postale 66, 50100 Florence, Italy. circ. 1,000.

709 707 CN ISSN 0081-6027
STRUCTURIST. 1960. biennial. $30 to institutions. Eli Bornstein, Ed. & Pub., Box 378, Sub. P.O. 6, University of Saskatchewan, Saskatoon, Sask. S7N 0W0, Canada. TEL 306-966-4198. Ed. Eli Bornstein. bk. rev. cum.index for nos. 1-20. circ. 1,350. (also avail. in microform from UMI; back issues avail.; reprint avail. from UMI) Indexed: Amer.Hum.Ind.

709 IT
STUDI DI STORIA DELLE ARTI. 1977. a. L.20,000($15) Istituto di Storia dell Arte, Universita di Genova, Via Balbi 4, 16126 Genoa, Italy. Ed. Prof. Gildo Fossati. circ. 1,000. (back issues avail.) Indexed: RILA.

709 701.18 IT
STUDI E TESTI DI STORIA E CRITICA DELL'ARTE. 1975. irreg., no.12, 1984. price varies. Societa Editrice Napoletana s.r.l., Corso Umberto I 34, 80138 Naples, Italy.

701 PL ISSN 0081-7104
STUDIA Z HISTORII SZTUKI. (Text in Polish; summaries in English, French and German) 1953. irreg., vol.36, 1986. price varies. (Polska Akademia Nauk, Instytut Sztuki) Ossolineum, Publishing House of the Polish Academy of Sciences, Rynek 9, 50-106 Wroclaw, Poland (Dist. by: Ars Polona-Ruch, Krakowskie Przedmiescie 7, Warsaw, Poland)

709 GW ISSN 0081-7228
STUDIEN ZUR DEUTSCHEN KUNSTGESCHICHTE. 1894. irreg., no.358, 1982. price varies. Verlag Valentin Koerner, H.-Sielcken-Str. 36, Postfach 304, D-7570 Baden-Baden 1, W. Germany (B.R.D.) circ. 1,000 (approx.)

700 GW ISSN 0081-7325
STUDIEN ZUR KUNST DES NEUNZEHNTEN JAHRHUNDERTS. 1966. irreg. price varies. Prestel-Verlag, Mandlstr. 26, 8000 Munich 40, W. Germany (B.R.D.)

709 950 GW ISSN 0170-3684
STUDIEN ZUR OSTASIATISCHEN SCHRIFTKUNST. vol.4, 1975. irreg. price varies. Franz Steiner Verlag Wiesbaden GmbH, Birkenwaldstr. 44, Postfach 347, D-7000 Stuttgart 1, W. Germany (B.R.D.) Ed. Dietrich Seckel.

700 913 US
STUDIES IN ANCIENT ART AND ARCHAEOLOGY. irreg. price varies. Cornell University Press, 124 Roberts Pl., Ithaca, NY 14850. TEL 607-257-7000.

700 200 US
STUDIES IN ART AND RELIGIOUS INTERPRETATION. 1982. irreg., vol.7, 1987. $39.95 per no. Edwin Mellen Press, Box 450, Lewiston, NY 14092.

700 US
STUDIES IN BRITISH ART. irreg., latest, 1981. price varies. Yale University Press, 92A Yale Sta., New Haven, CT 06520. TEL 203-432-0940.

700 720 US
STUDIES IN CISTERCIAN ART AND ARCHITECTURE. 1982. irreg. price varies. Cistercian Publications, WMU Sta., Kalamazoo, MI 49008. Ed. Meredith Parsons Lillich. circ. 1,000.

704 US
STUDIES IN ICONOGRAPHY. vol.9, 1983. a. $12 to individuals; institutions $26. Arizona State University, School of Art, Tempe, AZ 85287. Ed. Anthony Lacy Gully. Indexed: M.L.A. RILA.

740 US ISSN 0081-8178
STUDIES IN MANUSCRIPT ILLUMINATION. 1954. irreg., no.8, 1979. Princeton University Press, 3175 Princeton Pike, Lawrenceville, NJ 08648. TEL 609-896-1344. (reprint service avail. from UMI)

STUDIES IN PRE-COLUMBIAN ART AND ARCHAEOLOGY. see ARCHAEOLOGY

700 US
STUDIES IN THE FINE ARTS: ART PATRONAGE. irreg., vol.6, 1985. U M I Research Press, 300 N. Zeeb Rd., Ann Arbor, MI 48106. Ed. Linda Seidel.

700 US
STUDIES IN THE FINE ARTS: ART THEORY. vol.12, 1985. irreg. U M I Research Press, 300 N. Zeeb Rd., Ann Arbor, MI 48106. Ed. Donald Kuspit.

700 US
STUDIES IN THE FINE ARTS: AVANT-GARDE. vol.52, 1985. irreg. U M I Research Press, 300 N. Zeeb Rd., Ann Arbor, MI 48106. Ed. Stephen Foster.

700 US
STUDIES IN THE FINE ARTS: CRITICISM. vol.18, 1986. irreg. U M I Research Press, 300 N. Zeeb Rd., Ann Arbor, MI 48106. Ed. Donald Kuspit.

700 US
STUDIES IN THE FINE ARTS: ICONOGRAPHY. vol.10, 1985. irreg. U M I Research Press, 300 N. Zeeb Rd., Ann Arbor, MI 48106. Ed. Linda Seidel.

700 US
STUDIES IN THE FINE ARTS: STUDIES IN BAROQUE ART HISTORY. vol.5, 1982. irreg. U M I Research Press, 300 N. Zeeb Rd., Ann Arbor, MI 48106. Ed. Ann S. Harris.

700 US
STUDIES IN THE FINE ARTS: STUDIES IN RENAISSANCE ART HISTORY. vol.3, 1983. irreg. U M I Research Press, 300 N. Zeeb Rd., Ann Arbor, MI 48106. Ed. Ann S. Harris.

708 US ISSN 0091-7338
STUDIES IN THE HISTORY OF ART. 1971. a. $6.50 (approx.) ‡ National Gallery of Art, Washington, DC 20565 TEL 202-737-4215. (Distrib. by: Univ. Press of New England, Box 979, Hanover, NH 03755) charts. illus. circ. 6,000. Indexed: Curr.Cont. Arts & Hum.Cit.Ind. RILA. Formerly: Report and Studies in the History of Art (ISSN 0080-1240)

709 730 RM ISSN 0039-3983
STUDII SI CERCETARI DE ISTORIA ARTEI. SERIA ARTA PLASTICA. (Text in Romanian; summaries in English, French, German, Russian) 1954. a. $45. (Academia de Stiinte Sociale si Politice) Editura Academiei Republicii Socialiste Rumania, Calea Victoriei 125, 79717 Bucharest, Rumania (Subscr. to: ROMPRESFILATELIA, Calea Grivitei 64-66, P.O. Box 12-201, 78104 Bucharest, Rumania) Ed. V. Dragut. bk. rev. illus. index. Indexed: Numis.Lit. RILA.
History

SUEDOSTDEUTSCHES KULTURWERK, MUNICH. SCHRIFTENREIHEN. REIHE A. KULTUR UND DICHTUNG. see HISTORY — History Of Europe

SUOMEN MUINAISMUISTOYHDISTYKSEN AIKAKAUSKIRJA. see ARCHAEOLOGY

700 UK ISSN 0039-6168
SURREALIST TRANSFORMACTION. (Text in English, French) 1967. irreg. £4($5) British Surrealist Group, Transformaction, Peeks, Harpford, Sidmouth, Devon EX10 0NH, England. Ed. John Lyle. bk. rev. film rev. illus. circ. 1,000. (tabloid format)

700 658 US
SURVEY OF ARTS ADMINISTRATION TRAINING. 1975. biennial. $7.50. American Council for the Arts, 1285 6th Ave., 3rd Fl., Area M, Dept. 17, New York, NY 10019. TEL 212-245-4510. Ed. E. Arthur Prieve. circ. 1,500.

942 UK ISSN 0081-9751
SURVEY OF LONDON. vol.42, 1986. irreg. price varies. (Royal Commission on Historical Monuments) Athlone Press Ltd., 44 Bedford Row, London WC1R 4LY, England (Dist. in U.S. by: Athlone Press, Atlantic Highlands, NJ 07716) (reprint service avail. from AMS) Indexed: Br.Archaeol.Abstr.

700 NE
T A M BULLETIN. (Text in English) 1984. irreg. Travelling Art Mail, c/o T A M, Postbus 10388, 5000 JJ Tilburg, Netherlands. Ed. Ruud Janssen. bk. rev. illus. stats. circ. controlled.

701.18 AG
T & C. (Theorie et Critique); theory and criticism, teoria y critica. (Text in English, French and Spanish) 1979. irreg. International Association of Art Critics, Elpidio Gonzalez 4070, 1407 Buenos Aires, Argentina. Ed.Bd. circ. 3,000. Indexed: RILA.

TALOHA. see MUSEUMS AND ART GALLERIES

700 GW
TEMPO (HANAU); art & design. 1985. irreg. DM.100 per no. Guenter Gottlieb, Ed. & Pub., Postfach 1509, D-6450 Hanau, W. Germany (B.R.D.) Ed. Gunter Gottlieb. bk. rev. circ. 1,000.

TEXTILE MUSEUM JOURNAL. see TEXTILE INDUSTRIES AND FABRICS

THORVALDSENS MUSEUM. MEDDELELSER. see MUSEUMS AND ART GALLERIES

THRESHOLD. see ARCHITECTURE

700 RM
TIBISCUS. SERIA ARTA. (Text in Rumanian; summaries in German) irreg. Muzeul Banatului, Piata Huniade Nr. 1, Timisoara, Romania. Indexed: Numis.Lit.

TJUSTBYGDEN. see ARCHAEOLOGY

700 PL ISSN 0082-5514
TOWARZYSTWO NAUKOWE W TORUNIU. KOMISJA HISTORII SZTUKI. TEKA. (Subseries of Towarzystwo Naukowe w Toruniu. Wydzial Filologiczno-Filozoficzny. Prace) (Text in Polish; summaries in French) 1959. irreg., vol.6, 1976. price varies. Panstwowe Wydawnictwo Naukowe, Miodowa 10, 00-251 Warsaw, Poland (Dist. by: Ars Polona, Krakowskie Przedmiescie 7, 00-068 Warsaw, Poland) Ed. Artur Hutnikiewicz.

TRAVAUX D'HUMANISME ET RENAISSANCE. see HISTORY — History Of Europe

700 800 SP
TRAZA Y BAZA; cuadernos hispanos de simbologia, arte y literatura. 1972. a. $10. Ediciones el Albir, Calle de Los Angeles 8, Barcelona 1, Spain. bk. rev.

TRIBUS; Jarhbuch des Linden-Museums Stuttgart. see ANTHROPOLOGY

TRIERER ZEITSCHRIFT FUER GESCHICHTE UND KUNST DES TRIERER LANDES UND SEINER NACHBARGEBIETE. see ARCHAEOLOGY

TRIVIUM. see LITERATURE

700 GW
TUDUV-STUDIE. REIHEN KUNSTGESCHICHTE. 1979. irreg. price varies. Tuduv Verlagsgesellschaft mbH, Gabelsbergerstr. 15, 8000 Munich 2, W. Germany (B.R.D.)

700 US ISSN 0550-0850
UKRAINIAN ART DIGEST/NOTATKZ Z MISTETSTBA. (Text in Ukrainian) 1963. a. $10 per issue. Ukrainian Artist's Association in U.S.A., Philadelphia Branch - Obyednannia Mysttsiv Ukraintsiv v Amerytsi. Viddil u Filyadel'fii, 1022 N. Lawrence St., Philadelphia, PA 19123. TEL 215-922-2647. Ed. Petro Mehyk. bk. rev. illus. circ. 1, 000. Indexed: Amer.Bibl.Slavic & E.Eur.Stud.

700 IT
UMANA AVVENTURA. a. L.22000. Editoriale Jaca Book Spa, Via Aurelio Saffi 19, Milano, Italy.

700 US ISSN 0160-0699
UMBRELLA (GLENDALE) 1978. irreg. $15 to individuals; institutions $25. Umbrella Associates, Box 3692, Glendale, CA 91201. TEL 818-797-0514. Ed. Judith A. Hoffberg. adv. bk. rev. illus. circ. 500.

706 UK
UNITED SOCIETY OF ARTISTS. PUBLICATION. 1921. a. £1. United Society of Artists, Carlton House Terrace, London SW1Y 5BD, England. (Co-sponsor: Federation of British Artists)

700 US ISSN 0083-2103
U.S. NATIONAL ENDOWMENT FOR THE ARTS. ANNUAL REPORT. 1967. a. limited free distribution. National Endowment for the Arts, Public Information Office, Washington, DC 20506 TEL 202-682-5400. (Orders to: Supt. Doc., Washington, DC 20402)

700 AG
UNIVERSIDAD DE BUENOS AIRES. INSTITUTO DE ARTE AMERICANO E INVESTIGACIONES ESTETICAS. ANALES. 1948. a. Universidad de Buenos Aires, Instituto de Arte Americano e Investigaciones Esteticas, Buenos Aires, Argentina. illus.

700 946 SP ISSN 0213-392X
UNIVERSIDAD DE MURCIA. IMAFRONTE. DEPARTMENTO DE HISTORIA DEL ARTE. 1985. irreg., vol.1. ($1000) Universidad de Murcia, Secretariado de Publicaciones e Intercambio Cientifico, Santo Cristo, 1, 30001 Murcia, Spain. TEL 968 24 92 00.

700 860 MX ISSN 0076-7239
UNIVERSIDAD NACIONAL AUTONOMA DE MEXICO. INSTITUTO DE INVESTIGACIONES ESTETICAS. ANALES. 1937. a. price varies. ‡ Universidad Nacional Autonoma de Mexico, Instituto de Investigaciones Esteticas, Torre de Humanidades, Ciudad Universitaria, Mexico 20, D.F., Mexico. Ed. Xavier Moyssen.

700 MX
UNIVERSIDAD NACIONAL AUTONOMA DE MEXICO. INSTITUTO DE INVESTIGACIONES ESTETICAS. MONOGRAFIAS DE ARTE. 1977. irreg.; latest, 1979. price varies. Universidad Nacional Autonoma de Mexico, Instituto de Investigaciones Esteticas, Torre I de Humanidades, Ciudad Universitaria, Mexico 20, D.F., Mexico.

700 800 IT ISSN 0078-7728
UNIVERSITA DEGLI STUDI DI PADOVA. FACOLTA DI LETTERE E FILOSOFIA. OPUSCOLI ACCADEMICI. 1937. irreg., vol.13, 1979. price varies. Casa Editrice Leo S. Olschki, Casella Postale 66, 50100 Florence, Italy. circ. 1, 000.

700 800 IT ISSN 0078-7736
UNIVERSITA DEGLI STUDI DI PADOVA. FACOLTA DI LETTERE E FILOSOFIA. PUBBLICAZIONI. 1932. irreg., vol.61, 1984. price varies. Casa Editrice Leo S. Olschki, Casella Postale 66, 50100 Florence, Italy. circ. 1,000.

701.18 IT
UNIVERSITA DEGLI STUDI DI PARMA. ISTITUTO DI STORIA DELL'ARTE. CATALOGHI. (Each issue devoted to an individual artist) 1968. irreg. price varies. Universita degli Studi di Parma, Istituto di Storia dell'Arte, Piazzale della Pace 5, Palazzo Pilotta, 43100 Parma, Italy. bk. rev. bibl. illus. circ. 1,000.

707 IT ISSN 0557-3122
UNIVERSITA DEGLI STUDI DI ROMA.
SEMINARIO DI ARCHEOLOGIA E STORIA
DELL'ARTE GRECA E ROMANA. STUDI
MISCELLANEI. 1961. irreg., no.26, 1985. price
varies. Erma di Bretschneider, Via Cassiodoro, 19,
00193 Rome, Italy.

709 IT ISSN 0564-2477
UNIVERSITA DEGLI STUDI DI TRIESTE.
ISTITUTO DI STORIA DELL'ARTE
(PUBBLICAZIONI) 1954. irreg. price varies.
Edizioni dell' Ateneo S.p.A., P.O. Box 7216, 00100
Rome, Italy. illus. circ. 1,000.

709 GW
UNIVERSITAET BONN. SEMINAR FUER
ORIENTALISCHE KUNSTGESCHICHTE.
VEROEFFENTLICHUNGEN. REIHE B.
ANTIQUITATES ORIENTALES. 1977. irreg. price
varies. Dr. Rudolf Habelt GmbH, Am Buchenhang
1, 5300 Bonn 1, W. Germany (B.R.D.)

700 AU
UNIVERSITAET INNSBRUCK.
KUNSTGESCHICHTLICHE STUDIEN. (Subseries
of: Universitaet Innsbruck. Veroeffentlichungen)
1972. irreg. price varies. Oesterreichische
Kommissionsbuchhandlung, Maximilianstrasse 17,
A-6020 Innsbruck, Austria. Ed. Otto Lutterotti.

709 950 GW ISSN 0170-3692
UNIVERSITAET ZU KOELN.
KUNSTHISTORISCHES INSTITUT.
ABTEILUNG ASIEN. PUBLIKATIONEN. irreg.,
vol.5, 1985. price varies. Franz Steiner Verlag
Wiesbaden GmbH, Birkenwaldstr. 44, Postfach 347,
D-7000 Stuttgart 1, W. Germany (B.R.D.) Ed.Bd.
History

709 BE
UNIVERSITE CATHOLIQUE DE LOUVAIN.
INSTITUT SUPERIEUR D'ARCHEOLOGIE ET
D'HISTOIRE DE L'ART. DOCUMENTS DE
TRAVAIL. 1970. irreg., latest no.22, 1987. price
varies. Universite Catholique de Louvain, Institut
Superieur d'Archeologie et d'Histoire de l'Art, 1
place Blaise Pascal, 1348 Louvain-la-Neuve,
Belgium. Ed. T. Hackens.

709 913 MG
UNIVERSITE DE MADAGASCAR. MUSEE
D'ART ET D'ARCHEOLOGIE. TRAVAUX ET
DOCUMENTS. 1970. irreg., latest no.25, 1986.
FMG.3000. Universite de Madagascar, Musee d'Art
et d'Archeologie, B.P. 564 Isoraka, Antananarivo,
Malagasy Republic.

709 FR ISSN 0563-9794
UNIVERSITE DE TOULOUSE II (LE MIRAIL).
INSTITUT D'ART PREHISTORIQUE.
TRAVAUX. 1959. a. 85 F. Universite de Toulouse
II (le Mirail), Service des Publications, 56 rue du
Taur, 31069 Toulouse Cedex, France. Ed. C.
Barriere. (back issues avail.)

745 US ISSN 0068-628X
UNIVERSITY OF CALIFORNIA, LOS ANGELES.
MUSEUM OF CULTURAL HISTORY.
OCCASIONAL PAPERS. 1969. irreg., no.5, 1985.
price varies. University of California, Los Angeles,
Musuem of Cultural History, Los Angeles, CA
90024. TEL 213-825-4361.

700 378 US
UNIVERSITY OF ILLINOIS AT URBANA-
CHAMPAIGN. SCHOOL OF ART AND
DESIGN. NEWSLETTER. 1951. a. free. University
of Illinois at Urbana-Champaign, Continuing
Education and Public Service-Visual Arts, 123 Fine
and Applied Arts Bldg., Champaign, IL 61820. TEL
217-333-1000. Ed. Eugene C. Wicks.
 Formerly: University of Illinois at Urbana-
Champaign. Department of Art. Newsletter (ISSN
0073-5256)

700 PK ISSN 0080-9616
UNIVERSITY OF SIND. RESEARCH JOURNAL.
ARTS SERIES: HUMANITIES AND SOCIAL
SCIENCES. (Text in English) 1961. a. Rs.10.
University of Sind, Faculty of Arts, Jamshoro,
Hyderabad 6, Pakistan. Ed. Waheed Ali Farooqi.
bk. rev. circ. 1,000.

701 709 CS ISSN 0231-5025
UNIVERZITA J. E. PURKYNE. FILOZOFICKA
FAKULTA. SBORNIK PRACI. F: RADA
UMINOVEDNA. irreg., approx. a. Univerzita J. E.
Purkyne, Filozoficka Fakulta, A. Novaka 1, 602 00
Brno, Czechoslovakia.

700 913 780 CS ISSN 0083-4130
UNIVERZITA KOMENSKEHO. FILOZOFICKA
FAKULTA. ZBORNIK: MUSAICA. (Text in
Czech or Slovak; summaries in English and
German) 1961. irreg. exchange basis. Univerzita
Komenskeho, Filozoficka Fakulta, Gondova 2, 806
01 Bratislava, Czechoslovakia. Ed. Bohuslav
Novotny. circ. 700.

709 PL ISSN 0083-4424
UNIWERSYTET JAGIELLONSKI. ZESZYTY
NAUKOWE. PRACE Z HISTORII SZTUKI. (Text
in Polish; summaries in French and Russian) 1962.
irreg., no.157 1983. price varies. Panstwowe
Wydawnictwo Naukowe, Miodowa 10, 00-251
Warsaw, Poland (Dist. by: Ars Polona, Krakowskie
Przedmiescie 7, 00-068 Warsaw, Poland)

VEREIN FUER VOLKSKUNDE IN WIEN.
SONDERSCHRIFTEN. see *FOLKLORE*

709 BL
VIDA DAS ARTES. irreg. $50. Industrias Graficas
Libra, Rua Visconde de Carandai, 19, Jardim
Botanico, Rio de Janeiro, Brazil. illus.

700 300 370 320 CN
VIDEO OUT DISTRIBUTION CATALOGUE. 1983.
biennial. Satellite Video Exchange Society, 261
Powell St., Vancouver, B.C. V6A 1G3, Canada. Ed.
Jeannette Reinhardt.

700 US
VIDEOZINE. 1977. irreg. (Mamelle Inc.)
Contemporary Arts Press, Box 3123, San Francisco,
CA 94119. TEL 415-431-7672. (videotape)

700 US ISSN 0277-0490
VISUAL ARTS. 1978. a. National Endowment for the
Arts, 2401 E St., N.W., Washington, DC 20506.
TEL 202-682-5400.
 Formerly: Visual Arts Program (ISSN 0145-4013)

700 DK ISSN 0107-136X
VORE KUNSTNERE. vol.12, 1982/83. a. Kr.35.
Skolernes Kunstforening Alssund-Kredsen, Eksp.
Poul Berg, Roennebaervej 6, 6430 Nordborg,
Denmark. TEL 45- 445 06 70. Ed. Poul Berg. illus.
 Formerly: Skolernes Kunstforening Alssund-
Kredsen. Katalog.

709 GW
WALLRAF-RICHARTZ-JAHRBUCH;
WESTDEUTSCHES JAHRBUCH FUER
KUNSTGESCHICHTE. NEUE FOLGE. 1924. a.
DM.120. (Freunde des Wallraf-Richartz-Museums)
Wienand Verlag, Weyertal 59, D-5000 Cologne 41,
W. Germany (B.R.D.) Ed. Gerhard Bott. circ. 800.
Indexed: RILA.
 Formerly (until 1979): Wallraf-Richartz-Jahrbuch;
Westdeutsches Jahrbuch fuer Kunstgeschichte (ISSN
0083-7105)

709 US ISSN 0083-7148
WALTER W.S. COOK ALUMNI LECTURE. 1960.
irreg. $5. ‡ (New York University, Institute of Fine
Arts) J. J. Augustin, Inc., Locust Valley, NY 11560.
TEL 516-676-1510. index.

705 709 US ISSN 0083-7156
WALTERS ART GALLERY. JOURNAL. 1938. a.,
(occasionally biennial) $25. Walters Art Gallery,
600 N. Charles St., Baltimore, MD 21201. TEL
301-547-9000. Ed. Troy Moss. illus. circ. 1,000.
Indexed: Art Ind. Art & Archaeol.Tech.Abstr.
RILA.

WHO'S WHO IN ART. see *BIOGRAPHY*

700 658 UK ISSN 0266-707X
WHO'S WHO IN ARTS MANAGEMENT. 1984. a.
£8.95. Rhinegold Publishing Ltd., 239/241
Shaftesbury Ave., London WC2H 8EH, England.
Ed. Nichola Pritchett-Brown.

700 AU ISSN 0083-9981
WIENER JAHRBUCH FUER
KUNSTGESCHICHTE. (Text in English and
German) 1921. a. DM.112. (Institut fuer
Oesterreichische Kunstforschung) Hermann
Boehlaus Nachf., c/o Dr. Karl Lueger, Ring 12, A-
1010 Vienna, Austria. (Co-sponsor: Universitaet
Wien. Kunsthistorisches Institut) Eds. E. Frodl-
Kraft, G. Schmidt. bk. rev. illus. circ. 500. Indexed:
RILA.

709 943.6 GW
WIENER RINGSTRASSE-BILD EINER EPOCHE;
die Erweiterung der Inneren Stadt Wien unter
Kaiser Franz Joseph. irreg., vol.11, 1979. price
varies. (Fritz Thysson Stiftung) Franz Steiner Verlag
Wiesbaden GmbH, Birkenwaldstr. 44, Postfach 347,
D-7000 Stuttgart 1, W. Germany (B.R.D.)
Ed.Renate Wagner-Rieger.

WILBOUR MONOGRAPHS. see *HISTORY*

700 US
WINSLOW HOMER. 1986. a. Box 86, New Albany,
IN 47150. TEL 812-944-9386. Ed. Gene
Teitelbaum.

WINTERFARE. see *LITERATURE*

WITTENBERG REVIEW OF LITERATURE AND
ART. see *LITERATURE*

701 US
WORLD ART TRENDS. a. Harry N. Abrams, Inc.,
100 Fifth Ave., New York, NY 10011.
 Formerly: Art Actuel.

700 790 NE ISSN 0084-1498
WORLD COLLECTORS ANNUARY. (Text in
English) 1950. a. fl.240($100) World Collectors
Publishers, P.O. Box 263, 2270 AG Voorburg,
Netherlands. Ed. A.M.E. Van Eijk Van
Voorthuijsen. adv. cum.index (1946-1982) circ. 1,
000.

745 US ISSN 0084-1706
WORLD CRAFTS COUNCIL. GENERAL
ASSEMBLY. PROCEEDINGS OF THE
BIENNIAL MEETING.* 1964. biennial, 8th,
Kyoto, 1978. $4. (World Crafts Council) World
Crafts Foundation, 247 Centre St., New York, NY
10013. circ. 2,000.

WORLD CULTURAL GUIDES. see *TRAVEL AND
TOURISM*

700 PL ISSN 0084-2982
WROCLAWSKIE TOWARZYSTWO NAUKOWE.
KOMISJA HISTORII SZTUKI. ROZPRAWY.
(Text in Polish; summaries in English and French)
1960. irreg. price varies. Ossolineum, Publishing
House of the Polish Academy of Sciences, Rynek 9,
Wroclaw, Poland (Dist. by: Ars Polona-Ruch,
Krakowskie Przedmiescie 7, Warsaw, Poland) circ.
1,000.

WYDZIAL FILOLOGICZNO-FILOZOFICZNEGO.
PRACE. see *PHILOSOPHY*

700 US ISSN 0084-3415
YALE PUBLICATIONS IN THE HISTORY OF
ART. 1939. irreg., no.28, 1981. price varies. Yale
University Press, 92A Yale Sta., New Haven, CT
06520. TEL 203-432-0940.

709 YU ISSN 0514-616X
ZBORNIK ZASTITE SPOMENIKA KULTURE/
RECUEIL DES TRAVAUX SUR LA
PROTECTION DES MONUMENTS
HISTORIQUES. 1950. a. Republicki Zavod za
Zastitu Spomenika Kulture, Kalegdan 14, Belgrade,
Yugoslavia. Ed. Jovan Sekulic.

741 GW ISSN 0084-523X
ZEICHENWERK. 1970. irreg. DM.7.80. Georg
Kallmeyer Verlag, Grosser Zimmerhof 20, Postfach
1347, 3340 Wolfenbuettel, W. Germany (B.R.D.)
(looseleaf format)

700 GW
ZENTRALINSTITUTS FUER
KUNSTGESCHICHTE. JAHRBUCH. (Text in
English and German) 1985. a. DM.98. C.H. Beck'sche
Verlagsbuchhandlung, Wilhelmstr. 9, 8000 Munich
40, W. Germany (B.R.D.) circ. 120.

700 913   GR   ISSN 0252-8150
ZYGOS (1982); annual edition on the Hellenic fine arts. (Text in English) 1982. a. Dr.2000($30) Zygos Ltd., 33 Iofontos St., GR11634 Athens, Greece. Ed. Ion F. Frantzeskakis. adv. bk. rev. bibl. illus. cum.index. circ. 10,000.

ART — Abstracting, Bibliographies, Statistics

016.7   SZ
ART/KUNST; international bibliography of art books/ internationale bibliographie des kunstbuchs/ bibliographie internationale des livres d'art. (Text in English, French, and German) 1972. a. 36 Fr. W. Jaeggi AG, Postfach, CH-4001 Basel, Switzerland. Ed. W. Jaeggi. adv. bk. rev. circ. 4,500.

700 571 016   US   ISSN 0004-2994
ART AND ARCHAEOLOGY TECHNICAL ABSTRACTS; abstracts of the technical literature on archaeology and the fine arts. (Text in English; titles in English and original languages) 1955. s-a. $30 per vol. (2 nos. per vol.) Getty Conservation Institute, 4503 B Glencoe Ave., Marina del Rey, CA 90292-6466. TEL 213-822-2299. (Co-sponsor: International Institute for Conservation of Historic and Artistic Works (London)) Ed. Jessica S. Brown. index. cum.index every vol. circ. 4,500. Indexed: Chem.Abstr. Forest Prod.Abstr. Text.Tech.Dig. World Surf.Coat. RILA.
Formerly: I I C Abstracts.

016 700 720   US
ART AND ARCHITECTURE BIBLIOGRAPHIES. 1973. irreg., no.4, 1978. price varies. Hennessey & Ingalls, Inc., 8321 Campion Dr., Los Angeles, CA 90045. TEL 213-458-9074.

700 016   US
ART AND ARCHITECTURE INFORMATION GUIDE SERIES. 1974. irreg., vol.14, 1980. $65. Gale Research Company, Book Tower, Detroit, MI 48226. TEL 313-961-2242. Ed. Sydney Starr Keaveney.

700 016   UK   ISSN 0095-1420
ARTBIBLIOGRAPHIES CURRENT TITLES. 1972. bi-m. price varies. Clio Press Ltd., 55 St. Thomas' St., Oxford OX1 1JG, England (U.S. subscr. to: ABC-CLIO, Riviera Campus, 2040 Alameda Padre Serra, Santa Barbara, CA 93103) Ed. Tony Sloggett.

700 016   UK   ISSN 0300-466X
ARTBIBLIOGRAPHIES MODERN. 1969. s-a. price varies. Clio Press Ltd., 55 St. Thomas' St., Oxford OX1 1JG, England TEL (0865) 25033. (U.S. subscr. to: ABC-Clio, Riviera Campus, 2040 Alameda Padre Serra, Santa Barbara, CA 93104-4397) Ed. Tony Sloggett. abstr.
● Also available online. Vendors: DIALOG.
Formerly: L O M A Literature on Modern Art (ISSN 0090-7235)

709 016   DK
BIBLIOGRAFI OVER DANSK KUNST. 1971. a. free. Kunstakademiets Bibliotek - Academy of Fine Arts, Library, Kongens Nytorv 1, DK-1050 Copenhagen K, Denmark. Ed. Emma Salling. bk. rev. circ. 500.

097 016   DK
BIBLIOGRAFI OVER EUROPAEISKE KUNSTNERES EX LIBRIS/EUROPAEISCHE EX LIBRIS/EUROPEAN BOOK PLATES/EX LIBRIS D'EUROPE. (Text in Danish, English, French, German) 1967. a., latest combines 1976 and 1977 (pub. 1978) Kr.120. Klaus Roedel, Ed. & Pub., P.O. Box 109, DK-9900 Frederikshavn, Denmark. bibl. circ. 300.

700 016   GE   ISSN 0232-5810
BIBLIOGRAPHIE BILDENDE KUNST. 1973. a. Saechsische Landesbibliothek, Marienallee 12, 8060 Dresden, E. Germany (D.D.R.)

700 016   GE
BIBLIOGRAPHIE DER ANTIQUARIATS-, AUKTIONS- UND KUNSTKATALOGE. 1975. irreg. Karl-Marx-Universitaet, Universitaetsbibliothek, Beethovenstr. 6, 701 Leipzig, E. Germany (D.D.R.)

700 720   GW   ISSN 0173-1637
BIBLIOGRAPHIE ZUR KUNSTGESCHICHTLICHEN LITERATUR IN OST- UND SUEDOSTEUROPAEISCHEN ZEITSCHRIFTEN. 1970. a. Zentralinstitut fuer Kunstgeschichte in Muenchen, Meiserstr. 10, D-8000 Munich 2, W. Germany (B.R.D.) (Subscr. to: Buchhandlung Wasmuth KG, Hardenbergstr. 9A, D-1000 Berlin 12, W. Germany (B.R.D.)) circ. 200.

CANADIAN ART SALES INDEX. see *ART*

700 016   FR
LIVRE D'ART INFORMATION. irreg. free. Union des Editeurs Francais, 35 rue Mazarine, 75006 Paris, France. bk. rev.

700   US
R I L A NEWS. (Repertoire International de la Litterature de l'Art/International Repertory of the Literature of Art) irreg. (R I L A) J. Paul Getty Trust, c/o Sterling and Francine Clark Art Institute, Williamstown, MA 01267. TEL 413-458-8260.

790   UK
WORLD GUIDE TO PERFORMING ARTS PERIODICALS. 1982. a. £10. British I T I Centre, 31 Shelton St., London WC2H 9HT, England. Ed. Christopher Edwards.

ART — Computer Applications

621.3 001.6   US
SYMPOSIUM ON SMALL COMPUTERS IN THE ARTS. PROCEEDINGS. 1981. a. (Institute of Electrical and Electronics Engineers, Inc.) I E E E Computer Society Press, 1730 Massachusetts Ave., N.W., Washington, DC 20036 (And: 345 E. 47th St., New York, NY 10017)

ARTIFICIAL INTELLIGENCE

see *Computers — Artificial Intelligence*

ARTS AND HANDICRAFTS

745.5   UK   ISSN 0261-2135
CRAFTSMAN'S DIRECTORY. 1981. a. £4. S. & J. Lance Publications, Brook House, Mint St., Godalming, Surrey GU7 1HE, England. adv. circ. 2,500.

700   UK
CREATIVE HANDBOOK. 1973. a. £28. Creative Handbook, 100 St. Martins Ln., London WC2, England. circ. 9,000.

700   UK
CREATIVE HANDBOOK DIARY. 1979. a. £11.95. Creative Handbook, 100 St. Martins Ln., London WC2, England. Ed. Roy Capel.

700 770   AT   ISSN 0726-3589
CREATIVE SOURCE AUSTRALIA; the wizards of Oz. 1980. irreg. Aus.$55($55) Armadillo Publishers Pty. Ltd., 205-207 Scotchmer St., Fitzroy North, Vic. 3068, Australia. Ed. Elaine Howell. circ. 4,500. (back issues avail.)

745.5   AT
DIRECTORY OF CRAFT INFO. a. Crafts Council of N.S.W., 100 George St., The Rocks, N.S.W. 2000, Australia.

745.5 738   UK
EUROPEAN TABLEWARE BUYERS GUIDE. 1971. a. £27. International Trade Publications Ltd., Queensway House, 2 Queensway, Redhill, Surrey RH1 1QS, England. adv.
Former titles: Tableware Reference Book; Tableware and Pottery Gazette Reference Book (ISSN 0082-1438)

745.5   II
GLASS, POTTERIES AND CERAMIC ANNUAL. (Text in English) 1970. a. $15. Praveen Corp., Sayajiganj, Baroda 390005, India. Ed. C.M. Pandit.
Formerly: Glass, Potteries and Ceramic Journal (ISSN 0017-1042)

745.5   UA   ISSN 0255-0903
GROUPE INTERNATIONAL D'ETUDE DE LA CERAMIQUE EGYPTIENNE. BULLETIN DE LIAISON. (Text in English, French and German) 1975. a. Institut Francais d'Archeologie Orientale du Caire, 37 rue el Cheikh Aly Youssef, Mounira, Cairo, Egypt. Ed. Helen Jacquet-Gordon. circ. 200. (back issues avail.)
Ceramics

745.5   US   ISSN 0075-4250
JOURNAL OF GLASS STUDIES. 1959. a. $20. Corning Museum of Glass, One Museum Way, Corning, NY 14830-2253. TEL 607-937-5371. Ed. John H. Martin. cum.index: vols.1-15. circ. 1,150. (also avail. in microform from UMI; reprint service avail. from UMI) Indexed: Bull.Signal. Chem.Abstr. Curr.Cont. Art & Archaeol.Tech.Abstr. Art Ind. Arts & Hum.Cit.Ind. Br.Archaeol.Abstr. Numis.Lit. RILA.
Glass

745.5   UK
JOURNAL OF STAINED GLASS. 1924. a. £8.50. British Society of Master Glass Painters, 6 Queen Sq., London WC1, England. Eds. Peter Cormack, Jill Kerr. bk. rev. circ. 500. Indexed: Br.Hum.Ind. Br.Archaeol.Abstr. RILA.
Former titles: British Society of Master Glass Painters Journal; Journal of Stained Glass.

745.5   US   ISSN 0275-469X
NEW GLASS REVIEW. 1977. a. $5. Corning Museum of Glass, One Museum Way, Corning, NY 14830-2253. TEL 607-937-5371. (reprint service avail. from UMI)
Formerly: Contemporary Glass; Supersedes (1977-1979): Contemporary Glass Microfiche Program.
Glass

745.5 738.1   UK   ISSN 0032-5678
POTTERY QUARTERLY; a review of craft pottery. 1954. irreg., (approx. 4/yr.) £7 for 4 nos. Northfields Studio, Northfields, Tring, Herts., England. Ed. M. Fieldhouse. adv. bk. rev. illus. index. circ. 2,500. (also avail. in microform from UMI; reprint service avail. from UMI) Indexed: Br.Ceram.Abstr.

745.5   IT
QUADERNI DELL'EMILCERAMICA. a. L.8500. Faenza Editrice, Via Firenze 276, 48018 Faenza, Italy. Ed. Francesco Liverani.

745.5   US
QUILTMAKERS TIME. 1972. irreg., latest no.3, 1986. $3.95. Ed. Sally Goodspeed, 2318 N. Charles St., Baltimore, MD 21218. bk. rev. illus.
Quiltmaking

745.5   UK   ISSN 0144-1302
SCOTTISH POTTERY HISTORICAL REVIEW. 1980. a. Scottish Pottery Society, c/o Mr. G.D.R. Cruickshank, 21 Warrender Park Terrace, Edinburgh, Scotland. adv. bk. rev. circ. 300.

745.5   US   ISSN 0569-7468
SYMPOSIUM ON THE ART OF GLASSBLOWING PROCEEDINGS. 1956. a. price varies. American Scientific Glassblowers Society, 1507 Hagley Rd., Toledo, OH 43612. Ed. James E. Panczner. bibl. illus. circ. 1,000.
Glass

TEXTILE MUSEUM JOURNAL. see *TEXTILE INDUSTRIES AND FABRICS*

745.5   US
WILLIAMSBURG CRAFT SERIES. 1955. irreg. price varies. Colonial Williamsburg Foundation, Box C, Williamsburg, VA 23187. TEL 804-229-1000.

ASTROLOGY

133.5 US
ASTROLOGY (YEAR) 1972. 2/yr. plus 2 newsletters. $25. (National Astrological Society) Astrology Services International, 63 W. 38th St., No. 505, New York, NY 10018. Ed. Henry Weingarten. adv. charts. circ. 1,000 (controlled)
Formerly: N A S O Journal.

133.5 US
ASTROLOGY REFERENCE BOOK. 1972. a. $5.95. Symbols & Signs, Box 4536, N. Hollywood, CA 91607. Ed. Edith Waldron.
Formerly (until 1980): Astrology Annual Reference Book (ISSN 0363-4140)

133.5 US ISSN 0146-3365
C A O TIMES. 1975. irreg. $20 for 4 nos. C A O Times Inc., Box 75, Old Chelsea Sta., New York, NY 10113. Ed. Al H. Morrison. adv. bk. rev. circ. 1,100.

133.5 US
DAILY PLANET ALMANAC.* 1976. a. $3.95. Daily Planet, 1447 Ogden, Denver, CO 80218-1909. Ed. Terry Reim. adv. charts. illus. circ. 45,000. (back issues avail.)

133.5 US ISSN 0743-6408
DAILY PLANETARY GUIDE; an encyclopedia of practical astrological applications. 1978. a. $5.95. Llewellyn Publications, 213 E. 4th St., Box 64383, St. Paul, MN 55164. TEL 612-291-1970. Ed. Terry Buske. adv. (reprint service avail. from UMI)

133.5 US
FOURTH QUADRANT. 1979. irreg. free. Digicomp Research Corp., Terrace Hill, Ithaca, NY 14850. TEL 607-273-5900. Ed. Jeffrey Cox. adv. illus. circ. 400.

133.5 FR
GUIDE ASTROLOGIQUE. (Supplement to Astre) 1970. a. 10 F. G. Gourdon, Ed. and Pub., 10 rue de Crussol, 75011 Paris, France. adv. illus. circ. 120, 000.

J. GRUBER'S HAGERS-TOWN TOWN AND COUNTRY ALMANACK. see ENCYCLOPEDIAS AND GENERAL ALMANACS

133.5 II
JANMABHOOMI PANCHANG. (Text in Gujarati) 1945. a. Rps.100. Janmabhoomi Group of Newspapers, Janmabhoomi Bhavan, Ghoga St., Fort, Box 62, Bombay 400 001, India. Ed. Jyoti Bhatt. adv. circ. 46,000.

133.5 US ISSN 0085-2384
JOURNAL OF ASTROLOGICAL STUDIES. 1970. irreg. International Society for Astrological Research, Inc., 70 Melrose Pl., Montclair, NJ 07042. Ed. Julienne P. Mullette. charts. illus. stat. circ. 2,000.

133.5 640 II
KALNIRNAY. (Text in English, Hindi and Marathi) 1973. a. Rs.4.00($2) Sumangal Publishing Co., 172 M.M.G.S. Marg, Box 5547, Dadar, Bombay 400014, India. Ed. Jayant Salgaonkar. adv. circ. 2,500.

133.5 US
LAKEWOODS ASTROLOGICAL GUIDES. 1979. a. Lakewood Books, Box 857, Shelter Island, NY 11964. TEL 516-749-1122. Ed. Don Wigal. circ. 10, 000.

133 US ISSN 0145-8868
LLEWELLYN'S ASTROLOGICAL CALENDAR. 1931. a. $6.95. Llewellyn Publications, Box 64383, St. Paul, MN 55164. TEL 612-291-1970. Ed. Terry Buske. charts. circ. 50,000. (reprint service avail. from UMI)

133 US
LLEWELLYN'S MOON SIGN BOOK; gardening guide and lunar almanac. 1906. a. $3.95. Llewellyn Publications, 213 E. 4th St., Box 64383, St. Paul, MN 55164. TEL 612-291-1970. Ed. Terry Buske. adv. charts. tr.lit. circ. 60,000. (also avail. in microform from UMI; back issues avail.; reprint service avail. from UMI)
Formerly: Moonsign Book.

133.5 US
NEW AGE ASTROLOGY GUIDE (YEAR) 1972. a. $3. Milo Kovar, Ed. & Pub., 2640 Greenwich, No. 403, San Francisco, CA 94123. TEL 415-921-1192. adv. bk. rev. circ. 25,000. (back issues avail.)
Formerly: Astro Annual (ISSN 0277-9110)

133.5 US
SUN SIGN BOOK. 1983. a. $3.95. Llewellyn Publications, 213 E. 4th St., Box 64383, St. Paul, MN 55164. TEL 612-291-1970. Ed. Terry Buske. adv. circ. 21,000.

133.5 613.26 US
VEGETARIAN ASTROLOGER. irreg. 4216 Tod Ave., East Chicago, IN 46312. TEL 219-397-9297. Ed. Ted PanDeva.

ASTRONOMY

523.8 US
A A V S O BULLETIN--PREDICTED DATES OF MAXIMA AND MINIMA OF LONG PERIOD VARIABLE STARS. 1937. a. $20. American Association of Variable Star Observers, 25 Birch St., Cambridge, MA 02138. TEL 617-354-0484. Ed. Janet A. Mattei. circ. 1,500. (looseleaf format; back issues avail.) Indexed: Astron. & Astrophys.Abstr.
Formerly: A A V S O Bulletin (ISSN 0516-9518)

523.8 US
A A V S O REPORT. no.28, 1970. irreg. no.38, 1983. $30 per no. American Association of Variable Star Observers, 25 Birch St., Cambridge, MA 02138. TEL 617-354-0484. Ed. Janet A. Mattei. circ. 1,000. (back issues avail.) Indexed: Sci.Abstr. Astron. & Astrophys.Abstr.
Supersedes (1949-1966): American Association of Variable Star Observers. Quarterly Report.

ACADEMIE SERBE DES SCIENCES ET DES ARTS. CLASSE DES SCIENCES MATHEMATIQUES ET NATURELLES. BULLETIN. SCIENCES MATHEMATIQUES. see MATHEMATICS

520 US ISSN 0190-2717
ACADEMY OF SCIENCES OF THE U S S R. CRIMEAN ASTROPHYSICAL OBSERVATORY. BULLETIN. 1977. irreg. $57.50. Allerton Press, Inc., 150 Fifth Ave., New York, NY 10011. TEL 212-924-3950. Ed. A.B. Severnyi. Indexed: Sci.Abstr. Phys.Ber.

520 US ISSN 0190-2709
ACADEMY OF SCIENCES OF THE U S S R. SPECIAL ASTROPHYSICAL OBSERVATORY-NORTH CAUCASUS. BULLETIN. 1977. irreg. $55. Allerton Press, Inc., 150 Fifth Ave., New York, NY 10011. TEL 212-924-3950. Ed. I.M. Kopylov. Indexed: Sci.Abstr.

520 SP
AGRUPACION ASTRONOMICA DE SABADELL. CIRCULAR INFORMATIVA. no.267, 1981. irreg. (2-3/yr.) 5,700 ptas. Agrupacion Astronomica de Sabadell, Calle Font 1-1, Sabadell (Barcelona), Spain.
Formerly: Agrupacion Astronomica de Sabadell. Circular Mensual.

523.01 UR
AKADEMIYA NAUK KAZAKHSKOI S.S.R. ASTROFIZICHESKII INSTITUT. TRUDY. 1961. irreg., vol.28, 1976. 2.14 Rub. per no. Izdatel'stvo Nauka, Kazakhskoe Otdelenie, Ul.Shevchenko 28, 480021 Alma-Ata, Kazakh S.S.R., U.S.S.R. Ed. T. Omarov. abstr. bibl. illus. circ. 1,000. Indexed: Chem.Abstr. Math.R.

520 US ISSN 0191-3867
ALMANAC FOR COMPUTERS. 1977. a. price varies. U.S. Naval Observatory, Washington, DC 20392 TEL 202-653-1547. (Orders to: Superintendent of Documents, U.S. Government Printing Office, Washington, D.C. 20402)

520 PH ISSN 0569-0838
ALMANAC FOR GEODETIC ENGINEERS. (Text in English) a. P.5($1) Philippine Atmospheric, Geophysical and Astronomical Services Administration, 1424 Quezon Ave., Quezon City, Philippines. circ. 1,500.

528.6 SP ISSN 0210-735X
ALMANAQUE NAUTICO. 1792. a. 1380 ptas. Instituto y Observatorio de Marina, San Fernando (Cadiz), Spain. illus. circ. 5,500.

520 036 SP ISSN 0210-8046
ALMANAQUE NAUTICO REDUCIDO PARA USO CON MAQUINAS DE CALCULAR. 1979. a. 480 ptas.($35) Instituto y Observatorio de Marina, San Fernando, Cadiz, Spain. circ. 400.

AMERICAN SOCIETY FOR PHOTOGRAMMETRY AND REMOTE SENSING FALL CONVENTION. TECHNICAL PAPERS. see GEOGRAPHY

520 523.01 US ISSN 0066-4146
ANNUAL REVIEW OF ASTRONOMY AND ASTROPHYSICS. 1963. a. $44. Annual Reviews Inc., 4139 El Camino Way, Palo Alto, CA 94306. TEL 415-493-4400. Ed. Geoffrey Burbidge. bibl. index. cum.index. (back issues avail.; reprint service avail. from ISI) Indexed: Chem.Abstr. Curr.Cont. Sci.Abstr. Int.Aerosp.Abstr. Ind.Sci.Rev. M.M.R.I. Nucl.Sci.Abstr. Phys.Ber.

ANNUAL REVIEW OF EARTH AND PLANETARY SCIENCES. see EARTH SCIENCES

520 US
ANTARCTIC METEORITE NEWSLETTER. 1978. irreg. free. National Science Foundation, Division of Polar Programs, Antarctic Meteorite Working Group, Code SN2, Johnson Space Center, Houston, TX 77058. Eds. James L. Gooding, John D. Annexstad. circ. 600.

520 UK ISSN 0142-7253
ARCHAEOASTRONOMY. (Supplement to: Journal for the History of Astronomy) 1979. a. £10.50($21) Science History Publications Ltd., Halfpenny Furze, Chalfont St. Giles, Buck. HP8 4NR, England. Ed. Dr. M.A. Hoskin. adv. bk. rev. illus. index. circ. 700. (back issues avail.) Indexed: Sci.Abstr. Abstr.Anthropol. Br.Archaeol.Abstr.

520 GE ISSN 0570-6262
ARCHENHOLD-STERNWARTE. VORTRAEGE UND SCHRIFTEN. 1959. irreg., vol.7, no.64, 1984. M.4. Archenhold-Sternwarte, Alt-Treptow 1, 1193 Berlin-Treptow, E. Germany (D.D.R.) Ed. D.B. Herrmann. circ. 1,500.

522.1 FR ISSN 0249-7522
ASSOCIATION POUR LE DEVELOPPEMENT INTERNATIONAL DE L'OBSERVATOIRE DE NICE. BULLETIN. (Text in English and French) 1964. a. 50 F. Association pour le Developpement International de l'Observatoire de Nice, B.P. 139, F-06003 Nice, France. charts. illus. circ. 400.
Formerly (until 1974): Association pour le Developpement International de l'Observatoire de Nice. Bulletin d'Information (ISSN 0004-5861)

523 BU ISSN 0324-1459
ASTROFIZICHESKIE ISSLEDOVANIIA. (Text in Russian; summaries in English) 1975. irreg. 2 lv. per issue. (Bulgarska Akademiia na Naukite) Publishing House of the Bulgarian Academy of Sciences, Acad. G. Bonchev St., Bldg. 6, 1113 Sofia, Bulgaria. Ed. N. Nikolov. circ. 800. Indexed: Chem.Abstr. Sci.Abstr.

522.1 CN
ASTROLABE. 1979. irreg. University of Ottawa Press, 603 Cumberland, Ottawa, Ont. K1N 6N5, Canada. TEL 613-564-2270.

520 FR
ASTROLETTRE. 1984. irreg., approx. 5/yr. 6 F. per no. Philippe Bury, Ed. & Pub., 185 rue de Solignac, 87000 Limoges, France. adv. bk. rev.

520 PL ISSN 0554-8233
ASTRONOMIA. (Text in English or Polish; summaries in English) 1964. irreg., no.3,1976. price varies. Adam Mickiewicz University Press, Marchlewskiego 128, 61-874 Poznan, Poland.
Formerly: Uniwersytet im. Adama Mickiewicza w Poznaniu. Wydzial Matematyki, Fizyki i Chemii. Seria Astronomia.

ASTRONOMY

528 UK
ASTRONOMICAL ALMANAC. 1981. a. price varies. H.M.S.O., Box 569, London SE1 9NH, England. (Co-sponsors: H.M. Nautical Almanac Office; U.S. Naval Observatory, Washington, D.C.)
Supersedes: Astronomical Ephemeris (ISSN 0066-9962) & American Ephemeris and Nautical Almanac (ISSN 0065-8189); Nautical Almanac and Astronomical Ephemeris.

520 II ISSN 0066-9970
ASTRONOMICAL EPHEMERIS OF GEOCENTRIC PLACES OF PLANETS. (Text in English; summaries in Hindi) 1942. a. Rs.13. Shree Jiwaji Observatory, Ujain, Madhya Pradesh, India. Ed. Jyotishastracharya K. K. Joshi. circ. 500.

523 US ISSN 0083-2421
ASTRONOMICAL PHENOMENA. 1951. a. price varies. U.S. Naval Observatory, Department of the Navy, Washington, DC 20392 TEL 202-653-1547. (Orders to: Supt. of Documents, Government Printing Office, Washington, D.C. 20402.)

520 AT ISSN 0067-0006
ASTRONOMICAL SOCIETY OF VICTORIA. ASTRONOMICAL YEARBOOK. 1964. a. Aus.$6.50. Astronomical Society of Victoria, G.P.O. Box 1059J, Melbourne, Vic. 3001, Australia. Ed. C. Hyde. index. circ. 550.

520 BU ISSN 0068-3639
ASTRONOMICHESKI KALENDAR NA OBSERVATORIIATA V SOFIA. 1954. a. 1.26 lv. (Bulgarska Akademiia na Naukite, Sektsiia po Astronomiia) Publishing House of the Bulgarian Academy of Sciences, Acad. G. Bonchev St., Bldg. 6, 1113 Sofia, Bulgaria (Dist. by: Hemus, 6, Rouski Blvd., 1000 Sofia, Bulgaria) Ed. L. Levicharska. circ. 2,640.

520 GW ISSN 0067-0014
ASTRONOMISCHE GRUNDLAGEN FUER DEN KALENDER. 1949. a. DM.59. (Astronomisches Rechen-Institut) Verlag G. Braun GmbH, Karl-Friedrich-Str. 14, Postfach 1709, 7500 Karlsruhe 1, W. Germany (B.R.D.) Ed. T. Lederle. circ. 650.

520 US
ASTRONOMY THROUGH PRACTICAL INVESTIGATION. 1973. base modules plus approx. 1/yr. $0.75 per no. L.S.W. Publications, Inc., Box 82, Mattituck, NY 11952. Ed.Bd. circ. 1, 000.

520 523.01 NE ISSN 0067-0057
ASTROPHYSICS AND SPACE SCIENCE LIBRARY; a series of books on the developments of space science and of general astronomy and astrophysics published in connection with the journal Space Science Reviews. 1965. irreg. price varies. D. Reidel Publishing Co., P.O. Box 17, 3300 AA Dordrecht, Netherlands (And 190 Old Derby St., Hingham, MA 02043) Ed. C. de Jager. Indexed: Appl.Mech.Rev. Chem.Abstr. Math.R. GeoRef. Phys.Ber.

551.56 NO ISSN 0373-4854
AURORAL OBSERVATORY. MAGNETIC OBSERVATIONS. (Text in English) 1932. a. free. University of Tromsoe, Auroral Observatory, Box 953, 9001 Tromsoe, Norway. Ed. Steinar Berger.
Formerly (until 1965): Norske Institutt for Kosmisk Fysikk. Magnetic Observations.

520 GW ISSN 0340-7691
BAYERISCHE KOMMISSION FUER DIE INTERNATIONALE ERDMESSUNG. VEROEFFENTLICHUNGEN. 1896. irreg. price varies. Bayerische Kommission fuer die Internationale Erdmessung, Marstallplatz 8, D-8000 Munich 22, W. Germany (B.R.D.) Ed.Dd.

520 II
BHAGYAVATI PANCHANGA. (Text in Manipuri; summaries in major Indian languages) 1930. a. Rs.5. Bhagyavati Library, Sagolband Rd., Meino Lane, Manipur State, Imphal 795001, India. Ed. Shri Utsam Jatra Singh. adv. circ. 5,000.

520 UK ISSN 0068-130X
BRITISH ASTRONOMICAL ASSOCIATION. HANDBOOK. 1922. a. £6. British Astronomical Association, Burlington House, Piccadilly, London W1V 9AG, England. Ed. Gordon E. Taylor. adv. circ. 4,000.
Formerly: British Astronomical Association. Observer's Handbook.

529 FR ISSN 0068-4236
BUREAU INTERNATIONAL DE L'HEURE. RAPPORT ANNUEL. (Text in English) 1967. a. free to qualified personnel. (International Time Bureau) Observatoire de Paris, 61 Ave. de l'Observatoire, 75014 Paris, France. (Affiliate: International Astronomical Union) Dir. B. Guinot. circ. 4,800. Indexed: Astron. & Astrophys.Abstr.

CALIFORNIA INSTITUTE OF TECHNOLOGY. DIVISION OF GEOLOGICAL AND PLANETARY SCIENCES. REPORT ON GEOLOGICAL AND PLANETARY SCIENCES FOR THE YEAR. see EARTH SCIENCES — Geology

523.75 FR
CARTES SYNOPTIQUES DE LA CHROMOSPHERE SOLAIRE ET CATALOGUES DES FILAMENTS ET DES CENTRES D'ACTIVITE. 1919. biennial. free. Observatoire de Paris, Section d'Astrophysique de Meudon, Department Astronomie Solaire et Planetaire, 92190 Meudon, France. Ed. Mme. M.J. Martres. Indexed: Astron.Astrophys.Abstr.
Formerly: Cartes Synoptiques de la Chromosphere Solaire (ISSN 0085-4778)

520 US ISSN 0160-2500
CASE WESTERN RESERVE UNIVERSITY. WARNER SWASEY OBSERVATORY. PUBLICATIONS. 1971. irreg., 1-2/yr. available on exchange. ‡ Case Western University, Warner Swasey Observatory, Cleveland, OH 44106. TEL 216-368-3728. circ. 250(controlled) Indexed: Bull.Signal. Ref.Zh. Astron.& Astrophys.Abstr.

520 RM
CENTRE DE L'ASTRONOMIE ET DES SCIENCES SPATIALES. OBSERVATIONS SOLAIRES. (Text in French) 1956. a. (Observatorul Astronomic Din Bucuresti) Editura Academiei Republicii Socialiste Rumania, Calea Victoriei 125, 79717 Bucharest, Rumania (Subscr. to: ARTEXIM, Piata Scinteii nr.1, P.O. Box 33-16, 70055 Bucharest, Rumania) Ed. Emilia Tifrea. bk. rev. circ. 500. Indexed: Bull.Signal. Ref.Zh. Astron.&Astrophys.Abstr.
Formerly: Observatorul Astronomic din Bucuresti. Observations Solaires (ISSN 0068-3094)

522 RM
CENTRUL DE ASTRONOMIE SI STIINTE SPATIALE. ANUARUL ASTRONOMIC. 1940. a. (Observatorul Astronomic din Bucuresti) Editura Academiei Republicii Socialiste Rumania, Calea Victoriei 125, 79717 Bucharest, Rumania (Subscr. to: ARTEXIM, Piata Scinteii nr.1, P.O. Box 33-16, 70055 Bucharest, Rumania) Ed. G. Stanila. circ. 1, 600. Indexed: Bull.Signal. Ref.Zh. Astron. & Astrophys.Abstr.
Formerly: Observatorul Astronomie din Bucuresti. Anuarul (ISSN 0068-3086)

520 CK ISSN 0120-2758
COLOMBIA. OBSERVATORIO ASTRONOMICO NACIONAL. ANUARIO. a. $1.50 or exchange. Universidad Nacional de Colombia, Observatorio Astronomico Nacional, Aptdo. Aereo 2584, Bogota, Colombia.

522.1 CK ISSN 0067-9518
COLOMBIA. OBSERVATORIO ASTRONOMICO NACIONAL. PUBLICACIONES. (Text in Spanish or English; summaries in Spanish and English) 1967. irreg., no.5, 1971. Universidad Nacional de Colombia, Observatorio Astronomico Nacional, Aptdo. Aereo 2584, Bogota, Colombia. circ. 500.

520 551.6 CE
COLOMBO OBSERVATORY. REPORT. (Text in English) a. Colombo Observatory, Bauddhaloka Mawatha, Colombo 7, Sri Lanka. charts, illus, stat.

523.01 US ISSN 0146-2970
COMMENTS ON ASTROPHYSICS. 1969. 6/yr. (in 1 vol., 6 nos./vol.) $240 to individuals; academic institutions $148. Gordon and Breach Science Publishers, 50 W. 23rd St., New York, NY 10010. TEL 212-206-8900. Ed. B.F. Burke. adv. charts. illus. (also avail. in microform from MIM) Indexed: Chem.Abstr. Curr.Cont. Sci.Abstr. GeoRef. Phys.Ber.
Incorporating: Earth and Extraterrestrial Sciences (ISSN 0070-7902); Formerly: Comments on Astrophysics and Space Physics (ISSN 0010-2679)

551.6 FR ISSN 0181-3048
CONNAISSANCE DES TEMPS. (Supplement avail.) a. price varies. (Bureau des Longitudes) Etablissement Principal du Service Hydrographique et Oceanographique de la Marine, 13 rue du Chatelier, 29275 Brest, France. Ed. J. Chapront. circ. 1,000.

CURRENT PAPERS IN PHYSICS; containing about 78,000 titles of research articles from the world's physics journals. see PHYSICS — Abstracting, Bibliographies, Statistics

520 US ISSN 0732-4421
CURRENT TOPICS IN CHINESE SCIENCE. SECTION E: ASTRONOMY. 1983. a., latest vol.3, 1985. Gordon & Breach Science Publishers, 50 W. 23rd St., New York, NY 10010. TEL 212-206-8900.

520 UK ISSN 0260-7794
DARLINGTON ASTRONOMICAL SOCIETY. NEWSLETTER. 1980. irreg. membership. Darlington Astronomical Society, c/o Paul Tate, Ed., 59 Eden Cres., Darlington Co., Durham DL1 5TN, England. adv. bk. rev. illus.

520 629.4 NE
DEVELOPMENTS IN SOLAR SYSTEM AND SPACE SCIENCE. 1975. irreg., vol.4, 1979. price varies. Elsevier Science Publishers B.V., Box 211, 1000 AE Amsterdam, Netherlands. Eds. Z. Kopal, A.G.W. Cameron. Indexed: GeoRef.

DIRECTORY OF PHYSICS & ASTRONOMY STAFF (YEAR) see EDUCATION — Higher Education

520 IE ISSN 0070-7643
DUNSINK OBSERVATORY. PUBLICATIONS; communications of the Dublin Institute for Advanced Studies, Series C. 1960. irreg., vol.1, 1975. price varies. Dublin Institute for Advanced Studies, 10 Burlington Rd., Dublin 4, Ireland.

522.1 DK ISSN 0108-9358
E S O FOELGEFORSKNING;* bevillinger til stoette af astronomiske forskningsprojekter ved det europaeske Sydobservatorium. 1981. a. free. European Southern Observatory, Karl Schwarzschild Str. 2, 8046 Garching, W. Germany (B.R.D.) illus.

528 US ISSN 0071-0962
EPHEMERIS OF THE SUN, POLARIS AND OTHER SELECTED STARS WITH COMPANION DATA AND TABLES. 1910. a. U.S. Naval Observatory, Dept. of the Navy, Washington, DC 20392 TEL 202-653-1547. (Orders to: Supt. of Documents, Government Printing Office, Washington, D.C. 20402)

520 FR ISSN 0240-8376
EPIDECIDES LUNAIRES/LUNAR EPIDECIS. 1981. a. Service Hydrographique et Oceanographique de la Marine, 3 av. Octave Greard, 75200 Paris Naval, France (Subscr. address: EPSHOM, B.P. 426, 29275 Brest Cedex, France)

520 FR ISSN 0240-8368
EPIMENIDES/EPIMENIS. 1980. a. Service Hydrographique et Oceanographique de la Marine, 3 av. Octave Greard, 75200 Paris Naval, France (Subscr. address: EPSHOM, B.P. 426, 29275 Brest Cedex, France)

520 GW ISSN 0531-4496
EUROPEAN SOUTHERN OBSERVATORY. ANNUAL REPORT. (Text in English, French and German) 1964. a. free. European Southern Observatory, Karl-Schwarzschild-Str. 2, D-8046 Garching, W. Germany (B.R.D.) circ. 1,600.

520 UK
F A S HANDBOOK. 1977. a. £2. Federation of Astronomical Societies, 17 Havelock St., Thornton, Bradford, W. Yorkshire BD13 3HA, England. Ed. Brian Jones. adv. circ. 300.

520 SP ISSN 0210-8127
FENOMENOS ASTRONOMICOS. 1980. a. 180 ptas. Instituto y Observatorio de Marina, San Fernando, Cadiz, Spain. circ. 100.

ASTRONOMY

520 FR
FRANCE. BUREAU DES LONGITUDES.
ANNUAIRE: EPHEMERIDES. Cover title:
Ephemerides. (Supplement to: Astronomie) 1977. a.
price varies. (Bureau des Longitudes) Gauthier-
Villars, 77 Av. Denfert-Rochereau, 75014 Paris,
France.
   Supersedes (since 1977): Ephemerides
Astronomiques.

551   523.01   NE
GEOPHYSICS AND ASTROPHYSICS
MONOGRAPHS; a series of graduate-level
textbooks and monographs on plasma astrophysics
and geophysics, including magnetospheric, solar, and
stellar physics. (Text in English) 1972. irreg. price
varies. D. Reidel Publishing Co., P.O. Box 17, 3300
AA Dordrecht, Netherlands (And: 190 Old Derby
St., Hingham, MA 02043) Ed. B.M. McCormac.

GRADUATE PROGRAMS: PHYSICS,
ASTRONOMY, AND RELATED FIELDS. see
PHYSICS

520   UK   ISSN 0308-5074
GREAT BRITAIN. ROYAL GREEENWICH
OBSERVATORY. BULLETIN. 1956. irreg. price
varies. (Science and Engineering Research Council)
Royal Greenwich Observatory, c/o J. Dudley,
Librarian, Herstmonceux Castle, Hailsham, E. Essex
BN27 1RP, England. circ. 300.

520   UK   ISSN 0308-3322
GREAT BRITAIN. ROYAL GREENWICH
OBSERVATORY. ANNUAL REPORT. 1974-
1979/80; resumed 1985. irreg. price varies. (Science
and Engineering Research Council) Royal
Greenwich Observatory, Herstmonceux Castle,
Hailsham, East Essex BN27 1RP, England. circ.
200.

520   GR   ISSN 0072-7385
GREEK NATIONAL COMMITTEE FOR
ASTRONOMY. ANNUAL REPORTS OF THE
ASTRONOMICAL INSTITUTES OF GREECE.
(Text in English) 1960. a. available on exchange.
Greek National Committee for Astronomy,
Academy of Athens, 14 Anagnostopolou St., GR
106 73 Athens, Greece.

520   GW   ISSN 0439-1551
DAS HIMMELSJAHR. 1910. a. DM.11.80.
Franckh'sche Verlagshandlung, Pfizerstr. 5, Postfach
640, 7000 Stuttgart 1, W. Germany (B.R.D.) Ed.
H.U. Keller. adv. circ. 35,000.

520   551.22   YU
HVAR OBSERVATORY BULLETIN. (Text in
English; summaries in English and Serbo-Croatian)
1977. a. free. Hvar Observatory, Faculty of
Geodesy, Kaciceva 26, 41000 Zagreb, Yugoslavia.
Ed. Vladis Vujnovic. circ. 400. (back issues avail.)
Indexed: Astron.& Astrophys.Abstr.
Int.Aerosp.Abstr. Ref.Zh.
   Solar physics

528   II
INDIAN ASTRONOMICAL EPHEMERIS. 1958. a.
Rs.100. Meteorological Department, Lodi Rd., New
Delhi 110003, India (Subscr. to: Controller of
Publications, Government of India, Civil Lines,
Delhi 110054, India) index. circ. 550.
   Formerly: Indian Ephemeris and Nautical
Almanac (ISSN 0537-1546)

520   HU   ISSN 0374-0676
INFORMATION BULLETIN ON VARIABLE
STARS. (Text in English and French) 1961. irreg.,
approx. 200/yr. $20 per vol. (100 issues) Hungarian
Academy of Sciences, Konkoly Observatory,
International Astronomical Union, Box 67, H-1525
Budapest, Hungary. Eds. B. Szeidl, L. Szabados.
circ. 500. (back issues avail.) Indexed: Sci.Abstr.

520   621.38   MX
INSTITUTO NACIONAL DE ASTROFISICA,
OPTICA Y ELECTRONICA. BOLETIN. (Text in
English; summaries in Spanish) 1973. irreg. free.
Instituto Nacional de Astrofisica, Optica y
Electronica, Apartados Postales Nos. 216 y 51,
Puebla, C.P. 72000, Mexico. Ed. Dr. Jorge Ojeda-
Castaneda. illus. circ. 1,000. Indexed: Chem.Abstr.
Sci.Abstr.
   Formerly (1972-1978): Instituto de Tonantzintla.
Boletin (ISSN 0303-7584); Supersedes (1952-1972):
Mexico (City). Universidad Nacional. Observatorio
Astronomico, Tacubaya. Boletin de los
Observatorios Tonantzintla y Tacubaya (ISSN 0539-
6387)

528.6   SP   ISSN 0080-5971
INSTITUTO Y OBSERVATORIO DE MARINA.
EFEMERIDES ASTRONOMICAS. 1971. a.;
no.185, 1975. 960 ptas. Instituto y Observatorio de
Marina, San Fernando (Cadiz), Spain. circ. 600.

520   US   ISSN 0081-0304
INTERNATIONAL ASTRONOMICAL UNION.
CENTRAL BUREAU FOR ASTRONOMICAL
TELEGRAMS. CIRCULAR. 1922. irreg., no.4123,
1985. price varies. Smithsonian Institution
Astrophysical Observatory, 60 Garden St.,
Cambridge, MA 02138. TEL 617-495-7244. (Co-
sponsor: International Astronomical Union) Ed.
B.G. Marsden.
   Formerly (1922-1964): Union Astronomique
International. Bureau Central de Telegrammes
Astronomiques. Circulaire.

520   NE
INTERNATIONAL ASTRONOMICAL UNION.
GENERAL ASSEMBLY. HIGHLIGHTS. triennial,
7th, 1985. price varies. D. Reidel Publishing Co.,
Box 17, 3300 AA Dordrecht, Netherlands (And:
190 Old Derby St., Hingham, MA 02043)
   Formerly: International Astronomical Union.
General Assembly. Proceedings.

520   NE   ISSN 0074-1809
INTERNATIONAL ASTRONOMICAL UNION.
PROCEEDINGS OF SYMPOSIA. 1955. irreg.,
113th, 1985. price varies. D. Reidel Publishing Co.,
Box 17, 3300 AA Dordrecht, Netherlands (And:
190 Old Derby St., Hingham, MA 02043) Indexed:
Chem.Abstr.

520   NE   ISSN 0080-1372
INTERNATIONAL ASTRONOMICAL UNION.
TRANSACTIONS. (Issued in two parts: Part A:
Reports, Part B: Proceedings) 1922. triennial, 19th,
1985. price varies. D. Reidel Publishing Co., Box
17, 3300 AA Dordrecht, Netherlands (And 190 Old
Derby St., Hingham, MA 02043)
   Formerly: International Astronomical Union.
Transactions and Highlights; Incorporating: Reports
on Astronomy.

525.3   551   JA   ISSN 0074-7432
INTERNATIONAL POLAR MOTION SERVICE.
ANNUAL REPORT/KOKUSAI KYOKU-UNDO
KANSOKU JIGYO NENPO. (Text in English)
1964. a. available on exchange or request. ‡
International Polar Motion Service, Central Bureau
- Kokusai Kyoku-Undo Kansoku Jigyo Chuo-Kyoku,
International Latitude Observatory, Mizusawa 023,
Japan. (Affiliate: Federation of Astronomical and
Geophysical Services) Ed. S. Yumi. circ. 400
(approx.) (also avail. in microform)

520   UR   ISSN 0202-0742
ITOGI NAUKI I TEKHNIKI: ASTRONOMIYA.
vol.30, 1987. irreg. price varies. Vsesoyuznyi Institut
Nauchno-Tekhnicheskoi Informatsii (VINITI),
Baltiiskaya ul. 14, Moscow A-219, Russian S.F.S.R.,
U.S.S.R.

520   UR   ISSN 0202-0734
ITOGI NAUKI I TEKHNIKI: ISSLEDOVANIE
KOSMICHESKOGO PROSTRANSTVA. vol.26,
1987. irreg. price varies. Vsesoyuznyi Institut
Nauchno-Tekhnicheskoi Informatsii (VINITI),
Baltiiskaya ul. 14, Moscow A-219, Russian S.F.S.R.,
U.S.S.R. (Subscr. to: Mezhdunarodnaya Kniga,
Dimitrova ul. 39, 113095 Moscow, Russian S.F.S.R.,
U.S.S.R.) Indexed: Chem.Abstr. Sci.Abstr.

520   FR
JOURNEES DE STRASBOURG. 1968. a. 50 Fr. to
individuals; free to institutions. Observatoire de
Strasbourg, 11 rue de l'Universite, 67000 Strasbourg,
France. circ. 500.
   Formerly (until 1978): Observatoire de
Strasbourg. Publication (ISSN 0081-590X)

520   KO
KOREAN ASTRONOMICAL SOCIETY.
JOURNAL. (Text in English and Korean;
Summaries in English) 1967. a. 5000 Won($10)
(free to members) Korean Astronomical Society,
Astronomy Department, Seoul National University,
Shin-him Dong, Kwan-Ak KU, Seoul, S. Korea. circ.
500.

520   UR
KOSMICHESKAYA NAUKA I TEKHNIKA;
respublikanskii mezhvedomstvennyi sbornik
nauchnykh trudov. (Text in Russian) 1973. a.
(Akademiya Nauk Ukrainskoi S.S.R., Komissiya
Kosmicheskikh Issledovanii) Izdatel'stvo Naukova
Dumka, c/o Yu.A. Khramov, Dir, Ul. Repina, 3,
Kiev 252 601, Ukrainian S.S.R., U.S.S.R. (Subscr.
to: Mezhdunarodnaya Kniga, Moscow, G-200,
Russian S.F.S.R., U.S.S.R.) Ed. B.G. Bar'yakhtar.
   Formerly (until 1985): Kosmicheskie
Issledovaniya na Ukraine (ISSN 0321-4508)

522   US
L P I TECHNICAL REPORT. 1981. irreg. (4-8/yr.)
Lunar and Planetary Institute, 3303 NASA Rd.
One, Houston, TX 77058-4399. TEL 713-486-2135.
circ. 300.

520   US   ISSN 0075-7896
LANDOLT-BOERNSTEIN, ZAHLENWERTE UND
FUNKTIONEN AUS
NATURWISSENSCHAFTEN UND TECHNIK.
NEUE SERIE. GROUP 6: ASTRONOMY. 1965.
irreg., vol.2, 1982. Springer-Verlag, 175 Fifth Ave.,
New York, NY 10010 TEL 212-460-1500. (Also
Berlin, Heidelberg, Tokyo and Vienna) (reprint
service avail. from ISI)

520   US   ISSN 0075-9325
LICK OBSERVATORY. PUBLICATIONS. (At head
of title: University of California) 1892. irreg., vol.23,
1981. price varies. Lick Observatory, Library,
University of California, Santa Cruz, Santa Cruz,
CA 95064. TEL 408-429-2513. Ed.Bd. Indexed:
Astron. & Astrophys.Abstr.

520   US   ISSN 0024-7057
LOWELL OBSERVATORY BULLETIN. 1903. irreg.
‡ Lowell Observatory, Flagstaff, AZ 86002. TEL
602-774-3358. cum.index. circ. 300. (looseleaf
format) Indexed: Bull.Signal. Astron.Jahresber.
Int.Aerosp.Abstr.

520   551   UK
M E R I T NEWSLETTER. (Monitored Earth
Rotation and Intercompared Techniques) 1979.
irreg. free. (International Astronomical Union)
Royal Greenwich Observatory, c/o J. Dudley,
Librarian, Herstmonceux Castle, Hailsham, E.
Sussex BN27 1RP, England. (Co-sponsor:
International Union of Geodesy and Geophysics)
Ed. G.A. Wilkins. circ. 200.

520   US   ISSN 0141-1128
MONOGRAPHS ON ASTRONOMICAL
SUBJECTS. 1975. irreg., no.9, 1983. price varies.
Oxford University Press, 200 Madison Ave., New
York, NY 10016 TEL 212-679-7300. (And: Ely
House, 37 Dover St., London W1X 4AH, England)
Ed. A.J. Meadows.

MOZAMBIQUE. SERVICO METEOROLOGICO.
INFORMACOES DE CARACTER
ASTRONOMICO. see *EARTH SCIENCES —
Geophysics*

520   GE
NAUTISCHES JAHRBUCH. 1950. a. M.24.
Seehydrographischer Dienst, Dierkower Damm 45,
2540 Rostock 40, E. Germany (D.D.R.) (Subscr. to:
Buchexport, Leninstr. 16, 7000 Leipzig, E.
Germany) circ. 1,500.

528.3   GW   ISSN 0077-6211
NAUTISCHES JAHRBUCH, ODER
EPHEMERIDEN UND TAFELN. a. DM.30.
Deutsches Hydrographisches Institut, Bernhard-
Nocht-Str. 78, 2000 Hamburg 4, W. Germany
(B.R.D.) circ. 5,200.

ASTRONOMY

520   GW   ISSN 0078-2246
NOVA KEPLERIANA. NEUE FOLGE. (Subseries of: Bayerische Akademie der Wissenschaften. Mathematisch-Naturwissenschaftliche Klasse. Abhandlungen. Neue Folge) (Text in German; summaries partly in English) 1969. irreg., no.6, 1976. price varies. (Kepler-Kommission) C.H. Beck'sche Verlagsbuchhandlung, Wilhelmstr. 9, 8000 Munich 40, W. Germany (B.R.D.)

520   AE   ISSN 0065-6232
OBSERVATOIRE ASTRONOMIQUE D'ALGER. ANNALES. Variant title: Universite d'Alger. Observatoire Astronomique. Annales. irreg., no.5, 1979. Universite d'Alger, Observatoire Astronomique, Bouzareah, Algeria.

520   SZ   ISSN 0085-0942
OBSERVATOIRE DE GENEVE. PUBLICATIONS. SERIE A. (Text in English, French) 1928. irreg. (approx. a) 15 Fr. Observatoire de Geneve, CH-1290 Sauverny, Switzerland. Indexed: Bull.Signal. Astron.&Astrophys.Abstr.

520   SZ   ISSN 0435-2939
OBSERVATOIRE DE GENEVE. PUBLICATIONS. SERIE B. (Text in English and French) 1967. irreg. price varies. Observatoire de Geneve, CH-1290 Sauverny, Switzerland. Indexed: Bull.Signal. Astron. & Astrophys.Abstr.

522.1   SP   ISSN 0373-5125
OBSERVATORIO ASTRONOMICO DE MADRID. ANUARIO. 1860; N.S. 1907. a. 400 ptas. Observatorio Astronomico Nacional, Alfonso XII No. 3, 28014 Madrid, Spain.

520   AG   ISSN 0302-2277
OBSERVATORIO ASTRONOMICO MUNICIPAL DE ROSARIO. BOLETIN. (Text in Spanish; summaries in English) irreg. Observatorio Astronomico Municipal de Rosario, Parque Urquiza, Rosario, Argentina. illus.

522.1   BL
OBSERVATORIO NACIONAL RIO DE JANEIRO. EFEMERIDES ASTRONOMICAS. 1885. a. Cr.$20. Observatorio Nacional, Rua General Bruce, 586, Sao Cristovao, Rio de Janeiro, G.B., Brazil.
    Formerly (until 1977): Observatorio Nacional Rio de Janeiro. Anuario.

520 551   BL
OBSERVATORIO NACIONAL RIO DE JANEIRO. PUBLICACOES. (Text in English, French, Portuguese) 1977; N.S. 1980. irreg. free. Observatorio Nacional, Rue General Bruce 586, 10921 Rio de Janeiro RJ, Brazil.

520   PL   ISSN 0075-7047
OBSERWATORIUM KRAKOWSKI. ROCZNIK ASTRONOMICZNY. DODATEK MIEDZYNARODOWY. (Text in English, Polish and Russian) 1922. irreg., no.56, 1985. price varies. (Polska Akademia Nauk, Komitet Astronomii) Panstwowe Wydawnictwo Naukowe, Ul. Miodowa 10, 00-251 Warsaw, Poland (Dist. by: Ars Polona, Krakowskie Przedmiescie 7, 00-068 Warsaw, Poland) Ed. K. Rudnicki. circ. 680.

523   SP   ISSN 0210-8119
OCULTACIONES DE ESTRELLAS POR LA LUNA. 1964. irreg., no.39, 1973. Instituto y Observatorio de Marina, San Fernando (Cadiz), Spain.

520   AT   ISSN 0079-1067
PERTH OBSERVATORY. COMMUNICATIONS. 1964. irreg., no.3, 1977. exchange basis. ‡ (Perth Observatory) Western Australia Government Printer, Bickley, W.A. 6076, Australia. circ. 200. Indexed: Astron.& Astrophys.Abstr.

520   PH   ISSN 0115-1207
PHILIPPINE ASTRONOMICAL HANDBOOK. (Text in English) 1950. a. P.5($1) Philippine Atmospheric, Geophysical and Astronomical Services Administration, 1424 Quezon Ave., Quezon City, Philippines.

PHYSICS ABSTRACTS. see *PHYSICS — Abstracting, Bibliographies, Statistics*

PHYSICS AND CHEMISTRY IN SPACE. see *CHEMISTRY*

520   CS
PRACE ASTRONOMICKEHO OBSERVATORIA NA SKALNATOM PLESE/CONTRIBUTIONS OF THE ASTRONOMICAL OBSERVATORY ON SKALNATE PLESO. (Text in English; summaries in Russian and Slovak) vol.8, 1977. irreg. price varies. (Slovenska Akademia Vied) Veda, Publishing House of the Slovak Academy of Sciences, Klemensova 19, 814 30 Bratislava, Czechoslovakia (Subscr. to: Slovart, Gottwaldovo nam. 6, 817 64 Bratislava)

520   UK   ISSN 0267-1247
PROTOSTAR. 1984. irreg. free or exchange basis. Royal Observatory, Blackford Hill, Edinburgh EH9 3HJ, Scotland. Ed. A.S. Webster. circ. 200.

520   BE   ISSN 0072-4432
RIJKSUNIVERSITEIT TE GENT. STERRENKUNDIG OBSERVATORIUM. MEDEDELINGEN. (Text and summaries in Dutch, English or French) 1939. irreg. free. Rijksuniversiteit te Gent, Sterrenkundig Observatorium, Krijgslaan 281, 9000 Ghent, Belgium.

523   SP   ISSN 0210-6485
ROTACION DE LA TIERRA. 1970. a. Instituto y Observatorio de Marina, San Fernando (Cadiz), Spain.

522   CN   ISSN 0080-4193
ROYAL ASTRONOMICAL SOCIETY OF CANADA. OBSERVER'S HANDBOOK. 1908. a. $9. Royal Astronomical Society of Canada, 136 Dupont St., Toronto, Ont. M5R 1V2, Canada. TEL 416-924-7973. Ed. Dr. Roy L. Bishop. index. circ. 16,000. (also avail. in microform from UMI)

522.1   UK   ISSN 0309-099X
ROYAL OBSERVATORY. OCCASIONAL REPORTS. 1976. irreg. exchange basis. Royal Observatory, Blackford Hill, Edinburgh EH9 3HJ, Scotland.

522.1   UK   ISSN 0267-6281
ROYAL OBSERVATORY. RESEARCH AND FACILITIES. 1981. biennial. free or exchange basis. Royal Observatory, Blackford Hill, Edinburgh EH9 3HJ, Scotland.

520   FR   ISSN 0769-1033
SATELLITES GALILEENS DE JUPITER; phenomenes et configurations. (Text in English and French) 1979. a. 45 Fr. Bureau des Longitudes, 77 Ave. Denfert-Rochereau, F-75014 Paris, France (Subscr. addr.: 17 rue Deutsche-de-la-Meurthe, F-75014 Paris, France) Ed. J.E. Arlot.

523.01   US   ISSN 0081-0231
SMITHSONIAN CONTRIBUTIONS TO ASTROPHYSICS. 1956. irreg., no.17, 1974. Smithsonian Institution Press, 955 L'Enfant Plaza, Rm. 2100, Washington, DC 20560. TEL 202-287-3738. Ed. George B. Field. circ. 1,750. (reprint service avail. from UMI)

523.01   US   ISSN 0081-0320
SMITHSONIAN INSTITUTION. ASTROPHYSICAL OBSERVATORY. S A O SPECIAL REPORT. (Title varies slightly) (Text in English; summaries in English, French, Russian) 1957. irreg. free. Smithsonian Institution Astrophysical Observatory, 60 Garden St., Cambridge, MA 02138. TEL 617-495-7000. Ed. Irwin I. Shapiro. cum.index: 1957-1959. Indexed: GeoRef.

520   FR   ISSN 0081-0738
SOCIETE ASTRONOMIQUE DE BORDEAUX. BULLETIN.* 1961/62. a. price varies. Societe Astronomique de Bordeaux, Hotel des Societes Savantes, 71 rue du Loup, Bordeaux, France.

520   US   ISSN 0143-0432
SOVIET SCIENTIFIC REVIEWS. SECTION E: ASTROPHYSICS & SPACE PHYSICS REVIEWS. vol.3, 1984. 4/yr. (in 1 vol., 4 nos./vol.) $218 to individuals; academic price $134. Harwood Academic Publishers, 50 W. 23rd St., New York, NY 10010. Ed. R.A. Syunyaev. index. (back issues avail.)

520   PL   ISSN 0081-6701
STUDIA COPERNICANA. (Text in English, French, German) 1970. irreg., vol.26, 1985. price varies. (Polska Akademia Nauk, Instytut Historii Nauki, Oswiaty i Techniki) Ossolineum, Publishing House of the Polish Academy of Sciences, Rynek 9, Wroclaw, Poland (Dist. by: Ars Polona-Ruch, Krakowskie Przedmiescie 7, Warsaw Poland) Ed. Pawel Czartoryski. illus. Indexed: Math.R.

520   PL   ISSN 0082-5573
STUDIA SOCIETATIS SCIENTIARUM TORUNENSIS. SECTIO F. ASTRONOMIA. (Text in English; summaries in Polish) 1956. irreg. price varies. (Towarzystwo Naukowe w Toruniu) Panstwowe Wydawnictwo Naukowe, Miodowa 10, 00-251 Warsaw, Poland (Dist. by: Ars Polona, Krakowskie Przedmiescie 7, 00-068 Warsaw, Poland) Ed. Cecylia Iwaniszewska. charts. illus. index. circ. 650.

529   US
STUDY OF TIME. Represents: International Society for the Study of Time. Proceedings. (Text in English or German) 1972. irreg., vol.4, 1981. price varies. Springer-Verlag, 175 Fifth Ave., New York, NY 10010 TEL 212-460-1500. (Also Berlin, Heidelberg, Tokyo and Vienna) Ed.Bd. bibl. illus. (reprint service avail. from ISI)

522   PH   ISSN 0115-3307
TABLE OF SUNRISE, SUNSET, TWILIGHT, MOONRISE AND MOONSET. (Text in English) a. P.5($1) Philippine Atmospheric, Geophysical and Astronomical Services Administration, 1424 Quezon Ave., Quezon City, Philippines. circ. 300.
    Formerly: Philippines. Atmosphere, Geophysical and Astronomical Services Administration. Table of Sunrise, Sunset, Twilight, Moonrise and Moonset.

520   JA   ISSN 0082-4690
TOKYO ASTRONOMICAL BULLETIN. (Text in English and German) 1927-1946; N.S. 1947. irreg. available on exchange. Tokyo Astronomical Observatory - Tokyo Tenmondai, University of Tokyo, 2-21-1 Osawa, Mitaka, Tokyo 181, Japan. Indexed: Chem.Abstr. Sci.Abstr. Int.Aerosp.Abstr.

520   JA   ISSN 0082-4704
TOKYO ASTRONOMICAL OBSERVATORY. ANNALS. (Text in English and German) 1889. irreg. available on exchange. Tokyo Astronomical Observatory - Tokyo Tenmondai, University of Tokyo, 2-21-1 Osawa, Mitaka, Tokyo 181, Japan. Indexed: Chem.Abstr. Sci.Abstr. Int.Aerosp.Abstr.
    Supersedes (in 1922): Observatoire de Tokyo. Annales.

520   JA   ISSN 0374-4639
TOKYO ASTRONOMICAL OBSERVATORY. REPORT. (Text in Japanese) 1932. irreg. available on exchange basis only. Tokyo Astronomical Observatory - Tokyo Tenmondai, University of Tokyo, 2-21-1 Osawa, Mitaka, Tokyo 181, Japan. Indexed: Sci.Abstr.

520   JA   ISSN 0082-4712
TOKYO ASTRONOMICAL OBSERVATORY. REPRINTS. (Text in English and German) 1938. irreg. available on exchange basis. Tokyo Astronomical Observatory - Tokyo Tenmondai, University of Tokyo, 2-21-1 Osawa, Mitaka, Tokyo 181, Japan. Indexed: Int.Aerosp.Abstr.

520   UK   ISSN 0143-0599
U.K.I.R.T. NEWSLETTER. (United Kingdom Infrared Telescope) 1979. irreg., no.3, 1980. free. Royal Observatory, Blackford Hill, Edinburgh EH9 3HJ, Scotland. Ed. Dr. P.M. Williams. circ. 300. (back issues avail.)

520   UK   ISSN 0260-9983
U.K.I.R.T. REPORT. (United Kingdom Infrared Telescope) 1978. irreg., no.16, 1980. free or exchange basis. Royal Observatory, Blackford Hill, Edinburgh EH9 3HJ, Scotland.

520   UK   ISSN 0143-053X
U K S T U NEWSLETTER. (United Kingdom Schmidt Telescope Unit) 1978. irreg., no.2, 1979. free or exchange basis. Royal Observatory, Blackford Hill, Edinburgh EH9 3HJ, Scotland. Ed. S.B. Tritton. circ. 300. (back issues avail.)

528	US	ISSN 0083-243X
U.S. NAVAL OBSERVATORY. ASTRONOMICAL PAPERS PREPARED FOR USE OF AMERICAN EPHEMERIS AND NAUTICAL ALMANAC. 1882. irreg., vol.22, 1976. price varies. U.S. Naval Observatory, Washington, DC 20392 TEL 202-653-1547. (Orders to: Supt of Documents, Washington, DC 20402) index.

520	US	ISSN 0083-2448
U.S. NAVAL OBSERVATORY. PUBLICATIONS. SECOND SERIES. irreg. exchange basis. U.S. Naval Observatory, Department of the Navy, Washington, DC 20392. TEL 202-653-1547.

520	CL	ISSN 0069-3553
UNIVERSIDAD DE CHILE. DEPARTAMENTO DE ASTRONOMIA. PUBLICACIONES. (Text and summaries in Spanish and English) 1967. irreg. free or exchange. ‡ (Universidad de Chile, Departamento de Astronomia) Editorial Universitaria, Av. Maria Luisa Santander 0447, Santiago 9, Chile. Ed. Hugo Moreno. circ. 700. Indexed: Bull.Signal. Astron. & Astrophys. Abstr.

520	BL
UNIVERSIDADE DE SAO PAULO. INSTITUTO ASTRONOMICO E GEOFISICO. ANUARIO ASTRONOMICO. 1930-38; N.S. 1953; N.S. 1974. a. Cr.$130($6) ‡ Universidade de Sao Paulo, Instituto Astronomico e Geofisico, Biblioteca, Caixa Postal 30627, 01051 Sao Paulo, SP, Brazil. Ed. Paulo Benevides Soares. circ. 2,000. Indexed: Bull.Signal. Ref.Zh. Astron. & Astrophys.Abstr.
    Formerly: Sao Paulo, Brazil (State). Observatorio. Anuario Astronomico (ISSN 0080-6412)

UNIVERSIDADE DE SAO PAULO. INSTITUTO DE GEOCIENCIAS. BOLETIM. see EARTH SCIENCES

520	GW
UNIVERSITAET HANNOVER. ASTRONOMISCHE STATION. (VEROEFFENTLICHUNGEN) 1958. irreg. price varies. Universitaet Hannover, Institut fuer Erdmessung Geodaesie, Nienburger Str. 5, 3000 Hannover 1, W. Germany (B.R.D.) Ed. Guenter Seeber. circ. 150. Indexed: Astron.& Astrophys.Abstr. Astron.& Astrophys.Abstr.
    Formerly: Technische Universitaet Hannover. Astronomischer Station. (Veroeffentlichungen)

520	YU	ISSN 0350-3283
UNIVERSITY OF BELGRADE. FACULTY OF SCIENCES. DEPARTMENT OF ASTRONOMY. PUBLICATIONS. (Text and summaries in English, Russian) 1969. a. free. Univerzitet u Beogradu, Prirodno-Matematicki Fakultet, Katedra za Astronomiju, Studentski trg 16, 11000 Belgrade, Yugoslavia. Ed. Branislav Sevarlic. bibl. charts. illus. circ. 500.

UNIVERSITY OF BRITISH COLUMBIA. DEPARTMENT OF GEOPHYSICS AND ASTRONOMY. ANNUAL REPORT. see EARTH SCIENCES — Geophysics

UNIVERSITY OF BRITISH COLUMBIA, PHYSICS SOCIETY. JOURNAL. see PHYSICS

523.51	US	ISSN 0085-3968
UNIVERSITY OF NEW MEXICO. INSTITUTE OF METEORITICS. SPECIAL PUBLICATION. 1970. irreg., 2-3/yr. $5 per no. University of New Mexico, Institute of Meteoritics, Albuquerque, NM 87131. TEL 505-277-4202. Ed. Klaus Keil. circ. 1,000. (back issues avail.) Indexed: GeoRef.

520	US	ISSN 0276-1106
UNIVERSITY OF TEXAS PUBLICATIONS IN ASTRONOMY. 1969. irreg., no.23, 1984. price varies. University of Texas at Austin, Department of Astronomy, RLM 15.308, Austin, TX 78712. TEL 512-471-1313. circ. 200. Indexed: Astron.& Astrophys.Abstr.

522.1	VC	ISSN 0083-5293
VATICAN OBSERVATORY PUBLICATIONS. (Text in English) 1970. irreg. avail on exchange basis. ‡ Specola Vaticana, I-00120 Vatican City. Ed. George V. Coyne. cum.index in prep. circ. 500. Indexed: Astron. & Astrophys.Abstr.

520	GW	ISSN 0340-9821
VEROEFFENTLICHUNGEN DER ASTRONOMISCHEN INSTITUT DER UNIVERSITAET BONN. (Text in German; Summaries in English) 1930. irreg. price varies. (Astronomische Institut der Universitaet Bonn-Sternwarte) Ferd. Duemmlers Verlag, Kaiserstr. 31, D-5300 Bonn 1, W. Germany (B.R.D.)

523.01	CN	ISSN 0078-6950
VICTORIA, BRITISH COLUMBIA. DOMINION ASTROPHYSICAL OBSERVATORY. PUBLICATIONS. 1918. irreg. exchange basis. Dominion Astrophysical Observatory, National Research Council of Canada, Herzberg Institute of Astrophysics, Victoria, B.C., Canada. TEL 604-388-3157.

ASTRONOMY — Abstracting, Bibliographies, Statistics

520 523.01 016	US	ISSN 0067-0022
ASTRONOMY AND ASTROPHYSICS ABSTRACTS. 1969. irreg., vol.41, 1986. price varies. Springer-Verlag, 175 Fifth Ave., New York, NY 10010 TEL 212-460-1500. (Also Berlin, Heidelberg, Tokyo and Vienna) (reprint service avail. from ISI) Indexed: Phys.Ber.
    Supersedes: Astronomischer Jaresbericht.

METEOROLOGICAL AND GEOASTROPHYSICAL ABSTRACTS. see METEOROLOGY — Abstracting, Bibliographies, Statistics

520 016	UR	ISSN 0486-2236
REFERATIVNYI ZHURNAL. ASTRONOMIYA. 1953. m. 70 Rub. 90 Rub. with index. Vsesoyuznyi Institut Nauchno-Tekhnicheskoi Informatsii (VINITI), Baltiiskaya ul., 14, Moscow A-219, Russian S.F.S.R., U.S.S.R. (Subscr. to: Mezhdunarodnaya Kniga, Dimitrova ul. 39, 113095 Moscow, Russian S.F.S.R., U.S.S.R.)

629.13 016	UR	ISSN 0034-2408
REFERATIVNYI ZHURNAL. ISSLEDOVANIE KOSMICHESKOGO PROSTRANSTVA. 1964. m. 50 Rub. 60 Rub. including index. Vsesoyuznyi Institut Nauchno-Tekhnicheskoi Informatsii (VINITI), Baltiiskaya ul., 14, Moscow A-219, Russian S.F.S.R., U.S.S.R (Subscr. to: Mezhdunarodnaya Kniga, Dimitrova ul .39, 113095 Moscow, Russian S.F.S.R., U.S.S.R.)

U S S R REPORT: SPACE. see EARTH SCIENCES — Abstracting, Bibliographies, Statistics

AUTOMATION

see Computers — Automation

AUTOMOBILES

see Transportation — Automobiles

BAKERS AND CONFECTIONERS

see Food and Food Industries — Bakers and Confectioners

BALL GAMES

see Sports and Games — Ball Games

BANKING AND FINANCE

see Business and Economics — Banking and Finance

BEAUTY CULTURE

see also Beauty Culture — Perfumes and Cosmetics

646.7 668.5	DK	ISSN 0106-9918
AESTETIK; Koen og Kultur. a. Bibliotekscentralen, Telegrafvej 5, DK-2750 Ballerup, Denmark.

646.7	US	ISSN 0405-1157
BEAUTY & BARBER DEALERS WORLD. 1957. a. $10. Beauty World, Inc., c/o Patrick, 170 West End Ave., New York, NY 10023. Ed. Marion Rudoy.

343.794	US	ISSN 0094-4327
CALIFORNIA. STATE BOARD OF COSMETOLOGY. RULES AND REGULATIONS. 1929. irreg. free. State Board of Cosmetology, 1020 N St, Sacramento, CA 95814. TEL 916-445-7061. Key Title: Rules and Regulations - Board of Cosmetology (Sacramento)

646.7	US
COSMETICS: LATIN AMERICAN INDUSTRIAL REPORT. (Avail. for each of 22 Latin American countries) 1985. a. $435 per country report per industry covered. Aurora International, Box 9099, Bridgeport, CT 06601-2099. TEL 203-368-0579.

646.7	UK
INSTITUTE OF ELECTROLYSIS. LIST OF QUALIFIED OPERATORS. 1962. a. Institute of Electrolysis, 251 Seymour Grove, Manchester M16 ODS, Lancs, England.

646	US
MCCALL'S BEAUTY DIET & HEALTH GUIDE. 1981. a. $1.95. McCall Publishing Co., 230 Park Ave., New York, NY 10169.
    Formerly: McCall's Beauty Guide.

646 613	US	ISSN 0161-2190
VOGUE BEAUTY & HEALTH GUIDE. 1973. a. $2.75 per no. Conde Nast Publications Inc., Vogue, 350 Madison Ave., New York, NY 10017. TEL 212-880-8800. adv. illus. circ. 450,000. (reprint service avail. from UMI)

BEAUTY CULTURE — Perfumes And Cosmetics

AESTETIK; Koen og Kultur. see BEAUTY CULTURE

COSMETIC SCIENCE AND TECHNOLOGY SERIES. see MEDICAL SCIENCES

615	US	ISSN 0417-6383
DIRECTORY OF PROFESSIONAL ELECTROLOGISTS; geographically classified guide to permanent hair removal services. 1956. a. $2.50 (free to qualified personnel) Gordon Blackwell Publishing, Box 26, Eastchester, NY 10709. Ed. Gordon Blackwell. circ. 3,000.

DRUG AND COSMETIC CATALOG. see PHARMACY AND PHARMACOLOGY

GUIDE DE LA PARFUMERIE/GENERAL DIRECTORY OF THE PERFUME AND COSMETIC INDUSTRY. see BUSINESS AND ECONOMICS — Trade And Industrial Directories

668.5	NE
HANDBOEK VOOR PARFUMERIE EN SCHOONHEIDSSALON. 1982. a. fl.76.50 free with subscr. to Kosmetiek. Nijgh Periodieken B.V., Postbus 122, 3100 AC Schiedam, Netherlands. adv. circ. 3,256.

668.54 668.55   SP
N C P DOCUMENTA. (Noticias de Cosmetica y de
   Perfumeria) 1977. m. 600 ptas.($8) (or membership)
   (Sociedad Espanola de Quimicos Cosmeticos)
   Romargraf S.A., Juventud 55, Hospitalet del
   Llobregat, Barcelona, Spain. Ed.Bd. charts.

668.5   FR
PARFUMS-BEAUTE. 1931. a. 305 F. Editions Louis
   Johanet, 68 rue Boursault, 75017 Paris, France.

668.54   MX
PERFUMERIA MODERNA - DIRECTORIO DE
   PROVEEDORES/MODERN PERFUMIMG -
   DIRECTORY OF SUPPLIERS. 1971. a. $20.
   Bravo Grupo Editorial, S.A., Jose Maria Bustillos
   no. 49, Colonia Algarin, A.P. 27-433, Mexico 8,
   DF, Mexico. Ed. Antonio Bravo. adv. circ. 3,000.

668.55   JA
SHISEIDO ANNUAL REPORT. a. Shiseido Co. Ltd.,
   5-5 Ginza 7 Chome Chuo-ku, Tokyo, Japan.

668.5 667   GW   ISSN 0171-4341
WER UND WAS IN DER DEUTSCHEN
   KOERPERPFLEGE-, WASCH- UND
   REINIGUNGSMITTEL-INDUSTRIE. biennial.
   DM.108. B. Behr's GmbH & Co., Averhoffstr. 10,
   2000 Hamburg 76, W. Germany (B.R.D.)

BEVERAGES

see also Food and Food Industries;
Packaging

663.2   US   ISSN 0149-6778
AMERICAN WINE SOCIETY. BULLETIN. 1973.
   irreg. $3. American Wine Society, 3006 Latta Rd.,
   Rochester, NY 14612. TEL 716-225-7613. circ. 3,
   000. (back issues avail.)

663.2   US   ISSN 0149-676X
AMERICAN WINE SOCIETY MANUAL. irreg.
   price varies. American Wine Society, 3006 Latta
   Rd., Rochester, NY 14612. TEL 716-225-7613.
   (back issues avail.)

663   FR   ISSN 0066-2763
ANNUAIRE DES BOISSONS ET DES LIQUIDES
   ALIMENTAIRES/JAHRBUCH DER
   GETRAENKE UND FLUESSIGEN
   NAHRMITTEL. (Text in French, English, German)
   1945. a. Editions du Gonfalon, 29 Route de
   Dourdan, 91670 Angerville, France.

663.63   FR   ISSN 0066-3255
ANNUAIRE INTERNATIONAL DES JUS DE
   FRUITS. 1968. a. 120 F. International Federation of
   Fruit Juice Producers, 10 rue de Liege, 75009 Paris,
   France.

663   GT   ISSN 0066-8567
ASOCIACION NACIONAL DEL CAFE.
   DEPARTAMENTO DE ASUNTOS AGRICOLAS.
   INFORME ANUAL. 1962. a. free. Asociacion
   Nacional del Cafe, Departamento de Asuntos
   Agricolas, Edificio Etisa, Plazuela Espana, Zona 9,
   Guatemala, Guatemala.
      Formerly: Asociacion Nacional del Cafe.
   Departamento de Asuntos Agricolas. Annual
   Memory.

ASSAM DIRECTORY & TEA AREAS
   HANDBOOK. see *BUSINESS AND*
   ECONOMICS — Trade And Industrial Directories

663 664   II
BEVERAGE AND FOOD WORLD. (Text in
   English) vol.3, 1974. a. Rs.25($5) Amalgamated
   Press, Narang House, 41 Ambalal Doshi Marg,
   Bombay 400023, India. Ed. N.J. da Silva. circ. 3,
   000.
      Incorporating: Brewer/Distiller and Bottler.

663   US
BEVERAGE INDUSTRY ANNUAL MANUAL.
   1967. a. $45. Harcourt Brace Jovanovich, Inc., 7500
   Old Oak Blvd., Cleveland, OH 44130 TEL 216-243-
   8100. (Subscr. to: 1 E. First St., Duluth, MN
   55802) Ed. Gary Hemphill. adv. circ. 8,774.

338.47   US
BEVERAGE WORLD'S DATABANK. 1984. a. $47.
   Keller International Publishing Co., 150 Great Neck
   Rd., Great Neck, NY 11021. TEL 516-829-9210.
   Ed. N.L.H. Krauss. adv. circ. 20,890.
      Former titles: Beverage World's Daily Desk
   Reference Living Directory & Beverage World's
   Living Directory.

663   US
BEVERAGES: LATIN AMERICAN INDUSTRIAL
   REPORT. (Avail. for each of 22 Latin American
   countries) 1985. a. $435 per country report per
   industry covered. Aurora International, Box 9099,
   Bridgeport, CT 06601-2099. TEL 203-368-0579. Ed.
   Andres C. Aquino.

663.3   GW   ISSN 0068-0710
BRAUEREIEN UND MAELZEREIEN IN
   EUROPA. 1900. a. DM.265. Verlag Hoppenstedt
   und Co., Havelstr. 9, Postfach 4006, 6100
   Darmstadt, W. Germany (B.R.D.) adv.
   Brewing

BRAZIL. INSTITUTO DO ACUCAR E DO
   ALCOOL. CONSELHO DELIBERATIVO.
   PRESIDENCIA. COLETANEA DE RESOLUCOES (E)
   PRESIDENCIA. COLETANEA DE ATOS. see
   AGRICULTURE — Crop Production And Soil

663.3   US   ISSN 0006-971X
BREWERS DIGEST ANNUAL BUYERS GUIDE
   AND BREWERY DIRECTORY. 1926. a. $25.
   Siebel Publishing Co., Inc., 4049 W. Peterson Ave.,
   Chicago, IL 60646. TEL 312-463-3401. Ed. Dori
   Whitney. adv. circ. 3,104.

663.3   CN   ISSN 0068-094X
BREWING AND MALTING BARLEY RESEARCH
   INSTITUTE. ANNUAL REPORT. a. Brewing and
   Malting Barley Research Institute, 206 Grain
   Exchange Bldg., Winnipeg, Man., Canada. TEL
   201-942-1407. circ. controlled. Indexed: Food Sci.&
   Tech.Abstr.
   Brewing

663.2 658.8   UK
BRITAIN'S WINE INDUSTRY. 1985. irreg.
   £125($150) Jordan & Sons Ltd., Jordan House, 47
   Brunswick Place, London N1 6EE, England.

663.5   IT
CATALOGO DEI VINI D'ITALIA. 1969. irreg.
   L.120000. Giorgio Mondadori e Associati S.p.A.,
   Centro Direzionale, Palazzo Canova, 20090 Milan 2
   - Segrate, Italy. Ed. Paolo Levi. adv. illus.
      Formerly: Catalogo Bolaffi dei Vini Rossi d'Italia;
   Supersedes in part: Catalogo Bolaffi dei Vini d'Italia.
   Wine

663   US
COFFEE ANNUAL. a. $7. George Gordon Paton &
   Co., 161 Williams St., New York, NY 10038. TEL
   212-619-2900. adv. charts. illus. stat.

663.4   GW
DEUTSCHEN BRAUMEISTER- UND
   MALZMEISTER-BUNDES. 5/yr. (plus a. issue)
   DM.90 annual issue DM.50. Verlag Hans Carl
   GmbH, Breitegasse 58-60, Postfach 9110, D-8500
   Nuernberg 11, W. Germany.

DUTY & TAX-FREE SHOP WORLD GUIDE
   SERIES. VOL. 1: BEST "N" MOST IN WINES &
   SPIRITS. see *BUSINESS AND ECONOMICS —*
   International Commerce

663.2   GW
E W R; Schriftenreihe zum europaeischen Weinrecht.
   1979. irreg. (Institut fuer Weinrecht der Gesellschaft
   fuer Rechtspolitik, Trier) Deutscher Fachverlag,
   Postfach 100606, D-6000 Frankfurt 1, W. Germany
   (B.R.D.)

663.3   NE   ISSN 0071-2531
EUROPEAN BREWERY CONVENTION.
   PROCEEDINGS OF THE INTERNATIONAL
   CONGRESS. (Text in English, French, German)
   1950. biennial. price varies. Box 510, 2380 BB
   Zoeterwoude, Netherlands. Ed.Bd. circ. 1,500.
   Indexed: Chem.Abstr.
   Brewing

663   CK   ISSN 0084-7941
FEDERACION NACIONAL DE CAFETEROS DE
   COLOMBIA. BOLETIN DE INFORMACION
   ESTADISTICA SOBRE CAFE. a. Federacion
   Nacional de Cafeteros de Colombia, Departamento
   de Informacion Cafetera, Calle 73 No. 8-13, Bogota,
   D.E., Colombia.

FOOD AND DRINK TRADE HANDBOOK. see
FOOD AND FOOD INDUSTRIES

663   GW   ISSN 0072-422X
GESELLSCHAFT FUER DIE GESCHICHTE UND
   BIBLIOGRAPHIE DES BRAUWESENS.
   JAHRBUCH. 1928. a. DM.57. Gesellschaft fuer die
   Geschichte und Bibliographie des Brauwesens,
   Seestr. 13, D-1000 Berlin 65, W. Germany (B.R.D.)
   Ed. Hans G. Schultze-Berndt. bk. rev. circ. 800.

663.4   UK   ISSN 0265-0681
GOOD BEER GUIDE. 1974. a. £4.95. Campaign for
   Real Ale Ltd. (CAMRA), 34 Alma Rd., St. Albans,
   Herts AL1 3BW, England. TEL (0727) 67201. Ed.
   Neil Hanson. circ. 45,000. (back issues avail.)

663   UK
GOOD PUB GUIDE. a. £8.95. Consumers'
   Association, 14 Buckingham St., London WC2N
   6DS, England (Subscr. addr.: Castlemead, Gascoyne
   Way, Hertford SG13 7LZ, England) Ed. Alisdair
   Aird. circ. 30,000.

663.2   UK
HARPERS WINE AND SPIRIT ANNUAL. 1914. a.
   £20. Harper Trade Journals Ltd., Harling House,
   47-51 Great Suffolk St., London SE1 0BS, England.
   Ed. Tony Kirwood. adv. circ. 6,000.
      Former titles: Harpers Directory of the Wine and
   Spirit Trade; Harpers Directory and Manual of the
   Wine and Spirit Trade (ISSN 0073-0408)

338.47   US   ISSN 0882-6277
IMPACT (NEW YORK, 1983); beverage trends in
   America review and forecast. 1983. a. $695. M.
   Shanken Communications, Inc., 400 E. 51st St.,
   New York, NY 10022. TEL 212-751-6500.

663.4   US   ISSN 0198-9952
IMPACT AMERICAN BEER MARKET REVIEW
   AND FORECAST. 1980. a. $225. M. Shanken
   Communications, Inc., Attn.: Marilyn Schwartz, 400
   E. 51st St., New York, NY 10022. TEL 212-751-
   6500. Ed. Marvin R. Shanken. charts.

663.1   US   ISSN 0163-9536
IMPACT AMERICAN DISTILLED SPIRITS
   MARKET REVIEW AND FORECAST. 1976. a.
   $225. M. Shanken Communications, Inc., Attn.:
   Marilyn Schwartz, 400 E. 51st St., New York, NY
   10022. TEL 212-751-6500. Ed. Marvin R. Shanken.
   charts.
   Alcoholic

663.2   US   ISSN 0163-9544
IMPACT THE AMERICAN WINE MARKET
   REVIEW AND FORECAST. 1975. a. $195. M.
   Shanken Communications, Inc., Attn.: Marilyn
   Schwartz, 400 E. 51st St., New York, NY 10022.
   TEL 212-751-6500. Ed. Marvin R. Shanken. charts.
   (back issues avail.)
   Wine

IMPACT YEARBOOK; a directory of the U.S. wine
   & spirits industry. see *BUSINESS AND*
   ECONOMICS — Trade And Industrial Directories

663.3   UK
INCORPORATED BREWERS GUILD
   DIRECTORY. 1923. a. £9 to non-members.
   Brewers' Guild Publications Ltd., 8 Ely Pl., London
   EC1N 6SD, England. Ed. A. Duckworth. adv. circ.
   2,000.

663.93   BL
INSTITUTO BRASILEIRO DO CAFE.
   DEPARTAMENTO ECONOMICO. ANUARIO
   ESTATISTICO DO CAFE. a. free. ‡ Instituto
   Brasileiro do Cafe, Coordenadoria de Estudos da
   Economia Cafeeira - Brazilian Coffee Institute, Av.
   Rodrigues Alves, 129, 20081 Rio de Janeiro, Brazil.
   circ. 2,000.
      Formerly: Instituto Brasileiro do Cafe.
   Departamento Economico. Anuario Estatistico do
   Cafe. (ISSN 0073-988X)

BEVERAGES — ABSTRACTING, BIBLIOGRAPHIES, STATISTICS

663　　　　　　　BL
INSTITUTO BRASILEIRO DO CAFE. GRUPO EXECUTIVO DE RACIONALIZACAO DE CAFEICULTURA. RELATORIO DO GERCA. 1962. a. free. Instituto Brasileiro do Cafe, Grupo Executivo de Racionalizacao de Cafecultura, Av. Rodrigues Alves 129, 3 andar, 20081 Rio de Janeiro, Brazil. illus. circ. 1,000.

663　　　　　　　SZ　　ISSN 0074-9796
INTERNATIONAL BREWER'S DIRECTORY. (Text in English, French, German) 1928. every 6 yrs., 9th edt., 1986. 380 Fr. Verlag fuer Internationale Wirtschaftsliteratur GmbH, P.O. Box 108, CH-8047 Zurich, Switzerland. Ed. Walter Hirt.
Formerly: Internationales Firmenregister der Brauindustrie, Malzerien, Brennereien, Mineralwasser und Erfrischungsgetranke.

663.63　　　　　　FR　　ISSN 0074-5952
INTERNATIONAL FEDERATION OF FRUIT JUICE PRODUCERS. PROCEEDINGS OF CONGRESS. COMPTE-RENDU DU CONGRES. 1948. irreg., 9th, Munich, 1982. 170 F. International Federation of Fruit Juice Producers, 10 rue de Liege, 75009 Paris, France.

663.2　　　　　　IT　　ISSN 0374-5791
ISTITUTO SPERIMENTALE PER L'ENOLOGIA ASTI. ANNALI. (Text in Italian; summaries in English, German and French) 1970. a. L.40000. Istituto Sperimentale per l'Enologia, Via P. Micca 35, 14100 Asti, Italy. circ. 500. (back issues avail.) Indexed: Biol.Abstr.

338.47　　　　　　US
JOBSON'S LIQUOR HANDBOOK; statistics, trends and analysis for the distilled spirits industry. 1954. a. $89.95. Jobson Publishing Corp., 352 Park Ave. S., New York, NY 10010. TEL 212-685-4848. Ed. Nicolas Furlotte. adv. circ. 3,500.
Formerly: Liquor Handbook.

663.2　　　　　　US
JOBSON'S WINE MARKETING HANDBOOK; the comprehensive source for information on the wine business. 1971. a. $79.95. Jobson Publishing Corp., 352 Park Ave. S., New York, NY 10010. TEL 212-685-4848. Ed. Nicolas Furlotte. adv. circ. 3,500.
Formerly: Wine Marketing Handbook.

663.3　　　　　　JA　　ISSN 0075-6229
KIRIN BREWERY COMPANY, TOKYO. RESEARCH LABORATORY. REPORT/KIRIN BIRU K.K. SOGO KENKYUSHO KENKYU HOKOKU. (Text in English or German) 1958. a. free; available on exchange. Kirin Brewery Co. Ltd., Research Laboratories - Kirin Biru K. K. Sogo Kenkyusho, 26-1 Jingumae 6-chome, Shibuya-ku, Tokyo, Japan (Subscr. to: 3, Miyahara-cho, Takasaki-shi, Gunma 370-12, Japan) Ed.Bd. Indexed: Biol.Abstr.
Brewing

641　　　　　　　UK
LAKESCENE - GOOD PUBS IN CUMBRIA. 1976. a. £0.65. Border Press Agency Ltd., 12 Lonsdale St., Carlisle, Cumbria CA1 1DD, England. Ed. John Barker. adv.

663　　　　　　　US
LIQUOR INDUSTRY MARKETING. a. $39.95. Jobson Publishing Corp., 352 Park Ave. S., New York, NY 10010. TEL 212-685-4848. Ed. Nicolas Furlotte. (back issues avail.)

663.3　　　　　　US
LISTEN TO YOUR BEER. 1983. irreg. $12 for 4 nos. (Amateur Brewer Information Service) A B I S, Box 546, Portland, OR 97207. TEL 503-289-7596. Ed. Fred Eckhardt. adv. bk. rev. circ. 1,500. (back issues avail.)

663　　　　　　　FR　　ISSN 0085-221X
MEMENTO DE L'O.I.V. 1928. quinquennial; latest 1975. Office International de la Vigne et du Vin, 11 rue Roquepine, 75008 Paris, France. Indexed: Excerp.Med.

663.3　　　　　　US　　ISSN 0076-9932
MODERN BREWERY AGE BLUE BOOK. 1941. a. $95. Business Journals, Inc., 22 S. Smith St., Box 5550, Norwalk, CT 06856. TEL 203-853-6015. Ed. Howard Kelly.

663　　　　　　　US　　ISSN 0160-9580
NATIONAL BEVERAGE MARKETING DIRECTORY (YEAR) 1978. a. $345. Beverage Marketing Corporation, 2670 Commercial Ave., Mingo Junction, OH 43938. TEL 614-598-4133. Ed. Terry Welling. adv. circ. 2,300. (also avail. in magnetic tape)

PLANO DA SAFRA ACUCAR E ALCOOL. see AGRICULTURE — Crop Production And Soil

663　　　　　　　JA　　ISSN 0389-9136
RESEARCH INSTITUTE OF BREWING. REPORT. a. Research Institute of Brewing, Takinogawa, Kiat-Ku, Tokyo, Japan.

663　　　　　　　FR
SITUATION DE LA VITICULTURE DANS LE MONDE. 1980. a. 30 F. Office International de la Vigne et du Vin, 11 rue Roquepine, 75008 Paris, France.

663.53　　　　　　GW　　ISSN 0081-3729
SPIRITUOSEN-JAHRBUCH. 1950. a. DM.58.85. Versuchs- und Lehranstalt fuer Spiritusfabrikation und Fermentationstechnologie, Seestr. 13, 1000 Berlin 65, W. Germany (B.R.D.) circ. 4,500.

663.6　　　　　　US
STATISTICAL PROFILE OF THE SOFT DRINK INDUSTRY. 1974. irreg., approx. biennial. $50. National Soft Drink Association, 1101 16th St. N.W., Washington, DC 20036. TEL 202-463-6732. Ed. James G. Abert. circ. 1,500. (back issues avail.)

663　　　　　　　US　　ISSN 0081-931X
SUMMARY OF STATE LAWS AND REGULATIONS RELATING TO DISTILLED SPIRITS. biennial. $12. Distilled Spirits Council of the United States, Inc., 1250 Eye St., N.W., Washington, DC 20005. TEL 202-628-3544. circ. controlled.

SWEDEN. SOCIALSTYRELSEN. ALKOHOLSTATISTIK/ALCOHOL STATISTICS. see BEVERAGES — Abstracting, Bibliographies, Statistics

380.141　　　　　　II
TEA DIRECTORY. (Text in English) 1960. irreg., latest issue 1976. Rs.20. Tea Board, 14 Brabourne Rd., Calcutta 1, India. Ed. P.R. Sengupta.

663.94　　　　　　II
TEA RESEARCH ASSOCIATION. ADVISORY BULLETIN. 1971. irreg., no.10, 1982. Rs.4 per no. Tea Research Association, Tocklai Experimental Station, Jorhat 785008, Assam, India. cum.index every 5 yrs. Indexed: Hort.Abstr. Trop.Abstr.

663　633　　　　　II
TEA RESEARCH ASSOCIATION. MEMORANDUM. 1938. irreg., no.30, 1977. price varies. Tea Research Association, Tocklai Experimental Station, Jorhat 785008, Assam, India. charts. Indexed: Hort.Abstr. Trop.Abstr.

663　633　　　　　II
TEA RESEARCH ASSOCIATION. OCCASIONAL SCIENTIFIC PAPERS. (Text in English) no.12, 1982. irreg. price varies. Tea Research Association, Tocklai Experimental Sta., Jorhat 785008, Assam, India. bibl. charts. Indexed: Hort.Abstr.

663　630　　　　　II　　ISSN 0564-6723
TEA RESEARCH ASSOCIATION. TOCKLAI EXPERIMENTAL STATION. SCIENTIFIC ANNUAL REPORT. (Text in English) a. price varies. Tea Research Association, Tocklai Experimental Station, Jorhat 785008, Assam, India. Indexed: Biol.Abstr. Hort.Abstr. Trop.Abstr. Rev.Appl.Entomol. Rev.Plant Path.

663　　　　　　　FR　　ISSN 0082-5484
TOUTE LA BOISSON. INTERNATIONAL. a. 125 F. S E P Edition, 194-196 rue Marcadet, 75018 Paris, France.

663　　　　　　　GW　　ISSN 0171-4457
WER UND WAS IN DER DEUTSCHEN GETRAENKE-INDUSTRIE. biennial. DM.145. B. Behr's GmbH & Co., Averhoffstr. 10, 2000 Hamburg 76, W. Germany (B.R.D.)

663.2　　　　　　UK
WHICH? WINE GUIDE. a. £7.95. Consumers' Association, 14 Buckingham St., London WC2N 6DS, England (Subscr. to: Castlemead, Gascoyne Way, Hertford SG13 7LZ, England) Ed. Roger Voss. circ. 17,900.
Wine

WINE AND SPIRIT TRADE INTERNATIONAL YEAR BOOK. see BUSINESS AND ECONOMICS — International Commerce

663.2　　　　　　US　　ISSN 0882-7206
WINE SPECTATOR WINE MAPS; the complete guide to wineries, restaurants and lodging in California wine country. 1984. a. $5.20. Marvin R. Shanken Communications, Inc., 400 E. 51st St., New York, NY 10022. TEL 212-751-6500. Ed. Marvin R. Shanken. adv. index.

663.2　　　　　　UK
WINEMAKER'S DIARY. a. £3.20. Dataday Ltd., Dataday House, 8 Alexandra Rd., London SW19 7JZ, England.

663.1　　　　　　US
WINES AND VINES: DIRECTORY OF THE WINE INDUSTRY IN NORTH AMERICA. 1941. a. $35. Hiaring Co., 1800 Lincoln Ave., San Rafael, CA 94901. TEL 415-453-9700. circ. 5,000.
Supersedes: Wines and Vines - Annual Directory of the Wine Industry (ISSN 0084-0351)

663.2　　　　　　UK
WORLD GASTRONOMY. 1933. a. £7.95 to non-members. (International Wine and Food Society) New Perspectives Publishing Co., 19 Garrick St., London WC2, England. Ed. Jack Cooper. adv. bk. rev. circ. 9,000.
Formerly (until 1984): International Wine and Food Society Journal.

BEVERAGES — Abstracting, Bibliographies, Statistics

663.3　016　　　　UK
BREWING RESEARCH FOUNDATION. BULLETIN OF CURRENT LITERATURE. 1952. m. £50($50) non-members. Brewing Research Foundation, Lyttel Hall, Nutfield, Redhill, Surrey RH1 4RY, England. Ed. I.C. Macwilliam. bk. rev. circ. 400(controlled) Indexed: Agri.Eng.Abstr.
Formerly: Brewing Industry Research Foundation. Bulletin of Current Literature (ISSN 0300-4619)
Brewing

381　663　　　　　CN　　ISSN 0705-4319
CANADA. STATISTICS CANADA. CONTROL AND SALE OF ALCOHOLIC BEVERAGES IN CANADA/CONTROLE ET LA VENTE DES BOISSONS ALCOOLIQUES AU CANADA/ CONTROLE ET LA VENTE DES BOISSONS ALCOOLIQUES AU CANADA. (Catalogue 63-202) (Text and summaries in English and French) 1928. a. Can.$12($14) Statistics Canada, Communications Division, 3rd Floor, R.H. Coats Bldg., Ottawa, Ont. K1A 0T6, Canada TEL 613-993-7276. (Subscr. to: Publications Sales and Services, Ottawa, Ont. K1A 0T6, Canada) (also avail. in microform from MML)

663.42　016　　　　GW
MONATSSCHRIFT FUER BRAUWISSENSCHAFT. (Text in German; summaries in English and German) 1948. m. DM.118. (Technische Universitaet Muenchen und Berlin) Verlag Hans Carl GmbH & Co. KG, Breite Gasse 58-60, Postfach 9110, 8500 Nuernberg 11, W. Germany (B.R.D.) (Co-publisher: Westkreuz-Verlag) Eds. Karl-Ullrich Heyse, Wolfgang Popp. adv. bk. rev. abstr. bibl. charts. illus. tr.lit. index. cum.index. circ. 1,900. Indexed: Biol.Abstr. Chem.Abstr. Curr.Cont. Excerp.Med. Nutr.Abstr. Anal.Abstr. Curr.Pack.Abstr. Ind.Sci.Rev. VITIS.
Formerly: Brauwissenschaft (ISSN 0723-1520)

663.1 SW
SWEDEN. SOCIALSTYRELSEN.
ALKOHOLSTATISTIK/ALCOHOL STATISTICS.
(Subseries of: Sveriges Officiella Statistik) (Text in English and Swedish) 1873. a. Kr.30. (National Board of Health and Welfare) Allmaenna Foerlaget, Box 5227, 102 45 Stockholm, Sweden. stat.
Former titles: Rusdrycksfoersaeljningen; Accispliktiga Naeringar, Rusdrycksfoersaeljningen; Accispliktiga Naeringar, Braennvinsfoersaeljningen; Accispliktiga Naeringar; Braennvins Tillverkning och Foersaeljning Samt Socker-och Maltdryckstillverkningen; Braennvins Tillverkning och Foersaeljning Samt Hvitbetssocker-och Maltdryckstillverkningen; Braennvins Tillverkning och Foersaeljning Samt Hvitbetssockertillverkningen; Braenvins Tillverkning och Foersaeljning.
Alcoholic

663.2 016 GW ISSN 0042-7500
VITIS; Berichte ueber Rebenforschung mit Dokumentation der Weinbauforschung. (Text in English, French, German, Italian, Spanish) 1956. q. DM.36($9.) Bundesforschungsanstalt fuer Rebenzuechtung Geilweilerhof, 6741 Siebeldingen, W. Germany (B.R.D.) Ed.Bd. bk. rev. abstr. bibl. charts. illus. index. circ. 1,000. Indexed: Biol.Abstr. Chem.Abstr. Curr.Cont. Excerp.Med. Hort.Abstr. Plant Breed.Abstr. Soils & Fert. VITIS.
Wine

BIBLIOGRAPHIES

691.3 620.1 016 US ISSN 0084-6325
A C I BIBLIOGRAPHY. 1955. irreg., no.14, 1982. price varies. American Concrete Institute, Box 19150, Redford Sta., Detroit, MI 48219. TEL 313-532-2600. (reprint service avail. from UMI)

A M T I D: APPLICATION OF MODERN TECHNOLOGY TO INTERNATIONAL DEVELOPMENT. see *TECHNOLOGY: COMPREHENSIVE WORKS — Abstracting, Bibliographies, Statistics*

011 CN ISSN 0225-5170
A S T I S OCCASIONAL PUBLICATIONS. 1979. irreg. Arctic Science & Technology Information System, Arctic Institute of North America, University of Calgary, Calgary, Alta., Canada. Ed. C. Ross Goodwin. (also avail. in microfiche; back issues avail.)

ABORTION BIBLIOGRAPHY. see *BIRTH CONTROL — Abstracting, Bibliographies, Statistics*

011 SP
ACADEMIA ALFONSO X EL SABIO. CUADERNOS BIBLIOGRAFICOS. 1977. irreg. Academia Alfonso X el Sabio, Murcia, Spain.

013 BE ISSN 0065-0609
ACADEMIE ROYALE DES SCIENCES, DES LETTRES ET DES BEAUX ARTS DE BELGIQUE. INDEX BIOGRAPHIQUE DES MEMBRES, CORRESPONDANTS ET ASSOCIES. 1948. irreg. 100 Fr. Academie Royale des Sciences, des Lettres et des Beaux Arts de Belgique, Palais des Academies, 1 rue Ducale, 1000 Brussels, Belgium. circ. 350.

015 UK ISSN 0266-6731
AFRICA BIBLIOGRAPHY. 1985. a. price varies. (International African Institute) Manchester University Press, Oxford Rd., Manchester M13 9PL, England. TEL 061-273 5539. Ed. Hector Blackhurst.

AFRICAN BIBLIOGRAPHY SERIES. see *HISTORY — Abstracting, Bibliographies, Statistics*

015.6 UK ISSN 0306-9516
AFRICAN BOOKS IN PRINT. 1975. irreg. price varies. Mansell Publishing Ltd., 6 All Saints St., London N1 9RL, England (Dist. in U.S. by: H.W. Wilson Co., 950 University Ave., Bronx, NY 10452) Ed. H. Zell.

AFRICAN SPECIAL BIBLIOGRAPHIC SERIES. see *HISTORY — Abstracting, Bibliographies, Statistics*

960 016 US ISSN 0095-1080
AFRICANA JOURNAL; a bibliographic library journal and review annual. 1970. a. $30 to individuals; institutions $60. Africana Publishing Co. (Subsidiary of: Holmes & Meier Publishers, Inc) 30 Irving Pl., New York, NY 10003. TEL 212-254-4100. adv. bk. rev. Indexed: Lib.Lit. M.L.A. Bibl.Ind. Curr.Cont.Africa.
Formerly (until 1974): Africana Library Journal (ISSN 0002-0303)

011 JA
AICHI-KEN KYODO SHIRYO SOGO MOKUROKU. 1964. irreg., latest issue, 1973. 1000 Yen. Aichi Library Association - Aichi Toshokan Kyokai, 1-12-1 Higashisakura, Higashi-ku, Nagoya, Aichi, Japan. Ed. Aichi Toshokan Kyokai. bibl.

378.3 011 II
ALUMNI PUBLICATIONS: A CATALOGUE. (First Edition covers 1950-1975) (Text in English) 1976. quinquennial. free. United States Educational Foundation in India, Fulbright House, 12 Hailey Rd., New Delhi 110001, India. Ed. Dr. P.D. Sayal.

011 BL ISSN 0100-0977
AMAZONIA - BIBLIOGRAFIA. 1963. irreg. free. Instituto Brasileiro de Informacao em Ciencia e Tecnologia, SCRN 708/709 Bloco B Loja 18E 30, 70740 Brasilia DF, Brazil.

AMERICAN DISSERTATIONS ON FOREIGN EDUCATION; a bibliography with abstracts. see *EDUCATION — Abstracting, Bibliographies, Statistics*

AMERICAN HISTORY; a bibliographic review. see *HISTORY — Abstracting, Bibliographies, Statistics*

AMERICAN REFERENCE BOOKS ANNUAL. see *LIBRARY AND INFORMATION SCIENCES — Abstracting, Bibliographies, Statistics*

080 UN
ANNOTATED ACCESSIONS LIST OF STUDIES AND REPORTS IN THE FIELD OF SCIENCE STATISTICS. (Subseries of its (Document)) 1966. a. Unesco, Division of Statistics on Science and Technology, 7-9 Place de Fontenoy, 75700 Paris, France (Orders to: Bernan Associates-Unipub, 4611-F Assembly Dr., Lanham, MD 20706-4391) abstr. bibl. stat. circ. 1,000.

011 US ISSN 0748-5190
ANNOTATED BIBLIOGRAPHIES OF SERIALS: A SUBJECT APPROACH. no.5, 1986. irreg. price varies. Greenwood Press, 88 Post Rd. W., Box 5007, Westport, CT 06881. TEL 203-226-3571.

015 CH ISSN 0066-2445
ANNOTATED GUIDE TO TAIWAN PERIODICAL LITERATURE. (Text in Chinese and English: summaries in English) 1966. irreg., 3rd edt., 1986. Chinese Materials Center, Taipei Liaison Office, Box 22048, Taipei, Taiwan 100, Republic of China. Ed. Robert L. Irick. bk. rev. circ. 300.

ANNUAL BIBLIOGRAPHY OF COMPUTER-ORIENTED BOOKS. see *COMPUTERS — Abstracting, Bibliographies, Statistics*

ANNUAL BIBLIOGRAPHY OF VICTORIAN STUDIES. see *LITERATURE — Abstracting, Bibliographies, Statistics*

011 CK ISSN 0570-393X
ANUARIO BIBLIOGRAFICO COLOMBIANO. 1951. irreg., latest issue, no.20, 1982/83, 1985. Col.300($10) Instituto Caro y Cuervo, Seccion de Publicaciones, Apdo. Aereo 51502, Bogota, Colombia.

015 CR ISSN 0066-5010
ANUARIO BIBLIOGRAFICO COSTARRICENSE. 1956. irreg. free. Asociacion Costarricense de Bibliotecarios, Apartado 3308, San Jose, Costa Rica. circ. 500.

015 DR
ANUARIO BIBLIOGRAFICO DOMINICANO. a. Ediciones de la Biblioteca Nacional, Isabel la Catolica 309, Santo Domingo, Dominican Republic.

011 EC
ANUARIO BIBLIOGRAFICO ECUATORIANO. (Published as the 6th issue each year of Bibliografia Ecuatoriana) 1975. a. Universidad Central del Ecuador, Biblioteca General, Quito, Ecuador.

011 UY
ANUARIO BIBLIOGRAFICO URUGUAYO. (Suspended publication 1949: resumed 1968) 1946. irreg. donation or exchange requested. Biblioteca Nacional, Guayabo 1795, Casilla de Correo 452, Montevideo, Uruguay. circ. 600.

015 UY
ANUARIO - C B A - YEARBOOK. (Text in English, Spanish) 1968. a. $50. Eduardo Darino, Ed. & Pub., Casilla de Correo 1677, Montevideo, Uruguay (U.S. subscr. to: Darino, Box 1496-GCS, New York, NY 10163) adv. bk. rev. circ. 3,000.
Formerly: Comentarios Bibliograficos Americanos. Anuario (ISSN 0084-893X)

011 US ISSN 0195-7163
ARCADIA BIBLIOGRAPHICA VIRORUM ERUDITORUM. 1979. irreg., vol.9, 1986. Eurolingua, Box 101, Bloomington, IN 47402-0101.

ARCHITECTURE SERIES: BIBLIOGRAPHY. see *ARCHITECTURE — Abstracting, Bibliographies, Statistics*

982 015 AG
ARGENTINA. BIBLIOTECA DEL CONGRESO DE LA NACION. BOLETIN. 1918. a. exchange basis. Biblioteca del Congreso de la Nacion, Rivadavia 1850, 1033 Capital Federal, Buenos Aires, Argentina. TEL 40-5595. bibl. circ. 1,500.
Formerly: Argentina. Biblioteca del Congreso. Boletin (ISSN 0004-1009)

011 DK ISSN 0108-0261
ARTIKLER I BOEGER/DANISH NATIONAL BIBLIOGRAPHY. ARTICLES IN BOOKS. 1981. a. Kr.663.45 to individuals; libraries KR.612. Bibliotekscentralen, Tempovej 7-11, 2750 Ballerup, Denmark.

011 020 AT ISSN 0158-6610
AUCHMUTY LIBRARY PUBLICATION. 1979. irreg. Aus.$10. Auchmuty Library, University of Newcastle, N.S.W. 2308, Australia.

526 AT
AUSTRALIA. BUREAU OF MINERAL RESOURCES, GEOLOGY, AND GEOPHYSICS. PUBLICATIONS. (In two parts: Part 1: Publications; Part 2: Maps) irreg. free. Bureau of Mineral Resources, Geology, and Geophysics, Box 378, Canberra, A.C.T. 2601, Australia.
Cartography

015 AT ISSN 0067-1738
AUSTRALIAN BOOKS; a select list of recent publications and standard work in print. 1949. a. Aus.$6.50. National Library of Australia, Sales & Subscriptions Section, Canberra, A.C.T. 2600, Australia.

AUSTRALIAN FILMS; a catalogue of scientific, educational and cultural films. see *MOTION PICTURES*

526 016 AT ISSN 0045-0677
AUSTRALIAN MAPS. (Annual Cumulation) 1968. a. Aus.$24. National Library of Australia, Sales & Subscriptions Section, Canberra, A.C.T. 2600, Australia.

B C T V: BIBLIOGRAPHY ON CABLE TELEVISION. see *COMMUNICATIONS — Radio And Television*

001.3 015 CK ISSN 0006-6184
BANCO DE LA REPUBLICA. BIBLIOTECA LUIS ANGEL ARANGO. BOLETIN CULTURAL Y BIBLIOGRAFICO. 1958-1973; resumed 1978. irreg. Col.$700($10) Banco de la Republica, Biblioteca Luis Angel Arango, Barrio de la Candelaria, Calle 11 no. 4-14, Bogota, Colombia. Dir. Dario Jaramillo Agudelo. bk. rev. bibl. charts. illus. circ. 5,000. Indexed: M.L.A.

015 II
BANGIYA SAHITYAKOSHA. (Text in Bengali) vol.9, 1977. a. price varies. Bangla Bhasa Sahitya-o-Samskriti Gabessane Samastha, c/o Pustak Bipani, 27 Beniatola Ln., Calcutta 700009, India. Ed. Asokkumar Kundu. bk. rev. bibl. circ. 1,100.

BIBLIOGRAPHIES

015 BG
BANGLADESH NATIONAL BIBLIOGRAPHY.
(Text in Bengali, English) 1972. a. National Library
of Bangladesh, Directorate of Archives and
Libraries, Sher.-&-Bangla Nagar(agaigaon), Dhaka 7,
Bangladesh. Ed.Bd. circ. 2,000.

011 NE ISSN 0169-0477
BESCHREIBENDE BIBLIOGRAPHIEN. (Text in
western languages) 1971. irreg. Editions Rodopi
B.V., Keizersgracht 302-304, 1016 EX Amsterdam,
Netherlands. Ed. Cola Minis. circ. 500. (back issues
avail.) Indexed: M.L.A.

015 DK ISSN 0067-6543
BIBLIOGRAFI OVER DANMARKS OFFENTLIGE
PUBLIKATIONER. (Text in Danish and English)
1949. a. Kr.220. I.D.E., Danmarks Institut for
International Udveksling Af Videnskabelige
Publikationer, Amaliegade 38, DK-1256
Copenhagen K, Denmark (Sold on commission by:
Bibliotekscentralen, Telegrafvej 5, DK-2750
Ballerup, Denmark) Eds. Ulla Jensen, Gertrud
Nielsen. index. circ. 2,000.
 Bibliography of Danish government publications

BIBLIOGRAFIA BIBLIOGRAFII I NAUKI O
KSIAZCE/BIBLIOGRAPHY OF
BIBLIOGRAPHIES AND LIBRARY SCIENCE.
see LIBRARY AND INFORMATION
SCIENCES — Abstracting, Bibliographies,
Statistics

BIBLIOGRAFIA BRASILEIRA DE CIENCIAS
SOCIAIS. see SOCIAL SERVICES AND
WELFARE — Abstracting, Bibliographies, Statistics

BIBLIOGRAFIA BRASILEIRA DE DIREITO. see
LAW — Abstracting, Bibliographies, Statistics

BIBLIOGRAFIA BRASILEIRA DE ENGENHARIA.
see ENGINEERING — Abstracting,
Bibliographies, Statistics

BIBLIOGRAFIA BRASILEIRA DE FISICA. see
PHYSICS — Abstracting, Bibliographies, Statistics

BIBLIOGRAFIA BRASILEIRA DE MATEMATICA.
see MATHEMATICS — Abstracting,
Bibliographies, Statistics

BIBLIOGRAFIA BRASILEIRA DE MEDICINA. see
MEDICAL SCIENCES — Abstracting,
Bibliographies, Statistics

BIBLIOGRAFIA BRASILEIRA DE QUIMICA E
QUIMICA TECNOLOGICA. see BUSINESS
AND ECONOMICS — Abstracting, Bibliographies,
Statistics

BIBLIOGRAFIA BRASILEIRA DE ZOOLOGIA. see
BIOLOGY — Abstracting, Bibliographies, Statistics

BIBLIOGRAFIA DE LA LITERATURA
HISPANICA. see LITERATURE — Abstracting,
Bibliographies, Statistics

015 BL ISSN 0100-722X
BIBLIOGRAFIA DE PUBLICACOES OFICIAIS
BRASILEIRAS. 1981. irreg., vol.3, 1985. Camara
dos Deputados, Centro de Documentacao e
Informacao, Anexo 2, Palacio do Congresso
Nacional, 70160 Brasilia DF, Brazil.

016 940 RM
BIBLIOGRAFIA DOBROGEI. 1969. a. Biblioteca
Judeteana Constanta, Str. Muzeelor nr. 23,
Constanta, Romania.

011 SP ISSN 0523-1760
BIBLIOGRAFIA ESPANOLA (ANNUAL) 1958. a.
5000 ptas. Instituto Bibliografico Hispanico, Calle
de Atocha 106, Apartado 12311, Madrid 12, Spain.
Ed. Vicente Sanchez Munoz. bibl. circ. 1,000.

011 SP ISSN 0210-8372
BIBLIOGRAFIA ESPANOLA. SUPLEMENTO DE
PUBLICACIONES PERIODICAS. 1979. a.
Instituto Bibliografico Hispanico, Calle de Atocha
106, Apartado 12311, Madrid 12, Spain (Dist. by:
Editora Nacional, Torregalindo 10, Madrid 16,
Spain) Ed. Vicente Sanchez Munoz. bibl. circ. 1,
000.

BIBLIOGRAFIA GOSPODARKI I INZYNIERII
WODNEJ/BIBLIOGRAPHY OF WATER
MANAGEMENT AND ENGINEERING. see
EARTH SCIENCES — Hydrology

BIBLIOGRAFIA HYDROLOGII I OCEANOLOGII/
BIBLIOGRAPHY OF HYDROLOGY AND
OCEANOLOGY. see EARTH SCIENCES —
Abstracting, Bibliographies, Statistics

BIBLIOGRAFIA METEOROLOGII/
BIBLIOGRAPHY OF METEOROLOGY. see
METEOROLOGY

015 020 BU ISSN 0204-7373
BIBLIOGRAFIA NA BULGARSKATA
BIBLIOGRAFIIA/BIBLIOGRAPHY OF
BULGARIAN BIBLIOGRAPHIES. 1965. a. price
varies. Narodna Biblioteka Kiril i Metodii, 11,
Tolbukhin Blvd., Sofia, Bulgaria. Ed. K. Stavrev.
bibl. circ. 580.

200 016 AG ISSN 0326-6680
BIBLIOGRAFIA TEOLOGICA COMENTADA
DEL AREA IBEROAMERICANA. (Summaries in
English) 1973. a. $60. Instituto Superior Evangelico
de Estudios Teologicos, Camacua 282, 1406 Buenos
Aires, Argentina. Ed. Eduardo Bierzychudek. bk.
rev. bibl. index. circ. 1,000. (back issues avail.)

BIBLIOGRAFIA WYDAWNICTW CIAGLYCH/
BIBLIOGRAPHY OF POLISH SERIALS. see
LIBRARY AND INFORMATION SCIENCES —
Abstracting, Bibliographies, Statistics

015 UR
BIBLIOGRAFICHESKIE POSOBIYA
BELORUSSKOI S.S.R. a. Gosudarstvennaya
Knizhnaya Palata B.S.S.R., Parkovaya Magistral 11,
220600 Minsk, Byelorussian S.S.R., U.S.S.R.

057.86 015 CS ISSN 0323-1712
BIBLIOGRAFICKY KATALOG C S S R. CESKE
KNIHY. ZVLASTNI SESIT. CESKA GRAFIKA A
MAPY V ROCE. 1958. a. 25 Kcs. Statni Knihovna
C S R, Klementinum 190, 110 01 Prague 1,
Czechoslovakia. Ed. Eugenie Richterova.

057.86 015 CS ISSN 0323-1860
BIBLIOGRAFICKY KATALOG C S S R. CESKE
KNIHY. ZVLASTNI SESIT. SOUPIS CESKYCH
BIBLIOGRAFII. 1956. a. 6 Kcs. Statni Knihovna C
S R, Klementinum 190, 110 01 Prague 1,
Czechoslovakia. Ed. Eugenie Richterova.

057.86 015 CS ISSN 0232-041X
BIBLIOGRAFICKY KATALOG C S S R: CESKE
KNIHY. ZVLASTNI SESIT. CESKE
DISERTACE. 1964. a. $10.80 price varies. Statni
Knihovna C S R, Klementinum 190, 110 01 Prague
1, Czechoslovakia (Subscr. to: Artia, Ve Smeckach
30, 111 27 Prague 1, Czechoslovakia) Ed. Eugenie
Richterova.
 Formerly: Bibliograficky Katalog C S S R: Ceske
Knihy. Zvlastni Sesit. Ceskoslovenske Disertace
(ISSN 0323-1763)

010 CS ISSN 0067-6780
BIBLIOGRAFICKY ZBORNIK. (Text in Slovak;
summaries in English and German) 1957. a. price
varies. Matica Slovenska, Mudronova 35, 036 52
Martin, Czechoslovakia. bk. rev.

011 NE ISSN 0166-9966
BIBLIOGRAFIE VAN NEDERLANDSE
PROEFSCHRIFTEN/DUTCH THESES. 1924;
1966 N.S. irreg. price varies. (Rijksuniversiteit te
Utrecht, Bibliotheek) Swets Publishing Service
(Subsidiary of: Swets en Zeitlinger B.V.) Heereweg
347, 2126 CA Lisse, Netherlands (Dist. in the U.S.
and Canada by: Swets North America, Inc. Box
517, Berwyn, PA 19312)
 Formerly: Catalogus van Academische
Geschriften in Nederland Verschenen.

079 015 YU ISSN 0350-0349
BIBLIOGRAFIJA JUGOSLAVIJE. SERIJSKE
PUBLIKACIJE. 1959. a. $175 or avail. on
exchange. Jugoslovenski Bibliografski Institut,
Terazije 26, Belgrade, Yugoslavia. Ed. Miloje
Rakocevic. index.
 Formerly: Bibliografia Jugoslovenske Periodike
(ISSN 0006-1158)

015 YU ISSN 0350-9974
BIBLIOGRAFIJA PREVODA U S F R J. 1969. a.
$150 or avail. on exchange. Jugoslovenski
Bibliografski Institut, Terazije 26, Belgrade,
Yugoslavia. Ed. Miloje Rakocevic.

015 YU ISSN 0350-2562
BIBLIOGRAFIJA ZVANICNIH PUBLIKACIJA S F
R J. 1972. a. $75 or avail. on exchange.
Jugoslovenski Bibliografski Institut, Terazije 26,
Belgrade, Yugoslavia. Ed. Miloje Rakocevic.

BIBLIOGRAPHIA CARTOGRAPHICA; international
documentation of cartographical literature. see
GEOGRAPHY — Abstracting, Bibliographies,
Statistics

BIBLIOGRAPHIC GUIDE TO ART AND
ARCHITECTURE. see ARCHITECTURE —
Abstracting, Bibliographies, Statistics

BIBLIOGRAPHIC GUIDE TO BLACK STUDIES.
see ETHNIC INTERESTS — Abstracting,
Bibliographies, Statistics

011 US ISSN 0360-2729
BIBLIOGRAPHIC GUIDE TO CONFERENCE
PUBLICATIONS. (Text in various languages) 1974.
a. G.K. Hall & Co., 70 Lincoln St., Boston, MA
02111. TEL 617-423-3990.
 Formerly: Conference Publications Guide (ISSN
0091-7907)

BIBLIOGRAPHIC GUIDE TO DANCE. see
DANCE — Abstracting, Bibliographies, Statistics

BIBLIOGRAPHIC GUIDE TO EDUCATION. see
EDUCATION — Abstracting, Bibliographies,
Statistics

011 US ISSN 0360-2796
BIBLIOGRAPHIC GUIDE TO GOVERNMENT
PUBLICATIONS. (Text in various languages) a.
G.K. Hall & Co., 70 Lincoln St., Boston, MA
02111. TEL 617-423-3990.
 Formerly: Government Publications Guide (ISSN
0091-7915)

015 US ISSN 0360-280X
BIBLIOGRAPHIC GUIDE TO GOVERNMENT
PUBLICATIONS-FOREIGN. a. G.K. Hall & Co.,
70 Lincoln St., Boston, MA 02111. TEL 617-423-
3990.

BIBLIOGRAPHIC GUIDE TO LAW. see LAW —
Abstracting, Bibliographies, Statistics

BIBLIOGRAPHIC GUIDE TO MAPS AND
ATLASES. see GEOGRAPHY — Abstracting,
Bibliographies, Statistics

BIBLIOGRAPHIC GUIDE TO MUSIC. see
MUSIC — Abstracting, Bibliographies, Statistics

BIBLIOGRAPHIC GUIDE TO NORTH
AMERICAN HISTORY. see HISTORY —
Abstracting, Bibliographies, Statistics

BIBLIOGRAPHIC GUIDE TO PSYCHOLOGY. see
PSYCHOLOGY — Abstracting, Bibliographies,
Statistics

600 016 US ISSN 0360-2761
BIBLIOGRAPHIC GUIDE TO TECHNOLOGY.
1974. a. G.K. Hall & Co., 70 Lincoln St., Boston,
MA 02111. TEL 617-423-3990.
 Continues: Technology Book Guide (ISSN 0091-
7885)

010 UN
BIBLIOGRAPHICAL SERVICES THROUGHOUT
THE WORLD. no.6, 1984. quinquennial. price
varies. Unesco, 7 Place de Fontenoy, F-75700 Paris,
France (U.S. addr.: Bernan Associates-Unipub,
4611-F Assembly Dr., Lanham, MD 20706-4391)

010 CN ISSN 0067-687X
BIBLIOGRAPHICAL SOCIETY OF CANADA.
FACSIMILE SERIES. 1951. irreg. price varies.
Bibliographical Society of Canada - La Societe
Bibliographique du Canada, c/o W.P. Stoneman,
English Dept., University of Windsor, Windsor,
Ont. N9B 3P4, Canada. TEL 416-978-3897. circ.
360.

010 CN ISSN 0067-6888
BIBLIOGRAPHICAL SOCIETY OF CANADA.
MONOGRAPHS. 1957. irreg. price varies.
Bibliographical Society of Canada - La Societe
Bibliographique du Canada, c/o W.P. Stoneman,
English Dept., University of Windsor, Windsor,
Ont. N9B 3P4, Canada. TEL 416-978-3897. circ.
360.

010   CN   ISSN 0067-6896
BIBLIOGRAPHICAL SOCIETY OF CANADA.
PAPERS. (Text in English and French) 1962. a.
membership. Bibliographical Society of Canada -
La Societe Bibliographique du Canada, c/o W.P.
Stonemann, English Dept., University of Windsor,
Windsor, Ont. N9B 3P4, Canada. TEL 416-978-
3897. Ed. Patricia Stone. bk. rev. circ. 360.
 Supersedes: Bibliographical Society of Canada.
Newsletter.

015   MG   ISSN 0067-6926
BIBLIOGRAPHIE ANNUELLE DE
MADAGASCAR. 1964. a. 500 Fr.($2) Universite
de Madagascar, Bibliotheque Universitaire, B.P. 908,
Antananarivo, Malagasy Republic. index. circ. 1,
500.

BIBLIOGRAPHIE COURANTE D'ARTICLES DE
PERIODIQUES POSTERIEURS A 1944 SUR LES
PROBLEMES POLITIQUES, ECONOMIQUES
ET SOCIAUX/INDEX TO POST-1944
PERIODICAL ARTICLES ON POLITICAL,
ECONOMIC AND SOCIAL PROBLEMS. see
SOCIAL SCIENCES: COMPREHENSIVE
WORKS — Abstracting, Bibliographies, Statistics

BIBLIOGRAPHIE DER BERNER GESCHICHTE/
BIBLIOGRAPHIE DE L'HISTOIRE BERNOISE.
see HISTORY — Abstracting, Bibliographies,
Statistics

949.3 011   LU
BIBLIOGRAPHIE LUXEMBOURGEOISE. 1944/45.
a. 350 Fr. Bibliotheque Nationale, 37 Boulevard F.-
D. Roosevelt, 2450 Luxembourg. (back issues avail.)

370 016   GW   ISSN 0523-2678
BIBLIOGRAPHIE PAEDAGOGIK/
EDUCATIONAL BIBLIOGRAPHY. 1965. a. price
varies. (Dokumentationsring Paedagogik
(DOPAED)) K.G. Saur Verlag KG,
Poessenbacherstr. 12B, Postfach 711009, D-8000
Munich 71, W. Germany (B.R.D.), NY 10003 (U.S.
and Canadian subscr. to: K.G. Saur Inc., 175 Fifth
Ave., New York, NY 10010) circ. 1,000.
 Incorporated: Bibliographie Programmierter
Unterricht (ISSN 0067-7027)

913 016.9301   GE   ISSN 0232-4865
BIBLIOGRAPHIE ZUR ARCHAEO-ZOOLOGIE
UND GESCHICHTE DER HAUSTIERE. 1971. a.
exchange basis. Akademie der Wissenschaften der
DDR, Zentralinstitut fuer Alte Geschichte und
Archaeologie, Leipziger Str. 3-4, Postfach 1310,
DDR-1086 Berlin, E. Germany (D.D.R.) Ed.
Hanns-Hermann Mueller. Indexed:
Br.Archaeol.Abstr.

BIBLIOGRAPHIEN ZUR PHILOSOPHIE. see
PHILOSOPHY

BIBLIOGRAPHIES ANALYTIQUES SUR
L'AFRIQUE CENTRALE. see HISTORY —
Abstracting, Bibliographies, Statistics

BIBLIOGRAPHIES AND INDEXES IN
ECONOMICS AND ECONOMIC HISTORY. see
BUSINESS AND ECONOMICS — Abstracting,
Bibliographies, Statistics

011 800   US   ISSN 0749-470X
BIBLIOGRAPHIES OF MODERN AUTHORS.
1984. irreg., approx. 6/yr. $19.95 hardcover per no.;
paperback $9.95 per no. Borgo Press, Box 2845, San
Bernardino, CA 92406. TEL 714-884-5813.

011   GW   ISSN 0006-1506
BIBLIOGRAPHISCHE BERICHTE/
BIBLIOGRAPHICAL BULLETIN. (N.F.
Bibliographische Beihefte zur Zeitschrift fuer
Bibliothekswesen und Bibliographie) (Text in
English and German) 1959. a. DM.150 (approx.)
(Staatsbibliothek Preussischer Kulturbesitz) Vittorio
Klostermann, Frauenlobstr. 22, 6000 Frankfurt 90,
W. Germany (B.R.D.) adv. bibl. index. cum.index:
1959-1966; 1966-1970. circ. 1,400.

011   GE   ISSN 0070-3931
BIBLIOGRAPHISCHER INFORMATIONSDIENST
DER DEUTSCHEN BUECHEREI. 1963. irreg.
Deutsche Buecherei, Deutscher Platz 1, 7010
Leipzig, E. Germany(D.D.R.)

BIBLIOGRAPHY AND SUBJECT INDEX OF
SOUTH AFRICAN GEOLOGY. see EARTH
SCIENCES — Abstracting, Bibliographies,
Statistics

BIBLIOGRAPHY OF AGRICULTURE. see
AGRICULTURE — Abstracting, Bibliographies,
Statistics

015   CN   ISSN 0067-7175
BIBLIOGRAPHY OF CANADIAN
BIBLIOGRAPHIES. 1960. irreg., 2nd ed. 1972.
Can.$27.50. University of Toronto Press, Front
Campus, Toronto, Ont. M5S 1A6, Canada. TEL
613-667-7791. Ed. D.G. Lochhead.

011   GW   ISSN 0724-8415
BIBLIOGRAPHY OF CHINESE STUDIES; selected
articles on China in Chinese, English and German.
(Text in Chinese, English, German) 1983. a.
DM.18. (Institut fuer Asienkunde) Ostasien-Verlag
GmbH, Tempelhofer Damm 4, D-1000 Berlin 42,
W. Germany (B.R.D.) Ed. Yu-hsi Nieh. bibl. circ.
160. (back issues avail.)

BIBLIOGRAPHY OF DOCTORAL
DISSERTATIONS; NATURAL AND APPLIED
SCIENCES. see SCIENCES: COMPREHENSIVE
WORKS — Abstracting, Bibliographies, Statistics

BIBLIOGRAPHY OF DOCTORAL
DISSERTATIONS: SOCIAL SCIENCES AND
HUMANITIES. see SOCIAL SCIENCES:
COMPREHENSIVE WORKS — Abstracting,
Bibliographies, Statistics

BIBLIOGRAPHY OF ECONOMIC AND
STATISTICAL PUBLICATIONS ON
TANZANIA. see BUSINESS AND
ECONOMICS — Abstracting, Bibliographies,
Statistics

BIBLIOGRAPHY OF HOTEL AND RESTAURANT
ADMINISTRATION. see HOTELS AND
RESTAURANTS — Abstracting, Bibliographies,
Statistics

011   UK
BIBLIOGRAPHY OF ITALIAN PUBLICATIONS
PUBLISHED OR DISTRIBUTED IN GREAT
BRITAIN. 1985. a. £15.95. Magna Graecia's
Publishers, Office 8, Groundfloor, 38 Mount
Pleasant, London WC1X 0AP, England. Ed. Luigi
Gigliotti. circ. 15,000.

BIBLIOGRAPHY OF SKIING STUDIES. see
SPORTS AND GAMES — Abstracting,
Bibliographies, Statistics

016   SA   ISSN 0067-7256
BIBLIOGRAPHY OF SOUTH AFRICAN
GOVERNMENT PUBLICATIONS. (Text in
Afrikaans and English) 1969. irreg. Government
Printer, Bosman St., Private Bag X85, Pretoria 0001,
South Africa. (Prepared by: Department of National
Education, Division of Library Sciences)

016   SY   ISSN 0067-7302
BIBLIOGRAPHY OF THE MIDDLE EAST.*
(Subseries of Syrian Documentation Papers) a. $25.
Syrian Documentation Papers, P.O. Box 2712,
Damascus, Syria.

011   US
BIBLIOGRAPHY OF TOURISM AND TRAVEL
RESEARCH STUDIES, REPORTS AND
ARTICLES. 1980. irreg. $60 for 9 vols. (Business
Research Division) University of Colorado,
Graduate School of Business Administration,
Campus Box 420, Boulder, CO 80309. TEL 303-
492-8227. Ed. Charles R. Goeldner. circ. 500.

016   UK   ISSN 0067-7310
BIBLIOGRAPHY OF WORKS BY POLISH
SCHOLARS AND SCIENTISTS PUBLISHED
OUTSIDE POLAND IN LANGUAGES OTHER
THAN POLISH. 1964. irreg. Polish Society of Arts
and Sciences Abroad, 20 Princes Gate, London,
S.W.7, England.

BIBLIOGRAPHY ON COLD REGIONS SCIENCE
& TECHNOLOGY. see ENGINEERING —
Abstracting, Bibliographies, Statistics

015   IT   ISSN 0067-7418
BIBLIOTECA DI BIBLIOGRAFIA ITALIANA.
1923. irreg., vol.109, 1986. price varies. Casa
Editrice Leo S. Olschki, Casella Postale 66, 50100
Florence, Italy. circ. 1,000.

011   IT
BIBLIOTECA STATALE E LIBRERIA CIVICA DI
CREMONA. MOSTRE. 1978. irreg., no.13, 1983.
exchange basis. Biblioteca Statale e Libreria Civica
di Cremona, Via Ugolani Dati 4, Cremona, Italy.
Ed. Goffredo Dotti. circ. 1,780.

015   SP
BIBLIOTECA UNIVERSITARIA Y PROVINCIAL,
BARCELONA. BOLETIN DE NOTICIAS. irreg.
free. Universidad de Barcelona, Biblioteca, Gran Via
de les Corts Catalanes, 585, Barcelona-7, Spain.

010   IT   ISSN 0067-7531
BIBLIOTECONOMIA E BIBLIOGRAFIA. SAGGI E
STUDI. 1964. irreg., vol.21, 1985. price varies. Casa
Editrice Leo S. Olschki, Casella Postale 66, 50100
Florence, Italy. Ed. Francesco Barberi. circ. 1,000.

016   GW   ISSN 0067-7884
BIBLIOTHECA BIBLIOGRAPHICA AURELIANA.
(Text in English, French, German, Latin) 1959.
irreg., vol.109, 1987. price varies. Verlag Valentin
Koerner, H.-Sielcken-Str. 36, Postfach 304, D-7570
Baden-Baden 1, W. Germany (B.R.D.) index.

011   NE
BIBLIOTHECA BIBLIOGRAPHICA
NEERLANDICA. 1968. irreg., no.21, 1986. price
varies. De Graaf Publishers, Box 6, 2420 AA
Nieuwkoop, Netherlands.

015   UK   ISSN 0067-7914
BIBLIOTHECA CELTICA; A register of publications
relating to Wales and the Celtic peoples. 1909. a.,
price varies. National Library of Wales,
Aberystwyth, Dyfed SY23 3BU, Wales. index. circ.
450. Indexed: Br.Archaeol.Abstr.

011 200   GW
BIBLIOTHECA DISSIDENTIUM. (Subseries of:
Bibliotheca Bibliographica Aureliana) (Text in
English, French, German and Italian) 1980. irreg.
price varies. Verlag Valentin Koerner, Postfach 304,
D-7570 Baden-Baden 1, W. Germany (B.R.D.)
Ed.Bd. circ. 1,000.

011   US   ISSN 0342-4871
BIBLIOTHECA NOSTRATICA. 1977. irreg. price
varies. Eurolingua, Box 101, Bloomington, IN
47402-0101.

BIBLIOTHEQUE AFRICAINE. CATALOGUE DES
ACQUISITIONS. CATOLOGUS VAN DE
AANWINSTEN. see HISTORY — Abstracting,
Bibliographies, Statistics

015   BO
BIO-BIBLIOGRAFIA BOLIVIANA. 1962. a. $80.
Los Amigos del Libro, Casilla 450, Cochabamba,
Bolivia. Ed. Werner Guttentag. adv. bk. rev.
indexes. circ. 500.
 Formerly: Bibliografia Boliviana (ISSN 0067-
6578)

920   US
BIOGRAPHICAL DICTIONARIES AND
RELATED WORKS; an international bibliography
of collective biographies. 1967. irreg., latest 2nd
edt., 1986. $140. Gale Research Company, Book
Tower, Detroit, MI 48226. TEL 313-961-2242. Ed.
Robert B. Slocum.

011   DK   ISSN 0106-9713
BOERNEBIBLIOTEKSKATALOG. BOEGER Z
TIDSSKRIFTER EMNEKATALOG. 1975. a. (plus
supplements) Bibliotekscentralen, Tempovej 7-11,
DK-2750 Ballerup, Denmark.
 Continues in part: Katalog for Boerne- og
Skolebiblioteker.

011   DK   ISSN 0106-9691
BOERNEBIBLIOTEKSKATALOG. BOEGER Z
TIDSSKRIFTER FORFATTERKATALOG. 1975.
a. (plus supplements) Bibliotekscentralen, Tempovej
7-11, DK-2750 Ballerup, Denmark.
 Continues in part: Katalog for Boerne- og
Skolebiblioteker.

011   DK   ISSN 0106-9705
BOERNEBIBLIOTEKSKATALOG. BOEGER Z
TIDSSKRIFTER TITELKATALOG. 1975. a. (plus
supplements) Bibliotekscentralen, Tempovej 7-11,
DK-2750 Ballerup, Denmark.
 Continues in part: Katalog for Boerne- og
Skolebiblioteker.

010   PK   ISSN 0068-0206
BOOKS FROM PAKISTAN. (Text in English) 1967.
a. Rs.15. National Book Council of Pakistan,
Theosophical Hall, M.A. Jinnah Rd., Karachi,
Pakistan.
   Formerly: English Language Publications from
Pakistan.

016 892.7   CN   ISSN 0705-7172
BOOKS IN ARABIC. irreg. Metropolitan Toronto
Library Board, Regional Multilanguage Department,
789 Yonge St., Toronto, Ont. M4W 2G8, Canada.
TEL 416-393-7075.

016 891.992   CN   ISSN 0705-8209
BOOKS IN ARMENIAN. irreg. Metropolitan Toronto
Library Board, Regional Multilanguage Department,
789 Yonge St., Toronto, Ont. M4W 2G8, Canada.
TEL 416-393-7075.

016 890   CN   ISSN 0316-7437
BOOKS IN BENGALI. irreg. Metropolitan Toronto
Library Board, Regional Multilanguage Department,
789 Yonge St., Toronto, Ont. M4W 2G8, Canada.
TEL 416-393-7075. (processed)

016 890   CN
BOOKS IN CHINESE. irreg. Metropolitan Toronto
Library Board, Regional Multilanguage Department,
789 Yonge St., Toronto, Ont. M4W 2G8, Canada.
TEL 416-393-7075. (processed)

016 839   CN   ISSN 0705-2332
BOOKS IN DANISH. irreg. Metropolitan Toronto
Library Board, Regional Multilanguage Department,
789 Yonge St., Toronto, Ont. M4W 2G8, Canada.
TEL 416-393-7075.

016 839   CN   ISSN 0705-2294
BOOKS IN DUTCH. 1974. irreg. Metropolitan
Toronto Library Board, Regional Multilanguage
Department, 789 Yonge St., Toronto, Ont. M4W
2G8, Canada. TEL 416-393-7075.

016 894.541   CN   ISSN 0705-1883
BOOKS IN FINNISH. irreg. Metropolitan Toronto
Library Board, Regional Multilanguage Department,
789 Yonge St., Toronto, Ont. M4W 2G8, Canada.
TEL 416-393-7075.

016 890   CN   ISSN 0705-8373
BOOKS IN HINDI. irreg. Metropolitan Toronto
Library Board, Regional Multilanguage Department,
789 Yonge St., Toronto, Ont. M4W 2G8, Canada.
TEL 416-393-7075.

016 894.511   CN   ISSN 0705-6494
BOOKS IN HUNGARIAN. irreg. Metropolitan
Toronto Library Board, Regional Multilanguage
Department, 789 Yonge St., Toronto, Ont. M4W
2G8, Canada. TEL 416-393-7075.

015   US   ISSN 0068-0214
BOOKS IN PRINT. (Vols. 1-3 Authors; vols. 4-6
Titles; vol. 7, Publishers & Distributors) 1947. a. (q.
microfiche avail.) $249.95. R.R. Bowker Company,
Database Publishing Group, 245 W. 17th St., New
York, NY 10011. TEL 800-521-8110. (also avail. in
microfiche)
●Also available online. Vendors: BRS, DIALOG.

015   US   ISSN 0000-0310
BOOKS IN PRINT SUPPLEMENT; a mid-year
updating service listing new and forthcoming books,
price changes, and out-of-print titles. a. $139.95.
R.R. Bowker Company, Database Publishing Group,
245 W. 17th St., New York, NY 10011. TEL 800-
521-8110.
●Also available online. Vendors: BRS, DIALOG.

015   US   ISSN 0000-0906
BOOKS IN SERIES; original, reprinted, in-print, and
out-of-print books, published or distributed in the
U.S., in popular, scholarly, and professional series.
1977. irreg., 4th edt. 1985. $325. R.R. Bowker
Company, Database Publishing Group, 245 W. 17th
St., New York, NY 10011. TEL 800-521-8110.
   Formerly (until 3rd edt., 1980): Books in Series
in the United States (ISSN 0000-0515)

016 860   CN   ISSN 0705-7156
BOOKS IN SPANISH. irreg. Metropolitan Toronto
Library Board, Regional Multilanguage Department,
789 Yonge St., Toronto, Ont. M4W 2G8, Canada.
TEL 416-393-7075.

016 896   CN   ISSN 0705-825X
BOOKS IN URDU. 1972. irreg. Metropolitan Toronto
Library Board, Regional Multilanguage Department,
789 Yonge St., Toronto, Ont. M4W 2G8, Canada.
TEL 416-393-7075.

011   US   ISSN 0000-0736
BOOKS OUT OF PRINT. a. $99.95. R.R. Bowker
Company, Database Publishing Group, 245 W. 17th
St., New York, NY 10011. TEL 800-521-8110.
●Also available online. Vendors: BRS, DIALOG.

BORGO REFERENCE LIBRARY. see *HISTORY*

BOWKER'S LAW BOOKS AND SERIALS IN
PRINT. see *LAW — Abstracting, Bibliographies,
Statistics*

011   UK   ISSN 0263-1040
BRAD DIRECTORIES AND ANNUALS. 1961. a.
£10. Maclean Hunter Ltd., 76 Oxford St., London,
W1N 9FD, England. Ed. J. Redman. adv. circ. 922.

BRAILLE BOOKS (LARGE PRINT EDITION) see
BLIND — Abstracting, Bibliographies, Statistics

011   BL
BRAZIL. SERVICO SOCIAL DO COMERCIO.
COLECAO BIBLIOGRAFICA. 1970. a. free.
Servico Social do Comercio, Rua Voluntarios da
Patria 169, 22270 Rio de Janeiro, Brazil. Ed.Bd.

015   UK   ISSN 0068-1350
BRITISH BOOKS IN PRINT. 1874. a. £107. J.
Whitaker & Sons Ltd., 12 Dyott St., London WC1A
1DF, England (Dist. in U.S. by: R.R. Bowker Co.,
P.O. Box 1807, Ann Arbor, MI 48106) (also avail.
in microform)
●Also available online.

011   UK
BRITISH LIBRARY. DOCUMENT SUPPLY
CENTRE. SCIENCE REFERENCE AND
INFORMATION SERVICE. CURRENT SERIALS
RECEIVED. 1965. a. £37. British Library,
Document Supply Centre, Boston Spa, Wetherby,
West Yorkshire LS23 7BQ, England. circ. 2,500.
   Formerly (until 1986): British Library. Lending
Division. Current Serials Received (ISSN 0309-
0655)

016.05   UK
BRITISH RATE & DATA DIRECTORIES AND
ANNUALS. a. £7. Maclean-Hunter Ltd., 76 Oxford
St., London W1N 0HH, England. Ed. Jocelyn
Redman. adv. circ. 1,015.

016   GW   ISSN 0068-3043
DAS BUCH DER JUGEND. 1954. a. free.
(Arbeitskreis fuer Jugendliteratur)
Arbeitsgemeinschaft von Jugendbuchverlegern in der
BRD, Georgstr. 15, D-8000 Munich 40, W.
Germany (B.R.D.) Ed.Bd. bk. rev. circ. 220,000.

015 940   BU   ISSN 0323-9969
BULGARIA V CHUZHDATA LITERATURA/
BULGARIA IN FOREIGN LITERATURE. 1966.
a. 13.34 lv. Narodna Biblioteka Kiril i Metodii, 11,
Tolbukhin Blvd., Sofia, Bulgaria. Ed. N. Kukudova.
bibl. circ. 500.

015   BU
BULGARIAN ACADEMIC BOOKS. (Editions in
Bulgarian, English, Russian) 1969. a. free.
(Bulgarska Akademiia na Naukite) Publishing House
of the Bulgarian Academy of Sciences, Acad. G.
Bonchev St., Bldg. 6, 1113 Sofia, Bulgaria. bibl. circ.
1,000.

015   BU   ISSN 0323-9411
BULGARSKI DISERTACII. 1974. a. price varies.
Narodna Biblioteka Kiril i Metodii, 11. Tolbukhin
Blvd., 1504 Sofia, Bulgaria. Ed. T. Atanasova. bibl.
index. circ. 400.

070 015   BU   ISSN 0323-9764
BULGARSKI PERIODICHEN PECHAT/
BULGARIAN PERIODICALS; vestnitsi, spisaniia,
biuletini i periodichni sbornitsi. 1967. a. price varies.
Narodna Biblioteka Kiril i Metodii, 11, Tolbukhin
Blvd., Sofia, Bulgaria. Ed. S. Ivanov. bibl. circ. 700.

010   FR   ISSN 0076-0137
BULLETIN BIBLIOGRAPHIQUE THEMATIQUE;
informations bibliographiques-philosophie, religion,
sciences humaines. irreg. price varies. Union des
Editeurs Francais, 35 rue Mazarine, 75006 Paris,
France. circ. 35,000.
   Livres d'Aujourd'hui.

010   US   ISSN 0068-4309
BURT FRANKLIN BIBLIOGRAPHY AND
REFERENCE SERIES. (Text in various languages)
1949. irreg. price varies. Lenox Hill Publishing and
Distributing Corporation, 235 E. 44th St., New
York, NY 10017.

C.A.B. INTERNATIONAL. FORESTRY BUREAU.
ANNOTATED BIBLIOGRAPHIES. see *FORESTS
AND FORESTRY — Abstracting, Bibliographies,
Statistics*

011   CN   ISSN 0707-3747
C O N S E R MICROFICHE. (Conversion of Serials);
a computer-output-microfiche listing of serial
records created in the CONSER project and
authenticated by the National Library of Canada
and the Library of Congress. (Text in English and
French) 1979. a. National Library of Canada,
Canadiana Editorial Division, Acquisitions and
Bibliographic Services Branch, 395 Wellington St.,
Ottawa, Ont. K1A 0N4, Canada TEL 819-994-
6918. (Dist. in U.S. by: Library of Congress,
Cataloging Distribution Service, Washington, DC
20540) circ. 150. (microfiche)

011   US
CALIFORNIA PERIODICALS ON MICROFILM.
1978. a. $190 price includes California Periodicals
Index. Gabriel Micrographics (Subsidiary of:
Minnesota Scholarly Press, Inc.) Box 224, Mankato,
MN 56001. TEL 507-387-4964. Ed. Opal Kissinger.
(microfilm)

010   UK   ISSN 0068-6611
CAMBRIDGE BIBLIOGRAPHICAL SOCIETY.
TRANSACTIONS. 1949. a. £6. Cambridge
Bibliographical Society, c/o Cambridge University
Library, West Rd., Cambridge CB3 9DR, England.
Ed. David McKitterick. Indexed: Br.Hum.Ind.
Abstr.Engl.Stud.

016   UK   ISSN 0068-662X
CAMBRIDGE BIBLIOGRAPHICAL SOCIETY.
TRANSACTIONS. MONOGRAPH
SUPPLEMENTS. 1951. irreg. membership (non-
member price varies) Cambridge Bibliographical
Society, c/o Cambridge University Library, West
Rd., Cambridge CB3 9DR, England.

016   UK
CAMBRIDGE UNIVERSITY LIBRARY. GENIZAH
SERIES. irreg. £1 per no. Cambridge University
Press, Edinburgh Bldg., Shaftesbury Rd., Cambridge
CB2 2RY, England (And: 32 E. 57th St., New
York, NY 10022)

900 016   UK
CAMBRIDGE UNIVERSITY LIBRARY.
HISTORICAL BIBLIOGRAPHY SERIES. irreg. £1
per no. Cambridge University Press, Edinburgh
Bldg., Shaftesbury Rd., Cambridge CB2 2RY,
England (And: 32 E. 57th St., New York, NY
10022)

CANADIAN BOOKS FOR YOUNG PEOPLE/
LIVRES CANADIENS POUR LA JEUNESSE. see
*CHILDREN AND YOUTH — Abstracting,
Bibliographies, Statistics*

015   CN   ISSN 0068-8398
CANADIAN BOOKS IN PRINT. (Author & Title
Index & Companion Subject Index) 1967. q (cloth
Jan.; microfiche Apr., Jul., Oct.) price varies.
University of Toronto Press, Front Campus,
Toronto, Ont. M5S 1A6, Canada. TEL 613-667-
7791. Ed. M. Butler. circ. 3,500.

016 378   CN   ISSN 0068-9874
CANADIAN THESES/THESES CANADIENNES;
(microfiche) (Text in English and French) 1962. a.
price varies. ‡ National Library of Canada, Ottawa,
Ont. K1A 0N4, Canada TEL 613-995-7969.
(Subscr. to: Supply & Services Canada, Printing and
Publishing Division, Ottawa, Ont. K1A 0S9,
Canada) Ed. Helena Vesely. index. circ. 1,000. (also
avail. in microfilm)
   Incorporates: Candian Theses on Microfiche
(Supplement)

BIBLIOGRAPHIES

011 616.99 649 US
CANDLELIGHTERS CHILDHOOD CANCER FOUNDATION/ANNOTATED BIBLIOGRAPHY AND RESOURCE GUIDE. 1976. irreg., latest 1982, 1986 in prep. $1. Candlelighters Childhood Cancer Foundation, 2025 Eye St., N.W., Ste. 1011, Washington, DC 20006. TEL 202-659-5136. Ed. Minna Newman Nathanson. bk. rev. circ. 3,000.
 Formerly: Candlelighters Foundation Bibliography and Resource Guide.

011 MX
CATALOGO COLECTIVO DE PUBLICACIONES PERIODICAS EXISTENTES EN LAS BIBLIOTECAS DE LA UNIVERSIDAD. 1976. biennial. Mex.$40 (or exchange) Universidad Nacional Autonoma de Mexico, Direccion General de Bibliotecas, Villa Obregon, Ciudad Universitaria, Mexico 20, D.F., Mexico.

011 BL
CATALOGO COLETIVO NACIONAL DE PUBLICACOES PERIODICAS (IN MICROFICHES) biennial. $120. Instituto Brasileiro de Informacao em Ciencia e Tecnologia, SCRN 708/709 Bloco B Loja 18E 30, 70740 Brasilia DF, Brazil.
 Formerly: Catalogo Coletivo de Publicacoes Periodicas (in Microfiches)

CATALOGO DE PUBLICACIONES LATINOAMERICANAS SOBRE FORMACION PROFESIONAL. see *OCCUPATIONS AND CAREERS* — *Abstracting, Bibliographies, Statistics*

015 IT
CATALOGO DEI PERIODICI ITALIANI. 1981. irreg. L.60000. Editrice Bibliografica s.r.l., Viale Vittorio Veneto 24, 20124 Milan, Italy. Ed. Roberto Maini. adv. circ. 2,500.

011 JA
CATALOGUE OF BOOKS RECOMMENDED FOR LIBRARIES/SENTEI TOSHO SOMOKUROKU.
a. Japan Library Association - Nihon Toshokan Kyokai, 1-1-10 Taishido, Setagaya-ku, Tokyo 154, Japan.

282 011 US ISSN 0008-8307
CATHOLIC PRESS DIRECTORY; official media reference guide to Catholic newspapers and magazines of the United States and Canada. 1923. a. $25. Catholic Press Association, 119 North Park Ave., Rockville Centre, NY 11570. TEL 516-766-3400. Ed. James A. Doyle. adv. index. circ. 1,400.

011 327 US
CENTRAL ASIAN COLLECTANEA. irreg., no.13, 1984. 13833 Dowlais Dr., Rockville, MD 20853. Ed. Rudolf Loewenthal.

CENTRALNY KATALOG ZAGRANICZNYCH WYDAWNICTW CIAGLYCH W BIBLIOTEKACH POLSKICH. ALFABETYCZNY WYKAZ TYTULOW. see *LIBRARY AND INFORMATION SCIENCES* — *Abstracting, Bibliographies, Statistics*

944 015 FR
CENTRE INTERNATIONAL DE DOCUMENTATION OCCITANE. SERIE BIBLIOGRAPHIQUE. 1977. irreg. price varies. Centre International de Documentation Occitane, Boite Postale 4202, 34325 Beziers Cedex, France.

057.86 015 CS ISSN 0577-3490
CESKA BIBLIOGRAFIE; sbornik stati a materialu. (Text in Czech; summaries in English, French, German, Russian) 1959. a. price varies. Statni Knihovna C S R, Klementinum 190, 110 01 Prague 1, Czechoslovakia. Ed. Eugenie Richterova.

011 US
CHICOREL INDEX SERIES. 1970. irreg., vol.26, 1986. $125 per vol. American Library Publishing Co., Inc., 275 Central Park West, New York, NY 10024. TEL 212-362-1442. Ed. Marietta S. Chicorel. bk. rev. (also avail. in microform from MIM)

016 UK ISSN 0577-781X
CHILDREN'S BOOKS IN PRINT. 1972. a. £35. J. Whitaker & Sons Ltd., 12 Dyott St., London WC1A 1DF, England.

015 CL ISSN 0716-176X
CHILE. DIRECCION DE BIBLIOTECAS ARCHIVOS Y MUSEOS. BIBLIOGRAFIA CHILENA. 1877. a. Esc.2000($20) Direccion de Bibliotecas, Archivos y Museos, Biblioteca Nacional, Alameda 651, Santiago, Chile. bibl. circ. 1,000.
 Formerly (until 1981): Anuario de la Prensa Chilena.

011 BL
COLECAO DE ESTUDOS BIBLIOGRAFICOS. 1976. irreg. Fundacao Casa de Rui Barbosa, Rua Sao Clemente, 134, Botafogo 22260, Rio de Janeiro, RJ, Brazil. Dir. Olavo Brasil de Lima Junior.

COLLEGE ALUMNI PUBLICATIONS. see *COLLEGE AND ALUMNI* — *Abstracting, Bibliographies, Statistics*

500 016 BE ISSN 0080-0937
COMMISSION BELGE DE BIBLIOGRAPHIE, REPERTOIRE DES COMPTES-RENDUS DE CONGRES SCIENTIFIQUES. (Subseries of: Bibliographia Belgica) irreg. Commission Belge de Bibliographie, Rue des Tanneurs 80-84, B-1000 Brussels, Belgium.

010 UK ISSN 0306-1124
COMMONWEALTH BIBLIOGRAPHIES. 1974. irreg. Commonwealth Institute, Kensington High St., London W8 6NQ, England.

015 070.5 JA
CONTEMPORARY JAPANESE BOOKS. 1976. a. free. Publishers Association for Cultural Exchange, 2-1, Sarugaku-cho 1-chome, Chiyoda-ku, Tokyo 101, Japan. (back issues avail.)
 Formerly (until 1985): Annotated Catalogue of Books Published in Japan.

CORNELL UNIVERSITY. MODERN INDONESIA PROJECT PUBLICATIONS. MONOGRAPHS, TRANSLATIONS, BIBLIOGRAPHIES. see *ORIENTAL STUDIES*

CUMULATIVE BIBLIOGRAPHY OF LITERATURE EXAMINED BY THE RADIATION SHIELDING INFORMATION CENTER. see *PHYSICS* — *Abstracting, Bibliographies, Statistics*

655 011 US ISSN 0011-300X
CUMULATIVE BOOK INDEX; a world list of books in the English Language. 1898. 11/yr. (q. and a. cumulations) service basis. ‡ H. W. Wilson Co., 950 University Ave, Bronx, NY 10452. TEL 212-588-8400. Ed. Nancy Wong. (also avail. in microform from UMI; reprint service avail. from UMI; avail on CD-ROM)
 ●Also available online. Vendors: Wilsonline.

016 FR
CURIOSPRESS INTERNATIONAL; annuaire international des editeurs de publications etranges et curieuses. (Text in English, French, German, Italian, Spanish) 1974. biennial. 45 F. c/o Ed. Pierre Birukoff, INFOS al International, B.P. 127, 75563 Paris 12, France. illus.

CURRENT CHRISTIAN BOOKS. see *RELIGIONS AND THEOLOGY* — *Abstracting, Bibliographies, Statistics*

CURRENT CONTENTS/ARTS & HUMANITIES. see *HUMANITIES: COMPREHENSIVE WORKS* — *Abstracting, Bibliographies, Statistics*

011 JA ISSN 0386-7293
CURRENT CONTENTS OF ACADEMIC JOURNALS IN JAPAN. (Text in English) 1971. a. 9000 Yen. Center for Academic Publications Japan, Yayoi 2-chome, Bunkyo-ku, Tokyo 113, Japan. Ed. Ichiro Suzuki. circ. 1,000.

011 MY ISSN 0127-1555
CURRENT MALAYSIAN SERIALS (NON-GOVERNMENT)/TERBITAN BERSIRI KINI MALAYSIA (BUKAN KERAJAAN) (Text in English, Malay) 1976. irreg. M.$35. National Library of Malaysia - Perpustakaan Negara Malaysia, Wisma Thakurdas, Jalan Raja Laut, 51200 Kuala Lumpur, Malaysia (Orders to: Kedai Buku Koperatif, University Malaya, Bhd. No.7, Lorong 51A.227A, 46100 Petaling Jaya, Malaysia) Ed. Amanah Ahmad Omar. circ. 224.
 Formerly: Current Malaysian Serials/Terbitan Bersiri Kini Malaysia.

CURRENT RESEARCH IN FRENCH STUDIES AT UNIVERSITIES AND POLYTECHNICS IN THE UNITED KINGDOM. see *LINGUISTICS* — *Abstracting, Bibliographies, Statistics*

DANIA POLYGLOTTA; literature on Denmark in languages other than Danish and books of Danish interest published abroad. see *LITERATURE* — *Abstracting, Bibliographies, Statistics*

016 DK ISSN 0084-9715
DENMARK. RIGSBIBLIOTEKAREMBEDT. ACCESSIONSKATALOG; faelleskatalog over danske videnskabelige og faglige bibliotekers erhvervelser af udenlandsk litteratur. (Text in Danish and English) 1901. a. price varies. Rigsbibliotekarembedet, Nyhavn 31E, DK-1051 Copenhagen K, Denmark. Ed. Gerd Borgen Nielsen. circ. 500. (also avail. in microfiche)
 ●Also available online.

DEUTSCHER WETTERDIENST. BIBLIOGRAPHIEN. see *METEOROLOGY* — *Abstracting, Bibliographies, Statistics*

053 015 GW ISSN 0419-005X
DEUTSCHSPRACHIGE ZEITSCHRIFTEN DEUTSCHLAND - OESTERREICH - SCHWEIZ. 1956. a. DM.73.70. Verlag der Schillerbuchhandlung Hans Banger, Guldenbachstr. 1, D-5000 Cologne 41, W. Germany (B.R.D.)
 Formerly: Anschriften Deutschsprachiger Zeitschriften (ISSN 0066-460X)

020 011 US ISSN 0146-7085
DIRECTORY INFORMATION SERVICE; an annotated guide to business and industrial directories, professional and scientific rosters, directory databases, and other lists and guides of all kinds. (Supplement to: Directory of Directories) 1977. irreg. (2 every 18 months) $130. Gale Research Company, Book Tower, Detroit, MI 48226. Eds. Cecilia Ann Marlow, Robert C. Thomas. cum.index.

DIRECTORY OF AUSTRALIAN ASSOCIATIONS. see *ABSTRACTING AND INDEXING SERVICES*

011 020 338 US
DIRECTORY OF COMPUTERIZED DATA FILES. a. $48. U.S. National Technical Information Service, 5285 Port Royal Rd., Springfield, VA 22152. TEL 703-487-4650. (also avail. in microfiche; magnetic tape)

011 UK ISSN 0275-5580
DIRECTORY OF DIRECTORIES; an annotated guide to business and industrial directories, professional and scientific rosters, and other lists and guides of all kinds. (Supplement avail.: Directory Information Service) 1980. irreg., latest 4th edt., 1986. $185. Kogan Page Ltd., 120 Pentonville Rd., London N1 9JM, England (Dist. in U.S. and Canada by: Gale Research Company, Book Tower, Detroit, MI 48226) Eds. Cecilia Ann Marlow, Robert C. Thomas.

011 US
DIRECTORY OF DISTINGUISHED AMERICANS. 1982. a. $45. American Biographical Institute, Inc., Governing Board of Editors, Box 31226, 5126 Bur Oak Circle, Raleigh, NC 27622. Ed. J.M. Evans. circ. 5,000.

015 IR ISSN 0084-9960
DIRECTORY OF IRANIAN PERIODICALS. (Edition in Persian only) 1970. a. $20. National Library of Iran, 30 Tir St., Teheran, Iran. circ. 1,000.

DIRECTORY OF SMALL MAGAZINE/PRESS EDITORS AND PUBLISHERS. see *PUBLISHING AND BOOK TRADE* — *Abstracting, Bibliographies, Statistics*

010 US ISSN 0085-0020
DIRECTORY OF THE COLLEGE STUDENT PRESS IN AMERICA. 1965. quadrennial. $75. Oxbridge Communications, Inc., 150 Fifth Ave., New York, NY 10011. TEL 212-741-0231. Ed. Dario Politella.

BIBLIOGRAPHIES

016　　　　　　US　ISSN 0307-6075
DISSERTATION ABSTRACTS INTERNATIONAL. SECTION C: EUROPEAN ABSTRACTS. 1976. q. $345. University Microfilms International, 300 North Zeeb Road, Ann Arbor, MI 48106. TEL 313-761-4700. Indexed: Nutr.Abstr. Br.Archaeol.Abstr. Dairy Sci.Abstr. Field Crop Abstr. Food Sci.& Tech.Abstr. GeoRef. Geotech.Abstr. Herb.Abstr. Ind.Vet. Rural Recreat.Tour.Abstr. Vet.Bull. Weed Abstr. World Agri.Econ.& Rural Sociol.Abstr.

DOCTORAL DISSERTATIONS ON TRANSPORTATION. see *TRANSPORTATION — Abstracting, Bibliographies, Statistics*

016.33　　　　BL　ISSN 0101-4854
DOCUMENTACAO AMAZONICA; catalogo coletivo. 1974. irreg. free. Superintendencia do Desenvolvimento da Amazonia, Travessa Antonio Baena 1113, Cx. Postal 874, Belem, Para, Brazil. (Prepared by: Rede de Bibliotecas da Amazonia) stat.
Economic conditions in the Amazon valley

016　　　　　　IT　ISSN 0070-6906
DOCUMENTI SULLE ARTI DEL LIBRO. 1962. irreg., latest issue 1986. price varies. Edizioni Il Polifilo, Via Borgonuovo 2, 20121 Milan, Italy. Ed. Alberto Vigevani.

DRUG ABUSE BIBLIOGRAPHY. see *DRUG ABUSE AND ALCOHOLISM — Abstracting, Bibliographies, Statistics*

EAST ASIA BIBLIOGRAPHY; a review of new publications on China & the Far East. see *BUSINESS AND ECONOMICS — Abstracting, Bibliographies, Statistics*

011　　　　　　US
EAST ASIA LIBRARY SERIES. 1978. irreg., vol.5 in prep. (Hoover Institution, East Asian Collection) Stanford University, 219 Lou Henry Hoover Bldg., Stanford, IL 94305. TEL 415-497-4272. (Co-sponsor: University of California, Berkeley)

015　　　　　　BE
EDITEURS BELGES DE LANGUE FRANCAISE ET LEURS LIVRES. (Text in French) 1960. a. free. ‡ Association des Editeurs Belge, 111 Avenue du Parc, 1060 Brussels, Belgium. adv. circ. 17,000.
Former titles: Livres Belges de Langue Francaise; Livres Belges.

EGYPTIAN MUSEUM. LIBRARY. CATALOGUE. see *ARCHAEOLOGY — Abstracting, Bibliographies, Statistics*

ERLANGER BAUSTEINE ZUR FRAENKISCHEN HEIMATFORSCHUNG. see *HISTORY*

015　　　　　　GW　ISSN 0071-1462
ESSENER BIBLIOGRAPHIE. 1970. a. price varies. Stadtbibliothek Essen, Hindenburgstr. 25, Essen, W. Germany (B.R.D.) Ed. Alfred Peter. circ. 1,500.

ESTUARIES AND COASTAL WATERS OF THE BRITISH ISLES; an annual bibliography of recent scientific papers. see *BIOLOGY — Abstracting, Bibliographies, Statistics*

015　　　　　　ET　ISSN 0071-1772
ETHIOPIAN PUBLICATIONS: BOOKS, PAMPHLETS, ANNUALS AND PERIODICAL ARTICLES. 1963. a. $5. Addis Ababa University, Institute of Ethiopian Studies, Box 1176, Addis Ababa, Ethiopia. Eds. Degife Gabre-Tsadik, Mergia Diro. circ. 500. (back issues avail.)

ETUDES STRATEGIQUES ET MILITAIRES (COLLECTION) see *LINGUISTICS — Abstracting, Bibliographies, Statistics*

EUROPEAN BIBLIOGRAPHY OF SOVIET, EAST EUROPEAN AND SLAVONIC STUDIES/ BIBLIOGRAPHIE EUROPEENE DES TRAVAUX SUR L'URSS ET L'EUROPE DE L'EST/EUROPAISCHE BIBLIOGRAPHIE DER SOWJET- UND OESTEUROPASTUDIEN. see *HISTORY — Abstracting, Bibliographies, Statistics*

EUROPEAN ORGANIZATION FOR NUCLEAR RESEARCH. LISTE DES PUBLICATIONS SCIENTIFIQUES/LIST OF SCIENTIFIC PUBLICATIONS. see *PHYSICS — Abstracting, Bibliographies, Statistics*

010 060　　　　NE　ISSN 0071-3139
EUROPEAN YEARBOOK. 1956. a., except 1964. price varies. (Council of Europe, FR) Martinus Nijhoff Publishers, Postbus 163, 3300 AD Dordrecht, Netherlands. Ed. P. Drillien.

EXTENSION BIBLIOGRAFICA. see *SOCIAL SCIENCES: COMPREHENSIVE WORKS — Abstracting, Bibliographies, Statistics*

FARM AND GARDEN PERIODICALS ON MICROFILM. see *GARDENING AND HORTICULTURE — Abstracting, Bibliographies, Statistics*

016.05　　　　US　ISSN 0275-8466
FAXON LIBRARIANS' GUIDE TO SERIALS. 1931. a. $25 (free to qualified personnel) Faxon Company, Inc., Faxon Bldg., 15 Southwest Park, Westwood, MA 02090. TEL 617-329-3350. Ed. Kathleen B. Klesh. adv. illus. circ. 20,000. (also avail. in microfiche)
Former titles: Faxon Librarians' Guide (ISSN 0146-2660); Faxon Librarians' Guide to Periodicals (ISSN 0092-0487); Faxon Indexed Periodicals.

011 956 011　　　LE
FIHRIST; index to Arabic periodical literature. (Text in Arabic; occasionally in English, French, German, Spanish) 1981. q. £L500($200) Al-Fihrist Academic Research Institute, Abu Hishmah Bldg., Farabi St., Watwat (al-zarif), P.O. Box 14/5968, Beirut, Lebanon (Subcr. to: Syrian Lebanese Commerical Bank (Account no. for Al-Fihrist 20195), Hamra Branch, P.O. Box 118701, Beirut, Lebanon) Ed. Samir Shaykh. adv. bk. rev. index. circ. 1,500.

015　　　　　　FJ
FIJI NATIONAL BIBLIOGRAPHY. (Text in English) 1979. a. 5 F.($2.15) Ministry of Education, Library Service of Fiji, P.O. Box 2526, Government Bldg., Suva, Fiji. Ed. Humesh Prasad. index. circ. 600. (back issues avail.)

FILMATISEREDE BOEGER. see *MOTION PICTURES*

015　　　　　　FI　ISSN 0356-178X
FINK-S. (Text in English, Finnish, Swedish) 1974. a. Fmk.180. Helsingin Yliopiston Kirjasto, Box 312, 00171 Helsinki, Finland.

010　　　　　　FI　ISSN 0071-5298
FINLAND. POSTI-JA LENNATINLAITOS. KOTIMAISTEN SANOMALEHTIEN HINNASTO. INHEMSK TIDNINGSTAXA. (Text in Finnish and Swedish) 1855. a. Fmk.14. Posti- ja Lennatinlaitos - General Direction of Posts and Telegraphs, Mannerheimintie 11, SF-00100 Helsinki 10, Finland. index.

FOR YOUNGER READERS, BRAILLE AND TALKING BOOKS (LARGE PRINT EDITION) see *BLIND — Abstracting, Bibliographies, Statistics*

DIE FRAUENFRAGE IN DEUTSCHLAND. BIBLIOGRAPHIE. see *WOMEN'S INTERESTS — Abstracting, Bibliographies, Statistics*

016.054　　　　US　ISSN 0362-5044
FRENCH PERIODICAL INDEX/REPERTORIEX. (Text in French) 1974. a. $34. Ponchie & Co., c/o Jean-P. Ponchie, Ed., Chitwood Hall, Foreign Language Department, West Virginia University, Morgantown, WV 26506. bk. rev. circ. 400.

FRENCH 17; an annual descriptive bibliography of French seventeenth century studies. see *HISTORY — Abstracting, Bibliographies, Statistics*

016 840　　　　US　ISSN 0085-0888
FRENCH 20 BIBLIOGRAPHY; CRITICAL AND BIOGRAPHICAL REFERENCES FOR THE STUDY OF FRENCH LITERATURE SINCE 1885. 1949. a. $78. (French Institute-Alliance Francaise) Associated University Presses, 440 Forsgate Dr., Cranbury, NJ 08512. TEL 609-655-4770. Ed. Douglas W. Alden. circ. 1,200.
Supersedes: French 7 Bibliography, Critical and Biographical References for the Study of Contemporary French Literature.

FUNDHEFT FUER ARBEITS- UND SOZIALRECHT; systematischer Nachweis der deutschen Rechtsprechung, Zeitschriftenaufsaetze und selbstaendigen Schriften. see *LAW — Abstracting, Bibliographies, Statistics*

011　　　　　　US
GALE DIRECTORY OF PUBLICATIONS. 1869. a. Gale Research Co., Book Tower, Detroit, MI 48226. circ. 11,000.
Former titles (until 1987): I M S Directory of Publications; Until 1982: Ayer Directory of Publications (ISSN 0145-1642); Ayer Directory of Newspapers, Magazines, and Trade Publications (ISSN 0067-2696)

015　　　　　　GW
GERMANY (FEDERAL REPUBLIC, 1949-). DEUTSCHER BUNDESTAG. WISSENSCHAFTLICHE DIENSTE. BIBLIOGRAPHIEN. 1962. irreg. free. Deutscher Bundestag, Verwaltung, Hauptabteilung Wissenschaftliche Dienste, Bundeshaus, 5300 Bonn, W. Germany (B.R.D.)

015　　　　　　GW　ISSN 0344-9130
GERMANY (FEDERAL REPUBLIC, 1949-). DEUTSCHER BUNDESTAG. WISSENSCHAFTLICHE DIENSTE. MATERIALIEN. 1965. irreg. free. Deutscher Bundestag, Verwaltung, Hauptabteilung Wissenschaftliche Dienste, Bundeshaus, 5300 Bonn, W. Germany (B.R.D.)

013　　　　　　AU　ISSN 0072-4165
GESAMTVERZEICHNIS OESTERREICHISCHER DISSERTATIONEN. 1967. a. Verband der Wissenschaftlichen Gesellschaften Oesterreichs, Lindengasse 37, A-1070 Vienna, Austria.

015　　　　　　GH　ISSN 0072-4378
GHANA NATIONAL BIBLIOGRAPHY. 1965. a. $20. Ghana Library Board, Research Library on African Affairs, Box 2970, Accra, Ghana. circ. 200.

011　　　　　　DK　ISSN 0107-5209
GODE LYDBOEGER. 1981. a. Kr.442.61. Bibliotekscentralen, Tempovej 7-11, DK-2750 Ballerup, Denmark. illus.
Formerly: Lydbogskatalog.

015.73　　　　US　ISSN 0072-5188
GOVERNMENT REFERENCE BOOKS; a biennial guide to U.S. Government publications. 1968/69. biennial. $47.50. Libraries Unlimited, Inc., Box 263, Littleton, CO 80160. TEL 303-770-1220. Ed. Leroy C. Schwarzkopf.

GREAT BRITAIN. ROYAL COMMISSION ON HISTORICAL MANUSCRIPTS. ACCESSIONS TO REPOSITORIES AND REPORTS ADDED TO THE NATIONAL REGISTER OF ARCHIVES. see *HISTORY — Abstracting, Bibliographies, Statistics*

GREAT BRITAIN. ROYAL COMMISSION ON HISTORICAL MANUSCRIPTS. COMMISSIONERS' REPORTS TO THE CROWN. see *HISTORY — Abstracting, Bibliographies, Statistics*

GREAT BRITAIN. ROYAL COMMISSION ON HISTORICAL MANUSCRIPTS. JOINT PUBLICATION. see *HISTORY — Abstracting, Bibliographies, Statistics*

050　　　　　　IT
GUIDA DELLA STAMPA PERIODICA ITALIANA. 1969. irreg., 7th edt., 1984. L.30000. Unione della Stampa Periodica Italiana, Via Nazionale 163, 00184 Rome, Italy. adv.

016 658.8　　　US　ISSN 0533-5248
GUIDE TO AMERICAN DIRECTORIES. 1954. biennial. $55. B. Klein Publications, Box 8503, Coral Springs, FL 33065. TEL 305-752-1708. Ed. Bernard Klein.

GUIDE TO AMERICAN SCIENTIFIC AND TECHNICAL DIRECTORIES. see *TECHNOLOGY: COMPREHENSIVE WORKS — Abstracting, Bibliographies, Statistics*

GUIDE TO COLLECTIONS OF MANUSCRIPTS RELATING TO AUSTRALIA. see *HISTORY — Abstracting, Bibliographies, Statistics*

050 015　　　II　ISSN 0017-5285
GUIDE TO INDIAN PERIODICAL LITERATURE. (Text in English) 1964. q.(annual cumulation) Rs.700($95) (includes annual cumulation.) Indian Documentation Service, Patal Nagar, Post Box No. 13, Gurgaon 122 001, Haryana, India. Ed. Vijay Kumar Jain. adv.

011 020 070.5   US   ISSN 0164-0747
GUIDE TO MICROFORMS IN PRINT. AUTHOR,
TITLE. 1975. a. $129.50. Meckler Publishing, 11
Ferry Lane West, Westport, CT 06880. TEL 203-
226-6967. Ed. Ardis V. Carleton. adv. circ. 2,000.
　　Supersedes in part: Guide to Microforms in Print
(ISSN 0017-5293); Incorporates: International
Microforms in Print.

017   US   ISSN 0163-8386
GUIDE TO MICROFORMS IN PRINT. SUBJECT.
Variant title: Subject Guide to Microforms in Print.
1975. a. $149.50. Meckler Publishing, 11 Ferry
Lane West, Westport, CT 06880. TEL 203-226-
6967. Ed. Ardis V. Carleton. index. circ. 1,500.
　　Incorporates: International Microforms in Print.

011   US
GUIDE TO MICROFORMS IN PRINT.
SUPPLEMENT. 1979. a. $65. Meckler Publishing,
11 Ferry Lane West, Westport, CT 06880. TEL
203-226-6967. adv. bibl. circ. 1,000. (back issues
avail.)
　　Former titles: Microforms in Print. Supplement
(ISSN 0164-0739); Microlist (ISSN 0362-1014)

016 070   CN   ISSN 0315-7288
GUIDE TO PERIODICALS AND NEWSPAPERS
IN THE PUBLIC LIBRARIES OF
METROPOLITAN TORONTO. 1970. a.
Can.$29.50. Metropolitan Toronto Library Board,
789 Yonge St., Toronto, Ontario M4W 2G8,
Canada. TEL 416-824-5150.
　　Formerly: Toronto. Public Libraries. Guide to
Serials Currently Received in the Public Libraries of
Metropolitan Toronto.

011.02   US   ISSN 0072-8624
GUIDE TO REFERENCE BOOKS. 1902. irreg.,
latest 10th edt. 1986; supplement issued once every
2 years. price varies. American Library Association,
50 E. Huron St., Chicago, IL 60611. TEL 312-944-
6780. Ed. Eugene Sheehy.

GUIDE TO REFERENCE BOOKS FOR SCHOOL
MEDIA CENTERS. see LIBRARY AND
INFORMATION SCIENCES

011   UK   ISSN 0072-8640
GUIDE TO REFERENCE MATERIAL. 1959. irreg.,
4th edt. 1980. price varies. Library Association
Publishing Ltd., 7 Ridgmount St., London WC1E
7AE, England. Ed. A.J. Walford. index.

011   US   ISSN 0072-8667
GUIDE TO REPRINTS. (Text in English, French,
German, Italian, Latin and Spanish) 1967. a. $110.
Guide to Reprints, Inc., Box 249, Kent, CT 06757.
Ed. Ann S. Davis. adv. circ. 2,000.

GUIDE TO U S GOVERNMENT PUBLICATIONS.
see ABSTRACTING AND INDEXING
SERVICES

016 300   IS
HARRY S. TRUMAN RESEARCH INSTITUTE
FOR THE ADVANCEMENT OF PEACE.
REPRINT SERIES. (Text in English) 1971. irreg.
exchange basis. Hebrew University of Jerusalem,
Harry S. Truman Research Institute for the
Advancement of Peace, Mount Scopus, Jerusalem,
Israel. Ed. Norma Schneider. bibl. circ. 500.
　　Formerly: Harry S. Truman Research Institute,
Jerusalem. Occasional Papers.

026 059.992   US
HARVARD-YENCHING LIBRARY
BIBLIOGRAPHICAL SERIES. 1970. irreg.,
approx. every 4 or 5 yrs., latest 1981. price varies.
Harvard-Yenching Library, 2 Divinity Ave.,
Cambridge, MA 02138. TEL 617-495-3327. circ.
200.

015   US
HESSISCHE BIBLIOGRAPHIE. 1977. a. price varies.
(Stadt- und Universitatsbibliothek Frankfurt am
Main) K.G. Saur, Inc., 175 Fifth Ave., New York,
NY 10010.

015   GW   ISSN 0170-2408
HIERSEMANNS BIBLIOGRAPHISCHE
HANDBUECHER. 1979. irreg., vol.7, 1987. price
varies. Anton Hiersemann Verlag, Rosenbergstr.
113, Postfach 723, 7000 Stuttgart 1, W. Germany
(B.R.D.)

HIGHER EDUCATION ABSTRACTS; abstracts of
periodical literature, monographs and conference
papers on college students, faculty and
administration. see EDUCATION — Higher
Education

015   AT
HISTORICAL SOCIETY OF SOUTH AUSTRALIA.
GUIDESHEET. 1978. irreg. free. Historical Society
of South Australia Inc., Institute Bldg., 122 Kintore
Ave., Adelaide, SA 5000, Australia. Ed. B. Samuels.
circ. 1,994.

011   AG   ISSN 0073-327X
HONTANAR.* irreg. Editorial Universitaria de
Buenos Aires, Riva Davia 1571-1573, Buenos Aires,
Argentina.

001 011   GW   ISSN 0020-9201
I B Z. (International Bibliography of Periodical
Literature from all Fields of Knowledge) N.S. 1965.
12 vols./yr. DM.4700 (cloth bound) Felix Dietrich
Verlag, Jahnstr. 15, Postfach 1949, 4500
Osnabrueck, W. Germany (B.R.D.) Ed. Otto Zeller.
index.

016   II   ISSN 0073-6627
I N S D O C UNION CATALOGUE SERIES. irreg.,
no.16, 1976. Indian National Scientific
Documentation Centre, Hillside Rd., New Delhi
110012, India. Ed. S.N. Dutta.

297 016   UK   ISSN 0306-9524
INDEX ISLAMICUS. (Cumulates Quarterly Index
Islamicus) quinquennial. price varies. (University of
London, School of Oriental and African Studies)
Mansell Publishing Ltd., 6 All Saints St., London
N1 9RL, England (Dist. in U.S. by: H. W. Wilson
Co., 950 University Ave., Bronx, NY 10452)

050 016.5   IO   ISSN 0216-6216
INDEX OF INDONESIAN LEARNED
PERIODICALS/INDEKS MADJALAH ILMIAH.
(Text in Indonesian with English translations) 1960.
s-a. $15. Indonesian Institute of Sciences - Lembaga
Ilmu Pengetahuan Indonesia, Jalan Jenderal Gatot
Subroto, P.O. Box 3065/JKT, Indonesia. Ed.
Hendrarta Kusbandarrumsamsi. index. circ. 1,000.
Indexed: E.I.

015   US
INDEX TO COLORADO STATE PUBLICATIONS.
1977. q. with a. 5 yr. cum. $10 (microfiche only)
State Library, 201 E. Colfax Ave., Denver, CO
80203. TEL 303-866-6728. Ed. Barbara L. Wagner.
circ. 500. (also avail. in microfiche)
　　Formerly: COIN: Indexed Checklist to Colorado
State Publications.

016 059   PH   ISSN 0073-599X
INDEX TO PHILIPPINE PERIODICALS. 1946. s-a.
$18. University of the Philippines Library, Indexing
Section, Gonzalez Hall, Diliman, Quezon City 3004,
Philippines. circ. 1,000.
　　Formerly (until 1960): Index to Philippine
Periodical Literature.

011   US   ISSN 0161-4029
INDEX TO REVIEWS OF BIBLIOGRAPHICAL
PUBLICATIONS. 1976. a. price varies.
(Bibliographical society of Northern Illinois)
Whitston Publishing Co. Inc., Box 958, Troy, NY
12181. Ed. Thomas R. Liszka. circ. 200.

950   II   ISSN 0073-6090
INDIA: A REFERENCE ANNUAL. (Text in
English) 1953. a. $23. Ministry of Information and
Broadcasting, Research and Reference Division,
Publications Division, Patiala House, Tilak Marg,
New Delhi 110001, India (U.S. subscr. address: M/
S Inter Culture Associates, Thompson, CT 06277)
circ. 20,000.

011   II
INDIAN BOOKS IN PRINT. a. Rs.675. Indian
Bibliographies Bureau, 2153/2 Chah Indara,
Fountain, Delhi 110006, India (Dist. by: UBS
Publisher's Distributors Ltd., 5 Ansari Rd., New
Delhi 110002, India)

015   II   ISSN 0019-6002
INDIAN NATIONAL BIBLIOGRAPHY. (Sanskrit
fascicule in Devanagari script available for 1958-62,
1963-67) (Text in English) 1957. m. (q. before
1964); annual cumulations. Rs.360($129.40) price
varies for annual volumes. National Library, Central
Reference Library, Belvedere, Calcutta 700 027,
India. circ. 500.
　　Bibliographical record of current India
publications received by the National Library under
the Delivery of Books (Public Libraries) Act

015   II   ISSN 0073-6708
INDIAN STATISTICAL INSTITUTE. LIBRARY.
BIBLIOGRAPHIC SERIES.* (Text in English)
1959. irreg. price varies. Indian Statistical Institute,
Library, Asutosh Bldg., Calcutta 12, India.

617.6 016   AG   ISSN 0325-0679
INDICE DE LA LITERATURA DENTAL
PERIODICA EN CASTELLANO. Cover title:
Indice de la Literatura Dental en Castellano. 1950.
2/yr. $40. Asociacion Odontologica Argentina,
Junin 959, Buenos Aires, Argentina. bibl. circ. 300.
　　Continues: Indice de la Literatura Dental
Periodica en Castellano y Portugues.

011   US
INDIVIDUALLY PACED OR SELF TEACHING
INSTRUCTION SOURCE BOOK. 1985. a. or 2/
yr. $55.50. Carl H. Hendershot, Ed. & Pub., 4114
Ridgewood, Bay City, MI 48706. TEL 517-684-
3148. circ. 2,500. (back issues avail.)
　　Supersedes: Programmed Learning and
Individually Paced Instruction-Bibliography.

011   AT   ISSN 0310-6659
INDONESIAN ACQUISITIONS LIST/DAFTAR
PENGADAAN BAHAN INDONESIA. 1971.
irreg. Aus.$15. National Library of Australia, Sales
and Subscription Section, Canberra, A.C.T. 2600,
Australia. circ. 300.

010   FR   ISSN 0073-8034
INITIATION. SERIE TEXTES, BIBLIOGRAPHIES.
1959. irreg. price varies. Editions Cujas, 4,6,8, rue
de la Maison-Blanche, 75013 Paris, France.

011 020   BE
INSTITUT PROVINCIAL D'ETUDES ET
RECHERCHES BIBLIOTHECONOMIQUES.
MEMOIRES. 1978. irreg. Institut Provincial
d'Etudes et Recherches Bibliotheconomiques, 15 rue
des Croisiers, B-4000 Leige, Belgium. bk. rev. abstr.
bibl. circ. 1,000. (back issues avail.)

015   CK   ISSN 0073-991X
INSTITUTO CARO Y CUERVO. SERIE
BIBLIOGRAFICA. 1960. irreg., no.13, 1978. price
varies. Instituto Caro y Cuervo, Seccion de
Publicaciones, Apdo. Aereo 51502, Bogota,
Colombia.

INTERNATIONAL BOOKS IN PRINT; English-
language titles published outside the USA and Great
Britain. see PUBLISHING AND BOOK
TRADE — Abstracting, Bibliographies, Statistics

INTERNATIONAL DIRECTORY OF LITTLE
MAGAZINES AND SMALL PRESSES. see
PUBLISHING AND BOOK TRADE —
Abstracting, Bibliographies, Statistics

INTERNATIONAL OMBUDSMAN INSTITUTE
BIBLIOGRAPHY. see LAW — Abstracting,
Bibliographies, Statistics

INTERNATIONAL PERIODICALS AND
REFERENCE WORKS. see JOURNALISM —
Abstracting, Bibliographies, Statistics

010   GW   ISSN 0074-9672
INTERNATIONALE BIBLIOGRAPHIE DER
FACHADRESSBUECHER/INTERNATIONAL
BIBLIOGRAPHY OF SPECIAL DIRECTORIES.
1962. irreg., 7th edt., 1983. price varies. K.G. Saur
Verlag KG, Poessenbacherstr. 12 B, Postfach
711009, 8000 Munich 71, W. Germany (B.R.D.)
(U.S. and Canadian subscr. to: K.G. Saur Inc., 175
Fifth Ave., New York, N.Y. 10010) adv. (Reprint
service avail. from UMI, ISI)

BIBLIOGRAPHIES

011　　　　　　　　GE
INTERNATIONALE BIBLIOGRAPHIE ZUR DEUTSCHEN KLASSIK 1750-1850. 1960. a. DM.126. Zentralbibliothek der Deutschen Klassik, Platz der Demokratie 1, 5300 Weimar, E. Germany (D.D.R.) Eds. Hans Henning, Siegfried Seifert. adv. bk. rev. index. (back issues avail.)

016 020　　　　GW ISSN 0535-5079
INVENTARE NICHTSTAATLICHER ARCHIVE. 1952. irreg., no.25, 1981. price varies. (Landschaftsverband Rheinland, Archivberatungsstelle) Rheinland-Verlag, Kennedy-Ufer 2, 5000 Cologne 21, W. Germany (B.R.D.) (Distr. by: Rudolf Habelt Verlag, Am Buchenhang 1, 5300 Bonn, W. Germany (B.R.D.))

015　　　　IR　ISSN 0075-0522
IRANIAN NATIONAL BIBLIOGRAPHY. 1963. biennial. price varies. National Library of Iran, 30 Tir St., Teheran, Iran. Ed.Bd. circ. 2,000.

010　　　　US　ISSN 0000-0043
IRREGULAR SERIALS AND ANNUALS; an international directory. (Supplement avail.: Bowker International Serials Database Update) 1967. a. $159.95. R.R. Bowker Company, Database Publishing Group, 245 W. 17th St., New York, NY 10011. TEL 800-521-8110.
● Also available online. Vendors: BRS, DIALOG, European Space Agency.

015 781.7　　　IC
ISLENSK HLJODRITASKRA. (Supplement to Islensk Bokaskra) 1979. a. Landsbokasafn Islands, National Library of Iceland, Safnahusinu, Hverfisgotu 15, Reykjavik 101, Iceland. Ed. Helga Magnusson.

ISTITUTO CENTRALE PER LA PATOLOGIA DEL LIBRO "ALFONSO GALLO." BOLLETTINO. see *PUBLISHING AND BOOK TRADE — Abstracting, Bibliographies, Statistics*

JAHRESBIBLIOGRAPHIE MASSENKOMMUNIKATION. see *COMMUNICATIONS — Abstracting, Bibliographies, Statistics*

011　　　JA　ISSN 0910-7908
JAPAN ENGLISH PUBLICATIONS IN PRINT. (Text in English) 1985. irreg. 26.000 Yen($130) Japan Publications Guide, CPO Box 971, Tokyo 100-91, Japan. bibl.
Formed by the merger of: Japan English Magazine Directory (ISSN 0387-3935) & Japan English Books in Print (ISSN 0388-4201)

015　　　　JA
JAPANESE BOOKS IN PRINT (YEAR) 1977. a. 40000 Yen. Japan Book Publishers Association - Nihon Shoseki Shuppan Kyokai, 6 Fukuromachi, Shinjuku-Ku, Tokyo, Japan. Ed. Toshiyuki Hattori. circ. 7,000.

015.52　　　JA　ISSN 0385-3284
JAPANESE NATIONAL BIBLIOGRAPHY/ZEN NIHON SHUPPANBUTSU SOMOKUROKU. 1948. a. National Diet Library - Kokuritsu Kokkai Toshokan, 1-10-1 Nagata-cho, Chiyoda-ku, Tokyo 100, Japan.

JAZZ INDEX; bibliography of jazz literature in periodicals and collections. see *MUSIC — Abstracting, Bibliographies, Statistics*

956.96 016　　JO
JORDANIAN NATIONAL BIBLIOGRAPHY; annual register of book production in Jordan. (Text in Arabic and English) 1979. a. $20. Jordan Library Association, Box 6289, Amman, Jordan.

016.3　　　US　ISSN 0075-4951
KANSAS STATE UNIVERSITY. LIBRARY BIBLIOGRAPHY SERIES. 1964. irreg., no.15, 1982. price varies. Kansas State University, Library Publications, Manhattan, KS 66506 TEL 913-532-6516. (Order from: Chief Accountant's Office, Kansas State University Libraries, Manhattan, Kansas 66506)

011 370　　　DK　ISSN 0106-7591
KATALOG FOR SKOLEBIBLIOTEKER. EMNEKATOLOG. 1975. a. Kr.1093.30. Bibliotekscentralen, Tempovej 7-11, DK-2750 Ballerup, Denmark.
Supersedes in part: Katalog for Boerne- og Skolebiblioteker; Formerly: Katalog for Skolebiblioteker. Forfatterkatalog (ISSN 0106-7575)

011 370　　　DK　ISSN 0106-7583
KATALOG FOR SKOLEBIBLIOTEKER. TITELKATALOG. 1975. a. Kr.114.75. Bibliotekscentralen, Tempovej 7-11, DK-2750 Ballerup, Denmark.
Supersedes in part: Katalog for Boerne- og Skolebiblioteker.

015　　　YU　ISSN 0350-0411
KATALOG STRANIH SERIJSKIH PUBLIKACIJA U BIBLIOTEKAMA JUGOSLAVIJE. (In 2 vols.) 1972. a. $300 or avail. on exchange basis. Jugoslovenski Bibliografski Institut, Terazije 26, Belgrade, Yugoslavia. Ed. Miloje Rakocevic.

015　　　KE
KENYA. GOVERNMENT PRINTING AND STATIONERY DEPARTMENT. CATALOGUE OF GOVERNMENT PUBLICATIONS. a. or biennial. EAs.5($0.80) Government Printing and Stationery Department, P.O. Box 30128, Nairobi, Kenya.

KODALY INSTITUTE OF CANADA. MONOGRAPH; a selected bibliography of the Kodaly concept of music education. see *MUSIC — Abstracting, Bibliographies, Statistics*

011　　　DK　ISSN 0105-5046
KONGELIGE BIBLIOTEK. FAGBIBLIOGRAFER. 1975. irreg., latest no.15 1985. Kongelige Bibliotek - Royal Library, Christians Brygge 8, DK-1219 Copenhagen K, Denmark.

011　　　DK　ISSN 0105-8215
KONGELIGE BIBLIOTEK. SPECIALHJAELPMIDLER. 1978. irreg., latest no.13 1985. Kongelige Bibliotek - Royal Library, Christians Brygge 8, DK-1219 Copenhagen K, Denmark.

010　　　II　ISSN 0075-6970
KOTHARI'S WORLD OF REFERENCE WORKS. 1963. irreg., latest 1963. $1.50. Kothari Publications, 12 India Exchange Place, Calcutta 700001, India. Ed. H. Kothari. adv.

011　　　US
LARGE TYPE BOOKS IN PRINT. 5th edt. 1982. biennial. $69.95. R.R. Bowker Company, Database Publishing Group, 245 W. 17th St., New York, NY 10011. TEL 800-521-8110.

LATIN AMERICAN STUDIES IN THE UNIVERSITIES OF THE UNITED KINGDOM. see *HISTORY — Abstracting, Bibliographies, Statistics*

LATIN AMERICAN STUDIES IN THE UNIVERSITIES OF THE UNITED KINGDOM. STAFF RESEARCH IN PROGRESS OR RECENTLY COMPLETED IN THE HUMANITIES AND THE SOCIAL SCIENCES. see *HISTORY — Abstracting, Bibliographies, Statistics*

980 015　　SW
LATINOAMERICANA. (Text in Spanish and Swedish) 1978. irreg. free. Latinamerika-Institutet i Stockholm - Institute of Latin American Studies, Stockholm, S-106 91 Stockholm, Sweden.

860 015　　　CK
LEA. 1976. irreg. Carrera 44 no. 47-61, Apdo. Aereo 4307, Medellin, Colombia. Eds. Luis Amadeo Perez, German Suescun.

016　　　US
LEWIS CARROLL SOCIETY OF NORTH AMERICA. CHAPBOOK. Variant title: Carroll Studies. 1975. a. $20. Lewis Carroll Society of North America, 617 Rockford Rd., Silver Spring, MD 20902. Ed. Edward Guiliano. circ. 500.

015　　　CL
LIBRO CHILENO EN VENTA. 1975. biennial. $36. Servicio de Extension de Cultura Chilena, Portugal 12, Depto. 46, Santiago, Chile.

011　　　SP
LIBRORAMA INTERNACIONAL; periodico bibliografico. vol.2, 1976. irreg. free. Elvira 3, Madrid 28, Spain. Ed. Segundo Martin Macias. adv. bk. rev. circ. 40,000.

011　　　SP　ISSN 0377-0974
LIBROS ESPANOLES I S B N. 1973. a. 12.000 ptas.($65) Instituto Nacional del Libro Espanol, Agencia Espanola I S B N, Santiago Rusinol 8, Madrid 3, Spain. circ. 20,000.

015　　　UR
LITERATURA O SAKHALINSKOI OBLASTI. 1968. a. 0.30 Rub. (Sakhalinskaya Oblastnaya Biblioteka) Dal'nevostochnoe Knizhnoe Izdatel'stvo, Sakhalinskoe Otdelenie, Ul. Dzerzhinskogo, 34, Yuzhno-Sakhalinsk, Russian S.F.S.R., U.S.S.R.

016　　　PL　ISSN 0075-9945
LITERATURA PIEKNA. ADNOTOWANY ROCZNIK BIBLIOGRAFICZNY. 1954. a. 370 Zl.($26) (Biblioteka Narodowa-Instytut Bibliograficzny) Stowarzyszenie Bibliotekarzy Polskich, Konopczynskiego 5/7, Warsaw, Poland (Dist. by: Ars Polona-Ruch, Krakowskie Przedmiescie 7, Warsaw, Poland) circ. 5,500.

011　　　UK　ISSN 0265-5810
LITTLE RED BOOK; guide to international journals & periodicals. 1887. a. free. Wm. Dawson and Sons Ltd., Cannon House, Folkestone, Kent CT19 5EE, England.
Formerly: Guide to the Press of the World (ISSN 0072-8748)

016　　　FR
LIVRES DISPONIBLES. 1972. a.(6 vols.) 2900 F.($530) Editions du Cercle de la Librairie, 35 rue Gregoire de Tours, 75006 Paris Cedex 06, France.
Formed by the merger of: Catalogue de l'Edition Francaise (ISSN 0069-1089) & Repertoire des Livres de Langue Francaise Disponibles (ISSN 0080-1003)

400 800 016　　US　ISSN 0024-8215
M L A INTERNATIONAL BIBLIOGRAPHY OF BOOKS AND ARTICLES ON THE MODERN LANGUAGES AND LITERATURES. 1922. a. in 5 vols. $650. Modern Language Association of America, 10 Astor Place, New York, NY 10003. TEL 212-614-6314. Ed. Eileen M. Mackesy. bibl. index. circ. 32,500.
● Also available online. Vendors: DIALOG.

MABUA/FOUNTAIN; religious creation in literature, society and thought. see *LITERATURE*

016 960　　　CN　ISSN 0316-6570
MCGILL UNIVERSITY, MONTREAL. CENTRE FOR DEVELOPING-AREA STUDIES. BIBLIOGRAPHY SERIES. 1972. irreg., no.12, 1986. price varies. McGill University, Centre for Developing-Area Studies, 3715 Peel St. W., Montreal, Que. H3A 1X1, Canada. TEL 514-392-5327. Ed. Rosalind E. Boyd. circ. 800.

MADHYA PRADESH WHO'S WHO. see *BIOGRAPHY*

011　　　US
MAGAZINES FOR LIBRARIES; for the general reader and school, junior college, university and public libraries. 3rd edt. 1978. irreg., 4th edt. 1981; 5th edt. 1986. $95. R.R. Bowker Company, 245 W. 17th St., New York, NY 10011. TEL 800-521-8110. Eds. Bill Katz, Linda Sternberg Katz. Indexed: Bk.Rev.Ind.

016　　　HU　ISSN 0134-1464
MAGYAR IRODALOM ES IRODALOMTUDOMANY BIBLIOGRAFIAJA. 1976. a. 120 Ft. Orszagos Szechenyi Konyvtar, Budavari Palota F, H-1827 Budapest 1, Hungary. Ed. Gyorgy Pajkossy. circ. 600.

016　　　HU　ISSN 0133-3496
MAGYAR KONYVESZET (BUDAPEST. 1961) (Supplement to: Magyar Nemzeti Bibliografia. Konyvek Bibliografiaja (HU 0133-6843)) 1961. a. price varies. Orszagos Szechenyi Konyvtar, Budavari Palota F, H-1827 Budapest 1, Hungary. Ed. Marta Sipos. circ. 1,500.

016　　　HU　ISSN 0231-4592
MAGYAR NEMZETI BIBLIOGRAFIA. IDOSZAKI KIADVANYOK BIBLIOGRAFIAJA. 1981. a. 100 Ft. Orszagos Szechenyi Konyvtar, Budavari Palota F, H-1827 Budapest 1, Hungary. Ed. Nagy Zsoltne. circ. 1,320.
Supersedes in part: Magyar Nemzeti Bibliografia (ISSN 0373-1766); Also supersedes (1976-1980): Kurrens Idoszaki Kiadvanyok (ISSN 0134-0247)

BIBLIOGRAPHIES

015 HU ISSN 0541-9492
MAGYAR TUDOMANYOS AKADEMIA KONYVTARA KEZIRATTARANAK KATALOGUSAI. (Text in Hungarian; summaries in English, French, German) 1966. irreg., vol.15, 1984. exchange basis. Magyar Tudomanyos Akademia Konyvtara, Akademia u. 2, P.O. Box 7, 1361 Budapest 5, Hungary. circ. 800.

011 MW
MALAWI NATIONAL BIBLIOGRAPHY. 1967. a. mK. 5.00. National Archives, Mkulichi Rd., Box 62, Zomba, Malawi. Ed. Dick D. Najira. circ. 200 (controlled) (back issues avail.)

MARINE AFFAIRS BIBLIOGRAPHY; a comprehensive index to marine law and policy literature. see *LAW — Abstracting, Bibliographies, Statistics*

MARX KAROLY KOZGAZDASAGTUDOMANYI EGYETEM OKTATOINAK SZAKIRODALMI MUNKASSAGA. see *BUSINESS AND ECONOMICS — Abstracting, Bibliographies, Statistics*

MARYLAND. GENERAL ASSEMBLY. SUBJECT INDEX TO BILLS INTRODUCED IN THE SESSION. see *LAW*

011 US
MICROFORMS ANNUAL. 1973. biennial. $15 (free to libraries) Microforms International, Pergamon Press, Inc., Fairview Park, Elmsford, NY 10523. TEL 914-592-7700. adv. circ. 15,000.
   Formerly: M I M C Microforms Annual (ISSN 0362-4552)

011 US ISSN 0361-2635
MICROPUBLISHERS' TRADE LIST ANNUAL. Cover title: M T L A, the Micropublishers' Trade List Annual. 1978. a. $149. Chadwyck-Healey Inc., 1021 Prince St., Ste. 101, Alexandria, VA 22314 TEL 703-683-4890. (Distr. in U.K. by: Chadwyck-Healey Ltd., Cambridge Place, Cambridge CB2 1NR, England) index. circ. 300. (microfiche)

015 US ISSN 0748-2302
MINORITIES IN AMERICA. ANNUAL BIBLIOGRAPHY. 1985. irreg. $100. Pennsylvania State University Press, 215 Wagner Bldg., University Park, PA 16802. TEL 814-865-1327. Ed. Wayne Charles Miller.

015 UR
MOSKOVSKII UNIVERSITET. BIBLIOTEKA. RUKOPISNAYA I PECHATNAYA KNIGA V FONDAKH. 1973. irreg. 0.76 Rub. Moskovskii Universitet, Leninskie Gorki, Moscow V-234, Russian S.F.S.R., U.S.S.R. illus.

016 FR ISSN 0085-476X
MUSEUM NATIONAL D'HISTOIRE NATURELLE, PARIS. BIBLIOTHEQUE CENTRALE. LISTE DES PERIODIQUES FRANCAIS ET ETRANGERS. SUPPLEMENT. 1971. a. avail. only on exchange. Museum National d'Histoire Naturelle, Bibliotheque Centrale, 57 rue Cuvier, 75231 Paris 05, France. circ. controlled.

MUSIC & MUSICIANS: BRAILLE SCORES CATALOG - CHORAL (LARGE PRINT EDITION) see *BLIND — Abstracting, Bibliographies, Statistics*

MUSIC & MUSICIANS: BRAILLE SCORES CATALOG - INSTRUMENTAL. see *BLIND — Abstracting, Bibliographies, Statistics*

MUSIC & MUSICIANS: BRAILLE SCORES CATALOG - ORGAN (LARGE PRINT EDITION) see *BLIND — Abstracting, Bibliographies, Statistics*

MUSIC & MUSICIANS: BRAILLE SCORES CATALOG - PIANO (LARGE PRINT EDITION) see *BLIND — Abstracting, Bibliographies, Statistics*

MUSIC & MUSICIANS: BRAILLE SCORES CATALOG - VOCAL (LARGE PRINT EDITION) see *BLIND — Abstracting, Bibliographies, Statistics*

MUSIC & MUSICIANS: INSTRUCTIONAL CASSETTE RECORDINGS CATALOG (LARGE PRINT EDITION) see *BLIND — Abstracting, Bibliographies, Statistics*

MUSIC & MUSICIANS: INSTRUCTIONAL DISC RECORDINGS CATALOG (LARGE PRINT EDITION) see *BLIND — Abstracting, Bibliographies, Statistics*

MUSIC & MUSICIANS: LARGE-PRINT SCORES AND BOOKS CATALOG (LARGE PRINT EDITION) see *BLIND — Abstracting, Bibliographies, Statistics*

011 ZA
NATIONAL BIBLIOGRAPHY OF ZAMBIA. a. 1 n. National Archives, P.O. Box RW 50010, Ridgeway, Lusaka, Zambia. circ. 500. (looseleaf format; back issues avail.)

015 US ISSN 0090-0044
NATIONAL UNION CATALOG OF MANUSCRIPT COLLECTIONS. 1959/61. a. $100. U.S. Library of Congress, Special Materials Cataloging Division, 10 First St. S.E., Washington, DC 20540 TEL 202-287-6100. (Subscriptions to: Cataloging Distribution Service, Library of Congress, Washington, DC 20541)

016 978.9 US
NEW MEXICO; AN ANNOTATED DIRECTORY OF INFORMATION SOURCES. 1971. irreg. $15. Southwest Research and Information Center, P.O. Box 4524, Albuquerque, NM 87106. TEL 505-262-1862. Ed. Peter Montague. circ. 400.

050 011 US ISSN 0028-6680
NEW SERIAL TITLES. (Alphabetical arrangement) 1953. m. with q. and a. cums. $350. U.S. Library of Congress, Serial Record Division, Washington, DC 20540 TEL 202-287-6100. (Orders to: Cataloging Distribution Service, Library of Congress, Washington, DC 20541) (Prepared under the sponsorship of the Joint Committee on the Union List of Serials) circ. 2,250.
   Supersedes: National Register of Microform Masters.
   Supplements Union List of Serials, 3rd edt.

011 US
NEW YORK TIMES SCHOOL MICROFILM COLLECTION INDEX. irreg. University Microfilms International, 300 N. Zeeb Rd., Ann Arbor, MI 48106. Ed. Jack Heher. illus.
   Formerly: New York Times School Microfilm Collection Index by Reels (ISSN 0095-5663)

015 NZ ISSN 0028-8497
NEW ZEALAND NATIONAL BIBLIOGRAPHY. 1966. m. NZ.$100 (annual cum. NZ.$44) National Library of New Zealand, Private Bag, Wellington, New Zealand. circ. 650. (also avail. in microfiche; back issues avail.)

090 CN ISSN 0085-4166
NEWS FROM THE RARE BOOK ROOM. 1964. irreg., latest no.18, 1980. Can.$5 to individuals, free to institutions. ‡ University of Alberta Library, Bruce Peel Special Collections Library, Rutherford South, Edmonton, Alta. T6G 2JR, Canada. TEL 403-432-5998. Ed. John W. Charles. circ. 200. (processed offset)

016 JA
NIHON HAKUSHIROKU. 1955. irreg. 5800 Yen. Kojunsha, 2-9 Kitakarasuyama, Setagaya-ku, Tokyo, Japan. bibl.

015 NO ISSN 0029-1870
NORSK BOKFORTEGNELSE AARSKATALOG. 1903. a. (Universitetet i Oslo, Biblioteket, Norske Avdeling) Norske Bokhandlerforening, Oevre Vollgt. 15, Oslo 1, Norway.

011 US
NOTABLE BOOKS. a. $0.30 (quantity discounts avail.) American Library Association, 50 East Huron St., Chicago, IL 60611. TEL 312-944-6780.

NOTABLE CHILDREN'S TRADE BOOKS IN THE FIELD OF SOCIAL STUDIES. see *SOCIAL SCIENCES: COMPREHENSIVE WORKS — Abstracting, Bibliographies, Statistics*

NOVAYA LITERATURA PO TSENOOBRAZOVANIYU, OPUBLIKOVANNAYA V S.S.S.R; annotirovannyi ukazatel' see *BUSINESS AND ECONOMICS — Abstracting, Bibliographies, Statistics*

011 DK ISSN 0106-035X
NOVELLEREGISTER; titel- og forfatterindeks til novellesamlinger og antologier. 1971. a. Kr.450.80. Bibliotekscentralen, Tempovej 7-11, DK-2750 Ballerup, Denmark.

NUMISMATIC BOOKS IN PRINT. see *HOBBIES — Abstracting, Bibliographies, Statistics*

011 DK ISSN 0108-4321
NYERE DANSK FAGLITTERATUR. SUPPLEMENT. 1977. a. Kr.838.93. Bibliotekscentralen, Tempovej 7-11, DK-2750 Ballerup, Denmark.

011 DK ISSN 0107-5462
ODENSE UNIVERSITETSBIBLIOTEK. TIDSSKRIFTKATALOG. 1975. irreg. Kr.305. Odense Universitetsbibliotek, Campusvej 55, 5230 Odense M, Denmark.

016 US
ON CASSETTE; a comprehensive bibliography of spoken-word audio cassettes. 1985. a. $85. R.R. Bowker Company, Database Publishing Group, 245 W. 17th St., New York, NY 10011. TEL 800-521-8110.

010 US ISSN 0078-5768
OREGON STATE MONOGRAPHS. BIBLIOGRAPHIC SERIES. 1938. irreg., latest no.20. price varies. Oregon State University Press, 101 Waldo Hall, Corvallis, OR 97331. TEL 503-754-3166. (back issues avail.; reprint service avail. from UMI)

548 547 016 NE
ORGANIC AND ORGANOMETALLIC CRYSTAL STRUCTURES; BIBLIOGRAPHY.* (Subseries of Molecular Structures and Dimensions) 1971. irreg. Bohn, Scheltema en Holkema, Postbus 13079, 3507 LB Utrecht, Netherlands (Dist. by Polycrystal Book Service, Box 11567, Pittsburgh, PA. 15238)

330 016 FR ISSN 0474-5086
ORGANIZATION FOR ECONOMIC COOPERATION AND DEVELOPMENT. CATALOGUE OF PUBLICATIONS. a. free. ‡ Organisation for Economic Cooperation and Development, 2, rue Andre Pascal, 75775 Paris 16, France (U.S. orders to: O.E.C.D. Publications and Information Center, 1750 Pennsylvania Ave., N.W., Washington, D.C. 20006) (also avail. in microfiche)

050 FR
ORGANIZATION FOR ECONOMIC COOPERATION AND DEVELOPMENT. LIBRARY. CATALOGUE OF PERIODICALS/CATALOGUE DES PERIODIQUES. 1966. a. free. ‡ Organization for Economic Cooperation and Development, 2 rue Andre Pascal, 75775 Paris 16, France (U. S. orders to: O.E.C.D. Publications and Information Center, 1750 Pennsylvania Ave., N. W., Washington, D. C. 20006) (also avail. in microfiche)

ORGANIZATION FOR ECONOMIC COOPERATION AND DEVELOPMENT. LIBRARY. SPECIAL ANNOTATED BIBLIOGRAPHY: AUTOMATION. BIBLIOGRAPHIE SPECIALE ANALYTIQUE. see *COMPUTERS — Abstracting, Bibliographies, Statistics*

OUTSTANDING SCIENCE TRADE BOOKS FOR CHILDREN. see *CHILDREN AND YOUTH — Abstracting, Bibliographies, Statistics*

010 UK ISSN 0078-7124
OVERSEAS DIRECTORIES, WHO'S WHO, PRESS GUIDES, YEAR BOOKS AND OVERSEAS PERIODICAL SUBSCRIPTIONS. 1947. biennial. £18($55) New Product Newsletter Co. Ltd., 1A Chesterfield St., London W.I., England. Ed. H.R. Vaughan. adv. circ. 5,000. (also avail. in microfilm from UMI)

011 US ISSN 0163-7010
OXBRIDGE DIRECTORY OF NEWSLETTERS. 1979. biennial. $96. Oxbridge Communications, Inc., 150 Fifth Ave., New York, NY 10011. TEL 212-741-0231. Ed. Marge Domenech.

010 UK ISSN 0078-7175
OXFORD BIBLIOGRAPHICAL SOCIETY.
OCCASIONAL PUBLICATIONS. irreg. £7($17) to
individuals; £10 ($24) to institutions; subscr.
includes New Series publications. Oxford
Bibliographical Society, c/o Bodleian Library,
Oxford OX1 3BG, England. Ed.Bd.

010 UK ISSN 0078-7183
OXFORD BIBLIOGRAPHICAL SOCIETY.
PUBLICATIONS. NEW SERIES. 1949. irreg.
£7($17) to individuals; £10($24) to institutions;
subscr. includes Occasional publications. Oxford
Bibliographical Society, c/o Bodleian Library,
Oxford, OX1 3BG, England. Ed.Bd.

PACIFIC ISLANDS STUDIES AND NOTES. see
HISTORY — Abstracting, Bibliographies, Statistics

PANAMA. INSTITUTO DE INVESTIGACION
AGROPECUARIA. BIBLIOGRAFIA. see
*AGRICULTURE — Abstracting, Bibliographies,
Statistics*

015 SP
PANORAMAS BIBLIOGRAFICOS DE ESPANA.
no.2, 1976. irreg. no subscriptions avail. (Biblioteca
Nacional) Ministerio de Cultura, Of. del Secretario
General, Madrid, Spain.

011 II
PATRIKAPANJEE. (Text in Bengali) 1982. a. Rs.50.
Bangla Bhasa Shitya-o-Samaskriti Gabesana
Samastha, c/o Pustak Bipani, 27 Beniatola Lane,
Calcutta 700 009, India. Ed. Asok Kumar Kundu.
bibl. circ. 1,100.

010 KE
PERIODICALS IN EASTERN AFRICAN
LIBRARIES: A UNION LIST. 1965. biennial.
EAs.80($10) University of Nairobi, Library, Box
30197, Nairobi, Kenya.
 Formerly: Periodicals in East African Libraries: a
Union List (ISSN 0079-0877)

011 JA ISSN 0387-7000
PERIODICALS IN PRINT IN JAPAN/ZASSHI
SHIMBUN SOHKATAROGU. (Text in Japanese)
1978. a. 12,500 Yen. Media Research Center Inc.,
5-10-1 Shinjuku, Shinjuku-ku, Tokyo 160, Japan.
Ed. Li-chun Chow. adv. circ. 13,500. (back issues
avail.)
 ●Also available online.

015 PE
PERU. BIBLIOTECA NACIONAL. ANUARIO
BIBLIOGRAFICO PERUANO. 1943. irreg., latest
1972. $4. Biblioteca Nacional, Apartado 2335,
Lima, Peru. Ed. Lucila Valderrama. bk. rev. bibl.
illus. circ. 1,000.

015.599 PH ISSN 0303-190X
PHILIPPINE NATIONAL BIBLIOGRAPHY. 1974.
q. (with a. cumulations) price varies. National
Library, T. M. Kalaw St., Manila, Philippines. Ed.
Lily O. Orbase. circ. 1,000.

015 PH
PHILIPPINES. NATIONAL LIBRARY. T N L
RESEARCH GUIDE SERIES. (The National
Library) Short title: T N L Research Guide Series.
1971. irreg., approx. 2/yr. exchange basis. ‡
National Library, Bibliography Division, T. M.
Kalaw St., Manila, Philippines. Ed. Lily O. Orbase.
circ. 300. (processed)

PLAYWRIGHTS UNION OF CANADA
CATALOGUE OF CANADIAN PLAYS. see
THEATER — Abstracting, Bibliographies, Statistics

011 PL ISSN 0551-651X
POLITECHNIKA POZNANSKA. ZESZYTY
NAUKOWE. BIBLIOGRAFIA. 1962. irreg. price
varies. Politechnika Poznanska, Pl. Curie-
Sklodowskiej 5, Poznan, Poland. Ed. Stanislaw
Badon. circ. 150.

070 015 II ISSN 0445-6653
PRESS IN INDIA. (Issued in two parts) (Text in
English) 1957. a. price varies. Ministry of
Information and Broadcasting, Registrar of
Newspapers for India, Shastri Bhawan, New Delhi,
India (Order from: Controller of Publications,
Government of India, Civil Lines, Delhi 110054,
India) title index. circ. 1,000.
 Newpapers and periodicals

011 070.5 GW ISSN 0176-5248
PRESSE-PORTRAETS; das Angebot des
Pressehandels. 1978. a. DM.10. Presse Fachverlag,
Steindamm 87, D-2000 Hamburg 1, W. Germany
(B.R.D.) circ. 46,000.

013 UK ISSN 0079-5402
PRIVATE PRESS BOOKS; a checklist of books issued
by private presses in the past year. 1960. a.
£10($18) to non-members. Private Libraries
Association, Ravelston, South View Road, Pinner,
Middlesex, England. Ed. Philip Kerrigan. adv.
index. cum.index. circ. 900(approx.)

011 US
PROGRESSIVE PERIODICALS DIRECTORY
UPDATE. 1979. a. $8. Progressive Education, Box
120574, Nashville, TN 37212. Ed. Craig T. Canan.
circ. 1,000.
 Formerly: Southern Progressive Periodicals
Directory Update.

PSYCHOLOGY INFORMATION GUIDE SERIES.
see *PSYCHOLOGY — Abstracting, Bibliographies,
Statistics*

500 300 FR
PUBLICATIONS DE RECHERCHE
SCIENTIFIQUE EN FRANCE/SCHOLARLY
BOOKS IN FRANCE. (Text in English and
French) irreg. 103 bd. Saint Michel, 75005 Paris,
France.

011 020 070.5 US ISSN 0735-665X
PUBLISHERS' CATALOGS ANNUAL. 1979. a.
$190. Chadwyck-Healey Inc., 1021 Prince St., Ste.
101, Alexandria, VA 22314 TEL 703-683-4890.
(Distr. in U.K. by: Chadwyck-Healey Ltd.,
Cambridge Place, Cambridge CB2 1NR, England)
index. circ. 450. (microfiche)

070.5 US ISSN 0079-7855
PUBLISHERS' TRADE LIST ANNUAL; a buying
and reference guide to books and related products.
(In 5 vols.) 1872. a. $165. R.R. Bowker Company,
245 W. 17th St., New York, NY 10011. TEL 800-
521-8110. index.

016 CN ISSN 0706-2257
QUEBEC (PROVINCE) CENTRALE DES
BIBLIOTHEQUES. CHOIX: DOCUMENTATION
AUDIOVISUELLE. (Text in French) 1978. 10/yr.
(with annual cum.) Can.$40($52) Centrale des
Bibliotheques, 1685 Est, rue Fleury, Montreal, Que.
H2C 1T1, Canada. TEL 514-382-0895. circ. 400.
(also avail. in microfiche)
 Formed by the 1984 merger of: Quebec
(Province) Centrale des Bibliotheques. Choix
Jeunesse: Documentation Audiovisuelle (ISSN 0706-
2273)

016 CN ISSN 0706-2249
QUEBEC (PROVINCE) CENTRALE DES
BIBLIOTHEQUES. CHOIX: DOCUMENTATION
IMPRIMEE. (Text in French) 1978. 20/yr. (with
annual cum.) Can.$110($135) Centrale des
Bibliotheques, 1685 Est, rue Fleury, Montreal, Que.
H2C 1T1, Canada. TEL 514-382-0895. circ. 800.
(also avail. in microfiche)

011 CN
QUEBEC (PROVINCE) CENTRALE DES
BIBLIOTHEQUES. PRODUITS ET SERVICES
DOCUMENTAIRES. a. free. Centrale des
Bibliotheques, 1685 Est, rue Fleury, Montreal, Que.
H2C 1T1, Canada. TEL 514-382-0895. Ed.
Francoise Bray. circ. 9,000.
 Formerly: Quebec (Province) Centrale des
Bibliotheques. Services et Publications (ISSN 0227-
289X)

011 US
READER'S GUIDE SERIES. irreg. price varies.
Farrar, Straus & Giroux, Inc., 19 Union Square W.,
New York, NY 10003. TEL 212-741-6900.

RECHTSBIBLIOGRAPHIE/BIBLIOGRAPHIE
JURIDIQUE/LAW BIBLIOGRAPHY. see
LAW — Abstracting, Bibliographies, Statistics

200 016 US ISSN 0000-0868
RELIGIOUS AND INSPIRATIONAL BOOKS AND
SERIALS IN PRINT. 1978. biennial. $89. R.R.
Bowker Company, Database Publishing Group, 245
W. 17th St., New York, NY 10011. TEL 800-521-
8110.
 ●Also available online. Vendors: BRS, DIALOG.
 Formerly: Religious Books and Serials in Print
(ISSN 0000-0612)

016 UK ISSN 0305-960X
RELIGIOUS BOOKS IN PRINT. 1974. a. £25. J.
Whitaker & Sons Ltd., 12 Dyott St., London WC1A
1DF, England (Dist. in Canada by: Academic Press,
55 Barber Greene Rd., Don Mills, Ont. M3C 2AL,
Canada)

016 GW ISSN 0085-5499
REPERTOIRE BIBLIOGRAPHIQUE DES LIVRES
IMPRIMES EN FRANCE. 1968; N.S. vol.14,
1987. irreg. price varies. Verlag Valentin Koerner,
H.-Sielcken-Str. 36, Postfach 304, D-7570 Baden-
Baden 1, W. Germany (B.R.D.)

010 FR
REPERTOIRE DES ANNUAIRES. 1936. a. Syndicat
Professionnel Annuaire, Telematique,
Communication (ATC), 35 rue Gregoire de Tours,
75006 Paris, France.
 Formerly: Annuaire des Annuaires (ISSN 0066-
2720)

015 BE ISSN 0080-1224
REPERTORIUM VAN WERKEN, IN
VLAANDEREN UITGEGEVEN, OF DOOR
MONOPOLIEHOUDERS INGEVOERD. 1960. a.
950 Fr. Vereniging ter Bevordering van het Vlaamse
Boekwezen - Association of Publishers of Dutch
Language Books, Frankrijklei 93, 2000 Antwerp,
Belgium. circ. 1,500.

015 CL
REVISTA CHILENA EN VENTA. 1974. a. $18.
Servicio de Extension de Cultura Chilena, Portugal
12, Depto. 46, Santiago, Chile. Dir. Marta
Dominguez. (processed)

015 SP ISSN 0211-1993
REVISTAS ESPANOLAS CON ISSN. 1981. irreg.
1000 ptas. Instituto Bibliografico Hispanico, Calle
de Atocha 106, Apartado 12311, Madrid 12, Spain
(Dist. by: Editora Nacional, Torregalindo 10,
Madrid 16, Spain) Ed. Vicente Sanchez Munoz.
bibl. circ. 1,000.

015 UY ISSN 0085-5642
REVISTERO; el mas completo informe sobre las
publicaciones periodicas de America Latina. 1972. a.
$35. Eduardo Darino, Ed. & Pub., Casilla de Correo
1677, Montevideo, Uruguay (U.S. Subscr. to:
Darino, Box 1496-GCS, New York, NY 10163)
circ. 1,000.

REVUE BIBLIOGRAPHIQUE DE SINOLOGIE. see
HISTORY — Abstracting, Bibliographies, Statistics

015 BL
RIO DE JANEIRO. BIBLIOTECA NACIONAL.
COLECAO RODOLFO GARCIA. SERIE B.
CATALOGOS E BIBLIOGRAFIAS. irreg.
Biblioteca Nacional, Colecao Rodolfo Garcia, Av.
Rio Branco, Rio de Janeiro, Brazil.

015 BL
RIO DE JANEIRO, BRAZIL (STATE). INSTITUTO
ESTADUAL DO LIVRO. DIVISAO DE
BIBLIOTECAS. BOLETIM BIBLIOGRAFICO.
1977. irreg. Instituto Estadual do Livro, Divisao de
Bibliotecas, Av. Presidente Vargas 1261, Rio de
Janeiro, Brazil. circ. 1,000.

ROMANTIST. see *LITERATURE*

RUDOLF STEINER PUBLICATIONS. see
*PHILOSOPHY — Abstracting, Bibliographies,
Statistics*

011 IS
RUPPIN INSTITUTE LIBRARY. LIBRARY'S
ACCESSION LIST. (Text in English and Hebrew)
a. free. Ruppin Institute Library, Emek Hafer 60
960, Israel. TEL 053-685131.

S A L A L M BIBLIOGRAPHY AND REFERENCE
SERIES. (Seminar on the Acquisition of Latin
American Library Materials) see *LIBRARY AND
INFORMATION SCIENCES — Abstracting,
Bibliographies, Statistics*

BIBLIOGRAPHIES 131

015 SA ISSN 0036-0864
S A N B. (South African National Bibiography) (Text in Afrikaans, Bantu languages and English) 1959. q. with annual cum. R.40($36) State Library, Box 397, Pretoria 0001, South Africa. Ed. Barbara Kellermann. bibl. circ. 560. (back issues avail.)
Continues (from 1959): South Africa. State Library. Publications Received.

011 GE ISSN 0419-7305
SAECHSISCHE BIBLIOGRAPHIE. (Text in German) 1961. a. Saechsische Landesbibliothek, Marienalle 12, 8060 Dresden, E. Germany (D.D.R) Ed. Johannes Jandt.

011 US
SCARECROW AUTHOR BIBLIOGRAPHIES. 1969. irreg., no.77, 1986. price varies. Scarecrow Press, Inc., 52 Liberty St., Box 4167, Metuchen, NJ 08840. TEL 201-548-8600.

SCIENTIFIC SERIALS IN THAI LIBRARIES. see *SCIENCES: COMPREHENSIVE WORKS — Abstracting, Bibliographies, Statistics*

011 SW ISSN 0348-1093
SCRIPTA ACADEMICA. (Text in English, German, Swedish) 1977. a. University Library of Lund, P.O. Box 3, S-221 00 Lund, Sweden. (back issues avail.)

011 US
SELECTION GUIDE SERIES. irreg. Neal-Schuman Publishers, Inc., 23 Leonard St., New York, NY 10013. TEL 212-925-8650.

016.05 CN ISSN 0709-0536
SERIALS HOLDINGS IN NEWFOUNDLAND LIBRARIES. 1974. irreg. Can.$60 for main list; Can.$20 for supplements. Memorial University of Newfoundland Library, Periodicals Division, St. John's, Nfld. A1C 5S7, Canada. TEL 709-737-7438. Ed. S. Ellison. circ. controlled.
Former titles (until 1979): Serials Holdings in the Libraries of Memorial University of Newfoundland, St. John's Public Library and College of Trades and Technology (ISSN 0316-6597); Memorial University of Newfoundland. Library. Serials Holdings in the Libraries of Memorial University of Newfoundland and St. John's Public Library (ISSN 0316-6600)

011 UK
SERIALS IN C L W LIBRARY. 1981. a. £2.50. College of Librarianship Wales, Library, Llanbadarn Fawr, Aberystwyth SY23 3AS, Wales. Ed. R. Prichard.

011 YU ISSN 0350-3585
SLOVENSKA BIBLIOGRAFIJA. 1948. irreg. Narodna in Univerzitetna Knjiznica, Turjaska 1, 61001 Ljubljana, Yugoslavia. TEL 061-332-853.

016 CS
SLOVENSKA NARODNA BIBLIOGRAFIA SERIA B: PERIODIKA. (Text in Hungarian, Russian, Slovak; summaries in English, French, German, Slovak) 1985. a. Matica Slovenska, Mudronova 35, 036 52 Martin, Czechoslovakia (Subscr. addr.: Ustredna Expedicia a Dovoz Tlace, Gottwaldovo nam. 6, 813 81 Bratislava, Czechoslovakia) Ed. Anna Foldvariova. bibl. (back issues avail.)

016 CS
SLOVENSKA NARODNA BIBLIOGRAFIA SERIA D: DIZERTACNE PRACE. (Text in Czech, English, Russian, Slovak; summaries in English, French, German, Slovak) 1978. a. Matica Slovenska, Mudronova 35, 036 52 Martin, Czechoslovakia (Subscr. addr.: Ustredna Expedicia a Dovoz Tlace, Gottwaldovo nam. 6, 813 81 Bratislava, Czechoslovakia) Ed. Anna Foldvariova. (back issues avail.)

016 CS
SLOVENSKA NARODNA BIBLIOGRAFIA SERIA E: SPECIALNE TLACE. (Text in French, Hungarian; summaries in English, French, German, Slovak) 1985. a. Matica Slovenska, Mudronova 35, 036 52 Martin, Czechoslovakia (Subscr. addr.: Ustredna Expedicia a Dovoz Tlace, Gottwaldovo nam. 6, 813 81 Bratislava, Czechoslovakia) Ed. Anna Foldvariova. film rev. (back issues avail.)

016 CS
SLOVENSKA NARODNA BIBLIOGRAFIA SERIA F: FIREMNA LITERATURA. (Text in Czech, English, French, German, Hungarian, Russian, Slovenian, Spanish; summaries in English, French, German, Slovak) biennial. Matica Slovenska, Mudronova 35, 036 52 Martin, Czechoslovakia (Subscr. addr.: Ustredna Expedicia a Dovoz Tlace, Gottwaldovo nam. 6, 813 81 Bratislava, Czechoslovakia) Ed. Anna Foldvariova. tr.lit. (back issues avail.)

016 CS
SLOVENSKA NARODNA BIBLIOGRAFIA SERIA G: GRAFIKA. (Text in Czech, English, French, German, Russian, Slovak; summaries in English, French, German, Slovak) 1985. a. Matica Slovenska, Mudronova 35, 036 52 Martin, Czechoslovakia (Subscr. addr.: Ustredna Expedicia a Dovoz Tlace, Gottwaldovo nam. 6, 813 81 Bratislava, Czechoslovakia) Ed. Anna Voldvariova. (back issues avail.)

016 CS
SLOVENSKA NARODNA BIBLIOGRAFIA SERIA I: OFICIALNE DOKUMENTY. (Text in Russian, Slovak; summaries in English, French, German, Slovak) 1985. biennial. Matica Slovenska, Mudronova 35, 036 52 Martin, Czechoslovakia (Subscr. addr.: Ustredna Expedicia a Dovoz Tlace, Gottwaldovo nam. 6, 813 81 Bratislava, Czechoslovakia) Ed. Anna Foldvariova.

016 CS
SLOVENSKA NARODNA BIBLIOGRAFIA SERIA J: AUDIOVIZUALNE DOKUMENTY. (Text in English, French, Slovak; summaries in English, French, German, Slovak) 1984. a. Matica Slovenska, Mudronova 35, 036 52 Martin, Czechoslovakia (Subscr. addr.: Ustredna Expedicia a Dovoz Tlace, Gottwaldovo nam. 6, 813 81 Bratislava, Czechoslovakia) Ed. Anna Foldvariova. (back issues avail.)

SMALL PRESS RECORD OF BOOKS IN PRINT. see *PUBLISHING AND BOOK TRADE — Abstracting, Bibliographies, Statistics*

SOFTWARE ENCYCLOPEDIA. see *COMPUTERS — Software*

SOFTWARE PUBLISHERS' CATALOGS ANNUAL. see *COMPUTERS — Software*

SOLAR BIBLIOGRAPHY. see *ENERGY — Abstracting, Bibliographies, Statistics*

011 GE ISSN 0457-3900
SONDERBIBLIOGRAPHIEN DER DEUTSCHEN BUCHEREI. 1954. irreg. VEB Bibliographisches Institut, Gerichtsweg 26, 7010 Leipzig, E. Germany(D.D.R.) Indexed: Nutr.Abstr.

SOUTH AFRICAN INSTITUTE OF INTERNATIONAL AFFAIRS. BIBLIOGRAPHICAL SERIES/SUID-AFRIKAANSE INSTITUUT VAN INTERNASIONALE AANGELEENTHEDE. BIBLIOGRAFIESE REEKS. see *POLITICAL SCIENCE — Abstracting, Bibliographies, Statistics*

015.96 FJ
SOUTH PACIFIC BIBLIOGRAPHY. 1981. a. University of the South Pacific, Library, G.P.O. Box 1168, Suva, Fiji. (Co-Sponsor: Pacific Information Center) circ. 400.
Supersedes: University of the South Pacific. Library. Pacific Collection. Accession List; Incorporating: University of the South Pacific. Library. Legal Deposit Accessions.

015 FJ
SOUTH PACIFIC PERIODICALS INDEX. 1974. a. $15. University of the South Pacific, Library, G.P.O. Box 1168, Suva, Fiji. (Co-sponsor: Pacific Information Centre) Ed. Susil Bhan. circ. 170. (back issues avail.)
Formerly (until 1978): Bibliography of Periodical Articles Relating to the South Pacific.

996 FJ
SOUTH PACIFIC RESEARCH REGISTER. 1982. a. 13 F. University of the South Pacific, Library, G.P.O. Box 1168, Suva, Fiji. (Co-Sponsor: Pacific Information Centre)
Supersedes: Fiji Register of Research and Investigations.

010 US ISSN 0073-4977
SOUTHERN ILLINOIS UNIVERSITY, CARBONDALE. UNIVERSITY LIBRARIES. BIBLIOGRAPHIC CONTRIBUTIONS. 1964. irreg. price varies. Southern Illinois University, Carbondale, Morris Library, Carbondale, IL 62901. TEL 618-453-2683. Ed. Kenneth G. Peterson. circ. 600.

SPRINGER BOOKS ON PROFESSIONAL COMPUTING. see *COMPUTERS*

016 GW ISSN 0075-8728
STAMM LEITFADEN DURCH PRESSE UND WERBUNG/ANNUAL DIRECTORY THROUGH PRESS AND ADVERTISING. 1947. a. DM.118. Stamm Verlag GmbH, Goldammerweg 16, 4300 Essen 1, W. Germany (B.R.D.) Ed. Willy Stamm. adv. circ. 8,600.

050 US ISSN 0085-6630
STANDARD PERIODICAL DIRECTORY. 1963. biennial. $295. Oxbridge Communications, Inc., 150 Fifth Ave., New York, NY 10011. TEL 212-741-0231. Ed. Patricia Hagood.

310 015 UK ISSN 0309-5371
STATISTICS - ASIA & AUSTRALASIA: SOURCES FOR MARKET RESEARCH. 1974. irreg., 2nd, 1983. £48($145) C.B.D. Research Ltd., 154 High St., Beckenham, Kent BR3 1EA, England (Dist. in U.S. by: Gale Research Co., Penobscot Bldg., Detroit, MI 48226) Ed. Joan M. Harvey. circ. 2, 000.

STORIES: A LIST OF STORIES TO TELL AND TO READ ALOUD. see *CHILDREN AND YOUTH — Abstracting, Bibliographies, Statistics*

011 UR
STROIIZDAT: THE BEST-DESIGNED BOOKS. (Text in English) 1978. irreg. Stroiizdat, Shchousseva, rm.60, Moscow, Russian S.F.S.R., U.S.S.R. (Avail. from: Vneshtorgizdat, Bol'shaya Bronnaya 6a, Moscow, Russian S.F.S.R., U.S.S.R.)

STUDIES ON THE MORPHOLOGY AND SYSTEMATICS OF SCALE INSECTS. see *BIOLOGY — Entomology*

016 US ISSN 0000-0159
SUBJECT GUIDE TO BOOKS IN PRINT. (Issued in 3 vols.) 1956. a. $179.95. R.R. Bowker Company, Database Publishing Group, 245 W. 17th St., New York, NY 10011. TEL 800-521-8110.
●Also available online. Vendors: DIALOG.

016 US ISSN 0000-0167
SUBJECT GUIDE TO CHILDREN'S BOOKS IN PRINT. 1971. a. $75. R.R. Bowker Company, Database Publishing Group, 245 W. 17th St., New York, NY 10011. TEL 800-521-8110.
●Also available online.

016 949.6 GW ISSN 0081-9131
SUEDOSTEUROPA - BIBLIOGRAPHIE. (Text in European languages) 1956. irreg. price varies. Suedost-Institut, Guellstr. 7, 8000 Munich 2, W. Germany (B.R.D.) Ed. Gerhard Seewann.

015 SW ISSN 0586-0431
SVENSK TIDSKRIFTSFOERTECKNING/ CURRENT SWEDISH PERIODICALS. 1968. triennial with a. updates. (Kungliga Biblioteket, Bibliografiska Avdelningen - Royal Library) Tidnings AB Svensk Bokhandel, Box 1335, S-111 83 Stockholm, Sweden.

SWAZILAND NATIONAL BIBLIOGRAPHY. see *PUBLISHING AND BOOK TRADE — Abstracting, Bibliographies, Statistics*

TALKING BOOKS, ADULT (LARGE PRINT EDITION) see *BLIND — Abstracting, Bibliographies, Statistics*

TASCHENBUCH DES OEFFENTLICHEN LEBENS; Bundesrepublik Deutschland. see *PUBLIC ADMINISTRATION*

TAX FOUNDATION'S RESEARCH BIBLIOGRAPHY. see *BUSINESS AND ECONOMICS — Abstracting, Bibliographies, Statistics*

011   SW   ISSN 0345-0112
TEXT; Svensk tidskrift foer bibliografi. (Text in English and Swedish) 1974. irreg. (approx. 1/yr.) Kr.160 per vol. (4 issues) ‡ (Center for Bibliographical Studies, Uppsala) Dahlia Books, International Publishers and Booksellers, P.O. Box 1025, S-751 40 Uppsala, Sweden. Ed. Rolf E. Du Rietz. adv. bk. rev. circ. 200.

016 315   TH   ISSN 0082-3791
THAILAND. NATIONAL STATISTICAL OFFICE. STATISTICAL BIBLIOGRAPHY. (Text in English) 1961. irreg. price varies. National Statistical Office, Larn Luang Rd., Bangkok, Thailand. circ. 1,000.

013   DK   ISSN 0900-2278
THESES AND OTHER PUBLICATIONS OF THE UNIVERSITY OF COPENHAGEN. (Text in English) a. exchange basis. I.D.E., Danmarks Institut for International Udveksling Af Videnskabelige Publikationer, Amaliegade 38, DK-1256 Copenhagen K, Denmark. circ. controlled. (processed)

016 980   UK
THESES IN LATIN AMERICAN STUDIES AT BRITISH UNIVERSITIES IN PROGRESS OR RECENTLY COMPLETED. 1967. irreg. free. University of London, Institute of Latin American Studies, 31 Tavistock Square, London WC1H 9HA, England. Ed. D.F. Rodger. Indexed: CERDIC.
Formerly: Theses in Latin American Studies at British Universities in Progress and Completed (ISSN 0307-109X)

THOMAS SAY FOUNDATION MONOGRAPHS. see BIOLOGY — Entomology

011 370   DK   ISSN 0105-4090
TIDSSKRIFTINDEKS FOR SKOLEBIBLIOTEKER. 1972. a. Kr.166.40. Bibliotekscentralen, Tempovej 7-11, DK-2750 Ballerup, Denmark.

TOURISM COMPENDIUM. see TRAVEL AND TOURISM — Abstracting, Bibliographies, Statistics

U C L A MUSIC LIBRARY BIBLIOGRAPHY SERIES. (University of California, Los Angeles) see MUSIC — Abstracting, Bibliographies, Statistics

630 016   US
U S - CANADIAN RANGE MANAGEMENT; a selected bibliography on ranges, pastures, wildlife, livestock, and ranching. irreg. $55 for vol.2. Oryx Press, 2214 N. Central at Encanto, Ste. 103, Phoenix, AZ 85004. TEL 602-254-6156. Ed. John F. Vallentine.

011   DK   ISSN 0106-6633
UDENLANDSK LITTERATUR I DANSKE FOLKEBIBLIOTEKER FAGLITTERATUR. 1972. a. Kr.526.50. Bibliotekscentralen, Tempovej 7-11, DK-2750 Ballerup, Denmark.

011   US   ISSN 0000-0175
ULRICH'S INTERNATIONAL PERIODICALS DIRECTORY. (Supplement: Bowker International Serials Database Update) 1932. a., starting in 1980; previously biennial. $159.95 (in 2 vols.) R.R. Bowker Company, Database Publishing Group, 245 W. 17th St., New York, NY 10011. TEL 800-521-8110. index.
●Also available online. Vendors: BRS, DIALOG, European Space Agency.

016.912   UN
UNESCO. SCIENTIFIC MAPS AND ATLASES AND OTHER RELATED PUBLICATIONS. irreg. Unesco, 7-9 Place de Fontenoy, 75700 Paris, France. bibl. illus.

UNION CATALOGUE OF SOCIAL SCIENCE PERIODICALS/SERIALS. see SOCIAL SCIENCES: COMPREHENSIVE WORKS — Abstracting, Bibliographies, Statistics

013   SA   ISSN 0079-4325
UNION CATALOGUE OF THESES AND DISSERTATIONS OF THE SOUTH AFRICAN UNIVERSITIES. (Cumulated microfiche edition covers 1918-1977) (Text in Afrikaans and English) 1918. a. free. Potchefstroom University for Christian Higher Education, Potchefstroom, South Africa.

011 500   ZA
UNION LIST OF SCIENTIFIC AND TECHNICAL PERIODICALS IN ZAMBIA. 1980. irreg. K.4.50. National Council for Scientific Research, Box CH 158, Chelston, Lusaka, Zambia. Eds. W.C. Muship, J.C. Michello.

016   US
UNITED NATIONS DOCUMENTS AND PUBLICATIONS. CHECKLIST. 1946. a. Readex Microprint Corp., 58 Pine St., New Canaan, CT 06840. TEL 203-966-5906. Ed. Gwen Sloan. circ. 4,500. (also avail. in microfiche)
Former titles: United Nations Documents (ISSN 0191-8087); Readex Microprint Publications (ISSN 0079-984X)

358 016   US   ISSN 0082-8696
U.S. AIR FORCE ACADEMY LIBRARY. SPECIAL BIBLIOGRAPHY SERIES. 1957. irreg. United States Air Force Academy, Library, Colorado Springs, CO 80840. TEL 303-472-4406. circ. 500. (also avail. in microfiche from NTI)

U.S. DEPARTMENT OF STATE. LIBRARY. COMMERCIAL LIBRARY PROGRAM. PUBLICATIONS LIST. see LIBRARY AND INFORMATION SCIENCES — Abstracting, Bibliographies, Statistics

U.S. DEPARTMENT OF TRANSPORTATION. BIBLIOGRAPHIC LISTS. see TRANSPORTATION — Abstracting, Bibliographies, Statistics

U.S. ENVIRONMENTAL PROTECTION AGENCY. JOURNAL HOLDINGS REPORT. see ENVIRONMENTAL STUDIES — Abstracting, Bibliographies, Statistics

U.S. GENERAL SERVICES ADMINISTRATION. PUBLICATIONS. see PUBLIC ADMINISTRATION — Abstracting, Bibliographies, Statistics

011   VE
UNIVERSIDAD DE LOS ANDES. INSTITUTO DE INVESTIGACIONES LITERARIAS. SERIE ENSAYO Y CRITICA LITERARIA.* 1981. irreg. free. Universidad de los Andes, Instituto de Investigaciones Literarias, Via los Chorras de Milla, C.P. 5101, Merida, Venezuela. circ. 500.
Supersedes (1977-1978): Universidad de los Andes. Instituto de Investigaciones Literarias. Serie Bibliografico; Which was formerly (1971-1977): Universidad de los Andes. Centro de Investigaciones Literarias. Serie Bibliografico.

011   SP
UNIVERSIDAD DE NAVARRA. COLECCION BIBLIOGRAFIA. 1977. irreg. 7,250 ptas. (Universidad de Navarra, Facultad de Filosofia y Letras) Ediciones Universidad de Navarra, S.A., Apdo. 396, 31080 Pamplona, Spain.

020 011   MX   ISSN 0006-1719
UNIVERSIDAD NACIONAL AUTONOMA DE MEXICO. INSTITUTO DE INVESTIGACIONES BIBLIOGRAFICAS. BOLETIN. 1969. irreg., latest 1984. $20. Universidad Nacional Autonoma de Mexico, Instituto de Investigaciones Bibliograficas, Ciudad Universitaria, Coyoacan, Mexico 04510 D.F., Mexico. (Co-sponsor: Biblioteca Nacional) Ed. Ma. del Carmen Ruiz Castaneda. bibl. illus.
Supersedes: Biblioteca Nacional. Boletin.

010   MX   ISSN 0076-7468
UNIVERSIDAD NACIONAL AUTONOMA DE MEXICO. SEMINARIO DE INVESTIGACIONES BIBLIOTECOLOGICA. PUBLICACIONES. SERIE B. BIBLIOGRAFIA. 1960. irreg., no.4, 1967. ‡ Universidad Nacional Autonoma de Mexico, Seminario de Investigacions Bibliotecologicas, Torre de Ciencias, Ciudad Universitaria, Mexico 20, D.F., Mexico. Ed. Dr. Alicia Perales de Mercado. circ. controlled.
Theses by alumuni

025.2   AG   ISSN 0076-6399
UNIVERSIDAD NACIONAL DE CUYO. BIBLIOTECA CENTRAL. BOLETIN BIBLIOGRAFICO. 1940. irreg., no.52, 1982. exchange basis. ‡ Universidad Nacional de Cuyo, Biblioteca Central, Centro Universitario-C.C. 420, Mendoza, Argentina.

010   BL
UNIVERSIDADE DE SAO PAULO. FACULDADE DE ECONOMIA E ADMINISTRACAO. BIBLIOTECA. BOLETIM. 1965. irreg. exchange basis. Universidade de Sao Paulo, Faculdade de Economia e Administracao, Biblioteca, Cidade Universitaria Armando de Salles Oliveira, C.P. 11498, 01000 Sao Paulo, Brazil. bk. rev. circ. 250.
Formerly: Universidade de Sao Paulo. Faculdade de Ciencias Economicas e Administrativas. Biblioteca. Boletim.

013   GW   ISSN 0080-5173
UNIVERSITAET DES SAARLANDES. JAHRESBIBLIOGRAPHIE. 1968. a. exchange basis. Universitaet des Saarlandes, Universitaetsbibliothek, 6600 Saarbruecken 11, W. Germany (B.R.D.) Ed. Angelika Kussler.

UNIVERSITY MICROFILMS INTERNATIONAL NEWSLETTER. see LIBRARY AND INFORMATION SCIENCES — Abstracting, Bibliographies, Statistics

027 011   US   ISSN 0044-8877
UNIVERSITY OF ARIZONA LIBRARY. BIBLIOGRAPHIC BULLETIN. 1970. irreg. free to libraries. University of Arizona Library, Tucson, AZ 85721. bibl.

010   NZ   ISSN 0067-0499
UNIVERSITY OF AUCKLAND. LIBRARY. BIBLIOGRAPHICAL BULLETIN. 1964. irreg., no.13, 1984. exchange basis. ‡ University of Auckland Library, Auckland, New Zealand. circ. 93.

016 430   UK   ISSN 0260-5929
UNIVERSITY OF LONDON. INSTITUTE OF GERMANIC STUDIES. RESEARCH IN GERMANIC STUDIES. 1968. a. price varies. ‡ University of London, Institute of Germanic Studies, 29 Russell Square, London WC1B 5DP, England.
Formerly (until 1981): University of London. Institute of Germanic Studies. Theses in Progress at British Universities (ISSN 0082-4127)

011 020   UK   ISSN 0140-7260
UNIVERSITY OF LONDON. SCHOOL OF SLAVONIC AND EAST EUROPEAN STUDIES. LIBRARY. BIBLIOGRAPHICAL GUIDES. 1977. irreg. University of London, School of Slavonic and East European Studies, Senate House, Malet St., London WC1E 7HU, England. (back issues avail.)

013   US   ISSN 0078-1460
UNIVERSITY OF NORTH CAROLINA, GREENSBORO. FACULTY PUBLICATIONS. 1900. a. price varies. ‡ University of North Carolina at Greensboro, Greensboro, NC 27412. TEL 919-379-5000. circ. 1,000.

011   UK   ISSN 0143-0009
UNIVERSITY OF ST. ANDREWS. LIBRARY. CURRENT SERIALS. 1974. biennial. £1 also avail. on exchange to libraries. University of St. Andrews, Library, North St., St. Andrews, Fife KY16 9TR, Scotland. Ed. Mackenzie. circ. 300.

011   SA
UNIVERSITY OF THE WITWATERSRAND, JOHANNESBURG. LIBRARY. BIBLIOGRAPHICAL SERIES. 1958. irreg. (unnumbered) University of the Witwatersrand, Johannesburg, Library, Private Bag 31550, Braamfontein 2017, South Africa.

330 016   US
UNIVERSITY OF TOLEDO. BUSINESS RESEARCH CENTER. BIBLIOGRAPHIES. 1976. irreg., no.7, 1985. price varies. University of Toledo, College of Business Administration, 2801 W. Bancroft St., Toledo, OH 43606. TEL 419-537-2067.

015   GW   ISSN 0067-8899
VERZEICHNIS LIEFERBARER BUECHER/ GERMAN BOOKS IN PRINT. Short title: V L B. (Consists of five sections: Authors/Titles/Key-words (in three vols., 8th ed., 1978/79) and Schlagwortverzeichnis/Subject Index (in two vols., 1st ed., 1978/79)) 1971. a. price varies. (Buchhaendler-Vereinigung GmbH) K. G. Saur Verlag KG, Poessenbacherstr. 12 B, Postfach 711009, 8000 Munich 71, W. Germany (B.R.D.) (U.S. and Canadian subscr. to: K.G. Saur Inc., 175 Fifth Ave., New York, N.Y. 10010) index. (reprint service avail. from UMI, ISI)

VICTORIAN FICTION RESEARCH GUIDES. see
*LITERATURE — Abstracting, Bibliographies,
Statistics*

015   US   ISSN 0507-102X
VIRGINIA STATE PUBLICATIONS IN PRINT.
1965. a. $2. State Library, 11th St. at Capitol Sq.,
Richmond, VA 23219. TEL 804-786-2311. circ.
700.

011   UR
VOPROSY BIBLIOGRAFII. 1976. irreg. 0.78 Rub.
per issue. Akademiya Nauk S.S.S.R., Biblioteka,
Leningrad, Russian S.F.S.R., U.S.S.R. Ed. A.
Moiseeva.

VYBEROVA BIBLIOGRAFIA MUZEOLOGICKEJ
LITERATURY. see *MUSEUMS AND ART
GALLERIES — Abstracting, Bibliographies,
Statistics*

WELLCOME UNIT FOR THE HISTORY OF
MEDICINE. RESEARCH PUBLICATIONS. see
MEDICAL SCIENCES

016   UK   ISSN 0083-7911
WELSH BIBLIOGRAPHICAL SOCIETY.
JOURNAL. 1910. a. £1 to individuals; £2 to
institutions. Welsh Bibliographical Society, c/o B.
Jones, Ed., National Library of Wales, Aberystwyth,
Dyfed SY23 3BU, Wales. circ. 200.

WEST AFRICA RICE DEVELOPMENT
ASSOCIATION. CURRENT BIBLIOGRAPHY.
see *AGRICULTURE — Abstracting,
Bibliographies, Statistics*

010   US   ISSN 0512-4743
WEST VIRGINIA UNION LIST OF SERIALS.
1962. a. $55. West Virginia University Library,
Main Office, Box 6069, Morgantown, WV 26506-
6069. TEL 304-293-4040. Ed. Mildred Moyers.

016   UK   ISSN 0000-0213
WILLING'S PRESS GUIDE; a guide to the press of
the United Kingdom and to the principal
publications of Europe, Australasia, the Far East,
Middle East, and the Americas (incl. S. America)
1874. a. £43. Thomas Skinner Directories, Windsor
Court, East Grinstead House, East Grinstead, West
Sussex RH19 1XE, England. Ed. T. Taylor. adv.
subject index. circ. 7,500.

WINTERGREEN; a directory of progressive
periodicals. see *LITERARY AND POLITICAL
REVIEWS — Abstracting, Bibliographies, Statistics*

011   US   ISSN 8755-3759
WORDS ON TAPE. 1984. a. $29.95. Meckler
Publishing Corporation, 11 Ferry Lane West,
Westport, CT 06880-5808. TEL 203-220-6967.
(magnetic tape)
●Also available online. Vendors: BRS.

WORLD BIBLIOGRAPHY OF SOCIAL
SECURITY/BIBLIOGRAPHIE UNIVERSELLE
DE SECURITE SOCIALE. see *BUSINESS AND
ECONOMICS — Abstracting, Bibliographies,
Statistics*

WRITERS DIRECTORY. see *BIOGRAPHY*

910 011   CN
YUKON BIBLIOGRAPHY UPDATE. 1970. irreg.
price varies. Boreal Institute for Northern Studies,
CW 401 Bio Science Bldg., University of Alberta,
Edmonton, AB T6G 2E9, Canada. Ed. Geraldine A.
Cooke. cum.index. circ. 400. (back issues avail.)

Z G A BIBLIOGRAPHIC SERIES. (Zambia
Geographical Association) see *GEOGRAPHY —
Abstracting, Bibliographies, Statistics*

011   CS
ZAHRANICNE PERIODIKA V C S S R. (Hardcover
ceased in 1982) 1972. irreg. Univerzitna Kniznica,
Michalska 1, 885 17 Bratislava, Czechoslovakia.
(Co-sponsor: Czechoslovakia. Statni Knihovna) Ed.
Vincent Kutik. stat. circ. 1,000. (also avail. in
microfiche; back issues avail.)
●Available only online.

011   ZR
ZAIRE. BIBLIOTHEQUE NATIONALE.
BIBLIOGRAPHIE NATIONALE. (Text in French)
1971. irreg., latest 1975. Bibliotheque Nationale,
B.P. 3090, Kinshasa/Gombe, Zaire.

ZAMBIA. NATIONAL COUNCIL FOR
SCIENTIFIC RESEARCH. N C S R
BIBLIOGRAPHY. see *SCIENCES:
COMPREHENSIVE WORKS — Abstracting,
Bibliographies, Statistics*

015   RH
ZIMBABWE NATIONAL BIBLIOGRAPHY. 1961.
a. Z.$5. ‡ National Archives, Private Bag 7729,
Causeway, Harare, Zimbabwe. index. circ. 400.
Former titles (1967-1978): Rhodesia National
Bibliography (ISSN 0085-5677); (1961-1966):
Publications Deposited in the National Archives.

100 BOOKS ON ADVERTISING. see
*ADVERTISING AND PUBLIC RELATIONS —
Abstracting, Bibliographies, Statistics*

BICYCLES AND MOTORCYCLES

see *Sports and Games — Bicycles and
Motorcycles*

BIOGRAPHY

920   FR
A LA PREMIERE PERSONNE. 1980. irreg. price
varies. Editions Syros, 1 rue de Varenne, 75006
Paris, France.

A S C A P BIOGRAPHICAL DICTIONARY.
(American Society of Composers, Authors and
Publishers) see *MUSIC*

ALMANACH DU PEUPLE. see *ENCYCLOPEDIAS
AND GENERAL ALMANACS*

925 500   US   ISSN 0065-9347
AMERICAN MEN AND WOMEN OF SCIENCE.
PHYSICAL AND BIOLOGICAL SCIENCES.
1906. irreg., 16th edt., 1986. $595. (Jaques Cattell
Press) R.R. Bowker Company, Database Publishing
Group, 245 W. 17th St., New York, NY 10011.
TEL 800-521-8110. Indexed: Child.Auth.& Illus.
●Also available online. Vendors: BRS, DIALOG.

150 920   US   ISSN 0196-6545
AMERICAN PSYCHOLOGICAL ASSOCIATION.
DIRECTORY. 1916. quadrennial. $70 to non-
members; members $50. American Psychological
Association, 1200 17th St., N.W., Washington, DC
20036. TEL 202-955-7600. Ed. John A. Lazo. circ.
10,000.
Formerly: American Psychological Association.
Biographical Directory (ISSN 0090-9076)

920   US   ISSN 0569-714X
AMERICAN PSYCHOLOGICAL ASSOCIATION.
MEMBERSHIP REGISTER. (Supplement to:
American Psychological Association Biographical
Directory) 1967. a. $25 to non-members; members
$15. American Psychological Association, 1200 17th
St., N.W., Washington, DC 20036. TEL 202-955-
7600. Ed. John A. Lazo.

AMIS DE RAMUZ. BULLETIN. see *LITERATURE*

920   FR
ANNUAIRE MONDIAL DES CORSES. biennial.
350 F. Association Mondiale des Corses, 100 rue
Saint-Lazare, 75009 Paris, France. Ed. X. Moreschi.
adv. illus.

ARGENTINA. DEPARTAMENTO DE ESTUDIOS
HISTORICOS NAVALES. SERIE C:
BIOGRAFIAS NAVALES ARGENTINAS. see
MILITARY

920   US
AUTHOR BIOGRAPHICS MASTER INDEX. 1978.
irreg. $200. Gale Research Company, Book Tower,
Detroit, MI 48226. TEL 313-961-2242. Eds.
Barbara McNeil, Miranda C. Herbert.

AUTHORS IN THE NEWS; compilation of news
stories and feature articles from American
newspapers and magazines, covering prominent
writers in all fields. see *LITERATURE*

920   CS   ISSN 0067-8724
BIOGRAFICKE STUDIE. (Text in Slovak; summaries
in German and Russian) 1970. irreg., approx. a.
price varies. Matica Slovenska, Mudronova 35, 036
52 Martin, Czechoslovakia. bk. rev.

BIOGRAPHICAL DICTIONARIES AND
RELATED WORKS; an international bibliography
of collective biographies. see *BIBLIOGRAPHIES*

920   US   ISSN 0738-0097
BIOGRAPHY ALMANAC; a comprehensive
reference guide to more than 25,000 famous and
infamous newsmakers from biblical times to the
present. 1982. irreg., latest 3rd edt., 1986. price
varies. Gale Research Company, Book Tower,
Detroit, MI 48226. TEL 313-961-2242. Ed. Susan
Stetler.

920   UK
BIRMINGHAM POST & MAIL YEAR BOOK AND
WHO'S WHO. 1949. a. £11.50. Birmingham Post &
Mail Ltd., Colmore Circus, Birmingham, B4 6AX,
England. adv.
Formerly (until 1985): Birmingham Post Year
Book and Who's Who.

920   SA
BLACK WHO'S WHO OF SOUTHERN AFRICA.
(Text in English) a. R.25. African Business
Publications (Pty) Ltd., Box 2901, Johannesburg
2001, South Africa.

920   US   ISSN 0067-9240
BLUE BOOK: LEADERS OF THE ENGLISH-
SPEAKING WORLD. 1968. a. $120. Gale
Research Company, Book Tower, Detroit, MI
48226. circ. 10,000.

920 800   US   ISSN 0743-9628
BORGO BIOVIEWS. 1983. irreg., approx 4/yr. $12.95
(hardcover); $6.95 (paperback) per no. Borgo Press,
Box 2845, San Bernardino, CA 92406. TEL 714-
884-5813.

920   FR
BOTTIN MONDAIN; Tout Paris-Toute la France.
1903. a. $80. Societe Didot Bottin, 28, rue Docteur
Finlay, 75738 Paris Cedex 15, France.

BUILDERS OF INDIAN ANTHROPOLOGY. see
*SOCIAL SCIENCES: COMPREHENSIVE
WORKS*

CALIFORNIANS IN CONGRESS. see *PUBLIC
ADMINISTRATION*

920   CN   ISSN 0068-9963
CANADIAN WHO'S WHO. 1910. a. Can.$85.
University of Toronto Press, Front Campus,
Toronto, Ont. M5S 1A6, Canada. TEL 613-667-
7791. Ed. Kieran Simpson. circ. 5,000. Indexed:
Child.Auth.& Illus.
Formerly: Who's Who, The Canadian.

920 800   UK
CARLYLE NEWSLETTER. 1979. a. £7($12) for 3
nos. University of Edinburgh, Department of
English Literature, David Hume Tower, George
Square, Edinburgh EH8 9JX, Scotland. Ed. K.J.
Fielding. circ. 250. (back issues avail.) Indexed:
M.L.A.

CHEMISTS AND CHEMISTRY. see *CHEMISTRY*

CHINA DIRECTORY. see *PUBLIC
ADMINISTRATION*

CHIROPRACTIC HISTORY. see *MEDICAL
SCIENCES — Chiropractics, Homeopathy,
Osteopathy*

920   VE   ISSN 0069-5033
COLECCION "ANIVERSARIOS CULTURALES".
1965. irreg., no.4, 1968. Universidad Central de
Venezuela, Direccion de Cultura, Biblioteca, Piso
10, Ciudad Universitaria, Caracas, Venezuela.

920   VE
COLECCIONDINA MICA Y SIEMBRA.* no.2,
1976. irreg. Universidad Simon Bolivar, Apdo.
80659, Prados de Este, Caracas 1080, Venezuela.

BIOGRAPHY

012   US
COMMUNITY LEADERS OF AMERICA. 1967. a. $45. American Biographical Institute, Inc., Governing Board of Editors, Box 31226, 5126 Bur Oak Circle, Raleigh, NC 27602. TEL 919-832-2001. Ed. J.M. Evans. circ. 5,000.
   Formerly: Community Leaders and Noteworthy Americans (ISSN 0094-5587)

COMPOSERS OF THE AMERICAS/ COMPOSITORES DE AMERICA. see *MUSIC*

028.1 011   US   ISSN 0010-7468
CONTEMPORARY AUTHORS. 1962. irreg., vol.119, 1986. $90. Gale Research Company, Book Tower, Detroit, MI 48226. TEL 313-961-2242. Ed. Hal May. cum.index. Indexed: Child.Auth.& Illus.

920   US   ISSN 0748-0636
CONTEMPORARY AUTHORS AUTOBIOGRAPHY SERIES. 1984. a., latest vol.4, 1986. $74. Gale Research Company, Book Tower, Detroit, MI 48226. TEL 313-961-2242. Ed. Adele Sarkissian. circ. 1,500. (back issues avail.)

927   US   ISSN 0749-064X
CONTEMPORARY THEATRE, FILM & TELEVISION. 1984. irreg., latest vol.3, 1986. $95. ‡ Gale Research Company, Book Tower, Detroit, MI 48226. TEL 313-961-2242. Ed. Monica O'Donnell. cum.index. Indexed: Child.Auth.& Illus. Perf.Arts Biog.Master Ind.
   Incorporating (1912-1981): Who's Who in the Theatre (ISSN 0083-9833)

920 944   FR
CONTRIBUTIONS A LA CONNAISSANCE DES ELITES AFRICAINES. 1978. irreg. (Centre de recherche sur l'Afrique orientale, Laboratoire Peiresc) Editions du C N R S, 295 rue St. Jacques, 75005 Paris, France. Dir. Joseph Tubiana. illus.

CREATIVE CANADA. see *THEATER*

930.1   US   ISSN 0361-4735
CURRENT BIOGRAPHIES OF LEADING ARCHAEOLOGISTS. 1975. irreg. $7.95. Chesopiean Library of Archaeology, 7507 Pennington Rd., Norfolk, VA 23505.

920   US   ISSN 0084-9499
CURRENT BIOGRAPHY YEARBOOK. 1940. a. $42. ‡ H.W. Wilson Co., 950 University Avenue, Bronx, NY 10452. TEL 212-588-8400. Ed. Charles Moritz. cum.index: 1940-1970. Indexed: Amer.Bibl.Slavic & E.Eur.Stud. Child.Auth.& Illus.

DEBRETT'S HANDBOOK. see *GENEALOGY AND HERALDRY*

920   CN   ISSN 0070-4717
DICTIONARY OF CANADIAN BIOGRAPHY. 1966. irreg. University of Toronto Press, Front Campus, Toronto, Ont. M5S 1A6, Canada. TEL 613-667-7791. Ed. Frances Halpenny.

DICTIONARY OF CONTEMPORARY AMERICAN ARTISTS. see *ART*

920   UK   ISSN 0070-4733
DICTIONARY OF LATIN AMERICAN AND CARIBBEAN BIOGRAPHY. 1969. irreg. price varies. Melrose Press Ltd., 3 Regal Lane, Soham, Ely, Cambridgeshire CB7 5BA, England.

DICTIONARY OF LITERARY BIOGRAPHY YEARBOOK. see *LITERATURE*

920   UK
DICTIONARY OF SCANDINAVIAN BIOGRAPHY. 1972. irreg. price varies. Melrose Press Ltd., 3 Regal Lane, Soham, Ely, Cambridgeshire CB7 5BA, England. Ed. Ernest Kay.

920 967   MF
DICTIONNAIRE DE BIOGRAPHIE MAURICIENNE/DICTIONARY OF MAURITIAN BIOGRAPHY. (Text in English or French) no.31, 1969. irreg. Societe de l'Histoire de l'Ile Maurice, Rue de Froberville, Curepipe Road, Mauritius.

920   US   ISSN 0070-5101
DIRECTORY OF AMERICAN SCHOLARS. (In 4 vols.: Vol. 1: History; Vol. 2: English, Speech and Drama; Vol. 3: Foreign Languages, Linguistics and Philology; Vol. 4: Philosophy, Religion and Law) 1942. irreg., 8th edt., 1982. $90 per vol., $295 per set. (Jaques Cattell Press) R.R. Bowker Company, Database Publishing Group, 245 W. 17th St., New York, NY 10011. TEL 800-521-8110. index. (reprint service avail. from UMI) Indexed: Child.Auth.& Illus.

920 658   II   ISSN 0070-542X
DIRECTORY OF DIRECTORS. (Text in English) 1966. irreg., latest 1987. Rs.200($50) Kothari Publications, 12 India Exchange Place, Calcutta 700001, India. Ed. H. Kothari. adv.

DIRECTORY OF MEDICAL SPECIALISTS. see *MEDICAL SCIENCES*

354.438   US   ISSN 0090-9955
DIRECTORY OF POLISH OFFICIALS. irreg. U.S. Central Intelligence Agency, Washington, DC 20505 TEL 703-351-1100. (Dist. to Non-U.S. Government users by: Document Expediting (DOCEX) Project, Library of Congress, Washington, DC 20540) circ. controlled.

920 942   UK   ISSN 0070-7120
DORSET WORTHIES. 1962. irreg., no.18, 1984. Dorset County Museum, Dorchester, Dorset, England.

EUROPEAN COMMUNITIES AND OTHER EUROPEAN ORGANIZATIONS WHO'S WHO. see *BUSINESS AND ECONOMICS — Trade And Industrial Directories*

920 540 560   AG   ISSN 0325-4216
F A C E N A. (Text in Spanish; summaries in English) 1978. biennial. Arg.$200. Facultad de Ciencias Exactas y Naturales y Agrimensura, 9 de Julio 1449, 3400 Corrientes, Argentina. Ed.Bd. bk. rev. index. (back issues avail.) Indexed: Biol.Abstr. Chem.Abstr.

920   UK
FELLOWS OF THE ROYAL SOCIETY. BIOGRAPHICAL MEMOIRS. 1955. a. £53. Royal Society, 6 Carlton House Terrace, London SW1Y 5AG, England. circ. 1,420.

FIGURES DE WALLONIE. see *HISTORY — History Of Europe*

920   US
FILMORE BUNGLE. 1975. irreg. $2. Society for the Preservation & Enhancement of the Recognition of Millard Fillmore, Box 712, Cascade, CO 80809. TEL 303-684-2102. circ. 260.

920 831 282 360   GW   ISSN 0173-5543
FRAENKISCHER HAUSKALENDER UND CARITASKALENDER. 1949. a. DM.4.80. Echter Wuerzburg, Fraenkische Gesellschaftsdruckerei und Verlag GmbH, Juliuspromenade 64, 8700 Wuerzburg 1, W. Germany (B.R.D.) Ed. Max Roessler. circ. 18,000.

920   SA
GRAHAM'S TOWN SERIES. 1971. irreg., no.7, 1984. price varies. (Rhodes University) A.A. Balkema Ltd., P.O. Box 3117, Cape Town 8000, South Africa (And Box 1675, Rotterdam, Netherlands; in the U.S. and Canada, P.O. Box 230, Accord, MA 02018)

920   GW   ISSN 0072-7741
GROSSE NATURFORSCHER. 1947. irreg., vol.48, 1985. price varies. Wissenschaftliche Verlagsgesellschaft mbH, Postfach 40, 7000 Stuttgart 1, W. Germany (B.R.D.) Ed. Heinz Degen. Indexed: Biol.Abstr.

HAYDN-STUDIEN. see *MUSIC*

HISTORIC GUELPH; the royal city. see *HISTORY — History Of North And South America*

920 954   II   ISSN 0073-6244
INDIA WHO'S WHO. (Text in English) 1969. a. $32. (India News and Feature Alliance) I N F A Publications, Jeevan Deep Bldg., Parliament St., New Delhi 110001, India. adv. circ. 2,000.

INDIAN ARCHITECTS DIRECTORY. see *ARCHITECTURE*

920   II
INDIAN BIOGRAPHY. irreg. Rs.30. Centre for Asian Dokumentation, Box 11215, Calcutta 700014, India. Ed. S. Chaudhuri.

509   II
INDIAN NATIONAL SCIENCE ACADEMY. BIOGRAPHICAL MEMOIRS OF FELLOWS. (Text in English) irreg. price varies. Indian National Science Academy, 1 Bahadur Shah Zafar Marg, New Delhi 110002, India. bibl.
   Continues: National Institute of Sciences of India. Biographical Memoirs of Fellows (ISSN 0547-7557)

800   UK   ISSN 0143-8263
INTERNATIONAL AUTHORS AND WRITERS WHO'S WHO. 1934. triennial. price varies. Melrose Press Ltd., 3 Regal Lane, Soham, Ely, Cambridgeshire CB7 5BA, England TEL 313-961-2242. (Dist. in U.S. by: Gale Research Co., Book Tower, Detroit, MI 48226) Ed. Ernerst Kay. Indexed: Child.Auth.& Illus.
   Formerly: Author's and Writer's Who's Who (ISSN 0067-2386)

920 610   UK
INTERNATIONAL MEDICAL WHO'S WHO. 1980. irreg., 2nd edt., 1985. £195. Longman Group Ltd., Fourth Ave., Harlow, Essex CM19 5AA, England (Dist. in U.S. and Canada by: Gale Research Co. Ltd., Book Tower, Detroit, MI 48226)

920   UK   ISSN 0074-9613
INTERNATIONAL WHO'S WHO. 1935. a. $145. Europa Publications Ltd., 18 Bedford Sq., London WC1B 3JN, England. Indexed: Child.Auth.& Illus.

INTERNATIONAL WHO'S WHO IN ART AND ANTIQUES. see *ART*

INTERNATIONAL WHO'S WHO IN EDUCATION. see *EDUCATION*

920   UK
INTERNATIONAL WHO'S WHO IN ENGINEERING. 1984. irreg. price varies. Melrose Press Ltd., 3 Regal Lane, Soham, Ely, Cambridgeshire CB7 5BA, England.

920   UK
INTERNATIONAL WHO'S WHO IN MEDICINE. 1986. irreg. price varies. Melrose Press Ltd., 3 Regal Ln., Soham, Ely, Cambridgeshire CB7 5BA, England. Ed. Ernest Kay.

920   UK   ISSN 0261-0310
INTERNATIONAL WHO'S WHO IN THE ARAB WORLD. 1979. biennial. £124. International Who's Who of the Arab World Ltd., 169 Knightsbridge, London SW7 1DW, England.

920   UK
INTERNATIONAL YOUTH IN ACHIEVEMENT. 1981. irreg. price varies. Melrose Press Ltd., 3 Regal Lane, Soham, Ely, Cambridgeshire CB7 5BA, England.

920   UK   ISSN 0263-7022
JAMES HOGG SOCIETY. NEWSLETTER. 1982. a. £2. James Hogg Society, The Haldane Rm., Stirling University Library, Stirling FK9 4LA, Scotland. Ed. G.H. Hughes. bk. rev. circ. 100.

920   UK   ISSN 0075-6083
KINGS OF TOMORROW SERIES. 1967. irreg. price varies. Monarchist Press Association, 7 Sutherland Rd., West Ealing, London W13 0DX, England. circ. 3,500.

920   GW   ISSN 0454-1383
KOEPFE DES 20. JAHRHUNDERTS. 1957. irreg. DM.12.80. Colloquium Verlag, Unter den Eichen 93, 1000 Berlin 45, W. Germany (B.R.D.) circ. 3,000.

920   FI
KUKA KUKIN ON/WHO'S WHO IN FINLAND. 1909. every 4 yrs., latest edt. Fall 1986. Fmk.540. Kustannusosakeyhtio Otava, Uudenmaankatu 10, SF-00120 Helsinki, Finland.

BIOGRAPHY

920 943 GW
LEBENSBILDER AUS SCHWABEN UND FRANKEN. (Vols. 1-6: Schwaebische Lebensbilder) 1940. biennial. DM.48. Kommission fuer Geschichtliche Landeskunde in Baden-Wuerttemberg, Eugen-Str. 7, 7000 Stuttgart 1, W. Germany (B.R.D.) Ed. Robert Uhland.

LEITENDE MAENNER DER WIRTSCHAFT. see BUSINESS AND ECONOMICS — Management

MABUA/FOUNTAIN; religious creation in literature, society and thought. see LITERATURE

015 II
MADHYA PRADESH WHO'S WHO. (Text in English) 1978. a. Rs.30. New Era Publication, S.N.6, Char Bungalow Rd., Professor Colony, Bhopal 462001, India.

MAGILL'S LITERARY ANNUAL: HISTORY AND BIOGRAPHY. see LITERATURE

MEMOIRE DES FEMMES. see WOMEN'S INTERESTS

012 US ISSN 0461-7398
MEN AND WOMEN OF HAWAII. Variant title: Who's Who in Hawaii. 1918. every 7-10 yrs; 9th edt. 1972. $25. S B Printers, Inc., 420 Ward Ave., Honolulu, HI 96814. TEL 808-537-5353. Ed. Mrs. Betty Buker. circ. 3,000.

925 500 US ISSN 0077-2933
NATIONAL ACADEMY OF SCIENCES. BIOGRAPHICAL MEMOIRS. 1953. irreg. price varies. (National Academy of Sciences) National Academy Press, 2101 Constitution Ave., N.W., Washington, DC 20418. TEL 202-334-3318. Indexed: Biol.Abstr. GeoRef.

920 US ISSN 0077-5371
NATIONAL REGISTER OF PROMINENT AMERICANS AND INTERNATIONAL NOTABLES. 1966. biennial. $30. National Register of Prominent Americans, Drawer 100, Nokomis, FL 33555. Ed. William Smith. bk. rev. (also avail. in microform from UMI; reprint service avail. from UMI)

920 808.8 US ISSN 0077-6475
NEGRO AMERICAN BIOGRAPHIES AND AUTOBIOGRAPHIES. 1969. irreg., no.8, 1985. price varies. University of Chicago Press, 5801 S. Ellis Ave., Chicago, IL 60637. TEL 312-962-7700. Ed. John Hope Franklin. (reprint service avail. from UMI,ISI)

NEW ZEALAND BUSINESS WHO'S WHO. see BUSINESS AND ECONOMICS — Trade And Industrial Directories

NOUVELLE BIBLIOTHEQUE NERVALIENNE. see LITERATURE

920 659.2 US ISSN 0191-0051
O'DWYER'S DIRECTORY OF PUBLIC RELATIONS EXECUTIVES. 1979. triennial, next edt. 1986. $70. J.R. O'Dwyer Co., Inc., 271 Madison Ave., New York, NY 10016. TEL 212-679-2471. Ed. Jack O'Dwyer.

OESTERREICHISCHE KOMPONISTEN DES 20. JAHRHUNDERTS. see MUSIC

920 UK ISSN 0079-0729
PEOPLE FROM THE PAST SERIES. 1964. irreg., no.15, 1977. £4.95. ‡ Dobson Books Ltd., 80 Kensington Church St., London W8 4BZ, England. Ed. Egon Larsen.

920 AG
PERFILES CONTEMPORANEOS. no.2, 1976. irreg. Editorial Plus Ultra, Viamonte 1755, 1055 Buenos Aires, Argentina. Ed. Jose Isaacson.

PERFIS PARLAMENTARES. see PUBLIC ADMINISTRATION

920 UK
POLITICAL PORTRAITS. 1987. irreg. price varies. University of Wales Press, 6 Gwennyth St., Cathays, Cardiff CF2 4YD, Wales. Ed. K.O. Morgan.

920 943 GW ISSN 0080-2670
RHEINISCHE LEBENSBILDER. 1961. irreg., vol.8, 1980. price varies. Rheinland-Verlag, Kennedy-Ufer 2, 5000 Cologne 21, W. Germany (B.R.D.) (Distr. by: Rudolf Habelt Verlag, Am Buchenhang 1, 5300 Bonn, W. Germany (B.R.D.)) Ed. Bernhard Poll.

ROMANSERIER OG SELVBIOGRAFISKE SERIER. see LITERATURE

920 500 UK ISSN 0080-4606
ROYAL SOCIETY OF LONDON. BIOGRAPHICAL MEMOIRS OF FELLOWS OF THE ROYAL SOCIETY. (Continues: Obituary Notices of Fellows of the Royal Society, 9 Vols. (1932-54)) 1955. a. price varies. Royal Society of London, 6 Carlton House Terrace, London S.W.1, England. (reprint service avail. from ISI)

920 658 NZ ISSN 0557-4161
ROYAL SOCIETY OF NEW ZEALAND. PROCEEDINGS. 1868. a. NZ.$18. Royal Society of New Zealand, Private Bag, Wellington, New Zealand. Indexed: Biol.Abstr. GeoRef. Rev.Appl.Entomol.

SAGE YEARBOOKS IN WOMEN'S POLICY STUDIES. see WOMEN'S INTERESTS

920 UK
ST. DAVID'S DAY BILINGUAL SERIES. (Text in English and Welsh) 1928. a. price varies. University of Wales Press, 6 Gwennyth St., Cathays, Cardiff CF2 4YD, Wales.

920 BL
SOCIEDADE BRASILEIRA. 1974. a. Livraria Francisco Alves Editora, Rua Sete de Setembro 177, 20050 Rio de Janeiro RJ, Brazil. adv.
Social register

920 968 SA ISSN 0085-6363
SOUTH AFRICAN BIOGRAPHICAL AND HISTORICAL STUDIES. 1970. irreg., no.27, 1984. price varies. A.A. Balkema Ltd., P.O. Box 3117, Cape Town 8000, Cape Town, South Africa (And Box 1675, Rotterdam, Netherlands; in the U.S. and Canada, P.O. Box 230, Accord, MA 02018)

920 778.5 IT
STELLE FILANTI. 1978. irreg. Gremese Editore S.R.L., 88 Via Virginia Agnelli, 00151 Rome, Italy. Eds. Claudio G. Fava, Orio Caldiron.

SVERIGES FOERFATTARFOERBUND. MEDLEMSFOERTECKNING. see LITERATURE

920 SZ
SWISS BIOGRAPHICAL INDEX OF PROMINENT PERSONS/ANNUAIRE SUISSE DU MONDE ET DES AFFAIRES/WER IST WER IN DER SCHWEIZ UND IM FUERSTENSTUM LICHTENSTEIN/CHI E CHI IN SVIZZERA? 1972/73. biennial. 120 Fr.($60) Editions International Registry of Who's Who S.A. (Geneva), 23, Ch. du Lausanne, CH-1005 Lausanne, Switzerland. Ed.Bd. adv. circ. 3,000.

920 GW
TUDUV-STUDIEN. REIHE BAYERN PRIVAT. 1984. irreg. price varies. Tuduv Verlagsgesellschaft mbH, Gabelsbergerstr. 15, 8000 Munich 2, W. Germany (B.R.D.)

920 914.3 NE
VIENNA CIRCLE COLLECTION. 1973. irreg. price varies. D. Reidel Publishing Co., Box 17, 3300 AA Dordrecht, Netherlands (And 190 Old Derby St., Hingham, MA 02043) Ed.Bd.

VSPOMOGATEL'NYE ISTORICHESKIE DISTSIPLINY. see HISTORY — History Of Europe

920.01 UK ISSN 0083-937X
WHO'S WHO; an annual biographical dictionary. 1849. a. £52. A. & C. Black (Publishers) Ltd., 35 Bedford Row, London WC1R 4JH, England (Dist. in U.S. by: St. Martin's Press, 175 Fifth Ave., New York, NY 10010)

920 US
WHO'S WHO AMONG AMERICAN HIGH SCHOOL STUDENTS. (In 10 vols., by region) 1967. a. $28.50 per vol. Educational Communications, Inc., 721 N. McKinley, Lake Forest, IL 60045. TEL 312-295-6650. Ed. Paul C. Krouse. illus. stat.

920 US ISSN 0362-5753
WHO'S WHO AMONG BLACK AMERICANS. 1976. every 3-4 yrs. $90. Educational Communications, Inc., 721 N. McKinley Rd., Lake Forest, IL 60045. TEL 312-295-6650. Ed. William C. Matney. Indexed: Child.Auth.& Illus.

780 US ISSN 0362-3750
WHO'S WHO AMONG MUSIC STUDENTS IN AMERICAN HIGH SCHOOLS; a biographical dictionary of outstanding music students in American high schools. 1975. irreg. Randall Publishing Co., Box 2029, Tuscaloosa, AL 35401. TEL 205-349-2990.

378 920 US ISSN 0511-8891
WHO'S WHO AMONG STUDENTS IN AMERICAN JUNIOR COLLEGES. 1966/67. a. $23.80. Randall Publishing Co., Box 2029, Tuscaloosa, AL 35401. TEL 205-349-2990.

920 379 US
WHO'S WHO AMONG STUDENTS IN AMERICAN UNIVERSITIES AND COLLEGES. a., 41st 1975. $23.80. Randall Publishing Co., Box 2029, Tuscaloosa, AL 35401. TEL 205-349-2990.

920 US ISSN 0083-9396
WHO'S WHO IN AMERICA. (Supplement avail.: (Year) Supplement to Who's Who in America) 1899. biennial. $250. Marquis Who's Who, Macmillan Directory Division, 3002 Glenview Rd., Wilmette, IL 60091. TEL 312-441-2387. Indexed: Child.Auth.& Illus.
●Also available online. Vendors: DIALOG.

927 700 US ISSN 0000-0191
WHO'S WHO IN AMERICAN ART. 1936. biennial. $94.50. (Jaques Cattell Press) R.R. Bowker Company, Database Publishing Group, 245 W. 17th St., New York, NY 10011. TEL 800-521-8110. index. Indexed: Child.Auth.& Illus.

920 296 US ISSN 0196-8009
WHO'S WHO IN AMERICAN JEWRY (LOS ANGELES)* 1980? a. Standard Who's Who, 1742 Reedvale Ln., Los Angeles, CA 90049-2517. Ed. Harold M. Glass.
Incorporating: Directory of American Jewish Institutions.

WHO'S WHO IN AMERICAN LAW. see LAW

920 US
WHO'S WHO IN AMERICAN MUSIC. 2nd edt. 1985. biennial. $129.95. (Jaques Cattell Press) R.R. Bowker Company, Database Publishing Group, 245 W. 17th St., New York, NY 10011. TEL 800-521-8110.

923.2 US ISSN 0000-0205
WHO'S WHO IN AMERICAN POLITICS. 1967. biennial. $149.95. (Jaques Cattell Press) R.R. Bowker Company, Database Publishing Group, 245 W. 17th St., New York, NY 10011. TEL 800-521-8110. index. Indexed: Child.Auth.& Illus.

920 700 UK
WHO'S WHO IN ART. 1927. biennial. £24. Art Trade Press, 9 Brockhampton Rd., Havant, Hants PO9 1NU, England. Ed. M. Hickey.

920 US ISSN 0511-8948
WHO'S WHO IN CALIFORNIA. 1928. a. $135. Who's Who Historical Society, Box 10658, Bainbridge Island, WA 98110. Ed. Sarah Vitale. circ. 6,000.
Supersedes (1950-1952): Who's Who in Los Angeles County.

920 CN
WHO'S WHO IN CANADIAN FILM AND TELEVISION. (Text in English, French) 1985. a. Can.$21.95. Academy of Canadian Cinema & Television, 653 Yonge St., 2nd Floor, Toronto, Ont. M4Y 1Z9, Canada. TEL 416-967-0315. Ed. Chapelle Jaffe. adv. circ. 3,000.

920 340 CN ISSN 0710-6629
WHO'S WHO IN CANADIAN LAW. 1981. a. Can.$59.95. Trans-Canada Press, 161 Davenport Rd., Toronto, Ont. M5E 1R2, Canada. TEL 416-968-2714. Ed. Kim G. Kofmec.

136   BIOGRAPHY — ABSTRACTING, BIBLIOGRAPHIES, STATISTICS

920   US   ISSN 0147-8265
WHO'S WHO IN CHIROPRACTIC,
INTERNATIONAL. 1977. biennial. $49.50. Who's
Who in Chiropractic, International Publishing Co.,
Inc., Box 2615, Littleton, CO 80161. Ed. Fern L.
Dzaman.

WHO'S WHO IN CONSULTING; a reference guide
to professional personnel engaged in consultation for
business, industry and government. see BUSINESS
AND ECONOMICS — Management

920 330   UK
WHO'S WHO IN CUMBRIA. a. £6.50. Border Press
Agency Ltd., 12 Lonsdale St., Carlisle CA1 1DD,
England.

920 332   TH
WHO'S WHO IN FINANCE AND BANKING IN
THAILAND.* (Text in English) vol.2, 1978/79.
biennial. B.300($15) Advance Media Co., Ltd., U
Chuliang Bldg., 968 Rama IV Rd., Bangkok,
Thailand. Ed. Cherachit Vatanavatin. bibl.

920 330   US   ISSN 0083-9523
WHO'S WHO IN FINANCE AND INDUSTRY.
1936. biennial. $165. Marquis Who's Who,
Macmillan Directory Division, 3002 Glenview Rd.,
Wilmette, IL 60091. TEL 312-441-2387. Indexed:
Child.Auth.& Illus.
 Formerly: World Who's Who in Commerce and
Industry.

635 920   US   ISSN 0511-8964
WHO'S WHO IN FLORICULTURE. 1955. a. $150 to
non-members. Society of American Florists, 1601
Duke St., Alexandria, VA 22314. TEL 703-836-
8700. Ed. Drew Gruenburg. adv. circ. 11,000.

920   FR   ISSN 0083-9531
WHO'S WHO IN FRANCE/QUI EST QUI EN
FRANCE. 1953. biennial, latest 18th edt., 1986.
1420 F.($150) Editions Jacques Lafitte, 38 rue de
Contantinople, 75008 Paris, France. adv. circ. 11,
000.

920   II
WHO'S WHO IN INDIA (BOMBAY) (Text in
English) 1985. a. Rs.250($50) Business Press, Maker
Tower "E", 18th Floor, Cuffe Parade, Bombay 400
005, India. adv. circ. 6,000.

920   II   ISSN 0301-5106
WHO'S WHO IN INDIA (CALCUTTA) (Text in
English) 1973. irreg., latest 1987. Rs.200($50)
Kothari Publications, 12 India Exchange Place,
Calcutta 700001, India. Ed. H. Kothari. adv.

920 600   II   ISSN 0083-9558
WHO'S WHO IN INDIAN ENGINEERING AND
INDUSTRY. 1962. irreg. Rs.30($9) Kothari
Publications, 12 India Exchange Place, Calcutta
700001, India. Ed. H. Kothari. adv.

500   II   ISSN 0083-9566
WHO'S WHO IN INDIAN SCIENCE. (Text in
English) 1964. irreg., latest 1987. Rs.100($30)
Kothari Publications, 12 India Exchange Place,
Calcutta 700001, India. Ed. H. Kothari. adv.

368   US   ISSN 0083-9574
WHO'S WHO IN INSURANCE. a. $75. Underwriter
Printing and Publishing Co., 50 E. Palisade Ave.,
Englewood, NJ 07631. TEL 201-569-8808. Ed.
Donald E. Wolff. circ. 10,000.

920 368   UK
WHO'S WHO IN INSURANCE. 1976. a. £12.
Graham & Trotman Ltd., Bond Street House, 14
Clifford St., London W1X 1RD, England. Ed. T.
Wilmot. adv.

920   IS   ISSN 0083-9590
WHO'S WHO IN ISRAEL. (Also issues in Hebrew
under title Mi Va-Mi Be-Yisrael) (Text in English
and Hebrew) 1950. biennial. $60. Bronfman
Publishers Ltd., Box 1109, Tel Aviv 61 010, Israel.
Ed. Itzhak Ben. adv. circ. 3,000.

920   LE   ISSN 0083-9612
WHO'S WHO IN LEBANON. (Text in English)
1963/64. biennial. $50. Publitec Publications,
Gedeon House, 135-137 John Kennedy St., Jisr el
Bacha, Box 5936, Beirut, Lebanon (Dist. in U.S. by:
Unipub, Box 433, Murray Hill Sta., New York, NY
10016) Ed. Charles G. Gedeon. adv. circ. 3,000.

WHO'S WHO IN LIBRARY AND INFORMATION
SERVICES. see LIBRARY AND INFORMATION
SCIENCES

920   MY   ISSN 0083-9620
WHO'S WHO IN MALAYSIA AND SINGAPORE.
(Text in English) 1956. biennial. $85. J. Victor
Morais, Ed. & Pub., Box 266, B.P. House, Jalan
Davidson, Kuala Lumpur 0505, Malaysia (Dist. by:
International Publications Service, 114 E. 32nd St.,
New York, N.Y. 10016) illus.

954.7 920   PK   ISSN 0083-9671
WHO'S WHO IN PAKISTAN. (Text in English)
1930. a. Rs.35($30) Barque & Company, 87 Sarah-e-
Liaquat Ali, Box 201, Lahore, Pakistan. Ed. A.M.
Barque. adv. circ. 12,000.

659.2 920   US   ISSN 0511-9022
WHO'S WHO IN PUBLIC RELATIONS
(INTERNATIONAL) 1959/60. irreg. P R
Publishing Co., Inc., Box 600, Exeter, NH 03833.
TEL 603-778-0514.

920.053   SU
WHO'S WHO IN SAUDI ARABIA. (Text in English)
1977. a? $45. Tihama Advertising, Public Relations
& Marketing, Residential Centre 312, Box 5455,
Jeddah 21422, Saudi Arabia.

920   SZ   ISSN 0083-9736
WHO'S WHO IN SWITZERLAND. 1951. biennial.
150 Fr.($126) Editions Nagel S.A., 5-7, rue de
l'Orangerie, 1211 Geneva 7, Switzerland. circ. 10,
000.

920   LE   ISSN 0083-9752
WHO'S WHO IN THE ARAB WORLD. (Text in
English) 1965/66. biennial. $135. Publitec
Publications, Gedeon House, 135-137 John Kennedy
St., Jisr el Bacha, Box 5936, Beirut, Lebanon (Dist.
in U.S. by: Unipub, Box 433, Murray Hill Station,
New York, NY 10016) Ed. Charles G. Gedeon.
circ. 5,000.

920   UK
WHO'S WHO IN THE COMMONWEALTH. 1982.
irreg. price varies. Melrose Press Ltd., 3 Regal Lane,
Soham, Ely, Cambridgeshire CB7 5BA, England.

920   US   ISSN 0083-9760
WHO'S WHO IN THE EAST. 1945. biennial. $154.
Marquis Who's Who, Macmillan Directory Division,
3002 Glenview Rd., Wilmette, IL 60091. TEL 312-
441-2387.

338.1 636 920   US   ISSN 0510-4130
WHO'S WHO IN THE EGG AND POULTRY
INDUSTRIES. 1929. a. $50. Watt Publishing Co.,
Mount Morris, IL 61504. TEL 815-734-4171. circ.
11,000.

920   US   ISSN 0083-9787
WHO'S WHO IN THE MIDWEST. 1946. biennial.
$165. Marquis Who's Who, Macmillan Directory
Division, 3002 Glenview Rd., Wilmette, IL 60091.
TEL 312-441-2387. Indexed: Child.Auth.& Illus.

920   US   ISSN 0083-9809
WHO'S WHO IN THE SOUTH AND SOUTHWEST.
1946. biennial. $154. Marquis Who's Who,
Macmillan Directory Division, 3002 Glenview Rd.,
Wilmette, IL 60091. TEL 312-441-2387. Indexed:
Child.Auth.& Illus.

920   US   ISSN 0083-9817
WHO'S WHO IN THE WEST. 1946. biennial. $154.
Marquis Who's Who, Macmillan Directory Division,
3002 Glenview Rd., Wilmette, IL 60091. TEL 312-
441-2387.

920   US   ISSN 0083-9825
WHO'S WHO IN THE WORLD. 1971. biennial, 8th
edt., 1986. $199. Marquis Who's Who, Macmillan
Directory Division, 3002 Glenview Rd., Wilmette,
IL 60091. TEL 312-441-2387.

WHO'S WHO IN TRAINING AND
DEVELOPMENT. see BUSINESS AND
ECONOMICS — Management

920   UK
WHO'S WHO IN WESTERN EUROPE. 1980. irreg.
£65. Melrose Press Ltd., 7 Regal Lane, Soham, Ely,
Cambridgeshire CB7 5BA, England.

920   US   ISSN 0083-9841
WHO'S WHO OF AMERICAN WOMEN. 1958.
biennial. $154. Marquis Who's Who, Macmillan
Directory Division, 3002 Glenview Rd., Wilmette,
IL 60091. TEL 312-441-2387.

920   US
WHO'S WHO OF EMERGING LEADERS IN
AMERICA. 1987. biennial. $165. Marquis Who's
Who, Macmillan Directory Division, 3002 Glenview
Ave., Wilmette, IL 60091. TEL 312-441-2387.

920   SA
WHO'S WHO OF SOUTHERN AFRICA
INCLUDING MAURITIUS, SOUTH WEST
AFRICA, ZIMBABWE AND NEIGHBORING
COUNTRIES. (Text in English) 1907. a. R.98.
Who's Who of Southern Africa CC, P.O. Box
81284, Parkhurst 2120, South Africa TEL 011-880-
2406. (Dist. by: International Publications Service,
114 E. 32nd St., New York, NY 10016) Ed. M.E.
Essberger. adv.
 Former titles: Who's Who of Southern Africa
Including Mauritius, South West Africa, Zimbabwe-
Rhodesia and Neighboring Countries; Who's Who
of Southern Africa Including Mauritius, South West
Africa, Rhodesia and Neighboring Countries; Who's
Who of Southern Africa (ISSN 0083-9876);
Incorporating: Who's Who of Rhodesia, Mauritius,
Central and East Africa (ISSN 0083-9868)

920   UK
WHO'S WHO ON THE SCREEN. 1983. biennial.
£6.95($21.35) Madeleine Productions, 15 Wallace
Ave., Worthing BN11 5RA, England. Ed. John
Walter Skinner. bibl. illus. stats. circ. 5,000.

WORLD WHO'S WHO OF WOMEN. see
WOMEN'S INTERESTS

920 011   US
WRITERS DIRECTORY. 1970. biennial. $75. St.
James Press Inc., 425 N. Michigan Ave., Chicago,
IL 60611. TEL 312-329-0806. circ. 7,500.

BIOGRAPHY — Abstracting, Bibliographies, Statistics

BIBLIOGRAPHIA FRANCISCANA. see
RELIGIONS AND THEOLOGY — Abstracting,
Bibliographies, Statistics

016   US
BIOGRAPHICAL DICTIONARIES AND
RELATED WORKS. SUPPLEMENT; an
international bibliography of collective biography.
1972. irreg., 2nd edt. $140 for set. Gale Research
Company, Book Tower, Detroit, MI 48226. TEL
313-961-2242. Ed. Robert B. Slocum.

920 016   US   ISSN 0730-1316
BIOGRAPHY AND GENEALOGY MASTER
INDEX. 1976. irreg., 2nd edt., 1987. price varies.
Gale Research Company, Book Tower, Detroit, MI
48226. TEL 313-961-2242. Eds. Miranda C.
Herbert, Barbara McNeil. (also avail. in microfiche)
● Also available online. Vendors: DIALOG.
 Formerly: Biographical Dictionaries Master
Index.

920 016   US   ISSN 0006-3053
BIOGRAPHY INDEX; a quarterly index to
biographical material in books and magazines. 1946.
q. (annual and 3 year cumulations) $70. H. W.
Wilson Co., 950 University Ave., Bronx, NY 10452.
TEL 212-588-8400. Ed. Walter Webb. (avail. on
CD-ROM) Indexed: Child.Auth.& Illus.
● Also available online. Vendors: Wilsonline.

920   US
CHILDREN'S AUTHORS AND ILLUSTRATORS;
an index to biographical dictionaries. 1977. biennial,
latest edt., 1986. $140. Gale Research Company,
Book Tower, Detroit, MI 48226. TEL 313-961-
2242. Ed. Joyce Nakamura.

920   US
DICTIONARY OF LITERARY BIOGRAPHY. 1978.
irreg., vol.55, 1986. $90 per vol. Gale Research
Company, Book Tower, Detroit, MI 48226. TEL
313-961-2242. Ed.Bd. Indexed: M.L.A.
Child.Auth.& Illus. Perf.Arts Biog.Master Ind.

920 JM
WHO'S WHO JAMAICA. a. Who's Who Publications, Ltd., 14 Half Way Tree Rd., Kingston 5, Jamaica. Ed.Bd.

BIOLOGICAL CHEMISTRY

see Biology—Biological Chemistry

BIOLOGY

see also Biology—Biological Chemistry; Biology—Biophysics; Biology—Botany; Biology—Cytology and Histology; Biology—Entomology; Biology—Genetics; Biology—Microbiology; Biology—Microscopy; Biology—Ornithology; Biology—Physiology; Biology—Zoology; Medical Sciences; Pharmacy and Pharmacology

574 550 GW ISSN 0515-2712
ACTA ALBERTINA RATISBONENSIA. 1846. irreg. DM.30. Naturwissenschaftlicher Verein, Wilhelm Str. 11, D-8400 Regensburg, W. Germany (B.R.D.) Ed. Helmuth Ackermann. bk. rev. circ. 1,200. (back issues avail.)

574 HU ISSN 0567-7327
ACTA BIOLOGICA DEBRECINA. (Text in English, German, Hungarian and Russian) 1962. irreg., vol.20, 1984. Kossuth Lajos Tudomanyegyetem, Novenytani Tanszek, Egyetem Ter 1, 4010 Debrecen, Hungary. bibl. illus. circ. 450. Indexed: Biol.Abstr. Chem.Abstr. GeoRef.

574 PL ISSN 0860-2441
ACTA BIOLOGICA SILESIANA. (Text in English, German, Polish; summaries in English, Polish and Russian) 1975. irreg. price varies. Uniwersytet Slaski w Katowicach, Ul. Bankowa 14, 40-007 Katowice, Poland.
Formerly: Acta Biologica (ISSN 0208-5046)

ACTA FACULTATIS MEDICAE UNIVERSITATIS BRUNENSIS. see MEDICAL SCIENCES

ACTA HUMBOLDTIANA. SERIES GEOLOGICA, PALAEONTOLOGICA ET BIOLOGICA. see EARTH SCIENCES — Geology

574 PL ISSN 0065-132X
ACTA HYDROBIOLOGICA. (Text and summaries in English and Polish) 1959. irreg., vols.25/26, 1984. (Polska Akademia Nauk, Zaklad Biologii Wod) Panstwowe Wydawnictwo Naukowe, Ul. Miodowa 10, 00-251 Warsaw, Poland (Dist. by: Ars Polona, Krakowskie Przedmiescie 7, 00-068 Warsaw, Poland) Ed. R. Sowa. illus. circ. 980. Indexed: Biol.Abstr. Chem.Abstr. Pollut.Abstr. Geo.Abstr. GeoRef. Sel.Water Res.Abstr. Vet.Bull.

610 576 DK ISSN 0108-0172
ACTA PATHOLOGICA, MICROBIOLOGICA ET IMMUNOLOGICA SCANDINAVICA. SECTION A: PATHOLOGY. SUPPLEMENTUM. irreg. free to subscribers. Munksgaard, 35 Noerre Soegade, DK-1370 Copenhagen, Denmark. Ed. Joergen Rygaard. (reprint service avail. from ISI) Indexed: Biol.Abstr. Chem.Abstr. Curr.Cont. Ind.Med. Dent.Ind. Helminthol.Abstr. Ind.Sci.Rev. Trop.Dis.Bull.
Formerly: Acta Pathologica et Microbiologica Scandinavica. Section A: Pathology. Supplementum.
Pathology

616.07 576 DK ISSN 0108-0199
ACTA PATHOLOGICA, MICROBIOLOGICA ET IMMUNOLOGICA SCANDINAVICA. SECTION B: MICROBIOLOGY. SUPPLEMENTUM. irreg. free to subscribers. Munksgaard, 35 Noerre Soegade, DK-1370 Copenhagen K, Denmark. Ed. Joergen Rygaard. (reprint service avail. from ISI) Indexed: Curr.Cont. Excerp.Med. Ind.Med. Dent.Ind.
Formerly: Acta Pathologica et Microbiologica Scandinavica. Section B: Microbiology. Supplementum (ISSN 0105-0656)

575 JA ISSN 0065-1621
ACTA RADIOBOTANIKA ET GENETIKA/ HOSHASEN IKUSHUJO KENKYU HOKOKU. (Text in English or Japanese) 1967. irreg., no.2, 1971. exchange basis. Institute of Radiation Breeding - Norin-sho Nogyo Seibutsu Shigen Kenkyusho, Omiya-Machi, Naka-gun, Ibaraki 319-22, Japan.

574 CS ISSN 0001-7124
ACTA UNIVERSITATIS CAROLINAE: BIOLOGICA. (Editions in English, French, German, Russian) 1954. irreg. (5-6/yr) 60 Kcs.($33) Universita Karlova, Prirodovedecka Fakulta, Vinicna 5, 128 44 Prague 2, Czechoslovakia (Or Exchange Library, Faculty of Natural Science, Vimicina 5, 12844 Prague 2, Czechoslovakia) Ed. M. Kunst. bibl. charts. illus. stat. index. circ. 800. Indexed: Biol.Abstr. Excerp.Med. Plant Breed.Abstr. VITIS. Soils & Fert.

574 HU ISSN 0563-0592
ACTA UNIVERSITATIS DE ATTILA JOZSEF NOMINATAE. ACTA BIOLOGICA. (Text in English) 1947; N.S. 1955. a. exchange basis. Attila Jozsef University, c/o E. Szabo, Exchange Librarian, Dugonics ter 13, P.O.B. 393, Szeged H-6701, Hungary (Subscr. to: Kultura, Box 149, H-1389 Budapest, Hungary) Ed. Gyula Farkas. circ. 500.

574 PL ISSN 0208-4449
ACTA UNIVERSITATIS NICOLAI COPERNICI. BIOLOGIA. 1956. irreg. price varies. Uniwersytet Mikolaja Kopernika, Fosa Staromiejska 3, Torun, Poland (Dist. by: Osrodek Rozpowszechniania Wydanictw Naukowych PAN, Palac Kultury i Nauki, 00-901 Warsaw, Poland) Indexed: Biol.Abstr.
Formerly: Uniwersytet Mikolaja Kopernika, Torun. Nauki Matematyczno-Przyrodnicze. Biologia (ISSN 0083-4521)

574.33 574.4 574.8 US ISSN 0301-5556
ADVANCES IN ANATOMY, EMBRYOLOGY AND CELL BIOLOGY. 1966. irreg., vol.101, 1986. Springer-Verlag, 175 Fifth Ave., New York, NY 10010 TEL 212-460-1500. (Also Berlin, Heidelberg, Tokyo and Vienna) (reprint service avail. from ISI) Indexed: Biol.Abstr. Ind.Med. Sci.Cit.Ind. Ind.Sci.Rev. Ind.Vet. Vet.Bull.

574 US ISSN 0360-9960
ADVANCES IN BIOENGINEERING. (Represents Proceedings of annual meetings a. $40 to non-members; members $20. American Society of Mechanical Engineers, 345 E. 47th St., New York, NY 10017. TEL 212-705-7722. Ed. L. Thibault. illus. Indexed: Biol.Abstr. Chem.Abstr.

574 619 US ISSN 0065-2598
ADVANCES IN EXPERIMENTAL MEDICINE AND BIOLOGY. 1967. irreg. price varies. Plenum Publishing Corp., 233 Spring St., New York, NY 10013. TEL 212-620-8047. Ed.Bd. Indexed: Biol.Abstr. Chem.Abstr. Ind.Med. Sci.Cit.Ind. Dent.Ind. Ind.Sci.Rev.

574.92 US ISSN 0065-2881
ADVANCES IN MARINE BIOLOGY. 1963. irreg., vol.22, 1985. $57. Academic Press Inc., Orlando, FL 32887. TEL 305-345-2000. Eds. J.H.S. Blaxter, F.S. Russell. index. Indexed: Biol.Abstr. Biol.& Agr.Ind. Chem.Abstr. Sci.Cit.Ind. Geo.Abstr. Helminthol.Abstr. Ind.Sci.Rev.
Marine

AEROSPACE MEDICINE & BIOLOGY (NASA) see MEDICAL SCIENCES

574.92 US ISSN 0090-8843
ALABAMA MARINE RESOURCES BULLETIN. 1963. irreg., no.13, 1982. free. Department of Conservation and Natural Resources, Marine Resources Division, Box 189, Dauphin Island, AL 36528. TEL 205-861-2882. Ed. Hugh A. Swingle. charts. illus. circ. 1,000. Indexed: Biol.Abstr. Curr.Cont.

574.92 GW ISSN 0342-1120
ALGOLOGICAL STUDIES; Archiv fuer Hydrobiologie, Supplementbaende. (Text in English, French and German) 1970. irreg. price varies. E. Schweizerbart'sche Verlagsbuchhandlung, Johannesstr. 3A, 7000 Stuttgart 1, W. Germany (B.R.D.) Ed. O. Lhotsky. bk. rev. Indexed: Biol.Abstr.

ALLIANCE FOR ENGINEERING IN MEDICINE AND BIOLOGY. PROCEEDINGS OF THE ANNUAL CONFERENCE. see MEDICAL SCIENCES

ALMANAK NUKLIR BIOLOGI DAN KIMIA. see PHYSICS — Nuclear Energy

574 GE ISSN 0232-5381
ALTENBURGER NATURWISSENSCHAFTLICHE FORSCHUNGEN. (Summaries in English and German) 1981. biennial. M.12.50. Naturkundliches Museum Mauritianum, Postfach 216, DDR-7400 Altenburg, E. Germany (D.D.R.) Ed. Norbert Hoeser. circ. 1,000.

574 JA ISSN 0065-6674
AMAKUSA MARINE BIOLOGICAL LABORATORY. CONTRIBUTIONS. (Collected reprints of papers) (Text and summaries in English or Japanese) 1958. biennial. not for sale; limited controlled circ. Kyushu University, Amakusa Marine Biological Laboratory - Kyushu Daigaku Rigakubu Fuzoku Amakusa Rinkai Jikkensho, 2231 Tomioka, Reihoku-cho, Amakusa-gun, Kumamoto-ken 863-25, Japan. Ed. Taiji Kikuchi. circ. 130(controlled)
Marine

574 JA ISSN 0065-6682
AMAKUSA MARINE BIOLOGICAL LABORATORY. PUBLICATIONS. (Text and summaries in English) 1966. a. exchange basis. Amakusa Marine Biological Laboratory, Tomioka, Reihoku-cho, Kumamota-ken 863-25, Japan. Ed. Taiji Kikuchi. circ. 450. Indexed: Biol.Abstr.

551.48 574.5 GW ISSN 0065-6755
AMAZONIANA; LIMNOLOGIA ET OECOLOGIA REGIONALIS SYSTEMAE FLUMINIS AMAZONAS. (Text and summaries in German and Portuguese) 1965. irreg. (4 issues per vol.) DM.18 per issue. Verlag Walter G. Muehlau, Holtenauer Str. 116, 2300 Kiel, W. Germany (B.R.D.) Eds. Djalma Batista, Harald Sioli. Indexed: Biol.Abstr. ASCA. Forest.Abstr. Forest Prod.Abstr. GeoRef. Soils & Fert.

AMERICAN ASSOCIATION OF PATHOLOGISTS AND BACTERIOLOGISTS. SYMPOSIUM. MONOGRAPHS. see MEDICAL SCIENCES

574 US ISSN 0065-9436
AMERICAN MIDLAND NATURALIST MONOGRAPH SERIES. 1944. irreg. University of Notre Dame, American Midland Naturalist, Notre Dame, IN 46556. TEL 219-239-7481.

ANATOMISCHER ANZEIGER; Zentralblatt fuer die gesamte wissenschaftliche Anatomie. see MEDICAL SCIENCES

574 PL ISSN 0066-2232
ANNALES UNIVERSITATIS MARIAE CURIE-SKLODOWSKA. SECTIO C. BIOLOGIA. (Text in Polish or English; summaries in English, French, German, Russian) 1946. a. price varies. Uniwersytet Marii Curie-Sklodowskiej, Plac Marii Curie-Sklodowskiej 5, 20-031 Lublin, Poland. Ed. Z. Lorkiewicz. circ. 950. Indexed: Biol.Abstr. Chem.Abstr. Field Crop Abstr. Forest.Abstr. Forest Prod.Abstr. Herb.Abstr. Hort.Abstr. Int.Abstr.Biol.Sci. Plant Breed.Abstr. Rev.Appl.Entomol.

574 US
ANNUAL EDITIONS: BIOLOGY. Variant title: Focus: Biology. 1972. a. $8.95. Dushkin Publishing Group, Inc., Sluice Dock, Guilford, CT 06437. TEL 203-453-4351. Ed. Ian Nielsen. illus.
Formerly: Annual Editions: Readings in Biology (ISSN 0090-4384)

155.3 306.7 US
ANNUAL EDITIONS: HUMAN SEXUALITY. 1975. a. $9.50. Dushkin Publishing Group, Inc., Sluice Dock, Guilford, CT 06437. TEL 203-453-4351. Ed. Ian Nielsen.
Former titles: Annual Editions: Readings in Human Sexuality (ISSN 0163-836X); Focus: Human Sexuality (ISSN 0147-0655)

ANNUAL STUDENT SYMPOSIUM ON MARINE AFFAIRS. PROCEEDINGS. see EDUCATION

BIOLOGY

574.92 333.91 US ISSN 0733-2076
AQUARICULTURE AND AQUATIC SCIENCES. JOURNAL. 1980. irreg. $45 to individuals; libraries $90. Written Word, 7601 E. Forest Lake Drive, Parkville, MO 64152. TEL 816-842-5936. Ed. John Farrell Kuhns. adv. bk. rev. abstr. bibl. charts. illus. index. circ. 1,000. (back issues avail.) Indexed: Biol.Abstr. Aqua.Sci. & Fish.Abstr. Zoo.Rec.
Formerly: Journal of Aquaculture.

574.92 US
AQUATIC TOXICOLOGY. 1982. irreg., no.2, 1984. price varies. Raven Press, 1185 Ave. of the Americas, New York, NY 10036. TEL 212-575-0335. Ed. Lavern J. Weber. (back issues avail.) Indexed: Biol.Abstr. Excerp.Med. Sci.Cit.Ind. Biotech.Abstr. Sel.Water Res.Abstr. Vet.Bull.

ARBEITEN AUS DEM PAUL-EHRLICH-INSTITUT, DEM GEORG-SPEYER-HAUS UND DEM FERDINAND-BLUM-INSTITUT. see *MEDICAL SCIENCES*

574 GE ISSN 0003-9365
ARCHIV FUER PROTISTENKUNDE; Protozoen-Algen-Pilze. (Text in English, French and German; summaries in English) 1902. irreg. (4-8/yr.) M.45 per vol. VEB Gustav Fischer Verlag, Villengang 2, Postfach 176, 6900 Jena, E. Germany (D.D.R.) Ed.Bd. bk. rev. bibl. charts. illus. index. cum.index: vols.1-50, 1902-1918 (in 2 vols.) (reprint service avail. from ISI) Indexed: Biol.Abstr. Chem.Abstr. Curr.Cont. Excerp.Med. Sci.Cit.Ind. Abstr.Hyg. Helminthol.Abstr. Trop.Dis.Bull. Vet.Bull.

574 611 FR ISSN 0003-9586
ARCHIVES D'ANATOMIE, D'HISTOLOGIE ET D'EMBRYOLOGIE; normales et experimentales. 1922. a. price varies. Editions Alsatia, 10 rue Bartholdi, 68001 Colmar, France. bk. rev. charts. illus. Indexed: Biol.Abstr. Chem.Abstr. Excerp.Med. Ind.Med. Anim.Breed.Abstr. Dent.Ind.
Anatomy and embryology

574 619 CL ISSN 0004-0533
ARCHIVOS DE BIOLOGIA Y MEDICINA EXPERIMENTALES. (Summaries in English) 1964. a. $45. Sociedad de Biologia de Chile, Casilla 16164, Santiago 9, Chile. Ed. Tito Ureta, M.D. adv. bk. rev. circ. 1,250. (also avail. in microfiche from UMI) Indexed: Biol.Abstr. Chem.Abstr. Curr.Cont. Excerp.Med. Ind.Med. Sci.Cit.Ind. Helminthol.Abstr. Ind.Sci.Rev.

574 560 AG ISSN 0325-3856
ARGENTINA. MUSEO PROVINCIAL DE CIENCIAS NATURALES. COMUNICACIONES. NUEVA SERIE. (Text in Spanish; summaries in English) 1967; N.S. 1983. irreg. exchange basis. Ministerio de Educacion y Cultura, Museo Provincial de Ciencias Naturales, Primera Junta 2859, Casilla Correo 555, 3000 Santa Fe, Argentina. Ed. Carlos Alberto Virasoro. circ. 1,000. (back issues avail.)
Supersedes: Argentina. Museo Provincial de Ciencias Naturales. Comunicaciones.

574 GW ISSN 0171-4090
ARTICULATA; Zeitschrift fuer Biologie, Systematik und Neubeschreibung von Gliedertieren. (Text in English and German) 1975. irreg., approx. 2/yr. DM.20. c/o Dr. Kurt Harz, Ed., Endsee 44, D-8801 Steinsfeld, W. Germany (B.R.D.) bk. rev. index. circ. 650. (back issues avail.) Indexed: Entomol.Abstr.

574 551 PR ISSN 0066-9571
ASSOCIATION OF ISLAND MARINE LABORATORIES OF THE CARIBBEAN. PROCEEDINGS. 1957. irreg., vol.15, 1980. $5. Association of Island Marine Laboratories of the Caribbean, University of Puerto Rico, Dept. of Marine Sciences, Mayaguez, Puerto Rico. Ed. Ernest H. Williams, Jr. circ. 500.

574 550 GW ISSN 0067-2858
BADISCHER LANDESVEREIN FUER NATURKUNDE UND NATURSCHUTZ, FREIBURG. MITTEILUNGEN. NEUE FOLGE. 1919. a. DM.30. Badischer Landesverein fuer Naturkunde und Naturschutz e.V, Gerberau 32, D-78 Freiburg i. Br., W. Germany (B.R.D.) Ed. K. Sauer. bk. rev. Indexed: Biol.Abstr.

574 US ISSN 0198-0068
BANBURY REPORTS. Variant title: Banbury Reports Series. 1979. irreg., vol.25, 1986. price varies. Cold Spring Harbor Laboratory, Box 100, Cold Spring Harbor, NY 11724. TEL 516-367-8432. Indexed: Biol.Abstr. Chem.Abstr.

574 598.2 UK ISSN 0408-5655
BARDSEY OBSERVATORY REPORT. 1953. a. £2.50. Bardsey Bird & Field Observatory, c/o R.G. Loxton, Pub., Baines Wing, Leeds University, Leeds LS2 9JT, England. Ed. P. Hope Jones. circ. 500. (back issues avail.) Indexed: Biol.Abstr.

574 US ISSN 0090-5542
BASIC LIFE SCIENCES. (Consists of the Proceedings of the International Latin American Symposia) 1973. irreg. price varies. Plenum Publishing Corp., 233 Spring St., New York, NY 10013. TEL 212-620-8047. Ed. Alexander Hollaender. Indexed: Biol.Abstr. Chem.Abstr. Ind.Med.

BASLER VEROEFFENTLICHUNGEN ZUR GESCHICHTE DER MEDIZIN UND DER BIOLOGIE. see *MEDICAL SCIENCES*

570 550 GW
BEITRAEGE ZUR NATURKUNDE IN OSTHESSEN. 1969. irreg., no.20, 1985. DM.20. (Verein fuer Naturkunde in Osthessen e.V.) Verlag Parzeller GmbH & Co. KG, Peterstor 18, Postfach 409, 6400 Fulda, W. Germany (B.R.D.) bk. rev. circ. 500.

574.9 BE
BELGIUM. STATION DE RECHERCHES FORESTIERES ET HYDROBIOLOGIQUES. TRAVAUX. SERIE D. HYDROBIOLOGIE. (Text in Dutch and French) 1941. irreg. Station de Recherches Forestieres et Hydrobiologiques, Duboislaan 14, Groenendaal, B-1990 Hoeilaart, Belgium.
Formerly: Belgium. Administration des Eaux et Forets. Station de Recherche des Eaux et Forets. Travaux. Serie D. Hydrobiologie (ISSN 0067-5369)

574 US
BENCHMARK PAPERS IN BIOLOGICAL CONCEPTS. (Each vol. has distinctive title) 1973. irreg., vol.3, 1977. price varies. Van Nostrand Reinhold Company, 7625 Empire Dr., Florence, KY 41042. TEL 606-525-6600. illus. index.

574.5 US ISSN 0095-4640
BENCHMARK PAPERS IN ECOLOGY. (Each vol. has distinctive title) 1974. irreg., vol.13, 1983. price varies. Van Nostrand Reinhold Company, 7625 Empire Dr., Florence, KY 41042. TEL 606-525-6600. Ed. F.B. Golley. illus. index. Indexed: Biol.Abstr.

575 574 US
BENCHMARK PAPERS IN SYSTEMATIC AND EVOLUTIONARY BIOLOGY. (Each vol. has distinctive title) 1975. irreg., vol.9, 1985. price varies. Van Nostrand Reinhold Company, 7625 Empire Dr., Florence, KY 41042. TEL 606-525-6600. Ed. C.J. Bajema. illus. index. Indexed: Biol.Abstr.

574 610 AU
BERICHTE NATURWISSENSCHAFTLICH-MEDIZINISCHEN VEREINS IN INNSBRUCK. (Text in English, French and German; summaries in English, French, German and Italian) 1870. a. price varies. Naturwissenschaftlich-Medizinischer Verein in Innsbruck, Innrain 52, Universitaet Innsbruck, Technikerstr. 25, A-6020 Innsbruck, Austria. Ed. Wolfgang Schedl. bk. rev. circ. 500. Indexed: Biol.Abstr.

BERLINER BOTANISCHER VEREIN. VERHANDLUNG. see *BIOLOGY — Botany*

BIBLIOTHECA ANATOMICA. see *MEDICAL SCIENCES*

574 581 JA
BIFIDOBACTERIA AND MICROFLORA. a. $15. (Japan Bifidus Foundation) Japan Scientific Societies Press (JSSP), 6-2-10 Hongo, Bunkyo-Ku, Tokyo 113, Japan.

DIE BINNENGEWAESSER; Einzeldarstellungen aus der Limnologie und ihren Grenzgebieten. see *EARTH SCIENCES — Hydrology*

574 IO ISSN 0126-0758
BIOINDONESIA. (Text and summaries in English and Indonesian) 1975. irreg? $3 per no. Lembaga Biologi Nasional National Biological Institute, Jl. Raya Juanda no. 18, P.O. Box 110, Bogor, Indonesia. Ed. I. Lubis. circ. 500. (back issues avail.) Indexed: Biol.Abstr.

574 DK ISSN 0108-1942
BIOLOGI; fagkatalog for laerere. 1982. biennial. Kr.54.30. Bibliotekscentralen, Tempovej 7-11, DK-2750 Ballerup, Denmark.

574 PL ISSN 0554-811X
BIOLOGIA. (Text in Polish; summaries in English) 1961. irreg. price varies. Adam Mickiewicz University Press, Marchlewskiego 128, 61-874 Poznan, Poland.
Formerly: Uniwersytet im. Adama Mickiewicza w Poznaniu. Wydzial Biologii i Nauk o Ziemi. Seria Biologia.

574 FI ISSN 0356-1062
BIOLOGICAL RESEARCH REPORTS FROM THE UNIVERSITY OF JYVASKYLA. 1975. irreg. exchange basis. Jyvaskylan Yliopisto - University of Jyvaskyla, Seminaarinkatu 15, 40100 Jyvaskyla 10, Finland. Ed. Pertti Eloranta. circ. 450.

574 UN
BIOLOGICAL SUBSTANCES; international standards, reference preparations and reference reagents. (Text in Arabic, English, French and Spanish) 1972. irreg., latest 1984. 11 Fr. World Health Organization, Distribution and Sales, 20 Avenue Appia, CH-1211 Geneva 27, Switzerland. TEL 91-21-11. circ. 6,000. Indexed: Biol.Abstr.

574 UR
BIOLOGICHESKIE NAUKI. 1971. irreg. 1.20 Rub. Kazakhskii Gosudarstvennyi Universitet, Ul. Lenina 18, Alma-Ata, Kazakh S.S.R., U.S.S.R. bk. rev. bibl. illus. Indexed: Biol.Abstr. Chem.Abstr. Ind.Med. Forest.Abstr. Forest Prod.Abstr. Helminthol.Abstr.

574 GW ISSN 0006-3282
BIOLOGISCHE ABHANDLUNGEN. (Summaries in English, French, German, Russian) 1949. irreg. (2-3/yr) DM.3.50 per. no. Biologie Verlag, Postfach 1449, 6200 Wiesbaden, W. Germany (B.R.D.) Ed. Herbert Bruns. charts. illus. index. Indexed: Biol.Abstr.

574 US
BIOLOGY SERIES (SEATTLE) 1967. irreg., latest 1977. price varies. University of Washington Press, Seattle, WA 98105. TEL 206-543-4050.

574 US ISSN 0067-8821
BIOMATHEMATICS. (Text in English) 1970. irreg., vol.17, 1986. price varies. Springer-Verlag, 175 Fifth Ave., New York, NY 10010 TEL 212-460-1500. (Also Berlin, Heidelberg, Tokyo and Vienna) (reprint service avail. from ISI) Indexed: Math.R. Sci.Cit.Ind.

BIOMEDICAL RESEARCH TECHNOLOGY PROGRAM; a research resources directory. see *BIOLOGY — Abstracting, Bibliographies, Statistics*

574 630 610 UK ISSN 0264-8725
BIOTECHNOLOGY AND GENETIC ENGINEERING REVIEWS. 1984. a. £80($120) Intercept Ltd., P.O. Box 2, Ponteland, Newcastle upon Tyne NE20 9EB, England. Ed. Gordon E. Russell. index. (back issues avail.) Indexed: Biol.Abstr. Curr.Cont.

574 614.7 JA ISSN 0289-0011
BIOTRONICS. (Text and Summaries in English) 1972. a. free. Ministry of Education, Biotron Institute, Kyushu University 12, Fukuoka 812, Japan. Ed. H. Eguchi. circ. 1,000.

574.92 BL ISSN 0067-9593
BOLETIM DE CIENCIAS DO MAR. (Text in English and Portuguese) 1961. irreg., no.25, 1974. $90 or available on exchange. Universidade Federal do Ceara, Laboratorio de Ciencias do Mar, Av. da Abolicao, 3207, Caixa Postal 1072, Fortaleza, Ceara, Brazil. Ed. Antonio Adauto Fonteles Filho. circ. 1,000. Indexed: Biol.Abstr. Ocean.Abstr. Aqua.Sci.& Fish Abstr. Curr.Tit.Ocean.
Formerly: Universidade Federal do Ceara. Estacao de Biologia Marinha. Boletim.

574 BL ISSN 0101-3580
BOLETIM DE ZOOLOGIA. (Text in English, French and Portuguese) 1937. a. exchange basis. Universidade de Sao Paulo, Departamento de Zoologia, Caixa Postal 20.520, 01498 Sao Paulo, SP, Brazil. (Co-sponsor: Instituto de Biologia Marinha) Ed. Gilberto Righi. circ. 500. Indexed: Biol.Abstr. Zoo.Rec.
    Supersedes in part (since 1976): Boletim de Zoologia e Biologia Marinha. Nova Serie (ISSN 0067-9623)

574 US
BOYCE THOMPSON INSTITUTE FOR PLANT RESEARCH. ANNUAL REPORT. no.48, 1971. a. free. Boyce Thompson Institute for Plant Research, Tower Rd., Cornell University, Ithaca, NY 14853. TEL 607-257-2030. Ed. D.C. Torgeson. charts. illus. circ. 1,000. Indexed: Rev.Plant Path.

BRAGANTIA. see *AGRICULTURE*

574 550 UK ISSN 0068-2306
BRITISH MUSEUM (NATURAL HISTORY) BULLETIN. HISTORICAL. 1953. a. £36. British Museum (Natural History), Cromwell Rd., London SW7 5BD, England. illus. index. circ. 500.

574 UK
BRITISH MUSEUM (NATURAL HISTORY) REPORT. 1969. triennial. price varies. British Museum (Natural History), Cromwell Rd., London SW7 5BD, England. bibl. illus. stat. Indexed: Br.Archaeol.Abstr.
    Formerly: British Museum (Natural History) Bulletin (ISSN 0524-6474)

574 US ISSN 0068-2799
BROOKHAVEN SYMPOSIA IN BIOLOGY. no.5, 1982. irreg., no.29, 1977. Brookhaven National Laboratory, Upton, NY 11973 TEL 516-282-2123. (Orders to: National Technical Information Service, 5285 Port Royal Rd., Springfield, VA 22151) Indexed: Biol.Abstr. Excerp.Med. Ind.Med. Anim.Breed.Abstr. Dairy Sci.Abstr. Helminthol.Abstr. Plant Breed.Abstr.

574 AG ISSN 0068-340X
BUENOS AIRES. CENTRO DE INVESTIGACION DE BIOLOGIA MARINA. CONTRIBUCION CIENTIFICA. (Text in Spanish; summaries in English) 1962. irreg., no.42, 1969. price varies. Centro de Investigacion de Biologia Marina, Libertad 1235, Buenos Aires, Argentina. Indexed: Nutr.Abstr. Ocean.Abstr.

574 600 US ISSN 0738-8551
C R C CRITICAL REVIEWS IN BIOTECHNOLOGY. 1983. irreg. $104. C R C Press, Inc., 2000 Corporate Blvd., N.W., Boca Raton, FL 33431. Eds. Graham G. Stewart, Inge Russell. Indexed: Helminthol.Abstr. Ind.Sci.Rev.

574 US
CALIFORNIA ACADEMY OF SCIENCES. MEMOIRS. 1868. irreg., vol.8, 1986. California Academy of Sciences, Golden Gate Park, San Francisco, CA 94118. TEL 415-750-7116. Ed. Daphne Fautin.

574.9 US ISSN 0068-5755
CALIFORNIA NATURAL HISTORY GUIDES. 1959. irreg. price varies. University of California Press, 2120 Berkeley Way, Berkeley, CA 94720. Ed. Ernest Callenbach.

574 UK ISSN 0068-6697
CAMBRIDGE MONOGRAPHS IN EXPERIMENTAL BIOLOGY. 1954. irreg., no.24, 1985. $24.95 for latest vol. Cambridge University Press, Edinburgh Bldg., Shaftesbury Rd., Cambridge CB2 2RU, England (and 32 E. 57th St., New York NY 10022) Indexed: Biol.Abstr.

574 UK
CAMBRIDGE STUDIES IN MATHEMATICAL BIOLOGY. 1980. irreg., no.5, 1982. $34.50 (cloth) $13.95 (paper) for latest vol. Cambridge University Press, Edinburgh Bldg., Shaftesbury Rd., Cambridge CB2 2RU, England (And 32 E. 57th St., New York, NY 10022) Indexed: Biol.Abstr. Math.R.

CANADIAN BULLETIN OF FISHERIES AND AQUATIC SCIENCES. see *FISH AND FISHERIES*

572 CN ISSN 0068-8681
CANADIAN FEDERATION OF BIOLOGICAL SOCIETIES. NEWSLETTER. (Text in English and French) 1959. a. $5. Canadian Federation of Biological Societies, 575 King Edward, Ottawa, Ont. K1N 6N5, Canada. Ed. B. Murphy.

572 CN
CANADIAN FEDERATION OF BIOLOGICAL SOCIETIES. PROGRAMME AND PROCEEDINGS OF THE ANNUAL MEETING. 1976. a. $10. Canadian Federation of Biological Societies, 575 King Edward, Ottawa, Ont. K1N 6N5, Canada. TEL 613-234-9555. author index. Indexed: Biol.Abstr.
    Formed by the merger of: Canadian Federation of Biological Societies. Proceedings (ISSN 0068-869X) & Canadian Federation of Biological Societies. Programme of the Annual Meeting (ISSN 0068-8703)

CANADIAN SPECIAL PUBLICATION OF FISHERIES AND AQUATIC SCIENCES. see *FISH AND FISHERIES*

CANADIAN TECHNICAL REPORT OF FISHERIES AND AQUATIC SCIENCES. see *FISH AND FISHERIES*

CANADIAN WILDLIFE SERVICE. REPORT SERIES. see *CONSERVATION*

CARIBBEAN RESEARCH INSTITUTE. REPORT. see *HISTORY — History Of North And South America*

CARNEGIE MUSEUM OF NATURAL HISTORY. ANNALS OF (THE) CARNEGIE MUSEUM. see *SCIENCES: COMPREHENSIVE WORKS*

CARNEGIE MUSEUM OF NATURAL HISTORY. BULLETIN. see *SCIENCES: COMPREHENSIVE WORKS*

574 AU
CATALOGUS FAUNAE AUSTRIA. irreg. price varies. Verlag der Oesterreichischen Akademie der Wissenschaften, Dr. Ignaz-Seipelpl. 2, 1010 Vienna, Austria. Indexed: Biol.Abstr.

574 US
CELL MEMBRANES, METHODS AND REVIEWS. 1974. irreg. price varies. Plenum Publishing Corp., 233 Spring St., New York, NY 10013. TEL 212-620-8000. Ed. Bd. Indexed: Biol.Abstr. Chem.Abstr. Excerp.Med. Ind.Sci.Rev.
    Supersedes (as of 1983): Methods in Membrane Biology (ISSN 0093-4771)

CENTRE D'ECOLOGIE FORESTIERE ET RURALE. COMMUNICATIONS. see *FORESTS AND FORESTRY*

574 SX ISSN 0590-6342
CIMBEBASIA. SERIES A: NATURAL HISTORY. (Text mainly in English; summaries in French or German) 1962. irreg., vol.7, no.8, 1985. price varies. State Museum, Box 1203, Windhoek, Southwest Africa. Ed. H. Rust. index. circ. 400. (back issues avail.) Indexed: Biol.Abstr. Ind.S.A.Per.

574.92 IT
CIVICA STAZIONE IDROBIOLOGICA DI MILANO. QUADERNI. (Summaries in English) 1970. irreg. Civica Stazione Idrobiologica di Milano, Viale Gadio, 2, 20121 Milan, Italy. bibl. charts. illus.

CLINICAL IMMUNOBIOLOGY. see *MEDICAL SCIENCES — Allergology And Immunology*

574.5 US
COASTAL SOCIETY. ANNUAL CONFERENCE. PROCEEDINGS. 1975. a. price varies. Coastal Society, 5410 Grosvenor Lane, Ste. 110, Bethesda, MD 20814. Ed. Susan Harvey. bk. rev. circ. 400. Indexed: GeoRef.

574 US ISSN 0084-8824
COLD SPRING HARBOR LABORATORY. ABSTRACTS OF PAPERS PRESENTED AT MEETINGS. irreg. (8-13/yr.) $85 per no. Cold Spring Harbor Laboratory, Box 100, Publications Department, Cold Spring Harbor, NY 11724. TEL 516-367-8432. circ. controlled. (processed)

574 US ISSN 0069-5009
COLD SPRING HARBOR LABORATORY. ANNUAL REPORT. 1924. a. Cold Spring Harbor Laboratory, Box 100, Publications Department, Cold Spring Harbor, NY 11724. TEL 516-367-8432. circ. controlled.

574 US ISSN 0091-7451
COLD SPRING HARBOR LABORATORY. SYMPOSIA ON QUANTITATIVE BIOLOGY. 1933. a. price varies. Cold Spring Harbor Laboratory, Box 100, Publications Department, Cold Spring Harbor, NY 11724. TEL 516-367-8432. bk. rev. illus. index. circ. 3,500. (back issues avail.) Indexed: Biol.Abstr. Curr.Cont. Excerp.Med. Ind.Med. Sci.Cit.Ind. Dent.Ind.

574 US ISSN 0270-1847
COLD SPRING HARBOR MONOGRAPH SERIES. 1970. irreg. price varies. Cold Spring Harbor Laboratory, Box 100, Publications Department, Cold Spring Harbor, NY 11724. TEL 516-367-8432. bk. rev. illus. index. Indexed: Biol.Abstr. Chem.Abstr. Sci.Cit.Ind.

574 SP
COLECCION CIENCIAS BIOLOGICAS. 1974. irreg., no.14, 1983. price varies. (Universidad de Navarra, Facultad de Ciencias) Ediciones Universidad de Navarra S.A., Apdo. 396, 31080 Pamplona, Spain.

574 US ISSN 0069-6285
COLUMBIA BIOLOGICAL SERIES. 1910. irreg., no.24, 1968. Columbia University Press, 562 W. 113th St., New York, NY 10025. TEL 212-678-6777.

574.1 EI
COMMISSION OF THE EUROPEAN COMMUNITIES. JOINT RESEARCH CENTRE, ISPRA. ANNUAL REPORT: PROGRAM BIOLOGY-HEALTH PROTECTION. (Text in English, French, German, and Italian) 1972. a. Office for Official Publications of the European Communities, P.O. Box 1003, L-2985 Luxembourg, Luxembourg (Dist. in the U.S. by: European Community Information Service, 2100 M St., N.W., Ste. 707, Washington, DC 20037)
    Formerly: Commission of the European Communities. Centre for Information and Documentation. Annual Report: Program Biology-Health Protection.

574 CL ISSN 0069-8784
CONFERENCIAS DE BIOQUIMICA.* 1967. a. Universidad de Chile, Instituto de Quimica Fisiologica y Patologica, Av. Bernardo O'Higgins 1058, Casilla 10-D, Santiago, Chile.

574 UK
CONTEMPORARY BIOLOGY. 1971. irreg. price varies. Edward Arnold (Publishers) Ltd., 41 Bedford Square, London WC1B 3DQ, England.

CONTEMPORARY TOPICS IN IMMUNOBIOLOGY. see *MEDICAL SCIENCES — Allergology And Immunology*

CONTRIBUTIONS IN BIOLOGY AND GEOLOGY. see *EARTH SCIENCES — Geology*

574.92 US
CONTRIBUTIONS IN MARINE SCIENCE. 1945. a. $8. University of Texas at Austin, Marine Science Institute, Port Aransas, TX 78373-1267. TEL 512-749-6723. Ed. Donald Wohlschlag. circ. 1,000. Indexed: Biol.Abstr. Biol.& Agr.Ind. Chem.Abstr. Excerp.Med. Nutr.Abstr. Ocean.Ind. Sci.Cit.Ind. Geo.Abstr. GeoRef. Ind.Sci.Rev.
    Former titles: University of Texas. Institute of Marine Science. Contributions (ISSN 0082-3449); University of Texas. Institute of Marine Science. Publications.

574 914.106 UK
CORNISH BIOLOGICAL RECORDS. 1977. irreg. £0.60 per no. to non-members. Institute of Cornish Studies, Biological Recording Unit, Trevenson House, Pool, Redruth, Cornwall TR15 3RE, England. Ed. S.M. Turk. circ. 100.

574 US
CROP PROTECTION MONOGRAPHS. 1986. irreg. price varies. Springer-Verlag, 175 Fifth Ave., New York, NY 10160 TEL 212-460-1500. (Also Berlin, Heidelberg, Tokyo, Vienna) (reprint service avail. from ISI)

574	US	ISSN 0070-2137
CURRENT TOPICS IN CELLULAR
  REGULATION. 1969. irreg., vol.27, 1985.
  Academic Press Inc., (Subsidiary of: Harcourt Brace
  Jovanovich) Orlando, FL 32887. TEL 305-345-
  2000. Eds. Bernard L. Horecker, Earl R. Stadtman.
  Indexed: Biol.Abstr. Chem.Abstr. Ind.Med.
  Sci.Cit.Ind. Ind.Sci.Rev.

CURRENT TOPICS IN COMPARATIVE
  PATHOBIOLOGY. see MEDICAL SCIENCES

574	US	ISSN 0070-2153
CURRENT TOPICS IN DEVELOPMENTAL
  BIOLOGY. 1966. irreg., vol.20, 1986. Academic
  Press, Inc., Orlando, FL 32887. TEL 305-345-2000.
  Eds. Alberto Monroy, A.A. Moscona. Indexed:
  Biol.Abstr. Chem.Abstr. Ind.Med. Nutr.Abstr.
  Sci.Cit.Ind. Ind.Sci.Rev.

CURRENT TOPICS IN MEMBRANES AND
  TRANSPORT. see BIOLOGY — Zoology

CURRENT TOPICS IN PATHOLOGY. see
  MEDICAL SCIENCES

574	II	ISSN 0378-7540
CURRENT TRENDS IN LIFE SCIENCES. irreg.,
  latest vol.13, 1986. $95. (University Grants
  Commission) Today and Tomorrow's Printers and
  Publishers, 24-B/5 Original Rd., Karol Bagh, New
  Delhi 110005, India (Dist. in U.S. by: Scholarly
  Publications, 7310 Elcresta Dr., Houston, Texas
  77083) (Alternate sponsor: Council of Agricultural
  Research) Indexed: Chem.Abstr.
  Incorporates: Aspects of Plant Science.

574.92	CS
CZECHOSLOVAK ACADEMY OF SCIENCES.
  INSTITUTE OF LANDSCAPE ECOLOGY.
  SECTION OF HYDROBIOLOGY. ANNUAL
  REPORT. (Text in English) 1960. a. exchange basis
  only. Czechoslovak Academy of Sciences, Institute
  of Landscape Ecology, Section of Hydrobiology,
  Vltavska 17, 151 05 Prague 5, Czechoslovakia. Ed.
  Jaroslav Hrbacek. (back issues avail.) Indexed:
  Biol.Abstr.
  Formerly: Czechoslovakia. Academy of Sciences.
  Hydrobiological Laboratory. Annual Report.

574	US
DAHLEM WORKSHOP REPORTS. LIFE
  SCIENCES RESEARCH REPORT. irreg., vol.37,
  1987. Springer-Verlag, 175 Fifth Ave., New York,
  NY 10010 TEL 212-460-1500. (Also Berlin,
  Heidelberg, Tokyo and Vienna)

DANA-REPORT. see EARTH SCIENCES —
  Oceanography

574.5 550	GW	ISSN 0416-833X
DECHENIANA-BEIHEFTE (BONN) (Text in
  German; summaries in English) 1955. irreg. DM.25.
  Naturhistorischer Verein, Nussallee 15a, 5300 Bonn
  1, W. Germany (B.R.D.) Ed. Hartmut Bick. (back
  issues avail.)
  Ecology

574	IT	ISSN 0416-928X
DELPINOA. (Summaries in English.) 1959. irreg.
  exchange basis. Universita degli Studi di Napoli,
  Istituto e Orto Botanico, Via Foria 223, 80139
  Naples, Italy. bibl. charts. illus. circ. 650. Indexed:
  Biol.Abstr.

DENMARK. FISKERIMINISTERIET.
  FORSOEGSLABORATORIUM.
  AARSBERETNING/ANNUAL REPORT. see
  FISH AND FISHERIES

DESERT TORTOISE COUNCIL. PROCEEDINGS
  OF SYMPOSIUM. see EARTH SCIENCES

DEUTSCHE GESELLSCHAFT FUER
  PATHOLOGIE. VERHANDLUNGEN. see
  MEDICAL SCIENCES

574	UK
DEVELOPMENTAL AND CELL BIOLOGY
  MONOGRAPHS. irreg., no.14, 1984. $64.50 for
  latest vol. Cambridge University Press, Edinburgh
  Bldg., Shaftesbury Rd., Cambridge CB2 2RU,
  England (And 32 E. 57th St., New York, NY
  10022) Eds. D.R. Newth, J.G. Torrey. illus.

574	NE
DEVELOPMENTS IN BIOENERGETICS AND
  BIOMEMBRANES. 1977. irreg., vol.6, 1983. price
  varies. Elsevier Science Publishers B.V., Box 211,
  1000 AE Amsterdam, Netherlands. Indexed:
  Chem.Abstr.

574	NE
DEVELOPMENTS IN CELL BIOLOGY. 1977.
  irreg., vol.8, 1981. price varies. Elsevier Science
  Publishers B.V., Box 211, 1000 AE Amsterdam,
  Netherlands.

574 551.4	NE
DEVELOPMENTS IN HYDROBIOLOGY. (Text in
  English) 1981. irreg. price varies. Dr. W. Junk
  Publishers, Spuiboulevard 50, 3311 GR Dordrecht,
  Netherlands (U.S. address: Kluwer Academic
  Publishers, 190 Old Derby St., Hingham, MA
  02043) Ed. H.J. Dumont. Indexed: Biol.Abstr.
  Chem.Abstr.

574	NE
DEVELOPMENTS IN IMMUNOLOGY. 1978. irreg.,
  vol. 18, 1985. price varies. Elsevier Science
  Publishers B.V., Box 211, 1000 AE Amsterdam,
  Netherlands. Indexed: Biol.Abstr. Chem.Abstr.

574	NE
DEVELOPMENTS IN TOXICOLOGY AND
  ENVIRONMENTAL SCIENCE. 1977. irreg.,
  vol.11, 1983. price varies. Elsevier Science
  Publishers B.V., P.O. Box 211, 1000 AE
  Amsterdam, Netherlands. Indexed: Chem.Abstr.
  Ind.Med.

DIRECTORY OF BRITISH BIOTECHNOLOGY. see
  AGRICULTURE

DIRECTORY OF PATHOLOGY TRAINING
  PROGRAMS. see MEDICAL SCIENCES

574.5 910	FR	ISSN 0335-5330
DOCUMENTS DE CARTOGRAPHIE
  ECOLOGIQUE. (Text in English, French, German
  and Italian) 1963. a. 150 F.($15) Universite de
  Grenoble I (Universite Scientifique et Medicale de
  Grenoble), Laboratoire de Biologie Vegetale,
  Domaine Universitaire de Saint-Martin-d'Heres,
  B.P. 68, 38402 St. Martin d'Heres Cedex, France.
  Ed. Paul Ozenda. bk. rev. illus. maps. circ. 900.
  (back issues avail.) Indexed: Biol.Abstr. Bull.Signal.
  Bibl.Cart.
  Formerly: Documents pour la Carte de la
  Vegetation des Alpes (ISSN 0419-5728)

574	DR
DOMINICAN REPUBLIC. CENTRO NACIONAL
  DE INVESTIGACIONES AGROPECUARIAS.
  LABORATORIO DE SANIDAD VEGETAL.
  SANIDAD VEGETAL.* irreg. (5-6/yr.) free.
  Centro Nacional de Investigaciones Agropecuarias,
  Laboratorio de Sanidad Vegetal, San Cristobal,
  Dominican Republic. circ. controlled. (processed)

574 550	GW
DORTMUNDER BEITRAEGE ZUR
  LANDESKUNDE. (Text in English, German)
  1967. a. Museum fuer Naturkunde, Muensterstr.
  271, D-4600 Dortmund, W. Germany (B.R.D.)
  Ed.Bd. circ. 600. (back issues avail.)

574.5	AT	ISSN 0070-8348
ECOLOGICAL SOCIETY OF AUSTRALIA.
  PROCEEDINGS. 1966. biennial. price varies.
  (Ecological Society of Australia) Blackwell Scientific
  Publications, P.O. Box 1564, Canberra, A.C.T.,
  2601, Australia (Subscr. to: Blackwell Scientific
  Book Distributors Pty. Ltd., 31 Advantage Rd.,
  Highett, Vic. 3190, Australia) Ed.Bd. bk. rev. circ.
  900. Indexed: Biol.Abstr. Field Crop Abstr.
  Herb.Abstr.

574.5	US	ISSN 0070-8356
ECOLOGICAL STUDIES; ANALYSIS AND
  SYNTHESIS. 1970. irreg., vol.62, 1987. price
  varies. Springer-Verlag, 175 Fifth Ave., New York,
  NY 10010 TEL 212-460-1500. (Also Berlin,
  Heidelberg, Tokyo and Vienna) (reprint service
  avail. from ISI) Indexed: Biol.Abstr. Chem.Abstr.
  Ecology

574.5	BU	ISSN 0204-7675
EKOLOGIIA. (Text in various languages) 1975. irreg.
  price varies. (Bulgarska Akademiia na Naukite)
  Publishing House of the Bulgarian Academy of
  Sciences, Acad. G. Bonchev St., Bldg. 6, 1113 Sofia,
  Bulgaria. circ. 430. Indexed: Chem.Abstr.
  Helminthol.Abstr. Soils & Fert.

574	UR
EKOLOGIYA PTITS LITOVSKOI S.S.R. 1977. irreg.
  Akademiya Nauk Litovskoi S.S.R., Institut Zoologii
  i Parazitologii, Vil'nius, Lithuanian S.S.R., U.S.S.R.
  Ed. M. Valyus.

ENVIRONMENTAL BIOLOGY. see
  ENVIRONMENTAL STUDIES

ERGEBNISSE DER LIMNOLOGIE/ADVANCES
  IN LIMNOLOGY. see EARTH SCIENCES —
  Hydrology

574.9	UK	ISSN 0071-1489
ESSEX NATURALIST. 1887; N.S. 1977. a. price
  varies. Essex Field Club, Passmore Edwards
  Museum, Romford Road, Stratford, London, E15,
  England. Ed. M.W. Hanson. adv. circ. 1,000. (also
  avail. in microfilm from UMI; reprint service avail.
  from UMI) Indexed: Biol.Abstr. Br.Hum.Ind.
  Br.Geol.Lit. Br.Archaeol.Abstr. Geo.Abstr.
  Zoo.Rec.

574.33	US
ETTORE MAJORANA INTERNATIONAL
  SCIENCE SERIES. LIFE SCIENCES. irreg.,
  no.20, 1987. Plenum Publishing Corp., 233 Spring
  St., New York, NY 10013. Ed. Antonino Zichichi.
  bibl. index. Indexed: Chem.Abstr.

574 573	US
EVOLUTIONARY MONOGRAPHS. 1979. irreg.
  price varies. University of Chicago, Biology
  Department, 915 E. 57th St., Chicago, IL 60637.
  TEL 312-702-9475. Ed. Leigh M. Van Valen. circ.
  200. Indexed: Biol.Abstr. GeoRef.

574 573	US	ISSN 0093-4755
EVOLUTIONARY THEORY; an international journal
  of fact and interpretation. 1973. irreg. $25.
  University of Chicago, Biology Department, 915 E.
  57th St., Chicago, IL 60637. TEL 312-702-9475.
  Eds. Leigh M. Van Valen, Virginia C. Maiorana. bk.
  rev. circ. 550. Indexed: Biol.Abstr. Bull.Signal.
  Curr.Cont. Anim.Breed.Abstr. Bibl.&Ind.Geol.
  GeoRef.

574 610	SZ	ISSN 0071-3384
EXPERIMENTAL BIOLOGY AND MEDICINE.
  (Text in English) 1967. irreg. (approx. 1/yr.) price
  varies. S. Karger AG, Allschwilerstrasse 10, P.O.
  Box, CH-4009 Basel, Switzerland. Ed. A. Wolsky.
  (reprint service avail. from ISI) Indexed: Biol.Abstr.
  Chem.Abstr. Curr.Cont. Ind.Med.

FACULTAD NACIONAL DE AGRONOMIA
  MEDELLIN. see AGRICULTURE

FAUNA ENTOMOLOGICA SCANDINAVICA. see
  BIOLOGY — Entomology

574 595.7 591	NZ	ISSN 0111-5383
FAUNA OF NEW ZEALAND. 1982. irreg. price
  varies. (Department of Scientific and Industrial
  Research) Science Information Publishing Center,
  P.O. Box 9741, Wellington, New Zealand. Ed. C.T.
  Duval. bibl. illus. (back issues avail.) Indexed:
  Biol.Abstr. Zoo.Rec.

FEDERAL-PROVINCIAL WILDLIFE
  CONFERENCE. TRANSACTIONS. see
  ENVIRONMENTAL STUDIES

574	DK	ISSN 0109-856X
FELTUNDERSOEGELSE; noter og meddelelser.
  1967. irreg. Midtsjaellands Naturhistoriske Forening,
  c/o Evald Larsen, Vermehrensvej 8, DK-4100
  Ringsted, Denmark.

574.92	DK	ISSN 0109-2529
FICHES D'IDENTIFICATION DU PLANCTON.
  (Text in English and French) 1939. irreg., no.177,
  1986. Kr.10 per no. International Council for the
  Exploration of the Sea, Palaegade 2-4, DK-1261
  Copenhagen K, Denmark (Subscr. to: C.A. Reitzels
  Boghandel, Noerregade 20, DK-1165, Copenhagen
  K, Denmark) Ed. Vagn Hansen. circ. 600. (back
  issues avail.) Indexed: Biol.Abstr.
  Formerly (until 1985): Fiches d'Identification du
  Zooplancton (ISSN 0443-9155)

FINNISH GAME RESEARCH/
RIISTATIETEELLISIA JULKAISUJA. see
CONSERVATION

551.2　　　　US　ISSN 0095-0157
FLORIDA MARINE RESEARCH PUBLICATIONS.
1973. irreg., approx. 5/yr. free. Department of
Natural Resources, Bureau of Marine Research, 100
8th Ave. S.E., St. Petersburg, FL 33701. Ed. K.A.
Steidinger. charts. illus. circ. 1,000. Indexed:
Biol.Abstr. Ocean.Abstr. Aqua.Sci.& Fish.Abstr.
Deep Sea Res.& Oceanogr.Abstr. Zoo.Rec.
　　Supersedes its Educational Series, Leaflet Series,
Professional Papers, Saltwater Fishery Leaflets,
Special Scientific Report, and Technical Series.

FOLIA BIOCHIMICA ET BIOLOGICA GRAECA.
see *BIOLOGY — Biological Chemistry*

FOLIA DENDROLOGICA. see *FORESTS AND
FORESTRY*

574　　　　CS
FOLIA FACULTATIS SCIENTIARUM
NATURALIUM UNIVERSITATIS
PURKYNIANAE BRUNENSIS: BIOLOGIA. irreg.
(7-12/yr.) price varies. Universita J. E. Purkyne,
Prirodovedecka Fakulta, Kotlarska 2, 611 37 Brno,
Czechoslovakia. Indexed: Biol.Abstr. Chem.Abstr.
Helminthol.Abstr.

574　　　　SW　ISSN 0367-2476
FOLIA LIMNOLOGICA SCANDINAVICA. (Text
in English) 1943. irreg. Kr.200. Almqvist & Wiksell,
P.O. Box 45160, S-101 20 Stockholm, Sweden. Ed.
Bjork Kristiensen.

574　540　614.7　634.9　CN
FOREST PEST MANAGEMENT INSTITUTE
PROGRAM REVIEW. (Text in English, French)
1982. a. free. Forest Pest Management Institute,
Canadian Forestry Service, 1219 Queen St. E., Sault
Ste. Marie, Ont. P6A 5M7, Canada. TEL 705-949-
9461. Ed. K. B. Jamieson. bibl. circ. 500.

574　　　　FR
FRANCE. MINISTERE DE L'INDUSTRIE ET DE
LA RECHERCHE. REPERTOIRE NATIONAL
DES LABORATOIRES; LA RECHERCHE
UNIVERSITAIRE. TOME 2: SCIENCES DE LA
VIE. 1966. irreg. Documentation Francaise, 29-31
Quai Voltaire, 75340 Paris 07, France.
　　Formerly: France. Delegation Generale a la
Recherche Scientifique et Technique. Repertoire
National des Laboratoires; la Recherche
Universitaire; Sciences Exactes et Naturelles. Tome
2: Biologie (ISSN 0071-8548)

574　　　　UK　ISSN 0374-7646
FRESHWATER BIOLOGICAL ASSOCIATION.
ANNUAL REPORT. 1932. a. £5. Freshwater
Biological Association, The Ferry House,
Ambleside, Cumbria LA22 0LP, England. Ed. R.T.
Clarke. circ. 3,000. (also avail. in microfiche; back
issues avail.) Indexed: Biol.Abstr.

574　　　　UK　ISSN 0308-6739
FRESHWATER BIOLOGICAL ASSOCIATION.
OCCASIONAL PUBLICATIONS. irreg. price
varies. Freshwater Biological Association, Ferry
House, Ambleside, Cumbria LA22 0LP, England.
Ed. J.E.M. Horne. circ. 400. (also avail. in
microfiche; back issues avail.) Indexed: Math.R.
Forest.Abstr. Soils & Fert.

574　　　　UK　ISSN 0367-1887
FRESHWATER BIOLOGICAL ASSOCIATION.
SCIENTIFIC PUBLICATIONS. price varies.
Freshwater Biological Association, The Ferry
House, Ambleside, Cumbria LA22 0LP, England.
Ed. J.E.M. Horne. circ. 2,500. (also avail. in
microfiche; back issues avail.) Indexed: Biol.Abstr.

574　　　　SZ　ISSN 0301-0155
FRONTIERS OF MATRIX BIOLOGY. (Text in
English) 1973. irreg. (approx. 1/yr.) price varies. S.
Karger AG, Allschwilerstrasse 10, P.O. Box, CH-
4009 Basel, Switzerland. Eds. L. Robert, B. Robert.
(reprint service avail. from ISI) Indexed: Biol.Abstr.

574　　　　US
FUNGAL GENETICS NEWSLETTER. 1962. a. $7.
Fungal Genetics Stock Center, University of Kansas
Medical School, Department of Microbiology,
Kansas City, KS 66103. TEL 913-588-7044. Ed.
Peter J. Russell. circ. 1,000. Indexed: Biol.Abstr.
Rev.Plant Path.
　　Formerly: Neurospora Newsletter (ISSN 0028-
3975)

574.1　612　　GW　ISSN 0340-0840
FUNKTIONSANALYSE BIOLOGISCHER
SYSTEME. (Text in English and German) 1974.
irreg., vol.15, 1986. price varies. (Akademie der
Wissenschaften und der Literatur, Mainz) Franz
Steiner Verlag Wiesbaden GmbH, Birkenwaldstr. 44,
Postfach 347, D-7000 Stuttgart 1, W. Germany
(B.R.D.) Ed. Gerhard Thews. Indexed: Chem.Abstr.

574　　　　CL　ISSN 0374-7999
GAYANA: MISCELANEA. (Text in English or
Spanish) 1971. irreg. (1/yr.) Universidad de
Concepcion, Facultad de Ciencias Biologicas y de
Recursos Naturales, Casilla 2407, Apdo. 10,
Concepcion, Chile (Subscr. to: Editorial Universidad
de Concepcion, Depto. Ventas, Cas. 1557,
Concepcion, Chile) Ed. Alberto Larrain. Indexed:
Biol.Abstr.

574　550　　II　ISSN 0253-3340
GEOBIOS NEW REPORTS. (Text in English) 1982.
biennial. $40. University of Jodhpur, Botany
Department, Box 14, Jodhpur 342001, Rajasthan,
India. Ed. David N. Sen. bk. rev.

570　　　　GW　ISSN 0368-2307
GESELLSCHAFT FUER NATURKUNDE IN
WUERTTEMBERG. JAHRESHEFTE. 1845. a.
DM.35 price varies. Gesellschaft fuer Naturkunde in
Wuerttemberg, Rosenstein 1, 7000 Stuttgart 1, W.
Germany (B.R.D.) Ed. Horst Janus. circ. 1,100.
Indexed: Biol.Abstr. GeoRef.
　　Formerly: Verein fuer Vaterlaendische
Naturkunde in Wuerttemberg. Jahresheft.

574　500　　UK　ISSN 0373-241X
GLASGOW NATURALIST. 1908. a. £4. Glasgow
Natural History Society, c/o Ronald M. Dobson,
Ed., Department of Zoology, University of Glasgow,
Glasgow G12 8QQ, Scotland. bk. rev. charts. illus.
cum.index every 6 years. circ. 500. Indexed:
Biol.Abstr.

GORTANIA; atti del Museo Friulano di Storia
Naturale. see *EARTH SCIENCES*

574　　　　UK　ISSN 0308-1125
GREAT BRITAIN. INSTITUTE OF TERRESTRIAL
ECOLOGY. REPORT. 1975. a. Institute of
Terrestrial Ecology, Monks Wood Experimental
Station, Huntingdon Cambs PE17 2LS, England.
Indexed: Field Crop Abstr. Herb.Abstr.
　　Incorporating: Merlewood Research Station.
Report; Monks Wood Experimental Station. Report
(ISSN 0077-0418)

574　　　　GW　ISSN 0085-1299
GRUNDBEGRIFFE DER MODERNEN
BIOLOGIE. 1967. irreg. price varies. Gustav
Fischer Verlag, Wollgrasweg 49, Postfach 720143,
7000 Stuttgart 70, W. Germany (B.R.D.) adv. bk.
rev.

GUIDE TO BIOMEDICAL STANDARDS. see
MEDICAL SCIENCES

GUNNERIA. see *ARCHAEOLOGY*

574　　　　US　ISSN 0073-1331
HAWAII INSTITUTE OF MARINE BIOLOGY.
TECHNICAL REPORTS. 1964. irreg., no.3, 1973.
free to qualified personnel. ‡ Hawaii Institute of
Marine Biology, University of Hawaii, Box 1346,
Kaneohe, HI 96744. TEL 808-247-6631. circ. 200.
Indexed: Ocean.Abstr.

HIROSHIMA UNIVERSITY. LABORATORY FOR
AMPHIBIAN BIOLOGY. SCIENTIFIC REPORT.
see *BIOLOGY — Zoology*

574.92　　　NO　ISSN 0073-4128
HVALRAADETS SKRIFTER/SCIENTIFIC
RESULTS OF MARINE BIOLOGICAL
RESEARCH. (Text mainly in English) 1931. irreg.
price varies. (Norske Videnskaps-Akademi -
Norwegian Academy of Science and Letters)
Norwegian University Press, Kolstadgt. 1, Box
2959-Toeyen, 0608 Oslo 6, Norway (U.S. address:
Publications Expediting Inc., 200 Meacham Ave.,
Elmont, NY 11003) Indexed: Biol.Abstr.

574　　　　BU　ISSN 0324-0924
HYDROBIOLOGY. (Text in Bulgarian, English,
French and Russian) 1975. irreg. 1.32 lv. per no.
(Bulgarska Akademiia na Naukite) Publishing House
of the Bulgarian Academy of Sciences, Acad. G.
Bonchev St., Bldg. 6, 1113 Sofia, Bulgaria (Dist. by:
Hemus, 6, Rouski Blvd., 1000 Sofia, Bulgaria) bibl.
illus. circ. 430.

574.5　　　MX　ISSN 0185-0369
I N I R E B INFORMA. 1976. irreg. (approx. 4/yr.)
Mex.$2,500($6) per no. Instituto Nacional de
Investigaciones sobre Recursos Bioticos, Apdo.
Postal 63, Xalapa, Veracruz, Mexico. index. circ. 1,
000. (back issues avail.)

574.9　　　US　ISSN 0073-490X
ILLINOIS. NATURAL HISTORY SURVEY.
BIOLOGICAL NOTES. 1933. irreg., no.125, 1986.
single copies free. ‡ Illinois Natural History Survey,
Natural Resources Bldg., 607 E. Peabody Dr.,
Champaign, IL 61820. TEL 217-333-6880. Ed.
Audrey Hodginsdski. Indexed: Biol.Abstr.
Rev.Plant Path. Wild Life Rev. Zoo.Rec.

ILLINOIS. STATE MUSEUM. SCIENTIFIC
PAPERS SERIES. see *SCIENCES:
COMPREHENSIVE WORKS*

574　　　　US　ISSN 0073-4748
ILLINOIS BIOLOGICAL MONOGRAPHS. 1914.
irreg. University of Illinois Press, 54 E. Gregory
Dr., Champaign, IL 61820. TEL 217-333-0950.
(also avail. in microform from UMI,JOH; reprint
service avail. from UMI) Indexed: Biol.Abstr.
Rev.Appl.Entomol.

574　　　　UK
INDEX FILICUM. 1906. irreg. price varies. (Royal
Botanic Gardens) Oxford University Press, Walton
St., Oxford OX2 6DP, England. Ed. B.S. Parris.

574　　　　UK
INDEX KEWENSIS. 1896. every 5 yrs. (Royal
Botanic Gardens, Herbarium) Oxford University
Press, Walton St., Oxford OX2 6DP, England. circ.
1,200. (also avail. in microfiche)

574　　　　GW　ISSN 0344-4430
INFORMATIONSAUFNAHME UND
INFORMATIONSVERARBEITUNG IM
LEBENDEN ORGANISMUS. 1971. irreg., vol.3,
1975. price varies. (Akademie der Wissenschaften
und der Literatur, Mainz, Mathematisch-
Naturwissenschaftliche Klasse) Franz Steiner Verlag
Wiesbaden GmbH, Birkenwaldstr. 44, Postfach 347,
D-7000 Stuttgart 1, W. Germany (B.R.D.) Ed.
Martin Lindauer.

INSTITUT FUER DEN WISSENSCHAFTLICHEN
FILM. PUBLIKATIONEN ZU
WISSENSCHAFTLICHEN FILMEN. SEKTION
BIOLOGIE. see *MOTION PICTURES*

574　614.7　　BE
INSTITUT ROYAL DES SCIENCES NATURELLES
DE BELGIQUE. BULLETIN. SERIE BIOLOGIE.
1930. irreg. (8-15/yr.) 1200 Fr.($25) Koninklijk
Belgische Instituut voor Natuurwetenschappen -
Institut Royal des Sciences Naturelles de Belgique,
Vautierstraat 29, 1040 Brussels, Belgium. abstr.
bibl. charts. illus. cum.index. circ. 1,500. (back
issues avail.) Indexed: Biol.Abstr. Bull.Signal.
Ref.Zh. Zoo.Rec.

574　　　　BE　ISSN 0374-6232
INSTITUT ROYAL DE SCIENCES NATURELLES
DE BELGIQUE. BULLETIN. SERIE
ENTOMOLOGIE. 1930. irreg. (10-20/yr.) 1500
Fr.($30) Koninklijk Belgisch Instituut voor
Natuurwetenschappen - Institut Royal des Sciences
Naturelles de Belgique, Vautierstraat 29, 1040
Brussels, Belgium. bibl. charts. illus. cum.index.
circ. 1,500. (back issues avail.) Indexed: Biol.Abstr.
Bull.Signal. Ref.Zh. Rev.Appl.Entomol. Zoo.Rec.

INSTITUTE OF ENVIRONMENTAL SCIENCES.
ANNUAL MEETING. PROCEEDINGS. see
ENVIRONMENTAL STUDIES

INSTITUTE OF ENVIRONMENTAL SCIENCES.
TUTORIAL SERIES. see *ENVIRONMENTAL STUDIES*

574　　　　　BL　ISSN 0020-3661
INSTITUTO BIOLOGICO DA BAHIA. BOLETIM.
(Summaries in English and Portuguese) 1954. irreg.
Instituto Biologico da Bahia, Av. Adhemar de
Barros-Ondina, Caixa Postal 553, 40000 Salvador,
Bahia, Brazil. Dir. Antonio A.J. da Silva. bibl.
charts. illus. Indexed: Biol.Abstr. Chem.Abstr.

INSTITUTO DE LA PATAGONIA. ANALES.
SOCIAL SCIENCIES. see *HISTORY — History Of North And South America*

574　　　　　RM
INSTITUTUL PEDAGOGIC ORADEA. LUCRARI
STIINTIFICE SERIA BIOLOGIC. (Continues in
part its Lucrari Stiintifice: Seria Educatie Fizica,
Biologie, Stiinte Medicale (1971-72), its Lucrari
Stuntifice: Seria A and Seria B (1969-70), and its
Lucrari Stiintifice (1967-68)) (Text in Rumanian,
occasionally in English or French; summaries in
English, French, German or Rumanian) 1967. a.
Institutul Pedagogic Oradea, Calea Armatei Rosii
Nr. 5, Oradea, Rumania.

INSTYTUT SADOWNICTWA I KWIACIARSTWA
W SKIERNIEWICACH. SERIA A: PRACE
DOSWIADCZALNE Z ZAKRESU
SADOWNICTWA. see *AGRICULTURE*

INTERNATIONAL ANATOMICAL CONGRESS.
PROCEEDINGS. see *MEDICAL SCIENCES*

INTERNATIONAL ASSOCIATION OF
THEORETICAL AND APPLIED LIMNOLOGY.
COMMUNICATIONS. see *EARTH SCIENCES — Hydrology*

INTERNATIONAL ASSOCIATION OF
THEORETICAL AND APPLIED LIMNOLOGY.
PROCEEDINGS/INTERNATIONALE
VEREINIGUNG FUER THEORETISCHE UND
ANGEWANDTE LIMNOLOGIE.
VERHANDLUNGEN. see *EARTH SCIENCES — Hydrology*

574　　　　　II　ISSN 0253-7206
INTERNATIONAL BIO-SCIENCES
MONOGRAPHS. 1975. irreg., latest vol.17, 1987.
$95. Today and Tomorrow's Printers and Publishers,
24-B/5 Original Rd., Karol Bagh, New Delhi
110005, India (Dist. in U.S. by: Scholarly
Publications, 7310 Elcresta Dr., Houston, Texas
77083)

574　　　　　UK
INTERNATIONAL BIOLOGICAL PROGRAMME
SERIES. 1975. irreg., no.26, 1981. $140 for latest
vol. Cambridge University Press, Edinburgh Bldg.,
Shaftesbury Rd., Cambridge CB2 2RU, England
(And 32 E. 57th St., New York, NY 10022)
Indexed: Biol.Abstr.

574　　　　　NE　ISSN 0074-2082
INTERNATIONAL BIOMETEOROLOGICAL
CONGRESS. SUMMARIES AND REPORTS
PRESENTED TO THE CONGRESS. triennial,
1975, 6th, College Park, MD, U.S.A. price varies.
International Society of Biometeorology, Inquire:
Dr. S.W. Tromp. Sec. Gen., Hofbrouckerlaan 54,
Oegstgeest, Leiden, Netherlands. circ. 1,200.
Indexed: Biol.Abstr. Curr.Cont.

574.92　639.3　　　DK　ISSN 0106-1003
INTERNATIONAL COUNCIL FOR THE
EXPLORATION OF THE SEA. ANNALES
BIOLOGIQUES. (Text in English or French) 1943.
a. price varies. International Council for the
Exploration of the Sea, Palaegade 2, DK-1261
Copenhagen K, Denmark (Subscr. to: C. A. Reitzels
Boghandel, Noerregade 20, DK-1165 Copenhagen
K, Denmark) Ed. B.B. Parrish. index. circ. 500.
(back issues avail.)
　　Marine

574　574.92　　　UN
INTERNATIONAL DIRECTORY OF MARINE
SCIENTISTS. (Text in English) 1970. irreg. price
varies. Food and Agriculture Organization of the
United Nations, Distribution and Sales Section, Via
delle Terme di Caracalla, 00100 Rome, Italy
(Subscr. to: Marine Information Centre, Division of
Marine Sciences, Unesco, 7 Place de Fontenoy,
75700 Paris, France) (Co-sponsor: United Nations
Educational, Scientific and Cultural Organization
(Unesco))

574　　　　　II　ISSN 0074-7033
INTERNATIONAL MONOGRAPHS ON
ADVANCED BIOLOGY AND BIOPHYSICS.
(Text in English) 1969. irreg. price varies.
Hindustan Publishing Corp., 6-U.B. Jawahar Nagar,
Delhi 110007, India.

574　615　　US　ISSN 0731-0358
INTERNATIONAL SYMPOSIUM ON QUANTUM
BIOLOGY AND QUANTUM
PHARMACOLOGY. PROCEEDINGS. 1974. a.
$30. John Wiley & Sons, Inc., 605 Third Ave., New
York, NY 10016. TEL 212-850-6000. Ed. Per-Olov
Lowdin.

570　　　　　FR
INTERNATIONAL UNION OF BIOLOGICAL
SCIENCES. GENERAL ASSEMBLIES.
PROCEEDINGS. triennial. $10. International
Union of Biological Sciences, 51 bd. E.
Montmorency, 75016 Paris, France.
　　Former titles: International Union of Biological
Sciences. Reports of General Assemblies (ISSN
0074-9362)

574.92　333.7　　UK　ISSN 0255-2760
INTERNATIONAL WHALING COMMISSION.
SPECIAL ISSUES. 1977. irreg. price varies.
International Whaling Commission, Red House
Station Rd., Histon, Cambridge CB4 4NP, England.
Ed. G.P. Donovan. bibl. illus. stat. circ. 750. (back
issues avail.) Indexed: Biol.Abstr. Zoo.Rec.

IRAQ NATURAL HISTORY MUSEUM.
PUBLICATION. see *SCIENCES: COMPREHENSIVE WORKS*

IRISH FISHERIES INVESTIGATIONS. SERIES A:
FRESHWATER. see *FISH AND FISHERIES*

IRISH FISHERIES INVESTIGATIONS. SERIES B:
MARINE. see *FISH AND FISHERIES*

574　　　　　US　ISSN 0160-3787
ISOZYMES: CURRENT TOPICS IN BIOLOGICAL
AND MEDICINE RESEARCH. 1977. irreg. price
varies. Alan R. Liss, Inc., 41 E. 11th St., New York,
NY 10003. TEL 212-475-7700. Indexed: Biol.Abstr.
Chem.Abstr. Ind.Med. Sci.Cit.Ind. Dent.Ind.
Ind.Sci.Rev.

574　　　　　IS
ISRAEL INSTITUTE FOR BIOLOGICAL
RESEARCH. SCIENTIFIC ACTIVITIES. 1970. a.
Israel Institute for Biological Research, P.O. Box 19,
Ness Ziona 70 450, Israel. TEL 054-81423.

574.92　　　　IT　ISSN 0374-9118
ISTITUTO ITALIANO DI IDROBIOLOGIA.
MEMORIE. (Text in English) 1942. a. exchange
basis. ‡ Istituto Italiano di Idrobiologia, Verbania
Pallanza, Novara, Italy. Ed. Riccardo de Bernardi.
circ. 800. Indexed: Biol.Abstr. Aqua.Sci. &
Fish.Abstr. Water Resour.Abstr.

574.88　　　　UR　ISSN 0202-7070
ITOGI NAUKI I TEKHNIKI:
MOLEKULYARNAYA BIOLOGIYA. irreg., latest
vol.23, 1987. price varies. Vsesoyuznyi Institut
Nauchno-Tekhnicheskoi Informatsii (VINITI), Ul.
Baltiiskaya 14, Moscow A-219, Russian S.F.S.R.,
U.S.S.R. (Subscr. to: Mezhdunarodnaya Kniga,
Dimitrova ul. 39, 113095 Moscow, Russian S.F.S.R.,
U.S.S.R.) Indexed: Chem.Abstr.

574　　　　　UR　ISSN 0203-5405
ITOGI NAUKI I TEKHNIKI: OBSHCHIE
PROBLEMY BIOLOGII. 1982. irreg., latest vol.6,
1987. price varies. Vsesoyuznyi Institut Nauchno-
Tekhnicheskoi Informatsii (VINITI), Ul. Baltiiskaya
14, Moscow A-219, Russian S.F.S.R., U.S.S.R.
(Subscr. to: Mezhdunarodnaya Kniga, Dimitrova ul.
39, 113095 Moscow, Russian S.F.S.R., U.S.S.R.)

ITOGI NAUKI I TEKHNIKI: ONKOLOGIYA. see
MEDICAL SCIENCES — Cancer

JAHRBUCH FUER BIOTECHNOLOGIE. see
BIOLOGY — Biophysics

JAPANESE COLLAGEN CLUB. PROCEEDINGS
OF THE ANNUAL MEETING. see *MEDICAL SCIENCES*

574　　　　　US　ISSN 0883-1394
JOURNAL OF INFERENTIAL AND DEDUCTIVE
BIOLOGY. 1985. irreg. $198. Danielli Associates,
185 Highland St., Worcester, MA 01609. Eds.
Roger V. Jean, Alejandro B. Engel. adv. bk. rev.

574　　　　　US　ISSN 0075-4404
JOURNAL OF ULTRASTRUCTURE RESEARCH.
SUPPLEMENT. 1959. irreg., no.12, 1973. incl. in
subscr. to Journal. Academic Press, Inc., Books
Division, 1250 Sixth Ave., San Diego, CA 92101.
TEL 619-230-1840.

JUGOSLAVENSKE AKADEMIJE ZNANOSTI I
UMJETNOSTI. RAZRED ZA PRIRODNE
ZNANOSTI. RAD. see *EARTH SCIENCES — Geology*

KAGAWA PREFECTIVE AGRICULTURAL
EXPERIMENT STATION. BULLETIN. see
AGRICULTURE

574　　　　　GW　ISSN 0340-5419
KARL-AUGUST-FORSTER-LECTURES;
Informationsgesteuerte Synthese /informational
directed synthesis. (Subseries (from vol. 13) of:
Research in Molecular Biology) 1971. irreg. price
varies. (Akademie der Wissenschaften und der
Literatur, Mainz, Mathematisch-
Naturwissenschaftliche Klasse) Franz Steiner Verlag
Wiesbaden GmbH, Birkenwaldstr. 44, Postfach 347,
D-7000 Stuttgart 1, W. Germany (B.R.D.) Ed.
Rudolf K. Zahn.

574　910　550　614.7　　FI　ISSN 0453-7831
KEVO SUBARCTIC RESEARCH INSTITUTE.
REPORTS. (Text in English, German; summaries in
English) 1964. irreg. price varies. University of
Turku, Kevo Subarctic Research Institute, SF-20500
Turku, Finland (Orders to: The Academic
Bookstore, SF-00100 Helsinki, Finland) Ed. Erkki
Haukioja. circ. 400. Indexed: Biol.Abstr. Curr.Cont.
Curr.Adv.Plant.Sci. Entomol.Abstr. Forest.Abstr.
Geo.Abstr. Rev.Appl.Entomol. Zoo.Rec.

574.92　　　　SU
KING ABDUL AZIZ UNIVERSITY. FACULTY OF
MARINE SCIENCE. JOURNAL. 1981. a. King
Abdul Aziz University, Faculty of Marine Science,
P.O. Box 1540, Jeddah, Saudi Arabia. Ed. A.K.
Behairy. illus.

KOBE UNIVERSITY. FACULTY OF
AGRICULTURE. SCIENCE REPORTS. see
AGRICULTURE

KOCHI UNIVERSITY. AGRICULTURAL
SCIENCE. RESEARCH REPORTS. see
AGRICULTURE

574　　　　　AU　ISSN 0075-6547
KOLEOPTEROLOGISCHE RUNDSCHAU. irreg.
price varies. Zoologisch-Botanische Gesellschaft,
Althanstr. 14, PF 287, A-1091 Vienna, Austria. circ.
180. Indexed: Biol.Abstr. Rev.Appl.Entomol.

570　　　　　DK　ISSN 0366-3612
KONGELIGE DANSKE VIDENSKABERNES
SELSKAB. BIOLOGISKE SKRIFTER. (Text
mostly in English) 1941. irreg., vol.24, 1985. price
varies. Kongelige Danske Videnskabernes Selskab -
Royal Danish Academy of Sciences and Letters,
H.C. Andersens Blvd. 35, DK-1553 Copenhagen V,
Denmark (Orders to: Munksgaard Export and
Subscription Service, Noerre Soegade 35, DK-1370
Copenhagen K, Denmark) bibl. illus. Indexed:
Biol.Abstr.

574　591　　　　BE
KONINKLIJK BELGISCH INSTITUUT VOOR
NATUURWETENSCHAPPEN.
STUDIEDOCUMENTEN/INSTITUT ROYAL
DES SCIENCES NATURELLES DE BELGIQUE.
DOCUMENTS DE TRAVAIL. (Text in Dutch,
English and French) 1963. irreg. 60 Fr.($1.25) per
no. Institut Royal des Sciences Naturelles de
Belgique, Vautierstraat 29, 1040 Brussels, Belgium.
bibl. charts. illus. (back issues avail.)

KUWAIT BULLETIN OF MARINE SCIENCE. see
FISH AND FISHERIES

574 JA ISSN 0454-7802
KYOTO UNIVERSITY. FACULTY OF SCIENCE.
MEMOIRS. SERIES OF BIOLOGY. (Text in
European languages) 1924; N.S. 1967. a. on
exchange basis. Kyoto University, Faculty of
Science - Kyoto Daigaku Rigakubu, Kitashirakawa
Oiwake-cho, Sakyo-ku, Kyoto 606, Japan. (back
issues avail.) Indexed: Biol.Abstr. Chem.Abstr.
Field Crop Abstr. Herb.Abstr.

574.92 JA ISSN 0023-6098
KYOTO UNIVERSITY. MISAKI MARINE
BIOLOGICAL INSTITUTE. BULLETIN.* 1962.
irreg. (approx. 2/yr.) Kyoto University, Qisaki
Marine Biological Institute, Yoshida-Honmachi,
Sakyo-ku, Kyoto 606, Japan. Ed. Kiyomatsu
Matsubara. Indexed: Biol.Abstr.
Marine

LECTURE NOTES IN BIOMATHEMATICS. see
MATHEMATICS

LECTURES ON MATHEMATICS IN THE LIFE
SCIENCES. see MATHEMATICS

580 590 LH
LIECHTENSTEIN. BOTANISCH-ZOOLOGISCHE
GESELLSCHAFT LIECHTENSTEIN SARGANS-
WERDENBERG. BERICHT. 1972. a. $20.
Botanisch-Zoologische Gesellschaft Liechtenstein-
Sargans-Werdenberg, Heiligkreuz 52, 9490 Vaduz,
Liechtenstein. Ed.Bd. adv. bk. rev. bibl. illus. circ.
1,000.

574 US
LINNAEAN SOCIETY. SYMPOSIA SERIES. 1976.
irreg., no.11, 1985. Academic Press Inc., Orlando,
FL 32887. TEL 305-345-2000. Indexed: Biol.Abstr.
Chem.Abstr. GeoRef.

LIVE AND LET LIVE. see PHILOSOPHY

574.9 UK ISSN 0076-0579
LONDON NATURALIST. 1915. a. £3. London
Natural History Society, Upper Flat, 65 Arthur Rd.,
London SW19 7DN, England. Ed. K.H. Hyatt. bk.
rev. circ. 2,000. (back issues avail.) Indexed:
Geo.Abstr. GeoRef.

570 US ISSN 0076-1044
LOUISIANA TECH UNIVERSITY. DIVISION OF
LIFE SCIENCES RESEARCH. RESEARCH
BULLETIN. 1967. a. free. Louisiana Tech
University, Division of Life Sciences Research, Box
10198, Tech. Sta., Ruston, LA 71272. TEL 318-
257-4331. Ed. John L. Murad. circ. 100.
Formerly: Louisiana. Polytechnic Institute,
Ruston. School of Agriculture and Forestry.
Research Bulletin.

574 JA ISSN 0439-3546
LOW TEMPERATURE SCIENCE. SERIES B.
BIOLOGICAL SCIENCE. (Notes: from No. 1-10
(1952-1956) Series A and B issued in 1 vol.) (Text
in English) 1954. a. exchange basis. Hokkaido
University, Institute of Low Temperature Science,
North 19, West 8, Kita-ku, Sapporo 060, Japan. Ed.
Akira Sakai. Indexed: Biol.Abstr. Chem.Abstr.
Hort.Abstr.
Formerly: Hokkaido University. Institute of Low
Temperature Science. Series B. Biological Science
(ISSN 0073-294X)

574.5 910 SW ISSN 0076-1478
LUND STUDIES IN GEOGRAPHY. SERIES B.
HUMAN GEOGRAPHY. (Text in English, French
and German) 1949. irreg., no.51, 1985. price varies.
(Lunds Universitet, Department of Geography)
Liber Forlag, S-205 10, Malmo, Sweden. index,
cum.index every 4 yrs.

574 US
M B L LECTURES IN BIOLOGY. 1980. irreg. price
varies. (Marine Biological Laboratory) Alan R. Liss,
Inc., 41 E. 11th St., New York, NY 10003. TEL
212-475-7700. Eds. Harlyn O. Halvorson, K.E. van
Holde. Indexed: Biol.Abstr. Chem.Abstr.

574.88 US
MAGNETIC RESONANCE IN BIOLOGY. irreg.,
vol.2, 1983. John Wiley & Sons, 605 Third Ave.,
New York, NY 10158. Ed. Jack S. Cohen. Indexed:
Chem.Abstr.

MAINE AGRICULTURAL EXPERIMENT
STATION. ANNUAL REPORT. see
AGRICULTURE

574.92 II ISSN 0025-3146
MARINE BIOLOGICAL ASSOCIATION OF
INDIA. JOURNAL. (Text mainly in English;
occasionally in French, German or Spanish) 1959. a.
$7. Marine Biological Association of India
(M.B.A.I.), Ernakulam, Cochin 682-011, Kerala,
India. Ed. P.V. Rao. adv. bk. rev. charts. illus.
index. circ. 700. Indexed: Biol.Abstr. Geo.Abstr.
Helminthol.Abstr.

574.92 UK
MARINE BIOLOGICAL ASSOCIATION OF THE
UNITED KINGDOM. OCCASIONAL
PUBLICATIONS. 1980. irreg. Marine Biological
Association of the United Kingdom, Citadel Hill,
Plymouth PL1 2PB, Devon, England. circ. 500.
Formerly: Marine Biological Association of the
United Kingdom. Occasional Papers (ISSN 0260-
2784)

574.92 JA
MARINE BIOLOGICAL STATION OF
ASAMUSHI. BULLETIN. 1946. a. avail. on
exchange basis. Marine Biological Station, Tohoku
University, Asamushi, Aomori 039-34, Japan. illus.
index.

574.92 US
MARINE ECOLOGY; a comprehensive, integrated
treatise on life in oceans and coastal waters. 1970.
irreg., vol.5, 1984. price varies. John Wiley & Sons,
Inc., 605 Third Ave., New York, NY 10016. TEL
212-850-6000. Ed. O. Kinne. Indexed: Chem.Abstr.
Sel.Water Res.Abstr.

574 591 NO
MARINE INVERTEBRATES OF SCANDINAVIA.
(Text in English) irreg. price varies. Norwegian
University Press, Postboks 2959 Toyen, N-0608
Oslo 6, Norway. Ed. J. Sneli.

574 US
MATHEMATICS IN BIOLOGY. 1981. irreg., vol.2,
1984. Academic Press Inc., Orlando, FL 32887.
TEL 305-345-2000. Eds. R. Sibson, J.E. Cohen.
Indexed: Math.R.

574 617.6 JA ISSN 0288-3317
MATSUMOTO DENTAL COLLEGE RESEARCH
BULLETIN. (Text in Japanese and European
languages) 1972. a. Matsumoto Dental College,
1780, Gobara, Hirooka, Shiojiri-Shi 399-07, Japan.
circ. 500.

574 NZ ISSN 0302-086X
MAURI ORA. 1973. a. NZ$6($6) University of
Canterbury, Department of Zoology, Private Bag,
Christchurch, New Zealand. Eds. W. Davison, C.E.
Franklin. bk. rev. circ. 450. Indexed: Biol.Abstr.
Excerp.Med. Ref.Zh. Zoo.Rec.

574 DK ISSN 0106-1054
MEDDELELSER OM GROENLAND,
BIOSCIENCE. 1979. irreg. (Kommissionen for
Videnskabelige Undersoegelser i Groenland, GL -
Commission for Scientific Research in Greenland)
Nyt Nordisk Forlag - Arnold Busck A-S,
Koebmagergade 49, DK-1150 Copenhagen K,
Denmark. Ed. Jean Just. charts. illus. Indexed:
Biol.Abstr. Chem.Abstr.
Formerly: Greenland Biosciences; Supersedes in
part (1878-1979): Meddelelser om Groenland (ISSN
0025-6676)

551.46 US ISSN 0085-0683
MEMOIRS OF THE HOURGLASS CRUISES. 1969.
irreg. free. Department of Natural Resources,
Bureau of Marine Research, 100-8th Ave. S.E., St.
Petersburg, FL 33701. Ed. K.A. Steidinger. charts.
illus. circ. 1,000. (tabloid format; back issues avail.)
Indexed: Biol.Abstr. Aqua.Sci.& Fish.Abstr. Deep
Sea Res.& Oceanogr.Abstr. Zoo.Rec. Ocean.Abstr.

574 II
MEMOIRS ON INDIAN ANIMAL TYPES. (Text in
English) 1983. irreg. price varies. Hindustan
Publishing Corporation, 6 UB Jawahar Nagar, Delhi
110007, India. Ed. M.L. Bhatia.

574 CN ISSN 0702-0007
MEMORIAL UNIVERSITY OF
NEWFOUNDLAND. OCCASIONAL PAPERS IN
BIOLOGY. (Text in English; summaries in English
and French) 1978. irreg., vol.9, 1984. price varies.
Memorial University of Newfoundland, Department
of Biology, St. John's, Newfoundland A1B 3X9,
Canada. Ed. Gordon F. Bennett. (back issues avail.)
Indexed: Biol.Abstr.

BIOLOGY 143

570 US ISSN 0076-8227
MICHIGAN STATE UNIVERSITY. MUSEUM
PUBLICATIONS. BIOLOGICAL SERIES. (Text in
English; summaries occasionally in German) 1957.
irreg. (approx. 1-2/yr.) price varies. ‡ Michigan
State University, Museum, East Lansing, MI 48824.
TEL 517-355-2370. circ. 1,850. Indexed: Biol.Abstr.
GeoRef.

574.92 GW ISSN 0342-3247
MIKROFAUNA DES MEERESBODENS. 1970.
irreg., vol.90, 1983. price varies. (Akademie der
Wissenschaften und der Literatur, Mainz,
Mathematisch-Naturwissenschaftliche Klasse) Franz
Steiner Verlag Wiesbaden GmbH, Birkenwaldstr. 44,
Postfach 347, D-7000 Stuttgart 1, W. Germany
(B.R.D.) Ed. Peter Ax. Indexed: Biol.Abstr.

574 US ISSN 0076-9436
MISSISSIPPI ACADEMY OF SCIENCE.
JOURNAL. 1940. a. $5. Mississippi Academy of
Sciences, Inc., 520 N. President St., Jackson, MS
39201. TEL 601-353-6527. Ed. Allan G. Wehr. circ.
1,000. (also avail. in microform from UMI) Indexed:
Biol.Abstr. Chem.Abstr. GeoRef. Hort.Abstr.

574 US
MODERN BIOLOGY SERIES. irreg. price varies.
Holt, Rinehart and Winston, Inc., 383 Madison
Ave., New York, NY 10017. TEL 212-688-9100.

574 US
MOLECULAR BIOLOGY; an international series of
monographs and textbooks. 1961. irreg., no.53,
1986. Academic Press, Inc., Orlando, FL 32887.
Indexed: Helminthol.Abstr.

500.9 574 NE ISSN 0077-0639
MONOGRAPHIAE BIOLOGICAE. 1957. irreg.,
vol.58, 1985; vols. 59-60 in prep. price varies. Dr.
W. Junk Publishers, P.O. Box 13713, 2501 ES The
Hague, Netherlands (U.S. address: Kluwer
Academic Publishers, 190 Old Derby St., Hingham,
MA 02043) Ed. M. Dumont. Indexed: Biol.Abstr.

574 US
MONOGRAPHS IN EPIDEMIOLOGY AND
BIOSTATISTICS. irreg. price varies. Oxford
University Press, 200 Madison Ave., New York,
NY 10016 TEL 212-679-7300. (And Ely House, 37
Dover St., London W1X 4AH, England)

574 US
MONOGRAPHS IN PRIMATOLOGY. 1983. irreg.,
vol.8, 1985. price varies. Alan R. Liss, Inc., 41 E.
11th St., New York, NY 10003. Indexed:
Biol.Abstr.

MONTANA ACADEMY OF SCIENCES.
PROCEEDINGS. see SCIENCES:
COMPREHENSIVE WORKS

574 591 US
MOUNT DESERT ISLAND BIOLOGICAL
LABORATORY. BULLETIN. 1960. a. $5 to non-
members. Mount Desert Island Biological
Laboratory, Salsbury Cove, ME 04672. TEL 207-
288-3605. Ed. Arnost Kleinzeller. charts. illus.
index. circ. 1,000. Indexed: Biol.Abstr. Curr.Cont.

574.5 AG ISSN 0524-9481
MUSEO ARGENTINO DE CIENCIAS
NATURALES "BERNARDINO RIVADAVIA."
INSTITUTO NACIONAL DE INVESTIGACION
DE LAS CIENCIAS NATURALES. REVISTA.
ECOLOGIA. 1963. irreg., latest vol.3, no.3, 1984.
Museo Argentino de Ciencias Naturales "Bernardino
Rivadavia", Instituto Nacional de Investigacion de
las Ciencias Naturales, Avda. Angel Gallardo 470,
Casilla de Correo 220-Sucursal 5, Buenos Aires,
Argentina. Indexed: GeoRef.
Ecology

574.92 AG ISSN 0524-9503
MUSEO ARGENTINO DE CIENCIAS
NATURALES "BERNARDINO RIVADAVIA."
INSTITUTO NACIONAL DE INVESTIGACION
DE LAS CIENCIAS NATURALES. REVISTA.
HIDROBIOLOGIA. 1963. irreg., latest vol.4, no.5,
1981. Museo Argentino de Ciencias Naturales
"Bernardino Rivadavia", Instituto Nacional de
Investigacion de las Ciencias Naturales, Avda.
Angel Gallardo 470, Casilla de Correo 220-Sucursal
5, Buenos Aires, Argentina. Indexed: GeoRef.
Marine

574　　　　　　　　　RM　ISSN 0068-3078
MUZEUL DE ISTORIE NATURALA "GR.
ANTIPA." TRAVAUX. (Text in English, French,
German, Russian; summaries in Rumanian; abstracts
in English and French) 1957. a. 90 lei. Muzeul de
Istorie Naturala "Grigore Antipa", Soseaua Kiseleff
Nr. 1, 9744 Bucharest, Rumania. Ed. M. Bacescu.
bk. rev. index. circ. 900. Indexed: Ocean.Abstr.

570　　　　　　　　　PL　ISSN 0068-466X
MUZEUM GORNOSLASKIE W BYTOMIU.
ROCZNIK. SERIA PRZYRODA. (Text in Polish;
summaries in German and Russian) 1962. irreg.
price varies. Muzeum Gornoslaskie, Pl. Thaelmanna
2, 41-902 Bytom, Poland (Dist. by: Ars Polona-
Ruch, Krakowskie Przedmiescie 7, Warsaw, Poland)

574.92 540 639.2　　　KO
NATIONAL FISHERIES UNIVERSITY OF PUSAN.
INSTITUTE OF MARINE SCIENCES.
CONTRIBUTIONS. (Text in Korean; summaries in
English) 1968. a. 12000 Won($15) National
Fisheries University of Pusan, Institute of Marine
Sciences, Haewundae, Pusan 607-04, South Korea.
Ed. Pyung Chin. circ. 800. (back issues avail.)
　　Formerly (until 1983): National Fisheries
University of Pusan. Institute of Marine Sciences.
Publications.

574 610　　　　　　　JA　ISSN 0386-5541
NATIONAL INSTITUTE OF POLAR RESEARCH.
MEMOIRS. SERIES E: BIOLOGY AND
MEDICAL SCIENCE. (Text and Abstracts in
English) 1959. irreg., no.37, 1986. exchange basis.
National Institute of Polar Research - Kokuritsu
Kyokuchi Kenkyujo, 9-10, Kaga 1-chome, Itabashi-
ku, Tokyo 173, Japan. Ed. Tatsuro Matsuda. circ. 1,
000. Indexed: Biol.Abstr. Curr.Antarc.Lit.
　　Supersedes: Japanese Antarctic Research
Expedition, 1956-1962. Scientific Reports. Series E.
Biology (ISSN 0075-3394)

574.9 930 574　　　　　GW　ISSN 0077-6025
NATUR UND MENSCH:
JAHRESMITTEILUNGEN DER
NATURHISTORISCHEN GESELLSCHAFT
NUERNBERG. 1965. a. price varies.
Naturhistorische Gesellschaft Nuernberg e.V.,
Gewerbemuseumsplatz 4, Luitpoldhaus, 8500
Nuernberg 1, W. Germany (B.R.D) circ. 2,500.
Indexed: Biol.Abstr.
　　Formerly (until 1969): Naturhistorische
Gesellschaft Nuernberg. Mitteilungen und
Jahresbericht.

574　　　　　　　　　DK　ISSN 0077-6033
NATURA JUTLANDICA. (Text in English) 1947/48.
irreg. free or exchange basis. Naturhistorisk
Museum - Natural History Museum,
Universitetsparken, Building 210, DK-8000 Aarhus,
Denmark. Ed. Birger Jensen. illus. circ. 350.
Indexed: Biol.Abstr.

574 560　　　　　　　CN　ISSN 0707-3887
NATURAL HISTORY CONTRIBUTIONS. 1978.
irreg., latest vol.7, 1984. free. Saskatchewan
Museum of Natural History, Wascana Park, College
Ave. & Albert St., Regina, Sask. S4P 3V7, Canada.
TEL 306-787-2808. circ. 300. (back issues avail.)

574　　　　　　　　　US
NATURAL HISTORY MISCELLANEA. 1954. irreg.,
no.215, 1981. price varies. Chicago Academy of
Sciences, 2001 N. Clark St., Chicago, IL 60614.
TEL 312-549-0606. Ed. Paul G. Heltne. circ. 1,000.
(back issues avail.) Indexed: Biol.Abstr.

574　　　　　　　　　BL　ISSN 0101-1944
NATURALIA. 1975-1978; resumed 1980. a. $30 or
exchange basis. Universidade Estadual Paulista, Av.
Vicente Ferreira 1278, Caixa Postal 603, 17.500
Marilia SP, Brazil. Ed.Bd. circ. 1,000. Indexed:
Biol.Abstr. Math.R. Sociol.Abstr.
Abstr.Anthropol. GeoRef. Zoo.Rec.

574　　　　　　　　　US
NATURALISTS' DIRECTORY AND ALMANAC
INTERNATIONAL. 1877. irreg., vol.44, 1985.
price varies. E J Brill-Flora and Fauna Publications
(Subsidiary of: E.J. Brill) 225 W. 57th St., Ste. 404,
New York, NY 10019. TEL 212-757-7628. Ed.
Ross H. Arnett, Jr. adv. bk. rev. bibl. circ. 5,000.
(back issues avail.)
　　Formerly: Naturalists' Directory International
(ISSN 0277-609X)

574 550　　　　　　　GW　ISSN 0374-6054
NATURHISTORISCHE GESELLSCHAFT
HANNOVER. BEIHEFTE ZU DEN
BERICHTEN. (Text in German; summaries in
English and German) 1928. irreg. DM.20.
Naturhistorische Gesellschaft Hannover, Postfach
510153, Stillweg 2, D-3000 Hannover 51, W.
Germany (B.R.D.) bibl. charts. illus. circ. 850.

NATURHISTORISCHE GESELLSCHAFT
NUERNBERG. ABHANDLUNGEN. see
ARCHAEOLOGY

570　　　　　　　　　GW
NATURWISSENSCHAFTLICHER VEREIN IN
HAMBURG. ABHANDLUNGEN. 1937. a.
DM.60. Verlag Paul Parey, Spitalerstr. 12, 2000
Hamburg 1, W. Germany (B.R.D.) Ed. Otto Kraus.
bk. rev. bibl. illus. index. (reprint service avail. from
ISI) Indexed: Biol.Abstr. Chem.Abstr. GeoRef.
　　Supersedes in part: Naturwissenschaftlicher
Verein in Hamburg. Abhandlungen und
Verhandlungen (ISSN 0173-749X)

570　　　　　　　　　GW　ISSN 0173-7481
NATURWISSENSCHAFTLICHER VEREIN IN
HAMBURG. VERHANDLUNGEN. a. Verlag Paul
Parey, Spitalerstr. 12, 2000 Hamburg 1, W.
Germany (B.R.D.) adv. bk. rev. bibl. illus. index.
　　Supersedes in part: Naturwissenschaftlicher
Verein in Hamburg. Abhandlungen und
Verhandlungen (ISSN 0173-749X)

574 560　　　　　　　NE　ISSN 0374-955X
NATUURHISTORISCH GENOOTSCHAP IN
LIMBURG. PUBLICATIES. (Text in Dutch and
English; summaries in English) 1946. irreg. price
varies. Natuurhistorisch Genootschap in Limburg,
De Bosquetplein 6-7, 6211 KJ Maastricht,
Netherlands. Ed. Douwe Th. de Graaf. circ. 750.
(back issues avail.) Indexed: Biol.Abstr. GeoRef.
Rev.Appl.Entomol.

NAUKOVE TOVARYSTVO IMENI
SHEVCHENKA. PROCEEDINGS OF THE
SECTION OF CHEMISTRY, BIOLOGY AND
MEDICINE. see CHEMISTRY

NEUE DENKSCHRIFTEN DES
NATURHISTORISCHEN MUSEUMS IN WIEN.
see EARTH SCIENCES

574 639.2　　　　　　US　ISSN 0077-8397
NEW HAMPSHIRE. FISH AND GAME
DEPARTMENT. GAME MANAGEMENT AND
RESEARCH DIVISION. BIOLOGICAL SURVEY
BULLETIN. no.3, 1938. irreg., no.10, 1968. Fish
and Game Department, Game Management and
Research Division, 34 Bridge St., Concord, NH
03301. TEL 603-271-3421.

574　　　　　　　　　US　ISSN 0077-8370
NEW HAMPSHIRE. FISH AND GAME
DEPARTMENT. GAME MANAGEMENT AND
RESEARCH DIVISION. BIOLOGICAL SURVEY
SERIES. 1938. irreg., no.9, 1970. ‡ Fish and Game
Department, Game Management and Research
Division, 34 Bridge St., Concord, NH 03301. Ed.
Hilbert R. Siegler.

574　　　　　　　　　US　ISSN 0077-8389
NEW HAMPSHIRE. FISH AND GAME
DEPARTMENT. GAME MANAGEMENT AND
RESEARCH DIVISION. TECHNICAL
CIRCULAR SERIES. 1937. irreg., no.22a, 1968.
Fish and Game Department, Game Management
and Research Division, 34 Bridge St., Concord, NH
03301.

574　　　　　　　　　UN　ISSN 0077-8877
NEW TRENDS IN BIOLOGY TEACHING. (Text in
English and French; summaries in Spanish) 1966.
irreg., vol.4, 1977. $1650. Unesco, 7-9 Place de
Fontenoy, 75700 Paris, France (Dist. in U.S. by:
Bernan Associates-Unipub, 4611-F Assembly Dr.,
Lanham, MD 20706-4391)

574.5　　　　　　　　NZ　ISSN 0110-6465
NEW ZEALAND JOURNAL OF ECOLOGY. 1953.
a. NZ.$20. New Zealand Ecological Society, Inc.,
P.O. Box 12-019, Wellington, New Zealand. Ed.
N.G. Barlow. bk. rev. 21 year cum.index. circ. 700.
(also avail. in microfiche from IDC) Indexed:
Biol.Abstr. Chem.Abstr. Excerp.Med. Herb.Abstr.
Field Crop Abstr. Forest.Abstr. Forest Prod.Abstr.
Geo.Abstr. Sel.Water Res.Abstr. Vet.Bull.
　　Formerly: New Zealand Ecological Society.
Proceedings (ISSN 0077-9946)

574.92 551.46　　　　　NZ　ISSN 0028-842X
NEW ZEALAND MARINE SCIENCES
NEWSLETTER. 1961. a. NZ.$12. New Zealand
Marine Sciences Society, Oceanographic Institute,
P.O. Box 12346, Wellington, New Zealand. Eds. D.
Gordon, R.M.C. Thompson. bk. rev. bibl. circ.
300(controlled) (processed)
Marine

574　　　　　　　　　JA　ISSN 0371-2672
NIIGATA UNIVERSITY. FACULTY OF SCIENCE.
SCIENCE REPORTS. SERIES D: BIOLOGY.
(Text in English; summaries in European languages)
1964. a. exchange basis. Niigata University, Faculty
of Science - Niigata Daigaku Rigakubu, 8050
Igarashi Nino-cho, Niigata-shi 950-21, Japan.
Indexed: Biol.Abstr. Soils & Fert.

574.5 631　　　　　　JA　ISSN 0029-0874
NOGAKU KENKYU. (Text in Japanese; summaries
in English) 1918. irreg. exchange basis. Okayama
University, Institute for Agricultural and Biological
Sciences, Cho-2-20-1, Kurashiki 710, Japan. Ed.
Isao Aoyama. circ. 714.

574　　　　　　　　　FI　ISSN 0356-0910
NORDENSKIOLD-SAMFUNDETS TIDSKRIFT.
(Text in Swedish) 1941. a. Fmk.50. Nordenskiold-
Samfundet i Finland, Snellmaninkatu 9-11, 00170
Helsingfors, Finland. Ed. Carl-Adam Haeggstrom.
bk. rev. circ. 650.

574 614.7 312　　　NO
NORSK VILTFORSKNING. MEDDELESER. (Text
in English, Norwegian; summaries in English) 1935.
irreg. free. Directorate for Nature Management,
Tungasletta 2, N-7000 Trondheim, Norway. Ed.
Sveinn Myrberget. circ. 1,250. (back issues avail.)
Indexed: Biol.Abstr.

574.9　　　　　　　　AT　ISSN 0078-1630
NORTH QUEENSLAND NATURALIST. 1932.
irreg., vol.40, 1973. Aus.$4.50 (membership) North
Queensland Naturalists Club, Box 991, Cairns, N.
Queensland 4870, Australia. Ed.Bd. bk. rev. circ.
220. Indexed: Biol.Abstr.

NUKADA INSTITUTE FOR MEDICAL AND
BIOLOGICAL RESEARCH. REPORTS. see
MEDICAL SCIENCES

NUTRITION AND THE BRAIN. see NUTRITION
AND DIETETICS

OCEANOGRAPHY AND MARINE BIOLOGY: AN
ANNUAL REVIEW. see EARTH SCIENCES —
Oceanography

574　　　　　　　　　US　ISSN 0078-3986
OHIO BIOLOGICAL SURVEY. BIOLOGICAL
NOTES. 1964. irreg., no.17, 1982. price varies.
Ohio Biological Survey, 484 W. 12th Ave,
Columbus, OH 43210. TEL 614-422-9645. Ed.
Veda M. Cafazzo. circ. 1,000. Indexed: Biol.Abstr.
Rev.Plant Path.

574　　　　　　　　　US　ISSN 0078-3994
OHIO BIOLOGICAL SURVEY. BULLETIN. NEW
SERIES. 1913; N.S. 1959. irreg., latest 1985. price
varies. (Ohio Biological Survey) Ohio State
University, College of Biological Sciences, 484 W.
12th Ave, Columbus, OH 43210. TEL 614-422-
9645. Ed. Veda M. Cafazzo. circ. 1,000. Indexed:
Biol.Abstr.

574　　　　　　　　　US　ISSN 0270-5443
OHIO BIOLOGICAL SURVEY. INFORMATIVE
CIRCULAR. 1973. irreg., latest 1985. price varies.
484 W. 12th Ave., Columbus, OH 43210. TEL 614-
422-9645. Ed. Veda M. Cafazzo. circ. 1,000.
Indexed: Biol.Abstr. Rev.Plant Path.

574　　　　　　　　　US
OHIO STATE UNIVERSITY ANNUAL
BIOSCIENCES COLLOQUIA. 1975. a. price
varies. (Ohio State University, College of Biological
Sciences) Ohio State University Press, 1050
Carmack Rd., Columbus, OH 43210. TEL 614-292-
6930. Indexed: Chem.Abstr.

OKAYAMA UNIVERSITY. BERICHTE DES
OHARA INSTITUTS FUER
LANDWIRTSCHAFTLICHE BIOLOGIE. see
AGRICULTURE — Agricultural Economics

ORANGE FREE STATE. NATURE CONSERVATION BRANCH. MISCELLANEOUS PUBLICATIONS SERIES. see *CONSERVATION*

574　　　　US　ISSN 0553-0342
ORGANIZATION OF AMERICAN STATES. DEPARTMENT OF SCIENTIFIC AFFAIRS. SERIE DE BIOLOGIA: MONOGRAFIAS. (Text in Spanish) 1965. irreg., no.20, 1978. $3.50 per no. Organization of American States, Department of Publications, Washington, DC 20006. TEL 703-941-1617. circ. 3,000.

574　581　　JA　ISSN 0389-9047
OSAKA MUSEUM OF NATURAL HISTORY. SPECIAL PUBLICATIONS/OSAKA-SHIRITSU-SHIZENSHI-HAKUBUTSUKAN-SHUZO-SHIRYO-MOKUROKU. (Text in Japanese) 1969. a. Osaka Museum of Natural History, Nagai Park, Higashisumiyoshi-ku, Osaka, 546, Japan. Ed. Yasuhiko Shibata. circ. 1,000.

574　　　　US
OXFORD MONOGRAPHS ON BIOGEOGRAPHY. irreg. price varies. Oxford University Press, 200 Madison Ave., New York, NY 10016 TEL 212-679-7300. (And Ely House, 37 Dover St., London W1X 4AH, England)

P A S C A L THEMA. PART 215: BIOTECHNOLOGIES (EDITION FRANCAISE) see *MEDICAL SCIENCES — Abstracting, Bibliographics, Statistics*

P A S C A L THEMA. PART 216: BIOTECHNOLOGY (ENGLISH EDITION) see *MEDICAL SCIENCES — Abstracting, Bibliographies, Statistics*

PALEOBIOLOGIA. see *ANTHROPOLOGY*

PATHOBIOLOGY ANNUAL. see *MEDICAL SCIENCES*

PEDOBIOLOGIA. see *AGRICULTURE — Crop Production And Soil*

PERSPECTIVES IN PRIMATE BIOLOGY. see *ANTHROPOLOGY*

PETERSON'S GRADUATE PROGRAMS IN THE BIOLOGICAL, AGRICULTURAL AND HEALTH SCIENCES. see *EDUCATION — Guides To Schools And Colleges*

574.92　　　　TH
PHYKET MARINE BIOLOGICAL CENTER. RESEARCH BULLETIN. 1973. irreg. (3-4/yr.) Phuket Marine Biological Center, P.O. Box 60, Phuket, Thailand. illus.

POLLICHIA. MITTEILUNGEN. see *EARTH SCIENCES*

574.5　　　　PL　ISSN 0860-4045
POLSKI KLUB EKOLOGICZNEY OKREGU MALOPOLSKA. PRACE NAUKOWE. (Text in Polish; summaries in English and French) 1986. irreg., vol.3, 1986. price varies. Wydawnictwo A G H, Manifestu Lipcowego 16, 31-109 Krakow, Poland (Dist. by Ars Polona, Krakowskie Przedmiescie 7, 00-068 Warsaw, Poland) circ. 2,000.

574　　　　PO　ISSN 0032-5147
PORTUGALIAE ACTA BIOLOGICA. (Text in English, French, German, Portuguese) 1944. irreg. price varies. Universidade de Lisboa, Faculdade de Ciencias, Instituto Botanico, Lisbon 2, Portugal. (Co-sponsor: Laboratorio de Patologia Vegetal Verissimo de Almeida) bk. rev. circ. 500. Indexed: Biol.Abstr. Chem.Abstr. Field Crop Abstr. Herb.Abstr. Hort.Abstr. Rev.Plant Path.

574　　　　PL　ISSN 0079-4619
POZNANSKIE TOWARZYSTWO PRZYJACIOL NAUK. KOMISJA BIOLOGICZNA. PRACE. (Text in Polish; summaries in English) 1921. irreg., vol.69, 1981. price varies. (Poznanskie Towarzystwo Przyjaciol Nauk, Komisja Biologiczna) Panstwowe Wydawnictwo Naukowe, Ul. Miodowa 10, Warsaw, Poland (Dist. by Ars Polona-Ruch, Krakowskie Przedmiescie 7, 00-068 Warsaw, Poland) Ed.Bd. Indexed: Biol.Abstr. Chem.Abstr.

PREHISTORIC ARCHAEOLOGY AND ECOLOGY. see *ARCHAEOLOGY*

574　　　　YU　ISSN 0373-2134
PRIRODNJACKI MUZEJ U BEOGRADU. GLASNIK. SERIJA B: BIOLOSKE NAUKE. 1949. irreg. Prirodnjacki Muzej u Beogradu, Njegoseva 51, Belgrade, Yugoslavia. Ed. Zivomir Vasic. Indexed: GeoRef.

574　　　　YU　ISSN 0448-0147
PRIRODOSLOVNA ISTRAZIVANJA: ACTA BIOLOGICA. (Text and summaries in Croatian, English, French and German) 1957. biennial. $25. Jugoslavenska Akademija Znanosti i Umjetnosti - Yugoslav Academy of Sciences and Arts, Brace Kavurica 1, 41000 Zagreb, Yugoslavia. Ed. Mirko Malez. Indexed: Biol.Abstr.

574　　　　CS
PROBLEMY BIOLOGIE KRAJINY/QUESTIONES GEOBIOLOGICAE. irreg., vol.20, 1977. price varies. (Slovenska Akademia Vied) Veda, Publishing House of the Slovak Academy of Sciences, Klemensova 19, 814 30 Bratislava, Czechoslovakia (Subscr. to: Slovart, Gottwaldovo nam. 6, 817 64 Bratislava) Ed. M. Ruzicka.

574　　　　UR
PROBLEMY BIONIKI. vol.18, 1977. irreg. (Khar'kovskii Institut Radioelektroniki) Izdatel'stvo Vysshaya Shkola, Khar'kovskoe Otdelenie, Universitetskaya 16, 310000 Kharkov, Ukrainian S.S.R., U.S.S.R. Ed. Yu. Shabanov-Kushnarenko. Indexed: Biol.Abstr. Chem.Abstr. Sci.Abstr.

574　　　　US　ISSN 0172-6625
PROCEEDINGS IN LIFE SCIENCES. 1976. irreg., latest 1986. Springer-Verlag, 175 Fifth Ave., New York, NY 10010 TEL 212-460-1500. (Also Berlin, Heidelberg, Tokyo and Vienna) Eds. D.G. Weiss, A.Gorio.

PROGRESS IN CLINICAL AND BIOLOGICAL RESEARCH. see *MEDICAL SCIENCES*

574.5　　　　II　ISSN 0253-665X
PROGRESS IN ECOLOGY. 1973. irreg., vol.9, 1985. $32. Today and Tomorrow's Printers & Publishers, 24-B/5, Original Rd., Karol Bagh, New Delhi 110005, India (Dist. in U.S. by: Scholarly Publications, 7310 Elcresta Dr., Houston, Texas 77083) Indexed: Chem.Abstr.

574.192　574.88　　US　ISSN 0079-6603
PROGRESS IN NUCLEIC ACID RESEARCH AND MOLECULAR BIOLOGY. 1963. irreg., vol.32, 1985. $49.50. Academic Press, Inc, Orlando, FL 32887. TEL 305-345-2000. Ed. Waldo E. Cohn. Indexed: Biol.Abstr. Chem.Abstr. Ind.Med.

574　　　　US　ISSN 0079-6859
PROGRESS IN THEORETICAL BIOLOGY. 1967. irreg., vol.6, 1981. Academic Press, Inc., Orlando, FL 32887. TEL 305-345-2000. Eds. Robert Rosen, Fred M. Snell. Indexed: Biol.Abstr.

574.2　　　　US　ISSN 0736-4547
PROTEIN ABNORMALITIES. 1982. irreg., vol.3, 1983. price varies. Alan R. Liss, Inc., 41 E. 11th St., New York, NY 10003. TEL 212-475-7700. Indexed: Biol.Abstr. Chem.Abstr.

574　　　　US　ISSN 0079-7065
PROTIDES OF THE BIOLOGICAL FLUIDS. 1953. a. $210. Pergamon Press, Inc., Journals Division, Maxwell House, Fairview Park, Elmsford, NY 10523 TEL 914-592-7700. (U.K. Office: Pergamon Press Ltd., Headington Hill Hall, Oxford 0X3 0BW, England) Ed. H. Peeters. (also avail. in microform from MIM,UMI) Indexed: Biol.Abstr. Chem.Abstr.

574.92　639　　CN
QUEBEC (PROVINCE) DIRECTION GENERALE DES PECHES MARITIMES. CAHIER D'INFORMATION. 1960. irreg., no.115, 1986. free; avail. on exchange. ‡ Ministere de l'Agriculture, des Pecheries et de l'Alimentation, Bureau des Echanges, C.P. 340, Grande-Riviere, Cte de Gaspe, Que. G0C 1V0, Canada. TEL 418-385-2251. circ. 1,200. Indexed: Biol.Abstr. Ocean.Ind.
Formerly: Quebec (Province) Marine Biological Station, Grande-Riviere. Cahiers d'Information (ISSN 0079-8762)

574.92　639　　CN　ISSN 0318-8779
QUEBEC (PROVINCE) DIRECTION GENERALE DES PECHES MARITIMES. DIRECTION DE LA RECHERCHE. RAPPORT ANNUEL. (Text in French) 1953. a. free. ‡ Ministere de l'Agriculture, des Pecheries et de l'Alimentation, Bureau des Echanges, C.P. 340, Grande-Riviere, Cte de Gaspe, Que. G0C 1V0, Canada. Indexed: Biol.Abstr. Ocean.Ind.
Supersedes (since 1969): Quebec (Province) Marine Biological Station, Grande-Riviere. Rapport (ISSN 0079-8754)

574　　　　CN
QUEBEC (PROVINCE). MINISTERE DE L'AGRICULTURE, PECHERIES ET ALIMENTATION. DIRECTION GENERALE DES PECHES MARITIMES. TRAVAUX SUR LES PECHERIES. 1964. irreg. (3-4/yr.) exchange basis. Ministere de l'Agriculture, des Pecheries et de l'Alimentation, Bureau des Echanges, C.P. 340, Grande Riviere, Cte. de Gaspe, Que. G0C 1V0, Canada. circ. 1,300.

574.9　　　　AT　ISSN 0079-8843
QUEENSLAND NATURALIST. 550. irreg. (approx. a.) Aus.$4.50. Queensland Naturalists' Club, Box 1220 G.P.O., Brisbane, Qld. 4001, Australia. Ed. Joan Cribb. circ. 450. Indexed: Biol.Abstr. GeoRef. Zoo.Rec.

QUETICO-SUPERIOR WILDERNESS RESEARCH CENTER, ELY, MINNESOTA. ANNUAL REPORT. see *CONSERVATION*

574　554　　SP
REAL SOCIEDAD ESPANOLA DE HISTORIA NATURAL. BOLETIN DE GEOLOGIA Y BIOLOGIA. (Text in Spanish; summaries in English, French) 1871. a. free. Real Sociedad Espanola de Historia Natural, Ciudad Universitaria, Madrid 3, Spain. Indexed: Biol.Abstr.

574　　　　HU　ISSN 0079-9955
RECENT DEVELOPMENTS OF NEUROBIOLOGY IN HUNGARY. (Text in English) 1967. irreg., vol.10, 1982. price varies. (Magyar Tudomanyos Akademia) Akademiai Kiado, Publishing House of the Hungarian Academy of Sciences, P.O. Box 24, H-1363 Budapest, Hungary. Ed. K. Lissak. Indexed: Biol.Abstr. Chem.Abstr.

REICHORUI KENKYUJO NENPO/KYOTO UNIVERSITY. PRIMATE RESEARCH INSTITUTE. ANNUAL REPORT. see *ANTHROPOLOGY*

574.16　301.426　　PH
REPRODUCTIONS. (Text in English) 1970. irreg. (15-20/yr.) P.5($4) University of Santo Tomas, Institute for the Study of Human Reproduction, Faculty of Medicine, Espana St., Manila, Philippines. Ed. Vicente J.A. Rosales, M.D. bk. rev. circ. 5,000. (looseleaf format)

RESOURCE AND ENVIRONMENTAL SCIENCE SERIES. see *ENVIRONMENTAL STUDIES*

574　　　　US
REVIEWS OF HEMATOLOGY. 1980. irreg. $39.95. P J D Publications Ltd., Box 966, Westbury, NY 11590. TEL 516-626-0650. Ed. Dr. Julian L. Ambrus. (back issues avail.) Indexed: Biol.Abstr. Chem.Abstr. Curr.Cont.

574　　　　UY　ISSN 0304-971X
REVISTA DE BIOLOGIA DEL URUGUAY. (Text in Spanish; summaries in English) 1973. a. $10. Fernando Mane-Garzon, Ed. & Pub., Casilla de Correo 157, Montevideo, Uruguay. illus. index. circ. 1,500. (back issues avail.) Indexed: Biol.Abstr.

574.92　　　　EC
REVISTA PACIFICA SUR.* 1911. a. free. Comision Permanente del Pacifico Sur, Secretaria General, Gen. Ulpiano Pacz, 370 y Gral Franciso Robles, Quito 6, Ecuador. circ. 1,000. (back issues avail.) *Marine*

574　　　　FR　ISSN 0398-4346
REVUE ARACHNOLOGIQUE. (Text in French; summaries in English and French) 1977. irreg. 150 F. J.C. Ledoux, Ed. & Pub., 43 rue Paul Bert, F.30390 Aramon, France. (back issues avail.) Indexed: Biol.Abstr. Zoo.Rec.

574   FR
REVUE DES SCIENCES NATURELLES
D'AUVERGNE. (Text in French) 1921. a. 50 F.
Societe d'Histoire Naturelle d'Auvergne, Faculte de
Botanique, 4 rue Ledru, 63000 Clermont-Ferrand,
France. (back issues avail.)

ROYAL COLLEGE OF PATHOLOGISTS OF
AUSTRALASIA. BROADSHEETS. see *MEDICAL
SCIENCES*

574 590 551   IE   ISSN 0035-8983
ROYAL IRISH ACADEMY. PROCEEDINGS.
SECTION B: BIOLOGICAL, GEOLOGICAL
AND CHEMICAL SCIENCES. 1836. irreg. price
varies. Royal Irish Academy, 19 Dawson St., Dublin
2, Ireland. Ed. B. Young. charts. illus. index.
cum.index. circ. 600. Indexed: Biol.Abstr.
Chem.Abstr. Curr.Cont. Excerp.Med. Ind.Med.
Sci.Abstr. Sci.Cit.Ind. Aqua.Sci. & Fish.Abstr.
Br.Geol.Lit. Geo.Abstr. GeoRef. Ind.Vet.
Phys.Ber. RILA. Vet.Bull.

560 590   CN   ISSN 0384-8159
ROYAL ONTARIO MUSEUM. LIFE SCIENCES.
CONTRIBUTIONS. 1928. irreg. price varies. Royal
Ontario Museum, Publication Services, 100 Queen's
Park, Toronto, Ont. M5S 2C6, Canada. TEL 416-
586-5581. Ed.Bd. Indexed: Biol.Abstr. Zoo.Rec.
GeoRef.

574.9   CN   ISSN 0082-5093
ROYAL ONTARIO MUSEUM. LIFE SCIENCES.
MISCELLANEOUS PUBLICATIONS. 1963. irreg.
price varies. Royal Ontario Museum, Publication
Services, 100 Queen's Park, Toronto, Ont. M5S
2C6, Canada. TEL 416-586-5581. Indexed:
Biol.Abstr. Zoo.Rec. GeoRef.

574   CN   ISSN 0082-5107
ROYAL ONTARIO MUSEUM. LIFE SCIENCES.
OCCASIONAL PAPERS. 1935. irreg. price varies.
Royal Ontario Museum, Publication Services, 100
Queen's Park, Toronto, Ont. M5S 2C6, Canada.
TEL 416-586-5581. Ed.Bd. Indexed: Biol.Abstr.
Zoo.Rec. GeoRef.

574   UK   ISSN 0080-4622
ROYAL SOCIETY OF LONDON.
PHILOSOPHICAL TRANSACTIONS. SERIES B.
BIOLOGICAL SCIENCES. irreg. £87 per vol.
Royal Society of London, 6 Carlton House Terrace,
London, S.W.1, England. (reprint service avail. from
ISI) Indexed: Biol.Abstr. Chem.Abstr.
Excerp.Med. Ind.Med. Nutr.Abstr. Ocean.Abstr.
Br.Geol.Lit. Br.Archaeol.Abstr. Dairy Sci.Abstr.
Dent.Ind. Field Crop Abstr. Forest Prod.Abstr.
Forest.Abstr. GeoRef. Geo.Abstr.
Helminthol.Abstr. Herb.Abstr. Ind.Vet. Plant
Breed.Abstr. Petrol.Abstr. Rev.Plant Path. Soils &
Fert. Vet.Bull.

574   UK   ISSN 0080-4649
ROYAL SOCIETY OF LONDON. PROCEEDINGS.
SERIES B. BIOLOGICAL SCIENCES. 1832. irreg.
£42 per vol. Royal Society of London, 6 Carlton
House Terrace, London S.W.1, England. (reprint
service avail. from ISI) Indexed: Biol.Abstr.
Chem.Abstr. Curr.Cont. Eng.Ind. Excerp.Med.
Ind.Med. Nutr.Abstr. Anim.Breed.Abstr.
Br.Geol.Lit. Br.Archaeol.Abstr. Dairy Sci.Abstr.
Dent.Ind. Field Crop Abstr. Forest.Abstr.
Geo.Abstr. Helminthol.Abstr. Herb.Abstr.
Ind.Vet. Plant Breed.Abstr. Rev.Appl.Entomol.
Vet.Bull. Trop.Dis.Bull. Weed Abstr.

574   JA
SADO MARINE BIOLOGICAL STATION.
REPORT/NIIGATA DAIGAKU RIGAKUBU
FUZOKU SADO RINKAI JIKKENJO KENKYU
HOKOKU. (Text and summaries in English) 1971.
a. exchange basis. Niigata University, Sado Marine
Biological Station - Niigata Daigaku Rigakubu
Fuzoku Sado Rinkai Jikkenjo, 2-8050 Igarashi,
Niigata 950-21, Japan. Ed. Yoshiharu Honma. bibl.
circ. controlled. Indexed: Biol.Abstr.
    Formerly: Sado Marine Biological Station.
Annual Report (ISSN 0388-0117)

574   NO   ISSN 0036-4827
SARSIA. (Text in English, French, German) 1961.
irreg. price varies. (Universitetet i Bergen)
Norwegian University Press, Kolstadgt 1, Box 2959-
Toeyen, 0608 Oslo 6, Norway (U.S. address:
Publications Expediting Inc., 200 Meacham Ave.,
Elmont, NY 11003) Indexed: Biol.Abstr.
Chem.Abstr. Curr.Cont. Excerp.Med.
Ocean.Abstr. ASCA. Geo.Abstr.
Helminthol.Abstr. Sel.Water Res.Abstr.

333.7   FI   ISSN 0356-276X
SAVON LUONTO. (Text in Finnish; summaries in
English) 1969. a. Fmk.30. Kuopion Luonnon
Ystavain Yhdistys - Kuopio Naturalists' Society,
Kuopio Museum, Department of Natural History,
Kauppak 23, SF-70100 Kuopio 10, Finland. Ed.
Mikko Harri. charts. illus. stat. (back issues avail.)

333.7   FI   ISSN 0356-3189
SAVONIA. (Text in English) 1972. a. exchange basis.
Kuopion Luonnon Ystavain Yhdistys - Kuopio
Naturalists' Society, Kuopio Museum, Department
of Natural History, Kauppak. 23, SF-70100 Kuopio
10, Finland. Ed. Lauri Karenlampi. charts. illus.
stat. (back issues avail.)

SCIENCE AND NATURE; the annual of Marxist
philosophy for natural scientists. see *PHILOSOPHY*

574   FR
SCIENCE EXACTES ET TECHNOLOGIE.
SCIENCES DE LA VIE. LEXIQUE/EXACT
SCIENCE AND TECHNOLOGY. LIFE
SCIENCES. LEXICON. (Text in English and
French) 1978. a. 990 F.($157) Centre National de
la Recherche Scientifique, Centre de Documentation
Scientifique et Technique, 26 rue Boyer, 75971
Paris Cedex 20, France.

574.92   UK   ISSN 0375-2062
SCOTTISH MARINE BIOLOGICAL
ASSOCIATION. ANNUAL REPORT. 1896. a. £3.
Scottish Marine Biological Association,
Dunstaffnage Marine Research Laboratory, P.O.
Box 3, Oban, Argyll, Scotland. circ. 1,000. (also
avail. in microfiche) Indexed: Biol.Abstr.

574.92 551.46   US
SEARS FOUNDATION FOR MARINE
RESEARCH. MEMOIRS. 1948. irreg., no.1, pt.8,
1982. $50. Yale University, Sears Foundation for
Marine Research, Box 6666, 170 Whitney Ave.,
New Haven, CT 06511. TEL 203-436-4771. Ed.
Keith S. Thomson.

SENCKENBERGIANA MARITIMA. ZEITSCHRIFT
FUER MEERESGEOLOGIE UND
MEERESBIOLOGIE. see *EARTH SCIENCES —
Oceanography*

SENEGAL. CENTRE DE RECHERCHE
OCEANOGRAPHIQUE. DOCUMENT
SCIENTIFIQUE. see *EARTH SCIENCES —
Oceanography*

547   KO
SEOUL NATIONAL UNIVERSITY. FACULTY
PAPERS. BIOLOGY AND AGRICULTURE
SERIES. (Text in English) 1971. a. Seoul National
University, Seoul, S. Korea. Indexed: Excerp.Med.

574.92   JA   ISSN 0389-6609
SETO MARINE BIOLOGICAL LABORATORY.
SPECIAL PUBLICATION SERIES. (Text in
English) 1959. irreg. exchange basis. Kyoto
University, Seto Marine Biological Laboratory -
Kyoto Daigaku Rigakubu Fuzoku Seto Rinkai
Jikkensho, Shirahama-cho, Nishimuro-gun,
Wakayama-ken 649-22, Japan. Ed.Bd. circ. 460.
Indexed: Biol.Abstr.
    Formerly: Seto Marine Biological Laboratory.
Special Publications (ISSN 0080-9098)

574 591 551.46 639.2 JA   ISSN 0385-1109
SHIMA MARINELAND. SCIENCE REPORT. (Text
in English and Japanese) 1972. irreg. Shima
Marineland, Kashikojima, Ago-cho, Shima-gun, Mie
517-05, Japan. Ed. T. Tsujii. circ. 1,500. Indexed:
Biol.Abstr.

574 638   JA   ISSN 0583-0648
SHINSHU UNIVERSITY. FACULTY OF TEXTILE
SCIENCE AND TECHNOLOGY. JOURNAL.
SERIES A: BIOLOGY. (Text in English) 1951.
irreg. exchange basis. Shinshu University, Faculty of
Textile Science and Technology - Shinshu Daigaku
Sen'i Gakubu, 3-15-1 Tokida, Ueda, Nagano 386,
Japan. Indexed: Biol.Abstr. JCT. World
Text.Abstr.

574   JA   ISSN 0559-9822
SIEBOLDIA ACTA BIOLOGICA/SHIBORUDIA.
(Text in Japanese and English) 1952. irreg.
exchange basis. Kyushu University, College of
General Education, Biological Laboratory - Kyushu
Daigaku Kyoyobu Seibutsugaku Kyoshitsu, 4-2-1
Ropponmatsu, Chuo-ku, Fukuoka 810, Japan.
(reprint service avail. from UMI) Indexed:
Biol.Abstr.

574   US   ISSN 0270-2614
SKENECTADA. 1979. a. $15. Pine Bush Historic
Preservation Project, Inc., Box 22820, 1400
Washington Ave., Albany, NY 12222. Ed. Don
Rittner. bk. rev. abstr. charts. illus. circ. 1,000.
(back issues avail.) Indexed: Biol.Abstr. Zoo.Rec.

574   CS   ISSN 0037-6930
SLOVENSKA AKADEMIA VIED. BIOLOGICKE
PRACE/SLOVAK ACADEMY OF SCIENCES.
TREATISES ON BIOLOGY. (Text in English,
German or Slovak; summaries in English, German,
Russian) 1955. irreg. 20 Kcs.($5) Veda, Publishing
House of the Slovak Academy of Sciences,
Klemensova 19, 814 30 Bratislava, Czechoslovakia
(Subscr. to: Slovart, Gottwaldovo nam. 6, 817 64
Bratislava) charts. illus. circ. 500. Indexed:
Biol.Abstr.

500.9   BO
SOCIEDAD BOLIVIANA DE HISTORIA
NATURAL. REVISTA. (Text in Spanish;
summaries occasionally in English) 1974. irreg.
Sociedad Boliviana de Historia Natural, Casilla de
Correo 538, Cochabamba, Bolivia. illus. Indexed:
Biol.Abstr.

574   SP   ISSN 0212-4173
SOCIEDAD DE ESTUDIOS VASCOS.
CUADERNOS DE SECCION. CIENCIAS
NATURALES. 1983. irreg. (Sociedad de Estudios)
Eusko Ikaskuntza, S.A., Churruca, 7 - 2, 20004
Donostia, Spain.

570 580   PO   ISSN 0081-0665
SOCIEDADE BROTERIANA. MEMORIAS. (Text
in European languages; summaries in English,
French and Portuguese) 1930. irreg. (approx. 1/yr.)
Esc.3000($25) ‡ Sociedade Broteriana, Arcos do
Jardim, 3049 Coimbra, Portugal. (Co-sponsor:
Universidade de Coimbra. Instituto Botanico) Eds.
J.F. Mesquita, J.A.R. Paiva. circ. 1,000. Indexed:
Biol.Abstr. Excerp.Bot. Forest.Abstr. Forest
Prod.Abstr.

574   IT
SOCIETA DEI NATURALISTI IN NAPOLI.
BULLETIN. (Text in Italian; summaries in English)
1887. a. L.40000($20) Via Mezzocannone 8, 80134
Naples, Italy. Indexed: Biol.Abstr. Chem.Abstr.

574   NE
SOCIETAS INTERNATIONALIS
ODONATOLOGICA. RAPID
COMMUNICATIONS. 1980. irreg. price varies.
Societas Internationalis Odonatologica, c/o Dept. of
Animal Cytogenetics & Cytotaxonomy, Universiteit
van Utrecht, Box 80061, 3508 TB Utrecht,
Netherlands. Ed.Bd. bk. rev. charts. circ. 500.
Indexed: Biol.Abstr. Ref.Zh. Entomol.Abstr.
Genet.Abstr. Zoo.Rec.

574 554   SP   ISSN 0583-7405
SOCIETAT D'HISTORIA NATURAL DE
BALEARES. BOLETIN. (Text mainly in English,
French, German, Spanish; occasionally in Italian)
1955. a. 1,000 ptas. Societat d'Historia Natural de
Baleares, San Roque, 8, Estudio General Luliano,
Palma de Mallorca, Spain. Ed. Juan Cuerda. bk. rev.
circ. 1,000.

574　　　　　　PL　ISSN 0079-4570
SOCIETE DES AMIS DES SCIENCES ET DES LETTRES DE POZNAN. BULLETIN. SERIE D: SCIENCES BIOLOGIQUES. (Text in English, French and German) 1960. a. price varies. (Poznanskie Towarzystwo Przyjaciol Nauk) Poznanskie Twarzystwo Przyjaciol Nauk, Ul. S. Mielzynskiego 27/29, 61-725 Poznan, Poland (Dist by: Ars Polona-Ruch, Krakowskie Przedmiescie 7, Warsaw, Poland) Ed. Aleksandra Hoffmannowa. bibl. charts. illus. Indexed: Biol.Abstr. Chem.Abstr. GeoRef.

574　550　　　　LU　ISSN 0304-9620
SOCIETE DES NATURALISTES LUXEMBOURGEOIS. BULLETIN; publication de la societe botanique/annee de la Fauna. (Text and summaries in English, French and German) 1890. a. 400 Fr.($6) Societe des Naturalistes Luxembourgeois, B.P. 327, L-2013 Luxembourg, Luxembourg. circ. 850. (back issues avail.)

574　　　　　　US　ISSN 0583-9009
SOCIETY FOR DEVELOPMENTAL BIOLOGY. SYMPOSIUM. (Since 1967 issued as supplement to Journal of Developmental Biology) no.41, 1983. irreg., no.43, 1986. price varies. Alan R. Liss, Inc., 41 E. 11th St., New York, NY 10003. TEL 212-475-7700. Indexed: Biol.Abstr. Chem.Abstr. Ind.Med.

574　　　　　　UK
SOCIETY FOR EXPERIMENTAL BIOLOGY. SEMINAR SERIES. irreg., no.28, 1985. $34.50 for latest vol. Cambridge University Press, Edinburgh Bldg., Shaftesbury Rd., Cambridge CB2 2RU, England (And 32 E. 57th St., New York, NY 10022) index. Indexed: Biol.Abstr.

574　　　　　　UK　ISSN 0081-1386
SOCIETY FOR EXPERIMENTAL BIOLOGY. SYMPOSIA. 1947. irreg., no.36, 1984. £33($60) Cambridge University Press, Edinburgh Bldg., Shaftesbury Rd., Cambridge CB2 2PU, England (U.S. distr. addr.: 32 E. 57th St., New York, NY 10022) Ed. K. Bowler. Indexed: Biol.Abstr. Chem.Abstr. Ind.Med. ASCA.

SOCIETY OF WILDLIFE ARTISTS. PUBLICATION. see ART

591　　　　　　US　ISSN 0361-6525
SOCIOBIOLOGY. 1976. irreg., approx. a. $30. California State University, Chico, Department of Biological Sciences, Chico, CA 95926. Ed. David H. Kistner. adv. bk. rev. illus. index. circ. 500. (back issues avail.) Indexed: Biol.Abstr. Bull.Signal. Curr.Cont. ASCA. Entomol.Abstr. Zoo.Rec.

574　　　　　　BU　ISSN 0081-1823
SOFIISKI UNIVERSITET. BIOLOGICHESKI FAKULTET. GODISHNIK. irreg., vol.71, 1977/78. price varies. Publishing House of the Bulgarian Academy of Sciences, Acad. G. Bonchev St., Bldg. 6, 1113 Sofia, Bulgaria. Ed. I. Penev. circ. 550. Indexed: Biol.Abstr. Chem.Abstr.

574　610　　　　SA
SOUTH AFRICAN INSTITUTE FOR MEDICAL RESEARCH. PUBLICATION. (Text in English) 1917. irreg. South African Institute for Medical Research, P.O. Box 1038, Johannesburg 2000, South Africa. circ. 150. (back issues avail.)

574　　　　　　US
SOUTHERN BIOMEDICAL ENGINEERING CONFERENCE. PROCEEDINGS. 1982. irreg. Pergamon Press, Inc., Journals Division, Maxwell House, Fairview Park, Elmsford, NY 10523. TEL 914-592-7700.

574　　　　　　UK　ISSN 0143-0424
SOVIET SCIENTIFIC REVIEWS. SECTION D: BIOLOGICAL REVIEWS. 1980. a. Harwood Academic, 61 Grays' Inn Rd., London WC1X 8TL, England. Indexed: Biol.Abstr.

SPEZIELLE PATHOLOGISCHE ANATOMIE. see MEDICAL SCIENCES

570　　　　　　US　ISSN 0172-6226
SPRINGER ADVANCED TEXTS IN LIFE SCIENCES. irreg. price varies. Springer Verlag, 175 Fifth Ave., New York, NY 10010 TEL 212-460-1500. (And Berlin, Heidelberg, Tokyo and Vienna) (reprint service avail. from ISI)

574　　　　　　US
SPRINGER SERIES IN MOLECULAR BIOLOGY. 1982. irreg., latest 1986. Springer-Verlag, 175 Fifth Ave., New York, NY 10010 TEL 212-460-1500. (Also Berlin, Heidelberg, Tokyo and Vienna)

574　　　　　　HU　ISSN 0076-244X
STUDIA BIOLOGICA ACADEMIAE SCIENTIARUM HUNGARICAE. (Text in English and German) 1964. irreg., vol.19-20, 1986. price varies. (Magyar Tudomanyos Akademia) Akademiai Kiado, Publishing House of the Hungarian Academy of Sciences, P.O. Box 24, H-1363 Budapest, Hungary. Indexed: Biol.Abstr.

574　610　　　　PL　ISSN 0081-6582
STUDIA I MATERIALY Z DZIEJOW NAUKI POLSKIEJ. SERIA B. HISTORIA NAUK BIOLOGICZNYCH I MEDYCZNYCH. (Text in Polish; summaries in English and Russian) 1957. irreg., vol.30, 1980. price varies. (Polska Akademia Nauk, Zaklad Historii Nauki, Oswiaty i Techniki) Panstwowe Wydawnictwo Naukowe, Miodowa 10, 00-251 Warsaw, Poland (Dist. by: Ars Polona, Krakowskie Przedziescie 7, 00-068 Warsaw, Poland) Ed. E. Olszewski.
History

574　　　　　　RM　ISSN 0039-3398
STUDIA UNIVERSITATIS "BABES-BOLYAI". BIOLOGIA. (Text in Rumanian; summaries in English, French, German, Russian) 1958. a. exchange basis. Universitatea "Babes-Bolyai", Biblioteca Centrala Universitara, Str. Clinicilor Nr. 2, Cluj-Napoca, Rumania. bk. rev. charts. illus. Indexed: Biol.Abstr. Chem.Abstr. Excerp.Med. Field Crop Abstr. Herb.Abstr. Rev.Plant Path. Soils & Fert. VITIS.

574　　　　　　UK　ISSN 0537-9024
STUDIES IN BIOLOGY. 1966. irreg. price varies. Edward Arnold (Publishers) Ltd., 41 Bedford Square, London WC1B 3DQ, England. Indexed: Biol.Abstr. Nutr.Abstr.

574.5　　　　　　US
STUDIES IN ECOLOGY. irreg., vol.10, 1983. price varies. University of California Press, 2120 Berkeley Way, Berkeley, CA 94720. TEL 415-642-4247. Indexed: Biol.Abstr.

574.09　　　　　　US　ISSN 0149-6700
STUDIES IN HISTORY OF BIOLOGY. 1977. a. Johns Hopkins University Press, 701 W. 40th St., Ste. 275, Baltimore, MD 21211. TEL 301-338-6900. Eds. W. Coleman, C. Limoges. illus. (reprint service avail. from UMI)

SURFACTANT SCIENCE SERIES. see *CHEMISTRY*

574　　　　　　US　ISSN 0081-9697
SURVEY OF BIOLOGICAL PROGRESS. 1952. irreg., vol.4, 1961. Academic Press, Inc Orlando, FL 32887. TEL 305-345-2000. Ed. G.S. Avery, Jr. index.

574.92　　　　　　SW　ISSN 0346-8666
SWEDEN. FISHERY BOARD. INSTITUTE OF MARINE RESEARCH. REPORT. (Text in English, German and Swedish; summaries in English) 1975. irreg. price varies. Fishery Board of Sweden, Institute of Marine Research, S-453 00 Lysekil, Sweden. Ed. A. Lindquist. index. circ. 1, 000. Indexed: Biol.Abstr.
Formed by the merger of (1950-1972): Sweden. Institute of Marine Research. Series Biology. Reports (ISSN 0076-1710) & Sweden. Fisheries Board. Series Hydrography. Reports (ISSN 0562-8490)

574　　　　　　HU　ISSN 0082-0695
SYMPOSIA BIOLOGICA HUNGARICA. (Text in English and German) 1960. irreg., vol.31, 1986. price varies. (Magyar Tudomanyos Akademia) Akademiai Kiado, Publishing House of the Hungarian Academy of Sciences, P.O. Box 24, H-1363 Budapest, Hungary. Indexed: Biol.Abstr. Chem.Abstr.

574　540　　　　JA　ISSN 0371-5167
TAKEDA RESEARCH LABORATORIES. JOURNAL. (Text in Japanese or English; summaries in English) 1936. a. 2000 Yen. Takeda Chemical Industries, Ltd., Central Research Division, 17-85 Jusohonmachi 2-chome, Yodogawa-Ku, Osaka 532, Japan. Ed.Bd. circ. 1,500. (back issues avail.) Indexed: Excerp.Med.

574　　　　　　US
TELEGEN REPORTER. 1982. m. $895. E I C Intelligence, 48 W. 38th St., New York, NY 10018. TEL 212-944-8500. Ed. Jane Williams. (also avail. in microform)
●Also available online. Vendors: DIALOG, European Space Agency.

TETHYS. see *EARTH SCIENCES — Oceanography*

TEXAS TECH UNIVERSITY. GRADUATE STUDIES. see *HUMANITIES: COMPREHENSIVE WORKS*

574　551　　　　SP　ISSN 0212-5919
THALASSAS; revista de ciencias del mar. (Text and summaries in English and Spanish) 1983. a. 1600 ptas. Universidad de Santiago, Servicio de Publicaciones e Intercambio Cientifico, Campus Universitario, 15706 Santiago de Compostela, Spain. charts. illus. circ. 600. (back issues avail.)

574　　　　　　US　ISSN 0082-3945
THEORETICAL AND EXPERIMENTAL BIOLOGY; an international series of monographs. 1961. irreg., vol.6, 1967. Academic Press Inc., Orlando, FL 32887. TEL 305-345-2000. Ed. J.F. Danielli. Indexed: Biol.Abstr.

574.5　　　　　　HU　ISSN 0563-587X
TISCIA; dissertationes biologiae a collegio exploratorum fluminis Tisciae editae. (Text in English) 1965. a. exchange basis. Attila Jozsef University, c/o E. Szabo, Exchange Librarian, Dugonics ter 13, P.O.B. 393, H-6701 Szeged, Hungary (Subscr. to: Kultura, P.O. Box 149, H-1389 Budapest, Hungary) (Tisza Kutato Bizottsag) Ed. Gyorgy Bodrogkozi. charts. illus. circ. 300. Indexed: Biol.Abstr. Chem.Abstr. GeoRef. Sel.Water Res.Abstr.
Ecology

TOPICS IN GEOBIOLOGY. see *EARTH SCIENCES — Geology*

574　510　　　　FI　ISSN 0082-6979
TURUN YLIOPISTO. JULKAISUJA. SARJA A. II. BIOLOGICA- GEOGRAPHICA- GEOLOGICA. (Latin title: Annales Universitatis Turkuensis) (Text in English, Finnish, French and German) 1957. irreg. price varies. Turun Yliopisto - University of Turku, SF-20500 Turku 50, Finland (Dist. by: Akateeminen Kirjakauppa, SF-00100 Helsinki 10, Finland)

574　　　　　　US　ISSN 0735-9543
U C L A SYMPOSIUM SERIES ON MOLECULAR AND CELLULAR BIOLOGY. N.S., 1982. irreg., vol.40, 1986. price varies. (University of California, Los Angeles) Alan R. Liss, Inc., 41 E. 11th St., New York, NY 10003. TEL 212-475-7700. Indexed: Biol.Abstr. Chem.Abstr.

574　　　　　　US
U S-I B P SYNTHESIS SERIES. (International Biological Program) 1976. irreg., vol.16, 1981. price varies. Van Nostrand Reinhold Company, 7625 Empire Dr., Florence, KY 41042. TEL 606-525-6600. Ed. P.G. Risser. illus. index. Indexed: Biol.Abstr.

574.92　　　　　　UN
UNESCO REPORTS IN MARINE SCIENCE. 1977. irreg. (3-5/yr.) free. Unesco, Marine Information Centre, 7 Place de Fontenoy, 75700 Paris, France.

UNESCO TECHNICAL PAPERS IN MARINE SCIENCE. see *EARTH SCIENCES — Oceanography*

UNIVERSIDAD DE BOGOTA JORGE TADEO LOZANO. MUSEO DEL MAR. BOLETIN. see *EARTH SCIENCES — Oceanography*

574.92　　　　　　CK
UNIVERSIDAD DE BOGOTA JORGE TADEO LOZANO. MUSEO DEL MAR. INFORME. (Text in Spanish; summaries in English) 1971. irreg. price varies. Universidad de Bogota Jorge Tadeo Lozano, Museo del Mar, Calle 23 No. 4-47, Bogota, Colombia. Dir. Jorge Barreto Soulier. bibl.
Marine biology

BIOLOGY

574   UY   ISSN 0250-653X
UNIVERSIDAD DE LA REPUBLICA. FACULTAD DE HUMANIDADES Y CIENCIAS. REVISTA. SERIE CIENCIAS BIOLOGICAS. N.S. 1978. irreg. exchange basis. Universidad de la Republica, Facultad de Humanidades y Ciencias, Seccion Revista, Tristan Narvaja 1674, Montivideo, Uruguay. Dir. Beatriz Martinez Osorio.
   Formerly: Universidad de la Republica. Facultad de Humanidades y Ciencias. Revista. Serie Ciencias; Supersedes in part: Universidad de la Republica. Facultad de Humanidades y Ciencias. Revista.

574   SP
UNIVERSIDAD DE MURCIA. ANALES DE BIOLOGIA. (Consists of 5 subseries, also numbered individually) 1984. irreg., latest vol.8, 1986. Universidad de Murcia, Secretariado de Publicaciones e Intercambio Cientifico, Santo Cristo, 1, 30001 Murcia, Spain. TEL 968 24 92 00.

574   614.7   SP   ISSN 0213-4004
UNIVERSIDAD DE MURCIA. ANALES DE BIOLOGIA. SECCION BIOLOGIA AMBIENTAL. (Subseries of: Anales de Biologia) 1984. irreg., latest vol.8, 1986. ($1500) Universidad de Murcia, Secretariado de Publicaciones e Intercambio Cientifico, Santo Cristo, 1, 30001 Murcia, Spain. TEL 968 24 92 00.

574   SP   ISSN 0213-5442
UNIVERSIDAD DE MURCIA. ANALES DE BIOLOGIA. SECCION BIOLOGIA GENERAL. (Subseries of: Anales de Biologia) 1984. irreg., latest vol.5, 1985. ($1500) Universidad de Murcia, Secretariado de Publicaciones e Intercambio Cientifico, Santo Cristo, 1, 30001 Murcia, Spain. TEL 068 24 92 00.

574   SP   ISSN 0213-3938
UNIVERSIDAD DE MURCIA. ANALES DE BIOLOGIA. SECCION ESPECIAL. (Subseries of: Anales de Biologia) 1984. irreg., latest vol.2, 1984. ($3000) Universidad de Murcia, Secretariado de Publicaciones e Intercambio Cientifico, Santo Cristo, 1, 30001 Murica, Spain. TEL 968 24 92 00.

574   SP
UNIVERSIDAD DE NAVARRA. PUBLICACIONES DE BIOLOGIA. 1980. irreg., no.20, 1986. price varies. (Universidad de Navarra, Facultad de Ciencias) Ediciones Universidad de Navarra, S.A., Apdo. 396, 31080 Pamplona, Spain. (back issues avail.)

574   SP   ISSN 0212-8977
UNIVERSIDAD DE OVIEDO. REVISTA DE BIOLOGIA. (Abstracts in English and Spanish) 1982. a. 2500 ptas. Universidad de Oviedo, Facultad de Biologia, c/o Carlos Lastra, Redactor, Departamento de Zoologia, Oviedo, Spain (Orders to: Servicio de Publicaciones, Un. de Oviedo, c/o J. Arias de Velasco, 33005 Oviedo, Principado de Asturias, Spain) Indexed: Biol.Abstr.

574.92   BL   ISSN 0374-0412
UNIVERSIDADE FEDERAL DE PERNAMBUCO. DEPARTAMENTO DE OCEANOGRAFIA. CENTRO DE TECNOLOGIA. TRABALHOS OCEANOGRAFICOS. (Text in English, French and Portuguese; summaries in English) 1959. irreg. exchange. Universidade Federal de Pernambuco, Departamento de Oceanografia, Centro de Tecnologia, Av. Bernardo Vieira de Melo 986, Piedade, 5000 Recife, Pernambuco, Brazil. circ. 900. Indexed: Biol.Abstr.
   Former titles (1963-1966): Universidade Federal de Pernambuco. Instituto Oceanografico. Trabalhos (ISSN 0080-0236); (1960-1963): Universidade do Recife. Instituto Oceanografico. Trabalhos; (1959-1960): Instituto de Biologia Marinha e Oceanografia. Trabalhos.

574   IT   ISSN 0085-0950
UNIVERSITA DEGLI STUDI DI GENOVA. BOLLETINO DEI MUSEI E DEGLI ISTITUTI BIOLOGICI. (Text in Italian; summaries in English) 1891. a. exchange basis. Universita degli Studi di Genova, Istituto di Zoologia, Via Balbi 5, Genoa, Italy. Ed.Bd. circ. 500. Indexed: Biol.Abstr.

574   AU
UNIVERSITAET INNSBRUCK. ALPIN-BIOLOGISCHE STUDIEN. (Subseries of: Universitaet Innsbruck. Veroeffentlichungen) 1970. irreg., vol.6, 1974. price varies. Oesterreichische Kommissionsbuchhandlung, Maximilian Str. 17, A-6020 Innsbruck, Austria. Ed. Heinz Janetschek.

574   RM   ISSN 0041-9133
UNIVERSITATEA "AL. I. CUZA" DIN IASI. ANALELE STIINTIFICE. SECTIUNEA 2A: BIOLOGIE. (Text in French, German, Rumanian or Russian) 1955. a. 35 lei. Universitatea "Al. I. Cuza" din Iasi, Calea 23 August Nr. 11, Jassy, Rumania (Subscr. to: ILEXIM, Str. 13 Decembrie Nr. 3, P.O. Box 136-137, Bucharest, Rumania) Ed. C. Toma. bk. rev. abstr. charts. illus. circ. 550. Indexed: Biol.Abstr. Chem.Abstr. Math.R.

UNIVERSITATEA DIN BRASOV. BULETINUL. SERIA C. STIINTE ALE NATURRI SI PEDAGOGIE. see *MATHEMATICS*

574   630   RM
UNIVERSITATEA DIN CRAIOVA. ANALE. SERIA: BIOLOGIE, AGRONOMIE, HORTICULTURA. (Text in Rumanian; summaries in English, French and German) 1972. a. 80 lei($15) Universitatea din Craiova, Str. A.I. Cuza nr. 13, 1100 Craiova, Rumania. circ. 300.

574   581   TU   ISSN 0256-7865
UNIVERSITE D'ANKARA. FACULTE DES SCIENCES. COMMUNICATIONS SERIE C. BIOLOGIE. (Text in English, French and German) 1983. a. exchange basis. University of Ankara, Faculty of Sciences, Besevler, Ankara, Turkey. index. circ. 250. (back issues avail.)

574   TG
UNIVERSITY DU BENIN. ANNALES. SERIE SCIENCE. (Text in French; summaries in English and French) 1975. a. 2000 F.($5) Universite du Benin, B.P. 1515, Lome, Togo.

574   US   ISSN 0568-8604
UNIVERSITY OF ALASKA. BIOLOGICAL PAPERS. 1955. irreg., no.21, 1983. University of Alaska, Institute of Arctic Biology, 301 Irving, Fairbanks, AK 99701. TEL 907-474-7655. Ed. Bd. bibl. illus. circ. 500. Indexed: Biol.Abstr.

574   US   ISSN 0161-3243
UNIVERSITY OF ALASKA. BIOLOGICAL PAPERS. SPECIAL REPORTS. 1975. irreg., no.4, 1984. University of Alaska, Institute of Arctic Biology, 301 Irving, Fairbanks, AK 99701. TEL 907-474-7655. Ed. David W. Norton. (back issues avail.) Indexed: Biol.Abstr.

574.92   US   ISSN 0084-6147
UNIVERSITY OF ALASKA. INSTITUTE OF MARINE SCIENCE. OCCASIONAL PUBLICATION. 1971. irreg., no.5, 1980. price varies. ‡ University of Alaska, Institute of Marine Science, Fairbanks, AK 99701. TEL 907-474-7825. Ed. Helen K. Stockholm. Indexed: GeoRef.

574.92   US   ISSN 0065-5929
UNIVERSITY OF ALASKA. INSTITUTE OF MARINE SCIENCE. TECHNICAL REPORT. irreg. University of Alaska, Institute of Marine Science, Fairbanks, AK 99701. TEL 907-474-7825.

574   IQ   ISSN 0067-2890
UNIVERSITY OF BAGHDAD. BIOLOGICAL RESEARCH CENTRE. BULLETIN.* (Text in English; summaries in Arabic and English) 1965. a. exchange basis. University of Baghdad, Biological Research Centre, Baghdad, Iraq. Ed. Iyad A. Nader. Indexed: Biol.Abstr.

UNIVERSITY OF COLORADO. INSTITUTE OF ARCTIC AND ALPINE RESEARCH. OCCASIONAL PAPERS. see *SCIENCES: COMPREHENSIVE WORKS*

574.9   500.9   US   ISSN 0075-5028
UNIVERSITY OF KANSAS. MUSEUM OF NATURAL HISTORY. MISCELLANEOUS PUBLICATIONS. 1946. irreg., no.79, 1986. price varies. ‡ University of Kansas, Museum of Natural History, Lawrence, KS 66045. TEL 913-864-4540. Ed. Joseph T. Collins. circ. 1,000. (reprint service avail. from UMI) Indexed: Biol.Abstr. GeoRef. Key Title: Miscellaneous Publications - University of Kansas, Museum of Natural History.

574   500.9   US   ISSN 0085-2465
UNIVERSITY OF KANSAS. MUSEUM OF NATURAL HISTORY. MONOGRAPHS. 1970. irreg., latest no.7, 1979. price varies. ‡ University of Kansas, Museum of Natural History, Lawrence, KS 66044. TEL 913-864-4540. Ed. Joseph T. Collins. circ. 1,000. Indexed: Biol.Abstr.
Natural history

574   500.9   US
UNIVERSITY OF KANSAS. MUSEUM OF NATURAL HISTORY. PUBLIC EDUCATION SERIES. 1974. irreg., latest no.9, 1982. price varies. University of Kansas, Museum of Natural History, Lawrence, KS 66045. Ed. Joseph T. Collins.

574   500.9   US
UNIVERSITY OF KANSAS. MUSEUM OF NATURAL HISTORY. SPECIAL PUBLICATIONS. irreg., no.16, 1986. price varies. University of Kansas, Museum of Natural History, Lawrence, KS 66045. Ed. Joseph T. Collins.

574.92   SJ
UNIVERSITY OF KHARTOUM. HYDROBIOLOGICAL RESEARCH UNIT. ANNUAL REPORT. (Text in English) a. University of Khartoum, Hydrobiological Research Unit, Box 321, Khartoum, Sudan.

UNIVERSITY OF OSAKA PREFECTURE. BULLETIN. SERIES B: AGRICULTURE AND BIOLOGY/OSAKA-FURITSU DAIGAKU KIYO, B NOGAKU, SEIBUTSUGAKU. see *AGRICULTURE*

UNIVERSITY OF RHODE ISLAND. GRADUATE SCHOOL OF OCEANOGRAPHY. MARINE TECHNICAL REPORTS. see *EARTH SCIENCES — Oceanography*

574.92   JA   ISSN 0493-4334
UNIVERSITY OF TOKYO. FACULTY OF SCIENCE. MISAKI MARINE BIOLOGICAL STATION. CONTRIBUTIONS. (Text in English and Japanese) 1940. a. exchange basis. University of Tokyo, Misaki Marine Biological Station - Tokyo Daigaku Rigakubu Fuzoku Rinkai Jikkensho, Hongo, Tokyo, Japan.
Marine

UNIVERSITY OF TORONTO. FACULTY OF FORESTRY. RESEARCH REPORT. see *FORESTS AND FORESTRY*

UNIVERSITY OF WAIKATO. ANTARCTIC RESEARCH UNIT. REPORT. see *EARTH SCIENCES — Geology*

574   CN   ISSN 0317-3348
UNIVERSITY OF WATERLOO BIOLOGY SERIES. 1971. irreg. price varies. University of Waterloo, Department of Biology, Waterloo, Ont. N2L 3G1, Canada. TEL 519-885-1211.

574   PL
UNIWERSYTET GDANSKI. WYDZIAL BIOLOGII, GEOGRAFII I OCEANOLOGII. ZESZYTY NAUKOWE. BIOLOGIA. (Text in Polish; summaries in English and Russian) 1979. irreg. price varies. Uniwersytet Gdanski, Wydzial Biologii, Geografii i Oceanologii, Ul. Armii Czerwonej 110, 81-824 Sopot, Poland. Ed. Hanna Piotrowska.
   Formerly: Uniwersytet Gdanski. Wydzial Biologii i Nauk o Ziemi. Zeszyty Naukowe. Biologia (ISSN 0208-4961)

574.88   PL   ISSN 0137-2351
UNIWERSYTET JAGIELLONSKI. ZESZYTY NAUKOWE. PRACE Z BIOLOGII MOLEKULARNEJ. (Text in Polish; summaries in English) 1974. irreg., 1984. 42 Zl. per issue. (Instytut Biologii Molekularnej) Panstwowe Wydawnictwo Naukowe, Miodowa 10, 00-251 Warsaw, Poland (Dist. by: Ars Polona, Krakowskie Przedmiescie 7, 00-068 Warsaw, Poland) Ed. Z. Zak. bibl. illus. circ. 420. Indexed: Chem.Abstr.

574   SW   ISSN 0347-3236
VAEXTSKYDDSRAPPORTER. (Text in Swedish; summaries in English or German) 1977. irreg. price varies. Sveriges Lantbruksuniversitet - Swedish University of Agricultural Sciences, Research Information Centre/Plant Protection, Konsulentavdelningen/Vaextskydd, Box 7044, S-750 07 Uppsala, Sweden. Ed. Goeran Kroeker. charts. illus. Indexed: Rev.Appl.Entomol. Rev.Plant Path. Soils & Fert.

574.92   US   ISSN 0083-6427
VIRGINIA INSTITUTE OF MARINE SCIENCE, GLOUCESTER POINT. EDUCATIONAL SERIES. 1943. irreg., no.35, 1985. price varies. Virginia Institute of Marine Science, Gloucester Point, VA 23062. TEL 804-642-7175. (also avail. in microfiche)

574.92   US   ISSN 0083-6435
VIRGINIA INSTITUTE OF MARINE SCIENCE, GLOUCESTER POINT. MARINE RESOURCES ADVISORY SERIES. 1970. irreg., no.32, 1986. free. Virginia Institute of Marine Science, Gloucester Point, VA 23062. TEL 804-642-7170. (also avail. in microfiche)

574.92   US   ISSN 0083-6443
VIRGINIA INSTITUTE OF MARINE SCIENCE, GLOUCESTER POINT. SPECIAL SCIENTIFIC REPORT. 1948. irreg., no.115, 1983. price varies. Virginia Institute of Marine Science, Gloucester Point, VA 23062. TEL 804-642-7116. (also avail. in microfiche) Indexed: Biol.Abstr. Ocean.Abstr.

574.92   US   ISSN 0083-6397
VIRGINIA INSTITUTE OF MARINE SCIENCE, GLOUCESTER POINT. TRANSLATION SERIES. 1961. irreg., no.32, 1985. $1. Virginia Institute of Marine Science, Gloucester Point, VA 23062. TEL 804-642-7116. (also avail. in microfiche)

VOPROSY RADIOBIOLOGII I BIOLOGICHESKOGO DEISTVIYA TSITOSTATICHESKIKH PREPARATOV. see MEDICAL SCIENCES — Radiology And Nuclear Medicine

VYSKUMNY USTAV LESNEHO HOSPODARSTVA VO ZVOLENE. LESNICKE STUDIE. see FORESTS AND FORESTRY

VYSKUMNY USTAV RASTINNEJ VYROBY V PIESTANOCH. VEDECKE PRACE. see AGRICULTURE

574   AT
WESTERN AUSTRALIAN INSTITUTE OF TECHNOLOGY. SCHOOL OF BIOLOGY. BULLETIN. 1980. irreg. free. Western Australian Institute of Technology, School of Biology, Bentley, W.A., Australia. Ed. J.D. Majer. circ. 150.
   Formerly: Western Australian Institute of Technology. Department of Biology. Bulletin (ISSN 0158-3301)

574 600   US   ISSN 0888-5982
WHO'S WHO IN BIOTECHNOLOGY. 1979. biennial. $545. Research Publications, Inc. (Woodbridge), 12 Lunar Dr., Drawer AB, Woodbridge, CT 06525. TEL 203-297-2600.

574.5   US   ISSN 0084-0122
WILDLIFE BEHAVIOR AND ECOLOGY. 1971. irreg., latest 1982. price varies. University of Chicago Press, 5801 S. Ellis Ave., Chicago, IL 60637. TEL 312-962-7700. Ed. George B. Schaller. (reprint service avail. from UMI,ISI)

574   GE   ISSN 0084-0963
WISSENSCHAFTLICHE TASCHENBUECHER. REIHE BIOLOGIE. 1963. irreg. price varies. Akademie-Verlag, Leipziger Str. 3-4, 1086 Berlin, E. Germany (D.D.R.) Indexed: Biol.Abstr.

WOOLHOPE NATURALISTS' FIELD CLUB, HEREFORDSHIRE. TRANSACTIONS. see ARCHAEOLOGY

574 610   US   ISSN 0883-5527
WORLD BIOLICENSING REPORT. (Included with subscr. to: BioEngineering News) 1985. 10/yr. Deborah J. Mysiewicz Publishers, Inc., Box 1210, Port Angeles, WA 98362. TEL 206-928-3176.

574.1 612   IE   ISSN 0084-1641
WORLD CONGRESS ON FERTILITY AND STERILITY. PROCEEDINGS. (Format and publisher of Proceedings vary) 1923. triennial, 1968, 6th, Tel Aviv; 1971, 7th, Tokyo; 10th, 1980? International Federation of Fertility Societies, c/o Prof. R.F. Harrison, TCD Dept. of Obstetrics & Gynecology, Rotunda Hospital, Dublin 1, Ireland. Indexed: Biol.Abstr. Anim.Breed.Abstr.

574   JA
YOKOHAMA NATIONAL UNIVERSITY. SCIENCE REPORTS. SECTION 2: BIOLOGICAL AND GEOLOGICAL SCIENCES. (Text in European languages and Japanese) 1952. a. exchange basis only. Yokohama National University, Faculty of Education - Yokohama Kokuritsu Daigaku Kyoikugakubu, Tokiwadai 156, Hodogaya-ku, Yokohama 240, Japan. illus. Indexed: Biol.Abstr. GeoRef. Rev.Plant Path.
   Formerly: Yokohama National University. Science Reports. Section 2: Biological Sciences (ISSN 0513-5613)

ZENTRALBLATT FUER ALLGEMEINE PATHOLOGIE UND PATHOLOGISCHE ANATOMIE/GENERAL PATHOLOGY, PATHOLOGICAL ANATOMY. see MEDICAL SCIENCES

574   GW   ISSN 0174-2795
ZENTRALINSTITUT FUER VERSUCHSTIERZUCHT. JAHRESBERICHT. English edition: Annual Report (ISSN 0174-2787) (Editions in English, German) 1971. a. Zentralinstitut fuer Versuchstierzucht, Hermann-Ehlers-Allee 57, 3000 Hannover 91, W. Germany (B.R.D.) circ. 2,300 (Eng. edt. 1,300) (back issues avail.) Indexed: Biol.Abstr.

574.9   CL   ISSN 0084-554X
ZONARIDA.* 1961. irreg. Universidad de Chile-Zona Norte, Departamento de Investigaciones Cientificos, Avda. Universidad de Chile s/n, Casilla 1363, Antofagasta, Chile.

591.5 574.5   US   ISSN 0720-1842
ZOOPHYSIOLOGY. (Text in English) 1971. irreg., vol.19, 1986. price varies. Springer-Verlag, 175 Fifth Ave., New York, NY 10010 TEL 212-460-1500. (Also Berlin, Heidelberg, Tokyo and Vienna) Ed. D.S. Farne. (reprint service avail. from ISI) Indexed: Biol.Abstr.
   Formerly (until 1977): Zoophysiology and Ecology (ISSN 0084-5663)
   Ecology

BIOLOGY — Abstracting, Bibliographies, Statistics

581 016   BE   ISSN 0066-9784
A.E.T.F.A.T. INDEX; releve des travaux de phanerogamie systematique et des taxons nouveaux concernant l'Afrique au sud du Sahara et Madagascar. (Text in English and French) 1953. a. $8.50. Association pour l'Etude Taxonomique de la Flore d'Afrique Tropicale, 136 rue de la Hulpe, 1331 Rossieres, Belgium. cum.index: 1953-1976.

591.15 016   UK   ISSN 0003-3499
ANIMAL BREEDING ABSTRACTS; a monthly abstract of world literature. (Former name of issuing body: Commonwealth Agricultural Bureaux) 1933. m. £193($343) to non-members. C.A.B. International, Farnham House, Farnham Royal, Slough SL2 3BN, England (U.S. subscr. to: C.A.B. International, North American Office, 845 North Park Ave., Tucson, AR 85719) adv. bk. rev. abstr. index. circ. 1,400. (also avail. in microfiche; back issues avail.) Indexed: Nutr.Abstr. Dairy Sci.Abstr. Field Crop Abstr. Herb.Abstr. Rural Recreat.Tour.Abstr. World Agri.Econ.& Rural Sociol.Abstr. Vet.Bull.
   ●Also available online. Vendors: BRS, CISTI, DIMDI, DIALOG, European Space Agency.
   Stock and stock-breeding

597 016   CN
ATLANTIC SALMON REFERENCES. 1973. irreg. free. Maritimes Regional Library, Box 550, Halifax, N.S. B3J 2S7, Canada. cum.index. circ. 500.

590 016   BL   ISSN 0067-6691
BIBLIOGRAFIA BRASILEIRA DE ZOOLOGIA. 1950. irreg. Cr.$600($25) Instituto Brasileiro de Informacao em Ciencia e Tecnologia, SCRN 708/709 Bloco B Loja 18E 30, 70740 Brasilia DF, Brazil.

576 016   US
BIBLIOGRAPHY OF GERMFREE RESEARCH. 1962. a. $2.50. (Gnotobiotic Society) Ave Marie Press, c/o B.A. Teah, Ed., Dept. of Microbiology, Lobund Laboratory, University of Notre Dame, Notre Dame, IN 46556. TEL 219-239-5000. index. circ. controlled. (tabloid format; back issues avail.)

574 630 016   US   ISSN 0006-3177
BIOLOGICAL AND AGRICULTURAL INDEX; a subject index to periodicals in the fields of biology and agriculture and related sciences. 1964. m., except Aug. (quarterly and annual cumulations) service basis. H.W. Wilson Co., 950 University Ave., Bronx, NY 10452. TEL 212-588-8400. Ed. Rita Goetz.
   ●Also available online. Vendors: Wilsonline.
   Formerly: Agriculture Index.

574   US
BIOMEDICAL RESEARCH TECHNOLOGY PROGRAM; a research resources directory. 1977. biennial. free. U.S. National Institutes of Health, Division of Research Resources, Bldg. 31, Rm. 5B-10, 9000 Rockville Pike, Bethesda, MD 20205. TEL 301-496-5545. circ. 9,000.
   Formerly: Biotechnology Resources.

574 016   US
BIOSIS SEARCH GUIDE; BIOSIS previews edition. 1977. biennial. $90. BioSciences Information Service (BIOSIS), 2100 Arch St., Philadelphia, PA 19103-1399. TEL 215-587-4800. (looseleaf format; reprint service avail.)

574   US   ISSN 0733-5709
BIOTECHNOLOGY RESEARCH ABSTRACTS. m. $614. Cambridge Scientific Abstracts, 5161 River Rd., Bethesda, MD 20816. Ed. David Jackson. Indexed: Cal.Tiss.Abstr. Chemorec.Abstr. Oncol.Abstr.
   ●Also available online. Vendors: DIALOG, Orbit Information Technologies.
   Formerly: Biotechnology Abstracts.

016 581   DK   ISSN 0900-2367
BOTANISK CENTRALBIBLIOTEK. FORTEGNELSE OVER LOEBENDE PERIODICA. 1977. irreg. free. Botanisk Centralbibliotek, Soelvgade 83, 1307 Copenhagen K, Denmark. Ed. Annelise Hartmann.

612 016   US   ISSN 0008-0586
CALCIFIED TISSUE ABSTRACTS. 1969. q. $268. Cambridge Scientific Abstracts, 5161 River Rd., Bethesda, MD 20816. TEL 301-951-1400. Ed. Pam Clare. adv. bk. rev. abstr. index. (also avail. in magnetic tape) Indexed: Cal.Tiss.Abstr. Chemorec.Abstr. Oncol.Abstr.
   ●Also available online. Vendors: DIALOG.

595.7 011   FR   ISSN 0085-2783
CENTRE INTERNATIONAL DE DOCUMENTATION ARACHNOLOGIQUES. LISTE DES TRAVAUX ARACHNOLOGIQUES. 1968. a. 90 F.($13.50) ‡ Centre International de Documentation Arachnologique, 61 rue de Buffon, 75005 Paris, France. adv. bibl. index. (also avail. in record)

311   US
CORNELL UNIVERSITY. NEW YORK STATE COLLEGE OF AGRICULTURE AND LIFE SCIENCES. BIOMETRICS UNIT. ANNUAL REPORT. 1949. a. free. ‡ New York State College of Agriculture and Life Sciences, Department of Plant Breeding and Biometry, Cornell University, 337 Warren Hall, Ithaca, NY 14853. Ed. Shayle R. Searle. circ. controlled.

581 016   US   ISSN 0306-4484
CURRENT ADVANCES IN PLANT SCIENCE. 1972. m. $395. Pergamon Press, Inc., Journals Division, Maxwell House, Fairview Park, Elmsford, NY 10523 TEL 914-592-7700. (And Headington Hill Hall, Oxford OX3 0BW, England) Ed. H. Smith. adv. bk. rev. abstr. index. circ. 1,200. (also avail. in microform from MIM,UMI; back issues avail.) Indexed: Weed Abstr.

574 016   US   ISSN 0733-4443
CURRENT AWARENESS IN BIOLOGICAL
SCIENCES. 1954. 144/yr. $2000. Pergamon Press,
Inc., Journals Division, Maxwell House, Fairview
Park, Elmsford, NY 10523 TEL 914-592-7700.
(And Headington Hill Hall, Oxford OX3 0BW,
England) Ed. H. Smith. adv. abstr. index. circ. 1,
000. (also avail. in microform from MIM,UMI; back
issues avail.) Indexed: Biol.Abstr. Chem.Abstr.
Nutr.Abstr. Ind.Vet. Vet.Bull.
●Also available online. Vendors: Pergamon Infoline.
Formerly (until 1983): International Abstracts of
Biological Sciences (ISSN 0020-5818)

574 630 615 016   KO
CURRENT BIBLIOGRAPHIES ON SCIENCE &
TECHNOLOGY: BIOLOGY, PHARMACY &
FOOD SCIENCE. 1962. m. $107. Korea Institute
for Economics and Technology, P.O.B. 205, Seoul,
S. Korea. circ. 300. (reprint service avail. from
UMI)
Formerly: Current Index to Journals in Science
and Technology: Biology, Agriculture, Pharmacy;
Which superseded in part: Current Bibliography on
Science and Technology.

574 500   UK
CURRENT BIOTECHNOLOGY ABSTRACTS.
1983. m. £225($435) Royal Society of Chemistry,
University of Nottingham, Nottingham NG7 2RD,
England. Ed. E. C. Oliver. adv.
●Also available online. Vendors: Data-Star,
European Space Agency, Orbit Information
Technologies, Pergamon Infoline.

574 020 015   UK   ISSN 0267-1956
CURRENT RESEARCH IN BRITAIN.
BIOLOGICAL SCIENCES. 1980. a. £59. British
Library, Document Supply Centre, Boston Spa,
Wetherby, West Yorkshire LS23 7BQ, England. Ed.
A. Young.
Formerly: Research in British Universities
Polytechnics and Colleges. Vol.2: Biological
Sciences (ISSN 0143-0734)

595.7 016   US   ISSN 0013-8924
ENTOMOLOGY ABSTRACTS. 1969. m. $465.
Cambridge Scientific Abstracts, 5161 River Rd.,
Bethesda, MD 20816. TEL 301-951-1400. Ed. Pam
Clare. adv. index. (also avail. in magnetic tape)
Indexed: Cal.Tiss.Abstr. Chemorec.Abstr.
Oncol.Abstr.
●Also available online. Vendors: DIALOG.

574.92 016   UK   ISSN 0261-0663
ESTUARIES AND COASTAL WATERS OF THE
BRITISH ISLES; an annual bibliography of recent
scientific papers. no.3, 1979. a. £9.50. Marine
Biological Association of the United Kingdom,
Library and Information Services, Citadel Hill,
Plymouth PL1 2PB, England. Ed. E.K. Roberts.
circ. 200. (also avail. in microform) Indexed:
Aqua.Sci.& Fish.Abstr.
Formerly: Estuaries of the British Isles.

EXCERPTA MEDICA. SECTION 1: ANATOMY,
ANTHROPOLOGY, EMBRYOLOGY &
HISTOLOGY. see MEDICAL SCIENCES —
Abstracting, Bibliographies, Statistics

EXCERPTA MEDICA. SECTION 2:
PHYSIOLOGY. see MEDICAL SCIENCES —
Abstracting, Bibliographies, Statistics

EXCERPTA MEDICA. SECTION 4:
MICROBIOLOGY: BACTERIOLOGY,
MYCOLOGY AND PARASITOLOGY. see
MEDICAL SCIENCES — Abstracting,
Bibliographies, Statistics

EXCERPTA MEDICA. SECTION 5: GENERAL
PATHOLOGY AND PATHOLOGICAL
ANATOMY. see MEDICAL SCIENCES —
Abstracting, Bibliographies, Statistics

EXCERPTA MEDICA. SECTION 27: BIOPHYSICS,
BIO-ENGINEERING AND MEDICAL
INSTRUMENTATION. see MEDICAL
SCIENCES — Abstracting, Bibliographies,
Statistics

EXCERPTA MEDICA. SECTION 29: CLINICAL
BIOCHEMISTRY. see MEDICAL SCIENCES —
Abstracting, Bibliographies, Statistics

EXCERPTA MEDICA. SECTION 47: VIROLOGY.
see MEDICAL SCIENCES — Abstracting,
Bibliographies, Statistics

575.1 016   US   ISSN 0016-674X
GENETICS ABSTRACTS. 1968. m. $563. Cambridge
Scientific Abstracts, 5161 River Rd., Bethesda, MD
20816. TEL 301-951-1400. Ed. Pam Clare. adv. bk.
rev. abstr. (also avail. in magnetic tape) Indexed:
Anim.Breed.Abstr. Cal.Tiss.Abstr.
Chemorec.Abstr. Oncol.Abstr. Weed Abstr.
●Also available online. Vendors: DIALOG.

HELMINTHOLOGICAL ABSTRACTS. SERIES A:
ANIMAL AND HUMAN HELMINTHOLOGY.
see AGRICULTURE — Abstracting,
Bibliographies, Statistics

HELMINTHOLOGICAL ABSTRACTS. SERIES B:
PLANT NEMATOLOGY. see
AGRICULTURE — Abstracting, Bibliographies,
Statistics

I M B I S; Information fuer medizinisch-biologische
Statistik und deren Grenzgebiete. see MEDICAL
SCIENCES — Abstracting, Bibliographies,
Statistics

574.191 016   US
INTERNATIONAL BIOPHYSICS CONGRESS.
ABSTRACTS. 1961. irreg. $10. Massachusetts
Institute of Technology, International Biophysics
Congress, Cambridge, MA 02139 (Orders to: Room
20B-221) Ed. Walter Rosenelith.

574.92 551.46 016   UN   ISSN 0025-3308
MARINE SCIENCE CONTENTS TABLES. (Text in
English, French, Russian, Spanish) 1966-19??;
resumed 19?? m. free. Food and Agriculture
Organization of the United Nations, Distribution
and Sales Section, Via delle Terme di Caracalla,
00100 Rome, Italy. (Co-sponsor: Unesco Division of
Marine Sciences) Ed. G. Landi. circ. 3,200.
Indexed: Helminthol.Abstr.

P A S C A L EXPLORE. PART 84: GENIE
BIOMEDICAL. INFORMATIQUE
BIOMEDICALE. see MEDICAL SCIENCES —
Abstracting, Bibliographies, Statistics

PLANT BREEDING ABSTRACTS. see
GARDENING AND HORTICULTURE —
Abstracting, Bibliographies, Statistics

PLANT PROTECTION ABSTRACTS. see
AGRICULTURE — Abstracting, Bibliographies,
Statistics

581 016   UR
RASTITEL'NYI MIR SIBIRI I DAL'NEGO
VOSTOKA; tekushchii ukazatel' literatury. 1975.
irreg. 1 Rub. Akademiya Nauk S.S.S.R., Sibirskoe
Otdelenie, Prospekt Nauki, 21, Novosibirsk, Russian
S.F.S.R., U.S.S.R.
Formerly: Rastitel'nye Resursy Sibiri i Dal'nego
Vostoka.

REFERATIVNYI ZHURNAL. RADIATSIONNAYA
BIOLOGIYA. see MEDICAL SCIENCES —
Abstracting, Bibliographies, Statistics

589.2   UK   ISSN 0034-6438
REVIEW OF PLANT PATHOLOGY; consisting of
abstracts and reviews of current literature on plant
pathology. 1922. m. £172($308) to non-members.
C.A.B. International, Mycological Institute,
Farnham House, Farnham Royal, Slough SL2 3BN,
England. adv. bk. rev. abstr. index. circ. 1,950.
Indexed: Biol.Abstr. Abstr.Hyg. Field Crop Abstr.
Forest.Abstr. Forest Prod.Abstr. Helminthol.Abstr.
Herb.Abstr. Plant Breed.Abstr. Rev.Appl.Entomol.
Trop.Dis.Bull. Weed Abstr.
●Also available online. Vendors: BRS, CISTI,
DIMDI, DIALOG, European Space Agency.
Formerly: Review of Applied Mycology.
Mycology

574 016   US   ISSN 0162-2048
SERIAL SOURCES FOR THE BIOSIS DATA
BASE. 1938. a. $50. BioSciences Information
Service (BIOSIS), 2100 Arch St., Philadelphia, PA
19103-1399. TEL 215-587-4800. (reprint service
avail.)
Formerly: Biosis: List of Serials (ISSN 0067-
8937)

595.7 576   FR
STATION BIOLOGIQUE DE BESSE EN
CHANDESSE. ANNALES. (Text in English,
French and German) 1966. a. 100 F.($15)
Universite Clermont II, Station Biologique Besse,
BP 45, 63170 Aubiere, France. Ed.Bd. (back issues
avail.) Indexed: Biol.Abstr. Bull.Signal.

VIROLOGY ABSTRACTS. see MEDICAL
SCIENCES — Abstracting, Bibliographies,
Statistics

590 016   US   ISSN 0084-5604
ZOOLOGICAL RECORD. (Includes 27 separate
sections of individual titles) 1864. a. £1800.
(Zoological Society of London) BioSciences
Information Service (BIOSIS) U.K. Ltd., Garforth
House, 54 Micklegate, Boston Spa, York YO1 1LF,
England. Eds. H. Gwynne Vevers, Marcia A.
Edwards. index. (also avail. in microform from UMI;
back issues avail.) Indexed: Helminthol.Abstr.
●Also available online. Vendors: BRS, DIALOG.

BIOLOGY — Biological Chemistry

574.192 574.191   PL   ISSN 0208-614X
ACTA UNIVERSITATIS LODZIENSIS: FOLIA
BIOCHIMICA ET BIOPHYSICA. (Text in Polish;
summaries in various languages) 1955; N.S. 1981.
irreg. Uniwersytet Lodzki, Drukarnia Wojskowa, Ul.
Gdanska 130, Lodz, Poland (Dist. by: Ars Polona-
Ruch, Krakowskie Przedmiescie 7, Warsaw, Poland)
Supersedes in part: Uniwersytet Lodzki. Zeszyty
Naukowe. Seria 1: Nauki Matematyczno-
Przyrodnicze.

ADVANCES IN BIOCHEMICAL ENGINEERING.
see ENGINEERING

ADVANCES IN CARBOHYDRATE CHEMISTRY
AND BIOCHEMISTRY. see CHEMISTRY —
Organic Chemistry

574.19 615   US   ISSN 0065-2423
ADVANCES IN CLINICAL CHEMISTRY. 1958.
irreg., vol.25, 1986. $38. Academic Press, Inc.,
Orlando, FL 32887. TEL 305-345-2000. Eds. Harry
Sobotka, C.P. Stewart. index. cum.index: vols.1-5,
1958-1962; in vol.5 (1962) Indexed: Biol.Abstr.
Ind.Med. Sci.Cit.Ind. Ind.Sci.Rev.

612.015   SZ   ISSN 0250-4197
ADVANCES IN CLINICAL ENZYMOLOGY. (Text
in English) 1979. irreg. price varies. S. Karger AG,
P.O. Box, CH-4009 Basel, Switzerland. Eds. D.W.
Moss, Ellen Schmidt, F.W. Schmidt. Indexed:
Biol.Abstr. Chem.Abstr. Nutr.Abstr.

ADVANCES IN COMPARATIVE PHYSIOLOGY
AND BIOCHEMISTRY. see BIOLOGY —
Physiology

574.192   US
ADVANCES IN CYCLIC NUCLEOTIDE
RESEARCH AND PROTEIN
PHOSPHORYLATION RESEARCH. 1972. irreg.,
vol.11, 1979. price varies. Raven Press, 1185 Ave.
of the Americas, New York, NY 10036. TEL 212-
575-0335. Eds. Paul Greengard, G. Alan Robison.
Indexed: Biol.Abstr. Chem.Abstr. Curr.Cont.
Ind.Med. Sci.Cit.Ind. Ind.Sci.Rev.
Formerly: Advances in Cyclic Nucleotide
Research (ISSN 0084-5930)

574.192   US   ISSN 0065-258X
ADVANCES IN ENZYMOLOGY AND RELATED
AREAS OF MOLECULAR BIOLOGY. 1942.
irreg., vol.61, 1987. price varies. John Wiley & Sons,
Inc., 605 Third Ave., New York, NY 10016. TEL
212-850-6000. Ed. F.F. Nord. Indexed: Biol.Abstr.
Chem.Abstr. Ind.Med. Sci.Cit.Ind. Dairy
Sci.Abstr. Ind.Sci.Rev. Trop.Dis.Bull.
Formerly: Advances in Enzymology and Related
Subjects of Biochemistry.

574.192   US   ISSN 0065-2849
ADVANCES IN LIPID RESEARCH. 1963. irreg.,
vol.21, 1985. $69. Academic Press, Inc., Orlando,
FL 32887. TEL 305-345-2000. Eds. R. Paoletti, D.
Kritchevsky. index. Indexed: Biol.Abstr.
Chem.Abstr. Ind.Med. Nutr.Abstr. Sci.Cit.Ind.
Dairy Sci.Abstr. Food Sci.& Tech.Abstr.
Ind.Sci.Rev.

BIOLOGY — BIOLOGICAL CHEMISTRY

612.8   US   ISSN 0098-6089
ADVANCES IN NEUROCHEMISTRY. 1975. irreg. price varies. Plenum Publishing Corp., 233 Spring St., New York, NY 10013. TEL 212-620-8047. Eds. B.W. Agranoff, M.H. Aprison. Indexed: Biol.Abstr. Chem. Abstr.

612.015   US   ISSN 0160-2179
ADVANCES IN POLYAMINE RESEARCH. 1978. irreg., vol.2, 1978. Raven Press, 1185 Ave. of the Americas, New York, NY 10036. TEL 212-575-0335. Indexed: Biol.Abstr. Curr.Cont. Ind.Sci.Rev.

574.192   US   ISSN 0065-3233
ADVANCES IN PROTEIN CHEMISTRY. 1944. a., vol.38, 1986. Academic Press, Inc., Orlando, FL 32887. TEL 305-345-2000. Eds. M.L. Anson, John T. Edsall. Indexed: Biol.Abstr. Chem.Abstr. Ind.Med. Nutr.Abstr. Sci.Cit.Ind. Abstr.Hyg. Dairy Sci.Abstr. Food Sci.& Tech.Abstr. Ind.Sci.Rev. Trop.Dis.Bull.

574.192 615   US
ADVANCES IN STEROID BIOCHEMISTRY AND PHARMACOLOGY (YEAR) 1970. irreg., vol.7, 1980. Academic Press Inc., Orlando, FL 32887. TEL 305-345-2000. Eds. M.H. Briggs, A. Corbin. Indexed: Biol.Abstr. Ind.Med. Nutr.Abstr.
Former titles: Advances in Steroid Biochemistry; Advances in Steroid Biochemistry and Pharmacology (ISSN 0065-339X)

574.192   UK   ISSN 0306-0004
AMINO-ACIDS, PEPTIDES, AND PROTEINS. 1968. a. price varies. Royal Society of Chemistry, Burlington House, London W1V OBN, England (Subscr. to: Distribution Centre, Blackhorse Road, Letchworth, Herts SG6 1HN, England) Ed. J. Jones. charts. illus. index. Indexed: Chem.Abstr. Food Sci.& Tech.Abstr.

ANNALI DI MICROBIOLOGIA ED ENZIMOLOGIA. see *BIOLOGY — Microbiology*

574.192   US   ISSN 0066-4154
ANNUAL REVIEW OF BIOCHEMISTRY. 1932. a. $33. Annual Reviews Inc., 4139 El Camino Way, Palo Alto, CA 94306. TEL 415-493-4400. Ed. Charles C. Richardson. bibl. index, cum.index. (back issues avail.; reprint service avail. from ISI) Indexed: Biol.Abstr. Biol.& Agr.Ind. Chem.Abstr. Curr.Cont. Excerp.Med. Ind.Med. Nutr.Abstr. Anim.Breed.Abstr. Abstr.Bull.Inst.Pap.Chem. Biotech.Abstr. Dairy Sci.Abstr. Field Crop Abstr. Food Sci.& Tech.Abstr. Helminthol.Abstr. Herb.Abstr. Hort.Abstr. Ind.Sci.Rev. M.M.R.I. Plant Breed.Abstr. Soils & Fert. Trop.Dis.Bull. VITIS. Weed Abstr.

612.015   US
ANNUAL REVIEW OF CLINICAL BIOCHEMISTRY. 1981. irreg., vol.3, 1982. John Wiley & Sons Inc., 605 Third Ave., New York, NY 10016. TEL 212-850-6000. Ed. D.M. Goldberg. Indexed: Chem.Abstr.
Former titles: Clinical Biochemistry Reviews (ISSN 0272-9881); Annual Review of Clinical Biochemistry (ISSN 0195-8488)

574.192   AT   ISSN 0067-1703
AUSTRALIAN BIOCHEMICAL SOCIETY. PROCEEDINGS. 1968. a. Aus.$20. (Australian Biochemical Society, CSIRO-Division of Human Nutrition) D.A. Book Australia Pty. Ltd., 11 Station St., Mitcham, Vic. 3132, Australia. Ed. M.G. Clark. adv. circ. 1,400. Indexed: Biol.Abstr. Curr.Cont. Nutr.Abstr. Dairy Sci.Abstr. Helminthol.Abstr.
Formerly: Australian Biochemical Society. Programme and Abstracts.

574.192   US
BENCHMARK PAPERS IN BIOCHEMISTRY. (Each vol. has distinctive title) 1981. irreg., vol.4, 1982. price varies. Van Nostrand Reinhold Company, 7625 Empire Dr., Florence, KY 41042. TEL 606-525-6600. Ed. H.C. Friedman. illus. index. Indexed: Biol.Abstr.

574.192   II   ISSN 0365-9429
BIOCHEMICAL REVIEWS. (Text in English) vol.43, 1972. a. Society of Biological Chemists, Dept. of Biochemistry, Indian Institute of Science, Bangalore 560012, India. Indexed: Biol.Abstr. Chem.Abstr.

574.192   US
BIOCHEMICAL SOCIETY SYMPOSIA. 1963. irreg., vol.35, 1973. Academic Press, Inc., Orlando, FL 32887. Indexed: Ind.Med.

574.192   US   ISSN 0067-8678
BIOCHEMISTRY OF DISEASE. 1971. irreg., vol.12, 1986. price varies. Marcel Dekker, Inc., 270 Madison Ave., New York, NY 10016. TEL 212-696-9000. Eds. M. Farber, M. Pitot. Indexed: Biol.Abstr.
Formerly: Biochemical Pathology.

574   US   ISSN 0194-0538
BIOCHEMISTRY: SERIES OF MONOGRAPHS. 1980. irreg., latest 1985. price varies. John Wiley & Sons, Inc., 605 Third Ave., New York, NY 10158. TEL 212-850-6000. Ed. Alton Meister.

591.192 612.015   UR   ISSN 0136-9377
BIOKHIMIYA ZHIVOTNYKH I CHELOVEKA; respublikanskii mezhvedomstvennyi sbornik nauchnykh trudov. (Text in Russian) 1977. a. (Akademiya Ukrainskoi S.S.R., Institut Biokhimii im. A.V. Palladina) Izdatel'stvo Naukova Dumka, c/o Yu.A. Khramov, Dir, Ul. Repina, 3, Kiev 252 601, Ukrainian S.S.R., U.S.S.R. (Subscr. to: Mezhdunarodnaya Kniga, Moscow, G-200, Russian S.F.S.R., U.S.S.R.) Ed. B.K. Lishko. Indexed: Chem.Abstr.

CANCER BIOCHEMISTRY - BIOPHYSICS. see *MEDICAL SCIENCES — Cancer*

574.192   UK   ISSN 0069-0732
CAROTENOIDS OTHER THAN VITAMIN A. (Text in English) 1967. irreg., 3rd, 1972, Cluj, Romania; price varies. International Union of Pure and Applied Chemistry, c/o Dr. M. Williams, Secy., Bank Court Chambers, 2-3 Pound Way, Cowley Centre, Oxford OX4 3YF, England.

574.192   NE
CELL SURFACE REVIEWS. (Text and summaries in English) 1976. a., vol.8, 1982. price varies. Elsevier Science Publishers B.V., Biomedical Division, Postbus 211, 1000 AE Amsterdam, Netherlands. Eds. G. Poste, G.L. Nicolson. (back issues avail.) Indexed: Biol.Abstr. Chem.Abstr. Ind.Med. Sci.Cit.Ind. Ind.Sci.Rev.

574.192 576   GW   ISSN 0366-7154
CHEMIE MIKROBIOLOGIE TECHNOLOGIE DER LEBENSMITTEL. irreg. Verlag Hans Carl, Postfach 9110, Breite Gasse 58060, D-8500 Neurnburg 1, W. Germany (B.R.D.)

574.192   US   ISSN 0069-3111
CHEMISTRY AND BIOCHEMISTRY OF AMINO ACIDS, PEPTIDES, AND PROTEINS. 1971. irreg., vol.7, 1983. price varies. Marcel Dekker, Inc., 270 Madison Ave., New York, NY 10016. TEL 212-696-9000. Ed. B. Weinstein. Indexed: Chem.Abstr.

574.192 612.015 543   US   ISSN 0095-4861
CLINICAL AND BIOCHEMICAL ANALYSIS. 1974. irreg., vol.22, 1986. price varies. Marcel Dekker, Inc., 270 Madison Ave., New York, NY 10016. TEL 212-696-9000. Ed. M.K. Schwartz. Indexed: Biol.Abstr. Chem.Abstr.

612.015   US
CLINICAL BIOCHEMISTRY; contemporary theories and techniques. irreg., vol.3, 1984. Academic Press, Inc., Orlando, FL 32887. TEL 305-345-2000. Ed. Herbert E. Speigel. Indexed: Nutr.Abstr. Sci.Cit.Ind.

574.192   US   ISSN 0366-5887
COLLOQUIUM MOSBACH. Represents: Gesellschaft fuer Biologische Chemie, Mosbach. Colloquium. (Contributions in English, French and German) 1951. irreg., no.37, 1987. price varies. Springer-Verlag, 175 Fifth Ave., New York, NY 10010 TEL 212-460-1500. (Also Berlin, Heidelberg, Tokyo and Vienna) (reprint service avail. from ISI) Indexed: Biol.Abstr.
Formerly: Gesellschaft fuer Physiologische Chemie, Mosbach. Colloquium (ISSN 0072-4246)

574.192   AT   ISSN 0314-254X
COMMONWEALTH SCIENTIFIC AND INDUSTRIAL RESEARCH ORGANIZATION. DIVISION OF PROTEIN CHEMISTRY. ANNUAL REPORT. 1975/76. a. Aus.$2. C S I R O, 314 Albert St., East Melbourne, Vic. 3002, Australia. Ed. Peter Beck. circ. 1,000. Indexed: Biol.Abstr. Aus.Sci.Ind.

CONFERENCIAS DE BIOQUIMICA. see *BIOLOGY*

612.015   SZ   ISSN 0300-1725
CURRENT PROBLEMS IN CLINICAL BIOCHEMISTRY. 1968. irreg. price varies. Verlag Hans Huber, Laenggassstr. 76, CH-3000 Berne 9, Switzerland (Subscr. to: Hans Huber Publ. Inc., 14 Bruce Park Ave., Toronto, Ont. M4P 253, Canada) Ed.Bd. Indexed: Biol.Abstr. Chem.Abstr. Ind.Med. Dent.Ind.
Formerly: Aktuelle Probleme in der Klinischen Biochemie (ISSN 0065-5597)

574.192   NE
DEVELOPMENTS IN BIOCHEMISTRY. 1978. irreg., vol.27, 1985. price varies. Elsevier Science Publishers B.V., Box 211, 1000 AE Amsterdam, Netherlands. Indexed: Biol.Abstr. Chem.Abstr.

019   MX
DICCIONARIO DE ESPECIALIDADES BIOQUIMICAS. 1985. a. $100. Ediciones P L M, S.A. de C.V., San Bernardino 17, Col. de Valle, 03100 Mexico, D.F., Mexico. Ed. Federico Garcia Ortega. adv. circ. 7,000.

574.192   US   ISSN 0094-8500
ENZYME ENGINEERING. irreg., latest 8th edt. New York Academy of Sciences, 2 E. 63rd St., New York, NY 10021. TEL 212-838-0230. Ed. Bill Boland.

574.192   US   ISSN 0071-1365
ESSAYS IN BIOCHEMISTRY. 1965. a., vol.21, 1986. $18. (Biochemical Society) Academic Press Inc., Orlando, FL 32887. TEL 305-345-2000. Eds. P.N. Campbell, R.D. Marshall. Indexed: Biol.Abstr. Chem.Abstr. Ind.Med. Nutr.Abstr. Sci.Cit.Ind. Ind.Sci.Rev.

574.192   UK   ISSN 0071-4402
FEDERATION OF EUROPEAN BIOCHEMICAL SOCIETIES. (PROCEEDINGS OF MEETING) 1964. irreg., 12th, 1978. Federation of European Biochemical Societies, c/o Prof. H.M. Keir, Dept. of Biochemistry, Marischal College, Aberdeen AB9 1AS, Scotland. Indexed: Biol.Abstr.

574.192   GR   ISSN 0015-5489
FOLIA BIOCHIMICA ET BIOLOGICA GRAECA. (Text in English, French, German and Greek) 1964. irreg., 3-4/yr. exchange basis. (Hellenic Society of Marine Molecular Biology) Institute of Marine Molecular Biology, 2 Lampsaku St., Athens 611, Greece. Ed. A. Christomanos. Indexed: Biol.Abstr. Chem.Abstr. Excerp.Med.

574   US
G W U M C. DEPARTMENT OF BIOCHEMISTRY. ANNUAL SPRING SYMPOSIA SERIES. 1982. irreg. price varies. Plenum Publishing Corp., 233 Spring St., New York, NY 10013. TEL 212-620-8047. Ed.Bd.

574.192 581   JA   ISSN 0441-084X
HOKKAIDO FISHERIES EXPERIMENTAL STATION. SCIENTIFIC REPORTS. (Text in Japanese; summaries in English) 1963. a. Hokkaido Central Fisheries Experimental Station, Hamanaka-cho, Yoichi-machi, Hokkaido, Japan. Indexed: Biol.Abstr. Ind.Vet. Vet.Bull.

574.192 574.191   US   ISSN 0096-2708
HORIZONS IN BIOCHEMISTRY AND BIOPHYSICS. 1974. irreg., vol.5, 1978. price varies. Addison-Wesley Publishing Co., Advanced Book Program, Reading, MA 01867. TEL 617-944-3700. Ed.Bd. Indexed: Biol.Abstr. Chem.Abstr. Ind.Med. Sci.Abstr. Dent.Ind.

574.192   JA   ISSN 0074-3534
INTERNATIONAL CONGRESS OF BIOCHEMISTRY. PROCEEDINGS. 1949. triennial, 1967, 7th, Tokyo. $5. Japanese Biochemical Society - Nihon Seikagakkai, c/o Ishikawa Bldg. 3F, 25-16 Hongo 5, Bunkyo-ku, Tokyo 113, Japan. Indexed: Biol.Abstr.
Proceedings published in host country

574.192 574.1   FI   ISSN 0074-3690
INTERNATIONAL CONGRESS OF HISTOCHEMISTRY AND CYTOCHEMISTRY. PROCEEDINGS. 1960. quadrennial. price varies. University of Helsinki, Department of Anatomy, c/o Dr. Pertti Panula, Siltavuorenpenger 20A, 00170 Helsinki 17, Finland. adv. circ. 1,000.

574.192 AU ISSN 0074-4042
INTERNATIONAL CONGRESS ON CLINICAL
CHEMISTRY. ABSTRACTS. triennial, 11th, 1981,
Vienna; 12th, 1984, Rio de Janeiro. International
Federation of Clinical Chemistry, c/o Dr. M.M.
Mueller, Division of Clinical Biochemistry, 2nd
Dept. of Surgery, University of Vienna, Spitelgasse
23, A-1090 Vienna, Austria. Ed. M. Roth.

574.192 AU ISSN 0074-4069
INTERNATIONAL CONGRESS ON CLINICAL
CHEMISTRY. PAPERS. triennial since 1963; 10th,
1978, Mexico City; 11th, 1981, Vienna.
International Federation of Clinical Chemistry, c/o
Dr. M.M. Mueller, Division of Clinical
Biochemistry, 2nd Dept. of Surgery, University of
Vienna, Spitelgasse 23, A-1090 Vienna, Austria.

574.192 UR ISSN 0202-795X
ITOGI NAUKI I TEKHNIKI: BIOLOGICHESKAYA
KHIMIYA. irreg., latest vols.23-26. price varies.
Vsesoyuznyi Institut Nauchno-Tekhnicheskoi
Informatsii (VINITI), Ul. Baltiiskaya 14, Moscow
A-219, Russian S.F.S.R., U.S.S.R. (Subscr. to:
Mezhdunarodnaya Kniga, Dimitrova ul. 39, 113095
Moscow, Russian S.F.S.R., U.S.S.R.) Indexed:
Chem.Abstr.

574.192 IT ISSN 0075-4447
JOURNEES BIOCHIMIQUES LATINES.
RAPPORTS.* (Text in French and Italian) every 2-
3 years, 1968, 9th, Monaco. Inquire: Prof. A.
Bonsignore, University of Genoa, Italy.

574.192 US ISSN 0076-6879
METHODS IN ENZYMOLOGY. 1955. irreg.,
vol.131, 1986. Academic Press Inc., Orlando, FL
32887. TEL 305-345-2000. Eds. S.P. Colowick,
N.O. Kaplan. Indexed: Biol.Abstr. Chem.Abstr.
Ind.Med. Nutr.Abstr. Abstr.Hyg. Dent.Ind.
Ind.Sci.Rev.

574.192 543 US ISSN 0076-6941
METHODS OF BIOCHEMICAL ANALYSIS. 1954.
irreg., vol.32, 1987. price varies. John Wiley & Sons,
Inc., 605 Third Ave, New York, NY 10016. TEL
212-850-6000. Ed. David Glick. Indexed:
Biol.Abstr. Chem.Abstr. Ind.Med. Math.R.
Nutr.Abstr. Abstr.Hyg. Biotech.Abstr.
Comput.Rev. Ind.Sci.Rev.

574.192 US
MOLECULAR AND CELLULAR
BIOCHEMISTRY. 1983. irreg. $260. Martinus
Nijhoff Publishers, Kluwer Academic, 101 Philip
Dr., Assinippi Park, Norwell, MA 02061. Ed.
Michael Young. circ. 300. Indexed: Biol.Abstr.
Biotech.Abstr.
 Formerly: Developments in Molecular and
Cellular Biochemistry.

MOLECULAR BIOLOGY, BIOCHEMISTRY AND
BIOPHYSICS. see *BIOLOGY — Cytology And
Histology*

574.192 PL ISSN 0077-0485
MONOGRAFIE BIOCHEMICZNE. 1962. irreg.,
vol.32, 1982. price varies. (Polskie Towarzystwo
Biochemiczne) Panstwowe Wydawnictwo Naukowe,
Miodowa 10, 00-251 Warsaw, Poland (Dist by: Ars
Polona, Krakowskie Przedmiescie 7, 00-068
Warsaw, Poland) Ed. Konstancja Raczynska-
Bojanowska. bibl.

574 SZ ISSN 0077-0825
MONOGRAPHS IN DEVELOPMENTAL
BIOLOGY. (Text in English) 1969. irreg. (approx.
1/yr.) price varies. S. Karger AG, Allschwilerstrasse
10, P.O. Box, CH-4009 Basel, Switzerland. Ed.
H.W. Sauer. (reprint service avail. from ISI)
Indexed: Biol.Abstr. Chem.Abstr. Curr.Cont.
Ind.Med.

574.19 612 US ISSN 0094-8950
MONOGRAPHS IN LIPID RESEARCH. 1974. irreg.
price varies. Plenum Publishing Corp., 233 Spring
St., New York, NY 10013. TEL 212-620-8047. Ed.
David Kritchevsky.

MONOGRAPHS ON PHYSICAL BIOCHEMISTRY.
 see *CHEMISTRY — Physical Chemistry*

574.192 NE
NEW COMPREHENSIVE BIOCHEMISTRY. 1962.
irreg., vol.35, 1983. price varies. Elsevier Science
Publishers B.V., Box 211, 1000 AE Amsterdam,
Netherlands. Eds. L.L.M. van Deenen, A.
Neuberger. Indexed: Sci.Cit.Ind. Ind.Sci.Rev.
 Formerly: Comprehensive Biochemistry (ISSN
0069-8032)

574.192 541.3 JA ISSN 0078-6705
OSAKA UNIVERSITY. INSTITUTE FOR PROTEIN
RESEARCH. MEMOIRS. (Text in English) 1959.
a. exchange basis. ‡ Osaka University, Institute for
Protein Research - Osaka Daigaku Tanpakushitsu
Kenkyusho, 3-2 Yamadaoka, Suita, Osaka 565,
Japan. Ed. Yukiteru Katsube. circ. 500. Indexed:
Nutr.Abstr.

574.192 US
PAN AMERICAN ASSOCIATION OF
BIOCHEMICAL SOCIETIES SYMPOSIUM. 1972.
irreg., vol.2, 1972. (Pan-American Association of
Biochemical Societies) Academic Press, Inc.,
Orlando, FL 32887. TEL 305-345-2000. Indexed:
Biol.Abstr. Chem.Abstr.
 Formerly: P A A B S Symposium Series (ISSN
0364-2801)

574.192 UK
PHYTOCHEMICAL SOCIETY OF EUROPE.
ANNUAL PROCEEDINGS. a. £30($60) Oxford
University Press, Walton Street, Oxford QX2 6DP,
England. Ed. Peter J. Lea. adv. Indexed:
Chem.Abstr.

574.192 610 US
PROGRESS IN CLINICAL BIOCHEMISTRY AND
MEDICINE. 1984. irreg., vol.4, 1986. price varies.
Springer-Verlag, 175 Fifth Ave, New York, NY
10010 TEL 212-460-1500. (Also Berlin, Heidelberg,
Tokyo, Vienna) (reprint service avail. from ISI)

574 GW ISSN 0079-6336
PROGRESS IN HISTOCHEMISTRY AND
CYTOCHEMISTRY. (Text in English, French,
German) 1970. irreg. price varies. Gustav Fischer
Verlag, Wollgrasweg 49, Postfach 720143, 7000
Stuttgart 70, W. Germany (B.R.D.) Indexed:
Biol.Abstr. Chem.Abstr. Excerp.Med. Ind.Med.
Ind.Med.

591.192 US
RESEARCH METHODS IN NEUROCHEMISTRY.
1972. irreg. price varies. Plenum Publishing Corp.,
233 Spring St., New York, NY 10013. TEL 212-
620-8047. Eds. Neville Marks, Richard Rodnight.
Indexed: Biol.Abstr. Chem.Abstr.

574.192 US ISSN 0163-7673
REVIEWS IN BIOCHEMICAL TOXICOLOGY.
1979. a., vol.7, 1985. Elsevier Science Publishing
Co., Inc. (New York), 52 Vanderbilt Ave., New
York, NY 10017. TEL 212-916-1150. Ed. E.
Hodgson. Indexed: Chem.Abstr.

REVIEWS OF PHYSIOLOGY, BIOCHEMISTRY
AND EXPERIMENTAL PHARMACOLOGY. see
BIOLOGY — Physiology

ROTHAMSTED EXPERIMENTAL STATION.
REPORT. see *AGRICULTURE — Crop
Production And Soil*

615 574 SZ ISSN 0253-035X
SCHWEIZERISCHE GESELLSCHAFT FUER
KLINISCHE CHEMIE. BULLETIN. (Text in
English, French, German and Italian) 1960. irreg, 4-
6/yr. free to members. Schweizerische Gesellschaft
fuer Klinische Chemie - Societe Suisse de Chimie
Clinique (Societa Svizzera di Chimica Clinica), c/o
Dr. M. Rossier, Laboratoire, Hopital de Zone, CH-
1110 Morges, Switzerland. Eds. Michelle Rossier,
Peter Hagemann. adv. bk. rev. charts. circ. 650.
(looseleaf format) Indexed: Chem.Abstr.
 Formerly: Schweizerische Vereinigung fuer
Klinische Chemie. Bulletin (ISSN 0036-7788)

574.192 II ISSN 0300-0486
SOCIETY OF BIOLOGICAL CHEMISTS.
PROCEEDINGS. (Text in English) a. Society of
Biological Chemists, Department of Biochemistry,
Indian Institute of Science, Bangalore 560012, India.
Indexed: Biol.Abstr.

574.192 US ISSN 0306-0225
SUB CELLULAR BIOCHEMISTRY. 1971. a. price
varies. Plenum Publishing Corp., 233 Spring St.,
New York, NY 10013. TEL 212-620-8047. Ed.
D.B. Roodyn. adv. bk. rev. charts. illus. index.
Indexed: Biol.Abstr. Chem.Abstr. Curr.Cont.
Excerp.Med. Ind.Med.
 Supersedes (1972-1975): Journal Subcelluar
Biochemistry.

574.192 JA ISSN 0371-6813
TOKYO GAKUGEI UNIVERSITY. BULLETIN.
1949. a. free. Tokyo Gakugei University, Publication
Committee, 4-1-1 Nukui-Kita-Machi, Koganei,
Tokyo, Japan. Ed. Jun Inamori. circ. 600.

574.192 UK
TOPICS IN ANTIBIOTIC CHEMISTRY. 1977. irreg.
£30. Ellis Horwood Ltd., Market Cross House,
Cooper St., Chichester, West Sussex, England. (Co-
sponsor: Halsted Press (U.S.)) Ed. P.G. Sammes.
(back issues avail.) Indexed: Biol.Abstr.

574.192 US
TOPICS IN BIOELECTROCHEMISTRY AND
BIOENERGETICS. 1977. irreg., vol.5, 1983. price
varies. John Wiley & Sons, Inc., 605 Third Ave,
New York, NY 10016. TEL 212-850-6000. Ed. G.
Milazzo. Indexed: Chem.Abstr.

574.192 UK ISSN 0140-0835
TOPICS IN ENZYME AND FERMENTATION
BIOTECHNOLOGY. irreg. Ellis Harwood Ltd.,
Market Cross House, Cooper St., Chichester, West
Sussex PO19 1EB, England.

574.192 610 US ISSN 0272-9075
UNIVERSITY OF CALIFORNIA. LAWRENCE
BERKELEY LABORATORY. BIOLOGY AND
MEDICINE DIVISION. ANNUAL REPORT. a.
(University of California, Lawrence Berkeley
Laboratory, Biology and Medicine Division) U.S.
National Technical Information Service, 5285 Port
Royal Rd., Springfield, VA 22161. TEL 703-487-
4600.

WALTER AND ANDREE DE NOTTBECK
FOUNDATION SCIENTIFIC REPORTS. see
BIOLOGY — Microbiology

BIOLOGY — Biophysics

ACTA UNIVERSITATIS LODZIENSIS: FOLIA
BIOCHIMICA ET BIOPHYSICA. see
BIOLOGY — Biological Chemistry

574.191 610 US ISSN 0065-2245
ADVANCES IN BIOLOGICAL AND MEDICAL
PHYSICS. 1948. irreg., vol.17, 1980. Academic
Press, Inc., Orlando, FL 32887. TEL 305-345-2000.
Eds. John H. Lawrence, J.G. Hamilton. index.
Indexed: Biol.Abstr. Ind.Med. Nutr.Abstr.

574.191 US ISSN 0065-3292
ADVANCES IN RADIATION BIOLOGY. 1964.
irreg., vol.11, 1984. price varies. Academic Press,
Inc., Orlando, FL 32887. TEL 305-345-2000.
Ed.Bd. index. Indexed: Biol.Abstr. Sci.Cit.Ind.
Ind.Sci.Rev.

574.191 US ISSN 0883-9182
ANNUAL REVIEW OF BIOPHYSICS AND
BIOPHYSICAL CHEMISTRY. 1972. a. $47.
Annual Reviews Inc., 4139 El Camino Way, Palo
Alto, CA 94306. TEL 415-493-4400. Ed. Donald
M. Engelman. bibl. index. cum.index every 5 yrs.
(back issues avail.; reprint service avail. from ISI)
Indexed: Biol.Abstr. Chem.Abstr. Curr.Cont.
Ind.Med. Sci.Abstr. Sci.Cit.Ind. Ind.Sci.Rev.
M.M.R.I. Nucl.Sci.Abstr.
 Formerly (until vol.14, 1985): Annual Review of
Biophysics and Bioengineering (ISSN 0084-6589)

BIOMEKHANIKA/BIOMECHANICS. see
PHYSICS — Mechanics

574.191 UR ISSN 0374-6569
BIONIKA; respublikanskii mezhvedomstvennyi sbornik nauchnykh trudov. (Text in Russian) 1965. a. (Akademiya Nauk Ukrainskoi S.S.R, Institut Gidromekhaniki) Izdatel'stvo Naukova Dumka, c/o Yu.A. Khramov, Dir, Ul. Repina, 3, Kiev 252 601, Ukrainian S.S.R., U.S.S.R. (Subscr. to: Mezhdunarodnaya Kniga, Moscow, G-200, Russian S.F.S.R., U.S.S.R.) Ed. G.V. Logvinovich. Indexed: Sci.Abstr.

574.191 574 US ISSN 0067-8910
BIOPHYSICAL SOCIETY. ABSTRACTS. 1958. a. included with subscr. to Biophysical Journal. Rockefeller University Press, 1230 York Ave., New York, NY 10021. TEL 212-570-8552. (reprint service avail. from ISI, UMI) Indexed: Biol.Abstr. Supersedes: Biophysical Society. Symposium Proceedings (ISSN 0520-1985)

CANCER BIOCHEMISTRY - BIOPHYSICS. see MEDICAL SCIENCES — Cancer

574.191 US ISSN 0070-2129
CURRENT TOPICS IN BIOENERGETICS. 1966. irreg., vol.14, 1985. Academic Press, Inc., Orlando, FL 32887. TEL 305-345-2000. Ed. D.R. Sanadi. Indexed: Biol.Abstr. Nutr.Abstr. Sci.Cit.Ind. Ind.Sci.Rev.

574.191 JA
ELECTROPHYSIOLOGY/DENKI SEIRIGAKU. (Text in English) 1951. irreg. exchange basis. Showa University, School of Medicine, 1-5-8 Hatanodai, Shinagawa-ku, Tokyo 142, Japan. Indexed: Biol.Abstr.

574.191 US ISSN 0073-0475
HARVARD BOOKS IN BIOPHYSICS. 1965. irreg., no.3, 1983. price varies. ‡ (Harvard University Medical School, Department of Biophysics) Harvard University Press, 79 Garden St., Cambridge, MA 02138. TEL 617-495-2600. Indexed: Biol.Abstr. Chem.Abstr.

HORIZONS IN BIOCHEMISTRY AND BIOPHYSICS. see BIOLOGY — Biological Chemistry

574.191 II
INDIAN BIOPHYSICAL SOCIETY. PROCEEDINGS. irreg. Indian Biophysical Society, c/o Saha Institute of Nuclear Physics, 92 Acharya Prafulla Chandra Rd., Calcutta 700009, India.

INSTYTUT BADAN JADROWYCH. ZAKLAD RADIOBIOLOGII I OCHRONY ZDROWIA. PRACE DOSWIADCZAINE. see MEDICAL SCIENCES — Radiology And Nuclear Medicine

INTERNATIONAL MONOGRAPHS ON ADVANCED BIOLOGY AND BIOPHYSICS. see BIOLOGY

574.191 UR ISSN 0234-2979
ITOGI NAUKI I TEKHNIKI: BIOFIZIKA MEMBRAN. irreg., latest vols.4-5, 1987. price varies. Vsesoyuznyi Institut Nauchno-Tekhnicheskoi Informatsii (VINITI), Ul. Baltiiskaya 14, Moscow A-219, Russian S.F.S.R., U.S.S.R. (Subscr. to: Mezhdunarodnaya Kniga, Dimitrova ul. 39, 113095 Moscow, Russian S.F.S.R., U.S.S.R.)
Formerly: Itogi Nauki i Tekhniki: Biofizika (ISSN 0202-7003)

574.191 GW
JAHRBUCH FUER BIOTECHNOLOGIE. a. Carl Hanser Verlag, Kolbergerstr. 22, Postfach 860420, D-8000 Munich, W. Germany (B.R.D.) Ed.Bd.

574.875 US ISSN 0160-2462
MEMBRANE TRANSPORT PROCESSES. 1978. irreg., no.3, 1979. Raven Press, 1185 Ave. of the Americas, New York, NY 10036. TEL 212-575-0335. Ed. Joseph F. Hoffman.

MOLECULAR BIOLOGY, BIOCHEMISTRY AND BIOPHYSICS. see BIOLOGY — Cytology And Histology

541 UR
MOLEKULYARNAYA FIZIKA I BIOFIZIKA VODNYKH SISTEM. 1973. irreg. 1.03 Rub. (Leningradskii Universitet) Lenizdat, Fontanka, 59, Leningrad, Russian S.F.S.R., U.S.S.R. illus. Indexed: Chem.Abstr.
Supersedes: Struktura i Rol' Vody v Zhivom Organizme (ISSN 0585-4393)

NON-IONIZING RADIATION; r.f., microwaves, infra-red, lasers. see MEDICAL SCIENCES — Radiology And Nuclear Medicine

574.191 US
SPRINGER SERIES IN BIOPHYSICS. 1986. irreg. price varies. Springer-Verlag, 175 Fifth Ave., New York, NY 10160 TEL 212-460-1500. (Also Berlin, Heidelberg, Tokyo, Vienna) (reprint service avail. from ISI)

BIOLOGY — Botany

see also Agriculture—Crop Production and Soil; Forests and Forestry; Gardening and Horticulture

A L P R NEWS. (Association for Arid Lands Studies) see AGRICULTURE

581 DK ISSN 0105-4236
AARHUS UNIVERSITY. BOTANICAL INSTITUTE. REPORTS. 1976. irreg. price varies. University of Aarhus, Botanical Institute - Aarhus Universitet, Nordlandsvej 68, 8240 Risskov, Denmark. Ed. B. Oellgaard. illus. circ. 300.

581 PL ISSN 0065-0951
ACTA AGROBOTANICA. (Text in Polish and English; summaries in English, French or Polish) 1953. irreg., vol.34, 1982. price varies. (Polskie Towarzystwo Botaniczne) Panstwowe Wydawnictwo Naukowe, Miodowa 10, 00-251 Warsaw, Poland (Dist. by: Ars Polona, Krakowskie Przedmiescie 7, 00-068 Warsaw, Poland) Ed. M. Saniewski. illus. circ. 300. Indexed: Biol.Abstr. Chem.Abstr. Excerp.Med. Field Crop Abstr. Herb.Abstr. Hort.Abstr. Helminthol.Abstr. Rev.Plant Path. Weed Abstr.

581 BL ISSN 0301-2123
ACTA BIOLOGICA PARANAENSE. (Summaries in English and French) 1960. irreg., 1-2/yr. free. Universidade Federal do Parana, Setor de Ciencias Biologicas, Cx. Postal 441, 80000 Curitiba, Parana, Brazil. Ed. Dr. Clotilde de Lourdes Branco Germiniani. index. circ. 1,000. Indexed: Biol.Abstr. Curr.Cont. GeoRef. Lib.Sci.Abstr.
Supersedes in part: Universidade Federal do Parana. Departamento de Botanica. Boletim & Zoologia (ISSN 0044-5053); Formerly: Universidade do Parana. Departamento do Botanica e Farmacognosia. Boletim (ISSN 0041-8900)

581 SP ISSN 0210-7597
ACTA BOTANICA BARCINONENSIA. (Text in various languages) 1964. irreg. exchange basis. Universitat de Barcelona, Facultat de Biologia, Departament de Botanica, Barcelona, Spain. TEL 3-230 88 51-135. Ed. Xavier Llimona. circ. 1,000. Indexed: Biol.Abstr.
Supersedes (since 1978): Acta Geobotanica Barcinonensia (ISSN 0065-1222)

581 CU
ACTA BOTANICA CUBANA. irreg. Academia de Ciencias de Cuba, Instituto de Botanica, Industria 452, Havana, Cuba. bibl. illus. Indexed: Biol.Abstr.
Formerly: Acta Botanica Cuba.

ACTA BOTANICA HORTI BUCURESTIENSIS. see GARDENING AND HORTICULTURE

581 IC
ACTA BOTANICA ISLANDICA/TIMARIT UM ISLENZKA GRASAFRAEDI. (Text in English, French, German; summaries in English) 1972. irreg. $10. Natturugripasafnio a Akureyri - Akureyri Museum of Natural History, Box 580, Akureyri, Iceland. Ed. Horour Kristinsson. bk. rev. bibl. illus. circ. 250. Indexed: Biol.Abstr.
Continues (1963-68): Flora.

581 CS
ACTA BOTANICA SLOVACA. (Text in Slovak; summaries in English, German and Russian) irreg. price varies. (Slovenska Akademia Vied) Veda, Publishing House of the Slovak Academy of Sciences, Klemensova 19, 814 30 Bratislava, Czechoslovakia (Subscr. to: Slovart, Gottwaldovo nam. 6, 817 64 Bratislava)
Former titles: Acta Botanica; Acta Instituti Botanici.

581 VE ISSN 0084-5906
ACTA BOTANICA VENEZUELICA. (Text and summaries in English and Spanish) 1965. irreg. price varies. Ministerio de Agricultura y Cria, Instituto Botanico, Apartado 2156, Caracas, Venezuela. Ed. Tobias Lasser. charts. illus. circ. 1,000. (processed) Indexed: Biol.Abstr. Field Crop Abstr. Forest.Abstr. Herb.Abstr.

ACTA MANILANA. see CHEMISTRY — Organic Chemistry

589.2 PL ISSN 0001-625X
ACTA MYCOLOGICA. (Text and summaries in English, French, German & Polish) 1965. irreg., vol.19, 1983. price varies. (Polskie Towarzystwo Botaniczne - Polish Botanical Society) Panstwowe Wydawnictwo Naukowe, Miodowa 10, 00-251 Warsaw, Poland (Dist. by: Ars Polona, Krakowskie Przedmiescie 7, 00-068 Warsaw, Poland) Ed. A. Skirgiello. bk. rev. bibl. charts. illus. circ. 320. Indexed: Biol.Abstr. Chem.Abstr. Excerp.Bot. Rev.Plant Path.
Mycology

581 IC ISSN 0365-4850
ACTA NATURALIA ISLANDICA. (Text in English) 1946. a. price varies. Icelandic Museum of Natural History, P.O. Box 5320, 125 Reykjavik, Iceland. Ed. Erling Olafsson. Indexed: Biol.Abstr.

561 PL ISSN 0001-6594
ACTA PALAEOBOTANICA. (Text and summaries in English, Polish) 1960. irreg., vol.24, 1984. price varies. (Polska Akademia Nauk, Instytut Botaniki) Panstwowe Wydawnictwo Naukowe, Miodowa 10, 00-251 Warsaw, Poland (Dist. by: Ars Polona, Krakowskie Przedmiescie 7, 00-068 Warsaw, Poland) Ed. Andrzej Srodon. bibl. charts. illus. circ. 550. Indexed: Biol.Abstr. Excerp.Bot. Geo.Abstr. GeoRef. Plant Breed.Abstr.

581.9 SW ISSN 0084-5914
ACTA PHYTOGEOGRAPHICA SUECICA. (Text and summaries in English, German or Swedish) 1929. a. Kr.65 price varies. Svenska Vaextgeografiska Saellskapet - Swedish Society of Plant Geography, c/o Vaextbiologiska Institutionen, Box 559, S-751 22 Uppsala, Sweden. Ed. Erik Sjoegren. Indexed: Biol.Abstr. Field Crop Abstr. Forest.Abstr. Forest Prod.Abstr. Geo.Abstr. Plant Breed.Abstr. Soils & Fert.

581 GW ISSN 0065-1567
ACTA PHYTOMEDICA; Supplements to Journal of Phytopathology. (Text in English or German; summaries in English and German) 1973. irreg. price varies. Verlag Paul Parey (Berlin), Lindenstr. 44-47, 1000 Berlin 61, W. Germany (B.R.D.) Indexed: Biol.Abstr. Rev.Plant Path.

581 SW ISSN 0347-4917
ACTA REGIAE SOCIETATIS SCIENTIARUM ET LITTERARUM GOTHOBURGENSIS. BOTANICA. 1972. irreg., latest no.2, 1982. price varies; also exchange basis. Kungliga Vetenskaps-och Vitterhets-Samhaellet i Goeteborg, c/o Goeteborgs Universitetsbibliotek, Box 5096, S-402 22 Goeteborg, Sweden (Dist. in U.S., Canada, and Mexico by: Humanities Press, Inc., 171 First Ave., Atlantic Highlands, NJ 07716)
Supersedes in part: Goeteborgs Kungliga Vetenskaps- och Vitterhets- Samhaelle. Handlingar.

581 370 PL
ACTA UNIVERSITATIS LODZIENSIS: FOLIA BOTANICA. (Text in Polish; summaries in various languages) irreg. Uniwersytet Lodzki, Drukarnia Wojskowa, Ul. Gdanska 130, Lodz, Poland (Dist. by: Ars Polona-Ruch, Krakowskie Przedmescie 7, Warsaw, Poland)

581 635.9 AT ISSN 0313-4083
ADELAIDE BOTANIC GARDENS. JOURNAL. 1976. irreg. Aus.$40. Adelaide Botanic Gardens, North Terrace, Adelaide, S.A. 5000, Australia. Ed. H.R. Toelken. bk. rev. circ. 200. (back issues avail.) Indexed: Biol.Abstr. Hort.Abstr. Plant Breed.Abstr.

BIOLOGY — BOTANY

581 US ISSN 0065-2296
ADVANCES IN BOTANICAL RESEARCH. 1963. irreg., vol.12, 1986. Academic Press Inc., Orlando, FL 32887. TEL 305-345-2000. Ed. H.W. Woolhouse. Indexed: Biol.Abstr. Biol.& Agr.Ind. Chem.Abstr. Sci.Cit.Ind. Field Crop.Abstr. Forest.Abstr. Forest Prod.Abstr. Herb.Abstr. Ind.Sci.Rev. Plant Breed.Abstr. Soils & Fert. Weed Abstr.

581 US ISSN 0741-8280
ADVANCES IN ECONOMIC BOTANY. 1983. irreg., latest no.3. price varies. New York Botanical Garden, Scientific Publications Department, Bronx, NY 10458. TEL 212-220-8721. Ed. Dr. C. Padoch. (back issues avail.)

581 US
ADVANCES IN PLANT PATHOLOGY. 1982. irreg., vol.4, 1986. Academic Press Inc., Orlando, FL 32887. TEL 305-345-2000. Eds. D.S. Ingram, P.H. Williams. Indexed: Chem.Abstr.

581 II ISSN 0376-480X
ADVANCES IN POLLEN SPORE RESEARCH. 1976. a. $25. Today and Tomorrow's Printers and Publishers, 24B/5 Original Rd., Karol Bagh, New Delhi 110005, India (Dist. in U.S. by: Scholarly Publications, 7310 Elcresta Dr., Houston, Texas 77083) Ed. P.K.K. Nair.

581 NE ISSN 0376-7329
ADVANCES IN RESEARCH AND TECHNOLOGY OF SEEDS. 1975. irreg., part 10, 1986. price varies. (International Seed Testing Association) Centre for Agricultural Publishing and Documentation, Box 4, 6700 AA Wageningen, Netherlands. illus. Indexed: Biol.Abstr. Chem.Abstr. Field Crop.Abstr. Herb.Abstr.

581 NE
ADVANCES IN VEGETATION SCIENCE. (Text in English) 1980. irreg. price varies. Dr. W. Junk Publishers, Spuiboulevard 50, 3311 GR Dordrecht, Netherlands (U.S. address: Kluwer Academic Publishers, 190 Old Derby St., Hingham, MA 02043) Indexed: Biol.Abstr.

AGLINK LEAFLETS. see *AGRICULTURE*

581 631.5 SW ISSN 0002-1172
AGRI HORTIQUE GENETICA. (Text in English, German, Swedish; summaries in English, German) 1942. irreg. (1-2/yr.) exchange basis. (Weibullsholm Plant Breeding Institute) W. Weibull AB, Box 520, S-261 24 Landskrona, Sweden. Eds. Goeran Ewertson, Peder Weibull. charts. illus. circ. 600. Indexed: Biol.Abstr. Chem.Abstr. Field Crop.Abstr. Food Sci.& Tech.Abstr. Helminthol.Abstr. Herb.Abstr. Plant Breed.Abstr. VITIS.

AGRONOMIA MOCAMBICANA. see *AGRICULTURE*

AKADEMIA ROLNICZA W SZCZECINIE. ZESZYTY NAUKOWE. ROLNICTWO. SERIA PRZYRODNICZA. see *AGRICULTURE*

581 551.4 JA
AKITA PREFECTURAL COLLEGE OF AGRICULTURE. BULLETIN. (Text and summaries in English and Japanese) 1975. a. Akita Prefectural College of Agriculture, 2-2 Ohgata-Mura, Akita Pref., 010-04, Japan. circ. 550. (back issues avail.) Indexed: Biol.Abstr. Excerp.Med. Nutr.Abstr. Field Crop Abstr. Herb.Abstr. Ind.Vet. Plant Breed.Abstr. Soils & Fert. Vet.Bull.

ALGOLOGICAL STUDIES; Archiv fuer Hydrobiologie, Supplementbaende. see *BIOLOGY*

581 US
ALLERTONIA; a series of occasional papers. 1975. irreg., vol.2, 1981. price varies per no. Pacific Tropical Botanical Garden, Box 340, Lawai, Kauai, HI 96765. Indexed: Biol.Abstr. Chem.Abstr.

580 IT ISSN 0065-6429
ALLIONIA. (Text in Italian; summaries in English) 1952. a. (Istituto Botanico di Torino) Levrotto e Bella, Universita di Torino, Corso Vittorio Emanuele 28, 10125 Turin, Italy. circ. 500. Indexed: Biol.Abstr. Chem.Abstr. Mycol.Abstr. Field Crop Abstr. Forest.Abstr. Forest Prod.Abstr. Herb.Abstr.

581 632 US ISSN 0569-6992
AMERICAN PHYTOPATHOLOGICAL SOCIETY. MONOGRAPHS. 1961. irreg., latest 1986. price varies. American Phytopathological Society, 3340 Pilot Knob Rd., St. Paul, MN 55121. TEL 612-454-7250. Indexed: Biol.Abstr. Plant Breed.Abstr. Rev.Plant Path.

581 GW ISSN 0721-6513
ANDRIAS. (Text in German; summaries in English) 1981. irreg. Landessammlungen fuer Naturkunde, Erbprinzenstr. 13, Postfach 3949, 7500 Karlsruhe 1, W. Germany (B.R.D.)

580 IO ISSN 0517-8452
ANNALES BOGORIENSES; journal of tropical general botany. (Text in English) 1950. irreg., vol.8, no.2, 1984. price varies. National Biological Institute, Treub Laboratory, c/o Kebun Raya, Bogor, Indonesia. Ed. Susono Saono. charts. illus. circ. 315. Indexed: Biol.Abstr. Chem.Abstr. Field Crop Abstr. Herb.Abstr. Hort.Abstr. Soils & Fert.

581 IT
ANNALI DI BOTANICA. (Text in various European languages; summaries in English & Italian) 1902. a. L.16000. Universita degli Studi di Roma, Istituto di Botanica, Biblioteca, Piazzale Aldo Moro N.5, 00185 Rome, Italy. Ed.Bd. bk. rev. charts. illus. index. circ. 500. Indexed: Biol.Abstr. Chem.Abstr.
Supersedes (1885-1901): Istituto Botanico di Roma. Annuario.

581 632 US ISSN 0066-4286
ANNUAL REVIEW OF PHYTOPATHOLOGY. 1963. a. $31. Annual Reviews Inc., 4139 El Camino Way, Palo Alto, CA 94306. TEL 415-493-4400. Ed. R. James Cook. bibl. index. cum.index. (back issues avail.; reprint service avail. from ISI) Indexed: Biol.Abstr. Biol.& Agr.Ind. Chem.Abstr. Curr.Cont. Excerp.Med. Sci.Cit.Ind. Biotech.Abstr. Field Crop Abstr. Forest.Abstr. Forest Prod.Abstr. Helminthol.Abstr. Herb.Abstr. Hort.Abstr. Ind.Sci.Rev. M.M.R.I. Plant Breed.Abstr. Rev.Plant Path. Soils & Fert. VITIS. Weed Abstr.

581 US ISSN 0066-4294
ANNUAL REVIEW OF PLANT PHYSIOLOGY. 1950. a. $31. Annual Reviews Inc., 4139 El Camino Way, Palo Alto, CA 94306. TEL 415-493-4400. Ed. Winslow R. Briggs. bibl. index. cum.index. (back issues avail.; reprint service avail. from ISI) Indexed: Biol.Abstr. Biol.& Agr.Ind. Chem.Abstr. Curr.Cont. Psychol.Abstr. Sci.Cit.Ind. Abstr.Bull.Inst.Pap.Chem. Biotech.Abstr. Field Crop Abstr. Forest.Abstr. Forest Prod.Abstr. Helminthol.Abstr. Herb.Abstr. Hort.Abstr. Ind.Sci.Rev. M.M.R.I. Plant Breed.Abstr. Rev.Plant Path. Soils & Fert. VITIS. Vet.Bull. Weed Abstr.

581 GE
ARBEITSGEMEINSCHAFT SAECHSISCHER BOTANIKER. BERICHTE. 1959. a. Technische Universitaet Dresden, Botanischer Garten, Stuebelallee 2, DDR 8019 Dresden, E. Germany (D.D.R.) illus. circ. 800. Indexed: Biol.Abstr.

582 PL ISSN 0066-5878
ARBORETUM KORNICKIE. (Text in English and Polish; summaries in English and Russian) 1955. a. price varies. (Polska Akademia Nauk, Instytut Dendrologii) Panstwowe Wydawnictwo Naukowe, Miodowa 10, 00-251 Warsaw, Poland (Dist. by: Ars Polona, Krakowskie Przedmiescie 7, 00-068 Warsaw, Poland) (Co-sponsor: Arboretum Kornickie) Ed. W. Bugata. bibl. charts. illus. circ. 540. Indexed: Biol.Abstr. Chem.Abstr. Forest.Abstr. Forest Prod.Abstr. Hort.Abstr. Soils & Fert.
Formerly: Kornik, Poland. Zaklad Dendrologii i Pomologii. Prace.

581 FR ISSN 0066-8184
ARVERNIA BIOLOGICA: BOTANIQUE; recueil des travaux des laboratoires de botanique de la Faculte des Sciences de Clermont-Ferrand et de la Station Biologique de Besse. 1930. irreg. exchange basis only. Universite de Clermont II, Laboratoire de Biologie Vegetale, 4, rue Ledru, F-63038 Clermont-Ferrand Cedex 2, France. Ed.Bd. Indexed: VITIS.

581 II
ASPECTS OF PLANT SCIENCE. 1976. irreg., vol.9, 1986. $39. Today and Tomorrow's Printers and Publishers, 24B/5, Original Rd., Karol Bagh, New Delhi 110005, India (Dist. in U.S. by: Scholarly Publications, 7310 Elcresta Dr, Houston, Texas 77083) Indexed: Biol.Abstr.

551.5 FI
ATLAS FLORAE EUROPAEAE. (Text in English) 1972. irreg., vol.7, 1986. price varies. Societas Biologica Fennica Vanamo, P. Rautatiekatu 13, SF-00100 Helsinki, Finland (Subscr. to: Akateeminen Kirjakauppa (Academic Bookstore), Keskuskatu 1, SF-00100 Helsinki, Finland) (Co-sponsor: Committee for Mapping the Flora of Europe) Eds. Jaakko Jalas, Juha Suominen. Indexed: Bibl.Agri. Biol.Abstr. Bull.Signal. Chem.Abstr. Curr.Cont. Pollut.Abstr.

581 PL ISSN 0067-0294
ATLAS FLORY POLSKIEJ I ZIEM OSCIENNYCH/FLORAE POLONICAE TERRARUNIQUE ADIACENTIUM SCONOGRAPHIA. (Text in Latin and Polish) 1960. irreg., vol.6, 1983. price varies. (Polska Akademia Nauk, Instytut Botaniki) Panstwowe Wydawnictwo Naukowe, Miodowa 10, 00-251 Warsaw, Poland. Ed. J. Madalski. Indexed: Biol.Abstr.

580 PL ISSN 0067-0324
ATLAS ROZMIESZCZENIA DRZEW I KRZEWOW W POLSCE. (Text in Polish, English and Russian) 1963. irreg., vol.32, 1982. price varies. (Polska Akademia Nauk, Zaklad Dendrologii) Panstwowe Wydawnictwo Naukowe, Ul. Miodowa 10, 00-251 Warsaw, Poland (Dist. by: Ars Polona, Krakowskie Przedmiescie 7, 00-068 Warsaw, Poland) Ed. Kazimierz Browicz.

581 PL
BADANIA FIZJOGRAFICZNE NAD POLSKA ZACHODNIA. SERIA B. BOTANIKA. (Text in Polish; summaries in English, French or German) 1948. irreg., vol.34, 1983. price varies. (Poznanskie Towarzystwo Przyjaciol Nauk) Panstwowe Wydawnictwo Naukowe, Ul. Miodowa 10, Warsaw, Poland (Dist. by: Ars Polona-Ruch, Krakowskie Przedmiescie 7, Warsaw, Poland) Ed. J. Wislocki. illus. charts. circ. 300.
Formerly: Badania Fizjograficzne nad Polska Zachodnia. Seria B. Biologia (ISSN 0067-2815)

581 635 US ISSN 0005-4003
BAILEYA; a journal of horticultural taxonomy. 1953. irreg., vol.21, 1981. $7.50 per vol. or exchange. L. H. Bailey Hortorium, Cornell University, Ithaca, NY 14853. TEL 607-256-1000. Ed. W.J. Dress. bk. rev. bibl. charts. illus. index. circ. 600. (also avail. in microform from UMI; reprint service avail. from UMI) Indexed: Biol.Abstr. Hort.Abstr. Plant Breed.Abstr.

581 US
BARLEY GENETICS NEWSLETTER; an international communication medium. 1971. a. $5. (International Barley Genetics Symposium) Colorado State University, Department of Agronomy, c/o T. Tsuchiya, Ed., Fort Collins, CO 80523. Ed.Bd. circ. 600(controlled) Indexed: Plant Breed.Abstr.

581 US ISSN 0198-7356
BARTONIA. 1909. a. $12.50. Philadelphia Botanical Club, c/o Academy of Natural Sciences of Philadelphia, 19th St. and the Parkway, Philadelphia, PA 19103. TEL 215-299-1000. Ed. Alfred E. Schuyler. bk. rev. circ. 350. Indexed: Biol.Abstr.

581 SZ ISSN 0067-4605
BAUHINIA. (Text mainly in German; occasionally in English, French and Italian) 1955. irreg. (1/yr.) (Basler Botanische Gesellschaft) Verlag Wepf und Co., Eisengasse 5, 4001 Basel, Switzerland. Ed. R. Leuschner. circ. 500. Indexed: Biol.Abstr. GeoRef. Plant Breed.Abstr.

581 GW ISSN 0373-7640
BAYERISCHE BOTANISCHE GESELLSCHAFT. BERICHTE. 1891. a. price varies. Bayerische Botanische Gesellschaft, Menzinger Str. 67, D-8000 Munich 19, W. Germany (B.R.D.) Ed. Wolfgang Lippert. bk. rev. circ. 900. Indexed: Biol.Abstr. Excerp.Bot.

BIOLOGY — BOTANY

581.08   NE
BELMONTIA. N.S. 1974. irreg., vol.9, 1978. exchange basis. Landbouwhogeschool, Laboratory of Plant Taxonomy and Geography - State Agricultural University, Generaal Foulkesweg 37, 6700 ED Wageningen, Netherlands.

581   574.5   GW   ISSN 0724-3111
BERLINER BOTANISCHER VEREIN. VERHANDLUNG. 1859. a. DM.30. Berliner Botanischer Verein e.V., Koenigin-Luise-Str. 6-8, 1000 Berlin 33, W. Germany (B.R.D.) Ed.Bd. bk. rev. Indexed: Biol.Abstr.

581   GW
BIBLIOGRAPHIA PHYTOSOCIOLOGICA SYNTAXONOMICA. 1971. irreg. (2-8 nos./yr.) price varies. J. Cramer in Gebrueder Borntraeger Verlagsbuchhandlung, Johannesstr. 3A, D-7000 Stuttgart 1, W. Germany (B.R.D.) Ed. R. Tuexen. Indexed: Biol.Abstr.

581   GW   ISSN 0067-7892
BIBLIOTHECA BOTANICA; Originalabhandlungen aus dem Gesamtgebiet der Botanik. 1886. irreg. price varies. E. Schweizerbart'sche Verlagsbuchhandlung, Johannesstr. 3A, 7000 Stuttgart 1, W. Germany (B.R.D.) Ed.Bd.

581   GW
BIBLIOTHECA LICHENOLOGICA. (Text in English, French and German) 1973. irreg. price varies. J. Kramer in Gebrueder Borntraeger Verlagsbuchhandlung, Johannesstrasse 3A, 7000 Stuttgart 1, W. Germany (B.R.D.) Eds. J. Poelt, V. Wirth.

589.2   GW   ISSN 0067-8066
BIBLIOTHECA MYCOLOGICA. 1967. irreg. price varies. J. Cramer in Gebrueder Borntraeger Verlagsbuchhandlung, Johannesstr. 3A, D-7000 Stuttgart 1, W. Germany (B.R.D.) Eds. A. Bresinsky, H. Butin, H.-0. Schwantes. circ. 300. Indexed: Biol.Abstr.

581   GW   ISSN 0067-8112
BIBLIOTHECA PHYCOLOGICA. 1967. irreg. price varies. J. Cramer in Gebrueder Borntraeger Verlagsbuchhandlung, Johannesstr. 3A, D-7000 Stuttgart 1, W. Germany (B.R.D.) Eds. L. Kies, R. Schnetter. circ. 300. Indexed: Biol.Abstr.

BIFIDOBACTERIA AND MICROFLORA. see *BIOLOGY*

581   US   ISSN 0887-2236
BIOLOGICAL AND CULTURAL TESTS FOR CONTROL OF PLANT DISEASES. Short title: B and C Tests. 1986. a. $18. American Phytopathological Society, 3340 Pilot Knob Rd., St. Paul, MN 55121. TEL 800-328-7560. Ed. John R. Hartman. circ. 550. (back issues avail.)

BOCAGIANA. see *BIOLOGY — Zoology*

581   AG   ISSN 0524-0476
BONPLANDIA. (Text in Spanish) 1960. a. exchange. Instituto de Botanica del Nordeste, Sargento Cabral 2131, Casilla de Correo 209, 3400 Corrientes, Argentina. circ. 700. (looseleaf format; back issues avail.) Indexed: VITIS.

581   SW   ISSN 0068-0370
BOTANICA GOTHOBURGENSIA. (Subseries of Acta Universitatis Gothoburgensis) (Text in English, German, Norwegian, Swedish) 1963. irreg., no.7, 1978. price varies; also exchange basis. Acta Universitatis Gothoburgensis, Box 5096, S-402 22 Goeteborg, Sweden (Dist. in U. S., Canada, and Mexico by: Humanities Press, Inc., 171 First Ave., Atlantic Highlands, NJ 07716) Ed.Bd.

580   US
BOTANICAL MONOGRAPHS. irreg. price varies. University of California Press, 2120 Berkeley Way, Berkeley, CA 94720. Indexed: Biol.Abstr. Sci.Cit.Ind.

581   US   ISSN 0006-8098
BOTANICAL MUSEUM LEAFLETS. 1932. irreg. (10 nos. to vol.) $20 per vol. Harvard University, Botanical Museum, Oxford St., Cambridge, MA 02138. Ed. Richard Evans Schultes. illus. index to each vol. (approx. 2 years) circ. 275. Indexed: Biol.Abstr. Chem.Abstr. Field Crop Abstr. Herb.Abstr. Plant Breed.Abstr.
Plants useful or harmful to man

581   US
BOTANICAL SOCIETY OF AMERICA. DIRECTORY. biennial. $12. Botanical Society of America Inc., c/o Dr. David L. Ditcher, Dept. of Biology, Indiana University, Bloomington, IN 47405. TEL 812-335-9455.
Formerly: Botanical Society of America. Yearbook (ISSN 0068-0400)

581   UK   ISSN 0374-6607
BOTANICAL SOCIETY OF EDINBURGH TRANSACTIONS. 1836. a. £5 to non-members. Botanical Society of Edinburgh, Royal Botanic Garden, Inverleith Row, Edinburgh EH3 5LR, Scotland. Ed. J.A. Ratter. bibl. charts. illus. circ. 450. Indexed: Biol.Abstr. Geo.Abstr. Hort.Abstr. Sel.Water Res.Abstr. Rev.Plant Path.
Formerly (until vol.40, 1970): Botanical Society of Edinburgh. Transactions and Proceedings.

581   II
BOTANICAL SURVEY OF INDIA. OCCASIONAL PUBLICATIONS. irreg. price varies. Botanical Survey of India, P.O. Botanic Garden, Howrah 71103, India.

581   SA
BOTANICAL SURVEY OF SOUTH AFRICA. MEMOIRS. 1919. irreg., no.55, 1987. Botanical Research Institute, Department of Agriculture and Water Supply, Private Bag X101, Pretoria 0001, South Africa. circ. 1,000. Indexed: Biol.Abstr. Forest.Abstr. Forest Prod.Abstr. GeoRef. Soils & Fert.

581   GW   ISSN 0006-8179
BOTANISCHE STAATSSAMMLUNG MUENCHEN. MITTEILUNGEN. (Text in English, French and German; summaries in English) 1950. irreg. (1-2/yr.) exchange basis. Botanische Staatssammlung Muenchen, Menzinger Str. 67, 8000 Munich 19, W. Germany (B.R.D.) Ed. Dr. H. Hertel. charts. illus. index. circ. controlled. (processed) Indexed: Biol.Abstr. Plant Breed.Abstr.

581   SA   ISSN 0006-8241
BOTHALIA. 1921. irreg., vol.16, no.2, 1986. R.20. Botanical Research Institute, Department of Agriculture and Water Supply, Private Bag X101, Pretoria 0001, South Africa. Ed. O.A. Leistner. illus. index. circ. 400. Indexed: Biol.Abstr. Excerp.Bot. Field Crop Abstr. Forest.Abstr. Forest Prod.Abstr. Geo.Abstr. Herb.Abstr. Ind.S.A.Per. Rev.Plant Path. Soils & Fert.

581   BL   ISSN 0084-800X
BRADEA; boletin de herbarium bradeanum. (Text in Portuguese; summaries in English) 1969. irreg. $25. Herbarium Bradeanum, C.P. 15005, CEP 20031 Rio de Janeiro, RJ, Brazil. (Co-sponsor: Museu Nacional do Rio de Janeiro) abstr. bibl. charts. illus. index. circ. 400(controlled) Indexed: Biol.Abstr. Ash.G.Bot.Per.

581   UK   ISSN 0068-2292
BRITISH MUSEUM (NATURAL HISTORY) BULLETIN. BOTANY. 1951. a. £130. British Museum (Natural History), Cromwell Rd., London SW7 5BD, England. illus. index. circ. 750. Indexed: Biol.Abstr. GeoRef.

581   UK   ISSN 0301-9195
BRITISH PTERIDOLOGICAL SOCIETY. BULLETIN. 1973. a. £12 including "Fern Gazette" and "Pteridologist". British Pteridological Society, c/o British Museum (Nat. History), Cromwell Rd., London SW7 5BD, England. Ed. A.R. Busby. circ. 700. Indexed: Biol.Abstr.
Supersedes: British Pteridological Society. Newsletter (ISSN 0068-2403)

582   AU
BUNDESANSTALT FUER PFLANZENBAU, VIENNA. JAHRBUCH. (Text in German; summaries in English and German) 1948. a. price varies. Bundesanstalt fuer Pflanzenbau, Alliierten Str. 1, Postfach 64, A-1201 Vienna, Austria. Ed. R. Meinx. index. cum.index. circ. 750.
Formerly: Bundesanstalt fuer Pflanzenbau und Samenpruefung, Vienna. Jahrbuch (ISSN 0068-421X)

581   UK
C.A.B. INTERNATIONAL. MYCOLOGICAL INSTITUTE. PHYTOPATHOLOGICAL PAPERS. (Former name of issuing body: Commonwealth Agricultural Bureaux) 1956. irreg. price varies. ‡ C.A.B. International, Mycological Institute, Farnham House, Farnham Royal, Slough SL2 3BN, England. Indexed: Biol.Abstr. Helminthol.Abstr. Hort.Abstr. Rev.Plant Path.
Formerly: Commonwealth Mycological Institute. Phytopathological Papers (ISSN 0069-7141)

CANADA. NATIONAL MUSEUMS, OTTAWA: PUBLICATIONS IN NATURAL SCIENCE/ PUBLICATIONS DE SCIENCES NATURELLES. see *BIOLOGY — Zoology*

581   NZ   ISSN 0110-5892
CANTERBURY BOTANICAL SOCIETY. JOURNAL. 1968. a. price varies. Canterbury Botanical Society Inc., P.O. Box 8212, Christchurch, New Zealand. Ed. Ross Elder. bk. rev. circ. 250.

581   US
CAREERS IN BOTANY. 1965. irreg., latest 1982. $0.25. Botanical Society of America Inc., c/o School of Biological Sciences, University of Kentucky, Lexington, KY 40506.
Former titles: Botany as a Profession (ISSN 0068-0397) & Botanical Society of America. Miscellaneous Publications.

CAROLINEA; Beitraege zur Naturkundliche Forschung in Sueddeutschland. see *EARTH SCIENCES*

581   CK
CATALOGO ILUSTRADO DE LAS PLANTAS DE CUNDINAMARCA. 1966. irreg. $6 or exchange basis. Universidad Nacional de Colombia, Instituto de Ciencias Naturales, Apdo. 7495, Bogota, Colombia. Ed. Santiago Diaz-Piedrahita. bibl. illus. circ. 1,000. Indexed: Biol.Abstr. Bull.Signal. Ref.Zh. Excerp.Bot.

CENTRAL PLANTATION CROPS RESEARCH INSTITUTE. ANNUAL REPORT. see *AGRICULTURE*

589.2   IT
CENTRO MICOLOGICO FRIULANO. BOLLETINO. 1976. a. Centro Micologico Friulano, Via Beato Odorico da Pordenone 3, 33100 Udine, Italy.

581   US
CHEMIE DER PFLANZENSCHUTZ- UND SCHAEDLINGSBEKAEMPFUNGSMITTEL. (Text in German) 1970. irreg., vol.8, 1982. price varies. Springer-Verlag, 175 Fifth Ave., New York, NY 10010 TEL 212-460-1500. (Also Berlin, Heidelberg, Tokyo and Vienna) Ed. R. Wegler. (reprint service avail. from ISI)

CHEMISTRY OF PLANT PROTECTION. see *CHEMISTRY*

581   SP   ISSN 0010-0730
COLLECTANEA BOTANICA. (Text in various languages) 1946. a. $15 or exchange basis. Institut Botanic de Barcelona, Parc de Montjuic, Avinguda dels Muntanyans, 08004 Barcelona, Spain. Ed. O. de Bolos. bk. rev. bibl. circ. 1,050. Indexed: Biol.Abstr. Field Crop Abstr. Herb.Abstr. Ref.Zh. Zoo.Rec.

581   GW
COLLOQUES PHYTOSOCIOLOGIQUES. (Text in English, French and German) 1975. irreg., no.8, 1981. price varies. Gebrueder Borntraeger Verlagsbuchhandlung, c/o J. Cramer, Johannesstr. 3a, D-7000 Stuttgart 1, W. Germany (B.R.D.) Ed. J.M. Gehu. charts. illus. (back issues avail.) Indexed: Biol.Abstr.

COMMONWEALTH SCIENTIFIC AND INDUSTRIAL RESEARCH ORGANIZATION. DIVISION OF TROPICAL CROPS AND PASTURES. ANNUAL REPORT. see *AGRICULTURE — Crop Production And Soil*

COMMONWEALTH SCIENTIFIC AND INDUSTRIAL RESEARCH ORGANIZATION. DIVISION OF TROPICAL CROPS AND PASTURES. TECHNICAL PAPER. see *AGRICULTURE — Crop Production And Soil*

BIOLOGY — BOTANY

581   IS
CONSPECTUS FLORAE ORIENTALIS. (Text in English) 1980. irreg. Israel Academy of Sciences and Humanities, P.O. Box 4040, Jerusalem.

581   RM   ISSN 0069-9616
CONTRIBUTII BOTANICE. 1958. a. exchange basis only. Universitatea Gradina Botanica, Str. Republicii nr. 42, Cluj-Napoca, Rumania. Ed. Onoriu Ratiu. Indexed: Chem.Abstr. Rev.Plant Path.

581   US   ISSN 0736-0509
CONTRIBUTIONS FROM THE NEW YORK BOTANICAL GARDEN. 1898-1931; resumed 1984. irreg., latest no.16, 1986. price varies. New York Botanical Garden, Scientific Publications Department, Bronx, NY 10458. TEL 212-220-8721. Ed. W. Buck. (back issues avail.)

581   SZ
CRYPTOGAMICA HELVETICA. (Text in French, German and Italian) 1898. irreg., vol.15, 1977. price varies. (Schweizerische Naturforschende Gesellschaft) F. Flueck-Wirth, Krypto, P.O. Box, CH-9053 Teufen, Switzerland. Ed. K. Ammann. bibl. charts. illus. index. (back issues avail.) Indexed: Biol.Abstr.
Formerly: Beitraege zur Kryptogamenflora der Schweiz.

581   615   CU   ISSN 0138-8037
CUBA. CENTRO DE INFORMACION Y DOCUMENTACION AGROPECUARIO. BOLETIN DE RESENAS. SERIE: PLANTAS MEDICINALES. (Abstracts in English) 1983. irreg. exchange basis. Centro de Informacion y Documentacion Agropecuario, Gaveta Postal 4149, Havana 4, Cuba (Dist. by: Ediciones Cubanas, Obispo No. 461, Aptdo. 605, Havana, Cuba) Indexed: Agrindex.
Formerly: Cuba. Centro de Informacion y Divulgacion Agropecuario. Boletin de Resenas. Serie: Plantas Medicinales.

581   AT   ISSN 0727-9620
CUNNINGHAMIA; ecological contributions from the National Herbarium of New South Wales. 1981. biennial. exchange. Royal Botanic Gardens Sydney, Mrs Macquaries Road, Sydney, N.S.W. 2000, Australia. Eds. Dr. Jocelyn Powell, Matthew Stevens. circ. 1,000.

581   DK   ISSN 0416-6906
DANSK DENDROLOGISK ARSSKRIFT. (Text in Danish, Norwegian or Swedish; summaries in English, French or German) 1949. a. Kr.70($9.50) Dansk Dendrologisk Forening, Raadvad 32, DK 2800, Denmark. Ed. P.M. Plum. bk. rev. circ. 800. Indexed: Biol.Abstr. Forest.Abstr. Forest Prod.Abstr.

581   DK   ISSN 0109-3142
DANSKE PLANTEVAERNSKONFERENCE. 1984. a. free. Statens Plantaevlsforsoeg - Danish Research Service for Plant and Soil Science, Lyngby, Denmark (Subscr.to: Plantevaernscentret, Institut for Ukrudbekaempelse, Flakkebjerg, 4200 Slagelse, Denmark) illus.

581   634.9   GW   ISSN 0070-3958
DEUTSCHE DENDROLOGISCHE GESELLSCHAFT. MITTEILUNGEN. 1893. a. free. Deutsche Dendrologische Gesellschaft, Hawstr. 28, D-5500 Trier, W. Germany (B.R.D.) TEL (0651)3 30 61. Ed. Horst Bartels. bk. rev. cum.index. circ. 1,500.

581   GW   ISSN 0070-6728
DISSERTATIONES BOTANICAE. 1967. irreg. price varies. J. Kramer in Gebrueder Borntraeger Verlagsbuchhandlung, Johannesstr. 3A, 7000 Stuttgart 1, W. Germany (B.R.D.) circ. 500. Indexed: Biol.Abstr.

581.1   US
ENCYCLOPEDIA OF PLANT PHYSIOLOGY. NEW SERIES. 1975. irreg., vol.19, 1986. Springer Verlag, 175 Fifth Ave., New York, NY 10010 TEL 212-460-1500. (Also Berlin, Heidelberg, Tokyo and Vienna) Eds. A. Pirson, M.H. Zimmermann. (reprint service avail. from ISI) Indexed: Chem.Abstr.

581   GW   ISSN 0170-4818
ENGLERA. (Text and summaries in English, German) 1979. irreg. price varies. Botanischer Garten und Botanisches Museum Berlin-Dahlem, Koenigin-Luise-Str. 6-8, D-1000 Berlin 33, W. Germany (B.R.D.) Ed. H. Scholz. circ. 800. (back issues avail.)

ERLANGER BAUSTEINE ZUR FRAENKISCHEN HEIMATFORSCHUNG. see *HISTORY*

581   VE   ISSN 0252-8274
ERNSTIA. (Text mainly in Spanish, also French, Portuguese; summaries in English and Spanish) 1981. irreg. (approx. 7/yr.) exchange basis. Universidad Central de Venezuela, Facultad de Agronomia, Instituto de Botanica Agricola, Herbario, Apdo. 4579, Maracay- Edo. Aragua 2101, Venezuela. Ed. Carmen E.B. de Rojas. circ. 200. (back issues avail.)

ESTACION EXPERIMENTAL DE AULA DEI. ANALES. see *AGRICULTURE — Crop Production And Soil*

631.5   581   NE   ISSN 0071-2221
EUCARPIA. Represents: European Association for Research on Plant Breeding. Report of the Congress. 1956. triennial, 10th, 1983, Wageningen, Netherlands. price varies. PUDOC, Postbus 4, 6700 AA Wageningen, Netherlands. Ed.Bd. circ. 1,250. Indexed: Plant.Breed.Abstr.

581   GW   ISSN 0014-4037
EXCERPTA BOTANICA. SECTIO A: TAXONOMICA ET CHOROLOGICA. (Text in English, French and German) 1959. irreg., 7 nos. per vol. DM.278 per vol. Gustav Fischer Verlag, Wollgrasweg 49, Postfach 720143, 7000 Stuttgart 70, W. Germany (B.R.D.) Ed. Frau Follmann-Schrag. adv. bk. rev. cum.index. circ. 550. Indexed: Rev.Plant Path.

581   GW   ISSN 0014-4045
EXCERPTA BOTANICA. SECTIO B: SOCIOLOGICA. (Text in English, French and German) 1959. irreg., 4 nos. per vol. DM.178 per vol. Gustav Fischer Verlag, Wollgrasweg 49, Postfach 720143, 7000 Stuttgart 70, W. Germany (B.R.D.) Ed. R. Tuexen. adv. bibl. index. circ. 550.

581   US   ISSN 0071-3392
EXPERIMENTAL BOTANY; AN INTERNATIONAL SERIES OF MONOGRAPHS. 1964. irreg., vol.19, 1984. Academic Press Inc., Orlando, FL 32887. TEL 305-345-2000. Eds. J.F. Sutcliffe, J. Cronshaw. Indexed: Biol.Abstr.

FAUNA & FLORA. see *CONSERVATION*

581   UK   ISSN 0308-0838
FERN GAZETTE. 1909. a. £12 including "Bulletin" and "Pteridologist". British Pteridological Society, c/o British Museum (Natural History), Cromwell Rd., London SW7 5BD, England. Ed. M. Gibby. index. circ. 700. Indexed: Biol.Abstr. Geo.Abstr.
Formerly (until): British Fern Gazette (ISSN 0524-5826)

581   US   ISSN 0015-0746
FIELDIANA: BOTANY. 1895. irreg. price varies. Field Museum of Natural History, Division of Publications, Roosevelt Rd. at Lake Shore Dr., Chicago, IL 60605-2496. TEL 312-922-9410. Ed. Timothy Plowman. bibl. charts. illus. index. circ. 450. (back issues avail.; reprint service avail. from UMI) Indexed: Biol.Abstr. Chem.Abstr. Forest.Abstr. Forest Prod.Abstr. GeoRef.

581   BU   ISSN 0324-0975
FITOLOGIJA. (Text in Bulgarian; summaries in English, French, German and Russian) vol.20, 1982. a. (Akademiia na Selskostopanskite Nauki) Publishing House of the Bulgarian Academy of Sciences, Acad. G. Bonchev St., Bldg. 6, 1113 Sofia, Bulgaria. Ed. Bogdan Kuzmanov. circ. 480. (back issues avail.) Indexed: Biol.Abstr.

581   BL   ISSN 0100-4204
FITOSSANIDADE. 1974. irreg. Rua Livreiro Edesio, 612/401, 60.000 Fortaleza, Ceara, Brazil. Ed. Fernando Montenegro de Sales. bibl. charts. illus. *Botany*

500.9   EC   ISSN 0015-380X
FLORA. (Text in English and Spanish) 1937. irreg. exchange basis. Instituto Ecuatoriano de Ciencias Naturales, Apartado 408, Quito, Ecuador. Ed. M. Acosta-Solis. bk. rev. abstr. bibl. charts. illus. circ. 2,000. Indexed: Biol.Abstr. Ind.Sci.Rev.

581   GE   ISSN 0367-2530
FLORA; Morphologie, Geobotanik, Oekophysiologie. (Text in English, French and German: summaries in English) 1818. irreg. (6-12/yr.) M.180 per vol. VEB Gustav Fischer Verlag, Villengang 2, Postfach 176, 6900 Jena, E. Germany (D.D.R.) Ed.Bd. bk. rev. bibl. charts. illus. index. (reprint service avail. from ISI) Indexed: Biol.Abstr. Chem.Abstr. Curr.Cont. Excerp.Med. Forest.Abstr. Forest Prod.Abstr. Geo.Abstr.

581   CK   ISSN 0120-4351
FLORA DE COLOMBIA. 1983. irreg. $15 or exchange basis. Universidad Nacional de Colombia, Instituto de Ciencias Naturales, Apdo. 7495, Bogota, Colombia. Ed. Polidoro Pinto Escobar. circ. 2,000.

581   BL   ISSN 0071-5751
FLORA ECOLOGICA DE RESTINGAS DO SUDESTE DO BRASIL. 1960. irreg., no.23, 1978. exchange only. Museu Nacional, Quinta da Boa Vista, 20940 Rio de Janeiro, RJ, Brazil. bibl. illus.

581   GW   ISSN 0071-576X
FLORA ET VEGETATIO MUNDI. (Text in English, French and German) 1960. irreg., no.8, 1981. price varies. J. Cramer in Gebrueder Borntraeger Verlagsbuchhandlung, Johannesstr. 3A, D-7000 Stuttgart 1, W. Germany (B.R.D.) Ed. R. Tuexen. circ. 100. Indexed: Biol.Abstr.

581   NE   ISSN 0071-5786
FLORA MALESIANA. SERIES 2: PTERIDOPHYTA. (Text in English) 1959. irreg. price varies. (Foundation Flora Malesiana) Martinus Nijhoff Publishers, Box 163, 3300 AD Dordrecht, Netherlands. (Co-sponsor: Rijksherbarium) index. circ. 1,300. Indexed: Biol.Abstr. Forest.Abstr.

581   US   ISSN 0071-5794
FLORA NEOTROPICA. 1968. irreg., latest no.45, 1986. price varies. (Organization for Flora Neotropica) New York Botanical Garden, Scientific Publications Department, Bronx, NY 10458. TEL 212-220-8721. Ed. James L. Luteyn. (back issues avail.)

581   SW
FLORA OF ECUADOR. (Text in English) 1973. irreg. price varies. Publishing House of the Swedish Research Councils, Box 6710, S-113 85 Stockholm, Sweden. (Co-sponsor: Lund Botanical Society) Eds. Gunnar Harling, Benkt Sparre. circ. 500. Indexed: Biol.Abstr.
Formerly: Opera Botanica. Series B. Flora of Ecuador.

581   SA
FLORA OF SOUTHERN AFRICA. 1963. irreg., latest vol.18, no.3. Botanical Research Institute, Department of Agriculture and Water Supply, Private Bag X101, Pretoria 0001, South Africa. Ed. O.A. Leistner. illus. index. circ. 300.

581   IS
FLORA OF THE U.S.S.R. (Text in English) irreg. Israel Program for Scientific Translations, Box 7145, Jerusalem, Israel (And Keter Inc., 440 Park Ave. South, New York, NY 10016)

581   IS
FLORA PALAESTINA. (Text in English) 1966. irreg. Israel Academy of Sciences and Humanities, P.O. Box 4040, Jerusalem 91 040, Israel.

581   PL   ISSN 0071-5816
FLORA POLSKA; ROSLINY NACZYNIOWE POLSKI I ZIEM OSCIENNYCH. 1927. irreg., vol.14, 1980. price varies. (Polska Akademia Nauk, Instytut Botaniki) Panstwowe Wydawnictwo Naukowe, Miodowa 10, 00-251 Warsaw, Poland (Dist. by: Ars Polona, Krakowskie Przedmiescie 7, 00-068 Warsaw, Poland) Ed. A. Jasiewicz. Indexed: Biol.Abstr.

BIOLOGY — BOTANY

581   PL   ISSN 0071-5824
FLORA POLSKA: ROSLINY ZARODNIKOWE POLSKI I ZIEM OSCIENNYCH. 1957. irreg., vol.4, 1970. price varies. (Polska Akademia Nauk, Instytut Botaniki) Panstwowe Wydawnictwo Naukowe, Miodowa 10, Warsaw 5, Poland.

581   PL   ISSN 0071-5840
FLORA SLODKOWODNA POLSKI. 1963. irreg., vol.5, 1980. price varies. (Polska Akademia Nauk, Instytut Botaniki) Panstwowe Wydawnictwo Naukowe, Ul. Miodowa 10, 00-251 Warsaw, Poland (Dist. by: Ars Polona, Krakowskie Przedmiescie 7, 00-068 Warsaw, Poland) Ed. Karol Starmach. circ. 800.

581   BE
FLORE D'AFRIQUE CENTRALE (ZAIRE - RWANDA - BURUNDI) (Issued in several subseries) irreg. price varies. Jardin Botanique National de Belgique - Nationale Plantentuin van Belgie, Domaine de Bouchout, B-1860 Meise, Belgium. Ed. P. Bamps. Indexed: Forest.Abstr. Forest Prod.Abstr.
    Formerly: Flore du Congo, du Rwanda et du Burundi.

581   FR   ISSN 0430-666X
FLORE DE LA NOUVELLE CALEDONIE ET DEPENDANCES. 1967. irreg., no.13, 1984. Museum National d'Histoire Naturelle, Laboratoire de Phanerogamie, 16 rue Buffon, 75005 Paris, France. Ed.Bd.

581   FR
FLORE DE MADAGASCAR ET DES COMORES. 1937. irreg., no.125, 1986. Museum National d'Histoire Naturelle, Laboratoire de Phanerogamie, 16 rue Buffon, 75005 Paris, France. Ed.Bd.

581   FR   ISSN 0071-5867
FLORE DU CAMBODGE, DU LAOS ET DU VIETNAM. 1960. irreg., no.22, 1985. price varies. Museum National d'Histoire Naturelle, Laboratoire de Phanerogamie, 16 rue Buffon, 75005 Paris, France. Ed.Bd.

581   CM   ISSN 0071-5875
FLORE DU CAMEROUN. 1963. irreg., no.22, 1981. price varies. Ministere de l'enseignement Superieur et de la Recherche Scientifique, Herbier National, B.P. 1601, Yaounde, Cameroun. Eds. B. Satabie, C. Cusset. adv. bk. rev. circ. 550.

581   FR   ISSN 0071-5883
FLORE DU GABON. 1961. irreg., no.29, 1986. price varies. Museum National d'Histoire Naturelle, Laboratoire de Phanerogamie, 16 rue Buffon, 75005 Paris, France. Eds. J.F. Leroy, A. le Thomas.

581   630   US   ISSN 0071-5948
FLORIDA. DIVISION OF PLANT INDUSTRY. BIENNIAL REPORT. 1916. biennial. one copy free to Florida residents. ‡ Department of Agriculture and Consumer Services, Division of Plant Industry, Box 1269, Gainesville, FL 32602. TEL 904-372-3505. Ed. S.A. Alfieri, Jr. circ. 3,000. Indexed: Biol.Abstr. Rev.Plant Path.

635   613.7   152   US
FLOWER ESSENCE SOCIETY NEWSLETTER. 1981. irreg. (3-4/yr.) $20 membership. Earth-Spirit, Inc., Box 459, Nevada City, CA 95959. TEL 916-265-9163. Ed. Patricia Kaminski. bk. rev. illus. circ. 2,500.
    Formerly: Flower Essence Society Members' Newsletter.

581   SA   ISSN 0015-4504
FLOWERING PLANTS OF AFRICA. (Text in Afrikaans and English) 1921. a. R.15. ‡ Botanical Research Institute, Department of Agriculture and Water Supply, Private Bag X101, Pretoria 0001, South Africa. Ed. D.J.B. Killick. illus. cum.index. circ. 450. Indexed: Biol.Abstr.
    Formerly: Flowering Plants of South Africa.

581   595   AG   ISSN 0074-025X
FUNDACION MIGUEL LILLO. MISCELANEA. (Text in Spanish; summaries in English, French, German) 1937. irreg., no.77, 1982. ‡ (Ministerio de Cultura y Educacion) Fundacion Miguel Lillo, Miguel Lillo 251, 4000 Tucuman, Argentina. Ed. Jose A. Haedo Rossi. charts. illus. circ. 500. (back issues avail.) Indexed: Biol.Abstr. Ref.Zh.

581   333.7   AG
FUNDACION MIGUEL LILLO. SERIE CONSERVACION DE LA NATURALEZA. 1979. irreg., vol.2, 1982. Fundacion Miguel Lillo, Miguel Lillo 251, 4000 Tucuman, Argentina. Ed. Jose A. Haedo Rossi. bibl. charts. illus. circ. 500.

581   589.2   CN   ISSN 0823-0552
FUNGI CANADENSES. (Text in English or French) 1973. irreg. free. Agriculture Canada, Biosystematics Research Centre, Ottawa, Ont. K1A 0C6, Canada. TEL 613-996-1665. Ed. S.A. Redhead. cum.index. circ. 450. (back issues avail.) Indexed: Biol.Abstr. Mycol.Abstr. Rev.Plant Path.

581   CL   ISSN 0016-5301
GAYANA: BOTANICA. (Text in English of Spanish) 1961. a. Universidad de Concepcion, Facultad de Ciencias Biologicas y de Recursos Naturales, Casilla 2407, Apdo. 10, Concepcion, Chile (Subscr. address: Editorial Universidad de Concepcion, Depto. Ventas, Cas. 1557, Concepcion, Chile) Ed. Alberto Larrain. circ. 1,000. Indexed: Biol.Abstr.

581   US   ISSN 0072-0879
GENTES HERBARUM; occasional papers on the kinds of plants. 1920. irreg., vol.12, 1981. $25 per vol. or exchange. L. H. Bailey Hortorium, Cornell University, Ithaca, NY 14853. TEL 607-256-1000. Ed. M.D. Whelan. index. circ. 240. (also avail. in microform from UMI; reprint service avail. from UMI) Indexed: Biol.Abstr.

581   SZ   ISSN 0373-7896
GEOBOTANISCHES INSTITUT ETH, STIFTUNG RUEBEL, ZURICH. BERICHTE. (Text in English, German) 1928. a. 33 Fr.($16) per no. Geobotanisches Institut ETH, Stiftung Ruebel, Zurichbergstr. 38, CH-8044 Zurich, Switzerland. Ed. Elias Landolt. circ. 2,000. (back issues avail.) Indexed: Biol.Abstr. Curr.Cont.

581   SZ   ISSN 0254-9433
GEOBOTANISCHES INSTITUT ETH, STIFTUNG RUEBEL, ZURICH. VEROEFFENTLICHUNGEN. 1923. irreg. (3-6/yr.) price varies. Geobotanisches Institut ETH, Zurichbergstr. 38, CH-8044 Zurich, Switzerland. Ed. Elias Landolt. circ. 600. (back issues avail.) Indexed: Biol.Abstr. Curr.Adv.Plant Sci. Curr.Cont. Ecol.Abstr. Excerp.Bot. Excerp.Med. Field Crop Abstr. Forest.Abstr. Herb.Abstr. Soils & Fert.

581   IE   ISSN 0332-0235
GLASRA. 1976. a. exchange basis. National Botanic Gardens, Glasnevin, Dublin 9, Ireland. Ed. Aidan Brady. bk. rev. circ. 200.
    Formerly: National Botanic Gardens. Contributions.

581   II
GLIMPSES IN PLANT RESEARCH. a. $39. Today & Tomorrow's Printers & Publishers, 24B/5 Original Rd., Krol Bagh, New Delhi 110005, India. Ed. P.K.K. Nair.

581   GW   ISSN 0340-4145
GOETTINGER FLORISTISCHE RUNDBRIEFE; Zeitschrift fuer Arealkunde, Floristik und Systematik. 1967. irreg. DM.10. Ruhr-Universitaet Bochum, Spezielle Botanik, Universitaetsstr. 150, Postfach 102148, D-4630 Bochum 1, W. Germany (B.R.D.) Ed. H. Haeupler. bk. rev. circ. 1,200. (back issues avail.)

581   US
GRAY HERBARIUM. CONTRIBUTIONS. 1891. irreg., no.214. price varies. Harvard University, Gray Herbarium, 22 Divinity Ave., Cambridge, MA 02138. TEL 617-495-2368. Ed. Donald H. Pfister. circ. 500. Indexed: Biol.Abstr. Plant Breed.Abstr.

581   591   US
GREAT BASIN NATURALIST MEMOIRS. 1976. irreg., no.7,1982. Brigham Young University, 290 Life Science Museum, Provo, UT 84602. TEL 801-378-5053. Ed. Stephen L. Wood. circ. 500. (back issues avail.) Indexed: Biol.Abstr. Zoo.Rec.

635   AT
GROWING NATIVE PLANTS. 1971. a. price varies. (Department of Arts, Heritage and Environment, Australian National Botanic Gardens) Australian Government Publishing Service, Canberra, A.C.T. 2601, Australia. Ed. M.A. Fagg. cum.index. circ. 30, 000.

GUIDE TO GRADUATE STUDY IN BOTANY FOR THE UNITED STATES AND CANADA. see EDUCATION — Guides To Schools And Colleges

GUNNERIA. see ARCHAEOLOGY

581   US
HAROLD L. LYON ARBORETUM LECTURE. 1970. a. Harold L. Lyon Arboretum, 3860 Manoa Rd., Honolulu, HI 96822 TEL 808-988-3177. (Orders to: University of Hawaii Press, 2840 Kolowalu St., Honolulu, HI 96822) Ed. Yoneo Sagawa. circ. 1,000. Indexed: Biol.Abstr.

581   US
HERBERTIA. (Includes: Amaryllis Yearbook) 1934. a. membership. American Plant Life Society, Box 150, La Jolla, CA 92037. Ed. R. Mitchel Beauchamp. bk. rev. bibl. charts. illus. circ. 500. Indexed: Biol.Abstr.
    Formerly: Plant Life (ISSN 0032-0846)

581   AG   ISSN 0325-3732
HICKENIA; boletin del Darwinion. (Text in English and Spanish; summaries in English) 1976. irreg. $31. (Academia Nacional de Ciencias Exactas, Fisicas y Naturales) Instituto de Botanica Darwinion, Labarden y del Campo, Casilla Correo 22, San Isidro 1642, Buenos Aires, Argentina. (Co-sponsor: Consejo Nacional de Investigaciones Cientificas y Tecnicas) Ed. Angel L. Cabrera. bk. rev. illus. circ. 600. (back issues avail.) Indexed: Biol.Abstr. VITIS.

581   JA   ISSN 0046-7413
HIKOBIA. (Text and summaries in English and Japanese) 1950. a. 4000 Yen. (Hiroshima Botanical Club - Hikobia-kai) Hiroshima University, Botanical Institute, Higashisenda-cho, Hiroshima 730, Japan. Ed. Hyoji Suzuki. bk. rev. illus. stat. circ. 400. (back issues avail.) Indexed: Biol.Abstr. Field Crop Abstr. Forest.Abstr. Herb.Abstr.

581   BL   ISSN 0073-2877
HOEHNEA. (Text and summaries in English and Portuguese) 1971. irreg., no.11, 1984. price varies. ‡ Instituto de Botanica, Caixa Postal 4005, 01000 Sao Paulo, SP, Brazil. (back issues avail.) Indexed: Biol.Abstr.
    Supersedes in part: Arquivos de Botanica do Estado de Sao Paulo.

HOKKAIDO FISHERIES EXPERIMENTAL STATION. SCIENTIFIC REPORTS. see BIOLOGY — Biological Chemistry

581   JA   ISSN 0368-2145
HOKKAIDO UNIVERSITY. FACULTY OF SCIENCE. JOURNAL. SERIES 5: BOTANY. (Text in English) 1930. irreg. exchange basis. Hokkaido University, Faculty of Science - Hokkaido Daigaku Rigakubu, Nishi-8-chome, Kita-10-jo, Kita-ku, Sapporo 060, Japan. Ed. K. Saho. circ. 550. (back issues avail.) Indexed: Biol.Abstr. Chem.Abstr. Plant Breed.Abstr. Rev.Plant Path.

HOKKAIDO UNIVERSITY. INSTITUTE OF ALGOLOGICAL RESEARCH. SCIENTIFIC PAPERS/HOKKAIDO DAIGAKU RIGAKUBU KAISO KENKYUSHO OBUN HOKOKU. see EARTH SCIENCES — Oceanography

581   UK
HOOKER'S ICONES PLANETARIUM. (Text in English and Latin) 1837. irreg., latest vol. 40. price varies. Bentham-Moxon Trust, Royal Botanic Gardens, Kew, Richmond, Surrey TW9 3AB, England. Ed. P.S. Green. circ. 600.

581   US   ISSN 0073-4071
HUNTIA; a journal of botanical history. 1963. irreg., vol.6, 1985. $50. Carnegie-Mellon University, Hunt Institute for Botanical Documentation, 5000 Forbes Ave., Pittsburgh, PA 15213. TEL 412-268-2434. Ed. R.W. Kiger. bk. rev. circ. 350.

581   SG   ISSN 0073-4403
ICONES PLANTARUM AFRICANARUM. 1953. a. 12 Fr. Institut Fondamental d'Afrique Noire, Boite Postale 206, Dakar, Senegal, Senegal.

581 BL ISSN 0073-4705
IHERINGIA. SERIE BOTANICA. (Text in English, French, German, Portuguese and Spanish) 1958. irreg., no. 32, 1984. price varies. Fundacao Zoobotanica do Rio Grande do Sul, Museu de Ciencias Naturais, Caixa Postal 1188, 90.000 Porto Alegre, Rio Grande do Sul, Brazil. Ed. Arno A. Lise. bibl. illus. circ. 600. Indexed: Biol.Abstr.

591 BL
IHERINGIA. SERIE MISCELANEA. 1985. irreg. price varies. Fundacao Zoobotanica do Rio Grande do Sul, Museu de Ciencias Naturais, Caixa Postal 1188, 90.00 Porto Alegre, Rio Grande do Sul, Brazil. Ed. Arno A. Lise. bibl. illus. circ. 800.

581 GW ISSN 0073-5787
INDEX HEPATICARUM. (Text in English) 1962. irreg. price varies. J. Cramer in Gebrueder Borntraeger Verlagsbuchhandlung, Johannesstr. 3A, D-7000 Stuttgart 1, W. Germany (B.R.D.) Ed.Bd. circ. 500.

581 IS
INDEX SEMINUM. (Text in English) a. free. Tel Aviv University, Department of Botany, Ramat Aviv, Tel Aviv 69 978, Israel. TEL 03-420151. Ed. Yeduha Tankus.

581 NE ISSN 0073-6007
INDEX TO PLANT CHROMOSOME NUMBERS.* (Subseries of Regnum Vegetabile) 1956. irreg. price varies. (International Association for Plant Taxonomy) Bohn, Scheltema en Holkema, Pb 13079, 3507 LB Utrecht, Netherlands. Ed. R.J. Moore. circ. 1,000.

581 II ISSN 0073-6376
INDIAN FOREST RECORDS (NEW SERIES) BOTANY. (Text in English) 1937. irreg., vol.6, no.1, 1980. price varies. ‡ Forest Research Institute & Colleges, P.O. New Forest, Dehra Dun, India. circ. 500. Indexed: Biol.Abstr. Forest.Abstr. Forest Prod.Abstr. Indian Sci.Abstr. Rev.Appl.Entomol.

581.2 II ISSN 0537-2410
INDIAN PHYTOPATHOLOGICAL SOCIETY. BULLETIN. 1963. irreg. Indian Phytological Society, c/o Indian Agricultural Research Institute, Division of Mycology, New Delhi 110012, India. Indexed: Biol.Abstr. Rev.Plant Path.

581 CU
INFORMACION EXPRESS. SERIE: PLANTAS MEDICINALES Y FLORES. 1985. a. exchange basis. Centro de Informacion y Documentacion Agropecuario, Gaveta Postal 4149, Havana 4, Cuba (Dist. by: Ediciones Cubanas, Obispo No. 461, Aptdo. 605, Havana, Cuba) Indexed: Agrindex.

581 FR ISSN 0073-7917
INFORMATIONS ANNUELLES DE CARYOSYSTEMATIQUE ET CYTOGENETIQUE.* 1967. a. price varies. Institut de Botanique, Strasbourg, 8 rue Goethe, Strasbourg, France.

581 GW
INSTITUT FUER ALLGEMEINE BOTANIK UND BOTANISCHER GARTEN. MITTEILUNGEN. (Text in German; summaries in English) 1914. irreg., vol.20, 1986. exchange basis. ‡ Universitaet Hamburg, Institut fuer Allgemeine Botanik und Botanischer Garten, Ohnhorststr. 18, D-2000 Hamburg 52, W. Germany (B.R.D.) Eds. M. Bottger, H.-D. Ihlenfeldt. illus. Indexed: Biol.Abstr. Chem.Abstr. Rev.Plant Path.

581 II
INTERNATIONAL BIOSCIENCE SERIES. 1975. irreg., latest vol.11, 1986. $27. Today and Tomorrow's Printers & Publishers, 24B/5, Original Rd., Karol Bagh, New Delhi 110005, India (Dist. in U.S. by: Scholary Publications, 7310 Elcresta Dr., Houston, Texas 77083)

580 AT ISSN 0074-2090
INTERNATIONAL BOTANICAL CONGRESS. ABSTRACTS OF PAPERS. every 6 years. price varies. International Botanical Congress, c/o W.J. Cram, Exec. Sec., Australian Academy of Science, Box 783, Canberra, A.C.T. 2601, Australia.

580 AT
INTERNATIONAL BOTANICAL CONGRESS. PROCEEDINGS. every 6 years. price varies. International Botanical Congress, c/o W.J. Cram, Exec. Sec., Australian Academy of Science, Box 783, Canberra, A.C.T. 2601, Australia. Indexed: Biol.Abstr. Field Crop Abstr. Herb.Abstr. Weed Abstr.

589.2 588.2 GW ISSN 0723-3353
INTERNATIONAL JOURNAL OF MYCOLOGY AND LICHENOLOGY. (Text in English and German) irreg. (3-4/yr.) DM.90. J. Cramer in Gebrueder Borntraeger Verlagsbuchhandlung, Johannesstr. 3A, D-7000 Stuttgart 1, W. Germany (B.R.D.) Ed. W. Juelich.

589.45 NO ISSN 0074-7874
INTERNATIONAL SEAWEED SYMPOSIUM. PROCEEDINGS. (Published by host country) 1952. triennial, 11th, 1983, Qingdao, China. International Seaweed Symposium, c/o Dr. B. Larsen, Institute of Biotechnology, 7034 Trondheim NTH, Norway. (Co-sponsor: International Seaweed Association) circ. 400. Indexed: Biol.Abstr.

581 II ISSN 0539-0346
INTERNATIONAL SOCIETY OF PLANT MORPHOLOGISTS. YEARBOOK. (Text in English) 1951. a. International Society of Plant Morphologists, University of Delhi, Department of Botany, Delhi 110007, India. bk. rev. circ. 1,500.

581 UR ISSN 0202-716X
ITOGI NAUKI I TEKHNIKI: RASTENIEVODSTVO. irreg., latest vol.7, 1986. price varies. Vsesoyuznyi Institut Nauchno-Tekhnicheskoi Informatsii (VINITI), Ul. Baltiiskaya 14, Moscow A-219, Russian S.F.S.R., U.S.S.R (Subscr. to: Mezhdunarodnaya Kniga, Dimitrova ul. 39, 113095 Moscow, Russian S.F.S.R., U.S.S.R.)

581 635 BL
JARDIM BOTANICO DO RIO DE JANEIRO. ARQUIVOS. 1915. a. Cr.$20000. Instituto Brasileiro de Desenvolvimento Florestal, Jardim Botanico do Rio de Janeiro, Rua Jardim Botanico 1008, 22460 Gavea-RJ, Rio de Janeiro-RJ, Brazil. circ. 1,000.

581 UK
JODRELL LABORATORY. NOTES. 1964. irreg. free. Jodrell Laboratory, Royal Botanic Gardens, Kew, Richmond, Surrey TW9 3DS, England. Ed. M. Gregory. circ. 350. (back issues avail.) Indexed: Biol.Abstr.

581 II ISSN 0256-436X
JOURNAL OF PLANT ANATOMY AND MORPHOLOGY. (Text and summaries in English) 1980. a. $70. Scientific Publishers, Mann Bhawan, Ratanada Road, Jodhpur 342001, India. Ed. J.A. Inamdar. adv. bk. rev. circ. 450. (back issues avail.) Indexed: Biol.Abstr. Excerp.Bot. Weed Abstr.
 Formerly: Journal of Economic and Taxonomic Botany.

581.1 GW
JOURNAL OF PLANT PHYSIOLOGY. (Text in German; summaries in German and English) 1909. irreg. (5 nos. per vol.) DM.258 per vol. Gustav Fischer Verlag, Wollgrasweg 49, Postfach 720143, 7000 Stuttgart 70, W. Germany (B.R.D.) Ed. W. Larcher. adv. bk. rev. abstr. charts. illus. index. circ. 850. Indexed: Biol.Abstr. Chem.Abstr. Curr.Cont. ASCA. Abstr.Bull.Inst.Pap.Chem. Biotech.Abstr. Field Crop Abstr. Forest.Abstr. Forest Prod.Abstr. Geo.Abstr. Herb.Abstr. Hort.Abstr. Ind.Sci.Rev. Plant Breed.Abstr. Soils & Fert. VITIS. Weed Abstr.
 Formerly (until 1984): Zeitschrift fuer Pflanzenphysiologie (ISSN 0044-328X)

581 US ISSN 0453-1388
KALMIA; a botanic journal. (Text and summaries in English, Latin and Spanish) 1969. a. $5. Dr. Edward Murray, Ed. & Pub., Box 93215, Hollywood, CA 90093. TEL 213-871-9300. cum.index: vols.1-15, 1985. circ. 800. Indexed: Biol.Abstr. Agri.Ind. Excerp.Bot.

589.2 II ISSN 0379-5179
KAVAKA/FUNGUS; being transactions of the Mycological Society of India. (Text in English) 1973. a. Rs.25($6) individuals; institutions Rs.50 ($12) Mycological Society of India, 6/A Cunningham Rd., Bangalore 560052, India. Ed. C.V. Subramanian. bibl. illus. Indexed: Biol.Abstr. Rev.Plant Path.
 Mycology

581 UK ISSN 0075-5974
KEW BULLETIN. 1946. irreg. price varies. H.M.S.O., P.O. Box 569, London SE1 9NH, England (Subscr. avail. from: H.M.S.O. Books, P.O. Box 276, London SW8 5DT England) bk. rev. illus. circ. 550. (also avail. in microform from UMI) Indexed: Biol.Abstr. Field Crop Abstr. Forest.Abstr. Forest Prod.Abstr. Herb.Abstr. Hort.Abstr. Plant Breed.Abstr. Rev.Plant Path. Soils & Fert.

581 UK ISSN 0075-5982
KEW BULLETIN. ADDITIONAL SERIES. 1958. irreg. H.M.S.O., P.O. Box 569, London SE1 9NH, England (Subscr. avail. from: H.M.S.O. Books, P.O. Box 276, London SW8 5DT, England) circ. 500. Indexed: Biol.Abstr.

581 UK
KEW RECORD OF TAXONOMIC LITERATURE RELATING TO VASCULAR PLANTS. 1971. a. £90. H.M.S.O., Royal Botanic Gardens, Kew, Richmond, Surrey TW9 3AE, England. circ. 550. Indexed: Forest.Abstr. Forest Prod.Abstr.

581 JA
KINKI SHOKUBUTSU DOKOKAI KAISHI. (Text in Japanese) 1950. biennial. 1000 Yen($7) Kinki Shokubutsu Dokokai, Kunio Matsumoto - Kinki Botanical Society, 2-1-16 Yamamoto-Kita, Yao City 581, Osaka, Japan. Ed. Masaji Kuwashima. (back issues avail.)

581 RH ISSN 0451-9930
KIRKIA; the journal of botany of Zimbabwe. 1960. a. Rhod.$1.50($5) Ministry of Lands, Agriculture and Rural Resettlemen, Research and Specialist Services, Information Services, Box 8108, Causeway, Harare, Zimbabwe. Ed. S.J. Swift. bk. rev. circ. 600. (back issues avail.) Indexed: Biol.Abstr. Field Crop Abstr. Excerp.Bot. Forest.Abstr. Forest Prod.Abstr. Herb.Abstr. Rev.Plant Path.

581 NO ISSN 0332-8090
KONGELIGE NORSKE VIDENSKABERS SELSKAB MUSEET. RAPPORT. BOTANISK SERIE. (Text in English, Norwegian; summaries in English) irreg. Kongelige Universitetet i Trondheim, Norske Videnskabers Selskab Museet, Erl. Skakkes gt. 47, N-7000 Trondheim, Norway. Indexed: Biol.Abstr.

581 NO ISSN 0333-3124
KRISTIANSAND MUSEUM. AARBOK. 1965. a. Kr.50. Kristiansand Museum, P.O. Box 479, N-4601 Kristiansands, Norway. Ed. Per Arvid Asen. circ. 900.

581 GE ISSN 0075-7209
KULTURPFLANZE. 1953. irreg., vol.33, 1985. (Akademie der Wissenschaften der DDR, Zentralinstitut fuer Genetik und Kulturpflanzenforschung Gatersleben) Akademie-Verlag, Leipziger Str. 3-4, 1086 Berlin, E. Germany (D.D.R.) Indexed: Biol.Abstr. Chem.Abstr. Field Crop Abstr. Herb.Abstr. Plant Breed.Abstr. Rev.Plant Path. Soils & Fert. VITIS.

581 AG ISSN 0075-7314
KURTZIANA. (Text in English and Spanish; summaries in English) 1961. a. $15. Universidad Nacional de Cordoba, Museo Botanico, Direccion de Publicaciones, Casilla de Correo 495, 5000 Cordoba, Argentina. Ed. Armando T. Hunziker. bk. rev. circ. 400. Indexed: Biol.Abstr. Field Crop Abstr. Herb.Abstr.

581 AU
LANDESMUSEUM JOANNEUM. ABTEILUNG FUER BOTANIK. MITTEILUNGEN. 1972. irreg. price varies. Landesmuseum Joanneum, Abteilung fuer Botanik, Raubergasse 10, A-8010 Graz, Austria. Ed. Detlef Ernet. bk. rev. bibl. illus. circ. 600.

581 NE
LEIDEN BOTANICAL SERIES. 1975. irreg., vol.8, 1984. price varies. E.J. Brill Publishers, P.O. Box 9000, 2300 PA Leiden, Netherlands. Indexed: Biol.Abstr.

BIOLOGY — BOTANY

581   BE   ISSN 0457-4184
LEJEUNIA; revue de botanique. (Text in French; summaries in English and French) N.S. 1961. irreg. price varies. Botanical Society in Liege, Universite de Liege, Departement de Botanique, Sart Tilman, B-4000 Liege, Belgium. Ed. J. Lambinon. (back issues avail.) Indexed: Biol.Abstr. Bull.Signal. Agri.Ind. Field Crop Abstr. Herb.Abstr.

581   AG   ISSN 0075-9481
LILLOA; revista de botanica. (Text in Latin, Spanish; summaries in English, French, German, Italian) 1937. irreg., vol.36, no.2, 1985. price varies. Fundacion Miguel Lillo, Centro de Informacion Geo-Biologico, Miguel Lillo 251, 4000 San Miguel de Tucuman, Argentina. Ed. Jose A. Haedo Rossi. charts. illus. bibl. (back issues avail.) Indexed: Biol.Abstr. Bull.Signal. Ref.Zh. Field Crop Abstr. Forest.Abstr. Forest Prod.Abstr. Herb.Abstr. Hort.Abstr. Plant Breed.Abstr. Rev.Plant Path.

635 580   US
LONGWOOD PROGRAM SEMINARS. 1969. a. free. (Longwood Program in Public Horticulture Administration) University of Delaware, College of Agricultural Sciences, 157 Townsend Hall, Newark, DE 19717-1303. TEL 302-451-2517. Eds. Lynn Hershey Chesson, James E. Swasey. circ. 800(controlled)

581   AG   ISSN 0076-0897
LORENTZIA. 1970. irreg. $1. ‡ Universidad Nacional de Cordoba, Museo Botanico, Direccion de Publicaciones, Casilla de Correo 495, 5000 Cordoba, Argentina. Ed. Armando T. Hunziker. bk. rev. circ. 1,000. Indexed: Biol.Abstr. Sci.Abstr. Excerp.Bot.

581   SW   ISSN 0348-2456
LUNDS UNIVERSITET. VAEXTEKOLOGISKA INSTITUTIONEN. MEDDELANDEN. (Text in English, German or Swedish; summaries in English) 1973. irreg. price varies. Lund University, Department of Plant Ecology, Oestra Vallgaten 14, S-223 61 Lund, Sweden. Ed. Sture Wijk. charts. illus. index. circ. 350. (back issues avail.) Indexed: Biol.Abstr. Ecol.Abstr.

581 630 635   US
LYONIA. 1974. irreg., vol.2, 1986. price varies. Harold L. Lyon Arboretum, 3860 Manoa Rd., Honolulu, HI 96822. TEL 808-988-3177. Ed. Yoneo Sagawa. (back issues avail.) Indexed: Biol.Abstr.

581   US   ISSN 0099-8400
MCILVAINEA. 1972. a. $15. North American Mycological Association, 4245 Redinger Rd., Portsmouth, OH 45662. TEL 614-354-2018. Ed. Walter Litten. bk. rev. circ. 1,500. Indexed: Biol.Abstr. Rev.Plant Path.
Formerly: Journal McIlvanea.

581   HU   ISSN 0076-2482
MAGYARORSZAG KULTURFLORAJA. (Text in Latin and Hungarian) 1956. irreg., no.56, 1985. price varies. (Magyar Tudomanyos Akademia) Akademiai Kiado, Publishing House of the Hungarian Academy of Sciences, Box 24, H-1363 Budapest, Hungary (Subscr. to: Kultura, Box 149, H-1389 Budapest, Hungary) Indexed: Biol.Abstr.

MARSCHENRAT ZUR FOERDERUNG DER FORSCHUNG IM KUESTENGEBIET DER NORDSEE. NACHRICHTEN. see *SCIENCES: COMPREHENSIVE WORKS*

581   CS   ISSN 0076-6984
METODICKE PRIRUCKY EXPERIMENTALNI BOTANIKY/METHODS OF EXPERIMENTAL BOTANY. (Text in Czech; contents page also in English and Russian) 1965. irreg., no. 3, 1974. price varies. (Ceskoslovenska Akademie Ved) Academia, Publishing House of the Czechoslovak Academy of Sciences, Vodickova 40, 112 29 Prague 1, Czechoslovakia. Ed. B. Slavik. Indexed: Biol.Abstr.

581   PL   ISSN 0077-0655
MONOGRAPHIAE BOTANICAE. (Text in English and Polish; summaries in English and German) 1953. irreg., vol.64, 1983. price varies. (Polskie Towarzystwo Botaniczne) Panstwowe Wydawnictwo Naukowe, Miodowa 10, 00-251 Warsaw, Poland (Dist. by: Ars Polona, Krakowskie Przedmiescie 7, 00-068 Warsaw, Poland) Ed. M. Kostyniuk. bibl. Indexed: Biol.Abstr. Field Crop Abstr. Herb.Abstr. Plant Breed.Abstr. Rev.Plant Path.

581   IE   ISSN 0332-4273
MOOREA. 1982. a. membership. Irish Garden Plant Society, c/o National Botanical Gardens, Glasnevin, Dublin 9, Ireland. Ed. Dr. E. Charles Nelson. bk. rev. circ. 350(controlled)

581   AT   ISSN 0077-1813
MUELLERIA. 1955. a. available on exchange basis. ‡ National Herbarium of Victoria, South Yarra, Victoria 3141, Australia. Ed. H.I. Aston. index. circ. 600. Indexed: Biol.Abstr. Field Crop Abstr. Herb.Abstr. Plant Breed.Abstr.

581   AG   ISSN 0376-2793
MUSEO ARGENTINO DE CIENCIAS NATURALES "BERNARDINO RIVADAVIA." INSTITUTO NACIONAL DE INVESTIGACION DE LAS CIENCIAS NATURALES. REVISTA. BOTANICA. 1948. irreg., latest vol. 6, no. 3, 1983. free. Museo Argentino de Ciencias Naturales Bernardino Rivadavia, Avda. Angel Gallardo 470, Casilla de Correo 220-Sucursal 5, Buenos Aires, Argentina. illus.
Continues: Buenos Aires. Museo Argentino de Ciencias Naturales Bernardino Rivadavia. Instituto Nacional de Investigacion de las Ciencias Naturales. Revista. Ciencias Botanicas.

581   UY   ISSN 0027-0121
MUSEO NACIONAL DE HISTORIA NATURAL. COMMUNICACIONES BOTANICAS. (Text in English, French and Spanish) 1942. irreg. (4-6/yr.) exchange basis only. Museo Nacional de Historia Natural, Casilla de Correos 399, Montevideo, Uruguay. illus. cum.index. circ. 1,200.

581   BL
MUSEU BOTANICO MUNICIPAL. BOLETIM. (Text in English, German and Portuguese; summaries in English and German) 1971. irreg. Museu Botanico Municipal, Caixa Postal 1142, 80000 Curitiba, Parana, Brazil. circ. 1,000. (back issues avail.) Indexed: Biol.Abstr.

581   BL   ISSN 0080-3197
MUSEU NACIONAL, RIO DE JANEIRO. BOLETIM. NOVA SERIE. BOTANICA. 1944. irreg., no. 53, Mar. 1979. exchange only. Museu Nacional, Quinta da Boa Vista, 20940 Rio de Janeiro RJ, Brazil. illus. Indexed: Biol.Abstr.

581   FR   ISSN 0078-9755
MUSEUM NATIONAL D'HISTOIRE NATURELLE, PARIS. MEMOIRES. NOUVELLE SERIE. SERIE B. BOTANIQUE. 1950. irreg. price varies. Museum National d'Histoire Naturelle, 38 rue Geoffroy Saint-Hilaire, 75005 Paris, France. Indexed: Biol.Abstr. Forest.Abstr. Forest Prod.Abstr.

589.2   UK   ISSN 0077-2364
MUSHROOM SCIENCE. (Text and summaries in English, French, German) 1950. triennial, 1968, 2nd Symposium and 7th Congress, Hamburg. Mushroom Growers' Association, Agriculture House, Knightsbridge, London SW1X 7NJ, England. Indexed: Biol.Abstr. Rev.Plant Path.
Represents: International Congress on Mushroom Science. Proceedings & Scientific Symposium on the Cultivated Mushroom. Proceedings.
Mycology

581   CK   ISSN 0027-5123
MUTISIA; acta botanica colombiana. (Text in English, French, German, Spanish) 1952. irreg. $5 or exchange basis. Universidad Nacional de Colombia, Instituto de Ciencias Naturales, Apdo. 7495, Bogota, Colombia. Ed. Santiago Diaz-Piedrahita. bibl. illus. circ. 1,000. Indexed: Biol.Abstr. Bull.Signal. Ref.Zh. Excerp.Bot.

589.2   UK   ISSN 0027-5522
MYCOLOGICAL PAPERS. 1925. irreg. price varies. C.A.B. International, Mycological Institute, Farnham House, Farnham Royal, Slough SL2 3BN, England. Indexed: Rev.Plant Path.

589.2   US
MYCOLOGY SERIES. 1979. irreg., vol.6, 1985. price varies. Marcel Dekker, Inc., 270 Madison Ave., New York, NY 10016. TEL 212-696-9000. Indexed: Chem.Abstr.

581 635   UK
N T C WORKSHOP REPORT SERIES. 1983. irreg. National Turfgrass Council, 3 Ferrands Park Way, Harden, Bingley, W. Yorks. BD16 1HZ, England. Ed. J.P. Shildrick.

581   SA
NATIONAL BOTANIC GARDENS. REPORT. (Text in Afrikaans and English) 1913. a. free. National Botanic Gardens, Kirstenbosch, Private Bag X7, Claremont, South Africa. Ed. J.N. Eloff. circ. 500.
Formerly: National Botanic Gardens of South Africa. Report.

581   II
NATIONAL BOTANIC GARDENS, LUCKNOW. PROGRESS REPORT. (Text in English) 1966. a. free. ‡ National Botanical Research Institute, Lucknow. Progress Report, Lucknow 226001, India. (Affiliate: Council of Scientific and Industrial Research) circ. controlled. Indexed: Biol.Abstr. Chem.Abstr.
Former titles: National Botanic Gardens, Lucknow. Progress Report; National Botanic Gardens, Lucknow. Annual Report (ISSN 0076-1400)

581   II   ISSN 0076-1419
NATIONAL BOTANICAL RESEARCH INSTITUTE, LUCKNOW. BULLETIN. (Text in English) 1956. irreg. price varies. ‡ National Botanical Research Institute, Lucknow 226001, India. (Affiliate: Council of Scientific and Industrial Research) Indexed: Biol.Abstr. Chem.Abstr.
Formerly: National Botanic Gardens, Lucknow. Bulletin.

581 591 551   GW   ISSN 0547-9789
NATURWISSENSCHAFTLICHER VEREIN WUPPERTAL. JAHRESBERICHTE. (Text in German; summaries in English) 1851. a. DM.19. Naturwissenschaftlicher Verein Wuppertal, Cordulastr. 10, D-5600 Wuppertal 1, W. Germany (B.R.D.) Ed. Wolfgang Kolbe. index. circ. 1,000. (back issues avail.)

581 615.19   NP
NEPAL. DEPARTMENT OF MEDICINAL PLANTS. ANNUAL REPORT. (Text in English) 1969. a. free. Ministry of Forests, Department of Medicinal Plants, Thapathali, Katmandu, Nepal. circ. 500.

581   US   ISSN 0077-8931
NEW YORK BOTANICAL GARDEN. MEMOIRS. 1900. irreg, latest no.41, 1986. price varies. New York Botanical Garden, Scientific Publications Department, Bronx, NY 10458. TEL 212-220-8721. Ed. C. Rogerson. index. (back issues avail.) Indexed: Biol.Abstr. Rev.Plant Path.

581   NR   ISSN 0078-0715
NIGERIAN INSTITUTE FOR OIL PALM RESEARCH. JOURNAL. 1953. irreg. $1.40. Nigerian Institute for Oil Palm Research, P.M.B. 1030, Benin City, Nigeria. Ed. S.U. Remison. adv. bk. rev. indexes. circ. 1,000. Indexed: Biol.Abstr. Hort.Abstr. Plant Breed.Abstr. Rev.Plant Path. Soils & Fert.

581   US   ISSN 0078-1312
NORTH AMERICAN FLORA. 1905; series 2. irreg., latest no.12, 1986. price varies. New York Botanical Garden, Scientific Publications Department, Bronx, NY 10458. TEL 212-220-8721. Ed. C. Rogerson. (back issues avail.) Indexed: Biol.Abstr.

581   UK   ISSN 0080-4274
NOTES FROM THE ROYAL BOTANIC GARDEN, EDINBURGH. 1900. irreg., vol. 37, 1978/79. price varies. H.M.S.O. (Scotland), 13a Castle St., Edinburgh EH2 3AR, Scotland. Ed. Dr. J.A. Ratter. bk. rev. illus. circ. 550. (reprint service avail. from UMI) Indexed: Biol.Abstr. Excerp.Bot.

581   VE   ISSN 0085-4387
NOTICIERO TUBEROSAS.* (Text in Spanish; summaries in Spanish, occasionally in English and Portuguese) 1971. irreg. free to members. Sociedad Latinoamericana de Tuberosas, Box 97, Maracay, Venezuela. Ed. Alvaro Montaldo. abstr. circ. 250. (processed; also avail. in cards)

581   AU
NOTIZEN ZUR FLORA DER STEIERMARK. 1974. irreg. price varies. Florostisch-geobotanische Arbetisgemeinschaft des Naturwissenschaftlichen Vereins fuer Steiermark und Landesmuseeum Joanneum, Abteilung fuer Botanik, Raubergasse 10, A-8010 Graz, Austria. (Co-sponsor: Amt der Steiermarkischen Landesregierung) Ed. Detlaf Ernet.

BIOLOGY — BOTANY

581 595.7 IT
NOTIZIARIO SULLE MALATTIE DELLE PIANTE. (Text in English and Italian; summaries in English) 1952. a. L.60000. Societa Italiana di Fitoiatria, Via Celoria 2, 20133 Milan, Italy. Ed. Elio Baldacci. bk. rev. Indexed: Biol.Abstr.

581 GW ISSN 0078-2238
NOVA HEDWIGA, BEIHEFTE. (Text in English, French, German) 1962. irreg. price varies. J. Cramer in Gerbrueder Borntraeger Verlagsbuchhandlung, Johannesstr. 3A, D-7000 Stuttgart 1, W. Germany (B.R.D.) Ed. Johannes Gerloff. circ. 400. Indexed: Biol.Abstr. GeoRef.

581 AT ISSN 0085-4417
NUYTSIA. 1970. irreg. Aus.$10 per issue. Department of Agriculture, Western Australian Herbarium, Baron Hay Court, South Perth, W.A. 6151, Australia. circ. 600. Indexed: Biol.Abstr. CALL. Forest.Abstr. Plant Breed.Abstr.

581 595.7 GW ISSN 0171-7936
OFFENBACHER VEREIN FUER NATURKUNDE. ABHANDLUNGEN. (Text in German; summaries in English, German) 1970. irreg. Offenbacher Verein fuer Naturkunde, Parkstrasse 60, 6050 Offenbach am Main, W. Germany (B.R.D.) (back issues avail.) Indexed: Biol.Abstr.

581 595.7 GW ISSN 0343-2793
OFFENBACHER VEREIN FUER NATURKUNDE. BERICHT. (Text in German; summaries in English, German) 1860. a. Offenbacher Verein fuer Naturkunde, Parkstrasse 60, 6050 Offenbach am Main, W. Germnay (B.R.D.) (back issues avail.) Indexed: Biol.Abstr. VITIS.

581 DK ISSN 0078-5237
OPERA BOTANICA. (Supplements: Nordic Journal of Botany) (Text in English) 1953. irreg., no.75, 1984. Kr.30 (per 16 published pages) (Council for Nordic Publications in Botany) Nordic Journal of Botany, The Secretary, O Farimagsgade 2D, DK-1353 Copenhagen K, Denmark. Ed. Morten Lange. adv. bk. rev. index. circ. 500. (also avail. in microform from UMI; reprint service avail. from UMI; back issues avail.) Indexed: Biol.Abstr. Curr.Cont. Sci.Cit.Ind. Field Crop.Abstr. Forest.Abstr. Herb.Abstr. Plant Breed.Abstr. Soils & Fert. Weed Abstr.
Incorporating (as of 1981): Dansk Botanisk Arkiv (ISSN 0011-6211)

581 591 AG ISSN 0078-5245
OPERA LILLOANA. (Text in Spanish; summaries in English, French, German, Italian) 1957. irreg., vol.35, 1985. ‡ (Ministerio de Cultura y Educacion) Fundacion Miguel Lillo, Centro de Informacion Geo-Biologico, Miguel Lillo 251, 4000 San Miguel de Tucuman, Argentina. Ed. Jose Antonio Haedo Rossi. bibl. illus. circ. 500. (back issues avail.) Indexed: Biol.Abstr. Bull.Signal. Ref.Zh. GeoRef.

653.934 MX ISSN 0300-3701
ORQUIDEA (MEXICO) (Text in English and Spanish) 1971. irreg. Mex.$2500($30) ‡ Asociacion Mexicana de Orquideologia, A.C., Apdo. Postal 53-123, 11320 Mexico, D.F., Mexico. Ed. Eric Hagsater. adv. bk. rev. illus. index. circ. 600. Indexed: Biol.Abstr. Ash.G.Bot.Per. Excerpt.Bot.
Orchids

OSAKA MUSEUM OF NATURAL HISTORY. SPECIAL PUBLICATIONS/OSAKA-SHIRITSU-SHIZENSHI-HAKUBUTSUKAN-SHUZO-SHIRYO-MOKUROKU. see *BIOLOGY*

634.8 587.33 IT ISSN 0552-9506
OSSERVATORIO REGIONALE PER LE MALATTIE DELLA VITE. OSSERVAZIONI DI METEOROLOGIA, FENOLOGIA E PATOLOGIA DELLA VITE.* 1966. irreg. Osservatorio Regionale per le Malattie della Vite, Palermo, Italy. illus.

581 DK ISSN 0107-8801
OVERSIGT OVER DE METEOROLOGISKE FORHOLD PAA FORSOEGSSTATIONERNE. 1981. a. Statens Planteavlsforsoeg, Statens Planteavlskontor, Virumgaard, Kongevejen 83, 2800 Lyngby, Denmark.

581 UK ISSN 0264-861X
OXFORD SURVEYS OF PLANT MOLECULAR AND CELL BIOLOGY. 1984. a. £20($45) Oxford University Press, Walton St., Oxford OX2 6DP, England. Ed. B.J. Miffin. adv.

581 US
PALEO DATA BANKS; for the improvement of communication in palynology, paleobotany, and related sciences. 1977. irreg. $10. (University of Arizona, Department of Geology) Palynodata, 101 N. Avenida Carolina, Tucson, AZ 85711. TEL 602-621-6063. Ed. Dr. Gerhard O.W. Kremp. bk. rev. cum.index: circ. 450. (back issues avail.) Indexed: GeoRef.

581 BL ISSN 0553-8475
PESQUISAS: PUBLICACOES DE BOTANICA. (Numbering is in continuation of articles published in Pesquisas) no. 8, 1960. irreg. price varies or exchange. (Universidade do Vale do Rio dos Sinos, Instituto Anchietano de Pesquisas) Unisinos, Av. Unisinos, 950, 93000 Sao Leopoldo RS, Brazil.
Supersedes in part: Pesquisas.

581 GW ISSN 0079-1369
PHANEROGAMARUM MONOGRAPHIAE. 1969. irreg., vol. 14, 1981. price varies. J. Kramer Gebrueder Borntraeger Verlagsbuchhandlung, Johannesstr. 3A, D-7000 Stuttgart 1, W. Germany (B.R.D.) circ. 200. Indexed: Biol.Abstr.

581 US
PHYTOCHEMICAL SOCIETY. PROCEEDINGS. 1965. irreg., vol.22, 1984. $75. (Phytochemical Society) Academic Press Inc., Orlando, FL 32887. TEL 305-345-2000. Indexed: Biol.Abstr.
Formerly: Phytochemical Society Symposia Series. Proceedings.

581 US ISSN 0031-9430
PHYTOLOGIA; designed to expedite botanical and phytoecological publication. 1933. irreg., several vols. per year. $18 to individuals; libraries $16. ‡ H.N. & A.L. Moldenke, Eds. & Pubs., 590 Hemlock Ave. N.W., Corvallis, OR 97330. TEL 503-758-1079. bk. rev. abstr. bibl. charts. illus. index. circ. 450. Indexed: Biol.Abstr. Excerp.Bot. Forest.Abstr. Hort.Abstr. Plant Breed.Abstr. Rev.Plant Path.

581 AU ISSN 0079-2047
PHYTON. ANNALES REI BOTANICAE. 1949. a. S.800. Verlag Ferdinand Berger und Soehne OHG, Wienerstr. 21-23, 3580 Horn, Austria. Eds. O. Haertel, H. Teppner. Indexed: Curr.Cont.

581 DK ISSN 0107-6167
PLANT DISEASES AND PESTS IN DENMARK. vol. 97, 1980. a. free. Ministry of Agriculture, Danish State Committee of Crop Husbandry, DK-2800 Lyngby, Denmark (Subscr. to: Statens Plantvaernscenter, Lottenbergvej 2, DK-2800 Lyngby, Denmark) (Co-sponsors: National Plant Pathology Institute, National Pesticide Research Institute) Ed. O. Wagn. circ. 800. Indexed: Rev.Appl.Entomol. Rev.Plant Path.
Formerly: Plantesygdomme i Danmarks Aargangstaelling.

581 US
PLANT PATHOLOGY BULLETINS. irreg. Department of Agriculture and Consumer Services, Division of Plant Industry, Box 1269, Gainesville, FL 32602. TEL 904-372-3505.

581.1 US ISSN 0079-2241
PLANT PHYSIOLOGY. SUPPLEMENT ABSTRACTS OF ANNUAL MEETING. Variant title: American Society of Plant Physiologists. Proceedings of Annual Meeting. 1926 (Plant Physiology) a. $5 or with subscr. to Plant Physiology. American Society of Plant Physiologists, 15501-A Monona Dr., Rockville, MD 20855. index. circ. 5,400. (also avail. in microfilm; microfiche; reprint service avail. from UMI) Indexed: Biol.Abstr. Chem.Abstr.

POLLEN SCIENCE. see *AGRICULTURE — Crop Production And Soil*

581 PL ISSN 0080-357X
POLSKIE TOWARZYSTWO BOTANICZNE. SEKCJA DENDROLOGICZNA. ROCZNIK. (Text in English, or Polish; summaries in English, German, Polish, Russian) 1926. irreg. price varies. Panstwowe Wydawnictwo Naukowe, Ul. Miodowa 10, 00-251 Warsaw, Poland (Dist. by: Ars Polona, Krakowskie Przedmiescie 7, 00-068 Warsaw, Poland) Ed. Tadeusz Gorczynski. illus. Indexed: Biol.Abstr.

581 US ISSN 0340-4773
PROGRESS IN BOTANY. 1949. irreg., vol.45, 1983. price varies. Springer-Verlag, 175 Fifth Ave., New York, NY 10010 TEL 212-460-1500. (Also Berlin, Heidelberg, Tokyo and Vienna) (reprint service avail. from ISI) Indexed: Biol.Abstr. Chem.Abstr. Field Crop Abstr. GeoRef. Herb.Abstr. Plant Breed.Abstr. Rev.Plant Path. Soils & Fert. VITIS. Weed Abstr.
Formerly: Fortschritte der Botanik (ISSN 0071-7878)

581 US
PTERIDOLOGIA. 1979. irreg. price varies. American Fern Society, Inc., U.S. National Herbarium NHB-166, Smithsonian Institution, Washington, DC 20560. TEL 202-357-2568. Ed. D.B. Lellinger. circ. 750. (back issues avail.) Indexed: Biol.Abstr.

581 UK ISSN 0266-1640
PTERIDOLOGIST. 1984. a. £12 including "Bulletin" and "Fern Gazette". British Pteridological Society, c/o British Museum (Nat. History), Cromwell Rd., London SW7 5BD, England. Ed. M. Rickard. bk. rev. circ. 700.

PYMATUNING SYMPOSIA IN ECOLOGY. see *ENVIRONMENTAL STUDIES*

581 JA ISSN 0285-0850
RAIKEN/LICHEN. (Text in Japanese) 1972. irreg. 100 Yen. Lichenological Society of Japan, c/o Department of Botany, National Science Museum, 3-23-1 Hyakunin-cho, Shijuku-ku, Tokyo 160, Japan. Ed. Na M. Oshio. circ. 250.

580 NE ISSN 0080-0694
REGNUM VEGETABILE;* a series of publications for the use of plant taxonomists and plant geographers. irreg. price varies. (International Association for Plant Taxonomy) Bohn, Scheltema en Holkema, Postbus 13079, 3507 LB Utrecht, Netherlands. Ed. F. A. Stafleu. circ. 1,000-2,000. Indexed: Biol.Abstr. Ref.Zh. Bibl.Agri. Excerp.Bot.

581 IO ISSN 0034-365X
REINWARDTIA; a journal on taxonomic botany, plant sociology and ecology. (Text in English, French and German) 1950. irreg. price varies. Herbarium Bogoriense, LBN-LIPI, Jalan Ir. H. Juanda 22-24, Bogor, Indonesia. Ed.Bd. bk. rev. index. circ. 400. Indexed: Biol.Abstr. Zoo.Rec.

582.14 SZ ISSN 0486-4271
REPERTORIUM PLANTARUM SUCCULENTARUM. 1951. a. $4.25 price varies. International Organization for Succulent Plant Study, c/o U. Eggli, Lerchenbergstr. 19, CH-8703 Erlenbach ZH, Switzerland. Eds. N.P. Taylor, U. Eggli. circ. 500.

581 550 IC
RESEARCH INSTITUTE NEDRI AS. BULLETIN. (Text in English, German, Icelandic; summaries in English) 1969. irreg. Research Institute Nedri As., Hveragerdi, Iceland. Ed.Bd. Indexed: Biol.Abstr.

581 II ISSN 0254-1300
REVIEW OF TROPICAL PLANT PATHOLOGY. 1984. a. $95. Today & Tomorrow's Printers & Publishers, 24B/5 Original Rd., Karol Bagh, New Delhi 110005, India (Distr. in U.S. by: Scholarly Publications, 7310 El Cresta Dr., Houston, TX 77083) Eds. S.P. Raychadhuri, J.P. Verma.

581 MX
REVISTA MEXICANA DE MICOLOGIA. (Text in Spanish; summaries in English and French) 1968. a. $15 (or exchange) Sociedad Mexicana de Micologia, c/o Instituto Nacional de Investigaciones sobre Recursos Bioticos, Apdo. Postal 63, Xalapa, Veracruz, Mexico 91000. Ed. Gaston Guzman. adv. bk. rev. bibl. charts. illus. index. cum.index. circ. 800. (processed; also avail. in microform from UMI; reprint service avail. from UMI) Indexed: Biol.Abstr. Ind.Vet. Rev.Plant Path. Vet.Bull.
Former titles (until 1985): Sociedad Mexicana de Micologia. Boletin (ISSN 0085-6223) & Sociedad Mexicana de Micologia. Boletin Informativo.

BIOLOGY — BOTANY

581.87 FR ISSN 0181-7582
REVUE DE CYTOLOGIE ET DE BIOLOGIE VEGETALES-LA BOTANISTE. 1934. a. (in 4 parts) 660 Fr. Laboratoire de Biologie Vegetale Appliquee, 61 rue de Buffon, 75005 Paris, France. Ed. Jean Louis Hamel. bk. rev. charts. illus. index. circ. 11,350. Indexed: Biol.Abstr. Chem.Abstr. Field Crop Abstr. Herb.Abstr. Plant Breed.Abstr. Rev.Plant Path.
Formed by the merger of: Botaniste (ISSN 0045-2637) & Revue de Cytologie et de Biologie Vegetales (ISSN 0035-1067)

581 BL ISSN 0080-3014
RICKIA. (Text and summaries in English and Portuguese) 1962. irreg., no. 11, 1981. price varies. Instituto de Botanica, Caixa Postal 4005, 01000 Sao Paulo, SP, Brazil. (back issues avail.) Indexed: Biol.Abstr. Rev.Plant Path.
Supersedes in part: Archivos de Botanica do Estado de Sao Paulo.

ROYAL BOTANICAL GARDENS, HAMILTON, ONT. SPECIAL BULLETIN. see *GARDENING AND HORTICULTURE*

581 635 CN ISSN 0072-9655
ROYAL BOTANICAL GARDENS, HAMILTON, ONT. TECHNICAL BULLETIN. 1957. irreg. limited distribution; price varies. Royal Botanical Gardens, Box 399, Hamilton, Ont. L8N 3H8, Canada. TEL 416-527-1158. Ed. Dr. Peter F. Rice. circ. 1,000. (back issues avail.)

501 SP ISSN 0212-9108
RUIZIA; monografias del real jardin botanico. 1984. a. 2400 ptas. exchange basis. Real Jardin Botanico, C.S.I.C., Plaza de Murillo 2, 28014 Madrid, Spain (Subscr. to: Oficina de Publicaciones del C.S.I.C., Vitrubio 8, 28006 Madrid, Spain) Dir. Santiago Castroviejo. bibl. illus. index. circ. 1,000. (back issues avail.) Indexed: Bull.Signal. Excerp.Bot.

581.05 SZ ISSN 0373-2525
SAUSSUREA. 1970. a. 50 F. to libraries and institutions. ‡ Societe Botanique de Geneve, Conservatoire et Jardin Botaniques, Bibliotheque, Case Postale 60, CH-1292 Chambesy/GE, Switzerland. Ed. Patrick Perret. adv. illus. circ. 400. Indexed: Biol.Abstr.
Supersedes: Societe Botanique de Geneve. Travaux (ISSN 0583-8177)

581 GW ISSN 0085-5960
SCHRIFTENREIHE FUER VEGETATIONSKUNDE. 1966. irreg., no. 12, 1979. price varies. (Bundesforschungsanstalt fuer Naturschutz und Landschaftsoekologie) Landwirtschaftsverlag GmbH, Huelsbrockstr. 2, Postfach 480249, 4400 Muenster-Hiltrup, W. Germany (B.R.D.) charts. illus. stat. Indexed: Biol.Abstr.

590 GW ISSN 0341-3772
SCRIPTA GEOBOTANICA. 1970. irreg. price varies. (Universitaet Goettingen, Lehrstuhl fuer Geobotanik) Verlag Erich Goltze GmbH und Co. KG, Stresemannstr. 28, 3400 Goettingen, W. Germany (B.R.D.) Ed. Hans Heller.

581 US ISSN 0361-185X
SELBYANA. 1976. a. $35 to individuals; institutions $55. Marie Selby Botanical Gardens, c/o Mrs. Ruby Hollis, 811 S. Palm Ave., Sarasota, FL 33577. TEL 813-366-5730. Ed. W. John Kress. illus. circ. 500. Indexed: Biol.Abstr.

581 BL ISSN 0375-1651
SELLOWIA; anais botanicos do herbario "Barbosa Rodrigues". (Text and summaries in English, German and Portuguese.) 1949. a. $10. Herbario "Barbosa Rodrigues", Avenida Marcos Konder 800, 88300-Itajai, Santa Catarina, Brazil. Ed.Bd. circ. 1, 000.

581 JA ISSN 0385-3985
SENNKE/NEWS OF THE TOHOKU PLANT ASSOCIATION. (Text in Japanese) 1973. biennial. 1.500 Yen. (Miyakonojo-Shi Toshokan (Library)) Tohoku Shokubutsu Aikokai, 7-22 Himegi-Cho, Miyakonojo-Shi 885, Japan. Ed. Itsuo Ogura. circ. 150.

581 SP
SERIE BOTANICA. 1982. irreg., no.5, 1986. price varies. (Universidad de Navarra, Facultad de Ciencias) Ediciones Universidad de Navarra, S.A., Apdo. 396, 31080 Pamplona, Spain.

581 CS
SEVEROCESKOU PRIRODOU. 1969. irreg., no.18, 1985. 15 Kcs. Okresni Vlastivedne Muzeum, Mirove nam. 171, 412 01 Litomerice, Czechoslovakia. Ed. Karel Kubat.

581 SI
SINGAPORE NATIONAL ACADEMY OF SCIENCE. JOURNAL. (Text in English) 1977. a. S.30($15) Singapore National Academy of Science, National University of Singapore, Botany Department, Lower Kent Ridge Rd., Singapore 0511. Ed. A.N. Rao. Indexed: Biol.Abstr.

581 US ISSN 0081-024X
SMITHSONIAN CONTRIBUTIONS TO BOTANY. 1969. irreg., no.64, 1986. Smithsonian Institution Press, 955 L'Enfant Plaza, Rm. 2100, Washington, DC 20560. TEL 202-287-3738. Ed. Barbara T. Spann. circ. 1,400. (reprint service avail. from UMI) Indexed: Biol.Abstr. Forest.Abstr. Forest Prod.Abstr. Geo.Abstr.

581 MX
SOCIEDAD BOTANICA DE MEXICO. BOLETIN. 1941. a. membership. Sociedad Botanica de Mexico, Apdo. Postal 70-383, Mexico 20, D.F., Mexico. charts. illus. cum.index: 1941-1975. Indexed: Biol.Abstr. Forest.Abstr. Forest Prod.Abstr.

581 PO
SOCIEDADE BROTERIANA. ANUARIO. (Text in European languages; summaries in English, French and Portuguese) 1935. a. Esc.500($15) ‡ Sociedade Broteriana, Arcos do Jardim, 3049 Coimbra, Portugal. (Co-sponsor: Universidade de Coimbra. Instituto Botanico) Eds. J.F. Mesquita, Rosette Batarda Fernandes. circ. 750. Indexed: Biol.Abstr. Excerp.Bot.

581 PO ISSN 0081-0657
SOCIEDADE BROTERIANA. BOLETIM. (Text in European languages; summaries in English, French, and Portuguese) 1880/81. a. Esc.3000($20) ‡ Sociedade Broteriana, Arcos do Jardim, 3049 Coimbra, Portugal. (Co-sponsor: Universidade de Coimbra. Instituto Botanico) Eds. A. Fernandes, J.F. Mesquita. circ. 1,100. Indexed: Biol.Abstr. Excerp.Bot.

581 IT
SOCIETA ITALIANA DI FITOSOCIOLOGIA. NOTIZARIO. (Text in English, French, Italian; summaries in English and French) 1964. irreg., no. 19, 1984. L.40000($35) per issue to non-members. Societa Italiana di Fitosociologia, Via Scopoli 22/24, 27100 Pavia, Italy. Ed. G.G. Lorenzoni. bk. rev. illus. circ. 350. (back issues avail.) Indexed: Biol.Abstr.

SOCIETA SARDA DI SCIENZE NATURALI. BOLLETTINO. see *BIOLOGY — Ornithology*

SPAIN. INSTITUTO NACIONAL DE INVESTIGACIONES AGRARIAS. COMUNICACIONES. SERIE: GENERAL. see *AGRICULTURE*

581 595.7 US
STATE BIOLOGICAL SURVEY OF KANSAS. TECHNICAL BULLETIN. 1976. irreg. price varies. Biological Survey, Nichols Hall, 2291 Irving Hill Dr., Lawrence, KS 66045-2969. Ed. Ralph E. Brooks. circ. 500.

581 SP ISSN 0370-923X
STUDIA BOTANICA. Universidad de Salamanca, Departamento de Botanica, Facultad de Farmacia, Apartado de Correos 325, 37080 Salamanca, Spain. TEL 923 25 33 88.

580 PL ISSN 0082-5557
STUDIA SOCIETATIS SCIENTIARUM TORUNENSIS. SECTIO D. BOTANICA. (Text in Polish; summaries in English, German) 1951. irreg. price varies. (Towarzystwo Naukowe w Toruniu) Panstwowe Wydawnictwo Naukowe, Miodowa 10, 00-251 Warsaw, Poland (Dist. by: Ars Polona, Krakowskie Przedmiescie 7, 00-068 Warsaw, Poland) Ed. Jan Kopcewicz. Indexed: Biol.Abstr.

589.2 NE ISSN 0166-0616
STUDIES IN MYCOLOGY. (Text in English) 1972. irreg. price varies. Centraalbureau voor Schimmelcultures, Box 273, 3740 AG Baarn, Netherlands. Ed.Bd. Indexed: Biol.Abstr. Chem.Abstr. Curr.Cont. ASCA. Rev.Plant Path.

581.9 SW ISSN 0282-8677
STUDIES IN PLANT ECOLOGY. (Text and summaries in English, German or Swedish) 1972. irreg., no.15, 1982. price varies. Svenska Vaextgeografiska Saellskapet - Swedish Society of Plant Geography, c/o Vaextbiologiska Institutionen, Box 559, S-751 22 Uppsala, Sweden. Ed. Erik Sjoegren.
Formerly: Vaextekologiska Studier (ISSN 0346-735X)

581 SW ISSN 0375-2038
SVENSKA LINNE-SALLSKAPET AARSSKRIFT/ SWEDISH LINNEUS SOCIETY. YEARBOOK. (Text in English and Swedish; summaries in English) 1918. a. Kr.60($15) Linne-Sallskapet, Uppsala, Sweden. Ed. G. Broberg. circ. 800.

589.2 AU ISSN 0082-0598
SYDOWIA: ANNALES MYCOLOGICI; editii in notitiam scientiae mycologicae universalis. (Supplement: Beihefte zur Sydowia: Annales Mycologici, Ser. II) (Text in English, German and Latin) 1947. a. S.890. Verlag Ferdinand Berger und Soehne OHG, Wienerstr. 21-23, 3580 Horn, Austria. Ed. E. Horak. Indexed: Biol.Abstr. Plant Breed.Abstr. Rev.Plant Path.
Mycology

581 SW ISSN 0082-0644
SYMBOLAE BOTANICAE UPSALIENSES. (Since vol. 20 issued as part of Acta Universitatis Upsaliensis) (Text and summaries in English, French, German) 1932. irreg., vol. 23, 1980. price varies. (Botaniske Institutionerna, Uppsala - Botanical Institute, Upsala) Almqvist & Wiksell International, Box 62, S-101 20 Stockholm, Sweden. Ed. J. A. Nannfeldt. Indexed: Biol.Abstr. Field Crop Abstr. Geo.Abstr. Herb.Abstr. Rev.Plant Path. Weed Abstr.

581 JA
SYOKUBUTSU BUNRUI GAKKAI NYUSU/JAPAN SOCIETY OF PLANT TAXONOMIST. NEWS. (Text in Japanese) 1971. irreg. members only. Japan Society of Plant Taxonomists, c/o Department of Botany, National Science Museum, 3-23-1 Hyakunin-cho, Shinjuku-ku, Tokyo 160, Japan. Ed. H. Kashiwadani. circ. 350.

581 US
T I P S Y. (The International Permaculture Species Yearbook) a. $15. Yankee Permaculture, Box 202, Orange, MA 01364. TEL 617-544-7810. Ed. Dan Hemenway.

TAIWAN AGRICULTURAL RESEARCH INSTITUTE. RESEARCH SUMMARY. see *AGRICULTURE*

581 CH ISSN 0065-1125
TAIWANIA. Also known as: Acta Botanica Taiwanica. (Text and summaries in Chinese and English) 1948. a. exchange only. National Taiwan University, College of Science, Botany Department, Taipei, Taiwan 107, Republic of China. Ed.Bd. circ. 450. Indexed: Biol.Abstr. Chem.Abstr. Field Crop Abstr. Herb.Abstr. Hort.Abstr. Plant Breed.Abstr. Rev.Plant Path. Soils & Fert.

581 AT ISSN 0312-9764
TELOPEA. 1975. irreg. available on exchange; free to qualified personnel. ‡ National Herbarium of New South Wales, Royal Botanic Gardens, Ms Macquaries Road, Sydney, N.S.W. 2000, Australia. Ed. K.L. Wilson. illus. circ. 1,000. Indexed: Biol.Abstr. Excerp.Bot. Field Crop Abstr. Herb.Abstr.
Supersedes: New South Wales National Herbarium. Contributions (ISSN 0077-8753)

632 US
TENNESSEE ECONOMIC PEST REPORT. 1968. a. free. Department of Agriculture, Division of Plant Industries, Insect Survey Comm, Box 40627, Melrose Station, Nashville, TN 37204. TEL 615-360-0130. Ed. Michael E. Cooper. illus. circ. 400.
Formerly: Tennessee Cooperative Economic Insect Survey Report: Annual Summary.

581 591 333.91 IT
THALASSIA SALENTINA. (Text in English, French, Italian) 1966. a. exchange. Universita degli Studi di Lecce, Stazione di Biologia Marina di Porto Cesareo, C.P. 193, 73100 Lecce, Italy. (back issues avail.) Indexed: Biol.Abstr.

581   DK   ISSN 0040-7135
TIDSSKRIFT FOR PLANTEAVL/DANISH
JOURNAL OF PLANT AND SOIL SCIENCE.
(Text in Danish and English; summaries in English)
1895. irreg. (4-6/yr.) Kr.190. Danish State
Committee on Crop Husbandry, Kongevejen 83,
2800 Lyngby, Denmark. Ed. O. Wagn. circ. 1,100.
Indexed: Biol.Abstr. Chem.Abstr. Excerp.Med.
Nutr.Abstr. Field Crop Abstr. Forest.Abstr.
Forest Prod.Abstr. Helminthol.Abstr. Herb.Abstr.
Hort.Abstr. Plant Breed.Abstr. Rev.Plant Path.
Soils & Fert. Weed Abstr.

581   US   ISSN 0041-2198
TREE-RING BULLETIN. 1935. a. $15 to individuals;
institutions $20. Tree-Ring Society, Tucson, AZ
85721. TEL 602-621-2191. Ed. Valmore C.
LaMarche. charts. illus. maps. cum.index. circ.
350. Indexed: Biol.Abstr. Br.Archaeol.Abstr.
Forest.Abstr. Forest Prod.Abstr. GeoRef.

581   NP
TRIBHUVAN UNIVERSITY. NATURAL HISTORY
MUSEUM. JOURNAL. (Text in English) 1977.
irreg. $30. Tribhuvan University, Natural History
Museum, Swoyambhu, Kathmandu, Nepal. Ed. R.
L. Shresta. circ. 500.

TROPICAL DEVELOPMENT & RESEARCH
INSTITUTE. CROP AND PRODUCT SERIES.
see *AGRICULTURE — Crop Production And Soil*

581   GW   ISSN 0302-9417
TROPISCHE UND SUBTROPISCHE
PFLANZENWELT. 1973. irreg., vol.58, 1986. price
varies. (Akademie der Wissenschaften und der
Literatur, Mainz, Mathematisch-
Naturwissenschaftliche Klasse) Franz Steiner Verlag
Wiesbaden GmbH, Birkenwaldstr. 44, Postfach 347,
D-7000 Stuttgart 1, W. Germany (B.R.D.) Ed.
Werner Rauh.

581   MX
UNIVERSIDAD DE GUADALAJARA. INSTITUTO
DE BOTANICA. BOLETIN INFORMATIVO.
no.8, 1978. irreg. exchange. Universidad de
Guadalajara, Instituto de Botanica, Apdo. Postal
139, Zapopan, Jalisco, Mexico. bibl. illus.

581   SP   ISSN 0580-468X
UNIVERSIDAD DE MADRID. DEPARTAMENTO
DE BOTANICA Y FISIOLOGIA VEGETAL.
TRABAJOS. 1968. irreg. Universidad Complutense
de Madrid, Departmento de Botanica y Fisiologia
Vegetal., Ciudad Universitaria, Madrid 3, Spain.
bibl. illus.

581   SP   ISSN 0213-5450
UNIVERSIDAD DE MURCIA. ANALES DE
BIOLOGIA. SECCION BIOLOGIA VEGETAL.
(Subseries of: Anales de Biologia) 1984. irreg., latest
vol.6, 1985. Universidad de Murcia, Secretariado de
Publicaciones e Intercambio Cientifico, Santo Cristo,
1, 30001 Murcia, Spain. TEL 968 24 92 00.

581   MX
UNIVERSIDAD NACIONAL AUTONOMA DE
MEXICO. INSTITUTO DE BIOLOGIA.
ANALES: SERIE BOTANICA. (Text in Spanish;
summaries in English, Spanish) 1967. biennial.
Mex.$1298($12) Universidad Nacional Autonoma
de Mexico, Instituto de Biologia, Apdo. Postal 70-
233, Ciudad Universitaria 04510, Mexico, D.F.,
Mexico (Subscr. to: Instituto de Biologia. Biblioteca,
Apdo. Postal 70-233, Ciudad Universitaria 04510,
Mexico, D.F., Mexico) circ. 1,000. (back issues
avail.)
  Formerly: Universidad Nacional Autonoma de
Mexico. Instituto de Biologia. Anales (ISSN 0076-
7174)

581   BL   ISSN 0302-2439
UNIVERSIDADE DE SAO PAULO.
DEPARTAMENTO DE BOTANICA. BOLETIM
DE BOTANICA. (Text in English, Portuguese)
1973. irreg., vol. 6, 1978. $5. Universidade de Sao
Paulo, Departamento de Botanica, Caixa Postal
11461, 05421 Sao Paulo, Brazil. (Co-sponsor:
Instituto de Biociencias) Ed. E.C. de Oliveira. illus.
circ. 800. Indexed: Curr.Cont.
  Supersedes (1937-1969): Universidade de Sao
Paulo. Faculdade de Filosofia, Ciencias y Letras.
Botanica.

581   IT   ISSN 0079-0265
UNIVERSITA DEGLI STUDI DI PAVIA.
ISTITUTO BOTANICO. ATTI. 1889. a. price
varies. ‡ Universita degli Studi di Pavia, Istituto
Botanico, Casella Postale 230, 27100 Pavia, Italy.
Ed. Augusto Pirola. circ. 400. Indexed: Biol.Abstr.

UNIVERSITE D'ANKARA. FACULTE DES
SCIENCES. COMMUNICATIONS SERIE C.
BIOLOGIE. see *BIOLOGY*

581   FR   ISSN 0069-469X
UNIVERSITE DE CLERMONT-FERRAND II.
ANNALES SCIENTIFIQUES. SERIE BIOLOGIE
VEGETALE. 1965. irreg. price varies. Universite de
Clermont-Ferrand II, Unite d'Enseignement et de
Recherche de Sciences Exactes et Naturelles, B.P.
45, 63170 Aubiere, France. circ. 250.

581   UA   ISSN 0068-5313
UNIVERSITY OF CAIRO. HERBARIUM.
PUBLICATIONS. (Text in English) 1968. a. free to
botanical institutions and interested botanists.
University of Cairo, Botany Department,
Herbarium, Giza, Egypt. Ed. Vivi Taerkholm. circ.
1,500.

581   US   ISSN 0068-6395
UNIVERSITY OF CALIFORNIA PUBLICATIONS
IN BOTANY. 1902. irreg. price varies. University
of California Press, 2120 Berkeley Way, Berkeley,
CA 94729. TEL 415-642-4247. Indexed: Biol.Abstr.
Plant Breed.Abstr.

581   TZ
UNIVERSITY OF DAR ES SALAAM. BOTANY
DEPARTMENT. DEPARTMENTAL
HERBARIUM PUBLICATIONS. 1971. irreg. price
varies. ‡ University of Dar es Salaam, Botany
Department, P.O. Box 35060, Dar es Salaam,
Tanzania.

581   US   ISSN 0580-6097
UNIVERSITY OF MICHIGAN. HERBARIUM.
CONTRIBUTIONS. (Text in English and Spanish;
summaries in English) 1939. irreg., latest no. 15.
price varies. ‡ University of Michigan, Herbarium,
North University Building, Ann Arbor, MI 48109.
TEL 313-764-1817. cum.index: 1939-1942; 1966-
1972. circ. 250(approx.) Indexed: Biol.Abstr.
Forest.Abstr.

581   JA   ISSN 0368-2196
UNIVERSITY OF TOKYO. FACULTY OF
SCIENCE. JOURNAL. SECTION 3: BOTANY/
TOKYO DAIGAKU RIGAKUBU KIYO, DAI-3-
RUI, SHOKUBUTSUGAKU. (Text in European
languages) 1887. a. price varies. University of
Tokyo, Faculty of Science - Tokyo Daigaku
Rigakubu, Hongo, Tokyo, Japan TEL 03-814-2625.
(Order from Maruzen Co. Ltd., 2-3-10 Nihonbashi,
Chou-Ku, Tokyo 103, Japan or their Import and
Export Dept., Box 5050, Tokyo International,
Tokyo 100-31, Japan) Ed. Kunio Iwatsuki. circ. 440.
(also avail. in microform) Indexed: Biol.Abstr.
Rev.Plant Path.

UNIVERSITY OF WAIKATO. ANTARCTIC
RESEARCH UNIT. REPORT. see *EARTH
SCIENCES — Geology*

580   YU
UNIVERZITET U BEOGRADU. INSTITUT ZA
BOTANIKU I BOTANICKE BASTE. GLASNIK.
vol. 10, n.s., 1975. a. Univerzitet u Beogradu,
Institut za Botaniku i Botanicke Baste, Takovska 43,
Belgrade, Yugoslavia. Ed. Milorad M. Jankovic.

581   PL   ISSN 0302-8585
UNIWERSYTET JAGIELLONSKI. ZESZYTY
NAUKOWE. PRACE BOTANICZNE. (Text and
summaries in English, Polish) 1973. irreg. price
varies. Panstwowe Wydawnictwo Naukowe,
Miodowa 10, 00-251 Warsaw, Poland (Dist. by: Ars
Polona, Krakowskie Przedmiescie 7, 00-068
Warsaw, Poland) Indexed: Biol.Abstr. Chem.Abstr.

581   US   ISSN 0083-5269
VASCULAR FLORA OF OHIO. 1967. irreg. price
varies. Ohio State University Press, 1050 Carmack
Rd., Columbus, OH 43210. TEL 614-292-6930.

581 634.9   HU   ISSN 0083-5323
DIE VEGETATION UNGARISCHER
LANDSCHAFTEN. (Text in German) 1957. irreg.,
vol.7, 1977. price varies. (Magyar Tudomanyos
Akademia) Akademiai Kiado, Publishing House of
the Hungarian Academy of Sciences, P.O. Box 24,
H-1363 Budapest, Hungary.

581   II   ISSN 0378-9454
VISTAS IN PLANT SCIENCES. 1975. a. $14. Today
and Tomorrow's Printers and Publishers, 24B/5
Original Rd., Karol Bagh, New Delhi 110005, India
(Dist. in U.S. by: Scholarly Publications, 7310
Elcresta Dr., Houston, Texas 77083)

WELSH PLANT BREEDING STATION. ANNUAL
REPORT. see *AGRICULTURE — Crop
Production And Soil*

581   AT
WESTERN AUSTRALIAN HERBARIUM.
RESEARCH NOTES. 1978. irreg. Aus.$5 per issue.
Department of Agriculture, Western Australian
Herbarium, Baron Hay Court, South Perth, W.A.
6151, Australia. Indexed: Biol.Abstr.

632 581   US   ISSN 0091-4487
WESTERN SOCIETY OF WEED SCIENCE.
PROCEEDINGS. 1938. a. $12. Western Society of
Weed Science, c/o J. Lamar Anderson, Department
of Plant Science, Utah State University, Logan, UT
84322-4820. TEL 801-750-2236. Indexed:
Chem.Abstr. Biotech.Abstr. Hort.Abstr. Plant
Breed.Abstr. Soils & Fert. Weed Abstr.

632 581   US   ISSN 0090-8142
WESTERN SOCIETY OF WEED SCIENCE.
RESEARCH PROGRESS REPORT. 1952. a. $12.
Western Society of Weed Science, c/o J. Lamar
Anderson, Department of Plant Science, Utah State
University, Logan, UT 84322-4820. TEL 801-750-
2236. Indexed: Biotech.Abstr. Plant Breed.Abstr.

580 590   AU   ISSN 0084-5639
ZOOLOGISCH-BOTANISCHE GESELLSCHAFT,
VIENNA. ABHANDLUNGEN. irreg. Zoologisch-
Botanische Gesellschaft, Althanstr. 14, PF 287, A-
1091 Vienna, Austria.

580 590   AU   ISSN 0084-5647
ZOOLOGISCH-BOTANISCHE GESELLSCHAFT,
VIENNA. VERHANDLUNGEN. 1851. irreg. price
varies. Zoologisch-Botanische Gesellschaft,
Althanstr. 14, PF 287, A-1091 Vienna, Austria. bk.
rev. circ. 900. Indexed: Biol.Abstr. GeoRef.
Rev.Appl.Entomol.

BIOLOGY — Cytology And Histology

574.8 591   US
ACTUALITES PROTOZOOLOGIQUES. (Published
in host country) 1974. quadrennial, latest 1978.
International Congress of Protozoology, c/o Dr.
Hunter, Hawkins Laboratories, Pace University,
Pace Plaza, New York, NY 10038. TEL 212-285-
3000. Indexed: Bio.Abstr. Chem.Abstr. Curr.Cont.

ADVANCES IN ANATOMY, EMBRYOLOGY
AND CELL BIOLOGY. see *BIOLOGY*

574.87   US   ISSN 0275-6358
ADVANCES IN CELL CULTURE. 1981. a., latest,
vol.4, 1985. Academic Press, Inc., Orlando, FL
32887. TEL 305-345-2000. Ed. Karl Maramorosch.
Indexed: Biol.Abstr. Chem.Abstr.

574.8   US   ISSN 0084-5949
ADVANCES IN CYTOPHARMACOLOGY. Vol. 1
represents: International Symposium on Cell Biology
and Cytopharmacology. Proceedings. 1971. irreg.,
vol.3, 1979. Raven Press, 1185 Ave. of the
Americas, New York, NY 10036. TEL 212-575-
0335. Ed. F. Clementi. Indexed: Biol.Abstr.
Chem.Abstr. Curr.Cont. Ind.Med.

574.87   US   ISSN 0743-4634
ANNUAL REVIEW OF CELL BIOLOGY. 1985. a.
$31. Annual Reviews Inc., 4139 El Camino Way,
Palo Alto, CA 94306. TEL 415-493-4400. Ed.
George E. Palade. illus. index.

ARCHIVES D'ANATOMIE, D'HISTOLOGIE ET
D'EMBRYOLOGIE; normales et experimentales.
see *BIOLOGY*

574.87 UR ISSN 0301-2425
BIOFIZIKA ZHIVOI KLETKI. 1970. irreg. 1 Rub.
Akademiya Nauk S.S.S.R, Institut Biologicheskoi
Fiziki, Akademgorodok, 142292 Pushchino, Russian
S.F.S.R., U.S.S.R. Ed. G.M. Frank. illus. circ. 1,500.
Indexed: Ref.Zh.

574.875 US ISSN 0067-8864
BIOMEMBRANES. 1971. irreg. price varies. Plenum
Publishing Corp., 233 Spring St., New York, NY
10013. TEL 212-620-8047. Ed. L. A. Manson.
Indexed: Chem.Abstr. Ind.Med.

574.8 UK
BRITISH SOCIETY FOR CELL BIOLOGY.
SYMPOSIA. 1976. irreg., no.5, 1982. $79.50 for
latest vol. Cambridge University Press, Edinburgh
Bldg., Shaftesbury Rd., Cambridge CB2 2RU,
England (And 32 E. 57th St., New York, NY
10022) Indexed: Biol.Abstr.

574.8 US ISSN 0172-4665
CELL BIOLOGY MONOGRAPHS. 1977. irreg.,
vol.13, 1986. Springer-Verlag, 175 Fifth Ave., New
York, NY 10010 TEL 212-460-1500. (Also Berlin,
Heidelberg, Tokyo and Vienna) (reprint service
avail. from ISI) Indexed: Biol.Abstr.
Supersedes: Protoplasmologia; Handbuch der
Protoplasmaforschung (ISSN 0079-7073)

574.88
COLUMBIA SERIES IN MOLECULAR BIOLOGY.
irreg., latest 1976. price varies. Columbia University
Press, 562 W. 113th St., New York, NY 10025.
TEL 212-678-6777.

ELECTRON MICROSCOPY OF PROTEINS. see
BIOLOGY — Microscopy

INTERNATIONAL CONGRESS OF
HISTOCHEMISTRY AND CYTOCHEMISTRY.
PROCEEDINGS. see BIOLOGY — Biological
Chemistry

574.8 US ISSN 0074-767X
INTERNATIONAL REVIEW OF CONNECTIVE
TISSUE RESEARCH. 1963. irreg., vol.10, 1983.
Academic Press, Inc., Orlando, FL 32887. TEL
305-345-2000. Eds. David A. Hall, D.S. Jackson.
index. Indexed: Biol.Abstr. Excerp.Med. Ind.Med.
Nutr.Abstr. Sci.Cit.Ind. Dent.Ind. Ind.Sci.Rev.

574.8 US ISSN 0074-7696
INTERNATIONAL REVIEW OF CYTOLOGY.
1952. irreg., vol.104, 1986. Academic Press, Inc.,
Orlando, FL 32887. TEL 305-345-2000. Eds. G.H.
Bourne, J.F. Danielli. index. cum.index: vols.1-9
(1952-1960) in vol.10 (1960) Indexed: Biol.Abstr.
Chem.Abstr. Excerp.Med. Ind.Med. Sci.Cit.Ind.
Abstr.Hyg. Anim.Breed.Abstr. Ind.Sci.Rev. Plant
Breed.Abstr. Trop.Dis.Bull.

574.8 US ISSN 0091-679X
METHODS IN CELL BIOLOGY. 1964. irreg., vol.
27, 1986. Academic Press, Inc, Orlando, FL 32887.
TEL 305-345-2000. Ed. Leslie Wilson. illus.
Indexed: Biol.Abstr. Chem.Abstr. Excerp.Med.
Ind.Med. Nutr.Abstr. Ind.Sci.Rev. Rev.Plant
Path.
Continues: Methods in Cell Physiology.

574.8 616 UK ISSN 0307-5494
MICROBIOS LETTERS; a prestige international
biomedical journal for the rapid publication of
biomedical communications. 1976. irreg., (3-4/yr.)
$375. Faculty Press, 88 Regent St., Cambridge,
England. Ed.Bd. adv. bk. rev. abstr. bibl. charts.
illus. index. Indexed: Chem.Abstr. Excerp.Med.
Curr.Cont. Biol.Dig. Microbiol.Abstr. Ind.Vet.
Ref.Zh. Rev.Plant Path. Vet.Bull.

574.88 US
MILES INTERNATIONAL SYMPOSIUM.
(Publisher varies) a. price varies. (Miles Laboratories
Inc.) Raven Press, 1185 Ave. of the Americas, New
York, NY 10036. TEL 212-575-0335. Indexed:
Chem.Abstr.
Formerly (until 1971): International Symposium
on Molecular Biology Publications.

574 US ISSN 0077-0221
MOLECULAR BIOLOGY, BIOCHEMISTRY AND
BIOPHYSICS. 1967. irreg., vol.36, 1986. Springer-
Verlag, 175 Fifth Ave., New York, NY 10010 TEL
212-460-1500. (Also Berlin, Heidelberg, Tokyo and
Vienna) (reprint service avail. from ISI) Indexed:
Biol.Abstr. Chem.Abstr. Ind.Med.

MONOGRAPHS IN CLINICAL CYTOLOGY. see
MEDICAL SCIENCES

574.87 US
N A T O ADVANCED STUDY INSTITUTE.
SERIES H: CELL BIOLOGY. 1986. irreg., vol.2,
1986. price varies. Springer-Verlag, 175 Fifth Ave.,
New York, NY 10160 TEL 212-460-1500. (Also
Berlin, Heidelberg, Tokyo, Vienna) (reprint service
avail. from ISI)

PROGRESS IN HISTOCHEMISTRY AND
CYTOCHEMISTRY. see BIOLOGY — Biological
Chemistry

574.8 US ISSN 0079-6484
PROGRESS IN MOLECULAR AND
SUBCELLULAR BIOLOGY. 1969. irreg., vol.9,
1985. price varies. Springer-Verlag, 175 Fifth Ave.,
New York, NY 10010 TEL 212-460-1500. (Also
Berlin, Heidelberg, Tokyo and Vienna) Ed. F.E.
Hahn. (reprint service avail. from ISI) Indexed:
Biol.Abstr. Chem.Abstr.

574.8 GW ISSN 0340-5400
RESEARCH IN MOLECULAR BIOLOGY. 1973.
irreg., vol.11, 1982. price varies. (Akademie der
Wissenschaften und der Literatur, Mainz,
Mathematisch-Naturwissenschaftliche Klasse) Franz
Steiner Verlag Wiesbaden GmbH, Birkenwaldstr. 44,
Postfach 347, D-7000 Stuttgart 1, W. Germany
(B.R.D.) Ed. Rudolf K. Zahn. Indexed: Chem.Abstr.

574.8 US ISSN 0080-1844
RESULTS AND PROBLEMS IN CELL
DIFFERENTIATION. 1968. irreg., vol.13, 1986.
Springer-Verlag, 175 Fifth Ave., New York, NY
10010 TEL 212-460-1500. (Also Berlin, Heidelberg,
Tokyo and Vienna) (reprint service avail. from ISI)
Indexed: Biol.Abstr. Chem.Abstr. Ind.Med.

574.8 US
U C L A SYMPOSIUM ON MOLECULAR
BIOLOGY PROCEEDINGS. (University of
California, Los Angeles) 1972. irreg., no.26, 1983.
(International Chemical and Nuclear Corp.)
Academic Press, Inc., Orlando, FL 32887. TEL
305-345-2000. (Co-sponsor: University of California
at Los Angeles, Molecular Biology Institute) Eds. C.
Fred Fox, William S. Robinson. Indexed: Biol.Abstr.
Formerly: I C N-U C L A Symposium on
Molecular Biology Proceedings.

574.8 578 619 US ISSN 0730-6482
ULTRASTRUCTURAL PATHOLOGY
PUBLICATION. 1984. irreg. price varies.
Hemisphere Publishing Corporation, 79 Madison
Ave., New York, NY 10016. Eds. Jan Vincents
Johannessen, Victor Gould. bibl. charts. illus.
index. (back issues avail.)

BIOLOGY — Entomology

see also Agriculture—Crop Production and
Soil; Engineering—Chemical Engineering

595.7 IT ISSN 0065-0757
ACCADEMIA NAZIONALE ITALIANA DI
ENTOMOLOGIA. RENDICONTI. 1952. irreg.,
vol. 26/27, 1979. price varies. Accademia Nazionale
Italiana di Entomologia, Istituto di Entomologia
Agraria, Borgo XX Giugno, 06100 Perugia, Italy.

595.7 CS
ACTA ENTOMOLOGICA. (Text in English, French
and German) 1923. irreg., vol.41, 1984. price varies.
Narodni Muzeum, Prirodovedecke Muzeum,
Vitezneho Unora 74, 115 79 Prague 1,
Czechoslovakia (Subscr. to: P N S - Ustredni
Ezpedice a Dovoz Tisku Prague, Zavod 01,
Administrace Vyvozu Tisku, Kafkova 19, 160 00
Prague 6, Czechoslovakia) Ed. Jan Jezek.

595.7 FI ISSN 0001-561X
ACTA ENTOMOLOGICA FENNICA. (Text in
English, French and German) 1947. irreg. Fmk.110.
Entomological Society of Finland, P. Rautatiekatu
13, 00100 Helsinki 10, Finland (Distr. by:
Akateeminen Kirjakauppa, PL 128, SF-00101
Helsinki, Finland) (Co-sponsor: Societas
Entomologica Helsingforsiensis) Ed. W. Hackman.
circ. 700. Indexed: Biol.Abstr. Rev.Appl.Entomol.
Hort.Abstr.

595.7 CS ISSN 0554-9264
ACTA FAUNISTICA ENTOMOLOGICA. (Text in
English, German and Russian) 1956. irreg., no.16,
1980; vol.17, 1984. price varies. Narodni Muzeum,
Prirodovedecke Museum, Vitezneho Unora 74, 115
79 Prague 1, Czechoslovakia (Subscr. to: P N S -
Ustredni Expedice a Dovoz Tisku Prague, Zavod
01, Administrace Vyvozu Tisku, Kafkova 19, 160 00
Prague 6 Czechoslovakia) Ed. Josef Jelinek.
Indexed: Biol.Abstr. Rev.Appl.Entomol.

595.7 US ISSN 0065-2806
ADVANCES IN INSECT PHYSIOLOGY. 1963.
irreg., vol.18, 1985. Academic Press Inc., Orlando,
FL 32887. TEL 305-345-2000. Ed.Bd. Indexed:
Biol.Abstr. Biol.& Agr.Ind. Chem.Abstr.
Sci.Cit.Ind. Abstr.Hyg. Ind.Sci.Rev.
Rev.Appl.Entomol. Trop.Dis.Bull.

595.7 US ISSN 0065-6143
ALDRICH ENTOMOLOGY CLUB. NEWSLETTER.
1962. irreg., vol. 11, 1980. free. University of Idaho,
Department of Entomology, Moscow, ID 83843.
TEL 208-885-6276. Ed. Donald Wimmer. circ. 150.

595.7 US ISSN 0569-4450
AMERICAN ENTOMOLOGICAL INSTITUTE.
CONTRIBUTIONS. 1964. irreg. $40. American
Entomological Institute, 3005 S.W. 56th Ave.,
Gainesville, FL 32608. TEL 904-377-6458. Ed.
Henry K. Townes. circ. 200. (back vols. avail.)
Indexed: Biol.Abstr. Rev.Appl.Entomol.

595.7 US ISSN 0065-8162
AMERICAN ENTOMOLOGICAL INSTITUTE.
MEMOIRS. 1961. irreg. price varies. American
Entomological Institute, 3005 S.W. 56th Ave.,
Gainesville, FL 32608. TEL 904-377-6458. Ed.
Henry K. Townes. index. circ. 200. (back vols.
avail.) Indexed: Biol.Abstr.

595.7 US ISSN 0065-8170
AMERICAN ENTOMOLOGICAL SOCIETY.
MEMOIRS. 1916. irreg., no. 35, 1986. price varies.
American Entomological Society, Academy of
Natural Sciences, 1900 Race St., Philadelphia, PA
19103. TEL 215-561-3978. Ed. Selwyn S. Roback.
index. Indexed: Biol.Abstr.

595.7 FR ISSN 0066-2739
ANNUAIRE DES ARACHNOLOGISTES
MONDIAUX; acarologistes exceptes. 1968.
triennial. 150 F.($20) Centre International de
Documentation Arachnologique, 61 rue de Buffon,
75005 Paris, France.

595.7 US ISSN 0066-4170
ANNUAL REVIEW OF ENTOMOLOGY. 1956. a.
$31. Annual Reviews Inc., 4139 El Camino Way,
Box 10139, Palo Alto, CA 94303-0897. TEL 415-
493-4400. Ed. Thomas E. Mittler. bibl. index.
cum.index every 5 yrs. (back issues avail.; reprint
service avail. from ISI) Indexed: Biol.Abstr. Biol.&
Agr.Ind. Chem.Abstr. Curr.Cont. Excerp.Med.
Ind.Med. Sci.Cit.Ind. Abstr.Hyg. Apic.Abstr.
Biotech.Abstr. Forest.Abstr. Helmintol.Abstr.
Hort.Abstr. Ind.Sci.Rev. M.M.R.I. Plant
Breed.Abstr. Rev.Appl.Entomol. Rev.Plant Path.
Soils & Fert. Trop.Dis.Bull. VITIS. Weed Abstr.

595.7 576 591 TU
ARASTIRMA ESERLERI SERISI. (Text in Turkish;
summaries in English, French or German) 1952.
irreg. free. Ministry of Agriculture, Forest and Rural
affairs, Regional Plant Protection Research Institute,
Mudurlugu, Fatih Callesi 37, Kalaba, Ankara,
Turkey. index. circ. 600. (back issues avail.)
Indexed: Biol.Abstr.

595.2 US ISSN 0066-8036
ARTHROPODS OF FLORIDA AND
NEIGHBORING LAND AREAS. 1965. irreg.,
vol.11, 1984. free to Florida residents on request.
Department of Agriculture and Consumer Services,
Division of Plant Industry, Box 1269, Gainesville,
FL 32602. TEL 904-372-3505. Ed. Dr. H. Weems.
(back issues avail.) Indexed: Biol.Abstr. Bibl.Agri.
Zoo.Rec.

595.7 AT
AUSTRALIAN ENTOMOLOGICAL SOCIETY.
MISCELLANEOUS PUBLICATIONS. irreg. price
varies. Australian Entomological Society,
Entomology Branch, Department of Primary
Industries, Meiers Rd., Indooroopilly, Qld. 4068,
Australia. Indexed: Biol.Abstr.

BIOLOGY — ENTOMOLOGY

595.7   IT   ISSN 0366-2403
BOLLETTINO DI ZOOLOGIA AGRARIA E DI BACHICOLTURA. (Text in English, French, German, Italian; summaries in English and Italian) 1928. biennial. L.25000. Universita degli Studi di Milano, Istituto di Entomologia Agraria, Via Celoria 2, 20133 Milan, Italy. Ed.Bd. circ. 160. (back issues avail.) Indexed: Biol.Abstr.

595.7   UK   ISSN 0524-6431
BRITISH MUSEUM (NATURAL HISTORY). BULLETIN. ENTOMOLOGY. 1949. a. £230. British Museum (Natural History), Cromwell Rd., London SW7 5BD, England. illus. index. circ. 750. Indexed: Biol.Abstr. Rev.Appl.Entomol.

595.7   US   ISSN 0068-5631
CALIFORNIA INSECT SURVEY. BULLETIN. 1950. irreg. price varies. University of California Press, 2120 Berkeley Way, Berkeley, CA 94720. TEL 415-642-4247. Indexed: Biol.Abstr. Abstr.Hyg. Rev.Appl.Entomol. Trop.Dis.Bull.

595.1   BE
CATALOGUE DES COLEOPTERES DE BELGIQUE. irreg. price varies. Societe Royale Belge d'Entomologie, 29 rue Vautier, 1040 Brussels, Belgium.

595.7   AT   ISSN 0069-732X
COMMONWEALTH SCIENTIFIC AND INDUSTRIAL RESEARCH ORGANIZATION. DIVISION OF ENTOMOLOGY. REPORT. 1960/61. biennial. free. C S I R O, Division of Entomology, Box 1700, Canberra City, A.C.T. 2601, Australia. Ed. A. Frodsham. circ. 1,000. Indexed: Rev.Appl.Entomol. Weed Abstr.

595.7   AT   ISSN 0069-7338
COMMONWEALTH SCIENTIFIC AND INDUSTRIAL RESEARCH ORGANIZATION. DIVISION OF ENTOMOLOGY. TECHNICAL PAPER. 1957. irreg. price varies. C.S.I.R.O, Editorial and Publications Service, P.O. Box 89, East Melbourne, Vic. 3002, Australia. Indexed: Biol.Abstr. Rev.Appl.Entomol.

595.7   US   ISSN 0097-0905
CONNECTICUT. AGRICULTURAL EXPERIMENT STATION, NEW HAVEN. BULLETIN. 1877. irreg., no.826, 1985. free. Agricultural Experiment Station, 123 Huntington St., Box 1106, New Haven, CT 06504-1106. TEL 203-789-7272. Ed. Paul Gough. circ. 6,000. (back issues avail.) Indexed: Biol.Abstr. Chem.Abstr. Forest.Abstr. Forest Prod.Abstr. Helminthol.Abstr. Hort.Abstr.

595.7   US   ISSN 0070-7333
DROSOPHILA INFORMATION SERVICE. 1934. irreg., approx. a. $5. c/o Dr. Philip Hedrick, Ed., Division of Biological Sciences, University of Kansas, Lawrence, KS 66045. TEL 913-864-2700. circ. 1,200.

595.7   US   ISSN 0734-9874
ENTOMOGRAPHY. 1982. a. $40. Entomography Publications, 1722 J St., Ste 19, Sacramento, CA 95814. Eds. Charles S. Papp, Thomas D. Eichlin. Indexed: Biol.Abstr.

595.7   CN   ISSN 0071-0709
ENTOMOLOGICAL SOCIETY OF ALBERTA. PROCEEDINGS. 1953. a. Can.$4 to individuals; libraries Can.$6. ‡ Entomological Society of Alberta, c/o University of Alberta, Dept. of Entomology, Edmonton, Alta. T6G 2E3, Canada. TEL 403-432-3237. cum.index every 10 years. circ. 125.

595.7   US   ISSN 0071-0717
ENTOMOLOGICAL SOCIETY OF AMERICA. MISCELLANEOUS PUBLICATIONS. 1959. irreg., vol. 58, 1984. $7.50 per issue to non-members; members 4.50. Entomological Society of America, c/o David M. Lerner, Sales Manager, 4603 Calvert Rd., College Park, MD 20740. TEL 301-864-1334. Ed. Morris Rockstein. circ. 250. (also avail. in microform from UMI) Indexed: Biol.Abstr. Chem.Abstr. Rev.Appl.Entomol.

595.7   CN   ISSN 0071-0733
ENTOMOLOGICAL SOCIETY OF BRITISH COLUMBIA. JOURNAL. 1906. a. Can.$15. Entomological Society of British Columbia, c/o L. Humble, Sect. Treasurer, 506 West Burnside Rd., Victoria, B.C. V8Z1M5, Canada. Ed. H.R. MacCarthy. adv. bk. rev. circ. 250. (also avail. in microform from UMI)

595.7   CN   ISSN 0071-075X
ENTOMOLOGICAL SOCIETY OF CANADA. MEMOIRS. (Text in English or French) 1956. irreg. (1-8 per yr.) Can.$24.50. Entomological Society of Canada, 1320 Carling Ave., Ottawa, Ont. K1Z 7K9, Canada. TEL 613-725-2619. Ed. A.B. Ewan. circ. 1,100. Indexed: Biol.Abstr. Entomol.Abstr. Hort.Abstr. Rev.Appl.Entomol.

595.7   CN   ISSN 0315-2146
ENTOMOLOGICAL SOCIETY OF MANITOBA. PROCEEDINGS. 1945. a. Can.$8. Entomological Society of Manitoba, Inc., 195 Dafoe Rd., Winnipeg. Man. R3T 2M9, Canada. TEL 204-269-2100. Ed. R.E. Roughley. circ. 250. Indexed: Biol.Abstr.

595.7   NZ   ISSN 0110-4527
ENTOMOLOGICAL SOCIETY OF NEW ZEALAND. BULLETIN. 1972. irreg. price varies. Entomological Society of New Zealand, Entomology Division, D.S.I.R., Private Bag, Auckland, New Zealand. Indexed: Biol.Abstr.

595.7   CN   ISSN 0071-0768
ENTOMOLOGICAL SOCIETY OF ONTARIO. PROCEEDINGS; annual publication of entomological research in Ontario. 1871. a. ‡ Entomological Society of Ontario, University of Guelph, Dept. of Environmental Biology, Graham Hall, Guelph, Ont., Canada. TEL 519-824-4120. Ed. P.G. Kevan. bk. rev. index. circ. 1,000. (also avail. in microform from UMI) Indexed: Biol.Abstr. Chem.Abstr. Curr.Cont. Sci.Cit.Ind. Apic.Abstr. Helminthol.Abstr. Rev.Appl.Entomol. Zoo.Rec.

595.7   US   ISSN 0071-0776
ENTOMOLOGICAL SOCIETY OF PENNSYLVANIA. NEWSLETTER. 1965. a. membership. Entomological Society of Pennsylvania, 103 Patterson Bldg., University Park, PA 16802. TEL 814-863-4640. circ. 215.

595.7   SA
ENTOMOLOGICAL SOCIETY OF SOUTHERN AFRICA. MEMOIRS. irreg., no.14, 1981. Entomological Society of Southern Africa, Box 102, Pretoria 0001, South Africa. Indexed: Biol.Abstr. Curr.Cont. Entomol.Abstr. Herb.Abstr. Ind.S.A.Per. Rev.Appl.Entomol. Soils & Fert. Weed Abstr. Zoo.Rec.

595.7   SA
ENTOMOLOGICAL SOCIETY OF SOUTHERN AFRICA. PROCEEDINGS OF THE CONGRESS. 1974. irreg., approx. every 3 years. Entomological Society of Southern Africa, Box 103, Pretoria 0001, South Africa. abstr. Indexed: Biol.Abstr. Curr.Cont. Entomol.Abstr. Ind.S.A.Per. Zoo.Rec.

595.7   CS   ISSN 0071-0792
ENTOMOLOGICKE PROBLEMY. (Text in German or Slovak; summaries in English, German, Russian) 1961. irreg. price varies. (Slovenska Akademia Vied, Slovenska Entomologicka Spolocnost) Veda, Publishing House of the Slovak Academy of Sciences, Klemensova 19, 814 30 Bratislava, Czechoslovakia (Subscr. to: Slovart, Gottwaldovo nam. 6, 817 64 Bratislava) Ed. Ilja Okali. Indexed: Biol.Abstr. Rev.Appl.Entomol.

595.7   BL
ENTOMOLOGY NEWSLETTER. 1974. biennial. free. International Society of Sugar Cane Technologists, c/o IAA/Planalsucar, Caixa Postal 153/158, 13600 Araras SP, Brazil. Ed. P.S.M. Botelho. circ. 150. Indexed: Biol.Abstr. Rev.Appl.Entomol.

595.7   JA   ISSN 0071-1268
ESAKIA. (Text in English, French and German) 1960. irreg. exchange basis only. Kyushu University, Entomological Laboratory, Fukuoka 812, Japan. Ed.Bd. bk. rev. charts. illus. Indexed: Biol.Abstr. Entomol.Abstr. Rev.Appl.Entomol. Zoo.Rec.

595.7 574   DK   ISSN 0106-8377
FAUNA ENTOMOLOGICA SCANDINAVICA. (Text in English) 1973. irreg. (2-5/yr.) price varies. Scandinavian Science Press Ltd., Langasen 4, Ganlose, 2760 Malov, Denmark. Ed. Leif Lyneborg. illus. (back issues avail.) Indexed: Biol.Abstr.

FAUNA OF NEW ZEALAND. see *BIOLOGY*

595.7   GW
FLIES OF THE NEARCTIC REGION. (Text in English, German) 1980. irreg. E. Schweizerbart'sche Verlagsbuchhandlung, Johannesstr. 3A, D-7000 Stuttgart 1, W. Germany (B.R.D.) Ed. Graham C.D. Griffiths.

595.7   US   ISSN 0885-5943
FLORIDA STATE COLLECTION OF ARTHROPODS. OCCASIONAL PAPERS. 1981. irreg., vol.3, 1985. Department of Agriculture and Consumer Services, Division of Plant Industry, Box 1269, 1911 S.W. 34 St., Gainesville, FL 32602. TEL 904-372-3505. Ed. Howard Weems. bibl. (back issues avail.)

FOREST PEST MANAGEMENT INSTITUTE. INFORMATION REPORT SERIES. see *FORESTS AND FORESTRY*

FOREST PEST MANAGEMENT INSTITUTE. TECHNICAL NOTE SERIES. see *FORESTS AND FORESTRY*

595.7   JA   ISSN 0429-2871
FRAGMENTA COLEOPTEROLOGICA. (Text in English) 1961. irreg. (approx. a.) $2. Miyazaki Sangyo-Keiei University, Maruo 100, Furujo-cho, Miyazaki-shi 880, Japan. circ. 100. Indexed: Biol.Abstr.

595.7   IT   ISSN 0429-288X
FRAGMENTA ENTOMOLOGICA. (Text in Italian, English, French, German; summaries in Italian, English) 1951. s-a. avail. only on exchange. Universita degli Studi di Roma la Sapienza, Via Catone 34, 00192 Rome, Italy. Ed. A. Vigna-Taglianti. bk. rev. Indexed: Biol.Abstr. Entomol.Abstr. Zoo.Rec. Forest.Abstr. Rev.Appl.Entomol. VITIS.

FUNDACION MIGUEL LILLO. MISCELANEA. see *BIOLOGY — Botany*

595.7   AT   ISSN 0158-0760
GENERAL AND APPLIED ENTOMOLOGY. 1964. a. Aus.$6. Entomological Society of New South Wales, Entomology Department, Australian Museum, College St., Sydney N.S.W. 2000, Australia. Ed. D. Hales. adv. bk. rev. circ. 210. Indexed: Biol.Abstr. Chem.Abstr. Aus.Sci.Abstr. Ind.Vet. Rev.Appl.Entomol. Vet.Bull.
Formerly (until vol. 10, 1978): Entomological Society of Australia (N.S.W.) Journal (ISSN 0071-0725)

595.7   IT   ISSN 0392-7296
GIORNALE ITALIANO DI ENTOMOLOGIA. (Text in Italian and English) 1982. 3/yr. L.54000 to individuals; institutions L.65000. Casella Postale 188, I-26100 Cremona, Italy. Ed. Marco Berra. adv. charts. illus. cum.index. circ. 1,000. Indexed: Entomol.Abstr. Zoo.Rec.

595.7   US
HAWAIIAN ENTOMOLOGICAL SOCIETY. PROCEEDINGS. 1906. a. $10. (Hawaiian Entomological Society) University of Hawaii, c/o Entomology Dept., 3050 Maile Way, Honolulu, HI 96822. TEL 808-948-7076. Ed. C. Ray Joyce. circ. 600. (reprint service avail. from UMI)

595.7   GW   ISSN 0724-1348
HETEROCERA SUMATRANA. (Text in English and German) 1982. irreg. price varies. Verlag Erich Bauer, Luisenplatz 2, Postfach 4747, D-6200 Wiesbaden, W. Germany (B.R.D.) Ed. E.W. Diehl. (back issues avail.) Indexed: Entomol.Abstr.

595.7   II   ISSN 0073-6392
INDIAN FOREST RECORDS (NEW SERIES) ENTOMOLOGY. (Text in English) 1935. irreg., vol. 14, no. 2. 1981. price varies. ‡ Forest Research Institute & Colleges, P.O. New Forest, Dehra Dun, India. circ. 500. Indexed: Biol.Abstr. Forest.Abstr. Indian Sci.Abstr. Rev.Appl.Entomol.

BIOLOGY — ENTOMOLOGY

595.7   JA   ISSN 0020-1804
INSECTA MATSUMURANA. (Text mainly in English) 1926. N.S. 1973. irreg. exchange basis. Hokkaido University, Faculty of Agriculture, Entomological Institute - Hokkaido Daigaku Nogakubu Konchugaku Kyoshitsu, Nishi-9-chome, Kita-9-jo, Kita-ku, Sapporo 060, Japan. charts. illus. Indexed: Biol.Abstr. Rev.Appl.Entomol.

595.7   US   ISSN 0276-3656
INSECTICIDE AND ACARICIDE TESTS. 1976. a. $33 to non-members; members $15. Entomological Society of America, c/o David M. Lerner, Sales Manager, 4603 Calvert Rd., College Park, MD 20740. TEL 301-864-1334. Ed. A.C. York. Indexed: Rev.Appl.Entomol.

595.7   US   ISSN 0073-8115
INSECTS OF MICRONESIA. (Most issues in English only; a few issues in French or German only) 1954. irreg. price varies. Bishop Museum Press, Box 19000-A, Honolulu, HI 96817. TEL 808-947-3511. Indexed: Biol.Abstr.

595.7   US   ISSN 0098-1222
INSECTS OF VIRGINIA. (Subseries of: Virginia Polytechnic Institute and State University. Research Division. Bulletins) 1969. irreg. exchange basis only. Virginia Polytechnic Institute and State University, Department of Entomology, Blacksburg, VA 24061. TEL 703-961-5163. Ed. Mary C. Holliman. illus.

595.7   634.9   MX   ISSN 0185-2361
INSTITUTO NACIONAL DE INVESTIGACIONES FORESTALES. BOLETIN DIVULGATIVO. (Text in Spanish; summaries in English and Spanish) 1961. irreg. price varies. Instituto Nacional de Investigaciones Forestales Y Agropecuarias, Centro de Documentacion Cientifica y Tecnologica, Av. Progreso No. 5, Col. Coyoacan, Delegacion Coyoacan, 04110 Mexico, D.F., Mexico. TEL 658-43-33. (back issues avail.) Indexed: Biol.Abstr. Forest.Abstr. Forest Prod.Abstr.

595.7   634.9   MX   ISSN 0185-2310
INSTITUTO NACIONAL DE INVESTIGACIONES FORESTALES. BOLETIN TECNICO. (Text in Spanish; summaries in English and Spanish) 1961. irreg. price varies. Instituto Nacional de Investigaciones Forestales Y Agropecuarias, Centro de Documentacion Cientifica y Tecnologica, Av. Progreso No. 5, Col. Coyoacan, Delegacion Coyoacan, 04110 Mexico, D.F., Mexico. TEL 658-43-33. Indexed: Biol.Abstr. Forest.Abstr. Forest Prod.Abstr.

595.7   634.9   MX   ISSN 0185-2566
INSTITUTO NACIONAL DE INVESTIGACIONES FORESTALES. PUBLICACION ESPECIAL. (Text in Spanish; summaries in English and Spanish) 1961. irreg. price varies. Instituto Nacional de Investigaciones Forestales Y Agropecuarias, Centro de Documentacion Cientifica y Tecnologica, Av. Progreso No. 5, Col. Coyoacan, Delegacion Coyoacan, 04110 Mexico, D.F., Mexico. TEL 658-43-33. Indexed: Biol.Abstr. Forest.Abstr. Forest Prod.Abstr.

INSTITUTUL DE CERCETARI PENTRU PROTECTIA PLANTELOR. ANALELE/ RESEARCH INSTITUTE FOR PLANT PROTECTION. ANNALS. see *AGRICULTURE*

595.7   UK   ISSN 0074-364X
INTERNATIONAL CONGRESS OF ENTOMOLOGY. 1910. quadrennial, 16th. 1980, Kyoto, Japan; 17th. 1984, Hamburg, W. Germany. price varies. Council for International Congresses of Entomology, c/o British Museum (Natural History), Cromwell Rd., London, S.W. 7, England. Indexed: Biol.Abstr.

595.7   IS   ISSN 0075-1243
ISRAEL JOURNAL OF ENTOMOLOGY. (Text in English) 1966. a. $18. Entomological Society of Israel, Box 6, Bet-Dagan 50-200, Israel. Ed.Bd. adv. bk. rev. circ. 200. Indexed: Biol.Abstr. Chem.Abstr. Entomol.Abstr. Rev.Appl.Entomol. Biotech.Abstr.

616.968   US   ISSN 0146-6631
JOURNAL OF MEDICAL ENTOMOLOGY. SUPPLEMENT. 1976. irreg. price varies. (Bishop Museum, Department of Entomology) Bishop Museum Press, Box 19000-A, Honolulu, HI 96817. TEL 808-847-3511. Eds. Dr. Frank Radorsky, Dr. JoAnn Tenorio. Indexed: Biol.Abstr. Ind.Med.

591   PL   ISSN 0075-6350
KLUCZE DO OZNACZANIA OWADOW POLSKI. 1954. irreg., no.131, 1984. price varies. (Polskie Towarzystwo Entomologiczne) Panstwowe Wydawnictwo Naukowe, Ul. Miodowa 10, 00-251 Warsaw, Poland (Dist. by: Ars Polona, Krakowskie Przedmiescie 7, 00-068 Warsaw, Poland) Ed. A. Warchalowski. bibl. circ. 800. Indexed: Biol.Abstr. Rev.Appl.Entomol.

595.7   IT   ISSN 0304-0658
LABORATORIO DI ENTOMOLOGIA AGRARIA. BOLLETTINO. (Text and summaries in English and Italian) 1937. a. exchange basis only. Universita degli Studi di Napoli, Istituto di Entomologia Agraria, Via Universita 100, 80055 Portici, Italy. Ed. E. Tremblay. bk. rev. circ. 500. Indexed: Biol.Abstr. Entomol.Abstr. Hort.Abstr. Rev.Appl.Entomol.

595.78   US   ISSN 0024-0966
LEPIDOPTERIST'S SOCIETY. JOURNAL. 1947. a. membership. ‡ Lepidopterists Society, c/o Ron Leuschner, Publ. Coord., 1900 John St., Manhattan Beach, CA 90266. Ed. Dr. William E. Miller. bk. rev. bibl. charts. illus. index. circ. 1,200. Indexed: Biol.Abstr.

595.7   US   ISSN 0075-8795
LEPIDOPTERISTS' SOCIETY. MEMOIRS. 1964. irreg., latest 1981. Lepidopterists' Society, c/o Ron Leuschner, Publ. Coord., 1900 John St., Manhattan Beach, CA 90266. Ed. C.V. Covell Jr.

LIMNOBIOS. see *BIOLOGY — Zoology*

595.7   US
M E S NEWSLETTER. irreg. (3-4/yr.) $5 or membership. Michigan Entomological Society, c/o Dept. of Entomology, Michigan State University, East Lansing, MI 48824.

595.7   US   ISSN 0076-6224
MELANDERIA. 1969. irreg., no.43, 1985. price varies. ‡ Washington State Entomological Society, Department of Entomology, Washington State University, Pullman, WA 99164-6432. TEL 509-335-8128. Eds. Roger D. Akre, Richard S. Zack. circ. 950. (back issues avail.) Indexed: Biol.Abstr. Apic.Abstr.

595.7   US   ISSN 0076-6321
MELSHEIMER ENTOMOLOGICAL SERIES. 1967. irreg., approx. 2/yr., latest no. 35. $8 per no. Entomological Society of Pennsylvania, 103 Patterson Bldg., University Park, PA 16802. TEL 814-863-4640. Eds. Michael Blumenthal, Mark Ticehurst. circ. 215. Indexed: Biol.Abstr. Rev.Appl.Entomol.

595.7   GW   ISSN 0077-0698
MONOGRAPHIEN ZUR ANGEWANDTEN ENTOMOLOGIE. (Text in German or English) 1917. irreg., no. 24, 1983. price varies. Verlag Paul Parey (Hamburg), Spitalerstr. 12, 2000 Hamburg 1, W. Germany (B.R.D.) Ed. W. Schwenke. illus. bibl. index. (reprint service avail. from ISI) Indexed: Biol.Abstr. Curr.Cont.

595.7   GW   ISSN 0077-1864
MUENCHNER ENTOMOLOGISCHE GESELLSCHAFT. MITTEILUNGEN. 1910. a. DM.45. Muenchener Entomologische Gesellschaft, Muenchhausenstr. 21, 8000 Munich 60, W. Germany (B.R.D.) Ed. Roland Gerstmeier. bk. rev. circ. 1,200. Indexed: Biol.Abstr.

595.7   AG   ISSN 0524-949X
MUSEO ARGENTINO DE CIENCIAS NATURALES "BERNARDINO RIVADAVIA." INSTITUTO NACIONAL DE INVESTIGACION DE LAS CIENCIAS NATURALES. REVISTA. ENTOMOLOGIA. 1964. irreg.; latest vol. 4, no. 4, 1981. Museo Argentino de Ciencias Naturales "Bernardino Rivadavia", Instituto Nacional de Investigacion de las Ciencias Naturales, Avda. Angel Gallardo 470, Casilla de Correo 220 Sucursal 5, Buenos Aires, Argentina. Indexed: Rev.Appl.Entomol.

595.7   NE   ISSN 0548-1163
NEDERLANDSE ENTOMOLOGISCHE VERENIGING. MONOGRAPHS. (Text in Dutch and English) 1964. irreg., no.10, 1983. price varies. Nederlandse Entomologische Vereniging, Plantage Middenlaan 64, 1018 DH Amsterdam, Netherlands. Ed. Dr. P. van Helsdingen. illus. Indexed: Biol.Abstr.

595.7   GW   ISSN 0722-3773
NEUE ENTOMOLOGISCHE NACHRICHTEN. 1982. irreg. DM.75. Verlag Erich Bauer, Luisenplatz 2, Postfach 4747, D-6200 Wiesbaden, W. Germany (B.R.D.) (back issues avail.) Indexed: Entomol.Abstr.

595.7   US
NEW JERSEY MOSQUITO CONTROL ASSOCIATION. PROCEEDINGS. Variant title: Annual Mosquito Review. 1914. a. $5. New Jersey Mosquito Control Association, Inc, c/o Managing Editor, 200 Parsonage Rd., Edison, NJ 08820. TEL 201-549-0665. Ed. Roderic F. Schmidt. index. cum.index: 1914-1916. circ. 1,500. (back issues avail.) Indexed: Biol.Abstr. Abstr.Hyg. Rev.Appl.Entomol. Trop.Dis.Bull.
Formerly (until 1975): New Jersey Mosquito Extermination Association. Proceedings.

595.7   NZ   ISSN 0077-9962
NEW ZEALAND ENTOMOLOGIST. 1951. a. NZ.$15. Entomological Society of New Zealand, Entomology Division, D.S.I.R., Private Bag, Auckland, New Zealand. Ed. T. K. Crosby. bk. rev. index in vols. 1-4. circ. 700. Indexed: Biol.Abstr. Rev.Appl.Entomol. Ind.Sci.Rev.

NOTIZIARIO SULLE MALATTIE DELLE PIANTE. see *BIOLOGY — Botany*

595.7   US   ISSN 0362-2622
OCCASIONAL PAPERS IN ENTOMOLOGY. 1959. irreg. exchange basis. Department of Food and Agriculture, Division of Plant Industry, Analysis & Identification, 1220 N St., Sacramento, CA 95814. TEL 916-445-5421. Ed. Fred G. Andrews. illus. circ. 200. Indexed: Biol.Abstr. Zoo.Rec.
Continues: California. Bureau of Entomology. Occasional Papers.

OFFENBACHER VEREIN FUER NATURKUNDE. ABHANDLUNGEN. see *BIOLOGY — Botany*

OFFENBACHER VEREIN FUER NATURKUNDE. BERICHT. see *BIOLOGY — Botany*

OPERA LILLOANA. see *BIOLOGY — Botany*

595.7   US   ISSN 0030-5316
ORIENTAL INSECTS; an international journal of systematic entomology of the old world tropics. (Text in English) 1967. a. $23 to individuals; institutions $46. Association for the Study of Oriental Insects, Box 13148, Gainesville, FL 32604-1148. TEL 904-392-9279. Eds. V. K. Gupta, M. S. Mani. adv. bk. rev. abstr. bibl. charts. illus. index. circ. 300. (back issues avail.; reprint service avail. from UMI) Indexed: Biol.Abstr. Curr.Cont. Entomol.Abstr. Indian Sci.Abstr. Zoo.Rec. Rev.Appl.Entomol. Soils & Fert.

595.7   US
ORIENTAL INSECTS MONOGRAPHS SERIES. (Text in English) 1972. irreg. $45 per vol. Association for the Study of Oriental Insects, Box 13148, Gainesville, FL 32604-1148. TEL 904-392-9279. Ed. V.K. Gupta. circ. 200. (back issues avail.; reprint service avail. from UMI)

OSAKA MUSEUM OF NATURAL HISTORY. SPECIAL PUBLICATIONS/OSAKA-SHIRITSU-SHIZENSHI-HAKUBUTSUKAN-SHUZO-SHIRYO-MOKUROKU. see *BIOLOGY*

595.7   UR
PARAZITY, PARAZITOZY TA SHLIAKHYIKH LIKVIDATSII. (Text in Ukrainian; summaries in Russian) 1972. irreg. 1.94 Rub. Akademiya Nauk Ukrainskoi S.S.R., Institut Zoologii, Ul. Lenina, 15, Kiev, Ukrainian S.S.R., U.S.S.R. illus.

PLANT PROTECTION RESEARCH INSTITUTE. ANNUAL REPORT. see *AGRICULTURE — Crop Production And Soil*

595.7   GE   ISSN 0070-7279
REICHENBACHIA; Schriftenreihe fuer taxonomische Entomologie. (Text in English, French, German) 1962. irreg. price varies. Staatliches Museum fuer Tierkunde in Dresden, Augustusstr. 2, 8010 Dresden, E. Germany (D.D.R.) Ed. Rainer Emmrich. bk. rev. circ. 350. Indexed: Biol.Abstr. Zoo.Rec.

BIOLOGY — GENETICS

595.7   BL   ISSN 0085-5626
REVISTA BRASILEIRA DE ENTOMOLOGIA. (Text in Portuguese and English; summaries in English) 1954. a. $30. Sociedade Brasileira de Entomologia, Caixa Postal 9063, 01051 Sao Paulo, Brazil. Ed. Ubirajara Ribeiro Martins de Souza. bk. rev. circ. 650. Indexed: Biol.Abstr. Bull.Signal. Entomol.Abstr. Rev.Appl.Entomol. Zoo.Rec.

595.7   CL   ISSN 0034-740X
REVISTA CHILENA DE ENTOMOLOGIA. (Text in English, German and Spanish) 1951. irreg. $15. Sociedad Chilena de Entomologia, Casilla 21132, Santiago 21, Chile. adv. bk. rev. bibl. charts. illus. circ. 500. Indexed: Biol.Abstr. Rev.Appl.Entomol.

595.7   PE   ISSN 0080-2425
REVISTA PERUANA DE ENTOMOLOGIA. (Text in English and Spanish; summaries in English) 1958. a. S.50000($8) Sociedad Entomologica del Peru, Apdo. 4796, Lima 100, Peru. Ed. Pedro G. Aguilar. adv. bk. rev. circ. 1,000. Indexed: Biol.Abstr. Rev.Appl.Entomol.

595.7   UK   ISSN 0080-4363
ROYAL ENTOMOLOGICAL SOCIETY OF LONDON. SYMPOSIA. 1961. biennial. Royal Entomological Society, 41 Queen's Gate, London SW7 5HU, England. circ. 2,000. Indexed: Biol.Abstr. Zoo.Rec. Rev.Appl.Entomol.

SERICULTURAL EXPERIMENT STATION. ANNUAL REPORT/SANSHI SHIKENJO, NEMPO. see *AGRICULTURE*

595.7   NE   ISSN 0080-8954
SERIES ENTOMOLOGICA. 1966. irreg., vol. 41, 1987. price varies. Dr. W. Junk Publishers, Spuiboulevard 50, 3311 GR Dordrecht, Netherlands (U.S. address: Kluwer Academic Publishers, 101 Phillip Drive, Assinippi Park, Norwell, MA 02061) Eds. E. Schimitschek, K. A. Spencer. Indexed: Biol.Abstr.

595.7   JA   ISSN 0037-3680
SHIKOKU ENTOMOLOGICAL SOCIETY. TRANSACTIONS/SHIKOKU KONCHU GAKKAI KAIHO. (Text in English) 1950. irreg. price varies. Shikoku Entomological Society - Shikoku Konchu Gakkai, c/o Eime University, College of Agriculture, Entomological Laboratory, 3-5-7 Tarumi, Matsuyama 790, Japan. bibl. charts. illus. circ. 450. Indexed: Biol.Abstr. Rev.Appl.Entomol.

595.7   UA   ISSN 0081-0983
SOCIETE ENTOMOLOGIQUE D'EGYPTE. BULLETIN/ENTOMOLOGICAL SOCIETY OF EGYPT. BULLETIN. 1908. a, vol. 60, 1976. £E6($11.66) Entomological Society of Egypt, Box 430, Cairo, Egypt. Indexed: Biol.Abstr. Rev.Appl.Entomol.

595.7   UA   ISSN 0081-0991
SOCIETE ENTOMOLOGIQUE D'EGYPTE. BULLETIN. ECONOMIC SERIES. 1966. a., latest vol. 9, 1975. £E3($5) Entomological Society of Egypt, Box 430, Cairo, Egypt. Indexed: Biol.Abstr.

595.7   CN   ISSN 0071-0784
SOCIETE ENTOMOLOGIQUE DU QUEBEC. MEMOIRES. (Text in French; summaries in English) 1968. irreg. Societe Entomologique du Quebec, Complex Scientifique, D-1-54, 2700 rue Einstein, Ste.-Foy, Quebec, Que. G1P 3W8, Canada. TEL 418-656-2131. illus. Indexed: Biol.Abstr.

595.1   BE
SOCIETE ROYALE BELGE D'ENTOMOLOGIE. MEMOIRES. irreg. price varies. Societe Royale Belge d'Entomologie, 29 rue Vautier, 1040 Brussels, Belgium. Indexed: Biol.Abstr. Rev.Appl.Entomol.

595.7   SA
SOUTH AFRICA. DEPARTMENT OF AGRICULTURE. ENTOMOLOGY MEMOIRS. 1923. irreg., (approx. 4/yr.) price varies. ‡ Department of Agriculture and Water Supply, Private Bag X144, Pretoria 0001, South Africa. Ed. P.J.J. Steyn. charts. illus. stat. circ. 700. Indexed: Biol.Abstr. Forest.Abstr. Forest Prod.Abstr. Rev.Appl.Entomol.
     Former titles: South Africa. Department of Agriculture and Fisheries. Entomology Memoirs; South Africa. Department of Agricultural Technical Services. Entomology Memoirs (ISSN 0013-8940)

595.7   US   ISSN 0172-6188
SPRINGER SERIES IN EXPERIMENTAL ENTOMOLOGY. 1979. irreg., latest 1986. Springer Verlag, 175 Fifth Ave., New York, NY 10010 TEL 212-460-1500. (Also Berlin, Heidelberg, Tokyo and Vienna) Ed. T. A. Miller. (reprint service avail. from ISI)

595.7   GE   ISSN 0373-8981
STAATLICHES MUSEUM FUER TIERKUNDE IN DRESDEN. ENTOMOLOGISCHE ABHANDLUNGEN. (Text in English, French and German) 1961. irreg. price varies. Staatliches Museum fuer Tierkunde in Dresden, Augustusstr. 2, 8010 Dresden, E. Germany (D.D.R.) Ed. Rainer Emmrich. bk. rev. circ. 550. Indexed: Biol.Abstr. Zoo.Rec.

STATE BIOLOGICAL SURVEY OF KANSAS. TECHNICAL BULLETIN. see *BIOLOGY — Botany*

STATION BIOLOGIQUE DE BESSE EN CHANDESSE. ANNALES. see *BIOLOGY — Abstracting, Bibliographies, Statistics*

595.7   US
STUDIES ON THE MORPHOLOGY AND SYSTEMATICS OF SCALE INSECTS. (Subseries of: Virginia Polytechnic Institute and State University. Research Division. Bulletins) 1969. irreg. exchange basis only. Virginia Polytechnic Institute and State University, Department of Entomology, Blacksburg, VA 24061. TEL 703-961-5163. Ed. Mary C. Holliman. illus. circ. 2,100.
     Formerly: Bulletin on Scale Insects.

TASMANIA. DEPARTMENT OF AGRICULTURE. INSECT PEST SURVEY. see *AGRICULTURE — Crop Production And Soil*

595.7   630   500   011   US
THOMAS SAY FOUNDATION MONOGRAPHS. 1916. irreg. price varies. Entomological Society of America, 4603 Calvert Rd., College Park, MD 20740. TEL 301-864-1334. Ed. Morris Rockstein. circ. 500. Indexed: Agri.Ind.

595.7   NE   ISSN 0040-7496
TIJDSCHRIFT VOOR ENTOMOLOGIE. (Text in Dutch, English, French and German) 1858. a. fl.300. Nederlandse Entomologische Vereniging, Plantage Middenlaan 64, 1018 DH Amsterdam, Netherlands. Ed.Bd. charts. illus. Indexed: Biol.Abstr. Rev.Appl.Entomol.

595.7   US   ISSN 0082-6391
TRIBOLIUM INFORMATION BULLETIN. 1958. a. $20 to individuals; institutions $25. California State University, San Bernardino, School of Natural Sciences, San Bernardino, CA 92407. TEL 714-887-7394. Ed. A. Sokoloff. circ. 125. (also avail. in microfilm)

595.7   US   ISSN 0068-6417
UNIVERSITY OF CALIFORNIA PUBLICATIONS IN ENTOMOLOGY. 1906. irreg. price varies. University of California Press, 2120 Berkeley Way, Berkeley, CA 94720. TEL 415-642-4247. Indexed: Biol.Abstr. Abstr.Hyg. Rev.Appl.Entomol. Trop.Dis.Bull.

595.7   US
VIRGINIA POLYTECHNIC INSTITUTE AND STATE UNIVERSITY. DEPARTMENT OF ENTOMOLOGY. OCCASIONAL PAPERS. 1976. irreg. Virginia Polytechnic Institute and State University, Department of Entomology, Blacksburg, VA 24061. TEL 703-961-6341.

595.7   US   ISSN 0043-0773
WASHINGTON STATE ENTOMOLOGICAL SOCIETY PROCEEDINGS. 1954. irreg., 1-2/yr. $5. ‡ Washington State Entomological Society, Washington State University, Dept. of Entomology, Pullman, WA 99164-6432. TEL 509-335-8128. Ed. Roger D. Akre. bk. rev. charts. illus. circ. 150.

BIOLOGY — Genetics

575.1   591.15   581.15   CS
ACTA MUSEI MORAVIAE. SCIENTIA NATURALES 3: FOLIA MENDELIANA. (Text in Czech, English, German; summaries in English) 1973. a. $2. Moravske Muzeum, Nam.25, Unora 6, 659 37 Brno, Czechoslovakia. Ed. Vitezslav Orel. Indexed: Biol.Abstr.
     Issued 1966-1972 as: Folia Mendeliana (ISSN 0085-0748)

ACTA RADIOBOTANIKA ET GENETIKA/ HOSHASEN IKUSHUJO KENKYU HOKOKU. see *BIOLOGY*

591.15   GW   ISSN 0344-208X
ADVANCES IN ANIMAL BREEDING AND GENETICS/FORSTSCHRITTE DER TIERZUETUNG UND ZUECHTUNGSBIOLOGIE. (Text and summaries in English, German) 1979. irreg., no.3, 1982. price varies. Verlag Paul Parey (Hamburg), Spitalerstr. 12, 2000 Hamburg 1, W. Germany (B.R.D.)

573.1   US   ISSN 0065-2660
ADVANCES IN GENETICS. 1947. irreg., vol.23, 1985. Academic Press, Inc., Orlando, FL 32887. TEL 305-345-2000. Ed. M. Demerec. Indexed: Biol.Abstr. Biol.& Agr.Ind. Ind.Med. Sci.Cit.Ind. Anim.Breed.Abstr. Abstr.Hyg. Ind.Sci.Rev. Plant Breed.Abstr. Trop.Dis.Bull.

573.21   US   ISSN 0065-275X
ADVANCES IN HUMAN GENETICS. 1970. irreg. price varies. Plenum Publishing Corp., 233 Spring St., New York, NY 10013. TEL 212-620-8047. Eds. K. Hirschhorn, H. Harris. Indexed: Biol.Abstr. Chem.Abstr. Ind.Med. Sci.Cit.Ind. Ind.Sci.Rev.

591.15   575.1   US   ISSN 0066-4197
ANNUAL REVIEW OF GENETICS. 1967. a. $31. Annual Reviews Inc., 4139 El Camino Way, Palo Alto, CA 94306. TEL 415-493-4400. Ed. Allan Campbell. bibl. index. cum.index. (back issues avail.; reprint service avail. from ISI) Indexed: Biol.Abstr. Biol.& Agr.Ind. Chem.Abstr. Curr.Cont. Ind.Med. Sci.Cit.ind. Abstr.Hyg. Anim.Breed.Abstr. Biotech.Abstr. Forest.Abstr. Forest Prod.Abstr. Helminthol.Abstr. Ind.Sci.Rev. M.M.R.I. Plant Breed.Abstr. Rev.Plant Path. Trop.Dis.Bull.

575.1   IT   ISSN 0066-9830
ASSOCIAZIONE GENETICA ITALIANA. ATTI. (Text and summaries in English or Italian) 1955. a. L.20.000($7) Associazione Genetica Italiana, c/o Istituto di Biologia Animale, Via Loredan 10, 35100 Padova, Italy. Ed. G.A. Danieli. circ. 300. Indexed: Biol.Abstr. Curr.Cont.

575.1   US
BENCHMARK PAPERS IN GENETICS. (Each vol. has distinctive title) 1974. irreg., vol. 14, 1984. price varies. Van Nostrand Reinhold Company, 7625 Empire Dr., Florence, KY 41042. TEL 606-525-6600. Ed. D. L. Jameson. illus. index. Indexed: Biol.Abstr.

BENCHMARK PAPERS IN SYSTEMATIC AND EVOLUTIONARY BIOLOGY. see *BIOLOGY*

591.15   AG   ISSN 0067-9720
BOLETIN GENETICO. (Text and summaries in English and Spanish) 1965. irreg., no. 13, 1985. $15 or exchange. Instituto Nacional de Tecnologia Agropecuaria, Centro de Investigaciones en Ciencias Agronomicas, Departamento de Genetica, Casilla de Correo No. 25, 1712 Castelar, Argentina. Indexed: Biol.Abstr. VITIS.

581   JA   ISSN 0574-9549
C I S. (Chromosome Information Service) (Text in English) 1960. s-a. $24. Society of Chromosome Research - Senshokutai Gakkai, c/o The Research Institute of Evolutionary Biology, 2-4 Kamiyoga, Setagaya-ku, Tokyo 158, Japan. Ed. T.H. Yosida. circ. 500. Indexed: Biol.Abstr. Anim.Breed.Abstr. Plant Breed.Abstr.

575   SZ   ISSN 0376-4230
CONTRIBUTIONS TO VERTEBRATE EVOLUTION. (Text in English) irreg. price varies. S. Karger AG, Allschwilerstrasse 10, P.O. Box, CH-4009 Basel, Switzerland. Eds. M.K. Hecht, F.S. Szalay. (reprint service avail. from ISI) Indexed: Biol.Abstr. GeoRef.

575.005 US ISSN 0071-3260
EVOLUTIONARY BIOLOGY. Variant title:
Monographs in Evolutionary Biology. 1967. irreg.,
vol. 11, 1978. price varies. Plenum Publishing Corp.,
233 Spring St., New York, NY 10013. TEL 212-
741-6680. Eds. Max Hecht, Bruce Wallace. Indexed:
Biol.Abstr. Sci.Cit.Ind. GeoRef. Ind.Sci.Rev.

GAMMA FIELD SYMPOSIA. see *AGRICULTURE*

575.1   576   US   ISSN 0196-3716
GENETIC ENGINEERING; principles and methods.
1981. irreg., vol. 4, 1983. Academic Press Inc.,
Orlando, FL 32887. TEL 305-345-2000. Ed. R.
Williamson. Indexed: Chem.Abstr. Biotech.Abstr.

575.1   GE
GENETIK; Grundlagen, Ergebnisse und Probleme in
Einzeldarstellungen. 1963. irreg. VEB Gustav
Fischer Verlag, Villengang 2, GDR-6900 Jena, E.
Germany (D.D.R.) Ed. Dr. H. Stubbe. (reprint
service avail. from ISI) Indexed: Biol.Abstr.

575.1   SZ   ISSN 0378-9861
HUMAN GENE MAPPING. (Former name of
sponsoring body: National Foundation, March of
Dimes) (Text in English) irreg. price varies. (March
of Dimes Birth Defects Foundation, US) S. Karger
AG, Allschwilerstrasse 10, P.O. Box, CH-4009
Basel, Switzerland. circ. 800. Indexed: Biol.Abstr.
Chem.Abstr. Curr.Cont. Ind.Med.

573.21   US   ISSN 0172-7699
HUMAN GENETICS. SUPPLEMENT. 1978. irreg.,
vol.2, 1981. price varies. Springer-Verlag, 175 Fifth
Ave., New York, NY 10010 TEL 212-460-1500.
(Also Berlin, Heidelberg, Tokyo and Vienna) (also
avail. in microform from UMI; reprint service avail.
from ISI) Indexed: Ind.Med.

I C H E INTERNATIONAL COMMISSION ON
HUMAN ECOLOGY. see *ANTHROPOLOGY*

I.C.R. SCIENTIFIC REPORT. see *MEDICAL
SCIENCES — Cancer*

630   II   ISSN 0374-826X
INDIAN JOURNAL OF HEREDITY. (Text in
English) 1969. irreg. (approx. q.) $38. Genetic
Association of India, Izatnagar-243122, India. Ed.
N.S. Sidhu. adv. bk. rev. circ. 500. (back issues
avail.) Indexed: Biol.Abstr. Chem.Abstr.
Excerp.Med. Anim.Breed.Abstr. Plant
Breed.Abstr.

INFORMATIONS ANNUELLES DE
CARYOSYSTEMATIQUE ET
CYTOGENETIQUE. see *BIOLOGY — Botany*

591.15   KE
INSTITUTE OF PRIMATE RESEARCH. ANNUAL
REPORT. 1981. a. Institute of Primate Research,
P.O. Box 114, Limuru, Kenya.

595.7   KE
INTERNATIONAL CENTRE OF INSECT
PHYSIOLOGY AND ECOLOGY. ANNUAL
REPORT. 1973. a. International Centre of Insect
Physiology and Ecology, Box 30772, Nairobi,
Kenya. illus.

575   UR   ISSN 0301-391X
ITOGI NAUKI I TEKHNIKI: GENETIKA
CHELOVEKA. irreg., latest vol.6, 1982. price
varies. Vsesoyuznyi Institut Nauchno-Tekhnicheskoi
Informatsii (VINITI), Ul. Baltiiskaya, 14, Moscow
A-219, Russian S.F.S.R., U.S.S.R. (Subscr. to:
Mezhdunarodnaya Kniga, Dimitrova ul. 39, 113095
Moscow, Russian S.F.S.R., U.S.S.R.)

574   575   US
JACKSON LABORATORY SCIENTIFIC REPORT.
a. free. Jackson Laboratory, 600 Main St., Bar
Harbor, ME 04609. TEL 207-288-3371. Ed. Dr.
Barbara H. Sanford. circ. 2,000.
Formerly: Jackson Laboratory Annual Report.

616.8   US
JAMES ARTHUR LECTURE ON THE
EVOLUTION OF THE HUMAN BRAIN. 1956.
irreg., no.47, 1977. price varies. American Museum
of Natural History, Central Park W. at 79th St.,
New York, NY 10024. TEL 212-873-1300. Ed.
Brenda Jones. circ. 100. Indexed: Biol.Abstr.

575.1   II   ISSN 0253-7605
JOURNAL OF CYTOLOGY AND GENETICS.
(Text in English) vol. 12, 1977. a. Rs.50($10)
Society of Cytologists and Geneticists, Department
of Botany, Karnatak University, Dharwar 580003,
India. Indexed: Chem.Abstr. Curr.Cont.
Helminthol.Abstr. Plant Breed.Abstr.

575.1   JA   ISSN 0080-8539
KIHARA SEIBUTSUGAKU KENKYUSHO.
SEIKEN ZIHO/KIHARA INSTITUTE FOR
BIOLOGICAL RESEARCH. REPORT. (Text in
Japanese and English) 1941. a. 1000 Yen($4)
membership. Kihara Institute for Biological
Research - Kihara Seibutsugaku Kenkyusho, 3-122-
21 Mutsukawa, Minami-Ku, Yokohama 232, Japan.
Ed. Hitoshi Kihara. Indexed: Biol.Abstr. VITIS.

KULTURPFLANZE. see *BIOLOGY — Botany*

613.9   SZ   ISSN 0077-0876
MONOGRAPHS IN HUMAN GENETICS. (Text in
English) 1966. irreg. (approx. 1/yr.) price varies. S.
Karger AG, Allschwilerstrasse 10, P.O. Box, CH-
4009 Basel, Switzerland. Ed. R.S. Sparks. (reprint
service avail. from ISI) Indexed: Biol.Abstr.
Chem.Abstr. Curr.Cont. Ind.Med.

575   US   ISSN 0341-5376
MONOGRAPHS ON THEORETICAL AND
APPLIED GENETICS. 1975. irreg., vol.9, 1984.
price varies. Springer Verlag, 175 Fifth Ave., New
York, NY 10010 TEL 212-460-1500. (Also Berlin,
Heidelberg, Tokyo and Vienna) Ed.Bd. (reprint
service avail. from ISI) Indexed: Biol.Abstr.

575   JA   ISSN 0077-4995
NATIONAL INSTITUTE OF GENETICS,
MISHIMA, JAPAN. ANNUAL REPORT/
KOKURITSU IDENGAKU KENKYUSHO,
MISHIMA, JAPAN. NENPO. (Text in English)
1949/50. a. free. National Institute of Genetics -
Monbu-Sho Kokuritsu Idengaku Kenkyusho, 1111
Yata, Mishima 411, Japan. circ. 600.

OXFORD MONOGRAPHS ON MEDICAL
GENETICS. see *MEDICAL SCIENCES*

575.1   UK   ISSN 0265-072X
OXFORD SURVEYS IN EVOLUTIONARY
BIOLOGY. 1984. a. £25($50) Oxford University
Press, Walton St., Oxford OX2 6DP, England. Ed.
Richard Dawkins. bk. rev.

375.1   UK   ISSN 0265-0738
OXFORD SURVEYS ON EUKARYOTIC GENES.
1984. a. £25($50) Oxford University Press, Walton
St., Oxford OX2 6DP, England. Ed. Norman
Maclean.

575.1   SZ   ISSN 0301-0139
PIGMENT CELL. (Text in English) 1973. irreg.
(approx. 1/yr.) price varies. S. Karger AG,
Allschwilerstrasse 10, P.O. Box, CH-4009 Basel,
Switzerland. Ed. R.M. Mackie. (reprint service avail.
from ISI) Indexed: Biol.Abstr. Chem.Abstr.

575   US   ISSN 0733-9003
PROGRESS AND TOPICS IN CYTOGENETICS.
1981. irreg., vol.6, 1985. price varies. Alan R. Liss,
Inc., 41 E. 11th St., New York, NY 10003. TEL
212-475-7700. Indexed: Biol.Abstr. Chem.Abstr.

575.1   US   ISSN 0081-4148
STADLER GENETICS SYMPOSIUM.
PROCEEDINGS. 1971. a. price varies. Plenum
Publishing Corp., 233 Spring St., New York, NY
10013. TEL 212-620-8047. Ed. J.P. Gustafson.
Indexed: Biol.Abstr. Chem.Abstr. Ref.Zh.
Anim.Breed.Abstr.

UNIVERSITY OF FLORIDA. SCHOOL OF
FOREST RESOURCES & CONSERVATION.
COOPERATIVE FOREST GENETICS
RESEARCH PROGRAM. PROGRESS REPORT.
see *FORESTS AND FORESTRY*

575.1   CS
UNIVERZITA KOMENSKEHO. PEDAGOGICKA
FAKULTA V TRNAVE. PRIRODNE VEDY:
BIOLOGIA-GENETIKA. irreg., approx. a. price
varies. Slovenske Pedagogicke Nakladatelstvo,
Sasinkova 5, 815 60 Bratislava, Czechoslovakia.

WHITE PAPER ON HUMAN ECOLOGY. see
ANTHROPOLOGY

BIOLOGY — Microbiology

ACTA MANILANA. see *CHEMISTRY — Organic
Chemistry*

ACTA PATHOLOGICA, MICROBIOLOGICA ET
IMMUNOLOGICA SCANDINAVICA. SECTION
B: MICROBIOLOGY. SUPPLEMENTUM. see
BIOLOGY

576   FI   ISSN 0355-3221
ACTA UNIVERSITATIS OULUENSIS. SERIES D.
MEDICA. (Text in English) 1972. irreg.
Fmk.80($17) University of Oulu, Publications
Committee, 90100 Oulu 10, Finland. Ed. Leo
Hirvonen. cum.index. circ. 500. Indexed: Biol.Abstr.
D.A. Psychol.Abstr.

576   US   ISSN 0065-2164
ADVANCES IN APPLIED MICROBIOLOGY. 1959.
irreg., vol.31 1986. Academic Press Inc., Orlando,
FL 32887. TEL 305-345-2000. Ed. Wayne W.
Umbreit. index. Indexed: Biol.Abstr. Biol.&
Agr.Ind. Excerp.Med. Ind.Med. Sci.Cit.Ind.
Dairy Sci.Abstr. Food Sci.& Tech.Abstr.
Ind.Sci.Rev. Ind.Vet. Rev.Appl.Entomol. Plant
Breed.Abstr. Vet.Bull.

576   US   ISSN 0161-8954
ADVANCES IN AQUATIC MICROBIOLOGY.
1977. irreg., vol.3, 1986. Academic Press Inc.,
Orlando, FL 32887. TEL 305-345-2000. Eds. H. W.
Jannasch, P. J. Williams. Indexed: Biol.Abstr.
Ind.Vet. Vet.Bull.
Formerly: Advances in Microbiology of the Sea
(ISSN 0065-292X)

576   US   ISSN 0065-2911
ADVANCES IN MICROBIAL PHYSIOLOGY. 1967.
irreg., vol.27, 1986. Academic Press Inc., Orlando,
FL 32887. TEL 305-345-2000. Eds. A.H. Rose, J.G.
Morris. Indexed: Biol.Abstr. Chem.Abstr.
Ind.Med. Sci.Cit.Ind. Abstr.Hyg. Ind.Sci.Rev.
Trop.Dis.Bull.

576   US
ADVANCES IN MICROBIOAL ECOLOGY. 1977.
a. price varies. Plenum Publishing Corp., 233 Spring
St., New York, NY 10013. TEL 212-620-8047. Ed.
K.C. Marshall.

576   616   US   ISSN 0065-3527
ADVANCES IN VIRUS RESEARCH. 1953. irreg.,
vol.31, 1986. Academic Press, Inc., Orlando, FL
32887. TEL 305-345-2000. Eds. Kenneth M. Smith,
Max A. Lauffer. index. Indexed: Biol.Abstr.
Chem.Abstr. Excerp.Med. Ind.Med. Sci.Cit.Ind.
Abstr.Hyg. Forest.Abstr. Hort.Abstr. Ind.Sci.Rev.
Ind.Vet. Rev.Appl.Entomol. Rev.Plant Path.
Vet.Bull. Trop.Dis.Bull.

AMERICAN ASSOCIATION OF PATHOLOGISTS
AND BACTERIOLOGISTS. SYMPOSIUM.
MONOGRAPHS. see *MEDICAL SCIENCES*

576   589.9   US   ISSN 0094 8519
AMERICAN SOCIETY FOR MICROBIOLOGY.
ABSTRACTS OF THE ANNUAL MEETING.
1948. a. $15. American Society for Microbiology,
1913 I St., N.W., Washington, DC 20006. TEL 202-
833-9680. index. circ. 7,000. Indexed: Biol.Abstr.
Nutr.Abstr. Dairy Sci.Abstr. Food Sci.&
Tech.Abstr. Ind.Vet. Soils & Fert. Vet.Bull.
Weed Abstr.
Formerly: Bacteriological Proceedings (ISSN
0067-2777)

576   US
AMERICAN SOCIETY FOR MICROBIOLOGY.
EASTERN PENNSYLVANIA BRANCH.
SYMPOSIA. 1973. a. $16.50. Phenum Publishing
Corporation, 233 Spring St., New York, NY 10013.

576   US
AMERICAN TYPE CULTURE COLLECTION.
CATALOGUE OF ANIMAL AND PLANT
VIRUSES, CHLAMYDIAE, RICKETTSIAE AND
VIRUS ANTISERA. 1986. irreg. a. free. American
Type Culture Collection, 12301 Parklawn Dr.,
Rockville, MD 20852. TEL 302-881-2600. Ed. L.E.
Benade.
Supercedes in part: American Type Culture
Collection. Catalogue of Strains II, Animal Cell
Lines, Animal Viruses, Bacterial Viruses,
Mycoviruses, Plant Viruses, Rickettsiae,
Chlamydiae.

BIOLOGY — MICROBIOLOGY

576.64 589.9   US
AMERICAN TYPE CULTURE COLLECTION. CATALOGUE OF CELL LINES AND HYBRIDOMAS. (Plus annual supplements) irreg. free. American Type Culture Collection, 12301 Parklawn Dr., Rockville, MD 20852. TEL 301-881-2600. Ed. R. Hay.
Supersedes: American Type Culture Collection. Catalogue of Strains 2: Animal Cell Lines, Animal Viruses, Bacterial Viruses, Mycoviruses, Plant Viruses, Rickettsiae, Chlamydiae; Former titles: American Type Culture Collection. Catalogue of Strains 2: Animal Cell Lines, Animal Viruses, Bacterial Viruses, Mycoviruses, Rickettsiae, Chlamydiae; American Type Culture Collection. Catalogue of Strains: 2. Animal Viruses, Rickettsiae, Chlamydiae; American Type Culture Collection. Catalogue of Viruses, Rickettsiae, Chlamydiae (ISSN 0363-2989)

576.64   US
AMERICAN TYPE CULTURE COLLECTION. CATALOGUE OF FUNGI/YEASTS. (Plus annual supplements) 1986. irreg. free in U.S. American Type Culture Collection, 12301 Parklawn Dr., Rockville, MD 20852. TEL 301-881-2600. Eds. S.C. Jong, M.J. Gantt.
Supersedes in part: American Type Culture Collection. Catalogue of Strains 1: Algae, Bacteria, Bacteriophages, Plasmids, Fungi, Plant Viruses and Antisera and Protozoa.

576.64   US
AMERICAN TYPE CULTURE COLLECTION. CATALOGUE OF PROTISTS. ALGAE/PROTOZOA. (Plus annual supplements) 1986. irreg. free in U.S. American Type Culture Collection, 12301 Parklawn Dr., Rockville, MD 20852. TEL 301-881-2600. Eds. P.-M. Daggett, T. Nerad.
Supersedes in part: American Type Culture Collection. Catalogue of Strains 1: Algae, Bacteria, Bacteriophages, Plasmids, Fungi, Plant Viruses and Antisera and Protozoa.

576.64 589.9   US
AMERICAN TYPE CULTURE COLLECTION. CATALOGUE OF RECOMBINANT D N A COLLECTIONS. (Plus annual supplements) irreg. free. American Type Culture Collection, 12301 Parklawn Dr., Rockville, MD 20852. TEL 301-881-2600. Ed. R. Gherna.
Supercedes in part: American Type Culture Collection. Catalogue of Bacteria, Phages, and rD N A Vectors; American Type Culture Collection. Catalogue of Strains 1: Algae, Bacteria, Bacteriophages, Plasmids, Fungi, Plant Viruses and Antisea and Protozoa; Former titles: American Type Culture Collection. Catalogue of Strains 1: Algae, Bacteria, Bacteriophages, Fungi, Plant Viruses and Antisera and Protozoa; American Type Culture Collection. Catalogue of Strains: Algae, Bacteria, Bacteriophages, Fungi and Protozoa (ISSN 0363-2970)

576 574.192   IT   ISSN 0003-4649
ANNALI DI MICROBIOLOGIA ED ENZIMOLOGIA. (Text in Italian; summaries in English or French) 1940. a. L.18000. Universita degli Studi di Milano, Via Celoria 2, Milan, Italy. Ed. G. Ottogalli. bk. rev. bibl. charts. illus. index; cum.index. circ. 500. Indexed: Biol.Abstr. Chem.Abstr. Excerp.Med. Dairy Sci.Abstr. Food Sci.& Tech.Abstr. Helminthol.Abstr. Int.Abstr.Biol.Sci. VITIS.

576   US   ISSN 0066-4227
ANNUAL REVIEW OF MICROBIOLOGY. 1947. a. $31. Annual Reviews Inc., 4139 El Camino Way, Palo Alto, CA 94306. TEL 415-493-4400. Ed. L. Nicholas Ornston. bibl. index. cum.index. (back issues avail.; reprint service avail. from ISI) Indexed: Biol.Abstr. Chem.Abstr. Curr.Cont. Ind.Med. Nutr.Abstr. Sci.Cit.Ind. Abstr.Bull.Inst.Pap.Chem. Abstr.Hyg. Biotech.Abstr. Dairy Sci.Abstr. Food Sci.& Tech.Abstr. Forest.Abstr. Forest Prod.Abstr. Helminthol.Abstr. Hort.Abstr. Ind.Sci.Rev. Ind.Vet. M.M.R.I. Plant Breed.Abstr. Soils & Fert. VITIS. Vet.Bull. Trop.Dis.Bull.

576   US
APPLIED VIROLOGY RESEARCH. 1987. irreg. price varies. Plenum Publishing Corp., 233 Spring St., New York, NY 10013. TEL 212-620-8047. Ed. H.H. Draper.

ARASTIRMA ESERLERI SERISI. see BIOLOGY — Entomology

BAAS BECKING GEOBIOLOGICAL LABORATORY. ANNUAL REPORT. see EARTH SCIENCES — Geology

576   US
BENCHMARK PAPERS IN MICROBIOLOGY. (Each vol. has distinctive title) 1973. irreg., vol.21, 1985. price varies. Van Nostrand Reinhold Company, 7625 Empire Dr., Florence, KY 41042. TEL 606-525-6600. Ed. W. W. Umbreit. illus. index. Indexed: Biol.Abstr.

589.9   US
BERGEY'S MANUAL OF DETERMINATIVE BACTERIOLOGY. a. price varies. Williams and Wilkins, 428 E. Preston St., Baltimore, MD 21202. TEL 301-528-4000.

CHEMIE MIKROBIOLOGIE TECHNOLOGIE DER LEBENSMITTEL. see BIOLOGY — Biological Chemistry

COLLEGES AND UNIVERSITIES GRANTING DEGREES IN MICROBIOLOGY. see EDUCATION — Guides To Schools And Colleges

CONTRIBUTIONS TO MICROBIOLOGY AND IMMUNOLOGY. see MEDICAL SCIENCES — Allergology And Immunology

576   US   ISSN 0070-217X
CURRENT TOPICS IN MICROBIOLOGY AND IMMUNOLOGY. irreg., vol.134, 1986. price varies. Springer-Verlag, 175 Fifth Ave., New York, NY 10010 TEL 212-460-1500. (Also Berlin, Heidelberg, Tokyo and Vienna) (reprint service avail. from ISI) Indexed: Biol.Abstr. Chem.Abstr. Ind.Med. Sci.Cit.Ind. Abstr.Hyg. Ind.Sci.Rev. Ind.Vet. Vet.Bull. Trop.Dis.Bull.
Formerly: Ergebnisse der Mikrobiologie und Immunitaetsforschung.

DENMARK. STATENS HUSDYRBRUGSFORSOG. BERETNING. see AGRICULTURE — Poultry And Livestock

576   US
ECONOMIC MICROBIOLOGY. 1977. irreg., vol.8, 1983. Academic Press Inc., Orlando, FL 32887. TEL 605-345-2000. A. H. Rose. Indexed: Chem.Abstr. Food Sci.& Tech.Abstr.

576   US
EXPERIMENTAL VIROLOGY. 1978. irreg., vol.4, 1983. price varies. Academic Press Inc., Orlando, FL 32887. TEL 305-345-2000. Eds. T.W. Tinsley, F. Brown.

576   GW
FORTSCHRITTE DER MEDIZINISCHEN MIKROBIOLOGIE/PROGRESS IN MEDICAL MICROBIOLOGY. (Text in English or German; summaries in English) 1983. irreg. price varies. Gustav Fischer Verlag, Postfach 720143, Wollgrasweg 49, 7000 Stuttgart 70, W. Germany (B.R.D.) (North American subscr. to: VCH Publishers, 303 N.W. 12th Ave., Deerfield Beach, FL 334412-1705, U.S.A.) Ed. Dr. Ullmann. circ. 5,000. (back issues avail.)

GENETIC ENGINEERING; principles and methods. see BIOLOGY — Genetics

576.64 658   US
HANDBOOK ON HOSPITAL-ASSOCIATED INFECTIONS. irreg., vol.3, 1979. Marcel Dekker, Inc., 270 Madison Ave., New York, NY 10016.

576   US   ISSN 0092-6019
IMMUNOLOGY: AN INTERNATIONAL SERIES OF MONOGRAPHS AND TREATISES. 1971. irreg., vol.6, 1981. Academic Press Inc., Orlando, FL 32887. TEL 305-345-2000. Eds. F. J. Dixon, Jr., H. G. Kunkel.
Formerly: Monographs on Immunology (ISSN 0077-1023)

589.9   GE
INFEKTIONSKRANKHEITEN UND IHRE ERREGER; eine Sammlung von Monographien. 1965. irreg. VEB Gustav Fischer Verlag, Villengang 2, GDR-6900 Jena, E. Germany (D.D.R.) Ed.Bd. (reprint service avail. from ISI) Indexed: Biol.Abstr. Chem.Abstr.

INSTITUT PASTEUR D'ALGERIE. ARCHIVES. see MEDICAL SCIENCES — Communicable Diseases

576   SG
INSTITUT PASTEUR DE DAKAR. RAPPORT SUR LE FONCTIONNEMENT TECHNIQUE. (Text in French) 1938. a. exchange basis. Institut Pasteur Dakar, Box 220, 36 Avenue Pasteur, Dakar, Senegal. Ed. Jean-Pierre Digoutte. Indexed: Biol.Abstr.

INSTITUT PASTEUR HELLENIQUE. ARCHIVES. see MEDICAL SCIENCES — Communicable Diseases

576   JA   ISSN 0073-8751
INSTITUTE FOR FERMENTATION, OSAKA. RESEARCH COMMUNICATIONS/HAKKO KENKYUSHO HOKOKU. (Text and summaries in English) 1963. biennial; no.13, 1987. 1500 Yen per no. Institute for Fermentation - Hakko Kenkyusho, 2-17-85 Juso-honmachi, Yodogawa-ku, Osaka 532, Japan. Ed. Teiji Iijima. cum.index. circ. 1,500. (back issues avail.) Indexed: Biol.Abstr. Rev.Plant Path.
Until no. 4 (1969): Institute for Fermentation, Osaka. Annual Report.

INSTITUTUL DE CERCETARI PENTRU PROTECTIA PLANTELOR. ANALELE/RESEARCH INSTITUTE FOR PLANT PROTECTION. ANNALS. see AGRICULTURE

576.64   US   ISSN 0276-1076
INTERFERON. 1979. irreg., vol.6, 1985. Academic Press Inc., Orlando, FL 32887. TEL 305-345-2000. Ed. I. Gresser.

576   US
INTERNATIONAL BIODETERIORATION SYMPOSIUM. PROCEEDINGS. BIODETERIORATION OF MATERIALS. irreg. $49.50. Halsted Press (Subsidiary of: John Wiley & Sons, Inc.) 605 Third Ave., New York, NY 10016. Eds. A. Harry Walters, E. H. Hueck-van der Plas. illus.

576   US   ISSN 0074-3097
INTERNATIONAL CONFERENCE ON GLOBAL IMPACTS OF APPLIED MICROBIOLOGY. PROCEEDINGS. 1965. irreg. 1970 latest. Halsted Press (Subsidiary of: John Wiley & Sons, Inc.) 605 Third Ave., New York, NY 10016.

576 615   US   ISSN 0733-6373
INTERSCIENCE CONFERENCE ON ANTIMICROBIAL AGENTS AND CHEMOTHERAPY. PROGRAM AND ABSTRACTS. Abbreviated title: I C A A C Program and Abstracts. 1961. a. $10. American Society for Microbiology, 1913 I St. N.W., Washington, DC 20006. TEL 202-833-9680.

576.64 574   JA   ISSN 0075-7357
KYOTO UNIVERSITY. INSTITUTE FOR VIRUS RESEARCH. ANNUAL REPORT/KYOTO DAIGAKU UIRUSU KENKYUSHO NENKAN KIYO. (Text in English) 1958. a. Kyoto University, Institute for Virus Research - Kyoto Daigaku Uirusu Kenkyusho, Shogoin Kawahara-cho, Kyoto 606, Japan. Ed. Seiich Matsumoto. circ. controlled. Indexed: Biol.Abstr. Chem.Abstr.

576   HU   ISSN 0076-2431
MAGYAR TUDOMANYOS AKADEMIA. MIKROBIOLOGIAI KUTATO INTEZET. PROCEEDINGS/HUNGARIAN ACADEMY OF SCIENCES. RESEARCH INSTITUTE FOR MICROBIOLOGY. PROCEEDINGS. 1966. irreg. price varies. Akademiai Kiado, Publishing House of the Hungarian Academy of Sciences, P.O. Box 24, H-1363 Budapest, Hungary. Ed. J.G. Weiszfeiler. Indexed: Biol.Abstr. Chem.Abstr. Excerp.Med.

METHODS IN VIROLOGY. see MEDICAL SCIENCES — Communicable Diseases

576.05   US   ISSN 0098-1540
MICROBIOLOGY (WASHINGTON) 1974. a. $38. American Society for Microbiology, 1913 I St., N.W., Washington, DC 20006. TEL 202-833-9680. Ed. Loretta Leive. (reprint service avail.) Indexed: Chem.Abstr. Dairy Sci.Abstr. Helminthol.Abstr.

589.9   US   ISSN 0300-8398
MICROBIOLOGY ABSTRACTS. SECTION B. BACTERIOLOGY. 1966. m. $561. Cambridge Scientific Abstracts, 5161 River Rd., Bethesda, MD 20816. TEL 301-951-1400. Ed. Pam Clare. adv. bk. rev. abstr. (also avail. in magnetic tape) Indexed: Cal.Tiss.Abstr. Chemorec.Abstr. Oncol.Abstr.
●Also available online. Vendors: DIALOG.

576 US
MICROBIOLOGY SERIES. irreg., vol.18, 1986. price varies. Marcel Dekker, Inc., 270 Madison Ave., New York, NY 10016. TEL 212-889-9595. Ed. Allan I. Laskin. Indexed: GeoRef.

MICROSCOPIA ELECTRONICA AND BIOLOGIA CELULAR. see *BIOLOGY — Microscopy*

MONOGRAFIE PARAZYTOLOGICZNE. see *VETERINARY SCIENCE*

576 SZ ISSN 0077-0965
MONOGRAPHS IN VIROLOGY. (Text in English) 1967. irreg. (approx. 1/yr.) price varies. S. Karger AG, Allschwilerstrasse 10, P.O. Box, CH-4009 Basel, Switzerland. Ed. J.L. Melnick. (reprint service avail. from ISI) Indexed: Biol.Abstr. Chem.Abstr. Curr.Cont. Ind.Med.

576 US
PARASITIC DISEASES. 1981. irreg. price varies. Marcel Dekker, Inc., 270 Madison Ave., New York, NY 10016. TEL 212-696-9000.

576 NE ISSN 0555-3989
PROGRESS IN INDUSTRIAL MICROBIOLOGY. 1959. irreg., vol.22, 1985. price varies. Elsevier Science Publishers B.V., Box 211, 1000 AE Amsterdam, Netherlands. Eds. M.E. Bushell, M.J. Bull. Indexed: Biol.Abstr. Chem.Abstr.

PROGRESS IN MEDICAL VIROLOGY. see *MEDICAL SCIENCES — Communicable Diseases*

576 PY ISSN 0556-6908
REVISTA PARAGUAYA DE MICROBIOLOGIA. (Summaries in English) 1966. a. $10. Universidad Nacional de Asuncion, Facultad de Ciencias Medicas, Catedra de Bacteriologia y Parasitologia, Casilla de Correo 1102, Asuncion, Paraguay. Ed. Dr. Arquimedes Canese. illus. Indexed: Excerp.Med. Ind.Vet. Rev.Appl.Entomol. Vet.Bull. Trop.Dis.Bull.

576 FR ISSN 0081-1068
SOCIETE FRANCAISE DE MICROBIOLOGIE. ANNUAIRE. 1961. triennial. membership. Institut Pasteur, 28 rue du Docteur-Roux, Paris 75015, France.

576 US
SOCIETY FOR APPLIED BACTERIOLOGY. SYMPOSIUM SERIES. 1971. irreg., vol.12, 1984. Academic Press Inc., Orlando, FL 32887. TEL 305-345-2000. Indexed: Biol.Abstr. Chem.Abstr. Ind.Med.

576 US
SOCIETY FOR APPLIED BACTERIOLOGY. TECHNICAL SERIES. irreg., vol.21, 1985. $55. Academic Press Inc., Orlando, FL 32887. TEL 305-345-2000. Indexed: Biol.Abstr. Chem.Abstr.

576 US
SOCIETY FOR GENERAL MICROBIOLOGY. SPECIAL PUBLICATIONS. 1978. irreg., vol.16, 1985. $55. Academic Press Inc., Orlando, FL 32887. Indexed: Chem.Abstr.

576 UK ISSN 0081-1394
SOCIETY FOR GENERAL MICROBIOLOGY. SYMPOSIUM. 1961. irreg., no.36, 1984. $59.50 for latest vol. Cambridge University Press, Edinburgh Bldg., Shaftesbury Rd., Cambridge CB2 2RU, England (and 32 E. 57 St., New York NY 10022) index. Indexed: Biol.Abstr. Chem.Abstr. Rev.Plant Path.

576 US ISSN 0172-6331
SPRINGER SERIES IN MICROBIOLOGY. 1978. irreg., latest 1986. price varies. Springer-Verlag, 175 Fifth Ave., New York, NY 10010 TEL 212-460-1500. (Also Berlin, Heidelberg, Tokyo and Vienna) Ed. M.P. Starr. (reprint service avail. from ISI)

STATION BIOLOGIQUE DE BESSE EN CHANDESSE. ANNALES. see *BIOLOGY — Abstracting, Bibliographies, Statistics*

576 GW ISSN 0723-2020
SYSTEMATIC AND APPLIED MICROBIOLOGY. (Text in English, French and German) 1980. 3/yr. DM.298. Gustav Fischer Verlag, Wollgrasweg 49, D-7000 Stuttgart 70, W. Germany (B.R.D.) (Subscr. to: Verlag Chemie International, Inc., 1020 N.W. 6th St., Deerfield Beach, FL 33441) Ed. Dr. O. Kandler. circ. 800. (back issues avail.) Indexed: Biol.Abstr. Chem.Abstr. Excerp.Med. Ind.Med. ASCA. Abstr.Hyg. Dairy Sci.Abstr. Helminthol.Abstr. Ind.Vet. Rev.Appl.Entomol. Rev.Plant Path. Vet.Bull. Trop.Dis.Bull.
Formerly: Zentralblatt fuer Bakteriologie, Mikrobiologie und Hygiene (ISSN 0172-5564)

576 US ISSN 0082-2515
TECHNIQUES IN PURE AND APPLIED MICROBIOLOGY. 1969. irreg., unnumbered, latest, 1980. price varies. John Wiley & Sons, Inc., 605 Third Ave., New York, NY 10016. TEL 212-850-6000. Ed. Carl-Goeran Heden.

576 JA ISSN 0082-481X
UNIVERSITY OF TOKYO. INSTITUTE OF APPLIED MICROBIOLOGY. REPORTS. (Text in European languages) 1961. a. controlled free circ. University of Tokyo, Institute of Applied Microbiology - Tokyo Daigaku Oyo Biseibutsu Kenkyusho, 1-1-1 Yayoi, Bunkyo-ku, Tokyo 113, Japan. Ed. Hivea Saito. author index.

UNIVERSITY OF WAIKATO. ANTARCTIC RESEARCH UNIT. REPORT. see *EARTH SCIENCES — Geology*

576 616 US ISSN 0083-6591
VIROLOGY MONOGRAPHS/VIRUSFORSCHUNG IN EINZELDARSTELLUNGEN. 1968. irreg., vol.18, 1981. price varies. Springer-Verlag, 175 Fifth Ave., New York, NY 10010 TEL 212-460-1500. (Also Berlin, Heidelberg, Tokyo and Vienna) (reprint service avail. from ISI) Indexed: Biol.Abstr. Ind.Med.
Formerly: Handbuch der Virusforschung.

576 591.192 FI ISSN 0358-6758
WALTER AND ANDREE DE NOTTBECK FOUNDATION SCIENTIFIC REPORTS. (Text and summaries in English) 1976. irreg. Walter and Andree de Nottbeck Foundation, Tvarminne Zoological Station, SF-10900 Hangoenne, Finland (Subscr. to: c/o C.-A. Haeggstrom, Fabiansgatan 24A, SF-00100 Helsingfors, Finland) Ed. Carl-Adam Haeggstrom. circ. 250. (back issues avail.)

ZENTRALBLATT FUER BAKTERIOLOGIE, PARASITENKUNDE, INFEKTIONSKRANKHEITEN UND HYGIENE. SERIES A; MEDIZINISCHE MIKROBIOLOGIE UND PARASITOLOGIE. see *MEDICAL SCIENCES — Communicable Diseases*

BIOLOGY — Microscopy

A A F M PROCEEDINGS OF ANNUAL MEETING. (American Association of Feed Microscopists) see *MEETINGS AND CONGRESSES*

ADVANCES IN OPTICAL AND ELECTRON MICROSCOPY. see *PHYSICS — Optics*

578 574.8 UK
ELECTRON MICROSCOPY OF PROTEINS. 1981. irreg. price varies. Academic Press Inc. (London) Ltd., 24-28 Oval Rd., London NW1 7DX, England (Dist. in U.S. by: Academic Press, Inc., 111 Fifth Ave., New York, NY 10003) Eds. J.R. Harris, R. W. Horne.

578 US ISSN 0424-8201
ELECTRON MICROSCOPY SOCIETY OF AMERICA. PROCEEDINGS. (Proceedings 1-24 (1942-66) not published) 1967, 25th. a. $25. Claitors Publishing Division, 3165 S. Acadian, Box 3333, Baton Rouge, LA 70821. TEL 504-344-0476. Ed. William Bailey. circ. 700. Indexed: Chem.Abstr.

578 535.84 SA ISSN 0250-0418
ELECTRON MICROSCOPY SOCIETY OF SOUTHERN AFRICA. PROCEEDINGS/ ELEKTRONMIKROSKOPIEVERENIGING VAN SUIDELIKE AFRIKA. VERRIGTINGS. (Text mainly in English; some Afrikaans) 1971. a. R.17($15) Electron Microscopy Society of Southern Africa, c/o E.M. Veenstra, Department of Anatomy, University of the Witwatersrand, Box 1176, Johannesburg 2000, South Africa. circ. 200. (back issues avail.) Indexed: Biol.Abstr. Chem.Abstr. Excerp.Med.

578 IS ISSN 0071-2647
EUROPEAN CONGRESS ON ELECTRON MICROSCOPY. quadrennial; 6th, Jerusalem, 1976. (Israel Society of Electron Microscopy) Tal International, Inquire: Prof. D. Danon, Weizmann Institute of Science, Rehovot, Israel.
Proceedings published in host country

578 YU ISSN 0015-9298
FRAGMENTA BALCANICA MUSEI MACEDONICI SCIENTIARUM NATURALIUM.* 1954. irreg., (5-9/yr.) Prirodonaucen Muzej na Makedonija, Bulevar Ilinden 66, 91000 Skopje, Yugoslavia. Indexed: Biol.Abstr. Rev.Appl.Entomol.

JAHRBUCH FUER BIOTECHNOLOGIE. see *BIOLOGY — Biophysics*

578 GW ISSN 0076-6771
METHODENSAMMLUNG DER ELEKTRONENMIKROSKOPIE. 1970. irreg., no.11, 1984. DM.817 (DM 653.60 to members) (Deutsche Gesellschaft fuer Elektronenmikroskopie e.V.) Wissenschaftliche Verlagsgesellschaft mbH, Postfach 40, 7000 Stuttgart 1, W. Germany (B.R.D.) Eds. G. Schimmel, W. Vogell.

578.46 GW
MICROMORPHOLOGY OF DIATOM VALVES. (Text in English) 1961. a. DM.120. J. Cramer in Gebrueder Borntraeger Verlagsbuchhandlung, Johannesstr. 3A, D-7000 Stuttgart 1, W. Germany (B.R.D.) Ed. J.G. Helmcke. circ. 170.
Formerly: Diatomeenschalen im Elektronenmikroskopischen Bild (ISSN 0070-4687)

578 576 AG ISSN 0326-3142
MICROSCOPIA ELECTRONICA AND BIOLOGIA CELULAR. (Text in English, Portuguese, Spanish; abstracts in English) 1972. a. (in 2 vols.) Bs.135($30) to individuals; institutions $40. Instituto de Histologia y Embriologia, Facultad de Ciencias Medicas, Universidad Nacional de Cuyo, Casilla de Correo 56, 5500 Mendoza, Argentina (Subscr. addr.: Centro Regional de Investigaciones Cientificas y Tecnologicas, Casilla de Correo 131, 5500 Mendoza, Argentina) Eds. Mario H. Burgos, Ramon S. Piezzi. adv. charts. illus. index. circ. controlled. Indexed: Curr.Cont. Excerpta.Med. Ind.Med.
Formerly (until 1983): Revista de Microscopia Electronica.

578 GW ISSN 0342-958X
MICROSCOPICA ACTA. SUPPLEMENTA. irreg. price varies. S. Hirzel Verlag, Postfach 347, 7000 Stuttgart 1, W. Germany (B.R.D.)

578 CN
MICROSCOPICAL SOCIETY OF CANADA. PROCEEDINGS. (Text mainly in English; occasionally in French) 1974. a. Can.$15. Microscopical Society of Canada, 150 College St., Toronto, Ont. M5S 1A8, Canada. TEL 416-978-8896. Ed. G.N. Bance. adv. circ. 500. Indexed: Biol.Abstr. GeoRef.

ULTRASTRUCTURAL PATHOLOGY PUBLICATION. see *BIOLOGY — Cytology And Histology*

BIOLOGY — Ornithology

see also Agriculture–Poultry and Livestock; Pets

BIOLOGY — ORNITHOLOGY

598.2   PL   ISSN 0001-6454
ACTA ORNITHOLOGICA. (Text in English; summaries in English, Polish and Russian) irreg., vol.20 (no.3), 1984. price varies. (Polska Akademia Nauk, Instytut Zoologii) Panstwowe Wydawnictwo Naukowe, Miodowa 10, 00-251 Warsaw, Poland (Dist. by: Ars Polona, Krakowskie Przedmiescie 7, 00-068 Warsaw, Poland) Ed. M. Gramadzki. illus. circ. 810. Indexed: Biol.Abstr. Ref.Zh. Key Word Ind.Wildl.Res. Zoo Rec.

598.2   PL   ISSN 0137-1746
AKADEMIA ROLNICZA, POZNAN. ROCZNIKI. ORNITOLOGIA STOSOWANA. (Text in Polish; summaries in English and Russian) 1966. irreg. price varies. Akademia Rolnicza, Poznan, Ul. Wojska Polskiego 28, 60-637 Poznan, Poland. Indexed: Bibl.Agri.

598.2   GW   ISSN 0003-3154
ANGEWANDTE ORNITHOLOGIE/APPLIED ORNITHOLOGY. (Text mostly in German, occasionally in English, French, Italian) 1961. irreg. DM.16. Biologie-Verlag, Postfach 1449, 6200 Wiesbaden, W. Germany (B.R.D.) Ed. Herbert Bruns. Indexed: Biol.Abstr.

AQUILO. SER. ZOOLOGICA. see *BIOLOGY — Zoology*

598.2   GE
ATLAS DER VERBREITUNG PALAEARKTISCHER VOEGEL. 1960. irreg., latest 1985. (Akademie der Wissenschaften der DDR) Akademie-Verlag, Leipziger Str. 3-4, 1086 Berlin, E. Germany (D.D.R.) Eds. Heinrich Dalhe, I.A. Neufeldt.

BARDSEY OBSERVATORY REPORT. see *BIOLOGY*

598.2   UK
BIRD RESEARCH.* 1937. irreg. World Bird Research Station, Glanton, Northumberland NE66 4AH, England.

598.2   636   US
BIRD WATCH. 1973. irreg. $5. Kansas State University, Bird Populations Institute, Manhattan, KS 66506. TEL 913-532-6011. Ed. Robert LaShelle. bk. rev. circ. 2,400.

598.2   639.9   UK
BIRDWATCHER'S YEARBOOK AND DIARY. 1981. a. £8.25. Buckingham Press, 25 Manor Park, Maids Moreton, Buckingham, Bucks. MK18 1QX, England. Ed. John E. Pemberton. bk. rev. bibl. charts. illus. circ. 3,000.
     Formerly: Birdwatcher's Yearbook (ISSN 0144-364X)

598.2   DK   ISSN 0901-0637
BLAAVAND FUGLESTATION. RAPPORT. a. Kr.20. (Blaavand Fuglestation) Bibliotekscentralen, Telegrafvej 5, DK-2750 Ballerup, Denmark.

598.207   IT
BOLLETTINO DELL'ATTIVITA DI INANELLAMENTO/BULLETIN OF BIRD RINGING ACTIVITY. (Text in Italian) 1981. irreg. free. Istituto Nazionale di Biologia della Selvaggina, Via Stradelli Guelfi 23/A, 40064 Ozzano Emilia (Bo), Italy. Ed. Mario Spagnesi. stat. circ. 400. (back issues avail.)
     Bird-banding

598.2   UK   ISSN 0142-7660
BONNY MOOR HEN. 1978. a. Weardale Field Study Society, c/o Ian Forbes, Ed., Fieldfare, Wearhead, Co. Durham, England. charts. illus. circ. 300.

598.2   UK   ISSN 0068-2675
BRITISH TRUST FOR ORNITHOLOGY. ANNUAL REPORT. 1935. a. membership. British Trust for Ornithology, Beech Grove, Tring, England. Ed. J.J. Wolf. circ. 7,500.

CANADA. NATIONAL MUSEUMS, OTTAWA: PUBLICATIONS IN NATURAL SCIENCE/ PUBLICATIONS DE SCIENCES NATURELLES. see *BIOLOGY — Zoology*

CANADIAN WILDLIFE SERVICE. MONOGRAPH SERIES. see *CONSERVATION*

598.2   UK   ISSN 0262-7655
CHESHIRE ORNITHOLOGICAL ASSOCIATION. BIRD REPORT. 1968. a. £2.50. Cheshire Ornithological Association, c/o P.B. Perkins, 33 Sharston Crescent, Knutsford, Cheshire WA16 8AF, England. adv. illus. charts. circ. 900.

598.2   GW   ISSN 0589-686X
CORAX; Veroeffentlichungen der ornithologischen Arbeitsgemeinschaft fuer Schleswig-Holstein und Hamburg e.V. (Text in German; summaries sometimes in English) 1965. irreg., 2-4 yr. DM.40. Dr. Fridtjof Ziesemer, Ed. & Pub., Greifenberger Str. 11, D-2300 Kiel, W. Germany (B.R.D.) (Subscr. to: Peter Gloe, Muehlenstr. 10, D-2223 Meldorf, W. Germany (B.R.D.)) bk. rev. circ. 700. (back issues avail.) Indexed: Biol.Abstr.

598.2   US
CURRENT ORNITHOLOGY. 1983. irreg. price varies. Plenum Publishing Corp., 233 Spring St., New York, NY 10013. TEL 212-620-8047. Ed. Richard F. Johnson.

598.2   DK   ISSN 0011-6394
DANSK ORNITOLOGISK FORENINGS TIDSSKRIFT. (Text mainly in Danish; summaries in English) 1906. irreg., 2-4/yr. membership. Dansk Ornitologisk Forening - Danish Ornithological Society, Vesterbrogade 140, DK-1620 Copenhagen V, Denmark. Ed. Kaj Kampp. adv. bk. rev. bibl. illus. index. circ. 8,500. Indexed: Biol.Abstr. Key Word Ind.Wildl.Res. Wildlife Rev. Zoo.Rec.

598.2   CN   ISSN 0707-0942
DIRECTORY OF CO-OPERATIVE NATURALISTS' PROJECTS IN ONTARIO. 1976. biennial (with a. supplement) Can.$1.50. Long Point Bird Observatory, Box 160, Port Rowan, Ont. N0E 1M0, Canada. TEL 519-586-2909. Eds. Clive E. and Joy E. Goodwin. circ. 800.

598.2   CN   ISSN 0707-7165
ENVOL/FLIGHT. (Text in English and French) 1978. irreg. membership. Club d'Amateurs d'Oiseaux de Montreal, 228 de la Salle, Mont St. Hilaire, Que. J3H 3C2, Canada.

598.2   SW   ISSN 0283-2852
FAAGLAR I KVISMAREN. (Text in Swedish) 1962. a. Kr.40($5) Kvismare Faagelstation, Hidingsta, 705 90 Orebro, Sweden. Ed. Stattan Bensch. (back issues avail.)
     Formerly: Verksamheten vid Kvismare Faagelstation.

598.2   DK   ISSN 0107-3729
FUGLE. (Text in Danish) 1981. irreg. (4-6/yr.) membership. Dansk Ornitologisk Forening - Danish Ornithological Society, Vesterbrogade 140, DK-1620 Copenhagen V, Denmark. Ed. Joern Eskildsen. adv. illus. circ. 9,000. Indexed: Zoo.Rec.
     Formed by the merger of: Feltornithologen (ISSN 0046-3647) & Fuglevaern.

598.2   DK   ISSN 0108-7282
FUGLE I NORDJYLLAND. no. 18, 1981. a. Kr.42. Nordjysk Ornithologisk Kartotek, Volsted Bygade 25, Volsted, 9530 Stoevring, Denmark. illus.
     Formerly: Nordjysk Ornithologisk Kartotek. Rapport.

598.29   DK   ISSN 0109-9078
FUGLELIVET VED ROSKILDE FJORD. 1983. a. Kr.20. Rapportgruppen, c/o Bo Fisker, Knud den Stores Vej 47A, 4000 Roskilde, Denmark. illus.

GAME CONSERVANCY ANNUAL REVIEW. see *CONSERVATION*

598.2   GE
HANDBUCH DER OOLOGIE. 1960. irreg., latest 1985. Akademie-Verlag Berlin, Leipziger Str. 3-4, 1086 Berlin, E. Germany (D.D.R.) Ed. Wilhelm Meise.

598.2   AG   ISSN 0073-3407
HORNERO/OVEN BIRD. (Text in Spanish; occasionally articles in English, French or Portuguese) 1917. a. $8. Asociacion Ornitologica del Plata, 25 de Mayo 749, 1002 Buenos Aires, Argentina. bk. rev. index. circ. 800. Indexed: Biol.Abstr.

598.2   UK   ISSN 0277-1330
I C B P PARROT WORKING GROUP MEETING. PROCEEDINGS. 1980. irreg., 1st, 1980, St. Lucia. International Council for Bird Preservation, 219c Huntingdon Rd., Cambridge CB3 0DL, England (U.S. address: Smithsonian Institution Press, MNH 336, Washington, DC 20560)

598.2   UK   ISSN 0074-4263
INTERNATIONAL COUNCIL FOR BIRD PRESERVATION. BRITISH SECTION. REPORT. 1937. a. 50p. International Council for Bird Preservation, British Section, c/o Institute of Biology, 20 Queensberry Place, London SW7 2DZ, England. circ. 750.

598.2   UK   ISSN 0074-4271
INTERNATIONAL COUNCIL FOR BIRD PRESERVATION. PROCEEDINGS OF CONFERENCES. (Text in English, French, German; occasionally in Japanese and Spanish) irreg., 16th. 1974, Canberra, Australia; 18th, 1982, Cambridge, England. International Council for Bird Preservation, 219c Huntingdon Rd., Cambridge CB3 0DL, England.

598.2   IE   ISSN 0332-0111
IRISH BIRDS. 1977. a. £5. Irish Wildbird Conservancy, Southview, Church Rd., Greystones, Co. Wicklow, Ireland. TEL 01-875759. Ed. Hugh Brazier. bk. rev. illus. circ. 1,500. Indexed: Biol.Abstr.
     Incorporating: Irish Bird Report.

598.2   UK   ISSN 0261-5525
LINCOLNSHIRE BIRD REPORT. 1979. a. £5. Lincolnshire Bird Club, c/o A.L. Goodall, Ed., 42 Wolsey Way, Lincoln LN2 4QH, England. Ed. A.L. Goodall. circ. 500.
     Incorporating: Gibraltar Point Observatory Report.

598.2   UK   ISSN 0141-4348
LONDON BIRD REPORT. 1936. a. £3. London Natural History Society, Upper Flat, 65 Arthur Rd., London SW19 7DN, England. Ed. A. Moon. circ. 2,000. (back issues avail.)

598.2   US   ISSN 0550-4082
NUTTALL ORNITHOLOGICAL CLUB. PUBLICATIONS. 1957. irreg., no.20, 1983. price varies. Nuttall Ornithological Club, c/o Museum of Comparative Zoology, Harvard Univ., Cambridge, MA 02138. TEL 617-495-2471. Ed. R.A. Paynter, Jr. bibl. charts. illus. stat. circ. 1,000. Indexed: Zoo.Rec.

OFFENBACHER VEREIN FUER NATURKUNDE. ABHANDLUNGEN. see *BIOLOGY — Botany*

OFFENBACHER VEREIN FUER NATURKUNDE. BERICHT. see *BIOLOGY — Botany*

598.2   US   ISSN 0078-6594
ORNITHOLOGICAL MONOGRAPHS. 1964. irreg. American Ornithologists' Union, National Museum of Natural History, Smithsonian Institution, Washington, DC 20560. TEL 202-357-2051. Ed. David W. Johnston. circ. 1,000.

598.2   333.7   US
RAPTOR REPORT. 1973. a. $8 for 2 years. Society for the Preservation of Birds of Prey, Pacific Palisades, CA 90272. Ed. J. Richard Hilton. bk. rev. illus. stat. circ. 800.
     Supersedes: California Condor (ISSN 0045-3927)

RICERCHE DI BIOLOGIA DELLA SELVAGGINA. SUPPLEMENTO. see *BIOLOGY — Zoology*

598.2   UK   ISSN 0260-4736
SANDGROUSE. 1980. a. £5. Ornithological Society of the Middle East, c/o The Lodge, Sandy, Beds. SG19 2DL, England. Ed. Donald Parr. bk. rev. circ. 600. Indexed: Wild Life Rev. Zoo.Rec.
     Formerly: Turkish Bird Report.

598.2   CN   ISSN 0080-6552
SASKATCHEWAN NATURAL HISTORY SOCIETY. SPECIAL PUBLICATIONS. 1958. irreg. price varies. Saskatchewan Natural History Society, Box 414, Raymore, Sask. S0A 3J0, Canada. TEL 306-746-4544. Ed. Mary Gilliland. Indexed: Wild Life Rev.

BIOLOGY — PHYSIOLOGY   171

598.2   UK   ISSN 0036-9144
SCOTTISH BIRDS. 1958. a. £10 to non-members; £25 to libraries. ‡ Scottish Ornithologists Club, 21 Regent Terrace, Edinburgh EH7 5BT, Scotland. Ed. V.M. Thom. adv. bk. rev. charts. illus. index every 2 years. circ. 2,700. Indexed: Biol.Abstr. Geo.Abstr. Wild Life Rev. Zoo.Rec.

598.2   UK   ISSN 0267-9310
SEABIRD. 1969. a. £5.50 to individuals; libraries £7.50. Seabird Group, c/o R.S.P.B., The Lodge, Sandy, Beds. SG19 2DL, England. Ed. M. de L. Brooke. bk. rev. circ. 500.
  Former titles (until 1984): Seabird Report (ISSN 0080-8415) & Seabird Bulletin.

598.2   592 550 581   IT
SOCIETA SARDA DI SCIENZE NATURALI. BOLLETTINO. (Text in English, French and Italian; summaries in English and Italian) 1967. a. L.30000. c/o Istituto di Botanica dell'Universita, Via Muroni 25, 07100 Sassari, Italy. Ed.Bd. bk. rev. index. circ. 600. (back issues avail.) Indexed: Biol.Abstr.

598.2   UK   ISSN 0081-2048
SOMERSET BIRDS. 1924. a. £3. Somerset Ornithological Society, Barnfield, Tower Hill Rd., Crewkerne, Somerset, England. Ed. D.K. Ballance. circ. 500.

598.2 639.9   SA
SOUTHERN BIRDS. (Text in English) 1975. irreg. price varies. Southern African Ornithological Society, Witwatersrand Bird Club, Box 650284, Benmore, Transvaal 2010, South Africa. Ed. Carl J. Vernon. adv. bk. rev. abstr. bibl. circ. 600. (back issues avail.) Indexed: Biol.Abstr. Ind.S.A.Per.

598.2   NO   ISSN 0039-1247
STERNA. (Text in English and Norwegian, Summaries in English) 1951-1978, resumed 1985. a. Kr.30($5) exchange basis. Stavanger Museum, N-4000 Stavanger, Norway. Ed. Olav Runde. bk. rev. charts. illus. index. circ. 2,400. Indexed: Biol.Abstr.

598.2   DK   ISSN 0109-274X
STIGSNAES; rapport. 1981. a. Kr.30. Dansk Ornithologisk Forening i Vestsjaellands, Stigsnaes Fuglestation - Stignaes Bird Observatory, Aalehusvej 18, Raunstrup, 4160 Herlufmagle, Denmark. Ed. Bent Moeller Soerensen. illus.

598.2   US
STUDIES IN AVIAN BIOLOGY. 1978. irreg. price varies. Cooper Ornithological Society, Inc., c/o Martin L. Morton, Biology Department, Occidental College, Los Angeles, CA 90041.
  Supersedes (1900-1974): Pacific Coast Avifauna.

598.2   CN
TCHEBEC. 1970. a. membership. Quebec Society for the Protection of Birds, Box 43, Station B, Montreal, Que. H3B 3J5, Canada. Ed. Richard Yank. illus. stat. circ. 750. (back issues avail.)

598.2   US   ISSN 0040-4543
TEXAS ORNITHOLOGICAL SOCIETY. BULLETIN. 1967. a. $10 membership. Texas Ornithological Society, c/o Angelo State University, Department of Biology, San Angelo, TX 76909. Ed. Terry C. Maxwell. bk. rev. abstr. illus. circ. 800. Indexed: Biol.Abstr. Zoo.Rec.

639.9782   UK
THREATENED BIRDS OF AFRICA AND RELATED ISLANDS. 1985. irreg. latest vol.1, 1985. International Council for Bird Preservation, 219c Huntingdon Rd., Cambridge CB3 0DL, England.

598.2   IS
TORGOS. (Text in Hebrew; summaries in English) irreg. Society for the Protection of Nature, 4 Hashfela St., Tel Aviv 66 183, Israel. Ed. Ofer Bahat.

598.2   US
UNIVERSITY OF CALIFORNIA, DAVIS. GAME BIRD WORKSHOP. PROCEEDINGS. 1971. biennial. $1-3 per no. University of California, Davis, Department of Avian Sciences, Davis, CA 95616. TEL 916-752-3513. Ed. Dr. R. A. Ernst. circ. 175.

598.2   GW
VOGELKUNDLICHE HEFTE EDERTAL. 1975. a. DM.8. Hessische Gesellschaft fuer Ornithologie und Naturschutz, Arbeitskrais Edertal, c/o Karl Sperner, Am Griesfeld 2, 3590 Bad Wildungen-Wega, W. Germany (B.R.D.) Ed.Bd. circ. 750.

598.2   US   ISSN 0511-7542
WESTERN FOUNDATION OF VERTEBRATE ZOOLOGY. OCCASIONAL PAPERS. 1968. irreg. price varies. Western Foundation of Vertebrate Zoology, 1100 Glendon Ave., Ste. 1400, Los Angeles, CA 90024. TEL 213-208-8003. Ed. Jack C. von Bloeker, Jr. circ. 1,000. (back issues avail.) Indexed: Biol.Abstr. Zoo.Rec.

598.2   UK
WILDFOWL. 1948. a. membership. Wildfowl Trust, Slimbridge, Gloucester GL2 7BT, England. Eds. G.V.T. Mathews, M.A. Ogilvie. circ. 3,000. Indexed: Biol.Abstr. Ind.Vet. Vet.Bull. Wild Life Rev.

598.2   ZA
ZAMBIAN ORNITHOLOGICAL SOCIETY OCCASIONAL PAPERS. 1979. irreg., latest no.2, 1979. price varies. Zambian Ornithological Society, Box 33944, Lusaka, Zambia. circ. 300.

BIOLOGY — Physiology

see also Medical Sciences

574.1 612   US   ISSN 0065-244X
ADVANCES IN COMPARATIVE PHYSIOLOGY AND BIOCHEMISTRY. 1962. irreg., vol.8, 1982. Academic Press, Inc., Orlando, FL 32887. TEL 305-345-2000. Ed. O.E. Lowenstein. index. Indexed: Biol.Abstr. Ind.Med.

ADVANCES IN ENZYME REGULATION. see *MEDICAL SCIENCES*

ALFRED BENZON SYMPOSIUM. PROCEEDINGS. see *MEDICAL SCIENCES*

612.6   US   ISSN 0090-5348
ANNUAL EDITIONS: READINGS IN HUMAN DEVELOPMENT. Variant title: Annual Editions: Human Development. 1972. a. $9.50. Dushkin Publishing Group, Inc., Sluice Dock, Guilford, CT 06437. TEL 203-453-4351. Ed. Ian Nielsen. illus.

574.1   US   ISSN 0066-4278
ANNUAL REVIEW OF PHYSIOLOGY. 1939. a. $32. Annual Reviews Inc., 4139 El Camino Way, Palo Alto, CA 94306. TEL 415-493-4400. Ed. Robert M. Berne. bibl. index. cum.index. (back issues avail.; reprint service avail. from ISI) Indexed: Biol.Abstr. Biol.& Agr.Ind. Chem.Abstr. Curr.Cont. Excerp.Med. Ind.Med. Nutr.Abstr. Psychol.Abstr. SSCI. Sci.Cit.Ind. Abstr.Hyg. Anim.Breed.Abstr. Dairy Sci.Abstr. Dent.Ind. Helminthol.Abstr. Ind.Sci.Rev. Ind.Vet. M.M.R.I. Vet.Bull. Trop.Dis.Bull.

612   PO   ISSN 0066-7811
ARQUIVO DE ANATOMIA E ANTROPOLOGIA. (Text in Portuguese; summaries in English, French, German) 1912. a. $10. Universidade de Lisboa, Faculdade de Medicina, Avda. Egas Moniz, Lisbon 4, Portugal. bk. rev. circ. 300. Indexed: Biol.Abstr.

612   US   ISSN 0093-5557
BENCHMARK PAPERS IN HUMAN PHYSIOLOGY. (Each vol. has distinctive title) 1973. irreg., vol.17, 1983. price varies. Van Nostrand Reinhold Company, 7625 Empire Dr., Florence, KY 41042. TEL 606-525-6600. Ed. L.L. Langley. index. Indexed: Biol.Abstr.

612   UK   ISSN 0308-5384
BIOLOGICAL STRUCTURE AND FUNCTION. irreg., no.9, 1983. $69.50 for latest vol. Cambridge University Press, Edinburgh Bldg., Shaftesbury Rd., Cambridge CB2 2RU, England (And 32 E. 57th St., New York NY 10022) Eds. R.J. Harrison, R.M.H. McMinn.

574.1   UK
BRITISH SOCIETY FOR DEVELOPMENTAL BIOLOGY. SYMPOSIA. 1973. irreg., no.7, 1983. $85 for latest vol. Cambridge University Press, Edinburgh Bldg., Shaftesbury Rd., Cambridge CB2 2RU, England (And 32 E. 57th St., New York, NY 10022) Indexed: Biol.Abstr.

574.1   UK
CAMBRIDGE TEXTS IN THE PHYSIOLOGICAL SCIENCES. 1979. irreg., no.4, 1984. $29.95 (cloth) $12.95 (paper) for latest vol. Cambridge University Press, Edinburgh Bldg., Shaftesbury Rd., Cambridge CB2 2RU, England (And 32 E. 57th St., New York, NY 10022) Indexed: Biol.Abstr.

574.1   CH
CHINESE JOURNAL OF PHYSIOLOGY. (Text in English; summaries in English and Chinese) 1927. a. free. Chinese Physiological Society, National Taiwan University School of Medicine, Department of Physiology, Taipei, Taiwan, Republic of China. Ed.Bd. abstr. bibl. charts. illus. circ. 1,000. Indexed: Chem.Abstr. Excerp.Med. Ind.Med.

591.1   AT   ISSN 0155-7742
COMMONWEALTH SCIENTIFIC AND INDUSTRIAL RESEARCH ORGANIZATION. DIVISION OF ANIMAL PRODUCTION REPORT. irreg. C.S.I.R.O., Division of Animal Production, P.O. Box 239, Blacktown 2148, N.S.W., Australia. Indexed: Biol.Abstr.
  Formerly: Commonwealth Scientific and Industrial Research Organization. Division of Animal Physiology. Report. (ISSN 0069-7281)

591.1   AT
COMMONWEALTH SCIENTIFIC AND INDUSTRIAL RESEARCH ORGANIZATION. DIVISION OF ANIMAL PRODUCTION TECHNICAL REPORT. 1969. irreg. free. C.S.I.R.O., Division of Animal Production, Box 239, Blacktown N.S.W. 2148, Australia.
  Formerly: Commonwealth Scientific and Industrial Research Organization. Division of Animal Physiology. Technical Report (ISSN 0084-9014)

CONTRIBUTIONS TO HUMAN DEVELOPMENT. see *MEDICAL SCIENCES*

612   US   ISSN 0069-9705
CONTRIBUTIONS TO SENSORY PHYSIOLOGY. 1965. irreg., vol. 8, 1984. Academic Press, Inc., Orlando, FL 32887. TEL 305-345-2000. Ed. William D. Neff. index. Indexed: Biol.Abstr. Ind.Med.

DENMARK. STATENS HUSDYRBRUGSFORSOG. BERETNING. see *AGRICULTURE — Poultry And Livestock*

574.1   UR   ISSN 0533-1153
FIZIOLOGICHESKI AKTIVNYE VESHCHESTVA; respublikanskii mezhvedomstvennyi sbornik nauchnykh trudov. (Text in Russian) 1966. a. (Akademiya Nauk Ukrainskoi S.S.R., Institut Organicheskoi Khimii) Izdatel'stvo Naukova Dumka, c/o Yu.A. Khramov, Dir, Ul. Repina, 3, Kiev 252 601, Ukrainian S.S.R., U.S.S.R. (Subscr. to: Mezhdunarodnaya Kniga, Moscow, G-200, Russian S.F.S.R., U.S.S.R.) Ed. M.O. Lozinskii. Indexed: Chem.Abstr.

FUNKTIONSANALYSE BIOLOGISCHER SYSTEME. see *BIOLOGY*

574.1   US   ISSN 0072-9876
HANDBOOK OF PHYSIOLOGY. 1959. irreg. price varies. (American Physiological Society) Williams & Wilkins Co., 428 E. Preston St., Baltimore, MD 21202. TEL 301-528-4000. Ed. Victor E. Hall. Indexed: Biol.Abstr.

599.01   US
HAROLD C. MACK SYMPOSIUM. PROCEEDINGS.* irreg. latest issue, 1972. price varies. (Harper Hospital (Detroit), Department of Gynecology and Obstetrics) Charles C. Thomas, Publisher, 2600 S. First St., Springfield, IL 62717. TEL 217-789-8980. (Co-sponsor: Wayne State University) Eds. Harold C. Mack, Alfred I. Sherman.
  Continues: Symposium on the Physiology and Pathology of Human Reproduction (ISSN 0085-7076)

BIOLOGY — ZOOLOGY

574.191 FR ISSN 0073-8565
INSTITUT MICHEL PACHA. ANNALES. 1968. biennial. price varies. Institut Michel Pacha, Laboratoire Maritime de Physiologie, Tamaris-sur-Mer, France. Ed. G. Peres. bk. rev. Indexed: Biol.Abstr. Chem.Abstr. Bull.Signal.

612 US
INSTITUTE FOR ORGONOMIC SCIENCE. ANNALS. 1984. a. $15. Institute for Orgonomic Science, Box 304, Gwynedd Valley, PA 19437.

612 HU ISSN 0539-1113
INTERNATIONAL UNION OF PHYSIOLOGICAL SCIENCES. NEWSLETTER. 1964. irreg. $3. (International Union of Physiological Sciences) Akademiai Kiado, Publishing House of the Hungarian Academy of Sciences, P.O. Box 24, H-1363 Budapest, Hungary (c/o A. Kovach, Experimental Research Department, Semmelweis Medical University, Ulloi Ut 78/A, 1082 Budapest, Hungary) circ. 15,000.

574.1 FR ISSN 0074-946X
INTERNATIONAL UNION OF PHYSIOLOGICAL SCIENCES. PROCEEDINGS OF CONGRESS. irreg., 27th, 1977, Paris. International Union of Physiological Sciences, c/o Dr. J. Scherrer, Department of Physiology, U E R Pitie-Salpetriere, 91 Bd. de l'Hospital, 75634 Paris Cedex 13, France.

574.1 612 UR ISSN 0134-2673
ITOGI NAUKI I TEKHNIKI: FIZIOLOGIYA CHELOVEKA I ZHIVOTNYKH. irreg., latest vol.33, 1987. price varies. Vsesoyuznyi Institut Nauchno-Tekhnicheskoi Informatsii (VINITI), Baltiiskaya ul. 14, Moscow A-219, Russian S.F.S.R., U.S.S.R. (Subscr. to: Mezhdunarodnaya Kniga, Dimitrova ul. 39, 113095 Moscow, Russian S.F.S.R., U.S.S.R.)

612 FR ISSN 0075-4455
JOURNEES DE PHYSIOLOGIE APPLIQUEE AU TRAVAIL HUMAIN. 1959. irreg. 85 F. per no. (Societe d'Ergonomie de la Langue Francaise) N.E.B. Editions Scientifiques, B.P.3, 78350 Jouy-en-Josas, France.

LUNG BIOLOGY IN HEALTH AND DISEASE. see
MEDICAL SCIENCES — Respiratory Diseases

574.1 US ISSN 0079-2020
PHYSIOLOGICAL SOCIETY. MONOGRAPHS. 1953. irreg., no.6, 1985. Academic Press Inc., Orlando, FL 32887. TEL 305-345-2000. Ed.Bd. Indexed: Biol.Abstr. Ind.Med. Nutr.Abstr.

574.1 US
PHYSIOLOGICAL SOCIETY OF PHILADELPHIA. MONOGRAPHS. 1976. irreg. Halsted Press (Subsidiary of: John Wiley & Sons, Inc.) 605 Third Ave., New York, NY 10016. TEL 212-850-6000. Indexed: Biol.Abstr.

PROGRESS IN CLINICAL NEUROPHYSIOLOGY. see *MEDICAL SCIENCES — Psychiatry And Neurology*

574.16 SZ ISSN 0254-105X
PROGRESS IN REPRODUCTIVE BIOLOGY AND MEDICINE. (Text in English) 1976. irreg. (approx. 1/yr.) price varies. S. Karger AG, Allschwilerstrasse 10, P.O. Box, CH-4009 Basel, Switzerland. (reprint service avail. from ISI) Indexed: Biol.Abstr. Chem.Abstr. Curr.Cont. Dairy Sci.Abstr.
Formerly: Progress in Reproductive Biology (ISSN 0304-4262)

574.1 619 US
RAVEN PRESS SERIES IN EXPERIMENTAL PHYSIOLOGY. irreg. Raven Press, 1185 Ave. of the Americas, New York, NY 10036. TEL 212-575-0335.

574.1 540 615 US ISSN 0303-4240
REVIEWS OF PHYSIOLOGY, BIOCHEMISTRY AND EXPERIMENTAL PHARMACOLOGY. irreg., vol.105, 1986. price varies. Springer-Verlag, 175 Fifth Ave., New York, NY 10010 TEL 212-460-1500. (Also Berlin, Heidelberg, Tokyo and Vienna) (reprint service avail. from ISI) Indexed: Biol.Abstr. Chem.Abstr. Ind.Med.
Continues: Ergebnisse der Physiologie, Biologischen Chemie und Experimentellen Pharmakologie.

612 UK ISSN 0081-153X
SOCIETY FOR THE STUDY OF HUMAN BIOLOGY. SYMPOSIA. 1960. irreg., 1970, vol.14. price varies. (Society for the Study of Human Biology) Taylor & Francis Ltd., Rankline Rd., Basingstoke, Hampshire RG24 0PR, England. Ed.Bd. circ. 200. Indexed: Biol.Abstr.

612 UK
SOCIETY FOR THE STUDY OF INBORN ERRORS OF METABOLISM. SYMPOSIA. 1975. a. price varies. M T P Press Ltd., Falcon House, Queen Sq., Lancaster LA1 1RN, England. Indexed: Biol.Abstr. Chem.Abstr.

574.1 US
SOCIETY OF GENERAL PHYSIOLOGISTS. DISTINGUISHED LECTURE SERIES. 1978. irreg. price varies. Raven Press, 1185 Ave. of the Americas, New York, NY 10036. TEL 212-575-0335. Indexed: Biol.Abstr. Curr.Cont.

612 US ISSN 0094-7733
SOCIETY OF GENERAL PHYSIOLOGISTS SERIES. 1945? a. price varies. Raven Press, 1185 Ave. of the Americas, New York, NY 10036. TEL 212-575-0335. Indexed: Biol.Abstr. Chem.Abstr. Curr.Cont. Ind.Med. Sci.Cit.Ind.

574 PL ISSN 0082-5581
STUDIA SOCIETATIS SCIENTIARUM TORUNENSIS. SECTIO G. PHYSIOLOGIA. (Text in Polish; summaries in English, French, German) 1961. irreg., vol.3, 1977. price varies. (Towarzystwo Naukowe w Toruniu) Panstwowe Wydawnictwo Naukowe, Miodowa 10, 00-251 Warsaw, Poland (Dist. by: Ars Polona, Krakowskie Przedmiescie 7, 00-068 Warsaw, Poland) Ed. Juliusz Narebski. circ. 440. Indexed: Biol.Abstr.

574 JA ISSN 0564-7630
UNIVERSITY OF TOKYO. RESEARCH INSTITUTE OF LOGOPEDICS AND PHONIATRICS. ANNUAL BULLETIN. (Text in English) 1967. a. exchange basis. University of Tokyo Press, 7-3-1 Hongo, Bunkyo-ku, Tokyo 113-91, Japan. (back issues avail.) Indexed: Lang.& Lang.Behav.Abstr.

BIOLOGY — Zoology

see also Pets; Veterinary Science

598.1 UK ISSN 0142-5145
A S R A JOURNAL. 1979. a. membership. Association for the Study of Reptilia and Amphibia, c/o Cotswold Wild Life Park, Burford, Oxon, England. Ed. Dennis J. Wheatley. circ. 500.

591 CU
ACADEMIA DE CIENCIAS DE CUBA. INSTITUTO DE ZOOLOGIA. INFORME CIENTIFICO-TECNICO. (Text in Spanish; summaries in English) irreg., no. 68, Apr. 1978. Academia de Ciencias de Cuba, Instituto de Zoologia, Industria 452, Havana 2, Cuba.

591 CU
ACADEMIA DE CIENCIAS DE CUBA. INSTITUTO DE ZOOLOGIA. MISCELANEA ZOOLOGICA. irreg. exchange basis. Academia de Ciencias de Cuba, Instituto de Zoologia, Industria 452, Havana 2, Cuba.

591 GW ISSN 0567-672X
ACAROLOGIE; Schriftenreihe fuer vergleichende Milbenkunde. 1957. a. Hirschmann Verlag, Veitshoechheimer str. 14, 8500 Nuernberg 90, W. Germany (B.R.D.) (back issues avail.)

591 PL ISSN 0860-2603
ACTA ACADEMIAE AGRICULTURAE AC TECHNICAE OLSTENENSIS. ZOOTECHNICA/ ZOOTECHNICS. (Subseries of Its: Zeszyty Naukowe) (Text in Polish; summaries in English and Russian) 1956. irreg. price varies. Akademia Rolniczo-Techniczna, Blok 21, 10-957 Olsztyn-Kortowo, Poland (Dist. by: Ars Polona-Ruch, Krakowskie Przedmiescie 7, 00-901 Warsaw, Poland) illus.
Formerly: Zootechnika (ISSN 0324-9239)

597 YU ISSN 0579-7152
ACTA BIOLOGICA IUGOSLAVICA. SERIJA E: ICHTHYOLOGIA. 1969. a. 300 din. Unija Bioloskih Naucnih Drustava Jugoslavije, Nemanjina 6, 11080 Belgrade Zemun, Yugoslavia. Ed. Dobrila Habekovic. Indexed: Biol.Abstr. Helminthol.Abstr.

597 PL
ACTA ICHTHYOLOGICA ET PISCATORIA. 1970. irreg., no. 15, 1985. price varies. Akademia Rolnicza, Janosika 8, 71-424 Szczecin, Poland. Ed. Prof. Mieczyslaw Jasnowski. bk. rev. Indexed: Chem.Abstr. Nutr.Abstr. Field Crop Abstr.

ACTA NATURALIA ISLANDICA. see
BIOLOGY — Botany

590 SW ISSN 0072-4807
ACTA REGIAE SOCIETATIS SCIENTIARUM ET LITTERARUM GOTHOBURGENSIS. ZOOLOGICA. (Text in various languages) 1967. irreg., no.13, 1982. price varies; also exchange basis. Kungliga Vetenskaps- och Vitterhets-Samhaellet i Goeteborg, c/o Goeteborgs Universitetsbibliotek, P.O. Box 5096, S-402 22 Goeteborg, Sweden (Dist. in U.S., Canada, and Mexico by: Humanities Press, Inc., 171 First Ave., Atlantic Highlands, NJ 07716) circ. 700. Indexed: Biol.Abstr.
Supersedes in part: Goeteborgs Kungliga Vetenskaps- och Vitterhets-Samhaelle. Handlingar.

591 PL ISSN 0001-7051
ACTA THERIOLOGICA. (Text in English; summaries in Polish) 1954. irreg., vol.29, 1984. price varies. (Polska Akademia Nauk, Zaklad Badania Ssakow - Polish Academy of Sciences. Mammals Research Institute) Panstwowe Wydawnictwo Naukowe, Miodowa 10, 00-251 Warsaw, Poland (Dist. by Ars Polona, Krakowskie Przedmiescie 7, 00-068 Warsaw, Poland) Ed. Zdzislaw Pucek. bk. rev. bibl. charts. illus. index. circ. 900. Indexed: Biol.Abstr. Bull.Signal. Chem.Abstr. Curr.Cont. Key Word Ind.Wildl.Res. Ref.Zh. Sci.Cit.Ind. Anim.Breed.Abstr. ASCA. Biotech.Abstr. Wild Life Rev. Field Crop Abstr. Helminthol.Abstr. Herb.Abstr. Ind.Sci.Rev. Soils & Fert.

591 572 PL
ACTA UNIVERSITATIS LODZIENSIS: FOLIA ZOOLOGICA ET ANTHROPOLOGICA. (Text in Polish; summaries in various languages) irreg. Uniwersytet Lodzki, Drukarnia Wojskowa, Ul. Gdanska 130, Lodz, Poland (Dist. by: Ars Polona-Ruch, Krakowskie Przedmiescie 7, Warsaw, Poland)

591 BU ISSN 0324-0770
ACTA ZOOLOGICA BULGARICA. (Text in various languages) 1975. irreg. 1.60 lv. per no. (Bulgarska Akademiia na Naukite, Zoologicheski Institut) Publishing House of the Bulgarian Academy of Sciences, Acad. G. Bonchev St., Bldg. 6, 1113 Sofia, Bulgaria (Dist. by: Hemus, 6, Rouski Blvd., 1000 Sofia, Bulgaria) illus. circ. 520. Indexed: Biol.Abstr. Helminthol.Abstr. Soils & Fert.
Supersedes: Bulgarska Akademiia na Naukite, Sofia. Zoologicheski Institut S Muzei. Izvestiia (ISSN 0068-3981)

590 PL ISSN 0065-1710
ACTA ZOOLOGICA CRACOVIENSIA. (Text in English, French, German, Russian and Polish) 1956. irreg., vol.28, 1984. price varies. (Polska Akademia Nauk, Zaklad Zoologii Systematycznej i Daswiadczalnej) Panstwowe Wydawnictwo Naukowe, Ul. Miodowa 10, 00-251 Warsaw, Poland (Dist. by: Ars Polona, Krakowskie Przedmiescie 7, 00-068 Warsaw, Poland) Ed. K. Kowalski. bibl. charts. illus. circ. 800. Indexed: Biol.Abstr. Geo.Abstr. GeoRef.

591 BE ISSN 0001-7280
ACTA ZOOLOGICA ET PATHOLOGICA ANTVERPIENSIA. (Text in Dutch, English, French and German) irreg. (2-4/yr.) free to scientific institutions. Societe Royale de Zoologie d'Anvers - Koninklijke Maatschappij voor Dierkunde van Antwerpen, Koningin Astridplein 26, B-2018 Antwerp, Belgium. Ed. F.J. Daman. charts. illus. cum.index: 1953-1966. circ. 1,250. (also avail. in microfilm) Indexed: Biol.Abstr. Curr.Cont. Ind.Med. Abstr.Hyg. Helminthol.Abstr. Rev.Appl.Entomol. Trop.Dis.Bull. Vet.Bull. Zoo.Rec.
Formerly: Societe Royale de Zoologie d'Anvers. Bulletin.

BIOLOGY — ZOOLOGY

591   FI   ISSN 0001-7299
ACTA ZOOLOGICA FENNICA. 1926. irreg., (approx. 4/yr.) price varies. (Societas pro Fauna et Flora Fennica) Finnish Zoological Publishing Board, Rauhankatu 15B, SF-00170 Helsinki 10, Finland (Subscr. to: Akateeminen Kirjakauppa (Academic Bookstore), Keskuskatu 1, SF-00100 Helsinki 10, Finland) Ed. Samuel Panelius. illus. cum.index nos. 1-50; 51-100; 101-150. circ. 1,030. Indexed: Biol.Abstr. Ref.Zh. Key Word Ind.Wildl.Res. GeoRef. Rev.Appl.Entomol.
    Incorporating: Fauna Fennica (ISSN 0071-4054)

590   AG   ISSN 0065-1729
ACTA ZOOLOGICA LILLOANA. (Text in Spanish; summaries in English, French, German, Italian) 1943. irreg., vol.38, no.1,1981. (Ministerio de Cultura y Educacion) Fundacion Miguel Lillo, Miguel Lillo 251, 4000 Tucuman, Argentina. Ed. Jose A. Haedo Rossi. charts. bibl. illus. (back issues avail.) Indexed: Biol.Abstr. Bull.Signal. Chem.Abstr. Ref.Zh. Zoo.Rec. Anim.Behav.Abstr. Entomol.Abstr. Ecol.Abstr.

ACTUALITES PROTOZOOLOGIQUES. see *BIOLOGY — Cytology And Histology*

599.01   US   ISSN 0270-0794
ADVANCES IN CELLULAR NEUROBIOLOGY. 1980. a., vol.5, 1984. Academic Press Inc., Orlando, FL 32887. TEL 305-345-2000. Indexed: Biol.Abstr. Chem.Abstr.

591   GW   ISSN 0301-2808
ADVANCES IN ETHOLOGY/FORTSCHRITTE DER VERHALTENSFORSCHUNG. (Supplement to: Ethology) (Text and summaries in English, French, German) 1953. irreg. price varies. Verlag Paul Parey (Berlin), Lindenstr. 44-47, 1000 Berlin 61, W. Germany (B.R.D.) Indexed: Biol.Abstr. Curr.Cont. Psychol.Abstr.

597 551.46   JA
ADVANCES IN FISHERIES OCEANOGRAPHY. (Text in English) 1966. irreg., latest 1973. exchange basis. Japanese Society of Fisheries Oceanography - Suisan Kaiyo Kenkyu-kai, c/o Laboratory of Fisheries Oceanography, Tokyo University of Fisheries, 5-7 Konan 4-chome, Minato-ku, Tokyo 108, Japan. Ed. Syoiti Tanaka. adv.

578 616.9   US   ISSN 0065-308X
ADVANCES IN PARASITOLOGY. 1963. irreg., vol.25, 1986. Academic Press Inc., Orlando, FL 32887. TEL 305-345-2000. Ed.Bd. index. Indexed: Biol.Abstr. Ind.Med. Nutr.Abstr. Sci.Cit.Ind. Abstr.Hyg. Helminthol.Abstr. Ind.Sci.Rev. Ind.Vet. Rev.Appl.Entomol. Vet.Bull. Trop.Dis.Bull.

591   UK   ISSN 0269-0543
AGRICULTURAL ZOOLOGY REVIEWS. 1986. a. £50($75) Intercept Ltd., P.O. Box 2, Ponteland, Newcastle upon Tyne NE20 9EB, England. Ed. Gordon E. Russell. index.

591   PL   ISSN 0137-1703
AKADEMIA ROLNICZA, POZNAN. ROCZNIKI. ARCHEOZOOLOGIA. (Text in Polish; summaries in English and Russian) 1975. irreg, price varies. Akademia Rolnicza, Poznan, Ul. Wojska Polskiego 28, 60-637 Poznan, Poland. Indexed: Bibl. Agri.

636   PL   ISSN 0137-1770
AKADEMIA ROLNICZA, POZNAN. ROCZNIKI. ZOOTECHNIKA. (Text in Polish; summaries in English and Russian) 1959. irreg. price varies. Akademia Rolnicza, Poznan, Ul. Wojska Polskiego 28, 60-637 Poznan, Poland. Indexed: Bibl.Agri.

590.744   US   ISSN 0090-4473
AMERICAN ASSOCIATION OF ZOOLOGICAL PARKS AND AQUARIUMS. PROCEEDINGS. ANNUAL A A Z P A CONFERENCE. a. $40. American Association of Zoological Parks and Aquariums, Oglebay Park, Wheeling, WV 26003. TEL 304-242-2160. illus. Indexed: Biol.Abstr. Key Title: Proceedings. Annual A.A.Z.P.A. Conference.

591   US   ISSN 0569-8219
AMERICAN SOCIETY OF MAMMALOGISTS. SPECIAL PUBLICATIONS. 1967. irreg., no.8, 1985. price varies. American Society of Mammalogists, c/o Dr. H. Duane Smith, Sec.-Treas., Department of Zoology, Brigham Young University, Provo, UT 84602 TEL 801-378-2492. (Dist. by: Allen Press, Inc., Box 368, Lawrence, KS 66044) (reprint service avail. from UMI) Indexed: Biol.Abstr.

591 610   US
ANIMALS FOR RESEARCH - A DIRECTORY OF SOURCES. 1954. irreg., vol. 10, 1979. $7.75. (National Research Council, Institute of Laboratory Animal Resources) National Academy Press, 2101 Constitution Ave., N.W., Washington, DC 20418. TEL 202-334-3113.
    Formerly: Animals for Research.

591   PL   ISSN 0003-4541
ANNALES ZOOLOGICI. (Text in various languages) 1922. irreg., vol.38 (no.14), price varies. (Polska Akademia Nauk, Instytut Zoologii) Panstwowe Wydawnictwo Naukowe, Miodowa 10, 00-251 Warsaw, Poland (Dist. by: Ars Polona, Krakowskie Przedmiescie 7, 00-068 Warsaw, Poland) Ed. J. Nast. charts. index. circ. 770. Indexed: Biol.Abstr. Rev.Appl.Entomol. Soils & Fert.

591 598.2   FI   ISSN 0570-5177
AQUILO. SER. ZOOLOGICA. (Text in English and German) 1950. s-a. price varies. Societas Amicorum Naturae Ouluensis, Department of Zoology, University of Oulu, Linnanmaa, 90570 Oulu 57, Finland. Ed. Eino Erkĭnaro. circ. 350. (back issues avail.) Indexed: Biol.Abstr. Chem.Abstr. Ecol.Abstr. Geo.Abstr.

ARASTIRMA ESERLERI SERISI. see *BIOLOGY — Entomology*

594   IS   ISSN 0334-326X
ARGAMON; Israel journal of malacology. (Text in English) 1970. irreg. $11 subscr. includes Levantina. Israel Malacological Society, Netzer Sereni, 70-395, Israel. (Co-sponsor: Nahariya Municipal Malacological Museum) Ed. H. K. Mienis. bk. rev. bibl. charts. illus. index. circ. 525. (back issues avail. from vol. 4) Indexed: Zoo.Rec.

591   BL   ISSN 0066-7870
ARQUIVOS DE ZOOLOGIA. (Text in English, Portuguese and other languages) 1940. irreg. $25. Universidade de Sao Paulo, Museu de Zoologia, Caixa Postal 7172, 01051 Sao Paulo SP, Brazil. Ed. P.E. Vanzolini. circ. 600. (back issues avail.) Indexed: Biol.Abstr. Rev.Appl.Entomol. Zoo.Rec.

599   AT   ISSN 0310-0049
AUSTRALIAN MAMMALOGY. 1972. irreg. (1-2/yr.) price varies. Australian Mammal Society Inc., Flinders University, School of Biological Sciences, Bedford Park, S.A. 5042, Australia. Ed. C. Kemper. bk. rev. circ. 2,000. Indexed: Biol.Abstr. Aus.Sci.Ind. GeoRef.

591   PL   ISSN 0137-6683
BADANIA FIZJOGRAFICZNE NAD POLSKA ZACHODNIA. SERIA C. ZOOLOGIA. (Text in Polish; summaries in English) 1948. irreg., vol.34. price varies. (Poznanskie Towarzystwo Przyjaciol Nauk) Panstwowe Wydawnictwo Naukowe, Miodowa 10, 00-251 Warsaw, Poland. Ed. W. Rzepka. bibl. circ. 300.

591   NE   ISSN 0067-4745
BEAUFORTIA; series of miscellaneous publications. (Text in English, French or German) 1951. irreg., vol.36, 1986. DM.130 per no. Universiteit van Amsterdam, Zoologisch Museum, Instituut voor Taxonomische Zoologie, P.O. Box 20125, 1000 HC Amsterdam, Netherlands. Indexed: Biol.Abstr. Zoo.Rec. GeoRef.

590   NE
BEHAVIOUR. SUPPLEMENTS; an international journal of comparative ethology. 1950. irreg., vol. 20, 1977. price varies. E.J. Brill, P.O. Box 9000, 2300 PA Leiden, Netherlands.

591   US
BENCHMARK PAPERS IN BEHAVIOR. (Each vol. has distinctive title) 1974. irreg., vol.18, 1985. price varies. Van Nostrand Reinhold Company, 7625 Empire Dr., Florence, KY 41042. TEL 606-525-6600. Eds. M.W. Schein, S.W. Porges. illus. index. Formerly: Benchmark Papers in Animal Behavior (ISSN 0093-4720)

591   GE   ISSN 0067-6098
BERLINER TIERPARK-BUCH. 1957. irreg., no. 26, 1974. price varies. Tierpark Berlin, Am Tierpark 125, 1136 Berlin, E. Germany (D.D.R)

580 590   PO
BOCAGIANA. 1959. irreg., no.80, 1984. exchange basis. (Camara Municipal do Funchal) Museu Municipal Funchal, Rua da Mouraria, 31, 9000 Funchal, Madeira, Portugal. Eds. Manuel J. Biscoito, G.E. Maul. circ. 450. Indexed: Biol.Abstr. Zoo.Rec.

590   GW   ISSN 0302-671X
BONNER ZOOLOGISCHE MONOGRAPHIEN. (Text in English, French and German) 1971. irreg. (1-2/yr.) Zoologisches Forschungsinstitut und Museum A. Koenig, Adenauerallee 150-164, 5300 Bonn, W. Germany (B.R.D.) Ed. Goetz Rheinwald. circ. 400. Indexed: Biol.Abstr.

591   GW   ISSN 0174-3384
BRAUNSCHWEIGER NATURKUNDLICHE SCHRIFTEN. 1980. a. exchange basis. J. Cramer in Gebrueder Borntraeger Verlagsbuchhandlung, Johannsstr. 3A, D-7000 Stuttgart 1, W. Germany (B.R.D.)

591   US   ISSN 0006-9698
BREVIORA. 1952. irreg., no.487, 1986. price varies. Harvard University, Museum of Comparative Zoology, Cambridge, MA 02138. TEL 617-495-2988. Ed. Laura Ferguson. bibl. charts. illus. circ. 700. (back issues avail.) Indexed: Biol.Abstr. GeoRef.

591   UK   ISSN 0007-1498
BRITISH MUSEUM (NATURAL HISTORY) BULLETIN. ZOOLOGY. 1949. irreg. £160. British Museum (Natural History), Cromwell Rd., London SW7 5BD, England. illus. stat. circ. 750. Indexed: Biol.Abstr. Zoo.Rec. GeoRef. Helminthol.Abstr.

591   US   ISSN 0068-2780
BROOKFIELD BANDARLOG. 1949. irreg. membership. Chicago Zoological Society, Zoological Park, Brookfield, IL 60513. TEL 312-485-0263. Ed. George B. Rabb.

591   US   ISSN 0108-0326
BRYOZOA. (Text in English) 1980. a. membership. International Bryozoology Association, c/o Department of Geology, University of Illinois, Urbana, DK-2100 Copenhagen, Denmark, IL 61801. Ed. Daniel B. Blake. circ. 250.

590.744   AT   ISSN 0084-8182
BULLETIN OF ZOO MANAGEMENT. 1969. a. contr. free circ. Royal Zoological Society of South Australia, Inc., Zoological Gardens, Frome Road, Adelaide, S.A. 5000, Australia. Ed. David Langdon. bk. rev. circ. 250.

587   US
CALIFORNIA COOPERATIVE OCEANIC FISHERIES INVESTIGATIONS REPORTS. (Editions in English and Spanish) 1950. a. free. California Cooperative Oceanic Fisheries Investigations, Scripps Institution of Oceanography, A-027, La Jolla, CA 92093. TEL 619-534-4236. Ed. Julie Olfe. circ. 1,500. (back issues avail.) Indexed: Sci.Abstr. Ocean Ind.

591 581 598.2   CN   ISSN 0714-0983
CANADA. NATIONAL MUSEUMS, OTTAWA: PUBLICATIONS IN NATURAL SCIENCE/PUBLICATIONS DE SCIENCES NATURELLES. (Text in English and French) 1983. irreg., no.6, 1986. (National Museum of Natural Sciences) National Museums of Canada, Ottawa, Ont. K1A 0M8, Canada. Ed.Bd. abstr. charts. illus. circ. 1, 000. Indexed: Biol.Abstr.

CANADIAN WILDLIFE SERVICE. MONOGRAPH SERIES. see *CONSERVATION*

CAROLINEA; Beitraege zur Naturkundliche Forschung in Sueddeutschland. see *EARTH SCIENCES*

BIOLOGY — ZOOLOGY

594   US   ISSN 0084-862X
CATALOG OF DEALERS' PRICES FOR MARINE SHELLS. (Text in English and Latin) 1965. biennial. $9.50. Of Sea & Shore Publications, Box 219, Port Gamble, WA 98364. TEL 206-297-2426. Ed. Thomas C. Rice. circ. 2,000. (reprint service avail. from UMI)

591   US
CATALOGUE OF AMERICAN AMPHIBIANS AND REPTILES. 1963. irreg., approx. 20/yr. $15 to non-members; members $10. Society for the Study of Amphibians and Reptiles, Department of Zoology, Ohio University, Athens, OH 45701. TEL 614-594-5816. Ed. Jaime Villa. circ. 900. Indexed: Biol.Abstr.

591   AG
CENTRO PANAMERICANO DE ZOONOSIS. BOLETIN INFORMATIVO. BRUCELLOSIS EN LAS AMERICAS. (Editions in English and Spanish) 1974. a. free. Centro Panamericano de Zoonosis, Casilla 3092-C.C., 1000 Buenos Aires, Argentina. circ. 1,450 (Spanish edt.); 750 (English edt.)
   Supersedes in part (since 1978): Centro Panamericano de Zoonosis. Boletin Informativo.

591   PO
CIENCIA BIOLOGICA: BIOLOGIA MOLECULAR E CELULAR. (Text in English, French, German, Portuguese; summaries in two languages) 1934. a. $10. Universidade de Coimbra, Departamento de Zoologia, Coimbra, Portugal. Dir. A.P. Carvalho. bk. rev. charts. illus. index. cum.index. circ. 800(controlled) Indexed: Biol.Abstr. Chem.Abstr. Helminthol.Abstr. Rev.Appl.Entomol.
   Former titles: Universidade de Coimbra. Museum Zoologico. Memorias e Estudos (ISSN 0041-8765) & Universidade de Coimbra. Departamento de Zoologia. Ciencia Biologica.

COMMONWEALTH SCIENTIFIC AND INDUSTRIAL RESEARCH ORGANIZATION. DIVISION OF ANIMAL PRODUCTION REPORT. see *BIOLOGY — Physiology*

591   636.089   SZ   ISSN 0304-5374
COMPARATIVE ANIMAL NUTRITION. (Text in English) 1976. irreg. price varies. S. Karger AG, Allschwilerstrasse 10, P.O. Box, CH-4009 Basel, Switzerland. (reprint service avail. from ISI) Indexed: Biol.Abstr. Nutr.Abstr.

594   UK   ISSN 0144-9826
CONCHOLOGICAL SOCIETY SPECIAL PUBLICATION. 1980. irreg. Conchological Society of Great Britain and Ireland, c/o Mrs. E.B. Rands, 51 Wychwood Ave., Lutton, Bedfordshire LU2 7HT, England.

572   599.8   SZ   ISSN 0301-4231
CONTRIBUTIONS TO PRIMATOLOGY. (Text in English) 1962. irreg., approx. 1/yr. price varies. S. Karger AG, Allschwilerstrasse 10, P.O. Box, CH-4009 Basel, Switzerland. Ed. F.S. Szalay. (reprint service avail. from ISI) Indexed: Biol.Abstr. Chem.Abstr. Curr.Cont. GeoRef.
   Formerly: Bibliotheca Primatologica (ISSN 0067-8139)

591   NE
CRUSTACEANA. SUPPLEMENTS; international journal of Crustacean research. 1968. irreg., vol.10, 1986. price varies. E. J. Brill, P.O. Box 9000, 2300 PA Leiden, Netherlands. Indexed: Biol.Abstr. Ind.Sci.Rev.

591   US   ISSN 0736-7023
CRYPTOZOOLOGY. 1982. q. $35 to institutions; individuals $25. International Society of Cryptozoology, Box 43070, Tucson, AZ 85733. TEL 602-884-8369. Ed. J. Richard Greenwell. adv. bk. rev. circ. 800. (back issues avail.)

575.1   CU
CUBA. CENTRO DE INFORMACION Y DOCUMENTACION AGROPECUARIO. BOLETIN DE RESENAS. SERIE: MEJORAMIENTO ANIMAL. (Abstracts in English) 1974. irreg. exchange basis. Centro de Informacion y Documentacion Agropecuario, Gaveta Postal 4149, Havana 4, Cuba. Indexed: Agrindex.
   Formerly: Cuba. Centro de Informacion y Divulgacion Agropecuario. Boletin de Resenas. Serie: Genetica y Reproduccion.

591   US
CURRENT MAMMOLOGY. 1987. irreg. price varies. Plenum Publishing Corp., 233 Spring St., New York, NY 10013. TEL 212-620-8047. Ed. Hugh H. Genoways.

591   574   US   ISSN 0070-2161
CURRENT TOPICS IN MEMBRANES AND TRANSPORT. 1970. irreg., vol.27, 1986. price varies. Academic Press Inc., Orlando, FL 32887. TEL 305-345-2000. Eds. Felix Bronner, Arnest Kleinzeller. Indexed: Biol.Abstr. Chem.Abstr. Nutr.Abstr. Sci.Cit.Ind. Ind.Sci.Rev.

591   560   US   ISSN 0886-3806
CYPRIS; international ostracoda newsletter. 1983. a. membership. (International Research Group on Ostracoda) Northeast Louisiana University, Department of Geosciences, Monroe, LA 71209. TEL 318-342-4100. Eds. Mervin Kontrovitz, Eileen Kontrovitz. bibl. circ. 400.

590   DK   ISSN 0374-7344
DANISH REVIEW OF GAME BIOLOGY. (Text in English; summaries in Russian and Danish) 1945. irreg. price varies. Ministry of agriculture, Game Biology Station - Vildbiologisk Station, Kaloe, 8410 Roende, Denmark. Ed. Ib Clausager. circ. 2,200. Indexed: Biol.Abstr. Nutr.Abstr. Geo.Abstr. Key Word Ind.Wildl.Res. Wildlife Rev. Zoo.Rec.

590   GW   ISSN 0070-4342
DEUTSCHE ZOOLOGISCHE GESELLSCHAFT. VERHANDLUNGEN. a. price varies. Gustav Fischer Verlag, Wollgrasweg 49, Postfach 720143, 7000 Stuttgart 70, W. Germany (B.R.D.) Indexed: Biol.Abstr. Chem.Abstr. Anim.Breed.Abstr. Helminthol.Abstr. Rev.Appl.Entomol.

591   NE
DEVELOPMENT IN MAMMALS. 1977. irreg., vol.5, 1983. price varies. Elsevier Science Publishers B.V., Box 211, 1000 AE Amsterdam, Netherlands. Ed. M.H. Johnson. Indexed: Biol.Abstr.

591   NE
DEVELOPMENTS IN AQUACULTURE AND FISHERIES SCIENCE. 1976. irreg., vol.15, 1985. price varies. Elsevier Science Publishers B.V., Box 211, 1000 AE Amsterdam, Netherlands.

DIVREI HA-AKADEMIA HA-LEUMIT HA-YISRAELIT LEMADAIM-HA-HATIVA LE-MADAEI HA-TEVA. see *PHYSICS*

597   NE   ISSN 0378-1909
ENVIRONMENTAL BIOLOGY OF FISHES. (Text in English) 1976. irreg. (8-12/yr.) fl.720($175) to individuals; institutions $255. Dr. W. Junk Publishers (Subsidiary of: Kluwer Academic Publishers Group) P.O. Box 163, 3300 AD Dordrecht, Netherlands (Orders to: Kluwer Academic Publishers Group, Distribution Center: Box 322, 3300 AH Dordrecht, Netherlands) Ed.Bd. adv. bk. rev. circ. 700. Indexed: Biol.Abstr. Chem.Abstr. Curr.Cont. Excerp.Med. Ocean.Abstr. Geo.Abstr. Helminthol.Abstr.x. Sel.Water Res.Abstr.

FAR SEAS FISHERIES RESEARCH LABORATORY. BULLETIN. see *FISH AND FISHERIES*

FAR SEAS FISHERIES RESEARCH LABORATORY. SERIES. see *FISH AND FISHERIES*

FAUNA & FLORA. see *CONSERVATION*

591   NO   ISSN 0332-768X
FAUNA NORVEGICA SERIES A. NORWEGIAN FAUNA EXCEPT ENTOMOLOGY AND ORNITHOLOGY. (Text in English) 1980. a. Kr.40($6) Norsk Zoologisk Tidsskriftsentral, Zoological Museum, Sarsgt.1, N-0562 Oslo 5, Norway. Ed. Edvard K. Barth. cum.index (every 3 years) (back issues avail.)

FAUNA OF NEW ZEALAND. see *BIOLOGY*

591   IS
FAUNA OF RUSSIA AND ADJACENT COUNTRIES. (Text in English) irreg. Israel Program for Scientific Translations, Box 7145, Jerusalem, Israel (U.S. Distributor: Keter Inc., 440 Park Ave. South, New York, NY 10016)

591   IS
FAUNA OF THE U.S.S.R. (Text in English) irreg. Israel Program for Scientific Translations, Box 7145, Jerusalem, Israel (US Distributor: Keter Inc., 440 Park Ave. S., New York, NY 10016)

591   IS
FAUNA PALAESTINA. (Text in English) 1975. irreg. Israel Academy of Science and Humanities, P.O. Box 4040, Jerusalem 91 040, Israel.

591   PL   ISSN 0071-4089
FAUNA SLODKOWODNA POLSKI. (Text in Polish) 1935. irreg., vol.8, 1980. price varies. (Polska Akademia Nauk, Zaklad Biologii Rolnej) Panstwowe Wydawnictwo Naukowe, Miodowa 10, 00-251 Warsaw, Poland (Dist. by: Ars Polona, Krakowskie Przedmiescie 7, 00-068 Warsaw, Poland)

597   DK   ISSN 0109-2510
FICHES D'IDENTIFICATION DES MALADIES ET PARASITES DES POISSONS, CRUSTACES ET MOLLUSQUES/IDENTIFICATION LEAFLETS FOR DISEASES AND PARASITES OF FISH AND SHELLFISH. (Text in English and French) 1984. irreg., latest no.30, 1985. Kr.15 per no. International Council for the Exploration of the Sea, Palaegade 2-4, DK-1261 Copenhagen K, Denmark (Subscr. to: C.A. Reitzels Boghandel, Noerregade 20, DK-1165 Copenhagen K, Denmark) Eds. C.J. Sindermann, C. Maurin. circ. 600. (back issues avail.)

591   US   ISSN 0015-0754
FIELDIANA: ZOOLOGY. 1895. irreg. price varies. Field Museum of Natural History, Division of Publications, Roosevelt Rd. at Lake Shore Dr., Chicago, IL 60605-2496. TEL 312-922-9410. Ed. Dr. Timothy Plowman. bibl. charts. illus. stat. circ. 500. (back issues avail.; reprint service avail. from UMI) Indexed: Biol.Abstr. Chem.Abstr.

FISHERIES BULLETIN. see *FISH AND FISHERIES*

FOCUS ON RENEWABLE NATURAL RESOURCES. see *FORESTS AND FORESTRY*

591   GW   ISSN 0071-7991
FORTSCHRITTE DER ZOOLOGIE/PROGRESS IN ZOOLOGY. (Text in English, French, German) 1935. irreg. price varies. (Deutsche Zoologische Gesellschaft) Gustav Fischer Verlag, Wollgrasweg 49, Postfach 720143, 7000 Stuttgart 70, W. Germany (B.R.D.) Ed. M. Lindauer. Indexed: Biol.Abstr. Chem.Abstr. Sci.Cit.Ind. Ind.Sci.Rev. VITIS.
   Supersedes: Ergebnisse und Fortschritte der Zoologie.

FORTSCHRITTE IN DER TIERPHYSIOLOGIE UND TIERERNAEHRUNG/ADVANCES IN ANIMAL PHYSIOLOGY AND ANIMAL NUTRITION. see *AGRICULTURE — Poultry And Livestock*

591   PL   ISSN 0015-9301
FRAGMENTA FAUNISTICA. (Text mainly in Polish; occasionally in English, French, German and Russian; summaries in same languages) 1930. irreg., vol.28, 1984. price varies. (Polska Akademia Nauk, Instytut Zoologii) Panstwowe Wydawnictwo Naukowe, Miodowa 10, 00-251 Warsaw, Poland. Ed. W. Szelegiewicz. bibl. charts. illus. index. circ. 550. Indexed: Biol.Abstr. Rev.Appl.Entomol. Rev.Plant Path.

591   CL   ISSN 0016-531X
GAYANA: ZOOLOGICA. (Text in English or Spanish) 1961. a. Universidad de Concepcion, Facultad de Ciencias Biologicas y de Recursos Naturales, Casilla 2407, Apdo. 10, Concepcion, Chile (Subscr. address: Editorial Universidad de Concepcion, Depto. Ventas, Cas.1557, Concepcion, Chile) Ed. Alberto Larrain. circ. 1,000. Indexed: Biol.Abstr. GeoRef.

591   CS
GAZELLA. ANNUAL REPORT AND SCIENTIFIC ARTICLES. (Text and summaries in Czech and English) 1969. a. exchange basis. Zoologicka Zahrada v Praze - Zoological Garden of Prague, 171 00 Prague, Czechoslovakia. Eds. Jiri Volf, Jan Hora.
   Formerly: Zoologicka Zahrada v Praze. Vyrocni Zprava.

GREAT BASIN NATURALIST MEMOIRS. see *BIOLOGY — Botany*

BIOLOGY — ZOOLOGY 175

591 UK ISSN 0065-4507
GREAT BRITAIN. INSTITUTE OF ANIMAL PHYSIOLOGY. REPORT. 1960/61. biennial. £2. Agricultural and Food Research Council, 160 Great Portland St., London W1N 6DT, England (Avail. from: The Government Bookshop, 49 High Holborn, London WC1V 6HB, England) illus. circ. 1,500. Indexed: Anim.Breed.Abstr.

595 GW ISSN 0072-9612
HAMBURGISCHES ZOOLOGISCHES MUSEUM UND INSTITUT. MITTEILUNGEN. 1883. a. price varies. Universitaet Hamburg, Zoologisches Institut, Martin-Luther-King-Platz 3, 2000 Hamburg 13, W. Germany (B.R.D.) (Co-sponsor: Zoologisches Museum der Universitaet Hamburg) Ed. Gisela Rack. circ. 600. Indexed: Biol.Abstr. Entomol.Abstr. Rev.Appl.Entomol.

594 US ISSN 0073-0807
HARVARD UNIVERSITY. MUSEUM OF COMPARATIVE ZOOLOGY. DEPARTMENT OF MOLLUSKS. OCCASIONAL PAPERS ON MOLLUSKS. 1945. irreg. ‡ Harvard University, Museum of Comparative Zoology, Mollusk Department, Cambridge, MA 02138. TEL 617-495-2468. Ed. Kenneth J. Boss. circ. 225. (back issues avail.) Indexed: Biol.Abstr.

591 SA ISSN 0441-6651
HERPETOLOGICAL ASSOCIATION OF SOUTH AFRICA. JOURNAL. (Text in English) 1965. irreg. R.9($10) Herpetological Association of South Africa, c/o National Museum, P.O. Box 266, 9300 Bloemfontein, South Africa. Ed. W.R. Branch. adv. bk. rev. circ. 300. Indexed: Zoo.Rec.

591 JA
HIROSHIMA UNIVERSITY. JOURNAL OF SCIENCE. SERIES B. DIVISION 1: ZOOLOGY/ HIROSHIMA DAIGAKU RIKA KIYO, DOBUTSUGAKU. (Text in English and European languages) 1937. a. exchange basis. Hiroshima University, Faculty of Science, Higashisenda-cho, Hiroshima 730, Japan. Ed.Bd. circ. 400. Indexed: Biol.Abstr. VITIS.

590 574 JA
HIROSHIMA UNIVERSITY. LABORATORY FOR AMPHIBIAN BIOLOGY. SCIENTIFIC REPORT. (Text in English) 1972. a. exchange basis. Hiroshima University, Laboratory for Amphibian Biology, 1-89 1-chome Higashisenda-cho, Hiroshima 730, Japan. Indexed: Biol.Abstr.

591 JA ISSN 0368-2188
HOKKAIDO UNIVERSITY. FACULTY OF SCIENCE. JOURNAL. SERIES 6: ZOOLOGY. (Text in English) 1930. irreg. exchange basis. Hokkaido University, Faculty of Science - Hokkaido Daigaku Rigakubu, Nishi-8-chome, Kita-10-jo, Kita-ku, Sapporo 060, Japan. Ed. H. Iwata. circ. 400. (back issues avail.) Indexed: Biol.Abstr. Chem.Abstr. GeoRef.

I C L A R M CONFERENCE PROCEEDINGS. (International Center for Living Aquatic Resources Management) see FISH AND FISHERIES

IHERINGIA. SERIE MISCELANEA. see BIOLOGY — Botany

591 BL ISSN 0073-4721
IHERINGIA. SERIE ZOOLOGIA. (Text in English, French, German, Italian, Latin, Portuguese and Spanish) 1957. irreg., no.64, 1984. price varies. Fundacao Zoobotanica do Rio Grande do Sul, Museu de Ciencias Naturais, Caixa Postal 1188, 90.000 Porto Alegre, Rio Grande do Sul, Brazil. Ed. Arno A. Lise. bibl. illus. circ. 600. Indexed: Biol.Abstr. Zoo.Rec.

593 US
ILLUSTRATED GUIDE TO THE PROTOZOA. 1983. irreg. $80. (Society of Protozoologists) Allen Press, Inc., Box 368, Lawrence, KS 66044. Ed.Bd. Formerly (until 1985): Society of Protozoologists. Special Publication.

591 II ISSN 0537-0744
INDIA. ZOOLOGICAL SURVEY. ANNUAL REPORT. a. Zoological Survey of India, 34 Chittaranjan Ave., Calcutta 12, India.

591 II
INDIA. ZOOLOGICAL SURVEY. NEWSLETTER. (Text in English) 197? irreg. Zoological Survey of India, 34 Chittaranjan Ave., Calcutta 12, India.

INDIAN JOURNAL OF FISHERIES. see FISH AND FISHERIES

597 US ISSN 0736-0460
INDO-PACIFIC FISHES. 1982. irreg. price varies. (Bishop Museum, Division of Ichthyology) Bishop Museum Press, Box 19000-A, Honolulu, HI 96817. Eds. Dr. John Randall, Helen Randall.

591 562 US ISSN 0073-7240
INDO-PACIFIC MOLLUSCA. 1959. irreg., no.17, 1976. price varies. Delaware Museum of Natural History, Box 3937, Greenville, DE 19807. TEL 302-658-9111. Indexed: Biol.Abstr.

INSTITUTE OF PRIMATE RESEARCH. ANNUAL REPORT. see BIOLOGY — Genetics

590 BL ISSN 0073-9901
INSTITUTO BUTANTAN. MEMORIAS. (Text and summaries in English and Portuguese) 1918. a. ‡ Instituto Butantan, Caixa Postal 65, Sao Paulo, Brazil. Ed.Bd. author index. cum.index: 1918-1974. circ. 800. Indexed: Biol.Abstr. Chem.Abstr. Ind.Med. Abstr.Hyg. Bull.Inst.Pasteur. Ind.Vet. Trop.Dis.Bull. Vet.Bull. Zoo.Rec.

591 PO ISSN 0020-4021
INSTITUTO DE ZOOLOGIA "DR. AUGUSTO NOBRE". PUBLICACOES. (Text in English, French, German and Portuguese; summaries occasionally in English or French) 1940. irreg. (3-5/yr.) exchange basis. Instituto de Zoologia "Dr. Augusto Nobre", Universidade do Porto, Faculdade de Ciencias, Porto, Portugal. bibl. charts. illus. stat. circ. 1,000. Indexed: Biol.Abstr. Zoo.Rec.

594 MX ISSN 0026-1777
INSTITUTO POLITECNICO NACIONAL. ESCUELA NATIONAL DE CIENCIAS BIOLOGICAS. ANALES. (Text in English; occasionally in other languages) 1938. a. Mex.$40($4) Instituto Politecnico Nacional, Escuela Nacional de Ciencias Biologicas, Carpio y Plan de Ayala, Col. Santo Tomas, Apartado Postal 42-186, 11340, Mexico, D.F., Mexico. Ed. Martha Eugenia Perez V. circ. 1,000.

INSTITUTUL DE CERCETARI PENTRU PROTECTIA PLANTELOR. ANALELE/ RESEARCH INSTITUTE FOR PLANT PROTECTION. ANNALS. see AGRICULTURE

597.58 333.7 SP ISSN 0377-368X
INTERNATIONAL COMMISSION FOR THE CONSERVATION OF ATLANTIC TUNAS. REPORT. (Published in 2 parts for even and odd numbered years) (Editions in English, French and Spanish) biennial. International Commission for the Conservation of Atlantic Tunas, Principe de Vergara 17, 28001 Madrid, Spain. Ed. P.M. Miyake.

576 IT ISSN 0074-3860
INTERNATIONAL CONGRESS OF PARASITOLOGY. PROCEEDINGS. 1964. quadrennial; 5th, Toronto, 1982. price varies. World Federation of Parasitologists, c/o A. Mantovani, Sec., Facolta di Medicina Veterinaria, Via S. Giacomo 9/2, I-40126 Bologna, Italy.

INTERNATIONAL CONGRESS OF PRIMATOLOGY. PROCEEDINGS. see ANTHROPOLOGY

591 US ISSN 0074-7734
INTERNATIONAL REVIEW OF GENERAL AND EXPERIMENTAL ZOOLOGY. 1964. irreg., vol.4, 1970. Academic Press, Inc., Orlando, FL 32887. TEL 305-345-2000. Eds. William J. L. Felts, Richard J. Harrison. index. Indexed: Biol.Abstr.

INTERNATIONAL WHALING COMMISSION. REPORT. see FISH AND FISHERIES

591 UK ISSN 0074-9664
INTERNATIONAL ZOO YEARBOOK. 1960. a. price varies. Zoological Society of London, Regent's Park, London NW1 4RY, England. Ed. Peter Olney. index. cum.index. Indexed: Biol.Abstr. Anim.Breed.Abstr. Dairy Sci.Abstr. Ind.Vet. Vet.Bull.

591 UR ISSN 0202-702X
ITOGI NAUKI I TEKHNIKI: ZOOLOGIYA POZVONOCHNYKH. irreg., latest vol.14, 1986. price varies. Vsesoyuznyi Institut Nauchno-Tekhnicheskoi Informatsii (VINITI), Baltiiskaya ul. 14, Moscow A-219, Russian S.F.S.R., U.S.S.R. (Subscr. to: Mezhdunarodnaya Kniga, Dimitrova ul. 39, 113095 Moscow, Russian S.F.S.R., U.S.S.R.) Vertebrates

591 SA ISSN 0073-4381
J L B SMITH INSTITUTE OF ICHTHYOLOGY. ICHTHYOLOGICAL BULLETIN. (Text in English) 1956. irreg. $20 price varies. ‡ J L B Smith Institute of Ichthyology, Private Bag 1015, Grahamstown 6140, South Africa. (Co-sponsors: South African Council for Scientific and Industrial Research; South Africa Department of National Education) Ed. Phillip C. Heemstra. cum.index. circ. 1,000 (controlled) Indexed: Zoo.Rec.

591 SA ISSN 0075-2088
J L B SMITH INSTITUTE OF ICHTHYOLOGY. SPECIAL PUBLICATION. (Continues numbering of publication issued under former name of body, Dept. of Ichthyology, Rhodes University) (Text in English) 1967. irreg. $20. J L B Smith Institute of Ichthyology, Private Bag 1015, Grahamstown 6140, South Africa. (Co-sponsors: South African Council for Scientific and Industrial Research; South Africa Department of National Education) Ed. Phillip C. Heemstra. index. circ. 1,500(controlled) Indexed: Biol.Abstr. Ocean.Abstr. Zoo.Rec.

594 US ISSN 0075-3920
JOHNSONIA; monographs of the marine mollusks of the Western Atlantic. 1941. irreg. price varies. ‡ Harvard University, Museum of Comparative Zoology, Department of Mollusks, Cambridge, MA 02138. TEL 617-495-2468. Ed. Kenneth J. Boss. Indexed: Biol.Abstr.

594 US ISSN 0730-8000
JOURNAL OF SHELLFISH RESEARCH. 1981. a. $18 to individuals; institutions $20. ‡ National Shellfisheries Association, Inc., 2510 Ridgewood Rd., Ocean Springs, MS 39564. TEL 601-872-4250. Ed. Dr. Edwin W. Cake, Jr. bk. rev. index. cum.index: 1930-1972. circ. 550. Indexed: Biol.Abstr. Chem.Abstr. Nutr.Abstr.
Formerly: National Shellfisheries Association. Proceedings (ISSN 0077-5711)

591 PL ISSN 0075-5230
KATALOG FAUNY PASOZYTNICZEJ POLSKI. (Text in Polish) 1970. irreg., vol.3, 1972. price varies. (Polskie Towarzystwo Parazytologiczne) Panstwowe Wydawnictwo Naukowe, Miodowa 10, 00-251 Warsaw, Poland (Dist. by: Ars Polona, Krakowskie Przedmiescie 7, 00-068 Warsaw, Poland)

591 PL ISSN 0453-3623
KATALOG FAUNY POLSKI. (Text in Polish) 1960. irreg., no.38, 1983. price varies. (Polska Akademia Nauk, Instytut Zoologii) Panstwowe Wydawnictwo Naukowe, Ul. Miodowa 10, 00-251 Warsaw, Poland (Dist. by: Ars Polona, Krakowskie Przedmiescie 7, 00-068 Warsaw, Poland) Ed. M. Mroczkowski. bibl. circ. 550. Indexed: Biol.Abstr. Rev.Appl.Entomol.

KEY WORD INDEX OF WILDLIFE RESEARCH. see SCIENCES: COMPREHENSIVE WORKS — Abstracting, Bibliographies, Statistics

KONINKLIJK BELGISCH INSTITUUT VOOR NATUURWETENSCHAPPEN. STUDIEDOCUMENTEN/INSTITUT ROYAL DES SCIENCES NATURELLES DE BELGIQUE. DOCUMENTS DE TRAVAIL. see BIOLOGY

KUWAIT BULLETIN OF MARINE SCIENCE. see FISH AND FISHERIES

591 AU
LANDESMUSEUM JOANNEUM. ABTEILUNG FUER ZOOLOGIE. MITTEILUNGEN. (Text and summaries in German and English) 1972. irreg. (2-4/yr.) price varies. Landesmuseum Joanneum, Abteilung fuer Zoologie, Raubergasse 10, A-8010 Graz, Austria. Ed. Erich Kreissl. bk. rev. illus. tr.lit. index. circ. 600.

BIOLOGY — ZOOLOGY

591 595.7 AG ISSN 0325-7592
LIMNOBIOS. 1976. a. price varies. Instituto de Limnologia "Dr. Raul A. Ringuelet", Casilla de Correo 55, 1923 Berisso, Argentina. Ed. Andres Boltovskoy. adv. bk. rev. index. circ. 400. (back issues avail.) Indexed: Biol.Abstr. Ref.Zh. Aqua.Sci.& Fish Abstr. Zoo.Abstr.

591 CK ISSN 0085-2899
LOZANIA; acta zoologica Colombiana. (Text in Spanish, French, German and English) 1952. irreg. $5 or exchange basis. Universidad Nacional de Colombia, Instituto de Ciencias Naturales, Apdo. 7495, Bogota, Colombia. (Co-sponsor: Museo de Historia Natural) Ed. Santiago Diaz-Piedrahita. bibl. illus. circ. 1,000. Indexed: Biol.Abstr. Bull.Signal. VITIS.

599 NE ISSN 0024-7634
LUTRA. (Summaries in English, French or German) irreg., vol.27, 1984. fl.25. (Vereniging voor Zoogdierkunde - Society for the Study and Protection of Mammals) E. J. Brill, P.O. Box 9000, 2300 PA Leiden, Netherlands. bk. rev. charts. illus. Indexed: Biol.Abstr.

599 CS ISSN 0024-7774
LYNX; novitates mammaliologicae. (Text in Czech, English, German, Russian, Slovak) 1962. irreg. price varies. Narodni Muzeum, Prirodovedecke Muzeum, Vitezneho Unora 74, 115 79 Prague 1, Czechoslovakia (Subscr. to: P N S - Ustredni Expedice a Dovoz Tisku Prague, Zavod 01, Administrace Vyvozu Tisku, Kafkova 19, 160 00 Prague 6, Czechoslovakia) Ed. Ivan Heran. bk. rev. bibl. cum.index. Indexed: Biol.Abstr.

591 US
M C Z NEWSLETTER. 1971. irreg. (2-3/yr.) $3.50. Harvard University, Museum of Comparative Zoology, Cambridge, MA 02138. TEL 617-495-1910. Ed. Gabrielle Dundon. circ. 1,000. (looseleaf format)

591 HU ISSN 0076-2474
MAGYARORSZAG ALLATVILAGA/FAUNA HUNGARIAE. 1960. irreg., vol.161, 1986. price varies. (Magyar Tudomanyos Akademia) Akademiai Kiado, Publishing House of the Hungarian Academy of Sciences, P.O. Box 24, H-1363 Budapest, Hungary. Indexed: Biol.Abstr.

591 594 US ISSN 0076-2997
MALACOLOGIA. (Text in English, French, German, Spanish) 1962. irreg., vol.28, 1987. $17 to individuals; institutions $27. Institute of Malacology, c/o Department of Malacology, Academy of Natural Sciences of Philadelphia, 19th St., and the Parkway, Philadelphia, PA 19103. TEL 215-299-1130. (Co-sponsor: Institute of Malacology) Eds. G. M. Davis, R. Robertson. index. circ. 700. Indexed: Biol.Abstr. Chem.Abstr. Curr.Cont. GeoRef. Helminthol.Abstr. Ind.Sci.Rev.

591 US ISSN 0076-3004
MALACOLOGICAL REVIEW. (Text usually in English; occasionally in French or German) 1968. a. $15 to individuals; institutions $30. Society for Experimental and Descriptive Malacology, Box 3037, Ann Arbor, MI 48106. TEL 313-665-6228. Ed. J.B. Burch. bk. rev. index. circ. 700. Indexed: Biol.Abstr. GeoRef. Helminthol.Abstr. Zoo.Rec.

594 AT ISSN 0085-2988
MALACOLOGICAL SOCIETY OF AUSTRALIA. JOURNAL. 1957. a. Aus.$18 to individuals; institutions AUS$25. Malacological Society of Australia, c/o Zoology Department, University of Queensland, St. Lucia, Brisbane, Qld. 4067, Australia. TEL 328-4411. Ed. Dr. F.E. Wells. bk. rev. circ. 650. Indexed: Biol.Abstr. GeoRef.

591 GW ISSN 0301-2778
MAMMALIA DEPICTA. (Supplement to: Zeitschrift fuer Saeugetierkunde) (Text and summaries in German, English, French) 1966. irreg., no.11, 1979. price varies. Verlag Paul Parey (Hamburg), Spitalerstr. 12, 2000 Hamburg 1, W. Germany (B.R.D.) Eds. Wolf Herre, Manfred Roehrs. bibl. illus. index. (reprint service avail, from ISI) Indexed: Biol.Abstr.

591.4 US ISSN 0076-3519
MAMMALIAN SPECIES. 1969. irreg. $10. American Society of Mammalogists, c/o Dr. H. Duane Smith, Sec.-Treas., Department of Zoology, Brigham Young University, Provo, UT 84602. TEL 801-378-2492. Ed. B.J. Verts. circ. 1,400. (processed) Indexed: Biol.Abstr. GeoRef.

MARINE INVERTEBRATES OF SCANDINAVIA. see *BIOLOGY*

595.146 CN ISSN 0380-9633
MEGADRILOGICA. (Text in English and French; summaries in English, French, German and Spanish) 1968. irreg. Can.$5.00 per no. Oligochaetology Laboratory, 39 Pembroke Cres., Fredericton, N.B. E3B 2V1, Canada. TEL 506-459-3669. (Co-sponsor: Timbers Research Station) Ed. Dr. J.W. Reynolds. bibl. circ. 1,000. (back issues avail.) Indexed: Biol.Abstr. Bibl.Agri. Forest Abstr. Zoo.Rec.
Earthworms

591 PL ISSN 0076-6372
MEMORABILIA ZOOLOGICA. (Text in Polish; summaries in English, French and Russian) 1958. irreg. (1-2/yr.) price varies. (Polska Akademia Nauk, Instytut Zoologii) Ossolineum, Publishing House of the Polish Academy of Sciences, Rynek 9, Wroclaw, Poland (Dist. by: Ars Polona-Ruch, Krakowskie Przedmiescie 7, Warsaw, Poland) circ. 1,000. Indexed: Biol.Abstr. Rev.Appl.Entomol.

597 JA
MIE UNIVERSITY. FISHERIES RESEARCH LABORATORY. REPORT. (Editions in English and Japanese) 1978. irreg. Mie University, Fisheries Research Laboratory, 4190-172 Wagu, Shima-Cho, Shima-Gun, Mie-Ken 517-07, Japan. Ed. Washiro Kida. circ. 500.

591 GE ISSN 0076-8839
MILU: WISSENSCHAFTLICHE UND KULTURELLE MITTEILUNGEN AUS DEM TIERPARK BERLIN. 1960. irreg., vol.3, 1973. M.15. (Tierpark Berlin) Tierpark Berlin, Am Tierpark 41, 1136 Berlin, E. Germany (D.D.R.) Ed. H. Dathe. index.

591 SP ISSN 0211-6529
MISCELLANEA ZOOLOGICA. (Text in Catalan, English, French, German, Italian, Spanish) 1958. a. 1200 ptas. or exchange. ‡ Museu de Zoologia, Ajuntament de Barcelona, Attn: Dr. Anna Omedes, Apdo. 593, Parc de la Ciutadella, 08003 Barcelona, Spain. TEL 319-69-12. Ed. R. Nos. bibl. charts. illus. circ. 1,500. Indexed: Biol.Abstr. Ocean.Abstr. Ref.Zh. Acoust.Abstr. Anim.Behav.Abstr. Aqua.Sci.& Fish.Abstr. Behav.Abstr. Ecol.Abstr. Entomol.Abstr. Genet.Abstr. Helminthol.Abstr. Mar.Sci.Cont.Tab. Zoo.Rec.

591 IT ISSN 0391-1632
MONITORE ZOOLOGICO ITALIANO. MONOGRAFIE/ITALIAN JOURNAL OF ZOOLOGY. MONOGRAPHS. 1975. irreg., no.2, 1980. price varies. Universita degli Studi di Firenze, Dipartimento di Biologia Animale e Genetica, c/o L. Pardi, Ed., Via Romana 17, 50125 Florence, Italy. index. cum.index. (back issues avail.; reprint service avail. from ISI) Indexed: Biol.Abstr. Chem.Abstr. Curr.Cont.

591 IT ISSN 0374-9444
MONITORE ZOOLOGICO ITALIANO. SUPPLEMENTO/ITALIAN JOURNAL OF ZOOLOGY. SUPPLEMENT. 1966. a. L.58000. Universita degli Studi di Firenze, Dipartimento di Biologia Animale e Genetica, c/o L. Pardi, Ed., Via Romana 17, 50125 Florence, Italy. index. cum.index. (back issues avail.; reprint service avail. from ISI) Indexed: Biol.Abstr. Chem.Abstr. Curr.Cont.

591 PL
MONOGRAFIE FAUNY POLSKI. (Text in Polish, English, French and German; summaries also in Russian) 1973. irreg., vol.13, 1983. price varies. (Polska Akademia Nauk, Zaklad Zoologii Systematycznej i Doswiadczalnej) Panstwowe Wydawnictwo Naukowe, Miodowa 10, 00-251 Warsaw, Poland (Dist. by: Ars Polona, Krakowskie Przedmiescie 7, 00-068 Warsaw, Poland) bibl. circ. 900. Indexed: Biol.Abstr.

591 BE
MUSEE ROYAL DE L'AFRIQUE CENTRALE. ANNALES. SERIE IN 8. SCIENCES ZOOLOGIQUES/KONINKLIJK MUSEUM VOOR MIDDEN-AFRIKA. ANNALEN. REEKS IN 8. ZOOLOGISCHE WETENSCHAPPEN. 1948. irreg., no.248, 1986. price varies. Musee Royal de l'Afrique Centrale, 13 Steenweg op Leuven, B-1980 Tervuren, Belgium. charts. illus. Indexed: Biol.Abstr. Forest.Abstr. Rev.Appl.Entomol.

591 BE
MUSEE ROYAL DE L'AFRIQUE CENTRALE. DOCUMENTATION ZOOLOGIQUE/ KONINKLIJK MUSEUM VOOR MIDDEN-AFRIKA. ZOOLOGISCHE DOCUMENTATIE. 1961. irreg., no.20, 1984. Musee Royal de l'Afrique Centrale, 13 Steenweg op Leuven, B-1980 Tervuren, Belgium. Indexed: Biol.Abstr.

591 AG ISSN 0373-9066
MUSEO ARGENTINO DE CIENCIAS NATURALES "BERNARDINO RIVADAVIA." INSTITUTO NACIONAL DE INVESTIGACION DE LAS CIENCIAS NATURALES. REVISTA. ZOOLOGIA. 1948. irreg., vol.11, no.3, 1982. Museo Argentino de Ciencias Naturales "Bernardino Rivadavia", Instituto Nacional de Investigacion de las Ciencias Naturales, Avda. Angel Gallardo 470, Casilla de Correo 220-Sucursal 5, Buenos Aires, Argentina.
Continues its Revista, Ciencias Zoologicas.

591 UY ISSN 0027-0113
MUSEO NACIONAL DE HISTORIA NATURAL. COMMUNICACIONES ZOOLOGICAS. (Text in English, French and Spanish) 1943. irreg. (6-8/yr.) exchange basis only. Museo Nacional de Historia Natural, Casilla de Correos 399, Montevideo, Uruguay. illus. circ. 1,200. Indexed: Biol.Abstr.

591 SP
MUSEU DE ZOOLOGIA. COLLECCIONES. irreg. (1-2/yr.) Museu de Zoologia, Ajuntament de Barcelona, Attn: Dr. Anna Omedes, Apdo. 593, Parc de la Ciutadella, 08003 Barcelona, Spain.

591 BL ISSN 0080-312X
MUSEU NACIONAL, RIO DE JANEIRO. BOLETIM. NOVA SERIE. ZOOLOGIA. (Text in Portuguese; summaries mainly in English, occasionally in French and German) 1942. irreg., no.293, Feb. 1979. exchange only. Museu Nacional, Quinta da Boa Vista, 20940 Rio de Janeiro RJ, Brazil. bibl. charts. Indexed: Biol.Abstr.

590 FR ISSN 0078-9747
MUSEUM NATIONAL D'HISTOIRE NATURELLE, PARIS. MEMOIRES. NOUVELLE SERIE. SERIE A. ZOOLOGIE. 1950. irreg. price varies. Museum National d'Histoire Naturelle, 38 rue Geoffroy Saint-Hillaire, 75005 Paris, France. Indexed: Biol.Abstr. GeoRef.

591 US ISSN 0027-4100
MUSEUM OF COMPARATIVE ZOOLOGY. BULLETIN. 1863. irreg., vol.151, no.4, 1986. price varies. Harvard University, Museum of Comparative Zoology, Cambridge, MA 02138. TEL 617-495-2988. Ed. Laura Ferguson. bibl. illus. circ. 900. (back issues avail.) Indexed: Biol.Abstr. GeoRef.
Formerly: Harvard University. Museum of Comparative Zoology. Bulletin.

591 GW ISSN 0580-3896
MYOTIS; Mitteilungsblatt fuer Fledermauskundler. (Text in English, German) 1963. a. price varies. Zoologisches Forschungsinstitut und Musaeum Alexander Koenig, Adenauerallee 150-164, D-5300 Bonn 1, W. Germany (B.R.D.) Ed.Bd. Indexed: Biol.Abstr.

591 SA ISSN 0304-0798
NATAL MUSEUM. ANNALS/ANNALE VAN DIE NATALSE MUSEUM. (Text in English) 1906. a. R.60. Natal Museum, Loop St., Pietermaritzburg, 3201, South Africa. Ed. J. Londt. cum.index. circ. 320. (back issues avail.) Indexed: Biol.Abstr. GeoRef. Ind.S.A.Per. Zoo.Rec.

NATIONAL MUSEUM. MEMOIRS. see *ARCHAEOLOGY*

NATURWISSENSCHAFTLICHER VEREIN WUPPERTAL. JAHRESBERICHTE. see *BIOLOGY — Botany*

NEUE DENKSCHRIFTEN DES
NATURHISTORISCHEN MUSEUMS IN WIEN.
see EARTH SCIENCES

590   UK   ISSN 0078-0952
NOMENCLATOR ZOOLOGICUS. 1939. irreg.,
vol.7, 1975. £20. Zoological Society of London,
Regent's Park, London NW1 4RY, England. Eds.
Marcia A. Edwards, H. Gwynne Vevers.

591   US   ISSN 0078-1304
NORTH AMERICAN FAUNA. 1889. irreg., latest
no.74, 1982. U.S. Fish and Wildlife Service,
Department of the Interior, Washington, DC 20240
TEL 303-226-9403. (Orders to: Supt. of Documents,
Washington, DC 20402) Indexed: Biol.Abstr.

591   US   ISSN 0278-3274
NOVITATES ARTHROPODAE. (Text in English;
summaries in French and German) 1980. irreg. J-B
Publishing Co., 430 Ivy Ave., Crete, NE 68333. Ed.
William F. Rapp. Indexed: Biol.Abstr. Zool.Rec.

OPERA LILLOANA. see BIOLOGY — Botany

591   NZ
OTAGO MUSEUM BULLETIN: ZOOLOGY. 1967.
irreg., no.5, 1979. Otago Museum Trust Board,
Great King St., Dunedin, New Zealand.

599.01   US   ISSN 0260-0854
OXFORD REVIEWS OF REPRODUCTIVE
BIOLOGY. 1979. a. $79. Oxford University Press,
200 Madison Ave., New York, NY 10016 TEL 212-
679-7300. (And Ely House, 37 Dover St., London,
W1X 4AH, England) Ed. C. A. Finn. illus. (also
avail. in microform from UMI) Indexed:
Chem.Abstr. Ind.Vet. Vet.Bull.

591   BL   ISSN 0031-1049
PAPEIS AVULSOS DE ZOOLOGIA. (Text in
various languages) 1941. irreg. $15. Universidade de
Sao Paulo, Museu de Zoologia, Caixa Postal 7172,
01051 Sao Paulo SP, Brazil. Ed. P.E. Vanzolini.
illus. index. circ. 800. (back issues avail.) Indexed:
Biol.Abstr. Abstr.Bull.Inst.Pap.Chem.
Rev.Appl.Entomol. Zoo.Rec.

591   BL   ISSN 0553-8505
PESQUISAS: PUBLICACOES DE ZOOLOGIA.
(Numbering is in continuation of articles published
in Pesquisas) no. 6, 1960. irreg. price varies (or
exchange) (Universidade do Vale do Rio dos Sinos,
Instituto Anchietano de Pesquisas) Unisinos, Av.
Unisinos, 950, 93000 Sao Leopold RS, Brazil.
Supersedes in part: Pesquisas.

598.1 614.7   US
PHILADELPHIA HERPETOLOGICAL SOCIETY.
BULLETIN.* 1952. a. $6. Philadelphia
Herpetological Society, c/o Skaroff, 1548 Pratt St.,
Philadelphia, PA 19124-1923. Ed. Robert C. Feuer.
adv. bk. rev. circ. 300. (back issues avail.) Indexed:
Biol.Abstr. Wild Life Rev. Zoo.Rec.

574   CU
POEYANA. (Published under the title "Poeyana" from
January 1964 to August 1970, and again since
March 1974.) (Text in Spanish; abstracts in English)
1964. irreg., no.322, 1986. ‡ Academia de Ciencias
de Cuba, Instituto de Zoologia, Industria 452,
Havana 2, Cuba. bibl. charts. illus. circ. 2,000.
Indexed: Biol.Abstr. Rev.Appl.Entomol.
Formerly: Serie Poeyana (ISSN 0032-2229)

591 639.9   SZ
POLAR BEARS. Represents: Working Meeting of the
Polar Bear Specialist Group. Proceedings. no.5,
1975, St. Prex, Switzerland (pub. 1976) biennial.
$10. International Union for Conservation of Nature
and Natural Resources, Ave. du Mont-Blanc, CH-
1196 Gland, Switzerland (Dist. in the U.S. by:
Unipub, Inc., 345 Park Ave. S., New York, NY
10010)

597 639.3   PO   ISSN 0870-1245
PORTUGAL. INSTITUTO NACIONAL DE
INVESTIGACAO DAS PESCAS. BOLETIM.
(Text in English, French and Portuguese; summaries
in English and French) 1979. irreg. exchange basis.
‡ Instituto Nacional de Investigacao das Pescas, Av.
de Brasilia, 1400 Lisbon, Portugal. Ed. Lidia Nunes.
circ. 500. Indexed: Aqua.Sci.& Fish.Abstr.
Supersedes (1952-1979): Notas e Estudos, Serie
Recursos e Ambiente Aquaticos; Lisbon. Instituto
de Biologia Maritima. Notas e Estudos (ISSN 0020-
3777)
Marine

599.8   US   ISSN 0032-8324
PRIMATE NEWS. 1963. irreg. $5 contribution.
Oregon Regional Primate Research Center, 505
N.W. 185th Ave., Beaverton, OR 97006. TEL 503-
645-1141. Ed. James Parker. charts. illus. circ. 1,
000.

599   US   ISSN 0079-5100
PRIMATES; comparative anatomy and taxonomy.
1955. irreg., vol.8, 1970. price varies. Halsted Press
(Subsidiary of: John Wiley & Sons, Inc.) 605 Third
Ave., New York, NY 10016. TEL 212-850-6000.
Ed. W.C.O. Hill. Indexed: Chem.Abstr.

591   PK
PUNJAB UNIVERSITY JOURNAL OF ZOOLOGY.
1931-47; N.S. 1967. irreg. price varies. University of
the Punjab, Department of Zoology, New Campus,
Lahore, Pakistan. Ed. Dr. Shahzad A. Mufti. circ.
300. Indexed: Biol.Abstr.
Formerly: University of the Punjab. Department
of Zoology. Bulletin. New Series (ISSN 0079-8045)

591   IS
RE'EM. (Text in Hebrew) a. (Israel Mammal
Information Center) Society for the Protection of
Nature, 3 Hashfela St., Tel Aviv 66 183, Israel.
TEL 03-335063.

591   US
RESEARCH NOTES IN ANIMAL BEHAVIOR.*
1983. irreg. Pitman Publishing Inc., c/o Longman
Inc., 95 Church St., White Plains, NY 10601-1505.

REVISTA INVESTIGACIONES MARINAS. see
EARTH SCIENCES — Oceanography

REVISTA PARAGUAYA DE MICROBIOLOGIA.
see BIOLOGY — Microbiology

591   IT
RICERCHE DI BIOLOGIA DELLA
SELVAGGINA. (Text in Italian; summaries in
English, French, German and Italian) 1930. irreg.,
approx. 2/yr. exchange basis. ‡ Istituto Nazionale di
Biologia della Selvaggina, Via Stradelli Guelfi 23/A,
40064 Ozzano Emilia (Bologna), Italy. circ. 2,000.
Indexed: Biol.Abstr. Zoo.Rec.
Formerly: Ricerche di Zoologia Applicata alla
Caccia (ISSN 0044-5061)

591   IT
RICERCHE DI BIOLOGIA DELLA
SELVAGGINA. SUPPLEMENTO. (Text and
summaries in English, German and Italian) 1939.
irreg. Istituto Nazionale di Biologia della Selvaggina,
Via Stradelli Guelfi 23/A, 40064 Ozzano Emilia
(Bologna), Italy.
Formerly: Ricerche di Zoologia Applicata alla
Caccia. Supplemento.

591   NE   ISSN 0459-1801
RIJKSMUSEUM VAN NATUURLIJKE HISTORIE.
ZOOLOGISCHE BIJDRAGEN. (Text in Dutch,
English, German; summaries in English) 1955. irreg.
price on request. Rijksmuseum van Natuurlijke
Historie, Postbus 9517, 2300 RA Leiden,
Netherlands (Subscr. addr.: E. J. Brill, Postbus 9000,
2300 PA Leiden, Netherlands) circ. 550. (back
issues avail.) Indexed: Zoo.Rec.

591   NE   ISSN 0024-0672
RIJKSMUSEUM VAN NATUURLIJKE HISTORIE.
ZOOLOGISCHE MEDEDELINGEN. (Text
mainly in English, French or German; occasionally
in Dutch) 1915. irreg. price on request.
Rijksmuseum van Natuurlijke Historie, Postbus
9517, 2300 RA Leiden, Netherlands (Subscr. addr.:
E. J. Brill, Postbus 9000, 2300 PA Leiden,
Netherlands) charts. illus. circ. 550. (back issues
avail.) Indexed: Biol.Abstr. Zoo.Rec.

591   NE   ISSN 0024-1652
RIJKSMUSEUM VAN NATUURLIJKE HISTORIE.
ZOOLOGISCHE VERHANDELINGEN. (Text in
English, French, German; summaries in English)
1948. irreg. price on request. Rijksmuseum van
Natuurlijke Historie, Postbus 9517, 2300 RA
Leiden, Netherlands (Subscr. addr.: E. J. Brill,
Postbus 9000, 2300 PA Leiden, Netherlands) circ.
550. Indexed: Biol.Abstr. Zoo.Rec.

ROYAL ONTARIO MUSEUM. LIFE SCIENCES.
CONTRIBUTIONS. see BIOLOGY

591   UK
ROYAL ZOOLOGICAL SOCIETY OF
SCOTLAND. ZOO GUIDE. 1958. irreg. 60p. ‡
Royal Zoological Society of Scotland, Scottish
National Zoological Park, Murrayfield, Edinburgh
EH12 6TS, Scotland. adv. circ. 100,000. (tabloid
format)

591   UK
SCOTTISH SOCIETY FOR PREVENTION OF
VIVISECTION. ANNUAL REPORT. 1912. a. free.
Scottish Society for Prevention of Vivisection, 10
Queensferry St., Edinburgh, EH2 4PG, Scotland.
Ed. Clive Hollads. adv. circ. 10,000.

594   US   ISSN 0085-607X
SHELLER'S DIRECTORY OF CLUBS, BOOKS,
PERIODICALS AND DEALERS. 1968. biennial.
$4.95. Of Sea & Shore Publications, Box 219, Port
Gamble, WA 98364. TEL 206-297-2426. Ed.
Thomas C. Rice. adv. circ. 2,000. (reprint service
avail. from UMI)

SHIMA MARINELAND. SCIENCE REPORT. see
BIOLOGY

591   RH   ISSN 0250-300X
SMITHERSIA. 1956; N.S. 1983. irreg. price varies.
National Museums and Monuments of Zimbabwe,
P.O. Box 240, Bulawayo, Zimbabwe. Ed. H.D.
Jackson. index. circ. 200. Indexed: GeoRef.
Ind.S.A.Per. Rev.Appl.Entomol.
Supersedes: National Museums and Monuments
Administration. Occasional Papers. Series B:
Natural Sciences; Which was formerly: National
Museums and Monuments of Rhodesia. Occasional
Papers. Series B: Natural Sciences (ISSN 0304-
5315); Which superseded in part: National Museums
and Monuments of Rhodesia. Occasional Papers
(ISSN 0027-9730)

590   US   ISSN 0081-0282
SMITHSONIAN CONTRIBUTIONS TO
ZOOLOGY. 1969. irreg., no.441, 1986. Smithsonian
Institution Press, 955 L'Enfant Plaza, Rm. 2100,
Washington, DC 20560. TEL 202-287-3738. Ed.
Barbara T. Spann. circ. 2,000. (reprint service avail.
from UMI) Indexed: Biol.Abstr. Ocean.Abstr.
Pollut.Abstr. Abstr.Hyg. GeoRef.
Rev.Appl.Entomol.

SOCIETA SARDA DI SCIENZE NATURALI.
BOLLETTINO. see BIOLOGY — Ornithology

591   SZ   ISSN 0366-3469
SOCIETE NEUCHATELOISE DES SCIENCES
NATURELLES. BULLETIN. (Text in French;
summaries in English, German) 1843. a. 20 Fr.
Universite de Neuchatel, Institut de Botanique,
Chantemerle 22, 2000 Neuchatel 7, Switzerland.
Indexed: Biol.Abstr. Helminthol.Abstr.

590   GW   ISSN 0341-8391
SPIXIANA JOURNAL OF ZOOLOGY. (Includes:
Spixiana Supplemente) 1950. irreg., latest, vol.18.
DM.100. Zoologische Staatssammlung Muenchen,
Muenchhausenstrasse 21, 8000 Munich 60, W.
Germany (B.R.D.) Ed.Bd. Indexed: Biol.Abstr.
Formerly: Zoologische Staatssammlung,
Muenchen. Veroeffentlichungen (ISSN 0077-2135)

591   GE   ISSN 0375-2135
STAATLICHES MUSEUM FUER TIERKUNDE IN
DRESDEN. FAUNISTISCHE
ABHANDLUNGEN. (Text in English, French,
German) 1963. irreg. price varies. Staatliches
Museum fuer Tierkunde in Dresden, Augustusstr. 2,
8010 Dresden, E. Germany (D.D.R.) Ed. Rainer
Emmrich. bk. rev. circ. 400. Indexed: Biol.Abstr.
Zoo.Rec.

594   GE   ISSN 0070-7260
STAATLICHES MUSEUM FUER TIERKUNDE IN
DRESDEN. MALAKOLOGISCHE
ABHANDLUNGEN. (Text in English, French,
German) 1964. irreg. price varies. Staatliches
Museum fuer Tierkunde in Dresden, Augustusstr. 2,
8010 Dresden, E. Germany (D.D.R.) Ed. Rainer
Emmrich. bk. rev. circ. 250. (back issues avail.)
Indexed: Biol.Abstr. Zoo.Rec.

BIOLOGY — ZOOLOGY

591   GE   ISSN 0070-7287
STAATLICHES MUSEUM FUER TIERKUNDE IN DRESDEN. ZOOLOGISCHE ABHANDLUNGEN. (Text in English, French, German) 1961. irreg. price varies. Staatliches Museum fuer Tierkunde in Dresden, Augustusstr. 2, 8010 Dresden, E. Germany (D.D.R.) Ed. Rainer Emmrich. bk. rev. circ. 750. Indexed: Biol.Abstr. Zoo.Rec.

STATE BIOLOGICAL SURVEY OF KANSAS. TECHNICAL BULLETIN. see *BIOLOGY — Botany*

591   DK   ISSN 0375-2909
STEENTRUPIA. (Text and summaries in English) 1970. irreg. Kr.200. Zoologisk Museum, Universitetsparken 15, DK-2100 Copenhagen, Denmark. Ed. Henrik Enghoff. index. (back issues avail.) Indexed: Biol.Abstr. Zool.Rec.

591   PL   ISSN 0082-5565
STUDIA SOCIETATIS SCIENTIARUM TORUNENSIS. SECTIO E. ZOOLOGIA. (Text in Polish; summaries in English, French, German) 1948. irreg. price varies. (Towarzystwo Naukowe w Toruniu) Panstwowe Wydawnictwo Naukowe, Miodowa 10, 00-251 Warsaw, Poland (Dist. by: Ars Polona, Krakowskie Przedmiescie 7, 00-068 Warsaw, Poland) Indexed: Biol.Abstr.

590 591.9   NE   ISSN 0300-5488
STUDIES ON THE FAUNA OF SURINAME AND OTHER GUYANAS. (Subseries of: Natuurwetenschappelijke Studiekring voor Suriname en de Nederlandse Antillen. Uitgaven) 1957. irreg., vol.16, 1975. price varies. Natuurwetenschappelijke Studiekring voor Suriname en de Nederlandse Antillen - Foundation for Scientific Research in Surinam and the Netherlands Antilles, Zoological Laboratory, Plompetorengracht 9, 3512 CA Utrecht, Netherlands. Eds. P. Wagenaar Hummelinck, D.C. Geijskes. illus. circ. 800. Indexed: Biol.Abstr.

591   US   ISSN 0082-1101
SYNOPSES OF THE BRITISH FAUNA. 1970. irreg., no. 18, 1981. price varies. (Linnean Society of London, UK) Academic Press Inc., Orlando, FL 32887. TEL 305-345-2000. Eds. Doris Kermach, R. S. K. Barnes. Indexed: Biol.Abstr. GeoRef.

591   US
SYSTEMATICS ASSOCIATION. SPECIAL VOLUMES. 1940. irreg., latest vol.27, 1985. Academic Press Inc., Orlando, FL 32887. TEL 305-345-2000. Ed. D.L. Hawksworth. Indexed: Biol.Abstr. Chem.Abstr. GeoRef.

THALASSIA SALENTINA. see *BIOLOGY — Botany*

591   GW   ISSN 0040-7305
DAS TIERREICH; eine Zusammenstellung und Kennzeichnung der rezenten Tierformen. (Text in English, French and German) 1897. irreg. price varies. Walter de Gruyter und Co., Genthiner Str. 13, 1000 Berlin 30, W. Germany (B.R.D.) (U.S. adress: Walter de Gruyter, Inc., 200 Saw Mill Rd., Hawthorne, N.Y. 10532) Eds. H. Wermuth, E. Moehn. bibl. illus. circ. 250(approx.)

590   GE   ISSN 0082-4305
TIERWELT DEUTSCHLANDS. irreg., vol. 66, 1979. price varies. VEB Gustav Fischer Verlag, Villengang 2, Postfach 176, 6900 Jena, E. Germany (D.D.R.) Eds. K. Senglaub, H.-J. Hannemann, H. Schumann. (reprint service avail. from ISI)

591   CU   ISSN 0563-9425
TORREIA. N.S. 1967. irreg., latest no.37. exchange basis. ‡ Direccion Nacional de Zoologicos y Acuarios, Parque Zoologico Nacional, Apdo. de Correo 7097, Havana, Cuba. Ed. Abelardo Moreno. bibl. charts. illus. circ. 900. Indexed: Biol.Abstr. Nutr.Abstr.

591   SP
TREBALLS DEL MUSEU DE ZOOLOGIA. a. Museu de Zoologia, Ajuntament de Barcelona, Attn: Dr. Anna Omedes, Apdo. 593, Parc de la Ciutadella, 08003 Barcelona, Spain.

570   IO   ISSN 0082-6340
TREUBIA; a journal of zoology of the Indo-Australian archipelago. (Text in English) 1919. irreg. price varies. Balai Penelitian dan Pengembangan Biologi, Jalan Ir. H. Juanda 3, Bogor, Indonesia. (Co-sponsor: Pusat Penelitian dan Pengembangan Zoologi) Ed.Bd. index. circ. 500. Indexed: Biol.Abstr. Zoo.Rec.

591   SP   ISSN 0213-3997
UNIVERSIDAD DE MURCIA. ANALES DE BIOLOGIA. SECCION BIOLOGIA ANIMAL. (Subseries of: Anales de Biologia) 1984. irreg., vol.7, 1986. ($1500) Universidad de Murcia, Secretariado de Publicaciones e Intercambio Cientifico, Santo Cristo, 1, 30001 Murcia, Spain. TEL 968 24 92 00.

591   MX   ISSN 0368-8720
UNIVERSIDAD NACIONAL AUTONOMA DE MEXICO. INSTITUTO DE BIOLOGIA. ANALES: SERIE ZOOLOGIA. (Text in Spanish; summaries in English, Spanish) 1967. a. Mex.$1298($12) Universidad Nacional Autonoma de Mexico, Instituto de Biologia, Apdo. Postal 70-233, Ciudad Universitaria 04510, Mexico, D.F., Mexico. circ. 1,500. (back issues avail.) Indexed: Rev.Appl.Entomol.
Supersedes in part: Universidad Nacional Autonoma de Mexico. Instituto de Biologia. Anales (ISSN 0076-7174)

UNIVERSITE D'ANKARA. FACULTE DES SCIENCES. COMMUNICATIONS SERIE C. BIOLOGIE. see *BIOLOGY*

591   FR   ISSN 0069-4681
UNIVERSITE DE CLERMONT-FERRAND II. ANNALES SCIENTIFIQUES. SERIE BIOLOGIE ANIMALE. 1963. irreg. price varies. Universite de Clermont-Ferrand II, Unite d'Enseignement et de Recherche de Sciences Exactes et Naturelles, B.P. 45, 63170 Aubiere, France. circ. 250. (back issues avail.)

591.1   FR   ISSN 0069-4746
UNIVERSITE DE CLERMONT-FERRAND II. ANNALES SCIENTIFIQUES. SERIE PHYSIOLOGIE ANIMALE. 1967. irreg. price varies. Universite de Clermont-Ferrand II, Unite d'Enseignement et de Recherche de Sciences Exactes et Naturelles, B.P. 45, 63170 Aubiere, France. circ. 250.

591   NE   ISSN 0066-1325
UNIVERSITEIT VAN AMSTERDAM. ZOOLOGISCH MUSEUM. BULLETIN. (Text in English, French, German) 1966. irreg., vol.10, 1985. fl.50 per vol. Universiteit van Amsterdam, Zoologisch Museum, P.O. Box 20125, 1000 HC Amsterdam, Netherlands, Netherlands. Indexed: Biol.Abstr. Zoo.Rec. GeoRef.

590   US   ISSN 0068-6506
UNIVERSITY OF CALIFORNIA PUBLICATIONS IN ZOOLOGY. 1902. irreg. price varies. University of California Press, 2120 Berkeley Way, Berkeley, CA 94720. TEL 415-642-4247. Indexed: Biol.Abstr. Abstr.Hyg. Rev.Appl.Entomol. Trop.Dis.Bull.

590   US   ISSN 0076-8405
UNIVERSITY OF MICHIGAN. MUSEUM OF ZOOLOGY. MISCELLANEOUS PUBLICATIONS. 1916. irreg., approx. 2/yr. price varies. University of Michigan, Museum of Zoology, Ann Arbor, MI 48109. TEL 313-764-0476. Ed. Gerald R. Smith. circ. 1,200. Indexed: Biol.Abstr. Rev.Appl.Entomol.

590   US   ISSN 0076-8413
UNIVERSITY OF MICHIGAN. MUSEUM OF ZOOLOGY. OCCASIONAL PAPERS. 1913. irreg., approx. 10/yr. price varies. University of Michigan, Museum of Zoology, Ann Arbor, MI 48109. TEL 313-764-0473. Ed. Gerald R. Smith. cum.index. circ. 1,200. Indexed: Biol.Abstr. Rev.Appl.Entomol. Key Title: Occasional Papers of the Museum of Zoology, University of Michigan.

591   JA   ISSN 0368-220X
UNIVERSITY OF TOKYO. FACULTY OF SCIENCE. JOURNAL. SECTION 4: ZOOLOGY/ TOKYO DAIGAKU RIGAKUBU KIYO, DAI-4-RUI, DOBUTSUGAKU. (Text in English) 1926. a. $14.50. University of Tokyo, Faculty of Science - Tokyo Daigaku Rigakubu, Hongo, Tokyo, Japan. TEL 03-812-2111. Ed. Tsugio Shiroya. circ. 690. (also avail. in microform) Indexed: Biol.Abstr. Chem.Abstr.

591   PL   ISSN 0083-4416
UNIWERSYTET JAGIELLONSKI. ZESZYTY NAUKOWE. PRACE ZOOLOGICZNE. (Text in English and Polish; summaries in English and Russian) 1957. a. price varies. (Uniwersytet Jagiellonski) Panstwowe Wydawnictwo Naukowe, Miodowa 10, 00-251 Warsaw, Poland (Dist. by: Ars Polona, Krakowie Przedmiescie 7, 00-068 Warsaw, Poland) Ed. Czeslaw Jura. bibl. illus.

VERSUCHSTIERKUNDE. see *MEDICAL SCIENCES — Experimental Medicine, Laboratory Technique*

591   CS   ISSN 0506-7847
VERTEBRATOLOGICKE ZPRAVY/NOTULAE VERTEBRATOLOGICAE. (Text in Czech; summaries in English and German) 1967. a. price varies. Ceskoslovenska Akademie Ved, Ustav pro Vyzkum Obratlovcu, Kvetna 8, 603 65 Brno, Czechoslovakia. Ed. Jiri Havlin. bk. rev. bibl. circ. 1,000. (back issues avail)

591   NZ   ISSN 0375-5363
VICTORIA UNIVERSITY OF WELLINGTON ZOOLOGY PUBLICATIONS. 1949. irreg. no.75, 1981. exchange basis. Victoria University of Wellington, Zoology Department, Private Bag, Wellington, New Zealand. Ed. Prof. J.B.J. Wells. cum.index. circ. 400. Indexed: Biol.Abstr. Zoo.Rec.

594   US   ISSN 0361-1175
WESTERN SOCIETY OF MALACOLOGISTS. ANNUAL REPORT. 1968. a. $10. Western Society of Malacologists, c/o Margaret Mulliner, 5283 Vickie Dr., San Diego, CA 92109. illus. circ. 250. Indexed: Biol.Abstr. Key Title: Annual Report - Western Society of Malacologists.
Continues: Western Society of Malacologists. Echo; Abstracts and Proceedings of the Annual Meeting.

599   JA   ISSN 0083-9086
WHALES RESEARCH INSTITUTE, TOKYO, JAPAN. SCIENTIFIC REPORTS/GEIRUI KENKYUSHO EIBUN HOKOKU. (Text in English) 1948. a. price varies. Whales Research Institute - Geirui Kenkyusho, 3-32-11, Ojima, Koto-ku, Tokyo 136, Japan. Ed. Hideo Omura. index. circ. 500. Indexed: Biol.Abstr. Ocean.Abstr. Pollut.Abstr.

WILDLIFE - A REVIEW. see *CONSERVATION*

591   NE
WORLD ANIMAL SCIENCE. 1981. irreg. price varies. Elsevier Science Publishers B.V., Box 211, 1000 AE Amsterdam, Netherlands.

591   PL
WYZSZA SZKOLA PEDAGOGICZNA, KRAKOW. PRACE ZOOLOGICZNE. (Summaries in English and Russian) 1967. irreg. 112.00 Zl. Wyzsza Szkola Pedagogiczna, Krakow, Podchorazych 2, 30-084 Krakow, Poland. bibl. illus.

591   SA
Z S S A NEWSLETTER. a. Zoological Society of Southern Africa, Department of Zoology, University of Port Elizabeth, P.O. Box 1600, Port Elizabeth 6000, South Africa.

591   PL   ISSN 0554-8136
ZOOLOGIA. (Text in Polish; summaries in English) 1962. irreg. price varies. Adam Mickiewicz University Press, Marchlewskiego 128, 61-874 Poznan, Poland.
Formerly: Uniwersytet im. Adama Mickiewicza w Poznaniu. Wydzial Biologii i Nauk o Ziemi. Seria Zoologia.

591   US
ZOOLOGICAL PARKS & AQUARIUMS IN THE AMERICAS. 1930. biennial. $25 libraries; $50 non-members; $15 members. American Association of Zoological Parks & Aquariums, Oglebay Park, Wheeling, WV 26003. TEL 304-242-2160. Ed. Linda Boyd. adv. stat. index. circ. 3,000.
Formerly: Zoos and Aquariums in the Americas (ISSN 0740-7610)

591   US   ISSN 0084-5612
ZOOLOGICAL SOCIETY OF LONDON. SYMPOSIA. 1966. irreg., vol.52, 1984. Academic Press Inc., Orlando, FL 32887. TEL 305-345-2000. Indexed: Biol.Abstr. Chem.Abstr. Anim.Breed.Abstr. GeoRef. Ind.Vet. Vet.Bull.

591 574   II   ISSN 0379-3540
ZOOLOGICAL SURVEY OF INDIA. MEMOIRS.
(Text in English) 1907. irreg. price varies.
Zoological Survey of India, 34, Chittaranjan Ave.,
Calcutta 700012, India. circ. 450. (back issues
avail.) Indexed: Biol.Abstr. Rev.Appl.Entomol.

ZOOLOGISCH-BOTANISCHE GESELLSCHAFT,
VIENNA. ABHANDLUNGEN. see *BIOLOGY —
Botany*

ZOOLOGISCH-BOTANISCHE GESELLSCHAFT,
VIENNA. VERHANDLUNGEN. see
BIOLOGY — Botany

591   GW   ISSN 0044-5150
ZOOLOGISCHE BEITRAEGE; Neue Folge. (Text
and summaries in English and German) 1883. irreg.
price varies. Duncker und Humblot GmbH,
Dietrich-Schaefer-Weg 9, 1000 Berlin 41, W.
Germany (B.R.D.) Ed.Bd. charts. illus. index per
vol. Indexed: Biol.Abstr. Rev.Appl.Entomol.

591   GE   ISSN 0044-5177
ZOOLOGISCHE JAHRBUECHER. ABTEILUNG
FUER ANATOMIE UND ONTOGENIE DER
TIERE. (Text in English, French and German;
summaries in English) 1886. irreg. (4-6/yr.) M.180
per vol. VEB Gustav Fischer Verlag, Villengang 2,
Postfach 176, 6900 Jena, E. Germany (D.D.R.)
Ed.Bd. bk. rev. bibl. charts. illus. index. (reprint
service avail. from ISI) Indexed: Biol.Abstr.
Chem.Abstr. Curr.Cont. VITIS.

591   DK   ISSN 0084-5655
ZOOLOGY OF ICELAND. (Text in English) 1938.
irreg. price varies. Munksgaard, 35 Noerre Soegade,
DK-1370 Copenhagen K, Denmark. Eds. A.
Fridriksson, S. L. Tuxen. index. circ. 400. (reprint
service avail. from ISI) Indexed: Curr.Cont.

BIOPHYSICS

see Biology — Biophysics

BIRTH CONTROL

see also Population Studies

613.7   BG
BANGLADESH ASSOCIATION FOR
VOLUNTARY STERILIZATION. ANNUAL
REPORT. (Text in English) a. Tk.25. Bangladesh
Association for Voluntary Sterilization, 526
Dhanmondi Residential Area, Rd. No. 8, Dacca,
Bangladesh.

613.9   US
BIOMEDICAL BULLETIN. 1980. irreg. free.
Association for Voluntary Surgical Contraception,
Inc., 122 E. 42nd St., New York, NY 10168. TEL
212-573-8350. Ed. Douglas Huber, M.D. circ. 3,
000. (back issues avail.)
  Formerly: A V S Biomedical Bulletin (ISSN
0271-6771)

301.4   PK
F P A P BIENNIAL REPORT. (Text in English)
1964. biennial. Family Planning Association of
Pakistan, 3-A Temple Rd., Lahore, Pakistan. Ed.Bd.
circ. 1,500.
  Formerly: Family Planning Association of
Pakistan. Annual Report (ISSN 0071-3759)

301.42   II   ISSN 0377-7774
FAMILY PLANNING ASSOCIATION OF INDIA.
REPORT. (Text in English) 1950. a. free. Family
Planning Association of India, Bajaj Bhavan,
Nariman Point, Bombay 400021, India. illus. circ.
500.

301.42   KE
FAMILY PLANNING ASSOCIATION OF KENYA.
ANNUAL REPORT. 1971. a. free. Family Planning
Association of Kenya, Phoenix House, Kenyatta
Ave., P.O. Box 30581, Nairobi, Kenya. Ed. Insuberi
John. illus. Key Title: Annual Report - Family
Planning Association of Kenya.

362.8   US   ISSN 0095-3121
FAMILY PLANNING PROGRAMS IN
OKLAHOMA; annual statistical report. 1971. a.
Department of Health, Maternal and Child Health
Service, Oklahoma City, OK 73105. TEL 405-271-
4470. illus. circ. 450.

301.4   UK
I P P F ANNUAL REPORT. 1974. a. free.
International Planned Parenthood Federation,
Regent's College, Inner Circle, Regent's Park,
London NW1 4NS, England. illus.
  Former titles: I P P F in Action; International
Planned Parenthood Federation. Annual Report
(ISSN 0307-6857)

I U S S P PAPERS/U I E S P DOCUMENTS DE
L'UNION. (International Union for the Scientific
Study of Population) see *POPULATION STUDIES*

613.94   EC
INFORME ANUAL DE LAS ACTIVIDADES DE
LAS UNIDADES OPERATIVAS DE SALUD EN
EL PROGRAMA DE PLANIFICACION
FAMILIAR DEL MINISTERIO DE SALUD. a.
Ministerio de Salud Publica, Departamento
Nacional de Poblacion, Quito, Ecuador.

301.426   II
INSTITUTE OF ECONOMIC RESEARCH.
PUBLICATIONS ON FAMILY PLANNING.
(Text in English) irreg. price varies. Institute of
Economic Research, Director, Vidyagiri, Dharwar
580004, Karnataka, India.

INTERNATIONAL POPULATION
CONFERENCE. PROCEEDINGS. see
POPULATION STUDIES

613.9   IS
ISRAELI FAMILY PLANNING ASSOCIATION.
BULLETIN. 1979. irreg. Israeli Family Planning
Association, Rehov Boogershuv 66, Tel Aviv 63429,
Israel. TEL 03-281228.

301.42   II   ISSN 0077-4944
N I F P GENERAL SERIES. 1965. irreg., no.22,
1977. free (also available on exchange) National
Institute of Health and Family Welfare, New
Mehrauli Rd., Munirka, New Delhi 110067, India.
Ed. S. Pramanik. circ. 3,000.

301.42   II   ISSN 0077-4952
N I F P MANUAL SERIES. 1966. irreg. free;
available on exchange. National Institute of Health
and Family Welfare, New Mehrauli Rd., Munirka,
New Delhi 110067, India. Ed. S. Pramanik. circ. 3,
000.

301.42   II   ISSN 0077-4960
N I F P MONOGRAPH SERIES. 1966. irreg., no.19,
1973. free; available on exchange. National Institute
of Health and Family Welfare, New Mehrauli Rd.,
Munirka, New Delhi 110067, India. Ed. S.
Pramanik. circ. 3,000.

301.42   II   ISSN 0077-4979
N I F P REPORT SERIES. 1966. irreg., no.12, 1973.
avail. on exchange. National Institute of Health and
Family Welfare, New Mehrauli Rd., Munirka, New
Delhi 110067, India. Ed. S. Pramanik. circ. 3,000.

301.42   II   ISSN 0077-4987
N I F P TECHNICAL PAPER SERIES. 1966. irreg.,
no.17, 1973. avail. on exchange. National Institute
of Health and Family Welfare, New Mehrauli Rd.,
Munirka, New Delhi 110067, India. Ed. S.
Pramanik. circ. 3,000.

312 301.426   SI
NATIONAL FAMILY PLANNING AND
POPULATION SURVEY IN SINGAPORE.
REPORT. 1974. a., 2nd 1977 (pub. 1979) S.$15.
Family Planning and Population Board, 26 Dunearn
Rd., Singapore 11, Singapore. charts. stat.

362.8   NP
NEPAL FAMILY PLANNING AND MATERNAL
CHILD HEALTH BOARD. ANNUAL REPORT.
(Text in English) a. Family Planning Association of
Nepal, Box 486, Katmandu, Nepal. stat.

613.9 618   US
NETWORK (RESEARCH TRIANGLE PARK)
(Annual eds. in French, Spanish) 1979. q. free.
Family Health International, 1 Triangle Dr.,
Research Triangle Park, NC 27709. Ed. Elizabeth
T. Robinson. circ. 2,700. (back issues avail.)

312 618.2   US
NORTH CAROLINA REPORTED ABORTIONS. a.
Department of Human Resources, Division of
Health Services, State Center for Health Statistics,
Box 2091, Raleigh, NC 27602.

POPULATION AND FAMILY PLANNING
PROGRAMS. see *POPULATION STUDIES —
Abstracting, Bibliographies, Statistics*

618 614   US
U.S. CENTERS FOR DISEASE CONTROL.
ABORTION SURVEILLANCE. ANNUAL
SUMMARY. a. free. U.S. Center for Disease
Control, 1600 Clifton Rd., N.E., Atlanta, GA
30333. TEL 404-329-3311. Indexed:
Curr.Lit.Fam.Plan.
  Formerly: Abortion Surveillance (ISSN 0300-
6972)

362.8   US   ISSN 0094-4424
U.S. CENTERS FOR DISEASE CONTROL.
FAMILY PLANNING SERVICES: ANNUAL
SUMMARY. a. U.S. Center for Disease Control,
Atlanta, GA 30333. TEL 404-329-3311. stat. Key
Title: Family Planning Services; Annual Survey.

301.4   UK   ISSN 0535-1774
WORLD LIST OF FAMILY PLANNING
AGENCIES. 1952. irreg. free. International Planned
Parenthood Federation, Regent's College, Inner
Cirle, Regent's Park, London NW1 4NS, England.

BIRTH CONTROL — Abstracting, Bibliographies, Statistics

618 016   US   ISSN 0092-9522
ABORTION BIBLIOGRAPHY. 1970. a. price varies.
Whitston Publishing Co. Inc., Box 958, Troy, NY
12181. TEL 518-283-4363. Ed. Polly Goode.

613.9 016   US   ISSN 0092-6000
CURRENT LITERATURE IN FAMILY
PLANNING. 1972. m. $25. Planned Parenthood
Federation of America, Inc., Katharine Dexter
McCormick Library, 810 Seventh Ave., New York,
NY 10019. TEL 212-603-4637. Eds. G.A. Roberts,
Z.D. Modig. bk. rev. bibl. circ. 600. (also avail. in
microfiche from BLH) Indexed: P.A.I.S. Popul.Ind.

011 613.9   UK   ISSN 0308-8774
LATEST LITERATURE IN FAMILY PLANNING.
1974. bi-m. £4 to individuals; institutions £6. Family
Planning Information Service, 27-35 Mortimer St.,
London W1N 7RJ, England. Ed. A. Belfield. bk.
rev. bibl. circ. 400.
Planned parenthood

301   US   ISSN 0095-3105
NEBRASKA STATISTICAL REPORT OF
ABORTIONS. a. free. Bureau of Vital Statistics,
Lincoln, NE 68500. TEL 402-471-2871.

301.4   DK   ISSN 0106-7729
STATISTIK OM PRAEVENTION OG ABORTER.
(Text in Danish; summaries in English) 1978.
biennial. Kr.20. Sundhedsstyrelsen, St. Kongensgade
1, 1264 Copenhagen K, Denmark (Subscr. to:
Statens Informationtjeneste, Bredgade 20, 1260
Copenhagen, Denmark)
  Formerly: Statistik om Legale Aborter.

BLIND

see also Social Services and Welfare

371.911   DK   ISSN 0901-4306
BLINDES JUL. 1985. a. Kr.15. Moellebrovej 9, 9320
Klotterholm, Denmark. Ed. J. Kildegaard Hansen.

362   CN   ISSN 0068-9378
CANADIAN NATIONAL INSTITUTE FOR THE
BLIND. NATIONAL ANNUAL REPORT. (Text
in English and French) 1919. a. ‡ Canadian
National Institute for the Blind, National Office -
Institut National Canadien pour les Aveugles, 1931
Bayview Ave., Toronto, Ont. M4G 4C8, Canada.
TEL 416-480-7580. circ. 1,500.

027.663　　　　　　US　ISSN 0363-9029
CASSETTE BOOKS. 1977. a. free. U. S. Library of Congress, National Library Service for the Blind and Physically Handicapped, 1291 Taylor St., N.W., Washington, DC 20542. TEL 202-287-5100. bk. rev. index.

362.41　　　　　　US　ISSN 0732-1341
DIRECTORY OF AGENCIES SERVING THE VISUALLY HANDICAPPED IN THE U.S. biennial, with periodic supplements. American Foundation for the Blind, Inc., 15 W. 16th St., New York, NY 10011. TEL 212-620-2000. (also avail. in microform from UMI; audio cassette; reprint service avail. from UMI)

DIRECTORY OF FEDERAL AID FOR THE HANDICAPPED. see SOCIAL SERVICES AND WELFARE

DIRECTORY OF INFORMATION RESOURCES FOR THE HANDICAPPED. see EDUCATION — Special Education And Rehabilitation

362.4　　　　　　SA
DIRECTORY OF SERVICES FOR VISUALLY HANDICAPPED SOUTH AFRICANS. 1985. biennial. R.12.50. South African National Council for the Blind, P.O. Box 11149, Brooklyn, Pretoria 0011, South Africa. Ed. Anne Hadley.
　Formerly: Directory of Services Available to Visually Handicapped South Africans.

808.068　　　　　US
EXPECTATIONS. 1948. a. free to qualified personnel. ‡ Braille Institute of America, Inc., 741 N. Vermont Ave., Los Angeles, CA 90029. TEL 213-663-1111. Ed. Jody Avery. illus. index. circ. 3,000. (Braille)

371.911　　　　　　US
H K I REPORT. 1978. irreg. free. Helen Keller International, 15 W. 16th St., New York, NY 10011. TEL 212-620-2100. Ed. Lila S. Rosenblum. circ. 5,000. (back issues avail.)

011　　　　　　　　GE
HOERBUCHVERZEICHNIS. a. Zentralbuecherei fuer Blinde, Gustav-Adolf-Str. 7, 701 Leipzig, E. Germany (D.D.R.) bibl.

I G E NEWS. (International Guiding Eyes) see PETS

371.911　371.9　617.7　GW
JAHRBUCH FUER BLINDENFREUNDE. a. DM.55. Deutscher Blindenverand e.V., Bismarckallee 30, 5300 Bonn 2, W. Germany (B.R.D.) Ed.Bd. circ. 30,000. (back issues avail.)

362.41　　　　　　US
JEWISH BRAILLE INSTITUTE OF AMERICA. DIRECTORY OF SERVICES. a. Jewish Braille Institute of America, Inc., 110 E. 30 St., New York, NY 10016.

052　　　　　　　　KE
KENYA SOCIETY FOR THE BLIND. ANNUAL REPORT AND ACCOUNTS. a. Kenya Society for the Blind, P.O. Box 46656, Nairobi, Kenya.

LIBRARY RESOURCES FOR THE BLIND AND PHYSICALLY HANDICAPPED (LARGE PRINT EDITION) see LIBRARY AND INFORMATION SCIENCES

371.911　　　　　　US
LIGHT: ANNUAL REPORT. 1929. a. Braille Institute of America, Inc., 741 N. Vermont Ave., Los Angeles, CA 90029. TEL 213-663-1111. Ed. Margi Stapleton. charts. illus. stats. circ. 66,000. (back issues avail.)

647.9654　　　　　II
NATIONAL ASSOCIATION FOR THE BLIND. ANNUAL REPORT. (Text in English) 1955. a. National Association for the Blind, 11 Khan Abdul Gaffar Khan Road, Worli Seaface, Bombay 400025, India. Ed. Suresh C. Ahuja. stat. circ. 1,000.

362.41　371　　　JA　ISSN 0285-1350
NATIONAL REHABILITATION CENTER FOR THE DISABLED. RESEARCH BULLETIN. (Text in English, Japanese) 1980. a. free. National Rehabilitation Center for the Disabled, 4-1 Namiki, Tokorozawa, Saitama, Japan. Eds. I. Tanaka, Y. Hatsuyama. circ. 500.

371　　　　　　　　US　ISSN 0270-4234
NATIONAL SOCIETY TO PREVENT BLINDNESS. REPORT. a. National Society to Prevent Blindness, 500 E. Reminton Rd., Schaumburg, IL 60173. Key Title: Report - National Society to Prevent Blindness.
　Formerly: National Society for the Prevention of Blindness. Report.

REHABILITATION GAZETTE; international journal of independent living for the disabled. see EDUCATION — Special Education And Rehabilitation

362　　　　　　　　UK　ISSN 0080-4479
ROYAL NATIONAL INSTITUTE FOR THE BLIND. INFORMATION LEAFLETS. irreg. free. Royal National Institute for the Blind, Braille House, 338-346 Goswell Rd., London EC1V 7JE, England.

362.61　　　　　　UK
ST. DUNSTAN'S ANNUAL REPORT. 1916. a. free. St. Dunstan's for Men and Women Blinded on War Service, P.O. Box 4XB, 12-14 Harcourt St., London W1A 4XB, England. Ed. D.A. Castleton. illus. circ. controlled.

362.41　　　　　　US
SEEING EYE ANNUAL REPORT. 1939. a. free. ‡ Seeing Eye Inc., Box 375, Morristown, NJ 07960. TEL 201-539-4425. Ed. Catherine Swan. charts. illus. circ. 26,545.

362.41　　　　　　SA
SOUTH AFRICAN NATIONAL COUNCIL OF THE BLIND. BIENNIAL REPORT; with a summary of services available to the visually handicapped. (Editions in Afrikaans and English) 1932. biennial. ‡ South African National Council for the Blind, P.O. Box 11149, Brooklyn, Pretoria 0011, South Africa. circ. 1,500. (also avail. in Braille)

TALKING BOOKS IN THE PUBLIC LIBRARY SYSTEMS OF METROPOLITAN TORONTO. see LIBRARY AND INFORMATION SCIENCES

027.663　　　　　　US　ISSN 0193-113X
VOLUNTEERS WHO PRODUCE BOOKS; braille, tape, large type. 1970? biennial. free. U.S. Library of Congress, National Library Service for the Blind and Physically Handicapped, 1291 Taylor St., NW, Washington, DC 20542. TEL 202-287-5100. (also avail. in Braille)

BLIND — Abstracting, Bibliographies, Statistics

371.911　　　　　　US　ISSN 0277-5247
BRAILLE BOOKS (LARGE PRINT EDITION) 1966. biennial. free. U.S. Library of Congress, National Library Service for the Blind and Physically Handicapped, 1291 Taylor St., N.W., Washington, DC 20542. TEL 202-287-5100. bk. rev. index. (also avail. in Braille)
　Formerly: Press Braille, Adult (ISSN 0079-502X)

371.911　　　　　　US　ISSN 0093-2825
FOR YOUNGER READERS, BRAILLE AND TALKING BOOKS (LARGE PRINT EDITION) 1967. biennial. free. U.S. Library of Congress, National Library Service for the Blind and Physically Handicapped, 1291 Taylor St., N.W., Washington, DC 20542. TEL 202-287-5100. bk. rev. index. (also avail. in Braille)

LARGE TYPE BOOKS IN PRINT. see BIBLIOGRAPHIES

027.663　016　780　US　ISSN 0145-3173
MUSIC & MUSICIANS: BRAILLE SCORES CATALOG - CHORAL (LARGE PRINT EDITION) irreg. free. U.S. Library of Congress, National Library Service for the Blind and Physically Handicapped, Music Section, 1291 Taylor St., N.W., Washington, DC 20542. TEL 202-287-5100. (also avail. in Braille)

780　　　　　　　　US　ISSN 0145-3165
MUSIC & MUSICIANS: BRAILLE SCORES CATALOG - INSTRUMENTAL. irreg. U.S. Library of Congress, National Library Service for the Blind & Physically Handicapped, Music Section, 1291 Taylor St. N.W., Washington, DC 20542. TEL 202-287-5100. Ed. (also avail. in Braille)

027.663　016　780　US　ISSN 0145-3149
MUSIC & MUSICIANS: BRAILLE SCORES CATALOG - ORGAN (LARGE PRINT EDITION) irreg. free. U.S. Library of Congress, National Library Service for the Blind and Physically Handicapped, Music Section, 1291 Taylor St., N.W., Washington, DC 20542. TEL 202-287-5100. (also avail. in Braille)

027.663　016　780　US　ISSN 0145-3130
MUSIC & MUSICIANS: BRAILLE SCORES CATALOG - PIANO (LARGE PRINT EDITION) irreg. free. U.S. Library of Congress, National Library Service for the Blind and Physically Handicapped, Music Section, 1291 Taylor St., N.W., Washington, DC 20542. TEL 202-287-5100. (also avail. in Braille)

027.663　016　780　US
MUSIC & MUSICIANS: BRAILLE SCORES CATALOG - VOCAL (LARGE PRINT EDITION) irreg. free. U.S. Library of Congress, National Library Service for the Blind and Physically Handicapped, Music Section, 1291 Taylor St., N.W., Washington, DC 20542. TEL 202-287-5100. (also avail. in Braille)
　Formerly: Music & Musicians: Braille Scores Catalog - Voice (ISSN 0145-3157)

027.663　016　780　US　ISSN 0145-2525
MUSIC & MUSICIANS: INSTRUCTIONAL CASSETTE RECORDINGS CATALOG (LARGE PRINT EDITION) irreg. free. U.S. Library of Congress, National Library Service for the Blind and Physically Handicapped, Music Section, 1291 Taylor St., N.W., Washington, DC 20542. TEL 202-287-5100. (also avail. in audio cassette)

027.663　016　780　US　ISSN 0145-2517
MUSIC & MUSICIANS: INSTRUCTIONAL DISC RECORDINGS CATALOG (LARGE PRINT EDITION) irreg. free. U.S. Library of Congress, National Library Service for the Blind and Physically Handicapped, Music Section, 1291 Taylor St., N.W., Washington, DC 20542. TEL 202-287-5100. (also avail. in record)

027.663　016　780　US
MUSIC & MUSICIANS: LARGE-PRINT SCORES AND BOOKS CATALOG (LARGE PRINT EDITION) 1977. irreg. free. U.S. Library of Congress, National Library Service for the Blind and Physically Handicapped, Music Section, 1291 Taylor St., N.W, Washington, DC 20542. TEL 202-287-5100.
　Formerly: Music and Musicians: Large Print Scores and Books Catalog for the Blind and Physically Handicapped (ISSN 0363-8472)

027.6　016　362.4　US　ISSN 0484-1506
RECORDING FOR THE BLIND. CATALOG OF RECORDED BOOKS. 1960. irreg. $14. Recording for the Blind, Inc., 20 Roszel Rd., Princeton, NJ 08540. TEL 609-452-0606. Ed. John Kelly. circ. 15,000.

026　　　　　　　　US　ISSN 0082-1519
TALKING BOOKS, ADULT (LARGE PRINT EDITION) 1935. biennial. free. U.S. Library of Congress, National Library Service for the Blind and Physically Handicapped, 1291 Taylor St., N.W., Washington, DC 20542. TEL 202-287-5100. bk. rev. index.

BOATS AND BOATING

see Sports and Games — Boats and Boating

BOTANY

see Biology — Botany

BUILDING AND CONSTRUCTION

see also Building and
Construction — Carpentry and
Woodwork; Building and
Construction — Hardware; Architecture;
Engineering — Civil Engineering; Heating,
Plumbing and Refrigeration; Housing
and Urban Planning

690 BL
A B C: ANUARIO BRASILEIRO DA
CONSTRUCAO. 1961. a. ENGETEC, Rua Capitao
Prudente 160, CEP 05422 Sao Paulo, SP, Brazil.
Ed. M.R. Carril. adv. circ. 10,298.

691.3 US ISSN 0065-7875
A C I MANUAL OF CONCRETE PRACTICE. (In 5
Vols.) 1967. a. $265 per set. American Concrete
Institute, Box 19150, Redford Station, Detroit, MI
48219. TEL 313-532-2600.

A E M S SEMINAR (PAPERS) (American
Engineering Model Society) see ENGINEERING

A R T B A OFFICIALS AND ENGINEERS
DIRECTORY, TRANSPORTATION AGENCY
PERSONNEL. (American Road and Transportation
Builders Association) see TRANSPORTATION —
Roads And Traffic

A S C MINI-FILE. see ARCHITECTURE

690 VE
A - Z DE LA CONSTRUCCION Y LA
DECORACION. 1975. a. Publicaciones Araguaney,
Calle 8, Edificio Lec, piso 3, Las Urbina, Caracas
107, Venezuela.

690 DK ISSN 0105-8185
AALBORG UNIVERSITETSCENTER.
INSTITUTTET FOR BYGNINGSTEKNIK.
NOTE. irreg. price varies. Aalborg
Universitetscenter, Instituttet for Bygningsteknik -
Institute of Building Technology and Structural
Engineering, Sohngaardsholmvej 57, DK-9000
Aalborg, Denmark. illus.

690 DK ISSN 0105-7421
AALBORG UNIVERSITETSCENTER.
INSTITUTTET FOR BYGNINGSTEKNIK.
RAPPORT. 1977. irreg. price varies. Aalborg
Universitetscenter, Instituttet for Bygningsteknik -
Institute of Building Technology and Strustural
Engineering, Sohngaardsholmvej 57, DK-9000
Aalborg, Denmark. illus.

ACTA ACADEMIAE AGRICULTURAE AC
TECHNICAE OLSTENENSIS. AEDIFICATIO
ET MECHANICA/MECHANICS AND
BUILDING ENGINEERING. see
ENGINEERING — Mechanical Engineering

ACTA POLYTECHNICA SCANDINAVICA. CIVIL
ENGINEERING AND BUILDING
CONSTRUCTION SERIES. see
ENGINEERING — Civil Engineering

691.3 US ISSN 0065-7646
AMERICAN CEMENT DIRECTORY; directory of
companies and personnel, North, Central, and South
America. 1910. a. $46. Bradley Pulverizer Co., Box
1318, 123 S. Third St., Allentown, PA 18105. TEL
215-434-5191. Ed. Valerie A. Madea. adv. index.
circ. 1,800.

625.84 691 US ISSN 0517-0745
AMERICAN CONCRETE INSTITUTE.
COMPILATION. 1962. irreg. price varies.
American Concrete Institute, Box 19150, Redford
Sta., Detroit, MI 48219. TEL 313-532-2600.

691 US ISSN 0097-4145
AMERICAN CONCRETE INSTITUTE.
PROCEEDINGS. Published in American Concrete
Institute Journal. 1905. a. $72. American Concrete
Institute, Box 19150, Redford Sta., Detroit, MI
48219. TEL 513-532-2600. (also avail. in microform
from UMI) Indexed: Geotech.Abstr.

691 US ISSN 0065-7891
AMERICAN CONCRETE INSTITUTE. SPECIAL
PUBLICATION. 1962. irreg., latest 1985. price
varies. American Concrete Institute, Box 19150,
Redford Sta., Detroit, MI 48219. TEL 513-532-
2600. Indexed: Chem.Abstr.

690 US ISSN 0065-9940
AMERICAN RAILWAY BRIDGE AND
BUILDING ASSOCIATION. PROCEEDINGS.
vol. 74, 1969. a. membership. American Railway
Bridge and Building Association, Cary Bldg., 18154
Harwood Ave., Homewood, IL 60430. adv. circ.
800.

AMERICAN SOCIETY FOR TESTING AND
MATERIALS. COMPILATION OF A S T M
STANDARDS IN BUILDING CODES. see
ENGINEERING — Engineering Mechanics And
Materials

ANCIENT MONUMENTS SOCIETY
TRANSACTIONS. see ARCHITECTURE

690 624 FR
ANNUAIRE BATIMENT ET TRAVAUX PUBLICS.
a. Saint Lambert Editeur, B.P.72, 13673 Aubagne
Cedex, France.

ANNUAL BOOK OF A S T M STANDARDS.
VOLUME 04.01. CEMENT; LIME; GYPSUM. see
ENGINEERING — Engineering Mechanics And
Materials

ANNUAL BOOK OF A S T M STANDARDS.
VOLUME 04.02. CONCRETE AND MINERAL
AGGREGATES (INCLUDING MANUAL OF
AGGREGATE AND CONCRETE TESTING) see
ENGINEERING — Engineering Mechanics And
Materials

ANNUAL BOOK OF A S T M STANDARDS.
VOLUME 04.05. CHEMICAL-RESISTANT
MATERIALS; VITRIFIED CLAY, CONCRETE;
MASONRY; MORTARS; FIBER-CEMENT
PRODUCTS. see ENGINEERING — Engineering
Mechanics And Materials

ANNUAL BOOK OF A S T M STANDARDS.
VOLUME 04.06. THERMAL INSULATION;
ENVIRONMENTAL ACOUSTICS. see
ENGINEERING — Engineering Mechanics And
Materials

ANNUAL BOOK OF A S T M STANDARDS.
VOLUME 04.08. SOIL AND ROCK; BUILDING
STONES. see ENGINEERING — Engineering
Mechanics And Materials

ANNUAL BOOK OF A S T M STANDARDS.
VOLUME 08.04. PLASTIC PIPE AND
BUILDING PRODUCTS. see ENGINEERING —
Engineering Mechanics And Materials

690 UN
ANNUAL BULLETIN OF HOUSING AND
BUILDING STATISTICS FOR EUROPE. (Text in
English, French, and Russian) 1957. a., latest vol.28,
1984. price varies. Economic Commission for
Europe (ECE), Palais des Nations, 1211 Geneva,
Switzerland (Or United Nations Publications, Rm.
DC2-853, New York, NY 10017) stat. (processed)
Indexed: Geo.Abstr.
Formerly: U.N. Quarterly Housing Construction
Summary for Europe (ISSN 0041-7424)

690 UK
ARABIAN CONSTRUCTION. a. $65. Beacon
Publications PLC., York House, Newton Close,
Park Farm, Wellingborough, Northamptonshire
NN8 3UW, England.

692 US ISSN 0066-6157
ARCHITECTS, CONTRACTORS & ENGINEERS
GUIDE TO CONSTRUCTION COSTS. 1968. a.
$19. A.C. and E. Publishing Co., 4820 Pleasant
Ave., Minneapolis, MN 55409. TEL 612-824-1166.
Ed. D. Roth.

ARCHITECTURAL & BUILDING DIRECTORY OF
INDIA. see BUSINESS AND ECONOMICS —
Trade And Industrial Directories

666.95 CN ISSN 0478-4049
ASBESTOS PRODUCER/PRODUCTEUR
D'AMIANTE.* (Text in English and French) 1954.
irreg. Quebec Asbestos Mining Association, c/o
Quebec Metal Mining Assn., 704, 2 Quebec Place,
Quebec, P.Q. G1R 2B5, Canada. TEL 514-844-
4751. illus.

621.9 US ISSN 0164-0593
ASSOCIATED EQUIPMENT DISTRIBUTORS.
RENTAL RATES COMPILATION; nationally
averaged rental rates for construction equipment
including complete model specifications. 1944. a.
$27.50. Associated Equipment Distributors, 615 W.
22nd St., Oak Brook, IL 60521. TEL 312-574-0650.
Ed. David Loftus. illus. circ. 20,000. Key Title:
Rental Rates Compilation.
Formerly: Associated Equipment Distributors.
Rental Compilation (ISSN 0364-8893)

690 AU
AUSTRIA. BUNDESMINISTERIUM FUER
BAUTEN UND TECHNIK. ABTEILUNG
BAUKOORDINIERUNG. VORSCHAU. 1969. a.
S.350. Bundesministerium fuer Bauten und Technik,
Beirat fuer Bauwirtschaft, Stubenring 1, A-1011
Vienna, Austria. Ed. Franz Pachner. stat. index.
circ. controlled.

690 UK ISSN 0261-2933
B M C I S BUILDING MAINTENANCE PRICE
BOOK. 1980. a. £16. Building Maintenance Cost
Information Service, 85-87 Clarence St., Kingston
upon Thames, Surrey KT1 1RB, England. Ed. N.
Farager. adv. bk. rev. circ. 3,000.

690 340 US
B O C A BASIC NATIONAL BUILDING CODE.
triennial. $35. Building Officials and Code
Administrators International, 4051 W. Flossmoor
Rd., Country Club Hill, IL 60477-5795.

343 US
B O C A BASIC-NATIONAL EXISTING
STRUCTURES CODE. triennial. $26. Building
Officials and Code Administrators International,
4051 West Flossmoor Rd., Country Club Hills, IL
60477-5795.
Formerly: B O C A Basic Housing-Property
Maintenance Code (ISSN 0525-0110)

343 US
B O C A BASIC-NATIONAL MECHANICAL
CODE. triennial. $26. Building Officials and Code
Administrators International, 4051 West Flossmoor
Rd., Country Club Hills, IL 60477-5795. illus.
Formerly: B O C A Basic Mechanical Code
(ISSN 0360-4152)

690 JA ISSN 0453-4972
B R I RESEARCH PAPERS/KENCHIKU
KENKYUSHO CHOSA SHIKEN KENKYU
GAIYO HOKOKU. (Text in English; Summaries in
English and Japanese) 1960. irreg. exchange basis.
Building Research Institute, Ministry of
Construction - Kensetsu-sho Kenchiku Kenkyusho,
1 Tatehara, Oho-machi, Tsukuba-gun, Ibaraki-
Prefecture, 305, Japan. Ed. Yuji Ishiyama. circ. 400.

690 624 UK
B S HANDBOOK 3. SUMMARIES OF BRITISH
STANDARDS FOR BUILDING. 1985. a. £249.25.
British Standards Institution, Linford Wood, Milton
Keynes MK14 6LE, England.

690 DK ISSN 0107-6779
B T B. (Branchevejviser for Traelast og
Byggemarkeder) a. Kr.42.70. Osgard Reklame,
Roenvej 10, 2600 Glostrup, Denmark. illus.

BARBOUR COMPENDIUM BUILDING
PRODUCTS. see INTERIOR DESIGN AND
DECORATION

691 GW
BAUEN MIT ALUMINUM. 1965. a. DM.57.
(Aluminium-Zentrale e.V.) Aluminium-Verlag
GmbH, Koenigsallee 30, Postfach 1207, 4000
Duesseldorf 1, W. Germany (B.R.D.) adv. circ. 22,
000.

690 GW ISSN 0067-4664
BAUWELT KATALOG. 1929. a. DM.29.80 plus
postage. Bertelsmann Fachzeitschriften GmbH, Carl
Bertelsmann-Str. 270, 4830 Guetersloh 1, W.
Germany (B.R.D.) adv.

690 720 SA
BEFORE YOU BUILD. 1983. a. R.11.50. Peer
Publications, 7 Rutland Rd., Parkwood,
Johannesburg, South Africa. Ed. Colin Ainsworth
Sharp. circ. 12,000. (back issues avail.)

BUILDING AND CONSTRUCTION

960 US
BERGER BUILDING & DESIGN COST FILE. UNIT PRICES. VOL. 1: GENERAL CONSTRUCTION TRADES. a. Building Cost File, Inc., 2906 Anthony St., Wantagh, NY 11793-2330.
Formed by the 1981 merger of: Berger Design Cost File & Berger Building Cost File; which was formerly titled: Building Cost File (ISSN 0091-3499)

690 US
BERGER BUILDING & DESIGN COST FILE. UNIT PRICES. VOL. 2: MECHANICAL AND ELECTRICAL TRADES. a. Building Cost File, Inc., 2906 Anthony St., Wantagh, NY 11793-2330.
Formed by the 1981 merger of: Berger Design Cost File & Berger Building Cost File; which was formerly titled: Building Cost File (ISSN 0091-3499)

620.135 GW
BETON-KALENDER. 1906. a. DM.118. Wilhelm Ernst und Sohn, Hohenzollerndamm 170, 1000 Berlin 31, W. Germany (B.R.D.) Ed. G. Franz. circ. 22,000.

690 DK ISSN 0109-291X
BETON- OG KONSTRUKTIONSINSTITUTTET. RAPPORT. 1982. irreg. price varies. Beton- og Konstruktionsinstituttet, Elektrovej, Bygning 371, 2800 Lyngby, Denmark. illus.

691.3 GW ISSN 0409-2740
BETONTECHNISCHE BERICHTE. (Text in German; summaries English and French) 1960. biennial. DM.49.80. (Verein Deutscher Zementwerke e.V.) Beton-Verlag GmbH, Duesseldorfer Str. 8, Postfach 110134, 4000 Duesseldorf 11, W. Germany (B.R.D.) Ed. Gert Wischers. index. cum.index. circ. 1,500. Indexed: Ref.Zh.
Concrete

692.8 US
BIG BOOK; building industry guide. 1974. a. $70. Slater Publications, Inc., 163 Highland Ave., Needham Heights, MA 02194. TEL 617-449-3916. Ed. Robert T. Slater. adv. circ. 10,000. (also avail. in magnetic tape; back issues avail.)

690 US ISSN 0195-8461
BLUE BOOK OF MAJOR HOME BUILDERS. 1965. a. $140. L S I Systems Inc., 11-A Village Green, Crofton, MD 21114. TEL 301-261-6363. Ed. Donald F. Spear. charts. stat. circ. 900.

690 720 UK ISSN 0084-8026
BRITISH BUILDING PRODUCTS CATALOGUE; a catalogue of British building products available to architects overseas. 1950. a. Standard Catalogue Information Services Ltd., Medway Wharf Rd., Tonbridge, Kent TN9 1QR, England. Ed. D. Dottridge. index.

691 683 CN ISSN 0227-0595
BUILDCORE INDEX; construction materials, equipment & furniture available in Canada. 1974. a. Can.$74($71) Buildcore Inc., 1 Sparks Ave., Willowdale, Ont. M2H 2W1, Canada. TEL 416-493-2280. Ed. S. Klechek. adv. tr.lit. circ. 14,000.

690 UK ISSN 0084-814X
BUILDING AND ENGINEERING REVIEW.* 1965. a. 50p. c/o J. Woods, 10 Kingsberry Park, Rosetta, Belfast BT6 OHT, Northern Ireland.

691 UK ISSN 0068-3523
BUILDING BOARD DIRECTORY. 1959. biennial. £14. Benn Publications Ltd., 25 New Street Square, London EC4A 3JA, England (Orders to: Directories Dept., Sovereign Way, Tonbridge, Kent TN9 1RW, England) Ed. John Topham. adv. circ. 3,000.

692 US ISSN 0068-3531
BUILDING CONSTRUCTION COST DATA. 1942. a. $44.95. R.S. Means Company, Inc., 100 Construction Plaza, Kingston, MA 02364. TEL 617-747-1270. Ed. William D. Mahoney. index.

BUILDING SOCIETIES ASSOCIATION. REPORT OF THE COUNCIL. see *REAL ESTATE*

690 JM
BUILDING SOCIETIES ASSOCIATION OF JAMAICA FACTBOOK. 1974. a. free. Building Societies Association of Jamaica, Ltd., 73-75 Half Way Tree Rd., P.O.Box 141, Kingston 10, Jamaica. circ. 500.

690 DK
BYGGE NYTS LEVERANDOERREGISTER. a. Thomson Communications (Scandinavia) A-S, Struenseegade 7-9, DK-2200 Copenhagen N, Denmark. adv. circ. 11,914.

690 DK ISSN 0107-119X
BYGGE- OG BOLIGPOLITISKE OVERSIGT. 1971. a. free. Boligministeriet - Ministry of Housing, Slotsholmsgade 12, 1216 Copenhagen K, Denmark. bk. rev. circ. 300.
Formerly: Bygge- og Boligpolitiske Udvikling.

624 DK ISSN 0106-3715
BYGNINGSSTATISKE MEDDELELSER. (Text in Danish and English) 1929. irreg. (approx. 4/yr.) Kr.230. Dansk Selskab for Bygningsstatik, Bygning 118, Lundtoftevej 100, 2800 Lyngby, Denmark. Ed. L. Pilegaard Hansen. bibl. charts. illus. circ. 950. Indexed: Appl.Mech.Rev.

C A L U S RESEARCH REPORTS. (Centre for Advanced Land Use Studies) see *REAL ESTATE*

691 UK
C & C A TECHNICAL REPORT. 1954. irreg., latest Nov. 1986. Cement and Concrete Association, Wexham Springs, Slough SL3 6PL, Buckinghamshire, England. circ. 750. (back issues avail.) Indexed: HRIS.

691 SW ISSN 0346-6906
C B I FORSKNING/RESEARCH. (Text in English and Swedish; summaries in English) 1974. irreg. (approx. 6/yr.) Cement- och Betonginstitutet - Swedish Cement and Concrete Research Institute, S-100 44 Stockholm, Sweden.
Cement and concrete

691 SW ISSN 0346-8240
C B I RAPPORTER/REPORTS. (Text in English and Swedish; summaries in English) 1974. irreg. (approx. 6/yr.) Cement- och Betonginstitutet - Swedish Cement and Concrete Research Institute, S-100 44 Stockholm, Sweden.
Cement and concrete

C I R I A ANNUAL REPORT. (Construction Industry Research and Information Association) see *ENGINEERING — Civil Engineering*

C I R I A REPORT. (Construction Industry Research and Information Association) see *ENGINEERING — Civil Engineering*

C I R I A TECHNICAL NOTE. (Construction Industry Research and Information Association) see *ENGINEERING — Civil Engineering*

690 UK
C I T E NEWS. 1979. irreg. free. University of Strathclyde, Construction Information-Training Education Project, 131 Rottenrow, Glasgow G4 0NG, Scotland. Ed. Michael Munday. bk. rev. circ. 600.
Formerly: C I E News (ISSN 0143-7364)

690 CK
CAMARA COLOMBIANA DE LA CONSTRUCCION. ASAMBLEA NACIONAL. DOCUMENTO. 1957. a. $20. Camara Colombiana de la Construccion (CAMACOL), Carrera 10 No. 19-65, Piso 10, Apdo. 28588, Bogota D.E., Colombia. adv. circ. 10,000.

690.06 CN ISSN 0316-9375
CANADIAN CONSTRUCTION ASSOCIATION. DOCUMENTATION DE REFERENCE. (English edition available) (Text in French) 1972. irreg. Canadian Construction Association - Association Canadienne de la Construction, 85 Albert St., 2nd Fl., Ottawa, Ont. K1P 6A4, Canada. TEL 613-236-9455. illus. circ. 17,000. (processed) Key Title: Documentation de Reference - Association Canadienne de la Construction.

690 CN ISSN 0068-984X
CANADIAN TECHNICAL ASPHALT ASSOCIATION. PROCEEDINGS OF THE ANNUAL CONFERENCE. 1956. a. Can.$24.50 per no. to non-members. (Canadian Technical Asphalt Association) Polyscience Publications Inc., 555 Legendre E, Suite 24, Montreal, Quebec H2M 1G2, Canada. Ed. J. Clusiau. circ. 600.

690 AT
CARPENTER AND JOINER. 1960. irreg. (Building Workers' Industrial Union of Australia, Victorian Branch) Industrial Printing and Publicity Co. Ltd., 122 Dover St., Richmond, Vic. 3121, Australia. Ed. A. Zeeno.

CATALOG OF MODEL SERVICES AND SUPPLIES. see *ENGINEERING*

690 NE
CATALOGUS BOUWWERELD. a. Nijgh Periodieken B.V., Postbox 122, 3100 AC Schiedam, Netherlands. circ. 6,500.

691.5 YU ISSN 0008-882X
CEMENT; casopis industrije cementa jugoslavije. (Text in Croatian; summaries in English, French and German) 1957. irreg. $20. J.U.C.E.M.A. - Association of the Yugoslav Cement and Asbestos-Cement Producers, Prilaz JA 30, Zagreb, Yugoslavia. Ed. S. Keglevic. adv. bk. rev. charts. illus. index. circ. 650. Indexed: Chem.Abstr.

691.3 UK ISSN 0143-1560
CEMENT & CONCRETE ASSOCIATION. DEVELOPMENT REPORT. 1978. irreg. Cement & Concrete Association, Wexham Springs, Slough SL3 6PL, England.
Concrete

693 JA
CEMENT ASSOCIATION OF JAPAN. REVIEW OF THE GENERAL MEETING. (Text in English) 1947. a. 3,000 Yen. Cement Association of Japan, c/o Hattori Bldg., 1-1 Kyobashi, Chuo-ku, Tokyo 104, Japan. abstr.

620.1 JA
CEMENT ASSOCIATION OF JAPAN. REVIEW OF THE GENERAL MEETING. TECHNICAL SESSION. (Text in English) 1973. a. 3,500 Yen. Cement Association of Japan, c/o Hattori Bldg., 1-1 Kyobashi, Chuo-ku, Tokyo 104, Japan. abstr.

690 US
CEMENT: LATIN AMERICAN INDUSTRIAL REPORT. (Avail. for each of 22 Latin American countries) 1985. a. $435 per country report per industry covered. Aurora International, Box 9099, Bridgeport, CT 06601-2099. TEL 203-368-0579. Ed. Andres C. Aquino.

693 FR
CEMENT STANDARDS OF THE WORLD. irreg. 600 F. Cembureau, 2 rue Saint Charles, 75740 Paris Cedex 15, France.

691 AG ISSN 0008-8927
CEMENTO PORTLAND. 1944. a. contr. circ. Instituto del Cemento Portland Argentino, Calle San Martin 1137, Buenos Aires, Argentina. Ed. Carlos E. Duvoy. bk. rev. bibl. charts. illus. circ. 30,000.
Cement and concrete

690 II
CENTRAL BUILDING RESEARCH INSTITUTE. BUILDING RESEARCH NOTE. (Text in English) 1963; N.S. 1982. irreg. Rs.5 for 5 issues. Central Building Research Institute, Roorkee, Uttar Pradesh, India.
Formerly (until 1982): Central Building Research Institute. Building Digest (ISSN 0557-319X)

016 690 II ISSN 0557-322X
CENTRAL BUILDING RESEARCH INSTITUTE. LIST OF PUBLICATIONS. (Text in English) irreg. free. Central Building Research Institute, Roorkee, Uttar Pradesh, India.

690 UK ISSN 0260-7727
CHARTERED INSTITUTE OF BUILDING. YEAR BOOK. 1967/68. a. £30. Chartered Institute of Building, Englemere, Kings Ride, Ascot, Berks, SL5 8BJ, England. adv. circ. 3,000. (reprint service avail. from UMI)
Formerly: Chartered Institute of Building. Year Book and Directory of Members (ISSN 0073-9014)

CHARTERED INSTITUTE OF PUBLIC FINANCE AND ACCOUNTANCY. DIRECT LABOUR STATISTICS. ACTUALS. see *BUILDING AND CONSTRUCTION — Abstracting, Bibliographies, Statistics*

CIVIC TRUST AWARDS. see *ARCHITECTURE*

BUILDING AND CONSTRUCTION

690 AT
COMMONWEALTH SCIENTIFIC AND INDUSTRIAL RESEARCH ORGANIZATION. DIVISION OF BUILDING RESEARCH. TECHNICAL PAPER. 1954. irreg. price varies. C.S.I.R.O., Division of Building Research, Graham Rd., Highett, Vic. 3190, Australia. Indexed: Biol.Abstr.

691.3 UK
CONCRETE SOCIETY. TECHNICAL REPORT. no.2, 1970. irreg., latest no.28, 1985. Concrete Society, Devon House, 12-15 Dartmouth St., London SW1H 9BL, England. Indexed: HRIS.
Concrete

691.3 UK ISSN 0069-8288
THE CONCRETE YEAR BOOK. 1924. a. £32($96) Palladian Publications Ltd., 11 Grosvenor Crescent, London SW1X 7EE, England. Ed. Josephine Smith. adv. circ. 1,200. (reprint service avail. from UMI)

690 BE ISSN 0045-8023
CONFEDERATION NATIONALE DE LA CONSTRUCTION. ANNUAIRE. (Text in Dutch and French) 1948. a. 1400 Fr. Confederation Nationale de la Construction, Lombardstraat 34-42, 1000 Brussels, Belgium. Ed.Bd. adv. circ. 2,400.

331.83 690 US
CONNECTICUT HOUSING PRODUCTION AND PERMIT AUTHORIZED CONSTRUCTION. 1982. a. Department of Housing, 1179 Main St., Hartford, CT 06103-1089. TEL 203-566-5264. Ed. Sandy Bergin. circ. 2,000.
Formed by the merger of: Housing Units in Connecticut. Annual Summary & Connecticut. Department of Community Affairs Division of Research and Program Evaluation. Construction Activity Authorized by Building Permits. Summary (ISSN 0069-9020)

690 GW
CONSTRUCTION ANNUAL. (Text in Arabic, English, French) 1984. a. DM.12. Vogel-Verlag KG, Max-Planck-Str. 7/9, Postfach 67 40, D-8700 Wuerzburg 1, W. Germany (B.R.D.) Ed. Arnold Metzner. adv. circ. 12,000(controlled)

690 001.642 US
CONSTRUCTION COMPUTER APPLICATIONS DIRECTORY. a. $45. Construction Industry Press, 58 Paul Dr., Ste. F, San Rafael, CA 94903. TEL 415-499-7674. Ed. Paul Levin.

690 634.9 622 US
CONSTRUCTION EQUIPMENT BUYERS GUIDE. vol.72, 1985. a. $25 per no. (included in subscr. to: Construction Equipment) Cahners Publishing Co., Inc., Building and Construction Group, Division of Reed Publishing USA, Cahners Plaza, 1350 E. Touhy Ave., Box 5080, Des Plaines, IL 60017-5080 TEL 312-635-8800. (Subscr. to: 44 Cook St., Denver, CO 80206) Ed. Kirk Landers. circ. 80,000.

CONSTRUCTION HISTORY. see ARCHITECTURE

338.4 US ISSN 0069-9187
CONSTRUCTION IN HAWAII. 1967. a. free. Bank of Hawaii, Economics Department, Box 2900, Honolulu, HI 96846. TEL 808-537-8307. Ed. David L. Ramsour. (back issues avail.)
Formerly: Housing Activity in Hawaii.

690 II
CONSTRUCTION INDUSTRIES AND TRADE ANNUAL. a. Praveen Corp., Sayajiganj, Baroda 390005, India. Ed. C.M. Pandit.
Formerly: Construction Industries and Trade Journal (ISSN 0010-6828)

CONSTRUCTION INDUSTRIES OF MASSACHUSETTS DIRECTORY; a directory and catalog of highway and heavy construction in New England. see BUSINESS AND ECONOMICS — Trade And Industrial Directories

690 UK
CONSTRUCTION INDUSTRY EUROPE. 1974. irreg. £18. House Information Services Ltd., 178-202 Gt. Portland St., London W1N 6NH, England.

690 US
CONSTRUCTION: LATIN AMERICAN INDUSTRIAL REPORT. (Avail. for each of 22 Latin American countries) 1985. a. $435 per country report per industry covered. Aurora International, Box 9099, Bridgeport, CT 06601-2099. TEL 203-368-0579. Ed. Andres C. Aquino.

CONSTRUCTION LAW REPORTS. see LAW

690 UK
CONSTRUCTION SURVEYORS INSTITUTE DIARY. a. Welbecson Ltd., 3 Thomas St., Hull, Humberside HU9 1EJ, England.

690 US ISSN 0069-9217
CONSTRUCTION WRITERS ASSOCIATION. NEWSLETTER. 1953. irreg., (approx. q.) Construction Writers Association, Box 259, Poolesville, MD 20837. circ. 100.

690 HK
CONTRACTORS PLANT AND EQUIPMENT (HONG KONG CATALOGUE) 1976. a. HK.$40. Far East Tade Press Ltd., 15/F Lockhart Centre, 301 Lockhart Rd., Hong Kong, Hong Kong. adv. circ. 4,000.

690 AT
CORDELL'S WHO'S WHO IN BUILDING: HOUSING. a. (plus quarterly updates) Aus.$195. Thomson Publications (Australia) Pty. Ltd. (Subsidiary of: Cordell Building Publications) 160 Sailors Bay Rd., Northbridge, N.S.W. 2063, Australia.

690 AT
CORDELL'S WHO'S WHO IN BUILDING: NON-HOUSING. a. (plus quarterly updates) Aus.$195. Thomson Publications (Australia) Pty. Ltd. (Subsidiary of: Cordell Building Publications) 160 Sailors Bay Rd, Northbridge, N.S.W. 2063, Australia.

690 721 AT
CORDELL'S WHO'S WHO IN DESIGN SPECIFYING. a. Aus.$195. Thomson Publications (Australia) Pty Ltd. (Subsidiary of: Cordell Building Publications) 160 Sailors Bay Rd., Northbridge, N.S.W. 2063, Australia.

690 US
COUNCIL OF AMERICAN BUILDING OFFICIALS. ONE AND TWO FAMILY DWELLING CODE. (Includes supplements) 1971. a. prices vary. Council of American Building Officials, 5360 South Workman Mill Rd., Whittier, CA 90601.
Formerly (until 1983): International Conference of Building Officials. One and Two Family Dwelling Code.

690.028 UK ISSN 0260-745X
CRANES TODAY HANDBOOK. 1974. a. £25($57) United Trade Press Ltd., 33-35 Bowling Geen Lane, London EC1R 2DA, England. Ed. Graham Brent. adv. circ. 5,000.

692.8 US ISSN 0161-7257
CURRENT CONSTRUCTION COSTS.* 1963. a. $31.95. Lee Saylor, Inc., 1420 Willow Pass Rd., Concord, CA 94520. circ. 8,000.

690 US
CURRENT CONSTRUCTION REPORTS. (Published in several monthly, quarterly, and annual series issued separately.) U.S. Bureau of the Census, Customer Services, Washington, DC 20233 TEL 301-763-4100. (Subscr. to: Supt. of Documents, Washington, DC 20402) (also avail. in microfiche)

CURRENT CONSTRUCTION REPORTS: HOUSING UNITS AUTHORIZED BY BUILDING PERMITS; states and selected standard metropolitan statistical areas. see HOUSING AND URBAN PLANNING

690 CY ISSN 0253-8725
CYPRUS. DEPARTMENT OF STATISTICS AND RESEARCH. CONSTRUCTION AND HOUSING REPORT. (Text in English) a. cyprus pounds 3. Department of Statistics and Research, Ministry of Finance, Nicosia, Cyprus.

690 DK ISSN 0105-7871
DANMARKS INGENIOERAKADEMI. BYGNINGSAFDELNINGEN. DIALOG. 1976. irreg. price varies. Danmarks Ingenioerakademi, Bygningsafdelningen, Bygn. 373, 2800 Lyngby, Denmark.

690 DK ISSN 0108-0571
DANMARKS TEKNISKE HOEJSKOLE. AFDELINGEN B. irreg., no. 85, 1980. price varies. Danmarks Tekniske Hoejskole, Afdelingen for Baerende Konstruktioner, Bygning 118, DK-2800 Lyngby, Denmark.

690 DK ISSN 0108-058X
DANMARKS TEKNISKE HOEJSKOLE. AFDELINGEN FOR BAERENDE KONSTRUKTIONER. SERIE I. 1970. irreg., latest no.80, 1985. free. Danmarks Tekniske Hoejskole, Afdelingen for Baerende Konstruktioner, Bygning 118, DK-2800 Lyngby, Denmark. illus.

DANSKE BYGGEMARKEDER. see BUSINESS AND ECONOMICS — Marketing And Purchasing

690 DK ISSN 0108-9803
DENMARK. BOLIGMINISTERIET. BUILDING REGULATIONS. 1977. irreg. Boligministeriet - Ministry of Housing, Slotsholmsgade 12, 1216 Copenhagen K, Denmark.

690 DK ISSN 0109-0321
DENMARK. STATENS BYGGEFORSKNINGSINSTITUT. PROGRAM RESUMEER. Cover title: Programresumeer. 1983. a. free. Statens Byggeforskningsinstitut, Hoersholm, Denmark.

690 UK
DIRECTORY OF CONTRACTORS AND PUBLIC WORKS ANNUAL & CONSTRUCTION INDUSTRIES BUYERS GUIDE. 1889. a. £35. Biggar & Co. (Publishers) Ltd., 23 Rodney Rd., Cheltenham, Gloucestershire, England. Ed. Peter Miers. adv. bk. rev. circ. 5,000.
Formerly: Directory of Contractors and Construction Industries Buyers Guide.

690 US
DIRECTORY OF LICENSED PRODUCTS. 1961. a. free. Air Movement and Control Association, 30 W. University Dr., Arlington Heights, IL 60004. TEL 312-394-0150. Ed. Prasad Bhatt. circ. 10,000.

690 UK ISSN 0263-5437
DO-IT-YOURSELF REPORT. 1978. irreg. £95. Euromonitor Publications Ltd., 87-88 Turnmill St., London EC1M 5QU, England.
Formerly: Euromonitor Reports on D I Y and Home Improvement Markets (ISSN 0260-6542)

690 US
DODGE ASSEMBLIES COST DATA. a. $64.50. Dodge Cost Systems (Subsidiary of: McGraw-Hill Information Systems Co.) Box 28, Princeton, NJ 08543. TEL 609-426-7300.
Formerly: Dodge Construction Systems Costs.

624 US
DODGE HEAVY CONSTRUCTION COST DATA. 1968. a. $59.50. Dodge Cost Systems (Subsidiary of: McGraw-Hill Information Systems Co.) Box 28, Princeton, NJ 08543. TEL 609-426-7300.
Formerly: Dodge Guide to Public Works and Heavy Construction Costs.

690 US
DODGE REMODELLING & RETROFIT COST DATA. 1986. a. $45. Dodge Cost Information System, (Subsidiary of: McGraw-Hill Information Systems Co.) Box 28, Princeton, NJ 08543. TEL 609-426-7300. circ. 3,000.

690 US
DODGE SQUARE FOOT COST DATA. a. $186.50. Dodge Cost Systems (Subsidiary of: McGraw-Hill Information Systems Co.) Box 28, Princeton, NJ 08543. TEL 609-426-7300.
Formerly: Dodge Digest of Building Costs and Specifications.

690 US
DODGE UNIT COST DATA. 1966. a. $55. Dodge Cost Systems (Subsidiary of: McGraw-Hill Information Systems Co.) Box 28, Princeton, NJ 08543. TEL 609-426-7300.
Formerly: Dodge Manual for Building Construction Pricing and Scheduling.

BUILDING AND CONSTRUCTION

692.8   US   ISSN 0098-6453
E N R DIRECTORY OF CONTRACTORS. 1974. biennial. $32.50. McGraw-Hill Information Systems Co., 1221 Ave. of the Americas, New York. TEL 212-512-4634. Ed. James H. Webber. illus. circ. 11,000. Indexed: PROMT.

E N R DIRECTORY OF DESIGN FIRMS. see *ENGINEERING*

690   330   FR
ECONOMIE FRANCAISE EN PERSPECTIVES SECTORIELLES: FILIERE BATIMENT, GENIE CIVIL, MATERIAUX DE CONSTRUCTION. a. membership. Bureau d'Informations et de Previsions Economiques, 122 Av. Charles de Gaulle, 92522 Neuilly sur Seine, France.
    Formerly: Prevision a Un An de la Filiere Construction; Supersedes in part: Prevision a Un An de l'Economie Francaise.

EDUCATION FOR THE CONSTRUCTION INDUSTRY IN THE REGION. see *EDUCATION — Higher Education*

690   UN
EDUCATIONAL BUILDING DIGEST. 1973. irreg. (5-6/yr.) free or on exchange basis. Unesco, Principal Regional Office for Education in Asia and the Pacific, G.P.O. Box 1425, Bangkok 10501, Thailand. charts. illus. circ. 3,000. (looseleaf format)
    Formerly: School Building Digest.

692.8   FR   ISSN 0014-9373
ENTREPRISE EUROPEENNE. (Text in English, French and German) 1954. irreg. 50 F. ‡ (Federation Europeenne de la Construction) Societe d'Editions et de Publications Internationales du Batiment et des Travaux Publics, 33 Av. Kleber, 75116 Paris, France. adv. bk. rev. charts. illus. circ. 3,000.
    Former titles: International Federation of European Contractors of Building and Public Works Review (ISSN 0020-6687); International Federation of Building and Public Works Review.

690   UK
FACULTY OF BUILDING. REGISTER OF MEMBERS.* 1972. irreg. £5 per no. (Faculty of Building) Millbank Publications Ltd., 25 Catherine St., London WC2B 5JW, England. adv. circ. 5,500.

FENCE INDUSTRY/ACCESS CONTROL DIRECTORY. see *BUSINESS AND ECONOMICS — Trade And Industrial Directories*

690   GW   ISSN 0071-4585
DER FERTIGHAUS-KATALOG. 1965. a. DM.24.80. Fachschriften-Verlag GmbH, Hoehenstr. 17, Postfach 1329, 7012 Fellbach, W. Germany (B.R.D.)

FLORIDA BUILDERS AND CONTRACTORS DIRECTORY. see *BUSINESS AND ECONOMICS — Trade And Industrial Directories*

690   FR   ISSN 0291-8897
FRANCE. DIRECTION DES AFFAIRES ECONOMIQUES ET INTERNATIONALES. INFORMATIONS RAPIDES. 1980. irreg. free. (Direction des Affaires Economiques et Internationales) Documentation Francaise, 29-31 Quai Voltaire, 75340 Paris Cedex 07, France (Subscr. to: Documentation Francaise, 124 rue Henri Barbusse) (also avail. in microfiche; back issues avail.)

690   747   643.3   AT
GABRIEL'S HOME IMPROVEMENT ANNUAL. 1980. a. Hay Street Publications Pty Ltd, 405-411 Sussex St, Sydney, NSW 2000, Australia. Ed. Barry Cooke. circ. 110,000.

690   747   643.3   AT
GABRIEL'S KITCHENS AND BATHROOMS ANNUAL. 1985. a. Hay Street Publications Pty Ltd, 405-411 Sussex St, Sydney, NSW 2000, Australia. Ed. Barry Cooke. circ. 70,000.

690   US   ISSN 0195-847X
GOLD BOOK OF MULTIHOUSING. 1979. a. $140. L S I Systems Inc., 11-A Village Green, Crofton, MD 21114. TEL 301-261-6363. Ed. Donald F. Spear. charts. stat. circ. 450.

690   796.352   380   US
GOLF COURSE BUILDERS OF AMERICA DIRECTORY. a. free. Golf Course Builders of America, 4361 Northlake Blvd., P.B. Gardens, FL 33410. TEL 305-694-2977. circ. 2,000.

691   YU   ISSN 0350-1701
GRADJEVINSKI FAKULTET. INSTITUT ZA MATERIJALE I KONSTRUKCIJE. ZBORNIK ISTRAZIVACKIH RADOVA. 1972. a. 400 din. Univerzitet u Sarajevu, Gradjevinski Fakultet, Institut za Materijale i Konstrukcije, Stjepana Tomica 5, Sarajevo, Yugoslavia. Ed. Nadezda Knezevic Vuksanovic. circ. 750.

690   UK   ISSN 0068-354X
GREAT BRITAIN. BUILDING RESEARCH ESTABLISHMENT. ANNUAL REPORT. a. price varies. Building Research Establishment, Garston, Watford WD2 7JR, England. (also avail. in microform from UMI; reprint service avail. from UMI) Indexed: Met.Abstr. Fluidex.
    Former titles: Forest Products Research; Fire Research Annual Reports (ISSN 0071-5433)

GREAT BRITAIN. BUILDING RESEARCH ESTABLISHMENT. REPORTS. see *FIRE PREVENTION*

GREAT BRITAIN. DEPARTMENT OF THE ENVIRONMENT. METRICATION IN THE CONSTRUCTION INDUSTRY. see *METROLOGY AND STANDARDIZATION*

690   UK
GREAT BRITAIN. H.M.S.O. GOVERNMENT PUBLICATIONS SECTIONAL LISTS. irreg. free. H.M.S.O., Box 569, London SE1 9NH, England. (reprint service avail. from UMI)

690   747   UK
GUIDE TO RESTORATION EXPERTS. 1980. every 18 mos. £8.50($14.50) (Guild of Master Craftsmen) G M C Publications Ltd., 166 High St., Lewes, E. Sussex, England. Ed. Mairi M. Baker. adv. bk. rev. circ. 5,000.

691   US
GUIDE TO STABILITY DESIGN CRITERIA FOR METAL STRUCTURES. (Former name of issuing body: Column Research Council) 1976. irreg.; latest, 3rd edition. $63.95. (Structural Stability Research Council) John Wiley & Sons, Fritz Engineering Laboratory No. 13, Lehigh University, Bethlehem, PA 18015. Ed. B. G. Johnston.
    Formerly: Guide to Design Criteria for Metal Structures.

690.24   UK
GUILD OF MASTER CRAFTSMEN DIRECTORY OF MEMBERS. 1978. a. £6.95. (Guild of Master Craftsman) Guild of Master Craftsman Publications Ltd., 166 High St., Lewes, E. Sussex BN7 1YE, England. TEL (0273) 477374. Ed. Mairi Baker. circ. 5,000. (back issues avail.)

690   DK
HAANDBOG FOR BYGNINGSINDUSTRIEN. biennial. Nyt Nordisk Forlag - Arnold Busck A-S, Koebmagergade 49, 1150 Copenhagen K, Denmark. adv. circ. 8,200.

690   GW   ISSN 0017-7202
HANDBUCH DES BAUHERRN; Neubau - Umbau - Modernisierung. 1964. a. membership. Heinze GmbH, Bremer Weg 184, Postfach 505, 3100 Celle, W. Germany (B.R.D.) Ed. Juergen Wolf. adv. circ. 600,000.

690   340   GW
HANDBUCH DES GRUNDSTUECKS- UND BAURECHTS. irreg. DM.176. Werner-Verlag GmbH, Berliner Allee 11A, Postfach 8529, 4000 Duesseldorf 1, W. Germany (B.R.D.) (looseleaf format)

338.4   US
HISTORICAL PLANT COST AND ANNUAL PRODUCTION EXPENSES FOR SELECTED ELECTRIC PLANTS. a. U.S. Energy Information Administration, Forrestal Bldg., Washington, DC 20585 TEL 202-252-8800. (Orders to: Supt. Doc., Washington, DC 20402)
    Former titles: Thermal-Electric Plant Construction Cost and Production Expenses & Steam Electric Plant Construction Cost and Annual Production Expenses (ISSN 0083-0852)

HONG KONG ARCHITECTS & DESIGNERS CATALOGUE. see *ARCHITECTURE*

338.4   HK
HONG KONG BUILDER DIRECTORY. (Text in Chinese, English) a. HK.$280. Far East Trade Press Ltd. (Subsidiary of: Tradenews Asia Ltd.) 15/F Lockhart Centre, 301-307A Lockhart Centre, Hong Kong, Hong Kong. Eds. Iris Stoner. adv. illus. circ. 8,000.

690   UK
HOUSE'S GUIDE TO THE CONSTRUCTION INDUSTRY. 1968. a. £14. Van Nostrand Reinhold (UK) Co. Ltd., Molly Millar's Lane, Wokingham, Berkshire RG11 2PY, England.
    Former titles: Construction Industry U.K; House's Guide to the Construction Industry; House's Guide to the Building Industry (ISSN 0073-361X)

690   UK
HOUSING CONSTRUCTION CATALOGUE. a. Standard Catalogue Information Services Ltd., Medway Wharf Rd., Tonbridge, Kent TN9 1QR, England. circ. 20,000.

690   HU   ISSN 0018-7720
HUNGARIAN BUILDING BULLETIN. Russian edition: Vengerskii Stroitel'nyi Byulleten' (ISSN 0505-1983) (Editions in English and Russian) 1958. q. free. Epitesugyi Tajekoztatasi Kozpont, Harsfa u. 21, 1074 Budapest, Hungary. Ed. P. Hamvay. bk. rev. abstr. bibl. index. circ. 400. Indexed: Br.Ceram.Abstr.

691   US
HUTTON'S BUILDING PRODUCTS CATALOG. 1978. a. contr. circ. Hutton Publishing Co., Inc., 375 N. Broadway, Jericho, NY 11753. TEL 516-935-2740. adv. circ. 14,407.
    Formerly: B P C (Building Products Catalog) (ISSN 0161-6293)

690.24   US
HUTTON'S MECHANICAL PRODUCTS CATALOG. 1963. a. contr. circ. Hutton Publishing Co., Inc., 375 N. Broadway, Jericho, NY 11753. TEL 516-935-2740. circ. 15,053.

690   AU   ISSN 0018-8697
I B NACHRICHTEN. 1963. irreg. free. Oesterreichisches Institut fuer Bauforschung, An den Langen Luessen 1/6, A-1190 Vienna, Austria. Ed. Gertraud Winkler. bk. rev. abstr. charts. illus. circ. 1,000.

690   US
I E E E CEMENT INDUSTRY TECHNICAL CONFERENCE. RECORD. a. price varies. (I E E E, Industry Applications Society) Institute of Electrical and Electronics Engineers, Inc., 345 E. 47th St., New York, NY 10017 TEL 212-705-7900. (Subscr. address: 445 Hoes Lane, Piscataway, NJ 08854)
    Formerly: Cement Industry Technical Conference. Record (ISSN 0069-1402)

691   US
ILLINOIS DEALER DIRECTORY AND BUYER'S GUIDE. 1932. a. $20. Illinois Lumber and Material Dealers Association, 150 Leland Building, Springfield, IL 62701. TEL 217-544-5405. adv. circ. 750.
    Formerly: Illinois Directory and Suppliers Listing (ISSN 0073-4799)

INCOME-EXPENSE ANALYSIS: CONVENTIONAL APARTMENTS. see *REAL ESTATE*

691   BE
INDUSTRIE CIMENTIERE BELGE/BELGISCHE CEMENTNIJVERHEID. (Text and summaries in Dutch and French) 1976. a. free. Federation de l'Industrie Cimentiere - Verbond der Cementmijverheid, 46 rue Cesar Franck, 1050 Brussels, Belgium. stat. circ. 400-550.

690   VE
INFORMADOR DE LA CONSTRUCCION Y DE LA INDUSTRIA/CONSTRUCTION AND INDUSTRY BULLETIN. 1957. a. $50. Publicaciones Sangar CA, Apdo. 2323, Caracas, Venezuela. Ed. Santiago Garcia Bartolme. adv. circ. 10,000.

BUILDING AND CONSTRUCTION

690　　　　　　UK　ISSN 0073-9073
INSTITUTE OF CLERK OF WORKS OF GREAT BRITAIN INCORPORATED. YEAR BOOK.* 1930. a. 52.5p. G.W. Harris, 43 Leopold Road, Willesden, London, NW10, England.

690　　　　　　UK　ISSN 0267-2030
INSTITUTE OF MAINTENANCE AND BUILDING MANAGEMENT. REFERENCE BOOK AND LIST OF MEMBERS. 1985. a. £25. Millbank Publications, 25 Catherine St., London WC2B 5JW, England. TEL 01-379-3036. Ed. K.J. Allen. adv. circ. 2,500.

690　　　　　　NE
INSTITUTE T N O FOR BUILDING MATERIALS AND BUILDING STRUCTURES. ANNUAL REPORT. (Text in Dutch) 1954. a. Institute T N O for Building Materials and Building Structures, Lange Kleiweg 5, Rijswijk ZH, Netherlands (Mailing address: Postbus 49, 2600 AA Delft, Netherlands) Ed. F.K. Ligtenberg. bibl. charts. illus. circ. 2,500.

690　　　　　　UK
INSULATION HANDBOOK. a. £11.50. Turret-Wheatland Ltd., 12 Greycaine Rd., Watford, Herts. WD2 4JP, England.

690　　　　　　US　ISSN 8755-7541
INTERIOR COST DATA (YEAR) 1984. a. $45.95. R.S. Means Company, Inc., 100 Construction Plaza, Kingston, MA 02364. TEL 617-747-1270. Ed. William D. Mahoney.

690　　　　　　US
INTERNATIONAL CONFERENCE OF BUILDING OFFICALS. ACCUMULATIVE SUPPLEMENT TO THE UNIFORM CODES. a. $10 to members; non-members $13. International Conference of Building Officials, 5360 S. Workman Mill Rd., Whittier, CA 90601. TEL 213-699-0541.
　Formerly: International Conference of Building Officials. Accumulative Supplements to the Codes.

690　　　　　　US
INTERNATIONAL CONFERENCE OF BUILDING OFFICIALS. ANALYSIS OF REVISIONS TO THE UNIFORM BUILDING CODE. triennial. $7.70 to members; non-members $10. International Conference of Building Officials, 5360 S. Workman Mill Rd., Whittier, CA 90601. TEL 213-699-0541.

690　　　　　　US
INTERNATIONAL CONFERENCE OF BUILDING OFFICIALS. BUILDING DEPARTMENT ADMINISTRATION. 1973. irreg. $37.40 to non-members; members $28.75. International Conference of Building Officials, 5360 S. Workman Mill Rd., Whittier, CA 90601. TEL 213-699-0541.

690　　　　　　US　ISSN 0579-3769
INTERNATIONAL CONFERENCE OF BUILDING OFFICIALS. CODE CHANGES COMMITTEE. ANNUAL REPORT.* a. International Conference of Building Officials, 5360 S. Workman Mill Rd., Whittier, CA 90601.

690　　　　　　US
INTERNATIONAL CONFERENCE OF BUILDING OFFICIALS. DWELLING CONSTRUCTION UNDER THE UNIFORM BUILDING CODE. triennial. $7.65 to members; non-members $10. International Conference of Building Officials, 5360 S. Workman Mill Rd., Whittier, CA 90601. TEL 213-699-0541.

690　　　　　　US　ISSN 0082-7584
INTERNATIONAL CONFERENCE OF BUILDING OFFICIALS. UNIFORM BUILDING CODE. 1927. triennial. $36.30 to members; non-members $47.20. International Conference of Building Officials, 5360 S. Workman Mill Road, Whittier, CA 90601. TEL 213-699-0541. Ed. Beverly J. Eicholtz.

690　　　　　　US
INTERNATIONAL CONFERENCE OF BUILDING OFFICIALS. UNIFORM CODE FOR THE ABATEMENT OF DANGEROUS BUILDINGS. triennial. $6.20 to members; non-members $8.05; bulk rates avail. International Conference of Building Officials, 5360 S. Workman Mill Rd., Whittier, CA 90601. TEL 213-699-0541.

690　　　　　　US
INTERNATIONAL CONFERENCE OF BUILDING OFFICIALS. UNIFORM FIRE CODE. triennial. $22.80 to members; non-members $29.60; bulk rates avail. International Conference of Building Officials, 5360 S. Workman Mill Rd., Whittier, CA 90601. TEL 213-699-0541.

690　692　　　　US　ISSN 0501-1213
INTERNATIONAL CONFERENCE OF BUILDING OFFICIALS. UNIFORM HOUSING CODE. 1955. triennial. $6.20 to members; non-members $8.05; bulk rates avail. International Conference of Building Officials, 5360 S. Workman Mill Rd., Whittier, CA 90601. TEL 213-699-0541.

690　　　　　　US
INTERNATIONAL CONFERENCE OF BUILDING OFFICIALS. UNIFORM MECHANICAL CODE. triennial. $26 to members; non-members $29.70; bulk rates avail. International Conference of Building Officials, 5360 S. Workman Mill Rd., Whittier, CA 90601. TEL 213-699-0541.

690　　　　　　UK
INTERNATIONAL DIRECTORY OF BUILDING RESEARCH, INFORMATION AND DEVELOPMENT ORGANIZATIONS. 1959. irreg., latest issue 1986. £39.50. International Council for Building Research, Studies and Documentation, 11 New Feler Lane, London EC4P 4EE, England.
　Formerly: C I B Directory of Building Research Information and Development Organizations (ISSN 0419-2281)

690　　　　　　UK
INTERNATIONAL HEALTH CARE CONSTRUCTION & EQUIPMENT. a. Standard Catalogue Information Services Ltd., Medway Wharf Rd., Tonbridge, Kent TN9 1QR, England. circ. 12,500.

691　　　　　　FI
INTERNATIONAL TRADE CONFERENCE OF WORKERS OF THE BUILDING, WOOD AND BUILDING MATERIALS INDUSTRIES. (BROCHURE) irreg, 7th, 1975. Trade Unions International of Workers of the Building, Wood and Building Materials Industries, Box 281, 00101 Helsinki 10, Finland.

690　　　　　　IS　ISSN 0069-9195
ISRAEL. CENTRAL BUREAU OF STATISTICS. CONSTRUCTION IN ISRAEL/HA-BINUI BE-YISRAEL. (Subseries of the Bureau's Special Series) (Text in English, Hebrew) 1960/63. irreg. price varies. Central Bureau of Statistics, Box 13015, Jerusalem, Israel.

690　　　　　　IS
ISRAEL INSTITUTE OF TECHNOLOGY-TECHNION. RESEARCH REPORTS. (Text in English) biennial. free. Israel Institute of Technology-Technion, Building Research Station, Technion City, Haifa 32 000, Israel. TEL 04-292242.

693　　　　　　TH　ISSN 0125-1759
JOURNAL OF FERROCEMENT. 1976. q. $36 to individuals; institutions US$70. International Ferrocement Information Centre, Box 2754, Bangkok, Thailand. Ed. Ricardo P. Pama. adv. bk. rev. abstr. illus. index. circ. 700. (reprint service avail. from UMI) Indexed: Appl.Mech.Rev. BMT. C.R.I. Abstr.
　Former titles: N Z F C M A Bulletin; N Z F C M A Newsletter.
　Cement and concrete

K B S TEKNISKA FOERESKRIFTER/K B S TECHNICAL REGULATIONS; krav och raad/ requirements and recommendations. see *HOUSING AND URBAN PLANNING*

690　　　　　　US　ISSN 0075-6768
KONSTRUKTIONSBUECHER. (Text in German) 1955. irreg., vol.35, 1985. price varies. Springer-Verlag, 175 Fifth Ave., New York, NY 10010 TEL 212-460-1500. (Also Berlin, Heidelberg, Tokyo and Vienna) (reprint service avail. from ISI)

690　　　　　　SW　ISSN 0075-6776
KONTROLLRAADET FOER BETONGVAROR. MEDDELANDE. 1950. a. free. Kontrollraadet foer Betongvaror - Swedish Council for Precast Concrete Control, Kronobergsgatan 49, S-112 33 Stockholm, Sweden. Ed. Ivar Magnusson. circ. 5,000.

KUNST AM BAU. see *ARCHITECTURE*

692　331　　　　US　ISSN 0098-3608
LABOR RATES FOR THE CONSTRUCTION INDUSTRY. 1973. a. $100. R.S. Means Company, Inc., 100 Construction Plaza, Kingston, MA 02364. TEL 617-747-1270. Ed. William D. Mahoney.

691　　　　　　UK
LAXTON'S NATIONAL BUILDING PRICE BOOK. a. £33. Thomas Skinner Directories, Windsor Court, East Grinstead, West Sussex RH19 1XB, England. adv. stat. circ. 11,000.
　Formerly: Laxton's Building Price Book (ISSN 0305-6589)

691.3　　　　　US　ISSN 0075-9457
LIGHTWEIGHT CONCRETE INFORMATION SHEETS. 1952. irreg. free. Expanded Shale, Clay and Slate Institute, 6218 Montrose Rd., Rockville, MD 20852. Ed. Harry C. Robinson. circ. 20,000.
　Technical data sheets on lightweight concrete and on lightweight concrete masonry

LOG HOUSE. see *ARCHITECTURE*

MADERA Y SU USO EN LA CONSTRUCCION. see *FORESTS AND FORESTRY — Lumber And Wood*

MAINTENANCE SUPPLIES. see *BUSINESS AND ECONOMICS — Trade And Industrial Directories*

690　620　　　　CN
MANITOBA CONSTRUCTION INDUSTRY DIRECTORY. PURCHASING GUIDE. 1966. a. Can.$12. Sanford Evans Communications Ltd., 1077 St. James St., Box 6900, Winnipeg, Man. R3C 3B1, Canada. TEL 204-775-0201. adv. circ. 6,017.

690　　　　　　CN
MANITOBA/WINNIPEG BUILDING & CONSTRUCTION TRADES COUNCIL YEARBOOK. 1971. a. Naylor Communications Ltd., 100 Sutherland Ave., Winnipeg, Man. R2W 3C7, Canada. TEL 204-947-0222. Ed. Theresa Harrison. circ. 1,825.

691　　　　　　US
MEANS ASSEMBLIES COSTS. 1976. a. $49.95. R.S. Means Company, Inc., 100 Construction Plaza, Kingston, MA 02364. Ed. William D. Mahoney.
　Formerly: Means Systems Costs.

691　　　　　　US
MEANS CONCRETE COST DATA. 1982. a. $45.95. R.S. Means Company, Inc., 100 Construction Plaza, Kingston, MA 02364. TEL 617-747-1270. Ed. William D. Mahoney. bk. rev. circ. 3,000. (back issues avail.)
　Formerly: Concrete and Masonry Cost Data (ISSN 0739-8298)

690　　　　　　US　ISSN 0277-8610
MEANS HISTORICAL COST INDEXES. a. $26.95. R.S. Means Company, Inc., 100 Construction Plaza, Kingston, MA 02364-0800. TEL 617-747-1270. Ed. William D. Mahoney. charts. stat. circ. 250. (back issues avail.)

691　　　　　　US　ISSN 0734-8479
MEANS SITE WORK COST DATA. 1982. a. $46.95. R.S. Means Company, Inc., 100 Construction Plaza, Kingston, MA 02364. Ed. William D. Mahoney.

MEANS SQUARE FOOT COSTS; residential, commercial, industrial, institutional. see *REAL ESTATE*

690　　　　　　US　ISSN 0748-2698
MECHANICAL COST DATA. 1978. a. $46.95. R.S. Means Company, Inc., 100 Construction Plaza, Duxbury, MA 02364. Ed. William D. Mahoney.
　Formerly: Mechanical and Electrical Cost Data (ISSN 0193-1954)

690　658　　　　SA
MERKELS' BUILDERS' PRICING AND MANAGEMENT MANUAL. 1948. a. R.180. Thomson Publications S. A. (Pty) Ltd., Thomson House, Cnr. Will Scarlet & Hendrik Verwoerd, Randburg, P.O. Box 56182, Pinegowrie 2123, South Africa. adv.

BUILDING AND CONSTRUCTION

690   UK
MIDDLE EAST CONSTRUCTION CATALOGUE (BUILDING PRODUCTS EDITION) 1979. a. £40. Standard Catalogue Information Services Ltd., Medway Wharf Rd., Tonbridge, Kent, England. circ. 7,000.

DAS MODERNE HEIM; mit der "Internationalen Bauchronik". see *ARCHITECTURE*

691   DK   ISSN 0108-8602
MURERHAANDBOG. 1963. a. Kr.5. Kalk- og Teglinformation, Teglbaekvej 20, 8361 Hassselager, Denmark. illus.

690   CN   ISSN 0380-8599
N B C/N F C NEWS. (National Building Code/National Fire Code) (Text in English and French) 1957. irreg. free. (Associate Committee on the National Building Code, Division of Building Research) National Research Council of Canada, Ottawa, Ont. K1A OR6, Canada. TEL 613-993-9960. (Co-sponsor: Associate Committee on the National Fire Code) Ed. L. Saint-Martin. circ. 27,000.
    Formerly: N B C News (ISSN 0027-612X)

695   UK
N F R C YEARBOOK. 1979. a. National Federation of Roofing Contractors, 15 Soho Square, London W1V 5FB, England. Ed. A. Watts. adv.
    Roofing

690   FI   ISSN 0078-1126
N K B SKRIFTSERIE/N K B PUBLICATION SERIES. (Text in Danish, English, Norwegian, and Swedish) 1964. irreg., no.36, 1978. free. Nordiske Komite for Bygningsbestemmelsei, Eerikinkatu 24, SF-00100 Helsinki, Finland. circ. 500.

691.3   US   ISSN 0077-5355
N R M C A PUBLICATION. 1931. irreg., 1973, no. 144. price varies. National Ready Mixed Concrete Association, 900 Spring St., Silver Spring, MD 20910. TEL 301-587-1400. Ed. R.D. Gaynor. circ. 2,000. Indexed: Concr.Abstr.

691   UK
NATIONAL ASSOCIATION OF SCAFFOLDING CONTRACTORS YEAR BOOK. 1979. a. Comprint Ltd., 177 Hagden Lane, Watford, Herts. WD1 8LW, England.

666.8   II
NATIONAL COUNCIL FOR CEMENT AND BUILDING MATERIALS. ANNUAL REPORT. (Text in English) a. National Council for Cement and Building Materials, M-10 South Extension II, Ring Rd., New Delhi 110049, India. illus.
    Formerly: Cement Research Institute of India. Annual Report.

690   UK
NATIONAL FEDERATION OF BUILDING TRADES EMPLOYERS' NORTH WESTERN REGION YEAR BOOK AND DIRECTORY. 1908. a. £1.50. National Federation of Building Trades Employers, 2 Conyngham Rd., Victoria Park, Manchester M14 5SH, England. circ. 3,000.

691   UK   ISSN 0077-4480
NATIONAL FEDERATION OF PLASTERING CONTRACTORS. YEAR BOOK. 1958. a. free. Comprint Ltd., 177 Hagden Lane, Watford, Herts WD1 8LW, England. Ed. K. Williams. adv. circ. 2,500.

690   CN   ISSN 0701-5216
NATIONAL RESEARCH COUNCIL, CANADA. DIVISION OF BUILDING RESEARCH. BUILDING PRACTICE NOTE. (Editions in English, French) 1976. irreg. free. National Research Council of Canada, Institute for Research in Construction, Ottawa, Ont., K1A OR6, Canada. TEL 613-993-2463. Eds. L. Hayes, A.M. Dorais. circ. 1,900(English edit.); 500(French edit.) (back issues avail.)

690   CN   ISSN 0077-5460
NATIONAL RESEARCH COUNCIL, CANADA. DIVISION OF BUILDING RESEARCH. BUILDING RESEARCH NOTE. (Text in English) 1950. irreg. free. National Research Council of Canada, Division of Building Research, Ottawa, Ont. K1A OR6, Canada. TEL 613-993-2463. Eds. L. Hayes, A.M. Dorais.

690   CN   ISSN 0381-4319
NATIONAL RESEARCH COUNCIL, CANADA. DIVISION OF BUILDING RESEARCH. D B R PAPER. (Text in English) 1975. irreg. price varies. National Research Council of Canada, Division of Building Research, Ottawa, Ont. K1A OR6, Canada. TEL 613-993-2463. Eds. L. Hayes, A.M. Dorais.

690   CN
NATIONAL RESEARCH COUNCIL, CANADA. DIVISION OF BUILDING RESEARCH. PROCEEDINGS. (Editions in English, French) 1976. irreg. price varies. National Research Council of Canada, Division of Building Research, Ottawa, Ont. K1A OR6, Canada. TEL 613-993-2463. Eds. L. Hayes, A.M. Dorais.

690   CN   ISSN 0077-5517
NATIONAL RESEARCH COUNCIL, CANADA. DIVISION OF BUILDING RESEARCH. RESEARCH PROGRAM. a. free. National Research Council of Canada, Division of Building Research, Ottawa, Ont. K1A OR6, Canada. TEL 613-993-2463. Eds. L. Hayes, A.M. Dorais.

690   CN   ISSN 0701-5208
NATIONAL RESEARCH COUNCIL, CANADA. DIVISION OF BUILDING RESEARCH. SPECIAL TECHNICAL PUBLICATION. (Editions in English, French) 1973. irreg. price varies. National Research Council of Canada, Division of Building Research, Ottawa, Ont. K1A OR6, Canada. TEL 613-993-2463. Ed. A.M. Dorais.

690   NO   ISSN 0065-0226
NORGES LANDBRUKSHOEGSKOLE. INSTITUTT FOR BYGNINGSTEKNIKK. AARSMELDING/ANNUAL REPORT. (Text in Norwegian; summaries in English) 1964. a. free. Norges Landbrukshoegskole, Institutt for Bygningsteknikk, Box 15, N-1432 Aas-NLH, Norway.

NORGES LANDBRUKSHOEGSKOLE. INSTITUTT FOR BYGNINGSTEKNIKK. BYGGEKOSTNADSINDEKS FOR DRIFTSBYGNINGER I JORDBRUKET. PRISUTVIKLINGEN. see *AGRICULTURE*

690   NO   ISSN 0065-0234
NORGES LANDBRUKSHOEGSKOLE. INSTITUTT FOR BYGNINGSTEKNIKK. MELDING. (Text in Norwegian; summaries in English) 1951. irreg., no.111, 1985. free. Norges Landbrukshoegskole, Institutt for Bygningsteknikk, Box 15, N-1432 Aas-NLH, Norway.

691 674   US
NORTHWESTERN LUMBERMENS ASSOCIATION DEALER REFERENCE MANUAL. a. $70. ‡ Northwestern Lumbermens Association, 1405 Lilac Dr., N., Ste. 130, Minneapolis, MN 55422-4505. TEL 612-544-6822. (Co-sponsor: Iowa Lumbermens Association) Ed. Lori Kyllo. adv. index. circ. 2,050.
    Formerly: Northwestern-Iowa Dealer Reference Manual (ISSN 0078-1800)

690   AT   ISSN 0300-371X
NOTES ON THE SCIENCE OF BUILDING. 1949. irreg. price varies. (National Building Technology Centre) Australian Government Publishing Service, P.O. Box 30, Chatswood, N.S.W. 2067, Australia. illus. cum.index. circ. 6,000.

OEFFENTLICHE BAUMAPPE DER OSTSCHWEIZ. see *ARCHITECTURE*

729 691   US   ISSN 0271-7220
OLD-HOUSE JOURNAL CATALOG. 1976. a. $13.95. Old-House Journal Corporation, 69A Seventh Ave., Brooklyn, NY 11217. TEL 718-636-4514. Ed. Patricia Poore. adv. illus. circ. 25,000.
    Formerly: Old-House Journal Buyers' Guide.

690   US   ISSN 0883-8127
OPEN SHOP BUILDING CONSTRUCTION COST DATA (YEAR) 1985. a. $48.95. R.S. Means Company, Inc., 100 Construction Plaza, Kingston, MA 02364. TEL 617-747-1270. Ed. William Mahoney.

690   UK   ISSN 0030-7432
OVERSEAS BUILDING NOTES. 1950. irreg. £1 per issue. ‡ Building Research Establishment, Garston, Watford WD2 7JR, England. Ed. W. Kinniburgh. bk. rev. bibl. charts. illus. index. circ. 2,500. Indexed: Abstr.Hyg. Trop.Dis.Bull.

691 720   BL
P & T. (Produtos e Tecnicas) a. Editora Pini Ltda., Rua Anhaia 964, Bom Retiro, 01130 Sao Paulo, Brazil. adv.

690   UK   ISSN 0267-2049
PLANT MANAGER'S DIRECTORY (YEAR) 1985. a. £19.95. Millbank Publications, 25 Catherine St., London WC2B 5JW, England. TEL 01-379-3036. Ed. K.J. Allen. adv. charts. circ. 3,000.

POLITECHNIKA GDANSKA. ZESZYTY NAUKOWE. BUDOWNICTWO LADOWE. see *ENGINEERING* — *Civil Engineering*

POLITECHNIKA LODZKA. ZESZYTY NAUKOWE. BUDOWNICTWO. see *ENGINEERING* — *Civil Engineering*

691   PL
POLITECHNIKA WARSZAWSKA. INSTYTUT TECHNOLOGII I ORGANIZACJI PRODUKCJI BUDOWLANEJ. PRACE. (Text in Polish; summaries in English and Russian) 1971. irreg. price varies. Politechnika Warszawska, Plac Jednosci Robotniczei 1, 00-661 Warsaw, Poland. illus. circ. 460.

690   PL   ISSN 0324-9883
POLITECHNIKA WROCLAWSKA. INSTYTUT BUDOWNICTWA. PRACE NAUKOWE. KONFERENCJE. (Text in Polish and English; summaries in Russian) 1974. irreg., no.11, 1985. price varies. Politechnika Wroclawska, Wybrzeze Wyspianskiego 27, 50-370 Wroclaw, Poland (Dist. by: Ars Polona-Ruch, Krakowskie Przedmiescie 7, Warsaw, Poland) Ed. Jerzy Ciekot. circ. 475.

690   PL   ISSN 0324-9875
POLITECHNIKA WROCLAWSKA. INSTYTUT BUDOWNICTWA. PRACE NAUKOWE. MONOGRAFIE. (Text in Polish; summaries in English and Russian) 1985. irreg., no.18, 1985. price varies. Politechnika Wroclawska, Wybrzeze Wyspianskiego 27, 50-370 Wroclaw, Poland (Dist. by: Ars Polona-Ruch, Krakowskie Przedmiescie 7, Warsaw, Poland) Ed. Jerzy Ciekot. Indexed: Chem.Abstr.

690   PL   ISSN 0137-6241
POLITECHNIKA WROCLAWSKA. INSTYTUT BUDOWNICTWA. PRACE NAUKOWE. STUDIA I MATERIALY. (Text in Polish; summaries in English and Russian) 1971. irreg., no.14, 1982. price varies. Politechnika Wroclawska, Wybrzeze Wyspianskiego 27, 50-370 Wroclaw, Poland (Dist. by: Ars Polona-Ruch, Krakowskie Przedmiescie 7, Warsaw, Poland) Ed. Marian Kloza.

POLITECHNIKA WROCLAWSKA. INSTYTUT INZYNIERII CHEMICZNEJ I URZADZEN CIEPLNYCH. PRACE NAUKOWE. STUDIA I MATERIALY. see *ENGINEERING* — *Chemical Engineering*

690   UR   ISSN 0203-7343
POLUTEHNILINE INSTITUUT TALLINN. TEORIYA I RASCHET TONKOSTENNYKH I PROSTRANSTVENNYKH KONSTRUKTSII. (Subseries of Its Toimetised) (Text in Russian; summaries in English or German) irreg. price varies. Polutehniline Instituut Tallinn, Ehitajate tee 5, Tallinn, Estonian S.S.R., U.S.S.R.

690   GW   ISSN 0085-5154
PRIVATES BAUSPARWESEN. 1950. a. DM.25.60. Domus-Verlag GmbH, Dottendorfer Str. 82, Postfach 150137, 5300 Bonn 1, W. Germany (B.R.D.) Ed. Joachim Degner.

690   IT
PROGETTARE & COSTRUIRE. 1981. a. L.55000. Antonio Ghiorzo Ed. & Pub., Via Casella 16, 20156 Milan, Italy. adv. circ. 8,000.

690   VE
PRONTUARIO TECNICO DE LA CONSTRUCCION. 1975. a. Prontuario Tecnico Comercial, Av. Miquel Angel, Prolonga-Lion el Casquillito, Resd. Hilton, P.O. Box, Ofc. No. 1 Colinas de Bella Monte, Caracas 105, Venezuela. adv.

R I B A COMPUTER SOFTWARE SELECTOR. (Royal Institute of British Architects) see *COMPUTERS* — *Software*

BUILDING AND CONSTRUCTION

690 UK ISSN 0267-0801
R I B A INTERIOR DESIGN PRODUCT SELECTOR. 1985. a. £15. (Royal Institute of British Architects) R I B A Services Ltd., 66 Portland Place, London W1N 4AD, England. Ed. David Clegg. adv. circ. 5,000.

690 UK ISSN 0265-8739
R I B A PRODUCT SELECTOR. 1982. a. £33. (Royal Institute of British Architects) R I B A Services Ltd., 66 Portland Place, London W1N 4AD, England. Ed. David Clegg. adv. circ. 20,000.

690 FI ISSN 0355-550X
RAKENTAJAIN KALENTERI. 1917. a. Fmk.215. Rakentajain Kustannus Oy - Building Publications Ltd., P.O. Box 141, 00101 Helsinki 10, Finland. Ed. Markku Haikala. adv. circ. 11,000.

691 US ISSN 0149-7642
RED BOOK OF HOUSING MANUFACTURERS. 1974. a. $140. L S I Systems Inc., 11-A Village Green, Crofton, MD 21114. TEL 301-261-6363. Ed. Donald F. Spear. circ. 400.

691 US ISSN 0569-8057
REINFORCED CONCRETE RESEARCH COUNCIL. BULLETINS. 1950. irreg., no. 22. price varies; some free. ‡ American Society of Civil Engineers, Portland Cement Association, Reinforced Concrete Research Council, c/o Dr. A.E. Fiorato, 5420 Old Orchard Rd., Skokie, IL 60077. TEL 312-966-6200. circ. 500. (back issues avail.)
Cement and concrete

691 US ISSN 0271-5945
REPAIR AND REMODELING COST DATA. 1980. a. $47.95. R.S. Means Company, Inc., 100 Construction Plaza, Kingston, MA 02364. Ed. William D. Mahoney.

REPERTOIRE DE MATERIAUX ET ELEMENTS CONTROLES DU BATIMENT. see *METROLOGY AND STANDARDIZATION*

692.8 US
RESIDENTIAL CONSTRUCTION COSTS. 1982. a. $31.95. Lee Saylor, Inc., 1855 Olympic Blvd., Walnut Creek, CA 94596. TEL 415-933-6000. Ed. Paul Felber. circ. 4,000.

691 US ISSN 0733-6403
RESIDENTIAL /LIGHT COMMERCIAL COST DATA. 1982. a. $46.95. R.S. Means Company, Inc., 100 Construction Plaza, Kingston, MA 02364. Ed. William D. Mahoney.

690 US
RESTON SERIES IN CONSTRUCTION TECHNOLOGY.* 1971. irreg. price varies. Reston Publishing Company, Inc., c/o Prentice Hall, Englewood Cliffs, NJ 07632-3501. Ed. David Dusthimer. adv. bk. rev.

690 DK ISSN 0107-900X
S B I AARSBERETNING. 1949. a. free. Statens Byggeforskningsinstitut, Hoersholm, Denmark. illus.
Formerly: Denmark. Statens Byggeforskningsinstitut. Aarsberetning.

690 FR
SAGERET: ANNUAIRE GENERAL DU BATIMENT ET DES TRAVAUX PUBLICS. (In 5 vols.) 1809. a. 270 F. Sageret, 5 et 7 rue Plumet, 75015 Paris, France.

690 CN
SASKATCHEWAN BUILDING TRADES YEARBOOK. 1972. a. (South Saskatchewan Building and Construction Trades Council) Naylor Communications Ltd., 100 Sutherland Ave., Winnipeg, Man. R2W 3C7, Canada. Ed. Aaron Bushhowsky. circ. 2,000. (back issues avail.)

690 620 CN
SASKATCHEWAN CONSTRUCTION INDUSTRY DIRECTORY. PURCHASING GUIDE. 1975. a. Can.$12. Sanford Evans Communications Ltd., 1077 St. James St., Box 6900, Winnipeg, Man. R3C 3B1, Canada. TEL 204-775-0201. Ed. Bev Jolicoeur. adv. circ. 5,183.

690 624 UK ISSN 0085-6002
SCOTTISH BUILDING & CIVIL ENGINEERING YEAR BOOK. 1960. a. $16. ‡ Edinburgh Pictorial Ltd., Smiths Place House, Edinburgh 6, Scotland. Ed. C.C. Cumming. adv. circ. 3,000. (processed)

690 683 UK ISSN 0080-8059
SCOTTISH HARDWARE AND DRYSALTERS ASSOCIATION. YEARBOOK. 1967. a. membership. Scottish Hardware and Drysalters Association, 16 Royal Terrace, Glasgow, C3, Scotland.

690 UK ISSN 0080-8717
SELL'S BUILDING INDEX. 1923. a. £30. Sell's Publications Ltd., 55 High St., Epsom, Surrey KT19 8DW, England. adv. bk. rev. circ. 5,000.

690 SI
SOUTHEAST ASIA BUILDING ANNUAL. a. Q A F Publications & Exhibitions Pty. Ltd., 510 Thomson Road, No. 08-01 Block A, SLF Complex, Singapore 1129, Singapore.

SOUTHWEST BUILDERS AND CONTRACTORS DIRECTORY. see *BUSINESS AND ECONOMICS — Trade And Industrial Directories*

690 797.2 US
SPA DATA AND REFERENCE ANNUAL. 1933. a. $21.95. Communication Channels, Inc., 6255 Barfield Rd., Atlanta, GA 30328. TEL 404-256-9800. Ed. Terri Simmons. (reprint service avail. from UMI)
Former titles: Swimming Pool Age Data and Reference Annual; Swimming Pool Weekly/Age - Data and Reference Annual.

690 US
SPEC-DATA MANU-SPEC PROGRAM INDEX; listing of current systems participants. 1968. a. $50. Construction Specifications Institute, 601 Madison St., Alexandria, VA 22314. TEL 703-684-0300. Ed. Tamara L. Haynes. adv. circ. 22,068. (also avail. in microfiche)
Former titles: Spec-Data Manu-Spec System Index & Spec-Data Manu-Spec Index.

690 SA
SPECIFILE BUILDING COMPENDIUM. (Text in Afrikaans and English) 1965. a. Communications Group Specifile, Information Services Division, Handel Rd. & Northern Pkwy., Box 7870, Johannesburg 2000, South Africa. Ed. V. Shapiro. adv. circ. 5,500.

690 UK ISSN 0306-3046
SPON'S ARCHITECTS' & BUILDERS' PRICE BOOK. 1873. a. £28.95. E. & F.N. Spon Ltd., 11 New Fetter Lane, London EC4P 4EE, England. Ed.Bd. adv. stat. circ. 13,000.

690 UK
SPON'S LANDSCAPE & EXTERNAL WORKS PRICEBOOK. 1972. a. £27.50. E. & F.N. Spon Ltd., 11 New Fetter Lane, London EC4P 4EE, England. Ed. Derek Lovejoy & Partners. illus. circ. 2,500.
Former titles: Spon's Landscape Pricebook (ISSN 0144-8404) & Spon's Landscape Handbook (ISSN 0306-3054)

STUDIES IN CONSTRUCTION ECONOMY. see *REAL ESTATE*

690 FI
SUOMEN BETONITEOLLISUUDEN KESKUSJARJESTO. JULKAISU/ASSOCIATION OF THE CONCRETE INDUSTRY OF FINLAND. PUBLICATION. irreg. price varies. Suomen Betoniteollisuuden Keskusjarjesto, Iso Roobertinkatu 30, SF-00120 Helsinki, Finland.

690 SW ISSN 0586-6766
SWEDEN. STATENS RAAD FOER BYGGNADSFORSKNING. DOCUMENT. (Text in English; abstracts in English and Swedish) irreg. Statens Raad Foer Byggnadsforskning - Swedish Council for Building Research, Sankt Goeransgatan 66, S-112 33 Stockholm, Sweden (Orders to: Svensk Byggtjaenst, Box 7853, S-103 99 Stockholm, Sweden)

690 SW
SWEDEN. STATENS RAAD FOER BYGGNADSFORSKNING. RAPPORT. (Text in Swedish; abstracts in English and Swedish) irreg. Statens Raad foer Byggnadsforskning - Swedish Council for Building Research, Sankt Goeransgatan 66, S-112 33 Stockholm, Sweden (Orders to: Svensk Byggtjaenst, Box 7853, S-103 99 Stockholm, Sweden)

690 SW
SWEDEN. STATENS RAAD FOER BYGGNADSFORSKNING. SUMMARIES. (Text in English) 1977. irreg. free. Statens Raad Foer Byggnadsforskning - Swedish Council for Building Research, Sankt Goeransgatan 66, S-112 33 Stockholm, Sweden.

690 SW
SWEDEN. STATENS RAAD FOER BYGGNADSFORSKNING. SYNOPSES. (Text in English) 1977. irreg. (8-10/yr.) free. Statens Raad Foer Byggnadsforskning - Swedish Council for Building Research, Sankt Goeransgatan 66, S-112 33 Stockholm, Sweden.

690 SW
SWEDEN. STATENS RAAD FOER BYGGNADSFORSKNING. VERKSAMHETSPLAN. a. Statens Raad Foer Byggnadsforskning - Swedish Council for Building Research, Sankt Goeransgatan 66, S-112 33 Stockholm, Sweden.

690 SW
SWEDISH BUILDING RESEARCH NEWS. (Text in English) 1976. irreg. (2-3/yr.) free. Statens Raad Foer Byggnadsforskning - Swedish Council for Building Research, Sankt Goeransgatan 66, S-112 33 Stockholm, Sweden. Indexed: Br.Ceram.Abstr.

690 CN ISSN 0082-0431
SWEET'S CANADIAN CONSTRUCTION CATALOGUE FILE. (Text in English and French) 1966. a. ‡ McGraw-Hill Information Systems Company of Canada Ltd., 330 Progress Ave., Scarborough, Ont. M1P 2Z5, Canada. TEL 416-293-1931. Ed. D.J. Cahill. circ. 7,000(controlled)

690 US
SWEET'S GENERAL BUILDING AND RENOVATION FILE. 1906. a. $150. Sweet's Catalog Files (Subsidiary of: McGraw-Hill Information Systems Co.) 1221 Ave. of the Americas, New York, NY 10020. TEL 212-512-4303. circ. 23,000.
Formerly: Sweet's General Building Catalog File.

690 US
SWEET'S HOMEBUILDING AND REMODELING FILE. a. $40. Sweet's Catalog Files (Subsidiary of: McGraw-Hill Information Systems Co.) 1221 Ave. of the Americas, New York, NY 10020. TEL 212-512-4303. circ. 29,000.

690 US
SWEET'S INDUSTRIAL CONSTRUCTION AND RENOVATION FILE. a. free to qualified personnel. Sweet's Catalog Files (Subsidiary of: McGraw-Hill information Systems Co.) 1221 Ave. of the Americas, New York, NY 10020. TEL 212-512-4303. circ. 25,000.

690 US
SWEET'S INTERNATIONAL CONSTRUCTION FILE. a. free to qualified personnel. Sweet's Catalog Files (Subsidiary of: McGraw-Hill Information Systems Co.) 1221 Ave. of the Americas, New York, NY 10020. TEL 212-512-4303.

690 338.4 US ISSN 0197-6753
T M R TRAVEL MARKETING REPORT; North American directory of engineering, architectural & construction companies. 1981. biennial. $500. Travel Marketing Report, Box 66323, O'Hare International Airport, Chicago, IL 60666.

690 624 FR
TABLEAU DE BORD DU BATIMENT, GENIE CIVIL ET MATERIAUX DE CONSTRUCTION. a. membership. Bureau d'Informations et de Previsions Economiques, 122 Av Charles de Gaulle, 92522 Neuilly-sur-Seine, France.

TEXAS BUILDERS AND CONTRACTORS DIRECTORY. see *BUSINESS AND ECONOMICS — Trade And Industrial Directories*

691 FR
U N I C E M ANNUAIRE OFFICIEL. 1945. a. 168 F. (Union Nationale des Industries de Carrieres et Materiaux de Construction) Union Francaise d'Annuaires Professionnels (UFAP), B.P. 36, 78192 Trappes Cedex, France. Dir. Jean Lhespitau. adv. circ. 5,000.

BUILDING AND CONSTRUCTION — ABSTRACTING, BIBLIOGRAPHIES, STATISTICS

U.S. BUREAU OF STANDARDS. BUILDING TECHNOLOGY PUBLICATIONS. see *BUILDING AND CONSTRUCTION — Abstracting, Bibliographies, Statistics*

690   US   ISSN 0082-934X
U.S. BUREAU OF THE CENSUS. CENSUS OF CONSTRUCTION INDUSTRIES. (Issued in Area, Industry and Special Report Series) 1930. quinquennial. price varies. U.S. Bureau of the Census, Customer Services, Washington, DC 20233 TEL 301-763-4100. (Orders to: Supt. of Documents, Washington DC 20402) (also avail. in microform)

690   US   ISSN 0083-1794
U.S. NATIONAL BUREAU OF STANDARDS. BUILDING SCIENCE SERIES. irreg. price varies. U.S. National Bureau of Standards, Gaithersburg, MD 20899 TEL 301-975-3058. (Orders to: Supt. of Documents, Washington, DC 20402)

690   US
U.S. NATIONAL BUREAU OF STANDARDS. CENTER FOR BUILDING TECHNOLOGY. BUILDING TECHNOLOGY PROJECT SUMMARIES. 1968. a. price varies. U.S. National Bureau of Standards, Gaithersburg, MD 20899 TEL 301-975-3058. (Orders to: Supt. Docs., Govt. Printing Office, Washington, DC 20402) Eds. Noel Raufaste, Michael Olmert.

690   US
UNIVERSITY OF ILLINOIS. SMALL HOMES COUNCIL. BUILDING RESEARCH COUNCIL. COUNCIL NOTES. 1945. irreg. $4. ‡ University of Illinois at Urbana-Champaign, Small Homes Council - Building Research Council, 1 E. St. Mary's Rd., Champaign, IL 61820. TEL 217-333-1801. Ed. H.R. Spies. circ. 3,900.
Formerly: University of Illinois. Small Homes Council. Building Research Council. Circulars (ISSN 0073-5396)

690   US   ISSN 0073-540X
UNIVERSITY OF ILLINOIS. SMALL HOMES COUNCIL. BUILDING RESEARCH COUNCIL. RESEARCH REPORT. 1948. irreg. price varies. ‡ University of Illinois at Urbana-Champaign, Small Homes Council, Building Research Council, 1 E. St. Mary's Rd., Champaign, IL 61820. TEL 217-333-1801. Ed. H.R. Spies.

690   US   ISSN 0073-5426
UNIVERSITY OF ILLINOIS. SMALL HOMES COUNCIL. BUILDING RESEARCH COUNCIL. TECHNICAL NOTES. 1966. irreg., no.17, 1985. University of Illinois at Urbana-Champaign, Small Homes Council, Building Research Council, 1 E. St. Mary's Rd., Champaign, IL 61820. TEL 217-333-1801. Ed. H.R. Spies.

UNIVERSITY OF STRATHCLYDE. DEPARTMENT OF ARCHITECTURE & BUILDING SCIENCE. RESEARCH BULLETIN. see *ARCHITECTURE*

V OG S PRISER. ANLEG. see *BUSINESS AND ECONOMICS — Marketing And Purchasing*

690   DK   ISSN 0108-0229
V OG S PRISER. BYGNINGSDELE. 1982. a. Kr.1190. V og S Byggedata A-S, Fredrikssundvej 194, 2700 Broenshoej, Denmark.

V OG S PRISER. HUSBYGNING. see *BUSINESS AND ECONOMICS — Marketing And Purchasing*

690   GW   ISSN 0507-6714
VEREIN DEUTSCHER ZEMENTWERKE. FORSCHUNGSINSTITUT DER ZEMENTINDUSTRIE. TAETIGKEITSBERICHT. 1948. triennial. free. Verein Deutscher Zementwerke e.V., Tannenstr. 2, 4000 Duesseldorf 30, W. Germany (B.R.D.) circ. 2,000.

VIRGINIA POLYTECHNIC INSTITUTE AND STATE UNIVERSITY. PALLET AND CONTAINER RESEARCH LABORATORY. SPECIAL REPORT. see *FORESTS AND FORESTRY — Lumber And Wood*

693   AT
WALLING REVIEW. 1981. irreg. price varies. Concrete Masonry Association of Australia, 25 Berry St., North Sydney, N.S.W. 2060, Australia. circ. 1,000.

690   GW
WIR BAUEN UNSER HAUS SELBST. 1973. a. DM.14.80. Fachschriften-Verlag GmbH, Hoehenstr. 17, Postfach 1329, 7012 Fellbach, W. Germany (B.R.D.)

690   GW
DER WOCHENEND-, FERIEN- UND ZWEITHAUS-KATALOG. 1971. biennial. DM.19.80. Fachschriften-Verlag GmbH, Hoehenstrasse 17, Postfach 1329, 7012 Fellbach, W. Germany (B.R.D.) Ed. Eberhard Wolf.

693   FR
WORLD CEMENT DIRECTORY. irreg. Cembureau, 2 rue Saint Charles, 75740 Paris Cedex 15, France. illus.
Cement and concrete

690   AU
ZEMENT UND BETON. 1955. irreg. (4-6/yr.) S.200. Verein der Oesterreichischen Zementfabrikanten, Mentergasse 3, A-1070 Vienna, Austria. (Co-sponsor: Oesterreichischer Betonverein) Ed. Alfred Boehm. bk. rev. abstr. illus. circ. 1,800. Indexed: Chem.Abstr.
Cement and concrete

BUILDING AND CONSTRUCTION — Abstracting, Bibliographies, Statistics

ABSTRACTS OF BULGARIAN SCIENTIFIC LITERATURE. INDUSTRY, BUILDING AND TRANSPORT. see *BUSINESS AND ECONOMICS — Abstracting, Bibliographies, Statistics*

AMERICAN IRON AND STEEL INSTITUTE. ANNUAL STATISTICAL REPORT. see *ENGINEERING — Abstracting, Bibliographies, Statistics*

690   IT   ISSN 0075-1804
ANNUARIO STATISTICO DELL'ATTIVITA EDILIZIA E DELLE OPERE PUBBLICHE. irreg. price varies. Istituto Centrale di Statistica, Via Cesare Balbo 16, 00100 Rome, Italy.

690   AU
AUSTRIA. STATISTISCHES ZENTRALAMT. BAUSTATISTIK. (Subseries of its Beitreage zur Oesterreichischen Statistik) a. S.480 part I 1985; part II 1984, S450. Oesterreichisches Statistisches Zentralamt, Hintere Zollamtsstr. 2b, 1033 Vienna, Austria.

331   314   AU   ISSN 0067-2300
AUSTRIA. STATISTISCHES ZENTRALAMT. DIE WOHNBAUTAETIGKEIT. (Subseries of: Beitreage zur Oesterreichischen Statistik) 1956. a. S.100. ‡ Hintere Zollamtsstr. 2b, 1033 Vienna, Austria. circ. 400.

690   314   GW   ISSN 0084-7739
BAUSTATISTISCHES JAHRBUCH. 1960. a. DM.20. Hauptverband der Deutschen Bauindustrie, Abraham-Lincoln-Str. 30, Postfach 2966, 6200 Wiesbaden, W. Germany (B.R.D.) Ed.Bd.

690   331.83   BE
BELGIUM. INSTITUT NATIONAL DE STATISTIQUE. STATISTIQUES DE LA CONSTRUCTION ET DU LOGEMENT. (Text in Dutch and French) irreg. (1-2/yr.) 430 Fr. per no. Institut National de Statistique, 44 rue de Louvain, 1000 Brussels, Belgium.
Formerly: Belgium. Institut National de Statistique. Batiments et Logements (ISSN 0067-544X)

690   016   CS   ISSN 0007-3326
BUILDING ABSTRACTS SERVICE C I B.* 1959. 2-4/yr. free. Vyzkumny Ustav Vystavby a Architektury, Letenska 3, 118 45 Prague 1, Czechoslovakia. bibl. circ. 100. (looseleaf format)

338.4   CN   ISSN 0575-7975
CANADA. STATISTICS CANADA. BUILDING PERMITS. ANNUAL SUMMARY/PERMIS DE BATIR. (Catalog 64-203) (Text in English and French) 1966. a. Can.$50($51) Statistics Canada, Communications Division, 3rd Floor, R.H. Coats Bldg., Ottawa, Ont. K1A 0T6, Canada TEL 613-993-7276. (Subscr. to: Publications Sales and Services, Ottawa, Ont. K1A 0T6, Canada) (also avail. in microform from MML)

690   CN   ISSN 0527-4974
CANADA. STATISTICS CANADA. CONSTRUCTION IN CANADA/CONSTRUCTION AU CANADA. (Catalogue 64-201) (Text in English, French) 1951. a. Can.$35($36) Statistics Canada, Communications Division, 3rd Floor, R.H. Coats Bldg., Ottawa, Ont. K1A 0T6, Canada TEL 613-993-7276. (Subscr. to: Publications Sales and Services, Ottawa, Ont. K1A 0T6, Canada) (also avail. in microform from MML)

CANADA. STATISTICS CANADA. ELECTRICAL CONTRACTING INDUSTRY/ENTREPRENEURS D'INSTALLATIONS ELECTRIQUES. see *ELECTRICITY AND ELECTRICAL ENGINEERING — Abstracting, Bibliographies, Statistics*

CANADA. STATISTICS CANADA. MECHANICAL CONTRACTING INDUSTRY/LES ENTREPRENEURS D'INSTALLATIONS MECANIQUES. see *ENGINEERING — Abstracting, Bibliographies, Statistics*

690   CN   ISSN 0703-7295
CANADA. STATISTICS CANADA. NON-RESIDENTIAL GENERAL BUILDING CONTRACTING INDUSTRY/INDUSTRIE DES ENTREPRISES GENERALES EN CONSTRUCTION NON DOMICILIAIRE. (Catalog 64-207) (Text in English and French) 1971. a. Can.$15($16) Statistics Canada, Communications Division, 3rd Floor, R.H. Coats Bldg., Ottawa, Ont. K1A 0T6, Canada TEL 613-993-7276. (Subscr. to: Publications Sales and Services, Ottawa, Ont. K1A 0T6, Canada) (also avail. in microform from MML)

690   016   CN   ISSN 0008-3089
CANADIAN BUILDING ABSTRACTS. (Text in English and French) 1960. 3/yr. free. National Research Council of Canada, Division of Building Research, Ottawa, Ont. K1A 0R6, Canada. TEL 613-993-2463. Ed. A.M. Dorais. abstr. circ. 10,000. Indexed: Agri.Eng.Abstr.

690   UK   ISSN 0263-2977
CHARTERED INSTITUTE OF PUBLIC FINANCE AND ACCOUNTANCY. DIRECT LABOUR STATISTICS. ACTUALS. 1982. a. £18. Chartered Institute of Public Finance and Accountancy, 3 Robert St., London WC2N 6BH, England. (back issues avail.)

690   UK   ISSN 0262-5334
COMMERCIAL AND INDUSTRIAL FLOORSPACE STATISTICS. 1981. a. £5. Welsh Office, Economic and Statistical Services Division, New Crown Bldg., Cathays Park, Cardiff CF1 3NQ, Wales. Ed. E. Swires-Hennessy. stat. circ. 300.

690.3   016   US   ISSN 0045-8007
CONCRETE ABSTRACTS. 1972. bi-m. $128 to non-members. American Concrete Institute, P.O. Box 19150, Detroit, MI 48219. TEL 513-532-2600. Ed. Robert E. Wilde. circ. 800. (also avail. in microfiche; back issues avail.)
Concrete

690   DK   ISSN 0108-7568
DENMARK. DANMARKS STATISTIK. BYGNINGSOPGOERELSEN /STOCK OF BUILDING. 1977. every 4 years. Kr.34. Danmarks Statistik, Sejroegade 11, 2100 Copenhagen OE, Denmark.
Supersedes in part: Denmark. Danmarks Statistik. Folke- og Boligtaellingen.

690   FR
EUROPEAN CEMENT ASSOCIATION. EUROPEAN ANNUAL REVIEW. 1951. a. 200 F. (European Cement Association) Cembureau, 2 rue St. Charles, 75740 Paris Cedex 15, France. stat.
Formerly: Cement Market and Outlook.

338 690 FR
EUROPEAN CEMENT ASSOCIATION. WORLD STATISTICAL REVIEW. 1959. a. 200 F. (European Cement Association) Cembureau, 2 rue St. Charles, 75740 Paris Cedex 15, France.
Formerly: European Cement Association. Statistical Review.

690 FJ
FIJI. BUREAU OF STATISTICS. CENSUS OF BUILDING AND CONSTRUCTION. a. $1. Bureau of Statistics, Box 2221, Suva, Fiji.

690 314 GW ISSN 0072-1735
GERMANY (FEDERAL REPUBLIC, 1949-). STATISTISCHES BUNDESAMT. FACHSERIE 5, BAUTAETIGKEIT UND WOHNUNGEN, REIHE 1: BAUTAETIGKEIT. a. DM.11.80. W. Kohlhammer-Verlag GmbH, Abt. Veroeffentlichungen des Statistischen Bundesamtes, Philipp-Reis-Str. 3, Postfach 421120, 6500 Mainz 42, W. Germany (B.R.D.)

690 314 GW ISSN 0072-1743
GERMANY (FEDERAL REPUBLIC, 1949-). STATISTISCHES BUNDESAMT. FACHSERIE 5, BAUTAETIGKEIT UND WOHNUNGEN, REIHE 2: BEWILLIGUNGEN IM SOZIALEN WOHNUNGSBAU. a. price varies. W. Kohlhammer-Verlag GmbH, Abt. Veroeffentlichungen des Statistischen Bundesamtes, Philipp-Reis-Str. 3, Postfach 421120, 6500 Mainz 42, W. Germany (B.R.D.)

690 314 GW ISSN 0072-1751
GERMANY (FEDERAL REPUBLIC, 1949-). STATISTISCHES BUNDESAMT. FACHSERIE 5, BAUTAETIGKEIT UND WOHNUNGEN, REIHE 3: BESTAND AN WOHNUNGEN. a. DM.7.40. W. Kohlhammer-Verlag GmbH, Abt. Veroeffentlichungen des Statistischen Bundesamtes, Philipp-Reis-Str. 3, Postfach 421120, 6500 Mainz 42, W. Germany (B.R.D.)

690 314 GW
GERMANY (FEDERAL REPUBLIC, 1949-). STATISTISCHES BUNDESAMT. FACHSERIE 4, PRODUZIERENDES GEWERBE, REIHE 5. (Consists of three subseries: Reihe 5.1: Beschaeftigung, Umsatz und Geraetebestand der Betriebe im Baugewerbe; Reihe 5.2: Umsatz und Investitionen der Unternehmen im Baugewerbe; Reihe 5.3: Kostenstruktuer der Unternehem im Baugewerbe) a. price varies. W. Kohlhammer-Verlag GmbH, Abt. Veroeffentlichungen des Statistischen Bundesamtes, Philipp-Reis-Str. 3, Postfach 421120, 6500 Mainz 42, W. Germany (B.R.D.)
Formerly: Germany (Federal Republic, 1949-) Statistisches Bundesamt. Fachserie 4, Reihe 5: Beschaeftigung, Umsatz, Investitionen und Kosten Struktur im Baugewerbe (ISSN 0072-1727)

690 HU ISSN 0139-3510
HUNGARY. KOZPONTI STATISZTIKAI HIVATAL. BERUHAZASI, EPITOIPARI, LAKASEPITESI ZSEBKONYV. a. 30 Ft. Statisztikai Kiado Vallalat, Kaszasdulo u. 2, 1033 Budapest 3, Hungary (Subscr. to: Kultura, Box 149, H-1389 Budapest, Hungary) circ. 1,500.

338.47 HU ISSN 0237-0298
HUNGARY. KOZPONTI STATISZTIKAI HIVATAL. EPITOIPARI ARAK ALAKULASA. 1970. irreg. 120 Ft. Statisztikai Kiado Vallalat, Kaszasdulo u. 2, P.O. Box 99, 1300 Budapest, Hungary (Subscr. to: Kultura, Box 149, H-1389 Budapest, Hungary) stat.

690 314 HU ISSN 0236-9524
HUNGARY. KOZPONTI STATISZTIKAI HIVATAL. LAKASSTATISZTIKAI EVKONYU. a. 150 Ft. Statisztikai Kiado Vallalat, Kaszasdulo u. 2, P.O.B. 99, 1300 Budapest 3, Hungary (Subscr. to: Kultura, Box 149, H-1389 Budapest, Hungary)
Formerly: Hungary. Kozponti Statisztikai Hivatal. Lakasepites es Megszunes (ISSN 0209-5513)

330 IE
IRELAND. CENTRAL STATISTICS OFFICE. BUILDING AND CONSTRUCTION: AVERAGE EARNINGS AND HOURS WORKED. a. Central Statistics Office, Ardee Road, Dublin 6, Ireland. (processed)

330 IE
IRELAND. CENTRAL STATISTICS OFFICE. BUILDING AND CONSTRUCTION PLANNING PERMISSIONS. a. Central Statistics Office, Ardee Road, Dublin 6, Ireland. (processed)

330 IE
IRELAND. CENTRAL STATISTICS OFFICE. CENSUS OF BUILDING AND CONSTRUCTION. a. Central Statistics Office, Ardee Road, Dublin 6, Ireland. (processed)

690 LY ISSN 0075-9279
LIBYA. CENSUS AND STATISTICAL OFFICE. REPORT OF THE SURVEY OF LICENSED CONSTRUCTION UNITS. (Text in Arabic and English) 1967. a. free. Census and Statistical Department, Ministry of Planning, Tripoli, Libya.

690 315 MY ISSN 0085-3046
MALAYSIA. DEPARTMENT OF STATISTICS. SURVEY OF CONSTRUCTION INDUSTRIES: PENINSULAR MALAYSIA. (Text in English and Malay) 1963. a., latest 1974. M.$5. Department of Statistics - Jabatan Perangkaan, Jalan Young, Kuala Lumpur 10-01, Malaysia. stat. circ. 400.

N B O ABSTRACTS. (National Buildings Organisation) see ENGINEERING — Abstracting, Bibliographies, Statistics

690 016 SA ISSN 0077-3581
NATIONAL BUILDING RESEARCH INSTITUTE. COMPLETE LIST OF N B R I PUBLICATIONS. 1980. a. R.45. National Building Research Institute, Council for Scientific and Industrial Research, Box 395, Pretoria 0001, South Africa.

690 016 CN ISSN 0085-3828
NATIONAL RESEARCH COUNCIL, CANADA. DIVISION OF BUILDING RESEARCH. BIBLIOGRAPHY. (Text in English) 1951. irreg. free. National Research Council of Canada, Division of Building Research, Ottawa, Ont. K1A 0R6, Canada. TEL 613-993-2463. bk. rev.

338.4 NZ ISSN 0110-3490
NEW ZEALAND. DEPARTMENT OF STATISTICS. BUILDING STATISTICS. a. NZ.$7.15. Department of Statistics, Wellington, New Zealand (Subscr. to: Government Printing Office, Publications, Private Bag, Wellington, New Zealand) illus. stat.

690 NZ ISSN 0110-4640
NEW ZEALAND. DEPARTMENT OF STATISTICS. CENSUS OF BUILDING AND CONSTRUCTION. quinquennial. NZ.$3.96. Department of Statistics, Private Bag, Wellington, New Zealand (Subscr. to: Government Printing Office, Publications, Private Bag, Wellington, New Zealand)

690 310 NR
NIGERIA. FEDERAL OFFICE OF STATISTICS. BUILDING AND CONSTRUCTION SURVEY. a. £N3. Federal Office of Statistics, P.M.B. 12528, Lagos, Nigeria.

R I C S LIBRARY INFORMATION SERVICE ABSTRACTS AND REVIEWS. (Royal Institution of Chartered Surveyors) see ENGINEERING — Abstracting, Bibliographies, Statistics

690 310 SA
SOUTH AFRICA. CENTRAL STATISTICAL SERVICE. BUILDING PLANS PASSED AND BUILDINGS COMPLETED. (Report No. 05-44) a. Central Statistical Service, Private Bag X44, Pretoria 0001, South Africa (Orders to: Government Printer, Bosman St., Private Bag X85, Pretoria 0001, South Africa)
Formerly: South Africa. Department of Statistics. Building Plans and Buildings Completed.

690 310 SP ISSN 0561-4902
SPAIN. MINISTERIO DE LA VIVIENDA. ESTADISTICA DE LA INDUSTRIA DE LA CONSTRUCCION. (Subseries of Spain. Ministerio de la Vivienda. Documentos Informativos) a. Ministerio de la Vivienda, Secretaria General Tecnica, Madrid, Spain.

690 314 SW ISSN 0085-6991
SWEDEN. STATISTISKA CENTRALBYRAAN. STATISTISKA MEDDELANDEN. SUBGROUP BO (HOUSING AND CONSTRUCTION) (Text in Swedish; tables heads and summaries in English) N.S. 1963. irreg. Kr.830. Statistiska Centralbyraan, Distribution, S-701 89 Oerebro, Sweden. circ. 1,375.

690 US
U.S. BUREAU OF STANDARDS. BUILDING TECHNOLOGY PUBLICATIONS. 1975. a. price varies. U.S. National Bureau of Standards, Gaithersburg, MD 20899. TEL 301-975-3058.

BUILDING AND CONSTRUCTION — Carpentry And Woodwork

694 GW
BIRKNER EUROLIGNUM; the European timber market. (Text in English, French, German, Italian, Portuguese, Spanish) 1985. a. DM.140. Birkner & Co. Verlag, Winsbergring 38, Postfach 540750, D-2000 Hamburg 54, W. Germany (B.R.D.) Ed. Harry von Hofmann. adv.

694 UK
MODELLING AND MINIATURE CRAFTS. 1983. a. £4.25($9.50) (Guild of Master Craftsmen) Guild of Master Craftsman Publications Ltd., 166 High St., Lewes, East Sussex BN7 1YE, England. TEL (0273) 477374. Ed. M.M. Baker. adv. circ. 6,000.

698.3 NE
NEDERLANDSE HOUTBOND. JAARVERSLAG. irreg. Nederlandse Houtbond, Keizersgracht 298, Amsterdam, Netherlands.

694 674 DK
TRAE NYTS LEVERANDOERREGISTER. a. Thomson Communications (Scandinavia) A-S, Struenseegade 7-9, DK-2200 Copenhagen N, Denmark. adv. circ. 11,586.

694 674 US
WHERE TO BUY HARDWOOD PLYWOOD AND VENEER. 1960. a. $5. Hardwood Plywood Manufacturers Association, 1825 Michael Faraday Dr., Box 2789, Reston, VA 22090. TEL 703-435-2900. Ed. Clark E. McDonald. circ. 5,000.
Formerly: Where to Buy Hardwood Plywood.

BUILDING AND CONSTRUCTION — Hardware

AUTO AFTERMARKET SUPPLIERS. see BUSINESS AND ECONOMICS — Trade And Industrial Directories

683 UK
B H F DIRECTORY. a. £15. British Hardware Federation, 20 Harborne Rd., Edgbaston, Birmingham B15 3AB, England.

683 GW ISSN 0067-4583
BAUBESCHLAG-TASCHENBUCH. 1952. a. DM.36. Gert Wohlfarth GmbH Verlag Fachtechnik und Mercator-Verlag, Stresemannstr. 20-22, 4100 Duisburg 1, W. Germany (B.R.D.) Ed. Siegmund Vorpahl. adv. bk. rev. circ. 5,000.

683 UK ISSN 0261-1465
BENN'S HARDWARE DIRECTORY & D-I-Y BUYERS GUIDE; the year book of the Hardware Trade Journal. 1913. a. £26. Benn Business Information Services Ltd., P.O. Box 20, Sovereign Way, Tonbridge, Kent TN9 1RQ, England. index. circ. 3,500.
Formerly: Benn's Hardware Directory (ISSN 0067-5725)

683 UK
BENN'S INTERNATIONAL HARDWARE EXPORTER. (Supplement to "Hardware Trade Journal") a. Benn Publications Ltd., 25 New Street Square, London EC4A 3JA, England. Ed. Allen Barrett. adv. illus. stat. circ. 8,000.

BUILDCORE INDEX; construction materials, equipment & furniture available in Canada. see BUILDING AND CONSTRUCTION

BUSINESS AND ECONOMICS

679.6   UK   ISSN 0070-5179
DIRECTORY OF BRUSH AND ALLIED TRADES.
a. $45 includes subscription to Brushes International. Wheatland Journals Ltd., Penn House, Penn Place, Arickmansworth, Herts. WD3 1SN, England. Ed. Joan Barraclough. adv. circ. 1,500.

DIRECTORY OF HARDWARE AND HOUSEWARES DISTRIBUTORS. see *BUSINESS AND ECONOMICS — Trade And Industrial Directories*

FASTENER TECHNOLOGY BUYERS' GUIDE. see *BUSINESS AND ECONOMICS — Trade And Industrial Directories*

HARDWARE AGE "WHO MAKES IT" BUYERS' GUIDE. see *BUSINESS AND ECONOMICS — Trade And Industrial Directories*

680   AT
HARDWARE RETAILER NEWS.* 1966. irreg. Aus.$3. (Hardware Retailers Association of New South Wales) Hardware Retailer Publishing Co., c/o Robert D. Jameson, Beecroft, NSW 2119, Australia. Ed. John Hector.

683   US   ISSN 0273-625X
LOCKSMITH LEDGER/SECURITY GUIDE & DIRECTORY.* 1939. a. $28. Nickerson & Collins Co., 850 Busse Hwy, Park Ridge, IL 60068-5980. Ed. Bill Reed. adv. circ. 20,000. (reprint service avail. from UMI)

683   FR   ISSN 0025-9055
MEMENTO GENERAL TEQUI QUINCAILLERIE. 1965. a. 360 F. Union Francaise d'Annuaires Professionnels, 13 av. Vladimir Komarov, B.P. 36, 78192 Trappes Cedex, France.
Incorporating: Memento General de la Quincaillerie & Repertoire Tequi Quincaillerie.

683 627   JA
NAVAL ARCHITECTURE AND OCEAN ENGINEERING. (Text in English) a. 4000 Yen. Society of Naval Architects of Japan, 15-16 Toranomon 1-chome, Minato-ku, Tokyo 105, Japan.

683   DK   ISSN 0900-0275
NORMTALSUNDERSOEGELSEN FOR ISENKRAMBRANCHEN. 1983. a. Kr.305. Danamrks Isenkraemmerforeningen, Naverland 34, 2600 Glostrup, Denmark.
Formerly: Regnskabsundersoegelsen for Isenkrambranchen.

SCOTTISH HARDWARE AND DRYSALTERS ASSOCIATION. YEARBOOK. see *BUILDING AND CONSTRUCTION*

683   UK   ISSN 0143-0971
SHOP EQUIPMENT DISPLAY & SHOPFITTING DIRECTORY. 1958. a. £7. A G B Business Publications Ltd., Audit House, Field End Rd., Eastcote, Middx HA4 9XE, England. Ed. Philip de Ville. adv.
Former titles: Shop Equipment and Materials Guide; Shop Equipment and Shopfitting Directory (ISSN 0080-9381)

683   US
TOOLS & HARDWARE: LATIN AMERICAN INDUSTRIAL REPORT. (Avail. for each of 22 Latin American countries) 1985. a. $435 per country report per industry covered. Aurora International, Box 9099, Bridgeport, CT 06601-2099. TEL 203-368-0579.

BUSINESS AND ECONOMICS

see also *Advertising and Public Relations; Business and Economics — Accounting; Business and Economics — Banking and Finance; Business and Economics — Banking and Finance — Computer Applications; Business and Economics — Chamber of Commerce Publications; Business and Economics — Computer Applications; Business and Economics — Cooperatives; Business and Economics — Domestic Commerce; Business and Economics — Economic Situation and Conditions; Business and Economics — Economic Systems and Theories, Economic History; Business and Economics — International Commerce; Business and Economics — International Development and Assistance; Business and Economics — Investments; Business and Economics — Labor and Industrial Relations; Business and Economics — Macroeconomics; Business and Economics — Management; Business and Economics — Marketing and Purchasing; Business and Economics — Office Equipment and Services; Business and Economics — Personnel Management; Business and Economics — Production of Goods and Services; Business and Economics — Public Finance, Taxation; Business and Economics — Small Business; Business and Economics — Trade and Industrial Directories; Consumer Education and Protection; Insurance; Labor Unions; Occupations and Careers; Real Estate;*

also specific industries

330   PL   ISSN 0860-2948
ACTA ACADEMIAE AGRICULTURAE AC TECHNICAE OLSTENENSIS. OEKONOMIKA/ECONOMICS. (Subseries of its: Zeszyty Naukowe) (Text in Polish; summaries in English and Russian) 1959. irreg. price varies. Akademia Rolniczo-Techniczna, Blok 21, 10-718 Olsztyn-Kortowo, Poland (Dist. by: Ars Polona-Ruch, Krakowskie Przedmiescie 7, 00-901 Warsaw, Poland) Ed.Bd. illus.
Formerly: Ekonomika (ISSN 0324-9166)

330   HU   ISSN 0324-6256
ACTA MARXISTICA LENINISTICA. POLITIKAI GAZDASAGTAN TANULMANYOK. (Text in Hungarian, occasionally German, Russian) 1962. irreg., vol.30, 1984. Kossuth Lajos Tudomanyegyetem, Egyetem Ter 1, 4010 Debrecen, Hungary. Ed. Jozsef Darai.

330 370   PL
ACTA UNIVERSITATIS LODZIENSIS: FOLIA OECONOMICA. (Text in Polish; summaries in various languages) irreg. Uniwersytet Lodzki, Drukarnia Wojskowa, Ul. Gdanska 130, Lodz, Poland (Dist. by: Ars Polona-Ruch, Krakowskie Przedmiescie 7, Warsaw, Poland)

330   PL   ISSN 0208-5305
ACTA UNIVERSITATIS NICOLAI COPERNICI. EKONOMIA. 1972. irreg. price varies. Uniwersytet Mikolaja Kopernika, Fosa Staromiejska 3, Torun, Poland (Dist. by Osrodek Rozpowszechniania Wydawnictw Naukowych PAN, Palac Kultury i Nauki, 00-901 Warsaw, Poland)

330   HU   ISSN 0563-0622
ACTA UNIVERSITATIS SZEGEDIENSIS DE ATTILA JOZSEF NOMINATAE. SECTIO OECONOMICO-POLITICA. POLITIKAI GAZDASAGTAN. (Subseries of: Acta Universitatis Szegediensis de Attila Jozsef Nominatae. Sectio Oeconomico-Politica. HU 0554-5374) (Text in German, Hungarian and Russian; summaries in English, German or Russian) 1959. a. exchange basis. Attila Jozsef University, c/o E. Szabo, Exchange Librarian, Dugonics ter 13, P.O.B. 393, Szeged H-6701, Hungary (Subscr. to: Kultura, Box 149, H-1389 Budapest, Hungary) Ed. Lajos Nagy. circ. 200.

330   NE
ADVANCED TEXTBOOKS IN ECONOMICS. 1971. irreg., vol.23, 1986. price varies. Elsevier Science Publishers B.V., Box 211, 1000 AE Amsterdam, Netherlands. Eds. C.J. Bliss, M.D. Intriligator. Indexed: Math.r.

330   US   ISSN 0731-9053
ADVANCES IN ECONOMETRICS. 1981. a. $28.75 to individuals; institutions $57.50. J A I Press Inc., Box 1678, 36 Sherwood Pl., Greenwich, CT 06836. TEL 203-661-7602. Eds. R.L. Basmann, George F. Rhodes, Jr.

330   GW
AFRIKA STUDIEN. 1964. irreg. price varies. I F O Institut fuer Wirtschaftsforschung, Poschingerstr. 5, 8000 Muenchen 80, W. Germany (B.R.D.) circ. 650. Indexed: Geo.Abstr.

330   US
AFTERMARKET BUSINESS A P A A SHOW DAILY. 1969. a. (in 3 eds.) free to show attendees. Harcourt Brace Jovanovich, Inc., 7500 Old Oak Blvd., Cleveland, OH 44130. TEL 216-243-8100. Ed. Richard Weinberg. circ. 12,500.
Formerly: Home & Auto A P A A Show Daily.

330   US
AFTERMARKET BUSINESS BIG "I" SHOW DAILY. a. (in 3 eds.) free to show attendees. Harcourt Brace Jovanovich, Inc., 7500 Old Oak Blvd., Cleveland, OH 44130. TEL 216-243-8100. Ed. Richard Weinberg. circ. 15,000.
Formerly: Home & Auto Big "I" Show Daily.

330   IT   ISSN 0065-4264
AGENDA DEL DIRIGENTE DI AZIENDA.* a. Editoriale Emme Elle s.r.l., Via Reno, 30, Rome, Italy.

330   PL   ISSN 0208-7944
AKADEMIA EKONOMICZNA, KRAKOW. ZESZYTY NAUKOWE. (Text in Polish; summaries in English and Russian) 1955. irreg. price varies. Akademia Ekonomiczna, Krakow, Ul. Rakowicka 27, 31-510 Krakow, Poland. circ. 275. Indexed: Chem.Abstr.
Formerly: Wyzsza Szkola Ekonomiczna. Zeszyty Naukowe (ISSN 0075-5125)

330   PL   ISSN 0209-1674
AKADEMIA EKONOMICZNA, KRAKOW. ZESZYTY NAUKOWE. SERIA SPECJALNA: MONOGRAFIE. (Text in Polish; summaries in English and Russian) 1961. irreg. price varies. Akademia Ekonomiczna, Krakow, Ul. Rakowicka 27, 31-510 Krakow, Poland. circ. 275.
Formerly: Wyzsza Szkola Ekonomiczna, Krakow. Zeszyty Naukowe. Seria Specjalna: Monografie.

330   PL   ISSN 0079-4546
AKADEMIA EKONOMICZNA, POZNAN. ZESZYTY NAUKOWE. SERIA 1. (Former name of issuing body Wyzsza Szkola Ekonomiczna) 1961. irreg. price varies. Akademia Ekonomiczna, Poznan, Marchlewskiego 146, 60-967 Poznan, Poland. circ. 300. Indexed: Chem.Abstr.

330   PL   ISSN 0079-4554
AKADEMIA EKONOMICZNA, POZNAN. ZESZYTY NAUKOWE. SERIA 2. PRACE HABILITACYJNE I DOKTORSKIE. (Former name of issuing body Wyzsza Szkola Ekonomiczna) 1957. irreg. price varies. Akademia Ekonomiczna, Poznan, Marchlewskiego 146, 60-967 Poznan, Poland. circ. 200.

330   PL
AKADEMIA EKONOMICZNA WE WROCLAWIU. PRACE NAUKOWE. irreg. 9 Zl. Akademia Ekonomiczna, Wroclaw, Komandorska 118-120, 50-950 Wroclaw, Poland. illus.
Formerly: Wyzsza Szkola Ekonomiczna we Wroclawiu. Prace Naukowe.

330   PL
AKADEMIA ROLNICZA W SZCZECINIE. ZESZYTY NAUKOWE. EKONOMIKA, ORGANIZACJA I KIEROWANIE. 1975. irreg., no. 50, 1975. price varies. Akademia Rolnicza, Janosika 8, 71-424 Szczecin, Poland. Ed. Prof. Mieczyslaw Jasnowsi. bk. rev. Indexed: Chem.Abstr. Nutr.Abstr. Field Crop Abstr.

BUSINESS AND ECONOMICS

330   GE   ISSN 0138-3469
AKADEMIE DER WISSENSCHAFTEN DER D.D.R. ZENTRALINSTITUT FUER WIRTSCHAFTSWISSENSCHAFTEN. SCHRIFTEN. 1955. irreg., no. 21, 1984. price varies. Akademie-Verlag, Leipziger Str. 3-4, 1086 Berlin, E. Germany (D.D.R.) bibl. charts. illus.

330   FR
ALTERNATIVES ECONOMIQUES. 1982. irreg. price varies. Editions Syros, 1 rue de Varenne, 75006 Paris, France.

650   378   US
AMERICAN ASSEMBLY OF COLLEGIATE SCHOOLS OF BUSINESS. MEMBERSHIP DIRECTORY. a. $5. American Assembly of Collegiate Schools of Business, 605 Old Ballas Rd., Ste. 220, St. Louis, MO 63141-7011. Ed. Sharon L. Barber.
     Formerly: American Assembly of Collegiate Schools of Business. Accredited Schools, Officers, Committees (ISSN 0065-7131)

330   DK   ISSN 0109-7822
AMTERNES OEKONOMI. 1984. a. Kr.75. Amtsraadsforeningen i Danmark, Landermarket 102, DK-1119 Copenhagen K, Denmark.
     Formerly: Amtskommunernes Oekonomi.

330   650   SP
ANALES DE LA UNIVERSIDAD HISPALENSE. SERIE: EMPRESARIALES. Variant title: Anales de la Universidad Hispalense. Serie: Economicas y Empresariales. vol.2, 1976. irreg., latest no.24. price varies (or exchange) Universidad de Sevilla, San Fernando 4, Seville, Spain.

330   FR
ANNALES ECONOMIQUES DE CLERMONT-FERRAND. 1971. irreg., latest no.17, 1981. 40 F. Editions Cujas, 4,6, 8 rue de la Maison Blanche, 75013 Paris, France.

330   PL   ISSN 0459-9586
ANNALES UNIVERSITATIS MARIAE CURIE-SKLODOWSKA. SECTIO H. OECONOMIA. (Text in English, French, German, Polish; summaries in English, French, German, Polish, Russian) 1967. a. price varies. Uniwersytet Marii Curie-Sklodowskiej, Plac Marii Curie-Sklodowskiej 5, 20-031 Lublin, Poland. Ed. R. Orlowski. circ. 350.

330   GW
ANNALES UNIVERSITATIS SARAVIENSIS. WIRTSCHAFTSWISSENSCHAFTLICHE ABTEILUNG. SCHRIFTENREIHE. 1962. irreg., vol.119, 1986. price varies. (Universitaet des Saarlandes, Wirtschaftswissenschaftliche Fakultaet) Carl Heymanns Verlag KG, Luxemburgerstr. 449, 5000 Cologne 41, W. Germany (B.R.D.)

330   FR
ANNUAIRE DES ADMINISTRATEURS ET DES SOCIETES. vol.62, 1978. a. 1040 F. Societe de Documentation et d'Analyses Financieres, 7 rue Bergere, 75009 Paris, France.
     Formerly: Annuaire Desfosses.

330   FR
ANNUAIRE ECONOMIQUE. a, 23rd ed., 1985. Euro-Publi Marcel Puget, 9 Bd. des Italiens, 75002 Paris, France.

330   US   ISSN 0090-4309
ANNUAL EDITIONS: BUSINESS/MANAGEMENT. 1973/74. a. 9.95. Dushkin Publishing Group, Inc., Sluice Dock, Guilford, CT 06437. TEL 203-453-4351. illus.
     Former titles: Business Management (ISSN 0276-3923); Annual Editions: Readings in Business.

330   US
ANNUAL EDITIONS: ECONOMICS. 1971. a. $9.50. Dushkin Publishing Group, Inc., Sluice Dock, Guilford, CT 06437. TEL 203-453-4351. Ed. Ian Nielsen. illus.
     Formerly: Annual Editions: Readings in Economics (ISSN 0090-4430)

ARCHIVUM TREBONENSE. see *HISTORY — History Of Europe*

330   US
AREA DEVELOPMENT INDUSTRIAL DEVELOPMENT DIRECTORY OF CANADA. 1982. a. Halcyon Business Publications, Inc., 525 Northern Blvd., Great Neck, NY 11021. TEL 516-829-8990. Ed. G. Gambale. adv. tr.lit. circ. 21,700.

330   II
ARTHA VIJNANA REPRINT SERIES. (Text in English) irreg., no. 5, 1981. price varies. Gokhale Institute of Politics and Economics, Poona 411004, India.

330   NE
ASEPELT SERIES. 1962. irreg., vol. 5, 1976. price varies. Elsevier Science Publishers B.V., Box 211, 1000 AE Amsterdam, Netherlands.

330   HK
ASIA YEARBOOK. 1960. a. HK.$195($24.95) Far Eastern Economic Review Ltd., Box 160, Hong Kong, Hong Kong. Ed. Donald Wise. adv. Indexed: Gdlns.
     Formerly: Far Eastern Economic Review. Yearbook (ISSN 0071-3821)

330   AG
ASOCIACION DE ECONOMISTAS ARGENTINOS. COLECCION INSTITUTO SUPERIOR. irreg, no.3, 1976. Editorial el Coloquio, Junin 735, Buenos Aires, Argentina. charts, stat.

330   CN   ISSN 0319-003X
ATLANTIC CANADA ECONOMICS ASSOCIATION. ANNUAL CONFERENCE: A C E A PAPERS. no.4, 1975. a. Can.$10. Atlantic Canada Economics Association, c/o Prof. R.L. Comeau, Ed., Department of Economics, Dalhousie University, Halifax, N.S. B3H 3J5, Canada. TEL 902-424-2026. charts. stat. circ. 150.

AUCTION PRICES OF AMERICAN ARTISTS-VOLUME 5. see *ART*

330   AT   ISSN 0156-3394
AUSTRALIA. BUREAU OF INDUSTRY ECONOMICS. RESEARCH REPORT. 1978. irreg. Australian Government Publishing Service, G.P.O. Box 84, Canberra, A.C.T. 2601, Australia.

330   BG
BAMLADESA ARTHANAITIKA JARIPA. (Text in Bengali) 1971. a. Ministry of Finance, Economic Adviser's Wing, Bangladesh Secretariat, Shed No. 27, Dacca 2, Bangladesh.
     Formerly (until 1974/75): Bangladesh Economic Survey (ISSN 0070-8704)

330   UK   ISSN 0306-9338
BANGOR OCCASIONAL PAPERS IN ECONOMICS. 1973. irreg. price varies. University of Wales Press, 6 Gwennyth St., Cathays, Cardiff CF2 4YD, Wales. Ed. Jack Revell.

BARRON'S GUIDE TO GRADUATE BUSINESS SCHOOLS. see *EDUCATION — Higher Education*

330   GW
BEITRAEGE ZUR OEKONOMISCHEN FORSCHUNG. 1974. irreg. Vandenhoeck & Ruprecht, Robert-Bosch-Breite 6, Postfach 3753, D-3400 Goettingen, W. Germany (B.R.D.) Ed. Hans K. Schneider.

330   CN   ISSN 0706-7852
BENEFITS FOR SASKATCHEWAN INDUSTRY FROM RESOURCE DEVELOPMENT.* 1979. irreg. Government Printing Co., 2005 8th St., Regina, Sask. S4P 2Y9, Canada. TEL 306-566-9393.

330   SZ   ISSN 0067-6128
BERNER BEITRAEGE ZUR NATIONALOEKONOMIE. 1965. irreg., vol.49, 1985. price varies. Paul Haupt AG, Falkenplatz 14, CH-3001 Berne, Switzerland. Ed.Bd.

BERNER STUDIEN ZUM FREMDENVERKEHR. see *TRAVEL AND TOURISM*

330   RM   ISSN 0067-8082
BIBLIOTHECA OECONOMICA. (Text in Rumanian; summaries in English, French and Russian) 1967. irreg., vol.40, 1984. (Institutul Central de Cercetari Economice) Editura Academiei Republicii Socialiste Rumania, Calea Victoriei 125, 79717 Bucharest, Rumania (Subscr. to: ARTEXIM, Export-Import Presa, Str. Piata Scinteii nr.1, P.O.Box 33-16, 70055 Bucharest, Rumania)

330   UK
BIRKBECK COLLEGE DISCUSSION PAPERS IN ECONOMICS. 1972. irreg. free. University of London, Birkbeck College, 7-15 Gresse St., London W1P 1PA, England. Ed. B. Lockwood. circ. 200.

BLACK WHO'S WHO OF SOUTHERN AFRICA. see *BIOGRAPHY*

330   EC
BOLETIN TRIMESTRAL DE INFORMACION ECONOMICA. 1946. irreg? Universidad Central del Ecuador, Instituto de Investigaciones Economicas, Casilla 1088, Quito, Ecuador.

330   US   ISSN 0068-0354
BOSTWICK PAPER. 1968. irreg., no.5, 1985. $5. Bostwick Press, 5 Bostwick Ln., Richmond, VA 23226-3106. Ed. Thomas S. Berry. circ. 500. Indexed: Vert.File Ind.

338.9   BL   ISSN 0100-2910
BRAZILIAN ECONOMIC STUDIES. (Text in English) 1975. irreg. price varies. Instituto de Planejamento Economico e Social, Av. Presidente Antonio Carlos, 51/13 andar, CEP 20.020 Rio de Janeiro, RJ, Brazil. Ed. Michal Gartenkraut. bk. rev. circ. 1,000. Indexed: P.A.I.S. Hisp.Amer.Per.Ind.

330   UK
BRITISH-NORTH AMERICAN COMMITTEE PUBLICATIONS. 1970. irreg. price varies. British-North American Research Association, 35-37 Grosvenor Gardens House, Grosvenor Gardens, London SW1W 0BS, England. Ed.Bd. bibl. charts.
     Formerly: British-North American Research Association. Committee Publications.

330   UK
BRITISH-NORTH AMERICAN RESEARCH ASSOCIATION. OCCASIONAL PAPERS. 1972. irreg. price varies. British-North American Research Association, 35-37 Grosvenor Gardens House, Grosvenor Gardens, London SW1W 0BS, England. bibl. charts.

330   300   MR   ISSN 0007-4586
BULLETIN ECONOMIQUE ET SOCIAL DU MAROC. (Editions in Arabic and English) 1936. irreg. DH.50 for 4 numbers. Societe d'Etudes Economiques Sociales et Statistiques du Maroc, B.P. 535, Rabat-Chellah, Morocco. Ed. Abdelkhebir Khatibi. bk. rev. cum.index. circ. 1,300.

BURT FRANKLIN ESSAYS IN HISTORY, ECONOMICS, AND SOCIAL SCIENCES. see *HISTORY*

330   UK
BUSI BUSINESS SERVICES INDEX.* 1984. q. £6. Chambers & Gould Ltd., South Bank House, Black Prince Rd., London SE1 7SJ, England.

330   US
BUSINESS AND ECONOMIC HISTORY. 1975. a. price varies. University of Illinois at Urbana-Champaign, Bureau of Economic and Business Research, 428 Commerce W., 1206 S. Sixth St., Champaign, IL 61820. TEL 217-333-2330. Ed. Jeremy Atack. circ. 300.

330   UK   ISSN 0007-6538
BUSINESS ARCHIVES. 1934. a. £12 to individuals; institutions £15. Business Archives Council, 185 Tower Bridge Rd., London SE1 2UF, England. Ed. J. Armstrong. adv. bk. rev. cum.index. circ. 600(controlled) (back issues avail.)

330   US   ISSN 0146-4744
BUSINESS ASSISTANCE MONOGRAPH SERIES. irreg. Federal Reserve Bank of Boston, Urban Affairs Section, Boston, MA 02106.

BUSINESS AND ECONOMICS

650 SA
BUSINESS BLUE BOOK OF S.A. (Text in English) 1949. a. R.84. Communications Group, Group Marketing Division, P.O. Box 2735, Johannesburg 2000, South Africa. Ed. Dick Hutton. adv. circ. 5, 500.
Former titles: Blue Book of S.A. Business & Business Blue-Book of Southern Africa (ISSN 0068-4406)

330 US
BUSINESS ECONOMICS AND FINANCE SERIES. 1974. irreg., vol.12, 1980. Marcel Dekker, Inc., 270 Madison Ave., New York, NY 10016.

330 370 US
BUSINESS EDUCATION FILMS CATALOG. 1950. biennial. free. Business Education Films, Dartnell Films Circular, 7820-20 Ave., Brooklyn, NY 11214. Ed. Paul Weinberg. circ. 20,000.

330 US
BUSINESS INFORMATION FOR DALLAS. 1976. irreg. free. Dallas Public Library, Business and Technology Division, 1515 Young St., Dallas, TX 75201. TEL 214-749-4321. Ed. Marian I. Waite. bk. rev. circ. 2,000.

338 020 UK
BUSINESS INFORMATION SOURCEBOOK. 1983. base vol. plus q. updates. £49.95($98) Headland Press, Freepost 22, London EC1A 7QT, England. Ed. Gerry Smith.

BUSINESS LAW REPORTS. see *LAW*

330 UK
BUSINESS MONITOR. irreg. price varies. Department of Trade and Industry, Business Statistics Office, Cardiff Rd., Newport, Gwent NP9 1XG, England (Avail. from: H.M.S.O., P.O. Box 276, London SW8 5DT, England)

330 GW
BUSINESS REPORT (ABRIDGED VERSION) (Text in various languages) 1952. a. Bayer AG, D-5090 Leverkusen, W. Germany (B.R.D.) circ. 420,000.

330 GW
BUSINESS REPORT (UNABRIDGED VERSION) (Text in English, French and German) 1951. a. Bayer AG, D-5090 Leverkusen, W. Germany (B.R.D.) circ. 37,000.

330 IE
BUSINESS STUDIES SERIES. 1979. irreg. price varies. Confederation of Irish Industry, Confederation House, Kildare St., Dublin 2, Ireland. Ed. Tony Donohoe.

BUSINESS TRAVELER'S CITY GUIDE. see *TRAVEL AND TOURISM*

338 UK ISSN 0268-2273
C B I ANNUAL REPORT. a. 2. Confederation of British Industry, 103 New Oxford St., London WC1A 1DU, England.

330 CN ISSN 0824-8001
C.D. HOWE INSTITUTE COMMENTARY. 1982. irreg. Can.$2 per issue. C.D. Howe Institute, 125 Adelaide St. East, Toronto, Ont. M5C 1L7, Canada. Indexed: G.Soc.Sci.& Rel.Per.Lit.

330 CN ISSN 0826-9939
C.D. HOWE INSTITUTE. POLICY REVIEW AND OUTLOOK. 1974. a. C.D. Howe Institute, 125 Adelaide St. East, Toronto, Ont. M5C 1L7, Canada. TEL 416-865-1904. (also avail. in microform from MML)
Formerly: C. D. Howe Research Institute. Policy Review and Outlook.

330.1 BE
C E P S PAPERS. (Text in English) 1983. irreg. 2200 Fr. Centre for European Policy Studies, 33 rue Ducale, 1000 Brussels, Belgium. Ed. Helen Bloom. (back issues avail.)

330 330.1 BE
C E P S WORKING DOCUMENTS (ECONOMIC) (Text in English) 1983. irreg. 2008 Fr. Centre for European Policy Studies, 33 rue Ducale, 1000 Brussels, Belgium. Ed. Helen Bloom. (back issues avail.)

C R S PERSPECTIVES. (Centre for Resource Studies) see *MINES AND MINING INDUSTRY*

330 BL
CADASTRO DELTA; Brazil, its industry and exportation. 1943. a. $145. Albeisa do Brasil Editores Ltda., Rua Barao de Itapetininga 255, Andar 7, Conj. 705, CEP 01042, Sao Paulo, Brazil. Ed. Maria de Fatima Barros Besio. adv. circ. 200, 000.

CAHIERS ECONOMIQUES ET MONETAIRES. see *BUSINESS AND ECONOMICS — Banking And Finance*

330 US ISSN 0271-6615
CALIFORNIA SERVICES REGISTER. 1979. biennial. $195. Times Mirror Press, Box 23951, 1115 S. Boyle Ave., Los Angeles, CA 90023-0951. TEL 213-265-6767. Ed. Terry Gutierrez. circ. 500.

330 UK
CAMBRIDGE ECONOMIC HANDBOOKS. NEW SERIES. irreg. price varies. Cambridge University Press, Edinburgh Bldg., Shaftesbury Rd., Cambridge CB2 2RU, England (And 32 E. 57th St., New York NY 10022) Ed. F.H. Hahn.

330 UK ISSN 0068-6832
CAMBRIDGE UNIVERSITY. DEPARTMENT OF APPLIED ECONOMICS. MONOGRAPHS. 1948. irreg., no.27, 1980. price varies. Cambridge University Press, Edinburgh Bldg., Shaftesbury Rd., Cambridge CB2 2RU, England (And 32 E. 57th St., New York, NY 10022)

330 UK ISSN 0068-6840
CAMBRIDGE UNIVERSITY. DEPARTMENT OF APPLIED ECONOMICS. OCCASIONAL PAPERS. 1964. irreg., no.54, 1982. price varies. Cambridge University Press, Edinburgh Bldg., Shaftesbury Rd., Cambridge CB2 2RU, England (and 32 E. 57 St., New York, NY 10022)

330 AQ
CARIBBEAN HANDBOOK. 1983. a. $42. F T Caribbean, P.O. Box 1037, St. John's, Antiqua, W.I. TEL 809-462-3392. (Subscr. addrress: 3A Sloane Ave., London, SW3 3JD, England) Ed. Jeremy Taylor. adv. bk. rev. circ. 9,000.

330 DK ISSN 0107-5586
CASESAMLING. 1976. a. (Handelshoejskolen i Koebenhavn, Institut for Informatik og Oekonomistyring) Bibliotekscentralen, Telegrafvej 5, DK-2750 Ballerup, Denmark.

330 UK ISSN 0069-0937
CASS LIBRARY OF INDUSTRIAL CLASSICS. 1966. irreg., no.28, 1969. price varies. Frank Cass & Co. Ltd., Gainsborough House, 11 Gainsborough Rd., London E11 1RS, England (Dist. in U.S. by: Biblio Distribution Center, 81 Adams Drive, Totowa, N.J. 07512)

330 FR ISSN 0071-8343
CENTRE NATIONAL DE LA RECHERCHE SCIENTIFIQUE. SEMINAIRE D'ECONOMETRIE. CAHIERS. 1951. a. price varies. Centre National de la Recherche Scientifique, Seminaire d'Econometrie, 15 Quai Anatole-France, 75700 Paris, France.

330 FR ISSN 0071-8270
CENTRE NATIONAL DE LA RECHERCHE SCIENTIFIQUE. SEMINAIRE D'ECONOMETRIE. MONOGRAPHIES. 1960. irreg. price varies. Centre National de la Recherche Scientifique, Seminaire d'Econometrie, 15 Quai Anatole-France, 75700 Paris, France.

330 US ISSN 0196-7525
CHICAGO M B A; a journal of selected papers. 1977. a. $3. University of Chicago, Graduate School of Business, 1101 E. 58th St., Chicago, IL 60637. TEL 312-962-7743. Ed. Sanford Goodman. Indexed: Bus.Ind.

330 US
CHINA REPORT: ECONOMIC AFFAIRS. irreg. (approx. 130/yr.) $5 per no. U.S. Joint Publications Research Service, 1000 N. Glebe Rd., Arlington, VA 22201 TEL 703-487-4630. (Orders to: NTIS, Springfield, VA 22161)

330 BL
CIENCIAS ECONOMICAS. irreg. Ordem dos Economistas de Sao Paulo, Viaduto 9 de Julho, 26, Sao Paulo, Brazil. illus.
Continues: Revista de Ciencias Economicas: Economia, Financas, Administracao, Estatistica (ISSN 0484-6796)

330 GW ISSN 0170-5679
CIRET STUDIEN. 1963. irreg. price varies. I F O Institut fuer Wirtschaftsforschung, Poschingerstr. 5, 8000 Muenchen 80, W. Germany (B.R.D.) circ. 500.

COLECCAO HORIZONTE UNIVERSITARIO. see *POLITICAL SCIENCE*

330 SP
COLECCION TABLERO. irreg., no. 8, 1982. Editorial Planeta, S.A., Corcega, 273-277, Barcelona-8, Spain.

330 SZ
COLLOQUES ECONOMIQUES. (Text in French or German) 1974. a. price varies. Editions Universitaires de Fribourg, 42 Bd. de Perolles, CH-1700 Fribourg, Switzerland.

330 368 CK
COLOMBIA. SUPERINTENDENCIA BANCARIA. SEGUROS Y CAPITALIZACION. 1969. a. free. Superintendencia Bancaria, Bogota, Colombia. circ. 1,600.

330 US ISSN 0069-6331
COLUMBIA STUDIES IN ECONOMICS. 1968. irreg., no. 10, 1979. Columbia University Press, 562 W. 113th St., New York, NY 10025. TEL 212-678-6777.

650 US
COLUMBIA UNIVERSITY GRADUATE SCHOOL OF BUSINESS. DISSERTATIONS SERIES. irreg. price varies. (Columbia University, Graduate School of Business) Free Press, c/o Macmillan, 866 Third Ave., New York, NY 10022. TEL 212-935-2000.

330.9 US
COMMONWEALTH OF KENTUCKY. ANNUAL ECONOMIC REPORT (YEAR); an economic and governmental finance profile of Kentucky. 1972. a. $10. Kentucky Council of Economic Advisors, Center for Business & Economics Research, 301 Mathews Bldg., College of Business and Economics, University of Kentucky, Lexington, KY 40506-0047. TEL 606-257-7675. Ed. Carolyn Loof. circ. 800. (also avail. in microfiche; back issues avail.)
Formerly: Kentucky. Council of Economic Advisors. Annual Report (ISSN 0270-238X)

338 020 UK
COMPANY INFORMATION SOURCEBOOK. 1986. base vol. plus s-a. updates. £49.95($98) Headland Press, Freepost 22, London EC1A 7QT, England. Ed. Gerry Smith.

330 US ISSN 0739-1862
COMPANY THESAURUS. a. $225. Predicasts, Inc., 11001 Cedar Ave., Cleveland, OH 44106. TEL 800-321-6388.
Formerly: Corporate Thesaurus.

330 SA
CONDENSER. 1947. a. Tongaat-Hulett Group Ltd., P.O. Box 3, Maidstone 4400, Natal, South Africa. Ed. R.D. Kemp. circ. 15,000.

338 US ISSN 0146-0986
CONFERENCE BOARD. ANNUAL SURVEY OF CORPORATE CONTRIBUTIONS. (Subseries of: Conference Board. Report) $125 to non-members; members $25. ‡ Conference Board, Inc., 845 Third Ave, New York, NY 10022. TEL 212-759-0900. Indexed: B.P.I. P.A.I.S.
Formerly: Conference Board. Report on Company Contributions (ISSN 0069-8369)

650 330 US ISSN 0069-8350
CONFERENCE BOARD CUMULATIVE INDEX. 1963. a. free. Conference Board, Inc., 845 Third Ave., New York, NY 10022. TEL 212-759-0900. Ed. Ellen Ackerman. circ. 15,000.

330 ES
CONGRESO NACIONAL DE PROFESIONALES EN CIENCIAS ECONOMICAS. MEMORIA. 1972. irreg. Congreso Nacional de Profesionales en Ciencias Economicas, San Salvador, El Salvador.

BUSINESS AND ECONOMICS

CONSULTING RATES AND BUSINESS PRACTICES. ANNUAL SURVEY. see *OCCUPATIONS AND CAREERS*

CONSUMER CREDIT CONTROL. see *LAW*

330 332 US
CONTEMPORARY STUDIES IN ECONOMIC AND FINANCIAL ANALYSIS; an international series of monographs. 1976. irreg., vol.55, 1986. $22.50 to individuals; institutions $45. J A I Press Inc., Box 1678, 36 Sherwood Pl., Greenwich, CT 06836. TEL 203-661-7602. Eds. Edward Altman, Ingo Walter. charts. stat.

330 BL
CONTRIBUICOES EM ECONOMIA. 1977. irreg. Editora Campus Ltda. (Subsidiary of: Elsevier North-Holland, Inc.) Rua Barao de Itapagipe 55, Rio Comprido, 20261 Rio de Janeiro RJ, Brazil. Ed. Claudio M. Rothmuller. illus.

330 658 DK ISSN 0900-1808
COPENHAGEN SCHOOL OF ECONOMICS AND BUSINESS ADMINISTRATION. RESEARCH PAPER. irreg. (Copenhagen School of Economics and Business Administration, Marketing Institute) Bibliotekscentralen, Telegrafvej 5, DK-2750 ballerup, Denmark.

330 CK
CORPORACION FINANCIERA COLOMBIANA. EJERCICIO. a. Corporacion Financiera Colombiana, Carrera nos. 26-45, Apdo Aereo 11843, Bogota, Colombia.

330 US ISSN 0163-3031
CORPORATE FINANCE SOURCEBOOK. 1980. a. $212. N R P C (Subsidiary of: Macmillan Publishing Company) 3004 Glenview Rd., Wilmette, IL 60091. TEL 312-256-6067. Ed. Robert Weicherding. adv. tr.lit. circ. 10,122.

330 332.6 US ISSN 0145-692X
CORPORATE PROFILES FOR EXECUTIVES & INVESTORS. a. $14.50. Rand McNally & Co., 8225 N. Central Pk., Skokie, IL 60076. TEL 312-673-9100. charts.

330 US
COWLES FOUNDATION MONOGRAPHS. 1970. irreg., no.27, 1981. price varies. Yale University Press, 92A Yale Sta., New Haven, CT 06520. TEL 203-432-4969.
Formerly: Cowles Foundation for Research in Economics at Yale University. Monographs (ISSN 0084-9413)

330 US
CRAIN'S DETROIT BUSINESS. a. $20 in US; Canada & other foreign $32. Crain Communications, Inc. (Detroit), 1400 Woodbridge, Detroit, MI 48207.

330 PY
CUADERNOS B P D. SERIE: ECONOMIA. 1981. irreg. Banco Paraguayo de Datos, Casilla Postal 1140, MacArthur 250, Asuncion, Paraguay.

330 SP
CUADERNOS DE SECCION. CINENCIAS SOCIALES Y ECONOMICAS. 1986. irreg. (Sociedad de Estudios Vascos) Eusko Ikaskuntza, S.A., Churruca, 7 - 2, 20004 Donostia, Spain. TEL 425111.

330 380.5 UK
CUMBRIA & NORTH LANCASHIRE INDUSTRY AND BUILDING INDUSTRY YEAR BOOK. a. Border Press Agency Ltd., 12 Lonsdale St., Carlisle CA1 1DD, England.
Former titles: Cumbria and North Lancashire Industry Year Book & Cumbria and North Lancashire Industry and Transport Year Book.

330 CS ISSN 0590-5001
CZECHOSLOVAK ECONOMIC PAPERS. (Text in English) 1959. irreg. price varies. (Ceskoslovenska Akademie Ved, Ekonomicky Ustav) Academia, Publishing House of the Czechoslovak Academy of Sciences, Vodickova 40, 112 29 Prague 1, Czechoslovakia. bk. rev. bibl.

D J OE F - HAANDBOGEN; opslagsbog for tillidsrepraesentanter i D J OE F. (Danmarks Juris- og Oekonomforbund) see *LAW*

D S I R DISCUSSION PAPER. (Department of Scientific and Industrial Research) see *SCIENCES: COMPREHENSIVE WORKS*

330 CN ISSN 0317-6207
DAIRY FACTS AND FIGURES AT A GLANCE. a. free. Dairy Farmers of Canada, 75 Albert St., Ste. 1101, Ottawa, Ont. K1P 5E7, Canada.

330 CN ISSN 0318-2967
DAIRY POLICY. (Text in English and French) a. free. Dairy Farmers of Canada, 111 Sparks St., Ottawa, Ont. K1P 5B5, Canada.

338 DK ISSN 0106-4967
DENMARK. JORDBRUGSOEKONOMISK INSTITUT. AARSBERETNING.* 1979. a. Kr.18. Jordbrugsoekonomisk Institut, Valby Langgade 19, DK-2500 Valby, Denmark.

338 DK ISSN 0106-1291
DENMARK. JORDBRUGSOEKONOMISK INSTITUT. LANDBRUGETS OEKONOMI.* 1979. a. Kr.18. Jordbrugsoekonomisk Institut, Valby Langgade 19, DK-2500 Valby, Denmark.

330 II
DIRECTORY OF ECONOMIC RESEARCH CENTRES IN INDIA. (Supplements issued annually) 1972. irreg., 2nd edition, 1975. Rs.85($13.20) Information Research Academy, 37 Amir Ali Ave., Calcutta 700019, India. Ed. Partha Subir Guha. adv. circ. 2,500.

650 370.58 US
DIRECTORY OF EDUCATIONAL INSTITUTIONS. 1956. a. $3.50. Association of Independent Colleges and Schools, Accrediting Commission, One Dupont Circle, N.W., Ste. 350, Washington, DC 20036. TEL 202-659-2460. Ed. Mary Lou Klaric. circ. 20,000.
Former titles: Directory of Accredited Institutions & Directory of Business Schools (ISSN 0070-5187)

330 US ISSN 0278-0119
DIRECTORY OF INDUSTRY DATA SOURCES, U.S. AND CANADA. 1981. a. Ballinger Publishing Co., 54 Church St., Cambridge, MA 02138. abstr. bibl. stat.

330 US
DIRECTORY OF JAPANESE FIRMS, OFFICES AND OTHER ORGANIZATIONS IN THE UNITED STATES.* 1969. triennial. $16.90. Japan External Trade Organization (JETRO), Japan Trade Center, 401 N. Michigan, Ste. 660, Chicago, IL 60611 (Dist. by California Business Corporation, 900 Wilshire Blvd., Suite 414, Los Angeles, CA 90017)
Formerly: Directory of Japanese Firms, Offices and Subsidiaries in the United States.

650 US ISSN 0070-640X
DIRECTORY OF STATE AND FEDERAL FUNDS AVAILABLE FOR BUSINESS DEVELOPMENT. 1966. irreg., latest edt. 1985. $5. Pilot Books, 103 Cooper St., Babylon, NY 11702. TEL 516-422-2225.

330 US
DIRECTORY OF V A RS; value added resellers. a. $249. Chain Store Guide, 425 Park Ave., New York, NY 10022. TEL 212-371-9400.

330 US
DISTRIBUTOR MANUFACTURER NEWS B B S I CONVENTION DAILY. 1949. a. (in 3 eds.) free to convention attendees. Harcourt Brace Jovanovich, Inc., 7500 Old Oak Blvd., Cleveland, OH 44130 TEL 216-243-8100. (Subscr. address: 1 E. First St., Duluth, MN 55802) Ed. Jody Bryne. circ. 3,200.

330 FR
DOSSIER DE L'INDUSTRIE AFRICAINE.* 1980. a. 1300 F. Ediafric-la Documentation Africaine, 57 Ave. d'Iena, 75016 Paris, France.

330 US
DOW JONES-IRWIN BUSINESS AND INVESTMENT ALMANAC. 1977. a. $25. Dow Jones-Irwin, Homewood, IL 60430. TEL 312-798-6000. Eds. Sumner N. Levine, Caroline Levine.
Formerly: Dow Jones-Irwin Business Almanac (ISSN 0146-6534)

330 DK ISSN 0106-9535
DRIFTSOEKONOMI; regnskabsresultater. Spine title: D H Driftsoekonomi. 1972. a. free. Driftsoekonomiudvalget Danske Husmandsforeninger, c/o Det Faglige Landscenter, Kongsgaardsvej 28, 8260 Viby J., Denmark. Ed. Kofoed Hansen. bk. rev. illus. circ. 11,000.
Supersedes in part: Landbrugsregnskaber.

330 SA
DURBAN METROPOLITAN ECONOMY PROJECT; a survey of educational facilities & social rates of return. (Text in English) 1984. irreg. R.3. University of Natal, Department of Economics, King Goerge V Ave., Durban, South Africa. Ed. Gavin Grant Maasdorp. circ. 300.

330 NE
DYNAMIC ECONOMICS: THEORY AND APPLICATIONS (SERIES) 1976. irreg., vol.4, 1985. price varies. Elsevier Science Publishers B.V., P.O. Box 211, 1000 AE Amsterdam, Netherlands. Ed. Maurice Wilkinson. Indexed: Math.R.
Formerly: Dynamic Economics Series.

330 650 SA ISSN 0250-0027
DYNAMICA. (Text in Afrikaans and English) 1964. a. R.1.30. University of South Africa, Department of Business Economics, Box 392, Pretoria 0001, South Africa. Ed. A.E. Annandale. adv. bk. rev. circ. 3, 170. (back issues avail.)

330 CN
E.S. WOODWARD LECTURES IN ECONOMICS. irreg. University of British Columbia, Department of Economics, 1873 East Mall, Suite 997, University Campus, Vancouver, B.C. V6T 1Y2, Canada. TEL 604-228-2211.

330 US
EAST WEST EUROPEAN ECONOMIC INTERACTION. 1976. irreg., no.4, 1978. Springer-Verlag, 175 Fifth Ave., New York, NY 10010 TEL 212-460-1500. (Also Berlin, Heidelberg, Vienna) (reprint service avail. from ISI)

330 CK
ECONOMIA. 1959. irreg. Compania Editoria Continente, Edificio Morulanda, Carrera 6a, 14-74, Bogota, Colombia. Dir. E. Fierro Forero. bibl. illus.

330 MX
ECONOMIA MEXICANA. 1979. a. Centro de Investigacion y Docencia Economicas, Departamento de Economia, Apartado Postal 41-655, Mexico 10, D.F., Mexico.

330 HO ISSN 0424-2483
ECONOMIA POLITICA. 1962; N.S. 1972. irreg. $2. Universidad Nacional Autonoma de Honduras, Instituto de Investigaciones Economicas y Sociales, Ciudad Universitaria, Tegucigalpa, Honduras. Ed. Victor Meza. bk. rev. circ. 1,000.

ECONOMIC ANALYSIS OF NORTH AMERICAN SKI AREAS. see *SPORTS AND GAMES — Outdoor Life*

330.1 II ISSN 0070-8437
ECONOMIC AND SCIENTIFIC RESEARCH FOUNDATION. ANNUAL REPORT. 1967. a. Economic and Scientific Research Foundation, Federation House, New Delhi 110001, India. circ. 1,000.

330 UK ISSN 0140-0061
ECONOMIC AND SOCIAL HISTORY SURVEYS. 1977. irreg. Loughborough University of Technology, Department of Economics, Loughborough, Leics. LE11 3TU, England.

330 IE
ECONOMIC AND SOCIAL RESEARCH INSTITUTE. POLICY SERIES. irreg. price varies. Economic and Social Research Institute, 4 Burlington Rd., Dublin 4, Ireland. Indexed: Rural Recreat.Tour.Abstr. World Agri.Econ. & Rural Sociol.Abstr.

330 IE ISSN 0070-8755
ECONOMIC AND SOCIAL RESEARCH INSTITUTE. PUBLICATIONS SERIES. PAPER. (No. 1-35 issued by the institute under an earlier name: Economic Research Institute) 1961. irreg. price varies. Economic and Social Research Institute, 4 Burlington Rd., Dublin 4, Ireland. Indexed: Geo.Abstr. Rural Recreat.Tour.Abstr. World Agri.Econ.& Rural Sociol.Abstr.

BUSINESS AND ECONOMICS

330   CN   ISSN 0225-8013
ECONOMIC COUNCIL OF CANADA.
DISCUSSION PAPERS. 1973. irreg. free.
Economic Council of Canada, Information Division,
Box 527, Ottawa, Ont. K1P 5V6, Canada. TEL 613-993-1894. Ed.Bd. bibl. circ. 1,000.

330   US
ECONOMIC OUTLOOK FOR NEW JERSEY. a.
free. Office of Economic Policy, One W. State St.,
Trenton, NJ 08625.

330   BG   ISSN 0070-8631
ECONOMIC REVIEW.* (Text in English) 1964/65.
a. University of Dacca, Economics Association, c/o
Dept. of Economics, Ramna, Dacca 2, Bangladesh.

330   US
ECONOMIC ROAD MAPS. 1919. irreg. membership.
Conference Board, Inc., 845 Third Ave, New York,
NY 10022. TEL 212-759-0900. Ed. Eva Culen.
charts. stat. circ. 40,000. Indexed: Key to Econ.Sci.
PROMT.
    Formerly: Road Maps of Industry (ISSN 0035-7227)

330.1   FR   ISSN 0070-8801
ECONOMIE ET SOCIETE. 1970. irreg. price varies.
Editions du Seuil, 27 rue Jacob, 75261 Paris Cedex
06, France. Ed. Edmond Blanc. Indexed: Curr.Cont.
Key to Econ.Sci.

ECONOMIE FRANCAISE EN PERSPECTIVES
SECTORIELLES: FILIERE BATIMENT, GENIE
CIVIL, MATERIAUX DE CONSTRUCTION. see
BUILDING AND CONSTRUCTION

331   FR   ISSN 0068-4821
ECONOMIES ET SOCIETES. SERIE A B.
ECONOMIE DU TRAVAIL. 1960. irreg., latest
issue, 1983. 300 F. Presses Universitaires de
Grenoble, B.P. 47 X, 38040 Grenoble, France. Dir.
H. Bartoli. circ. 1,600.

330   FR   ISSN 0068-483X
ECONOMIES ET SOCIETES. SERIE G.
ECONOMIE PLANIFIEE. 1956. irreg. 300 F.
Presses Universitaires de Grenoble, B.P. 47 X,
38040 Grenoble, France. Eds. Henri Chambre, M.
Lavigne.

330.1   FR   ISSN 0068-4872
ECONOMIES ET SOCIETIES. SERIE T.
INFORMATION - RECHERCHE
INNOVATION. 1959. irreg. 300 F. Presses
Universitaires de Grenoble, B.P. 47 X, 38040
Grenoble, France. Dir. F. Russo. circ. 1,600.

330   EC   ISSN 0070-8925
ECUADOR ECONOMICO.* a. Universidad Central
del Ecuador, Instituto de Investigaciones
Economicas, Casilla 1088, Quito, Ecuador.

330   US
ELIOT JANEWAY LECTURES ON HISTORICAL
ECONOMICS. 1974. irreg. price varies. (Princeton
University, Woodrow Wilson School) Princeton
University Press, 3175 Princeton Pike, NJ 08648.
TEL 609-896-1344. (reprint service avail. from
UMI)

338   DK   ISSN 0105-6662
ERHVERVSNOEGLEN. 1978. a. Kr.130.
Noegleforlaget, Haslevej 12-14, 6000 Kolding,
Denmark. Ed. R. Poulsen. circ. 4,000.

330.9   FR   ISSN 0757-6714
ETAT DU MONDE; annuaire economique et
geopolitique mondial. (Text and summaries in
French) 1982. a. price varies. Editions La
Decouverte, 1 place Paul Painleve, 75005 Paris,
France. Ed.Bd. circ. 45,000. (back issues avail)

382   FR   ISSN 0302-0622
EURO COOPERATION; ECONOMIC STUDIES
ON EUROPE. irreg. free. Banco di Roma, 5,
Avenue du Coq, F-750009 Paris, France. (Co-Sponsors: Commerzbank; Credit Lyonnais) stat.

330   UK
EURO KOMPASS U K INDUSTRIAL SECTIONS.
1978. a. (in 6 vols.) Kompass Publishers Ltd.,
Windsor Court, East Grinstead House, East
Grinstead, West Sussex RH19 1XD, England. circ.
6,000.

EUROPE FOR BUSINESS TRAVELERS. see
TRAVEL AND TOURISM

330   301   UN
F A O ECONOMIC AND SOCIAL
DEVELOPMENT PAPER. 1978. irreg., no.59,
1986. price varies. Food and Agriculture
Organization of the United Nations, Distribution
and Sales Section, Via delle Terme di Caracalla,
Rome, Italy (Dist. in the U.S. by: Bernan
Associates-Unipub, 4611-F Assembly Drive,
Lanham, MD 20706-4391)

330   US
F & S JAPANESE INDUSTRY LETTER. irreg. Frost
& Sullivan, Inc., 106 Fulton St., New York, NY
10038. TEL 212-233-1080. Ed. Hiro Shibuya.

330   US
F & S REPORTS. irreg. Frost & Sullivan, Inc., 106
Fulton St., New York, NY 10038. TEL 212-233-1080. Ed. Henry M. Berler.

330   GW   ISSN 0071-769X
F I W - SCHRIFTENREIHE. 1962. irreg., vol.121,
1986. price varies. (Forschunginstitut fuer
Wirtschaftsverfassung und Wettbewerb e.V.) Carl
Heymanns Verlag KG, Luxemburgerstr. 449, 5000
Cologne 449, W. Germany (B.R.D.) adv. bk. rev.

330   US
FEDERAL RESERVE BANK OF ATLANTA.
WORKING PAPER SERIES. 1976. irreg. free.
Federal Reserve Bank of Atlanta, Box 1731,
Atlanta, GA 30301. TEL 404-586-8500. (back
issues avail.)

330   CN
FINANCIAL POST REPORT ON THE NATION;
Canada: outlook. 1984. a. Can.$5. MacLean-Hunter
Ltd., Business Publication Division, MacLean
Hunter Bldg., 777 Bay St., Toronto, Ont. M5W
1A7, Canada. TEL 416-596-5147. Ed. Anne Bower.
circ. 180,000.

330   CN
FINANCIAL POST SURVEY OF PREDECESSOR
AND DEFUNCT COMPANIES. 1981. biennial.
Can.$39.50. (Financial Post) Maclean Hunter Ltd.,
Business Publication Division, Maclean-Hunter
Bldg., 777 Bay St., Toronto, Ont. M5W 1A7,
Canada. TEL 416-596-5585. Ed. John Byrne. adv.
circ. 6,000.
    *Aids in tracing mergers, amalgamations, name
changes or charter cancellations of Canadian
companies*

330   PL   ISSN 0071-674X
FOLIA OECONOMICA CRACOVIENSIA. (Text in
Polish; summaries in English and Russian) 1960. a.
price varies. (Polska Akademia Nauk, Oddzial w
Krakowie, Komisja Nauk Ekonomicznych)
Ossolineum, Publishing House of the Polish
Academy of Sciences, Rynek 9, Wroclaw, Poland
(Dist. by Ars Polona-Ruch, Krakowskie
Przedmiescie 7, Warsaw, Poland) Ed. Aleksander
Zelias. circ. 530.

330   650   IT
FONDAZIONE GIOVANNI AGNELLI.
PROGETTO POLITICA INDUSTRIALE.
QUADERNO DI RICERCA. no.2, 1975. irreg.
(Fondazione Giovanni Agnelli) Editorale Valentino,
Via G. Giacosa 38, Turin 10125, Italy.

330   MX
FONDO DE CULTURA. SERIE DE LECTURAS.
1973. irreg. Mex.$4,000($35) per no. Fondo de
Cultura Economica, Av. Universidad 975, 03100
Mexico, D.F., Mexico. Ed. Carlos Bazdresch. adv.
bk. rev. bibl. circ. 5,000.

330   DK   ISSN 0109-4955
FORTEGNELSE OVER DANSK
UDVIKLINGSFORSKNING. 1984. a. (Roskilde
Universitetscenter, Foreningen af Aktive
Udviklingsforskere) Bibliotekscentralen, Telegrafvej
5, DK-2750 Ballerup, Denmark.

650   UK
FOUNDATION FOR BUSINESS
RESPONSIBILITIES. DIALOGUES. irreg., no.2,
1972. ‡ Foundation for Business Responsibilities, 40
Doughty St., London WC1N 2LF, England.
    Formerly: Industrial Educational and Research
Foundation. Dialogues.

650   UK   ISSN 0073-7410
FOUNDATION FOR BUSINESS
RESPONSIBILITIES. DISCUSSION PAPER.
1965. irreg. price varies. Foundation for Business
Responsibilities, 40 Doughty St., London WC1N
2LF, England. bk. rev.

650   UK   ISSN 0073-7429
FOUNDATION FOR BUSINESS
RESPONSIBILITIES. OCCASIONAL PAPERS.
1965. irreg. price varies. Foundation for Business
Responsibilities, 40 Doughty St., London WC1N
2LF, England. bk. rev.

658   UK   ISSN 0073-7437
FOUNDATION FOR BUSINESS
RESPONSIBILITIES. RESEARCH PAPER. 1965.
irreg. price varies. Foundation for Business
Responsibilities, 40 Doughty St., London WC1N
2LF, England. bk. rev.

330   FR
FRANCE. MINISTERE DE L'ECONOMIE ET DES
FINANCES. STATISTIQUES ET ETUDES
FINANCIERES. FINANCES PUBLIQUES.
SERIE ROUGE. vol.29, 1977. irreg. 100 F.
Ministere de l'Economie et des Finances, 93 rue de
Rivoli, 75056 Paris, France (Dist. by: Imprimerie
Nationale, 2 rue Paul Hervieu, Paris 15, France)
charts.

310   658.5   FR
FRANCE. SERVICE D'ETUDE DES STRATEGIES
ET DES STATISTIQUES INDUSTRIELLES.
SOCIETES D'ETUDES ET DE CONSEILS,
INGENIEURS-CONSEILS. 1968. a. 64 F. Service
d'Etude des Strategies et des Statistiques
Industrielles, 83/85 bd. du Montparnasse, 75270
Paris Cedex 06, France.
    Formerly: France. Service du Traitement de
l'Information et des Statistiques Industrielles.
Societe d'Etudes et de Conseils, Ingenieurs-Conseils.

647   US
FRANCHISE LAW REVIEW. 1986. irreg. (2-3/yr.)
$15. International Franchise Association, 1350 New
York Ave., N.W. Ste. 900, Washington, DC 20005.
Ed. Neil A. Simon.

330   GW   ISSN 0067-5938
FREIE UNIVERSITAET BERLIN. OSTEUROPA-INSTITUT.
WIRTSCHAFTSWISSENSCHAFTLICHE
VEROEFFENTLICHUNGEN. 1954. irreg. price
varies. Freie Universitaet Berlin, Osteuropa-Institut,
Garystr. 55, 1000 Berlin 33 (Dahlem), W. Germany
(B.R.D.) Ed.Bd. circ. 500.

FRUIT AND VEGETABLE TRUCK RATE AND
COST SUMMARY. see *AGRICULTURE*

FUNDACAO CENTRO DE PESQUISAS
ECONOMICAS E SOCIAIS DO PIAUI.
RELATORIO DE ATIVIDADES. see
SOCIOLOGY

665.7   FR   ISSN 0072-0046
G; DOCUMENTATION TECHNIQUE ET
COMMERCIALE DES VENDEURS DE GAZ.
1970. irreg. Gaz de France, Direction Commerciale,
23 rue Philibert-Delorme, 75017 Paris, France. circ.
3,000.
    Replaces: Gaz et L'Industrie.
    House organ

330   US   ISSN 0196-1098
GEORGIA. OFFICE OF PLANNING AND
BUDGET. STATE INVESTMENT PLAN. a.
Office of Planning and Budget, 270 Washington St.,
Atlanta, GA 30334. TEL 404-656-3820.

330   US   ISSN 0722-2416
GERMAN YEARBOOK ON BUSINESS HISTORY.
1981. a. price varies. Springer-Verlag, 175 Fifth
Ave., New York, NY 10010 TEL 212-460-1500.
(Also Berlin, Heidelberg, Tokyo and Vienna) Ed.Bd.

330   GH
GHANA ECONOMIC REVIEW. a. $2.47. Editorial
and Publishing Services, Box 5743, Accra, Ghana.
Ed. Moses Danquah. adv. charts. illus. stat.

GOKHALE INSTITUTE MIMEOGRAPH SERIES.
see *POLITICAL SCIENCE*

GOKHALE INSTITUTE OF POLITICS AND
ECONOMICS. STUDIES. see *POLITICAL
SCIENCE*

BUSINESS AND ECONOMICS 195

330 VE
GUIA INDUSTRIAL DE VENEZUELA. 1955. a. Editorial Guia Industrial, Apdo. 60772, Caracas 101, Venezuela.

330 GW ISSN 0072-9566
HAMBURGER JAHRBUCH FUER WIRTSCHAFTS- UND GESELLSCHAFTSPOLITIK. 1956. a. price varies. Verlag J. C. B. Mohr (Paul Siebeck), Wilhelmstr. 18, Postfach 2040, 7400 Tuebingen, W. Germany (B.R.D.) Ed.Bd.

330 DK ISSN 0105-533X
HANDELSHOEJSKOLEN I AARHUS. INSTITUT FOR MARKEDSOEKONOMI. SKRIFTSERIE E. irreg., no.13, 1984. price varies. Handelshoejskolen i Aarhus, Institut for Markedsoekonomi, Aarhus, Denmark (Subscr. to: Handelsvidenskabelig Boghandel, Fuglesangs Alle 20, 8210 Aarhus V, Denmark)

330 370 DK ISSN 0900-2472
HANDELSHOEJSKOLEN I KOEBENHAVN. CENTER FOR UDDANNELSES FORSKNING. ARBEJDSNOTE. 1984. irreg. free. Handelshoejskolen i Koebenhavn, Center for Uddannelsesforskning, Copenhagen, Denmark. Ed. christian knudsen. circ. 300.

330 378 DK ISSN 0109-5587
HANDELSHOEJSKOLEN I KOEBENHAVN. H A-CENTER. RAPPORT. 1984. irreg. free. Handelshoejskolen i Koebenhavn, H A-Center, Copenhagen, Denmark.

330 DK
HANDELSHOEJSKOLEN I KOEBENHAVN. INSTITUT FOR TRAFIK-, TURIST- OG REGIONALOEKONOMI. PUBLIKATION. 1984. irreg. free. Copenhagen School of Economics and Business Administration, Copenhagen, Denmark. Ed. Tage Skjoett-Larsen. illus. circ. 100.

330 DK ISSN 0106-4363
HANDELSHOESKOLEN I AARHUS. INSTITUTE FOR ERHVERVS- OG SAMFUNDSBESKRIVELSE. SKRIFTSERIE C. no.6, 1983. irreg. price varies. Handelshoejskolen i Aarhus, Institute for Erhvervs- og Samfundsbeskrivelse - Institut for Applied Economics, Aarhus, Denmark (Orders to: Handelsvidenskabelig Boghandel, Fuglesangalle 4, 8210 Aarhus V, Denmark) circ. 200.

330 US
HARVARD BUSINESS SCHOOL. ANNUAL REPORT. a. Harvard Business School, Annual Report Office, Gallatin Hall E, Boston, MA 02163. TEL 617-495-6466.

330 US
HARVARD BUSINESS SCHOOL. BAKER LIBRARY. KRESS LIBRARY OF BUSINESS AND ECONOMICS. PUBLICATIONS. 1939. irreg., no. 24, 1984. price varies. Harvard Business School, Soldiers Field Rd., Boston, MA 02163. TEL 617-495-6360. (back issues avail.)
Formerly: Harvard University. Graduate School of Business Administration. Baker Library. Kress Library of Business and Economics. Publications (ISSN 0073-0777)

330 US ISSN 0073-0505
HARVARD ECONOMIC STUDIES. irreg., latest vol.158, 1986. price varies. Harvard University Press, 79 Garden St., Cambridge, MA 02138.

HARVEST BOOK SERIES. see SOCIOLOGY

330 FI
HELSINGIN KAUPPAKORKEAKOULU. F-SARJA. TYOEPAPEREJTA- WORKING PAPERS. (Text in English and Finnish) irreg. Helsinki School of Economics, Runeberginkatu 22-24, 00100 Helsinki 10, Finland.

330 FI
HELSINGIN KAUPPAKORKEAKOULU. JULKAISUSARJA B. TUTKIMUKSIA. (Text in English and Finnish) irreg. Helsinki School of economics, Runeberginkatu 22-24, 00100 Helsinki 10, Finland.

330 FI
HELSINGIN KAUPPAKORKEAKOULU. JULKAISUSARJA C. OPPIKIRJOJA. (Text in French and Finnish) irreg. Helsinki School of Economics, Runeberginkatu 22-24, 00100 Helsinki 10, Finland.

330 FI
HELSINGIN KAUPPAKORKEAKOULU. JULKAISUSARJA E. SELVITYKSIAE. (Text in English and Finnish) irreg. Helsinki School of Economics, Runeberginkatu 22-24, 00100 Helsinki 10, Finland.

330 FI ISSN 0358-2973
HELSINGIN KAUPPAKORKEAKOULU. JULKAISUSARJA F. TYOPAPEREITA. (Text in English and Finnish) 1980. irreg. exchange basis. Helsingin Kaupakorkeakoulu, Kirjasto - Helsinki School of Economics, Runebergintatu 22-24, 00100 Helsinki 10, Finland. circ. 100.

330 JA ISSN 0018-280X
HITOTSUBASHI JOURNAL OF ECONOMICS. 1960. a. Hitotsubashi University, Hitotsubashi Academy, 2-1 Naka, Kunitachi, Tokyo 186, Japan. Eds. A. Ono, R. Minami. bibl. charts. illus. stat. index. circ. 1,200. Indexed: Curr.Cont. P.A.I.S. SSCI. Key to Econ.Sci.

330 UK ISSN 0073-2818
HOBART PAPERS. 1960. irreg. $55 (combined subscription for all series) Institute of Economic Affairs, 2 Lord North St., London S.W.1, England (Dist. in North America by: Transatlantic Arts, Inc., Box 6086, Albuquerque, NM 87197) (also avail. in microfiche)

650 US ISSN 0073-2907
HOFSTRA UNIVERSITY YEARBOOK OF BUSINESS. (Each number has also a distinctive title) 1964. irreg., latest ser.21, vol.1, 1986. $30. Hofstra University, School of Business, 111 Heger Hall, Hempstead, NY 11550. TEL 516-560-5678.

330.08 JA ISSN 0441-7410
HOKUDAI ECONOMIC PAPERS. (Text in English) 1969. a. free. Hokkaido University, Faculty of Economics - Hokkaido Daigaku Keizaigakubu, North 9, West 7, Kitaku, Sapporo 060, Japan.
Formerly: Hokkaido Economic Papers.

659.1 HO
HONDURAS. CONSEJO SUPERIOR DE PLANIFICACION ECONOMICA. PLAN OPERATIVO ANUAL. SECTOR INDUSTRIAL. a. Consejo Superior de Planificacion Economica, Secretaria Tecnica, Tegucigalpa, Honduras.

HONDURAS. CONSEJO SUPERIOR DE PLANIFICACION ECONOMICA. PLAN OPERATIVO ANUAL. SECTOR TURISMO. see TRAVEL AND TURISM

330 HK ISSN 0018-4578
HONG KONG ECONOMIC PAPERS. 1961. a. $5. Hong Kong Economic Association, Box 4004, Hong Kong, Hong Kong (Subscr. to: Shun Po Ltd., 4A North Point Industrial Bldg., 499 King's Road, Hong Kong) adv. bk. rev. circ. 1,000.

330 HK
HONG KONG ECONOMIC YEARBOOK. (Text in Chinese) a. Economic Information & Agency, 342 Hennessy Rd., 10th Fl., Hong Kong, Hong Kong. adv. circ. 9,800.

HOTEL & MOTEL MANAGEMENT SHOW DAILY. see HOTELS AND RESTAURANTS

330 338 US
HOW TO FIND COMPANY INTELLIGENCE IN STATE DOCUMENTS. 1976. a. $50. Washington Researchers Publishing, 2612 P St., N.W., Washington, DC 20007. TEL 202-333-3533.
Formerly: Sources of State Information on Corporations.

330 338 US
HOW TO FIND INFORMATION ABOUT COMPANIES; the corporate intelligence source book. a. $95. Washington Researchers Publishing, 2612 P St., N.W., Washington, DC 20007. TEL 202-333-3533.

330 338 US
HOW TO FIND INFORMATION ABOUT JAPANESE COMPANIES AND INDUSTRIES. 1984. irreg. $100. Washington Researchers Publishing, 2612 P St., N.W., Washington, DC 20007. TEL 202-333-3533.

330 II ISSN 0419-0432
HUKERIKAR MEMORIAL LECTURE SERIES. (Text in English) 1964. irreg. price varies. Institute of Economic Research, Director, Vidyagiri, Dharwar 580004, Karnataka, India.

338 JA ISSN 0537-9202
I.D.E. OCCASIONAL PAPERS SERIES. (Text in English) irreg. Institute of Developing Economies - Ajia Keizai Kenkyusho, 42 Ichigaya-Hommura-cho, Shinjuku-ku, Tokyo 162, Japan.
Formerly (until 1969): I.A.E.A. Occasional Papers (Institute of Asian Economic Affairs)

330 GW
I F O FORSCHUNGSBERICHTE DER ABTEILUNG ENTWICKLUNGSLAENDER. 1965. irreg. price varies. I F O Institut fuer Wirtschaftsforschung, Poschingerstr. 5, 8000 Munich 80, W. Germany (B.R.D.) circ. 250.

330 GW ISSN 0170-5695
I F O INSTITUT FUER WIRTSCHAFTSFORSCHUNG. STUDIEN ZU HANDELS- UND DIENSTLEISTUNGSFRAGEN. 1962. irreg., no.26, 1985. price varies. I F O Institut fuer Wirtschaftsforschung, Poschingerstr. 5, 8000 Munich 80, W. Germany (B.R.D.) circ. 500.
Formerly: I F O Institut fuer Wirtschaftsforschung. Studien zu Handelsfragen (ISSN 0073-4268)

330 GW
I F O STUDIEN ZUR ENTWICKLUNGSFORSCHUNG. 1976. irreg. price varies. I F O Institut fuer Wirtschaftsforschung, Poschingerstr. 5, 8000 Munich 80, W. Germany (B.R.D.) circ. 650.

330 BL
I P E A SERIE P N P E. 1982. irreg. price varies. Instituto de Planejamento Economico e Social, Programa Nacional de Pequisa Economico, Caixa Postal 2672, Rio de Janeiro, RJ, Brazil. Ed. Michal Gartenkraut. circ. 1,000.

330 BL
I P E A SERIE PENSAMENTO ECONOMICO BRASILEIRO. 1975. irreg. price varies. Instituto de Planejamento Economico e Social, Caixa Postal 2672, Rio de Janeiro, Brazil.

330 US
I S E R RESEARCH NOTES. 1968. irreg., latest issue, 1982. $2. University of Alaska, Institute of Social and Economic Research, 3211 Providence Dr., Anchorage, AK 99508. TEL 907-786-7710. Ed. Linda Leask.
Formerly: I S E G R Research Notes (ISSN 0065-5945)

331 FI
I U I YEARBOOK. (Industriens Utredningsinstitut); microeconometrics. (Text in English) a. Industrial Institute for Economic and Social Research - Industriens Utredningsinstitut, Grevgatan 34, 5 tr., S-11453 Stockholm, Sweden. charts. illus.

338 II
INDIA. MINISTRY OF HEAVY INDUSTRY. REPORT. (Text in English) 1973. irreg. Ministry of Heavy Industry, New Delhi, India.

330 380 KE
INDUSTRIAL & TRADE DIRECTORY. a. EAs.200. Translinkers Publishing Co., Box 44169, Nairobi, Kenya. Ed. George C. Kimani. adv. bk. rev. circ. 60,000.
Formerly (until 1981): Kenya Enterprise.

330 US
INDUSTRIAL DEVELOPMENT AND THE SOCIAL FABRIC; an international series of historical monographs. 1979. irreg., vol.7, 1984. $22.50 to individuals; institutions $45. J A I Press Inc., Box 1678, 36 Sherwood Pl., Greenwich, CT 06836. TEL 203-661-7602. Ed. John P. McKay.

BUSINESS AND ECONOMICS

330   RH
INDUSTRIAL REVIEW. a. $30. Thomson Publications (Pvt) Ltd., P.O. Box 1683, Harare, Zimbabwe.

330   CN   ISSN 0824-801X
INFLATION MONITOR. 1983. irreg. Inflation Monitor, 125 Adelaide St. East, Toronto, Ont. M5C 1L7, Canada. TEL 605-865-1904.

330   UK   ISSN 0073-909X
INSTITUTE OF ECONOMIC AFFAIRS. OCCASIONAL PAPERS. 1963. irreg. $55 (combined subscription for all series) Institute of Economic Affairs, 2 Lord North St., London SW1, England (Dist. in North America by: Transatlantic Arts. Inc., Box 6086, Albuquerque, NM 87197) (also avail. in microfiche)

330   UK   ISSN 0073-9103
INSTITUTE OF ECONOMIC AFFAIRS. RESEARCH MONOGRAPHS. 1966. irreg. $55 (combined subscription for all series) Institute of Economic Affairs, 2 Lord North St., London S.W.1, England (Dist. in North America by: Transatlantic Arts, Inc., Box 6086, Albuquerque, NM 87197) (also avail. in microfiche)

330   II
INSTITUTE OF ECONOMIC RESEARCH. PUBLICATIONS ON ECONOMICS. (Text in English) irreg. price varies. Institute of Economic Research, Director, Vidyagiri, Dharwar 580004, Karnataka, India.

330   US
INSTITUTE OF SOCIAL AND ECONOMIC RESEARCH. REPORTS. 1963. irreg., no.58, 1985. price varies. University of Alaska, Institute of Social and Economic Research, 3211 Providence Dr., Anchorage, AK 99508. TEL 907-786-7710. Ed. Linda Leask.
    Formerly: Institute of Social, Economic and Government Research. Reports (ISSN 0065-5937)

330   BE   ISSN 0074-1752
INTERNATIONAL ASSOCIATION OF STUDENTS IN ECONOMICS AND MANAGEMENT. INTERNATIONAL COMPENDIUM. ANNUAL REPORT. 1949. a. membership. International Association of Students in Economics and Management, International A I E S E C Secretariat, International Associations Centre, 40 rue Washington, Box 10, 1050 Brussels, Belgium. Ed.Bd. circ. 6,000.

330   CN   ISSN 0704-7584
INTERNATIONAL DEVELOPMENT RESEARCH CENTRE. ANNUAL REPORT/CENTRE DE RECHERCHES POUR LE DEVELOPPEMENT INTERNATIONAL. RAPPORT ANNUEL. (Text in English and French) 1971. a. International Development Research Centre, Box 8500, Ottawa, Ont. K1G 3H9, Canada. TEL 613-236-6163. illus.

330   UK   ISSN 0074-4646
INTERNATIONAL ECONOMIC ASSOCIATION. PROCEEDINGS OF THE CONFERENCES AND CONGRESSES. 1956. irreg. Macmillan Press Ltd. (Subsidiary of: Macmillan Publishers Ltd.) 4 Little Essex St., London WC2R 3LF, England.

330   US
INTERNATIONAL ECONOMIC STUDIES INSTITUTE. CONTEMPORARY ISSUES. 1975. irreg. International Economic Studies Institute, 1400 Eye St. N.W., Ste. 510, Washington, DC 20005-2293. TEL 202-898-2022. Ed. Timothy W. Stanley. circ. 7,000.

330   II   ISSN 0074-7068
INTERNATIONAL MONOGRAPHS ON STUDIES IN INDIAN ECONOMICS. (Text in English) 1969. irreg. price varies. Hindustan Publishing Corp., 6-U.B. Jawahar Nagar, Delhi 110007, India.

330   CN
INVENTORY OF INDUSTRIAL PARKS IN QUEBEC.* 1977. a. free. Department of Industry and Commerce, Industrial Infrastructure Division, 1 Place Ville-Maria, 23rd Floor, Montreal, Que. H3B 3M6, Canada. TEL 514-873-3548. circ. 2,500.

330   IE   ISSN 0790-6080
IRELAND. CENTRAL STATISTICS OFFICE. CENSUS OF INDUSTRIAL PRODUCTION. 1984. a. £4.45. Government Publications Office, Trade and Postal Sales, Bishop St., Dublin 8, Ireland. TEL 01-781-666.

330   IT   ISSN 0075-1529
ISTITUTO MOBILIARE ITALIANO. ANNUAL REPORT. (Editions in English and Italian) 1932. a. ‡ Istituto Mobiliare Italiano, 25 Viale dell' Arte, 00144 Rome, Italy. circ. 2,400.

330 340 336.2   GW   ISSN 0075-2886
JAHRESFACHKATALOG RECHT-WIRTSCHAFT-STEUERN. 1949. a. DM.39.80. Werbegemeinschaft Elwert und Meurer, Hauptstr. 101, 1000 Berlin 62, W. Germany (B.R.D.) adv. bk. rev.

650   US
JOSEPH I. LUBIN MEMORIAL LECTURES. 1961. a. price varies. (New York University, College of Business & Public Administration) New York University Press, 24 W. Fourth St., New York, NY 10003. TEL 212-598-2234. Ed. Dean Daniel E. Diamond. circ. 2,000.
    Formerly (until 1984): Charles C. Moskowitz Lectures (ISSN 0084-8727)

330.9   TZ
JOURNAL OF ECONOMIC REFLECTIONS. 1972. irreg. University of Dar es Salaam, Department of Economics, Box 35184, Dar es Salaam, Tanzania. bk. rev.
    Supersedes: Economic Reflections.

330   US   ISSN 0361-6576
JOURNAL OF ECONOMICS (VERMILLION) 1975. a. $11. Missouri Valley Economic Association, c/o D.A. Johnson, School of Business, University of South Dakota, Vermillion, SD 57069. TEL 605-677-5552. Ed. J. Kirker Stephens. bk. rev. circ. 350.

330   JA
K K C BRIEF. irreg. Keizai Koho Center, Japan Institute for Social and Economic Affairs, Otemachi Bldg. 6-1, Otemachi 1-chome, Chiyoda-ku, Tokyo 100, Japan.

650   JA   ISSN 0453-4557
KEIO BUSINESS REVIEW. (Text in English) vol.15, 1978. a. price varies. Keio University Society of Business and Commerce, c/o Faculty of Business and Commerce, Mita Minato-ku, Tokyo 108, Japan (Dist. by: Japan Publications Trading Co., Ltd., P.O. Box 5030 Tokyo International, Tokyo, Japan) Ed. Tadahiro Yamamasu. charts. stat. Indexed: P.A.I.S. Account.& Data Proc.Abstr.

650   JA   ISSN 0075-5346
KEIO MONOGRAPHS OF BUSINESS AND COMMERCE. 1967. irreg. price varies. (Keio University Society of Business and Commerce) Japan Publications Trading Co. Ltd., Box 5030, Tokyo International, Tokyo 100-31, Japan (Or 1255 Howard St., San Francisco, CA 94103)

330   UK
KEY BRITISH ENTERPRISES. a. $210. Dun & Bradstreet Ltd., 26-32 Clifton St., London EC2P 2LY, England. Ed. Urselle Morris.
    ●Also available online. Vendors: Pergamon Infoline.

330   JA   ISSN 0075-6415
KOBE ECONOMIC AND BUSINESS RESEARCH SERIES. (Text in English) 1962. irreg. exchange basis. Kobe University, Research Institute for Economics and Business Administration, Rokko, Nada, Kobe, Japan. Ed.Bd. circ. 500.

330   JA   ISSN 0075-6407
KOBE ECONOMIC AND BUSINESS REVIEW. (Text in English) 1953. a. exchange basis. Kobe University, Research Institute for Economics and Business Administration, Rokko, Nada, Kobe, Japan. Ed.Bd. circ. 500.

330   JA   ISSN 0454-1111
KOBE UNIVERSITY ECONOMIC REVIEW. (Text in English) 1955. a. Kobe University, Faculty of Economics, Rokkodai-cho, Nadu-ku, Kobe, Japan. circ. 650. Indexed: Key to Econ.Sci.

330   DK   ISSN 0574-0045
KOEBENHAVNS UNIVERSITET. OEKONOMISKE INSTITUT. MEMO. no.107, 1981. irreg. Koebenhavns Universitet, Oekonomiske Institut, Studiestraede 6, DK-1455 Copenhagen K, Denmark. illus.

332 338   FR
KOMPASS REGIONAUX. (19 separate volumes for each region) (Text in French) 1976. a. price varies per regional volume. Societe Nouvelle d'Editions pour l'Industrie, 22 Avenue Franklin D. Roosevelt, 75008 Paris, France. charts. stat.
    Formerly: Inventaires Economiques et Industriels Regionaux.

330   DK   ISSN 0109-3533
KONSULENTORDNINGEN; byerhvervenes og arbejdsmarkedets konsulenter og deres arbejdsopgaver ultimo. 1983. a. free. Teknologistyrelsen, Tagensvej 135, 2200 Copenhagen N, Denmark.

330   HU   ISSN 0075-6989
KOZGAZDASAGI ERTEKEZESEK. 1962. irreg., vol.31, 1984. price varies. (Magyar Tudomanyos Akademia) Akademiai Kiado, Publishing House of the Hungarian Academy of Sciences, Box 24, H-1363 Budapest, Hungary.

338   NO   ISSN 0452-7208
KRISTOFER LEHMKUHL FORELESNING. 1958. a. free. Norges Handelshoeyskole - Norwegian School of Economics and Business Administration, Helleveien 30, 5035 Bergen-Sandviken, Norway. circ. 500.

330   DK   ISSN 0107-7163
LANDOEKONOMISK OVERSIGT. 1954. irreg. free. (Danske Landboforeningen) Bibliotekscentralen, Telegrafvej 5, DK-2750 Ballerup, Denmark.

LAWN CARE INDUSTRY SHOW EXTRA. see *GARDENING AND HORTICULTURE*

LECTURE NOTES IN ECONOMICS AND MATHEMATICAL SYSTEMS; operations research, computer science, social science. see *MATHEMATICS*

LEGAL CONNECTION: CORPORATIONS AND LAW FIRMS; a directory of publicly-held corporations and their law firms. see *LAW*

LEONARD'S ANNUAL INDEX OF ART AUCTIONS (YEAR) see *ART*

330   LY
LIBYAN ECONOMIC AND BUSINESS REVIEW. (Text in English) biennial. L.1000($2.80) University of Libya, Center of Economic and Business Research, Benghazi, Libya. Ed. Misbah Oreibi.

338   FI   ISSN 0356-7850
LIIKEARKISTO. (Text in Finnish; summaries in English) 1964. irreg. (3-4/yr.) Fmk.40($7) Liikearkistoyhdistys r.y. - Finnish Business Archives Association, Box 271, 00101 Helsinki 10, Finland. Ed. Ossi Jokimies. adv. bk. rev. circ. 400.

338   FI
LIIKEARKISTOYHDISTYS. JULKAISUJA. 1963. irreg., no.4, 1986. price varies. Liikearkistoyhistys r.y. - Finnish Business Archives Association, Box 271, SF-00101 Helsinki 10, Finland. Ed. Penti Laiva-Koivisto. adv.

338   UK
LOCAL AREA HOUSING STATISTICS. 1985. irreg., (approx. 1-2/m.) free. Nationwide Building Society, New Oxford House, High Holborn, London WC1V 6PW, England. Ed. Barry Bissett. circ. 8, 500. (back issues avail.)

330   UK
LOUGHBOROUGH OCCASIONAL PAPERS IN ECONOMICS. irreg. free. Loughborough University of Technology, Department of Economics, Loughborough, Leics. LE11 3TU, England. circ. 50(controlled) (back issues avail.)

330 650   MH
MACAU INDUSTRY. 1977. a. Macau Business Centre, Edificio Ribeiro, P.O. Box 138, Macao. stat.

330 MW
MALAWI DEVELOPMENT CORPORATION. ANNUAL REPORT. (Text in English) a. Malawi Development Corporation, Box 566, Blantyre, Malawi.

330 US
MANAGEMENT INFORMATION SYSTEMS. irreg., vol.4, 1983. U M I Research Press, 300 N. Zeeb Rd., Ann Arbor, MI 48106. Ed. Gary Dickson.

330 UR ISSN 0130-9404
MATEMATICHESKIE METODY V EKONOMIKE. 1967. irreg. 0.75 Rub. approx. (Akademiya Nauk Latviiskoi S.S.R., Institut Ekonomiki) Izdatel'stvo Zinatne, Turgeneva Iela, 19, Riga 226018, Latvian S.S.R., U.S.S.R. bibl. charts. circ. 800.

330 IS ISSN 0333-7839
MAURICE FALK INSTITUTE FOR ECONOMIC RESEARCH IN ISRAEL. REPORT AND DISCUSSION PAPER SERIES. (Editions in English and Hebrew) 1964/66. irreg. free. Maurice Falk Institute for Economic Research in Israel, P. Naphtali Bldg., The Hebrew University, Mt. Scopus, 91905 Jerusalem, Israel. circ. 500.
   Formerly: Maurice Falk Center for Economic Research in Israel. Report. (ISSN 0076-5473)

338.7 II ISSN 0376-5423
MEGHALAYA INDUSTRIAL DEVELOPMENT CORPORATION. ANNUAL REPORT. (Text in English) 1972. a. Meghalaya Industrial Development Corporation, Additional Civil Secretariat Bldg., Shillong 1, India. Key Title: Annual Report - Meghalaya Industrial Development Corporation.

330 US
MELLEN STUDIES IN BUSINESS. 1986. irreg., vol.2. $39.95 per no. Edwin Mellen Press, Box 450, Lewiston, NY 14092.

330 US
MERGER AND ACQUISITION SOURCEBOOK. a. Quality Services Co., 5290 Overpass Rd., Santa Barbara, CA 93111. TEL 805-964-7841. Ed. Dr. Walter Jurek.

650 US ISSN 0076-7840
MICHIGAN BUSINESS PAPERS. 1937. irreg., no.67, 1985. price varies. University of Michigan, Graduate School of Business Administration, Division of Research, Ann Arbor, MI 48109. TEL 313-764-1366. Ed. Jemadari Kamara. (reprint service avail. from UMI)

650 US ISSN 0076-7859
MICHIGAN BUSINESS REPORTS. 1938. irreg., no.60, 1979. price varies. University of Michigan, Graduate School of Business Administration, Division of Research, Ann Arbor, MI 48109. TEL 313-764-1366. Ed.Bd. (reprint service avail. from UMI)

650 US ISSN 0076-7867
MICHIGAN BUSINESS STUDIES. 1926; N.S. 1975. irreg., vol.2, 1982. price varies. University of Michigan, Graduate School of Business Administration, Division of Research, Ann Arbor, MI 48109. TEL 313-764-1366. Ed. Bd. (reprint service avail. from UMI)

650 US ISSN 0076-7972
MICHIGAN INTERNATIONAL BUSINESS STUDIES. 1963. irreg. price varies. University of Michigan, Graduate School of Business Administration, Division of Research, Ann Arbor, MI 48109. TEL 313-764-1366. Ed.Bd. (reprint service avail. from UMI)

MIDWEST LAW REVIEW. see *LAW*

338.9 AG
MIRADOR; panorama de la civilizacion industrial. (Text in Spanish, summaries in English, French and Portuguese) 1958. irreg. Editorial Mirador, Santiago del Estero 315, Buenos Aires, Argentina. Ed. C. Levin. bk. rev. illus.

330 MY
MONOGRAPH SERIES ON MALAYSIAN ECONOMIC AFFAIRS. 1971. irreg., no.6, 1987. price varies. University of Malaya, Faculty of Economics & Administration, Lembah Pantai, Kuala Lumpur 22-11, Malaysia. bibl. circ. 1,000.

330 DK ISSN 0107-492X
MONOPOLTILSYNETS AARSBERETNING. a. Bibliotekscentralen, Telegrafvej 5, DK-2750 Ballerup, Denmark.

330 BE
MUSEE ROYAL DE L'AFRIQUE CENTRALE. DOCUMENTATION ECONOMIQUE/ KONINKLIJK MUSEUM VOOR MIDDEN-AFRIKA. ECONOMISCHE DOCUMENTATIE. 1961. irreg., no.5, 1983. price varies. Musee Royal de l'Afrique Centrale, 13 Steenweg op Leuven, B-1980 Tervuren, Belgium.

N A B T E REVIEW. (National Association for Business Teacher Education) see *EDUCATION — Higher Education*

N I S E R OCCASIONAL PAPERS. (Nigerian Institute of Social and Economic Research) see *SOCIAL SCIENCES: COMPREHENSIVE WORKS*

338 MY
N S T ANNUAL. a. M.$8. Berita Publishing Sdn. Bhd., 22 Jalan Liku, 59100 Kuala Lumpur, Malaysia.

330.72 US
NATIONAL BUREAU OF ECONOMIC RESEARCH. WORKING PAPER. irreg., approx. 300/yr. $300. National Bureau of Economic Research, 1050 Massachusetts Ave., Cambridge, MA 02138.

320 330 US
NATIONAL DIRECTORY OF CORPORATE PUBLIC AFFAIRS. 1983. a. $55. Columbia Books, Inc., 1350 New York Ave., Ste. 207, Washington, DC 20005. TEL 202-737-3777. Eds. Arthur C. Close, John Gregg.

330 301 UK ISSN 0070-8453
NATIONAL INSTITUTE OF ECONOMIC AND SOCIAL RESEARCH, LONDON. ECONOMIC AND SOCIAL STUDIES. 1946. irreg., no.33, 1982. price varies. Cambridge University Press, Edinburgh Bldg., Shaftesbury Rd., Cambridge CB2 2RU, England (and 32 E. 57 St., New York, NY 10022) index.

330 UK ISSN 0077-4928
NATIONAL INSTITUTE OF ECONOMIC AND SOCIAL RESEARCH, LONDON. OCCASIONAL PAPERS. 1946. irreg., no.37, 1984. price varies. Cambridge University Press, Edinburgh Bldg., Shaftesbury Rd., Cambridge CB2 2RU, England (and 32 E. 57 St., New York NY 10022)

330 PL ISSN 0137-1428
NAUKI EKONOMICZNE. (Text in Polish; summaries in various languages) 1974. irreg. price varies. Adam Mickiewicz University Press, Marchlewskiego 128, 61-874 Poznan, Poland.

NEW AFRICAN YEARBOOK: EAST AND SOUTH. see *POLITICAL SCIENCE*

NEW AFRICAN YEARBOOK: WEST AND CENTRAL. see *POLITICAL SCIENCE*

330 US
NEW JERSEY. OFFICE OF ECONOMIC POLICY. ECONOMIC REPORT OF THE GOVERNOR. 1982. a. free. Office of Economic Policy, One W. State St., Trenton, NJ 08625. Ed. Joseph Seneca. circ. 2,000.

330 330.9 NZ ISSN 0112-2061
NEW ZEALAND. ECONOMIC MONITORING GROUP REPORT. 1983. irreg. New Zealand Planning Council, P.O. Box 5066, Wellington, New Zealand. (back issues avail.)

330 NZ ISSN 0077-9954
NEW ZEALAND ECONOMIC PAPERS. 1967. a. NZ.$15. ‡ New Zealand Association of Economists, Box 568, Wellington, New Zealand. Ed. P. Wooding. bk. rev. circ. 800. Indexed: Rural Recreat.Tour.Abstr. World Agri.Econ.& Rural Sociol.Abstr.

330 NZ ISSN 0078-0057
NEW ZEALAND INSTITUTE OF ECONOMIC RESEARCH. ANNUAL REPORT. 1960. a. NZ.$5. New Zealand Institute of Economic Research, Private Bag, Wellington, New Zealand.

330 NZ
NEW ZEALAND INSTITUTE OF ECONOMIC RESEARCH. CONTRACT RESEARCH. 1969. irreg., no.19, 1984. price varies. New Zealand Institute of Economic Research, Private Bag, Wellington 1, New Zealand.

330 NZ ISSN 0078-0049
NEW ZEALAND INSTITUTE OF ECONOMIC RESEARCH. DISCUSSION PAPER. 1961. a. price varies. New Zealand Institute of Economic Research, Private Bag, Wellington 1, New Zealand.

330 NZ ISSN 0112-1170
NEW ZEALAND INSTITUTE OF ECONOMIC RESEARCH. MEDIUM TERM REVIEW. 1983. a. New Zealand Institute of Economic Research, Private Bag, Wellington 1, New Zealand. Ed. J. Gallacher.

330 NZ ISSN 0078-0065
NEW ZEALAND INSTITUTE OF ECONOMIC RESEARCH. RESEARCH PAPER. 1961. irreg., no. 29, 1983. price varies. New Zealand Institute of Economic Research, Private Bag, Wellington, New Zealand.

338.1 NR ISSN 0331-0361
NIGERIAN ECONOMIC SOCIETY. PROCEEDINGS OF THE ANNUAL CONFERENCE. 1973. a. included in subscription to Nigerian Journal of Economic & Social Studies. Nigerian Economic Society, c/o Dept. of Economics, University of Ibadan, Ibadan, Nigeria. Ed. S. Ibi Ajayi. circ. 800.

NIGERIAN INSTITUTE OF SOCIAL AND ECONOMIC RESEARCH. ANNUAL REPORT. see *SOCIAL SCIENCES: COMPREHENSIVE WORKS*

338 NE
NIJENRODE STUDIES IN BUSINESS. 1977. irreg. price varies. Kluwer Nijhoff Publishing, 190 Old Derby St., Hingham, MA 02043 (Foreign distr.: Kluwer Academic Publishers Group, Box 322, 3300 AH Dordrecht, Netherlands)

330.1 NO ISSN 0078-1029
NORD-NORGE NAERINGSLIV OG OEKONOMI. 1948. irreg. price varies. Studieselskapet for Nord-Norsk Naeringsliv, Sjoegaten 15, 8001 Bodoe, Norway. cum.index: nos. 1-41 in vol.41.

NORDISK KOMITE FOR TRANSPORTOEKONOMISK FORSKNING. PUBLIKATION. see *TRANSPORTATION*

330 UK
NORTH STAFFORDSHIRE POLYTECHNIC. DEPARTMENT OF ECONOMICS. DISCUSSION PAPERS. 1980. irreg. (approx. 5/yr.) free. North Staffordshire Polytechnic, Department of Economics, Leek Rd., Stoke-on-Trent ST4 2DF, England. Ed. P. Reynolds.

330 CN ISSN 0826-9947
OBSERVATION. 1974. irreg. C.D. Howe Institute, 125 Adelaide St. East, Toronto, Ont. M5C 1L7, Canada. TEL 416-865-1904. (also avail. in microform from MML) Indexed: Can. B.P.I. PROMT.
   Formerly (until 1980): H R I Observations (ISSN 0381-5250)

330 320 DK ISSN 0109-0976
ODENSE UNIVERSITET. INSTITUT FOR OFFENTLIG OEKONOMI OG POLITIK. OCCASIONAL PAPER. 1982. irreg., latest no.16 1984. Odense Universitet, Institut for Erhvervsret og Politologi - Odense University, Department of Commercial Law and Political Science, Odense Universitetsbibliotek, Campusvej 5, 5230 Odense, Denmark. illus.

330 US ISSN 0149-1091
O'DWYER'S DIRECTORY OF CORPORATE COMMUNICATIONS. 1975. a. $90. J.R. O'Dwyer Co., Inc., 271 Madison Ave., New York, NY 10016. TEL 212-679-2471. Ed. Jack O'Dwyer. adv. stat. index.

330 US ISSN 0078-3390
OEKONOMETRIE UND
UNTERNEHMENSFORSCHUNG/
ECONOMETRICS AND OPERATIONS
RESEARCH. (Text in German; occasionally in English) 1962. irreg., no.21, 1976. price varies. Springer-Verlag, 175 Fifth Ave., New York, NY 10010 TEL 212-460-1500. (also Berlin, Heidelberg, Vienna) (reprint service avail. from ISI) Indexed: Biol.Abstr.

330 GE ISSN 0233-0946
OEKONOMIEHISTORISCHE TEXTE. 1959. irreg. price varies. (Akademie der Wissenschaften der DDR, Zentralinstitut fuer Wirtschaftswissenschaften) Akademie-Verlag, Leipziger Str. 3-4, 1086 Berlin, E. Germany (D.D.R.)
Formerly: Oekonomische Studientexte (ISSN 0078-3404)

330 DK ISSN 0109-7725
OEKONOMISK ANALYSE, SOMMERREGNSKABER; regnskabsresultatet opnaaet af landmaend. 1982. a. free. Dritsoekonomiudvalget, Danske Husmandsforeninger, Kongaardsvej 28, 8260 Viby J., Denmark. Ed. Per Koford Hansen. bk. rev. circ. 11,000.

330 DK ISSN 0108-6464
OEKONOMISKE UDVIKLING PAA FAEROERNE. 1973. irreg. Raadgivende Udvalg Vedroerende Faeroerne, Statsministeriet, Copenhagen, Denmark (Orders to: Soeren Skafte, Christianborg, 1218 Copenhagen K, Denmark) circ. 500.

330 AU ISSN 0078-3595
OESTERREICHISCHES WIRTSCHAFTSINSTITUT FUER STRUKTURFORSCHUNG UND STRUKTURPOLITIK. SCHRIFTENREIHE. 1968. irreg. free. Oesterreichisches Wirtschaftsinstitut fuer Strukturforschung und Strukturpolitik, Hessenplatz, A-4020 Linz, Austria. Klaus Zerbs. circ. 2,000.
Formerly: Oesterreichisches Institut fuer Mittelstandspolitik. Schriftenreihe.

333 JA ISSN 0287-0916
OITA UNIVERSITY. RESEARCH INSTITUTE OF ECONOMICS. BULLETIN. (Text in Japanese) 1967. a. (Oita University, Research Institute of Economics) Oita University, Economic Society - Oita Daigaku Keizai Gakkai, Oita, Japan. circ. 600.

330 650 US
OKLAHOMA STATE UNIVERSITY. COLLEGE OF BUSINESS ADMINISTRATION. WORKING PAPERS. 1966. irreg., latest no.86-12. free. Oklahoma State University, College of Business Administration, Office of Business and Economic Research, Stillwater, OK 74078-0555. TEL 405-624-5125.
Supersedes: Oklahoma State University. College of Business Administration. Extension Service. Business Papers (ISSN 0078-4427)

330 332 DK ISSN 0900-8187
OM STATSREGNSKABET. a. (Finansministeriet, Statens Regnskabdirektoratet) Bibliotekscentralen, Telegrafvej 5, DK-2750 Ballerup, Denmark.

338 020 UK
ONLINE BUSINESS SOURCEBOOK. 1986. base vol. plus q. updates. £55($109) Headland Press, Freepost 22, London EC1A 7QT, England. Eds. Allan Foster, Gerry Smith.

330 CN
ONTARIO ECONOMIC COUNCIL. RESEARCH STUDIES. 1975. irreg. price varies. University of Toronto Press, Toronto, Ont., Canada. TEL 613-667-7791.

658 CN ISSN 0078-5083
ONTARIO RESEARCH FOUNDATION. ANNUAL REPORT. 1928. a. free. Ontario Research Foundation, Dept. of Marketing, Sheridan Park, Ont. L5K 1B3, Canada. TEL 416-822-4111.

330 PL ISSN 0474-2893
OPOLSKIE ROCZNIKI EKONOMICZNE. 1968. a. price varies. (Polskie Towarzystwo Ekonomiczne, Oddzial w Opolu) Panstwowe Wydawnictwo Naukowe, Miodowa 10, 00-251 Warsaw, Poland (Dist. by: Ars Polona, Krakowskie Przedmiescie 7, 00-068 Warsaw, Poland) Ed. J. Kroszel. bibl. circ. 1, 060.

330 DK ISSN 0107-2064
ORGANISATORISKE FRAGMENTER. 1973. a. Kr.70. Handelshoejskolen i Aarhus, Institut for Organisation og Virksomhedsledelse, Ryhavevej 8, 8210 Aarhus V., Denmark. illus. circ. 300.

330 JA ISSN 0078-6640
OSAKA CITY UNIVERSITY ECONOMIC REVIEW.* (Text in English, French, German and other languages) 1965. a. 1000 Yen. Osaka City University, Faculty of Economics, 459 Sugimoto-cho, Sumiyoshi-ku, Osaka 558, Japan.

P S I DISCUSSION PAPERS. (Policy Studies Institute) see *SOCIAL SCIENCES: COMPREHENSIVE WORKS*

P S I: REPORT SERIES. (Policy Studies Institute) see *POLITICAL SCIENCE*

338.9 PK ISSN 0078-821X
PAKISTAN INSTITUTE OF DEVELOPMENT ECONOMICS. REPORT. (Text in English) 1962. irreg. Pakistan Institute of Development Economics, Box No. 1091, Islamabad, Pakistan. circ. 1,000.

338.9 PK ISSN 0078-8228
PAKISTAN INSTITUTE OF DEVELOPMENT ECONOMICS. RESEARCH REPORT. (Text in English) 1963. irreg. price varies. Pakistan Institute of Development Economics, P.O. Box 1091, Islamabad, Pakistan. circ. controlled.

PAPER SALES CONVENTION NEWS. see *PAPER AND PULP*

330 US
PENNSYLVANIA CONFERENCE OF ECONOMISTS. PROCEEDINGS OF THE ANNUAL MEETING. 1951. a. $15. Pennsylvania Conference of Economists, c/o Alexander Garvin, Economics Dept, Indiana University of Pennsylvania, Indiana, PA 15701. TEL 412-357-2640. Ed. Joseph Horton. charts. circ. 500. (back issues avail.)

330 PH
PERFORMANCE AND PROSPECTS; International Economy/Domestic Economy. irreg. Private Development Corporation of the Philippines, P.O. Box 757, Rizal 3117, Philippines.

330 FR
PERSPECTIVES DE L'ECONOMIQUE. SERIE 2. ECONOMIE CONTEMPORAINE. 1969. irreg. price varies. Editions Calmann-Lévy, 3 rue Auber, 75009 Paris, France. Ed. Christian Schmidt.

330 FR
PERSPECTIVES DE L'ECONOMIQUE. SERIE 3. CRITIQUE. 1969. irreg. price varies. Editions Calmann-Lévy, 3 rue Auber, 75009 Paris, France. Ed. Christian Schmidt.

PLANNING FOR SOCIAL CHANGE. see *SOCIOLOGY*

330 338.91 FR
PLANS DE DEVELOPPEMENT DES PAYS DE L'AFRIQUE NOIRE. irreg. 1.190 Fr. Ediafric, 10 rue Vineuse, 75016 Paris, France.

330 CN ISSN 0832-7912
POLICY STUDY. 1986. irreg. C.D. Howe Institute, 125 Adelaide St. East, Toronto, Ont. M5C 1L7, Canada. TEL 416-865-1904.

330 PL
POLITECHNIKA GDANSKA. ZESZYTY NAUKOWE. EKONOMIA. (Text in Polish; summaries in English and Russian) 1967. irreg. price varies. Politechnika Gdanska, Majakowskiego 11/12, 81-952 Gdansk 6, Poland (Dist. by: Osrodek Rozpowszechniania Wydawnictw Naukowych Pan, Palac Kultury i Nauki, 00-901 Warsaw, Poland)

330 PL ISSN 0548-0442
POLITECHNIKA KRAKOWSKA. ZESZYTY NAUKOWE. NAUKI EKONOMICZNE. (Text in Polish; summaries in English, French, German, Russian) 1967. irreg. price varies. Politechnika Krakowska, Ul. Warszawska 24, 31-155 Krakow, Poland (Dist. by: Ars Polona-Ruch, Krakowskie Przedmiescie 7, 00-068 Warsaw, Poland) bibl. charts. illus. circ. 200.

POLITECHNIKA LODZKA. ZESZYTY NAUKOWE. ORGANIZACJA I ZARZADZANIE. see *SOCIAL SCIENCES: COMPREHENSIVE WORKS*

330 PL ISSN 0137-6306
POLITECHNIKA WROCLAWSKA. OSRODEK BADAN PROGNOSTYCZNYCH. PRACE NAUKOWE. KONFERENCJE. (Text in Polish; summaries in English and Russian) 1975. irreg., no.7, 1980. price varies. Politechnika Wroclawska, Wybrzeze Wyspianskiego 27, 50-370 Wroclaw, Poland (Dist. by: Ars Polona-Ruch, Krakowskie Przedmiescie 7, Warsaw, Poland) Ed. Marian Kloza.

330 PL ISSN 0079-3353
POLSKA AKADEMIA NAUK. ODDZIAL W KRAKOWIE. KOMISJA NAUK EKONOMICZNYCH. PRACE. (Text in Polish; summaries in English) 1960. irreg. price varies. Ossolineum, Publishing House of the Polish Academy of Sciences, Rynek 9, 50-106 Wroclaw, Poland (Dist. by: Ars Polona-Ruch, Krakowskie Przedmiescie 7, Warsaw, Poland)

330 US
PRACTICAL GUIDE TO COUNTERTRADE. 1985. irreg. $40. Metal Bulletin Inc., 220 Fifth Ave., New York, NY 10001. Eds. Peter Harben, Henry Cooke.

330 FR
PREVISIONS GLISSANTES DETAILLEES HORIZON 1990. a. Bureau d'Informations et de Previsions Economiques, 122 Av Charles de Gaulle, 92522 Neuilly-sur-Seine, France.
Former titles: Previsions Glissantes Detaillees 1979-1984 & Previson a Moyen Terme de l'Economie Francaise & Prevision Glissante a Cinq Ans.

330 510 US ISSN 0079-5240
PRINCETON STUDIES IN MATHEMATICAL ECONOMICS. 1964. irreg., latest, no.7. price varies. Princeton University Press, 3175 Princeton Pike, Lawrenceville, NJ 08540. TEL 609-896-1344. Ed.Bd. (reprint service avail. from UMI)

330 US ISSN 0079-5291
PRINCETON UNIVERSITY. ECONOMETRIC RESEARCH PROGRAM. RESEARCH MEMORANDUM. 1957. irreg., no.318, 1985. $35. Princeton University, Econometric Research Program, Attn.: Pia Ellen, Program Secretary, Department of Economics, 207 Dickinson Hall, Princeton, NJ 08544. TEL 609-452-4030. Ed. Gregory C. Chow. circ. 250. (back issues avail.)

330 US
PROGRAMME FOR GROWTH SERIES. 1964. irreg., vol.12, 1974. price varies. Halsted Press (Subsidiary of: John Wiley & Sons, Inc.) 605 Third Ave, New York, NY 10016. TEL 212-850-6000. Ed. R. Stone.

330 TH
QUARTERLY AND ANNUAL INDUSTRIAL PRODUCTION INDEXES. (Text in English, Thai) 1972. a. price varies. National Statistical Office, Economic Survey Division, Krung Kasem Road, Bangkok Metropolis 10100, Thailand. Ed.Bd.

QUEBEC (PROVINCE). MINISTERE DE L'INDUSTRIE ET DU COMMERCE. DIRECTION DE L'ANALYSE ET DE LA PREVISION ECONOMIQUES. see *TRANSPORTATION*

330 CN ISSN 0316-5078
QUEEN'S UNIVERSITY. INSTITUTE FOR ECONOMIC RESEARCH. DISCUSSION PAPER. 1969. irreg. Can.$350. Queen's University, Institute for Economic Research, Kingston. Ont. K7L 3N6, Canada. TEL 613-545-6348. bibl. circ. 200.

R.B.R.R. KALE MEMORIAL LECTURES. see *POLITICAL SCIENCE*

RAND MCNALLY BUSINESS TRAVELER'S ROAD ATLAS; and guide to major cities. see *TRAVEL AND TOURISM*

330 UK ISSN 0305-814X
READING IN POLITICAL ECONOMY. 1967.
irreg., no.25, 1980. $55 (combined subscription for
all series) Institute of Economic Affairs, 2 Lord
North St., London S.W.1, England (Dist. in North
America by: Transatlantic Arts, Inc., Box 6086,
Albuquerque, NM 89197) adv. bk. rev. (also avail.
in microfiche)
Formerly: Readings in Political Economy (ISSN
0079-9874)

330 UK
RECOMMENDATION FOR SURVIVAL IN
BUSINESS. 1981. irreg. £4.50. Marcus, Tobias &
Co., 65 Shakespeare Dr., Shirley, Solihull B90 2AN,
England.

330 CN ISSN 0826-8983
RESEARCH AND DEVELOPMENT IN THE
CANADIAN CORPORATE SECTION; a survey
of attitudes and spending intentions. 1985. a.
Can.$10 to non-members. Conference Board of
Canada, 255 Smyth Road, Ottawa, Ont. K1H 8M7,
Canada. TEL 613-526-3280.

330 US
RESEARCH FOR BUSINESS DECISIONS. irreg.,
vol.89, 1986. U M I Research Press, 300 N. Zeeb
Rd., Ann Arbor, MI 48106. Ed. Richard Farmer.

330 US
RESEARCH IN BUSINESS ECONOMICS AND
PUBLIC POLICY. irreg., vol.10, 1985. U M I
Research Press, 300 N. Zeeb Rd., Ann Arbor, MI
48106. Ed. Fred Bateman.

330 US ISSN 0191-1937
RESEARCH IN CORPORATE SOCIAL
PERFORMANCE AND POLICY; an annual
compilation of research. 1978. a. $24.75 to
individuals; institutions $49.50. J A I Press Inc., 36
Sherwood Pl., Box 1678, Greenwich, CT 06836-
1678. TEL 203-661-7602. Ed. Lee Preston.

330.05 340 US ISSN 0193-5895
RESEARCH IN LAW AND ECONOMICS; a
research annual. (Supplement avail.: Economics of
Nonproprietory Organizations) 1979. a. $23.75 to
individuals; institutions $47.50. J A I Press Inc.,
Box 1678, 36 Sherwood Pl., Greenwich, CT 06836.
TEL 203-661-7602. Ed. Richard O. Zerbe, Jr.
Indexed: Leg.Per. C.L.I. L.R.I.

330 II
REVIEW OF COMMERCE STUDIES. 1972. a.
Rs.10($2.50) University of Delhi, School of
Economics, Department of Commerce, Delhi
110007, India. Ed. R.A. Sharma. (back issues avail)

330 VE
REVISTA DE ECONOMIA.* 1961. a. Universidad de
Los Andes, Facultad de Economia, Via los Chorras
de Milla, C. P. 5101, Merida, Venezuela.
Formerly: Economia (ISSN 0070-8399)

330 DR
REVISTA DE ESTUDIOS ECONOMICOS. 1982.
irreg., latest vol.3, no.1, 1984. $2. Banco Central de
la Republica Dominicana, Apdo. Postal 1347, Santo
Domingo, Dominican Republic.

330 BE
RIJKSUNIVERSITEIT TE GENT. FACULTEIT
VAN DE ECONOMISCHE WETENSCHAPPEN.
WERKEN. irreg. Rijksuniversiteit te Gent, Faculteit
van de Economische Wetenschappen, Hoveniersberg
4, B-9000 Ghent, Belgium. Eds. E. de Lembre, W.
Georges.

330 PL ISSN 0080-343X
ROCZNIK EKONOMICZNY. 1961. a. price varies.
(Polskie Towarzystwo Ekonomiczne, Oddzial w
Szczecinie) Panstwowe Wydawnictwo Naukowe, Ul.
Miodowa 10, 00-251 Warsaw, Poland (Dist. by: Ars
Polona, Krakowskie Przedmiescie 7, 00-068
Warsaw, Poland) Ed.Bd. adv. bk. rev. circ. 650.

330 DK ISSN 0105-8827
ROSKILDE UNIVERSITETSCENTER. INSTITUT
FOR SAMFUNDSOEKONOMI OG
PLANLAEGNING. RESEARCH REPORT. 1981.
irreg. free. Roskilde Universitetscenter, Institut for
Samfundsoekonomi og Planlaegning, Roskilde,
Denmark.

330 650 US ISSN 0068-5836
SAN DIEGO STATE UNIVERSITY. BUREAU OF
BUSINESS AND ECONOMIC RESEARCH.
MONOGRAPHS. irreg. price varies. San Diego
State University, Bureau of Business and Economic
Research, School of Business Administration, San
Diego, CA 92182. TEL 619-265-5200.

330 650 US ISSN 0068-5844
SAN DIEGO STATE UNIVERSITY. BUREAU OF
BUSINESS AND ECONOMIC RESEARCH.
RESEARCH STUDIES AND POSITION
PAPERS. no. 2,1965. irreg., no.18, 1968. price
varies. San Diego State University, Bureau of
Business and Economic Research, School of
Business Administration, San Diego, CA 92182.
TEL 619-265-5200.

330 UG
SCARCITY. (Text in English) vol.2, 1968. irreg.
(approx. a.) Makerere Economics Society, Box
7062, Kampala, Uganda.

SCOTTISH ECONOMIC AND SOCIAL HISTORY.
see SOCIAL SCIENCES: COMPREHENSIVE
WORKS

330 KO
SEOUL NATIONAL UNIVERSITY. ECONOMIC
REVIEW. (Text in English, French and German)
1967. a. free. Seoul National University, Institute of
Economic Research, 19 Jongam-Dong Sungbuk-Gu,
Seoul, S. Korea (Subscr. to: Publishing Center of
Seoul National University, 199 Dongsung-Dong
Jongro-Gu, Seoul, S. Korea) bk. rev. charts. illus.
stat. circ. 700. Indexed: Geo.Abstr. Rural
Recreat.Tour.Abstr. World Agri.Econ.& Rural
Sociol.Abstr.

650 UK
SIR FREDERIC HOOPER AWARD ESSAY. 1969.
a. membership. Foundation for Business
Responsibilities, 40 Doughty St., London WC1N
2LF, England.

338 320 UK ISSN 0080-9780
SIR GEORGE EARLE MEMORIAL LECTURE ON
INDUSTRY AND GOVERNMENT. 1966. a. price
varies. Foundation for Business Responsibilities, 40
Doughty St., London WC1N 2LF, England. bk. rev.

SKATTEN. ERHVERV. see BUSINESS AND
ECONOMICS — Public Finance, Taxation

330 NE ISSN 0560-3641
SOCIAAL-ECONOMISCHE RAAD.
JAARVERSLAG/SOCIAAL-ECONOMISCHE
RAAD. ANNUAL REPORT. a. fl.25. Sociaal-
Economische Raad, Postbus 90405, 2509 LK The
Hague, Netherlands. bk. rev.

330 US ISSN 0737-7762
SOCIAL CONCEPT. 1983. biennial. $12 to
individuals; institutions $25. Social Concept Inc., c/
o Julie Matthaei, 1266 Boulevard, New Haven, CT
06511. Ed.Bd. adv. bk. rev. circ. 300.

340 BL
SOCIEDADES POR ACOES. 1977. irreg. Editora
Resenha Universitaria, Rua Quatinga 12, 04140 Sao
Paulo, Brazil.

330.1 339 CH
SOOCHOW JOURNAL OF ECONOMICS AND
BUSINESS. (Text in Chinese and English) 1977. a.
$15 per no. Soochow University, Lane 129, Yeng
Ping S. Road, Taipei, Taiwan, Republic of China.
Ed.Bd. circ. 1,000.

330 SP
SPAIN. INSTITUTO NACIONAL DE INDUSTRIA.
INFORME ANUAL. (Text in English and Spanish)
1981. a. free. Instituto Nacional de Industria, Plaza
de Salamanca 8, 28006 Madrid, Spain. TEL 341-401
40 04. charts, stat.
Formerly: Spain. Instituto Nacional de Industria.
Memoria I N I (Year)

330 SP
SPAIN. INSTITUTO NACIONAL DE INDUSTRIA.
PROGRAMA DE INVESTIGACIONES
ECONOMICAS: SERIE E. no.8, 1977. irreg.
Instituto Nacional de Industria, Programa de
Investigaciones Economicas, Plaza del Marque de
Salamanca 8-30, Madrid 6, Spain.

332.1 US ISSN 0081-3559
SPECIAL PAPERS IN INTERNATIONAL
ECONOMICS. 1955. irreg., no.14, 1980. $30
(includes Essays in International Finance; Reprints
in International Finance; Studies in International
Finance) ‡ Princeton University, International
Finance Section, Dept. of Economics, Dickinson
Hall, Princeton, NJ 08544. TEL 609-452-4048. Dir.
Peter B. Kenen. circ. 2,000. (back issues avail.;
reprint service avail. from UMI)

330 330.9 EI
STATISTICAL OFFICE OF THE EUROPEAN
COMMUNITIES. COMPARISON IN REAL
TERMS OF E S A AGGREGATES. (Editions in
English, French, German and Italian) 1977.
quinquennial. 1000 Fr.($21) Statistical Office of the
European Communities, B.P. 1903, 2920
Luxembourg, Luxembourg. Ed.Bd. circ. 4,100.

330 GW
STIFTUNG VOLKSWAGENWERK.
SCHRIFTENREIHE. 1967. irreg. Vandenhoeck &
Ruprecht, Robert-Bosch-Breite 6, Postfach 3753, D-
3400 Goettingen, W. Germany (B.R.D.) Ed.Bd.

330 PL ISSN 0081-6930
STUDIA SPOLECZNO-EKONOMICZNE. 1968.
irreg., latest issue 1986, no.13. 200 Zl. Instytut
Slaski, Instytut Naukowo-Badawczy, Piastowska 17,
45 082 Opole, Poland.

330 RM ISSN 0578-5472
STUDIA UNIVERSITATIS "BABES-BOLYAI."
OECONOMICA. (Text in Rumanian; summaries in
English, French, German, Russian) 1960. a.
exchange basis. Universitatea "Babes-Bolyai",
Biblioteca Centrala Universitara, Str. Clinicilor nr.
2, Cluj-Napoca, Rumania.

330 GW ISSN 0170-5687
STUDIEN ZUR BAUWIRTSCHAFT. 1974. irreg.
price varies. I F O Institut fuer
Wirtschaftsforschung, Poschingerstr. 5, 0000
Munich 80, W. Germany (B.R.D.) circ. 500.

330 GW ISSN 0721-0086
STUDIEN ZUR BEVOELKERUNGSOEKONOMIE.
1981. irreg. price varies. I F O Institut fuer
Wirtschaftsforschung, Poschingerstr. 5, 8000
Munich 80, W. Germany (B.R.D.) circ. 500.

330 GW ISSN 0170-7779
STUDIEN ZUR ENERGIEWIRTSCHAFT. 1978.
irreg. price varies. I F O Institut fuer
Wirtschaftsforschung, Poschingerstr. 5, 8000
Munich 80, W. Germany (B.R.D.) circ. 500.

330 GW ISSN 0170-5660
STUDIEN ZUR INDUSTRIEWIRTSCHAFT. 1967.
irreg. price varies. I F O Institut fuer
Wirtschaftsforschung, Poschingerstr. 5, 8000
Munich 80, W. Germany (B.R.D.) circ. 500.

330 GW ISSN 0170-5652
STUDIEN ZUR VERKEHRSWIRTSCHAFT. 1972.
irreg. price varies. I F O Institut fuer
Wirtschaftsforschung, Poschingerstr. 5, 8000
Munich 80, W. Germany (B.R.D.) circ. 500.

330 NE
STUDIES IN BAYESIAN ECONOMETRICS AND
STATISTICS. 1980. irreg., vol.5, 1984. price varies.
Elsevier Science Publishers B.V., Box 211, 1000 AE
Amsterdam, Netherlands. Eds. Arnold Zellner,
Joseph B. Kadane.
Formerly: Studies in Bayesian Econometrics.

650 US ISSN 0081-7635
STUDIES IN BUSINESS AND SOCIETY. 1965.
irreg., latest 1981. price varies. (University of
Chicago, Graduate School of Business) University of
Chicago Press, 5801 S. Ellis Ave., Chicago, IL
60637. TEL 312-962-7700. (reprint service avail.
from UMI,ISI)

330 UK ISSN 0081-7856
STUDIES IN ECONOMICS. 1970. irreg., no. 11,
1976. price varies. George Allen & Unwin
(Publishers) Ltd., 40 Museum St., London W.C.1,
England (U.S. addr.: Allen & Unwin In., 8
Winchester Place, Winchester, MA 01890)

330 NE
STUDIES IN INTERNATIONAL ECONOMICS.
1974. irreg., vol.8, 1984. price varies. Elsevier
Science Publishers B.V., Box 211, 1000 AE
Amsterdam, Netherlands. Eds. J.N. Bhagwati, J.S.
Chipman.

330 NE
STUDIES IN PRODUCTION AND
ENGINEERING ECONOMICS. 1981. irreg.,
vol.4, 1985. price varies. Elsevier Science Publishers
B.V., Box 211, 1000 AE Amsterdam, Netherlands.
Ed. R.W. Grubbstroem.

330 NE
STUDIES IN PUBLIC ECONOMICS. 1979. irreg.,
vol. 2, 1979. price varies. Elsevier Science
Publishers B.V., Box 211, 1000 AE Amsterdam,
Netherlands. Eds. M. Feldstein, E. Sheshinski.

330 301 US
STUDIES IN SOCIAL ECONOMICS. 1967. irreg.,
no.25, 1986. price varies. Brookings Institution,
1775 Massachusetts Ave. N.W., Washington, DC
20036. TEL 202-797-6258.

STUDIES IN THE POLITICAL ECONOMY OF
CANADA. see *POLITICAL SCIENCE*

330 US
STUDIES IN WAGE-PRICE POLICY. 1967. irreg.,
no.6, 1983. price varies. Brookings Institution, 1775
Massachusetts Ave. N.W., Washington, DC 20036.
TEL 202-797-6258.

STUDIES ON THE MORPHOLOGY AND
SYSTEMATICS OF SCALE INSECTS. see
BIOLOGY — Entomology

STUDY OF FINANCIAL RESULTS AND
REPORTING TRENDS IN THE GAMING
INDUSTRY. see *SPORTS AND GAMES*

330 FI ISSN 0355-6034
SUOMEN PANKKI. JULKAISUJA. SARJA A/
BANK OF FINLAND. PUBLICATIONS. SERIES
A/FINLANDS BANK. PUBLIKATIONER. SERIE
A. (Vols. 1-35, in Finnish and Swedish, were pub.
annually) (Text in English, Finnish or Swedish)
1942. irreg., no.63, 1986. Fmk.60. Suomen Pankki -
Bank of Finland, Information Department, Box 160,
SF-00101 Helsinki, Finland. Eds. Annikki
Leukkunen, Marja Hirvensalo. circ. 1,200.
Formerly (until 1972): Suomen Pankki
Taloustieteellinen Tutkimuslaitos. Julkaisuja. Series
A: Taloudellisia Selvityksia (ISSN 0081-9476)

330 FI ISSN 0357-4776
SUOMEN PANKKI. JULKAISUJA. SARJA B/
BANK OF FINLAND. PUBLICATIONS. SERIES
B/FINLANDS BANK. PUBLIKATIONER. SERIE
B. (Text in Finnish or Swedish; summaries in
English) 1943. irreg., no.41, 1986. Fmk.80. Suomen
Pankki - Bank of Finland, Information Department,
Box 160, SF-00101 Helsinki, Finland. Eds. Annikki
Leukkunen, Marja Hirvensalo. circ. 1,000.
Formerly (until no.31, 1969): Suomen Pankki.
Taloustieteellinen Tutkimuslaitos. Julkaisuja. Series
B (ISSN 0081-9484)

330 FI ISSN 0081-9492
SUOMEN PANKKI. JULKAISUJA. SARJA C/
BANK OF FINLAND. PUBLICATIONS. SERIES
C/FINLANDS BANK. PUBLIKATIONER. SERIE
C. (Text mainly in Finnish, occasionally in Swedish)
1962. irreg., no.7, 1984. Fmk.25. Suomen Pankki -
Bank of Finland, Information Department, Box 160,
SF-00101 Helsinki, Finland. Ed. Annikki
Leukkunen. circ. 300.

330 FI ISSN 0355-6042
SUOMEN PANKKI. JULKAISUJA. SARJA D/
BANK OF FINLAND. PUBLICATIONS. SERIES
D/FINLANDS BANK. PUBLIKATIONER.
SERIE D. (Text in Finnish, Swedish or English)
1963. irreg., no.62, 1986. Fmk.60. Suomen Pankki -
Bank of Finland, Information Department, Box 160,
SF-00101 Helsinki, Finland. Eds. Annikki
Leukkunen, Marja Hirvensalo. circ. 600.
Formerly: Suomen Pankki, Taloustieteellinen
Tutkimuslaitos. Series D. Mimeographed Series
(ISSN 0081-9506)

330 UK ISSN 0081-9670
SURREY PAPERS IN ECONOMICS. 1967. irreg.
£0.50 per no. University of Surrey, Bookshop,
Guildford, Surrey GU2 5XH, England. Eds. R.P.
Troeller, S.F. Frowen.
Formerly: International Economics.

339 US
SURVEYS OF APPLIED ECONOMICS. 1973. irreg.
price varies. Saint Martins Press, 175 Fifth Avenue,
New York, NY 10010.

330 SW ISSN 0082-0067
SWEDEN. KONJUNKTURINSTITUTET.
OCCASIONAL PAPER. (Text in English) 1964.
irreg., no.12, 1980. price varies.
(Konjunkturinstitutet - National Institute of
Economic Research) Allmaenna Foerlaget, Box
5227, 102 45 Stockholm, Sweden.

330 SZ
SWITZERLAND. KOMMISSION FUER
KONJUNKTURFRAGEN. ALLFAELLIGE
STUDIEN. French edition: Switzerland.
Commission pour les Questions Conjoncturelles.
Etudes Occasionnelles. (Supplement to: Switzerland.
Eidgenoessisches Volkswirtschaftsdepartement.
Volkswirtschaft and to Schweizerische
Nationalbank. Monatsbericht) irreg., no.300, 1986.
Eidgenoessisches Volkswirtschaftsdepartement,
Kommission fuer Konjunkturfragen, Belpstr. 53,
3003 Berne, Switzerland.

T.I. (Technical Information for Industry) see
TECHNOLOGY: COMPREHENSIVE WORKS

330 FR ISSN 0291-8692
TABLEAUX ECONOMIQUES DE MIDI-
PYRENEES. (Text in French) 1981. a. 35 Fr. per
issue. Institut National de la Statistique et des
Etudes Economiques (INSEE), Direction Regionale
de Toulouse, 36 rue des 36 Ponts, 31054 Toulouse,
France. Ed. Louis Amiel.

330 TZ
TANZANIA INDUSTRIAL STUDIES AND
CONSULTING ORGANISATION. ANNUAL
REPORT AND ACCOUNTS. 1978. a. free.
Tanzania Industrial Studies and Consulting
Organisation (TISCO), Box 2650, Dar es Salaam,
Tanzania. Ed. E.M. Ntabaye. circ. 2,500. (back
issues avail.) Indexed: Met.Abstr.

TEMADOKUMENTACIOS KIADVANYOK/
THEMATICAL REVIEWS. see *TECHNOLOGY:
COMPREHENSIVE WORKS*

330 340 AG
TENDENCIAS ECONOMICAS: LEGISLACION
ECONOMICAS ARGENTINA/BUSINESS
TRENDS: ARGENTINE ECONOMIC
LEGISLATION. (Text in English and Spanish)
1960. a. Esmeralda 320, Buenos Aires, Argentina.
Ed. Jose Luis Blanco. adv. Indexed: Key to
Econ.Sci.

330.9 TH ISSN 0857-2984
THAILAND INDUSTRIAL BUYER'S GUIDE. 1981.
a. $40 per no. Business Publications (1985) Co.
Ltd., 9/42 Soi Kingpetch, Petchburi Road, P.O. Box
2729, Bangkok 10400, Thailand.

330.1 FR ISSN 0082-3988
THEORIE DE LA PRODUCTION. 1970. irreg.,
latest no.16, 1980. price varies. (Institut de
Recherches en Economie de la Production) Editions
Cujas, 4,6,8, rue de la Maison-Blanche, 75013 Paris,
France. Dir. Jacques De Bandt.

330 US
TRADESHOW CONVENTION GUIDE. 1964. a.
Billboard Publications, Inc., Amusement Business
Division, Box 24970, Nashville, TN 37202. TEL
615-748-8100. adv. circ. 11,183.

TRAFIKOEKONOMISKE ENHEDSPRISER. see
TRANSPORTATION — Roads And Traffic

330 HU ISSN 0133-7769
TRENDS IN WORLD ECONOMY. (Text in English,
French, German, Hungarian, Russian, Spanish)
1971. irreg. (4-6/yr.) price varies. Vilaggazdasagi
Tudomanyos Tanacs, Kallo esperes u. 15, P.O.B. 36,
1531 Budapest, Hungary. Ed. B. Balkay. circ. 1,000.
(processed)

380 US
TRINET DIRECTORY OF LEADING U S
COMPANIES: SECOND 1,500. 1980. a. $175.
Trinet, Inc., 9 Campus Dr., Parsippany, NJ 07054.
TEL 201-267-3600.
Formerly: Second 1,500 Companies (ISSN 0275-
7443)

380 US
TRINET DIRECTORY OF LEADING U S
COMPANIES: TOP 1,500. 1980. a. $175. Trinet,
Inc., 9 Campus Dr., Parsippany, NJ 07054. TEL
201-267-3600.
Former titles: Top 1,500 Companies (ISSN 0275-
7435); E I S Directory of Top 1,500 Companies
(Economic Information Systems)

380 US
TRINET DIRECTORY OF LEADING U S
COMPANIES: TOP 1,500 PRIVATE. 1980. a.
$175. Trinet, Inc., 9 Campus Dr., Parsippany, NJ
07054. TEL 201-267-3600.
Former titles: Top 1,500 Private Companies
(ISSN 0275-7427); E I S Directory of Top 1,500
Private Companies; E I S Directory of Top 500
Private and Foreign Owned Companies.

650 US
TRY US; national minority business directory. 1969. a.
$32. National Minority Business Directories, 65
22nd Ave., N.E., Minneapolis, MN 55418. TEL
612-781-6819.
Formerly: National Minority Business Directory
(ISSN 0077-5231)

338 650 US ISSN 0082-7126
U C L A BUSINESS FORECAST FOR THE
NATION AND CALIFORNIA. 1960. a. $35.
University of California, Los Angeles, Graduate
School of Management, U.C.L.A. Business
Forecasting Project, 405 Hilgard Ave., Los Angeles,
CA 90024. TEL 213-825-7935. Ed. Robert M.
Williams. circ. 2,000.

U S A FOR BUSINESS TRAVELERS. see *TRAVEL
AND TOURISM*

U S REAL ESTATE REGISTER. see
ADVERTISING AND PUBLIC RELATIONS

330 650 330.9 US
U S S R REPORT: NATIONAL ECONOMY. 1969.
irreg. (approx. 100/yr.) $5 per no. U.S. Joint
Publications Research Service, 1000 N. Glebe Rd.,
Arlington, VA 22201 TEL 703-841-1050. (Orders
to: NTIS, Springfield, VA 22161)
Former titles: U S S R Report: Economic Affairs;
Translations on U S S R Economic Affair.

330 327 US
U S S R REPORT: WORLD ECONOMY AND
INTERNATIOAL RELATIONS. irreg. (approx.
15/yr.) $5 per no. U.S. Joint Publications Research
Service, 1000 N. Glebe Rd., Arlington, VA 22201
TEL 703-487-4630. (Orders to: NTIS, Springfield,
VA 22161)

330 338.91 UN
UNITED NATIONS. ECONOMIC COMMISSION
FOR AFRICA. PROPOSALS FOR
PROGRAMME BUDGET. biennial. Economic
Commission for Africa, Addis-Ababa, Ethiopia.

330 CL
UNIVERSIDAD DE CHILE. FACULTAD DE
CIENCIAS ECONOMICAS Y
ADMINISTRATIVAS. DESARROLLO. irreg.
Universidad de Chile, Facultad de Ciencias
Economicas y Administrativas, Santiago, Chile.

330 SP
UNIVERSIDAD DE DEUSTO. PUBLICACIONES.
ECONOMIA. 1972. irreg., no. 4, 1976. Universidad
Comercial de Deusto, Bilbao, Spain.

330 UY
UNIVERSIDAD DE LA REPUBLICA. FACULTAD
DE CIENCIAS ECONOMICAS Y DE
ADMINISTRACION. REVISTA. 1940; N.S. 1950.
irreg. Universidad de la Republica, Facultad de
Ciencias Economicas y de Administracion,
Montivideo, Uruguay. bibl. charts.

330 SP
UNIVERSIDAD DE SEVILLA. INSTITUTO
GARCIA OVIEDO. CUADERNOS. irreg. price
varies. Universidad de Sevilla, Instituto Garcia
Oviedo, San Fernando 4, Seville, Spain.

330　　　　　　　　AG
UNIVERSIDAD NACIONAL DEL LITORAL. FACULTAD DE CIENCIAS ECONOMICAS COMERCIALES Y POLITICAS. 1926. irreg. Universidad Nacional del Litoral, Facultad de Ciencias Economicas Comerciales y Politicas, Santa Fe, Argentina.

330　　　　　　　　PE
UNIVERSIDAD NACIONAL MAYOR DE SAN MARCOS. FACULTAD DE CIENCIAS ECONOMICAS Y COMERCIALES. REVISTA. 1929. irreg. Universidad Nacional Mayor de San Marcos, Facultad de Ciencias Economicas y Comerciales, Casilla 2631, Lima, Peru. bibl.
　　Formerly: Revista Economica y Financiera.

330　　　　　　　　PO
UNIVERSIDADE DE COIMBRA. FACULDADE DE DIREITO. BOLETIM DE CIENCIAS ECONOMICAS. (Text in Portuguese, summaries in English) 1952. a. $18. Universidade de Coimbra, Faculdade de Direito, Rua Ferreira Borges, Coimbra, Portugal. bk. rev. charts. stat. circ. 1,000.

330　　　　　　　　IT
UNIVERSITA DEGLI STUDI DI PARMA. FACOLTA DI ECONOMIA E COMMERCIO. STUDI E RICERCHE. 1964. a. Universita degli Studi di Parma, Facolta di Economia e Commercio, Parma, Italy.

330　　　　　　　　IT
UNIVERSITA DI SASSARI. FACOLTA DI GIURISPRUDENZA. PUBBLICAZIONI. SERIE ECONOMICA. 1984. irreg. Casa Editrice Dott. A. Giuffre, Via B. Arsizio 40, 20151 Milan, Italy.

330　　　　　　　　GW
UNIVERSITAET HAMBURG. SEMINAR FUER ALLGEMEINE BETRIEBSWIRTSCHAFTLEHRE. SCHRIFTENREIHE. 1978. irreg. Vandenhoeck & Ruprecht, Robert-Bosch-Breite 6, Postfach 3753, D-3400 Goettingen, W. Germany (B.R.D.)

330　　　　　　　　GW
UNIVERSITAET HAMBURG. STUDIEN ZUR ANGEWANDTES WIRTSCHAFTSFORSCHUNG UND OEKONOMETRIE. 1975. irreg. (Universitaet Hamburg) Vandenhoeck & Ruprecht, Verlagsbuchhandlung, Robert-Bosch-Breite 6, Postfach 3753, D-3400 Goettingen, W. Germany (B.R.D.) Eds. H. Gollnick, H. Scherf.

330　　　　GW　ISSN 0531-0318
UNIVERSITAET ZU KOELN. INSTITUT FUER HANDELSFORSCHUNG. MITTEILUNGEN. SONDERHEFTE. 1954. irreg., no. 35, 1987. price varies. Verlag Otto Schwartz und Co., Annastr. 7, 3400 Goettingen, W. Germany (B.R.D.) Ed. Edmund Sundhoff.

330　　　　RM　ISSN 0379-7864
UNIVERSITATEA "AL. I. CUZA" DIN IASI. ANALELE STIINTIFICE. SECTIUNEA 3C: STIINTE ECONOMICE. (Text in English, French, Rumanian) a. 35 lei. Universitatea "Al. I. Cuza" din Iasi, Calea 23 August Nr.11, Jassy, Rumania (Subscr. to: ILEXIM, Str. 13 Decembrie Nr. 3, P.O. Box 136-137, Bucharest, Rumania) Ed. M. Todosia. bk. rev. abstr. charts. illus. circ. 250.

UNIVERSITY OF ALASKA. INSTITUTE OF SOCIAL AND ECONOMIC RESEARCH. RESEARCH SUMMARY. see *SOCIOLOGY*

330　　　　　　　　CN
UNIVERSITY OF BRITISH COLUMBIA. DEPARTMENT OF ECONOMICS. DISCUSSION PAPER. 1968. irreg. University of British Columbia, Department of Economics, 1873 East Mall, Suite 997, University Campus, Vancouver, B.C. V6T 1Y2, Canada. TEL 604-228-2211.

330　　　　CN　ISSN 0381-0410
UNIVERSITY OF BRITISH COLUMBIA. DEPARTMENT OF ECONOMICS. RESOURCES PAPER. 1976. irreg. University of British Columbia, Department of Economics, 1873 East Mall, Suite 997, University Campus, Vancouver, B.C. V6T 1Y2, Canada. TEL 604-228-2211.

330　338　　US　ISSN 0068-6077
UNIVERSITY OF CALIFORNIA. INSTITUTE OF BUSINESS AND ECONOMIC RESEARCH. PUBLICATIONS. 1948. irreg. price varies. University of California Press, 2120 Berkeley Way, Berkeley, CA 94720. TEL 415-642-4247.

650　　　　US　ISSN 0069-3359
UNIVERSITY OF CHICAGO. GRADUATE SCHOOL OF BUSINESS. SELECTED PAPERS. 1962. irreg. University of Chicago, Graduate School of Business, Chicago, IL 60637. TEL 312-962-7743. Dir. Betty E. McGuire. circ. 10,000(controlled)

330　　　　　　　　TZ
UNIVERSITY OF DAR ES SALAAM. ECONOMIC RESEARCH BUREAU. OCCASIONAL PAPER. Short title: E R B Occasional Paper Series. 1966. irreg. price varies. University of Dar es Salaam, Economic Research Bureau, Box 35096, Dar es Salaam, Tanzania. circ. 100.

330　　　　TZ　ISSN 0418-3746
UNIVERSITY OF DAR ES SALAAM. ECONOMIC RESEARCH BUREAU. PAPERS. Short title: E R B Papers. 1966. irreg. $3 per no. University of Dar es Salaam, Economic Research Bureau, Box 35096, Dar es Salaam, Tanzania.

330　　　　　　　　SA
UNIVERSITY OF NATAL. LOW-INCOME HOUSING SERIES. (Text in English) 1983. irreg. University of Natal, Department of Economics, King George V Ave., Durban, South Africa. Ed. Gavin Grant Maasdorp.

330　　　　　　　　SA
UNIVERSITY OF NATAL. MONOGRAPH SERIES; transport policies and economic development in Southern Africa. (Text in English) 1984. irreg. R.15. University of Natal, Department of Economics, King George V Ave., Durban, South Africa. Ed. Gavin Grant Maasdorp. circ. 300.

330　　　　　　　　SA
UNIVERSITY OF NATAL. OCCASIONAL PAPERS; distribution of personal wealth in South Africa. (Text in English) 1982. irreg. R.1.50. University of Natal, Department of Economics, King George V Ave., Durban, South Africa. Ed. Gavin Grant Maasdorp. circ. 300.

650　　　　US　ISSN 0077-7943
UNIVERSITY OF NEVADA. BUREAU OF BUSINESS AND ECONOMIC RESEARCH. RESEARCH REPORT. 1961. irreg. price varies. University of Nevada, Bureau of Business and Economic Research, Reno, NV 89557-0016. TEL 702-784-6877.

330　382　346　JA　ISSN 0473-4637
UNIVERSITY OF OSAKA PREFECTURE. BULLETIN. SERIES D: SCIENCES OF ECONOMY, COMMERCE AND LAW. 1957. a. exchange basis. University of Osaka Prefecture - Osaka-furitsu Daigaku, 4-804 Mozuume-machi, Sakai-shi, Osaka 591, Japan.

330　　　　US　ISSN 0081-8437
UNIVERSITY OF PENNSYLVANIA. WHARTON SCHOOL OF FINANCE AND COMMERCE. STUDIES IN QUANTITATIVE ECONOMICS. 1966. irreg. price varies. University of Pennsylvania Wharton School of Finance and Commerce, Economics Research Unit, 3718 Locust Walk, Philadelphia, PA 19104. TEL 215-898-7601.

338　　　　　　　　SI
UNIVERSITY OF SINGAPORE. ECONOMIC RESEARCH CENTRE. OCCASIONAL PAPERS. 1977. irreg. Chopmen Enterprises, Katong Shopping Centre, Mountbatten Road 05-28, Singapore 1543, Singapore.

330　　　　　　　　US
UNIVERSITY OF SOUTH CAROLINA. BUREAU OF BUSINESS AND ECONOMIC RESEARCH. OCCASIONAL STUDIES. 1972. irreg., no.15, 1983. University of South Carolina, College of Business Administration, Division of Research, Columbia, SC 29208. TEL 803-777-3176. Ed. Jan C. Stucker. charts. illus. circ. 1,900(controlled)

330　　　　UK　ISSN 0306-7408
UNIVERSITY OF STRATHCLYDE, FRASER OF ALLANDER INSTITUTE FOR RESEARCH ON THE SCOTTISH ECONOMY. RESEARCH MONOGRAPH. 1975. irreg. price varies. University of Strathclyde, Fraser of Allander Institute for Research on the Scottish Economy, Curran Bldg., 100 Cathedral St., Glasgow G4 0LN, Scotland. bibl. Indexed: Rural Recreat.Tour.Abstr. World Agri.Econ.& Rural Sociol.Abstr.

330　　　　　　　　AT
UNIVERSITY OF SYDNEY. FACULTY OF ECONOMICS. INFORMATION AND RESEARCH MONOGRAPH. no.2, 1976. irreg. University of Sydney, Faculty of Economics, Sydney, N.S.W. 2006, Australia. bibl.

650　　　　US　ISSN 0495-2634
UNIVERSITY OF TEXAS, AUSTIN. BUREAU OF BUSINESS RESEARCH. PUBLICATIONS. a. University of Texas at Austin, Bureau of Business Research, Box 7459, Austin, TX 78713. TEL 512-471-1616. (reprint service avail. from UMI) Key Title: Publications-Bureau of Business Research, the University of Texas at Austin.

650　　　　　　　　US
UNIVERSITY OF TEXAS, AUSTIN. BUREAU OF BUSINESS RESEARCH. RESEARCH REPORT SERIES. 1928. irreg., latest, 1980. price varies. University of Texas at Austin, Bureau of Business Research, Box 7459, Austin, TX 78713. TEL 512-471-1616. (reprint service avail. from UMI)
　　Formerly: University of Texas, Austin. Bureau of Business Research. Research Monograph (ISSN 0082-3279)

UNIVERSITY OF THE WEST INDIES. INSTITUTE OF SOCIAL AND ECONOMIC RESEARCH. WORKING PAPERS. see *SOCIOLOGY*

UNIVERSITY OF TOLEDO. BUSINESS RESEARCH CENTER. BIBLIOGRAPHIES. see *BIBLIOGRAPHIES*

650　　　　　　　　US
UNIVERSITY OF TOLEDO. BUSINESS RESEARCH CENTER. MISCELLANEOUS PAPERS. 1968. irreg., latest 1986. price varies. University of Toledo, College of Business Administration, 2801 W. Bancroft St., Toledo, OH 43606. TEL 419-537-2067.

650　　　　　　　　US
UNIVERSITY OF TOLEDO. BUSINESS RESEARCH CENTER. OCCASIONAL PAPERS. (Subseries of Toledo Business Report) 1963. irreg., no.24, 1977. price varies. University of Toledo, College of Business Administration, 2801 W. Bancroft St., Toledo, OH 43606. TEL 419-537-2067. circ. 800.

650　382　　　　US
UNIVERSITY OF TOLEDO. BUSINESS RESEARCH CENTER. STUDIES IN INTERNATIONAL BUSINESS. 1979. irreg., latest 1986. price varies. University of Toledo, College of Business Administration, 2801 Bancroft St., Toledo, OH 43606. TEL 419-537-2067. Ed. Alan B. Flaschner.

301　330　　　　CN
UNIVERSITY OF TORONTO. INSTITUTE FOR POLICY ANALYSIS. ANNUAL REPORT. 1976. irreg. ‡ University of Toronto, Institute for Policy Analysis, 150 St. George St., Toronto, Ont. M5S 1A1, Canada. TEL 416-978-8623.
　　Supersedes: University of Toronto. Institute for the Quantitative Analysis of Social and Economic Policy. News Letter (ISSN 0082-5271)

301　330　　CN　ISSN 0829-4909
UNIVERSITY OF TORONTO. INSTITUTE FOR POLICY ANALYSIS. WORKING PAPER SERIES. irreg. free. ‡ University of Toronto, Institute for Policy Analysis, 150 St. George St., Toronto, Ont. M5S 1A1, Canada. TEL 416-978-8623. (Co-sponsor: Department of Economics)
　　Formerly: University of Toronto. Institute for the Quantitative Analysis of Social and Economic Policy. Working Paper Series (ISSN 0082-5301)

UNIVERZITA KOMENSKEHO. USTAV MARXIZMU-LENINIZMU. ZBORNIK: MARXISTICKA FILOZOFIA. see *POLITICAL SCIENCE*

330 YU
UNIVERZITET VO SKOPLJE. EKONOMSKIOT FAKULTET. GODISNIK/UNIVERSITE DE SKOPJE. FACULTE DES SCIENCES ECONOMIQUE. ANNUAIRE. (Text in Macedonian; summaries in English, French, German and Russian) 1956. a. Univerzitet vo Skopje, Ekonomskiot Fakultet, Skopje, Yugoslavia. circ. 500.

330 335 PL ISSN 0208-4813
UNIWERSYTET GDANSKI. WYDZIAL EKONOMIKI TRANSPORTU. ZESZYTY NAUKOWE. INSTYTUT EKONOMII POLITYCZNEJ. PRACE I MATERIALY. (Text in Polish; summaries in English and Russian) 1971. irreg. price varies. Uniwersytet Gdanski, Ul. Czerwonej Armii 110, 81-824 Sopot, Poland.

330 DK ISSN 0107-2013
VEDROERENDE UDVIKLINGEN I DE EUROPAEISKE FAELLESSKABER. BERETNING. 1973. irreg. (Departementet for Udenrigsoekonomi) Underigsministeriet, Markedsafdelningen, Asiatisk Plads 2, 1448 Copenhagen, Denmark.

330 UR
VOPROSY EKONOMIKI NARODNOGO KHOZYAISTVA MURMANSKOI OBLASTI. irreg. 0.48 Rub. Akademiya Nauk S.S.S.R., Kol'skii Filial, Otdel Ekonomicheskikh Issledovanii, Apatity, Akademgorodok, Russian S.F.S.R., U.S.S.R. illus.

330 US
WARD'S DIRECTORY OF LARGEST U S COMPANIES; the all-purpose marketing and financial directory. (In 3 volumes: Largest U.S. Companies (0882-7990); Major U.S. Private Companies (0882-8008); Major International Companies (0882-8016)) 1961. a. $900. Information Access Company, 11 Davis Dr., Belmont, CA 94002. TEL 415-591-2333. Ed. Henry Dugan. (also avail. in magnetic tape)
Former titles (until 1981): Ward's Directory of 55,000 Largest U S Corporations; 50,000 Leading U S Corporations (ISSN 0730-3130); 30,000 Leading U S Corporations; 7500 Leading U S Manufacturers.

330 UK ISSN 0083-7350
WARWICK ECONOMIC RESEARCH PAPERS. 1968. irreg. (approx. 20/yr.) free. ‡ University of Warwick, Department of Economics, Coventry CV4 7AL, England. circ. 250. (also avail. in microfilm)

650 UK
WARWICK PAPERS IN MANAGEMENT. 1982. irreg. £3($6) ‡ University of Warwick, Insitut for Management Research and Development, Coventry, Warwickshire CV4 7AL, England. Ed. R.C. Tomlinson. circ. 200.
Formerly: Warwick Papers in Industry, Business and Administration (ISSN 0263-5976); Supersedes: Warwick Industrial Economic and Business Research Papers; Warwick Research Industrial and Business Studies (ISSN 0083-7369)

330 JA
WASEDA BUSINESS AND ECONOMIC STUDIES. (Text in English) 1965. a. free. Waseda University, Graduate School of Commerce, 1-6-1 Nishi-Waseda, Shinjuku-ku, Tokyo 160, Japan. charts. illus. circ. 500.

WELTWIRTSCHAFT AM JAHRESWECHSEL. see HISTORY — History Of Europe

330 GW
WER LEITET; das Middle Management der deutschen Wirtschaft. a. DM.240. Verlag Hoppenstedt & Co., Havelstr. 9, P.O. Box 4006, 6100 Darmstadt, W. Germany (B.R.D.)

330 US ISSN 0068-4392
WEST VIRGINIA UNIVERSITY. BUSINESS AND ECONOMIC STUDIES. 1949. irreg., vol.13, 1976. $3.50. West Virginia University, Bureau of Business Research, Box 6025, Morgantown, WV 26506. TEL 304-293-5837. index; cum. index; 1949-1976. Indexed: P.A.I.S. Vert.File Ind.

330 AT
WESTERN AUSTRALIA. BASIC INFORMATION FOR INDUSTRIALISTS. 1971. a. Department of Industrial Development, 170 St. George's Terrace, Perth. W.A. 6000, Australia. circ. 7,500.

330 020 US
WHO KNOWS ABOUT INDUSTRIES AND MARKETS. a. $40. Washington Researchers Publishing, 2612 P St., N.W., Washington, DC 10007. TEL 202-333-3533.
Formerly: Industry Analysis in the Federal Government.

WHO'S WHO IN CUMBRIA. see BIOGRAPHY

WHO'S WHO IN FINANCE AND INDUSTRY. see BIOGRAPHY

330 US ISSN 0084-0246
WILLIAM K. MCINALLY LECTURE. 1966. a. University of Michigan, Graduate School of Business Administration, Division of Research, Tappan and Monroe Sts., Ann Arbor, MI 48109. TEL 313-764-1366. (reprint service avail. from UMI)

330 AU ISSN 0259-0719
WIRTSCHAFTSUNIVERSITAET WIEN. DISSERTATIONEN. 1969. irreg., no.47, 1986. price varies. Verband der Wissenschaftlichen Gesellschaften Oesterreichs, Lindengasse 37, A-1070 Vienna, Austria.
Formerly: Hochschule fuer Welthandel in Wien. Dissertationen.

330 GW ISSN 0083-7113
WIRTSCHAFTSWISSENSCHAFTLICHE UND WIRTSCHAFTSRECHTLICHE UNTERSUCHUNGEN. 1962. irreg. price varies. (Walter Eucken Institut) Verlag J.C.B. Mohr (Paul Siebeck), Wilhelmstr. 18, Postfach 2040, 7400 Tuebingen, W. Germany (B.R.D.)

650 US ISSN 0084-0513
WISCONSIN BUSINESS MONOGRAPHS. 1968. irreg., no.12, 1981. price varies. ‡ University of Wisconsin-Madison, Bureau of Business Research, 110 Commerce Building, 1155 Observatory Dr., Madison, WI 53706. TEL 608-262-1550.
Formerly: University of Wisconsin. Bureau of Business Research and Service. Monographs (ISSN 0512-0918)

330 US ISSN 0084-0599
WISCONSIN ECONOMY STUDIES. 1967. irreg., no.21, 1985. price varies. ‡ University of Wisconsin-Madison, Bureau of Business Research, 110 Commerce Building, 1155 Observatory Dr., Madison, WI 53706. TEL 608-262-1550.
Formerly: Wisconsin Commerce Studies.

330 PL ISSN 0084-2974
WROCLAWSKI ROCZNIK EKONOMICZNY. 1968. a. price varies. (Polskie Towarzystwo Ekonomiczne) Biuro Wydawnictw i Bibliotek PAN, P.O. Box 24, 00-901 Warsaw, Poland (Dist. by: Ars Polona, Krakowskie Przedmiescie 7, 00-068 Warsaw, Poland) Ed.Bd. circ. 750.

330 US
YALE UNIVERSITY. ECONOMIC GROWTH CENTER. ANNUAL REPORT. 1961. a. free. Yale University, Economic Growth Center, Yale Sta., Box 1987, New Haven, CT 06520. TEL 203-436-8414. circ. 500.

330 US
YEARBOOK ON CORPORATE MERGERS, JOINT VENTURES AND CORPORATE POLICY; merger yearbook. 1978. a. $142. Cambridge Corporation, Drawer 670, Ipswich, MA 01938. TEL 617-356-0072. Ed. Andrew D. Clapp. adv. charts. stat. index. (back issues avail.)

YOUR (YEAR) GUIDE TO SOCIAL SECURITY BENEFITS. see SOCIAL SERVICES AND WELFARE

330 ZA
ZAMBIA. CENTRAL STATISTICAL OFFICE. INDUSTRY MONOGRAPHS. irreg. K.4. Central Statistical Office, P.O. Box 31908, Lusaka, Zambia.

330 020 ZA
ZAMBIA. MINISTRY OF LEGAL AFFAIRS. ANNUAL REPORT. (Text in English) a. (Ministry of Legal Affairs) Government Printer, Government Printing Department, P.O. Box 30136, Lusaka, Zambia. circ. 750.

330 US
ZEROWORK. 1975. irreg., no.3, 1983. $4.50. Social Science Division, State University of New York, Purchase, NY 10577. TEL 914-253-5000. Ed.Bd. adv. bk. rev. film rev. bibl. cum.index. circ. 3,000. (back issues avail.)

BUSINESS AND ECONOMICS —
Abstracting, Bibliographies, Statistics

330 340 016 BU ISSN 0204-6032
ABSTRACTS OF BULGARIAN SCIENTIFIC LITERATURE. ECONOMICS AND LAW. (Economics section in English; Law section in French) 1958. q. 3.44 lv. Bulgarska Akademiia na Naukite, Centur za Nauchna Informaciia - Scientific Information Centre of Bulgarian Academy of Sciences, 7 Noemvri St. 1, 1040 Sofia, Bulgaria (Dist. by: RP, Klokotnica St., No.2A, Sofia 1202, Bulgaria) Ed.Bd. bk. rev. abstr. index. circ. 460.

016 338 690 BU ISSN 0204-5265
ABSTRACTS OF BULGARIAN SCIENTIFIC LITERATURE. INDUSTRY, BUILDING AND TRANSPORT. (Editions in English and Russian) 1957. q. 3.44 lv. per no. (Bulgarska Akademiya of Naukite) Publishing House of the Bulgarian Academy of Sciences, 7 Noemvri St. 1, 1040 Sofia, Bulgaria (Dist. by: Hemus, 6 Rouski Blvd., 1000 Sofia, Bulgaria) Ed. B. Balev. abstr. circ. 230. Indexed: Chem.Abstr.

657 US ISSN 0748-7975
ACCOUNTANTS' INDEX. 1920. q. with a. cum. $160. American Institute of Certified Public Accountants, 1211 Ave. of the Americas, New York, NY 10036-8775. TEL 212-575-5515.
●Also available online. Vendors: Orbit Information Technologies.

ACCOUNTING & DATA PROCESSING ABSTRACTS. see COMPUTERS — Abstracting, Bibliographies, Statistics

330 CN ISSN 0319-4264
ALBERTA ECONOMIC ACCOUNTS. 1976. a. Bureau of Statistics, Alberta Treasury, Sir. F.W. Haultain Bldg., 7th Floor, 9811-109 St., Edmonton, Alta. T5K 0C8, Canada. TEL 403-427-3058.

330 317 US ISSN 0066-0736
AMERICAN STATISTICAL ASSOCIATION. BUSINESS AND ECONOMIC STATISTICS SECTION. PROCEEDINGS. 1954. a. $28 to non-members; members $23. American Statistical Association, 806 15th St., N.W., Suite 640, Washington, DC 20005. TEL 202-393-3253. (also avail. in microform from UMI)

650 016 UK ISSN 0261-0108
ANBAR MANAGEMENT PUBLICATIONS BIBLIOGRAPHY. 1961. a. £8.50. Anbar Publications Ltd., Box 23, Wembley HA9 8DJ, England. Ed. A.C. Ede.
Formerly: Anbar Management Services Bibliography (ISSN 0003-2808)

382 316 AO ISSN 0066-1848
ANGOLA. DIRECCAO DOS SERVICOS DE ESTATISTICA. ESTATISTICAS DO COMERCIO EXTERNO. (Text in Portuguese) 1938. irreg. Direccao dos Servicos de Estatistica, Caixa Postal 1215, Luanda, Angola. stat. circ. 750.

382 316 TG
ANNUAIRE DES STATISTIQUES DU COMMERCE EXTERIEUR DU TOGO. a., latest 1977. 4000 Fr.CFA. Direction de la Statistique, Boite Postale 118, Lome, Togo.

317 650 US ISSN 0066-4375
ANNUAL SUMMARY OF BUSINESS STATISTICS, NEW YORK STATE. 1948. a. free. Department of Commerce, One Commerce Plaza, Albany, NY 12245. Ed. William Grainger. circ. 1,500.

382 318 GT ISSN 0570-426X
ANUARIO ESTADISTICO CENTROAMERICANO DE COMERCIO EXTERIOR. 1964. a. $15. General Treaty on Central American Economic Integration, Permanent Secretariat - Tratado General de Integracion Econonica Centroamericana, 4a Avenida 10-25, Zona 14, Guatemala City, Guatemala.

330 318 VE ISSN 0066-5185
ANUARIO ESTADISTICO DE LOS ANDES; VENEZUELA.* 1966. a. Universidad de Los Andes, Instituto de Investigaciones Economicas, Via los Chorras de Milla, C.P. 5101, Merida, Venezuela.

016 331 DK ISSN 0107-9018
ARBEJDERBEVAEGELSENS BIBLIOTEK OG ARKIV/LABOUR MOVEMENT LIBRARY AND ARCHIVE, DENMARK; liste over loebende tidsskrifter og aarboeger paa A B A. (Text in Danish and English) 1976. irreg. free. Rejsbygade 1, 1759 Copenhagen V, Denmark. circ. 600.

330 DK ISSN 0107-444X
ARBEJDSFORMIDLINGSSTATISTIK FOR ERHVERVSHAEMMEDE. 1978. a. free. Arbejdsdirektoratet, Adelgade 13, 1304 Copenhagen K, Denmark.

330 317 US ISSN 0518-6242
ARIZONA STATISTICAL REVIEW. 1945. a. Valley National Bank of Arizona, Economic Planning Division, Box 29514, 241 N. Central Ave., Phoenix, AZ 85038. TEL 602-261-1492. Ed. Joanne M. Stroud. adv. stat. circ. 50,000.
Formerly: Statistical Review of Arizona.

382.6 319 AT ISSN 0705-0534
AUSTRALIA. BUREAU OF STATISTICS. AUSTRALIAN EXPORTS, COUNTRY BY COMMODITY. 1958/59. a. subscription price on application. Australian Bureau of Statistics, Box 10, Belconnen, A.C.T. 2616, Australia. circ. 1,000.
Formerly: Australia. Bureau of Statistics. Australian Exports Bulletin (ISSN 0067-186X)

338 AT
AUSTRALIA. BUREAU OF STATISTICS. AUSTRALIAN NATIONAL ACCOUNTS: GROSS PRODUCT BY INDUSTRY. a. free. Australian Bureau of Statistics, Box 10, Belconnen, A.C.T. 2616, Australia. circ. 1,500.
Former titles: Australia. Bureau of Statistics. Estimates of Gross Product by Industry at Current and Constant Prices; Australia. Bureau of Statistics. Australian National Accounts: Gross Product by Industry at Current and Constant Prices.

339.394 AT ISSN 0312-6250
AUSTRALIA. BUREAU OF STATISTICS. AUSTRALIAN NATIONAL ACCOUNTS - NATIONAL INCOME AND EXPENDITURE. a. Aus.$3.60. Australian Bureau of Statistics, Box 10, Belconnen, A.C.T. 2616, Australia. illus. stat. circ. 2,000.

336 AT ISSN 0045-0111
AUSTRALIA. BUREAU OF STATISTICS. BALANCE OF PAYMENTS, AUSTRALIA. 1957/58. a. Aus.$2,90. Australian Bureau of Statistics, Box 10, Belconnen, A.C.T. 2616, Australia. circ. 2, 000.

331.2 319 AT
AUSTRALIA. BUREAU OF STATISTICS. DISTRIBUTION AND COMPOSITION OF EMPLOYEE EARNINGS & HOURS. a. free. Australian Bureau of Statistics, Box 10, Belconnen, A.C.T. 2616, Australia. circ. 2,500.
Formerly: Australia. Bureau of Statistics. Earnings and Hours of Employment.

382 319 AT
AUSTRALIA. BUREAU OF STATISTICS. FOREIGN TRADE, AUSTRALIA, PART 1: EXPORTS AND IMPORTS. 1904. a. price on request. Australian Bureau of Statistics, Box 10, Belconnen, A.C.T. 2616, Australia. circ. 1,500.
Formerly: Australia. Bureau of Statistics. Overseas Trade, Australia, Part 1: Exports and Imports (ISSN 0705-0518)

382 AT ISSN 0705-0526
AUSTRALIA. BUREAU OF STATISTICS. FOREIGN TRADE, AUSTRALIA. PART 2: COMPARATIVE AND SUMMARY TABLES. a. price varies. Australian Bureau of Statistics, Box 10, Belconnen, A.C.T. 2616, Australia. circ. 1,500.
Formerly: Australia. Bureau of Statistics. Overseas Trade, Australia. Part 2: Comparative and Summary Tables.

319.4 AT
AUSTRALIA. BUREAU OF STATISTICS. GOVERNMENT FINANCIAL ESTIMATES, AUSTRALIA. 1974. a. Aus.$2.30. Australian Bureau of Statistics, Box 10, Belconnen, A.C.T. 2616, Australia. stat. circ. 1,500.
Formerly: Australia. Bureau of Statistics. Public Authority Finance. Public Authority Estimates.

331 319 AT
AUSTRALIA. BUREAU OF STATISTICS. LABOUR STATISTICS, AUSTRALIA. 1912. a. Aus.$7.80. Australian Bureau of Statistics, Box 10, Belconnen, A.C.T. 2616, Australia. circ. 1,500.
Continues: Australia. Bureau of Statistics. Labour Report (ISSN 0067-0812)

336 319.4 AT
AUSTRALIA. BUREAU OF STATISTICS. QUEENSLAND OFFICE. GOVERNMENT FINANCE, QUEENSLAND. a. free. Australian Bureau of Statistics, Queensland Office, 313 Adelaide St., Brisbane, Qld. 4000, Australia.
Formerly: Australia. Bureau of Statistics. Queensland Office. Public Finance: Government Authorities.

338 319 AT
AUSTRALIA. BUREAU OF STATISTICS. SOUTH AUSTRALIAN OFFICE. MANUFACTURING ESTABLISHMENTS, DETAILS OF OPERATIONS BY INDUSTRY. a. Aus.$3.10. Australian Bureau of Statistics, South Australian Office, Box 2272, G. P. O., Adelaide, S. A. 5001, Australia.
Former titles: Australia. Bureau of Statistics. South Australian Office. Manufacturing Establishments (ISSN 0310-0871); Australia. Bureau of Census and Statistics. South Australian Office. Factories (ISSN 0067-0928)

336 AT
AUSTRALIA. BUREAU OF STATISTICS. STATE AND LOCAL GOVERNMENT FINANCE, AUSTRALIA. (Text in English) 1971. a. Aus.$4.50. Australian Bureau of Statistics, Box 10, Belconnen, A.C.T. 2616, Australia. stat. circ. 1,150.
Formerly: Australia. Bureau of Statistics. Public Authority Finance. State and Local Authorities.

331.2 319 AT ISSN 0814-9593
AUSTRALIA. BUREAU OF STATISTICS. TASMANIAN OFFICE. LABOUR FORCE STATISTICS. 1969. a. free. Australian Bureau of Statistics, Tasmanian Office, Box 66A, G.P.O., Hobart, Tasmania 7001, Australia. index. circ. 560.
Formerly: Australia. Bureau of Statistics. Tasmanian Office. Labour, Wages and Prices (ISSN 0067-1045)

336 319 AT ISSN 0312-7850
AUSTRALIA. BUREAU OF STATISTICS. TASMANIAN OFFICE. LOCAL GOVERNMENT FINANCE. 1974. a. Aus.$1.90. Australian Bureau of Statistics, Tasmanian Office, Box 66A, G.P.O., Hobart, Tasmania 7001, Australia. circ. 460. (processed)
Supersedes: Australia. Bureau of Statistics. Tasmanian Office. Finance (ISSN 0067-1037)

331.88 AT ISSN 0312-1437
AUSTRALIA. BUREAU OF STATISTICS. TRADE UNION STATISTICS, AUSTRALIA. a. free. Australian Bureau of Statistics, Box 10, Belconnen, A.C.T. 2616, Australia. illus. circ. 2,000.

338.4 319 AT
AUSTRALIA. BUREAU OF STATISTICS. WESTERN AUSTRALIAN OFFICE. CENSUS OF MANUFACTURING ESTABLISHMENTS. SUMMARY OF OPERATIONS BY INDUSTRY CLASS. a. free. Australian Bureau of Statistics, Western Australian Office, 1-3 St. George's Terrace, Perth, W.A. 6000, Australia. circ. 500.
Formerly: Australia. Bureau of Statistics. Western Australian Office. Economic Censuses: Manufacturing Establishments: Summary of Operations by Industry Class.

614.85 319 AT
AUSTRALIA. BUREAU OF STATISTICS. WESTERN AUSTRALIAN OFFICE. INDUSTRIAL ACCIDENTS. 1962-63. a. free. Australian Bureau of Statistics, Western Australian Office, 1-3 St. George's Terrace, Perth, W.A. 6000, Australia. circ. 600. (processed)
Supersedes in part: Australia. Bureau of Statistics. Western Australian Office. Industrial Accidents.

336.2 319 AT ISSN 0067-1444
AUSTRALIA. DEPARTMENT OF THE TREASURY. INCOME TAX STATISTICS. Title varies: Commonwealth Income Tax Statistics. 1963-64. a. price varies. Australian Government Publishing Service, G.P.O. Box 84, Canberra, A.C.T. 2601, Australia.

330.9 319 AT
AUSTRALIA. DEPARTMENT OF THE TREASURY. ROUND-UP. irreg. Department of the Treasury, Publishing Branch, G.P.O. Box 84, Canberra, A.C.T. 2601, Australia. stat.
Formerly: Australia. Department of the Treasury. Round-Up of Economic Statistics (ISSN 0815-1881)

336.2 319 AT ISSN 0519-6035
AUSTRALIA. DEPARTMENT OF THE TREASURY. TAXATION BRANCH. TAXATION STATISTICS. 1959/60. a. Department of the Treasury, G.P.O. Box 84, Canberra, A.C.T. 2601, Australia. stat.

314.3 331.7 AU
AUSTRIA. STATISTISCHES ZENTRALAMT. ERHEBUNG DER LAND UND FORSTWIRTSCHAFTLICHEN ARBEITSKRAEFTE. irreg. Hintere Zollamtstr. 2b, 1033 Vienna, Austria.

338 314 AU
AUSTRIA. STATISTISCHES ZENTRALAMT. GEWERBESTATISTIK PART 2. (Subseries of its Beitraege zur Oesterreichischen Statistik) 1965. a. S.520. Oesterreichisches Statistisches Zentralamt, Hintere Zollamtstr. 2b, 1033 Vienna, Austria.

338 314 AU
AUSTRIA. STATISTISCHES ZENTRALAMT. INDUSTRIE UND GEWERBESTATISTIK PART 1. (Subseries of its Beitraege zur Oesterreichischen Statistik) 1954. a. S.320. Oesterreichisches Statistisches Zentralamt, Hintere Zollamtstr. 2b, 1033 Vienna, Austria.
Former titles: Austria. Statistisches Zentralamt. Industrie Statistik und Gewerb & Austria. Statistisches Zentralamt. Industrie Statistik.

338.7 314 AU ISSN 0081-5233
AUSTRIA. STATISTISCHES ZENTRALAMT. STATISTIK DER AKTIENGESELLSCHAFTEN IN OESTERREICH. 1962. a. S.230. (Oesterreichisches Statistisches Zentralamt) Oesterreichische Staatsdruckerei, Rennweg 120, 1037 Vienna, Austria.

330 BF
BAHAMAS. DEPARTMENT OF STATISTICS. ANNUAL REVIEW OF PRICES: REPORT. 1974. a. Department of Statistics, Box N 3904, Nassau, Bahamas.

318 382 BF
BAHAMAS. DEPARTMENT OF STATISTICS. EXTERNAL TRADE. a. $6. Department of Statistics, Box N 3904, Nassau, Bahamas.

331.1 339 318 BF
BAHAMAS. DEPARTMENT OF STATISTICS. HOUSEHOLD INCOME REPORT. 1973. irreg. $5. Department of Statistics, Box N 3904, Nassau, Bahamas. illus.
Incorporating (since 1975): Bahamas. Department of Statistics. Labour Force and Income Distribution.

330.0212 310 CR ISSN 0522-098X
BANCO CENTRAL DE COSTA RICA. ESTADISTICAS ECONOMICAS. 1971. a. free. Banco Central de Costa Rica, Departamento de Investigaciones y Estadistica, Apdo. 10058, San Jose, Costa Rica. charts. circ. 300.

BANCO CENTRAL DE HONDURAS. SECCION DE SEGUROS. BOLETIN DE ESTADISTICAS DE SEGUROS. see INSURANCE — Abstracting, Bibliographies, Statistics

330.9 318 VE ISSN 0522-1153
BANCO CENTRAL DE VENEZUELA. SECCION A.L.A.L.C. ALGUNAS ESTADISTICAS DE LOS PAISES DE A.L.A.L.C. 1966. irreg. Banco Central de Venezuela, Seccion Asociacion Latinoamericana de Libre Comercio, Departamento de Investigaciones Economicas, Caracas, Venezuela.

BUSINESS AND ECONOMICS — ABSTRACTING, BIBLIOGRAPHIES, STATISTICS

332.1 330   EC
BANCO CENTRAL DEL ECUADOR. BALANZA DE PAGOS. (Text in English and Spanish) a. free. Banco Central del Ecuador, Av. 10 de Agosto (Plaza Bolivar), La Alameda, Quito, Ecuador. circ. 15,000.

330 382 336 310   BG
BANGLADESH BANK. STATISTICS DEPARTMENT. ANNUAL BALANCE OF PAYMENTS. (Text in English) 1974/75. a. Bangladesh Bank, Department of Public Relations and Publications, Motijheel Commercial Area, Dacca 2, Bangladesh. stat.

382 316   BG
BANGLADESH BANK. STATISTICS DEPARTMENT. ANNUAL IMPORT PAYMENTS. (Text in English) 1973/74. a. Bangladesh Bank, Department of Public Relations and Publications, Motijheel Commercial Area, Dacca 2, Bangladesh. stat.

332.1   IS   ISSN 0334-4541
BANK OF ISRAEL. ANNUAL STATISTICS OF ISRAEL'S BANKING SYSTEM. 1978. a. $15. Bank of Israel, Kiryat Ben Gurion, Box 780, Jerusalem, Israel.

330 315   JA   ISSN 0070-8666
BANK OF JAPAN. ECONOMIC STATISTICS ANNUAL. Title varies: Economic Statistics of Japan. (Text and title in English and Japanese) a. price varies. Bank of Japan, Research and Statistics Department - Nippon Ginko, 2-2-1 Hongoku-Cho, Nihonbashi, Chuo-ku, Toyko 103, Japan (Order from: Japan Publications Trading Co., Ltd., Box 5030, Tokyo International, Tokyo, Japan; or 1255 Howard St., San Francisco, CA 94103)

382 316   SJ   ISSN 0522-246X
BANK OF SUDAN. FOREIGN TRADE STATISTICAL DIGEST. (Text in English) 1968. a. Bank of Sudan, Statistics Department, Box 313, Khartoum, Sudan.

319   BB   ISSN 0067-4125
BARBADOS. STATISTICAL SERVICE. OVERSEAS TRADE REPORT. 1957. a. Statistical Service, National Insurance Building, 3rd Fl., Fairchild St., Bridgetown, Barbados, W. Indies.

011   US
BARRON'S INDEX. irreg. University Microfilms International, 300 N. Zeeb Rd., Ann Arbor, MI 48106. TEL 313-761-4700.

016.331   BE
BELGIUM. OFFICE NATIONAL DE L'EMPLOI. LISTE DES INFORMATIONS STATISTIQUES ET DES PUBLICATIONS DE L'O N E M. (Subseries of: Belgium. Office National de l'Emploi. Collection "Notes Documentaires") irreg. Office National de l'Emploi, Bd. de l'Empereur 7, 1000 Brussels, Belgium.

540 016   BL   ISSN 0100-0756
BIBLIOGRAFIA BRASILEIRA DE QUIMICA E QUIMICA TECNOLOGICA. 1972. irreg. Cr.$600($25) Instituto Brasileiro de Informacao em Ciencia e Tecnologia, SCRN 708/709 Bloco B Loja 18E 30, 70740 Brasilia DF, Brazil. bk. rev.
Supersedes: Bibliografia Brasileira de Quimica (ISSN 0067-6683) & Bibliografia Brasileira de Quimica Tecnologia (ISSN 0405-721X)

330 015   MX
BIBLIOGRAFIA ECONOMICA DE MEXICO. LIBROS. 1955. irreg., latest 1981-1983. free. Banco de Mexico, Direccion de Investigacion Economica, Apdo. 98 bis, Mexico 1, D.F., Mexico. bibl.
Formerly (until 1981): Bibliografia Economica de Mexico (ISSN 0006-100X)

016   US   ISSN 0749-1786
BIBLIOGRAPHIES AND INDEXES IN ECONOMICS AND ECONOMIC HISTORY. 1984. irreg. price varies. Greenwood Press, 88 Post Rd. W., Box 5007, Westport, CT 06881. TEL 203-226-3571.

330 016.3309   TZ
BIBLIOGRAPHY OF ECONOMIC AND STATISTICAL PUBLICATIONS ON TANZANIA. 1967. irreg. Bureau of Statistics, Box 796, Dar es Salaam, Tanzania.

330 315   II
BIBLIOGRAPHY OF PUBLICATIONS FROM ECONOMIC RESEARCH CENTRES IN INDIA. (Supplements issued annually) 1973. irreg., latest edition, 1974. Rs.85($13.20) Information Research Academy, 37 Amir Ali Ave., Calcutta 700019, India. Ed. Partha Subir Guha. adv. circ. 1,700.

310 382   BO
BOLIVIA. INSTITUTO NACIONAL DE ESTADISTICA. ANUARIO DE COMERCIO EXTERIOR. 1910. a. $17. Instituto Nacional de Estadistica, Casilla de Correo No. 6129, La Paz, Bolivia.

310 338   BO
BOLIVIA. INSTITUTO NACIONAL DE ESTADISTICA. ANUARIO DE ESTADISTICAS INDUSTRIALES. 1939. a. $15. Instituto Nacional de Estadistica, Casilla de Correo No. 6129, La Paz, Bolivia.

339 318   BO
BOLIVIA. INSTITUTO NACIONAL DE ESTADISTICA. INDICE DE PRECIOS AL CONSUMIDOR. (Monthly edition avail.) 1974. a. $43. Instituto Nacional de Estadistica, Casilla de Correo No. 6129, La Paz, Bolivia.

332.6   LU
BOND MARKET IN LUXEMBURG FRANCS AND IN ECU. (Text in English, French) 1984. a. free. Societe de la Bourse de Luxembourg, B.P. Box 165, 11 Avenue de la Porte Neuve, 2011 Luxembourg, Luxembourg. circ. 2,500.
Formed by the merger of: Marche des Emprunts Internationaux en Ecu & Marche National des Emprunts Obligataires.

331.1 316   BS
BOTSWANA. CENTRAL STATISTICS OFFICE. EMPLOYMENT SURVEY. (Text in English) a. R.2. Central Statistics Office, Ministry of Finance and Development Planning, Private Bag 0024, Gaborone, Botswana (Orders to: Government Printer, Box 87, Gaborone, Botswana)

338 318   BL
BRAZIL. COMISSAO DE FINANCIAMENTO DA PRODUCAO. ANUARIO ESTATISTICO. 1973. a. free. Comissao de Financiamento da Producao, Avda. W-3 Norte Quadra 514, Bloco "B" Lote 7, 70000 Brasilia, D.F., Brazil.

338.9 314   UK   ISSN 0068-1210
BRITISH AID STATISTICS; STATISTICS OF U.K. ECONOMIC AID TO DEVELOPING COUNTRIES. 1966. a. £5.75. Overseas Development Administration, Library, Abercrombie House, Eaglesham Rd., East Kilbride, Glasgow G75 8EA, Scotland.

319   VB
BRITISH VIRGIN ISLANDS. STATISTICS OFFICE. BALANCE OF PAYMENTS. irreg. Statistics Office, Finance Department, Road Town, Tortola, British Virgin Islands.

319   VB
BRITISH VIRGIN ISLANDS. STATISTICS OFFICE. NATIONAL INCOME AND EXPENDITURE. irreg. $3.50. Statistics Office, Finance Department, Road Town, Tortola, British Virgin Islands.

BUILDING SOCIETY FACTBOOK (YEAR) see *REAL ESTATE*

330.9 316   UV
BURKINA FASO. INSTITUT NATIONAL DE LA STATISTIQUE ET DE LA DEMOGRAPHIE. BULLETIN ANNUAIRE D'INFORMATION STATISTIQUE ET ECONOMIQUE. no.16, 1975. a. Institut National de la Statistique et de la Demographie, Ouagadougou, Burkina Faso.
Formerly: Upper Volta. Institut National de la Statistique et de la Demographie. Bulletin Annuaire d'Information Statistique et Economique; Supersedes: Upper Volta. Direction de la Statistique et de la Mecanographie. Bulletin Mensuel d'Information Statistique et Economique; Upper Volta. Directions de la Statistique et de la Mecanographie. Bulletin Annuaire Statistique et Economiques.

650 016 330   US   ISSN 0007-6961
BUSINESS PERIODICALS INDEX; a cumulative subject index to English language periodicals in the fields of accounting, advertising and public relations, automation, banking, communications, economics, finance and investments, insurance, labor, management, etc. 1958. m. (plus q. and a. cum.) service basis. H. W. Wilson Co., 950 University Ave., Bronx, NY 10452. TEL 212-588-8400. Ed. Bettie Jane Third. cum.index. (avail. on CD-ROM)
●Also available online. Vendors: Wilsonline.
Formerly: Industrial Arts Index.

316.7   CM
CAMEROUN. DIRECTION DE LA STATISTIQUE ET DE LA COMPTABILITE NATIONALE. NOTE ANNUELLE DE STATISTIQUE. 1974. a. 4000 Fr.CFA. Direction de la Statistique et de la Comptabilite Nationale - Department of Statistics and National Accounts, Boite Postale 660, Yaounde, Cameroon. stat.

338 317   CN   ISSN 0317-7882
CANADA. STATISTICS CANADA. AGGREGATE PRODUCTIVITY MEASURES/MESURES GLOBALES DE PRODUCTIVITE. (Catalogue 14-201) (Text in English and French) 1946. a. Can.$15($16) Statistics Canada, Communications Division, 3rd Floor, R.H. Coats Bldg., Ottawa, Ont. K1A 0T6, Canada TEL 613-993-7276. (Subscr. to: Publications Sales and Services, Ottawa, Ont. K1A 0T6, Canada) (also avail. in microform from MML)
Former titles: Canada. Statistics Canada. Aggregate Productivity Trends/Tendances de la Productivite des Agregats (ISSN 0068-7073); Indexes of Output per Person Employed and per Man-Hour in Canada, Commercial Industries (ISSN 0073-6082)

236 317   CN   ISSN 0575-8254
CANADA. STATISTICS CANADA. CONSOLIDATED GOVERNMENT FINANCE: FISCAL YEAR ENDED NEAREST TO DECEMBER 31/FINANCES PUBLIQUES CONSOLIDEES: ANNEE FINANCIERE TERMINEE LE PLUS PRES DE 31 DECEMBRE. (Catalogue 68-202) (Text in English and French) 1954. a. Can.$20($21) Statistics Canada, Communications Division, 3rd Floor, R.H. Coats Bldg., Ottawa, Ont. K1A 0T6, Canada TEL 613-993-7276. (Subscr. to: Publications Sales and Services, Ottawa, Ont. K1A 0T6, Canada) (also avail. in microform from MML)

332   CN   ISSN 0575-8262
CANADA. STATISTICS CANADA. CORPORATION FINANCIAL STATISTICS. (Catalogue 61-207) (Text in English and French) 1965. a. Can.$50($51.50) Statistics Canada, Communications Division, 3rd Floor, R.H. Coats Bldg., Ottawa, Ont. K1A 0T6, Canada TEL 613-993-7276. (Subscr. to: Publications Sales and Services, Ottawa, Ont. K1A 0T6, Canada)

336   CN   ISSN 0576-0119
CANADA. STATISTICS CANADA. CORPORATION TAXATION STATISTICS. (Catalogue 61-208) (Text in English and French) 1965. a. Can.$60($61.50) Statistics Canada, Communications Division, 3rd Floor, R.H. Coats Bldg., Ottawa, Ont. K1A 0T6, Canada TEL 613-993-7276. (Subscr. to: Publications Sales and Services, Ottawa, Ont. K1A 0T6, Canada)

332   CN   ISSN 0576-0100
CANADA. STATISTICS CANADA. CREDIT UNIONS. (Catalogue 61-209) (Text in English and French) 1966. a. Can.$50($51.50) Statistics Canada, Communications Division, 3rd Floor, R.H. Coats Bldg., Ottawa, Ont. K1A 0T6, Canada TEL 613-993-7276. (Subscr. to: Publications Sales and Services, Ottawa, Ont. K1A 0T6, Canada)

658.8 317   CN   ISSN 0590-5702
CANADA. STATISTICS CANADA. DIRECT SELLING IN CANADA/VENTE DIRECTE AU CANADA. (Catologue 63-218) (Text in English and French) 1966. a. Can.$15($16) Statistics Canada, Communications Division, 3rd Flood, R.H. Coats Bldg., Ottawa, Ont. K1A 0T6, Canada TEL 613-993-7276. (Subscr. to: Publications Sales and Services, Ottawa, Ont. K1A 0T6, Canada) (also avail. in microform from MML)

382 CN ISSN 0317-5375
CANADA. STATISTICS CANADA. EXPORTS-MERCHANDISE TRADE/EXPORTATIONS-COMMERCE DE MERCHANDISES. (Catalogue 65-202) (Text in English and French) 1939. a. Can.$150($169.50) Statistics Canada, Communications Division, 3rd Floor, R.H. Coats Bldg., Ottawa, Ont. K1A 0T6, Canada TEL 613-993-7276. (Subscr. to: Publications Sales and Services, Ottawa, Ont. K1A 0T6, Canada) (also avail. in microform from MML)

312 CN ISSN 0703-7368
CANADA. STATISTICS CANADA. FAMILY INCOMES (CENSUS FAMILIES) /REVENUS DES FAMILLE (FAMILLES DE RECENSEMENT) (Catalogue 13-208) (Text in English and French) 1971. a. Can.$12($13) Statistics Canada, Communications Division, 3rd Floor, R.H. Coats Bldg., Ottawa, Ont. K1A 0T6, Canada TEL 613-993-7276. (Subscr. to: Publications Sales and Services, Ottawa, Ont. K1A 0T6, Canada) (also avail. in microform from MML)

CANADA. STATISTICS CANADA. FEDERAL GOVERNMENT EMPLOYMENT IN METROPOLITAN AREAS/EMPLOI DANS L'ADMINISTRATION FEDERALE REGIONS METROPOLITAINES. see *PUBLIC ADMINISTRATION — Abstracting, Bibliographies, Statistics*

336 317 CN ISSN 0575-8521
CANADA. STATISTICS CANADA. FEDERAL GOVERNMENT FINANCE: REVENUE AND EXPENDITURE, ASSETS AND LIABILITIES/FINANCES PUBLIQUES FEDERALES: RECETTES AND DEPENSES, ACTIF ET PASSIF. (Catalogue 68-211) (Text in English and French) 1953. a. Can.$20($21) Statistics Canada, Communications Division, 3rd Floor, R.H. Coats Bldg., Ottawa, Ont. K1A 0T6, Canada TEL 613-993-7276. (Subscr. to: Publications Sales and Services, Ottawa, Ont. K1A 0T6, Canada) (also avail. in microform from MML)

331.11 317 CN ISSN 0703-2684
CANADA. STATISTICS CANADA. HISTORICAL LABOUR FORCE STATISTICS, ACTUAL DATA, SEASONAL FACTORS, SEASONALLY ADJUSTED DATA/STATISTIQUES CHRONOLOGIQUES SUR LA POPULATION ACTIVE, CHIFFRES REELS, FACTEURS SAISONNIERS ET DONNEES DESAISONNALISEES. (Catalogue 71-201) (Text in English and French) 1953. a. Can.$50($60) Statistics Canada, Communications Division, 3rd Floor, R.H. Coats Bldg., Ottawa, Ont. K1A 0T6, Canada TEL 613-993-7276. (Subscr. to: Publications Sales and Services, Ottawa, Ont. K1A 0T6, Canada) (also avail. in microform from MML)

382 CN ISSN 0380-1349
CANADA. STATISTICS CANADA. IMPORTS-MERCHANDISE TRADE/IMPORTATIONS-COMMERCE DE MARCHANDISES. (Catalogue 65-203) (Text in English and French) 1939. a. Can.$150($169.50) Statistics Canada, Communications Division, 3rd Floor, R.H. Coats Bldg., Ottawa, Ont. K1A 0T6, Canada TEL 613-993-7276. (Subscr. to: Publications Sales and Services, Ottawa, Ont. K1A 0T6, Canada) (also avail. in microform from MML)

338 317 CN ISSN 0382-4012
CANADA. STATISTICS CANADA. MANUFACTURING INDUSTRIES OF CANADA: SUB-PROVINCIAL AREAS/INDUSTRIES MANUFACTURES DU CANADA: NIVEAU INFRAPROVINCIAL/INDUSTRIES MANUFACTURIERES DU CANADA: NIVEAU INFRAPROVINCIAL. (Catalog 31-209) (Text in English and French) 1946. a. Can.$70($80) Statistics Canada, Communications Division, 3rd Floor, R.H. Coats Bldg., Ottawa, Ont. K1A 0T6, Canada TEL 613-993-7276. (Subscr. to: Publications Sales and Services, Ottawa, Ont. K1A 0T6, Canada) (also avail. in microform from MML)

658 CN ISSN 0590-9325
CANADA. STATISTICS CANADA. MARKET RESEARCH HANDBOOK. (Catalogue 63-224) (Text in English and French) 1975. a. Statistics Canada, Communications Division, 3rd Floor, R.H. Coats Bldg., Ottawa, Ont. K1A 0T6, Canada TEL 613-993-7276. (Subscr. to: Publications Sales and Services, Ottawa, Ont. K1A 0T6, Canada) (also avail. in microform from MML)

338 CN ISSN 0575-9021
CANADA. STATISTICS CANADA. MISCELLANEOUS MANUFACTURING INDUSTRIES/INDUSTRIES MANUFACTURIERES DIVERSES. (Catalogue 47-205) (Text in English and French) 1930. a. Can.$20($21) Statistics Canada, Communications Division, 3rd Floor, R.H. Coats Bldg., Ottawa, Ont. K1A 0T6, Canada TEL 613-993-7276. (Subscr. to: Publications Sales and Services, Ottawa, Ont. K1A 0T6, Canada) (also avail. in microform from MML)

339 317 CN ISSN 0823-065X
CANADA. STATISTICS CANADA. PRIVATE AND PUBLIC INVESTMENT IN CANADA. INTENTIONS/INVESTISSEMENTS PRIVES ET PUBLICS AU CANADA. PERSPECTIVES. (Catalogue 61-205) (Text in English and French) 1968. a. Can.$25($26) Statistics Canada, Communications Division, 3rd Floor, R.H. Coats Bldg., Ottawa, Ont. K1A 0T6, Canada TEL 613-993-7276. (Subscr. to: Publications Sales and Services, Ottawa, Ont. K1A 0T6, Canada) (also avail. in microform from MML)
Formerly: Canada. Statistics Canada. Private and Public Investment in Canada. Outlook/Investissements Prives et Publics au Canada. Perspectives (ISSN 0318-2274)

339 317 CN ISSN 0823-0668
CANADA. STATISTICS CANADA. PRIVATE AND PUBLIC INVESTMENT IN CANADA. REVISED INTENTIONS/INVESTISSEMENTS PRIVES ET PUBLICS AU CANADA. PERSPECTIVE REVISEE. (Catalogue 61-206) (Text in English and French) 1968. a. Can.$25($26) Statistics Canada, Communications Division, 3rd Floor, R.H. Coats Bldg., Ottawa, Ont. K1A 0T6, Canada TEL 613-993-7276. (Subscr. to: Publications Sales and Services, Ottawa, Ont. K1A 0T6, Canada) (also avail. in microform from MML)
Formerly: Canada. Statistics Canada. Private and Public Investment in Canada, Mid-Year Review/Investissements Prives et Publics au Canada. Revue de la Mi-Annee (ISSN 0707-9559)

338.4 317 CN ISSN 0575-9455
CANADA. STATISTICS CANADA. PRODUCTS SHIPPED BY CANADIAN MANUFACTURERS/PRODUITS LIVRES PAR LES FABRICANTS CANADIENS. (Catalogue 31-211) (Text in English and French) 1961. a. Can.$40($41.50) Statistics Canada, Communications Division, 3rd Floor, R.H. Coats Bldg., Ottawa, Ont. K1A 0T6, Canada TEL 613-993-7276. (Subscr. to: Publications Sales and Services, Ottawa, Ont. K1A 0T6, Canada) (also avail. in microform from MML)

336 CN ISSN 0575-9463
CANADA. STATISTICS CANADA. PROVINCIAL GOVERNMENT ENTERPRISE FINANCE: INCOME AND EXPENDITURE, ASSETS, LIABILITIES AND NET WORTH/REVENUS ET DEPENSES, ACTIF, PASSIF ET VALEUR NETTE. (Catalogue 61-204) (Text in English and French) 1958. a. Can.$25($26.50) Statistics Canada, Communications Division, 3rd Floor, R.H. Coats Bldg., Ottawa, Ont. K1A 0T6, Canada TEL 613-993-7276. (Subscr. to: Publications Sales and Services, Ottawa, Ont. K1A 0T6, Canada) (also avail. in microform from MML)

336 317 CN ISSN 0710-1023
CANADA. STATISTICS CANADA. PROVINCIAL GOVERNMENT FINANCE: ASSETS, LIABILITIES, SOURCE AND APPLICATION OF FUNDS. (Catalogue 68-209) (Text in English and French) 1950. a. Can.$25($26) Statistics Canada, Communications Division, 3rd Floor, R.H. Coats Bldg., Ottawa, Ont. K1A 0T6, Canada TEL 613-993-7276. (Subscr. to: Publications Sales and Services, Ottawa, Ont. K1A 0T6, Canada) (also avail. in microform from MML)
Formerly: Canada. Statistics Canada. Provincial Government Finance: Assets, Liabilities, Sources and Uses of Funds (ISSN 0318-8876)

658.8 317 CN ISSN 0227-017X
CANADA. STATISTICS CANADA. RETAIL CHAIN AND DEPARTMENT STORES. (Catalogue 63-210) (Text in English and French) 1933. a. Can.$25($26) Statistics Canada, Communications Division, 3rd Floor, R.H. Coats Bldg., Ottawa, Ont. K1A 0T6, Canada TEL 613-993-7276. (Subscr. to: Publications Sales and Services, Ottawa, Ont. K1A 0T6, Canada) (also avail. in microform from MML)
Formerly: Canada. Statistics Canada. Retail Chain Stores/Magasins de Detail a Succursales (ISSN 0380-7878)

332.6 317 CN
CANADA. STATISTICS CANADA. SYSTEM OF NATIONAL ACCOUNTS, CANADA'S INTERNATIONAL INVESTMENT POSITION/SYSTEME DE COMPTABILITE NATIONALE BILAN CANADIEN DES INVESTISSEMENTS INTERNATIONAUX. (Catalogue 67-202) (Text in English and French) 1926. a. Can.$35($36.50) Statistics Canada, Communications Division, 3rd Floor, R.H. Coats Bldg., Ottawa, Ont. K1A 0T6, Canada TEL 613-593-7276. (Subscr. to: Publications Sales and Services, Ottawa, Ont. K1A 0T6, Canada) (also avail. in microform from MML)
Formerly: Canada's International Investment Position/Bilan Canadien des Investissements Internationaux (ISSN 0318-8868)

331 317 CN ISSN 0575-9978
CANADA. STATISTICS CANADA. TRUSTEED PENSION PLANS-FINANCIAL STATISTICS/REGIMES DE PENSIONS EN FIDUCIE STATISTIQUE FINANCIERE. (Catalogue 74-201) (Text in English and French) 1957. a. Can.$35($36) Statistics Canada, Communications Division, 3rd Floor, R.H. Coats Bldg., Ottawa, Ont. K1A 0T6, Canada TEL 613-993-7276. (Subscr. to: Publications Sales and Services, Ottawa, Ont. K1A 0T6, Canada) (also avail. in microform from MML)

658.8 317 CN ISSN 0527-6411
CANADA. STATISTICS CANADA. VENDING MACHINE OPERATORS/EXPLOITANTS DE DISTRIBUTEURS AUTOMATIQUES. (Catalogue 63-213) (Text in English and French) 1958. a. Can.$15($16) Statistics Canada, Communications Division, 3rd Floor, R.H. Coats Bldg., Ottawa, Ont. K1A 0T6, Canada TEL 613-993-7276. (Subscr. to: Publications Sales and Services, Ottawa, Ont. K1A 0T6, Canada) (also avail. in microform from MML)

016 338 CN ISSN 0227-8669
CANADIAN BUSINESS INDEX. 1975. m. Can.$850. Micromedia Ltd., 158 Pearl St., Toronto, Ont. M5H 1L3, Canada. TEL 416-593-5211. Ed. Virve Wiland. index.
●Also available online. Vendors: CISTI, DIALOG, IST-INFORMATHEQUE, QL Systems Ltd.
Formerly: Canadian Business Periodicals Index (ISSN 0318-6717)

310 330 UK ISSN 0263-2985
CAPITAL EXPENDITURE AND DEBT FINANCING STATISTICS. 1946. a. £18. Chartered Institute of Public Finance and Accountancy, 3 Robert St., London WC2N 6BH, England. stat. (back issues avail.)
Formerly: Return of Outstanding Debt (ISSN 0143-103X)
Analysis of local authority debt in England and Wales and Scotland

CASES IN PUBLIC POLICY AND MANAGEMENT; an annotated bibliography. see *PUBLIC ADMINISTRATION — Abstracting, Bibliographies, Statistics*

338 316 ZA ISSN 0069-1429
CENSUS OF INDUSTRIAL PRODUCTION IN ZAMBIA. 1962. a., latest 1980. K.3. Central Statistical Office, P.O. Box 31908, Lusaka, Zambia.

310 FJ
CENSUS OF PRIVATE NON-PROFIT MAKING INSTITUTIONS IN FIJI. A REPORT. irreg., latest 1981. $1 per no. Bureau of Statistics, Box 2221, Suva, Fiji.

381 CY
CENSUS OF WHOLESALE AND RETAIL TRADE. (Text in English) 1981. irreg. £C2.00. Ministry of Finance, Department of Statistics and Research, Nicosia, Cyprus.
Formerly: Census of Distribution.

BUSINESS AND ECONOMICS — ABSTRACTING, BIBLIOGRAPHIES, STATISTICS

319　　　　　　BB　ISSN 0255-8432
CENTRAL BANK OF BARBADOS. BALANCE OF PAYMENTS. Variant title: Balance of Payments of Barbados. (Formerly issued by Barbados Statistical Service) 1976. a. Central Bank of Barbados, Research Department, P.O. Box 1016, Treasury Building, Bridgetown, Barbados, W.I. circ. 500.

332　　　　　　IE　ISSN 0332-2696
CENTRAL BANK OF IRELAND. IRISH ECONOMIC STATISTICS. 1973. a. free. Central Bank of Ireland, P.O. Box 559, Dame Street, Dublin 2, Ireland. TEL 716666. stat. circ. 8,200.

338　310　　　　FR
CENTRE D'ENQUETES STATISTIQUES DE CAEN. ENQUETE ANNUELLE D'ENTREPRISE: INDUSTRIES DIVERSES. a. (Ministere du Travail) Documentation France, 29-31 Quai Voltaire, 75340 Paris 07, France. illus.

332　310　　　　UK　ISSN 0263-2276
CHARTERED INSTITUTE OF PUBLIC FINANCE AND ACCOUNTANCY. FINANCIAL GENERAL & RATING STATISTICS. 1978. a. £18. Chartered Institute of Public Finance and Accountancy, 3 Robert St., London WC2N 6BH, England. (back issues avail.)
　Formerly: Chartered Institute of Public Finance and Accountancy. Return of Rates.

336.2　310　　　　UK　ISSN 0260-5546
CHARTERED INSTITUTE OF PUBLIC FINANCE AND ACCOUNTANCY. RATE COLLECTION STATISTICS. ACTUALS. 1935. a. £18. Chartered Institute of Public Finance and Accountancy, 3 Robert St., London WC2N 6BH, England. (back issues avail.)

382　318　　　　CL
CHILE. INSTITUTO NACIONAL DE ESTADISTICAS. COMERCIO EXTERIOR. 1915. a. $9. Instituto Nacional de Estadisticas, Av. Bulnes 418, Casilla 498, Correo 3-Santiago, Chile.

339　318　　　　CL
CHILE. INSTITUTO NACIONAL DE ESTADISTICAS. INDICE DE PRECIOS AL CONSUMIDOR. 1928. m. $5. Instituto Nacional de Estadisticas, Av. Bulnes 418, Casilla 498, Correo 3-Santiago, Chile.

332　336　318　　　CK
COLOMBIA. DEPARTAMENTO ADMINISTRATIVO NACIONAL DE ESTADISTICA. ANUARIO DE ESTADISTICAS FISCALES Y FINANCIERAS. 1960. a. $5. Departamento Administrativo Nacional de Estadistica, Banco Nacional de Datos, Avenida Eldorado, Centro Administrativo Nacional, Apdo. Aereo 80043, Bogota, Colombia. Ed. Dr. Saul Ojeda Gomez. adv. bk. rev.

382　314　　　　GR
COMMERCE EXTERIEUR DE LA GRECE. (Text in French and Greek) a. $30. National Statistical Service, Publications and Information Division, 14-16 Lycourgou St., 10166 Athens, Greece.
　Formerly (until 1965): Foreign Trade of Greece (ISSN 0071-738X)

317　　　　　　GT　ISSN 0588-912X
COMPENDIO ESTADISTICO CENTROAMERICANO. 1957. a. $14. General Treaty on Central American Economic Integration, Permanent Secretariat - Tratado General de Integracion Economica Centroamericana, 4a Avenida 10-25, Zona 14, Guatemala City, Guatemala.

330　　　　　　GP
COMPTES ECONOMIQUES DE LA GUADELOUPE. 1968. a. 5 F. Institut National de la Statistique et des Etudes Economiques, B.P.96, 97102 Basse Terre, Guadeloupe. stat. circ. 530.

330　318　　　　MQ
COMPTES ECONOMIQUES DE LA MARTINIQUE. 1968. irreg., latest, 1973. 5 F. Institut National de la Statistique et des Etudes Economiques, 18, Bd A. Pinard, Route de Schoelcher, B.P.605, 97261 Fort de France Cedex, Martinique. adv. stat. circ. 600.

330　316　　　　FR
COMPTES ECONOMIQUES DU TERRITOIRE FRANCAIS DES AFARS ET DES ISSAS. irreg. 5 F. Institut National de la Statistique et des Etudes Economiques, 18 bd A. Pinard, 75675 Paris 14, France. stat. circ. 600.

381　　　　　　RW
COMPTES ECONOMIQUES NATIONAUX DU RWANDA. 1976. a. 500 F. Direction Generale de la Statistique, B.P. 46, Kigali, Rwanda.

339　314　　　　BE　ISSN 0069-8075
COMPTES NATIONAUX DE LA BELGIQUE. (Text in Dutch and French) a. Institut National de Statistique, 44 rue de Louvain, 1000 Brussels, Belgium.

330　016　　　　UK　ISSN 0045-8368
CONTENTS OF RECENT ECONOMICS JOURNALS. Short title: C O R E J. 1971. 50/yr. £62.50. H.M.S.O., Department of Trade and Industry, 1 Victoria St., London SW1H 0ET, England. Ed. P.C. McShane. circ. 1,000. (reprint service avail. from UMI)

650　016　　　　UK　ISSN 0306-3224
CONTENTS PAGES IN MANAGEMENT. 1972. fortn. £70. Manchester Business School, Booth St. West, Manchester M15 6PB, England. Ed. D. Ross. author index, cum.index. circ. 250.
　Formerly: Current Contents in Management.

318　331.11　　　CR
COSTA RICA. DIRECCION GENERAL DE ESTADISTICA Y CENSOS. ENCUESTA DE HOGARES, EMPLEO Y DESEMPLEO: AREA METROPOLITANA DE SAN JOSE. 1976. irreg., latest 1984. Direccion General de Estadistica y Censos, Apartado 10163, San Jose, Costa Rica.

330.9　310　　　CU
CUBA EN CIFRAS. a. Comite Estatal de Estadisticas, Centro de Informacion Cientifico-Tecnica, Gaveta Postal 6016, Havana, Cuba. charts. stat.

011　　　　　　UK
CURRENT ASIAN & AUSTRALASIAN DIRECTORIES; a guide to directories published in or relating to all countries in Asia, Australasia & Oceania. 1978. irreg. £27($85) C.B.D. Research Ltd., 15 Wickham Rd., Beckenham, Kent BR3 2JS, England. Ed. I.G. Anderson.

016　　　　　　UK　ISSN 0070-1858
CURRENT BRITISH DIRECTORIES. 1953. irreg., latest no.10, 1985. £60($110) ‡ C.B.D. Research Ltd., 15 Wickham Rd., Beckenham, Kent BR3 2JS, England (Dist. in U.S. by: Gale Research Co., Penobscot Bldg., Detroit, MI 48226) Ed. C.A.P. Henderson. adv. index. circ. 4,000.

011　　　　　　UK　ISSN 0070-1955
CURRENT EUROPEAN DIRECTORIES. 1969. irreg., 2nd, 1981. £45($140) ‡ C.B.D. Research Ltd., 15 Wickham Rd., Beckenham, Kent BR3 2JS, England (Dist. in U.S. by: Gale Research Co., Penobscot Bldg., Detroit, MI 48226) Ed. G.P. Henderson. adv. index. circ. 2,000.

331.1　　　　　US　ISSN 0091-9209
CURRENT GOVERNMENTS REPORTS: CITY EMPLOYMENT. (Series GE-2) 1948. a. price varies. U.S. Bureau of the Census, Customer Services, Washington, DC 20233 TEL 301-763-4100. (Subscr. to: Supt. of Documents, Washington, DC 20402) Ed. Alan V. Stevens. (also avail. in microfiche) Key Title: City Employment.

336.73　317　　　US　ISSN 0090-5895
CURRENT GOVERNMENTS REPORTS: STATE GOVERNMENT FINANCES. (Series GF-3) a. price varies. U.S. Bureau of the Census, Customer Services, Washington, DC 20233 TEL 301-763-4100. (Subscr. to: Supt. of Documents, Washington, DC 20402) Ed. Vance Kane. (also avail. in microfiche) Key Title: State Government Finances.
　Continues: U.S. Bureau of the Census. State Finances.

310　　　　　　CY
CYPRUS. DEPARTMENT OF STATISTICS AND RESEARCH. CENSUS OF INDUSTRIAL PRODUCTION. (Text in English) 1954. quinquennial. £C3. Ministry of Finance, Department of Statistics and Research, Nicosia, Cyprus.

330　314　　　　CY　ISSN 0070-2412
CYPRUS. DEPARTMENT OF STATISTICS AND RESEARCH. ECONOMIC REPORT. (Title varies, 1955-62, Economic Review) (Text in English) 1954. a. £C3. Department of Statistics and Research, Ministry of Finance, Nicosia, Cyprus.

310　　　　　　CY
CYPRUS. DEPARTMENT OF STATISTICS AND RESEARCH. HOUSEHOLD EXPENDITURE SURVEY. (Text in English) 1971. quinquennial. cyprus pounds 6. Ministry of Finance, Department of Statistics and Research, Nicosia, Cyprus.

382　314　　　　DK　ISSN 0070-2781
DANMARKS VAREINDFOERSEL OG-UDFOERSEL/EXTERNAL TRADE OF DENMARK. (Text in Danish; notes in English) 1883. a. Kr.206.56. Danmarks Statistik, Sejroegade 11, 2100 Copenhagen OE, Denmark.

331.11　314　　　DK　ISSN 0070-346X
DENMARK. DANMARKS STATISTIK. ARBEJDSLOESHEDEN/UNEMPLOYMENT. (Text in Danish; notes in English) 1910-1985, ceased. a. Kr.33.61. Danmarks Statistik, Sejroegade 11, 2100 Copenhagen OE, Denmark.

336.2　314　　　DK　ISSN 0107-105X
DENMARK. DANMARKS STATISTIK. INDKOMSTER OG FORMUER /INCOME AND PROPERTY ASSESSMENTS. (Text in Danish; notes in English) 1975. a. Kr.90.16. Danmarks Statistik, Sejroegade 11, 2100 Copenhagen OE, Denmark.
　Supersedes: Denmark. Danmarks Statistik. Indkomster og Formuer Ved Slutligningen; Denmark. Danmarks Statistik. Indkomstansaettelser til Staten (ISSN 0070-3524)

338　314　　　　DK　ISSN 0070-3532
DENMARK. DANMARKS STATISTIK. INDUSTRISTATISTIK/INDUSTRIAL STATISTICS. (Text in Danish; notes in English) 1905. a. Kr.43.44. Danmarks Statistik, Sejroegade 11, 2100 Copenhagen OE, Denmark.

331　　　　　　DK　ISSN 0107-8771
DENMARK. DANMARKS STATISTIK. LOEN- OG INDKOMSTATISTIK. 1982. irreg., (4-6/yr.) Kr.96.72. Danmarks Statistik, Sejroegade 11, 2100 Copenhagen OE, Denmark.

332.7　　　　　DK　ISSN 0108-5476
DENMARK. DANMARKS STATISTIK. PENGE OG KAPITALMARKED. irreg. Kr.50.82. Danmarks Statistik, Sejroegade 11, 2100 Copenhagen OE, Denmark.
　Formerly: Denmark. Danmarks Statistik. Kreditmarkedsstatistik. (ISSN 0107-3095)

338　　　　　　DK　ISSN 0108-738X
DENMARK. DANMARKS STATISTIK. REGNSKABSSTATISTIK FOR INDUSTRIEN / INDUSTRIAL ACCOUNTS STATISTICS. (Text in Danish and English) 1981. a. Kr.68.85. Danmarks Statistik, Sejroegade 11, 2100 Copenhagen OE, Denmark.
　Formerly: Denmark. Danmarks Statistik. Driftsregnskabsstatistik for Industrien.

336　　　　　　DK　ISSN 0105-1164
DENMARK. DANMARKS STATISTIK. SKATTER OG AFGIFTER/TAXES AND DUTIES. OVERSIGT. (Text in Danish; Notes in English) a. Kr.68.85. Danmarks Statistik, Sejroegade 11, 2100 Copenhagen OE, Denmark.
　Supersedes in part: Denmark. Danmarks Statistik. Ejendoms- og Selskabsbeskatningen i Skatteaaret.

382　314　　　　DK　ISSN 0108-5506
DENMARK. DANMARKS STATISTIK. UDENRIGSHANDEL/EXTERNAL TRADE. (Text in Danish; notes in English) 1980. irreg. Kr.143.44. Danmarks Statistik, Sejroegade 11, 2100 Copenhagen OE, Denmark.
　Formerly: Denmark. Danmarks Statistik. Handelsstatistike Meddelelser. Maanedsstatistik over Udenrigshandelen-Monthly Bulletin of External Trade (ISSN 0017-7342)

BUSINESS AND ECONOMICS — ABSTRACTING, BIBLIOGRAPHIES, STATISTICS

314   DK   ISSN 0107-7031
DENMARK. DANMARKS STATISTIK. VARESTATISTIK FOR INDUSTRI/MANUFACTURERS' SALES OF COMMODITIES. (Text in Danish and English) 1980. a. Kr.90.16. Danmarks Statistik, Sejroegade 11, 2100 Copenhagen OE, Denmark.
    Supersedes in part: Denmark. Danmarks Statistik. Kvartalsstatistik for Industrien. Varestatistik, 4. Kvartal og Aaret.

338.91   UN   ISSN 0254-2412
DEVELOPMENT INFORMATION ABSTRACTS. (Text in English, French, Spanish; summaries in English) 1981. bi-m. free. U.N. Department of International Economic and Social Affairs, Information Systems Unit, 2 United Nations Plaza, Rm. DCII-1772, New York, NY 10017. TEL 212-754-4836. Ed. Luciana Marulli-Koening. abstr. bibl. circ. 1,800. (back issues avail.)

339 314   YU   ISSN 0300-2527
DRUSTVENI PROIZVOD I NARODNI DOHODAK. (Subseries of Statisticki Bilten) 1969/70. a. 30 din.($1.67) Savezni Zavod za Statistiku, Kneza Miloso 20, Belgrade, Yugoslavia. stat.

011 330   NE   ISSN 0255-9900
E C INDEX; publications and documents of the European Communities. Variant title: European Communities Index. (Editions in English and French) 1985. m. $1207. Europe Data, Bredestraat 24, 621 HC Maastricht, Netherlands. Ed. Ruud Warnar. bibl. index.

330 016   SW
E F I NYTT/E F I NEWS. (Text in Swedish; summaries in English) 1973. irreg. free. Handelshoegskolan i Stockholm, Ekonomiska Forskningsinstitutet - Economic Research Institute at the Stockholm School of Economics, Box 6501, 113 83 Stockholm, Sweden. Ed. Rune Castenaes. bk. rev. circ. 4,000.

330 011   UK
EAST ASIA BIBLIOGRAPHY; a review of new publications on China & the Far East. 1979. irreg. £8 for 4 nos. East Asia Co., 103 Camden High St., London NW1 7JN, England. adv. bk. rev. circ. 2, 000.

330 016   NE   ISSN 0303-4879
ECONOMIC TITLES/ABSTRACTS; semi-monthly providing concise information of interest to business, trade, industry, economic libraries and research institutes. (Text in Dutch, English, French, German) 1974. 24/yr. fl.1053($407) (Ministerie van Economische Zaken, Economische Voorlichtingsdienst - Ministry of Economic Affairs, Economic Information Service) Martinus Nijhoff Publishers, Postbus 163, 3300 AD Dordrecht, Netherlands (Orders to: Kluwer Academic Publishers Group, Distribution Center, Box 322, 3300 AH Dordrecht, Netherlands) (also avail. in microform) Indexed: Key to Econ.SCi.
●Also available online. Vendors: BELINDIS, Data-Star, DIALOG.
    Formerly: Economic Titles.

330   EC
ECUADOR. DEPARTAMENTO DE ESTADISTICAS FISCALES. ESTADISTICAS FISCALES. irreg. Departamento de Estadisticas Fiscales, Subsecretaria de Presupuesto y Credito Publico, Quito, Ecuador.

331.2   US   ISSN 0271-4787
EMPLOYMENT AND EARNINGS: UNITED STATES. a. U.S. Bureau of Labor Statistics, Dept. of Labor, 441 G St. N.W., Washington, DC 20212 TEL 202-655-4000. (Orders to: Supt. of Documents, Washington, DC 20402) (also avail. in microform from UMI) Indexed: PROMT. Pers.Lit. Text.Tech.Dig.
    Formerly: Employment and Earnings Statistics for the United States (ISSN 0071-013X)

338 318   VE
ENCUESTA INDUSTRIAL: RESULTADOS NACIONALES. 1974. a. Oficina Central de Estadistica e Informatica, Apdo. de Correos 4593, San Martin, Caracas 101, Venezuela. stat.

338   PR
ESTABLECIMIENTOS MANUFACTURERAS EN PUERTO RICO. a. free. Department of Labor, Bureau of Labor Statistics, 505 Munoz Rivera Ave., Hato Rey, PR 00918. index. circ. 775.

382 314   SP   ISSN 0071-1527
ESTADISTICA DEL COMERCIO EXTERIOR DE ESPANA. m. (with annual summary) 1350 ptas. Editorial Pueyo, Arenal 6, Madrid, Spain.

332.6 318   PN
ESTADISTICA PANAMENA. INVERSIONES DIRECTAS EXTRANJERAS EN PANAMA. 1960. irreg. Bl.0.75. Direccion de Estadistica y Censo, Contraloria General, Apdo. 5213, Panama 5, Panama. stat. circ. 1,000.

330 318   PN   ISSN 0379-4245
ESTADISTICA PANAMENA. SITUACION ECONOMICA. SECCION 321 Y 325. INDUSTRIA ENCUESTA. 1957. a. Bl.0.75. Direccion de Estadistica y Censo, Contraloria General, Apdo. 5213, Panama 5, Panama. circ. 1, 700.

338 310   PN
ESTADISTICA PANAMENA. SITUACION ECONOMICA. SECCION 323. INDICE DE VOLUMEN FISICO DE LA PRODUCCION INDUSTRIAL. 1968. a. Bl.0.75. Direccion de Estadistica y Censo, Contraloria General, Apartado 5213, Panama 5, Panama. circ. 700.
    Former titles: Estadistica Panamena. Situacion Economica. Indice de Volumen Fisico de la Produccion Industrial; Estadistica Panamena. Situacion Economica. Seccion 323. Produccion Manufacturera (ISSN 0379-0754)

318   PN
ESTADISTICA PANAMENA. SITUACION ECONOMICA. SECCION 331-COMERCIO. ANUARIO DE COMERCIO EXTERIOR. 1958. a. Bl.4. Direccion de Estadistica y Censo, Contraloria General, Apdo. 5213, Panama 5, Panama. charts. stat. circ. 1,200.
    Formerly: Estadistica Panamena. Situacion Economica. Seccion 331-Comercio. Comercio Exterior (Annual) (ISSN 0379-4261)

318   PN   ISSN 0378-4983
ESTADISTICA PANAMENA. SITUACION ECONOMICA. SECCION 331. COMERCIO EXTERIOR (PRELIMINARY REPORT) 1958. a. Bl.1.50. Direccion de Estadistica y Censo, Contraloria General, Apdo. 5213, Panama 5, Panama. charts. stat. circ. 1,200.

318   PN   ISSN 0378-6730
ESTADISTICA PANAMENA. SITUACION ECONOMICA. SECCION 343-344. HACIENDA PUBLICA Y FINANZAS. 1958. a. Bl.1.00. Direccion de Estadistica y Censo, Contraloria General, Apartado 5213, Panama 5, Panama. circ. 1, 300.

318   PN   ISSN 0378-4991
ESTADISTICA PANAMENA. SITUACION ECONOMICA. SECCION 352. HOJA DE BALANCE DE ALIMENTOS. 1960. a. Bl.0.75. Direccion de Estadistica y Censo, Contraloria General, Apartado 5213, Panama 5, Panama. circ. 1, 200.

338 318   PN   ISSN 0379-072X
ESTADISTICA PANAMENA. SITUACION SOCIAL. SECCION 441. ESTADISTICAS DEL TRABAJO. 1963. a. Bl.0.75. Direccion de Estadistica y Censo, Contraloria General, Apartado 5213, Panama 5, Panama. circ. 1,500.
    Formerly: Estadistica Panamena. Situacion Social. Seccion 441-Trabajo y Salarios. Estadisticas del Trabajo; Incorporating: Panama. Direccion de Estadistica y Censo. Estadistica Panamena Serie M: Empleo.

338.09 314   SP
ESTADISTICAS DE PRODUCCION INDUSTRIAL; analisis y resultados. a. Servicio Sindical de Estadisticas, Huertas 73, Madrid, Spain.

382.09 318   VE
ESTADISTICAS DEL COMERCIO EXTERIOR DE VENEZUELA. PERIODICIDAD ANUAL. a. Oficina Central de Estadistica e Informatica, Apdo. de Correos 4593, San Martin, Caracas 101, Venezuela.
    Formerly: Estadisticas del Comercio Exterior de Venezuela. Boletin.

382 316   ET   ISSN 0425-4309
ETHIOPIA. CUSTOMS HEAD OFFICE. EXTERNAL TRADE STATISTICS. (Text in English) 1946. a. Eth.$6($2.90) Customs Head Office, Box 3248, Addis Ababa, Ethiopia. charts. stat. index.

338 016   UK   ISSN 0071-2582
EUROPEAN COMPANIES; a guide to sources of information. 1961. irreg. ‡ C.B.D. Research Ltd., 15 Wickham Rd., Beckenham, Kent BR3 2JS, England (Dist. in U.S. by: Gale Research Co., Penobscot Bldg., Detroit, MI 48226) Ed. G.P. Henderson. adv. circ. 2,000.

310   AF
EXPORT STATISTICS OF AFGHANISTAN/IHSA'IYAH-I AMUAL-I SADIRATI-I AFGHANISTAN. (Text in English or Persian) a. $20. Central Statistical Office, Nader Shah Minah, Block No. 4, Box 2002, Kabul, Afghanistan. stat.

382 316   GM
EXTERNAL TRADE STATISTICS OF GAMBIA. Variant title: Gambia. Central Statistics Department. Annual Report of External Trade Statistics. (Formerly issued by Central Statistics Division) 1973. a. d. 25. Central Statistics Department, Wellington St., Banjul, Gambia.

332   US
FED IN PRINT; business and banking topics. 1969. s-a. free. Federal Reserve Bank of Philadelphia, Philadelphia, PA 19105. TEL 215-574-6000. Ed. Deborah Naulty. circ. 1,800.

338 319   FJ
FIJI. BUREAU OF STATISTICS. CENSUS OF DISTRIBUTION AND SERVICES. 1971. irreg., vol.2, 1976. $2.50 per no. Bureau of Statistics, Box 2221, Suva, Fiji.

338   FJ
FIJI. BUREAU OF STATISTICS. CENSUS OF INDUSTRIAL PRODUCTION. 1968. a. $1. Bureau of Statistics, Box 2221, Suva, Fiji.

FIJI. BUREAU OF STATISTICS. ECONOMIC AND FUNCTIONAL CLASSIFICATION OF GOVERNMENT ACCOUNTS. see *BUSINESS AND ECONOMICS — Public Finance, Taxation*

331.11   FJ
FIJI. BUREAU OF STATISTICS. EMPLOYMENT SURVEY OF FIJI. 1969. a. $1. Bureau of Statistics, Box 2221, Suva, Fiji.

315 339   FJ
FIJI. BUREAU OF STATISTICS. FIJI HOUSEHOLD INCOME AND EXPENDITURE SURVEY. 1973. irreg., latest 1977. $3. Bureau of Statistics, Box 2221, Suva, Fiji. stat.

380   FJ
FIJI. BUREAU OF STATISTICS. SURVEY OF DISTRIBUTIVE TRADE. (Text in English) irreg.? Bureau of Statistics, P.O. Box 2221, Government Buildings, Suva, Fiji Islands.

382   FJ
FIJI. BUREAU OF STATISTICS. TRADE REPORT. 1939. a. $13. Bureau of Statistics, Box 2221, Suva, Fiji.

330   FJ
FIJI FACTS AND FIGURES. 1975. a. free. Bureau of Statistics, Box 2221, Suva, Fiji.

331.86 370   FI   ISSN 0357-2625
FINLAND. TILASTOKESKUS. AMMATILLISET OPPILAITOKSET/FINLAND. STATISTIKCENTRALEN. YRKESUTBILDNINGSANSTALTERNA/FINLAND. CENTRAL STATISTICAL OFFICE. VOCATIONAL EDUCATION. (Section X B of Official Statistics of Finland) (Text in English, Finnish and Swedish) 1979. a. Fmk.40. Central Statistical Office, P.O. Box 504, SF-00101 Helsinki, Finland.

BUSINESS AND ECONOMICS — ABSTRACTING, BIBLIOGRAPHIES, STATISTICS

336 314 FI ISSN 0359-081X
FINLAND. TILASTOKESKUS. KUNTIEN TALOUS/FINLAND. STATISTIKCENTRALEN. KOMMUNERNAS EKONOMI/FINLAND. CENTRAL STATISTICAL OFFICE. MUNICIPAL FINANCES. (Section XXXI of Official Statistics of Finland) (Text in Finnish and Swedish; summaries in English) 1927. a. Fmk.50. Tilastokeskus, Annankatu 44, SF-00100 Helsinki 10, Finland (Subscr. to: Government Printing Centre, Box 516, SF-00100 Helsinki 10, Finland)
Formerly: Finland. Tilastokeskus. Kuntien Finanssitilasto (ISSN 0430-5566)

312.2 610 FI ISSN 0355-2144
FINLAND. TILASTOKESKUS. KUOLEMANSYYT/ FINLAND. STATISTIKCENTRALEN. DOEDSORSAKER/FINLAND. CENTRAL STATISTICAL OFFICE. CAUSES OF DEATH IN FINLAND. (Section VI B of Official Statistics of Finland) (Text in English, Finnish and Swedish) 1939. a. Fmk.90. Tilastokeskus, Annankatu 44, SF-00100 Helsinki 10, Finland (Subscr. to: Government Printing Centre, Box 516, SF-00100 Helsinki 10, Finland)

314 332 FI ISSN 0355-2454
FINLAND. TILASTOKESKUS. PANKIT/ FINLAND. STATISTIKCENTRALEN. BANKERNA/FINLAND. CENTRAL STATISTICAL OFFICE. BANKS. (Section VII C of Official Statistics of Finland) (Text in English, Finnish and Swedish) 1974. a. Fmk.40. Tilastokeskus, Annankatu 44, SF-00100 Helsinki 10, Finland (Subscr. to: Government Printing Centre, Box 516, SF-00100 Helsinki 10, Finland)
Formed by the merger of: Finland. Tilastokeskus. Osuuspankkitilasto & Finland. Tilastokeskus. Saastopankkitilasto & Finland. Tilastokeskus. Liikepankit ja Kiinnitys Luottolaitokset.

338 314 FI ISSN 0071-5344
FINLAND. TILASTOKESKUS. TEOLLISUUSTILASTO/FINLAND. CENTRAL STATISTICAL OFFICE. INDUSTRIAL STATISTICS. (Section XVIII A of Official Statistics of Finland) (Text in Finnish and Swedish; summaries in English) 1884. a. Fmk.275. Tilastokeskus, Annankatu 44, SF-00101 Helsinki 10, Finland (Subscr. to: Government Printing Centre, Box 516, SF-00100 Helsinki 10, Finland)

311 FI
FINLAND. TILASTOKESKUS. TILASTOLLISIA TIEDONANTOJA. KOTITALOUSTIEDUSTELU/ FINLAND. STATISTIKCENTRALEN. STATISTISKA MEDDELANDEN. HUSHAALLSBUDGETUNDERSOEKNINGEN/ FINLAND. CENTRAL STATISTICAL OFFICE. STATISTICAL SURVEYS. HOUSEHOLD SURVEY. (Text in English, Finnish and Swedish) 1906. irreg. (every 5 years), latest 1981. price varies. Tilastokeskus, Annankatu 44, SF-00100 Helsinki 10, Finland (Subscr. to: Government Printing Centre, Box 516, SF-00100 Helsinki 10, Finland)
Continues in part (1906-1972): Finland. Tilastokeskus. Tilastollisia Tiedonantoja (ISSN 0355-208X)

332 FI ISSN 0355-2276
FINLAND. TILASTOKESKUS. TILASTOTIEDOTUS KT. KANSANTALOUDEN TILINPITO/NATIONAL RAEKENSKAPER/ NATIONAL ACCOUNTS. (Subseries of Finland. Tilastokeskus. Tilastoitiedotus) (Text in English, Finnish and Swedish) irreg. (approx. 8/yr.) Fmk.90 per vol. Tilastokeskus, Annankatu 44, SF-00100 Helsinki 10, Finland (Subscr. to: Government Printing Centre, Box 516, SF-00100 Helsinki 10, Finland)

314 339 FI ISSN 0780-9352
FINLAND. TILASTOKESKUS. TULO- JA VARALLISUUSTILASTO/FINLAND. STATISTIKCENTRALEN. INKOMST- OCH FOERMOEGENHETSTATISTIK/FINLAND. CENTRAL STATISTICAL OFFICE. STATISTICS OF INCOME AND PROPERTY. (Section IV B of Official Statistics of Finland) (Text in English, Finnish and Swedish) 1926. a. Fmk.45. Tilastokeskus, Annankatu 44, SF-00100 Helsinki 10, Finland (Subscr. to: Government Printing Centre, Box 516, SF-00100 Helsinki 10, Finland)
Formerly: Finland. Tilastokeskus. Tulo- ja Omaisuustilasto (ISSN 0355-211X)

331 FI ISSN 0358-2825
FINLAND. TILASTOKESKUS. TULONJAKOTILASTO/FINLAND. STATISTIKCENTRALEN. INKOMSTFOERDELNINGSSTATISTIK/ FINLAND. CENTRAL STATISTICAL OFFICE. INCOME DISTRIBUTION STATISTICS. (Section XLI of Official Statistics of Finland) (Text in English, Finnish and Swedish) 1980. a. Fmk.49. Tilastokeskus, Annankatu 44, SF-00100 Helsinki 10, Finland (Subscr. to: Government Printing Centre, Box 516, SF-00101 Helsinki 10, Finland)

314 338 FI ISSN 0355-2071
FINLAND. TILASTOKESKUS. TUTKIMUKSIA/ FINLAND. STATISTIKCENTRALEN. UNDERSOEKNINGAR/FINLAND. CENTRAL STATISTICAL OFFICE. STUDIES. 1966. irreg. price varies. Tilastokeskus, Annankatu 44, SF-00100 Helsinki 10, Finland (Subscr. to: Government Printing Centre, Box 516, SF-00100 Helsinki 10, Finland)

331.11 FI ISSN 0781-5611
FINLAND. TILASTOKESKUS. TYOVOIMATUTKIMUS/FINLAND. STATISTIKCENTRALEN. ARBETSKRAFTSUNDERSOKNINGEN/ FINLAND. CENTRAL STATISTICAL OFFICE. LABOUR FORCE SURVEY. (Section XL of Official Statistics of Finland) (Text in English, Finnish and Swedish) 1977. a. Fmk.45. Tilastokeskus, Annankatu 44, SF-00100 Helsinki 10, Finland (Subscr. to: Government Printing Centre, Box 516, SF-00101 Helsinki 10, Finland)
Formerly: Finland. Tilastokeskus. Tyovoimatiedustelu (ISSN 0356-3316)

382 316 UN ISSN 0071-7398
FOREIGN TRADE STATISTICS OF AFRICA. SERIES A: DIRECTION OF TRADE. (Text in English and French) 1962. irreg., latest no.25, 1977. price varies. United Nations Economic Commission for Africa - Commission Economique pour l'Afrique, Box 3001, Addis Ababa, Ethiopia (Dist. by: United Nations Publications, Room LX-2300, New York, NY 10017; or Distribution and Sales Section, Palais des Nations, CH-1211 Geneva 10, Switzerland)

382 316 UN ISSN 0071-7401
FOREIGN TRADE STATISTICS OF AFRICA. SERIES B: TRADE BY COMMODITY. (Text in English and French) 1962. irreg., latest no.31, 1978. price varies. United Nations Economic Commission for Africa - Commission Economique pour l'Afrique, Box 3001, Addis Ababa, Ethiopia (Dist. by: United Nations Publications, Room LX-2300, New York, NY 10017; or Distirbution and Sales Section, Palais des Nations, CH-1211 Geneva 10, Switzerland)

382 UN
FOREIGN TRADE STATISTICS OF AFRICA. SERIES C: SUMMARY TABLES/STATISTIQUES AFRICAINES DU COMMERCE EXTERIEUR. SERIE C: TABLEAUX RECAPITULATIFS. 1977. irreg., no.3, 1980. United Nations Economic Commission for Africa, Box 3001, Addis Ababa, Ethiopia.

382 315 UN ISSN 0252-4538
FOREIGN TRADE STATISTICS OF ASIA AND THE PACIFIC. SERIES A. 1969. a. price varies. United Nations Economic and Social Commission for Asia and the Pacific, United Nations Bldg., Rajadamnern Ave., Bangkok 2, Thailand (Dist. by: United Nations Publications, Room DC2-0853, New York, NY 10017; or Distribution and Sales Section, Palais des Nations, CH-1211 Geneva 10, Switzerland)

382 315 UN ISSN 0252-4546
FOREIGN TRADE STATISTICS OF ASIA AND THE PACIFIC. SERIES B. 1977. a. United Nations Economic and Social Commission for Asia and the Pacific, United Nations Bldg., Rajadamnern Ave., Bangkok 2, Thailand (Dist. by: United Nations Publications, Room DC2-0853, New York, NY 10017; or Distribution and Sales Section, Palais des Nations, CH-1211 Geneva 10, Switzerland)

315 BG
FOREIGN TRADE STATISTICS OF BANGLADESH. (Text in English) 1961/63. a. Tk.100($35) Bangladesh Bureau of Statistics, Secretariat, Dacca 2, Bangladesh.
Formerly: Annual Foreign Trade Statistics of Bangladesh (ISSN 0071-7371)

382 315 IR ISSN 0075-0492
FOREIGN TRADE STATISTICS OF IRAN. YEARBOOK.* (Text in Arabic and English) a. Ministry of Finance and Economic Affairs, Teheran, Iran.

382 315 PH
FOREIGN TRADE STATISTICS OF THE PHILIPPINES. a. P.60($20) National Census and Statistics Office, Ramon Magsaysay Blvd., Box 779, Manila, Philippines.

382 315 YE
FOREIGN TRADE STATISTICS OF YEMEN ARAB REPUBLIC. (Text in English) a. Central Bank of Yemen, Research Department, Box 59, Sana'a, Yemen. stat.

FORSCHUNGSDOKUMENTATION ZUR ARBEITSMARKT- UND BERUFSFORSCHUNG. see BUSINESS AND ECONOMICS — Labor And Industrial Relations

382 314 FR ISSN 0071-8688
FRANCE. DIRECTION GENERALE DES DOUANES ET DROITS INDIRECTS. STATISTIQUES DU COMMERCE EXTERIEUR: IMPORTATIONS- EXPORTATIONS. NOMENCLATURE: N.G.P. (NOMENCLATURE GENERALE DES PRODUITS) a. 135 F. Imprimerie Nationale, Service des Ventes, 59128 Flers en Escrebieux, France.

330 310 FR ISSN 0533-0793
FRANCE. INSTITUT NATIONAL DE LA STATISTIQUE ET DES ETUDES ECONOMIQUES. COLLECTIONS. SERIE C, COMPTES ET PLANIFICATION. (Text in French; summaries in English and Spanish) 1969. irreg. 555 F. for 8 nos. Institut National de la Statistique et des Etudes Economiques, 18 bd. A. Pinard, 75675 Paris 14, France. circ. 2,400. Indexed: P.A.I.S.For.Lang.Ind.

330 314 FR ISSN 0533-0815
FRANCE. INSTITUT NATIONAL DE LA STATISTIQUE ET DES ETUDES ECONOMIQUES. COLLECTIONS. SERIE E, ENTERPRISES. irreg. 555 F. for 8 nos. Institut National de la Statistique et des Etudes Economiques, 18 bd. A. Pinard, 75675 Paris 14, France. stat. circ. 2,400. Indexed: P.A.I.S.For.Lang.Ind.

330 310 FR ISSN 0533-0823
FRANCE. INSTITUT NATIONAL DE LA STATISTIQUE ET DES ETUDES ECONOMIQUES. COLLECTIONS. SERIE M, MENAGES. (Text in French; summaries in English and Spanish) 1969. irreg. 690 F. for 10 nos. Institut National de la Statistique et des Etudes Economiques, 18 bd. A. Pinard, 75675 Paris 14, France. circ. 2,400. Indexed: P.A.I.S.For.Lang.Ind.

314 FR ISSN 0533-0831
FRANCE. INSTITUT NATIONAL DE LA STATISTIQUE ET DES ETUDES ECONOMIQUES. COLLECTIONS. SERIE R, REGIONS. 1969. irreg. 300 F. for 4 nos. Institut National de la Statistique et des Etudes Economiques, 18 bd. A. Pinard, 75675 Paris 14, France. circ. 2,400. Indexed: P.A.I.S.For.Lang.Ind.

334 FR ISSN 0336-6979
FRANCE. INSTITUT NATIONAL DE LA STATISTIQUE ET DES ETUDES ECONOMIQUES. DOCUMENTS DIVERS. irreg. Institut National de la Statistique et des Etudes Economiques, 18 bd. A. Pinard, 75675 Paris Cedex 14, France.

BUSINESS AND ECONOMICS — ABSTRACTING, BIBLIOGRAPHIES, STATISTICS

338 310 FR
FRANCE. MINISTERE DE L'INDUSTRIE, DES P & T ET DU TOURISME. ENQUETE ANNUELLE D'ENTREPRISE. 1968. a. 71 F. Ministere de l'Industrie, des P & T et du Tourisme, Service d'Etude des Strategies et des Statistiques Industrielles, 85 bd. Montparnasse, 75270 Paris Cedex 06, France. illus. circ. 800. (also avail. in microfiche)
Formerly: France. Ministere de Redeploiement Industriel et du Commerce Exterieur. Enquete Annuelle.

331 314 FR
FRANCE. MINISTERE DES AFFAIRES SOCIALES ET DE LA SOLIDARITE NATIONALE. BULLETIN MENSUEL DE STATISTIQUES DU TRAVAIL. SUPPLEMENT. irreg. 45 F. per no. (Ministere des Affaires Sociales et de la Solidarite Nationale, Service des Etudes et de la Statistique Travail-Emploi) Documentation Francaise, 29-31 Quai Voltaire, 75340 Paris Cedex 07, France. (also avail. in microfiche)
Formerly: France Ministere du Travail. Bulletin de Statistiques du Travail. Supplement.

338 314 FR
FRANCE. SERVICE D'ETUDE DES STRATEGIES ET DES STATISTIQUES INDUSTRIELLES. ANNUAIRE DE STATISTIQUE INDUSTRIELLE. 1947. a. 350 F. Service d'Etude des Strategies et des Statistiques Industrielles, 83/85 Bd. du Montparnasse, 75270 Paris Cedex 06, France.
Former titles: France. Service du Traitement de l'Information et des Statistiques Industrielles. Annuaire de Statistique Industrielle (ISSN 0071-8211) & France. Bureau Centrale de Statistique Industrielle. Annuaire de Statistique Industrielle.

338 311 FR ISSN 0244-7118
FRANCE. SERVICE D'ETUDE DES STRATEGIES ET DES STATISTIQUES INDUSTRIELLES. COLLECTIONS: TRAITS FONDAMENTAUX DU SYSTEME INDUSTRIEL FRANCAIS. 1974. irreg., no.14, 1977. 64 F. Service d'Etude des Strategies et des Statistiques Industrielles, 83/85 Bd. du Montparnasse, 75006 Paris, France.
Former titles: France. Service d'Etude des Strategies et des Statistiques Industrielles. Recueil Statistiques; France. Service du Traitement de l'Information et des Statistiques Industrielles. Recueil Statistiques.

317 US ISSN 0085-1043
GEORGIA STATISTICAL ABSTRACT. 1951. biennial. $22.50. University of Georgia, College of Business Administration, Division of Research, Athens, GA 30602. TEL 404-542-4085. Ed. Lorena Akioka. circ. 1,200.

331.11 314 GW
GERMANY (FEDERAL REPUBLIC, 1949-). BUNDESANSTALT FUER ARBEIT. BERUFSBERATUNG. ERGEBNISSE DER BERUFSBERATUNGSSTATISTIK. (Beilage Zu den Amtlichen Nachrichten der Bundesanstalt fuer Arbeit) 1953. a. DM.9. ‡ Bundesanstalt fuer Arbeit, Regensburger Str. 104, 8500 Nuernberg 1, W. Germany (B.R.D.) index.

331 314 GW ISSN 0341-7840
GERMANY (FEDERAL REPUBLIC, 1949-). BUNDESMINISTERIUM FUER ARBEIT UND SOZIALORDNUNG. HAUPTERGEBNISSE DER ARBEITS- UND SOZIALSTATISTIK. 1952. a. DM.12. Bundesministerium fuer Arbeit und Sozialordnung, Postfach 140280, 5300 Bonn 1, W. Germany (B.R.D.) Ed.Bd. bk. rev. circ. 1,700.

382 310 GW ISSN 0072-1638
GERMANY (FEDERAL REPUBLIC, 1949-). STATISTISCHES BUNDESAMT. ALPHABETISCHES LAENDERVERZEICHNIS FUER DIE AUSSENHANDELSSTATISTIK. irreg. DM.7.40 each. W. Kohlhammer-Verlag GmbH, Abt. Veroeffentlichungen des Statistischen Bundesamtes, Philipp-Reis-Str. 3, Postfach 421120, 6500 Mainz 42, W. Germany (B.R.D.)

382 314 GW ISSN 0072-1654
GERMANY (FEDERAL REPUBLIC, 1949-). STATISTISCHES BUNDESAMT. FACHSERIE 7, AUSSENHANDEL, REIHE 2: AUSSENHANDEL NACH WAREN UND LAENDERN (SPEZIALHANDEL) m. (plus a. cumulation) DM.324. W. Kohlhammer-Verlag GmbH, Abt. Veroeffentlichungen des Statistischen Bundesamtes, Philipp-Reis-Str. 3, Postfach 421120, 6500 Mainz 42, W. Germany (B.R.D.)

382 314 GW
GERMANY (FEDERAL REPUBLIC, 1949-). STATISTISCHES BUNDESAMT. FACHSERIE 7, AUSSENHANDEL, REIHE 4. AUSSENHANDEL MIT AUSGEWAEHLTEN WAREN; Reihe 4.1: Ein- und Ausfuhr von Mineraloel (Generalhandel) m. (plus a. cum.) DM.96. W. Kohlhammer-Verlag GmbH, Abt. Veroeffentlichungen des Statistischen Bundesamtes, Philipp-Reis-Str. 3, Postfach 421120, 6500 Mainz 42, W. Germany (B.R.D.)

382 314 GW ISSN 0072-1697
GERMANY (FEDERAL REPUBLIC, 1949-). STATISTISCHES BUNDESAMT. FACHSERIE 7, AUSSENHANDEL, REIHE 6: DURCHFUHR IM SEEVERKEHR UND SEEUMSCHLAG. a. DM.8.90. W. Kohlhammer-Verlag GmbH, Abt. Veroeffentlichungen des Statistischen Bundesamtes, Philipp-Reis-Str. 3, Postfach 421120, 6500 Mainz 42, W. Germany (B.R.D.)

382 314 GW ISSN 0072-1700
GERMANY (FEDERAL REPUBLIC, 1949-). STATISTISCHES BUNDESAMT. FACHSERIE 7, AUSSENHANDEL, REIHE 7: SONDERBEITRAEGE. irreg. price varies. W. Kohlhammer-Verlag GmbH, Abt. Veroeffentlichungen des Statistischen Bundesamtes, Philipp-Reis-Str. 3, Postfach 421120, 6500 Mainz 42, W. Germany (B.R.D.)

331 314 GW ISSN 0072-1832
GERMANY (FEDERAL REPUBLIC, 1949-). STATISTISCHES BUNDESAMT. FACHSERIE 1, BEVOELKERUNG UND ERWERBSTAETIGKEIT, REIHE 4: ERWERBETAETIGKEIT. irreg. price varies. W. Kohlhammer-Verlag GmbH, Abt. Veroeffentlichungen des Statistischen Bundesamtes, Philipp-Reis-Str. 3, Postfach 421120, 6500 Mainz 42, W. Germany (B.R.D.)

380 314 GW ISSN 0072-1964
GERMANY (FEDERAL REPUBLIC, 1949-). STATISTISCHES BUNDESAMT. FACHSERIE 6, HANDEL, GASTGEWERBE, REISEVERKEHR; REIHE 1: GROSSHANDEL. a. price varies. W. Kohlhammer-Verlag GmbH, Abt. Veroeffentlichungen des Statistischen Bundesamtes, Philipp-Reis-Str. 3, Postfach 421120, 6500 Mainz 42, W. Germany (B.R.D.)

380 314 GW ISSN 0072-1972
GERMANY (FEDERAL REPUBLIC, 1949-). STATISTISCHES BUNDESAMT. FACHSERIE 6, HANDEL, GASTGEWERBE, REISEVERKEHR; REIHE 3: EINZELHANDEL. (Consists of several subseries) a. price varies. W. Kohlhammer-Verlag GmbH, Abt. Veroeffentlichungen des Statistischen Bundesamtes, Philipp-Reis-Str. 3, Postfach 421120, 6500 Mainz 42, W. Germany (B.R.D.)

381 314 GW
GERMANY (FEDERAL REPUBLIC, 1949-). STATISTISCHES BUNDESAMT. FACHSERIE 6, HANDEL, GASTGEWERBE, REISEVERKEHR; REIHE 5: WAHRENVERKEHR MIT BERLIN (WEST) a. DM.2.90. W. Kohlhammer-Verlag GmbH, Abt. Veroeffentlichungen des Statistischen Bundesamtes, Philipp-Reis-Str. 3, Postfach 421120, 6500 Mainz 42, W. Germany (B.R.D.)

338 314 GW
GERMANY (FEDERAL REPUBLIC, 1949-). STATISTISCHES BUNDESAMT. FACHSERIE 4, PRODUZIERENDES GEWERBE, REIHE 3.1: PRODUKTION GEWERBE DES IN- UND AUSLANDES. (Consists of several subseries) 1951. irreg. DM.82.40. W. Kohlhammer-Verlag GmbH, Abt. Veroeffentlichungen des Statistischen Bundesamtes, Philipp-Reis-Str. 3, Postfach 421120, 6500 Mainz 42, W. Germany (B.R.D.)

338 314 GW ISSN 0072-2073
GERMANY (FEDERAL REPUBLIC, 1949-). STATISTISCHES BUNDESAMT. FACHSERIE 4, PRODUZIERENDES GEWERBE, REIHE 5: SONDERBEITRAEGE. 1951. irreg. price varies. W. Kohlhammer-Verlag GmbH, Abt. Veroeffentlichungen des Statistischen Bundesamtes, Philipp-Reis-Str. 3, Postfach 421120, 6500 Mainz 42, W. Germany (B.R.D.)

338 314 GW ISSN 0072-2103
GERMANY (FEDERAL REPUBLIC, 1949-). STATISTISCHES BUNDESAMT. FACHSERIE 4, PRODUZIERENDE GASTGEWERBE, REIHE 7: HANDWERK. BESCHAEFTIGTE UM UMSATZ IM HANDWERK. irreg. DM.25.60. W. Kohlhammer-Verlag GmbH, Abt. Veroeffentlichungen des Statistischen Bundesamtes, Philipp-Reis-Str. 3, Postfach 421120, 6500 Mainz 42, W. Germany (B.R.D.)

338 314 GW
GERMANY (FEDERAL REPUBLIC, 1949-). STATISTISCHES BUNDESAMT. FACHSERIE 2, UNTERNEHMEN UND ARBEITSSTATTEN, REIHE 2.1: ABSCHLUESSE DER KAPITALGESELLSCHAFTEN. 1971. a. DM.14.70. W. Kohlhammer-Verlag GmbH, Abt. Veroeffentlichungen des Statistischen Bundesamtes, Philipp-Reis-Str. 3, Postfach 421120, 6500 Mainz 42, W. Germany (B.R.D.)

338 314 GW
GERMANY (FEDERAL REPUBLIC, 1949-). STATISTISCHES BUNDESAMT. FACHSERIE 2, UNTERNEHMEN UND ARBEITSSTATTEN, REIHE 3: ABSCHLUESSE DER OEFFENTLICHEN VERSORGUNGS- UND VERKEHRSUNTERNEHMEN. 1959. a. DM.12. W. Kohlhammer-Verlag GmbH, Abt. Veroeffentlichungen des Statistischen Bundesamtes, Philipp-Reis-Str. 3, Postfach 421120, 6500 Mainz 42, W. Germany (B.R.D.)

336 314 GW
GERMANY (FEDERAL REPUBLIC, 1949-). STATISTISCHES BUNDESAMT. FACHSERIE 14: FINANZEN UND STEUERN. (Consists of several subseries) 1959. irreg. price varies. W. Kohlhammer-Verlag GmbH, Abt. Veroeffentlichungen des Statistischen Bundesamtes, Philipp-Reis-Str. 3, Postfach 421120, 6500 Mainz 42, W. Germany (B.R.D.)

331.2 310 GW
GERMANY (FEDERAL REPUBLIC, 1949-). STATISTISCHES BUNDESAMT. FACHSERIE 16, LOEHNE UND GEHAELTER, REIHE 5.2: TARIFLOEHNE UND GEHAELTER DES AUSLANDES. 1950/51. a. price varies. W. Kohlhammer-Verlag GmbH, Abt. Veroeffentlichungen des Statistischen Bundesamtes, Philipp-Reis-Str. 3, Postfach 421120, 6500 Mainz 42, W. Germany (B.R.D.)

331.2 338.1 314 GW
GERMANY (FEDERAL REPUBLIC, 1949-). STATISTISCHES BUNDESAMT. FACHSERIE 16, REIHE 1: ARBEITERVERDIENSTE IN DER LANDWIRTSCHAFT. a. DM.1.60. W. Kohlhammer-Verlag GmbH, Abt. Veroeffentlichungen des Statistischen Bundesamtes, Philipp-Reis-Str. 3, Postfach 421120, 6500 Mainz 42, W. Germany (B.R.D.)
Supersedes: Germany (Federal Republic, 1949-). Statistisches Bundesamt. Loehne und Gehaelter. Reihe 1: Arbeiterverdienste in der Landwirtschaft.

330 314 GW ISSN 0072-4009
GERMANY (FEDERAL REPUBLIC, 1949-). STATISTISCHES BUNDESAMT. FACHSERIE 18, VOLKSWIRTSCHAFTLICHE GESAMTRECHNUNGEN, REIHE 1: KONTEN UND STANDARDTABELLEN. a. price varies. W. Kohlhammer-Verlag GmbH, Abt. Veroeffentlichungen des Statistischen Bundesamtes, Philipp-Reis-Str. 3, Postfach 421120, 6500 Mainz 42, W. Germany (B.R.D.)

382 314   GW
GERMANY (FEDERAL REPUBLIC, 1949-). STATISTISCHES BUNDESAMT. FREMDSPRACHIGE VEROEFFENTLICHUNGEN NR. 6370010: FOREIGN TRADE ACCORDING TO THE STANDARD INTERNATIONAL TRADE CLASSIFICATION (SITC) - SPECIAL TRADE. a. DM.22.50. W. Kohlhammer-Verlag GmbH, Abt. Veroeffentlichungen des Statistischen Bundesamtes, Philipp-Reis-Str. 3, Postfach 421120, 6500 Mainz 42, W. Germany (B.R.D.)

314   GW   ISSN 0072-4106
GERMANY (FEDERAL REPUBLIC, 1949-) STATISTISCHES BUNDESAMT. WARENVERZEICHNIS FUER DIE AUSSENHANDELSSTATISTIK. a. DM.45. W. Kohlhammer-Verlag GmbH, Abt. Veroeffentlichungen des Statistischen Bundesamtes, Philipp-Reis-Str. 3, Postfach 421120, 6500 Mainz 42, W. Germany (B.R.D.)

330 316   GH   ISSN 0072-4335
GHANA. CENTRAL BUREAU OF STATISTICS. ECONOMIC SURVEY. 1951. irreg., latest 1982. $20. Central Bureau of Statistics, Box 1098, Accra, Ghana.

331.2 314   UK
GREAT BRITAIN. DEPARTMENT OF EMPLOYMENT. STATISTICS DIVISION. TIME RATES OF WAGES AND HOURS OF WORK. a. £39. Department of Employment, Statistics Division, HQ Stats A1, Watford WD1 8FP, England.
    Incorporates: Great Britain. Department of Employment. Changes in Rates of Wages and Hours of Work (ISSN 0534-0500)

338 314   UK
GREAT BRITAIN. DEPARTMENT OF TRADE AND INDUSTRY. BUSINESS STATISTICS OFFICE REPORT ON THE CENSUS OF PRODUCTION. (Issued in parts. Subseries of the Business Monitor) 1970. a. price varies. Department of Trade and Industry, Business Statistics Office, Cardiff Road, Newport, Gwent NP9 1XG, England (Order from: H.M.S.O., P.O. Box 276, London SW8 5DT, England) stat.
    Former titles: Great Britain. Department of Industry. Business Statistics Office Report on the Census of Production; Great Britain. Department of Trade and Industry. Business Statistics Office. Report on the Census of Production.

338 314   GR   ISSN 0072-7393
GREECE. NATIONAL STATISTICAL SERVICE. ANNUAL INDUSTRIAL SURVEY. (Text in English and Greek) 1958. a. $7. National Statistical Service, Publications and Information Division, 14-16 Lycourgou St., 10166 Athens, Greece.
    Formerly: Greece. National Statistical Service. Results of the Annual Industrial Survey.

331.1   GR   ISSN 0256-3576
GREECE. NATIONAL STATISTICAL SERVICE. LABOUR FORCE SURVEY. a. $3. National Statistical Service, Publications and Information Division, 14-16 Lycourgou St., 10166 Athens, Greece.
    Formerly (until 1980): Greece. National Statistical Service. Employment Survey Conducted in Urban and Semi-Urban Areas (ISSN 0256-3614)

336 314   GR
GREECE. NATIONAL STATISTICAL SERVICE. PUBLIC FINANCE STATISTICS. (Text in English and Greek) 1962. a. $4. National Statistical Service, Publications and Information Division, 14-16 Lycourgou St., 10166 Athens, Greece.
    Formerly (until 1972): Greece. National Statistical Service. Statistical Yearbook of Public Finance (ISSN 0072-7431)

336   GR   ISSN 0302-1416
GREECE. NATIONAL STATISTICAL SERVICE. STATISTICS ON THE DECLARED INCOME OF LEGAL ENTITIES AND ITS TAXATION. (Text in Greek) 1959. a. $2.50. National Statistical Service, Publications and Information Division, 14-16 Lycourgou St., 10166 Athens, Greece.

336   GR   ISSN 0302-1114
GREECE. NATIONAL STATISTICAL SERVICE. STATISTICS ON THE DECLARED INCOME OF PHYSICAL PERSONS AND ITS TAXATION. (Text in Greek) 1960. a. $4. National Statistical Service, Publications and Information Division, 14-16 Lycourgou St., 10166 Athens, Greece.

338 318   GT
GUATEMALA. INSTITUTO NACIONAL DE ESTADISTICA. DIRECTORIO NACIONAL DE ESTABLECIMIENTOS INDUSTRIALES. (Former name of issuing body: Direccion General de Estadistica) a. $10. Instituto Nacional de Estadistica, Ministerio de Economia, 8A Calle no. 9-55, Zona 1, Guatemala, Guatemala.

658 016   US
H B S CASE BIBLIOGRAPHY. a. price varies. Harvard University, Graduate School of Business Administration, Soldiers Field Post Office, Boston, MA 02163. TEL 617-495-6117. bibl. circ. 1,000. (back issues avail.)
    Supersedes (1975-1980): Intercollegiate Bibliography. New Cases in Administration. (ISSN 0095-490X)

331 317   US
HANDBOOK OF OKLAHOMA EMPLOYMENT STATISTICS. 1952. a. (in 2 vols.) free. ‡ Employment Security Commission, Research Division, 310 Will Rogers Bldg., Oklahoma City, OK 73105. Ed. O.V. Richardson. stat. circ. 750.

650 016   US
HARVARD BUSINESS SCHOOL. BAKER LIBRARY. CORE COLLECTION, AN AUTHOR AND SUBJECT GUIDE. 1969/70. a. $15. Harvard Business School, Soldiers Field, Boston, MA 02163. TEL 617-495-6405.
    Formerly: Harvard University. Graduate School of Business Administration. Baker Library. Core Collection, An Author and Subject Guide.

016 650   US
HARVARD BUSINESS SCHOOL. BAKER LIBRARY. CURRENT PERIODICAL PUBLICATIONS IN BAKER LIBRARY. 1971/72. a. $30. ‡ Harvard Business School, Soldiers Field Rd., Boston, MA 02163. TEL 617-495-6405.
    Formerly: Harvard University. Graduate School of Business Administration. Baker Library. Current Periodical Publications in Baker Library.

330 016   FI   ISSN 0356-8164
HELSINGIN KAUPPAKORKEAKOULU. JULKAISUSARJA D. LAITOSJULKAISUJA. (Text in English and Finnish) 1975. irreg., latest no.77, 1986. price varies. Helsingin Kauppakorkeakoulu - Helsinki School of Economics, Runeberginkatu 22-24, 00100 Helsinki 10, Finland. Ed.Bd. bibl. circ. 300.
    Supersedes: Helsingin Kauppakorkeakoulu. Kirjasto. Julkaisusarja.

330.9 352   GW
HERNE IN ZAHLEN. JAHRESVEROEFFENTLICHUNGEN. a. DM.4($1.26) Stadt Herne -Amt fuer Stadtentwicklung, Stadtforschung und Statistik, Postfach 1820, 4690 Herne 1, W. Germany (B.R.D.) stat. circ. 250.

339 315   HK
HONG KONG. ESTIMATES OF GROSS DOMESTIC PRODUCT. (Text in English) 1966. a. HK.$20. Census and Statistics Department, Kai Tak Commercial Bldg., 317 Des Voeux Rd., Central, Hong Kong, Hong Kong (Subscr. to: Director of Information Services, Information Services Department, Beaconsfield House, Queen's Rd., Central, Hong Kong, Hong Kong)

330 314   HU   ISSN 0209-6919
HUNGARY. KOZPONTI STATISZTIKAI HIVATAL. AGAZATI KAPCSOLATOK MERLEGE. irreg. 245 Ft. Statisztikai Kiado Vallalat, Kaszasdulo u. 2, P.O. Box 99, 1300 Budapest 3, Hungary (Subscr. to: Kultura, Box 149, H-1389 Budapest, Hungary)

381 314   HU   ISSN 0134-1138
HUNGARY. KOZPONTI STATISZTIKAI HIVATAL. BELKERESKEDELMI EVKONYV. a. 262 Ft. Statisztikai Kiado Vallalat, Kaszasdulo u. 2, P.O. Box 99, 1300 Budapest 3, Hungary (Subscr. to: Kultura, Box 149, H-1389 Budapest, Hungary)

331.2 314   HU   ISSN 0133-543X
HUNGARY. KOZPONTI STATISZTIKAI HIVATAL. FOGLALKOZTATOTTSAG ES KERESETI ARANYOK. a. 150 Ft. Statisztikai Kiado Vallalat, Kaszasdulo u. 2, P.O.B. 99, 1300 Budapest 3, Hungary (Subscr. to: Kultura, Box 149, H-1389 Budapest, Hungary)

314 338   HU   ISSN 0133-8684
HUNGARY. KOZPONTI STATISZTIKAI HIVATAL. IPARI ZSEBKONYV. a. 26 Ft. Statisztikai Kiado Vallalat, Kaszasdulo u. 2, P.O.B.99, 1300 Budapest 3, Hungary (Subscr. to: Kultura, Box 149, H-1389 Budapest, Hungary) circ. 2,200.

338 314   HU   ISSN 0209-4002
HUNGARY. KOZPONTI STATISZTIKAI HIVATAL. IPARSTATISZTIKAI EVKONYV. a. 250 Ft. Statisztikai Kiado Vallalat, Kaszasdulo u. 2, P.O.B. 99, 1300 Budapest 3, Hungary (Subscr. to: Kultura, Box 149, H-1389 Budapest, Hungary)

382 314   HU   ISSN 0139-3634
HUNGARY. KOZPONTI STATISZTIKAI HIVATAL. KULKERESKEDELMI STATISZTIKAI EVKONYV. 1971. a. 360 Ft. (Kozponti Statisztikai Hivatal) Statisztikai Kiado Vallalat, Kaszasdulo u. 2, P.O.B.99, 1300 Budapest 3, Hungary (Subscr. to: Kultura, Box 149, H-1389 Budapest, Hungary)

310   AF
IMPORTS STATISTICS OF AFGHANISTAN/ IHSA'IYAH-I AMUAL-I VARIDATI-I AFGHANISTAN. (Text in English or Persian) a. $20. Central Statistical Office, Nader Shah Minah, Block No. 4, Box 2002, Kabul, Afghanistan. stat.

011 330 500   MR
INDEX DOCUMENTATION-ECONOMIE-SCIENCE-TECHNIQUE. Short title: I D E S T. (Text in French) 1972. irreg. (3-4/yr.) DH.400. Centre National de Documentation, B.P. 826, Rabat, Morocco. Ed. Mohamed Mamdouh. adv. bk. rev. circ. 1,000. (also avail. in microfiche)

330 016   US
INDEX OF ECONOMIC ARTICLES IN JOURNALS AND COLLECTIVE VOLUMES. 1961. irreg., vol.20, 1978. $50. ‡ American Economic Association, 1313 21st. Ave. So., Nashville, TN 37212 TEL 615-322-2595. (Order from: Richard D. Irwin, Inc., 1818 Ridge Rd., Homewood, IL 60430) (back issues avail.)
●Also available online. Vendors: DIALOG.

331 016   CN   ISSN 0226-1537
INDEX OF INDUSTRIAL RELATIONS LITERATURE. 1976. a. Can.$75. Queen's University, Industrial Relations Center, Kingston, Ont. K7L 3N6, Canada. TEL 613-545-2193. circ. 300.

382   UK   ISSN 0266-0180
INDEX TO BUSINESS REPORTS. 1978. 2/yr. £16.95($32.95) Quarry Press, 14 Plantation Rd., Harrogate, N. Yorkshire HG2 0DB, England. Ed. N.R. Hunter. circ. 400(controlled)

338 315   II   ISSN 0073-6139
INDIA. CENTRAL STATISTICAL ORGANIZATION. ANNUAL SURVEY OF INDUSTRIES/UDYOGEN KA VARSHIKA SARVEKSHANA. (Text in English and Hindi) 1973/74. a. Rs.31.50($11.34) Central Statistical Organization, Sardar Patel Bhavan, Parliament St., New Delhi 110001, India. circ. 500.

331 315   II
INDIA. LABOUR BUREAU. POCKET BOOK OF LABOUR STATISTICS. 1959. a. Rs.15($5.40) Labour Bureau, Simla 171004, India (Order from: Controller of Publications, Government of India, Civil Lines, Delhi 110054, India) stat. circ. 2,700.

315.98   IO   ISSN 0376-9984
INDONESIA STATISTICS. (Text in English) a. First National City Bank, Jl. Thamrin 45, Box 2463, Jakarta, Indonesia.

331 016   US   ISSN 0070-0142
INDUSTRIAL AND LABOR RELATIONS BIBLIOGRAPHY SERIES. 1952. irreg., no.16, 1982. price varies. (New York State School of Industrial and Labor Relations) I L R Press, Cornell University, Ithaca, NY 14851-0952. TEL 607-255-3061. Indexed: E.I.

BUSINESS AND ECONOMICS — ABSTRACTING, BIBLIOGRAPHIES, STATISTICS

338.9 016   UN   ISSN 0378-2654
INDUSTRIAL DEVELOPMENT ABSTRACTS; U N I D O industrial information system (I N D I S) 1971. irreg., (2-4/yr.) price varies. United Nations Industrial Development Organization, Box 300, A-1400 Vienna, Austria.

330 310   UN
INDUSTRIAL STATISTICS YEARBOOK. 1950. a. United Nations, Department of Economic and Social Affairs, Secretariat, New York, NY 10017.
  Former titles (until 1981): Yearbook of Industrial Statistics; Until 1973: Growth of World Industry.

338 314   YU
INDUSTRIJSKI PROIZVODI. (Subseries of Statisticki Bilten) a. 30 din.($1.67) Savezni Zavod za Statistiku, Kneza Milosa 20, Belgrade, Yugoslavia. stat. circ. 1,000.

310   FR   ISSN 0252-2683
INFORMATIONS RECENTES SUR LES COMPTES NATIONAUX DES PAYS EN DEVELOPPMENT/LATEST INFORMATION ON NATIONAL ACCOUNTS OF DEVELOPING COUNTRIES. (Text in English and French) 1967. a. free. Organization for Economic Co-operation & Development, 2 rue Andre Pascal, 75016 Paris, France. adv. circ. 2,000. (back issues avail.)

330 016   US   ISSN 0085-204X
INTERNATIONAL BIBLIOGRAPHY OF THE SOCIAL SCIENCES. ECONOMICS. Title page also reads: International Bibliography of Economics. 1952. a. $110. (Unesco, UN) Methuen Inc., 29 W. 35th St., New York, NY 10001-2291. circ. 2,000.

332 310   UN   ISSN 0020-6725
INTERNATIONAL FINANCIAL STATISTICS. French edition (ISSN 0252-2977); Spanish edition (ISSN 0252-3078) 1948. m.(plus annual issue) $100 ($50 to university libraries, faculty and students) International Monetary Fund, Publications Unit, 700 19th St., N.W., Washington, DC 20431. TEL 202-623-7430. Ed. Werner Dannemann. mkt. stat. charts. circ. 12,500. (also avail. in microfilm from UMI; magnetic tape; reprint service avail. from UMI) Indexed: P.A.I.S. Int.Manage.Inform. Key to Econ.Sci. PROMT.

310 658   UK   ISSN 0308-2938
INTERNATIONAL MARKETING DATA AND STATISTICS. 1975. a. £87. Euromonitor Publications Ltd., 87-88 Turnmill St., London EC1M 5QU, England.

332.1 310   UN   ISSN 0250-7374
INTERNATIONAL MONETARY FUND. GOVERNMENT FINANCE STATISTICS YEARBOOK. 1977. a. $20 ($10.00 to university libraries, faculty and students) International Monetary Fund, Publications Unit, 700 19th St., N.W., Washington, DC 20431. TEL 202-623-7430. Ed. Werner Dannemann. charts. stat. circ. 3,000. (also avail. in microform from UMI; back issues avail.)

382 310   UN   ISSN 0084-3822
INTERNATIONAL TRADE STATISTICS YEARBOOK. 1950. a. (in 2 vols.), latest 1984. $80 for 2 vols. (United Nations Statistical Office) United Nations Publications, Room DC2-853, New York, NY 10017 (Or Distribution and Sales Section, CH-1211 Geneva 10, Switzerland) (also avail. in microfiche)

332.67 314   YU
INVESTICIJE. (Subseries of Statisticki Bilten) 1966. a. 100 din.($3.24) Savezni Zavod za Statistiku, Uzun Mirkova 1, Belgrade, Yugoslavia. stat. circ. 1,000.

331   US
IOWA. BUREAU OF LABOR. BIENNIAL REPORT. 1885. biennial. free. Bureau of Labor, Research and Statistics Division, 307 E. Seventh St., Des Moines, IA 50319. TEL 515-281-3606. stat. circ. 300. (processed)

330 315   IR
IRAN. MINISTRY OF ECONOMY. BUREAU OF STATISTICS. SERIES.* no.49, 1969. irreg? Ministry of Finance and Economic Affairs, Bureau of Statistics, Director General of Statistics, Main Palace, Tehran, Iran. Ed. A. Sh. Shaheen. charts. stat.

381 315   IR
IRAN. MINISTRY OF ECONOMY. INTERNAL WHOLESALE TRADE STATISTICS.* (Text in English) a. free. Ministry of Finance and Economic Affairs, Teheran, Iran. stat. circ. controlled. (also avail. in record)

382 315   IR
IRAN. MINISTRY OF ECONOMY. INTERNATIONAL TRADE STATISTICS.* (Text in English) irreg. (approx. 1/yr.) free. Ministry of Finance and Economic Affairs, Teheran, Iran. stat. circ. controlled. (also avail. in record)

338 315   IR   ISSN 0075-0506
IRANIAN INDUSTRIAL STATISTICS.* (Text in English and Persian) 1962. a. free. Ministry of Finance and Economic Affairs, Bureau of Statistics, Tehran, Iran.

338 315   IQ
IRAQ. CENTRAL STATISTICAL ORGANIZATION. RESULTS OF THE INDUSTRIAL SURVEY OF LARGE ESTABLISHMENTS IN IRAQ. (Edition in Arabic and English) 1957. a. ID.1500. Central Statistical Organization, Baghdad, Iraq.

382 315   IQ   ISSN 0021-0900
IRAQ. CENTRAL STATISTICAL ORGANIZATION. SUMMARY OF FOREIGN TRADE STATISTICS. (Text and title in Arabic and English) 1960. a. ID.250. Central Statistical Organization, Baghdad, Iraq. circ. 500.

330   IE
IRELAND. CENTRAL STATISTICS OFFICE. ANALYSIS OF EXTERNAL TRADE BY PORTS. a. Central Statistics Office, Earlsfort Terrace, Dublin 2, Ireland. (processed)

336   IE
IRELAND. CENTRAL STATISTICS OFFICE. BALANCE OF INTERNATIONAL PAYMENTS. a. Central Statistics Office, Earlsfort Terrace, Dublin 2, Ireland.
  Stencilled release

IRELAND. CENTRAL STATISTICS OFFICE. BUILDING AND CONSTRUCTION: AVERAGE EARNINGS AND HOURS WORKED. see BUILDING AND CONSTRUCTION — Abstracting, Bibliographies, Statistics

IRELAND. CENTRAL STATISTICS OFFICE. BUILDING AND CONSTRUCTION PLANNING PERMISSIONS. see BUILDING AND CONSTRUCTION — Abstracting, Bibliographies, Statistics

IRELAND. CENTRAL STATISTICS OFFICE. CENSUS OF BUILDING AND CONSTRUCTION. see BUILDING AND CONSTRUCTION — Abstracting, Bibliographies, Statistics

IRELAND. CENTRAL STATISTICS OFFICE. CENSUS OF INDUSTRIAL PRODUCTION. see BUSINESS AND ECONOMICS

330   IE
IRELAND. CENTRAL STATISTICS OFFICE. ESTIMATED NUMBERS AND EXPENDITURE OF VISITORS TO IRELAND AND IRISH VISITORS ABROAD. a. Central Statistics Office, Earlsfort Terrace, Dublin 6, Ireland. (processed)

331   IE   ISSN 0790-5866
IRELAND. CENTRAL STATISTICS OFFICE. LABOUR FORCE SURVEY. FIRST RESULTS. a. £2.20. Central Statistics Office, Ardee Road, Rathmines, Dublin 6, Ireland (Subscr. to: Government Publications Office, Trade and Postal Sales, Bishop St., Dublin 8, Ireland)

330   IE
IRELAND. CENTRAL STATISTICS OFFICE. ROAD FREIGHT TRANSPORT SURVEY. a. £2.20. Central Statistics Office, Earlsfort Terrace, Dublin 2, Ireland (Subscr. to: Govermnent Publications Office, Trade and Postal Sales, Bishop St., Dublin 8, Ireland)

382 315   IS
ISRAEL. CENTRAL BUREAU OF STATISTICS. ANNUAL FOREIGN TRADE STATISTICS. (Part 1-Imports; Part 2-Exports; by Commodity and Country) (Text in English and Hebrew) 1975. a. $30. Central Bureau of Statistics, Box 13015, Jerusalem, Israel. stat.
  Supersedes: Israel. Central Bureau of Statistics. Foreign Trade Statistics Quarterly (ISSN 0021-1990); Israel. Central Bureau of Statistics. Monthly Foreign Trade Statistics.

331 315   IS   ISSN 0075-1049
ISRAEL. CENTRAL BUREAU OF STATISTICS. LABOUR FORCE SURVEYS. (Subseries of its Special Series) (Text in English and Hebrew) 1954. irreg., latest issue, no.738, 1982. price varies. Central Bureau of Statistics, Box 13015, Jerusalem, Israel.

330 314   IT   ISSN 0075-1723
ITALY. ISTITUTO CENTRALE DI STATISTICA. ANNUARIO DI STATISTICHE INDUSTRIALI. a. L.11000. Istituto Centrale di Statistica, Via Cesare Balbo 16, 00100 Rome, Italy. charts. illus. stat. circ. 1,500.

382 314   IT
ITALY. ISTITUTO CENTRALE DI STATISTICA. ANNUARIO STATISTICO DEL COMMERCIO INTERNO E DEL TURISMO. a. L.8500. Istituto Centrale di Statistica, Via Cesare Balbo 16, 00100 Rome, Italy. circ. 1,200.
  Formerly: Italy. Istituto Centrale di Statistica. Annuario Statistico del Commercio Interno (ISSN 0075-1782).

382 314   IT   ISSN 0390-6558
ITALY. ISTITUTO CENTRALE DI STATISTICA. STATISTICA ANNUALE DEL COMMERCIO CON L'ESTERO. TOMO 1. a. L.13000. Istituto Centrale di Statistica, Via Cesare Balbo 16, 00100 Rome, Italy. circ. 1,100.
  Supersedes in part: Italy. Istituto Centrale di Statistica. Statistica Annuale del Commercio con l'Estero (ISSN 0075-1871)

382 314   IT   ISSN 0390-6566
ITALY. ISTITUTO CENTRALE DI STATISTICA. STATISTICA ANNUALE DEL COMMERCIO CON L'ESTERO. TOMO 2. a. L.23000. Istituto Centrale di Statistica, Via Cesare Balbo 16, 00100 Rome, Italy. circ. 1,100.
  Supersedes in part: Italy. Istituto Centrale di Statistica. Statistica Annuale del Commercio con l'Estero (ISSN 0075-1871)

330 314   GW   ISSN 0021-4027
JAHRBUECHER FUER NATIONALOEKONOMIE UND STATISTIK. (Text and summaries in German or English) 1863. irreg., 6 nos./vol. DM.258. Gustav Fischer Verlag, Wollgrasweg 49, Postfach 720143, 7000 Stuttgart 70, W. Germany (B.R.D.) Ed.Bd. bk. rev. charts. index; cum.index. circ. 900. Indexed: P.A.I.S.For.Lang.Ind. SSCI. Key to Econ.Sci.

330 300   JA
JAPAN. MINISTRY OF HEALTH AND WELFARE. STATISTICS AND INFORMATION DEPARTMENT. REPORT ON SURVEY OF SOCIO-ECONOMIC ASPECTS ON VITAL EVENTS. a. 2.700 Yen. Ministry of Health and Welfare, Statistics and Information Department, 7-3 Ichigaya-Honmura cho, Shinjuk-ku, Tokyo 162, Japan (Order from: Health & Welfare Statistics Association, c/o Mezon Azabu, 5-13-14 Roppongi, Minato-ku, Tokyo, Japan)

331 315   JA
JAPAN. MINISTRY OF LABOUR. YEARBOOK OF LABOUR STATISTICS. (Text in English and Japanese) 1948. a. 8000 Yen. Ministry of Labour, Statistics and Information Department - Nihon Rodosho, Minister's Secretariat, Tokyo 100, Japan. charts.stat. circ. 800.

331.11 315   JA
JAPAN. STATISTICS BUREAU. EMPLOYMENT STATUS SURVEY. (Includes: Employment Statistics) 1956. quinquennial. price varies. Statistics Bureau - Management and Coordination Agency, 19-1 Wakamatsu-cho, Shinjuku-ku, Tokyo 162, Japan (Subscr. to: Government Publications Service Centre, 1-2-1 Kasumigaseki, Chiyoda-ku, Tokyo 100, Japan)

212   BUSINESS AND ECONOMICS — ABSTRACTING, BIBLIOGRAPHIES, STATISTICS

330 016   JA   ISSN 0448-8709
JAPAN SCIENCE REVIEW: ECONOMIC SCIENCES. (Text in English and Japanese) 1953. a. (Japan Union of Associations of Economic Sciences) Japan Society for the Promotion of Science, 2-1-2 Hitotsubashi, Chiyoda-ku, Tokyo 101, Japan. stat. author index.

382 315   JO   ISSN 0075-4021
JORDAN. DEPARTMENT OF STATISTICS. EXTERNAL TRADE STATISTICS. 1965. a. $30 incl. its Annual Statistical Yearbook. Department of Statistics, Amman, Jordan.

658   UK   ISSN 0142-5951
JOURNAL CONTENTS IN QUANTITATIVE METHODS. 1979. m. £65($110) University of Manchester, Institute of Science and Technology, Department of Management Sciences, P.O. Box 88, Manchester M60 1QD, England. Ed. Simon Conrad.

330.9 317   US
KENTUCKY ECONOMIC STATISTICS. 1952. a. $4. Department of Economic Development, Division of Research and Planning, Capitol Plaza Tower, Frankfort, KY 40601. TEL 502-564-4886. Ed. Ron Decker. circ. 2,500.
    Formerly: Kentucky Deskbook of Economic Statistics (ISSN 0361-591X)

316 331   KE
KENYA. CENTRAL BUREAU OF STATISTICS. EMPLOYMENT AND EARNINGS IN THE MODERN SECTOR. irreg., latest 1979. price varies. Central Bureau of Statistics, Ministry of Finance & Planning, Box 30266, Nairobi, Kenya (Orders to: Government Printing and Stationery Office, Box 30128, Nairobi, Kenya)

338 316   KE
KENYA. CENTRAL BUREAU OF STATISTICS. REGISTER OF MANUFACTURING FIRMS. 1970. irreg. EAs.10. Central Bureau of Statistics, Ministry of Finance & Planning, Box 30226, Nairobi, Kenya (Orders to: Government Printing and Stationery Department, Box 30128, Nairobi, Kenya)
    Formerly: Kenya. Ministry of Finance and Economic Planning. Statistics Division. Register of Manufacturing Firms.

316.76 338   KE
KENYA. CENTRAL BUREAU OF STATISTICS. STATISTICAL ABSTRACT. 1961. a. Central Bureau of Statistics, Ministry of Finance & Planning, Box 30266, Nairobi, Kenya (Orders to: Government Printing and Stationery Department, Box 30128, Nairobi, Kenya)
    Formerly: Kenya. Ministry of Economic Planning and Development. Statistics Division. Statistical Abstract (ISSN 0075-5850)

330 016   NE   ISSN 0165-4748
KEY TO ECONOMIC SCIENCE; semi-monthly review of abstracts on economics, finance, trade, industry, foreign aid, management, marketing, labour. (Text in Dutch, English, French and German; Dutch abstracts summarized in English) 1953. 24/yr. fl.168($63.50) (Ministerie van Economische Zaken, Economische Voorlichtingsdienst - Netherlands. Ministry of Economic Affairs. Economic Information Service) Martinus Nijhoff Publishers, Spuiboulevard 50, 3311 GR Dordrecht, Netherlands (Orders to: Kluwer Academic Publishers Group, Distribution Center, Box 322, 3300 AH Dordrecht, Netherlands) abstr. index. Indexed: Key to Econ.Sci.
    ●Also available online. Vendors: BELINDIS, Data-Star, DIALOG.
    Formerly: Economic Abstracts (ISSN 0012-9917)

339 315   KO   ISSN 0075-6822
KOREA (REPUBLIC). NATIONAL BUREAU OF STATISTICS. ANNUAL REPORT ON THE FAMILY INCOME AND EXPENDITURE SURVEY/TOSI GAGYE YONBO. (Text in English and Korean) 1963. a. 7830 Won. National Bureau of Statistics, Economic Planning Board, Gyeongun-Dong, Jongro-Gu, Seoul, S. Korea. Ed. Myong Hyun Sohn. circ. 400.

338.9 315   KO   ISSN 0075-6830
KOREA (REPUBLIC). NATIONAL BUREAU OF STATISTICS. ANNUAL REPORT ON THE PRICE SURVEY/MULGA YONBO. (Text in English and Korean) 1969. a. 7830 Won. National Bureau of Statistics, Economic Planning Board, Gyeongun-Dong, Jongro-Gu, Seoul, S. Korea. Ed. Myong Hyun Sohn. circ. 450.

KOREA (REPUBLIC). NATIONAL BUREAU OF STATISTICS. REPORT ON MINING AND MANUFACTURING SURVEY/ KWANGGONGUP TONGGYE ZO SA BOGO SEO. see MINES AND MINING INDUSTRY — Abstracting, Bibliographies, Statistics

380 315   KO   ISSN 0075-6857
KOREA (REPUBLIC). NATIONAL BUREAU OF STATISTICS. WHOLESALE AND RETAIL TRADE CENSUS REPORT/TOSOMAEUP CENSUS BOGO SEO. (Text in English and Korean) 1968. triennial. 17,400 Won. National Bureau of Statistics, Economic Planning Board, Gyeongun-Dong, Jongro-Gu, Seoul, S. Korea. Ed. Myong Hyun Sohn. circ. 700.

331.1 016   II   ISSN 0075-756X
LABOUR LITERATURE: A BIBLIOGRAPHY. (Text in English) 1957; N.S. 1971. a. free. ‡ Ministry of Labour, Library, Sharam Shakti Bhavan, Rafi Marg, New Delhi, India. Ed. S.P. Kulshresth. circ. 250. (processed)

331   CY
LABOUR STATISTICS REPORT. (Text in English) a. cyprus pounds 4. Ministry of Finance, Department of Statistics and Research, Nicosia, Cyprus.
    Supersedes: Annual Report on Unemployment.

330 315   LE   ISSN 0075-837X
LEBANON. DIRECTION CENTRALE DE LA STATISTIQUE. COMPTES ECONOMIQUES.* (Text in Arabic and French) a. Direction Centrale de la Statistique, Ministere du Plan, Beirut, Lebanon.

658   GE
LEITUNG UND PLANUNG VON WISSENSCHAFT UND TECHNIK. 1969. a. M.104. Zentralinstitut fuer Information und Dokumentation, Koepenicker Str. 80/82, 1020 Berlin, E. Germany (D.D.R.) circ. 850.

382 316   LY   ISSN 0075-9228
LIBYA. CENSUS AND STATISTICAL OFFICE. EXTERNAL TRADE STATISTICS. (Text in English and Arabic) 1954. q & a. free. Census and Statistical Department, Ministry of Planning, Tripoli, Libya.

338 316   LY   ISSN 0075-9244
LIBYA. CENSUS AND STATISTICAL OFFICE. INDUSTRIAL CENSUS. (Text in Arabic and English) 1964. decennial. free. Census and Statistical Department, Ministry of Planning, Tripoli, Libya.

338 316   LY   ISSN 0075-9252
LIBYA. CENSUS AND STATISTICAL OFFICE. REPORT OF THE ANNUAL SURVEY OF LARGE MANUFACTURING ESTABLISHMENTS. (Text in Arabic and English) 1965. a. free. Census and Statistical Department, Ministry of Planning, Tripoli, Libya.

331.2 314   YU   ISSN 0300-2535
LICNI DOHOCI. (Subseries of Statisticki Bilten) a. 30 din.($1.67) Savezni Zavod za Statistiku, Kneza Milosa 20, Belgrade, Yugoslavia. stat. circ. 1,000.

331 016   GW
LITERATURDOKUMENTATION ZUR ARBEITSMARKT- UND BERUFSFORSCHUNG. 1972. a. DM.20. Bundesanstalt fuer Arbeit, Institut fuer Arbeitsmarkt- und Berufsforschung, Regensburger Str. 104, 8500 Nuremberg, W. Germany (B.R.D.) index.cum.index: 1972-1974. circ. 5,000.

314 330   LU   ISSN 0076-1575
LUXEMBOURG. SERVICE CENTRAL DE LA STATISTIQUE ET DES ETUDES ECONOMIQUES. ANNUAIRE STATISTIQUE. 1955. a. 1000 Fr. Service Central de la Statistique et des Etudes Economiques, 19-21 Boulevard Royal, B.P. 304, 2013 Luxembourg, Luxembourg.
    Before 1962: Luxembourg. Office de la Statistique Generale. Annuaire Statistique.

312 330   LU
LUXEMBOURG. SERVICE CENTRAL DE LA STATISTIQUE ET DES ETUDES ECONOMIQUES. ANNUAIRE STATISTIQUE RETROSPECTIF. (Subseries of its Annuaire Statistique) 1960. every 10 yrs.; latest 1973. 800 Fr. Service Central de la Statistique et des Etudes Economiques, 19-21 Boulevard Royal, B.P. 304, 2013 Luxembourg, Luxembourg.

330 314   LU   ISSN 0076-1583
LUXEMBOURG. SERVICE CENTRAL DE LA STATISTIQUE ET DES ETUDES ECONOMIQUES. BULLETIN DU STATEC. 1955. irreg. (8-10/yr.) 680 Fr. Service Central de la Statistique et des Etudes Economiques, 19-21 Boulevard Royal, B.P. 304, 2013 Luxembourg, Luxembourg.

310 330   LU   ISSN 0076-1591
LUXEMBOURG. SERVICE CENTRAL DE LA STATISTIQUE ET DES ETUDES ECONOMIQUES. COLLECTION D ET M: DEFINITIONS ET METHODES. 1966. irreg. 100 Fr. per no. Service Central de la Statistique et des Etudes Economiques, 19-21 Boulevard Royal, B.P. 304, 2013 Luxembourg, Luxembourg.

330 314   LU   ISSN 0070-881X
LUXEMBOURG. SERVICE CENTRAL DE LA STATISTIQUE ET DES ETUDES ECONOMIQUES. CAHIERS ECONOMIQUES. SERIE A: ECONOMIE LUXEMBOURGEOISE. 1950. biennial. price varies. Service Central de la Statistique et des Etudes Economiques, 19-21 Boulevard Royal, B.P. 304, 2013 Luxembourg, Luxembourg.

330 314   LU
LUXEMBOURG. SERVICE CENTRAL DE LA STATISTIQUE ET DES ETUDES ECONOMIQUES. CAHIERS ECONOMIQUES. SERIE B: COMPTES NATIONAUX. irreg. price varies. Service Central de la Statistique et des Etudes Economiques, 19-21 bd. Royal, B.P. 304, 2013 Luxembourg, Luxembourg.

338 314   LU
LUXEMBOURG. SERVICE CENTRAL DE LA STATISTIQUE ET DES ETUDES ECONOMIQUES. CAHIERS ECONOMIQUES. SERIE C: APERCUS SUR L'INDUSTRIE. irreg. price varies. Service Central de la Statistique et des Etudes Economiques, 19-21 Boulevard Royal, B.P. 304, 2013 Luxembourg, Luxembourg.

330 314   LU
LUXEMBOURG. SERVICE CENTRAL DE LA STATISTIQUE ET DES ETUDES ECONOMIQUES. CAHIERS ECONOMIQUES. SERIE D: ETUDES DIVERSES. irreg. price varies. Service Central de la Statistique et des Etudes Economiques, 19-21 Boulevard Royal, B.P. 304, 2013 Luxembourg, Luxembourg.

330   HU   ISSN 0133-0152
MAGYAR KOZGAZDASAGI IRODALOM/ HUNGARIAN ECONOMIC LITERATURE. 1972. a. price varies or exchange basis. Marx Karoly Kozgazdasagtudomanyi Egyetem, Dimitrov Ter 8, Budapest 9, Hungary. Ed. Agnes Demmler. index. circ. 500.

338   MG
MALAGASY REPUBLIC. INSTITUT NATIONAL DE LA STATISTIQUE ET DE LA RECHERCHE ECONOMIQUE. RECENSEMENT INDUSTRIEL. 1969. irreg. FMG.6460. Direction Generale de la Banque des Donnees de l'Etat, Presidence de la republique, B.P. 485, Antananarivo, Malagasy Republic.

382 316   MW   ISSN 0076-325X
MALAWI. NATIONAL STATISTICAL OFFICE. ANNUAL STATEMENT OF EXTERNAL TRADE. 1964. a. K.18. ‡ National Statistical Office, Box 333, Zomba, Malawi.

BUSINESS AND ECONOMICS — ABSTRACTING, BIBLIOGRAPHIES, STATISTICS

330 316   MW   ISSN 0076-3241
MALAWI. NATIONAL STATISTICAL OFFICE. ANNUAL SURVEY OF ECONOMIC ACTIVITIES. (Issued in 1966 as: Census of Industrial Production) 1966. a. K.5.50($3.90) ‡ National Statistical Office, Box 333, Zomba, Malawi.

331 316   MW
MALAWI. NATIONAL STATISTICAL OFFICE. REPORTED EMPLOYMENT AND EARNINGS: ANNUAL REPORT. a. K.3.00. National Statistical Office, Box 333, Zomba, Malawi. stat.

330 316   ML
MALI. DIRECTION NATIONALE DE LA STATISTIQUE ET DE L'INFORMATIQUE. ANNUAIRE STATISTIQUE.* 1962. a. price varies. Direction Nationale de la Statistique et de la Informatique, Bamako, Mali. index.
   Former titles: Mali. Service de la Statistique Generale, de la Comptabilite Nationale et de la Mecanographie. Annuaire Statistique (ISSN 0076-3411); Before 1962 issued as: Chambre de Commerce d'Agriculture et d'Industrie de Bamako, Mali. Annuaire Statistique (ISSN 0069-2522)

336 316   ML
MALI. SERVICE DE LA STATISTIQUE GENERALE, DE LA COMTABILITE NATIONALE ET DE LA MECANOGRAPHIE. STATISTIQUES DOUANIERES DU COMMERCE EXTERIEUR.* irreg. Direction Nationale de la Statistique et de L'informatique, B.P. 12, Bamako, Mali.

338 314   MM   ISSN 0076-3462
MALTA. CENTRAL OFFICE OF STATISTICS. CENSUS OF INDUSTRIAL PRODUCTION REPORT. a. L.2. Central Office of Statistics, Auberge d'Italie, Valletta, Malta (Subscr. to: Information Division, Auberge de Castille, Valletta, Malta)
   Formerly: Malta. Central Office of Statistics. Census of Production Report.

658 016   II
MANAGEMENT ABSTRACTS. 1972. q. Rs.30($7) All India Management Association, Management Research and Information Division, 14, Institutional Area Lodi Rd., New Delhi 110003, India. Ed. Paul Zackariah. circ. 2,000.

338 016   TR
MANAGEMENT ABSTRACTS. 1973. bi-m. free. Management Development Centre, Library, Salvatori Building, Box 1301, Port-of-Spain, Trinidad, W.I. Ed. Joyce H. Williams. bk. rev. circ. 850.

658.8 016   US   ISSN 0308-2172
MANAGEMENT AND MARKETING ABSTRACTS. 1972. m. $400. (Paper Printing & Packaging Industries Research Association, UK) Pergamon Press, Inc., Journals Division, Maxwell House, Fairview Park, Elmsford, NY 10523 TEL 914-592-7700. (And: Headington Hill Hall, Oxford OX3 0BW, England) Ed. Marie Rushton. bk. rev. abstr. index. (also avail. in microform from MIM, UMI)
   ●Also available online. Vendors: Pergamon Infoline.
   Formerly: Marketing Abstracts (ISSN 0307-0794)

016 658   US   ISSN 0360-2400
MANAGEMENT CONTENTS; semi-monthly compilation of tables of contents from more than 320 business magazines and journals. 1975. bi-w. $95. Find-S V P, 500 Fifth Ave., New York, NY 10110. TEL 212-354-2424. Ed. Karen O'Connor. adv. bk. rev. circ. 2,000. (back issues avail.)
   ●Also available online. Vendors: BRS, DIALOG, Mead Data Central, Orbit Information Technologies.

658.8 016   UK   ISSN 0025-3596
MARKET RESEARCH ABSTRACTS. 1963. s-a. £40 to non-members. Market Research Society, 175 Oxford St., London W1R 1TA, England. Ed. Mrs. M. Rumble. circ. 700. (also avail. in microfilm from UMI)

382   US
MARKET SHARE REPORTS. irreg. country reports $11; commodity reports $7.50. U.S. National Technical Information Service, 5285 Port Royal Road, Springfield, VA 22161. TEL 703-487-4600. stat.

658.8 016   UK   ISSN 0305-0661
MARKETING & DISTRIBUTION ABSTRACTS. 1971. 8/yr (plus index) £102.50. (Institute of Marketing) Anbar Publications Ltd, P.O. Box 23, Wembley, England. Ed. A.C. Ede. (looseleaf format)

330   HU   ISSN 0521-4211
MARX KAROLY KOZGAZDASAGTUDOMANYI EGYETEM: DOKTORI ERTEKEZESEK. 1969. biennial. exchange basis. Marx Karoly Kozgazdasagtudomanyi Egyetem, Dimitrov Ter 8, Budapest 9, Hungary. Ed. Klara Liptai. index. circ. 300.
   ●Also available online. Vendors: DIALOG.

330   HU   ISSN 0133-5162
MARX KAROLY KOZGAZDASAGTUDOMANYI EGYETEM OKTATOINAK SZAKIRODALMI MUNKASSAGA. 1968. biennial. exchange basis. Marx Karoly Kozgazdasagtudomanyi Egyetem, Dimitrov Ter 8, Budapest 9, Hungary. Ed. Zsuzsa Nagy. index. circ. 1,000.

381   MF
MAURITIUS. CENTRAL STATISTICAL OFFICE. NATIONAL ACCOUNTS OF MAURITIUS. 1983. a. Rs.100. Central Statistical Office, Rose Hill, Mauritius (Orders to: G.P.O., Elizabeth II, Port Louis, Mauritius)

338 318   MX   ISSN 0071-1543
MEXICO. DIRECCION GENERAL DE ESTADISTICA. ESTADISTICA INDUSTRIAL ANUAL. 1963. irreg., latest 1974. free. Secretaria de Programacion y Presupuesto, Articulo 123 no. 88, Mexico 1, D.F., Mexico (Orders to: Direccion General de Estudios del Territorio Nacional, Balderas 71, Col. Centro, Mexico 1, D.F., Mexico)

331 318   MX   ISSN 0076-7492
MEXICO. SECRETARIA DE PROGRAMACION Y PRESUPUESTO. 1938. a. free. Secretaria de Programacion y Presupuesto, Departamento de Estadisticas Industriales, Articulo 123 no. 88, Mexico 1, D.F., Mexico (Orders to: Direccion General de Estudios del Territorio Nacional, Balderas 71, Col. Centro, Mexico 1, D.F., Mexico)

330 016   US   ISSN 0091-9047
MICHIGAN BUSINESS AND ECONOMIC RESEARCH BIBLIOGRAPHY. irreg. free. University of Michigan, Institute of Science & Technology, Division of Research, 851 Senda Plata, Venice, FL 33595. TEL 313-764-1817. Ed. A.W. Swinyard.

331.2   AT
MONASH UNIVERSITY. CAREERS & APPOINTMENTS SERVICE. SURVEY OF GRADUATE STARTING SALARIES AS OF 30 APRIL (YEAR) 1979. a. Monash University, Careers & Appointments Service, Wellington Road, Clayton, Vic 3168, Australia. Ed. Jennifer Baldwin. circ. 2,000.

382   MJ
MONTSERRAT. STATISTICS OFFICE. DIGEST OF STATISTICS. no.2, 1975. a. $10. Statistics Office, Plymouth, Montserrat.
   Formerly: Montserrat. Statistics Office. Digest of Overseas Trade Statistics.

336 315   PH
N E D A STATISTICAL YEARBOOK OF THE PHILIPPINES. (Text in English) 1974. a. National Economic and Development Authority, Box 1116, Manila, Philippines.

339.373   US   ISSN 0361-3895
NATIONAL INCOME AND PRODUCT ACCOUNTS OF THE UNITED STATES: STATISTICAL TABLES. 1965. irreg. $12.50. U.S. Department of Commerce, Office of Business Economics, Washington, DC 20203 TEL 202-377-2000. (Order from: NTIS, 5285 Port Royal Rd., Springfield, VA 22161)

339 315   TH
NATIONAL INCOME OF THAILAND. (Text in English, Thai) 1964. a. free. National Economic And Social Development Board, Office of the Prime Minister, Bangkok 10100, Thailand. charts.
   Formerly: National Income Statistics of Thailand (ISSN 0077-4723)

016 338.9   UK
NEDDY BOOKS AND VIDEOS. 1970. a. free. National Economic Development Office, Millbank Tower, Millbank, London SW1P 4QX, England. Ed. J. Collinson. bibl. circ. 10,000.
   Former titles: Neddy Books; N.E.D.O. in Print.

338 314   YU   ISSN 0300-2497
NEKI POKAZATELJI TEHNICKOG RAZVOJA PRIVREDE JUGOSLAVIJE. (Subseries of Statisticki Bilten. Continues Statistika Nove Tehniki. Issued also in English) a. 10 din.($1.11) Savezni Zavod za Statistiku, Kneza Milosa 20, Belgrade, Yugoslavia. circ. 1,000.

016 338.9   NP
NEPAL DOCUMENTATION; occasional bibliography. (Text in English and Nepali) 1972. irreg. Rs.10($4) Centre for Economic Development and Administration, Box 797, Kirtipur Campus, Kathmandu, Nepal. index. (back issues avail.)

338.9 315   NP   ISSN 0077-6564
NEPAL INDUSTRIAL DEVELOPMENT CORPORATION. STATISTICAL ABSTRACTS. (Text in English) irreg. Nepal Industrial Development Corporation, N.I.D.C. Bldg., Durbar Marg, Box 10, Kathmandu, Nepal.

332.75 314   NE   ISSN 0077-6793
NETHERLANDS. CENTRAAL BUREAU VOOR DE STATISTIEK. FAILLISSEMENTSSTATISTIEK. BANKRUPTCIES. (Text in Dutch and English) 1951. fl.15. Centraal Bureau voor de Statistiek, Prinses Beatrixlaan 428, Voorburg, Netherlands (Orders to: Staatsuitgeverij, Christoffel Plantijnstraat, The Hague, Netherlands)

332 314   NE   ISSN 0168-4590
NETHERLANDS. CENTRAAL BUREAU VOOR DE STATISTIEK. HYPOTHEKEN. STATISTICS OF MORTGAGES. (Text in Dutch and English) 1965. a. fl.13.70. Centraal Bureau voor de Statistiek, Prinses Beatrixlaan 428, Voorburg, Netherlands (Orders to: Staatsuitgeverij, Christoffel Plantijnstraat, The Hague, Netherlands)
   Formerly: Netherlands. Centraal Bureau voor de Statistiek. Hypotheken en Hypotheekbanken. Statistics of Mortgages (ISSN 0077-6823)

382 314   NE
NETHERLANDS. CENTRAAL BUREAU VOOR DE STATISTIEK. NAAMLIJSTEN VOOR DE STATISTIEK VAN DE BUITENLANDSE HANDEL. LIST OF GOODS FOR THE STATISTICS OF FOREIGN TRADE. 1969. a. fl.50. Centraal Bureau voor de Statistiek, Prinses Beatrixlaan 428, Voorburg, Netherlands (Orders to: Staatsuitgeverij, Christoffel Plantijnstraat, The Hague, Netherlands)

382 314   NE   ISSN 0168-4094
NETHERLANDS. CENTRAAL BUREAU VOOR DE STATISTIEK. NAAMLIJSTEN VOOR DE STATISTIEK VAN DE BUITENLANDSE HANDEL. SUPPLEMENT. LIST OF GOODS FOR THE STATISTICS OF FOREIGN TRADE. SUPPLEMENT. 1962. a. fl.28.50. Centraal Bureau voor de Statistiek, Prinses Beatrixlaan 428, Voorburg, Netherlands (Orders to: Staatsuitgeverij, Christoffel Plantijnstraat, The Hague, Netherlands)

663   NE   ISSN 0168-5767
NETHERLANDS. CENTRAAL BUREAU VOOR DE STATISTIEK. PRODUKTIESTATISTIEKEN: ALCOHOLFABRIEKEN, BIERBROUWERIJEN EN MOUTERIJEN, DISTILLEERDERIJEN EN FRISDRANKENINDUSTRIE. a. fl.14.40. Centraal Bureau voor de Statistiek, Prinses Beatrixlaan 428, Voorburg, Netherlands (Orders to: Staatsuitgeverij, Christoffel Plantijnstraat, The Hague, Netherlands)
   Former titles: Netherlands. Centraal Bureau voor de Statistiek. Produktiestatistieken: Bierbrouwerijen en Mouterijen, Alcoholfabrieken, Distilleerderijen en Frisdrankenindustrie; Netherlands. Centraal Bureau voor de Statistiek. Produktiestatistieken: Bierbrouwerijen en Mouterijen, Distilleerderijen en Likeurstokerijen, Frisdrankindustrie; Netherlands. Centraal Bureau voor de Statistiek. Produktiestatistieken: Distilleerderijen en Likeurstokerijen.

BUSINESS AND ECONOMICS — ABSTRACTING, BIBLIOGRAPHIES, STATISTICS

331 338.1 314   NE   ISSN 0077-6963
NETHERLANDS. CENTRAAL BUREAU VOOR DE STATISTIEK. STATISTIEK DER LONEN IN DE LANDBOUW. STATISTICS OF WAGES IN AGRICULTURE. (Text in Dutch and English) 1958. irreg. fl.4. Centraal Bureau voor de Statistiek, Prinses Beatrixlaan 428, Voorburg, Netherlands (Orders to: Staatsuitgeverij, Christoffel Plantijnstraat, The Hague, Netherlands)

382 314   NE   ISSN 0168-4876
NETHERLANDS. CENTRAAL BUREAU VOOR DE STATISTIEK. STATISTIEK VAN DE AAN-, AF- EN DOORVOER. GOEDERENVERVOER VAN EN NAAR NEDERLAND. STATISTICS OF THE INTERNATIONAL GOODS TRAFFIC. (Text in Dutch and English) 1963. a. fl.24.05. Centraal Bureau voor de Statistiek, Prinses Beatrixlaan 428, Voorburg, Netherlands (Orders to: Staatsuitgeverij, Christoffel Plantijnstraat, The Hague, Netherlands)
    Formerly: Netherlands. Centraal Bureau voor de Statistiek. Statistiek van het Internationaal Goederenvervoer. Statistics of the International Goods Traffic (ISSN 0077-7293)

332   NE   ISSN 0168-7956
NETHERLANDS. CENTRAAL BUREAU VOOR DE STATISTIEK. STATISTIEK VAN DE INVESTERINGEN IN VASTE ACTIVA IN DE NIJVERHEID. STATISTICS ON FIXED CAPITAL FORMATION IN INDUSTRY. (Text in Dutch and English) 1951/52. a. fl.12.45. Centraal Bureau voor de Statistiek, Prinses Beatrixlaan 428, Voorburg, Netherlands (Orders to: Staatsuitgeverij, Christoffel Plantijnstraat, The Hague, Netherlands)
    Formerly: Netherlands. Centraal Bureau voor de Statistiek. Statistiek van de Investeringen in Vaste Activa in de Industrie (ISSN 0077-7110)

332 314   NE   ISSN 0168-3330
NETHERLANDS. CENTRAAL BUREAU VOOR DE STATISTIEK. STATISTIEK VAN DE SPAARGELDEN. STATISTICS OF SAVINGS. (Text in Dutch and English) 1965. a. price varies. Centraal Bureau voor de Statistiek, Prinses Beatrixlaan 428, Voorburg, Netherlands (Orders to: Staatsuitgeverij, Christoffel Plantijnstraat, The Hague, Netherlands)

331 314   NE   ISSN 0168-3667
NETHERLANDS. CENTRAAL BUREAU VOOR DE STATISTIEK. STATISTIEK WERKZAME PERSONEN. a. fl.16. Centraal Bureau voor de Statistiek, Prinses Beatrixlaan 428, Voorburg, Netherlands (Orders to: Staatsuitgeverij, Christoffel Plantijnstraat, The Hague, Netherlands)

330 310   NE
NETHERLANDS. CENTRAAL BUREAU VOOR DE STATISTIEK. STATISTISCHE ONDERZOEKINGEN. (Text in Dutch and English) 1947. irreg. price varies. Centraal Bureau voor de Statistiek, Prinses Beatrixlaan 428, Voorburg, Netherlands (Orders to: Staatsuitgeverij, Christoffel Plantijnstraat, The Hague, Netherlands)
    Formerly: Netherlands. Centraal Bureau voor de Statistiek. Statistische en Econometrische Onderzoekingen. Statistical and Econometric Studies (ISSN 0077-7048)

339 314   NE   ISSN 0168-3888
NETHERLANDS. CENTRAAL BUREAU VOOR DE STATISTIEK. VERMOGENSVERDELING. REGIONALE GEGEVENS. DISTRIBUTION OF PERSONAL WEALTH. REGIONAL DATA. (Text in Dutch and English) 1951. irreg. fl.18.10. Centraal Bureau voor de Statistiek, Prinses Beatrixlaan 428, Voorburg, Netherlands (Orders to: Staatsuitgeverij, Christoffel Plantijnstraat, The Hague, Netherlands)

338 314   NE   ISSN 0077-751X
NETHERLANDS. CENTRAAL BUREAU VOOR DE STATISTIEK. WINSTSTATISTIEK DER GROTERE NAAMLOZE VENNOOTSCHAPPEN. PROFIT-STATISTICS OF THE LIMITED LIABILITY COMPANIES. (Text in Dutch and English) 1939-51. a. fl.7. Centraal Bureau voor de Statistiek, Prinses Beatrixlaan 428, Voorburg, Netherlands (Orders to: Staatsuitgeverij, Christoffel Plantijnstraat, The Hague, Netherlands)

331.1 317   US   ISSN 0550-6638
NEW YORK (STATE). DEPARTMENT OF LABOR. STATISTICS ON OPERATIONS. ANNUAL REPORT. a. Department of Labor, Division of Research and Statistics, One Main St., 9th Fl., Brooklyn, NY 11201 TEL 718-797-7703. (Dist. by: Office of Communications, State Campus, Albany, N.Y. 12240) Ed. Eileen DeVeau. illus. stat.

382 319   NZ   ISSN 0110-2184
NEW ZEALAND. DEPARTMENT OF STATISTICS. EXPORTS. a. NZ.$13.20. Department of Statistics, Private Bag, Wellington, New Zealand (Subscr. to: Government Printing Office, Publications, Private Bag, Wellington, New Zealand) (also avail. in microfiche)

382.5 319   NZ   ISSN 0110-3741
NEW ZEALAND. DEPARTMENT OF STATISTICS. IMPORTS. a. NZ.$13.20. Department of Statistics, Wellington, New Zealand (Subscr. to: Government Printing Office, Publications, Private Bag, Wellington, New Zealand) (also avail. in microfiche)

336   NZ   ISSN 0110-3776
NEW ZEALAND. DEPARTMENT OF STATISTICS. INCOMES AND INCOME TAX STATISTICS. a. NZ.$5. Department of Statistics, Private Bag, Wellington, New Zealand (Subscr. to: Government Printing Office, Publications, Private Bag, Wellington, New Zealand)

382 339 319   NZ   ISSN 0112-5117
NEW ZEALAND. DEPARTMENT OF STATISTICS. OVERSEAS BALANCE OF PAYMENTS. a. NZ.$5.50. Department of Statistics, Private Bag, Wellington, New Zealand (Subscr. to: Government Printing Office, Publications, Private Bag, Wellington, New Zealand)
    Formerly: New Zealand. Department of Statistics. Balance of Payments (ISSN 0110-4616)

331 319   NZ   ISSN 0110-5019
NEW ZEALAND. DEPARTMENT OF STATISTICS. PART A: PRICES. a. NZ.$7. Department of Statistics, Private Bag, Wellington, New Zealand (Subscr. to: Government Printing Office, Publications, Private Bag, Wellington, New Zealand)
    Supersedes in part: New Zealand. Department of Statistics. Prices, Wages and Labour (ISSN 0077-9911)

382 319   NZ   ISSN 0077-9806
NEW ZEALAND. DEPARTMENT OF STATISTICS. REPORT AND ANALYSIS OF EXTERNAL TRADE. a. NZ.$8.80. Department of Statistics, Private Bag, Wellington, New Zealand (Subscr. to: Government Printing Office, Publications, Private Bag, Wellington, New Zealand)

336   NZ   ISSN 0112-3998
NEW ZEALAND. DEPARTMENT OF STATISTICS. STATISTICS OF INCOMES AND INCOME TAX OF COMPANIES. biennial. NZ.$5.50. Department of Statistics, Private Bag, Wellington, New Zealand (Subscr. to: Government Printing Office, Publications, Private Bag, Wellington, New Zealand)

336   NZ   ISSN 0112-3939
NEW ZEALAND. DEPARTMENT OF STATISTICS. STATISTICS OF INCOMES AND INCOME TAX OF PERSONS. irreg. NZ.$7.15. Department of Statistics, Private Bag, Wellington, New Zealand (Subscr. to: Government Printing Office, Publications, Private Bag, Wellington, New Zealand)

319 339   NZ   ISSN 0112-6601
NEW ZEALAND HOUSEHOLD EXPENDITURE AND INCOME SURVEY. 1974. a. NZ.$13.75. Department of Statistics, Wellington, New Zealand (Subscr. to: Government Printing Office, Publications, Private Bag, Wellington, New Zealand) stat.
    Former titles: New Zealand Household Survey (ISSN 0110-392X); New Zealand. Department of Statistics. Household Sample Survey.

338   NQ
NICARAGUA. INSTITUTO NACIONAL DE ESTADISTICAS Y CENSOS. ENCUESTA ANUAL INDUSTRIA MANUFACTURERE. a. Instituto Nacional de Estadisticas y Censos, Apdo. Postal 4031, Managua, Nicaragua.

338 310   NR
NIGERIA. FEDERAL OFFICE OF STATISTICS. INDUSTRIAL SURVEY. a. £N3. Federal Office of Statistics, P.M.B. 12528, Lagos, Nigeria.

658 310   NR
NIGERIA. FEDERAL OFFICE OF STATISTICS. REPORT ON RURAL CONSUMER SURVEY. a. £N2. Federal Office of Statistics, P.M.B. 12528, Lagos, Nigeria.

330.9 310   NR
NIGERIA. FEDERAL OFFICE OF STATISTICS. REPORT ON RURAL ECONOMIC SURVEY. a. £N2. Federal Office of Statistics, P.M.B. 12528, Lagos, Nigeria.

658 310   NR
NIGERIA. FEDERAL OFFICE OF STATISTICS. REPORT ON URBAN CONSUMER SURVEY. a. £N2. Federal Office of Statistics, P.M.B. 12528, Lagos, Nigeria.

316 382   NR   ISSN 0078-0634
NIGERIA. FEDERAL OFFICE OF STATISTICS. REVIEW OF EXTERNAL TRADE.* (Text in English) 1964. a. £N5s. Federal Office of Statistics, P.M.B. 12528, Lagos, Nigeria.

330   NR   ISSN 0794-2877
NIGERIA BUSINESS GUIDE ANNUAL; a practical guide for businessmen and foreign investors in Nigeria. (Text in English) 1986. a. $25. Comprehensive Guide Ltd., P.O. Box 3323, Lagos, Nigeria. Ed. Joseph Ajiboye. adv. bk. rev. circ. 250,000.

029   NO   ISSN 0558-0439
NORSK SENTER FOR INFORMATIKK. ARTIKKEL INDEKS. 1948. m. (10/yr.) Kr.5900 (includes annual General-Indeks) Norsk Senter for Informatikk, Forskningsveien 1, Oslo 3, Norway. Ed. Geirr I. Leistad. abstr.

331 314   NO   ISSN 0078-1878
NORWAY. STATISTISK SENTRALBYRAA. ARBEIDSMARKEDSTATISTIKK/LABOUR MARKET STATISTICS. (Subseries of its Norges Offisielle Statistikk) (Text in English and Norwegian) 1967. a. Kr.40. Statistisk Sentralbyraa, Box 8131 Dep., 0033 Oslo 1, Norway. circ. 1,600.

338 314   NO   ISSN 0800-580X
NORWAY. STATISTISK SENTRALBYRAA. INDUSTRISTATISTIKK/INDUSTRIAL STATISTICS. VOL.1. (Subseries of its Norges Offisielle Statistikk) (Text in English and Norwegian) 1961. a. Kr.50. Statistisk Sentralbyraa, Box 8131 Dep., 0033 Oslo 1, Norway. circ. 1,800.
    Supersedes in part (after 1982): Norway. Statistisk Sentralbyraa. Industristatistikk/Industrial Statistics (ISSN 0078-1886)

338 314   NO   ISSN 0800-5818
NORWAY. STATISTISK SENTRALBYRAA. INDUSTRISTATISTIKK/INDUSTRIAL STATISTICS. VOL.2. a. Kr.50. Statistisk Sentralbyraa, P.O. Box 8131 Dep., 0033 Oslo 1, Norway. circ. 1,800.
    Supersedes in part (as from 1982): Norway. Statistisk Sentralbyraa. Industristatistikk/Industrial Statistics (ISSN 0078-1886)

332.1 314   NO   ISSN 0078-1908
NORWAY. STATISTISK SENTRALBYRAA. KREDITTMARKED STATISTIKK/CREDIT MARKET STATISTICS. (Subseries of its Norges Offisielle Statistikk) (Text in English and Norwegian) 1955. a. Kr.30. Statistisk Sentralbyraa, Box 8131 Dep., 0033 Oslo 1, Norway.

331 314   NO   ISSN 0078-1916
NORWAY. STATISTISK SENTRALBYRAA. LOENNSSTATISTIKK/WAGE STATISTICS. (Subseries of its Norges Offisielle Statistikk) (Text in English and Norwegian) 1950. a. Kr.45. Statistisk Sentralbyraa, Box 8131 Dep., 0033 Oslo 1, Norway. circ. 1,400.

314   NO
NORWAY. STATISTISK SENTRALBYRAA. NASJONALREGNSKAP/NATIONAL ACCOUNTS. (Subseries of its Norges Offisielle Statistikk) 1965. a. Kr.55. Statistisk Sentralbyraa, Box 8131 Dep., 0033 Oslo 1, Norway. circ. 2,000.

BUSINESS AND ECONOMICS — ABSTRACTING, BIBLIOGRAPHIES, STATISTICS 215

330 314 NO ISSN 0078-1924
NORWAY. STATISTISK SENTRALBYRAA.
OEKONOMISK UTSYN/ECONOMIC SURVEY.
(Subseries of its Norges Offisielle Statistikk) (Text in Norwegian; summaries in English) 1936. quadrennial. price varies. Statistisk Sentralbyraa, Box 8131 Dep., 0033 Oslo 1, Norway. circ. 6,100.

382 314 NO ISSN 0078-1940
NORWAY. STATISTISK SENTRALBYRAA.
UTENRIKSHANDEL/EXTERNAL TRADE.
(Subseries of its Norges Offisielle Statistikk) (Text in English and Norwegian) 1961. a. Kr.70. Statistisk Sentralbyraa, Box 8131 Dep., 0033 Oslo 1, Norway. circ. 2,000.

381 314 NO ISSN 0078-1959
NORWAY. STATISTISK SENTRALBYRAA.
VAREHANDELSSTATISTIKK/WHOLESALE
AND RETAIL TRADE STATISTICS. (Subseries of its Norges Offisielle Statistikk) (Text in English and Norwegian) 1966. a. Kr.50. Statistisk Sentralbyraa, Box 8131 Dep., 0033 Oslo 1, Norway. circ. 1,450.

330 016 UR
NOVAYA LITERATURA PO TSENOOBRAZOVANIYU, OPUBLIKOVANNAYA V S.S.S.R; annotirovannyi ukazatel' 1970. irreg. 0.42 Rub. Nauchno-Issledovatel'skii Institut po Tsenoobrazovaniyu, Vtoraya Yaroslavskaya ul., 3, Moscow, Russian S.F.S.R., U.S.S.R.

332 310 FR ISSN 0304-3371
O E C D FINANCIAL STATISTICS/
STATISTIQUES FINANCIERES DE L'O C D E.
(In 3 Parts Plus the Methodological Supplement; Part 1: Monthly Financial Statistics; Part 2: Financial Accounts, Part 3: Non-Financial Enterprises Financial Statements) (Text in English and French) 1971. m.(Part 1); 3/yr.(Part 2); a.(Part 3 and supplement) 500 F.($100) combined subscription with Financial Market Trends 360F($72) Organization for Economic Cooperation and Development, 2 rue Andre-Pascal, 75775 Paris Cedex 16, France (U.S. orders to: O.E.C.D. Publications and Information Center, 1750 Pennsylvania Ave., N.W., Washington, DC 20006) (also avail. in microfiche)

339 314 AU ISSN 0085-4433
OESTERREICHS VOLKSEINKOMMEN. 1952. a. S.240. Oesterreichisches Statistisches Zentralamt, Hintere Zollamtsstr. 2b, 1033 Vienna, Austria.

331 317 US
OKLAHOMA. EMPLOYMENT SECURITY COMMISSION. ACTUARIAL DIVISION.
HANDBOOK OF EMPLOYMENT SECURITY PROGRAM STATISTICS. 1952. a. free. Employment Security Commission, Actuarial Division, Will Rogers Bldg., Oklahoma City, OK 73105. TEL 405-521-3735. Ed. Dennis O. Martin. stat. circ. 500.

331 US
OKLAHOMA. EMPLOYMENT SECURITY COMMISSION. RESEARCH DIVISION.
COUNTY EMPLOYMENT AND WAGE DATA. 1952. a. free. Employment Security Commission, Research Division, 310 Will Rogers Bldg., Oklahoma City, OK 73105. Ed. Dennis Martin. stat. circ. 800.
Formerly: Oklahoma. Employment Security Commission. Research and Planning Division. County Employment and Wage Data.

OPERATIONS RESEARCH/MANAGEMENT SCIENCE; international literature digest service. see *ABSTRACTING AND INDEXING SERVICES*

382 FR ISSN 0474-540X
ORGANIZATION FOR ECONOMIC COOPERATION AND DEVELOPMENT.
FOREIGN TRADE BY COMMODITIES.
(Editions in English and French) 1975. a. 150 F.($30) Organization for Economic Cooperation and Development, 2 rue Andre-Pascal, 75775 Paris Cedex 16, France (U.S. orders to: O.E.C.D. Publications and Information Center, 1750 Pennsylvania Ave., N.W., Washington, DC 20006) (also avail. in microfiche)
Former titles: Organization for Economic Cooperation and Development. Statistics of Foreign Trade. Series C: Tables by Commodities. Imports and Exports/Statistiques du Commerce Exterieur. Serie C: Tableaux par Produits; Organization for Economic Cooperation and Development. Statistics of Foreign Trade. Series C: Trade by Commoditiess. Market Summaries. Imports and Exports/ Statistiques du Commerce Exterieur. Serie C: Exchange Par Produits. Resume Par Marches. Importations et Exportations & O E C D Foreign Trade Statistics. Serie C.

311.11 310 FR ISSN 0474-5515
ORGANIZATION FOR ECONOMIC COOPERATION AND DEVELOPMENT.
LABOUR FORCE STATISTICS (YEARBOOK) / STATISTIQUES DE LA POPULATION ACTIVE. (Text in English and French) 1950. a. (with q. supplements) price varies. Organization for Economic Cooperation and Development, Chateau de la Muette, 2 rue Andre Pascal, 75775 Paris 16, France (U.S. orders to: O.E.C.D. Publications and Information Center, 1750 Pennsylvania Ave., N.W., Washington, DC 20006) (also avail. in microfiche)

338.9 310 FR
ORGANIZATION FOR ECONOMIC COOPERATION AND DEVELOPMENT. MAIN ECONOMIC INDICATORS. HISTORICAL STATISTICS. STATISTIQUES RETROSPECTIVES. (Text in English and French) 1966. irreg. $17. Organization for Economic Cooperation and Development, 2 rue Andre Pascal, 75775 Paris 16, France (U.S. orders to: O.E.C.D Publications and Information Center, 1750 Pennsylvania Ave., N.W., Washington, DC 20006) (also avail. in microfiche)
Formerly: Organization for Economic Cooperation and Development. Historical Statistics. Statistiques Retrospectives (ISSN 0474-5442)

336.2 FR
ORGANIZATION FOR ECONOMIC COOPERATION AND DEVELOPMENT.
REVENUE STATISTICS OF O.E.C.D. MEMBER COUNTRIES. (Text in English and French) 1965. a. $27. Organization for Economic Cooperation and Development, 2 rue Andre - Pascal, 75775 Paris Cedex 16, France (U.S. orders to: O.E.C.D. Publications and Information Center, 1750 Pennsylvania Ave., N.W., Washington, DC 20006) (also avail. in microfiche)

330.9 016 300.9 US
P A I S BULLETIN. (Also avail. on CD-ROM) 1915. m. (cumulated 4/yr.) $295. Public Affairs Information Service, Inc., 11 W. 40th St., New York, NY 10018-2693. TEL 212-869-6186. Ed. Lawrence J. Woods. (reprint service avail.)
●Also available online. Vendors: BRS, Data-Star, DIALOG.
Formerly: Public Affairs Information Service. Bulletin (ISSN 0033-3409)

320 016 US
P A I S FOREIGN LANGUAGE INDEX. (Includes 3 cum. q. issues and annual vol.; also avail. on CD-ROM) (Text in English; indexes material in Italian, Portuguese, Spanish) 1972. q. $495. Public Affairs Information Service, Inc., 11 W. 40th St., New York, NY 10018. TEL 212-869-6186. Ed. Lawrence J. Woods. author index. (reprint service avail.)
●Also available online. Vendors: BRS, Data-Star, DIALOG.
Formerly: Public Affairs Information Service Foreign Language Index (ISSN 0048-5810)

336 PK
PAKISTAN. FINANCE DIVISION. PUBLIC FINANCE STATISTICS. (Text in English) 1975/76. a. Finance Division, Islamabad, Pakistan.

338.9 315 PK
PAKISTAN INSTITUTE OF DEVELOPMENT ECONOMICS. STATISTICAL PAPERS. 1967. irreg. price varies. Pakistan Institute of Development Economics, Box 1091, Islamabad, Pakistan. Ed.Bd. stat. circ. 1,000.

319 330 PP
PAPUA NEW GUINEA. BUREAU OF STATISTICS. STATISTICAL BULLETIN: NATIONAL ACCOUNTS STATISTICS. (Text in English) a. free. National Statistical Office, P.O. Wards Strip, Papua New Guinea. Ed. J.J. Shadlow.

319 330 PP
PAPUA NEW GUINEA. BUREAU OF STATISTICS. STATISTICAL BULLETIN: SURVEY OF RETAIL SALES AND SELECTED SERVICES. (Text in English) a. free. National Statistical Office, P.O. Wards Strip, Papua New Guinea. Ed. J.J. Shadlow.
Formerly: Papua New Guinea. Bureau of Statistics. Statistical Bulletin: Census of Retail Sales and Selected Services.

338 315 PP ISSN 0078-7701
PAPUA NEW GUINEA. NATIONAL STATISTICAL OFFICE. RURAL INDUSTRIES. 1959. a. free. National Statistical Office, P.O. Wards Strip, Papua New Guinea. Ed. J.J. Shadlow. circ. 884.

338 315 PP ISSN 0078-9321
PAPUA NEW GUINEA. NATIONAL STATISTICAL OFFICE. RURAL INDUSTRIES. PRELIMINARY STATEMENT. 1968. a. free. National Statistical Office, P.O. Wards Strip, Papua New Guinea. Ed. J.J. Shadlow. circ. 884.

338 315 PP ISSN 0078-9313
PAPUA NEW GUINEA. NATIONAL STATISTICAL OFFICE. SECONDARY INDUSTRIES (FACTORIES AND WORKS). PRELIMINARY STATEMENT. 1966/67. a. free. National Statistical Office, P.O. Wards Strip, Papua New Guinea. Ed. J.J. Shadlow. circ. 758.

338 315 PP ISSN 0078-933X
PAPUA NEW GUINEA. NATIONAL STATISTICAL OFFICE. SECONDARY INDUSTRIES. 1959. a. free. National Statistical Office, P.O. Wards Strip, Papua New Guinea. Ed. J.J. Shadlow. circ. 758.

338 319 PP ISSN 0078-9259
PAPUA NEW GUINEA. NATIONAL STATISTICAL OFFICE. STATISTICAL BULLETIN: CAPITAL EXPENDITURE BY PRIVATE BUSINESSES. 1968. a. free. National Statistical Office, P.O. Wards Strip, Papua New Guinea. Ed. J.J. Shadlow. circ. 652.

381 319 PP
PAPUA NEW GUINEA. NATIONAL STATISTICAL OFFICE. STATISTICAL BULLETIN: SURVEY OF RETAIL SALES AND SELECTED SERVICES. (Text in English) 1967/68. a. National Statistical Office, P.O. Wards Strip, Papua New Guinea. circ. 612.

336.2 319 PP ISSN 0078-9372
PAPUA NEW GUINEA. NATIONAL STATISTICAL OFFICE. TAXATION STATISTICS. PRELIMINARY BULLETIN. 1966/67. a. free. National Statistical Office, P.O. Wards Strip, Papua New Guinea. Ed. J.J. Shadlow. circ. 590.

338 318 PY ISSN 0085-4743
PARAGUAY. MINISTERIO DE INDUSTRIA Y COMERCIO. DIVISION DE REGISTRO Y ESTADISTICA INDUSTRIAL. ENCUESTA INDUSTRIAL. irreg. free. Ministerio de Industria y Comercio, Division de Registro y Estadistica Industrial, Av. Espana 475, Asuncion, Paraguay. stat. (processed)

330.9 318 BL
PARANA, BRAZIL. SECRETARIA DE ESTADO PARA OS NEGOCIOS DA FAZENDA; estatistica economico-financeira. 1972. irreg. free. Secretaria de Estado das Financas, Curitiba, Brazil. illus.

BUSINESS AND ECONOMICS — ABSTRACTING, BIBLIOGRAPHIES, STATISTICS

658.3 016   UK   ISSN 0305-067X
PERSONNEL & TRAINING ABSTRACTS. 1971. 8/yr. (plus index) £102.50. (Institute of Personnel Management) Anbar Publications Ltd., Box 23, Wembley, England. Ed. A.C. Ede. (looseleaf format)
Supersedes in part: Anbar Management Services Abstracts (ISSN 0003-2794)

350 658.3 016   US   ISSN 0031-5753
PERSONNEL LITERATURE. 1941. m. $21. U.S. Office of Personnel Management, Library, Washington, DC 20415 TEL 202-655-4000. (Orders to: Supt. of Documents, Washington, DC 20402) bibl. index. circ. 3,800. (also avail. in microform from UMI; reprint service avail. from UMI)

658.3 016   US   ISSN 0031-577X
PERSONNEL MANAGEMENT ABSTRACTS. 1955. q. $55 (includes index) Personnel Management Abstracts, 704 Island Lake Rd., Chelsea, MI 48118. TEL 313-475-1979. Ed. Gloria Reo. adv. bk. rev. abstr. index. circ. 1,200. (also avail. in microform from UMI; reprint service avail. from UMI) Indexed: P.A.I.S.

330.9   PE
PERU: COMPENDIO ESTADISTICO. 1980. a. $30. Instituto Nacional de Estadistica, Ave. 28 de Julio 1056, Lima, Peru. bk. rev. circ. 1,200.

331.1 315   PH   ISSN 0115-1851
PHILIPPINES. LABOR STATISTICS SERVICE. YEAR BOOK OF LABOR STATISTICS. (Text in English) 1973. quadrennial. Labor Statistics Service, Mole Building, Intramuros, Manila, Philippines. stat.

381   PH
PHILIPPINES. NATIONAL CENSUS AND STATISTICS OFFICE. ANNUAL SURVEY OF ESTABLISHMENTS. (In 8 parts) 1973. a, latest 1974. National Census and Statistics Office, Ramon Magsaysay Blvd., Box 779, Manila, Philippines.

381 315   PH
PHILIPPINES. NATIONAL CENSUS AND STATISTICS OFFICE. ANNUAL SURVEY OF WHOLESALE AND RETAIL ESTABLISHMENTS. a, latest 1969. P.9($3) National Census and Statistics Office, Ramon Magsaysay Blvd., Box 779, Manila, Philippines.

382 315   PH
PHILIPPINES. NATIONAL CENSUS AND STATISTICS OFFICE. COASTWISE TRADE REPORT. a, latest 1974. P.50($14) National Census and Statistics Office, Ramon Magsaysay Blvd., Box 779, Manila, Philippines.

381 315   PH
PHILIPPINES. NATIONAL CENSUS AND STATISTICS OFFICE. DIRECTORY OF LARGE ESTABLISHMENTS. irreg., latest 1975. P.45($13) National Census and Statistics Office, Ramon Magsaysay Blvd., Box 779, Manila, Philippines.

332.1 314   PL   ISSN 0079-2640
POLAND. GLOWNY URZAD STATYSTYCZNY. ROCZNIK STATYSTYCZNY FINANSOW. YEARBOOK OF FINANCE STATISTICS. (Subseries of its: Statystyka Polski) 1968. irreg., latest 1982. Glowny Urzad Statystyczny, Al. Niepodleglosci 208, 00-925 Warsaw, Poland.

382 314   PL   ISSN 0079-2683
POLAND. GLOWNY URZAD STATYSTYCZNY. ROCZNIK STATYSTYCZNY HANDLU WEWNETRZNEGO/YEARBOOK OF INTERNATIONAL TRADE STATISTICS. (Subseries of its: Statystyka Polski) 1969. irreg., latest 1981. 55 Zl. Glowny Urzad Statystyczny., Al. Niepodleglosci 208, 00-925 Warsaw, Poland.

338 314   PL   ISSN 0079-2705
POLAND. GLOWNY URZAD STATYSTYCZNY. ROCZNIK STATYSTYCZNY INWESTYCJI I SRODKOW TRWALYCH. YEARBOOK OF INVESTMENT AND FIXED ASSETS STATISTICS. (Issued in its Seria Roczniki Branzowe. Branch Yearbooks) a. Glowny Urzad Statystyczny, Al. Niepodleglosci 208, 00-925 Warsaw, Poland.

338 314   PL   ISSN 0079-2764
POLAND. GLOWNY URZAD STATYSTYCZNY. ROCZNIK STATYSTYCZNY PRZEMYSLU. YEARBOOK OF INDUSTRY STATISTICS. (Issued in its Seria Roczniki Branzowe. Branch Yearbooks) a. Glowny Urzad Statystyczny, Al. Niepodleglosci 208, 00-925 Warsaw, Poland.

382 314   PL   ISSN 0079-2691
POLAND. GLOWNY URZAD STATYSTYCZNY. ROCZNIK STATYSTYKI HANDLU ZAGRANICZNEGO. (Subseries of its: Statystyka Polski) (Text in Polish with English translation) 1966. irreg., latest 1986. 56 Zl. Glowny Urzad Statystyczny, Al. Niepodleglosci 208, Warsaw, Poland.

331 314   PL   ISSN 0079-2896
POLAND. GLOWNY URZAD STATYSTYCZNY. ZATRUDNIENIE W GOSPODARCE NARODOWEJ. (Subseries of its: Statystyka Polski) 1969. a. 24 Zl. Glowny Urzad Statystyczny, Al. Niepodleglosci 208, 00-925 Warsaw, Poland.

POLISH TECHNICAL AND ECONOMIC ABSTRACTS. see *TECHNOLOGY: COMPREHENSIVE WORKS — Abstracting, Bibliographies, Statistics*

338 314   PO   ISSN 0377-2314
PORTUGAL. ESTATISTICAS INDUSTRIAIS: CONTINENTE, ACORES E MADEIRA. VOLUME 1: INDUSTRIAS EXTRACTIVAS, ELECTRICIDADE, GAS, AGUA/PORTUGAL. STATISTIQUES INDUSTRIELLES: CONTINENT, ACORES ET MADERE. VOLUME 1: INDUSTRIES EXTRACTIVES, ELECTRICITE, GAZ, EAU. (Text in French and Portuguese) 1943. a. Esc.450. Instituto Nacional de Estatistica, Av. Antonio Jose de Almeida, 1078 Lisbon Codex, Portugal (Orders to: Imprensa Nacional, Casa da Moeda, Direccao Comercial, rua D. Francisco Manuel de Melo 5, 1000 Lisbon, Portugal)
Former titles: Portugal. Estatisticas Industrias. Continente e Ilhas Adjacentes; Portugal. Instituto Nacional de Estatistica. Estatistica Industrial.

330   PO   ISSN 0079-418X
PORTUGAL. ESTATISTICAS INDUSTRIAIS: CONTINENTE, ACORES E MADEIRA. VOLUME 2: INDUSTRIAS TRANSFORMADORAS/PORTUGAL. STATISTIQUES INDUSTRIELLES: CONTINENT, ACORES ET MADERE. VOLUME 2: INDUSTRIES MANUFACTURIERES. 1971. a. Esc.3450. Instituto Nacional de Estatistica, Av. Antonio Jose de Almeida, 1078 Lisbon Codex, Portugal (Orders to: Impresa Nacional, Casa da Moeda, Direccao Comercial, Rua D. Francisco Manuel de Melo 5, 1000 Lisbon, Portugal)
Former titles: Portugal. Estatisticas Industriais: Continente e Ilhas Adjacentes; Portugal. Instituto Nacional de Estatistica. Estatistica Industrial.

336.2 314   PO
PORTUGAL. INSTITUTO NACIONAL DE ESTATISTICA. ESTATISTICAS DAS CONTRIBUICOES E IMPOSTOS. CONTINENTE, ACORES E MADEIRA. 1877. a. Esc.825. Instituto Nacional de Estatistica, Av. Antonio Jose de Almeida, 1078 Lisbon Codex, Portugal (Orders to: Imprensa Nacional, Casa da Moeda, Direccao Comercial, rua D. Francisco Manuel de Melo 5, 1000 Lisbon, Portugal)
Formerly: Portugal. Instituto Nacional de Estatistica. Estatisticas das Contribucoes e Impostos (ISSN 0079-4120)

336 314   PO
PORTUGAL. INSTITUTO NACIONAL DE ESTATISTICA. ESTATISTICAS DAS FINANCAS PUBLICAS. CONTINENTE, ACORES E MADEIRA. (Text in French and Portuguese) 1968. a. Esc.540. Instituto Nacional de Estatistica, Av. Antonio Jose de Almeida, 1078 Lisbon Codex, Portugal (Orders to: Imprensa Nacional, Casa da Moeda, Direccao Comercial, rua D. Francisco Manuel de Melo 5, 1000 Lisbon, Portugal)
Formerly: Portugal. Instituto Nacional de Estatistica. Estatisticas das Financas Publicas (ISSN 0377-2276)

382 314   PO
PORTUGAL. INSTITUTO NACIONAL DE ESTATISTICA. ESTATISTICAS DO COMERCIO EXTERNO. CONTINENTE, ACORES E MADEIRA. (Text in French and Portuguese) 1914. a. Esc.3000. Instituto Nacional de Estatistica, Av. Antonio Jose de Almeida, 1078 Lisbon Codex, Portugal (Orders to: Imprensa Nacional, Casa da Moeda, Direccao Comercial, Rua D. Francisco Manuel de Melo 5, 1000 Lisbon, Portugal)
Formerly: Portugal. Instituto Nacional de Estatistica. Estatisticas do Comercio Externo (ISSN 0079-4147)

338 314   PO
PORTUGAL. INSTITUTO NACIONAL DE ESTATISTICA. SERVICOS CENTRAIS. ESTATISTICAS DAS SOCIEDADES: CONTINENTE, ACORES E MADEIRA. (Text in French, Portuguese) 1939. a. Esc.560. Instituto Nacional de Estatistica, Av. Antonio Jose de Almeida, 1078 Lisbon Codex, Portugal.
Formerly: Portugal. Instituto Nacional de Estatistica. Servicos Centrais. Estatisticas das Sociedades. Continente e Ilhas Adjacentes (ISSN 0870-3205)

331.11 314   PO
PORTUGAL. MINISTERIO DO TRABALHO. SERVICO DE ESTATISTICAS. ESTATISTICAS DO TRABALHO. (Text in Portuguese; summaries in English, French) 1975. irreg. Ministerio do Trabalho, Servico de Estatisticas, Servico de Informacao Cientifica e Tecnica, Rua D. Filipa de Vilhena 17, Lisbon 1, Portugal.

338 016   US   ISSN 0551-9276
PREDI-BRIEFS. 1961. m. $180 per topic (29 topics avail.) Predicasts, Inc., 200 University Circle Research Center, 11001 Cedar Ave., Cleveland, OH 44106. TEL 216-795-3000. Indexed: Resour.Ctr.Ind.

338 016   US   ISSN 0270-4536
PREDICASTS F & S INDEX EUROPE. 1978. m. with q. and a. cumulations. $700. Predicasts, Inc., 200 University Circle Research Center, 11001 Cedar Ave., Cleveland, OH 44106. TEL 216-795-3000. abstr. bibl. stat. tr.lit.
●Also available online. Vendors: BRS, DIALOG.
Former titles: F and S Index Europe (ISSN 0199-5219) & F and S Europe (ISSN 0193-1229)

338 016   US   ISSN 0270-4528
PREDICASTS F & S INDEX INTERNATIONAL. 1967. m. with q. and a. cumulations. $700. Predicasts, Inc., 200 University Circle Research Center, 11001 Cedar Ave., Cleveland, OH 44106. TEL 216-795-3000.
●Also available online. Vendors: BRS, DIALOG.
Formerly: F and S International (ISSN 0014-5661)

338   US   ISSN 0744-2785
PREDICASTS F & S INDEX OF CORPORATE CHANGE. 1972. q. (plus a. cumulation) $225. Predicasts Inc., 200 University Circle Research Center, 11001 Cedar Ave., Cleveland, OH 44106. TEL 216-795-3000. abstr. bibl. index.
●Also available online. Vendors: BRS, DIALOG.
Former titles (until 1981): Predicasts Index of Corporate Change (ISSN 0273-3994); F and S Index of Corporate Change (ISSN 0163-6693)

338 016   US   ISSN 0270-4544
PREDICASTS F & S INDEX UNITED STATES. 1960. m. with q. and a. cumulations. $700 ($825 with w. supplements) Predicasts, Inc., 200 University Circle Research Center, 11001 Cedar Ave., Cleveland, OH 44106. TEL 216-795-3000. index.
●Also available online. Vendors: BRS, DIALOG.
Formerly: F and S Index of Corporations and Industries (ISSN 0014-567X)

338 016   US   ISSN 0278-0135
PREDICASTS FORECASTS. 1960. q. $725. Predicasts, Inc., 200 University Circle Research Center, 11001 Cedar Ave., Cleveland, OH 44106. TEL 216-795-3000. Ed. Eileen Gazzuolo. charts. mkt. tr.lit. index.
●Also available online. Vendors: DIALOG.
Formerly: Predicasts (ISSN 0032-7166)
Economic and market forecast abstracts arranged by product

BUSINESS AND ECONOMICS — ABSTRACTING, BIBLIOGRAPHIES, STATISTICS

338 016   US   ISSN 0092-7767
PREDICASTS SOURCE DIRECTORY. 1973. a. $135 with 3 quarterly supplements. Predicasts, Inc., 200 University Circle Research Center, 11001 Cedar Ave., Cleveland, OH 44106. TEL 216-795-3000. bibl. Key Title: Source Directory of Predicasts, Inc.

382   UK
PUBLISHED DATA ON EUROPEAN INDUSTRIAL MARKETS. 1971. irreg. £35. I A L Consultants Ltd., 14 Buckingham Palace Rd., London SW1W 0QP, England.

382   UK
PUBLISHED DATA ON MIDDLE & FAR EAST INDUSTRIAL MARKETS. 1983. irreg. £35. I A L Consultants Ltd., 14 Buckingham Palace Rd., London SW1W 0QP, England.

331.1 016   CN   ISSN 0075-613X
QUEEN'S UNIVERSITY AT KINGSTON. INDUSTRIAL RELATIONS CENTRE. BIBLIOGRAPHY SERIES. 1965. irreg., no. 6, 1975. price varies. ‡ Queen's University, Industrial Relations Centre, Kingston, Ont. K7L 3N6, Canada. TEL 613-545-2193.

310 330   II   ISSN 0079-9564
RAJASTHAN, INDIA. DIRECTORATE OF ECONOMICS AND STATISTICS. BASIC STATISTICS. (Text in English and Hindi) 1956. a. Rs.3. Directorate of Economics and Statistics, Krishi Bhawan, Jaipur, Rajasthan, India.

330 016   UK   ISSN 0034-5296
RESEARCH INDEX. 1965. fortn. (quarterly cumulative no.) £149. Business Surveys Ltd., P.O. Box 21, Dorking, RH5 4EE, Surrey, England. Ed. Derek Denman. adv. (also avail. in microfiche) Indexed: Curr.Cont.
●Also available online. Vendors: Pergamon Infoline.

381 310   US   ISSN 0361-0020
RETAILING IN TENNESSEE. irreg. Department of Revenue, Sales and Use Tax Division, Nashville, TN 37219. TEL 615-741-3581. stat.

658 011   UK   ISSN 0141-5077
S C I M P. (Selective Cooperative Index of Management Periodicals); European index of management periodicals. 1978. 10/yr. £75. European Business School Librarians Group, Manchester Business School Library, Booth St. West, Manchester M15 6PB, England. Ed. Bram Oort. cum.index. circ. 200.
●Also available online.

S E C I N ABSTRACTS. JOURNAL. (Socio-Economic Information Network) see *SOCIOLOGY — Abstracting, Bibliographies, Statistics*

658.8 310   US
SALES & MARKETING MANAGEMENT SURVEY OF BUYING POWER (PART I) 1929. a. $65. Bill Communications, Inc., 633 Third Avenue, New York, NY 10017. TEL 212-986-4800. Ed. Robert H. Albert. adv. charts. stat. circ. 50,000. (reprint service avail. from UMI)
Formerly: Sales Management Survey of Buying Power (Part I)

658.8 310   US
SALES & MARKETING MANAGEMENT SURVEY OF BUYING POWER (PART II) 1973. a. $35. Bill Communications, Inc., 633 Third Avenue, New York, NY 10017. TEL 212-986-4800. Ed. Robert H. Albert. adv. charts. stat. circ. 50,000. (reprint service avail. from UMI)
Formerly: Sales Management Survey of Buying Power (Part II)

658.8 310   US
SALES & MARKETING MANAGEMENT SURVEY OF SELLING COSTS. 1973. a. $35. Bill Communications, Inc., 633 Third Avenue, New York, NY 10017. TEL 212-986-4800. Ed. Robert H. Albert. adv. charts. stat. circ. 50,000. (reprint service avail. from UMI)
Formerly: Sales Management Survey of Selling Costs.

658.8 310   US
SALES & MARKETING MANAGEMENT SURVEY OF U.S. INDUSTRIAL & COMMERCIAL BUYING POWER. 1974. a. $35. Bill Communications, Inc., 633 Third Ave., New York, NY 10017. Ed. Robert H. Albert. adv. charts. stat. circ. 50,000. (reprint service avail. from UMI)
Former titles: Sales and Marketing Management Survey of Industrial and Commercial Buying Power; Sales and Marketing Management Survey of Industrial Purchasing Power; Sales Management Survey of Industrial Purchasing Power.

330.95   UN   ISSN 0125-0027
SAMPLE SURVEYS IN THE ESCAP REGION. a. United Nations Economic and Social Commission for Asia and the Pacific, The United Nations Building, Rajadamnern Ave., Bangkok 2, Thailand. stat. Indexed: GeoRef.
Formerly: United Nations. Economic Commission for Asia and the Far East. Sample Surveys in the ECAFE Region.

382 315   MY   ISSN 0080-6455
SARAWAK EXTERNAL TRADE STATISTICS. (Text in English) 1954. a. M.$20. ‡ Department of Statistics, Federal Complex, Jalan Simpang Tiga, Kuching, Sarawak, Malaysia.

382 319   SU
SAUDI ARABIA. CENTRAL DEPARTMENT OF STATISTICS. FOREIGN TRADE STATISTICS. (Text in Arabic and English) a. s.R.100. Central Department of Statistics, Box 3735, Riyadh 11118, Saudi Arabia.

330 315.6   SU
SAUDI ARABIA. CENTRAL DEPARTMENT OF STATISTICS. STATISTICAL INDICATOR. (Text in Arabic and English) 1976. a. free. Central Department of Statistics, Box 3735, Riyadh 11118, Saudi Arabia. charts. stat.

658 011   FI   ISSN 0782-2987
SCANP. (Scandinavian Periodicals Index in Economics and Business) (Text in Danish, English, Norwegian and Swedish) 1977. q. Fmk.550. Helsinki School of Economics Library, Runeberginkatu 22-24, 00100 Helsinki, Finland. circ. 125. (back issues avail)

016 330.9   US
SELECTED BIBLIOGRAPHY OF RECENT ECONOMIC DEVELOPMENT PUBLICATIONS. irreg., latest 1975/76. Vanderbilt University, Graduate Program in Economic Development, Nashville, TN 37235. TEL 615-322-2486.

SEYCHELLES. DEPARTMENT OF FINANCE. VISITOR SURVEY. see *TRAVEL AND TOURISM — Abstracting, Bibliographies, Statistics*

310   SE
SEYCHELLES. PRESIDENT'S OFFICE. STATISTICS DIVISION. HOUSEHOLD EXPENDITURE SURVEY. irreg., latest 1984. Rs.45. President's Private Office, Statistics Division, Box 206, Mahe, Seychelles. stat.

316   SE
SEYCHELLES. PRESIDENT'S OFFICE. STATISTICS DIVISION. STATISTICAL ABSTRACT. a. Rs.60. President's Office, Statistics Division, Box 206, Mahe, Seychelles.

338 315   SI   ISSN 0080-9675
SINGAPORE. DEPARTMENT OF STATISTICS. REPORT ON THE CENSUS OF INDUSTRIAL PRODUCTION. a. S.$9.20. Department of Statistics, Maxwell Road PO Box 3010, Singapore 9050, Republic of Singapore.

318   BL   ISSN 0100-1345
SINOPSE ESTATISTICA DO BRASIL/ STATISTICAL ABSTRACT OF BRAZIL. (Summarizes data from Statistical Yearbook-Anuario Estatistico do Brasil) (Text in English or Portuguese) 1971. biennial. $25. Fundacao Instituto Brasileiro de Geografia e Estatistica, Centro de Servicos Graficos, Av. Brasil 15671, CEP 21241 Rio de Janeiro, Brazil. charts. illus. stat. circ. 3,000. (back issues avail.)

330 016   AG   ISSN 0080-9772
SINTESIS BIBLIOGRAFICA. 1964. irreg., no.9, 1972. free. Universidad Nacional de la Plata, Facultad de Ciencias Economicas, Biblioteca, 6 Esq. 47, La Plata, Argentina.
Formerly: Boletin Hemerografico.

331.1   SA
SOUTH AFRICA. CENTRAL STATISTICAL SERVICE. LABOUR STATISTICS: WAGE RATES, EARNINGS AND AVERAGE HOURS WORKED IN THE PRINTING AND NEWSPAPER INDUSTRY, ENGINEERING INDUSTRY, BUILDING INDUSTRY AND COMMERCE. (Report No. 01-20) a. R.2.50. Central Statistical Service, Private Bag X44, Pretoria 0001, South Africa (Orders to: Government Printer, Bosman St., Private Bag X85, Pretoria 0001, South Africa)
Formerly: South Africa. Department of Statistics. Labour Statistics: Wage Rates, Earnings and Average Hours Worked in the Printing and Newspaper Industry, Engineering Industry, Building Industry and Commerce.

339   SA
SOUTH AFRICA. CENTRAL STATISTICAL SERVICE. REPORT ON PRICES. (Report No. 11-01) a. Central Statistical Service, Private Bag X44, Pretoria 0001, South Africa (Orders to: Government Printer, Bosman St., Private Bag X85, Pretoria 0001, South Africa)
Formerly: South Africa. Department of Statistics. Report on Prices.

338.23   SA
SOUTH AFRICA. CENTRAL STATISTICAL SERVICE. SURVEY OF THE ACCOUNTS OF COMPANIES. PART 1. SECONDARY AND TERTIARY INDUSTRIES. (Report No. 09-01) a., latest 1984-85. Central Statistical Service, Private Bag X44, Pretoria 0001, South Africa (Orders to: Government Printer, Bosman St., Private Bag X85, Pretoria 0001, South Africa)
Supersedes in part: South Africa. Department of Statistics. Survey of the Accounts of Companies in Secondary and Tertiary Industries; Incorporates: South Africa. Department of Statistics. Survey of the Accounts of Mining Companies.

338.23   SA
SOUTH AFRICA. CENTRAL STATISTICAL SERVICE. SURVEY OF THE ACCOUNTS OF COMPANIES. PART 2. MINING. (Report No.09-01) a. Central Statistical Service, Private Bag X44, Pretoria 0001, South Africa (Orders to: Government Printer, Bosman St., Private Bag X85, Pretoria 0001, South Africa)
Superseded in Part: South Africa. Department of Statistics. Survey of the Accounts of Companies in Secondary and Tertiary Industries.

382 316   SA
SOUTH AFRICA. COMMISSIONER FOR CUSTOMS AND EXCISE. FOREIGN TRADE STATISTICS. a. price varies. Commissioner for Customs and Excise, Private Bag X47, Pretoria 0001, South Africa (Orders to: Government Printer, Private Bag X85, Pretoria 0001, South Africa)
Formerly: South Africa. Department of Customs and Excise. Foreign Trade Statistics (ISSN 0081-2196)

336.2 317   US   ISSN 0085-6460
SOUTH DAKOTA. DEPARTMENT OF REVENUE. ANNUAL STATISTICAL REPORT. 1952. a. Department of Revenue, Kneip Bldg., Pierre, SD 57501. TEL 605-773-3311. Ed. Dwight McElhaney. charts. circ. 450. (processed)
Formerly: South Dakota Department of Revenue. Annual Report.

338 314   SP   ISSN 0081-3354
SPAIN. INSTITUTO NACIONAL DE ESTADISTICA. ESTADISTICA INDUSTRIAL. a. 1200 ptas. Instituto Nacional de Estadistica, P de la Castellana, 183, Madrid 16, Spain.

336 314   SP   ISSN 0081-3435
SPAIN. MINISTERIO DE HACIENDA. INFORMACION ESTADISTICA.* a. Ministerio de Hacienda, Madrid, Spain.

SPORTING GOODS MARKET. see *SPORTS AND GAMES — Abstracting, Bibliographies, Statistics*

BUSINESS AND ECONOMICS — ABSTRACTING, BIBLIOGRAPHIES, STATISTICS

330.9   CE
SRI LANKA YEARBOOK. (Text in English, Sinhala and Tamil) 1948. irreg. price varies. Department of Census and Statistics, Box 563, Colombo 7, Sri Lanka (Order from: Superintendent, Government Publications Bureau, Colombo, Sri Lanka) circ. 4,640.
Continues: Ceylon Yearbook.

350 336   II
STATE DOMESTIC PRODUCT OF HIMACHAL PRADESH. (Text in English) 1963. a. Directorate of Economics and Statistics, Simla, Himachal Pradesh, India. circ. 700.
Supersedes: State Income of Himachal Pradesh.

317 650   US   ISSN 0191-0310
STATISTICAL ABSTRACT OF OKLAHOMA. 1956. biennial. $20. University of Oklahoma, Center for Economic and Management Research, College of Business Administration, 307 W. Brooks St., Rm. 4, Norman, OK 73019. TEL 405-325-2931. circ. 1,000.

332.1 315   TH
STATISTICAL DATA ON COMMERCIAL BANKS IN THAILAND. (Text in English) 1964. a. free. Bangkok Bank Ltd., Economic Research Division, 9 Suapa Rd., Bangkok, Thailand. illus.

960   UN
STATISTICAL INFORMATION BULLETIN FOR AFRICA/BULLETIN D'INFORMATION STATISTIQUE POUR L'AFRIQUE. (Text in English or French) irreg., no.13, 1980. United Nations Economic Commission for Africa, Box 3001, Addis Ababa, Ethiopia.
Continues: Statistical and Economic Information Bulletin for Africa.

382 318   JM
STATISTICAL INSTITUTE OF JAMAICA. EXTERNAL TRADE ANNUAL REVIEW. 1970. a. Jam.$47. Statistical Institute of Jamaica, 9 Swallowfield Rd., Kingston 5, Jamaica. stat.
Formerly: Jamaica. Department of Statistics. External Trade Annual Review.

332   JM
STATISTICAL INSTITUTE OF JAMAICA. MONETARY STATISTICS REPORT. 1957. a. Jam.$13. Statistical Institute of Jamaica, 9 Swallowfield Rd., Kingston 5, Jamaica. (processed)
Formerly: Jamaica. Department of Statistics. Monetary Statistics (ISSN 0026-9638)

318 330   JM
STATISTICAL INSTITUTE OF JAMAICA. NATIONAL INCOME AND PRODUCT. 1975. a. Jam.$18. Statistical Institute of Jamaica, 9 Swallowfield Road, Kingston 5, Jamaica.
Formerly: Jamaica. Department of Statistics. National Income and Product.

382.094 314   EI   ISSN 0586-4925
STATISTICAL OFFICE OF THE EUROPEAN COMMUNITIES. AUSSENHANDEL: ANALITISCHE UBERSICHTEN. FOREIGN TRADE: ANALYTICAL TABLES. (Text in English) a. $416. Rue Alcide de Gasperi, B.P. 1907, Luxembourg, Luxembourg (Dist. in the U.S. by: European Community Information Service, 2100 M St., NW, Suite 707, Washington, DC 20037)

314   EI   ISSN 0081-4873
STATISTICAL OFFICE OF THE EUROPEAN COMMUNITIES. BASIC STATISTICS. (Text in Dutch, English, French, German, and Italian) 1961. a. $3.80. Rue Alcide de Gasperi, B.P. 1907, Luxembourg, Luxembourg (Dist. in the U.S. by: European Community Information Service, 2100 M St., NW, Suite 707, Washington, DC 20037)

382 314   EI   ISSN 0081-4881
STATISTICAL OFFICE OF THE EUROPEAN COMMUNITIES. COMMERCE EXTERIEUR: PRODUCTS C E C A. (Avail. only on microfiche) (Text in Dutch, French, German, Italian) irreg. Rue Alcide de Gasperi, B.P. 1907, Luxembourg, Luxembourg (Dist. in the U.S. by: European Community Information Service, 2100 M St., NW, Suite 707, Washington, DC 20037) (also avail. in microfiche)

382 314   EI   ISSN 0081-4903
STATISTICAL OFFICE OF THE EUROPEAN COMMUNITIES. FOREIGN TRADE: STANDARD COUNTRY CLASSIFICATION. (Text in Dutch, English, French, German, Italian) a. Rue Alcide de Gasperi, B.P. 1907, Luxembourg, Luxembourg (Dist. in the U.S. by: European Community Information Service, 2100 M St., NW, Suite 707, Washington, DC 20037)

339 314   EI   ISSN 0081-4911
STATISTICAL OFFICE OF THE EUROPEAN COMMUNITIES. NATIONAL ACCOUNTS. YEARBOOK. (Text in Dutch, English, French, German, Italian) a. Rue Alcide de Gasperi, B.P. 1907, Luxembourg, Luxembourg (Dist. in the U.S. by: European Community Information Service, 2100 M St., NW, Suite 707, Washington, DC 20037)

338.4 314   EI   ISSN 0081-4970
STATISTICAL OFFICE OF THE EUROPEAN COMMUNITIES. STATISTIQUES INDUSTRIELLES ANNUAIRE. (Text in Dutch, French, German, Italian) a. 600. Rue Alcide de Gasperi, B.P. 1907, Luxembourg, Luxembourg (Dist. in the U.S. by: European Community Information Service, 2100 M St., NW, Suite 707, Washington, DC 20037)

330 314   EI   ISSN 0081-4997
STATISTICAL OFFICE OF THE EUROPEAN COMMUNITIES. YEARBOOK OF REGIONAL STATISTICS. (Text in English) 1981. a. $27.40. Rue Alcide de Gasperi, B.P. 1907, Luxembourg, Luxembourg (Dist. in the U.S. by: European Community Information Service, 2100 M St., NW, Suite 707, Washington, DC 20037)

330 315   JA   ISSN 0081-5047
STATISTICAL SURVEY OF ECONOMY OF JAPAN.* 1955. a. 1400 Yen. Economic and Foreign Affairs Research Association, Seno Bldg., 14-9, 3-chome, Roppongl, Minato-ku, Tokyo 106, Japan. (Co-sponsor: Ministry of Foreign Affairs)

338.9 316   KE
STATISTICAL SURVEY OF THE EAST AFRICAN COMMUNITY INSTITUTIONS. 1973. a. EAs.7.50. East African Community, Statistical Department, Box 30462, Nairobi, Kenya.

336 315   CH
STATISTICAL YEARBOOK OF THE REPUBLIC OF CHINA. 1975. a. Directorate-General of Budget, Accounting, and Statistics, Executive Yuan, 1, Chung Hsiao East Rd., Sec. 1, Taipei, Taiwan, Republic of China. stat.

314   UK   ISSN 0081-5098
STATISTICS - AFRICA; sources for market research. 1970. irreg., 2nd, 1978. £25($80) ‡ C.B.D. Research Ltd., 15 Wickham Rd., Beckenham, Kent BR3 2JS, England (Dist. in U.S. by: Gale Research Co., Penobscot Bldg., Detroit, MI 48226) Ed. Joan M. Harvey. index. circ. 2,000.

317 318   UK   ISSN 0309-5452
STATISTICS - AMERICA; sources for market research (North, Central & South America) 1973. irreg., 2nd, 1980. £43.50($135) ‡ C.B.D. Research Ltd., 15 Wickham Rd., Beckenham, Kent BR3 2JS, England (Dist. in U.S. by: Gale Research Co., Penobscot Bldg., Detroit, MI 48226) Ed. Joan M. Harvey. circ. 2,000.

314   UK   ISSN 0081-5101
STATISTICS - EUROPE; sources for market research. 1968. irreg., 5th, 1987. £42.50($130) ‡ C.B.D. Research Ltd., 15 Wickham Rd., Beckenham, Kent BR3 2JS, England (Dist. in U.S. by: Gale Research Co., Penobscot Bldg., Detroit, MI 48226) Ed. Joan M. Harvey. index. circ. 2,000.

382 315   SY   ISSN 0081-5136
STATISTICS OF FOREIGN TRADE OF SYRIA; classified according to United Nations standard international trade classification. (Text in Arabic and English) 1964. a. $46. Central Bureau of Statistics, Damascus, Syria.

330.9 310   MX
STATISTICS ON THE MEXICAN ECONOMY. 1977. a. Nacional Financiera S.N.C., Gerencia de Investigaciones Industriales e Informacion Tecnica, Isabel la Catolica 51, Delegacion Cuauhtemoc, 06008 Mexico, D.F., Mexico.

382 314   YU   ISSN 0084-4373
STATISTIKA SPOLJNE TRGOVINE SFR JUGOSLAVIJE. 1949. a. 500 din.($22.22) Savezni Zavod za Statistiku, Kneza Miloso 20, Belgrade, Yugoslavia. circ. 1,500.

382.5 316   IV   ISSN 0081-5276
STATISTIQUES DU COMMERCE EXTERIEUR DE COTE D'IVOIRE. 1961. a. Service des Statistiques Douanieres, Abidjan, Ivory Coast.

382 316   AE
STATISTIQUES DU COMMERCE EXTERIEUR DE L'ALGERIE. (Text in French) 1963. m. (plus q. and a. cum.) price varies. Direction des Douanes, 19, rue du Docteur Saadane, Algiers, Algeria.

382 316   TI   ISSN 0081-5292
STATISTIQUES DU COMMERCE EXTERIEUR DE LA TUNISIE. a. Institut National de la Statistique, 70 rue Echcham, Tunis, Tunisia.

382 316   MG   ISSN 0081-5306
STATISTIQUES DU COMMERCE EXTERIEUR DE MADAGASCAR. 1965. a. FMG.5920. Direction Generale de la Bnaque des Donnees de l'Etat, Presidence de la Republique, B.P. 485, Antananarivo, Malagasy Republic.

330   GW   ISSN 0531-9323
STATISTISCHE STUDIEN. irreg., vol.10, 1982. price varies. (Universitaet Erlangen-Nuernberg, Institut fuer Statistik) Franz Steiner Verlag Wiesbaden GmbH, Birkenwaldstr. 44, Postfach 347, D-7000 Stuttgart 1, W. Germany (B.R.D.) Ed. Ingeborg Esenwein-Rothe. Indexed: Key to Econ.Sci.

318.8 388   SR
SURINAM. ALGEMEEN BUREAU VOOR DE STATISTIEK. KWARTAAL STATISTIEK VAN DE INDUSTRIELE PRODUKTIE. (Text in Dutch) irreg. Algemeen Bureau voor de Statistiek, Paramaribo, Surinam.

338 316   SQ
SWAZILAND. CENTRAL STATISTICAL OFFICE. CENSUS OF INDUSTRIES. (Not published in 1968, 1969, 1974, 1975) 1967. a. free. Central Statistical Office, Box 456, Mbabane, Swaziland.
Formerly: Swaziland. Central Statistical Office. Census of Industrial Production.

331.1 314   SW
SWEDEN. STATISTISKA CENTRALBYRAAN. ARBETSKRAFTUNDERSOEKNINGEN. ARSMEDELTAL. 1963. irreg. Statistiska Centralbyraan, Distribution, S-701 89 Oerebro, Sweden. illus. stat.

338 314   SW   ISSN 0082-0172
SWEDEN. STATISTISKA CENTRALBYRAAN. INDUSTRI. (Text in Swedish; summaries in English) 1911. a. (in 2 vols.) Kr.270. Statistiska Centralbyraan, Distribution, S-701 89 Oerebro, Sweden. circ. 1,500.

658.3 314   SW   ISSN 0082-0202
SWEDEN. STATISTISKA CENTRALBYRAAN. KOMMUNAL PERSONAL. (In 2 parts: Del 1, Landstingspersonal; Del 2, Primarkommunal Personal) (Text in Swedish; title heads in English) 1968. a. Kr.90. Statistiska Centralbyraan, Distribution, S-701 89 Oerebro, Sweden. circ. 600.

331.2 314   SW   ISSN 0082-0210
SWEDEN. STATISTISKA CENTRALBYRAAN. LOENER. 1929. a. Kr.180. Statistiska Centralbyraan, Distribution, S-701 89 Oerebro, Sweden. circ. 900.

314 331   SW   ISSN 0082-0237
SWEDEN. STATISTISKA CENTRALBYRAAN. STATISTISKA MEDDELANDEN. SUBGROUP AM (LABOR MARKET) (Text in Swedish; table heads and summaries in English) N.S. 1963. irreg. Kr.1200. Statistiska Centralbyraan, Distribution, S-701 89 Oerebro, Sweden. circ. 1,250.

338 314   SW   ISSN 0082-027X
SWEDEN. STATISTISKA CENTRALBYRAAN. STATISTISKA MEDDELANDEN. SUBGROUP I (MANUFACTURING) (Text in Swedish; table heads and summaries in English) N.S. 1963. irreg. Kr.750. Statistiska Centralbyraan, Distribution, S-701 89 Oerebro, Sweden. circ. 1,300.

BUSINESS AND ECONOMICS — ABSTRACTING, BIBLIOGRAPHIES, STATISTICS

336 314   SW   ISSN 0082-0296
SWEDEN. STATISTISKA CENTRALBYRAAN. STATISTISKA MEDDELANDEN. SUBGROUP N (NATIONAL ACCOUNTS AND FINANCE) (Text in Swedish; table heads and summaries in English) N.S. 1963. irreg. Kr.320. Statistiska Centralbyraan, Distribution, S-701 89 Oerebro, Sweden. circ. 1,500.

338 381 314   SW   ISSN 0082-0261
SWEDEN. STATISTISKA CENTRALBYRAAN. STATISTISKA MEDDELANDEN. SUBGROUP H (TRADE) (Text in Swedish; table heads and summaries in English) N.S. 1963. irreg. Kr.950. Statistiska Centralbyraan, Distribution, S-701 89 Oerebro, Sweden. circ. 2,000.

330 314   SW   ISSN 0082-030X
SWEDEN. STATISTISKA CENTRALBYRAAN. STATISTISKA MEDDELANDEN. SUBGROUP P (PRICES AND PRICE INDICES) (Text in Swedish; table heads and summaries in English) N.S. 1963. irreg. Kr.850. Statistiska Centralbyraan, Distribution, S-701 89 Oerebro, Sweden. circ. 2,150.

382 314   SZ
SWITZERLAND. DIRECTORATE GENERAL OF CUSTOMS. ANNUAL REPORT. (2 parts) (Text in French and German) a. 31 Fr. (includes Part 1 and Part 2) Eidgenoessische Oberzolldirektion, Abteilung Handelsstatistik, Monbijoustr. 40, 3003 Berne, Switzerland.

382 314   SZ   ISSN 0081-525X
SWITZERLAND. DIRECTORATE GENERAL OF CUSTOMS. ANNUAL STATISTICS. (3 volumes) (Text in French and German) a. 100 Fr. (vols. 1 and 2); 37 Fr. (vol. 3) Eidgenoessische Oberzolldirektion, Abteilung Handelsstatistik, Monbijoustr. 40, 3003 Berne, Switzerland.

330.9   CH
TAIWAN STATISTICAL DATA BOOK. (Text in English) 1960. a. free. Council for Economic Planning and Development, 87 Nanking E. Road, 9th floor, Sec. 2, Taipei 100, Taiwan 10408, Republic of China.

338 316   TZ
TANZANIA. BUREAU OF STATISTICS. SURVEY OF INDUSTRIAL PRODUCTION. 1965. a. Bureau of Statistics, Box 796, Dar es Salaam, Tanzania (Orders to: Government Publications Agency, Box 1801, Dar es Salaam, Tanzania)
    Formerly: Tanzania. Central Statistical Bureau. Survey of Industrial Production (ISSN 0564-6545)

016 336.2   US   ISSN 0496-974X
TAX FOUNDATION'S RESEARCH BIBLIOGRAPHY. 1959. irreg. price varies. Tax Foundation, Inc., One Thomas Circle, N.W., Ste. 500, Washington, DC 20005. TEL 202-822-9050.

330   US
TEXAS FACT BOOK. biennial. $6. University of Texas at Austin, Bureau of Business Research, Box 7459, Austin, TX 78713. TEL 512-471-1616. bibl. illus. stat. index. circ. 5,000. (back issues avail., reprint service avail. from UMI)

315 338   TH
THAILAND. NATIONAL STATISTICAL OFFICE. REPORT OF INDUSTRIAL SURVEY IN NORTHEAST REGION/THAILAND. SAMNAKNGAN SATHITI HAENG CHAT. (Text in English and Thai) 1972. irreg. price varies. National Statistical Office, Larn Luang Rd., Bangkok, Thailand. charts. stat.

382   TH
THAILAND'S FOREIGN TRADE STATISTICS. (Text mainly in English and Thai; some Chinese) irreg. B.250. Interstate Publications, Box 5-85, Pathumwan, Bangkok 5, Thailand.

658 016   UK   ISSN 0049-4100
TOP MANAGEMENT ABSTRACTS. 1971. 8/yr., (plus index) £102.50. (British Institute of Management) Anbar Publications Ltd., Box 23, Wembley HA9 8DJ, England. Ed. A.C. Ede. (looseleaf format)
    Supersedes in part: Anbar Management Services Abstracts (ISSN 0003-2794)

330.9   UK   ISSN 0260-6372
TRADING STANDARDS AND CONSUMER PROTECTION STATISTICS. ACTUALS. 1978. a. £2.25. Society of County Treasurers, c/o Honorary Treasurer, County Hall, Northallerton DL7 8AL, England.

318 330.9   TR
TRINIDAD AND TOBAGO. CENTRAL STATISTICAL OFFICE. BUSINESS SURVEYS. irreg., latest 1978. T.T.$4. Central Statistical Office, P.O. Box 98, 23 Park St., Port-of-Spain, Trinidad, W.I.

332 318   TR   ISSN 0082-6529
TRINIDAD AND TOBAGO. CENTRAL STATISTICAL OFFICE. FINANCIAL STATISTICS. 1966. a. T.T.$4. Central Statistical Office, P.O. Box 98, 23 Park St., Port-of-Spain, Trinidad, W.I. (Orders to: Government Printing Office, 48 St. Vincent St., Port of Spain, Trinidad, W.I.)

317.29 331.1   TR
TRINIDAD AND TOBAGO. CENTRAL STATISTICAL OFFICE. LABOUR FORCE BY SEX. (Subseries of: Continuous Sample Survey of Population) irreg., latest issue 1982. T.T.$1.50. Central Statistical Office, P.O. Box 98, 23 Park St., Port-of-Spain, Trinidad, W.I. (Orders to: Government Printing Office, 48 St. Vincent St., Port of Spain, Trinidad, W.I.) illus. stat.

382 318   TR   ISSN 0082-6545
TRINIDAD AND TOBAGO. CENTRAL STATISTICAL OFFICE. OVERSEAS TRADE. ANNUAL REPORT. (Issued in three parts) 1951. a. $20 (pt.A), $10 (pt.B), $10 (pt.C) Central Statistical Office, P.O. Box 98, 23 Park St., Port-of-Spain, Trinidad, W.I. (Orders to: Government Printing Office, 48 St. Vincent St., Port of Spain, Trinidad, W.I.)

338.5 314   BU
TSENI. 1969. a. 1.45 lv. Ministerstvo na Informatsiiata i Suobshteniiata, 18, Ul. Graf Ignatiev, Sofia, Bulgaria. (Co-sponsor: Tsentralno Statistichesko Upravlenie) stat. circ. 280.

382 318   TU   ISSN 0082-6901
TURKEY. DEVLET ISTATISTIK ENSTITUSU. DIS TICARET YILLIK ISTATISTIK/STATISTIQUE ANNUELLE DU COMMERCE EXTERIEUR/ ANNUAL FOREIGN TRADE STATISTICS. (Text in English and Turkish) 1926. a. free or on exchange basis. State Institute of Statistics, Necatibey Caddesi 114, Ankara, Turkey.

382 339 016   UN   ISSN 0041-5227
U N C T A D GUIDE TO PUBLICATIONS. (Text in English, French, and Spanish) a. free. (United Nations Conference on Trade and Development (UNCTAD)) United Nations Publications, Reference Unit, Palais des Nations, CH-1211 Geneva 10, Switzerland (Or United Nations Publications, Rm. DC2-853, New York, NY 10017)

UNESCO. STATISTICS ON SCIENCE AND TECHNOLOGY/STATISTIQUES RELATIVES AUX SCIENCE ET A LA TECHNOLOGIE/ ESTADISTICAS RELATIVAS A LA CIENCIA Y A LA TECNOLOGIA. see *SCIENCES: COMPREHENSIVE WORKS — Abstracting, Bibliographies, Statistics*

339   UN
UNITED NATIONS. NATIONAL ACCOUNTS STATISTICS. (Supplement avail.: National Accounting Practices in Seventy Countries) (Text in English) 1957. a. $125. United Nations Publications, Room DC2-853, New York, NY 10017 (Or Distribution and Sales Section, CH-1211 Geneva 10, Switzerland) (also avail. in microfiche)
    Formerly (until 1981): Yearbook of National Account Statistics (ISSN 0084-3881)

331.2 317   US
U.S. BUREAU OF LABOR STATISTICS. AREA WAGE SURVEYS. irreg. throughout the year for individual areas. $103. U.S. Bureau of Labor Statistics, 441 G St. N.W., Washington, DC 20212 TEL 202-655-4000. (Orders to: Supt. of Documents, Washington, DC 20402)

331.1 317   US   ISSN 0082-9056
U.S. BUREAU OF LABOR STATISTICS. HANDBOOK OF LABOR STATISTICS. (Subseries of its Bulletins) 1924/26. irreg. price varies. U.S. Bureau of Labor Statistics, 441 G St., N.W., Washington, DC 20210 TEL 202-655-4000. (Orders to: Supt. of Documents, Washington, DC 20402)

331 317   US
U.S. BUREAU OF LABOR STATISTICS. MAJOR PROGRAMS. irreg. free. U.S. Bureau of Labor Statistics, 441 G St., Washington, DC 20212. TEL 202-655-4000.

331.2 317   US   ISSN 0501-7041
U.S. BUREAU OF LABOR STATISTICS. NATIONAL SURVEY OF PROFESSIONAL, ADMINISTRATIVE, TECHNICAL AND CLERICAL PAY. a. price varies. U.S. Bureau of Labor Statistics, 441 G. Street, N.W., Washington, DC 20212 TEL 202-655-4000. (Orders to: Supt. of Documents, Washington, DC 20402) (also avail. in microform)

U.S. BUREAU OF LABOR STATISTICS. OCCUPATIONAL OUTLOOK HANDBOOK. see *OCCUPATIONS AND CAREERS — Abstracting, Bibliographies, Statistics*

331.11 317   US
U.S. BUREAU OF LABOR STATISTICS. PRODUCTIVITY MEASURES FOR SELECTED INDUSTRIES. a. price varies. U.S. Bureau of Labor Statistics, 441 G Street, N.W., Washington, DC 20212 TEL 202-523-9244. (Orders to: Supt. of Documents, Washington, DC 20402) (also avail. in microform)
    Former titles: U.S. Bureau of Labor Statistics. Productivity Indexes for Selected Industries & U.S. Bureau of Labor Statistics. Indexes of Output per Man-Hour; Selected Industries.

330 016   US   ISSN 0277-7207
U.S. DEPARTMENT OF COMMERCE. PUBLICATIONS CATALOG. 1950. a. $5.50. U.S. Department of Commerce, Office of Publications, Washington, DC 20230 TEL 202-377-2000. (Orders to: Supt. of Documents, Washington, DC 20402) Eds. E. Neil Sawyer & Doris H. Gerhoff. bibl. Key Title: Publications Catalog of the U.S. Department of Commerce.
    Former titles: U.S. Department of Commerce. Publications; a Catalog and Index Supplement (ISSN 0091-9039); U.S. Department of Commerce. Publications. Supplement (ISSN 0499-0994)

332.1 317   US   ISSN 0083-0666
U.S. FEDERAL DEPOSIT INSURANCE CORPORATION. BANK OPERATING STATISTICS. 1967. a. U.S. Federal Deposit Insurance Corporation., 550 17th St., N.W., Washington, DC 20429. TEL 202-389-4221.

U.S. FOREIGN AGRICULTURAL TRADE STATISTICAL REPORT, CALENDAR YEAR. see *AGRICULTURE — Abstracting, Bibliographies, Statistics*

U.S. FOREIGN AGRICULTURAL TRADE STATISTICAL REPORT, FISCAL YEAR. see *AGRICULTURE — Abstracting, Bibliographies, Statistics*

330.9 016   AG
UNIVERSIDAD DE BUENOS AIRES. INSTITUTO DE ECONOMIA. BIBLIOGRAFIA SOBRE ECONOMIA NACIONAL. 1950. Universidad de Buenos Aires, Instituto de Economia, Buenos Aires, Argentina. Ed. J. Broide.

330 310   GH
UNIVERSITY OF GHANA. INSTITUTE OF STATISTICAL, SOCIAL AND ECONOMIC RESEARCH. TECHNICAL PUBLICATION SERIES. 1966. irreg., no.46, 1984. University of Ghana, Institute of Statistical, Social and Economic Research, Box 74, Legon, Ghana.
    Formerly: University of Ghana. Institute of Statistical, Social and Economic Research. Technical Research Monographs (ISSN 0072-4416)

330 016   US
UNIVERSITY RESEARCH IN BUSINESS AND ECONOMICS: A BIBLIOGRAPHY OF (YEAR) PUBLICATIONS. Variant title: A U B E R Bibliography. 1956. a. $25. (Association for University Business and Economic Research) West Virginia University, Bureau of Business Research, Box 6025, Morgantown, WV 26506-6025. TEL 304-293-5837. Eds. Stanley J. Kloc, Lenley Lewis. cum.index: 1957-81. circ. 700. (also avail. in microfiche; back issues avail.)
Formerly: Bibliography of Publications of University Bureaus of Business and Economic Research (ISSN 0066-8761)

330.9   US
UTAH STATISTICAL ABSTRACT. 1947. triennial. $25. University of Utah, Bureau of Economic and Business Research, Salt Lake City, UT 84112. TEL 801-581-6333.

338   UK   ISSN 0262-8309
WELSH ECONOMIC TRENDS. irreg. (approx. biennial) £7.50. Welsh Office, Economic and Statistical Services Division, New Crown Bldg., Cathays Park, Cardiff CF1 4NQ, Wales. Ed. E. Swires-Hennessy. stat. circ. 700.

336 310   II
WEST BENGAL. ANNUAL FINANCIAL STATEMENT (BUDGET) a. West Bengal Government Press, Publication Branch, 38 Gopal Nagar Rd., Alipore, Calcutta 27, India.

315.4 330   II   ISSN 0511-5493
WEST BENGAL. BUREAU OF APPLIED ECONOMICS AND STATISTICS. STATISTICAL HANDBOOK. (Issuing body varies) (Text in English) 1960. a. price varies. Bureau of Applied Economics and Statistics, 1 Kiron Sankar Roy Rd., Calcutta 700001, India. stat.

382 315   MY   ISSN 0085-8080
WEST MALAYSIA ANNUAL STATISTICS OF EXTERNAL TRADE. (Text in English & Malay) 1962. a. Department of Statistics - Jabatan Perangkaan, Jalan Young, Kuala Lumpur 10-01, Malaysia. circ. 1,400.

381   CY
WHOLESALE AND RETAIL TRADE SURVEY. (Text in English) 1982. a. cyprus Pounds 2. Ministry of Finance, Department of Statistics and Research, Nicosia, Cyprus.

314 330.9   AU   ISSN 0510-5609
WIRTSCHAFTSZAHL. 1961. irreg. (1-2/yr.) Handelskammer Niederoesterreich, Herrengasse 10, A-1014 Vienna, Austria. Ed. Friedel Stratjel. charts. circ. 1,000.

331 016 658.3   US   ISSN 0273-3234
WORK RELATED ABSTRACTS. 1950. m. $390. Information Coordinators, Inc., 1435-37 Randolph St., Detroit, MI 48226. TEL 313-962-9720. Ed. Sonja Hempseed. bk. rev. abstr. cum.index. circ. 500. (looseleaf format)
Formerly: Employment Relations Abstracts (ISSN 0013-6875)
Guide to current material on labor relations and personnel management

658 016   UK   ISSN 0305-0653
WORK STUDY & O AND M ABSTRACTS. 1973. 8/yr. (plus index) £102.50. (Institute of Management Services) Anbar Publications Ltd., P.O. Box 23, Wembley HA9 8DJ, England. Ed. A.C. Ede. (looseleaf format)
Supersedes in part: Anbar Management Services Abstracts (ISSN 0003-2794)

338.9   UN
WORLD BANK RESEARCH PROGRAM: ABSTRACTS OF CURRENT STUDIES. 1974. a. World Bank, 1818 H St., N.W., Washington, DC 20433. TEL 202-477-1234.

332.1 310   UK
WORLD BANKING (YEAR) Variant title: World Banking Statistical Annual Survey. a. Financial Times Business Information, 102 Clerkenwell Road, London EC1M 5SA, England. charts. illus. stat. circ. 12,000.

368.4 016   SZ   ISSN 0006-1476
WORLD BIBLIOGRAPHY OF SOCIAL SECURITY/BIBLIOGRAPHIE UNIVERSELLE DE SECURITE SOCIALE. (Text in English, French, German and Spanish) 1963. s-a. 50 Fr. International Social Security Association, Box 1, 1211 Geneva 22, Switzerland. circ. 1,800. Indexed: P.A.I.S.
Social security

330 310   UN   ISSN 0257-1870
YEARBOOK OF INTERNATIONAL COMMODITY STATISTICS. 1984. a. $52. (United Nations Conference on Trade and Development (UNCTAD)) United Nations Publications, Palais des Nations, 1211 Geneva 10, Switzerland (Or United Nations Publications, Rm. DC2-853, New York, NY 10017)

331 310   UN   ISSN 0084-3857
YEAR BOOK OF LABOUR STATISTICS. (Text in English, French and Spanish) 1935/36. a. 130 Fr.($74.10) International Labour Office - Bureau International du Travail, Publications Sales Service, CH 1211 Geneva 22, Switzerland (U.S. distributor: I L O Branch Office, 1750 New York Ave. N.W., Washington, DC 20006) circ. 6,000. (also avail. in microfiche)

331.1 314   YU
YUGOSLAVIA. SAVEZNI ZAVOD ZA STATISTIKU. ANKETA O OSTVARIVANJU PRAVA RADNIKA IZ RADNOG ODNOSA. (Subseries of Statisticki Bilten) irreg. 10 din.($0.60) Savezni Zavod za Statistiku, Kneza Milosa 20, Belgrade, Yugoslavia. stat.

339.4 314   YU
YUGOSLAVIA. SAVEZNI ZAVOD ZA STATISTIKU. ANKETA O PORODICNIM BUDZETIMA RADNICKIH DOMACINSTAVA. (Subseries of: Yugoslavia. Savezni Zavod Statistiku. Statisticki Bilten) (Issued also in English) irreg. 15 din. Savezni Zavod za Statistiku, Kneza Milosa 20, Belgrade, Yugoslavia. stat.

314 338   YU
YUGOSLAVIA. SAVEZNI ZAVOD ZA STATISTIKU. INDUSTRIJSKE ORGANIZACIJE. (Subseries of: Yugoslavia. Savezni Zavod za Statistiku. Statisticki Bilten) irreg. 15 din. Savezni Zavod za Statistiku, Kneza Milosa 20, Belgrade, Yugoslavia. stat.

331 314   YU
YUGOSLAVIA. SAVEZNI ZAVOD ZA STATISTIKU. SAMOUPRAVLJANJE U PRIVREDI. (Subseries of its Statisticki Bilten) irreg. 20 din.($1.11) Savezni Zavod za Statistiku, Kneza Milosa 20, Belgrade, Yugoslavia. stat. circ. 1,000.

658 331 314   YU
YUGOSLAVIA. SAVEZNI ZAVOD ZA STATISTIKU. SAMOUPRAVLJANJE U USTANOVAMA DRUSTVENIH SLUZBI. (Subseries of: Yugoslavia. Savezni Zavod za Statistiku. Statisticki Bilten) irreg. 10 din. Savezni Zavod za Statistiku, Kneza Milosa 20, Belgrade, Yugoslavia. stat.

331 314   YU   ISSN 0513-0883
YUGOSLAVIA. SAVEZNI ZAVOD ZA STATISTIKU. ZAPOSLENO OSOBLJE. (Subseries of its Statisticki Bilten) 20 din.($1.11) Savezni Zavod za Statistiku, Kneza Milosa 20, Belgrade, Yugoslavia. circ. 1,000.

382 316   ZA   ISSN 0084-4489
ZAMBIA. CENTRAL STATISTICAL OFFICE. ANNUAL STATEMENT OF EXTERNAL TRADE. (Published in 2 vols: Vol. 1, Imports, Exports and Re-Exports by S.I.T.C. Grouping; Vol. 2, Major Country Analysis) 1964. a. K.4 per vol. Central Statistical Office, Box 31908, Lusaka, Zambia.

382.1 336   ZA
ZAMBIA. CENTRAL STATISTICAL OFFICE. BALANCE OF PAYMENTS STATISTICS. a. K.3. Central Statistical Office, P.O. Box 31908, Lusaka, Zambia.

316 331   ZA   ISSN 0084-4500
ZAMBIA. CENTRAL STATISTICAL OFFICE. EMPLOYMENT AND EARNINGS. 1969. irreg., latest 1980. K.3. Central Statistical Office, P.O. Box 31908, Lusaka, Zambia.

316 650   ZA   ISSN 0084-4519
ZAMBIA. CENTRAL STATISTICAL OFFICE. FINANCIAL STATISTICS OF PUBLIC CORPORATIONS. 1965. a. K.0.30. Central Statistical Office, P.O. Box 31908, Lusaka, Zambia.

331.11   ZA
ZAMBIA. CENTRAL STATISTICAL OFFICE. MANPOWER SURVEY. (Text in English) 1975. a. K.3. Central Statistical Office, P.O. Box 31908, Lusaka, Zambia.

539.7 016   GE
ZIDIS. (Text in English) 1979. irreg. Akademie der Wissenschaften der DDR, Zentralinstitut fuer Isotopen- und Strahlenforschung, Permoserstr. 15, 705 Leipzig, E. Germany (D.D.R.) (Subscr. to: Buchexport, P.F. 160, 701 Leipzig, E. Germany (D.D.R.)) Ed. R. Schroeter. bibl. circ. 450. (also avail. in microfiche)
Formed by the merger of: Isotype Titles (ISSN 0047-1550) & Zidis-Information (ISSN 0323-4290)

338 330   RH
ZIMBABWE. CENTRAL STATISTICAL OFFICE. CENSUS OF PRODUCTION. 1962. a. Rhod.$1. Central Statistical Office, Box 8063, Causeway, Salisbury, Zimbabwe. circ. 220.

336   RH
ZIMBABWE. CENTRAL STATISTICAL OFFICE. INCOME TAX STATISTICS; analysis of assessments and loss statements. a. Rhod.$0.50. Central Statistical Office, Box 8063, Causeway, Salisbury, Zimbabwe. circ. 250.

BUSINESS AND ECONOMICS — Accounting

657   US
A I C P A PROFESSIONAL STANDARDS. (In 3 parts: Accounting; Ethics; Auditing) 1974. base vols. plus updates. $208. (American Institute of Certified Public Accountants) Commerce Clearing House, Inc., 4025 W. Peterson Ave., Chicago, IL 60646. TEL 312-583-8500. (looseleaf format)

657   UK   ISSN 0263-0974
ACCOUNTANTS' & ADMINISTRATORS' HANDBOOK. 1982. a. £10.50. Gee & Co. (Publishers) Ltd., Alhambra House, 27-31 Charing Cross Rd., London WC2H 0LR, England. Ed. C.R. Pearce.
Formerly: Handbook for Accountants' and Administrators.

657   US
ACCOUNTING AND AUDITING UPDATE SERVICE. irreg. (approx. 1-6/m.) $175. Warren, Gorham and Lamont, Inc., 210 South St., Boston, MA 02111. TEL 800-922-0066.

657   MY   ISSN 0126-625X
ACCOUNTING JOURNAL. (Text in English) 1971. a. M.$4. University of Malaya Accounting Club, Faculty of Economics and Administration, University of Malaya, Lembah Pantai, Kuala Lumpur 22-11, Malaysia. Ed.Bd. adv. bibl. charts. circ. 750.

657   US
ADVANCES IN ACCOUNTING. 1984. a. $23.75 to individuals; institutions $47.50. J A I Press Inc., 36 Sherwood Pl., Box 1678, Greenwich, CT 06836-1678. TEL 301-661-7602. Ed. Bill N. Schwartz.

657   US   ISSN 0360-8840
AMERICAN ACCOUNTING ASSOCIATION. SOUTHEAST REGIONAL GROUP. COLLECTED PAPERS OF THE ANNUAL MEETING. a. American Accounting Association, c/o Paul Gerhardt, Admin. Sec., 5717 Bessie Dr., Sarasota, FL 33583. TEL 813-921-7797. illus. Key Title: Collected Papers of the Annual Meeting, Southeast Regional Group, American Accounting Association.

BUSINESS AND ECONOMICS — ACCOUNTING

657   336.2   US   ISSN 0065-874X
AMERICAN INSTITUTE OF CERTIFIED PUBLIC ACCOUNTANTS. DIVISION OF FEDERAL TAXATION. STATEMENTS ON RESPONSIBILITIES IN TAX PRACTICE. 1964. irreg. membership. American Institute of Certified Public Accountants, Division of Federal Taxation, 1211 Ave. of the Americas, New York, NY 10036. TEL 212-575-6200. circ. 160,000. (also avail. in microfiche from UMI)

657   US
AMERICAN INSTITUTE OF CERTIFIED PUBLIC ACCOUNTANTS. PUBLIC OVERSIGHT BOARD. ANNUAL REPORT. 1979. a. American Institute of Certified Public Accountants, Public Oversight Board, 540 Madison Ave., New York, NY 10022. TEL 212-486-2448. Ed. Louis Matusiak. circ. 8,000.

657   378   UK   ISSN 0263-1768
APPROVED COURSES FOR ACCOUNTANCY EDUCATION. 1981. a. Board of Accreditation of Educational Courses, 399 Silbury Blvd., Witan Gate East, Milton Keynes MK9 2HL, England.
    Formerly: Degree Studies and the Accountancy Profession.

657   US   ISSN 0146-9819
AUDITING RESEARCH MONOGRAPHS. 1972. irreg., no.6, 1984. price varies. American Institute of Certified Public Accountants, 1211 Ave. of the Americas, New York, NY 10036-8775. TEL 212-575-6200.

657   AT
AUSTRALIAN ACCOUNTING RESEARCH FOUNDATION. RESEARCH STUDIES. 1970. irreg. price varies. Australian Accounting Research Foundation, 170 Queen St., Melbourne, Vic. 3000, Australia. (Co-sponsors: Australian Society of Accountants; Institute of Chartered Accountants in Australia) Ed.Bd. circ. 3,000.
    Formerly: Accountancy Research Foundation, Melbourne. Accounting and Auditing Research Committee. Research Studies (ISSN 0084-5884)

657   SA   ISSN 0067-6349
BESTUURLIKE INFORMASIE/MANAGERIAL INFORMATION. (Text in Afrikaans and English) 1969. a. Potchefstroom University for Christian Higher Education, Department Kosteberekening, Posbus 368, Bedryfsrekeningkunde, Potchetstroom, South Africa. Ed. J.E. Sorgorager D'Econ.

657   AG
BOLETIN INTERAMERICANO DE CONTABILIDAD. irreg. $10. Asociacion Interamericana de Contabilidad, Av. Cordoba 1261, Buenos Aires, Argentina. (Co-sponsor: Federacion Argentina de Colegios de Graduados en Ciencias Economicas) circ. 15,000.

657   CN   ISSN 0068-8983
C I C A HANDBOOK. (Editions in English and French) 1968. irreg. Can.$42 (base vol.) Can.$30 (supplements) Canadian Institute of Chartered Accountants, 150 Bloor St. W., Toronto, Ont. M5S 2Y2, Canada. TEL 416-962-1242. circ. 71,000.

657   382   CN
CANADIAN CERTIFIED GENERAL ACCOUNTANTS' RESEARCH FOUNDATION. STUDY PAPERS. (Text in English, French) 1981. irreg. free. Certified General Accountants' Association of Canada, Canadian Certified General Accountants' Research Foundation, 740-1176 West Georgia St., Vancouver, BC V6E 4A2, Canada. TEL 604-669-3555. circ. 700. (back issues avail.)

657   CN   ISSN 0713-357X
CANADIAN INSTITUTE OF CHARTERED ACCOUNTANTS. UNIFORM FINAL EXAMINATION REPORT; contains UFE questions and approaches to answering the uniform final examination. French edition (ISSN 0820-0386) (Editions in English and French) a. price varies. ‡ Canadian Institute of Chartered Accountants, 150 Bloor St. W., Toronto, Ont. M5S 2Y2, Canada. TEL 416-962-1242. circ. 10,000.
    Former titles: Canadian Institute of Chartered Accountants. Uniform Final Examination Handbook; Canadian Institute of Chartered Accountants. Intermediate and Final Examinations.

657   UK
CHARTERED INSTITUTE OF PUBLIC FINANCE AND ACCOUNTANCY. CONFERENCE HANDBOOK. 1890. a. membership. Chartered Institute of Public Finance and Accountancy, 3 Robert St., London WC2N 6BH, England.

657.6   US
CIRCULATION AUDITING AROUND THE WORLD; memorandum report by the secretary-general. 1962. a. $2. International Federation of Audit Bureau of Circulations, 900 N. Meacham Rd., Schaumburg, IL 60173-4968. Ed. M. David Keil. circ. controlled.

COST ENGINEERS' NOTEBOOK. see ENGINEERING

657.025   CN   ISSN 0527-9275
DIRECTORY OF CANADIAN CHARTERED ACCOUNTANTS. biennial. price varies. Canadian Institute of Chartered Accountants, 150 Bloor St. W., Toronto, Ont. M5S 2Y2, Canada. TEL 416-962-1242. circ. 4,000.

657   DK   ISSN 0109-0305
EMNEREGISTER, SELSKABS- OG HOVEDAKTIONAERFORHOLD M.V. 1981. a. Kr.120. Foreningen af Statsautoriserede Revisorer, Revisorernes Hus, Kronprinsessegade 8, 1306 Copenhagen K, Denmark.

657.6   US
FEDERAL AUDIT GUIDES. irreg., (in 4 base vols., plus updates) $330. Commerce Clearing House, Inc., 4025 W. Peterson Ave., Chicago, IL 60646. TEL 312-583-8500.

657   CN   ISSN 0071-5115
FINANCIAL REPORTING IN CANADA. 1953. biennial. price varies. Canadian Institute of Chartered Accountants, 150 Bloor St. W., Toronto, Ont. M5S 2Y2, Canada. TEL 416-962-1242. Ed. G. Lew. circ. 3,500.

657   FR
FRANCE. INSTITUT NATIONAL DE LA STATISTIQUE ET DES ETUDES ECONOMIQUES. SERIE C: COMPTES ET PLANIFICATION. 1968. a. 510 F. Institut National de la Statistique et des Etudes Economiques, 18 bd. A Pinard, 75675 Paris 14, France.

657   US   ISSN 0275-8911
GEORGIA JOURNAL OF ACCOUNTING. 1980. a. free. University of Georgia, J.M. Tull School of Accounting, Athens, GA 30602. TEL 404-542-1616. circ. 2,500.

657   AU
HOCHSCHULE FUER WELTHANDEL, WIEN. INSTITUT FUER ORGANISATION UND REVISIONSWESEN. VEROEFFENTLICHUNGEN. 1953. irreg. price varies. Manzsche Verlags- und Universitaetsbuchhandlung, Kohlmarkt 16, A-1014 Vienna, Austria. Ed. L. Illetschko.
    Formerly: Hochschule fuer Welthandel, Wien. Institut fuer Organisation und Revisionswesen. Verhandlungen.

HORSE OWNERS AND BREEDERS TAX MANUAL. see SPORTS AND GAMES — Horses And Horsemanship

657   FR
INSTITUT FRANCAIS DES EXPERTS COMPTABLES. CAHIERS. 1970. irreg. (approx. 4/yr.) included in subscr. to Economie et Comptabilite. Institut Francais des Experts Comptables, 139 rue du Faubourg Saint-Honore, 75008 Paris, France. circ. 5,000.

657   AT
INSTITUTE OF CHARTERED ACCOUNTANTS IN AUSTRALIA. ANNUAL REPORT AND ACCOUNTS. a. Institute of Chartered Accountants in Australia, Box 3921, Sydney, N.S.W. 2001, Australia.

657   UK
INSTITUTE OF CHARTERED ACCOUNTANTS IN ENGLAND AND WALES. EXPOSURE DRAFTS AND STATEMENTS OF STANDARD ACCOUNTING PRACTICE. irreg. price varies. Institute of Chartered Accountants in England and Wales, P.O. Box 433, Moorgate Place, London EC2P 2BJ, England.
    Formerly: Institute of Chartered Accountants in England and Wales. Practice Administration Series, Exposure Drafts and Statements of Standard Accounting Practice (ISSN 0073-9049)

657   UK   ISSN 0073-9030
INSTITUTE OF CHARTERED ACCOUNTANTS IN ENGLAND AND WALES. MANAGEMENT INFORMATION SERIES. 1968. irreg. price varies. Institute of Chartered Accountants in England and Wales, P.O. Box 433, Moorgate Place, London EC2P 2BJ, England.

657   GY   ISSN 0380-4011
INSTITUTE OF CHARTERED ACCOUNTANTS OF GUYANA. NEWSLETTER. irreg. Institute of Chartered Accountants of Guyana, 10 Water St., Kingston, Guyana.

657   UK   ISSN 0073-9057
INSTITUTE OF CHARTERED ACCOUNTANTS OF SCOTLAND. OFFICIAL DIRECTORY. 1896. a. £20. Institute of Chartered Accountants of Scotland, 27 Queen Street, Edinburgh, EH2 1LA, Scotland. adv. circ. 1,500.

657   UK
INSTITUTE OF COST AND MANAGEMENT ACCOUNTANTS. FRAMEWORK SERIES IN ACCOUNTING. 1983. irreg. £3.50 per no. Institute of Cost and Management Accountants, 63 Portland Place, London W1N 4AB, England.

657   UK
INSTITUTE OF COST AND MANAGEMENT ACCOUNTANTS. OCCASIONAL PAPERS SERIES. irreg. price varies. Institute of Cost and Management Accountants, 63 Portland Place, London W1N 4AB, England.

657   IS
ISRAEL C P A. (Text in English) 1971. irreg., no.3, 1975. price varies. Institute of Certified Public Accountants in Israel, P.O. Box 29281, 1 Montefiore St., Tel Aviv, Israel.

657   658   GW
JAHRBUCH FUER BETRIEBSWIRTE. 1975. a. DM.36.80. Taylorix-Fachverlag Stiegler & Co., Moenchstrasse 29, 7000 Stuttgart 1, W. Germany (B.R.D.) Eds. Heinz Stehle, Werner Roessle, Norbert Leuz.

657   GW
JAHRBUCH FUER PRAKTIKER DES RECHNUNGSWESENS. 1956. a. DM.19.80. Taylorix-Fachverlag Stiegler & Co., Moenchstrasse 29, 7000 Stuttgart 1, W. Germany (B.R.D.) Eds. W. Alt, Leiselotte Kotsch-Fasshauer, Norbert Leuz. circ. 6,000.
    Formerly: Taschenbuch fuer den Buchhalter (ISSN 0082-1853)

657   IS
JERUSALEM CONFERENCE ON ACCOUNTANCY.* (Text in English) 1971. triennial. price varies. Institute of Certified Public Accountants in Israel, P.O. Box 29281, 1 Montefiore St., Tel Aviv, Israel.

657   US
JOURNAL OF ACCOUNTING RESEARCH. SUPPLEMENT. 1966. a. $26 includes journal. University of Chicago, Graduate School of Business, Institute of Professional Accounting, Chicago, IL 60637. TEL 312-962-7743. Ed. Nicholas Dopuch. charts.
    Formerly (until 1973): Empirical Research in Accounting, Selected Studies (ISSN 0424-9283)

MAIN HURDMAN & CRANSTOUN NEWS SUMMARY. see BUSINESS AND ECONOMICS — Public Finance, Taxation

BUSINESS AND ECONOMICS — BANKING AND FINANCE

657   NZ
MASSEY UNIVERSITY. FACULTY OF BUSINESS STUDIES. OCCASIONAL PAPERS. 1972. irreg., (approx. bi-m.) NZ.$5. Massey University, Faculty of Business Studies, Palmerston North, New Zealand. Ed. Prof. C.T. Heazlewood. circ. controlled. (back issues avail.)

657   US   ISSN 0077-3360
N A M F ACCOUNTING MANUAL;* a uniform accounting system for metal finishers. 1968. irreg. $100 to non-members; members $15. National Association of Metal Finishers, 111 E. Wacker Dr., Chicago, IL 60601. TEL 312-644-6610. Ed. J.D. Carey.

657   US
OREGON. STATE BOARD OF ACCOUNTANCY. CERTIFIED PUBLIC ACCOUNTANTS, PUBLIC ACCOUNTANTS, AND ACCOUNTANTS AUTHORIZED TO CONDUCT MUNICIPAL AUDITS IN OREGON. a. $5. Department of Commerce, Board of Accountancy, 403 Labor & Industries Bldg., Salem, OR 97310. TEL 503-378-4181. circ. 4,000.
     Former titles: Oregon. State Board of Accountancy. Certified Public Accountants, Public Accountants, Professional Corporations, and Accountants Authorized to Conduct Municipal Audits in Oregon (ISSN 0090-6735); Oregon: State Board of Accountancy. Roster of Accountants Authorized to Conduct Municipal Audits (ISSN 0471-8356)

RAILWAY ACCOUNTING RULES. see *TRANSPORTATION — Railroads*

657   UK
RECOMMENDATION FOR ACCOUNTANTS AND AUDITORS. 1980. irreg. £4.50. Marcus, Tobias & Co., 65 Shakespeare Dr., Shirley, Solihull B90 2AN, England.

657   US
RESEARCH IN GOVERNMENTAL AND NON-PROFIT ACCOUNTING. 1985. a. $23.75 to individuals; institutions $47.50. J A I Press Inc., 36 Sherwood Pl., Box 1678, Greenwich, CT 06836-1678. TEL 203-661-7602. Ed. James L. Chan.

657   DK   ISSN 0108-3716
REVISORHAANDBOGEN. 1982. a. Kr.85. Foreningen af Statsautoriserede Revisorer, Revisorernes Hus, Kronprinsessegade 8, 1306 Copenhagen K, Denmark.

S E C ACCOUNTING RULES. see *BUSINESS AND ECONOMICS — Investments*

657   DK   ISSN 0108-688X
SKATTEBEREGNINGEN. 1982. a. Kr.115. Foreningen af Statsautoriserede Revisorer, Revisorernes Hus, Kronprinsessegade 8, 1306 Copenhagen K, Denmark.

STRATEGY AND EXECUTIVE ACTION. see *BUSINESS AND ECONOMICS — Management*

657   US   ISSN 0586-5050
STUDIES IN ACCOUNTING RESEARCH. 1969. irreg. price varies. American Accounting Association, c/o Paul A. Gerhardt, Admin. Sec., 5717 Bessie Dr., Sarasota, FL 33583. TEL 813-921-7797.

657   US
TAX SAVING OPPORTUNITIES SERIES. 1983. irreg. Laventhol & Horwath, 919 Third Ave., New York, NY 10022.

657   US
TAX TIMES. a. $76. Tax Times, Information Services Order Department Services, 200 Old Tappan Rd., Old Tappan, NJ 07675. TEL 800-562-0245. (Co-publishers: Rosenfeld, Emanuel Inc; Prentice-Hall Information Services)

657   US   ISSN 0071-6065
UNIVERSITY OF FLORIDA. DEPARTMENT OF ACCOUNTING. ACCOUNTING SERIES. 1963. irreg., no.12, 1982. price varies. University Presses of Florida, 15 N.W. 15th St., Gainesville, FL 32603. Ed. A. Rashad Abdel-Khalik.

657   US   ISSN 0073-5191
UNIVERSITY OF ILLINOIS AT URBANA-CHAMPAIGN. CENTER FOR INTERNATIONAL EDUCATION AND RESEARCH IN ACCOUNTING. MONOGRAPHS. 1964. irreg., latest no.11. price varies. University of Illinois at Urbana-Champaign, Center for International Education and Research in Accounting, 320 Commerce Bldg. (West), Box 109, 1206 S. Sixth St., Champaign, IL 61820-6271. TEL 217-333-4545. Ed. V.K. Zimmerman. adv. circ. 700.

657   NZ
VICTORIA UNIVERSITY OF WELLINGTON. DECISION RESEARCH CENTRE. WORKING PAPER SERIES. 1982. irreg. NZ.$3 per no. Victoria University of Wellington, Department of Accountancy, Private Bag, Wellington, New Zealand. Ed. S.P. Keef. charts. circ. 50.

BUSINESS AND ECONOMICS — Banking And Finance

see also *Business and Economics—Economic Situation and Conditions; Business and Economics—Investments; Insurance*

332.1   US   ISSN 0084-5833
A D C A: AMERICAN DIRECTORY OF COLLECTION AGENCIES AND ATTORNEYS. 1918. a. $30.95. Service Publishing Co., 722 Park Lane Bldg., 2025 I St. N.W., Washington, DC 20006. TEL 202-872-0082. adv.

621.9   US
A T M DIRECTORY. (Automated Teller Machines) 1982. a. $25. Bank Administration Institute, 60 Gould Center, Rolling Meadows, IL 60008. TEL 312-228-6200. Ed. R. Gerald Fox. adv. tr.lit. circ. 25,000. (reprint service avail.)

332   US
ADVANCES IN FINANCIAL PLANNING AND FORECASTING. 1985. irreg. $23.75 to individuals; institutions $47.50. J A I Press Inc., 36 Sherwood Pl., Box 1678, Greenwich, CT 06836-1678. TEL 203-661-7602. Ed. Cheng F. Lee.

AFFAIRES ET GENS D'AFFAIRES. see *HISTORY — History Of Europe*

332   KE
AFRICAN CONFEDERATION OF SAVINGS AND CREDIT COOPERATIVES. ANNUAL REPORT. (Text in English) a. African Confederation of Savings and Credit Cooperatives, Box 43278, Nairobi, Kenya.
     Formerly: Africa Cooperative Savings and Credit Association. Annual Report.

AGRICULTURAL DEVELOPMENT BANK OF PAKISTAN. ANNUAL REPORT AND STATEMENT OF ACCOUNTS. see *AGRICULTURE — Agricultural Economics*

332   SP
AGRUPACION SINDICAL NACIONAL DE EMPRESAS DE FINANCIACION. CENSO. irreg. Agrupacion Sindical Nacional de Empresa de Financiacion, Paseo del Prado 18 y 20, Madrid, Spain.

332   KU
ALAHLI BANK OF KUWAIT K.S.C. ANNUAL REPORT AND BALANCE SHEET. a. Alahli Bank of Kuwait K.S.C., Mubarak Al-Kabir Street, P.O. Box 1387, Safat, Kuwait. charts. illus. stat.

332   CN   ISSN 0318-3971
ALBERTA OPPORTUNITY COMPANY. ANNUAL REPORT. 1974. a. Alberta Opportunity Co., P.O. Box 1860, Ponoka, Alta. T0C 2H0, Canada, Canada. TEL 403-427-2140.

332   US
ALMANAC OF BUSINESS AND INDUSTRIAL FINANCIAL RATIOS. 1971. a. $39.95. Prentice-Hall, Inc., Englewood Cliffs, NJ 07632. TEL 201-592-2000. Ed. Dr. Leo Troy. charts. stat. index. circ. 5,000.

332.1   US
AMERICAN BANKERS ASSOCIATION KEY TO ROUTING NUMBERS. 1911. a. $40. Rand McNally & Co., Financial Publishing Division, 8255 N. Central Park, Skokie, IL 60076 TEL 312-673-9100. (Orders to: Box 7600, Chicago, IL 60680) (also avail. in magnetic tape)

332.2   US
AMERICAN SAVINGS DIRECTORY. 1981. a. $80. McFadden Business Publications, 6195 Crooked Creek Rd., Norcross, GA 30092. TEL 404-448-1011. Ed. Dan Erwin. adv. circ. 5,200.

332.1   NE   ISSN 0066-1309
AMSTERDAM-ROTTERDAM BANK. ANNUAL REPORT. 1964. a. Amsterdam-Rotterdam Bank N.V., Herengracht 595, Amsterdam, Netherlands.

332   US   ISSN 0421-9910
ANALYSIS OF PUBLIC UTILITY FINANCING. 1950. w., q., and a. $350 for all issues; $235 for q. & a., $195 for annual only. Ebasco Business Consulting Co., 2 World Trade Center, New York, NY 10048. TEL 212-839-1268. Ed. H. Genzale.

332   FR
ANNUAIRE DU RESEAU ECUREUIL. biennial. price varies. Editions de l' Epargne, 174 Bld. Saint-Germain, 75297 Paris cedex 06, France.
     Formerly: Annuaire des Caisses d'Epargne; France et Outre-Mer (ISSN 0066-278X)

332 334   US
ANNUAL INSTITUTE ON SECURITIES REGULATION. 1969. a. $85. Practising Law Institute, 810 Seventh Ave., New York, NY 10019. TEL 212-765-5700. Ed.Bd. (back issues avail.)

332.1 340   US   ISSN 0739-2451
ANNUAL REVIEW OF BANKING LAW. 1982. a. $70. Butterworth Legal Publishers, 84 Montvale Ave., Stoneham, MA 02180. TEL 617-438-2451.

332   AQ
ANTIGUA COMMERCIAL BANK. ANNUAL REPORT. a. Antigua Commercial Bank, Thames and St. Mary St., St. John's, Antigua.

ANUARIO FINANCIERO Y DE SOCIEDADES ANONIMAS DE ESPANA. see *BUSINESS AND ECONOMICS — Production Of Goods And Services*

338.91 330   SJ
ARAB BANK FOR ECONOMIC DEVELOPMENT IN AFRICA. ANNUAL REPORT. 1975. a. Arab Bank for Economic Development in Africa, Box 2640, Khartoum, Sudan. Ed.Bd. charts. illus. stat.

332.1   BA
ARAB BANKING AND FINANCE HANDBOOK. (Text in English) 1983. a. $80. Falcon Publishing, Box 5028, Manama, Bahrain. Ed. S. Ganguly. adv. stat. circ. 5,500.

332.1   HK
ASIABANKING ALMANAC. 1980. a. $90. Asiamedia Company Limited, 2 Wellington St., 16th floor, Hong Kong. Ed. Irene Suen. adv. bk. rev. circ. 5,000.
     Formerly: Asian Banking Directory (ISSN 0252-1024)

332.1 338.9   PH   ISSN 0066-8370
ASIAN DEVELOPMENT BANK. ANNUAL REPORT. (Text in English) 1967. a. Asian Development Bank, Box 789, Manila 2800, Philippines. circ. 17,000.

ASIAN DEVELOPMENT BANK. BOARD OF GOVERNORS. SUMMARY OF PROCEEDINGS (OF THE) ANNUAL MEETING. see *BUSINESS AND ECONOMICS — International Development And Assistance*

332.1 338.9   PH
ASIAN DEVELOPMENT BANK. KEY INDICATORS OF DEVELOPING MEMBER COUNTRIES OF A D B. (Text in English) 1969. a. free. Asian Development Bank, Economic Office, Box 789, Manila 2800, Philippines.

332 338.9   PH   ISSN 0066-8397
ASIAN DEVELOPMENT BANK. OCCASIONAL PAPERS. 1969. irreg., 1978, no. 12. contr. free circ. Asian Development Bank, P.O. Box 789, Manila 2800, Philippines.

BUSINESS AND ECONOMICS — BANKING AND FINANCE

332 UK
ASIA'S 7500 LARGEST COMPANIES. (Text in English) 1985. a. £85. E.L.C. International, Sinclair House, The Avenue, West Ealing, London W13 8NT, England. Ed. E. Blaufeld. circ. 1,000.

332 CK
ASOCIACION NACIONAL DE INSTITUCIONES FINANCIERAS. SIMPOSIO SOBRE MERCADO DE CAPITALES.* no.3, 1974. a. Asociacion Bancaria de Colombia, Carrera 7 no.17-09, Piso 3, Bogota, D.E., Colombia.

332.1 LE
ASSOCIATION DES BANQUES DU LIBAN. BILANS DES BANQUES.* irreg. Association of Banks in Lebanon, Rue de l'Armee, Box 967, Beirut, Lebanon. stat.

332.1 BL
B N H RELATORIO DE ATIVIDADES. a. Banco Nacional da Habitacao, Secretaria de Divulgacao, Av. Republica do Chile 230, Rio de Janeiro RJ, Brazil. charts. illus. stat.

332 BL ISSN 0005-4585
BANAS; revista industrial e financeira. (Annual no. in English) 1959. m. Cr.$400. Editora Banas, S.A., Av. Presidente Castelo Branco 6241, CEP 05038, Sao Paulo, Brazil. Ed. Elizabeth Banas. adv. bk. rev. charts. illus. pat. stat. circ. 34,000. (tabloid format)
Formerly: Banas Informa; Incorporating: Banas-Classificado Industrial Brasileiro & Brasil Industrial (ISSN 0068-0699) & Imagem do Brasil e da America Latina & Brasil Financeiro e Grandes Companhias.

332.1 IT ISSN 0067-3161
BANCA D'ITALIA. ASSEMBLEA GENERALE ORDINARIA DEI PARTECIPANTI. (Editions in English, Italian) 1894. a. free. Banca d'Italia, Servizio Studi, Via Nazionale, 91, Rome, Italy. circ. 7,500.

332 IT
BANCA D'ITALIA. SERVIZIO STUDI. TEMI DI DISCUSSIONE. 1979. irreg. free. Banca d'Italia, Servizio Studi, Via Nationale, 91, 00184 Rome, Italy. circ. 2,800. (back issues avail.)

382 332 RM
BANCA ROMANA DE COMERT EXTERIOR. ANNUAL BULLETIN. (Text in English) a. Banca de Comert Exterior, Calea Victoriei Nr.22-24, Bucharest, Rumania.

332.1 330.9 CL ISSN 0716-2448
BANCO CENTRAL DE CHILE, SANTIAGO. MEMORIA ANUAL. 1926. a. $18. Banco Central de Chile, Departamento de Publicaciones e Informaciones, Casilla 967, Santiago, Chile. TEL 56-2-696-2281. circ. 1,200 (Spanish edt.; English edt. 900)

332.1 CR ISSN 0067-320X
BANCO CENTRAL DE COSTA RICA. MEMORIA ANUAL. 1950. a. free. Banco Central de Costa Rica, San Jose, Costa Rica. charts. stat.

332.1 AG
BANCO CENTRAL DE LA REPUBLICA ARGENTINA. CENTRO DE ESTUDIOS MONETARIOS Y BANCARIOS. DISCUSSION PAPER. (Text in English) 1976. irreg., no.13, June 1983. Banco Central de la Republica Argentina, Centro de Estudios Monetarios y Bancarios, Reconquista 266-78, Buenos Aires, Argentina. circ. 250.

332.1 AG
BANCO CENTRAL DE LA REPUBLICA ARGENTINA. CENTRO DE ESTUDIOS MONETARIOS Y BANCARIOS. SERIE DE COMPUTACION. 1975. irreg., no.4, May 1977. Banco Central de la Republica Argentina, Centro de Estudios Monetarios y Bancarios, Reconquista 266-78, Buenos Aires, Argentina.

332.1 AG
BANCO CENTRAL DE LA REPUBLICA ARGENTINA. CENTRO DE ESTUDIOS MONETARIOS Y BANCARIOS. SERIE DE ESTUDIOS TECNICOS. 1975. irreg., no.65, Feb. 1986. Banco Central de la Republica Argentina, Centro de Estudios Monetarios y Bancarios, Reconquista 266-78, Buenos Aires, Argentina.

332.1 AG
BANCO CENTRAL DE LA REPUBLICA ARGENTINA. CENTRO DE ESTUDIOS MONETARIOS Y BANCARIOS. SERIE DE INFORMACION PUBLICA. 1976. irreg., no.18, Oct. 1986. Banco Central de la Republica Argentina, Centro de Estudios Monetarios y Bancarios, Reconquista 266-78, Buenos Aires, Argentina.

332 DR
BANCO CENTRAL DE LA REPUBLICA DOMINICANA. MEMORIA. a. Banco Central de la Republica Dominicana, Apdo. Postal 1347, Santo Domingo, Dominican Republic.

332 NQ
BANCO CENTRAL DE NICARAGUA. BIBLIOTECA Y SERVICIOS DE INFORMACION. BARRICADA INDICE TEMATICO Y ONOMASTICO.* a. Ministerio de Comercio Exterior (MICE), Apdo. 2412, Managua, Nicaragua.

332 NQ
BANCO CENTRAL DE NICARAGUA. BOLETIN ANUAL.* 1936. a. free. Ministerio de Comercio Exterior (MICE), Apdo. 2412, Managua, Nicaragua. Ed. Ramon Cabrales. bk. rev. charts. stat. circ. 2,500.
Former titles: Banco Central de Nicaragua. Boletin Semestral & Banco Central de Nicaragua. Boletin Trimestral (ISSN 0005-4690)

332.1 NQ ISSN 0067-3226
BANCO CENTRAL DE NICARAGUA. INFORME ANUAL.* 1961. a. Ministerio de Comercio Exterior (MICE), Apdo. 2412, Managua, Nicaragua. Dir. Noel Lacayo Baretto.

332.1 ES
BANCO CENTRAL DE RESERVA DE EL SALVADOR. MEMORIA.* 1934. a. Banco Central de Reserva de el Salvador, Calle Poniente y 7A, Avda Norte, San Salvador, El Salvador. Dir. Guillermo Hidalgo Quehl. charts. stat. circ. 3,100.

332 PE
BANCO CENTRAL DE RESERVA DEL PERU. MEMORIA. 1922. a. Banco Central de Reserva del Peru, Apartado 1958, Lima, Peru. charts. stat.

332 VE
BANCO CENTRAL DE VENEZUELA. ANUARIO DE CUENTAS NACIONALES. a. Banco Central de Venezuela, Apdo. Postal 2017, Esquina de las Carmelitas, Caracas, Venezuela.

332.1 VE ISSN 0067-3269
BANCO CENTRAL DE VENEZUELA. MEMORIA. 1940. a. free. Banco Central de Venezuela, Esquina de las Carmelitas, Caracas, Venezuela. circ. 2,000.

BANCO CENTRAL DEL ECUADOR. BALANZA DE PAGOS. see BUSINESS AND ECONOMICS — Abstracting, Bibliographies, Statistics

332.1 EC ISSN 0067-3277
BANCO CENTRAL DEL ECUADOR. MEMORIA DEL GERENTE GENERAL.* 1948. irreg. free. Banco Central del Ecuador, Av. 10 de Agosto, La Alameda-Quito, Ecuador. TEL 210-340. charts. illus. stat.

332.1 PY ISSN 0067-3285
BANCO CENTRAL DEL PARAGUAY. MEMORIA.* (Title varies) 1952. a. free. Banco Central del Paraguay, Independencia Nacional y 25 de Mayo, Paraguay.

332.1 UY
BANCO CENTRAL DEL URUGUAY. RESENA DE LA ACTIVIDAD ECONOMICO-FINANCIERA. irreg. Banco Central del Uruguay, Departamento de Investigaciones Economicas, Cerrito 351, Montevideo, Uruguay. stat.

332.1 SP
BANCO DE BILBAO. AGENDA FINANCIERA. vol.14, 1975. a. Banco de Bilbao, Gran Via 12, Bilbao 1, Spain.

332 SP
BANCO DE BILBAO. INFORME - MEMORIA. a. Banco de Bilbao, Servicio de Estudios, Gran Via 12, Bilbao, Spain. charts. illus. stat.
Formerly: Banco de Bilbao. Memoria.

332.1 SP ISSN 0067-3315
BANCO DE ESPANA. INFORME ANUAL. 1962. a. free to qualified personnel. Banco de Espana, Negociado de Publicaciones, Alcala 50, Madrid 28014, Spain.

332 GT
BANCO DE GUATEMALA. ESTUDIO ECONOMICO Y MEMORIA DE LABORES. 1945. a. Banco de Guatemala, Seccion de Servicios Auxiliares, 7 Avda. No. 22-01, Zona 1, Guatemala City, Guatemala.
Continues (after 1967): Banco de Guatemala. Memoria.

332.1 330.9 MX ISSN 0067-3374
BANCO DE MEXICO. INFORME ANUAL. a. Banco de Mexico, Subdireccion de Investigacion Economica y Bancaria, Apdo. 98 Bis, Mexico 1, D.F., Mexico. charts. (also avail. in microfiche)

332.1 BL ISSN 0101-0646
BANCO DO BRASIL. ANNUAL REPORT. (Text in English) a. Banco do Brasil S.A., Setor Bancario Sul, Bloco A, Edificio Sede do Banco do Brasil, 70073 Brasilia, Brazil. Ed.Bd. charts. illus. stat.

332.1 BL
BANCO DO ESTADO DE PERNAMBUCO. BANDEPE RELATORIO. (Summary in English) 1969. a. free. Banco do Estado de Pernambuco, Cais do Apolo, 222, Recife, Brazil. illus. stat. circ. 3,000.

332 BO
BANCO MINERO DE BOLIVIA. MEMORIA. a. Banco Minero de Bolivia, Casilla No. 1410, La Paz, Bolivia.

332 MX
BANCO NACIONAL DE COMERCIO EXTERIOR, MEXICO. ANNUAL REPORT. Spanish edition: Informe Anual. 1938. irreg., latest 1983. free. Banco Nacional de Comercio Exterior S.A., Gerencia de Publicaciones, Malintzin 28, Col. del Carmen, Coyacan Mexico D.F. 04100, Mexico. illus. stat. Indexed: Key to Econ.Sci.

332.1 HO
BANCO NACIONAL DE DESARROLLO AGRICOLA. MEMORIA ANUAL. 1950. a. free. Banco National de Desarrollo Agricola, Unidad de Estudios Economicos, Tegucigalpa, Honduras. charts. illus. stat. circ. 2,000.
Formerly (until 1979): Banco Nacional de Fomento, Tegucigalpa. Memoria Anual (ISSN 0067-3390)

332.1 PN
BANCO NACIONAL DE PANAMA. ASESORIA ECONOMICA. MEMORIA ANUAL. 1906. a. free. Banco Nacional de Panama, Apdo 5220, Panama 5, Panama. circ. 1,500.

332 PN
BANCO NACIONAL DE PANAMA. INFORME DEL GERENTE GENERAL. 1904. Banco Nacional de Panama, Apdo. 5220, Panama City, Panama.

332 BL
BANCO NACIONAL DO DESENVOLVIMENTO ECONOMICO. ANNUAL REPORT. (Portuguese edition available) (Text in English) a. Banco Nacional do Desenvolvimento Economico, Av. Rio Branco 53, Rio de Janeiro RJ, Brazil. charts. illus. stat.

332.1 AG
BANCO SINDICAL. MEMORIA Y BALANCE GENERAL. no.10, 1978. a. Banco Sindical, Reconquista 319-27, Buenos Aires, Argentina.

332.1 BG
BANGLADESH BANK. ANNUAL REPORT. (Text in English) a. Bangladesh Bank, Department of Public Relations and Publications, Motijheel Commercial Area, Dacca 2, Bangladesh.

332 DK ISSN 0108-7177
BANK. 1980. a. free. Handelsbanken, Staunings Plads 1-3, 1643 Copenhagen V, Denmark. illus.

332.1 CN ISSN 0045-1436
BANK DIRECTORY OF CANADA. a. (plus bi-m. supplements) Can.$17. Canadian Payments Association, P.O. Box 348, 2 First Canadian Place, Toronto, Ont. M5X 1E1, Canada. TEL 613-238-4173. Ed. Mrs. Whitney Curtis. circ. 9,000.

BUSINESS AND ECONOMICS — BANKING AND FINANCE

332   US
BANK DIRECTORY OF NEW ENGLAND. 1913. a. $20. Shawmut Bank of Boston, N.A., Correspondent Banking Group, One Federal St., Boston, MA 02211. TEL 617-292-2298. circ. controlled.

332.1   US
BANK DIRECTORY OF THE NINTH FEDERAL RESERVE DISTRICT. 1918. a. $31. Commercial West, 7535 Office Ridge Circle, Eden Prairie, Minneapolis, MN 55344. TEL 612-941-5823. adv. circ. 5,000.

330.9   IO   ISSN 0302-6795
BANK EKSPOR IMPOR INDONESIA. ANNUAL REPORT/LAPORAN TAHUNAN. (Text in English and Indonesian) a. Bank Ekspor Impor Indonesia, Jl. Lapagan Setasium 1, Box 32, Jakarta, Indonesia. illus. stat.

332.1   CN
BANK FACTS: CHARTERED BANKS OF CANADA. (Editions in English and French) 1968. a. free. Canadian Bankers' Association, Box 348, 2 First Canadian Place, Toronto, Ont. M5X 1E1, Canada. TEL 416-362-6092. circ. 64,000.
    Formerly: Factbook: Chartered Banks of Canada.

332.1   SZ   ISSN 0067-3560
BANK FOR INTERNATIONAL SETTLEMENTS. ANNUAL REPORT. (Text in English, French, German and Italian) a. not for sale; avail. to limited qualified personnel. Bank for International Settlements, 7 Centralbahnstrasse, Case Postale 262, CH-4002 Basel, Switzerland. charts. stat. index. circ. controlled.

332   PK
BANK GUIDE. (Text in English) 1977. a. Barque & Company, Barque Chambers, Barque Square, 87 Sharah e-Liquat Ali, Box 201, Lahore, Pakistan.

338.8   US   ISSN 0519-1572
BANK HOLDING COMPANY FACTS. 1960. a. free. Association of Bank Holding Companies, 730 15th St. N.W., Washington, DC 20005. TEL 202-393-1158. Ed J.L. More. stat. circ. 600.

332.1   336   US
BANK INCOME TAX RETURN MANUAL. 1983. a. $79.50. Warren, Gorham & Lamont, Inc., 210 South St., Boston, MA 02111. TEL 800-922-0066.

332.1   CN   ISSN 0067-3587
BANK OF CANADA. ANNUAL REPORT. 1935. a. free. Bank of Canada, Public Information Division, Secretary's Dept., Ottawa K1A 0G9, Canada. TEL 613-563-8111.

332.1   CN   ISSN 0713-7931
BANK OF CANADA. TECHNICAL REPORTS. 1969. irreg. free. Bank of Canada, Distribution Section, Secretary's Dept., Ottawa K1A 0G9, Canada. TEL 613-563-8111.
    Formerly (until 1973): Bank of Canada. Staff Research Studies (ISSN 0067-3595)

330.9   CE
BANK OF CEYLON. ANNUAL REPORT AND ACCOUNTS. (Text in English) a. Bank of Ceylon, 41 Bristol St., Colombo 1, Sri Lanka. illus.
    Former titles: Bank of Ceylon. Annual Report; (1939-19??): Central Bank of Ceylon. Report and Accounts (ISSN 0067-3617)

332.1   UK   ISSN 0308-5279
BANK OF ENGLAND. REPORT AND ACCOUNTS. a. free. Bank of England, Economics Division, Threadneedle St., London EC2, England. (reprint service avail.)
    Formerly: Bank of England. Report (ISSN 0067-3625)

332   FI   ISSN 0081-945X
BANK OF FINLAND. ANNUAL STATEMENT. Finnish Edition (ISSN 0355-595X); Swedish Edition (ISSN 0585-9573) 1866. a. Fmk.10. Suomen Pankki - Bank of Finland, Information Department, Box 160, SF-00101 Helsinki, Finland. Ed. Annikki Leukkunen. circ. 4,500 (all edts.)

332   FI   ISSN 0081-9468
BANK OF FINLAND. YEARBOOK. Finnish edition: Suomen Pankki. Vuosikirja (ISSN 0355-5925); Swedish edition: Finlands Bank. Aarsbok (ISSN 0355-5933) (Editions in Finnish, Swedish and English) 1914. a. Fmk.60. Suomen Pankki - Bank of Finland, Information Department, Box 160, SF-00101 Helsinki, Finland. Ed. Annikki Leukkunen. circ. 3,400 (all edts.)

332.1   IS   ISSN 0067-365X
BANK OF ISRAEL. ANNUAL REPORT. (Editions in English and Hebrew) a. $15. Bank of Israel, Kiryath Ben Gurion, Box 780, Jerusalem, Israel.

BANK OF ISRAEL. ANNUAL STATISTICS OF ISRAEL'S BANKING SYSTEM. see *BUSINESS AND ECONOMICS — Abstracting, Bibliographies, Statistics*

BANK OF ISRAEL. ECONOMIC REVIEW. see *BUSINESS AND ECONOMICS — Economic Situation And Conditions*

332.1   IS   ISSN 0334-2093
BANK OF ISRAEL. ISRAEL'S BANKING SYSTEM. (Editions in English and Hebrew) a. $10. Bank of Israel, Kiryath Ben Gurion, Box 780, Jerusalem, Israel.

332.1   IS   ISSN 0067-3641
BANK OF ISRAEL. MAIN POINTS OF THE ANNUAL REPORT. a. $2. Bank of Israel, Kiryath Ben Gurion, Box 780, Jerusalem, Israel.

332   JM   ISSN 0067-3668
BANK OF JAMAICA. REPORT AND STATEMENT OF ACCOUNTS. a. free. Bank of Jamaica, P.O. Box 621, King St., Kingston, Jamaica.

332.1   JA
BANK OF JAPAN. ANNUAL REPORT. (Text in English) a. free. Bank of Japan, Foreign Department - Nihon Ginko, C.P.O. Box 203, Tokyo 100-91, Japan. charts. stat.
    Formerly: Bank of Japan. Annual Report of the Policy Board (ISSN 0067-3676)

332.1   KO   ISSN 0067-3706
BANK OF KOREA. ANNUAL REPORT. a. Bank of Korea, Research Department, Seoul 100, S. Korea. Ed. Han Do Huh.

332.1   MF   ISSN 0067-3722
BANK OF MAURITIUS. ANNUAL REPORT. (Text in English) 1968. a. free. Bank of Mauritius, P.O. Box 29, Port Louis, Mauritius. circ. 1,000.

332.1   PP
BANK OF PAPUA NEW GUINEA. REPORT AND FINANCIAL STATEMENTS. (Text in English) 1974. a. free. Bank of Papua New Guinea, Economics Department, Douglas St., Port Moresby, Papua New Guinea. illus. stat. circ. 2,000.

332   KO
BANK OF SEOUL AND TRUST COMPANY. ECONOMIC REVIEW. no.5,6, 1977. irreg. Bank of Seoul and Trust Company, Seoul, S. Korea.

332.1   SL
BANK OF SIERRA LEONE. ANNUAL REPORT AND STATEMENT OF ACCOUNTS. a. free. Bank of Sierra Leone, P.O. Box 30, Freetown, Sierra Leone.
    Formerly: Bank of Sierra Leone. Annual Report (ISSN 0067-3730)

332.1   SJ   ISSN 0067-3749
BANK OF SUDAN. REPORT. a. free. Bank of Sudan, Box 313, Khartoum, Sudan.

BANK OF TANZANIA. ECONOMIC AND OPERATIONS REPORT. see *BUSINESS AND ECONOMICS — Economic Situation And Conditions*

332   JA
BANK OF TOKYO ANNUAL REPORT. 1978. a. Bank of Tokyo Ltd., 1-6-3 Hongokucho, Nihombashi, Chuo-ku, Tokyo 103, Japan. charts. cum. index covering 2 yrs. circ. 12,000.
    Formerly: Bank of Tokyo Semiannual Report (ISSN 0005-5360)

332.1   TO
BANK OF TONGA. ANNUAL REPORT. a. Bank of Tonga, Head Office, P.O. Box 924, Nukualofa, Tonga.

332.1   ZA
BANK OF ZAMBIA. REPORT AND STATEMENT OF ACCOUNTS. (Text in English) a. Bank of Zambia, Box 30080, Lusaka, Zambia.

332   IO   ISSN 0408-4632
BANK PEMBANGUNAN INDONESIA. ANNUAL REPORT. (Text in English) 1960. a. free. Bank Pembangunan Indonesia - Development Bank of Indonesia, Box 140, Jakarta, Indonesia. Ed.Bd. charts. illus. stat.

332.1   UK
BANK SORTING CODE NUMBERS. 1967. a. £2.50. (Association for Payment Clearing Services) Thomas Skinner Directories, East Grinstead House, East Grinstead, W. Sussex RH19 1ZB, England. circ. 120,000.

332   DK   ISSN 0108-9129
BANKER OG SPAREKASSER; beretning om bankers og sparekassers. 1976. a. free. Tilsynet med Banker og Sparekasser, Noerre Voldgade 94/5, 1358 Copenhagen K, Denmark. circ. 3,500.

332.1   UK   ISSN 0067-379X
BANKERS ALMANAC AND YEAR BOOK. 1886. a. $175. Thomas Skinner Directories, Windsor Court, East Grinstead House, East Grinstead, W. Sussex RH19 1XE, England. adv. circ. 20,000.

321.1   UK
BANKERS' ALMANAC WORLD RANKING. a. £60. Thomas Skinner Directories, Windsor Court, East Grinstead House, East Grinstead, W. Sussex RH19 1XE, England.

332.1   US
BANKERS DIARY AND GUIDE. a. $38. Warren, Gorham and Lamont, Inc., 210 South St., Boston, MA 02111. TEL 800-922-0066.

332   HK
BANKERS HANDBOOK FOR ASIA. 1976. a. Asian Finance Publications Ltd., Suite D, 9th Floor, Hyde Centre, 223 Gloucester Rd., Hong Kong, Hong Kong. Ed. T.K. Seshadri. adv. charts. illus. circ. 10,000.

332.1   II   ISSN 0067-3803
BANKERS' WHO'S WHO. (Text in English) 1962/63. irreg. £15. Business Publications International, United India Life Building, Box 548, F-Block, Connaught Place, New Delhi 1, India. Ed. K. L. Sahgal. adv. bk. rev. circ. 10,000. (back issues avail.)

332.1   US
BANKING GUIDES - ASIA, AUSTRALIA, NEW ZEALAND WITH PRINCIPAL HOTELS AND BANK HOLIDAYS. Cover title: Asian Banking Guide. a. Manufacturers Hanover Trust Co., International Division, 350 Park Ave., New York, NY 10022.

332   UK
BANKING IN THE E E C; structures and sources of finance. irreg. £76($109) Financial Times Business Information, 102 Clerkenwell Rd., London EC1M 5SA, England.
    Formerly: Banking Structures and Sources of Finance in the European Community.

332   US
BANKING: LATIN AMERICAN INDUSTRIAL REPORT. (Avail. for each of 22 Latin American countries) 1985. a. $435 per country report per industry covered. Aurora International, Box 9099, Bridgeport, CT 06601-2099. TEL 203-368-0579. Ed. Andres C. Aquino.

332.1   340   US   ISSN 0737-2159
BANKING LAW ANTHOLOGY. 1983. a. $99.95. Book Publishers, Inc., 7315 Wisconsin Ave., Ste. 229 E, Bethesda, MD 20814. Ed. Allison P. Zabriskie. Indexed: Leg.Per.

332.1   340   US
BANKING LAW JOURNAL DIGEST (SUPPLEMENT) a. to update set of 2 base volumes. $98 for base vols. plus supp. Warren, Gorham and Lamont, Inc., 210 South St., Boston, MA 02111. TEL 800-922-0066.

BUSINESS AND ECONOMICS — BANKING AND FINANCE

332.1 PK ISSN 0067-3811
BANKING STATISTICS OF PAKISTAN. (Text in English) 1948/57. a. Rs.20($5) State Bank of Pakistan, Central Directorate, Public Relations Department, I.I. Chundrigar Rd., Box 4456, Karachi, Pakistan. circ. 470.

332 UK
BANKING STRUCTURES AND SOURCES OF FINANCE IN THE FAR EAST. irreg. £51.50. Financial Times Business Information, 102 Clerkenwell Rd., London EC1M 5SA, England.

332.1 MG
BANKIN'NY INDOSTRIA. RAPPORT ANNUEL. 1964. a. free. Bankin'Ny Indostria - Bank Nationale pour le Developpement Industriel, B.P. 174, 101 Antananarivo, Malagasy Republic. Ed.Bd. circ. 1, 416.
   Formerly (until 1977): Banque Nationale Malagasy de Developpement. Rapport d'Activite (ISSN 0067-401X)

332 SI
BANKS AND FINANCIAL INSTITUTIONS IN SINGAPORE; Consulton report. (Text and summaries in English) 1976. a. S.140($70) Consulton (Private) Ltd, 1 Colombo Court 09-10, Singapore 0617, Singapore. Ed. B.J. Fernandes. circ. 2,000. (back issues avail.)

332.1 SZ ISSN 0067-382X
BANKWIRTSCHAFTLICHE FORSCHUNGEN. 1969. irreg., no.100,1986. price varies. (Universitaet Zuerich, Institut fuer Schweizerisches Bankwesen) Paul Haupt AG, Falkenplatz 14, CH-3001 Berne, Switzerland. (Co-sponsor: Hochschule St. Gallen fuer Wirtschafts- und Sozialwissenschaften, Institut fuer Bankwirtschaft)

332.1 TI ISSN 0067-3854
BANQUE CENTRALE DE TUNISIE. BULLETIN.* 1959. irreg. Banque Centrale de Tunisie, 7 Place de la Monnaie, Tunis, Tunisia.

332.1 TI ISSN 0067-3862
BANQUE CENTRALE DE TUNISIE. RAPPORT D'ACTIVITE.* (Title varies: Rapport Annuel) 1958/59. a. Banque Centrale de Tunisie, 7 Place de la Monnaie, Tunis, Tunisia.

332 SG ISSN 0067-3889
BANQUE CENTRALE DES ETATS DE L'AFRIQUE DE L'OUEST. RAPPORT ANNUEL. 1962. a. free. Banque Centrale des Etats de l'Afrique de l'Ouest, 3 Ave. W. Ponty, B.P. 1398, Dakar, Senegal (Provisional address: 29 rue de Colisee, Paris (8e), France) circ. 2,000. Indexed: P.A.I.S.For.Lang.Ind.

332.1 SG ISSN 0067-3897
BANQUE CENTRALE DES ETATS DE L'AFRIQUE DE L'OUEST. RAPPORT D'ACTIVITE. 1963. a. Banque Centrale des Etats de l'Afrique de l'Ouest, 3 Ave. W. Ponty, B.P. 1398, Senegal, France (Provisional address: 29 rue de Colisee, Paris (8e), France)

332.1 ZR
BANQUE COMMERCIALE ZAIROISE. REPORTS AND BALANCE SHEETS. a. Banque Commerciale Zairoise, B.P. 2798, Kinshasa, Zaire.

332.1 BE
BANQUE DE BRUXELLES LAMBERT. RAPPORTS DE L'EXERCICE/BANK BRUSSEL LAMBERT. ANNUAL REPORT. 1935. a. free. Banque de Bruxelles Lambert SA - Bank Brussel Lambert NV., 24 av. Marnix, B-1050 Brussels, Belgium. Ed. Daniel Cardon. circ. 27,000.
   Formerly: Banque de Bruxelles. Rapport Annuel (ISSN 0067-3919)

332.3 BD
BANQUE DE CREDIT DE BUJUMBURA. RAPPORTS ET BILAN. (Text in French) 1965. a. Banque de Credit de Bujumbura, B.P. 300, Bujumbura, Burundi. circ. 700.

332.1 FR ISSN 0067-3927
BANQUE DE FRANCE. COMPTE-RENDU. a. free. Banque de France, Service de l'Information, 43 rue de Valois, 75049 Paris Cedex 1, France.

332.1 BD ISSN 0067-3935
BANQUE DE LA REPUBLIQUE DU BURUNDI. RAPPORT ANNUEL. (Text in French) 1964. a. 1300 Fr.CFA($40) Banque de la Republique du Burundi, Department des Etudes, de l'Organisation et de l'Informatique, B.P. 705, Bujumbura, Burundi. circ. 500.

332.1 CM ISSN 0067-3900
BANQUE DES ETATS DE L'AFRIQUE CENTRALE. RAPPORT D'ACTIVITE. 1973. a. free. Banque des Etats de l'Afrique Centrale, Direction des Etudes et de la Documentation, Services Centraux, B.P. 1917, Yaounde, Cameroun. circ. 1,500.

332.1 MR ISSN 0067-396X
BANQUE DU MAROC. RAPPORT ANNUEL. a. free. Banque du Maroc, 277 Ave. Mohammed V, Rabat, Morocco.

332.1 ZR ISSN 0300-1172
BANQUE DU ZAIRE. RAPPORT ANNUEL. a. K.66.85 per no. Banque du Zaire, B.P. 2697, Kinshasa, Zaire.
   Formerly: Banque Nationale du Congo. Rapport Annuel (ISSN 0067-4001)

332.1 MR
BANQUE MAROCAINE DU COMMERCE EXTERIEUR. ANNUAL REPORT. 1961. a. Banque Marocaine du Commerce Exterieur, 140 Avenue Hassan II, Casablanca, Morocco.

332.1 BE ISSN 0067-3978
BANQUE NATIONALE DE BELGIQUE. RAPPORT SUR LES OPERATIONS. (Editions in Dutch, English and French) a. Banque Nationale de Belgique, 5 Bd. de Berlaimont, B-1000 Brussels, Belgium.

332.1 BD
BANQUE NATIONALE DE DEVELOPPEMENT ECONOMIQUE DU BURUNDI. RAPPORT ANNUEL. a. Banque Nationale de Developpement Economique du Burundi, B.P. 1620, Bujumbura, Burundi.

332.1 RW
BANQUE NATIONALE DU RWANDA. RAPPORT D'ACTIVITES. a. $25. Banque Nationale du Rwanda, B.P. 531, Kigali, Rwanda. stat.
   Farmerly (until 1986): Banque Nationale du Rwanda. Rapport Annuel.

332.1 MG
BANQUE NATIONALE POUR LE DEVELOPPEMENT RURAL. RAPPORT ANNUEL. a. Banque Nationale pour le Developpement Rural, B.P. 183, Antananarivo, Malagasy Republic.

332.1 RW
BANQUE RWANDAISE DE DEVELOPPEMENT. RAPPORT ANNUEL. (Text in French) a. Banque Rwandaise de Developpement, B.P. 1341, Kigali, Rwanda. charts. stats.

332.1 TG
BANQUE TOGOLAISE DE DEVELOPPEMENT. RAPPORT D'ACTIVITES. (Text in French) a. Banque Togolaise de Developpement, B.P. 65, Lome, Togo.
   Formerly: Banque Togolaise de Developpement. Rapport Annuel (ISSN 0067-4036)

332.1 BB
BARBADOS NATIONAL BANK. ANNUAL REPORT & STATEMENT OF ACCOUNTS. a. Barbados National Bank, James St., Bridgetown, Barbados, W. Indies.

BAWL STREET JOURNAL; annual lampoon of the financial community. see LITERARY AND POLITICAL REVIEWS

332.7 NE ISSN 0005-9110
BERICHTEN VAN DE AFDELING VOLKSKREDIETWEZEN. 1964. irreg., no.26, 1976. free. Ministerie van Welzijn, Volksgezondheid en Cultuur, Steenvoordelaan 370, Rijswijk (Z.H.), Netherlands. charts. stat.

BOERSE. see BUSINESS AND ECONOMICS — Investments

332 UK ISSN 0068-3566
BUILDING SOCIETIES. YEAR BOOK. 1927. a. £30. Franey and Co. Ltd., 7 Swallow Place, London W1R 7AA, England. Ed. Jean Amos. adv.

BUILDING SOCIETY FACTBOOK (YEAR) see REAL ESTATE

330.9 KU
BURGAN BANK. ANNUAL REPORT. 1977. a. Burgan Bank, Abdulla al-Salem St., Box 5389 Safat, Kuwait.

332 UK ISSN 0068-4457
BUSINESS MONITOR: MISCELLANEOUS SERIES. M3 COMPANY FINANCE. a. price varies. Department of Industry, 29 Great Peter St., London SW1P 3LW, England (Avail. from H.M.S.O., c/o Liaison Officer, Atlantic House, Holborn Viaduct, London EC1P 1BW, England) Indexed: Int.Packag.Abstr. Paper & Bd.Abstr.

332 US ISSN 0734-0486
C M R E MONOGRAPHS. 1971. irreg., latest no.46. $3 per no. Committee for Monetary Research and Education, Inc., Box 1630, Greenwich, CT 06836. TEL 203-661-2533. circ. 3,000.
   Former titles: C M R E Monetary Tracts; C M R E Money Tracts.

332.1 EC
C O F I E C. INFORME ANUAL. a. Compania Financiera Ecuatoriana de Desarrollo, Box 411, Quito, Ecuador. illus. stat.

332 FR
CAHIERS ECONOMIQUES ET MONETAIRES. irreg. price varies. Banque de France, Service de l'Information, 43 rue de Valois, 75049 Paris Cedex 01, France. Ed. R. Raymond. charts. stat. circ. 3, 000. Indexed: P.A.I.S. P.A.I.S.For.Lang.Ind.

332.1 LU
CAISSE D'EPARGNE DE L'ETAT DU GRAND-DUCHE DE LUXEMBOURG. RAPPORTS ET BILANS. 1901. a. free. Caisse d'Epargne de l'Etat du Grand-Duche de Luxembourg - Banque de l'Etat, 1 Place de Metz, Luxembourg, Luxembourg. Ed.Bd. circ. 3,000.

332 SP ISSN 0409-9192
CAJA DE AHORROS Y MONTE DE PIEDAD DE LAS BALEARES. MEMORIA. irreg. Caja de Ahorros y Monte de Piedad de las Baleares, C. Ramon Llull 2, Palma de Mallorca, Spain. Dir. Carlos Blanes Nouvilas. illus. charts. stat.

CANADA. DEPARTMENT OF INSURANCE. REPORT. CO-OPERATIVE CREDIT ASSOCIATIONS. see INSURANCE

CANADA. DEPARTMENT OF INSURANCE. REPORT. SMALL LOANS COMPANIES AND MONEY-LENDERS. see INSURANCE

CANADA. DEPARTMENT OF INSURANCE. REPORT. TRUST AND LOAN COMPANIES. see INSURANCE

332 CN
CANADA. TREASURY BOARD. ACCESS REGISTER. (Editions in English, French) a. Can.$10. Treasury Board, 140 O'Connor St., Ottawa, Ont. K1A 0R5, Canada. TEL 613-957-2400.
   Supersedes in part: Canada. Treasury Board. Index of Federal Information Banks.

332 CN
CANADA. TREASURY BOARD. INDEX TO PERSONAL INFORMATION. (Editions in English, French) a. Can.$10. Treasury Board, 140 O'Connor St., Ottawa, Ont. K1A 0R5, Canada. TEL 613-957-2400.
   Supersedes in part: Canada. Treasury Board. Index of Federal Information Banks.

332 BB ISSN 0255-8440
CENTRAL BANK OF BARBADOS. ANNUAL STATISTICAL DIGEST. 1975. a. free. Central Bank of Barbados, Research Department, P.O. Box 1016, Treasury Bldg., Bridgetown, Barbados, W. Indies. TEL 809-436-6870. charts. stat. circ. 1,200.

BUSINESS AND ECONOMICS — BANKING AND FINANCE

332.1   CE   ISSN 0069-1496
CENTRAL BANK OF CEYLON. ANNUAL REPORT. (Text in English, Sinhalese and Tamil) 1950. a. $3. ‡ Central Bank of Ceylon, Janadhipathi Mawatha, Colombo 1, Sri Lanka.

332.1   CH   ISSN 0069-150X
CENTRAL BANK OF CHINA. ANNUAL REPORT. (Editions in Chinese and English) 1962. a. Central Bank of China, Taipei, Taiwan, Republic of China. circ. 3,500 (Chinese edt.); 2,000 (English edt.)

332.1   CY   ISSN 0069-1518
CENTRAL BANK OF CYPRUS. ANNUAL REPORT. (Text in English) 1965. a. free. Central Bank of Cyprus, Box 5529, Nicosia, Cyprus. circ. 940.

332.1   UA
CENTRAL BANK OF EGYPT. ANNUAL REPORT. 1961. a. free. Central Bank of Egypt, Research Department, 31 Sharia Kasr-el Nil, Cairo, Egypt. Ed. Khairy Sourial Bishay. circ. 2,600.
    Formerly: Central Bank of Egypt. Board of Directors. Report (ISSN 0069-1526)

332   IQ   ISSN 0069-1534
CENTRAL BANK OF IRAQ, BAGHDAD. REPORT. (Text in Arabic and English) 1951. a. free. ‡ Central Bank of Iraq, Statistics and Research Department, P.O. Box 64, Baghdad, Iraq. circ. 2,000.

332.1   IE   ISSN 0069-1542
CENTRAL BANK OF IRELAND. ANNUAL REPORT. (Includes Spring Quarterly Bulletin) 1943. a. free. Central Bank of Ireland, P.O. Box 559, Dame St, Dublin 2, Ireland. TEL 716666. circ. 6,400.

CENTRAL BANK OF IRELAND. IRISH ECONOMIC STATISTICS. see BUSINESS AND ECONOMICS — Abstracting, Bibliographies, Statistics

332   JO   ISSN 0069-1550
CENTRAL BANK OF JORDAN. ANNUAL REPORT/BANK AL-MARKAZI AL-URDUNI. ANNUAL REPORT. a. Central Bank of Jordan, Department of Research and Studies, Box 37, Amman, Jordan. charts. stat.

332.1   KE   ISSN 0069-1569
CENTRAL BANK OF KENYA. ANNUAL REPORT. 1966/67. a. Central Bank of Kenya, Box 60000, Nairobi, Kenya.

332   KU
CENTRAL BANK OF KUWAIT. ANNUAL REPORT. (Editions in Arabic and English) a. free. Central Bank of Kuwait, Box 526, Kuwait.

332   MM   ISSN 0577-0653
CENTRAL BANK OF MALTA. ANNUAL REPORT. 1968. a. free. Central Bank of Malta, Research Department, Castille Square, Valletta, Malta. circ. 1,600.

332.1   NR   ISSN 0069-1577
CENTRAL BANK OF NIGERIA. ANNUAL REPORT AND STATEMENT OF ACCOUNTS. 1960. a. Central Bank of Nigeria, P.M.B. 12194, Tinubu Square, Lagos, Nigeria. circ. 4,000.

332.1   SO
CENTRAL BANK OF SOMALI. ANNUAL REPORT AND STATEMENT OF ACCOUNTS. (Text in English) 1961. a. free. Central Bank of Somali, Economic Research and Statistics Department, Box 11, Mogadishu, Somalia.
    Former titles (until no. 14, 1974): Somali National Bank. Annual Report and Statement of Accounts; Somali National Bank. Report and Balance Sheet (ISSN 0067-3188)

332.1   SQ
CENTRAL BANK OF SWAZILAND. ANNUAL REPORT. 1974. a. Central Bank of Swaziland, P.O. Box 546, Mbabane, Swaziland. illus. circ. 400.

354   BF
CENTRAL BANK OF THE BAHAMAS. ANNUAL REPORT AND STATEMENT OF ACCOUNTS. 1974. a. Central Bank of the Bahamas, P.O. Box N4868, Nassau, Bahamas. illus. stat. circ. 800.

332.1   GM
CENTRAL BANK OF THE GAMBIA. ANNUAL REPORT. 1971. a. Central Bank of the Gambia, Economic Research Department, 1-2 Buckle St., Banjul, Gambia.

332.1   PH   ISSN 0069-1585
CENTRAL BANK OF THE PHILIPPINES. ANNUAL REPORT. (Statistical Appendix avail.) 1949. a. $6 per no. Central Bank of the Philippines, A. Mabini corner Vito Cruz Streets, Manila, Philippines. Eds. Luisita S. Itchon, Purita Neri. circ. 3,000.

332   TU
CENTRAL BANK OF THE REPUBLIC OF TURKEY. ANNUAL REPORT. 1931. a. Central Bank of the Republic of Turkey - Turkiye Cumhuriyet Merkez Bankasi, General Directorate of Planning and Research, Directorate of Documentation, Ankara, Turkey. stat. circ. 2,000.

332.1   TR   ISSN 0069-1593
CENTRAL BANK OF TRINIDAD AND TOBAGO. REPORT. 1965. a. free. ‡ Central Bank of Trinidad and Tobago, Eric Williams Plaza, St. Vincent St., P.O. Box 1250, Port-of-Spain, Trinidad, West Indies. circ. 1,000.

332   YE   ISSN 0301-6625
CENTRAL BANK OF YEMEN. ANNUAL REPORT. (Text in Arabic and English) 1971/72. a. free. Central Bank of Yemen, Box 59, San'a, Yemen.

332.1   MX   ISSN 0577-2451
CENTRO DE ESTUDIOS MONETARIOS LATINOAMERICANOS. ENSAYOS. 1963. irreg. price varies. Centro de Estudios Monetarios Latinoamericanos, Durango 54, 06700 Mexico, D.F., Mexico. circ. 1,000.

332   CH
CHIAO T'UNG YIN HANG. ANNUAL REPORT. (Text in English) 1961. a. Bank of Communications, 91 Heng Yang Road, Taipei, Taiwan, Republic of China. TEL (02)361-3000. Ed. H.L. Huang. circ. 2,000.

332   FR
COLLECTION RADIOGRAPHIE DU CAPITAL - LES LIAISONS FINANCIERES. (In 2 vols.: Tome I - Societes Francaises; Tome II - Societes Francaises a Participations Etrangeres) 1966. a. 1234 F. DAFSA Documentation, 7 rue Bergere, 75009 Paris, France. adv.
    Formerly: Liaisons Financieres en France (ISSN 0075-8957)

332   CK
COLOMBIA. SUPERINTENDENCIA BANCARIA. INFORME DE LABORES. 1924. a. free. Superintendencia Bancaria, Bogota, Colombia. circ. 1,400.

332   ET   ISSN 0588-6694
COMMERCIAL BANK OF ETHIOPIA. ANNUAL REPORT. a. free. Commercial Bank of Ethiopia, P.O. Box 255, Addis Ababa, Ethiopia. charts. illus. stat.

332.1   GR
COMMERCIAL BANK OF GREECE. REPORT. a. Commercial Bank of Greece, 11 Sophocleous St., 102 35 Athens, Greece.

332.1   GR   ISSN 0424-9402
COMMERCIAL BANK OF GREECE. REPORT OF THE CHAIRMAN OF THE BOARD OF DIRECTORS. (Text in English) a. free. Commercial Bank of Greece, Public Relations Department, 11 Sofokleous St., 102 35 Athens, Greece. illus, stat. charts.

332   KU
COMMERCIAL BANK OF KUWAIT. ANNUAL REPORT OF THE BOARD OF DIRECTORS AND ACCOUNTS. a. Commercial Bank of Kuwait, Box 2861, Mubarak al-Kabir St., Safat, Kuwait.

332   US
COMMERCIAL WEST BANK DIRECTORY. a. $36 to individuals; Commercial West subscribers $31. Financial Communications Inc, 7535 Office Ridge Circle, Eden Prairie, MN 55344. TEL 612-941-5823. adv. circ. 5,000.

332.1   FR
COMMISSION BANCAIRE. RAPPORT ANNUEL. a. 140 F. price varies. (Commission Bancaire) Banque de France, Service de l'Information, 43 rue de Valois, 75001 Paris, France (Or Commission Bancaire, 73 rue de Richelieu, 75002 Paris, France)
    Formerly: Commission de Controle des Banques. Rapport Annuel.

334.2   US
COMPARATIVE DIGEST OF CREDIT UNION ACTS. 1959. biennial. $20. Credit Union National Association, Inc., Box 431, Madison, WI 53701. TEL 608-231-4000. Ed. Robert W. Davis.

332.1   US   ISSN 0084-9154
CONFERENCE ON BANK STRUCTURE AND COMPETITION. PROCEEDINGS. 1964. a. price varies. ‡ Federal Reserve Bank of Chicago, Public Information Center, Research Dept., Box 834, Chicago, IL 60690. TEL 312-322-5112. (reprint service avail.)

332   658.8   UK
CONSUMER CREDIT ASSOCIATION OF THE UNITED KINGDOM. MEMBERSHIP DIRECTORY.* 1912. a. £2.25. Consumer Credit Association of the United Kingdom, Queens House, Chester CH1 3BQ, England. adv. circ. 1,500.
    Formerly: Retail Credit Federation Membership Directory (ISSN 0080-1852)

CONTEMPORARY STUDIES IN ECONOMIC AND FINANCIAL ANALYSIS; an international series of monographs. see BUSINESS AND ECONOMICS

332.1   KE
CO-OPERATIVE BANK OF KENYA. ANNUAL REPORT & ACCOUNTS. 1969. a. free. Co-operative Bank of Kenya Ltd., Box 48231, Nairobi, Kenya. Ed. G.M. Sila. circ. 3,000.
    Formerly: Co-operative Bank of Kenya. Annual Report and Statement of Accounts.

332.1   CH
COOPERATIVE BANK OF TAIWAN. ANNUAL REPORT/TAI-WAN SHENA HO TSO CHIN KU. ANNUAL REPORT. 1957. a. free. Cooperative Bank of Taiwan, 75-1 Kuan Chien Rd., Taipei, Taiwan, Republic of China. illus. stat.

332.1   DK
COPENHAGEN HANDELSBANK. REPORT AND ACCOUNTS. (Editions in English and German) a. Copenhagen Handelsbank A-S - Aktieselskabet Kjoebenhavns Handelsbank, Holmens Kanal 2, DK-1091 Copenhagen K, Denmark. charts. stat.
    Formerly: Copenhagen Handelsbank. Annual Report.

CORPORATE FINANCE BLUEBOOK. see BUSINESS AND ECONOMICS — Trade And Industrial Directories

332   US
CORPORATE FUND RAISING DIRECTORY (YEAR)* 1980. a. $79.50. Public Service Materials Center, 5130 Macarthur Blvd., N.W., Apt. 200, Washington, DC 20016-3316.
    Formerly: Corporate Fund Raising Directory.

332.1   US   ISSN 0091-3855
COST OF PERSONAL BORROWING IN THE UNITED STATES. 1971. a. $112.95. ‡ Financial Publishing Company, 82 Brookline Ave, Boston, MA 02215. TEL 617-262-4040. Ed. James C. Senay. charts. circ. 625.

CRAWFORD'S DIRECTORY OF CITY CONNECTIONS. see BUSINESS AND ECONOMICS — Trade And Industrial Directories

658.15   US   ISSN 0070-1467
CREDIT MANUAL OF COMMERCIAL LAWS. 1898. a. $50 to non-members. National Association of Credit Management, 520 Eighth Ave.., New York, NY 10018. TEL 212-947-5070.

BUSINESS AND ECONOMICS — BANKING AND FINANCE

334.2   US   ISSN 0092-4954
CREDIT UNION DIRECTORY AND BUYERS' GUIDE. 1973. a. $77 (or in subscr. to complete Credit Union Information Service, $197) United Communications Group, Credit Union Information Service, 8701 Georgia Ave., Ste. 800, Silver Spring, MD 20910. TEL 301-589-8875. Ed. David Rohde. adv. circ. 6,500.
    Formerly: C U I S Credit Union Directory and Buyers' Guide.

310   US
CREDIT UNION NATIONAL ASSOCIATION. CREDIT UNION REPORT. a. $5. Credit Union National Association, Inc., P.O. Box 431, 5710 Mineral Pt. Rd., Madison, WI 53701. TEL 608-231-4000. Ed. Terri Hanke. circ. 9,000. (back issues avail.)

334.2   US   ISSN 0074-4468
CREDIT UNION YEARBOOK. 1954. a. free. Credit Union National Association, Inc., Box 431, Madison, WI 53701. TEL 608-231-4000. circ. 50,000.
    Formerly: International Credit Union Yearbook.

332.3   AU
CREDITANSTALT-BANKVEREIN. ANNUAL REPORT. (Text in English) a. Creditanstalt-Bankverein, Schottengasse 6, A-1010 Vienna, Austria.
    Continues: Creditanstalt-Bankverein. Report.

332.1   US
CURRENT ISSUES IN BANKS & THRIFT INSTITUTIONS. 1983. a. free. Ernst & Whinney, 2000 National City Center, Cleveland, OH 44114. TEL 216-861-5000. stat. circ. 19,420.
    Formerly: Current Issues in Banking; Supersedes: Current Issues in Savings Institutions.

332   CY
CYPRUS DEVELOPMENT BANK. ANNUAL REPORT. 1953. a. Cyprus Development Bank, Nicosia, Cyprus. circ. 1,100.

332   DK   ISSN 0108-6979
DANMARKS NATIONALBANK. BERETNING OG REGNSKAB (DANSK UDGAVE) English edition: Denmarks Nationalbank. Reports and Accounts (ISSN 0108-6995) 1819. a. free. Danmarks Nationalbank, Havnegade 5, DK 1093 Copenhagen K, Denmark. illus.

332.1   DK   ISSN 0108-6995
DANMARKS NATIONALBANK. REPORT AND ACCOUNTS FOR THE YEAR (YEAR) 1945. a. Danmarks Nationalbank, Havnegade 5, DK-1093 Copenhagen K, Denmark.

332.1   DK
DANSKE BANK AF 1871. ANNUAL REPORT. (Text in English) 1871. a. Danske Bank af 1871 A-S, 12, Holmens Kanal, DK-1092 Copenhagen K, Denmark. illus.
    Formerly (until 1976): Danske Landmandsbank. Annual Report (ISSN 0070-2838)

332.1   US
DESKTOP BANK DIRECTORY. 1985. a. $74.95. Rand McNally & Co., 8255 N. Central Pk., Skokie, IL 60076 TEL 312-673-9100. (Subscr. to: Box 7600, Chicago, IL 60680) Ed. Anne Burke.

332.1   GW   ISSN 0070-394X
DEUTSCHE BUNDESBANK. GESCHAEFTSBERICHT. English Edition: Deutsche Bundesbank. Report (ISSN 0418-8306) (Editions in German and English) 1948. a. Deutsche Bundesbank, Postfach 100602, 6000 Frankfurt 1, W. Germany (B.R.D.) circ. 60,300 (62,000 German edt.; 7,000 English edt.)

332 331.8   GW
DEUTSCHES BANKEN-HANDBUCH (YEAR) a. DM.69.40. Walhalla-und Praetoria-Verlag, Dolomitenstr. 1, Postfach 301, 8400 Regensburg 1, W. Germany (B.R.D.) Ed. Hannelore Grill, G. Haker. bk. rev.
    Formerly: Bankangestellte (ISSN 0067-3781)

332.1   MF
DEVELOPMENT BANK OF MAURITIUS. REPORT AND ACCOUNTS. (Text in English) 1965. a. Development Bank of Mauritius, Box 157, Port Louis, Mauritius.

332 338.9   BP
DEVELOPMENT BANK OF SOLOMON ISLANDS. ANNUAL REPORT. 1978. a. Development Bank of Solomon Islands, Madingley Rd., Honiara, British Solomon Islands.

332.1   ZA
DEVELOPMENT BANK OF ZAMBIA. ANNUAL REPORT. (Text in English) a. Development Bank of Zambia, Box 33955, Lusaka, Zambia.

332   KE
DEVELOPMENT FINANCE COMPANY OF KENYA. ANNUAL REPORT AND STATEMENT OF ACCOUNTS. (Text in English) a. Development Finance Company of Kenya Ltd., Box 30483, Bima House, Harambee Ave., Nairobi, Kenya.

332.1   GW
DG BANK DEUTSCHE GENOSSENSCHAFTSBANK. BERICHT UEBER DAS GESCHAEFTSJAHR. (Editions in English, French, German) a. DG Bank Deutsche Genossenschaftsbank, Am Platz der Republik, 6000 Frankfurt 1, W. Germany (B.R.D.) charts. stat.
    Formerly: Deutsche Genossenschaftsbank. Bericht.

332   US
DIGEST OF CHANGES IN C U S I P. (Committee on Uniform Security Procedures) a. $150. (American Bankers Association) Standard & Poor's Corporation, 25 Broadway, New York, NY 10004. TEL 212-208-8000. Ed. John Frei.

332   CK
DIRECTORIO DE INSTITUCIONES FINANCIERAS. a. Col.3000($10) Corporacion Editorial Interamericana, Avda. Jimenez 403 (of 907), Apdo. 14965, Bogota 1, Colombia.

332.3   US   ISSN 0070-5098
DIRECTORY OF AMERICAN SAVINGS AND LOAN ASSOCIATIONS. 1955. a. $50. T.K. Sanderson Organization, 1115 E. 30th St., Baltimore, MD 21218. TEL 301-235-3383. Ed. T.K. Sanderson.

332.1 378   US   ISSN 0084-9855
DIRECTORY OF BANKERS SCHOOLS. biennial. $45 to non-members; members $29.50. ‡ American Bankers Association, 1120 Connecticut Ave. N.W., Washington, DC 20036. TEL 202-663-5087.

332.1   CN   ISSN 0070-5225
DIRECTORY OF CANADIAN TRUST COMPANIES. 1953. a. ‡ Trust Companies Association of Canada Inc., Suite 400, Board of Trade Bldg., 11 Adelaide St., W., Toronto, Ont. M5H 1L9, Canada. TEL 416-364-1207.

332.1   US   ISSN 0093-951X
DIRECTORY OF TRUST INSTITUTIONS. 1962. a. $29.50. Communication Channels, Inc., 6255 Barfield Rd., Atlanta, GA 30328. TEL 404-256-9800. Ed. Barbara Kalinsky. adv. illus. circ. 16,500.
    Continues: Directory of Trust Institutions of United States and Canada.

332.1   DR
DOMINICAN REPUBLIC. SUPERINTENDENCIA DE BANCOS. ANUARIO ESTADISTICO. a. Superintendencia de Bancos, Santo Domingo, Dominican Republic.

332.1   UG
EAST AFRICAN DEVELOPMENT BANK. ANNUAL REPORT. (Text in English) 1968. a. East African Development Bank, Box 7128, Kampala, Uganda.

332   FR
ECONOMIES ET SOCIETES. SERIE MO. ECONOMIE MONETAIRE. 1978. irreg. 300 F. Presses Universitaires de Grenoble, B.P. 47 X, 38040 Grenoble, France. Ed. C. de Boisseiu.

332   EC
ECUADOR. SUPERINTENDENCIA DE BANCOS. BOLETIN. 1938. a. Superintendencia de Bancos, Avda. 12 de Octubre, Casilla 424, Quito, Ecuador. charts. stat.

332   EC
ECUADOR. SUPERINTENDENCIA DE BANCOS. DOCUMENTOS. irreg., no.7, 1978. Superintendencia de Bancos, Avda 10 de Agosto, No. 251, Casilla 424, Quito, Ecuador. charts. stat.

332   EC
ECUADOR. SUPERINTENDENCIA DE BANCOS. INVERSIONES EXTRANJERAS EN EL ECUADOR. a. Superintendencia de Bancos, Avda. 10 de Agosto No. 251, Apartado 424, Quito, Ecuador.

332   EC
ECUADOR. SUPERINTENDENCIA DE BANCOS. MEMORIA. a. Superintendencia de Bancos, Avda 10 de Agosto no. 251, Casilla 424, Quito, Ecuador. charts. stat.

EL SALVADOR. SUPERINTENDENCIA DE BANCOS Y OTRAS INSTITUCIONES FINANCIERAS. ESTADISTICAS: SEGUROS, FINANZAS, BANCOS. see *INSURANCE*

332   US   ISSN 0071-142X
ESSAYS IN INTERNATIONAL FINANCE. 1943. irreg., no.155, 1984. $12 (includes Reprints in International Finance) Princeton University, International Finance Section, Dept. of Economics, Dickinson Hall, Princeton, NJ 08544. TEL 609-452-4048. Dir. Peter B. Kenen. circ. 3,000. (also avail. in microfilm from UMI; back issues avail.; reprint service avail. from UMI)

332.2   EI
EUROPEAN ECONOMIC COMMUNITY SAVINGS BANK GROUP. REPORT. (Editions in English, French and German) 1966. biennial. $10. European Economic Community Savings Banks Group, Ave. de la Renaissance, 12, 1040 Brussels, Belgium. Eds. K. Meyer-Horn, M. Focan. circ. 3,000.

332.1   BE   ISSN 0071-2787
EUROPEAN FEDERATION OF FINANCE HOUSE ASSOCIATIONS. ANNUAL REPORT. (Text in English, French, German) 1963. a. membership. European Federation of Finance House Associations, 267 av. de Tervuren, Boite 10, 1150 Brussels, Belgium. M. Baert. circ. controlled.

332.1   BE   ISSN 0071-2795
EUROPEAN FEDERATION OF FINANCE HOUSE ASSOCIATIONS. CONFERENCE PROCEEDINGS. (Text in English, French, German) 1961. a. membership (includes Annual Report and Newsletters) European Federation of Finance House Associations, 267 av. de Tervuren, Boite 10, 1150 Brussels, Belgium. Ed. M. Baert. circ. controlled.

332.6   EI   ISSN 0071-2868
EUROPEAN INVESTMENT BANK. ANNUAL REPORT. (Text in English, Danish, Dutch, French, German, Greek, Italian, Portuguese and Spanish) 1958. a. free. European Investment Bank, 100 Bd. Konrad Adenauer, L-2950 Luxembourg, Luxembourg (Dist. in U.S. by: European Community Information Service, 2100 M St., NW, Suite 707, Washington, DC 20037)

332   UK
EXPATRIATE SURVIVAL KIT. 1982. a. £13.50($22.50) Financial Times Business Information, 102 Clerkenwell Rd., London EC1M 5SA, England.

332   UK
EXPATRIATE'S GUIDE TO RETIRING ABROAD. 1982. a. Financial Times Business Information, 102 Clerkenwell Rd., London EC1M 5SA, England.

EXPORT-IMPORT BANK OF JAPAN. ANNUAL REPORT. see *BUSINESS AND ECONOMICS — International Commerce*

332.1   US   ISSN 0270-5109
EXPORT-IMPORT BANK OF THE UNITED STATES. ANNUAL REPORT. 1945. a. free. Export-Import Bank of the United States, 811 Vermont Ave., N.W., Washington, DC 20571. TEL 202-566-8860. circ. 15,000.
    Former titles: Export-Import Bank of the United States. Statement of Conditions (ISSN 0270-5087); Export-Import Bank of the United States. Summary of Operations (ISSN 0071-3511); Export-Import Bank of the United States. Report to Congress.

BUSINESS AND ECONOMICS — BANKING AND FINANCE

332.1 US
EXPORT-IMPORT BANK OF THE UNITED STATES. REPORT TO CONGRESS ON EXPORT CREDIT COMPETITION AND THE EXPORT-IMPORT BANK OF THE UNITED STATES. 1972. a. free. Export-Import Bank of the United States, 811 Vermont Ave., N.W., Washington, DC 20571. TEL 202-566-8860. circ. 3,500.
Formerly: Export-Import Bank of the United States. Semiannual Report to Congress on Export Credit Competition and the Export-Import Bank of the United States.

332 UK ISSN 0308-8499
EXTEL ISSUING HOUSE YEAR BOOK. a. Extel Financial Ltd., 37-45 Paul St., London EC2A 4PB, England. (back issues avail.)

332 332.1 PH
FACTBOOK ON THE PHILIPPINE FINANCIAL SYSTEM. (Text and summaries in English) 1976. a. P.80. Central Bank of the Philippines, A. Mabini St., Malate, Manila, Philippines. circ. 500. (back issues avail.)

332.7 US
FAIR CREDIT REPORTING MANUAL. 1971. irreg., 2nd edt. 1977; supplements issued annually to update base vol. $84 for base vol. plus supp. Warren, Gorham and Lamont, Inc., 210 South St., Boston, MA 02111. TEL 800-922-0066. Ed. Ralph C. Clontz, Jr.

332 CN ISSN 0071-3864
FARM CREDIT CORPORATION CANADA. ANNUAL REPORT. 1960. a. free. Farm Credit Corporation Canada, Box 2314, Postal Station D, Ottawa, Ont. K1P 6J9, Canada. TEL 613-996-6606.

332.1 CN ISSN 0071-3872
FARM CREDIT CORPORATION CANADA. FEDERAL FARM CREDIT STATISTICS/ STATISTIQUES DU CREDIT AGRICOLE FEDERAL. a. Farm Credit Corporation Canada, Box 2314, Postal Station D, Ottawa, Ont. K1P 6J9, Canada. TEL 613-996-6606.

320 CN
FARM CREDIT IN THE CANADIAN FINANCIAL SYSTEM/FINANCEMENT DE L'AGRICULTURE CANADIENNE. (Text in English and French) biennial. free. Farm Credit Corporation Canada, Box 2314, Postal Station D, Ottawa, Ont. K1P 6J9, Canada. TEL 613-996-6606.

332 CN
FEDERAL BUSINESS DEVELOPMENT BANK. ANNUAL REPORT. a. Federal Business Development Bank, 800 Victoria Square, Montreal, Que. H4Z 1L4, Canada. TEL 514-283-5904.

332.1 US
FEDERAL HOME LOAN BANK OF ATLANTA. ANNUAL REPORT. a. Federal Home Loan Bank of Atlanta, Box 56527, Peachtree Center Sta., Atlanta, GA 30343-0527. TEL 404-522-2450. illus. stat.

332.1 US
FEDERAL HOME LOAN BANK OF CHICAGO. ANNUAL REPORT. 1933. a. Federal Home Loan Bank of Chicago, 111 E. Wacker Dr., Chicago, IL 60601. circ. 500.

332.1 US
FEDERAL HOME LOAN BANK OF DALLAS. ANNUAL REPORT. 1932. a. Federal Home Loan Bank of Dallas, 500 E. John Carpenter Freeway, Box 619026, Dallas/Ft. Worth, TX 75261-9026. Ed. Rebecca A. Vail.

332.1 US
FEDERAL HOME LOAN BANK OF DES MOINES. ANNUAL REPORT. a. Federal Home Loan Bank of Des Moines, 907 Walnut St., Des Moines, IA 50309.

332.1 US
FEDERAL HOME LOAN BANK OF INDIANAPOLIS. ANNUAL REPORT.* a. Federal Home Loan Bank of Indianapolis, Box 60, Indianapolis, IN 46206-0060.

332.1 US
FEDERAL HOME LOAN BANK OF LITTLE ROCK. ANNUAL REPORT. a. Federal Home Loan Bank of Little Rock, 1400 Tower Bldg., Little Rock, AR 72201. TEL 501-372-7141.

332.3 US ISSN 0098-2830
FEDERAL HOME LOAN BANK OF SAN FRANCISCO. ANNUAL REPORT. a. free. Federal Home Loan Bank of San Francisco, Box 7948, 600 California St., San Francisco, CA 94120. TEL 415-393-1210. illus. Key Title: Annual Report - Federal Home Loan Bank of San Francisco.

332.1 US
FEDERAL HOME LOAN BANK OF SAN FRANCISCO. PROCEEDINGS OF THE ANNUAL CONFERENCE. 1975. a. price varies. Federal Home Loan Bank of San Francisco, Box 7948, 600 California St., San Francisco, CA 94120. TEL 415-393-1210.

332.1 US
FEDERAL HOME LOAN BANK OF SEATTLE. ANNUAL REPORT.* a. 1501 4th Ave., Ste. 1800, Seattle, WA 98101-1693.

332.1 US
FEDERAL HOME LOAN BANK OF TOPEKA. ANNUAL REPORT. a. Box 176, 120 E. Sixth St., KS 66601.

332.1 US ISSN 0094-7156
FEDERAL HOME LOAN MORTGAGE CORPORATION. REPORT. a. Federal Home Loan Mortgage Corporation, 311 First St., N.W., Washington, DC 20001. TEL 202-789-4700. illus. stat. Key Title: Report of the Federal Home Loan Mortgage Corporation.

FEDERAL INCOME TAXATION OF BANKS AND FINANCIAL INSTITUTIONS (SUPPLEMENT) see BUSINESS AND ECONOMICS — Public Finance, Taxation

332 368 US
FEDERAL RESERVE BANK OF CLEVELAND. WORKING PAPER. irreg. (approx. 9/yr) free. Federal Reserve Bank of Cleveland, Research Department, Box 6387, Cleveland, OH 44101. TEL 216-579-2000.

332.1 US ISSN 0743-6351
FEDERAL RESERVE BANK OF KANSAS CITY. BANKING STUDIES. 1983. irreg. free. Federal Reserve Bank of Kansas City, Division of Bank Supervision & Structure, 925 Grand Ave., Kansas City, MO 64198. TEL 816-881-2879. Ed. Forest Myers. circ. 4,000.

332.4 US ISSN 0361-8013
FEDERAL RESERVE BANK OF MINNEAPOLIS. ANNUAL REPORT. a. Federal Reserve Bank of Minneapolis, Research Department, 250 Marquette Ave., Minneapolis, MN 55480. TEL 612-340-2345.

332.1 US
FEDERAL RESERVE BANK OF NEW YORK. ANNUAL REPORT. 1928? a. Federal Reserve Bank of New York, Research Publications, 33 Liberty St., Rm. 901, New York, NY 10045. TEL 212-791-5502. Ed.Bd. circ. 43,500. (back issues avail.)

332 FR ISSN 0071-4380
FEDERATION NATIONALE DU CREDIT AGRICOLE. ANNUAIRE DU CREDIT AGRICOLE MUTUEL.* 1960, 3rd ed. a. Federation Nationale du Credit Agricole, 48 rue la Boetie, 75008 Paris, France.

332 334 SW
FEDERATION OF SWEDISH CO-OPERATIVE BANKS. ANNUAL REPORT. a. Sveriges Foereningsbankers Foerbund, Box 30144, S-104 25 Stockholm, Sweden. (Co-sponsor: Foereningsbankernas Bank)

332
FINANCE FACTS YEARBOOK. 1961. a. $15 to non-members; members $10. American Financial Services Association, 1101 14 St., N.W., 4th Fl., Washington, DC 20005. Eds. Thomas A. Durkin, Ysabel Burns McAleer. circ. 12,000.

332 US
FINANCE: LATIN AMERICAN INDUSTRIAL REPORT. (Avail. for each of 20 Latin American countries) 1985. a. $235 per country report. Aurora International, Box 9099, Bridgeport, CT 06601-2099. TEL 203-368-0579. Ed. Andres C. Aquino.

332 NE
FINANCIAL AND MONETARY POLICY STUDIES. no.4, 1979. irreg. price varies. Martinus Nijhoff Publishers, Postbus 163, 3300 AD Dordrecht, Netherlands.
Formerly: Financial and Monetary Studies.

332 UK
FINANCIAL DIRECTORIES OF THE WORLD. irreg. price varies. International Business Communications Ltd., Bath House, 56 Holborn Viaduct, London EC1A 2EX, England.

332.1 US ISSN 0362-1405
FINANCIAL INDUSTRY NUMBER STANDARD DIRECTORY. 1976. irreg. Depository Trust Company, 55 Water St., New York, NY 10041. TEL 212-558-8000.

332 UK
FINANCIAL OUTLOOK. irreg. Gower Publishing, Gower House, Croft Rd., Aldershot, Hants. GU11 3HR, England.

332.1 332.6 CN
FINANCIAL POST EIGHT YEAR PRICE RANGE. 1979. a. (Financial Post Information Service) MacLean Hunter Ltd., Financial Post Division, Maclean Hunter Bldg., 777 Bay St., Toronto, Ont. M5W 1A7, Canada. TEL 516-596-5585.
Formerly: Financial Post Corporation Service. Eight Year Price Range.

332 US ISSN 0066-5363
FINANCIAL REVIEW. 1966. a. $5. Eastern Finance Association, c/o Geoffrey Booth, Ed., College of Business Administration, University of Rhode Island, Kingston, RI 02881. TEL 401-792-1000. adv. bk. rev. circ. 1,100. Indexed: J.of Econ.Lit. Bus.Ind. PROMT.
Formerly: Appalachian Financial Review.

332.3 US ISSN 0278-6567
FINANCIAL STATEMENTS AND OPERATING RATIOS FOR THE MORTGAGE BANKING INDUSTRY. 1963. a. $55 to non-members; members $35. Mortgage Bankers Association of America, Economics and Education Department, 1125 15th St., N.W., Washington, DC 20005. TEL 202-681-6500.
Former titles: Mortgage Banking: Financial Statements and Operating Ratios (ISSN 0095-9308); Mortgage Banking: Trends, Financial Statements and Operating Ratios (ISSN 0077-1546)

332 JA ISSN 0289-1522
FINANCIAL STATISTICS OF JAPAN. 1952. a. free. Ministry of Finance, Institute of Fiscal and Monetary Policy, 3-1-1 Kasumigaseki, Chiyoda-ku, Tokyo 100, Japan.
Formerly: Japan. Finance Department. Bulletin of Financial Statistics.

332.1 US ISSN 0363-8987
FINANCIAL STUDIES OF THE SMALL BUSINESS. 1976. a. $52. Financial Research Associates, Box 2502, Winter Haven, FL 33883-2502. TEL 813-299-3969. Ed. Karen Goodman. circ. 4,000.

332.1 US
FINANCING AND INSURING EXPORTS: A USER'S GUIDE TO EXIMBANK AND F.C.I.A. PROGRAMS. 1985. a. $55. Export-Import Bank of the United States, 811 Vermont Ave., N.W., Washington, DC 20571. TEL 202-566-8860. circ. 1,500.

332 CS ISSN 0322-9653
FINANCNI ZPRAVODAJ. 1956. irreg. (approx. 15/yr) 15 Kcs. for 5 nos. Ministerstvo Financi CSR, Letenska 15, Prague 1, Czechoslovakia. Ed. Anna Mrazova. charts. index.
Formerly: Federalni Ministerstvo Financi. Vestnik (ISSN 0042-4641)

332.1 US
FIRST EMPIRE STATE CORPORATION. INTERIM REPORT. irreg. First Empire State Corporation, One M & T Plaza, Buffalo, NY 14240. TEL 716-842-2153.

BUSINESS AND ECONOMICS — BANKING AND FINANCE

332.1   LB
FIRST NATIONAL CITY BANK, LIBERIA. ANNUAL REPORT. a. First National City Bank, P.O. Box 280, Monrovia, Liberia. illus. stat.

332.1   CH
FLOW OF FUNDS IN TAIWAN DISTRICT, REPUBLIC OF CHINA. (Text in Chinese and English) 1968. a. Central Bank of China, Taipei, Taiwan, Republic of China. circ. 1,200.

332.31   FR   ISSN 0071-8254
FRANCE. CAISSE NATIONALE DE CREDIT AGRICOLE. RAPPORT SUR LE CREDIT AGRICOLE MUTUEL. English edition: Credit Agricole Annual Report. 1975. a. free. Caisse Nationale de Credit Agricole, 91-93 Boulevard Pasteur, 75015 Paris, France. circ. 5,710 (4,000 French edt.; 1,710 English edt.)

332.7   FR
FRANCE. CONSEIL NATIONAL DU CREDIT. RAPPORT ANNUEL. a. 65 Fr. Banque de France, Service de l'Information, 43 rue de Valois, 75001 Paris, France.

332.2   FR
FRANCE. MINISTERE DE L'ECONOMIE ET DES FINANCES. CAISSES D'EPARGNE ORDINAIRE. irreg. Ministere de l'Economie et des Finances, Service d'Edition et de Vente des Publications Officielles, 39 rue de la Convention, 75015 Paris, France.

332 339   DR
FUENTES Y USOS DE FONDOS. 1976. biennial. RD.$2. Banco Central de la Republica Dominica, Departamento de Estudios Economicos, Apdo. 1347, Santo Domingo, Dominican Republic. circ. 1,000. (looseleaf format)

332   UK   ISSN 0072-5633
GREAT BRITAIN. DEPARTMENT OF TRADE. BANKRUPTCY: GENERAL ANNUAL REPORT. a. H.M.S.O., P.O. Box 569, London SE1 9NH, England. (reprint service avail. from UMI)

332   FR   ISSN 0066-2933
GROUPEMENT DES SOCIETES IMMOBILIERES D'INVESTISSEMENT. ANNUAIRE. 1966. triennial. Groupement des Societes Immobilieres d'Investissement, 18 rue de Vienne, 75008 Paris, France. Ed. Raymond Long. charts. stat.

322   GW
GRUNDLAGEN UND PRAXIS DES BANK- UND BOERSENWESENS. 1976. irreg. price varies. Erich Schmidt Verlag GmbH Bielefeld), Viktoriastr. 44A, 4800 Bielefeld, W. Germany (B.R.D.)

332.1   US
GUIDE TO FEDERAL INCOME TAXES FOR SAVINGS INSTITUTIONS. 1982. irreg. $20. Ernst & Whinney, 2000 National City Center, Cleveland, OH 44114. TEL 216-861-5000. stat. circ. 1,050.

332.4   UK   ISSN 0306-3933
HAMBRO EUROMONEY DIRECTORY. a. $95. Euromoney Publications Ltd., Nestor House, Playhouse Yard, London EC4V 5EX, England.

332   DK   ISSN 0105-4058
HANDELSHOEJSKOLEN I AARHUS. INSTITUT FOR FINANSIERING OG KREDITVAESEN. KOMPENDIUM D. no. 8, 1981. irreg. Handelshoejskolen i Aarhus, Institut for Finansiering og Kreditvaesen, Aarhus, Denmark. illus.

332.1   AU
HAUPTVERBAND DER OESTERREICHISCHEN SPARKASSEN. JAHRESBERICHT. (Text in German; summaries in English, French and German) 1912. a. free. Hauptverband der Oesterreichischen Sparkassen, P.O. Box 256, A-1011 Vienna, Austria. charts. stat. circ. 4,000.

332.1   US
HISTORICAL CHART BOOK. a. $1.25 (or included in subscr. to Federal Reserve Chart Book) U.S. Federal Reserve System, Board of Governors, Publications Services, Rm. MS-138, Washington, DC 20551. TEL 202-452-3000.

332.7   HK
HONG KONG EXPORT CREDIT INSURANCE CORPORATION. ANNUAL REPORT. a. Hong Kong Export Credit Insurance Corporation, South Seas Centre, Tower 1, 2nd Floor, 75 Mody Rd., Tsimshatsui East, Kowloon, Hong Kong.

332   HK
HONG KONG INTERBANK DIRECTORY. 1980. a. $20. Techni-Press Asia Ltd., GPO Box 3894, Hong Kong, Hong Kong. circ. 1,000.

HOUSING FINANCE COMPANY OF KENYA. ANNUAL REPORT AND ACCOUNTS. see *HOUSING AND URBAN PLANNING*

330.1   US   ISSN 0424-2769
HOW TO AVOID FINANCIAL TANGLES. 1969. irreg., vol.24, 1984. $5 per no. ‡ American Institute for Economic Research, Great Barrington, MA 01230. TEL 413-528-1216. Ed. Bruce H. French.
    Incorporates: How to Avoid Financial Tangles: Section B. Wills and Trusts, Taxes, and Help for the Widow; How to Avoid Financial Tangles: Section A. Elementary Property Problems and Financial Relationships.

332.3   KU
INDUSTRIAL BANK OF KUWAIT. ANNUAL REPORT. (Text in English) 1975. a. free. Industrial Bank of Kuwait - Bank al-Kuwayt al-Sinai, Box 3146, Safat, Kuwait. circ. 1,500.

332.1   SJ   ISSN 0073-7356
INDUSTRIAL BANK OF SUDAN. BOARD OF DIRECTORS. ANNUAL REPORT. (Text in English and Arabic) 1962. a. free. Industrial Bank of Sudan, Research Department, P.O. Box 1722, Khartoum, Sudan. Ed. Mohamed Amara.

332.1   JO
INDUSTRIAL DEVELOPMENT BANK. ANNUAL REPORT AND BALANCE SHEET/BANK AL-INMA AL-SINAI. ANNUAL REPORT AND BALANCE SHEET. 1967. a. free. Industrial Development Bank, Majlis al-Ommah St., Box 1982, Amman, Jordan. charts. illus. circ. 2,000.

332.1   KE
INDUSTRIAL DEVELOPMENT BANK LIMITED. ANNUAL REPORT AND ACCOUNTS. a. Industrial Development Bank Limited, Bima House, P.O. Box 44036, Nairobi, Kenya. illus. stat.

332.1   II   ISSN 0073-7372
INDUSTRIAL DEVELOPMENT BANK OF INDIA. ANNUAL REPORT. (Text in English; occasionally in Hindi) 1964/65. a. free. Industrial Development Bank of India, Mittal Court , B Wing, 224 Backbay Reclamation, Nariman Point, Bombay 400021, India.

332.1   IS   ISSN 0073-7380
INDUSTRIAL DEVELOPMENT BANK OF ISRAEL LIMITED. REPORT. (Text in English & Hebrew) a. Industrial Development Bank of Israel Limited, Tel Aviv, Israel.

332.1   PK   ISSN 0073-7399
INDUSTRIAL DEVELOPMENT BANK OF PAKISTAN. REPORT. (Text in English) 1961/62. a. Industrial Development Bank of Pakistan, State Life Bldg., Wallace Rd., Karachi, Pakistan.

332.1   TU   ISSN 0073-7402
INDUSTRIAL DEVELOPMENT BANK OF TURKEY. ANNUAL STATEMENT. (Text in English) a. Industrial Development Bank of Turkey - Turkiye Sinai Kalkinma Bankasi, Meclisi Mebusan Cad. 137, Box 59, Findikli, Istanbul, Turkey.

332 336.1   GW   ISSN 0067-9941
INSTITUT "FINANZEN UND STEUERN." GRUENE BRIEFE. 1954. irreg., no.261, 1986. price varies. Institut "Finanzen und Steuern." e.V., Markt 10, Postfach 1808, 5300 Bonn, W. Germany (B.R.D.) index, cum.index. (back issues avail.)

332 336.1   GW   ISSN 0067-995X
INSTITUT "FINANZEN UND STEUERN." SCHRIFTENREIHE. 1950. irreg., no.124, 1986. price varies. Institut "Finanzen und Steuern." e.V., Markt 10, Postfach 1808, 5300 Bonn, W. Germany (B.R.D.) index, cum.index. (back issues avail.)

332   DK
INSTITUT FOR FINANSIERING OG KREDITVAESEN. KOMPENDIUM. irreg., no.10, 1982. price varies. Institut for Finansiering og Kreditvaesen, Handelshoejskolen i Aarhus, Aarhus, Denmark (Order to: Handelsvidenskabelig Boghandel, Fuglesangs Alle 4, 8210 Aarhus V. Denmark)) illus.

332   TZ
INSTITUTE OF FINANCE MANAGEMENT. PROSPECTUS. (Text in English) a. Institute of Finance Management, Box 3918, Dar es Salaam, Tanzania.

332.1 338.9   US
INTER-AMERICAN DEVELOPMENT BANK. ANNUAL REPORT. Spanish edition: Inter-American Development Bank. Informe Anual. (Editions also in French & Portuguese) 1960. a. Inter-American Development Bank, 808 17th St., N.W., Washington, DC 20577. TEL 202-634-6000.
    Formerly: Inter-American Development Bank. Report (ISSN 0074-087X); Incorporating: Inter-American Development Bank. Statement of Loans.

332.1 338.9   US   ISSN 0074-0861
INTER-AMERICAN DEVELOPMENT BANK. BOARD OF GOVERNORS. PROCEEDINGS OF THE MEETING. Spanish edition: Inter-American Development Bank. Board of Governors. Anales (de la) Reunion (ISSN 0538-3102) (Editions in English, Portuguese, Spanish and French) 1960. a. Inter-American Development Bank, 808 17th St., N.W., Washington, DC 20577. TEL 202-634-6000.

332.1   UK
INTERNATIONAL BUSINESS OPPORTUNITIES. TOP AFRICAN BANKS. 1984. irreg. £90($180) I.C. Publications Ltd., P.O. Box 261, Carlton House, 69 Gt. Queen St., London WC2B 5BN, England.

332.1   UK
INTERNATIONAL BUSINESS OPPORTUNITIES. TOP 200 ARAB BANKS. 1985. irreg. £90($180) I.C. Publications Ltd., P.O. Box 261, Carlton House, 69 Gt. Queen St., London WC2B 5BN, England.

332.1   CH
INTERNATIONAL COMMERCIAL BANK OF CHINA. ANNUAL REPORT. (Text in English) 1960. a. free. International Commercial Bank of China, Economic Research Department, 100 Chi Lin Rd., Taipei 104, Taiwan, Republic of China. Ed. H.M. Su. stat. circ. 2,500.
    Continues: Chung-Kuo Yin Hang. Annual Report.

332   UN   ISSN 0074-6061
INTERNATIONAL FINANCE CORPORATION. REPORT. 1956/57. a. International Finance Corporation, 1818 H St., N.W., Washington, DC 20433.

332   UN   ISSN 0250-7498
INTERNATIONAL MONETARY FUND. ANNUAL REPORT OF THE EXECUTIVE BOARD. French edition (ISSN 0250-7501); German edition (ISSN 0250-7528); Spanish edition (ISSN 0250-751X) (Editions in English, French, German and Spanish) 1947. a. (September) free. International Monetary Fund, Publications Unit, 700 19th K St., N.W., Washington, DC 20431. TEL 202-623-7430. (also avail. in microform from UMI; reprint service avail. from UMI)
    Formerly: International Monetary Fund. Annual Report of the Executive Directors (ISSN 0085-2171)

332   UN   ISSN 0250-7366
INTERNATIONAL MONETARY FUND. ANNUAL REPORT ON EXCHANGE ARRANGEMENTS AND EXCHANGE RESTRICTIONS. (Text in English) 1950. a. free ($12 per additional copy) International Monetary Fund, Publications Unit, 700 19th St., N.W., Washington, DC 20431. (also avail. in microform from UMI; reprint service avail. from UMI)
    Formerly: International Monetary Fund. Annual Report on Exchange Restrictions (ISSN 0085-2163)

332   UN   ISSN 0251-6365
INTERNATIONAL MONETARY FUND. OCCASIONAL PAPERS. 1980. irreg., no.51, 1987. $7.50 ($4.50 to university libraries, faculty and students) International Monetary Fund, Publications Unit, 700 19th St., Washington, DC 20431. TEL 202-623-7430. (also avail. in microform from UMI; back issues avail.)

BUSINESS AND ECONOMICS — BANKING AND FINANCE

332   UN   ISSN 0538-8759
INTERNATIONAL MONETARY FUND. PAMPHLET SERIES. French edition (ISSN 0252-2985); Spanish edition (ISSN 0252-2993) 1964. irreg., no.42, 1984. free. International Monetary Fund, Publications Unit, 700 19th St., N.W., Washington, DC 20431. TEL 202-623-7430. Ed. Ian S. McDonald. (also avail. in microform from UMI; reprint service avail. from UMI)

332.1   UN   ISSN 0094-1735
INTERNATIONAL MONETARY FUND. SELECTED DECISIONS OF THE INTERNATIONAL MONETARY FUND AND SELECTED DOCUMENTS. French edition (ISSN 0250-7285); Spanish edition (ISSN 0250-7293) 1972. irreg. free. International Monetary Fund, Publications Unit, 700 19th St., N.W., Washington, DC 20431. TEL 202-623-7430. index. (reprint service avail. from UMI)
    Continues: International Monetary Fund. Selected Decisions of the Executive Directors and Selected Documents.

330   UN   ISSN 0074-7025
INTERNATIONAL MONETARY FUND. SUMMARY PROCEEDINGS OF THE ANNUAL MEETING OF THE BOARD OF GOVERNORS. (Includes list of members of delegations) 1946. a. free. International Monetary Fund, Publications Unit, 700 19th St., N.W., Washington, DC 20431. TEL 202-623-7430. (also avail. in microform from UMI; reprint service avail. from UMI)

332   SZ
INTERNATIONAL SAVINGS BANKS INSTITUTE. REPORT. (Text in English, French, German) 1970. biennial. free. International Savings Banks Institute, 1-3 rue Albert-Gos, 1206 Geneva, Switzerland. Ed. J.M. Pesant. circ. 5,000.

332   US   ISSN 0074-9370
INTERNATIONAL UNION OF BUILDING SOCIETIES AND SAVINGS ASSOCIATIONS. CONGRESS PROCEEDINGS. (Text in French, German, English, Spanish) 1914. triennial, 1977, 14th, San Francisco. International Union of Building Societies and Savings Associations, c/o Don F. Geyer, Sec.-Gen., 111 E. Wacker Dr., 25th Fl., Chicago, IL 60601. TEL 312-726-6676.

332   YU
INVESTBANKA. ANNUAL REPORT. 1956. a. free. Investbanka, Terazije 9, Box 152, 11001 Belgrade, Yugoslavia. Ed. Ljubisa K. Plavsic. circ. 1,700.
    Formerly: Yugoslovenska Investiciona Banka. Annual Report (ISSN 0075-4536)

332.1   MW
INVESTMENT AND DEVELOPMENT BANK OF MALAWI. ANNUAL REPORT AND ACCOUNTS. (Text in English) 1973. a. Investment and Development Bank of Malawi, Box 358, Blantyre, Malawi.

658.8 332   IE   ISSN 0075-0573
IRELAND (EIRE) CENTRAL STATISTICS OFFICE. HIRE-PURCHASE AND CREDIT SALES. a. Central Statistics Office, Ardee Rd., Dublin 6, Ireland.
    Stencilled releases

332   SU
ISLAMIC DEVELOPMENT BANK. ANNUAL REPORT. 1975. a. free. Islamic Development Bank, Box 5925, Jeddah, Saudi Arabia. circ. 5,000.

332.1   IS   ISSN 0075-1146
ISRAEL DISCOUNT BANK. REPORT. (Text in English) 1955. a. free. Israel Discount Bank Limited, 27-29 Yehuda Ha-Levi St., Tel Aviv, Israel.

JOURNAL CONTENTS IN QUANTITATIVE METHODS. see *BUSINESS AND ECONOMICS — Abstracting, Bibliographies, Statistics*

332 378   US   ISSN 0093-3961
JOURNAL OF FINANCIAL EDUCATION. 1972. a. $5 to individuals; institutions $6. Florida Atlantic University, College of Business and Public Administration, Boca Raton, FL 33431. TEL 305-393-3995. Ed. Daniel E. McCarty. adv. circ. 800. (back issues avail.)
    Formerly: Financial Education (ISSN 0190-7654)

332.1   KE
KENYA COMMERCIAL BANK. DIRECTOR'S REPORT AND ACCOUNTS AND EXECUTIVE CHAIRMAN'S STATEMENT. a. Kenya Commercial Bank, Box 48400, Nairobi, Kenya.

332.1   KO   ISSN 0075-6806
KOREA DEVELOPMENT BANK; ITS FUNCTIONS AND ACTIVITIES. (Text in English) 1965. a. free. Korea Development Bank, Research Department, Box 28, Seoul, S. Korea. Ed. Min Beoung Yun.

332   KU
KUWAIT INVESTMENT COMPANY. (REPORT) a. Kuwait Investment Company, Box 1005, Safat, Kuwait.

332   PH
LAND BANK OF THE PHILIPPINES. ANNUAL REPORT.* 1974. a. Land Bank of the Philippines, B.F. Condominium, 6th Fl., Aduana St., Manila, Philippines. Ed.Bd. charts. illus. stat. circ. 6,000.

332.1   SZ
LEADING EUROPEAN BANKS; a comparative analysis of 100 leading European banks. 1974. a. (St. Gall Institute of Banking Studies) Paul Haupt AG, Falkenplatz 14, CH-3001 Berne, Switzerland.
    Formerly: 100 European Banks.

332.1   LO
LESOTHO BANK. REPORT AND ACCOUNTS. Cover title: Lesotho Bank. Annual Report. a. Lesotho Bank, Lesotho Development Bank, Lesotho Bank Centre, Kingways St., P.O. Box 999, Maseru 100, Lesotho. Ed.Bd.

332.2   BL
LINHAS DE FINANCIAMENTO DO B N H. vol.3, 1978. a. Banco Nacional da Habitacao, Secretaria de Divulgacao, Assessoria de Planejamento e Coordenacao, Av. Republica do Chile 230, Rio de Janeiro RJ, Brazil. Dir. Luiz Sande. charts. stat.

332.3   US   ISSN 0277-1497
LOANS CLOSED AND SERVICING VOLUME FOR THE MORTGAGE BANKING INDUSTRY. 1971. a. $55 to non-members; members $25. Mortgage Bankers Association of America, Economics and Education Department, 1125 15th St., N.W., Washington, DC 20005. TEL 202-861-6500.
    Formerly: Mortgage Banking: Loans Closed and Servicing Volume (ISSN 0363-1710)

332.1   II   ISSN 0076-2563
MAHARASHTRA STATE FINANCIAL CORPORATION. ANNUAL REPORT. (Text in English) 1963. a. free. Maharashtra State Financial Corporation, New Excelsior Building, 7, 8 & 9th Floors, Amrit Keshav Nayak Marg, Fort, Bombay 400001, India. charts. stat.

MAJOR BANKS, FINANCE & INVESTMENT COMPANIES OF CONTINENTAL EUROPE. see *BUSINESS AND ECONOMICS — Trade And Industrial Directories*

332.1   MW   ISSN 0076-3322
MALAWI. POST OFFICE SAVINGS BANK. ANNUAL REPORT. 1964. a. Post Office Savings Bank, Box 521, Blantyre, Malawi. circ. 300.

332   CN
MANITOBA. CO-OPERATIVE LOANS AND LOANS GUARANTEE BOARD. ANNUAL REPORT. 1971. a. free. Co-Operative Loans and Loans Guarantee Board, 800-215 Garry St., Winnipeg, Man. R3C 3P3, Canada. Ed.Bd. circ. 100.

334   CN
MANITOBA. DEPARTMENT OF CO-OPERATIVE DEVELOPMENT. REPORT/RAPPORT. (Text in English and French) 1972. a. Department of Co-Operative Development, Winnipeg, Man., Canada. TEL 204-944-3682. illus.
    Continues: Manitoba Credit Unions: Annual Report.

332.1   IS   ISSN 0076-4515
MARITIME BANK OF ISRAEL. ANNUAL REPORT/BANK HA-SAPANUT LE-YISRAEL. ANNUAL REPORT. (Text in English and Hebrew) a. free. Maritime Bank of Israel, Ltd, P.O. Box 1529, Tel Aviv 61000, Israel.

338.5   US   ISSN 0025-6137
MAY TRENDS. 1967. irreg., vol.17, 1987. free. ‡ George S. May International Company, Management Consultants, 111 S. Washington St., Park Ridge, IL 60068-9975. TEL 312-825-8806. Ed. J.E. McArdle. adv. circ. 30,000.

332   UK   ISSN 0266-2094
MIDDLE EAST FINANCIAL DIRECTORY. 1975. a. £60($90) Middle East Economic Digest Ltd., 21 John St., London WC1N 2BP, England. Ed. Anna Krajewska. adv. index. (back issues avail.)

332   US
MONEY MARKET DIRECTORY OF PENSION FUNDS AND THEIR INVESTMENT ADVISORS. 1971. a. $485. ‡ Money Market Directories, Inc., 300 E. Market St., Charlottesville, VA 22901. TEL 804-977-1450. Ed. T.H. Fitzgerald, Jr. adv. index. circ. 6,500. (magnetic tape)
    Formerly: Money Market Directory (ISSN 0077-0388)

332   FR
LA MONNAIE EN (YEAR) 1970. a. free. Banque de France, Service de l'information, 43 rue de Valois, 75001 Paris, France.

MONNAIES, PRIX, CONJONCTURE. see *HISTORY*

332   MX   ISSN 0185-4968
NACIONAL FINANCIERA. ANNUAL REPORT. a. Nacional Financiera, S.N.C., Isabel La Catolica, 06008 Mexico, Mexico.

332.1   TZ
NATIONAL BANK OF COMMERCE. ANNUAL REPORT AND ACCOUNTS. (Text in English and Swahili) 1967. a. free. National Bank of Commerce, P.O. Box 1255, Dar es Salaam, Tanzania. circ. 3, 000.

332.1   GR   ISSN 0077-3514
NATIONAL BANK OF GREECE. ANNUAL REPORT/ETHNIKE TRAPEZA TES HELLADOS. APOLOGISMOS. (Editions in English & Greek) 1843. a. free. National Bank of Greece, Economic Research Department, 86 Eolou St., Athens 121, Greece. circ. 21,000 (12,500 Greek edt.; 8,500 English edt.)

332   KU
NATIONAL BANK OF KUWAIT. ANNUAL REPORT OF THE BOARD OF DIRECTORS AND ACCOUNTS. 1953. a. National Bank of Kuwait S.A.K., Economics and Planning Division, Abdullah al-Salim St., Box 95, Kuwait.

332.1   LB
NATIONAL BANK OF LIBERIA. ANNUAL REPORT. 1974. a. National Bank of Liberia, Box 2048, E.G. King Plaza, Broad St., Monrovia, Liberia. stat.

332   PK
NATIONAL BANK OF PAKISTAN. ANNUAL REPORT. (Text in English) a. National Bank of Pakistan, I.I. Chundrigar Rd., Karachi 2, Pakistan.

332.1   PK   ISSN 0077-3522
NATIONAL BANK OF PAKISTAN. REPORT AND STATEMENT OF ACCOUNTS. (Text in English) a. National Bank of Pakistan, I. I. Chundrigar Rd., Karachi 2, Pakistan.

NATIONAL BANK OF YUGOSLAVIA. ANNUAL REPORT. see *BUSINESS AND ECONOMICS — Economic Situation And Conditions*

332.3   DQ
NATIONAL COMMERCIAL & DEVELOPMENT BANK. ANNUAL REPORT AND FINANCIAL STATEMENTS. a. National Commercial & Development Bank, 64 Hillsborough St., Roseau, Dominica, West Indies. (Affiliate: A I D Bank) illus.
    Formerly: Dominica Agricultural and Industrial Development Bank. Annual Report and Financial Statements.

332.1   US
NATIONAL COUNCIL OF SAVINGS INSTITUTIONS. ANNUAL REPORT OF THE PRESIDENT. a. National Council of Savings Institutions, 1101 15th., N.W., Washington, DC 20005. TEL 202-857-3100.
    Formerly: National Association of Mutual Banks of the United States. Report.

BUSINESS AND ECONOMICS — BANKING AND FINANCE

332.2 US
NATIONAL COUNCIL OF SAVINGS INSTITUTIONS DIRECTORY. 1924. a. $59 to non-members; members and institutions $25. National Council of Savings Institutions, 1101 15th St., N.W., Rm. 400, Washington, DC 20005. TEL 202-857-3100. Ed. Martha B. Roberts.
Formerly (until 1984): Directory of the Mutual Savings Banks of the United States (ISSN 0092-6132) Continues: Directory and Guide to the Mutual Savings Banks of the United States.

332.1 SL
NATIONAL DEVELOPMENT BANK. ANNUAL REPORT AND ACCOUNTS. (Text in English) 1969. a. free. ‡ National Development Bank, Leone House, 21/23 Siaka Stevens St., Freetown, Sierra Leone. stat. circ. 450.

332.1 US ISSN 8756-9043
NATIONAL FACT BOOK OF SAVINGS INSTITUTIONS. a. $25. National Council of Savings Institutions, 1101 15th St., N.W., Rm. 400, Washington, DC 20005. TEL 202-857-3100.
Formerly: National Fact Book of Savings Banking (ISSN 0738-260X)

332.1 GH
NATIONAL INVESTMENT BANK, GHANA. ANNUAL REPORT. Short title: N I B Annual Report. 1963. a. ‡ National Investment Bank, 37 Liberty Ave., P.O. Box 3726, Accra, Ghana. illus. stat. circ. controlled.
Formerly: National Investment Bank, Ghana. Report of the Directors (ISSN 0077-5061)

332 NE ISSN 0167-3998
NEDERLANDSCHE BANK N.V. ANNUAL REPORT. 1981. a. fl.42($16) (Dutch Central Bank) Martinus Nijhoff Publishers, Postbus 163, 3300 AD Dordrecht, Netherlands (Orders to: Kluwer Academic Publishers Group, Distribution Center, Box 322, 3300 AH Dordrecht, Netherlands)

332 NP
NEPAL BANK LIMITED. ANNUAL REPORT AND BALANCE SHEET. (Text in English) a. Nepal Bank Limited, Dharma Path, Kathmandu, Nepal. charts. stat.

332.1 NP
NEPAL RASTRA BANK. ANNUAL REPORT. (Text in English) 1957. a. free. Nepal Rastra Bank, Research Department, Baluwatar, Kathmandu, Nepal.
Formerly: Nepal Rastra Bank. Report of the Board of Directors (ISSN 0077-6580)

332.1 338.9 NE ISSN 0077-7560
NETHERLANDS INVESTMENT BANK FOR DEVELOPING COUNTRIES. ANNUAL REPORT. (Text in English) 1965. a. Netherlands Investment Bank for Developing Countries - Nederlandse Investeringsbank voor Ontwikkelingslanden N.V., The Hague, Netherlands. circ. 2,000.

332.1 US
NEW JERSEY. DEPARTMENT OF BANKING. ANNUAL REPORT. 1895. a. $10. Department of Banking, Box CN040, Trenton, NJ 08625. TEL 609-292-7272. Ed. Gerald Trimble. circ. 1,300.
Formed by the merger of: New Jersey. Division of Savings and Loan Associations. Annual Report (ISSN 0098-8073) & New Jersey. Division of Banking. Annual Report (ISSN 0098-7409)

332.1 NR ISSN 0549-2734
NIGERIAN INDUSTRIAL DEVELOPMENT BANK. ANNUAL REPORT AND ACCOUNTS. 1971. a. free. Nigerian Industrial Development Bank, 63171 Broad St., P.O. Box 2357, Lagos, Nigeria. illus. circ. 2,000.

332 JA
NIHON KAIHATSU GINKO. CHOSABU. CHOSA GEPPO. 1973. irreg. free. Japan Development Bank - Nihon Kaihatsu Ginko, 1-9-1- Otemachi, Chiyoda-ku, Tokyo, Japan. circ. 2,300.

332.1 NO ISSN 0078-1185
NORGES BANK. REPORT AND ACCOUNTS. Cover title: Norges Bank. Annual Report. (Text in English) a. Norges Bank, P.O.Box 1179 Sentrum, N-01071 Oslo 1, Norway.

332.1 NO
NORSKE CREDITBANK. Caption title: Norske Creditbank. Report of the Board of Directors. a. Norske Creditbank, Kirkegaten 21, Oslo 1, Norway.
Formerly: Norske Creditbank. Annual Report.

332 US
OCCASIONAL PAPERS IN METROPOLITAN BUSINESS AND FINANCE. irreg. $10 per no. New York University, Salomon Brothers Center for the Study of Financial Institutions, Graduate School of Business Administration, 90 Trinity Pl., New York, NY 10006. TEL 212-598-1212.

332.1 AU
OESTERREICHISCHE BANKWISSENSCHAFTLICHE GESELLSCHAFT. SCHRIFTENREIHE. 1953. irreg., vol.62, 1984. price varies. Manzsche Verlags- und Universitaetsbuchhandlung, Kohlmarkt 16, A-1014 Vienna, Austria. Ed. Wilhelm Buehler.

332.1 AU ISSN 0078-3528
OESTERREICHISCHE NATIONALBANK. BERICHT UEBER DAS GESCHAEFTSJAHR MIT RECHNUNGSABSCHLUSS. (Editions in English and German) 1956. a. free. Oesterreichische Nationalbank, Otto-Wagner-Platz 3, A-1090 Vienna, Austria. Ed. Alfred Kanitz. circ. 2,250.

OM STATSREGNSKABET. see BUSINESS AND ECONOMICS

382 332 FR ISSN 0474-5655
ORGANIZATION FOR ECONOMIC COOPERATION AND DEVELOPMENT. COUNCIL. CODE DE LA LIBERATION DES MOUVEMENTS DE CAPITAUX. CODE OF LIBERALISATION OF CAPITAL MOVEMENTS. (Editions in English and French) irreg. price varies. Organisation for Economic Cooperation and Development, 2 rue Andre Pascal, 75775 Paris 16, France (U.S. orders to: O.E.C.D. Publications and Information Center, 1750 Pennsylvania Ave., N.W., Washington, DC 20006) (also avail. in microfiche)

332.1 PK ISSN 0078-7884
PAKISTAN BANKING DIRECTORY.* (Text in English) 1966/67. a. Sanaullah Publications, Box 4186, Karachi, Pakistan.

332 NO ISSN 0332-5598
PENGER OG KREDITT. 1973. irreg., no.15, 1985. free. Norges Bank, Information Section, P.O. Box 1179 Sentrum, N-0107 Oslo 1, Norway. Ed. Hermod Skaanland.

332 US ISSN 0079-0761
PER JACOBSSON FOUNDATION. PROCEEDINGS. (Editions in English, French, Spanish) 1964. a. free. Per Jacobsson Foundation, International Monetary Fund Bldg., Washington, DC 20431. TEL 202-477-3366. (Affiliate: International Monetary Fund) Ed. Gordon Williams. circ. 24,000 (20,000 English edt.; 2,500 French edt.; 1,500 Spanish edt.)
Formerly: Per Jacobsson Memorial Lecture (ISSN 0079-077X)

378 US
PETERSON'S COLLEGE MONEY HANDBOOK (YEAR); the complete guide to expenses, scholarships, loans, jobs, and special aid programs at four-year colleges. 1983. a. $15.95. Peterson's Guides, 166 Bunn Dr., Box 2123, Princeton, NJ 08543-2123. TEL 609-924-5338. Ed. Andrea E. Lehman. (also avail. in microform)

332 380 320 PH
PHILIPPINES YEARBOOK OF THE FOOKIEN TIMES. (Text in English) 1936. a. P.200($25) Fookien Times Yearbook Publishing Co., Inc., Cor. 13th and Railroad Streets, Port Area, Manila, Philippines. Ed. Betty Go Belmonte. adv. circ. 20,000. (back issues avail.) Indexed: Ind.Phil.Per.

332 382 US ISSN 0887-7637
POLITICAL CLIMATE FOR INTERNATIONAL BUSINESS; a forecast of risk in 85 countries. 1981. a. $315. Frost & Sullivan, Inc., Political Risk Services, 106 Fulton St., New York, NY 10038. TEL 212-233-1080. Eds. William D. Coplin, Michael K. O'Leary.

332 382 US ISSN 0889-2725
POLITICAL RISK YEARBOOK. 1987. a. $1000. Frost & Sullivan, Inc., Political Risk Services, 106 Fulton St., New York, NY 10038. TEL 212-233-1080. Eds. William D. Coplin, Michael K. O'Leary.

332.1 US ISSN 0085-4999
POLK'S WORLD BANK DIRECTORY. INTERNATIONAL EDITION. 1894. a. $101.25. R.L. Polk & Co., Bank Services Division, 2001 Elm Hill Pike, Box 1340, Nashville, TN 37202. TEL 615-889-3350. adv. bk. rev. charts. stat. circ. 17,500.

332.1 MF
POST OFFICE SAVINGS BANK. ANNUAL REPORT. (Text in English) a., latest 1978/79. Government Printing Office, Elizabeth II Ave., Port Louis, Mauritius.

332.7 FR
PRINCIPAUX MECANISMES DE DISTRIBUTION DE CREDIT. irreg., vol.9, 1985. 35 F. Banque de France, Service de l'Information, 43 rue de Valois, 75001 Paris, France.

332 PR
PUERTO RICO. GOVERNMENT DEVELOPMENT BANK. ANNUAL REPORT. 1978. a. (Government Development Bank) Publishing Resources, Inc., Box 41307, San Juan, PR 00940. Ed. Anne W. Chevako. circ. 7,500.
Formerly: Puerto Rico. Government Development Bank. Report of Activities.

332.1 II ISSN 0304-8101
PUNJAB NATIONAL BANK. ANNUAL REPORT. (Text in English) a. Punjab National Bank, Ltd., 5 Parliament St., New Delhi 10001, India. Key Title: Annual Report - Punjab National Bank.

332 QA
QATAR NATIONAL BANK (S.A.Q.). REPORT OF THE DIRECTORS AND BALANCE SHEET. a. Qatar National Bank (S.A.Q.), Box 1000, Doha, Qatar.

332 650 US ISSN 0080-3340
R M A ANNUAL STATEMENT STUDIES. 1923. a. $32.50 to non-members; members $10. ‡ Robert Morris Associates, 1616 Philadelphia National Bank Bldg., Philadelphia, PA 19107. TEL 215-665-2850. index. circ. 30,000.

332.3 US
RAND MCNALLY CREDIT UNION DIRECTORY. 1986. a. $54.95. Rand McNally & Co., 8255 N. Central Pk., Skokie, IL 60076. TEL 312-673-9100. stat.

332 IS
RASHUT NAYEROT HAERECH. ANNUAL REPORT. (Text in Hebrew) a. Rashut Nayerot Haerech, P.O. Box 7450, Jerusalem, Israel. TEL 02-245288.

332 US
REPORT ON DOMESTIC AND INTERNATIONAL COMMERCIAL LOAN CHARGE-OFFS. 1972. a. $15 to non-members; members $10. Robert Morris Associates, 1616 Philadelphia National Bank Bldg., Philadelphia, PA 19107. TEL 215-665-2850.
Former titles: Domestic and International Commercial Loan Charge-Offs (ISSN 0192-7639); Commercial Loan Charge-Offs.

332 US ISSN 0080-1380
REPRINTS IN INTERNATIONAL FINANCE. 1965. irreg., no.23, 1983. $12 (includes Essays in International Finance) ‡ Princeton University, International Finance Section, Dept. of Economics, Dickinson Hall, Princeton, NJ 08544. TEL 609-452-4048. Ed. Peter B. Kenen. circ. 3,000. (back issues avail.)

332 US ISSN 0196-3821
RESEARCH IN FINANCE. (Supplement avail.: Management Under Government Intervention: The View from Mount Scopus) 1979. a. $26.25 to individuals; institutions $52.50. J A I Press Inc., Box 1678, 36 Sherwood Pl., Greenwich, CT 06836. TEL 203-661-7602. Ed. Haim Levy.

BUSINESS AND ECONOMICS — BANKING AND FINANCE

332.1   AT   ISSN 0080-1771
RESERVE BANK OF AUSTRALIA. ANNUAL REPORT. 1960. a. free. Reserve Bank of Australia, 65 Martin Place, Box 3947 G.P.O., Sydney, N.S.W. 2001, Australia. circ. 20,000.

332.1   330.9   AT   ISSN 0080-178X
RESERVE BANK OF AUSTRALIA. OCCASIONAL PAPERS. 1970. irreg. price varies. Reserve Bank of Australia, 65 Martin Place, Box 3947 G.P.O., Sydney, N.S.W. 2001, Australia. circ. 6,000.

332   II   ISSN 0080-1801
RESERVE BANK OF INDIA. ANNUAL REPORT. (Text in English) 1936. a. price varies. Reserve Bank of India, Division of Reports, Reviews & Publications, Department of Economic Analysis & Policy, New Central Office Bldg., 9th floor, P.O. Box 1036, Bombay 400 023, India. TEL 2862524. circ. 7,500.

332   MW   ISSN 0486-5383
RESERVE BANK OF MALAWI. REPORT AND ACCOUNTS. a. free. Reserve Bank of Malawi, Research Department, Box 30063, Lilongwe 3, Malawi.
     Formerly: Reserve Bank of Malawi. Annual Report and Statement of Account.

332.1   UK
RETAIL BANKER'S YEARBOOK. 1983. a. £75($105) Lafferty Publications Ltd., 2 Pear Tree Court, London EC1R 0DS, England (U.S. subscr. addr.: Lafferty Publications (U.S.), 3065 Canal Towpath, Georgetown NW, Washington DC 20007) Ed. Susan Bevan. (back issues avail.)

332.1   US
REVIEW OF BANK PERFORMANCE. a. Salomon Brothers Inc., Securities Department, One New York Plaza, New York, NY 10004. TEL 212-747-7000.

332   BL
REVISTA DO B I N D E. English edition: B I N D E Annual Report. 1963. a. Banco Nacional do Desenvolvimento Economico, Av. Rio Branco, 53, Rio de Janeiro, Brazil. bibl. charts. stat.
     Former title: Banco Nacional do Desenvolvimento Economico. Relatorio Anual.

332   MX   ISSN 0556-6835
REVISTA MEXICANA DE FIANZAS. 1964. a. Mex.$2000($5) (Mexican Bond Companies and Bancomer, S.N.C.) Fernando Castaneda Alatorre Ed. & Pub., Puebla 383, Col. Roma, Deleg. Cuauhtemoc, 06700 Mexico, D.F., Mexico. adv. circ. 1,000.

332.1   SZ   ISSN 0080-2611
REVUE INTERNATIONALE D'HISTOIRE DE LA BANQUE. 1968. a. price varies. (Banco di Napoli, IT) Librarie Droz, 11 rue Massot, 1211 Geneva 12, Switzerland. bk. rev.

332.1   SW
RIKSGAELDKONTORET. STATISTISK AARSBOK. 1920. a. free. Riksgaeldkontoret - National Debt Office, Box 16306, 103 26 Stockholm, Sweden. Ed. Lars Kalderen. circ. 1,000.
     Formerly (until 1980): Riksgaeldkontoret. Aarsbok (ISSN 0082-0091)

332   TR
ROYAL BANK OF TRINIDAD AND TOBAGO. ANNUAL REPORT. a. Royal Bank of Trinidad and Tobago, 36 Chancery Lane, Port of Spain, Trinidad and Tobago.

332   SZ
S B C BOOKLET. (Text in English) irreg. Schweizerischer Bankverein - Swiss Bank Corporation, 6 Aeschenplatz, CH-4002 Basel, Switzerland.

332.1   US
S E C ANNUAL REPORTS. BANKING SUPPLEMENT. 1983. irreg. free. Ernst & Whinney, 2000 National City Center, Cleveland, OH 44114. TEL 216-861-5000. stat. circ. 3,675.
     Formerly: S E C Annual Reports.

332   XI
ST. KITTS-NEVIS-ANGUILLA NATIONAL BANK LIMITED AND ITS SUBSIDIARIES. ANNUAL REPORT AND ACCOUNTS. a. St. Kitts-Nevis-Anguilla National Bank Limited, Church St., Basseterre, St. Kitts, W. Indies.

332   US   ISSN 0276-2021
SALOMON BROTHERS CENTER FOR THE STUDY OF FINANCIAL INSTITUTIONS. MONOGRAPH SERIES. Variant title: Monograph Series in Finance and Economics. 1928; N.S. 1975. irreg. (4-5/yr.); latest 1984. $10 to qualified personnel; others $20. New York University, Salomon Brothers Center for the Study of Financial Institutions, Graduate School of Business Administration, 90 Trinity Pl., New York, NY 10006. Ed. Anthony Saunders.
     Formerly: New York University Institute of Finance. Bulletin (ISSN 0077-9466)

332   US
SALOMON BROTHERS CENTER FOR THE STUDY OF FINANCIAL INSTITUTIONS. OCCASIONAL PAPERS. 1979. irreg., no.6, 1985. $10 per no. New York University, Salomon Brothers Center for the Study of Finance, Graduate School of Business Administration, 90 Trinity Pl., New York, NY 10006. Ed. A.W. Sametz. circ. 1, 000.

332   US
SALOMON BROTHERS CENTER FOR THE STUDY OF FINANCIAL INSTITUTIONS. WORKING PAPER. 1971. irreg., no.382, 1986. $60. New York University, Salomon Brothers Center for the Study of Financial Institutions, Graduate School of Business Adminstration, 90 Trinity Pl., New York, NY 10006. Ed. A.W. Sametz. circ. 500.

332   SU   ISSN 0581-8672
SAUDI ARABIAN MONETARY AGENCY. STATISTICAL SUMMARY. a. Saudi Arabian Monetary Agency, Research and Statistics Department, Box 2992, Riyadh, Saudi Arabia. charts. stat.

332   US   ISSN 0731-0935
SAVINGS AND LOAN SOURCEBOOK. 1954. a. $2.50. United States League of Savings Institutions, 111 E. Wacker Dr., Chicago, IL 60601. TEL 312-644-3100. Ed. Nancy Lapp. circ. 24,000.
     Supersedes in part: Savings and Loan Fact Book (ISSN 0581-8761)

332   346.066   SZ
SCHRIFTENREIHE FINANZWIRTSCHAFT UND FINANZRECHT. 1970. irreg., no.49, 1986. price varies. Paul Haupt AG, Falkenplatz 14, CH-3001 Berne, Switzerland.

332.1   SZ
SCHWEIZERISCHE BANKWESEN. (Text in German) a. (Schweizerische Nationalbank) Orell Fuessli Graphische Betriebe AG, Dietzingerstr. 3, CH-8036 Zurich, Switzerland. stat.

332   340   US   ISSN 0080-8474
SECURITIES LAW REVIEW. 1969. a. $70. ‡ Clark Boardman Company, Ltd., 435 Hudson St., New York, NY 10014. Ed. Donald C. Langevoort.
Indexed: Leg.Per. C.L.I. L.R.I.

332.1   US
SERVICE CORPORATION DIRECTORY. 1976. a. $80 to non-members; members $40. U S League of Savings Institutions, 111 E. Wacker Dr., Chicago, IL 60601. TEL 312-644-3100. Ed. H. Olin. circ. 1, 000.

332.4   SI
SINGAPORE. BOARD OF COMMISSIONERS OF CURRENCY. ANNUAL REPORT AND ACCOUNTS. 1967. a. $5. Board of Commissioners of Currency, 79 Robinson Rd. 01-01, Singapore 0106, Singapore. circ. 700.
     Formerly: Singapore. Board of Commissioners of Currency. Annual Report.

335   368   SI
SINGAPORE BANKING, FINANCE & INSURANCE. 1979. a. S.$7. Times Directories Private Ltd., 422 Thomson Rd., Singapore 1129, Singapore.

332.1   KO
SMALL AND MEDIUM INDUSTRY BANK, SEOUL. ANNUAL REPORT. 1962. a. free. Small and Medium Industry Bank, Seoul, S. Korea. Ed. Kwan-Heng Chough. circ. 1,000.
     Formerly: Medium Industry Bank, Seoul. Report (ISSN 0076-6143)

332.1   BE
SOCIETE GENERALE DE BANQUE. RAPPORT. a. Societe Generale de Banque, Montagne du Parc 3, B-1000 Brussels, Belgium.

332   BE   ISSN 0081-1114
SOCIETE GENERALE DE BELGIQUE. RAPPORT/REPORT. (Editions in English and French) 1822. a. free. Societe Generale de Belgique, External Relations Department, 30 rue Royale, B-1000 Brussels, Belgium.

332   UK
SORTING CODE NUMBERS; directory of bank branches and other financial institutions to which code numbers have been allocated. 1961. a. £2.40. Thomas Skinner Directories, East Grinstead House, East Grinstead, West Sussex RH19 1XE, England. circ. 105,000.

332.1   SA
SOUTH AFRICAN RESERVE BANK. REPORT OF THE ORDINARY GENERAL MEETING/SUID-AFRIKAANSE RESERWEBANK. VERSLAG VAN DIE GEWONE ALGEMENE VERGADERING. (Text in Afrikaans and English) 1922. a. free. South African Reserve Bank, P.O. Box 427, Pretoria 0001, South Africa. circ. 3,120.

SPECIAL PAPERS IN INTERNATIONAL ECONOMICS. see BUSINESS AND ECONOMICS

332   US
STANDARD & POOR'S DIVIDEND RECORD (ANNUAL) a. $18.50. Standard & Poor's Corporation, 25 Broadway, New York, NY 10004. Ed. Anthony Onofrio. (looseleaf format; also avail. in microfiche)

332   II
STATE BANK OF INDIA. ANNUAL REPORT. (Text in English) 1955. a. State Bank of India, Economic Research Department, Central Office, Bombay 400 021, India.
     Supersedes: State Bank of India. Report of the Central Board of Directors (ISSN 0585-0991); Report for the Half Year of the Imperial Bank of India.

STATISTICAL SUMMARY OF THAILAND. see AGRICULTURE — Abstracting, Bibliographies, Statistics

332.1   CS   ISSN 0081-539X
STATNI BANKA CESKOSLOVENSKA. BULLETIN. 1967. a. free. Statni Banka Ceskoslovenska, Na Prikope 28, 110 03 Prague 1, Czechoslovakia.

332   GW   ISSN 0081-7279
STUDIEN ZUR FINANZPOLITIK. 1964. irreg., no.32, 1984. price varies. I F O Institut fuer Wirtschaftsforschung, Poschingerstr. 5, 8000 Munich 80, W. Germany (B.R.D.) circ. 500.

332   US   ISSN 0081-8070
STUDIES IN INTERNATIONAL FINANCE. 1950. irreg., no.54, 1984. $30 (includes Essays in International Finance; Reprints in International Finance; Special Papers in International Economics) ‡ Princeton University, International Finance Section, Dept. of Economics, Dickinson Hall, Princeton, NJ 08544. TEL 609-452-4048. Dir. Peter B. Kenen. circ. 2,000. (back issues avail.; reprint service avail. from UMI)

332   NE
STUDIES IN MONETARY ECONOMICS. 1976. irreg., vol.8, 1983. price varies. Elsevier Science Publishers B.V., Box 211, 1000 AE Amsterdam, Netherlands. Eds. Karl Brunner, Stanley Fisher. charts. stat.

332   SJ
SUDAN COMMERCIAL BANK. REPORT OF THE BOARD OF DIRECTORS. irreg. Sudan Commercial Bank, Box 1116, Khartoum, Sudan.

BUSINESS AND ECONOMICS — BANKING AND FINANCE

332 UK
SUNDAY TELEGRAPH BUSINESS FINANCE DIRECTORY: THE GUIDE TO SOURCES OF U K CORPORATE FINANCE. 1984. a. £35 paperback; £44 hardback. Graham & Trotman Ltd., Sterling House, 66 Wilton Rd., London SW1V 1DE, England. Eds. G.C. Bricault, J.C. Carr. adv.
Former titles: Sunday Telegraph U K Finance Directory: A Guide to Sources of U K Corporate Finance; Sunday Telegraph U K Finance Directory: A Directory of Sources of U K Corporate Finance; U K Finance Directory: A Directory of Sources of U K Corporate Finance.

332 SW
SVENSK OBLIGATIONSBOK. 1913. a. Kr.420($45) Svenska Bankfoereningen - Swedish Bankers Association, Box 7603, S-103 94 Stockholm, Sweden. Ed. Sture Braasjoe.

332.1 SW ISSN 0081-9913
SVENSKA HANDELSBANKEN. ANNUAL REPORT. Variant title: Svenska Handelsbanken. Annual Report and Auditors' Report. Swedish Version: 1871; English Version: 1955. a. free. Svenska Handelsbanken, Kungstraedgaardsgatan 2, S-103 28 Stockholm, Sweden. circ. 8,000.

332.1 SW ISSN 0347-3198
SVERIGES RIKSBANK. FOERVALTNINGSBERAETTELSE. English edition: Central Bank of Sweden. Annual Report (ISSN 0347-5042) a. Sveriges Riksbank, Box 16283, S-103 25 Stockholm, Sweden.

332.1 SW ISSN 0348-7342
SVERIGES RIKSBANK. STATISTISK AARSBOK/ CENTRAL BANK OF SWEDEN. STATISTICAL YEARBOOK. (Tables in English and Swedish) 1908. a. Sveriges Riksbank, Box 16283, S-103 25 Stockholm, Sweden.
Formerly (until 1979): Sveriges Riksbank. Aarsbok.

332 SQ
SWAZILAND. MINISTRY OF FINANCE. CAPITAL FUND ESTIMATES. a. free. Ministry of Finance, Box 456, Mbabane, Swaziland.
Formerly: Swaziland. Central Statistical Office. Capital Fund Estimates.

332 SZ
SWISS BANK CORPORATION. REPORT OF THE BOARD OF DIRECTORS TO THE ANNUAL GENERAL MEETING OF SHAREHOLDERS. a. Schweizerischer Bankverein - Swiss Bank Corporation, 6 Aeschenplatz, CH-4002 Basel, Switzerland.

332.1 TZ
TANZANIA HOUSING BANK. ANNUAL REPORT AND STATEMENT OF ACCOUNTS/ BENKI YA NYUMBA TANZANIA. RIPOTI YA MWAKA. (Text in English and Swahili) 1974. a. Tanzania Housing Bank, Public Relations Department, Box 1723, Dar es Salaam, Tanzania. Ed.Bd. circ. 1,500.

332.1 TZ
TANZANIA INVESTMENT BANK. ANNUAL REPORT. (Text in English and Swahili) 1971. a. Tanzania Investment Bank, Box 9373, Dar es Salaam, Tanzania.

332.1 TZ
TANZANIA RURAL DEVELOPMENT BANK. ANNUAL REPORT AND ACCOUNTS. (Text in English and Swahili) 1972. a. Tanzania Rural Development Bank, Box 268, Dar es Salaam, Tanzania.

332 UK
TECHNICAL BUDGET REPRESENTATIONS. a. £3. Confederation of British Industry, 103 New Oxford St., London WC1A 1DU, England.

332.1 US
TEXAS BANKING RED BOOK. 1946. a. $21. Bankers Digest, Inc., 6440 N. Central Expressway, Dallas, TX 75206. TEL 214-373-4544. Ed. Bonnie Blackman. adv. circ. 18,500. (looseleaf format)

332 US
THORNDIKE ENCYCLOPEDIA OF BANKING AND FINANCIAL TABLES (SUPPLEMENT) annual supplement to update base vol. $84 for base vol. plus supp. Warren, Gorham and Lamont, Inc., 210 South St., Boston, MA 02111. TEL 800-922-0066.

332.6 330.9 CN
TORONTO STOCK EXCHANGE FACT BOOK. a. free. Toronto Stock Exchange, Exchange Tower, 2 First Canadian Pl., Toronto, Ont. M5X 1J2, Canada. TEL 416-947-4700. index.

332.1 TU
TURKIYE SINAI KALKINMA BANKASI. ANNUAL REPORT. 1950. a. Turkiye Sinai Kalkinma Bankasi, Meclisi Mebusan Caddesi, No.137, P.K. 17, Karakoy, Istanbul, Turkey. illus.

TWENTIETH CENTURY FUND. NEWSLETTER. see POLITICAL SCIENCE — International Relations

332 SZ
U B S PUBLICATIONS ON BUSINESS, BANKING AND MONETARY PROBLEMS. irreg., no.100, 1986. Union de Banques Suisses - Union Bank of Switzerland, Bahnhofstrasse 45, 8021 Zurich, Switzerland.

U C B INVESTOR'S HANDBOOK. (Uganda Commercial Bank) see BUSINESS AND ECONOMICS — Investments

332 UK
U.K.'S 7500 LARGEST COMPANIES. (Text in English) 1985. a. £90. E.L.C. International, Sinclair House, The Avenue, West Ealing, London W13 8NT, England. Ed. A. Humphris. circ. 1,000.

332.3 US
U S SAVINGS AND LOAN DIRECTORY. 1982. a. $105. (United States League of Savings Institutions) Rand McNally & Co., Financial Publishing Division, 8255 N. Central Park, Skokie, IL 60076 TEL 312-673-9100. (Orders to: Box 7600, Chicago, IL 60680) adv.

332.1 UG
UGANDA COMMERCIAL BANK. ANNUAL REPORT. (Text in English) 1966. a. Uganda Commercial Bank, Box 973, Kampala, Uganda. circ. 2,000.

332 MR
UNION BANCARIA HISPANO MARROQUI. ASSEMBLEE GENERALE ORDINAIRE DES ACTIONNAIRES. RAPPORT. a. Union Bancaria Hispano Marroqui, Assemblee Generale Ordinaire des Actionnaires, 69 rue du Prince Moulay Abdallah, Casablanca, Morocco.

332 FI ISSN 0355-0133
UNION BANK OF FINLAND. ANNUAL REPORT. 1952. a. Union Bank of Finland, P.B. 868, 00101 Helsinki 10, Finland.

332 UK ISSN 0503-2628
UNIT TRUST YEARBOOK. 1964. a. £19.50($30) (Association of Unit Trust Managers) Financial Times Business Information, 102 Clerkenwell Road, London EC1M 5SA, England. adv. circ. 3,500. (tabloid format)
Supersedes: Directory of Unit Trusts.

U.S. FEDERAL DEPOSIT INSURANCE CORPORATION. ANNUAL REPORT. see INSURANCE

332.1 US ISSN 0083-0674
U.S. FEDERAL DEPOSIT INSURANCE CORPORATION. CHANGES AMONG OPERATING BANKS AND BRANCHES. a. U.S. Federal Deposit Insurance Corporation., 550 17th St., N.W., Washington, DC 20429. TEL 202-389-4221.

332 US
U.S. FEDERAL DEPOSIT INSURANCE CORPORATION. FEDERAL DEPOSIT INSURANCE ACT, RULES AND REGULATIONS, AND RELATED LAWS. (Looseleaf Supplements) irreg. $50 for yearly service. Prentice-Hall, Inc., Box 500, Englewood Cliffs, NJ 07632 TEL 201-592-2000. (Orders to: FDIC, 550 17th St., N.W., Washington, DC 20429)

332 US
U.S. FEDERAL DEPOSIT INSURANCE CORPORATION. NEWS RELEASES. irreg. U.S. Federal Deposit Insurance Corporation, 550 17th St. N.W., Washington, DC 20429. TEL 202-389-4221.

332 US
U.S. FEDERAL DEPOSIT INSURANCE CORPORATION. OPERATING BANKING OFFICES. a. U.S. Federal Deposit Insurance Corporation, 550 17th St., N.W., Washington, DC 20429. TEL 202-389-4221.
Formerly: U.S. Federal Deposit Insurance Corporation. Operating Bank Offices.

332 US ISSN 0278-5692
U.S. FEDERAL DEPOSIT INSURANCE CORPORATION. TRUST ASSETS OF BANKS AND TRUST COMPANIES. a. U.S. Federal Deposit Insurance Corporation, 550 17th St., N.W., Washington, DC 20429. TEL 202-389-4221.
Formerly: U.S. Federal Deposit Insurance Corporation. Trust Assets of Insured Commercial Banks (ISSN 0149-8274)

332.7 US ISSN 0083-0720
U.S. FEDERAL HOME LOAN BANK BOARD. REPORT.* (Included in the April issue of the Federal Home Loan Bank Board Journal from 1971) 1947. a. free. U.S. Federal Home Loan Bank Board, Office of Communications, Box 37248, Washington, DC 20013. circ. 10,600.

332.7 US ISSN 0083-0747
U.S. FEDERAL HOME LOAN BANK BOARD. TRENDS IN THE SAVINGS AND LOAN FIELD.* a. U.S. Federal Home Loan Bank Board, Office of Communications, Box 37248, Washington, DC 20013. Ed. Elizabeth Miller. circ. 600.

332.1 US ISSN 0083-0887
U.S. FEDERAL RESERVE SYSTEM. ANNUAL REPORT. 1914. a. free. U.S. Federal Reserve System, Board of Governors, Publications Services, Rm. MS-138, Washington, DC 20551. TEL 202-452-3000. circ. 10,000.

332.1 US
U.S. FEDERAL RESERVE SYSTEM. ANNUAL STATISTICAL DIGEST. a. price varies. U.S. Federal Reserve System, Board of Governors, Publications Services, Rm. MS-138, Washington, DC 20551. TEL 202-452-3000.

334.2 US
U.S. NATIONAL CREDIT UNION ADMINISTRATION. ANNUAL REPORT. a. free. U.S. National Credit Union Administration, 1776 G St., N.W., Washington, DC 20456. TEL 202-537-1000.
Credit unions

332.4 US
U.S. TREASURY DEPARTMENT. UNITED STATES MINT. ANNUAL REPORT OF THE DIRECTOR OF THE MINT. 1873. a. $1.25. U.S. Department of the Treasury, United States Mint, 633 3rd St., N.W., Washington, DC 20220 TEL 202-566-2000. (Orders to: Superintendent of Documents, Washington, DC 20402)
Formerly: U.S. Treasury Department. Bureau of the Mint. Annual Report of the Director of the Mint.

332 AU
UNIVERSITAET INNSBRUCK. FINANZWISSENSCHAFTLICHE STUDIEN. (Subseries of: Universitaet Innsbruck. Veroeffentlichungen) 1969. irreg., vol.9, 1970. price varies. Oesterreichische Kommissionsbuchhandlung, Maximilianstr. 17, A-6020 Innsbruck, Austria. Ed. Clemens August Andreae.

332 US
UNIVERSITY OF TOLEDO. BUSINESS RESEARCH CENTER. STUDIES IN FINANCIAL INSTITUTIONS. 1971. irreg., no.12, 1987. price varies. University of Toledo, College of Business Administration, 2801 W. Bancroft St., Toledo, OH 43606. TEL 419-537-2067.

332 FR
V.I.P. DE LA FINANCE ET DE LA BANQUE. 1978. biennial. 490 F. Publications Professionnelles Francaises, 15 Square de Vergennes, 75015 Paris, France. (Affiliate: France Expansion)

332   VE
VENEZUELA. MINISTERIO DE HACIENDA. MEMORIA. a. Ministerio de Hacienda, Oficina de Relaciones Publicas, Oficina 312, Centro Simon Bolivar-Edificio Norte, Venezuela. Ed.Bd. stat.

332.1   US   ISSN 0083-5730
VERMONT. COMMISSIONER OF BANKING AND INSURANCE. ANNUAL REPORT OF THE BANK COMMISSIONER. 1880. a. free. ‡ Department of Banking and Insurance, Division of Banking, 120 State St., Montpelier, VT 05602. TEL 802-828-3301. Ed. W.H. Rockford, Jr. circ. 700.

WALL STREET JOURNAL INDEX. see *BUSINESS AND ECONOMICS — Investments*

332.1   US   ISSN 0272-5371
WESTERN BANK DIRECTORY. 1950. a. $21.50. Western Banker Publications, Inc., 824 W. Franklin, Boise, ID 83702. Ed. John L. Gannon. adv.

332   UK
WHO OWNS WHAT IN WORLD BANKING. a. Financial Times Business Information, 102 Clerkenwell Rd., London EC1M 5SA, England. adv. stat.

332   UK
WHO'S WHO IN BANKING IN EUROPE. irreg. price varies. International Business Communications Ltd., Bath House, 56 Holborn Viaduct, London EC1A 2EX, England.

WHO'S WHO IN FINANCE AND BANKING IN THAILAND. see *BIOGRAPHY*

332   UK
WORKING ABROAD (LONDON, 1977); the expatriate's guide. 1977. irreg. £12.50($21) Financial Times Business Information, 102 Clerkenwell Road, London EC1M 5SA, England.

332.1   UK
WORLD BANKING.* a. £32($15) Financial Times Business Information, 102 Clerkenwell Rd., London WC1M 5SA, England. illus.

332   US
WORLD COUNCIL OF CREDIT UNIONS. STATISTICAL REPORT & DIRECTORY. (Text in English, French, Spanish) a. World Council of Credit Unions, 5810 Mineral Pt. Rd., Box 391, Madison, WI 53701. TEL 608-231-7130. Ed. Jim Jerving. charts. illus. stat. circ. 6,000.
    Former titles: World Council of Credit Unions. International Annual Report; World Council of Credit Unions Yearbook.

332   US   ISSN 0743-5363
WORLD CURRENCY YEARBOOK. 1955. a. $225. International Currency Analysis, Inc., 7239 Ave. N., Brooklyn, NY 11234-5826. Ed. Philip cowitt. charts. stat. index. circ. 1,000. (also avail. in microform)
    Formerly: Pick's Currency Yearbook (ISSN 0079-2063)

332.1   TU
YAPI VE KREDI BANKASI. ANNUAL REPORT. (Text in English) a. Yapi ve Kredi Bankasi, Istiklal Caddesi, Korsan Cikmazi 1, Box 250, Beyoglu, Istanbul, Turkey.

BUSINESS AND ECONOMICS — Banking And Finance–computer Applications

see also Computers–Electronic Data Processing

332.1   001.64   US   ISSN 0095-5396
AMERICAN BANKERS ASSOCIATION. NATIONAL OPERATIONS & AUTOMATION CONFERENCE. PROCEEDINGS. 1963. a. price varies. American Bankers Association, Operations and Automation Division, 1120 Connecticut Ave., N.W., Washington, DC 20036. TEL 202-663-5430.
    Formerly: American Bankers Association. National Automation Conference. Proceedings (ISSN 0065-7441)

332.1   001.64   US   ISSN 0363-2539
AMERICAN BANKERS ASSOCIATION. OPERATIONS AND AUTOMATION DIVISION. RESULTS OF THE NATIONAL OPERATIONS & AUTOMATION SURVEY. 1975. triennial. $225 to non-members; members $150. American Bankers Association, 1120 Connecticut Ave., N.W., Washington, DC 20036. TEL 202-663-5087. Key Title: Results of the National Operations & Automation Survey.
    Continues: American Bankers Association. Operations and Automation Division. Results of the National Automation Survey.

001.64   US
DATAPRO REPORTS ON BANKING AUTOMATION. 1 base vol. (plus bi-m. updates) $580. Datapro Research Corporation (Subsidiary of: McGraw-Hill) 1805 Underwood Blvd., Delran, NJ 08075. TEL 609-764-0100.

332.1   US   ISSN 0741-336X
STANDARD FOR AUDITING COMPUTER APPLICATIONS.* 1984. a. (with s-a. updates) $75. Auerbach Publishers, Inc. (Subsidiary of: International Thomson Organization Ltd.) One Penn Plaza, New York, NY 10119.

BUSINESS AND ECONOMICS — Chamber Of Commerce Publications

382   MR   ISSN 0065-7689
A M C H A M MOROCCO. Cover title: American Chamber of Commerce in Morocco. Annual Review. (Text in English and French) 1966. a. free. American Chamber of Commerce in Morocco, 53 rue Allal Ben Abdallah, Casablanca, Morocco. adv.

963   ET
ADDIS ABABA CHAMBER OF COMMERCE. CHAMBER NEWS. (Text in Amharic and English) 1981. irreg. free. Addis Ababa Chamber of Commerce, Box 2458, Addis Ababa, Ethiopia. Ed. Solomon Asfaow. adv. circ. 2,500.

338   US   ISSN 0145-4048
ALABAMA DIRECTORY OF MINING AND MANUFACTURING. biennial. $35. Development Office, c/o State Capitol, Montgomery, AL 36130. TEL 205-263-0048. Ed. Richard W. McLaney. adv. index. circ. 5,000.
    Supersedes (as of 1976): Industrial Alabama (ISSN 0073-7321)

381   CN
ALBERTA CHAMBER OF COMMERCE. LEGISLATIVE REPORT. 1979. irreg., (24-26/yr.) Can.$65. Alberta Chamber of Commerce, No. 800, 10179-105 St., Edmonton, Alba. T5J 1E2, Canada. Ed. Don Marlett.

382   BL   ISSN 0065-7662
AMERICAN CHAMBER OF COMMERCE FOR BRAZIL. ANNUAL DIRECTORY. 1917. a. membership. American Chamber of Commerce for Brazil, Praca Pio X No. 15, 5th Fl., Caixa Postal 916-ZC-00, 20.001 Rio de Janeiro, Brazil. adv. circ. 1,500.

382   FR   ISSN 0065-7670
AMERICAN CHAMBER OF COMMERCE IN FRANCE. DIRECTORY. 1894. a. 450 F. American Chamber of Commerce in France, 21 Av. George V, 75008 Paris, France. adv. circ. 1,800.
    Incorporating: List of American Firms in France.

382   IT   ISSN 0569-3667
AMERICAN CHAMBER OF COMMERCE IN ITALY. DIRECTORY. 1964. a. L.80000($70) American Chamber of Commerce in Italy, Via Cantu 1, 20123 Milan, Italy. Ed. Gabriella Gabet. adv. circ. 4,500.

382   TH
AMERICAN CHAMBER OF COMMERCE IN THAILAND. HANDBOOK DIRECTORY. biennial. $20. American Chamber of Commerce in Thailand, 140 Wireless Rd., Bangkok, Thailand.

338   US
AMERICAN SUBSIDIARIES OF GERMAN FIRMS. 1968. a. $65 to non-members; members $40. German American Chamber of Commerce, 666 Fifth Ave., New York, NY 10103. TEL 212-974-8830. Ed. Benigna Kirsten. adv. circ. 1,700.

381   FR   ISSN 0066-2798
ANNUAIRE DES CHAMBRES DE COMMERCE ET D'INDUSTRIE. 1963. a. 20 F. Assemblee Permanente des Chambres de Commerce et d'Industrie (APCCI), 45 av. d'Iena, 75116 Paris, France. adv.

330   ML   ISSN 0080-0988
ANNUAIRE DES ENTREPRISES DU MALI. Title varies: Repertoire des Entreprises Financieres, Commerciales Industrielles Exercant en Republique du Mali. 1964. irreg. 150 FM. Chambre de Commerce et d'Industrie du Mali, B.P. 46, Bamako, Mali. circ. 150.

382   ZR
ANNUAIRE DES ENTREPRISES DU ZAIRE. (Text in French) 1984. a. Association Nationale des Entreprises du Zaire, 10 av. des Aviateurs, B.P. 7247, Kinshasa, Zaire. Ed.Bd. adv. circ. 1,500.

382   FR   ISSN 0066-3115
ANNUAIRE FRANCO-ITALIEN. 1963/64. biennial. 150 F. Chambre de Commerce Italienne de Paris, 134 rue du Faubourg Saint-Honore, 75008 Paris, France. adv. circ. 2,000.

650   FR   ISSN 0066-3743
ANNUAIRES FRANCAIS ET LISTES D'ADRESSES SUSCEPTIBLES D'INTERESSER LE COMMERCE ET L'INDUSTRIE. 3rd edt., 1974. irreg. 60 F. Chambre de Commerce et d'Industrie de Paris, 27 av. de Friedland, 75008 Paris, France.

380   CN
ANNUAL SURVEY OF CLERICAL EMPLOYEES. (Text in English and French) 1945. a. Can.$35 to non-members; members Can.$25. Montreal Board of Trade, 1080 Beaver Hall Hill, Montreal, Que. H2Z 1S9, Canada. TEL 514-878-4651. circ. 600.

382   US
ASIAN AMERICAN TRADE DIRECTORY. 1964. irreg. $15. (Association of Asian-American Chambers of Commerce) Seamark Publications (Subsidiary of: Intercontinental Media Services) Box 1933, Washington, DC 20013. adv. bk. rev. film rev. illus. pat. stat. tr.lit. index. circ. 10,000.

970   BF
BAHAMAS. CHAMBER OF COMMERCE. ANNUAL DIRECTORY. (Text in English) 1960. a. $5. Chamber of Commerce, P.O.Box N665, Nassau, Bahamas. Ed. B.J. Clancey-Deveaux. adv. circ. 10,000.

382   US
BELGIAN AMERICAN TRADE DIRECTORY. biennial. $55. Belgian American Chamber of Commerce in the U.S., 350 Fifth Ave., Ste. 703, New York, NY 10118-0110.

381   UK   ISSN 0307-0158
BIRMINGHAM & WEST MIDLANDS CHAMBERS OF COMMERCE DIRECTORY. a. £40. Guardian Communications Ltd., Albany House, Hurst St., Birmingham B5 4BD, England.

380   AG
BOLSA. (Supplements avail.) vol.56, 1960. irreg. $3 per no. Bolsa de Comercio de Buenos Aires, Sarmiento 299, Buenos Aires, Argentina. adv. illus. mkt. stat.
    Formerly: Bolsa de Comercio de Buenos Aires. Boletin (ISSN 0006-6923)

380   AG   ISSN 0006-6931
BOLSA DE COMERCIO DE ROSARIO. REVISTA. 1913. a. free. Bolsa de Comercio de Rosario, Rosario, Santa Fe, Argentina. Ed. Victor M. Cabanellas. adv. mkt. stat. circ. 5,000.

941   UK
BRISTOL CHAMBER OF COMMERCE AND INDUSTRY DIRECTORY. a. £15. (Bristol Chamber of Commerce & Industry) Kemps Group (Printers & Publishers) Ltd., Westbury House, 701-705 Warwick Rd., Solihull West Midlands B91 3DA, England.

947   BU
BULGARIAN CHAMBER OF COMMERCE AND INDUSTRY. STATISTICAL REFERENCE BOOK. a. Bulgarian Chamber of Commerce and Industry, 11-a Stamboliiski Blvd., Sofia, Bulgaria.

BUSINESS AND ECONOMICS — CHAMBER OF COMMERCE PUBLICATIONS

960   SA
C C I YEAR BOOK & DIRECTORY. 1940. a. R.5. Cape Chamber of Industries, Broadway Industries Centre, Heerengracht, Box 1536, Cape Town 8000, South Africa. Ed. C.E. McCarthy. adv. circ. 1,250.

381   VE   ISSN 0008-1876
CAMARA DE COMERCIO DE LA GUAIRA. BOLETIN ESTADISTICO. 1946. a. free. Camara de Comercio de la Guaira, Frente a la Plaza el Consul, Edificio "Camara de Comercio", Maiquetia, Apdo. 150, La Guaira, Venezuela. adv. charts. illus. stat. circ. 2,000.

382   VE
CAMARA VENEZOLANO BRITANICA DE COMERCIO E INDUSTRIA. ANUARIO. (Text in English and Spanish) 1972. a. Bs.35. Camara Venezolano Britanica de Comercio e Industria, Edificio Blandin, Chacaito, Apdo. 5713, Caracas 101, Venezuela. Dir. Teddy A. Phocas. adv. circ. 2,000.
    Formerly: Asociacion Venezolano Britanica de Comercio e Industria. Anuario (ISSN 0084-6848)

381   IT
CAMERA DI COMMERCIO, INDUSTRIA ARTIGIANATO E AGRICOLTURA DI MILANO. SCAMBI COMMERCIALI CON L'ESTERO. a. (in 2 vols.) L.10000 (per vol.) Camera di Commercio Industria Artigianato e Agricoltura di Milano, Via Meravigli, 20123 Milan, Italy. charts. stat.

381   IT
CAMERA DI COMMERCIO, INDUSTRIA, ARTIGIANATO E AGRICOLTURA DI PADOVA. NOTIZIARIO ESTERO. irreg. free. Camera di Commercio, Industria, Artigianato e Agricoltura di Padova, Via E. Filiberto 34, Padua, Italy.

382   UK   ISSN 0309-0329
CANADA-U.K. YEAR BOOK. 1925. a. £10.60. (Canada-U.K. Chamber of Commerce) Rank Zerox Ltd., 2 Brewers Green, Victoria SW1H 0RH, England. Ed. G.F. Bacon. circ. 550.

946.9   SP
CATALOGO DE EXPORTADORES. 1942. irreg. Camara Oficial de Comercio, Industria y Navegacion de Valencia, Poeta Querol 15, Valencia 2, Spain. adv.

946.9   SP
CATALOGO DE IMPORTADORES. 1982. irreg. Camara Oficial de Comercio, Industria y Navegacion de Valencia, Poeta Querol 15, Valencia 2, Spain.

382   SP   ISSN 0069-1178
CATALUNA EXPORTA. 1983. a. 1500 ptas. Camara Oficial de Comercio, Industria y Navegacion de Barcelona, Ample, 11-13, 08002 Barcelona, Spain. circ. 1,000.

381   CN
CENTRE DE COMMERCE MONDIAL DE MONTREAL. REPERTOIRE DES ASSOCIATIONS. 1963. a. Can.$17. Centre de Commerce Mondial de Montreal, 772 rue Sherbrooke Ouest, Montreal, Que. H3A 1G1, Canada. TEL 514-288-9090. Ed. Louise Lauzon. adv. stat. tr.lit. circ. 7,000.

381   CE
CEYLON CHAMBER OF COMMERCE. ANNUAL REVIEW OF BUSINESS AND TRADE. (Text in English) 1839. a. $20. Ceylon Chamber of Commerce, Box 274, 127, Lower Chatham St., Colombo 1, Sri Lanka. Ed.Bd. charts. stat.

381   CE
CEYLON CHAMBER OF COMMERCE. DIRECTORY OF IMPORTERS. (Text in English) 1983. irreg. $15. Ceylon Chamber of Commerce, Chamber of Commerce Bldg., Box 274, Colombo 1, Sri Lanka.

381   CE
CEYLON CHAMBER OF COMMERCE. REGISTER OF MEMBERS. (Text in English) 1981. irreg. $15. Ceylon Chamber of Commerce, Chamber of Commerce Building, Box 274, Colombo 1, Sri Lanka.

380.1   IO
CHAMBER OF COMMERCE AND INDUSTRY IN WEST JAVA. MEMBER LIST/KAMAR DAGANG DAN INDUSTRI DI JAWA BARAT. DAFTAR ANGGOTA. (Text in English and Indonesian) a. Chamber of Commerce and Industry in West Java, Jl. Sunaiaraja 3, Bandung, West Java, Indonesia.

381   SL   ISSN 0080-9527
CHAMBER OF COMMERCE OF SIERRA LEONE. JOURNAL. (Text in English) 1965. a. Le.1.50. Chamber of Commerce of Sierra Leone, P.O. Box 502, Freetown, Sierra Leone. Ed. (Mrs.) F. Iscandari. adv. circ. 1,000.

380.1   PH
CHAMBER OF COMMERCE OF THE PHILIPPINES. TRADE DIRECTORY. a. Chamber of Commerce of the Philippines, Magallanes Drive, Manila 2801, Philippines. illus.

381   UV
CHAMBRE DE COMMERCE, D'INDUSTRIE ET D'ARTISANAT DU BURKINA FASO. ANNUAIRE. 1980. a. free. Chambre de Commerce, d'Industrie et d'Artisanat du Burkina Faso, Box 502, Ouagadougou, Burkina Faso. adv. bk. rev. circ. 2,500.
    Formerly: Chambre de Commerce, d'Artisanat et d'Industrie de Haute-Volta. Annuaire.

380.1   CM
CHAMBRE DE COMMERCE, D'INDUSTRIE ET DES MINES DU CAMEROUN. COMPTE-RENDU D'ACTIVITES. irreg. Chambre de Commerce, d'Industrie et des Mines du Cameroun, B.P. 4011, Douala, Cameroon.

381 330   ML   ISSN 0067-3110
CHAMBRE DE COMMERCE ET D'INDUSTRIE DU MALI. PRECIS FISCAL, COMMERCIAL, DES CHANGES ET DES ECHANGES. 1964. a. price varies. ‡ Chambre de Commerce et d'Industrie du Mali, B.P. 46, Bamako, Mali. circ. 200.

382   FR   ISSN 0069-2557
CHAMBRE DE COMMERCE FRANCO-ASIATIQUE. ANNUAIRE DES MEMBRES. (Special number of: Asie Nouvelle) 1968. a. Chambre de Commerce Franco-Asiatique, 94 rue St. Lazare, 75009 Paris, France.

382   FR   ISSN 0069-2565
CHAMBRE DE COMMERCE JAPONAISE EN FRANCE. ANNUAIRE.* 1967/68. a. Chambre de Commerce Japonaise en France, 1 av. Friedland, 75008 Paris, France.

382   FR   ISSN 0069-2581
CHAMBRE OFFICIELLE FRANCO ALLEMANDE DE COMMERCE ET D'INDUSTRIE. LISTE DES MEMBRES/OFFIZIELLE DEUTSCH-FRANZOESISCHE INDUSTRIE- UND HANDELSKAMMER. MITGLIDERLISTE. 1966. a. 60 Fr. Chambre Officielle Franco Allemande de Commerce et d'Industrie, 18 rue Balard, 75015 Paris, France.

381   FR
CHAMBRE REGIONALE DE COMMERCE ET D'INDUSTRIE D'ALSACE. RAPPORT SUR LES ACTIVITES. a. Chambre Regionale de Commerce et d'Industrie d'Alsace, 10, Place Gutenberg, 67081 Strasbourg, France.

CHRISTIAN CHAMBER OF COMMERCE. CLASSIFIED MEMBERSHIP DIRECTORY. see *ADVERTISING AND PUBLIC RELATIONS*

382   FR
COMMERCE EXTERIEUR DES REGIONS PROVENCE, COTE D'AZUR ET CORSE. 1968. a. 15 F. per no. Chambre de Commerce et d'Industrie de Marseille, Palais de la Bourse, 13231 Marseille Cedex 1, France. Ed. A.L. Paul. illus. circ. 2,000.

381   CK
CONFEDERACION COLOMBIANA DE CAMARAS DE COMERCIO. ASAMBLEA GENERAL. INFORME FINAL.* 1970. irreg. free. Confederacion Colombiana de Camaras de Comercio, Carrera 13, no. 27-47, Oficina 502, Apdo. 29750, Bogota, Colombia. circ. 1,000.

980   ES
DIRECTORIO COMERCIAL E INDUSTRIAL. (Text and summaries in English and Spanish) 1970. a. $12. (Camara de Comercio e Industria de El Salvador) Ediciones Culturales Publicitarias, S.A., 57 Avenida Norte No. 114, Colonia Escalon, San Salvador, El Salvador (Subscr. to: 9a Avenida Norte y 5a, Calle Poniente, San Salvador) adv. index. circ. 2,000.

381   CE
DIRECTORY OF EXPORTERS. (Text in English) 1975. a. $20. Ceylon Chamber of Commerce, Export Section, Chamber of Commerce Bldg., Box 274, Colombo 1, Sri Lanka. adv.

954 670   CE
DIRECTORY OF GARMENT MANUFACTURERS. (Text in English) 1979. a. $8. Ceylon Chamber of Commerce, Chamber of Commerce Bldg., Box 274, Colombo 1, Sri Lanka.

381   UK
DUNDEE AND TAYSIDE CHAMBER OF COMMERCE AND INDUSTRY. BUYER'S GUIDE AND TRADE DIRECTORY. 1958. a. £6. Dundee and Tayside Chamber of Commerce and Industry, Panmure St., Dundee DD1 1ED, Scotland. Ed. W.D. Shaw. adv. circ. 1,800 (controlled)
    Formerly: Dundee Chamber of Commerce. Buyer's Guide and Trade Directory.

381   UK   ISSN 0263-404X
EAST MIDLANDS CHAMBERS OF COMMERCE REGIONAL DIRECTORY. 1983. a. £38. Guardian Communications Ltd., Albany House, Hurst St., Birmingham B5 4BD, England.

330.9   SP   ISSN 0568-8876
ECONOMIA ALAVESA. a. 1350 ptas. Camara Oficial de Comercio e Industria de Alava, Dato 38, Vitoria, Spain. Ed. D. Lorenzo Bergareche Capa. index. circ. 1,000.

941   UK
EDINBURGH CHAMBER OF COMMERCE AND MANUFACTURES DIRECTORY. 1948. a. £2.90. Edinburgh Chamber of Commerce and Manufactures, 3 Randolph Crescent, Edinburgh EH3 7UD, Scotland.

330   ML   ISSN 0071-0008
ELEMENTS DU BILAN ECONOMIQUE. 1961. irreg., latest issue, 1965. ‡ Chambre de Commerce et d'Industrie du Mali, B.P. 46, Bamako, Mali. circ. 200.

960   IV
L'ENTREPRISE IVOIRIENNE. a. Chambre d'Industrie de Cote d'Ivoire, B.P. 1758, Abidjan, Ivory Coast.

963   ET
ETHIOPIAN CHAMBER OF COMMERCE. STATISTICAL DIGEST. 1967. a. $2.45. Ethiopian Chamber of Commerce, Box 517, Addis Ababa, Ethiopia. (reprint service avail. from ISI)

381   PK   ISSN 0071-4429
FEDERATION OF PAKISTAN CHAMBERS OF COMMERCE INDUSTRY. BRIEF REPORT OF ACTIVITIES. (Text in English) a. Rs.100. Federation of Pakistan Chambers of Commerce and Industry, St-28, Block 5, Scheme-V, Share-Firdousi Kehkashan, Clifton, Karachi, Pakistan.

975   US
FLORIDA AND THE OTHER FORTY-NINE. 1976. a. free. Department of Commerce, Secretary of Commerce, 107 W. Gaines St., Tallahassee, FL 32301. TEL 904-488-1234. stat. circ. controlled.

975   US
FLORIDA COUNTY COMPARISONS. 1980. a. free. Department of Commerce, Secretary of Commerce, 107 W. Gaines St., Tallahassee, FL 32301. TEL 904-488-1234. stat. circ. controlled.

975   US
FLORIDA COUNTY PROFILES. 1979. a. free. Department of Commerce, Secretary of Commerce, 107 W. Gaines St., Tallahassee, FL 32301. TEL 904-488-1234. stat. circ. controlled.
    Formerly: Florida Community-County Comparison.

BUSINESS AND ECONOMICS — CHAMBER OF COMMERCE PUBLICATIONS

975　　　　　　　　US
FLORIDA ECONOMY; its growth and development. 1977. biennial. free. Department of Commerce, Secretary of Commerce, 107 W. Gaines St., Tallahassee, FL 32301. TEL 904-488-1234. stat. circ. controlled.
　　Formerly (1977-1986): Florida's Economy.

382　　　　　　　　FR
FRANCO-BRITISH CHAMBER OF COMMERCE AND INDUSTRY. YEAR BOOK. 1874. a. 200 F. Franco-British Chamber of Commerce and Industry, 8 rue Cimarosa, 75016 Paris, France. adv. circ. 2,000.
　　Formerly: British Chamber of Commerce in France. Year Book (ISSN 0068-1415)

382　　　　UK　　ISSN 0071-917X
FRANCO BRITISH TRADE DIRECTORY. 1883. a. £40. French Chamber of Commerce in Great Britain, 54 Conduit St., London W.1., England. Ed. R. Clark. circ. 2,000.

382　　　　UA　　ISSN 0072-1433
GERMAN ARAB TRADE. irreg. membership. Deutsch-Arabische Handelskammer - German-Arab Chamber of Commerce, 2 Sherif St., Cairo, Egypt.

382　　　　　　　　TH
GERMAN-THAI CHAMBER OF COMMERCE HANDBOOK. a. $6. German-Thai Chamber of Commerce, 699 Silom Rd., Kongboonma Bldg., Bangkok, Thailand. Ed. Wayne Morrison.

380　　　　　　　　UK
GLASGOW CHAMBER OF COMMERCE. ANNUAL REPORT. a. Glasgow Chamber of Commerce, 30 George Sq., Glasgow G2 1EQ, Scotland. Ed.Bd. charts. illus.

380.1　　　　　　　　SW
GOTHENBURG AND WESTERN SWEDEN CHAMBER OF COMMERCE. MEMBERSHIP DIRECTORY. 1953. irreg., latest 1986. free. Gothenburg and Western Sweden Chamber of Commerce - Vaestsvenska Handelskammaren, Box 5253, S-402 25 Goethenburg, Sweden. adv. circ. 5,000.
　　Formerly: Trade Directory of Western Sweden.

949.5　　　　　　　　GR
GREEK EXPORT DIRECTORY. (Text in English) 1970. triennial. free. Athens Chamber of Commerce and Industry, 7 Acadimias St., 106 71 Athens, Greece. adv. illus. circ. 5,000.

380　　　　　　　　SP
GUIA DEL COMERCIO Y DE LA INDUSTRIA (YEAR) 1960. biennial. 5000 ptas.($31) Camara Oficial de Comercio e Industria de Madrid, Huertas 13, 28012 Madrid, Spain. adv. circ. 2,000.
　　Former titles (until 1980): Guia del Comercio y de la Industria de Madrid (ISSN 0528-2438); Catalogo de la Industria de Madrid.

382　　　　FR　　ISSN 0072-7962
GUIDE ANNUAIRE DU COMMERCE FRANCO-ALLEMAND/JAHRBUCH FUER DEN DEUTSCH-FRANZOESISCHEN HANDEL.* (Text in French and German) 1961/62. irreg., 2nd edt., 1965. Chambre Officielle Franco Allemande de Commerce et d'Industrie, 18 rue Balard, 75015 Paris, France.

381　　　　　　　　US
HERE IS YOUR INDIANA GOVERNMENT. 1944. biennial. $4. Indiana State Chamber of Commerce, One North Capitol, Ste. 200, Indianapolis, IN 46204. TEL 317-634-6407. Ed. Carl Henn. circ. 20,000.

380.1　　　　　　　　HK
HONG KONG JUNIOR CHAMBER. ANNUAL REVIEW.* a. Hong Kong Junior Chamber, 23 Ice House St., Hong Kong, Hong Kong. illus.

382　330.1　　　　　　　FR
I C C ANNUAL REVIEW. (Editions in English, French, German and Spanish) 1977. a. International Chamber of Commerce, 38 Cours Albert 1er, 75008 Paris, France. TEL 1-45 62 34 56. illus.

338　380　　　　　　　GW
INDUSTRIE- UND HANDELSKAMMER HANNOVER-HILDESHEIM. YEARBOOK - INFORMATION KOMMENTAIRE. 1949. a. free. Industrie- und Handelskammer Hannover-Hildesheim, Schiffgraben 49, 3000 Hannover 1, W. Germany (B.R.D.) Ed. Wolfram Linsenmann. adv. bk. rev. stat. tr.lit. index. circ. 13,000.
　　Formerly: Industrie- und Handelskammer Hannover-Hildesheim. Information-Kommentaire.

946.9　　　　SP　　ISSN 0211-8734
INFORME ECONOMICO REGIONAL. 1972. a. 500 ptas. Camara Oficial de Comercio, Industria y Navegacion de Valencia, Poeta Querol 15, Valencia 2, Spain. (Co-sponsors: Camaras de Comercio, Industria y Navegacion de Alcoy, Alicante, Castellon, Orihuela) Ed. Federico Domenech. bk. rev. circ. 1,000.

380.1　　　　　　　　FR
INTERNATIONAL CHAMBER OF COMMERCE. HANDBOOK. (Editions in English and French) a. International Chamber of Commerce, 38 Cours Albert 1er, 75008 Paris, France. TEL 1-45 62 34 56.

382　　　　　　　　IR
IRAN CHAMBER OF COMMERCE, INDUSTRIES AND MINES. DIRECTORY. biennial. Iran Chamber of Commerce, Industries and Mines, 254 Takht Jamshid Ave., Teheran, Iran.

330　　　　JM　　ISSN 0021-4094
JAMAICA CHAMBER OF COMMERCE JOURNAL. vol.29, 1973. irreg. free. (Jamaica Chamber of Commerce) Cara Publications Ltd., Box 172, 7-8 East Parade, Kingston, Jamaica, W. Indies. Ed. Avis Henriques. adv. bk. rev. illus. circ. 2,000.

381　　　　　　　　NE
KAMER VAN KOOPHANDEL EN FABRIEKEN VOOR AMSTERDAM. JAARREDE. 1812. a. Kamer van Koophandel en Fabrieken voor Amsterdam - Chamber of Commerce, Koningin Wilhelminaplein 13, 1062 HH Amsterdam, Netherlands. circ. 5,000.

338　　　　PK　　ISSN 0075-5079
KARACHI. CHAMBER OF COMMERCE AND INDUSTRY. ANNUAL REPORT. (Text in English) a. free. Chamber of Commerce and Industry, Aiwan-e-Tijarat, Box 4158, Nicol Rd., Karachi 2, Pakistan.
　　Formrely: Karachi. Chamber of Commerce and Industry. Report.

380.1　　　　　　　　KE
KENYA NATIONAL CHAMBER OF COMMERCE AND INDUSTRY. ANNUAL REPORT. a. Kenya National Chamber of Commerce and Industry, Nairobi, Kenya. stat.

941　　　　　　　　UK
LANCASHIRE CHAMBERS OF COMMERCE & INDUSTRY DIRECTORY. a. £15. (Lancashire Chambers of Commerce) Kemps Group (Printers & Publishers) Ltd., Westbury House, 701-705 Warwick Rd., Solihull, West Midlands B91 3DA, England.

977　　　　　　　　US
LARGE EMPLOYERS DIRECTORY OF METROPOLITAN ST. LOUIS. 1957. biennial. $30. St. Louis Regional Commerce and Growth Association, 10 Broadway, St. Louis, MO 63102. TEL 314-231-5555. Ed. W.M. Julius. circ. 3,600.

381　　　　　　　　UK
LEEDS. CHAMBER OF COMMERCE AND INDUSTRY. CLASSIFIED TRADE DIRECTORY OF MEMBERS. a. £6.50. Chamber of Commerce and Industry, 2 St. Alban's Place, Wade Lane, Leeds LS2 8HZ, England. Ed. R.G. Taylor. circ. 2,500.

381　　　　　　　　UK
LEEDS CHAMBERS OF COMMERCE & INDUSTRY DIRECTORY. a. £35. Guardian Communications Ltd., Albany House, Hurst St., Birmingham B5 4BD, England.

LIVING IN VENEZUELA. see *TRAVEL AND TOURISM*

381　　　　　　　　UK
LONDON CHAMBER OF COMMERCE. ANNUAL REVIEW. 1882. a. membership. London Chamber of Commerce, 69 Cannon St., London, EC4N 5AB, England. adv. circ. 8,200.
　　Formerly: London Chamber of Commerce and Industry. Annual Review.

381　　　　UK　　ISSN 0142-9728
LONDON CHAMBER OF COMMERCE AND INDUSTRY. DIRECTORY. 1882. a. £40. Guardian Communications Ltd., Albany House, Hurst St., Birmingham B5 4BD, England. adv.
　　Formerly: London Chamber of Commerce and Industry. Annual Report and Annual Directory (ISSN 0076-0528)

974　　　　　　　　US
MADISON, CONNECTICUT - A PICTORIAL GUIDE. 1982. biennial. Madison Chamber of Commerce, Inc., 786 Boston Post Rd., Box 953, Madison, CT 06443. TEL 203-245-8211. Ed. Margaret M. Sprague. adv. illus. circ. 10,000.

976　　　　　　　　US
MAJOR EMPLOYERS DIRECTORY. a. $7 per no. Birmingham Area Chamber of Commerce, 600 Commerce Center, 2027 First Ave. N., Birmingham, AL 35202. TEL 205-323-5461.

381　　　　　　　　UK
MANCHESTER CHAMBER OF COMMERCE AND INDUSTRY. REGIONAL BUSINESS DIRECTORY. (Text in English, French and German, Spanish) a. (Manchester Chamber of Commerce and Industry) Kemps Group (Printers & Publishers) Ltd., Westbury House, 701-705 Warwick Rd., Solihull, West Midlands B91 3DA, England. adv. illus. tr.lit.

380.1　　　　UK　　ISSN 0306-5758
MANCHESTER CHAMBER OF COMMERCE AND INDUSTRY. YEARBOOK.* (Text in English, French and German) a. (Manchester Chamber of Commerce and Industry) Kemps Group (Printers & Publishers) Ltd., 1-5 Bath St., London EC1V 9QA, Englang. illus.

967　　　　　　　　MF
MAURITIUS CHAMBER OF COMMERCE AND INDUSTRY. ANNUAL REPORT. (Text in English) 1950. a. free. Mauritius Chamber of Commerce and Industry, 3 Royal Street, Port Louis, Mauritius. TEL 08-3301. Ed.Bd. circ. 800.

380.1　　　　UK　　ISSN 0302-4148
MERSEYSIDE CHAMBER OF COMMERCE AND INDUSTRY. DIRECTORY. a. £23. Industrial Newspapers Ltd., Queensway House, Queensway, Redhill, Surrey RH1 1QS, England (Distr. by: Guardian Communications Ltd., Albany House, Hurst St., Birmingham B5 4BD, England) (reprint service avail. from UMI)

382　　　　　　　　US
MOBILE AREA CHAMBER OF COMMERCE MEMBERSHIP DIRECTORY AND BUYER'S GUIDE. a. $20 to non-members. ‡ Mobile Area Chamber of Commerce, Box 2187, Mobile, AL 36652. TEL 205-433-6951. Ed. Walter A. Underwood. adv. circ. 5,000.
　　Formerly (since 1979): Who's Who in the Mobile Area.

382　　　　　　　　NE
NETHERLANDS-AMERICAN TRADE DIRECTORY. (Text in English) 1969. biennial. fl.160($70) to members; non-members fl. 210 ($93) American Chamber of Commerce in the Netherlands, Carnegieplein 5, The Hague, Netherlands.

382　　　　UK　　ISSN 0308-1273
NETHERLANDS-BRITISH TRADE DIRECTORY. 1961. a. £15 to non-members. Netherlands-British Chamber of Commerce, The Dutch House, 307/308 High Holborn, London WC1V 7LS, England. adv. circ. 5,000.

974　　　　　　　　US
NIAGARA FALLS AREA CHAMBER OF COMMERCE.BUSINESS/INDUSTRIAL DIRECTORY. a. $15. Niagara Falls Area Chamber of Commerce, 345 Third St., Niagara Falls, NY 14303. TEL 716-285-9141. Ed. Fred Caso. circ. 2,000.

BUSINESS AND ECONOMICS — CHAMBER OF COMMERCE PUBLICATIONS

380 NR ISSN 0189-5036
NIGERIAN BUSINESS JOURNAL. (Text in English) 1950. a. £N.10. Lagos Chamber of Commerce and Industry, 1 Idowu Taylor St., Victoria Island, P.O. Box 109, Lagos, Nigeria. Ed. S.B. Akande. adv. bk. rev. circ. 5,000.
Formerly: Commerce in Nigeria (ISSN 0069-6633)

338 UK
NORTH WEST ENGLAND DIRECTORY OF INDUSTRY AND COMMERCE. a. $45. Kemps Group (Printers & Publishers) Ltd., Westbury House, 701-705 Warwick Rd., Solihull, West Midlands B91 3DA, England. adv. illus. tr.lit.
Formerly: North West England Industrial Classified Directory (ISSN 0260-0587)

382 UK ISSN 0305-0998
NORWEGIAN CHAMBER OF COMMERCE. YEAR BOOK AND DIRECTORY OF MEMBERS. (Text in English) 1908. a. free to members. ‡ Norwegian Chamber of Commerce (London) Inc., 21-24 Cockspur St., London S.W.1, England. Ed. Oeystein Grahammm-Flateboe. adv. circ. 1,800.

941 UK ISSN 0261-880X
NORWICH AND NORFOLK CHAMBER OF COMMERCE AND INDUSTRY. DIRECTORY. 1981. a. £5. Norwich and Norfolk Chamber of Commerce, 112 Barrack St., Norwich, Norfolk NR3 1UB, England. Ed. Jan Jeeves. adv. illus. circ. 3,500.

330 GW ISSN 0720-4868
OSTSEEJAHRBUCH. 1934. a. price varies. Industrie- und Handelskammer zu Luebeck, Breite Strasse 6-8, 2400 Luebeck, W. Germany (B.R.D.) Ed. Hans-Jochen Arndt. circ. 1,200.
Former title: Wirtschaft im Ostseeraum (ISSN 0084-0483)

338 PK
PAKISTAN DIRECTORY OF TRADE AND INDUSTRY. (Text in English) 1976. a. Lahore Chamber of Commerce and Industry, P.O. Box 597, 11 Aiwan-i-Tijarat, Lahore, Pakistan.

381 US
PENNSYLVANIA CHAMBER OF COMMERCE. STATE & REGIONAL DIRECTORY. a. $13.25. Pennsylvania Chamber of Commerce, 222 N. Third St., Harrisburg, PA 17101. TEL 717-255-3258. Ed. John Eichorn. circ. 650.
Formerly: Pennsylvania Chamber of Commerce. Directory of State, Regional and Commercial Organizations (ISSN 0098-5368)

330.9 SP
PROVINCIA DE ZARAGOZA. INFORME ECONOMICO. a. price varies. Camara Oficial de Comercio e Industria de Zaragoza, D. Jaime I No. 18, Zaragoza 1, Spain. circ. 1,000.
Formerly (until 1976): Desarrollo Industrial y Mercantil en la Provincia de Zaragoza.

381 US ISSN 0033-6068
QUEENSBOROUGH. 1914. a. membership. Queens Chamber of Commerce, 29-15 Bridge Plaza N., Long Island City, NY 11101. adv. illus. circ. 1,500.

330 FR
REGARDS SUR L'ECONOMIE DE LA HAUTE-NORMANDIE. 1984. a. 50 F. Chambre Regionale de Commerce et d'Industrie de Haute-Normandie, Palais des Consuls, Quai de la Bourse, Rouen, France. Ed. Robert Querret. adv. circ. 1,500.
Formerly: Activite Economique de la Haute-Normandie (ISSN 0065-1788)

946.9 SP ISSN 0211-8866
REGION EXPORTA; Alicante, Castellon, Valencia. 1973. a. 500 ptas. Camara Oficial de Comercio, Industria y Navegacion de Valencia, Poeta Querol 15, Valencia 2, Spain. (Co-sponsors: Camaras Oficiales de Comercio, Industria y Navegacion de Alcoy, Alicante, Castellon, Orihuela)

381 330 ML ISSN 0080-1011
REPERTOIRE DES PRINCIPAUX TEXTES LEGISLATIFS ET REGLEMENTAIRES PROMULGUES EN REPUBLIQUE DU MALI. 1959. a. ‡ Chambre de Commerce et d'Industrie du Mali, B.P. 46, Bamako, Mali. circ. 100.

382 BL
SAO PAULO YEARBOOK. 1946. a. $43. American Chamber of Commerce for Brazil, Praca Pio X no. 15, 5th Fl., Caixa Postal 916-ZC-00, 20.001 Rio de Janeiro, Brazil. Ed. Diana Slusser. adv. circ. 2,500.

380 UK
SCOTLAND CHAMBERS OF COMMERCE. DIRECTORY. a. £25. Glasgow Chamber of Commerce, 30 George Square, Glasgow G2 1EQ, Scotland. adv. index. circ. 10,000.
Former titles: Glasgow Chamber of Commerce. Regional Directory & Glasgow Chamber of Commerce. Industrial Index to Glasgow & West of Scotland.

338.9 UK ISSN 0266-5441
SCOTLINK. 1959. a. free. Junior Chamber Scotland, 31 Woodlands Rd., Kirkcawy, Fife KY2 5YU, Scotland. (Affiliate: Jaycees International) Ed. Neil M. Bruce. adv. circ. 2,000.
Formerly: Scotland Tomorrow (ISSN 0080-7923)

941 UK
SCOTTISH CHAMBERS OF COMMERCE NATIONAL DIRECTORY. a. £18. (Scottish Chamber of Commerce) Kemps Group (Printers & Publishers) Ltd., Westbury House, 701-705 Warwick Rd., Solihull, West Midlands B91 3DA, England.
Formerly: Glasgow Chamber of Commerce and Manufactures Regional Directory.

381 UK
SHEFFIELD & SOUTH YORKSHIRE CHAMBERS OF COMMERCE DIRECTORY. a. £32. Guardian Communications Ltd., Albany House, Hurst St., Birmingham B5 4BD, England. (Co-sponsor: South Yorkshire Chamber of Commerce)

382 SI ISSN 0377-449X
SINGAPORE INTERNATIONAL CHAMBER OF COMMERCE. ANNUAL REPORT. 1837. a. S.$30 per no. ‡ Singapore International Chamber of Commerce, 6 Raffles Quay, 05-00, Denmark House, Singapore 0104, Singapore. Ed. Roderick Maclean. stat. circ. 1,000.
Formerly: Singapore International Chamber of Commerce. Report (ISSN 0583-3736)

382 SI
SINGAPORE INTERNATIONAL CHAMBER OF COMMERCE. EXPATRIATE LIVING COSTS IN SINGAPORE. (Text in English) 1970. irreg. S.$6 per no. Singapore International Chamber of Commerce, 6 Raffles Quay, 05-00, Denmark House, Singapore 0104, Singapore. Ed. Roderick Maclean. circ. 5,000.

382 SI
SINGAPORE INTERNATIONAL CHAMBER OF COMMERCE. INVESTORS GUIDE TO THE ECONOMIC CLIMATE OF SINGAPORE. (Text in English) 1973. a. S.$15 per no. Singapore International Chamber of Commerce, 6 Raffles Quay, 05-00, Denmark House, Singapore 0104, Singapore. charts. stat.
Formerly: Singapore International Chamber of Commerce. Investor's Guide (ISSN 0129-5276)

338 UK
SOUTH BUCKS & EAST BERKS CHAMBER OF COMMERCE & INDUSTRY DIRECTORY. a. £18. Kemps Group (Printers & Publishers) Ltd., Westbury House, 701-705 Warwick Rd., Solihull, West Midlands B91 3DA, England. adv. illus. tr.lit.

338 UK
SOUTHAMPTON CHAMBER OF COMMERCE REGIONAL DIRECTORY. a. $45. Kemps Group (Printers & Publishers) Ltd., Westbury House, 701-705 Warwick Rd., Solihull, West Midlands B91 3DA, England.

SOUTHERN CALIFORNIA BUSINESS DIRECTORY AND BUYERS GUIDE. see BUSINESS AND ECONOMICS — Trade And Industrial Directories

338 UK
SOUTHERN HOME COUNTIES CHAMBER OF COMMERCE DIRECTORY. a. $45. Kemps Group (Printers & Publishers) Ltd., Westbury House, 701-705 Warwick Rd., Solihull, West Midlands B91 3DA, England.
Former titles: Southern Home Counties Directory & Croydon Chamber of Commerce and Industry Directory (ISSN 0144-2996)

381 CE
SRI LANKA IN BRIEF. (Text in English) 1977. a. $5. Ceylon Chamber of Commerce, Chamber of Commerce Bldg., Box 274, Colombo 1, Sri Lanka.

650 380 JA ISSN 0585-0444
STANDARD TRADE INDEX OF JAPAN. Title varies: Japan Register of Merchants, Manufacturers and Shippers. (Text in English) 1957. a. $164. Japan Chamber of Commerce and Industry, Rm. 505, World Trade Center Bldg., 4-1 Himamatsu-cho 2-chome, Minato-ku, Tokyo 105, Japan.

382.5 II ISSN 0537-1120
SURVEY OF INDIA'S EXPORTS. (Text in English) 1962. a. Rs.25. Indian Chamber of Commerce, Calcutta, World Trade Department, India Exchange, 4 India Exchange Place, Calcutta 700001, India. adv. circ. 500.

380 US ISSN 0069-2441
SURVEY OF LOCAL CHAMBERS OF COMMERCE. biennial. $30. Chamber of Commerce of the U.S., 1615 H St., N.W., Washington, DC 20062. TEL 202-659-6000.

382 US ISSN 0502-5842
UNITED STATES-ITALY TRADE DIRECTORY. 1950. a. $90. Italy-America Chamber of Commerce, Inc., 350 Fifth Ave., New York, NY 10118. TEL 212-279-5520. adv. circ. 4,000.

970 CN
VANCOUVER BOARD OF TRADE ROSTER AND PURCHASERS' GUIDE. a. Can.$50. (Vancouver Board of Trade) Naylor Communications, 124 W. 8th St., N. Vancouver, B.C., Canada.

382 VE
VENEZUELAN - AMERICAN CHAMBER OF COMMERCE AND INDUSTRY. YEARBOOK AND MEMBERSHIP DIRECTORY. 1961. a. Bs.200($30) Venezuelan-American Chamber of Commerce and Industry - Camara Venezolano Americana de Comercio e Industria, Apdo. 5181, Caracas 1010A, Venezuela. adv. circ. 3,000. (reprint service avail. from UMI)
Formerly: American Chamber of Commerce of Venezuela. Yearbook and Membership Directory (ISSN 0065-7697)

338 UK
WALES BUSINESS DIRECTORY. a. $45. (Federation of Welsh Chambers of Commerce Inc. & Welsh Development Agency) Kemps Group (Printers & Publishers) Ltd., Westbury House, 701-705 Warwick Rd., Solihull, West Midlands B91 3DA, England.
Formerly: Available from Wales.

338 UK
WALSALL CHAMBER OF COMMERCE & INDUSTRY DIRECTORY. a. Kemps Group (Printers & Publishers) Ltd., Westbury House, 701-705 Warwick Rd., Solihull, West Midland B91 3DA, England.

975 US
WEST VIRGINIA: AN ECONOMIC-STATISTICAL PROFILE. 1982. irreg. (every 3-4 yrs) $50. West Virginia Chamber of Commerce, Box 2789, Charleston, WV 25330. TEL 304-342-1115. stat. circ. 1,500. (back issues avail.)

338 UK
WESTMINSTER CHAMBER OF COMMERCE DIRECTORY. a. $45. Kemp's Group (Printers & Publishers) Ltd., Westbury House, 701-705 Warwick Rd., Solihull, West Midlands B91 3DA, England. illus.
Formerly: City of Westminster Chamber of Commerce Directory.

381 AT
WHO'S WHO IN U.S. BUSINESS IN AUSTRALIA. 1974. a. Aus.$48.50. American Chamber of Commerce in Australia, 50 Pitt St., Third Floor, Sydney, N.S.W. 2000, Australia. Ed. K. Bannon. adv. circ. 2,000.

380 US ISSN 0084-2478
WORLD WIDE CHAMBER OF COMMERCE DIRECTORY. 1967. a. $15.50. Johnson Publishing Co. (Loveland), 504 W. Eisenhower, Box 1029, Loveland, CO 80537. TEL 303-663-3231. circ. 8,000.

BUSINESS AND ECONOMICS —
Computer Applications

658　001.6　　　　　US
BETRIEBS- UND WIRTSCHAFTSINFORMATIK. irreg., vol.11, 1984. Springer-Verlag, 175 Fifth Ave., New York, NY 10010 TEL 212-460-1500. (And Berlin, Heidelberg, Tokyo and Vienna) Ed.Bd.

338　001.6　　　FR　ISSN 0294-0701
GUIDE EUROPEEN DES PROGICIELS. Added title: G.E.P.L. 1976. a. 2107.92 F. Centre d'Experimentation des Progiciels (CXP), 5 rue de Monceau, 75008 Paris, France.
　　Formerly: Guide Europeen des Produits Logiciels (ISSN 0395-2061)

I E E E SYMPOSIUM ON MASS STORAGE SYSTEMS. DIGEST OF PAPERS. see *COMPUTERS*

001.6　330　　　UK　ISSN 0308-9541
JOURNAL OF APPLIED SYSTEMS ANALYSIS. 1969. a. £10($22) to individuals; £20($36) to institutions. University of Lancaster, Department of Systems, Bailrigg, Lancaster LA1 4YX, England. Ed. P.B. Checkland. bk. rev. charts. stat. circ. 500. (also avail. in microfilm from UMI; reprint service avail. from UMI) Indexed: Chem.Abstr. Sci.Abstr. Anbar. BMT. Oper.Res.Manage.Sci. Ergon.Abstr.
　　Formerly (until vol.5, no.1, Nov. 1976): Journal of Systems Engineering (ISSN 0022-4820)

JYVASKYLA STUDIES IN COMPUTER SCIENCE, ECONOMICS AND STATISTICS. see *COMPUTERS*

658　　　　　NE　ISSN 0378-3766
NORTH-HOLLAND/T I M S STUDIES IN THE MANAGEMENT SCIENCES. Title varies: T I M S Studies in Management Science. (Text in English) 1975. irreg., vol.21, 1985. price varies. Elsevier Science Publishers B.V., Box 211, 1000 AE Amsterdam, Netherlands. Ed. R.E. Machol. bibl. charts. (also avail. in microfilm from MIM) Indexed: Intl.Abstr.Oper.Res.

BUSINESS AND ECONOMICS —
Cooperatives

ALTERNATIVE TRADING NEWS. see *BUSINESS AND ECONOMICS — International Development And Assistance*

334　　　　US　ISSN 0065-793X
AMERICAN COOPERATION YEARBOOK.* 1925. a. $14.50 hardcover; softcover $12. American Institute of Cooperation, 50 F St., N.W., Ste. 900, Washington, DC 20001. TEL 202-296-6825. Ed. Mary Kay Bidlack. index. circ. 4,750.

334　　　　　FR　ISSN 0071-4356
ANNUAIRE DE LA COOPERATION F.N.C.C. 1914. irreg., latest 1984. 10 F. (Federation Nationale des Cooperatives de Consommateurs) Societe Cooperative d'Edition et de Librairie, 27-33 Quai Le Gallo, 92100 Boulogne sur Seine, France. Ed. E. Deslandes. circ. 600.

334　　　　　BS
BOTSWANA. MINISTRY OF AGRICULTURE. DIVISION OF CO-OPERATIVE DEVELOPMENT. ANNUAL REPORT. a. Ministry of Agriculture, Division of Co-Operative Development, Private Bag 0033, Gaborone, Botswana. illus. stat.

334　　　　　FR
CAISSE CENTRALE DE COOPERATION ECONOMIQUE. RAPPORT ANNUEL. 1947. a. free. Caisse Centrale de Cooperation Economique, Cite du Retiro, 35-37 rue Boissy d'Anglas, 75379 Paris Cedex 08, France. illus. circ. 8,000.
　　Formerly: Caisse Centrale de Cooperation Economique. Rapport d'Activite (ISSN 0575-1632)

CO-OPERATIVE COMMUNICATIONS. see *AGRICULTURE — Agricultural Economics*

334　　　　　UK
CO-OPERATIVE STATISTICS. 1879. a. £50. Co-operative Union Ltd., Holyoake House, Hanover St., Manchester M60 0AS, England. circ. 700.

334　　　II　ISSN 0069-9837
COOPERATIVE TRADE DIRECTORY FOR SOUTHEAST ASIA. (Text in English) 1964. irreg., 3rd edt, 1970. supplement. Rs.20($3) per set. International Co-Operative Alliance, Regional Office and Education Centre for South-East Asia, Box 3312, 43 Friends Colony, New Delhi 110014, India. Ed. M.V. Madane. circ. 300.

CREDIT UNION DIRECTORY AND BUYERS' GUIDE. see *BUSINESS AND ECONOMICS — Banking And Finance*

CREDIT UNION NATIONAL ASSOCIATION. CREDIT UNION REPORT. see *BUSINESS AND ECONOMICS — Banking And Finance*

CREDIT UNION YEARBOOK. see *BUSINESS AND ECONOMICS — Banking And Finance*

330.9　　　　UN
CUADERNOS DE LA C E P A L. (Text in Spanish; occasionally in English) 1981. irreg., latest no.54, 1986. price varies. Comision Economica para America Latina (CEPAL), Casilla 179-D, Santiago, Chile (Subscr. to: United Nations Publications, Sales Section, Rm. DC2-0853, New York, NY 10017; or DIstribution and Sales Section, Palais des Nations, 1211 Geneva 10, Switzerland) (back issues avail.)

334　　　　　CS
CZECHOSLOVAK COOPERATIVE MOVEMENT IN FIGURES. 1957. a. free. Ustredni Rada Druzstev, Tesnov 5, 110 06 Prague 1, Czechoslovakia. charts. stat. circ. 5,000.

334　　　　　CK
DIRECTORIO NACIONAL DE ENTIDADES COOPERATIVOS. irreg. Departamento Administrativo Nacional de Estadistica, Division de Edicion, Avda. Eldovado, Bogota, Colombia.

FARM CREDIT ADMINISTRATION. ANNUAL REPORT. see *AGRICULTURE — Agricultural Economics*

334　658.8　　　SZ　ISSN 0071-4410
FEDERATION OF MIGROS COOPERATIVES. ANNUAL REPORT; Report of the Board of Directors to the Assembly of Delegates. (Editions in English, French, German, Italian) 1941 French and German edts., 1956 English edt., 1982 Italian edt. a. free. ‡ Federation of Migros Cooperatives, Limmatstrasse 152, Box 266, CH-8031 Zurich, Switzerland. circ. 4,000. (tabloid format)

FEDERATION OF SWEDISH CO-OPERATIVE BANKS. ANNUAL REPORT. see *BUSINESS AND ECONOMICS — Banking And Finance*

334　　　　　GW
DIE GENOSSENSCHAFTEN IN DER BUNDESREPUBLIK DEUTSCHLAND. 1965. biennial. DM.35. DG Bank Deutsche Genossenschaftsbank, Am Platz der Republik, 6000 Frankfurt, W. Germany (B.R.D.) illus. stat. circ. 1, 500.

334　381　338　647.94　GE　ISSN 0138-5410
GERMAN DEMOCRATIC REPUBLIC. CONSUMER CO-OPERATIVE SOCIETIES. MAGAZINE. (Text in English) 1967. a. DM.3. Postfach 1269, DDR-1086 Berlin, E. Germany (D.D.R.) (Subscr. to: Buchexport, Postfach 160, DDR-7010 Leipzig, E. Germany (D.D.R.)) Ed.Bd. circ. 3,000.

334　　　　　IS
HAIFA UNIVERSITY. INSTITUTE FOR STUDY AND RESEARCH OF THE KIBBUTZ AND THE COOPERATIVE IDEA. DISCUSSION PAPERS. (Text in English and Hebrew) irreg. Haifa University, Institute for Study and Research of the Kibbutz and the Cooperative Idea, Hacarmel, Haifa 31 999, Israel.

334　378　　　　UK
I C T C REVIEW. no.2, 1982. a. International Co-operative Training Centre, Co-operative College, Stanford Hall, Loughborough, Leics., England. Ed. Clare Bishop. bk. rev. circ. 600.

334　301　　　UK　ISSN 0309-3298
IN THE MAKING; directory of radical cooperation. 1973. biennial. £1($6) 44 Albion Rd., Sutton, Surrey SM2 5TF, England. Ed. D. Bollen. bk. rev. circ. 2, 000.

334　　　　　BL
INSTITUTO NACIONAL DE COLONIZACAO E REFORMA AGRARIA. COORDENADORIA REGIONAL DO PARANA. SINOPSE DO COOPERATIVISMO NO PARANA. 1970. irreg. Instituto Nacional de Colonizacao e Reforma Agraria, Coordenadoria Regional do Parana, Curitiba, Brazil. illus.

334　　　　NG　ISSN 0534-4697
INTER-AFRICAN CONFERENCE ON CO-OPERATIVE SOCIETIES MEETING. REUNION.* irreg. (Commission for Technical Co-Operation in Africa, South of the Sahara) Maison de l'Afrique, Bp. 878, Niamey, Niger.

334　　　　SZ　ISSN 0074-4247
INTERNATIONAL COOPERATIVE ALLIANCE. CONGRESS REPORT. 1895. quadrennial; 28th, 1984, Hamburg. 17 Fr. International Co-Operative Alliance, Rte. des Morillons 15, 1218 Grand Saconnex, Geneve, Switzerland. (reprint service avail. from UMI)

334　　　　II　ISSN 0074-4255
INTERNATIONAL COOPERATIVE ALLIANCE. COOPERATIVE SERIES.* (Text in English) 1965. irreg. International Cooperative Alliance, Regional Office for South-East Asia, Bonow House, 43 Friends' Colony East, New Delhi 110 065, India. circ. 2,000.

334　　　　IS　ISSN 0080-1313
ISRAEL. MINISTRY OF LABOUR. REGISTRAR OF COOPERATIVE SOCIETIES. REPORT ON THE COOPERATIVE MOVEMENT IN ISRAEL. (Text in English) 1964. a. Ministry of Labour and Social Affairs, Registrar of Cooperative Societies, 10 Yad Harutzim St., Talpiot, Box 1260, Jerusalem, Israel. circ. 1,200.

334　　　　　IS
KIBBUTZ (EFAL) (Text in French) 1983. a. Yad Tabenkin, Efal 52 960, Israel.

MANITOBA. DEPARTMENT OF CO-OPERATIVE DEVELOPMENT. REPORT/RAPPORT. see *BUSINESS AND ECONOMICS — Banking And Finance*

334　　　　　MF
MAURITIUS. MINISTRY OF CO-OPERATIVES AND CO-OPERATIVE DEVELOPMENT. ANNUAL REPORT. (Text in English) irreg. Government Printing Office, Elizabeth II Ave., Port Louis, Mauritius.

630　338.91　　　UK　ISSN 0143-8484
PLUNKETT DEVELOPMENT SERIES. 1980. irreg. price varies. Plunkett Foundation for Co-Operative Studies, 31 St. Giles St., Oxford OX1 3LF, England. Indexed: Rural Recreat.Tour.Abstr. World Agri.Econ.& Rural Sociol.Abstr.

334　　　　UK　ISSN 0142-5005
PLUNKETT FOUNDATION FOR CO-OPERATIVE STUDIES. STUDY SERIES. 1978. irreg. price varies. Plunkett Foundation for Co-Operative Studies, 31 St. Giles St., Oxford OX1 3LF, England.

334.099　　　AT　ISSN 0481-3375
QUEENSLAND. REGISTRAR OF CO-OPERATIVE AND OTHER SOCIETIES. REPORT.* a. Government Printer, Brisbane, Australia. illus.

334　　　　CN　ISSN 0080-097X
REPERTOIRE DES COOPERATIVES DU QUEBEC.* 1969. a. free. Editeur Officiel du Quebec, 1283 Bd. Charest ouest, Quebec G1N 2C9, Canada. circ. 1,500.

334　　　　　II
SAHYOG. a. Cooperative Training College, Vallabh Vidyanagar, Gujarat, India.

334　　　　GW　ISSN 0080-7028
SCHRIFTEN ZUR KOOPERATIONSFORSCHUNG. BERICHTE. 1968. irreg. price varies. (Forschungsgesellschaft fuer Genossenschaftswesen, Muenster) Verlag J.C.B. Mohr (Paul Siebeck), Wilhelmstr. 18, Postfach 2040, 7400 Tuebingen, W. Germany (B.R.D.)

334   GW   ISSN 0080-7036
SCHRIFTEN ZUR KOOPERATIONSFORSCHUNG. STUDIEN. 1951. irreg. price varies. (Forschungsgesellschaft fuer Genossenschaftswesen, Muenster) Verlag J.C.B. Mohr (Paul Siebeck), Wilhelmstr. 18, Postfach 2040, 7400 Tuebingen, W. Germany (B.R.D.)
 Formerly: Quellen und Studien.

334   GW   ISSN 0080-7044
SCHRIFTEN ZUR KOOPERATIONSFORSCHUNG. VORTRAEGE. 1950. irreg. price varies. (Forschungsgesellschaft fuer Genossenschaftswesen, Muenster) Verlag J.C.B. Mohr (Paul Siebeck), Wilhelmstr. 18, Postfach 2040, 7400 Tuebingen, W. Germany (B.R.D.)
 Formerly: Vortraege und Aufsaetze.

334   US   ISSN 0038-4003
SOUTHERN COOPERATOR.* 1970. irreg. $5. Federation of Southern Cooperatives, Education Dept., Box 95, Epes, AL 35460. Ed. Alice Paris. adv. charts. illus. circ. 6,000.

U.S. NATIONAL CREDIT UNION ADMINISTRATION. ANNUAL REPORT. see BUSINESS AND ECONOMICS — Banking And Finance

330   CN
UNIVERSITE DE SHERBROOKE. I R E C U S. CAHIERS DE LA COOPERATION. 1969. irreg, latest no.3, 1972. price varies. Universite de Sherbrooke, Institut de Recherche et d'Enseignement pour les Cooperatives, Sherbrooke, Que. J1K 2R1, Canada. TEL 819-821-7202. Ed.Bd.

330   CN
UNIVERSITE DE SHERBROOKE. I R E C U S. DOSSIERS SUR LES COOPERATIVES. 1973. irreg, latest no.4, 1977. price varies. Universite de Sherbrooke, Institut de Recherche et d'Enseignement pour les Cooperatives, Sherbrooke, Que. J1K 2R1, Canada. TEL 819-821-7202. circ. 200.

334   FI   ISSN 0356-1364
UNIVERSITY OF HELSINKI. DEPARTMENT OF COOPERATIVE STUDIES. PUBLICATIONS. (Text in English and Finnish) 1967. irreg. price varies. Helsingin Yliopisto, Department of Cooperative Studies, Franzeninkatu 13, 00500 Helsinki 50, Finland. circ. 150.

VAIKUNTH MEHTA NATIONAL INSTITUTE OF COOPERATIVE MANAGEMENT. PUBLICATIONS. see BUSINESS AND ECONOMICS — Management

YEAR BOOK OF AGRICULTURAL CO-OPERATION. see AGRICULTURE — Agricultural Economics

334 334   ZA   ISSN 0514-5430
ZAMBIA. DEPARTMENT OF COOPERATIVES. ANNUAL REPORT. a. 20 n. Government Printer, Box 136, Lusaka, Zambia. stat.

BUSINESS AND ECONOMICS — Domestic Commerce

AFRICAN TRADE/COMMERCE AFRICAIN. see BUSINESS AND ECONOMICS — International Commerce

381   FR   ISSN 0066-3182
ANNUAIRE GENERAL DES COOPERATIVES FRANCAISES ET DE LEURS FOURNISSEURS; FRANCE, AFRIQUE ET MARCHE COMMUN. 1956. a. 550 F. Office des Cooperatives et des Collectivites, 49 rue de Richelieu, 75001 Paris, France. adv.

380.1   II
ANNUAL REPORT ON THE WORKING AND AFFAIRS OF MYSORE SALES INTERNATIONAL LIMITED. (Text in English) 1967. a. Mysore Sales International Ltd, Bangalore, India. Ed. Janasdhan Roye. circ. 2,500.
 Government business enterprises

381   IT   ISSN 0084-6627
ANNUARIO GENERALE ITALIANO. a. L.200000. Guida Monaci, Via Francesco Crispi 10, 00187 Rome, Italy.

BARGAIN SHOPPER'S GUIDE TO MELBOURNE. see CONSUMER EDUCATION AND PROTECTION

BARGAIN SHOPPERS GUIDE TO SYDNEY. see CONSUMER EDUCATION AND PROTECTION

BUSINESS LAWS OF ARAB EMIRATES. see LAW

BUSINESS LAWS OF EGYPT. see LAW

BUSINESS LAWS OF IRAQ. see LAW

BUSINESS LAWS OF KUWAIT. see LAW

BUSINESS LAWS OF OMAN. see LAW

BUSINESS LAWS OF SAUDI ARABIA. see LAW

381   UK   ISSN 0261-796X
BUSINESS LOCATION HANDBOOK. 1981. a. $22.50. Beacon Publications PLC, York House, Newton Close, Park Farm, Wellingborough, Northamptonshire NN8 3UW, England.

CAMARA DE COMERCIANTES EN ARTEFACTOS PARA EL HOGAR. REVISTA. see INTERIOR DESIGN AND DECORATION — Furniture And House Furnishings

381   FR   ISSN 0069-1100
CATALOGUE DES PRODUITS AGREES PAR QUALITE-FRANCE. 2nd edt., 1963. irreg. 3 F. Association Nationale pour la Promotion et le Controle de la Qualite, 18 rue Volney, 75002 Paris, France.

381   AT
CHEAP EATS IN SYDNEY. biennial. Horan, Wall & Walker, P.O. Box 8, Surry Hills, NSW 2010, Australia.

381   CN
COMMERCE. LE POINT; une revue annuel de l'economie du Quebec. a. Can.$20($35) included in subscr. to Commerce. Publications Les Affaires Inc., 465 St. Jean St., Suite 908, Montreal, Que. H2Y 2R6, Canada. TEL 514-844-1511. Ed. Michel Lord. adv. circ. 38,413.

381   II   ISSN 0591-1710
COMMERCE YEARBOOK OF PUBLIC SECTOR. (Text in English) 1970. a. Rs.125. Commerce Publications Limited, NKM International House, 178 Backbay Reclamation, Bombay 400020, India. Ed. Vadilal Dagli.

381.45   US   ISSN 0277-1969
DIRECTORY OF COOPERATIVES, VOLUNTARIES AND WHOLESALE GROCERS. a. $179. Chain Store Guide (Subsidiary of: Lebhar-Friedman, Inc.) 425 Park Ave., New York, NY 10022. TEL 212-371-9400. (also avail. in magnetic tape)
 Former titles: Directory of Retailer Owned Cooperative Chains, Wholesaler Sponsored Voluntary Chains, Wholesale Grocers (ISSN 0271-8006); Retailer Owned Cooperative Chains, Voluntary Chains and Wholesale Grocers (ISSN 0196-1810)

381   US
DIRECTORY OF HARDLINES DISTRIBUTORS. a. $159. Chain Store Guide, 425 Park Ave., New York, NY 10022. TEL 212-371-9400.

DOMESTIC WATERBORNE TRADE OF THE UNITED STATES. see TRANSPORTATION — Ships And Shipping

381   EC
ECUADOR. MINISTERIO DE INDUSTRIAS, COMERCIO E INTEGRACION. DOCUMENTO. 1975. a. Ministerio de Industrias, Comercio e Integracion, Quito, Ecuador.

381   EC
ECUADOR. MINISTERIO DE INDUSTRIAS, COMERCIO E INTEGRACION. INFORME A LA NACION. 1974. a. Ministerio de Industrias, Comercio e Integracion, Quito, Ecuador. illus.

ELECTRICAL MACHINERY: LATIN AMERICAN INDUSTRIAL REPORT. see ELECTRICITY AND ELECTRICAL ENGINEERING

380.1   TG
ENQUETE SUR LES ENTERPRISES INDUSTRIELLES ET COMMERCIALES DU TOGO. a. 3000 Fr.CFA. Direction de la Statistique, Boite Postale 118, Lome, Togo. stat.

381   AT   ISSN 0085-0268
ENTERPRISE.* 1963. a. free. University of New South Wales, Commerce Society, P.O. Box 1, Kensington, N.S.W. 2033, Australia.

381   PN
F O B COLON FREE ZONE. (Text in English and Spanish) 1979. a. $5. (Colon Free Zone Users Association) Focus Publications, S.A., Apdo. 6-3287, El Dorado, Panama City, Panama. Ed. Kenneth J. Jones. adv. circ. 20,000.
 Formerly: Colon Free Zone Directory.

381 658   US   ISSN 0547-8804
FINANCIAL AND OPERATING RESULTS OF DEPARTMENT AND SPECIALTY STORES. a. $69.50 to non-members; members $37.50. National Retail Merchants Association, Financial Executives Division, 100 W. 31st St., New York, NY 10001. TEL 212-244-8780.

381   FR   ISSN 0071-8483
FRANCE. COMMISSION CENTRALE DES MARCHES. GUIDE DU FOURNISSEUR DE L'ETAT ET DES COLLECTIVITES LOCALES. 1964. irreg., latest issue 1972. 26 Fr. (Ministere de l'Economie et des Finances, Commission Centrale des Marches) Moniteur des Travaux Publics et du Batiment, 17 rue d'Uzes, 75065 Paris, France. circ. 12,000.
 Formerly: France. Commission Centrale des Marches. Guide du Fournisseur de l'Etat.

381 658   FR   ISSN 0071-8386
FRANCE-COLLECTIVITES: GUIDE NATIONAL DES CHEFS DES SERVICES D'ACHATS ET DES FOURNISSEURS DE COLLECTIVITES. 1962/63. a. 330 F. Office des Cooperatives et des Collectivites, 49 rue de Richelieu, 75001 Paris, France.

GERMAN DEMOCRATIC REPUBLIC. CONSUMER CO-OPERATIVE SOCIETIES. MAGAZINE. see BUSINESS AND ECONOMICS — Cooperatives

380.1   GU
GUAM. DEPARTMENT OF COMMERCE. OCCASIONAL PAPER. irreg., no.6, 1979. Department of Commerce, 590 S. Marine Dr., GITC Bldg. Ste. 601, Tamuning, Guam 96911.

338   FI   ISSN 0356-5092
HINNAT JA KILPAILU/PRISER OCH KONKURRENS. (Text in Finnish and Swedish) 1977. irreg. (3-4/yr.) free. Elinkeinohallitus - National Board of Trade and Consumer Interests, Haapaniemenkatu 4 A, 00530 Helsinki, Finland. Ed. Matti Purasjoki. index. circ. 2,200.
 Formerly (until 1977): Kilpailunvapauslehti (ISSN 0023-1401)

380   SZ   ISSN 0080-603X
HOCHSCHULE ST. GALLEN FUER WIRTSCHAFTS- UND SOZIALWISSENSCHAFTEN. FORSCHUNGSINSTITUT FUER ABSATZ UND HANDEL. SCHRIFTENREIHE. 1960. irreg., vol.16, 1976. price varies. Paul Haupt AG, Falkenplatz 14, CH-3001 Berne, Switzerland.

381   KE
INDUSTRIAL AND COMMERCIAL DEVELOPMENT CORPORATION. ANNUAL REPORT AND ACCOUNTS. (Text in English) a. Industrial and Commercial Development Corporation, Box 45519, Nairobi, Kenya.

381   IR   ISSN 0074-1213
INTERNAL TRADE OF IRAN.* (Text in English and Persian) 1965. a. free. Ministry of Finance and Economic Affairs, Bureau of Statistics, Tehran, Iran.

381   KE
K I R D I ANNUAL REPORT AND STATEMENT OF ACCOUNTS. 1982. a. Kenya Industrial Research and Development Institute, Box 30650, Nairobi, Kenya. circ. 1,000.

BUSINESS AND ECONOMICS — ECONOMIC SITUATION AND CONDITIONS

381   KE
KENYA NATIONAL TRADING CORPORATION. ANNUAL REPORT. (Title varies slightly) (Text in English) a. Kenya National Trading Corporation Ltd., Box 30587, Nairobi, Kenya.

381   UK   ISSN 0260-6526
LARGE STORES DIRECTORY. 1980. a. £15 to members; non-members £25. Institute of Grocery Distribution, Letchmore Heath, Watford WD2 8DQ, England.

LATIN AMERICAN METAL MECHANIC & ELECTRONIC INDUSTRY DIRECTORY. see *MACHINERY*

381   MY
MALAYSIA. DEPARTMENT OF INLAND REVENUE. ANNUAL REPORT/MALAYSIA. JABATAN HASIL DALAM NEGERI. LAPURAN TAHUNAN. (Text in Malay) 1972. a. Department of Inland Revenue, Kuala Lumpur, Malaysia.

MARKETING CALIFORNIA DRIED FRUITS: PRUNES, RAISINS, DRIED APRICOTS & PEACHES. see *AGRICULTURE — Agricultural Economics*

MEDICAL PRODUCTS MARKETERS DIRECTORY. see *MEDICAL SCIENCES*

353.9   US
MICHIGAN. DEPARTMENT OF COMMERCE. ANNUAL REPORT. 1963. a. free. Department of Commerce, Lansing, MI 48913. TEL 517-373-0488. Ed. Russell Barnes. illus. stat. circ. 150,000.
Formerly: Michigan. Department of Commerce. Annual Report Summary (ISSN 0094-3479)

381.41   SA
NATIONAL FRESH PRODUCE MARKET, JOHANNESBURG. ANNUAL REPORT OF THE DIRECTOR. (Report year ends June 30) 1913. a. free. National Fresh Produce Market, Box 577, Johannesburg 2000, South Africa. circ. 350. (processed)

381   SA   ISSN 0077-5894
NATIONAL TRADE-INDEX OF SOUTHERN AFRICA. 1928. a. R.65. Intratex, P.O. Box 1405, Pinetown 3600, South Africa. Ed. A. Stagg. adv.

381   US   ISSN 0077-9156
NEW YORK (STATE) DEPARTMENT OF COMMERCE. RESEARCH BULLETIN. 1960-197??; resumed 19?? irreg., no.53, 1983. price varies. Department of Commerce, Bureau of Business Research, Statistics Unit, 99 Washington Ave., Albany, NY 12245. Ed. William E. Zimmerman. circ. 1,500.

381   NQ   ISSN 0078-0510
NICARAGUA. DIRECCION GENERAL DE ADUANAS. MEMORIA. 1918. a. $7. Direccion General de Aduanas, Managua, Nicaragua. stat. circ. 200.

381   GW
NORDFRIESLAND; Chronik in Wort und Bild; Handbuch fuer den Kreis Nordfriesland. a. DM.5. Flensburger Zeitungsverlag GmbH, Nikolaistr. 7, 2390 Flensburg, W. Germany (B.R.D.) illus.

380   NO
NORWAY. MINISTRY OF INDUSTRY AND HANDICRAFT. REPORTS TO THE STORTING. irreg. price varies. Ministry of Industry and Handicraft, Akersgaten 42, Box 8014-Dep., Oslo 1, Norway.

OFFICE - DATA PROCESSING MACHINES: LATIN AMERICAN INDUSTRIAL REPORT. see *COMPUTERS — Computer Industry*

381.3   FR
ORGANIZATION FOR ECONOMIC COOPERATION AND DEVELOPMENT. CONSUMER POLICY IN O.E.C.D. COUNTRIES. (Text in English) a. 15. Organisation for Economic Cooperation and Development, 2 rue Andre-Pascal, 75775 Paris Cedex 16, France (U.S. orders to: O.E.C.D. Publications and Information Center, 1750 Pennsylvania Ave., N.W., Washington, DC 20006) (also avail. in microfiche)
Formerly: Organization for Economic Cooperation and Development. Annual Reports on Consumer Policy in O.E.C.D. Member Countries.

381   918.6   US
PANAMA NOW. (Editions in English, Spanish) 1986. biennial. $30. Focus Publications International, S.A., Apdo. 6-3287, El Dorado, Panama City, Panama. Ed. Kenneth J. Jones. adv. circ. 10,000.

PETROLEUM: LATIN AMERICAN INDUTRIAL REPORT. see *PETROLEUM AND GAS*

PHARMACEUTICAL: LATIN AMERICAN INDUSTRIAL REPORT. see *PHARMACY AND PHARMACOLOGY*

PHILIPPINES. MINISTRY OF TRADE. ANNUAL REPORT. see *BUSINESS AND ECONOMICS — International Commerce*

381   332.6   II
PONDICHERRY INDUSTRIAL PROMOTION, DEVELOPMENT AND INVESTMENT CORPORATION. ANNUAL REPORTS AND ACCOUNTS. (Text in English) 1975. a. Pondicherry Industrial Promotion, Development and Investment Corporation Ltd., 38 Romain Rolland St, Pondicherry 605001, India. circ. controlled.

PRINTING & PUBLISHING: LATIN AMERICAN INDUSTRIAL REPORT. see *PUBLISHING AND BOOK TRADE*

RETAIL TRADE DEVELOPMENTS IN GREAT BRITAIN. see *BUSINESS AND ECONOMICS — Trade And Industrial Directories*

381   PH
S E C BULLETIN. 1972. irreg. P.25 per no. Securities and Exchange Commission, P.O. Box 104, Greenhills, Mandaluyong, Metro Manilla, Philippines. Ed. Angelita A. Ledesma. circ. 1,000.

380   GW   ISSN 0080-7001
SCHRIFTEN ZUR HANDELSFORSCHUNG. N.S. 1951. irreg., no.75, 1987. price varies. (Universitaet zu Koeln, Institut fuer Handelsforschung) Verlag Otto Schwartz und Co., Annastr. 7, 3400 Goettingen, W. Germany (B.R.D.)

SPORTS TRADER BUYER'S GUIDE. see *BUSINESS AND ECONOMICS — Marketing And Purchasing*

381   SJ
SUDAN. DEPARTMENT OF STATISTICS. INTERNAL TRADE AND OTHER STATISTICS. (Text in English) a. Department of Statistics, Box 700, Khartoum, Sudan.

381   AU
SURVEY OF THE AUSTRIAN ECONOMY/ OESTERREICHS WIRTSCHAFT IM UEBERBLICK. 1972. a. S.100. Wirtschafts-Studio des Oesterreichen Gesellschafts und Wirtschaftsmuseums, c/o Josef Docekal, Vogelsanggasse 36, A-1050 Vienna, Austria. Ed. Josef Docekal.

TOBACCO: LATIN AMERICAN INDUSTRIAL REPORT. see *TOBACCO*

381   688.72   UK
TOY TRADER DAILY NEWS (EARLS COURT) 1978. a. free. Wheatland Journals Ltd., Penn House, Penn Place, Rickmansworth, Herts. WD3 1SN, England. Ed. Caroline Fysh. adv.
Formerly: Toy Fayre Earls Court Newspaper.

381   688.72   UK
TOY TRADER DAILY NEWS (HARROGATE) 1948. a. free. Wheatland Journals Ltd., Penn House, Penn Place, Rickmansworth, Herts. WD3 1SN, England. Ed. Caroline Fysh. adv.
Formerly: Toy Fayre Harrogate Newspaper.

TRANSPORTATION: LATIN AMERICAN INDUSTRIAL REPORT. see *TRANSPORTATION*

380   US   ISSN 0082-5956
TRANSPORTATION STATISTICS IN THE UNITED STATES. 1954. irreg. price varies. U.S. Interstate Commerce Commission, 12th St. and Constitution Ave., N.W., Washington, DC 20423 TEL 202-655-4000. (Orders to: Supt. of Docs., Washington, DC 20402)

381   630   UK
UNITED FARMERS TRADING AGENCY YEAR BOOK AND DIARY. a. Welbecson Ltd., Strawberry St., Hull, Humberside HU9 1EX, England.

381   US   ISSN 0083-0917
U.S. FEDERAL TRADE COMMISSION. ANNUAL REPORT.* 1915. a. price varies. U.S. Federal Trade Commission, Office of Public Affairs, Sixth St. & Pennsylvania Ave., N.W., Washington, DC 20580 TEL 202-655-4000. (Orders to: Supt. of Documents, Washington, DC 20402) Key Title: Annual Report of the Federal Trade Commission.

381   US
U.S. FEDERAL TRADE COMMISSION. COURT DECISIONS PERTAINING TO THE FEDERAL TRADE COMMISSION.* a. price varies. U.S. Federal Trade Commission, Office of Public Affairs, Sixth St. & Pennsylvania Ave., N.W., Washington, DC 20580 TEL 212-655-4000. (Orders to: Supt. of Documents, Washington, DC 20402)
Formerly: U.S. Federal Trade Commission. Statutes and Court Decisions Pertaining to the Federal Trade Commission. Supplements (ISSN 0083-0933)

381   US   ISSN 0083-0925
U.S. FEDERAL TRADE COMMISSION. FEDERAL TRADE COMMISSION DECISIONS, FINDINGS, ORDERS AND STIPULATIONS.* 1915. a. price varies. U.S. Federal Trade Commission, Office of Public Affairs, Sixth St. & Pennsylvania Ave., N.W., Washington, DC 20580 TEL 202-655-4000. (Orders to: Supt. of Documents, Washington, DC 20402)

381   US   ISSN 0083-1514
U.S. INTERSTATE COMMERCE COMMISSION. ANNUAL REPORT. 1887. a. price varies. U.S. Interstate Commerce Commission, 12th St. and Constitution Ave., N.W., Washington, DC 20423 TEL 202-655-4000. (Orders to: Supt. of Docs., Washington, DC 20402)

381   US   ISSN 0083-1522
U.S. INTERSTATE COMMERCE COMMISSION. INTERSTATE COMMERCE ACTS ANNOTATED. 1930. irreg. price varies. U.S. Interstate Commerce Commission, 12th St. and Constitution Ave., N.W., Washington, DC 20423 TEL 202-655-4000. (Orders to: Supt. of Docs., Washington, DC 20402)

381   US   ISSN 0083-1530
U.S. INTERSTATE COMMERCE COMMISSION. INTERSTATE COMMERCE COMMISSION REPORTS. DECISIONS OF THE INTERSTATE COMMERCE COMMISSION OF THE UNITED STATES. 1887. irreg. price varies. U.S. Interstate Commerce Commission, 12th St. and Constitution Ave., N.W., Washington, DC 20423 TEL 202-655-4000. (Orders to: Supt. of Docs., Washington, DC 20402)

UNIVERSITY OF OSAKA PREFECTURE. BULLETIN. SERIES D: SCIENCES OF ECONOMY, COMMERCE AND LAW. see *BUSINESS AND ECONOMICS*

381   CN   ISSN 0083-517X
VANCOUVER BOARD OF TRADE. ANNUAL REPORT. 1887. a. free. Board of Trade, Suite 400, 999 Canada Place, Vancouver, B.C. V6C 3K1, Canada. TEL 604-681-2111. adv. circ. 5,000.

381   AT   ISSN 0726-9501
WESTERN AUSTRALIA. DEPARTMENT OF INDUSTRIAL DEVELOPMENT. BUILDING INVESTMENT. 1977. irreg., latest 1984. free. Department of Industrial Development, Research Section, 170 St. George's Terrace, Perth, W.A. 6000, Australia. Ed.Bd. charts. stat. circ. 1,000.

BUSINESS AND ECONOMICS — Economic Situation And Conditions

330   BO
ACADEMIA BOLIVIANA DE CIENCIAS ECONOMICAS. REVISTA. 1980. irreg. $6 per vol. (Amigos del Libro) Academia Boliviana de Ciencias Economicas, Casilla 450, Cochabamba, Bolivia. Ed. Juan L. Cariaga. adv. bk. rev. circ. 1,000.

BUSINESS AND ECONOMICS — ECONOMIC SITUATION AND CONDITIONS

ADVANCES IN BEHAVIORAL ECONOMICS. see *PSYCHOLOGY*

AFRICA INSTITUTE. OCCASIONAL PUBLICATIONS. see *HISTORY — History Of Africa*

320 338 UK
AFRICA REVIEW. 1977. a. $59. World of Information, 21 Gold St., Saffron Walden, Essex CB10 1EJ, England. Ed. Richard Green. adv. illus. stat. circ. 9,000.
 Formerly (until 1985): Africa Guide (ISSN 0308-678X)

AFRICA SOUTH OF THE SAHARA. see *HISTORY — History Of Africa*

AGRICULTURAL REVIEW FOR EUROPE. see *AGRICULTURE — Agricultural Economics*

AGRICULTURAL TRADE IN EUROPE. see *AGRICULTURE — Agricultural Economics*

330.9 US
ALABAMA ECONOMIC OUTLOOK. 1983. biennial. $10. Development Office, c/o State Capitol, Montgomery, AL 36130. TEL 205-284-8910.

330.9 US ISSN 0162-5403
ALASKA REVIEW OF SOCIAL AND ECONOMIC CONDITIONS. 1964. irreg. free. University of Alaska, Institute of Social and Economic Research, 3211 Providence Dr., Anchorage, AK 99508-4614. TEL 907-786-7710. Ed. Linda Leask. charts. illus. index. circ. 3,000. Indexed: P.A.I.S. Rural Recreat.Tour.Abstr. World Agri.Econ.& Rural Sociol.Abstr.
 Former titles (until Dec. 1977): Alaska Review of Business and Economic Conditions (ISSN 0034-6462); Review of Business and Economic Conditions in Alaska.

ALBANIA REPORT. see *POLITICAL SCIENCE*

330.9 CN
ALBERTA. DEPARTMENT OF INDUSTRY AND COMMERCE. EXECUTIVE REPORT. a. Department of Industry and Commerce, Economic Research Branch, Edmonton, Alta. T5K 2C8, Canada.
 Formerly: Alberta. Department of Industry and Commerce. Economic Research Branch. Executive Report.

338.9 CN ISSN 0080-1534
ALBERTA RESEARCH COUNCIL. CONTRIBUTION SERIES. 1942. irreg. free. Alberta Research Council, Publications Dept., P.O. Box 8330, Sta. F, Edmonton, Alta. T6H 5X2, Canada. TEL 403-450-5111.

330 IT ISSN 0065-6151
ALESSANDRIA, ITALY. CENTRO DOCUMENTAZIONE E RICHERCHE ECONOMICO-SOCIALI. QUADERNI CEDRES. 1963. irreg., no.119, 1982. free. Amministrazione Provinciale, Alessandria, Italy. Dir. Carlo Beltrame. bk. rev. circ. 1,000.

330 TI ISSN 0066-3042
ANNUAIRE ECONOMIQUE DE LA TUNISIE. English edition: Economic Yearbook of Tunisia (ISSN 0070-8747) 1964. biennial. $20. Union Tunisienne de l'Industrie, du Commerce et de l'Artisanat, 32 rue Charles de Gaulle, Tunis, Tunisia. adv. circ. 5,000.

330.9 ET
ANNUAIRE ECONOMIQUE DES PAYS MEMBRES DE L'ORGANISATION DE L'UNITE AFRICAINE/ECONOMIC YEARBOOK OF MEMBER STATES OF THE ORGANIZATION OF AFRICAN UNITY.* (Text in English and French) a. Organization for African Unity, Library - Organisation de l'Unite Africaine, P.O. Box 3246, Addis Ababa, Ethiopia.

330 RH
ANNUAL ECONOMIC REVIEW. a. free. Government Printer, Box 8062, Causeway, Zimbabwe.
 Former titles (1981): Economic Survey of Rhodesia; Until 1965: Review of the Economy of Rhodesia (ISSN 0080-1992)

330.9 JA
ANNUAL REPORT ON NATIONAL ACCOUNT. (Text in Japanese) a. 2300 Yen. Ministry of Finance, Economic Planning Agency, 2-1, 1-chome, Kasumigaseki, Chiyoda-ku, Tokyo, Japan.

330.9 MX
ANUARIO DE LA ECONOMICA MEXICANA/ MEXICAN ECONOMY ANNUAL. 1965. a. Expansion, S.A., Sinaloa No. 149-9, Mexico 7, D.F., Mexico. Ed. Carlos Gelis G. adv. circ. 8,500.

330.9 KU
ARABIAN YEAR BOOK; commercial directory. (Text in English) 1978. a. $120. Dar Al Seyyassah Est., P.O. Box 42480, Shuwaikh, Kuwait. Ed. Ahmed Z. Al Talleh. adv. circ. 15,000.
 Formerly: Arabian Trade Digest.

ARBEITSGEMEINSCHAFT FUER LEBENSNIVEAUVERGLEICHE. SCHRIFTENREIHE. see *SOCIAL SCIENCES: COMPREHENSIVE WORKS*

330.9 AG
ARGENTINE ECONOMIC DEVELOPMENT. (Text in English & French) biennial. Ministerio de Economia, Balcarce 136, Buenos Aires, Argentina.

330.9 320 UK
ASIA & PACIFIC REVIEW. 1980. a. $59. World of Information, 21 Gold St., Saffron Walden, Essex CB10 1EJ, England. Ed. Richard Green. adv. illus. stat. circ. 9,000.
 Former titles (until 1985): Asia and Pacific (ISSN 0262-5407); Until 1981: Asia and Pacific Annual Review.

330.9 HK
ASIA CORPORATE PROFILE AND NATIONAL FINANCE. a. Asian Finance Publications Ltd., Suite D, 9th Floor, Hyde Centre, 223 Gloucester Rd., Hong Kong, Hong Kong. Ed. T.K. Seshadri.

330.9 LE
ASSOCIATION DES BANQUES DU LIBAN. RAPPORT DU CONSEIL. Cover title: Association des Banques du Liban. Rapport Annuel. (Text in French) irreg. Association of Banks in Lebanon, Rue de l'Armee, Box 967, Beirut, Lebanon. stat.

330.1 CN ISSN 0067-0162
ATLANTIC PROVINCES ECONOMIC COUNCIL. ANNUAL REPORT. 1966. a. membership. Atlantic Provinces Economic Council, 5121 Sackville St., Suite 500, Halifax, N.S. B3J 1K1, Canada. TEL 902-422-6516. circ. 1,000. (reprint service avail. from UMI)

350 AT ISSN 0158-1309
AUSTRALIA. DEPARTMENT OF PRIMARY INDUSTRY. ANNUAL REPORT. 1979. a. free. Department of Primary Industry, Edmund Barton Bldg., Broughton St., Barton, A.C.T. 2600, Australia.

330.9 BF
BAHAMAS HANDBOOK. 1960. a. $14.95. Etienne Dupuch Jr. Publications, P.O. Box N7513, Nassau, Bahamas. Ed. S.P. Dupuch. adv. index.
 Formerly: Bahamas Handbook and Businessman's Annual (ISSN 0067-2912)

330.9 330.1 IT
BANCA D'ITALIA. CONTRIBUTI ALLA ANALISI ECONOMICA. 1971. a. free. Banca d'Italia, Servizio Studi, Via Nazionale 91, Rome, Italy. Ed. Franco Cotula.
 Formerly: Banca d'Italia. Contributi alla Ricerca Economica (ISSN 0392-4661)

330.9 IT
BANCA NAZIONALE DEL LAVORO. CONDENSED STATEMENT OF CONDITION. a. Banca Nazionale del Lavoro, Via Vittorio Veneto 119, 00187 Rome, Italy. Indexed: P.A.I.S.

BANCO CENTRAL DE CHILE, SANTIAGO. MEMORIA ANUAL. see *BUSINESS AND ECONOMICS — Banking And Finance*

330.9 CR
BANCO CENTRAL DE COSTA RICA. BALANZA DE PAGOS. 1950. a. free. Banco Central de Costa Rica, Departamento de Investigaciones y Estadistica, Apdo. 10058, San Jose, Costa Rica. circ. 1,500.

330.9 CR ISSN 0408-3172
BANCO CENTRAL DE COSTA RICA. INFORMACION ECONOMICA SEMANAL. 1950. w. free. Banco Central de Costa Rica, Division de Asuntos Economicos, San Jose, Costa Rica. charts. stat.

330.9 CR
BANCO CENTRAL DE COSTA RICA. SERIE "COMENTARIOS SOBRE ASUNTOS ECONOMICOS". 1972. irreg., no.64, 1986. free. Banco Central de Costa Rica, Departamento de Investigaciones y Estadistica, Apdo. 10058, San Jose, Costa Rica. stat. circ. 300.

330 HO
BANCO CENTRAL DE HONDURAS. INFORME ECONOMICO. 1960. a. Banco Central de Honduras, Departamento de Estudios Economicos, Tegucigalpa, Honduras. charts. stat.

330.9 HO ISSN 0067-3218
BANCO CENTRAL DE HONDURAS. MEMORIA. 1950. a. Banco Central de Honduras, Departamento de Estudios Economicos, Tegucigalpa, Honduras. charts. stat.

330.9 NQ
BANCO CENTRAL DE NICARAGUA. DEPARTEMENTO DE ESTUDIOS ECONOMICOS. INDICADORES ECONOMICOS.* 1976. irreg. Ministerio de Comercio Exterior (MICE), Apdo. 2412, Managua, Nicaragua. charts. stat.

330 VE ISSN 0067-3250
BANCO CENTRAL DE VENEZUELA. INFORME ECONOMICO. 1962. a. Banco Central de Venezuela, Esquina de las Carmelitas, Caracas, Venezuela.

330.9 EC
BANCO CENTRAL DEL ECUADOR. BOLETIN-ANUARIO. 1978. a. free or exchange basis. Banco Central del Ecuador, Av. 10 de Agosto (Plaza Bolivar), La Alameda, Quito, Ecuador. Ed. Aurelio Salas. charts. illus. stat. circ. 8,000.
 Incorporating: Banco Central de Ecuador. Memoria Anual de Actividades.

330.9 918.6 EC
BANCO CENTRAL DEL ECUADOR. DIVISION TECNICA. CUENTAS NACIONALES DEL ECUADOR. irreg. Banco Central del Ecuador, Division Tecnica, Gerencia de Estudios Economicos, Av. 10 de Agosto (Plaza Bolivar), La Alameda, Quito, Ecuador. TEL 210-340. circ. 6,000.

330 UY
BANCO CENTRAL DEL URUGUAY. INDICADORES DE LA ACTIVIDAD ECONOMICO-FINANCIERA. irreg. Banco Central del Uruguay, Montevideo, Uruguay. stat. charts.

330.9 SP
BANCO DE BILBAO. ECONOMIC REPORT. (Text in English) a. Banco de Bilbao, Economic Research Department, Bilbao, Spain. charts. stat.

330.9 SP ISSN 0522-1315
BANCO DE BILBAO. INFORME ECONOMICO. 1950. a. Banco de Bilbao, Servicio de Estudios, Apartado 21, Bilbao, Spain. charts. stat.

330.9 GT
BANCO DE GUATEMALA. ESTADISTICAS DEL SECTOR EXTERNO. no.3, 1975. irreg. Banco de Guatemala, Departamento de Estudios Economicos, 7 Av. No. 22-01, Zona 1, Guatemala City, Guatemala. stat.

BANCO DE MEXICO. INFORME ANUAL. see *BUSINESS AND ECONOMICS — Banking And Finance*

338.9 BL
BANCO DO NORDESTE DO BRASIL. SERIE ESTUDOS ECONOMICOS E SOCIAIS. 1975. irreg. $3. Banco do Nordeste do Brasil, Rua Senador Pompeu 834, Galeria Pedro Jorge, 60000 Fortaleza - Ceara, Brazil.

330.9 EC
BANCO NACIONAL DE FOMENTO. INFORME DE LABORES. a. Banco Nacional de Fomento, Departamento de Relaciones Publicas, Apdo. 685, Quito, Ecuador. charts. illus. stat.

BUSINESS AND ECONOMICS — ECONOMIC SITUATION AND CONDITIONS

330   PN
BANCO NACIONAL DE PANAMA. ASESORIA ECONOMICA Y PLANIFICACION. CARTA ECONOMICA. 1971. irreg. (2-3/yr.) free. Banco Nacional de Panama, Asesoria Economica y Planificacion, Apdo. 5220, Panama 5, Panama. bk. rev. charts. illus. stat. circ. 1,500.

330.9   BL
BANCO NACIONAL DO DESENVOLVIMENTO ECONOMICO. RELATORIO DAS ATIVIDADES. English edition: Banco Nacional do Desenvolvimento Economico. Annual Report. a. Banco Nacional do Desenvolvimento Economico, Av. Rio Branco 53, Rio de Janeiro RJ, Brazil. charts. illus. stat.

330.9   BL
BANCO REGIONAL DE DESENVOLVIMENTO DO EXTREMO SUL. ANNUAL REPORT. 1965. a. free. Banco Regional de Desenvolvimento do Extremo Sul, Caixa Postal 139, 90100 Porto Alegre RS, Brazil. illus. circ. 1,000.
    Former by the merger of: Banco Regional de Desenvolvimento do Extremo Sul. Relatorio da Directoria (ISSN 0522-2079) & Banco Regional de Desenvolvimento do Extremo Sul. Relatorio Annal.

338.9   BG
BANGLADESH. PLANNING COMMISSION. ANNUAL DEVELOPMENT PROGRAMME. Bengali edition: Barshika Unnayana Karmasuci. (Text in English) a. Planning Commission, Dacca, Bangladesh.

332   IS
BANK OF ISRAEL. ECONOMIC REVIEW. (Editions in English and Hebrew) 1955. irreg. IS.4500($9) Bank of Israel, Research Department, Kiryath Ben Gurion, Box 780, Jerusalem, Israel. Eds. Yehuda Shulewitz, Susanne Freund. stat. circ. 1,000. Indexed: Ind.Heb.Per. P.A.I.S. Key to Econ.Sci.
    Formerly: Bank of Israel. Bulletin (ISSN 0005-5220)

330   JA   ISSN 0067-3692
BANK OF JAPAN. SPECIAL PAPER. (Text in English) 1961. irreg. Bank of Japan, Research and Statistics - Nihon Ginko, C.P.O. Box 203, Tokyo 100-91, Japan. charts.

330.9   LY   ISSN 0067-3714
BANK OF LIBYA. ANNUAL REPORT OF THE BOARD OF DIRECTORS.* (Editions in Arabic and English) 1957. a. free. Bank of Libya, Economic Research Division, Box 1103, Tripoli, Libya.

330 332   TZ   ISSN 0067-3757
BANK OF TANZANIA. ECONOMIC AND OPERATIONS REPORT. a. free. Bank of Tanzania, Research and Statistics Department, Box 2939, Dar es Salaam, Tanzania. circ. 3,000.
    Formerly: Bank of Tanzania. Economic Report (ISSN 0067-3765)

330   TH   ISSN 0067-3773
BANK OF THAILAND. ANNUAL ECONOMIC REPORT. a. $6.50. Bank of Thailand, Department of Economic Research, Bang Khunprom, Bangkok, Thailand. circ. 1,850.

330.9   TH
BANK OF THAILAND. PAPER. 1974/75. irreg. Bank of Thailand, Department of Economic Research, Bangkok, Thailand.

338.9   FR
BANQUE DE FRANCE. DIRECTION DE LA CONJONCTURE. SITUATION FINANCIERE DES REGIONS EN (YEAR); operations des guichets bancaires. 1966. a. free. Banque de France, Service de l'Information, 43 rue de Valois, 75049 Paris Cedex 1, France. stat.
    Formerly: Banque de France. Direction de la Conjoncture. Structure et Evolution Financiere des Regions de Province (ISSN 0522-3199)

330.9   FR
BANQUE DE FRANCE. LA ZONE FRANC EN (YEAR) a. 90 Fr. Banque de France, Services des Relations avec la Zone Franc, Service de l'Information, 43 rue de Valois, 75049 Paris Cedex 1, France.
    Formerly: Banque de France. Comite Monetaire de la Zone Franc. Secretariat. Rapport.

332   LU
BANQUE INTERNATIONALE A LUXEMBOURG. CAHIERS ECONOMIQUES. 1975. irreg. free. Banque Internationale a Luxembourg, 2 Boulevard Royal, Luxembourg, Luxembourg. circ. 5,000.

330.9   FR
BANQUE INTERNATIONALE POUR L'AFRIQUE OCCIDENTALE. CONSEIL D'ADMINISTRATION. RAPPORT ET RESOLUTIONS, RAPPORT DES COMMISSAIRES AUX COMPTES. a. Banque Internationale pour l'Afrique Occidentale, Conseil d'Administration, 9 av. de Messine, 75008 Paris, France. illus.

330.9   BB
BARBADOS. MINISTRY OF FINANCE AND PLANNING. ECONOMIC REPORT. 1977. a. Ministry of Finance and Planning, Government Printery, Bay St., St. Michael, Barbados, W. Indies. circ. 500.

330   UK   ISSN 0307-4552
BARCLAYS COUNTRY REPORTS. irreg. free. Barclays Bank PLC, Economics Department, 54 Lombard St., London EC3P 3AH, England. (looseleaf format)

330.9   US   ISSN 0094-1115
BASIC ECONOMIC DATA FOR IDAHO. a. Department of Employment, Bureau of Research and Analysis, Box 35, Boise, ID 83735. TEL 208-334-2765. stat.

330.943   GW
BERLINER WIRTSCHAFTSDATEN. 1973. irreg. Senator fuer Wirtschaft und Arbeit, Martin Luther Str. 105, 1000 Berlin 62, W. Germany (B.R.D.) Ed. Dr. Walter Hagemann. circ. 350. (looseleaf format)

330.9   BL
BRAZIL. SUPERINTENDENCIA DO DESENVOLVIMENTO DO NORDESTE. RELATORIO ANUAL. irreg. exchange basis. Superintendencia do Desenvolvimento do Nordeste, Av. Prof. Moraes Rego s/n, Edificio SUDENE, Cidade Universitaria, 50000 Recife, Pernambuco, Brazil. charts. stat.

338.9   EI   ISSN 0068-4120
BULLETIN OF THE EUROPEAN COMMUNITIES. SUPPLEMENT. (Text in Danish, Dutch, English, French, German, Greek, Italian, Spanish and Portuguese) 1968. irreg. (Commission of the European Communities) Office for Official Publications of the European Communities, 2 Rue Mercier, 2985 Luxembourg, Luxembourg (Dist. in U.S. by: European Community Information Service, 2100 M St., N.W., Ste. 707, Washington, DC 20037) Indexed: GeoRef.

330.9   SP
BUSINESS OPPORTUNITIES IN SPAIN. (Editions in English, French, Spanish) a. Banco de Santander, Publicidad y Estudios, Paseo de Pereda, 9/12, Santander 2, Spain.

330.9   MY
BUSINESS TRENDS ASIA REPORT: INDONESIA. 1979. irreg. $20. M P R C (Asia) Sdn. Berhad, 132-B Jalan Kasah, Damansara Heights, 50490 Kuala Lumpur, Malaysia. Ed. Paul Markandan. bk. rev. stat. circ. controlled.

330.9   CK
C.E.D.E. COLECCION-DEBATES. 1980. irreg. price varies. Universidad de los Andes, Centro de Estudios sobre Desarrollo Economico, Apdo. Aereo 4976, Bogota 3, Colombia.

330   CK
C.E.D.E. DOCUMENTOS DE TRABAJO. 1973. irreg. Universidad de los Andes, Centro de Estudios sobre Desarrollo Economico, Calle 18A Carrera 1e, Apdo. Aereo 4976, Bogota, Colombia. Ed.Bd. bibl. charts. stat.

330.9   CN
CALGARY IN FACT. 1977. a. Calgary Economic Development Authority, 237 8th Ave. S.E., Box 2100, Sta. M, Calgary, Alb. T2P 2M5, Canada. Ed. Henri Niet. circ. 15,000.

330.9   CN
CANADA. DEPARTMENT OF CONSUMER AND CORPORATE AFFAIRS. DIRECTOR OF INVESTIGATIONS AND RESEARCH. REPORT. (Text in English and French) a. free. Department of Consumer and Corporate Affairs, Ottawa, Ont. K1A 0C9, Canada. TEL 613-997-3284.

330   TR   ISSN 0069-0481
CARIBBEAN ECONOMIC ALMANAC; a collection of economic and statistical data covering the Caribbean area. 1962. irreg. price varies. Economic and Business Research Information and Advisory Service, P.O. Box 780, Port of Spain, Trinidad. Ed. Max B. Ifill. bk. rev. circ. 1,000.

330.9   BB   ISSN 0304-6796
CENTRAL BANK OF BARBADOS. ANNUAL REPORT. 1973. a. free. Central Bank of Barbados, P.O. Box 1016, Treasury Bldg., Bridgetown, Barbados, W.I. TEL 809-436-6870. charts. stat. circ. 1,400.

330.9   CE
CENTRAL BANK OF CEYLON. REVIEW OF THE ECONOMY/ARTHIKA VIVARANAYA. (Text in English) 1975. a. Rs.10($6) Central Bank of Ceylon Department of Economic Research, Deputy Director of Information, Janadhipathi Mawathi, Colombo 1, Sri Lanka.

330.9   KU
CENTRAL BANK OF KUWAIT. ECONOMIC CHART BOOK. (Text in Arabic and English) 1979. a. free. Central Bank of Kuwait, Research Department, Box 526, Kuwait. charts. circ. 2,000.

330.9   KU
CENTRAL BANK OF KUWAIT. ECONOMIC REPORT. (Editions in Arabic and English) a. free. Central Bank of Kuwait, Research Department - Bank al-Kuwayt al-Markazi, Box 526, Kuwait. charts. stat.

330.9   NR   ISSN 0008-9281
CENTRAL BANK OF NIGERIA. ECONOMIC AND FINANCIAL REVIEW. 1963. irreg., vol.16, no.2, 1978. free. Central Bank of Nigeria, P.M.B. 12194, Tinubu Square, Lagos, Nigeria. charts. stat. circ. 4,000. Indexed: Key to Econ.Sci.

CENTRO DE ESTUDIOS DE LA REALIDAD ECONOMICA Y SOCIAL. SERIE COCHABAMBA. see *SOCIOLOGY*

330.9 301   BO
CENTRO DE ESTUDIOS DE LA REALIDAD ECONOMICA Y SOCIAL. SERIE ESTUDIOS REGIONALES. irreg., no.4, 1982. Centro de Estudios de la Realidad Economica y Social, Casilla 10018, La Paz, Bolivia.

CENTRO DE ESTUDIOS DE LA REALIDAD ECONOMICA Y SOCIAL. SERIE ESTUDIOS URBANOS. see *SOCIOLOGY*

CENTRO DE ESTUDIOS DE LA REALIDAD ECONOMICA Y SOCIAL. SERIE MOVIMIENTOS SOCIALES. see *SOCIOLOGY*

330.9 340 320   CL   ISSN 0716-1123
CENTRO DE ESTUDIOS PUBLICOS. DOCUMENTO DE TRABAJO. (Text in Spanish; occasionally in English) 1981. irreg. Centro de Estudios Publicos, Monsenor Sotero Sanz No. 175, Providencia, Santiago - 9, Chile. Ed. Arturo Fontaine Talavera. adv. circ. 1,000.

330.9   BO
CENTRO DE INVESTIGACION Y PROMOCION DEL CAMPESINADO. CUADERNOS DE INVESTIGACION. 1973. irreg. Centro de Investigacion y Promocion del Campesinado, Casilla 5854, La Paz, Bolivia.

330.9   BL
COLECAO ECONOMIA. irreg. Editora Paz e Terra, Rua Sao Jose 90, Centro, Rio de Janeiro, Brazil. Ed.Bd.

330.9   BL
COLECAO EM CIMA DO FATO. 1983. irreg. Editora Codecri, Ltda., Rua Saint Roman, 142, Rio de Janeiro, RJ, Brazil.

BUSINESS AND ECONOMICS — ECONOMIC SITUATION AND CONDITIONS

330.9   SP ISSN 0210-1432
COMENTARIO SOCIOLOGICO. 1973. irreg. 4.500 ptas. Confederacion Espanola de Cajas de Ahorros, Servicio de Estudios Sociologicos, Caballero de Gracia, 30, 28014 Madrid, Spain. circ. 5,000.

330.9   PY
COMITE DE IGLESIAS. CUADERNOS DE INVESTIGACION. irreg., no.9, 1983. Comite de Iglesias para Ayudas de EMergencia, Gral Diaz 429, Asuncion, Paraguay.

330   CN ISSN 0069-7842
COMMUNITY IMPROVEMENT CORPORATION. ANNUAL REPORT/SOCIETE D'AMENAGEMENT REGIONAL. RAPPORT ANNUEL. (Text in English and French) 1967. a. free contr. circ. Community Improvement Corporation, 377 York St., Fredericton, N.B., Canada. TEL 506-453-2277. Ed. Elsie Gardner. circ. 1,000.

330.9   US
CONFERENCE ON AMERICAN ECONOMIC ENTERPRISE. PAPERS. irreg., latest 1981. Sleepy Hollow Restorations, Inc., Tarrytown, NY 10591.

330.9 320   UK
CONTRIBUTIONS TO POLITICAL ECONOMY. 1984. a. $26. (Cambridge Political Economy Society) Academic Press Inc. (London) Ltd., 24-28 Oval Rd., London NW1 7DX, England. Ed.Bd. Indexed: SSCI.

341.7   EI
COUNCIL OF THE EUROPEAN COMMUNITIES. REVIEW OF THE COUNCIL'S WORK. a. price varies. Office for Official Publications of the European Communities, P.O. Box 1003, L-2985 Luxembourg, Luxembourg (Dist. in the U.S. by: European Community Information Service, 2100 M St., N.W., Ste. 707, Washington, DC 20037)

330.9   US
COUNTY ECONOMIC INDICATORS. a. $3. Economic Development Department, 595 Cottage St., N.E., Salem, OR 97301. TEL 503-373-1200.

650   US
CURRENT BUSINESS REPORTS. (In several series of retail and wholesale trade reports, issued separately) a. U.S. Bureau of the Census, Customer Services, Washington, DC 20233 TEL 301-763-4100. (Subscr. to: Supt. of Documents, Washington, DC 20402) (also avail. in microfiche)

330.9   CY
CYPRUS. FIVE YEAR PLANS. Variant title: Emergency Economic Action Plans. (Text in English and Greek) 1961. quinquennial. free. Government Printing Office, Nicosia, Cyprus (Subscr. to: Director-General, Planning Bureau, Nicosia, Cyprus) circ. 2,000.

338.9   CN ISSN 0381-7024
DALHOUSIE UNIVERSITY. INSTITUTE OF PUBLIC AFFAIRS. OCCASIONAL PAPERS. 1977. irreg. Dalhousie University, Henson College of Public Affairs and Continuing Education, Halifax, N.S. B3H 3J5, Canada. TEL 902-424-2526. Ed. Margaret Dingley.

330.9   CR
DATOS SOCIO-ECONOMICOS DE COSTA RICA. 1974. a. free. Banco Central de Costa Rica, Apdo. 10058, 1000 San Jose, Costa Rica. charts. stat. circ. 1,500.

330.9   BL
DEBATE. 1984. irreg. Centro de Projetos e Estudos, Av. Luiz Viana Filho, CEP 40.000, Salvador, Bahia, Brazil. Ed. Valdomiro Santana. circ. 2,000.
  Supersedes (as of 1986): Debates/Cenpes.

330.9   DK ISSN 0418-6745
DENMARK REVIEW. French edition: Realites Danoises (ISSN 0107-5810); German edition: Daenische Revue (ISSN 0107-5799); Spanish edition: Revista Danesa (ISSN 0107-5837) 1961. irreg. free. Udenrigsministeriet - Ministry of Foreign Affairs, Asiatisk Plads 2, DK-1448 Copenhagen K, Denmark. Eds. Preben Hansen, Thorkild Borre. Indexed: Key to Econ.Sci.   PROMT.

382   IE
DEVELOPMENTS IN THE EUROPEAN COMMUNITIES. REPORT. 1973. irreg., latest no.27. £4.10. Government Publications Sales Office, Sun Alliance House, Molesworth St., Dublin 2, Ireland.

330.9   BL
DIAGNOSTICOS A P E C. (Text in English and Portuguese) irreg. Associacao Promotora de Estudos de Economia, Rua Sorocaba 295, Rio de Janeiro, Botafogo, Brazil. Ed. Victor da Silva Alves Filho.

330.9   DQ
DOMINICA. MINISTRY OF FINANCE AND DEVELOPMENT. STATISTICAL DIVISION. DIGEST. quinquennial. Ministry of Finance and Development, Bath Rd., Roseau, Dominica, West Indies.
  Formerly: Dominica. Ministry of Finance and Development. Statistical Digest.

330.9   DQ
DOMINICA. MINISTRY OF FINANCE AND DEVELOPMENT. VITAL STATISTICS REPORT. quinquennial. e.c. $2. Ministry of Finance and Development, Roseau, Dominica, West Indies.

330.9   FR
DOSSIER SAHEL.* 1978. a. 550 F. Ediafric-la Documentation Africaine, 57 ave. d'Iena, 75016 Paris, France.

330.9   FR ISSN 0291-8706
DOSSIERS ANTILLES GUYANE. ETUDES DIVERSES. (Text in French) irreg. Institut National de la Statistique et des Etudes Economiques (INSEE), Service Interregional Antilles. Guyane, Tour Secid 7th & 8th Fl., B.P. 863, 07675 Pointe a Pitre, Guadeloupe. circ. 500.

330   UK ISSN 0424-3331
E I U WORLD OUTLOOK. 1969. a. £75($147) (Economist Intelligence Unit) Economist Publications Ltd., 40 Duke St., London W1M 5DG, England (U.S. address: 10 Rockefeller Plaza, New York, NY 10020)

330.9   KE
EAST AFRICA REPORT ON TRADE AND INDUSTRY. a. (Kenya Association of Manufacturers) News Publishers Ltd., Norwich Union House, Mama Ngina St., P.O. Box 30339, Nairobi, Kenya. Ed. Henry Reuter. adv. circ. 2,500.

338.9   BL
ECONOMIA BRASILEIRA E SUAS PERSPECTIVAS - A P E C A O. (Text in English and Portuguese) 1962. a. $75. Associacao Promotora de Estudos de Economia, Rua Sorocaba 295, Botafogo, Rio de Janeiro, Brazil. Eds. Victor da Silva, Mircea Buescu. circ. 10,000.

330.9   CU
ECONOMIA CUBANA. English edition: Cuban Economy. a. Comite Estatal de Estadisticas, Centro de Informacion Cientifico-Tecnico, Av. Tercera no. 4411, Municipio de Playa, Havana, Cuba. stat.

330   ES ISSN 0012-9860
ECONOMIA SALVADORENA.* 1952. a. $5. Universidad de El Salvador, Instituto de Estudios Economicas, Ciudad Universitaria, Final 25 Av. Norte, San Salvador, El Salvador. adv. bibl. charts. circ. 1,500.

330.9   US ISSN 0095-2850
ECONOMIC AND SOCIAL PROGRESS IN LATIN AMERICA; ANNUAL REPORT. Spanish edition: Progreso Economico y Social en America Latina. Informe. (Editions also in Portuguese and French) 1961. a. exchange basis. Inter-American Development Bank, 1300 New York Ave., N.W., Washington, DC 20577. TEL 202-634-6000. charts. Key Title: Economic and Social Progress in Latin America.
  Continues: Socio-Economic Progress in Latin America; Annual Report (ISSN 0074-0888)

338.9   UN ISSN 0252-5704
ECONOMIC AND SOCIAL SURVEY OF ASIA AND THE PACIFIC. (Text in English and French) 1948. a. price varies. United Nations Economic and Social Commission for Asia and the Pacific, United Nations Bldg., Rajadamnern Ave., Bangkok 10200, Thailand (Dist. by: United Nations Publications, Room DC2-0853, New York, NY 10017; or Distribution and Sales Section, Palais des Nations, CH-1211 Geneva 10, Switzerland)
  Formerly: Economic Survey of Asia and the Far East (ISSN 0070-8690)

330   TH
ECONOMIC CONDITIONS IN/AND OUTLOOK FOR THAILAND. 1978. a. free. Bank of Thailand, Department of Economic Research, Bangkok, Thailand. circ. 4,800.

330   CN ISSN 0070-847X
ECONOMIC COUNCIL OF CANADA. ANNUAL REPORT. (Text in English and French) 1964. a. free. Economic Council of Canada, Information Division, P.O. Box 527, Ottawa, Ont. K1P 5V6, Canada. TEL 613-993-1894.

330   CN ISSN 0070-8488
ECONOMIC COUNCIL OF CANADA. ANNUAL REVIEW. (Text in English and French) 1964. a. price varies. Economic Council of Canada, Information Division, P.O. Box 527, Ottawa, Ont. K1P 5V6, Canada. TEL 819-997-2560.

330   US
ECONOMIC REPORT OF THE PRESIDENT. 1947. a. $8.50. U.S. Executive Office of the President, Council of Economic Advisers, Washington, DC 20500 TEL 202-395-7332. (Orders to: Supt. of Documents, Washington, DC 20402) circ. 50,000.
  Formerly: U.S. Executive Office of the President. Economic Report of the President.

330.9   JM ISSN 0259-9171
ECONOMIC REVIEW (YEAR) 1985. a. Jam.$8($1.45) Private Sector Organisation of Jamaica, 14 Hope Rd., P.O. Box 236, Kingston 10, Jamaica, W. Indies. TEL (809) 92-93804. (back issues avail.)

330.9   PO
ECONOMIC SITUATION IN THE YEAR (YEAR) 1976. a. free. Ministerio das Financas e do Plano, Departamento Central de Planeamento, Avenida D. Carlos I, 126, 1200 Lisbon, Portugal. circ. 500.
  Former titles: Portugal. Ministerio das Financas e do Plano. Departamento Central de Planeamento. Plano; Portugal. Ministerio do Plano e da Coordenacao Economica. Departamento Central de Planeamento. Plano.

338.9   UN ISSN 0070-8712
ECONOMIC SURVEY OF EUROPE. (Text in English, French and Russian) 1948. a., latest 1984/85. price varies. Economic Commission for Europe (ECE), Palais des Nations, 1211 Geneva, Switzerland (Or United Nations Publications, Rm. DC2-853, New York, NY 10017)

330   JA ISSN 0021-4833
ECONOMIC SURVEY OF JAPAN. English edition of: Annual Economic White Paper of Economic Planning Agency, Japan. (Text in English) 1969. a. 3900 Yen($23) (Economic Planning Agency) Japan Times, Ltd., 4-5-4 Shibaura, Minato-ku, Tokyo 108, Japan. charts. mkt. stat. (processed)
  Supersedes: Japanese Economic Statistics.

338.9   UN
ECONOMIC SURVEY OF LATIN AMERICA AND THE CARIBBEAN. (Editions in English and Spanish) 1948. a. price varies. Comision Economica para America Latina (CEPAL), Casilla 179-D, Santiago, Chile (Subscr. to: United Nations Publications, Sales Section, Rm. DC2-0853, New York, NY 10017; or Distribution and Sales Section, Palais des Nations, 1211 Geneva 10, Switzerland) stat. index. (back issues avail.)
  Formerly (until 1983): Economic Survey of Latin America (ISSN 0070-8720)

330.9   LB ISSN 0303-853X
ECONOMIC SURVEY OF LIBERIA. (Text in English) a., latest 1981. $5. Ministry of Planning and Economic Affairs, Box 9016, Monrovia, Liberia. stat.

BUSINESS AND ECONOMICS — ECONOMIC SITUATION AND CONDITIONS

330   II
ECONOMIC SURVEY OF MAHARASHTRA. (Text in English and Marathi) 1962. a. free. Directorate of Economics and Statistics, D.D. Building, Old Custom House, Bombay 400023, India. Ed. S.M. Vidwans.
Former titles: Economic Survey of India; Maharashtra: An Economic Review (ISSN 0076-2539)

330.9   SI   ISSN 0376-8791
ECONOMIC SURVEY OF SINGAPORE. (Text in English) 1974. a. S.$35. Ministry of Trade and Industry, CPF Bldg., 40-00, 79 Robinson Rd., Singapore 0106, Singapore (Orders to: Singapore National Printers, Box 485, Singapore, Singapore) circ. 7,300.

330   TI   ISSN 0070-8747
ECONOMIC YEARBOOK OF TUNISIA. (Text in Arabic, English and French) 1964. biennial. $6. Union Tunisienne de l'Industrie, du Commerce et de l'Artisanat, 32 rue Charles de Gaulle, Tunis, Tunisia. adv. circ. 5,000.

330.9   FR
ECONOMIE ALGERIENNE.* 1978. a. 990 F. Ediafric-la Documentation Africaine, 57 ave. d'Iena, 75016 Paris, France.

330   BE
ECONOMIE BELGE EN (YEAR)/BELGISCHE ECONOMIE IN (YEAR) (Supplement avail.) 1947. a. 500 Fr. Ministere des Affaires Economiques, 6 rue de l'Industrie, 1040 Brussels, Belgium. illus. stat.

330.9   FR
ECONOMIE CAMEROUNAISE.* 1979. a. 990 F. Ediafric-la Documentation Africaine, 57 ave. d'Iena, 75016 Paris, France.

330   TI   ISSN 0070-878X
ECONOMIE DE LA TUNISIE EN CHIFFRES. (Text in Arabic and French) 1960. a. Institut National de la Statistique, 70 rue Echcham, Tunis, Tunisia.

330.9   FR
ECONOMIE DES PAYS D'AFRIQUE NOIRE.* 1979. a. 635 F. Ediafric-la Documentation Africaine, 57 ave. d'Iena, 75016 Paris, France.

330.9   FR
ECONOMIE FRANCAISE EN (YEAR) 1959. a. Bureau d'Informations et de Prevision Economique, 122 Ave. Charles de Gaulle, 92522 Neuilly sur Seine, France. circ. 450.

330.9   FR
ECONOMIE FRANCAISE EN DONNEES D'ENCADREMENT. (Volume 1 of 5) a. membership. Bureau d'Informations et de Previsions Economiques, 122 Av. Charles de Gaulle, 92522 Neuilly sur Seine, France.
Supersedes in part: Prevision a Un An de l'Economie Francaise.

ECONOMIE FRANCAISE EN PERSPECTIVES SECTORIELLES: FILIERE BATIMENT, GENIE CIVIL, MATERIAUX DE CONSTRUCTION. see *BUILDING AND CONSTRUCTION*

338   FR
ECONOMIE FRANCAISE EN PERSPECTIVES SECTORIELLES: INDUSTRIES DE BIENS DE CONSOMMATION. (Volume 2 of 5) a. membership. Bureau d'Informations et de Previsions Economiques, 122 Av. Charles de Gaulle, 92522 Neuilly sur Seine Cedex, France. stat.
Supersedes in part: Prevision a Un a de l'Economie Francaise.

338   FR
ECONOMIE FRANCAISE EN PERSPECTIVES SECTORIELLES: INDUSTRIES DE BIENS D'EQUIPEMENT. (Volume 3 of 5) a. membership. Bureau d'Informations et de Previsions Economiques, 122 Av. Charles de Gaulle, 92522 Neuilly sur Seine Cedex, France. stat.
Supersedes in part: Prevision a Un An de l'Economie Francaise.

338   FR
ECONOMIE FRANCAISE EN PERSPECTIVES SECTORIELLES: INDUSTRIES DE BIENS INTERMEDIAIRES. (Volume 4 of 5) a. membership. Bureau d'Informations et de Previsions Economiques, 122 Av Charles de Gaulle, 92522 Neuilly sur Seine Cedex, France. stat.
Supersedes in part: Prevision a Un An de l'Economie Francaise.

330.9   FR
ECONOMIE GABONAISE.* 1977. a. 470 F. Ediafric-la Documentation Africaine, 57 ave. d'Iena, 57016 Paris, France.

330.9   FR
ECONOMIE IVOIRIENNE.* (Numero special du Bulletin de l'Afrique Noire) 1970. a. 990 F. Ediafric - la Documentation Africaine, 57 ave. d'Iena, 75016 Paris, France. illus.

330   LH
ECONOMY OF THE PRINCIPALITY OF LIECHTENSTEIN. (Text in English, French and German) 1962. irreg. Press and Information Office, Government Palace, FL-9490 Vaduz, Liechtenstein. circ. 4,000.
Formerly: Liechtenstein Economy.

330.9   EC
ECUADOR. CORPORACION FINANCIERA NACIONAL. BOLETIN ESTADISTICO. no.6, 1978. irreg. Corporacion Financiera Nacional, Robles 731 y Amazonas, Apartado de Correos 163, Quito, Ecuador. charts.

330.9   FR
EDIAFRIC - LA DOCUMENTATION AFRICAINE. PLANS DE DEVELOPPEMENT.* 1977. a. 635 F. Ediafric-la Documentation Africaine, 57 ave. d'Iena, 75016 Paris, France.

334   IO
EDISI CHUSUS BULLETIN KOPERASI. 1971. irreg. Rps.350 per no. Department of Trade, Directorate General of Cooperative Office, Jl. Haryonon MT, Kebayoran Baru, Jakarta, Indonesia. charts. stat.

330.9   ES
EL SALVADOR. MINISTERIO DE PLANIFICACION Y COORDINACION DEL DESARROLLO ECONOMICO Y SOCIAL. MEMORIA DE LABORES. 1976. irreg. Ministerio de Planificacion y Coordinacion del Desarrollo Economico y Social, Biblioteca Tecnica "Hector Humberto Zelaya", 10 Av. Sur y Calle Mexico, 1505 Barrio San Jacinto, San Salvador, El Salvador.

330.9   ES
EL SALVADOR, INFORME ECONOMICO Y SOCIAL. 1975. a. free. Ministerio de Planificacion y Coordinacion del Desarrollo Economico y Social, Biblioteca Tecnica "Hector Humberto Zelaya", 10 Av. Sur y Calle Mexico, 1505 Barrio San Jacinto, San Salvador, El Salvador. stat. circ. 88. (processed)
Continues: Economia Salvodorena.
Includes comparative data for previous years

330.9   GW   ISSN 0340-8744
EMPIRICA; Austrian economic papers. 1974. irreg. (2 nos. per vol.) DM.105 per vol. (Oesterreichisches Institut fuer Wirtschaftsforschung, AU) Gustav Fischer Verlag, Postfach 720143, 7000 Stuttgart 70, W. Germany (B.R.D.) Eds. H. Seidel, K. Aiginger. adv. circ. 800. Indexed: P.A.I.S.For.Lang.Ind.

330.9   UK   ISSN 0267-8128
ENGLAND. ECONOMIC AND SOCIAL RESEARCH COUNCIL. RESEARCH PROGRAMME BULLETIN. 1985. irreg. Economic and Social Research Council, 1 Temple Ave., London EC4Y 0BD, England. Ed. Dr. Angela Williams.

330.9   BL
ENSAYOS E C I E L. (Text and summaries in English, Spanish & Portuguese) 1974. irreg., vol.7, 1980-81. free. Programa de Estudios Conjuntos para la Integracion Economica Latinoamericano, Caixa Postal 740, Rio de Janeiro, Brazil. adv. circ. 2,000.

330.9 300   SJ
ESSAYS ON THE ECONOMY AND SOCIETY OF THE SUDAN. 1977. irreg. Economic and Social Research Council, Box 1166, Khartoum, Sudan. Ed. Ali Mohamed el Hassan. bibl.

132   SP   ISSN 0213-2699
ESTUDIOS ECONOMICOS. 1972. irreg. 300 ptas. Banco de Espana, Negociado de Publicaciones, Alcala 50, Madrid 28014, Spain.

330.9   BL
ESTUDOS SOBRE O NORDESTE. irreg. Editora Paz e Terra, Rua Sao Jose 90, Centro, Rio de Janeiro, Brazil. Ed.Bd.

320   UK
EUROPE REVIEW. 1985. a. $59. World of Information, 21 Gold St., Saffron Walden, Essex CB10 1EJ, England. Ed. Richard Green. adv. illus. stat. circ. 7,000.

330.9   UK
EUROPEAN REGIONAL INCENTIVES. 1980. a. £40. Centre for the Study of Public Policy, University of Strathclyde, Livingstone Tower, 26 Richmond St., Glasgow, G1 1XH, England. TEL 041-552-4400 Ext. 3909. Eds. Douglas Yuill, Kevin Allen. circ. 500.

330.9   US
EXPLORATIONS IN THE WORLD ECONOMY. 1982. irreg. $29.95 cloth; paper $14.95. Sage Publications, Inc., 2111 W. Hillcrest Dr., Newbury Park, CA 91320. TEL 805-499-0721. Ed. Immanuel Wallerstein. (back issues avail.)

330.9   US
EXTRAORDINARY CONTRACTUAL RELIEF REPORTER. a. $230. Federal Publications Inc., 1120 20 St., N.W., Washington, DC 20036. TEL 202-377-7000.
Government contracts

FAR EAST AND AUSTRALASIA. see *HISTORY — History Of Australasia And Other Areas*

330.9   US
FEDERAL RESERVE BANK OF ATLANTA. RESEARCH PAPER SERIES. 1976. irreg., no.6, 1979. free. Federal Reserve Bank of Atlanta, Atlanta, GA 30303. circ. 2,000.

330.9   US   ISSN 0361-8714
FEDERAL RESERVE BANK OF BOSTON. CONFERENCE SERIES. 1969. a. ‡ Federal Reserve Bank of Boston, Research Department, 600 Atlantic Ave., Boston, MA 02106. TEL 617-973-3000. Ed. J. Poskanzer. bibl. charts. tr.lit. circ. 10,000. (also avail. in microform from UMI; reprint service avail. from UMI)

FEDERATION DES INDUSTRIES CHIMIQUES DE BELGIQUE. RAPPORT ANNUEL. see *ENGINEERING — Chemical Engineering*

330.9   FJ
FIJI. BUREAU OF STATISTICS. VITAL STATISTICS. 1976. irreg. $2. Bureau of Statistics, Box 2221, Suva, Fiji.

330.9   UK
FINANCE FOR NEW PROJECTS IN UK; guide to private and public sector initiatives and grants. 1975. biennial. Peat Marwick Mitchell & Co., 1 Puddle Dock, Blackfriars, London EC4V 3PD, England. Ed. Peat Marwick. circ. 20,000.
●Also available online.

330   FI   ISSN 0071-5271
FINLAND. KANSANTALOUSOSASTO. TALOUDELLINEN KATSAUS. ECONOMIC SURVEY. (Supplement to the Budget) (Text in English, Finnish, Swedish) 1948. a. Fmk.26. Valtion Painatuskeskus - Government Printing Centre; Ministry of Finance, Annankatu 44, 00100 Helsinki 10, Finland.

338.9   DK   ISSN 0901-8735
FIRMENGRUENDUNG IN DAENEMARK. English edition: Setting up in Denmark. (Text in German) 1979. biennial. free. Copenhagen Handelsbank A-S - Kjoebenhavns Handelsbank, Holmens Kanal 2, DK-1091 Copenhagen K, Denmark. charts. illus. stat.

338.5   JA
FIVE YEAR ECONOMIC FORECAST/GOKANEN KEIZAI YOSOKU. (Text in Japanese; summaries in English) 1975. a. Japan Economic Research Center, Economic Analysis Division - Nihon Keizai Kenkyu Senta, 1-9-5 Otemachi, Chiyoda-ku, Tokyo 100, Japan. circ. controlled.

BUSINESS AND ECONOMICS — ECONOMIC SITUATION AND CONDITIONS

338.9 US ISSN 0071-7282
FORECAST. 1964. a. free. United California Bank, Research and Planning Division, Box 3666 Terminal Annex, Los Angeles, CA 90051. TEL 213-614-4111. circ. 40,000. Indexed: Mag.Ind.

330.9 US ISSN 0090-9467
FOREIGN ECONOMIC TRENDS AND THEIR IMPLICATIONS FOR THE UNITED STATES. irreg. $90. U.S. National Technical Information Service, 5285 Port Royal Rd., Springfield, VA 22161 TEL 202-377-2000. (Orders to: Supt. of Documents, Washington, DC 20402) illus. stat. (also avail. in microform from UMI; reprint service avail. from UMI) Indexed: Ind.U.S.Gov.Per. Key to Econ.Sci.
Continues: Economic Trends and Their Implications for the United States.

330 FR ISSN 0071-8505
FRANCE. COMMISSION DE LA CONCURRENCE. RAPPORTS ECONOMIQUES. 1954. a. Commission de la Concurrence, 75 av. des Champs Elysees, 75008 Paris, France. circ. controlled.

FRANCE. INSTITUT NATIONAL DE LA STATISTIQUE ET DES ETUDES ECONOMIQUES. SERIE C: COMPTES ET PLANIFICATION. see *BUSINESS AND ECONOMICS — Accounting*

330.9 FR
FRANCE. INSTITUT NATIONAL DE LA STATISTIQUE ET DES ETUDES ECONOMIQUES. SERIE R: REGIONS. 1968. a. 275 F. Institut National de la Statistique et des Etudes Economiques, 18 bd. A. Pinard, 75675 Paris 14, France.

330.9 GE ISSN 0071-9412
FREIBERGER FORSCHUNGSHEFTE. MONTANWISSENSCHAFTEN. REIHE D: ECONOMIC SCIENCES. 1951. irreg. price varies. (Bergakademie Freiberg) VEB Deutscher Verlag fuer Grundstoffindustrie, Karl-Heine-Str. 27, 7031 Leipzig, E. Germany (D.D.R.)

338.9 DR
FUNDACION DOMINICANA DE DESARROLLO. INFORME ANUAL. a. Fundacion Dominicana de Desarrollo, Calle Mercedes 4, Santo Domingo, Z. P. No. 1, Dominican Republic. charts. illus.

330 EI ISSN 0069-6749
GENERAL REPORT ON THE ACTIVITIES OF THE EUROPEAN COMMUNITIES. (Supersedes the General Report on the Activities of the Community published individually by the European Coal and Steel Community. High Authority; European Economic Community. Commission; European Atomic Energy Community. Commission) (Text in Dutch, English, French, German, and Italian) 1968. a. 225 Fr. Commission of the European Communities, Service des Renseignements, 200 rue de la Loi, Brussels 4, Belgium (Dist. in U.S. by: European Community Information Service, 2100 M St., N.W., Ste. 707, Washington, DC 20037)

330.9 GH ISSN 0304-1190
GHANA. (Text in English) irreg. Information Services Department, Box 745, Accra, Ghana. illus. Key Title: Estimates of Consolidated Fund Expenditure.

330.9 GH ISSN 0435-9348
GHANA COMMERCIAL BANK. ANNUAL REPORT. a. free. Ghana Commercial Bank, Research Department, P.O. Box 134, Accra, Ghana.

330.9 II
GOA, DAMAN, AND DIU. DIRECTORATE OF ECONOMICS, STATISTICS, AND EVALUATION. EVALUATION REPORT. 1969. irreg. Directorate of Economics, Statistics, and Evaluation, Panaji, Goa, India. stat. circ. 150.

330.9 UK
GOVERNMENT SUPPORT FOR BRITISH BUSINESS. 1981. a. £25. University of Strathclyde, Center for the Study of Public Policy, Livingstone Tower, 26 Richmond Street, Glasgow G1 1XH, Scotland. TEL 041-552-4400. Ed.Bd. circ. 1,000.
●Also available online.
Formerly: Industrial Aids in the UK - A Businessman's Guide.

330 CH
GRAPHICAL SURVEY OF THE ECONOMY OF TAIWAN DISTRICT, REPUBLIC OF CHINA. (Text in Chinese and English) 1972. a. not for sale. Central Bank of China, Taipei, Taiwan, Republic of China. circ. 2,000.

380.1 GU
GUAM ANNUAL ECONOMIC REVIEW. 1963. a. $2.50 per no. (free locally) Department of Commerce, 590 S. Marine Dr., GITC Bldg., Ste. 601, Tamuning, Guam 96911.
Incorporating: Guam. Department of Commerce. Statistical Abstract; Former titles: Guam Economic Annual Review; Guam. Department of Commerce. Quarterly Review of Business Conditions.

330 BL
GUANABARA: O BALANCO ECONOMICO. 1972. a. free. Instituto de Desenvolvimento da Guanabara, Av. Calogeras, 15 - 3. andar, Rio de Janeiro, Brazil. illus. stat. circ. 1,000.

GUATEMALA. BANCO NACIONAL DE DESARROLLO AGRICOLA. MEMORIA. see *AGRICULTURE — Agricultural Economics*

338 BO
GUIA BOLIVIA; industria, comercio, ganaderia. 1976. irreg. Editora Nacional, Bolivar 3235, Cochabamba, Bolivia.

330 UY
GUIA PARA INVERSIONES EN EL URUGUAY. 1976. irreg. Comision Coordinadora para el Desarrollo Economico, Av. Rondeau 1908, Montevideo, Uruguay.

HARRY BROWNE'S SPECIAL REPORTS. see *BUSINESS AND ECONOMICS — Investments*

330.9 US ISSN 0067-3633
HAWAII ANNUAL ECONOMIC REVIEW. 1968. a. single copies free. Bank of Hawaii, Economics Department, Box 2900, Honolulu, HI 96846. TEL 808-537-8307. Ed. David L. Ramsour. stat. circ. 7,500. (back issues avail.) Indexed: B.P.I. P.A.I.S.
Formerly: Economy of Hawaii.

HERNE IN ZAHLEN. JAHRESVEROEFFENTLICHUNGEN. see *BUSINESS AND ECONOMICS — Abstracting, Bibliographies, Statistics*

330.9 HK
HONG KONG ANNUAL REPORT. a. Government Information Services, Beaconsfield House, Queen's Rd., Central, Victoria, Hong Kong, Hong Kong.

330.9 HK
HONG KONG SOCIAL AND ECONOMIC TRENDS. (Text in English) 1968. triennial. HK.$30. Census and Statistics Department, Kai Tak Commercial Bldg., 317 Des Voeux Rd., Central, Hong Kong, Hong Kong (Subscr. to: Director of Information Services, Information Services Department, Beaconsfield House, Queen's Rd., Central, Hong Kong)

HUNTER VALLEY RESEARCH FOUNDATION. WORKING PAPERS. see *STATISTICS*

330 GW ISSN 0170-3617
I F O SPIEGEL DER WIRTSCHAFT; Struktur und Konjunktur in Bild und Zahl. 1973. a. DM.120. I F O-Institut fuer Wirtschaftsforschung, Poschingerstr. 5, 8000 Munich 80, W. Germany (B.R.D.)
Formerly: Wirtschaftsbilderheft BRD und Ausland (ISSN 0019-1566)

330 II
I S E C MONOGRAPH. no.4, 1976. irreg. Rs.20($4.50) (Institute for Social and Economic Change) World Press Ltd., 37A College St., Calcutta 700073, India. Ed. F. Rao.

I S E R OCCASIONAL PAPERS. (Institute of Social and Economic Research) see *SOCIAL SCIENCES: COMPREHENSIVE WORKS*

330 US
IDAHO OCCUPATION WAGE SURVEY. 1979. a. Department of Employment, 317 Main St., Boise, ID 83735. TEL 208-334-2757. circ. 2,000.

330 US ISSN 0093-9552
ILLINOIS STATE AND REGIONAL ECONOMIC DATA BOOK. 1970. irreg. free. Department of Commerce and Community Affairs, 620 E. Adams, Springfield, IL 62701. TEL 217-782-1438. Ed. W. Biermann. stat. circ. 2,000(controlled)

330.9 318 BL
INDICE DO BRASIL/BRAZILIAN INDEX YEARBOOK. irreg. Cr.$2500 per no. Indice-O Banco de Dados, Rua Alcindo Guanabara 24, 20038 Rio de Janeiro, Brazil. illus.

330.9 US
INDUSTRY NORMS AND KEY BUSINESS RATIOS. LIBRARY EDITION. a. $295. Dun & Bradstreet Corporation, Credit Services, One Diamond Hill Rd., Murry Hill, NJ 07974. TEL 800-342-2477.

330.9 BL
INFORMATION ON PARANA. Portuguese edt.: Parana Informacoes. 1973. irreg. free. ‡ Banco de Desenvolvimento do Parana, S.A., Av. Vicente Machado, 445, Cx. Postal 6042, Curitiba, Parana, Brazil. Ed. Luiz Fernando Osti Magalhaes. illus.

330.9 FR
INSTITUT D'ECONOMIE REGIONALE BOURGOGNE-FRANCHE-COMTE. CAHIERS. irreg. no.35, 1985. 60 F. Institut d'Economie Regionale Bourgogne-Franche-Comte, 4 bd. Gabriel, 21000 Dijon, France.

330.9 DK ISSN 0106-8628
INSTITUT FOR GRAENSEREGIONSFORSKNING. ARBEJDSPAPIR. no.14, 1982. irreg. price varies. Institut for Graenseregionsforskning, Persillegade 6, 6200 Aabenraa, Denmark. illus.

330.9 SI
INSTITUTE OF SOUTHEAST ASIAN STUDIES. PROCEEDINGS OF INTERNATIONAL CONFERENCES. (Text in English) 1973. irreg., no.30, 1987. price varies. Institute of Southeast Asian Studies, Heng Mui Keng Terrace, Pasir Panjang, Singapore 0511, Singapore.

330.9 VE
INSTITUTO DE CREDITO AGRICOLA Y PECUARIO. INFORME ANUAL. 1975. a. Instituto de Credito Agricola y Pecuario, Barquisimeto, Venezuela.
Continues: Banco Agricola y Pecuario. Informe.

338.9 PE
INSTITUTO DE ESTUDIOS PERUANOS. ANALISIS ECONOMICO. 1964. irreg., latest no.10. price varies. I E P Ediciones, Horacio Urteaga 694 (Campo de Marte), Lima 11, Peru.

330 CK
INTEGRACION FINANCIERA; pasado, presente y futuro de las finanzas en Colombia y el mundo. 1984. irreg. (?) Medios & Medios Publicidad Cia Ltda., Cr. 10 No. 60-11 P. 6, Apdo. 036943, Bogota, Colombia.

INTELLECTUAL ACTIVIST. see *POLITICAL SCIENCE*

330.9 US ISSN 0738-1425
INTERNATIONAL DEVELOPMENT RESOURCE BOOKS. 1984. irreg. price varies. Greenwood Press, 88 Post Rd. W., Box 5007, Westport, CT 06881. TEL 203-226-3571.

330.9 UN ISSN 0250-7463
INTERNATIONAL FINANCIAL STATISTICS YEARBOOK. French edition (ISSN 0252-029X); Spanish edition (ISSN 0252-3043) 1976. a. $25. International Monetary Fund, Publications Unit, 700 19th St., N.W., Washington, DC 20431. TEL 202-623-7430.

330 UN
INTERNATIONAL LABOUR OFFICE. P R E A L C. INVESTIGACIONES SOBRE EMPLEO. 1978. irreg., no.26, 1985. $7 per no. International Labour Office, Programa Regional del Empleo para America Latina y el Caribe, Casilla 618, Santiago, Chile. adv. bk. rev. stat. circ. 1,000. (looseleaf format; back issues avail.)

BUSINESS AND ECONOMICS — ECONOMIC SITUATION AND CONDITIONS

330.9   IR
IRAN TRADE & INDUSTRY ANNUAL REVIEW. (Text in English) a. Echo Publications, Ave. Shiras, Kuche Khalhali No. 4, P.O. Box 2008, Teheran, Iran. adv.

330   IT   ISSN 0075-1995
ITALY. MINISTERO DEL BILANCIO E DELLA PROGRAMMAZIONE ECONOMICA. RELAZIONE GENERALE SULLA SITUAZIONE ECONOMICA DEL PAESE. 1951. a. free. Ministero del Bilancio, Rome, Italy.

330   AU
JAHRBUCH DER OESTERREICHISCHEN WIRTSCHAFT. 1975. a. Bundeskammer der Gewerblichen Wirtschaft, Wiedner Hauptstr. 63, A-1045 Vienna, Austria. Ed. Werner Filek-Wittinghausen.

330   GW   ISSN 0449-5225
JAHRBUCH DER WIRTSCHAFT OSTEUROPAS/ YEARBOOK OF EAST-EUROPEAN ECONOMICS. (Editions in English and German) 1970. a. DM.96. (Osteuropa-Institut, Munich) Guenter Olzog Verlag, Thierschstr. 11/15, 8000 Munich 22, W. Germany (B.R.D.) Ed. Hans Raupach. bk. rev. circ. 800.

330.9   JA
JAPAN. ANNUAL REPORT ON NATIONAL LIFE. (Text in English) a. price varies. Ministry of Finance, Economic Planning Agency, 2-1, 1-chome, Kasumigaseki, Chiyoda-ku, Tokyo, Japan. Ed.Bd. (back issues avail.)

JAPAN ECONOMIC ALMANAC; an annual in-depth report on the state of the Japanese economy. see BUSINESS AND ECONOMICS — Production Of Goods And Services

330   JA   ISSN 0075-3238
JAPAN ECONOMIC RESEARCH CENTER. CENTER PAPER SERIES. (Text in English) 1965. irreg. Japan Economic Research Center, General Administration Division - Nihon Keizai Kenkyu Senta, 1-9-5 Otemachi, Chiyoda-ku, Tokyo 100, Japan. (back issues avail.)

330   AT
JOURNAL OF AUSTRALIAN POLITICAL ECONOMY. 1977. irreg. (approx. 3/yr.) Aus.$12 to individuals; institutions Aus.$20. Australian Political Economy Movement, P.O. Box 112, Parkville, Victoria 3052, Australia. Ed.Bd. adv. bk. rev. circ. 1,000.

330.9   PE
JUNTA DEL ACUERDO DE CARTAGENA. PUBLICACIONES. irreg., no.3, 1982. Junta del Acuerdo de Cartagena, Departamento de Comunicaciones e Informacion, San Isidro, Lima, Peru.

K K C BRIEF. see BUSINESS AND ECONOMICS

330   JA
KEIDANREN KEIZAI SHIRYO. (Text in Japanese) 1947. irreg. $2. Japan Federation of Economic Organizations - Keizai Dantai Rengokai (KEIDANREN), 9-4 Otemachi, 1-Chome, Chiyoda-ku, Tokyo 100, Japan. charts. illus. stat. circ. 3,500.

330   JA
KEIDANREN PAMPHLET. (Text in Japanese) 1950. irreg. $2. Japan Federation of Economic Organizations - Keizai Dantai Rengokai (KEIDANREN), 9-4 Otemachi, 1-Chome, Chiyoda-ku, Tokyo 100, Japan. charts. illus. stat. circ. 3,500.

330   JA
KEIDANREN POCKET SERIES. (Text in Japanese) 1975. irreg. free. Japan Federation of Economic Organizations - Keizai Dantai Rengokai (KEIDANREN), 9-4 Otemachi, 1-Chome, Chiyoda-ku, Tokyo 100, Japan. circ. 10,000.

330.9   US   ISSN 0270-515X
KENTUCKY. COUNCIL OF ECONOMIC ADVISORS. POLICY PAPERS SERIES. 1977. irreg. (4-5/yr.) $5. Kentucky Council of Economic Advisors, College of Business and Economics, 302 Mathews Bldg., University of Kentucky, Lexington, KY 40506. TEL 606-258-7675. circ. 600. Indexed: P.A.I.S.

330.9   KE
KENYA. CENTRAL BUREAU OF STATISTICS. ECONOMIC SURVEY. 1960. a. price varies. Central Bureau of Statistics, Ministry of Finance & Planning, Box 30266, Nairobi, Kenya (Orders to: Government Printing and Stationery Department, Box 30128, Nairobi, Kenya)
    Formerly: Kenya. Ministry of Economic Planning and Development. Economic Survey (ISSN 0075-5842)

330.9   UK
KENYA YEARBOOK. a. £10($30) New Product Newsletter Co. Ltd., 1A Chesterfield St., London W.1., England. adv. charts. illus.

330.9   II   ISSN 0453-7440
KERALA; AN ECONOMIC REVIEW. (Text in English) 1959. a. price varies. Kerala State Planning Board, Trivandrum 4, India. circ. 2,000.

330.9   GW   ISSN 0342-0787
KIELER ARBEITSPAPIERE. (Text in English or German) 1973. irreg. DM.10 per no. Kiel Institut fuer Weltwirtschaft, Duesternbrooker Weg 120, 2300 Kiel 1, W. Germany (B.R.D.) circ. 150. Indexed: Rural Recreat.Tour.Abstr. World Agri.Econ.& Rural Sociol.Abstr.

KOREA POLICY SERIES. see POLITICAL SCIENCE

330.9   320.253   US
KOREAN AFFAIRS REPORT. 1966. 60/yr. $5 per no. U.S. Joint Publications Research Service, 1000 N. Glebe Rd., Arlington, VA 22201 TEL 703-487-4630. (Orders to: NTIS, Springfield, VA 22161)
    Formerly: Translations on North Korea.

330.9   MY
LAPORAN KETUA ODIT NEGARA. KERAJAAN PERSEKUTUAN. a. Jabatan Percetakan Negara, Kuala Lumpur, Malaysia.

330.9   320   UK
LATIN AMERICA & CARIBBEAN REVIEW. 1979. a. $59. World of Information, 21 Gold St., Saffron Walden, Essex CB10 1EJ, England. Ed. Richard Green. adv. illus. stat. circ. 5,000.
    Former titles (until 1985): Latin America and Caribbean (ISSN 0262-5415); Until 1981: Latin America Annual Review and the Caribbean.

330.9   LO
LESOTHO NATIONAL DEVELOPMENT CORPORATION. NEWSLETTER. irreg. Lesotho National Development Corporation, Box 666, Maseru, Lesotho.

330.9   IS   ISSN 0334-9160
LEUMI REVIEW; Israel: macroperspectives. (Text in English) 1952. irreg. (approx. 4/yr.) free. Bank Leumi Le-Israel, P.O. Box 2, 61 000 Tel Aviv, Israel. Ed. G. Shifron. charts. mkt. stat. circ. 8,000.
    Formed by the merger of: Bank Leumi Israel Macroperspectives & Bank Leumi Economic Review (ISSN 0034-6519); Formerly: Review of Economic Conditions in Israel.

330.9   UK   ISSN 0267-7164
LIBERTARIAN ALLIANCE. ECONOMIC NOTES. 1985. irreg. £5($10) Libertarian Alliance, 3 Langley Court, Covent Garden, London WC2E 9JY, England. Ed.Bd. adv. bk. rev. bibl. film rev. circ. 1,000. (back issues avail.)

330.9   UR   ISSN 0207-1266
LITUANISTIKA V S.S.S.R. EKONOMIKA; nauchno-referativnyi sbornik. (Text in Russian) 1978. a. 0.60 Rub. Akademiya Nauk Litovskoi S.S.R., Nauchno-Informatsionnyi Tsentr, Michurino g-ve 1/46, Vilnius, Lithuanian S.S.R., U.S.S.R. Ed. A. Balsys. circ. 300.

330.9   JA
LONG-TERM ECONOMIC FORECAST. (Text in Japanese; summaries in English) 1970. a. Japan Economic Research Center - Nihon Keizai Kenkyu Senta, 1-9-5 Otemachi, Chiyoda-ku, Tokyo 100, Japan.

330.9   MY
M P R C REPORT ON FINANCE, COMMERCE, INDUSTRY: INDONESIA. 1972. irreg. $30. ‡ M P R C (Asia) Sdn. Berhad, 132-B Jalan Kasah, Damansara Heights, 50490 Kuala Lumpur, Malaysia. Ed. Paul Markandan. bk. rev. stat. circ. controlled.

330.9   MY
M P R C REPORT ON FINANCE, COMMERCE, INDUSTRY: INDONESIA. SUPPLEMENT. 1974. irreg. $15. M P R C (Asia) Sdn. Berhad, 132-B Jalan Kasah, Damansara Heights, 50490 Kuala Lumpur, Malaysia. Ed. Paul Markandan. bk. rev. stat.

330.9   MY
M P R C REPORT ON FINANCE, COMMERCE, INDUSTRY: SINGAPORE. 1972. irreg. $15. ‡ M P R C (Asia) Sdn. Berhad, 132-B Jalan Kasah, Damansara Heights, 50490 Kuala Lumpur, Malaysia. Ed. Paul Markandan. bk. rev. stat. circ. controlled.

330.9   MY
M P R C REPORT ON FINANCE, COMMERCE, INDUSTRY: SOUTH EAST ASIA. 1977. irreg. $50. M P R C (Asia) Sdn. Berhad, 132-B Jalan Kasah, Damansara Heights, 50490 Kuala Lumpur, Malaysia. Ed. Paul Markandan. bk. rev. stat. circ. (controlled)

330.9   MY
M P R C REPORT ON FINANCE, COMMERCE, INDUSTRY: THAILAND. 1973. irreg. $30. ‡ M P R C (Asia) Sdn. Berhad, 132-B Jalan Kasah, Damansara Heights, 50490 Kuala Lumpur, Malaysia. Ed. Paul Markandan. bk. rev. stat. circ. controlled.

MACHINERY: LATIN AMERICAN INDUSTRIAL REPORT. see MACHINERY

330.1   MW   ISSN 0076-3101
MALAWI ECONOMIC REPORT. a. K.2.75. Government Printer, P.O. Box 37, Zomba, Malawi.

330.9   MM
MALTA. CENTRAL OFFICE OF STATISTICS. ECONOMIC SURVEY. a. Office of the Prime Minister, Economic Division, Valletta, Malta (Subscr. to: Information Division, Auberge de Castille, Valletta, Malta)

330   AT   ISSN 0816-2484
MANAGEMENT REPORTS ON THE AUSTRALIAN ECONOMY. 1965. a. Aus.$150. Coopers & Lybrand W.D. Scott, Box 1815, North Sydney, N.S.W. 2060, Australia.
    Formerly: Australian Economy; Business Forecast (ISSN 0084-7348)

330   CN
MANITOBA. ECONOMIC DEVELOPMENT NETWORK. COMMUNITY PROFILE INFORMATION SYSTEM. 1959. a. Can.$99. ‡ Economic Development Network, 20 3rd St. NE, Portage la Prairie, Man. R1N 1N4, Canada. TEL 204-857-8736. stat. circ. controlled.
    Formerly (until 1982): Manitoba Community Reports (ISSN 0318-6415)

330.9   350   310   US
MASSACHUSETTS TAXPAYERS FOUNDATION. STATE BUDGET TRENDS. 1973. a. $3.50. Massachusetts Taxpayers Foundation, Inc., 24 Province St., Boston, MA 02108. TEL 617-720-1000. (back issues avail.)

330.9   FR
MEMENTO DE L'ECONOMIE AFRICAINE.* 1980. a. 990 F. Ediafric-la Documentation Africaine, 57 Ave. d'Iena, 75016 Paris, France.

MEMO FROM BELGIUM. see POLITICAL SCIENCE

977   US
METROPOLITAN MILWAUKEE ECONOMIC FACT BOOK. Title varies: Economic Fact Book on Metropolitan Milwaukee. 1965. a. $75. Metropolitan Milwaukee Association of Commerce, 756 N. Milwaukee St., Milwaukee, WI 53202. TEL 414-273-3000. circ. 300.
    Formerly: Metropolitan Milwaukee Association of Commerce. Economic Studies (ISSN 0076-7077)

972 MX ISSN 0543-7741
MEXICO;* facts, figures, trends. Spanish edition: Mexico; Hechos, Cifras, Tendencias. 1960. irreg.; latest issue 1976. $8 spanish edition; $12 English edition. ‡ Banco Nacional de Comercio Exterior, S.A., Departamento de Publicaciones, Venustiano Carranza 32, Mexico 1, D.F., Mexico.

MEXICO. INSTITUTO NACIONAL DE INVESTIGACIONES FORESTALES, AGRICOLAS Y PECUARIAS. FOLLETOS DE INVESTIGACION. see *AGRICULTURE*

330.9 UK ISSN 0305-3210
MIDDLE EAST REVIEW. 1974. a. $59. World of Information, 21 Gold St., Saffron Walden, Essex CB10 1EJ, England. Ed. Richard Green. adv. illus. stat. circ. 10,500. Indexed: P.A.I.S. HR Rep.
Formerly (until 1981): Middle East Annual Review.

330.9 US
MIDDLE TENNESSEE STATE UNIVERSITY, MURFREESBORO. BUSINESS AND ECONOMIC RESEARCH CENTER. CONFERENCE PAPER. irreg. price varies. Middle Tennessee State University, Murfreesboro, Business and Economic Research Center, Box 102, Murfreesboro, TN 37132. TEL 615-898-2610.

MINERALS: LATIN AMERICAN INDUSTRY REPORT. see *MINES AND MINING INDUSTRY*

330.9 320 US
MONGOLIA REPORT. irreg. (approx. 5/yr.) $5 per no. U.S. Joint Publications Research Service, 1000 N. Glebe Rd., Arlington, VA 22201 TEL 703-487-4630. (Orders to: NTIS, Springfield, VA 22161)
Formerly: Translations on Mongolia.

330.9 KE
NATION ECONOMIC SURVEY. (Text in English) 1976/77. a. Nation Newspapers Ltd., Nation House, Tom Mboya St., Box 49010, Nairobi, Kenya.

330.9 ET
NATIONAL BANK OF ETHIOPIA. ANNUAL REPORT. 1964. a. free. National Bank of Ethiopia, c/o Research Library, Box 5550, Addis Ababa, Ethiopia.

330 YU ISSN 0077-2798
NATIONAL BANK OF YUGOSLAVIA. ANNUAL REPORT. (Text in English) 1958. a. Narodna Banka Jugoslavije, Bulevar Revolucije 15, Box 1010, 11001 Belgrade, Yugoslavia. circ. 1,200.

330.9 IR ISSN 0572-5941
NATIONAL INCOME OF IRAN. 1974. irreg., latest 1977. free. Bank Markazi Iran, Economic Statistics Department - Central Bank of Iran, Ave. Ferdowsi, Teheran, Iran.

330.9 NP
NEPAL. RASHTRIYA PANCAYATA. ARTHIKA SAMITI. (Text in Nepali) a. Rashtriya Panchayat Sachivalaya, Rashtriya Panchayat Bhavan, Singhdarbar, Kathmandu, Napal.

330.9 US
NEW JERSEY. DEPARTMENT OF LABOR. LABOR MARKET REVIEW. SOUTHERN N.J. REGION. 1981. a. free. Department of Labor, Division of Planning and Research, Office of Planning and Management, Trenton, NJ 08625-0056. TEL 609-292-7567. Ed. David R. Crane. circ. 1,000.

650 US ISSN 0077-9083
NEW YORK STATE BUSINESS FACT BOOK. PART 1: BUSINESS AND MANUFACTURING. 1947. approx. every 5 years. free. Department of Commerce, One Commerce Plaza, Albany, NY 12245. Ed. Raymond G. Paolino. circ. 5,000.

650 US ISSN 0077-9105
NEW YORK STATE BUSINESS FACT BOOK. SUPPLEMENT. 1961. a. free. Department of Commerce, One Commerce Plaza, Albany, NY 12245. Ed. Raymond G. Paolino. circ. 4,000.

NEW ZEALAND. ECONOMIC MONITORING GROUP REPORT. see *BUSINESS AND ECONOMICS*

330.9 NE
NIJENRODE STUDIES IN ECONOMICS. 1976. irreg. $22.50. Martinus Nijhoff Publishers, Postbus 163, 3300 AD Dordrecht, Netherlands.

338 US ISSN 0549-8368
NORTH DAKOTA GROWTH INDICATORS. 1959. irreg. free. Economic Development Commission, Liberty Memorial Bldg., Bismarck, ND 58505.

330.9 VE
NUEVA CIENCIA.* 1975. irreg. $10. Universidad Central de Venezuela, Facultad de Ciencias Economicas y Sociales, Ciudad Universitaria, Caracas, Venezuela.

NYLON FILAMENT & POLYESTER FILAMENT GROWTH. see *TEXTILE INDUSTRIES AND FABRICS*

O E C S ANNUAL DIGEST OF STATISTICS. (Organisation of Eastern Caribbean States) see *STATISTICS*

O E C S NATIONAL ACCOUNT DIGEST. (Organisation of Eastern Caribbean States) see *STATISTICS*

O E C S STATISTICAL POCKET DIGEST. (Organisation of Eastern Caribbean States) see *STATISTICS*

O E C S TRADE DIGEST. (Organisation of Eastern Caribbean States) see *STATISTICS*

330 US
OREGON, A STATISTICAL PROFILE. a. $3. Economic Development Department, 595 Cottage St. N.E., Salem, OR 97310. TEL 503-373-1200. charts.
Formerly: Oregon, an Economic Profile.

330 FR ISSN 0474-5124
ORGANIZATION FOR ECONOMIC COOPERATION AND DEVELOPMENT. ECONOMIC SURVEYS: AUSTRIA. 1959. a. Organisation for Economic Cooperation and Development, 2 rue Andre Pascal, 75775 Paris 16, France (U.S. orders to: O.E.C.D. Publications and Information Center, 1750 Pennsylvania Ave., N.W., Washington, DC 20006) (also avail. in microfiche)
Supersedes in part: Organization for Economic Cooperation and Development. Economic Conditions in Austria and Switzerland.

330.9 FR
ORGANIZATION FOR ECONOMIC COOPERATION AND DEVELOPMENT. ECONOMIC SURVEYS: AUSTRALIA. a. $5. Organisation for Economic Cooperation and Development, 2 rue Andre-Pascal, 75775 Paris 16, France (U.S. orders to: O.E.C.D. Publications and Information Center, 1750 Pennsylvania Ave., N.W., Washington, D.C. 20006) illus. stat. (also avail. in microfiche)

330 FR ISSN 0474-5132
ORGANIZATION FOR ECONOMIC COOPERATION AND DEVELOPMENT. ECONOMIC SURVEYS: BELGIUM-LUXEMBOURG ECONOMIC UNION. 1960. a. Organisation for Economic Cooperation and Development, 2 rue Andre Pascal, 75775 Paris 16, France (U.S. orders to: O.E.C.D. Publications and Information Center, 1750 Pennsylvania Ave., N.W., Washington, DC 20006) (also avail. in microfiche)

330 FR ISSN 0474-5140
ORGANIZATION FOR ECONOMIC COOPERATION AND DEVELOPMENT. ECONOMIC SURVEYS: CANADA. 1959. a. Organisation for Economic Cooperation and Development, 2 rue Andre Pascal, 75775 Paris 16, France (U.S. orders to: O.E.C.D. Publications and Information Center, 1750 Pennsylvania Ave., N.W., Washington, D.C. 20006) (also avail. in microfiche)

330.9 FR ISSN 0474-5159
ORGANIZATION FOR ECONOMIC COOPERATION AND DEVELOPMENT. ECONOMIC SURVEYS: DENMARK. 1960. a. Organisation for Economic Cooperation and Development, 2 rue Andre Pascal, 75775 Paris 16, France (U.S. orders to: O.E.C.D. Publications and Information Center, 1750 Pennsylvania Ave., N.W., Washington, D.C. 20006) (also avail. in microfiche)

330 FR ISSN 0474-5167
ORGANIZATION FOR ECONOMIC COOPERATION AND DEVELOPMENT. ECONOMIC SURVEYS: FRANCE. 1953. a. Organization for Economic Cooperation and Development, 2 rue Andre Pascal, 75775 Paris 16, France (U.S. orders to: O.E.C.D. Publications and Information Center, 1750 Pennsylvania Ave., N.W., Washington, D.C. 20006) (also avail. in microfiche)

330.9 FR
ORGANIZATION FOR ECONOMIC COOPERATION AND DEVELOPMENT. ECONOMIC SURVEYS: FINLAND. a. Organization for Economic Cooperation and Development, 2 rue Andre Pascal, 75775 Paris 16, France (U.S. orders to: O.E.C.D. Publications and Information Center, 1750 Pennsylvania Ave. N.W., Washington, DC 20006) (also avail. in microfiche)

330 FR ISSN 0474-5175
ORGANIZATION FOR ECONOMIC COOPERATION AND DEVELOPMENT. ECONOMIC SURVEYS: GERMANY. 1953. a. Organization for Economic Cooperation and Development, 2 rue Andre Pascal, 75775 Paris 16, France (U.S. orders to: O.E.C.D. Publications and Information Center, 1750 Pennsylvania Ave. N.W., Washington, D.C. 20006) (also avail. in microfiche)

330 FR ISSN 0474-5183
ORGANIZATION FOR ECONOMIC COOPERATION AND DEVELOPMENT. ECONOMIC SURVEYS: GREECE. 1954. a. Organization for Economic Cooperation and Development, 2 rue Andre Pascal, 75775 Paris 16, France (U.S. orders to: O.E.C.D. Publications and Information Center, 1750 Pennsylvania Ave., N.W., Washington, DC 20006) (also avail. in microfiche)

330.9 FR ISSN 0474-5191
ORGANIZATION FOR ECONOMIC COOPERATION AND DEVELOPMENT. ECONOMIC SURVEYS: ICELAND. 1960. a. Organization for Economic Cooperation and Development, 2 rue Andre Pascal, 75775 Paris 16, France (U.S. orders to: O.E.C.D. Publications and Information Center, 17750 Pennsylvania Ave., N.W., Washington, D.C. 20006) (also avail. in microfiche)

330 FR ISSN 0474-5205
ORGANIZATION FOR ECONOMIC COOPERATION AND DEVELOPMENT. ECONOMIC SURVEYS: IRELAND. 1960. a. Organization for Economic Cooperation and Development, 2 rue Andre Pascal, 75775 Paris 16, France (U.S. orders to: O.E.C.D. Publications and Information Center, 1750 Pennsylvania Ave., N.W., Washington, D.C. 20006) (also avail. in microfiche)

330 FR ISSN 0474-5213
ORGANIZATION FOR ECONOMIC COOPERATION AND DEVELOPMENT. ECONOMIC SURVEYS: ITALY. (Not published in 1978) 1953. a. Organization for Economic Cooperation and Development, 2 rue Andre Pascal, 75775 Paris 16, France (U.S. orders to: O.E.C.D Publications and Information Center Pennsylvania Ave., N.W., Washington, D.C. 20006) (also avail. in microfiche)

330 FR ISSN 0474-5221
ORGANIZATION FOR ECONOMIC COOPERATION AND DEVELOPMENT. ECONOMIC SURVEYS: JAPAN. 1964. a. Organization for Economic Cooperation and Development, 2 rue Andre Pascal, 75775 Paris 16, France (U.S. orders to: O.E.C.D. Publications and Information Center, 1750 Pennsylvania Ave., N.W., Washington, DC 20006) (also avail. in microfiche)

330 FR ISSN 0474-523X
ORGANIZATION FOR ECONOMIC COOPERATION AND DEVELOPMENT. ECONOMIC SURVEYS: NETHERLANDS. 1954. a. Organization for Economic Cooperation and Development, 2 rue Andre Pascal, 75775 Paris 16, France (U.S. orders to: O.E.C.D. Publications and Information Center, 1750 Pennsylvania Ave., N.W., Washington, D.C. 20006) (also avail. in microfiche)

248 BUSINESS AND ECONOMICS — ECONOMIC SITUATION AND CONDITIONS

330 FR ISSN 0474-5248
ORGANIZATION FOR ECONOMIC
COOPERATION AND DEVELOPMENT.
ECONOMIC SURVEYS: NORWAY. 1960. a.
Organization for Economic Cooperation and
Development, 2 rue Andre Pascal, 75775 Paris 16,
France (U.S. orders to: O.E.C.D. Publications and
Information Center, 1750 Pennsylvania Ave., N.W.,
Washington, D.C. 20006) (also avail. in microfiche)

330 FR ISSN 0474-5256
ORGANIZATION FOR ECONOMIC
COOPERATION AND DEVELOPMENT.
ECONOMIC SURVEYS: PORTUGAL. 1960. a.
Organization for Economic Cooperation and
Development, 2 rue Andre Pascal, 75775 Paris 16,
France (U.S. orders to: O.E.C.D. Publications and
Information Center, 1750 Pennsylvania Ave., N.W.,
Washington, D.C. 20006) (also avail. in microfiche)

330 949.7 FR ISSN 0474-5264
ORGANIZATION FOR ECONOMIC
COOPERATION AND DEVELOPMENT.
ECONOMIC SURVEYS: SOCIALIST FEDERAL
REPUBLIC OF YUGOSLAVIA. 1962. a. $5.
Organization for Economic Cooperation and
Development, 2 rue Andre Pascal, 75775 Paris 16,
France (U.S. orders to: O.E.C.D. Publications and
Information Center, 1750 Pennsylvania Ave., N.W.,
Washington, D.C. 20006) (also avail. in microfiche)

330 FR ISSN 0474-5272
ORGANIZATION FOR ECONOMIC
COOPERATION AND DEVELOPMENT.
ECONOMIC SURVEYS: SPAIN. 1958. a.
Organization for Economic Cooperation and
Development, 2 rue Andre Pascal, 75775 Paris 16,
France (U.S. orders to: O.E.C.D. Publications and
Information Center, 1750 Pennsylvania Ave., N.W.,
Washington, D.C. 20006) (also avail. in microfiche)

330 FR ISSN 0474-5280
ORGANIZATION FOR ECONOMIC
COOPERATION AND DEVELOPMENT.
ECONOMIC SURVEYS: SWEDEN. 1954. a.
Organization for Economic Cooperation and
Development, 2 rue Andre Pascal, 75775 Paris 16,
France (U.S. orders to: O.E.C.D. Publications and
Information Center, 1750 Pennsylvania Ave., N.W.,
Washington, D.C. 20006) (also avail. in microfiche)

330 FR ISSN 0474-5299
ORGANIZATION FOR ECONOMIC
COOPERATION AND DEVELOPMENT.
ECONOMIC SURVEYS: SWITZERLAND. 1959.
a. Organization for Economic Cooperation and
Development, 2 rue Andre Pascal, 75775 Paris 16,
France (U.S. orders to: O.E.C.D. Publications and
Information Center, 1750 Pennsylvania Ave. N.W.,
Washington, D.C. 20006) (also avail. in microfiche)

330 FR ISSN 0474-5302
ORGANIZATION FOR ECONOMIC
COOPERATION AND DEVELOPMENT.
ECONOMIC SURVEYS: TURKEY. (Not
published in 1978) 1954. a. Organization for
Economic Cooperation and Development, 2 rue
Andre Pascal, 75775 Paris 16, France (U.S. orders
to: O.E.C.D. Publications and Information Center,
1750 Pennsylvania Ave., N.W., Washington, D.C.
20006) (also avail. in microfiche)

330 FR ISSN 0474-5310
ORGANIZATION FOR ECONOMIC
COOPERATION AND DEVELOPMENT.
ECONOMIC SURVEYS: UNITED KINGDOM.
1953. a. Organization for Economic Cooperation
and Development, 2 rue Andre Pascal, 75775 Paris
16, France (U.S. orders to: O.E.C.D. Publications
and Information Center, 1750 Pennsylvania Ave.,
N.W., Washington, D.C. 20006) (also avail. in
microfiche)

330 FR ISSN 0376-6438
ORGANIZATION FOR ECONOMIC
COOPERATION AND DEVELOPMENT.
ECONOMIC SURVEYS: NEW ZEALAND. a.
Organization for Economic Cooperation and
Development, 2 rue Andre Pascal, 75775 Paris 16,
France (U.S. orders to: O.E.C.D. Publications and
Information Center, 1750 Pennsylvania Ave. N.W.,
Washington, DC 20006) (also avail. in microfiche)

330 FR ISSN 0474-5329
ORGANIZATION FOR ECONOMIC
COOPERATION AND DEVELOPMENT.
ECONOMIC SURVEYS: UNITED STATES. 1953.
a. Organization for Economic Cooperation and
Development, 2 rue Andre Pascal, 75775 Paris 16
(U.S. orders to: O.E.C.D. Publications and
Information Center, 1750 Pennsylvania Ave., N.W.,
Washington, DC 20006) (also avail. in microfiche)

330.9 II
ORISSA, INDIA. FINANCE DEPARTMENT.
ANNUAL FINANCIAL STATEMENT. a. Orissa
Government Press, Cuttack, Orissa, India.

330.9 II
ORISSA, INDIA. FINANCE DEPARTMENT.
WHITE PAPER ON THE ECONOMIC
CONDITIONS AND THE DEVELOPMENTAL
ACTIVITIES IN ORISSA. (Text in English) a.
(Finance Department) Orissa Government Press,
Cuttack, Orissa, India.
    Continues: Orissa, India. Finance Department.
White Paper on Departmental Activities,
Government of Orissa (ISSN 0472-0989)

330.9 BL
P N P E. SERIE. 1982. irreg., no.11, 1985. price
varies. Instituto de Planejamento Economico e
Social, Programa Nacional de Pesquisa Economica,
Caixa Postal 2672, Rio de Janeiro,RJ, Brazil. Ed.
Eustaquio J. Reis. circ. 1,000.

P R E A L C NEWSLETTER. (Programa Regional
del Empleo para America Latina y el Caribe) see
OCCUPATIONS AND CAREERS

320 UK
PACIFIC BUSINESS GUIDE. 1984. a. $15. World of
Information, 21 Gold St., Saffron Walden, Essex
CB10 1EJ, England. Ed. Richard Green. adv. illus.
stat. circ. 7,000.

330 PK ISSN 0078-8082
PAKISTAN ECONOMIC SURVEY. (Text in
English) 1962. a. price varies. Finance Division,
Islamabad, Pakistan (Order from: Manager of
Publications, Government of Pakistan, 2nd Floor,
Ahmad Chamber, Tariq Rd., P.E.C.H.S., Karachi
29, Pakistan) index.

330.9 PN
PANAMA. MINISTERIO DE PLANIFICACION Y
POLITICA ECONOMICA. INFORME
ECONOMICO. a. Ministerio de Planificacion y
Politica Economica, Direccion de Planificacion
Economica y Social, Panama, Panama. stat.

330.9 RE
PANORAMA DE L'ECONOMIE DE LA
REUNION. 1981. a. price varies. (Institut National
de la Statistique et des Etudes Economiques
(INSEE)) Observatoire Economique de la Reunion,
4 rue de l'Ecole, 97490 Ste. Clotilde, Reunion. bk.
rev. circ. 2,500.

330.9 US
PERFORMANCE REPORT OF THE ALASKA
ECONOMY. Cover title: Alaska Economy; Year-
End Performance Report. 1972. a. Office of the
Governor, Division of Budget and Management,
Pouch AM, Juneau, AK 99811. illus. stat.

338.9 PE ISSN 0085-4840
PERU. OFICINA REGIONAL DE DESARROLLO
DEL NORTE. ANALISIS GENERAL DE
SITUACION DE LA REGION NORTE.* 1969.
irreg. Oficina Regional de Desarrollo del Norte, Av.
Luis Gonzalez No 1915, Chiclayo, Peru.

330.9 PH
PHILIPPINE DEVELOPMENT REPORT. (Text in
English) a. National Economic and Development
Authority, Box 1116, Manila, Philippines. stat.
    Formerly (until 1977): Philippines. National
Economic and Development Authority. Report on
the Economy.

330.9 PL ISSN 0137-6314
POLITECHNIKA WROCLAWSKA. OSRODEK
BADAN PROGNOSTYCZNYCH. PRACE
NAUKOWE. MONOGRAFIE. 1978. irreg., no.6,
1984. price varies. Politechnika Wroclawska,
Wybrzeze Wyspianskiego 27, 50-370 Wroclaw,
Poland. Ed. Jerzy Ciekot.

330.9 PL ISSN 0137-6322
POLITECHNIKA WROCLAWSKA. OSRODEK
BADAN PROGNOSTYCZNYCH. PRACE
NAUKOWE. STUDIA I MATERIALY. (Text in
Polish; summaries in English and Russian) 1977.
irreg., no.3, 1978. price varies. Politechnika
Wroclawska, Wybrzeze Wyspianskiego 27, 50-370
Wroclaw, Poland (Dist. by: Ars Polona, Krakowski
Przedmiescie 7, 00-068 Warsaw, Poland) Ed.
Marian Kloza. circ. 475.

330.9 PL ISSN 0137-6330
POLITECHNIKA WROCLAWSKA. OSRODEK
BADAN PROGNOSTYCZNYCH. PRACE
NAUKOWE. WSPOLPRACA/
SOTRUDNICHESTVO. Short title: Wspolpraca.
(Text in Russian) 1973. irreg., no.2, 1974. price
varies. Politechnika Wroclawska, Wybrzeze
Wyspianskiego 27, 50-370 Wroclaw, Poland (Dist.
by: Ars Polona, Krakowskie Przedmiescie 7, 00-068
Warsaw, Poland) circ. 480.

330.9 EC
PONTIFICIA UNIVERSIDAD CATOLICA DEL
ECUADOR. INSTITUTO DE
INVESTIGACIONES ECONOMICAS.
DOCUMENTOS. 1983. irreg. Pontificia
Universidad Catolica del Ecuador, Instituto de
Investigaciones Economicas, Casilla 2184, Quito,
Ecuador.

330.9 ZR
PORTEFEUILLE; revue des entreprises. 1971. irreg.
Department du Portefeuille, B.P. 3473, Kinhasa/
Gombe, Zaire. Ed. Atunaku Adunagow. Indexed:
P.A.I.S.

330.9 PL
PRACE POPULARNONAUKOWE. EKONOMIA I
ORGANIZACJA. irreg. price varies. Towarzystwo
Naukowe w Toruniu, Ul. Wysoka 16, 87-100 Torun,
Poland (Dist. by: Ars-Polona Ruch, Krakowskie
Przedmiescie 7, 00-068 Warsaw, Poland)
    Supersedes in part: Prace Popularnonaukowe
(ISSN 0079-4805)

PRICES OF AGRICULTURAL PRODUCTS AND
SELECTED INPUTS IN EUROPE AND NORTH
AMERICA. see AGRICULTURE — Agricultural
Economics

330 IT ISSN 0033-1902
PROVINCIA DI FORLI IN CIFRE. (Supplement to
Rassegna Economica) 1959. irreg. L.15000 includes
Rassegna Economica. Camera di Commercio,
Industria, Artigianato e Agricoltura di Forli, Corso
della Repubblica 5, 47100 Forli, Italy. Ed. Luciano
Castrucci.

330.9 US
PRUDENTIAL INSURANCE COMPANY OF
AMERICA. ECONOMIC FORECAST. vol.31,
1982. a. Prudential Insurance Co. of America,
Economic & Investment Research Dept., 5 Plaza,
Newark, NJ 07101. TEL 201-877-6000. charts.

330 PR ISSN 0079-7871
PUERTO RICO. DEPARTMENT OF THE
TREASURY. ECONOMY & FINANCES. 1955. a.
free. Department of the Treasury, Office of
Economic Affairs, Box 4515, San Juan, PR 00905.
Ed. Ting Chen Hsu. charts. stat. circ. 6,000.

330.9 US ISSN 0091-5696
QUALITY OF LIFE IN IOWA; an economic and
social report to the Governor. 1970. a. Office for
Planning and Programming, Capitol Hill Annex, 523
E. 12 St., Des Moines, IA 50319. TEL 515-281-
3711. Ed. Ronald Sagraves. illus. stat.

330 SY ISSN 0079-9696
RAPPORT ANNUEL SUR L'ECONOMIE
SYRIENNE. (Text in French) 1963/64. a. $95.
Office Arabe de Presse et de Documentation, P.O.
Box 3550, 67 Place Chanbandar, Damascus, Syria.

338.9 PE
REALIDAD PERUANA. no.3, 1975. irreg. price
varies. Editorial Horizonte, Av. Nicolas de Pierola
995, Casilla 2118, Lima 1, Peru. charts. stat.

388 US ISSN 0080-0449
REFERENCE BOOK-ARGENTINA. (Issued in 2
vols) (Text in Spanish) a. Dun & Bradstreet, Inc., 99
Church St., New York, NY 10007 TEL 212-285-
7000. (And Florida 234, Buenos Aires, Argentina)

BUSINESS AND ECONOMICS — ECONOMIC SITUATION AND CONDITIONS

380 US ISSN 0080-0457
REFERENCE BOOK-REPUBLIC OF SOUTH AFRICA. (Published in 4 provincial editions: Sec. 1: Orange Free State, Sec. 2: Cape Province, Sec. 3: Natal, Sec. 4: Transvaal) a. not available to libraries. Dun & Bradstreet, Inc., 99 Church St., New York, NY 10007 TEL 212-285-7000. (And 91 Kerk St., Johannesburg, South Africa)

RESERVE BANK OF AUSTRALIA. OCCASIONAL PAPERS. see *BUSINESS AND ECONOMICS — Banking And Finance*

330.9 NZ ISSN 0110-523X
RESERVE BANK OF NEW ZEALAND. RESEARCH PAPERS. 1971. irreg. free. Reserve Bank of New Zealand, Economic Dept., Box 2498, Wellington, New Zealand. bibl. stat. circ. 2,500.

330 VE
REVISTA DE HACIENDA. 1936. a. free. Ministerio de Hacienda, Direccion de Investigaciones Economicas, Centro Simon Bolivar, Edificio Norte, Caracas, Venezuela. Ed. Antonio Aguirre S.J. charts. circ. 1,500. Indexed: P.A.I.S.For.Lang.Ind.

RIVERLANDER NOTES. see *CONSERVATION*

330.9 GW
RUND UM DIE BOERSE. a. Commerzbank AG, Neue Mainzer Str. 32-36, 6000 Frankfurt, W Germany (B.R.D.) circ. 75,000.

330.9 RW
RWANDA. DIRECTION GENERALE DE LA STATISTIQUE. SITUATION ECONOMIQUE DE LA REPUBLIQUE RWANDAISE AU 31 DECEMBRE. 1973 (N.S.) $7. Direction Generale de la Statistique, B.P. 46, Kigali, Rwanda.
Formerly: Rwanda. Direction Generale de la Documentation et de la Statistique Generale. Situation Economique de la Republique Rwandaise au 31 Decembre.

330.9 CE
SAMVARDHANA. (Text in English or Sinhalese) irreg. Rs.3.75 per no. 27/3 M Housing Scheme, Kiribathgoda, Kelaniya, Sri Lanka.
Economic and developmental studies of Sri Lanka

338.9 CN ISSN 0080-6676
SASKATCHEWAN ECONOMIC AND FINANCIAL POSITION. 1954. a. free. Department of Finance, 2350 Albert St., Regina, Saskatchewan, Canada. TEL 306-787-6765. circ. 2,500.

330.9 CN ISSN 0558-6976
SASKATCHEWAN ECONOMIC REVIEW. 1951. a. Bureau of Statistics, Rm. 207, Walter Scott Bldg., 3085 Albert St., Regina, Sask. S4S 0B1, Canada. TEL 306-565-6327. circ. 5,000.

336 SZ
SCHWEIZERISCHE KONJUNKTUR UND VORAUSSCHAU. French edition: Conjoncture Suisse et Perspectives. (Supplement to: Switzerland. Eidgenoessisches Volkswirtschafts Departement. Volkswirtschaft and to Wirtschaftsspiegel) a. Eidgenoessisches Volkswirtschaftsdepartement, Kommission fuer Konjunkturfragen, Belpstr. 53, 3003 Berne, Switzerland.
Formerly: Schweizerische Konjunktur und ihre Aussichten.

330.9 SG
SENEGAL. MINISTERE DE L'ECONOMIE ET DES FINANCES. COMPTES ECONOMIQUES DE LA NATION. a. 5000 Fr.CFA. Ministere de l'Economie et des Finances, Direction de la Statistique, B.P. 116, Dakar, Senegal.

330.9 FR
SERIE E O/INTERNATIONAL. irreg. Editions d' Organisation, 5 rue Rouss elet, 75007 Paris, France. Eds. Gerard le Pan de Ligny, Luc Boyer.

338.9 DK ISSN 0901-800X
SETTING UP IN DENMARK; a survey of economic, legal and financial aspects of foreign investment in Denmark. German edition: Firmengruendung in Daenemark. 1972. biennial. free. Copenhagen Handelsbank A-S - Aktieselskabet Kjoebenhavns Handelsbank, Holmens Kanal 2, DK-1091 Copenhagen K, Denmark. charts. illus. stat.

388 US ISSN 0080-9756
SINOPSIS DUN - BRAZIL. (Text in Portuguese) a. not available to libraries. Dun & Bradstreet, Inc., 99 Church St., New York, NY 10007 TEL 212-285-7000. (And Avenida Sao Joao 473, 1st Fl., Sao Paulo, Brazil)

330.1 IV ISSN 0080-9829
SITUATION ECONOMIQUE DE COTE D'IVOIRE.* 1960. irreg. Service de la Statistique, B.P. 222, Abidjan, Ivory Coast.

330 MR ISSN 0080-9845
SITUATION ECONOMIQUE DU MAROC. (Text in Arabic and French) a. DH.27.50. Direction de la Statistique, B.P. 178, Rabat, Morocco. (also avail. in microfiche)

330 SG ISSN 0080-9853
SITUATION ECONOMIQUE DU SENEGAL. 1962. a., latest 1983. 7000 Fr.CFA. Ministere de l'Economie et des Finances, Direction de la Statistique, B.P. 116, Dakar, Senegal.

330.9 FR
SITUATION ECONOMIQUE ET PERSPECTIVES D'AVENIR. 1962. irreg. Chambre de Commerce et d'Industrie de Pau, 21 rue Louis Barthou, Pau, France. Ed.Bd. circ. 6,000.

330.9 FR
SITUATION FINANCIERE DES REGIONS DE PROVINCE EN (YEAR); operations des residents. a. (Conseil National du Credit) Banque de France, Service de l'Information, 43 rue de Valois, 75001 Paris, France.
Formerly: Etude sur la Situation Financiere des Regions.

330.9 FR
SOCIETES ET FOURNISSEURS D'AFRIQUE NOIRE.* 1980. a. 950 F. Ediafric-la Documentation Africaine, 57 Ave. d'Iena, 75016 Paris, France.

315.4 330.9 II
SOCIO-ECONOMIC REVIEW OF PUNJAB. (Subseries of the Organisation's Publication) a. Economic and Statistical Organisation, Chandigarh, Punjab, India. stat.

330.9 SA
SOUTH AFRICA COMPARED. 1978. a. R.2. South Africa Foundation, Box 7006, Johannesburg 2000, South Africa. Ed. M.R. Christie.

330.9 SA
SOUTH AFRICA FOUNDATION. INFORMATION DIGEST (YEAR) Afrikaans edition: Beknopte Feitebron. German edition: Kurze Ubersicht. Italian edition: Questo e il Sud Africa. (Editions in Afrikaans, English, German, Italian) 1969. a. R.2.50. South Africa Foundation, Box 7006, Johannesburg 2000, South Africa. Ed. J. Opland. stats. circ. 40,000.

332 SA ISSN 0081-2528
SOUTH AFRICAN RESERVE BANK. ANNUAL ECONOMIC REPORT/SUID-AFRIKAANSE RESERWEBANK. JAARLIKSE EKONOMIESE VERSLAG. (Editions in English and Afrikaans) 1961. a. R.3.50. South African Reserve Bank, Box 427, Pretoria 0001, South Africa. circ. 2,800 (English edt.); 1,200 (Afrikaans edt.)

330.9 320 US
SOUTHEAST ASIA REPORT. irreg. (approx. 220/yr.) $5 per no. U.S. Joint Publications Research Service, 1000 N. Glebe Rd., Arlington, VA 22201 TEL 703-487-4630. (Orders to: NTIS, Springfield, VA 22161)
Former titles: South and East Asia Report; Translations on South and East Asia.

330.9 CE
SRI LANKA. MINISTRY OF PLANNING AND ECONOMIC AFFAIRS. DIVISION OF EXTERNAL RESOURCES. ECONOMIC INDICATORS. a. Ministry of Planning and Economic Affairs, Division of External Resources, Box 277, Ceylingo House, 2nd Floor, Colombo 1, Sri Lanka. charts. stat.

338.9 US ISSN 0073-1080
STATE OF HAWAII DATA BOOK. 1962. a. $15. Department of Planning and Economic Development, Box 2359, Honolulu, HI 96804. TEL 808-548-4025. Ed. Robert C. Schmitt. stat. circ. 2,500.
Formerly: Statistical Abstract of Hawaii.

STATISTICAL OFFICE OF THE EUROPEAN COMMUNITIES. COMPARISON IN REAL TERMS OF E S A AGGREGATES. see *BUSINESS AND ECONOMICS*

STATISTICAL OFFICE OF THE EUROPEAN COMMUNITIES. GAS PRICES. see *ENERGY*

STATISTISCHES JAHRBUCH DER STADT NUERNBERG. see *STATISTICS*

330.9 IT ISSN 0391-6103
STUDI D'ECONOMIA. 1976. irreg., no.14, 1982. price varies. Liguori Editore s.r.l., Via Mezzocannone 19, 80134 Naples, Italy. TEL 081/20 6077. Ed. D.W. Pearce.

330.9 NE
STUDIES IN REGIONAL SCIENCE AND URBAN ECONOMICS. 1977. irreg., vol.14, 1985. price varies. Elsevier Science Publishers B.V., Box 211, Amsterdam, Netherlands. Eds. Ake Andersson, Walter Isard. Indexed: Math.R.

330.9 320 US
SUB-SAHARAN AFRICA REPORT. irreg. (approx. 125/yr.) $5 per no. U.S. Joint Publications Research Service, 1000 N. Glebe Rd., Arlington, VA 22201 TEL 703-487-4630. (Orders to: NTIS, Springfield, VA 22161)
Former titles: Translations on Subsaharan Africa; Translations on Africa.

SUDAN. ECONOMIC AND SOCIAL RESEARCH COUNCIL. BULLETIN. see *SOCIAL SCIENCES: COMPREHENSIVE WORKS*

SUDAN. ECONOMIC AND SOCIAL RESEARCH COUNCIL. OCCASIONAL PAPER. see *SOCIAL SCIENCES: COMPREHENSIVE WORKS*

SUDAN. ECONOMIC AND SOCIAL RESEARCH COUNCIL. RESEARCH REPORT. see *SOCIAL SCIENCES: COMPREHENSIVE WORKS*

330 SJ
SUDAN. MINISTRY OF FINANCE AND NATIONAL ECONOMY. ECONOMIC AND FINANCIAL RESEARCH SECTION. ECONOMIC SURVEY. a. Ministry of Finance and National Economy, Economic and Financial Research Section, Box 2092, Khartoum, Sudan.
Supersedes: Sudan. National Planning Commission. Economic Survey (ISSN 0081-9050)

330.9 SJ
SUDAN TRADE DIRECTORY. a. Arthur H. Thrower Ltd., 44-46 S. Ealing Rd., London W.5., England. adv.

330.9 SQ
SWAZILAND. DEPARTMENT OF ECONOMIC PLANNING AND STATISTICS. ECONOMIC REVIEW. 1970. a. Department of Economic Planning and Statistics, P.O. Box 602, Mbabane, Swaziland. illus.
Formerly: Swaziland. Economic Planning Office. Economic Review.

330.9 SZ
SWISS FINANCIAL YEAR BOOK. 1977. a. 95 Fr. Elvetica Edizioni SA, Via Livio 4, Casella Postale 694, CH-6830 Chiasso, Switzerland. Ed. M.G. Grosso. adv. circ. 5,000.

330.9 FR
TABLEAUX DE L'ECONOMIE FRANCAISE. 1956. a. 38 F. Institut National de la Statistique et des Etudes Economiques, 18 bd. A. Pinard, 75675 Paris 14, France. stat. circ. 20,000. (processed)

330.9 FR
TABLEAUX ECONOMIQUES DE L'ILE-DE-FRANCE. a. 28 Fr. Conseil Regional d'Ile-de-France, Direction Regionale de Paris, 12 rue Boulitte, 75675 Paris cedex 14, France. index. (back issues avail.)

250 BUSINESS AND ECONOMICS — ECONOMIC SYSTEMS AND THEORIES, ECONOMIC HISTORY

TORONTO STOCK EXCHANGE FACT BOOK. see *BUSINESS AND ECONOMICS — Banking And Finance*

TRAVEL BUSINESS ANALYST. see *TRAVEL AND TOURISM*

U S S R REPORT: NATIONAL ECONOMY. see *BUSINESS AND ECONOMICS*

U S S R REPORT: PROBLEMS OF THE FAR EAST. see *POLITICAL SCIENCE — International Relations*

330.9 320   US
U S S R REPORT: U S A. ECONOMICS, POLITICS, IDEOLOGY. English translation of Russian: S Sh A: Ekonomika, Politika, Ideologiya. 1970. irreg., (approx. 12/yr.) $5 per no. U.S. Joint Publications Research Service, 1000 N. Glebe Rd., Arlington, VA 22201 TEL 703-487-4630. (Orders to: NTIS, Springfield, VA 22161)
    Formerly: U S A: Economics, Politics, Ideology.

UNITED NATIONS. ECONOMIC AND SOCIAL COUNCIL. OFFICIAL RECORDS. see *POLITICAL SCIENCE — International Relations*

650   US
U.S. BUREAU OF THE CENSUS. CENSUS OF RETAIL TRADE. 1929. quinquennial. price varies. U.S. Bureau of the Census, Customer Services, Washington, DC 20233 TEL 301-763-4100. (Orders to: Supt. of Documents, Washington, DC 20402)
    Supersedes in part: U.S. Bureau of the Census. Census of Retail Trade, Wholesale Trade and Selected Service Industries; U.S. Bureau of the Census. Census of Business (ISSN 0082-9323)

330.9   US
U.S. BUREAU OF THE CENSUS. CENSUS OF SERVICE INDUSTRIES. quinquennial. price varies. U.S. Bureau of the Census, Customer Services, Washington, DC 20233 TEL 301-763-4100. (Orders to: Supt. of Documents, Washington, DC 20402)
    Supersedes in part: U.S. Bureau of the Census. Census of Retail Trade, Wholesale Trade and Selected Service Industries; U.S. Bureau of the Census. Census of Business (ISSN 0082-9323)

330.9   US
U.S. BUREAU OF THE CENSUS. CENSUS OF WHOLESALE TRADE. quinquennial. price varies. U.S. Bureau of the Census, Customer Services, Washington, DC 20233 TEL 301-763-4100. (Orders to: Supt. of Documents, Washington, DC 20504) (also avail. in microfiche)
    Supersedes in part: U.S. Bureau of the Census. Census of Retail Trade, Wholesale Trade and Selected Service Industries; U.S. Bureau of the Census. Census of Business (ISSN 0082-9323)

650   US   ISSN 0082-9463
U.S. BUREAU OF THE CENSUS. COUNTY BUSINESS PATTERNS. (Consists of 1 report per state and a U.S. summary) 1946. a. price varies. U.S. Bureau of the Census, Customer Services, Washington, DC 20233 TEL 301-763-4100. (Orders to: Supt. of Documents, Washington, DC 20402) (also avail. in microfiche)

330.9   SP
UNIVERSIDAD DE SEVILLA. INSTITUTO DE DESARROLLO REGIONAL. EDICIONES. irreg. price varies. Universidad de Sevilla, Instituto de Desarrollo, San Fernando 4, Seville, Spain. charts. illus.

UNIVERSITY OF NAIROBI. INSTITUTE FOR DEVELOPMENT STUDIES. DISCUSSION PAPERS. see *HISTORY — History Of Africa*

UNIVERSITY OF NAIROBI. INSTITUTE FOR DEVELOPMENT STUDIES. WORKING PAPERS. see *HISTORY — History Of Africa*

330.9   SA
UNIVERSITY OF PORT ELIZABETH. INSTITUTE FOR PLANNING RESEARCH. FACT PAPER SERIES/UNIVERSITEIT VAN PORT ELIZABETH. INSTITUUT VIR BEPLANNINGSNAVORSING. FEITESTUK REEKS. 1971. irreg., no.21, 1977. University of Port Elizabeth, Institute for Planning Research, Box 1600, Port Elizabeth 6000, South Africa.

330.9   SA
UNIVERSITY OF PORT ELIZABETH. INSTITUTE FOR PLANNING RESEARCH. INFORMATION BULLETIN SERIES/UNIVERSITEIT VAN PORT ELIZABETH. INSTITUUT VIR BEPLANNINGSNAVORSING. INLIGTINGSBULLETIN REEKS. 1971. irreg. University of Port Elizabeth, Institute for Planning Research, Box 1600, Port Elizabeth 6000, South Africa.

330   US
UPPER MIDWEST COUNCIL. (REPORTS) 1960. irreg. price varies. Upper Midwest Council, 250 Marquette Ave., Minneapolis, MN 55480.
    Supersedes (as of 1964): Upper Midwest Economic Study. Progress Report (ISSN 0083-4610) & Upper Midwest Economic Study. Technical Paper (ISSN 0083-4637) & Upper Midwest Economic Study. Urban Report (ISSN 0083-4645)

330.5   US
VALLEY BUSINESS PERSPECTIVES. 1976. irreg. (approx. 2/yr.) $8. California State University, Fresno, School of Business and Administrative Sciences, Valley Business Center, Fresno, CA 93740. TEL 209-294-2352. Ed. Charlotte Hiatt. adv. circ. 2,000.
    Formerly (until 1985): San Joaquin Valley Business Perspectives.

330.1   GW   ISSN 0085-7661
VERBAENDE, BEHOERDEN, ORGANISATIONEN DER WIRTSCHAFT. a. DM.141. Verlag Hoppenstedt und Co., Havelstr. 9, Postfach 4006, 6100 Darmstadt, W. Germany (B.R.D.)

WATER & WASTE TREATMENT: LATIN AMERICAN INDUSTRIAL REPORT. see *ENGINEERING — Civil Engineering*

330.9 320   US
WEST EUROPE REPORT. 1968. irreg. (approx. 125/yr.) $5 per no. U.S. Joint Publications Research Service, 1000 N. Glebe Rd., Arlington, VA 22201 TEL 703-487-4630. (Orders to: NTIS, Springfield, VA 22161)
    Former titles: Western Europe Report; Translations on Western Europe.

WESTERN AUSTRALIAN POCKET YEARBOOK. see *HISTORY — History Of Australasia And Other Areas*

WESTERN AUSTRALIAN YEARBOOK. NEW SERIES. see *HISTORY — History Of Australasia And Other Areas*

330   JA
WHITE PAPER ON JAPANESE ECONOMY. (Text in English) 1970. a. $39. (Economic Planning Agency) Business Intercommunication, Inc., C.P.O. Box 587, Tokyo 100-02, Japan.

330   UN   ISSN 0084-1714
WORLD ECONOMIC SURVEY. (Text in English, French and Spanish) 1986. a. $29. United Nations Publications, Rm. DC2-853, New York, NY 10017 (Or Distribution and Sales Section, CH-1211 Geneva 10, Switzerland) (also avail. in microfiche)

WORLD LEASING YEARBOOK. see *BUSINESS AND ECONOMICS — Investments*

330.9   PL   ISSN 0474-2966
WYZSZA SZKOLA PEDAGOGICZNA, OPOLE. ZESZYTY NAUKOWE. SERIA A. EKONOMIA. (Text in Polish; summaries in English) 1965. irreg., vol.9, 1983. price varies; avail. on exchange basis. Wyzsza Szkola Pedagogiczna, Opole, Oleska 48, 45-052 Opole, Poland (Dist. by: Ars Polona-Ruch, Krakowskie Przedmiescie 7, Warsaw, Poland) Ed. Zbigniew Mikolajewicz.

330.9   US
YALE UNIVERSITY. ECONOMIC GROWTH CENTER. CENTER DISCUSSION PAPER. irreg., no.499, 1985. $2. Yale University, Economic Growth Center, Yale Sta., Box 1987, New Haven, CT 06520. TEL 203-436-8414. Indexed: Geo.Abstr. Popul.Ind.

YUGOSLAV FACTS AND VIEWS. see *POLITICAL SCIENCE — International Relations*

330.9   ZA
ZAMBIA. NATIONAL COMMISSION FOR DEVELOPMENT PLANNING. ECONOMIC REPORT. a. 4 Fr.CFA. National Commission for Development Planning, Lusaka, Zambia.

330.9   RH
ZIMBABWE, A FIELD FOR INVESTMENT. 1961. a. Z.$15. ‡ Thomson Publications Zimbabwe (Pvt) Ltd., P.O. Box 1683, Harare, Zimbabwe. Ed. Angus Shaw. adv. illus. stat. circ. 3,000(controlled)

330.9   RH
ZIMBABWE IN FIGURES. (Text in English) 1982. a. Zimbabwe Banking Corporation, P.O. Box 3198, Harare, Zimbabwe. circ. 3,000.

330.9   FR
ZONE FRANC ET L'AFRIQUE.* 1979. a. 550 F. Ediafric-la Documentation Africaine, 57 Ave. d'Iena, 75016 Paris, France.

BUSINESS AND ECONOMICS — Economic Systems And Theories, Economic History

330.1   GW
ABHANDLUNGEN ZU DEN WIRTSCHAFTLICHEN STAATSWISSENSCHAFTEN. 1968. irreg. Vandenhoeck & Ruprecht, Robert-Bosch-Breite 6, Postfach 3753, D-3400 Goettingen, W. Germany (B.R.D.) Ed. Horst C. Recktenwald.

330.9   YU
ACTA HISTORICO-OECONOMICA IUGOSLAVIAE; casopis za ekonomsku istoriju jugoslavije. (Text in Serbo-Croatian; summaries in English and German) 1974. a. 42 din.($5.40) Komisija za Ekonomsku Historiju Jugoslavije, Strossmayerov trg 2, Zagreb, Yugoslavia (Subscr. to: Mladost, Export-Import of Books and Journals, 41000 Zagreb, Kaptol 294, Yugoslavia) Ed. Ivan Erceg. bk. rev. circ. 1,000. Indexed: Hist.Abstr. Amer.Hist.& Life.

330.1   FI   ISSN 0355-2667
ACTA WASAENSIA. (Text and summaries in English) 1971. irreg., no.21, 1985. price varies. Vaasan Korkeakoulu - University of Vaasa, Raastuvankatu 31, 65100 Vaasa 10, Finland. Ed. Kauko Mikkonen. circ. 200.

330.1   US   ISSN 0278-0984
ADVANCES IN APPLIED MICROECONOMICS; a research annual. 1981. a. $23.75 to individuals; institutions $47.50. J A I Press Inc., 36 Sherwood Pl., Box 1678, Greenwich, CT 06836-1678. TEL 203-661-7602. Ed. V. Kerry Smith.

AFRICA SEMINAR: COLLECTED PAPERS. see *HISTORY — History Of Africa*

330.9 960   US   ISSN 0145-2258
AFRICAN ECONOMIC HISTORY. (Text in English and French) 1976. a. $10 to individuals; institutions $15. University of Wisconsin-Madison, African Studies Program, 1454 Van Hise, 1220 Linden Dr., Madison, WI 53706. TEL 608-262-2380. adv. bk. rev. circ. 450. (reprint service avail. from ISI) Indexed: Curr.Cont. Hist.Abstr. SSCI. Arts & Hum.Cit.Ind. Amer.Hist.& Life. Curr.Cont.Africa.
    Formerly: African Economic History Review (ISSN 0360-6333)

AKADEMIA ROLNICZA W SZCZECINIE. ZESZYTY NAUKOWE. NAUK SPOLECZNYCH I EKONOMICZNYCH. see *SOCIAL SCIENCES: COMPREHENSIVE WORKS*

330.1   HK
ALMANAC OF CHINA'S FOREIGN RELATIONS AND TRADE. (Text in Chinese and English) 1984. a. HK.$400($85) China Resources Trade Consultancy Co. Ltd., China Resources Bldg., 49th Fl., 26 Harbour Rd., Wanchai, Hong Kong. stat. circ. 18,083. (back issues avail.)

330.1   GW
ANGEWANDTE STATISTIK UND OEKONOMETRIE. (Text in English, German) 1975. a. Vandenhoeck & Ruprecht, Robert-Bosch-Breite 6, Postfach 3753, D-3400 Goettingen, W. Germany (B.R.D.) Ed.Bd.

330.1 II
ASSAM ECONOMIC JOURNAL. (Text in English) vol.3, 1977. a. Rs.10($2) Dibrugarh University, Department of Economics, Dibrugarh 786001, India.

BANCA D'ITALIA. CONTRIBUTI ALLA ANALISI ECONOMICA. see *BUSINESS AND ECONOMICS — Economic Situation And Conditions*

330.1 SP
BANCO DE ESPANA. ESTUDIOS DE HISTORIA ECONOMICA. irreg., no.8, 1983. Banco de Espana, Negociado de Publicaciones, Alcala 50, Madrid 14, Spain.

330.1 SZ ISSN 0522-7216
BEITRAEGE ZUR WIRTSCHAFTSPOLITIK. 1965. irreg., no.45, 1986. price varies. Paul Haupt AG, Falkenplatz 14, CH-3001 Berne, Switzerland.

330 US
C E P REPORTS AND C E P STUDIES. 1969. bi-m. $100 to libraries. Council on Economic Priorities, 30 Irving Pl., New York, NY 10003. Indexed: P.A.I.S.
Formerly: Economic Priorities Report.

C E P S PAPERS. (Centre for European Policy Studies) see *BUSINESS AND ECONOMICS*

C E P S WORKING DOCUMENTS (ECONOMIC) (Centre for European Policy Studies) see *BUSINESS AND ECONOMICS*

330.1 FR
CAHIERS D'ECONOMIE POLITIQUE. 1974. irreg., no.8, 1982. (Universite de Picardie) Presses Universitaires de France, 108 bd. Saint Germain, 75279 Paris Cedex 6, France (Orders to: Service des Periodiques, 12 rue Jean de Beauvais, 75005 Paris) (reprint service avail. from KTO)

330 UK
CAMBRIDGE STUDIES IN ECONOMIC HISTORY. irreg. price varies. Cambridge University Press, Edinburgh Bldg., Shaftesbury Rd., Cambridge CB2 2RU, England (And 32 E. 57th St., New York NY 10022) Ed.Bd.

CAPITALISMO E SOCIALISMO. see *POLITICAL SCIENCE*

330.1 SP
COLECCION DE ECONOMIA. 1976. irreg., no.5, 1978. price varies. (Universidad de Navarra, Instituto de Estudios Superiores de la Empresa) Ediciones Universidad de Navarra S.A., Apdo. 396, 31080 Pamplona, Spain.

330 US ISSN 0069-6323
COLUMBIA ESSAYS ON THE GREAT ECONOMISTS. 1971. irreg., no.6, 1976. Columbia University Press, 562 W. 113th St., New York, NY 10025. TEL 212-678-6777.

330.1 CN ISSN 0319-7549
COMMON SENSE ECONOMICS. 1974. a. $12. University of Waterloo, Department of Economics, Waterloo, Ont. N2L 3G1, Canada. TEL 519-885-1211. Ed. R.R. Kerton. adv. bk. rev. charts. illus. circ. 700. (back issues avail.)

330.1 US ISSN 0084-9235
CONTRIBUTIONS IN ECONOMICS AND ECONOMIC HISTORY. 1970. irreg. price varies. Greenwood Press, 88 Post Rd. W., Box 5007, Westport, CT 06881. TEL 203-226-3571. Ed. Robert Sobel.

330 NE ISSN 0573-8555
CONTRIBUTIONS TO ECONOMIC ANALYSIS. 1952. irreg., vol.155, 1985. price varies. Elsevier Science Publishers B.V., Box 211, 1000 AE Amsterdam, Netherlands. Ed.Bd. Indexed: Math.R.

330.1 FR ISSN 0070-1572
CROISSANCE URBAINE ET PROGRES DES NATIONS. 1969. irreg. price varies. Editions Cujas, 4,6,8 rue de la Maison-Blanche, 75013 Paris, France. Dir. Andre Piatter.

330 IT ISSN 0070-8402
ECONOMIA E STORIA. (Contributions in English, French, German and Italian) 1972. irreg. (latest issue no.64, 1984) price varies. Edizioni dell' Ateneo, S.p.A., Box 7216, 00100 Rome, Italy. Ed. Oscar Nuccio. circ. 1,000. Indexed: Hist.Abstr. Amer.Hist.& Life.
Reprints

330.1 BG
ECONOMICUS. (Text in English) vol.2, Apr. 1976. irreg. Tk.2. Chittagong University, Department of Economics, Chittagong, Bangladesh.

330 FR ISSN 0068-4864
ECONOMIES ET SOCIETES. SERIE AF. HISTOIRE QUANTITATIVE DE L'ECONOMIE FRANCAISE. 1961. irreg. 300 F. Presses Universitaires de Grenoble, B.P. 47 X, 38040 Grenoble, France. Ed. J. Marczewski. circ. 1,600.

330 FR ISSN 0013-0567
ECONOMIES ET SOCIETES. SERIE EM. ECONOMIE MATHEMATIQUE ET ECONOMETRIE. 1971. irreg. 300 F. Presses Universitaires de Grenoble, B.P. 47 X, 38040 Grenoble, France. Dir. R. Vallee. adv. bk. rev.

330.1 FR ISSN 0068-4880
ECONOMIES ET SOCIETES. SERIE M. PHILOSOPHIE - SCIENCES SOCIALES ECONOMIE. irreg. 300 F. Presses Universitaires de Grenoble, B.P. 47 X, 38040 Grenoble, France. Dir. Jean Lacroix. circ. 1,600.

335 FR ISSN 0068-4856
ECONOMIES ET SOCIETES. SERIE S. ETUDES DE MARXOLOGIE. 1959. irreg. 300 F. Presses Universitaires de Grenoble, B.P. 47 X, 38040 Grenoble, France. Dir. M. Rubel. bk. rev. circ. 1, 600.

949 330.1 NE
ECONOMISCH- EN SOCIAAL-HISTORISCH JAARBOEK. 1916. a. price varies. (Nederlandsch Economisch-Historisch Archief) Uitgeverij S.M. Ontwikkeling, Box 33, 2300 AA Leiden, Netherlands. Indexed: Hist.Abstr. Amer.Hist.& Life.
Supersedes: Economisch-Historisch Jaarboek.

330 UR
EKONOMIKO-MATEMATICHESKIE METODY V PLANIROVANII NARODNOGO KHOZYAISTVA. irreg. 0.97 Rub. Akademiya Nauk Tadzhikskoi S.S.R., Institut Ekonomiki, Prospekt Lenina 37, Dushanbe, Tadzhik S.S.R., U.S.S.R. illus.

330.1 US
ESSAYS IN ECONOMIC AND BUSINESS HISTORY. 1979. biennial. $21. University of Southern California, Department of History, Los Angeles, CA 90089-0034. TEL 213-743-2368. (Co-sponsor: Economic and Business Historical Society) Ed. Edwin J. Perkins. circ. 200. (back issues avail.)

330 BE ISSN 0071-1977
ETUDES D'HISTOIRE ECONOMIQUE ET SOCIALE.* 1941. irreg. price varies. Institut Historique Belge de Rome, c/o Archives Generales du Royaume, 2-6 Rue de Ruysbroeck, B-1000 Brussels, Belgium. circ. controlled.

330.1 GW
FINANZWISSENSCHAFTLICHE SCHRIFTEN. irreg., no.2, 1976. Verlag Peter Lang GmbH, Hinter den Ulmen 19, D-6000 Frankfurt/Main 50, W. Germany (B.R.D.)

330.1 GE ISSN 0138-5100
FORSCHUNGEN ZUR WIRTSCHAFTSGESCHICHTE. 1971. irreg., vol.23, 1986. (Akademie der Wissenschaften der DDR) Akademie Verlag Berlin, Leipziger Str. 3-4, 1086 Berlin, E. Germany (D.D.R.)

330 US ISSN 0071-8106
FOUNDATION FOR THE STUDY OF CYCLES. RESEARCH BULLETIN. 1950. irreg. price varies. ‡ Foundation for the Study of Cycles, 124 South Highland Ave., Pittsburgh, PA 15206. TEL 412-441-1666. Ed. G. Shirk.

330.1 FR
FRANCE. INSTITUT NATIONAL DE LA STATISTIQUE ET DES ETUDES ECONOMIQUES. SERIE E: ENTREPRISES. 1968. a. 510 F. Institut National de la Statistique et des Etudes Economiques, 18 bd A. Pinard, 75675 Paris 14, France.

330 HU ISSN 0072-033X
GAZDASAGTORTENETI ERTEKEZESEK. (Text in Hungarian; occasional summaries in German or Russian) 1958. irreg. price varies. (Magyar Tudomanyos Akademia) Akademiai Kiado, Publishing House of the Hungarian Academy of Sciences, P.O. Box 24, H-1363 Budapest, Hungary.

330 SW ISSN 0072-5080
GOETEBORGS UNIVERSITET. EKONOMISK-HISTORISKA INSTITUTIONEN. MEDDELANDEN. (Text in Swedish; occasionally in English; occasional summaries in English or French) 1958. irreg., no.49, 1982. price varies; also available on exchange from University of Gothenburg Library. Goeteborgs Universitet, Ekonomisk-Historiska Institutionen, Stora Nygatan 23-25, S-411 08 Goeteborg, Sweden. circ. 600.

330.1 SW ISSN 0434-2410
GOETEBORGS UNIVERSITET. NATIONALEKONOMISKA INSTITUTIONEN. EKONOMISKA STUDIER. 1978. irreg., no.14, 1983. Goeteborgs Universitet, Nationalekonomiska Institutionen - University of Goeteborg, Department of Economics, Viktoriagatan 30, S-411 25 Goeteborg, Sweden. circ. 500.

330.1 HT
HAITI. SECRETAIRE D'ETAT DU PLAN. PLAN ANNUEL ET BUDGET DE DEVELOPPEMENT. a. Secretaire d'Etat du Plan, Port-au-Prince, Haiti.
Formerly: Haiti. Conseil National de Developpement et de Planification. Plan Annuel et Budget de Developpement.

650 US ISSN 0073-067X
HARVARD STUDIES IN BUSINESS HISTORY. 1931. irreg., latest vol.38, 1987. price varies. (Harvard University Graduate School of Business Administration) Harvard University Press, 79 Garden St., Cambridge, MA 02138. TEL 617-495-2600. Ed. Alfred D. Chandler, Jr.

330 UK ISSN 0309-1783
HOBART PAPERBACKS; studies in the translation of economic ideas into practical policy and the economics of government. 1971. irreg. $55 (combined subscription for all series) Institute of Economic Affairs, 2 Lord North St., London SW1P 3LB, England (Dist. in North America by: Transatlantic Arts, Inc., Box 6086, Albuquerque, NM 87197)

I C C ANNUAL REVIEW. (International Chamber of Commerce) see *BUSINESS AND ECONOMICS — Chamber Of Commerce Publications*

330.07 SW
INDUSTRIAL INSTITUTE FOR ECONOMIC AND SOCIAL RESEARCH. CURRENT RESEARCH PROJECTS. (Text in English) 1969. a. free. Industrial Institute for Economic and Social Research - Industriens Utredningsinstitut, Grevgatan 34, S-114 53 Stockholm, Sweden. circ. 10,000.

330.1 BO
INSTITUTO DE INVESTIGACIONES ECONOMICAS. REVISTA. 1950. a. Universidad Tecnica de Oruro, Facultad de Ciencias Economicas y Financieras, Casilla 264, Oruro, Bolivia. Dir. Freddy Sanjines Montan.

INTERNATIONAL LABOUR OFFICE. P R E A L C. INVESTIGACIONES SOBRE EMPLEO. (Programa Regional del Empleo para America Latina y el Caribe) see *BUSINESS AND ECONOMICS — Economic Situation And Conditions*

330 GE ISSN 0075-2800
JAHRBUCH FUER WIRTSCHAFTSGESCHICHTE. 1960. a. (in four parts) M.112. (Akademie der Wissenschaften der DDR, Institut fuer Wirtschaftsgeschichte) Akademie-Verlag, Leipziger Str. 3-4, 1086 Berlin, E. Germany (D.D.R.) Indexed: Hist.Abstr. P.A.I.S.For.Lang.Ind. Amer.Hist.& Life.

JOURNAL OF AUSTRALIAN POLITICAL ECONOMY. see *BUSINESS AND ECONOMICS* — *Economic Situation And Conditions*

330   510   GW
MATHEMATICAL SYSTEMS IN ECONOMICS. 1972. irreg., vol.102, 1985. price varies. Verlag Anton Hain GmbH, Adelheidstr. 2, Postfach 1220, 6240 Koenigstein, W. Germany (B.R.D.) Ed.Bd. Indexed: Math.R.

330.1   US
MICROECONOMIC STUDIES. 1986. irreg. price varies. Springer-Verlag, 175 Fifth Ave., New York, NY 10160 TEL 212-460-1500. (Also Berlin, Heidelberg, Tokyo, Vienna) (reprint service avail. from ISI)

330.1   NO   ISSN 0085-431X
NORWAY. STATISTISK SENTRALBYRAA. ARTIKLER/ARTICLES. (Text in Norwegian; summaries in English) 1957. irreg. price varies. Statistisk Sentralbyraa, Box 8131 Dep., 0033 Oslo 1, Norway. circ. 1,800. Indexed: Popul.Ind.

330   300   UK   ISSN 0078-3013
OCCASIONAL PAPERS IN ECONOMIC AND SOCIAL HISTORY. 1969. irreg. individually priced. Hull University Press, Hull HU6 7RX, England. Ed. John Saville. Indexed: SSCI.

330   FR   ISSN 0079-0982
PERSPECTIVES DE L'ECONOMIQUE. SERIE 1. FONDATEURS DE L'ECONOMIE. 1969. irreg. price varies. Editions Calmann-Levy, 3 rue Auber, 75009 Paris, France. Ed. Christian Schmidt.

330.1   US
POLITICAL ECONOMY AND PUBLIC POLICY; an international series of monographs in law, economics, history of economic thought and public finance. 1983. irreg., vol.4, 1985. $22.50 to individuals; institutions $45. J A I Press Inc., Box 1678, 36 Sherwood Pl., Greenwich, CT 06836. Eds. William Brelt, Kenneth G. Elzinga. index.

330.1   320   US
POLITICAL ECONOMY OF WORLD-SYSTEMS ANNUALS. 1978. a. $29.95 for hardcover; softcover $14.95. Sage Publications, Inc., 2111 W. Hillcrest Dr., Newbury Park, CA 91320 TEL 805-499-0721. (And Sage Publications, Ltd., 28 Banner St., London EC1Y 8QE, England) Ed. Immanuel Wallerstein. (back issues avail.)

330   UK
READINGS IN ECONOMIC HISTORY AND THEORY.* 1974. irreg. price varies. J.M. Dent & Sons Ltd., 33 Welbeck St., London W1M 8LX, England.

330   US   ISSN 0363-3268
RESEARCH IN ECONOMIC HISTORY; an annual compilation of research. 1976. a. $22.50 to individuals; institutions $45. J A I Press Inc., Box 1678, 36 Sherwood Pl., Greenwich, CT 06836. TEL 203-661-7602. Ed. Paul Uselding. bibl. charts. stat. Indexed: SSCI.

330.1   US   ISSN 0193-2306
RESEARCH IN EXPERIMENTAL ECONOMICS; a research annual. (Supplement avail.: An Experiment in Non-Cooperative Oligopoly) 1979. a. $23.75 to individuals; institutions $47.50. J A I Press Inc., Box 1678, 36 Sherwood Pl., Greenwich, CT 06836. TEL 203-661-7602. Ed. Vernon L. Smith.

330.1   320   US   ISSN 0161-7230
RESEARCH IN POLITICAL ECONOMY; an annual compilation of research. 1978. a. $23.75 to individuals; institutions $47.50. J A I Press Inc., Box 1678, 36 Sherwood Pl., Greenwich, CT 06836. TEL 203-661-7602. Ed. Paul Zarembka.

330.1   US
RESEARCH IN THE HISTORY OF ECONOMIC THOUGHT AND METHODOLOGY. 1983. a. $23.75 to individuals; institutions $47.50. J A I Press Inc., 36 Sherwood Pl., Box 1678, Greenwich, CT 06836-1678. Ed. Warren J. Samuels.

330.1   US
REVIEW OF AUSTRALIAN ECONOMICS. 1986. Auburn University, Ludwig von Mises Institute, Auburn, AL 36849. TEL 205-826-2500. adv.

330.1   BU   ISSN 0204-9627
SOFIISKI UNIVERSITET. KATEDRA PO POLITICESKA IKONOMIYA. GODISNIK. (Text in Bulgarian; summaries in English and Russian) irreg., vol.16, 1978. price varies. (Sofiiski Universitet., Katedra po Politicheska Ikonomiya) Publishing House of the Bulgarian Academy of Sciences, Acad. G. Bonchev St., Bldg. 6, 1113 Sofia, Bulgaria. Ed.Bd.

SOOCHOW JOURNAL OF ECONOMICS AND BUSINESS. see *BUSINESS AND ECONOMICS*

SOUNDVIEW EXECUTIVE BOOK SUMMARIES. see *BUSINESS AND ECONOMICS* — *Management*

320.1   SA
SOUTH AFRICAN JOURNAL OF ECONOMIC HISTORY. (Text in English; summaries in Afrikaans) 1982. biennial. R.20 to individuals; institutions R.40. Economic History Society of Southern Africa, University of the Witwatersrand, Division of Economic History, Johannesburg, South Africa. Ed. A.B. Lumby. bk. rev. circ. 250.
Formerly: Perspectives in Economic History.

330.1   AU
SOZIAL- UND WIRTSCHAFTSHISTORISCHE STUDIEN. 1972. irreg. price varies. Verlag fuer Geschichte und Politik, Neulinggasse 26, A-1030 Vienna, Austria. Ed. Herbert Knittler, Michael Mitterauer.

330.1   PL   ISSN 0081-6485
STUDIA HISTORIAE OECONOMICA. (Text in English, French and German) 1966. irreg., vol.11, 1976. price varies. Adam Mickiewicz University Press, Marchlewskiego 128, 61-874 Poznan, Poland. Ed. Jerzy Topolski. circ. 1,500.

330.1   US   ISSN 0344-824X
STUDIEN UEBER WIRTSCHAFT-UND SYSTEMVERGLEICHE. (Text in English or German) 1971. irreg., vol.11, 1984. price varies. Springer-Verlag, 175 Fifth Ave., New York, NY 10010 TEL 212-460-1500. (Also Berlin, Heidelberg, Tokyo and Vienna) Ed. F. Nemschak. (reprint service avail. from ISI)

STUDIEN ZUR RECHTS-, WIRTSCHAFTS- UND KULTURGESCHICHTE. see *LAW*

330.1   US
STUDIES IN CONTEMPORARY ECONOMICS. 1982. irreg., vol.15, 1985. Springer-Verlag, 175 Fifth AVe., New York, NY 10010 TEL 212-460-1500. (Also Berlin, Heidelberg, Tokyo and Vienna) Ed.Bd.

330.1   IT   ISSN 0391-3295
TEORIE ECONOMICHE. 1977. irreg., no.14, 1984. price varies. Liguori Editore s.r.l., Via Mezzocannone 19, 80134 Naples, Italy. TEL 081/20 6077. Eds. Bruno Jossa, Salvatore Vinci.

330.1   510   US
TEXTS AND MONOGRAPHS IN ECONOMICS AND MATHEMATICAL SYSTEMS. 1983. irreg., latest 1986. Springer-Verlag, 175 Fifth Ave., New York, NY 10010 TEL 212-460-1500. (Also Berlin, Heidelberg, Tokyo, Vienna) (reprint service avail. from ISI)

330.1   CM
UNIVERSITE DE YAOUNDE. FACULTE DE DROIT ET DES SCIENCES ECONOMIQUES. ECONOMIE GENERALE. irreg. Universite de Yaounde, Faculte de Droit et des Sciences Economiques, B.P. 337, Yaounde, Cameroon.

UNIVERSITY OF CALIFORNIA, BERKELEY. INSTITUTE OF INTERNATIONAL STUDIES. RESEARCH SERIES. see *POLITICAL SCIENCE*

330.1   FI   ISSN 0358-870X
UNIVERSITY OF VAASA. PROCEEDINGS. DISCUSSION PAPERS. 1979. irreg., no.75, 1985. Vaasan Korkeakoulu - University of Vaasa, Raastuvank. 31, 65100 Vaasa 10, Finland. Ed. Kauko Mikkonen.
Formerly (until 1980): Vaasa School of Economics. Proceedings. Discussion Papers (ISSN 0357-3486)

330.1   332.2   301   CS
UNIVERZITA J. E. PURKYNE. FILOZOFICKA FAKULTA. SBORNIK PRACI. G: RADA SOCIALNEVDNA. irreg., approx. a. Univerzita J. E. Purkyne, Filozoficka Fakulta, A. Novaka 1, 602 00 Brno, Czechoslovakia.

330.1   SW   ISSN 0346-6493
UPPSALA STUDIES IN ECONOMIC HISTORY. (Subseries of Acta Universitatis Upsaliensis) 1974. irreg. (Uppsala Universitet) Almqvist & Wiksell International, Box 62, S-101 20 Stockholm, Sweden. Ed. Bo Gustafsson.
Continues: Ekonomisk-Historiska Studier.

330.1   FI   ISSN 0358-9110
VAASAN KORKEAKOULU. JULKAISUJA. OPETUSMONISTEITA/UNIVERSITY OF VAASA. PROCEEDINGS. TEACHING AID SERIES. 1972. irreg., no.35, 1985. Vaasan Korkeakoulu - University of Vaasa, Raastuvankatu 31, 65100 Vaasa 10, Finland. Ed. Kauko Mikkonen.
Formerly (until 1980): Vaasan Kauppakorkeakoulu. Julkaisuja. Opetusmonisteita (ISSN 0355-2624)

330.1   FI   ISSN 0358-9080
VAASAN KORKEAKOULU. JULKAISUJA. TUTKIMUKSIA/UNIVERSITY OF VAASA. PROCEEDINGS. RESEARCH PAPERS. 1970. irreg., no.113, 1985. price varies. Vaasan Korkeakoulu - University of Vaasa, Raastuvankatu 31, 65100 Vaasa 10, Finland. Ed. Kauko Mikkonen.
Formerly (until 1980): Vaasan Kauppakorkeakoulu. Julkaisuja. Tutkimuksia (ISSN 0355-2632)

VIERTELJAHRSCHRIFT FUER SOZIAL- UND WIRTSCHAFTSGESCHICHTE. BEIHEFTE. see *SOCIAL SCIENCES: COMPREHENSIVE WORKS*

330.1   US   ISSN 0172-5963
WIRTSCHAFTSPOLITISCHE STUDIEN. (Text in German) 1976. irreg. price varies. Springer-Verlag, 175 Fifth Ave., New York, NY 10010 TEL 212-460-1500. (Also Berlin, Heidelberg, Tokyo and Vienna) (reprint service avail. from ISI)

330.1   309   GW   ISSN 0170-3579
WISSENSCHAFTLICHE PAPERBACKS; Sozial- und Wirtschaftsgeschichte. irreg., vol.23, 1986. DM.24. Franz Steiner Verlag Wiesbaden GmbH, Birkenwaldstr. 44, Postfach 347, D-7000 Stuttgart 1, W. Germany (B.R.D.) Ed. Hans Pohl.
History

330   US
WORLD ECONOMIC HISTORY. irreg. Cornell University Press, 124 Roberts Place, Ithaca, NY 14850. TEL 607-257-7000.

330.9   US
YALE SERIES IN ECONOMIC HISTORY. irreg., latest, 1976. Yale University Press, 92A Yale Sta., New Haven, CT 06520. TEL 203-432-0940.

330.1   GW   ISSN 0342-3956
ZEITSCHRIFT FUER UNTERNEHMENSGESCHICHTE. BEIHEFTE. irreg., vol.48, 1987. price varies. (Gesellschaft fuer Unternehmensgeschichte e.V., Koeln) Franz Steiner Verlag Wiesbaden GmbH, Birkenwaldstr. 44, Postfach 347, D-7000 Stuttgart 1, W. Germany (B.R.D.) Eds. W. Treue, H. Pohl.

BUSINESS AND ECONOMICS — International Commerce

382   UA
A B C - ARAB TRADE REFERENCE: ARAB & MIDDLE EAST COUNTRIES. (Text in Arabic, English, French, German, and Italian) 1973. irreg. 99 Shari Ramsis, Al-Qahirah, Egypt. illus.

382   GW   ISSN 0065-003X
A B C EUROPE PRODUCTION. (In 2 vols.) (Text in German; indexed in English, French, German, Italian, Portuguese, Spanish) 1960. a. prices on request. A B C-Verlagshaus Darmstadt, Berliner Allee 8, 6100 Darmstadt, W. Germany (B.R.D.) (Dist. by: International Publications Service, 114 E. 32nd St., New York, NY 10016) adv. circ. 18,000.

BUSINESS AND ECONOMICS — INTERNATIONAL COMMERCE

658 US
ADVANCES IN INTERNATIONAL COMPARATIVE MANAGEMENT. 1984. a. $24.75 to individuals; institutions $49.50. J A I Press Inc., 36 Sherwood Pl., Box 1678, Greenwich, CT 06836-1678. TEL 203-661-7602. Ed. Richard N. Farmer.

380 UN
AFRICAN TRADE/COMMERCE AFRICAIN. (Text and summaries in French and English) 1976. irreg. avail. only on exchange. United Nations Economic Commission for Africa - Commission Economique pour l'Afrique, Box 3001, Addis Ababa, Ethiopia. charts. illus. tr. lit. circ. 4,500. (back issues avail.)
First issue (May 1976) called: African Trader/Commercant Africain.
Intro-African trade literature

382 AE
ALGERIA. INSTITUT NATIONAL ALGERIEN DU COMMERCE EXTERIEUR. ANNUAIRE DES EXPORTATEURS. (Text in Arabic, English and French) 1976. a. 80 din. Institut National Algerien du Commerce Exterieur - Algerian National Institute for Foreign Trade, 6 blvd. Amilcar Cabral, Algiers, Algeria.

ALTERNATIVE TRADING NEWS. see *BUSINESS AND ECONOMICS — International Development And Assistance*

382.6 US ISSN 0272-1163
AMERICAN EXPORT REGISTER. (Index in Arabic, Chinese, English, French, German, Japanese, Portuguese and Spanish) 1945. a. $112. Thomas Publishing Co., One Penn Plaza, 250 W. 34th St., New York, NY 10119. TEL 212-290-7343. illus. index.
Formerly: American Register of Exporters and Importers (ISSN 0065-9967)

382 FR
ANNUAIRE DES AGENTS COMMERCIAUX COURTIERS ET REPRESENTANTS DE COMMERCE-FRANCE ET MARCHE COMMUN. 1972. irreg. D.A.G., 65 rue de Rivoli, 75001 Paris, France. adv.

382 FR
ANNUAIRE DES ENTREPRISES ET ORGANISMES D'OUTRE-MER. 1910. a. 560 Fr. Rene Moreux et Cie, 190 bd. Haussmann, 75008 Paris, France.
Formerly: Annuaire des Entreprises d'Afrique Noire, des Organismes Officiells et Professionels d'Outre-Mer, des Organismes de Cooperation Francais, Etrangers et Internationaux (ISSN 0066-2828)

382 HT
ANNUAIRE DU COMMERCE EXTERIEUR D'HAITI: IMPORTATIONS, EXPORTATIONS. a. Administration Generale des Douanes, Port-au-Prince, Haiti. stat.

382 UK ISSN 0072-5846
ANNUAL STATEMENT OF THE OVERSEAS TRADE OF THE UNITED KINGDOM. a. price varies. Customs and Excise Department, King's Beam House, 39-41 Mark Lane, London EC1R 7HE, England (Avail. from H.M.S.O., c/o Liaison Officer, Atlantic House, Holborn Viaduct, London EC1P 1BN, England)

382 UY
ANUARIO DE IMPORTACION - EXPORTACION DEL URUGUAY. 1957. a. $55. Centro de Estadisticas Nacionales y Comercio Internacional del Uruguay, Misiones 1361, Casilla de Correo 1510, Montevideo, Uruguay. Ed. C. Vetesi. adv. circ. 2,500.

382 AG ISSN 0066-5118
ANUARIO DEL COMERCIO EXTERIOR LATINO-AMERICANO; guide to the industry and foreign trade of Latin America. 1966. a. $30 free to advertisers. (Latin American Free Trade Association) E.P.I.S.A., Rivadavia 825, 2 Piso, Buenos Aires, Argentina. Ed. E.F. Cappagli. index.
Formerly: Anuario de los Paises de A L A L C (ISSN 0571-3846)

382 UK ISSN 0140-1874
ARAB BUSINESS YEARBOOK. 1976. a. £32($51) paperback; £40($64) hardback. Graham & Trotman Ltd., Sterling House, 66 Wilton Rd., London SW1V 1DE, England. adv.

382 US
ARGENTINE-AMERICAN BUSINESS REVIEW DIRECTORY.* 1978. biennial. $25. Motivational Communications, Inc. (New York), 10261 Chardon Rd., Chardon, OH 44024-9725. Ed. Barry V. Conforte. adv. circ. 15,000.

ARIZONA DIRECTORY OF EXPORTS. see *BUSINESS AND ECONOMICS — Trade And Industrial Directories*

382 II ISSN 0066-8230
ASIA - AFRICA WORLD TRADE REGISTER. (Text in English; classified headings in English, French, German and Spanish) 1970. irreg. £7. Business Publications International, United India Life Building, Box 548, F-Block, Connaught Place, New Delhi 1, India. Ed. K.L. Sahgal. adv. circ. 10, 000.
Classified business directory on countries of Asia-Africa with international section

382 UK ISSN 0268-2257
ASIAN LIVING COSTS. 1979. irreg. £18. Confederation of British Industry, 103 New Oxford St., London WC1A 1DU, England.

ASPIS; the classified Greek commercial directory. see *BUSINESS AND ECONOMICS — Trade And Industrial Directories*

350 382 AT
AUSTRALIA. DEPARTMENT OF PRIMARY INDUSTRY. CONDITIONS FOR EXPORT OF EXPERIMENTAL SHIPMENTS. 1972. a. free. Department of Primary Industry, Quarantine and Inspection Service, Edmund Barton Bldg., Broughton St., Barton, A.C.T. 2600, Australia.

350 382 AT
AUSTRALIA. DEPARTMENT OF PRIMARY INDUSTRY. CONDITIONS FOR EXPORT OF GRAPES. 1972. a. free. Department of Primary Industry, Quarantine and Inspection Service, Edmund Barton Bldg., Broughton ST., Barton, A.C.T. 2600, Australia.

350 382 AT
AUSTRALIA. DEPARTMENT OF PRIMARY INDUSTRY. CONDITIONS FOR EXPORT OF PRIMARY PRODUCTS. 1972. a. free. Department of Primary Industry, Quarantine and Inspection Service, Edmund Barton Bldg., Broughton St., Barton, A.C.T. 2600, Australia.
Formerly (until 1987): Australia. Department of Primary Industry. Conditions for Export of Pears.

382 US
AUSTRALIAN-AMERICAN BUSINESS REVIEW.* 1980. biennial. $25. Motivational Communications, Inc. (New York), 10261 Charon Rd., Chardon, OH 44024-9725. TEL 212-741-0800. Ed. Barry V. Conforte. circ. 50,000.

382 AT
AUSTRALIAN EXPORTS. 1964. a. Aus.$55. Peter Isaacson Publications, 45-50 Porter St., Prahran, Vic. 3181, Australia (Dist. by: Croner Publications, Inc., 211-05 Jamaica Ave., NY 11428) Ed. John F. Ross.
Formerly: Australian Directory of Exports (ISSN 0084-7305)

382 338 AT ISSN 0155-7009
AUSTRALIAN IMPORTS. 1978. a. Aus.$40. Peter Isaacson Publications, 45-50 Porter St., Prahran, Vic. 3181, Australia (Dist. by: Croner Publications, Inc., 211-05 Jamaica Ave., NY 11428) adv.

382 GW ISSN 0415-7508
B D I DEUTSCHLAND LIEFERT/B D I GERMANY SUPPLIES/B D I L'ALLEMAGNE FOURNIT/B D I ALEMANIA SUMINISTRA; official export register of the Federation of German Industries. (Text in English, French, German and Spanish) 1952. a. DM.180. (Bundesverband der Deutschen Industrie) Verlag W. Sachon GmbH & Co., Schloss Mindelburg, 8948 Mindelheim, W. Germany (B.R.D.) Ed. Werner Sachon. adv. circ. 15,139.

382 US
B I MIDDLE EAST MARKETING CONDITIONS: EGYPT. a. $650. Business International Corporation, One Dag Hammarskjold Plaza, New York, NY 10017. TEL 212-750-6300.

382.1 JM
BALANCE OF PAYMENTS OF JAMAICA. a. free. Bank of Jamaica, Research Dept., Box 621, Kingston, Jamaica. illus. stat.

BALANCE OF PAYMENTS OF SIERRA LEONE. see *BUSINESS AND ECONOMICS — Public Finance, Taxation*

BALANCE OF PAYMENTS OF TRINIDAD AND TOBAGO. see *BUSINESS AND ECONOMICS — Public Finance, Taxation*

BALANZA DE PAGOS DE ESPANA. see *BUSINESS AND ECONOMICS — Public Finance, Taxation*

BANCA ROMANA DE COMERT EXTERIOR. ANNUAL BULLETIN. see *BUSINESS AND ECONOMICS — Banking And Finance*

380 NQ
BANCO CENTRAL DE NICARAGUA. COMERCIO EXTERIOR DE NICARAGUA POR PRODUCTOS Y PAISES.* a. Ministerio de Comercio Exterior (MICE), Apdo. 2412, Managua, Nicaragua. stat. circ. 3,000.

382 EC
BANCO CENTRAL DEL ECUADOR. ACUERDOS INTERNACIONALES DE COMERCIO Y PAGOS. irreg. free. Banco Central del Ecuador, Av. 10 de Agosto (Plaza Bolivar), La Alameda, Quito, Ecuador.

BANGLADESH BANK. STATISTICS DEPARTMENT. ANNUAL BALANCE OF PAYMENTS. see *BUSINESS AND ECONOMICS — Abstracting, Bibliographies, Statistics*

382 JA
BANK OF JAPAN. PRICE INDEXES ANNUAL. (Text in Japanese and English) a. price varies. Bank of Japan, Research and Statistics Department - Nippon Ginko, 2-2-1 Hogoku-cho, Nihonbashi, Chuo-ku, Tokyo 103, Japan (Order from: Japan Publications Trading Co., Ltd., Box 5030, Tokyo International, Tokyo, Japan; or 1255 Howard St., San Francisco, CA 94103)
Formerly: Bank of Japan. Export and Import Price Indexes Annual.

BANK OF LIBYA. BALANCE OF PAYMENTS. see *BUSINESS AND ECONOMICS — Public Finance, Taxation*

382 BE ISSN 0067-561X
BELGIUM. OFFICE BELGE DU COMMERCE EXTERIEUR. BIJVOEGSEL B B H. REEKS B. irreg. Office Belge du Commerce Exterieur, 162 Boulevard Emile Jacqmain, 1210 Brussels, Belgium.

BIRMINGHAM INTERNATIONAL TRADE DIRECTORY. see *BUSINESS AND ECONOMICS — Trade And Industrial Directories*

382 UK
BRITISH EXPORTS/EXPORTATIONS BRITANNIQUES/BRITISCHER EXPORT/EXPORTACIONES BRITANICAS. (Text in English; indexes in French, German, Spanish) 1969. a. £65. Kompass Publishers Ltd., Windsor Court, East Grinstead House, East Grinstead, West Sussex RH19 1XD, England. adv. circ. 12,000.
●Also available online.
Former titles: British Exports. Export Services. (ISSN 0305-7682); British Exports (ISSN 0068-1970)

382 UK
BRITISH INVISIBLE EXPORTS COUNCIL. ANNUAL REPORT. 1968. a. free. British Invisible Exports Council, 6th Fl., Dunster House, 37 Mincing Lane, London EC3R 7BQ, England. TEL 01-929 0918. illus. stat.
Formerly: Committee on Invisible Exports. Annual Report (ISSN 0308-4892)

BUSINESS AND ECONOMICS — INTERNATIONAL COMMERCE

382   UK   ISSN 0068-4465
BUSINESS MONITOR: MISCELLANEOUS SERIES. M4 OVERSEAS TRANSACTIONS. a. price varies. Department of Industry, 29 Great Peter St., London SW1P 3LW, England (Avail. from: H.M.S.O., c/o Liaison Officer, Atlantic House, Holborn Viaduct, London EC1P 1BW, England) Indexed: Paper & Bd.Abstr.

382   US   ISSN 0263-3701
C O M E C O N DATA. (Council for Mutual Economic Assistance) biennial; alternates with C O M E C O N Foreign Trade Data. $45. (Vienna Institute for Comparative Economic Studies) Greenwood Press, 88 Post Rd. West, Box 5007, Westport, CT 06881. TEL 203-226-3571.

382   US
C O M E C O N FOREIGN TRADE DATA. (Council for Mutual Economic Assistance) 1980. biennial; alternates with C O M E C O N Data. $45. (Vienna Institute for Comparative Economic Studies) Greenwood Press, Box 5007, 88 Post Road West, Westport, CT 06881. TEL 203-226-3571. charts. (back issues avail.)

382   614.7   CN
CANADA. CANADIAN IMPORT TRIBUNAL. ANNUAL REPORT. (Text in English and French) 1969. a. Supply and Services Canada, Canadian Import Tribunal, Ottawa, Ont. K1A 0G5, Canada. TEL 613-593-4601.
    Formerly: Canada. Anti-Dumping Tribunal. Annual Report.

CANADA. GRAIN COMMISSION. ECONOMICS AND STATISTICS DIVISION. CANADIAN GRAIN EXPORTS. see *AGRICULTURE — Feed, Flour And Grain*

382.097   CN   ISSN 0702-0333
CANADA-JAPAN, THE EXPORT-IMPORT PICTURE. 1964. biennial. Canada-Japan Trade Council, Fuller Bldg., Suite 903, 75 Albert St., Ottawa, Ont. K1P 5E7, Canada. TEL 613-233-4047. Ed. J.E. Struthers. charts. stat. circ. 4,800.

CANADIAN CERTIFIED GENERAL ACCOUNTANTS' RESEARCH FOUNDATION. STUDY PAPERS. see *BUSINESS AND ECONOMICS — Accounting*

382   US
CHASE WORLD GUIDE FOR EXPORTERS. (Includes supplementary bulletins) a. $295. Chase Trade Information Corporation, Box 245, 78th Fl., New York, NY 10048. TEL 212-432-8000.

382   660   II   ISSN 0531-5980
CHEMICALS AND ALLIED PRODUCTS EXPORT PROMOTION COUNCIL. EXPORTERS DIRECTORY. (Text in English) a. Chemicals and Allied Products Export Promotion Council, World Trade Centre, 14/1B Ezra St, Calcutta 700001, India.

380   US   ISSN 0577-7259
CHICAGO MERCANTILE EXCHANGE YEARBOOK. 1984. a. $10 per no. Chicago Mercantile Exchange, Statistics Department, 30 S. Wacker Dr., Chicago, IL 60606. TEL 312-930-1000. circ. 300.
    Incorporates (1972-1983): International Monetary Market Yearbook.

CHILE. INSTITUTO NACIONAL DE ESTADISTICAS. COMERCIO EXTERIOR. see *BUSINESS AND ECONOMICS — Abstracting, Bibliographies, Statistics*

382   CH
CHINA, REPUBLIC. EXPORT PROCESSING ZONE ADMINISTRATION. EXPORTS OF E P Z. (Text in Chinese and English) a. Export Processing Zone Administration, Kaohsiung, Taiwan, Republic of China.

382   HK
CHINA'S EXPORTS. 1984. irreg. (4-6/yr.) HK.$80($12) Grossource Ltd., Tien Chu Commercial Bldg., 10th Fl., 173-174 Gloucester Rd., Hong Kong, Hong Kong. circ. 45,000.

382   CK
COLOMBIA. DEPARTAMENTO ADMINISTRATIVO NACIONAL DE ESTADISTICA. ANUARIO DE COMERCIO EXTERIOR. a. Departamento Administrativo Nacional de Estadistica, Bogota, Colombia.

382   BE
COMMERCE EXTERIEUR DE L'U.E.B.L. AVEC LES PAYS D'AFRIQUE. (Text in Dutch and French) 1967. a. Office Belge du Commerce Exterieur, 162 Boulevard Emile Jacqmain, 1210 Brussels, Belgium.
    Each issue includes comparative figures for previous two years on commerce of the Union Economique Belgo-Luxemburgeoise

382   BE
COMMERCE EXTERIEUR DE L'U.E.B.L. AVEC LES PAYS D'AMERIQUE LATINE/BUITENLANDSE HANDEL VAN DE B.L.E.U. MET DE LANDEN VAN LATIJNS AMERIKA BRUXELLES. a. Office Belge du Commerce Exterieur, 162 Boulevard Emile Jacqmain, 1210 Brussels, Belgium. stat.
    Each issue includes comparative figures for previous two years on commerce of the Union Economique Belgo-Luxemburgeoise

382   BE
COMMERCE EXTERIEUR DE L'U.E.B.L. AVEC LES PAYS D'ASIE/BUITENLANDSE HANDEL VAN DE B.L.E.U. MET DE LANDEN VAN AZIE BRUXELLES. a. Office Belge du Commerce Exterieur, 162 Boulevard Emile Jacqmain, 1210 Brussels, Belgium. stat.
    Each issue includes comparative figures for previous two years on commerce of the Union Economique Belgo-Luxembourgeoise

382   BE
COMMERCE EXTERIEUR DE L'U.E.B.L. AVEC LES PAYS DE L'EST/BUITENLANDSE HANDEL VAN DE B.L.E.U. MET DE OOSTLANDEN BRUXELLES. a. Office Belge du Commerce Exterieur, 162 Boulevard Emile Jacqmain, 1210 Brussels, Belgium. stat.
    Each issue includes comparative figures for previous two years on commerce of the Union Economique Belgo-Luxembourgeoise

382   BE
COMMERCE EXTERIEUR DE L'U.E.B.L. AVEC LES PAYS DE LA C.E.E/BUITLANDSE HANDEL VAN DE B.L.E.U. MET DE E.E.G.-LIDSTATEN BRUXELLES. a. Office Belge du Commerce Exterieur, 162 Boulevard Emile Jacqmain, 1210 Brussels, Belgium. stat.
    Each issue includes comparative figures for previous two years on commerce between the European Economic Community and the Union Economique Belgo-Luxembourgeoise

382   BE
COMMERCE EXTERIEUR DE L'U.E.B.L. AVEC LES PAYS INDUSTRIALISES (AUTRE QUE LES PAYS DE LA C.E.E. ET L'A.E.L.E.)/BUITENLANDSE HANDEL VAN DE B.L.E.U. MET DE INDUSTRIELANDEN (NIET E.E.G.-EN E.V.A.-LIDSTATEN BRUXELLES) a. Office Belge du Commerce Exterieur, 162 Boulevard Emile Jacqmain, 1210 Brussels, Belgium. stat.
    Each issue includes comparative figures for previous two years on commerce between the Union Economique Belgo-Luxembourgeoise and the European Economic community and European Free Trade Association

382   IV
COMMERCE EXTERIEUR DE LA COTE D'IVORIE: RESULTATS ET EVOLUTION. irreg. Direction des Affaires Economiques et des Relations Economiques Exterieures, Abidjan, Ivory Coast. stat.

382   341   EI
COMMISSION OF THE EUROPEAN COMMUNITIES. COLLECTION OF AGREEMENTS. (Editions in Danish, Dutch, English, French, German, Italian) 1977. irreg. price varies. European Communities, Office of Official Publications of the European Communities, 2 rue Mercier, 2985 Luxembourg, Luxembourg (Distr. in the U.S. by: European Community Information Service, 2100 M St., N.W. Ste. 707, Washington, D.C. 20037)

COMMISSION OF THE EUROPEAN COMMUNITIES. REPORT ON COMPETITION POLICY/RAPPORT SUR LA POLITIQUE DE CONCURRENCE. see *BUSINESS AND ECONOMICS — Production Of Goods And Services*

382   BE
COMPAGNIE FINANCIERE EUROPEENNE ET D'OUTRE-MER. FINOUTREMER. RAPPORT ANNUEL. 1972. a. free. Compagnie Financiere Europeene et d'Outre-Mer, 30 rue Royale, 1000 Brussels, Belgium.
    Former titles: Compagnie Europeenne et d'Outre-Mer. Rapports; Compagnie du Congo pour le Commerce et l'Industrie. Assemblee Generale. Rapports.

382   US   ISSN 0070-2250
CUSTOM HOUSE GUIDE. 1862. a. $259. North American Publishing Co., 401 N. Broad St., Philadelphia, PA 19108. Ed. Joseph Douress. index. circ. 5,600.

382   AT
CUSTOMS OFFICER'S ASSOCIATION OF AUSTRALIA. FOURTH DIVISION. FOURTH DIVISION CUSTOMS OFFICER. 1968. irreg. Aus.$0.05 per no. Percival Publishing Co. Pty. Ltd., 862-870 Elizabeth St., Sydney, N.S.W. 2000, Australia.

382.7   CY
CYPRUS. DEPARTMENT OF CUSTOMS AND EXCISE. ANNUAL REPORT. (Text in English) a. Department of Customs and Excise, Nicosia, Cyprus. stat.

382   CY   ISSN 0070-2420
CYPRUS. DEPARTMENT OF STATISTICS AND RESEARCH. STATISTICS OF IMPORTS AND EXPORTS. (Text in English) 1961. a. £C6. Department of Statistics and Research, Ministry of Finance, Nicosia, Cyprus.

CYPRUS. TOURISM ORGANISATION. ANNUAL REPORT. see *TRAVEL AND TOURISM*

382   DK   ISSN 0108-3910
DANMARK EXPORT: FOOD & BEVERAGES/PRODUITS ALIMENTAIRES & BOISSONS/LEBENSMITTEL & GETRAENKE. (Text in Arabic, English, French, German and Italian) 1982. a. free. Fakto Press, Transformervej 20, 2730 Herlev, Denmark. illus.

DANSK TEKSTIL EXPORTGUIDE/DANISH TEXTILE EXPORT GUIDE. see *TEXTILE INDUSTRIES AND FABRICS*

DIGEST OF COMMERCIAL LAWS OF THE WORLD. see *LAW — International Law*

382   PH
DIMENSIONS OF PHILIPPINE EXPORTS.* (Text in English) 1974. a. Ministry of Trade, Trade & Industry Bldg., 361 Gil J. Puyat Ave. Ext., Makati, Metro Manila, Philippines. Ed. Socorro B. Ramos. stat.

382   US   ISSN 0070-5071
DIRECTORY OF AMERICAN FIRMS OPERATING IN FOREIGN COUNTRIES. 1955/56. irreg., 10th edt., 1984. $150. World Trade Academy Press, Inc., 50 E. 42nd St., New York, NY 10017. TEL 212-697-4999.

DIRECTORY OF EXPORT BUYERS IN THE U.K. see *BUSINESS AND ECONOMICS — Trade And Industrial Directories*

382   II
DIRECTORY OF INDIAN EXPORTERS. (Continues: Directory of Exporters of Indian Produce and Manufactures) (Text in English) 1919. triennial. price varies. ‡ Department of Commercial Intelligence and Statistics, 1 Council House St., Calcutta 700001, India (Order from: Controller of Publications, Civil Lines, New Delhi 110054, India) adv.
    Formerly: Indian Export Directory.

382   US
DIRECTORY OF INTERNATIONAL TRADE. 1984. a. $25. Produce Marketing Association, 700 Barksdale Plaza, Newark, DE 19711. TEL 302-738-7100. Ed. Steve Ahiberg. adv. circ. 1,500.

BUSINESS AND ECONOMICS — INTERNATIONAL COMMERCE 255

382 US
DIRECTORY OF MIDDLE EAST IMPORTERS.
2nd edt., 1981. irreg. $110. Inter-Crescent
Publishing Co., Inc., 12021 Nieta Dr., Garden
Grove, CA 92640. TEL 714-537-1000.
Formerly: Directory of Middle East Imports.

382 US ISSN 0070-6531
DIRECTORY OF UNITED STATES IMPORTERS.
1966. biennial. $275. Journal of Commerce, Inc.,
110 Wall St., New York, NY 10005. TEL 212-425-
1616. Ed. E.S. Boccia. adv. index.

382 DQ ISSN 0417-9382
DOMINICA. MINISTRY OF FINANCE AND
DEVELOPMENT. ANNUAL OVERSEAS
TRADE REPORT. (Former Name of Issuing Body:
Treasury Department) a. $3. Ministry of Finance
and Development, Roseau, Dominica, West Indies.

382 DR
DOMINICAN REPUBLIC. CENTRO
DOMINICANO DE PROMOCION DE
EXPORTACIONES. BOLETIN ESTADISTICO.
1972. a. $10. Centro Dominicano de Promocion de
Exportaciones, Apdo. 192-2, Plaza de la
Independencia, Santo Domingo, Dominican
Republic. illus.
Former titles: Dominican Republic. Centro
Dominicano de Promocion de Exportaciones.
Memoria Anual & Dominican Republic. Centro
Dominicano de Promocion de Exportaciones.
Informe de Labores.

382 SW ISSN 0349-2737
DUTY & TAX-FREE SHOP WORLD GUIDE
SERIES. VOL. 1: BEST "N" MOST IN WINES &
SPIRITS. (Text in English) 1980. a. $85. Generation
Publications, P.O. Box 234, S-891 01
Oernskoeldsvik, Sweden. Ed. Yngve Bia. adv.
charts. stat. index. (back issues avail.)
Formerly: Duty and Tax-Free Shop World
Review. Vol. 1: Best "N" Most in Liquors.

382 SW ISSN 0349-2737
DUTY & TAX-FREE SHOP WORLD GUIDE
SERIES. VOL. 3: BEST "N" MOST IN
CIGARETTES, CIGARS AND TOBACCO. (Text
in English) 1980. a. $85. Generation Publications,
P.O. Box 234, S-891 01 Oernskoeldsvik, Sweden.
Ed. Yngve Bia. adv. charts. stat. index. (back issues
avail.)
Formerly: Duty and Tax-Free Shop World
Review. Vol. 3. Best "N" Most in Cigarettes, Cigars
and Pipe Tobaccos.

382 SW
DUTY & TAX-FREE SHOP WORLD GUIDE
SERIES. VOL. 4: BEST "N" MOST IN D F S.
(Text in English) 1980. a. $85. Generation
Publications, P.O. Box 234, S-891 01
Oernskoeldsvik, Sweden. Ed. Yngve Bia. adv.
charts. stat. index. (back issues avail.)
Formerly: Duty and Tax-Free Shop World
Review. Vol. 4: Best "N" Most Special Edition.

382 SZ ISSN 0531-4119
E F T A TRADE. (Text in English, French and
German) a. free. European Free Trade Association,
9-11 rue de Varembe, 1211 Geneva 20, Switzerland.

382 DK ISSN 0108-7509
EKSPORTKREDIT, EKSPORTFREMME:
AARSBERETNINGER. 1982. a. free. Ministry of
Industry, Danish Trade Fund, Codanhus, Gl.
Kongevej 60, 1850 Frederiksberg C, Denmark. illus.
Formed by the merger of: Eksportkreditraadet.
Beretning & Eksportfremmeraadet. Beretning.

382 FR
ESSOR; French industrial companies database. (Text
in French) a. $1800. Union Francaise d'Annuaires
Profesionnels (U.F.A.P.), 13 Avenue Komarov,
78190 Trappes, France. circ. 40,000.
●Also available online.

ESTADISTICA PANAMENA. SITUACION
ECONOMICA. SECCION 341. BALANZA DE
PAGOS. see BUSINESS AND ECONOMICS —
Public Finance, Taxation

382 SZ ISSN 0531-4127
EUROPEAN FREE TRADE ASSOCIATION.
ANNUAL REPORT. French edition: Rapport
Annuel (ISSN 0258-0756); German edition:
Jahresbericht (ISSN 0258-3852) (Editions in
English, French and German) 1960/61. a. free.
European Free Trade Association, 9-11 rue de
Varembe, 1211 Geneva 20, Switzerland.

330 338 US
EUROPEAN MARKETS: A GUIDE TO
COMPANY AND INDUSTRY INFORMATION
SOURCES. 1983. irreg. $150. Washington
Researchers Publishing, 2612 P St., N.W.,
Washington, DC 20007. TEL 202-333-3533.

EXPORT CANADA; the marketing directory of
Canadian trade. see BUSINESS AND
ECONOMICS — Trade And Industrial Directories

382.6 UK
EXPORT DATA; export document requirements of all
countries. 1917. a. £20. Benn Publications Ltd., 25
New Street Square, London EC4A 3JA, England.
Ed. Cynthia Patey. adv. index. circ. 3,000.
Formerly: Export Data Exporters Year Book
(ISSN 0071-3554)

382 DK
EXPORT DIRECTORY OF DENMARK. (Text in
English, French, German and Spanish; summaries in
English) 1927. a. Kr.455. Kraks Legat, Nytorv 17,
DK-1450 Copenhagen K, Denmark. circ. 20,000.

382 UK
EXPORT GUIDE TO EUROPE (YEAR) a. £65.
Globe Book Services Ltd., Brunel Rd., Houndmills,
Basingstoke, Hants. RG21 2XS, England.

382 332.1 JA ISSN 0071-3503
EXPORT-IMPORT BANK OF JAPAN. ANNUAL
REPORT. 1951. a. free. Export-Import Bank of
Japan, 1-4-1 Ohtemachi, Chiyoda-ku, Tokyo, Japan.
Ed. Masahiko Agata. circ. 7,000.

332.1 KO
EXPORT-IMPORT BANK OF KOREA. ANNUAL
REPORT. (Text in English) a. Export-Import Bank
of Korea, Box 4009, Seoul 100, S. Korea. charts.
illus. stat.

382.7 PR ISSN 0270-5184
EXPORT-IMPORT MARKETS; Puerto Rico Edition.
(Text & summaries in English and Spanish) 1982. a.
free. Whitney Marketing Inc., Apdo. 2631, Old San
Juan, PR 00903. TEL 809-725-7373. Ed. Hugo
Miranda. adv. stat.
Formerly: Exporter Guide - Caribbean and Latin
America.

382 UK
EXPORT SERVICES. 1972. a. free. Kompass
Publishers Ltd., Windsor Court, East Grinstead
House, East Grinstead, West Sussex RH19 1XD,
England. circ. 6,000.

382 JA
EXPORT STATISTICAL SCHEDULE OF JAPAN
(YEAR) (Text in English and Japanese) 1965. a.
3400 Yen($36) Japan Tariff Association, c/o Jibiki
Daini Bldg., 4-7-8 Kojimachi, Chiyoda-ku, Tokyo,
Japan.
Supersedes in part: Commodity Classification for
Foreign Trade Statistics: Japan (ISSN 0546-0786)

382 US
EXPORTERS DIRECTORY/U.S. BUYING GUIDE.
biennial. $250. Journal of Commerce, Inc., 110 Wall
St., New York, NY 10005 TEL 201-859-1300.
(Subscr. addr.: Journal of Commerce, 445 Marshall
St., Phillipsburg, NJ 08865)
Formerly: Export Directory/U.S. Buying Guide.

382.6 US ISSN 0732-0159
EXPORTERS' ENCYCLOPAEDIA. 1904. a. (with s-
m. updates) $365. Dun's Marketing Services
(Subsidiary of: Dun & Bradstreet Corporation) 49
Old Bloomfield Rd., Mtn. Lakes, NJ 07046. TEL
201-455-0900. Ed. Robert D. Tmars. adv. index.
circ. 5,100.
Former titles: Dun and Bradstreet Exporters'
Encyclopaedia - World Marketing Guide (ISSN
0149-8118); Exporters' Encyclopaedia-World
Marketing Guide (ISSN 0071-3546)

382 US ISSN 0556-3585
EXPORTS BY PENNSYLVANIA
MANUFACTURERS. 1972. irreg. free. ‡
Department of Commerce, Bureau of Policy,
Planning & Systems Development, 474 Forum Bldg.,
Harrisburg, PA 17120. TEL 717-787-7532. Ed.
W.R. Kresge.

382 CH ISSN 0301-9217
EXPORTS OF THE REPUBLIC OF CHINA. 1970/
71. a. $100. ‡ China External Trade Development
Council, 201 Tunhwa North Rd., Taipei, Taiwan,
Republic of China. circ. 5,000.

382.5 LB
EXTERNAL TRADE OF LIBERIA: IMPORT AND
EXPORT. (Text in English) a., latest 1980. $5.
Ministry of Planning and Economic Affairs, Box
9016, Monrovia, Liberia.

382 UK
FINNISH BUYER'S GUIDE. vol.5, 1983. irreg.
British Industrial Publicity Overseas Ltd., Walter
House, Bedford St., London WC2R 0QB, England.

382 CK
FONDO DE PROMOCION DE
EXPORTACIONES. DIRECTORIO DE
EXPORTADORES/EXPORT DIRECTORY. (Text
in English, Spanish) 1976. a. free. Proexpo Fondo
de Promocion de Exportaciones, Calle 15 No. 8-68,
Piso 7, Bogota, Colombia. adv. illus. circ. 15,000.

FOOD AND AGRICULTURE ORGANIZATION
OF THE UNITED NATIONS. TRADE
YEARBOOK. see AGRICULTURE — Agricultural
Economics

382 340 BL
FOREIGN INVESTMENTS IN BRAZIL.
LEGISLATION. 1967. irreg. $30. Banco Central do
Brasil - Central Bank of Brazil, Departamento de
Fiscalizacao e Registro de Capitais Estrangeiros/
DIPLA, SBS, Ed. Sede, 4 andar, 70074 Brasilia,
DF, Brazil (Subscr to: DEMAP/DISUP/SECRE,
SBS Ed. Sede, 2 subsolo, 70074 Brasilia DF, Brazil)
circ. 2,000.
Formerly: Foreign Investments in Brazil.

382 US
FOREIGN TRADE MARKETPLACE. 1977. irreg.
$120. Gale Research Company, Book Tower,
Detroit, MI 48226. Ed. George J. Schultz.

382 665 US ISSN 0363-6798
FOREIGN TRADE REPORTS. BUNKER FUELS.
(Series FT-810) 1948. m. and a. $19. U.S. Bureau of
the Census, Foreign Trade Division, Washington,
DC 20233 TEL 301-763-4100. (Subscr. to: Supt. of
Documents, Washington, DC 20402) (also avail. in
microform)

382 US ISSN 0361-0047
FOREIGN TRADE REPORTS. SUMMARY OF U.S.
EXPORT AND IMPORT MERCHANDISE
TRADE. (Series FT-900) 1945. m. and a. $55
(includes series: FT-975, 985, 986) U.S. Bureau of
the Census, Foreign Trade Division, Washington,
DC 20233 TEL 301-763-4100. (Subscr. to: Supt. of
Documents, Washington, DC 20402) (also avail. in
microform)

382 US ISSN 0095-7771
FOREIGN TRADE REPORTS. U.S. AIRBORNE
EXPORTS AND GENERAL IMPORTS. (Series
FT 986) m. $55 (includes series: FT-900, 975, 985)
U.S. Bureau of the Census, Foreign Trade Division,
Washington, DC 20233 TEL 301-763-4100. (Subscr.
to: Supt. of Documents, Washington, DC 20402)

382 US
FOREIGN TRADE REPORTS. U.S. IMPORTS FOR
CONSUMPTION AND GENERAL IMPORTS-T
S U S A COMMODITY BY COUNTRY OF
ORIGIN: ANNUAL (YEAR) (Tariff Schedules of
the United States Annotated) (Series FT-246) 1965.
a. price varies. U.S. Bureau of the Census, Foreign
Trade Division, Washington, DC 20233 TEL 301-
763-4100. (Subscr. to: Supt. of Documents,
Washington, DC 20402)
Formerly: Foreign Trade Reports. U.S. Imports
for Consumption and General Imports; Tariff
Schedules Annotated by Country (ISSN 0565-1190)

BUSINESS AND ECONOMICS — INTERNATIONAL COMMERCE

382   US   ISSN 0565-1204
FOREIGN TRADE REPORTS. U.S. TRADE WITH PUERTO RICO AND U.S. POSSESSIONS. (Series FT-800) 1943. m. and a. $34. U.S. Bureau of the Census, Foreign Trade Division, Washington, DC 20233 TEL 301-763-4100. (Subscr. to: Supt. of Documents, Washington, DC 20402)

382   US   ISSN 0095-0890
FOREIGN TRADE REPORTS. U.S. WATERBORNE EXPORTS AND GENERAL IMPORTS; trade area, district, port, type service and U.S. flag. (Series FT 985) 1952. m. and a. $55 (includes Series FT-900, 975, 986) U.S. Bureau of the Census, c/o Customer Services Section (Publications), Washington, DC 20233 TEL 301-763-4100. (Subscr. to: Supt. of Documents, Washington, DC 20402)

382   US
FOREIGN TRADE REPORTS. VESSEL ENTRANCES AND CLEARANCES. (Series FT 975) 1945. a. (m. until 1951) $55 (includes series: FT-900, 985, 986) U.S. Bureau of the Census, Washington, DC 20233 TEL 301-763-4100. (Subscr. to: Supt. of Documents, Washington, DC 20402)

382   FR   ISSN 0071-8645
FRANCE. DIRECTION GENERALE DES DOUANES ET DROITS INDIRECTS. COMMENTAIRES ANNUELS DES STATISTIQUES DU COMMERCE EXTERIEUR. irreg. Imprimerie Nationale, Service des Ventes, 59128 Flers en Escrebieux, 75732 Paris Cedex 15.

382   FR   ISSN 0071-8726
FRANCE. DIRECTION NATIONALE DES DOUANES ET DROITS INDIRECTS. TABLEAU GENERAL DES TRANSPORTS. 1964. a. price varies. Imprimerie Nationale, Service des Ventes, 59128 Flers en Escrebieux, 75732 Paris Cedex, France.

382   FR   ISSN 0071-8718
FRANCE. DIRECTION NATIONALE DES DOUANES ET DROITS INDIRECTS. TRANSPORT DU COMMERCE EXTERIEUR. a. price varies. Imprimerie Nationale, Service des Ventes, 59128 Flers en Escrebieux, 75732 Paris Cedex, France.

FRANCE. MINISTERE DE L'ECONOMIE ET DES FINANCES. BALANCE DES PAIEMENTS ENTRE LA FRANCE ET L'EXTERIEUR. see *BUSINESS AND ECONOMICS — Public Finance, Taxation*

FRANCO BRITISH TRADE DIRECTORY. see *BUSINESS AND ECONOMICS — Chamber Of Commerce Publications*

382   UN
G A T T STUDIES IN INTERNATIONAL TRADE. (Editions in English, French and Spanish) 1971. irreg., no.8, 1980. price varies. General Agreement on Tariffs and Trade, Centre William Rappard, 154 rue de Lausanne, 1211 Geneva 21, Switzerland (Dist. in U.S. by: Bernan Associates-UNIPUB, 4611-F, Assembly Drive, Lanham, MD 20706-4391) circ. 5,800 (comb. circ.)

382   UN   ISSN 0072-0623
GENERAL AGREEMENT ON TARIFFS AND TRADE. BASIC INSTRUMENTS AND SELECTED DOCUMENTS SERIES. SUPPLEMENT. (Editions in English, French and Spanish) 1952. a. price varies. General Agreement on Tariffs and Trade, Centre William Rappard, 154 rue de Lausanne, 1211 Geneva 21, Switzerland (Dist. in U.S. by: Bernan Associates-UNIPUB, 4611-F, Assembly Drive, Lanham, MD 20706-4391) cum.index. circ. 4,700 (comb. circ.)

382   UN   ISSN 0072-615X
GENERAL AGREEMENT ON TARIFFS AND TRADE. G A T T ACTIVITIES IN (YEAR) (Editions in English, French and Spanish) 1959/60. a. price varies. General Agreement on Tariffs and Trade, Centre William Rappard, 154 rue de Lausanne, 1211 Geneva 21, Switzerland (Dist. in U.S. by: Bernan Associates-UNIPUB, 4611-F, Assembly Drive, Lanham, MD 20706-4391) circ. 7, 700 (comb.circ.)

382   UN   ISSN 0072-064X
GENERAL AGREEMENT ON TARIFFS AND TRADE. INTERNATIONAL TRADE. (Editions in English, French and Spanish) 1953. a. price varies. General Agreement on Tariffs and Trade, Centre William Rappard, 154 rue de Lausanne, 1211 Geneva 21, Switzerland (Dist. in U.S. by: Bernan Associates-UNIPUB, 4611-F, Assembly Drive, Lanham, MD 20706-4391) circ. 7,200 (comb. circ.)

382   US
GLOBAL MARKET SURVEYS. irreg. $0.50 per issue. U.S. Department of Commerce, International Trade Association, Market Research Division, Washington, DC 20230. Indexed: Amer.Stat.Ind.

382   327   US   ISSN 0739-4640
GLOBAL RISK ASSESSMENTS; issues, concepts and applications. irreg., vol.3, 1987. $32.50. Global Risk Assessments, Inc., 3638 University Ave., Ste. 215, Riverside, CA 92501. TEL 714-788-0672. Ed. Jerry Rogers.

382   US   ISSN 0017-2588
GOVERNMENT BUSINESS WORLDWIDE REPORTS. 1969. irreg. price varies. J.H. Wagner, Ed. & Pub., Box 5997, Washington, DC 20016. TEL 202-966-6379. charts. illus. stat.

GREAT BRITAIN. DEPARTMENT OF TRADE. EXPORT OF WORKS OF ART. see *ART*

382   UK   ISSN 0072-5676
GREAT BRITAIN. DEPARTMENT OF TRADE. IMPORT DUTIES ACT 1958. ANNUAL REPORT. a. H.M.S.O., P.O. Box 569, London SE1 9NH, England. (reprint service avail. from UMI)

382   MX
GUIA DEL COMERCIO EXTERIOR MEXICANO. 1972. a. Av. Revolucion 534-603, Mexico 18, DF, Mexico. Ed. Alejandro Hernandez Romo. circ. 10, 000.

382   US
GUIDE TO WORLD COMMODITY MARKETS. 1977. irreg. $50. Nichols Publishing, Box 96, New York, NY 10024. TEL 212-580-8079. Ed. Gerald Roberts.

382   GY   ISSN 0533-991X
GUYANA. STATISTICAL BUREAU. ANNUAL ACCOUNT RELATING TO EXTERNAL TRADE. 1954. a. $3. Statistical Bureau, Georgetown, Guyana.

382   UK
HARRY G. JOHNSON MEMORIAL LECTURES. 1979. a. Trade Policy Research Centre, 1 Gough Square, London EC4A 3DE, England.

382   UK
HINTS TO EXPORTERS.* irreg. Export Services and Promotions Division, Department of Trade and Industry, 1 Victoria St., London, SW1H 0ET, England.

382   NE   ISSN 0073-3032
HOLLAND EXPORTS. (Consists of four publications: Industrial Products, Consumer Goods/Non Food, Consumer Goods/Food, Commercial Gardening and Farming) (Text in English, French, German and Spanish) 1952. a. free. A B C voor Handel en Industrie C. V., Koningin Wilhelminalaan 16, P.O. Box 190, 2000 AD Haarlem, Netherlands. adv. circ. 31,500.

382   HK
HONG KONG REVIEW OF OVERSEAS TRADE. (Text in English) 1964. a. HK$21. Census and Statistics Department, Kai Tak Commercial Bldg., 317 Des Voeux Rd., Central, Hong Kong, Hong Kong (Subscr. to: Director of Information Services, Information Services Department, Beaconsfield House, Queen's Rd., Central, Hong Kong) charts. stat.

HORTICULTURAL TRADES ASSOCIATION MEMBERS' REFERENCE BOOK. see *GARDENING AND HORTICULTURE*

382   BE   ISSN 0067-5628
I C E SUPPLEMENT. SERIE C. irreg. Office Belge du Commerce Exterieur, 132 Boulevard Emile Jacqmain, 1210 Brussels, Belgium.

382   II   ISSN 0073-6546
I I T C DIRECTORY. (Text in English) 1969. a. free to qualified personnel. Indian International Trade Center, 59 Jolly Maker Chambers I, Nariman Point, Bombay 400020, India.

382   JA
IMPORT STATISTICAL SCHEDULE OF JAPAN (YEAR) (Text in English and Japanese) 1987. a. Japan Tariff Association, c/o Jibiki Daini Bldg., 4-7-8 Kojimachi, Chiyoda-ku, Tokyo.
Supersedes in part: Commodity Classification for Foreign Trade Statistics: Japan (ISSN 0546-0786)

382   II   ISSN 0536-9983
IMPORT TRADE CONTROL: HANDBOOK OF RULES AND PROCEDURES. (Text in English) a. Ministry of Commerce, New Delhi, India (Order from: Controller of Publications, Government of India, Civil Lines, Delhi 110054, India)

382   II   ISSN 0536-9061
IMPORT TRADE CONTROL POLICY. (Issued in two volumes) (Text in English) a. price varies. Ministry of Commerce, New Delhi, India (Order from: Controller of Publications, Government of India, Civil Lines, Delhi 110054, India)

382   US   ISSN 0073-5604
IMPORTERS AND EXPORTERS TRADE PROMOTION GUIDE. 1967. irreg. $5. World Wide Trade Service, Box 283, Medina, WA 98039. Ed. George Lucas.

382   CN   ISSN 0383-6304
IMPORTFILE.* 1973. irreg. (2-3/yr.) Canadian Importers Association Inc., World Trade Centre, 60 Harbour St., Toronto, Ont. M5J 1B7, Canada.

IMPORTING WOOD PURCHASING GUIDE. see *FORESTS AND FORESTRY — Lumber And Wood*

382   CH
IMPORTS OF THE REPUBLIC OF CHINA; list of select Taiwan import commodities & leading importers. 1973/74. a. $100. China External Trade Development Council, 201 Tunhwa North Rd., Taipei, Taiwan, Republic of China. circ. 4,000.

INDEX TO BUSINESS REPORTS. see *BUSINESS AND ECONOMICS — Abstracting, Bibliographies, Statistics*

382   II
INDIAN EXPORT YEAR BOOK. (Text in English) 1975. a. $40. Sales Overseas, D-20 Green Park, New Delhi 110 016, India. TEL 666 279. Ed. H.R. Suri. circ. 10,000.

382   II   ISSN 0073-6473
INDIAN INSTITUTE OF FOREIGN TRADE. REPORT. (Text in English) a. price varies. Indian Institute of Foreign Trade, Ashok Bhawan, 93 Nehru Pl., New Delhi 110024, India.

382   US
INDIANA INTERNATIONAL TRADE DIRECTORY. a. Department of Commerce, International Trade Division, State House, Indianapolis, IN 46204. TEL 317-232-8845.

382   II
INDIA'S PRODUCTION, EXPORTS, AND INTERNAL CONSUMPTION OF COIR. (Text and summaries in English) 1967. a. Rs.50. ‡ Coir Board, Cochin 682016, Kerala, India. stat. circ. 500.
Formerly: India's Exports and Internal Consumption of Coir and Coir Goods.

382   IO   ISSN 0126-3714
INDONESIA. EXPORT BY COMMODITY, COUNTRY OF DESTINATION AND PORT OF EXPORT. 1967. a. $9. Central Bureau of Statistics, Jl. Dr Sutomo 8, Jakarta Pusat, Indonesia. circ. 1, 000.

382   IO   ISSN 0126-4419
INDONESIA. IMPORT BY COMMODITY AND COUNTRY OF ORIGIN. (Text in English) 1963. a. $11. Central Bureau of Statistics, Jl. Dr Sutomo 8, Jakarta, Indonesia. circ. 1,000.

INDONESIAN IMPORTERS. see *BUSINESS AND ECONOMICS — Trade And Industrial Directories*

BUSINESS AND ECONOMICS — INTERNATIONAL COMMERCE

382 US ISSN 0196-3643
INFORMATION CHICAGO. 1979. a. $25.
Information Consultants, 26 E. Huron St., Chicago,
IL 60611. TEL 312-787-2677. Ed. Arnie Matanky.
adv. circ. 5,000.

INTERNATIONAL AUCTION RECORDS. see *ART*

382 UK
INTERNATIONAL BUSINESS OPPORTUNITIES.
EGYPT. irreg. £60($100) I.C. Publications Ltd.,
P.O. Box 261, Carlton House, 69 Gt. Queen St.,
London WC2B 5BN, England.

382 UK
INTERNATIONAL BUSINESS OPPORTUNITIES.
IRAQ. irreg. £60($100) I.C. Publications Ltd., P.O.
Box 261, Carlton House, 69 Gt. Queen St., London
WC2B 5BN, England.

382 UK
INTERNATIONAL BUSINESS OPPORTUNITIES.
SAUDI ARABIA. irreg. £60($100) I.C. Publications
Ltd., P.O. Box 261, Carlton House, 69 Gt. Queen
St., London WC2B 5BN, England.

INTERNATIONAL COAL. see *MINES AND MINING INDUSTRY*

INTERNATIONAL CUSTOMS JOURNAL/
BULLETIN INTERNATIONAL DES DOUANES.
see *BUSINESS AND ECONOMICS — Public Finance, Taxation*

382 980 US
INTERNATIONAL DIRECTORY OF IMPORTERS:
AFRICA. 1983/84. a. Blytmann International, 195
Dry Creek Rd., Healdsburg, CA 95448. TEL 707-433-3900.

382 980 US
INTERNATIONAL DIRECTORY OF IMPORTERS:
SOUTH/CENTRAL AMERICA. 1983/84. a. $110.
Blytmann International, 195 Dry Creek Rd.,
Healdsburg, CA 95448. TEL 707-433-3900.

INTERNATIONAL MONETARY FUND.
BALANCE OF PAYMENTS STATISTICS. see
BUSINESS AND ECONOMICS — Macroeconomics

382 UK ISSN 0263-5488
INTERNATIONAL TAX-FREE TRADE BUYERS
GUIDE & DIRECTORY. a. $72. International
Trade Publications Ltd., Queensway House, 2
Queensway, Redhill, Surrey RH1 1QS, England. Ed.
Julian Fox.

382 US
INTERNATIONAL TRADE ADMINISTRATION
REPORTS. irreg. $2 per no. U.S. Industry and
Trade Administration, Bureau of International
Commerce, Market Research Division, Rm. 1204,
Washington, DC 20230. TEL 202-377-3334.
 Formed by the merger of: Foreign Market
Airgrams & Foreign Market Reports.

382 SZ ISSN 0251-9461
INTERNATIONAL TRADE AND
DEVELOPMENT STATISTICS. HANDBOOK/
STATISTIQUES DU COMMERCE
INTERNATIONAL ET DU DEVELOPMENT.
MANUEL. (Text in English and French) 1969.
irreg. $50. United Nations Conference on Trade and
Development, Palais des Nations, 1211 Geneva 10,
Switzerland (Susbcr.to: United Nations Publications,
New York, N.Y. 10017) circ. 5,200. (back issues
avail.)

382 US ISSN 0021-003X
INVESTING, LICENSING & TRADING
CONDITIONS ABROAD. 1965. base vol. plus m.
supplements. $1075. Business International Corp.,
One Hammarskjold Plaza, New York, NY 10017.
TEL 212-750-6300. Ed. Tom Ehrbar.
 Formerly: Investing, Licensing and Trading
Conditions in 5 Countries.

382 IS ISSN 0075-1154
ISRAEL EXPORT DIRECTORY. (Text in English,
French, German and Spanish) 1941. a. $40. Israel
Export Institute, 14 Chissin St., P.O. Box 11586,
Tel Aviv 61114, Israel. (Co-sponsor: Israel
Company for Fairs and Exhibitions) Ed. Z. Peltz.
adv. bk. rev. circ. 12,000.

382 IS
ISRAEL INDUSTRY/COMMERCE AND EXPORT
NEWS.* (Text in English) 1980. a. Israel
Publications Ltd., P.O. Box 11587, Tel Aviv, Israel.
Ed. O. Field. adv. illus. stat. circ. 6,000.

ITALY. ISTITUTO CENTRALE DI STATISTICA.
ANNUARIO STATISTICO DEL COMMERCIO
INTERNO E DEL TURISMO. see *BUSINESS AND ECONOMICS — Abstracting, Bibliographies, Statistics*

ITALY. ISTITUTO CENTRALE DI STATISTICA.
STATISTICA ANNUALE DEL COMMERCIO
CON L'ESTERO. TOMO 1. see *BUSINESS AND ECONOMICS — Abstracting, Bibliographies, Statistics*

ITALY. ISTITUTO CENTRALE DI STATISTICA.
STATISTICA ANNUALE DEL COMMERCIO
CON L'ESTERO. TOMO 2. see *BUSINESS AND ECONOMICS — Abstracting, Bibliographies, Statistics*

382 GW ISSN 0075-224X
JAHRBUCH DER EXPORT- UND
VERSANDTLEITER. 1952. a. DM.62. K. O.
Storck Verlag, Stahltwiete 7, 2000 Hamburg 50, W.
Germany (B.R.D.) adv.

382 JM
JAMAICAN EXPORTER. 1972. a. free. Jamaica
Exporters' Association, 13 Dominica Dr., Kingston
5, Jamaica. Ed. Fred Wilmot. adv.

382 JA
JAPAN'S ECONOMY AND JAPAN-U S TRADE.
1982. a. (Japan-US Study Group) Japan Times Ltd.,
5-4 Shibaura, 4-Chome, Minato-ku, Tokyo 1D8,
Japan.
 Formerly: Japan's Economy and Trade.

382 PK
KARACHI. CHAMBER OF COMMERCE AND
INDUSTRY. PATTERN OF FOREIGN TRADE
OF PAKISTAN. (Text in English) irreg. Rs.250.
Karachi Chamber of Commerce and Industry,
Aiwan-e-Tijarat, Box 4158, Nicol Rd., Karachi 2,
Pakistan.

382 KE
KENYA. COMMISSIONER OF CUSTOMS AND
EXCISE. ANNUAL TRADE REPORT. a.
EAs.150. Customs and Excise Department,
Statistical Branch, Box 40160, Nairobi, Kenya. Ed.
V. Da. Costa.
 Supersedes in part: Annual Trade Report of
Tanzania, Uganda and Kenya.

382 KE
KENYA EXPORT DIRECTORY. 1977? irreg., latest
1985. K.100. (Kenya External Trade Authority)
News Publisher, Box 43137, Nairobi, Kenya. Ed.
Joe Rodrigues. adv. circ. 4,000.

382 GW ISSN 0340-6989
KIELER STUDIEN. irreg., vol.203, 1986. price varies.
(Universitaet Kiel, Institut fuer Weltwirtschaft)
Verlag J.C.B. Mohr (Paul Siebeck), Wilhelmstr. 18,
Postfach 2040, 7400 Tuebingen, W. Germany
(B.R.D.) D. Herbert Giersch. Indexed: M.L.A.

382 DK ISSN 0106-1135
KOMPASS SELECT EXPORT. BUILDING
CONSTRUCTION, CONTRACTORS.* Cover
title: Euro Kompass Denmark. Construction. (Text
in Danish, English, French, German and Spanish)
1981. a. included in subscr. to: Kompass. Kompas-
Denmark, c/o Kompass Information Center, Lyngby
Hovedgade 4, 2800 Lyngby, Denmark. illus.
 Formerly: Kompass Select Denmark.
Construction.

382 DK ISSN 0106-1100
KOMPASS SELECT EXPORT. BUSINESS
SERVICES. Cover title: Euro Kompass Denmark.
Services. (Text in Danish, English, French, German
and Spanish) 1981. a. included in subscr. to:
Kompass. Kompas-Danmark, c/o Kompass
Information Center, Lyngby Hovedgade 4, 2800
Lyngby, Denmark. illus.
 Formerly: Kompass Select Denmark. Business
Services.

382 DK ISSN 0106-1119
KOMPASS SELECT EXPORT. CHEMICAL
INDUSTRY. Cover title: Euro Kompass Denmark.
Chemicals. (Text in Danish, English, French,
German and Spanish) 1981. a. included in subscr.
to: Kompass. Kompas-Danmark, c/o Kompass
Information Center, Lyngby Hovedgade 4, 2800
Lyngby, Denmark. illus.
 Formerly: Kompass Select Denmark. Chemicals.

382 DK ISSN 0106-1143
KOMPASS SELECT EXPORT. ELECTRICAL AND
ELECTRONIC EQUIPMENT. Cover title: Euro
Kompass Denmark. Electrical and Electronic
Equipment. (Text in Danish, English, French,
German and Spanish) 1981. a. included in subscr.
to: Kompass. Kompas-Danmark, c/o Kompass
Information Center, Lyngby Hovedgade 4, 2800
Lyngby, Denmark. illus.
 Formerly: Kompass Select Denmark. Electrical
and Electronic Equipment.

382 DK ISSN 0106-1151
KOMPASS SELECT EXPORT. FOOD INDUSTRY.
Cover title: Euro Kompass Denmark. Foods and
Beverages. (Text in Danish, English, French,
German and Spanish) 1981. a. included in subscr.
to: Kompass. Kompas-Danmark, c/o Kompass
Information Center, Lyngby Hovedgade 4, 2800
Lyngby, Denmark. illus.
 Formerly: Kompass Select Denmark. Food and
Beverages.

382 DK ISSN 0106-116X
KOMPASS SELECT EXPORT. FURNITURE. Cover
title: Euro Kompass Denmark. Furniture. (Text in
Danish, English, French, German and Spanish)
1981. a. included in subscr. to: Kompass. Kompas-
Danmark, c/o Kompass Information Center, Lyngby
Hovedgade 4, 2800 Lyngby, Denmark. illus.
 Formerly: Kompass Select Denmark. Furniture.

382 DK ISSN 0106-1186
KOMPASS SELECT EXPORT. MACHINE
INDUSTRY. Cover title: Euro Kompass Denmark.
Machinery. (Text in Danish, English, French,
German and Spanish) 1981. a. included in subscr.
to: Kompass. Kompas-Danmark, c/o Kompass
Information Center, Lyngby Hovedgade 4, 2800
Lyngby, Denmark. illus.
 Formerly: Kompass Select Denmark. Machinery.

382 DK ISSN 0106-1194
KOMPASS SELECT EXPORT. METAL
PRODUCTS. Cover title: Euro Kompass Denmark.
Metal. (Text in Danish, English, French, German
and Spanish) 1981. a. included in subscr. to:
Kompass. Kompas-Danmark, c/o Kompass
Information Center, Lyngby Hovedgade 4, 2800
Lyngby, Denmark. illus.
 Formerly: Kompass Select Denmark. Metal.

382 DK ISSN 0106-1208
KOMPASS SELECT EXPORT. PAPER INDUSTRY,
GRAPHIC ARTS. Cover title: Euro Kompass
Denmark. Paper and Graphic Arts. (Text in Danish,
English, French, German and Spanish) 1980. a.
included in subscr. to: Kompass. Kompas-Danmark,
c/o Kompass Information Center, Lyngby
Hovedgade 4, 2800 Lyngby, Denmark. illus.
 Formerly: Kompass Select Denmark. Paper and
Printing.

382 DK ISSN 0106-1216
KOMPASS SELECT EXPORT. RUBBER
INDUSTRY, PLASTICS INDUSTRY. Cover title:
Euro Kompass Denmark. Plastics and Rubber. (Text
in Danish, English, French, German and Spanish)
1981. a. included in subscr. to: Kompass. Kompas-
Danmark, c/o Kompass Information Center, Lyngby
Hovedgade 4, 2800 Lyngby, Denmark. illus.
 Formerly: Kompass Select Denmark. Plastics and
Rubber.

382 DK ISSN 0106-1178
KOMPASS SELECT EXPORT. SCIENTIFIC AND
INDUSTRIAL INSTRUMENTS, WATCH
INDUSTRY. Cover title: Euro Kompass Denmark.
Scientific and Industrial Instruments. (Text in
Danish, English, French, German and Spanish)
1981. a. included in subscr. to: Kompass. Kompas-
Danmark, c/o Kompass Information Center, Lyngby
Hovedgade 4, 2800 Lyngby, Denmark. illus.
 Formerly: Kompass Select Denmark. Instruments.

BUSINESS AND ECONOMICS — INTERNATIONAL COMMERCE

382   DK   ISSN 0106-1224
KOMPASS SELECT EXPORT. TEXTILES, CLOTHING AND FOOTWEAR. Cover title: Euro Kompass Denmark. Textiles, Clothing and Footwear. (Text in Danish, English, French, German and Spanish) 1981. a. included in subscr. to: Kompass. Kompas-Danmark, c/o Kompass Information Center, Lyngby Hovedgade 4, 2800 Lyngby, Denmark. illus.
    Formerly: Kompass Select Denmark. Textiles-Clothing and Footwear.

382   DK   ISSN 0106-1232
KOMPASS SELECT EXPORT. TRANSPORT EQUIPMENT. Cover title: Euro Kompass Denmark. Transport Equipment. (Text in Danish, English, French, German and Spanish) 1981. a. included in subscr. to: Kompass. Kompass-Danmark, c/o Kompass Information Center, 2800 Lyngby, Denmark. illus.
    Formerly: Kompass Select Denmark. Transport Equipment.

382   DK   ISSN 0106-1240
KOMPASS SELECT EXPORT. WOOD INDUSTRY. Cover title: Euro Kompass Denmark. Wood Industry. 1981. a. included in subscr. to: Kompass. Kompas-Danmark, c/o Kompass Information Center, Lyngby Hovedgade 4, Denmark. illus.
    Formerly: Kompass Select Denmark. Wood.

382   DK   ISSN 0108-4291
KONTAKTKALENDER; danske repraesentationer i udlandet. 1973. a. Udenrigsministeriet, Handelsafdelningen, Copenhagen, Denmark. adv. circ. 6,000.

382   KO   ISSN 0023-3943
KOREA TRADE. (Editions in Arabic, English, French, Japanese and Spanish) 1962. irreg. (8/yr.) free. Korea Trade Promotion Corp., C.P.O. Box 1621, Seoul, S. Korea. TEL 753-4181-9. Ed. Kwang Ho Ahn. adv. illus. tr.lit. Indexed: P.A.I.S.

382   DK   ISSN 0106-3812
LANDBRUGSEKSPORTEN. 1960. irreg. free. Landbrugets Afsaetningsudvalg, Afdeling for Markedsanalyse, Axelborg, Axeltorn 3, 1609 Copenhagen V, Denmark. circ. 1,100.

382   341   US
LAW REPRINTS: TRADE REGULATION SERIES.* 1967. irreg. $245. Congressional Information Service, Inc., 4520 East-West Hwy., Ste. 800, Bethesda, MD 20814. TEL 800-638-8380. index.
    Former titles: B N A's Law Reprints: Trade Regulation Series (ISSN 0275-6978); Law Reprints. Trade Regulation Series (ISSN 0075-8256)

LICENSING LAW HANDBOOK. see LAW

382   FR   ISSN 0459-3871
LIGUE INTERNATIONALE CONTRE LA CONCURRENCE DELOYALE. ANNUAIRE. a. International League Against Unfair Competition, Secretariat General, 2 rue Fabert, 75007 Paris, France.

382   UK
LONDON CREATIVE LISTINGS. 1985. a. £15. Kogan Page, 120 Pentonville Rd., London N1 9JN, England. adv.

M T I A N E G'S EXPORT NOTE PAD. (Metal Trades Industry Association National Export Group) see METALLURGY

382   310   MH
MACAO. REPARTICAO DOS SERVICOS DE ESTATISTICA. ANUARIO DO COMERCIO EXTERNO. (Text in Chinese, English and Portuguese) a. free. Reparticao dos Servicos de Estatistica, Box 471, Macao. circ. 500.

382   336   CN   ISSN 0076-1990
MCGOLDRICK'S HANDBOOK OF CANADIAN CUSTOMS TARIFF AND EXCISE DUTIES. 1921. a. Can.$60. McMullin Publishers Ltd., 417 St. Pierre St., Montreal, Que. H2Y 2M4, Canada. TEL 514-849-1424. Ed. D.J. Callaghan. adv. bk. rev. circ. 20,000.

382   BL
MADE IN BRAZIL; Brazilian export market. no.6, 1977. a. Assessoria de Promocao e Cultura Editora Ltda., Avda Brigadeiro Luis Antonio 402, P.O. Box 5390, 01318 Sao Paulo, Brazil. (Co-sponsors: Ministerio da Industria; Banco do Brasil) Ed. Jose L. Ribeiro Leite. adv. charts. illus. stat.

382   GW   ISSN 0172-2182
MADE IN EUROPE BUYERS' GUIDE. (Text in English) 1954. a. free to subscribers of Made in Europe. Made in Europe Marketing Organization GmbH & Co. KG, Unterlindau 21-29, 6000 Frankfurt 1, W. Germany (B.R.D.) (U.S. Subscr. to: Made in Europe, 150 Green St., Brooklyn, NY 11222) Ed. H.E. Reisner. adv.

382   HU   ISSN 0209-4401
MADE IN HUNGARY YEARBOOK. (Text in English and German) 1974. a. Magyar Tavirati Iroda, Box 3, H-1426 Budapest, Hungary. Ed. Gyoergy Blasiks. adv. circ. 6,000.

MALAWI. NATIONAL STATISTICAL OFFICE. BALANCE OF PAYMENTS. see BUSINESS AND ECONOMICS — Public Finance, Taxation

382   MR   ISSN 0076-4655
MAROC EN CHIFFRE. (Text in Arabic and French) 1961. a. DH.22. Direction de la Statistique, B.P. 178, Rabat, Morocco. (Co-sponsor: Banque Marocaine du Commerce Exterieur, Direction du Developpement) (also avail. in microfiche)

382   GW   ISSN 0076-6208
MEIER-DUDY/MEIER'S DIRECTORY OF EXPORTERS AND IMPORTERS; Meier's Addressbuch der Exporteure und Importeure. (Text in English, French, Spanish) 1903. a. DM.75. Verlag von Meier's Adressbuch der Exporteure Rudolf Dudy KG, Neue Kirohgasse 10-12, 6394 Graevenwiesbach 5, W. Germany (B.R.D.) (Dist. by: Intl. Publications Service, 114 E. 32nd St., New York, N.Y. 10016) Ed. Christa Reichel. adv. bk. rev. circ. 3,500.

382   MX
MERCADO COMUN LATINO-AMERICANO (EDICION ESPECIAL) (Monthly no longer published; only special issues avail.) 1959. irreg. $36. Ediciones Especiales, Apartado Postal 170, Admon 1, Mexico 1, D.F., Mexico. Ed. Luigi Mercuri Seri. adv. charts. illus. stat. circ. 37,300.
    Formerly (until 1981): Mercado Comun Latino-Americano.

382   FR
MICROTABLES IMPORTS-EXPORTS OF O.E.C.D. COUNTRIES. a. 1500 F.($300) Organisation for Economic Cooperation and Development, 2 rue Andre Pascal, 75775 Paris Cedex 16, France (U.S. orders to: O E C D Publications Center, 1750 Pennsylvania Ave. N.W., Washington, DC 20006) (microfiche)

382   UK   ISSN 0140-7953
MIDDLE EAST LIVING COSTS. 1977. irreg. £18. Confederation of British Industry, 103 New Oxford St., London WC1A 1DU, England.

382   US
MINNESOTA INTERNATIONAL BUSINESS SERVICES DIRECTORY. a. free. Trade Office, 90 W. Plato Blvd., St. Paul, MN 55107. TEL 612-297-4222. circ. 2,000.
    Formerly: Minnesota Exporter's Assistance Guide.

382   AT   ISSN 0311-0273
MITSUI NEWS. 1973. irreg. Mitsui and Co. Australia, Ltd., Royal Exchange Building, 56 Pitt St., Sydney, N.S.W. 2000, Australia.

MONTSERRAT. STATISTICS OFFICE. DIGEST OF STATISTICS. see BUSINESS AND ECONOMICS — Abstracting, Bibliographies, Statistics

382   910.202   US   ISSN 0093-7487
MULTINATIONAL EXECUTIVE TRAVEL COMPANION. 1970. a. $50 ($70 foreign) Guides to Multinational Business, Inc., Harvard Sq., Box 92, Cambridge, MA 02238. TEL 617-868-2288. Ed. Chriss Traeff. adv. charts. stat. tr.lit. circ. 250, 000(controlled) (back issues avail.)

382   US   ISSN 0149-0818
MULTINATIONAL INDUSTRIAL RELATIONS SERIES. 1977. a. irreg. University of Pennsylvania, Wharton School, Industrial Research Unit, 3733 Vance Hall, Philadelphia, PA 19104-6358. TEL 215-898-5605.

382   BE
N A T O. ANNUAL ECONOMIC COLLOQUIA. PROCEEDINGS. 1975. a. free. North Atlantic Treaty Organization, Economics Directorate, Information Service, B-1110 Brussels, Belgium. circ. 2,500. (also avail. in microfiche)
    Formerly: North Atlantic Treaty Organization. Directorate of Economic Affairs. Colloquium. Series.

NATIONAL ACCOUNTS OF RHODESIA. see BUSINESS AND ECONOMICS — Public Finance, Taxation

382.7   NZ
NEW ZEALAND. DEPARTMENT OF TRADE AND INDUSTRY. IMPORT LICENSING SCHEDULE. 1938. irreg. price varies. Department of Trade and Industry, Private Bag, Wellington, New Zealand. Ed. J.F. Clark. circ. 4,000.

382   NZ
NEW ZEALAND EXPORT-IMPORT CORPORATION. REPORT. 1975. a. New Zealand Export-Import Corporation, Wellington, New Zealand.

382   NR   ISSN 0078-0650
NIGERIA TRADE SUMMARY. a. Federal Office of Statistics, P.M.B. 12528, Lagos, Nigeria.

382   NO
NORDISK HANDELS KALENDER. a. Scan-Inform A-S, Noeisomhedsvn. 36, N-6400 Molde, Norway. adv. circ. 6,500.

382   NO   ISSN 0549-6233
NORDISK HANDELS KALENDER: SKANDINAVISK ADDRESSEBOG/KEY TO SCANDINAVIA: DANMARK, NORGE, SVERIGE, FINLAND, ISLAND. (Text in English, German and Norwegian) 1903. a. Kr.440. Scan-Inform A-S, Noeisomhedsvn. 36, N-6400 Molde, Norway. illus.

382   UK   ISSN 0268-2281
NORTH AMERICAN LIVING COSTS. 1984. irreg. £10. Confederation of British Industry, 103 New Oxford St., London WC1A 1DU, England.

382   JA
NOW IN JAPAN. no.22, 1976. irreg. Japan External Trade Organization, 2-5 Toranomon 2-Chome, Minato-Ku, Tokyo 105, Japan. (processed) Indexed: World Text.Abstr.

OFFICE EQUIPMENT EXPORTER. see BUSINESS AND ECONOMICS — Office Equipment And Services

382   UK
OILS AND FATS INTERNATIONAL DIRECTORY. a. $75. International Trade Publications Ltd., Queensway House, 2 Queensway, Redhill, Surrey RH1 1QS, England.

382   US   ISSN 0731-9096
OREGON INTERNATIONAL TRADE DIRECTORY. biennial. Economic Development Department, 1500 S.W. First Ave., Ste. 620, Portland, OR 97201. TEL 503-229-5625.

ORGANIZATION FOR ECONOMIC COOPERATION AND DEVELOPMENT. COUNCIL. CODE DE LA LIBERATION DES MOUVEMENTS DE CAPITAUX. CODE OF LIBERALISATION OF CAPITAL MOVEMENTS. see BUSINESS AND ECONOMICS — Banking And Finance

382   US
OWEN'S BUSINESS DIRECTORY AND TRAVEL GUIDE. 1953. a. $80. Owens Publications Inc., 6565 E. 42nd St., Tulsa, OK 74145 TEL 918-664-8293. (And Owens S.A., Case 248, 1630 Bulle, Switzerland) Ed. Roy Price. adv. bk. rev. circ. 6, 000.
    Former titles: Owen's Trade Directory and Business Travel Guide: Middle East-Africa-Asia-Mediterranean; Owen's Commerce and Travel and International Register (ISSN 0078-7167)

BUSINESS AND ECONOMICS — INTERNATIONAL COMMERCE

382 UK
P R WEEK MARKETING AND PUBLIC RELATIONS HANDBOOK. 1985. a. £12.95. (P R Week) Kogan Page, 120 Pentonville Rd., London N1 9JN, England. Ed. Geoff Lace. adv.

PACIFIC COAST COUNCIL ON LATIN AMERICAN STUDIES. PROCEEDINGS. see HISTORY — History Of North And South America

382 PK ISSN 0078-8104
PAKISTAN. EXPORT PROMOTION BUREAU. EXPORT GUIDE SERIES. irreg. Export Promotion Bureau, National Assembly Bldg., Court Rd., Karachi, Pakistan.

338.1 382 PK ISSN 0078-8112
PAKISTAN. EXPORT PROMOTION BUREAU. FRESH FRUITS.* (Text in English) a. Export Promotion Bureau, National Assembly Bldg., Court Rd., Karachi, Pakistan.

332 382 PK ISSN 0078-8058
PAKISTAN CUSTOMS TARIFF. (Text in English) 1960. irreg. price varies. Central Board of Revenue, Islamabad, Pakistan (Order from: Manager of Publications, Government of Pakistan, 2nd Floor, Ahmad Chamber, Tariq Rd., P.E.C.H.S., Karachi 29, Pakistan) Ed. M.I. Said. bk. rev. circ. 6,000.

382 PK ISSN 0078-8090
PAKISTAN EXPORT DIRECTORY. (Text in English) 1966/67. a. (Export Promotion Bureau) Trade and Industry Publications Limited, Trade and Industry House, 14 West Wharf Road, Box 4611, Karachi 2, Pakistan. Ed. G. Naseeruddin.

382 PK
PAKISTAN TRADE DIRECTORY - EXPORTERS AND MANUFACTURERS. (Text in English) 1952. irreg. Rs.400($42) Publishers International, Bandukwala Bldg., No. 4, I.I. Chundrigar Rd, Karachi, Pakistan. Ed. Kamaluddin Ahmed. adv. circ. 10,000.
   Former titles: Directory of Exporters and Manufacturers & Directory of Pakistan Exporters.

PAKISTAN'S BALANCE OF PAYMENTS. see BUSINESS AND ECONOMICS — Public Finance, Taxation

382 PY
PARAGUAY. CENTRO DE PROMOCION DE LAS EXPORTACIONES. DIRECTORIO DE EXPORTADORES/EXPORT DIRECTORY. a. Ministerio de Industria y Comercio, Centro de Promocion de las Exportaciones, Avda. Espana 374, C.C. 1772, Asuncion, Espana. TEL 204-880-44 231 33.

382 381 PH
PHILIPPINES. MINISTRY OF TRADE. ANNUAL REPORT.* (Text in English) 1948. a. free. Ministry of Trade, Trade & Industry Bldg., 361 Gil J. Puyat Ave. Ext, Makati, Metro Manila, Philippines.
   Formerly: Philippines. Department of Commerce and Industry. Annual Report (ISSN 0079-1539)

382 PH
PHILIPPINES. MINISTRY OF TRADE. TREND ANALYSIS OF THE TWENTY LEADING EXPORTS AND PROSPECTS IN THE YEAR AHEAD.* (Text in English) 1974. irreg. Ministry of Trade, Trade & Industry Bldg., 361 Gil J. Puyat Ave. Ext, Makati, Metro Manila, Philippines. Ed. Socorro B. Ramos.

382 PH
PHILIPPINES. MINISTRY OF TRADE. TWENTY LEADING IMPORTS.* (Text in English) 1974. irreg. Ministry of Trade, Trade & Industry Bldg., 361 Gil J. Puyat Ave. Ext, Makati, Metro Manila, Philippines. Ed. Socorro B. Ramos.

POLITICAL CLIMATE FOR INTERNATIONAL BUSINESS; a forecast of risk in 85 countries. see BUSINESS AND ECONOMICS — Banking And Finance

POLITICAL RISK YEARBOOK. see BUSINESS AND ECONOMICS — Banking And Finance

PORT OF SEATTLE. ANNUAL REPORT. see TRANSPORTATION — Ships And Shipping

382.7 EI
PRACTICAL GUIDE TO THE USE OF THE EUROPEAN COMMUNITIES' SCHEME OF GENERALIZED TARIFF PREFERENCES. (Text in Danish, Dutch, English, French, German and Italian) a. price varies. (Commission of the European Communities, Directorate-General for External Relations) Office for Official Publications of the European Communities, P.O. Box 1003, L-2985 Luxembourg, Luxembourg (Dist. in U.S. by: European Community Information Service, 2100 M St., N.W., suite 707, D.C. 20037) charts. stat.

PRINCIPAL INTERNATIONAL BUSINESSES; the world marketing directory. see BUSINESS AND ECONOMICS — Marketing And Purchasing

PROBLEMY PRAWNE HANDLU ZAGRANICZNEGO. see LAW

PUBLISHED DATA ON EUROPEAN INDUSTRIAL MARKETS. see BUSINESS AND ECONOMICS — Abstracting, Bibliographies, Statistics

PUBLISHED DATA ON MIDDLE & FAR EAST INDUSTRIAL MARKETS. see BUSINESS AND ECONOMICS — Abstracting, Bibliographies, Statistics

382 UK ISSN 0141-1780
QUEEN'S AWARD MAGAZINE. 1965. a. £8($10) Magazine Co-Partnership, 100 Fleet St., London EC4Y 1DE, England. Ed. Nicholas Goodison. adv. circ. 20,000. (back issues avail.)

650 FR ISSN 0079-9262
QUI REPRESENTE QUI. (Text and summaries in English, French, German, Spanish) 1956. a. 650 F. Societe Nouvelle d'Editions pour l'Industrie, 22 av. F.D. Roosevelt, 75008 Paris, France. adv. illus.
   Lists 15829 branches or foreign representatives of importers in France

382 FR ISSN 0080-1070
REPERTOIRE DES SOCIETES DE COMMERCE EXTERIEUR FRANCAISES. 1969. biennial. 320 F. (Federation Nationale des Syndicats de Societes de Commerce Exterieur) Editions Techniques Professionnelles (E.T.P.), 31 Ave. Pierre I de Serbie, 75784 Paris Cedex 16, France. circ. 3,000.

382 FR ISSN 0080-1119
REPERTOIRE FRANCAIS DU COMMERCE EXTERIEUR/FRENCH FOREIGN TRADE DIRECTORY. 1950. a. 600 Fr.($98) Union Francaise d'Annuaires Professionnels (U.F.A.P.), 13 Avenue Komarov, 78190 Trappes, France.

330 US ISSN 0275-5319
RESEARCH IN INTERNATIONAL BUSINESS AND FINANCE; an annual compilation of research. 1979. a. $23.75 to individuals; institutions $47.50. J A I Press Inc., Box 1678, 36 Sherwood Pl., Greenwich, CT 06836. TEL 203-661-7602. Ed. H. Peter Grey.

382 387 GW ISSN 0170-5253
ROLL ON ROLL OFF IN EUROPE; international guide for roll-on/roll off shipping. 1972. a. DM.268. Walter Stork-Edition, Hamburg, Postfach 106011, D-2000 Hamburg 1, W. Germany (B.R.D.) Ed. Walter W. Stork. circ. 5,000.

382 UK
RUSSIAN BUYERS' GUIDE. (Text in Russian) vol.27, 1983. a. British Industrial Publicity Overseas Ltd., Walter House, Bedford St., London WC2, England. circ. controlled.

382 SA ISSN 0081-2552
S A F T O ANNUAL REPORT/SUID-AFRIKAANSE BUITELANDSE HANDELSARGONISASIE JAARVERSLAG. (Text in Afrikaans and English) a. free. South African Foreign Trade Organization, Libridge, 12th Fl., 25 Ameshoff St., P.O. Box 9039, Johannesburg 2000, South Africa.

382 US
SAUDI ARABIA MARKET CONDITIONS. 1982. a. $650. Business International Corp., One Dag Hammarskjold Plaza, New York, NY 10017. TEL 212-750-6300.
   Formerly: B I Middle East Marketing Conditions: Saudi Arabia; Supersedes in part: B I/Memo.

382 UK
SELL'S BRITISH EXPORTERS. 1916. a. £30. Sell's Publications Ltd., 55 High St., Epsom, Surrey KT19 8DW, England. adv. bk. rev. circ. 5,000.
   Former titles: British Exporters (ISSN 0140-5772); Sell's British Exporters (ISSN 0080-8709)

382 SG
SENEGAL. MINISTERE DE L'ECONOMIE ET DES FINANCES. ANALYSE DU COMMERCE EXTERIEUR. 1975. a. 4000 Fr.CFA. Ministere de l'Economie et des Finances, Direction de la Statistique, B.P. 116, Dakar, Senegal.
   Formerly (until 1982): Commerce Exterieur du Senegal.

382 SE
SEYCHELLES TRADE REPORT. a., latest 1983. Rs.60. President's Office, Department of Finance, Statistics Division, Box 206, Mahe, Seychelles.

382 US
SOURCES OF AFRICAN AND MIDDLE-EASTERN ECONOMIC INFORMATION. 1982. irreg. Greenwood Press, 88 Post Rd. West, Westport, CT 06881. TEL 203-226-3571. Eds. Euan Blauvelt, Jennifer Durlacher.

381 SA
SOUTH AFRICAN EXPORTERS/EXPORTATEURS SUD-AFRICAINS/SUEDAFRIKANISCHE EXPORTEURE/EXPORTADORES DE SUD AFRICA. (Text in English, French, German and Spanish) 1978. a. free to qualified personnel. South African Foreign Trade Organization, Libridge, 12th Fl., 25 Ameshoff St., P.O. Box 9039, Johannesburg 2000, South Africa. stat.

382 CE ISSN 0069-2360
SRI LANKA EXPORT DIRECTORY. a. Ministry of Trade and Shipping, Colombo 3, Sri Lanka.

382 EI
STATISTICAL OFFICE OF THE EUROPEAN COMMUNITIES. COMMERCE EXTERIEUR: NOMENCLATURE DES PAYS. (Multilingual text) irreg. Rue Alcide de Gasperi, B.P. 1907, Luxembourg, Luxembourg (Dist. in the U.S. by: European Community Information Service, 2100 M St., N.W., Ste. 707, Washington, DC 20037)

382 679 II
STATISTICS OF MARINE PRODUCTS EXPORTS. (Text in English) 1973. a. $5. Marine Products Export Development Authority, Collis Estate, M. G. Rd., P.B. 1708, Cochin 682016, India. charts. illus. stat.
   Formerly: Marine Products Export Review.

382 PL ISSN 0137-3587
STUDIA MARITIMA. (Text in English, French and German) 1979. a. price varies. Ossolineum, Publishing House of the Polish Academy of Sciences, Rynek 9, Wroclaw, Poland (Dist. by: Ars Polona-Ruch, Krakowskie Przedmiescie 7, Warsaw, Poland) Ed. E. Cieslak.

283 US
STUDIES IN INTERNATIONAL ECONOMICS. 1984. irreg., no.3, 1985. price varies. Brookings Institution, 1775 Massachusetts Ave., N.W., Washington, DC 20036. TEL 202-797-6258.

380.5 FR ISSN 0181-5334
SYSTEME D'INFORMATION SUR LES TRANSPORTS DE MARCHANDISES: RESULTATS GENERAUX, TRAFIC INTERIEUR ET INTERNATIONAL. a. Departement des Statistiques de Transport, Ministere des Transports, 55-57 rue Brillat-Savarin, 75658 Paris Cedex 13, France.
   Formerly: Systeme d'Information sur les Transports de Marchandises: Resultats Generaux, Trafic International.

382.6 CH ISSN 0494-5336
TAIWAN EXPORTS. (Text mainly in English) 1957. irreg. Board of Foreign Trade, 1 Hu Kou St., Taipei, Taiwan, Republic of China. illus.

382 TZ
TANZANIA IMPORT AND EXPORT DIRECTORY. 1975. irreg. 1800 F. National Bank of Commerce, Directorate of International Operations, Box 6826, Dar es Salaam, Tanzania. adv. illus. circ. 3,000.

BUSINESS AND ECONOMICS — INTERNATIONAL COMMERCE

TASMANIA. DEPARTMENT OF THE TREASURY. COMMONWEALTH GRANTS TO TASMANIA. see *BUSINESS AND ECONOMICS — Public Finance, Taxation*

382   FI
TECHNIK AUS FINNLAND. (Text in German) 1936. a. Fmk.24($4) Finnish Foreign Trade Association, Arkadiankatu 4-6B, 00100 Helsinki 10, Finland. illus. circ. 15,000.
Former Titles: Technik und aus Finnland; Technik aus Finnland (ISSN 0359-7008); Finnische Handelsrundschau (ISSN 0015-2420)

TECHNOLOGY TRANSFER SOCIETY. INTERNATIONAL SYMPOSIUM PROCEEDINGS. see *BUSINESS AND ECONOMICS — Management*

382   TH
THAILAND TRADE INDEX. (Text in English and Thai) 1976. a. Interstate Publications, Box 5-85, Pathumwan, Bangkok 5, Thailand. adv. illus. stat.

382   UK
THAMES ESSAYS. 1970. irreg. (approx 6/yr.) Gower Publishing Company Ltd., Gower House, Croft Rd., Aldershot, Hampshire GU11 3HR, England.

382 338.91   UN   ISSN 0252-5216
TRADE AND DEVELOPMENT: AN U N C T A D REVIEW. 1979. irreg. price varies. (United Nations Conference on Trade and Development (UNCTAD)) United Nations Publications, Palais Des Nations, 1211 Geneva 10, Switzerland (Or United Nations Publications, Rm. DC2-853, New York, NY 10017) Indexed: P.A.I.S.

382 338.91   UN
TRADE AND DEVELOPMENT REPORT. 1981. a. price varies. (United Nations Conference on Trade and Development (UNCTAD)) United Nations Publications, Palais des Nations, 1211 Geneva 10, Switzerland (Or United Nations Publications, Rm. DC2-853, New York, NY 10017)

382   CH   ISSN 0082-5778
TRADE OF CHINA; Taiwan district. (Subseries of its Maritime Customs. I. Statistical Series) (Text in English and Chinese) 1950. a. 56($58) Inspectorate General of Customs, Statistical Department, 4th Story, 131 Nanking Road E. Sect. 3, Taipei, Taiwan, Republic of China. Ed.Bd. circ. 620.

382   UK
TRADE POLICY RESEARCH CENTRE. SPECIAL REPORTS. 1981. irreg. Trade Policy Research Centre, 1 Gough Square, London EC4A 3DE, England.

382   AT
TRAVELTRADE VISA GUIDE. 1977. a. Business Press International Pty. Ltd., 162 Goulburn St., Darlinghurst N.S.W. 2010, Australia. Ed. Kaye Tanner. circ. 2,500.

382   US
U S/CHINA TRADE STATISTICS. 1974. a. $25. National Council for U.S.-China Trade, 1818 'N' St., N.W., Ste. 500, Washington, DC 20036. TEL 202-429-0340. (back issues avail.)
Formerly: Sino-United States Trade Statistics.

UNITED NATIONS COMMISSION ON INTERNATIONAL TRADE LAW. YEARBOOK. see *LAW — International Law*

382 338.91   UN
UNITED NATIONS CONFERENCE ON TRADE AND DEVELOPMENT: PROCEEDINGS. irreg., latest (6th, Belgrade, 1983) price varies. United Nations Publications, Room DC2-0853, New York, NY 10017 (Or Distribution and Sales Section, Palais des Nations, 1211 Geneva 10, Switzerland)

382   US   ISSN 0082-9846
U.S. BUREAU OF DOMESTIC AND INTERNATIONAL BUSINESS ADMINISTRATION. OVERSEAS BUSINESS REPORTS. irreg. $44. U.S. Department of Commerce, International Trade Administration, Washington, DC 20230 TEL 202-377-2000. (Orders to: Supt. of Documents, Washington, DC 20402)
Continues the same title issued by the U.S. Bureau of International Commerce.

382   US   ISSN 0094-8411
U.S. BUREAU OF EAST-WEST TRADE. EXPORT ADMINISTRATION REGULATIONS. 1941. a. $30 includes updating Export Administration Bulletins. U.S. Industry and Trade Administration, Bureau of East-West Trade, U.S. Dept. of Commerce, Washington, DC 20203 TEL 202-377-2000. (Subscr. to: Supt. of Documents, Washington, DC 20402) (looseleaf format)
Formerly: Export Control Regulations (ISSN 0082-8947)

382   US   ISSN 0082-8939
U.S. BUREAU OF INTERNATIONAL COMMERCE. ANNUAL REPORTS. a. U.S. Industry and Trade Administration, Bureau of International Commerce, Washington, DC 20203 TEL 202-377-2000. (Orders to: Supt. of Documents, Washington, DC 20402)

382   US   ISSN 0565-0933
U.S. BUREAU OF THE CENSUS. GUIDE TO FOREIGN TRADE STATISTICS. irreg. price varies. U.S. Bureau of the Census, Foreign Trade Division, Washington, DC 20233 TEL 301-763-4100. (Orders to: Supt. of Documents, Washington, DC 20402) (also avail. in microfiche)

382   US
U.S. DEPARTMENT OF COMMERCE. TRADE LISTS. irreg. price varies. U.S. Department of Commerce, International Trade Administration, Office of Trade Information Services, Washington, DC 20230. TEL 202-377-2000.
Formerly: U.S. Bureau of International Commerce. Trade Lists (ISSN 0082-8963)

353.1 382   US   ISSN 0083-002X
U.S. DEPARTMENT OF STATE. COMMERCIAL POLICY SERIES. (Subseries of its Departmental Series) 1934. irreg. price varies. U.S. Department of State, Bureau of Public Affairs, 2201 C St. N.W., Washington, DC 20520 TEL 202-632-1394. (Subscr. to: Supt. of Documents, Washington, DC 20402)

U.S. FOREIGN AGRICULTURAL SERVICE. FOOD AND AGRICULTURAL EXPORT DIRECTORY. see *AGRICULTURE — Agricultural Economics*

382   US
U.S. INTERNATIONAL TRADE COMMISSION. ANNUAL REPORT. 1917. a. U.S. International Trade Commission, 701 E St., N.W., Washington, DC 20436. TEL 202-523-0161. circ. 3,000.
Formerly: U.S. Tariff Commission. Annual Report (ISSN 0083-3428)

382   US   ISSN 0083-3436
U.S. INTERNATIONAL TRADE COMMISSION. IMPORTS OF BENZENOID CHEMICALS AND PRODUCTS. 1945. a. U.S. International Trade Commission, 701 E St., N.W., Washington, DC 20436. TEL 202-523-0151.

350.827   US   ISSN 0083-3444
U.S. INTERNATIONAL TRADE COMMISSION. OPERATION OF THE TRADE AGREEMENTS PROGRAM. 1934/48. a. U.S. International Trade Commission, 701 E St., N.W., Washington, DC 20436. TEL 202-523-0161.

UNIVERSITY OF TOLEDO. BUSINESS RESEARCH CENTER. STUDIES IN INTERNATIONAL BUSINESS. see *BUSINESS AND ECONOMICS*

382   PL   ISSN 0208-4864
UNIWERSYTET GDANSKI. WYDZIAL EKONOMIKI TRANSPORTU. ZESZYTY NAUKOWE. EKONOMIKA HANDLU ZAGRANICZNEGO. PRACE I MATERIALY. (Text in Polish; summaries in English and Russian) 1971. irreg. price varies. Uniwersytet Gdanski, Ul. Czerwonej Armii 110, 81-824 Sopot, Poland. circ. 300.
Formerly: Uniwersytet Gdanski. Wydzial Ekonomiki Transportu. Zeszyty Naukowe. Instytut Handlu Zagranicznego. Prace i Materialy.

382   UY
URUGUAY. DIRECCION GENERAL DE COMERCIO EXTERIOR. ESTADISTISTICAS DE COMERCIO EXTERIOR. 1977. a. Direccion General de Comercio Exterior, Montevideo, Uruguay. circ. 1,000.

382   NN
VANUATU. NATIONAL PLANNING AND STATISTICS OFFICE. OVERSEAS TRADE/ COMMERCE EXTERIEUR. (Text in English and French) 1971. a. Informations Department, Statistics Division, NP 50, Port-Vila, Vanuatu. stat. circ. 400.
Formerly: Vanuatu. Bureau of Statistics. Overseas Trade/Commerce Exterieur.

382   GW   ISSN 0042-966X
W G A GESCHAEFTSBERICHT. 1947. a. free. Wirtschaftsvereinigung Gross- und Aussenhandel, Gotenstr. 21, 2000 Hamburg 1, W. Germany (B.R.D.) Ed. Hans-Juergen Mueller. adv. bk. rev. illus. circ. 2,000.

380.1   IS   ISSN 0302-5489
WE REPRESENT IN ISRAEL AND ABROAD. (Text in English) 1969. irreg. $33. Tanne Advertising Ltd., 68 Shlomo Hamelech St., P.O.B. 29322, Tel Aviv, Israel. Ed. Milo Ewas. adv. circ. 8,000.

382   UK   ISSN 0142-646X
WEST EUROPEAN LIVING COSTS. 1972. a. £18. Confederation of British Industry, 103 New Oxford St., London WC1A 1DU, England.

382   JA
WHITE PAPER ON INTERNATIONAL TRADE: JAPAN. (Text in English) a. $75. Japan External Trade Organization, 2-5 Toranomon 2-Chome, Minato-Ku, Tokyo 105, Japan. circ. 5,000.

382   UK
WINE AND SPIRIT TRADE INTERNATIONAL YEAR BOOK. 1898. a. £19.50. Evro Publishing Co. Ltd., 55 Heath Rd., Twickenham, Middlesex TW1 4AW, England. adv.

382   II   ISSN 0084-1501
WORLD COMMERCE ANNUAL. (Text in English) 1967. a. £9. Business Publications International, United India Life Building, Box 548, F-Block, Connaught Place, New Delhi 1, India. Ed. K.L. Saghal. adv. circ. 10,000. (back issues avail.)

WORLD STAINLESS STEEL STATISTICS. see *METALLURGY — Abstracting, Bibliographies, Statistics*

382   US   ISSN 0512-3739
WORLD TRADE ANNUAL. 1963. a. price varies. (United Nations Statistical Office, UN) Walker & Co., 720 Fifth Ave., New York, NY 10019. TEL 212-265-3632.

382   US   ISSN 0512-3747
WORLD TRADE ANNUAL SUPPLEMENT. 1964. a. price varies. (United Nations Statistical Office, UN) Walker & Co., 720 Fifth Ave., New York, NY 10019. TEL 212-265-3632.

WORLD WROUGHT COPPER STATISTICS. see *METALLURGY — Abstracting, Bibliographies, Statistics*

382   US
WORLDWIDE ECONOMIC INDICATORS. 1975. a. $180 to individuals; libraries and institutions $135. Business International Corp., One Dag Hammarskjold Plaza, New York, NY 10017. circ. 1,000.

382 387   IS   ISSN 0084-3830
YEARBOOK OF ISRAEL PORTS STATISTICS/ SHENATON STATISTI: LE NEMLEI ISRAEL. (Absorbed its English edition Yearbook of Israel Ports Statistics with no.3, 1965-66) (Text in English and Hebrew) 1963/64. a., latest no.18, 1982. Israel Ports Authority, P.O. Box 20121, Tel-Aviv, Israel.

382   US
YEARBOOK OF U S - JAPAN ECONOMIC RELATIONS. 1977. a. $6. Japan Economic Institute, 1000 Connecticut Ave., N. W., Washington, DC 20036. TEL 202-296-5633. circ. 6,000.

382   YU   ISSN 0084-4349
YUGOSLAV EXPORT - IMPORT DIRECTORY. (Not issued in 1977) (Text in English and German) 1956. irreg. $5. (Privredna Komora) Yugoslaviapublic, Knez Mihailova 10, Box 447, 11001 Belgrade, Yugoslavia. adv. circ. 5,000.

BUSINESS AND ECONOMICS — INTERNATIONAL DEVELOPMENT AND ASSISTANCE

382   RH
ZIMBABWE. CENTRAL STATISTICAL OFFICE. STATEMENT OF EXTERNAL TRADE. a. Z.$2($2.72) Central Statistical Office, Box 8063, Causeway, Zimbabwe. circ. 300. (tabloid format)

BUSINESS AND ECONOMICS — International Development And Assistance

A P O ANNUAL REPORT. (Asian Productivity Organization) see BUSINESS AND ECONOMICS — Production Of Goods And Services

338.9   IV   ISSN 0568-1308
AFRICAN DEVELOPMENT BANK. REPORT BY THE BOARD OF DIRECTORS/BANQUE AFRICAINE DE DEVELOPPEMENT. RAPPORT DU CONSEIL D'ADMINISTRATION. Cover title: African Development Bank. Annual Report. French cover title: Banque Africaine de Developpement. Rapport Annuel. 1966. a. African Development Bank, B.P. No. 1387, Abidjan 01, Ivory Coast.

338.91   IV
AFRICAN DEVELOPMENT FUND. ANNUAL REPORT/FONDS AFRICAIN DE DEVELOPPEMENT. RAPPORT ANNUEL. 1974. a. free. African Development Fund, B.P. 1387, Abidjan, Ivory Coast. circ. 5,000.

338.9   SG
AFRICAN INSTITUTE FOR ECONOMIC DEVELOPMENT AND PLANNING. PROGRAMME. (Text in English and French) 1972. a. free. African Institute for Economic Development and Planning, B.P. 3186, Dakar, Senegal.

330.9   SG
AFRICAN INSTITUTE FOR ECONOMIC DEVELOPMENT AND PLANNING. SERIES IN ECONOMIC AND SOCIAL DEVELOPMENT/ INSTITUT AFRICAIN DE DEVELOPPEMENT ECONOMIQUE ET DE PLANIFICATION. COLLECTION D'ETUDES SUR LE DEVELOPPEMENT ECONOMIQUE ET SOCIAL. irreg. 500 Fr. African Institute for Economic Development and Planning, Dakar, Senegal. illus.

338.91 334 327   US
ALTERNATIVE TRADING NEWS. 1975. irreg. $10. Friends of Third World, Inc., 611 W. Wayne St., Ft. Wayne, IN 46802-2125. TEL 219-422-6821. Ed. Jim Goetsch. bk. rev. bibl. circ. 12,000. (looseleaf format)
    Formerly: Friends in Action.

338.9   FR   ISSN 0396-2156
ANNUAIRE DU TIERS MONDE. a. $40.95. Imprimerie et Librairie Berger-Levrault, 5 rue Auguste-Compte, Paris 6e, France.

338.9   CN
ANNUAL AID REVIEW; memorandum of Canada to the Development Assistance Committee of the Organization for Economic Co-operation and Development. (Editions in English and French) 1972. a. free. Canadian International Development Agency, Public Affairs Branch, 200 Promenade du Portage, Hull, Que K1A 0G4, Canada. TEL 819-997-5456.

338.91   NZ
ANNUAL DEVELOPMENT ASSISTANCE REVIEW, MEMORANDUM OF NEW ZEALAND. Cover title: Review of the New Zealand Aid Programme. 1974. a. Ministry of Foreign Affairs, Wellington, New Zealand.
    Formerly: Annual Aid Review, Memorandum of New Zealand.

338.91   UN
ANNUAL REPORT ON DEVELOPMENT ASSISTANCE TO MAURITIUS. (Text in English) a. United Nations Development Programme, Office of the Resident Representative for Mauritius and the Seychelles, Box 253, Port Louis, Mauritius.

338.91   UN
ANNUAL REPORT ON DEVELOPMENT ASSISTANCE TO THE SEYCHELLES. (Text in English) a. United Nations Development Programme, 1 U.N. Plaza, New York, NY 10017.

ARAB BANK FOR ECONOMIC DEVELOPMENT IN AFRICA. ANNUAL REPORT. see BUSINESS AND ECONOMICS — Banking And Finance

338.9   KU   ISSN 0304-6729
ARAB FUND FOR ECONOMIC AND SOCIAL DEVELOPMENT. ANNUAL REPORT. (Text in Arabic and English) 1973. a. free. Arab Fund for Economic and Social Development, P.O. Box 21923, Safat, Kuwait. illus.

ASIAN DEVELOPMENT BANK. ANNUAL REPORT. see BUSINESS AND ECONOMICS — Banking And Finance

332.1   PH   ISSN 0066-8389
ASIAN DEVELOPMENT BANK. BOARD OF GOVERNORS. SUMMARY OF PROCEEDINGS (OF THE) ANNUAL MEETING. 1968. a. non-priced. Asian Development Bank, P.O. Box 789, Manila 2800, Philippines. circ. 1,000.

ASIAN DEVELOPMENT BANK. KEY INDICATORS OF DEVELOPING MEMBER COUNTRIES OF A D B. see BUSINESS AND ECONOMICS — Banking And Finance

ASIAN DEVELOPMENT BANK. OCCASIONAL PAPERS. see BUSINESS AND ECONOMICS — Banking And Finance

338.91   AT   ISSN 0729-0691
AUSTRALIA. DEPARTMENT OF FOREIGN AFFAIRS. DEVELOPMENT ASSISTANCE BUREAU. ANNUAL REVIEW. a. Department of Foreign Affairs, Development Assistance Bureau, Canberra, A.C.T. 2600, Australia.

BOCHUMER MATERIALEN ZUR ENTWICKLUNGSFORSCHUNG UND ENTWICKLUNGSPOLITIK. see POLITICAL SCIENCE — International Relations

BOCHUMER SCHRIFTEN ZUR ENTWICKLUNGSFORSCHUNG UND ENTWICKLUNGSPOLITIK. see POLITICAL SCIENCE — International Relations

338.91   BL
BRAZIL. DEPARTAMENTO NACIONAL DO SERVICO SOCIAL DO COMERCIO. CENTRO DE ESTUDOS E INFORMACAO. BOLETIN BIBLIOGRAFICO. 1969. biennial. free. Departamento Nacional do Servico Social do Comercio, Centro de Estudos e Informacao, Rua Voluntarios da Patria 169, 22270 Rio de Janeiro, Brazil. circ. 500.

BRITISH COLUMBIA. MINISTRY OF AGRICULTURE AND FOOD. AGRICULTURAL AID TO DEVELOPING COUNTRIES. see AGRICULTURE

338.9   US   ISSN 0069-682X
C E D NEWSLETTER. 1966. a. free. Committee for Economic Development, 477 Madison Ave., New York, NY 10022. TEL 212-688-2063. circ. 25,000. (reprint service avail. from UMI)

338.9   CN
CANADIANS IN THE THIRD WORLD. Canadiens dans le Tiers Monde. (Editions in English and French) 1969. a. free. Canadian International Development Agency, Public Affairs Branch, 200 Promenade du Portage, Hull, Que. K1A 0G4, Canada. TEL 819-997-5456. charts. illus. stat. circ. controlled. (back issues avail.)
    Fomerly: C.I.D.A. Annual Review.

332.1 016   UN   ISSN 0095-5434
CATALOG OF WORLD BANK PUBLICATIONS. Variant title: World Bank Catalog of Publications. 1973. a. free. World Bank, 1818 H St., N.W., Washington, DC 20433. index.
    Formerly (1973-1974): World Bank Catalog. Accession List.

338   CE
COLOMBO PLAN BUREAU. THE COLOMBO PLAN COUNCIL REPORT. (Text in English) 1951. a. free. Colombo Plan Bureau, 12 Melbourne Ave., Box 596, Colombo 4, Sri Lanka. TEL 581813. circ. 1,500.
    Formerly: Colombo Plan Bureau. Technical Cooperation Under the Colombo Plan. Report (ISSN 0069-5947)

338.9   CE
COLOMBO PLAN FOR CO-OPERATIVE ECONOMIC AND SOCIAL DEVELOPMENT IN ASIA AND THE PACIFIC. CONSULTATIVE COMMITTEE. PROCEEDINGS AND CONCLUSIONS. (Text in English) 1952. biennial. free. Colombo Plan Bureau, 12 Melbourne Ave., Box 596, Colombo 4, Sri Lanka. TEL 581813. index. cum.index: 1952-1972. circ. 1,500.
    Former titles: Colombo Plan for Co-operative Economic and Social Development in Asia and the Pacific. Consultative Committee. Report; Colombo Plan for Co-operative Economic Development in South and South-East Asia. Report of the Consultative Committee (ISSN 0069-5963)

338.9   CE
COLOMBO PLAN FOR CO-OPERATIVE ECONOMIC AND SOCIAL DEVELOPMENT IN ASIA AND THE PACIFIC. DEVELOPMENT PERSPECTIVES. COUNTRY ISSUES PAPERS BY MEMBER GOVERNMENTS TO THE CONSULTATIVE COMMITTEE. (Text in English) 1980. biennial. free. Colombo Plan Bureau, 12 Melbourne Ave., Box 596, Colombo 4, Sri Lanka. TEL 581813. cum.index. circ. 1,500.
    Formerly: Colombo Plan for Co-operative Economic Development in South and South East Asia. Country Issues Papers.

338.9   UK
COMECON DATA (YEAR) (Published in alternate years with: Comecon Foreign Trade Data (Year)) (Text in German; with English key and index) 1968. a. £30. (Wiener Institut fuer Internationale Wirtschaftsvergleiche, AU - Vienna Insitute for Comparative Economic Studies) Macmillan Press Ltd., 4 Little Essex St., London WC2R 3LF, England. circ. 1,200.
    Formerly (until 1979): R G W in Zahlen.

338.91   EI
COMMISSION OF THE EUROPEAN COMMUNITIES. EUROPEAN REGIONAL DEVELOPMENT FUND. ANNUAL REPORT. (Text in various languages) 1974. a. price varies. Office for Official Publications of the European Communities, P.O. Box 1003, L-2985, Luxembourg, Luxembourg (Dist. in U.S. by: European Community Information Service, 2100 M St., NW, Suite 707, Washington, DC 20037)

338.91   UN
COMPENDIUM ON DEVELOPMENT ASSISTANCE TO KENYA. (Text in English) a. United Nations Development Programme, 1 U.N. Plaza, New York, NY 10017.
    Formerly (until Dec. 1976): Report on Development Assistance to Kenya.

338.9   GT   ISSN 0553-6863
CONVENIOS CENTROAMERICANOS DE INTEGRATION ECONOMICA. (Text in English and Spanish) 1963. irreg., latest, vol.11. $5. General Treaty on Central American Economic Integration, Permanent Secretariat - Tratado General del Integracion Economica Centroamericana, 4a Avenida 10-25, Zona 14, Guatemala City, Guatemala.

338.91   DK
DANMARKS DELTAGELSE I DET INTERNATIONALE UDVIKLIGSSAMARBEJDE. a. Danida, Ministry of Foreign Affairs - Danish International Development Agency, Asiatisk Plads 2, DK-1448 Copenhagen K, Denmark. illus. stat.

338.91   DK
DENMARK'S DEVELOPMENT ASSISTANCE. ANNUAL REPORT. 1974. a. free. Danida, Ministry of Foreign Affairs - Danish International Development Agency, Asiatisk Plads 2, DK-1448 Copenhagen K, Denmark. stat.

BUSINESS AND ECONOMICS — INTERNATIONAL DEVELOPMENT AND ASSISTANCE

338.91 UK
DEVELOPING WORLD HEALTH. 1986. a. $24.95. Grosvenor Press International, West Garden Place, Kendal St., London W2 2AQ, England. Ed. Richard Parkes. adv. circ. 15,000.

338.91 UN
DEVELOPMENT ASSISTANCE TO MALAWI; ANNUAL REPORT. (Text in English) a. United Nations Development Programme, 1 U.N. Plaza, New York, NY 10017.

DEVELOPMENT BANK OF SOLOMON ISLANDS. ANNUAL REPORT. see *BUSINESS AND ECONOMICS — Banking And Finance*

370.91 SG
DIRECTORY OF DEVELOPMENT AND TRAINING INSTITUTES IN AFRICA. (Text in English and French) 1983. a. $35. Council for the Development and Social Research in Africa (CODESRIA), B.P. 3304, Dakar, Senegal. Ed. A.S. Bujra. circ. 1,000.

DIRECTORY OF THE NATIONAL PRODUCTIVITY ORGANIZATIONS IN A P O MEMBER COUNTRIES. see *BUSINESS AND ECONOMICS — Production Of Goods And Services*

338.91 UN
DIRECTORY: ORGANIZATIONS OF THE UNITED NATIONS SYSTEM IN THE UNITED REPUBLIC OF TANZANIA. a. United Nations Development Programme, Tanzania, Box 9182, Dar es Salaam, Tanzania.
Former titles: Directory of International Personnel in Tanzania; List of International Personnel in Tanzania.

338.9 FR ISSN 0068-4813
ECONOMIES ET SOCIETES. SERIE F. DEVELOPPEMENT, CROISSANCE, PROGRES DES PAYS EN VOIE DE DEVELOPPEMENT. 1955. irreg. 300 F. Presses Universitaires de Grenoble, B.P. 47 X, 38040 Grenoble, France. Ed. Pierre Pascallon. circ. 1,600.

338.91 610 551 GW ISSN 0722-0111
ENTWICKLUNGSLAENDER-STUDIEN; Verzeichnis entwicklungslaenderbezogener Forschungsarbeiten. 1966. a. Deutsche Stiftung fuer Internationale Entwicklung, Hans-Boeckler-Str. 5, 5300 Bonn 3, W. Germany (B.R.D.) Ed.Bd. index. (back issues avail.)

338.91 UN
ESTUDIOS E INFORMES DE LA C E P A L/C E P A L STUDIES AND REPORTS. (Text mainly in Spanish) 1980. irreg., no.62, 1986. price varies. Comision Economica para America Latina (CEPAL), Casilla 179-D, Santiago, Chile (Subscr. to: United Nations Publications, Room DC2-0853, New York, NY 10017; or Distribution and Sales Section, Palais des Nations, 1211 Geneva 10, Switzerland) (back issues avail.)

338.9 EI
EUROPEAN COAL AND STEEL COMMUNITY. CONSULTATIVE COMMITTEE. HANDBOOK. French edt.: Communaute Europeenne du Charbon et de l'Acier. Commission des Communautes Europeennes. Comite Consultatif. Manuel. (Text in Dutch, Danish, English, German and Italian) 1953. irreg. free. European Coal and Steel Community, Consultative Committee, Secretariat, B.-P. 1907, Luxembourg, Luxembourg. circ. controlled.

338.9 EI ISSN 0423-6831
EUROPEAN COAL AND STEEL COMMUNITY. CONSULTATIVE COMMITTEE. YEARBOOK. French edt.: Communaute Europeenne du Charbon et de l'Acier. Comite Consultatif. Annuaire. German edt.: Europaeische Gemeinschaft fuer Kohle und Stahl. Beratender Ausschuss. Jahrbuch. 1954. a. free. European Coal and Steel Community, Consultative Committee, Secretariat, B.P. 1907, Luxembourg, Luxembourg. circ. controlled.

338.9 BE ISSN 0071-2884
EUROPEAN LEAGUE FOR ECONOMIC COOPERATION. PUBLICATIONS. (Text in English or French) 1949. irreg. free. ‡ European League for Economic Cooperation, Ave. de la Toison d'Or 1-Bte. 11, 1060 Brussels, Belgium.

336 BE ISSN 0531-7436
EUROPEAN LEAGUE FOR ECONOMIC COOPERATION. REPORT OF THE SECRETARY GENERAL ON THE ACTIVITIES OF E.L.E.C. a. free. European League for Economic Cooperation, Ave. de la Toison d'Or 1-Bte. 11, 1060 Brussels, Belgium.

338.9 BE ISSN 0071-2892
EUROPEAN LEAGUE FOR ECONOMIC COOPERATION. REPORTS OF THE INTERNATIONAL CONGRESS. (Issued in the League's Publications) irreg., 1969, 6th, Brussels. free. European League for Economic Cooperation, Ave. de la Toison d'Or-Bte.11, B-1060 Brussels, Belgium.

FACTS & FIGURES; a comparative statistical analysis. see *ENERGY*

338.9 FR
FRANCE. SECRETARIAT D'ETAT AUX AFFAIRES ETRANGERES CHARGE DE LA COOPERATION. DIRECTION DE L'AIDE AU DEVELOPPEMENT. COTE D'IVOIRE. DOSSIER D'INFORMATION ECONOMIQUE. 1969. irreg. free. Secretariat d'Etat aux Affaires Etrangeres Charge de la Cooperation, Direction de l'Aide au Developpement, 37 Quai d'Orsay, 757000 Paris, France. circ. 500. (processed)

338.9 FR
FRANCE. SECRETARIAT D'ETAT AUX AFFAIRES ETRANGERES CHARGE DE LA COOPERATION. DIRECTION DE L'AIDE AU DEVELOPPEMENT. MALI. DOSSIER D'INFORMATION ECONOMIQUE. 1971. irreg. free. Secretariat d'Etat aux Affaires Etrangeres Charge de la Cooperation, Direction de l'Aide au Developpement, 37 Quai d'Orsay, 75700 - Paris, France. circ. 500. (processed)

338.9 FR
FRANCE. SECRETARIAT D'ETAT AUX AFFAIRES ETRANGERES CHARGE DE LA COOPERATION. DIRECTION DE L'AIDE AU DEVELOPPEMENT. NIGER. DOSSIER D'INFORMATION ECONOMIQUE. 1970. irreg. free. Secretariat d'Etat aux Affaires Etrangeres Charge de la Cooperation, Direction de l'Aide au Developpement, 37 Quai d'Orsay, 75700 - Paris, France. abstr. charts. stat. circ. 500. (processed)

338.9 GT ISSN 0553-6898
GENERAL TREATY FOR CENTRAL AMERICAN ECONOMIC INTEGRATION. PERMANENT SECRETARIAT. NEWSLETTER. 1963. irreg. General Treaty on Central American Economic Integration, Permanent Secretariat - Tratado General del Integracion Economica Centroamericana, 4a Avenida 10-25, Zona 14, Guatemala City, Guatemala.

338.9 FR
GEOGRAPHICAL DISTRIBUTION OF FINANCIAL FLOWS TO DEVELOPING COUNTRIES. (DISBURSEMENT) 1966. a. price varies. Organisation for Economic Cooperation and Development, 2 rue Andre Pascal, 75775 Paris 16, France (U.S. orders to: O.E.C.D. Publications and Information Center, 1750 Pennsylvania Ave., N. W., Washington, D. C. 20006) (also avail. in microfiche)
Formerly: Geographical Distribution of Financial Flows to Less Developed Countries. (Disbursements) (ISSN 0474-5434); Supersedes: Organization for Economic Cooperation and Development. Flow of Financial Resources to Less Developed Countries.

338.9 UK ISSN 0309-1082
GREAT BRITAIN. LAND RESOURCES DEVELOPMENT CENTRE. PROGRESS REPORT. 1975. biennial. free. Overseas Development Administration, Land Resources Development Centre, Tolworth Tower, Surbiton, Surrey KT6 7DY, England. Ed. C.S. Griffin. illus. circ. 600. Indexed: Biol.Abstr.
Formerly: Great Britain. Land Resources Division. Progress Report.

338.9 UK ISSN 0950-9593
GREAT BRITAIN. OVERSEAS DEVELOPMENT ADMINISTRATION. REPORT ON RESEARCH AND DEVELOPMENT. 1983. a. £6.95. Overseas Development Administration, Eland House, Stag Place, London SW1E 5DH, England TEL 01-213 3000. (Subscr. to: Publications Desk, Library, Overseas Development Administration, Abercrombie House, Eaglesham Rd., East Kilbride, Glasgow G75 8EA, Scotland) circ. controlled. (also avail. in microfiche)

338.91 UK
HANDBOOK OF NATIONAL DEVELOPMENT PLANS. a. (plus s-a. supplements) £60($96) Graham & Trotman Ltd., Sterling House, 66 Wilton Rd., London SW1V 1DE, England (Distr. in U.S. and Canada by: Graham & Trotman Inc., 13 Park Ave., Gaithersburg, MD 20877) Ed. G. Tewson.

338.91 JA
I.D.E. SYMPOSIUM PROCEEDINGS. (Text in English) 1974. irreg., latest 1983. Institute of Developing Economies - Ajia Keizai Kenkyusho, 42 Ichigaya-Hommura-cho, Shinjuku-ku, Tokyo 162, Japan (Subscr. to: Maruzen Co., Ltd., Box 5050, Tokyo International 100-31, Japan) circ. 1,000.

339 GW
I F O MITTEILUNGEN DER ABTEILUNG ENTWICKLUNGSLAENDER. (Text in German; summaries occasionally in English) 1965. a. free. I F O Institut fuer Wirtschaftsforschung, Poschingerstr. 5, 8000 Munich 80, W. Germany (B.R.D.) Ed. Axel J. Halbach. adv. bk. rev. abstr. charts. illus. circ. 400.
Former titles: I F O Mitteilungen: Entwicklungslaender - Afrika Studienstelle; Informationen der Afrika-Studienstelle (ISSN 0046-9394)

338.91 DK ISSN 0901-6171
I F U ANNUAL REPORT. 1978. a. free. Industrialiserings Fonden for Udviklingslandene - Industrialization Fund for Developing Countries, Bremerholm 4, 1069 Copenhagen K, Denmark.
Formerly: I F U's Participation in Joint Ventures (ISSN 0108-1969)

I I E P SEMINAR PAPERS. (International Institute for Educational Planning) see *EDUCATION — International Education Programs*

338.9 IS ISSN 0047-1216
I T C C REVIEW. (International Technical Cooperation Centre) (Text in English) 1972. irreg. $35. Association of Engineers and Architects in Israel, 200 Dizengoff Rd., P.O. Box 3082, Tel Aviv, Israel. adv. bk. rev. bibl. charts. illus. circ. 1,000. (also avail. in microform from MIM) Indexed: Excerp.Med. Geo.Abstr. Rural Recreat.Tour.Abstr. Soils & Fert. World Agri.Econ.& Rural Sociol.Abstr.

338 UN ISSN 0252-4481
INDUSTY AND TECHNOLOGY DEVELOPMENT NEWS - ASIA AND THE PACIFIC. 1962. irreg., latest no.15, 1985. United Nations Economic and Social Commission for Asia and the Pacific, Division of Industry, Housing and Technology, United Nations Bldg., Rajadamnern Ave., Bangkok 2, Thailand (Dist. by: United Nations Publications, Room DC2-0853, New York, NY 10017; or Distribution and Sales Section, Palais des Nations, CH-1211 Geneva 10, Switzerland)
Former titles (until 1983): Industrial Development News - Asia and the Pacific; until 1977: Asian Industrial Development News (ISSN 0572-4171)

INFOTERRA INTERNATIONAL; directory of sources for environmental information. see *ENVIRONMENTAL STUDIES*

330 FR ISSN 0073-8247
INSTITUT D'EMISSION D'OUTRE MER, PARIS. RAPPORT D'ACTIVITE. 1967. a. free. ‡ Institut d'Emission d'Outre Mer, Paris., 1 Cite du Retiro, 75008 Paris, France.

338.9 FR
INSTITUT D'ETUDES DU DEVELOPPEMENT. CAHIERS. 1975. irreg. price varies. (Institut d'Etudes du Developpement, SZ) Presses Universitaires de France, 108 bd. Saint Germain, 75279 Paris Cedex 6, France (Service des Periodiques, 12 rue Jean de Beauvais, 75005 Paris) (reprint service avail. from KTO)

BUSINESS AND ECONOMICS — INTERNATIONAL DEVELOPMENT AND ASSISTANCE

INSTITUT FUER IBEROAMERIKA-KUNDE. SCHRIFTENREIHE. see *POLITICAL SCIENCE — International Relations*

338.91 658   CM
INSTITUT PANAFRICAIN POUR LE DEVELOPPEMENT. CENTRE D'ETUDES ET DE RECHERCHES APPLIQUEES. EVALUATION DU SEMINAIRE SUR LA METHODOLOGIE DU MANAGEMENT DES PROJETS. a. $25. Institut Panafricain pour le Developpement, Centre de Documentation, B.P. 4078, Douala, Cameroon. Ed. Adovi John-Bosco. bk. rev. circ. 1,500.

338.91 658   CM
INSTITUT PANAFRICAIN POUR LE DEVELOPPEMENT. CENTRE DE FORMATION AU MANAGEMENT DES PROJETS. BILAN DES ACTIVITES. irreg.? Institut Panafricain pour le Developpement, Centre de Documentation, B.P. 4078, Douala, Cameroon.

INSTITUT PANAFRICAIN POUR LE DEVELOPPEMENT. TRAVAUX MANUSCRITS. see *AGRICULTURE — Agricultural Economics*

330.06   JA
INSTITUTE OF DEVELOPING ECONOMIES. ANNUAL REPORT. (Text in English) a. Institute of Developing Economies, 42 Ichigaya-Hommura-cho, Shinjuku-ku, Tokyo 162, Japan.

338.9   UK
INSTITUTE OF DEVELOPMENT STUDIES. ANNUAL REPORT. a. Institute of Development Studies, University of Sussex, Brighton, Sussex BN1 9RE, England.

380 338   UY   ISSN 0538-3048
INTER-AMERICAN COUNCIL OF COMMERCE AND PRODUCTION. URUGUAYAN SECTION. PUBLICACIONES. 1951. irreg. Inter-American Council of Commerce and Production, Misiones 1400, Montevideo, Uruguay.

INTER-AMERICAN DEVELOPMENT BANK. ANNUAL REPORT. see *BUSINESS AND ECONOMICS — Banking And Finance*

INTER-AMERICAN DEVELOPMENT BANK. BOARD OF GOVERNORS. PROCEEDINGS OF THE MEETING. see *BUSINESS AND ECONOMICS — Banking And Finance*

338.9   AG   ISSN 0538-3110
INTER-AMERICAN DEVELOPMENT BANK. INSTITUTE FOR LATIN AMERICAN INTEGRATION. ANNUAL REPORT. (Edition in English and Spanish) 1965. a. $14. Banco Interamericano de Desarrollo, Instituto para la Integracion de America Latina, Esmeralda 130, Buenos Aires. TEL 394-2059. circ. controlled.

330   US
INTER-AMERICAN FOUNDATION ANNUAL REPORT. (Text in English, Spanish, and Portuguese) a. free. Inter-American Foundation, 1515 Wilson Blvd., Rosslyn, VA 22209. TEL 703-841-3800. circ. 12,000. (back issues avail.)

INTERNATIONAL TRADE AND DEVELOPMENT STATISTICS. HANDBOOK/ STATISTIQUES DU COMMERCE INTERNATIONAL ET DU DEVELOPMENT. MANUEL. see *BUSINESS AND ECONOMICS — International Commerce*

338.096   UN
INVESTMENT AFRICA. 1973. irreg. avail. only on exchange. United Nations Economic Commission for Africa - Commission Economique pour l'Afrique, Box 3001, Addis Ababa, Ethiopa. stat. circ. 1,500.
Formerly: Investment Promotion Newsletter.

IRISH STUDIES IN INTERNATIONAL AFFAIRS. see *POLITICAL SCIENCE — International Relations*

338.91   JA
JAPAN INTERNATIONAL COOPERATION AGENCY. ORGANIZATION AND FUNCTIONS. (Text in English) 1975. a. free. Japan International Cooperation Agency, P.O. Box 216, 2-1-1 Nishi-shinjuku, Shinjuku-ku, Tokyo 163, Japan. circ. 2,000.

338.9   UN   ISSN 0085-2392
JOURNAL OF DEVELOPMENT PLANNING. (Editions in English, French, Spanish) 1972. irreg, latest no.16. price varies. (Department of International Economic and Social Affairs (DIESA)) United Nations Publications, Room DC2-853, New York, NY 10017 (Or Distribution and Sales Section, Palais des Nations, CH-1211 Geneva 10, Switzerland) Indexed: P.A.I.S. E.I.

JOURNAL OF HIMALAYAN STUDIES AND REGIONAL DEVELOPMENT. see *ANTHROPOLOGY*

338.91   GW
JOURNALISTENHANDBUCH ENTWICKLUNGSPOLITIK. 1974. a. Karl Marx Str. 4-6, 5300 Bonn 1, W. Germany (B.R.D.)

338.91   UN
LIST OF E C A DOCUMENTS ISSUED/LISTE DES DOCUMENTS PUBLIES PAR LA C E A. irreg., no.70, 1980. United Nations Economic Commission for Africa, Box 3001, Addis Ababa, Ethiopia.

338.9   UN   ISSN 0252-5348
MEKONG BULLETIN. (Text in English) 1968. a. free. United Nations Economic and Social Commission for Asia and the Pacific, Mekong Committee, United Nations Bldg., Rajadamnern Ave., Bangkok 10200, Thailand.
Formerly: Mekong Monthly Bulletin (ISSN 0047-6668)

338.9   PK   ISSN 0544-8433
MONOGRAPHS IN THE ECONOMICS OF DEVELOPMENT. no.18, 1972. irreg. price varies. Pakistan Institute of Development Economics, Box 1091, Islamabad, Pakistan. Ed.Bd. circ. 1,500.

NETHERLANDS INVESTMENT BANK FOR DEVELOPING COUNTRIES. ANNUAL REPORT. see *BUSINESS AND ECONOMICS — Banking And Finance*

338.9   NO
NORGES OG UTVIKLINGSLANDENE. a. Royal Norwegian Ministry of Development Cooperation, Norwegian Agency for International Development, Box 8142 Dep. 0033, Oslo 1, Norway. illus.
Formerly: Norges Samarbeid med Utviklingslandene.

338   NO   ISSN 0048-0541
NORKONTAKT. 1965. irreg. (6-8/yr.) free. Royal Norwegian Ministry of Development Cooperation - Norwegian Agency for International Development, Box 8142, 0033 Oslo1, Norway. Ed. Halle Joern Hanssen. bk. rev. charts. illus. stat. circ. 10,000.

338.9   AU   ISSN 0078-3536
OESTERREICHISCHE SCHRIFTEN ZUR ENTWICKLUNGSHILFE. 1963. irreg., vol.12, 1985. price varies. Verlag Ferdinand Berger und Soehne OHG, Wienerstr. 21-23, A-3580 Horn, Austria. Ed. Leopold Scheidl.

330   FR
ORGANIZATION FOR ECONOMIC COOPERATION AND DEVELOPMENT. ACTIVITIES OF O.E.C.D.: REPORT BY THE SECRETARY GENERAL. 1971. a. Organisation for Economic Cooperation and Development, 2 rue Andre-Pascal, 75775 Paris 16, France (U.S. orders to: O.E.C.D Publication and Information Center, 1750 Pennsylvania Ave., N.W., Washington, D.C. 20006) (also avail. in microfiche)

ORGANIZATION FOR ECONOMIC COOPERATION AND DEVELOPMENT. COUNCIL. CODE DE LA LIBERATION DES MOUVEMENTS DE CAPITAUX. CODE OF LIBERALISATION OF CAPITAL MOVEMENTS. see *BUSINESS AND ECONOMICS — Banking And Finance*

338.9   FR   ISSN 0474-5663
ORGANIZATION FOR ECONOMIC COOPERATION AND DEVELOPMENT. DEVELOPMENT COOPERATION; efforts and policies of the members of the Development Assistance Committee. (Editions in English and French) a. $34. Organisation for Economic Cooperation and Development, 2 rue Andre - Pascal, 75775 Paris Cedex 16, France (U.S. orders to: O.E.C.D. Publications and Information Center, 1750 Pennsylvania Ave., N.W., Washington, DC 20006) (also avail. in microfiche)

338.91   US   ISSN 0092-7643
OVERSEAS DEVELOPMENT COUNCIL. ANNUAL REPORT. 1971. a. no subscriptions avail. Overseas Development Council, 1717 Massachusetts Ave., N.W., Ste. 501, Washington, DC 20036. TEL 202-234-8701. Ed. Valeriana Kallab. illus. Key Title: Annual Report - Overseas Development Council.

338.91   US
OVERSEAS DEVELOPMENT COUNCIL. WORKING PAPERS. no.7, 1982. irreg. no subscriptions avail. Overseas Development Council, 1717 Massachusetts Ave., N.W., Ste. 501, Washington, DC 20036. TEL 202-234-8701.

338.9   JA
OVERSEAS ECONOMIC COOPERATION FUND. ANNUAL REPORT/KAGAI KEIZAI KYORYOKU KIKIN NENPO. (Text in English, French, Spanish) 1972. a. free. Overseas Economic Cooperation Fund - Kagai Keizai Kyoryoku Kikin, Takebashi Godo Bldg, 4-1, Ohtemachi 1-chome, Chiyoda-ku, Tokyo 100, Japan.

PAKISTAN INSTITUTE OF DEVELOPMENT ECONOMICS. REPORT. see *BUSINESS AND ECONOMICS*

PAKISTAN INSTITUTE OF DEVELOPMENT ECONOMICS. RESEARCH REPORT. see *BUSINESS AND ECONOMICS*

980   US   ISSN 0552-9913
PAN AMERICAN DEVELOPMENT FOUNDATION. ANNUAL REPORT. 1964. a. free. Pan-American Development Foundation, 1889 F St.,N.W., Washington, DC 20006. TEL 202-789-3969. circ. 2,500.

338.91   UK   ISSN 0268-4020
PAPERS IN THE ADMINISTRATION OF DEVELOPMENT. irreg. (2-3/yr.) price varies. Geo Books, Regency House, 34 Duke St., Norwich NR3 3AP, England. (back issues avail.) Indexed: Geo.Abstr.

338.91   UN
PERSONNEL DES NATIONS UNIES ET DES AGENCES SPECIALISEES EN REPUBLIQUE DE RWANDA. (Text in French) a. United Nations Development Programme, Rwanda, B.P. 445, Kigali, Rwanda.

PLANS DE DEVELOPPEMENT DES PAYS DE L'AFRIQUE NOIRE. see *BUSINESS AND ECONOMICS*

338.91   US   ISSN 8755-9412
POLICY NOTES. 1975. irreg. $12. Interfaith Action for Economic Justice, 110 Maryland Ave., N.E., Washington, DC 20002. TEL 202-543-2800. Ed. Stephen Clapp. circ. 800. (looseleaf format; back issues avail.)
Formerly (until Aug. 1983): Food Policy Notes.

PROGRESS & ENGINEERING. DEVELOPING COUNTRIES EDITION. see *ENGINEERING — Mechanical Engineering*

338.91   UN
RAPPORT ANNUEL SUR L'ASSISTANCE AU DEVELOPPEMENT: RWANDA. (Text in French) a. United Nations Development Programme, Rwanda, B.P. 445, Kigali, Rwanda.

338.91　　　　　UN
RAPPORT ANNUEL SUR LA COOPERATION AU DEVELOPPEMENT - BURUNDI. (Text in French) a. United Nations Development Program, Programme des Nations Unies pour le Developpement au Burundi, c/o Ms. Linda Schrieber, Chief, Documentation and Statistics Office, BPPE, UNDP, New York, NY 10017. circ. controlled.
　　Formerly (until 1984): Rapport Annuel sur l'Assistance au Developpement: Burundi.

338.9　　　　　PK　　ISSN 0557-8280
READINGS IN DEVELOPMENT ECONOMICS. 1970. irreg. price varies. Pakistan Institute of Development Economics, Box 1091, Islamabad, Pakistan. bibl. charts. stat. circ. 1,000.

338.9　　　　　SG　　ISSN 0850-4008
REGISTER DEVELOPMENT RESEARCH PROJECTS AFRICA. (Text in English, French) 1973. a. $35. Council for the Development of Economic and Social Research in Africa (CODESRIA), B.P. 3304, Dakar, Senegal. Ed. A.S. Bujra. bibl.
　　Formerly (until 1983): Africa Development Research Annual/Annuaire des Recherches Africaines sur les Problemes de Developpement.

338.9　　　　　UN
REPORT ON DEVELOPMENT ASSISTANCE TO ETHIOPIA. (Text in English) a. United Nations Development Programme, Office of the Resident Representative in Ethiopia, Box 5580, Addis Ababa, Ethiopia.

338.91　　　　　UN
REPORT ON DEVELOPMENT COOPERATION TO THE DEMOCRATIC REPUBLIC OF THE SUDAN. (Text in English) a. United Nations Development Programme, Sudan, Box 913, Khartoum, Sudan.
　　Formerly: Development Assistance to the Democratic Republic of the Sudan.

338　　　　　HO
REVISTA DE LA INTEGRACION Y EL DESARROLLO DE CENTROAMERICA. 1976. s-a. Banco Centroamericano de Integracion Economica, Apdo. Postal 772, Tegucigalpa, Honduras.
　　Formerly: Revista de la Integracion Centroamericana.

338.91　360　　　　　SG
ROSTER OF AFRICA SOCIAL SCIENTISTS. (Text in English and French) 1981. a. $35. Council for the Development of Economic and Social Research in Africa (CODESRIA), B.P. 3304, Dakar, Senegal. Ed. A.S. Bujra.

338.91　　　　　US
RURAL RECONSTRUCTION REVIEW. 1979. a. International Institute of Rural Reconstruction, 1775 Broadway, Ste. 619, New York, NY 10019. TEL 212-245-2680. Ed. Jaime P. Ronquillo. adv. bk. rev. circ. 2,000.

338.91　　　　　SW　　ISSN 0349-0874
S A R E C ANNUAL REPORT. (Text in English) 1977. a. Swedish Agency for Research Cooperation with Developing Countries, S-10525 Stockholm, Sweden. charts. circ. 4,000.

338.91　320　960　　　　　US
SAGE SERIES ON AFRICAN MODERNIZATION AND DEVELOPMENT. (Not published in 1977) 1976. a. $29.95 for hardcover; $14.95 for softcover. Sage Publications, Inc., 2111 W. Hillcrest Dr.1, Newbury Park, CA 91320 TEL 805-499-0721. (And Sage Publications, Ltd., 28 Banner St., London EC1Y 8QE, England) Ed. Peter E. Lovejoy. (back issues avail.)

338.91　　　　　US　　ISSN 0195-7988
SOCIAL PLANNING, POLICY & DEVELOPMENT ABSTRACTS. 1979. s-a. $65 to individuals; libraries $137. Sociological Abstracts Inc., Box 22206, San Diego, CA 92122. Ed. Miriam Chall.
　●Also available online. Vendors: BRS, DIALOG.
　　Formerly: Social Welfare, Social Planning, Policy and Social Development.

338.9　　　　　MY
SOUTHEAST ASIA DEVELOPMENT CORPORATION BERHAD. REPORTS AND ACCOUNTS. a. Southeast Asia Development Corporation Berhad, G.P.O. Box 2171, Kuala Lumpur 01-20, Malaysia. charts. stat.

338.9　　　　　UN　　ISSN 0085-6908
STUDIES ON SELECTED DEVELOPMENT PROBLEMS IN VARIOUS COUNTRIES IN THE MIDDLE EAST. 1967. a., latest 1973. price varies. United Nations Economic Commission for Western Asia, United Nations Building, Box 4656, Bir Hassan, Beirut, Lebanon (Dist. by: Distribution and Sales Section, Palais des Nations, CH-1211 Geneva 10, Switzerland)

338.91　　　　　UN
SURVEY OF ECONOMIC AND SOCIAL CONDITIONS IN AFRICA. French edition: Etude des Conditions Economiques et Sociales en Afrique. a. United Nations Economic Commission for Africa, Box 3001, Addis Ababa, Ethiopia.
　　Continues: Survey of Economic Conditions in Africa.

338.91　　　　　UK
THIRD WORLD DEVELOPMENT. 1983. a. $40. Grosvenor Press International, West Garden Place, Kendal St., London W2 2AQ, England. Ed. Richard Parkes. adv. circ. 25,000.

338.9　　　　　FR
TIERS-MONDE EN MARCHE. 1976. irreg. 160 F. Imprimerie et Librairie Berger-Levrault, 5 rue Auguste-Compte, Paris 6e, France. Eds. Pierre-Francois Gonidec, Edmond Jouve. bibl. illus.

TRADE AND DEVELOPMENT: AN U N C T A D REVIEW. (United Nations Conference on Trade and Development (UNCTAD)) see BUSINESS AND ECONOMICS — International Commerce

TRADE AND DEVELOPMENT REPORT. see BUSINESS AND ECONOMICS — International Commerce

338.91　　　　　UN
U N C R D BULLETIN. (Text in English) 1979. a. free. United Nations, Centre for Regional Development, Nagono 1-47-1, Nakamura-ku, Nagoya 450, Japan. Ed.Bd. charts. illus. circ. 2,000. Regional planning

338.91　　　　　US
U S AND WORLD DEVELOPMENT: AGENDA. 1973. a. no subscriptions avail. Overseas Development Council, 1717 Massachusetts Ave. N.W., Washington, DC 20036. TEL 202-234-8701. Ed. Valeriana Kallab.
　　Formerly: U S and the Developing World: Agenda for Action.

338.9　　　　　UN
UNITED NATIONS. CONFERENCE ON TRADE AND DEVELOPMENT. TRADE AND DEVELOPMENT BOARD. OFFICIAL RECORDS. (Supplements avail.) irreg. price varies. (United Nations Conference on Trade and Development (UNCTAD)) United Nations Publications, Palais des Nations, 1211 Geneva 10, Switzerland (Or United Nations Publications, Room LX-2300, New York, NY 10017)
　　Formerly: United Nations. Trade and Development Board. Official Records (ISSN 0082-8475)

338.91　　　　　UN
UNITED NATIONS. DEVELOPMENT PROGRAMME. COMPENDIUM OF APPROVED PROJECTS. a. $10. United Nations Development Programme, Information Division, One U.N. Plaza, Rm. 1972, New York, NY 10017.

UNITED NATIONS. ECONOMIC COMMISSION FOR AFRICA. PROPOSALS FOR PROGRAMME BUDGET. see BUSINESS AND ECONOMICS

UNITED NATIONS CONFERENCE ON TRADE AND DEVELOPMENT: PROCEEDINGS. see BUSINESS AND ECONOMICS — International Commerce

338.91　　　　　UN
UNITED NATIONS ECONOMIC COMMISSION FOR AFRICA. ANNUAL REPORT. (Text in English) a. United Nations Economic Commission for Africa, Box 3001, Addis Ababa, Ethiopia.

338.91　　　　　UN　　ISSN 0250-801X
UNITED NATIONS INDUSTRIAL DEVELOPMENT ORGANIZATION. DEVELOPMENT AND TRANSFER OF TECHNOLOGY SERIES. (Editions in English, French, Spanish; occasionally in Chinese and Russian) 1977. irreg. price varies. United Nations Industrial Development Organization, P.O. Box 300, A-1400 Vienna, Austria.

338.9　　　　　US　　ISSN 0083-0062
U.S. DEPARTMENT OF STATE. ECONOMIC COOPERATION SERIES. 1948. irreg. price varies. U.S. Department of State, Bureau of Public Affairs, 2201 C St. N.W., Washington, DC 20520 TEL 202-632-1394. (Orders to Supt. of Documents, Washington, DC 20402)

338.91　　　　　US　　ISSN 0276-6469
U.S. INTERNATIONAL DEVELOPMENT COOPERATION AGENCY. CONGRESSIONAL PRESENTATION, FISCAL YEAR. 1982. a. U.S. International Development Cooperation Agency, Office of Public Affairs, Washington, DC 20523. TEL 202-653-2920. Key Title: Congressional Presentation, Fiscal Year.
　　Supersedes: U.S. Agency for International Development. Congressional Presentation, Fiscal Year.

338.91　300　　　　　SJ
UNIVERSITY OF KHARTOUM. DEVELOPMENT STUDIES AND RESEARCH CENTRE. DISCUSSION PAPERS. irreg. University of Khartoum, Development Studies and Research Centre, Faculty of Economic & Social Studies, Khartoum, Sudan.

338.91　　　　　SJ
UNIVERSITY OF KHARTOUM. DEVELOPMENT STUDIES AND RESEARCH CENTRE. MONOGRAPH SERIES. irreg. University of Khartoum, Development Studies and Research Centre, Box 321, Khartoum, Sudan. Ed. Sadig Rasheed. Indexed: Geo.Abstr.

338.91　　　　　SJ
UNIVERSITY OF KHARTOUM. DEVELOPMENT STUDIES AND RESEARCH CENTRE. OCCASIONAL PAPERS. 1979. irreg. University of Khartoum, Development Studies and Research Centre, Box 321, Khartoum, Sudan. Ed. Sadig Rasheed.

309.2　　　　　KE
UNIVERSITY OF NAIROBI. INSTITUTE FOR DEVELOPMENT STUDIES. OCCASIONAL PAPER. 1967. irreg., no.31, 1979. price varies. ‡ University of Nairobi, Institute for Development Studies, Box 30197, Nairobi, Kenya. bibl. illus. stat. circ. 200 (approx.)
　　Continues: University College, Nairobi. Institute for Development Studies. Occasional Papers (ISSN 0547-1796)

W I D FORUM. (Office of Women in International Development) see SOCIOLOGY

338.9　　　　　AU
WIENER INSTITUT FUER INTERNATIONALE WIRTSCHAFTSVERGLEICHE. FORSCHUNGSBERICHTE. 1972. irreg. Wiener Institut fuer Internationale Wirtschaftsvergleiche, Postfach 87, A-1103 Vienna, Austria. Ed. G. Fink. circ. 700.

338.9　　　　　AU
WIENER INSTITUT FUER INTERNATIONALE WIRTSCHAFTSVERGLEICHE. REPRINT SERIE. irreg., no.16, 1972. As.2400 (with Forschungsberichte) ‡ Wiener Institut fuer Internationale Wirtschaftsvergleiche, Postfach 87, A-1103 Vienna, Austria. Ed. G. Fink. charts. stat. circ. 400.

338.91 301.412 US
WORKING PAPERS ON WOMEN IN INTERNATIONAL DEVELOPMENT. 1981. irreg., no.107, 1985. Michigan State University, Office of Women in International Development, 202 International Center, E. Lansing, MI 48824-1035. TEL 517-353-5040. Ed. Rita S. Gallin. circ. 1,000. Indexed: P.A.I.S. Popul.Ind. Vert.File.Ind.
Formerly: W I D Working Papers.

338.9 UN
WORLD BANK. ANNUAL REPORT. (Text in Arabic, Chinese, English, French, German, Japanese, Spanish) 1947. a. free. World Bank, 1818 H St., N.W., Washington, DC 20433. TEL 202-477-1234. charts. stat.

338.9 UN ISSN 0251-401X
WORLD BANK. COMMODITY TRADE AND PRICE TRENDS. (Text in English, French and Spanish) 1970. biennial. $20. World Bank, 1818 H St., N.W., Washington, DC 20433 TEL 202-477-1234. (Avail. from Johns Hopkins University Press (Journals Division), 2539 St. Paul Street, Baltimore, MD 21218) Ed. Shamsher Singh. circ. 375.

332.1 912 UN ISSN 0512-2457
WORLD BANK ATLAS. 1967. a. ‡ World Bank, 1818 H St., N.W., Washington, DC 20433. TEL 202-477-1234.

338.91 UN ISSN 0253-2859
WORLD DEBT TABLES. a. with supplements. $100. World Bank, 1818 H St., N.W., Washington, DC 20433.

338.91 US ISSN 0163-5085
WORLD DEVELOPMENT REPORT. 1978. a. (World Bank) Oxford University Press, 200 Madison Ave., New York, NY 10016 TEL 212-679-7300. (And Ely House, 37 Dover St., London W1X 4AH, England)

BUSINESS AND ECONOMICS — Investments

332.6 UK ISSN 0266-2132
AIRFINANCE ANNUAL. 1984. a. £40($90) Airfinance Journal Ltd., Laxfield House, 2 Church St., Coggeshall, Essex CO6 1TU, England. circ. 5,000. (back issues avail.)

332.6 350 US ISSN 0092-6736
ALASKA. DEPARTMENT OF REVENUE. STATE INVESTMENT PORTFOLIO. (Report year ends Jun. 30) a. Department of Revenue, Box SB, Juneau, AK 99811. TEL 907-465-2173. stat. Key Title: State Investment Portfolio. (Juneau)

ALMANAC OF BUSINESS AND INDUSTRIAL FINANCIAL RATIOS. see BUSINESS AND ECONOMICS — Banking And Finance

ALMANAC OF CHINA'S FOREIGN RELATIONS AND TRADE. see BUSINESS AND ECONOMICS — Economic Systems And Theories, Economic History

332.6 US
AMERICAN STOCK EXCHANGE. AMEX FACT BOOK. 1968. irreg., latest issue 1985. $5. American Stock Exchange, Inc, 86 Trinity Pl., New York, NY 10006. TEL 212-306-1386. Dir. of Pub. Vincent A. Green. circ. 7,500.
Former titles (until 1982): American Stock Exchange. AMEX Databook (ISSN 0066-0760); American Stock Exchange. AMEX Statistical Review.

332.6 US ISSN 0066-0779
AMERICAN STOCK EXCHANGE. ANNUAL REPORT. a. American Stock Exchange Inc., 86 Trinity Place, New York, NY 10006. TEL 212-306-1000.

332.6 US
AMERICAN STOCK EXCHANGE DIRECTORY. a. $8. Commerce Clearing House, Inc., 4025 W. Peterson Ave., Chicago, IL 60646. TEL 312-583-8500. Ed. A.E. Schechter.

332.6 NE
AMSTERDAM STOCK EXCHANGE. (Text in English) 1969. a. Amsterdam Stock Exchange, Beursplein 5, Amsterdam 1001, Netherlands. charts. illus. stat. circ. 5,000.

332.6 US
ANALYSTS HANDBOOK. 1964. a. $550. Standard & Poor's Corporation, 25 Broadway, New York, NY 10004. TEL 212-208-8000. Ed. Roy Anderson. stat.

332.6 FR ISSN 0066-9008
ASSOCIATION DES SOCIETES ET FONDS FRANCAIS D'INVESTISSEMENT. ANNUAIRE. 1963. a. Association des Societes et Fonds Francais d'Investissement, 1 rue d'Astorg, 75008 Paris, France. abstr. stat. cum.index. circ. 2,500.

332.66 658.91 793 US
ATLANTIC CITY ACTION. 1978. a. $125. Glasco Associates, Inc., 33 S. Presbyterian Ave., Atlantic City, NJ 08404 TEL 609-347-1225. (Subscr. to: Box 5059, Atlantic City, NJ 08404) Ed. Al Glasgow. circ. 2,800. (back issues avail.)

332.6 AT
AUSTRALIA. FOREIGN INVESTMENT REVIEW BOARD. REPORT. a. Australian Government Publishing Service, G.P.O. Box 84, Canberra, A.C.T. 2601, Australia.

338.01 US ISSN 0067-1959
AUSTRALIAN MARKET GUIDE. biennial. not available for sale to libraries. Dun & Bradstreet, Inc., 99 Church St., New York, NY 10007 TEL 212-285-7000. (And 24 Albert Rd., Melbourne South 3205, Australia)

332.6 SZ
BASLER EFFEKTENBOERSE. JAHRESBERICHT/ RAPPORT ANNUEL/ANNUAL REPORT. (Text in English and German) 1961. a. Basler Effektenboerse - Basel Stock Exchange, Aeschenplatz 7, Postfach, 400201258588x, Switzerland. charts.

332.6 BE
BELGIUM. MINISTERE DES AFFAIRES ECONOMIQUES. RAPPORT ANNUEL SUR LES INVESTISSEMENTS ETRANGERS EN BELIQUE/JAARLIJKS RAPPORT OVER DE BUITENLANDSE INVESTERINGEN. a. free. Ministere des Affaires Economiques, 23 Square de Meeus, 1040 Brussels, Belgium.
Formerly (until 1984): Investissements Etrangers en Belgique (ISSN 0075-0247)

332.6 SZ
BERNER BOERSENVEREIN. JAHRESBERICHT. (Text in German) a. membership. Berner Boersenverein - Berne Stock Exchange, Aarbergergasse 30, 3011 Berne, Switzerland.

332.6 US ISSN 0362-8701
BEST'S INSURANCE SECURITIES RESEARCH SERVICE. 1968. irreg. $2000. A.M. Best Co., Oldwick, NJ 08858. TEL 201-439-2200. illus. (looseleaf format)

BIBLIOGRAPHY OF APPRAISAL LITERATURE. see REAL ESTATE — Abstracting, Bibliographies, Statistics

332.6 US
BLUE CHIP STOCKS. 1972. a. Elton Stephens Investments, 4016 S. Michigan St., Box 476, South Bend, IN 46624-0476. TEL 219-291-3823. Ed. Elton Stephens. (looseleaf format; back issues avail.)

332.6 332 AU
BOERSE. a. Girozentrale Vienna, Schubertring 5, 1010 Vienna, Austria. Ed. Michael Briem. circ. 2,000.

332.64 SP
BOLSA DE BARCELONA. MEMORIA. a. Colegio de Agentes de Cambio y Bolsa de Barcelona, Servicio de Estudios e Informacion, Paseo Isabel II s/n, 08003 Barcelona, Spain.
Formerly: Bolsa de Barcelona. Estadisticas.

332.64 PE
BOLSA DE VALORES DE LIMA. MEMORIA. 1975. a. free. Bolsa de Valores de Lima, Miro Quesada 265, Lima, Peru.

332.64 EC
BOLSA DE VALORES DE QUITO. INFORMES Y MEMORIA ANUAL. a. Bolsa de Valores de Quito, Av. 6 de Diciembre y Pazmino 245, Apartado 3272, Quito, Ecuador.

332.6 BL
BOLSA DE VALORES DE SAO PAULO. RELATORIO. (Text in Portuguese) a. free. Bolsa de Valores de Sao Paulo, Rua Alvares Penteado 151, Sao Paulo, Brazil. stat.

332.6 BL ISSN 0557-0506
BOLSA DE VALORES DO RIO DE JANEIRO. RESUMO ANUAL. 1964. a. Cr.$7($2) Bolsa de Valores do Rio de Janeiro - Rio de Janeiro Stock Exchange, Praca 15 de Novembro, 20, Rio de Janeiro, Brazil. circ. 500.

332.63 US
BOND MARKET: ANALYSIS AND OUTLOOK. a. Salomon Brothers Inc., One New York Plaza, New York, NY 10004. TEL 212-747-7000.

BOND MARKET IN LUXEMBURG FRANCS AND IN ECU. see BUSINESS AND ECONOMICS — Abstracting, Bibliographies, Statistics

332.6 BL
BRAZIL. SUPERINTENDENCIA DO DESENVOLVIMENTO DO NORDESTE. NORDESTE, OPORTUNIDADES DE INVESTIMENTOS. 1975. a. Superintendencia do Desenvolvimento do Nordeste, Edificio Entreposto Federal de Pesca, Cais de Santa Rita, 8 Andar, Recife, Brazil.

332.6 CN ISSN 0068-161X
BRITISH COLUMBIA MUNICIPAL YEARBOOK. 1949. a. Can.$10. (British Columbia Bond Dealers Association) JSB Productions Ltd., Box 46475, Station G, Vancouver, B.C. V6R 4G7, Canada. TEL 604-736-6754. Ed. Joan Stewart. adv. circ. 4,000.

BRITISH SECURITY COMPANIES. see BUSINESS AND ECONOMICS — Trade And Industrial Directories

332.6 US
C U S I P CORPORATE DIRECTORY. a. $590. (American Bankers Association, Committee on Uniform Security Identification Procedures) Standard & Poor's Corporation, 25 Broadway, New York, NY 10004. TEL 212-208-8000.
Formerly: American Bankers Association. Committee on Uniform Security Identification Procedures. C U S I P Directory: Corporate Directory (ISSN 0091-3804)

332.6 US
C U S I P MASTER DIRECTORY. 1969. a. $960. (American Bankers Association, Committee on Uniform Security Identification Procedures) Standard & Poor's Corporation, 25 Broadway, New York, NY 10004. TEL 212-208-8000.
Formerly: American Bankers Association. Committee on Uniform Security Identification Procedures. C U S I P Directory (ISSN 0569-2954)

332.6 CN
CANADA. INVESTMENT CANADA. ANNUAL REPORT. 1975/76. a. Investment Canada Agency, Box 2800 Station D, Ottawa, Ont. K1P 6A5, Canada. TEL 613-995-9449.
Formerly (until 1985): Canada. Foreign Investment Review Agency. Annual Report.

332.65 US ISSN 0577-571X
CAPITAL INVESTMENTS OF THE WORLD PETROLEUM INDUSTRY. 1946. a. free. Chase Manhattan Bank, Energy Economics Division, One Chase Manhattan Plaza, New York, NY 10015. TEL 212-425-0616. Ed. Richard Dobias. circ. 30,000.

332.6 UK ISSN 0308-9088
CITY DIRECTORY. a. £35. Woodhead-Faulkner (Publishers) Ltd., Fitzwilliam House, 32 Trumpington St., Cambridge CB2 1QY, England. adv.

332.6 US
COMMODITY PRICES. 1974. irreg. $44. Gale Research Company, Book Tower, Detroit, MI 48226. TEL 313-961-2242. Ed. Paul Wasserman.

BUSINESS AND ECONOMICS — INVESTMENTS

338   US   ISSN 0069-6862
COMMODITY YEAR BOOK. 1939. a. $46.95.
Commodity Research Bureau (Subsidiary of: Knight-Ridder) 100 Church St., Ste. 1850, New York, NY 10007. TEL 212-406-4545. Ed. Susan G. Buchanan. index.

332.678   US   ISSN 0741-1995
CONCERNED INVESTORS GUIDE; non-financial corporate data. 1983. a. $167 to individuals; libraries $117. Resource Publishing Group, Inc., 1401 Wilson Blvd. Ste. 101, Arlington, VA 22209. TEL 703-524-0815. Ed. Sharen D. Knight.

332.6   US
CONTRARY OPINION LIBRARY. a. Fraser Publishing Co. (Subsidiary of: Fraser Management Associates, Inc.) 309 S. Willard St., Box 494, Burlington, VT 05402. circ. 30,000.

CORPORATE PROFILES FOR EXECUTIVES & INVESTORS. see BUSINESS AND ECONOMICS

332.6   US   ISSN 0149-6581
DIRECTORY OF COMPANIES REQUIRED TO FILE ANNUAL REPORTS WITH THE SECURITIES AND EXCHANGE COMMISSION UNDER THE SECURITIES EXCHANGE ACT OF 1934; alphabetically and by industry groups. 1950. a. $4.75. U.S. Securities and Exchange Commission, Office of Economic Research, 500 N. Capitol St., Washington, DC 20549 TEL 202-655-4000. (Orders to: Supt. of Documents, Washington, DC 20402) Ed. N.B. Marshall. index. circ. 5,000. (reprint service avail. from UMI)
Formerly (until 1976): Directory of Companies Filing Annual Reports with the Securities and Exchange Commission Under the Securities Exchange Act of 1934.

332.67   AT
DIRECTORY OF PROPERTY INVESTORS AND DEVELOPERS. irreg. Davies and Dalziel Investment Service, G.P.O. Box 1392m, Melbourne, Vic. 3001, Australia.

DIRECTORY OF PUBLIC HIGH TECHNOLOGY CORPORATIONS. see BUSINESS AND ECONOMICS — Trade And Industrial Directories

332.6   US   ISSN 0886-0521
DIRECTORY OF WALL STREET RESEARCH. 1976. a. $149. W.R. Nelson & Co., 11 Elm Pl., Box 689, Rye, NY 10580-9990. Ed. Walter R. Nelson. adv. stat.
Former titles: Investment Decisions Directory of Wall Street Research & Nelson's Directory of Wall Street Research (ISSN 0740-8714); National Directory of Wall Street Research; Directory of Securities Research (ISSN 0277-8343); Nelson Directory of Securities Research (ISSN 0272-5355)

332.6   US
DOW JONES INVESTOR'S HANDBOOK. 1982. a. $10.95 paper. Dow Jones-Irwin, Homewood, IL 60430. Ed. Phyllis Pierce.

332.6   US   ISSN 0098-2466
DUN & BRADSTREET'S GUIDE TO YOUR INVESTMENTS. 17th edt., 1973. a. $10.95 paperback; hardcover $16.95. Harper & Row, Publishers, Inc., 10 E. 53rd St., New York, NY 10022. TEL 212-207-7000.
Formerly: Your Investments: How to Increase Your Capital and Income.

332.6   UK   ISSN 0263-1229
EXPATRIATE'S GUIDE TO SAVINGS AND INVESTMENT. 1980. a. Financial Times Business Information, 102-108 Clerkenwell Rd., London EC1M 5SA, England. Ed. J. Stone. adv.

332.65   US
FINANCIAL ANALYSIS OF A GROUP OF PETROLEUM COMPANIES. 1945. a. free. Chase Manhattan Bank, Energy Economics Division, One Chase Manhattan Plaza, New York, NY 10015. TEL 212-425-0616. Ed. Richard Dobias. circ. 30,000.

332.6   US
FINANCIAL CORPORATE MUNICIPAL BOND TRANSFER SERVICE. 1972. a. with m. supplements. $615. Financial Information, Inc., 30 Montgomery St., Jersey City, NJ 07302. TEL 201-332-5400.
Formerly: Financial Corporate Bond Transfer Service (ISSN 0360-5825)

FINANCIAL POST EIGHT YEAR PRICE RANGE. see BUSINESS AND ECONOMICS — Banking And Finance

332.6   CN   ISSN 0071-5050
FINANCIAL POST SURVEY OF INDUSTRIALS. 1927. a. Can.$43.95. Maclean Hunter Ltd., Financial Post Division, Maclean Hunter Bldg., 777 Bay St., Toronto, Ont. M5W 1A7, Canada. TEL 416-596-5585. Ed. John Byrne. adv. circ. 11,000.
Investment and statistical data on public Canadian industrial securities

332.678   US   ISSN 0364-0752
FINANCIAL STOCK GUIDE SERVICE. DIRECTORY OF ACTIVE STOCKS. a. (with m. supplements) $640 includes Directory of Obsolete Securities. Financial Information, Inc., 30 Montgomery St., Jersey City, NJ 07302. TEL 201-332-5400.

332.6   US   ISSN 0085-0551
FINANCIAL STOCK GUIDE SERVICE. DIRECTORY OF OBSOLETE SECURITIES. 1927. a. $325 to qualified personnel. Financial Information, Inc., 30 Montgomery St., Jersey City, NJ 07302. TEL 201-332-5400.

FORECAST OF SHOP RENTS. see REAL ESTATE

332.6   FR
FRANCE. COMMISSION DES OPERATIONS DE BOURSE. RAPPORT AU PRESIDENT DE LA REPUBLIQUE. irreg. France. Direction des Journaux Officiels, 26 rue Desaix, 75732 Paris Cedex 15, France.

332.6   US   ISSN 0746-2468
FUTURES MAGAZINE REFERENCE GUIDE TO FUTURES MARKETS. 1972. a. $34. Futures Magazine, Inc. (Subsidiary of: Oster Communications Co.) 250 S. Wacker Dr., Ste. 950, Chicago, IL 60606. TEL 312-977-0999. Ed. Darrell Jobman. adv. bk. rev. stat. tr.lit. circ. 75,000. (also avail. in microfiche; back issues avail.) Indexed: BPIA. Bus.Ind.
Formerly: Commodities Magazine Reference Guide to Futures Markets (ISSN 0275-9489)

332.6   NE   ISSN 0072-4467
GIDS BIJ DE PRIJSCOURANT. 1894. a. fl.169.50. J.H. de Bussy, P.O. Box 162, 1000 AD Amsterdam, Netherlands. Ed. O. Blikslager. circ. 1,600.

332.6   UK   ISSN 0072-5692
GREAT BRITAIN. DEPARTMENT OF TRADE. PARTICULARS OF DEALERS IN SECURITIES AND OF TRUST UNITS. a. H.M.S.O., P.O. Box 569, London SE1 9NH, England. (reprint service avail. from UMI)

332.6   BE
GROUPE BRUXELLES LAMBERT. ANNUAL REPORTS. 1979. a. Groupe Bruxelles Lambert, S.A., 24 Avenue Marnix, 1050 Brussels, Belgium.

GRUNDLAGEN UND PRAXIS DES BANK- UND BOERSENWESENS. see BUSINESS AND ECONOMICS — Banking And Finance

332.6   IT
GUIDA DEL MERCATO RISTRETTO. 1962. a. L.70000. (Databank S.p.A., Stock Market Division) Edizioni S A S I P, Via dei Piatti, 11, 20123 Milan, Italy.

332.6   US   ISSN 0736-6264
HANDBOOK FOR NO-LOAD FUND INVESTORS. 1981. a. $36. No-Load Fund Investor, Inc., Box 283, Hastings-on-Hudson, NY 10706. TEL 914-693-7420. charts. stat.

332.6   US   ISSN 0072-9892
HANDBOOK OF SECURITIES OF THE UNITED STATES GOVERNMENT AND FEDERAL AGENCIES AND RELATED MONEY MARKET INSTRUMENTS. 1922. biennial. $10 (free to qualified institutions) First Boston Corp., Park Ave. Plaza, New York, NY 10055. TEL 212-909-2000. circ. 60,000.

332.6   330.9   US
HARRY BROWNE'S SPECIAL REPORTS. irreg. $225. Harry Browne's Special Reports, Inc., Box 5586, Austin, TX 78763. TEL 512-453-7313. Ed. Harry Browne. charts. stat. index. (looseleaf format; back issues avail.)

332.64   GR
HELLENIC INDUSTRIAL DEVELOPMENT BANK. INVESTMENT GUIDE. Spine title: E T B A Investment Guide. (Supplements avail.) (Text in English and Greek) 1961. irreg. Dr.500($5) Hellenic Industrial Development Bank, 18 E. Venizelos St., Athens 135, Greece. circ. 3,000.

332.6   HK
HONG KONG INDUSTRIAL INVESTMENT. (Editions in English, French, German and Japanese) 1968. a. free to qualified personnel. Department of Industry, Fire Brigade, Hong Kong, Hong Kong. Ed. Robert Sun. illus. stat. circ. 15,000.

332.6   GW   ISSN 0073-3342
HOPPENSTEDT VADEMECUM DER INVESTMENTFONDS. 1961. biennial. DM.148. Verlag Hoppenstedt und Co., Havelstr. 9, Postfach 4006, 6100 Darmstadt, W. Germany (B.R.D.) adv. bk. rev.

HORSE OWNERS AND BREEDERS TAX MANUAL. see SPORTS AND GAMES — Horses And Horsemanship

332.6   333.33   US
HOW TO BUY AND SELL BUSINESS OPPORTUNITIES. 1979. biennial. $28.95. (Society of Certified Business Opportunity Appraisers) American Business Consultants, Inc., 1540 Nuthatch, Sunnyvale, CA 94087. TEL 408-738-3011. Ed. Wilfred F. Tetreault. circ. 10,000. (back issues avail.)

332.6   BL
HOW TO INVEST IN BRAZIL. (Text in English) a., with q. supplements. $100. ESTEPE, Publishing Department, Rua Senador Dantas 19 Grupo 707, ZC-06 20000 Rio de Janeiro, Brazil.

332.6   US
INCOME STOCKS. 1972. a. Elton Stephens Investments, 4016 S. Michigan St., Box 476, South Bend, IN 46624-0476. TEL 219-291-3823. Ed. Elton Stephens. (looseleaf format; back issues avail.)

332.6   341   US   ISSN 0074-2163
INTERNATIONAL CENTRE FOR SETTLEMENT OF INVESTMENT DISPUTES. ANNUAL REPORT. (Editions also in French and Spanish) 1966/67. a. free. International Centre for Settlement, 1818 H St., N.W., Washington, DC 20433. TEL 202-477-1234. circ. 5,000.

332   KO
INTRODUCTION TO THE KOREAN SECURITIES MARKET. (Text in English) irreg. free. Korea Stock Exchange, 33, Yoido-dong, Youngdeungpo-ku, Seoul, S. Korea. illus. circ. 1,500.
Formerly: Securities Market in Korea.

332.6   EC
INVEST IN ECUADOR. (Text in English, French, German and Spanish) a. free. Banco Central del Ecuador, Secretaria General, Casill 339, Quito, Ecuador. circ. 30,000.

332.67   PN
INVEST IN PANAMA. (Text in English) vol.3, 1979. irreg. Banco Nacional de Panama, Via Espana-Torre B.N.P., P.O. Box 5220, Panama 5, Panama.

INVESTERING I PRODUKTION. see BUSINESS AND ECONOMICS — Production Of Goods And Services

332.6   DK   ISSN 0109-9426
INVESTERINGSFORENINGER TILSYNET. 1985. a. free. Industriministeren, Investeringforeninger, Norre Volgade 94, DK-1358 Copenhagen K, Denmark.

332.6   UK
INVESTING FOR BEGINNERS. 1983. a. £8.75($16) Financial Times Business Information, 102-108 Clerkenwell Rd., London EC1M 5SA, England.
Formerly: Beginners Please.

332.6   US   ISSN 0075-0271
INVESTMENT COMPANIES; mutual funds and other types. Variant title: Wiesenberger Investment Companies Service. 1941. a. with m. & q. updating. $345. (Wiesenberger Services, Inc.) Warren, Gorham and Lamont, Inc., 210 South St., Boston, MA 02111. TEL 800-922-0066. Ed. Paul A. Johnston.

BUSINESS AND ECONOMICS — INVESTMENTS

332.67   US
INVESTOR RESPONSIBILITY RESEARCH CENTER. ANNUAL REPORT. 1973. a. Investor Responsibility Research Center, Inc., 1755 Massachusetts Ave., N.W., Ste. 600, Washington, DC 20036-2102. TEL 202-939-6500. Ed. Margaret Carroll.

332.6   NP
INVESTORS' GUIDE TO NEPAL. (Text in English) 1975. irreg. Industrial Services Centre, Box 1318, Kathmandu, Nepal. adv. circ. 3,000.

332.6   UK
INVESTORS GUIDE TO THE STOCKMARKET. irreg. £8.75($16) Financial Times Business Information, 102-108 Clerkenwell Rd., London EC1M 5SA, England.

332.6   IV
IVORY COAST. DIRECTION DES INVESTISSEMENTS. BUDGET SPECIAL D'INVESTISSEMENT ET D'EQUIPEMENT. RAPPORT DE PRESENTATION.* a. Direction du Budget Special d'Investissement et d'Equipement, Abidjan, Ivory Coast.

332.63   AT   ISSN 0075-3785
JOBSON'S YEAR BOOK OF PUBLIC COMPANIES. 1920. a. Aus.$175. Dun & Bradstreet (Australia) Pty. Ltd., 24 Albert Rd., Melbourne, Vic. 3205, Australia. adv. illus. circ. 5, 000.
    Formerly: Jobson's Investment Digest of Australia and New Zealand (ISSN 0021-7093)

332.678   PK
KARACHI. CHAMBER OF COMMERCE AND INDUSTRY. GUIDE FOR INDUSTRIAL INVESTMENT IN PAKISTAN. (Text in English) irreg. Rs.100. Karachi Chamber of Commerce and Industry, Aiwan-e-Tijarat, Box 4158, Nicol Rd., Karachi 2, Pakistan.

KENYA: THE GATEWAY TO AFRICA; guidelines to investors. see *BUSINESS AND ECONOMICS — Trade And Industrial Directories*

332.6   DK
KOEBENHAVNS FONDSBOERS. AARSRAPPORT/COPENHAGEN STOCK EXCHANGE. ANNUAL REPORT. 1963. a. Koebenhavns Fondsboers - Copenhagen Stock Exchange, Nikolaj Plads 6, 1067 Copenhagen K, Denmark. stat. circ. 2,000.

332.64   KO
KOREA STOCK EXCHANGE. FACT BOOK. (Text in English) 1979. a. free. Korea Stock Exchange, 33, Yoido-dong, Youngdeungpo-ku, Seoul, S. Korea. circ. 1,000.

KOTHARI'S INDUSTRIAL DIRECTORY OF INDIA. see *BUSINESS AND ECONOMICS — Trade And Industrial Directories*

332.6   MY   ISSN 0126-7558
KUALA LUMPUR STOCK EXCHANGE. COMPANIES HANDBOOK. (Text in English) 1974. a. M.30. Kuala Lumpur Stock Exchange, Damansara Centre, Ground Floor, Block 'C', Damansara Heights, P.O. Box 11023, 50732 Kuala Lumpur, Malaysia. Ed. Qua Gek Kim. adv. stat. circ. 4,000.

LAW REPRINTS: SECURITIES REGULATION SERIES. see *LAW*

338   332.6   US   ISSN 0278-6524
MARKET GUIDE CONTINENTAL EUROPE. a. not avail. to libraries in U.S. Dun & Bradstreet International, International Marketing Services, 99 Church St., New York, NY 10007. TEL 212-312-6816.
    Formerly: International Market Guide - Continental Europe (ISSN 0074-6908)

353.9   332.6   US   ISSN 0090-9912
MONTANA. OFFICE OF THE LEGISLATIVE AUDITOR. STATE OF MONTANA BOARD OF INVESTMENTS. REPORT ON EXAMINATION OF FINANCIAL STATEMENTS. (Report year ends June 30) a. free. Office of the Legislative Auditor, State Capitol, Rm. 135, Helena, MT 59620. TEL 406-444-3122. stat. Key Title: State of Montana Investment Program. Report on Audit.

332.6   US   ISSN 0027-0814
MOODY'S BANK & FINANCE MANUAL. a. $760 (includes fortn. Moody's Bank & Finance News Reports) Moody's Investors Service, Inc., 99 Church St., New York, NY 10007. TEL 212-553-0300. Ed. Robert Hanson.

332.6   US   ISSN 0545-0217
MOODY'S INDUSTRIAL MANUAL. 1900. a. $760 price includes bi-weekly news reports. Moody's Investors Service, 99 Church St., New York, NY 10007. TEL 212-553-0300. Ed. Robert Hanson. stat. index.

332.678   US
MOODY'S INTERNATIONAL MANUAL. 1981. a. $1,095. Moody's Investors Service, 99 Church St., New York, NY 10007. TEL 212-553-0300. Ed. Robert Hanson.

332.6   US   ISSN 0545-0233
MOODY'S MUNICIPAL & GOVERNMENT MANUAL. a. $985 price includes bi-weekly news report. Moody's Investors Service, 99 Church St., New York, NY 10007. TEL 212-553-0300. Ed. Robert Hanson. stat. index.

332.6   US
MOODY'S O T C INDUSTRIAL MANUAL. a. $690 (includes fortnightly Moody's O T C Industrial News Report) Moody's Investors Service, 99 Church St., New York, NY 10007. TEL 212-553-0300. Ed. Robert Hanson.

332.6   US   ISSN 0545-0241
MOODY'S PUBLIC UTILITY MANUAL. a. $650 (includes fortn. Moody's Public Utility News Reports) Moody's Investors Service, 99 Church St., New York, NY 10007. TEL 212-553-0300. Ed. Robert Hanson.

332.6   US
MOODY'S TRANSPORTATION MANUAL. a. $650 (includes weekly Moody's Transportation News Reports) Moody's Investors Service, 99 Church St., New York, NY 10007. TEL 212-553-0300. Ed. Robert Hanson.

332.6   US
MUTUAL FUND FACT BOOK. a. $4. Investment Company Institute, 1600 M St., N.W., Washington, DC 20036. TEL 202-293-7700.

332.6   US   ISSN 0076-4175
MUTUAL FUNDS ALMANAC. 1969. a. $23 soft cover. Donoghue Organization, Box 540, Holliston, MA 01746. TEL 617-429-5930. Ed. Connie Bugbee. adv. circ. 10,000.
    Formerly: Manual of Mutual Funds.

332.6   US   ISSN 0077-5703
NATIONAL SECURITIES AND RESEARCH CORPORATION. ANNUAL FORECAST. Variant title: National's Forecast For (Year) 1948. a. free. ‡ National Securities & Research Corp., 605 Third Ave., New York, NY 10016. TEL 212-661-3000.

332.6   US   ISSN 0092-4679
NATIONAL SECURITY TRADERS ASSOCIATION. TRADERS' ANNUAL. 1961. a. $5. Investment Dealers' Digest (IDD) Inc., 150 Broadway, New York, NY 10038. TEL 212-227-1200. illus. circ. 5,000.

332.6   314   NE
NETHERLANDS. CENTRAAL BUREAU VOOR DE STATISTIEK. INSTITUTIONELE BELEGGERS. INSTITUTIONAL INVESTORS. (Text in Dutch and English) 1966. a. fl.9.50. Centraal Bureau voor de Statistiek, Prinses Beatrixlaan 428, Voorburg, Netherlands (Orders to: Staatsuitgeverij, Christoffel Plantijnstraat, The Hague, Netherlands)
    Formerly: Netherlands. Centraal Bureau voor de Statistiek. Beleggingen van Institutionele Beleggers. Investments of Institutional Investors (ISSN 0168-3381)

332.6   NO   ISSN 0085-4565
OSLO BOERS. BERETNING. 1896. a. free. Oslo Boers - Oslo Stock Exchange, Tollbugt. 2, Oslo 1, Norway. circ. 1,600.

332.6   US   ISSN 0196-1276
OVERSEAS PRIVATE INVESTMENT CORPORATION. ANNUAL REPORT. 1971. a. free. Overseas Private Investment Corporation, 1615 M St., N.W., Washington, DC 20527. Ed. Robert L. Jordan. circ. 30,000. Key Title: Annual Report - Overseas Private Investment Corporation.

332.6   US
PACIFIC STOCK EXCHANGE. ANNUAL REPORT. a. Pacific Stock Exchange, 301 Pine St., San Francisco, CA 94104. TEL 415-393-4000.

332.6   PK   ISSN 0078-8198
PAKISTAN INDUSTRIAL CREDIT AND INVESTMENT CORPORATION. ANNUAL REPORT. (Text in English) 1962. a. Pakistan Industrial Credit and Investment Corporation, Economic and Research Department, State Life Building No. 1, P.O. Box 5080, I.I. Chundrigar Rd., Karachi 2, Pakistan. Ed. Abdul Hafeez Khan. charts. stat.

332.6327   PY
PARAGUAY. MINISTRY OF INDUSTRY AND TRADE. INVESTMENT GUIDE. irreg. Ministry of Industry and Trade - Ministerio de Industria y Comercio, Gabinete Tecnico, Avda. Espana N. 323, Asuncion, Paraguay. TEL 204 795.

332.63   PH
PHILIPPINE STANDARD COMMODITY CLASSIFICATION. irreg. National Economic and Development Authority, Box 1116, Manila, Philippines.

332.6   PH   ISSN 0079-1504
PHILIPPINES. BOARD OF INVESTMENTS. ANNUAL REPORT. 1968. a. free. ‡ Board of Investments, MCC P.O. Box 676, Makati, Metro Manila-3117, Philippines. circ. 3,000.

POLITICAL CLIMATE FOR INTERNATIONAL BUSINESS; a forecast of risk in 85 countries. see *BUSINESS AND ECONOMICS — Banking And Finance*

POLITICAL RISK YEARBOOK. see *BUSINESS AND ECONOMICS — Banking And Finance*

PONDICHERRY INDUSTRIAL PROMOTION, DEVELOPMENT AND INVESTMENT CORPORATION. ANNUAL REPORTS AND ACCOUNTS. see *BUSINESS AND ECONOMICS — Domestic Commerce*

332.6   US
PRATT'S GUIDE TO VENTURE CAPITAL SOURCES. 1970/71. a. $99. Venture Economics, Inc., 16 Laurel Ave., Wellesley Hills, MA 02181 (Orders to: Box 348, Wellesley Hills, MA 02181) bibl.
    Formerly: Guide to Venture Capital Sources.

332.6   PH
PRIVATE DEVELOPMENT CORPORATION OF THE PHILIPPINES. ANNUAL PDCP SURVEY ON BUSINESS PERFORMANCE. (Text in English) 1977. a. $120. Private Development Corporation of the Philippines - Pribadong Korporasyon Sa Pagpapaunlad Ng Pilipinas, P.O. Box 757, Makati, Metro Manila 3117, Philippines.

332.67   341   US   ISSN 0090-9742
PRIVATE INVESTORS ABROAD; problems and solutions in international business. 1967. a. $70. (Southwestern Legal Foundation, International and Comparative Law Center) Matthew Bender & Co., Inc., 235 E. 45 St., New York, NY 10017. TEL 212-661-5050. Indexed: Leg.Per. C.L.I. L.R.I.

332.6   UK
PRIVATE INVESTOR'S LEDGER. a. £5.95. Financial Times Business Publishing, Greystoke Pl., Fetter Ln., London EC4A 1ND, England.

332.6   US   ISSN 0094-3134
PROBE DIRECTORY OF FOREIGN DIRECT INVESTMENT IN THE UNITED STATES. 1974. irreg., 6th edt., 1983, latest edt. 1986. $125. Probe International, Inc., Box 3364, Stamford, CT 06905. TEL 203-329-9595. Ed. Benjamin Weiner.

R.E.I.T. FACT BOOK. (National Association of Real Estate Investment Trusts) see *REAL ESTATE*

BUSINESS AND ECONOMICS — INVESTMENTS

332.6   TZ   ISSN 0856-0382
RASILIMALI; Tanzania investment outlook. (Text in English) 1972. irreg., no.10, 1983. Tanzania Investment Bank, Box 9373, Dar es Salaam, Tanzania.

332.6   657   US
S E C ACCOUNTING RULES. 1968. base vol. plus updates. $205. Commerce Clearing House, Inc., 4025 W. Peterson Ave., Chicago, IL 60646. TEL 312-583-8500. (looseleaf format)

332.6   US
S I E GUIDE TO INVESTMENT SERVICES. 1967. a. $1. Select Information Exchange, 2095 Broadway, New York, NY 10023. TEL 212-874-6408. Ed. George H. Wein. adv. bk. rev. bibl. circ. 125,000.
    Former titles: S I E Sophisticated Investor & Investment Sources and Ideas (ISSN 0085-6355); Sources and Ideas; Incorporating: Sophisticated Investor.

332.6   GW   ISSN 0080-5572
SALING AKTIENFUEHRER. 1872. a. DM.132. Verlag Hoppenstedt und Co., Havelstr. 9, Postfach 4006, 6100 Darmstadt, W. Germany (B.R.D.) adv.

332.6   TH
SECURITIES EXCHANGE OF THAILAND. HANDBOOK. 1975. irreg. Securities Exchange of Thailand, Siam Center, 4th Floor (Rm. 412), 965 Ram I Rd., Bangkok, Thailand.

332.6   US
SECURITIES INDUSTRY YEARBOOK. 1981. a. $85 to non-members; members $50. Securities Industry Association, Inc., 120 Broadway, New York, NY 10271. TEL 212-608-1500. Ed. Rosalie Pepe. circ. 4,000.
    Formerly: Security Industry Yearbook (ISSN 0730-5796)

338.7   US   ISSN 0094-467X
SECURITIES INVESTOR PROTECTION CORPORATION. ANNUAL REPORT. 1971. a. free. Securities Investor Protection Corp., 900 17th St. N.W., Suite 800, Washington, DC 20006. TEL 202-223-8400. Ed. Jeffrey R. McCord. stat. circ. 15,000. Key Title: Annual Report - Securities Investor Protection Corporation.

332.6   JA
SECURITIES MARKET IN JAPAN. (Text in English) 1973. biennial. 4750 Yen. Japan Securities Research Institute, Shokenkaikan, 1-5-8 Nihonbashi Kayaba-cho, Chuo-ku, Tokyo 103, Japan. illus. stat.

332.6   AT   ISSN 0037-3311
SHAREHOLDER. 1966. irreg. membership. Australian Shareholders Association, N.S.W. Branch, 51 Pitt St., Sydney, N.S.W. 2000, Australia. adv. charts. illus.

332.6   LU
SOCIETE DE LA BOURSE DE LUXEMBOURG. RAPPORT ANNUEL. Luxembourg Stock Exchange. Annual Report. (Text in English and French) 1950. a. free. Societe de la Bourse de Luxembourg, B.P. Box 165, 11 Avenue de la Porte Neuve, 2011 Luxembourg, Luxembourg. circ. 3,000.

332.678   SA
SOUTH AFRICA: A GUIDE TO FOREIGN INVESTORS. a. Erudita Publications (Pty) Ltd., Crn. 11th Ave. & Main Rd., P.O. Box 29159, Melville, Johannesburg 2109, South Africa. adv.

332.6   US
STANDARD AND POOR'S DIRECTORY OF BOND AGENTS. Short title: Directory of Bond Agents. (Includes bimonthly cum. supplement) 1975. irreg. $700. Standard & Poor's Corporation, 25 Broadway, New York, NY 10004. TEL 212-208-8000. Ed. Vito Calbi.

332.6   US
STARTING RIGHT IN YOUR NEW BUSINESS. 1981. biennial. $9.95. (Society of Certified Business Opportunity Appraisers) American Business Consultants, Inc., 1540 Nuthatch, Sunnyvale, CA 94087. TEL 408-738-3011. Ed. Wilfred F. Tetreault. circ. 40,000.

332.6   PK   ISSN 0081-4466
STATE BANK OF PAKISTAN. INDEX NUMBERS OF STOCK EXCHANGE SECURITIES. (Text in English) 1963. a. Rps.12($4.40) State Bank of Pakistan, Central Directorate, Public Relations Department, I.I. Chundrigar Rd., Box 4456, Karachi, Pakistan.

332.6   UK   ISSN 0305-1129
STOCK EXCHANGE, LONDON. MEMBERS AND FIRMS OF THE STOCK EXCHANGE. Cover title: Members of the Stock Exchange. 1802. a. £50. ‡ Council of the Stock Exchange, London EC2N 1HP, England. circ. 8,000.

332.6   SI
STOCK EXCHANGE OF SINGAPORE. HANDBOOK. (Text in English) 1966. a. Stock Exchange of Singapore Ltd., Hong Leong Bldg., Rm. 1603, Raffles Quay, Singapore 0104, Singapore. adv. circ. 6,000.

332.6   UK   ISSN 0076-0684
STOCK EXCHANGE OFFICIAL YEAR BOOK. 1875. a. £67.50($134) Macmillan Press Ltd., 4 Little Essex St., London WC2R 3LF, England. Eds. Gavin Harrap Fryer, David Martin Michael Davies. adv. circ. 6,750.

332.6   US
STOCK TRADER'S ALMANAC. 1968. a. $24.45 soft cover. ‡ Hirsch Organization Inc., 6 Deer Trail, Old Tappan, NJ 07675. TEL 201-664-3400. Ed. Yale Hirsch. circ. 30,000.

336.2   332.6   US   ISSN 0081-5624
STOCK VALUES AND DIVIDENDS FOR TAX PURPOSES. a. $12. Commerce Clearing House, Inc., 4025 W. Peterson Ave., Chicago, IL 60646. TEL 312-583-8500.

332.6   SW
STOCKHOLMS FONDBOERS. BERAETTELSE/ STOCKHOLM STOCK EXCHANGE. REPORT. a. Stockholms Fondboers, Kaellargraend, S-111 29 Stockholm, Sweden.

332.6   US
SUGESTIVE LOW PRICED STOCKS. 1972. a. Elton Stephens Investments, 4016 S. Michigan St., Box 476, South Bend, IN 46624-0476. TEL 219-291-3823. Ed. Elton Stephens. (looseleaf format; back issues avail.)

332.6   FI   ISSN 0781-4437
SUOMEN JOUKKOVELKAKIRJALAINAT/ FINNISH BOND ISSUES/FINLANDSKA MASSKULDEVREVSLAN. (Text in English, Finnish and Swedish) a. Fmk.50. Suomen Pankki - Bank of Finland, Information Department, Box 160, SF-00101 Helsinki, Finland. Ed. Kaiju Kallio. circ. 700.
    Formerly: Suomen Obligaatiokirja (ISSN 0585-9581)

332.6   AT
SYDNEY STOCK EXCHANGE. RESEARCH DEPARTMENT, COMPANY REVIEW SERVICE. (Text and summaries in English) 1938. a. Aus.$2,500. ‡ Sydney Stock Exchange, Research Department, 20 Bond St, Sydney, N.S.W., Australia. Ed. P.M. Nothman. stat. index. circ. controlled. (looseleaf format)
    Former titles: Sydney Stock Exchange. Research and Statistical Department. Company Review Service; Sydney Stock Exchange. Research and Statistical Department. Company Statistical Service.

332.6   IT   ISSN 0082-1446
TACCUINO DELL'AZIONISTA. 1935. a. L.240000. Edizioni S A S I P, Via dei Piatti, 11, 20123 Milan, Italy. Ed. Carlo Colombi. index. circ. 5,000.

336   340   US   ISSN 0731-5821
TAX SHELTERED INVESTMENTS HANDBOOK. a. $85. Clark Boardman Company, Ltd., 435 Hudson St., New York, NY 10014. TEL 212-929-7500.

TORONTO STOCK EXCHANGE FACT BOOK. see BUSINESS AND ECONOMICS — Banking And Finance

332.6   332   UG
U C B INVESTOR'S HANDBOOK. 1983. biennial. Uganda Commercial Bank, Box 973, Kampala, Uganda. circ. 1,500.

332.6   US
UNITED & BABSON GRAPHIC GUIDE. 1965. a. $20. ‡ Babson-United Investment Advisors, Inc., 210 Newbury St., Boston, MA 02116. TEL 617-267-8855. Ed. Donald Chun. charts.
    Formerly: United Graphic Guide (ISSN 0082-7916)

332.63   US   ISSN 0083-3215
U.S. SECURITIES AND EXCHANGE COMMISSION. ANNUAL REPORT. 1935. a. price varies. U.S. Securities and Exchange Commission, 500 N. Capitol St., Washington, DC 20549 TEL 202-655-4000. (Orders to: Supt. of Documents, Washington, DC 20402) (reprint service avail. from UMI)

332.63   US   ISSN 0083-3223
U.S. SECURITIES AND EXCHANGE COMMISSION. DECISIONS AND REPORTS. 1934. irreg. price varies. U.S. Securities and Exchange Commission, 500 N. Capitol St., Washington, DC 20549 TEL 202-655-4000. (Orders to: Supt. of Documents, Washington, DC 20402) (also avail. in microform from UMI; reprint service avail. from UMI)

332.63   US   ISSN 0083-3231
U.S. SECURITIES AND EXCHANGE COMMISSION. JUDICIAL DECISIONS. 1934/39. irreg. price varies. U.S. Securities and Exchange Commission, 500 N. Capitol St., Washington, DC 20549 TEL 202-655-4000. (Orders to: Supt. of Documents, Washington, DC 20402) (reprint service avail. from UMI)

332.6   PE
VADEMECUM BURSATIL. 1979. a. Bolsa de Valores de Lima, Miro Quesada 265, Lima, Peru. (Co-sponsor: Banco Continental) circ. 1,000.

332.6   CN   ISSN 0083-520X
VANCOUVER STOCK EXCHANGE. ANNUAL REPORT. 1908. a. Can.$5.50. Vancouver Stock Exchange, Stock Exchange Tower, 609 Granville St., P.O. Box 10333, Vancouver, B.C. V7Y 1H1, Canada. TEL 604-689-3334. Ed. Joyce Courtney. circ. 5,000.

VENTURE CAPITAL REPORT. see BUSINESS AND ECONOMICS — Small Business

332.6   US   ISSN 0092-749X
WALKER'S MANUAL OF WESTERN CORPORATIONS. 1909. a. $345. Walker's Manual, 14032 Lake St., Ste. 101, Garden Grove, CA 92643. TEL 714-636-2952. Ed. Carol T. Honey. adv. index. (back issues avail.)
    Formerly: Walker's Manual of Western Corporations & Securities.

332.6   US   ISSN 0083-7075
WALL STREET JOURNAL INDEX. 1958. a. and m. $305 for annual; $550 for m. plus a.; $333 for m. only. Dow Jones & Co., Inc., 200 Liberty St., New York, NY 10281 TEL 413-592-7761. (Subscr. to: Box 455, Chicopee, MA 01021) Ed. Sharon Russin. (microfiche)
●Also available online.

332.6   US
WALL STREET RESEARCH REPORTS. irreg. Frost & Sullivan, Inc., 106 Fulton St., New York, NY 10038. TEL 212-233-1080.

332.6   US
WHITE'S TAX EXEMPT BOND MARKET RATINGS. 1954. a. $300. Delta Press, 100 Ave. of the Americas, New York, NY 10013. TEL 212-285-6400. Ed. Wilson White, Jr.

332.6   US   ISSN 0090-418X
WHO'S WHO IN THE SECURITIES INDUSTRY. (Published for the annual convention of the Securities Industry Association as a part of the Economist SIA convention editions. Issued formerly as part of Economist I.B.A. convention editions) 1912. a. $18. ‡ (Securities Industry Association) Economist Publishing Co., 311 W. Superior St., Ste. 316, Chicago, IL 60610. Ed. George R. Stearns. adv. illus. circ. 6,000.

332.6   AU   ISSN 0042-4250
WIENER BOERSEKAMMER. VERORDNUNGSBLATT. 1870. irreg., several times a week. Wiener Boersekammer, Wipplingerstr 34, A-1011 Vienna 1, Austria. index. (looseleaf format)

BUSINESS AND ECONOMICS — LABOR AND INDUSTRIAL RELATIONS

332.67   US
WIESENBERGER SALESMAN'S PACKAGE. 1941. a. with q. updates. $225. Warren, Gorham & Lamont, Inc., 210 South St., Boston, MA 02111. TEL 800-922-0066.

332.6   US
WISCONSIN. COMMISSIONER OF SECURITIES. BIENNIAL REPORT. 1924. biennial since 1967. free. ‡ Commissioner of Securities, Box 1768, Madison, WI 53701. TEL 608-266-3431. circ. 1,000.
    Formerly: Wisconsin. Commissioner of Securities. Annual Report (ISSN 0084-0548)

332.6   330.9   UK   ISSN 0264-0732
WORLD LEASING YEARBOOK. 1980. a. £40($90) Hawkins Publishers Ltd., Laxfield House, 2 Church St., Coggeshall, Essex CO6 1TU, England. Ed. Adrian Hornbrook. adv. circ. 7,000. (back issues avail.)

332.6   LE   ISSN 0075-8361
YEAR-BOOK OF THE LEBANESE JOINT-STOCK COMPANIES/ANNUAIRE DES SOCIETES LIBANAISES PAR ACTION. (Text in French; index in Arabic, English and French) 1964. biennial. $45. Middle East Commercial Information Center, P.O. Box 6466, Beirut, Lebanon (Dist. by Bernan Associates-Unipub, 4611-F Assembly Dr., Lanham, MD 20706-4391) Ed. Charles G. Gedeon. adv. circ. 2,000.

332.6   LE
YEAR-BOOK OF THE LEBANESE LIMITED LIABILITY COMPANIES/ANNUAIRE DES SOCIETES LIBANAISES A RESPONSIBILITE LIMITEE. (Text in French) 1973. a, latest 1977. $45. Middle East Commercial Information Center, Box 6466, Beirut, Lebanon (Dist. by: Bernan Associates-Unipub, 4611-F Assembly Dr., Lanham, MD 20706-4391) Ed. Charles C. Gadeon. adv. index. circ. 2,000.

332.6   SZ
ZUERCHER BOERSE. JAHRESBERICHT. 1877. a. free. (Zurich Stock Exchange) Effektenboersenverein Zuerich, Bleicherweg 5, 8001 Zurich, Switzerland. charts. illus. stat. circ. 12,000.

BUSINESS AND ECONOMICS — Labor And Industrial Relations

see also Labor Unions

331.2   658   US
A M S DATA PROCESSING SALARIES REPORT. 1983. a. $75 to members; non-members $115. Association for Management Success, 2360 Maryland Rd., Willow Grove, PA 19090. TEL 215-659-4300. Ed. Cindy Latessa.
    Formerly: A M S Systems and Processing Salaries Report.

331.2   US   ISSN 0278-1506
A M S GUIDE TO MANAGEMENT COMPENSATION. 1973. a. $75 to members; non-members $115. Association for Management Success, 2360 Maryland Rd., Willow Grove, PA 19090. TEL 215-659-4300.

331.2   US
A M S OFFICE SALARIES REPORT; salary & benefits information for office employees in the U.S. and Canada. (Former name of issuing body: Administrative Management Society) 1946. a. $75 to members; non-members $115. Association for Management Success, 2360 Maryland Rd., Willow Grove, PA 19090. TEL 215-659-4300. Ed. Linda Garges.
    Formerly: A M S Directory of Office Salaries.

658.31   US
A S T D BUYERS GUIDE AND CONSULTANTS DIRECTORY.* a. $9.95 to non-members. American Society for Training and Development, 1630 Duke St., No. 1443, Alexandria, VA 22314. Ed. Oliver E. Ellis.
    Former titles: Training Resources; A S T D Consultant Directory (ISSN 0098-5619)

AARBOG FOR ARBEJDERBEVAEGELSENS HISTORIE. see *HISTORY — History Of Europe*

331   SW
AARET SOM GAATT; Verksamhetsberaettelse foer T C O. 1944. a. Tjaenstemaennens Central Organisation - Swedish Central Organization of Salaried Employees, Linnegatan 14, Box 5252, 102 45 Stockholm, Sweden. circ. 15,000.
    Formerly: Tjaenstemaennens Central Organisation. Aarsrapport (ISSN 0082-4542)

331   CN
ABORDAGE. 1974. irreg. Syndicat Canadien de la Fonction Publique, Local 1575, Universite du Quebec a Rimouski, 300 Ave. des Ursulines, Rimouski, Que. G5L 3A1, Canada. TEL 418-681-6024. bk. rev. circ. 290. (looseleaf format; back issues avail.)

331.1   US
ADVANCES IN INDUSTRIAL AND LABOR RELATIONS. 1983. a. $23.75 to individuals; institutions $47.50. J A I Press Inc., Box 1678, 36 Sherwood Pl., Greenwich, CT 06836. TEL 203-661-6702. Ed. David B. Lipsky.

331   US   ISSN 0148-8147
AFFIRMATIVE ACTION COMPLIANCE MANUAL FOR FEDERAL CONTRACTORS. 1975. irreg. $196. The Bureau of National Affairs, Inc., 1231 25th St., N.W., Washington, DC 20037. TEL 202-452-4200. Ed. Michael Levin-Epstein. index. (looseleaf format)

AGRICULTURAL WAGES IN INDIA. see *AGRICULTURE — Agricultural Economics*

331.1   US
ALABAMA. DEPARTMENT OF INDUSTRIAL RELATIONS. ANNUAL PLANNING INFORMATION. 1976. a. free. Department of Industrial Relations, Research and Statistics Division, Montgomery, AL 36130. TEL 205-832-6106. illus. stat. circ. 350.
    Formerly: Alabama. Department of Industrial Relations. Annual Manpower Planning Report (ISSN 0361-297X)

AMERICAN ASSOCIATION OF ENGINEERING SOCIETIES. ENGINEERING MANPOWER COMMISSION. ENGINEERING AND TECHNOLOGY ENROLLMENTS. see *ENGINEERING*

AMERICAN ASSOCIATION OF ENGINEERING SOCIETIES. ENGINEERING MANPOWER COMMISSION. ENGINEERS' SALARIES: SPECIAL INDUSTRY REPORT. see *ENGINEERING*

AMERICAN ASSOCIATION OF ENGINEERING SOCIETIES. ENGINEERING MANPOWER COMMISSION. PROFESSIONAL INCOME OF ENGINEERS. see *ENGINEERING*

331   US
AMERICAN COMPANESATION ASSOCIATION. CONFERENCE HIGHLIGHTS. a. $15. American Compensation Association, 6619 N. Scottsdale Rd., Box 92312, Phoenix, AZ 85038-9312. TEL 602-951-9191.

331   US
AMERICAN COMPENSATION ASSOCIATION. CONFERENCE. PROCEEDINGS. 1956. a. $10. American Compensation Association, 6619 N. Scottsdale Rd., Scottsdale, AZ 85253-7802. TEL 602-951-9191. Ed. Kathy Davidson. circ. 10,000.
    Formerly: American Compensation Association. National Conference. Proceedings.

331   368   DK   ISSN 0109-1107
ANKENAEVNET FOR ARBEJDSLOESHEDSFORSIKRINGEN. BERETNING. 1972. a. free. Ankenaevnet for Arbejdsloeshedsforsikringen, Amaliegade 25, 1256 Copenhagen K, Denmark. circ. 3,600.

331   US   ISSN 0193-3418
ANNUAL NATIONAL CONFERENCE ON LABOR AT NEW YORK UNIVERSITY. PROCEEDINGS. 1948. a. price varies. (New York University, Institute of Labor Relations) Matthew Bender & Co., Inc., 235 E. 45 St, New York, NY 10017. TEL 212-661-5050. Ed. Richard Adelman. cum.index: 1973-1983. (back issues avail.) Indexed: Leg.Per. C.L.I. L.R.I.
    Supersedes (1948-1976): Conference on Labor, New York University. Proceedings (ISSN 0069-8563)

331.11   US
ANNUAL PLANNING INFORMATION BRIDGEPORT-NORWALK-STAMFORD-VALLEY SERVICE DELIVERY AREA. a. Labor Department, Employment Security Division, 200 Folly Brook Blvd., Wethersfield, CT 06109. TEL 203-566-3462. Ed. Roger Skelly. circ. 325.
    Former titles: Annual Planning Information for Stamford Labor Market Area & Stamford Annual Planning Information.

331.11   US
ANNUAL PLANNING INFORMATION: SACRAMENTO METROPOLITAN STATISTICAL AREA. 1980. a. Health and Welfare Agency, Employment Development Department, Employment Data and Research Division, 800 Capitol Mall, Sacramento, CA 95814. TEL 916-322-8791. circ. 500.
    Formerly: Annual Planning Information: Sacramento Standard Metropolitan Statistical Area.

331.2   AU
ARBEITSKOSTEN IN DER INDUSTRIE OESTERREICHS. 1960. triennial. free. Bundeskammer der Gewerblichen Wirtschaft, Abteilung fuer Statistik und Dokumentation, Wiedner Hauptstr. 63, Postfach 182, A-1045 Vienna, Austria. Ed. Guenther Herget. stat. circ. 2, 000.

331   AU   ISSN 0587-1689
ARBEITSMARKT POLITIK. 1969. irreg. price varies. Hochschule fuer Sozial- und Wirtschaftswissenschaften, Linz, Oesterreichisches Institut fuer Arbeitsmarkt Politik, 4045 Auhof, A-4045 Linz/Donau, Austria.

331.15   340   GW   ISSN 0066-586X
ARBEITSRECHT DER GEGENWART. 1963. a. price varies. Erich Schmidt Verlag GmbH, Viktoriastr. 44A, Postfach 7330, 4800 Bielefeld 1, W. Germany (B.R.D.) Ed. Gerhard Mueller. adv. bk. rev.

331   SZ   ISSN 0003-777X
ARBEITSRECHT UND ARBEITSLOSENVERSICHERUNG. (Text in French and German) 1953. irreg. (3-4/yr.) 25 Fr. (Bundesamt fuer Industrie, Gewerbe und Arbeit) Schulthess Polygraphischer Verlag AG, Zwingliplatz 2, 8022 Zurich, Switzerland. adv. index. circ. 1,677.

ARBEJDERBEVAEGELSENS BIBLIOTEK OG ARKIV/LABOUR MOVEMENT LIBRARY AND ARCHIVE, DENMARK; liste over loebende tidsskrifter og aarboeger paa A B A. see *BUSINESS AND ECONOMICS — Abstracting, Bibliographies, Statistics*

331   DK   ISSN 0107-4628
ARBEJDERBEVAEGELSENS BIBLIOTEK OG ARKIV. BIBLIOGRAFISKE SERIE. 1973. irreg. Arbejderbevaegelsens Bibliotek og Arkiv, Rejsbygade 1, Folkets Hus, DK-1759 Copenhagen V, Denmark. circ. 700.

331   DK   ISSN 0108-9625
ARBEJDERBEVAEGELSENS ERHVERVSRAAD. BERETNING. 1982. a. free. Arbejderbevaegelsens Erhvervsraad, Faellessekretariat, Kooperationens Hus, Reventlowsgade 14/2, 1651 Copenhagen V, Denmark. illus. circ. 2,500.

331   DK
ARBEJDERHISTORIE; meddelelser om forskning i arbejderbevaegelsens historie. 1973. biennial. Selskabet til Forskning i Arbejderbevaegelsens Historie, Rejsbygade, DK-1759 Copenhagen V, Denmark. bk. rev. bibl. circ. 1,100. Indexed: Hist.Abstr. Amer.Hist.& Life.

331   DK   ISSN 0109-1158
ARBEJDERMUSEET. AARBOG. 1983. a. Kr.10. Arbejdermuseet, Roemersgade 22, 1362 Copenhagen K, Denmark. Ed. Peter Ludvigsen. illus. circ. 5,000.

331   DK   ISSN 0109-1514
ARBEJDSDIREKTORATET BERETNING OM ARBEJDSFORMIDLIGEN OG ARBEJDSLOESHEDSFORSIKRINGEN. 1978. a. Arbejdsdirektoratet, Adelgade 13, 1304 Copenhagen K, Denmark. illus.

BUSINESS AND ECONOMICS — LABOR AND INDUSTRIAL RELATIONS

331 DK ISSN 0107-9735
ARBEJDSMARKEDET OG
ARBEJDSMARKEDSPOLOTIK/LABOR
MARKET AND LABOR MARKET POLICY.
1978. a. Arbejdsministeriet, Oekonomisk-Statistisk
Konsulent, Laksegade 19, 1063 Copenhagen K,
Denmark. circ. 600.

331 DK ISSN 0106-7826
ARBEJDSMARKEDSOVERSIGT; nationalt forloeb,
regionale fordelinger. 1978. a. free.
Arbejdsdirektoratet, Adelgade 13, 1304 Copenhagen
K, Denmark. illus.

331 DK ISSN 0108-7150
ARBEJDSRETLIGT TIDSSKRIFT; arbejdsrettens
domme, arbejdsretlige kendelser. 1980. a. Kr.335.
Jurist- og Oekonomforbundets Forlag, Gothersgade
133, D-1123 Copenhagen K, Denmark. Eds. C. Ove
Christensen, Ole Hasselbalch.
Formed by the merger of: Arbejdsretlige Domme
& Arbejdsretlige Kendelser.

331 948 SW
ARBETARROERELSENS AARSBOK. 1926. a.
Upplandsgatan 5, 111 81 Stockholm, Sweden.
Indexed: Hist.Abstr. Amer.Hist.& Life.
Formerly: Arbetarnas Kulturhistoriskap. Notiser.

331.1 340 US
ARBITRATION & THE LAW. 1981. a. $50.
American Arbitration Association, Office of General
Counsel, 140 W. 51st St., New York, NY 10020.
TEL 212-484-4110. Ed. Michael F. Hoellering.
abstr. index. circ. 600.

331.09 AU ISSN 0003-8849
ARCHIV. 1961. a. S.100 or membership. Verein fuer
Geschichte der Arbeiterbewegung, Albertgasse 23,
A-1080 Vienna, Austria. Ed. Wolfgang
Maderthaner. bk. rev. bibl. illus. index. circ. 1,000.

331 US
ARCHIVES OF LABOR AND URBAN AFFAIRS
NEWSLETTER. 1971. irreg. free. Wayne State
University, Archives of Labor and Urban Affairs,
Walter Reuther Library, 5401 Cass Ave., Detroit,
MI 48202. TEL 313-577-2424. Ed. Malvina H.
Abonyl. bibl. circ. 3,000. (back issues avail.)
Formerly: Archives of Labor History and Urban
Affairs Newsletter (ISSN 0044-8729)

331.1 US
ARKANSAS COVERED EMPLOYMENT AND
EARNINGS. 1948. irreg. free. Employment
Security Division, Research and Analysis Section,
Box 2981, Little Rock, AR 72203. TEL 501-371-
1541. circ. 300.
Formerly: Arkansas Average Covered
Employment and Earnings by County and Industry
(ISSN 0092-2889)

331 JA
ASIAN REGIONAL CONFERENCE ON
INDUSTRIAL RELATIONS. PROCEEDINGS.
(Text in English) 1965. biennial. price varies. Japan
Institute of Labour - Nihon Rodo Kyokai, Chutaikin
Bldg, 7-6 Shibakoen 1-chome, Minato-ku, Tokyo
105, Japan. circ. 700.
Formerly: Japan Institute of Labour. Proceedings.

331.1 341.57 IO
ATMA JAYA RESEARCH CENTRE.
INTERNATIONAL CONTRACT LABOUR. 1983.
irreg. Atma Jaya Research Centre - Pusat Penelitian
Atma Jaya, Jalan Jenderal Sudirma 49a, Box 2639,
Jakarta 10001, Indonesia.

AVERAGE WAGE RATES OF FARM WORKERS
IN THE PHILIPPINES. see AGRICULTURE —
Agricultural Economics

331 GW ISSN 0342-3875
BEIHEFTE ZUR INTERNATIONALEN
WISSENSCHAFTLICHEN KORRESPONDENZ
ZUR GESCHICHTE DER DEUTSCHEN
ARBEITERBEWEGUNG. 1973. irreg. price varies.
(Historiche Kommission zu Berlin) Colloquium
Verlag, Unter den Eichen 93, 1000 Berlin 45, W.
Germany (B.R.D.) Ed. Henryk Skrzypczak. circ. 1,
000.

331 BE
BELGIUM. OFFICE NATIONAL DE L'EMPLOI.
ETUDES ECONOMIQUES ET SOCIALES. 1935.
a. 650 Fr. Office National de l'Emploi, Bd. de
l'Empereur 7, 1000 Brussels, Belgium. circ. 3,000.
Incorporating: Belgium. Office National de
l'Emploi. Rapport Annuel (ISSN 0067-5644)

331 DK ISSN 0106-7052
BERETNING OVER ARBEJDSMILJOEFONDETS
VIRKSOMHED. 1977. a. free. Ministry of Labor,
Arbejdsmiljoefondet, Vesterbrogade 69, DK-1620
Copenhagen V, Denmark. Ed. Carsten Faelling.

331 II ISSN 0067-9917
BOMBAY LABOUR JOURNAL.* (Text in English)
1960. a. free. Bombay Labour Institute, Dadabhai
Chamarbaugwala Rd., Parel, Bombay 12, India. Ed.
Mrs. S.A. Vaidya.

331 BL
BRAZIL. MINISTERIO DO TRABALHO E
PREVIDENCIA SOCIAL. CENTRO DE
DOCUMENTACAO E INFORMATICA.
MERCADO DE TRABALHO: FLUTUACAO.*
1972. irreg. Ministerio do Trabalho e Previdencia
Social, Centro de Documentacao e Informatica,
Avenida Pres. A. Carlos 251, 13 andar, ZC-P2000
Rio de Janeiro, Brazil.

331 CN ISSN 0319-0404
BRITISH COLUMBIA. LABOUR RELATIONS
BOARD. ANNUAL REPORT. 1974. a. Can.$5.
Labour Relations Board, 1275 W. 6th Ave.,
Vancouver, B.C. V6H 1A6, Canada. TEL 604-660-
1300. circ. 500.

331.2 CN ISSN 0705-9698
BRITISH COLUMBIA. MINISTRY OF LABOUR.
ANNUAL REPORT. 1918. a. free. Ministry of
Labour, Victoria, B.C., Canada. TEL 604-389-3067.
Ed. George Dobie. illus. circ. 3,000.
Formerly: British Columbia. Department of
Labour. Annual Report (ISSN 0381-2898)

331.2 CN ISSN 0703-0665
BRITISH COLUMBIA. MINISTRY OF LABOUR.
NEGOTIATED WORKING CONDITIONS. a.
Can.$15. Ministry of Labour, Policy and Planning
Branch, Victoria, B.C., Canada. TEL 604-389-3831.
illus.
Formerly: Working Conditions in British
Columbia Industry.

331 NE
BULLETIN OF COMPARATIVE LABOUR
RELATIONS. (Text in English) irreg. (1-2/yr.)
price varies. (Rijksuniversiteit Te Leuven, Institute
for Labour Relations, BE) Kluwer Law and
Taxation Publishers, Postbus 23, 7400 GA
Deventer, Netherlands. Ed. R. Blanpain. Indexed:
BPIA.

331.1 US ISSN 0362-4129
CALIFORNIA. DEPARTMENT OF INDUSTRIAL
RELATIONS. ANNUAL REPORT. 1883. a.
Department of Industrial Relations, Box 603, San
Francisco, CA 94101. TEL 415-557-4070. Ed.
Richard Stephens. illus. Key Title: Annual Report
for the Department of Industrial Relations.

331.1 US ISSN 0008-1191
CALIFORNIA INDUSTRIAL RELATIONS
REPORTS. 1953. irreg. free. Department of
Industrial Relations, Division of Labor Statistics and
Research, Box 603, San Francisco, CA 94101. TEL
415-557-2184. charts. stat.

CALIFORNIA WORK INJURIES AND
ILLNESSES. see INDUSTRIAL HEALTH AND
SAFETY — Abstracting, Bibliographies, Statistics

331.11 331.4 US
CALIFORNIA YOUTH AUTHORITY'S STATUS
OF FEMALE EMPLOYEES. REPORT. 1981.
irreg. Department of Youth Authority, 4241
Williamsborough Dr., Sacramento, CA 95823. TEL
916-445-4673. circ. 1,200.

330 UK
CAMBRIDGE UNIVERSITY. DEPARTMENT OF
APPLIED ECONOMICS. PAPERS IN
INDUSTRIAL RELATIONS AND LABOUR.
1975. irreg., no.6, 1981. price varies. Cambridge
University Press, Edinburgh Bldg., Shaftesbury Rd.,
Cambridge CB2 2RU, England (And 32 E. 57th St.,
New York, NY 10022)

331 CN
CANADA. LABOUR CANADA. ANNUAL
REVIEW. a. free. Labour Canada, Ottawa, Ont.
K1A 0J2, Canada TEL 613-997-2617. (Subscr. to:
Canadian Government Publishing Centre, Supply
and Services Canada, Ottawa, Ont. K1A 0S9,
Canada) (reprint service avail. from MML)

331 CN ISSN 0068-743X
CANADA. LABOUR CANADA. WAGE RATES,
SALARIES AND HOURS OF LABOUR. (Text in
English and French) 1916. a. Labour Canada,
Ottawa, Ont. K1A 0J2, Canada TEL 613-997-2617.
(Subscr. to: Canadian Government Publishing
Centre, Supply and Services Canada, Ottawa, Ont.
K1A 0S9, Canada) (reprint service avail. from
MML)

331 CN ISSN 0711-849X
CANADA. LABOUR RELATIONS BOARD.
ANNUAL REPORT. 1980/81. a. free. Labour
Relations Board, 400 University Ave., Toronto, Ont.
M7A 1V4, Canada. TEL 416-965-4151. Ed. Colleen
Edwards. circ. 1,150.

CANADA. PENSION REVIEW BOARD.
REPORTS/RECUEIL DES ARRETS DU
CONSEIL DE REVISION DES PENSIONS. see
MILITARY

331.4 340 CN
CANADA. WOMEN'S BUREAU. WOMEN IN THE
LABOUR FORCE. (Text in English and French)
1968. a. free. Labour Canada, Women's Bureau,
Ottawa K1A 0J2, Ont., Canada. circ. 10,000.
Formerly (until 1979): Canada. Women's Bureau.
Women in the Labour Force: Facts and Figures
(ISSN 0068-7448)

331 CN ISSN 0068-905X
CANADIAN LABOUR TERMS. irreg., 8th ed., 1984.
Can.$5. C C H Canadian Ltd., 6 Garamond Ct.,
Don Mills, Ont. M3C 1Z5, Canada. TEL 416-441-
2992. Indexed: Bus.Ind.

331.2 CN ISSN 0705-6680
CANADIAN PERSPECTIVE. 1976. irreg. $25 (free
to members) Association of Canadian Pension
Management, 2 Bloor St. W., Rm. 503, Toronto,
Ont. M4W 3E2, Canada. TEL 416-964-1260.

331 US ISSN 0361-5057
COLLEGE RECRUITING REPORT. 1972. a. $110.
Abbott, Langer & Associates, 548 First St., Crete,
IL 60417. TEL 312-672-4200. Ed. Steven Langer.
circ. 500.

331 368.4 CK
COLOMBIA. MINISTERIO DE TRABAJO Y
SEGURIDAD SOCIAL. MEMORIA. 1967. a.
Ministerio de Trabajo y Seguridad Social, Seccion
Biblioteca & Publicaciones, Bogota, Colombia.
Supersedes: Colombia. Ministerio de Trabajo,
Higiene y Prevision Social. Memoria.

331 US ISSN 0278-0992
COMPENSATION IN MANUFACTURING -
ENGINEERS AND MANAGERS. 1976. biennial.
$110. (Society of Manufacturing Engineers) Abbott,
Langer and Associates, 548 First St., Crete, IL
60417. TEL 312-672-4200. Ed. Steven Langer.

331 US
COMPENSATION IN THE ACCOUNTING/
FINANCIAL FIELD. 1980. a. $175. Abbott,
Langer & Associates, 548 First St., Crete, IL 60417.
TEL 312-672-4200. Ed. Steven Langer.
Formerly: Accounting/Financial Report.

331 US
COMPENSATION IN THE M I S/D P FIELD.
(Management Information Systems/Data
Processing) 1984. a. $250. Abbott, Langer &
Associates, 548 First St., Crete, IL 60417. TEL 312-
672-4200. Ed. Steven Langer.

331 US
COMPENSATION IN THE SECURITY/LOSS
PREVENTION FIELD. 1978. biennial. $110.
(American Society for Industrial Security) Abbott,
Langer & Associates, 548 First St., Crete, IL 60417.
TEL 312-672-4200. Ed. Steven Langer.
Formerly: Security Report.

BUSINESS AND ECONOMICS — LABOR AND INDUSTRIAL RELATIONS

331 US
COMPENSATION IN TRAINING & DEVELOPMENT. 1981. a. $110. (American Society for Training & Development) Abbott, Langer & Associates, 548 First St., Crete, IL 60417. TEL 312-672-4200. Ed. Steven Langer.
Formerly: Compensation in Human Resources Development.

331 US
COMPENSATION OF ATTORNEYS (NON-LAW FIRMS) 1979. a. $175. Abbott, Langer & Associates, 548 First St., Crete, IL 60417. TEL 312-672-4200. Ed. Steven Langer.

331 US
COMPENSATION OF INDUSTRIAL ENGINEERS. 1972. a. $90. (Institute of Industrial Engineers) Abbott, Langer & Associates, 548 First St., Crete, IL 60417 TEL 312-672-4200. (Norcross, GA 30092) Ed. Steven Langer.

331.1 II ISSN 0069-8555
CONFERENCE ON HUMAN RELATIONS IN INDUSTRY. PROCEEDINGS. (Text in English) 1959. a. $4. ‡ South India Textile Research Association, Coimbatore 641014, India. Ed. P.V. Veeraraghavan. bk. rev. circ. 600.

331.4 US ISSN 0146-3608
CONTRIBUTIONS IN LABOR HISTORY. 1977. irreg., no.14, 1983. price varies. Greenwood Press, 88 Post Rd. W., Box 5007, Westport, CT 06881. TEL 203-226-3571. Eds. Milton Cantor, Bruce Laurie.

331.1 US ISSN 0070-0029
CORNELL INTERNATIONAL INDUSTRIAL AND LABOR RELATIONS REPORTS. 1954. irreg., no.13, 1987. price varies. (New York State School of Industrial and Labor Relations) I L R Press, Cornell University, Ithaca, NY 14851-0952. TEL 607-255-3061.

331.1 US ISSN 0070-0053
CORNELL STUDIES IN INDUSTRIAL AND LABOR RELATIONS. 1951. irreg., no.22, 1982. price varies. (New York State School of Industrial and Labor Relations) I L R Press, Cornell University, Ithaca, NY 14851-0952. TEL 607-255-3061.

331 US
COVERED EMPLOYMENT TRENDS IN NEW JERSEY. 1944. a. free. ‡ Department of Labor, Division of Planning and Research, Office of Demographic and Economic Analysis, CN-383, Trenton, NJ 08625. TEL 609-292-6225. circ. 1,100.
Former titles: Covered Employment Trends in New Jersey by Geographical Areas of the State & New Jersey Covered Employment Trends by Geographical Areas of the State (ISSN 0092-1459)

CURRENT GOVERNMENTS REPORTS: COUNTY EMPLOYMENT. see *PUBLIC ADMINISTRATION*

CURRENT GOVERNMENTS REPORTS: FINANCES OF EMPLOYEE RETIREMENT SYSTEMS OF STATE AND LOCAL GOVERNMENTS. see *BUSINESS AND ECONOMICS — Public Finance, Taxation*

331 US
CURRENT GOVERNMENTS REPORTS: PUBLIC EMPLOYMENT. (Series GE-1) 1940. a. price varies. U.S. Bureau of the Census, Customer Services, Washington, DC 20233. TEL 301-763-4100. (also avail. in microfiche)

331.1 CN ISSN 0318-952X
CURRENT INDUSTRIAL RELATIONS SCENE IN CANADA. 1973. a. Can.$100. Queen's University, Industrial Relations Centre, Kingston, Ont. K7L 3N6, Canada. TEL 613-545-2193. circ. 1,000.

368.4 331 CY ISSN 0070-2390
CYPRUS. MINISTRY OF LABOUR AND SOCIAL INSURANCE. ANNUAL REPORT. (Text in Greek; summary in English available) 1943. a. free. Ministry of Labour and Social Insurance, Nicosia, Cyprus.

331 DK ISSN 0106-6838
DENMARK. ARBEJDSTILSYNET. RAPPORT. no.1, 1978. irreg. Kr.25. Arbejdstilsynet, Tryksagsafdelningen, Landskronagade 33-35, 2100 Copenhagen OE, Denmark. (Co-sponsor: Arbejdsmiljoeinstituttet) illus.

331 DK ISSN 0900-6885
DENMARK. DIREKTORATET FOR ARBEJDSTILSYNET. ARBEJDSTILSYNETS AARSBERETNING. (Text in Danish; summaries in English) a. (Direktoratet for Arbejdstilsynet) Bibliotekscentralen, Telegrafvej 5, DK-2750 Ballerup, Denmark.

331 US
DIRECTORY OF CAREER RESOURCES FOR MINORITIES; a guide to career resources and opportunities for minorities. 1980. a? $37.50. Ready Reference Press, Box 5169, Santa Monica, CA 90405. Ed. Alvin Renetzky.

331 UK
DIRECTORY OF EMPLOYERS ASSOCIATIONS, TRADE UNIONS, JOINT ORGANIZATIONS ETC. irreg. H M S O, Standing Orders, P.O. Box 276, Cornwall House, London SW8 5DT, England. circ. 1,325.

331 US ISSN 0735-3707
DIRECTORY OF OUTPLACEMENT FIRMS. 1980. irreg., 4th edt., 1986. price varies. Kennedy & Kennedy, Inc., Templeton Rd., Fitzwilliam, NH 03447. Ed. James H. Kennedy.

331 EI
DOCUMENTATION EUROPEENNE - SERIE SYNDICALE ET OUVRIERE. (Editions also in Dutch, German and Italian) 1968. irreg. free. ‡ Commission of the European Communities, Direction Generale de la Presse et Information, Rue de la Loi 200, 1049 Brussels, Belgium (Dist. in U.S. by European Community Information Service, 2100 M St. N.W., Suite 707, Washington, DC 20037) circ. controlled.

331.1 US
E E O C COMPLIANCE MANUAL. 1975. irreg. $128. The Bureau of National Affairs, Inc., 1231 25th St., N.W., Washington, DC 20037. TEL 202-452-4200. Ed. Michael Levin-Epstein. (looseleaf format)

331 UK ISSN 0142-4866
E O C RESEARCH BULLETIN. 1978. irreg. free. Equal Opportunities Commission, Research Unit, Overseas House, Quay St., Manchester, England. Ed. E. Puttick. circ. 2,000.

ECONOMIES ET SOCIETES. SERIE A B. ECONOMIE DU TRAVAIL. see *BUSINESS AND ECONOMICS*

331.1 PR ISSN 0555-6635
EMPLEO Y DESEMPLEO EN PUERTO RICO/ EMPLOYMENT AND UNEMPLOYMENT IN PUERTO RICO: CALENDAR YEARS. (Text in English and Spanish) 1967. a. free. Department of Labor & Human Resources, Hato Rey, PR 00917.

331.2 CN ISSN 0701-1539
EMPLOYEE BENEFIT COSTS IN CANADA. 1953. biennial. Can.$295. Stevenson, Kellogg, Ernst & Whinney, 2300 Yonge St., Ste. 1800, Toronto, Ont. M4P 1G2, Canada. TEL 416-483-4313. Ed. D. Scott MacCrimmon. circ. 300.
Formerly: Fringe Benefit Costs in Canada (ISSN 0071-9625)

EXECUTIVE COMPENSATION SERVICE. REPORTS ON INTERNATIONAL COMPENSATION. BRAZIL. see *BUSINESS AND ECONOMICS — Management*

EXECUTIVE COMPENSATION SERVICE. TECHNICIAN REPORT. see *BUSINESS AND ECONOMICS — Management*

331.4 AT
FACTS ON WOMEN AT WORK IN AUSTRALIA. 1979. a. Aus.$1.90. Australian Government Publishing Service, Box 84, Canberra, ACT 2600, Australia. circ. 900.

331.11 US
FEDERAL CIVILIAN WORK FORCE STATISTICS. AFFIRMATIVE EMPLOYMENT STATISTICS. 1965. biennial. ‡ U.S. Office of Personnel Management, Personnel Systems and Oversight Group, Work Force Analysis and Statistics Division, Washington, DC 20415 TEL 202-655-4000. (Subscr. to Supt. of Docs., Govt. Printing Off., Washington, DC 20402) circ. 2,000. (also avail. in microfilm) Indexed: C.I.S.Ind.
Former titles: Federal Civilian Work Force Statistics. Equal Employment Opportunity Statistics; Federal Civilian Work Force Statistics. Minority Group Employment in the Federal Government; Federal Civilian Manpower Statistics. Minority Group Employment in the Federal Government; Minority Group Employment in the Federal Government; Study of Minority Group Employment in the Federal Government.

331 US
FEDERAL CIVILIAN WORK FORCE STATISTICS. OCCUPATIONS OF FEDERAL WHITE-COLLAR AND BLUE-COLLAR WORKERS. 1956. biennial. ‡ U.S. Office of Personnel Management, Personnel Systems and Oversight, Work Force Analysis and Statistics Division, 1900 E St. N.W., Washington, DC 20415 TEL 202-632-5417. (Subscr. to: National Technical Information Service, 5285 Port Royal Rd., Springfield, VA 22161) (also avail. in microfilm) Indexed: C.I.S.Ind.
Former titles: Federal Civilian Work Force Statistics. Occupations of Federal White-Collar Workers (ISSN 0146-4906); Occupations of Federal White-Collar Workers; Federal White-Collar Workers. Their Occupations and Salaries.

331.2 US
FEDERAL CIVILIAN WORK FORCE STATISTICS. PAY STRUCTURE OF THE FEDERAL CIVIL SERVICE. 1947. a. U.S. Office of Personnel Management, Personnel Systems and Oversight, Work Force Analysis and Statistics Division, Washington, DC 20415 TEL 202-632-4921. (Subscr. to: National Technical Information Service, 5285 Port Royal Rd., Springfield, VA 22161) charts. stat. circ. 900(controlled) Indexed: C.I.S.Ind.
Former titles: Federal Civilian Manpower Statistics. Pay Structure of the Federal Civil Service; Pay Structure of the Federal Civil Service.

331 US ISSN 0277-3325
FEDERAL CIVILIAN WORK FORCE STATISTICS. WORK YEARS AND PERSONNEL COSTS. EXECUTIVE BRANCH, UNITED STATES GOVERNMENT. 1970. a. U.S. Office of Personnel Management, Personnel Systems and Oversight, Work Force Analysis and Statistics Division, 1900 E St., N.W., Washington, DC 20415 TEL 202-632-4921. (Subscr. to: National Technical Information Service, 5285 Port Royal Rd., Springfield, VA 22161) charts. stat. circ. 400(controlled)
Former titles: Work-Years and Personnel Costs. Executive Branch of the United States Government; Work-Years and Personnel Costs. Executive Branch, U.S. Government; Man-Years and Personnel Costs. Executive Branch, U.S. Government.

331 FJ
FIJI. BUREAU OF STATISTICS. NATIONWIDE UNEMPLOYMENT SURVEY. 1973. irreg. $2. Bureau of Statistics, Box 2221, Suva, Fiji.

331.11 FJ
FIJI CLASSIFICATION & DICTIONARY OF OCCUPATIONS. 1975. irreg. $5. Bureau of Statistics, Box 2221, Suva, Fiji.

331 FI ISSN 0430-5280
FINLAND. TYOVOIMAMINISTERIO. TYOVOIMAKATSAUS/FINLAND. MINISTRY OF LABOUR. LABOUR REPORTS. (Text in English or Finnish) 1957. irreg. Fmk.80. Central Statistical Office, P.O. Box 504, SF-00101 Helsinki, Finland. Ed. Oiva Loennberg. illus. circ. 2,000.

331 374 GW ISSN 0340-8973
FORSCHUNGSDOKUMENTATION ZUR ARBEITSMARKT- UND BERUFSFORSCHUNG. 1970. irreg. (2-3/yr.) DM.80. Bundesanstalt fuer Arbeit, Institut fuer Arbeitsmarkt- und Berufsforschung, Regensburger Str. 104, 8500 Nuremberg, W. Germany (B.R.D.) circ. 5,000. (back issues avail.)

BUSINESS AND ECONOMICS — LABOR AND INDUSTRIAL RELATIONS

331.11   FR
FRANCE. CENTRE D'DTUDES DE L'EMPLOI. CAHIERS. 1972. irreg., no. 29, 1986. price varies. Centre d'Etudes de l'Emploi, 51 rue de la Chaussee d'Antin, 75009 Paris Cedex 14, France.

331   FR
FRANCE. CENTRE D'ETUDES DE L'EMPLOI. DOSSIERS DE RECHERCHE. 1981. irreg., no.16, 1986. price varies. Centre d'Etudes de l'Emploi, 51 Ave de la Chaussee d'Antin, 75009 Paris Cedex 14, France.

FRANCE. INSTITUT NATIONAL DE LA STATISTIQUE ET DES ETUDES ECONOMIQUES. COLLECTIONS. SERIE D, DEMOGRAPHIE ET EMPLOI. see *POPULATION STUDIES — Abstracting, Bibliographies, Statistics*

331.2   UK   ISSN 0308-1419
GREAT BRITAIN. DEPARTMENT OF EMPLOYMENT. NEW EARNINGS SURVEY. 1970. a. £40. Department of Employment, Caxton House, Tothill St., London SW1H 9NF, England (Avail. from: H.M.S.O., 49 High Holborn, London WC1V 6HB, England)

331.1   UK
GREAT BRITAIN. DEPARTMENT OF EMPLOYMENT. RESEARCH. 1972/73. a. free. Department of Employment, Research Administration, Steel House, Tothill St., London SW1H 9NF, England (Avail. from: H.M.S.O., 49 High Holborn, London WC1V 6HB, England)

331.11   UK   ISSN 0072-6532
GREAT BRITAIN. MANPOWER RESEARCH UNIT. MANPOWER STUDIES. 1964. irreg. price varies. H.M.S.O., P.O.B. 569, London SE1 9NH, England. (reprint service avail. from UMI)

331.1   US   ISSN 0072-8853
GUIDEBOOK TO LABOR RELATIONS. a. $10.50. Commerce Clearing House, Inc., 4025 W. Peterson Ave., Chicago, IL 60646. TEL 312-583-8500.

331   US
HANDBOOK OF LABOR FORCE DATA FOR SELECTED AREAS OF OKLAHOMA. 1966. a. Employment Security Commission, Research Division, 310 Will Rogers Bldg., Oklahoma City, OK 73105. Ed. Wayne Hugus. stat. circ. 300.

331   DK   ISSN 0107-4458
HANDELSHOEJSKOLEN I KOEBENHAVN. INSTITUT FOR ORGANISATION OG ARBEJDSSOCIOLOGI. H D STUDIET I ORGANISATION; haandbog for studerende. vol.15, 1981. a. Kr.38. Handelshoejskolen i Koebenhavn, Institut for Organisation og Arbejdssociologi, Copenhagen, Denmark (Orders to: Danske Boghandleres Kommissionsanstalt, Siljangade 6, 2300 Copenhagen-S Denmark) circ. 700.
Formerly: Haandbog for Studerende ved H D Studiet i Organisation.

331   US   ISSN 0194-7818
HANDICAPPED REQUIREMENTS HANDBOOK. 1978. base vol. plus m. updates. $95. Thompson Publishing Group, Federal Programs Advisory Service, 1725 K St., N.W., Ste. 200, Washington, DC 20006. TEL 202-872-1766. Ed. Darla Fera. bk. rev.

HOGE RAAD VOOR DE MIDDENSTAND. JAARVERSLAG. see *PUBLIC ADMINISTRATION*

HUNGARY. KOZPONTI STATISZTIKAI HIVATAL. FOGLALKOZTATOTTSAG ES KERESETI ARANYOK. see *BUSINESS AND ECONOMICS — Abstracting, Bibliographies, Statistics*

331   II   ISSN 0418-5633
I.A.M.R. REPORTS. (Text in English) 1963. irreg. price varies. Institute of Applied Manpower Research, Indrapastha Estate, Mahatma Gandhi Marg, New Delhi 110002, India. Ed.Bd.

331.1   US   ISSN 0070-0177
I L R PAPERBACKS. 1967. irreg., no.18, 1983. price varies. (New York State School of Industrial and Labor Relations) I L R Press, Cornell University, Ithaca, NY 14851. TEL 607-255-3061.

331   GW
I-PUNKT. a. Echter Wuerzburg Fraenk. Gesellschaftsdruckerei u. Verlag GmbH, Postfach 55 60, Juliuspromenade 64, 8700 Wuerzburg 1, W. Germany (B.R.D.) circ. controlled.

331.12   US
IDAHO. DEPARTMENT OF EMPLOYMENT. ANNUAL PLANNING REPORT. 1972. a. free. Department of Employment, Research and Analysis, 317 Main, Boise, ID 83735. TEL 208-334-2959. Ed. Carol Johnston. circ. 1,200.

353.9   US   ISSN 0362-3912
IDAHO. DEPARTMENT OF LABOR AND INDUSTRIAL SERVICES. ANNUAL REPORT. 1974. a. Department of Labor and Industrial Services, 317 Main St., Rm. 400, Boise, ID 83720. TEL 208-334-2320. stat. Key Title: Annual Report of the Idaho Department of Labor and Industrial Services.

331   US
INCOME IN SALES/MARKETING MANAGEMENT. 1978. a. $125. (Sales & Marketing Executives-International) Abbott, Langer & Associates, 548 First St., Crete, IL 60417. TEL 312-672-4200. Ed. Steven Langer.

331   II
INDIA. MINISTRY OF LABOUR. ANNUAL REPORT. (Text in English) a. Ministry of Labour, New Delhi, India.
Supersedes (1974): India. Department of Labour and Employment. Annual Report (ISSN 0579-3238)

331   DK   ISSN 0109-4319
INDSATSEN MOD UNGDOMSARBEJDSLOESHEDEN. 1979. a. Kr.35. Arbejdsministeriet, Laksegade 19, 1063 Copenhagen K, Denmark. (Co-sponsors: Indenrigsministeriet, Undervisningsministeriet) circ. 2,700.

614.85   CN   ISSN 0073-7313
INDUSTRIAL ACCIDENT PREVENTION ASSOCIATION. GUIDE TO SAFETY. 1965. a. Can.$2.95 free to member firms. Industrial Accident Prevention Association, 2 Bloor St., Toronto, Ont. M4W 3N8, Canada. TEL 416-965-8888. circ. 60, 000.

331   AT   ISSN 0155-2589
INDUSTRIAL ARBITRATION REPORTS, NEW SOUTH WALES. 1900. irreg. Aus.$42.50. Department of Industrial Relations & Technology, 50 Phillip St., Sydney, NSW 2000, Australia (Subscr. to: Government Printing Office, 390-422 Harris St., Ultimo, N.S.W. 2007, Australia) Ed. A.K. Buckley.

331.1   US
INDUSTRIAL RELATIONS RESEARCH ASSOCIATION. ANNUAL RESEARCH VOLUME. 1947. a. $36. Industrial Relations Research Association, 7226 Social Science Bldg., University of Wisconsin, Madison, WI 53706. TEL 608-262-2762. Ed.Bd.

331   US
INDUSTRIAL RELATIONS RESEARCH ASSOCIATION. PROCEEDINGS OF THE ANNUAL MEETING. a. membership. Industrial Relations Research Association, 7226 Social Science Bldg., University of Wisconsin, Madison, WI 53706. TEL 608-262-2762. Indexed: BPIA. Bus.Ind.
Former titles: Industrial Relations Research Association. Proceedings of the Annual Winter Meeting (ISSN 0277-7347) & Industrial Relations Research Association. Proceedings of Annual Winter Meeting (ISSN 0275-3081)

331   US
INDUSTRIAL RELATIONS RESEARCH ASSOCIATION. PROCEEDINGS OF THE ANNUAL SPRING MEETING. a. membership. Industrial Relations Research Association, 7226 Social Science Bldg., University of Wisconsin, Madison, WI 53706. TEL 608-262-2762. Indexed: BPIA.

331.1   CN   ISSN 0073-7593
INDUSTRIAL RELATIONS RESEARCH IN CANADA/RECHERCHE SUR LES RELATIONS INDUSTRIELLES AU CANADA. (Text in English and French) 1969. a. free. Labour Canada, Ottawa, Ont. K1A 0J2, Canada TEL 613-997-2617. (Subscr. to: Canadian Government Publishing Centre, Supply and Services Canada, Ottawa, Ont. K1A 0S9, Canada) circ. 1,500. (reprint service avail. from MML)
Formerly: Canada. Department of Labor. Labour and Industrial Relations Research in Canada. Progress Report.

331.2   ZR
INSTITUT NATIONAL DE PREPARATION PROFESSIONNELLE. CAHIER.* irreg. 1. Institut National de Preparation Professionnelle, B.P. 7248, Kinshasa 1, Zaire. illus.

331.1   US   ISSN 0073-9421
INSTITUTE OF LABOR AND INDUSTRIAL RELATIONS. POLICY PAPERS IN HUMAN RESOURCES AND INDUSTRIAL RELATIONS. 1967. irreg., no.23, 1975. price varies. ‡ (Institute of Labor and Industrial Relations) Institute of Labor and Industrial Relations Publication, University of Michigan, Victor Vaughn Bldg., 1111 E. Catherine, Ann Arbor, MI 48109-2054. Ed. Louis A. Ferman. (reprint service avail. from UMI)

331   NG   ISSN 0538-2807
INTER-AFRICAN LABOUR CONFERENCE REPORTS, RECOMMENDATIONS AND CONCLUSIONS.* irreg. (Commission for Technical Co-Operation in Africa South of the Sahara) Maison de l'Afrique, B.P. 878, Niamey, Niger.

331   US
INTER-CITY WAGE & SALARY DIFFERENTIALS. 1978. a. $110. Abbott, Langer & Associates, 548 First St., Crete, IL 60417. TEL 312-672-4200. Ed. Steven Langer.

331   CN
INTERNATIONAL CONFERENCE ON TRENDS IN INDUSTRIAL AND LABOUR RELATIONS. no. 2, 1976. irreg. McGill University, Industrial Relations Centre, Montreal, Que. H3A 1G5, Canada. TEL 514-392-3077. Ed. Prof. Frances Bairstow.

331   UN
INTERNATIONAL INSTITUTE FOR LABOUR STUDIES. PUBLIC LECTURE SERIES. 1975. irreg. 5 Fr. International Institute for Labour Studies, C.P. 6, CH-1211 Geneva 22, Switzerland.

331   UK   ISSN 0074-6509
INTERNATIONAL INSTITUTE FOR LABOUR STUDIES. PUBLICATIONS. 1966. irreg. Macmillan Press Ltd. (Subsidiary of: Macmillan Publishers Ltd.) Little Essex St., London WC2R 3LF, England.

331   UN
INTERNATIONAL INSTITUTE FOR LABOUR STUDIES. RESEARCH SERIES. 1976. irreg. price varies. International Institute for Labour Studies, Box 6, CH-1211 Geneva 22, Switzerland.

331   UN   ISSN 0074-6673
INTERNATIONAL LABOUR CONFERENCE. REPORTS TO THE CONFERENCE AND RECORD OF PROCEEDINGS. (Editions in English, French, German, Spanish and Russian) 1919. a. 350 Fr.($199.50) covering 14 to 18 vols. per conference. International Labour Office - Bureau International du Travail, Publications Sales Service, CH-1211 Geneva 22, Switzerland (Dist. in U.S. by: I L O Branch Office, 1750 New York Ave., N.W., Washington, DC 20006) (back vols. avail. in microform)

INTERNATIONAL LABOUR LAW REPORTS. see *LAW*

BUSINESS AND ECONOMICS — LABOR AND INDUSTRIAL RELATIONS

331   UN   ISSN 0378-5882
INTERNATIONAL LABOUR OFFICE. OFFICIAL BULLETIN. SERIES A. (Editions in English, French and Spanish) 1920. irreg., approx. 3/yr. 75 Fr.($42.75) both series. International Labour Office - Bureau International du Travail, Publications Sales Service, CH-1211 Geneva 22, Switzerland (U.S. Dist: ILO Branch Office, 1750 New York Ave., N.W., Washington, DC 20006) bibl. index. circ. 2,500. (also avail. in microform) Indexed: C.I.S. Abstr.
Supersedes in part: International Labour Office. Official Bulletin (ISSN 0020-7772)

331   UN   ISSN 0378-5890
INTERNATIONAL LABOUR OFFICE. OFFICIAL BULLETIN. SERIES B. (Editions in English, French and Spanish) 1920. irreg., (2-3/yr.) 75 Fr.($42.75) both series. International Labour Office - Bureau International du Travail, Publications Sales Service, CH-1211 Geneva 22, Switzerland (U.S. dist.: ILO Branch Office, 1750 New York Ave., N.W., Washington, D.C. 20006) bibl. index. circ. 2,500. (also avail. in microform)
Supersedes in part: International Labour Office. Official Bulletin (ISSN 0020-7772)

331   US
INTERNATIONAL SERIES ON THE QUALITY OF WORKING LIFE.* 1976. irreg. price varies. Kluwer Nijhoff Publishing, 101 Philip Dr., Assinippi Park, Norwell, MA 02061 (Foreign orders to: Kluwer Academic Publishers Group, Distribution Center, Box 322, 3300 AH Dordrecht, Netherlands) Ed. Hans van Beinum.

331.1   US   ISSN 0149-449X
IOWA. DEPARTMENT OF JOB SERVICE. ANNUAL REPORT. 1938. a. contr. free circ. Department of Job Service, 1000 E. Grand Ave., Des Moines, IA 50319. TEL 515-281-3201. circ. 2,000.
Formerly: Iowa. Employment Security Commission. Annual Report.

331   JA
JAPAN STATISTICAL ASSOCIATION. ANNUAL REPORT ON THE INTERNAL MIGRATION IN JAPAN DERIVED FROM THE BASIC RESIDENT REGISTERS. (Text in English and Japanese) a. Japan Statistical Association, 95 Wakamatucho, Shinjyuku-ku, Tokyo, Japan (Subscr. to: Government Publications Service Center, 2-1, 1-chome, Kasumigaseki, Chiyoda-ku, Tokyo, Japan)

331   JA
JAPAN STATISTICAL ASSOCIATION. ANNUAL REPORT ON THE LABOUR FORCE SURVEY. (Text in English and Japanese) a. Japan Statistical Association, 95 Wakamatucho, Shinjyuku-ku, Tokyo, Japan (Subscr. to: Government Publications Service Center, 2-1, 1-chome, Kasumigaseki, Chiyoda-ku, Tokyo, Japan)

331   JA
JAPAN STATISTICAL ASSOCIATION. ANNUAL REPORT ON THE RETAIL PRICE SURVEY. (Text in English and Japanese) a. Japan Statistical Association, 95 Wakamatucho, Shinjyuku-ku, Tokyo, Japan (Subscr. to: Government Publications Service Center, 2-1, 1-chome Kasumigaseki, Chiyoda-ku, Tokyo, Japan)

331   JA
JAPAN STATISTICAL ASSOCIATION. ANNUAL REPORT ON THE UNINCORPORATED ENTERPRISE SURVEY. (Text in English and Japanese) a. Japan Statistical Association, 95 Wakamatucho, Shinjyuku-Ku, Tokyo, Japan (Subscr. to: Government Publications Center, 2-1, 1-chome, Kasumigaseki, Chiyoda-Ku, Tokyo, Japan)

331.11   US
JOB SERVICE NORTH DAKOTA. ANNUAL REPORT. 1937. a. free. Job Service North Dakota, 1000 E. Divide Ave., Box 1537, Bismarck, ND 58502. TEL 701-224-2825. Ed. Tom Pederson. circ. 200.
Formerly: North Dakota. Employment Security Bureau. Annual Report (ISSN 0078-155X)

331.11   US
JOB SERVICE NORTH DAKOTA. BIENNIAL REPORT TO THE GOVERNOR. 1964. biennial. free. Job Service North Dakota, 1000 E. Divide Ave., Box 1537, Bismarck, ND 58502. TEL 701-224-2825. Ed. Lyle Halvorson. circ. 75.
Formerly: North Dakota. Employment Security Bureau. Biennial Report to the Governor (ISSN 0078-1568)

331.2   US
JOINT GOVERNMENTAL SALARY SURVEY: ARIZONA. 1975. a. free. ‡ Department of Administration, Personnel Division, 1831 W. Jefferson, Phoenix, AZ 85007. TEL 602-255-5482. Ed. George L. Morawski. charts. stat. circ. controlled.
Supersedes: Survey of Salaries and Employee Benefits of Private and Public Employers in Arizona. (ISSN 0091-5599)

331   KO   ISSN 0454-7543
KOREA (REPUBLIC). ECONOMIC PLANNING BOARD. ANNUAL REPORT ON THE ECONOMICALLY ACTIVE POPULATION. (Text in Korean, English) 1963. a. 7830 Won. National Bureau of Statistics, Economic Planning Board, Gyeongun-Dung, Jongro-Gu, Seoul, S. Korea. Ed. Myong Hyun Sohn. circ. 400.

331   US
LABOR FORCE IN IDAHO. a. free. Department of Employment, Bureau of Research and Analysis, Box 35, Boise, ID 83735. TEL 208-334-2765. stat.

331.1   US   ISSN 0362-3793
LABOR FORCE STATUS OF INDIANA RESIDENTS. a. Employment Security Division, Indianapolis, IN 46204. TEL 317-232-7670.

LABOR RATES FOR THE CONSTRUCTION INDUSTRY. see *BUILDING AND CONSTRUCTION*

331.1   US
LABOR RELATIONS AND PUBLIC POLICY SERIES. 1968. irreg. University of Pennsylvania, Wharton School, Industrial Research Unit, 3733 Vance Hall, Philadelphia, PA 19104-6358. TEL 215-898-5605.
Formerly: University of Pennsylvania. Wharton School of Finance and Commerce. Labor Relations and Public Policy Series. Reports (ISSN 0075-7470)

331   PK
LABOUR CODE OF PAKISTAN. (Text in English) 1953. a. $60 (update service $10 annually) Bureau of Labour Publications, 8, Business Centre, Dunolly Rd., P.O. Box 5833, Karachi-2, Pakistan. Ed. M. Shafi.

331   II   ISSN 0377-077X
LABOUR IN THE PUBLIC SECTOR UNDERTAKINGS: BASIC INFORMATION. 1968. irreg. price varies. Ministry of Labour, Implementation and Evaluation Division, New Delhi, India (Order from: Controller of Publications, Government of India, Civil Lines, Delhi 110054, India) stat.

331   340   PK
LABOUR LAW CASES. (Text in English) 1947. a. Rs.285($57) Bureau of Labour Publications, 8, Business Centre, P.O. Box 5833, Karachi-2, Pakistan. Ed. M. Shafi. abstr. (back issues avail.)

331   340   CN   ISSN 0383-3372
LABOUR LEGISLATION IN NOVA SCOTIA. irreg. Department of Labour, Box 697, Halifax, N.S. B3J 2T8, Canada. TEL 902-424-4313.

331   UN   ISSN 0538-8325
LABOUR-MANAGEMENT RELATIONS SERIES. irreg. price varies. International Labour Office - Bureau International du Travail, Publications Sales Service, CH-1211 Geneva 22, Switzerland (U.S. distributors: I L O Branch Office, 1750 New York Ave. N.W., Washington, DC 20006)

331   CN   ISSN 0075-7586
LABOUR STANDARDS IN CANADA. NORMES DU TRAVAIL AU CANADA. (Text in English and French) 1951. a. Can.$6.25($7.50) Labour Canada, Ottawa, Ont., Canada TEL 613-997-2617. (Subscr. to: Canadian Government Publishing Centre, Supply and Services Canada, Ottawa, Ont. K1A 0S9, Canada) circ. 1,500. (reprint service avail. from MML)

331   US
LAW REPRINTS: LABOR LAW SERIES. 1967. irreg. $245. Congressional Information Service, Inc., 4520 East-West Hwy, Ste. 800, Bethesda, MD 20814. TEL 800-638-8380. index.
Former titles: B N A's Law Reprints: Labor Law Series (ISSN 0275-6994); Law Reprints: Labor Series.

331   UK   ISSN 0262-1452
LINCOLNSHIRE INFORMATION. EMPLOYMENT. 1981. a. Lincolnshire County Council, Director of Highways and Planning, County Offices, Lincoln, England. charts. illus.

331   UK   ISSN 0306-0837
LLAFUR. 1972. a. membership. Society for the Study of Welsh Labour History, c/o Dr. Deian Hopkin, Ed., Department of History, University College, Aberystwyth SY23 3DY, Wales. adv. bk. rev. circ. 1,500. (back issues avail.) Indexed: Hist.Abstr. Amer.Hist.& Life.

331.1   US   ISSN 0076-0870
LOOKING FORWARD;* a series of occasional papers. 1964. irreg. no.18, 1971; latest 1978. League for Industrial Democracy, 181 Hudson St., No. 3A, New York, NY 10013-1804.

331   669   AT   ISSN 0085-3321
M.T.I.A. ANNUAL REPORT. 1970. a. Aus.$5. Metal Trades Industry Association of Australia, 105 Walker St., North Sydney, N.S.W. 2060, Australia. Ed. L.R. Davies. circ. 2,000.

331.1   CN   ISSN 0076-194X
MCGILL UNIVERSITY, MONTREAL. INDUSTRIAL RELATIONS CENTRE. ANNUAL CONFERENCE PROCEEDINGS. no.12, 1976. a. price varies. McGill University, Industrial Relations Centre, 1001 Sherbrooke St. W., Montreal, P.Q. H3A 1G5, Canada. TEL 514-392-3077.

331   MY
MALAYSIAN EMPLOYERS FEDERATION ANNUAL REPORT. (Text in English) 1962. a. Malaysian Employers Federation Persekutuan Majikan Majikan Malaysia, P.O. Box 11026, Kuala Lumpur 01-02, Malaysia. circ. 1,000.

350.1   CN   ISSN 0706-3792
MANITOBA. MUNICIPAL EMPLOYEES BENEFITS BOARD. ANNUAL REPORT. 1977. a. Municipal Employees Benefits Board, 200-400 Tache Ave., Winnipeg, Man. R2H 3C3, Canada. TEL 204-944-2194.

331.1   CN   ISSN 0076-3853
MANITOBA LABOUR - MANAGEMENT REVIEW COMMITTEE. ANNUAL REPORT. 1965. a. free. Department of Labour, Room 606, Norquay Bldg., Winnipeg, Man. R3C 0V8, Canada. TEL 204-944-3411.

331   US   ISSN 0149-080X
MANPOWER AND HUMAN RESOURCES STUDIES. 1962. irreg. University of Pennsylvania, Wharton School, Industrial Research Unit, 3733 Vance Hall, Philadelphia, PA 19104-6358. TEL 215-898-5605.

331.2   US
MASS RETAILERS' EXECUTIVE PERQUISITE REPORT. biennial. $48 to non-members; members $38. National Mass Retailing Institute, 570 Seventh Ave., NY 10018. TEL 212-354-6600.

331.2   US
MASS RETAILERS' MERCHANDISING REPORT. a. $80 to non-members; members $65. National Mass Retailing Institute, 570 Seventh Ave., New York, NY 10018. TEL 212-354-6600.
Incorporating: Operating Results of Self-Service Discount Department Stores.

BUSINESS AND ECONOMICS — LABOR AND INDUSTRIAL RELATIONS

331 US ISSN 0076-4922
MASSACHUSETTS. DIVISION OF EMPLOYMENT SECURITY. EMPLOYMENT AND WAGES IN ESTABLISHMENTS SUBJECT TO THE MASSACHUSETTS EMPLOYMENT SECURITY LAW. STATE SUMMARY. 1970. a. free. Division of Employment Security, Job Market Research, Charles F. Hurley Bldg., Government Center, Boston, MA 02114. TEL 617-727-6360. circ. 700.
Former titles: Massachusetts. Division of Employment Security. Employment and Wages in Establishments Subject to the Massachusetts Employment Security Law (ISSN 0360-8301); Massachusetts. Division of Employment Security. Employment and Wages for the Year.

331 MF
MAURITIUS. MINISTRY OF LABOUR AND INDUSTRIAL RELATIONS. ANNUAL REPORT. (Text in English) a. Government Printing Office, Elizabeth II Ave., Port Louis, Mauritius.
Formerly (until 1975/76): Mauritius. Ministry of Labour. Annual Report.

ME'ASEF; studies in the history and problems of the Israeli labor movement. see HISTORY — History Of The Near East

331.86 AU
MENSCH UND ARBEIT; internationale Zeitschrift fuer Arbeitspaedagogik, Arbeitspsychologie, Arbeitstechnik und Betriebswirtschaft. 1947. irreg. S.95. (Arbeitsgemeinschaft fuer Psychotechnik in Oesterreich) Psychotechnisches Institut, Vegagasse 4, A-1190 Vienna, Austria. Ed. Dr. Guido Hackl. bk. rev. circ. 2,000. Indexed: C.I.S. Abstr.

331.1 US
MICHIGAN. EMPLOYMENT SECURITY COMMISSION. ANNUAL PLANNING REPORT. 1972. a. free. Employment Security Commission, 7310 Woodward Ave., Detroit, MI 48202. TEL 313-876-5000. illus. stat. circ. 1,000.
Formerly: Michigan. Employment Security Commission. Labor Market Analysis Section. Annual Manpower Planning Report: Detroit Labor Market Area (ISSN 0090-8401)

353.9 US ISSN 0092-9212
MICHIGAN STATE EMPLOYEES' RETIREMENT SYSTEM FINANCIAL AND STATISTICAL REPORT. 1953. a. free. ‡ State Employees Retirement System, Stevens T. Mason Building, 2nd Floor, West Wing, Lansing, MI 48913. TEL 517-373-1004. stat. circ. 1,100. Key Title: Michigan State Employees' Retirement System.

331 US
MINNESOTA. DEPARTMENT OF ECONOMIC SECURITY. ANNUAL REPORT. 1936. a. free. Department of Economic Security, 390 N. Robert St., St. Paul, MN 55101. TEL 612-296-2536. Ed. Warren C. Johnson. circ. 1,500.
Former titles (until 1979): Minnesota. Department of Employment Services. Annual Report (ISSN 0364-717X); (1969-1974): Minnesota. Department of Manpower Services. Annual Report (ISSN 0076-9126); Before 1969: Minnesota. Department of Employment Security. Annual Report.

MONOGRAPHS IN ORGANIZATIONAL BEHAVIOUR AND INDUSTRIAL RELATIONS. see SOCIAL SCIENCES: COMPREHENSIVE WORKS

331.2 US ISSN 0092-5950
N M R I COMPENSATION IN MASS RETAILING, SALARIES AND INCENTIVES. 1972. biennial. $70 to non-members; members $60. ‡ National Mass Retailing Institute, 570 Seventh Ave., New York, NY 10018. TEL 212-354-6600. illus.
Formerly: M R I Compensation in Mass Retailing, Salaries and Incentives.

331.1 US
NATIONAL ACADEMY OF ARBITRATORS. ANNUAL MEETING. PROCEEDINGS. 1948. a. $33. The Bureau of National Affairs, Inc., B N A Books, 2550 M St., N.W., Ste. 699, Washington, DC 20037 TEL 201-225-1900. (Subscr. to: BNA Books Distribution Center, 300 Raritan Center Pkwy, CN 94, Edison, NJ 08818) Ed. Walter Gershenfeld.

331 US ISSN 0077-3735
NATIONAL CIVIL SERVICE LEAGUE. ANNUAL REPORT.* a. free. National Civil Service League, 3600 Gunston Rd., Alexandria, VA 22302.

331 CN ISSN 0226-3882
NEGOTIATED WORKING CONDITIONS FROM COLLECTIVE AGREEMENTS IN NOVA SCOTIA. irreg. Department of Labour, Research Division, Box 697, Halifax, N.S. B3J 2T8, Canada. TEL 902-424-4125.

331 JA
NEMPO NIHON NO ROSHI KANKEI. 1968. a. 3000 Yen. Japan Institute of Labour - Nihon Rodo Kyokai, Chutaikin Bldg., 1-7-6 Shibakoen, Minato-ku, Tokyo, Japan.

331.2 US
NEVADA WAGE SURVEY. Variant title: Nevada Statewide Wage Survey. 1973. a. free. Employment Security Department, 500 E. Third St., Carson City, NV 89713. TEL 702-885-4550. circ. 2,500.
Formerly: State of Nevada Wage Report (ISSN 0081-4563)

331 CN
NEW BRUNSWICK. DEPARTMENT OF LABOUR AND HUMAN RESOURCES. ANNUAL REPORT. (Text in English and French) 1944. a. free. Department of Labour and Human Resources, P.O. Box 6000, Fredericton, N.B. E3B 5H1, Canada. TEL 506-453-2303. Ed. Marg Carfra. circ. 900.
Former titles: New Brunswick. Department of Labour and Manpower. Annual Report & New Brunswick. Department of Labour. Annual Report (ISSN 0077-8052)

331 US
NEW LABOR REVIEW. 1978. irreg., no.4, 1981. free. San Francisco State University, Labor Studies Forum, Division of Cross Disciplinary Programs in the Behavioral and Social Sciences, 1600 Holloway Ave., San Francisco, CA 94132. TEL 415-469-2055. Ed.Bd. adv. bk. rev. circ. 1,000. (also avail. in microform from UMI)

331.1 US ISSN 0093-5034
NEW YORK (STATE) DEPARTMENT OF LABOR. DIVISION OF RESEARCH AND STATISTICS. LABOR RESEARCH REPORT. irreg. Department of Labor, Division of Research and Statistics, One Main St., 9th Fl., Brooklyn, NY 11201 TEL 718-797-7703. (Dist. by: Division of Research and Statistics, State Campus, Albany, N.Y. 12240) Ed. Eileen DeVeau. stat. Key Title: Labor Research Report (Albany)
Continues: New York (State) Division of Employment. Research and Statistics Office. Research Bulletin.

331 US ISSN 0070-0134
NEW YORK STATE SCHOOL OF INDUSTRIAL AND LABOR RELATIONS. BULLETIN. (Supersedes its Extension Bulletin and Research Bulletin) 1951. irreg., no.54, 1984. price varies. (New York State School of Industrial and Labor Relations) I L R Press, Cornell University, Ithaca, NY 14851-0952. TEL 607-255-3061.

331 US
NEW YORK STATE SCHOOL OF INDUSTRIAL AND LABOR RELATIONS. INSTITUTE OF PUBLIC EMPLOYMENT. MONOGRAPH. 1973. irreg., no. 10, 1982. price varies. (New York State School of Industrial and Labor Relations, Institute of Public Employment) I L R Press, Cornell University, Ithaca, NY 19851. TEL 607-255-3061.

331 US ISSN 0070-0185
NEW YORK STATE SCHOOL OF INDUSTRIAL AND LABOR RELATIONS. KEY ISSUES SERIES. 1967. irreg., no.30, 1986. price varies. (New York State School of Industrial and Labor Relations) I L R Press, Cornell University, Ithaca, NY 14851-0952. TEL 607-255-3061.

331.11 NR
NIGERIA. NATIONAL MANPOWER BOARD. MANPOWER STUDIES. 1963. irreg. (1-2/yr.) price varies. National Manpower Board, 5 Oil Mills St., Lagos, Nigeria. Ed. B.O. Oshuntolu. stat. circ. 500.

331.1 CN ISSN 0830-0763
NON-WAGE PROVISIONS IN SASKATCHEWAN COLLECTIVE AGREEMENTS. (Text in English) 1973. a. free. Department of Labour, Policy Planning and Research Branch, 1870 Albert St., Regina, Saskatchewan S4P 3V7, Canada. TEL 306-787-3369. circ. 1,000.
Formerly (until 1985): Study of Saskatchewan Collective Bargaining Agreements (ISSN 0701-6794)

331 UK
NORTH EAST LABOUR HISTORY BULLETIN. 1967. a. £3 to individuals; institutions £4.50. Newcastle Upon Tyne Polytechnic, Department of English and History, Lipman Building, Newcastle Upon Tyne NE1 8ST, England. Ed.Bd. adv. bk. rev. bibl. charts. stat. circ. 250.
Formerly: North East Group for the Study of Labour History Bulletin (ISSN 0029-2818)
History

331 NO ISSN 0078-1835
NORWAY. ARBEIDSDIREKTORATET. AARSMELDING.* (Text in Norwegian, summary in English) a. Arbeidsdirektoratet, Postboks 8127, Oslo 1, Norway.

331.1 340 PR ISSN 0029-4195
NOTICIAS DEL TRABAJO. vol.31, 1970. irreg. free. ‡ U.S. Department of Labor, Bureau of Labor Statistics, Avenida Barbosa 414, Hato Rey, PR 00917. charts. stat. circ. 15,000.

331.2 CN ISSN 0380-5689
NOVA SCOTIA. DEPARTMENT OF LABOUR. ANNUAL REPORT. 1935. a. Department of Labour, Box 697, Halifax, N.S., Canada. TEL 902-424-4125.

331 CN
NOVA SCOTIA. DEPARTMENT OF LABOUR. COMPENDIUM OF GRIEVANCE ARBITRATION DECISIONS. 1978. a. free. Department of Labour, Research Division, Box 697, Halifax, N.S. B3J 2T8, Canada. TEL 902-424-4313. circ. 300.
Formerly: Nova Scotia. Department of Labour and Manpower. Compendium of Grievance Arbitration Decisions (ISSN 0226-3890)

331.2 CN ISSN 0550-1741
NOVA SCOTIA. DEPARTMENT OF LABOUR. ECONOMICS AND RESEARCH DIVISION. WAGE RATES, SALARIES AND HOURS OF LABOUR IN NOVA SCOTIA. 1967. a. free. Department of Labour, Economics and Research Division, Box 697, Halifax, Nova Scotia, Canada. TEL 902-424-4125. charts. (processed)

331 NZ ISSN 0078-3064
OCCASIONAL PAPERS IN INDUSTRIAL RELATIONS. 1966. irreg. price varies. Victoria University of Wellington, Industrial Relations Centre, Private Bag, Wellington, New Zealand.

OCCUPATIONAL DISEASE IN CALIFORNIA. see INDUSTRIAL HEALTH AND SAFETY — Abstracting, Bibliographies, Statistics

331 US
OKLAHOMA. EMPLOYMENT SECURITY COMMISSION. RESEARCH DIVISION. ANNUAL REPORT TO THE GOVERNOR. 1939. a. free. ‡ Employment Security Commission, Research Division, 310 Will Rogers Bldg., Oklahoma City, OK 73105. Ed. Dennis Martin. charts. stat. circ. 1,200.
Formerly: Oklahoma. Employment Security Commission. Research and Planning Division. Annual Report ot the Governor.

ONTARIO EDUCATION RELATIONS COMMISSION. ANNUAL REPORT. see EARTH SCIENCES

331.4 BE ISSN 0078-5164
OPEN DOOR INTERNATIONAL FOR THE EMANCIPATION OF THE WOMAN WORKER. REPORT OF CONGRESS. 1929. irreg., 1966, 13th, London. free. ‡ Open Door International, 16 rue Americain, B-1050 Brussels, Belgium. Ed. Adele Hauwel.

BUSINESS AND ECONOMICS — LABOR AND INDUSTRIAL RELATIONS

331.11 FR ISSN 0473-6788
ORGANIZATION FOR ECONOMIC COOPERATION AND DEVELOPMENT. REVIEWS OF MANPOWER AND SOCIAL POLICIES. 1963. irreg. Organization for Economic Cooperation and Development, 2 rue Andre Pascal, 75775 Paris 16, France (U.S. orders to: O.E.C.D. Publications and Information Center, 1750 Pennsylvania Ave., N.W., Washington, D.C. 20006) (also avail. in microfiche)

331 PP
PAPUA NEW GUINEA. MANPOWER PLANNING UNIT. MANPOWER STUDIES.* (Text in English) no.9, 1974. irreg. (2-3/yr.) Manpower Planning Unit, Box 3618, Port Moresby, Papua New Guinea. charts. stat.

331 FR
PARTICIPATION. (Supplement to France. Ministere du Travail. Bulletin Mensuel des Statistiques du Travail) irreg. Ministere du Travail, 127 rue de Grenelle, 75700 Paris, France.

331 US
PENNSYLVANIA. LABOR RELATIONS BOARD. REPORT. 1937. a. free. Department of Labor and Industry, 1617 Labor & Industry Bldg., Seventh & Forster Sts., Harrisburg, PA 17120. TEL 717-787-1091. Ed. George Knehr. charts. stat. circ. 1,000.

331.11 US
PITTSBURGH SERIES IN LABOR AND SOCIAL HISTORY. 1974. irreg. price varies. University of Pittsburgh Press, 127 N. Bellefield Ave., Pittsburgh, PA 15260. TEL 412-624-4110. Ed. Maurine Weiner Greenwald.
Formerly: Pittsburgh Series in Labor History.

331.11 PO
PORTUGAL. MINISTERIO DO TRABALHO. SERVICO DE INFORMACAO CIENTIFICA E TECNICA. BOLETIM DO TRABALHO E EMPREGO. irreg. Esc.600. Ministerio do Trabalho, Servico de Informacao Cientifica e Tecnica, Praca de Londres 2, Lisbon, Portugal.

331 CN ISSN 0085-512X
PRINCE EDWARD ISLAND. DEPARTMENT OF LABOUR. ANNUAL REPORT. 1967. a. free. ‡ Department of Labour, Box 2000, Charlottetown, P.E.I. C1A 7N8, Canada. TEL 902-892-3416. Eds. Glenda Stewart. circ. 250.
Formerly: Prince Edward Island. Department of Fisheries and Labour. Annual Report.

331.1 US ISSN 0079-5305
PRINCETON UNIVERSITY. INDUSTRIAL RELATIONS SECTION. RESEARCH REPORT. 1926 (as Report series) irreg., no. 124, 1984. ‡ Princeton University, Industrial Relations Section, Firestone Library, Princeton, NJ 08544. TEL 609-452-4040. circ. 1,000.

331 NE
PROJECT PERSONEELSVOORZIENING KWARTAIRE SECTOR. BULLETIN. 1979. irreg., no.3, 1982. Centraal Planbureau, Van Stolkweg 14, 2585 JR The Hague, Netherlands. (Co-sponsor: Sociaal en Cultureel Planbureau) charts. stat.

331.1 US
PROVISIONS OF CALIFORNIA COLLECTIVE BARGAINING AGREEMENTS. 1977. biennial. free. Department of Industrial Relations, Division of Labor Statistics and Research, Box 603, San Francisco, CA 94101. TEL 415-557-2184. Ed. Maria Yeftimovich. circ. 2,000. (back issues avail.)

331 943.7 CS
PRUMYSLOVE OBLASTI. 1967. a. Nakladatelstvi Profil, Cihlarska 51, 701 00 Ostrava 1, Czechoslovakia (Subscr. to: Artia, Ve Smeckach 30, 111 27 Prague 1, Czechoslovakia) charts. illus. Indexed: Hist.Abstr.
Formerly: Vznik a Vyvoj Prumyslovych Oblasti.

331 AT
PUBLIC RELATIONS HANDBOOK FOR MANAGERS AND EXECUTIVES. 1984. biennial. Aus.$19.50. Margaret Gee, 17 Queen St., Melbourne, Vic. 3000, Australia. Ed. Jim Macnamara.

331.11 US
PURDUE UNIVERSITY. OFFICE OF MANPOWER STUDIES. MANPOWER & TECHNICAL EDUCATION REQUIREMENTS REPORTS. 1965. irreg. $3.50. Purdue University, Office of Manpower Studies, Knox Hall, West Lafayette, IN 47907. TEL 317-494-5600. Ed. J.P. Lisack. circ. 21,000. Indexed: ERIC.
Formerly: Purdue University. Office of Manpower Studies. Manpower Report (ISSN 0079-8134)

331.1 CN ISSN 0317-2546
QUEEN'S UNIVERSITY. INDUSTRIAL RELATIONS CENTRE. RESEARCH AND CURRENT ISSUES SERIES. 1964. irreg., no.47, 1986. price varies. ‡ Queen's University, Industrial Relations Centre, Kingston, Ont. K7L 3N6, Canada. TEL 613-545-2193. circ. 1,000.
Formerly: Queen's University. Industrial Relations Centre. Research Series (ISSN 0075-6164)

331.1 CN ISSN 0075-6148
QUEEN'S UNIVERSITY AT KINGSTON. INDUSTRIAL RELATIONS CENTRE. REPORT OF ACTIVITIES. irreg. free. ‡ Queen's University, Industrial Relations Centre, Kingston, Ont. K7L 3N6, Canada. TEL 613-545-2193.

331.1 CN ISSN 0075-6156
QUEEN'S UNIVERSITY AT KINGSTON. INDUSTRIAL RELATIONS CENTRE. REPRINT SERIES. 1961. irreg., no.63, 1986. price varies. ‡ Queen's University, Industrial Relations Centre, Kingston, Ont. K7L 3N6, Canada. TEL 613-545-2193.

331 AT ISSN 0158-9830
RESEARCH DISCUSSION PAPERS. 1979. irreg. Aus.$15. Australian Chamber of Manufactures, 370 St. Kilda Rd., Melbourne 3004, Australia. Ed. Michael Connell. circ. 300. (back issues avail.)

331 US ISSN 0194-3057
RESEARCH IN LABOR ECONOMICS; a research annual evaluating manpower training programs. 1977. a. $28.75 to individuals; institutions $57.50. J A I Press Inc., Box 1678, 36 Sherwood Pl., Greenwich, CT 06836-1678. TEL 203-661-7602. Ed. Ronald G. Ehrenberg.

301.1 US ISSN 0277-2833
RESEARCH IN THE SOCIOLOGY OF WORK. 1981. $24.75 to individuals; institutions $47.50. J A I Press Inc., Box 1678, 36 Sherwood Pl., Greenwich, CT 06836-1678. TEL 203-661-7602. Eds. Ida Harper Simpson, Richard L. Simpson. Indexed: Lang.& Lang.Behav.Abstr.

331 361.1 HT ISSN 0482-8062
REVUE DU TRAVAIL. 1951. a. Departement du Travail et du Bien-Etre Social, Port-au-Prince, Haiti. stat. Indexed: P.A.I.S.For.Lang.Ind.

RUHR-UNIVERSITAET. INSTITUT ZUR GESCHICHTE DER ARBEITERBEWEGUNG. MITTEILUNGSBLATT. see LABOR UNIONS

331 UK ISSN 0261-5649
RUSKIN COLLEGE, OXFORD. LIBRARY. OCCASIONAL PUBLICATION. 1979. irreg. price varies. Ruskin College, Library, Oxford OX1 2HE, England. Ed. D. Horsfield.

331 DK ISSN 0108-5417
S D A - NYT. 1978. irreg. (4-6/yr.) Samnordisk Dokumentationscentral for Arbejdsmiljoe, Landskronagade 33-35, 2100 Copenhagen OE, Denmark. Ed. Max Meedom. circ. 2,000.

331 US
SALARIES & BONUSES IN PERSONNEL/ INDUSTRIAL RELATIONS FUNCTIONS. 1979. a. $150. (Personnel Journal) Abbott, Langer & Associates, 548 First St., Crete, IL 60417. TEL 312-672-4200. Ed. Steven Langer.
Formerly: Personnel/Industrial Relations Report, Parts 1 and 2.

331 US
SALARIES & RELATED MATTERS IN THE SERVICE DEPARTMENT. 1973. a. $125. (National Association of Service Managers) Abbott, Langer & Associates, 548 First St., Crete, IL 60417. TEL 312-672-2400. Ed. Steven Langer.

331.2 US
SALARY BUDGET SURVEY. a. $10. American Compensation Association, 6619 N. Scottsdale Rd., Box 29312, Phoenix, AZ 85038-9312. TEL 605-951-9191.

331.1 CN ISSN 0706-4926
SASKATCHEWAN. DEPARTMENT OF LABOUR. WAGES AND WORKING CONDITIONS BY OCCUPATION. 1974. a. free. Department of Labour, Policy Planning and Research Branch, 1870 Albert St., Regina, Sask. S4P 3V7, Canada. TEL 306-787-2169. Ed. J. Boyd. circ. 2,000.

331 UK
SCOTTISH INDUSTRIAL POLICY SERIES. 1982. irreg. Edinburgh University Press, 22 George Square, Edinburgh EH8 9LF, Scotland. Ed. Neil Hood.

331 943 UK
SCOTTISH LABOUR HISTORY SOCIETY. JOURNAL. 1969. a. Aberdeen Scottish Labour History Society, c/o Department of History, University of Strathclyde, McCance Bldg., 16 Richmond St., Glasgow G1 1XQ, Scotland. Ed. Ian S. Wood. Indexed: Hist.Abstr. Amer.Hist.& Life.

331.11 338 PE ISSN 0250-9814
SERIE PRAXIS. 1973. irreg. $5 per no. Centro de Estudios y Promocion del Desarrollo (DESCO), Av. Salaverry 1945, Lima 14, Peru (Subscr. to: PUBLIREC S.A., Jr. Miguel Zamora 146, Lima 1, Peru) circ. 2,000.

331 SI ISSN 0129-6310
SINGAPORE. MINISTRY OF LABOUR. ANNUAL REPORT. (Text in English) 1946. a. price varies. Ministry of Labour, Havelock Rd., Singapore 0105, Singapore. Ed.Bd. charts. stat. circ. 500.

SINGAPORE. MINISTRY OF SCIENCE AND TECHNOLOGY. NATIONAL SURVEY OF SCIENTIFIC MANPOWER. see SCIENCES: COMPREHENSIVE WORKS

SOUTH AFRICA. UNEMPLOYMENT INSURANCE FUND. REPORT/SOUTH AFRICA. WERKLOOSHEIDVERSEKERINGSFONDS. VERSLAG. see INSURANCE

331 AT ISSN 0311-0702
SOUTH AUSTRALIA. DEPARTMENT OF LABOUR. GUIDE TO LEGISLATION. 1972. irreg. free. Department of Labour, G.P.O. Box 465, Adelaide, SA 5001, Australia. circ. 5,000.

310 331 US
SOUTH CAROLINA. DEPARTMENT OF LABOR. ANNUAL REPORT. 1936. a. free. Department of Labor, Box 11329, 3600 Forest Dr., Columbia, SC 29211. TEL 803-734-9600. Ed. James Knight.

STAT A PRAVO. see LAW

331.1 US ISSN 0095-6430
STATE OF FLORIDA COMPREHENSIVE MANPOWER PLAN. a. State Manpower Planning Council, Atkins Bldg., Rm. 204, 1320 Executive Center Dr., Tallahassee, FL 32301. TEL 904-488-8213.

331.8 CN ISSN 0081-5985
STRIKES AND LOCKOUTS IN CANADA/ GREVES ET LOCK-OUT AU CANADA. (Text in English and French) 1913. a. Can.$6. Labour Canada, Ottawa, Ont. K1A 0J2, Canada TEL 613-997-2617. (Subscr. to: Canadian Government Publishing Centre, Supply and Services Canada, Ottawa, Ont. K1A 0S9, Canada) circ. 1,700. (reprint service avail. from MML)

331 DK ISSN 0108-2469
STUDIES IN LABOR MARKET DYNAMICS. 1981. irreg. price varies. Aarhus School of Economics, Fueglsangs Alle 4, 8210 Aarhus V, Denmark, Denmark. Ed. Peder J. Pedersen. illus. circ. 400.

331.2 SQ
SWAZILAND. CENTRAL STATISTICAL OFFICE. EMPLOYMENT AND WAGES. 1969. a. free. Central Statistical Office, Box 456, Mbabane, Swaziland.

BUSINESS AND ECONOMICS — LABOR AND INDUSTRIAL RELATIONS

331.116   SW
SWEDEN. STATENS ARBETSGIVARVERK. ARBETSGIVARVERKET INFORMERAR. 1965. irreg. (4-6/yr.) Kr.4. Statens Arbetsgivarverket - National Swedish Agency for Government Employers, Box 2243, S-103 16 Stockholm, Sweden. Ed. Bertil Drougge.
    Former titles (until 1979): Sweden. Statens Avtalsverk. Information Fraan S A V (ISSN 0036-0996); Sweden. Statens Avtalsverk. Aktuellt.

TANZANIA. BUREAU OF STATISTICS. SURVEY OF EMPLOYMENT. see *STATISTICS*

331   US
TENNESSEE ANNUAL AVERAGE LABOR FORCE ESTIMATES.* 1970. a. free. Department of Employment Security, Research and Statistics Section, 536 Cordell Hull Bldg., 436 6th Ave., N., Nashville, TN 37219. TEL 615-741-2131. stat. circ. controlled.
    Formed by the merger of: Tennessee Civilian Work Force Estimates (ISSN 0085-7165) & Tennessee Annual Average Work Force Estimates.

331   US
TENNESSEE LABOR MARKET INFORMATION DIRECTORY.* a. Department of Employment Security, Research & Statistics Section, 536 Cordell Hull Bldg., 436 6th Ave., N., Nashville, TN 37219. TEL 615-741-2131.

331   TH
THAILAND STANDARD INDUSTRIAL CLASSIFICATION. (Text in English and Thai) 1972. irreg. Department of Labour, Bangkok, Thailand.

331.88   IC
TIMARIT IDNADARMANNA. 1927. a. membership. Landssamband Idnadarmanna - Federation of Icelandic Crafts and Industries, Hallveigarstig 1, Box 102, Reykjavik, Iceland. Ed. Thorleifur Jonsson. circ. 4,000.

331.4   US
TIME OF CHANGE: HANDBOOK ON WOMEN WORKERS. (Subseries of Women's Bureau Bulletin) 1948. irreg. price varies. U.S. Department of Labor, Women's Bureau, 200 Constitution Ave. N.W., Washington, DC 20210 TEL 202-523-6667. (Orders to: Supt. of Documents, Washington, DC 20402)
    Former titles: Handbook of Women Workers (ISSN 0083-3622) & Time of Change.

331   CK
TRABAJO. 1950. irreg. Ministerio del Trabajo, Oficina No. 42, Bogota, Colombia. Ed. I. Reyes Rosada.

331.11   UG   ISSN 0082-724X
UGANDA. MINISTRY OF PLANNING AND ECONOMIC DEVELOPMENT. STATISTICS DIVISION. ENUMERATION OF EMPLOYEES. 1959. a. price varies. ‡ Ministry of Planning and Economic Development, Statistics Division, P.O. Box 13, Entebbe, Uganda (Subscr. to: Government Printer, Box 33, Entebbe, Uganda)

331.11   US
UNION LABOR IN CALIFORNIA. 1939. biennial since 1975. free. Department of Industrial Relations, Division of Labor Statistics and Research, Box 603, San Francisco, CA 94101. TEL 415-557-2184. Ed. Lynette Tang.

331   US   ISSN 0082-9021
U.S. BUREAU OF LABOR STATISTICS. BULLETINS. 1913. irreg. price varies. U.S. Bureau of Labor Statistics, 441 G St. N.W., Washington, DC 20212 TEL 202-655-4000. (Orders to: Supt. of Documents, Washington, DC 20402)

331   US
U.S. BUREAU OF LABOR STATISTICS. EMPLOYEE BENEFITS IN MEDIUM AND LARGE FIRMS. a. 4.75. U.S. Bureau of Labor Statistics, 441 G St., N.W., Rm. 916, Washington, DC 20212 TEL 202-523-1944. (Subscr. to: Publications Sales Center, Box 2145, Chicago, IL 60690) Ed. Jorden N. Pfuntner. charts. stat. circ. 3,500. (also avail. in magnetic tape; back issues avail.)

331.1   US
U.S. BUREAU OF LABOR STATISTICS. EMPLOYMENT AND EARNINGS: STATES AND AREAS. (Subseries of its Bulletin Series) 1939. a. U.S. Bureau of Labor Statistics, 441 G St., N.W., Washington, DC 20212 TEL 202-655-4000. (Orders to: Supt. of Documents, Washington, DC 20402)
    Formerly: U.S. Bureau of Labor Statistics. Employment and Earnings Statistics for States and Areas (ISSN 0082-9048)

331.1   US   ISSN 0082-9064
U.S. BUREAU OF LABOR STATISTICS. INDUSTRY WAGE SURVEYS. (Subseries of its Bulletin Series) issued irreg. throughout the year. U.S. Bureau of Labor Statistics, 441 G St., N.W., Washington, DC 20212 TEL 202-655-4000. (Orders to: Supt. of Documents, Washington, DC 20402)

344.73   US   ISSN 0271-1567
U.S. DEPARTMENT OF LABOR. EMPLOYEE RETIREMENT INCOME SECURITY ACT. REPORT TO CONGRESS. 1975. a. free. Department of Labor, Pension and Welfare Benefits Administration, 200 Constitution Ave. N.W., Washington, DC 20216. TEL 202-523-8921. Ed. William C. Russell. circ. 3,000. Key Title: Employee Retirement Income Security Act. Report to Congress.
    Formerly: Administration of the Employee Retirement Income Security Act (ISSN 0146-7352)

331   US   ISSN 0083-0526
U.S. EQUAL EMPLOYMENT OPPORTUNITY COMMISSION. ANNUAL REPORT. Title varies: Equal Employment Opportunity Report. 1968. a. U.S. Equal Employment Opportunity Commission., 2401 E. St., N.W., Washington, DC 20507 TEL 202-655-4000. (Orders to: Supt. of Documents, Washington, DC 20402)

331.15   US   ISSN 0083-0771
U.S. FEDERAL MEDIATION AND CONCILIATION SERVICE. ANNUAL REPORT. 1948. a. price varies. U.S. Federal Mediation and Conciliation Service., 2100 K St. N.W., Washington, DC 20427 TEL 202-655-4000. (Orders to: Supt. of Documents, Washington, DC 20402)

331.1   US
U.S. NATIONAL COMMISSION FOR EMPLOYMENT POLICY. ANNUAL REPORT. 1973. a. U.S. National Commission for Employment Policy, 1522 K St. N.W., Suite 300, Washington, DC 20005. TEL 202-724-1545. circ. 5,000.
    Formerly: U.S. National Commission for Manpower Policy. Annual Report to the President and the Congress (ISSN 0361-7440)

331.155   US   ISSN 0083-2200
U.S. NATIONAL LABOR RELATIONS BOARD. ANNUAL REPORT. 1936. a. price varies. U.S. National Labor Relations Board, 1717 Pennsylvania Ave. N.W., Washington, DC 20572 TEL 202-275-2091. (Orders to: Supt. of Documents, Washington, DC 20402)

331.156   US   ISSN 0083-2219
U.S. NATIONAL LABOR RELATIONS BOARD. COURT DECISIONS RELATING TO THE NATIONAL LABOR RELATIONS ACT. 1939. irreg., latest vol.30. $28. U.S. National Labor Relations Board, 1717 Pennsylvania Ave. N.W., Washington, DC 20570 TEL 202-275-2091. (Orders to: Supt. of Documents, Washington, DC 20402)

331.154   US   ISSN 0083-2286
U.S. NATIONAL MEDIATION BOARD. ANNUAL REPORT. 1935. a. $5. U.S. National Mediation Board, 1425 K St. N.W., Washington, DC 20572. TEL 202-523-5920.

331   US   ISSN 0083-2278
U.S. NATIONAL MEDIATION BOARD. (REPORTS OF EMERGENCY BOARDS) irreg. (3-4/yr.) $10.00 subscription includes Annual Reports, Emergency Board Reports, Certifications and Dismissals, Determinations of Craft or Class, Findings upon Investigation, other NMB information releases. U.S. National Mediation Board, 1425 K St. N.W., Washington, DC 20572. TEL 202-523-5920.

332.6   US
U.S. RAILROAD RETIREMENT BOARD. ANNUAL REPORT. 1936. a. price varies. U.S. Railroad Retirement Board, 844 Rush St., Chicago, IL 60611 TEL 312-751-4700. (Order from: Supt. of Documents, Washington, DC 20402) circ. 1,700.

331   US   ISSN 0739-439X
UNIVERSITY OF CALIFORNIA, LOS ANGELES. INSTITUTE OF INDUSTRIAL RELATIONS. MONOGRAPH AND RESEARCH SERIES. 1953. irreg., no.45, 1985. price varies. University of California, Los Angeles, Institute of Industrial Relations, Los Angeles, CA 90024. TEL 213-825-9191. Ed. Jane Wildhorn. circ. 500.
    Formerly: University of California, Los Angeles. Institute of Industrial Relations. Monograph Series (ISSN 0068-6255)

331   US   ISSN 0073-1226
UNIVERSITY OF HAWAII. INDUSTRIAL RELATIONS CENTER. OCCASIONAL PUBLICATIONS. 1948. irreg., no.146, 1983. price varies. University of Hawaii, Industrial Relations Center, 2425 Campus Rd., Honolulu, HI 96822. TEL 808-948-8132.

331.1   US   ISSN 0073-5353
UNIVERSITY OF ILLINOIS AT URBANA-CHAMPAIGN. INSTITUTE OF LABOR AND INDUSTRIAL RELATIONS. REPRINT SERIES. 1950. irreg. free to qualified personnel. University of Illinois at Urbana-Champaign, Institute of Labor and Industrial Relations, 504 E. Armory Ave., Champaign, IL 61820. TEL 217-333-1480. Ed. Alice Vernon. circ. 400.

331   TR
UNIVERSITY OF THE WEST INDIES, TRINIDAD. INSTITUTE OF SOCIAL & ECONOMIC RESEARCH. OCCASIONAL PAPERS: HUMAN RESOURCES SERIES. 1977. irreg. price varies. University of the West Indies, Institute of Social & Economic Research, St. Augustine, Trinidad, West Indies. Ed. Jack Harewood. charts. stat. circ. 220. (back issues avail.)

VICTORIAN WORKERS COMPENSATION PRACTICE GUIDE. see *LAW*

331   US
VIRGINIA. EMPLOYMENT COMMISSION. ANNUAL PLANNING REPORT.* a. Employment Commission, Richmond, VA 23219.

331   US
VIRGINIA. EMPLOYMENT COMMISSION. ANNUAL REPORT.* a. Employment Commission, Richmond, VA 23219. stat.

331   US
VIRGINIA. EMPLOYMENT COMMISSION. ANNUAL RURAL MANPOWER REPORT. a. Employment Commission, Richmond, VA 23219. TEL 804-523-2121. stat.

331   US
VIRGINIA. EMPLOYMENT COMMISSION. LABOR MARKET TRENDS. irreg. Employment Commission, Economic Information Services Division, Box 1358, Richmond, VA 23211. TEL 804-786-7496. charts.

331   CN   ISSN 0382-1242
WAGE RATES, SALARIES AND HOURS OF LABOUR IN NOVA SCOTIA. a. Department of Labour, Research Division, Box 697, Halifax, N.S. B3J 2T8, Canada. TEL 902-424-4125.

331   SW   ISSN 0280-4743
WAGES AND TOTAL LABOUR COSTS FOR WORKERS: INTERNATIONAL SURVEY. 1966. a. Kr.80. Svenska Arbetsgivarefoereningen - Swedish Employers' Confederation, 103 30 Stockholm, Sweden. Ed. Maerta Finne. circ. 1,000.

380   GW
WERBE - MITTEL KATALOG. a. DM.24.05. Goeller Verlag, Hauptstr. 4, Postfach 240, 7570 Baden-Baden, W. Germany (B.R.D.) Ed. H.-J. Goeller. adv. circ. 10,000.

331   US
WERTHEIM PUBLICATIONS IN INDUSTRIAL RELATIONS. irreg., latest 1983. Harvard University Press, 79 Garden St., Cambridge, MA 02138. TEL 617-495-2600.

BUSINESS AND ECONOMICS — MACROECONOMICS

331   II   ISSN 0043-3071
WEST BENGAL LABOUR GAZETTE. (Text in English) 1957. irreg. (Department of Labour) West Bengal Government Press, Publication Branch, 38 Gopal Nagar Rd., Alipore, Calcutta 27, India. stat.

331.11   US
WEST VIRGINIA EMPLOYMENT AND EARNINGS TRENDS: ANNUAL SUMMARY. 1968. a. free. Department of Employment Security, Labor and Economic Research, 112 California Ave., Charleston, WV 25305. TEL 304-348-2660. circ. 400.

344.73   US   ISSN 0097-9171
WISCONSIN. EMPLOYMENT RELATIONS COMMISSION. REPORTER.* irreg. Industrial Relations Service Bureau, 3420 Heritage Dr., Minneapolis, MN 55435. Key Title: Industrial Relations Service Bureau's Wisconsin Employment Relations Commission, Reporter.

331   910.202   UK
WORKING ABROAD (LONDON) a. £6.95. Kogan Page Ltd., 120 Pentonville Rd., London N1 9JN, England. Ed. Godfrey Golzen. adv.

331   CN   ISSN 0084-1307
WORKING CONDITIONS IN CANADIAN INDUSTRY/CONDITIONS DE TRAVAIL DANS L'INDUSTRIE CANADIENNE. (Text in English and French) 1957. a. Can.$6. Labour Canada, Ottawa, Ont. K1A 0J2, Canada TEL 613-997-2617. (Subscr. to: Canadian Government Publishing Centre, Supply and Services Canada, Ottawa, Ont. K1A 0S9, Canada) circ. 1,800. (reprint service avail. from MML)

331   UK
WORKING FOR YOURSELF. a. £7.95. Kogan Page Ltd., 120 Pentonville Rd., London N1 9JN, England. Ed. Godfrey Golzen. adv.

331   US
WYOMING. DEPARTMENT OF LABOR AND STATISTICS. ANNUAL REPORT. 1977. a. Department of Labor and Statistics, Herschler Bldg., Cheyenne, WY 82002. TEL 307-777-7261. charts. illus. stat.

331   US
WYOMING. EMPLOYMENT SECURITY COMMISSION. ANNUAL REPORT. 1973. a. Employment Security Commission, Box 2760, Casper, WY 82601. TEL 307-335-3200. Ed. Philip J. McAulay. circ. 150.

331   US
WYOMING ANNUAL PLANNING REPORT. 1940? a. free. Employment Security Commission, Research & Analysis Section, Box 2760, Casper, WY 82602. TEL 307-235-3200. circ. 250.
    Formerly: Wyoming. Employment Security Commission. Research and Analysis Section. Annual Planning Report.

331   SA
YOUNG WORKER. 1976. irreg. R.1. Y.C.W. Publications, Box 47160, Greyville 4023, South Africa. Ed. M.G. Cloete. circ. 10,000.

331   ZA   ISSN 0084-4632
ZAMBIA. DEPARTMENT OF LABOUR. REPORT. a. 60 n. Government Printer, P.O. Box 136, Lusaka, Zambia.

331.1   YU
ZAPOSLENI PO OBCINAH. irreg. 20 din. Zavod SR Slovenije za Statistiko, Vozarski Pot 12, Ljubljana, Yugoslavia. Ed. Mlinar Branko.

BUSINESS AND ECONOMICS — Macroeconomics

337   US
ANNUAL EDITIONS: MACROECONOMICS. 1975. a. Dushkin Publishing Group, Inc., Sluice Dock, Guilford, CT 06437. TEL 203-453-4351. Ed. Ian Nielsen.

339   UY
BANCO CENTRAL DEL URUGUAY. DEPARTAMENTO DE ESTADISTICAS ECONOMICAS. PRODUCTO E INGRESO NACIONALES. a. Banco Central del Uruguay, Departamento de Estadisticas Economicas, Cerrito 351, Montevideo, Uruguay. charts.
    Formerly: Banco Central del Uruguay. Division Asesoria Economica y Estudios. Producto e Ingreso Nacionales. Actualizacion de las Principales Variables.

339   US   ISSN 0008-588X
CAPITAL GOODS REVIEW. 1950. irreg. ‡ Machinery and Allied Products Institute, 1200 18th St., N.W., Washington, DC 20036. TEL 202-331-8430. Ed. Richard R. MacNabb. charts. circ. 4,500. Indexed: P.A.I.S.

339   CH
CHINA, REPUBLIC. DIRECTORATE-GENERAL OF BUDGET, ACCOUNTING AND STATISTICS. REPORT ON THE SURVEY OF PERSONAL INCOME DISTRIBUTION IN TAIWAN AREA. (Text in English and Chinese) 1974. a. Directorate-General of Budget, Accounting and Statistics, Executive Yuan, Taipei, Taiwan, Republic of China. charts. illus. stat.

339   CK
COLOMBIAN ECONOMY. (Text in English) 1978. $35. Camara de Comercio Colombo-Americana, Apdo. Aereo 8008, Bogota, Colombia. Ed. Oscar A. Bradford. adv. charts. circ. 1,000.

312   339   US
CURRENT POPULATION REPORTS: CONSUMER INCOME. (Series P-60) 1948. irreg. U.S. Bureau of the Census, Customer Services, Washington, DC 20233 TEL 301-763-4100. (Orders to: Supt. of Documents, Washington, DC 20402)

339   US
CURRENT POPULATION REPORTS: CONSUMER INCOME. MONEY INCOME OF HOUSEHOLDS, FAMILIES AND PERSONS IN THE UNITED STATES (YEAR) (Part of series P-60) a. price varies. U.S. Bureau of the Census, Customer Services, Washington, DC 20233 TEL 301-763-4100. (Orders to: Supt. of Documents, Washington, DC 20402)
    Former titles: Current Population Reports: Consumer Income. Money Income in (Year) of Families and Persons in the United States; Money Income in (Year) of Families, Unrelated Individuals and Persons in the United States (ISSN 0073-5698)

339   TU
ECONOMIC INDICATORS OF TURKEY. (Editions in English and Turkish) a. Turkiye Is Bankasi, Economic Research Department, Ataturk Bulvari 191, Kavaklidere, Ankara, Turkey. stat. circ. 3,500 (English edt.); 5,800 (Turkish edt.)

339   SZ   ISSN 0070-9514
EIDGENOESSISCHE ZUKUNFT: BAUSTEINE FUER DIE KOMMENDE SCHWEIZ. 1963. irreg., no.15, 1978. price varies. Paul Haupt AG, Falkenplatz 14, CH-3001 Berne, Switzerland. Ed. Friedrich Salzmann.

339   GE
FRAGEN DES SOZIALISTISCHEN WELTSYSTEMS. (Text in German, Polish and Russian) a. Akademie fuer Staats- und Rechtswissenschaft, August-Bebel-Str. 89, 1502 Potsdam-Babelsberg, E. Germany (D.D.R.)

FUENTES Y USOS DE FONDOS. see BUSINESS AND ECONOMICS — Banking And Finance

GREAT BRITAIN. BOARD OF INLAND REVENUE. THE SURVEY OF PERSONAL INCOMES. see BUSINESS AND ECONOMICS — Public Finance, Taxation

339   UK   ISSN 0072-5927
GREAT BRITAIN. DEPARTMENT OF EMPLOYMENT. FAMILY EXPENDITURE SURVEY. 1957. a. £15.25. Department of Employment, Caxton House, Tothill St., London SW2H 9NF, England (Avail. from: H.M.S.O., 49 High Holborn, London WC1V 6HB, England)

338   UN
I L P E S CUADERNOS. (In 3 sections) (Text in Spanish) 1967. irreg., latest no.30. price varies. Instituto Latinamericano de Planificacion Economica y Social - Latin American Institute for Economic and Social Planning, Edificio Naciones Unidas, Av. Dag Hammarskjold, Casilla 1567, Santiago, Chile (Dist. in U.S. by Economic Commission for Latin America, 1801 K St. N.W., Suite 1261, Washington, DC 20006)
Study and teaching

330   II
INDIA. CENTRAL STATISTICAL ORGANISATION. NATIONAL ACCOUNTS STATISTICS: SOURCES AND METHODS. 1980. irreg. Rs.16.50($5.94) Central Statistical Organisation, Sardar Patel Bhavan, Sansad Marg, New Delhi 110001, India.

330   II
INDIA. CENTRAL STATISTICAL ORGANIZATION. NATIONAL ACCOUNTS STATISTICS. 1948/49. a Rs.60.45($21.75) Central Statistical Organization, Sardar Patel Bhavan, Sansad Marg, New Delhi 110001, India.
    Formerly: India. Central Statistical Organization. Estimates of National Income (ISSN 0073-6147)

339   PE
INSTITUTO NACIONAL DE ESTADISTICA. BOLETIN ANUAL. 1983. irreg. Instituto Nacional de Estadistica, Oficina Regional de Estadistica del Cusco, Direccion General de Indicadores Economicos y Sociales, Av. 28 de Julio No. 1056, Lima, Peru. Ed.Bd. circ. 500.

332   UN   ISSN 0252-3051
INTERNATIONAL MONETARY FUND. BALANCE OF PAYMENTS STATISTICS. Yearbook issue (ISSN 0252-3035) 1949. m.(plus yearbook) $38 ($19.00 to university libraries, faculty, and students) International Monetary Fund, Publications Unit, 700 19th St., N.W., Washington, DC 20431. TEL 202-623-7430. Ed. Werner Dannemann. stat. circ. 4,000. (also avail. in microform from UMI; magnetic tape; reprint service avail. from UMI)
    Formerly (until 1981): Balance of Payments Yearbook (ISSN 0378-2662)

IRELAND (EIRE) CENTRAL STATISTICS OFFICE. NATIONAL INCOME AND EXPENDITURE. see BUSINESS AND ECONOMICS — Public Finance, Taxation

336   JO   ISSN 0449-1513
JORDAN. DEPARTMENT OF STATISTICS. NATIONAL ACCOUNTS. (Text in English) 1960. a. $10. Department of Statistics, Amman, Jordan.

339   KU
KUWAIT. CENTRAL STATISTICAL OFFICE. ANNUAL BULLETIN FOR PRICES AND INDEX NUMBERS. (Text in Arabic and English) a. Central Statistical Office, P.O. Box 26188, Safat 13122, Kuwait.

339.368   BS   ISSN 0302-2056
NATIONAL ACCOUNTS OF BOTSWANA. a., latest 1978/1979. R.1.50. Central Statistics Office, Ministry of Finance and Development Planning, Private Bag 0024, Gaborone, Botswana (Orders to: Government Printer, Box 87, Gaborone, Botswana) stat.

330   US
NATIONAL PLANNING ASSOCIATION REPORTS. no.135, 1974. irreg. latest no.222. membership. National Planning Association, 1616 P St., N.W., Ste. 400, Washington, DC 20036. TEL 202-265-7685. Ed. Martha L. Benz. bibl. charts. stat. circ. 2,000.

339.2   US   ISSN 0079-0907
PERSONAL INCOME IN COUNTIES OF NEW YORK STATE. 1961. a. free. Department of Commerce, One Commerce Plaza, Albany, NY 12245. Ed. William Grainger. circ. 1,500.

339   PH
PHILIPPINES. NATIONAL ECONOMIC AND DEVELOPMENT AUTHORITY. NATIONAL INCOME SERIES. (Text in English) irreg., no.8, 1978. price varies. National Economic and Development Authority, Box 1116, Padre Faura St., Manila, Philippines. illus.

BUSINESS AND ECONOMICS — MANAGEMENT

339   SZ
PRICES AND EARNINGS AROUND THE GLOBE. (Editions in English, French, German, Italian and Spanish) 1970. irreg, 6th edt., 1985. free. Union de Banques Suisses, Bahnhofstrasse 45, 8021 Zurich, Switzerland. circ. 38,000 (English edt.); 168,000 (all edts.)

339   US   ISSN 0194-3960
RESEARCH IN HUMAN CAPITAL AND DEVELOPMENT; a research annual. 1979. a. $23.75 to individuals; institutions $47.50. J A I Press Inc., Box 1678, 36 Sherwood Pl., Greenwich, CT 06836-1678. TEL 203-661-7602. Ed. Ismail Sirageldin.

SOOCHOW JOURNAL OF ECONOMICS AND BUSINESS. see BUSINESS AND ECONOMICS

339.2   US
STUDIES IN INCOME AND WEALTH. 1937. irreg., no.51, 1986. price varies. National Bureau of Economic Research, 1050 Massachusetts Ave., Cambridge, MA 02138 TEL 617-868-3900. (Orders to: University of Chicago Press, 11030 S. Langley Ave., Chicago, IL 60628)
    Formerly: Conference on Research in Income and Wealth (ISSN 0069-8652)

339   UK   ISSN 0081-864X
STUDIES IN THE NATIONAL INCOME AND EXPENDITURE OF THE UNITED KINGDOM. 1966. irreg., no.7, 1977. $22.95 for latest vol. (National Institute of Economic and Social Research) Cambridge University Press, Edinburgh Bldg., Shaftesbury Rd., Cambridge CB2 2RU, England (and 32 E. 57 St., New York NY 10022) (Co-sponsor: Cambridge University, Department of Applied Economics) Ed. Richard Stone.

STUDIES IN WAGE-PRICE POLICY. see BUSINESS AND ECONOMICS

339.2   SJ
SUDAN. DEPARTMENT OF STATISTICS. NATIONAL INCOME ACCOUNTS AND SUPPORTING TABLES. (Text in Arabic and English) a. Department of Statistics, National Income Division, Box 700, Khartoum, Sudan. illus. stat.

309.2   SA
UNIVERSITY OF PORT ELIZABETH. INSTITUTE FOR PLANNING RESEARCH. ANNUAL REPORT/UNIVERSITEIT VAN PORT ELIZABETH. INSTITUUT VIR BEPLANNINGSNAVORSING. JAARVERSLAG. (Text in Afrikaans and English) 1970. a. free. University of Port Elizabeth, Institute for Planning Research, Box 1600, Port Elizabeth 6000, South Africa. circ. 400 (controlled) (back issues avail.)

339   VE
VENEZUELA. MINISTERIO DE HACIENDA. CUENTA GENERAL DE INGRESOS Y GASTOS PUBLICOS, BIENES NACIONALES, INCLUSIVE MATERIAS: INGRESOS Y GASTOS.* a. Ministerio de Hacienda, Caracas, Venezuela.

BUSINESS AND ECONOMICS — Management

808.5 301.16   US   ISSN 0360-0939
A C A BULLETIN. 1972. q. $40 to individuals; libraries $20. Association for Communication Administration, 5105 Blacklick Rd., Annandale, VA 22003. Ed. Robert N. Hall. adv. bk. rev. circ. 700. (also avail. in microfilm; reprint service avail. from UMI) Indexed: C.I.J.E. High.Educ.Curr.Aware.Bull.
    Continues: Association of Departments and Administrators in Speech Communication. Bulletin.

650   US
A M A MANAGEMENT BRIEFINGS. 1971. irreg., approx. 12/yr. $7.50 to members; others $10. American Management Associations, 135 W. 50th St., New York, NY 10020 TEL 212-586-8100. (Subscr. to: Box 319, Saranac Lake, N.Y. 12983) charts. illus. circ. controlled.

650   US
A M A SURVEY REPORTS. 1973. irreg. (approx 3/yr.) $13.50 per no. to non-members; members $10. American Management Associations, 135 W. 50th St., New York, NY 10020 TEL 212-586-8100. (Subscr. to: Box 319, Saranac Lake, N.Y. 12983) charts. illus. stat.

A M S DATA PROCESSING SALARIES REPORT. (Association for Management Success) see BUSINESS AND ECONOMICS — Labor And Industrial Relations

A M S GUIDE TO MANAGEMENT COMPENSATION. (Association for Management Success) see BUSINESS AND ECONOMICS — Labor And Industrial Relations

A M S OFFICE SALARIES REPORT; salary & benefits information for office employees in the U.S. and Canada. (Association for Management Success) see BUSINESS AND ECONOMICS — Labor And Industrial Relations

658.01   UK   ISSN 0066-9709
A T M OCCASIONAL PAPERS. 1965. irreg. price varies. Association of Teachers of Management, c/o M. Greatorex, Polytechnic of Central London, 35 Marylebone Road, London NW1 5LS, England.

658   US   ISSN 0065-0668
ACADEMY OF MANAGEMENT. PROCEEDINGS. 1938. a. $15. Academy of Management, Box KZ, Mississippi State University, MS 39762. TEL 601-325-3928. Ed.Bd. illus. index. circ. 1,800. (also avail. in microform from UMI; back issues avail; reprint service avail. from UMI) Indexed: Bus.Ind. BPIA.

658   US
ACCORD. irreg. free. Accord Association, 1898 S. Flatiron Ct., Boulder, CO 80302. TEL 303-444-5080. Eds. W. John D. Kennedy, Henry Lansford. circ. 6,000.
    Formerly: Romcoe Forum.

658.4   CN
ADMINISTRATIVE SCIENCES ASSOCIATION OF CANADA. PROCEEDINGS, ANNUAL CONFERENCE. 1973. a. Can.$120. Administrative Sciences Association of Canada, School of Business, Queen's University at Kingston, Kingston, Ont. K7L 3N6, Canada. TEL 613-545-2336. Ed. Donald Nightingale. illus. circ. 700.
    Former titles: Canadian Association of Administrative Sciences. Proceedings, Annual Conference (ISSN 0318-5036); Association of Canadian Schools of Business. Proceedings of the Annual Conference (ISSN 0066-9490)

658   US
ADVANCES IN APPLIED BUSINESS STRATEGY. 1984. a. $24.75 to individuals; institutions $49.50. J A I Press Inc., 36 Sherwood Pl., Box 1678, Greenwich, CT 06836-1678. Ed. Robert B. Lamb.

ADVANCES IN INTERNATIONAL COMPARATIVE MANAGEMENT. see BUSINESS AND ECONOMICS — International Commerce

658   US
ADVANCES IN STRATEGIC MANAGEMENT. 1983. a. $24.75 to individuals; institutions $49.50. J A I Press Inc., Box 1678, 36 Sherwood Pl., Greenwich, CT 06836-1678. TEL 203-661-7602. Ed. Robert Lamb.

658   IT
AGENDA EDIZIONE GUIDA MONACI. S.P.A. a. L.60000. Guida Monaci, Via F. Crispi 10, 00187 Rome, Italy. adv.

330   GW   ISSN 0065-5384
AKADEMIE FUER FUEHRUNGSKRAEFTE DER WIRTSCHAFT. TASCHENBUECHER ZUR BETRIEBSPRAXIS. irreg. price varies. Verlag fuer Wissenschaft, Wirtschaft und Technik GmbH und Co. KG, Amsbergstr. 22, 3388 Bad Harzburg 1, 3388 Bad Harzburg, W. Germany (B.R.D.)

ALCAN FACTS - AUSTRALIA (YEAR) see HISTORY

658   SP
ALTA DIRECCION. MONOGRAFIAS. irreg. 1200 ptas. Ediciones Nauta, S.A., Loreto 16, 08029 Barcelona, Spain. Ed. Juan L. Gutierrez Ducons.

658   US
AMERICAN INSTITUTE FOR DECISION SCIENCES. ANNUAL MEETING PROCEEDINGS. 1970. a. $17. Decision Sciences Institute, University Plaza, Atlanta, GA 30303. TEL 404-658-4000. circ. 2,000. (also avail. in microform) Indexed: BPIA.
    Formerly: American Institute for Decision Sciences. National Conference Proceedings.

658   US   ISSN 0360-7100
AMERICAN INSTITUTE FOR DECISION SCIENCES. SOUTHEAST SECTION. PROCEEDINGS. 1971. a. $10. American Institute for Decision Sciences, Southeast Section, Department of Business Administration, Virginia Polytechnic Institute and State University, Blacksburg, VA 24061. TEL 203-961-6601. Ed. Bernard W. Taylor, III. abstr. charts. pat. index. circ. 400.

658   US   ISSN 0065-9185
AMERICAN MANAGEMENT ASSOCIATION. RESEARCH STUDIES. irreg. $7.50 to non-members; members $5. American Management Associations, 135 W. 50 St., New York, NY 10020 TEL 312-586-8100. (Subscr. to: Box 319, Saranac Lake, N.Y. 12983)

658   US   ISSN 0065-9193
AMERICAN MANAGEMENT ASSOCIATION. SEMINAR PROGRAM. 1963. irreg. American Management Associations, 135 W. 50th St., New York, NY 10020 TEL 212-586-8100. (Subscr. to: Box 319, Saranac Lake, N.Y. 12983)

658   US
AMERICAN PRODUCTION AND INVENTORY CONTROL SOCIETY. ANNUAL INTERNATIONAL CONFERENCE PROCEEDINGS. 1960. a. $30 to non-members. American Production and Inventory Control Society, Inc., 500 W. Annandale Rd., Falls Church, VA 22046-4274. TEL 703-237-8344. circ. 51,000. (reprint service avail. from UMI)
    Former titles: American Production and Inventory Control Society. Annual Conference Proceedings (ISSN 0191-1783); A P I C S Annual Conference Proceedings (ISSN 0065-9819); A P I C S International Technical Conference Proceedings (ISSN 0190-8340)

658   UK   ISSN 0307-0409
ANBAR YEARBOOK. 1972. a. £85. Anbar Publications Ltd., P.O. Box 23, Wembley HA9 8DJ, England. Ed. A.C. Ede. abstr. bibl. index.

658   US   ISSN 0276-8976
APPLICATIONS OF MANAGEMENT SCIENCE. (Supplement avail.: Management Science Implementation) 1981. a. $24.75 to individuals; institutions $49.50. J A I Press Inc., Box 1678, 36 Sherwood Pl., Greenwich, CT 06836. TEL 203-661-7602. Eds. Randall L. Schultz, Michael J. Ginsburg.

658   SZ
B I/P E R S EXECUTIVE COMPENSATION REPORT. (Text in English) 1981. a. $600. Business International S A, 12-14 chemin Rieu, 1208 Geneva 17, Switzerland. Ed. Lars Andersson. (looseleaf format; back issues avail.)
    Formerly: B I/P E R S Annual Compensation Survey.

B O M A EXPERIENCE EXCHANGE REPORT; income/expense analysis for office buildings. (Building Owners and Managers Association International) see REAL ESTATE

658.1   US   ISSN 0360-8743
BEST IN ANNUAL REPORTS. (Subseries of: Print Casebooks) 1975. a. $19.50. R C Publications, Inc., 104 Fifth Ave., 9th Fl., New York, NY 10011 TEL 301-229-9040. (Subscr. to: 6400 Goldsboro Rd, Bethesda, MD 20817) illus.

658 378   US   ISSN 0361-1108
BRICKER'S INTERNATIONAL DIRECTORY OF UNIVERSITY EXECUTIVE PROGRAMS. 1969. a. $100. Samuel A. Pond, Ed. & Pub., 425 Family Farm Rd., Woodside, CA 94062. TEL 415-851-3090. (back issues avail.)
    Former titles: Bricker's International Directory of University Executive Development Programs (ISSN 0277-7312); Bricker's International Directory of University-Sponsored Executive Development Programs (ISSN 0191-2682)

BUSINESS AND ECONOMICS — MANAGEMENT

658   FR   ISSN 0078-950X
BUREAU UNIVERSITAIRE DE RECHERCHE OPERATIONNELLE. CAHIERS. 1957. irreg. 200 F. for 4 numbers. Bureau Universitaire de Recherche Operationnelle, 4 Place Jussieu, 75230 Paris, France. circ. 1,000.

658   UK   ISSN 0308-0455
BUSINESS GRADUATES ASSOCIATION ADDRESS BOOK. 1969. a. £50 to non-members. (Business Graduates Association Ltd.) A P Books, 33 Ashbourne Ave., London NW11 0DU, England. Ed. Alan Philipp. adv. bk. rev. circ. 3,500. Indexed: Anbar.

658   II   ISSN 0078-5261
C O R S I BULLETIN.* (Text in English) 1968. a. $3. (Operational Research Society of India, Calcutta Branch) Macneill & Barry Ltd., Ed. P. K. Ghosh, Research and Development Mgr., 9/3 Mandeville Gardens, Calcutta 700029, India. index.

658   II   ISSN 0068-5356
CALCUTTA MANAGEMENT ASSOCIATION. ANNUAL REPORT. (Text in English) 1959. a. membership. Calcutta Management Association, 1 Shakespeare Sarani, Calcutta 700071, India.

658   CN   ISSN 0068-8320
CANADIAN ASSOCIATION OF MANAGEMENT CONSULTANTS. ANNUAL REPORT.* 1963. a. free. Canadian Association of Management Consultants, 45 Charles St., E., Toronto, Ont. M4Y 1S2, Canada. TEL 416-231-4122. circ. 1,800.

658   US
CENTER FOR CREATIVE LEADERSHIP. TECHNICAL REPORT. irreg., no.20, 1982. Center for Creative Leadership, 5000 Laurinda Dr., Greensboro, NC 27402. Ed. Robert E. Kaplan.

658   US   ISSN 0009-8434
CLASSIFICATION MANAGEMENT. 1965. a. $18. ‡ National Classification Management Society, 6116 Roseland Dr., Rockville, MD 20852. TEL 301-231-9191. Ed. E.J. Suto. circ. 1,200. (also avail. in microfiche)

658   SP
COLECCION DIRECCION DE EMPRESAS Y ORGANIZACIONES. 1976. irreg., no.7, 1979. price varies. (Universidad de Navarra, Instituto de Estudios Superiores de la Empresa) Ediciones Universidad de Navarra S.A., Apdo. 396, 31080 Pamplona, Spain.

658   SP
COLECCION LA EMPRESA Y SU ENTORNO. SERIE A C. 1967. irreg., no.7, 1975. price varies. Ediciones Universidad de Navarra, S.A., Apdo. 396, 31080 Pamplona, Spain.
Formerly: Universidad de Navarra. Instituto de Estudios Superiores de la Empresas. Coleccion I E S E. Serie AC (ISSN 0078-8716)

658   SP
COLECCION LA EMPRESA Y SU ENTORNO. SERIE L. 1970. irreg., no.14, 1981. price varies. Ediciones Universidad de Navarra, S.A., Apdo. 396, 31080 Pamplona, Spain.
Formerly: Universidad de Navarra. Instituto de Estudios Superiores de la Empresa. Coleccion I E S E. Serie L (ISSN 0078-8708)

658   FR
COLLECTION E F G. (Economie-Formation-Gestion) irreg. Editions d' Organisation, 5 rue Rousselet, 75007 Paris, France. Ed. Michel Bernard.

658   FR   ISSN 0069-651X
COMITE NATIONAL DE L'ORGANISATION FRANCAISE. ANNUAIRE. 1950. a. Association Francaise de Management, 119 rue de Lille, F-75007 Paris, France.

658   FR
CONSEIL NATIONAL DU PATRONAT FRANCAIS. ANNUAIRE. a. 132 F. 31 av. Pierre 1er de Serbie, 75784 Paris, France. index.

658   US   ISSN 0196-1292
CONSULTANTS AND CONSULTING ORGANIZATIONS DIRECTORY; a reference guide to concerns and individuals engaged in consultation for business, industry and government. irreg., 7th edt., 1986. $365. Gale Research Company, Book Tower, Detroit, MI 48226. TEL 313-961-2242. Ed. Janice McLean. index.
Formerly: Consultants and Consulting Organizations (ISSN 0589-4859)

658   US
CORPORATE 1000; a directory of who runs the top 1000 U.S. corporations. 1985. a. $95. Washington Monitor, Inc., 1301 Pennsylvania Ave., N.W., Ste. 1000, Washington, DC 20004. TEL 202-347-7757. Ed. Bill Wade. circ. 8,000. (back issues avail.)

658   DK   ISSN 0107-8216
D M C INFORMATION. 1977. irreg. (1-3/yr.) free. Dansk Management Center, Kristianiagade 7, 2100 Copenhagen OE, Denmark. illus.

D S I R INDUSTRIAL INFORMATION SERIES. see ENGINEERING

658   US
DECISION RESEARCH; a series of monographs. 1984. irreg., vol.2, 1986. $24.75 to individuals; institutions $49.50. J A I Press Inc., Box 1678, 36 Sherwood Pl., Greenwich, CT 06836-1678. TEL 203-661-7602. Ed. Howard Thomas.

658   II   ISSN 0070-5322
DIRECTORY OF COMPANY SECRETARIES. (Text in English) 1969. irreg. Rs.30($9) Kothari Publications, 12 India Exchange Place, Calcutta 700001, India. Ed. H. Kothari. adv.

DIRECTORY OF DIRECTORS. see BIOGRAPHY

658   UK   ISSN 0070-5438
DIRECTORY OF DIRECTORS. 1878. a. £64. Thomas Skinner Directories, East Grinstead House, East Grinstead, W. Sussex RH19 1ZB, England. adv. circ. 4,750.

658.31   US   ISSN 0090-6484
DIRECTORY OF EXECUTIVE RECRUITERS. 1971. a. $21 per no. ‡ Consultants News, Templeton Road, Fitzwilliam, NH 03447. TEL 603-585-2200. Ed. James H. Kennedy.

658.3   US
DIRECTORY OF MANAGEMENT CONSULTANTS. 1976. irreg., 4th edt., 1985. $58.50 per no. Consultants News, Templeton Rd., Fitzwilliam, NH 03447. TEL 603-585-2200. Ed. James H. Kennedy.

658   UK
DIRECTORY OF MANAGEMENT CONSULTANTS IN THE UK. 1983. a. £35. Alan Armstrong & Associates Ltd., 76 Park Rd., London NW1 4SH, England.

DIRECTORY OF PLANS, EXECUTIVES, POLICIES FOR PCS, OFFICE AUTOMATION, DATACOM, ELECTRONIC MAIL. see COMMUNICATIONS

658   FR
ECONOMIES ET SOCIETES. SERIE S G. SCIENCE DE GESTION. irreg. 300 F. Presses Universitaires de Grenoble, B.P. 47 X, 38040 Grenoble, France. Ed. Henri Savall.

338 658.5   UR
EKONOMIKO-MATEMATICHESKIE METODY PLANIROVANIYA I UPRAVLENIYA. 1972. irreg. 0.72 Rub. Akademiya Nauk S.S.S.R., Dal'nevostochnyi Nauchnyi Tsentr, Ul. Leninskaya 50, Vladivostok, Russian S.F.S.R., U.S.S.R.

650   US   ISSN 0071-0210
ENCYCLOPEDIA OF BUSINESS INFORMATION SOURCES. irreg., 6th edt., 1986. $210. Gale Research Company, Book Tower, Detroit, MI 48226. TEL 313-961-2242. Ed. James Woy.
Formerly: Executives Guide to Information Sources.

658   US
ENCYCLOPEDIA OF ECONOMICS. 1973/74. irreg., latest 1985. $9.95 price varies. Dushkin Publishing Group, Inc., Sluice Dock, Guilford, CT 06437. TEL 203-453-4351. illus.
Formerly: Economics: Encyclopedia (ISSN 0090-4422)

658   PK
EXECUTIVE.* (Text in English) 1975. a. Institute of Business Administration, University of Karachi, University Campus, Krachi 32, Pakistan. illus.

658   US   ISSN 0095-4144
EXECUTIVE COMPENSATION SERVICE. REPORTS ON INTERNATIONAL COMPENSATION. ARGENTINA.* a. $170 to participants; others $340. American Management Associations, Executive Compensation Service, c/o Fulfillment Dept., Trudeau Rd., Saranac Lake, NY 12983 (Subscr. to: Box 319, Saranac Lake, N.Y. 12983) illus. stat. Key Title: Reports on International Compensation. Argentina.

331.2   US
EXECUTIVE COMPENSATION SERVICE. REPORTS ON INTERNATIONAL COMPENSATION. BRAZIL.* a. $170 to participants; others $340. American Management Associations, Executive Compensation Service, c/o Fulfillment Dept., Trudeau Rd, Saranac Lake, NY 12983 (Subscr. to: Box 319, Saranac Lake, NY 12983)

331.2   US   ISSN 0090-9971
EXECUTIVE COMPENSATION SERVICE. REPORTS ON INTERNATIONAL COMPENSATION. PUERTO RICO.* a. $170 to participants; others $340. American Management Associations, Executive Compensation Service, c/o Fulfillment Dept., Trudeau Rd., Saranac Lake, NY 12983 (Subscr. to: Box 319, Saranac Lake, N.Y. 12983) stat. Key Title: Reports on International Compensation. Puerto Rico.

330   US   ISSN 0093-8750
EXECUTIVE COMPENSATION SERVICE. TECHNICIAN REPORT.* 1973. a. $80 to participants; others $180. American Management Associations, Executive Compensation Service, c/o Fulfillment Dept., Trudeau Rd., Saranac Lake, NY 12983 (Subscr. to: Box 319, Saranac Lake, NY 12983) Ed. Michael D. Marvin.

658   UK
EXECUTIVE GRAPEVINE; the directory of executive recruitment consultants UK. 1979. a. £29 hardback; soft cover £24. Executive Grapevine, 79 Manor Way, Blackheath, London SE3 9XG, England (Subscr. addr.: 575 Madison Ave., Ste. 1006, New York, NY 10022, U.S.A.) Ed. Robert B. Baird.

658   FR
FICHES E O - FORMATION PERMANENTE. irreg. price varies. Editions Organisation, 5 rue Rousselet, 75007 Paris, France. Ed. Armand Dayan. bibl. (cards)

658   CN   ISSN 0071-5042
FINANCIAL POST DIRECTORY OF DIRECTORS. 1931. a. Can.$74.95. Maclean Hunter Ltd., Financial Post Division, Mclean Hunter Bldg., 777 Bay St., Toronto, Ont. M5W 1A7, Canada. TEL 416-596-5585. Ed. Jean Graham. adv. circ. 6,000.

658   NO   ISSN 0071-7630
FORRETNINGS- OG BEDRIFTSLEDEREN. 1959. a. Kr.168. Forlaget Tanum-Norli A-S, Kr. Augustsgt. 7A, Oslo 1, Norway. Ed. Nil M. Apeland. circ. 3,900.

658   SZ   ISSN 0071-9765
FUEHRUNG UND ORGANISATION DER UNTERNEHMUNG. 1961. irreg., no.38, 1983. price varies. (Hochschule St. Gallen fuer Wirtschafts- und Sozialwissenschaften, Institut fuer Betriebswirtschaft) Paul Haupt AG, Falkenplatz 14, CH-3001 Berne, Switzerland.

658   IT
GESTIONE INFORMATA. no.2, 1978. irreg., no.3, 1984. price varies. Liguori Editore s.r.l., Via Mezzocannone 19, 80134 Naples, Italy. TEL 081/20 6077. Ed. Lucio Potito.

BUSINESS AND ECONOMICS — MANAGEMENT

658   GW   ISSN 0073-0122
HANDBUCH DER RATIONALISIERUNG. 1958. irreg. DM.390. (Rationalisierungskuratorium der Deutschen Wirtschaft) Industrie-Verlag Carlheinz Gehlsen, Dechenstr. 7, Postfach 287, 5300 Bonn, W. Germany (B.R.D.)

650   658.01   US   ISSN 0073-0785
HARVARD UNIVERSITY. GRADUATE SCHOOL OF BUSINESS ADMINISTRATION. PROGRAM FOR MANAGEMENT DEVELOPMENT. PUBLICATION. 1960. a. price varies. Harvard University, Graduate School of Business Administration, Boston, MA 02163. TEL 617-495-6000.

658   SZ
HOCHSCHULE ST. GALLEN FUER WIRTSCHAFTS- UND SOZIALWISSENSCHAFTEN. VEROEFFENTLICHUNGEN. SCHRIFTENREIHE BETRIEBSWIRTSCHAFT. 1973. irreg., no.13, 1984. price varies. Paul Haupt AG, Falkenplatz 14, CH-3001 Berne, Switzerland.

658   GW   ISSN 0173-0665
I D - INFORMATIONSDIENST FUER DIE PERSONALABTEILUNG. 1979. DM.152.80. Verlag Dr. Peter Deubener GmbH, Furst-Pueckler-Str. 30, Postfach 41 04 68, 5000 Cologne, W. Germany (B.R.D.) TEL 0221-40320. index.

658   II
I F M R PUBLICATIONS. no. 12, 1975. irreg. Institute for Financial Management and Research, Madras 600034, India (Dist. by: Vora & Co., Publishers, 3 Round Bldg., Kalbadevi, Bombay 400002, India)

658   UK   ISSN 0304-4270
INSEAD ADDRESS BOOK. 1968. a. £50($75) to non-members. ‡ (INSEAD Alumni Association) A P Books, 33 Ashbourne Ave., London NW11 0DU, England. Ed. Alan Phillip. adv. circ. 6,000.

658   FR
INSTITUT FRANCAIS DES SCIENCES ADMINISTRATIVES. (PUBLICATIONS) 1967. irreg., latest no.20, 1981. 120 F. Editions Cujas, 4,6, 8 rue de la Maison Blanche, 75013 Paris, France.

INSTITUT PANAFRICAIN POUR LE DEVELOPPEMENT. CENTRE D'ETUDES ET DE RECHERCHES APPLIQUEES. EVALUATION DU SEMINAIRE SUR LA METHODOLOGIE DU MANAGEMENT DES PROJETS. see *BUSINESS AND ECONOMICS — International Development And Assistance*

INSTITUT PANAFRICAIN POUR LE DEVELOPPEMENT. CENTRE DE FORMATION AU MANAGEMENT DES PROJETS. BILAN DES ACTIVITES. see *BUSINESS AND ECONOMICS — International Development And Assistance*

658.007   IO
INSTITUTE FOR MANAGEMENT EDUCATION AND DEVELOPMENT. REPORT. (Text in English) 1980. a. $20. Institute for Management Education and Development - Lembaga Pendidikan dan Pembinaan Management, Jalan Mentang Raya 9, Jakarta, Indonesia. Ed. A. Winoto Doeriat. circ. 10,000.

309.2   TZ
INSTITUTE OF DEVELOPMENT MANAGEMENT. REPORT OF THE ACTIVITIES OF THE INSTITUTE. 1973. a. Institute of Development Management, Box 1, Mzumbe, Morogoro, Tanzania. circ. 500.

658.5   UK   ISSN 0260-373X
INSTITUTE OF MANAGEMENT CONSULTANTS. YEARBOOK. 1982. a. £20. (Institute of Management Consultants) Sterling Publications Ltd., 86-88 Edgware Rd., London W2 2YW, England. adv. circ. 3,600.

658   JA   ISSN 0085-2120
INTERNATIONAL COUNCIL FOR SCIENTIFIC MANAGEMENT. PROCEEDINGS OF WORLD CONGRESS. 1924, Prague. triennial since 1951; 1969, 15th, Tokyo. price varies; $18 for 15th. International Management Association of Japan, Mori 10th Building, Toranomon 1-18-1 Minato-ku, Tokyo 105, Japan (Inquire: World Council of Management, Box 20, 1211 Geneva 20, Switzerland)
Proceedings published by organizing committee

658   UK   ISSN 0267-7717
INTERNATIONAL EXECUTIVE TRANSFERS; Europe, USA, the Middle East. a. £275($367) (Economist Intelligence Unit) Economist Publications Ltd., 40 Duke St., London W1A 1DW, England.

150   US   ISSN 0160-7146
JACOB MARSCHAK INTERDISCIPLINARY COLLOQUIUM ON MATHEMATICS IN THE BEHAVIORAL SCIENCES. 1959. a. $5.50. University of California, Los Angeles, Graduate School of Management, 405 Hilgard Ave., Los Angeles, CA 90024. TEL 213-825-1581. (Co-sponsor: Western Management Sciences Institute) circ. 100.

JAHRBUCH FUER BETRIEBSWIRTE. see *BUSINESS AND ECONOMICS — Accounting*

658   II
JODHPUR MANAGEMENT JOURNAL. 1971. a. Rs.15($5) University of Jodhpur, Faculty of Commerce, Jodhpur 342001, Rajasthan, India. Ed. K. Agarwala. adv. bk. rev. circ. 1,000.

658   US
JOINT FINANCIAL MANAGEMENT IMPROVEMENT PROGRAM. ANNUAL REPORT. a. Joint Financial Management Improvement Program, 666 Eleventh St., N.W., Ste. 705, Washington, DC 20001.

658.2   JA
JOURNAL OF INDUSTRY AND MANAGEMENT/SANGYO KEIEI KENKYUSHOHO. (Text in Japanese) irreg. Kyushu Sangyo University - Kyushu Sangyo Daigaku, 2-327 Shokadai, Higashi-ku, Tokyo, Japan.

658   CE
KALAMANAKARANAYA; management. (Text in Sinhalese) 1977. irreg? Rs.1.50. University of Sri Lanka, Vidyodaya Campus, Management Studies Society, Gangodawila, Nugegoda, Sri Lanka.

658   JA   ISSN 0085-2570
KOBE UNIVERSITY. SCHOOL OF BUSINESS ADMINISTRATION. ANNALS. (Text in English) 1957. a. exchange basis. ‡ Kobe University, School of Business Administration, Rokkodai-cho, Nada-ku, Kobe 657, Japan. Ed.Bd. bibl. charts. circ. controlled. (back issues avail.)

658   UK
KOMPASS U.K. MANAGEMENT REGISTER. a. £20. Kompass Publishers Ltd., Windsor Court, East Grinstead House, East Grinstead, West Sussex RH19 1XD, England. circ. 14,000.

658   US
L R I GUIDES TO MANAGEMENT. MONOGRAPHS.* 1965. irreg., latest no. 7. price varies. Leadership Resources Inc., Box 2226, Merrifield, VA 22116-2226. Ed. Ronald E. Kieloch.
Formerly: Management Monographs (ISSN 0076-3640)

658   US   ISSN 0195-9204
LEADERSHIP. 1980. a. $4 per no. American Society of Association Executives, 1575 Eye St., N.W., Washington, DC 20005. TEL 202-626-2735. Ed. James O. Sample. adv. circ. 40,000. Indexed: Chr.Per.Ind. Rel.Ind.One.

920   650   GW   ISSN 0075-871X
LEITENDE MAENNER DER WIRTSCHAFT. 1940. a. DM.367. Verlag Hoppenstedt und Co., Havelstr. 9, Postfach 4006, 6100 Darmstadt, W. Germany (B.R.D.) adv.

658.5   US   ISSN 0024-8509
M T M/JOURNAL OF METHODS-TIME MEASUREMENT. 1955. a. $8. Methods-Time Measurement Association for Standards and Research, 16-01 Broadway, Fair Lawn, NJ 07410. TEL 201-791-7720. Ed. James P. O'Brien. charts. illus. index. circ. 2,200. (also avail. in microform from UMI) Indexed: Account.& Data Proc.Abstr. BPIA. Bus.Ind. Key to Econ.Sci.

658   629.13   US   ISSN 0565-7199
MANAGEMENT (BALTIMORE); a bibliography for N A S A managers. 1968. a. U.S. National Aeronautics and Space Administration, Scientific and Technical Information Facility, Box 8757, Baltimore/Washington International Airport, MD 21240 TEL 301-621-0153. (Order from: N T I S, Springfield, VA 22161) index.

658   UK
MANAGEMENT AND INDUSTRIAL RELATIONS SERIES. 1982. irreg., no.6, 1984. price varies. Cambridge University Press, Edinburgh Bldg., Shaftesbury Rd., Cambridge CB2 2RU, England (And 32 E. 57th St., New York, NY 10022)

658   UN   ISSN 0074-6703
MANAGEMENT DEVELOPMENT SERIES. irreg. price varies. International Labour Office - Bureau International du Travail, Publications Sales Service, CH-1211 Geneva 22, Switzerland (U.S. distributors: I L O Branch Office, 1750 New York Ave. N. W., Washington, DC 20006)

629.8   US   ISSN 0076-3624
MANAGEMENT GUIDE TO N C. 1964. irreg., no.2, 1971. $11.50. Numerical Control Society, Box 1234, Beloit, WI 53511. TEL 608-364-7949. Ed. M. De Vries.

658.4   UG   ISSN 0300-2144
MANAGEMENT JOURNAL. Short title: Management. 1968. a. S.2. ‡ Management Training and Advisory Centre, P.O. Box 4655, Kampala, Uganda. adv. illus. circ. 2,500.
Formerly: M T A C Journal.

658   SZ
MANAGEMENT PRAXIS. 1958. irreg. price varies. (Hochschule St. Gallen fuer Wirtschafts- und Sozialwissenschaften, Institut fuer Betriebswirtschaft) Paul Haupt AG, Falkenplatz 14, CH-3001 Berne, Switzerland. Indexed: Excerp.Med. Account.& Data Proc.Abstr.
Formerly: Betriebswirtschaftliche Mitteilungen (ISSN 0067-639X)

658   II
MANAGEMENT TRAINING AND RESEARCH CENTRES IN INDIA. DIRECTORY. 1982. irreg. Rs.150($20) Information Research Academy, 37 Amir Ali Ave., Flat 9, Calcutta 700019, India. Ed. Partha Subir Guhe.

658   UK
MANAGEMENT TRAINING DIRECTORY; a selected guide to post-experience courses and centres in the UK and US. 1980. a. £29.50. Alan Armstrong & Associates Ltd., 76 Park Rd., London NW1 4SH, England.

658   GW
MANAGEMENT WISSEN JAHRBUCH. 1974. a. DM.28. Vogel-Verlag KG, Postfach 6740, Max-Planck-Str. 7-9, 8700 Wuerzburg 1, W. Germany (B.R.D.) adv.

658   SJ
MANAGER. (Text in English) 1975. irreg. (1-2/yr.) Management Development Centre, Box 2308, Khartoum, Sudan. Ed. Sowar El Dabab Ahmed.

658   378   UK   ISSN 0260-4388
MANCHESTER TRAINING HANDBOOKS. 1981. irreg. price varies. University of Manchester, Department of Administrative Studies, Crawford House, Precinct Centre, Oxford Rd., Manchester M13 9QS, England.

658   BG
MANEGGIARE. (Text in English or Bengali) 1977. irreg. Tk.10. University of Chittagong, Department of Management, Chittagong, Bangladesh. Ed. Abdul Mannan. adv. circ. 1,200.

MEDICAL GROUP MANAGEMENT ASSOCIATION. DIRECTORY. see *MEDICAL SCIENCES*

BUSINESS AND ECONOMICS — MANAGEMENT

658 381 FR ISSN 0076-8812
MILLESIME. 1953. a. 25 F.($5) Association des Anciens Eleves de l'Ecole Superieur de Commerce de Paris, 79 Avenue de la Republique, Paris 11, France. adv. bk. rev. circ. 8,000.

658.4 MY ISSN 0126-8392
NATIONAL PRODUCTIVITY CENTRE, MALAYSIA. ANNUAL REPORT/PUSAT DAYA PENGELUARAN NEGARA. LAPURAN TAHUNAN. (Text in English and Malay) 1962. a. free. National Productivity Centre, Sultan St., Box 64, Petaling Jaya, Malaysia. circ. 5,000.

658 DK ISSN 0108-8165
ODENSE UNIVERSITET. INSTITUT FOR VIRKSOMHEDSLEDELSE. SKRIFTER. 1982. irreg., no.3, 1983. Odense Universitet, Institut for Virksomhedsledelse, Odense, Denmark.

OEKONOMETRIE UND UNTERNEHMENSFORSCHUNG/ ECONOMETRICS AND OPERATIONS RESEARCH. see BUSINESS AND ECONOMICS

658 CN
OFFICE PRODUCT NEWS DIRECTORY. a. Southam Communications Ltd., 1450 Don Mills Rd., Don Mills, Ont. M3B 2X7, Canada. TEL 416-445-6641. adv.
Formerly: Administrative Digest Business Directory.

658 378 US
OFFICIAL GUIDE FOR G M A T REVIEW. (Graduate Management Admission Test) 1972. biennial. $9.95. (Graduate Management Admission Council) Educational Testing Service, Princeton, NJ 08541. TEL 609-734-5221. (back issues avail.)
Former titles: Official Guide to G M A T; Guide to Graduate Management Education.

658 378 US
OFFICIAL GUIDE TO M B A PROGRAMS. (Master of Business Administration) 1972. biennial. $9.95. (Graduate Management Admission Council) Educational Testing Service, Princeton, NJ 08541. TEL 609-734-5221. Ed. Charlotte Kurst.

OPERATING RESULTS OF INDEPENDENT SUPERMARKETS. see BUSINESS AND ECONOMICS — Small Business

001.4 658 GW ISSN 0078-5318
OPERATIONS RESEARCH - VERFAHREN/ METHODS OF OPERATIONS RESEARCH. (Text in English, German) 1963. irreg., vol.55, 1985. price varies. Verlag Anton Hain GmbH, Adelheid Str. 2, Postfach 1220, 6240 Koenigstein, W. Germany (B. R. D.) Ed.Bd. circ. 300-700. Indexed: Math.R. Sci.Abstr. Int.Abstr.Oper.Res.

658 GW ISSN 0048-2129
ORDO; Jahrbuch fuer die Ordnung von Wirtschaft und Gesellschaft. 1948. a. price varies. Gustav Fischer Verlag, Wollgrasweg 49, 7000 Stuttgart 70, W. Germany (B.R.D.)

658 US ISSN 0149-1644
ORGANIZATIONAL COMMUNICATIONS; abstracts, analysis, and overview. a. $36 hardcover; paperback $17.95. (American Business Communication Association) Sage Publications, Inc, 2111 W. Hillcrest Dr., Newbury Park, CA 91320. TEL 805-499-0721. (Co-sponsor: International Communication Association, Austin, Texas.) (reprint service avail. from UMI)
Formerly: Organizational Communications Abstracts (ISSN 0160-5852)

658 UR
ORGANIZATSIYA UPRAVLENIYA. 1971. irreg. 0.81 Rub. Izdetel'stvo Ekonomika, Berezhkovskaya nab., 6, 121864 Moscow, Russian S.F.S.R., U.S.S.R.

658 CN ISSN 0710-362X
P E M: PLANT ENGINEERING AND MAINTENANCE SOURCEBOOK. a. Can.$12. Clifford - Elliot Ltd., 277 Lakeshore Road E., No. 209, Oakville, Ont. L6J 6J3, Canada. Ed. Lee Scott. circ. 17,000.

658 SZ ISSN 0079-2276
PLANUNG UND KONTROLLE IN DER UNTERNEHMUNG. 1966. irreg. vol.9, 1986. price varies. (Hochschule St. Gallen fuer Wirtschafts- und Sozialwissenschaften, Institut fuer Betriebswirtschaft) Paul Haupt AG, Falkenplatz 14, CH-3001 Berne, Switzerland.

658 PL ISSN 0324-9484
POLITECHNIKA WROCLAWSKA. INSTYTUT ORGANIZACJI I ZARZADZANIA. PRACE NAUKOWE. KONFERENCJE. (Text in Polish; summaries in English and Russian) 1973. irreg., no.17, 1986. price varies. Politechnika Wroclawska, Wybrzeze Wyspianskiego 27, 50-370 Wroclaw, Poland (Dist. by: Ars Polona-Ruch, Krakowskie Przedmiescie 7, Warsaw, Poland) Ed. Jerzy Ciekot.

658 PL ISSN 0324-9492
POLITECHNIKA WROCLAWSKA. INSTYTUT ORGANIZACJI I ZARZADZANIA. PRACE NAUKOWE. MONOGRAFIE. (Text in Polish; summaries in English and Russian) 1970. irreg., no.13, 1985. price varies. Politechnika Wroclawska, Wybrzeze Wyspianskiego 27, 50-370 Wroclaw, Poland (Dist. by: Ars Polona-Ruch, Krakowskie Przedmiescie 7, Warsaw, Poland) Ed. Jerzy Ciekot.

658 PL ISSN 0324-9468
POLITECHNIKA WROCLAWSKA. INSTYTUT ORGANIZACJI I ZARZADZANIA. PRACE NAUKOWE. STUDIA I MATERIALY. (Text in Polish; summaries in English and Russian) 1970. irreg., no.14, 1985. price varies. Politechnika Wroclawska, Wybrzeze Wyspianskiego 27, 50-370 Wroclaw, Poland (Dist. by: Ars Polona-Ruch, Krakowskie Przedmiescie 7, Warsaw, Poland) Ed. Jery Ciekot.

POLITICAL CLIMATE FOR INTERNATIONAL BUSINESS; a forecast of risk in 85 countries. see BUSINESS AND ECONOMICS — Banking And Finance

POLITICAL RISK YEARBOOK. see BUSINESS AND ECONOMICS — Banking And Finance

658 338 US ISSN 0079-3825
POOR'S REGISTER OF CORPORATIONS, DIRECTORS AND EXECUTIVES. 1928. a. with q. supplements. $398. Standard & Poor's Corporation, 25 Broadway, New York, NY 10004. TEL 212-208-8000. Ed. T. Lupo. (also avail. in magnetic tape)

650 658 SZ ISSN 0079-4880
PRAKTISCHE BETRIEBSWIRTSCHAFT. 1958. irreg., vol.10, 1982. price varies. (Hochschule St. Gallen fuer Wirtschafts- und Sozialwissenschaften, Institut fuer Betriebswirtschaft) Paul Haupt AG, Falkenplatz 14, CH-3001 Berne, Switzerland.

658 US ISSN 0741-6466
PRODUCTIVITY DIGEST. 1984. a. $20 members; non-members $30. American Productivity Center, 123 N. Post Oak Ln., Houston, TX 77024. TEL 713-681-4020.

658 US ISSN 0741-6458
PRODUCTIVITY PERSPECTIVES. 1980. a. $15 members; non-members $25. American Productivity Center, 123 N. Post Oak Ln., Houston, TX 77024. TEL 713-681-4020.

658 SZ ISSN 0079-7111
PRUEFEN UND ENTSCHEIDEN. 1958. irreg., no.9, 1983. price varies. (Universitaet Bern, Institut fuer Betriebswirtschaft) Paul Haupt AG, Falkenplatz 14, CH-3001 Berne, Switzerland.

658 GW
QUANTITATIVE METHODEN DER UNTERNEHMUNGSPLANUNG. 1975. irreg., no.20, 1985. price varies. Verlag Anton Hain GmbH, Adelheidstr. 2, Postfach 1220, 6240 Koenigstein, W. Germany (B.R.D.) Eds. H. Goeppl, D. Opitz.

QUI REPRESENTE QUI. see BUSINESS AND ECONOMICS — International Commerce

658 US
REFERENCE BOOK OF CORPORATE MANAGEMENTS. 1967. a. ‡ Dun & Bradstreet, Inc., 99 Church St., New York, NY 10007. TEL 212-285-7000. circ. 3,500.
Former titles (until 1981): Dun and Bradstreet Reference Book of Corporate Managements (ISSN 0070-7627); Moody's Handbook of Corporate Managements (ISSN 0545-0209)

RESEARCH IN DOMESTIC AND INTERNATIONAL AGRIBUSINESS MANAGEMENT; a research annual. see AGRICULTURE — Agricultural Economics

RESEARCH IN PUBLIC POLICY AND MANAGEMENT. see PUBLIC ADMINISTRATION

ROYAL SOCIETY OF NEW ZEALAND. PROCEEDINGS. see BIOGRAPHY

658 US ISSN 0193-4201
SIGNIFICANT ISSUES FACING DIRECTORS. 1977. a. $36.50. Directors Publications, Inc., Box 5198, Westport, CT 06881. TEL 203-226-7565. Ed. Thomas Connor. (back issues avail.)

SIR FREDERIC HOOPER AWARD ESSAY. see BUSINESS AND ECONOMICS

658 UN
SMALL INDUSTRY BULLETIN FOR ASIA AND THE PACIFIC. 1965. a. price varies. Economic Commission for Asia and the Pacific (ESCAP), United Nations Bldg., Rajadamnern Ave., Bangkok 3, Thailand (Dist. by: United Nations Publications, Room DC2-0853, New York, NY 10017; or Distribution and Sales, Palais des Nations, CH-1211 Geneva 10, Switzerland)

658 658 JA
SOPHIA UNIVERSITY. INSTITUTE OF COMPARATIVE CULTURE. BUSINESS SERIES. (Text in English) 1960. 5-6/yr. 1.000 Yen per copy. Sophia University, Institute of Comparative Culture, 4 Yonbancho, Chiyoda-Ku, Tokyo 102, Japan. Ed. Robert J. Ballon. circ. 800. (back issues avail.)

658 US ISSN 0195-1718
SOUNDVIEW EXECUTIVE BOOK SUMMARIES. 1979. irreg. (2-3/mo.) $82. Bristol Publishing Inc., 5 Main St., Bristol, UT 05443. TEL 203-655-6795. Ed. Cynthia Folino. adv. bk. rev. circ. 22,000.
Formerly: Soundview Summaries.

658 657 US ISSN 0743-2542
STRATEGY AND EXECUTIVE ACTION. 1984. irreg. (2-3/yr.) $15 for 4 nos. University of Mississippi, School of Business Administration, 300 LaBauve A, University, MS 38677. TEL 601-232-7481. Ed. Nolan Waller. circ. 600.

658 NE
STUDIES IN MANAGEMENT SCIENCE AND SYSTEMS. 1975. irreg., vol.11, 1985. price varies. Elsevier Science Publishers B.V., Box 211, 1000 AE Amsterdam, Netherlands. Ed. B. V. Dean. Indexed: Math.R.

658 NE ISSN 0081-8194
STUDIES IN MATHEMATICAL AND MANAGERIAL ECONOMICS. 1964. irreg., vol.33, 1984. price varies. Elsevier Science Publishers B.V., Box 211, 1000 AE Amsterdam, Netherlands. Eds. H. Theil, H. Glejser. Indexed: Math.R. Int.Abstr.Oper.Res.

658 US
STUDIES IN MEDIA MANAGEMENT.* irreg. price varies. Communication Arts Books (Subsidiary of: Hastings House Publishers) 260 Fifth Ave., New York, NY 10001.

SURVEY OF ARTS ADMINISTRATION TRAINING. see ART

658 382 600 US
TECHNOLOGY TRANSFER SOCIETY. INTERNATIONAL SYMPOSIUM PROCEEDINGS. 1980. a. $45. Technology Transfer Society, 279 S. Beverly Dr., Ste. 1078, Beverly Hills, CA 90212. TEL 213-274-3815. bk. rev. cum.index. circ. 500. (back issues avail.)

282 BUSINESS AND ECONOMICS — MARKETING AND PURCHASING

658 UK
THAMESMAN PUBLICATIONS. OCCASIONAL PAPERS. 1978. irreg. £1. Oxford Polytechnic, Department of Management and Business Studies, Lady Spencer-Churchill College, Wheatley, Oxon. QX9 1HX, England. Ed. R.D. Bennett.

658 US
TOP EXECUTIVE COMPENSATION. (Subseries of: Conference Board. Report) 1960. a. $150 to non-members; members $30. Conference Board, Inc., 845 Third Ave., New York, NY 10022. TEL 212-759-0900. illus. stat.

658 US
TRAINING AND DEVELOPMENT ORGANIZATIONS DIRECTORY; a reference work describing firms, institutes, and other agencies offering training programs for business, industry and government. 1978. irreg., latest 3rd edt. $270. Gale Research Company, Book Tower, Detroit, MI 48226. TEL 313-961-2242. Eds. Paul Wasserman, Janice McLean.

658 650 UY
UNIVERSIDAD DE LA REPUBLICA. INSTITUTO DE ADMINISTRACION. BOLETIN. 1976. irreg., no.4, 1979. Universidad de la Republica, Instituto de Administracion, Montevideo, Uruguay.

658 UY ISSN 0077-1287
UNIVERSIDAD DE LA REPUBLICA. INSTITUTO DE ADMINISTRACION. CUADERNO. 1956. irreg., no.80, 1979. price varies. Universidad de la Republica, Instituto de Administracion, 18 de Julio 1953 4p, Montevideo, Uruguay.

UNIVERSIDAD DE SEVILLA. INSTITUTO GARCIA OVIEDO. PUBLICACIONES. see *LAW*

658 SZ
UNIVERSITAET ZUERICH. INSTITUT FUER BETRIEBSWIRTSCHAFTLICHE FORSCHUNG. SCHRIFTENREIHE. 1970. irreg., no.52, 1986. price varies. Paul Haupt AG, Falkenplatz 14, CH-3001 Berne, Switzerland.

658 US
UNIVERSITY OF TOLEDO. BUSINESS RESEARCH CENTER. WORKING PAPERS. 1969. irreg., latest 1987. price varies. University of Toledo, College of Business Administration, 2801 W. Bancroft St., Toledo, OH 43606. TEL 419-537-2067.
 Formerly: University of Toledo. Business Research Center. Working Papers in Operations Analysis (ISSN 0094-1565)

658 CN
UNIVERSITY OF TORONTO. FACULTY OF MANAGEMENT STUDIES. WORKING PAPER SERIES.* 1971. irreg. Can.$5 or on exchange basis. University of Toronto, Faculty of Management Studies, 246 Bloor St. W., Toronto, Ont. M5S 1V4, Canada. TEL 613-978-2011. Ed. Frank Mathewson.

658 PL ISSN 0208-4791
UNIWERSYTET GDANSKI. WYDZIAL EKONOMIKI PRODUKCJI. ZESZYTY NAUKOWE. ORGANIZACJA PRACY I ZARZADZANIE. (Text in Polish; summaries in English and Russian) 1974. irreg. price varies. Uniwersytet Gdanski, Ul. Czerwonej Armii 110, 81-824 Sopot, Poland. Ed. Alfred Czerminski.

658 SZ ISSN 0083-4548
UNTERNEHMUNG UND UNTERNEHMUNGSFUEHRUNG. 1968. irreg., vol.14, 1985. price varies. (Hochschule St. Gallen fuer Wirtschafts- und Sozialwissenschaften, Institut fuer Betriebswirtschaft) Paul Haupt AG, Falkenplatz 14, 3001 Berne, Switzerland.

658 FR
V.I.P. DU CONSEIL. 1978. biennial. 490 F. Publications Professionnelles Francaises, 15 Square de Vergennes, 75015 Paris, France. (Affiliate: France Expansion) Ed. Zina Avril. circ. 1,000.

658 II ISSN 0083-5102
VAIKUNTH MEHTA NATIONAL INSTITUTE OF COOPERATIVE MANAGEMENT. PUBLICATIONS. irreg. price varies. Vaikunth Mehta National Institute of Cooperative Management, University Road, Poona 411 007, India.

330 658 FR ISSN 0083-6095
VIE DES AFFAIRES;* bulletin consacre a l'analyse des avis emis par les dirigeants d'entreprise a l'egard du droit economique et des politiques gouvernementales. 1970. irreg. price varies. Agence Legislative, 22 rue de Chateaudun, Paris 11e, France.

658.562 US ISSN 0083-8217
WEST COAST RELIABILITY SYMPOSIUM. 5th, 1964. irreg., 12th, 1971. American Society for Quality Control, Los Angeles Section, 310 W. Wisconsin Ave., Milwaukee, WI 53203.

658 US
WHAT IT COSTS TO RUN AN AGENCY. 1955. biennial. $18. Rough Notes Co., Inc., 1200 N. Meridian, Box 564, Indianapolis, IN 46206. TEL 317-634-1541.

658 338 UK ISSN 0083-9302
WHO OWNS WHOM. CONTINENTAL EUROPE. (In 2 vols.) (Text in English, French and German) 1961. a. $285. Dun & Bradstreet Ltd., 26-32 Clifton St., London EC2P 2LY, England. index.

WHO'S WHO IN ARTS MANAGEMENT. see *ART*

658 920 US ISSN 0083-9485
WHO'S WHO IN CONSULTING; a reference guide to professional personnel engaged in consultation for business, industry and government. 1968. irreg., 2nd edt., 1982. $175. Gale Research Company, Book Tower, Detroit, MI 48226. TEL 313-961-2242. Eds. Paul Wasserman, Janice McLean.

658.31 920 US ISSN 0092-4598
WHO'S WHO IN TRAINING AND DEVELOPMENT.* 1970. a. $35 to non-members. American Society for Training and Development, 1630 Duke St., No. 1443, Alexandria, VA 22314. adv. illus. circ. 25,000.
 Formerly: American Society for Training and Development. Membership Directory (ISSN 0569-776X)

650 US
WILEY SERIES ON SYSTEMS AND CONTROLS FOR FINANCIAL MANAGEMENT. 1971. irreg., unnumbered, latest 1985. price varies. John Wiley & Sons, Inc., 605 Third Ave., New York, NY 10016. TEL 212-850-6000. Ed. Steven G. Silverberg.

658 US ISSN 0275-276X
YEAR-END REGULATORY REVIEW. 1978. a. $17.50. Directors Publications, Inc., Box 5198, Westport, CT 06881. TEL 203-226-7565. Ed. Thomas Connor.

BUSINESS AND ECONOMICS — Marketing And Purchasing

see also Advertising and Public Relations

A L A WORLDWIDE DIRECTORY AND FACT BOOK. (American Logistics Association) see *MILITARY*

658 011 GW ISSN 0721-2720
A U M A KALENDER AUSLAND. a. free. Ausstellungs und Messe-Ausschuss des Deutschen Wirtschaft, Lindenstr. 8, D-5000 Cologne 1, W. Germany (B.R.D.) Ed. Kornelia Gelhausen. circ. 10,000. (back issues avail.)

658 011 GW ISSN 0721-2747
A U M A KALENDER REGIONAL. 1973. a. free. Ausstellungs und Messe-Ausschuss des Deutschen Wirtschaft, Lindenstr. 8, D-5000 Cologne 1, W. Germany (B.R.D.) Ed. Kornelia Gelhausen. circ. 5,300. (back issues avail.)

658 GW ISSN 0724-0554
A U M A ZAHLENSPIEGEL MESSEPLATZ DEUTSCHLAND. 1967. a. free. Ausstellungs- und Messe-Ausschuss der Deutschen Wirtschaft E.V., Lindenstr. 8, 5000 Cologne 1, W. Germany (B.R.D.) Ed. Harald Koetter. circ. 8,000.
 Formerly: Deutsche Messen und Ausstellungen - Ein Zahlenspiegel (ISSN 0084-9766)

658 011 GW ISSN 0724-0457
A U M A ZAHLENSPIEGEL REGIONAL. 1982. a. free. Ausstellungs und Messe-Ausschuss des Deutschen Wirtschaft, Lindenstr. 8, D-5000 Cologne 1, W. Germany (B.R.D.) Ed. Harald Koetter. circ. 2,700. (back issues avail.)

658.8 UK ISSN 0260-6488
A - Z OF U.K. MARKETING DATA. 1980. irreg. £35. Euromonitor Publications Ltd., 87-88 Turnmill St., London EC1M 5QU, England.

ADVANCED MANUFACTURING TECHNOLOGY. see *ENGINEERING — Mechanical Engineering*

658 US ISSN 0098-9258
ADVANCES IN CONSUMER RESEARCH. 1974. a. $29. Association for Consumer Research, Brigham Young University, Graduate School of Management, 632 TNRB, Provo, UT 84602. TEL 801-378-2080. circ. 1,500. Indexed: BPIA. Manage.Cont.

658 US
ADVANCES IN NONPROFIT MARKETING. 1985. a. $23.75 to individuals; institutions $47.50. J A I Press Inc., 36 Sherwood Pl., Box 1678, Greenwich, CT 06836-1678. Ed. Russell W. Belk.

658 US
AFTERMARKET BUSINESS BUYER'S GUIDE. 1974. a. $6. Harcourt Brace Jovanovich, Inc, 7500 Old Oak Blvd., Cleveland, OH 44130 TEL 216-243-8100. (Subscr. to: 1 E. First St., Duluth, MN 55802) Ed. Richard Weinberg. adv. circ. 22,455.
 Formerly: Home & Auto Buyer's Guide (ISSN 0162-8801)

658 US ISSN 0739-2958
ALL ABOUT MAIL ORDER. biennial. $19.95 per no. N T C Business Books, 4255 W. Touhy Ave., Lincolnwood, IL 60646-1975. Ed. Lou Smith.
 Formerly: United States Mail Order Industry Annual Report.

658.8 US
AMERICAN MARKETING ASSOCIATION. ANNUAL MARKETING EDUCATORS' CONFERENCE. PROCEEDINGS. 1921. a. American Marketing Association, 250 S. Wacker Dr., Ste. 200, Chicago, IL 60606. index. Indexed: BPIA. Bus.Ind.
 Supersedes: American Marketing Association. Proceedings (ISSN 0065-9231); Incorporating: A M A Combined Proceedings Series; A M A Papers of the Conferences; Formerly: A M A Abstracts of Papers of the Conferences (ISSN 0065-9215)

658.8 US
AMERICAN MARKETING ASSOCIATION. INTERNATIONAL MEMBERSHIP DIRECTORY AND MARKETING SERVICES GUIDE. a. $100 to non-members. American Marketing Association, 250 S. Wacker Dr., Ste. 200, Chicago, IL 60606. TEL 312-648-0536. circ. 30,000.
 Former titles: American Marketing Association. Membership Roster and Directory of International Marketing Service Organizations; American Marketing Association. Membership Roster Including the Advertising Section of Marketing Service Organizations; American Marketing Association. Marketing Service Organization and Membership Roster; American Marketing Association. Directory of Marketing Services and Membership Roster (ISSN 0093-1454)

380.1 II ISSN 0376-5512
ANDHRA PRADESH STATE TRADING CORPORATION LIMITED. ANNUAL REPORT. (Text in English) a. Andhra Pradesh State Trading Corporation Limited, 5-10-174 Fatchmaiden Rd., Hyderabad 500004, India. Key Title: Annual Report-Andhra Pradesh State Trading Corporation Limited.

658.8 FR ISSN 0066-300X
ANNUAIRE DU MARKETING. 1964/65. a. 410 F. Association Nationale du Marketing, Recherche, Strategie, Action, 30 rue d'Astorg, 75008 Paris, France. adv. bk. rev. circ. 3,000.

658.8 FR ISSN 0066-3077
ANNUAIRE EUROPEEN DES DIRECTEURS COMMERCIAUX ET DE MARKETING. 1958. a. 150 F. Dirigeants Commerciaux de France, 30 rue d'Astorg, 75008 Paris, France. adv.

BUSINESS AND ECONOMICS — MARKETING AND PURCHASING

658.8　　　　US　ISSN 0730-2606
ANNUAL EDITIONS: MARKETING. 1973. a. $9.50. Dushkin Publishing Group, Inc., Sluice Dock, Guilford, CT 06437. TEL 203-453-4351. Ed. Ian Nielsen. illus.
　Former titles: Readings in Marketing; Annual Editions: Readings in Marketing.

658　　　　AT
AUSTRALIA'S TOP 500 COMPANIES. 1986. a. Aus.$230. R.G. Riddell Pty. Ltd., P.O. Box 282, 100 Alexander St., Crows Nest, N.S.W. 2065, Australia. Eds. J.W. Wilson, R.J. Findlay. adv. circ. 2,500.

B T H A BUYERS GUIDE. (British Toy & Hobby Manufacturers Association) see *GIFTWARE AND TOYS*

658.8　　　　UK
BENN'S DIRECT MARKETING SERVICE. 1980. a. £50. Benn Business Information Services Ltd., P.O. Box 20, Sovereign Way, Tonbridge, Kent TN9 1RQ, England. adv.

BOOK MARKETS IN WESTERN AND EASTERN EUROPE. see *PUBLISHING AND BOOK TRADE*

BOOK PUBLISHERS. see *PUBLISHING AND BOOK TRADE*

BOOKSELLERS ASSOCIATION OF GREAT BRITAIN AND IRELAND. CHARTER GROUP. ECONOMIC SURVEY. see *PUBLISHING AND BOOK TRADE*

658.8　　　　US　ISSN 0068-063X
BRADFORD'S DIRECTORY OF MARKETING RESEARCH AGENCIES AND MANAGEMENT CONSULTANTS IN THE UNITED STATES AND THE WORLD. 1943. a. $48. Bradford's Directory, Box 276, Fairfax, VA 22030. TEL 703-830-4646. Ed. William W. Denlinger. adv. circ. 5,000.

BRITAIN'S D I Y INDUSTRY. see *COMPUTERS — Hardware*

BRITAIN'S DATA COMMUNICATIONS EQUIPMENT SUPPLIERS. see *BUSINESS AND ECONOMICS — Office Equipment And Services*

BRITAIN'S FIRE PROTECTION INDUSTRY. see *FIRE PREVENTION*

BRITAIN'S FREIGHT-FORWARDING INDUSTRY. see *TRANSPORTATION*

BRITAIN'S WINE INDUSTRY. see *BEVERAGES*

BRITISH JEWELLERS ASSOCIATION. BUYER'S GUIDE. see *JEWELRY, CLOCKS AND WATCHES*

658　　　　AT　ISSN 0311-5070
BUSINESS WHO'S WHO AUSTRALIAN BUYING REFERENCE. 1967. a. Aus.$175. R.G. Riddell Pty. Ltd., P.O. Box 282, 100 Alexander St., Crows Nest, N.S.W. 2065, Australia. Ed. D. Williams. adv. circ. 2,000.
　Formerly: Riddell's Australian Purchasing Yearbook (ISSN 0085-5715)

CADEAU ET L'ENTREPRISE; les techniques de stimulation des ventes. see *ADVERTISING AND PUBLIC RELATIONS*

658.7　　　　US
CALIFORNIA. DEPARTMENT OF CONSUMER AFFAIRS. ANNUAL REPORT. 1975. a. Department of Consumer Affairs, 1020 N St., Sacramento, CA 95814. Ed. Virginia Herald. circ. 250.

658.7　　　　CN
CANADIAN DIRECTORY OF SHOPPING CENTRES. 1975. a. 215. Maclean-Hunter Ltd., Business Publication Division, Maclean-Hunter Bldg., 777 Bay St., Toronto, Ont. M5W 1A7, Canada. TEL 416-596-5939. Ed. Maureen Cavanaugh.

658　011　　　　CN　ISSN 0829-8629
CANADIAN GOVERNMENT BUYER. 1986. 10/yr. C.$25. Momentum Magazines, 100 Rexdale Blvd., Ste. 100, Rexdale, Ont. M9W 1N7, Canada. TEL 416-746-8270. Ed. Franca Intrevado. adv. circ. 25,000. (back issues avail.)

658　　　　CN　ISSN 0829-4836
CANADIAN JOURNAL OF MARKETING RESEARCH. 1980. a. $15. Professional Marketing Research Society, 2323 Yonge St., Suite 806, Toronto, Ont. M4P 2C9, Canada. TEL 416-487-4893. Ed. Chuck Chakrapani. adv. bk. rev. circ. 1,200. (back issues avail.)

CATERING (LONDON, 1984) see *HOTELS AND RESTAURANTS*

658.8　　　　US　ISSN 0734-8169
CHILDREN'S MEDIA MARKET PLACE. 1978. irreg., 3rd edt. 1987. $39.95. Neal-Schuman Publishers, Inc., 23 Leonard St., New York, NY 10013. TEL 212-925-8650. Ed. Delores Jones.

COMPUTER SERVICES. SOFTWARE. see *BUSINESS AND ECONOMICS — Office Equipment And Services*

658.8　　　　US　ISSN 0573-665X
CONNECTICUT MARKET DATA. 1957. biennial. Department of Economic Development, 210 Washington St., Hartford, CT 06106. TEL 203-566-5437.

CONSUMER CREDIT ASSOCIATION OF THE UNITED KINGDOM. MEMBERSHIP DIRECTORY. see *BUSINESS AND ECONOMICS — Banking And Finance*

658.8　　　　UK　ISSN 0308-4353
CONSUMER EUROPE. 1977. biennial. £225. Euromonitor Publications Ltd., 87-88 Turnmill St., London EC1M 5QU, England.

CO-OPERATIVE COMMUNICATIONS. see *AGRICULTURE — Agricultural Economics*

658.8　　　　DK　ISSN 0109-3401
COPENHAGEN SCHOOL OF ECONOMICS AND BUSINESS ADMINISTRATION. MARKETING INSTITUTE. WORKING PAPERS. 1983. irreg. free. Handelshoejskolen i Koebenhavn, Marketing Institute, Howitzvej 60, 2000 Copenhagen F, Denmark. charts. cum.index. circ. 200.

COPENHAGEN SCHOOL OF ECONOMICS AND BUSINESS ADMINISTRATION. RESEARCH PAPER. see *BUSINESS AND ECONOMICS*

CREDIT MANUAL OF COMMERCIAL LAWS. see *BUSINESS AND ECONOMICS — Banking And Finance*

CROSS AND TALK; for communications between you and the world. see *ADVERTISING AND PUBLIC RELATIONS*

658.7　　　　DK　ISSN 0106-1941
DANSKE BYGGEMARKEDER. 1978. biennial. Kr.150. Fagbladet Byggemarkedet, Fagbladsafdelingen, Kontorhuset, Naverland 34, 2600 Glostrup, Denmark. illus.

658.8　　　　DK　ISSN 0109-5013
DATA OM MARKEDET/DATA ON THE MARKET. (Text in Danish and English) a. free. Markeds-Data, Ahlefeldsgade 16, 1359 Copenhagen K, Denmark.

658　　　　US　ISSN 0149-7421
DEVELOPMENTS IN MARKETING SCIENCE. 1977. a. Academy of Marketing Science, School of Business Administration, University of Miami, Box 248505, Coral Gables, FL 33124. TEL 305-284-2510. adv. (reprint service avail. from UMI)

658　659.1　　　　UK
DIRECT MAIL DATABOOK. 1976. irreg. (every 2-3 yrs.) £35($63) Gower Publishing Co. Ltd., Gower House, Croft Rd., Aldershot Hants GU11 3HR, England. Ed. Jennifer Durlacher.

658　　　　US　ISSN 0192-3137
DIRECT MARKETING MARKET PLACE; the directory of the direct marketing industry. 1980. a. $85. Hilary House Publishers, Inc., 1033 Channel Dr., Hewlett, NY 11557. TEL 516-295-2376. Ed. Edward L. Stern. adv. stat. tr.lit. index. circ. 4,800. (back issues avail.)

658.8　　　　UK
DIRECTORY OF EUROPEAN RETAILERS & INTERNATIONAL BUYING AGENTS. 1953. biennial. £65. Newman Books Ltd., 48 Poland St., London W1V 4PP, England. Ed. Karen Rasmussen. adv.
　Formerly: Stores of the World Directory (ISSN 0081-5829)

650　658.8　　　　US　ISSN 0070-556X
DIRECTORY OF FRANCHISING ORGANIZATIONS. 1959. a. $5. Pilot Books, 103 Cooper St., Babylon, NY 11702. TEL 516-422-2225. Ed. S. Small.

DIRECTORY OF MAJOR MALLS; lists existing and planned shopping centers in the United States and Canada over 250,000 sq. ft. of gross leasable area. see *REAL ESTATE*

658.8　　　　US　ISSN 0196-8262
DIRECTORY OF PREMIUM, INCENTIVE AND TRAVEL BUYERS. 1970. a., with s-a supplements. $130. Salesman's Guide, Inc., 1140 Broadway, New York, NY 10001. TEL 212-684-2985.
　Formerly: Directory of Premium and Incentive Buyers (ISSN 0070-6124)

658.7　　　　US
DIRECTORY OF SHOP-BY-MAIL BARGAIN SOURCES. 1978. irreg., latest 1986. $3.95. Pilot Books, 103 Cooper St., Babylon, NY 11702. TEL 516-422-2225. Eds. Margaret A. Boyd, Sue Scott-Martin.
　Purchasing

658　　　　US　ISSN 0737-0903
DISTRIBUTION MANAGEMENT.* 1983. a. (plus m. updates) $140. Auerbach Publishers, Inc. (Subsidiary of: International Thomson Organization Ltd.) One Penn Plaza, New York, NY 10119.

DO-IT-YOURSELF REPORT. see *BUILDING AND CONSTRUCTION*

DOG VOLUME 3. ADMINISTRATION, MANAGEMENT, MARKETING AND SALES. see *OCCUPATIONS AND CAREERS*

DROP SHIPPING SOURCE DIRECTORY OF MAJOR CONSUMER PRODUCT LINES. see *BUSINESS AND ECONOMICS — Trade And Industrial Directories*

DRUG STORE MARKET GUIDE; a detailed distribution analysis of chain and wholesale drug store industry. see *BUSINESS AND ECONOMICS — Trade And Industrial Directories*

658.8　　　　US　ISSN 0070-7821
E I A GUIDE. 1946. a. $30. Directories of Industry, Inc., 9371 Kramer, Unit 1, Westminster, CA 92683. TEL 714-892-4468. Ed. Billa Wann. adv. circ. 25,000.
　Formerly: Western Industrial Purchasing Guide and Electronic/Sources.

070.5　　　　US
EDITOR & PUBLISHER MARKET GUIDE. 1924. a. $60. Editor & Publisher Co., Inc., 11 W. 19th St., New York, NY 10011. TEL 212-675-4380. adv. circ. 3,968. (also avail. in microfiche from BLH, UMI; reprint service avail. from UMI)

ELECTRONIC MARKET DATA BOOK. see *ELECTRICITY AND ELECTRICAL ENGINEERING*

658.8　　　　US　ISSN 0071-0695
ENTERTAINMENT INDUSTRY SERIES. 1961. irreg. (approx. 1/yr.) price varies. Seven Arts Press, Inc., 6253 Hollywood Blvd., Suite 1100, Hollywood, CA 90028. TEL 213-469-1095. Ed. Walter E. Hurst. bk. rev. circ. 3,000.

658.8　　　　UK　ISSN 0071-2930
EUROPEAN MARKETING DATA AND STATISTICS. 1962. a. £87. Euromonitor Publications Ltd., 87-88 Turnmill St., London EC1M 5QU, England.

BUSINESS AND ECONOMICS — MARKETING AND PURCHASING

658 US
EXPOSITION WORLD. 1982. irreg. Louisiana World Exposition, Inc., Box 1984, New Orleans, LA 70158. TEL 504-566-1984. Ed. Winston Lill.

658 US ISSN 0071-3716
FAIRCHILD'S FINANCIAL MANUAL OF RETAIL STORES. 1923. a. $60. Fairchild Books (Subsidiary of: Fairchild Publications Inc.) 7 E. 12th St., New York, NY 10003. TEL 212-741-4280. Ed. Robert Benjamin. stat. circ. 2,000. (back issues avail.)

658 IT
FIERA DI MILANO. 1947. a. L.35000 per no. Fiera di Milano, Largo Domodossola 1, 20145 Milan, Italy. Eds. Gino Colombo, Vittorio Reali. adv.

658 IT
FIERE NEL MONDO. 1981. a. L.45000. Centro Italiano Pubblicita s.r.l., Via G. Bruzzesi 35, Milan, Italy. Ed. Bonisolli Lanfranco. adv.

658.8 CN ISSN 0227-6038
FINANCIAL POST CANADIAN MARKETS. 1925. a. Can.$75. Maclean Hunter Ltd., Financial Post Division, Maclean Hunter Bldg., 777 Bay St., Toronto, Ont. M5W 1A7, Canada. TEL 416-596-5585. Ed. Jean Graham. adv. circ. 6,000.
Formerly: Financial Post Survey of Markets (ISSN 0071-5077)

658.8 US ISSN 0273-4125
FINDEX; directory of market research reports, studies and surveys. 1979. a. (with mid-year suppl.) $255. National Standards Association, Inc., 1561 River Rd., Bethesda, MD 20816. TEL 301-951-1389. Ed. Susan DeGange. circ. 5,000.
●Also available online. Vendors: DIALOG.

FOOD PROCESSING. see FOOD AND FOOD INDUSTRIES

658.8 US
FRANCHISING OPPORTUNITIES HANDBOOK. a. $9.50 per copy. U.S. Department of Commerce, I T A-Service Industries Division, Washington, DC 20230 TEL 202-377-0342. (Orders to: Supt. of Documents, Washington, DC 20402)

FRASER'S CANADIAN TRADE DIRECTORY. see BUSINESS AND ECONOMICS — Trade And Industrial Directories

FREELANCERS OF NORTH AMERICA. see PUBLISHING AND BOOK TRADE

658 US
GREEN BOOK: INTERNATIONAL DIRECTORY OF MARKETING RESEARCH HOUSES AND SERVICES. 1963. a. $50. American Marketing Association (New York), 310 Madison Ave., No. 1211, New York, NY 10017-6009. TEL 212-687-3280. Ed. Pat Ryan. circ. 6,000.
Formerly: Green Book: International Directory of Marketing Research Houses (ISSN 8756-534X)

GUIA VENEZOLANA DE PUBLICIDAD Y MERCADEO. see ADVERTISING AND PUBLIC RELATIONS

HANDBOOK OF ADVERTISING AND MARKETING SERVICES. see ADVERTISING AND PUBLIC RELATIONS

HANDBOOK OF CANADIAN CONSUMER MARKETS. see CONSUMER EDUCATION AND PROTECTION

658 US
HONG KONG BARGAIN GUIDE TO FACTORY OUTLETS. 1986. biennial. $10. Howard Spriggle Publishers, Box 550, Ocean View, DE 19970-9801. Ed. Kenwood Spriggle. circ. 2,500.

658 338 US ISSN 0739-6821
ILLUSTRATED BUYERS GUIDE TO EXHIBITS; directory of portable and modular displays. 1983. a. $30. Exhibitor Publications, Inc., 745 Marquette Bank, Rochester, MN 55904. TEL 506-289-6556. Ed. Lee Knight. adv. circ. 4,000.

INCOME IN SALES/MARKETING MANAGEMENT. see BUSINESS AND ECONOMICS — Labor And Industrial Relations

658 380 US
INSIDE THE LEADING MAIL ORDER HOUSES. 1982. biennial. $89.95 per volume. (Crain Books) N T C Business Books, 4255 W. Touhy Ave., Lincolnwood, IL 60646. TEL 312-679-5500. Ed. Maxwell Sroge. (back issues avail.)

658.8 DK ISSN 0108-1489
INSTITUT FOR AFSAETNINGSOEKONOMI. NYT. 1974. irreg. (approx. 8/yr) Handelshøjskolen i Koebenhavn, Institut for Afsaetningsoekonomi - Copenhagen School of Economics and Business Administration, Rosenoerns Alle 31,4.sal, 1970 Copenhagen V, Denmark. illus. circ. 250.

658.8 FR ISSN 0074-1582
INTERNATIONAL ASSOCIATION OF CHAIN STORES. REPORT OF PLENARY SESSION. 1952. irreg., 1976, 19th, Rio de Janeiro. membership. International Association of Chain Stores, c/o Gen. Frederic C. Treidell, 61 Quai d'Orsay, 75007 Paris, France.

658.8 US ISSN 0074-459X
INTERNATIONAL DIRECTORY OF MARKETING RESEARCH HOUSES AND SERVICES. 1962. a. $50. ‡ (American Marketing Association, New York Chapter) Aalborg Tulane, Box 310, New Berlin, NY 13411. Ed. Pat Ryan. adv. circ. 6,000.

658.8 US
INTERNATIONAL VENDING BUYER'S GUIDE AND DIRECTORY. 1946. a. $12.50. Vending Times, Inc., 545 Eighth Ave., New York, NY 10018. TEL 212-714-0101. Ed. Arthur E. Yohalem. adv. circ. 15,000.
Absorbed: Vending Buyer's Guide.

658 GW
INTERNATIONALE BEITRAEGE ZUR MARKT-, MEINUNGS- UND ZUKUNFTSFORSCHUNG. irreg. price varies. Wickert Institute Tuebingen, 7919 Illereichen, W. Germany (B.R.D.)

IRELAND (EIRE) CENTRAL STATISTICS OFFICE. HIRE-PURCHASE AND CREDIT SALES. see BUSINESS AND ECONOMICS — Banking And Finance

JAHRBUCH FUER BETRIEBSWIRTE. see BUSINESS AND ECONOMICS — Accounting

JOURNAL CONTENTS IN QUANTITATIVE METHODS. see BUSINESS AND ECONOMICS — Abstracting, Bibliographies, Statistics

658.8 378 US
JOURNAL OF MARKETING FOR HIGHER EDUCATION. 1987. biennial. $24 to individuals; institutions $32; libraries $42. Haworth Press, Inc., 28 E. 22nd St., New York, NY 10010-6194. Ed. James A. Burns.

658.8 US
JOURNAL OF PUBLIC POLICY & MARKETING. a. $15. University of Michigan, Graduate School of Business Administration, Ann Arbor, MI 48109. TEL 313-764-1366. Ed. Thomas C. Kinnear.
Formerly: Journal of Marketing and Public Policy (ISSN 0743-9156)

658 GW
LAGERTECHNIK. 1967. a. free. Europa Fachpresse-Verlag GmbH (Subsidiary of: Sueddeutscher Verlag) Hackenstr. 7, D-8000 Munich 2, W. Germany (B.R.D.) Ed. Peter Scherr. adv. circ. 14,400.

658 UK ISSN 0140-3206
LONDON SHOP SURVEYS. 1974. biennial. £28. Newman Books Ltd., 48 Poland St., London W1V 4PP, England. Ed. Caroline Page. adv.

658.8 US ISSN 0092-4857
M E I MARKETING ECONOMICS GUIDE. 1973. a. $25. Marketing Economics Institute, Ltd., 108 W. 39th St., New York, NY 10018. Ed. Alfred Hong. illus. stat. (also avail. in magnetic tape)

658 US
M R A RESEARCH SERVICE DIRECTORY. 1973. a. $40 to members; non-members $85. Marketing Research Association, Inc., 111 E. Wacker Dr., Ste. 600, Chicago, IL 60601. TEL 312-644-6610. circ. 2,500.

658.8 US ISSN 0085-2953
MAIL ORDER BUSINESS DIRECTORY. 1955. a. $65. B. Klein Publications, Box 8503, Coral Springs, FL 33065. TEL 305-752-1708.

658.8 UK ISSN 0076-4523
MARKET RESEARCH SOCIETY. YEARBOOK. 1968. a. £35. Market Research Society, 175 Oxford St., London W1R 1TA, England. Ed. Phyllis Vangelder. adv. circ. 6,000.

658.8 UK
MARKET RESEARCH SOURCEBOOK. 1984. a. £49.95($98) Headland Press, Freepost 22, London EC1A 7QT, England. Ed. Tricia Walters.

MARKETING CALIFORNIA STRAWBERRIES. see AGRICULTURE

658.8 US ISSN 0098-1397
MARKETING ECONOMICS KEY PLANTS; guide to industrial purchasing power. 1960. biennial. $100. Marketing Economics Institute, Ltd., 108 W. 39th St., New York, NY 10018. Ed. Alfred Hong. stat. (also avail. in magnetic tape)
Formerly: Market Statistics Key Plant Directory (ISSN 0076-4531)

658 UK
MARKETING EXECUTIVE HANDBOOK. 1984. a. £14.95($25) Kirbypark Ltd., 11-13 Cricklewood Lane, London NW2 1ET, England. Ed. Kim O'Brien. adv. bk. rev. circ. 3,000.

658 US
MARKETPULSE. 1985. irreg. (approx. 4/yr.) free to qualified personnel. (Dependable Lists, Inc.) D L I Communications, Inc., 33 Irving Pl., New York, NY 10003. TEL 212-677-6760. Ed. Ray Lewis.

658.8 UK ISSN 0076-4647
MARKETS YEAR BOOK. 1955. a. £5.50. ‡ World's Fair Ltd., 2 Daltry St., Oldham, Lancs, England. circ. 30,000.

658.8 UK
MARKETSEARCH. 1976. a. $148. Arlington Publications Ltd., 87 Jermyn St., London SW1Y 6JD, England. Ed. Kathleen Mann.
Formerly: International Directory of Published Market Research (ISSN 9066-1605)

658.7 UK ISSN 0142-114X
MATERIALS HANDLING BUYERS GUIDE. 1963. a. $20. Turret-Wheatland Ltd., 12 Greycaine Rd., Watford, Herts. WD2 4JP, England. adv. index.
Formerly: Manual of Materials Handling and Ancilliary Equipment (ISSN 0076-4167)

658.8 US
MERCHANDISE & OPERATING RESULTS OF DEPARTMENT AND SPECIALTY STORES. a. $69.50 to non-members; members $37.50. National Retail Merchants Association, Financial Executives Division, 100 W. 31st. St., New York, NY 10001. TEL 212-244-8780.

658 380 US
MERCHANDISE MART BUYERS GUIDE. 1952. a. free. Directory Publications (Chicago) (Subsidiary of: Merchandise Mart Properties, Inc.) 470 Merchandise Mart, Chicago, IL 60654. Ed. Jim DeSeno. adv. circ. 60,000.
Formerly (until 1979): Merchandise Mart Directory (ISSN 0539-3876)

658 669 ZA
METAL MARKETING CORPORATION OF ZAMBIA. ANNUAL REPORT. (Text in English) a. Metal Marketing Corporation of Zambia, Box 34570, Lusaka, Zambia.

670 US ISSN 0736-2889
MICHIGAN MANUFACTURERS DIRECTORY. 1937. a. $133. Pick Publications, Inc., 28715 Greenfield Rd., Southfield, MI 38076. TEL 313-443-1799. Ed. P.S. Pickell. adv. circ. 5,000.
Formerly: Directory of Michigan Manufacturers (ISSN 0070-5845)

MICHIGAN STATE HORTICULTURAL SOCIETY. ANNUAL REPORT. see FOOD AND FOOD INDUSTRIES

BUSINESS AND ECONOMICS — MARKETING AND PURCHASING

658.8 US
MILLION DOLLAR DIRECTORY. 1959. a. $11955 to institutions; libraries $990. Dun's Marketing Services (Subsidiary of: Dun and Bradstreet, Inc.) 49 Old Bloomfield Rd., Mtn. Lakes, NJ 07046. TEL 201-455-0900. (also avail. in magnetic tape)
● Also available online.
Formerly: Dun and Bradstreet Million Dollar Directory (ISSN 0734-2861); Incorporating: Dun and Bradstreet Middle Market Directory (ISSN 0070-7600)

658 615 US
N A R D ALMANAC AND HEALTH GUIDE. 1915. a. National Association of Retail Druggists, 205 Daingerfield, Alexandria, VA 22314. TEL 703-683-8200. circ. 1,125,250 (controlled)
Formerly: N A R D Almanac.

381.1 US ISSN 0196-3171
N A R D A'S COSTS OF DOING BUSINESS SURVEY.* 1947. a. $25. National Association of Retail Dealers of America, 10 E. 22nd St., No. 310, Lombard, IL 60148-4915. Ed. Jules Steinberg. circ. 4,000.

658.8 US
N C P D M ANNUAL CONFERENCE PROCEEDINGS. (Supplement to: Bibliography on Physical Distribution Management) vol.13, 1975. a. $25. National Council of Physical Distribution Management, 2803 Butterfield Rd., Ste. 380, Oak Brook, IL 60521. Ed. Elaine M. Winter. bk. rev. charts. circ. 7,500.
Former titles: National Council of Physical Distribution Management. Annual Conference Proceedings; National Council of Physical Distribution Management. Annual Meeting Proceedings.

658.8 US
NATIONAL ICE CREAM RETAILERS ASSOCIATION. YEARBOOK. 1941. a. National Ice Cream Retailers Association, 1800 Pickwick Ave., Glenview, IL 60025. Ed. David L. Stumph. adv. illus. circ. 800.

NATIONAL SPORTING GOODS ASSOCIATION BUYING GUIDE. see *SPORTS AND GAMES*

NATIONWIDE DIRECTORY OF SPORTING GOODS BUYERS. see *SPORTS AND GAMES*

NYLON FILAMENT & POLYESTER FILAMENT GROWTH. see *TEXTILE INDUSTRIES AND FABRICS*

658 900 US
OFFICIAL DIRECTORY OF FESTIVALS, SPORTS & SPECIAL EVENTS. 1984. biennial. $65. Special Events Report, Inc., 213 W. Institute Pl., No. 303, Chicago, IL 60610. TEL 312-944-1727. Ed. Lesa Ukman. adv. circ. 5,000.
Formerly: International Directory of Special Events and Festivals (ISSN 0743-4170)

658.87 US
P O S I S.* (Point-of-Sale Information Service) 1976. irreg. $95. Price Waterhouse, Retail Automation Research Office, 300 Hamilton, No. 400, Palo Alto, CA 94301. Ed. Thomas L. Arnett. circ. 500.

PHARMACEUTICAL MARKETERS DIRECTORY. see *PHARMACY AND PHARMACOLOGY*

658.8 US
PORTFOLIO OF SALES AND MARKETING PLANS. a. Sales and Marketing Management, (Subsidiary of: Bill Communications, Inc.) 633 Third Ave., New York, NY 10017.

658 US
POTENTIALS MART. 1983. a. $48. Lakewood Publications, Inc., 50 S. 9th St., Minneapolis, MN 55402. TEL 612-333-0471. Ed. R.W. Anderson. adv. circ. 40,740.
Premiums and gifts

658.8 382 US ISSN 0097-6288
PRINCIPAL INTERNATIONAL BUSINESSES; the world marketing directory. 1974. a. $425. Dun & Bradstreet International, 1 World Trade Center, Ste. 9069, New York, NY 10048. TEL 212-938-8400.

658 US
PROMOTION POWER; sales promotion newsletter. 1978. irreg. free. Donnelley Directory (New York), 287 Bowman Ave., Purchase, NY 10577. TEL 914-933-6718. Ed. Tibor Taraba.

910 658.8 US
RAND MCNALLY COMMERCIAL ATLAS AND MARKETING GUIDE. 1876. a. $185. Rand McNally & Co., 8255 N. Central Park, Skokie, IL 60076 TEL 312-673-9100. (Orders to: Box 7600, Chicago, IL 60680) Ed. Dawn Checchin. charts. stat. index. circ. 5,000.

658 US
RESEARCH IN CONSUMER BEHAVIOR; a research annual. 1985. a. $23.75 to individuals; institutions $47.50. J A I Press Inc., Box 1678, 36 Sherwood Pl., Greenwich, CT 06836-1678. TEL 203-661-7602. Ed. Jagdish N. Sheth.

658.8 US ISSN 0191-3026
RESEARCH IN MARKETING; an annual compilation of research. (Supplement avail.: Choice Models for Buyer Behavior) 1978. a. $23.75 to individuals; institutions $47.50. J A I Press Inc., Box 1678, 36 Sherwood Pl., Greenwich, CT 06836. TEL 203-661-7602. Ed. Jagdish N. Sheth. Indexed: Psychol.Abstr. BPIA.

658 CN
RETAIL COUNCIL OF CANADA. OPERATING SURVEY OF CANADIAN RETAILING. a. Can.$55. Retail Council of Canada, 210 Dundas St. W., Ste. 600, Toronto, Ont. M5G 2E8, Canada. TEL 416-598-4684.

658 CN
RETAIL COUNCIL OF CANADA. SHRINKAGE SURVEY. a. Can.$25. Retail Council of Canada, 210 Dundas St. W., Ste. 600, Toronto, Ont. M5G 2E8, Canada. TEL 416-598-4684.

658.8 UK
RETAIL DIRECTORY. 1939. a. £68. Newman Books Ltd., 48 Poland St., London W1V 4PP, England. Eds. Karen Rasmussen, Caroline Page. adv.
Former titles: Stores, Shops, Hypermarkets Retail Directory (ISSN 0305-4012); Stores and Shops Retail Directory (ISSN 0081-5810)

658.83 UK
RETAIL TRADE INTERNATIONAL. 1975. biennial. £290. Euromonitor Publications Ltd., 87-88 Turnmill St., London EC1M 5QU, England.
Formerly: Retail Trade Europe.

S N DISTRIBUTION STUDY OF GROCERY STORE SALES. see *FOOD AND FOOD INDUSTRIES*

SAN FRANCISCO FRESH FRUIT AND VEGETABLE WHOLESALE MARKET PRICES. see *AGRICULTURE*

658.8 SZ ISSN 0302-2048
SCHWEIZERISCHE GESELLSCHAFT FUER MARKTFORSCHUNG. GESCHAEFTSBERICHT. (Text in German) irreg., no.37, 1977. Schweizerische Gesellschaft fuer Marktforschung, Bleicherweg 21, 8022 Zurich, Switzerland. stat.

658.7 UK
SCOTTISH TRADES AND SHOPS HOLIDAYS. a. £1. Wm. Culross & Son Ltd., Coupar Angus, Pershshire, Scotland.

658 US
SHOP-AT-HOME DIRECTORY. 1987. a. Belcaro Group, Inc., 650 S. Cherry St., Ste. 440, Denver, CO 80222. TEL 303-377-2535. adv. circ. 1,000,000.

658 CN ISSN 0226-7551
SHOPPING CENTRE CANADA. 1979. a. Can.$18. Maclean Hunter Ltd., Business Publication Division, Maclean Hunter Bldg., 777 Bay St., Toronto, Ont. M5W 1A7, Canada. TEL 416-596-5987. Ed. Tim Dickson. illus.

658.7 UK
SHOPPING IN EDINBURGH. 1981. a. £0.95. Pastime Publications Ltd., 15 Dublin Street Lane South, Edinburgh EH1 3PX, Scotland. adv. circ. 50,000.

658 KE
SOKONI: OFFICIAL NEWSLETTER OF THE MARKETING SOCIETY OF KENYA. irreg. Marketing Society of Kenya, P.O. Box 74759, Nairobi, Kenya.

SOPHIA UNIVERSITY. INSTITUTE OF COMPARATIVE CULTURE. BUSINESS SERIES. see *BUSINESS AND ECONOMICS — Management*

380 790.1 UK
SPORTS TRADER BUYER'S GUIDE. a. £15 free to qualified personnel. Benn Publications Ltd., Sovereign Way, Tonbridge, Kent TN9 1RW, England. adv.

STRATEGY AND EXECUTIVE ACTION. see *BUSINESS AND ECONOMICS — Management*

658 UN
STUDIES IN THE PROCESSING, MARKETING AND DISTRIBUTION OF COMMODITIES. 1984. irreg. price varies. (United Nations Conference on Trade and Development (UNCTAD)) United Nations Publications, Room DC2-0853, New York, NY 10017 (Or Distribution and Sales Sections, Palais des Nations, 1211 Geneva 10, Switzerland)

658.8 US ISSN 0081-9662
SURPLUS DEALERS DIRECTORY.* 1950. a. $12.50 includes monthly bulletin. Institute of Surplus Dealers, 230-11a Linden Blvd., Cambria Heights, NY 11411. TEL 718-723-8158. Ed. Fred D. Reder.

658 II
TEA TRADING CORPORATION OF INDIA. ANNUAL REPORT. (Text in English) a. Tea Trading Corporation of India Ltd., 225-F Acharya Jagadish Bose Rd., Calcutta 700020, India.

658.8 US
TEST AND MEASUREMENT WORLD YEARBOOK. a. $995. Market Intelligence Research Company, 4000 Middlefield Rd., Palo Alto, CA 94303. TEL 415-856-8200.

658.8 US
THOMAS REGISTER OF AMERICAN MANUFACTURERS AND THOMAS REGISTER CATALOG FILE. (19 vol. set) 1905. a. $190. Thomas Publishing Co., One Penn Plaza, 250 W. 34th St., New York, NY 10119. TEL 212-695-0500. Ed. Ronald Duchaine. index.
● Also available online. Vendors: DIALOG.
Formerly: Thomas Register of American Manufacturers (ISSN 0082-4216)

658 US
TRADESHOW WEEK DATA BOOK. 1985. a. $175. Tradeshow Week, 12233 W. Olympic Blvd., Ste. 236, Los Angeles, CA 90064. TEL 213-826-5696. (Co-sponsor: Trade Show Bureau)

658.8 UK
U.K. MARKETING HANDBOOK. 1982. a. £35. Creative Handbook, 100 St. Martins Ln., London WC2, England. Ed. Susan Scott Parkis. adv. circ. 6,000.

658.8 US
U.S. DEPARTMENT OF COMMERCE. CONSUMER GOODS AND SERVICES DIVISION. FRANCHISE OPPORTUNITIES HANDBOOK. 1965. a. price varies. U.S. Department of Commerce, Room 1104, Washington, DC 20230 TEL 202-377-2000. (Orders to Supt. of Documents, Washington, DC 20402)

658 659.1 FR
V.I.P. DU MARKETING ET DE LA PUBLICITE. 1976. biennial. 490 F. Publications Professionnelles Francaises, 15 Square de Vergennes, 75015 Paris, France. (Affiliate: France Expansion)

658.7 690 DK
V OG S PRISER. ANLEG. 1973. a. Kr.598. V og S Byggedata A-S, Frederikssundsvej 194, 2700 Broenshoej, Denmark.
Formerly: V og S Priser (ISSN 0105-421X)

658.7 690 DK ISSN 0105-4201
V OG S PRISER. HUSBYGNING. 1974. a. Kr.561. V og S Byggedata A-S, Frederikssundsvej 194, 2700 Broenshoej, Denmark.

BUSINESS AND ECONOMICS — OFFICE EQUIPMENT AND SERVICES

VANUATU. NATIONAL PLANNING AND STATISTICS OFFICE. CONSUMER PRICES INDEXES/INDICES DES PRIX A LA CONSOMMATION. see *CONSUMER EDUCATION AND PROTECTION*

658.8   UK   ISSN 0143-4381
VENDING INTERNATIONAL MANUAL; the handbook of vending. 1969. a. £12. Weald of Kent Publications (Tonbridge) Ltd., 47 High St., Tonbridge, Kent, England. Ed. Patrick Crawford. adv.
   Vending machines

658.8   UK   ISSN 0083-9175
WHERE TO BUY. (Composed of 4 volumes: Chemicals; Building; Electrical; Agricultural and Horticultural) 1930. a. £4 plus postage for each vol. Industrial Newspapers Ltd., Queensway House, 2 Queensway, Redhill, Surrey RH1 1QS, England. Ed. F. Loader. (reprint service avail. from UMI)

658.8   UK   ISSN 0083-9310
WHO OWNS WHOM, NORTH AMERICA. 1969. a. $225. Dun & Bradstreet Ltd., 26-32 Clifton St., London EC2P 1LY, England. index.
●Also available online. Vendors: Pergamon Infoline.

WOLFF'S GUIDE TO THE LONDON METAL EXCHANGE. see *METALLURGY*

YEAR BOOK OF AGRICULTURAL CO-OPERATION. see *AGRICULTURE — Agricultural Economics*

BUSINESS AND ECONOMICS —
Office Equipment And Services

651   FR
ANNUAIRE DE LA MECANOGRAPHIE, MATERIEL DE BUREAU, INFORMATIQUE. 1972. a. 340 F. Editions Louis Johanet, 68 rue Boursault, 75017 Paris, France.

651   658.8   UK
BRITAIN'S DATA COMMUNICATIONS EQUIPMENT SUPPLIERS. 1985. irreg. £95($150) Jordan & Sons Ltd., Jordan House, 47 Brunswick Place, London N1 6EE, England.

651   380.14   UK
COMPUTER SERVICES. SOFTWARE. 1984. irreg. £95($150) Jordan & Sons Ltd., Jordan House, 47 Brunswick Place, London N1 6EE, England.

COMPUTER USERS HANDBOOK. see *COMPUTERS — Hardware*

COMPUTERS & OFFICE EQUIPMENT: LATIN AMERICAN INDUSTRIAL REPORT. see *COMPUTERS*

651   VE
E P O: CATALOGO DE EQUIPOS PARA OFICINA. 1976. a. M.G. Ediciones Especializadas, Av. Maturin, No. 15, Urb. Los Cedros, El Bosque, Caracas 1050, Venezuela. Ed. Montserrat Giol. adv.

651   US   ISSN 0072-4327
GEYER'S WHO MAKES IT DIRECTORY. 1877. a. avail. only with subscription to Geyer's Dealer Topics. Geyer-McAllister Publications, Inc., 51 Madison Ave., New York, NY 10010. TEL 212-689-4411. Ed. R. Rauch. adv. circ. 15,700.

I E E E SYMPOSIUM ON MASS STORAGE SYSTEMS. DIGEST OF PAPERS. see *COMPUTERS*

651.2   SZ
I F O S A. MINUTES OF THE GENERAL MEETING.* 1962. a. free. International Federation of Stationers' Associations, P.B. 130, 8021 Zurich, Switzerland. Ed. Hanni Felix.

651.07   II   ISSN 0304-7083
INSTITUTE OF SECRETARIAT TRAINING AND MANAGEMENT. ANNUAL REPORT. (Text in English) a. Institute of Secretariat Training and Management, West Block 1, Wing 5, R.K. Puram, New Delhi 110022, India. Key Title: Annual Report - Institute of Secretariat Training and Management.

651.2   US   ISSN 0020-6288
INTERNATIONAL BUSINESS EQUIPMENT. (Text in English, French and German) 1964. a. $10 for 3 nos. Office Publications, Inc., 1600 Summer St., Stamford, CT 06904. TEL 203-327-9670. Ed. William R. Schulhof. adv. bk. rev. charts. illus. tr.lit. circ. 56,000. (also avail. in microform from UMI; reprint service avail. from UMI) Indexed: Sci.Abstr. BMT.

651   IT
MOBILI PER UFFICIO. a. L.10000. Compagnia Pubblicazioni Internazionali, Viale Stelvio 21, 20159 Milan, Italy. Ed. Giuseppe Vallardi. adv. circ. 25,000.

NATIONAL BUSINESS EDUCATION YEARBOOK. see *EDUCATION — Teaching Methods And Curriculum*

651   US   ISSN 0077-572X
NATIONAL SHORTHAND REPORTERS ASSOCIATION. PROCEEDINGS OF THE ANNUAL CONVENTION. a. National Shorthand Reporters Association, 118 Park St., S.E., Vienna, VA 22180. Ed. Mary Louise Gilman. circ. 3,500.

380.1   NR   ISSN 0331-0973
NIGERIAN YELLOW PAGES. 1971. a. I C I C (Directory Publishers) Ltd., P.M.B. 3204, Surulere, Lagos, Nigeria. Ed. Olu Adeyemi.
   Formerly (until 1979): Nigerian Office and Residential Directory; Nigerian Office and Quarters Directory (ISSN 0085-4190)

651.2   382   US   ISSN 0471-1424
OFFICE EQUIPMENT EXPORTER. 1946. a. Office Publications, Inc., 1600 Summer St., Stamford, CT 06904. TEL 203-327-9670. Ed. William R. Schulhof. adv. circ. 17,000.

651   US   ISSN 0085-445X
OFICINA; REVISTA DE EQUIPOS PARA OFICINAS. (Text and summaries in Spanish) 1940. a. Office Publications, Inc., 1600 Summer St., Stamford, CT 06904. TEL 203-327-9670. Ed. William Schulhof. circ. 13,000. (reprint service avail. from UMI)

651   VE
PROOFICINAS. 1978. a. Publicaciones Araguaney, Calle 8, Edificio Lec, piso 3, La Urbina, Caracas 107, Venezuela. adv.

651.2   US
RESOURCE CENTER INDEX. (Former name of issuing body: National Micrographics Association) 1974. s-a. $25 to non-members. Association for Information and Image Management, Resource Center, 1100 Wayne Ave., Ste. 1100, Silver Spring, MD 20910. TEL 301-587-8202. (also avail. in microfiche)
   Formerly: Micrographics Index.

338   UK   ISSN 0081-461X
STATIONERY TRADE REFERENCE BOOK AND BUYERS GUIDE. 1954. a. £25. Whitehall Press Ltd., Earl House, Maidstone, Kent ME14 1PE, England.

651.2   US   ISSN 0739-2966
TELECONFERENCING RESOURCES DIRECTORY. 1983. a. $47.50. Knowledge Industry Publications, Inc., 701 Westchester Ave., White Plains, NY 10604. TEL 914-328-9157. Ed. Margaret Csenge.

651.2   651   US
TOP 100 DATA PROCESSING ALMANAC. 1979. a. $375. Gartner Group, 22 Cummings Point Rd., Stamford, CT 06902. TEL 203-964-0096.

BUSINESS AND ECONOMICS —
Personnel Management

A S T D BUYERS GUIDE AND CONSULTANTS DIRECTORY. see *BUSINESS AND ECONOMICS — Labor And Industrial Relations*

658.3   US
ANNUAL EXECUTIVE COMPENSATION REPORT. 1964. a. $205. Sibson & Company, Inc., 212 Carnegie Center, CN 5323, Princeton, NJ 08543-5323. TEL 609-520-2700. Ed. Ed Emerman. circ. 1,000. (back issues avail.)
   Formerly: Annual Executive Compensation Study.

658.3   GW   ISSN 0174-6200
BASISTEXTE PERSONALWESEN. 1983. irreg., no.6, 1985. price varies. Ferdinand Enke Verlag, Postfach 1304, D 7000 Stuttgart 1, W. Germany (B.R.D.) Ed. O. Neuberger.

CANADIAN CASES ON EMPLOYMENT LAW REPORTS. see *LAW*

658.3   352   US   ISSN 0732-5282
COMPENSATION (WASHINGTON); an annual report on local government executive salaries and fringe benefits. 1982. a. $120. International City Management Association, 1120 G St., N.W., STe. 300, Washington, DC 20005. TEL 202-626-4600. circ. 900.

658.3   FR   ISSN 0071-2493
EUROPEAN ASSOCIATION FOR PERSONNEL MANAGEMENT. CONGRESS REPORTS. 1963. irreg., 1977, Madrid. European Association for Personnel Management, 29 av. Hoche, 75008 Paris, France.

658.3   US   ISSN 0163-7665
FEDERAL PERSONNEL GUIDE. 1979. a. $3. Federal and Military Personnel Publications (Subsidiary of: Uniformed Services Almanac, Inc.) Box 274, Washington, DC 20044. TEL 703-532-1635. Ed. Lee E. Sharff. circ. 100,000. Indexed: Pers.Lit.

658.3   336   US
FINANCIAL INSTITUTIONS RETIREMENT FUND. ANNUAL REPORT. a. Financial Institutions Retirement Fund, 5 Corporate Park Dr., White Plains, NY 10604. TEL 914-694-1300.

658.3   US
FRANKLIN FOUNDATION LECTURE SERIES. 1976. a. $8.50. (John and Mary Franklin Foundation) Georgia State University, College of Business Administration, University Plaza, Atlanta, GA 30303. Eds. Carl A. Bramlette, Jr., & Michael H. Mescon. (back issues avail., reprint service avail. from UMI)

658.4   US   ISSN 0092-4989
INTERNATIONAL DIRECTORY OF EXECUTIVE RECRUITERS. 1973. irreg., 4th edt., 1984. $27.95 per no. ‡ Consultants News, Templeton Road, Fitzwilliam, NH 03447. TEL 603-585-2200. Ed. James H. Kennedy.

INTERNSHIPS; 35,000 on-the-job training opportunities for all types of careers. see *OCCUPATIONS AND CAREERS*

658.3   UK
KNOW YOUR TRAINING FILMS. 1975. a. £47.95 for two vols. Management Update Ltd., 43 Brodrick Rd., London SW17 7DX, England. TEL 01-767-7542. Ed. H. Johannsen. adv. film rev. circ. 2,000.

658.311   US   ISSN 0076-0889
LOOKING INTO LEADERSHIP SERIES.* 1961. irreg. price varies. ‡ Leadership Resources Inc., Box 2226, Merrifield, VA 22116-2226.

658.3   US   ISSN 0077-3441
NATIONAL ASSOCIATION OF SUGGESTION SYSTEMS. STATISTICAL REPORT. 1943. a. membership. National Association of Suggestion Systems, 230 N. Michigan, Ste. 1200, Chicago, IL 60601. TEL 312-372-1770. circ. 1,000.

338   US
NORTH CAROLINA. DEPARTMENT OF HUMAN RESOURCES. ANNUAL REPORT. a. Department of Human Resources, 325 N. Salisbury St., Raleigh, NC 27611.

658.3   US   ISSN 0078-4001
OHIO. DIVISION OF STATE PERSONNEL. ANNUAL REPORT. 1960/61. a. free. Division of State Personnel, Department of Administrative Services, 30 E. Broad St, Columbus, OH 43215. TEL 614-466-6341.

BUSINESS AND ECONOMICS — PRODUCTION OF GOODS AND SERVICES

658.3 US
OKLAHOMA. PUBLIC EMPLOYEES RETIREMENT SYSTEM. ANNUAL REPORT. a. Public Employees Retirement System, 580 Jim Thorpe Bldg., Box 53007, Oklahoma City, OK 73152. TEL 405-521-2381.

658.3 US
PERSONNEL POLICIES AND BENEFITS FOR THE APPAREL INDUSTRY.* biennial. $62 to non-members; members $25. American Apparel Manufacturers Association, 2500 Wilson Blvd., Ste. 301, Arlington, VA 22201-3816.
Supersedes in part: Apparel Plant Wages and Personnel Policies (ISSN 0084-6678)

331 PO
PORTUGAL. MINISTERIO DAS CORPORACOES E PREVIDENCIA SOCIAL. GABINETE DE PLANEAMENTO. INGUERITO EMPREGO. (Subseries of its Serie Estatistica) (Summaries in English and French) irreg. Ministerio das Corporacoes e Previdencia Social, Gabinete de Planeamento, Lisbon, Portugal. stat.

QUEBEC (PROVINCE). REGIE DES RENTES DU QUEBEC. STATISTICAL OUTLOOK. see *INSURANCE*

658.3 BL
R I: REVISTA DOS RECURSOS HUMANOS NA EMPRESA. irreg. Associacao Brasileira de Administracao de Pessoal, Servicos Editoriais, Rua Cardoso de Almeida 163, Sao Paulo, Brazil. illus.

658.3 US
RESEARCH IN PERSONNEL AND HUMAN RESOURCES MANAGEMENT. 1983. a. $26.25 to individuals; institutions $52.50. J A I Press Inc., Box 1678, 36 Sherwood Pl., Greenwich, CT 06836. TEL 203-661-7602. Eds. Kendrith M. Rowland, Gerald R. Ferris.

SALARIES & BONUSES IN PERSONNEL/ INDUSTRIAL RELATIONS FUNCTIONS. see *BUSINESS AND ECONOMICS — Labor And Industrial Relations*

SOUNDVIEW EXECUTIVE BOOK SUMMARIES. see *BUSINESS AND ECONOMICS — Management*

TOP EXECUTIVE COMPENSATION. see *BUSINESS AND ECONOMICS — Management*

331 AT
TOP MANAGEMENT REMUNERATION REVIEW. 1975. a. Aus.$1355. Cullen Egan Dell Australia Pty. Ltd., 280 George St, Sydney, N.S.W. 2000, Australia. Ed. Chris D. Hart. circ. 350.

658.3 US ISSN 0361-6797
U.S. CIVIL SERVICE COMMISSION. BUREAU OF PERSONNEL MANAGEMENT EVALUATION. EVALUATION METHODS SERIES. 1975. irreg. U.S. Office of Personnel Management, Washington, DC 20415. TEL 202-655-4000. stat. Key Title: Evaluation Methods Series.

353.001 658.3 US ISSN 0093-366X
U.S. CIVIL SERVICE COMMISSION. PERSONNEL RESEARCH AND DEVELOPMENT CENTER. TECHNICAL STUDY. 1974. irreg. free. ‡ U.S. Office of Personnel Management, 1900 E. St., N.W., Washington, DC 20415. TEL 202-655-4000. Key Title: Technical Study - U.S. Civil Service Commission. Personnel Research and Development Center.

BUSINESS AND ECONOMICS —
Production Of Goods And Services

338.9 UN ISSN 0066-846X
A P O ANNUAL REPORT. (Text in English) 1962. a. free. Asian Productivity Organization, 8-4-14 Akasaka, Minato-ku, Tokyo 107, Japan. Ed. S. Nazim Zaidi. circ. 5,000.

338 PK
ALL PAKISTAN TEXTILE MILLS ASSOCIATION. CHAIRMAN'S REVIEW. (Text in English) a. free. All Pakistan Textile Mills Association, Muhammadi House, 3rd Floor, I.I. Chundrigar Rd., Karachi 2, Pakistan.
Formerly: All Pakistan Textile Mills Association. Annual Report.

650 FR ISSN 0066-3379
ANNUAIRE NATIONAL DES FOURNISSEURS DES ADMINISTRATIONS FRANCAISES. 2nd edt., 1962. a. Edition et Publicite Jean Vanvert, 32 rue Yves-Toudic, 75010 Paris, France.

338 660 UN ISSN 0251-0081
ANNUAL BULLETIN OF TRADE IN CHEMICAL PRODUCTS. 1974. a. $30. (Economic Commission for Europe (ECE)) United Nations Publications, Room DC2-0853, New York, NY 10017 (Or Distributions and Sales Section, Palais des Nations, 1211 Geneva 10, Switzerland)

338 660 UN ISSN 0255-4291
ANNUAL REVIEW OF THE CHEMICAL INDUSTRY. 1971. a. $30. (Economic Commission for Europe (ECE)) United Nations Publications, Room DC2-0853, New York, NY 10017 (Or Distribution and Sales Section, Palais des Nations, 1211 Genenva 10, Switzerland)

338 IT
ANNUARIO OTTICO ITALIANO. biennial. Edizioni Ariminum, Via Negroli 51, Milan 20133, Italy.

338.9 BL
ANUARIO A B D I B.* (Text in English, French, Portuguese, Spanish) a. (Associacao Brasileira para o Desenvolvimento das Industrias de Base) Diagrama Comunicacoes, 129 av. Churc, Rio de Janeiro, Brazil. illus.

338 BL
ANUARIO DAS INDUSTRIAS DO ESTADO DO RIO GRANDE DO SUL. 1976. a. Secretaria da Industria e Comercio, Porto Alegre, Brazil. (Co-sponsor: Federacao das Industrias do Estado do Rio Grande do Sul)

330 SP ISSN 0301-7443
ANUARIO FINANCIERO Y DE SOCIEDADES ANONIMAS DE ESPANA. 1916. a. 4000 ptas. Editorial S O P E C S.A., Mauricio Legendre 27, Madrid 16, Spain. circ. 3,500.

338 BA
ARAB INDUSTRY REVIEW. 1984. a. $35. Falcon Publishing, Box 5028, Manama, Bahrain. Ed. Roger Turney. circ. 10,000.

338 GW ISSN 0003-9314
ARCHIV FUER OEFFENTLICHE UND FREIGEMEINNUETZIGE UNTERNEHMEN; Zeitschrift fuer Strukturlehre der Einzelwirtschaften und fuer Einzelwirtschaftspolitik. 1954. irreg. price varies. (Universitaet zu Koeln, Forschungsinstitut fuer Sozialpolitik) Verlag Otto Schwartz und Co., Annastr. 7, 3400 Goettingen, W. Germany (B.R.D.) Ed. Theo Thiemeyer. adv. bk. rev. bibl. circ. 800(controlled)

338 US
ASSOCIATED INDUSTRIES OF NEW YORK STATE. BULLETIN.* irreg. Associated Industries of New York State, Inc., 152 Washington Ave., Albany, NY 12210.

338.994 AT
AUSTRALIA. INDUSTRIES ASSISTANCE COMMISSION. ANNUAL REPORT. 1974. a. price varies. Australian Government Publishing Service, G.P.O. 84, Canberra, A.C.T. 2601, Australia. illus.

338 US
B A R - B R I BAR REVIEW. TRUSTS. a. B A R-B R I Bar Review, 11801 W. Olympic Blvd., Los Angeles, CA 90064. TEL 213-477-2542.

338.9 BE
B E N E L U X ECONOMIC UNION. CONSEIL CENTRAL DE L'ECONOMIE. RAPPORT DU SECRETAIRE SUR L'ACTIVITE DU CONSEIL. 1950. biennial. free. B E N E L U X Economic Union, Central Economic Council, Rue de la Regence 39, 1000 Brussels, Belgium.
Formerly: Benelux Economic Union. Conseil Consultatif Economique et Social Rapport du Secretaire Concernant les Activites du Conseil (ISSN 0522-8948)

338 BL
BANCO NACIONAL DO DESENVOLVIMENTO ECONOMICO. PLANO DE ACAO/BANCO NACIONAL DO DESENVOLVIMENTO ECONOMICO. PLAN OF ACTION. (Editions in Spanish and English) triennial. Banco Nacional do Desenvolvimento Economico, Ave. Rio Branco 53, Rio de Janeiro, Brazil.

330.9 MR
BANQUE NATIONALE POUR LE DEVELOPPEMENT ECONOMIQUE. RAPPORT ANNUEL. (Text in French, Arabic) 1960. a. free. Banque Nationale pour le Developpement Economique, B.P. 407, Place des Alaouites, Rabat, Morocco. illus. stat. circ. 4,000.

338 US ISSN 0093-8025
BASEBOOK. Title varies: Predicasts Basebook. 1973. a. $500. Predicasts, Inc., 200 University Circle Research Center, 11001 Cedar Ave., Cleveland, OH 44106. TEL 800-321-6388.

338.8 US ISSN 0196-7622
BELGIAN AMERICAN CHAMBER OF COMMERCE IN THE UNITED STATES. DIRECTORY; listing of U.S. firms in Belgium & Luxembourg. Variant title: U S Belgium Trade Directory. irreg., latest 1985. Belgian American Chamber of Commerce in the U.S., 350 Fifth Ave., Ste. 703, New York, NY 10118-0110.

338.7 BS
BOTSWANA DEVELOPMENT CORPORATION. ANNUAL REPORT. 1971. a. Botswana Development Corporation, P.O. Box 438, Gaborone, Botswana. Ed.Bd. circ. 1,500.

338 BL ISSN 0045-2742
BRAZIL. SUPERINTENDENCIA DO DESENVOLVIMENTO DA AMAZONIA. S U D A M DOCUMENTA. (Text in Portuguese; summaries in Portuguese and English) 1970. irreg. free. Superintendencia do Desenvolvimento da Amazonia, Travessa Antonio Baena 1113, Caixa Postal 874, Belem-Para, Brazil. adv.

338.981 BL
BRAZIL DEVELOPMENT SERIES/SERIES DESENVOLVIMENTO BRASILEIRO. (Text in English and Portuguese) 1971. a. $20. (Brazilian Institute of Economic Studies) TELEPRESS Servicos de Imprensa, Ltda., Rua Albuquergque Lins, 1315, 01230 Sao Paulo, S.P., Brazil. Ed. Olavo G. Otero. illus. circ. 10,000.

C E D NEWSLETTER. (Committee for Economic Development) see *BUSINESS AND ECONOMICS — International Development And Assistance*

338 BL
CADASTRO INDUSTRIAL DO PARA. irreg. Federacao das Industrias, Av. Nazare, 759, Belem, Para, Brazil.

338.7 CM
CAMEROON DEVELOPMENT CORPORATION. ANNUAL REPORT AND ACCOUNTS/ RAPPORT ANNUEL ET COMPTE-RENDU FINANCIER. (Text in English and French) 1947. a. free. Cameroon Development Corporation, Bota, Victoria, Cameroon. illus. circ. 5,000. Key Title: Annual Report and Accounts-Cameroon Development Corporation.

CANADIAN ENGINEERING & INDUSTRIAL YEAR BOOK. see *ENGINEERING*

CAPITAL GOODS REVIEW. see *BUSINESS AND ECONOMICS — Macroeconomics*

BUSINESS AND ECONOMICS — PRODUCTION OF GOODS AND SERVICES

338   US   ISSN 0090-7111
CENSUS OF MAINE MANUFACTURES. (Subseries of: Maine. Bureau of Labor Standards. B L S Bulletin) 1948. a. free. Department of Labor, State House Station 45, Augusta, ME 04333. TEL 207-289-4313. Ed. William A. Peabody. charts. stats. circ. 600. Indexed: Vert.File Ind.

338.47   PR   ISSN 0552-5276
CENSUS OF MANUFACTURING INDUSTRIES OF PUERTO RICO. (Text in English and Spanish) a. free. Department of Labor, Bureau of Labor Statistics, 505 Munoz Rivera Ave., Hato Rey, PR 00918. stat. circ. 1,000. (tabloid format)

338.9   US   ISSN 0069-1674
CENTRAL NAUGATUCK VALLEY REGIONAL PLANNING AGENCY. ANNUAL REPORT. 1960. a. $5 contribution. ‡ Central Naugatuck Valley Regional Planning Agency, 20 E. Main St., Waterbury, CT 06702. TEL 203-757-0535. circ. 500. (processed)

338.9   EC
CENTRO DE DESARROLLO INDUSTRIAL DEL ECUADOR. NOTICIAS TECNICAS. 1973. a. (with m. bulletins) free. Ministry of Industry, Centro de Desarrollo Industrial, Box 5833, Guayaquil, Ecuador. circ. 1,200.

338   CH
CHINA DEVELOPMENT CORPORATION. ANNUAL REPORT.* (Vols. for 1959-72 issued by the body under its English form of name) 1959. a. China Development Corporation, 131 Nanking East Road, Section 5, Taipei, Taiwan, Republic of China. illus. stat.

338   CR
CIFRAS SOBRE PRODUCCION INDUSTRIAL. 1977. a. free. Banco Central de Costa Rica, Departamento de Investigaciones y Estadistica, Apdo. 10058, San Jose, Costa Rica. charts. stat. circ. 300.

338   CK
COLOMBIA. DEPARTAMENTO ADMINISTRATIVO NACIONAL DE ESTADISTICA. ANUARIO DE ESTADISTICAS INDUSTRIALES. 1972. a. Departamento Administrativo Nacional de Estadistica, Banco Nacional de Datos, Apdo. Nacional 80043, Bogota D.E., Colombia.
    Supersedes: Colombia. Departamento Administrativo Nacional de Estadistica. Industria Manufacturera Nacional.

338.6   EI
COMMISSION OF THE EUROPEAN COMMUNITIES. REPORT ON COMPETITION POLICY/RAPPORT SUR LA POLITIQUE DE CONCURRENCE. (Text in Dutch, English, French, German and Italian) 1972. a. price varies. Office for Official Publications of the European Communities, P.O. Box 1003, L-2985 Luxembourg, Luxembourg (Dist. in the U.S. by: European Community Information Service, 2100 M St., N.W., Ste. 707, Washington, DC 20037) Indexed: Chem.Abstr.

338.9   AT
COMMITTEE FOR ECONOMIC DEVELOPMENT OF AUSTRALIA. C E D A INFORMATION PAPERS (IP SERIES) 1979. irreg. price varies. Committee for Economic Development of Australia, 186 Exhibition St., Melbourne, Vic. 3000, Australia. Indexed: GeoRef.

338.9   AT
COMMITTEE FOR ECONOMIC DEVELOPMENT OF AUSTRALIA. C E D A "M" SERIES. 1961. irreg. price varies. Committee for Economic Development of Australia, 186 Exhibition St., Melbourne, Vic. 3000, Australia. Ed.Bd.

338   AT
COMMITTEE FOR ECONOMIC DEVELOPMENT OF AUSTRALIA. C E D A "P" SERIES; policy statements. 1965. irreg. price varies. Committee for Economic Development of Australia, 186 Exhibition St, Melbourne, Vic. 3000, Australia. Ed.Bd.

COMMONWEALTH SCIENTIFIC AND INDUSTRIAL RESEARCH ORGANIZATION. DIVISION OF WATER AND LAND RESOURCES. see *AGRICULTURE — Agricultural Economics*

338.6   FR
COMPETITION POLICY IN O E C D COUNTRIES. (Text in English) 1972. irreg. price varies. Organisation for Economic Cooperation and Development, 2 rue Andre-Pascal, 75775 Paris 16, France (U.S. orders to: O.E.C.D. Publications and Information Center, 1750 Pennsylvania Ave. N.W., Washington, DC 20006) (also avail. in microfiche)
    Formerly: Annual Reports on competition in O E C D Member Countries (ISSN 0300-1547)

CONNAISSANCE DE L'OUEST. see *GEOGRAPHY*

338   CR
CORPORACION COSTARRICENSE DE FINANCIAMIENTO INDUSTRIAL. MEMORIA ANUAL. a. Corporacion Costarricense de Financiamiento Industrial, Apartado 10067, San Jose, Costa Rica.

338   US   ISSN 0498-8477
CURRENT INDUSTRIAL REPORTS. m., q., and annual reports. U.S. Bureau of the Census, Customer Services, Department of Commerce, Washington, DC 20233 TEL 301-763-4100. (Subscr. to: Supt. of Documents, Washington, DC 20402) (also avail. in microform) Indexed: Abstr.Bull.Inst.Pap.Chem. Curr.Pack.Abstr.

338   CY   ISSN 0253-8598
CYPRUS. DEPARTMENT OF STATISTICS AND RESEARCH. SERVICES SURVEY. (Text in English) a. cyprus pounds 2. Department of Statistics and Research, Ministry of Finance, Nicosia, Cyprus.

D S I R INDUSTRIAL INFORMATION SERIES. see *ENGINEERING*

338   DK   ISSN 0106-9977
DANMARKS 200 STOERSTE VIRKSOMHEDER. 1975. a. Kr.50. A-S Forlaget Boersen, Vognmagergade 2, Box 2103, 1120 Copenhagen K, Denmark.

338   DK   ISSN 0106-9985
DANMARKS 2000 STOERSTE VIRKSOMHEDER/ 2000 LARGEST COMPANIES IN DENMARK. (Text in Danish and English) 1967. a. Kr.340. Teknisk Forlag A-S, Skelbaekgade 4, DK-1717 Copenhagen V, Denmark. Ed. H. Reinvaldt. adv. circ. 3,000.
    Former titles: Danmarks 1000 Stoerste Virkomheder; Danmarks 500 Stoerste Virksomheder (ISSN 0419-9472)

309.2   US
DELAWARE VALLEY REGIONAL PLANNING COMMISSION. ANNUAL REPORT. Cover title: D.V.R.P.C. Annual Report. a. free. Delaware Valley Regional Planning Commission, Bourse Bldg., 21 S. Fifth St., Philadelphia, PA 19103. TEL 215-592-1800. illus.
    Formerly: Delaware Valley Regional Planning Commission. Biennial Report (ISSN 0098-6232)

338   PH
DEVELOPMENT ACADEMY OF THE PHILIPPINES. PRESIDENT'S REPORT TO THE BOARD OF TRUSTEES. (Text in English) 1974. a. Development Academy of the Philippines, Office of Special Services, Box 5160 MCC, Makati, Metro Manila, Philippines. illus. circ. controlled.
    Formerly: Development Academy of the Philippines. Annual Report.

DICTIONNAIRE DE L'INDUSTRIE FRANCAISE. see *BUSINESS AND ECONOMICS — Trade And Industrial Directories*

338   SI   ISSN 0217-8311
DIRECTORY OF CERTIFIED PRODUCTS IN SINGAPORE. (Text in English) 1976. a. Singapore Institute of Standards and Industrial Research, 179 River Valley Road, Singapore 0617, Singapore. circ. 3,800.

309.2   US
DIRECTORY OF MISSOURI'S REGIONAL PLANNING COMMISSIONS. (Vols. for 1972/73 prepared by the Department of Community Affairs) Office of Administration, Division of Budget and Planning, Capitol Bldg., Rm. B-9, Box 809, Jefferson City, MO 65101. TEL 314-751-2345. illus.
    Formerly: Directory of Missouri's Regional Planning System (ISSN 0090-7812)

DIRECTORY OF OIL WELL SUPPLY COMPANIES. see *PETROLEUM AND GAS*

338.7   II   ISSN 0376-8546
DIRECTORY OF PUBLIC ENTERPRISES IN INDIA. (Text in English) 1974. a. National Forum of Public Enterprises, C-40 South Extension II, New Delhi 49, India. illus.

338   UN
DIRECTORY OF THE NATIONAL PRODUCTIVITY ORGANIZATIONS IN A P O MEMBER COUNTRIES. (Text in English) 1962. irreg. Asian Productivity Organization, 8-4-14 Akasaka, Minato-ku, Tokyo 107, Japan. Ed. S. Nazim Zaidi. circ. 2,000.
    Former titles: Profiles of the National Productivity Organizations in A P O Member Countries; Asian Productivity Organization. Review of Activities of National Productivity Organizations (ISSN 0571-3005)

338   AO
DIVULGACAO. 1969. a. Camara Municipal du Lobito, Caixa Postal Tres, Lobito, Angola. charts. illus.

338.9   SA   ISSN 0070-8518
ECONOMIC DEVELOPMENT PROGRAMME FOR THE REPUBLIC OF SOUTH AFRICA. 1964. irreg. Government Printer, Bosman St., Private Bag X85, Pretoria 0001, South Africa. (Prepared by: Department of the Prime Minister, Economic Planning Branch)

ECONOMIE FRANCAISE EN PERSPECTIVES SECTORIELLES: INDUSTRIES DE BIENS DE CONSOMMATION. see *BUSINESS AND ECONOMICS — Economic Situation And Conditions*

ECONOMIE FRANCAISE EN PERSPECTIVES SECTORIELLES: INDUSTRIES DE BIENS D'EQUIPEMENT. see *BUSINESS AND ECONOMICS — Economic Situation And Conditions*

ECONOMIE FRANCAISE EN PERSPECTIVES SECTORIELLES: INDUSTRIES DE BIENS INTERMEDIAIRES. see *BUSINESS AND ECONOMICS — Economic Situation And Conditions*

338   FR   ISSN 0068-4902
ECONOMIES ET SOCIETES. SERIE P. RELATIONS ECONOMIQUES INTERNATIONALES. 1944. irreg. 300 F. Presses Universitaires de Grenoble, B.P. 47 X, 38040 Grenoble, France. Dir. Jean Weiller. circ. 1,600.

338   EC   ISSN 0070-8887
ECUADOR. CENTRO DE DESARROLLO INDUSTRIAL. INFORME DE LABORES. 1959. a., latest issue 1973. free. Centro de Desarrollo Industrial, Av. Orellana 1297, Box 2321, Quito, Ecuador. circ. 600.

338   EC
ECUADOR. MINISTERIO DE INDUSTRIAS, COMERCIO E INTEGRACION. BOLETIN DE INFORMACION DE LAS EMPRESAS ACOGIDAS A LA LEY DE FOMENTO INDUSTRIAL. 1974. a. Ministerio de Industrias, Comercio e Integracion, Quito, Ecuador.

338.3   UR
EKONOMIKA PROMYSLOVOSTI. (Subseries of: Kharkivskyi Politekhnichnyi Instytut. Vestnik) irreg. 0.53 Rub. Kharkivskyi Politekhnichnyi Instytut, Ul. Frunze, 21, Kharkov, Ukrainian S.S.R., U.S.S.R. illus.

338.4   FR
ENGINEERING INDUSTRIES IN O E C D MEMBER COUNTRIES: NEW BASIC STATISTICS. (Only avail. in microfiche since 1985) (Text in English and French) a. $9.50 price varies. Organization for Economic Cooperation and Development, 2 rue Andre-Pascal, 75775 Paris, France (U.S. orders to: O.E.C.D. Publications and Information Center, 1750 Pennsylvania Ave. N.W., Washington, D.C. 20006) (also avail. in microfiche)

ENQUETE SUR LES ENTERPRISES INDUSTRIELLES ET COMMERCIALES DU TOGO. see *BUSINESS AND ECONOMICS — Domestic Commerce*

BUSINESS AND ECONOMICS — PRODUCTION OF GOODS AND SERVICES

338.9   SP   ISSN 0084-5132
ESCUELA DE GERENTES DE COOPERATIVAS. CARTILLAS DE COOPERACION. 1971. irreg., latest issue, 1978. 25 ptas. (Escuela de Gerentes de Cooperativas) Centro Nacional de Educacion Cooperativa, Palacio de la Cooperacion, Apdo. de Correos 15, San Felix 9, Zaragoza, Spain. (Affiliate: Federacion Nacional de Cooperativas de Espana) Ed. Joaquin Mateo.

338.9   SP   ISSN 0084-5159
ESCUELA DE GERENTES DE COOPERATIVAS. COLECCION TEXTOS. irreg. price varies. Escuela de Gerentes de Cooperativas, Palacio de la Cooperacion, Apdo. de Correos 15, San Felix 9, Zaragoza, Spain. (Co-sponsor: Centro Nacional de Educacion Cooperativa) Ed. Joaquin Mateo.

338.9   SP   ISSN 0084-5167
ESCUELA DE GERENTES DE COOPERATIVAS. CUADERNOS DE PRACTICAS. irreg. 100 ptas. Escuela de Gerentes de Cooperativas, Palacio de la Cooperacion, Apdo. de Correos 15, San Felix 9, Zaragoza, Spain. (Co-sponsor: Centro Nacional de Educacion Cooperativa) Ed. Joaquin Mateo.

338.9   SP   ISSN 0084-5175
ESCUELA DE GERENTES DE COOPERATIVAS. SERIE ESPECIAL. irreg. 200 ptas. Escuela de Gerentes de Cooperativas, Palacio de la Cooperacion, Apdo. de Correos 15, San Felix 9, Zaragoza, Spain. (Co-sponsor: Centro Nacional de Educacion Cooperativa)

338   UK   ISSN 0800-0638
EUROPE'S 15000 LARGEST COMPANIES. 1975. a. $145. E.L.C. International, Sinclair House, the Avenue, London W13 8NT, England (Dist. in the U.S. by: Dun's Marketing Services, 3 Century Drive, Parsippany, NJ 07054) Ed. P. Cowan. circ. 4,000.
Former titles (until 1985): Europe's 10000 Largest Companies; (until 1984): Europe's 5000 Largest Companies.

338   640.73   BE
FEDERATION DES ENTREPRISES DE BELGIQUE. RAPPORT ANNUEL/VERBOND VAN BELGISCHE ONDERNEMINGEN. JAARLYKS VERSLAG. a. Federation des Entreprises de Belgique - Verbond van Belgische Ondernemingen, 4 Ravenstein, B-1000 Brussels, Belgium.
Formerly: Federation des Industries Belges. Rapport Annuel (ISSN 0071-4178)

338   US   ISSN 0171-5062
FERTIGUNG UND BETRIEB. (Text in German) 1974. irreg., vol.15, 1982. price varies. Springer-Verlag, 175 Fifth Ave., New York, NY 10010 TEL 212-460-1500. (Also Berlin, Heidelberg, Tokyo and Vienna) (reprint service avail. from ISI)
Supersedes: Werkstattbuecher fuer Betriebsfachleute Konstrukteure und Studenten (ISSN 0083-8055)

338.9   FI   ISSN 0355-8878
FINLAND. VALTIONEUVOSTON KANSLIAN. JULKAISUJA. 1972. irreg. price varies. Valtion Painatuskeskus - Government Printing Centre; Council of State, Annankatu 44, 00100 Helsinki 10, Finland.
Formerly (1960-1971): Finland. Valtakunnansuunnittelutoimisto. Julkaisuja. Sarja A (ISSN 0071-5360)

330   FR   ISSN 0071-6847
FONDS DE DEVELOPPMENT ECONOMIQUE ET SOCIAL. CONSEIL DE DIRECTION. RAPPORT. a. (Ministere de l'Economie et des Finances) Imprimerie Nationale, Service des Ventes, 59128 Flers en Escrebieux, France.

338   PH   ISSN 0085-0802
FOREIGN INVESTMENT OPPORTUNITIES IN THE PHILIPPINES. (Text and summaries in English) 1968. a. free. ‡ Board of Investments, MCC P.O. Box 676, Makati, Metro Manila-3117, Philippines. circ. 3,000.

338   US
FORTUNE DIRECTORY; the 500 largest industrials & 500 largest service co's. in the U.S. 1955; expanded 1970. a. $8. ‡ Time Inc., Fortune Division, Time & Life Bldg., Rockefeller Center, New York, NY 10020. TEL 212-586-1212. stat.
Formerly: Fortune Double 500.

338   FR   ISSN 0071-870X
FRANCE. DIRECTION GENERALE DE LA CONCURRENCE ET DES PRIX. BULLETIN OFFICIEL DES SERVICES DES PRIX. 1941. irreg. 6.50 F. (Direction General de la Concurrence et des Prix) France. Direction des Journaux Officiels, 26 rue Desaix, 75732 Paris, France.

330   FR
FRANCE. MINISTERE DE L'ECONOMIE, DES FINANCES ET DU BUDGET. RAPPORT DU CONSEIL DE DIRECTION DU FOND DE DEVELOPPEMENT ECONOMIQUE ET SOCIAL. 1955. a. 80 F. Ministere de l'Economie, des Finanaces et du Budget, Direction du Tresor, 151 rue St. Honore, 75001 Paris, France. circ. 1,000.
Formerly: France. Ministere de l'Economie. Rapport du Conseil de Direction du Fonds de Developpement Economique et Social (ISSN 0071-8920)

338   US
GENERAL MOTORS PUBLIC INTEREST REPORT. 1971. a. free. General Motors Corp., Detroit, MI 48202. TEL 313-556-5000. Ed. Thomas F. Macan. circ. 70,000.

GERMAN DEMOCRATIC REPUBLIC. CONSUMER CO-OPERATIVE SOCIETIES. MAGAZINE. see *BUSINESS AND ECONOMICS — Cooperatives*

330   GW   ISSN 0072-159X
GERMANY (FEDERAL REPUBLIC, 1949-). SACHVERSTAENDIGENRAT ZUR BEGUTACHTUNG DER GESAMTWIRTSCHAFTLICHEN ENTWICKLUNG. JAHRESGUTACHTEN. 1964. a. DM.35. (Sachverstaendigenrat zur Begutachtung der Gesamtwirtschaftlichen Entwicklung) W. Kohlhammer Verlag GmbH, Abt. Veroeffentlichungen des Statistischen Bundesamtes, Philipp-Reis-Str. 3, Postfach 421120, 6500 Mainz 42, W. Germany (B.R.D.) circ. 3,300.

338   US   ISSN 0072-5137
GOVERNMENT CONTRACTS DIRECTORY. 1964. a. $79.50. Government Data Publications, 1120 Connecticut Ave., N.W., Washington, DC 20036. Ed. Siegfried Lobel.

338   UK   ISSN 0072-565X
GREAT BRITAIN. DEPARTMENT OF TRADE. COMPANIES: GENERAL ANNUAL REPORT. a. H.M.S.O., P.O. Box 569, London SE1 9NH, England. (reprint service avail. from UMI)

338   GU
GROSS ISLAND PRODUCT OF GUAM. (Text in English) 1978. irreg. Department of Commerce, 590 S. Marine Dr., GITC Bldg. Ste. 601, Tamuning, Guam 96911.

338   AT   ISSN 0085-1280
GROWTH. 1961. irreg. price varies. Committee for Economic Development of Australia, 186 Exhibition St., Melbourne, Vic 3000, Australia. Indexed: Biol.Abstr. Aus.P.A.I.S.

338   SP
GRUPO I N I (RESUMEN DE ACTIVIDADES) a. free. Instituto Nacional de Industria, Plaza de Salamanca, 8, 28006 Madrid, Spain. TEL 341-401 40 04. illus.
Former titles: Resumen de Actividades I N I (Year); Spain. Instituto Nacional de Industria. Resumen de Actividades.

330.9   SG
GUIDE DE L'INVESTISSEUR INDUSTRIEL AU SENEGAL. irreg. 3000 Fr.CFA. Societe Nationale d'Etude et de Promotion Industrielle, 14, rue Maunoury, B.P. 100, Dakar, Senegal. illus.

338   II
GUJARAT INDUSTRIAL DEVELOPMENT CORPORATION. ANNUAL REPORT. (Text in English) a. Gujarat Industrial Development Corporation, Ashram Rd., Ahmedabad 9, India. illus. stat.

338   GW   ISSN 0073-0068
HANDBUCH DER GROSSUNTERNEHMEN. (In 2 vols.) 1940. a. DM.550 for 2 vols. Verlag Hoppenstedt and Co., Havelstr. 9, Postfach 4006, 6100 Darmstadt, W. Germany (B.R.D.) adv.

338.9   US   ISSN 0073-1072
HAWAII. DEPARTMENT OF PLANNING AND ECONOMIC DEVELOPMENT. ANNUAL REPORT. 1962. a. free. Department of Planning and Economic Development, P.O. Box 2359, Honolulu, HI 96804. TEL 808-548-4025. circ. 1,500.

338   HK
HONG KONG PRODUCTIVITY COUNCIL & CENTRE ANNUAL REPORT. (Text in Chinese, English) 1968. annual. Hong Kong Productivity Council, 12/F World Commerce Centre, Harbour City, 11 Canton Rd., Tsimshatsui, Kowloon, Hong Kong. Ed. Andy Ng. circ. 3,000.

HUNGARY. KOZPONTI STATISZTIKAI HIVATAL. IPARSTATISZTIKAI EVKONYV. see *BUSINESS AND ECONOMICS — Abstracting, Bibliographies, Statistics*

I.D.E. OCCASIONAL PAPERS SERIES. (Institute of Developing Economies) see *BUSINESS AND ECONOMICS*

338.9   BL
I P E A ESTUDOS PARA O PLANEJAMENTO. 1972. irreg. price varies. Instituto de Planejamento Economico e Social, Caixa Postal 2672, Rio de Janeiro, Brazil.

339   BL
I P E A SERIE MONOGRAFICA. 1971. irreg. price varies. Instituto de Planejamento Economico e Social, Caixa Postal 2672, Rio de Janeiro, Brazil.

338   US   ISSN 0495-145X
INDUSTRIAL DEVELOPMENT IN THE T.V.A. AREA. 1959. a. Tennessee Valley Authority, Industrial Development Staff, 34B Old City Hall, Knoxville, TN 37902. TEL 615-632-6867. Ed. Larry W. Colaw. illus. stat. circ. 3,000.

338   US   ISSN 0099-1872
INDUSTRIAL GROWTH IN TENNESSEE, ANNUAL REPORT. a. free. Department of Economic and Community Development, Rachel Jackson Bldg., 8th fl., Nashville, TN 37219. TEL 615-741-1995. stat.

338   JA
INDUSTRIAL LOCATION HANDBOOK/KOGYO RITCHI HANDOBUKKU. (Text in Japanese) 1966. triennial. Japan Industrial Location Center - Nihon Kogyo Ritchi Senta, 2-1 Shiba-Kotohiramachi, Minato-ku, Tokyo, Japan. charts. illus.

338   CN   ISSN 0073-7569
INDUSTRIAL LOCATIONS IN CANADA. 1966. a. free to subscribers of the Financial Times of Canada. Financial Times of Canada, Ste. 500, 920 Yonge St., Toronto, Ont. M4W 3L5, Canada. TEL 416-922-1133. adv. circ. 106,000.

338   UK   ISSN 0263-7952
INDUSTRIAL RESEARCH IN UNITED KINGDOM. 1946. biennial, 11th edt., 1985. £105. ‡ Longman Group Ltd., Fourth Ave., Harlow, Essex CM19 5AA, England (Dist. in U.S. and Canada by: Gale Research Co. Ltd., Book Tower, Detroit, MI 48226) index.

658   UK
INDUSTRIAL SOCIETY. HANDBOOK AND DIARY. 1960. a. £1.50. Industrial Society, Peter Runge House, 3 Carlton House Terrace, London SW1 5DG, England. bibl. stat. circ. 20,000.

338   II   ISSN 0073-7666
INDUSTRIAL STRUCTURE OF RAJASTHAN. (Text in English) 1958. a. Rs.5. Directorate of Economics and Statistics, Krishi Bhawan, Jaipur, Rajasthan, India.

338   CM
INDUSTRIE CAMEROUNAISE. a. Syndicat des Industries du Cameroun, B. P. 673, Douala, Cameroon.

338   JA   ISSN 0446-1266
INDUSTRIES OF JAPAN. (Text in English) 1958. a. 800 Yen. (Mainichi Daily News) Mainichi Newspapers, 1-1-1 Hitotsubashi, Chiyoda-ku, Tokyo 100, Japan. stat.

BUSINESS AND ECONOMICS — PRODUCTION OF GOODS AND SERVICES

338 916.76　　KE　ISSN 0073-781X
INDUSTRY IN EAST AFRICA. 1962/63. a. $10.
United Africa Press Ltd., Box 1237, Nairobi, Kenya.
Ed. C.N. Bhatt.

338　　　　　　DK　ISSN 0446-2491
INGENIOEREN INDKOEBSBOG. 1960. a. Kr.215.
Teknisk Forlag A-S, Skelbaekgade 4, DK-1717
Copenhagen V, Denmark. adv. circ. 6,000.

INTERNATIONAL TRENDS IN
MANUFACTURING TECHNOLOGY. see
TECHNOLOGY: COMPREHENSIVE WORKS

338　　　　　　DK　ISSN 0108-2329
INVESTERING I PRODUKTION. 1982. a. free.
Egnsudviklingsraadet, Soendergade 25, 8600
Silkeborg, Denmark. circ. 5,000.
　　Formerly: Denmark. Egnsudviklingsraadet.
Beretning.

338　　　　　　IS　ISSN 0081-9743
ISRAEL. MINISTRY OF COMMERCE AND
INDUSTRY. SURVEYS AND DEVELOPMENT
PLANS OF INDUSTRY IN ISRAEL/TA'ASIYAH
HA-YISRA'ELIT. (Hebrew and English Editions)
1964. a. free. Ministry of Industry and Trade,
Jerusalem, Israel. Ed. T. Ben-Yosef. circ. 1,000.
　　Formerly: Survey of Industry in Israel.

338　　　　　　IT　ISSN 0075-1987
ITALY. ISTITUTO NAZIONALE PER LO STUDIO
DELLA CONGIUNTURA. QUADERNI
ANALITICI. irreg., (approx. 37/yr.) L.5500 per no.
Istituto Nazionale per Lo Studio della Congiuntura,
Rome, Italy. Ed. Almerina Ipsevich. charts. stat.
circ. 550.

338　　　　　　JA
JAPAN. GOVERNMENT INDUSTRIAL
DEVELOPMENT LABORATORY, HOKKAIDO.
ANNUAL REPORT/HOKKAIDO KOGYO
KAIHATSU SHIKENJO NEMPO. 1961. a.
Government Industrial Development Laboratory,
Hokkaido - Hokkaido Kogyo Kaihatsu Shikenjo, 41-
2 Higashi-tsukisamu, Toyohira-ku, Sapporo 061-01,
Hokkaido, Japan. abstr.

338　　　　　　JA
JAPAN. GOVERNMENT INDUSTRIAL
RESEARCH INSTITUTE, KYUSHU ANNUAL
REPORT/KYUSHU KOGYO GIJUTSU
SHIKENJO NEMPO. (Text in Japanese) a.
Government Industrial Research Institute, Kyushu,
807-1 Shukumachi, Tosu-Kyushu 841, Japan. abstr.

600 330　　　　JA
JAPAN ECONOMIC ALMANAC; an annual in-
depth report on the state of the Japanese economy.
(Text in English) 1962. a. 9.800 Yen($48.50) Japan
Economic Journal - Nihon Keizai Shinbunsha, 1-9-5
Otemachi, Chiyoda-ku, Tokyo 100, Japan.
　　Formerly (until 1985): Industrial Review of Japan
(ISSN 0537-5452)

338.9　　　　　KE
KENYA. CENTRAL BUREAU OF STATISTICS.
DEVELOPMENT ESTIMATES. a. EAs.50.
Central Bureau of Statistics, Ministry of Finance &
Planning, Box 30266, Nairobi, Kenya (Orders to:
Government Printing and Stationery Department,
Box 30128, Nairobi, Kenya)
　　Formerly: Kenya. Ministry of Economic Planning
and Development. Statistics Division. Development
Estimates (ISSN 0075-5818)

338.9　　　　　KE
KENYA. CENTRAL BUREAU OF STATISTICS.
ESTIMATES OF RECURRENT
EXPENDITURES. 1959. a. EAs.15. Ministry of
Finance, Box 30007, Nairobi, Kenya (Orders to:
Government Printing and Stationery Department,
Box 30128, Nairobi, Kenya)
　　Formerly: Kenya. Ministry of Economic Planning
and Development. Statistics Division. Estimates of
Recurrent Expenditures (ISSN 0075-5834)

338.9　　　　　KE
KENYA. CENTRAL BUREAU OF STATISTICS.
ESTIMATES OF REVENUE EXPENDITURES.
1959. a. EAs.3. Central Bureau of Statistics,
Ministry of Finance & Planning, Box 30266,
Nairobi, Kenya (Orders to: Government Printing
and Stationery Department, Box 30128, Nairobi,
Kenya)
　　Formerly: Kenya. Ministry of Economic Planning
and Development. Estimates of Revenue
Expenditures (ISSN 0075-5826)

338　　　　　　KE
KENYA. CENTRAL BUREAU OF STATISTICS.
SURVEYS OF INDUSTRIAL PRODUCTION.
irreg. EAs.50 per no. Central Bureau of Statistics,
Ministry of Finance and Planning, Box 30266,
Nairobi, Kenya (Orders to: Government Printing
and Stationery Office, Box 30128, Nairobi, Kenya)

KENYA ASSOCIATION OF MANUFACTURERS.
MEMBERS LIST AND INTERNATIONAL
STANDARD INDUSTRIAL CLASSIFICATION.
see *BUSINESS AND ECONOMICS — Trade And
Industrial Directories*

338.9　　　　　KO
KOREA (REPUBLIC). ECONOMIC PLANNING
BOARD. ANNUAL REPORT ON CURRENT
INDUSTRIAL PRODUCTION SURVEY. (Text in
English and Korean) 1971. a. 11,310 Won. National
Bureau of Statistics, Economic Planning Board,
Gyeongun-Dung, Jongro-Gu, Seoul, S. Korea. Ed.
Myong Hyun Sohn. circ. 500.

KOTHARI'S INDUSTRIAL DIRECTORY OF
INDIA. see *BUSINESS AND ECONOMICS —
Trade And Industrial Directories*

338 380.5　　　LB
LIBERIA. MINISTRY OF COMMERCE,
INDUSTRY AND TRANSPORTATION.
ANNUAL REPORT. a. Ministry of Commerce,
Industry and Transportation, Box 9041, Monrovia,
Liberia.

338　　　　　　LB
LIBERIA. MINISTRY OF PLANNING AND
ECONOMIC AFFAIRS. ANNUAL REPORT TO
THE PEOPLE'S REDEMPTION COUNCIL.
1965/66. a., latest 1980. $5. Ministry of Planning
and Economic Affairs, Box 9016, Monrovia, Liberia.
　　Formerly: Liberia. Ministry of Planning and
Economic Affairs. Annual Report to the Session of
the Legislature of the Republic of Liberia (ISSN
0459-2182); Which continues: Liberia. Department
of Planning and Economic Affairs. Annual Report.

338　　　　　　II　ISSN 0076-0269
LOCATIONS OF INDUSTRIES IN GUJARAT
STATE. (Text in English) 1956. irreg. Rs.7.30.
Bureau of Economics and Statistics, Sector No. 18,
Gandhinagar, India.

338　　　　　　II　ISSN 0541-5357
M B I'S INDIAN INDUSTRIES ANNUAL. (Text in
English) 1963. a. Rs.20. Chary Publications, 14 Sidh
Prasad, Ghatkopar Mahul Rd., Tilak Nagar, Bombay
400089, India.

338　　　　　　US
MAJOR INDUSTRIAL RESEARCH UNIT
STUDIES. 1928. irreg. University of Pennsylvania,
Wharton School, Industrial Research Unit, 3733
Vance Hall, Philadelphia, PA 19104-6358. TEL
215-898-5601.
　　Formerly: University of Pennsylvania. Wharton
School of Finance and Commerce. Industrial
Research Unit Studies (ISSN 0083-9094)

338　　　　　　US　ISSN 0736-8313
MANUFACTURING RESOURCE PLANNING.*
1981. a. (plus m. updates) $140. Auerbach
Publishers, Inc. (Subsidiary of: International
Thomson Organization Ltd.) One Penn Plaza, New
York, NY 10119.

338　　　　　　US　ISSN 0736-8259
MASTER PRODUCTION SCHEDULING.* 1981. a.
(plus m. updates) $140. Auerbach Publishers, Inc.
(Subsidiary of: International Thomson Organization
Ltd.) One Penn Plaza, New York, NY 10119.

338　　　　　　US　ISSN 0736-8321
MATERIAL REQUIREMENTS PLANNING.* 1982.
a. (plus m. updates) $140. Auerbach Publishers, Inc.
(Subsidiary of: International Thomson Organization
Ltd.) One Penn Plaza, New York, NY 10119.

338　　　　　　GW　ISSN 0341-759X
MEISTER - ZEITUNG. 1971. m. DM.50. Vogel-
Verlag KG, Max-Planck-Str. 7/9, 8700 Wuerzburg
1, W. Germany (B.R.D.) Ed. Claus Martin Stotz.
adv. circ. 12,000(controlled)

338　　　　　　BL
MELHORES E MAIORES. (Special edition of :
Exame) 1974. a. $3.59 per no. Editora Abril S a,
Av. Otaviano Alves de Lima, 4400, Sao Paulo,
Brazil. Ed.Bd. adv. charts. illus. stat. circ. 50,000.

338　　　　　　US　ISSN 0540-4193
MISSOURI'S NEW AND EXPANDING
INDUSTRIES. 1952. a. free. Department of
Economic Development, Box 118, Jefferson City,
MO 65102. TEL 314-751-3674. Ed. J. Kormann.
circ. 1,000.

338　　　　　　US
MODERN CORPORATION CHECKLISTS
(SUPPLEMENT) loose-leaf supplements issued
annually to update base volume. $76 for base vol.
plus supp. Warren, Gorham and Lamont, Inc., 210
South St., Boston, MA 02111. TEL 800-922-0066.

338　　　　　　US　ISSN 0077-040X
MONITOR;* the voice of industry in New York State.
1914. irreg. free to qualified personnel. Associated
Industries of New York State, Inc., 152 Washington
Ave., Albany, NY 12210. Ed. Lavina Finin.
Indexed: Biol.Dig. Ind.U.S.Gov.Per.

338.9　　　　　NP　ISSN 0077-6548
NEPAL INDUSTRIAL DEVELOPMENT
CORPORATION. ANNUAL REPORT. (Text in
English) 1959/60. a. free. Nepal Industrial
Development Corporation, N.I.D.C. Bldg., Durbar
Marg, Box 10, Kathmandu, Nepal.

338.9　　　　　NP　ISSN 0077-6556
NEPAL INDUSTRIAL DEVELOPMENT
CORPORATION. INDUSTRIAL DIGEST. (Text
in English) 1966. a. Rs.30($5) Nepal Industrial
Development Corporation, N.I.D.C. Bldg., Durbar
Marg, Box 10, Kathmandu, Nepal. Ed. Ramesh
Nath Dhungel.

330　　　　　　NE　ISSN 0077-7536
NETHERLANDS. CENTRAAL PLANBUREAU.
CENTRAAL ECONOMISCH PLAN. (Includes the
National Budget) a. price varies. Staatsuitgeverij,
Chr. Plantijnstr., The Hague, Netherlands. (Prepared
by: Centraal Planbureau)

338　　　　　　US
NEW AND EXPANDING INDUSTRIES REPORT
FOR ALABAMA. 1962. a. free. Development
Office, c/o State Capitol, Montgomery, AL 36130.
TEL 205-263-0048. Ed. Richard W. McLaney.
index.

338.9　　　　　CN　ISSN 0077-8117
NEW BRUNSWICK. RESEARCH AND
PRODUCTIVITY COUNCIL. REPORT. 1962. a.
free. Research and Productivity Council,
Fredericton, New Brunswick, Canada. TEL 506-
452-8994. Ed. Dr. D. Abbott. circ. 1,000.

338.9　　　　　US　ISSN 0077-8478
NEW JERSEY. ECONOMIC POLICY COUNCIL.
ANNUAL REPORT OF ECONOMIC POLICY
COUNCIL AND OFFICE OF ECONOMIC
POLICY. 1968. a. free. ‡ Office of Economic
Policy, One W. State St., Trenton, NJ 08625. Ed.
Joseph Seneca. circ. 2,000.

338　　　　　　NR
NEW NIGERIA DEVELOPMENT COMPANY
LIMITED. ANNUAL REPORT AND
ACCOUNTS. 1969. a. free. New Nigeria
Development Company Ltd., P.M.B. 2120, Kaduna,
Nigeria.
　　Supersedes: Northern Nigeria Development
Corporation. Report.

338　　　　　　DK　ISSN 0108-1497
NEW PRODUCTS FROM DENMARK. German
edition: Neue Produkte aus Daenemark (ISSN
0108-1705); French edition: Productions Nouvelles
du Danemark (ISSN 0108-1713); Spanish edition:
Productos Nuevos de Dinamarca (ISSN 0108-1721)
(Text in English) 1982. irreg. free.
Udenrigsministeriet - Ministry of Foreign Affairs,
Asiatisk Plads 2, DK-1448 Copenhagen K,
Denmark. Eds. Preben Hansen, Thorkild Borre.
illus.

338　　　　　　FR　ISSN 0078-0960
NOMENCLATURE DES ENTREPRISES
NATIONALES A CARACTERE INDUSTRIEL
OU COMMERCIAL ET DES SOCIETES
D'ECONOMIE MIXTE D'INTERET
NATIONAL. irreg. price varies; 1975, two volumes
77F. (Ministere de l'Economie et des Finances)
Imprimerie Nationale, Service des Ventes, 59128
Flers en Escrebieux, France.

BUSINESS AND ECONOMICS — PRODUCTION OF GOODS AND SERVICES

NORTH CAROLINA. DEPARTMENT OF HUMAN RESOURCES. ANNUAL REPORT. see *BUSINESS AND ECONOMICS — Personnel Management*

341.1　　　　　FR　ISSN 0029-7038
ORGANIZATION FOR ECONOMIC COOPERATION AND DEVELOPMENT. LIAISON BULLETIN BETWEEN RESEARCH AND TRAINING INSTITUTES. (Editions in English and French) irreg. price varies. Organization for Economic Cooperation and Development, 2 rue Andre-Pascal, 75775 Paris Cedex 16, France (U.S. orders to: O.E.C.D. Publications and Information Center, 1750 Pennsylvania Ave., N.W., Washington, DC 20006) (also avail. in microfiche; back issues avail.)

338　　　　　NR
OYO STATE. MINISTRY OF ECONOMIC PLANNING AND COMMUNITY DEVELOPMENT. ANNUAL REPORT.* a. Ministry of Economic Planning and Community Development, Ibadan, Nigeria (Orders to: Oyo State Government Printer, Ibadan, Nigeria)
　　Formerly: Western State. Ministry of Economic Planning and Community Development. Annual Report.

338　　　　　PK　ISSN 0078-8392
PAKISTAN. OFFICE OF THE ECONOMIC ADVISER. GOVERNMENT SPONSORED CORPORATIONS AND OTHER INSTITUTIONS. (Text in English) 1965. a. free; limited distribution. Office of the Economic Adviser, Islamabad, Pakistan.

338.9　　　　　PK　ISSN 0078-8414
PAKISTAN. PLANNING AND DEVELOPMENT DIVISION. DEVELOPMENT PROGRAMME. (Text in English) a. Planning and Development Division, P Block, Islamabad, Pakistan.

338.9　　　　　PK　ISSN 0078-8201
PAKISTAN INDUSTRIAL DEVELOPMENT CORPORATION. REPORT. (Text in English) 1952/53. a. Pakistan Industrial Development Corporation, PIDC House, Dr. Ziauddin Ahmad Rd., Karachi 4, Pakistan.

338.9　　　　　JA
PEOPLE AND NATIONAL LAND POLICY/HITO TO KOKUDO. (Text in Japanese.) 1975. irreg. 450 Yen. Kokudo Keikaku Kyokai, 21 Kotohiracho, Minato-ku, Tokyo 105, Japan. illus.

338　　　　　US　ISSN 0554-2731
PLANT LOCATION; the industrial & economic development workbook. 1959. a. $40. Simmons-Boardman Publishing Corporation, 345 Hudson St., New York, NY 10014. TEL 212-620-7200. Ed. Pam Lunt. adv. bibl. stat. circ. 42,000(controlled) (also avail. in microform from UMI; reprint service avail. from UMI)

338.9　　　　　GW　ISSN 0079-2284
PLANUNGSSTUDIEN. 1969. irreg., vol.18, 1982. price varies. Nomos Verlagsgesellschaft mbH und Co. KG, Waldseestr. 3-5, Postfach 610, 7570 Baden-Baden, W. Germany (B.R.D.) Ed. Joseph H. Kaiser.

PLASTICS: LATIN AMERICAN INDUSTRIAL REPORT. see *PLASTICS*

338　　　　　PL　ISSN 0239-9423
POLITECHNIKA POZNANSKA. INSTYTUT NAUK EKONOMICZNYCH I SPOLECZNYCH. ZESZYTY NAUKOWE. 1975. irreg. price varies. Politechnika Poznanska, Pl. Curie-Sklodowskiej 5, Poznan, Poland. Ed. Marian Frackowiak.
　　Formerly: Politechnika Poznanska. Instytut Nauk Ekonomicznych i Spolecznych. Prace Naukowe (ISSN 0239-0094)

338　　　　　PL
POLITECHNIKA POZNANSKA. ZESZYTY NAUKOWE. ORGANIZACJA I ZARZADZANIE. 1969. irreg. price varies. Politechnika Poznanska, Pl. Curie Sklodowskiej 5, Poznan, Poland. Ed. Leszek Pacholski. circ. 250.
　　Formerly: Politechnika Poznanska. Zeszyty Naukowe. Ekonomika i Organizacja Przemyslu (ISSN 0137-690X)

338　　　　　PL　ISSN 0324-8046
POLITECHNIKA SLASKA. ZESZYTY NAUKOWE. ORGANIZACJA. (Text in Polish; summaries in English and Russian) 1972. irreg. price varies. Politechnika Slaska, W. Pstrowskiego 7, 44-100 Gliwice, Poland (Dist. by: Ars Polona, Krakowskie Przedmiescie 7, 00-068 Warsaw, Poland) Ed. Waldemar Pindur.

338　　　　　UR
POLUTEHNILINE INSTITUUT TALLINN. IZUCHENIE EFFEKTIVNOSTI PROIZVODSTVA. (Subseries of its Toimetised) (Text in Russian; summaries in English or German) irreg. price varies. Polutehniline Instituut Tallinn, Ehitajate tee 5, Tallinn, Estonian S.S.R., U.S.S.R.

338　621.9　　　　　UR
POLUTEHNILINE INSTITUUT TALLINN. PROBLEMY EKONOMIKI MASHINOSTROENIYA I METALLOOBRABOTKI ESTONSKOI S.S.R. (Subseries of Its Toimetised) (Text in Russian; summaries in English or German) irreg. price varies. Polutehniline Instituut Tallinn, Ehitajate tee 5, Tallinn, Estonian S.S.R., U.S.S.R.

338　　　　　UR
POLUTEHNILINE INSTITUUT TALLINN. SOVERSHENSTVOVANIE METODIKI UCHETA I EKONOMICHESKOGO ANALIZA V PROMYSHLENNOSTI. (Subseries of Its Toimetised) (Text in Russian; summaries in English or German) irreg. price varies. Polutehniline Instituut Tallinn, Ehitajate tee 5, Tallinn, Estonian S.S.R., U.S.S.R.

POOR'S REGISTER OF CORPORATIONS, DIRECTORS AND EXECUTIVES. see *BUSINESS AND ECONOMICS — Management*

338.7　　　　　CN
PRINCE EDWARD ISLAND DEVELOPMENT AGENCY. ANNUAL REPORT. 1966. a. ‡ Prince Edward Island Development Agency, Charlottetown, P.E.I. C1E 1B0, Canada. TEL 902-566-4222.
　　Formerly (until 1985): Industrial Entreprises Incorporated. Annual Report.

338　　　　　IV
PRINCIPALES INDUSTRIES INSTALLEES EN COTE D'IVOIRE. 1968. a. free. Chambre d'Industrie de Cote d'Ivoire, B.P. 1758, Abidjan, Ivory Coast.
　　Formerly: Principales Industries Ivoiriennes.

338　　　　　PL　ISSN 0079-581X
PROBLEMY REJONOW UPRZEMYSLAWIANYCH. (Text in Polish; summaries in English, Russian) 1968. irreg. price varies. (Polska Akademia Nauk) Panstwowe Wydawnictwo Naukowe, Miodowa 10, 00-251 Warsaw, Poland (Dist. by: Ars Polona, Krakowskie Przedmiescie 7, 00-068 Warsaw, Poland) Ed. A. Stelmachowski. bibl.

338　　　　　SW
PROCORDIA. AARSREDOVISNING/ PROCORDIA. ANNUAL REPORT. a. free. Procordia AB, Box 2278, S-103 17 Stockholm, Sweden. illus.
　　Formerly: Stastfoeretag. Aarsredovising.

388　622　　　　　CL
PRODUCCION Y EXPORTACIONES CHILENAS DE COBRE. irreg. exchange basis. Comision Chilena del Cobre, Subdireccion de Estudios y Relaciones Internacionales, Augustina 1161, 4 Piso, Santiago, Chile.

658.2　　　　　US
PRODUCTION'S MANUFACTURING PLANBOOK.* 1973. a. $7.50. Production Publishing Co., Inc., Box 101, Bloomfield Hills, MI 48303-0101. TEL 313-647-8300. adv. circ. 80,000. (reprint service avail. from UMI)

338　　　　　PE　ISSN 0032-9908
PRODUCTIVIDAD. 1961. a. free. Ministerio de Trabajo y Promocion Social, Centro Nacional de Productividad, Jiron Zepita 423, Apdo. 5442, Edificio Ferrand, Piso 5, Lima, Peru. Dir. Alfonso Luna-Victoria Sanchez. adv. abstr. charts. illus. circ. 2,500.

338　　　　　IT　ISSN 0555-4810
PROSPETTIVE DELL'INDUSTRIA ITALIANA. (Subseries of Collana de Studi e Documentazione) 1964. a. L.22000. Servizio Italiano Pubblicazioni Internazionali s.r.l., Viale L. Pasteur, 6, 00144 Rome, Italy.

333.7　　　　　US　ISSN 0079-7634
PUBLIC POLICY ISSUES IN RESOURCE MANAGEMENT. 1965. irreg., vol.5, 1973. price varies. (University of Washington, Graduate School of Public Affairs) University of Washington Press, Seattle, WA 98105. TEL 206-543-4050.

338.7　　　　　II
PUNJAB STATE INDUSTRIAL DEVELOPMENT CORPORATION. ANNUAL REPORT.* (Text in English) a. Punjab State Industrial Development Corporation, United Commercial Bank Bldg., 3rd Floor, Sector 17-B, Chandigarh, India. illus. stat.

354　　　　　AT
QUEENSLAND. DEPARTMENT OF INDUSTRY DEVELOPMENT. ANNUAL REPORT. 1972. a. free. Department of Industry Development, G.P.O. 1141, Brisbane, Qld. 4001, Australia. illus. circ. 7,000.
　　Formerly: Queensland. Department of Commercial and Industrial Development. Annual Report.

338.7　　　　　II
RAJASTHAN STATE WAREHOUSING CORPORATION. ANNUAL REPORT AND ACCOUNTS. (Text in English) a. Rajasthan State Warehousing Corporation, Govind Bhavan, Subhash Marg, C-Scheme, Jaipur 1, India. stat.

338　　　　　DK　ISSN 0107-8666
RAPPORT OM KONTROLLEN MED KONSUMMAELKPRODUKTER. 1980. a. free. Veterinaerdirektoratet - Danish State Veterinary Service, Frederiksgade 21, 1265 Copenhagen K, Denmark. Ed. E. Malling Olsen.
　　Formerly: Kontrollen med Konsummaelkprodukter.

338.9　　　　　UR
REGIONAL'NAYA NAUKA O RAZMESHCHENII PROIZVODITEL'NYKH SIL; sbornik referativnykh rabot. irreg. 0.67 Rub. Akademiya Nauk S.S.S.R., Sibirskoe Otdelenie, Institut Ekonomiki i Organizatsii Promyshlennogo Proizvodstva, Novosibirsk, Akademgorodok, Russian S.F.S.R., U.S.S.R. illus.

REHABILITATION INDUSTRIES CORPORATION. ANNUAL REPORT. see *EDUCATION — Special Education And Rehabilitation*

338　650　　　　　FR　ISSN 0080-1089
REPERTOIRE DICTIONNAIRE INDUSTRIEL.* 1956. a. Service de Renseignements du Repertoire Industriel, 13 rue de Marivaux, 75002 Paris, France.

338.767　　　　　II
REPUBLIC FORGE COMPANY. ANNUAL REPORT. (Text in English) 14th, 1971/72. a. Republic Forge Company, Maula Ali, Hyderabad 40, India. stat. Key Title: Annual Report - Republic Forge Company.

338　　　　　UK
SCANDINAVIA'S 5000 LARGEST COMPANIES. 1986. a. E.L.C. International, Sinclair House, The Avenue, West Ealing, London W13 8NT, England (Distr. in U.S. by: Dun's Marketing Services, Parsippany, NJ) circ. 1,000.

338.7　　　　　GW　ISSN 0724-2557
SCHRIFTEN DES WERKSARCHIVS. 1969. irreg. free. Henkel KGaA, Postfach 1100, 4000 Duesseldorf 1, W. Germany (B.R.D.) Ed. Manfred Schoene. illus.

338　　　　　ZR　ISSN 0377-5135
SCIENCES, TECHNIQUES, INFORMATIONS C R I A C. irreg. Centre de Recherches Industrielles en Afrique Centrale, B.P. 54, Lubumbashi, Zaire. illus.
　　Formerly: Centre de Recherche Industrielles en Afrique Centrale. Bulletin d'Information.

338　380　　　　　BL
SEMINARIO NACIONAL DE CONTROLE DE QUALIDADE. ANAIS. 1973. irreg. Federacao das Industrias do Estado do Rio Grande do Sul, Porto Alegre, Brazil.

SERIE PRAXIS. see *BUSINESS AND ECONOMICS — Labor And Industrial Relations*

338.9   SI   ISSN 0080-9683
SINGAPORE. ECONOMIC DEVELOPMENT BOARD. ANNUAL REPORT. (Text in English) 1962. a. S.14. ‡ Economic Development Board, 1 Maritime Square, World Trade Centre 10-4, Singapore 0409, Singapore. Ed. Mary Kwan. circ. 10,000.

338   SI   ISSN 0129-6256
SINGAPORE STANDARDS YEARBOOK. (Text in English) 1977. biennial. Singapore Institute of Standards & Industrial Research, 179 River Valley Road, Singapore 0617, Singapore. circ. 1,500.

SOLAR COLLECTOR MANUFACTURING ACTIVITY. see *ENERGY*

338   SP
SPAIN. MINISTERIO DE INDUSTRIA. RESULTADOS DE LA ENCUESTA DE COYUNTURA INDUSTRIAL: SECTOR INDUSTRIAL. 1963. irreg. included with the review Economia Industrial. Ministerio de Industria, Paseo de la Castellana 160, Madrid 16, Spain. bk. rev. circ. 10,000.

338   GR   ISSN 0072-7458
STATE OF GREEK INDUSTRY IN (YEAR) (Text in English) 1940-1977; resumed 1984. a. free. Federation of Greek Industry, 5 Xenophontos Str., 105 57 Athens, Greece. circ. 4,000.

STUDIES IN PRODUCTION AND ENGINEERING ECONOMICS. see *BUSINESS AND ECONOMICS*

STUDIES ON TAXATION AND ECONOMIC DEVELOPMENT. see *BUSINESS AND ECONOMICS — Public Finance, Taxation*

338.9   FI   ISSN 0355-6050
SUOMEN PANKKI. JULKAISUJA. KASVUTUTKIMUKSIA/BANK OF FINLAND. PUBLICATIONS. STUDIES ON FINLAND'S ECONOMIC GROWTH. Short English title: Studies on Finland's Economic Growth. (Text in Finnish; summaries in English) 1966. irreg., no.12, 1986. Fmk.40. Suomen Pankki - Bank of Finland, Information Department, Box 160, SF-00101 Helsinki, Finland. Ed. Heikki Elonen. circ. 750.
Formerly (until 1971): Suomen Pankki. Taloustieteellinen Tutkimuslaitos. Julkaisuja. Series Kasvututkimuksia (ISSN 0081-9514)

338   II
TAMIL NADU INDUSTRIAL DEVELOPMENT CORPORATION. ANNUAL REPORT. (Report year ends Mar. 31) (Text in English) 7th edt., 1972. a. Tamil Nadu Industrial Development Corporation, Local Library Authority Building, 3rd Floor, 150-A Anna Salai, Madras, India. illus. stat.

TAMIL NADU TOURISM DEVELOPMENT CORPORATION. ANNUAL REPORT. see *TRAVEL AND TOURISM*

338   TZ
TANZANIA. MINISTRY OF PLANNING AND ECONOMIC AFFAIRS. HALI YA UCHUMI WA TAIFA/ANNUAL ECONOMIC SURVEY. 1973. a. $3. ‡ Ministry of Planning and Economic Affairs, Economic Policy Division, P.O. Box 9242, Dar es Salaam, Tanzania (Subscr. to: Government Publications Agency, P.O. Box 1801, Dar es Salaam, Tanzania) stat. circ. 1,000.
Formerly: Tanzania. Ministry of Economic Affairs and Developement Planning. Hali Ya Uchumi Wa Taifa/Annual Economic Survey.

338   US   ISSN 0361-2597
TEXAS. INDUSTRIAL COMMISSION. ANNUAL REPORT. 1962. a. free. Industrial Commission, Box 12728, Capital Sta., Austin, TX 78711. TEL 512-472-5059. illus. stat. circ. 750.

650   UK   ISSN 0082-4429
TIMES 1000; lists leading companies in Britain and Overseas. 1966. a. £18.50. Times Books Ltd., 16 Golden Square, London W1R 4BN, England. Ed. Margaret Allen. adv. circ. 9,000.

338   SA   ISSN 0563-8895
TOP COMPANIES. (Supplement to: Financial Mail) 1967. a. (South African Associated Newspapers) Financial Mail, Box 9959, Johannesburg, South Africa. illus.

338.9   TU   ISSN 0082-6944
TURKEY. DEVLET PLANAMA TESKILATI. YILI PROGRAMI UCUNCU BES YIL/ANNUAL PROGRAM OF THE FIVE YEAR DEVELOPMENT PLAN. 1963. a. State Planning Organization - Devlet Planlama Teskilati, Ankara, Turkey.

354   UG
UGANDA ESTIMATES OF DEVELOPMENT EXPENDITURES. a., latest 1977/78. EAs.20 price varies. Government Printer, Box 33, Entebbe, Uganda.

338   US   ISSN 0082-9307
U.S. BUREAU OF THE CENSUS. ANNUAL SURVEY OF MANUFACTURES. 1949. a., except for years covered by Census of Manufactures. price varies. U.S. Bureau of the Census, Customer Services, Washington, DC 20233. TEL 301-763-4100. (also avail. in microfiche)

338   US   ISSN 0082-9374
U.S. BUREAU OF THE CENSUS. CENSUS OF MANUFACTURES. (Issued in 3 series: Geographic Area Series, Industry Series, and Subject Series) 1810. quinquennial; census reports issued periodically. price varies. U.S. Bureau of the Census, Customer Services, Washington, DC 20233 TEL 301-763-4100. (Order forms and announcements available from the Bureau; publication orders to: Supt. of Documents, Washington, DC 20402) (also avail. in microform)

650   US
U.S. INDUSTRIAL OUTLOOK (YEAR) 1960. a. $21. U.S. Department of Commerce, International Trade Administration, Room 1211-HCHB, Washington, DC 20230 TEL 212-377-4356. (Orders to: Supt. of Documents, Washington, DC 20402) Ed. Peter J. Reynolds. charts. illus. stat. index. circ. 25,000. (also avail. in microfiche)
Former titles: U.S. Industrial Outlook for 350 Industries with 5-Year Projections; U.S. Industrial Outlook for 250 Industries with Projections for (Year); U.S. Industrial Outlook (ISSN 0083-1344)

338   AG   ISSN 0457-1673
UNIVERSIDAD NACIONAL DE LA PLATA. INSTITUTO DE LA PRODUCCION. SERIE CONTRIBUCIONES. 1960. irreg. Universidad Nacional de la Plata, Instituto de la Produccion, Calle 53, No. 419, La Plata, Argentina. Ed. Servando R.M. Dozo. charts. stat.

338   US   ISSN 0518-6544
UNIVERSITY OF ARKANSAS. INDUSTRIAL RESEARCH AND EXTENSION CENTER. ANNUAL REPORT. 1956. a. free. University of Arkansas, Industrial Research and Extension Center, Box 3017, Little Rock, AR 72203. TEL 501-569-3470. Ed. William G. Conley. circ. 1,200.

UNIVERSITY OF NAIROBI. INSTITUTE FOR DEVELOPMENT STUDIES. OCCASIONAL PAPER. see *BUSINESS AND ECONOMICS — International Development And Assistance*

338   PL   ISSN 0208-4783
UNIWERSYTET GDANSKI. WYDZIAL EKONOMIKI PRODUKCJI. ZESZYTY NAUKOWE. ZAGADNIENIA EKONOMIKI PRZEMYSLU. (Text in Polish; summaries in English and Russian) 1972. irreg. price varies. Uniwersytet Gdanski, Ul. Czerwonej Armii 110, 81-824 Sopot, Poland. Ed. Jsan Wojewnik. illus.

338   PL   ISSN 0208-4775
UNIWERSYTET GDANSKI. WYDZIAL EKONOMIKI PRODUKCJI. ZESZYTY NAUKOWE. ZAGADNIENIA FINANSOWE. (Text in Polish; summaries in English and Russian) 1974. irreg. price varies. Uniwersytet Gdanski, Ul. Armii Czerwonej 110, 81-824 Sopot, Poland.

338   US
UPDATE (ALBANY)* irreg. Associated Industries of New York State Inc., 152 Washington Ave., Albany, NY 12210.

338   FI   ISSN 0356-8091
VALTIONYHTIOT. 1969. a. Fmk.35. Valtionyhtioiden Neuvottelukunta, Aleksanterinkatu 10, Helsinki 17, Finland. Wd. Ritva Hainari. circ. 8, 000.

338   US   ISSN 0363-2067
VERMONT INDUSTRIAL DEVELOPMENT AUTHORITY. ANNUAL REPORT. 1975. a. Vermont Industrial Development Authority, 58 E. State St., Montpelier, VT 05602. TEL 802-223-7226. circ. 100. Key Title: Annual Report - Vermont Industrial Development Authority.

WHO OWNS WHOM. CONTINENTAL EUROPE. see *BUSINESS AND ECONOMICS — Management*

338.9689   ZA
ZAMBIA. MINISTRY OF PLANNING AND FINANCE. ANNUAL REPORT. 1971. a. 20 n. Ministry of Planning and Finance, Box RW 62, Lusaka, Zambia (Orders to: Government Printer, Box 136, Lusaka, Zambia)
Formed by the merger of: Zambia. Ministry of Development and National Guidance. Annual Report & Zambia. Ministry of Finance. Annual Report (ISSN 0084-4896)

338   SP
132 EXPRES. 1973. a. free. Subdireccion de Estudios Economicos y Marketing, Avenida Generalisimo, 146, Madrid-16, Spain. charts. illus. stat. tr.lit. (tabloid format)

BUSINESS AND ECONOMICS —
Public Finance, Taxation

336   US   ISSN 0163-1241
ABINGDON CLERGY INCOME TAX GUIDE. 1972. a. $5.95. Abingdon, 201 Eighth Ave. S., Box 801, Nashville, TN 37202. TEL 615-749-6347.
Formerly (until 1978): Clergy's Federal Income Tax Guide (ISSN 0090-9866)

ALASKA. DEPARTMENT OF REVENUE. STATE INVESTMENT PORTFOLIO. see *BUSINESS AND ECONOMICS — Investments*

336   UK
ALLIED DUNBAR TAX GUIDE. a. Longman Professional, 21-27 Lamb's Conduit St., London WC1N 3EN, England.

AMERICAN INSTITUTE OF CERTIFIED PUBLIC ACCOUNTANTS. DIVISION OF FEDERAL TAXATION. STATEMENTS ON RESPONSIBILITIES IN TAX PRACTICE. see *BUSINESS AND ECONOMICS — Accounting*

336.2   US
ANALYSIS OF OREGON PERSONAL INCOME. 1969. a. $10. 371-2244, Department of Revenue, Revenue Bldg., Salem, OR 97310.
Former titles: Personal Income Tax Analysis (ISSN 0092-6655) & Analysis of Oregon's Personal Income Tax Returns.

336   II
ANDHRA PRADESH STATE FINANCIAL CORPORATION. REPORT AND ACCOUNTS. (Text in English) 1956. a. Andhra Pradesh State Financial Corporation, 5-9-194 Chirag Ali Lane, Hyderabad 500001, India. stat.
Continues: Andhra Pradesh State Financial Corporation. Report.

336   AG
ARGENTINA. SECRETARIA DE ESTADO DE HACIENDA. MEMORIA. 1860. a. Secretaria de Estado de Hacienda, Buenos Aires, Argentina.

336   AT
AUSTRALIA. BUREAU OF STATISTICS. VICTORIAN OFFICE. LOCAL GOVERNMENT FINANCE, VICTORIA. 1958. a. Aus.$2.90. Australian Bureau of Statistics, Victorian Office, Box 2796Y, G.P.O. Melbourne, Victoria 3001, Australia. circ. 800.
Formerly: Australia. Bureau of Statistics. Victorian Office. Government Finance (ISSN 0067-1142)

BUSINESS AND ECONOMICS — PUBLIC FINANCE, TAXATION

336.1 AT
AUSTRALIA. COMMONWEALTH GRANTS COMMISSION. GRANTS COMMISSION REPORT ON FINANCIAL ASSISTANCE FOR LOCAL GOVERNMENT. 1974. irreg. price varies. Australian Government Publishing Service, G.P.O. Box 84, Canberra, A.C.T. 2601, Australia. illus. stat.
Former titles: Australia. Grants Commission. Grants Commission Report on Financial Assistance for Local Government; Australia. Grants Commission. Grants Commission Report on Special Assistance for States.

336.2 AT ISSN 0728-6856
AUSTRALIA. DEPARTMENT OF INDUSTRY, TECHNOLOGY AND COMMERCE. ANNUAL REPORT. 1954. a. free. Department of Industry, Technology and Commerce, Public Relations Section, Barton, A.C.T. 2600, Australia. Ed.Bd. circ. 8,000.
Former titles (until 1981): Australia. Department of Police and Customs. Review of Activities; Australia. Department of Industry and Commerce. Annual Report (ISSN 0067-1347)

336 AT
AUSTRALIA. DEPARTMENT OF THE TREASURY. TREASURY ECONOMIC PAPER. 1972. a. Department of the Treasury, G.P.O. Box 84, Canberra, A.C.T. 2601, Australia. charts. stat.

336.2 AT
AUSTRALIAN INCOME TAX ASSESSMENT ACT AND REGULATIONS; including regulations, rates and international agreements. 1969. a. Aus.$29. C C H Australia Ltd., P.O. Box 230, North Ryde, NSW 2113, Australia.
Formerly: Australian Income Tax Assessment Act.

336.2 AT
AUSTRALIAN MASTER TAX GUIDE. a. Aus.$39. C C H Australia Ltd., Box 230, North Ryde, N.S.W. 2113, Australia.

336.2 AT
AUSTRALIAN SALES TAX GUIDE. 1973. irreg., (approx. 6/yr.) Aus.$388. C C H Australia Ltd., P.O. Box 230, North Ryde, N.S.W. 2113, Australia. index.

336 340 AT
AUSTRALIAN TAX CASES. 1969. fortn. Aus.$318. C C H Australia Ltd., P.O. Box 230, North Ryde, NSW 2113, Australia. Indexed: Curr.Aus.N.Z.Leg.Lit.Ind.

336.2 AT
AUSTRALIAN TAXPAYER'S ASSOCIATION. ANNUAL TAXATION SUMMARY. 1919. a. Aus.$5. Australian Taxpayer's Association, 343 Little Collins St., Melbourne, Australia. Ed. Eric Risstrom. circ. 40,000.
Formerly: Federated Taxpayer's Association of Australia. Annual Taxation Summary.

336 BA
BAHRAIN. MONETARY AGENCY. ANNUAL REPORT. a. Monetary Agency, Box 27, Manama, Bahrain. charts. stat.

336 382 SL ISSN 0067-2998
BALANCE OF PAYMENTS OF SIERRA LEONE. a. free. Bank of Sierra Leone, P.O. Box 30, Freetown, Sierra Leone.

336 382 TR ISSN 0067-3005
BALANCE OF PAYMENTS OF TRINIDAD AND TOBAGO. a., latest issue 1979/85. T.T.$5. Central Statistical Office, P.O. Box 98, 23 Park St., Port-of-Spain, Trinidad, W.I. (Orders to: Government Printing Office, 48 St. Vincent St., Port of Spain, Trinidad, W.I.)

336 382 SP ISSN 0067-3021
BALANZA DE PAGOS DE ESPANA. 1971. a. $4.50. Ministerio de Economia y Hacienda, Secretaria General de Comercio, Castellana 162, Planta 16, Madrid 28046, Spain. circ. 1,500.

336 PN
BANCO NACIONAL DE PANAMA. INFORMACION ECONOMICA Y FINANCIERA DE LA REPUBLICA DE PANAMA. 1978. irreg., latest 1986. free. Banco Nacional de Panama, Asesoria Economica, Apdo. 5220, Panama 5, Panama. charts. stat.

BANGLADESH BANK. STATISTICS DEPARTMENT. ANNUAL BALANCE OF PAYMENTS. see BUSINESS AND ECONOMICS — Abstracting, Bibliographies, Statistics

BANK INCOME TAX RETURN MANUAL. see BUSINESS AND ECONOMICS — Banking And Finance

336 382 LY ISSN 0075-921X
BANK OF LIBYA. BALANCE OF PAYMENTS. (Text in Arabic and English) 1954. a. free. Bank of Libya, Box 1103, Tripoli, Libya.

336.2 NE ISSN 0077-670X
BELASTINGDRUK IN NEDERLAND/BURDEN OF TAXES IN THE NETHERLANDS. (Text in Dutch and English) 1943. a. fl.18.65. Centraal Bureau voor de Statistiek, Prinses Beatrixlaan 428, Voorburg, Netherlands (Orders to: Staatsuitgeverij, Christoffel Plantijnstraat, The Hague, Netherlands)

336 US ISSN 0741-8477
BOSTON UNIVERSITY JOURNAL OF TAX LAW. 1983. a. $20. Boston University, School of Law, Alumni Center, 765 Commonwealth Ave., Boston, MA 02215. Ed. Harold Adrion. abstr. bibl. Indexed: Leg.Per.

336 BS ISSN 0068-0451
BOTSWANA. ANNUAL STATEMENTS OF ACCOUNTS. a., latest 1979/1980. p.11. Government Printer, Private Bag 0081, Gaborone, Botswana.

336.2 BS
BOTSWANA. DEPARTMENT OF INCOME TAX. ANNUAL REPORT. 1972. a. Department of Income Tax, Gaborone, Botswana.

336.68 BS ISSN 0524-1448
BOTSWANA. ESTIMATES OF REVENUE AND EXPENDITURE. (Continues the publication with the same title issued by Beuchanaland (Protectorate)) a., latest 1981/1982. p.2. Government Printer, Private Bag 0081, Gaborone, Botswana. stat.

336 PK
BUDGET OF THE GOVERNMENT OF PAKISTAN. DEMANDS FOR GRANTS AND APPROPRIATIONS. (Text in English) a. free to qualified personnel. Finance Division, Islamabad, Pakistan.
Supersedes: Pakistan. Ministry of Finance. Budget of the Central Government (ISSN 0078-8317)

336 UK ISSN 0268-2265
BUDGET REPRESENTATIONS TO THE CHANCELLOR. 1965. a. £3. Confederation of British Industry, 103 New Oxford St., London WC1A 1DU, England.

336.2 UK ISSN 0525-3063
BUTTERWORTHS BUDGET TAX TABLES. 1966. a. Butterworth & Co. (Publishers) Ltd., c/o John Lord, Promo. Mgr., 88 Kingsway, London WC2B 6AB, England. Ed. Derek Bond. circ. 13,000.

336 US ISSN 0068-5801
CALIFORNIA. STATE BOARD OF EQUALIZATION. ANNUAL REPORT. 1879. a. free. State Board of Equalization, Box 1799, Rm. 130, Sacramento, CA 95808. TEL 916-445-6188. Ed. Mary L. Claus. circ. 4,000.

336.02 CN
CANADA. DEPARTMENT OF NATIONAL REVENUE. REPORT: CUSTOMS, EXCISE AND TAXATION. (Text in English and French) a. Department of National Revenue, Finance Directorate, 191 Laurier Ave. W., Ottawa, Ont. K1A OL5, Canada. TEL 613-995-6447.

336.2 CN
CANADIAN INCOME TAX FOR BUSINESSMEN AND ACCOUNTANTS. irreg., 14th edt., 1984. Can.$29.50. C C H Canadian Ltd., 6 Garamond St., Don Mills, Ont. M3C 1Z5, Canada. TEL 416-441-2992.

336.2 CN
CANADIAN MASTER TAX GUIDE. a. Can.$19.75 paperback; Can.$26.50 hardbound. C C H Canadian Ltd., 6 Garamond Ct., Don Mills, Ont. M3C 1Z5, Canada. TEL 416-441-2992.

336.2 CN ISSN 0317-946X
CANADIAN TAX FOUNDATION. PROVINCIAL AND MUNICIPAL FINANCES. 1963. biennial. price varies. Canadian Tax Foundation, Suite 1900, 130 Adelaide St. W., Toronto, Ont. M5H 3P5, Canada. TEL 416-863-9784.
Until 1969: Canadian Tax Foundation. Provincial Finances (ISSN 0068-9823)

336.2 CN ISSN 0316-3571
CANADIAN TAX FOUNDATION. TAX CONFERENCE. REPORT OF PROCEEDINGS. 1947. a. Canadian Tax Foundation, Suite 1900, 130 Adelaide St. W., Toronto, Ont. M5H 3P5, Canada. TEL 416-863-9784.

336.2 CN ISSN 0008-512X
CANADIAN TAX PAPERS. irreg., no.78, 1986. price varies. Canadian Tax Foundation, Suite 1900, 130 Adelaide St. W., Toronto, Ont. M5H 3P5, Canada. TEL 416-863-9784.

336.2 CN
CANADIAN TAXATION OF MINING INCOME. 1978. irreg. Can.$28. C C H Canadian Ltd., 6 Garamond St., Don Mills, Ont. M3C 1Z5, Canada. TEL 416-441-2992.

336 CJ
CAYMAN ISLANDS. CURRENCY BOARD. REPORT. 1972. a. Currency Board, Grand Cayman, Cayman Islands, British W.I. illus. circ. 250.

336.73 US ISSN 0272-6017
CHANGING PUBLIC ATTITUDES ON GOVERNMENTS AND TAXES; a commission survey. a. $3 per no. U.S. Advisory Commission on Intergovernmental Relations, 1111 20th St., N.W., Ste. 2000, Washington, DC 20575. TEL 202-655-4000.

336 UK
CHECK YOUR TAX. a. £1.75. W. Foulsham & Co. Ltd., Yeovil Rd., Slough SL1 4JH, England.

336 CL
CHILE. DIRECCION DE PRESUPUESTOS. CALCULO DE ENTRADAS DE LA NACION.* a. Direccion de Presupuestos, Piso 12, Of. 27, Teatinos 120, Santiago, Chile. charts.

336 CL
CHILE. DIRECCION DE PRESUPUESTOS. DEPARTAMENTO DE ESTUDIOS FINANCIEROS. FINANZAS PUBLICAS.* 1957. a. contr.circ. Direccion de Presupuestos, Departamento de Estudios Financieros, Teatinos 120, Piso 12, Of. 27, Santiago, Chile. bibl. charts. stat.

336 CL
CHILE. DIRECCION DE PRESUPUESTOS. EXPOSICION SOBRE EL ESTADO DE LA HACIENDA PUBLICA.* 1914. a. Direccion de Presupuestos, Piso 12, Of. 27, Teatinos 120, Santiago, Chile. charts. stat.

336 CL
CHILE. DIRECCION DE PRESUPUESTOS. INSTRUCCIONES PARA LA EJECUCION DE LA LEY DE PRESUPUESTOS.* a. Direccion de Presupuestos, Piso 12, Of. 27, Teatinos 120, Santiago, Chile. charts.

336 CL
CHILE. DIRECCION DE PRESUPUESTOS. LEY DE PRESUPUESTOS.* 1884. a. Direccion de Presupuestos, Piso 12, Of. 27, Teatinos 120, Santiago, Chile. charts.

336 CN ISSN 0831-7496
CITY OF OTTAWA. CORPORATE FINANCIAL AND STATISTICAL INFORMATION. (Text in English and French) 1975. a. Can.$15($12) Corporation of the City of Ottawa, 111 Sussex Dr., Ottawa, Ont. K1N 5A1, Canada. TEL 613-564-3575. stat. (back issues avail.)
Formerly: City of Ottawa. Financial and Other Statistics.

336 DR
COLECCION MANUALES DE FINANZAS PUBLICAS. 1980. irreg., no.16, 1982. price varies. Secretaria de Estado de Finanza, Instituto de Capacitacion Tributaria, Apartado Postal 20216, Santo Domingo, Dominican Republic. adv.

BUSINESS AND ECONOMICS — PUBLIC FINANCE, TAXATION

336   CK
COLOMBIA. DIRECCION GENERAL DEL PRESUPUESTO. PROYECTO DE PRESUPUESTO. a. Direccion General del Presupuesto, Bogota, Colombia.

336.2   EI
COMMISSION OF THE EUROPEAN COMMUNITIES. DIRECTORATE OF TAXATION. INVENTORY OF TAXES. (Text in English; some also in Dutch, French, German, or Italian) irreg. Office for Official Publications of the European Communities, P.O. Box 1003, L-2985 Luxembourg, Luxembourg (Dist. in the U.S. by: European Community Information Service, 2100 M St., N.W., Ste. 707, Washington, DC 20037)

336   EI   ISSN 0590-6571
COMMISSION OF THE EUROPEAN COMMUNITIES. FINANCIAL REPORT. (Editions in Dutch, French, German, Italian) 1956. a. Commission of the European Communities, Services de Renseignement et de Diffusion des Documents, Rue de la Loi 200, 1049 Brussels, Belgium (Dist. in the U.S. by: European Community Information Service, 2100 M St., N.W., Ste. 707, Washington, DC 20037) circ. controlled.

354.67   CM
COMPTES NATIONAUX DU CAMEROUN. a., latest 1977/1978. 4000 Fr.CFA. Direction de la Statistique et de la Comptabilite Nationale - Department of Statistics and National Accounts, Boite Postale 660, Yaounde, Cameroon.

CONGRESS OF MICRONESIA. JOINT COMMITTEE ON PROGRAM AND BUDGET PLANNING. PUBLIC HEARINGS ON HIGH COMMISSIONER'S PRELIMINARY BUDGET. see *PUBLIC ADMINISTRATION*

353.9   US   ISSN 0099-0108
CONNECTICUT. TREASURY DEPARTMENT. ANNUAL REPORT. a. free. Treasury Department, 20 Trinity St., Hartford, CT 06106. TEL 203-566-5050. illus. Key Title: Annual Report of the Treasurer, State of Connecticut.

350   US
CONSOLIDATED TAX RETURN (SUPPLEMENT) a. $96 for base volume. Warren, Gorham and Lamont, Inc., 210 South St., Boston, MA 02111. TEL 800-922-0066.

336   SP   ISSN 0069-9292
CONTABILIDAD NACIONAL DE ESPANA. a. Instituto Nacional de Estadistica, P de la Castellana, 183, Madrid 16, Spain.

336.2   BL
COORDENACAO DO SISTEMA DE TRIBUTACAO, BRAZIL. PARECERES NORMATIVOS. (Subseries of Biblioteca Mapa Fiscal) 1970. irreg. Bol.$2200. Mapa Fiscal Editora S.A., Rua Miguel Teles Jr., 382 a 394, Sao Paulo, Brazil. Eds. J. Goncalves, J. Vallim. bk. rev. index. circ. 15,000.

336.2   CN   ISSN 0070-0282
CORPORATE MANAGEMENT TAX CONFERENCE. 1959-60. a. price varies. Canadian Tax Foundation, Suite 1900, 130 Adelaide St. W., Toronto, Ont. M5H 3P5, Canada. TEL 416-863-9784. Indexed: C.L.I. L.R.I.

336   CR
COSTA RICA. DIRECCION GENERAL DE LA TRIBUTACION DIRECTA. ESTADISTICA DEMOGRAFIA FISCAL DEL IMPUESTO SOBRE LA RENTA. PERIODOS. no.71, 1974. irreg. free. Direccion General de Tributacion Directa, San Jose, Costa Rica. circ. 250.

336   CR   ISSN 0070-0576
COSTA RICA. MINISTERIO DE HACIENDA OFICINA DEL PRESUPESTO. INFORME.* a. Ministerio de Hacienda, Oficina del Presupuesto, San Jose, Costa Rica.

336   NR
CROSS RIVER STATE. MINISTRY OF ECONOMIC DEVELOPMENT AND RECONSTRUCTION. STATE DEVELOPMENT PLAN.* 1970/74. irreg. 5p. Ministry of Economic Development and Reconstruction, Calabar, Nigeria (Dist. by: Cross River State Government Printer, Calabar, Nigeria) illus. stat.
Formerly: South-Eastern State. Ministry of Economic Development and Reconstruction. State Development Plan.

336   US   ISSN 0360-2508
CURRENT GOVERNMENTS REPORTS: CHART BOOK ON GOVERNMENT DATA. ORGANIZATION, FINANCES AND EMPLOYMENT. (Series GF-7) 1966. a. price varies. U.S. Bureau of the Census, Washington, DC 20233. TEL 301-763-4100. (also avail. in microfiche)
Formerly: U.S. Bureau of the Census. Recurrent Reports on Governments. Chart Book on Government Finances and Employment (ISSN 0082-9420)

336.73   US   ISSN 0082-9439
CURRENT GOVERNMENTS REPORTS: CITY GOVERNMENT FINANCES. (Series GF-4) 1965. a. price varies. U.S. Bureau of the Census, Customer Services, Washington, DC 20233. TEL 301-763-4100. (also avail. in microfiche)

336   US   ISSN 0098-678X
CURRENT GOVERNMENTS REPORTS: COUNTY GOVERNMENT FINANCES. (Series GF-8) a. price varies. U.S. Bureau of the Census, Customer Services, Washington, DC 20233. TEL 301-763-4100. (also avail. in microfiche)

336 331 350   US   ISSN 0096-3224
CURRENT GOVERNMENTS REPORTS: FINANCES OF EMPLOYEE RETIREMENT SYSTEMS OF STATE AND LOCAL GOVERNMENTS. (Series GF-2) a. price varies. U.S. Bureau of the Census, Customer Services, Washington, DC 20233. TEL 301-763-4100. (also avail. in microfiche)

336   US   ISSN 0095-3741
CURRENT GOVERNMENTS REPORTS: GOVERNMENTAL FINANCES. (Series GF-5) a. price varies. U.S. Bureau of the Census, Customer Services, Washington, DC 20233. TEL 301-763-4100. (also avail. in microfiche) Key Title: Governmental Finances (Washington)

336   US
CURRENT GOVERNMENTS REPORTS: LOCAL GOVERNMENT FINANCES IN SELECTED METROPOLITAN AREAS AND LARGE COUNTIES. (Series GF-6) a. price varies. U.S. Bureau of the Census, Customer Services, Washington, DC 20233. TEL 301-763-4100. (also avail. in microfiche)

336   US   ISSN 0501-7718
CURRENT GOVERNMENTS REPORTS: QUARTERLY SUMMARY OF STATE AND LOCAL TAX REVENUE. (Series GT) q. $11. U.S. Bureau of the Census, Customer Services, Washington, DC 20233 TEL 301-763-4100. (Subscr. to: Supt. of Documents, Washington, DC 20402) (also avail. in microfiche)

336.2   US
CURRENT GOVERNMENTS REPORTS: STATE AND LOCAL GOVERNMENT SPECIAL STUDIES. (Series GSS) irreg. U.S. Bureau of the Census, Customers Services, Washington, DC 20233 TEL 301-763-4100. (Orders to: Supt. of Documents, Washington, D.C. 20402) (also avail. in microfiche)

336   US   ISSN 0270-0808
CURRENT GOVERNMENTS REPORTS: STATE GOVERNMENT TAX COLLECTIONS. (Series GF-1) a. price varies. U.S. Bureau of the Census, Customer Services, Washington, DC 20233. TEL 301-763-4100. (also avail. in microform) Key Title: State Government Tax Collections.
Formerly: State Tax Collections (ISSN 0095-4152)

336   US
CUT YOUR OWN TAXES AND SAVE (YEAR) a. World Almanac Publications (Subsidiary of: United Media Enterprises) 200 Park Ave., New York, NY 10166. TEL 212-692-3700. Ed. Daril Bentley. circ. 200,000.

336   CY   ISSN 0070-2323
CYPRUS. BUDGET: ESTIMATES OF REVENUE AND EXPENDITURE. (Text in English) a. Mils.600($12) Government Printing Office, Nicosia, Cyprus.

336   CY   ISSN 0084-9510
CYPRUS. DEVELOPMENT ESTIMATES. a. Mils.400($8) Government Printing Office, Nicosia, Cyprus.

336   CY   ISSN 0574-8305
CYPRUS. LOAN COMMISSIONERS. ACCOUNTS AND STATISTICS FOR THE YEAR. 1954. a. $0.75. Loan Commissioners, Nicosia, Cyprus. circ. 350.

336   UK
DAILY MAIL INCOME TAX GUIDE. 1951. a. £1.25. Associated Newspapers Group Ltd., Carmelite House, London EC4Y 0JA, England.

336   US   ISSN 0084-9685
DELAWARE. STATE TREASURER. ANNUAL REPORT. a. free. State Treasurer, Thomas Collins Building, Dover, DE 19901. TEL 302-736-4231. circ. controlled.

336.2   DK   ISSN 0109-6672
DENMARK. DIREKTORATET FOR TOLDVAESENET. TOLDVAESENETS AARSBERETNING. 1971. a. free. Direktoratet for Toldvaesenet, Amaliegade 44, DK-1256 Copenhagen K, Denmark. Ed. Kaj Nielsen. illus. circ. 3,200.
Former Titles: Denmark. Direktoratet for Toldvaesenet. Toldvaesenet Aktiviteter & Denmark. Direktoratet for Toldvaesenet. Toldvaesenet.

336   DK   ISSN 0106-3006
DENMARK. FINANSMINISTERIET. BUDGETDEPARTMENTET. BUDGETREDEGOERELSE. 1979. a. Kr.50. (Finansministeriet, Budgetdepartmentet) Official Danish Information Service, P.O. Box 1103, Bredgade 20, 1009 Copenhagen K, Denmark (Subscr.to: Danske Boghendleres Kommissionsanstalt, Siljangade 6, 2300 Copenhagen S, Denmark)

336   DK   ISSN 0106-4908
DENMARK. STATSSKATTEDIREKTORATET OG LIGNINGSRAADET. MEDDELELSER 1. HAEFTE: INDKOMST- OG FORMUEANSAETTELSER. 1976. a. Kr.30. Statsskattedirektoratet og Ligningsraadet, Copenhagen, Denmark (Orders to: Danske Boghandlers Kommissionsanstalt, Siljangade 6, 2300 Copenhagen S, Denmark)
Formerly: Denmark. Statens Ligningsdirektorat og Ligningsraadet. Indkomst- og Formueskat.

336   DK
DENMARK. STATSSKATTEDIREKTORATET OG LIGNINGSRAADET. MEDDELELSER 2. HAEFTE: VURDERING AF FAST EJENDOM. 1976. a. Kr.40. Statsskattedirektoratet og Ligningsraadet, Copenhagen, Denmark (Orders to: Danske Boghandlers Kommissionsanstalt, Siljangade 6, 2300 Copenhagen S, Denmark)
Formerly: Denmark. Statsskatedirektoratet og Ligningsraadet. Vurdering af Fast Ejendom.

336   EC
ECUADOR. CORPORACION FINANCIERA NACIONAL. MEMORIA. a. free. Corporacion Financiera Nacional, Direccion de Relaciones Publicas, Casilla Postal 163, Quito, Ecuador. charts. illus. stat.
Formerly (until 1977): Ecuador. Comision de Valores. Corporacion Financiera Nacional. Memoria (ISSN 0589-7688)

336   EC
ECUADOR. DIRECCION GENERAL DE RECAUDACIONES. BOLETIN.* irreg. Direccion General de Recaudaciones, Quito, Ecuador. charts. stat.

336 382   PN   ISSN 0378-7397
ESTADISTICA PANAMENA. SITUACION ECONOMICA. SECCION 341. BALANZA DE PAGOS. 1954/58. a. Bl.0.75. Direccion de Estadistica y Censo, Contraloria General, Apdo. 5213, Panama 5, Panama. circ. 2,200.

BUSINESS AND ECONOMICS — PUBLIC FINANCE, TAXATION

336 LO
ESTIMATES OF THE REVENUE AND EXPENDITURE OF THE KINGDOM OF LESOTHO. a. Government Printer, Maseru, Lesotho.

336.73 US ISSN 0071-3678
FACTS AND FIGURES ON GOVERNMENT FINANCE. 1941. a. $75. ‡ Tax Foundation, Inc., One Thomas Circle, N.W., Ste. 500, Washington, DC 20005. TEL 202-822-9050. Ed. Elsie Watters. stat. (also avail. in microform)

353 US
FEDERAL ESTATE AND GIFT TAXATION (SUPPLEMENT) s-a. supplements to base vol. $96. Warren, Gorham and Lamont, Inc., 210 South St., Boston, MA 02111. TEL 800-922-0066.
Formerly: Stephens, Maxfield and Lind's Federal Estate and Gift Taxation (Supplement)

336.2 US ISSN 0092-6531
FEDERAL ESTATE AND GIFT TAXES EXPLAINED, INCLUDING ESTATE PLANNING. irreg., latest 1985. $14.50. Commerce Clearing House, Inc., 4025 W. Peterson Ave., Chicago, IL 60646. TEL 312-583-8500. Key Title: Federal Estate and Gift Taxes Explained.

336.2 US ISSN 0071-4135
FEDERAL GRADUATED WITHHOLDING TAX TABLES. a. $6 pap. Commerce Clearing House, Inc., 4025 W. Peterson Ave., Chicago, IL 60646. TEL 312-583-8500.

336.1 US ISSN 0361-1582
FEDERAL GRANT-IN-AID ACTIVITY IN FLORIDA: A SUMMARY REPORT. 1974. a. $2.22. Department of Administration, Division of State Planning, Bureau of Intergovernmental Relations, 660 Apalachee Pkwy., Tallahassee, FL 32304. stat.

343.730 US ISSN 0196-1349
FEDERAL INCOME TAX GUIDE. 1979? a. Ace Books (Subsidiary of: Charter Communications) c/o Grosset & Dunlap, 51 Madison Ave., New York, NY 10010.

353 US
FEDERAL INCOME TAX LAW. a. $48. Warren, Gorham and Lamont, Inc., 210 South St., Boston, MA 02111. TEL 800-922-0066.
Former titles: Federal Income Tax Law (Supplement) & Stanley and Kilcullen's Federal Income Tax Law (Supplement)

353 332 US
FEDERAL INCOME TAXATION OF BANKS AND FINANCIAL INSTITUTIONS (SUPPLEMENT) q. supplements to base vol. $98 for base vol. plus supp. Warren, Gorham and Lamont, Inc., 210 South St., Boston, MA 02111. TEL 800-922-0066.

350 347 US
FEDERAL TAX LITIGATION (SUPPLEMENT) a. $96. Warren, Gorham and Lamont, Inc., 210 South St., Boston, MA 02111. TEL 800-922-0066.
Former titles: Federal Tax Litigation; Tax Court Practice (Supplement)

336.2 US
FEDERAL TAX MANUAL WITH MONTHLY REPORTS. 1960. a. $175. Commerce Clearing House, Inc., 4025 W. Peterson Ave., Chicago, IL 60646. TEL 312-583-8500. (looseleaf format)
Former titles: Federal Tax Compliance Reports; Federal Tax Compliance Manual; Federal Tax Return Manual (ISSN 0071-4143)

336.2 NE
FED'S FISCALE BROCHURES. 1964. irreg., approx. 6/yr. price varies. Uitgeverij FED B. V., Staverenstraat 3201 5, Deventer, Netherlands. Ed.Bd.

336 FJ
FIJI. BUREAU OF STATISTICS. ECONOMIC AND FUNCTIONAL CLASSIFICATION OF GOVERNMENT ACCOUNTS. 1968. irreg. $1.50 per no. Bureau of Statistics, Box 2221, Suva, Fiji.

336 FJ
FIJI. CENTRAL MONETARY AUTHORITY. ANNUAL REPORT. 1975. a. 5. Central Monetary Authority, Minister of Finance, P.O. Box 1220, Suva, Fiji. charts. stat. circ. 720.

FINANCIAL INSTITUTIONS RETIREMENT FUND. ANNUAL REPORT. see *BUSINESS AND ECONOMICS — Personnel Management*

336 FI ISSN 0071-5255
FINLAND. KANSANTALOUSOSASTO. KANSANTALOUDEN KEHITYSARVIO. SUMMARY: NATIONAL BUDGET FOR FINLAND. (Text in Finnish; summaries in English) 1966. a. Fmk.15. Valtion Painatuskeskus - Government Printing Centre; Ministry of Finance, Annankatu 44, 00100 Helsinki 10, Finland.

332 FR
FISCALITE EUROPEENNE. (Includes supplements) 1968. irreg. price varies. Cahiers Fiscaux Europeens, 51 Avenue Victoria, 06000 Nice, France. Ed. Pierre Fontaneau. (looseleaf format)

353.9 US ISSN 0094-8551
FLORIDA. BUREAU OF LOCAL GOVERNMENT FINANCE. ANNUAL LOCAL GOVERNMENT FINANCIAL REPORT. a. free. Bureau of Local Government Finance, 111 Carlton Bldg., Tallahassee, FL 32304. Key Title: Annual Local Government Financial Report, State of Florida.

336.2 FR
FRANCE. CONSEIL DES IMPOTS. RAPPORT AU PRESIDENT DE LA REPUBLIQUE. irreg. price varies. France. Direction des Journaux Officiels, 26 rue Desaix, 75732 Paris Cedex 15, France. (Co-sponsor: Ministere de l'Environnement et du Cadre de Vie) (also avail. in microfiche)

336 FR ISSN 0071-8637
FRANCE. DIRECTION GENERALE DES DOUANES ET DROITS INDIRECTS. ANNUAIRE ABREGE DE STATISTIQUES. irreg. Imprimerie Nationale, Service des Ventes, 59128 Flers en Escrebieux, 75732 Paris Cedex 15.

336 340 FR
FRANCE. DIRECTION GENERALE DES IMPOTS. PRECIS DE FISCALITE. 1980. a. 5 F. Direction Generale des Impots, Service des Domaines, 17 rue Scribe, 75436 Paris, Cedex 09, France.

336 FR ISSN 0071-8742
FRANCE. INSPECTION GENERALE DES FINANCES. ANNUAIRE. 1952. a. Imprimerie Nationale, S.E.V.P.O., 39 rue de la Convention, 75732 Paris Cedex 15, France.

336 382.1 FR ISSN 0071-8890
FRANCE. MINISTERE DE L'ECONOMIE ET DES FINANCES. BALANCE DES PAIEMENTS ENTRE LA FRANCE ET L'EXTERIEUR. a. Ministere de l'Economie et des Finances, Direction du Tresor, 93 rue de Rivoli, 75056 Paris, France. circ. controlled.

336 FR ISSN 0071-8904
FRANCE. MINISTERE DU BUDGET. BUDGET. 1952. a. price varies. Ministere du Budget, Service de l'Information, 93 rue de Rivoli, 75056 Paris, France (Dist. by: Documentation Francaise, 29-31 Quai Voltaire, Paris Cedex 07, France)
Formerly: France. Ministere de l'Economie et des Finances. Budget.

354.67 GO
GABON. DIRECTION GENERALE DES FINANCES ET DU BUDGET. PROJET DU BUDGET GENERAL. irreg. Direction Generale des Finances et du Budget, Ministere de l'Economie et des Finances, Libreville, Gabon. stat.

354.667 GH
GHANA. SUPREME MILITARY COUNCIL. BUDGET PROPOSALS. a. NC.1. Supreme Military Council, Ministry of Finance, Accra, Ghana. stat.

336 US ISSN 0072-5161
GOVERNMENT FINANCE BRIEF. NEW SERIES. 1965. irreg., no.31, 1981. price varies. ‡ Tax Foundation, Inc., One Thomas Circle, N.W., Ste. 500, Washington, DC 20005. TEL 202-822-9050. Ed. Elsie Watters.

339.4 UK
GREAT BRITAIN. BOARD OF INLAND REVENUE. THE SURVEY OF PERSONAL INCOMES. irreg. £4.95. H.M.S.O., Publications Centre, P.O. Box 276, London SW8 5DT, England (Avail. from H.M.S.O., c/o Liaison Officer, Atlantic House, Holborn Viaduct, London EC1P 1BN, England) stat.

GREAT BRITAIN. DEPARTMENT OF THE ENVIRONMENT. LOCAL GOVERNMENT FINANCIAL STATISTICS: ENGLAND AND WALES. see *PUBLIC ADMINISTRATION — Municipal Government*

336.1 UK
GREAT BRITAIN. DEPARTMENT OF THE ENVIRONMENT. RATE REBATES IN ENGLAND AND WALES. (Joint publication with the Welsh Office) a. price varies. H.M.S.O., Box 569, London SE1 9NH, England.

336.1 UK
GREAT BRITAIN. DEPARTMENT OF THE ENVIRONMENT. RATES AND RATEABLE VALUES IN ENGLAND AND WALES. (Joint publication with the Welsh Office) 1970/1971. irreg. price varies. H.M.S.O., Box 569, London SE1 9NH, England.

336 UK
GREAT BRITAIN. TREASURY. SUPPLY ESTIMATES. 1850. a. price varies. H.M. Treasury, 51 Nine Elms Lane, London SW8 5DR, England (Avail. from H.M.S.O., P.O. Box 569, Stamford St., London SE1 9NH, England) stat. index.

336.2 GU ISSN 0072-7873
GUAM. DEPARTMENT OF REVENUE AND TAXATION. REPORT. 1969. a. $2. Department of Revenue and Taxation, Office of the Director, 855 West Marine Dr., Agana, GU 96910. TEL 671-477-1040. circ. 100.

336 CN
GUIDE DU CONTRIBUABLE CANADIEN. a. Can.$29.95. C C H Canadian Ltd., 6 Garamond Crt., Don Mills, Ont. M3C 1Z5, Canada. TEL 416-441-2992.

GUIDE TO FEDERAL FUNDING FOR EDUCATION. see *EDUCATION — School Organization And Administration*

336.2 JA ISSN 0072-8551
GUIDE TO JAPANESE TAXES. (Text in English) 1965. a. $20. Zaikei Shoho Sha, 1-2-14 Higashi Shimbashi, Minato-ku, Tokyo, Japan (Dist. in U.S. by: Fred B. Rothman & Co., 10368 W. Centennial Rd., Littleton, CO 80123) Ed. Yuji Gomi. circ. 6,000.

336.2 US ISSN 0072-8837
GUIDEBOOK TO CALIFORNIA TAXES. 1950. a. $15. Commerce Clearing House, Inc., 4025 W. Peterson Ave., Chicago, IL 60646. TEL 312-583-8500.

336.2 US ISSN 0093-8637
GUIDEBOOK TO FLORIDA TAXES. a. $15. Commerce Clearing House, Inc., 4025 W. Peterson Ave., Chicago, IL 60646. TEL 312-583-8500.

336.2 US ISSN 0072-8845
GUIDEBOOK TO ILLINOIS TAXES. 1971. a. $16. Commerce Clearing House, Inc., 4025 W. Peterson Ave., Chicago, IL 60646. TEL 312-583-8500.

336.2 US ISSN 0072-8861
GUIDEBOOK TO MASSACHUSETTS TAXES. 1967. a. $15. Commerce Clearing House, Inc., 4025 W. Peterson Ave., Chicago, IL 60646. TEL 312-583-8500.

336.2 US ISSN 0072-887X
GUIDEBOOK TO MICHIGAN TAXES. 1968. a. $15. Commerce Clearing House, Inc., 4025 W. Peterson Ave., Chicago, IL 60646. TEL 312-583-8500.

336.2 US ISSN 0072-8888
GUIDEBOOK TO NEW JERSEY TAXES. 1969. a. $15. Commerce Clearing House, Inc., 4025 W. Peterson Ave., Chicago, IL 60646. TEL 312-583-8500.

BUSINESS AND ECONOMICS — PUBLIC FINANCE, TAXATION

336.2 US ISSN 0072-8896
GUIDEBOOK TO NEW YORK TAXES. 1965. a. $15. Commerce Clearing House, Inc., 4025 W. Peterson Ave., Chicago, IL 60646. TEL 312-583-8500.

336.2 US ISSN 0091-1186
GUIDEBOOK TO NORTH CAROLINA TAXES. 1972. a. $15. Commerce Clearing House, Inc., 4025 W. Peterson Ave., Chicago, IL 60646. TEL 312-583-8500.

336.2 US ISSN 0091-4010
GUIDEBOOK TO OHIO TAXES. 1972. a. $15. Commerce Clearing House, Inc., 4025 W. Peterson Ave., Chicago, IL 60646. TEL 312-583-8500.

336.2 US ISSN 0072-890X
GUIDEBOOK TO PENNSYLVANIA TAXES. 1965. a. $15. Commerce Clearing House, Inc., 4025 W. Peterson Ave., Chicago, IL 60646. TEL 312-583-8500.

336.2 US ISSN 0093-8645
GUIDEBOOK TO WISCONSIN TAXES. irreg. $15. Commerce Clearing House, Inc., 4025 W. Peterson Ave., Chicago, IL 60646. TEL 312-583-8500.

336 II ISSN 0533-649X
GUJARAT STATE FINANCIAL CORPORATION. ANNUAL REPORT. (Text in English) a. Gujarat State Financial Corporation, Jaladarshan Bldg., Ashram Rd., Navrangpura, Box 4030, Ahmedabad 380009, India. illus. stat.

336 UK
H M CUSTOMS AND EXCISE OFFICIAL V A T GUIDES. irreg. Longman Professional, 21-27 Lambs Conduit St., London WC1N 3NJ, England. (looseleaf format)

336 US ISSN 0163-4615
HANDBOOK OF BUSINESS FINANCE AND CAPITAL SOURCES. 1979. every 18 mos. $95. Interfinance Corporation, 511 11th Ave., Box 15553, Minneapolis, MN 55415. Ed. Dileep Rao.

336.2 NE
HANDBOOK ON THE U.S. - GERMAN TAX CONVENTION. (Text in English and German) 1966. irreg. fl.880 incl. base vol. International Bureau of Fiscal Documentation, Box 20237, 1000 HE Amsterdam, Netherlands. (looseleaf format)

336 GW
HANDBUCH DER STEUERVERANLAGUNGEN: EINKOMMENSTEUER, KOERPERSCHAFTSTEUER, GEWERBESTEUER, UMSATZSTEUER. (Subseries of the institute's Schriften) 1964. a. price varies. (Deutsches Wissenschaftliches Steuerinstitut der Steuerberater und Steuerbevollmaechtigten e.V.) C.H. Beck'sche Verlagsbuchhandlung, Wilhelmstr. 9, 8000 Munich 40, W. Germany (B.R.D.)

336 UK
HARRISON'S INLAND REVENUE INDEX TO TAX CASES. irreg. Longman Professional, 21-27 Lambs Conduit St., London WC1N 3NJ, England. (looseleaf format)

HAWAII. LEGISLATIVE AUDITOR. SPECIAL REPORTS. see PUBLIC ADMINISTRATION

HORSE OWNERS AND BREEDERS TAX MANUAL. see SPORTS AND GAMES — Horses And Horsemanship

336 NE
I F A CONGRESS SEMINAR SERIES. 1977. a. price varies. Kluwer Law and Taxation Publishers, Box 23, 7400 AG Deventer, Netherlands (Orders to: Kluwer Academic Publishers Group, Distribution Center, Box 322, 3300 AH Dordrecht, Netherlands)

336 US
ILLINOIS PROPERTY TAX STATISTICS. 1940. a. free. Department of Revenue, 101 W. Jefferson St., Springfield, IL 62708. Ed. Sharon Logsdon. stat. circ. 1,200.

336.2 US
INCOME, EMPLOYMENT, ESTATE AND GIFT TAX PROVISIONS: INTERNAL REVENUE CODE. a. $25 paperback. Commerce Clearing House, Inc., 4025 W. Peterson Ave., Chicago, IL 60646. TEL 312-583-8500.
 Formerly: Income, Estate and Gift Tax Provisions: Internal Revenue Code (ISSN 0073-5671)

336.2 II ISSN 0073-6120
INDIA. CENTRAL BOARD OF REVENUE. CENTRAL EXCISE MANUAL.* (Text in English) a. Rs.6.25($2.85) Central Board of Revenue, Ministry of Finance, New Delhi, India.

336 II
INDIA. FINANCE DEPARTMENT. BUDGET OF THE CENTRAL GOVERNMENT. a. Finance Department, New Delhi, India. charts. stat.
 Supersedes: India. Ministry of Finance. Budget (ISSN 0536-9290)

336 UK
INLAND REVENUE CLEARANCES. irreg. Longman Professional, 21-27 Lambs Conduit St., London WC1N 3NJ, England. (looseleaf format)

336 UK
INLAND REVENUE OFFICIAL TAX GUIDES. irreg. Longman Professional, 21-27 Lambs Conduit St., London WC1N 3NJ, England.

336 UK
INLAND REVENUE PRACTICES AND CONCESSIONS. irreg. Longman Professional, 21-27 Lambs Conduit St., London WC1N 3NJ, England.

INSTITUT "FINANZEN UND STEUERN." GRUENE BRIEFE. see BUSINESS AND ECONOMICS — Banking And Finance

INSTITUT "FINANZEN UND STEUERN." SCHRIFTENREIHE. see BUSINESS AND ECONOMICS — Banking And Finance

336 UK ISSN 0260-6496
INSTITUTE OF CHARTERED ACCOUNTANTS IN ENGLAND AND WALES. TAX DIGEST. 1980. irreg. Institute of Chartered Accountants in England and Wales, P.O. Box 433, Moorgate Place, London EC2P 2BJ, England.

336 US
INTERNAL REVENUE CODE. Cover title: Complete Internal Revenue Code. a. $19.50. Research Institute of America, Inc., 90 Fifth Ave., New York, NY 10011. TEL 212-645-4800.

336 SZ ISSN 0074-1744
INTERNATIONAL ASSOCIATION OF STATE LOTTERIES. (REPORTS OF CONGRESS) 1974. biennial, 12th, 1976, Nairobi. 8 Fr.($300) International Association of State Lotteries, Hirschengraben 62, Box 644, 8021 Zurich, Switzerland. adv. bk. rev. circ. 1,000.
 Reports published in host country

336 NE ISSN 0074-2104
INTERNATIONAL BUREAU OF FISCAL DOCUMENTATION. ANNUAL REPORT. (Text in English) 1953. a. free. International Bureau of Fiscal Documentation, Box 20237, 1000 HE Amsterdam, Netherlands. Ed. Dir. J. van Hoorn, Jr.

336 NE ISSN 0074-2112
INTERNATIONAL BUREAU OF FISCAL DOCUMENTATION. PUBLICATION. irreg., no.38, 1985. price varies. International Bureau of Fiscal Documentation, Box 20237, 1000 HE Amsterdam, Netherlands.

336.2 BE ISSN 0074-4476
INTERNATIONAL CUSTOMS JOURNAL/ BULLETIN INTERNATIONAL DES DOUANES. (Text in English, French, German, Italian, Spanish) 1891. irreg. price varies. International Customs Tariffs Bureau - Bureau International des Tarifs Douaniers, Rue de l'Association 38, B-1000 Brussels, Belgium (Dist. in the U.S. by: National Technical Information Service, U.S. Department of Commerce, Springfield, VA 22161) circ. 4,500.

332 NE
INTERNATIONAL FISCAL HARMONIZATION SERIES. 1969. irreg., no.3, 1975. price varies. International Bureau of Fiscal Documentation, Box 20237, 1000 HE Amsterdam, Netherlands.

336 US ISSN 0074-6533
INTERNATIONAL INSTITUTE OF PUBLIC FINANCE. PAPERS AND PROCEEDINGS. (Text in English, French, German) 1938. a. price varies. ‡ (International Institute of Public Finance) Wayne State University Press, Leonard N. Simons Bldg., 5959 Woodward Ave., Detroit, MI 48202. TEL 313-577-4603. circ. 600.

336 UK
INTERNATIONAL TAX SYSTEMS AND PLANNING TECHNIQUES. irreg. Longman Professional, 21-27 Lambs Conduit St., London WC1N 3NJ, England.

336 IE ISSN 0075-0603
IRELAND (EIRE) CENTRAL STATISTICS OFFICE. NATIONAL INCOME AND EXPENDITURE. 1958. a. £3.35. Government Publications Office, Trade and Postal Sales, Bishop Street, Dublin 8, Ireland (Published by: The Stationery Office, Waterloo Rd., Dublin 4, Ireland) circ. 2,000.
 Supersedes in part: Irish Statistical Survey.

336 IE ISSN 0075-0670
IRELAND (EIRE) DEPARTMENT OF FINANCE. FINANCIAL STATEMENT OF THE MINISTER FOR FINANCE. a. Department of Finance, Dublin, Ireland.

336 IS
ISRAEL. DEPARTMENT OF CUSTOMS AND V A T. YALKUT. (Value Added Tax) (Text in Hebrew; occasional summaries in English and other languages) 1955. irreg. IS.30($20) Department of Customs and V A T, Publication & Instruction Section, 32 Agron St., Box 320, Jerusalem 91002, Israel. Ed. Asher Joseph. circ. 1,500.
 Formerly: Israel. Department of Customs and Excise. Yalkut (ISSN 0578-8250)

336 IS
ISRAEL. KNESSET. VA'ADAT HA-KESAFIM MISPARIM AL VA'ADAT HA-KESAFIM/ ISRAEL. KNESSET. FINANCE COMMITTEE. DATA ON ACTIVITIES. 1972/73. a. ‡ Knesset, Finance Committee, Jerusalem, Israel. Ed. Ivor Kershner. circ. controlled. (processed)

336 IS
ISRAEL TAX LAW LETTER. (Text in English) 1980. irreg. (approx. 15/yr.) $35 for 12 issues. A G Publications Ltd., Box 7422, 31070 Haifa, Israel. circ. 250.

336 IV
IVORY COAST. MINISTERE DE L'ECONOMIE, DES FINANCES ET DU PLAN. COMPTES DE LA NATION. 1966. a. $20. Ministere de l'Economie, des Finances et du Plan, B. P. 5-65, Abidjan, Ivory Coast.
 Formerly: Ivory Coast. Ministere du Plan. Comptes de la Nation.

336.24 US ISSN 0084-4314
J.K. LASSER'S YOUR INCOME TAX. 1937. a. $8.95. (J.K. Lasser Institute) Prentice Hall Press, One Gulf & Western Plaza, New York, NY 10023. TEL 212-373-8500. Ed. Bernard Greisman.

336.2 US ISSN 0075-2061
J.K. LASSER'S YOUR INCOME TAX, PROFESSIONAL ED. 1962. a. $29.95. (J.K. Lasser Institute) Prentice Hall Press, One Gulf & Western Plaza, New York, NY 10023. TEL 212-373-8500.

336 GW
JAHRBUCH DER FACHANWAELTE FUER STEUERRECHT. a. DM.76. Verlag Neue Wirtschafts-Briefe GmbH, Eschstrasse 22, 4690 Herne 1, W. Germany (B.R.D.) (back issues avail.)

JAHRESFACHKATALOG RECHT-WIRTSCHAFT-STEUERN. see BUSINESS AND ECONOMICS

336 II
KARNATAKA. FINANCE DEPARTMENT. ANNUAL REPORT. (Text in English) a. Finance Department, Bangalore, Karnataka, India.
 Supersedes: Mysore. Finance Department. Annual Report.

BUSINESS AND ECONOMICS — PUBLIC FINANCE, TAXATION

336.3   US   ISSN 0095-1498
KENTUCKY LOCAL DEBT REPORT. 1971. a. Commonwealth of Kentucky, New Capitol Annex Bldg., Frankfort, KY 40601. TEL 502-564-2382.

LAW REPRINTS: TAX LAW SERIES. see *LAW*

336   LO   ISSN 0075-8817
LESOTHO. TREASURY. REPORT ON THE FINANCES AND ACCOUNTS. a. R.4. Treasury, P.O. Box 401, Maseru, Lesotho.

336   LB   ISSN 0304-727X
LIBERIA. MINISTRY OF FINANCE. ANNUAL REPORT. 1972. a. Ministry of Finance, Broad St., Monrovia, Liberia. charts. stat.

336.666   LB
LIBERIA. MINISTRY OF PLANNING AND ECONOMIC AFFAIRS. GOVERNMENT ACCOUNTS. a, latest 1980. $3. Ministry of Planning and Economic Affairs, Box 9016, Monrovia, Liberia. stat.

336   US   ISSN 0085-2821
LOCAL GOVERNMENT FINANCES IN MARYLAND. 1948. a. Department of Fiscal Services, Division of Fiscal Research, 90 State Circle, Annapolis, MD 21401. stat. circ. controlled. (processed; also avail. in microfiche from CRS)

336.2   CN
LOI DE L'IMPOT SUR LE REVENU DU CANADA. 12th edt., 1983. a. Can.$31.25 paperbound; Can.$ 38.50 hardbound. C.C.H. Canadian Ltd., 6 Garamond Ct., Don Mills, Ont. M3C 1Z5, Canada. TEL 416-441-2992. index.
Formerly: Loi de l'Impot sur le Revenu Canadien (ISSN 0076-048X)

336.17   CN
LOTO - QUEBEC. RAPPORT ANNUEL. (Editions in English and French) 1970. a. Societe des Loteries et Courses du Quebec, Public Affairs, 500 Sherbrooke St. W., Montreal, Que. H3A 3G6, Canada. TEL 514-282-8000. illus. circ. 3,000.

336   LU   ISSN 0076-1559
LUXEMBOURG. MINISTERE DES FINANCES. BUDGET DE L'ETAT. a. contr. free circ. Ministere des Finances, 3 rue de la Congregation, 1352 Luxembourg, Luxembourg.

336   LU
LUXEMBOURG. MINISTERE DES FINANCES. PROJET DE LOI CONCERNANT LE BUDGET DES RECETTES ET DES DEPENSES DE L'ETAT. a. contr. free circ. Ministere des Finances, 3 rue de la Congregation, 1352 Luxembourg, Luxembourg.

MCGOLDRICK'S HANDBOOK OF CANADIAN CUSTOMS TARIFF AND EXCISE DUTIES. see *BUSINESS AND ECONOMICS — International Commerce*

336   II   ISSN 0076-2555
MAHARASHTRA STATE BUDGET IN BRIEF. (Text in English and Marathi) 1960/61. a. free. Directorate of Economics and Statistics, D.D. Bldg., Old Custom House, Bombay 400023, India. Ed. S.M. Vidwans. circ. controlled.

657.46   336.2   US
MAIN HURDMAN & CRANSTOUN NEWS SUMMARY. irreg? Main Hurdman & Cranstoun (Certified Public Accountants), 55 E. 52nd St., New York, NY 10055. TEL 212-909-5000.

336.2   US
MAIN HURDMAN & CRANSTOUN TAX NEWSLETTER. irreg? Main Hurdman & Cranstoun (Certified Public Accountants), 55 E. 52nd St., New York, NY 10055. TEL 212-909-5000.

336.2   US
MAINE. BUREAU OF PROPERTY TAXATION. ANNUAL REPORT. 1974. a. Bureau of Property Taxation, Rm. 202, State Office Bldg., Augusta, ME 04333. TEL 207-289-2011. charts. stat.
Formerly (until 1976): Maine. Bureau of Property Taxation. Biennial Report (ISSN 0361-3550)

336   MW   ISSN 0076-3020
MALAWI. ACCOUNTANT GENERAL. REPORT. a., latest 1982. K.8. Government Printer, P.O. Box 37, Zomba, Malawi.

336   MW
MALAWI. DEPARTMENT OF TAXES. ANNUAL REPORT OF THE COMMISSIONER OF TAXES. (Text in English) a. Government Printer, Box 37, Zomba, Malawi.

MALAWI. ECONOMIC PLANNING DIVISION. MID-YEAR ECONOMIC REVIEW. see *PUBLIC ADMINISTRATION*

336   MW   ISSN 0076-3195
MALAWI. MINISTRY OF FINANCE. BUDGET STATEMENT. a. Government Printer, P.O. Box 37, Zomba, Malawi.

336   MW
MALAWI. MINISTRY OF FINANCE. FINANCIAL STATEMENT. (Subseries of its Budget Document) a. Government Printer, Box 37, Zomba, Malawi.

336   382   MW   ISSN 0085-3003
MALAWI. NATIONAL STATISTICAL OFFICE. BALANCE OF PAYMENTS. 1964. a. K.5.50($2.80) ‡ National Statistical Office, Box 333, Zomba, Malawi.

336   MW   ISSN 0076-3314
MALAWI. OFFICE OF THE AUDITOR GENERAL. REPORT. a. K.2. Government Printer, P.O. Box 37, Zomba, Malawi.

336.2   US   ISSN 0362-868X
MASSACHUSETTS TAX PRIMER. 1968. biennial, latest 1986. $4.50. Massachusetts Taxpayers Foundation, Inc., 24 Province St., Boston, MA 02108. TEL 617-720-1000. circ. 5,000. (back issues avail.)

336   US
MASTER FEDERAL TAX MANUAL. Cover title: Research Institute Master Federal Tax Manual. 1975. a. $12.95. Research Institute of America, Inc., 90 Fifth Ave., New York, NY 10011. TEL 212-645-4800. Ed.Bd.

336   MF   ISSN 0076-549X
MAURITIUS. CUSTOMS AND EXCISE DEPARTMENT. ANNUAL REPORT. 1938. a, latest 1978. Rs.225. Customs and Excise Department, Port Louis, Mauritius (Orders to: Government Printing Office, Elizabeth II Ave., Port Louis, Mauritius) circ. 350.

336   MF   ISSN 0543-1565
MAURITIUS. DIRECTOR OF AUDIT. REPORT. 1912. a. Rs.55. Audit Department, Port Louis, Mauritius. circ. 500.

336   MF   ISSN 0076-5562
MAURITIUS. PUBLIC ACCOUNTS COMMITTEE. REPORT.* a. price varies. Government Printing Office, Elizabeth II Ave., Port Louis, Mauritius.

336.776   US   ISSN 0095-0645
MINNESOTA. DEPARTMENT OF REVENUE. BIENNIAL REPORT. 1940. biennial. Department of Revenue, Centennial Office Bldg., St. Paul, MN 55145. TEL 612-296-3781. stat. Key Title: Biennial Report - State of Minnesota, Department of Revenue.
Continues: Minnesota. Department of Taxation. Biennial Report.

336.2   US
MINNESOTA SALES AND USE TAX ANNUAL REPORT BULLETIN. 1971. a. Department of Revenue, Research Division 230, Box 64446, MI 55164. charts. stat.
Formerly: Minnesota Sales and Use Tax Quarterly Report Bulletin.

366.778   US
MISSOURI. DEPARTMENT OF REVENUE. ANNUAL COMBINED FINANCIAL REPORT. 1919. a. price varies. Department of Revenue, Office of Legislation and Regulations, Box 629, Jefferson City, MO 65105. TEL 314-751-2110. (Co-Sponsor: Missouri State Treasurer) Ed. Leslie Beckham. stat. circ. 300.

336.2   UK   ISSN 0267-8829
MOORES & ROWLAND'S TAX GUIDE. 1978. a. Butterworth & Co. (Publishers) Ltd., 88 Kingsway, London WC2B 6AB, England. Ed. N.A. Eastaway.
Formerly: Rowland's Tax Guide (ISSN 0143-280X)

336   382   RH
NATIONAL ACCOUNTS OF RHODESIA. 1946. a., latest 1978. Rhod.$1. ‡ Central Statistical Office, P.O. Box 8063, Causeway, Salisbury, Zimbabwe. circ. 300.
Formerly: National Accounts and Balance of Payments of Rhodesia (ISSN 0077-2941)

336   MM   ISSN 0077-295X
NATIONAL ACCOUNTS OF THE MALTESE ISLANDS. a. Central Office of Statistics, Auberge d'Italie, Valletta, Malta (Subscr. to: Information Division, Auberge de Castille, Valletta, Malta)

336   CN   ISSN 0077-4529
NATIONAL FINANCES: AN ANALYSIS OF THE REVENUES AND EXPENDITURES OF THE GOVERNMENT OF CANADA. 1954/55. a. price varies. Canadian Tax Foundation, Suite 1900, 130 Adelaide St. W., Toronto, Ont. M5H 3P5, Canada. TEL 416-863-9784.

336.2   US   ISSN 0069-8687
NATIONAL TAX ASSOCIATION - TAX INSTITUTE OF AMERICA. PROCEEDINGS OF THE ANNUAL CONFERENCE. 1907. a. $20 (or membership) National Tax Association - Tax Institute of America, 21 E. State St., Columbus, OH 43215. TEL 614-224-8352. Ed. Stanley J. Bowers. index. circ. 2,000.
Formerly: Conference on Taxation. Proceedings.

336   NE   ISSN 0168-3489
NETHERLANDS. CENTRAAL BUREAU VOOR DE STATISTIEK. NATIONALE REKENINGEN. NATIONAL ACCOUNTS. (Text in Dutch and English) 1948/50. a. fl.38.75. Centraal Bureau voor de Statistiek, Prinses Beatrixlaan 428, Voorburg, Netherlands (Orders to: Staatsuitgeverij, Christoffel Plantijnstraat, The Hague, Netherlands)

336   US
NEW ENGLAND WAR TAX RESISTANCE NEWSLETTER. 1968. a. free. New England War Tax Resistance, Box 174, MIT Branch P.O., Cambridge, MA 02139. Ed.Bd. circ. 500.

336   US
NEW JERSEY. DIVISION OF TAXATION. ANNUAL REPORT. a. Division of Taxation, Office of Tax Analysis, 50 Barracks St., Trenton, NJ 08646. TEL 609-292-7169.

336   US
NEW YORK UNIVERSITY. INSTITUTE ON FEDERAL TAXATION. CONFERENCE ON CHARITABLE FOUNDATIONS. 1955. biennial. $40. (New York University, School of Continuing Education in Law and Taxations) Matthew Bender & Co., Inc., 235 E. 45th St., New York, NY 10017. TEL 212-661-5050. Ed. Nicolas Liakas. index. cum.index: vols. 1-10. (back issues avail.) Indexed: C.L.I. L.R.I.

336   346.066   NZ
NEW ZEALAND INCOME TAX LEGISLATION. 1984. irreg. NZ.$275. Commerce Clearing House, 127 Sunnybrae Rd., Auckland 10, New Zealand.

336   NZ
NEW ZEALAND LOTTERY BOARD. REPORT. (Title varies slightly) 1963. a. price varies. (New Zealand Lottery Board) Government Printing Office, Private Bag, Wellington, New Zealand. stat. circ. 200.
Formerly (until 1977): New Zealand. Lottery Board of Control. Report (ISSN 0545-7297)

336   NO   ISSN 0333-1423
NORSK SKATTELOVSAMLING. a. Norwegian University Press, Postboks 2959, Toeyen, N-0608 Oslo 6, Norway.

336.2   US
NORTH CAROLINA. DEPARTMENT OF REVENUE. FRANCHISE TAX AND CORPORATE INCOME TAX RULES AND REGULATIONS. 1964. irreg., latest 1983. free. Department of Revenue, Corporate Income and Franchise Tax Division, Box 25000, Raleigh, NC 27640. TEL 919-733-3166. circ. 7,500.
Formerly (until 1976?): North Carolina. Department of Revenue. Franchise Tax and Corporate Income Tax Bulletins for Taxable Years (ISSN 0078-138X)

BUSINESS AND ECONOMICS — PUBLIC FINANCE, TAXATION

336   SZ
OFFENTLICHE FINANZEN DER SCHWEIZ/ FINANCES PUBLIQUES EN SUISSE. (Text in French and German) 1972. a. Bundesamt fuer Statistik, Hallwylstr. 15, CH-3003 Berne, Switzerland.

336.2   US
OKLAHOMA. AD VALOREM TAX DIVISION. PROGRESS REPORT TO THE LEGISLATURE ON PROPERTY REVALUATION. 1968. a. free. ‡ Tax Commission, Ad Valorem Tax Division, 2501 Lincoln Blvd., Oklahoma City, OK 73194. TEL 405-521-3178. Ed. Robert L. Hartman. stat. circ. 500. (processed)

336   DK   ISSN 0108-9722
OPGAVESAMLING I SKAT 1. Cover title: Opgavesamling i Skatteret I. 1980. a. Kr.150. Alternativ Revision's Forlag, Riddergade 7, 4700 Naestved, Denmark.

336   DK   ISSN 0108-9730
OPGAVESAMLING I SKAT 2 OG ERHVERVSJURA. Cover title: Opgavesamling i Skatteret II og Erhvervsjura. 1980. a. Kr.150. Alternativ Revision's Forlag, Riddergade 7, 4700 Naestved, Denmark.

336.2   US
OREGON PROPERTY TAX STATISTICS. 1970. a. $9. Department of Revenue, Revenue Bldg., Salem, OR 97310. TEL 503-378-4977.
     Formerly: Oregon. Department of Revenue. Summary of Levies and Statistics.

336.2   US
OREGON RATIO AND ASSESSMENT DATA ROLL. 1971. a. $5. Department of Revenue, Revenue Bldg., Salem, OR 97310. TEL 503-378-4977.
     Formerly: Oregon. Department of Revenue. Sales Ratio Study.

336   FR
ORGANIZATION FOR ECONOMIC COOPERATION AND DEVELOPMENT. AGRICULTURAL POLICY REPORTS. (Only avail. on microfiche) irreg. Organization for Economic Cooperation and Development, 2 rue Andre Pascal, 75775 Paris Cedex 16, France (U.S. orders to: O.E.C.D. Publications Center, 1750 Pennsylvania Ave., N.W., Washington D.C. 20006) (also avail. in microfiche)

336.2   JA   ISSN 0078-7094
OUTLINE OF JAPANESE TAX. 1953. a. 3500 Yen. Ministry of Finance, Seifu Kankobutsu Service Centre, 1-2 Kasumigaseki, Chiyoda-ku, Tokyo 100, Japan.

OWNER OCCUPIED HOUSING STATISTICS FROM HOMESTEAD REBATE AND INCOME TAX DATA MATCH. see *HOUSING AND URBAN PLANNING*

336   PK
PAKISTAN. FINANCE DIVISION. ANNUAL BUDGET STATEMENT (FINAL) (Text in English) a. Finance Division, Islamabad, Pakistan. stat.

336   PK
PAKISTAN. FINANCE DIVISION. BUDGET IN BRIEF. (Text in English) 1964/65. a. free to qualified personnel. Finance Division, Islamabad, Pakistan.
     Formerly: Pakistan. Ministry of Finance. Budget in Brief (ISSN 0078-8309)

336   PK
PAKISTAN. FINANCE DIVISION. ECONOMIC ANALYSIS OF THE BUDGET. (Text in English) a. free to qualified personnel. Finance Division, Islamabad, Pakistan.
     Continues: Pakistan. Ministry of Finance. Economic Analysis of the Central Government (ISSN 0078-8325)

338.9   PK
PAKISTAN. FINANCE DIVISION. ESTIMATES OF FOREIGN ASSISTANCE. (Text in English) irreg. Finance Division, Islamabad, Pakistan.
     Supersedes (1976-1977): Pakistan. Ministry of Finance Estimates of Foreign Assistance (ISSN 0555-8786)

336   PK
PAKISTAN. FINANCE DIVISION. SUPPLEMENTARY DEMANDS FOR GRANTS AND APPROPRIATIONS. (Text in English) 1973/74. irreg. free to qualified personnel. Finance Division, Islamabad, Pakistan. charts. stat. circ. controlled.

336   PK   ISSN 0078-7892
PAKISTAN BASIC FACTS. (Text in English) a. Rs.5. Office of the Economic Adviser, Islamabad, Pakistan.
     Formerly: Pakistan. Ministry of Finance. Basic Facts About the Budget (ISSN 0078-8295)

PAKISTAN CUSTOMS TARIFF. see *BUSINESS AND ECONOMICS — International Commerce*

336   382   PK   ISSN 0078-852X
PAKISTAN'S BALANCE OF PAYMENTS. (Text in English) 1948/59. a. Rs.10($3) State Bank of Pakistan, Central Directorate, Public Relations Department, I.I. Chundrigar Rd., Box 4456, Karachi, Pakistan.

336   AT
PAPUA NEW GUINEA INCOME TAX LEGISLATION. 1976. irreg. Aus.$238. C H Australia Ltd., P.O. Box 230, North Ryde, N.S.W. 2113, Australia.

336   US
PENNSYLVANIA. STATE TAX EQUALIZATION BOARD. ANNUAL CERTIFICATION. vol.28, 1975. a. State Tax Equalization Board, Harrisburg, PA 17126. TEL 717-787-5950.

336   US
PERSPECTIVES ON LOCAL PUBLIC FINANCE AND PUBLIC POLICY. 1983. a. $24.75 to individuals; institutions $49.50. J A I Press Inc., Box 1678, 36 Sherwood Pl., Greenwich, CT 06836. TEL 203-661-7602. Ed. John M. Quigley.

336.2   PH   ISSN 0079-1547
PHILIPPINES. NATIONAL TAX RESEARCH CENTER. REPORT. 1960. a. National Tax Research Center, First BF Condominium, Aduana St., Intramuros, Manila, Philippines. circ. 1,000.
     Formerly: Philippines. Joint Legislative-Executive Tax Commission. Report.

336   PO   ISSN 0079-4201
PORTUGAL. MINISTERIO DAS FINANCAS. RELATORIO DO ORCAMENTO GERAL DO ESTADO.* a. price varies. Ministerio das Financas, Lisbon 2, Portugal.

POSTBUECHL. see *COMMUNICATIONS — Postal Affairs*

336   HU   ISSN 0230-9718
PUBLIC FINANCE IN HUNGARY. (Text in English) 1982. irreg. price varies. Secreteriate of the Ministry of Finance, 1051 Jozsef nador ter 2-4, Budapest, Hungary. Ed.Bd.

336   UK
PUBLIC LEDGER COMMODITY YEAR BOOK. 1980. a. £36. Turret-Wheatland Ltd., 12 Greycaine Rd., Watford, Herts. WD2 4JP, England. Ed. John Buckley.

336   PR
PUERTO RICO. OFICINA DE PRESUPUESTO Y GERENCIA. RESOLUCIONES CONJUNTAS DEL PRESUPUESTO GENERAL Y DE PRESUPUESTOS ESPECIALES. a. free; limited distribution. Oficina de Presupuesto - Puerto Rico. Office of Budget and Management, Box 3228, San Juan, PR 00904.
     Formerly: Puerto Rico. Negociado del Presupuesto. Resoluciones Conjuntas del Presupuesto General y de Presupuestos Especiales (ISSN 0079-7863)

336.2   340   CN
QUEBEC CORPORATION AND INCOME TAX LEGISLATION. irreg., 21st edt., 1984. Can.$13.56. C H Canadian Ltd., 6 Garamond St., Don Mills, Ont. M3C 1Z5, Canada. TEL 416-441-2992.

336   II   ISSN 0079-9556
RAJASTHAN, INDIA. DIRECTORATE OF ECONOMICS AND STATISTICS. BUDGET STUDY. (Text in English and Hindi) 1959. a. free. Directorate of Economics and Statistics, Krishi Bhawan, Jaipur, Rajasthan, India.

336   SY   ISSN 0080-0309
RECUEIL COMPLET DES BUDGETS DE LA SYRIE. a. $45. Office Arabe de Presse et de Documentation, P.O. Box 3550, 67 Place Chahbandar, Damascus, Syria.

336   FR   ISSN 0080-0945
REPERTOIRE COMPLEMENTAIRE ALPHABETIQUE DES VALEURS MOBILIERES FRANCAISES ET ETRANGERES NON COTEES EN FRANCE. a. 993,72 F. Editions Financieres Alphabetiques, 3 av. Trudaine, 75009 Paris, France.

336   FR   ISSN 0080-1127
REPERTOIRE GENERAL ALPHABETIQUE DES VALEURS COTEES EN FRANCE ET DES VALEURS NON COTEES. (Suppl. available: la Vie des Societes) 36th edt., 1953. a. 958,44 F. Editions Financieres Alphabetiques, 3 av. Trudaine, 75009 Paris, France.

336   LO   ISSN 0085-2740
REPORT BY THE AUDITOR GENERAL ON THE ACCOUNTS OF LESOTHO. 1966. a., latest issue 1972-73. $0.50. ‡ Auditor General, Box 502, Maseru, Lesotho.

336   TR
REPORT OF THE AUDITOR GENERAL ON THE ACCOUNTS OF TRINIDAD AND TOBAGO. a., latest issue 1983. $1.80. (Auditor General of Trinidad and Tobago) Government Printery, Sales Section, 48 St. Vincent St., Port-of-Spain, Trinidad, West Indies. stat.

336.1   US   ISSN 0091-8695
REPORT ON FEDERAL FUNDS RECEIVED IN IOWA. (Continues its Report on Federal Grants-in-Aid in Iowa) 1971. a. free. Office for Planning and Programming, 523 E. 12th St., Des Moines, IA 50319. TEL 515-281-3711. Ed. A. Thomas Wallace.

332.1   SU   ISSN 0558-7220
SAUDI ARABIAN MONETARY AGENCY. ANNUAL REPORT. 1961. a. Saudi Arabian Monetary Agency, Research and Statistics Department, Box 2992, Riyadh, Saudi Arabia. charts.

336.2   NE
SELECTED MONOGRAPHS ON TAXATION. (Text in English) 1974. irreg., no.5, 1980. price varies. International Bureau of Fiscal Documentation, Box 20237, 1000 HE Amsterdam, Netherlands. (Co-sponsor: Harvard Law School International Tax Program)

336   NE
SERIES ON INTERNATIONAL TAXATION. 1980. irreg. price varies. Kluwer Law and Taxation Publishers, Box 23, 7400 GA Deventer, Netherlands.

352.1   US   ISSN 0272-8362
SETTING MUNICIPAL PRIORITIES. (Subseries of: Landmark Studies) 1980. a. Allanheld, Osmun & Co. (Subsidiary of: Littlefield, Adams & Co.) 81 Adams Dr., Box 327, Totowa, NJ 07511. Eds. R.D. Horton, C. Brecher.

336   SE
SEYCHELLES. OFFICE OF THE PRESIDENT. BUDGET ADDRESS. (Text in Creole, English and French) a. President's Office, Victoria, Mahe, Seychelles.

336   SL
SIERRA LEONE. MINISTRY OF FINANCE. BUDGET SPEECH. a. Ministry of Finance, Freetown, Sierra Leone.

332   SI
SINGAPORE TRADE CLASSIFICATION & CUSTOMS DUTIES. (Text in English) 1967. irreg. S.$10($8.86) per no. Singapore Trade Development Board, 1 Maritime Square 03-01, World Trade Centre, Telok Blangah Road, Singapore 0409. circ. 6,000.

336   DK
SKATTEBVE; til studiebrug. 1983. a. Kr.106.15. Skattekartotek, Palaegade 4, 1261 Copenhagen K, Denmark.

BUSINESS AND ECONOMICS — PUBLIC FINANCE, TAXATION

336   DK   ISSN 0108-6022
SKATTELOVE; gaeldende indkomst- og formueskattelove. 1958. a. Kr.415. Foreningen af Statsautoriserede Revisorer, Kronprinsessegade 8, 1306 Copenhagen K, Denmark.

336   DK   ISSN 0106-8024
SKATTEN. 1946. a. Kr.38. Bibliotekscentralen, Telegrafvej 5, DK-2750 Ballerup, Denmark.

336   DK   ISSN 0107-3885
SKATTEN. ERHVERV. 1981. a. Kr.36. Aktuelle Boeger, c/o Danske Boghendleres Kommissionanstalt, Siljangade 6, 2300 Copenhagen S, Denmark. Ed. Jens Stubkjaer.
    Formerly: Afskrivning m.v.

336   SP   ISSN 0081-3451
SPAIN. INSTITUTO DE CREDITO OFICIAL. MEMORIA DEL CREDITO OFICIAL. (Supplement avail.) 1963. a. free. ‡ Ministerio de Economia y Hacienda, Instituto de Credito Oficial, Paseo del Prado, 4, 28014 Madrid, Spain. TEL 221 93 80. charts. stat. circ. 3,000.

336   SP
SPAIN. MINISTERIO DE ECONOMIA Y HACIENDA. DIRECCION GENERAL DE SEGUROS. BALANCES Y CUENTAS; seguros privados. (Former name of issuing body: Ministerio de Hacienda) 1981. a. free. Ministerio de Economia y Hacienda, Direccion General de Seguros, Madrid, Spain. charts.
    Formerly: Spain. Ministerio de Hacienda. Memoria (ISSN 0081-3443)

336   US   ISSN 0162-3494
STANDARD FEDERAL TAX REPORTS. a. revision plus w. update. $1075 includes Taxes on Parade Newsletter. Commerce Clearing House, Inc., 4025 W. Peterson Ave., Chicago, IL 60646. TEL 312-583-8500.

336.2   NZ   ISSN 0111-9370
STAPLES' GUIDE TO NEW ZEALAND INCOME TAX PRACTICE. 1936. a. NZ.$31.50. Sweet & Maxwell (N.Z.) Ltd., Private Bag, Auckland, New Zealand (Dist. by Carswell Co. Ltd., 2330 Midland Ave., Agincourt 742, Ont., Canada) adv. circ. 8,200.
    Formerly: Guide to New Zealand Income Tax Practice (ISSN 0072-8616)

336.2   US   ISSN 0081-4598
STATE TAX HANDBOOK. 1964. a. $15 pap. Commerce Clearing House, Inc., 4025 W. Peterson Ave., Chicago, IL 60646. TEL 312-583-8500.

336   DK   ISSN 0106-2905
STATENS OG KOMMUNERNES BUDGETTER. 1986. a. Budgetdepartementet, Direktoratet for Statens Indkoeb, Copenhagen, Denmark.

336   NE   ISSN 0168-373X
STATISTIEK DER RIJKSFINANCIEN/STATISTICS OF THE STATE FINANCES OF THE NETHERLANDS. (Text in Dutch and English) 1943-44. irreg. fl.26.60. Centraal Bureau voor de Statistiek, Prinses Beatrixlaan 428, Voorburg, Netherlands (Orders to: Staatsuitgeverij, Christoffel Plantijnstraat, The Hague, Netherlands)

336.2 331.8   GW
STEUER-GEWERKSCHAFTS-HANDBUCH. a. DM.65. (Bund Deutscher Steuerbeamten) Walhalla- und Praetoria-Verlag, Dolomitenstr. 1, Postfach 301, 8400 Regensburg 1, W. Germany (B.R.D.) (Co-sponsor: Deutsche Steuer-Gewerkschaft)

336.2   GW
STEUER-TELEX; Spezialdienst fuer den Steuerfachmann. 1974. a. DM.468. Verlag Dr. Peter Deubner GmbH, Fuerst-Pueckler-Str. 30, Postfach 41 02 68, 5000 Cologne 41, W. Germany (B.R.D.) bk. rev. index.
    Supersedes: Aktuelle Steuer-Informationen (ISSN 0002-385X)

336.2   SZ
STEUERBELASTUNG IN DER SCHWEIZ/CHARGE FISCALE EN SUISSE. (Text in French and German) a. Bundesamt fuer Statistik, Hallwylstrasse 15, 3003 Berne, Switzerland.

336.2   GW   ISSN 0081-5519
STEUERBERATER-JAHRBUCH; zugleich Bericht ueber den jaehrlich stattfindenden Fachkongress der Steuerberater der B R D. 1950. a. DM.90. (Fachinstitut der Steuerberater) Verlag Dr. Otto Schmidt KG, Unter den Ulmen 96-98, 5000 Cologne 51, W. Germany (B.R.D.)

STOCK VALUES AND DIVIDENDS FOR TAX PURPOSES. see BUSINESS AND ECONOMICS — Investments

336   US
STUDIES IN FEDERAL TAXATION. 1969. irreg., no.6, 1983. price varies. ‡ American Institute of Certified Public Accountants, 1211 Ave. of the Americas, New York, NY 10036-8775. TEL 212-575-6200.
    Formerly: Studies in Federal Taxation. Tax Study (ISSN 0081-7929)

336   US
STUDIES OF GOVERNMENT FINANCE: SECOND SERIES. 1975. irreg., no.22, 1985. price varies. Brookings Institution, 1775 Massachusetts Ave., N.W., Washington, DC 20036. TEL 202-797-6258.

336.2 338   NE   ISSN 0071-2191
STUDIES ON TAXATION AND ECONOMIC DEVELOPMENT. (Text in English) 1961. irreg., no.7, 1980. price varies. International Bureau of Fiscal Documentation, Box 20237, 1000 HE Amsterdam, Netherlands.

336   SW   ISSN 0347-7169
SWEDEN. FINANSDEPARTMENTET. REGERINGENS BUDGETFOERSLAG. a. Kr.25. (Ministry of Finance) Allmaenna Foerlaget, Box 5227, 102 45 Stockholm, Sweden.

336   SW
SWEDEN. MINISTRY OF FINANCE. REVISED FINANCE BILL. (Text in English) a. Ministry of Finance, Roedbodgatan 6, S-10333 Stockholm, Sweden. stats.

336   SW   ISSN 0082-0393
SWEDISH BUDGET. (Text in English) 1962/63. a. free. Ministry of Finance, Roedbodgatan 6, S-10333 Stockholm, Sweden.

336.2   FR
SYNDICAT GENERAL DES IMPOTS. GUIDE FONCIER. 1957. a. Euro-Publi Marcel Puget, 9 bd. des Italiens, 75002 Paris, France.
    Formerly: Syndicat General des Impots. Guide National de l'Enregistrement et des Domaines (ISSN 0082-1055)

336   FR   ISSN 0082-1209
SYSTEMES-DECISIONS. SECTION II. GESTION FINANCIERE ET COMPTABILITE. 1970. irreg. price varies. Presses Universitaires de France, 108 bd. Saint Germain, 75279 Paris Cedex 6, France (Dist. by: Service des Periodiques, 12 rue Jean de Beauvais, 75005 Paris, France) (reprint service avail. from KTO)

336   FR
TABLEAUX FISCAUX EUROPEENS. irreg. 1400 Fr. Cahiers Fiscaux Europeens, 51 Avenue Victoria, 06000 Nice, France. Ed. Pierre Fontaneau. (looseleaf format)

350.827   US   ISSN 0082-173X
TARIFF SCHEDULES OF THE UNITED STATES ANNOTATED. irreg. $45. U.S. International Trade Commission, E St. between 7th & 8th Sts., N.W., Washington, DC 20436 TEL 202-523-0161. (Order from: U.S. Govt. Printing Office, Washington, DC 20402)

336.1   AT
TASMANIA. DEPARTMENT OF THE TREASURY. COMMONWEALTH GRANTS TO TASMANIA. (At head of title, 1972- : Parliament of Tasmania) irreg. Tasmanian Government Printer, c/o A.B. Caudell, GPO Box 307-C, Hobart, Tas. 7011, Australia. stat.

336.946   AT
TASMANIA. DEPARTMENT OF THE TREASURY. CONSOLIDATED REVENUE FUND; summary of estimated expenditure (including expenditure reserved by law) and estimated revenue. Tasmanian Government Printer, c/o A.B. Caudell, Hobart, Tas. 7011, Australia. stat.

336   PN
TAX ADMINISTRATION REVIEW. (Text in English, Spanish) 1985. a. $20. Inter-American Center of Tax Administrators, Apdo. 2129, Panama 9A, Panama. (Co-sponsor: Institute of Fiscal Studies of Spain)

TAX BURDEN ON TOBACCO. see TOBACCO — Abstracting, Bibliographies, Statistics

336   UK
TAX CASE REPORT. irreg. £30. H.M.S.O., P.O. Box 276, London SW8 5DT, England. circ. 5,250.

336   US
TAX FOUNDATION. ANNUAL MEMORANDUM. a. $5. Tax Foundation, Inc., One Thomas Circle, N.W., Ste. 500, Washington, DC 20005. TEL 202-822-9050.

336.2   US   ISSN 0082-2159
TAX FOUNDATION. RESEARCH PUBLICATIONS. NEW SERIES. 1965. irreg., no.35, 1982. price varies. ‡ Tax Foundation, Inc., One Thomas Circle, N.W., Ste. 500, Washington, DC 20005. TEL 202-822-9050. Ed. Elsie Watters.

350   US
TAX FRAUD AND EVASION (SUPPLEMENT) supplements issued annually to update base volume. $115 for base volume. Warren, Gorham and Lamont, Inc., 210 South St., Boston, MA 02111. TEL 800-922-0066.

336.2   CN
TAX MEMO. 1954. a. price varies. Canadian Tax Foundation, Suite 1900, 130 Adelaide St. W., Toronto, Ont. M5H 3P5, Canada. TEL 416-863-9784. charts. stat.

350   US
TAX PRACTICE DESKBOOK (SUPPLEMENT) a. suppl. to update base vol. $88. Warren, Gorham and Lamont, Inc., 210 South St., Boston, MA 02111. TEL 800-922-0066.
    Formerly: Freeman and Freeman's Tax Practice Deskbook (Supplement)

336.2   UK   ISSN 0269-3720
TAX PRACTITIONER'S DIARY. a. Butterworth & Co. (Publishers) Ltd., 88 Kingsway, London WC2B 6AB, England.

336.2   CN   ISSN 0227-1265
TAX PRINCIPLES TO REMEMBER. French edition: Elements Fondamentaux de l'Impot (ISSN 0227-1273) (Editions in English and French) 1972. a. price varies. Canadian Institute of Chartered Accountants, 150 Bloor St. W., Toronto, Ont. M5S 2Y2, Canada. TEL 416-962-1242. circ. 13,000.

TAX SHELTERED INVESTMENTS HANDBOOK. see BUSINESS AND ECONOMICS — Investments

336   US
TAX YEAR IN REVIEW. 1978. a. $29.50. Research Institute of America, Inc., 90 Fifth Ave., New York, NY 10011. TEL 212-645-4800. Ed.Bd.

336.2   US   ISSN 0068-581X
TAXABLE SALES IN CALIFORNIA (SALES AND USE TAX) 1960. q. and a. free. State Board of Equalization, Box 1799, Sacramento, CA 95808. TEL 916-445-0840. Ed. Jeff Reynolds. circ. 5,000.
    Formerly: Trade Outlets and Taxable Retail Sales in California.

336   US
TAXATION DIGEST. JOURNAL. 1981. a. $39.50. Warren, Gorham & Lamont, Inc., 210 South St., Boston, MA 02111. TEL 800-922-0066. Ed. Brian E. Comerford.

350   US
TAXATION OF THE CLOSELY HELD CORPORATION (SUPPLEMENT) supplements issued 2/yr. to update base volume. $96 for base volume. Warren, Gorham and Lamont, Inc., 210 South St., Boston, MA 02111. TEL 800-922-0066.
    Formerly: Taxation of Closely Held Corporations (Supplement)

336.2   PK
TAXATION STRUCTURE OF PAKISTAN. (Text in English) 1974/75. a. Finance Division, Islamabad, Pakistan.

BUSINESS AND ECONOMICS — PUBLIC FINANCE, TAXATION

336.2   NZ   ISSN 0082-2175
TAXATION TABLES. 1936. a. NZ.$12. Sweet and Maxwell (N.Z.) Ltd., Box 37-549, 13 Cheshire St., Auckland 1, New Zealand (Dist. by: Carswell Co. Ltd., 2330 Midland Ave., Agincourt, Ont. M1S, 1P7, Canada) circ. 5,000.

336   TH
THAILAND'S BUDGET IN BRIEF. (Text in English and Thai) 1960 (Thai edt.); 1962 (Eng. edt.) irreg. free. Bureau of the Budget, Bangkok, Thailand. circ. 1,500.

TIMBER TAX JOURNAL. see *FORESTS AND FORESTRY*

336.2   UK
TOLLEY'S CAPITAL GAINS TAX (YEAR) a. £13.50. Tolley Publishing Co. Ltd., 17 Scarbrook Rd., Croydon, Surrey CR0 1SQ, England.

336.2   UK
TOLLEY'S CORPORATION TAX (YEAR) a. £12.25. Tolley Publishing Co. Ltd., 17 Scarbrook Rd., Croydon, Surrey CR0 1SQ, England. Ed. E.L. Harvey.

336.2   UK   ISSN 0305-8921
TOLLEY'S INCOME TAX (YEAR) a. £14.95. Tolley Publishing Co. Ltd., 17 Scarbrook Rd., Croydon, Surrey CR0 1SQ, England.

336.2   UK
TOLLEY'S INHERITANCE (YEAR) a. £14.50. Tolley Publishing Co. Ltd., 17 Scarbrook Rd., Croydon, Surrey CR0 1SQ, England.
Formerly: Tolley's Capital Transfer Tax.

336.2   UK   ISSN 0262-4583
TOLLEY'S TAX DATA (YEAR) 1981. a. £6.95. Tolley Publishing Co. Ltd., 17 Scarbrook Rd., Croydon, Surrey CR0 1SQ, England.

336.2   UK   ISSN 0307-6687
TOLLEY'S TAX TABLES (YEAR) a. £5.25. Tolley Publishing Co. Ltd., 17 Scarbrook Rd., Croydon, Surrey CR0 1SQ, England. stat.

336   341.57   UK
TOLLEY'S TAXATION IN THE REPUBLIC OF IRELAND (YEAR) 1973. a. £11.95. Tolley Publishing Co. Ltd., 17 Scarbrook Rd., Croydon, Surrey CR0 1SQ, England. Eds. Glyn Saunders, Eric Harvey. (back issues avail.)

336.2   US   ISSN 0564-4402
TULANE TAX INSTITUTE. 1951. a. $945. Claitors Publishing Division, 3165 S. Acadian at Interstate 10, Box 3333, Baton Rouge, LA 70821. TEL 504-344-0476. (also avail. in microfilm from WSH; back issues avail.) Indexed: Leg.Per. C.L.I.

336   TI   ISSN 0082-6820
TUNISIA. MINISTERE DU PLAN. BUDGET ECONOMIQUE. a. free. Ministere du Plan, Tunis, Tunisia.

336.2   US   ISSN 0083-0534
U S EXCISE TAX GUIDE. a. $12 paperback. Commerce Clearing House, Inc., 4025 W. Peterson Ave., Chicago, IL 60646. TEL 312-583-8500.

336.2   US   ISSN 0083-1700
U S MASTER TAX GUIDE. a. $15.50 paperback. Commerce Clearing House, Inc., 4025 W. Peterson Ave., Chicago, IL 60646. TEL 312-583-8500.

330.9   TS
UNITED ARAB EMIRATES. CENTRAL BANK. ANNUAL REPORT. (Text in Arabic and English) a. Central Bank, Box 854, Abu Dhabi Town, Abu Dhabi, United Arab Emirates.

336.3   US   ISSN 0091-3553
U.S. COMMUNITY SERVICES ADMINISTRATION. FEDERAL OUTLAYS IN SUMMARY. 1967. a. U.S. Community Services Administration, 1200 Nineteenth St., N.W., Washington, DC 20506 TEL 202-244-5840. (Orders to: National Technical Information Service, Springfield, VA 22151) stat. (also avail. in microfiche from NTI) Key Title: Federal Outlays in Summary.
Formerly: U.S. Office of Economic Opportunity. Federal Outlays in Summary.

336   US   ISSN 0083-1476
U.S. INTERNAL REVENUE SERVICE. ANNUAL REPORT. 1863. a. U.S. Internal Revenue Service., 1111 Constitution Ave., N.W., Washington, DC 20224 TEL 202-488-3100. (Orders to: Supt. Doc., Washington, DC 20402)

336.2   US   ISSN 0083-1484
U.S. INTERNAL REVENUE SERVICE. TAX GUIDE FOR SMALL BUSINESS. 1956. a. U.S. Internal Revenue Service, 1111 Constitution Ave., N.W., Washington, DC 20224 TEL 202-488-3100. (Orders to: Supt. Doc., Washington, DC 20402)

336   US   ISSN 0362-9163
U.S. OFFICE OF MANAGEMENT AND BUDGET. SPECIAL ANALYSIS: BUDGET OF THE UNITED STATES GOVERNMENT.* 1976/77. a. U.S. Office of Management and Budget, Executive Office Bldg., Washington, DC 20503. TEL 202-395-3000. (also avail. in microform from UMI) Key Title: Special Analysis: Budget of the United States Government.

336   US
U.S. TREASURY DEPARTMENT. BUREAU OF GOVERNMENT FINANCIAL OPERATIONS. TREASURY COMBINED STATEMENT OF RECEIPTS, EXPENDITURES AND BALANCES OF THE UNITED STATES. a. U.S. Department of the Treasury, Bureau of Government Financial Operations, Washington, DC 20226 TEL 202-566-2000. (Orders to: Supt. of Documents, Washington, DC 20402) (back issues avail.)
Formerly: U.S. Treasury Department. Combined Statement of Receipts, Expenditures and Balances of the United States Government.

336   UK
V A T GUIDE AND CASEBOOK. (Value Added Tax) irreg. Longman Professional, 21-27 Lambs Conduit St., London WC1N 3NJ, England. (looseleaf format)

336.2   634.9   US
WASHINGTON (STATE). DEPARTMENT OF REVENUE. FOREST TAX SECTION. FOREST TAX ANNUAL REPORT. a. Department of Revenue, General Administration Bldg. AX-02, Olympia, WA 98504. TEL 206-753-2871.
Former titles: Washington (State). Department of Revenue. Forest Tax Annual Report; Washington (State). Department of Revenue. Forest Tax Report (ISSN 0362-7462)

336.2   US
WASHINGTON (STATE). DEPARTMENT OF REVENUE. RESEARCH SECTION. COMPARATIVE STATE/LOCAL TAXES. 1967. a. Department of Revenue, General Administration Bldg. AX-02, Olympia, WA 98504. TEL 206-753-2087. stat. circ. controlled.
Formerly: Washington (State). Department of Revenue. Research and Information Division. Comparative State/Local Taxes.

336.2   US
WASHINGTON (STATE). DEPARTMENT OF REVENUE. RESEARCH SECTION. PROPERTY TAX LEVY AND COLLECTION STATISTICS. 1970. a. Department of Revenue, General Administration Bldg. AX-02, Olympia, WA 98504. TEL 206-753-2087. stat. circ. controlled. (tabloid format)
Formerly: Washington (State). Department of Revenue. Research and Information Division. Property Tax Levy and Collection Statistics.

336   US   ISSN 0091-6102
WEST VIRGINIA RESEARCH LEAGUE. STATISTICAL HANDBOOK; a digest of selected data on state and local government in West Virginia. 1970. a. $6. West Virginia Research League Inc., 1107 Charleston National Plaza, Charleston, WV 25301. TEL 304-346-9451. Ed. Sarah F. Roach. charts. stat. circ. controlled.

336   US
WEST VIRGINIA TAX CALENDAR. 1950. a. $25. West Virginia Chamber of Commerce, Box 2789, Charleston, WV 25330. TEL 304-342-1115.

336.2   PR   ISSN 0083-9132
WHAT YOU SHOULD KNOW ABOUT TAXES IN PUERTO RICO. (Not Published for 1977 and 1978) 1956. a. free. Department of the Treasury, Office of Economic Affairs, Box S-4515, San Juan, PR 00905. circ. 1,500.

336.2   UK   ISSN 0260-3926
WHILLANS'S TAX TABLES. 1948. a. ‡ Butterworth & Co. (Publishers) Ltd., 88 Kingsway, London WC2B 6AB, England. Ed. Sheila Parrington. circ. 24,000.
Formerly: Whillan's Tax Tables and Tax Reckoner (ISSN 0308-7948)

336.3   US   ISSN 0363-4795
WORLD MILITARY AND SOCIAL EXPENDITURES. 1974. a. $4. World Priorities, Inc., Box 25140, Washington, DC 20007. TEL 202-965-1661. Ed. Ruth Leger Sivard. circ. 25,000.

336   US
WORLD TAX SERIES. irreg. $440. Commerce Clearing House, Inc., 4025 W. Peterson Ave., Chicago, IL 60646. TEL 312-583-8500. (back issues avail.)

336.2   US   ISSN 0094-9019
WYOMING. DEPARTMENT OF REVENUE AND TAXATION. ANNUAL REPORT. 1973. a. free. Department of Revenue and Taxation, Herschler Bldg., Cheyenne, WY 82002-0110. TEL 307-777-7961. stat. circ. 300. Key Title: Annual Report of the Department of Revenue and Taxation of the State of Wyoming.

336   SZ
ZAHLUNGSBILANZ DER SCHWEIZ. French edition: Balance Suisse des Paiements. (Supplement to Switzerland. Eidgenoessisches Volkswirtschaftsdepartement. Volkswirtschaft und Schweizerische Nationalbank. Monatsbericht) a. Eidgenoessisches Volkswirtschaftsdepartement, Kommission fuer Konjunkturfragen, Belpstr. 53, 3003 Berne, Switzerland.
Formerly: Ertragsbilanz der Schweiz.

336   ZA
ZAMBIA. CENTRAL STATISTICAL OFFICE. NATIONAL ACCOUNTS. 1965. a. K.5. Central Statistical Office, P.O. Box 31908, Lusaka, Zambia.

336   ZA
ZAMBIA. DEPARTMENT OF CUSTOMS AND EXCISE. ANNUAL REPORT OF THE CONTROLLER OF CUSTOMS AND EXCISE. (Text in English) a. Government Printer, Box 30136, Lusaka, Zambia.

336.2   ZA   ISSN 0084-4675
ZAMBIA. DEPARTMENT OF TAXES. ANNUAL REPORT OF THE COMMISSIONER OF TAXES. 1964/65. a. 10 n. Government Printer, P.O. Box 136, Lusaka, Zambia.

336   ZA   ISSN 0084-4683
ZAMBIA. DEPARTMENT OF THE ADMINISTRATOR-GENERAL AND OFFICIAL RECEIVER. REPORT. 1964. a. 10 n. Government Printer, P.O. Box 136, Lusaka, Zambia.

336   ZA   ISSN 0084-4497
ZAMBIA. OFFICE OF THE AUDITOR-GENERAL. REPORT OF THE AUDITOR-GENERAL. 1963. a. 30 n. Government Printer, P.O. Box 136, Lusaka, Zambia.

336.2   JA
ZEIMU TOKEI KARA MITA HOJIN KIGYO NO JITTAI. Short title: Hojin Kigyo No Jittai. (Text in Japanese) 1963. a. Ministry of Finance, Seifu Kankobutsu Service Centre, 1-2 Kasumigaseki, Chiyoda-ku, Tokyo 100, Japan.

ZIMBABWE. CENTRAL STATISTICAL OFFICE. INCOME TAX STATISTICS; analysis of assessments and loss statements. see *BUSINESS AND ECONOMICS — Abstracting, Bibliographies, Statistics*

336   RH
ZIMBABWE. ESTIMATES OF EXPENDITURE. a., latest 1983/84. Rhod.$2.10. Government Printer, Box 8062, Causeway, Zimbabwe.

336   RH
ZIMBABWE. MINISTRY OF FINANCE. FINANCIAL STATEMENT. 1940. a. Rhod.$0.50 per no. Ministry of Finance, Private Bag 7705, Causeway, Zimbabwe (Subscr. to: Government Printer, Box 8062, Causeway, Zimbabwe) circ. 1, 200.
Formerly: Rhodesia. Ministry of Finance. Budget Statement.

336   GW
ZOLLKALENDER. a. DM.65. (Bund der Deutschen Zollbeamten) Walhalla- und Praetoria-Verlag Georg Zwichenpflug, Dolomitenstr. 1, Postfach 301, 8400 Regensburg 1, W. Germany (B.R.D.) Ed. Gunter Engel.

336.2   US
1040 PREPARATION. a. $24.50. Commerce Clearing House, Inc., 4025 W. Peterson Ave., Chicago, IL 60646. TEL 312-583-8500. illus.
     Formerly: Practical Guide to Individual Income Tax Return Preparation (ISSN 0098-1575)

BUSINESS AND ECONOMICS — Small Business

338.6   BE   ISSN 0067-5393
BELGIUM. CONSEIL SUPERIEUR DES CLASSES MOYENNES. RAPPORT ANNUEL DU SECRETAIRE GENERAL. Dutch edition: Belgium. Hoge Raad voor de Middenstand. Jaarverslag van de Secretaris Generaal. (Editions in French and Dutch) 1951. a. free. Conseil Superieur des Classes Moyennes, 24 rue de la Charite, 1040 Brussels, Belgium.

338 346.066   US
BUSINESS FRANCHISE GUIDE. base vol. plus m. reports. $430. Commerce Clearing House, Inc., 4025 W. Peterson Ave., Chicago, IL 60646. TEL 312-583-8500.

338.9   CK
CAJA DE CREDITO AGRARIO, INDUSTRIAL Y MINERO. FINANCIAMENTO DE LA PEQUENA Y MEDIANA INDUSTRIA. 1973. a. Caja de Credito Agrario, Industrial y Minero, Bogota, Colombia. charts. stat.

338   CN
CANADA. DEPARTMENT OF INDUSTRY, TRADE AND COMMERCE. SMALL BUSINESS LOANS ACT. ANNUAL REPORT. (Text in English and French) 1961. a. Department of Industry, Trade and Commerce, Small Business Loans Act, Ottawa, Ont., Canada. TEL 613-995-5771. Ed. W.S.D. Hendry. circ. 7,800.
     Formerly: Canada. Department of Finance. Small Business Loans Act. Annual Report (ISSN 0527-687X)

338   DK   ISSN 0108-5255
DISCOUNTBUTIKKER (YEAR) 1982. a. Kr.355. Per Press, Frederik d. VI's Alle 5, 2000 Frederiksberg, Denmark.
     Formerly: Lavprisbutikker.

338   CN
ECONOMIC REVIEW AND OUTLOOK. 1945. a. free. Ministry of Industry and Small Business Development, 1405 Douglas St., Victoria, B.C. V8W 3C1, Canada. TEL 604-387-5095. Ed. F. Blassetti. circ. 6,500.
     Former titles: British Columbia Economic Activity; British Columbia Economic Outlook Survey (ISSN 0319-0412)

338.7   NE   ISSN 0070-8836
ECONOMISCH INSTITUUT VOOR HET MIDDEN- EN KLEINBEDRIJF. YEAR REPORT. 1961. a. free. Research Institute for Small & Medium Sized Businesses, Postbus 7001, 2701 AA Zoetermeer, Netherlands.

338   US
FRANCHISING IN THE ECONOMY. (Formerly issued by U.S. Bureau of Industrial Economics) a. $4.75 per copy. U.S. Department of Commerce, I T A Service Industries Division, Washington, DC 20230 TEL 202-566-8611. (Orders to: Supt. of Documents, Washington DC 20402)

ILLUSTRATED BUYERS GUIDE TO EXHIBITS; directory of portable and modular displays. see BUSINESS AND ECONOMICS — Marketing And Purchasing

338   II
K V I C ANNUAL REPORT. (Editions in English and Hindi) 1957. a. Khadi and Village Industries Commission, Directorate of Publicity, Gramodaya, Irla Rd., Vile Parle (West), Bombay 400056, India. charts. illus. stat.
     Formerly: India. Khadi and Village Industries Commission. Report (ISSN 0073-6198)

338   GW   ISSN 0177-7491
MAERKTE IM SAARLAND. 1947. a. DM.6. Statistisches Amt des Saarland, Hardenbergstr. 3, Postfach 409, 6600 Saarbruecken, W. Germany (B.R.D.) circ. 600.

338   DK   ISSN 0107-8305
MARKEDS-BOG. 1982. a. Kr.30. Dixit, c/o Torben Kahr, Postboks 29, 8653 Them, Denmark. illus.
     Formerly: Markedskalender.

338 380.1   US
NATIONAL DIRECTORY OF MINORITY-OWNED BUSINESS FIRMS. 1985. a. $195. Business Research Services, 2 E. 22nd St., Ste. 308, Lombard, IL 60148. TEL 312-495-8787. Ed. Elisabeth Eubank. adv. (also avail. in magnetic tape)

338 658   US
OPERATING RESULTS OF INDEPENDENT SUPERMARKETS. a. $50. Food Marketing Institute, 1750 K St., N.W., Washington, DC 20006. TEL 202-429-8298.

338   US
PRESIDENTIAL ADVISORY COMMITTEE ON SMALL AND MINORITY BUSINESS OWNERSHIP. ANNUAL REPORT. a. Presidential Advisory Committee on Small Minority Business Ownership, 1441 L St., N.W., Rm. 602, Washington, DC 20416.

338   UK
SMALL BUSINESS BIBLIOGRAPHY. 1980. a. £25. London Business School, Sussex Place, Regent's Park, London NW1 4SA, England. Ed. Helen Edwards. circ. 600.

330.9   US
SMALL BUSINESS REPORTER. 1958. irreg. (4-6/yr.) $2 per no. Bank of America, Small Business Reporter Department, Box 37000, San Francisco, CA 94137. TEL 415-622-3456. Ed. Judith Sherard.

338   TZ
SMALL INDUSTRIES DEVELOPMENT ORGANIZATION. ANNUAL REPORT. (Editions in English and Swahili) 1975. a. Small Industries Development Organization (SIDO), Box 2476, Dar es Salaam, Tanzania. Ed.Bd. circ. 1,000.

338   II
SMALL INDUSTRIES GUIDE.* irreg., no.2, 1969. Rs.02 per issue. Ministry of Industrial Development, Development Commissioner-Small Scale Industries, Internal Trade and Company Affairs, New Delhi, India. charts. stat.

338   NR
SMALL-SCALE INDUSTRIES: SOUTH EASTERN AND BENUE PLATEAU STATES OF NIGERIA. a. University of Nigeria, Department of Economics, Nsukka, Nigeria. Eds. E.C. Iwuji, A.E. Okorafor.

338   US
SMALL TIME OPERATOR; how to start your own small business, keep your books, pay your taxes and stay out of trouble. 1976. a. $10.95. Bell Springs Publishing, Box 640, Laytonville, CA 95454. TEL 707-984-6746. Ed. Bernard Kamoroff. bk. rev. circ. 40,000.

658   US   ISSN 0081-4415
STARTING AND MANAGING SERIES. irreg. price varies. U.S. Small Business Administration, 1441 L St., N.W., Washington, DC 20416 TEL 202-653-6914. (Orders to: Supt. of Documents, Washington, DC 20402)

338   US
STATES AND SMALL BUSINESS: PROGRAMS AND ACTIVITIES. a. U.S. Small Business Administration, Office of the Chief Counsel for Advocacy, 1441 L St., N.W., Washington, DC 20516. TEL 202-634-6098.

U.S. INTERNAL REVENUE SERVICE. TAX GUIDE FOR SMALL BUSINESS. see BUSINESS AND ECONOMICS — Public Finance, Taxation

658   US   ISSN 0083-3266
U.S. SMALL BUSINESS ADMINISTRATION. ADMINISTRATIVE MANAGEMENT COURSE PROGRAM. TOPICS. irreg. U.S. Small Business Administration, 1441 L St., N.W., Washington, DC 20416 TEL 202-653-6914. (Orders to: Supt. of Documents, Washington, DC 20402)

338   US   ISSN 0083-3274
U.S. SMALL BUSINESS ADMINISTRATION. ANNUAL REPORT. (Supersedes its Report to the President and Congress) 1953. a. free. U.S. Small Business Administration, 1441 L St., N.W., Washington, DC 20416. TEL 202-653-6914.

338 332.6   UK   ISSN 0265-6248
VENTURE CAPITAL REPORT. 1978. a. £180($270) Venture Capital Report Ltd., 20 Baldwin St., Bristol BS1 1SE, England. Ed. Lucius Cary. adv. bk. rev. charts. illus. index. cum.index. circ. 1,000. (back issues avail.)

BUSINESS AND ECONOMICS — Trade And Industrial Directories

380.1   HK   ISSN 0532-9175
A.A.'S FAR EAST BUSINESSMAN'S DIRECTORY. Title varies: Far East Businessman's Directory. (Text in English) a. Artists Associates, G.P.O. Box 1623, Hong Kong, Hong Kong. illus.

380   GW
A B C DER DEUTSCHEN WIRTSCHAFT; Quellenwerk fuer Einkauf-Verkauf. a. prices on request. A B C-Verlagshaus Darmstadt, Berliner Allee 8, 6100 Darmstadt, W. Germany (B.R.D.) circ. 23,000.

380   YU
A B C PRIVREDE JUGOSLAVIJE. 1973. a. (Chamber of Economy Croatia) Privredni Vjesnik, Rooseveltov Trg 2, Box 631, Zagreb, Yugoslavia. TEL 011- 692-089. Ed. Ante Gavranovic. adv. circ. 4,500.

380   US
A P D U MEMBERSHIP DIRECTORY. 1976. a. $200. Association of Public Data Users, 87 Prospect Ave., Princeton, NJ 08520. TEL 609-452-6025. Ed. Jacqueline McGee. cum.index 1976-1985. circ. 230.

338 387   UK   ISSN 0267-7377
ABERDEEN PORT HANDBOOK. 1985. a. £10. Charter Publications, Bank Chambers, Downham Market, Norfolk PE38 9BU, England. Ed. James Moriarty. circ. 6,000.

338   UK
ADHESIVES EURO-GUIDE. 1981. irreg. £30. I A L Consultants Ltd., 14 Buckingham Palace Rd., London SW1W 0QP, England.

380.1   UK   ISSN 0568-062X
AEROSOL REVIEW. 1965. a. £17. Morgan-Grampian (Publishers) Ltd., 30 Calderwood St., London SE18 6QH, England. Ed. Neil Eisberg. adv. circ. 1,500.

338   US
AFFILIATES & OFFICES OF JAPANESE FIRMS IN THE U.S.A. DIRECTORY.* a. $70. PressAid Center, 2975 Wilshire Blvd., No. 603, Los Angeles, CA 90020.

338 677   II
ALL INDIA TEXTILES DIRECTORY. (Text in English) a. Rs.250($50) Business Press, Maker Tower "E", 18th Floor, Cuffe Parade, Bombay 400 005, India. adv. circ. 2,500.

380   CN
ALMANACH MODERNE. (Text in French) 1956. a. Can.$4.50. Quebecmag Inc., 3510 St. Laurent, Suite 300, Montreal, Que. H2X 2V2, Canada. Ed. Denis Levesque. adv. bk. rev. circ. 125,000.

051   US
ALTERNATE CELEBRATIONS CATALOGUE. First and second editions issued as: Alternate Christmas Catalogue. 1972. 2-3/yr. $8.95 per no. Pilgrim Press, 132 W. 31st St., New York, NY 10001 TEL 212-594-8555. (Orders to: Alternatives, Box 1707, Forest Park, GA 30051) Ed. Milo Shannon-Thornberry. circ. 45,000.

BUSINESS AND ECONOMICS — TRADE AND INDUSTRIAL DIRECTORIES

338   AG
AMERICAN BUSINESS IN ARGENTINA. 1974. a. $50. American Chamber of Commerce in Argentina, Av. Roque Saenz Pena 567, 1352 Buenos Aires, Argentina. adv. illus.
    Formerly: Directory of American Business in Argentina.

382   GR   ISSN 0065-8537
AMERICAN-HELLENIC CHAMBER OF COMMERCE. BUSINESS DIRECTORY. SPECIAL ISSUE. (Text in English) 1960. biennial. $40. American-Hellenic Chamber of Commerce, 17 Valaoritou St., 106 71 Athens, Greece. TEL 36 18 385-36 36 407. Ed. Symeon G. Tsomokos. adv. circ. 5,000.
    Supplement to: American-Hellenic Chamber of Commerce. Business Directory (ISSN 0065-8529)

AMERICAN MARKETING ASSOCIATION. INTERNATIONAL MEMBERSHIP DIRECTORY AND MARKETING SERVICES GUIDE. see *BUSINESS AND ECONOMICS — Marketing And Purchasing*

AMERICAN SHOEMAKING DIRECTORY. see *SHOES AND BOOTS*

AMERICAN SOCIETY FOR INFORMATION SCIENCE. HANDBOOK AND DIRECTORY. see *LIBRARY AND INFORMATION SCIENCES*

382   US   ISSN 0740-4018
AMERICA'S CORPORATE FAMILIES AND INTERNATIONAL AFFILIATES. a. $305. Dun's Marketing Services (Subsidiary of: Dun & Bradstreet, Inc.) 49 Old Bloomfield Rd., Mountain Lakes, NJ 07046. TEL 201-455-0900.

380   FR
ANNUAIRE DES CENTRALES ET GROUPEMENTS D'ACHATS; le livre d'or de la distribution francaise. 1969. biennial. 470 F. Societe d'Edition et de Promotion Agro-Alimentaire, Industrielles et Commerciales, 42 rue du Louvre, B.P. 551, 75027 Paris Cedex 01, France. bk. rev. bibl. circ. 5,000. (tabloid format)

382   FR
ANNUAIRE DES EXPORTATEURS FRANCAIS COMMERCANT AVEC L'U.R.S.S. 1976. a. 270 F. to non-members. Chambre de Commerce Franco-Sovietique, 22 av. F.D. Roosevelt, 75008 Paris, France. adv. circ. 3,500.

380   FR
ANNUAIRE DES HYPERMARCHES. 1973. biennial. 370 F. Societe d'Edition et de Promotion Agro-Alimentaires, Industrielles et Commerciales, 42 rue du Louvre, B.P. 551, 75027 Paris Cedex 01, France. adv. circ. 5,000.
    Formerly: Hyperguide des Hypermarches.

670   FR
ANNUAIRE DESECHALIERS. (Text in French; table of contents and subtitles in English and German) 1975. a. 140 F. Periodiques Parisiens, 150 Champs Elysees, 75008 Paris, France.

380   AT
ANNUAIRE FRANCAIS D'AUSTRALIE. (Text in French) 1957. biennial. Aus.$20. Courrier Australien, 396 Kent St., Sydney, N.S.W. 2000, Australia. Ed. J.P. Sourdin. circ. 6,000. (back issues avail)

380   US
ANNUAL FRANCHISE HANDBOOK DIRECTORY. a. Information Press, Inc., 728 Center St., Box 550, Lewiston, NY 14092. TEL 716-754-4669.

380.1 666   IT   ISSN 0392-5978
ANNUARIO DEI FORNITORI. a. Faenza Editrice S.p.A., Via Pier de Crescenzi n. 44, 48018 Faenza, Italy. adv.
    Ceramics

670 666   IT
ANNUARIO DELLE CERAMICHE ITALIANE PER L'EDILIZIA. a. Faenza Editrice S.p.A., Via Pier de Crescenzi no.44, 48018 Faenza, Italy. adv.
    Ceramics

ANTWERP HANDBOOK 1984. see *TRANSPORTATION — Ships And Shipping*

338   BE
ANTWERP PORT ANNUAL. 1905. a. 900 Fr. Lloyd Anversois S.A., Eiermarkt 23, B-2000 Antwerp, Belgium. Ed. B. Verbruggen. adv. illus. circ. 5,000.
    Formerly: Annuaire Maritime.

380.1   SP
ANUARIO DE EMPRESAS EXPORTADORAS. 1974. a. Organizacion Sindical Espanola, Servicio de Accion Exterior Empresarial, Casa Sindical, Paseo del Prado 18, Madrid, Spain.

338   CK
ANUARIO EMPRESARIAL DE COLOMBIA; registro nacional de comerciantes. 1972. a. Col.2500($50) (Confederacion Colombiana de Camaras de Comercio) Editorial Prensa Moderna, Carrera 13-No. 27-47, Of.502, Bogota, Colombia. Ed. Gaston E. Abello. circ. 15,000. (magnetic tape; microfiche)

677   NZ
APPAREL BUYERS GUIDE YEAR BOOK. 1980. a. NZ.$12. Apparel Publishing Ltd., Box 56-071, Dominion Rd., Auckland 3, New Zealand. Ed. Val Blomfield. adv. circ. 4,000.

382   FR   ISSN 0066-5398
APPEL SERVICE; REPERTOIRE D'ADRESSES UTILES POUR LE COMMERCE ET L'INDUSTRIE.* 1968. irreg. price varies. Editions Publiplast, 55 rue du Faubourg-Montmartre, 75009 Paris, France.

380   US
APPLIANCE MANUFACTURER BUYERS GUIDE. 1953. a. $45. Corcoran Communications, Inc., 6200 S.O.M. Center Rd., No. C14, Solon, OH 44139. TEL 216-349-3060. Ed. Norman C. Remich. adv. circ. 32,829.

380   UK
ARAB BUYERS' GUIDE TO BRITISH INDUSTRY. 1951. a. British Industrial Publicity Overseas Ltd., Walter House, Bedford Street, London, WC2, England.

380   UK
ARAB TRADE DIRECTORY. (Text in Arabic, English and French) biennial. $120. New Product Newsletter Co. Ltd., 1A Chesterfield St., London W1, England. adv.

380   UK
ARABIAN YEARBOOK. 1978. a. $135. New Product Newsletter Co. Ltd., 1A Chesterfield St., London W1, England (Dist. by: Croner Publications, Inc., 211-05 Jamaica Ave., NY 11428)

338 720   II
ARCHITECTURAL & BUILDING DIRECTORY OF INDIA. (Text in English) 1980. a. Rs.200($45) Business Press, Maker Tower "E", 18th Floor, Cuffe Parade, Bombay 400 005, India. adv. bk. rev. illus. circ. 7,500.

382   US
ARIZONA DIRECTORY OF EXPORTS. 1977. every 18 mos. Department of Commerce, 1700 W. Washington Ave., Phoenix, AZ 85007. TEL 602-255-5371. circ. 5,000.
    Formerly: Arizona U S A International Trade Directory.

ASIAN AMERICAN TRADE DIRECTORY. see *BUSINESS AND ECONOMICS — Chamber Of Commerce Publications*

380.1   ES
ASOCIACION SALVADORENA DE INDUSTRIALES DIRECTORIO DE ASOCIADOS. (Text in Spanish) a. Asociacion Salvadorena de Industriales, Apartado Postal No. (06) 48, Calles Roma y Liverpool, Colonia Roma, San Salvador, El Salvador.

382   UK   ISSN 0260-2474
ASPIS; the classified Greek commercial directory. (Text in English and Greek) 1980. a. Aspis Publications, 89 Tottenham Ln., London N8 9BE, England. illus.

380.1 663.6   II
ASSAM DIRECTORY & TEA AREAS HANDBOOK. 1928. a. Rs.120. Assam Review Publishing Co., 29 Waterloo St., Calcutta 700 069, India. Ed. J.N. Banerjee. adv. bk. rev. circ. 7,500.
    Formerly: Assam Directory of Tea Areas.

ASSOCIATED BRITISH PORTS HANDBOOK. see *TRANSPORTATION — Ships And Shipping*

AUSTRALASIAN SOLAR INDEX AND BUYERS GUIDE. see *ENERGY*

380.1 645   AT
AUSTRALIAN CONTRACT FURNISHING CYCLOPAEDIA. 1971. a. Aus.$29. Furnishing Media Pty Ltd., 162 Williams Rd., Prahran, Vic. 3181, Australia. circ. 3,500.

AUSTRALIAN IMPORTS. see *BUSINESS AND ECONOMICS — International Commerce*

338   AT   ISSN 0311-2667
AUSTRALIAN KEY BUSINESS DIRECTORY. Short title: K B D. 1973. a. Aus.$375. Dun and Bradstreet (Australia) Pty. Ltd., 24 Albert St., South Melbourne, Vic. 3205, Australia. Ed. David M. Newbold. adv. circ. 5,000.

380 340   AT   ISSN 0155-297X
AUSTRALIAN LEGAL DIRECTORY. 1977. a. Aus.$47. (Law Council of Australia) Australian Document Exchange Pty. Ltd., 130 Phillip Street, 1st floor, Sydney, N.S.W. 2000, Australia. Ed. Hamish Grieve. circ. 2,000.

AUSTRALIAN MARKET GUIDE. see *BUSINESS AND ECONOMICS — Investments*

381.45   US   ISSN 0736-0452
AUTO AFTERMARKET SUPPLIERS. 1973. biennial. $169. Chain Store Guide (Subsidiary of: Lebhar-Friedman, Inc.) 425 Park Ave., New York, NY 10022.
    Former titles: Directory of Auto Supply Chains (ISSN 0730-2533) Supersedes in part: Directory: Home Centers and Hardware Chains, Auto Supply Chains (ISSN 0094-8667); Directory-Hardware and Home Improvement Center Chains, Auto Supply Chains (ISSN 0092-1483); Directory-Auto Supplies and Hardware Chains.

380   US
AUTOMOTIVE DISMANTLERS AND RECYCLERS BUYERS GUIDE/MEMBERSHIP ROSTER. a. $150 to non-members; free to members. Automotive Dismantlers and Recyclers Association, 1133 15th St. N.W., Ste. 1000, Washington, DC 20005. TEL 202-293-2372. Ed. David Peiffer. adv. circ. 2,000.

AUTORIDADES E EXECUTIVOS. see *COMMUNICATIONS*

380   UK
B.A.I.E. MEMBERSHIP DIRECTORY. 1978. a. £109. British Association of Industrial Editors, 3 Locks Yard., High St, Sevenoaks, Kent TN13 1LT, England. adv. circ. 1,000.
    Former titles: Who's Who in Industrial Editing (ISSN 0068-1296) & British Association of Industrial Editors. B A I E Directory of Members.

380   BA   ISSN 0408-215X
BAHRAIN TRADE DIRECTORY. (Text in Arabic and English) a. Box 524, Manama, Bahrain. Ed. A.E. Ashir.

664.752   US
BAKING DIRECTORY/BUYERS GUIDE. a. $50. Sosland Publishing Co., 9000 W. 67 St., Merriam, KS 66202. TEL 913-236-7300. Ed. Laurie Gorton.

380   II
BANGLADESH DIRECTORY AND YEAR BOOK. (Text in English) 1976. a. Rs.75($15) Associated Book Promoters, 9/2A Ekbalpur Ln., Calcutta 700023, India.

382   BB
BARBADOS. EXPORT DIRECTORY. 1982. irreg. Export Promotion Corporation, Pelican Industrial Park, St. Michael, Barbados, W.I. TEL 809-427-5752/55.

381   PK   ISSN 0067-4230
BARQUE'S PAKISTAN TRADE DIRECTORY AND WHO'S WHO. (Text in English) 1949-50. a. $65.40. Barque & Company, Barque Chambers, Barque Sq., 87 Shahrah e-Liaquat Ali, Box 201, Lahore, Pakistan. Ed. A.M. Barque. adv. circ. 15,000.

BUSINESS AND ECONOMICS — TRADE AND INDUSTRIAL DIRECTORIES

650 382　　　　GW　ISSN 0067-6063
BERLINER HANDELSREGISTER VERZEICHNIS. a. DM.76. Addressbuch-Gesellschaft Berlin mbH, Friedrichstr. 210, 1000 Berlin 61, W. Germany (B.R.D.) adv. index.

338　　　　　　US
BIOTECHNOLOGY DIRECTORY. 1984. a. $140. Stockton Press, 15 E. 26th St., New York, NY 10010 (Distr. in U.K. by: Macmillan Publishers Ltd., 4 Little Essex St., London WC2R 3LF, England) Ed. Jim Coombs. adv.
   Formerly: International Biotechnology Directory (ISSN 0265-3877)

382 382　　　　US
BIRMINGHAM INTERNATIONAL TRADE DIRECTORY. 1982. quadrennial. $15 per no. Birmingham Area Chamber of Commerce, Research and Trade Division, 600 Commerce Center, 2027 First Ave. N., Birmingham, AL 35202. TEL 205-323-5461.

BOAT & MOTOR DEALER. see *SPORTS AND GAMES — Boats And Boating*

796.9 387　　　　US
BOATING INDUSTRY MARINE BUYERS GUIDE. 1929. a. $25 per copy. (Boating Industry Magazine) Whitney Communications Co., 850 Third Ave., New York, NY 10022. TEL 212-715-2600. Ed. Olga E. Badillo-Sciortino. adv. circ. 29,784. (also avail. in microfiche)

338 387　　UK　ISSN 0267-2243
BOSTON SEA AND AIR PORT HANDBOOK. 1985. a. £5. Charter Publications, Bank Chambers, Downham Market, Norfolk PE38 9BU, England. Ed. James Moriarty. circ. 6,000.

BOTTIN AUTO-CYCLE-MOTO. see *TRANSPORTATION — Automobiles*

338　　　　　　FR
BOTTIN PROFESSIONS. 1895. a. (6 vols.) $265. Societe Didot Bottin, 28 rue du Docteur Finlay, 75738 Paris Cedex 15, France. index.

338　　　　SA　ISSN 0520-7010
BRABY'S BLOEMFONTEIN DIRECTORY. (Text in English) a. R.13. A.C. Braby (Pty) Ltd., P.O. Box 1426, Pinetown 3600, South Africa. Ed. A. Stagg.

338　　　　　　SA
BRABY'S BUSINESS DIRECTORY OF JOHANNESBURG. a. R.25. A.C. Braby (Pty) Ltd., P.O. Box 1426, Pinetown 3600, South Africa. adv.

338　　　　SA　ISSN 0378-9179
BRABY'S CAPE PROVINCE DIRECTORY. (Text in English) a. R.32. A.C. Braby (Pty) Ltd., P.O. Box 1426, Pinetown 3600, South Africa. Ed. A. Stagg.

380　　　　　　SA
BRABY'S COMMERCIAL DIRECTORY OF SOUTH, EAST & CENTRAL AFRICA. a. R.69. A.C. Braby (Pty) Ltd., P.O. Box 1426, 10 Caversham Road, Pinetown 3600, South Africa. adv.

380　　　　　　SA
BRABY'S COMMERCIAL DIRECTORY OF SOUTHERN AFRICA. a. R.80. A.C. Braby (Pty) Ltd., P.O. Box 1426, 10 Caversham Road, Pinetown 3600, South Africa. Ed. A. Stagg. adv.
   Formerly: Commercial Directory of South Africa.

338　　　　SA　ISSN 0378-9217
BRABY'S EAST LONDON DIRECTORY. (Text in English) a. R.13. A.C. Braby (Pty) Ltd., P.O. Box 1426, Pinetown 3600, South Africa. Ed. A. Stagg.

338　　　　　　SA
BRABY'S NATAL DIRECTORY. (Text in English) a. R.57. A.C. Braby (Pty) Ltd., P.O. Box 1426, Pinetown 3600, South Africa. Ed. A. Stagg. adv.

338　　　　SA　ISSN 0378-9292
BRABY'S ORANGE FREE STATE DIRECTORY. (Text in English) a. R.20. A.C. Braby (Pty) Ltd., P.O. Box 1426, Pinetown 3600, South Africa. Ed. A. Stagg.

338　　　　SA　ISSN 0520-7037
BRABY'S PIETERMARITZBURG DIRECTORY. (Text in English) a. R.17. A.C. Braby (Pty) Ltd., P.O. Box 1426, Pinetown 3600, South Africa. Ed. A. Stagg.

338　　　　SA　ISSN 0068-0621
BRABY'S TRANSVAAL DIRECTORY. a. R.58. A.C. Braby (Pty) Ltd., P.O. Box 1426, Pinetown 3600, South Africa. Ed. A. Stagg.

380.1　　　　　　US
BRAZIL - U.S. BUSINESS LISTING; companies in the United States and their subsidiaries and affiliates in Brazil. 1980. triennial. Brazilian-American Chamber of Commerce, Inc., 22 W. 48th St., Ste.404, New York, NY 10036-1886. TEL 212-575-9030.

BREWERS DIGEST ANNUAL BUYERS GUIDE AND BREWERY DIRECTORY. see *BEVERAGES*

380　　　　　　UK
BRITAIN'S PRIVATELY OWNED COMPANIES: THE SECOND 2000. a. £60. Jordan & Sons Ltd., Jordan House, 47 Brunswick Pl., London N1 6EE, England.
   Supersedes in part: Britain's Top Private Companies. The First and Second Thousand.

380　　　　　　UK
BRITAIN'S PRIVATELY OWNED COMPANIES: THE TOP 2000. a. £60. Jordan & Sons Ltd., Jordan House, 47 Brunswick Pl., London N1 6EE, England. adv. bk. rev. charts. stat. circ. 2,000.
   Supersedes in part: Britiain's Top Private Companies. The First and Second Thousand; Former titles: Britain's Top 2000 Private Companies; Britain's Top 1000 Private Companies (ISSN 0263-3671)

380.1　　　　UK　ISSN 0263-242X
BRITAIN'S TOP 1000 FOREIGN-OWNED COMPANIES. 1979. irreg. £25. Jordan & Sons Ltd., Jordan House, 47 Brunswick Pl., London N1 6EE, England.

380.1 621.3　　UK　ISSN 0263-2446
BRITAIN'S TOP 500 ELECTRONIC COMPANIES. 1979. biennial. £95. Jordan & Sons Ltd., Jordan House, 47 Brunswick Pl., London N1 6EE, England.

BRITISH ALTERNATIVE THEATRE DIRECTORY. see *THEATER*

380.1 540　　UK　ISSN 0263-2438
BRITISH CHEMICAL INDUSTRY. 1978. biennial. £125. Jordan & Sons Ltd., Jordan House, 47 Brunswick Pl., London N1 6EE, England.

BRITISH COLUMBIA PORTS HANDBOOK 1984. see *TRANSPORTATION — Ships And Shipping*

670　　　　　　UK
BRITISH CONSTRUCTION EQUIPMENT AND CRANES. DIRECTORY. (Text in Arabic, English, French, and Spanish) a. Federation of Manufacturers of Construction Equipment and Cranes, Carolyn House, 22-26 Dingwall Rd., Croydon CR9 2PL, England. adv. circ. 10,000.

380.1 647.94　　UK　ISSN 0263-368X
BRITISH HOTEL INDUSTRY. 1980. biennial. £125. Jordan & Sons Ltd., Jordan House, 47 Brunswick Pl., London N1 6EE, England.

380.1 332.64　　UK　ISSN 0263-3655
BRITISH SECURITY COMPANIES. 1978. biennial. £125. Jordan & Sons Ltd., Jordan House, 47 Brunswick Pl., London N1 6EE, England.

BRITISH THEATRE DIRECTORY. see *THEATER*

338　　　　　　UK
BUILDING SOCIETIES WHO'S WHO. 1949. biennial. £18. Franey and Co. Ltd., 7 Swallow Place, London W1R 7AA, England.

382　　　　FI　ISSN 0355-0346
BUSINESS CONTACTS IN FINLAND. 1974. irreg. free. Yritystieto Oy, Box 148, 00181 Helsinki 18, Finland. Ed. Borje Thilman. adv. circ. 15,000.

338.4　　　　　　HK
BUSINESS DIRECTORY OF HONG KONG. (Text in English) 1977. a. $65. Current Publications Ltd, 1501 Enterprise Bldg., 228 Queen's Road Central, Box 9848, Hong Kong, Hong Kong. Ed. Charles Lau. adv.

338　　　　　　IO
BUSINESS GUIDE BOOK TO JAKARTA. (Text in English) 1969. a. $7.50. Gabungan Importir Nasional Seluruh Indonesia - National Importers Association of Indonesia, Wisma Nusantara Bldg., Jalan Majapahit No. 1, Jakarta, Indonesia (Foreign correspondence to: EKON Advertising Agency, Box 2744, Jakartta, Indonesia) Ed.Bd. adv. illus. circ. 10, 000.
   Continues: Djakarta Business Guide Book.

380　　　　　　US
BUSINESS ORGANIZATIONS, AGENCIES, AND PUBLICATIONS DIRECTORY. 1980. irreg., 3rd edt., 1986. $290. Gale Research Company, Book Tower, Detroit, MI 48226. TEL 313-961-2242. Eds. Kay Gill, Donald P. Boyden.
   Formerly: Business Organizations and Agencies Directory.

658.8　　　　AT　ISSN 0068-4503
BUSINESS WHO'S WHO OF AUSTRALIA. 1964. a. Aus.$225. R.G. Riddell Pty. Ltd., 100 Alexander St., Crowns Nest, N.S.W. 2065, Australia. Ed. D. Williams. adv. circ. 5,500.
   ●Also available online. Vendors: AUSINET.
   Formerly: Business Who's Who of Australia and Australian Purchasing Yearbook.

338　　　　　　PH
BUSINESSDAY'S CORPORATE PROFILES. 1981. a. P.300($70) Businessday Corporation, 113 West Ave., Quezon City 3010, Philippines. circ. 8,400.

380.1　　　　　　CH
BUSINESSMAN'S DIRECTORY, THE REPUBLIC OF CHINA. (Text in English and Chinese) 1971. a. $25. Taiwan Enterprise Press, Ltd., P.O. Box 73-4, Taipei, Republic of China. Ed. Henry K.C. Lee. adv. bk. rev. circ. 30,000.

382　　　　II　ISSN 0304-968X
BUY FROM INDIA; world trade directory & handbook. (Text in English) 1974. biennial. Rs.150($43) per no. Buy from India, 10 Mangal Baugh, Pushpa Park, Malad, Bombay 400064, India. Ed. Shri L.S. Varma. adv. illus.

380　　　　　　US
BUYER'S GUIDE TO THE NEW YORK MARKET. 1930. a. free. Earnshaw Publications, Inc., 393 Seventh Ave., New York, NY 10001. Ed. Thomas W. Hudson, Sr. adv. circ. 20,000.

C A A P DIRECTORY: WHOLESALERS OF ORGANIC PRODUCE & PRODUCTS. (California Agrarian Action Project) see *AGRICULTURE*

C P I PRODUCT PROFILES. see *CHEMISTRY*

C P I PURCHASING CHEMICALS DIRECTORY. see *ENGINEERING — Chemical Engineering*

338　　　　　　SA
C.T. DIRECTORY OF SOUTH AFRICA. (Cape Town) (Text in English) a. R.75. Intratex (PTY) Ltd., 10 Caversham Road, Pinetown 3600, South Africa. Ed. A. Stagg.

670 338　　US　ISSN 0068-5739
CALIFORNIA MANUFACTURERS REGISTER. 1948. a. $125. (California Manufacturers Association) Times Mirror Press, 1115 S. Boyle Ave., Box 23951, Los Angeles, CA 90023. TEL 213-265-6700. Ed. Phyllis Freiburger. adv. tr.lit. circ. 6,800.

770　　　　　　JA
CAMERART PHOTO TRADE DIRECTORY. 1958. a. $32. CamerArt, Inc., C.P.O. Box 620, Tokyo, Japan. illus.

CAMP DIRECTORS PURCHASING GUIDE. see *SPORTS AND GAMES — Outdoor Life*

796.51　　　　UK　ISSN 0068-6948
CAMPING CARAVANNING AND SPORTS EQUIPMENT TRADES DIRECTORY. 1966. a. £40. Camping and Sports Equipment Ltd., 4 Spring St., London W2 3RA, England. Ed. P. Moloney. adv. circ. 3,500.
   Formerly: Camping and Sports Equipment Trades Directory.

BUSINESS AND ECONOMICS — TRADE AND INDUSTRIAL DIRECTORIES

330 658 CN
CANADIAN AUTOMOTIVE AFTERMARKET DIRECTORY/MARKETING GUIDE. a. Can.$25. Wadham Publications, Ltd., 109 Vanderhoof Ave., Toronto, Ont. M4G 2J2, Canada. TEL 416-425-9021. Ed. Bob Blans. adv. circ. 4,500.

670 CN ISSN 0068-8452
CANADIAN CHEMICAL, PHARMACEUTICAL AND PRODUCT DIRECTORY. 1948. a. Can.$25($35) Lloyd Publications of Canada, Box 262, West Hill, Ont. M1E 4R5, Canada. TEL 416-686-2131. Ed. J. Lloyd. adv. index. circ. 7,000.
Formerly: Canadian Chemical Directory.

670 664 CN ISSN 0068-8754
CANADIAN FOOD AND PACKAGING DIRECTORY. 1924. a. Can.$25($35) Lloyd Publications of Canada, Box 262, West Hill, Ont. M1E 4R5, Canada. TEL 416-686-2131. Ed. J. Lloyd. adv. index. circ. 8,500.

380.1 685 CN ISSN 0068-8762
CANADIAN FOOTWEAR & LEATHER DIRECTORY. 1924. a. Can.$18($28) Lloyd Publications of Canada, Box 262, West Hill, Ont. M1E 4R5, Canada. TEL 416-686-2131. Ed. J. Lloyd. adv. index. circ. 5,500.

380.1 749 CN ISSN 0068-8789
CANADIAN FURNITURE & FURNISHINGS DIRECTORY. 1924. a. Can.$18($28) Lloyd Publications of Canada, Box 262, West Hill, Ont. M1E 4R5, Canada. TEL 416-686-2131. Ed. J. Lloyd. adv. index. circ. 5,700.

380 621.3 683.8 CN ISSN 0456-3867
CANADIAN HARDWARE, ELECTRICAL & BUILDING SUPPLY DIRECTORY. 1949. a. Can.$25($35) Lloyd Publications of Canada, Box 262, West Hill, Ont. M1E 4R5, Canada. TEL 416-686-2131. Ed. J. Lloyd. adv. index. circ. 8,500.

647.9 CN ISSN 0381-5765
CANADIAN HOTEL, RESTAURANT, INSTITUTION & STORE EQUIPMENT DIRECTORY. 1925. a. Can.$25($35) Lloyd Publications of Canada, Box 262, West Hill, Ont. M1E 4R5, Canada. TEL 416-686-2131. Ed. J. Lloyd. adv. index. circ. 8,300.

380.1 658.8 CN ISSN 0068-9041
CANADIAN JEWELLERY & GIFTWARE DIRECTORY. 1924. a. Can.$25($35) Lloyd Publications of Canada, Box 262, West Hill, Ont. M1E 4R5, Canada. TEL 416-686-2131. Ed. J. Lloyd. adv. index. circ. 7,000.

338 CN ISSN 0315-0879
CANADIAN KEY BUSINESS DIRECTORY. 1974. a. $380. Dun & Bradstreet Canada Ltd. Lee., 84 Carlton St., Toronto, Ont. M5B 1L6, Canada. Ed. Elizabeth Bryant.

780 CN ISSN 0381-5730
CANADIAN MUSIC DIRECTORY. 1926. a. Can.$18($28) Lloyd Publications of Canada, Box 262, West Hill, Ont. M1E 4R5, Canada. TEL 416-686-2131. Ed. J. Lloyd. adv. index. circ. 5,300.

670 790.1 CN ISSN 0316-7771
CANADIAN SPORTING GOODS & PLAYTHINGS. DIRECTORY. 1949. a. Can.$25($35) Lloyd Publications of Canada, Box 262, West Hill, Ont. M1E 4R5, Canada. TEL 416-686-2131. Ed. J. Lloyd. adv. index. circ. 8,000.

677 CN ISSN 0068-9858
CANADIAN TEXTILE DIRECTORY. 1924. a. Can.$25($35) Lloyd Publications of Canada, Box 262, West Hill, Ont. M1E 4R5, Canada. TEL 416-686-2131. Ed. J. Lloyd. adv. index. circ. 7,500.

380 CN ISSN 0068-9904
CANADIAN TRADE INDEX. (Text in English; glossary in French and Spanish) 1900. a. Can.$107. Canadian Manufacturers Association, One Yonge St., Ste. 1400, Toronto, Ont. M5E 1J9, Canada. TEL 416-363-7261. Ed. Nancy L. McDonald. adv. index. circ. 13,000.

380.1 CN ISSN 0068-9955
CANADIAN VARIETY MERCHANDISE DIRECTORY. 1924. a. Can.$25($35) Lloyd Publications of Canada, Box 262, West Hill, Ont. M1E 4R5, Canada. TEL 416-686-2131. Ed. J. Lloyd. adv. index. circ. 6,000.
Formerly: Canadian Toy, Notion and Stationery Directory.

CANARY ISLANDS SHIPPING HANDBOOK 1983/4. see TRANSPORTATION — Ships And Shipping

664.15 380.1 US
CANDY BUYERS DIRECTORY. 1932. a. $25. Manufacturing Confectioner Publishing Co., Directory Division, 175 Rock Rd., Glen Rock, NJ 07452. TEL 201-652-2655. Ed. Allen R. Allured. adv. circ. 11,000. (tabloid format)
Including: Directory of Candy Brokers.

338 SA
CAPE TIMES PENINSULA DIRECTORY. (Text in English) a. R.75. Intratex (PTY) Ltd., 10 Caversham Road, Pinetown 3600, South Africa. Ed. A. Stagg.

CAPTAIN LILLIE'S COAST GUIDE AND RADIOTELEPHONE DIRECTORY. see TRANSPORTATION — Ships And Shipping

338 US ISSN 0275-2883
CARIBBEAN/AMERICAN DIRECTORY. 1982. a. $100. 1377 K St., N.W., Washington, DC 20005. Ed. Herbert L. Cooper. adv. circ. 5,000.

338 XK
CARIBBEAN DIRECTORY. 1979. a. Caribbean Publishing Co. Ltd., P.O. Box 104, Castries, St. Lucia. adv. circ. 20,000.

380 MX
CATALOGO PRODUCTOS Y SERVICIOS DEL ESTADO DE MEXICO. 1973. a. Asociacion de Industriales del Estado de Mexico, Diagonal Jose T. Cuellar 99 A, Mexico 8, D.F., Mexico.

338 CJ
CAYMAN ISLANDS HANDBOOK AND BUSINESSMAN'S GUIDE. 1973. a. $25. Northwester Company Ltd., Box 243, George Town, Grand Cayman, B.W.I. Ed. Desmond Seales. adv. illus.

338 670 MW
CHAMBER OF COMMERCE AND INDUSTRY OF MALAWI. INDUSTRIAL AND TRADE DIRECTORY. 1974. biennial, 6th 1982. K.3.50. Chamber of Commerce and Industry of Malawi, P.O. Box 258, Blantyre, Malawi. adv. circ. 10,000.
Formerly: Industrial Directory and Brand Names Index of Malawi.

380 PK
CHAMBER'S TRADE DIRECTORY. (Text in English) irreg. Rs.150. Chamber of Commerce and Industry, Aiwan-e-Tijarat, Box 4158, Nicol Rd., Karachi 2, Pakistan.

660 US
CHEM SOURCES - U.S.A. 1958. a. $200 initial subscription. Directories Publishing Company, Inc., Box 1372, Ormond Beach, FL 32075 TEL 904-673-1241. (Subscr. address: Box 1824, Clemson, SC 29633 (803-646-7840)) Ed. Christa L. Gandenberger.
●Also available online.

670 CN ISSN 0069-2891
CHEMICAL BUYERS GUIDE. 1917. a. Can.$50. Southam Communications Ltd., 1450 Don Mills Rd., Don Mills, Ont. M3B 2X7, Ont. M3B 2X7, Canada. TEL 416-445-6641. Ed. Arthur Kendrick. adv. circ. 11,082.

338 387 UK ISSN 0268-649X
CHERBOURG PORT HANDBOOK. (Text in English, French) 1985. a. £10. Charter Publications, Bank Chambers, Downham Market, Norfolk PE38 9BU, England. Ed. John Ison. circ. 6,000.

658 338 US ISSN 0069-3251
CHICAGO, COOK COUNTY AND ILLINOIS INDUSTRIAL DIRECTORY. 1953. a. $95. Registry Publications, Ltd., 425 Huehl Rd., Bldg. 15B, North Brook, IL 60062. TEL 312-498-4010. Ed. M.L. Mounts. adv. circ. 6,000.

670 US ISSN 0748-8548
CHICAGO GEOGRAPHIC DIRECTORY. Variant title: Chicago Geographic Edition. biennial. $65. Manufacturers' News, Inc., 4 E. Huron St., Chicago, IL 60611. TEL 312-337-1084. adv. illus.

380 KO
CHONGUK KIOPCHE CHONGNAM/ DIRECTORY OF KOREAN BUSINESS. (Text in Korean) 1970. irreg. 28000($35) Taehan Sanggong Hoeuiso, Korea Chamber of Commerce & Industry, Seoul, S. Korea. Ed. Soo Chang Chung. adv. circ. 2,500.

380 AT
CHRISTIAN REFERDEX. 1979. a. free. Christian Referdex Pty. Ltd., 640 Ann St., Fortitude Valley, Australia. Ed. K.D. Robinson. adv. circ. 35,000.
Formerly: Interdom Christian Referdex (ISSN 0158-0140)

CITY HANDBOOK; guide to the shipping services of the City of London. see TRANSPORTATION — Ships And Shipping

380 UK ISSN 0266-9064
CITY OF BIRMINGHAM DIRECTORY OF INDUSTRY & COMMERCE. 1985. a. £30. Guardian Communications Ltd., Albany House, Hurst St., Birmingham B5 4BD, England.

338 UK ISSN 0142-5072
CITY OF LONDON DIRECTORY & LIVERY COMPANIES GUIDE. 1863. a. £13.50. City Press Ltd., Fairfax House, Colchester, Essex C01 1RJ, England. Ed. Patricia M. Hetherington. adv. circ. 1,500.

670 US ISSN 0069-4525
CLASSIFIED DIRECTORY OF WISCONSIN MANUFACTURERS. 1921. a. $80. (Wisconsin Manufacturers & Commerce) W M C Service Corporation, 501 E. Washington Ave., Box 352, Madison, WI 53701-0352. Ed. Elaine Rohrs. adv. index. circ. 3,500.

382 HK
CLASSIFIED INTERNATIONAL BUSINESS DIRECTORY FOR CHINA. 1981. biennial. HK.$180. China Council for the Promotion of International Trade, G.P.O. Box 3724, Hong Kong, Hong Kong. Ed. Richard L.C. Wong. adv. bk. rev. circ. 40,000.

338 IT
COLLANA DI STUDI E DOCUMENTAZIONE. 1962. irreg., na 47, 1981. price varies. Servizio Italiano Pubblicazioni Internazionali s.r.l., Viale L. Pasteur n. 6, 00144 Rome, Italy.

380.1 ET
COMMERCIAL BANK OF ETHIOPIA. TRADE DIRECTORY. irreg. free. Commercial Bank of Ethiopia, P.O. Box 255, Addis Ababa, Ethiopia.

380.1 US ISSN 0270-2460
COMMERCIAL NEWS U S A. NEW PRODUCTS ANNUAL DIRECTORY; international marketing information for the foreign service. a. U.S. Department of Commerce, Fourteenth St. between Constitution and E. St., N.W., Washington, DC 20230. TEL 202-377-2000.

380 US
COMPLETE COMMODITY FUTURES DIRECTORY. 1930. irreg. $75. Christopher Resources, Inc., 34 N. White St., Box E, Frankfort, IL 60423. TEL 312-655-4923. Ed. Michael C. Marasco. (looseleaf format; back issues avail.)

COMPOSITE CATALOG OF OIL FIELD EQUIPMENT & SERVICES. see PETROLEUM AND GAS

COMPUTER SECURITY BUYERS GUIDE. see COMPUTERS — Computer Security

670 US
CONNECTICUT AND RHODE ISLAND DIRECTORY OF MANUFACTURERS.* 1979. a. $62.50. Manufacturers' News, Inc., 4 E. Huron St., Chicago, IL 60611. TEL 312-337-1084. adv.

BUSINESS AND ECONOMICS — TRADE AND INDUSTRIAL DIRECTORIES

380 625.7 690 US
CONSTRUCTION INDUSTRIES OF MASSACHUSETTS DIRECTORY; a directory and catalog of highway and heavy construction in New England. 1948. a. $15. Construction Industries of Massachusetts, Inc., 1500 Providence Highway, Ste. 14, Box 667, MA 02062.
Former titles: Construction Directory; New England Road Builders Association. N E R B A Annual Directory (ISSN 0077-8281)

CONSULTANTS AND CONSULTING ORGANIZATIONS DIRECTORY; a reference guide to concerns and individuals engaged in consultation for business, industry and government. see *BUSINESS AND ECONOMICS — Management*

CONTAINER CONTACTS. see *TRANSPORTATION*

380 UK ISSN 0309-2143
CONVERTER DIRECTORY;* suppliers and services to the U.K. converting industry. a. Faversham House Group Ltd., 111 St. James's Rd., Croydon, Surrey CR9 2TH, England. (reprint service avail. from UMI)

COOPERATIVE TRADE DIRECTORY FOR SOUTHEAST ASIA. see *BUSINESS AND ECONOMICS — Cooperatives*

338.4 660 US ISSN 0574-1181
CORPORATE DIAGRAMS AND ADMINISTRATIVE PERSONNEL OF THE CHEMICAL INDUSTRY. 1958. irreg. $150 for 14th edt. Chemical Economic Services, Box 468, Palmer Sq., Princeton, NJ 08540. TEL 609-921-8468. Ed. Kenneth R. Kern. index. (back issues avail.)

380.1 332 US ISSN 0740-2546
CORPORATE FINANCE BLUEBOOK. 1983. a. Zehring Publishing, 40 Central Park S., New York, NY 10019. TEL 212-759-1972. Ed. Karen Zehring.

380 US ISSN 0589-7920
CORPORATE REPORT FACT BOOK; a directory of publicly held companies in the Ninth Federal Reserve District. 1968. a. plus supplement. $64. Dorn Communications Inc., 7831 E. Bush Lake Rd., Minneapolis, MN 55435. TEL 612-835-6855. Ed. Jean Goble.
Incorporating: Corporate Report Who's Who in Upper Midwest Business.

380 US
CORPORATE REPORT FACT BOOK WISCONSIN; a directory of publicly held companies in the state of Wisconsin. 1984. a. $34. Dorn Communications, Inc., 7831 E. Bush Lake Rd., Minneapolis, MN 55435. TEL 612-835-6855.

CORPORATE 500: THE DIRECTORY OF CORPORATE PHILANTHROPY. see *SOCIAL SERVICES AND WELFARE*

332 UK
CRAWFORD'S DIRECTORY OF CITY CONNECTIONS. 1973. a. £95($185) (Economist Intelligence Unit) Economist Publications Ltd., 40 Duke St., London W1A 1DW, England. Ed. Janet Dignan. adv. circ. 3,000.

380 NA
CURACAO TRADE AND INDUSTRY DIRECTORY.* (Text in Dutch, English or Spanish.) a. (Curacao Trade and Industry Association) Citroen-Daal, Pietermaai 21, P.O.B. 49, Willemstad, Curacao, Netherlands Antilles. illus.

380 942 UK
CURLEY'S STREETS & TRADES DIRECTORIES OF WEMBLEY, MIDDLESEX & SELBY, YORKSHIRE. 1948. biennial. £4.80. Curley's Directories Ltd., 49 Woodfield Ave., Wembley HA0 3NP, England.

338 UK
CUSTOM CHEMICAL SYNTHESIS SERVICES IN FRANCE. 1984. irreg. £95. I A L Consultants Ltd., 14 Buckingham Palace Rd., London SW1W 0QP, England.

338 UK
CUSTOM CHEMICAL SYNTHESIS SERVICES IN THE U.K. 1981. irreg. £95. I A L Consultants Ltd., 14 Buckingham Palace Rd., London SW1W 0QP, England.

338 UK
CUSTOM CHEMICAL SYNTHESIS SERVICES IN WEST GERMANY. 1983. irreg. £95. I A L Consultants Ltd., 14 Buckingham Palace Rd., London SW1W 0QP, England.

381 CY ISSN 0070-2331
CYPRUS CHAMBER OF COMMERCE AND INDUSTRY DIRECTORY;* guide to commerce, industry, tourism and agriculture. (Text in English) 1967. irreg., 2nd edt., 1970. $25. D. Couvas & Sons Ltd., Box 35, Limasol, Cyprus (Dist. by: International Publications Service, 114 E. 32nd St., New York, NY 10016)

338 US
DALTON'S NEW YORK METROPOLITAN DIRECTORY: BUSINESS/INDUSTRY. 1984. a. $95. Dalton Directory, 410 Lancaster Ave., Haverford, PA 19041. TEL 215-649-2680. Ed. Patrick Dalton.

338 US
DALTON'S PHILADELPHIA METROPOLITAN DIRECTORY: BUSINESS/INDUSTRY. 1964. a. $79.50. Dalton Directories, 410 Lancaster Ave., Haverford, PA 19041. TEL 215-649-2680.

338 387 UK ISSN 0268-6503
DARWIN PORT HANDBOOK. 1985. a. £10. Charter Publications, Bank Chambers, Downham Market, Norfolk PE38 9BU, England. Ed. Gerry Cansdale. circ. 6,000.

DEFENSE ELECTRONICS. MARKETING DIRECTORY AND BUYERS GUIDE. see *ELECTRICITY AND ELECTRICAL ENGINEERING*

380 US ISSN 0272-8117
DELAWARE DIRECTORY OF COMMERCE AND INDUSTRY. 1950. biennial. $53. (Delaware State Chamber of Commerce) Manufacturers News, Inc., 4 E. Huron St., Chicago, IL 60611. TEL 312-337-1084. Ed. Steven J. Simcock. adv.
Formerly: Directory of Manufacturers, State of Delaware.

380 UK
DERBY AREA TRADES UNION COUNCIL DIRECTORY. 1970. a. £1. Derby Area Trades Union Council, Cedar House, Leicester Rd., Glenfield, Leicester LE3 3HF, England.

659.1 745.2 US ISSN 0195-4326
DESIGN DIRECTORY; a listing of firm and consultants in industrial, graphic, interior and environmental design. 1979. a. $41. Wefler & Associates, Inc., Box 1591, Evanston, IL 60204. TEL 312-454-1940. Ed. W. Daniel Wefler. (back issues avail.)

380 GW ISSN 0170-284X
DEUTSCHE BRANCHEN-FERNSPRECHBUCH; firms classified according to trades. (Index in English and French) 1926. a. DM.210. Deutscher Adressbuch-Verlag, Holzhofallee 38, Postfach 11 03 20, D-6100 Darmstadt, W. Germany (B.R.D.) adv. circ. 6,000.

338 380 GW ISSN 0418-8381
DAS DEUTSCHE FIRMEN-ALPHABET; Industrie, Handel, Verkehr, Organisationen. a. DM.101. Deutscher Adressbuch-Verlag, Holzhofallee 38, Postfach 110320, 6100 Darmstadt, W. Germany (B.R.D.) adv. circ. 7,000.

338 GW ISSN 0343-589X
DEUTSCHES BUNDES-ADRESSBUCH: INDUSTRIE, GROSS- UND AUSSENHANDEL, DIENSTLEISTUNGEN, ORGANISATIONEN. a. DM.105. Deutscher Adresbuch-Verlag, Holzhofallee 38, Postfach 110320, 6100 Darmstadt, W. Germany (B.R.D.) adv. illus. circ. 5,000.
Continues: Deutsches Bundes-Adressbuch der Firmen aus Industrie, Handel und Verkehr.

338 JA ISSN 0910-1780
DIAMOND'S JAPAN BUSINESS DIRECTORY. variant Title: Japan Business Directory. (Text in English) 1970. a. 60.000($350) Diamond Lead Co., Ltd., 4-2 Kasumigaseki 1-chome, Chiyoda-ku, Tokyo 100, Japan. Ed. Tetsuji Yamada. adv. circ. 30,000. (back issues avail.)

670 338 FR
DICTIONNAIRE DE L'INDUSTRIE FRANCAISE. a. Union Francaise d'Annuaires Professionels, 13 av. Vladimir Komarov, B.P. 36, 78192 Trappes Cedex, France.

338 US ISSN 0094-209X
DIRECTORIES OF HAWAII. irreg. free. Department of Planning and Economic Development, Information Office, Box 2359, Honolulu, HI 96804. TEL 808-548-4025. bibl.

380 PN
DIRECTORIO COMERCIAL E INDUSTRIAL DE PANAMA/COMERCIAL AND INDUSTRIAL DIRECTORY OF PANAMA. 1958. a. Camara de Comercio, Industria y Agricultura de Panama, P.O. Box 74, Panama City 1, Panama. adv. circ. 2,000.

380.1 LB
DIRECTORY AND WHO'S WHO IN LIBERIA. 1971. irreg. A & A Enterprises Inc., Box 103, Monrovia, Liberia. adv. illus.

DIRECTORY OF AMERICAN FIRMS OPERATING IN FOREIGN COUNTRIES. see *BUSINESS AND ECONOMICS — International Commerce*

670 US
DIRECTORY OF ARKANSAS MANUFACTURERS. 1955. a. $30. Arkansas Industrial Development Foundation, Box 1784, Little Rock, AR 72203. TEL 501-371-1121. Ed. Patricia F. Brown. adv. illus. circ. 3,000.
Formerly: Directory of Manufacturers in Arkansas (ISSN 0361-2996)

DIRECTORY OF ARTS CENTRES. see *ART*

DIRECTORY OF CARDAMOM PLANTERS. see *AGRICULTURE — Crop Production And Soil*

382 US
DIRECTORY OF CENTRAL AMERICA ORGANIZATIONS. 1984. a. $15. Central America Resource Center, Box 2327, Austin, TX 78768. TEL 512-476-9841. adv. circ. 1,000. (back issues avail.)

670 917.5 US
DIRECTORY OF CENTRAL ATLANTIC STATES. 1912? biennial, latest 1987/1988. $73. Manufacturers' News, Inc., 4 E. Huron St., Chicago, IL 60611. TEL 312-337-1084.

670 US ISSN 0070-5241
DIRECTORY OF CENTRAL ATLANTIC STATES MANUFACTURERS. MARYLAND, DELAWARE, VIRGINIA, WEST VIRGINIA, NORTH CAROLINA, SOUTH CAROLINA. Variant title: Central Atlantic States Manufacturers Directory. 1950. a. $69. George D. Hall Co. Inc., 50 Congress St., Boston, MA 02109.

647.95 US ISSN 0411-7085
DIRECTORY OF CHAIN RESTAURANT OPERATORS. a. $199. Chain Store Guide (Subsidiary of: Lebhar-Friedman, Inc.) 425 Park Ave., New York, NY 10022. TEL 212-371-9400. Ed. James Tierney.

380 HK ISSN 0259-1146
DIRECTORY OF CHINESE EXTERNAL ECONOMIC ORGANIZATIONS & INDUSTRIAL/COMMERCIAL ENTERPRISES. 1982. irreg. HK.$450($78) (China United Advertising Corporation, CC) Economic Information & Agency, 342 Hennessy Rd., 10th Fl., Hong Kong, Hong Kong.

338 US ISSN 0084-9898
DIRECTORY OF COLORADO MANUFACTURERS. 1948. a. $50. University of Colorado, Graduate School of Business Administration, Boulder, CO 80309. TEL 303-492-8227. Ed. Gerald L. Allen. circ. 2,500.

BUSINESS AND ECONOMICS — TRADE AND INDUSTRIAL DIRECTORIES

380 SY
DIRECTORY OF COMMERCE & INDUSTRY. 1979. a. $60. Arab Advertising Organization, 28 Mountanabbi St., P.O. Box 2842, Damascus, Syria. Ed. Haitham Bashir. adv. circ. 20,000.

670 915.5 US
DIRECTORY OF CONNECTICUT MANUFACTURERS. every 18 months. $42. Manufacturers' News, Inc., 4 E. Huron St., Chicago, IL 61611.

DIRECTORY OF CONSULTING ENGINEERING SERVICES IN NORTH CAROLINA. see *ENGINEERING*

670 747 US
DIRECTORY OF CONTRACT WALLCOVERINGS AND SPECIFICATIONS. 1984. a. $15.95. Tapis Publishing Co., Inc., 570 7th Ave., Ste. 500, New York, NY 10018. Ed. Janet Verdeguer. adv. circ. 9,000.

338 US ISSN 0419-2508
DIRECTORY OF DEPARTMENT STORES; includes mail order firms. a. $189. Chain Store Guide (Subsidiary of: Lebhar-Friedman, Inc.) 425 Park Ave., New York, NY 10022. TEL 212-371-9400. (also avail. in magnetic tape)

DIRECTORY OF DEVELOPMENT AND TRAINING INSTITUTES IN AFRICA. see *BUSINESS AND ECONOMICS — International Development And Assistance*

658.8 US
DIRECTORY OF DISCOUNT STORES; including catalog showrooms, consumer electronics retailers and distributors. 1961. a. $189. Chain Store Guide (Subsidiary of: Lebhar-Friedman, Inc.) 425 Park Ave., New York, NY 10022.
Former titles: Directory of Discount Department Stores (ISSN 0736-931X); Directory of Discount Centers (ISSN 0070-5446)

338 US ISSN 0730-2703
DIRECTORY OF DRUG STORE AND H B A CHAINS; includes drug wholesalers. 1945. a. $189. Chain Store Guide (Subsidiary of: Lebhar-Friedman, Inc.) 425 Park Ave., New York, NY 10022. TEL 212-371-9400. stat. (also avail. in magnetic tape)
Formerly: Directory of Drug Store Chains.

DIRECTORY OF ELECTRIC LIGHT AND POWER COMPANIES. see *ELECTRICITY AND ELECTRICAL ENGINEERING*

380.1 US
DIRECTORY OF ELECTRICAL WHOLESALE DISTRIBUTORS. 1930. irreg. $595. McGraw-Hill Publications, 1221 Ave. of the Americas, New York, NY 10020.

DIRECTORY OF ENGINEERING/ ARCHITECTURAL MINORITY AND WOMEN OWNED FIRMS. see *ENGINEERING*

338 UK
DIRECTORY OF ENGINEERING CAPACITY. 1958. a. $14. Coventry Chamber of Commerce & Industry, 123 St. Nicholas St., Coventry CV1 4FD, England. Ed. June Morden. adv. circ. 5,000.

DIRECTORY OF ENGINEERING SOCIETIES AND RELATED ORGANIZATIONS. see *ENGINEERING*

DIRECTORY OF ENGINEERS AND LAND SURVEYORS REGISTERED IN SOUTH CAROLINA. see *ENGINEERING*

011 UK
DIRECTORY OF EUROPEAN INDUSTRIAL & TRADE ASSOCIATIONS. 1971. irreg., 4th, 1986. £62.50($150) C.B.D. Research Ltd., 15 Wickham Rd., Beckenham, Kent BR3 2JS, England (Dist. in U.S. by: Gale Research Co., Penobscot Bldg., Detroit, MI 48226) Ed. I.G. Anderson. circ. 4,000.
Formerly: Directory of European Associations. Part 1: National Industrial Trade and Professional Associations (ISSN 0070-5500)

DIRECTORY OF EUROPEAN RETAILERS & INTERNATIONAL BUYING AGENTS. see *BUSINESS AND ECONOMICS — Marketing And Purchasing*

382 UK ISSN 0142-4769
DIRECTORY OF EXPORT BUYERS IN THE U.K. 1978. a. Trade Research Publications, 6 Beech Hill Court, Berkhamsted, Herts. HP4 2PR, England.

338 600 US
DIRECTORY OF FEDERAL LABORATORIES. biennial. $10. High Tech Publishing Company, 10 Ridge Rd., Box 360, Ridge, NY 11961. TEL 516-924-6168.
●Also available online.

338 US
DIRECTORY OF FLORIDA INDUSTRIES. 1935. a. $49.95. Florida Chamber of Commerce Management Corp., Inc., Box 11309, Tallahassee, FL 32302. TEL 904-222-2831. Ed. Frank Ryll, Jr. adv. circ. controlled.

DIRECTORY OF GARMENT MANUFACTURERS. see *BUSINESS AND ECONOMICS — Chamber Of Commerce Publications*

DIRECTORY OF GAS UTILITY COMPANIES. see *PETROLEUM AND GAS*

338 US ISSN 0731-6925
DIRECTORY OF GENERAL MERCHANDISE, VARIETY CHAINS AND SPECIALTY STORES. a. $179. Chain Store Guide (Subsidiary of: Lebhar-Friedman, Inc.) 425 Park Ave., New York, NY 10022. TEL 212-371-9400. (also avail. in magnetic tape)
Formerly: Directory of General Merchandise, Mail Order Firms and Family Centers (ISSN 0277-1985)

338 658.8 US ISSN 0070-5594
DIRECTORY OF GOVERNMENT PRODUCTION PRIMECONTRACTORS. 1966. a. $15. Government Data Publications, 1120 Connecticut Ave., N.W., Washington, DC 20036. Ed. Siegfried Lobel.

683 US ISSN 0882-536X
DIRECTORY OF HARDWARE AND HOUSEWARES DISTRIBUTORS. biennial. $149. Chain Store Guide (Subsidiary of: Lebhar-Friedman, Inc.) 425 Park Ave., New York, NY 10022. TEL 212-371-9400. (also avail. in magnetic tape)
Formerly: Directory of Hardware Distributors (ISSN 0736-9573)

DIRECTORY OF HAZARDOUS WASTE SERVICES. see *ENVIRONMENTAL STUDIES*

338.4 HK
DIRECTORY OF HONG KONG INDUSTRIES. (Text in English) 1976. a. $65. Hong Kong Productivity Council, T S T P.O. Box 99027, Kowloon, Hong Kong. adv. circ. 3,000.

382.45 621 II ISSN 0417-5964
DIRECTORY OF INDIAN ENGINEERING EXPORTERS. 1957. irreg., 8th edt., 1977. price varies. Engineering Export Promotion Council, World Trade Centre, 3rd Fl., 14/1B Ezra St., Calcutta 700001, India. adv. illus. circ. 5,000.

338 PK
DIRECTORY OF INDUSTRIAL ESTABLISHMENTS IN PUNJAB. (Text in English) 1975. a. Rs.40. Directorate of Industries and Mineral Development, Lahore, Punjab, Pakistan.

DIRECTORY OF INDUSTRIAL LABORATORIES IN ISRAEL. see *ENGINEERING*

670 338 US ISSN 0075-0379
DIRECTORY OF IOWA MANUFACTURERS. 1948. biennial. $25. Iowa Department of Economic Development, 200 E. Grand Ave., Des Moines, IA 50309. TEL 515-281-3925. index.

669.14 US
DIRECTORY OF IRON AND STEEL WORKS OF THE UNITED STATES AND CANADA. triennial. price varies. American Iron and Steel Institute, 1000 16th St., N.W., Washington, DC 20036. TEL 202-452-7100.

330 IS
DIRECTORY OF ISRAEL. (Text in English) 1953. a. $45. N.A. Etrogy Publishing Company, Box 815, Tel-Aviv, Israel (Dist. by International Publications Service, 303 Park Ave. S., New York, N.Y. 10010) Ed. A. Etrogy. adv. bk. rev.
Formerly: Directory of Israeli Merchants and Manufacturers (ISSN 0070-5705)

670 US ISSN 0070-5721
DIRECTORY OF KANSAS MANUFACTURERS AND PRODUCTS. 1940/41. a. $35. Department of Economic Development, 400 W. 8th St., Topeka, KS 66603. TEL 913-296-3483. Ed. Lisa M. Kraemer. index of products. circ. 2,000.

380 US
DIRECTORY OF LEADING CHAIN STORES. a. Chain Store Guide, 425 Park Ave., New York, NY 10022. TEL 212-371-9400.

670 338 US ISSN 0275-1089
DIRECTORY OF LOUISIANA MANUFACTURERS. 1942. a. $35. ‡ Department of Commerce, Box 94185, Capitol Station, Baton Rouge, LA 70804-9185. TEL 504-342-5359. Ed. Ivan M. Nott. index. circ. 3,500.
Formerly: Louisiana Directory of Manufacturers (ISSN 0076-1028)

659.1 US ISSN 0419-2923
DIRECTORY OF MAILING LIST HOUSES. 1955. irreg. $65. B. Klein Publications, Box 8503, Coral Springs, FL 33065. TEL 305-752-1708. Ed. Bernard Klein.

380 659.1 US
DIRECTORY OF MAILING LIST HOUSES (NEW YORK) a. $65. Todd Publications, Box 92, Lenox Hill Sta., New York, NY 10021. Ed. Barry Klein. adv. circ. 5,000.

670 US
DIRECTORY OF MANUFACTURERS - MINNESOTA. biennial. $65. Nelson Marketing Services, Inc., 11300 Rupp Dr., Burnsvilee, MN 55337. TEL 612-894-9494. circ. 3,500.

670 US ISSN 0070-5802
DIRECTORY OF MARYLAND MANUFACTURERS. 1963. biennial. $30. Department of Economic and Community Development, Business Directories, 45 Calvert St., Annapolis, MD 21401. TEL 301-269-2041. Ed. Marilyn Corbett. adv. circ. 5,500.

670 US
DIRECTORY OF MASSACHUSETTS MANUFACTURERS. a. $30. Associated Industries of Massachusetts, 441 Stuart St., Box 763, Boston, MA 02116. TEL 617-262-1180.

670 US ISSN 0070-5926
DIRECTORY OF NEBRASKA MANUFACTURERS. 1960. biennial. $20. Department of Economic Development, Box 94666, Lincoln, NE 68509. TEL 402-471-3111. Ed. Shirley Kling. circ. 5,000.

670 US
DIRECTORY OF NEW ENGLAND MANUFACTURERS. a. $104. Associated Industries of Massachusetts, 411 Stuart St., Box 763, Boston, MA 02117. TEL 617-267-1180.

670 US
DIRECTORY OF NEW YORK MANUFACTURERS. a. $57. Associated Industries of Massachusetts, 411 Stuart St., Box 763, Boston, MA 02117. TEL 617-262-1180.

670 US ISSN 0090-5577
DIRECTORY OF NORTH DAKOTA MANUFACTURERS. 1959. biennial. free. ‡ Economic Development Commission, Liberty Memorial Bldg., Bismarck, ND 58505. Ed. David R. Torkelson. circ. 1,500.
Formerly: Directory of North Dakota Industrial and Manufacturing Plants.

DIRECTORY OF OIL WELL DRILLING CONTRACTORS. see *PETROLEUM AND GAS*

DIRECTORY OF OIL WELL SUPPLY COMPANIES. see *PETROLEUM AND GAS*

BUSINESS AND ECONOMICS — TRADE AND INDUSTRIAL DIRECTORIES

670 US
DIRECTORY OF OREGON MANUFACTURERS. biennial. $60. Economic Development Department, 595 Cottage St., N.E., Salem, OR 97310. TEL 503-373-1200.

380.1 PH
DIRECTORY OF PHILIPPINE EXPORTERS AND IMPORTERS. a. Directory of Philippine Industries, Box 2653, Manila, Philippines.

670 PH
DIRECTORY OF PHILIPPINE MANUFACTURERS AND PRODUCERS. a. Directory of Philippine Industries, Box 2653, Manila, Philippines.

DIRECTORY OF PREMIUM, INCENTIVE AND TRAVEL BUYERS. see BUSINESS AND ECONOMICS — Marketing And Purchasing

338 352 US
DIRECTORY OF PRIMES. 1983. a. $15. Government Data Publications, 1120 Connecticut Ave., N.W., Washington, DC 20036.

DIRECTORY OF PRODUCERS AND DRILLING CONTRACTORS: CALIFORNIA. see PETROLEUM AND GAS

DIRECTORY OF PRODUCERS AND DRILLING CONTRACTORS: KANSAS. see PETROLEUM AND GAS

DIRECTORY OF PRODUCERS AND DRILLING CONTRACTORS: LOUISIANA, ARKANSAS, FLORIDA, GEORGIA. see PETROLEUM AND GAS

DIRECTORY OF PRODUCERS AND DRILLING CONTRACTORS: MICHIGAN, INDIANA, ILLINOIS, KENTUCKY. see PETROLEUM AND GAS

DIRECTORY OF PRODUCERS AND DRILLING CONTRACTORS: OKLAHOMA. see PETROLEUM AND GAS

DIRECTORY OF PRODUCERS AND DRILLING CONTRACTORS: ROCKY MOUNTAIN REGION, WILLISTON BASIN, FOUR CORNERS NEW MEXICO. see PETROLEUM AND GAS

DIRECTORY OF PRODUCERS AND DRILLING CONTRACTORS: TEXAS. see PETROLEUM AND GAS

338 US ISSN 0738-7369
DIRECTORY OF PUBLIC HIGH TECHNOLOGY CORPORATIONS. 1983. a. $195. American Investor Information Services, 311 Bainbridge St., Philadelphia, PA 19147-1543. TEL 215-925-2761. Ed. Ronald P. Smolin. adv. circ. 1,500.
●Also available online.

DIRECTORY OF RESTAURANT & FAST FOOD CHAINS IN CANADA. see FOOD AND FOOD INDUSTRIES

338 380.1 CN
DIRECTORY OF RETAIL CHAINS IN CANADA. 1975. a. Can.$210. Maclean Hunter Ltd., Business Publication Division, 777 Bay St., Toronto, Ont. M5W 1A7, Canada. Ed. Maureen Cavanaugh.

338 US
DIRECTORY OF SHOPPING CENTERS IN THE UNITED STATES. 1960. a. $285. National Research Bureau, Inc., 310 S. Michigan Ave., Ste. 1150, Chicago, IL 60604. TEL 312-663-5580. Ed. Nancy D. Veatch. adv. circ. 5,000.

380 CE
DIRECTORY OF STATE CORPORATIONS. (Text in English) a. Rs.10. Sri Lanka Institute for the Study of State Corporations, 380 Bauddhaloka Mawatha, Colombo 7, Sri Lanka.

338 672 US ISSN 0070-6426
DIRECTORY OF STEEL FOUNDRIES IN THE UNITED STATES, CANADA AND MEXICO. 1930. biennial. $30. Steel Founders' Society of America, 455 State St., Des Plaines, IL 60016. TEL 312-299-9160. Ed. Jack D. McNaughton. circ. 1, 500.

380.1 658.8 US ISSN 0196-1845
DIRECTORY OF SUPERMARKET, GROCERY & CONVENIENCE STORE CHAINS. a. $189. Chain Store Guide (Subsidiary of: Lebhar-Friedman, Inc.) 425 Park Ave., New York, NY 10022. TEL 212-371-9400.

670 US ISSN 0070-6450
DIRECTORY OF TEXAS MANUFACTURERS. 1933. a. $110 (Includes Texas Industrial Expansion) University of Texas at Austin, Bureau of Business Research, Box 7459, Austin, TX 78713. TEL 512-471-1616. Ed. Ida M. Lambeth. circ. 5,000. (back issues avail.; reprint service avail. from UMI)

664 US
DIRECTORY OF THE CANNING, FREEZING, PRESERVING INDUSTRIES. 1966. biennial. $90. Edward E. Judge & Sons, Inc., Box 866, Westminster, MD 21157. TEL 301-876-2052. Ed. Daniel P. Judge. (back issues avail.)

674 US ISSN 0070-6477
DIRECTORY OF THE FOREST PRODUCTS INDUSTRY. 1919. biennial. Miller Freeman Publications, Inc., 500 Howard St., San Francisco, CA 94105. TEL 415-397-1881. Ed. Vincent M. Ridley. (reprint service avail. from UMI)

DIRECTORY OF THE SCIENTISTS, TECHNOLOGISTS, AND ENGINEERS OF THE P C S I R. (Pakistan Council of Scientific and Industrial Research) see SCIENCES: COMPREHENSIVE WORKS

380.1 530 US
DIRECTORY OF THE SOLAR INDUSTRY. 1976. a. $20. Solar Data, 13 Evergreen Rd., Hampton, NH 03842. TEL 603-926-8082. Ed. Richard N. Livingstone.

DIRECTORY OF THE SPANISH COTTON-SYSTEM TEXTILE ENTERPRISES/ DIRECTORIO EMPRESAS TEXTILES DE PROCESO ALGODONERO/DIRECTORI EMPRESES TEXTILS DE PROCES COTONER/ DIRECTOIRE ENTERPRISES TEXTILES DE PROCESSUS COTONNIER. see TEXTILE INDUSTRIES AND FABRICS

380.1 551.4 UK
DIRECTORY OF U K FLUID POWER DISTRIBUTORS. 1980. a. Applied Technology Publications Ltd., 15 Coombe Rd., New Malden, Surrey KT3 4PX, England. Ed. Raymond Hey. circ. 4,500.

DIRECTORY OF UNITED STATES IMPORTERS. see BUSINESS AND ECONOMICS — International Commerce

338 US
DIRECTORY OF WIRE COMPANIES OF NORTH AMERICA. 1973. a. $65. Business Information Services, Inc., 7 Hampden Rd., Stafford Springs, CT 06076-9310. TEL 203-684-2471. Ed. Richard J. Callahan. adv. circ. 5, 000.

DIRECTORY OF WOOL, HOSIERY AND FABRICS. see TEXTILE INDUSTRIES AND FABRICS

540 US ISSN 0196-0555
DIRECTORY OF WORLD CHEMICAL PRODUCERS. 1980. a. $295. Chemical Information Services, Ltd., Box 61, Oceanside, NY 11572.

338 SA ISSN 0416-2706
DONALDSON'S PORT ELIZABETH , UITENHAGE AND DESPATCH DIRECTORY. (Text in English) a. R.17. A.C. Braby (Pty) Ltd., P.O. Box 1426, Pinetown 3600, South Africa. Ed. A. Stagg.
Formerly: Donaldson's Port Elizabeth Directory.

DOVER PORT HANDBOOK. see TRANSPORTATION — Ships And Shipping

380 658.8 US
DROP SHIPPING SOURCE DIRECTORY OF MAJOR CONSUMER PRODUCT LINES. 1977. a. $6. Consolidated Marketing Services, Inc., Box 1361, New York, NY 10163. TEL 212-688-8797. Ed. Nicholas T. Scheel.

670 330 US ISSN 0277-3716
DRUG STORE MARKET GUIDE; a detailed distribution analysis of chain and wholesale drug store industry. 1981. a. $189. Melnor Publishing, Inc., 1739 Horton Ave., Mohegan Lake, NY 10547. TEL 914-528-7147. Ed. Melanie R. Buse.

338 US
DUN & BRADSTREET STANDARD REGISTER. Variant title: Dun and Bradstreet/Seyd's Register. (Published in 5 volumes: Vol.1, Northern Counties, Vol.2. Midlands, Vol.3. London, Vol.4. Southern Counties and Wales, Vol.5. Scotland and North Ireland) 1965. a. L.1.24 not available to libraries. Dun & Bradstreet, Inc., 99 Church St., New York, NY 10007 TEL 212-285-7000. (And 26-32 Clifton St., London EC2P 2LY, England)
Former titles: Dun and Bradstreet Register (ISSN 0070-7635); Bradstreet's Register; Incorporating: Seyd's Commercial Lists (ISSN 0080-911X)

380 US ISSN 0734-2845
DUN'S BUSINESS RANKINGS. 1982. a. $295. Dun's Marketing Services (Subsidiary of: Dun & Bradstreet Corporation) 49 Old Bloomfield Rd., Mountain Lakes, NJ 07046. TEL 201-299-8016.

DUN'S INDUSTRIAL GUIDE/METALWORKING DIRECTORY. see METALLURGY

DUNCAN'S RADIO MARKET GUIDE. see COMMUNICATIONS — Radio And Television

DUNDEE AND TAYSIDE CHAMBER OF COMMERCE AND INDUSTRY. BUYER'S GUIDE AND TRADE DIRECTORY. see BUSINESS AND ECONOMICS — Chamber Of Commerce Publications

338 SA
DURBAN CORPORATION DIRECTORY. (Text in English) a. R.25. Directory Publications (Pty) Ltd., P.O. Box 1426, Pinetown 3600, South Africa. Ed. A. Stagg. adv.

380 CN
DURHAM CLASSIFIED BUSINESS DIRECTORY & CONSUMERS' GUIDE. 1976. a. Can.$15($25) Lloyd Local Directory (Subsidiary of: Lloyd Publications of Canada) Box 262, West Hill, Ont. M1E 4R5, Canada. TEL 416-686-2131. Ed. J. Lloyd. adv. index. circ. 30,000.
Formerly: Durham Yellow Directory.

E B G. (Electronics Buyers Guide) see ELECTRICITY AND ELECTRICAL ENGINEERING

E C A YEAR BOOK DESK DIARY. (Electrical Contractors' Association) see ELECTRICITY AND ELECTRICAL ENGINEERING

621.38 US ISSN 0423-9938
E E M. (Electronic Engineers Master) 1957. a. $75. Hearst Business Communications, Inc., 645 Stewart Ave., Garden City, NY 11530. TEL 516-222-2500. Ed. Astrid Spector. adv. circ. 102,187.

E N R DIRECTORY OF DESIGN FIRMS. see ENGINEERING

338 KE
EAST AFRICA DIRECTORY. 1960. a. P.O. Box 41237, Nairobi, Kenya. Ed. G.C. Kimani. adv. circ. 20,000.

380 EC
ECUADOR. MINISTERIO DE INDUSTRIAS, COMERCIO E INTEGRACION. EMPRESAS ACOGIDAS A LA LEY DE FOMENTO INDUSTRIAL. DIRECTORIO INDUSTRIAL. 1957. irreg. Ministerio de Industrias, Comercio e Integracion, Quito, Ecuador.

338 380 GW ISSN 0343-5881
EINKAUFS 1X1 DER DEUTSCHEN INDUSTRIE. 1961. a. DM.107. Deutscher Adressbuch-Verlag, Holzhofallee 38, Postfach 110320, 6100 Darmstadt, W. Germany (B.R.D.) adv. index in English and French. circ. 10,000.

537 US
ELECTRONIC DESIGN'S GOLD BOOK. 1974. a. $50. Hayden Publishing Co., Inc., 10 Mulholland Dr., Hasbrouck Heights, NJ 07604. TEL 201-288-7520. Ed. George Weingarten. adv.

BUSINESS AND ECONOMICS — TRADE AND INDUSTRIAL DIRECTORIES

380.1   621.3   US   ISSN 0091-9519
ELECTRONIC INDUSTRIES ASSOCIATION. TRADE DIRECTORY AND MEMBERSHIP LIST. a. $80 to non-members; members $40. Electronic Industries Association, 2001 Eye St., N.W., Washington, DC 20006. TEL 202-457-4905. Ed. Carol S. Cedrone.
   Continues: Electronic Industries Association. Membership List.

338   621.3   US   ISSN 0422-9053
ELECTRONIC INDUSTRY TELEPHONE DIRECTORY. 1963. a. $40. Harris Publishing Co. (Twinsburg), 2057-2 Aurora Rd., Twinsburg, OH 44087. TEL 216-425-9000. Ed. Lonetta Witt. adv. circ. 110,000.

338   621.3   US
ELECTRONIC REPRESENTATIVES DIRECTORY. 1949. a. $25. Harris Publishing Co. (Twinsburg), 2057-2 Aurora Rd., Twinsburg, OH 44087. TEL 216-425-9000. Ed. Kathi Graeser. adv. circ. 8,500.

ELECTRONICS BUYERS' GUIDE. see *ELECTRICITY AND ELECTRICAL ENGINEERING*

ELEKTRONIKINDUSTRIENS INDKOEBSBOG. see *ELECTRICITY AND ELECTRICAL ENGINEERING*

EMBROIDERY DIRECTORY. see *TEXTILE INDUSTRIES AND FABRICS*

338   BL
EMPRESAS JAPONESAS NO BRASIL. ANNUARIO/BURAJIRU NIKKEI KIGYO NENKAN. (Text in Japanese and Portuguese) a. Selecoes Economicas, Av. Paulista 807, Sao Paulo, Brazil.

ENGINEER BUYERS GUIDE. see *ENGINEERING*

ENGINEERING INDUSTRIES ASSOCIATION. CLASSIFIED DIRECTORY AND BUYERS GUIDE. see *ENGINEERING*

621.3   670   US
EQUIPMENT DIRECTORY OF AUDIO-VISUAL, COMPUTER AND VIDEO PRODUCTS. 1953. a. $37 to commercial non-members; users $25. International Communications Industries Association, Inc., 3150 Spring St., Fairfax, VA 22031. TEL 703-273-7200. Ed. Mary Stevens. adv. charts. illus. stat. index. circ. 14,000. (processed)
   Formerly: Audio-Visual Equipment Directory (ISSN 0571-8759)

382   920   BE   ISSN 0771-7911
EUROPEAN COMMUNITIES AND OTHER EUROPEAN ORGANIZATIONS WHO'S WHO. (Text in English, French and German) 1978. biennial. 2490 Fr. Editions Delta, 92-94 Square E. Plasky, 1040 Brussels, Belgium. Ed. G. Francis Seingry. adv. circ. 6,000. (back issues avail.)

EUROPEAN MARKETS: A GUIDE TO COMPANY AND INDUSTRY INFORMATION SOURCES. see *BUSINESS AND ECONOMICS — International Commerce*

EUROPEAN RESEARCH CENTRES; a directory of organizations in science, technology, agriculture and medicine. see *SCIENCES: COMPREHENSIVE WORKS*

EUROPEAN RIG- AND SUPPLY SHIP OWNERS. see *TRANSPORTATION — Ships And Shipping*

380   CN   ISSN 0708-1332
EXPORT CANADA; the marketing directory of Canadian trade. 1978. a. Can.$55($48) Canex Enterprises, Inc., Box 1048, Sta. A., Surrey, B.C. V3S 4P5, Canada. TEL 604-596-9426. Ed. M. Butchard. adv. illus. circ. 10,000.

380   CL
EXPORT DIRECTORY CHILE/DIRECTORIO DE LA EXPORTACION. (Text in English, French, German, Spanish) 1976. a. free. ProChile, Pedro de Baldivia 0193, 2nd Floor, Santiago, Chile. adv. circ. 15,000.

382   BL
EXPORT DIRECTORY OF BRAZIL/GUIA BRASILEIRO DE EXPORTACAO. (Text in English, French, Portuguese, and Spanish) 1964. a. Cr.$50. Banco do Brasil, Eixo Rodoviario Sul, Sector Bancario Sul, Lote 23, C.P. 562, Brazilia, D.F., Brazil. (Co-sponsor: Emprendimentos Brasileiros de Informacoes Dirigidas Ltda.) Ed. Gilberto Huber. bk. rev. illus. circ. 25,000.
   Formerly: G B E: Export Directory of Brazil.

380.1   620   UK
F I D I C INTERNATIONAL DIRECTORY OF CONSULTING ENGINEERS. 1979. biennial. $42. (Federation Internationale des Ingenieurs Conseils) Rhys Jones Marketing, The Lodge, Diamond Terrace, London SE10 8QN, England. Ed. Rod Rhys Jones. circ. 5,000.

380   IC
F I S FRETTABREF. no.1, vol.5, 1969. irreg. (approx. 6/yr.) membership. Felag Islenzkra Storkaupmanna - Association of Icelandic Wholesalers and Importers, Tjarnargata 14, Box 476, Reykjavik, Iceland. Ed. Arni Reynisson. circ. 250 (controlled)

FALMOUTH PORT AND INDUSTRY HANDBOOK 1984. see *TRANSPORTATION — Ships And Shipping*

683   US
FASTENER TECHNOLOGY BUYERS' GUIDE. 1982. a. International Thomson Industrial Press, Inc., 6521 Davis Industrial Parkway, Solon, OH 44139. TEL 216-248-1125. Ed. Frank W. Akstens.

FEDERATION DES INDUSTRIES CHIMIQUES DE BELGIQUE. ANNUAIRE. see *ENGINEERING — Chemical Engineering*

382   PK
FEDERATION OF PAKISTAN CHAMBERS OF COMMERCE AND INDUSTRY. DIRECTORY OF EXPORTERS. (Text in English) 1977. a. Rs.150($20) Federation of Pakistan Chambers of Commerce and Industry, St-28, Block 5, Scheme-V, Share-Firdousi Kehkashan, Clifton, Karachi, Pakistan.

FEED INDUSTRY RED BOOK; reference book and buyers' guide for the feed manufacturing industry. see *AGRICULTURE — Feed, Flour And Grain*

690   US
FENCE INDUSTRY/ACCESS CONTROL DIRECTORY. 1958. a. $21.95. Communication Channels Inc., 6255 Barfield Rd., Atlanta, GA 30328. TEL 404-256-9800. Ed. Barbara Katinsky. adv.
   Formerly: Fence Industry Directory.

380   CE
FERGUSON'S SRI LANKA DIRECTORY. (Text in English) 1859. biennial. $26. Associated Newspapers of Ceylon Ltd., Box 1195, Lake House, Colombo 10, Sri Lanka. Ed. T.C.L. Ferdinando. adv. stat. circ. 10,000.
   Formerly: Ferguson's Ceylon Directory.

FIJI CLASSIFICATION & DICTIONARY OF OCCUPATIONS. see *BUSINESS AND ECONOMICS — Labor And Industrial Relations*

338   US   ISSN 0276-8208
FLORIDA BUILDERS AND CONTRACTORS DIRECTORY. a. Gulfstream Publishing Co., Inc., 300 S. Pine Island Rd., Ft. Lauderdale, FL 33324.

917.502   US
FLORIDA MANUFACTURERS REGISTER. a. $79. Manufacturers' News, Inc., 4 E. Huron St., Chicago, IL 60611. TEL 312-337-1084. adv. illus.

FLUID POWER HANDBOOK & DIRECTORY. see *ENGINEERING — Engineering Mechanics And Materials*

380   JA
FOOD ECONOMICS YEARBOOK/SHOKURYO KEIZAI NENKAN.* a. 2500 Yen. Shokuryo Keizai Shimbun Sha, 35-12 Ishigatsujimachi, Tennoji-ku, Osaka 543, Japan. illus.
   Continues: Sogo Keizai Nenkan.

664   338   US
FOOD INDUSTRY DIRECTORY. 1974. a. Gro Com Group, Box 10378, Clearwater, FL 33517. circ. 25,000.

670   PH
FOREIGN BUYERS OF PHILIPPINE COTTAGE INDUSTRY PRODUCTS. a. Directory of Philippine Industries, Box 2653, Manila, Philippines.

FORTH PORTS HANDBOOK 1984. see *TRANSPORTATION — Ships And Shipping*

338.4   US   ISSN 0197-7792
FORTUNE WORLD BUSINESS DIRECTORY; the 500 largest industrials, 50 largest commercial banks outside the U.S. and 50 largest world industrials. 1957; expanded 1976. a. $7. Time Inc., Fortune Division, Time & Life Building, Rockefeller Center, New York, NY 10020 TEL 212-586-1212. (Order from: Fortune Directories, 250 W. 49th St., New York, NY 10019) charts. stat.
   Formerly: Fortune Directory.

670   FR
LA FRANCE DE L'INDUSTRIE ET SES SERVICES. Variant title: Kompass France. (Text in French; classifications and summaries in English, French, German, Spanish) 1923. a. 1900 F. Societe Nouvelle d'Editions pour l'Industrie, 22 Avenue Franklin D. Roosevelt, 75008 Paris, France. adv. illus. circ. 10,000. (also avail. in magnetic tape)
   Former titles: Repertoire General de la Production Francaise (ISSN 0337-5714) & Annuaire Industriel. Repertoire General de la Production Francaise (ISSN 0075-6652)

338   011   FR   ISSN 0244-710X
FRANCEXPORT. (Text in English, French, German and Spanish) 1980. m. 650 Fr.($95) Librairie du Commerce International, 24 Bd. de l'Hopital, B.P. 438, 75233 Paris Cedex 05, France (Subscr. to: Addor Associates Inc., P.O. Box 2128, Westport, CT 06880) circ. 32,000.

338   US   ISSN 0318-8752
FRANCHISE ANNUAL; complete handbook and directory. 1969. a. $24.95. (International Franchise Opportunities) Info Press, Inc., 728 Center St., Box 550, NY 14092. TEL 716-754-4669. Ed. E.L. Dixon, Jr. bk. rev. index. circ. 15,000.

380.1   658   CN   ISSN 0071-9277
FRASER'S CANADIAN TRADE DIRECTORY. 1913. a. Can.$110. Maclean-Hunter Ltd., Business Publication Division, Maclean-Hunter Bldg., 777 Bay St., Toronto, Ont. M5W 1A7, Canada. TEL 416-596-5086.

FREELANCE EDITORS' ASSOCIATION OF CANADA. DIRECTORY OF MEMBERS. see *PUBLISHING AND BOOK TRADE*

380   FR
FRENCH COMPANY HANDBOOK; for evaluating key French companies. (Text in English) 1981. a. $49. International Business Development, 56 rue Lemercier, 75017 Paris, France (U.S. subscr. to: Addor Associates, Inc., Box 2128, 115 Roseville Rd., Westport, CT 06880) (Co-publisher: International Herald Tribune) Eds. Barton Reichert, Irving Sedar. circ. 15,000.

380.1   GM
GAMBIA. CENTRAL STATISTICS DEPARTMENT. DIRECTORY OF ESTABLISHMENTS. (Formerly issued by Central Statistics Division) a. d.8. Central Statistics Department, Wellington St., Banjul, Gambia.

GAYELLOW PAGES; classified directory of gay U S A and Canada organizations and businesses. see *HOMOSEXUALITY*

338   387   UK
GENOA PORT AND SHIPPING HANDBOOK. 1985. a. £10. Charter Publications, Bank Chambers, Downham Market, Norfolk PE38 9BU, England. Ed. John Ison. circ. 6,000.

670   US   ISSN 0272-1074
GEORGE D. HALL'S NEW YORK MANUFACTURERS DIRECTORY. 1980. biennial. $57. George D. Hall Co. Inc., 50 Congress St., Boston, MA 02109. TEL 617-523-3745.

330   US   ISSN 0435-5482
GEORGIA MANUFACTURING DIRECTORY. biennial. $40. Department of Industry and Trade, 230 Peachtree St., Box 1776, Atlanta, GA 30301. TEL 404-656-3607. Ed. Deborah Battle. circ. 5,500.

380.1 688   US   ISSN 0148-9437
GIFT AND TABLEWARE REPORTER. GIFT
GUIDE; a buyers' guide. a. $10. Gralla Publications,
1515 Broadway, New York, NY 10036. TEL 212-
869-1300. Ed. Jack McDermott.

GOLF COURSE BUILDERS OF AMERICA
DIRECTORY. see BUILDING AND
CONSTRUCTION

GOOLE PORT HANDBOOK. see
TRANSPORTATION — Ships And Shipping

664.752   US
GRAIN GUIDE/NORTH AMERICAN GRAIN
YEARBOOK. a. $35. Sosland Publishing Co., 9000
W. 67 St., Merriam, KS 66202. TEL 913-236-7300.
Ed. Sue Robinson.
    Supersedes: Grain Directory/Buyers's Guide.

380.1   630   CN
GRAINLIST (YEAR) 1985. a. Can.$40. Canada
Grains Council, 760-360 Main St., Winnipeg,
Manitoba R3C 3Z3, Canada. TEL 204-942-2254.

GREAT YARMOUTH PORT AND INDUSTRY
HANDBOOK. see TRANSPORTATION — Ships
And Shipping

670   US
GREATER BUFFALO BUSINESS DIRECTORY. a.
$40. Greater Buffalo Chamber of Commerce, 107
Delaware Ave., Buffalo, NY 14202. TEL 716-852-
7100. adv. circ. 8,500.
    Former titles: Western New York Business
Directory & Western New York Buyer's Guide and
Roster; Directory-Metropolitan Buffalo; Buffalo
Area Chamber of Commerce Buyer's Guide.

380   352   AT
GREEK GOLDEN GUIDE. (Text in Greek) 1979. a.
free. Golden Guide Publishing, 187 Collins St.,
Melbourne, Vic. 3000, Australia.

380   DK
GREENS; haandbogen om dansk erhvervsliv.
(Summaries in French, English and German) 1884.
a. Kr.1435. A-S Forlaget Boersen, Moentergade 19,
Box 2103, 1014 Copenhagen K, Denmark. Ed. John
Johansson. circ. 3,000.

338   GU   ISSN 0072-7865
GUAM BUSINESS DIRECTORY. (Text in English)
1954. irreg. free contr. circ. in Guam; $2.50 in the
U.S. Department of Commerce, Economic Research
Center, 590 S. Marine Dr., GITC Bldg., Ste. 601,
Tamuning, Guam 96911.

380   GU
GUAM TRADE WITH THE UNITED STATES
AND FOREIGN COUNTRIES. (Text in English)
1976. a. $1.50. Department of Commerce, Office of
Trade Statistics, GITC Bldg., 590 S. Marine Dr.,
Ste. 601, Tammuning, GU 96911. Ed.Bd. circ. 300.

GUIA DAS EDITORAS BRASILEIRAS. see
PUBLISHING AND BOOK TRADE

380   PY
GUIA DE LA INDUSTRIA: REPUBLICA DEL
PARAGUAY. irreg., no.2, 1983. Editora Guia de la
Industria, Alberdi 454, 1 piso, Of. 10, Edif.
Cardinal, Asuncion, Paraguay.

380.1   666   SP
GUIA GENERAL DE LAS INDUSTRIAS
AZULEJERAS Y AUXILIARES DE ESPANA. a.
Faenza Editrice Iberia S.L., Calle Navarra 85,
Castellon de la Flora, Spain. adv.
    Ceramics

382   IT
GUIDA DELLE REGIONI D'ITALIA. 1971. a.
L.150000. Sispr-Societa Italiana Studio Problemi
Regionali, Via della Scrofa 14, 00186 Rome, Italy.
Ed. Enzo Marraro. adv. circ. 10,000.

380   668.55   FR   ISSN 0072-7989
GUIDE DE LA PARFUMERIE/GENERAL
DIRECTORY OF THE PERFUME AND
COSMETIC INDUSTRY. (Text in English and
French) 1948. biennial. 250 F. Editions Publi-Guid,
195 Quai de la Gourdine, 77400 Lagny, France. Ed.
Gilbert Hieblot. adv. index in English and French.
circ. 3,000.

338.0961   TI   ISSN 0330-9290
GUIDE ECONOMIQUE DE LA TUNISIE. 1976. a.
$50. Societe I E A, 16 rue de Rome, Tunis, Tunisia.
illus.

674   US
GUIDE FOR BUYERS OF QUALITY
HARDWOODS. a. Hardwood Manufacturer's
Association, 805 Stevick Bldg., Memphis, TN
38103. TEL 901-743-3466. Ed. J.H. Lee. circ. 10,
000.

380   US
GUIDE TO KEY BRITISH ENTERPRISES I AND
II. a. Dun & Bradstreet, Inc., 99 Church St., New
York, NY 10007 TEL 212-285-7000. (And 26-32
Clifton St., London EC2P 2LY, England)
    Formerly: British Middle Market Directory
(ISSN 0068-2268)

338   US
GUIDE TO OBTAINING MINORITY BUSINESS
DIRECTORIES. a. $6. National Minority Business
Directories, 65 22nd Ave., N.E., Minneapolis, MN
55418. TEL 612-781-6819.
    Formerly: Guide to Minority Business Directories
(ISSN 0362-3459)

GUIDOR. (Guide Annuaire Officiel du Complexe de
Rungis) see FOOD AND FOOD INDUSTRIES —
Grocery Trade

382   UK
GUYANA TRADE DIRECTORY. 1981. a. £1.
Arthur H. Thrower Ltd., 44-46 South Ealing Rd.,
London W5, England.

380   AU
HANDELSREGISTER OESTERREICH; mit dem
genauen Wortlaut der amtlichen Protokollierung.
1947. a. S.1950. Jupiter Verlag GmbH, Robertgasse
2, A-1020 Vienna, Austria.

683   670   US
HARDWARE AGE "WHO MAKES IT" BUYERS'
GUIDE. 1922. a. $25 free w/subscription to
Hardware Age. Chilton Co., Chilton Way, Radnor,
PA 19089. TEL 215-964-4284. Ed. George A.
Headley. adv. tr.lit. circ. controlled. (reprint service
avail. from UMI)
    Formerly: Hardware Age "Who Makes It"
Directory.

HARPERS GUIDE TO SPORTS TRADE. see
SPORTS AND GAMES

338   670   US
HARRIS INDIANA INDUSTRIAL DIRECTORY
(YEAR) 1924. a. $59. Harris Publishing Co.
(Twinsburg), 2057-2 Aurora Rd., Twinsburg, OH
44087. TEL 216-425-9000. Ed. Irene Amick.
    Formerly: Harris Indiana Marketers Industrial
Directory & Indiana Industrial Directory (ISSN
0073-6910)

338.4   US
HARRIS MICHIGAN INDUSTRIAL DIRECTORY.
1974. a. $89. Harris Publishing Co. (Twinsburg),
2057-2 Aurora Rd., Twinsburg, OH 44087. TEL
216-425-9000. Ed. Maryellen Smith.
    Former titles: Harris Michigan Marketers
Industrial Directory; Harris Michigan Manufacturers
Industrial Directory (ISSN 0363-1869)

670   US
HARRIS OHIO INDUSTRIAL DIRECTORY. 1918.
a. $89. ‡ Harris Publishing Co. (Twinsburg), 2057-2
Aurora Rd., Twinsburg, OH 44087. TEL 216-425-
9000. Ed. Fran Carlsen.
    Former titles: Harris Ohio Marketers Industrial
Directory (ISSN 0733-4664) & Ohio Industrial
Directory (ISSN 0161-4878); Ohio Manufacturers
Industrial Directory; Directory of Ohio
Manufacturers (ISSN 0070-5985)

382   US
HARRIS PENNSYLVANIA INDUSTRIAL
DIRECTORY. 1913. a. $89. Harris Publishing Co.
(Twinsburg), 2057-2 Aurora Rd., Twinsburg, OH
44087. TEL 216-425-9000. Ed. Fran Segulin.
    Former titles: Pennsylvania Industrial Directory &
Harris Pennsylvania Marketing Directory (ISSN
0734-8541) & Industrial Directory of the
Commonwealth of Pennsylvania.

HAZARDOUS CARGO CONTACTS. see
TRANSPORTATION — Ships And Shipping

380   338   AU   ISSN 0531-5824
HEROLD EXPORT-ADRESSBUCH VON
OESTERREICH/AUSTRIAN EXPORT
DIRECTORY/ANNUAIRE D'EXPORTATION
DE L'AUTRICHE/ANUARIO DE
EXPORTACION DE AUSTRIA. (Text in English,
German, French and Spanish) 1950. a. S.390($20)
Herold Vereinigte Anzeigen-Gesellschaft M.B.H.,
Wipplingerstr. 14, A-1013 Vienna, Austria.

670   US
HIGH TECH & MANUFACTURING DIRECTORY
OF IDAHO. 1972. biennial. $35. University of
Idaho, Center for Business Development and
Research, College of Business and Economics,
Moscow, ID 83843. TEL 208-885-6611. Ed. Joy
Passanante Williams. circ. 2,000.
    Formerly (until 1982): Manufacturing Directory
of Idaho.

380.1   US   ISSN 0272-0167
HOME CENTER OPERATORS & HARDWARE
CHAINS (YEAR) 1948. a. $189. Chain Store
Guide (Subsidiary of: Lebhar-Friedman, Inc.) 425
Park Ave., New York, NY 10022. TEL 212-371-
9400. (also avail. in magnetic tape)
    Supersedes in part: Directory: Home Centers and
Hardware Chains, Auto Supply Chains (ISSN 0094-
8667)

640   380.1   US
HOME SEWING INDUSTRY RESOURCE
DIRECTORY. 1963. a. $4. Homesewing Trade
News, 330 Sunrise Highway, Box 286, Rockville
Centre, NY 11571. TEL 516-766-1226. Ed. Senta
Mead. adv. circ. 13,575.

382   HK   ISSN 0073-3245
HONG KONG MANUFACTURERS AND
EXPORTERS REGISTER. 1963. irreg., 8th edt.,
1975. $18. Oriental Publicity Service, P.O. Box
4366, N.P., Hong Kong, Hong Kong. Ed. Anthony
Leung. adv. circ. 5,000.

HOW TO FIND COMPANY INTELLIGENCE IN
STATE DOCUMENTS. see BUSINESS AND
ECONOMICS

HOW TO FIND INFORMATION ABOUT
COMPANIES; the corporate intelligence source
book. see BUSINESS AND ECONOMICS

HOW TO FIND INFORMATION ABOUT
JAPANESE COMPANIES AND INDUSTRIES.
see BUSINESS AND ECONOMICS

380.1   613.7   US
I D E A INDUSTRY DIRECTORY. 1984. a. $25.
International Dance-Exercise Association, 4501
Mission Bay Dr., Ste. 2F, San Diego, CA 92109.
TEL 619-274-2770. Ed. Patricia Ryan.

380.1   658.8   US   ISSN 0731-518X
I D HANDBOOK OF FOODSERVICE
DISTRIBUTION. (Institutional Distribution) 1981.
a. $199. Bill Communications, Inc., 633 Third Ave.,
New York, NY 10017. TEL 212-986-4800. Ed.
Edith Fried Walker. circ. 1,000.

380   UK
I W S A YEAR BOOK. (Text in English and French)
1979. a. £18. International Water Supply
Association, c/o L.R. Bays, Sec. Gen., 1 Queen
Ann's Gate, London SW1H 9BT, England. Ed. L.R.
Bays. adv. circ. 5,000.
    Formerly: International Who's Who in Water
Supply (ISSN 0260-4604)

670   US   ISSN 0160-3302
ILLINOIS MANUFACTURERS DIRECTORY. 1912.
a. $122. Manufacturers' News, Inc., 4 E. Huron St.,
Chicago, IL 60611. TEL 312-337-1084. adv. illus.

670   US   ISSN 0092-3818
ILLINOIS SERVICES DIRECTORY. 1985.
Manufacturers' News, Inc., 4 E. Huron St., Chicago,
IL 60611. TEL 312-337-1084. adv. illus.

380.01   663.1   US   ISSN 0749-7946
IMPACT YEARBOOK; a directory of the U.S. wine
& spirits industry. 1985. a. $105. M. Shanken
Communications, Inc., 400 E. 51 St., New York,
NY 10022. TEL 212-751-6500. Ed. Marvin R.
Shanken. adv. stat. index.

INDIAN HOSIERY DIRECTORY. see CLOTHING
TRADE

BUSINESS AND ECONOMICS — TRADE AND INDUSTRIAL DIRECTORIES

670 US ISSN 0735-2417
INDIANA MANUFACTURERS DIRECTORY. a. $88. Manufacturers' News, Inc., 4 E. Huron St., Chicago, IL 60611. TEL 312-337-1084. adv. illus.

380.1 382 IO ISSN 0216-1052
INDONESIAN IMPORTERS. (Text in English) 1978. biennial. $50. Gabungan Importir Nasional Seluruh Indonesia - National Importers Association of Indonesia, Jalan Majapahit 1, Box 2744, Jakarta Pusat, Indonesia. Eds. Zahri Achmad, S. Hoesin. circ. 3,000.

338 382 II
INDUSTRIAL AND BUSINESS DIRECTORY KERALA (YEAR) a. National Publishers, P.O. Box 263, Kottayam, Kerala, India. Ed. C.J. Mani.

INDUSTRIAL & TRADE DIRECTORY. see *BUSINESS AND ECONOMICS*

338.7 UK
INDUSTRIAL DIRECTORY OF WALES. irreg. £4. Wales Investment Location, Pearl Assurance House, Greyfriars Rd., Cardiff CF1 3AG, Wales. Ed. Mrs. G. Grace. adv. circ. 2,500.

670 AU ISSN 0073-7712
INDUSTRIE COMPASS OESTERREICH. 1867. a. S.1300. (Austrian Chamber of Commerce) Compass-Verlagsgesellschaft Rudolf Hanel & Sohn, Wipplingerstrasse 32, A-1013 Vienna, Austria. adv. circ. 3,000.

381 II ISSN 0073-7763
INDUSTRIES DIRECTORY, CAPITALS.* irreg. Rs.30. J.K. Publications, 16 Park Area, New Delhi 5, India. Ed. J.K. Jain.

381 II ISSN 0073-7771
INDUSTRIES DIRECTORY, DELHI.* irreg. Rs.5. J.K. Publications, 16 Park Area, New Delhi 5, India. Ed. J.K. Jain.

381 II ISSN 0073-7798
INDUSTRIES DIRECTORY, NORTHERN INDIA.* irreg. Rs.15. J.K. Publications, 16 Park Area, New Delhi 5, India. Ed. J.K. Jain.

INFORMATION MOSCOW, WESTERN EDITION. see *TRAVEL AND TOURISM*

INGENIOEREN INDKOEBSBOG. see *BUSINESS AND ECONOMICS — Production Of Goods And Services*

INSIDE THE LEADING MAIL ORDER HOUSES. see *BUSINESS AND ECONOMICS — Marketing And Purchasing*

747 US
INTERIOR DESIGN BUYERS GUIDE. 1970. a. $10. Cahners Publishing Co., Inc., Interior Design Group, Division of Reed Publishing USA, 249 W. 17th St., New York, NY 10011. TEL 212-645-0067. Ed. Neil H. Feinstein. adv. tr.lit. index. (back issues avail.)
Formerly: Interior Design Directory.

382 UK
INTERNATIONAL BUSINESSMEN'S WHO'S WHO. 1967. irreg. Melrose Press Ltd., 3 Regal Ln., Soham, Ely, Cambs. CB7 5BA, England.

INTERNATIONAL C A D/C A M INDUSTRY DIRECTORY. see *COMPUTERS — Computer Graphics*

INTERNATIONAL DIRECTORY OF ARTS (YEAR) see *ART*

380 US
INTERNATIONAL DIRECTORY OF CORPORATE AFFILIATIONS. 1981. a. $267. National Register Publishing Co., 3004 Glenview Rd., Wilmette, IL 60091. TEL 312-256-6067. Ed. Margaret Deuson. adv. stat. index. circ. 2,500. (also avail. in magnetic tape)

INTERNATIONAL DIRECTORY OF IMPORTERS: AFRICA. see *BUSINESS AND ECONOMICS — International Commerce*

INTERNATIONAL DIRECTORY OF IMPORTERS: SOUTH/CENTRAL AMERICA. see *BUSINESS AND ECONOMICS — International Commerce*

INTERNATIONAL DIRECTORY OF MARKETING RESEARCH HOUSES AND SERVICES. see *BUSINESS AND ECONOMICS — Marketing And Purchasing*

380.1 US
INTERNATIONAL DIRECTORY OF PRIVATE PRESSES. 1978. a. $30. Press of Arden Park, 861 Los Molinos Way, Sacramento, CA 95864. TEL 916-481-7881. Ed. Budd Westreich. (back issues avail.)

INTERNATIONAL FOOD DIRECTORY. see *FOOD AND FOOD INDUSTRIES*

338.1 US ISSN 0074-6193
INTERNATIONAL GREEN BOOK; directory of U.S. and Latin American processors of cottonseed, soybean, linseed and peanuts. 1910. a. $22.50. (Haughton Publishing Co. of Texas) Cotton Gin and Oil Mill Press, Box 18536, Dallas, TX 75218. TEL 214-288-7511. Ed. Don Swanson. adv. circ. 500. (also avail. in microform from UMI)

INTERNATIONAL INDUSTRIAL SENSOR DIRECTORY. see *ENGINEERING*

665.5 380 US
INTERNATIONAL OIL SCOUTS ASSOCIATION DIRECTORY. 1956. a. $25. International Oil Scouts Association, Box 272949, Houston, TX 77277-2949. circ. 400.

INTERNATIONAL PULP & PAPER DIRECTORY. see *PAPER AND PULP*

INTERNATIONAL REFRACTORIES HANDBOOK & DIRECTORY. see *CERAMICS, GLASS AND POTTERY*

380.1 GW ISSN 0302-2196
INTERNATIONALES VERZEICHNIS DER WIRTSCHAFTSVERBAENDE/WORLD GUIDE TO TRADE ASSOCIATIONS. irreg., 3rd edt., 1985. $200. K.G. Saur Verlag KG, Poessenbacherstr. 12 B, Postfach 711009, 8000 Munich 71, W. Germany (B.R.D.) (U.S. and Canadian subscr. to: K.G. Saur Inc., 175 Fifth Ave., New York, N.Y. 10010) (reprint service avail. from UMI, ISI)

338 US
INTERSTATE MANUFACTURERS AND INDUSTRIAL DIRECTORY BUYERS GUIDE. 1977. a. Bell Directory Publishers Inc., 1995 Broadway, New York, NY 10023.

338 NR
INVESTMENTS AND CREDIT CORPORATION OF OYO STATE. INDUSTRIAL DIRECTORY. 1970. irreg. Investments and Credit Corporation of Oyo State, P.M.B. 5085, Ibadan, Nigeria.
Formerly: Western Nigeria Development Corporation. Industrial Directory.

380.1 US
IOWA INTERNATIONAL DIRECTORY. biennial. free. Iowa Department of Economic Development, 200 E. Grand Ave., Des Moines, IA 50309. TEL 515-281-3925.
Former titles: Iowa Manufacturer's Export Directory; Iowa Directory of Exporting Companies; Iowa International Directory.

670 US ISSN 0737-7940
IOWA MANUFACTURERS REGISTER. a. $48. Manufacturers' News, Inc., 4 E. Huron St., Chicago, IL 60611. TEL 312-337-1084. adv. illus.

380 UK ISSN 0269-2716
IPSWICH & SUFFOLK DIRECTORY OF INDUSTRY & COMMERCE. a. £28. Guardian Communications Ltd., Albany House, Hurst St., Birmingham B5 4BD, England.

IPSWICH PORT HANDBOOK 1984. see *TRANSPORTATION — Ships And Shipping*

IRELAND PORTS & SHIPPING HANDBOOK. see *TRANSPORTATION — Ships And Shipping*

670 676 IS
ISRAEL INSTITUTE OF PACKAGING. PACKAGING DIRECTORY. 1976. irreg. Israel Centerefor Packaging and Product Design, P.O. Box 20038, Tel Aviv, Israel. TEL 03-254402. Ed. Zvi Ben-Nun. adv.

380 352 AT
ITALIAN GOLDEN GUIDE. (Text in Italian) 1979. a. free. Golden Guide Publishing, 187 Collins St., Melbourne, Vic. 3000, Australia. circ. 60,000.

338.0962 UA
ITTIHAD AL-SINAAT AL-MISRIYAH. YEARBOOK. Vols. for 1971-72 issued by the body under its English form of name: Federation of Egyptian Industries. Yearbook. (Text in English) 1961. a. £E5. Federation of Egyptian Industries, 26a, Sherif Pasha St., Cairo, Egypt. Ed. Gamil el Sabban. adv. stat. circ. 900.
Continues: Ittihad al-Sinaat al-Bal-Jumhuriyah al-Arabiyah al-Muttahidah. Yearbook.

338.7 IO
JAKARTA BUSINESS DIRECTORY. (Text in English or Indonesian) 1974. irreg. Kamar Dagang dan Industri Jakarta, Jalan W. Jakarta Fair, Tromol Post 3077, Jakarta, Indonesia. illus.

380.1 IO
JAKARTA METROPOLITAN BUYERS' GUIDE. (Text in English) a. C.V. Taro & Co., Jalan Samanhudi ZB, Box 3472, Jakarta, Indonesia.

382 629.1 JA ISSN 0286-0635
JAPAN AVIATION DIRECTORY. (Text in English) 1968. a. $45. Wing Aviation Press, 2nd Gomi Bldg., 14-5, Ginza 1-chome, Tokyo 104, Japan. Eds. Hitoshi Ohashi, Akihiko Takao. adv. circ. 18,000.

338 JA ISSN 0075-322X
JAPAN DIRECTORY. (Text in English) 1931. a. 45.000 Yen($225) Japan Press, Ltd., C.P.O. Box 6, Tokyo, Japan (Or 2-12-8 Kita Aoyama, Minato-ku, Tokyo 107, Japan) Ed. Yoshio Wada. adv. circ. 25,000.

670 537.5 US
JAPAN ELECTRONICS BUYERS' GUIDE. (Avail. in 4 vols.) a. $143 per set; $43 for ea. vol. Dempa Publications, Inc., 400 Madison Ave., New York, NY 10017. TEL 212-752-3003. Ed. Hideo Hirayama. adv.

382 JA
JAPAN TIMES DIRECTORY. a. 4000 Yen. Japan Times, Ltd., 4-5-4 Shibaura, Minato-ku, Tokyo 108, Japan.
Names, addresses, phone numbers of foreign residents in Japan, and leading enterprises, foreign and Japanese

382 JA
JAPAN TRADE DIRECTORY/NIHON BOEKI SHINKOKAI. (Text in English) 1982. a. 230. Japan External Trade Organization, Publication Department, 2-5 Toranomon, 2-chome, Minato-ku, Tokyo 105, Japan. Ed. Jun Sasaki. adv. circ. 10,000.

670 338 UK
KELLY'S BUSINESS DIRECTORY; list of manufacturers and merchants (alphabetical and classified) 1877. a. Kelly's Directories, Windsor Court, East Grinstead House, East Grinstead, West Sussex RH19 1XB, England. adv. circ. 10,750.
●Also available online.
Formerly: Kelly's Manufacturers and Merchants Directory (ISSN 0075-5370)

910.2 UK
KELLY'S POST OFFICE LONDON BUSINESS DIRECTORY; comprehensive list of trades in London (classified and alphabetical) 1799. a. Kelly's Directories, Windsor Court, East Grinstead Hous, East Grinstead, West Sussex RH19 1XB, England. adv. circ. 30,000.
Formerly: Kelly's Post Office London Directory (ISSN 0075-5389)

338 UK
KELLY'S U.K. EXPORTS TO EUROPE. a. £40. Kelly's Directories, Windsor Court, East Grinstead House, East Grinstead, West Sussex RH19 1XB, England. circ. 19,500.
●Also available online.
Formerly: Kelly's British Industry and Services in the Common Market.

KEMPS PROPERTY INDUSTRY YEARBOOK. see *REAL ESTATE*

BUSINESS AND ECONOMICS — TRADE AND INDUSTRIAL DIRECTORIES

670　　　　　US　ISSN 0075-5494
KENTUCKY DIRECTORY OF
  MANUFACTURERS. 1948. a. $25. ‡ Department
  of Economic Development, Capital Plaza Tower,
  Frankfort, KY 40601. TEL 502-564-4886. Ed.
  Mildred J. Keefer. circ. 5,500.
  Formerly: Kentucky Industrial Directory (ISSN
  0075-5516)

338　　　　　US　ISSN 0363-5198
KENTUCKY DIRECTORY OF SELECTED
  INDUSTRIAL SERVICES. 1970. biennial. $10.
  Department of Economic Development, Capital
  Plaza Tower, Frankfort, KY 40601. TEL 502-564-
  4886. Ed. Mildred Keefer. circ. 1,000.

670　　　　　US　ISSN 0741-9031
KENTUCKY MANUFACTURERS REGISTER. a.
  $44. Manufacturers' News, Inc., 4 E. Huron St.,
  Chicago, IL 60611. TEL 312-337-1084. adv. illus.

338.4　　　　KE
KENYA. CENTRAL BUREAU OF STATISTICS.
  DIRECTORY OF INDUSTRIES. irreg., latest
  1977. EAs.15. Central Bureau of Statistics, Ministry
  of Finance & Planning, Box 30128, Nairobi, Kenya
  (Orders to: Government Printing and Stationery
  Office, Box 30128, Nairobi, Kenya)
  Continues: Kenya. Ministry of Finance and
  Economic Planning. Statistics Division. Register of
  Manufacturing Firms.

338　　　　　KE
KENYA ASSOCIATION OF MANUFACTURERS.
  MEMBERS LIST AND INTERNATIONAL
  STANDARD INDUSTRIAL CLASSIFICATION.
  1959. a. $20. Kenya Association of Manufacturers,
  Box 30225, Nairobi, Kenya. adv. circ. 500.
  Formerly: Kenya Association of Manufacturers.
  Industrial Index & Members List.

380　332.6　　KE
KENYA: THE GATEWAY TO AFRICA; guidelines
  to investors. irreg. free. Ministry of Industry,
  Industrial Promotion Department, Box 30418,
  Nairobi, Kenya.
  Formerly: Guidelines for Industrial Investors in
  Kenya.

380.1　　　　KE
KENYA, UGANDA, TANZANIA, EAST AFRICAN
  COMMUNITY DIRECTORY; TRADE
  COMMERCE INDEX. 1959/60. irreg. East
  African Directory Company, Box 41237, Nairobi,
  Kenya. illus.
  Continues: Kenya, Uganda, Tanzania, Zambia,
  Malawi and Ethiopia Directory; Trade and
  Commercial Index (ISSN 0453-6525)

338.2　　　　US
KEYSTONE COAL INDUSTRY MANUAL. 1918. a.
  $120. McGraw-Hill Publications Co., 1221 Ave. of
  the Americas, New York, NY 10020. Ed. George F.
  Nielsen. adv.

338.4　　　　US
KNITTING TIMES BUYERS' GUIDE &
  KNITWEAR APPAREL DIRECTORY. a. $15.
  National Knitwear and Sportswear Association, 386
  Park Ave. S., New York, NY 10016. TEL 212-683-
  7520.
  Former titles: Knitting Times Buyer's Guide and
  Knitwear Directory; Knitting Times Buyers' Guide
  Directory; Knitted Outerwear Times Buyer's Guide
  Directory.

670　　　　　DK
KOMPAS DANMARK; indeks over Danmarks
  industri og naegringsliv. (Text in Danish;
  classifications in Danish, German, French, English,
  Spanish; summaries in Danish, English, German)
  1961. a. Bibliotekscentralen, SZ , Tempovej 7-11,
  DK-2750 Ballerup, Denmark (Dist. in the U.S. by:
  Croner Publications, Inc., 211-03 Jamaica Ave.,
  Queens Village, NY 11428) adv. bk. rev. circ. 6,000.
  Formerly: Kompas Danmark (ISSN 0075-661X)

670　　　　　AT
KOMPASS AUSTRALIA. 1970. a. Aus.$265.
  (Associated Chambers of Manufacturers of
  Australia) Peter Isaacson Publications, 45-50 Porter
  St., Prahran Victoria 3181, Australia.
  Formerly: Kompass Register; Kompass Australia
  (ISSN 0075-6628)

670　　　　　BE　ISSN 0075-6636
KOMPASS BELGIUM/LUXEMBOURG; repertoire
  de l'economie de la Belgique et du Luxembourg.
  (Text in Dutch and French; classifications in Dutch,
  English, French, German; summaries in Dutch,
  English, French, German) 1961. a. free. (Foundation
  for Promoting International Economic Information,
  SZ) Kompass Belgium S.A., Av. Moliere 256, 1060
  Brussels, Belgium (Dist. in the U.S. and Canada by:
  Croner Publications, 211-03 Jamaica Ave., Queens
  Village, NY 11428) Ed. M.J. Cocquyt. adv. circ. 4,
  700.
  ●Also available online.

670　　　　　SP　ISSN 0075-6644
KOMPASS ESPANA; repertorio general de la
  economia espanola. (Text in Spanish; classifications
  in English, French, German, Italian, Spanish;
  summaries in English, French, German, Spanish)
  1960. a. $60. (Foundation for Promoting
  International Economic Information, SZ) Kompass
  Espana SA, Av. del General Peron 26, Madrid, 20,
  Spain (Croner Publications Inc., 211-03 Jamaica
  Ave., Queens Village, NY 11428)

670　　　　　NE　ISSN 0075-6660
KOMPASS HOLLAND; informatiewerk over het
  Nederlandse Bedrijfsleven. (Text in Dutch;
  classifications and summaries in Dutch, German,
  French, English, Spanish) 1964. a. fl.325.
  (Foundation for Promoting International Economic
  Information, SZ) Kompass Nederland BV,
  Hogehilweg 15, 1101 CB Amsterdam Z.O.,
  Netherlands (Subscr. to Croner Publications, Inc.,
  211-03 Jamaica Ave., Queens Village, NY 11428)
  adv. bk. rev. circ. 8,600.

670　　　　　IT　ISSN 0075-6687
KOMPASS ITALIA; repertorio generale dell'economia
  Italiana. (Text in Italian; classifications and
  summaries in Italian, French, English, German,
  Spanish) 1962. a. L.300000. (Kompass International
  S.A., SZ) Seat, Via A. Saffi, 18, 10138 Turin, Italy.
  adv. circ. 10,000.

670　　　　　MR　ISSN 0075-6695
KOMPASS MAROC; register of Moroccan industry
  and commerce. (Text and classifications in French;
  summaries in English and French) 1966. a. $120.
  (Foundation for Promoting International Economic
  Information, SZ) Kompass Maroc-Veto, Boite
  Postale 11100, MA Casablanca, Morocco (Dist. in
  U.S. and Canada by: Croner Publications, 211-03
  Jamaica Ave., Queens Village, NY 11428) (Affiliate:
  Kompass International AG, Zurich) Ed. Eric
  Verdavainne. adv. circ. 6,000.

380　　　　　NO　ISSN 0075-6709
KOMPASS NORGE; indeks over Norges industri og
  Naeringsliv. (Text in English, French, German,
  Norwegian, Spanish; summaries in English, German,
  Norwegian) 1970. a. Kr.825. (Export Council of
  Norway and Federation of Norwegian Industries,
  SZ) Kompass Norge A-S, Lokkeveien 87, N-4000
  Stavanger, Norway (Dist. in the U.S. by: Croner
  Publications, Inc. 211-03 Jamaica Ave., Queens
  Village, NY 11428) adv. circ. 5,000.

670　664　　　FR
KOMPASS PROFESSIONELS. (Text and
  summaries in English, French, German and Spanish)
  1974. a. price varies. Societe Nouvelle d'Editions
  pour l'Industrie, 22 Avenue F.D. Roosevelt, 75008-
  Paris, France. adv. illus.
  Formerly: Kompass Alimentation.

670　　　　　SZ　ISSN 0075-6717
KOMPASS SCHWEIZ/LIECHTENSTEIN;
  informationswerk der Schweizerischen. Wirtschaft.
  (Text in French, German, Italian; classifications in
  English, French, German, Italian; summaries in
  English, French, and German) 1947. a. $150.
  Schweiz Verlag AG, In Grosswiesen 14, 8044
  Zurich, Switzerland (Dist. in the U.S. and Canada
  by: Croner Publications, Inc., 211-03 Jamaica Ave.,
  Queens Village, NY 11428) adv. circ. 10,000.

380　　　　　FR
KOMPASS SPECIAL SERVICES. 1934? a. 360 F.
  Societe Nouvelle d'Editions pour l'Industrie, 22
  Ave. F.D. Roosevelt, 75008 Paris, France.

670　　　　　SW　ISSN 0075-6725
KOMPASS SVERIGE; handbok oever Sveriges
  industri og Naeringsliv. (Text in Swedish;
  classifications in Swedish, English, French, German,
  Spanish; summaries in Swedish, English, German)
  1958. a. Kr.460. (Foundation for Promoting
  International Economic Information, SZ) Kompass
  Sweden, Sveavagen 56, Box 3159, 10363 Stockholm,
  Sweden (Dist. in U.S. and Canada by: Croner
  Publications, 211-03 Jamaica Ave., Queens Village,
  NY 11428)

670　687　　　FR
KOMPASS TEXTILE ET HABILLEMENT. (Text
  and Summaries in English, French, German and
  Spanish) 1974. a. 480 F. Societe Nouvelle
  d'Editions pour l'Industrie, 22 Ave. F.D. Roosevelt,
  75008 Paris, France. adv. illus.

670　　　　　UK
KOMPASS UNITED KINGDOM; register of British
  industry and commerce. (Text in English;
  classifications in English, French, German, Italian,
  Spanish) 1962. a. £70. (Confederation of British
  Industry) Kompass Publishers Ltd., Windsor Court,
  East Grinstead House, East Grinstead, West Sussex
  RH19 1XD, England (Dist. by: Croner Publications,
  Inc., 211-05 Jamaica Ave., NY 11428) adv. circ. 9,
  000.
  ●Also available online.
  Formerly: Kompass United Kingdom/CBI (ISSN
  0075-6733)

380.1　　　　SA
KONTAK IN TENDERING. (Text in English) 1981.
  a. R.65. Mildenhall Publications (Pty) Ltd., Box
  1022, Johannesburg 2000, South Africa. Ed. Pat
  Gaffney. adv. circ. 2,000.

338　　　　　PH
KONTAKS. (Supplement to Philippines Business
  Directory) a. P.60($10) Philippines Business
  Directory, Box 3199, Manila, Philippines. adv.

380　659　　　KO
KOREA ANNUAL. Korean edition: Hapdong
  Yongam (ISSN 0073-0335) (Text in Korean) 1958.
  a. $45. Hapdong News Agency, 108-4, Soosong-
  Dong, Chongro-Ku, Box Kwangwhamoon 145,
  Seoul, S. Korea. Ed. Park Yong-kon. circ. 16,000.

380　659　　　US　ISSN 0075-6814
KOREA DIRECTORY. 1958. a. $73. (Korea
  Directory Company) Croner Publications, Inc., 211-
  05 Jamaica Ave., Queens Village, NY 11428. adv.

338　332.6　　II
KOTHARI'S INDUSTRIAL DIRECTORY OF
  INDIA. (Text in English) 1936. every 18 mos.
  Rs.350($95) Kothari Enterprises, 114
  Nungambakkam High Rd., Madras 600034, India.
  Ed. A.C. Fernando. adv. circ. 5,000.
  Formerly: Kothari's Economic and Industrial
  Guide of India; Continues: Kothari's Economic
  Guide and Investor's Handbook of India.

338　　　　　DK
KRAK; industrial and trade directory for Denmark.
  (Issued in 5 vols.) 1770. a. Kr.1122.40. Kraks Legat,
  Nytorv 17, DK-1450 Copenhagen K, Denmark. adv.
  circ. 14,000.

338　　　　　SA　ISSN 0378-9268
LADYSMITH DIRECTORY. (Text in English) a.
  R.8. A.C. Braby (PTY) Ltd., P.O. Box 1426,
  Pinetown 3600, South Africa. Ed. A. Stagg.

380　　　　　US
LAMBERT'S WORLD OF TRADE, FINANCE
  AND ECONOMIC DEVELOPMENT.* (Vol.1:
  Africa and the Americas; Vol.2: Asia, Europe,
  Australasia, Oceania) 1984. a. $250. Lambert
  Publications, Inc., Box 21008, Washington, DC
  20009-0508. TEL 202-332-0973.

380　　　　　CR
LATIN-AMERICAN IMPORT-EXPORT
  DIRECTORY. (Text in English, Spanish) 1983. a.
  $23.50. International Trade Council, Box 73, San
  Jose - 1007, Costa Rica. TEL 33-8697.

338　　　　　SA
LAWRIE'S DURBAN STREET DIRECTORY. (Text
  in English) a. R.53. Allan Laurie (Pty) Ltd., P.O.
  Box 1426, Pinetown 3600, South Africa. Ed. A.
  Stagg. adv. circ. 20,000.

312   BUSINESS AND ECONOMICS — TRADE AND INDUSTRIAL DIRECTORIES

LEATHER MANUFACTURER'S DIRECTORY. see *LEATHER AND FUR INDUSTRIES*

670   LE   ISSN 0075-8353
LEBANESE INDUSTRIAL AND COMMERCIAL DIRECTORY/ANNUAIRE DES PROFESSIONS AU LIBAN. (Text in French; index in Arabic, English and French) 1953. biennial. $30. Middle East Commercial Information Center, Box 6466, Beirut, Lebanon (Dist. by UNIPUB, 345 Park Ave. S., New York, NY 10010) Ed. Charles G. Gedeon. adv. circ. 10,000.

LEEDS. CHAMBER OF COMMERCE AND INDUSTRY. CLASSIFIED TRADE DIRECTORY OF MEMBERS. see *BUSINESS AND ECONOMICS — Chamber Of Commerce Publications*

382.025   LB
LIBERIAN TRADE DIRECTORY; basic trade information, exporters & importers. irreg. Ministry of Commerce, Industry and Transportation, Director of Foreign Trade, Box 9041, Monrovia, Liberia.

380.1   US
LINEAL INDUSTRIAL DISTRIBUTORS REGISTERS. (Text in English and Spanish) 1983. irreg. $225. Lineal Publishing Co., Inc., 2425 E. Commercial Blvd., Ft. Lauderdale, FL 33308. TEL 305-776-7308.

380   UK
LIST OF BONDED WAREHOUSES. irreg. price varies. H.M.S.O., Box 569, London SE1 9NH, England.

666   US
LITTLE BLACK BOOK; annual directory of ceramic mold manufacturers in the United States. 1973. a. $1.95. Daisy Publishing Inc., Box 67A, Mukilteo, WA 98275. TEL 206-624-8921. Ed. Dale Swant. adv. circ. 11,000.

380   UK
LONDON DIRECTORY FOR TRADE & INDUSTRY. a. £42. Guardian Communications Ltd., Albany House, Hurst St., Birmingham B5 4BD, England.

670   UK
LONDON DIRECTORY OF INDUSTRY AND COMMERCE. a. $36. Kemps Group (Printers & Publishers) Ltd., 1-5 Bath St., London EC1V 9QA, England. adv.
Former titles: London Directory; Trades Register of London (ISSN 0082-5808)

LONDON PORT HANDBOOK 1984. see *TRANSPORTATION — Ships And Shipping*

LONDON SHIPPING CONTACTS. see *TRANSPORTATION — Ships And Shipping*

LOS ANGELES PORT AND SHIPPING HANDBOOK. see *TRANSPORTATION — Ships And Shipping*

380   US   ISSN 0733-5016
MACRAE'S ALABAMA STATE INDUSTRIAL DIRECTORY. irreg., latest 1984. $85. MacRae's Blue Book, Inc., 817 Broadway, New York, NY 10003. TEL 800-622-7237. Ed. Barry Lee.
Formerly: Alabama State Industrial Directory (ISSN 0740-431X)

338.0025   US   ISSN 0739-8476
MACRAE'S ARIZONA/NEW MEXICO STATE INDUSTRIAL DIRECTORY. irreg., latest 1984. $85. MacRae's Blue Book, Inc., 817 Broadway, New York, NY 10003. TEL 800-622-7237. Ed. Barry Lee.
Formed by the merger of: MacRae's Arizona State Industrial Directory (ISSN 0731-6704); which was formerly titled: Arizona State Industrial Directory (ISSN 0195-7082) & MacRae's New Mexico State Industrial Directory (ISSN 0275-1836) ; which was formerly titled: New Mexico State Industrial Directory.

380   US   ISSN 0740-4670
MACRAE'S ARKANSAS STATE INDUSTRIAL DIRECTORY. irreg., latest 1985. $75. MacRae's Blue Book, Inc., 817 Broadway, New York, NY 10003. TEL 800-622-7237. Ed. Barry Lee.
Formerly: Arkansas State Industrial Directory (ISSN 0197-3800)

338   US
MACRAE'S BLUE BOOK. 1890. a. $125. MacRae's Blue Book, Inc., 817 Broadway, New York, NY 10003. TEL 800-622-7237. Ed. Barry Lee.
Former titles: MacRae's Industrial Directory (ISSN 0749-5986) & MacRae's Blue Book (ISSN 0076-2067)

380   US   ISSN 0740-4638
MACRAE'S CALIFORNIA STATE INDUSTRIAL DIRECTORY. irreg., latest 1985. $110. MacRae's Blue Book, Inc., 817 Broadway, New York, NY 10003. TEL 800-622-7237. Ed. Barry Lee.
Formerly: California State Industrial Directory.

380   US   ISSN 0740-6126
MACRAE'S COLORADO/UTAH/NEVADA STATE INDUSTRIAL DIRECTORY. irreg., latest 1985. $95. MacRae's Blue Book, Inc., 817 Broadway, New York, NY 10003. TEL 800-622-7237. Ed. Barry Lee.
Formed by the merger of: MacRae's Colorado State Industrial Directory (ISSN 0732-4197); which was formerly titled: Colorado State Industrial Directory & MacRae's Nevada State Industrial Directory (ISSN 0734-015X); which was formerly titled: Nevada State Industrial Directory (ISSN 0195-7139) & MacRae's Utah State Industrial Directory. Which was formerly titled: Utah State Industrial Directory.

338   US   ISSN 0740-2937
MACRAE'S CONNECTICUT STATE INDUSTRIAL DIRECTORY. 1972. a. $85. MacRae's Blue Book, Inc., 817 Broadway, New York, NY 10003. TEL 800-622-7237. Ed. Barry Lee.
Formerly: Connecticut State Industrial Directory (ISSN 0098-6186)

650   US   ISSN 0749-1093
MACRAE'S DIRECTORY OF FIRMS MARKETING THROUGH MANUFACTURERS' REPRESENTATIVES. 1956. irreg. $85. ‡ MacRae's Blue Book, Inc., 817 Broadway, New York, NY 10003. TEL 800-622-7237. Ed. Barry Lee.
Formerly: MacRae's Manufacturers' Agents Guide (ISSN 0076-4213)

380   US   ISSN 0740-4697
MACRAE'S FLORIDA STATE INDUSTRIAL DIRECTORY. irreg., latest 1985. $95. MacRae's Blue Book, Inc., 817 Broadway, New York, NY 10003. TEL 800-622-7237. Ed. Barry Lee.
Formerly: Florida State Industrial Directory (ISSN 0163-4712)

380   US   ISSN 0733-4982
MACRAE'S GEORGIA STATE INDUSTRIAL DIRECTORY. irreg., latest 1984. $85. MacRae's Blue Blook, Inc., 817 Broadway, New York, NY 10003. TEL 800-622-7237.
Formerly: Georgia State Industrial Directory (ISSN 0161-8571)

380   US   ISSN 0740-6088
MACRAE'S IDAHO/MONTANA/WYOMING STATE INDUSTRIAL DIRECTORY. irreg., latest 1985. $95. MacRae's Blue Book, Inc., 817 Broadway, New York, NY 10003. TEL 800-622-7237. Ed. Barry Lee.
Formed by the merger of: MacRae's Idaho State Industrial Directory (ISSN 0732-4200); which was formerly titled: Idaho State Industrial Directory & MacRae's Montana State Industrial Directory (ISSN 0732-4189); which was formerly titled: Montana State Industrial Directory (ISSN 0195-7120) & MacRae's Wyoming State Industrial Directory (ISSN 0275-1852) Which was formerly titled: Wyoming State Industrial Directory.

380   US   ISSN 0740-4336
MACRAE'S ILLINOIS STATE INDUSTRIAL DIRECTORY. irreg., latest 1984. $110. MacRae's Blue Book, Inc., 817 Boradway, New York, NY 10003. TEL 800-622-7237. Ed. Barry Lee.
Formerly: Illinois State Industrial Directory.

380   US   ISSN 0740-6045
MACRAE'S INDIANA STATE INDUSTRIAL DIRECTORY. irreg., latest 1985. $99. MacRae's Blue Book, Inc., 817 Broadway, New York, NY 10003. TEL 800-622-7237. Ed. Barry Lee.
Formerly: Indiana State Industrial Directory (ISSN 0190-1362)

380   US   ISSN 0740-428X
MACRAE'S IOWA/NEBRASKA STATE INDUSTRIAL DIRECTORY. irreg., latest 1984. $95. MacRae's Blue Book, Inc., 817 Broadway, New York, NY 10003. TEL 800-622-7237. Ed. Barry Lee.
Formed by the merger of: MacRae's Nebraska State Industrial Directory (ISSN 0731-6720); which was formerly: Nebraska State Industrial Directory (ISSN 0197-3835) & MacRae's Iowa State Industrial Directory (ISSN 0732-4170); which was formerly: Iowa State Industrial Directory.

380   US   ISSN 0740-6118
MACRAE'S KANSAS STATE INDUSTRIAL DIRECTORY. irreg., latest 1985. $80. MacRae's Blue Book, Inc., 817 Broadway, New York, NY 10003. TEL 800-622-7237. Ed. Barry Lee.
Formerly: Kansas State Industrial Directory.

380   US   ISSN 0740-4328
MACRAE'S KENTUCKY/WEST VIRGINIA STATE INDUSTRIAL DIRECTORY. irreg., latest 1984. $95. MacRae's Blue Book, Inc., 817 Broadway, New York, NY 10003. TEL 800-622-7237. Ed. Barry Lee.
Formed by the merger of: MacRae's West Virginia State Industrial Directory (ISSN 0733-3692); which was formerly: West Virginia State Industrial Directory (ISSN 0160-7391) & MacRae's Kentucky State Industrial Directory; which was formerly: Kentucky State Industrial Directory (ISSN 0190-1354)

380   US   ISSN 0733-3234
MACRAE'S LOUISIANA STATE INDUSTRIAL DIRECTORY. irreg., latest 1984. $70. MacRae's Blue Book, Inc., 817 Broadway, New York, NY 10003. TEL 800-622-7237. Ed. Barry Lee.
Formerly: Louisiana State Industrial Directory (ISSN 0190-129X)

338   US   ISSN 0740-2945
MACRAE'S MAINE/NEW HAMPSHIRE/ VERMONT STATE INDUSTRIAL DIRECTORY. 1974. irreg., latest 1986. $95. MacRae's Blue Book, Inc., 817 Broadway, New York, NY 10003. TEL 800-622-7237. Ed. Barry Lee.
Formed by the merger of: MacRae's Maine State Industrial Directory (ISSN 0731-6739); which was formerly titled: Maine State Industrial Directory (ISSN 0098-6194) & MacRae's New Hampshire State Industrial Directory (ISSN 0733-4974); which was formerly titled: New Hampshire State Industrial Directory (ISSN 0098-6216) & MacRae's Vermont State Industrial Directory. Which was formerly titled: Vermont State Industrial Directory (ISSN 0098-6208)

380   US
MACRAE'S MARYLAND/D.C./DELAWARE STATE INDUSTRIAL DIRECTORY. irreg., latest 1986. $95. MacRae's Blue Book, Inc., 817 Broadway, New York, NY 10003. TEL 800-622-7237. Ed. Barry Lee.
Formed by the merger of: MacRae's Maryland State Industrial Directory (ISSN 0732-9695); which was formerly: Maryland State Industrial Directory (ISSN 0148-5660) & MacRae's Delaware State Industrial Directory (ISSN 0733-2947); which was formerly: Delaware State Industrial Directory (ISSN 0148-5652)

380   US   ISSN 0740-4689
MACRAE'S MASSACHUSETTS/RHODE ISLAND STATE INDUSTRIAL DIRECTORY. irreg., latest 1987. $110. MacRae's Blue Book, Inc., 817 Broadway, New York, NY 10003. TEL 800-622-7237. Ed. Barry Lee.
Formed by the merger of: MacRae's Rhode Island State Industrial Directory (ISSN 0733-4451); which was formerly: Rhode Island State Industrial Directory (ISSN 0148-5679) & MacRae's Massachusetts State Industrial Directory (ISSN 0732-1112); which was formerly: Massachusetts State Industrial Directory (ISSN 0148-7558)

380   US   ISSN 0733-4958
MACRAE'S MICHIGAN STATE INDUSTRIAL DIRECTORY. irreg., latest 1985. $99. MacRae's Blue Book, Inc., 817 Broadway, New York, NY 10003. TEL 800-622-7237. Ed. Barry Lee.
Formerly: Michigan State Industrial Directory (ISSN 0190-1338)

BUSINESS AND ECONOMICS — TRADE AND INDUSTRIAL DIRECTORIES

380   US   ISSN 0740-6061
MACRAE'S MINNESOTA STATE INDUSTRIAL DIRECTORY. irreg., latest 1985. $85. MacRae's Blue Book, Inc., 817 Broadway, New York, NY 10003. TEL 800-622-7237. Ed. Barry Lee.
Formerly: Minnesota State Industrial Directory (ISSN 0195-7112)

380   US   ISSN 0740-4654
MACRAE'S MISSISSIPPI STATE INDUSTRIAL DIRECTORY. irreg., latest 1985. $70. MacRae's Blue Book, Inc., 817 Broadway, New York, NY 10003. TEL 800-622-7237. Ed. Barry Lee.
Formerly: Mississippi State Industrial Directory (ISSN 0190-1346)

380   US   ISSN 0740-607X
MACRAE'S MISSOURI STATE INDUSTRIAL DIRECTORY. irreg., latest 1985. $85. MacRae's Blue Book, Inc., 817 Broadway, New York, NY 10003. TEL 800-622-7237. Ed. Barry Lee.

338   US   ISSN 0733-3684
MACRAE'S NEW JERSEY STATE INDUSTRIAL DIRECTORY. 1901. a. $135 hardbound; $110 paperbound. MacRae's Blue Book, Inc., 817 Broadway, New York, NY 10003. TEL 800-622-7237. Ed. Barry Lee.
Formerly: New Jersey State Industrial Directory (ISSN 0098-6224)

338   US   ISSN 0740-2953
MACRAE'S NEW YORK STATE INDUSTRIAL DIRECTORY. 1953. a. $135 hardbound; $110 paperbound. MacRae's Blue Book, Inc., 817 Broadway, New York, NY 10003. TEL 800-622-7237. Ed. Barry Lee. stat.
Former titles: Greater New York Industrial Directory (ISSN 0733-3552) & New York State Industrial Directory (ISSN 0548-9067)

380   US
MACRAE'S NORTH CAROLINA/SOUTH CAROLINA/VIRGINIA. irreg., latest 1986. $95. MacRae's Blue Book, Inc., 817 Broadway, New York, NY 10003. TEL 800-622-7237. Ed. Barry Lee.
Former titles: MacRae's North Carolina State Industrial Directory (ISSN 0739-845X) & North Carolina State Industrial Directory (ISSN 0161-4738)

380   US   ISSN 0739-8468
MACRAE'S NORTH DAKOTA/SOUTH DAKOTA STATE INDUSTRIAL DIRECTORY. irreg., latest 1984. $90. MacRae's Blue Book, Inc., 817 Broadway, Plainview, NY 10003. TEL 800-622-7237. Ed. Barry Lee.
Formed by the merger of: MacRae's South Dakota State Industrial Directory; which was formerly: South Dakota State Industrial Directory & MacRae's North Dakota State Industrial Directory; which was formerly: North Dakota State Industrial Directory (ISSN 0197-3827)

380   US   ISSN 0733-4176
MACRAE'S OHIO STATE INDUSTRIAL DIRECTORY. irreg., latest 1985. $99. MacRae's Blue Book, Inc., 817 Broadway, New York, NY 10003. TEL 800-622-7237. Ed. Barry Lee.
Formerly: Ohio State Industrial Directory.

380   US   ISSN 0740-4662
MACRAE'S OKLAHOMA STATE INDUSTRIAL DIRECTORY. irreg., latest 1985. $75. MacRae's Blue Book, Inc., 817 Broadway, New York, NY 10003. TEL 800-622-7237. Ed. Barry Lee.
Formerly: Oklahoma State Industrial Directory.

380   US   ISSN 0740-610X
MACRAE'S OREGON STATE INDUSTRIAL DIRECTORY. irreg., latest 1985. $85. MacRae's Blue Book, Inc., 817 Broadway, New York, NY 10003. TEL 800-622-7237. Ed. Barry Lee.
Formerly: Oregon State Industrial Directory (ISSN 0195-7147)

338   US   ISSN 0740-4298
MACRAE'S PENNSYLVANIA STATE INDUSTRIAL DIRECTORY. 1969. irreg., latest 1986. $135 hardbound; $110 softbound. MacRae's Blue Book, Inc., 817 Broadway, New York, NY 10003. TEL 800-622-7237. Ed. Barry Lee.
Formerly: Pennsylvania State Industrial Directory (ISSN 0553-6065)

380   US   ISSN 0740-4646
MACRAE'S TENNESSEE STATE INDUSTRIAL DIRECTORY. irreg., latest 1985. $80. MacRae's Blue Book, Inc., 817 Broadway, New York, NY 10003. TEL 800-622-7237. Ed. Barry Lee.
Formerly: Tennessee State Industrial Directory (ISSN 0190-1311)

380   US   ISSN 0739-8484
MACRAE'S TEXAS STATE INDUSTRIAL DIRECTORY. irreg., latest 1984. $99. MacRae's Blue Book, Inc., 817 Broadway, New York, NY 10003. TEL 800-622-7237. Ed. Barry Lee.
Formerly: Texas State Industrial Directory.

338   US
MACRAE'S VERIFIED DIRECTORY OF MANUFACTURERS' REPRESENTATIVES. 1957. irreg. $75. ‡ MacRae's Blue Book, Inc., 817 Broadway, New York, NY 10003. TEL 800-622-7237. Ed. Barry Lee.
Former titles: MacRae's Directory of Manufacturers' Representatives (ISSN 0738-4599) & Verified Directory of Manufacturers' Representatives (ISSN 0083-5692)

380   US   ISSN 0740-6134
MACRAE'S WASHINGTON STATE INDUSTRIAL DIRECTORY. irreg., latest 1985. $85. MacRae's Blue Book, Inc., 817 Broadway, New York, NY 10003. TEL 800-622-7237. Ed. Barry Lee.
Formerly: Washington State Industrial Directory.

380   US   ISSN 0740-6053
MACRAE'S WISCONSIN STATE INDUSTRIAL DIRECTORY. irreg., latest 1985. $80. MacRae's Blue Book, Inc., 817 Broadway, New York, NY 10003. TEL 800-622-7237. Ed. Barry Lee.
Formerly: Wisconsin State Industrial Directory (ISSN 0195-7155)

380   AU   ISSN 0076-2105
MADE IN AUSTRIA. (Text in English, French, German) 1966. a. S.720. Jupiter Verlag GmbH, Robertgasse 2, A-1020 Vienna, Austria. index.

670   TI
MADE IN TUNISIA; guide des industries tunisiennes. 1974. biennial. $30. CERES Productions, 6 Ave Montplaisir, Tunis, Tunisia. Eds. Moncef Guellati, Leila Zghidi. adv. circ. 10,000.

380.1   659   IS
MADRIKH PIRSUM. 1976. a. Israel Advertising Association, 5 Hess St., P.O. Box 1719, Tel Aviv, Israel. Ed. Rama Lippman. adv. circ. 1,000.

338   FR
MAFOGRA.* 1963. a. 156.10 F. Societe des Editions de l' Imprimerie Nouvelle, 53 guai Seine 19e, Paris, France. Ed. M. Mauduit. circ. 6,000.

MAGAZINE INDUSTRY MARKET PLACE; the directory of American periodical publishing. see PUBLISHING AND BOOK TRADE

338   US
MAINE MANUFACTURING DIRECTORY. 1965. biennial. $27.50. (State Development Office) Tower Publishing Co., 34 Diamond St., Box 7220, Portland, ME 04112. TEL 207-774-9813.
Former titles: Maine Marketing Directory (ISSN 0145-9007); Directory of Maine Manufacturers.

670   US   ISSN 0197-1220
MAINE, VERMONT AND NEW HAMPSHIRE DIRECTORY OF MANUFACTURERS. 1979. a. $52.50. Commerce Register, Inc., 190 Godwin Ave., Midland Park, NY 07432. TEL 201-445-3000.

380.1   US
MAINTENANCE SUPPLIES. 1956. a. $20. MacNair-Dorland Company, 101 W. 31st St., New York, NY 10001. Ed. Dominic Mariani. adv. bk. rev. illus. tr.lit. index. circ. 11,500. (back issues avail.)
Formerly: Maintenance Supplies Buyers' Guide.

382   332   UK   ISSN 0268-232X
MAJOR BANKS, FINANCE & INVESTMENT COMPANIES OF CONTINENTAL EUROPE. 1985. a. £55($88) Graham & Trotman Ltd., Sterling House, 66 Wilton Rd., London SW1V 1DE, England (Distr. in U.S. and Canada by: Graham & Trotman Inc., 13 Park Ave., Gaithersburg, MD 20877) Ed. Ruth Whiteside.

382   UK
MAJOR COMPANIES OF ARGENTINA, BRAZIL, MEXICO AND VENEZUELA. 1981. irreg. £60 paperback; £67 hardback. Graham & Trotman Ltd., Sterling House, 66 Wilton Rd., London SW1V 1DE, England. Ed. S.J. Andrade. adv.

338   UK
MAJOR COMPANIES OF EUROPE. 1982. a. price varies. Graham & Trotman Ltd., Sterling House, 66 Wilton Rd., London SW1V 1DE, England. Ed. Ruth Whiteside. adv. (also avail. in microfiche)

382   UK   ISSN 0144-2740
MAJOR COMPANIES OF NIGERIA. 1979. a. £40($64) paperback; £49($78) hardback. Graham & Trotman Ltd., Sterling House, 66 Wilton Rd., London SW1V 1DE, England. Ed. J. Carr. adv.

382   UK
MAJOR COMPANIES OF THE ARAB WORLD. 1977. a. £120($192) paperback; £135($216) hardback. Graham & Trotman Ltd., Sterling House, 66 Wilton Rd., London SW1V 1DE, England. Ed. G.C. Bricault. adv. (also avail. in microfiche)

382   UK
MAJOR COMPANIES OF THE FAR EAST. 1983. a. price varies. Graham & Trotman Ltd., Sterling House, 66 Wilton Rd., London SW1V 1DE, England. Ed. J.C. Carr. adv.

382   UK   ISSN 0268-2338
MAJOR COMPANIES OF THE UNITED STATES OF AMERICA. 1986. a. £185($296) paperback; £199($318) hardback. Graham & Trotman Ltd., Sterling House, 66 Wilton Rd., London SW1V 1DE, England. Ed. Ruth Whiteside.

MAJOR ENERGY COMPANIES OF EUROPE. see ENERGY

MALAYSIA. DIRECTORY OF TIMBER TRADE. see FORESTS AND FORESTRY — Lumber And Wood

382   US   ISSN 0095-0688
MANHATTAN DIRECTORY OF COMMERCIAL & INDUSTRIAL PROPERTIES.* 1937. a. $110. Standard Abstract Corp., c/o Benjamin Scheckner, 70 E. 10th St., No. 12F, New York, NY 10003. adv.

380.1   CN   ISSN 0076-390X
MANITOBA TRADE DIRECTORY. 1956. a. Can.$25. Sanford Evans Communications Ltd., Box 6900, Winnipeg, Man. R3C 3B1, Canada. TEL 204-775-0201. Ed. Bev Jolicoeur. adv. circ. 12,500.

384   US   ISSN 0076-4418
MARCONI'S INTERNATIONAL REGISTER; international trade and communications directory. 1899. a. $85. Telegraphic Cable & Radio Registrations, Inc., 19 Dogwood Ln., Box 14, Larchmont, NY 10538. TEL 914-632-8171. Ed. L.G. Smith, Jr. adv. index. circ. 5,000.
Formerly: International Register of Telegraphic and Trade Addresses.

MARKET GUIDE CONTINENTAL EUROPE. see BUSINESS AND ECONOMICS — Investments

670   US   ISSN 0195-5810
MASSACHUSETTS DIRECTORY OF MANUFACTURERS. 1979. a. $62.50. Commerce Register, Inc., 190 Godwin Ave., Midland Park, NJ 07432. TEL 201-445-3000. adv.

670   US
MASSACHUSETTS SERVICE DIRECTORY. a. $57. Associated Industries of Massachusetts, 411 Stuart St., Box 763, Boston, MA 02117. TEL 617-262-1180.

MATERIALS RESEARCH CENTRES; a world directory of organizations and programmes in materials science. see ENGINEERING — Engineering Mechanics And Materials

380   HK   ISSN 0258-3038
MECHANICAL & ELECTRONIC INDUSTRIES YEARBOOK OF CHINA. (Text in English) 1986. a. HK.$350($60) Economic Information Agency, 342 Hennessy Rd., 10th Fl., Hong Kong, Hong Kong. (Co-sponsor: Ministry of Mechanical and Electronic Industries)

BUSINESS AND ECONOMICS — TRADE AND INDUSTRIAL DIRECTORIES

380 070 AT ISSN 0811-8892
MEDIA OWNERSHIP IN AUSTRALIA. a. Aus.$39. (Information Australia) Margaret Gee Media Group, 45 Flinders Lane, Melbourne, Vic. 3000, Australia. Ed. G.R. Brown.

338 US ISSN 0146-8022
MEDICAL AND HEALTHCARE MARKETPLACE GUIDE. 1975. a. $307. International Bio-Medical Information Service, Inc., 8525 S.W. 92 St., Ste. 3A, Box 560756, Miami, FL 33156. TEL 305-271-7272. Eds. Arthur B. Hale, Adeline B. Hale. circ. 5,000. (also avail. in microfiche; back issues avail.)

MEDICAL LABORATORY DIRECTORY (YEAR) see *LABOR UNIONS*

MEDICAL PRODUCT OF JAPAN; directory of medical equipment. see *MEDICAL SCIENCES*

MEDWAY PORTS SHIPPING HANDBOOK. see *TRANSPORTATION — Ships And Shipping*

338 387 UK ISSN 0267-7350
MELBOURNE PORT AND SHIPPING HANDBOOK. 1985. a. £10. Charter Publications, Bank Chambers, Downham Market, Norfolk PE38 9BU, England. Ed. Gerry Cansdale. circ. 6,000.

380 US
MEMBERSHIP DIRECTORY & BUYER'S GUIDE. 1985. a. Greater Washington Maryland Service Station and Automotive Repair Association, 9420 Annapolis Rd., Ste. 307, Lenham, MD 20706-3021. TEL 301-577-2875. circ. 7,000.

MERCHANDISE MART BUYERS GUIDE. see *BUSINESS AND ECONOMICS — Marketing And Purchasing*

MERSEY PORTS HANDBOOK (YEAR) see *TRANSPORTATION — Ships And Shipping*

METAL & ENGINEERING INDUSTRY YEAR BOOK. see *ENGINEERING*

669 US
METAL-CENTER NEWS' METAL DISTRIBUTION. 1975. a. $5. Fairchild Publications, Inc., Metal Center News, 7 E. 12th St., New York, NY 10003. TEL 212-741-4000. adv. circ. 11,800.

670 US
MICHIGAN DIRECTORY OF MANUFACTURERS. a. $82.50. Commerce Register, Inc., 190 Godwin Ave., Midland Park, NJ 07432. TEL 201-445-3000.

MICROCOMPUTER MARKET PLACE. see *COMPUTERS — Microcomputers*

338 UK ISSN 0261-2275
MID GLAMORGAN INDUSTRIAL DIRECTORY. 1978. a. Polytechnic of Wales, Rm. H001, Treforest, Pontypridd, Mid Glamorgan CF37 1DL, Wales.

633 US
MILLING DIRECTORY/BUYERS GUIDE. 1973. a. $35. Sosland Publishing Co., 9000 W. 67 St., Merriam, KS 66202. TEL 913-236-7300. Ed. Laure Jones. stat. circ. 9,200.

380 UK
MILTON KEYNES DIRECTORY OF BUSINESS & BUYING. 1981. a. £4. Holcot Press Ltd., Station House, Station Rd., Newport Pognell, Milton Keynes MK16 0AG, England. Eds. Richard Meredith, Colin Fox. circ. 7,500.

MINES & MINING EQUIPMENT AND SERVICE COMPANIES WORLDWIDE (YEAR) see *MINES AND MINING INDUSTRY*

338 US
MINNESOTA INTERNATIONAL TRADE DIRECTORY. Cover title: Minnesota U S A International Trade Directory. biennial. free. Trade Office, 90 W. Plato Blvd., St. Paul, MN 55107. TEL 612-297-4222. circ. 5,000.

670 US ISSN 0738-1514
MINNESOTA MANUFACTURERS REGISTER. a. $73. Manufacturers' News, Inc., 4 E. Huron St., Chicago, IL 60611. TEL 312-337-1084. adv. illus.

380.1 US
MINORITY SUPPLIERS REPORT AND DIRECTORY; industrial reference guide. 1971. a. $65. Project Magazine Inc., Box 8214, Philadelphia, PA 19101. TEL 215-387-1600. Ed. Emory Washington. index. (looseleaf format)
Formerly: Minority Suppliers Directory.

338 US ISSN 0076-9584
MISSOURI DIRECTORY OF MANUFACTURING AND MINING. Variant title: Missouri Directory of Manufacturers and Mining Operations. 1947. a. $70. Informative Data Co., 3546 Watson Rd., St. Louis, MO 63139. Ed. Dennis Schutte. adv. circ. 10,000.

670 917 US
MISSOURI MANUFACTURERS DIRECTORY. a. $75. Manufacturer's News, Inc., 4 Huron St., Chicago, IL 60611.

380.1 US ISSN 0276-0959
MODERN'S MARKET GUIDE. 1966. a. $50. Vance Publishing Corporation, 400 Knightsbridge Parkway, Lincolnshire, IL 60069. TEL 312-634-2600. adv. circ. 6,418.

670 US
MONTANA MANUFACTURERS & PRODUCTS DIRECTORY. 1955. biennial. $5 per no. Department of Commerce, Business Assistance Division, Capitol Sta., Helena, MT 59620. TEL 406-444-3923. stat. circ. 2,000. (back issues avail.)
Formerly: Directory of Montana Manufacturers (ISSN 0544-8794)

MONTREAL PORT AND SHIPPING HANDBOOK (YEAR) see *TRANSPORTATION — Ships And Shipping*

MONTSERRAT. STATISTICS OFFICE. OVERSEAS TRADE REPORT. see *STATISTICS*

629.227 US
MOTORCYCLE PRODUCT NEWS TRADE DIRECTORY. 1973. a. Freed Crown Lee Publishing, Inc., Box 2338, 6931 Van Nuys Blvd., Van Nuys, CA 91405. adv. circ. 14,400.

338.8 US ISSN 0363-4426
MULTINATIONAL MARKETING & EMPLOYMENT DIRECTORY. 7th edt., 1977. irreg., 8th edt. 1982. $90. World Trade Academy Press, Inc., 50 E. 42nd St., New York, NY 10017. TEL 212-697-4999.
Formed by the Merger of: Angel's National Directory of Personnel Managers & Multinational Corporations Operating Overseas; National and International Employment Handbook for Specialized Personnel.

N A S A SOFTWARE DIRECTORY. see *COMPUTERS — Software*

380 US
N A S C O CAMPUS CO-OP DIRECTORY. 1974. biennial. $2.50. North American Students of Cooperation, Box 7715, Ann Arbor, MI 48107. TEL 313-663-0889. adv. circ. 5,000.
Formerly: Cooperatives in Campus Areas of North America.

380 SA
NATAL CHAMBER OF INDUSTRIES. YEARBOOK & DIRECTORY. 1926. a. R.10. Natal Chamber of Industries, Industries House, 1 Victoria Embankment, Box 1300, Durban 4000, South Africa. Ed. I. Doyle. adv. circ. 2,500.
Former titles: Natal Chamber of Industries. Annual Report; Natal Manufacturers Association. Annual Report.

NATIONAL ASSOCIATION OF WASTE DISPOSAL CONTRACTORS. TRADE DIRECTORY. see *PUBLIC HEALTH AND SAFETY*

671 US
NATIONAL COIL COATERS ASSOCIATION. PRODUCT CAPABILITY DIRECTORY. a. first issue free; bulk rates avail. National Coil Coaters Association, 1900 Arch St., Philadelphia, PA 19103. TEL 215-564-3484. (back issues avail.)

NATIONAL DIRECTORY OF MINORITY-OWNED BUSINESS FIRMS. see *BUSINESS AND ECONOMICS — Small Business*

320 US ISSN 0095-3113
NATIONAL DIRECTORY OF STATE AGENCIES.* biennial. $85.50. National Standards Association, 5160 River Rd., Bethesda, MD 20816. TEL 301-951-1316.

380.1 US
NATIONAL TRADE AND PROFESSIONAL ASSOCIATIONS OF THE UNITED STATES AND LABOR UNIONS. Abbreviated title: N T P A Directory. 1966. a. $50. Columbia Books Inc., 1350 New York Ave., Ste. 207, Washinton, DC 20005. TEL 202-737-3777. Ed. John Russell. circ. 7,800.
Former titles (1975-1981): National Trade and Professional Associations of the United States and Canada and Labor Unions (ISSN 0094-8284); Directory of National Trade and Professional Associations of the United States (ISSN 0070-5918); National Trade and Professional Associations of the United States and Labor Unions (ISSN 0090-5038)

380 US
NEW HAMPSHIRE MANUFACTURING DIRECTORY. biennial. $27.50. Tower Publishing Co., 34 Diamond St., Box 7720, Portland, ME 04112. TEL 207-774-9813.
Formerly: New Hampshire Marketing Directory (ISSN 0276-2110)

670 US
NEW JERSEY DIRECTORY OF MANUFACTURERS. 1979. a. $82.50. Commerce Register, Inc, 190 Godwin Ave., Midland Park, NJ 07432. TEL 201-445-3000. adv. circ. 3,000.

670 622 US
NEW MEXICO MANUFACTURING DIRECTORY (YEAR) 1955/56. biennial. $20. ‡ Economic Development & Tourism Department, Santa Fe, NM 87503. TEL 505-827-6217. Ed. Carol Selleck. circ. 2,000.
Former titles: New Mexico Directory of Manufacturing; Directory of New Mexico Manufacturing and Mining (ISSN 0070-5934)

338 387 UK ISSN 0266-0652
NEW SOUTH WALES PORTS HANDBOOK. 1985. a. £10. Charter Publications, Bank Chambers, Downham Market, Norfolk PE38 9BU, England. Ed. Gerry Cansdale. circ. 6,000.

670 US
NEW YORK METROPOLITAN DIRECTORY OF MANUFACTURERS. 1981. a. $82.50. Commerce Register, Inc., 190 Godwin Ave., Midland Park, NJ 07432. TEL 201-445-3000. adv.

NEW YORK STATE BUSINESS FACT BOOK. PART 1: BUSINESS AND MANUFACTURING. see *BUSINESS AND ECONOMICS — Economic Situation And Conditions*

NEW YORK STATE BUSINESS FACT BOOK. SUPPLEMENT. see *BUSINESS AND ECONOMICS — Economic Situation And Conditions*

670 US
NEW YORK UPSTATE DIRECTORY OF MANUFACTURERS. 1981. a. $52.50. Commerce Register Inc., 190 Godwin Ave., Midland Park, NJ 07432. TEL 201-445-3000. adv.

650 NZ ISSN 0077-9571
NEW ZEALAND BUSINESS WHO'S WHO. 1935. a. NZ.$70. (F E P Productions Ltd.) Fourth Estate Holdings Ltd., Box 9143, Wellington, New Zealand. Ed. S.E. Carnihan. adv. circ. 7,000.

381 NR ISSN 0078-0596
NIGERIA BUSINESS DIRECTORY.* 1967. a. 7 Coates St., Ebute-Metta, Lagos, Nigeria.

338.4 NR
NIGERIA INDUSTRIAL DIRECTORY. 1975. irreg. £N3.50. Manufacturers Association of Nigeria, 37, Marina, Box 3835, Lagos, Nigeria. adv. circ. 5,000.
Formerly: Maufacturers Association of Nigeria. Industrial Directory.

BUSINESS AND ECONOMICS — TRADE AND INDUSTRIAL DIRECTORIES

380.1 338 NO ISSN 0078-1215
NORGES HANDELS-KALENDER/NORWEGIAN DIRECTORY OF COMMERCE/ANNUAIRE DU COMMERCE DU NORVEGE/NORWEGISCHE HANDELS-ADRESSBUCH; adressbok for handel, handverk og industri. (Text in Norwegian; explanations and headings in English, French and German) 1878. a. Kr.400($80) S.M. Bryde Forlag A S, Sognsveien 70, 0855 Oslo 8, Norway (Dist. in U.S. by: International Publications Service, 114 E. 32nd St., New York, NY 10016) adv. circ. 8,000.

380 US
NORTH CAROLINA DIRECTORY OF TRADE AND PROFESSIONAL ASSOCIATIONS. 1976. biennial. $13 per no. University of North Carolina at Greensboro, Center for Applied Research, 301 B & E Bldgs., Greensboro, NC 27412. TEL 919-334-3088. Ed. Robert Norton.

338 US
NORTH CAROLINA METALWORKING DIRECTORY. 1975. triennial. $15. North Carolina State University, Industrial Extension Service, Box 7902, Raleigh, NC 27695-7902. TEL 919-737-2358. Ed. Robert L. Edwards. circ. 1,000.

670 US ISSN 0737-0989
NORTH JERSEY REGIONAL INDUSTRIAL PURCHASING GUIDE. 1976. a. $35. Thomas Regional Directory Co., Inc., 330 W. 34th St., New York, NY 10001. TEL 212-290-7390. Ed. Mary Caputo. adv.

660.029 US ISSN 0276-539X
O P D CHEMICAL BUYERS DIRECTORY. 1913. a. Schnell Publishing Co., Inc., 100 Church St., New York, NY 10007-2601. TEL 212-723-9820. circ. 16,000.
 Formerly: Chemical Buyers Directory.

338 387 UK ISSN 0268-6481
OAKLAND PORT AND SHIPPING HANDBOOK. 1985. a. £10. Charter Publications, Bank Chambers, Downham Market, Norfolk PE38 9BU, England. Ed. James Moriarty. circ. 6,000.

OCCUPATIONAL HEALTH & SAFETY PURCHASING SOURCEBOOK. see INDUSTRIAL HEALTH AND SAFETY

O'DWYER'S DIRECTORY OF PUBLIC RELATIONS FIRMS. see ADVERTISING AND PUBLIC RELATIONS

338 US
OFFICIAL INTERNATIONAL BUSINESS DIRECTORY OF THE LATIN AMERICAN WORLD. (Text in English, Portuguses, Spanish) 1982. a. $150 per m. Aurora International, Box 9099, Bridgeport, CT 06601-2099. TEL 203-368-0579. Ed. Andres C. Aquino. adv.
 Formerly: Official International Business Directory of the Spanish Speaking World (ISSN 0735-5513)

OFFICIAL VIDEO DIRECTORY & BUYER'S GUIDE. see COMMUNICATIONS — Radio And Television

OFFSHORE SERVICE VESSELS; guide to the American fleet. see TRANSPORTATION — Ships And Shipping

OFFSHORE TUGS; guide to the American fleet. see TRANSPORTATION — Ships And Shipping

670 US
OHIO DIRECTORY OF MANUFACTURERS. 1983. a. $82.50. Commerce Register, Inc., 190 Godwin Ave., Midland Park, NJ 07432. TEL 201-445-3000.

670 US ISSN 0737-7495
OHIO MANUFACTURERS DIRECTORY. a. $99. Manufacturers' News, Inc., 4 E. Huron St., Chicago, IL 60611. TEL 312-337-1084. adv. illus.

OIL & GAS DIRECTORY. see PETROLEUM AND GAS

OIL DIRECTORY OF CANADA. see PETROLEUM AND GAS

OIL DIRECTORY OF COMPANIES OUTSIDE THE U.S. AND CANADA. see PETROLEUM AND GAS

OIL DIRECTORY OF HOUSTON, TEXAS. see PETROLEUM AND GAS

338 US
OKLAHOMA DIRECTORY OF MANUFACTURERS AND PRODUCTS. Cover title: Oklahoma Directory of Manufacturers. 1957. biennial. $35. Department of Commerce, 6601 Broadway Extension, Oklahoma City, OK 73116. Ed. Russ Peoples. circ. 4,500.

380 UK
OVERSEAS TRADE DIRECTORIES; who's who, press guides, year books. 1947. irreg. £38($50) New Product Newsletter Co. Ltd., 1A Chesterfield St., London W.1., England. Ed. H.R. Vaughan. adv. circ. 5,000. (also avail. in microfilm from UMI)

OWEN'S BUSINESS DIRECTORY AND TRAVEL GUIDE. see BUSINESS AND ECONOMICS — International Commerce

P E M: PLANT ENGINEERING AND MAINTENANCE SOURCEBOOK. see BUSINESS AND ECONOMICS — Management

382 659 UK
P R PLANNER - EUROPE. 1974. a. £141. Media Publishing Ltd., Hale House, 290-296 Green Lanes, London N13 5TP, England. (looseleaf format)

382 659 UK
P R PLANNER - U.K. 1966. a. £125. Media Publishing Ltd., Hale House, 290-296 Green Lanes, London N13 5TP, England. (looseleaf format)

380.1 770 US
P T N MASTER BUYING GUIDE & DIRECTORY. (Photographic Trade News) 1938. a. $10. P T N Publishing Corp., 210 Crossways, Park Dr., Woodbury, NY 11797. TEL 516-496-8000. Ed. Harold Johnson. adv. illus. circ. 10,000.

380.1 US ISSN 0555-8581
PACIFIC SOUTHWEST DIRECTORY. 1951. a. $40 to non-members. California Grain & Feed Association, Box 161027, Sacramento, CA 95816-1000. Ed. Anne Downs. adv. circ. 1,200.
 Covers Arizona, California, Hawaii, Nevada and Utah

667.6 380.1 US ISSN 0090-5402
PAINT RED BOOK; directory of the paint and coatings industry. 1968. a. $36.95. Communication Channels, Inc., 6255 Barfield Rd., Atlanta, GA 30328. TEL 404-256-9800. Ed. Barbara Katinsky.

PANAMA HANDBOOK 1983. see TRANSPORTATION — Ships And Shipping

676 US
PAPER YEAR BOOK. 1943. a. $50. Harcourt Brace Jovanovich, Inc., 7500 Old Oak Blvd., Cleveland, OH 44130 TEL 216-243-8100. (Subscr. to: One E. First St., Duluth, MN 55802) Ed. Roy Wirtzfeld. adv. circ. 1,771. Indexed: Abstr.Bull.Inst.Pap.Chem.

338 387 UK ISSN 0267-7369
PENANG PORT HANDBOOK. 1985. a. £10. Charter Publications, Bank Chambers, Downham Market, Norfolk PE38 9BU, England. Ed. Gerry Cansdale. circ. 6,000.

670 US ISSN 0733-5237
PENNSYLVANIA DIRECTORY OF MANUFACTURERS. 1980? a. $82.50. Commerce Register, Inc., 190 Godwin Ave., Midland Park, NJ 07432. TEL 201-445-3000. adv.

917.402 US
PENNSYLVANIA MANUFACTURERS REGISTER. a. $99. Manufacturers' News, Inc., 4 E. Huron St., Chicago, IL 60611. TEL 312-337-1084. adv. illus.

PERINATOLOGY-NEONATOLOGY BUYERS GUIDE. see MEDICAL SCIENCES — Obstetrics And Gynecology

PERIOD BUILDING RESTORATION TRADES & SUPPLIERS DIRECTORY. see ARCHITECTURE

670 615.19 JA
PHARMACEUTICAL MANUFACTURERS OF JAPAN. 1981. biennial. $88. Yakugyo Jiho Co., Ltd., 2-36 Kanda Jimbo-cho, Chiyoda-ku, Tokyo 101, Japan.

338 PH
PHILIPPINES BUSINESS DIRECTORY. a. P.300($75) Philippines Business Directory, Box 3199, Manila, Philippines. adv.

PHILIPPINES YEARBOOK OF THE FOOKIEN TIMES. see BUSINESS AND ECONOMICS — Banking And Finance

338 US
PIPELINE AND UNDERGROUND UTILITIES CONSTRUCTION. ANNUAL DIRECTORY. 1952. a. $30. Oildom Publishing Co. of Texas, Inc, 3314 Mercer St., Houston, TX 77027. TEL 713-622-0676. Ed. Oliver Klinger. circ. 15,000.

338 US
PLACES: A DIRECTORY OF PUBLIC PLACES FOR PRIVATE EVENTS AND PRIVATE PLACES FOR PUBLIC FUNCTIONS. 1978. biennial. $18.95 per no. Tenth House Enterprises, Inc., Box 810, Gracie Sta., New York, NY 10028. TEL 212-737-7536. Eds. Hannelore Hahn, Tatiana Stoumen. circ. 10,000.

380.1 US
POOL & SPA NEWS DIRECTORY. 1968. a. $24.95. Leisure Publications, Inc., 3923 W. 6 St., Los Angeles, CA 90020. TEL 213-385-3926. Ed. J. Field. adv. circ. 10,000.
 Formerly: Pool News Directory (ISSN 0194-1380)

POOLE HANDBOOK. see TRANSPORTATION — Ships And Shipping

PORT KELANG SHIPPING HANDBOOK. see TRANSPORTATION — Ships And Shipping

PORT RASHID: DUBAI SHIPPING HANDBOOK. see TRANSPORTATION — Ships And Shipping

656.3 US
POST'S PULP & PAPER DIRECTORY. 1884. a. Miller Freeman Publications, Inc., 500 Howard St., San Francisco, CA 94105. TEL 415-397-1881. Ed. Vincent M. Ridley. (reprint service avail. from UMI)

PRINTWORLD DIRECTORY OF CONTEMPORARY PRINTS (YEAR) see ART

380.1 US
PRIVATE LABEL DIRECTORY. 1981. a. $20. E.W. Williams Publishing Co., 80 Eighth Ave., New York, NY 10011. TEL 212-989-1101. Ed. Olga Gudal. adv. bk. rev. circ. 4,008.

PROBE DIRECTORY OF FOREIGN DIRECT INVESTMENT IN THE UNITED STATES. see BUSINESS AND ECONOMICS — Investments

PROCESS ENGINEERING DIRECTORY. see ENGINEERING — Chemical Engineering

382 670 SP ISSN 0079-5836
PRODEI; catalogue of Spanish Manufacturers, Exporters and Importers. (Text and summaries in English, French, German, Spanish) 1945. biennial. $90. Capel Editorial Distribuidora, S.A., Almirante 21, Madrid 4, Spain. adv. circ. 10,000.

PRODUCER'S MASTERGUIDE; the international production manual for motion pictures, television, commercials, cable and videotape industries in the United States, Canada, the United Kingdom, Ireland, Bermuda and the Caribbean Islands. see MOTION PICTURES

670 US
PRODUCT DIRECTORY OF THE REFACTORIES INDUSTRY OF THE UNITED STATES. 1921. quadrennial. $40. Refactories Institute, 301 Fifth Ave., Ste. 1517, Pittsburgh, PA 15222. TEL 412-281-6787. Ed. Charles G. Marvin. circ. 1,500. (looseleaf format)

PROFESSIONAL AND INDUSTRIAL PHOTOGRAPHIC EQUIPMENT. see PHOTOGRAPHY

650 338 II ISSN 0079-5925
PROFESSIONAL AND TRADE ORGANISATIONS IN INDIA. 1963. irreg., latest 1987. Rs.50($25) Kothari Publications, 12 India Exchange Place, Calcutta 700001, India. Ed. H. Kothari. adv.

BUSINESS AND ECONOMICS — TRADE AND INDUSTRIAL DIRECTORIES

380   621.3   US
PROFESSIONAL ELECTRONICS YEARBOOK. 1970. a. $10. National Sales and Service Dealers Association, 2708 W. Berry, Ft. Worth, TX 76109. TEL 817-921-9061. Ed. Kurt Bauer. adv. tr.lit. circ. 5,000.

380.1   770   UK
PROFESSIONAL PHOTOGRAPHER DIRECTORY AND BUYER'S GUIDE. 1961. a. £1.50. Maclaren Publishers Ltd., Maclaren House, Scarbrook Rd., Croydon, Surrey CR9 1QH, England. Ed. David Warr. adv. bk. rev. circ. 7,718. (also avail. in microfilm)

380.1   659.1
PUBLIC RELATIONS SOCIETY OF AMERICA DIRECTORY. Variant title: Public Relations Journal Register Issue. (Published as 13th issue of Public Relations Journal) 1945. a. $75. Public Relations Society of America, Inc., 845 Third Ave., New York, NY 10022. TEL 212-826-1750. Ed. Michael Winkleman. adv. bibl. circ. 11,800. Indexed: B.P.I. P.A.I.S.
  Formerly: Public Relations Register.

070.5   US   ISSN 0000-0671
PUBLISHERS, DISTRIBUTORS AND WHOLESALERS OF THE UNITED STATES. 1979. a. $85. R.R. Bowker Company, Database Publishing Group, 245 W. 17th St., New York, NY 10011. TEL 800-521-8110.
●Also available online. Vendors: DIALOG.
  Formerly: Publishers and Distributors of the United States (ISSN 0000-0620)

338   PR   ISSN 0090-3612
PUERTO RICO OFFICIAL INDUSTRIAL DIRECTORY. 1966. a. $90. (Economic Development Administration) Whitney Marketing Inc., Apdo. 2631, Old San Juan, PR 00903. TEL 809-725-7373. Ed. Hugo Miranda. adv. stat.

PULP & PAPER BUYERS GUIDE. see *PAPER AND PULP*

650   FR   ISSN 0079-9270
QUI VEND ET ACHETE QUOI; annuaire industriel de Haute Normandie. 1970. a. 240 F. Chambre Regionale de Commerce et d'Industrie de Haute-Normandie, Palais des Consuls, Quai de la Bourse, Rouen, France. circ. 2,500.

382   SP
QUIEN VENDE EN ESPANA LOS PRODUCTOS EXTRANJEROS/WHO SELLS FOREIGN PRODUCTS IN SPAIN. 1966. biennial. 12000 ptas. Prointer-Ediciones, Puerta del Sol 11, Madrid, Spain.

R S V P: DIRECTORY OF CREATIVE TALENT. (Repondez S'il Vous Plait) see *ART*

338   SA
RAND - PRETORIA DIRECTORY. (Text in English) a. R.57. Intratex (Pty) Ltd., 10 Caversham Road, Pinetown 3600, South Africa. Ed. A. Stagg.

670   US
RECOGNITION AND IDENTIFICATION BLUE BOOK. 1976. a. $15. D & F Publications, Box 1230, Brighton, MI 48116-1830. Ed. James J. Farrell. adv.
  Formerly: National Trophy Industry Directory of Manufacturers and Suppliers.

332   364   UK   ISSN 0080-0538
REGENCY INTERNATIONAL DIRECTORY; of private investigators, process servers, private detectives & debt collecting agencies. 1967. a. $45. (Regency International Publications Ltd.) Regency International Publications Ltd., Newstone House, 127 Sandgate Rd., Folkestone, Kent CT20 2BL, England. Ed. Alan L. Valle. adv. circ. controlled.

338   BL
REGISTRO INDUSTRIAL BRASILEIRO. 1979. a. $120. Publicacoes Industriais Ltda., Rua Brigadeiro Tobias 356, 5 Andar, 01032 Sao Paulo SP, Brazil. Ed. Raul Gonzales Simon. adv. illus. circ. 10,000. (back issues avail.)

670   MX
REGISTRO INDUSTRIAL MEXICANO. 1986. a. $55. Reportero Industrial Mexicano, S.A., Goldsmith 38-301, 11560 Mexico, D.F., Mexico. Ed. Marcos Garay. circ. 16,000.

380   CN   ISSN 0704-7940
REPERTOIRE DES PRODUITS FABRIQUES AU QUEBEC. (Text in French, glossary in English and French) 1978. a. Can.$46.95. Centre de Recherche Industrielle du Quebec, Box 9038, 333 rue Franquet, Sainte-Foy, Que. G1V 4C7, Canada. TEL 418-659-1550. adv. circ. 6,500.

RETAIL DIRECTORY. see *BUSINESS AND ECONOMICS — Marketing And Purchasing*

381   UK
RETAIL TRADE DEVELOPMENTS IN GREAT BRITAIN. 1976. irreg. £42($83) (Cambridge Information & Research Services Ltd.) Gower Publishing Co. Ltd., Gower House, Croft Rd., Aldershot, Hants GU11 3HR, England.

670   US
RHODE ISLAND DIRECTORY OF MANUFACTURERS. a. $10. Department of Economic Development, 7 Jackson Walkway, Providence, RI 02903. TEL 401-277-2601. circ. 5,000.
  Formerly: Rhode Island Directory of Manufacturers and List of Commercial Establishments (ISSN 0080-2743)

001.535   US
ROBOTICS WORLD DIRECTORY. 1984. a. $39.95. Communication Channels, Inc., 6255 Barfield Rd., Atlanta, GA 30328. TEL 404-256-9800.

338   387   UK   ISSN 0268-702X
ROUEN PORT AND SHIPPING HANDBOOK. 1985. a. £10. Charter Publications, Bank Chambers, Downham Market, Norfolk PE38 9BU, England. Ed. John Ison. circ. 6,000.

670   CN   ISSN 0080-6536
SASKATCHEWAN MANUFACTURERS GUIDE.* 1971. biennial. controlled circulation. Government Printing Co., 2005 8th St., Regina, Sask. S4P 3V7, Canada. TEL 306-566-9393.
  Formerly: Saskatchewan Index. Manufacturers' Edition & Saskatchewan Trade Directory.

330   CN
SASKATCHEWAN TRADE DIRECTORY. 1986. a. Can.$25. Sanford Evans Communications Ltd., Directory Division, 1077 St. James St., Box 6900, Winnipeg, Man. R3C 3B1, Canada. TEL 204-775-0201. Ed. Bev Jolicoeur. adv. circ. 10,500.

380   US
SATELLITE DIRECTORY. a. Telecommunications Alert, 1 Park Ave., New York, NY 10016. TEL 212-683-3899.

380.1   US
SAUDI ARABIA TRADE DIRECTORY. a. $125. Inter-Crescent Publishing Co., Inc., 12021 Nieta Dr., Garden Grove, CA 92640. TEL 714-537-1000.

338   CN
SCOTT'S INDUSTRIAL DIRECTORIES - ATLANTIC. 1977. biennial. Can.$87.50. Scott's Directories (Subsidiary of: Southam Communications Ltd.) 75 Thomas St., Oakville, Ont. L6J 3A3, Canada. TEL 416-845-8881.

338   CN
SCOTT'S INDUSTRIAL DIRECTORIES - ONTARIO. 1957. every 18 mos. Can.$159.95. Scott's Directories (Subsidiary of: Southam Communications Ltd.) 75 Thomas St., Oakville, Ont. L6J 3A3, Canada. TEL 416-845-8881.

338   CN
SCOTT'S INDUSTRIAL DIRECTORIES - QUEBEC. 1963. every 18 mos. Can.$147.50. Scott's Directories (Subsidiary of: Southam Communications Ltd.) 75 Thomas St., Oakville, Ont. L6J 3A3, Canada. TEL 416-845-8881.

338   CN   ISSN 0317-879X
SCOTT'S INDUSTRIAL DIRECTORIES - WESTERN. Spine title: Scott's Western. 1969. every 20 mos. Can.$147.50. Scott's Directories (Subsidiary of: Southam Communications Ltd.) 75 Thomas St., Oakville, Ont. L6J 3A3, Canada. TEL 416-845-8881.
  Continues: Scott's Industrial Directory. Western Provinces (ISSN 0317-8781)

380   CN
SCOTT'S TRADE DIRECTORY OF METROPOLITAN TORONTO. 1980. every 20 mos. Can.$169.95. Scott's Directories (Subsidiary of: Southam Communications Ltd.) 75 Thomas St., Oakville, Ont. L6J 3A3, Canada. TEL 416-845-8881.
  Incorporating (as of 1983): Scott's Trade Directory of Toronto Vicinity.

338   PH
SECURITIES & EXCHANGE COMMISSION. BUSINESS DAY'S 1000 TOP CORPORATIONS IN THE PHILIPPINES. (Text in English) 1969. a. 400p.($67) (Securities & Exchange Commission) Businessday Corporation, 113 West Ave., Quezon City, Philippines. circ. 25,000.
  Formerly: S E C - B D Top 1000 Corporations in the Philippines.

380.1   US
SECURITY DEALER PRODUCT DIRECTORY AND REFERENCE GUIDE. 1982. a. $15. P T N Publishing Corp., 210 Crossway Park Dr., Woodbury, NY 11797. TEL 516-496-8000. Ed. Harold Johnson. adv. illus. circ. 15,000.

338   GW
SEIBT EXPORT DIRECTORY OF GERMAN INDUSTRIES. (Editions in English, French, German, Spanish) 1921. a. DM.110. Seibt Verlag GmbH, Pilgersheimer Str. 38, D-8000 Munich 90, West Germany. adv. circ. 13,000.

338   UK   ISSN 0261-1584
SELL'S DIRECTORY. 1885. a. £40. Sell's Publications Ltd., 55 High St., Epsom, Surrey KT19 8DW, England. adv. bk. rev. circ. 5,000.
  Former titles: Sell's Directory of Products & Services (ISSN 0080-8725); Sell's Directory of British Industry and Commerce.

380   UK
SELL'S SCOTTISH DIRECTORY. 1984. a. £30. Sell's Publications Ltd., 55 High St., Epsom, Surrey KT19 8DW, England. bk. rev. circ. 5,000.
  Formerly: Scottish National Register of Classified Trades (ISSN 0080-8148)

338   387   UK   ISSN 0267-2316
SHARJAH PORTS HANDBOOK. 1985. a. £10. Charter Publications, Bank Chambers, Downham Market, Norfolk PE38 9BU, England. Ed. James Moriarty. circ. 6,000.

380   387   IO
SHIPPING & PORTS DIRECTORY OF INDONESIA. (Text in English) 1977. biennial. $50. Yayasan Media Pembangunan, Jalan Majapahit 1, Box 2744-JKT., Jakarta, Indonesia. Ed. Safari Hoesin.

SHOE FACTORY BUYERS GUIDE; directory of suppliers to the shoe manufacturing industry. see *SHOES AND BOOTS*

380.1   US   ISSN 0037-4210
SHOPPING CENTER DIRECTORY. 1957. a. $285. National Research Bureau, Inc., 310 S. Michigan Ave., Chicago, IL 60604. TEL 312-663-5580. Ed. Nancy Veatch.

658.8   US   ISSN 0049-0393
SHOPPING CENTER WORLD PRODUCT AND SERVICE DIRECTORY. 1975. a. $24.95. Communication Channels, Inc., 6255 Barfield Rd., Atlanta, GA 30328. TEL 404-256-9800. Ed. Barbara Katinsky. circ. 26,500.
  Former titles: Shopping Center World Product Directory.

380   UK
SHOWDATES. (Supplement to: Showman's Directory) 1981. a. £10 includes copy of Showman's Directory. Stephen & Jean Lance Publications, Brook House, Mint St., Godalming, Surrey GU7 1HE, England. circ. 2,500.

380   UK
SHOWMAN'S DIRECTORY. (Supplement avail.: Showdates) 1968. a. £4. Stephen & Jean Lance Publications, Brook House, Mint St., Godalming, Surrey GU7 1HE, England. circ. 5,500.

BUSINESS AND ECONOMICS — TRADE AND INDUSTRIAL DIRECTORIES

338 UK
SIGN MAKERS AND SUPPLIERS YEAR BOOK AND DIRECTORY. 1971. a. £4.10. A. E. Morgan Publications Ltd., Stanley House, 9 West St., Epsom, Surrey KT18 7RL, England. adv. illus. index.

330 SI ISSN 0129-4423
SINGAPORE BUSINESS YEARBOOK. (Text in English) 1972. a. S.$8. Times Periodicals Private Ltd., 1 New Industrial Rd., Singapore 1953, Singapore. adv. circ. 12,000.
Formerly: Singapore Trade & Industry Yearbook.

382 SI
SINGAPORE INDIAN CHAMBER OF COMMERCE. ANNUAL REPORT & DIRECTORY. (Text in English) a. S.$35. Singapore Indian Chamber of Commerce, 101 Cecil Street, No. 23-01 Tong Eng Bldg.(0106), Singapore 9020, Singapore.
Formerly: Singapore Indian Chamber of Commerce. Directory.

SKANDINAVISKE SKIPSREDERIER/YEARBOOK OF SCANDINAVIAN SHIPOWNERS. see TRANSPORTATION — Ships And Shipping

338 PK
SMAR'S INDUSTRIAL DIRECTORY OF PAKISTAN. (Text in English) 1971. a. Rs.25($20) Smar International, 6 Afshan Chambers, Tariq Rd., P.E.C.H.S., Karachi 29, Pakistan. Ed. Mahmud-Ul-Hassan. adv. circ. 5,000.

SOUTH AFRICAN FREIGHT MANUAL. see TRANSPORTATION

SOUTH BUCKS & EAST BERKS CHAMBER OF COMMERCE & INDUSTRY DIRECTORY. see BUSINESS AND ECONOMICS — Chamber Of Commerce Publications

338 US ISSN 0094-2758
SOUTH DAKOTA MANUFACTURERS & PROCESSORS DIRECTORY. 1975. biennial. $24.50. (Bureau of Industrial and Agricultural Development) Manufacturers' News, Inc., 4 E. Huron St., Chicago, IL 60611. Key Title: Manufacturers & Processors Directory (Pierre)
Continues: Directory of South Dakota Manufacturers and Processors.

338 387 UK ISSN 0268-6511
SOUTHAMPTON PORT HANDBOOK. 1985. a. £10. Charter Publications, Bank Chambers, Downham Market, Norfolk PE38 9BU, England. Ed. John Ison. circ. 6,000.

380 011 JA
SOUTHEAST/EAST ASIAN ENGLISH PUBLICATIONS IN PRINT. (Text in English) 1986. triennial. 25.000 Yen($145) Japan Publications Guide Service, CPO Box 971, Tokyo 100-91, Japan. adv. circ. 1,000.

380.1 US ISSN 0093-3090
SOUTHERN CALIFORNIA BUSINESS DIRECTORY AND BUYERS GUIDE. 1969. a. $128. ‡ (Los Angeles Area Chamber of Commerce) Civic-Data Corp., 523 Superior Ave., Newport Beach, CA 92663. TEL 714-646-1623. Ed. Marie F. O'Hora. adv. illus. circ. 10,000.

380 690 US
SOUTHWEST BUILDERS AND CONTRACTORS DIRECTORY. a. Gulfstream Publishing Co., Inc., 300 S. Pine Island Rd., Ft. Lauderdale, FL 33324.

STAGE MANAGERS DIRECTORY. see THEATER

STANDARD DIRECTORY OF ADVERTISERS. see ADVERTISING AND PUBLIC RELATIONS

335 US
STANDARD DIRECTORY OF INTERNATIONAL ADVERTISERS AND ADVERTISING AGENCIES. 1984. a. $177. National Register Publishing Co., 3004 Glenview Rd., Wilmette, IL 60091. TEL 312-441-2212. Ed. Linda Peterson. adv.

STOWAGE AND SEGREGATION TO I M D G CODE. see TRANSPORTATION — Ships And Shipping

380.1 665.5 531.64 UK
STRATHCLYDE OIL REGISTER. 1980. a. (Strathclyde Regional Council) Thomas Telford Ltd., Telford House, Box 101, 26-34 Old St., London EC1P 1JH, England. Ed.Bd. circ. 15,000.

670 FI
SUOMEN TEOLLISUUSLIITTO. JASENLUETTELO/FINLANDS INDUSTRIFOERBUND. MEDLEMSFOERTECKNING/FEDERATION OF FINNISH INDUSTRIES. LIST OF MEMBERS. (Text in English, Finnish and Swedish) irreg. Suomen Teollisuusliitto, Etelaranta 10, PL 220, 00131 Helsinki 13, Finland.

SURPLUS DEALERS DIRECTORY. see BUSINESS AND ECONOMICS — Marketing And Purchasing

SYDNEY PORTS HANDBOOK (YEAR) see TRANSPORTATION — Ships And Shipping

678.2 668.4 FR ISSN 0224-2435
SYNDICAT GENERAL DES COMMERCES ET INDUSTRIES DU CAOUTCHOUC ET DES PLASTIQUES. GUIDE. 1978. biennial. 165 F. Syndicat General du Caoutchouc et des Plastiques, 1 Square la Bruyere, 75009 Paris, France. Ed. P. Mercier. circ. 3,000.

338 670 CH ISSN 0082-1470
TAIWAN BUYERS' GUIDE; alphabetical and classified lists of 12000 Taiwan manufacturers, importers, exporters and services. (Editions in Chinese and English) 1958. a. NT.$3,600($150) China Productivity Center, Box 769, Taipei, Taiwan, Republic of China. Ed. John C.C. Du. adv. bk. rev. circ. 20,000.

382 CH
TAIWAN TRADE DIRECTORY. (Text in Chinese and English) 1963. a. Importers & Exporters Association of Taipei, Box 598, Taipei 104, Taiwan, Republic of China.

338 670 TZ
TANZANIA. BUREAU OF STATISTICS. DIRECTORY OF INDUSTRIES. 1968 (not published 1972-1974) irreg., latest 1975. Bureau of Statistics, Box 796, Dar es Salaam, Tanzania (Orders to: Government Publications Agency, Box 1801, Dar es Salaam, Tanzania)

670 AT
TASMANIAN MANUFACTURERS DIRECTORY. 1978. irreg. Aus.$5. Tasmanian Development Authority, G.P.O. Box 646G, Hobart, Tas. 7001, Australia. circ. 2,500.

TEES AND HARTLEPOOL PORTS. see TRANSPORTATION — Ships And Shipping

384 US
TELECOM FACTBOOK (NEW YORK) a. Telecommunications Alert, 1 Park Ave., New York, NY 10016. TEL 212-683-3899.

TELECOMMUNICATIONS SYSTEMS AND SERVICES DIRECTORY; an international descriptive guide to approximately 2,000 telecommunications organizations, systems, and services. see COMMUNICATIONS

380 UK
TELEKOMPASS. 1969. a. £10. Kompass Publishers Ltd., Windsor Court, East Grinstead House, East Grinstead, West Sussex RH19 1XD, England.
Formerly: Dial Industry.

338 CN
TELEX GOLD PAGES; Canada's business communications directory. (Text in English and French) 1976. a. free to subscribers to Telex. C N C P Telcommunications, 3300 Bloor St. West, Room 903, Toronto, Ont. M8X 2W9, Canada. TEL 416-232-6507. Ed. J.S. Brown. circ. 50,000.

380 690 US
TEXAS BUILDERS AND CONTRACTORS DIRECTORY. a. Gulfstream Publishing Co., Inc., 300 S. Pine Island Rd., Ft. Lauderdale, FL 33324.

670 US ISSN 0743-1163
TEXAS MANUFACTURERS REGISTER. a. $114. Manufacturers' News, Inc., 4 E. Huron St., Chicago, IL 60611. TEL 312-337-1084. adv. illus.

650 US
TEXAS TRADE AND PROFESSIONAL ASSOCIATIONS AND OTHER SELECTED ORGANIZATIONS. 1951. biennial. $8.50. University of Texas at Austin, Bureau of Business Research, Box 7459, Austin, TX 78713. TEL 512-471-1616. Eds. Laurie Gamel, Rita J. Wright. circ. 1,750. (back issues avail.; reprint service avail. from UMI)
Formerly: Selected Trade and Professional Associations in Texas (ISSN 0080-8644)

338 677 SA
TEXINFORM; information index for the textile industry. (Text in English) 1971. biennial. R.65. Kenneth Rosenthal (Pty) Ltd., Ste. 304, Rosepark North, 8 Sturdee Ave., Rosebank 2196, South Africa (Subscr. to: Box 52665, Saxonwold 2132, Johannesburg, South Africa) Ed. Kenneth Rosenthal. bk. rev. cum.index. circ. 550. (back issues avail.)

380.1 TH ISSN 0563-3400
THAI CHAMBER OF COMMERCE. BUSINESS DIRECTORY. (Text in English) irreg. $13. Thai Chamber of Commerce., 150 Rajbopitre Rd., Bangkok, Thailand. Ed. Phensri Hiraniri. illus.

382 TH
THAI INDUSTRIAL DIRECTORY. (Text in English and Thai) 1970. a. Advertising and Media Consultants Ltd., 12th Floor, Silom Condominium, 52/38 Soi Saladaeng 2, Bangkok, Thailand. Ed. Satish Sehgal. adv. circ. 15,000.

380.1 II
THAPAR'S INDIAN INDUSTRIAL DIRECTORY AND IMPORT AND EXPORT DIRECTORY OF THE WORLD. (Text in English) a. $60. Thapar International Industrial Information Services, Giriraj Bldg., 1st Fl., Flat E, 11, Altamount Rd., Cumballa Hill, Bombay 400026, India. Ed. Yash Pal Thapar. adv. circ. 50,000.
Formerly: Calcutta Market.

THOMAS REGISTER OF AMERICAN MANUFACTURERS AND THOMAS REGISTER CATALOG FILE. see BUSINESS AND ECONOMICS — Marketing And Purchasing

381 IE ISSN 0082-4224
THOM'S COMMERCIAL DIRECTORY. 1844. a. $60. Thom's Directories Ltd., 38 Merrion Sq., Dublin 2, Ireland. Ed. J.L. Wootton, Sr.

380.1 674 UK ISSN 0082-4372
TIMBER TRADES DIRECTORY. 1890. irreg. £25. Benn Publications Ltd., 25 New Street Sq., London EC4A 3JA, England. Ed. John Topham. adv. index. circ. 2,000.
Classified lists of firms engaged in timber and allied trades throughout the world

959.5 SI ISSN 0217-6009
TIMES BUSINESS DIRECTORY OF SINGAPORE. (Text in English) a. S.$60. Times Periodicals Private Ltd., 1 New Industrial Rd., Singapore 1953, Singapore. adv. bk. rev. circ. 45,000.
Formerly: Straits Times Directory of Singapore; Supersedes in part: Straits Times Directory of Malaysia and Singapore (ISSN 0585-3931)

338 NR
TIMES TRADE AND INDUSTRIAL DIRECTORY. 1972. irreg. £N2.10. Daily Times of Nigeria Ltd., Box 139, Lagos, Nigeria. illus.

338 US
TOLL-FREE DIGEST. 1976. a. $17.95. Toll-Free Digest Co., Inc., Box 800, Claverack, NY 12513. Ed. Paul R. Montana.

670 US
TOOLING AND MANUFACTURING ASSOCIATION. PURCHASING GUIDE. biennial. Tooling and Manufacturing Association, 1177 S. Dee Rd., Park Ridge, IL 60068. TEL 312-825-1120. Ed. Bruce Braker. circ. 15,000.
Formerly: Tool and Die Institute Purchasing Guide.

670 US
TRADE AND PROFESSIONAL ASSOCIATIONS IN CALIFORNIA: A DIRECTORY. 1979. irreg., no.4, 1986. $40 to individuals; libraries $25. California Institute of Public Affairs, 226 W. Foothill Blvd., Box 10, Claremont, CA 91711. TEL 714-624-5212.

BUSINESS AND ECONOMICS — TRADE AND INDUSTRIAL DIRECTORIES

650   UK   ISSN 0082-5689
TRADE ASSOCIATIONS AND PROFESSIONAL BODIES OF THE UNITED KINGDOM. 1962. irreg., 6th edt. 1976. price varies. Pergamon Press, Ltd., Headington Hill Hall, Oxford OX3 0BW, England (U.S. subscr. to: Maxwell House, Fairview Park, Elmsford, NY 10523)

381   060   MM
TRADE DIRECTORY (1985-86) 1968. a. $6. Chamber of Commerce (Malta), The Exchange, Republic St., Valletta, Malta. Ed. Joseph G. Vassallo. adv. bk. rev. circ. 1,500.
    Former titles: Malta Chamber of Commerce. Trade Directory; Malta Trade Directory (ISSN 0076-3446); Malta Chamber of Commerce Classified Directory.

382   UK
TRADE DIRECTORY OF GUYANA. 1974. a. £1.75. Arthur H. Thrower Limited, 44-46 South Ealing Rd., London W.5, England.

382   UK
TRADE DIRECTORY OF PAPUA NEW GUINEA. a. £1.75. Arthur H. Thrower Limited, 44-46 South Ealing Rd., London W.5, England.

380.1   SE
TRADE DIRECTORY OF SEYCHELLES. 1976. a. $7.25. Express Transport Company Ltd., Box 239, Mahe, Seychelles. charts. illus. stat.

382   UK   ISSN 0082-5735
TRADE DIRECTORY OF THE REPUBLIC OF THE SUDAN. 1957/58. a. £2.50. Arthur H. Thrower Limited, 44-46 South Ealing Rd., London W.5, England. Ed. Arthur H. Thrower.

670   SI   ISSN 0129-9867
TRADELINK - S M A ANNUAL DIRECTORY (YEAR) (Text in English) 1960. a. S.$30($15) Singapore Manufacturers' Association, 02-18 World Trade Centre, Telok Blangah Rd., Singapore 0409, Singapore, Singapore. Ed. Catherine Chua. adv. circ. 7,000.
    Former titles: Singapore Manufacturers' Association Directory; Directory of Singpore Manufacturers (ISSN 0070-6337)

380   011   JA   ISSN 0285-3809
TRADESCOPE. (Text in English) 1981. w. free. Japan External Trade Organization, 2-2-5, Toranomon, Minato-Ku, Tokyo 105, Japan. Ed. Yasuhiro Tashiro. circ. 5,000.

380.1   910.09   US
TRADESHOW & EXHIBIT MANAGER BUYERS GUIDE. a. $45. Brentwood Publishing Corp. (Subsidiary of: Simon & Schuster, unit of Gulf & Western, Inc.) 1640 5th St., Santa Monica, CA 90401 TEL 213-395-0234. (Subscr. to: Box 2178, Santa Monica, CA 90406-2178) Ed. Kris Kyes. adv. tr.lit. circ. 13,000. (back issues avail.)

382.6   II   ISSN 0082-5824
TRADO; ASIAN-AFRICAN DIRECTORY OF EXPORTERS, IMPORTERS AND MANUFACTURERS. (Text in English) 1956. a. $115. Trado Publications Pvt. Ltd., C-6 Safdarjung Development Area, Community Center, New Delhi 110016, India. Ed. J.K. Chug. adv. index. circ. 10,000.

380.5   US   ISSN 0447-9181
TRANSPORTATION TELEPHONE TICKLER. (Published in a national edition in 4 vols. and 10 regional editions) 1950. a. $45 per set. Journal of Commerce, Inc., 110 Wall St., New York, NY 10005 TEL 201-859-1300. (Subscr. address.: Journal of Commerce, 445 Marshall St., Phillipsburg, NJ 08865) adv. index. circ. 60,000.

670   NZ
TRAVEL EXECUTIVES OF NEW ZEALAND. 1968. a. NZ.$9. Mercantile Gazette Marketing, Box 20-034, Christchurch 5, New Zealand. Ed. B.M. Stoop. adv.

675.058   US
TRAVELWARE RESOURCES DIRECTORY. a. $20. Business Journals Inc., 22 S. Smith St., Box 5550, Norwalk, CT 06855. TEL 203-853-6015. illus.
    Former titles: Luggage and Travelware Directory and Market Guide; Luggage and Travelware Directory; Luggage and Leather Goods Directory.

382   UK   ISSN 0082-657X
TRINIDAD AND TOBAGO TRADE DIRECTORY. 1963/64. a. Arthur H. Thrower Ltd., 44-46 South Ealing Rd., London W.5, England. Ed. Arthur H. Thrower. index.

TRY US; national minority business directory. see BUSINESS AND ECONOMICS

TURKEY PORT AND SHIPPING HANDBOOK 1984. see TRANSPORTATION — Ships And Shipping

670   UK   ISSN 0082-7142
U K TRADE NAMES; including imported items. 1966. biennial. £48. Kompass Publishers Ltd., Windsor Court, East Grinstead House, East Grinstead, West Sussex RH19 1XD, England. circ. 2,500.
●Also available online.

338   US
U S INDUSTRIAL DIRECTORY. (In 4 vols.) 1940. a. $114. Cahners Publishing Co., Inc., Manufacturing Group (Stamford), Division of Reed Publishing USA, 8 Stamford Forum, Box 12077, Stamford, CT 06904 TEL 203-328-2500. (Subscr. to: 44 Cook St., Denver, CO 80206) adv. circ. 38,000.

382   DK   ISSN 0532-1360
UDENRIGS HANDELSKALENDEREN FOR DANMARK/TRADE DIRECTORY FOR DENMARK/DAENISCHER HANDELSKALENDER/ANNUAIRE DE L'EXPORTATION DU DANEMARK/ANUARIO DE LA EXPORTACION DE DINAMARCA. (Text in Danish, English, French, German and Spanish) 1957. biennial. Udenrigshandelens Informationsbureau, Hellerupvej 78, 2900 Hellerup, Denmark. illus.

650   338   AT
UNIVERSAL BUSINESS DIRECTORIES, ADELAIDE BUSINESS AND STREET DIRECTORY. 1942. a. Aus.$20. Universal Press Pty.Ltd., 64 Talavera Rd., Macquarie Park, N.S.W. 2113, Australia. adv.
    Formerly: Universal Business Directories, Adelaide and South Australia Country Trade and Business Directory (ISSN 0083-3797)

650   338   AT
UNIVERSAL BUSINESS DIRECTORIES, BRISBANE AND SUBURBAN BUSINESS AND STREET DIRECTORY. 1934. a. Aus.$25. Universal Press Pty. Ltd., 64 Talavera Rd., Macquarie Park, N,S.W. 2113, Australia. adv.
    Formerly: Universal Business Directories, Brisbane and Suburban Business and Trade Directory (ISSN 0083-369X)

650   338   AT   ISSN 0083-3746
UNIVERSAL BUSINESS DIRECTORIES, MELBOURNE AND SUBURBAN BUSINESS AND TRADE DIRECTORY. 1948. a. Aus.$45. Universal Press Pty. Ltd., 64 Talavera Rd., Macquarie Park, N.S.W. 2113, Australia. adv.

650   338   AT   ISSN 0083-3789
UNIVERSAL BUSINESS DIRECTORIES, PERTH AND FREMANTLE AND SUBURBS BUSINESS AND TRADE DIRECTORY. 1960. a. Aus.$17. Universal Press Pty. Ltd., 64 Talavera Rd., Macquarie Park, N.S.W. 2113, Australia.

338   650   AT
UNIVERSAL BUSINESS DIRECTORIES, SYDNEY AND SUBURBAN BUSINESS AND STREET DIRECTORY. 1948. a. Aus.$50. Universal Press Pty. Ltd., 64 Talavera Rd., Macquarie Park, N.S.W. 2113, Australia. adv.
    Formerly: Universal Business Directories, Sydney and Suburban Business and Trade Directory (ISSN 0083-3819)

338   650   AT
UNIVERSAL BUSINESS DIRECTORIES, TASMANIA BUSINESS AND STREET DIRECTORY. 1950. a. Aus.$10. Universal Press Pty. Ltd., 64 Talavera Rd., Macquarie Park, N.S.W. 2113, Australia. adv.
    Formerly: Universal Business Directories, Tasmania Business and Trade Directory (ISSN 0083-3827)

650   338   AT   ISSN 0083-3843
UNIVERSAL BUSINESS DIRECTORIES WESTERN AUSTRALIA COUNTRY BUSINESS AND TRADE DIRECTORY. 1940. a. Aus.$19. Universal Press Pty. Ltd., 64 Talavera Rd., Macquarie Park, N.S.W. 2113, Australia.

670   US
UTAH DIRECTORY OF BUSINESS AND INDUSTRY. 1951. a. $17. Department of Employment Security, Division of Economic Development, 6150 State Office Bldg., Salt Lake City, UT 84114. TEL 801-533-5325. circ. 2,500.
    Formerly: Directory of Utah Manufacturers (ISSN 0070-6566)

VANCOUVER PORT HANDBOOK. see TRANSPORTATION — Ships And Shipping

670   US
VERMONT DIRECTORY OF MANUFACTURERS. biennial. Agency of Development and Community Affairs, Pavilion Office Bldg., Montpelier, VT 05602. TEL 802-828-3231. Ed. George A. Donovan. circ. 8,000.

380   US
VERMONT MANUFACTURING DIRECTORY. biennial. $17.50. Tower Publishing Co., 34 Diamond St., Box 7720, Portland, ME 04112. TEL 207-774-9813.
    Formerly: Vermont Marketing Directory.

971.3   CN   ISSN 0317-2961
VERNON'S CITY OF GUELPH (ONTARIO) DIRECTORY. a. Vernon Directories, Hamilton, Ont., Canada.

778.55   US   ISSN 0190-3705
VIDEO REGISTER. 1979. a. $54.50. Knowledge Industry Publications, Inc., 701 Westchester Ave., White Plains, NY 10604. Ed. Margaret Csenge. adv.

622   622   US
VIRGINIA INDUSTRIAL DIRECTORY. 1940. biennial. $50 to members; non-members $60. Virginia Chamber of Commerce, 9 S. Fifth St., Richmond, VA 23219. TEL 804-644-1607. Ed. John R. Broadway. circ. 5,000.
    Formerly: Directory of Virginia Manufacturing and Mining (ISSN 0070-6574)

338   387   UK   ISSN 0266-7274
VIRGINIA PORTS AND SHIPPING HANDBOOK. 1985. a. £5. Charter Publications, Bank Chambers, Downham Market, Norfolk PE38 9BU, England. Ed. James Moriarty. circ. 6,000.

380.1   US   ISSN 0882-7990
WARD'S BUSINESS DIRECTORY OF LARGEST U S COMPANIES; approximately 45,000 largest U S public and private companies. 1961. a. $360. Information Access Company, 11 Davis Dr., Belmont, CA 94002. TEL 415-591-2333. Ed. Elissa A. Leidy. (also avail. in magnetic tape; avail. on floppy disk)

338   US   ISSN 0882-8016
WARD'S BUSINESS DIRECTORY OF MAJOR INTERNATIONAL COMPANIES; 15,000 leading worldwide corporations. 1985. a. $360. Information Access Company, 11 Davis Dr., Belmont, CA 94002. TEL 415-591-2333. Ed. Elissa A. Leidy. circ. 3,000. (also avail. in magnetic tape; avail. on floppy disk)

380.1   US   ISSN 0882-8008
WARD'S BUSINESS DIRECTORY OF MAJOR U S PRIVATE COMPANIES; approximately 45,000 U S private companies and subsidiaries not publicly traded. 1984. a. $360. Information Access Company, 11 Davis Dr., Belmont, CA 94002. TEL 415-591-2333. Ed. Elissa A. Leidy. (also avail. in magnetic tape; avail. on floppy disk)

380   US   ISSN 0737-4445
WARD'S DIRECTORY OF 49,000 PRIVATE U.S. COMPANIES. a. $195. Information Access Company, 11 Davis Dr., Belmont, CA 94002 (Orders to: Baldwin H. Ward Directories, Data Dept., 929 Petaluma Blvd. N., Petaluma, CA 94952)

670 US ISSN 0148-5687
WASHINGTON MANUFACTURERS REGISTER. 1965. biennial. $70. (Department of Commerce and Economic Development, Trade Development Division) Times Mirror Press, 1115 S. Boyle, Box 23951, Los Angeles, CA 90023. TEL 213-265-6700. Ed. John G. Davis. adv. circ. 2,900.
Former titles: Directory of Washington Manufacturers (ISSN 0148-3641); Directory of Washington State Manufacturers, Products, Industry, Location (ISSN 0419-3857)

670 GW
WER LIEFERT WAS? 1949. a. DM.70. Bezugsquellennachweis fuer den Einkauf "Wer Liefert Was?" GmbH, Novmannenweg 18-20, 2000 Hamburg 26, W. Germany (B.R.D.) adv. circ. 34, 400.
●Also available online.

670 GW
WER UND WAS IN DER DEUTSCHEN SUESSWARENINDUSTRIE; Suesswaren-Jahrbuch. 1974. a. DM.109.12. B. Behr's GmbH & Co, Averhoffstr. 10, 2000 Hamburg 76, W. Germany (B.R.D.) circ. 1,500.

670 US
WEST VIRGINIA MANUFACTURERS REGISTER. 1987. biennial. $39. Manufacturers' News, Inc., 4 E. Huron St., Chicago, IL 60611.

380 AT ISSN 0816-2271
WESTERN AUSTRALIAN RESOURCE DEVELOPEMENT SERVICES DIRECTORY. 1983. a. free. Confederation of Western Australian Industry, P.O. Box 6209, Hay St. East, Perth, W.A. 6000, Australia. Ed. J.C. Lenzo. adv. circ. 2,000.

WHERE TO BUILD - WHERE TO REPAIR. see *TRANSPORTATION — Ships And Shipping*

WHERE TO BUY. see *BUSINESS AND ECONOMICS — Marketing And Purchasing*

659.1 US ISSN 0511-8794
WHITMARK DIRECTORY; source book of talent, production and audio visual in the Southwest. 1967/68. a. $90. Whitmark Associates, 4120 Main St., Ste. 100, Dallas, TX 75226-1143. TEL 214-826-9400. adv. circ. 2,500. (back issues avail.)

338 UK ISSN 0302-4091
WHO OWNS WHOM. AUSTRALASIA AND FAR EAST. (In 2 vols.) 1971. a. $190. Dun & Bradstreet Ltd., 26-32 Clifton St., London EC2P 1LY, England. index.
Formerly: Who Owns Whom. Australia and Japan International.

658 UK ISSN 0140-4040
WHO OWNS WHOM. UNITED KINGDOM AND REPUBLIC OF IRELAND. (In 2 vols.) 1958. a. $285. Dun & Bradstreet Ltd., 26-32 Clifton St., London EC2P 1LY, England. Ed. S. Lanyon. index.
●Also available online. Vendors: Pergamon Infoline.
Formerly: Who Owns Whom. United Kingdom (ISSN 0083-9329)

WHO'S WHO IN ARTS MANAGEMENT. see *ART*

920 621.38 US ISSN 0083-9507
WHO'S WHO IN ELECTRONICS. 1949. a. $98. Harris Publishing Co. (Twinsburg), 2057-2 Aurora Rd., Twinsburg, OH 44087. TEL 216-425-9000. Eds. Kathi Graeser, Lonetta Witt. adv. index. circ. 35,000.

621.3 001.6 621.381 US ISSN 0888-5931
WHO'S WHO IN ELECTRONICS & COMPUTER SCIENCE. 1979. biennial. $545. Research Publications, Inc. (Woodbridge), 12 Lunar Dr., Drawer AB, Wooodbridge, CT 06525. TEL 203-297-2600.

WIE ERREICHE ICH WEN? see *TRANSPORTATION — Ships And Shipping*

WIRE JOURNAL INTERNATIONAL DIRECTORY/CATALOG. see *ENGINEERING*

671.84 010 US
WIRE TECHNOLOGY BUYER'S GUIDE. 1975. a. $25. International Thomson Industrial Press, Inc., 6521 Davis Industrial Pkwy., Solon, OH 44139. TEL 216-248-1125. Ed. Donald B. Dobbins. adv. circ. 6,000.

670 US ISSN 0738-0070
WISCONSIN MANUFACTURERS REGISTER. a. $85. Manufacturers' News, Inc., 4 E. Huron St., Chicago, IL 60611. TEL 312-337-1084. adv. illus.

382 UK
WORLD DIRECTORY OF MULTINATIONAL ENTERPRISES. biennial. £135. Globe Book Services, Ltd., Brunel Rd., Houndmills, Basingstoke, Hants. RG21 2XS, England.

WORLD DIRECTORY OF PHARMACEUTICAL MANUFACTURERS. see *PHARMACY AND PHARMACOLOGY*

382 UK
WORLD TRADE INDEX. 1975. a. £27($50) Eagle Publishing Co., 63B Lansdowne Place, Hove, E. Sussex BN3 1FL, England. Ed. A.M. Allen. adv. (back issues avail.)

338 540 UK
WORLDWIDE CHEMICAL DIRECTORY. 1976. a. £65($62.40) Chemical Intelligence Services, 39A Bowling Green Lane, London EC1R 0BJ, England. circ. 5,868.

WORLDWIDE GOVERNMENT DIRECTORY. see *PUBLIC ADMINISTRATION*

677 620 II
WORRALL'S TEXTILE & ENGINEERING DIRECTORY. (Text in English) a. Rs.100. Commerce Publications Limited, NKM International House, 178 Backbay Reclamation, Bombay 400020, India. Ed. Vadilal Dagli.
Formerly: Textile & Engineering Directory for India & Pakistan.

YUGOSLAV EXPORT - IMPORT DIRECTORY. see *BUSINESS AND ECONOMICS — International Commerce*

916.89 ZA
ZAMBIA DIRECTORY. (Text in English) a. B & D Directories Ltd., Box 1659, Ndola, Zambia. adv.

CANCER

see *Medical Sciences—Cancer*

CARDIOVASCULAR DISEASES

see *Medical Sciences—Cardiovascular Diseases*

CARPENTRY AND WOODWORK

see *Building and Construction—Carpentry and Woodwork*

CERAMICS, GLASS AND POTTERY

see also Art

666 PL
AKADEMIA GORNICZO-HUTNICZA IM. STANISLAWA STASZICA. ZESZYTY NAUKOWE. CERAMIKA. (Text in English and Polish; summaries in English, Polish, Russian) 1956. irreg., vol.49, 1984. price varies. (Akademia Gorniczo-Hutnicza im. Stanislawa Staszica) Wydawnictwo A G H, Manifestu Lipcowego 16, 31-109 Krakow, Poland (Dist. by: Ars. Polona, Krakowskie Przedmiescie 7, 00-068 Warsaw, Poland) abstr. bibl.
Formerly: Akademia Gorniczo-Hutnicza im. Stanislawa Staszica. Instytut Ceramiki Specjalnej i Ogniotrwalej. Prace Naukowe (ISSN 0075-7012)

666 IT ISSN 0003-2891
ANDAR PER CERAMICHE. (Text in Italian; summaries in English, French and German) 1969. a. L.2500. Via C. Cavour 24, 42013 Casalgrande, Reggio Emilia, Italy. Ed. Mirko A. Montanari. adv. index. cum.index. circ. 8,000(controlled)
Ceramics

ANNUAL BOOK OF A S T M STANDARDS. VOLUME 15.01. REFRACTORIES, MANUFACTURED CARBON AND GRAPHITE PRODUCTS; ACTIVATED CARBON. see *ENGINEERING — Engineering Mechanics And Materials*

ANNUARIO ARTICOLI CASALINGHI E ARTICOLI REGALO. see *INTERIOR DESIGN AND DECORATION — Furniture And House Furnishings*

666 BL ISSN 0100-8633
ANNUARIO BRASILEIRO DE CERAMICA. 1978. a. $15. Associacao Brasileira de Ceramica, Caixa Postal 30327, 01000 Sao Paulo, Brazil.
Ceramics

666 IT ISSN 0066-4472
ANNUARIO CERAMICA. 1970. a. L.6000($20) Casa Editrice Palazzo Vecchio, Via Vittorio Emanuele, 155, 50134 Florence, Italy. adv.
Ceramics

ANNUARIO DEI FORNITORI. see *BUSINESS AND ECONOMICS — Trade And Industrial Directories*

ANNUARIO DELLE CERAMICHE ITALIANE PER L'EDILIZIA. see *BUSINESS AND ECONOMICS — Trade And Industrial Directories*

ARCHITECTS' GUIDE TO GLASS, METAL & GLAZING. see *ARCHITECTURE*

666 BE ISSN 0447-9823
ASSOCIATION INTERNATIONALE POUR L'HISTOIRE DU VERRE. BULLETIN. (Text in English, French and German) 1962. irreg. price varies. Association Internationale pour l'Histoire du Verre, c/o P.C. Ritsema Van Eck, Rijksmuseum, P.O. Box 50673, 1007 DD Amsterdam, Netherlands. bk. rev. circ. 200. Indexed: Br.Archaeol.Abstr.

666 UK ISSN 0144-2147
BRITISH CERAMIC RESEARCH. SPECIAL PUBLICATIONS. 1948. irreg. (2-3/yr.); no.115, 1986. British Ceramic Research Ltd., Queen's Rd., Penkhull, Stoke-on-Trent ST4 7LQ, England. bibl. charts. illus. circ. 1,000. Indexed: Chem.Abstr. GeoRef.
Ceramics

666 UK ISSN 0144-3631
BRITISH CERAMIC RESEARCH ASSOCIATION. TECHNICAL NOTES. 1960. irreg. (1-6/m.) no.355, 1983. British Ceramic Research Association Ltd., Queens Rd., Penkhull, Stoke-on-Trent ST4 7LQ, England. charts. illus.
Ceramics

666 UK ISSN 0524-5141
BRITISH CERAMIC SOCIETY. PROCEEDINGS. irreg. price varies. British Ceramic Society, Shelton House, Stoke Rd., Shelton, Stoke-on-Trent ST4 2DR, England. Indexed: Chem.Abstr. Sci.Abstr. Br.Ceram.Abstr.
Ceramics

666.1 UK ISSN 0068-2020
BRITISH GLASS INDUSTRY RESEARCH ASSOCIATION. ANNUAL REPORT. 1955. a. membership or exchange basis. British Glass Industry Research Association, Northumberland Rd., Sheffield S10 2UA, England. Ed. P.J. Doyle. circ. 1,000.
Glass

666 CN ISSN 0068-8444
CANADIAN CERAMIC SOCIETY. JOURNAL. 1928. a. Can.$25($27) Canadian Ceramic Society, 2175 Sheppard Ave. E., Ste. 110, Willowdale, Ont, Canada. TEL 416-469-4257. adv. circ. 800. Indexed: Chem.Abstr. Curr.Cont. Br.Ceram.Abstr.
Ceramics

CERAMICS, GLASS AND POTTERY — ABSTRACTING, BIBLIOGRAPHIES, STATISTICS

666   US   ISSN 0363-8642
CEMENTS RESEARCH PROGRESS. 1974. a. $20. American Ceramic Society, Inc., 65 Ceramic Dr., Columbus, OH 43214. TEL 614-268-8645. Ed. Dr. James Clifton, Dr. Paul Brown. cum.index: 1974-1983. (back issues avail.)

666   US
CERAMIC DATA BOOK. 1922. a. $15. Corcoran Communications, Inc., 6200 S.O.M. Center Rd., No. C14, Solon, OH 44139 TEL 216-349-3060. (Subscr. address: 270 St. Paul St., Denver, CO 80206) Ed. Pat Janeway. adv. charts. circ. 12,930.
Ceramics

666   US   ISSN 8756-8187
CERAMIC SOURCE. 1985. a. $25. American Ceramic Society, Inc., 65 Ceramic Dr., Columbus, OH 43214. TEL 614-268-8645. Ed. W.J. Smothers. adv. charts. illus. circ. 11,907.

666   US
CERAMICS: LATIN AMERICAN INDUSTRIAL REPORT. (Avail. for each of 22 Latin American countries) 1985. a. $435 per country report per industry covered. Aurora International, Box 9099, Bridgeport, CT 06601-2099. TEL 203-368-0579. Ed. Andres C. Aquino.

666   658.8   US   ISSN 0069-3677
CHINA GLASS AND TABLEWARE RED BOOK DIRECTORY. (13th issue of monthly magazine China Glass and Tableware) 1906. a. $10 per no. (included in subscr. to monthly) Ebel-Doctorow Publications, Inc., 1115 Clifton Ave, Clifton, NJ 07013. TEL 201-779-1600. Ed. Amy Stavis. adv. circ. 6,000.

666   FR   ISSN 0069-830X
CONFEDERATION DES INDUSTRIES CERAMIQUES DE FRANCE. ANNUAIRE. 1953/54. biennial. 186 F. Septima, 14 rue Falguiere, 75015 Paris, France. adv.
Ceramics

666   GW
DEUTSCHE KERAMIK. 1973. triennial. 32. Verlagsabteilung des Westerwaldvereins e.V., Peter-Altmeier-Platz 1, 5430 Montabaur, W. Germany (B.R.D.)

666   GW
DEUTSCHE KERAMISCHE GESELLSCHAFT. FACHAUSSCHUSSBERICHTE. 1953. irreg., no.24, 1985. DM.38 to members; non-members DM.76. Deutsche Keramische Gesellschaft e.V., Menzenberger Str. 47, Postfach 1226, 5340 Bad Honnef 1, W. Germany (B.R.D.) TEL 02224-71038. (Subscr. to: Bauverlag GmbH, Subscription Dept., P.O Box 14 60, D-6200 Wiesbaden.) Ed.Bd. Indexed: Chem.Abstr.
Ceramics

666.1   GW
DEUTSCHER GLASERKALENDER; Ratgeber und Helfer fuer Glaser und Fensterbauer. 1950. a. DM.11.80. Verlag Karl Hofmann, Steinwasenstr. 6-8, Postfach 1360, 7060 Schorndorf, W. Germany (B.R.D.) adv. stat. circ. 5,500.
Glass

666   GW
EHRENPREIS DEUTSCHE KERAMIK. 1983. irreg. DM.48. Verlagsabteilung des Westerwaldvereins e.V., Kreishaus, Peter-Altmeier-Platz 1, 5430 Montabaur, W. Germany (B.R.D.) Ed.Bd.

666   UK   ISSN 0071-0547
ENGLISH CERAMIC CIRCLE. TRANSACTIONS. 1927. a. price varies. ‡ English Ceramic Circle, c/o Mrs. J. Bennett, Secy., 5 The Drive, Beckenham, Kent BR3 1EE, England. Ed. John Howell. index every 3, 4, or 5 yrs. circ. 500. Indexed: Art & Archaeol.Tech.Abstr. Br.Ceram.Abstr. Br.Archaeol.Abstr. RILA.
Ceramics

666.1   UK   ISSN 0306-204X
EUROPEAN GLASS DIRECTORY AND BUYER'S GUIDE. 1970/71. a. £32. (Glass Manufacturers Federation) Fuel & Metallurgical Journals Ltd., Queensway House, 2 Queensway, Redhill, Surrey RH1 1QS, England. Ed. R. Sansom. adv.
Formerly: Glass Directory and Buyer's Guide.

GIFT AND DECORATIVE ACCESSORIES BUYERS DIRECTORY. see *GIFTWARE AND TOYS*

666.1   UK   ISSN 0260-6321
GLASS AND GLAZING NEWS. 1980. irreg. (6-8/yr.) free. Glass and Glazing Federation, 44-48 Borough High St., London SE1 1XB, England. TEL 01-403-7177. Ed. B.H.K. Hern. illus. circ. 25,000.

666   US
GLASS: LATIN AMERICAN INDUSTRIAL REPORT. (Avail. for each of 22 Latin American countries) 1985. a. $435 per country report per industry covered. Aurora International, Box 9099, Bridgeport, CT 06601-2099. TEL 203-368-0579. Ed. Andres C. Aquino.

666.1   NE   ISSN 0271-2938
GLASS SCIENCE AND TECHNOLOGY. 1977. irreg., vol.7, 1984. price varies. Elsevier Science Publishers B.V., Box 211, 1000 AE Amsterdam, Netherlands. Indexed: Chem.Abstr.
Glass

GUIA GENERAL DE LAS INDUSTRIAS AZULEJERAS Y AUXILIARES DE ESPANA. see *BUSINESS AND ECONOMICS — Trade And Industrial Directories*

INDEX TO REPRODUCTIONS IN ART PERIODICALS. see *ABSTRACTING AND INDEXING SERVICES*

666   FR   ISSN 0074-218X
INTERNATIONAL CERAMIC CONGRESS. PROCEEDINGS. (Proceedings published by host country) irreg., 13th, 1974, Amsterdam. European Ceramic Association, 44 rue Copernic, 75016 Paris, France.
Ceramics

666   UK
INTERNATIONAL CERAMIC DIRECTORY. 1984. quadrennial. £40. London and Sheffield Publishing Co. Ltd., 5 Pond St., Hampstead, London NW3 2PN, England.

666   669   US   ISSN 0147-300X
INTERNATIONAL GLASS/METAL CATALOG. 1958. a. $30. (Artlee Catalog, Inc.) Ashlee Publishing Co., Inc., 310 Madison Ave., New York, NY 10017. TEL 212-682-7681. Ed. Charles B. Cumpston. adv. circ. 11,000.
Former titles (until 1973): Glass/Metal Catalog (ISSN 0072-4645); Glass/Metal Directory.

666   382   UK
INTERNATIONAL REFRACTORIES HANDBOOK & DIRECTORY. 1976. quadrennial. £35. London and Sheffield Publishing Co. Ltd., 5 Pond St., Hampstead, London NW3 2PN, England.

LITTLE BLACK BOOK; annual directory of ceramic mold manufacturers in the United States. see *BUSINESS AND ECONOMICS — Trade And Industrial Directories*

666   UK   ISSN 0260-1869
MANPOWER: GLASS INDUSTRY. 1979. a. price varies. Ceramics Glass & Mineral Products Industry Training Board, Bovis House, Northolt Rd., Harrow, Middx. HA2 0EF, England.

666   913   GW   ISSN 0076-5171
MATERIALIEN ZUR ROEMISCH-GERMANISCHEN KERAMIK. 1914. irreg., no.10, 1985. price varies. (Deutsches Archaeologisches Institut, Roemisch-Germanische Kommission) Dr. Rudolf Habelt GmbH, Am Buchenhang 1, 5300 Bonn 1, W. Germany (B.R.D.)

666   PL   ISSN 0079-3264
POLSKA AKADEMIA NAUK. ODDZIAL W KRAKOWIE. KOMISJA CERAMICZNA. PRACE: CERAMIKA. (Text in English and Polish; summaries in English and Russian) 1964. irreg., no.34, 1984. price varies. Ossolineum, Publishing House of the Polish Academy of Sciences, Rynek 9, Wroclaw, Poland (Dist. by: Ars Polona-Ruch, Krakowskie Przedmiescie 7, Warsaw, Poland) Ed. Roman Pampuch. circ. 520. Indexed: Chem.Abstr. Eng.Ind.

666.7   US   ISSN 0080-049X
REFRACTORY MATERIALS; a series of monographs. 1965. irreg., vol.7, 1971. Academic Press Inc., Orlando, FL 32887. TEL 305-345-2000. Ed. John L. Margrave.

666.1   HU
SCIENTIFIC SOCIETY OF THE SILICATE INDUSTRY. CONFERENCE ON SILICATE INDUSTRY AND SILICATE SCIENCE. (Text in English, German, Hungarian, Russian) 1973. quadrennial. $64. OMIKK Technoinform, Muzeum u. 17, Budapest VIII, Hungary (Subscr. to: OMIKK-Technoinform, H-1428 Budapest, Pf.12, Hungary) Ed. Maria Palocz. (also avail. in microfiche)
Glass

666.3   UK   ISSN 0260-7972
SCOTTISH POTTERY STUDIES. 1982. irreg. £1.95. Scottish Pottery Society, c/o Graeme Cruickshank, 21 Warrender Park Terrace, Edinburgh, Scotland. circ. 1,000.

748   US
SOCIETY OF GLASS DECORATORS. SEMINAR PROCEEDINGS. 1964. a. $100 to non-members; members $25. Society of Glass & Ceramic Decorators, 207 Grant St., Port Jefferson, NY 11777. TEL 516-473-0232. Ed. Frank S. Child. circ. 300.
Formerly: Society of Glass Decorators. Papers Presented at Annual Seminar (ISSN 0081-1602)
Glass

666   UK   ISSN 0082-0954
SYMPOSIUM ON SPECIAL CERAMICS, STOKE-ON-TRENT, ENGLAND. SPECIAL CERAMICS, PROCEEDINGS. 1959. irreg., no.7, 1980. £25. Institute of Ceramics, Shelton House, Stoke Rd., Shelton, Stoke-on-Trent, England.
Ceramics

999.1   943   GW   ISSN 0170-3447
VEROEFFENTLICHUNGEN ZUR GESCHICHTE DES GLASES UND DER GLASHUETTER IN DEUTSCHLAND; Historische Topographie. irreg., vol.4, 1977. price varies. Franz Steiner Verlag Wiesbaden GmbH, Birkenwaldstr. 44, Postfach 347, D-7000 Stuttgart 1, W. Germany (B.R.D.) Ed. Axel von Saldern.

VJESNIK ZA ARHEOLOGIJU I HISTORIJU DALMATINSKU/BULLETIN D'ARCHEOLOGIE ET D'HISTOIRE DALMATES. see *ARCHAEOLOGY*

666   UK   ISSN 0511-4063
WEDGWOOD SOCIETY. PROCEEDINGS. 1956. biennial. price varies. Wedgwood Society, c/o Mrs. T.B. Jarvis, Roman Villa, Rockbourne, Fordingbridge, Hants. SP6 3PG, England. Ed. Alison Kelly. illus.

CERAMICS, GLASS AND POTTERY — Abstracting, Bibliographies, Statistics

666   016   UK   ISSN 0300-4570
BRITISH CERAMIC ABSTRACTS. 1958. m. £89. British Ceramic Research Ltd., Queens Rd., Penkhull, Stoke-on-Trent ST4 7LQ, England. index. circ. 1,000. Indexed: Br.Ceram.Abstr. Int.Packag.Abstr.

338.4   CN
CANADA. STATISTICS CANADA. GLASS AND GLASS PRODUCTS INDUSTRIES/INDUSTRIES DU VERRE ET D'ARTICLES EN VERRE. (Catalog 44-207) (Text in English and French) 1927. a. Can.$20($21) Statistics Canada, Communications Division, 3rd Floor, R.H. Coats Bldg., Ottawa, Ont. K1A 0T6, Canada TEL 613-993-7276. (Subscr. to: Publications Sales and Services, Ottawa, Ont. K1A 0T6, Canada) (also avail. in microform from MML)
Formerly: Canada. Statistics Canada. Glass and Glass Products Manufacturers/Fabricants de Verre et d'Articles en Verre (ISSN 0575-8661)

666   US   ISSN 0095-9960
CERAMIC ABSTRACTS. 1922. bi-m. $185 incl. subscr. to Bulletin and Journal. American Ceramic Society, Inc., 65 Ceramic Dr., Columbus, OH 43214. TEL 614-268-8645. Ed. W.J. Smothers. circ. 4,000. (also avail. in microform from UMI; reprint service avail. from UMI) Indexed: Br.Ceram.Abstr.
●Also available online. Vendors: Orbit Information Technologies, Pergamon Infoline.

CHAMBER OF COMMERCE PUBLICATIONS

see Business and Economics — Chamber of Commerce Publications

CHEMICAL ENGINEERING

see Engineering — Chemical Engineering

CHEMISTRY

see also Chemistry — Analytical Chemistry;
Chemistry — Crystallography;
Chemistry — Electrochemistry;
Chemistry — Inorganic Chemistry;
Chemistry — Organic Chemistry;
Chemistry — Physical Chemistry

540   US   ISSN 0065-7719
A C S MONOGRAPHS. 1924. irreg., no.185, 1986. American Chemical Society, 1155 16th St., N.W., Washington, DC 20036. TEL 202-872-8065. Ed. Marjorie Caserio. Indexed: Biol.Abstr. Chem.Abstr.

540   US   ISSN 0097-6156
A C S SYMPOSIUM SERIES. 1974. irreg., no.235, 1983. price varies. American Chemical Society, 1155 16th St. N.W., Washington, DC 20036. TEL 202-872-8065. Ed. M. Joan Comstock. (reprint service avail. from ISI) Indexed: Biol.Abstr. Chem.Abstr. Sci.Cit.Ind. ASCA. API Abstr. Dairy Sci.Abstr. Food.Sci.& Tech.Abstr. GeoRef. Ind.Sci.Rev. Sel.Water Res.Abstr. Weed Abstr.

540   HU   ISSN 0075-5397
A KEMIA UJABB EREDMENYEI. 1970. irreg., vol.64, 1986. price varies. (Magyar Tudomanyos Akademia) Akademiai Kiado, Publishing House of the Hungarian Academy of Sciences, P.O. Box 24, H-1363 Budapest, Hungary. Ed. Bela Csakvari.

540   CH   ISSN 0001-3927
ACADEMIA SINICA. INSTITUTE OF CHEMISTRY. BULLETIN. 1959. a. exchange basis. Academia Sinica, Institute of Chemistry, Taipei, Taiwan, Republic of China. Ed.Bd. charts. illus. circ. 1,000. Indexed: Chem.Abstr. Plant Breed.Abstr.

540   HU   ISSN 0231-3146
ACTA CHIMICA HUNGARICA. (Text in English) 1951. 6/yr. (in 1 vol., 6 nos./vol.) $102. (Magyar Tudomanyos Akademia) Akademiai Kiado, Publishing House of the Hungarian Academy of Sciences, P.O. Box 24, H-1363 Budapest, Hungary. Eds. F. Marta, Gy. Deak. adv. bk. rev. bibl. charts. illus. index. cum.index. (also avail. in microform from MIM) Indexed: Biol.Abstr. Chem.Abstr. Curr.Cont. Excerp.Med. Met.Abstr. Sci.Cit.Ind. ASCA. Biotech.Abstr. Curr.Chem.React. Food Sci.& Tech.Abstr. Helminthol.Abstr. Ind.Chem. Ind.Sci.Rev. Mass Spectr.Bull. World Alum.Abstr.
Formerly: Academia Scientiarum Hungarica. Acta Chimica (ISSN 0001-5407)

ACTA PHYSICA ET CHIMICA DEBRECINA. see PHYSICS

669 540   FI   ISSN 0001-6853
ACTA POLYTECHNICA SCANDINAVICA. CHEMICAL TECHNOLOGY AND METALLURGY. (Text and summaries in English) irreg. (4-5/yr.) Fmk.130. Teknillisten Tieteiden Akatemia - Finnish Academy of Technical Sciences, Kansakoulukatu 10 A, SF-00100 Helsinki 10, Finland. Ed. Seppo Palosaari. index. cum index: 1958-1985. circ. 250. (also avail. in microfilm from UMI; back issues avail.; reprint service avail. from UMI) Indexed: Chem.Abstr. Curr.Cont. Sci.Abstr.

540 370   PL
ACTA UNIVERSITATIS LODZIENSIS: FOLIA CHIMICA. (Text in Polish; summaries in various languages) irreg. Uniwersytet Lodzki, Drukarnia Wojskowa, Ul. Gdanska 130, Lodz, Poland (Dist. by: Ars Polona-Ruch, Krakowskie Przedmiescie 7, Warsaw, Poland) Indexed: Chem.Abstr.

ADHESIVES EURO-GUIDE. see BUSINESS AND ECONOMICS — Trade And Industrial Directories

540   US   ISSN 0065-2393
ADVANCES IN CHEMISTRY SERIES. 1950. irreg., no.205, 1984. price varies. American Chemical Society, 1155 16th St., N.W., Washington, DC 20036. TEL 202-872-8065. Ed. M. Joan Comstock. (reprint service avail. from ISI) Indexed: Biol.Abstr. Chem.Abstr. Excerp.Med. Nutr.Abstr. Sci.Cit.Ind. API Abstr. Dairy Sci.Abstr. Food Sci.& Tech.Abstr. Geo.Abstr. GeoRef. Ind.Sci.Rev.

540   UK
ADVANCES IN DYNAMIC STEREOCHEMISTRY. (Text in English) 1985. a. $40. Freund Publishing House, Ltd., Suite 500, Chesam House, 150 Regent St., London W1R 5FA, England. Ed. Marcel Gielen. adv. circ. 1,000.

ADVANCES IN INORGANIC CHEMISTRY AND RADIOCHEMISTRY. see CHEMISTRY — Inorganic Chemistry

541.28   US   ISSN 0065-3276
ADVANCES IN QUANTUM CHEMISTRY. 1964. irreg., vol.18, 1986. $89. Academic Press, Inc., Orlando, FL 32887. TEL 305-345-2000. Ed. Per-Olav Lowdin. index. Indexed: Chem.Abstr. Sci.Cit.Ind. Ind.Sci.Rev. Phys.Ber.

AGROCHEMICALS HANDBOOK. see AGRICULTURE

540   PL   ISSN 0860-1100
AKADEMIA GORNICZO-HUTNICZA IM. STANISLAWA STASZICA. ZESZYTY NAUKOWE. CHEMIA. (Text in English and Polish; summaries in English, Polish, Russian) 1985. irreg., no.3, 1987. price varies. (Akademia Gorniczo-Hutnicza im. Stanislawa Staszica) Wydawnictwo A G H, Manifestu Lipcowego 16, 31-109 Krakow, Poland (Dist. by: Ars Polona, Krakowskie Przedmiescie 7, 00-068 Warsaw, Poland) Ed. Z. Kleczek. illus. circ. 300.

AKADEMIA ROLNICZA, POZNAN. ROCZNIKI. FIZYKA, CHEMIA. see PHYSICS

ALMANAK NUKLIR BIOLOGI DAN KIMIA. see PHYSICS — Nuclear Energy

540   US   ISSN 0065-7727
AMERICAN CHEMICAL SOCIETY. ABSTRACTS OF PAPERS (AT THE NATIONAL MEETING) 1937. biennial. $32 to non-members; ACS members $24; division members $22. American Chemical Society, Distribution Office, 1155 16 St., N.W., Washington, DC 20036. TEL 202-872-8065. Ed. Evalyn Fuller. circ. 3,000. (processed) Indexed: Biol.Abstr. Biotech.Abstr. Dairy Sci.Abstr. Food Sci.& Tech.Abstr. Mass Spectr.Bull.

540   US   ISSN 0065-7735
AMERICAN CHEMICAL SOCIETY. ABSTRACTS OF PAPERS (AT THE REGIONAL MEETINGS) irreg. American Chemical Society, Regional Meetings Office, 1155 16 St., N.W., Washington, DC 20036. TEL 202-872-8065. circ. controlled. (processed) Indexed: Nutr.Abstr. Mass Spectr.Bull.

AMERICAN CHEMICAL SOCIETY. DIRECTORY OF GRADUATE RESEARCH. see EDUCATION — Guides To Schools And Colleges

540   US
AMERICAN INSTITUTE OF CHEMISTS. PROFESSIONAL DIRECTORY. 1981. a. $35. American Institute of Chemists, Inc., 7315 Wisconsin Ave., Bethesda, MD 20814. TEL 301-652-2447. Ed. David A.H. Roethel. adv. circ. 6,000.
Formerly: American Institute of Chemists. Membership Directory (ISSN 0084-6376)

542   US
ANLEITUNG FUER DIE CHEMISCHE LABORATORIUMSPRAXIS/CHEMICAL LABORATORY PRACTICE. 1970. irreg., vol.21, 1984. price varies. Springer-Verlag, 175 Fifth Ave., New York, NY 10010 TEL 212-460-1500. (Also Berlin, Heidelberg, Tokyo and Vienna) Ed. H. Mayer-Kaupp. (reprint service avail. from ISI)
Formerly: Anleitung fuer die Chemische Laboratoriumspraxis (ISSN 0066-1910)

540   FI   ISSN 0066-1961
ANNALES ACADEMIAE SCIENTIARUM FENNICAE. SERIES A, II: CHEMICA. (Text in English, French, German) 1942. irreg. price varies. Suomalainen Tiedeakatemia - Academia Scientiarum Fennica, Snellmanink. 9-11, 00170 Helsinki, Finland. Ed. Jouko Koskikallio. circ. 525. (also avail. in microform; back issues avail.) Indexed: Biol.Abstr. Bull.Signal. Chem.Abstr. Excerp.Med. Ind.Med. Ref.Zh. Sci.Abstr. Anal.Abstr. Bibl.Agri. GeoRef. Hort.Abstr. Phys.Abstr.

540   PL   ISSN 0137-6853
ANNALES UNIVERSITATIS MARIAE CURIE-SKLODOWSKA. SECTIO AA. CHEMIA. (Text in English, French, Polish; summaries in English, Polish and Russian) 1946. a. price varies. Uniwersytet Marii Curie-Sklodowskiej, Plac Marii Curie-Sklodowskiej 5, 20-031 Lublin, Poland. Ed. Kazimierz Sykut. circ. 550. Indexed: Chem.Abstr.

ANNUAL BULLETIN OF TRADE IN CHEMICAL PRODUCTS. see BUSINESS AND ECONOMICS — Production Of Goods And Services

660.2   US   ISSN 0140-9115
ANNUAL REPORTS ON FERMENTATION PROCESSES. 1977. a. $42.50. Academic Press, Inc., Orlando, FL 32887. TEL 305-345-2000. Ed. D. Perlman. Indexed: Chem.Abstr.

ANNUAL REVIEW OF THE CHEMICAL INDUSTRY. see BUSINESS AND ECONOMICS — Production Of Goods And Services

ARCHEIA TES PHARMAKEUTIKES (ATHENS) see PHARMACY AND PHARMACOLOGY

ASSOCIATION OF ISLAND MARINE LABORATORIES OF THE CARIBBEAN. PROCEEDINGS. see BIOLOGY

540   US
BAKER SERIES IN CHEMISTRY. irreg. price varies. Cornell University Press, 124 Roberts Place, Ithaca, NY 14850. TEL 607-257-7000.

540   GW   ISSN 0301-0457
BEHRING INSTITUTE MITTEILUNGEN; Behring Institute Research Communications. (Text in English and Russian; summaries in English and German) 1907. irreg. (2-3/yr.) price varies. Medizinische Verlagsgesellschaft mbH, P.O. Box 17 32, 3550 Marburg 1, W. Germany (B.R.D.) TEL 06421-24044. Eds. F.R. Seiler, H.G. Schwick. circ. 4,000. (back issues avail.) Indexed: Chem.Abstr. Excerp.Med. Ind.Med.

540   US
BENCHMARK PAPERS IN POLYMER CHEMISTRY. (Each vol. has distinctive title) 1978. irreg. Van Nostrand Reinhold Company, 7625 Empire Dr., Florence, KY 41042. TEL 606-525-6600. illus. index.

540 660   II   ISSN 0067-9925
BOMBAY TECHNOLOGIST. (Text in English) 1951. a. Rs.4.($0.50) approx. Technological Association, University of Bombay, Department of Chemical Technology, Matunga, Bombay 19, India. Indexed: Biol.Abstr. Chem.Abstr.

BRAGANTIA. see AGRICULTURE

BRITISH CHEMICAL INDUSTRY. see BUSINESS AND ECONOMICS — Trade And Industrial Directories

540   CN
C P I PRODUCT PROFILES. a. Can.$70. Corpus Information Service, Division of Southam Communications Ltd., 1450 Don Mills Road, Don Mills, Ont. M3B 2X7, Canada. TEL 416-445-6641. Ed. Mary Mancini.

540   UK
CAMBRIDGE TEXTS IN CHEMISTRY AND BIOCHEMISTRY. irreg. price varies. Cambridge University Press, Edinburgh Bldg., Shaftesbury Rd., Cambridge CB2 2RU, England (And 32 E. 57th St., New York NY 10022) Ed.Bd.
Formerly: Cambridge Chemistry Texts.

540 CN
CANADIAN CHEMICAL INDUSTRY: A CORPUS SURVEY. irreg. Can.$225. Corpus Information Services, Division of Southam Communications Ltd., 1450 Don Mills Road, Don Mills, Ont. M3B 2X7, Canada. TEL 416-445-6641. Ed. Mary Mancini.

540 US
CARBON DIOXIDE REVIEW. a. Oxford University Press, 200 Madison Ave., New York, NY 10016 TEL 212-679-7300. (And Ely House, 37 Dover St., London W1X 4AH, England) Ed. William C. Clark.

660 US
CATALYSIS: SCIENCE AND TECHNOLOGY. 1981. irreg., vol.8, 1987. Springer-Verlag, 175 Fifth Ave., New York, NY 10010 TEL 212-460-1500. (Also Berlin, Heidelberg, Tokyo and Vienna) Eds. J.R. Anderson, M. Boudart. (reprint service avail. from ISI)

CHEM SOURCES - U.S.A. see BUSINESS AND ECONOMICS — Trade And Industrial Directories

540 US
CHEMCYCLOPEDIA. 1982. a. American Chemical Society, 1155 16th St., N.W., Washington, DC 20036. TEL 202-872-4600. Ed. Joseph Kuney. adv. circ. 61,906.

540 UK
CHEMFACTS: BELGIUM. 1977. irreg. £45. Chemical Intelligence Services, 39A Bowling Green Lane, London EC1R 0BJ, England.

540 UK
CHEMFACTS: CANADA. 1982. a. £65. Chemical Intelligence Services, 39A Bowling Green Lane, London EC1R 0BJ, England.

540 UK
CHEMFACTS: FEDERAL REPUBLIC OF GERMANY. 1976. biennial. £60. Chemical Intelligence Services, 39A Bowling Green Lane, London EC1R 0BJ, England.

540 UK
CHEMFACTS: FRANCE. 1978. irreg. £40. Chemical Intelligence Services, 39A Bowling Green Lane, London EC1R 0BJ, England.

540 UK
CHEMFACTS: ITALY. 1979. irreg. £40. Chemical Intelligence Services, 39A Bowling Green Lane, London EC1R 0BJ, England.

540 UK
CHEMFACTS: JAPAN. 1982. irreg. £70. Chemical Intelligence Services, 39A Bowling Green Lane, London EC1R 0BJ, England.

540 UK
CHEMFACTS: NETHERLANDS. 1978. biennial. £45. Chemical Intelligence Services, 39A Bowling Green Lane, London EC1R 0BJ, England.

540 UK
CHEMFACTS: SPAIN. 1978. a. £60. Chemical Intelligence Services, 39A Bowling Green Lane, London EC1R 0BJ, England.

540 UK
CHEMFACTS: UNITED KINGDOM. 1977. irreg. £60. Chemical Intelligence Serivices, 39A Bowling Green Lane, London EC1R 0BJ, England.

540 PL ISSN 0554-8241
CHEMIA. (Text in Polish; summaries in English) 1960. irreg. Adam Mickiewicz University Press, Marchlewskiego 128, 61-874 Poznan, Poland.
Formerly: Uniwersytet im. Adama Mickiewicza w Poznaniu. Wydzial Matematyki, Fizyki i Chemii. Seria Chemia.

540 UK
CHEMICAL COMPANY PROFILES: THE AMERICAS. 1978. a. £55. Chemical Intelligence Serivices, 39A Bowling Green Lane, London EC1R 0BJ, England.
Formerly: Chemical Industry of Americas.

540 US ISSN 0094-6249
CHEMICAL REFERENCE MANUAL. 1973. irreg. Em Science, 480 Democrat Rd., Gibbstown, NJ 08027. TEL 609-423-6300. adv. illus. circ. 100,000.

CHEMICAL REGULATION REPORTER; a weekly review of activity affecting chemical users and manufacturers. see ENVIRONMENTAL STUDIES

540 UK
CHEMICALS. (Text in English; introduction in French, German, Spanish) 1920. biennial. £8. ‡ Chemical Industries Association Ltd., Alembic House, 93 Albert Embankment, London SE1 7TU, England. Ed. E. Wilson. circ. 13,000.
Formerly: British Chemicals and Their Manufacturers.

CHEMICALS AND ALLIED PRODUCTS EXPORT PROMOTION COUNCIL. EXPORTERS DIRECTORY. see BUSINESS AND ECONOMICS — International Commerce

540 US
CHEMICALS: LATIN AMERICAN INDUSTRIAL REPORT. (Avail. for each of 22 Latin American countries) 1985. a. $435 per country report per country covered. Aurora International, Box 9099, Bridgeport, CT 06601-2099. TEL 203-368-0579. Ed. Andres C. Aquino.

540 AT
CHEMIST CATALOGUE. a. Aus.$150. Permail Pty. Ltd., P.O. Box 56, Artarmon, N.S.W. 2064, Australia.

540 615.19 US
CHEMISTRY AND PHARMACOLOGY OF DRUGS. 1982. irreg., latest 1986. John Wiley & Sons, Inc., 605 Third Ave., New York, NY 10158. Ed. Daniel Lednicer. Indexed: Chem.Abstr.

540 US ISSN 0069-3146
CHEMISTRY OF FUNCTIONAL GROUPS. 1965. irreg., unnumbered, latest 1986. price varies. John Wiley & Sons, Inc., 605 Third Ave., New York, NY 10016. TEL 212-850-6000. Ed. Saul Patai.

540 581 US
CHEMISTRY OF PLANT PROTECTION. 1986. irreg. price varies. Springer-Verlag, 175 Fifth Ave., New York, NY 10160 TEL 212-460-1500. (Also Berlin, Heidelberg, Tokyo, Vienna) (reprint service avail. from ISI)

540 920 NE
CHEMISTS AND CHEMISTRY. 1984. irreg. price varies. D. Reidel Publishing Company, Box 17, 3300 AA Dordrecht, Netherlands.

540 GE ISSN 0138-4074
COMMON NAME - KARTEI PFLANZENSCHUTZ- UND SCHAEDLINGSBEKAEMPFUNGSMITTEL. 1966. a. M.7. V E B Fahlberg-List, Direktion Forschung, Informationsstelle, Alt Salbke 60-63, DDR-3013 Magdeburg-SO, E. Germany (D.D.R.)

540 US
CONCEPTS IN CHEMISTRY. irreg. price varies. Houghton Mifflin Co., One Beacon St., Boston, MA 02107. TEL 617-725-5000.

540 CS
CONFERENCE ON COORDINATION CHEMISTRY PROCEEDINGS. irreg., 6th, 1976, Bratislava. price varies. Slovenska Vysoka Skola Technicka, Janska 1, 812 37 Bratislava, Czechoslovakia. Indexed: Chem.Abstr.

541.224 UK ISSN 0069-9845
COORDINATION CHEMISTRY. (Text in English; occasionally in French or German) 1968, 9th. irreg., 15th 1973, Moscow; 16th 1974, Dublin. price varies. International Union of Pure and Applied Chemistry, c/o Dr. M. Williams, Bank Court Chambers, 2-3 Pound Way, Cowley Centre, Oxford OX4 3YF, England.

540 630 615.19 UK ISSN 0263-5917
CRITICAL REPORTS ON APPLIED CHEMISTRY. 1980. irreg. (approx. a.) price varies. (Society of Chemical Industry) Blackwell Scientific Publications Ltd., Osney Mead, Oxford OX2 OEL, England. (back issues avail.)

540 US
CURRENT CHEMICAL CONCEPTS. 1969. irreg., vol.5, 1970. price varies. Academic Press, Inc., Orlando, FL 32887. TEL 305-345-2000. Ed. Louis Meites.

540 615.9 US ISSN 0275-2581
CURRENT TOPICS IN ENVIRONMENTAL AND TOXICOLOGICAL CHEMISTRY. 1981. a., latest vol.3, 1985. price varies. Gordon and Breach Science Publishers, 50 W. 23rd St., New York, NY 10010. TEL 212-206-8900.

CUSTOM CHEMICAL SYNTHESIS SERVICES IN FRANCE. see BUSINESS AND ECONOMICS — Trade And Industrial Directories

CUSTOM CHEMICAL SYNTHESIS SERVICES IN THE U.K. see BUSINESS AND ECONOMICS — Trade And Industrial Directories

CUSTOM CHEMICAL SYNTHESIS SERVICES IN WEST GERMANY. see BUSINESS AND ECONOMICS — Trade And Industrial Directories

DAHLEM WORKSHOP REPORTS. PHYSICAL AND CHEMICAL SCIENCES RESEARCH REPORT. see PHYSICS

DICCIONARIO AGROQUIMICO. see AGRICULTURE

660 US ISSN 0012-3277
DIRECTORY OF CHEMICAL PRODUCERS-U.S.A. 1961. a. (with s-a. supplements) S R I International, Chemical Industries Centers, Chemical Marketing Research Center, Menlo Park, CA 94025. TEL 415-859-3627. Ed. J. Hardy. charts. stat.

660 US
DIRECTORY OF CHEMICAL PRODUCERS- WESTERN EUROPE. 1978. a. (with s-a. supplements) S R I International, Chemical Industries Centers, Chemical Marketing Research Center, Menlo Park, CA 94025. TEL 415-859-3627. Ed. J. Hardy. charts. stat.

DIRECTORY OF WORLD CHEMICAL PRODUCERS. see BUSINESS AND ECONOMICS — Trade And Industrial Directories

DISTRICT MEMOIR. see EARTH SCIENCES — Geology

540 530 BL ISSN 0100-4670
ECLETICA QUIMICA; serie quimica. (Text in Portuguese; summaries in English and Portuguese) 1976. a. $30 or exchange basis. Universidade Estadual Paulista, Av. Vicente Ferreira 1278, Caixa Postal 603, 17.500 Marilia SP, Brazil. Ed.Bd. bibl. charts. circ. 1,000. Indexed: Biol.Abstr. Chem Abstr. Anal.Abstr.

614.7 UK ISSN 0305-7712
ENVIRONMENTAL CHEMISTRY. 1975. irreg. price varies. Royal Society of Chemistry, Burlington House, London W1V 0BN, England (Subscr. to: Distribution Centre, Blackhorse Rd., Letchworth, Herts. SG6 1HN, England) Ed. H.J. Bowen. charts. illus. index. Indexed: Chem.Abstr. GeoRef.

540 US ISSN 0071-1373
ESSAYS IN CHEMISTRY. 1970. a. $25. Academic Press Inc., Orlando, FL 32887. TEL 305-345-2000. Ed.Bd.

EUROPEAN DIRECTORY OF AGROCHEMICAL PRODUCTS. see AGRICULTURE

541.2 US ISSN 0093-1713
EXCITED STATES. 1973. irreg, vol 6, 1982. Academic Press, Inc., Orlando, FL 32887. TEL 305-345-2000. Ed. E.L. Lim. illus. Indexed: Chem.Abstr. Sci.Cit.Ind. Ind.Sci.Rev.

F A C E N A. (Facultad de Ciencias Exactas y Naturales y Agrimensura) see BIOGRAPHY

540 CS
FOLIA FACULTATIS SCIENTIARUM NATURALIUM UNIVERSITATIS PURKYNIANAE BRUNENSIS: CHEMIA. irreg. (7-12/yr.) price varies. Universita J. E. Purkyne, Prirodovedecka Fakulta, Kotlarska 2, 611 37 Brno, Czechoslovakia. Indexed: Biol.Abstr.

FOREST PEST MANAGEMENT INSTITUTE PROGRAM REVIEW. see BIOLOGY

CHEMISTRY

540 660   YU   ISSN 0367-4444
GLASNIK HEMICARA I TEHNOLOGA BOSNE I HERCEGOVINE. (Subseries of: Documenta Chemica Yugoslavica) irreg. 100 din. Akademija Nauka i Umjetnosti Bosne i Hercegovine, Hemijski Institut, Vojvode Putnika 43, Sarajevo, Yugoslavia. Ed. Franjo Krleza. Indexed: Chem.Abstr.

540   UK   ISSN 0072-6524
GREAT BRITAIN. LABORATORY OF THE GOVERNMENT CHEMIST. ANNUAL REPORT OF THE GOVERNMENT CHEMIST. 1959. a. price varies. H.M.S.O., P.O.B. 569, London SE1 9NH, England. (reprint service avail. from UMI)

540   FR
GUIDE DE LA CHIMIE INTERNATIONAL. a. 490 F. S.E.P Edition, 194-196 rue Marcadet, 75018 Paris, France. Ed. Robert Frappa.

GUIDE TO FLUORESCENCE LITERATURE. see *PHYSICS*

540 614.7   US
HANDBOOK OF ENVIRONMENTAL CHEMISTRY. 1980. irreg., vol.4, part A, 1986. Springer-Verlag, 175 Fifth Ave., New York, NY 10010. TEL 212-460-1500. (reprint service avail. from ISI)

540   GW   ISSN 0720-941X
HENKEL REFERATE; Veroeffentlichungen aus der Henkel-Forschung. English edition: Henkel Referate (ISSN 0720-9428) 1964. a. free. Henkel KGaA, Postfach 1100, D-4000 Duesseldorf 1, W. Germany (B.R.D.) Ed. Marianne Reinhardt. circ. 8,000.

671   US   ISSN 0146-4752
HIGH SOLIDS COATINGS; magazine and buyer's guide. 1976. a. $89 (foreign $99) Technology Marketing Corp., One Technology Plaza, Norwalk, CT 06854. TEL 203-852-6800. Ed. Robson Storey. bk. rev. (back issues avail.) Indexed: Chem.Abstr.

HINDUSTAN LATEX. VARSHIKA RIPORTA/ HINDUSTAN LATEX. ANNUAL REPORTS. see *PLASTICS*

540   UK
HOUSEHOLD CLEANING REPORT. 1980. biennial. £235. Euromonitor Publications Ltd., 87-88 Turnmill St., London EC1M 5QU, England.
Formerly: Household Chemical Market.

I L Z R O ANNUAL REVIEW. (International Lead Zinc Research Organization, Inc.) see *METALLURGY*

I L Z R O LEAD RESEARCH DIGEST. (International Lead Zinc Research Organization, Inc.) see *METALLURGY*

I L Z R O ZINC/CADIUM RESEARCH DIGEST. (International Lead Zinc Research Organization, Inc.) see *METALLURGY*

540   SP   ISSN 0210-508X
I.Q.S; trabajos de fin de carrera. 1971. a. $10. Instituto Quimico de Sarria, Barcelona 17, Spain. circ. controlled. (back issues avail.) Indexed: Chem.Abstr.

540   FR
IMAGES DE LA CHIMIE. 1973. irreg. Editions du C N R S, 295 rue St. Jacques, 75005 Paris, France.

INDIAN CHEMICAL DIRECTORY. see *ENGINEERING — Chemical Engineering*

540   RM
INSTITUTUL PEDAGOGIC ORADEA. LUCRARI STIINTIFICE SERIA CHIMIE. (Text in Rumanian, occasionally in English or French; summaries in English, French, German, or Rumanian) 1967. a. Institutul Pedagogic Oradea, Calea Armatei Rosii Nr. 5, Oradea, Rumania.
Continues in part its Lucrari Stiintifice: Seria Matematica, Fizica, Chimie (1971-72); its Lucrari Stiintifice: Seria A and Seria B (1969-70) and its Lucrari Stiintifice (1967-68)

540 660   UK   ISSN 0074-3925
INTERNATIONAL CONGRESS OF PURE AND APPLIED CHEMISTRY. (LECTURES) (Text in English; occasionally in French or German) 1960. biennial, 1973, 24th Hamburg; 1975, 25th, Jerusalem. (International Union of Pure and Applied Chemistry) Pergamon Press, Ltd., Headington Hill Hall, Oxford OX3 0BW, England (U.S. subscr. to: Maxwell House, Fairview Park, Elmsford, NY 10523) Indexed: Chem.Abstr.

INTERNATIONAL GUIDE TO SCIENTIFIC INSTRUMENTS & CHEMICALS. see *INSTRUMENTS*

540   II   ISSN 0074-7041
INTERNATIONAL MONOGRAPHS ON ADVANCED CHEMISTRY. (Text in English) 1965. irreg. price varies. Hindustan Publishing Corp., 6-U.B. Jawahar Nagar, Delhi 110007, India.

INTERNATIONAL POLYMER SCIENCE AND TECHNOLOGY. see *PLASTICS*

540   US
INTERNATIONAL SERIES OF MONOGRAPHS ON CHEMISTRY. irreg. price varies. Oxford University Press, 200 Madison Ave., New York, NY 10016 TEL 212-679-7300. (And Ely House, 37 Dover St., London W1X 4AH, England) Ed.Bd.

541.28
INTERNATIONAL SYMPOSIUM ON ATOMIC, MOLECULAR AND SOLID-STATE THEORY, COLLISION PHENOMENA AND COMPUTATIONAL METHODS. PROCEEDINGS. Represents: International Journal of Quantum Chemistry. Symposium. Variant title: Lowdin Symposia. 1967. irreg. $30. John Wiley & Sons, Inc., 605 Third Ave., New York, NY 10016. TEL 212-850-6000. Ed. Per-Olov Lowdin. (also avail. in microform from UMI; reprint service avail. from UMI) Indexed: Biol.Abstr. Chem.Abstr. Sci.Abstr.
Former titles (1974-1977): International Symposium on Atomic, Molecular and Solid-State Theory and Quantum Statistics. Proceedings (ISSN 0360-8832); (1969-1973): International Symposium on Atomic, Molecular and Solid-State Theory and Quantum Biology. Proceedings (ISSN 0076-1370); (1967): International Symposium on Atomic, Molecular and Solid-State Theory. Proceedings.

660   JA
INTERNATIONAL SYMPOSIUM ON THE CHEMISTRY OF CEMENT. PROCEEDINGS.* irreg., 5th, 1968, Tokyo. $22. Cement Association of Japan, Hattori Building, No. 1, 1-chome, Kyobashi, Chuo-Ku, Tokyo, Japan.

JOURNAL OF BALLISTICS; a communication journal. see *ENGINEERING — Mechanical Engineering*

540   UR   ISSN 0453-3585
KATALIZ I KATALIZATORY; respublikanskii mezhvedomstvennyi sbornik nauchnykh trudov. (Text in Russian) 1965. a. (Akademiya Nauk Ukrainskoi S.S.R, Institut Fizicheskoi Khimii im. L.V. Pisarzhevskogo) Izdatel'stvo Naukova Dumka, c/o Yu.A. Khramov, Dir, Ul. Repina, 3, Kiev 252 601, Ukrainian S.S.R., U.S.S.R. (Subscr. to: Mezhdunarodnaya Kniga, Moscow, G-200, Russian S.F.S.R., U.S.S.R.) Ed. V.M. Vlasenko. Indexed: Chem.Abstr.

540   DK   ISSN 0900-1646
KEMIKALIEKONTROLLEN AARSBERETNING. a. (Miljoestyrelsen) Bibliotekscentralen, Telegrafvej 5, DK-2750 Ballerup, Ballerup.

540 549   DK   ISSN 0105-9386
KEMISK ANALYSE AF MINERALER OG BJERGARTER. (Text in Danish, summaries in English) 1977. irreg. free. University of Copenhagen, Geologisk Centralinstitut, Oester voldgade 10, 1350 Copenhagen, Denmark. Ed. Niels Hansen. illus. circ. 100. Indexed: Chem.Abstr.

540   FI   ISSN 0356-7818
KEMISTIN KALENTERI. (Text in Finnish and Swedish) 1947. a. Suomen Kemistiliitto - Finnish Union of Chemists, Rautatielaisenkatu 6, 00520 Helsinki 52, Finland. Ed. Arja Junkkar. adv. circ. 3, 000.

540   MY
KIMIA. 1970. a. free to qualified personnel. ‡ Malaysian Institute of Chemistry, c/o Rubber Research Institute of Malaysia, Jalan Ampang, Box 150, Kuala Lumpur, Malaysia. Ed. M.M. Singh. adv. illus. circ. 1,500. Indexed: Chem.Abstr.

540   PH   ISSN 0115-2130
KIMIKA. 1961. a. $5 per no. Chemical Society of the Philippines, Bioanalytical Research Department, United Laboratories Inc., Mandaluyong, Metro Manila, Philippines. Ed. Benigno D. Peczon. adv. charts. illus. circ. 750. (processed) Indexed: Chem.Abstr.
Formerly: Chemists' Quarterly (ISSN 0045-6527)

540   JA   ISSN 0085-2635
KYUSHU UNIVERSITY. FACULTY OF SCIENCE. MEMOIRS. SERIES C: CHEMISTRY/KYUSHU DAIGAKU RIGAKUBU KIYO, C. KAGAKU. (Text in English) 1948. a. exchange basis. Kyushu University, Faculty of Science, Department of Chemistry - Kyushu Daigaku Rigakubu, 6-10-1 Hakozaki, Higashi-ku, Fukuoka 812, Japan. circ. 650. Indexed: Chem.Abstr. Sci.Abstr. JCT. Mass Spectr.Bull.

542   US   ISSN 0003-2700
LABORATORY GUIDE TO INSTRUMENTS, EQUIPMENT AND CHEMICALS. LAB GUIDE. (Special issue of Analytical Chemistry) 1955. a. $9. American Chemical Society, 1155 16th St. N.W., Washington, DC 20036. TEL 202-872-8065. Ed. George Morrison. adv. bk. rev. circ. 76,000.
Former titles: Laboratory Guide to Instruments, Equipment and Chemicals (ISSN 0458-595X); A C S Laboratory Guide (ISSN 0065-7700); Analytical Chemistry Buyers Guide.

540   US   ISSN 0342-4901
LECTURE NOTES IN CHEMISTRY. 1976. irreg., vol.44, 1986. price varies. Springer-Verlag, 175 Fifth Ave., New York, NY 10010 TEL 212-460-1500. (Also Berlin, Heidelberg, Tokyo and Vienna) Ed.Bd. (reprint service avail. from ISI) Indexed: Chem.Abstr.

591.2   US   ISSN 0277-013X
LYMPHOKINES. 1980. a., latest, vol.12, 1985. Academic Press, Inc., Orlando, FL 32887. TEL 305-345-2000. Indexed: Chem.Abstr.
Formerly: Lymphokine Reports (ISSN 0197-596X)

540   US
MCCUTCHEON'S EMULSIFIERS AND DETERGENTS. 1949. a. $45. M C Publishing Company, Inc., McCutcheon Division, 175 Rock Rd., Glen Rock, NJ 07452. TEL 201-652-2655. Ed. A. Allured. adv. circ. 5,300.

543   UK   ISSN 0305-9987
MASS SPECTROMETRY. 1971. biennial. price varies. Royal Society of Chemistry, Burlington House, London W1V 0BN, England (Subscr. to: Distribution Centre, Blackhorse Rd., Letchworth, Herts. SG6 1HN, England) Ed. R.A.W. Johnstone. charts. illus. Indexed: Chem.Abstr.

540 510   GW   ISSN 0340-6253
MATCH; informal communications in mathematical chemistry. (Text mostly in English; occasionally in French and German) 1975. irreg. DM.35 for 4 issues. Max-Planck-Institut fuer Stahlenchemie, Stiftstr. 34-36, 4330 Muelheim, W. Germany (B.R.D.) Ed.Bd. bk. rev. abstr. bibl. charts. index. Indexed: Chem.Abstr. Math.R.

MEIJERITIETEELLINEN AIKAKAUSKIRJA/ FINNISH JOURNAL OF DAIRY SCIENCE. see *AGRICULTURE — Dairying And Dairy Products*

MODELING AND SIMULATION ON MICROCOMPUTERS. see *ELECTRICITY AND ELECTRICAL ENGINEERING*

MONOGRAPHS ON THE PHYSICS AND CHEMISTRY OF MATERIALS. see *PHYSICS*

MUSEUM NATIONAL D'HISTOIRE NATURELLE, PARIS. MEMOIRES. NOUVELLE SERIE. SERIE D. SCIENCES PHYSICO-CHIMIQUES. see *PHYSICS*

CHEMISTRY

NAGOYA CITY UNIVERSITY. FACULTY OF PHARMACEUTICAL SCIENCE. ANNUAL REPORT/NAGOYA-SHIRITSU DAIGAKU YAKUGAKUBU KENKYU NEMPO. see *PHARMACY AND PHARMACOLOGY*

NATIONAL FISHERIES UNIVERSITY OF PUSAN. INSTITUTE OF MARINE SCIENCES. CONTRIBUTIONS. see *BIOLOGY*

540 574 610   US
NAUKOVE TOVARYSTVO IMENI SHEVCHENKA. PROCEEDINGS OF THE SECTION OF CHEMISTRY, BIOLOGY AND MEDICINE. (Text in English and Ukrainian) vol.7, 1973. irreg. $2. Shevchenko Scientific Society, 63 Fourth Ave., New York, NY 10003. TEL 202-254-5130.
  Supersedes in part its: Proceedings of the Section of Mathematics, Natural Sciences and Medicine (ISSN 0470-5017)

540   UN   ISSN 0077-8885
NEW TRENDS IN CHEMISTRY TEACHING. (Text in English and French) 1967. irreg., vol.5, 1981. Unesco, 7-9 Place de Fontenoy, 75700 Paris, France (Dist. in U.S. by: Bernan Associates-Unipub, 4611-F Assembly Dr., Lanham, MD 20706-4391) Ed. P. Farago.

540   JA
NIIGATA UNIVERSITY. FACULTY OF SCIENCE. SCIENCE REPORTS. SERIES C: CHEMISTRY. (Text in European languages) 1964. irreg. exchange basis. Niigata University, Faculty of Science - Niigata Daigaku Rigakubu, 8050 Igarashi Nino-cho, Niigata-shi 950-21, Japan.

NUCLEUS. see *PHYSICS — Nuclear Energy*

O P D CHEMICAL BUYERS DIRECTORY. see *BUSINESS AND ECONOMICS — Trade And Industrial Directories*

540   US   ISSN 0553-0377
ORGANIZATION OF AMERICAN STATES. DEPARTMENT OF SCIENTIFIC AFFAIRS. SERIE DE QUIMICA: MONOGRAFIAS. 1965. irreg., no.21, 1979. $3.50. Organization of American States, Department of Publications, Washington, DC 20006. TEL 703-941-1617. circ. 3,000.

540   SW
P K L KEMIKALIER. 1976. biennial. Kr.100. Plastoch Kemikalieleverantoerers Foerening - Swedish Plastics and Chemicals Suppliers Association, Box 5512, S-114 85 Stockholm, Sweden.

540   CS
PEDAGOGICKA FAKULTA V USTI NAD LABEM. SBORNIK: RADA CHEMICKA. (Text in Czech or German; summaries in Czech, English, German, Russian) irreg. 22 Kcs. Statni Pedagogicke Nakladatelstvi, Ostrovni 30, 113 01 Prague 1, Czechoslovakia. illus.

540   NE
PHARMACOCHEMISTRY LIBRARY. 1977. irreg., vol.8, 1985. price varies. Elsevier Science Publishers B.V., P.O. Box 211, 1000 AE Amsterdam, Netherlands. Indexed: Chem.Abstr.

540   UK   ISSN 0556-3860
PHOTOCHEMISTRY (LONDON) 1970. a. price varies. Royal Society of Chemistry, Burlington House, London W1V 0BN, England (Subscr. to: Distribution Centre, Blackhorse Rd., Letchworth, Herts. SG6 1HN, England) Ed. D. Bryce-Smith. charts. index. Indexed: Chem.Abstr.

540 530   US   ISSN 0079-1938
PHYSICS AND CHEMISTRY IN SPACE. 1970. irreg., no.14, 1986. price varies. Springer-Verlag, 175 Fifth Ave., New York, NY 10010 TEL 212-460-1500. (Also Berlin, Heidelberg, Tokyo and Vienna) Ed. F. Roederes. (reprint service avail. from ISI)

PHYSICS AND CHEMISTRY OF MATERIALS WITH LOW-DIMENSIONAL STRUCTURES. see *PHYSICS — Mechanics*

540   PL
POLITECHNIKA GDANSKA. RAPORT. WYDZIAL CHEMICZNY. 1982. a. price varies. Politechnika Gdanska, Ul. Majakowskiego 11/12, 80-952 Gdansk 6, Poland.

540   PL   ISSN 0416-7309
POLITECHNIKA GDANSKA. ZESZYTY NAUKOWE. CHEMIA. (Text in Polish; summaries in English and Russian) 1955. irreg. price varies. Politechnika Gdanska, Majakowskiego 11/12, 81-952 Gdansk 6, Poland (Dist. by: Osrodek Rozpowszechniania Wydawnictw Naukowych Pan, Palac Kultury i Nauki, 00-901 Warsaw, Poland) Indexed: Chem.Abstr.

540   PL   ISSN 0075-7055
POLITECHNIKA KRAKOWSKA. ZESZYTY NAUKOWE. CHEMIA. (Text in Polish; summaries in English, French, German, Russian) 1968. irreg. price varies. Politechnika Krakowska, Warszawska 24, 31-155 Krakow, Poland (Dist. by: Ars Polona-Ruch, Krakowskie Przedmiescie 7, 00-068 Warsaw, Poland) bibl. charts. illus. circ. 200. Indexed: Chem.Abstr.

540   PL   ISSN 0458-1555
POLITECHNIKA LODZKA. ZESZYTY NAUKOWE. CHEMIA. (Text in Polish; summaries in English and Russian) 1954. irreg. price varies. Politechnika Lodzka, Ul. Zwirki 36, 90-924 Lodz, Poland (Dist. by: Ars Polona-Ruch, Krakowskie Przedmiescie 7, Warsaw, Poland) Ed. Andrzej Cyganski. circ. 383. Indexed: Chem.Abstr.

540 660   PL   ISSN 0372-9494
POLITECHNIKA SLASKA. ZESZYTY NAUKOWE. CHEMIA. (Text in Polish; summaries in English and Russian) 1957. irreg. price varies. Politechnika Slaska, W. Pstrowskiego 7, 44-100 Gliwice, Poland (Dist. by: Ars Polona, Krakowskie Przedmiescie 7, 00-068 Warsaw, Poland) Ed. Genowefa Bienkiewicz. circ. 250. Indexed: Chem.Abstr. Met.Abstr.

540   NE
POLYMER SCIENCE LIBRARY. 1979. irreg., vol.3, 1985. price varies. Elsevier Science Publishers B.V., P.O. Box 211, 1000 AE Amsterdam, Netherlands. Ed. A.D. Jenkins.

540   NE
PROGRESS IN FILTRATION AND SEPARATION. 1979. irreg., vol.3, 1983. price varies. Elsevier Science Publishers B.V., P.O. Box 211, 1000 AE Amsterdam, Netherlands. Ed. R.J. Wakeman. Indexed: Chem.Abstr.

540 539   US   ISSN 0149-1970
PROGRESS IN NUCLEAR ENERGY (NEW SERIES) 1977. 6/yr. (in 2 vols., 3 nos./vol.) $280 (annual bound volume $276) Pergamon Press, Inc., Journals Division, Maxwell House, Fairview Park, Elmsford, NY 10523 TEL 914-592-7700. (And Headington Hill Hall, Oxford, Eng) Eds. Bal Raj Sahgal, M.M.R. Williams. (also avail. in microform from MIM,UMI) Indexed: Chem.Abstr. Curr.Cont. Excerp.Med. Sci.Abstr. Geo.Abstr. Risk Abstr.
  Supersedes (as of 1977): Progress in Nuclear Energy. Series 3 - Process Chemistry (ISSN 0079-6514); Progress in Nuclear Energy. Series 9 - Analytical Chemistry (ISSN 0079-6530)

540   US   ISSN 0197-8039
RADIATION CURING BUYER'S GUIDE. 1977. a. $22. Technology Marketing Corp., One Technology Plaza, Norwalk, CT 06854. TEL 203-852-6800. Ed.Bd.
  Formerly: U V Curing Buyer's Guide (ISSN 0146-5031)

540   US   ISSN 0080-181X
RESIDUE REVIEWS. (Text in English; occasionally in German or French) 1962. irreg., vol.97, 1986. Springer-Verlag, 175 Fifth Ave., New York, NY 10010 TEL 212-460-1500. (Also Berlin, Heidelberg, Tokyo and Vienna) (reprint service avail. from ISI) Indexed: Biol.Abstr. Biol.& Agr.Ind. Chem.Abstr. Excerp.Med. Ind.Med. Pollut.Abstr. Biotech.Abstr. Dairy Sci.Abstr. Hort.Abstr. Ind.Vet. Rev.Appl.Entomol. Rev.Plant Path. Soils & Fert. Vet.Bull. Weed Abstr.

ROYAL IRISH ACADEMY. PROCEEDINGS. SECTION B: BIOLOGICAL, GEOLOGICAL AND CHEMICAL SCIENCES. see *BIOLOGY*

540   UK   ISSN 0080-4428
ROYAL SOCIETY OF CHEMISTRY. MONOGRAPHS FOR TEACHERS. 1959. irreg. price varies. Royal Society of Chemistry, Burlington House, London W1V 0BN, England (Subscr. to: Distribution Centre, Blackhorse Rd., Letchworth, Herts. SG6 1HN, England) Ed. Michael Withers. Indexed: Chem.Abstr.
  Formerly: Royal Institue of Chemistry. Monographs for Teachers.

540   SI
S N I C BULLETIN. (Text in English) 1972. a. membership. Singapore National Institute of Chemistry, c/o Dept. of Chemistry, 23 Outram Park 03-129, Singapore 0316, Singapore. Ed. W.L. Kwik. adv. charts. circ. 1,000. Indexed: Chem.Abstr.
  Formerly: Singapore National Institute of Chemistry. Bulletin.

SAITAMA UNIVERSITY. SCIENCE REPORTS. SERIES A: MATHEMATICS. see *MATHEMATICS*

540 530   IT   ISSN 0391-3244
SCIENZE DELLA MATERIA. 1977. irreg., no.3, 1979. price varies. Liguori Editore s.r.l., Via Mezzocannone 19, 80134 Naples, Italy. TEL 081/20 6077. Ed. Giuseppe del Re.

540   FR
SOCIETE FRANCAISE DE CHIMIE. ANNUAIRE. a. 250 F. Societe Francaise de Chimie, 250 rue Saint-Jacques, 75005 Paris, France.

540   BU
SOFIISKI UNIVERSITET. KHIMICHESKI FAKULTET. GODISNIK. (Text in Bulgarian; summaries in English) irreg., vol.71. 1976/77. price varies. (Sofiiski Universitet, Khimicheski Fakultet) Publishing House of the Bulgarian Academy of Sciences, Acad. G. Bonchev St., Bldg. 6, 1113 Sofia, Bulgaria. Ed.Bd. circ. 550. Indexed: Chem.Abstr.

540   UK   ISSN 0584-8555
SPECTROSCOPIC PROPERTIES OF INORGANIC & ORGANOMETALLIC COMPOUNDS. 1968. a. price varies. Royal Society of Chemistry, Burlington House, London W1V 0BN, England (Subscr. to: Distribution Centre, Blackhorse Rd., Letchworth, Herts. SG6 1HN, England) Eds. E.A.V. Ebsworth, D.M. Adams. charts. illus. index. Indexed: Chem.Abstr.

540   US   ISSN 0172-6323
SPRINGER ADVANCED TEXTS IN CHEMISTRY. irreg. Springer-Verlag, 175 Fifth Ave., New York, NY 10010 TEL 212-460-1500. (Also Berlin, Heidelberg, Tokyo and Vienna) Ed. C. Cantor.

SPRINGER SERIES IN CHEMICAL PHYSICS. see *PHYSICS*

541   US   ISSN 0081-5993
STRUCTURE AND BONDING. (Text in English) 1966. irreg., vol.62, 1985. price varies. Springer-Verlag, 175 Fifth Ave., New York, NY 10010 TEL 212-460-1500. (Also Berlin, Heidelberg, Tokyo and Vienna) circ. 1,500. (reprint service avail. from ISI) Indexed: Biol.Abstr. ASCA.

540   RM   ISSN 0039-3401
STUDIA UNIVERSITATIS "BABES-BOLYAI". CHEMIA. (Text in Romanian; summaries in English, French, German or Russian) 1958. a. exchange basis. Universitatea "Babes-Bolyai", Biblioteca Centrala Universitara, Str. Clinicilor Nr. 2, Cluj-Napoca, Rumania. abstr. charts. illus. index. Indexed: Chem.Abstr. Psychol.Abstr. Anal.Abstr.

540 574   US   ISSN 0081-9603
SURFACTANT SCIENCE SERIES. 1966. irreg., vol.19, 1986. price varies. Marcel Dekker, Inc., 270 Madison Ave., New York, NY 10016. TEL 212-696-9000. Eds. M.J. Schick, F.M. Fowkes. Indexed: Biol.Abstr. Chem.Abstr.

540   US   ISSN 0081-976X
SURVEY OF PROGRESS IN CHEMISTRY. 1963. irreg., vol.10, 1983. Academic Press, Inc., Orlando, FL 32887. TEL 305-345-2000. Ed. Arthur F. Scott. index.

TAKEDA RESEARCH LABORATORIES. JOURNAL. see *BIOLOGY*

540 US ISSN 0082-2531
TECHNIQUES OF CHEMISTRY. 1971. irreg., vol.19, 1987. price varies. John Wiley & Sons, Inc., 605 Third Ave., New York, NY 10016. TEL 212-850-6000. Ed. A. Weissberger. Indexed: Chem.Abstr.
Incorporating: Technique of Inorganic Chemistry & Technique of Organic Chemistry (ISSN 0082-240X)

541 US ISSN 0082-3961
THEORETICAL CHEMISTRY; a series of monographs. 1965. irreg., vol.9, 1984. Academic Press Inc., Orlando, FL 32887. TEL 305-345-2000. Ed. D.P. Craig. Indexed: Chem.Abstr.

541.2 US ISSN 0361-0551
THEORETICAL CHEMISTRY: ADVANCES AND PERSPECTIVES. 1975. irreg., vol.68, 1981. Academic Press, Inc., Orlando, FL 32887. TEL 305-345-2000. Eds. Douglas Henderson, Henry Eyring.

540 US ISSN 0340-1022
TOPICS IN CURRENT CHEMISTRY. 1965. irreg., vol.138, 1986. price varies. Springer-Verlag, 175 Fifth Ave., New York, NY 10010 TEL 212-460-1500. (Also Berlin, Heidelberg, Tokyo and Vienna) Ed. F.L. Boschke. (reprint service avail. from ISI) Indexed: Biol.Abstr. Chem.Abstr. ASCA. Curr.Chem.React. GeoRef. Ind.Chem.
Formerly: Fortschritte der Chemischen Forschung (ISSN 0071-7894)

TOPICS IN INORGANIC AND GENERAL CHEMISTRY. see *CHEMISTRY — Inorganic Chemistry*

541.223 US ISSN 0082-500X
TOPICS IN STEREOCHEMISTRY. 1967. irreg., vol.17, 1987. price varies. John Wiley & Sons, Inc., 605 Third Ave., New York, NY 10016. TEL 212-850-6000. Eds. N.L. Allinger, E.L. Eliel. Indexed: Chem.Abstr. ASCA.

UNIVERSITATEA DIN CRAIOVA. ANALE. SERIA: MATEMATICA, FIZICA-CHIMIE. see *MATHEMATICS*

540 FR ISSN 0069-4703
UNIVERSITE DE CLERMONT-FERRAND II. ANNALES SCIENTIFIQUES. SERIE CHEMIE. 1960. irreg. price varies. Universite de Clermont-Ferrand II, Unite d'Enseignement et de Recherche de Sciences Exactes et Naturelles, B.P. 45, 63170 Aubiere, France. circ. 250.

UNIVERSITE LAVAL. CENTRE DE RECHERCHES SUR LES ATOMES ET LES MOLECULES. RAPPORT ANNUEL; physics and chemistry of atoms and molecules. see *PHYSICS — Nuclear Energy*

540 PL ISSN 0083-4319
UNIWERSYTET JAGIELLONSKI. ZESZYTY NAUKOWE. PRACE CHEMICZNE. (Text in English, Polish; summaries in English, Polish, Russian) no.5, 1959. irreg., vol.28, 1983. price varies. Panstwowe Wydawnictwo Naukowe, Miodowa 10, 00-251 Warsaw, Poland (Dist. by: Ars Polona, Krakowkie Przedmiescie 7, 00-068 Warsaw, Poland) bibl. illus. Indexed: Chem.Abstr.

URANIA UNIVERSUM. see *PHYSICS*

VEGYIPARI SZAKIRODALMI TAJEKOZTATO/ CHEMICAL ENGINEERING ABSTRACTS. see *CHEMISTRY — Abstracting, Bibliographies, Statistics*

VOM WASSER; ein Fachbuch fuer Wasserchemie und Wasserreinigungstechnik. see *WATER RESOURCES*

540 AT ISSN 0085-8153
WESTERN AUSTRALIA. GOVERNMENT CHEMICAL LABORATORIES. REPORT OF INVESTIGATIONS. 1968. irreg. free to qualified personnel. Government Chemical Laboratories, 125 Hay Street, Perth, W.A. 6000, Australia. circ. 50. Indexed: Chem.Abstr.

WHO'S WHO IN CHEMISTRY & PLASTICS. see *PLASTICS*

540 GE ISSN 0084-0971
WISSENSCHAFTLICHE TASCHENBUECHER. REIHE CHEMIE. 1962. irreg. price varies. Akademie-Verlag, Leipziger Str. 3-4, 1086 Berlin, E. Germany (D.D.R.) Indexed: Biol.Abstr.

540 US
WORLD AROMATICS AND DERIVATIVES. 1973. a. price on request. S R I International, World Petrochemicals Program, Menlo Park, CA 94025. TEL 415-326-6200. Ed. S.L. Soder. charts. stat.
●Also available online.
Formerly: Benzene-Toluene-Xylenes and Derivatives.

540 US
WORLD C4 HYDROCARBONS AND DERIVATIVES. 1974. a. S R I International, World Petrochemicals Program, Menlo Park, CA 94025. TEL 415-326-6200. Ed. S.L. Soder. charts. stat.
●Also available online.
Formerly: C4 Hydrocarbons and Derivatives.

540 US
WORLD ETHYLENE AND DERIVATIVES. 1973. a. S R I International, World Petrochemicals Program, Menlo Park, CA 94025. TEL 415-326-6200. Ed. S.L. Soder. charts. stat.
●Also available online.
Formerly: Ethylene and Derivatives.

660 US
WORLD FEEDSTOCKS. 1984. a. S R I International, World Petrochemicals Program, Menlo Park, CA 94025. TEL 415-326-6200. Ed. S.L. Soder. charts. stat.

540 US
WORLD METHANOL AND DERIVATIVES. 1981. a. S R I International, World Petrochemicals Program, Menlo Park, CA 94025. TEL 415-326-6200. Ed. S.L. Soder. charts. stat.
●Also available online.

540 US
WORLD PROPYLENE AND DERIVATIVES. 1973. a. S R I International, World Petrochemicals Program, Menlo Park, CA 94025. TEL 415-326-6200. Ed. S.L. Soder. charts. stat.
Formerly: Propylene and Derivatives.

WORLDWIDE CHEMICAL DIRECTORY. see *BUSINESS AND ECONOMICS — Trade And Industrial Directories*

540 PL ISSN 0324-9034
WYZSZA SZKOLA PEDAGOGICZNA, OPOLE. ZESZYTY NAUKOWE. SERIA A. CHEMIA. (Text in Polish; summaries in English) vol.5, 1981. irreg. price varies, avail. on exchange basis. Wyzsza Szkola Pedagogiczna, Opole, Oleska 48, 45-052 Opole, Poland (Dist. by: Ars Polona-Ruch, Krakowkie Przedmiescie 7, Warsaw, Poland) Indexed: Chem.Abstr.

CHEMISTRY — Abstracting, Bibliographies, Statistics

541.36 016 US ISSN 0149-2268
BULLETIN OF CHEMICAL THERMODYNAMICS (1977) 1958. a. $25 to individuals; institutions $40. (International Union of Pure and Applied Chemistry, Commission on Thermodynamics) Thermochemistry, Inc., Oklahoma State University, Department of Chemistry, Stillwater, OK 74078. TEL 405-624-6676. Ed. Robert D. Freeman. adv. bk. rev. circ. 500. Indexed: Chem.Abstr. Phys.Ber.
Former titles (1962-1976): Bulletin of Thermodynamics and Thermochemistry (ISSN 0068-4139); (1958-1961): Bulletin of Chemical Thermodynamics; Which supersedes: Thermochemical Bulletin and Bulletin of Unpublished Thermal Material.

540 016 US ISSN 0001-0634
CHEMICAL ABSTRACTS SERVICE SOURCE INDEX. Abbreviated title: C A S S I. 1969. base vol. (every 4-5 yrs.) updated with q. supplements. $800 base. vol.; q. supplements $200. (American Chemical Society) Chemical Abstracts Service, Box 3012, Columbus, OH 43210 TEL 614-421-3600. (Subscr. to: Customer Services Dept., 2540 Olentangy River Rd., Columbus, OH 43210) Ed. David W. Weisgerber.
●Also available online. Vendors: Orbit Information Technologies, STN International.

540 016 GW ISSN 0009-2975
CHEMISCHER INFORMATIONSDIENST. Short title: ChemInform. 1970. w. DM.2,185($1,204) (Gesellschaft Deutscher Chemiker, GW) V C H Verlagsgesellschaft mbH, Postfach 1260/1280, 6940 Weinheim, W. Germany (U.S. adress: V C H Publishers Inc., 220 East 23rd St., NY, NY, 10010-4606) (Co-sponsor: Fachinformationszentrum Chemie und Bayer AG) Ed.Bd. adv. index. circ. 1, 400. (reprint service avail. from ISI) Indexed: Chem.Abstr.
Supersedes: Chemisches Zentralblatt.

540 016 US ISSN 0300-1261
CHEMORECEPTION ABSTRACTS; chemical senses & applied techniques. 1973. q. $209. (European Chemoreception Organization) Cambridge Scientific Abstracts, 5161 River Rd., Bethesda, MD 20816. TEL 301-951-1400. Ed. Pam Clare. adv. bk. rev. abstr. index. (also avail. in magnetic tape) Indexed: Cal.Tiss.Abstr. Chemorec.Abstr. Oncol.Abstr.
●Also available online. Vendors: DIALOG.

540 016 US ISSN 0163-6278
CURRENT CHEMICAL REACTIONS. Short Title: C C R. 1979. m. $580. Institute for Scientific Information, 3501 Market St., Philadelphia, PA 19104 TEL 215-386-0100. (And 132 High St., Uxbridge, Middlesex, UB8 1DP, England) cum.index.

660 016 II ISSN 0037-9689
CURRENT TITLES IN ELECTROCHEMISTRY. (Text in English) 1969. m. Rs.50($50) for individuals; Rs.100 ($100) for institutions. ‡ Society for Advancement of Electrochemical Science and Technology, Karaikudi 623 006, Tamil Nadu, India. Ed. P.V. Vasudeva Rao. index. Indexed: Chem.Abstr.
Incorporating: Electrochemical News.

530 540 016 UK
EIGHT PEAK INDEX OF MASS SPECTRA. (In two versions: printed verson & computer readable version) vol.2, 1975. irreg., latest vol.3, 1984. £730($1400) Royal Society of Chemistry, Mass Spectrometry Data Centre, The University, Nottingham NG7 2RD, England. Ed. Steve Down. (also avail. in magnetic tape)

544.92 016 US ISSN 0072-8446
GUIDE TO GAS CHROMATOGRAPHY LITERATURE. 1964. irreg., vol.3, 1974. price varies. Plenum Publishing Corp., I.F.I.-Plenum Data Co., 233 Spring St., New York, NY 10013. TEL 212-741-6680.

540 016 US ISSN 0891-6055
INDEX CHEMICUS. Short title: I C. 1960. w. (plus q. and a. cum. of index section) $3,350 price varies. Institute for Scientific Information, 3501 Market St., Philadelphia, PA 19104 TEL 215-386-0100. (And 132 High St., Uxbridge, Middlesex, UB8 1DP, England) (also avail. in microform)
●Also available online. Vendors: Telesystemes - Questel.
Former titles: Current Abstracts of Chemistry and Index Chemicus (ISSN 0011-3158) & Index.

547 016 UK ISSN 0536-6518
INDEX OF REVIEWS IN ORGANIC CHEMISTRY. 1971. a. price varies. Royal Society of Chemistry, The University, Nottingham NG7 2RD, England (Subscr. to: Distribution Centre, Blackhorse Rd., Letchworth, Herts. SG6 1HN, England) index.

326 CHEMISTRY — ANALYTICAL CHEMISTRY

540 016   UK   ISSN 0025-4738
MASS SPECTROMETRY BULLETIN. 1966. m. £210($406) Royal Society of Chemistry, Mass Spectrometry Data Centre, University of Nottingham, Nottingham NG7 2RD, England (Subscr. to: Distribution Centre, Blackhorse Rd., Letchworth, Herts SG6 1HN, England) Ed. S. Down. adv. bk. rev. bibl. index. cum.index. circ. 500. (magnetic tape)
• Also available online. Vendors: European Space Agency, Pergamon Infoline.

NUCLEAR MAGNETIC RESONANCE SPECTROMETRY ABSTRACTS. see PHYSICS — Abstracting, Bibliographies, Statistics

PREDICASTS OVERVIEW OF MARKETS AND TECHNOLOGIES. see ENGINEERING — Abstracting, Bibliographies, Statistics

540   US
U S S R REPORT: CHEMISTRY. 1973. irreg. (approx. 17/yr.) $5 per no. U.S. Joint Publications Research Service, 1000 N. Glebe Rd., Arlington, VA 22201 TEL 703-487-4630. (Orders to: NTIS, Springfield, VA 22161)
Formerly: U S S R and Eastern Europe Scientific Abstracts: Chemistry; Which was formed by the merger of: U S S R Scientific Abstracts: Chemistry; East European Scientific Abstracts: Chemistry.

540 016 660   HU   ISSN 0231-0775
VEGYIPARI SZAKIRODALMI TAJEKOZTATO/ CHEMICAL ENGINEERING ABSTRACTS. 1949. m. 5600 Ft. Orszagos Muszaki Informacios Kozpont es Konyvtar (O.M.I.K.K.) - National Technical Information Centre and Library, Muzeum u. 17, Box 12, 1428 Budapest, Hungary (Subscr. to: Kultura, Box 149, H-1389 Budapest, Hungary) Ed. E. Vajda. abstr. index. circ. 520.
Supersedes (as from 1982): Muszaki Lapszemle. Kemia Vegyipar/Technical Abstracts. Chemistry, Chemical Industry (ISSN 0027-5026)

CHEMISTRY — Analytical Chemistry

544.92   US   ISSN 0065-2415
ADVANCES IN CHROMATOGRAPHY. 1966. irreg., vol.24, 1984. price varies. Marcel Dekker, Inc., 270 Madison Ave., New York, NY 10016. TEL 212-696-9000. Indexed: Biol.Abstr. Chem.Abstr. Ind.Med. Sci.Cit.Ind. Dairy Sci.Abstr. Dent.Ind. Food Sci.& Tech.Abstr. GeoRef. Ind.Sci.Rev.

543   US   ISSN 0003-2700
ANALYTICAL CHEMISTRY. 1929. s-m. plus Review Issue and Lab Guide. $37 to non-members; members $25. American Chemical Society, 1155 16th St., N.W., Washington, DC 20036. TEL 202-872-8065. Ed. George Morrison. adv. bk. rev. abstr. bibl. charts. illus. tr.lit. index. circ. 29,000. (also avail. in microform from UMI; reprint service avail. from ISI) Indexed: A.S.& T.Ind. Biol.Abstr. Ceram.Abstr. Chem.Abstr. Eng.Ind. Excerp.Med. I.P.A. Ind.Med. Met.Abstr. Nutr.Abstr. Ocean.Abstr. Pollut.Abstr. Sci.Abstr. Sci.Cit.Ind. API Abstr. Abstr.Bull.Inst.Pap.Chem. Anal.Abstr. Art & Archaeol.Tech.Abstr. Biotech.Abstr. Br.Ceram.Abstr. C.I.J.E. C.I.S.Abstr. CJPI. Dairy Sci.Abstr. Dent.Ind. Fuel & Energy Abstr. Gas Abstr. Gen.Sci.Ind. Hort.Abstr. Ind.Hyg.Dig. Ind.Sci.Rev. Lead Abstr. Mass Spectr.Bull. Petrol.Abstr. RAPRA. Risk Abstr. Sel.Water Res.Abstr. Soils & Fert. Text.Tech.Dig. World Alum.Abstr. World Text.Abstr.
• Also available online.
Formerly (1929-1946): Industrial and Analytical Chemistry. Analytical Edition (ISSN 0096-4484)

543   US
ANALYTICAL CHEMISTRY OF THE ELEMENTS SERIES. 1963. irreg., unnumbered, 1975 latest. price varies. Halsted Press (Subsidiary of: John Wiley & Sons, Inc.) 605 Third Ave., New York, NY 10016. TEL 212-850-6000.

544.92   NE
ANALYTICAL CHEMISTRY SYMPOSIA SERIES. 1979. irreg., vol.24, 1986. price varies. Elsevier Science Publishers B.V., P.O. Box 211, 1000 AE Amsterdam, Netherlands. Indexed: Biol.Abstr. Chem.Abstr.
Formerly: Chromatography Symposia Series.

543   UK   ISSN 0583-8894
ANALYTICAL SCIENCES MONOGRAPHS. 1973. irreg., no.8, 1981. price varies. Royal Society of Chemistry, Burlington House, London W1V 0BN, England (Subscr. to: Distribution Centre, Blackhorse Rd., Letchworth, Herts. SG6 1HN, England) bibl. charts. illus. Indexed: Biol.Abstr.

ANNUAL BOOK OF A S T M STANDARDS. VOLUME 03.05. CHEMICAL ANALYSIS OF METALS; METAL BEARING ORES. see ENGINEERING — Engineering Mechanics And Materials

ANNUAL BOOK OF A S T M STANDARDS. VOLUME 14.01. ANALYTICAL METHODS - SPECTROSCOPY; CHROMATOGRAPHY; TEMPERATURE MEASUREMENT; COMPUTERIZED SYSTEMS. see ENGINEERING — Engineering Mechanics And Materials

543   US   ISSN 0066-961X
ASSOCIATION OF OFFICIAL ANALYTICAL CHEMISTS. OFFICIAL METHODS OF ANALYSIS. 1920. quinquennial. $148.50. Association of Official Analytical Chemists, 1111 N. 19th St., Ste. 210, Arlington, VA 22209. TEL 703-522-3032. Ed. Sidney Williams. index. circ. 20,000. Indexed: Chem.Abstr.

543   US   ISSN 0145-5338
BENCHMARK PAPERS IN ANALYTICAL CHEMISTRY. (Each vol. has distinctive title) 1976. irreg., vol.3, 1981. price varies. Van Nostrand Reinhold Company, 7625 Empire Dr., Florence, KY 41042. TEL 606-525-6600. illus. index.

543   US   ISSN 0069-2883
CHEMICAL ANALYSIS; a series of monographs on analytical chemistry and its applications. 1953. irreg., vol.93, 1987. price varies. John Wiley & Sons, Inc., 605 Third Ave., New York, NY 10016. TEL 212-850-6000. Eds. P.J. Elving, J.D. Winefordner. index. Indexed: Biol.Abstr. Chem.Abstr. GeoRef.

543   US   ISSN 0069-3936
CHROMATOGRAPHIC SCIENCE SERIES. 1965. irreg., vol.32, 1985. price varies. Marcel Dekker, Inc., 270 Madison Ave., New York, NY 10016. Ed. J.C. Giddings. Indexed: Chem.Abstr.

CLINICAL AND BIOCHEMICAL ANALYSIS. see BIOLOGY — Biological Chemistry

542   GW   ISSN 0070-315X
DECHEMA MONOGRAPHIEN. irreg., vol.100, 1985. price varies. (Deutsche Gesellschaft fuer Chemisches Apparatewesen e.V. - DECHEMA) V C H Verlagsgesellschaft mbH, Postfach 1260/1280, 6940 Weinheim, W. Germany (B.R.D) (U.S. address: 220 East 23rd.St., New York, NY, 10010-4606) index. (reprint service avail. from ISI) Indexed: Chem.Abstr. Dairy Sci.Abstr. Food Sci.& Tech.Abstr.

543   US   ISSN 0070-9778
ELECTROANALYTICAL CHEMISTRY: A SERIES OF ADVANCES. (Subseries of Monographs in Electroanalytical Chemistry and Electrochemistry) 1966. irreg., vol.14, 1986. price varies. Marcel Dekker, Inc., 270 Madison Ave., New York, NY 10016. TEL 212-696-9000. Ed. A.J. Bard. Indexed: Sci.Cit.Ind. Ind.Sci.Rev.

543.08   US   ISSN 0270-8531
HIGH-PERFORMANCE LIQUID CHROMATOGRAPHY. 1980. irreg., vol.3, 1983. Academic Press, Inc., Orlando, FL 32887. TEL 305-345-2000.

544.92   NE
JOURNAL OF CHROMATOGRAPHY LIBRARY. 1973. irreg., vol.32, 1985. price varies. Elsevier Science Publishers B.V., P.O. Box 211, 1000 AE Amsterdam, Netherlands. Indexed: Biol.Abstr. Chem.Abstr.

545.3   SZ   ISSN 0022-0728
JOURNAL OF ELECTROANALYTICAL CHEMISTRY AND INTERFACIAL ELECTROCHEMISTRY; international journal dealing with all aspects of electroanalytical chemistry, including fundamental electrochemistry. (Text in English, French or German; summaries in English) 1959. irreg. (approx. 42/yr.) 4200 Fr. Elsevier Sequoia S.A., Box 564, CH-1001 Lausanne 1, Switzerland. Ed. R. Parsons. adv. bk. rev. charts. illus. index. circ. 1,200. (back issues avail.) Indexed: Chem.Abstr. Curr.Cont. Excerp.Med. Met.Abstr. Sci.Cit.Ind. Anal.Abstr. Fuel & Energy Abstr. Ind.Sci.Rev. Int.Aerosp.Abstr. World Alum.Abstr.
Formerly: Journal of Electroanalytical Chemistry. Electroanalytical

METHODS OF BIOCHEMICAL ANALYSIS. see BIOLOGY — Biological Chemistry

543   US   ISSN 0076-8642
MIKROCHIMICA ACTA. SUPPLEMENT. 1966. irreg., no.9, 1981. Springer-Verlag, 175 Fifth Ave., New York, NY 10010 TEL 212-460-1500. (also Berlin, Heidelberg, Vienna) (also avail. in microform from UMI; reprint service avail. from ISI) Indexed: Chem.Abstr.

643   US
MODERN MONOGRAPHS IN ANALYTICAL CHEMISTRY. 1981. irreg., vol.2, 1984. price varies. Marcel Dekker, Inc., 270 Madison Ave., New York, NY 10016. TEL 212-696-9000. Ed. George G. Guilbault.

MONOGRAPHS IN ELECTROANALYTICAL CHEMISTRY AND ELECTROCHEMISTRY SERIES. see CHEMISTRY — Electrochemistry

NIGERIAN STORED PRODUCTS RESEARCH INSTITUTE. ANNUAL REPORT. see AGRICULTURE — Agricultural Equipment

543 547   US   ISSN 0078-6136
ORGANIC ELECTRONIC SPECTRAL DATA. 1960. irreg., vol.21, 1985. price varies. (Organic Electronic Spectral Data, Inc.) John Wiley & Sons, Inc., 605 Third Ave, New York, NY 10016. TEL 212-850-6000. Ed.Bd.

544.66   US   ISSN 0092-0509
POWDER DIFFRACTION FILE SEARCH MANUAL. ALPHABETICAL LISTING. INORGANIC. (Subseries of the Committee's Publication SMA) a. $285. ‡ Joint Committee on Powder Diffraction Standards., International Centre for Diffraction Data, 1601 Park Lane, Swarthmore, PA 19081. TEL 215-328-9400. index.

544.66   US   ISSN 0092-1300
POWDER DIFFRACTION FILE SEARCH MANUAL. FINK METHOD. INORGANIC. (Subseries of the Committee's Publication SMF) a. $305. ‡ Joint Committee on Powder Diffraction Standards., International Centre for Diffraction Data, 1601 Park Lane, Swarthmore, PA 19081. TEL 215-328-9400. index.

544.66   US   ISSN 0092-1319
POWDER DIFFRACTION FILE SEARCH MANUAL. HANAWALT METHOD. INORGANIC. (Subseries of the Committee's Publication SMH) a. $225. ‡ Joint Committee on Powder Diffraction Standards., International Centre for Diffraction Data, 1601 Park Lane, Swarthmore, PA 19081. TEL 215-328-9400. index.

547.3   US
PRACTICAL SPECTROSCOPY SERIES. 1976. irreg., vol.4, 1980. price varies. Marcel Dekker, Inc., 270 Madison Ave., New York, NY 10016. TEL 212-696-9000. Indexed: Biol.Abstr.

PROGRESS IN NUCLEAR MAGNETIC RESONANCE SPECTROSCOPY. see PHYSICS — Nuclear Energy

R & D DIGEST. (Research & Development Division) see ENERGY

543   US
REAGENT CHEMICALS. irreg., approx. every 5 yrs. price varies. American Chemical Society, Committee on Analytical Reagents, 1155 16th St., N.W., Washington, DC 20036. TEL 202-872-8065.

543 NE
TECHNIQUES AND INSTRUMENTATION IN ANALYTICAL CHEMISTRY. 1978. irreg., vol.6, 1984. price varies. Elsevier Science Publishers B.V., P.O. Box 211, 1000 AE Amsterdam, Netherlands. Indexed: Chem.Abstr.

541.36 541.3   US   ISSN 0082-4046
THERMODYNAMICS RESEARCH CENTER. DATA PROJECT. SELECTED VALUES OF PROPERTIES OF CHEMICAL COMPOUNDS. CATEGORY A. TABLES OF SELECTED VALUES OF PHYSICAL AND THERMODYNAMIC PROPERTIES OF CHEMICAL COMPOUNDS. 1955. irreg., supplement A-51, 1984. $275 per supplement. Thermodynamics Research Center, Texas A & M University System, College Station, TX 77843-3111. TEL 409-845-4940. Ed. Kenneth R. Hall. circ. 230. (looseleaf format)

544.63   US   ISSN 0082-402X
THERMODYNAMICS RESEARCH CENTER. DATA PROJECT. SELECTED VALUES OF PROPERTIES OF CHEMICAL COMPOUNDS. CATEGORY B. SELECTED INFRARED SPECTRAL DATA. 1959. irreg., supplement B-23, 1983. $150 per supplement. Thermodynamics Research Center, Texas A & M University System, College Station, TX 77843-3111. TEL 409-845-4940. Ed. Kenneth R. Hall. circ. 122. (looseleaf format)

547.128   US
THERMODYNAMICS RESEARCH CENTER. DATA PROJECT. SELECTED VALUES OF PROPERTIES OF CHEMICAL COMPOUNDS. CATEGORY F. SELECTED 1H NUCLEAR MAGNETIC RESONANCE SPECTRAL DATA. 1960. irreg., F-31, 1982. $150 per supplement. Thermodynamics Research Center, Texas A & M University System, College Station, TX 77843-3111. TEL 409-845-4940. Ed. Kenneth R. Hall. circ. 114. (looseleaf format)
Formerly: Thermodynamics Research Center Data Project. Selected Values of Properties of Chemical Compounds. Category F. Selected Nuclear Magnetic Resonance Spectral Data (ISSN 0082-4070)

544.63   US
THERMODYNAMICS RESEARCH CENTER. HYDROCARBON PROJECT. SELECTED VALUES OF PROPERTIES OF HYDROCARBONS AND RELATED COMPOUNDS. CATEGORY B: SELECTED INFRARED SPECTRAL DATA. 1943. irreg., supplement B-81, 1983. $150 per supplement. (Texas Engineering Experiment Station) Thermodynamics Research Center System, Texas A & M University, College Station, TX 77843-3111. TEL 409-845-4940. Ed. Kenneth R. Hall. circ. 238. (looseleaf format)
Formerly: A P I Research Project 44. Selected Values of Properties of Hydrocarbons and Related Compounds. Category B: Selected Infrared Spectral Data (ISSN 0065-9649)

547.3 543.085   US
THERMODYNAMICS RESEARCH CENTER. HYDROCARBON PROJECT. SELECTED VALUES OF PROPERTIES OF HYDROCARBONS AND RELATED COMPOUNDS. CATEGORY C: SELECTED ULTRAVIOLET SPECTRAL DATA. 1945. irreg., supplement C-50, 1984. $150 per supplement. (Texas Engineering Experiment Station) Thermodynamics Research Center System, Texas A & M University, College Station, TX 77843-3111. TEL 409-845-4940. Ed. Kenneth R. Hall. circ. 227. (looseleaf format)
Formerly: A P I Research Project 44. Selected Values of Properties of Hydrocarbons and Related Compounds. Category C: Selected Ultraviolet Spectral Data (ISSN 0065-9657); Incorporating: Thermodynamics Research Center. Data Project. Selected Values of Properties of Chemical Compounds. Category C. Selected Ultraviolet Spectral Data.

547.3 543.085   US
THERMODYNAMICS RESEARCH CENTER. HYDROCARBON PROJECT. SELECTED VALUES OF PROPERTIES OF HYDROCARBONS AND RELATED COMPOUNDS. CATEGORY D: SELECTED RAMAN SPECTRAL DATA. 1948. irreg., supplement D-24, 1983. $150 per supplement. (Texas Engineering Experiment Station) Thermodynamics Research Center, Texas A & M University System, College Station, TX 77843-3111. TEL 409-845-4940. Ed. Kenneth R. Hall. circ. 159.
Formerly: A P I Research Project 44. Selected Values of Properties of Hydrocarbons and Related Compounds. Category D: Selected Raman Spectral Data (ISSN 0065-9665); Incorporating: Thermodynamics Research Center. Data Project. Selected Values of Properties of Chemical Compounds. Category D. Selected Raman Spectral Data (ISSN 0082-4038)

547.3 543.085   US
THERMODYNAMICS RESEARCH CENTER. HYDROCARBON PROJECT. SELECTED VALUES OF PROPERTIES OF HYDROCARBONS AND RELATED COMPOUNDS. CATEGORY E: SELECTED MASS SPECTRAL DATA. 1947. irreg., supplement E-60, 1984. $150 per supplement. (Texas Engineering Experiment Station) Thermodynamics Research Center, Texas A & M University System, College Station, TX 77843-3111. TEL 409-845-4940. Ed. Kenneth R. Hall. circ. 283. (looseleaf format)
Formerly: A P I Research Project 44. Selected Values of Properties of Hydrocarbons and Related Compounds. Category E: Selected Mass Spectral Data (ISSN 0065-9673); Incorporating: Thermodynamics Research Center. Data Project. Selected Values of Properties of Chemical Compounds. Category E. Selected Mass Spectral Data.

547.3   US
THERMODYNAMICS RESEARCH CENTER. HYDROCARBON PROJECT. SELECTED VALUES OF PROPERTIES OF HYDROCARBONS AND RELATED COMPOUNDS. CATEGORY F: SELECTED NUCLEAR MAGNETIC RESONANCE DATA. 1959. irreg., supplement F-28, 1984. $150 per supplement. (Texas Engineering Experiment Station) Thermodynamics Research Center, Texas A & M University System, College Station, TX 77843-3111. TEL 409-845-4940. Ed. Kenneth R. Hall. circ. 146. (looseleaf format)
Formerly: A P I Research Project 44. Selected Values of Properties of Hydrocarbons and Related Compounds. Category F: Selected Nuclear Magnetic Resonance Data (ISSN 0065-9681)

547.3 543.085   US
THERMODYNAMICS RESEARCH CENTER. HYDROCARBON PROJECT. SELECTED VALUES OF PROPERTIES OF HYDROCARBONS AND RELATED COMPOUNDS. CATEGORY G: SELECTED 13-C NUCLEAR MAGNETIC RESONANCE SPECTRAL DATA. 1975. irreg., supplement G-14, 1984. $150 per supplement. (Texas Engineering Experiment Station) Thermodynamics Research Center, Texas A & M University System, College Station, TX 77843-3111. TEL 409-845-4940. Ed. Kenneth R. Hall. circ. 140.
Formerly: A P I Research Project 44. Selected Values of Properties of Hydrocarbons and Related Compounds. Category G: Selected 13 C Nuclear Magnetic Resonance Spectral Data.

543   US   ISSN 0082-6243
TREATISE ON ANALYTICAL CHEMISTRY. PART 1: THEORY AND PRACTICE OF ANALYTICAL CHEMISTRY. 1959. irreg., vol.12, 1983. price varies. John Wiley & Sons, Inc., 605 Third Ave, New York, NY 10016. TEL 212-850-6000. Eds. I.M. Kolthoff, P.J. Elving.

543   US   ISSN 0082-6251
TREATISE ON ANALYTICAL CHEMISTRY. PART 2: ANALYTICAL CHEMISTRY OF THE ELEMENTS; ANALYTICAL CHEMISTRY OF INORGANIC AND ORGANIC COMPOUNDS. 1961. irreg., vol.17, 1980. price varies. John Wiley & Sons, Inc., 605 Third Ave, New York, NY 10016. TEL 212-850-6000. Eds. I.M. Kolthoff, P.J. Elving.

543   US   ISSN 0082-626X
TREATISE ON ANALYTICAL CHEMISTRY. PART 3: ANALYTICAL CHEMISTRY IN INDUSTRY. 1967. irreg., vol.3, 1976. price varies. John Wiley & Sons, Inc., 605 Third Ave, New York, NY 10016. TEL 212-850-6000. Eds. I.M. Kolthoff, P.J. Elving.

543   NE   ISSN 0069-8024
WILSON & WILSON'S COMPREHENSIVE ANALYTICAL CHEMISTRY. 1959. irreg., vol.14, 1982. price varies. Elsevier Science Publishers B.V., P.O. Box 211, 1000 AE Amsterdam, Netherlands. Ed. G. Svehla.

YAMAGUCHI-KEN KOGAI SENTA NENPO/ YAMAGUCHI PREFECTURAL ENVIRONMENTAL POLLUTION RESEARCH CENTER. ANNUAL REPORT. see *ENVIRONMENTAL STUDIES*

CHEMISTRY — Crystallography

548.9   US
ADVANCES IN LIQUID CRYSTALS. 1975. irreg., vol.6, 1983. Academic Press, Inc., Orlando, FL 32887. TEL 305-345-2000. Ed. G.H. Brown. Indexed: Biol.Abstr. Chem.Abstr. Sci.Cit.Ind. Ind.Sci.Rev. Phys.Ber.

548   US   ISSN 0514-8863
AMERICAN CRYSTALLOGRAPHIC ASSOCIATION. MONOGRAPHS. 1944. irreg., no.8, 1979. price varies. American Crystallographic Association, 335 E. 45th St., New York, NY 10017 (Distr. by: Polycrystal Book Service, Box 27, Western Springs, IL 60558) Ed. S.C. Abrahams. circ. 1,250. Indexed: Bull.Signal. Chem.Abstr. Phys.Abstr.

548   US   ISSN 0569-4221
AMERICAN CRYSTALLOGRAPHIC ASSOCIATION. PROGRAM & ABSTRACTS. 1950. a. $5. American Crystallographic Association, 335 E. 45th St., New York, NY 10017 (Distr. by: Polycrystal Book Service, Box 27, Western Springs, IL 60558) Ed. S.C. Abrahams. circ. 2,500. Indexed: Bull.Signal. Chem.Abstr. GeoRef. Phys.Abstr.

548   US   ISSN 0065-8006
AMERICAN CRYSTALLOGRAPHIC ASSOCIATION. TRANSACTIONS. 1965. a. $15. American Crystallographic Association, 335 E. 45th St., New York, NY 10017 TEL 212-661-9404. (Subscr. to: Polycrystal Book Service, Box 27, Western Springs, IL 60558) circ. 2,500. (back issues avail.) Indexed: Chem.Abstr. GeoRef.

548   US   ISSN 0172-5076
CRYSTALS: GROWTH, PROPERTIES AND APPLICATIONS. 1978. irreg., vol.10, 1984. price varies. Springer-Verlag, 175 Fifth Ave., New York, NY 10010 TEL 212-460-1500. (Also Berlin, Heidelberg, Tokyo and Vienna) (reprint service avail. from ISI) Indexed: Chem.Abstr.

DEFECTS IN SOLIDS. see *PHYSICS*

548   DK   ISSN 0074-9389
INTERNATIONAL UNION OF CRYSTALLOGRAPHY. ABSTRACTS OF THE TRIENNIAL CONGRESS. (Supplement to: Acta Crystallographica. Section A) (Text in English, French or German) 1960. triennial ; 1975, 10th General Assembly, Amsterdam. Munksgaard, Noerre Soegade 35, DK-1370 Copenhagen K, Denmark. (reprint service avail. from ISI)

548   UR   ISSN 0202-7984
ITOGI NAUKI I TEKHNIKI: KRISTALLOKHIMIYA. irreg., latest vol.20, 1986. price varies. Vsesoyuznyi Institut Nauchno-Tekhnicheskoi Informatsii (VINITI), Ul. Baltiiskaya 14, Moscow A-219, Russian S.F.S.R., U.S.S.R. Indexed: Chem.Abstr.

LANDOLT-BOERNSTEIN, ZAHLENWERTE UND FUNKTIONEN AUS NATURWISSENSCHAFTEN UND TECHNIK. NEUE SERIE. GROUP 3: CRYSTAL PHYSICS. see *PHYSICS*

548 NE ISSN 0377-2012
MOLECULAR STRUCTURES AND DIMENSIONS. 1970. irreg. price varies. D. Reidel Publishing Co., Box 17, 3300 AA Dordrecht, Netherlands (And 190 Old Derby St., Hingham, MA 02043) Ed. Olga Kennard.

548 NE ISSN 0166-6983
STRUCTURE REPORTS. SECTION A. vol.48, 1984. irreg. (International Union of Crystallography) D. Reidel Publishing Co., Box 17, 3300 AA Dordrecht, Netherlands (And 190 Old Derby St., Hingham, MA 02043)

548 NE ISSN 0166-7033
STRUCTURE REPORTS. SECTION B. vol.46, 1985. irreg. (International Union of Crystallography) D. Reidel Publishing Co., Box 17, 3300 AA Dordrecht, Netherlands (And 190 Old Derby St., Hingham, MA 02043)

CHEMISTRY — Electrochemistry

541.37 660 US ISSN 0567-9907
ADVANCES IN ELECTROCHEMISTRY AND ELECTROCHEMICAL ENGINEERING. 1961. irreg., vol.16, 1987. price varies. John Wiley & Sons, Inc., 605 Third Ave., New York, NY 10016. TEL 212-850-6000. Ed. P. Delahay. Indexed: Chem.Abstr.

541.37 UR
AKADEMIYA NAUK KAZAKHSKOI S.S.R. INSTITUT ORGANICHESKOGO KATALIZA I ELEKTROKHIMII. TRUDY. vol.15, 1977. irreg. 1.34 Rub. per no. Izdatel'stvo Nauka, Kazakhskoe Otdelenie, Ul. Shevchenko 28, 480021 Alma-Ata, Kazakh S.S.R., U.S.S.R. Ed. L. Kozin. abstr. bibl. illus. circ. 1,000. Indexed: Chem.Abstr.

541.37 AT ISSN 0155-6002
AUSTRALASIAN CORROSION ASSOCIATION. ANNUAL CONFERENCE PROCEEDINGS. 1960. a. Aus.$35($50) Australasia Corrosion Association, c/o Australasian Secretary, P.O. Box 233, Kingswood, S.A. 5062, Australia. bk. rev. circ. 350. Indexed: Chem.Abstr.

541.37 US
ELECTROCHEMICAL SOCIETY SERIES. 1948. irreg., unnumbered, latest 1984. $42.50. (Electrochemical Society, Inc.) John Wiley & Sons, Inc., 605 Third Ave., New York, NY 10016. TEL 212-850-6000.

541.37 UK ISSN 0305-9979
ELECTROCHEMISTRY. 1970. a. price varies. Royal Society of Chemistry, Burlington House, London W1V 0BN, England (Subscr. to: Distribution Centre, Blackhorse Road, Letchworth, Herts. SG6 1HN, England) Ed. D. Pletcher. Indexed: Chem.Abstr.

I L Z R O ANNUAL REVIEW. (International Lead Zinc Research Organization, Inc.) see *METALLURGY*

I L Z R O LEAD RESEARCH DIGEST. (International Lead Zinc Research Organization, Inc.) see *METALLURGY*

I L Z R O ZINC/CADIUM RESEARCH DIGEST. (International Lead Zinc Research Organization, Inc.) see *METALLURGY*

541.37 CI ISSN 0091-391X
INTERNATIONAL SYMPOSIUM ON SILICON MATERIALS SCIENCE AND TECHNOLOGY. PROCEEDINGS.* 1969. irreg., 1st., 1969, New York. $10. Electrochemical Society, Box 2071, Princeton, NJ 08540. Eds. Rolf R. Haberecht, Edward L. Kern.

541.37 UR ISSN 0202-8093
ITOGI NAUKI I TEKHNIKI: ELEKTROKHIMIYA. irreg., latest vols.24-25, 1987. price varies. Vsesoyuznyi Institut Nauchno-Tekhnicheskoi Informatsii (VINITI), Ul. Baltiiskaya 14, Moscow A-219, Russian S.F.S.R., U.S.S.R. (Subscr. to: Mezhdunarodnaya Kniga, Dimitrova ul. 39, 113095 Moscow, Russian S.F.S.R., U.S.S.R.) Indexed: Chem.Abstr. Met.Abstr.

541.37 US ISSN 0076-9924
MODERN ASPECTS OF ELECTROCHEMISTRY. no.3, 1964. irreg. price varies. Plenum Publishing Corp., 233 Spring St., New York, NY 10013. TEL 212-620-8047. Eds. B.E. Conway, J. Bockris. Indexed: Chem.Abstr.

543 541.37 US ISSN 0077-0833
MONOGRAPHS IN ELECTROANALYTICAL CHEMISTRY AND ELECTROCHEMISTRY SERIES. 1969. irreg., vol.4, 1984. price varies. Marcel Dekker, Inc., 270 Madison Ave., New York, NY 10016. TEL 212-696-9000. Ed. A.J. Bard.

CHEMISTRY — Inorganic Chemistry

546 US
ADVANCES IN INORGANIC AND BIOINORGANIC MECHANISMS. 1982. irreg., vol.4, 1986. Academic Press Inc., Orlando, FL 32887. TEL 305-345-6000. Ed. A.G. Sykes. Indexed: Chem.Abstr.

546 541.38 US ISSN 0065-2792
ADVANCES IN INORGANIC CHEMISTRY AND RADIOCHEMISTRY. 1959. irreg., vol.29, 1985. Academic Press, Inc., Orlando, FL 32887. TEL 305-345-2000. Eds. H.J. Emeleus, A.G. Sharpe. index. Indexed: Chem.Abstr. Sci.Cit.Ind. Ind.Sci.Rev.

546.34 US ISSN 0065-2954
ADVANCES IN MOLTEN SALT CHEMISTRY. 1971. irreg. price varies. Plenum Publishing Corp., 233 Spring St., New York, NY 10013. TEL 212-620-8047. Ed.Bd. Indexed: Chem.Abstr.

ANNUAL REPORTS IN INORGANIC AND GENERAL SYNTHESES. see *CHEMISTRY — Physical Chemistry*

546 US
BENCHMARK PAPERS IN INORGANIC CHEMISTRY. (Each vol. has distinctive title) 1972. irreg., vol.6, 1977. price varies. Van Nostrand Reinhold Company, 7625 Empire Dr., Florence, KY 41042. TEL 606-525-6600. illus. index.

546 530 AT ISSN 0725-3575
C.S.I.R.O. DIVISION OF MATERIALS SCIENCE. RESEARCH REPORT. 1948. biennial. Aus.$3. C.S.I.R.O, P.O. Box 89, East Melbourne, Vic. 3002, Australia. Ed. J.A. Spink. circ. 1,000.

546 US
CENTRIFUGAL PUMP SPECIFICATIONS. 1981. a. $29.95. Gordon Publications Inc., Reference Book Group, Box 1952, Dover, NJ 07801. TEL 201-267-6040. adv. charts. stat. circ. 4,000. (also avail. in magnetic tape; back issues avail.)

546 US ISSN 0740-3739
FINE CHEMICALS DIRECTORY. 1985. a. $450. Pergamon Journals, Inc., Maxwell House, Fairview Park, Elmsford, NY 10523 TEL 914-592-7700. (And Headington Hill Hall, Oxford, OX3 0BW, England) (also avail. in microform from MIM,UMI) ●Also available online. Vendors: Pergamon Infoline.

546 US ISSN 0172-7966
INORGANIC CHEMISTRY CONCEPTS. 1977. irreg., vol.9, 1986. price varies. Springer-Verlag, 175 Fifth Ave., New York, NY 10010 TEL 212-460-1500. (Also Berlin, Heidelberg, Tokyo and Vienna) Ed.Bd. (reprint service avail. from ISI) Supersedes (1949-1969): Anorganische und Allgemeine Chemie in Einzeldarstellungen (ISSN 0066-4553)

546 UR ISSN 0234-4483
IONNYE RASPLAVY I TVERDYE ELECTROLITY; respublikanskii mezhvedomstvennyi sbornik naychnykh trudov. 1986. a. (Akademiya Nauk Ukrainskoi S.S.R., Institut Obshchei i Neorganicheskoi Khimii) Izdatel'stvo Naukova Dumka, ul. Repina 3, Kiev 252601, Ukrainian S.S.R., U.S.S.R. Ed. Yu.K. Delimarskii.

ISSLEDOVANIYA V OBLASTI KHIMII REDKOZEMEL'NYKH ELEMENTOV. see *EARTH SCIENCES*

546 531.64 536 539.7 JA ISSN 0454-9244
KYOTO UNIVERSITY. RESEARCH REACTOR INSTITUTE. ANNUAL REPORTS. (Text and summaries in English) 1968. a. Kyoto University, Research Reactor Institute, Kumatori-Cho, Sennan-Gun, Osaka 590-14, Japan. Ed. K. Okano. circ. 1,000. (back issues avail.) Indexed: Chem.Abstr.

DIE MAKROMOLEKULARE CHEMIE. SUPPLEMENT. see *CHEMISTRY — Organic Chemistry*

546 US
MECHANISMS OF INORGANIC AND ORGANOMETALLIC REACTIONS. 1983. a. Plenum Publishing Corp., 233 Spring St., New York, NY 10013. Ed. M.V. Twigg. Indexed: Chem.Abstr.

546 US
METAL IONS IN BIOLOGICAL SYSTEMS. vol.14, 1982. irreg., vol.22, 1986. price varies. Marcel Dekker, Inc., 270 Madison Ave., New York, NY 10016. TEL 212-696-9000. Ed. Helmut Siegel. Indexed: Chem.Abstr. Ind.Sci.Rev.

546.536 JA ISSN 0388-0664
NIPPON TUNGSTEN REVIEW. (Text in English) 1968. a. free. Nippon Tungsten Co., Ltd., 20-31, Shimizu 2-Chome, Minami-Ku, Fukuoka 815, Japan. Ed. S. Takezaki. Indexed: Chem.Abstr.

546 PL ISSN 0324-9832
POLITECHNIKA WROCLAWSKA. INSTYTUT CHEMII NIEORGANICZNEJ I METALURGII PIERWIASTKOW RZADKICH. PRACE NAUKOWE. KONFERENCJE. (Text in Polish; summaries in English and Russian) 1973. irreg., no.10, 1984. price varies. Politechnika Wroclawska, Wybrzeze Wyspianskiego 27, 50-370 Wroclaw, Poland (Dist. by: Ars Polona-Ruch, Krakowskie Przedmiescie 7, Warsaw, Poland) Ed. Jerzy Ciekot. Indexed: Chem.Abstr.

546 PL ISSN 0324-9840
POLITECHNIKA WROCLAWSKA. INSTYTUT CHEMII NIEORGANICZNEJ I METALURGII PIERWIASTKOW RZADKICH. PRACE NAUKOWE. MONOGRAFIE. (Text in Polish; summaries in English and Russian) 1970. irreg., no.25, 1985. price varies. Politechnika Wroclawska, Wybrzeze Wyspianskiego 27, 50-370 Wroclaw, Poland (Dist. by: Ars Polona-Ruch, Krakowskie Przedmiescie 7, Warsaw, Poland) Ed. Jerzy Ciekot.

546 PL ISSN 0370-0755
POLITECHNIKA WROCLAWSKA. INSTYTUT CHEMII NIEORGANICZNEJ I METALURGII PIERWIASTKOW RZADKICH. PRACE NAUKOWE. STUDIA I MATERIALY. (Text in Polish; summaries in English and Russian) 1970. irreg., no.18, 1981. price varies. Politechnika Wroclawska, Wybrzeze Wyspianskiego 27, 50-370 Wroclaw, Poland (Dist. by: Ars Polona-Ruch, Krakowskie Przedmiescie 7, Warsaw, Poland) Ed. Marian Kloza.

546 UR ISSN 0320-3379
POLUTEHNILINE INSTITUUT TALLINN. NEORGANICHESKAYA KHIMIYA I TEKHNOLOGIYA. (Subseries of its Toimetised) (Text in Russian; summaries in English or German) irreg. price varies. Polutehniline Instituut Tallinn, Ehitajate tee 5, Tallinn, Estonian S.S.R., U.S.S.R.

POWDER DIFFRACTION FILE SEARCH MANUAL. ALPHABETICAL LISTING. INORGANIC. see *CHEMISTRY — Analytical Chemistry*

POWDER DIFFRACTION FILE SEARCH MANUAL. FINK METHOD. INORGANIC. see *CHEMISTRY — Analytical Chemistry*

POWDER DIFFRACTION FILE SEARCH MANUAL. HANAWALT METHOD. INORGANIC. see *CHEMISTRY — Analytical Chemistry*

546 US ISSN 0079-6379
PROGRESS IN INORGANIC CHEMISTRY. 1959. irreg., vol.33, 1985. price varies. John Wiley & Sons, Inc., 605 Third Ave., New York, NY 10016. TEL 212-850-6000. Ed. S.J. Lippard.

541.3 546   UK   ISSN 0260-1818
ROYAL SOCIETY OF CHEMISTRY. ANNUAL
REPORTS ON THE PROGRESS OF
CHEMISTRY. SECTION A: INORGANIC
CHEMISTRY. 1904. a. £60($118) Royal Society of
Chemistry, Burlington House, Piccadilly, London
W1V 0BN, England (Subscr. to: Distribution
Centre, Blackhorse Rd., Letchworth, Herts SG6
1HN, England) Ed. J. Donaldson. index.
cum.index: vols.1-46.
  Supersedes: Chemical Society. Annual Reports on
the Progress of Chemistry. Section A: Physical and
Inorganic Chemistry (ISSN 0308-6003); Which was
formerly: Chemical Society, London. Annual
Reports on the Progress of Chemistry. Section A:
General, Physical and Inorganic Chemistry (ISSN
0069-3022)

546   NE
STUDIES IN INORGANIC CHEMISTRY. 1978.
irreg., vol.6, 1985. price varies. Elsevier Science
Publishers B.V., P.O. Box 211, 1000 AE
Amsterdam, Netherlands. Indexed: Chem.Abstr.

536   HU   ISSN 0082-1306
SZILIKATKEMIAI MONOGRAFIAK. 1960. irreg.
price varies. (Magyar Tudomanyos Akademia)
Akademiai Kiado, Publishing House of the
Hungarian Academy of Sciences, Box 24, H-1363
Budapest, Hungary.

546   NE
TOPICS IN F-ELEMENT CHEMISTRY. 1985. irreg.
price varies. D. Reidel Publishing Company, Postbus
17, 3300 AA Dordrecht, Netherlands.

546 540   NE   ISSN 0082-495X
TOPICS IN INORGANIC AND GENERAL
CHEMISTRY. (Text in English) 1964. irreg.,
vol.20, 1985. price varies. Elsevier Science
Publishers B.V., P.O. Box 211, 1000 AE
Amsterdam, Netherlands. Eds. P.L. Robinson,
R.J.H. Clark.

546   NO
UNIVERSITETET I TRONDHEIM. NORGES
TEKNISKE HOEGSKOLE. INSTITUTT FOR
UORGANISK KJEMI. AVHANDLING. 1976.
irreg., no.44, 1985. Kr.300. Universitetet i
Trondheim, Norges Tekniske Hoegskole. Institutt
for Uorganisk Kjemi, 7034 Trondheim-NTH,
Norway. circ. 250.

CHEMISTRY — Organic Chemistry

547 581 576 616.99 PH   ISSN 0065-1370
ACTA MANILANA. (Text and summaries in
English) 1965. a. P.20($3) University of Santo
Tomas, Espana St., Manila D-403, Philippines. Ed.
Ciriaco Pedrosa. circ. 500. (back issues avail.)
Indexed: Biol.Abstr. Nutr.Abstr. Ind.Phil.Per.

547.5   US   ISSN 0065-2121
ADVANCES IN ALICYCLIC CHEMISTRY. 1966.
irreg., vol.3, 1971. Academic Press, Inc., Orlando,
FL 32887. TEL 305-345-2000. Eds. Harold Hart,
Gerasimos J. Karabatsos.

547.78 574.192   US   ISSN 0065-2318
ADVANCES IN CARBOHYDRATE CHEMISTRY
AND BIOCHEMISTRY. 1945. irreg., vol.43, 1985.
$55. Academic Press, Inc., Orlando, FL 32887. TEL
305-345-2000. Eds. Melville L. Wolfrom, R. Stuart
Tipson. Indexed: Biol.Abstr. Chem.Abstr.
Ind.Med. Nutr.Abstr. Abstr.Bull.Inst.Pap.Chem.
Curr.Chem.React. Food Sci.& Tech.Abstr.
Ind.Chem. Ind.Sci.Rev. Trop.Dis.Bull.
  Formerly (1945-1968): Advances in Carbohydrate
Chemistry (ISSN 0096-5332)

547.59   US   ISSN 0065-2725
ADVANCES IN HETEROCYCLIC CHEMISTRY.
(Supplements avail.) 1963. irreg., no.39, 1986. price
varies. Academic Press, Inc., Orlando, FL 32887.
TEL 305-345-2000. Ed. A.R. Katritzky. index.
Indexed: Sci.Cit.Ind. Curr.Chem.React. Ind.Chem.
Ind.Sci.Rev.

547   NE
ADVANCES IN INCLUSION SCIENCE. 1983.
irreg. price varies. D. Reidel Publishing Company,
Box 17, 3300 AA Dordrecht, Netherlands (And 190
Old Derby St., Hingham, MA 02043)

547 698   US
ADVANCES IN ORGANIC COATINGS SCIENCE
AND TECHNOLOGY. 1979. irreg. price varies.
Technomic Publishing Co., Inc., 851 New Holland
Ave., Box 3535, Lancaster, PA 17604. TEL 717-
291-5609. Eds. Geoffrey D. Parfitt, Angelos V.
Patsis.

547.05   US   ISSN 0065-3055
ADVANCES IN ORGANOMETALLIC
CHEMISTRY. 1964. irreg., vol.25, 1986. Academic
Press, Inc., Orlando, FL 32887. TEL 305-345-2000.
Eds. F.G.A. Stone, Robert West. index. Indexed:
Chem.Abstr. Sci.Cit.Ind. Curr.Chem.React.
Ind.Chem. Ind.Sci.Rev. Mass Spectr.Bull.

547   US   ISSN 0065-3195
ADVANCES IN POLYMER SCIENCE/
FORTSCHRITTE DER HOCHPOLYMEREN-
FORSCHUNG. (Contributions in English, French,
German) 1958. irreg., vol.81, 1986. price varies.
Springer-Verlag, 175 Fifth Ave., New York, NY
10010 TEL 212-460-1500. (Also Berlin, Heidelberg,
Tokyo and Vienna) (reprint service avail. from ISI)
Indexed: Biol.Abstr. Chem.Abstr. Sci.Cit.Ind.
Ind.Sci.Rev. World Text.Abstr.
  Polymers

547 660.284 668.4   US   ISSN 0044-6378
ADVANCES IN URETHANE SCIENCE AND
TECHNOLOGY. 1971. irreg. price varies.
Technomic Publishing Co., Inc., 851 New Holland
Ave., Box 3535, Lancaster, PA 17604. TEL 717-
291-5609. Eds. Kurt C. Frisch, Sidney L. Reegen.
charts. illus. stat. index. Indexed: Chem.Abstr.
Eng.Ind. Sci.Cit.Ind. Ind.Sci.Rev.
  Polymers

547   UR
AKADEMIYA NAUK KAZAKHSKOI S.S.R.
INSTITUT KHIMICHESKIKH NAUK. TRUDY.
vol.46, 1977. irreg. 1.88 Rub. per no. Izdatel'stvo
Nauka, Kazakhskoe Otdelenie, Ul.Shevchenko 28,
480021 Alma-Ata, Kazakh S.S.R., U.S.S.R. Ed. M.
Goryaev. abstr. bibl. illus. circ. 1,000. Indexed:
Biol.Abstr. Chem.Abstr. GeoRef.

547 615.7   US
ALKALOIDS; chemistry and pharmacology. 1950.
irreg., vol.28, 1986. Academic Press, Inc., Orlando,
FL 32887. TEL 305-345-2000. Indexed:
Chem.Abstr.

547   US
ANALYSIS OF ORGANIC MATERIALS: AN
INTERNATIONAL SERIES OF MONOGRAPHS.
1972. irreg., latest vol.14, 1982. Academic Press
Inc., Orlando, FL 32887. TEL 305-345-2000. Eds.
R. Belcher, S. Anderson. Indexed: Chem.Abstr.
  Formerly: Monographs in Organic Functional
Group Analysis (ISSN 0077-0906)

547   NE
ASPECTS OF HOMOGENEOUS CATALYSIS: A
SERIES OF ADVANCES. (Text in English) 1970.
irreg. price varies. D. Reidel Publishing Co., Box 17,
3300 AA Dordrecht, Netherlands (And 190 Old
Derby St., Hingham, MA 02043) Ed. Renato Ugo.

547   US   ISSN 0067-4915
BEILSTEINS HANDBUCH DER ORGANISCHEN
CHEMIE. FOURTH SUPPLEMENT. (The main
work was published: 1918-1937; First Supplement:
1928-1938; Second Supplement: 1941-1957; Third
Supplement: 1930-1949; Fourth Supplement: 1950-
1959; Fifth Supplement: 1960-1979) 1972. irreg.,
latest 1987. price varies. Springer-Verlag, 175 Fifth
Ave., New York, NY 10010 TEL 212-460-1500.
(Also Berlin, Heidelberg, Tokyo and Vienna)
(reprint service avail. from ISI)

547   US
BENCHMARK PAPERS IN ORGANIC
CHEMISTRY. (Each vol. has distinctive title) 1974.
irreg., vol.6, 1977. price varies. Van Nostrand
Reinhold Company, 7625 Empire Dr., Florence, KY
41042. TEL 606-525-6600. illus. index.

547   UK
CARBOHYDRATE CHEMISTRY. PART 1: MONO-,
DI-, & TRI-SACCHARIDES & THEIR
DERIVATIVES. 1983. a. price varies. Royal
Society of Chemistry, Burlington House, London
W1V 0BN, England (Subscr. to: Distribution
Centre, Blackhorse Rd., Letchworth, Herts. SG6
1HN, England) Ed. N.R. Williams. charts. illus.
index. Indexed: Chem.Abstr.
  Supersedes in part: Carbohydrate Chemistry
(ISSN 0576-7172)

547   UK
CARBOHYDRATE CHEMISTRY. PART 2:
MACROMOLECULES. 1983. a. price varies. Royal
Society of Chemistry, Burlington House, Piccadilly,
London W1V 0BN, England (Subscr. to:
Distribution Centre, Blackhorse Rd., Letchworth,
Herts. SG6 1HN, England) Ed. J.F. Kennedy.
charts. illus. index. Indexed: Chem.Abstr.
  Supersedes in part: Carbohydrate Chemistry
(ISSN 0576-7172)

547   NE
CATALYSIS BY METAL COMPLEXES. 1976. irreg.
price varies. D. Reidel Publishing Co., Box 17, 3300
AA Dordrecht, Netherlands (And 190 Old Derby
St., Hingham, MA 02043) Eds. Renato Ugo, B.R.
James. Indexed: Biol.Abstr. Chem.Abstr.
  Formerly: Homogeneous Catalysis in Organic and
Inorganic Chemistry.

547   US   ISSN 0069-3138
CHEMISTRY AND PHYSICS OF CARBON: A
SERIES OF ADVANCES. 1966. irreg., vol.19,
1984. price varies. Marcel Dekker, Inc., 270
Madison Ave., New York, NY 10016. TEL 212-
696-9000. Eds. P.L. Walker, Jr., P.A. Thrower.
Indexed: Chem.Abstr. Sci.Cit.Ind. GeoRef.
Ind.Sci.Rev.

547.59   US   ISSN 0069-3154
CHEMISTRY OF HETEROCYCLIC
COMPOUNDS; a series of monographs. 1951.
irreg., vol.46, 1986. John Wiley & Sons, Inc., 605
Third Ave., New York, NY 10016. TEL 212-850-
6000. Eds. Arnold Weissburger, Edward C. Taylor.
index. Indexed: Chem.Abstr.

547   UK   ISSN 0069-3162
CHEMISTRY OF NATURAL PRODUCTS. (Text in
English; occasionally in French or German) 1961.
irreg., 9th, 1974, Ottawa, pub. 1979. price varies.
International Union of Pure and Applied Chemistry,
c/o Dr. M. Williams, Bank Court Chambers, 2-3
Pound Way, Cowley Centre, Oxford OX4 3YF,
England.

664   NE
DEVELOPMENTS IN FOOD SCIENCE. 1978.
irreg., vol.11, 1985. price varies. Elsevier Science
Publishers B.V., Box 211, 1000 AE Amsterdam,
Netherlands. Indexed: Chem.Abstr. Food Sci.&
Tech.Abstr.

547   US   ISSN 0071-7886
FORTSCHRITTE DER CHEMIE ORGANISCHER
NATURSTOFFE/PROGRESS IN THE
CHEMISTRY OF ORGANIC NATURAL
PRODUCTS. 1938. irreg., vol.48, 1986. Springer-
Verlag, 175 Fifth Ave., New York, NY 10010 TEL
212-460-1500. (Also Berlin, Heidelberg, Tokyo and
Vienna) cum.index: vols.1-20, 1938-62; also avail.
separately. (reprint service avail. from ISI) Indexed:
Biol.Abstr. Chem.Abstr. Excerp.Med. Ind.Med.
Biotech.Abstr. VITIS.

547   UK   ISSN 0141-2140
GENERAL AND SYNTHETIC METHODS. 1978. a.
Royal Society of Chemistry, Burlington House,
London W1V 0BN, England (Subscr. to:
Distribution Centre, Blackhorse Rd., Letchworth,
Herts. SG6 1HN, England) Ed. G. Pattenden.
Indexed: Chem.Abstr.

547   UK   ISSN 0144-8773
HETEROCYCLIC CHEMISTRY. 1980. irreg. Royal
Society of Chemistry, Burlington House, London
W1V 0BN, England (Subscr. to: Distribution
Centre, Blackhorse Rd., Letchworth, Herts. SG6
1HN, England) Eds. H. Suschitzky, O. Meth-Cohn.
Indexed: Chem.Abstr.

INDIAN JOURNAL OF HEREDITY. see
  BIOLOGY — Genetics

INTERNATIONAL PROGRESS IN URETHANES.
see *PLASTICS*

CHEMISTRY — ORGANIC CHEMISTRY

547   NE
ISOTOPES IN ORGANIC CHEMISTRY. 1975. irreg., vol.6, 1984. Elsevier Science Publishers B.V., P.O. Box 211, 1000 AE Amsterdam, Netherlands. Eds. E. Buncel, C.C. Lee. Indexed: Chem.Abstr.

547   UR   ISSN 0137-0251
ITOGI NAUKI I TEKHNIKI: ORGANICHESKAYA KHIMIYA. irreg., latest vol.14, 1985. price varies. Vsesoyuznyi Institut Nauchno-Tekhnicheskoi Informatsii (VINITI), Ul. Baltiiskaya 14, Moscow A-219, Russian S.F.S.R., U.S.S.R. (Subscr. to: Mezhdunarodnaya Kniga, Dimitrova ul. 39, 113095 Moscow, Russian S.F.S.R., U.S.S.R.) Indexed: Chem.Abstr.

540 547   JA   ISSN 0075-2010
ITSUU LABORATORY, TOKYO. ANNUAL REPORT/ITSUU KENKYUSHO NENPO. (Text in English and German; summaries in Japanese) 1950. irreg. (a. or biennial) exchange basis. Itsuu Laboratory - Itsuu Kenkyusho, 2-28-10 Tamagawa, Setagaya-ku, Tokyo 173, Japan. Ed. M. Natsume.

547.84   US   ISSN 0360-8905
JOURNAL OF POLYMER SCIENCE. POLYMER SYMPOSIA EDITION. 1963. irreg., no.69, 1981. $13.95. John Wiley & Sons, Inc., 605 Third Ave., New York, NY 10016. TEL 212-850-6000. illus. (also avail. in microform from BLH,UMI; back issues avail. from UMI) Indexed: Chem.Abstr. Curr.Cont. Sci.Abstr. Abstr.Bull.Inst.Pap.Chem. Ind.Sci.Rev. World Text.Abstr.
    Supersedes: Journal of Polymer Science. Part C Polymer Symposia (ISSN 0449-2994)
Polymers

547   US
LECTURE NOTES IN BIO-ORGANIC CHEMISTRY. 1986. irreg. price varies. Springer-Verlag, 175 Fifth Ave., New York, NY 10160 TEL 212-460-1500. (Also Berlin, Heidelberg, Tokyo, Vienna) (reprint service avail. from ISI)

547.59   US   ISSN 0090-2268
LECTURES IN HETEROCYCLIC CHEMISTRY. (Suppl. issue of Journal of Heterocyclic Chemistry) 1971. biennial. $35. (Heterocyclic Chemistry Society) HeteroCorporation, Box 16000 MH, Tampa, FL 33687. Ed. Raymond N. Castle. circ. 400. Indexed: Chem.Abstr.

665.4   GW   ISSN 0076-891X
M W V JAHRESBERICHT. 1950. a. DM.70. Mineraloelwirtschafts Verband e.V., Steindamm 71, 2000 Hamburg 1, W. Germany (B.R.D.) Ed. R. Stubenvoll. circ. 6,000.
    Formerly: M W V /A E V Jahresbericht.

547   UK   ISSN 0144-2988
MACROMOLECULAR CHEMISTRY (LONDON); a review of the literature published during (year) 1980. a. Royal Society of Chemistry, Burlington House, London W1V 0BN, England (Subscr. to: Distribution Centre, Blackhorse Rd., Letchworth, Herts. SG6 1HN, England) Indexed: Chem.Abstr.

547   UK   ISSN 0076-2075
MACROMOLECULAR CHEMISTRY (OXFORD) (Text in English; occasionally in French or German) 1962. irreg., 4th, 5th, 6th, 1969, Prague. price varies. International Union of Pure and Applied Chemistry, c/o Dr. M. Williams, Secy., Bank Court Chambers, 2-3 Pound Way, Cowley Centre, Oxford OX4 3YF, England. Ed. B.C.L. Weedon.
1972, 8th, Helsinki

547 541.39   US   ISSN 0076-2091
MACROMOLECULAR SYNTHESES. 1963. irreg., vol.9, 1985. price varies. John Wiley & Sons, Inc., 605 Third Ave., New York, NY 10016. TEL 212-850-6000. Ed. C.G. Overberger.

547 546   SZ   ISSN 0253-5904
DIE MAKROMOLEKULARE CHEMIE. SUPPLEMENT. (Text in English, French and German) 1975. irreg. price varies. Huethig & Wepf Verlag, Eisengasse 5, CH-4001 Basel, Switzerland. Ed. Hartwig Hoecker. adv. Indexed: Chem.Abstr. Ind.Sci.Rev.
    Macromolecular Chemistry and Physics.

547   GW
MODERN SYNTHETIC METHODS. 1976. triennial. (Association of Swiss Chemists, SZ) Springer-Verlag, 175 Fifth Ave., New York, NY 10160 TEL 212-460-1500. (Subscr. to: Springer-Verlag Berlin, Heidelberger Platz 3, D-1000 Berlin 33, West Germany (B.R.D.)) Ed. R. Scheffold. (back issues avail.)

665   SP
OLEO; anuario espanol de aceites y grasas e industrias auxiliares. no.6, 1976. biennial. 3000 ptas.($20) Julian Yebenes Guerrero, Pub., Fernando VI, 27, 28004 Madrid, Spain. adv. stat. circ. 3,000.

ORGANIC AND ORGANOMETALLIC CRYSTAL STRUCTURES; BIBLIOGRAPHY. see *BIBLIOGRAPHIES*

547   US   ISSN 0078-611X
ORGANIC CHEMISTRY; a series of monographs. 1964. irreg., vol.12, 1986. Academic Press Inc., Orlando, FL 32887. TEL 305-345-2000. Ed. Alfred T. Blomquist.

547   UK   ISSN 0305-9812
ORGANIC COMPOUNDS OF SULPHUR, SELENIUM AND TELLURIUM. 1971. biennial. price varies. Royal Society of Chemistry, Burlington House, London W1V 0BN, England (Subscr. to: Distribution Centre, Blackhorse Road, Letchworth, Herts. SG6 1HN, England) Ed. D. Hogg. charts. illus. index. Indexed: Chem.Abstr.

ORGANIC ELECTRONIC SPECTRAL DATA. see *CHEMISTRY — Analytical Chemistry*

547 541.35   US   ISSN 0078-6152
ORGANIC PHOTOCHEMISTRY: A SERIES OF ADVANCES. 1967. irreg., vol.7, 1985. price varies. Marcel Dekker, Inc., 270 Madison Ave., New York, NY 10016. TEL 212-696-9000. Ed. O.L. Chapman. Indexed: Chem.Abstr.

547 541.39   US   ISSN 0078-6160
ORGANIC REACTION MECHANISMS. ANNUAL SURVEY. 1966. irreg., vol.19, 1985. price varies. John Wiley & Sons, Inc., 605 Third Ave, New York, NY 10016. TEL 212-850-6000. Ed.Bd. Indexed: Chem.Abstr.

547 541.39   US   ISSN 0078-6179
ORGANIC REACTIONS. 1942. irreg., vol.36, 1987. price varies. John Wiley & Sons, Inc., 605 Third Ave., New York, NY 10016. TEL 212-850-6000. Ed. W.G. Dauben. Indexed: Biol.Abstr. Chem.Abstr. Curr.Cont. Nutr.Abstr. Nutr.Abstr.& Rev.

547 541.39   US   ISSN 0078-6209
ORGANIC SYNTHESES. (Vols. 1-49 avail. only in: Organic Syntheses Collective Volumes) vol.64, 1986. a. price varies. John Wiley & Sons, Inc., 605 Third Ave., New York, NY 10016. TEL 212-850-6000. Indexed: Chem.Abstr. ASCA. Abstr.Bull.Inst.Pap.Chem.

547   US   ISSN 0078-6225
ORGANISCHE CHEMIE IN EINZELDARSTELLUNGEN. 1950. irreg., no.15, 1974. price varies. Springer-Verlag, 175 Fifth Ave., New York, NY 10010 TEL 212-460-1500. (Also Berlin, Heidelberg, Vienna) (reprint service avail. from ISI)

547.05   UK   ISSN 0301-0074
ORGANOMETALLIC CHEMISTRY. 1972. a. price varies. Royal Society of Chemistry, Burlington House, London W1V 0BN, England (Subscr. to: Distribution Centre, Blackhorse Road, Letchworth, Herts. SG6 1HN, England) Eds. E.W. Abel, F.G. Stone. charts. illus. index. Indexed: Chem.Abstr.

547.05 541.39   US
ORGANOMETALLIC REACTIONS AND SYNTHESES. 1971. irreg. price varies. Plenum Publishing Corp., 233 Spring St., New York, NY 10013. TEL 212-620-8000. Eds. E.I. Becker, M. Tsutsui.
    Formerly (until vol.6, 1977): Organometallic Reactions Series (ISSN 0078-6497)

547   UK   ISSN 0306-0713
ORGANOPHOSPHORUS CHEMISTRY. 1970. a. price varies. Royal Society of Chemistry, Burlington House, London W1V 0BN, England (Subscr. to: Distribution Centre, Blackhorse Rd. Letchworth, Herts. SG6 1HN England) Eds. D.W. Hutchinson, J.A. Miller. charts. illus. index. Indexed: Chem.Abstr.

541 547   PL   ISSN 0324-9824
POLITECHNIKA WROCLAWSKA. INSTYTUT CHEMII ORGANICZNEJ I FIZYCZNEJ. PRACE NAUKOWE. KONFERENCJE. (Text in Polish and English) 1974. irreg., no.7, 1981. price varies. Politechnika Wroclawska, Wybrzeze Wyspianskiego 27, 50-370 Wroclaw, Poland (Dist. by: Ars Polona-Ruch, Krakowskie Przedmiescie 7, Warsaw, Poland) Ed. Marian Kloza. circ. 325.

541 547   PL   ISSN 0324-9816
POLITECHNIKA WROCLAWSKA. INSTYTUT CHEMII ORGANICZNEJ I FIZYCZNEJ. PRACE NAUKOWE. MONOGRAFIE. (Text in Polish; summaries in English and Russian) 1969. irreg., no.15, 1986. price varies. Politechnika Wroclawska, Wybrzeze Wyspianskiego 27, 50-370 Wroclaw, Poland (Dist. by: Ars Polona-Ruch, Krakowskie Przedmiescie 7, Warsaw, Poland) Ed. Jerzy Ciekot.

541 547   PL   ISSN 0370-081X
POLITECHNIKA WROCLAWSKA. INSTYTUT CHEMII ORGANICZNEJ I FIZYCZNEJ. PRACE NAUKOWE. STUDIA I MATERIALY. (Text in Polish; summaries in English and Russian) 1970. irreg., no.8, 1978. price varies. Politechnika Wroclawska, Wybrzeze Wyspianskiego 27, 50-370 Wroclaw, Poland (Dist. by: Ars Polona-Ruch, Krakowskie Przedmiescie 7, Warsaw, Poland) Ed. Marian Kloza. Indexed: Chem.Abstr.

547   UR
POLUTEHNILINE INSTITUUT TALLINN. SVOISTVA RASTVOROV KISLORODOSODERZHASHCHIKH ORGANICHESKIKH SOEDINENII. (Subseries of its Toimetised) (Text in Russian; summaries in English or German) irreg. price varies. Polutehniline Instituut Tallinn, Ehitajate tee 5, Tallinn, Estonian S.S.R., U.S.S.R.

541.393   US   ISSN 0275-5777
POLYMER MONOGRAPHS. 1977. a. price varies. Gordon and Breach Science Publishers, 50 West 23rd St., New York, NY 10010. TEL 212-206-8900. Ed. Herbert Morawetz.
Polymers

547.3466   US   ISSN 0092-0576
POWDER DIFFRACTION FILE SEARCH MANUAL. ORGANIC. (Subseries of the Committee's Publication SMO) a. $215. ‡ Joint Committee on Powder Diffraction Standards., International Centre for Diffraction Data, 1601 Park Lane, Swarthmore, PA 19081. TEL 215-328-9400. index.

PROGRESS IN COLLOID AND POLYMER SCIENCE. see *CHEMISTRY — Physical Chemistry*

547   US   ISSN 0163-7827
PROGRESS IN LIPID RESEARCH. 1952. 4/yr. $140 (annual bound volume $156) Pergamon Press, Inc., Journals Division, Maxwell House, Fairview Park, Elmsford, NY 10523 TEL 914-592-7700. (And Headington Hill Hall, Oxford OX3 0BW, England) Ed. Ralph T. Holman. (also avail. in microform from MIM,UMI) Indexed: Biol.Abstr. Chem.Abstr. Ind.Med. Nutr.Abstr. Dairy Sci.Abstr.
    Formerly: Progress in the Chemistry of Fats and Other Lipids (ISSN 0079-6832)
Oils and fats

PROGRESS IN PHYSICAL ORGANIC CHEMISTRY. see *CHEMISTRY — Physical Chemistry*

547   US   ISSN 0079-6700
PROGRESS IN POLYMER SCIENCE. 1967. 4/yr. $135 (annual bound volume $132) Pergamon Press, Inc., Journals Division, Maxwell House, Fairview Park, Elmsford, NY 10523 TEL 914-592-7700. (And Headington Hill Hall, Oxford OX3 0BW, England) Eds. A.D. Jenkins, D. Vogl. index. (also avail. in microform from MIM,UMI) Indexed: Chem.Abstr. Sci.Abstr. HRIS.
Polymers

547 NE
PROGRESS IN THEORETICAL ORGANIC
CHEMISTRY. 1976. irreg., vol.3, 1982. price
varies. Elsevier Science Publishers B.V., P.O. Box
211, 1000 AE Amsterdam, Netherlands. Indexed:
Chem.Abstr.

547 UR ISSN 0079-6883
PROGRESS POLIMERNOI KHIMII. 1965. irreg.
Akademiya Nauk S.S.S.R., Institut
Elementoorganicheskikh Soedinenii, Ul. Vavilova,
14, Moscow, Russian S.F.S.R., U.S.S.R.

547 541.39 NE ISSN 0079-9823
REACTION MECHANISMS IN ORGANIC
CHEMISTRY. (Text in English) 1963. irreg.,
vol.10, 1975. price varies. Elsevier Science
Publishers B.V., P.O. Box 211, 1000 AE
Amsterdam, Netherlands. Eds. C. Eaborn, N.B.
Chapman.

547 US ISSN 0341-2377
REACTIVITY AND STRUCTURE: CONCEPTS OF
ORGANIC CHEMISTRY. 1975. irreg., vol.23,
1986. price varies. Springer-Verlag, 175 Fifth Ave.,
New York, NY 10010 TEL 212-460-1500. (Also
Berlin, Heidelberg, Tokyo and Vienna) Ed.Bd.
(reprint service avail. from ISI)

547 HU ISSN 0079-9947
RECENT DEVELOPMENTS IN THE CHEMISTRY
OF NATURAL CARBON COMPOUNDS. (Text
in English) 1965. irreg., vol.10, 1984. price varies.
(Magyar Tudomanyos Akademia) Akademiai Kiado,
Publishing House of the Hungarian Academy of
Sciences, P.O. Box 24, H-1363 Budapest, Hungary.
Indexed: Chem.Abstr.

547 US ISSN 0742-5996
RING SYSTEMS HANDBOOK. 1960. irreg. $300.
(American Chemical Society) Chemical Abstracts
Service, 2540 Olentangy River Rd., Box 3012,
Columbus, OH 43210. TEL 614-421-3600. Indexed:
Chem.Abstr.
 Former titles: Parent Compound Handbook; Ring
Index: A List of Ring Systems Used in Organic
Chemistry. Supplement (ISSN 0080-309X)

547 NE ISSN 0080-3758
RODD'S CHEMISTRY OF CARBON
COMPOUNDS. 1964. irreg., vol.4L, 1980. price
varies. Elsevier Science Publishers B.V., Box 211,
1000 AE Amsterdam, Netherlands. Ed. S. Coffey.

547 UK ISSN 0069-3030
ROYAL SOCIETY OF CHEMISTRY. ANNUAL
REPORTS ON THE PROGRESS OF
CHEMISTRY. SECTION B: ORGANIC
CHEMISTRY. 1904. a. £70($137) Royal Society of
Chemistry, Burlington House, Piccadilly, London
W1V OBN, England (Subscr. to: Distribution
Centre, Blackhorse Rd., Letchworth, Herts. SG6
1HN, England) Eds. A.G. Davies, P.G. Garrett.
index. cum.index: vols.1-46.

547 US
STUDIES IN ORGANIC CHEMISTRY SERIES.
1973. irreg., vol.11, 1987. price varies. Marcel
Dekker, Inc., 270 Madison Ave., New York, NY
10016. TEL 212-696-9000. Ed. P. Gassman.

547 541.39 SZ ISSN 0253-200X
SYNTHETIC METHODS OF ORGANIC
CHEMISTRY. cover title: Theilheimer's Synthetic
Methods of Organic Chemistry. (Text in English)
1946. a. price varies. S. Karger AG,
Allschwilerstrasse 10, CH-4009 Basel, Switzerland.
Ed. A.F. Finch. Indexed: Biol.Abstr. Chem.Abstr.
Curr.Cont. Ind.Med.

547 541.39 US ISSN 0082-2418
TECHNIQUES AND APPLICATIONS IN
ORGANIC SYNTHESIS SERIES. 1965. irreg.,
vol.6, 1979. price varies. Marcel Dekker, Inc., 270
Madison Ave., New York, NY 10016. TEL 212-
696-9000. Ed. R.L. Augustine.

THERMODYNAMICS RESEARCH CENTER.
INTERNATIONAL DATA SERIES. SELECTED
DATA ON MIXTURES. SERIES A.
THERMODYNAMIC PROPERTIES OF NON-
REACTING BINARY SYSTEMS OF ORGANIC
SUBSTANCES. see CHEMISTRY — Physical
Chemistry

CHEMISTRY — Physical Chemistry

ABSORPTION SPECTRA IN THE ULTRAVIOLET
AND VISIBLE REGION. see PHYSICS — Optics

541.395 US ISSN 0360-0564
ADVANCES IN CATALYSIS. 1948. irreg., no.33,
1985. Academic Press, Inc., Orlando, FL 32887.
TEL 305-345-2000. Ed. W.G. Frankenburg.
Indexed: Biol.Abstr. Chem.Abstr. Sci.Cit.Ind.
Curr.Chem.React. Ind.Chem. Ind.Rev.Sci.
 Formerly: Advances in Catalysis and Related
Subjects (ISSN 0065-2342)

ADVANCES IN CHEMICAL PHYSICS. see
PHYSICS

541.39 US ISSN 0065-2741
ADVANCES IN HIGH TEMPERATURE
CHEMISTRY. 1967. irreg., vol.4, 1974. Academic
Press, Inc., Orlando, FL 32887. TEL 305-345-2000.
Ed. Leroy Eyring.

543 541.35 US ISSN 0065-3152
ADVANCES IN PHOTOCHEMISTRY. 1963. irreg.,
vol.13, 1987. price varies. John Wiley & Sons, Inc.,
605 Third Ave., New York, NY 10016. TEL 212-
850-6000. Ed. A. Noyes. index.

547.1 US ISSN 0065-3160
ADVANCES IN PHYSICAL ORGANIC
CHEMISTRY. 1963. irreg., vol.21, 1985. Academic
Press Inc., Orlando, FL 32887. TEL 305-345-2000.
Eds. V. Gold, D. Bethell. Indexed: Chem.Abstr.
Sci.Cit.Ind. Ind.Sci.Rev.

ADVANCES IN SOLID STATE TECHNOLOGY.
see PHYSICS

541.39 546.1 US ISSN 0092-1335
ANNUAL REPORTS IN INORGANIC AND
GENERAL SYNTHESES. 1973. irreg., vol.5, 1977.
Academic Press, Inc., Orlando, FL 32887. TEL
305-345-2000. Eds. Kurt Niedenzu, Hans Zimmer.
illus.

547.1 541.39 US ISSN 0066-409X
ANNUAL REPORTS IN ORGANIC SYNTHESIS.
1971. irreg., vol.8, 1985. Academic Press Inc.,
Orlando, FL 32887. TEL 305-345-2000. Eds. John
McMurray, R. Bryan Miller.

541.3 US ISSN 0066-426X
ANNUAL REVIEW OF PHYSICAL CHEMISTRY.
1951. a. $32. Annual Reviews Inc., 4139 El Camino
Way, Palo Alto, CA 94306. TEL 415-493-4400. Ed.
Herbert L. Strauss. bibl. index. cum.index. (back
issues avail., reprint service avail. from ISI) Indexed:
Chem.Abstr. Sci.Abstr. Sci.Cit.Ind.
Abstr.Bull.Inst.Pap.Chem. Fuel & Energy Abstr.
Ind.Sci.Rev. M.M.R.I. Nucl.Sci.Abstr.

541.3 US
BENCHMARK PAPERS IN PHYSICAL
CHEMISTRY AND CHEMICAL PHYSICS. (Each
vol. has distinctive title) 1978. irreg., vol.5, 1982.
price varies. Van Nostrand Reinhold Company,
7625 Empire Dr., Florence, KY 41042. TEL 606-
525-6600. illus. index.

541.3 BL
BIOMASSA. 1979. a. Revista Brasileira de Tecnologia,
c/o G. Massarani, COPPE UFRJ, Caixa Postal
1191, 20000 Rio de Janeiro, RJ, Brazil. Ed.Bd.
Indexed: Gas Abstr.

541.36 US ISSN 0572-6921
BRIGHAM YOUNG UNIVERSITY. CENTER FOR
THERMOCHEMICAL STUDIES.
CONTRIBUTIONS.* irreg., no.66, 1975. price
varies. Brigham Young University, Center for
Thermochemical Studies, Provo, UT 84602.

CENTRO DE EDAFOLOGIA Y BIOLOGIA
APLICADA. ANUARIO. see AGRICULTURE —
Agricultural Economics

541.3 UK ISSN 0305-9723
COLLOID SCIENCE. 1970. biennial. price varies.
Royal Society of Chemistry, Burlington House,
London W1V OBN, England (Subscr. to:
Distribution Centre, Blackhorse Road, Letchworth,
Herts. SG6 1HN, England) Ed. D.H. Everett.
charts. illus. index. Indexed: Chem.Abstr.

541.3 NE ISSN 0069-8040
COMPREHENSIVE CHEMICAL KINETICS. (Text
in English) 1969. irreg., vol.25, 1985. price varies.
Elsevier Science Publishers B.V., P.O. Box 211,
1000 AE Amsterdam, Netherlands. Ed.Bd.

537 UR ISSN 0573-3022
CONFERENCE INTERNATIONALE SUR LES
PHENOMENES D'IONISATION DANS LES
GAZ. COMPTES RENDUS.* irreg., no.3, 1963.
Akademiya Nauk Belorusskoi S.S.R., Institut Fiziki
- B.S.S.R. Academy of Sciences. Institute of Physics,
Leninskii Prospekt 70, Minsk, Byelorussian S.S.R.,
U.S.S.R.

541.3 UK ISSN 0305-9758
ELECTRON SPIN RESONANCE. 1973. every 18
mos. price varies. Royal Society of Chemistry,
Burlington House, London W1V OBN, England
(Subscr. to: Distribution Centre, Blackhorse Rd.,
Letchworth, Herts SG6 1HN, England) Ed. P.B.
Ayscough. charts. illus. index. Indexed:
Chem.Abstr. Sci.Cit.Ind.

541.3 UK ISSN 0301-5696
FARADAY SYMPOSIA. 1968. a. price varies. Royal
Society of Chemistry, Burlington House, London
W1V OBN, England (Subscr. to: Distribution
Centre, Blackhorse Rd., Letchworth, Herts. SG6
1HN, England) charts. illus. index. Indexed: Biol.Abstr.
Chem.Abstr. Sci.Abstr. Sci.Cit.Ind. Mass
Spectr.Bull.
 Formerly: Symposia of the Faraday Society.

541 BU ISSN 0204-5958
FIZIKO-KHIMICHESKA MEKHANIKA/PHYSICO-
CHEMICAL MECHANICS. (Text in Bulgarian,
German, Russian; summaries in English, Russian)
1975. irreg. 1.15 lv. per no. (Bulgarska Akademiia
na Naukite) Publishing House of the Bulgarian
Academy of Sciences, Acad. G. Bonchev St., Bldg.
6, 1113 Sofia, Bulgaria (Dist. by: Hemus, 6, Rouski
Blvd., 1000 Sofia, Bulgaria) illus. circ. 480. Indexed:
Chem.Abstr.

541.3 UR ISSN 0367-2409
FIZIKO-KHIMICHESKAYA MEKHANIKA I
LIOFILNOST' DISPERSNYKH SISTEM;
respublikanskii mezhvedomstvennyi sbornik
nauchnykh trudov. (Text in Russian) 1968. a.
(Akademiya Nauk Ukrainskoi S.S.R., Institut
Kolloidnoi Khimii i Khimii Vody) Izdatel'stvo
Naukova Dumka, c/o Yu.A. Khramov, Dir, Ul.
Repina, 3, Kiev 252 601, Ukrainian S.S.R., U.S.S.R.
(Subscr. to: Mezhdunarodnaya Kniga, Moscow, G-
200, Russian S.F.S.R., U.S.S.R.) Ed. F.D.
Ovcharenko. Indexed: Chem.Abstr.

547.1 541.39 US ISSN 0073-8077
INORGANIC SYNTHESES SERIES. 1939. a.
$19.95. (Inorganic Syntheses, Inc.) McGraw-Hill
Book Co., 1221 Ave. of the Americas, New York,
NY 10020. TEL 212-997-1221. Ed. Robert Parry.
adv. bk. rev. index. cum.index: vols.1-10 in vol.10.
Indexed: Chem.Abstr. Sci.Cit.Ind. Ind.Sci.Rev.

541.3 US
INTERNATIONAL JOURNAL OF CHEMICAL
KINETICS. SYMPOSIUM. 1975. irreg. $49. John
Wiley & Sons, Inc., 605 Third Ave., New York, NY
10016. TEL 212-850-6000. Ed. Sidney W. Benson.

INTERNATIONAL SYMPOSIUM ON THE
PHARMACOLOGY OF
THERMOREGULATION. see PHARMACY AND
PHARMACOLOGY

541.372 US ISSN 0092-0193
ION EXCHANGE AND SOLVENT EXTRACTION;
a series of advances. 1966. irreg., vol.9, 1985.
Marcel Dekker, Inc., 270 Madison Ave., New York,
NY 10016. TEL 212-696-9000. Eds. J.A. Marinsky,
Y. Marcus. illus. (also avail. in microform from RPI)
Indexed: Chem.Abstr.
 Formed by the 1973 merger of: Ion Exchange; a
Series of Advances (ISSN 0075-0328) & Solvent
Extraction Reviews.

541.3 UR ISSN 0202-7968
ITOGI NAUKI I TEKHNIKI: KINETIKA.
KATALIZ. irreg., latest vol.16, 1987. 6 Rub.
Vsesoyuznyi Institut Nauchno-Tekhnicheskoi
Informatsii (VINITI), Ul. Baltiiskaya 14, Moscow
A-219, Russian S.F.S.R., U.S.S.R. (Subscr. to:
Mezhdunarodnaya Kniga, Dimitrova ul. 39, 113095
Moscow, Russian S.F.S.R., U.S.S.R.) Indexed:
Chem.Abstr.

541.3 NE ISSN 0075-3696
JERUSALEM SYMPOSIA ON QUANTUM CHEMISTRY AND BIOCHEMISTRY. 1969. irreg. price varies. (Israel Academy of Sciences and Humanities, Section on Sciences, IS) D. Reidel Publishing Co., Box 17, 3300 AA Dordrecht, Netherlands (And 190 Old Derby St., Hingham, MA 02043) Ed. B. Pullman. Indexed: Biol.Abstr. Chem.Abstr.

LASER FOCUS/ELECTRO OPTICS BUYERS' GUIDE. see PHYSICS — Optics

MACROMOLECULAR SYNTHESES. see CHEMISTRY — Organic Chemistry

574.192 541.3 US ISSN 0309-0698
MONOGRAPHS ON PHYSICAL BIOCHEMISTRY. irreg. price varies. Oxford University Press, 200 Madison Ave., New York, NY 10016 TEL 212-679-7300. (And Ely House, 37 Dover St., London W1X 4AH, England) Eds. W.F. Harrington, A.R. Peacocke.

541.3 UK ISSN 0305-9804
NUCLEAR MAGNETIC RESONANCE. 1972. a. price varies. Royal Society of Chemistry, Burlington House, London W1V OBN, England (Subscr. to: Distribution Centre, Blackhorse Road, Letchworth, Herts. SG6 1HN, England) Ed. G.A. Webb. charts. illus. index. Indexed: Chem.Abstr. GeoRef.

541.3 JA ISSN 0078-429X
OKAYAMA UNIVERSITY. RESEARCH LABORATORY FOR SURFACE SCIENCE. REPORTS. (Text in European languages) 1954. irreg. free or exchange basis. Okayama University, Research Laboratory for Surface Science - Okayama Daigaku Rigakubu Kaimen-kagaku Kenkyu Shisetsu, Faculty of Science, Tsushima, Okayama 700, Japan.

ORGANIC PHOTOCHEMISTRY: A SERIES OF ADVANCES. see CHEMISTRY — Organic Chemistry

ORGANIC REACTION MECHANISMS. ANNUAL SURVEY. see CHEMISTRY — Organic Chemistry

ORGANIC REACTIONS. see CHEMISTRY — Organic Chemistry

ORGANIC SYNTHESES. see CHEMISTRY — Organic Chemistry

ORGANOMETALLIC REACTIONS AND SYNTHESES. see CHEMISTRY — Organic Chemistry

541 JA ISSN 0474-7879
OSAKA (PREFECTURE). RADIATION CENTER, ANNUAL REPORT/OSAKA-FURITSU HOSHASEN CHUO KENKYUSHO NENPO. (Text in English) 1960. a. exchange basis. Radiation Center - Osaka-furitsu Hoshasen Chuo Kenkyusho, 704 Shinke-cho, Sakai 593, Japan. circ. 1,000. Indexed: Biol.Abstr. Chem.Abstr.

OSAKA UNIVERSITY. INSTITUTE FOR PROTEIN RESEARCH. MEMOIRS. see BIOLOGY — Biological Chemistry

541.35 UK ISSN 0079-1806
PHOTOCHEMISTRY (OXFORD) (Text in English; occasionally in French or German) 1964. irreg., 4th, 1972, Baden-Baden, W. Germany; 5th, 1974, Enschede, Netherlands. price varies. International Union of Pure and Applied Chemistry, c/o Dr. M. Williams, Secy., Bank Court Chambers, 2-3 Pound Way, Cowley Centre, Oxford OX4 3YF, England.

541.3 US ISSN 0079-1881
PHYSICAL CHEMISTRY; a series of monographs. 1952. irreg., vol.36, 1978. Academic Press Inc., Orlando, FL 32887. TEL 305-345-2000. Ed. Ernest M. Loebl.

541.3 NE
PHYSICAL SCIENCES DATA. 1978. irreg., vol.22, 1985. price varies. Elsevier Science Publishers B.V., P.O. Box 211, 1000 AE Amsterdam, Netherlands.

541.3 NE
PHYSICS AND CHEMISTRY OF MATERIALS WITH LOW DIMENSIONAL STRUCTURES. SERIES A. LAYERED STRUCTURES. 1976. irreg. price varies. D. Reidel Publishing Co., Box 17, 3300 AA Dordrecht, Netherlands (And 190 Old Derby St., Hingham, MA 02043) Ed. E. Mooser.

541.3 NE
PHYSICS AND CHEMISTRY OF MATERIALS WITH LOW DIMENSIONAL STRUCTURES. SERIES B: QUASI-ONE-DIMENSIONAL STRUCTURES. 1976. irreg. price varies. D. Reidel Publishing Co., Box 17, 3300 AA Dordrecht, Netherlands (And 190 Old Derby St., Hingham, MA 02043) Ed. F.A. Levy.

541.3 NE
PHYSICS AND CHEMISTRY OF MATERIALS WITH LOW DIMENSIONAL STRUCTURES. SERIES C. MOLECULAR STRUCTURES. 1976. irreg. price varies. D. Reidel Publishing Co., Box 17, 3300 AA Dordrecht, Netherlands (And 190 Old Derby St., Hingham, MA 02043) Ed. I. Zschokke.

PLASTICHEM. see ENGINEERING — Chemical Engineering

POLITECHNIKA WROCLAWSKA. INSTYTUT CHEMII ORGANICZNEJ I FIZYCZNEJ. PRACE NAUKOWE. KONFERENCJE. see CHEMISTRY — Organic Chemistry

POLITECHNIKA WROCLAWSKA. INSTYTUT CHEMII ORGANICZNEJ I FIZYCZNEJ. PRACE NAUKOWE. MONOGRAFIE. see CHEMISTRY — Organic Chemistry

POLITECHNIKA WROCLAWSKA. INSTYTUT CHEMII ORGANICZNEJ I FIZYCZNEJ. PRACE NAUKOWE. STUDIA I MATERIALY. see CHEMISTRY — Organic Chemistry

541.3 UR
POLUTEHNILINE INSTITUUT TALLINN. FIZICHESKAYA KHIMIYA SOEDINENII A2B6 I A4B6. (Subseries of Its Toimetised) (Text in Russian; summaries in English or German) irreg. price varies. Plutehniline Instituut Tallinn, Ehitajate tee 5, Tallinn, Estonian S.S.R., U.S.S.R.

541.3 UR ISSN 0203-9737
POLUTEHNILINE INSTITUUT TALLINN. PROBLEMY PODZEMNOI I OTKRYTOI RAZRABOTKI GORYUCHIKH SLANTSEV I NERUDNYKH MATERIALOV. (Subseries of Its Toimetised) (Text in Russian; summaries in English or German) irreg. price varies. Polutehniline Instituut Tallinn, Ehitajate tee 5, Tallinn, Estonian S.S.R., U.S.S.R.

541.3 547 US ISSN 0340-255X
PROGRESS IN COLLOID AND POLYMER SCIENCE. (Supplement to: Colloid and Polymer Science) 1909. irreg., vol.72, 1986. price varies. Springer-Verlag, 175 Fifth Ave., New York, NY 10160 TEL 212-460-1500. (Distr. in Germany by: Dr. Dietrich /Steinkopff Verlag, Darmstadt, West Germany (B.R.D.)) Eds. H.G. Kilian, G. Lacey. adv. circ. 2,000. (reprint service avail. from ISI) Indexed: Chem.Abstr. Curr.Cont. World Text.Abstr.

547.1 US ISSN 0079-6662
PROGRESS IN PHYSICAL ORGANIC CHEMISTRY. 1963. irreg., vol.16, 1987. price varies. John Wiley & Sons, Inc., 605 Third Ave., New York, NY 10016. TEL 212-850-6000. Eds. A. Streitwieser, Jr., R.W. Taft. Indexed: Chem.Abstr.

541.39 US ISSN 0079-6743
PROGRESS IN REACTION KINETICS. 1961. 4/yr. $125 (annual bound volume $120) Pergamon Press, Inc., Journals Division, Maxwell House, Fairview Park, Elmsford, NY 10523 TEL 914-592-7700. (And Headington Hill Hall, Oxford OX3 0BW, England) Ed.Bd. index. (also avail. in microform from MIM,UMI) Indexed: Biol.Abstr. Chem.Abstr.

541 US ISSN 0079-6786
PROGRESS IN SOLID STATE CHEMISTRY. 1964. 4/yr. $135 (annual bound volume $132) Pergamon Press, Inc., Journals Division, Maxwell House, Fairview Park, Elmsford, NY 10523 TEL 914-592-7700. (And Headington Hill Hall, Oxford OX3 0BW, England) Eds. Gerd M. Rosenblatt, Wayne L. Worrell. index. (also avail. in microform from MIM, UMI) Indexed: Chem.Abstr. Sci.Abstr. Mass Spectr.Bull.

541 US
PROGRESS IN SURFACE AND MEMBRANE SCIENCE. vol.4, 1971. irreg., vol.14, 1981. Academic Press Inc., Orlando, FL 32887. TEL 305-345-2000. Eds. D.A. Cadenhead, J.F. Danelli. Indexed: Biol.Abstr. Chem.Abstr.

541 JA ISSN 0441-2516
RADIOACTIVITY SURVEY DATA IN JAPAN. (Text in English) 1963. a. exchange basis. National Institute of Radiological Sciences - Hohasen Igaku Sogo Kenkyusho, 4-9-1 Anagawa, Chiba 280, Japan. Ed. H. Suzuki. circ. 1,300.

REACTION MECHANISMS IN ORGANIC CHEMISTRY. see CHEMISTRY — Organic Chemistry

541 US
RECENT PROGRESS IN SURFACE MEMBRANE SCIENCE. 1964. irreg., vol.14, 1981. Academic Press, Inc., Orlando, FL 32887. TEL 305-345-2000. Ed.Bd. index.
Formerly: Recent Progress in Surface Science (ISSN 0079-9971)

541.3 530 US ISSN 0080-1666
RESEARCH IN SURFACE FORCES. (Papers from Lab. of Surface Phenomena, Institute of Physical Chemistry, Academy of Sciences, U.S.S.R) (English translation of original Russian) 1963. irreg., vol.4, 1974. price varies. Consultants Bureau, Special Research Report (Subsidiary of: Plenum Publishing Corp.) 233 Spring St., New York, NY 10013. TEL 212-620-8443. Ed. B.V. Deryagin.

541.3 UK ISSN 0260-1826
ROYAL SOCIETY OF CHEMISTRY. ANNUAL REPORTS ON THE PROGRESS OF CHEMISTRY. SECTION C: PHYSICAL CHEMISTRY. a. £58($114) Royal Society of Chemistry, Burlington House, London W1V 0BN, England (Subscr. to: Distribution Centre, Blackhorse Rd., Letchworth, Herts. SG6 1HN, England) Ed. M.C.R. Symons.
Supersedes in part: Royal Society of Chemistry. Annual Reports on the Progress of Chemistry. Section A: Physical and Inorganic Chemistry.

541.36 NE
STUDIES IN MODERN THERMODYNAMICS. 1979. irreg., vol.4, 1982. price varies. Elsevier Science Publishers B.V., P.O. Box 211, 1000 AE Amsterdam, Netherlands. Indexed: Chem.Abstr.

541.3 NE
STUDIES IN PHYSICAL AND THEORETICAL CHEMISTRY. 1978. irreg., vol.38, 1985. price varies. Elsevier Science Publishers B.V., P.O. Box 211, 1000 AE Amsterdam, Netherlands. Indexed: Biol.Abstr. Chem.Abstr.

SURFACE SCIENCE; a journal devoted to the physics and chemistry of interfaces. see PHYSICS

541.36 536 US ISSN 0082-0784
SYMPOSIUM (INTERNATIONAL) ON COMBUSTION. Variant title: International Symposium on Combustion. Proceedings. (Research papers) biennial, 20th, 1985. $150. Combustion Institute, 5001 Baum Blvd., Pittsburgh, PA 15213. TEL 412-387-1366. cum.index in 10th issue. circ. 3, 500. Indexed: Chem.Abstr.

SYNTHETIC METHODS OF ORGANIC CHEMISTRY. see CHEMISTRY — Organic Chemistry

TECHNIQUES AND APPLICATIONS IN ORGANIC SYNTHESIS SERIES. see CHEMISTRY — Organic Chemistry

THERMODYNAMICS RESEARCH CENTER. DATA PROJECT. SELECTED VALUES OF PROPERTIES OF CHEMICAL COMPOUNDS. CATEGORY A. TABLES OF SELECTED VALUES OF PHYSICAL AND THERMODYNAMIC PROPERTIES OF CHEMICAL COMPOUNDS. see CHEMISTRY — Analytical Chemistry

547.1 US
THERMODYNAMICS RESEARCH CENTER. HYDROCARBON PROJECT. SELECTED VALUES OF PROPERTIES OF HYDROCARBONS AND RELATED COMPOUNDS. CATEGORY A: TABLES OF SELECTED VALUES OF PHYSICAL AND THERMODYNAMIC PROPERTIES OF HYDROCARBONS. 1942. irreg., supplement A-88, 1984. $275 per supplement. (Texas Engineering Experiment Station) Thermodynamics Research Center System, Texas A & M University, College Station, TX 77843-3111. TEL 409-845-4940. Ed. Kenneth R. Hall. circ. 319. (looseleaf format)
　　Formerly: A P I Research Project 44. Selected Values of Properties of Hydrocarbons and Related Compounds. Category A: Tables of Selected Values of Physical and Thermodynamic Properties of Hydrocarbons (ISSN 0065-9630)

541.3　547.1　　US　　ISSN 0147-1503
THERMODYNAMICS RESEARCH CENTER. INTERNATIONAL DATA SERIES. SELECTED DATA ON MIXTURES. SERIES A. THERMODYNAMIC PROPERTIES OF NON-REACTING BINARY SYSTEMS OF ORGANIC SUBSTANCES. 1973. irreg. $150. Thermodynamics Research Center, Texas A & M University System, College Station, TX 77843-3111. TEL 409-845-4940. Ed. Henry V. Kehiaian. circ. 128. Indexed: Chem.Abstr.

547.1　　UK
TOPICS IN PHYSICAL ORGANOMETALLIC CHEMISTRY. 1985. a. $40. Freund Publishing House, Ltd., Suite 500, Chesham House, 150 Regent St., London W1R 5FA, England. Ed. Marcel Gielen. adv. circ. 1,000.

541.3　　CN　　ISSN 0041-9370
UNIVERSITY OF ALBERTA. DEPARTMENT OF CHEMISTRY. DIVISION OF THEORETICAL CHEMISTRY. TECHNICAL REPORT. 1966. irreg. (5-10/yr.) free. ‡ University of Alberta, Department of Chemistry, Edmonton, Alta. T6G 2G2, Canada. TEL 403-432-3506. Ed. Serafin Fraga. circ. 150. (processed) Indexed: Bull.Signal. Chem.Abstr.

530　　NE　　ISSN 0090-1911
VIBRATIONAL SPECTRA AND STRUCTURE. 1972. irreg., vol.14, 1982. price varies. Elsevier Science Publishers B.V., P.O. Box 211, 1000 AE Amsterdam, Netherlands. Ed. J.R. Durig. charts. illus. index. Indexed: Chem.Abstr.

541　　UR
VOPROSY KHIMII I KHIMICHESKOI TEKHNOLOGII. vol.42, 1976. irreg. price varies. (Dnepropetrovskii Khimiko-Tekhnologicheskii Institut) Izdatel'stvo Vysshaya Shkola Khar'kovskogo Universiteta, Ul. Universitetskaya 16, Khar'kov 310003, Ukrainian S.S.R., U.S.S.R. Ed. M. Loshkarev. abstr. bibl. charts. illus. circ. 1,000. Indexed: Chem.Abstr.

WORLD PLASTICS. see *PLASTICS*

CHILDREN AND YOUTH — About

see also Education; Medical Sciences — Pediatrics

362.7　　US
ACTIVE PARENTING; the newsletter of video-based parenting education. vol.2, 1986. irreg. Active Parenting, Inc., 4669 Roswell Rd., N.E., Atlanta, GA 30342. TEL 800-235-7755. Ed. Karen Stephens. (also avail. in video cassette)

362.7　　US　　ISSN 0732-3565
ADVANCES IN LAW AND CHILD DEVELOPMENT. 1982. a. $23.75 to individuals; institutions $47.50. J A I Press Inc., Box 1678, 36 Sherwood Pl., Greenwich, CT 06836. TEL 203-661-7602. Ed. Robert L. Sprague. Indexed: Psychol.Abstr.

155.4　371.9　　US
ADVANCES IN LEARNING AND BEHAVIORAL DISABILITIES. 1982. a. $23.75 to individuals; institutions $47.50. J A I Press Inc., Box 1678, 36 Sherwood Pl., Greenwich, CT 06836. TEL 203-661-7602. Eds. Kenneth D. Gadow, Irv Bialer. Indexed: Psychol.Abstr.　Lang.& Lang.Behav.Abstr.

ADVANCES IN MOTOR DEVELOPMENT RESEARCH. see *PHYSICAL FITNESS AND HYGIENE*

370　649.1　　FR　　ISSN 0069-7761
ANNUAIRE DES COMMUNAUTES D'ENFANTS. 1954. a. 15 F. Association Nationale des Communautes d'Enfants, 145 bd. Magenta, 75010 Paris, France.

AUSTRALIAN EARLY CHILDHOOD ASSOCIATION. VICTORIAN BRANCH. NEWSLETTER. see *EDUCATION*

649　　UK
BABY BOOK. 1947. a. Newbourne Publications Ltd., Cambridge House, 373-375 Euston Rd., London NW1, England. Ed. Norman Morris. adv. circ. 575,000.

BOERNETANDPLEJEN I DANMARK. see *MEDICAL SCIENCES — Dentistry*

649　　UK
BOUNTY BABY BOOK.* 1974. a. free. Bounty Publications Ltd., 140 A Gloucester Mansions, Cambridge Circus, London WC2H 8HD, England. circ. 600,000.

BOY SCOUTS OF AMERICA. ANNUAL REPORT TO CONGRESS. see *CLUBS*

369.4　　CN　　ISSN 0045-334X
BUFFALO. 1946. irreg. free to members. Girl Guides of Canada, Manitoba Council, 872 St. James St., Winnipeg, Man. R3G 3K2, Canada. TEL 204-774-1939. Ed.Bd. circ. 1,800.

C B C FEATURES; containing news of the children's book world. (Children's Book Council, Inc.) see *PUBLISHING AND BOOK TRADE*

362.7　　US　　ISSN 0197-744X
CALIFORNIA. DEPARTMENT OF EDUCATION. ANNUAL REPORT ON PUBLICLY SUBSIDIZED CHILD CARE SERVICES. a. $2.50. Department of Education, 721 Capitol Mall, Sacramento, CA 95814. TEL 916-445-3878.

CARNEGIE-MELLON SYMPOSIA ON COGNITION. see *PSYCHOLOGY*

649　　US
CHILD CARE HANDBOOK. 1973. irreg. $6. American Home Economics Association, 2010 Massachusetts Ave. N.W., Washington, DC 20036. TEL 202-862-8300.
　　Care and hygiene

CHILD STUDY JOURNAL MONOGRAPH. see *EDUCATION*

CHILDHOOD IN POETRY. see *CHILDREN AND YOUTH — Abstracting, Bibliographies, Statistics*

364.36　　US
CHILDREN IN CUSTODY; a report on juvenile detention and correctional facility census. 1971. biennial. free. U.S. Department of Justice, Bureau of Justice Statistics, 633 Indiana Ave. N.W., Washington, DC 20531 TEL 800-638-8736. (Orders to: Box 6000, Rockville, MD 20850) circ. 12,000.
　　Supersedes: U.S. Department of Health, Education and Welfare. Statistics on Public Institutions for Delinquent Children (ISSN 0082-9935)

028.5　　UK
CITY SPARROWS. 1872. a. ‡ (Scottish Children's League) McMillan Martin Ltd., Charles Roe House, Chestergate, Macclesfield SK11 6DZ, Cheshire, England. adv. circ. 2,000.

155.5　　US
COMMON FOCUS; an exchange of information about early adolescence. 1978. irreg. free. University of North Carolina, Center for Early Adolescence, Ste. 223, Carr Mill Mall, Carrboro, NC 27510. TEL 919-966-1148. Ed. Monica D. Jacoby. bk. rev. film rev. abstr. bibl. circ. 20,000. (back issues avail.)

155.4　　US　　ISSN 0147-1082
CONTEMPORARY PROBLEMS OF CHILDHOOD; a bibliographic series. 1977. irreg. price varies. Greenwood Press, 88 Post Rd. W., Box 5007, Westport, CT 06881. TEL 203-226-3571. Ed. Carol Ann Winchell.

CONTRIBUTIONS TO RESIDENTIAL TREATMENT. see *PSYCHOLOGY*

155　　US　　ISSN 0273-124X
CONTRIBUTIONS TO THE STUDY OF CHILDHOOD AND YOUTH. 1982. irreg. price varies. Greenwood Press, 88 Post Rd. W., Box 5007, Westport, CT 06881. TEL 203-226-3571.

362.7　　NE
DIRECTIE KINDERBESCHERMING. biennial. ‡ Ministerie van Justitie, Postbus 20301, 2500 EH The Hague, Netherlands. stat. circ. 2,000.

DIRECTORY OF RESEARCH AND DEVELOPMENTAL PROJECTS. see *EDUCATION*

E R I C/C U E TRENDS AND ISSUES. see *EDUCATION*

E R I C CLEARINGHOUSE ON URBAN EDUCATION. DIGEST. see *EDUCATION*

348　　US
FIRST YEAR OF LIFE; a guide to your baby's growth and development month by month. 1977. a. Cahners Publishing Co., Inc., American Baby Group, Division of Reed Publishing USA, 249 W. 17th St., New York, NY 10011. TEL 212-645-0067. Ed. Judith Nolte. adv. circ. 3,000,000.

364　　UK　　ISSN 0072-6443
GREAT BRITAIN. HOME OFFICE. STUDIES IN THE CAUSES OF DELINQUENCY AND THE TREATMENT OF OFFENDERS. 1955. irreg. price varies. H.M.S.O., Box 569, London SE1 9NH, England. (reprint service avail. from UMI)

362.7　649　　FR
GUIDE DE LA JEUNE MAMAN. a. 17 rue Viete, 75017 Paris, France.

HAANBOG FOR BOERNE- OG UNGDOMINSTITUTIONER. DOEGNINSTITUTIONER. see *SOCIAL SERVICES AND WELFARE*

HAWAII. DEPARTMENT OF HEALTH. MENTAL HEALTH SERVICES FOR CHILDREN AND YOUTH; children's MH services branch. see *SOCIAL SERVICES AND WELFARE*

HUMAN STRESS CURRENT ADVANCES IN RESEARCH. see *PSYCHOLOGY*

362.7　　UK　　ISSN 0074-7416
I P A CONFERENCE REPORT. (Text in English, French or German) 1961. irreg., approx. every 3 yrs., 1984, Ljubljana. membership. ‡ International Association for the Child's Right to Play, c/o Mr. N.R. Balmforth, Play Board, Britannia House, 50 Great Charles St. Queensway, Birmingham B3 2LP, England. Ed. Robin C. Moore. bk. rev. circ. 1,500.

INTERNATIONAL CHILDREN'S CENTRE. PARIS. REPORT OF THE DIRECTOR-GENERAL TO THE EXECUTIVE BOARD. see *SOCIOLOGY*

INTERNATIONAL CHILDREN'S CENTRE. PARIS. TRAVAUX ET DOCUMENTS. see *SOCIOLOGY*

INVALID CHILDREN'S AID NATIONWIDE YEAR BOOK. see *SOCIAL SERVICES AND WELFARE*

JUNIOR AUTHORS AND ILLUSTRATORS SERIES. see *JOURNALISM*

796.1　910.4　　GW
KAKTUSBLUETE. 1973. irreg. DM.3. Kaktusbluete, Kapellenstr. 38, 5800 Hagen 1, W. Germany (B.R.D.) Ed. Friedhelm Kuhl. adv. bk. rev. film rev. circ. 1,000. (back issues avail.)

KINDEX; an index to legal periodical literature concerning children. see *LAW — Abstracting, Bibliographies, Statistics*

LIBERIA. MINISTRY OF LABOUR, YOUTH & SPORTS. ANNUAL REPORT. see *SOCIAL SERVICES AND WELFARE*

CHILDREN AND YOUTH —
Abstracting, Bibliographies, Statistics

028.5 010   US   ISSN 0067-9070
BLACK EXPERIENCE IN CHILDREN'S BOOKS. 1946. irreg., latest 1984. $3. New York Public Library, Office of Branch Libraries, 455 Fifth Ave., New York, NY 10016. TEL 212-340-0892. Ed. Barbara Rollock. index.
   Formerly: Books About Negro Life for Children.

778.5 028.52   DK   ISSN 0109-2030
BOERNEBIBLIOTEKSKATALOG. DIAS, FILM, VIDEO. 1983. a. Kr.205.45. Bibliotekscentralen, Tempovej 7-11, DK-2750 Ballerup, Denmark.
   Formerly: Boernebibliotekskatalog. Dias, Film.

028.52   DK   ISSN 0109-193X
BOERNEBIBLIOTEKSKATALOG. LYDBOEGER, BOG & BAAND. 1983. a. Kr.342.10. Bibliotekscentralen, Tempovej 7-11, DK-2750 Ballerup, Denmark.
   Formerly: Boernebibliotekskatalog. Lydboeger.

649 016
BREASTFEEDING ABSTRACTS. 1981. q. $9.50. La Leche League International, Inc., 9616 Minneapolis Ave., Box 1209, Franklin Park, IL 60131. TEL 312-455-7730. Ed. Kathleen Auerbach. bk. rev. abstr. circ. 1,100.
   Care and hygiene

028.5 011   CN
CANADIAN BOOKS FOR YOUNG PEOPLE/ LIVRES CANADIENS POUR LA JEUNESSE. (Text in English and French) 1976. biennial. Can.$15. University of Toronto Press, University of Toronto, Ont. M5S 1A6, Canada TEL 613-667-7791. (Subscr. to: Publications Order Department, 5201 Dufferin St., Downsview, Ont. M3H 5T8) Ed. Irma McDonough. circ. 1,500.

CANDLELIGHTERS CHILDHOOD CANCER FOUNDATION/ANNOTATED BIBLIOGRAPHY AND RESOURCE GUIDE. see *BIBLIOGRAPHIES*

612 016   US   ISSN 0009-3939
CHILD DEVELOPMENT ABSTRACTS AND BIBLIOGRAPHY. 1927. 3/yr. $50. (Society for Research in Child Development, Inc.) University of Chicago Press, 5801 S. Ellis Ave., Chicago, IL 60637 TEL 312-962-7600. (Orders to: Box 37005, Chicago, IL 60637) Ed. Hoben Thomas. bk. rev. abstr. bibl. index. circ. 5,700. (also avail. in microform from MIM,UMI; reprint service avail. from UMI,ISI) Indexed: C.I.J.E. Except.Child.Educ.Abstr.

028.5   US
CHILDHOOD IN POETRY. 1967. irreg., 3rd supp., 1980. $110. Gale Research Company, Book Tower, Detroit, MI 48226. TEL 313-961-2242. Ed. John Mackay Shaw. Indexed: Child.Auth.& Illus.

028.1   US
CHILDREN'S BOOK REVIEW INDEX. 1976. a. $82. Gale Research Company, Book Tower, Detroit, MI 48226. TEL 313-961-2242. Ed. Barbara Beach.

649   US
CHILDREN'S CATALOG. 1909. quinquennial, with a. supplements. $54. ‡ H. W. Wilson Co., 950 University Ave., Bronx, NY 10452. TEL 212-588-8400. Ed. Juliette Yaakov. bk. rev.

CHILDREN'S LITERATURE ABSTRACTS. see *PUBLISHING AND BOOK TRADE — Abstracting, Bibliographies, Statistics*

028.52   DK   ISSN 0109-8853
FOLKEBIBLIOTEKERNES UDENLANSKE BOERNEBOGSSAMLING. KATALOG. 1985. a. Kr.188.25. Bibliotekscentralen, Telegrafvej 5, 2750 Ballerup, Denmark.

GERMANY (FEDERAL REPUBLIC, 1949-). STATISTISCHES BUNDESAMT. FACHSERIE 13, SOZIALLEISTUNGEN, REIHE 6: JUGENDHILFE. see *SOCIAL SERVICES AND WELFARE — Abstracting, Bibliographies, Statistics*

649.1 614   FR   ISSN 0076-2814
MAISONS D'ENFANTS ET D'ADOLESCENTS DE FRANCE. ALBUM-ANNUAIRE NATIONAL; publication documentaire illustree des establishments de vacances, de repos, de soins, de cure et de prevention pour enfants et adolescents. a., latest edition 28th, 1976. 120 F. Editions Gaston Gorde, 45 Av. Paul Doumer, Roguebrune, France.

649 640   AT   ISSN 0813-4626
MY BABY. 1983. a. Aus.$5.95. Depin Pty. Ltd., 23 Willoughby Rd., P.O. Box 1067, Crows Nest, N.S.W. 2065, Australia. Ed. Carol Fallows. adv. bk. rev. circ. 35,000.

362   UK   ISSN 0302-1998
NATIONAL CHILDREN'S BUREAU. ANNUAL REVIEW. a. membership. National Children's Bureau, 8 Wakley St., Islington, London EC1V 7QE, England. (back issues avail.)

NATIONAL DEAF CHILDREN'S SOCIETY. YEAR BOOK AND ANNUAL ACCOUNTS. see *DEAF*

364.36   NE
NETHERLANDS. CENTRAAL BUREAU VOOR DE STATISTIEK. JUSTICIELE KINDERBESCHERMING. (Text in Dutch and English) 1950/51. a. fl.13.70. Centraal Bureau voor de Statistiek, Hoofdafdeling Statistieken van Criminaliteit en Rechtspleging, Prinses Beatrixlaan 428, Voorburg, Netherlands (Orders to: Staatsuitgeverij, Christoffel Plantijnstraat, The Hague, Netherlands)
   Formerly: Netherlands. Centraal Bureau voor de Statistiek. Toepassing der Kinderwetten. Application of Juvenile Law (ISSN 0077-7471)

649   UK
NEW BABY. 1972. a. $2 free in U.K. to health professionals. ‡ B. Edsall & Co. Ltd., 124 Belgrave Rd., London SW1V 2BL, England. Ed. P. Scowen. adv. illus. pat. circ. 650,000.

NEW BRUNSWICK. DEPARTMENT OF YOUTH. REPORT. see *CHILDREN AND YOUTH — For*

NEW YORK (STATE) ASSEMBLY. STANDING COMMITTEE ON CHILDREN AND FAMILIES. ANNUAL REPORT. see *SOCIAL SERVICES AND WELFARE*

OVERZICHT TIJDSCHRIFTARTIKELEN. see *ABSTRACTING AND INDEXING SERVICES*

PAPERS AND REPORTS ON CHILD LANGUAGE DEVELOPMENT. see *LINGUISTICS*

PHAEDRUS; international annual of children's literature research. see *LITERATURE*

PLAY SCHOOLS NEWSLETTER. see *EDUCATION*

028.5   UK
PLAYHOUR ANNUAL. a. £2.95 per no. Fleetway Annuals, Kings Reach Tower, Stamford St., London SE1 9LS, England. Ed. J. Smith.

RAINER FOUNDATION. ANNUAL REPORT. see *CRIMINOLOGY AND LAW ENFORCEMENT*

647 610   JA   ISSN 0386-8435
RESEARCH AND CLINICAL CENTER FOR CHILD DEVELOPMENT. ANNUAL REPORT. (Text and summaries in English) 1978. a. Hokkaido University, Research and Clinical Center for Child Development, Nishi-7-Chome, Kita-11-Jo, Kita-ku, Sapporo-Chi, 060, Japan. Ed. Kazuo Miyake. cum.index. circ. 500. (back issues avail.) Indexed: Psychol.Abstr.

155.4 370   US   ISSN 0091-3065
REVIEW OF CHILD DEVELOPMENT RESEARCH. (Vols. 1 & 2 published by Russell Sage Foundation) irreg., vol.7, 1984. price varies. (Society for Research in Child Development, Inc.) University of Chicago Press, 5801 S. Ellis Ave., Chicago, IL 60637. TEL 312-962-7700. adv. bk. rev. (reprint service avail. from UMI,ISI)

SAVE THE CHILDREN. ANNUAL REPORT. see *SOCIAL SERVICES AND WELFARE*

369.4   SZ
SCOUTING 'ROUND THE WORLD/SCOUTISME A TRAVERS LE MONDE; facts and figures on world scouting and on national scout organizations which are members of the World Organization of the Scout Movement. irreg. 10 Fr. (World Organization of the Scout Movement) World Scout Bureau, Case Postale 78, 1211 Geneva 4, Switzerland.
   Scouting

649 610   JA
SHONI NO HOKEN/HEALTH FOR CHILDREN. 1966. a. free. Osaka Children's Medical Center, 2-5-30, Higashinari-ku, Osaka 537, Japan. adv. bk. rev. circ. 1,000. (back issues avail.)

028.5   UK
SIGNAL SELECTION OF CHILDREN'S BOOKS. 1985. a. price varies. Thimble Press, Lockwood Station Rd., South Woodchester, Stroud, Glos. GL5 5EQ, England. Ed. Nancy Chambers. bk. rev.
   Supersedes: Signal Review (ISSN 0264-2212)
   Juvenile literature

155.4   US   ISSN 0037-976X
SOCIETY FOR RESEARCH IN CHILD DEVELOPMENT. MONOGRAPHS. 1935. irreg. (4-6/yr.) $50. University of Chicago Press, 5801 S. Ellis Ave., Chicago, IL 60637 TEL 312-962-7600. (Orders to: Box 37005, Chicago, IL 60637) Ed. Robert N. Emde. circ. 5,400. (also avail. in microform from UMI; reprint service avail. from UMI,ISI) Indexed: Biol.Abstr. Curr.Cont. Educ.Ind. Ind.Med. Psychol.Abstr. SSCI. Sci.Cit.Ind. Adol.Ment.Hlth.Abstr. C.I.J.E. Child Devel.Abstr. Lang.& Lang.Behav.Abstr.

028.5   US
SOURCEBOOK (KNOXVILLE); for high school seniors. a. 13-30 Corporation, 505 Market St., Knoxville, TN 37902. TEL 615-637-7621. Ed. Keith Bellows.

371.9
THEIR WORLD. 1970. a. $4. Foundation for Children with Learning Disabilities, 99 Park Ave., 6th Fl., New York, NY 10016. TEL 212-687-7211. Ed. Julie Gilligan. adv. bk. rev. abstr. circ. 70,000.

WORLD ALLIANCE OF Y M C A'S DIRECTORY. see *CLUBS*

369.433   UK   ISSN 0084-1412
WORLD ASSOCIATION OF GIRL GUIDES AND GIRL SCOUTS. REPORT OF CONFERENCE. 1930. triennial, 25th, 1985. World Association of Girl Guides and Girl Scouts, World Bureau, Olave Centre, 12 C Lyndhurst Rd., London NW3 5PQ, England. circ. 1,500.

369.43   SZ
WORLD SCOUT BUREAU REPORT. 1922. triennial. 2.25. (World Organization of the Scout Movement) World Scout Bureau, Case Postale 78, 1211 Geneva 4, Switzerland.
   Formerly: Boy Scouts World Bureau.
   Scouting

Y CANADA. see *CLUBS*

Y M C A'S OF THE WORLD. see *CLUBS*

649   SI
YOUNG PARENTS. 1986. a. S.$5. Times Periodicals Pte. Ltd., 1 New Industrial Road, Singapore 1953, Singapore. Ed. Betty Khoo. adv. illus. circ. 20,000.

649.1   UK
YOUR FIRST BABY. 1980. a. free. Newbourne Publications Ltd., Cambridge House, 373-375 Euston Rd., London NW1, England. Ed. Ruth Bennett. adv. circ. 350,000.

YOUTH SERVICES GUIDE. see *SOCIAL SERVICES AND WELFARE*

369.4 790.1   ZA
ZAMBIA. MINISTRY OF YOUTH AND SPORT. DEPARTMENT OF YOUTH DEVELOPMENT. ANNUAL REPORT. (Text in English) 1982. a. (Ministry of Youth and Sport, Department of Youth Development) Government Printer, Government Printing Department, P.O. Box 30136, Lusaka, Zambia. circ. 810.

CHILDREN AND YOUTH — For

362.7   US
INFORMATION SHARING INDEX. a. U.S. Department of Health and Human Services, Office of Child Support Enforcement, National Child Support Enforcement Reference Center, 6110 Executive Blvd., Rm. 820, Rockville, MD 20852. TEL 301-443-5106.

INTERNATIONAL DIRECTORY OF CHILDREN'S LITERATURE. see *PUBLISHING AND BOOK TRADE — Abstracting, Bibliographies, Statistics*

028.5   DK   ISSN 0107-4636
LAES OM; emne-og genredelt katalog for de 9-13 aarige. 1981. biennial. Kr.147.55. Bibliotekscentralen, Tempovej 7-11, DK-2750 Ballerup, Denmark. illus.

800 011 500   US
OUTSTANDING SCIENCE TRADE BOOKS FOR CHILDREN. 1971. a. (National Science Teachers Association, Joint Committee Project) Children's Book Council, Inc., 67 Irving Pl., New York, NY 10003. TEL 212-254-2666. Ed. Jeanette Brod.
Grades K-8

028.5   US
STORIES: A LIST OF STORIES TO TELL AND TO READ ALOUD. irreg., no.7, 1977. $3. New York Public Library, Office of Branch Libraries, 455 Fifth Ave., New York, NY 10016. TEL 212-340-0892. Ed. Marilyn Berg Iarusso.

028.5   DK   ISSN 0106-6625
UDENLANDSKE LITTERATUR I DANSKE FOLKEBIBLIOTEKER. BOERNEBOGER. 1974. a. Kr.622.95. Bibliotekscentralen, Telegrafvej 5, 2750 Ballerup, Denmark. (also avail. in microfiche)
Formerly: Udenlandske Boerneboeger i Danske Folkebiblioteker.

028.5   DK   ISSN 0108-6952
UNGE LAESER OM; emne- og genredelt katalog. 1983. triennial. Kr.116.40. Bibliotekscentralen, Tempovej 7-11, DK-2750 Ballerup, Denmark.

CHILDREN AND YOUTH — For

A A U JUNIOR OLYMPIC HANDBOOK. (Amateur Athletic Union of the United States) see *SPORTS AND GAMES*

200   DK
ALLE BOERNS JUL. 1982. a. Kr.13. Danmarks Folkekirkelige Soendagsskoler og Boernegudstjenester, Boernebladet, Korskaervej 25, 7000 Fredericia, Denmark. illus.
Formerly: Boernebladets Jul (ISSN 0105-709X)

ANNALS OF CHILD DEVELOPMENT. see *PSYCHOLOGY*

AUSTRALIAN ASSOCIATION FOR ADOLESCENT HEALTH. NEWSLETTER. see *MEDICAL SCIENCES*

028.5 157.61   AT
AUTUMN SCHOOL OF STUDIES ON ALCOHOL & DRUGS. PROCEEDINGS OF SEMINARS. 1966. a. Aus.$10. St. Vincent Hospital, Department of Community Medicine, Victoria Parade, Fitzroy, Vic. 3065, Australia. Ed. Joseph Santamaria. circ. 400. (back issues avail.)

DIE BARKE; Lehrer-Jahrbuch. see *LITERATURE*

028.5   NO
BARNE OG UNGDOMSLITTERATUR. UTVALG AV BOKER UTKOMMETI. a. free. Ministry of Culture and Scientific Affairs, Norwegian Directorate for Public and School Libraries - Statens Bibliotektilsyn, P.O. Box 8145 Dep., 0033 Oslo 1, Norway. Ed. Else Granheim. bk. rev. circ. 4,700. (back issues avail.)
Formerly: Utvalg for Skolebiblioteker av Boker Utkommet.

028.5   UK
BIG ENID BLYTON STORY ANNUAL. a. £1.75. Purnell Books (Subsidiary of: Macdonald Co. (Publishers) Ltd.) 3rd Fl., Greater London House, Hamstpead Rd., London ENW1 7QX, England.

028.5   II   ISSN 0006-3614
BIRBAL. (Text in Marathi) 1970. a. Prestige Publications, 461-1 Sadashiv Peth, Tilak Rd., Poona 411030, Maharashtra, India. Ed. Raja Mangalwedwkar. adv. circ. 2,000. Indexed: GeoRef. *Children and youth*

028.5   DK   ISSN 0106-8199
BOERNEBOGSSERIER TEGNESERIER. 1976. a. Kr.59.80. Bibliotekscentralen, Tempovej 7-11, 2750 Ballerup, Denmark.
Formerly: Boernebogsserier.

028.5 778.5   DK   ISSN 0105-1377
BOERNEFILMKATALOGET. 1976. a. Kr.317.65. Bibliotekscentralen, Tempovej 7-11, 2750 Ballerup, Denmark. illus.

BOERNEFILMKATALOGET. SUPPLEMENT. see *MOTION PICTURES — Abstracting, Bibliographies, Statistics*

301.58   UK   ISSN 0068-0605
BOYS' BRIGADE, LONDON. ANNUAL REPORT. 1883. a. £1. Boys' Brigade, Inc., Brigade House, Parsons Green, London SW6 4TH, England. circ. 4,000.

155.5   US
BRIDGING THE GAP: WHAT'S HAPPENING NOW. 1983. irreg. $3. (Emory University, Family Planning Program) Printed Matter, Inc., Box 15246, Atlanta, GA 30333. TEL 404-523-6522. Ed. Anne D. Mather. bibl. illus. circ. 60,000.

051   CN   ISSN 0316-8484
CANADIAN CHILDREN'S ANNUAL. 1975. a. Can.$9.95. Potlatch Publications Ltd., 99 John St. South, Hamilton, Ont. L8N 2C2, Canada. TEL 416-528-2302. Ed. Robert F. Nielsen. circ. 20,000.

028.5   US   ISSN 0163-1756
CHILDREN'S BOOKS INTERNATIONAL. PROCEEDINGS. a. Boston Public Library, Box 286, Boston, MA 02117. TEL 617-536-5400.
Formerly: Children's Book International. Proceedings and Book Catalog (ISSN 0364-264X)

CHILDREN'S BOOKS OF THE YEAR. see *PUBLISHING AND BOOK TRADE*

028.5 370 070.5   US
CHILDREN'S BOOKS OF THE YEAR (YEAR) 1916. a. $4. Child Study, Children's Book Committee at Bank Street, 610 W. 112th St., New York, NY 10025. TEL 212-663-7200. Ed.Bd. circ. 3,500. (back issues avail.)

028.52   US   ISSN 0362-4145
CHILDREN'S LITERATURE REVIEW. 1976. irreg., vol.11, 1986. $78. Gale Research Company, Book Tower, Detroit, MI 48226. TEL 313-961-2242. Ed. Gerard J. Senick. bk. rev. Indexed: Child.Auth.& Illus.

CHILDREN'S LITERATURE SERIES. see *LITERATURE*

028.5   US   ISSN 0735-6358
CHOICES: A CORE COLLECTION FOR YOUNG RELUCTANT READERS. 1983. triennial. $45. John Gordon Burke Publishers, Inc., Box 1492, Evanston, IL 60204-1492.

028.5   FR
COLLECTION KNOWLEDGE & TECHNIQUE: YOUTH. (Text in English) 1977. irreg. Editions Denoel, 19 rue de l'Universite, Paris 7e, France. Dir. Philippe Lorin.

EXPECTATIONS. see *BLIND*

FILM AUSTRALIA CATALOGUE. see *MOTION PICTURES*

028.5   DK   ISSN 0107-7503
FOREBYGGENDE; foranstaltninger for smaaboern. a. (Sundhedstyrelsen) Bibliotekscentralen, Telegrafvej 5, DK-2750 Ballerup, Denmark.

THE GOOD BOOK GUIDE TO CHILDREN'S BOOKS. see *PUBLISHING AND BOOK TRADE*

INDIAN COUNCIL FOR CHILD WELFARE. ANNUAL REPORT. see *SOCIAL SERVICES AND WELFARE*

028.5   AU
INITIATIVE. 1966. irreg. (4-6/yr.) membership. Junge Generation in der Volkspartei, Jugendklub Innere Stadt, Wollzeile 24, 1010 Vienna, Austria. Ed. Guenter Zillich. adv. illus. circ. 1,000.
Formerly (until 1972): Magazin Vier und Zwanzig (ISSN 0024-9785)

INTERAMERICAN CHILDREN'S INSTITUTE. REPORT OF THE GENERAL DIRECTOR. see *SOCIAL SERVICES AND WELFARE*

369.4   BE   ISSN 0074-5790
INTERNATIONAL FALCON MOVEMENT. CONFERENCE REPORTS. (Reports published in its monthly paper, the I F M-Bulletin) (Text in English, French, German, Spanish and Swedish) irreg., 11th, 1970, Germany. International Falcon Movement, Place du Samedi 13, 1000 Brussels, Belgium. Ed. Jacqui Cottyn.

028.5   US
KID'S CLUB MAGAZINE. (Children ages 6-12) 1986. irreg. Western Publishing Co., Inc., 1220 Mound Ave., Racine, WI 53804. TEL 714-966-9092. Ed. Don Lesinski. circ. 200,000.

028.5   GW
KINDER-UND JUGENDBUECHER. a. DM.1.70. Koch, Neff, Oetinger & Co., Schockenriedstr. 37, 7000 Stuttgart 80, W. Germany (B.R.D.)

560   UK
LET ME TELL YOU ABOUT - DINOSAURS. 1983. irreg. £1.99. World International Publishing Ltd., P.O. Box 111, Gt. Ducie St., Manchester M60 3BL, England. Ed. Mae Broadley. adv.

600   UK
LET ME TELL YOU ABOUT - HOW THINGS WORK. 1983. irreg. £1.99. World International Publishing Ltd., P.O. Box 111, Gt. Ducie St., Manchester M60 3BL, England. Ed. Mae Broadley. adv.

808.068   CN
LITTLE THINGS WORD LOOM. 1981. irreg. Word Loom, Box 20, 242 Montrose, Winnipeg, Man., Canada. Ed. Ronan Reinart. circ. 100.

MAAGALAI KAREYA. see *LITERATURE*

028.5   CY   ISSN 0025-5904
MATHITIKI ESTIA. (Text in English, French, Greek) 1950. irreg. (1-2/yr.) free. Ministry of Education, Nicosia School Committee, Nicosia, Cyprus. Ed. Chrysanthos St. Kyprianou. bk. rev. film rev. play rev. bibl. charts. illus. circ. controlled. (processed)

028.5   GW
N O W SCHUELERZEITUNG DER STAATLICHEN REALSCHULE SPEYER. 1970. a. Realschule im Georg-Friedrich-Kolb-Schulzentrum, 6720 Speyer, W. Germany (B.R.D.) circ. 400.

028.5   AU   ISSN 0028-3444
NEUE WEGE; Kulturzeitschrift junger Menschen. 1947. irreg. (7-8/yr.) S.60. Theater der Jugend, Batthianystiege Hofburg, A-1010 Vienna, Austria. Ed. Herman Mayer. bk. rev. film rev. play rev. illus. index. circ. 7,000. (tabloid format)

361   CN   ISSN 0077-8079
NEW BRUNSWICK. DEPARTMENT OF YOUTH. REPORT. a. Department of Youth, Fredericton, N.B., Canada. TEL 506-453-2412.
Formerly: New Brunswick. Department of Youth and Welfare. Report.

NEW YORK (CITY). DEPARTMENT OF JUVENILE JUSTICE. ANNUAL REPORT. see *LAW*

NOTABLE CHILDREN'S TRADE BOOKS IN THE FIELD OF SOCIAL STUDIES. see *SOCIAL SCIENCES: COMPREHENSIVE WORKS — Abstracting, Bibliographies, Statistics*

028.5   AU   ISSN 0078-3560
OESTERREICHISCHER BUCHKLUB DER JUGEND. JAHRBUCH. 1949. a. membership. Oesterreichischer Buchklub der Jugend, Mayerhofgasse 6, A-1040 Vienna, Austria. Ed.Bd.

336 CHIROPRACTICS, HOMEOPATHY, OSTEOPATHY

028.5   US
PATHWAYS (MIDDLETON) a. $8. Inky Trails Publications, Box 345, Middleton, ID 83644. Ed. Pearl Kirk.
   Formerly: Tots to Teens.

PETERSON'S SUMMER OPPORTUNITIES FOR KIDS AND TEENAGERS. see *OCCUPATIONS AND CAREERS*

028.5   UK
PLAYSCHOOL ANNUAL. a. World Distributors Ltd., Box 111, 12 Lever St., Manchester M6O 1TS, England. Ed. M. Broadley.

028.5   613.7   CR
SALUD PARA TODOS. 1977. a. free. Asociacion Demografica Costarricense, Apdo. Postal 10203, 1000 San Jose, Costa Rica. Ed. Lia Barth. illus. charts. circ. 125,000.

362.7   AU   ISSN 0080-701X
SCHRIFTEN ZUR JUGENDLEKTUERE. irreg. price varies. International Institute for Children's Literature and Reading Research, Mayerhofgasse 6, A-1040 Vienna, Austria.

028.5   SZ
SCHWEIZERISCHER BUND FUER JUGENDLITERATUR. JAHRESBERICHT/ LIGUE SUISSE POUR LA LITTERATURE DE LA JEUNESSE. RAPPORT ANNUEL. 1954. a. 20 Fr. membership. Schweizerischer Bund fuer Jugendliteratur, Zentralsekretariat, Herzogstr. 5, 3014 Berne, Switzerland.

028.5   UK   ISSN 0262-4206
SCOOP SPORT ANNUAL. 1980. a. £1.65. D.C. Thomson & Co. Ltd., Albert Sq., Dundee DD1 9QJ, Scotland. illus.

SCOTTISH YOUTH HOSTELS ASSOCIATION HANDBOOK. see *HOTELS AND RESTAURANTS*

369.4   UK
SCOUT ANNUAL. 1983. a. £3.25. World International Publishing Co. Ltd., Gt. Ducie St., Manchester M60 3BL, England. Ed. Mae Broadley. adv.

028.5   UR
SPUTNIK SEL'SKOI MOLODEZHI. a. 0.35 Rub. Izdatel'stvo Molodaya Gvardiya, Ul. Sushevskaya, 21, Moscow a-55, Russian S.F.S.R., U.S.S.R. illus.

808.068   028.5   SW   ISSN 0347-5387
SVENSKA BARNBOKSINSTITUTET. SKRIFTER/ SWEDISH INSTITUTE FOR CHILDREN'S BOOKS. STUDIES. 1971. irreg., no.21, 1986. Svenska Barnboksinstitutet - Swedish Institute for Children's Books, Odengatan 61, S-113 22 Stockholm, Sweden. Ed. Sonja Svensson.

028.5   AT   ISSN 0727-4327
SYDNEY FOR KIDS. 1982. biennial. Aus.$4.95. Horan, Wall and Walker, P.O. Box 8, Surry Hills, N.S.W. 2010, Australia.

028.5   CS
TABORTUZ. irreg. Socialisticky Svaz Mladeze C S S R - Socialist Union of Youth, Nam. M. Gorkeho 24, 116 47 Prague 1, Czechoslovakia.

028.5   DK   ISSN 0107-7783
UNGDOMSKALENDER; ideer til aaret skolen. 1983. a. Kr.2,500. Ole Camaae, Lerbjergstien 18, 3460 Birkenroed, Denmark. TEL 02 27 62 82. Ed. H.C. Kolstrup. adv. bk. rev. illus. circ. 2,500.

VIETNAM YOUTH. see *GENERAL INTEREST PERIODICALS — Vietnam*

808.836   UK
WALT DISNEY'S DONALD DUCK FUN ANNUAL. 1979. a. £1.75. Purnell Publishers Ltd., Paulton, Bristol, Avon BS18 5LQ, England.

808.836   UK
WALT DISNEY'S MICKEY MOUSE CLUB ANNUAL. a. £1.75. Purnell Publishers Ltd., Paulton, Bristol, Avon BS18 5LQ, England.

808.836   UK
WALT DISNEY'S WINNIE THE POOH ANNUAL. 1979. a. £1.75. Purnell Publishers Ltd., Paulton, Bristol, Avon BS18 5LQ, England.

028.5   371.42   IT
WORKING HOLIDAYS (YEAR) 1952. a. £4.80. Central Bureau, Seymour Mews Hosue, Seymour Mews, London W1H 9PE, England. TEL 01 486 5101. Ed. Hilary Sewell. circ. 10,000.

028.5   US
WRITE IN THERE. a. World Pen Pals, 1690 Como Ave., St. Paul, MN 55108. TEL 612-647-9566.
   Supersedes: Silver Lining.

371.42   US   ISSN 0163-1640
18 ALMANAC; a handbook for leaving high school. 1973. a. $2. 13-30 Corporation, 505 Market St., Knoxville, TN 37902. TEL 615-637-7621. Ed. Pam Beaver. adv. circ. 700,000.

CHIROPRACTICS, HOMEOPATHY, OSTEOPATHY

see *Medical Sciences — Chiropractics, Homeopathy, Osteopathy*

CIRCUITS

see *Computers — Circuits*

CIVIL DEFENSE

see also *Military*

350.755   DK   ISSN 0108-7193
DENMARK. FORSVARSMINISTERIET. FORSVARSMINISTERENS AARLIGE REDEGOERELSE. 1982. a. free. Forsvarsministeriet - Ministry of Defense, Slotsholmsgade 10, 1216 Copenhagen K, Denmark. Ed. R.W. Boelsen. illus. circ. 6,000.

350.755   FR
FRANCE. SERVICE INTERDEPARTEMENTAL DE LA PROTECTION CIVILE. BULLETIN. irreg., latest Feb., 1981. free. Service Interdepartemental de la Protection Civile, 12 Quai de Gesvres, Paris 4, France. bibl. charts. illus.
   Formerly: Bulletin de la Protection Civile de la Prefecture de Police.

355.623   GW
GERMANY (FEDERAL REPUBLIC, 1949-). BUNDESMINISTER DES INNERN. SCHUTZKOMMISSION. TAETIGKEITSBERICHT. 1965. a. free. Bundesministerium des Innern, Schutzkommission, 5300 Bonn, W. Germany (B.R.D.) illus. circ. 200.
   Formerly (until 1972): Germany (Federal Republic, 1949-). Bundesminister des Innern. Schutzkommission. Berichte der Fachausschuesse.

CIVIL ENGINEERING

see *Engineering — Civil Engineering*

CIVIL RIGHTS

see *Political Science — Civil Rights*

CLASSICAL STUDIES

see also *Archaeology; History; Linguistics; Literature; Museums and Art Galleries*

930   913   HU   ISSN 0567-7246
ACTA UNIVERSITATIS DE ATTILA JOZSEF NOMINATAE. ACTA ANTIQUA ET ARCHAEOLOGICA. (Supplement avail. in Hungarian) (Text in German, Greek or Latin; notes in French or German) 1958. a. exchange basis. Attila Jozsef University, c/o E. Szabo, Exchange Librarian, Dugonics ter 13, P.O. Box 393, Szeged H-6701, Hungary (Subscr. to: Kultura, Box 149, H-1389 Budapest, Hungary) Eds. Samu Szadeczky-Kardoss, Egon Maroti. circ. 600.
   Incorporating: Opuscula Byzantina (ISSN 0139-2751)

700   IT   ISSN 0065-681X
AMERICAN ACADEMY IN ROME. PAPERS AND MONOGRAPHS. 1919. irreg. price varies. American Academy in Rome, Via Angelo Masina 5, 00153 Rome, Italy.

AMERICAN PHILOLOGICAL ASSOCIATION. DIRECTORY OF MEMBERS. see *LINGUISTICS*

AMERICAN PHILOLOGICAL ASSOCIATION. SPECIAL PUBLICATIONS. see *LINGUISTICS*

880   AT   ISSN 0066-4774
ANTICHTHON. 1967. a. Aus.$18. University of Sydney, Australian Society for Classical Studies, Dept. of Greek, Sydney N.S.W. 2006, Australia. Eds. R.J. Mortley, G.R. Stanton. adv. circ. 400. Indexed: Aus.P.A.I.S. Numis.Lit.

870   UK   ISSN 0309-5541
ARCA; classical and medieval texts, papers and monographs. 1976. irreg. (1-5/yr.) price varies. Francis Cairns (Publications), P.O. Box 147, The University, Liverpool L69 3BX, England. Eds. Francis Cairns, Robin Seager.

ARCHEOLOGIA CLASSICA. see *ARCHAEOLOGY*

ARCHIWUM FILOLOGICZNE. see *LINGUISTICS*

489   FI   ISSN 0570-734X
ARCTOS; ACTA PHILOLOGICA FENNICA. (Text in English, French, German and Italian) 1954. a. Fmk.100($20) Klassillis - Filologinen Yhdistys, Hallituskatu 11-13, SF-00100 Helsinki 10, Finland (Dist. by: Academic Bookstore, P.O. Box 10128,SF-00100 Helsinki 10, Finland) Ed. H. Solin. bk. rev. circ. 30.

800   AG   ISSN 0325-4194
ARGOS. 1977. a. $12. Asociacion Argentina de Estudios Clasicos, Beruti 3199, 1425 Buenos Aires, Argentina. Ed. R. Buzon. adv. bk. rev. circ. 500.

930   880   US
ASPECTS OF GREEK AND ROMAN LIFE. irreg. price varies. Cornell University Press, 124 Roberts Place, Ithaca, NY 14850. TEL 607-257-7000.

B E F A R. PUBLICATION. (Bibliotheque des Ecoles Francaises d'Athenes et de Rome) see *ARCHAEOLOGY*

BERLINER BYZANTINISTISCHE ARBEITEN. see *HISTORY — History Of Europe*

800   BE
BIBLIOGRAPHIE PAPYROLOGIQUE SUR FICHES. 1941. irreg., approx. 6/yr. 600 Fr. Fondation Egyptologique Reine Elisabeth, Parc du Cinquantenaire 10, B-1040 Brussels, Belgium. Eds. M. Hombert, G. Nachtergael.

800   SP
BIBLIOTECA CLASICA GREDOS. 1976. irreg. Editorial Gredos, Sanchez Pacheco 81, Madrid 2, Spain.

800   950   IT
BIBLIOTECA DEGLI STUDI CLASSICI E ORIENTALI. 1974. irreg., no.12, 1978. price varies. Giardini Editori e Stampatori, Via Santa Bibbiana 28, 56100 Pisa, Italy.

800   SZ   ISSN 0067-7965
BIBLIOTHECA HELVETICA ROMANA. 1954. irreg., no.23, 1985. price varies. (Institut Suisse de Rome, IT) Librarie Droz, 11, rue Massot, 1211 Geneva 12, Switzerland.

CLASSICAL STUDIES

880 GW ISSN 0340-7853
BIBLIOTHEK DER GRIECHISCHEN LITERATUR. Abbreviated title: B G L. 1971. irreg., vol.22, 1986. price varies. Anton Hiersemann Verlag, Rosenbergstr. 113, Postfach 723, 7000 Stuttgart 1, W. Germany (B.R.D.) Eds. P. Wirth, W. Gessel.

870 UK
BRITANNIA MONOGRAPH SERIES. 1981. irreg. Society for the Promotion of Roman Studies, 31 Gordon Sq., London WC1H 0PP, England. Indexed: Br.Archaeol.Abstr.

880 FR ISSN 0007-4217
BULLETIN DE CORRESPONDANCE HELLENIQUE. 1877. a. (in two fascicules) price varies. (Ecole Francaise d'Athenes, GR) Diffusion de Boccard, 11 rue de Medicis, 75006 Paris, France. charts. illus. Indexed: Curr.Cont. M.L.A. Arts & Hum.Cit.Ind. Numis.Lit.

870 NE
BULLETIN DU CANGE. 1924. a. E.J. Brill, P.O. Box 9000, 2300 PA Leiden, Netherlands.

880 GR
BYZANTINA. (Text and summaries in English, French and Greek) 1969. a. $20. University of Thessaloniki, Byzantine Research Center, 71 Solonis St., Athens 143, Greece. Ed. Kas M. Grigori. Indexed: CERDIC.

870 UK
CAMBRIDGE CLASSICAL STUDIES. irreg. price varies. Cambridge University Press, Edinburgh Bldg., Shaftesbury Rd., Cambridge CB2 2RU, England (And 32 E. 57th St., New York NY 10022) Ed.Bd.

880 870 UK ISSN 0068-6638
CAMBRIDGE CLASSICAL TEXTS AND COMMENTARIES. 1965. irreg., no.25, 1984. $59.50 for latest vol. Cambridge University Press, Edinburgh Bldg., Shaftesbury Rd., Cambridge CB2 2RU, England (And 32 E. 57 St., New York, NY 10022) Ed.Bd. index.

400 UK ISSN 0068-6735
CAMBRIDGE PHILOLOGICAL SOCIETY. PROCEEDINGS. 1882. a. £8 for resident members. Cambridge Philological Society, c/o Dr. C. Austin, Trinity Hall, Cambridge CB2 1TJ, England. Eds. R.L. Hunter, M.M. McKenzie. circ. 700. Indexed: Curr.Cont. Arts & Hum.Cit.Ind. Numis.Lit.

400 UK ISSN 0068-6743
CAMBRIDGE PHILOLOGICAL SOCIETY. PROCEEDINGS. SUPPLEMENT. 1965. irreg., latest vol.12, 1987. £12.50. Cambridge Philological Society, c/o Dr. C. Austin, Trinity Hall, Cambridge CB2 1TJ, England. Eds. M.M. McKenzie, R.L. Hunter.

800 NE
CINCINNATI CLASSICAL STUDIES. NEW SERIES. 1977. irreg., vol.6, 1986. price varies. E.J. Brill, P.O. Box 9000, 2300 PA Leiden, Netherlands.

800 PO ISSN 0870-0141
CLASSICA; boletim de pedagogia e cultura. 1977. irreg. price varies. Universidade de Lisboa, Departamento de Estudos Classicos, Cidade Universitaria, 1699 Lisbon Codex, Portugal. circ. 350.

800 DK ISSN 0106-5815
CLASSICA ET MEDIAEVALIA; revue Danoise de philologie et d'histoire. (Text in English, French, German) 1938. a. Kr.350. (Dansk Selskab for Oldtids og Middelalderforskning) Museum Tusculanums Forlag, Njalsgade 94, DK-2300 Copenhagen S, Denmark. Ed. Otto Steen Due.

480 880 US ISSN 0278-6656
CLASSICAL ANTIQUITY. 1968. biennial. $20 to individuals; institutions $40. University of California Press, Journals Division, 2120 Berkeley Way, Berkeley, CA 94720. TEL 415-642-4191. Ed.Bd. adv. index. Indexed: Curr.Cont. Arts & Hum.Cit.Ind.
Formerly: California Studies in Classical Antiquity (ISSN 0068-5895)

800 US
CLASSICAL ASSOCIATION OF NEW ENGLAND. ANNUAL BULLETIN. 1906. a. membership only.
‡ Classical Association of New England, c/o Gilbert Lawall, Ed., 71 Sand Hill Rd., Amherst, MA 01002. bibl. illus. circ. 950.

800 NE
COLUMBIA STUDIES IN THE CLASSICAL TRADITION. 1976. irreg., vol.14, 1986. price varies. E.J. Brill, P.O. Box 9000, 2300 PA Leiden, Netherlands.

745 091 GW
CORPUS DER BYZANTINISCHEN MINIATURENHANDSCHRIFTEN (C B M) 1977. irreg., vol.3, 1983. price varies. (Oesterreichische Akademie der Wissenschaften, Kommission fuer Byzantinistik, AU) Anton Hiersemann Verlag, Rosenbergstr. 113, Postfach 723, 7000 Stuttgart 1, W. Germany (B.R.D.) Eds. Otto Demus, Irmgard Hutter.

954.82 II ISSN 0376-8090
DAMILICA. (Text in English or Tamil) 1970. irreg. Rs.18.50. Department of Archaeology, Madras, Tamil Nadu, India. bibl. illus.

489 BE ISSN 0070-4792
DIDACTICA CLASSICA GANDENSIA. 1962. a. 300 Fr. ‡ Rijksuniversiteit te Gent, Blandijnberg 2, B-9000 Ghent, Belgium (Orders to: Mrs. Verbeken-De Pauw, St.-Pietersnieuwstraat 109, B-9000 Ghent, Belgium) Eds. J. Veremans, F. Decreus.

489 BE ISSN 0070-685X
DOCUMENTATIO DIDACTICA CLASSICA. (Text in Latin) 1963. a. 200 Fr. Rijksuniversiteit te Gent, Blandijnberg 2, B-9000 Ghent, Belgium (Orders to: Mrs. Verbeken-De Pauw, St.-Pietersnieuwstraat 109, B-9000 Ghent, Belgium) Eds. J. Veremans, F. Decreus.
Classical philology

800 NE
EIRENE; studia graeca et latina. (Text in English, German and Russian) 1960. a. fl.90($43) John Benjamins Publishing Co., Amsteldijk 44, Box 52519, 1007 HA Amsterdam, Netherlands TEL 020-738156. (U.S. office: John Benjamins North America, Inc., One Buttonwood Sq., Philadelphia, PA 19130) bk. rev. (back issues avail.)

800 SZ ISSN 0071-0822
ENTRETIENS SUR L'ANTIQUITE CLASSIQUE. no.3, 1958. irreg., vol.32, 1986. price varies. (Fondation Hardt pour l'Etude de l'Antiquite Classique) Librarie Droz, 11 rue Massot, 1211 Geneva 12, Switzerland. Indexed: Rel.Ind.Two.

800 PO ISSN 0870-0133
EVPHROSYNE. (Text in English, French, German, Italian, Portuguese and Spanish) 1957. a. $35. Universidade de Lisboa, Centro Estudos Classicos, Cidade Universitaria, 1699 Lisbon Codex, Portugal (Subscr. to: Imprensa Nacional, Casa da Moeda, Rua D. Francisco Manuel de Melo, No. 5, 1000 Lisbon, Portugal) bk. rev. circ. 800.

FILOLOGIA KLASYCZNA. see LINGUISTICS

800 940 CN
FLORILEGIUM; annual papers on classical antiquity and the Middle Ages. 1979. a. Can.$12. Carleton University, Department of English, Ottawa, Ont., K1S 5B6, Canada. TEL 613-231-3847. Eds. D.J. Wurtele, R.C. Blockley. circ. 200. Indexed: M.L.A. RILA.

930 940 US ISSN 0072-7474
GREEK, ROMAN AND BYZANTINE MONOGRAPHS. 1959. irreg., no.10, 1984. price varies. Duke University, Department of Classical Studies, Box 4715, Duke Sta., Durham, NC 27706. TEL 919-684-6456. Ed. Keith Stanley. Indexed: New Test.Abstr. Numis.Lit.

930 940 US ISSN 0072-7482
GREEK, ROMAN, AND BYZANTINE STUDIES. SCHOLARLY AIDS. (Supplement to quarterly journal: Greek, Roman and Byzantine Studies) 1961. irreg., no.2, 1969. price varies. Duke University, Department of Classical Studies, Box 4715, Duke Sta., Durham, NC 27706. TEL 919-684-6456. Ed. Keith Stanley.

800 SP ISSN 0210-7694
HABIS. (Text in English, French, German, Spanish) 1970. a. Universidad de Sevilla, San Fernando 4, Sevilla 41004, Spain. charts, illus.

HARVARD STUDIES IN CLASSICAL PHILOLOGY. see LINGUISTICS

930 410 SZ ISSN 0073-0939
HAUTES ETUDES DU MONDE GRECO-ROMAIN. 1964. irreg., no.14, 1985. price varies. (Ecole Pratique des Hautes Etudes, Centre de Recherches d'Histoire et de Philologie, FR) Librarie Droz, 11, rue Massot, 1211 Geneva 12, Switzerland. circ. 1,000.

480 IT ISSN 0017-9981
HELIKON; revista di tradizione e cultura classica. 1961. irreg., vol.16, 1976. Universita degli Studi di Messina, Messina, Italy (Dist. by: Erma di Bretschneider, Via Cassiodor 19, 00193 Rome, Italy)

HERMES-EINZELSCHRIFTEN. see LINGUISTICS

930 BE
HUMANISTICA LOVANIENSIA; journal of Neo-Latin studies. 1968. a. price varies. (Katholieke Universiteit te Leuven, Seminarium Philologiae Humanisticae) Leuven University Press, Krakenstraat 3, 3000 Louvain, Belgium. bk. rev. circ. 750. (back issues avail.) Indexed: M.L.A.

930 BE
HUMANISTICA LOVANIENSIA. SUPPLEMENTA. 1978. irreg., vol.4, 1986. Leuven University Press, Krakerstraat 3, B-3000 Louvain, Belgium.

480 880 GW ISSN 0085-1671
HYPOMNEMATA; Untersuchungen zur Antike und zu ihrem Nachleben. 1962. irreg., no.81, 1984. price varies. Vandenhoeck und Ruprecht, Theaterstr. 13, Postfach 37 53, 3400 Goettingen, W. Germany (B.R.D.)

800 US ISSN 0363-1923
ILLINOIS CLASSICAL STUDIES. 1976. a. $25. (University of Illinois) Scholars Press, Box 1608, Decatur, GA 30031-1608. Ed. J.K. Newman. circ. 250.

480 880 IT ISSN 0073-5752
INCUNABULA GRAECA. 1961. irreg., no.87, 1986. price varies. Edizioni dell' Ateneo S.p.A., P.O. Box 7216, 00100 Rome, Italy. circ. 1,500.

870 200 BE
INSTRUMENTA LEXICOLOGIA LATINA. SERIES A & B. 1979. irreg., approx. 10/yr. (Cetedoc) N.V. Brepols I.G.P., Rue Baron Francois du Four 8, B-2300 Turnhout, Belgium.

INTERNATIONAL ASSOCIATION FOR CLASSICAL ARCHAEOLOGY. PROCEEDINGS OF CONGRESS. see ARCHAEOLOGY

950 IT
ISTITUTO UNIVERSITARIO ORIENTALE DI NAPOLI. SEMINARIO DI STUDI DEL MONDO CLASSICO. ANNALI. SEZIONE LINGUISTICA. 1978. irreg. $50. Herder Editrice e Libreria s.r.l., Piazza Montecitorio 117-121, 00186 Rome, Italy. Ed. Domenice Silvestri.

930 880 JA ISSN 0582-4524
JOURNAL OF CLASSICAL STUDIES/SEIYO KOTENGAKU KENKYU. (Extracts in English) 1928. a. (Classical Society of Japan) Iwanami Shoten Publishers, 2-5-5 Hitotsubashi, Chiyoda-ku, Tokyo 101, Japan.

880 UK ISSN 0075-4269
JOURNAL OF HELLENIC STUDIES. Issued with: Archaeological Reports (ISSN 0570-6084) 1880. a. £22($44) to institutions; members £17($34) Society for the Promotion of Hellenic Studies, 31-34 Gordon Square, London WC1H 0PP, England. Ed. C.B.R. Pelling. adv. bk. rev. circ. 3,000. (also avail. in microfilm from UMI; reprint service avail. from UMI) Indexed: Br.Hum.Ind. Curr.Cont. Hum.Ind. M.L.A. Arts & Hum.Cit.Ind. Ind.Bk.Rev.Hum. Numis.Lit. New Test.Abstr. Phil.Ind.

337

870   UK ISSN 0075-4358
JOURNAL OF ROMAN STUDIES. (Text in English, French, German, Greek and Latin) 1911. a. membership. Society for the Promotion of Roman Studies, 31-34 Gordon Sq., London WC1H 0PP, England. Ed. Averil Cameron. adv. bk. rev. cum.index: vols.1-40. circ. 2,800. Indexed: Br.Hum.Ind. Curr.Cont. Hum.Ind. Arts & Hum.Cit.Ind. Br.Archaeol.Abstr. Ind.Bk.Rev.Hum. Numis.Lit. New Test.Abstr.

KTEMA; civilisations de l 'Orient, de la Grece et de Rome Antiques. see *HISTORY — History Of Asia*

870   UK ISSN 0951-7391
LATIN AND GREEK TEXTS; classical and medieval. 1980. irreg. Francis Cairns (Publications), P.O. Box 147, The University, Liverpool L69 3BX, England.
 Formerly: Liverpool Latin Texts (ISSN 0144-9451)

480 880 GW ISSN 0024-7421
LUSTRUM; Internationale Forschungsberichte aus dem Bereich des Klassischen Altertums. 1956. irreg., no.26, 1984. price varies. Vandenhoeck und Ruprecht, Theaterstr. 13, Postfach 37 53, 3400 Goettingen, W. Germany (B.R.D.) Eds. Hans-Joachim Mette, Andreas Thierfelder. adv. circ. 1, 000.

870 880 US ISSN 0076-471X
MARTIN CLASSICAL LECTURES. (A series of lectures delivered annually at Oberlin College) 1931. irreg., latest vol.30, 1986. price varies. (Oberlin College) Harvard University Press, 79 Garden St., Cambridge, MA 02138. TEL 617-495-2600.

800   NE
MNEMOSYNE. SUPPLEMENTS; bibliotheca classica batava. 1938. irreg., vol.94, 1986. price varies. E.J. Brill, P.O. Box 9000, 2300 PA Leiden, Netherlands.

930   GW ISSN 0930-1127
MUENCHENER BEITRAEGE ZUR MEDIAEVISTIK UND RENAISSANCE-FORSCHUNG. (Text in English, German) 1967. irreg. Arbeo-Gesellschaft e.V., D-8049 Bachenhausen, W. Germany (B.R.D.) Ed. Gabriel Silagi. circ. 450. (back issues avail.) Indexed: M.L.A.

913   NR
MUSEUM AFRICUM; West African journal of classical and related studies. 1972. a. £N3. University of Ibadan, Department of Classics, Ibadan, Nigeria. Ed. L.A. Thompson. adv. bk. rev. circ. 500.
 Supersedes: Nigeria and the Classics (ISSN 0549-2629)

930   AU
MYKENISCHE STUDIEN. (Subseries of Oesterreichische Akademie der Wissenschaften. Philosophisch-Historische Klasse. Sitzungsberichte) 1972. irreg. price varies. (Oesterreichische Akademie der Wissenschaften, Kommission fuer Mykenische Forschung) Verlag der Oesterreichischen Akademie der Wissenschaften, Ignaz Seipel-Platz 2, A-1010 Vienna, Austria.

MYRTIA: REVISTA DE FILOLOGIA CLASICA. see *LINGUISTICS*

480   US ISSN 0077-6521
NEO-HELLENIKA.* (Text in English, French, German, Italian and Spanish) 1970. irreg., no.3, 1978. $20. University of Texas at Austin, Center for Neo-Hellenic Studies, Humanities Research Center, Rm. 3210, Austin, TX 78712. TEL 512-471-3434. adv. bk. rev. Indexed: M.L.A.

800   UK
NEW SURVEYS IN THE CLASSICS. 1966. a. membership; free to subscribers of "Greece and Rome". (Classical Association) Oxford University Press, Walton St., Oxford OX2 6DP, England. Ed.Bd. bibl.

870   SZ ISSN 0078-0936
NOCTES ROMANAE; Forschungen ueber die Kultur der Antike. 1949. irreg., vol.16, 1980. price varies. Paul Haupt AG, Falkenplatz 14, CH-3001 Berne, Switzerland. Ed. Georg Luck.

NOVA TELLUS. see *HUMANITIES: COMPREHENSIVE WORKS*

913   DK ISSN 0107-1378
ODENSE UNIVERSITY CLASSICAL STUDIES. (Text in English, French) 1971. irreg., no.12, 1981. price varies. Odense University Press, 36, Pjentedamsgade, DK-5000 Odense, Denmark. (back issues avail.)

OPUSCULA ATHENIENSIA. see *ARCHAEOLOGY*

930   GW ISSN 0078-5555
ORBIS ANTIQUUS. 1950. irreg. price varies. Aschendorffsche Verlagsbuchhandlung, Soester Str. 13, 4400 Muenster, W. Germany (B.R.D.) Ed. Max Wegner.

930   US
OXFORD CLASSICAL AND PHILOSOPHICAL MONOGRAPHS. irreg. price varies. Oxford University Press, 200 Madison Ave., New York, NY 10016 TEL 212-679-7300. (And Ely House, 37 Dover St., London W1X 4AH, England)

OXFORD MONOGRAPHS ON CLASSICAL ARCHAEOLOGY. see *ARCHAEOLOGY*

800   GW ISSN 0552-9638
PALINGENESIA; Monographien und Texte zur klassischen Altertumswissenschaft. (Text in English and German) irreg., vol.22, 1985. price varies. Franz Steiner Verlag Wiesbaden GmbH, Birkenwaldstr. 44, Postfach 347, D-7000 Stuttgart 1, W. Germany (B.R.D) Eds. P. Steinmetz, O. Lendle.

PHILOSOPHIA ANTIQUA. see *PHILOSOPHY*

930   AT ISSN 0726-4399
PRIMITIAE; a journal of classical studies. 1980. a. Aus.$5. Australian National University Classical Society, c/o Department of Classics, GPO Box 4, Canberra, ACT 2601, Australia. circ. 200. (back issues avail.)

870   GW ISSN 0721-6203
QUELLEN UND UNTERSUCHUNGEN ZUR LATEINISCHEN PHILOLOGIE DES MITTELALTERS. 1981. irreg., vol.9, 1987. price varies. Anton Hiersemann Verlag, Rosenbergstr. 113, Postfach 723, D-7000 Stuttgart 1, W. Germany (B.R.D.)

800   FR ISSN 0035-2004
REVUE DES ETUDES ANCIENNES. 1929. irreg. 150 F. Universite de Bordeaux III, Domaine Universitaire, 33405 Talence Cedex, France. bk. rev. abstr. bibl. charts. illus. index. Indexed: M.L.A. Br.Archaeol.Abstr. Numis.Lit.

880 480 FR ISSN 0035-2039
REVUE DES ETUDES GRECQUES. 1888. irreg., vol.99, 1986. 475 F. (Societe des Etudes Grecques) Societe d'Edition les Belles Lettres, 95 bd. Raspail, 75006 Paris, France. bk. rev. abstr. bibl. illus. index. circ. 2,000. Indexed: M.L.A. Numis.Lit.

930 400 FR
REVUE DES ETUDES LATINES. 1928. a. 250 F. (Societe des Etudes Latines) Societe d'Edition les Belles Lettres, 95 bd. Raspail, 75006 Paris, France. Ed. P. Grimal. bk. rev. bibl. cum.index every 5 yrs. circ. 2,000. Indexed: M.L.A. Br.Archaeol.Abstr.

880   IT ISSN 0080-3251
RIVISTA DI CULTURA CLASSICA E MEDIOEVALE. QUADERNI. 1960. irreg., no.16, 1983. price varies. Edizioni dell' Ateneo S.p.A., P.O. Box 7216, 00100 Rome, Italy. circ. 2,000.

ROEMISCHE HISTORISCHE MITTEILUNGEN. see *HISTORY — History Of Europe*

480   GW ISSN 0341-3209
ROMANISTIK IN GESCHICHTE UND GEGENWART. 1975. irreg., no.20, 1986. price varies. Verlag Helmut Buske, Schlueterstr. 14, 2000 Hamburg 13, W. Germany (B.R.D.) Ed.Bd.

870 930 IT
ROMANOBARBARICA. 1976. a. L.40000($30) (Universita degli Studi di Roma, Istituto di Lingua e Letteratura Latina) Herder Editrice e Libreria s.r.l., Piazza Montecitorio 120, 00186 Rome, Italy. Ed. Bruno Luiselli, Manlio Simonetti. Indexed: Numis.Lit.

930   US ISSN 0732-9814
RUTGERS UNIVERSITY STUDIES IN CLASSICAL HUMANITIES. 1982. biennial. $49.95. Transaction Books, Rutgers University, New Brunswick, NJ 08903. TEL 201-932-2280. Ed. William W. Fortenbaugh.

800 400 IT
SANDALION. 1978. a. L.28000($20) (Universita degli Studi di Sassari) Herder Editrice e Libreria s.r.l., Piazza Montecitorio 120, 00186 Rome, Italy. Ed.Bd.

800   US ISSN 0080-6684
SATHER CLASSICAL LECTURES. 1924. irreg., vol.48, 1982. price varies. University of California Press, 2120 Berkeley Way, Berkeley, CA 94720. TEL 415-642-4247.

870 880 GE ISSN 0138-595X
SCHRIFTEN ZUR GESCHICHTE UND KULTUR DER ANTIKE. 1970. irreg., vol.25, 1985. (Akademie der Wissenschaften der DDR) Akademie-Verlag Berlin, Leipziger Str.3-4, 1086 Berlin, E. Germany (D.D.R.)

400   IS
SCRIPTA CLASSICA ISRAELICA. (Text in English, German or Latin) 1974. a. $10. (Israel Society for the Promotion of Classical Studies) Jerusalem Academic Press, Box 3640, Jerusalem, Israel. illus.

870   IT ISSN 0080-8393
SCRIPTORES LATINI; collana di scrittori Latini ad uso accademica. 1965. irreg., no.19, 1984. price varies. Edizioni dell' Ateneo S.p.A., P.O. Box 7216, 00100 Rome, Italy. Ed. Antonio Traglia. circ. 1,000.

800   IT
SCRITTURA E CIVILTA. 1977. a. L.57000. (Universita degli Studi di Roma, Istituto di Paleografia) Bottega d'Erasmo, Via G. Ferrari 9, 10124 Turin, Italy. Ed. Armando Petrucci. adv. bk. rev. circ. 500.

930 950 IT ISSN 0081-6124
STUDI CLASSICI E ORIENTALI. 1951. irreg. L.36000($65) (Universita degli Studi di Pisa, Instituto per le Scienze dell'Antichita) Giardini Editori e Stampatori, Istituti per le Scienze dell'Antichita, 56100 Pisa, Italy. Ed. Graziano Arrighetti.

880   IT ISSN 0081-6159
STUDI DI METRICA CLASSICA. 1962. irreg., no.7, 1983. price varies. Edizioni dell' Ateneo S.p.A., P.O. Box 7216, 00100 Rome, Italy. Ed. Bruno Gentili. circ. 1,500.

480 470 SW ISSN 0081-6450
STUDIA GRAECA ET LATINA GOTHOBURGENSIA. (Subseries of Acta Universitatis Gothoburgensis) (Text in various languages) 1955. irreg., no.47, 1985. price varies; also exchange basis. Acta Universitatis Gothoburgensis, Box 5096, S-402 22 Goeteborg, Sweden (Dist. in U.S., Canada, and Mexico by: Humanities Press, Inc., 171 First Ave., Atlantic Highlands, NJ 07716) Eds. Cajus Fabricius, Tore Jansson.

880   BE
STUDIA HELLENISTICA. irreg. price varies. Eikenboslaan 19, B-3200 Kessel 10, Belgium.

932   GW ISSN 0340-2215
STUDIEN ZUR ALTAEGYPTISCHEN KULTUR. 1974. irreg., no.13, 1986. price varies. Verlag Helmut Buske, Schlueterstr. 14, 2000 Hamburg 13, W. Germany (B.R.D.) Eds. Hartwig Altenmueller, Dietrich Wildung.

800   NE ISSN 0167-6679
STUDIES IN CLASSICAL ANTIQUITY. 1979. irreg. price varies. Editions Rodopi B.V., Keizersgracht 302-304, 1016 EX Amsterdam, Netherlands.

800   GW ISSN 0081-7724
STUDIES IN CLASSICAL LITERATURE. 1966. irreg. price varies. Walter de Gruyter & Co., Mouton Publishers, Postfach 110240, D-1000 Berlin 11, W. Germany (B.R.D.) (U.S. addr.: Mouton Publishers, division of Walter de Gruyter, Inc., 200 Saw Mill River Road, Hawthorne, NY 10532)

STUDIES IN MEDITERRANEAN ARCHAEOLOGY. MONOGRAPH SERIES. see *ARCHAEOLOGY*

STUDIES IN MEDITERRANEAN ARCHAEOLOGY. POCKET-BOOK SERIES. see *ARCHAEOLOGY*

STUDIES IN MYCENAEAN INSCRIPTIONS AND DIALECT. see *LINGUISTICS*

489 890   RM   ISSN 0081-8844
STUDII CLASICE. (Text in English, French, German, Italian, Rumanian and Russian) 1959. a. $18. (Societatea de Studii Clasice din Republica Socialista Romania) Editura Academiei Republicii Socialiste Rumania, Calea Victoriei 125, 79717 Bucharest, Rumania (Subscr. to: ARTEXIM, Str. Piata Scinteii 1, P.O. Box 33-16, 70055 Bucharest, Rumania) Ed.Bd. bk. rev. circ. 900. Indexed: Numis.Lit.

STUDIUM. see *HISTORY — History Of Europe*

SVENSKA INSTITUTET I ATHEN. SKRIFTER. see *ARCHAEOLOGY*

SVENSKA INSTITUTET I ROM. SKRIFTER. ACTA SERIES PRIMA. see *ARCHAEOLOGY*

870   BE
SYMBOLAE. SERIES A. 1976. irreg., vol.15, 1986. Leuven University Press, Krakenstraat 3, B-3000 Louvain, Belgium.

800 400   NO   ISSN 0039-7679
SYMBOLAE OSLOENSES. (Text in Ancient Greek, English, French, German and Latin) 1922. a. $28. (Societatis Graeco-Latinae) Norwegian University Press, Kolstadgt. 1, Box 2959-Toeyen, 0608 Oslo 6, Norway (U.S. address: Publications Expediting Inc., 200 Meacham Ave., Elmont, NY 11003) Ed. Egil Kraggerud. illus. cum.index pub. in 1959 covering first 35 vols. circ. 350. Indexed: M.L.A.

480 880   PL   ISSN 0302-7384
SYMBOLAE PHILOLOGORUM POSNANIENSIUM. (Text in English, Latin and Polish; summaries in Latin) 1973. irreg. price varies. Adam Mickiewicz University Press, Marchlewskiego 128, 61-875 Poznan, Poland. Eds. Ioannes Wikarjak, Georgius Danielewicz.

880   CN   ISSN 0381-9361
TEIRESIAS; a review and continuing bibliography of Boiotian studies. 1971. a., plus supplements. Can.$7.50. ‡ Department of Classics, McGill University, 855 Sherbrooke St. W., Montreal, Que. H3A 2T7, Canada. TEL 514-392-5335. Ed.Bd. bibl. illus. circ. 300. Indexed: Can.Ind.
    Boiotian studies

TIRYNS. see *ARCHAEOLOGY*

489   FI   ISSN 0082-7029
TURUN YLIOPISTO. KLASSILLISEN FILOLOGIAN LAITOS. OPERA EX INSTITUTO PHILOLOGIAE CLASSICAE UNIVERSITATIS TURKUENSIS EDITA. (Subseries of Turun Yliopisto. Julkaisuja. Sarja B. Humaniora) (Text in English, French, German and Italian) 1969. irreg., no.7, 1986. price varies. Turun Yliopisto, Klassillisen Filologian Laitos - University of Turku, Department of Classical Philology, SF-20500 Turku 50, Finland. Ed. Heikki Koskenniemi. circ. 300.

930   MX
UNIVERSIDAD NACIONAL AUTONOMA DE MEXICO. CENTRO DE ESTUDIOS CLASICOS. CUADERNOS. 1975. irreg., no.20, 1985. Universidad Nacional Autonoma de Mexico, Centro de Estudios Clasicos, Ciudad Universitaria, Mexico, D.F., Mexico.

930   IT   ISSN 0393-1412
UNIVERSITA CATTOLICA. ISTITUTO DI STORIA ANTICA. RICERCHE. 1984. irreg., n.4, 1986. price varies. Editoriale Jaca Book s.p.a., Via Aurelio Saffi 19, 20123 Milan, Italy. TEL 498 23 41. Ed. Marta Sordi.

UNIVERSITA DEGLI STUDI DI GENOVA. ISTITUTO DI FILOLOGIA CLASSICA E MEDIEVALE. PUBBLICAZIONI. see *LINGUISTICS*

UNIVERSITA DEGLI STUDI DI MACERATA. FACOLTA DI LETTERE E FILOSOFIA. ANNALI. see *ARCHAEOLOGY*

UNIVERSITAETSBIBLIOTHEK GIESSEN. KURZBERICHTE AUS DEN PAPYRUS-SAMMLUNGEN. see *HISTORY*

800   HU   ISSN 0418-453X
UNIVERSITATIS SCIENTIARUM DEBRECENIENSIS. ACTA CLASSICA. (Text in various languages) 1965. irreg., vol.19, 1983. Kossuth Lajos Tudomanyegyetem, Klasszika Filologiai Tanszek, Egyetem Ter 1, 4010 Debrecen, Hungary. bibl.

880   US   ISSN 0068-6344
UNIVERSITY OF CALIFORNIA PUBLICATIONS. CLASSICAL STUDIES. 1965. irreg. price varies. University of California Press, 2120 Berkeley Way, Berkeley, CA 94720. TEL 415-642-4247.

489   UK   ISSN 0076-0730
UNIVERSITY OF LONDON. INSTITUTE OF CLASSICAL STUDIES. BULLETIN. (Supplement avail.) 1954. a. £15. University of London, Institute of Classical Studies, 31-34 Gordon Square, London WC1H OPY, England. TEL 01-387-7696. Ed. J.P. Barron. Indexed: Curr.Cont. Arts & Hum.Cit.Ind.

489   UK   ISSN 0076-0749
UNIVERSITY OF LONDON. INSTITUTE OF CLASSICAL STUDIES. BULLETIN SUPPLEMENT. 1955. irreg., no.45, 1986. price varies. University of London, Institute of Classical Studies, 31-34 Gordon Sq., London WC1H OPY, England. TEL 01-387-7696. Ed. J.P. Barron.

UNIVERZITA J. E. PURKYNE. FILOZOFICKA FAKULTA. SBORNIK PRACI. E: RADA ARCHEOLOGICKO-KLASICKA. see *ARCHAEOLOGY*

930 913 480 880   CS   ISSN 0083-4114
UNIVERZITA KOMENSKEHO. FILOZOFICKA FAKULTA. ZBORNIK: GRAECOLATINA ET ORIENTALIA. (Text in English, French, German, Latin; summaries in Slovak) 1969. a. exchange basis. (Univerzita Komenskeho, Filozoficka Fakulta) Slovenske Pedagogicke Nakladatelstvo, Sasinkova 5, 815 60 Bratislava, Czechoslovakia. Eds. Ladislaus Drozdik, Etela Simovicova. circ. 824.

VERBA SENIORUM. see *RELIGIONS AND THEOLOGY*

870   US
VERGILIAN SOCIETY NEWSLETTER. a. membership. Vergilian Society of America, University of Maryland, Classics Dept., College Park, MD 20742. TEL 301-454-2510. Ed. R.J. Rowland Jr. circ. 1,400.

809 016   US   ISSN 0506-7294
VERGILIUS. 1956. a. $10. Vergilian Society of America, University of Maryland, Classics Dept., College Park, MD 20742. TEL 301-454-2510. Ed. Ward W. Briggs, Jr. adv. bk. rev. circ. 1,400.

800   CN   ISSN 0316-2508
VEXILLUM. 1972. irreg. Can.$12 to non-members. (B.C. Association of Teachers of Classics) B.C. Teachers' Federation, 105-2235 Burrard St., Vancouver, B.C. V6J 3H9, Canada. TEL 604-731-8121. circ. 125.
    Formerly: B.C. Association of Teachers of Classics. Newsletter (ISSN 0045-2912)

880   UK   ISSN 0083-629X
VIRGIL SOCIETY. PROCEEDINGS. 1961/62. a. price varies. Virgil Society, c/o F. Robertson, Faculty of Letters, Reading University, Reading, England. Ed. H. Currie. bk. rev.

WIENER STUDIEN. ZEITSCHRIFT FUER KLASSISCHE PHILOLOGIE UND PATRISTIK. see *LINGUISTICS*

WUERZBURGER JAHRBUECHER FUER DIE ALTERTUMSWISSENSCHAFT. see *LINGUISTICS*

800   UK   ISSN 0084-330X
YALE CLASSICAL STUDIES. irreg., no.27, 1982. $49.50 for latest vol. (Yale University, Department of Classics, US) Cambridge University Press, Edinburgh Bldg., Shaftesbury Rd., Cambridge CB2 2RU, England (And 32 E. 57th St., New York NY 10022)

CLASSICAL STUDIES — Abstracting, Bibliographies, Statistics

800 016   FR
ANNEE PHILOLOGIQUE; bibliographie critique et analytique de l'antiquite greco-latine. (Text in all Occidental languages; summaries in English, French and German) 1924; N.S. 1928. a. 500 F. Societe International de Bibliographie Classique - International Society of Classical Bibliography, 11 av. Rene Coty, 75014 Paris, France (Dist. by: Societe d'Edition les Belles Lettres, 95 bd. Raspail, 75006 Paris, France) Ed. Juliette Ernst. bk. rev. circ. 2,000. Indexed: Br.Archaeol.Abstr.

CLEANING AND DYEING

see also *Textile Industries and Fabrics*

667.3   CS   ISSN 0009-0727
CESKOSLOVENSKY KOLORISTA.* 1960. irreg. (3-4/yr.) free. Sdruzeni pro Odbyt Dehtovych Barviv, Na Porici 24, Prague 2, Czechoslovakia. charts. circ. 1,500.

667.12   FR
FEDERATION DES ENTREPRENEURS DE NETTOYAGE DE FRANCE. ANNUAIRE OFFICIEL. a. 200 Fr. (Federation des Entrepreneurs de Nettoyage de France) Heral, 23 rue Tronchet, 75008 Paris, France. adv.

INTERNATIONAL FEDERATION OF ASSOCIATIONS OF TEXTILE CHEMISTS AND COLORISTS. REPORTS OF CONGRESS. see *TEXTILE INDUSTRIES AND FABRICS*

667   MX
LAVANDERIA MODERNA/MODERN CLEANING: DIRECTORY OF SUPPLIERS; directorio de proveedores. 1972. a. Jose Ma. Bustillos No. 49, Mexico 8, D.F., Mexico. Ed. Antonio Bravo. adv. circ. 3,000.

WER UND WAS IN DER DEUTSCHEN KOERPERPFLEGE-, WASCH- UND REINIGUNGSMITTEL-INDUSTRIE. see *BEAUTY CULTURE — Perfumes And Cosmetics*

CLOTHING TRADE

see also *Clothing Trade—Fashions; Leather and Fur Industries; Shoes and Boots; Textile Industries and Fabrics*

687   US
ACCESSORIES DIRECTORY. a. $12. Business Journals, Inc., 22 S. Smith St., Box 5550, Norwalk, CT 06856. TEL 203-853-6015. adv. circ. 11,645.

687   FR
ANNUAIRE DE LA MERCERIE, NOUVEAUTES, BONNETERIE, LINGERIE, CONFECTIONS. 1923. a. 130 F. Editions Duc, 10 rue de Lancry, 75010 Paris, France. adv.

687   US
APPAREL: LATIN AMERICAN INDUSTRIAL REPORT. (Avail. for each of 22 Latin American countries) 1985. a. $435 per country report per industry covered. Aurora International, Box 9099, Bridgeport, CT 06601-2099. TEL 203-368-0579. Ed. Andres C. Aquino.

APPAREL PLANT WAGES SURVEY. see *TEXTILE INDUSTRIES AND FABRICS*

687 677   GW
BEKLEIDUNGS-INDUSTRIE. JAHRBUCH. a. DM.44. Fachverlag Schiele und Schoen GmbH, Markgrafenstr. 11, 1000 Berlin 61, W. Germany (B.R.D.) Eds. W. Rieser, W. Schierbaum. charts. illus. stat.
    Formerly: Taschenbuch fuer die Bekleidungs-Industrie.

CLOTHING TRADE — ABSTRACTING, BIBLIOGRAPHIES, STATISTICS

687.2 US ISSN 0362-2452
BODY FASHIONS/INTIMATE APPAREL DIRECTORY. 1913. a. $20. Harcourt Brace Jovanovich, Inc., 7500 Old Oak Blvd., Cleveland, OH 44130 (Subscr. to: One E. First St., Duluth, MN 55802) Ed. Jill Gerson. adv. index. Indexed: Tr.& Indus.Ind. World Text.Abstr.
   Former titles: Body Fashions Directory and Source of Supply; Corset and Underwear Review Directory.

687 UK
BRITISH CLOTHING INDUSTRY YEARBOOK. 1974. a. £21. (British Knitting and Clothing Export Council) Kemps Group Ltd., 1-5 Bath St., London EC1V 9QA, England. adv. bk. rev. circ. 4,000.

687 685.31 UK
CLOTHING AND FOOTWEAR INSTITUTE YEAR BOOK AND MEMBERSHIP REGISTER. 1956. a. £15. Clothing and Footwear Institute, 71 Brushfield Street, London E1 6AA, England. adv. circ. 6,700.
   Formerly: Clothing Institute Year Book and Membership Register (ISSN 0307-8515)

687 US ISSN 0070-5195
DIRECTORY OF BUYING OFFICES AND ACCOUNTS. a. $45. Salesman's Guide, Inc., 1140 Broadway, New York, NY 10001. TEL 212-684-2985. circ. 5,000.
   Resident buying offices, corporate buying offices and merchandise brokers: New York, Chicago, Los Angeles

381 US ISSN 0277-9625
DIRECTORY OF MEN'S AND BOYS' WEAR SPECIALTY STORES. a. $149. Chain Store Guide (Subsidiary of: Lebhar-Friedman, Inc.) 425 Park Ave., New York, NY 10022. TEL 212-371-9400.
   Formerly: Directory of Men's and Boy's Specialty Stores (ISSN 0272-1112)

658 US ISSN 0277-9617
DIRECTORY OF WOMEN'S & CHILDREN'S WEAR SPECIALTY STORES. a. $149. Chain Store Guide (Subsidiary of: Lebhar-Friedman, Inc.) 425 Park Ave., New York, NY 10022. TEL 212-371-9400. (also avail. in magnetic tape)
   Former titles: Directory of Apparel Specialty Stores. Women's and Children's (ISSN 0272-1104)

FAIRCHILD'S TEXTILE & APPAREL FINANCIAL DIRECTORY. see *TEXTILE INDUSTRIES AND FABRICS*

687 US
FOCUS, AN ECONOMIC PROFILE OF THE APPAREL INDUSTRY.* biennial. $76.50 to non-members; members $30. American Apparel Manufacturers Association, 2500 Wilson Blvd., Ste. 301, Arlington, VA 22201-3816.

687 US
GARMENT MANUFACTURER'S INDEX. 1938. a. $8.95. Klevens Publications, Inc., 7600 Ave. V, Littlerock, CA 93543. TEL 805-944-4111. Ed. H.B. Schwartz. adv. tr.lit. circ. 18,684.

687 IT
GUIDA ALL'ABBIGLIAMENTO ITALIANO. 1978. a. L.75000. (Italian Apparel Association) Gesto s.r.l., Via Cesare Battisti 21, 20122 Milan, Italy. adv. circ. 15,000.

687.4 US
HAT LIFE YEARBOOK & DIRECTORY; directory of men's hat and cap industry. 1933. a. $7. 551 Summit Ave., Jersey City, NJ 07306. TEL 201-795-1582. Ed. Peter Annunziata. adv. circ. 7,000.
   Formerly: Hat Life Year Book (ISSN 0073-0904)

687.3 US
HOSIERY STATISTICS. 1934. a. $40. National Association of Hosiery Manufacturers, 447 S. Sharon Amity Rd., Charlotte, NC 28211. TEL 704-365-0913. Ed. Sarah Alexander. charts. stat. circ. 1,000 (controlled) (back issues avail.)

687 II
INDIAN HOSIERY DIRECTORY. (Text in English) 1950. a. Rs.20. Journal's Publication, Samrala Rd., Ludhiana 141008, India. Ed. Narinder Mohan.

KOMPASS TEXTILE ET HABILLEMENT. see *BUSINESS AND ECONOMICS — Trade And Industrial Directories*

687 US ISSN 0077-5983
NATIONWIDE DIRECTORY OF MEN'S AND BOYS' WEAR BUYERS (EXCLUSIVE OF NEW YORK METROPOLITAN AREA) 1965. a., with 2 supplements. $87. Salesman's Guide, Inc., 1140 Broadway, New York, NY 10001. TEL 212-684-2985. Ed. Edward R. Blank. index. (also avail. in magnetic tape)

658.8 687 US ISSN 0077-5991
NATIONWIDE DIRECTORY OF WOMEN'S AND CHILDREN'S WEAR BUYERS (EXCLUSIVE OF NEW YORK METROPOLITAN AREA) 1963. a., with 2 supplements. $87. Salesman's Guide, Inc., 1140 Broadway, New York, NY 10001. TEL 212-684-2985.

658.8 US ISSN 0077-6009
NATIONWIDE MAJOR MASS MARKET MERCHANDISERS (EXCLUSIVE OF NEW YORK METROPOLITAN AREA) 1964. a. $80. Salesman's Guide, Inc., 1140 Broadway, New York, NY 10001. Ed. Edward R. Blank. index. circ. 1,500. (reprint service avail. from UMI)

687 746
NECKWEAR INDUSTRY DIRECTORY. biennial. $7 per no. Neckwear Association of America, 151 Lexington Ave., New York, NY 10016. Ed. Gerald Andersen. circ. 25,000.

PATTERN MAKERS' JOURNAL. see *LABOR UNIONS*

687.11 US
SPECIAL STATISTICAL REPORT ON PRODUCTION SALES AND PROFIT TRENDS FOR THE MEN'S & BOY'S CLOTHING INDUSTRY. 1982. a. $20. Clothing Manufacturers Association of the U.S.A., 1290 Ave. of the Americas, New York, NY 10104. Ed. Robert A. Kaplan. circ. 500. (back issues avail.)
   Formerly: Special Report on Financial and Economic Data for the Men's and Boy's Clothing Industry.

687 US ISSN 0084-1056
WOMEN'S ACCESSORIES DIRECTORY; NEW YORK METROPOLITAN AREA. 1951. a. $16. Salesman's Guide, Inc., 1140 Broadway, New York, NY 10001. TEL 212-684-2985. index.

687.2 658.7 US ISSN 0043-7549
WOMEN'S INTIMATE APPAREL BUYERS. 1951. a. $16. Salesman's Guide, Inc., 1140 Broadway, New York, NY 10001. TEL 212-684-2985. adv. index. circ. 2,000.
   Formerly: Women's Intimate Apparel. Lingerie

687.12 US
WOMEN'S, MISSES & JR. COATS AND SUITS BUYERS DIRECTORY; NEW YORK METROPOLITAN AREA. 1951. a. $17. Salesman's Guide, Inc., 1140 Broadway, New York, NY 10001. TEL 212-684-2985. index.
   Formerly: Women's Coats and Suits Directory: New York Metropolitan Area (ISSN 0084-1064)

CLOTHING TRADE — Abstracting, Bibliographies, Statistics

338.4 CN ISSN 0527-5679
CANADA. STATISTICS CANADA. MEN'S CLOTHING INDUSTRIES/INDUSTRIE DES VETEMENTS POUR HOMMES. (Catalogue 34-216) (Text in English and French) 1918. a. Can.$20($21) Statistics Canada, Communications Division, 3rd Floor, R.H. Coats Bldg., Ottawa, Ont. K1A 0T6, Canada TEL 613-993-7276. (Subscr. to: Publications Sales and Services, Ottawa, Ont. K1A 0T6, Canada) (also avail. in microform from MML)

687 CN ISSN 0384-3769
CANADA. STATISTICS CANADA. MISCELLANEOUS CLOTHING INDUSTRIES/INDUSTRIES DIVERSES DE L'HABILLEMENT. (Catalogue 34-218) (Text in English and French) 1949. a. Can.$20($21) Statistics Canada, Communications Division, 3rd Floor, R.H. Coats Bldg., Ottawa, Ont. K1A 0T6, Canada TEL 613-993-7276. (Subscr. to: Publications Sales and Services, Ottawa, Ont. K1A 0T6, Canada) (also avail. in microform from MML)

338.4 CN ISSN 0384-4498
CANADA. STATISTICS CANADA. WOMEN'S AND CHILDREN'S CLOTHING INDUSTRIES/INDUSTRIES DES VETEMENTS POUR DAMES ET POUR ENFANTS. (Catalogue 34-217) (Text in English and French) 1918. a. Can.$20($21) Statistics Canada, Communications Division, 3rd Floor, R.H. Coats Bldg., Ottawa, Ont. K1A 0T6, Canada TEL 613-993-7276. (Subscr. to: Publications Sales and Services, Ottawa, Ont. K1A 2T6, Canada) (also avail. in microform from MML)

CLOTHING TRADE — Fashions

746.92 UK ISSN 0590-8876
COSTUME. 1967. a. membership. Costume Society, 3 Meadway Gate, London NW11 7LA, England. Ed. Ann Saunders. bk. rev. bibl. charts. illus. circ. 1,000. Indexed: Br.Hum.Ind. Br.Archaeol.Abstr. RILA. World Text.Abstr.

746.92 UK ISSN 0265-1092
DESIGN INTERNATIONAL. a. Emmet Microform, 57a Lion Lane, Haslemere, Surrey GU27 1JF, England. (also avail. in microfiche)

391 900 US ISSN 0361-2112
DRESS. 1975. a. membership. Costume Society of America, Box 761, 15 Little John Rd., Englishtown, NJ 07726. bk. rev. illus. circ. 1,100. Indexed: RILA.

659.152 UK ISSN 0142-2081
FASHION INDEX. 1979. irreg., vol.3, 1985. £15. (Newcastle upon Tyne Polytechnic Library) Newcastle upon Tyne Polytechnic Products Ltd., Ellison Building, Ellison Place, Newcastle upon Tyne NE1 8ST, England. TEL 091-2358148. Ed. F. Shepherd. (back issues avail.)

646.4 US
HOMESEWING RESOURCE DIRECTORY OF BRANDED LINE MERCHANDISE IN THE HOMESEWING INDUSTRY. 1963. a. $4. Homesewing Trade News, 330 Sunrise Hwy., Box 286, Rockville Centre, NY 11571. TEL 516-766-1226. Ed. Pat Kobishyn. adv. circ. 13,520.
   Formerly: Resource Directory of Branded Line Merchandise in the Homesewing Industry.

659.152 US
INTIMATE FASHION NEWS DIRECTORY. 1955. a. $7.50. Mackay Publishing Corp., 309 Fifth Ave., New York, NY 10016. TEL 212-679-6677. Ed. Milton Kristt. adv.

NECKWEAR INDUSTRY DIRECTORY. see *CLOTHING TRADE*

659.152 IT
SCIARE MODA. a. D M K Editrice s.r.l., Via Boscovich 14, 20124 Milan, Italy. Ed. Massimo di Marco. adv. circ. 100,000.

659.152 US
SHOWCASE. 1986. a. $60. Models & Photographers of America, Box 25099, Colorado Springs, CO 80936-5099. Ed. Ron Marshall. adv. bk. rev.

659.152 GE ISSN 0081-3672
SPEZIAL.* 1966. a. M.2.70. Verlag Fuer die Frau, Friedrich-Ebert-Str. 76-78, 701 Leipzig, E. Germany (D.D.R.)
   Blouses, skirts, combinations

CLUBS

see also *College and Alumni*

A L A WORLDWIDE DIRECTORY AND FACT BOOK. (American Logistics Association) see *MILITARY*

371.85 US
ADELPHIA LAW JOURNAL.* 1972-19??; resumed 1982. a. $10. Sigma Nu Phi Legal Fraternity, 625 Fourth Ave., S., Ste. 1500, Minneapolis, MN 55415. bk. rev. cum.index: 1982-1984. circ. 2,000. (back issues avail.)
   Formerly: Adelphia.

ANNEE SPORTIVE U.S.M.T. (Union Sportive Metropolitaine des Transports) see SPORTS AND GAMES

366.1   UK   ISSN 0066-7900
ARS QUATUOR CORONATORUM; transaction of the Quatuor Coronati Lodge of Research. 1888. a. membership. Q.C. Correspondence Circle Ltd., 60 Great Queen St., London WC2B 5BA, England. Ed. C.N. Batham. bk. rev. index. circ. 14,500.

367   VE   ISSN 0004-4792
ASOCIACION CULTURAL HUMBOLDT. BOLETIN. 1965. a. free. Asociacion Cultural Humboldt, Apdo. 60.501 Chacao, Caracas, Venezuela. Ed.Bd. circ. 1,000.

658   AT
AUSTRALIAN JAYCEES NATIONAL DIRECTORY. 1970. a. Australian Jaycees, 6 Thesiger Court, Deakin A.C.T. 2600, Australia.

371.83   UK
BENTHAM NEWSLETTER. 1978. a. £5. University College London, Bentham Committee, Gower St., London WC1E 6BT, England. Ed. F. Rosen. adv. bk. rev. circ. 600.

369.4   US
BOY SCOUTS OF AMERICA. ANNUAL REPORT TO CONGRESS. 1917. a. free. Boy Scouts of America, 1325 Walnut Hill Lane, Irving, TX 75038-3096. TEL 214-580-2000. Ed. Audrey Clough. circ. 4,000.

367   SP
BROTS DE COLLCEROLA. (Text in Catalan) 1970. irreg., latest no.46. Delegacion Vallvidrera del C. E. A., Mont d'Orsa 17, Barcelona 17, Spain. Ed. Vigens Fonolleda. play rev. abstr. illus. pat. circ. 150(controlled)

BUFFALO. see CHILDREN AND YOUTH — About

658.048   GW
BUND DEUTSCHER KRIEGSOPFER. JAHRBUCH. 1952. a. DM.5. (Bund Deutscher Kriegsopfer) Hallplatz 15, Postfach 364, 8500 Nuernberg, W. Germany (B.R.D.) Ed. H. Kless.

367   UK   ISSN 0262-9208
GIRL ANNUAL. a. £2.95 per no. Fleetway Annuals, IPC Magazines, Kings Reach Tower, Stamford St., London S.E.1, England. Ed. E. Cohen.

367   US
LAST MONTH'S NEWSLETTER. 1968. irreg. free to members. ‡ Procrastinators' Club of America, 1111 Broad-Locust Bldg., Philadelphia, PA 19102. Ed.Bd. circ. 3,500.

650   US
LEADER (CORAL GABLES) (Editions in Chinese, English, French, Japanese, Korean, Spanish) 1962. a. $5. Jaycees International, Inc., 400 University Dr., Coral Gables, FL 33114. TEL 305-446-7608. Ed. Peggy Fisher. adv. bk. rev. charts. illus. circ. 300,000. (also avail. in microform from UMI; reprint service avail. from UMI)
    Formerly: J C I World (ISSN 0021-3578)

810 366   US
OZIANA. 1971. a. $1. International Wizard of Oz Club, Inc., 220 N. 11th St., Escanaba, MI 49829. Ed. Robin Olderman. circ. 800.

658.048   AT
PENFRIEND & ETHNIC LINKUP INDEX. irreg. $1 with self-addressed return envelope. Penfriend Linkup Index, Box 70, Coburg, Vic. 3058, Australia. Ed. Bill Helem.

ROYAL SCOTTISH AUTOMOBILE CLUB OFFICIAL HANDBOOK. see SPORTS AND GAMES

658.048 910   US   ISSN 0162-5934
S W L. (Shortwave Listener) 1959. irreg. $16. American Shortwave Listeners Club, 16182 Ballad Ln., Huntington Beach, CA 92649-2204. TEL 714-846-1685. Ed. Stewart MacKenzie. adv. bk. rev. bibl. charts. illus. stat. circ. 600.

369.4   AT
SCOUT ASSOCIATION OF AUSTRALIA. ANNUAL REPORT. 1971. a. free. Scout Association of Australia, Brigadier R. Fullford, National Headquarters, Churchill House, 218 Northbourne Avenue, Braddon, A.C.T. 2601, Australia. Ed. R.J. Perryman. circ. 3,650.
    Formerly: Scout Association of Australia. Review of Progress (ISSN 0310-818X)

369.4   UK
WELSH ASSOCIATION OF YOUTH CLUBS. YEARBOOK OF ACTIVITIES; leaders handbook. 1965. a. £1. Welsh Association of Youth Clubs, Andrews Bldgs., 67 Queen St., Cardiff, Wales. Ed. D.G. Frost. adv. index. circ. 1,000. (tabloid format)

369.4   SZ   ISSN 0513-6032
WORLD ALLIANCE OF Y M C A'S DIRECTORY. 1920. biennial. 6.50 Fr. World Alliance of Young Men's Christian Associations, 37 Quai Wilson, 1201 Geneva, Switzerland. circ. 8,000.

367 267   CN   ISSN 0315-095X
Y CANADA. (Text in English and French) 1971. irreg. Young Men's Christian Association of Canada, 2160 Yonge St., Toronto, Ont. M4S 2A9, Canada. TEL 416-485-9447. illus.

267   SZ
Y M C A'S OF THE WORLD. 1958. irreg., latest 1977. 9 Fr. World Alliance of Young Men's Christian Associations, 37 Quai Wilson, 1201 Geneva, Switzerland.

369.5   US
YOUNG WOMEN'S CHRISTIAN ASSOCIATION OF THE UNITED STATES OF AMERICA. NATIONAL BOARD. ANNUAL REPORT. a. Young Women's Christian Association of the United States of America, National Board, 726 Broadway, New York, NY 10003. TEL 212-614-2700.

COLLEGE AND ALUMNI

see also Literary and Political Reviews; Literature

378.1   NE   ISSN 0001-8139
ADELAAR. 1948. irreg. (3-4/yr.) free. Sint Janscollege, c/o Editor, Colijnplein 9, 2555 HA The Hague, Netherlands. Ed. B.W. Dijkmans. bk. rev. film rev. illus. play rev. record rev. circ. 850. (tabloid format)

378   US
ALLIANCE (CHARLESTON) 1985. a. membership. Medical University of South Carolina, College of Health Related Proffesions, Alumni Association, 171 Ashley Ave., Charleston, SC 29425. Ed. Bonnie Jerdan Sayles. circ. 3,000.

ALPHA PSI OMEGA: PLAYBILL. see THEATER

378.1   CN
ARCH. 1949. irreg. (6-8/yr.) $4.50. Royal Military College of Canada, Kingston, Ont., Canada. TEL 613-545-5010. adv. bk. rev. film rev. illus. play rev. circ. 1,000. (newspaper)
    Formerly: Marker (ISSN 0025-3529)

378   US
ASSOCIATION OF COLLEGE HONOR SOCIETIES, BOOKLET OF INFORMATION. 1945. triennial, latest 1986. free. Association of College Honor Societies, c/o Dorothy I. Mitstifer, Sec.-Treas., 1257 Haslett Rd., Box 547, Haslett, MI 48840. Ed. Dion W.J. Shea. circ. 15,000.

BIG TEN FOOTBALL YEARBOOK. see SPORTS AND GAMES — Ball Games

378.1   UK   ISSN 0007-0157
BRIGHTONIAN. 1870. a. £1. Brighton College, Brighton BN2 2AL, Sussex, England. Ed. P.H.L. Chasseaud. adv. bibl. charts. illus. play rev. circ. 2,600.

CAPE OF GOOD HOPE IMVO/NEWS. see EDUCATION — Higher Education

378   US
CARROLL ALUMNI JOURNAL. 1960. irreg. (5-6/yr.) $260. John Carroll University, Alumni Association, University Heights, Cleveland, OH 44118. TEL 216-491-4321. Ed. Wally Guenther.

378.599   PH
CENTRALITE. irreg. $4.50. Central Philippine University, Box 231, Iloilo City, Philippines. illus.

CHIMES. see LITERATURE

378.1   HK   ISSN 0009-6261
CHUNG CHI BULLETIN. (Text in Chinese and English) 1951. a. Chinese University of Hong Kong, Chung Chi College, Shatin N.T., Hong Kong. Ed. Patrick Yin. bibl. charts. illus. circ. 3,800.
    Formerly: Chung Chi College Bulletin.

378.1   UK   ISSN 0010-0676
COLFEIAN. 1900. a. £1. ‡ Old Colfeians Association, Horn Park, Eltham Rd., London S.E. 12, England. Ed.Bd. adv. illus. circ. 1,750.

378   US
D M D. 1983. a. Medical University of South Carolina, College of Dental Medicine, Alumni Association, 171 Ashley Ave., Charleston, SC 29425. Ed. Bonnie Sayles. circ. 900.

378   AT
DEAKIN UNIVERSITY. GUIDE TO OFF CAMPUS STUDIES. 1978. a. Deakin University, Victoria 3217, Australia. circ. 18,000.

378.1   UK   ISSN 0012-5695
DOUAI MAGAZINE. 1894. a. £2.50. Douai Abbey, Woolhampton, Near Reading, Berkshire, England. Ed. D.E. Power. adv. bk. rev. illus. circ. 1,300.

378.1   UK   ISSN 0012-8643
EASTBOURNIAN. 1870. a. £1.50. ‡ Eastbourne College, Eastbourne, Sussex, England. Ed. N.L. Wheeler. adv. illus. circ. 1,200(controlled)

378.1   UK   ISSN 0046-3701
FETTESIAN. 1878. a. £2. Fettes College, Edinburgh, Scotland. Ed. A.F. Reeves. adv. circ. 1,200.

378.1   SA   ISSN 0015-8054
FORT HARE PAPERS. (Text in Afrikaans and English; summaries in English) 1945. irreg., vol.8, no.1, 1985. R.5 per no. Fort Hare University Press, Private Bag X1322, Alice, Republic of Ciskei, South Africa. Ed. M.J. Prins. charts. illus. circ. 1,500. (tabloid format) Indexed: Biol.Abstr. Chem.Abstr. Curr.Cont. M.L.A. Field Crop Abstr. Herb.Abstr. Ind.S.A.Per.

378   GW
GAESDONCKER BLATTER. 1949. a. DM.20. Collegium Augustinianum Gaesdonck, Gaesdoncker Str. 220, 4180 Goch 3, W. Germany (B.R.D.) circ. 1,500.

378.198   US
GENESIS. 1969. a. free. Nassau Community College, SUNY, Department of English, Garden City, NY 11530. TEL 516-222-7185. circ. 3,000.
    Formerly: Taking Shape.

378   CN
KEYSTONE. a. Can.$17. Wilfrid Laurier University Student Publications, W L U Student Publications, Waterloo, Ont. N2L 3C5, Canada. TEL 519-884-2990. Eds. Janice Farrell, Brenda Grimes. adv. circ. 750.

378   CN
MCGILL DAILY. (Text in English and French) 1910. irreg. (3-4/w.) Daily Publications Society, 3480 McTavish, Montreal, Que. H3A 1X9, Canada. TEL 514-392-8955. Ed. Joe Heath. adv. bk. rev. film rev. circ. 16,000. (tabloid format)

378.1   US
MARSHALL NEWS.* 1959. a. membership. Association of Marshall Scholars and Alumnae, c/o Institute for Ecumenical Research, Collegeville, MN 56321. circ. 550.
    Formerly: Association of Marshall Scholars and Alumni. Newsletter (ISSN 0004-573X)

COLLEGE AND ALUMNI — ABSTRACTING, BIBLIOGRAPHIES, STATISTICS

378   US   ISSN 0887-3887
MOBILE GRADUATE NEWS AND NOTES. 1986. irreg. $24. University of Maine at Presque Isle, Mobile Graduate Program, 112 Pullen Hall, Presque Isle, ME 04769 TEL 207-764-0311. (Subscr. to: Houlton Learning Corp., Box 323, Houlton, ME 04730-0323) Ed. Lloyd R. Chase. adv. bk. rev. circ. 350.

378.198   UK
NATIONAL YOUTH & STUDENT DISCOUNT HANDBOOK. 1980. a. £2.99. N U S Marketing Ltd., Box 190, London WC1E 7HR, England. Ed. John Faircloth. circ. 200,000.

NORTHWESTERN ENDICOTT REPORT; salary schedules and employment trends on the employment of college and university graduates in business and industry. see *OCCUPATIONS AND CAREERS*

378.1   US   ISSN 0031-2657
PASQUINO. 1921. irreg. (10-11/yr.) $1. Potomac State College, Journalism Dept., Keyser, WV 26726. TEL 304-788-3011. Ed. Fred Jacoby. adv. circ. 2,000. (also avail. in microform from BLH)

378   CN
PHAROS. a. Can.$15. Dalhousie University, Student Union, Halifax, N.S. B3H 4J2, Canada. TEL 902-424-2211.

371.85   US
PHI ETA SIGMA. FORUM. a. Auburn University at Montgomery, Montgomery, AL 36193. TEL 205-826-5856. circ. 20,000.

PHILIPPINES. MINISTRY OF EDUCATION & CULTURE. NATIONAL SCHOLARSHIP CENTER. DIRECTORY OF ALUMNI. see *EDUCATION*

PHILIPPINES. MINISTRY OF EDUCATION, CULTURE AND SPORTS. NATIONAL SCHOLARSHIP CENTER. ANNUAL REPORT. see *EDUCATION*

081   US   ISSN 0092-4318
PLATTE VALLEY REVIEW. 1973. a. $3. Kearney State College, Kearney, NE 68847. TEL 308-236-4141. Ed.Bd. illus. circ. 1,000. Indexed: M.L.A.

378.198   US
POINTER. 1922. irreg. (5-8/yr.) $20. United States Military Academy, Directorate of Cadet Activity, United States Corps Cadet, West Point, NY 10996. TEL 914-938-2780. adv. circ. 4,500. (back issues avail.)

378   EC
PONTIFICIA UNIVERSIDAD CATOLICA DEL ECUADOR. REVISTA. Cover title: Revista de la Universidad Catolica. vol. 5, 1977. irreg. S/30 per no. or exchange. Pontificia Universidad Catolica de Ecuador, Avda. 12 de Octubre 1076 y Carrion, Apdo. 2184, Quito, Ecuador. Ed. Ernesto Proano.

378   CN
PUBLI - P E Q. 1981. irreg. free. Presse Etudiante du Quebec, 1581 Dufresne, Montreal, QC H2K 3J6, Canada. TEL 514-526-0235. circ. 215,550. (tabloid format)

378   CN
QUAD. 1953. a. Can.$12. Bishop's University, Students' Association, Lennoxville, Que. J1M 1Z7, Canada. TEL 819-569-9551. Ed. Charles Cambell. adv. circ. 1,250.

371.83   UK   ISSN 0048-6809
RATCLIFFIAN. 1870. a. £4. (Ratcliffe College) Echo Press Ltd., Swan St., Loughborough, Leics., England. Ed. P.W. Mullen. adv. illus. index. circ. 1,000.

378.1   SA
RHODES REVIEW. (Text mainly in English; occasionally in Afrikaans) 1975. a. free. ‡ Rhodes University, Box 94, Grahamstown, South Africa. Ed. F. Denny. adv. bk. rev. circ. 14,000.
   Incorporating: Rhodes Newsletter (ISSN 0035-4678)

378   US
TALLADEGAN.* vol.93, 1975. a. free. Talladega College, 627 W. Battle St., Talladega, AL 35160. TEL 205-362-0206. Ed. Juliette Bowles. illus.

378   380   GW
TEST - INFO. 1980. a. free. Zentralstelle fuer die Vergabe von Studienplaetzen, Sonnenstr. 171, Postfach 8000, D-4600 Dortmund 1, W. Germany (B.R.D.) circ. 200,000.
   Formerly: T M S - Testbroschuere.

378   UK
THUNDERER. 1961. a. 50p. Royal Naval Engineering College, Manadon, Plymouth, England. Eds. Stuart Brooks, Gerry Thwaites. adv. illus. circ. 400 (controlled)

278   US
U.S. NAVAL ACADEMY ALUMNI ASSOCIATION. REGISTER OF ALUMNI. 1938. a. $22. U S Naval Academy Alumni Association, Inc., Alumni House, Annapolis, MD 21402. TEL 301-263-4448. Ed. Col. James W. Hammond. adv. index. circ. 1,800. (processed)

UNIVERSITY OF CHICAGO RECORD. see *EDUCATION — Higher Education*

378.1   SA
UNIVERSITY OF PRETORIA. ANNUAL REPORT/UNIVERSITEIT VAN PRETORIA. JAARVERSLAG. (Text in Afrikaans and English) 1954. a. free. University of Pretoria - Universiteit van Pretoria, Director of Public Relations, Pretoria 0002, South Africa. Ed. H.K. Myburgh. adv. bibl. circ. 18,000.
   Formerly (until 1983): Skakelblad (ISSN 0037-6051)

378   AT   ISSN 0157-2849
UNIVERSITY OF QUEENSLAND. CALENDAR. 1913. a. Aus.$25. University of Queensland, Registrar, St. Lucia, Qld. 4067, Australia (Subscr. to: University Bookshop, P.O. Box 86, St. Lucia, Qld. 4067) circ. 1,500.

378   AT   ISSN 0313-6906
UNIVERSITY OF WOLLONGONG. ANNUAL REPORT. a. free. University of Wollongong, Box 1144, Wollongong, N.S.W. 2500, Australia.

378   AT   ISSN 0726-4844
UNIVERSITY OF WOLLONGONG. LEGISLATION. irreg. free. University of Wollongong, Box 1144, Wollongong, N.S.W. 2500, Australia.
   Supersedes in part: University of Wollongong. Calendar (ISSN 0312-0007)

378   AT
UNIVERSITY OF WOLLONGONG. POSTGRADUATE HANDBOOK. a. Aus.$4. University of Wollongong, P.O. Box 1144, Wollongong, N.S.W. 2500, Australia.
   Formerly: University of Wollongong. Faculties Sector Postgraduate Handbook (ISSN 0726-1586); Supersedes in part: University of Wollongong. Calendar (ISSN 0312-0007)

378   AT   ISSN 0726-0717
UNIVERSITY OF WOLLONGONG. UNDERGRADUATE HANDBOOK. a. Aus.$7. University of Wollongong, P.O. Box 1144, Wollongong, N.S.W. 2500, Australia.
   Absorbed: University of Wollongong. Institute Sector Handbook (ISSN 0810-5294); Supersedes in part: University of Wollongong. Calendar (ISSN 0312-0007)

378   KE
VARSITY FOCUS. (Text in English) 1979. irreg., no.22, 1981. (University of Nairobi, Vice-Chancellor) Nairobi University Press, Box 30197, Nairobi, Kenya. bk. rev. circ. 2,000.

378   CN   ISSN 0229-9119
VARSITY STUDENT HANDBOOK. 1980. a. free. (Varsity Newspaper) Varsity Publications, 44 St. George St., Toronto, Ont. M5S 2E4, Canada. TEL 416-979-2831. Ed.Bd. adv. film rev. play rev. illus. circ. 25,000. (back issues avail.)

378.1   US   ISSN 0043-3136
WEST GEORGIA COLLEGE REVIEW. (Not published in 1976) 1968. a. free. West Georgia College, Learning Resources Committee, Carrollton, GA 30118. TEL 404-834-1355. Ed. Jimmy C. Stokes. bk. rev. bibl. circ. 600. Indexed: M.L.A.

378.1   UK
WOLVERHAMPTON POLYTECHNIC STUDENTS' UNION HANDBOOK. a. Wolverhampton Polytechnic Students' Union, St. Peter's Sq., Wolverhampton, England.

COLLEGE AND ALUMNI — Abstracting, Bibliographies, Statistics

378.18   011   US
COLLEGE ALUMNI PUBLICATIONS. 1980. biennial. $20 per no. Public Relations Publishing Company, 888 Seventh Ave., New York, NY 10106. TEL 212-315-8250.

378   US
MISSISSIPPI. BOARD OF TRUSTEES OF STATE INSTITUTIONS OF HIGHER LEARNING. ANNUAL REPORT. 1945. a. free. Mississippi Board of Trustees of State Institutions of Higher Learning, Box 2336, Jackson, MS 39205. TEL 601-982-6611. Ed. E.E. Thrash. charts. stat. circ. controlled. (processed)

COMMUNICABLE DISEASES

see *Medical Sciences — Communicable Diseases*

COMMUNICATIONS

see also *Communications — Computer Applications; Communications — Postal Affairs; Communications — Radio and Television; Communications — Telephone and Telegraph; Journalism*

A C A BULLETIN. (Association for Communication Administration) see *BUSINESS AND ECONOMICS — Management*

A I A A COMMUNICATIONS SATELLITE SYSTEMS CONFERENCE. TECHNICAL PAPERS. (American Institute of Aeronautics and Astronautics) see *AERONAUTICS AND SPACE FLIGHT*

301.16   384.55   GW
A V - BRANCHE (YEAR) 1981. a. DM.35. Medienreport Verlags GmbH, Hegnacher Str. 30, 7050 Waiblingen 7, W. Germany (B.R.D.) Ed. Rolf G. Lehmann. adv. circ. 4,000.

301.16   BL
ANUARIO BRASILEIRO DE MEDIA. 1967. a. Editora Meio e Mensagem Ltda., Rua Caetes 139, 05016 Sao Paulo, Brazil. Ed. J.C. Salles Neto. adv. circ. 7,500.

301.16   GW   ISSN 0570-751X
AREOPAG; Jahrbuch fuer Kultur and Kommunikation. 1980. a. DM.26. Verlag Gunther Neske, Postfach 7240, D-7417 Pfullingen, Kloster, W. Germany (B.R.D.) Ed.Bd.

301.16   VE
ASUNTO. 1975. irreg. Universidad del Zulia, Escuela de Comunicacion Social, Maracaibo, Venezuela.

384.5   UK
AUDIO VISUAL DIRECTORY. irreg. Maclaren Publishers Ltd., Box 109, Maclaren House, Scarbrook Rd., Croydon CR9 1QH, England.

621.38   384.554   AT
AUSTRALIAN FILM, TELEVISION AND RADIO SCHOOL. ANNUAL REPORT. 1972. a. free. Australian Film,Television and Radio School, PO Box 126, North Ryde, NSW 2113, Australia. Ed. Sandy George. circ. 1,500. (back issues avail.)
   Formerly: Australian Film and Television School. Annual Report.

621.38   338   BL
AUTORIDADES E EXECUTIVOS. irreg. Associacao Brasileira de Telecomunicacoes, Rua da Quitanda, 191, Rio de Janeiro, Brazil. illus.

B/P A A MEMBERSHIP DIRECTORY AND YELLOW PAGES. (Business Professional Advertising Association) see *ADVERTISING AND PUBLIC RELATIONS*

301.16 070.43 GW
BEITRAEGE ZUR KOMMUNIKATIONSWISSENSCHAFT UND MEDIENFORSCHUNG. 1975. irreg. Verlag Peter Lang GmbH, Hinter den Ulmen 19, D-6000 Frankfurt/Main 50, W. Germany (B.R.D.)

621.38 UK ISSN 0141-9471
BROADCAST ENGINEERING NOTES. 1978. irreg. free. Independent Broadcasting Authority, Engineering Information Service, Crawley Ct., Winchester, Hants. SO21 2QA, England.

301.16 SP
COLECCION COMUNICACION VISUAL. irreg. price varies. Editorial Gustavo Gili S.A., Rosellon 87-89, Apdo. de Correos 35.149, Barcelona 29, Spain. illus.

301.16 SZ
COMMUNICATIO PUBLICA. 1974. irreg., no.8, 1980. price varies. Paul Haupt AG, Falkenplatz 14, CH-3001 Berne, Switzerland.

301.16 US
COMMUNICATION RESEARCH REPORTS. 1984. a. World Communication Association, 516 Ulumu St., Kailua, HI 96825 (Subscr. to: c/o Dr. Ronald Applbaum, Pan American University, Edinburg, TX 77087) Ed. Virginia Richmond. circ. 1,500. (back issues avail.)

001.5 US ISSN 0069-777X
COMMUNICATIONS HANDBOOK.* 1963. a. $1.50. 7200 Corporate Center Dr., Ste. 610, Miami, FL 33126. Ed. Arthur P. Salsberg. adv. circ. 100, 000.

621 US
COMMUNICATIONS: LATIN AMERICAN INDUSTRIAL REPORT. (Avail. for each of 22 Latin American countries) 1985. a. $435 per country report per industry covered. Aurora International, Box 9099, Bridgeport, CT 06601-2099. TEL 203-368-0579. Ed. Andres C. Aquino.

301.16 VE
COMUNICACION. 1975. irreg. Centro de Comunicacion "Jesus M. Pellin.", Apdo. 4.838 Carmelitas, Caracas, Venezuela. Ed. Jose I. Rey. bk. rev. circ. 2,500.

CONFEDERACAO NACIONAL DOS TRABALHADORES EM COMUNICACOES E PUBLICIDADE. RELATORIO ANUAL. see *LABOR UNIONS*

621.38 383 PO
CORREIOS E TELECOMUNICACOES DE PORTUGAL. ANUARIO ESTATISTICO. 1975. a. Correios e Telecomunicacoes de Portugal, Rua Alexandre Herculano 100, Lisbon, Portugal. illus. circ. 1,000.

301.16 US
CRITICAL COMMUNICATIONS REVIEW. 1982. irreg. price varies. Ablex Publishing Corp., 335 Chestnut St., Norwood, NJ 07648. TEL 201-767-8450. Eds. Vincent Mosco, Janet Wasko.

621.38 DK ISSN 0105-8541
DANMARKS TEKNISKE HOEJSKOLE. INSTITUTTET FOR TELETEKNIK. RAPPORT I T. irreg., vol.68, 1982. Danmarks Tekniske Hoejskole, Instituttet for Teleteknik - Technical University of Denmark. Institute of Circuit Theory and Telecommunication, Bygn 343, 2800 Lyngby, Denmark. illus.

DANSK MEDIA INDEX. see *COMMUNICATIONS — Abstracting, Bibliographies, Statistics*

621 US
DICTIONARY OF NEW INFORMATION TECHNOLOGY ACRONYMS. 1984. irreg. $68. Gale Research Company, Book Tower, Detroit, MI 48226. Eds. Michael Gordon, Alan Singelton.

621.38 658 US
DIRECTORY OF PLANS, EXECUTIVES, POLICIES FOR PCS, OFFICE AUTOMATION, DATACOM, ELECTRONIC MAIL. 1983. a. $595. International Resource Development Inc., 6 Prowitt St., Norwalk, CT 06855. TEL 203-866-7800.
    Supersedes (as of 1982): Electronic Mail Executives Directory.

808.5 US
DIRECTORY OF SPEAKERS. 1981. irreg. $55. Oryx Press, 2214 N. Central at Encanto, Ste. 103, Phoenix, AZ 85004. TEL 602-254-6156. Ed. Howard J. Langer.

301.16 US ISSN 0173-170X
DISORDERS OF HUMAN COMMUNICATION. 1980. irreg., vol.8, 1984. price varies. Springer-Verlag, 175 Fifth Ave., New York, NY 10010 TEL 212-460-1500. (Also Berlin, Heidelberg, Tokyo and Vienna) Ed.Bd. (reprint service avail. from ISI)

070.172 US ISSN 0424-4923
EDITOR & PUBLISHER INTERNATIONAL YEAR BOOK; encyclopedia of the newspaper industry. 1924. a. $60. Editor & Publisher Co., Inc., 11 W. 19th St., New York, NY 10011. TEL 212-675-4380. Ed. Robert U. Brown. circ. 13,855. (also avail. in microform from UMI; reprint service avail. from UMI) Indexed: Bus.Ind. Tr.& Indus.Ind.

ELECTROSONIC WORLD. see *ELECTRICITY AND ELECTRICAL ENGINEERING*

301.16 371.42 US ISSN 0882-3316
EMERGING PATTERNS OF WORK AND COMMUNICATIONS IN AN INFORMATION AGE. 1985. irreg. price varies. Greenwood Press, Box 5007, 88 Post Rd. W., Westport, CT 06881. TEL 203-226-3571.

621.38 BL
EMPRESA BRASILEIRA DE TELECOMMUNICACOES. RELATORIO ANUAL. 1972. a. (Empresa Brasileira de Telecomunicacoes S.A., Assessoria de Comunicacao Social) P L V Assessoria e Design, Rua das Marrecas, 36 Sala 401, Rio de Janeiro, RJ, Brazil (Address of EMBRATEL: Av. Presidente Varga 1012, 20071 Rio de Janeiro, Brazil) circ. 6,000.

ESTADISTICA PANAMENA. SITUACION ECONOMICA. SECCION 333 Y 334. TRANSPORTE Y COMUNICACIONES. see *TRANSPORTATION*

301.16 US
GEBBIE PRESS ALL-IN-ONE MEDIA DIRECTORY. 1972. a. $70. Gebbie Press, Box 1000, New Paltz, NY 12561. TEL 914-255-7560. Ed. Amalia Gebbie. index.
    Formerly: Gebbie Press All-In-One Directory (ISSN 0097-8175)

HUTTON'S BUILDING SYSTEMS AND CONTROLS CATALOG. see *CRIMINOLOGY AND LAW ENFORCEMENT — Security*

621.38 US
I E E E GLOBAL TELECOMMUNICATIONS CONFERENCE. CONFERENCE RECORD. Short title: GLOBECOM. 1982. a. (I E E E, Communications Society) Institute of Electrical and Electronics Engineers, Inc., 345 E. 47th St., New York, NY 10017 TEL 212-705-7900. (Subscr. address: 445 Hoes Lane, Piscataway, NJ 08854)
    Supersedes: National Telecommunications Conference. Record; National Telemetering Conference. Record.
    Telecommunications

621.38 US ISSN 0536-1486
I E E E INTERNATIONAL CONFERENCE ON COMMUNICATIONS. CONFERENCE RECORD. 1965. a. price varies. (I E E E, Communications Society) Institute of Electrical and Electronics Engineers, Inc, 345 E. 47th St., New York, NY 10017 TEL 212-705-7900. (Subscr. address: 445 Hoes Lane, Piscataway, NJ 08854) bibl. illus.
    Formerly: International Conference on Communications. Conference Record.

I E E E POSITION LOCATION AND NAVIGATION SYMPOSIUM. RECORD. see *ELECTRICITY AND ELECTRICAL ENGINEERING*

301.16 II
I I M C BULLETIN. (Text in English) a. Rs.5. Indian Institute of Mass Communication, D-13, South Extension, Part II, New Delhi 110049, India.

380 II ISSN 0536-7506
INDIA. OFFICE OF THE COMPTROLLER AND AUDITOR-GENERAL. REPORT: UNION GOVERNMENT (POSTS AND TELEGRAPHS) 1970/71. a. $14.40. Office of the Comptroller and Auditor-General, Controller of Publications, Civil Lines, Delhi 110054, India. stat.

301.16 II
INDIAN INSTITUTE OF MASS COMMUNICATION. ANNUAL REPORT. (Text in English) a. Indian Institute of Mass Communication, D-13, South Extension, Part II, New Delhi 110049, India.

301.16 US ISSN 0740-5502
INFORMATION AND BEHAVIOR. 1985. a. $49.95. Transaction Books, Rutgers University, New Brunswick, NJ 08903. TEL 201-932-2280. Ed. Brent D. Ruben. circ. 4,000. (back issues avail.)

INFORMATION SOURCES. see *COMPUTERS*

621.38 PL ISSN 0020-451X
INSTYTUT LACZNOSCI. PRACE. (Text in Polish; summaries in English, French, German and Russian) 1954. irreg. price varies. Wydawnictwa Komunikacji i Lacznosci, Kazimierzowska 52, Warsaw, Poland. Ed. L. Kedzierski. (also avail. in microfilm) Indexed: Sci.Abstr. INSPEC.

301.16 US
INTERNATIONAL AND INTERCULTURAL COMMUNICATION ANNUAL. 1975? a. $29.95 cloth; $14.95 paper. Sage Publications, Inc., 2111 W. Hillcrest Dr., Newbury Park, CA 91320. TEL 805-499-0721. Ed. William Gudykunst. (reprint service avail. from UMI)

384 UK ISSN 0579-3742
INTERNATIONAL ASSOCIATION FOR MASS COMMUNICATIONS RESEARCH. LETTER FROM THE PRESIDENT. 1968. irreg. International Association for Mass Communications Research, c/o James D. Halloran, Centre for Mass Communications Research, University of Leicester, 104 Regent Rd., Leicester, England.

384 UK
INTERNATIONAL ASSOCIATION FOR MASS COMMUNICATIONS RESEARCH. MONOGRAPHS. biennial. International Association for Mass Communications Research, c/o Prof. James D. Halloran, Centre for Mass Communications Research, University of Leicester, 104 Regent Rd., Leicester, England.

621.38 531.64 US
INTERNATIONAL COMMUNICATIONS AND ENERGY CONFERENCE (PROCEEDINGS)/ CONFERENCE INTERNATIONALE SUR LES COMMUNICATIONS ET L'ENERGIE (PROCEEDINGS) 1970? biennial. Institute of Electrical and Electronics Engineers, Inc., 345 E. 47th St., New York, NY 10017 (Subscr. address: 445 Hoes Lane, Piscataway, NJ 08854)
    Former titles (until 1982): Canadian Communications and Energy Conference (Proceedings) /Conference Canadienne sur les Communications et l'Energie (Proceedings); 1974-1980: Canadian Communications and Power Conference; Until 1972: Canadian Communications and EHV Conference; Until 1970: Canadian Symposium on Communications. Symposium Digest.

INTERNATIONAL GEOSCIENCE AND REMOTE SENSING SYMPOSIUM DIGEST. see *ELECTRICITY AND ELECTRICAL ENGINEERING*

621.38 US
INTERNATIONAL PROFESSIONAL COMMUNICATION CONFERENCE. CONFERENCE RECORD. Short title: I P C C. 1981. a. Institute of Electrical and Electronics Engineers, Inc., 345 E. 47th St., New York, NY 10017 (Subscr. address: 445 Hoes Lane, Piscataway, NJ 08854)
    Formerly (until 1985): I E E E Professional Communication Society Conference. Record.

COMMUNICATIONS

621.38 629.1 US
INTERNATIONAL RADAR CONFERENCE. RECORD. Variant title: International Conference on Radar (Publication) (Alternately published by I E E E and I E E) 1973. irreg. price varies. (I E E E, Aerospace and Electronic Systems Society) Institute of Electrical and Electronics Engineers, Inc., 345 E. 47th St., New York, NY 10017. TEL 212-705-7900.

001.5 US
INTERNATIONAL TECHNICAL COMMUNICATION CONFERENCE PROCEEDINGS. 1956. a. $47. Society for Technical Communication, 815 15th St., N.W., Washington, DC 20005 (Orders to: Univelt, Inc., Box 28130, San Diego, CA 92128) bibl. circ. 1,500. (also avail. in microfiche; back issues avail.; reprint service avail. from UMI PMC) Indexed: Eng.Ind.

621.38 US
INTERNATIONAL TELECONFERENCING SYMPOSIUM (PROCEEDINGS) 1980. a. $400. Cross Information Company, 1881 9th St., Ste. 311, Boulder, CO 80301-5151. TEL 303-444-7799. Ed. Thomas B. Cross. (back issues avail.)

621.38 UR ISSN 0130-6804
ITOGI NAUKI I TEKHNIKI: ELEKTROSVYAZ' irreg., vol.17, 1987. price varies. Vsesoyuznyi Institut Nauchno-Tekhnicheskoi Informatsii (VINITI), Ul. Baltiiskaya 14, Moscow A-219, Russian S.F.S.R., U.S.S.R. (Subscr. to: Mezhdunarodnaya Kniga, Dimitrova ul. 39, 113095 Moscow, Russian S.F.S.R., U.S.S.R.)

JOURNALISTEN JAHRBUCH. see *JOURNALISM*

KEY ABSTRACTS - TELECOMMUNICATIONS. see *COMMUNICATIONS — Abstracting, Bibliographies, Statistics*

KOREAN PRESS ANNUAL/HANGUK SINMUN PANGSONG YONGAM. see *JOURNALISM*

621.38 LB
LIBERIA MINISTRY OF POSTS AND TELECOMMUNICATIONS. ANNUAL REPORT. a. Ministry of Posts and Telecommunications, Monrovia, Liberia.

301.16 016.3354 US ISSN 0098-9509
MARXISM AND THE MASS MEDIA; towards a basic bibliography. 1987. irreg. price varies. (International Mass Media Research Center, FR) International General, Box 350, New York, NY 10013 (And 173 Ave. de la Dhuys, 93170 Bagnolet, France) Ed. Seth Siegelaub. circ. 2,000.

301.16 US ISSN 0196-8017
MASS COMMUNICATION REVIEW YEARBOOK. 1980. a. $59.95. Sage Publications, Inc., 2111 W. Hillcrest Dr., Newbury Park, CA 91320 TEL 805-499-0721. (And Sage Publications, Ltd., 28 Banner St., London EC1Y 8QE, England) Eds. Michael Gurevitch, Mark R. Levy.

384 AT
MASS MEDIA REVIEW. irreg. Australian Society for Education in Film and Television, G.P.O. Box 252C, Hobart, Tas. 7001, Australia.

MASSACHUSETTS INSTITUTE OF TECHNOLOGY. RESEARCH LABORATORY OF ELECTRONICS. R L E PROGRESS REPORT. see *ELECTRICITY AND ELECTRICAL ENGINEERING*

808 US
MISSOURI SPEECH JOURNAL. 1970. a. $4. (Speech and Theatre Association of Missouri) Central Missouri State University, Warrensburg, MO 64093. TEL 816-429-4111. Ed. Dr. Jones Floyd. circ. 175.

NATIONAL CENTER FOR AUDIO TAPES ARCHIVE. CATALOG. see *EDUCATION — Teaching Methods And Curriculum*

301.16 US
NORTH AMERICAN ONLINE DIRECTORY. a. $85. R.R. Bowker Company, Database Publishing Group, 245 W. 17th St., New York, NY 10011. TEL 800-521-8110.
Former titles (until 1985): Information Industry Market Place (ISSN 0000-0450); Information Market Place.

384 CN ISSN 0078-3722
OFFICE DES COMMUNICATIONS SOCIALES, MONTREAL. CAHIERS D'ETUDES ET DE RECHERCHES. 1965. irreg. price varies. ‡ Office des Communications Sociales, 4005 rue de Bellechasse, Montreal, Que. H1X 1J6, Canada. TEL 514-729-6391. circ. 500-750.

420 US ISSN 0078-4052
OHIO SPEECH JOURNAL. 1962. a. $3. Speech Communication Association of Ohio, c/o Dr. James R. Phipps, Speech Department, Cedarville College, Box 601, Cedarville, OH 45314. TEL 513-766-2211. Ed. Sue DeWine. adv. bk. rev. circ. 400. Indexed: Lang.& Lang.Behav.Abstr.

OPTICAL MEMORY REPORT. see *PHYSICS — Optics*

301.16 US
OTHER NETWORKS. 1981. irreg., approx. 2/yr. $25 for 4 issues. Public Interest Media Project, Box 14066, Philadelphia, PA 19123. TEL 215-922-0227. Ed. Stan Pokras. bk. rev. circ. 1,000.

301.16 US
PEOPLE AND COMMUNICATION. 1977. irreg., vol.17, 1986. $28 cloth; $14 paper. Sage Publications, Inc., 2111 W. Hillcrest Dr., Newbury Park, CA 91320 TEL 805-499-0721. (And Sage Publications, Ltd., 28 Banner St., London EC1Y 8QE, England) Eds. F. Gerald Kline, Peter Clarke. bibl. (back issues avail.)

301.16 US
PEOPLE, COMMUNICATION ORGANIZATION. 1986. irreg. price varies. Ablex Publishing Corp., 355 Chestnut St., Norwood, NJ 07648. TEL 201-767-8450. Ed. Lee Thayer.

PRESSENS ARBOG. see *HISTORY — History Of Europe*

020 US ISSN 0163-5689
PROGRESS IN COMMUNICATION SCIENCES. 1979. a. price varies. Ablex Publishing Corp., 355 Chestnut St., Norwood, NJ 07648. TEL 201-767-8450. Eds. Brenda Derrin, Melvin Voigt. (reprint service avail. from ISI)

354 CN
QUEBEC (PROVINCE) MINISTERE DES COMMUNICATIONS. RAPPORT DES ACTIVITES. 1972. a. free. Ministere des Communications, Quebec, Canada. TEL 418-643-1529. illus. stat.

621.38 UK
RADAR SYSTEMS INTERNATIONAL. 1969. irreg. free. Marconi Radar Systems Ltd., Writtle Rd., Chelmsford CM1 3BN, England. circ. controlled.

001.5 UN ISSN 0080-1356
REPORTS AND PAPERS ON MASS COMMUNICATIONS. (Text in English and French) 1953. irreg., no.95, 1985. price varies. Unesco, 7-9 Place de Fontenoy, 75700 Paris, France (Dist. in U.S. by: Bernan Associates-Unipub, 4611-F Assembly Dr., Lanham, MD 20706-4391)

301.16 384.5 SA ISSN 0314-1357
RESEARCH LABORATORIES REVIEW OF ACTIVITIES. (Text in English) 1971. a. Telecom Australia, Research Laboratories, 770 Blackburn Rd., Clayton, Vic. 3168, Australia. Ed. F.W. Arter. circ. 3,000. (back issues avail)

384 US ISSN 0099-1414
SAGE ANNUAL REVIEWS OF COMMUNICATION RESEARCH. 1972. a. $14.95 for softcover; hardcover $29.95. Sage Publications, Inc., 2111 W. Hillcrest Dr., Newbury Park, CA 91320 TEL 805-499-0721. (And Sage Publications, Ltd., 28 Banner St., London EC1Y 8QE, England) Eds. James W. Carey, Peter Miller. (back issues avail.)

301.16 US
SAGE SERIES IN INTERPERSONAL COMMUNICATION. 1983. irreg., vol.5, 1984. $29.95 for hardcover; paperback $14.95. Sage Publications, Inc., 2111 W. Hillcrest Dr., Newbury Park, CA 91320. TEL 805-499-0721. Ed. Mark L. Knapp.

301.16 CE
SANNIVEDANA. (Text in English or Sinhalese) a. Rs.3.50. University of Sri Lanka, Vidyalankara Campus, Department of Mass Communications, Kelaniya, Sri Lanka.

301.16 SP ISSN 0213-0289
SOCIEDAD DE ESTUDIOS VASCOS. CUADERNOS DE SECCION. MEDIOS DE COMUNICACION. 1984. irreg. (Sociedad de Estudios Vascos) Eusko Ikaskuntza, S.A., Churruca, 7-2, 20004 Donostia, Spain.

808.2 US
SOCIETY FOR TECHNICAL COMMUNICATION ANTHOLOGY SERIES. 1973. irreg. price varies. (Society for Technical Communication) Univelt, Inc., Box 28130, San Diego, CA 92128. TEL 202-737-0035. (back issues avail.)

001.5 US ISSN 0081-5179
STATISTICS OF THE COMMUNICATIONS INDUSTRY IN THE UNITED STATES. 1939. a. price varies. U.S. Federal Communications Commission., 1919 M St., N.W., Washington, DC 20554 TEL 202-783-3238. (Orders to: Supt. of Documents, Washington, DC 20402)

301.16 US ISSN 0275-7982
STUDIES IN COMMUNICATIONS; a research annual. 1980. a. $23.75 to individuals; institutions $47.50. J A I Press Inc., Box 1678, Greenwich, CT 06830. TEL 203-661-7602. Ed. Thelma McCormack. Indexed: Lang.& Lang.Behav.Abstr.

001.5 US ISSN 0585-7031
STUDIES IN PUBLIC COMMUNICATION.* irreg. price varies. Communication Arts Books (Subsidiary of: Hastings House Publishers) 260 Fifth Ave., New York, NY 10001.

621.38 SW
SWEDISH TELECOM. ANNUAL REPORT. (Text in English) a. Televerket - Swedish Telecommunications Administration, Maarbackagatan 11, S-123 86 Farsta, Sweden. circ. 5,000. (back issues avail.)
Formerly: Sweden. Televerket. Annual Report (ISSN 0586-1926)

TALLER DE CULTURA Y MEDIOS DE COMUNICACION. DOCUMENTOS DE TRABAJO. see *SOCIOLOGY*

621.38 GW ISSN 0082-1764
TASCHENBUCH DER FERNMELDE-PRAXIS. 1963. a. DM.38. Fachverlag Schiele und Schoen GmbH, Markgrafenstr. 11, 1000 Berlin 61, W. Germany (B.R.D.) Ed. H. Pooch. adv. circ. 7,500.

301.16 AT
TELECOM AUSTRALIA. ANNUAL REPORT. 1975. a. Telecom Australia, Communications House, 199 William St., Melbourne, Vic 3000, Australia. Ed. R.W. Brack. circ. 16,000.

621.38 US
TELECOMMUNICATIONS (NEW YORK) 1977. irreg., vol.10, 1984. (Muenchner Kreis Supranational Association for Communications Research, GW) Springer-Verlag, 175 Fifth Ave., New York, NY 10010 TEL 212-460-1500. (Also Berlin, Heidelberg, Tokyo and Vienna)

621.38 001.6 600 338 US ISSN 0738-3045
TELECOMMUNICATIONS SYSTEMS AND SERVICES DIRECTORY; an international descriptive guide to approximately 2,000 telecommunications organizations, systems, and services. 1983. irreg., 2nd edt., 1985. Gale Research Company, Book Tower, Detroit, MI 48226. TEL 313-961-2242. Ed. Martin Connors. (also avail. in magnetic tape)

537 JA
TOHOKU UNIVERSITY. RESEARCH INSTITUTE OF ELECTRICAL COMMUNICATION. TECHNICAL REPORT. (Text in English) 1964. irreg. exchange basis. Tohoku University, Research Institute of Electrical Communication - Tohoku Daigaku Denki Tsushin Kenkyusho, 2-1-1 Katahira, Sendai 980, Japan.

621.38　　　　　　　JA
TOYO'S TECHNICAL BULLETIN/TOYO TSUSHINKI GIHO. (Text in Japanese) 1963. a. exchange basis. Toyo Communication Equipment Company - Toyo Tsushinki K. K., 3-484 Tsukagoshi, Saiwai-ku, Kawasaki-shi 210, Japan.

602.6　001.535　　　US
TRAC: GLOBAL YEARBOOK OF ISSUES, EVENTS, AND DISCOVERIES IN TELECOMMUNICATIONS, ROBOTICS, ARTIFICIAL INTELLIGENCE, CAD/CAM. 1987. a. $395. E I C - Intelligence, 48 W. 38th St., New York, NY 10018. TEL 212-944-8500.

TRANSPORT & COMMUNICATIONS BULLETIN FOR ASIA & THE PACIFIC. see *TRANSPORTATION*

301.16　　　　　　　GW
TUDUV-STUDIE. REIHE KOMMUNIKATIONSWISSENSCHAFTEN. 1986. irreg. price varies. Tuduv Verlagsgesellschaft mbH, Gabelsbergerstrasse 15, 8000 Munich 2, W. Germany (B.R.D.)

U.S. ADMINISTRATIVE OFFICE OF THE UNITED STATES COURTS. REPORT ON APPLICATIONS FOR ORDERS AUTHORIZING OR APPROVING THE INTERCEPTION OF WIRE OR ORAL COMMUNICATIONS. see *LAW*

001.5　　　　US　ISSN 0083-0607
U.S. FEDERAL COMMUNICATIONS COMMISSION. I N F BULLETINS. 1949. irreg., latest 1976? free. ‡ U.S. Federal Communications Commission, 1919 M St., N.W., Washington, DC 20554. TEL 202-632-7000.

001.5　　　　GW　ISSN 0341-3136
UNIVERSITAET BONN. INSTITUT FUER KOMMUNIKATIONSFORSCHUNG UND PHONETIK. FORSCHUNGSBERICHTE. 1966. irreg., vol.72, 1981. price varies. Verlag Helmut Buske, Schluetersr. 14, 2000 Hamburg 13, W. Germany (B.R.D.) Ed. Gerold Ungeheuer.

621.3　　　　　　　JA
UNIVERSITY OF ELECTROCOMMUNICATIONS. RESEARCH INSTITUTE FOR COMMUNICATION SCIENCES. ANNUAL REPORT/DENKI TSUSHIN DAIGAKU DENKI TSUSHIN KENKYU SHISETSU NENPO. (Text in English or Japanese) 1961. a. free. University of Electrocommunications, Research Institute for Communication Sciences., 1-5-1 Chofugaoka, Chofu-shi, Tokyo 181, Japan. illus.
　Formerly: University of Telecommunications. Research Laboratory of Communication Sciences. Annual Report.

UNIVERSITY OF TOKYO. ELECTRICAL AND ELECTRONIC ENGINEERING DEPARTMENT. BULLETIN. see *ELECTRICITY AND ELECTRICAL ENGINEERING*

621.38　　　　　　　UY
URUGUAY. ADMINISTRACION NACIONAL DE TELECOMUNICACIONES. MEMORIA ANUAL. a. Administracion Nacional de Telecomunicaciones, Paraguay 2431, Casilla Correo 909, Montevideo, Uruguay.
　Telecommunication

VIDEO SOURCE BOOK. see *MOTION PICTURES*

301.16　　　　II　ISSN 0043-7948
WORD. (Text in English) 1963. a. Rs.5($1) Bharatiya Vidya Bhavan, Kulapati K. M. Munshi Marg, Bombay 400007, India. Ed. G.S. Pohekar. adv. bk. rev. circ. 1,000.

621.38　　　　　　　US
WORLDWIDE REPORT: TELECOMMUNICATIONS POLICY. RESEARCH AND DEVELOPMENT. irreg., approx. 30/yr. $5 per no. U.S. Joint Publications Research Service, 1000 N. Glebe Rd., Arlington, VA 22201 TEL 703-487-4630. (Orders to: NTIS, Springfield, VA 22161)
　Formerly: Telecommunications Policy. Research and Development.

384.6　　　　　　　UN
YEARBOOK OF COMMON CARRIER TELECOMMUNICATION STATISTICS/ ANNUAIRE STATISTIQUE DES TELECOMMUNICATIONS DU SECTEUR PUBLIC. (Each vol. cumulative over 10 yrs.) (Text in English, French and Spanish) a. 58 Fr. International Telecommunication Union - Union Internationale des Telecommunications, Place de Nations, 1211 Geneva 20, Switzerland.
　Incorporating: Telecommunication Statistics.

COMMUNICATIONS — Abstracting, Bibliographies, Statistics

001.6　　　　JA　ISSN 0910-6510
ABSTRACTS ON SCIENCE AND TECHNOLOGY IN JAPAN: ELECTRONICS AND COMMUNICATION. (Text in English) 1985. q. 28.000 Yen. Japan Information Center of Science and Technology - Nihon Kagaku Gijutsu Joho Senta, 5-2, Nagata-cho, 2-Chome, Chiyoda-Ku, Tokyo 100, Japan. circ. 1,000.

384　　　　CN　ISSN 0703-7244
CANADA. STATISTICS CANADA. CABLE TELEVISION/TELEDISTRIBUTION. (Catalogue 56-205) (Text in English and French) 1967. a. Can.$22($23) Statistics Canada, Communications Division, 3rd Floor, R.H. Coats Bldg., Ottawa, Ont. K1A 0T6, Canada TEL 613-993-7276. (Subscr. to: Publications Sales and Services, Ottawa, Ont. K1A 0T6, Canada) (also avail. in microform from MML)
　Formerly: Canada. Statistics Canada. Community Antenna Television/Services de Television a Antenne Collective.

338.4　　　　CN　ISSN 0828-9824
CANADA. STATISTICS CANADA. COMMUNICATIONS AND OTHER ELECTRONIC INDUSTRIES/INDUSTRIES DE L'EQUIPEMENT ET D'AUTRE MATERIEL ELECTRONIQUE. (Catalogue 43-206) (Text in English and French) 1960. a. Can.$20($21) Statistics Canada, Communications Division, 3rd Floor, R.H. Coats Bldg., Ottawa, Ont. K1A 0T6, Canada TEL 613-993-7276. (Subscr. to: Publications Sales and Services, Ottawa, Ont. K1A 0T6, Canada) (also avail. in microform from MML)
　Formerly: Canada. Statistics Canada. Communications Equipment Meanufacturers/ Fabricants d'Equipement de Telecommunication (ISSN 0527-494X)

384.097　　　　CN　ISSN 0380-0334
CANADA. STATISTICS CANADA. COMMUNICATIONS SERVICE BULLETIN/ COMMUNICATIONS-BULLETIN DE SERVICE. (Catalogue 56-001) (Text in English and French) 1971. irreg. Can.$39($45) Statistics Canada, Communications Division, 3rd Floor, R.H. Coats Bldg., Ottawa, Ont. K1A 0T6, Canada TEL 613-993-7276. (Subscr. to: Publications Sales and Services, Ottawa, Ont. K1A 0T6, Canada) (also avail. in microform from MML)

384.54　　　　CN　ISSN 0575-9560
CANADA. STATISTICS CANADA. RADIO AND TELEVISION BROADCASTING/ RADIODIFFUSION ET TELEVISION. (Catalogue 56-204) (Text in English and French) 1961. a. Can.$22($23) Statistics Canada, Communications Division, 3rd Floor, R.H. Coats Bldg., Ottawa, Ont. K1A 0T6, Canada TEL 613-993-7276. (Subscr. to: Publications Sales and Services, Ottawa, Ont. K1A 0T6, Canada) (also avail. in microform from MML)

384　　　　CN　ISSN 0703-7252
CANADA. STATISTICS CANADA. TELECOMMUNICATIONS STATISTICS/ STATISTIQUE DES TELECOMMUNICATIONS. (Catalogue 56-201) (Text in English and French) 1917. a. Can.$10($11) Statistics Canada, Communications Division, 3rd Floor, R.H. Coats Bldg., Ottawa, Ont. K1A 0T6, Canada TEL 613-993-7276. (Subscr. to: Publications Sales and Services, Ottawa, Ont. K1A 0T6, Canada) (also avail. in microform from MML)

COLUMBIA. DEPARTAMENTO ADMINISTRATIVO NACIONAL DE ESTADISTICA. ANUARIO GENERAL DE ESTADISTICA - TRANSPORTES Y COMUNICACIONES. see *TRANSPORTATION — Abstracting, Bibliographies, Statistics*

016　　　　US　ISSN 0162-2811
COMMUNICATION ABSTRACTS. 1978. q. $60 to individuals; institutions $130. Sage Publications, Inc., 2111 W. Hillcrest Dr., Newbury Park, CA 91320 TEL 805-499-0721. (And: Sage Publications, Ltd., 28 Banner St., London EC1Y 8QE, England) Ed. Thomas F. Gordon. adv. abstr, bibl. index. (back issues avail.)

301.16　　　　US　ISSN 0732-4456
CONTRIBUTIONS TO THE STUDY OF MASS MEDIA AND COMMUNICATIONS. 1983. irreg. price varies. Greenwood Press, 88 Post Rd. W., Box 5007, Westport, CT 06881. TEL 203-226-3571. bibl. index.

016　　　　　　　DK
DANSK MEDIA INDEX. 1969. a. Kr.310. Dansk Media Komite, Norgesmindevej 15, 2900 Hellerup, Denmark. Ed. Sigurd Bennike. circ. 600.

621.38　016　　UK　ISSN 0013-5119
ELECTRONICS AND COMMUNICATIONS ABSTRACTS. 1961. m. £85($150) Multi-Science Publishing Co. Ltd., 107 High St., Brentwood, Essex CM14 4RX, England. Ed. A. Reynish. abstr. index.

621.38　016　　US　ISSN 0361-3313
ELECTRONICS AND COMMUNICATIONS ABSTRACTS JOURNAL; an abstract journal involving the theory, design and application of electronic devices and systems. 1967. bi-m. $462. Cambridge Scientific Abstracts, 5161 River Rd., Bethesda, MD 20816. TEL 301-951-1400. adv. bk. rev. abstr. index. cum.index. circ. 1,000. (also avail. in microfilm) Indexed: Cal.Tiss.Abstr. Chemorec.Abstr. Oncol.Abstr.
●Also available online. Vendors: DIALOG.
　Formerly: Electronics Abstracts Journal (ISSN 0013-5097)

GREECE. NATIONAL STATISTICAL SERVICE. TRANSPORT AND COMMUNICATION STATISTICS. see *TRANSPORTATION — Abstracting, Bibliographies, Statistics*

314　380.3　　　　HU
HUNGARY. KOZPONTI STATISZTIKAI HIVATAL. KOZLEKEDESI POSTA ES TAVKOZLESI. a. 130 Ft. Statisztikai Kiado Vallalat, Kaszasdulo u. 2, P.O.B.99, 1300 Budapest 3, Hungary (Subscr. to: Kultura, Box 149, H-1389 Budapest, Hungary)
　Formerly: Hungary. Kozponti Statisztikai Hivatal. Kozlekedesi es Hirkozlesi Evkonyv (ISSN 0133-9133)

384.554　　　　UK　ISSN 0143-5663
INTERNATIONAL INDEX TO TELEVISION PERIODICALS. 1983. biennial. £25. International Federation of Film Archives (F.I.A.F.), 90-94 Shaftesbury Ave., London S1V 7DH, England (Subscr. addr.: St. James Press, 425 N. Michigan Ave., Chicago 60611, U.S.A.) Ed. Michael Moulds. (also avail. in microfiche)

621.8　016　　　　UN
INTERNATIONAL TELECOMMUNICATION UNION. CENTRAL LIBRARY. LISTE DES PERIODIQUES. LIST OF PERIODICALS. LISTA DE REVISTAS. (Text in English, French, Spanish) 1967. a. International Telecommunication Union, Central Library - Union Internationale des Telecommunications, Place des Nations, 1211 Geneva 20, Switzerland. Ed. A.G. el-Zanati.

621.38　016　　　　UN
INTERNATIONAL TELECOMMUNICATION UNION. CENTRAL LIBRARY. LISTES DES PUBLICATIONS ANNUELLES. LIST OF ANNUALS. LISTA DE PUBLICACIONES ANUALES. (Text in English, French and Spanish) 1972. a. International Telecommunication Union, Central Library - Union Internationale des Telecommunications, Place des Nations, 1211 Geneva 20, Switzerland. Ed. A.G. el-Zanati. circ. 1, 000.

301.16 016 GW
JAHRESBIBLIOGRAPHIE
MASSENKOMMUNIKATION. (Text in various languages) 1974. a. DM.28. (Staats und Universitaetsbibliothek Bremen) WissenschaftsVerlag Volker Spiess GmbH, Potsdamer Str. 199, 1000 Berlin 30, W. Germany (B.R.D.) Ed. Wilbert Ubbens. bibl. index. circ. 2,500. (back issues avail.)

621 UK ISSN 0950-4761
KEY ABSTRACTS - ANTENNAS & PROPAGATION. 1987. m. $110 to non-members. INSPEC, I.E.E. Station House, Nightingale Rd., Hitchin, Herts. SG5 1RJ, England (U.S. addr.: 445 Hoes Lane, Piscataway, NJ 08854) index.

621.38 UK ISSN 0950-4826
KEY ABSTRACTS - OPTOELECTRONICS. 1987. m. $110 to non-members. INSPEC, I.E.E., Station House, Nightingale Rd., Hitchin, Herts. SG5 1RJ, England (U.S. addr.: 445 Hoes Lane, Piscataway, NJ 08854) index.

621.38 016 UK ISSN 0950-4877
KEY ABSTRACTS - TELECOMMUNICATIONS. 1975. m. $110 to non-members. INSPEC, I.E.E., Station House, Nightingale Rd., Hitchin, Herts. SG5 1RJ, England (U.S. addr.: 445 Hoes Lane, Piscataway, NJ 08854) index.
Formerly (until 1987): Key Abstracts - Communications Technology (ISSN 0306-5588)

301.16 DK ISSN 0105-1385
N O R D I C O M; bibliography of Nordic mass communication literature/bibliografi over Nordisk Massekommunikationslitteratur. 1976. a. Kr.40. Nordic Documentation Center for Mass Communication Research - Nordisk Dokumentationscentral for Masskommunikationsforskning, Statsbiblioteket, Universitetsparken, DK-8000 Aarhus C, Denmark. Ed. Claus Kragh Hansen. index. circ. 600.

NORWAY. STATISTISK SENTRALBYRAA. SAMFERDSELSSTATISTIKK/TRANSPORT AND COMMUNICATION STATISTICS. see TRANSPORTATION — Abstracting, Bibliographies, Statistics

384 314 NO ISSN 0800-2177
NORWAY. TELEVERKET. STATISTIKK. 1897. a. free. Televerket, Teledirektoratet, Box 6701, Oslo 1, Norway. bk. rev. circ. 1,350.
Continues: Norway. Televerket. Statistisk Arbok.

PERFORMING ARTS BIOGRAPHY MASTER INDEX. see THEATER — Abstracting, Bibliographies, Statistics

PORTUGAL. INSTITUTO NACIONAL DE ESTATISTICA. SERVICOS CENTRAIS. ESTATISTICAS DOS TRANSPORTES E COMMUNICACOES: CONTINENTE, ACORES E MADEIRA. see TRANSPORTATION — Abstracting, Bibliographies, Statistics

621.38 016 UR ISSN 0034-267X
REFERATIVNYI ZHURNAL. RADIOTEKHNIKA. 1955. m. 220 Rub. (280 Rub. including index) Vsesoyuznyi Institut Nauchno-Tekhnicheskoi Informatsii (VINITI), Baltiiskaya ul., 14, Moscow A-219, Russian S.F.S.R., U.S.S.R. (Subscr. to: Mezhdunarodnaya Kniga, Dimitrova ul. 39, 113095 Moscow, Russian S.F.S.R., U.S.S.R.)

SWEDEN. STATISTISKA CENTRALBYRAAN. STATISTISKA MEDDELANDEN. SUBGROUP T (TRANSPORT AND OTHER FORMS OF COMMUNICATION) see TRANSPORTATION — Abstracting, Bibliographies, Statistics

384 016 US
TELECOMMUNICATIONS ALERT; a unique monthly reporting and highlighting service covering all current developments in telecommunications. 1983. m. $187. Management Telecommunications Publishing, One Park Ave., New York, NY 10016. TEL 212-683-3899. Ed.Bd. abstr. circ. 4,000.

791.45 016 CS
VYBEROVA ANOTOVANA BIBLIOGRAFIE STUDIJNICH MATERIALU. 1968. biennial. free. Ceskoslovenska Televize, Odbor Vyzkumu Programu CST a Divaku CSR, Oddeleni Dokumentace a Odborne Informace, Jindrisska 16, 111 50 Prague 1, Czechoslovakia. Ed. Karel Lemberger. bibl. circ. 300.

COMMUNICATIONS — Computer Applications

ADVANCES IN SATELLITE COMMUNICATIONS SERIES. see ENGINEERING — Computer Applications

COMMUNICATION THEORY IN THE CAUSE OF HUMANITY; notes on the application of theory to the strengthening of democratic institutions. see HUMANITIES: COMPREHENSIVE WORKS — Computer Applications

380.3 621.381 US
DATA COMMUNICATIONS PRODUCT DIRECTORY. 1984. irreg. $124. Architecture Technology Corporation, Box 24344, Minneapolis, MN 55424. TEL 612-935-2035. (back issues avail.)

ELECTRICAL & ELECTRONICS ABSTRACTS. see ELECTRICITY AND ELECTRICAL ENGINEERING — Abstracting, Bibliographies, Statistics

ELECTRICAL ENGINEERING, TELECOMMUNICATIONS AND SIGNAL PROCESSING. see ENGINEERING — Computer Applications

380.3 US
I E E E INFOCOM. PROCEEDINGS. Variant title: Joint Conference of the I E E E Computer and Communications Societies. 1982. a. (Institute of Electrical and Electronics Engineers, Inc.) I E E E Computer Society Press, 1730 Massachusetts Ave., N.W., Washington, DC 10026-1903 (And 345 E. 47th St., New York, NY 10017) (Co-sponsor: I E E E Communications Society)
Formerly (until 1982): I N F O C O M Proceedings.

JAPAN ANNUAL REVIEWS IN ELECTRONICS, COMPUTERS & TELECOMMUNICATIONS. AMORPHOUS SEMICONDUCTOR TECHNOLOGIES & DEVICES. see ELECTRICITY AND ELECTRICAL ENGINEERING

JOURNAL OF HUMAN COMMUNICATIONS RESEARCH; a forum for bio-medical communications research. see HUMANITIES: COMPREHENSIVE WORKS — Computer Applications

380.3 384.554 US
OFFICIAL VIDEO SOFTWARE DIRECTORY. 1983. a. Home Viewer Publications, Inc., 11 N. 2nd St., Philadelphia, PA 19106. TEL 215-629-1558. Ed. Bruce Apar.

380.3 US
PHOENIX CONFERENCE ON COMPUTERS AND COMMUNICATIONS. CONFERENCE PROCEEDINGS. Variant title: Annual Phoenix Conference on Computers and Communications. Proceedings. 1982. a. (Institute of Electrical and Electronics Engineers, Inc.) I E E E Computer Society Press, 1730 Massachusetts Ave., N.W., Washington, DC 20036-1903 (And 345 E. 47th St., New York, NY 10017) (Co-sponsor: I E E E Communications Society)

COMMUNICATIONS — Postal Affairs

383 DK ISSN 0107-4350
ADRESSELOESE POSTFORSENDELSER. 1980. a. free. Generaldirektoratet for P & T, Tietgensgade 37 2, 1530 Copenhagen V, Denmark. illus.
Continues in part: Postomdeling af Reklamer.

383 DK ISSN 0107-4369
ADRESSEREDE BREVFORSENDELSER. 1980. a. free. Generaldirektoratet for P & T, Tietgensgade 37 2, 1530 Copenhagen V, Denmark. illus.

383 BE
BELGIUM. REGIE DES POSTES. RAPPORT D'ACTIVITE. 1954. a. Regie des Postes, Centre Monnaie, 1000 Brussels, Belgium. Ed.Bd. illus. circ. 2,700.

381 US ISSN 0068-4201
BULLINGER'S POSTAL AND SHIPPERS GUIDE FOR THE UNITED STATES AND CANADA. 1871. a. $200 yearly rental. Bullinger's Guides, Inc., 63 Woodland Ave., Box 501, Westwood, NJ 07675. Ed. Robert M. Hoyt. circ. 3,500.

383 CN
CANADA POSTAL GUIDE PART 1: POSTAL LAW AND REGULATIONS. irreg. Can.$12. Supply and Services Canada, Publishing Centre, Ottawa, Ont. K1A 0S9, Canada. TEL 613-997-2560. (looseleaf format)

383 CN
CANADA POSTAL GUIDE PART 2: INTERNATIONAL MAILS, RATES AND CONDITIONS. irreg. Can.$15. Supply and Services Canada, Publishing Centre, Ottawa, Ont. K1A 0S9, Canada. TEL 613-997-2560. (looseleaf format)

CORREIOS E TELECOMUNICACOES DE PORTUGAL. ANUARIO ESTATISTICO. see COMMUNICATIONS

383 US
DIRECTORY OF INTERNATIONAL MAIL. irreg. U.S. Postal Service, Public and Communications Department, Washington, DC 20260 TEL 202-245-4000. (Subscr. to: Supt. of Documents, Washington, DC 20402)

383 US
DIRECTORY OF MAIL DROPS IN THE UNITED STATES AND CANADA. 1976. biennial. $9.95. Loompanics Unlimited, Box 1197, Port Townsend, WA 98368. Ed. Michael Hoy. adv. bk. rev. circ. 2,500. (also avail. in microfiche)

383 US
DOMESTIC MAIL MANUAL. a. $28. U.S. Postal Service, Washington, DC 20260 TEL 202-245-4000. (Subscr. to: Supt. of Documents, Washington, DC 20402)

383 GW ISSN 0435-7329
GERMANY (FEDERAL REPUBLIC, 1949-). BUNDESMINISTERIUM FUER DAS POST- UND FERNMELDEWESEN. JAHRESRECHNUNG, NACHWEISUNG UEBER DIE EINNAHMEN UND AUSGABEN DER DEUTSCHEN BUNDESPOST. 1959. a. Bundesministerium fuer das Post-und Fernmeldewesen, Adenauerallee 81, 5300 Bonn, W. Germany (B.R.D.) circ. controlled.
Continues: Germany (Federal Republic). Bundesministerium fuer das Post- und Fernmeldewesen. Jahresnachweisung ueber die Einnahmen und Ausgaben der Deutschen Bundespost.

383 IS ISSN 0075-1308
ISRAEL. MINISTRY OF COMMUNICATIONS. STATISTICS/ISRAEL. MISRAD HA-TIKSHORET. STATISTIKAH. (Editions in English and Hebrew) 1955. a. Ministry of Communications, Jaffa Rd. 23, Jerusalem, Israel. circ. 300.

383 MF
MAURITIUS. POSTS AND TELEGRAPHS DEPARTMENT. ANNUAL REPORT. (Text in English) a., latest 1978/79. Government Printing Office, Elizabeth II Ave., Port Louis, Mauritius.

383 US ISSN 0731-9185
NATIONAL FIVE DIGIT ZIP CODE AND POST OFFICE DIRECTORY. a. $9. U.S. Postal Service, Washington, DC 20260 TEL 202-245-4000. (Orders to: Supt. of Documents, Washington, DC 20402)
Formerly: National Zip Code and Post Office Directory (ISSN 0191-6971); Formed by the 1979 merger of: National Zip Code Directory (ISSN 0160-6476) & Directory of Post Offices.

P T T BEDRIJF; denkbeelden, methoden, onderzoekingen. (Staatsbedrijf der Posterijen Telegrafie en Telefonie) see COMMUNICATIONS — Telephone And Telegraph

383 336 AU
POSTBUECHL. a. free. Steiger-Werbung Verlags- und Werbegesellschaft mbH, Hermanngasse 25, A-1070 Vienna, Austria. circ. 2,500,000.

SCOTTISH POSTMARK GROUP. HANDBOOK. see PHILATELY

383 UN
UNION POSTALE UNIVERSELLE. ACTES. 1874. quinquennial, 19th, Hamburg, 1984. 168 Fr. ‡ Universal Postal Union - Union Postale Universelle, Welpoststrasse 4, CH-3000 Berne 15, Switzerland.
Formerly: Universal Postal Union. Documents du Congres (ISSN 0083-3878)

383 UN ISSN 0085-7602
UNION POSTALE UNIVERSELLE. STATISTIQUE DES SERVICES POSTAUX. (Text in French) 1966. a., latest 1984. 75 Fr. ‡ Universal Postal Union - Union Postale Universelle, Welpoststrasse 4, CH-3000 Berne 15, Switzerland. circ. 750.

383.2 US
U.S. POSTAL SERVICE. REVENUE AND COST ANALYSIS REPORT. 1970/71. a. U.S. Postal Service, Rates and Classification Department, Washington, DC 20260. TEL 202-245-4000. stat.
Formerly: U.S. Postal Service. Support Group. Revenue and Cost Analysis (ISSN 0092-2765)

383 ZA
ZAMBIA. POSTS AND TELECOMMUNICATIONS CORPORATION. ANNUAL REPORT. 1963/64. a. 50 n. Government Printer, P.O. Box 136, Lusaka, Zambia.
Formerly (until 1974/75): Zambia. General Post Office. Annual Report of the Postmaster-General (ISSN 0084-5019)

383 384.6 US
ZIP/AREA CODE DIRECTORY. 1979. irreg., latest 1985. $3.50. Pilot Books, 103 Cooper St., Babylon, NY 11702. TEL 516-422-2225.

COMMUNICATIONS — Radio And Television

384 GW ISSN 0066-5746
A R D - JAHRBUCH. 1969. a. DM.14.80. Hans-Bredow-Institut, Heimhuder Str. 21, 2000 Hamburg 13, W. Germany (B.R.D.) Ed. Hans Bausch. circ. 13,000.

621.38 US ISSN 0190-3632
A R R L REPEATER DIRECTORY. a. $3. American Radio Relay League, Inc., 225 Main St., Newington, CT 06111. Ed. Bart J. Jahnke. circ. 55,000.

A V - BRANCHE (YEAR) see COMMUNICATIONS

791.4 PR
ALBUM DE RECUERDOS. a. Consolidated Publishers Inc., Avda. Pinero 1000, Rio Piedras, Puerto Rico (Orders to: Apdo. 71384, San Juan, PR 00936) adv. circ. 50,000.

384.54 FR ISSN 0066-247X
ANNUAIRE BIOGRAPHIQUE DU CINEMA ET DE LA TELEVISION EN FRANCE ET EN BELGIQUE.* 1953/54. irreg. Contact-Editions, 5 rue Robert-Estienne, Paris 8e, France.

384.554 FR ISSN 0066-3565
ANNUAIRE O.G.M. (Partie 1: Radio-Television-HiFi-Electronique-Electroacoustique; Partie 2: Musique) a. 330 F. per vol. (Office General de la Musique) Editions Louis Johanet, 68 rue Boursault, 75017 Paris, France. adv.

384 JA
ANNUAL WORLDWIDE T V SURVEY. (Text in English) 1964. a. $45. Movie TV Marketing, Box 30, Central Post Office, Tokyo 100-91, Japan. Ed. William J. Ireton. adv. circ. 100,000.

621.384 621.385 IT
ANNUARIO AUDIO & VIDEO. 1977. a. L.20000. Media Edizioni srl., Via Gaffurio 4, 20124 Milan, Italy. Ed. Edoardo Fleischner. adv. circ. 40,000.

AUSTRALIAN FILM, TELEVISION AND RADIO SCHOOL. ANNUAL REPORT. see COMMUNICATIONS

384.554 370 AT ISSN 0313-8461
AUSTRALIAN FILM, TELEVISION AND RADIO SCHOOL HANDBOOK. 1978. a. free. Australian Film, Television and Radio School, P.O. Box 126, North Ryde, N.S.W. 2113, Australia. Ed. Sandy George. circ. 2,000. (back issues avail.)
Formerly: Australian Film and Television School Handbook.

384 UK ISSN 0068-1377
B B C ANNUAL REPORT AND HANDBOOK. 1928. a. British Broadcasting Corp., 35 Marylebone High St., London W1M 4AA, England. index.

384.5 011 US ISSN 0742-4914
B C T V: BIBLIOGRAPHY ON CABLE TELEVISION. 1975. a. (plus bi-m updates) $35. Communications Institute, Communications Library, 1535 Francisco St., Lockbox 5891, San Francisco, CA 94101-5891. TEL 415-626-5050. index. cum.index: 1975-1985. (looseleaf format; back issues avail.)

BACKSTAGE T V FILM/TAPE & SYNDICATION DIRECTORY. see MOTION PICTURES

384.12 GW ISSN 0067-4966
BEITRAEGE ZUM RUNDFUNKRECHT. 1965. irreg., vol.35, 1986. price varies. (Arbeitsgemeinschaft der Oeffentlich-rechtlichen Rundfunkanstalten der Bundesrepublik Deutschland) Alfred Metzner Verlag, Zeppelinallee 43, D-6000 Frankfurt/Main 97, W. Germany (B.R.D.)

384.5 001.6 621.381 UK
BERNARDS AND BABANI PRESS RADIO & ELECTRONICS & COMPUTER BOOKS. 1971. irreg., no.5, 1972. Bernard Babani (Publishing) Ltd., The Grampians, Shepherds Bush Rd., London W6 7NF, England.
Formerly: Bernards and Babani Press Radio and Electronics Books.

384.55 YU
BIT INTERNATIONAL; television today. (Text in Croatian and English) 1968. irreg. $7. Galerije Grada Zagreba, Katarinin trg 2, 41000 Zagreb, Yugoslavia. Ed. Bozo Bek. illus. circ. 5,000.

621.38 UK
BLUE BOOK OF BRITISH BROADCASTING. 1974. a. £18. Tellex Monitors Ltd., 47 Gray's Inn Rd., London WC1X 8PR, England. Ed. Zabelle Stenton. adv. circ. 1,500.

621.38 US
BROADCAST ENGINEERING SPEC BOOK. (Special 13th issue of Broadcast Engineering) 1981. a. $20 free to qualified personnel. Intertec Publishing Corp., Box 12901, Overland Park, KS 66212. TEL 913-888-4664. Ed. Jerry Whitaker. circ. 35,327. (back issues avail.)

384 UK
BROADCAST YEARBOOK AND DIARY.* 1961. a. £25.50. International Thomson Publishing Ltd., 100 Avenue Rd.t., London NW3 3TP, England. adv. circ. 4,000.

791.4 US ISSN 0732-7196
BROADCASTING/CABLECASTING YEARBOOK. 1935. a. $85. Broadcasting Publications, Inc., 1735 DeSales St., Washington, DC 20036. TEL 202-638-1022. adv. circ. 19,373. (also avail. in microfilm)
Formerly: Broadcasting/Cable Yearbook (ISSN 0277-3678); Formed by the merger of: Broadcasting Cable Sourcebook (ISSN 0097-8132) & Broadcasting Yearbook (ISSN 0068-2713)

384.5 US
BUSINESS RADIO BUYERS GUIDE. 1971. a. $9.50. Cardiff Publishing Company, 6530 S. Yosemite, Englewood, CO 80111. TEL 303-694-1522. Ed. Terry Sweeney. adv. circ. 20,466. (reprint service avail. from UMI)

384.55 UK
C.A.T.S. REPORTS. 1973. irreg. £20. Centre for Advanced T V Studies, 42 Theobald's Rd., London WC18 XNW, England. Ed. John Hopkins. adv. bk. rev. circ. 600. (back issues avail.)
Supersedes (as of vol.8, 1980): J C A T S (ISSN 0308-6801)

C I N C O M: COURSES IN COMMUNICATIONS. (Communications Institute) see EDUCATION — Guides To Schools And Colleges

C.I.R.M. (Centro Internazionale Radio-Medico) see MEDICAL SCIENCES

C T V D: CINEMA - TV - DIGEST; a quarterly review of the serious, foreign-language cinema-TV-press. see MOTION PICTURES

791 US ISSN 0193-3639
CABLE AND STATION COVERAGE ATLAS AND 35-MILE ZONE MAPS. 1966. a. $205. Television Digest, Inc., 1836 Jefferson Place, N.W., Washington, DC 20036. TEL 202-872-9200. Ed. Albert Warren. index.
Formerly: C A T V and Station Coverage Atlas and 35-Mile Zone Maps (ISSN 0068-4694)

384.554 US ISSN 0736-8143
CABLE T V FINANCIAL DATABOOK; sourcebook for all key financial data on cable T V. 1980. a. $90. Paul Kagan Associates, Inc., 126 Clock Tower Place, Carmel, CA 93923. TEL 408-624-1536. Ed. Alice J. Schneider. adv. charts. stat. (back issues avail.)

384.55 US ISSN 0363-1915
CABLEFILE; the standard reference for the cable television industry. 1976. a. $129.95. International Thomson Communications Inc. (Subsidiary of: International Thomson Business Press) 600 Grant St., Ste. 600, Denver, CO 80217 TEL 303-860-0111. (Subscr. addr.: Box 5208, T. A., Denver. CO 80217) Ed. Kate Hampford. adv. stat. circ. 4,396.

384 CN
CANADA. CANADIAN RADIO-TELEVISION AND TELECOMMUNICATIONS COMMISSION. ANNUAL REPORT. (Editions in English and French) 1968/69. a. free. Canadian Radio-Television and Telecommunications Commission, Information Services, Ottawa, Ont. K1A ON2, Canada. TEL 613-997-0313. circ. 5,000.
Formerly: Canada. Radio-Television Commission. Annual Report (ISSN 0068-9556)

621.38 CN
CANADIAN AMATEUR ADVANCED STUDY GUIDE. 1976. a. Can.$15. C.A.R.F. Publications Ltd., Box 356, Kingston, Ont. K7L 4W2, Canada. TEL 613-544-6161. circ. 10,000.

621.38 CN
CANADIAN AMATEUR CERTIFICATE STUDY GUIDE. 1976. a. Can.$15. C.A.R.F. Publications Ltd., Box 356, Kingston, Ont. K7L 4W2, Canada. TEL 613-544-6161. circ. 15,000.

621.38 CN
CANADIAN AMATEUR RADIO REGULATIONS HANDBOOK. 1970. a. Can.$9.50. ‡ C.A.R.F. Publications Ltd., Box 356, Kingston, Ont. K7L 4W2, Canada. TEL 613-544-6161. Ed. A.P. Stark. circ. 10,000.

384 UK
CASE STUDIES ON BROADCASTING SYSTEMS. irreg. price varies. Routledge & Kegan Paul PLC, 11 New Fetter Lane, London EC4P 4EE, England (U.S. address: 9 Park St., Boston, MA 02108)

791 BE ISSN 0528-4759
CENTRE INTERNATIONAL DE LIAISON DES ECOLES DE CINEMA ET DE TELEVISION. BULLETIN D'INFORMATIONS. 1978. irreg. free. International Liaison Centre for Cinema and Television Schools - Centre International de Liaison des Ecoles de Cinema et de Television (CILECT), c/o Raymond Ravar, 8 rue Theresienne, B-1000 Brussels, Belgium. Ed. Henry Verhasset. bk. rev. circ. controlled.

CINEGUIA; annuario espanol del espectaculo y audiovisuales. see MOTION PICTURES

384.54 UK
COMMONWEALTH BROADCASTING ASSOCIATION. HANDBOOK. 1976. biennial. Commonwealth Broadcasting Association, Broadcasting House, London W1A 1AA, England.

COMMUNICATIONS — RADIO AND TELEVISION

621.38 UK ISSN 0305-3601
COMMUNICATION & BROADCASTING; information, practice, technique. (Text in English; summaries in French, German and Spanish) 1974. irreg. Marconi Co. Ltd., Marconi House, Chelmsford, Essex CM1 1PL, England. Ed. L. Simmonds. adv. charts. illus. index. circ. 7,500. (reprint service avail. from UMI) Indexed: Curr.Cont. Sci.Abstr.
 Formed by the merger of: Point to Point Communication (ISSN 0032-2334) & Sound and Vision (ISSN 0038-1829)
 Broadcast engineering

621.38 GW
COMMUNICATION RESEARCH AND BROADCASTING. (Text in English) 1979. irreg., vol.7, 1986) price varies. (Internationales Zentralinstitut fuer das Jugend- und Bildungsfernsehen) K. G. Saur Verlag KG, Peossenbacherstr. 2, 8000 Munich 71, W. Germany (B.R.D.) (U.S. and Canadian subscr. to: K.G. Saur Inc., 175 Fifth Ave., New York, N.Y. 10010) (reprint service avail. from UMI, ISI)

COMMUNICATOR (INDIANAPOLIS); a TV technicians newsletter. see *ELECTRICITY AND ELECTRICAL ENGINEERING*

384 CN ISSN 0708-0131
CONSEIL DE PRESSE DU QUEBEC. RAPPORT ANNUEL. (Text in English, French) 1977. a. free. Conseil de Presse du Quebec, 55 1/2, rue Saint Louis, Quebec, Canada. TEL 418-692-3008. circ. 2, 500.

384 GW ISSN 0084-9790
DEUTSCHLANDFUNK. JAHRBUCH. 1962. biennial. Deutschlandfunk, Raderbergguertel 40, 5000 Cologne 51, W. Germany (B.R.D.)

791.4 US ISSN 0736-7759
DIRECTORY OF FREE PROGRAMS, PERFORMING TALENT AND ATTRACTIONS. 1983. a. $75. Box 1288, Champlain, NY 12919-1288. Eds. Robert D. and Eileen E. Shelley. bk. rev. circ. 500,273.

621.38 UK ISSN 0262-9771
DIRECTORY OF INTERNATIONAL BROADCASTING. 1978. a. £30. B.S.O. Publications Ltd., 3/5 St. John St., London EC1M 4AE, England. Ed. M. Popiel, J. Stannard. circ. 1, 000.

384 371 US ISSN 0731-0331
DIRECTORY OF RELIGIOUS BROADCASTING. 1972. a. $49.95. National Religious Broadcasters, Inc., CN 1926, Morristown, NJ 07960. TEL 201-428-5400. Ed. Ben Armstrong. index. circ. 2,500.

384.54 380 US
DUNCAN'S RADIO MARKET GUIDE. a. $175. Duncan's American Radio Inc., Box 2966, Kalamazoo, MI 49003. TEL 616-342-1356. Ed. James H. Duncan.

384 SZ
E B U MONOGRAPHS, LEGAL AND ADMINISTRATIVE SERIES. (Editions in English and French) 1964. irreg. price varies. European Broadcasting Union, Ancienne Route 17A, Case Postale 67, CH-1218 Grand-Saconnex/Geneva, Switzerland.

384 SZ
E B U SEMINARS FOR PRODUCERS AND DIRECTORS OF EDUCATIONAL TELEVISION FOR SCHOOLS AND ADULTS. (Editions in English and French) 1962. a. 5 Fr. European Broadcasting Union, Ancienne Postale 17A, Case Postale 67, CH-1218 Grand-Saconnex/Geneva, Switzerland.

384 SZ
E B U WORKSHOPS FOR PRODUCERS AND DIRECTORS OF TELEVISION PROGRAMMES FOR CHILDREN AND YOUNG PEOPLE. (Editions in English and French) 1968. biennial. 8 Fr. European Broadcasting Union, Ancienne Route 17A, Case Postale 67, CH-1218 Grand Saconnex/Geneva, Switzerland.

384.55 PE
EMPRESA NACIONAL DE TELECOMMUNICACIONES DEL PERU. MEMORIA ANUAL. 1970. a. free. ENTEL Peru S.A., Las Begonias 475, San Isidro 27, Lima, Peru. illus. stat. circ. 3,000. (back issues avail.)

791.4 070.5 US ISSN 0739-1897
ENTERTAINMENT, PUBLISHING AND THE ARTS HANDBOOK. a. $45. Clark Boardman Company, Ltd., 435 Hudson St., New York, NY 10014. Eds. Michael Meyer, John David Viera.

EQUIPMENT DIRECTORY OF AUDIO-VISUAL, COMPUTER AND VIDEO PRODUCTS. see *BUSINESS AND ECONOMICS — Trade And Industrial Directories*

384.5 700 CN
FACE TO FACE WITH TALENT. 1970. biennial. Can.$40. Alliance of Canadian Cinema, Television and Radio Artists, 2239 Yonge St., Toronto, Ont. M4S 2B5, Canada. TEL 416-489-1311. Ed. Doug Coupar. circ. 2,500.

791.4 778.5 US
FILM ANGELS. a. $150. Leo Shull Publications, 1501 Broadway, New York, NY 10036. TEL 212-354-7600.

384 UK
FILMS ON VIDEO. 1982. a. £2.25. Argus Specialist Publications Ltd., 1 Golden Sq., London W1, England. Ed. Aiden Steer. adv. circ. 25,000.

384.12 FI
FINNISH BROADCASTING COMPANY. PLANNING AND RESEARCH DEPARTMENT. RESEARCH REPORTS. (Text in English) irreg. free. Finnish Broadcasting Company, Section for Long-Range Planning, Kesakatu 2, 00260 Helsinki 26, Finland. Ed. Matti Oksanen. circ. 400.
 Formerly: Finnish Broadcasting Company. Section for Long-Range Planning. Research Reports (ISSN 0084-4225)

621.384 US
FOREIGN CALLBOOK. 1920. a. $21 includes update Service Editions. Radio Amateur Callbook, Inc., 925 Sherwood Drive, Lake Bluff, IL 60044. TEL 312-234-6600. adv.
 Formerly: Foreign Radio Amateur Callbook Magazine (ISSN 0015-7260)
 Amateur

GADNEY'S GUIDE TO INTERNATIONAL CONTESTS, FESTIVALS & GRANTS IN FILM & VIDEO, PHOTOGRAPHY, TV-RADIO BROADCASTING, WRITING, POETRY, PLAYWRITING & JOURNALISM. see *MOTION PICTURES*

621.384 DK
GRUNDTVIG STUDIER. 1948. a. Kr.71. Grundtvig-Selskabet af 8. September 1947, c/o Danske Boghendleres Anstalt, Siljangade 6, 2300 Copenhagen S, Denmark (Subscr. to: Vartov, Farvergade 27, DK-1463 Copenhagen K, Denmark) Ed. Gustav Albeck. bk. rev. Indexed: M.L.A.

HOLLYWOOD REPORTER STUDIO BLU-BOOK DIRECTORY. see *MOTION PICTURES*

621.38 DK ISSN 0109-9140
HOMESERVICE STATIONS OUTSIDE THE TROPICAL BANDS. 1984. a. Kr.25. Danish Shortwave Clubs International, Tavleager 31, 2670 Greve Strand, Denmark.

384 UK ISSN 0308-423X
I B A TECHNICAL REVIEW. 1972. irreg., no.21, 1982. Independent Broadcasting Authority, 70 Brompton Rd., London SW3 1EY, England. charts. illus. Indexed: Sci.Abstr.

384.554
I N T V CENSUS. a. (Association of Independent Television Stations, Inc.) View Communications Corp., 80 Fifth Ave., New York, NY 10011. TEL 212-807-9595. Ed. William H. Dunlap. adv.

384.54 US ISSN 0093-1926
I.R.C.A. FOREIGN LOG. 1972. a. price varies. ‡ International Radio Club of America, Box 21074, Seattle, WA 98111. Ed. Bruce Portzer. circ. 300.

791.4 US ISSN 0074-7564
I R T S GOLD MEDAL ANNUAL. 1964. a. membership. International Radio and Television Society, Inc., 420 Lexington Ave., New York, NY 10017. TEL 212-867-6650. adv.
 Formerly: I R T S Gold Medal Journal.

384.54 UK ISSN 0309-0175
INDEPENDENT BROADCASTING AUTHORITY. ANNUAL REPORT AND ACCOUNTS. 1954/1955. a. £2.50. Independent Broadcasting Authority, 70 Brompton Rd., London SW3 1EY, England (Dist. by: H.M.S.O., 49 High Holborn, London WC1V 6HB, England)

621.38 UK ISSN 0266-1233
INFORMATION FROM THE VOLUNTEER CENTRE MEDIA PROJECT. 1977. a. £12.50. Volunteer Centre, Media Project, 29 Lower King's Rd., Berkhamsted, Herts HP4 2AB, England. Ed. Mike Hodgkinson. circ. 650.

384 US
INTERNATIONAL AND COMPARATIVE BROADCASTING. 1976. irreg. price varies. Temple University Press, Philadelphia, PA 19122. TEL 215-787-8787. Ed. John Lent.

384 SZ
INTERNATIONAL FORUM OF LIGHT MUSIC IN RADIO. (Editions in English and French) 1973. biennial. 5 Fr. European Broadcasting Union, Ancienne Route 17A, Case Postale 67, CH-1218 Grand-SacconnexGeneva, Switzerland.

INTERNATIONAL INDEX TO TELEVISION PERIODICALS. see *COMMUNICATIONS — Abstracting, Bibliographies, Statistics*

384.55 UK
INTERNATIONAL T V & VIDEO GUIDE. 1982. a. $13.95. Tantivy Press, 136-148 Tooley St., London SE1 2TT, England (Dist. in U.S. by: New York Zoetrope Inc., 838 Broadway, New York, NY 10003) Ed. Richard Paterson. adv. bk. rev.

621.385 US ISSN 0275-0473
INTERNATIONAL TELECOMMUNICATIONS ENERGY CONFERENCE. PROCEEDINGS. Short titles: I N T E L E C. (Published by other organizations when held outside of U.S.) 1978. a. (I E E E, Communications Society) Institute of Electrical and Electronics Engineers, Inc., 345 E. 47th St., New York, NY 10017. TEL 212-705-7900.
 Formerly: International Telephone Energy Conference. Proceedings.

384.55 US
INTERNATIONAL TELEVISION & VIDEO ALMANAC; reference tool of the television and home video industries. 1956. a. $55. Quigley Publishing Co., 159 W. 53 St., New York, NY 10019. TEL 212-247-3100. Ed. Richard Gertner.
 Formerly: International Television Almanac (ISSN 0539-0761)

791 SZ ISSN 0082-0776
INTERNATIONAL TELEVISION SYMPOSIUM AND TECHNICAL EXHIBITION, MONTREUX. (PAPERS) 1961. biennial. 150 Fr. ‡ International Television Symposium "System Record", Case Postale 97, 1820 Montreaux, Switzerland. Ed.Bd. adv. circ. 4,000.

621.38 BE ISSN 0074-9516
INTERNATIONAL UNION OF RADIO SCIENCE. PROCEEDINGS OF GENERAL ASSEMBLIES. (Text in English and French) 1928. triennial, 21st, 1984, Florence, Italy. $10. International Union of Radio Science, c/o J. Van Bladel, Sec. Gen., Ave. A. Lancaster 32, B-1180 Brussels, Belgium. circ. 1, 200.
 Formerly: International Scientific Radio Union. Proceedings of General Assemblies.

384 CN
INTERNATIONAL VIDEO EXCHANGE DIRECTORY. 1972. biennial. Can.$2. Satellite Video Exchange Society, 1160 Hamilton St., Vancouver, B.C. V6B 2S2, Canada. TEL 604-688-4336. Ed. Shawn Prews. bk. rev. bibl. circ. 5,000.
 Formerly: Video Exchange Directory.

COMMUNICATIONS — RADIO AND TELEVISION

384 621.38 GW ISSN 0535-4358
INTERNATIONALES HANDBUCH FUER RUNDFUNK UND FERNSEHEN. 1957. biennial. DM.89. Hans-Bredow-Institut, Heimhuder Str. 21, 2000 Hamburg 13, W. Germany (B.R.D.) adv. circ. 2,500.

622 UR ISSN 0202-0769
ITOGI NAUKI I TEKHNIKI: RADIOTEKHNIKA. irreg., vol.38, 1987. price varies. Vsesoyuznyi Institut Nauchno-Tekhnicheskoi Informatsii (VINITI), Ul. Baltiiskaya 14, Moscow A-219, Russian S.F.S.R., U.S.S.R. (Subscr. to: Mezhdunarodnaya Kniga, Dimitrova ul. 39, 113095 Moscow, Russian S.F.S.R., U.S.S.R.)

KEY ABSTRACTS - ANTENNAS & PROPAGATION. see *COMMUNICATIONS — Abstracting, Bibliographies, Statistics*

384.55 UK
LOOK-IN TELEVISION ANNUAL. a. £3.45. Independent Television Books Ltd., 247 Tottenham Court Rd., London W1P 0AU, England. Ed. Colin Shelbourn.

384.5 US
LOOK - LISTEN PROJECT REPORT. 1953. a. $6.50. National Telemedia Council, Inc., 120 E. Wilson St., Madison, WI 53703. TEL 608-257-7712. Ed. Marieli Rowe. circ. 400.
  Formerly: Look - Listen Opinion Poll Report.

384.5 MW
MALAWI BROADCASTING CORPORATION. ANNUAL REPORT AND STATEMENT OF ACCOUNTS. (Text in English) a. Malawi Broadcasting Corporation, Box 30133, Chichiri, Blantyre 3, Malawi.

621.38 II
MASS MEDIA IN INDIA. (Text in English) 1978. a. Rs.15. Ministry of Information and Broadcasting, Publications Division, Patiala House, Tilak Marg, New Delhi 110001, India.

384.54 US
MOBILE COMMUNICATIONS HANDBOOK. 1977. a. $59.95. R C R Pubications, 1725 Marion St., Denver, CO 80218. Ed. Carol A. Martin. adv. index. circ. 6,000.
  Formerly (until 1986): Mobile Radio Handbook.

384 AT
MORGAN INDEX ON TV AND RADIO. 1973. a. Aus.$6.50. Roy Morgan Research Centre Pty. Ltd., Box 2282U, Melbourne, Vic. 3001, Australia.

MOVIE/T V MARKETING GLOBAL MOTION PICTURE YEAR BOOK. see *MOTION PICTURES*

621.38 JA ISSN 0077-2631
N H K TECHNICAL MONOGRAPH. (Nippon Hoso Kyokai) (Text in English) 1963. a. exchange basis. Japan Broadcasting Corp. NHK, Science & Technical Research Laboratories, Information Services & Patents Division, 1-10-11 Kinuta, Setagaya-ku, Tokyo 157, Japan. circ. 1,100. Indexed: Chem.Abstr. Sci.Abstr. Elec.Eng.Abstr. JCT.
  Broadcast engineering

621.38 NZ ISSN 0110-5337
N.Z.A.R.T. AMATEUR RADIO CALLBOOK. 1928. a. NZ.$49.50 includes monthly Break-In. ‡ New Zealand Association of Radio Transmitters, Inc., P.O. Box 1733, Christchurch, New Zealand. Ed. C.R. Crawford. adv. bk. rev. circ. 4,000.

NEW YORK CASTING/SURVIVAL GUIDE; and datebook. see *THEATER*

384.5 US
NIELSEN REPORT ON TELEVISION. 1955. a. free. (Media Research Group) A. C. Nielsen Co., Nielsen Plaza, Northbrook, IL 60062. Ed. L. Frerk. circ. 23,000. (also avail. in microform)

OFFICE DES COMMUNICATIONS SOCIALES, MONTREAL. CAHIERS D'ETUDES ET DE RECHERCHES. see *COMMUNICATIONS*

621.38 US
OFFICIAL REGISTRY OF C B OPERATORS.* 1976. a. $5. Today Publications and News Service, Inc., 621 National Press Bldg., Washington, DC 20045. index.

384.554 380 US ISSN 0890-782X
OFFICIAL VIDEO DIRECTORY & BUYER'S GUIDE. 1987. a. $50. Palm Springs Media, Inc., Box 2740, Palm Springs, CA 92263. TEL 619-322-3050. Ed. Steve Tolin. adv. circ. 6,000.

OFFICIAL VIDEO SOFTWARE DIRECTORY. see *COMMUNICATIONS — Computer Applications*

384.554 770 GR
PHOTO, CINE, VIDEO BUYER'S GUIDE. (Text in Greek) 1983. biennial. Moressopulos & Associates, P.O. Box 30564, GR-100 33 Athens, Greece. Ed. Thomas Ginoudes. adv. circ. 12,000.

384.5 US
PHOTOFACT/COMPUTERFACTS ANNUAL INDEX. 1946. a., (with q. supplements) $3. Howard W. Sams & Co. Inc., 4300 W. 62nd St., Indianapolis, IN 46268. TEL 800-428-7267. adv. index. cum.index. circ. controlled.
  Formerly: Photofact Annual Index (ISSN 5006)

621.384 UR
POLUTEHNILINE INSTITUUT TALLINN. ISSLEDOVANIYA PO PRIKLADNOI KVANTOVOI ELEKTRONIKE. (Subseries of its Toimetised) (Text in Russian; summaries in English or German) irreg. price varies. Polutehniline Instituut Tallinn, Ehitajate tee 5, Tallinn, Estonian S.S.R., U.S.S.R.

PRESS RADIO AND T.V. GUIDE. see *JOURNALISM*

PRODUCER'S MASTERGUIDE; the international production manual for motion pictures, television, commercials, cable and videotape industries in the United States, Canada, the United Kingdom, Ireland, Bermuda and the Caribbean Islands. see *MOTION PICTURES*

621.38 UK ISSN 0266-2256
PROFESSIONAL VIDEO INTERNATIONAL YEARBOOK. 1977. a. £14. Link House Magazines Ltd., Link House, Dingwall Avenue, Croydon CR9 2TA, England. Ed. Sally Baker. adv. bk. rev. tr.lit. index. circ. 3,000. (back issues avail.)
  Formerly: International Video Yearbook (ISSN 0261-1910)

621.38 UK
R S G B AMATEUR RADIO CALL BOOK. 1951. a. Radio Society of Great Britain, Lambda House, Cranborne Rd., Potters Bar, Herts EN6 3JE, England. Ed. C.F. Drake. adv. circ. 15,000.

384.5 US
R T T Y JOURNAL. BEGINNERS HANDBOOK. 1975. irreg. $8 per no. R T T Y Journal, 9085 La Casita Ave., Fountain Valley, CA 92708. TEL 714-847-5050. Ed. Dale S. Sinner. adv. bk. rev. circ. 3,500.

384 AT
RADIO (YEAR) 1959. a. free. Federation of Australian Radio Broadcasters, Research and Promotion Division, Radio Marketing Bureau, 225 Miller St., North Sydney, N.S.W. 2060, Australia. Ed. R. Logie. circ. 12,000.
  Formerly: Radio Facts and Figures.

384.54 UK ISSN 0260-2423
RADIO ADVERTISERS' GUIDE.* 1980. irreg. £25. Hamilton House, Grooms Lane, Creaton, Northampton NN6 8NS, England. illus.

621.384 US ISSN 0079-9440
RADIO AMATEUR'S HANDBOOK. (Editions in English and Spanish) 1926. a. $27 hardcover; $18 paper. ‡ American Radio Relay League, Inc., 225 Main St., Newington, CT 06111. Ed. Mark Wilson. illus. index. circ. 60,000.

621.384 US ISSN 0079-9467
RADIO HANDBOOK. 1935. irreg. 23rd edt., 1986. $29.95. (Editors and Engineers Ltd.) Howard W. Sams & Co., Inc., 4300 W. 62nd St., Indianapolis, IN 46268. TEL 317-298-5400. Ed. William I. Orr.

629.135 US
RADIO TECHNICAL COMMISSION FOR AERONAUTICS. PROCEEDINGS OF THE ANNUAL ASSEMBLY MEETING. 1955. a. $25. Radio Technical Commission for Aeronautics, Suite 500, 1425 K St., N.W., Washington, DC 20005. Ed. Jodie Alcorn. circ. 750. (also avail. in microform)

621.38 384.5 US
REFERENCE DATA FOR ENGINEERS; radio, electronics, computer and communications. irreg. $69.95. Howard W. Sams & Co., Inc., 4300 West 62nd St., Indianapolis, IN 46268. TEL 317-298-5400.
  Formerly: Reference Data for Radio Engineers.

RESEARCH LABORATORIES REVIEW OF ACTIVITIES. see *COMMUNICATIONS*

S W L. (Shortwave Listener) see *CLUBS*

384 SZ
SCHWEIZERISCHE RADIO- UND FERNSEHGESELLSCHAFT. JAHRBUCH. (Text and summaries in French, German) 1931. a. free. Schweizerische Radio- und Fernsehgesellschaft, P.O. Box, CH-3000 Berne 15, Switzerland. (back issues avail.)

SCREEN INTERNATIONAL FILM AND T.V. YEARBOOK. see *MOTION PICTURES*

791.45 US
SERIES, SERIALS, AND PACKAGES. 1949. a. $249. National Video Clearinghouse, Inc., Broadcast Information Bureau, 100 Lafayette Dr., Syosset, NY 11791. TEL 516-496-3355. Ed. Avra Leah Fliegelman. adv. index.
  Formerly: T V Film Source Book. Series, Serials and Packages (ISSN 0082-1373)

384.54 SA
SOUTH AFRICAN BROADCASTING CORPORATION. ANNUAL REPORT. (Text in Afrikaans and English) a. South African Broadcasting Corporation, POB 8606, Johannesburg, South Africa. Ed. Des Celliers.

384.55 621.389 US
STEREO REVIEW'S VIDEO BUYERS GUIDE. 1984. a. $3.95 per no. C B S Magazines, Stereo Review Department, 1515 Broadway, New York, NY 10036. TEL 212-719-6000. Ed. William Burton. adv.

301.16 JA
STUDIES OF BROADCASTING; an international annual of broadcasting science. (Text in English) 1963-1970; resumed 1971. a. exchange basis. Japan Broadcasting Corp., Broadcasting Culture Research Institute, Theoretical Research Center - Nippon Hoso Kyokai, 2-1-1 Atago, Minato-ku, Tokyo 105, Japan. bk. rev. illus. circ. 1,000.

STUDIO SOUND'S PRO-AUDIO DIRECTORY. see *SOUND RECORDING AND REPRODUCTION*

791 UK
T V DETECTIVES ANNUAL. 1979. a. £1.95. Brown Watson Ltd., 44 Hill St., London W1X 84B, England.

791 371.3 US ISSN 0082-1357
T V FEATURE FILM SOURCE BOOK. 1949. a. (includes 2 supplements) $299. National Video Clearinghouse, Inc., Broadcast Information Bureau, 100 Lafayette Dr., Syosset, NY 11791. TEL 516-496-3355. Ed. Avra Leah Fliegelman. adv. index.

791.45 CN ISSN 0082-1365
T V - FILM FILEBOOK; information on Canadian TV-film industry. 1960. a. Can.$4. 2533 Gerrard St. E., Scarborough, Ont., Canada. Ed. A.C. Benson. adv. circ. 2,500.

TABS. see *THEATER*

791 US ISSN 0732-8648
TELEVISION AND CABLE FACTBOOK. (Vol. 1. Stations; Vol. 2. Cable & Services) 1944. a. $235. Television Digest, Inc., 1836 Jefferson Place, N.W., Washington, DC 20036. TEL 202-872-9200. Ed. Albert Warren. index. circ. 6,264.
  Formerly: Television Factbook (ISSN 0082-268X)

384.55 UK ISSN 0262-6470
TELEVISION & RADIO. 1963. a. £5.90. Independent Broadcasting Authority, 70 Brompton Rd., London SW3 1EY, England (Dist. by: Independent Television Publications, 247 Tottenham Court Rd., London W1P 0AU, England) Ed. Michael Melaniphy.
  Former titles: Guide to Independent Television and Independent Local Radio; I T V Guide to Independent Television (ISSN 0536-2121)

COMMUNICATIONS — TELEPHONE AND TELEGRAPH

384.55   US
TELEVISION CONTACTS. 1976. a. (plus m. updates) $217. Larimi Communications, Inc., 5 W. 37th St., New York, NY 10018. Ed. Bob Del Pazzo. circ. 5,000.

791.4   778.5   US
TELEVISION NETWORK MOVIES. a. $75. Television Index, Inc., 40-29 27th St., Long Island City, NY 11101. TEL 718-937-3990. Ed. Jerry Leichter.

791.4   UK
TELEVISION: THE NEW ERA; U.K. consumer electronics market. 1983. irreg. £135. Euromonitor Publications Ltd., 87-88 Turnmill St., London EC1M 5QU, England.
    Formerly: Home Entertainment (ISSN 0260-6534)

621.38   DK   ISSN 0106-1968
TROPICAL BANDS SURVEY. 1973. irreg. Kr.25. Danish Shortwave Clubs International, Tavleager 31, DK-2670 Greve Strand, Denmark. Ed. Bernhard Gruendl. circ. 1,500.

384.5   US
TUNE IN THE WORLD WITH HAM RADIO. a. $10. American Radio Relay League, Inc., 225 Main St., Newington, CT 06111.

621.38   US
U S CALLBOOK. 1920. a. $21. Radio Amateur Callbook, Inc., 925 Sherwood Dr., Lake Bluff, IL 60044. TEL 312-234-6600. adv.
    Formerly: Radio Amateur Callbook Magazine: U S Listings (ISSN 0033-7706)
    Amateur

621.384   CN   ISSN 0076-0587
UNIVERSITY OF WESTERN ONTARIO. CENTRE FOR RADIO SCIENCE. ANNUAL REPORT. 1968. a. ‡ University of Western Ontario, Centre for Radio Science, London, Ont. N6A 5C2, Canada. TEL 519-679-2111. circ. 100.

791.4   DK   ISSN 0109-7717
VIDEO. VAERD AT SE. 1985. a. Kr.64.50. Bibliotekscentralen, Telegrafvej 5, DK-2750 Ballerup, Denmark.

791.4   AT   ISSN 0729-1965
VIDEOWORLD BUYER'S GUIDE ANNUAL. 1982. a. Australian Hi-Fi Publications Pty. Ltd., Box 341, Mona Vale, N.S.W. 2103, Australia. Ed. Greg Borrowman.

791.4   UK
WHO'S WHO ON TELEVISION. biennial. £5.95. Independent Television Books Ltd., 247 Tottenham Court Rd., London W1P 0AU, England. Ed. Eddie Pedder.

COMMUNICATIONS — Telephone And Telegraph

384.1   CN
ANNUAL REVIEW AND PLANNING FRAMEWORK FOR TELECOMMUNICATION IN THE GOVERNMENT OF CANADA. (Text in English and French) 1976/77. a. free. Government Telecommunications Agency, Department of Communications, 300 Slater St., Ottawa, Ont. K1A 0C8, Canada. circ. 2,000.
    Forme titles: Annual Review and Planning Framework in the Government of Canada; Annual Review of Telecommunications in the Government of Canada.

384   AT   ISSN 0067-2181
AUSTRALIAN TELECOMMUNICATION MONOGRAPHS. 1963. irreg. Aus.$4 to non-members. Telecommunication Society of Australia, Box 4050, Melbourne, Vic. 3001, Australia. Ed. R. Keighley.

CANADIAN NATIONAL ANNUAL REPORT. see *TRANSPORTATION*

301.16   UK
DEVELOPING WORLD COMMUNICATIONS. 1986. a. $24.95. Grosvenor Press International, West Garden Place, Kendal St., London W2 2AQ, England. adv. circ. 15,000.

384.6   BA
GULF DIRECTORY. 1978. a. $53. Falcon Publishing, Box 5028, Manama, Bahrain. Ed. Marion McKechnie. adv. circ. 26,000.
    Formerly: Gulf Telephone Directory.

384.1   UN
INDICATORS FOR THE TELEGRAM RETRANSMISSION SYSTEM (TRS) - TELEX IDENTIFICATION CODES. (Text in English, French and Spanish) 1966. triennial. 84 Fr. International Telecommunication Union - Union Internationale des Telecommunications, Place des Nations, CH-1211 Geneva 20, Switzerland.
    Formerly: List of Destination Indicators and Telex Identification Codes (ISSN 0074-901X)

384.6   US
INDUSTRY GUIDE TO PRIVATE PAY TELEPHONES. a. $225. TeleStrategies Publishing, Inc., 1355 Beverly Rd., Ste. 100, McLean, VA 22101. TEL 703-734-7050.

384.6   US
INTERNATIONAL TELCOM DIRECTORY. a. Telecommunications Alert, 1 Park Ave., New York, NY 10016. TEL 212-683-3899.

384.1   UN   ISSN 0074-9044
INTERNATIONAL TELECOMMUNICATION UNION. LIST OF TELEGRAPH OFFICES OPEN FOR INTERNATIONAL SERVICE. (Preface in English, French and Spanish) 1869. quinquennial. 61 Fr. International Telecommunication Union - Union Internationale des Telecommunications, Distribution and Sales Section, Place des Nations, CH-1211 Geneva 20, Switzerland.

384.1   UN   ISSN 0085-2201
INTERNATIONAL TELECOMMUNICATION UNION. REPORT ON THE ACTIVITIES. (Editions in English, French, Spanish) 1948. a. 5 Fr. International Telecommunication Union - Union Internationale des Telecommunications, Place des Nations, CH-1211 Geneva 20, Switzerland.

INTERNATIONAL TELEPHONE DIRECTORY OF T D D USERS. see *DEAF*

384   AT   ISSN 0310-8031
INTERNATIONAL TELEX DIRECTORY. INTERNATIONAL SERVICE. 1972. a. Playfair Publishing Group, P.O. Box 52, Northbridge, N.S.W. 2063, Australia.

384.1   UN   ISSN 0074-9001
LIST OF CABLES FORMING THE WORLD SUBMARINE NETWORK. (Text in English, French and Spanish) 1877. irreg., 19th ed., 1977. 21 Fr. International Telecommunication Union - Union Internationale des Telecommunications, Place des Nations, CH-1211 Geneva 20, Switzerland.

384.1   UN   ISSN 0074-9028
LIST OF INTERNATIONAL TELEPHONE ROUTES. (Text in English, French and Spanish) 1961. a., 25th. edt., 1986. 45 Fr. International Telecommunication Union - Union Internationale des Telecommunications, Place des Nations, CH-1211 Geneva 20, Switzerland.

MARCONI'S INTERNATIONAL REGISTER; international trade and communications directory. see *BUSINESS AND ECONOMICS — Trade And Industrial Directories*

384   MF
MAURITIUS. TELECOMMUNICATIONS DEPARTMENT. ANNUAL REPORT. (Text in English) a. Government Printing Office, Elizabeth II Ave., Port Louis, Mauritius.

384.6   NG
NIGER. OFFICE DES POSTES ET TELECOMMUNICATIONS. ANNUAIRE OFFICIEL DES TELEPHONES. a. Office des Postes et Telecommunications, Niamey, Niger.

383   384   NE   ISSN 0030-8366
P T T BEDRIJF; denkbeelden, methoden, onderzoekingen. 1947. irreg. (3-4/yr.) free. Staatsbedrijf der Posterijen Telegrafie en Telefonie, Kortenaerkade 12, The Hague, Netherlands. Eds. K. Vredenbregt, C. Bakker. stat. index. cum.index every 10 vols. circ. (controlled) Indexed: Sci.Abstr.

384.6   US
PHONEFACTS. a. United States Telephone Association, 900 19th St. N.W., Ste. 800, Washington, DC 20006-2102. TEL 202-835-3100. charts. illus. stat.
    Formerly: Independent Phonefacts.

384   US
PLANNING GUIDE X-1. base vol. plus m. updates. $345. (Center for Communications Management Information) C C M I McGraw-Hill, McGraw-Hill Information Systems Co., 50 S. Franklin Tpk., Ramsey, NJ 07446. TEL 201-825-3311.
    Formerly: Guide to Communication Services.

384   US
PLANNING GUIDE 2. INTRA-L A T A TELECOMMUNICATIONS RATES AND SERVICES. base vol. plus m. updates. $650. (Center for Communications Management Information) C C M I McGraw-Hill, McGraw-Hill Information Systems Co., 50 S. Franklin Tpk., Ramsey, NJ 07446. TEL 201-825-3311.
    Formerly: Guide to Intra L A T A Communications Services.

384   US
PLANNING GUIDE 3. VALUE-ADDED NETWORKS AND DATA PRIVATE LINE. TELECOMMUNICATIONS RATES AND SERVICES. base vol. plus m. updates. $525. (Center for Communications Management Information) C C M I McGraw-Hill, McGraw-Hill Information Systems Co., 50 S. Franklin Tpk., Ramsey, NJ 07446. TEL 201-815-3311.
    Formerly: V A N and Resale Carrier Guide.

POLITECHNIKA WROCLAWSKA. INSTYTUT TELEKOMUNIKACJI I AKUSTYKI. PRACE NAUKOWE. KONFERENCJE. see *ELECTRICITY AND ELECTRICAL ENGINEERING*

POLITECHNIKA WROCLAWSKA. INSTYTUT TELEKOMUNIKACJI I AKUSTYKI. PRACE NAUKOWE. MONOGRAFIE. see *ELECTRICITY AND ELECTRICAL ENGINEERING*

POLITECHNIKA WROCLAWSKA. INSTYTUT TELEKOMUNIKACJI I AKUSTYKI. PRACE NAUKOWE. STUDIA I MATERIALY. see *ELECTRICITY AND ELECTRICAL ENGINEERING*

623.82   620.009   US   ISSN 0032-5015
PORTS O'CALL. 1968. quinquennial. free contr. circ. Society of Wireless Pioneers, Box 530, Santa Rosa, CA 95402. TEL 707-542-0898. Ed. William A. Breniman. bk. rev. bibl. illus. stat. circ. controlled.
    History

384   CN   ISSN 0080-6633
SASKATCHEWAN TELECOMMUNICATIONS. ANNUAL REPORT. 1947. a. free. ‡ Saskatchewan Telecommunications, 2121 Saskatchewan Dr., Regina, Sask. S4P 3Y2, Canada. TEL 306-347-2005. Ed. Evan Flude. circ. 2,000.

384.1   UN   ISSN 0074-9052
TABLE OF INTERNATIONAL TELEX RELATIONS AND TRAFFIC. (Text in English, French and Spanish) 1964. a. 103 Fr. International Telecommunication Union - Union Internationale des Telecommunications, Place des Nations, CH-1211 Geneva 20, Switzerland.

384   GW   ISSN 0082-190X
TASCHENBUCH DER POST- UND FERNMELDE-VERWALTUNG. 1970. a. DM.34. Fachverlag Schiele und Schoen GmbH, Markgrafenstr. 11, 1000 Berlin 61, W. Germany (B.R.D.) Ed. H. Bonson. adv. circ. 45,000.
    Formerly: Taschenbuch fuer Fernmelde-Verwaltung.

TELECOM FACTBOOK (NEW YORK) see *BUSINESS AND ECONOMICS — Trade And Industrial Directories*

384   US
TELECOM FACTBOOK (WASHINGTON) 1985. a. $125. Television Digest, Inc., 1836 Jefferson Pl., N.W., Washington, DC 20036. TEL 202-872-9200.

621.38 SI ISSN 0217-3891
TELECOMMUNICATION AUTHORITY OF
SINGAPORE. TELECOMS ANNUAL REPORT.
1974. a. price varies. Telecommunication Authority
of Singapore, Telecoms Headquarters, Comcentre,
31 Exeter Rd., Singapore 0923, Singapore. circ.
controlled.
　Formed by the 1974 merger of:
Telecommunication Authority of Singapore. T A S
Annual Report & Singapore Telephone Board
Annual Report.

384.1 US ISSN 0730-9872
TELECOMMUNICATIONS SOURCEBOOK. 1976.
a. $78. North American Telecommunications
Association, 2000 M St. N.W., Ste. 550,
Washington, DC 20036. Ed. Mary I. Bradshaw. adv.
circ. 10,000.

384.55 GW
TELEFAX INTERNATIONAL. INTERNATIONAL
TELEFAX DIRECTORY. 1985. a. $95. Telex-
Verlag Jaeger & Waldmann GmbH, Holzhofallee 38,
Postfach 111060, 6100 Darmstadt 11, W. Germany
(B.R.D.) (Dist. by: Universal Media Div., Shamgar
Inc., 212 Broadway, Box 45, Bethpage, NY 11714,
U.S.) adv.
　Formerly: Jaeger and Waldmann International
Telefax Directory.

384 621.385 US ISSN 0082-2655
TELEPHONE ENGINEER AND MANAGEMENT
DIRECTORY. 1937. a. $60. Harcourt Brace
Jovanovich, Inc. (Geneva), 124 S. First St., Geneva,
IL 60134. TEL 312-232-1400. Ed. Robert E.
Stoffels. adv. circ. 8,000.

384 US
TELEPHONY'S DIRECTORY & BUYER'S GUIDE
FOR THE TELECOMMUNICATIONS
INDUSTRY. 1895. a. $30. Telephony Publishing
(Subsidiary of: Intertec Publishing Corp.) 55 E.
Jackson Blvd., Chicago, IL 60604. TEL 312-922-
2435. Ed. Gerry Barrett. adv. circ. 11,000.
　Former titles: Telephony's Directory & Buyer's
Guide for the Telephone Industry & Telephony's
Directory of the Telephone Industry (ISSN 0082-
2671)

384.55 GW
TELEX & TELETEX INTERNATIONAL. TELEX
AND TELETEX DIRECTORY. 1952. a. $145
includes Telex Post International updating
supplements. Telex-Verlag Jaeger & Waldmann
GmbH, Holzhofallee 38, Postfach 111060, 6100
Darmstadt 11, W. Germany (B.R.D.) (Dist. by:
Universal Media Div., Shamgar, Inc., 212
Broadway, Box 45, Bethpage, NY 11714) adv.
　Former titles: Jaeger and Waldmann International
Telex and Teletex Directory; Jaeger and Waldmann
International Telex Directory; Jaeger and
Waldmann World Telex Directory.

384.1 DK ISSN 0109-8071
TELEX DANMARK/ANNUAIRE DES ABONNES
TELEX DU DANEMARK. 1973. a. Kr.32. Post og
Telegrafvaesenet, Farvergada 17, DK-1007
Copenhagen, Denmark.
　Formerly: Telexbog Danmark.

384.1 GW
TELEX UND TRAVEL INTERNATIONAL. a. $50.
Telex-Verlag Jaeger & Waldman GmbH,
Holzhofallee 38, Postfach 111060, 6100 Darmstadt
11, W. Germany (B.R.D.) (Dist. by: Universal
Media Div./Shamgar, Inc., 212 Broadway, Box 45,
Bethpage, NY 11714 USA) adv.

TOLL-FREE DIGEST. see BUSINESS AND
ECONOMICS — Trade And Industrial Directories

384 FR ISSN 0082-5980
TRANSTELEL; TRANSMISSIONS,
TELECOMMUNICATIONS, ELECTRONIQUE
EN FRANCE.* 1962. biennial. Bureau des
Relations Exterieures et Sociales, 30 rue Bergere,
Paris 9e, France.

384 US
UNITED STATES TELEPHONE ASSOCIATION.
ANNUAL STATISTICAL VOLUME. Cover title:
Telephone Statistics. (In 2 vols.) 1954. a. $45 to
non-members. United States Telephone Association,
900 19th St., N.W., Ste. 800, Washington, DC
20006-2102. TEL 202-835-3100. index. circ. 1,000.
　Formerly: United States Independent Telephone
Association. Annual Statistical Volume (ISSN 0083-
1298)

384.6 US
UNITED STATES TELEPHONE ASSOCIATION.
HOLDING COMPANY REPORT. 1963. a. $5.
United States Telephone Association, 900 19th St.,
N.W., Ste.800, Washington, DC 20006-2102. TEL
202-835-3100. circ. 3,000.
　Formerly: United States Independent Telephone
Association. Holding Company Report.

ZIP/AREA CODE DIRECTORY. see
COMMUNICATIONS — Postal Affairs

COMPUTER APPLICATIONS

see Aeronautics and Space
Flight — Computer Applications;
Agriculture — Computer Applications;
Archaeology — Computer Applications;
Art — Computer Applications; Business
and Economics — Computer Applications;
Communications — Computer
Applications; Education — Computer
Applications; Engineering — Computer
Applications; Humanities:
Comprehensive Works — Computer
Applications; Law — Computer
Applications; Library and Information
Sciences — Computer Applications;
Linguistics — Computer Applications;
Mathematics — Computer Applications;
Medical Sciences — Computer
Applications; Music — Computer
Applications; Publishing and Book
Trade — Computer Applications; Sciences:
Comprehensive Works — Computer
Applications; Transportation — Computer
Applications

COMPUTERS

see also Computers — Artificial Intelligence;
Computers — Automation;
Computers — Circuits;
Computers — Computer Architecture;
Computers — Computer Assisted
Instruction; Computers — Computer
Engineering; Computers — Computer
Graphics; Computers — Computer
Industry; Computers — Computer
Industry Directories;
Computers — Computer Music;
Computers — Computer Networks;
Computers — Computer Programming;
Computers — Computer Sales;
Computers — Computer Security;
Computers — Computer Simulation;
Computers — Computer Systems;
Computers — Cybernetics;
Computers — Data Base Management;
Computers — Data Communications and
Data Transmission Systems;
Computers — Electronic Data Processing;
Computers — Hardware;
Computers — Information Science and
Information Theory;
Computers — Microcomputers;
Computers — Minicomputers;
Computers — Personal Computers;
Computers — Software;
Computers — Theory of Computing;
Computers — Word Processing

001.6425 621.381 US
A C M ADMINISTRATIVE DIRECTORY OF
COLLEGE AND UNIVERSITY COMPUTER
SCIENCE/DATA PROCESSING PROGRAMS
AND COMPUTER FACILITIES. a. $12.
Association for Computing Machinery, Inc., 11 W.
42nd St., New York, NY 10036 (Subscr. to: A C M
Order Dept., Box 64145, Baltimore, MD 21264)
　Formerly: Administrative Directory of College
and University Computer Science Departments and
Computer Centers (ISSN 0190-6607)

621.381 US
A C M MONOGRAPH SERIES. 1968. irreg., vol.21,
1981. (Association for Computing Machinery)
Academic Press, Inc., Orlando, FL 32887. TEL
305-345-2000. Ed. Thomas A. Standish.

001.6 DK ISSN 0109-4157
A U D - NYT. 1981. irreg. free. Aalborg
Universitetsdatacenter, DK-9000 Aalborg, Denmark.
Ed. Uffe Moeller. circ. 1,000.
　Formerly: Data Center - Nyt (ISSN 0107-0533)

001.6 621.381 DK ISSN 0109-3770
AALBORG UNIVERSITETSDATACENTER.
PUBLIKATION. irreg. Kr.40. (Aalborg
Universitetsdatacenter) Bibliotekscentralen,
Telegrafvej 5, DK-2750 Ballerup, Denmark.

510 621.381 FI ISSN 0355-2713
ACTA POLYTECHNICA SCANDINAVICA.
MATHEMATICS AND COMPUTER SCIENCE
SERIES. (Texts and summaries in English) irreg. (2-
3/yr.) Fmk.130. Teknillisten Tieteiden Akatemia -
Finnish Academy of Technical Sciences,
Kansakoulukatu 10 A, SF-00100 Helsinki 10,
Finland. Ed. Reijo Sulonen. index. cum.index: 1958-
1985. circ. 250. (also avail. in microfilm from UMI;
back issues avail.; reprint service avail. from UMI)
Indexed: Curr.Cont. Math.R. Sci.Abstr.
Sci.Cit.Ind. ASCA. Comput.Cont. Compumath.
Soft.Abstr.Eng.
　Formerly: Acta Polytechnica Scandinavica.
Mathematics and Computing Machinery Series
(ISSN 0001-6861)

001.64 621.381 US ISSN 0065-2458
ADVANCES IN COMPUTERS. 1960. irreg., vol.25,
1986. Academic Press, Inc., Orlando, FL 32887.
TEL 305-345-2000. Ed. Marshall C. Yovits. index.
Indexed: Compumath.

001.6 621.381 US
ADVANCES IN COMPUTING RESEARCH. 1983.
a. $28.75 to individuals; institutions $57.50. J A I
Press Inc., 36 Sherwood Place, Greenwich, CT
06380. TEL 203-661-7602. Ed. Franco P. Preparata.
Indexed: ASCA.

621.381 551 US
ADVANCES IN GEOPHYSICAL DATA
PROCESSING; a research annual. 1984. a. $28.75
to individuals; institutions $57.50. J A I Press Inc.,
Box 1678, 36 Sherwood Pl., Greenwich, CT 06836.
TEL 203-661-7602. Ed. Marwan Simaan.

001.6 621.381 US
ADVANCES IN STATISTICAL ANALYSIS AND
STATISTICAL COMPUTING. 1985. a. $28.75 to
individuals; institutions $57.50. J A I Press Inc.,
Box 1678, 36 Sherwood Pl., Greenwich, CT 06836-
1678. TEL 203-661-7602. Ed. Roberto S. Mariano.

ALMANAC FOR COMPUTERS. see ASTRONOMY

001.6 621.381 US ISSN 8756-7016
ANNUAL REVIEW OF COMPUTER SCIENCE.
1986. a. $39. Annual Reviews Inc., 4139 El Camino
Way, Palo Alto, CA 94306. TEL 415-493-4400. Ed.
Joseph F. Traub.

001.6 621.381 JA
ANNUAL SURVEY OF COMPUTER USERS. 1966.
a. 10000 Yen. Japan Management Science Institute,
4-18-3-309 Minami-Aoyama, Minato-ku, Tokyo
107, Japan. Ed.Bd.

001.6 621.381 HK
ASIAN COMPUTER DIRECTORY. (Text in
English) 1976. a. $78. Computer Publications Ltd.,
19-27 Wyndham St., Wilson House, 3rd Fl., Hong
Kong, Hong Kong. Ed. Euan Barty. adv. bk. rev.
circ. 7,000.
　Formerly: Asian Computer Yearbook.

ASILOMAR CONFERENCE ON CIRCUITS,
SYSTEMS AND COMPUTERS. CONFERENCE
RECORD. see COMPUTERS — Circuits

621.381 001.6 US ISSN 0066-9091
ASSOCIATION FOR COMPUTING MACHINERY.
PROCEEDINGS OF NATIONAL
CONFERENCE. (Suspended 1953-1963) 1946. a.
price varies. Association for Computing Machinery,
11 W. 42nd St., New York, NY 10036 TEL 212-
869-7440. (Subscr. to: Box 64145, Baltimore, MD
21264) Indexed: Comput.Lit.Ind.

AUDIO-VIDEO I CS D.A.T.A. BOOK. see
COMPUTERS — Electronic Data Processing

BENCHMARK PAPERS IN ELECTRICAL
ENGINEERING & COMPUTER SCIENCE. see
ENGINEERING — Computer Applications

352 COMPUTERS

BERNARDS AND BABANI PRESS RADIO & ELECTRONICS & COMPUTER BOOKS. see *COMMUNICATIONS — Radio And Television*

001.64 621.381 UK
BRITISH COMPUTER SOCIETY. MICROFORM SPECIALIST GROUP. ANNUAL PROCEEDINGS. 1976. a. British Computer Society, Microform Specialist Group, 29 Portland Place, London W1N 4HU, England.

001.6 621.381 US
C M G CONFERENCE PROCEEDINGS. 1976. a. $55. Computer Measurement Group, Headquarters, 6397 Littel River Tnpk., Arlington, VA 22312-5002. Indexed: Comput.Lit.Ind.

621.381 001.6 UK
CAMBRIDGE COMPUTER SCIENCE TEXTS. 1972. irreg., no.20, 1984. $29.95 cloth; $12.95 paper for latest vol. Cambridge University Press, Edinburgh Bldg., Shaftesbury Rd., Cambridge CB2 2RU, England (And 32 E. 57th St., New York NY 10022) Ed.Bd.

001.6 IT ISSN 0392-0143
CENTRO DI RIFERIMENTO ITALIANO DIANE. NOTIZIARIO. 1980. irreg. free. Istituto di Studi sulla Ricerca e Documentazione Scientifica, Centro di Riferimento Italiano Diane, Via Cesare di Lollis 12, 00185 Rome, Italy. bk. rev. circ. 1,500.

COMPUTER & CONTROL ABSTRACTS. see *COMPUTERS — Abstracting, Bibliographies, Statistics*

001.6 621.381 UK ISSN 0267-1980
COMPUTER APPLICATIONS IN SOCIAL WORK AND ALLIED PROFESSIONS. irreg. City of Birmingham Polytechnic, Department of Sociology and Applied Social Studies, Perry Barr, Birmingham B42 2SU, England. Ed. Stuart Toole.

COMPUTER CONTENTS; semi-monthly compilation of tables of contents from more than 250 of the latest computer periodicals. see *COMPUTERS — Abstracting, Bibliographies, Statistics*

001.6 510 US
COMPUTER SCIENCE AND APPLIED MATHEMATICS. 1971. irreg., vol.52, 1986. $59. Academic Press, Inc., Orlando, FL 32887. TEL 305-345-2000. Ed. Werner Reinboldt. Indexed: Math.R.

001.6 621.381 US
COMPUTER SCIENCE TECHNICAL REPORT ANTHOLOGY. 1981. a. $2.75. University of Maryland, Computer Science Center, College Park, MD 20742. TEL 301-454-4255. Ed. Deborah J. Stoffel. bibl. index. cum.index: 1963-1983. circ. 250. (also avail. in microfiche; back issues avail.)

001.6 621.381 CN ISSN 0382-1005
COMPUTERS. French edition: Ordinateurs (ISSN 0382-1013) 1971. irreg. National Research Council of Canada, Division of Mechanical Engineering, Montreal Road Laboratories, Ottawa, Ont. K1A 0R6, Canada. circ. controlled.

001.6 621.381 651.2 US
COMPUTERS & OFFICE EQUIPMENT: LATIN AMERICAN INDUSTRIAL REPORT. (Avail. for each of 22 Latin American countries) 1985. a. $435 per country report per industry covered. Aurora International, Box 9099, Bridgeport, CT 06601-2099. TEL 203-368-0579.

001.6 150 US
COMPUTERS AND PEOPLE SERIES. 1980. irreg., vol.12, 1984. $26.50. Academic Press Inc., Orlando, FL 32887. TEL 305-345-2000. Ed. B. Gaines.

001.6 UK
COMPUTING DECISIONS. a. £29.50. (The National Computing Centre Ltd.) The Kemps Group (Printers & Publishers) Ltd., Westbury House, 701-705 Warwick Rd., Solihull, West Midlands B91 3DA, England.

001.6 621.381 US ISSN 0344-8029
COMPUTING SUPPLEMENTA. 1977. irreg., vol.5, 1984. Springer-Verlag, 175 Fifth Ave., New York, NY 10010 TEL 212-460-1500. (Also Berlin, Heidelberg, Tokyo and Vienna) (reprint service avail. from ISI)

001.6 CN
COMPUVIEWS. 1983. irreg. $8. J M G Software International, Inc., 801 Mohawk Rd. W., Hamilton, Ontario L9C 6C2, Canada. TEL 416-575-3200. Ed. George Geczy. illus. stat. (looseleaf format)

621.381 001.6 US ISSN 0734-757X
CONTRIBUTIONS TO THE STUDY OF COMPUTER SCIENCE. 1983. irreg. price varies. Greenwood Press, Box 5007, 88 Post Rd. West, Westport, CT 06881. TEL 203-226-3571.

DATALOGI O. see *COMPUTERS — Electronic Data Processing*

001.6 DK ISSN 0109-9779
DATALOGISKE SKRIFTER. 1985. irreg. free. Roskilde Universitetscenter, Computer Science Department, Box 260, 4000 Roskilde, Denmark.

DENSANKI RIYO NI KANSURU SHINPOJUMU KOENGAIYO/PROCEEDINGS OF THE SYMPOSIUM OF COMPUTER RESEARCH. see *ENGINEERING — Civil Engineering*

001.6 621.381 US
DESIGN COMPUDATA (YEAR) 1983. a. $95. Graphic Systems Inc., 180 Franklin St., Cambridge, MA 02139. TEL 617-492-1148. Ed. Alan Southerton. adv. index. circ. 3,000.

DIRECTORY OF COMPUTER & SOFTWARE RETAILERS. see *COMPUTERS — Computer Industry Directories*

001.6 621.381 US
E A T C MONOGRAPHS IN THEORETICAL COMPUTER SCIENCE. 1984. irreg., vol.8, 1987. Springer-Verlag, 175 Fifth Ave., New York, NY 10010 TEL 212-460-1500. (Also Berlin, Heidelberg, Tokyo, Vienna) (reprint service avail. from ISI)

ENCYCLOPEDIA OF INFORMATION SYSTEMS AND SERVICES. see *COMPUTERS — Computer Industry Directories*

001.6 621.381 US
EUROGRAPHIC SEMINARS. 1984. irreg., latest 1986. Springer-Verlag, 175 Fifth Ave., New York, NY 10010 TEL 212-460-1500. (Also Berlin, Heidelberg, Tokyo, Vienna) (reprint service avail. from ISI)

001.6 621.381 US
FACHBERICHTE SIMULATION. 1984. irreg., latest 1984. Springer-Verlag, 175 Fifth Ave., New York, NY 10010 TEL 212-460-1500. (Also Berlin, Heidelberg, Tokyo, Vienna) (reprint service avail. from ISI)

001.6 FR
FRANCE. INSTITUT NATIONAL DE RECHERCHE EN INFORMATIQUE ET EN AUTOMATIQUE. RAPPORTS DE RECHERCHE. (Text in English and French) 1974. irreg. free. Institut National de Recherche en Informatique et en Automatique, Domaine de Voluceau, Rocquencourt, B.P. 105, 78153 Le Chesnay, France. bk. rev. circ. 4,000.

001.64 621.381 NE
FUNDAMENTAL STUDIES IN COMPUTER SCIENCE. irreg., vol.9, 1984. price varies. Elsevier Science Publishers B.V., Box 211, 1000 AE Amsterdam, Netherlands.

001.6 AG
GAVI. 1980. a. Ing.Simon Pristupin, Suipach 128-2, Cuerpo-3, Piso K (1008), Buenos Aires, Argentina. adv. circ. 6,000.

GEOGRAPHICAL SOCIETY OF CHINA. BULLETIN. see *GEOGRAPHY*

001.64 651.8 UK ISSN 0072-582X
GREAT BRITAIN. DEPARTMENT OF EDUCATION AND SCIENCE. COMPUTER BOARD FOR UNIVERSITIES AND RESEARCH COUNCILS. REPORT. 1968. irreg. H.M.S.O., P.O. Box 569, London SE1 9NH, England.

658.8 US
GUIDE TO FREE COMPUTER MATERIALS. 1983. a. $30.25. Educators Progress Service, Inc., Randolph, WI 53956. TEL 414-326-3126. Ed. Kathleen Suttles Nehmer.

621.381 US
I E E E SYMPOSIUM ON MASS STORAGE SYSTEMS. DIGEST OF PAPERS. 4th, 1980. irreg. (Institute of Electrical and Electronics Engineers, Inc.) I E E E Computer Society Press, 1730 Massachusetts Ave. N.W., Washington, DC 20036-1903 (And 345 E. 47th St., New York, NY 10017)

001.6 IS
I L T A M TECHNICAL REPORTS. (Text in English) irreg. Corporation for Planning and Research, 78 Yirmeyahu St., Romena, Jerusalem, Israel.

001.6 621.381 CN
INFO GUIDE (YEAR); annual guide for E.D.P. and high technology. (Text in English and French; summaries in English, French, German) 1985. a., plus q. updates. Can.$445($420) Info Media International, 140 Cloverdale, No. 207, Dorval, PQ H9S 3H9, Canada. TEL 514-631-8438. Ed. Loren P. Villiers.

101.6 GW
INFORMATIK. 1969. irreg., vol.51, 1985. price varies. Bibliographisches Institut, Dudenstr. 6, Postfach 311, 6800 Mannheim 1, W. Germany (B.R.D.) Ed.Bd.

001.6 US ISSN 0343-3005
INFORMATIK-FACHBERICHTE. (Text in English or German) 1976. irreg., vol.129, 1986. price varies. Springer-Verlag, 175 Fifth Ave., New York, NY 10010 TEL 212-460-1500. (Also Berlin, Heidelberg, Tokyo and Vienna) Ed. W. Brauer. (reprint service avail. from ISI)

001.6 301.16 070.5
340 US ISSN 0734-9637
INFORMATION SOURCES. 1976. a. $79.95 non-members; members $39.95. Information Industry Association, 555 New Jersey Ave., N.W., Ste. 800, Washington, DC 20001. TEL 202-639-8262. Eds. Barbara Van Gorder, Ann K. Ellis. circ. 3,000.

331.1 621.381 US ISSN 0098-2431
INSTITUTE FOR THE CERTIFICATION OF COMPUTER PROFESSIONALS. ANNUAL REPORT. a. Institute for the Certification of Computer Professionals, 2200 E. Devon, Des Plaines, IL 60018-4503. circ. 1,500. Key Title: Annual Report - the Institute for Certification of Computer Professionals.

001.6 US
INTERNATIONAL LECTURE SERIES IN COMPUTER SCIENCE. 1981. a. Academic Press Inc., Orlando, FL 32887. TEL 305-345-2000. Indexed: Math.R.

621.3 US ISSN 0731-3071
INTERNATIONAL SYMPOSIUM ON FAULT-TOLERANT COMPUTING. DIGEST OF PAPERS. Short title: F T C S. 1971. a. price varies. (Institute of Electrical and Electronics Engineers, Inc.) I E E E Computer Society Press, 1730 Massachusetts Ave., N.W., Washington, DC 20036-1903 TEL 202-371-0101. (And 345 E. 47th St., New York, NY 10017)
Formerly: International Symposium on Fault-Tolerant Computing. Proceedings (ISSN 0363-8928); Supersedes: International Symposium on Fault-Tolerant Computing. Digest (ISSN 0074-882X)

INTERNATIONAL TEST CONFERENCE. PROCEEDINGS. see *COMPUTERS — Hardware*

001.6 UI
INTERNATIONAL TRACTS IN COMPUTER STUDIES. 1976. a. price varies. Advance Publications, Block D, Hirzell Court, St. Peter Port, Guernsey, Channel Islands. Eds. D. Evans, S. Chomet. circ. 1,000.

001.6 350 310 FI ISSN 0357-9921
JYVASKYLA STUDIES IN COMPUTER SCIENCE, ECONOMICS AND STATISTICS. (Text in English) 1980. irreg. price varies. Jyvaskylan Yliopisto - University of Jyvaskyla, Seminaarink. 15, 40100 Jyvaskyla 10, Finland. Ed. Heikki Laitinen. circ. 450.

001.6 DK ISSN 0107-8283
KOEBENHAVNS UNIVERSITET. DATALOGISK INSTITUT. RAPPORT. irreg. Kr.75. Koebenhavns Universitet, Datalogisk Institut, Sigurdsgade 41, 2200 Copenhagen N, Denmark.

001.6 US ISSN 0302-9743
LECTURE NOTES IN COMPUTER SCIENCE. 1973. irreg., vol.242, 1986. price varies. Springer-Verlag, 175 Fifth Ave., New York, NY 10010 TEL 212-460-1500. (Also Berlin, Heidelberg, Tokyo and Vienna) Eds. G. Goos, J. Hartmanis. (reprint service avail. from ISI) Indexed: Compumath.

001.6 629.8 IS
MAEDA VENITUNIM. 3/yr. I.B.M. Israel, I.B.M. House, 2 Weizmann St., Tel Aviv. TEL 03-618032. Ed. Yossi Shuval.

001.6 621.381 CN
MERCURY; newsletter of the computer centre. 1969. irreg, vol.16, 1985. free. University of Manitoba, Computer Services, Engineering Bldg., Rm. 603, Winnipeg, Man. R3T 2N2, Canada. TEL 204-474-8239. Ed. Pat Nichols. circ. 1,000.

001.6 621.381 BL
MONOGRAFIAS EM CIENCIA DA COMPUTACAO. (Text in English and Portuguese) 1969. irreg. free. ‡ Pontificia Universidade Catolica do Rio de Janeiro, Departamento de Informatica, Rua Marques de Sao Vicente 225 - Gavea, 22453 Rio de Janeiro RJ, Brazil. Ed. Antonio L. Furtado. circ. 200.
Formerly (until 1975): Monographs in Computer Science and Computer Applications.

001.6 621.381 US
N A T O ADVANCED STUDY INSTITUTE SERIES F: COMPUTER AND SYSTEM SCIENCES. 1983. irreg., vol.26, 1986. price varies. (North Atlantic Treaty Organization) Springer-Verlag, 175 Fifth Ave., New York, NY 10010 (Also Berlin, Heidelberg, Tokyo and Vienna)

001.64 621.381 US
NATIONAL COMPUTER CONFERENCE (PROCEEDINGS) (Subseries of: A F I P S Conference Proceedings) 1973. a. $80. American Federation of Information Processing Societies, 1899 Preston White Dr., Reston, VA 22091. TEL 703-620-8919. illus. (also avail. in microform; back issues avail.) Indexed: Sci.Abstr. Comput.Lit.Ind.
Formerly: National Computer Conference and Exposition (Proceedings) (ISSN 0095-6880)

001.6 UR
OBRABOTKA SIMVOL'NOI INFORMATSII. 1973. irreg. 0.47 Rub. Akademiya Nauk S.S.S.R., Vychislitel'nyi Tsentr, Ul. Vavilova, 40, Moscow V-333, Russian S.F.S.R., U.S.S.R. illus.

001.6 621.381 PL
POLISH ACADEMY OF SCIENCES. INSTITUTE OF COMPUTER SCIENCE. REPORTS. (Text in English, Polish and Russian) 1969. irreg., no.380, 1977. free. Polish Academy of Sciences, Institute of Computer Science, Box 22, 00-901 Warsaw, Poland. Ed. Andrzej Blikle. circ. 575. Indexed: Math.R. Ref.Zh. Graph.Arts Lit.Abstr.
Formerly: Polska Akademia Nauk. Centrum Obliczeniowe. Prace (ISSN 0079-3175)

001.6 621.381 PL ISSN 0860-1615
POLITECHNIKA WROCLAWSKA. CENTRUM OBLICZENIOWE. PRACE NAUKOWE. KONFERENCJE. (Text in Polish) 1985. irreg., no.2, 1985. price varies. Politechnika Wroclawska, Wybrzeze Wyspianskiego 27, 50-370 Wroclaw, Poland. Ed. Jerzy Ciekot.

001.6 621.381 PL ISSN 0860-1623
POLITECHNIKA WROCLAWSKA. CENTRUM OBLICZENIOWE. PRACE NAUKOWE. STUDIA I MATERIALY. 1980. irreg., no.2, 1983. price varies. Politechnika Wroclawska, Wybrzeze Wyspianskiego 27, 50-370 Wroclaw, Poland. Ed. Jerzy Ciekot.

001.6 621.381 US
PRINCETON UNIVERSITY. DEPARTMENT OF COMPUTER SCIENCE. TECHNICAL REPORT. 1960. irreg. ‡ Princeton University, Department of Computer Science, Princeton, NJ 08540. TEL 609-452-3000.
Formerly: Princeton University. Computer Sciences Laboratory. Technical Report (ISSN 0079-5283)

001.6 621.381 US
RESEARCH REPORTS ESPRIT - PROJECT 322: CAD INTERFACES. 1986. irreg. price varies. Springer-Verlag, 175 Fifth Ave., New York, NY 10160 TEL 212-460-1500. (Also Berlin, Heidelberg, Tokyo, Vienna) (reprint service avail. from ISI)

001.6 FR
SOCIETES DE SERVICE ET DE CONSEIL EN INFORMATIQUE. irreg., latest 1982. (Direction des Industries Electroniques et de l'Informatique) Documentation Francaise, 29-31 Quai Voltaire, 75340 Paris, France. stat.

001.6 621.381 011 US
SPRINGER BOOKS ON PROFESSIONAL COMPUTING. 1984. irreg., latest 1984. Springer-Verlag, 175 Fifth Ave., New York, NY 10010 TEL 212-460-1500. (Also Berlin, Heidelberg, Tokyo, Vienna) (reprint service avail. from ISI)

001.6 621.381 NE
SYSTEMICA. 1981. a. fl.50. Systeem Groep Nederland, Nerhoven 10, 5126 TB Gilze, Netherlands. Ed. H. Koppelaar. adv. bk. rev. circ. 600.

621.381 US
T E N C O N (I E E E REGION 10 CONFERENCE). PROCEEDINGS; an international conference on consumer & industrial electronics & applications. Variant Title: I E E E Trends in Electronics Conference. Proceedings. 1982. biennial. price varies. (I E E E, Region 10) Institute of Electrical and Electronics Engineers, Inc., 345 E. 47th St., New York, NY 10017. TEL 212-705-7900.

TELECOMMUNICATIONS SYSTEMS AND SERVICES DIRECTORY; an international descriptive guide to approximately 2,000 telecommunications organizations, systems, and services. see *COMMUNICATIONS*

001.6 621.381 US ISSN 0172-603X
TEXTS AND MONOGRAPHS IN COMPUTER SCIENCE. 1975. irreg., latest 1986. price varies. Springer-Verlag, 175 Fifth Ave., New York, NY 10010 TEL 212-460-1500. (Also Berlin, Heidelberg, Tokyo and Vienna) Eds. F.L. Bauer, D. Gries. Indexed: Math.R. Sci.Abstr.

001.6 621.381 CN ISSN 0829-5425
UNIVERSITY COMPUTING AND INFORMATION SERVICES NEWSLETTER. 1967. irreg. Dalhousie University, Computing Services, Halifax, N.S. B3H 4H8, Canada. TEL 902-424-3472. Ed. Ram Raju. adv. bk. rev. circ. 900. (looseleaf format)
Formerly: Dalhousie University. Computer Centre. Newsletter (ISSN 0384-8116)

001.6 621.381 CN ISSN 0316-4683
UNIVERSITY OF ALBERTA. DEPARTMENT OF COMPUTING SCIENCE. TECHNICAL REPORTS. 1965. irreg. Can.$2.50 or on exchange. ‡ University of Alberta, Department of Computing Science, Edmonton, Alta. T6G 2H1, Canada. TEL 403-432-3977. circ. 60.
Formerly: University of Alberta. Department of Computing Science. Publication (ISSN 0065-6062)

001.64 621.381 UK
UNIVERSITY OF NEWCASTLE-UPON-TYNE. COMPUTING LABORATORY. TECHNICAL REPORT SERIES. 1969. irreg. £30 for 15 nos. University of Newcastle-Upon-Tyne, Computing Laboratory, Claremont Tower, Newcastle-Upon-Tyne NE1 7RU, England. Ed. M.J. Elphick. bibl. circ. 112. (also avail. in microfiche; reprint service avail. from NTIS)

001.64 621.381 AT ISSN 0082-0547
UNIVERSITY OF SYDNEY. BASSER DEPARTMENT OF COMPUTER SCIENCE. TECHNICAL REPORT. 1957. irreg. free. ‡ University of Sydney, Basser Department of Computer Science, Sydney 2006, N.S.W., Australia. circ. 150.

001.6 621.381 CN ISSN 0042-0204
UNIVERSITY OF TORONTO. DEPARTMENT OF COMPUTER SCIENCE. TECHNICAL REPORTS. 1968. irreg., approx. 12/yr. exchange basis. ‡ University of Toronto, Department of Computer Science, Toronto, Ont. M5S 1A1, Canada. charts. illus. circ. 100. (processed)

001.6 621.381 UK
WHARTON'S COMPLETE OFFICE AUTOMATION GUIDE. 1975. a. £30. Wharton Publishing Ltd., 1st Fl., Regal House, Twickenham, Middlesex, TW1 3QS, England. Ed. Tina Dean. Indexed: Sci.Abstr.
Formerly: International Office Automation Guide.

WHO'S WHO IN ELECTRONICS & COMPUTER SCIENCE. see *BUSINESS AND ECONOMICS — Trade And Industrial Directories*

001.64 621.381 US
WILEY SERIES IN COMPUTING. 1972. irreg., unnumbered, latest 1986. price varies. John Wiley & Sons, Inc., 605 Third Ave., New York, NY 10016. TEL 212-850-6000. Ed. D.W. Barron. Indexed: Sci.Abstr.

WORKING SYMPOSIUM ON OCEANOGRAPHIC DATA SYSTEMS. PROCEEDINGS. see *EARTH SCIENCES — Oceanography*

001.6 621.381 US
WORKSHOP ON COMPUTER VISION REPRESENTATION AND CONTROL. PROCEEDINGS. 1982. biennial. price varies. (Institute of Electrical and Electronics Engineers, Inc.) I E E E Computer Society Press, 1730 Massachusetts Ave., N.W., Washington, DC 20036.

621.38 001.6 US
YANKEE INGENUITY. irreg. Yankee Group, Harvard Square, Box 43, Cambridge, MA 02138. TEL 617-542-0100.

COMPUTERS — Abstracting, Bibliographies, Statistics

001.64 016 US ISSN 0149-1199
A C M GUIDE TO COMPUTING LITERATURE. 1964. a. $150 to non-members; members $75. Association for Computing Machinery, 11 W. 42nd St., New York, NY 10036 TEL 212-869-7440. (Orders to: Box 64145, Baltimore, MD 21264) Ed. A. Finerman. circ. 2,200. (back issues avail.)
Formerly: Bibliography and Subject Index of Current Computing Literature (ISSN 0149-1202)

621.381 001.5 016 US
ABSTRACT NEWSLETTER: COMPUTERS, CONTROL & INFORMATION THEORY. w. $109. U.S. National Technical Information Service, 5285 Port Royal Rd., Springfield, VA 22161. TEL 703-487-4630. Ed. Linda J. LaGarde. index. (back issues avail.)
Former titles: Weekly Abstract Newsletter: Computers, Control and Information Theory; Weekly Government Abstracts. Computers, Control and Information Theory (ISSN 0364-796X)

657 651.8 016 UK ISSN 0001-4796
ACCOUNTING & DATA PROCESSING ABSTRACTS. 1970. 8/yr., (plus index) £102.50. (Institute of Chartered Accountants in England & Wales) Anbar Publications Ltd., Box 23, Wembley HA9 8DJ, England. Ed. A.C. Ede. (looseleaf format)
Supersedes in part: Anbar Management Services Abstracts (ISSN 0003-2794)

AMERICAN STATISTICAL ASSOCIATION. STATISTICAL COMPUTING SECTION. PROCEEDINGS (OF THE ANNUAL MEETING) see *STATISTICS*

001.6 011.7 US
ANNUAL BIBLIOGRAPHY OF COMPUTER-ORIENTED BOOKS. 1965. a. $9. Center for Cybernetics Systems Synergism, Box 7345, Colorado Springs, CO 80933. Ed. J.D. Couger. bk. rev.

COMPUMATH CITATION INDEX. see *MATHEMATICS — Abstracting, Bibliographies, Statistics*

651.8 016 UI ISSN 0010-4469
COMPUTER ABSTRACTS. Issued with: Computer News (ISSN 0010-4647) 1957. m. $310. Technical Information Co. Ltd., Box 59, St. Helier, Jersey, Channel Islands. Ed. B.A. Fancourt. bk. rev. abstr. pat. tr.lit. index. circ. 1,200. Indexed: Comput.Rev.

354   COMPUTERS — ARTIFICIAL INTELLIGENCE

651.8 629.8 016   UK   ISSN 0036-8113
COMPUTER & CONTROL ABSTRACTS.
   Alternative title: INSPEC, Section C. 1966. m.
$830. INSPEC, I.E.E., Station House, Nightingale
Rd., Hitchin, Herts. SG5 1RJ, England (U.S.
address: 445 Hoes Lane, Piscataway, NJ 08854)
adv. abstr.bibl. index. cum.index every 4 years. (also
avail. in microform) Indexed: Comput.Rev. Fluidex.
Ergon.Abstr.
   ●Also available online. Vendors: BRS, CEDOCAR,
CISTI, Data-Star, DIALOG, European Space
Agency, JICST, Orbit Information Technologies,
STN International, University of Tsukuba.

651.8 016   US   ISSN 0191-9776
COMPUTER AND INFORMATION SYSTEMS
ABSTRACT JOURNAL; an abstract journal
pertaining to the theory, design, fabrication and
application of computer and information systems.
1962. m. $651 incl. index. Cambridge Scientific
Abstracts, 5161 River Rd., Bethesda, MD 20816.
TEL 301-951-1400. adv. bk. rev. abstr. pat. index.
circ. 1,647. (also avail. in microfilm) Indexed:
Cal.Tiss.Abstr. Chemorec.Abstr. Oncol.Abstr.
   ●Also available online. Vendors: DIALOG.
   Former titles: Computer and Information Systems
(ISSN 0010-4507); Information Processing Journal
(ISSN 0362-8973)

001.6 011.7 621.381   US
COMPUTER CONTENTS; semi-monthly compilation
of tables of contents from more than 250 of the
latest computer periodicals. 1983. 24/yr. $115. Find
- S V P, 500 Fifth Ave., New York, NY 10110.
TEL 212-354-2424. Ed. Karen O'Connor. bk. rev.
circ. 1,000.
   ●Also available online. Vendors: DIALOG.

001.6 621.381 001.7   US   ISSN 0883-931X
COMPUTER INDUSTRY ABSTRACTS; the source
for market information on computers, peripherals,
and software. 1985. q. $250. Data Analysis Group,
4387 Valle Dr., La Mesa, CA 92041. TEL 619-464-
6888. Ed. Keith R. Parker. abstr. charts. stat.
cum.index. (back issues avail.; also avail. on disk)
   Incorporating (as of 1985): Computer Industry
Forecast (ISSN 0883-9301)

001.6   US   ISSN 0744-0081
COMPUTER INDUSTRY UPDATE. 1979. m. $295.
Industry Market Reports, Inc., Box 681, Los Altos,
CA 94023. TEL 415-941-6679. Ed. George Weiser.
abstr. (back issues avail.)

001.6 016 621.381   US   ISSN 0270-4846
COMPUTER LITERATURE INDEX. 1971. q. plus
annual cumulation. $148. Applied Computer
Research, Inc., Box 9280, Phoenix, AZ 85068. TEL
602-995-5929. Ed. Phillip C. Howard. bk. rev. abstr.
bibl. (also avail. in microfiche)
   Formerly (until 1979): Quarterly Bibliography of
Computers and Data Processing (ISSN 0048-6132)

001.6   US
COMPUTER READABLE DATABASES; a directory
and data sourcebook. 1978. irreg., approx.
e0138658xxyrs., with updates. American Library
Association, 50 E. Huron, Chicago, IL 60611. (Co-
publisher: Elsevier Scientific Publishing Co.) Eds.
Martha E. Williams. stat. (looseleaf format)
   ●Also available online. Vendors: DIALOG.
   Formerly: Computer Readable Bibliographic Data
Bases.

001.6 016   UK   ISSN 0309-8885
COMPUTING JOURNAL ABSTRACTS. 1969. bi-w.
£91.50 to non-members. National Computing
Centre Ltd., Oxford Rd., Manchester M1 7ED,
England. index. circ. 450. Indexed: BMT. Mgmt.&
Market.Abstr.

621.381 001.6 011.7   US   ISSN 0010-4884
COMPUTING REVIEWS. 1960. m. $95 to non-
members; members $30. Association for Computing
Machinery, 11 W. 42nd St., New York, NY 10036.
TEL 212-869-7440. Ed. A. Finerman. adv. bk. rev.
abstr. index. cum.index. circ. 8,500. (also avail. in
microform) Indexed: Chem.Abstr. Math.R.
Ergon.Abstr.

001.53 016   UK   ISSN 0011-4243
CYBERNETICS ABSTRACTS. English translation of:
Referativnyi Zhurnal-Kibernetika. 1964. m. $930.
Scientific Information Consultants Ltd., 661
Finchley Rd., London NW2 2HN, England. abstr.
   Formerly: Theoretical Cybernetics Abstracts.

070.5 011 001.6   US   ISSN 0739-2907
ELECTRONIC PUBLISHING ABSTRACTS. 1983.
m. $340. Pergamon Press, Inc., Journals Division,
Maxwell House, Fairview Park, Elmsford, NY
10523 TEL 914-592-7700. (And Headington Hill
Hall, Oxford, OX3 0BW, England) Ed. Dr. Avril
Jamieson. adv. (also avail. in microfilm from MIM,
UMI)
   ●Also available online. Vendors: Orbit Information
Technologies, Pergamon Infoline.

001.6 314   HU   ISSN 0139-3286
HUNGARY. KOZPONTI STATISZTIKAI
HIVATAL. SZAMITASTECHNIKAI
STATISZTIKAI EVKONYV. a. 88 Ft. Statisztikai
Kiado Vallalat, Kaszasdulo u. 2, P.O.B. 99, 1300
Budapest 3, Hungary (Subscr. to: Kultura, Box 149,
H-1389 Budapest, Hungary)
   Formerly: Szamitastechnikai Evkonyv (ISSN
0133-9559)

001.6 011.7 621.381   US   ISSN 0741-2355
I B M - P C INDEX.* 1983. bi-monthly plus annual
cumulation. $38. B P Publications, 465 Chestnut
Tree Hill Rd., Southbury, CT 06488-1955.

001.6 621.381 011.7   US
INDEX; the ultimate information index for all
personal computer users. 1981. biennial. $14.95.
Missouri Indexing, No. 7 Watch Hill Rd., St. Louis,
MO 63124. TEL 314-232-7953. Ed. W.H. Wallace.
circ. 5,000. (also avail. in magnetic tape; back issues
avail.)

001.429 016   NE   ISSN 0020-580X
INTERNATIONAL ABSTRACTS IN OPERATIONS
RESEARCH. 1973. 6/yr. fl.440($152)
(International Federation of Operational Research
Societies) Elsevier Science Publishers B.V., Box 211,
1000 AE Amsterdam, Netherlands. Ed. Graham K.
Rand. adv. abstr. index. cum.index. circ. 8,000.

001.6 621.381 001.7   US   ISSN 0890-1406
JAPAN COMPUTER TECHNOLOGY AND
APPLICATIONS ABSTRACTS. 1987. m. $425.
University Publications of America, 44 N. Market
St., Frederick, MD 21701. TEL 301-694-0100. Ed.
Daniel A. Stafford.

001.6 621.381 001.7 UK   ISSN 0950-4788
KEY ABSTRACTS - COMPUTER
COMMUNICATIONS AND STORAGE. 1987. m.
$110 to non-members. INSPEC, I.E.E., Station
House, Nightingale Rd., Hitchin, Herts. SG5 1RJ,
England (U.S. addr.: 445 Hoes Lane, Piscataway,
NJ 08854) index.

001.6 621.381 001.7 UK   ISSN 0950-4796
KEY ABSTRACTS - COMPUTING IN
ELECTRONICS & POWER. 1987. m. $110 to non-
members. INSPEC, I.E.E., Station House,
Nightingale Rd., Hitchin, Herts. SG5 1RJ, England
(U.S. addr.: 445 Hoes Lane, Piscataway, NJ 08854)
index.

001.6 621.381 001.7 UK   ISSN 0950-4869
KEY ABSTRACTS - SOFTWARE ENGINEERING.
1987. m. $110 to non-members. INSPEC, I.E.E.,
Station House, Nightingale Rd., Hitchin, Herts SG5
1RJ, England (U.S. addr.: 445 Hoes Lane,
Piscataway, NJ 08854)

001.6 011.7 621.381   US
MICROCOMPUTER INDEX. 1980. bi-m. $85.
Database Services Inc., 2685 Marine Way, Ste.
1305, Mountain View, CA 94043-1125. Ed. Frances
G. Spigai. bk. rev. abstr. index. (also avail. in
magnetic tape; back issues avail.)
   ●Also available online. Vendors: CISTI, DIALOG,
Mead Data Central, VU/TEXT Information
Services, Inc.

658.403 621.381   US   ISSN 0741-6016
MICROCOMPUTER INDUSTRY UPDATE; concise
news capsules for managers and executives. 1983.
m. $225. Industry Market Reports, Inc., Box 681,
Los Altos, CA 94022. TEL 415-941-6679. Ed.
George Weiser.

651.8 016   NE   ISSN 0028-6095
NEW LITERATURE ON AUTOMATION.
(Abstracts in English, French and German) 1960.
monthly (11/yr.) fl.175. Libresso B.V., Postbus 878,
7400 AW Deventer, Netherlands. Ed. M.J. Van den
Aa. bk. rev. abstr. bibl. index. cum.index: 1961-
1964; 1965-1968. circ. 1,150.
   Formerly: Literature on Automation.

629.8 016   FR   ISSN 0474-5868
ORGANIZATION FOR ECONOMIC
COOPERATION AND DEVELOPMENT.
LIBRARY. SPECIAL ANNOTATED
BIBLIOGRAPHY: AUTOMATION.
BIBLIOGRAPHIE SPECIALE ANALYTIQUE.
(Text in English and French) 1964. irreg.
Organization for Economic Cooperation and
Development, 2 rue Andre Pascal, 75775 Paris 16,
France (U.S. orders to: O.E.C.D. Publications and
Information Center, 1750 Pennsylvania Ave., N.W.,
Washington, D.C. 20006) (also avail. in microfiche)

001.6 621.381   US   ISSN 0743-2534
P C ABSTRACTS. 1983. s-a. $149. Garland
Publishing, Inc., 136 Madison Ave., New York, NY
10016. TEL 212-686-7492. Ed. Gary Kurtis.

001.535 011.7   US
ROBOMATIX ANNUAL INDEX. a. E I C
Intelligence, Inc., 48 W. 38th St., New York, NY
10018. TEL 212-944-8500.

001.535 011.7   US
ROBOMATIX REPORTER. 1983. m. $475 includes
cum.index. E I C Intelligence, Inc., 48 W. 38th St.,
New York, NY 10018. TEL 800-223-6275. Ed.
Barry Lenson. abstr. bibl. charts. illus. pat. stat.
index. cum.index. circ. 1,000. (also avail. in
microform)
   ●Also available online. Vendors: DIALOG,
European Space Agency.

001.53 001.6   US
U S S R REPORT: CYBERNETICS, COMPUTERS,
AND AUTOMATION TECHNOLOGY. 1973.
irreg., approx. 10/yr. $5 per no. U.S. Joint
Publications Research Service, 1000 N. Glebe Rd.,
Arlington, VA 22201 TEL 703-487-4630. (Orders
to: NTIS, Springfield, VA 22161)
   Formerly: U S S R and Eastern Europe Scientific
Abstracts: Cybernetics, Computers, and Automation
Technology; Which was formed by the merger of: U
S S R Scientific Abstracts: Cybernetics, Computers,
and Automation Technology; East European
Scientific Abstracts: Cybernetics, Computers, and
Automation Technology.

COMPUTERS — Artificial Intelligence

Includes: Robotics.

see also Computers — Cybernetics

001.535   US
ABLEX SERIES IN ARTIFICIAL INTELLIGENCE.
1985. irreg. price varies. Ablex Publishing Corp.,
355 Chestnut St., Norwood, NJ 07648. TEL 201-
767-8450. Ed. Jerry Hobbs.
   Formerly: Advances in Artificial Intelligence.

001.535 001.6 629.8 US
ADVANCES IN AUTOMATION AND ROBOTICS.
1985. irreg. $59.50. J A I Press Inc., 36 Sherwood
Pl., Greenwich, CT 06836.

ADVANCES IN SENSOR TECHNOLOGY. see
TECHNOLOGY: COMPREHENSIVE WORKS

001.535   US
CONFERENCE ON ARTIFICIAL INTELLIGENCE
APPLICATIONS. PROCEEDINGS. 1984. a. price
varies. (Institute of Electrical and Electronics
Engineers, Inc., Computer Society) I E E E
Computer Society Press, 1730 Massachusetts Ave.,
N.W., Washington, DC 20036-1903 TEL 202-371-
0101. (And: 345 E. 47th St., New York, NY 10017)

001.535   US
EXPERT SYSTEMS IN GOVERNMENT
SYMPOSIUM. Short title: E S I G. 1985. a. price
varies. (Institute of Electrical and Electronics
Engineers, Inc., Computer Society) I E E E
Computer Society Press, 1730 Massachusetts Ave.,
N.W., Washington, DC 20036-1903 TEL 202-371-
0101. (And: 345 E. 47th St., New York, NY 10017-
2394)

001.535 US
FALL JOINT COMPUTER CONFERENCE.
PROCEEDINGS. Short title: F J C C. 1986. a.
price varies. (Institute of Electrical and Electronics
Engineers, Inc., Computer Society) I E E E
Computer Society Press, 1730 Massachusetts Ave.,
N.W., Washington, DC 20036-1903 TEL 201-371-
0101. (And 345 E. 47th ST., New York, NY 10017-
2394) (Co-sponsor: Association for Computing
Machinery)

I E E E INTERNATIONAL CONFERENCE ON
ROBOTICS AND AUTOMATION.
PROCEEDINGS. see *COMPUTERS —
Automation*

001.535 621.381 US
INTERNATIONAL ROBOTICS INDUSTRY
DIRECTORY. 1981. a. $35. Technical Database
Corp., Box 720, Conroe, TX 77305. TEL 409-539-
9688. Ed. Philip Flora. adv. illus. stat. tr.lit. index.
circ. 6,000. (also avail. in microfilm; back issues
avail.)
 Formerly: Robotics Industry Directory (ISSN
0278-159X)

001.53 US ISSN 0076-2032
MACHINE INTELLIGENCE WORKSHOP. 1967. a.
price varies. Halsted Press (Subsidiary of: John
Wiley & Sons, Inc.) 605 Third Ave., New York, NY
10016. TEL 212-850-6000. Eds. D. Michie, B.
Meltzer.

001.535 US
NATIONAL CONFERENCE ON ARTIFICIAL
INTELLIGENCE. PROCEEDINGS. 1980. a.
(American Association for Artificial Intelligence)
Morgan Kaufmann, Publishers, 95 First St., Los
Altos, CA 94022. abstr. circ. 3,000.

001.535 US
PUBLISHING PROGRAM IN COMPUTER
SCIENCE: ARTIFICIAL INTELLIGENCE. irreg.,
vol.16, 1985. U M I Research Press, 300 N. Zeeb
Rd., Ann Arbor, MI 48106. Ed. Harold Stone.

ROBOTICS WORLD DIRECTORY. see *BUSINESS
AND ECONOMICS — Trade And Industrial
Directories*

621.38 001.5 GE
ROBOTRON TECHNISCHE MITTEILUNGEN.
(Text in German; summaries in English, French,
Russian) irreg. Robotron-Elektronik Radeberg,
Wilhelm-Pick-Str. 70, 8142 Radeberg, E. Germany
(D.D.R.) illus. charts.

621.381 001.535 UK
WORLD YEARBOOK OF FIFTH GENERATION
COMPUTING RESEARCH AND
DEVELOPMENT. 1987. a. £40. Kogan Page, 120
Pentonville Rd., London N1 9JN, England. Ed. Igor
Aleksander.

621.381 001.535 UK
WORLD YEARBOOK OF ROBOTICS RESEARCH
AND DEVELOPMENT. a. £48. Kogan Page Ltd.,
120 Pentonville Rd., London N1 9JN, England. Ed.
Peter Scott.
 Formerly: International Robotics Yearbook.

COMPUTERS — Automation

ABSTRACT NEWSLETTER: MANUFACTURING
TECHNOLOGY. see *TECHNOLOGY:
COMPREHENSIVE WORKS — Abstracting,
Bibliographies, Statistics*

ADVANCES IN AUTOMATION AND ROBOTICS.
see *COMPUTERS — Artificial Intelligence*

001.6 629.8 US ISSN 0748-8602
ADVANCES IN HUMAN/COMPUTER
INTERACTION. 1985. a. price varies. Ablex
Publishing Corp., 355 Chestnut Ave., Norwood, NJ
07648. TEL 201-767-8450. Ed. Rex Hartson.

001.6 629.8 US
ANNUAL AUTOMATION REPORT TO THE
ARIZONA LEGISLATURE.* a. State Department
of Administration, Data Processing Division,
Phoenix, AZ 85007. TEL 602-255-5216.

001.6 UK ISSN 0268-1188
AUTOMATED MANUFACTURING DIRECTORY.
1984. a. £30. Morgan-Grampian Book Publishing
Co., Ltd., Morgan-Grampian Hse, Calderwood St.,
London, SE18 6 QH, England. Ed. Phil Brown. adv.
circ. 1,250.
 Formerly (until 1985): Automation Directory.

AUTOMATED MATERIALS HANDLING AND
STORAGE. see *TRANSPORTATION*

629.8 001.6 UR
AVTOMATIZIROVANNYE SISTEMY
UPRAVLENIYA. 1974. irreg. 1.10 Rub.
Leningradskii Universitet, Universitetskaya nab. 7/9,
Leningrad B-164, Russian S.F.S.R., U.S.S.R. (Co-
sponsor: Ministerstvo Vysshego i Srednego
Spetsial'nogo Obrazovaniya) Indexed: Math.R.

001.6 629.8 US ISSN 0741-0042
C A D/C A M: MANAGEMENT STRATEGIES.*
1983. a. (plus monthly updates) $215. Auerbach
Publishers, Inc., One Penn Plaza, New York, NY
10119.

D L A BULLETIN. (Division of Library Automation)
see *LIBRARY AND INFORMATION
SCIENCES — Computer Applications*

001.6 629.8 US
I E E E INTERNATIONAL CONFERENCE ON
ROBOTICS AND AUTOMATION.
PROCEEDINGS. 1984. a. price varies. (Institute of
Electrical and Electronics Engineers, Inc., Computer
Society) I E E E Computer Society Press, 1730
Massachusetts Ave, N.W., Washington, DC 20036-
1903 TEL 202-371-0101. (And 345 E. 47th St.,
New York, NY 10017)
 Formerly: International Conference on Robotics.
Proceedings.

001.6 US
I E E E WORKSHOP ON LANGUAGES FOR
AUTOMATION (PROCEEDINGS) 1983. a. price
varies. (Institute of Electrical and Electronics
Engineers, Inc.) I E E E Computer Society Press,
1730 Massachusetts Ave., N.W., Washington, DC
20036-1903 (And 345 E. 47th St., New York, NY
10017)

001.6 629.8 US ISSN 0748-0059
IMAGE UNDERSTANDING. 1984. a. price varies.
Ablex Publishing Corp., 355 Chestnut St., Norwood,
NJ 07648. Eds. Shimon Ullman, Whitman Richards.

INDIAN SOCIETY OF STATISTICS AND
OPERATIONS RESEARCH. JOURNAL. see
STATISTICS

001.6 629.8 US
INTERNATIONAL COMPUTER VISION
DIRECTORY. 1984. a. $35. Technical Database
Corp., Box 720, Conroe, TX 77305. TEL 409-539-
9688. Ed. Philip Flora. adv. illus. stat. tr.lit. index.
circ. 3,000. (also avail. in microfilm)

629.8 001.6 UK ISSN 0074-3526
INTERNATIONAL CONGRESS OF AUTOMATIC
CONTROL. PROCEEDINGS. 1960. triennial.
(International Federation of Automatic Control)
Pergamon Press Ltd., Headington Hill Hall, Oxford
OX3 0BW, England.

001.6 629.8 US
INTERNATIONAL PROGRAMMABLE
CONTROLLERS DIRECTORY. 1984. a. $35.
Technical Database Corp., Box 720, Conroe, TX
77503. TEL 409-539-9688. Ed. Philip Flora. adv.
illus. stat. tr.lit. index. circ. 2,000. (also avail. in
microfilm)

651.8 CS
LORMATIC; informacni bulletin. irreg. price varies.
Institute for Application of Computing Technique in
Control, Revolucni 24, Prague 1, Czechoslovakia.

LOW COST C A D/C A M SYSTEMS. (Computer
Aided Design) see *COMPUTERS — Computer
Graphics*

629.8 JA ISSN 0374-4329
NAGOYA UNIVERSITY. FACULTY OF
ENGINEERING. AUTOMATIC CONTROL
LABORATORY. RESEARCH REPORTS/
NAGOYA DAIGAKU KOGAKUBU JIDO
SEIGYO. (Text in English) 1955. a. free. Nagoya
University, Faculty of Engineering, Automatic
Control Laboratory - Nagoya Daigaku Kogakubu
Fuzoku Jido Seigyo, Furo-cho, Chikusa-ku, Nagoya
464, Japan. abstr. charts. circ. controlled. (back
issues avail.)

001.6 629.8 PL ISSN 0434-0760
POLITECHNIKA SLASKA. ZESZYTY NAUKOWE.
AUTOMATYKA. (Text in Polish; summaries in
English and Russian) 1961. irreg. price varies.
Politechnika Slaska, W. Pstrowskiego 7, 44-100
Gliwice, Poland (Dist. by: Ars Polona-Ruch,
Krakowskie Przedmiescie 7, 00-068 Warsaw,
Poland) Ed. Anna Skrzywan-Kosek. circ. 270.

629.8 001.6 IT ISSN 0048-8291
RICERCHE DI AUTOMATICA. (Text in English)
1970. irreg. L.18000($18) (Consiglio Nazionale delle
Ricerche) Edizioni Scientifiche Inglesi Americane,
Via Palestro, 30, 00185 Rome, Italy. (Co-sponsor:
Associazione Italiane per il Calcalo Automatico) Ed.
Antonio Ruberti. bibl. charts. circ. 1,000. Indexed:
Math.R. Comput.& Contr.Abstr. Comput.Rev.
INSPEC.

001.6 629.8 US
ROBOTICS TECHNICAL DIRECTORY (YEAR)
1984. a. price varies. I S A Services, Inc., Box
12277, 67 Alexander Dr., Research Triangle Park,
NC 27709. Ed. William M. Rowe. adv. bk. rev.
tr.lit. circ. 10,000.
 Formerly: Robotics - C A D/C A M Directory.

629.8 001.6 PL
STUDIA Z AUTOMATYKI. (Text in Polish;
summaries in English) 1969. irreg., vol.9, 1983.
price varies. (Poznanskie Towarzystwo Przyjaciol
Nauk) Panstwowe Wydawnictwo Naukowe, Ul.
Miodowa 10, 00-251 Warsaw, Poland (Dist. by: Ars
Polona, Krakowskie Przedmiescie 7, 00-068
Warsaw, Poland) Ed. R. Knast. bibl. circ. 300.
Indexed: Math.R.
 Formerly: Poznanskie Towarzystwo Przyjaciol
Nauk. Komisja Automatyki. Prace (ISSN 0079-
4589)

629.8 001.6 NE
STUDIES IN AUTOMATION AND CONTROL.
1978. irreg., vol.5, 1984. price varies. Elsevier
Science Publishers B.V., Box 211, 1000 AE
Amsterdam, Netherlands.

629 629.8 UR
VOPROSY TEORII SISTEM
AVTOMATICHESKOGO UPRAVLENIYA. 1974.
irreg. 1 Rub. Leningradskii Universitet,
Universitetskaya nab. 7/9, Leningrad B-164, Russian
S.F.S.R., U.S.S.R. Indexed: Math.R.

COMPUTERS — Circuits

*see also Computers — Computer
Engineering*

ANALOG DIALOGUE; a forum for the exchange of
circuits, systems, and software for real-world signal
processing. see *COMPUTERS — Computer
Engineering*

621.381 US
ASILOMAR CONFERENCE ON CIRCUITS,
SYSTEMS AND COMPUTERS. CONFERENCE
RECORD. 1967. a. price varies. (Institute of
Electrical and Electronics Engineers, Inc.) I E E E
Computer Society Press, 1730 Massachusetts Ave.,
N.W., Washington, DC 20036-1903. Indexed:
Sci.Abstr.
 Formerly (until 1972): Asilomar Conference on
Circuits and Systems. Conference Record (ISSN
0571-3218)

COMPUTERS — Computer Architecture

001.6 621.381 US
DIGITAL & AUDIO-VIDEO DISCONTINUED DEVICES D.A.T.A. BOOK. 8th edt., 1978/79. a. $65. D.A.T.A., Inc. (Subsidiary of: International Thomson Organization) 9889 Willow Creek Rd., Box 26875, San Diego, CA 92126. TEL 619-578-7600.
Former titles: Discontinued I C's D.A.T.A. Book (ISSN 0730-2290); Discontinued Integrated Circuit D.A.T.A. Book (ISSN 0271-0129); D.A.T.A. Book of Discontinued Integrated Circuits (ISSN 0146-4825)

COMPUTERS — Computer Architecture

see also Computers—Computer Engineering

621.815 US
A C M/I E E E DESIGN AUTOMATION CONFERENCE. PROCEEDINGS. 1963? a. price varies. (Institute of Electrical and Electronics Engineers, Inc.) I E E E Computer Society Press, 1730 Massachusetts Ave., N.W., Washington, DC 20036-1903 (And 345 E. 47th St., New York, NY 10017) (Co-sponsor: Association for Computing Machinery, Special Interest Group on Design Automation) Indexed: Sci.Abstr.
Former titles (1975-1980): Design Automation Conference. Proceedings (ISSN 0146-7123); (until 1974): Design Automation Workshop. Proceedings (ISSN 0420-0098)

621.381 621.815 US
COMPUTER DESIGN AND ARCHITECTURE SERIES. 1976. irreg. Elsevier Science Publishing Co., Inc. (New York), 52 Vanderbilt Ave., New York, NY 10017. TEL 212-916-1150. Ed. Edward McCluskey.

621.815 US
I E E E COMPUTER SOCIETY WORKSHOP ON COMPUTER ARCHITECTURE FOR PATTERN ANALYSIS AND IMAGE DATABASE MANAGEMENT. PROCEEDINGS. Short title: C A P A I D M. 1981. biennial. price varies. (Institute of Electrical and Electronics Engineers, Inc.) I E E E Compute. Society Press, 1730 Massachusetts Ave., N.W., Washington, DC 20036-1903 TEL 301-589-8142. (And 345 E. 47th St., New York, NY 10017)

621.815 US ISSN 0149-7111
SYMPOSIUM ON COMPUTER ARCHITECTURE. CONFERENCE PROCEEDINGS. 1973. a. (Institute of Electrical and Electronics Engineers, Inc.) I E E E Computer Society Press, 1730 Massachusetts Ave., N.W., Washington, DC 20036-1903 TEL 202-371-0101. (And 345 E. 47th St., New York, NY 10017) (Co-publisher in alternate years: Association for Computing Machinery) Indexed: Sci.Abstr.

COMPUTERS — Computer Assisted Instruction

see also Education—Computer Applications

370.28 371.394 US ISSN 0147-9296
ASSOCIATION FOR EDUCATIONAL DATA SYSTEMS. ANNUAL CONVENTION PROCEEDINGS. 1973. a. $20. Association for Educational Data Systems, 1201 16th St., N.W., Washington, DC 20036. TEL 202-822-7845. (reprint service avail. from UMI) Indexed: Sci.Abstr.

371.394 US
C A L I C O. MONOGRAPH SERIES. 1986. irreg. $9.95. Computer Assisted Language & Instruction Consortium, 3078 JKHB, Brigham Young University, Provo, UT 84602. TEL 801-378-7079. Ed. Jerry W. Larson. charts. (back issues avail.)

371.394 US
COGNITION AND COMPUTING. 1987. irreg. price varies. Ablex Publishing Corporation, 355 Chestnut St., Norwood, NJ 07648. TEL 201-767-8450. Ed. John Black.

371.394 US
HUMAN/COMPUTER INTERACTION. 1982. irreg. price varies. Ablex Publishing Corp., 355 Chestnut St., Norwood, NJ 07648. TEL 201-767-8450. Ed. Ben Shneiderman.

COMPUTERS — Computer Engineering

see also Computers—Computer Architecture

621.381 US
ABLEX SERIES IN SOFTWARE ENGINEERING. 1987. irreg. price varies. Ablex Publishing Corporation, 355 Chestnut St., Norwood, NJ 07648. TEL 201-767-8450. Ed. Marvin Zelkowitz.

620 621.3 US ISSN 0161-3626
ANALOG DIALOGUE; a forum for the exchange of circuits, systems, and software for real-world signal processing. 1967. irreg., 2-3/yr. free to institutions, libraries, and qualified personnel. Analog Devices, Inc., 2 Technology Way, Box 280, Norwood, MA 02062. TEL 617-329-4700. Ed. Daniel H. Sheingold. bk. rev. bibl. charts. illus. tr.lit. circ. 90,000. (back issues avail.) Indexed: Sci.Abstr. INSPEC.

621.381 621.381 US ISSN 0736-8305
EXECUTION AND CONTROL SYSTEMS.* 1982. a., plus m. updates. $140. Auerbach Publishers, Inc. (Subsidiary of: International Thomson Organization Ltd.) One Penn Plaza, New York, NY 10119.

621.281 US
I E E E INTERNATIONAL CONFERENCE ON COMPUTER DESIGN. V L S I IN COMPUTERS. PROCEEDINGS. Short title: I C C D. 1983. a. (Institute of Electrical and Electronics Engineers, Inc.) I E E E Computer Society Press, 1730 Massachusetts Ave., N.W., Washington, DC 20036-1903 (And 345 E. 47th St., New York, NY 10017)
Supersedes in part (1980-1982): I E E E International Conference on Circuits and Computers. I C C C Proceedings.

621.381 US
INTERNATIONAL CONFERENCE ON DATA ENGINEERING (PROCEEDINGS) 1984. a. price varies. (Institute of Electrical and Electronics Engineers, Inc., Computer Society) I E E E Computer Society Press, 1730 Massachusetts Ave., N.W., Washington, DC 20036-1903 TEL 202-371-0101. (And: 345 E. 47th St., New York, NY 10017)

621.3 US ISSN 0195-623X
INTERNATIONAL SYMPOSIUM ON MULTIPLE-VALUED LOGIC. PROCEEDINGS. 1971. a. (Institute of Electrical and Electronics Engineers, Inc.) I E E E Computer Society Press, 1730 Massachusetts Ave., N.W., Washington, DC 20036-1903 TEL 202-371-0101. (And 345 E. 47th St., New York, NY 10017) Indexed: Sci.Abstr.
Formerly (1971-1972): Symposium on the Theory and Applications of Multiple-Valued Logic Design. Conference Record.

621.381 US
PUBLISHING PROGRAM IN COMPUTER SCIENCE: COMPUTER ARCHITECTURE AND DESIGN. irreg., vol.5, 1986. U M I Research Press, 300 N. Zeeb Rd., Ann Arbor, MI 48106. Ed. Harold Stone.

RADIO - ELECTRONICS EXPERIMENTERS HANDBOOK (YEAR) see ELECTRICITY AND ELECTRICAL ENGINEERING

621.381 US
WESTEX: I E E E WESTERN CONFERENCE ON KNOWLEDGE-BASED ENGINEERING AND EXPERT SYSTEMS. PROCEEDINGS. 1986. a. price varies. (Institute of Electrical and Electronics Engineers, Computer Society) I E E E Computer Society Press, 1730 Massachusetts Ave. N.W., Washington, DC 20036-1903 TEL 202-731-0101. (And 345 E. 47th St., New York, New York 10017-2394)

COMPUTERS — Computer Graphics

001.644 DK ISSN 0573-9985
COMPUTER AIDED DESIGN I DANMARK. a. (Statens Byggeforskningsinstitut) Bibliotekscentralen, Telegrafvej 5, DK-2750 Ballerup, Denmark.

001.644 US ISSN 0743-2836
COMPUTER GRAPHICS DIRECTORY. 1983. a. $80. PennWell Publishing Co., Box 1260, Tulsa, OK 74101. TEL 918-835-3161. adv.

001.6443 US ISSN 0278-2774
COMPUTER GRAPHICS MARKETPLACE. 1981. irreg. $35. Oryx Press, 2214 N. Central at Encanto, Ste, 103, Phoenix, AZ 85004. TEL 602-254-6156. Ed. John Cosentino.

001.644 US ISSN 0732-667X
GLITCHES; CompuGraphic user's newsletter. 1981. irreg. $36. (CompuGrahic Users Association) Maverick Publications, Drawer 5007, Bend, OR 97708. TEL 503-382-6978. Ed. Kenneth Asher. cum.index. circ. 1,200. (back issues avail.)

001.644 US
I E E E COMPUTER SOCIETY CONFERENCE ON COMPUTER VISION AND PATTERN RECOGNITION. PROCEEDINGS. Short title: C V P R. 1983. a. price varies. (Institute of Electrical and Electronics Engineers, Inc.) I E E E Computer Society Press, 1730 Massachusetts Ave., N.W., Washington, DC 20036-1903 TEL 202-371-0101. (And 345 E. 47th St., New York, NY 10017)
Supersedes (1977-1982): I E E E Computer Society Conference on Pattern Recognition and Image Processing. P R I P. Proceedings; Formerly (1975): Conference on Computer Graphics, Pattern Recognition, and Data Structure. Proceedings.

001.644 US
I E E E INTERNATIONAL CONFERENCE ON COMPUTER-AIDED DESIGN. PROCEEDINGS. Short title: I C C A D. 1983. a. (Institute of Electrical and Electronics Engineers, Inc.) I E E E Computer Society Press, 1730 Massachusetts Ave., N.W., Washington, DC 20036-1903 (And 345 E. 47th St., New York, NY 10017)
Supersedes in part (1980-1982): I E E E International Conference on Circuits and Computers. I C C C Proceedings.

001.644 620 US ISSN 0736-1823
INTERNATIONAL C A D/C A M INDUSTRY DIRECTORY. 1983. a. $40. Technical Database Corp., Box 720, Conroe, TX 77305. TEL 409-539-9688. Ed. Philip FLora. adv. tr.lit. index. circ. 5, 000. (also avail. in microfilm)
Formerly: C A D/C A M Industry Directory.

001.644 US
INTERNATIONAL COMPUTER GRAPHICS DIRECTORY. a. $35. Technical Database Corp., Box 720, Conroe, TX 77305. TEL 409-539-9688. Ed. Philip Flora. adv. illus. stat. tr.lit. index. circ. 3,000.

001.5 651.8 US
INTERNATIONAL CONFERENCE ON PATTERN RECOGNITION. PROCEEDINGS. 1973. biennial. price varies. (Institute of Electrical and Electronics Engineers, Inc.) I E E E Computer Society Press, 1730 Massachusetts Ave., N.W., Washington, DC 20036-1903 TEL 202-371-0101. (And 345 E. 47th St., New York, NY 10017)
Formerly (1973-1978): International Joint Conference on Pattern Recognition. Proceedings.

001.6 629.8 US
LOW COST C A D/C A M SYSTEMS. (Computer Aided Design) a. $99. Engineering Software Exchange, 41 Travers Ave., Yonkers, NY 10705. TEL 914-963-3695. Ed. Lidia Lopinto. circ. 500.
Formerly: C A D Systems Update.

001.644 621.381 US
S. KLEIN COMPUTER GRAPHICS REVIEW. 1985. a. $40. Technology & Business Communications, Inc., 730 Boston Post Rd., Box 915, Sudbury, MA 01776. TEL 617-443-4671. Ed. Bd. adv. circ. 22,000 (controlled)

S. KLEIN DIRECTORY OF COMPUTER GRAPHICS SUPPLIERS; hardware, software, systems & services. see COMPUTERS — Computer Industry Directories

001.644 US
SYMBOLIC COMPUTATION; artificial intelligence - computer graphics. 1982. irreg., latest 1986. Springer-Verlag, 175 Fifth Ave., New York, NY 10010 TEL 212-460-1500. (Also Berlin, Heidelberg, Tokyo, Vienna) (reprint service avail. from ISI)

COMPUTERS — Computer Industry

INSTITUTE FOR THE CERTIFICATION OF COMPUTER PROFESSIONALS. ANNUAL REPORT. see *COMPUTERS*

338   621.381   US
OFFICE - DATA PROCESSING MACHINES: LATIN AMERICAN INDUSTRIAL REPORT. 1985. a. $235 per country report. Aurora International, Box 9099, Bridgeport, CT 06601-2099. TEL 203-368-0579. Ed. Andres C. Aquino.

621.381   338   NE   ISSN 0167-6962
TRANSNATIONAL DATA REPORT; the international report on information politics and regulation. (Text in English) 1978. irreg. (approx. 12/yr., vol.8, 1985) fl.472. (Transnational Data Reporting Service, Inc., US) Elsevier Science Publishers B.V., Van Eeghenlaan 25, 1071 EN Amsterdam, Netherlands. Ed. G. Russel Pipe. adv. bk. rev. bibl. charts. illus. stat. tr.lit. index. Indexed: P.A.I.S. Sci.Abstr. Comput.Cont. Commun.Abstr. Comput.Lit.Ind. Key to Econ.Sci.

COMPUTERS — Computer Industry Directories

338   UK
ARABIAN COMPUTER GUIDE. a. £30. Beacon Publications PLC., York House, Newton Close, Park Farm, Wellingborough, Northamptonshire NN8 3UW, England.

001.6   GR
COMPU-DATA; the Greek computer market buyers' guide. (Text in Greek) 1985. a. Dr.1000. Compupress Ltd., 44 Syngrou Ave., 117 42 Athens, Greece. Ed. N. Manousos. adv. circ. 30,000.
Formerly: Data (Athens)

001.6   338   US
COMPUTER DIRECTORY AND BUYER'S GUIDE. (Supplement to: Computers and People) a. $35. Berkeley Enterprises, Inc., 815 Washington St., Newtonville, MA 02160. TEL 617-332-5453. Ed. J.P. Callahan. adv. illus.

COMPUTER READABLE DATABASES; a directory and data sourcebook. see *COMPUTERS — Abstracting, Bibliographies, Statistics*

338   US
DATAPRO WHO'S WHO IN MICROCOMPUTING. 1982? a? $39.95. Datapro Research Corporation, 1805 Underwood Blvd., Delran, NJ 08075.

338   001.642   621.381   US   ISSN 0738-839X
DIRECTORY OF COMPUTER & SOFTWARE RETAILERS. 1983. a. $249. Chain Store Guide (Subsidiary of: Lebhar-Friedman, Inc.) 425 Park Ave., New York, NY 10022. TEL 212-371-9400.

338   621.381   001.642   US
DIRECTORY OF COMPUTER INSTALLATIONS: MID-ATLANTIC STATE. 1985. a. $295. Computer Management Research, Inc., 20 Waterside Plaza, New York, NY 10010. TEL 212-683-0606.

DIRECTORY OF COMPUTERIZED DATA FILES. see *BIBLIOGRAPHIES*

658.8   UK   ISSN 0267-1441
DIRECTORY OF ELECTRONICS, INSTRUMENTS & COMPUTERS. 1965. a. £24. Morgan-Grampian Book Publishing Co. Ltd., 30 Calderwood St., London SE18 6QH, England. Ed. Phil Brown. adv. circ. 2,500.
Former titles (until 1984): Directory of Instruments, Electronics, Automation & Instruments, Electronics and Automation Purchasing Directory (ISSN 0074-0578)

338   IS
DIRECTORY OF SPECIAL DATABASES IN ISRAEL. (Text in English and Hebrew) 1986. irreg. $25. National Center of Scientific and Technological Information, Box 20125, Tel-Aviv, Israel. Ed. E. Hoffmann.

001.6   621.381   US   ISSN 0734-9068
ENCYCLOPEDIA OF INFORMATION SYSTEMS AND SERVICES. 7th edt., 1986. irreg. $210 U.S. vol.; Intl. vol. $185. Gale Research Company, Book Tower, Detroit, MI 48226. TEL 313-961-2242. Ed. Amy Lucas.

FAIRPLAY MARINE COMPUTING GUIDE. see *TRANSPORTATION — Ships And Shipping*

338   US
FEDERAL DATA BASE FINDER. 1984. every 18 months. $95. Information USA, 4701 Willard Ave., Ste. 1707, Chevy Chase, MD 20815. TEL 301-657-1200. Ed. Matthew Lesko. circ. 5,000.

338   US
GRADUATE ASSISTANTSHIP DIRECTORY IN COMPUTER SCIENCES. a. $15 to non-members; members $10. Association for Computing Machinery, 11 W. 42nd St., New York, NY 10036. TEL 212-869-7440.

INTEL YELLOW PAGES. see *COMPUTERS — Hardware*

MICROCOMPUTER MARKET PLACE. see *COMPUTERS — Microcomputers*

338   001.642   621.831   US
PERSONAL COMPUTER - AN INDUSTRY SOURCE BOOK. 1983. a. $495. Chromatic Communications Enterprises, Inc., Box 3249, Walnut Creek, CA 94598. TEL 415-945-1602. Ed. Robert Patrick.

001.64   US   ISSN 0732-9199
S. KLEIN DIRECTORY OF COMPUTER GRAPHICS SUPPLIERS; hardware, software, systems & services. 1980. a. $73. Technology & Business Communications, Inc., 730 Boston Post Rd., Box 915, Sudbury, MA 01776. TEL 617-443-4671. Ed. Mal Stiefel. adv. circ. 10,000. Indexed: Comp.Lit.Ind.
Formerly: Harvard Directory of Computer Graphics Suppliers.

338   US
SHOP BY MAIL DIRECTORY FOR PERSONAL COMPUTER USERS. 1986. irreg. $3.95. Pilot Books, 103 Cooper St., Babylon, NY 11702. TEL 516-422-2225. Ed. Mike LeFan.

COMPUTERS — Computer Industry, Vocational Guidance

see also *Education; Occupations and Careers*

COMPUTERS — Computer Music

see also *Music — Computer Applications*

C M E ANNUAL REPORT. (Center for Music Experiment) see *MUSIC*

COMPUTERS — Computer Networks

001.644   US
COMMUNITY MEMORY NEWS. 1983. a. $1. Community Memory Project, 2617 San Pablo, Berkeley, CA 94702. TEL 415-841-1114. Ed. Karen Paulsell. bk. rev. circ. 2,000. (back issues avail.)

001.644   US
COMPUTER NETWORKING SYMPOSIUM. PROCEEDINGS. 1977. a. price varies. (Institute of Electrical and Electronics Engineers, Inc.) I E E E Computer Society Press, 1730 Massachusetts Ave., N.W., Washington, DC 20036-1903 TEL 301-589-8142. (And 345 E. 47th St., New York, NY 10017) (Co-sponsor: U.S. National Bureau of Standards)

001.644   US
CONFERENCE ON LOCAL COMPUTER NETWORKS (PROCEEDINGS) 1976. a. (Institute of Electrical and Electronics Engineers, Inc.) I E E E Computer Society Press, 1730 Massachusetts Ave., N.W., Washington, DC 20036-1903. TEL 202-371-0101. (Co-sponsor: University of Minnesota. Computer Center)
Former titles: 1978: Conference on Local Computer Networking; In 1976: Conference on Experiments in New Approaches to Local Computer Networking.

001.644   CN   ISSN 0713-5424
GRAPHICS INTERFACE. PROCEEDINGS/ COMPTES RENDUS. Variant title: Graphic Interface Conference. Proceedings. (Text in English and French) 1969. a. Can.$25. Canadian Information Processing Society, 243 College St. 5th flr., Toronto, Ont. M5T 2Y1, Canada (Or National Research Council of Canada, Division of Electrical Engineering, Ottawa, Ont. K1A, 0R8) (Co-sponsors: Canadian Man-Computer Communications Society; National Computer Graphics Association of Canada) circ. 500. (back issues avail.)

001.644   UK
INTERNATIONAL ONLINE INFORMATION MEETING (PROCEEDINGS) 1977. a. Learned Information Ltd., Woodside, Hinksey Hill, Oxford OX1 5AU, England.

001.644   US   ISSN 0740-6932
LOCALNETTER DESIGNER'S HANDBOOK; the annual publication devoted solely to local network equipments. 1982. a. $102. Architecture Technology Corporation, Box 24344, Minneapolis, MN 55424. TEL 612-935-2035. Ed. Kenneth J. Thurber. adv. charts. illus. circ. 5,000. (back issues avail.)

001.644   US
NETWORK DATABASE SYSTEMS. irreg., latest 2nd edt. $215. Architecture Technology Corporation, Box 24344, Minneapolis, MN 55424. TEL 612-935-2035.

001.644   US   ISSN 0160-9742
NETWORK PLANNING PAPER. 1978. irreg., latest no.9. U.S. Library of Congress, Network Development and MARC Standards Office, Cataloging Distribution Service, Processing Services, Washington, DC 20540. TEL 202-287-1306. Ed. Sigrid G. Harriman. bibl. charts. circ. 1,500.

PERSONAL COMPUTER LOCAL NETWORKS REPORT. see *COMPUTERS — Personal Computers*

COMPUTERS — Computer Programming

see also *Computers — Software*

001.642   US
A P I C STUDIES IN DATA PROCESSING SERIES. 1961. irreg., vol.28, 1986. (Automatic Programming Information Centre) Academic Press Inc., Orlando, FL 32887. TEL 305-345-2000. Ed. F. Duncan.
Formerly: Automatic Programming Information Centre. Studies in Data Processing Series.

658.403   US   ISSN 0196-870X
ADVANCES IN COMPUTER PROGRAMMING MANAGEMENT. a. John Wiley & Sons, Inc., 605 Third Ave., New York, NY 10036. TEL 212-850-6000.

001.642   UK   ISSN 0084-6198
ALGOL BULLETIN. (Text in English) 1959. irreg., (1-2/yr.) $11 per 3 issues. International Federation for Information Processing, c/o Dr. C.H. Lindsey, Dept. of Computer Science, University of Manchester, Manchester MI3 9PL, England. Ed. C.H. Lindsey. bk. rev. circ. 400. (back issues avail.) Indexed: Ref.Zh. Sci.Abstr. Comput.Rev. Comput.Cont. Soft.Abstr.Eng.

001.642　　　　　　　US　ISSN 0066-4138
ANNUAL REVIEW IN AUTOMATIC
PROGRAMMING. 1960. a. $80. Pergamon Press,
Inc., Journals Division, Maxwell House, Fairview
Park, Elmsford, NY 10523 TEL 914-592-7700.
(And Headington Hill Hall, Oxford OX3 0BW,
England) Ed. P. Brown. (also avail. in microform
from MIM,UMI) Indexed: Sci.Abstr.

001.642　　　　　　　US　ISSN 0090-7383
CONFERENCE ON DATA SYSTEMS
LANGUAGES. DATA BASE TASK GROUP.
REPORT.* 1969. irreg., latest issue 1971. $8. ‡
Association for Computing Machinery,
Programming Language Committee, 11 W. 42nd St.,
New York, NY 10036 TEL 212-869-7440. (And
British Computer Society, 29 Portland Pl., London
WIN 4AP, England) illus. Key Title: Report -
C.O.D.A.S.Y.L. Data Base Task Group.

001.642　　　　　　　US
CURRENT TRENDS IN PROGRAMMING
METHODOLOGY. 1977. irreg., latest 1978.
$21.95. Prentice-Hall, Inc., Box 500, Englewood
Cliffs, NJ 07632. TEL 201-592-2000.

001.642　　　　　　　US
I E E E COMPUTER SOCIETY CONFERENCE
ON ADA APPLICATIONS AND
ENVIRONMENTS. 1984. biennial. price varies.
(Institute of Electrical and Electronics Engineers,
Inc., Computer Society, Computer Languages
Technical Committee) I E E E Computer Society
Press, 1730 Massachusetts Ave., N.W., Washington,
DC 20036-1903 TEL 202-371-0101. (And 345 E.
47th St., New York, NY 10017)

001.642　　　　　　　US
ICON NEWSLETTER. 1978. irreg., latest no.22. free.
University of Arizona, Department of Computer
Science, Tucson, AZ 85721. TEL 602-621-6613. Ed.
Ralph E. Griswold. circ. 2,000.

MICROPROGRAMMING WORKSHOP.
PROCEEDINGS. see COMPUTERS —
Microcomputers

001.642　　　　　　　UR
POLUTEHNILINE INSTITUUT TALLINN.
POSTROENIE TRANSLYATOROV,
OBRABOTKA DANNYKH, VOPROSY
PROGRAMMIROVANIYA. (Subseries of its
Toimetised) (Text in Russian; summaries in English
or German) irreg. price varies. Polutehniline
Instituut Tallinn, Ehitajate tee 5, Tallinn, Estonian
S.S.R., U.S.S.R.

001.6　621.381　　　US
SNOBOL4 INFORMATION BULLETIN. 1968.
irreg., latest no.30. free. University of Arizona,
Department of Computer Science, Tucson, AZ
85721. TEL 602-621-6613. Ed. Ralph E. Griswold.
circ. 800.

001.642　621.381　　GW
SOFTWAREFUEHRER FUER HOME-COMPUTER.
1985. a. DM.12.80. Dr. Lothar Rossipaul
Verlagsgesellschaft mbH, Bavariaring 24, 8000
Munich, W. Germany (B.R.D.) Ed. Rainer
Rossipaul. circ. 100,000.

001.642　621.381　　GW
SOFTWAREFUEHRER FUER PERSONAL-
COMPUTER. 1985. a. DM.28. Dr. Lothar
Rossipaul Verlagsgesellschaft mbH, Bavariaring 24,
8000 Munich, W. Germany (B.R.D.) Ed. Rainer
Rossipaul. circ. 60,000.

001.642　　　　　　　US
SYMPOSIUM ON LOGIC PROGRAMMING
PROCEEDINGS. 1984. a. price varies. (Institute of
Electrical and Electronics Engineers, Inc.) I E E E
Computer Society Press, 1730 Massachusetts Ave.,
N.W., Washington, DC 20036-1903 (And 345 E.
47th St., New York, NY 10017)
　Formerly (until 1984): International Symposium
on Logic Programming. Proceedings.

001.642　　　　DK　ISSN 0107-9352
UNIVERSITETETS STATISTISKE INSTITUT.
COMPUTER PROGRAMMES. 1982. irreg. free.
Universitetets Statistiske Institut, Studiestraede 6,
1455 Copenhagen K, Denmark. illus.

COMPUTERS — Computer Sales

see also Business and
　Economics—Marketing and Purchasing

DIRECTORY OF COMPUTER & SOFTWARE
　RETAILERS. see COMPUTERS — Computer
　Industry Directories

DIRECTORY OF ELECTRONICS, INSTRUMENTS
　& COMPUTERS. see COMPUTERS — Computer
　Industry Directories

SIN-TIME REVIEW BUYERS GUIDE. see
　COMPUTERS — Personal Computers

COMPUTERS — Computer Security

658.478　　　　　　　US　ISSN 0197-1514
ADVANCES IN COMPUTER SECURITY
MANAGEMENT. irreg. Heyden & Sons, Inc., c/o
John Wiley & Sons, 605 Third Ave., New York, NY
10016.

658.478　341　　　　CN
CANADA. PRIVACY COMMISSIONER. ANNUAL
REPORT. (Text in English and French) 1983. a.,
latest 1984-85. free. Privacy Commissioner, 112
Kent St., Ste. 1400, Ottawa, Ont. K1A 1H3,
Canada. TEL 613-995-2410. Ed. Sally Jackson. stat.
circ. 8,000. (back issues avail.)

658.478　　　　　　　US
COMPUTER SECURITY BUYERS GUIDE. a.
Computer Security Institute, 360 Church St.,
Northborough, MA 01532. TEL 617-393-2600. circ.
4,000. (looseleaf format)

DIRECTORY OF CRIMINAL JUSTICE
INFORMATION SOURCES. see LAW —
Computer Applications

658.478　　　　　　　US　ISSN 0278-7032
I E E E SYMPOSIUM ON SECURITY AND
PRIVACY. PROCEEDINGS. 1980. a. (Institute of
Electrical and Electronics Engineers, Inc.) I E E E
Computer Society Press, 1730 Massachusetts Ave.,
N.W., Washington, DC 20036-1903 (And 345 E.
47th St., New York, NY 10017)
　Formerly (1980-1985): Symposium on Security
and Privacy. Proceedings.

COMPUTERS — Computer Simulation

621.39　　　　　　　DK　ISSN 0106-357X
COMBINED SIMULATION. 1978. irreg. Koskilde
Universitetscenter, Datalogi, 4000 Roskilde,
Denmark.

621.319　　　　　　　US　ISSN 0198-0092
MODELING AND SIMULATION. 1969. a. price
varies. Instrument Society of America, 67 Alexander
Dr., Box 12277, Research Triangle Park, NC 27709.
(reprint service avail. from UMI, ISI and publisher)

001.6　621.319　　　US
SIMULATION (ANAHEIM) 1975. irreg., latest
Vancouver, 1986. $50 approx. (International
Associations of Science and Technology for
Development) Acta Press, Box 2481, Anaheim, CA
92804. Ed. M.H. Hamza. Indexed: ASCA.
Bk.Rev.Ind. Comput.Cont. Compumath.
Geo.Abstr. Lang.& Lang.Behav.Abstr.

001.6　621.319　　　US　ISSN 0272-4715
SIMULATION SYMPOSIUM. RECORD OF
PROCEEDINGS. 1968. a. price varies. (Institute of
Electrical and Electronics Engineers, Inc.) I E E E
Computer Society Press, 1730 Massachusetts Ave.,
N.W., Washington, DC 20036-1903 (And 345 E.
47th St., New York, NY 10017) (Co-sponsors:
Annual Simulation Symposium, Inc.; Society for
Computer Simulation)
　Formerly: Annual Simulation Symposium.
Proceedings.

001.64　621.319　　　US　ISSN 0094-7474
SUMMER COMPUTER SIMULATION
CONFERENCE. PROCEEDINGS. (Winter
Simulation Conference. Proceedings also published
annually; sponsoring body and publisher vary) 1969.
a. price varies. (Society for Computer Simulation)
Simulation Councils, Inc., Box 17900, San Diego,
CA 92117. TEL 614-277-3088. bk. rev. illus. index.
cum.index. (back issues avail.) Indexed:
Appl.Mech.Rev. Chem.Abstr. Comput.&
Cont.Abstr.

COMPUTERS — Computer Systems

see also Computers—Computer
　Architecture

621.381　　　　　　　US
ADVANCES IN LARGE SCALE SYSTEMS. 1984.
a. $28.75 to individuals; institutions $57.50. J A I
Press Inc., Box 1678, 36 Sherwood Pl., Greenwich,
CT 06836. TEL 203-661-7602. Ed. Jose B. Cruz, Jr.

001.535　621.381　　US
ADVANCES IN MAN-MACHINE SYSTEMS
RESEARCH. 1984. a. $28.75 to individuals;
institutions $57.50. J A I Press Inc., Box 1678, 36
Sherwood Pl., Greenwich, CT 06836. TEL 203-661-
7602. Ed. William B. Rouse.

ANALOG DIALOGUE; a forum for the exchange of
circuits, systems, and software for real-world signal
processing. see COMPUTERS — Computer
Engineering

ASILOMAR CONFERENCE ON CIRCUITS,
SYSTEMS AND COMPUTERS. CONFERENCE
RECORD. see COMPUTERS — Circuits

621.381　　　　　　　UK
COMPUTER SYSTEMS ENGINEERING. 1975.
irreg. price varies. Edward Arnold (Publishers) Ltd.,
41 Bedford Square, London WC1B 3DQ, England.
Indexed: Sci.Abstr.

651.8　　　　　　　　UK
COMPUTER USERS' YEAR BOOK. 1969. a. £85. V
N U Business Publications BV, 32-34 Broadwick St.,
London W1A 2HG, England. Ed. A. Murdoch. adv.
bk. rev. circ. 8,000.

DIRECTORY OF COMPUTER INSTALLATIONS:
MID-ATLANTIC STATE. see COMPUTERS —
Computer Industry Directories

EXECUTION AND CONTROL SYSTEMS. see
　COMPUTERS — Computer Engineering

621.381　　　　　　　US　ISSN 0073-1129
HAWAII INTERNATIONAL CONFERENCE ON
SYSTEM SCIENCES. PROCEEDINGS. 1968. a.
(University of Hawaii, College of Business
Administration) Western Periodicals Co., 13000
Raymer St., N. Hollywood, CA 91605. adv. circ.
400.

621.381　　　　　　　AU
I I A S A ANNUAL REPORT. (Text in English)
1973. a. free. International Institute for Applied
Systems Analysis, Laxenburg, Austria. Ed. J.
Anderer. illus. circ. 2,500. Indexed: Sci.Abstr.
Geo.Abstr.

INFO GUIDE (YEAR); annual guide for E.D.P. and
high technology. see COMPUTERS

621.381　　　　　　　US
INTERNATIONAL CONFERENCE ON
DISTRIBUTED COMPUTING SYSTEMS.
PROCEEDINGS. 1979. a. (Institute of Electrical
and Electronics Engineers, Inc.) I E E E Computer
Society Press, 1730 Massachusetts Ave., N.W.,
Washington, DC 20036-1903 (And 345 E. 47th St.,
New York, NY 10017)

621.381　　　　　　　US
INTERNATIONAL CONFERENCE ON
SUPERCOMPUTING SYSTEMS.
PROCEEDINGS. 1985. irreg. price varies.
(Institute of Electrical and Electronics Engineers,
Inc., Computer Society) I E E E Computer Society
Press, 1730 Massachusetts Ave., N.W., Washington,
DC 20036-1903 TEL 202-371-0101. (And: 345 E.
47th St., New York, NY 10017)

JOURNAL OF APPLIED SYSTEMS ANALYSIS.
see BUSINESS AND ECONOMICS — Computer Applications

621.381 US
L A N SOFTWARE DIRECTORY. (Local Area Network) 1985. irreg. (1-2/yr.) $137. Architect Technology Corp., Box 24344, Minneapolis, MN 55424. TEL 612-935-2035. Ed. Harvey A. Freeman.

621.381 US
PROGRAMMABLE CONTROLS TECHNICAL DIRECTORY (YEAR) 1987. a. price vaires. I S A Services, Inc., 67 Alexander Drive, Box 12277, Triangle Park, NC 27709. TEL 919-549-8411.

621.381 US
PUBLISHING PROGRAM IN COMPUTER SCIENCE: SYSTEMS PROGRAMMING. irreg., vol.21, 1984. U M I Research Press, 300 N. Zeeb Rd., Ann Arbor, MI 48106. Ed. Harold Stone.

621.381 US
REAL-TIME SYSTEMS SYMPOSIUM. PROCEEDINGS. 1981. a. (Institute of Electrical and Electronics Engineers, Inc.) I E E E Computer Society Press, 1730 Massachusetts Ave., N.W., Washington, DC 20036-1903 (And 345 E. 47th St., New York, NY 10017)

621.381 US ISSN 0094-2898
SOUTHEASTERN SYMPOSIUM ON SYSTEM THEORY. PROCEEDINGS. 1969. a. (Institute of Electrical and Electronics Engineers, Inc., Computer Society) I E E E Computer Society Press, 1730 Massachusetts Ave., N.W., Washington, DC 20036-1903 TEL 202-371-0101. (And 345 E. 47th St., New York, NY 10017) Key Title: Proceedings of the Annual Southeastern Symposium on System Theory.

VOPROSY TEORII SISTEM AVTOMATICHESKOGO UPRAVLENIYA. see COMPUTERS — Automation

001.6 621.381 US
YOURDON REPORT;* journal of structured systems development. 1976. irreg. free. Yourdon Press, 1501 Broadway, New York, NY 10036. Ed. Wendy Eakin. circ. 10,000.

COMPUTERS — Cybernetics

Includes: Bionics.

see also Computers—Artificial Intelligence

001.53 US ISSN 0066-0086
AMERICAN SOCIETY FOR CYBERNETICS. PROCEEDINGS OF THE ANNUAL SYMPOSIUM. 1967. irreg. price varies. American Society for Cybernetics, George Mason University, Department of Decision Sciences, Fairfax, VA 22030. circ. 100.
Cybernetics

001.53 FR
ASSOCIATION FRANCAISE POUR LA CYBERNETIQUE ECONOMIQUE ET TECHNIQUE. ANNUAIRE. 1968. irreg. Association Francaise pour la Cybernetique Economique et Technique, 156 bd. Pereire, 75017 Paris, France.
Formerly: Association Francaise d'Informatique et de Recherche Operationnelle. Annuaire (ISSN 0066-9296); Formed by the merger of: Societe Francaise de Recherche Operationelle. Annuaire & Association Francaise de Calcul et de Traitement d'Information. Annuaire.

001.53 US ISSN 0340-0034
COMMUNICATION AND CYBERNETICS. 1966. irreg., vol.17, 1978. price varies. Springer-Verlag, 175 Fifth Ave., New York, NY 10010 TEL 212-460-1500. (Also Berlin, Heidelburg, Tokyo and Vienna) (reprint service avail. from ISI)
Formerly: Kommunikation und Kybernetik in Einzeldarstellungen (ISSN 0075-6601)
Cybernetics

510 001.6 US
COMPUTATIONAL MATHEMATICS AND APPLICATIONS. 1977. irreg., latest vol.6, 1982. Academic Press Inc., Orlando, FL 32887. TEL 305-345-2000. Ed. J.R. Whiteman. Indexed: Math.R.

001.53 US ISSN 0883-4202
CYBERNETIC. 1967. irreg. $80. American Society for Cybernetics, c/o Department of Decision Science, George Mason University, Fairfax, VA 22030. Ed. Paul Trachtman. bk. rev. bibl. illus. circ. 250.
Former titles: A S C Cybernetics Forum; (until vol.8, 1975): A S C Forum; (until vol.10, 1981): A C S Newsletter.

001.53 BE
CYBERNETICS: WORKS IN PROGRESS/ CYBERNETICS: DOCUMENTS DE TRAVAIL. irreg., latest no.5. 800 Fr.($32) International Association for Cybernetics, Palais des Expositions, Place Andre Rijckmans, 5000 Namur, Belgium.

001.53 UR ISSN 0207-0111
GIBRIDNYE VYCHISLITEL'NYE MASHINY I KOMPLEKSY; respublikanskii mezhvedomstvennyi sbornik nauchnykh trudov. (Text in Russian) 1979. a. (Akademiya Nauk Ukrainskoi S.S.R, Institut Elektrodinamiki) Izdatel'stvo Naukova Dumka, c/o Yu.A. Khramov, Dir, Ul. Repina, 3, Kiev 252 601, Ukrainian S.S.R., U.S.S.R (Subscr. to: Mezhdunarodnaya Kniga, Moscow, G-200, Russian S.F.S.R., U.S.S.R.) Ed. V.V. Vasiliev.

001.53 US
I E E E INTERNATIONAL CONFERENCE ON SYSTEMS, MAN, AND CYBERNETICS. PROCEEDINGS. 1971. a. (I E E E, Systems, Man, and Cybernetics Society) Institute of Electrical and Electronics Engineers, Inc., 345 E. 47th St., New York, NY 10017 TEL 212-705-7900. (Subscr. address: 445 Hoes Lane, Piscataway, NJ 08854) illus.
Former titles (until 1983): International Conference on Cybernetics and Society. Proceedings (ISSN 0360-8913); (1976; 1985): I E E E International Conference on Cybernetics and Society. Proceedings; (1974): International Conference on Systems, Man and Cybernetics. Proceedings; I E E E Systems, Man, and Cybernetics Group. Annual Conference Record; (1971): I E E E Systems, Man, and Cybernetics Group. Annual Symposium Record.

001.53 GE ISSN 0232-1351
INFORMATIK - KYBERNETIC - RECHENTECHNIK. SCHRIFTENREIHE. 1981. irreg., vol.11, 1985. price varies. (Akademie der Wissenschaften der D.D.R., Zentralinstitut fuer Kybernetik und Informationsprozesse) Akademie-Verlag, Leipziger Str. 3-4, 1086 Berlin, E. Germany (D.D.R.) Ed.Bd. Indexed: Math.R.

001.53 BE ISSN 0074-3380
INTERNATIONAL CONGRESS FOR CYBERNETICS. PROCEEDINGS. ACTES. 1956. triennial, 11th, 1986. 9.000 Fr. International Association for Cybernetics - Association Internationale de Cybernetique, Palais des Expositions, Place Andre Rijckmans, 5000 Namur, Belgium.

001.53 UR ISSN 0130-6774
ITOGI NAUKI I TEKHNIKI: TEKHNICHESKAYA KIBERNETIKA. irreg., latest vol.22, 1987. price varies. Vsesoyuznyi Institut Nauchno-Tekhnicheskoi Informatsii (VINITI), Baltiiskaya ul. 14, Moscow A-219, Russian S.F.S.R., U.S.S.R. (Subscr. to: Mezhdunarodnaya Kniga, Dimitrova ul. 39, 113095 Moscow, Russian S.F.S.R., U.S.S.R.)

ITOGI NAUKI I TEKHNIKI: TEORIYA VEROYATNOSTEJ - MATEMATICHESKAYA STATISTIKA-TEORETICHESKAYA KIBERNETIKA. see MATHEMATICS

001.53 UR ISSN 0374-3896
NAUKOVEDENIE I INFORMATIKA; respublikanskii mezhvedomstvennyi sbornik nauchnykh trudov. (Text in Russian) 1969. a. (Akademiya Ukrainskoi S.S.R., Institut Kibernetiki) Izdatel'stvo Naukova Dumka, c/o Yu.A. Khramov, Dir, Ul. Repina, 3, Kiev 252 601, Ukrainian S.S.R., U.S.S.R. (Subscr. to: Mezhdunarodnaya Kniga, Moscow, G-200, Russian S.F.S.R., U.S.S.R.) Ed. G.M. Dobrov. Indexed: Sci.Abstr.

001.53 621.38 PL ISSN 0324-9794
POLITECHNIKA WROCLAWSKA. INSTYTUT CYBERNETYKI TECHNICZNEJ. PRACE NAUKOWE. KONFERENCJE. (Text in Polish; summaries in English and Russsian) 1973. irreg., no.29, 1985. price varies. Politechnika Wroclawska, Wybrzeze Wyspianskiego 27, 50-370 Wroclaw, Poland (Dist. by: Ars Polona-Ruch, Krakowskie Przedmiescie 7, 00-068 Warsaw, Poland) Ed. Jerzy Ciekot. Indexed: Math.R.

001.53 PL ISSN 0324-9786
POLITECHNIKA WROCLAWSKA. INSTYTUT CYBERNETYKI TECHNICZNEJ. PRACE NAUKOWE. MONOGRAFIE. (Text in Polish; summaries in English and Russian) 1974. irreg., no.13, 1986. price varies. Politechnika Wroclawska, Wybrzeze Wyspianskiego 27, 50-370 Wroclaw, Poland (Dist. by Ars Polona-Ruch, Krakowskie Przedmiescie 7, 00-068 Warsaw, Poland) Ed. Jerzy Ciekot. circ. 675. Indexed: Math.R.

001.53 621.38 PL ISSN 0324-9808
POLITECHNIKA WROCLAWSKA. INSTYTUT CYBERNETYKI TECHNICZNEJ. PRACE NAUKOWE. STUDIA I MATERIALY. (Text in Polish; summaries in English and Russian) 1972. irreg., no.30, 1983. price varies. Politechnika Wroclawska, Wybrzeze Wyspianskiego 27, 50-370 Wroclaw, Poland (Dist. by: Ars Polona-Ruch, Krakowskie Przedmiescie 7, 00-068 Warsaw, Poland) Ed. Jerzy Ciekot. Indexed: Math.R.

001.53 UR
POLUTEHNILINE INSTITUUT TALLINN. METODY OBRABOTKI I REGISTRATSII SIGNALOV. (Subseries of its Toimetised) (Text in Russian; summaries in English or German) irreg. price varies. Polutehniline Instituut Tallinn, Ehitajate tee 5, Tallinn, Estonian S.S.R., U.S.S.R.

001.53 UR ISSN 0134-3823
POLUTEHNILINE INSTITUUT TALLINN. RASCHET I PROEKTIROVANIE PRIBOROV, USTROISTV I SISTEM TEKHNICHESKOI KIBERNETIKI. (Subseries of its Toimetised) (Text in Russian; summaries in English or German) irreg. price varies. Polutehniline Instituut Tallinn, Ehitajate tee 5, Tallinn, Estonian S.S.R., U.S.S.R.

001.53 PL ISSN 0137-3595
POSTEPY CYBERNETYKI. (Summaries in English and Russian) 1965. q. $28. (Polskie Towarzystwo Cybernetyczne) Ossolineum, Publishing House of the Polish Academy of Sciences, Rynek 9, Wroclaw, Poland (Dist. by: Ars Polona-Ruch, Krakowskie Przedmiescie 7, Warsaw, Poland) Ed. Robert Staniszewski. Indexed: Math.R.
Formerly: Polskie Towarzystwo Cybernetyczne. Biuletyn (ISSN 0079-3655)

001.53 BU ISSN 0204-9848
PROBLEMI NA TEKHNICHESKATA KIBERNETIKA I ROBOTIKA/PROBLEMS OF ENGINEERING CYBERNETICS AND ROBOTICS. (Text in various languages) 1975. irreg. 0.89 lv. per no. (Bulgarska Akademiia na Naukite) Publishing House of the Bulgarian Academy of Sciences, Acad. G. Bonchev St., Bldg. 6, 1113 Sofia, Bulgaria. circ. 470. Indexed: Math.R.

001.53 US ISSN 0275-8717
PROGRESS IN CYBERNETICS AND SYSTEMS RESEARCH. 1975. irreg., vol.11, 1982. price varies. Hemisphere Publishing Corporation, 79 Madison Ave., New York, NY 10016. Ed. Robert Trappl. bibl. charts. illus. index. (back issues avail.) Indexed: Curr.Cont.

001.53 II
S C I M A SPECIAL SERIES. (Text in English) 1980. irreg. price varies. (Society of Management Science and Applied Cybernetics) South Asian Publishers Pvt. Ltd., 36 Netaji Subhash Marg, Daryaganj, New Delhi 110002, India. Ed. A. Ghosal. circ. 1,000.

001.53 US
SYMPOSIUM ON COMPUTER ARITHMETIC. PROCEEDINGS. 3rd, 1975. biennial. price varies. (Institute of Electrical and Electronics Engineers, Inc.) I E E E Computer Society Press, 1730 Massachusetts Ave., N.W., Washington, DC 20036-1903 (And 345 E. 47th St., New York, NY 10017)

COMPUTERS — DATA BASE MANAGEMENT

621.38 001.53   UR
TECHNINE KIBERNETIKA/TEKHNICHESKAYA KIBERNETIKA. (Text in Russian; summaries in English and Lithuanian) 1974. irreg. price varies. (Akademiya Nauk Litovskoi S.S.R., Institut Fiziko-Tekhnicheskikh Problem Energetiki) Izdatel'stvo Mokslas, Zvaigzdziu 23, Vilnius 232050, Lithuanian S.S.R., U.S.S.R. (Subscr. to: Mezhdunarodnaya Kniga, ul. Dimitrova 39/20, 113095 Moscow, Russian S.F.S.R., U.S.S.R.) Ed. A. Nemura. circ. 1,000. Indexed: Sci.Abstr.

001.53   PL   ISSN 0208-4805
UNIWERSYTET GDANSKI. WYDZIAL EKONOMIKI PRODUKCJI. ZESZYTY NAUKOWE. CYBERNETYKA EKONOMICZNA I INFORMATYKA. (Text in Polish; summaries in English and Russian) 1972. irreg. price varies. Uniwersytet Gdanski, Ul. Czerwonej Armii 110, 81-824 Sopot, Poland.

COMPUTERS — Data Base Management

ADVANCES IN COMPUTER PROGRAMMING MANAGEMENT. see *COMPUTERS — Computer Programming*

658.403   US   ISSN 0196-8718
ADVANCES IN DATA BASE MANAGEMENT. a. John Wiley & Sons, Inc., 605 Third Ave., New York, NY 10036. TEL 212-850-6000.

658.403   US   ISSN 0197-1476
ADVANCES IN DATA COMMUNICATIONS MANAGEMENT. irreg. Heyden & Sons, Inc., c/o John Wiley & Sons, 605 Third Ave., New York, NY 10016. TEL 215-382-6673.

ADVANCES IN DATA PROCESSING MANAGEMENT. see *COMPUTERS — Electronic Data Processing*

658.403   US   ISSN 0197-1433
ADVANCES IN DISTRIBUTED PROCESSING MANAGEMENT. irreg. Heyden & Sons, Inc., c/o John Wiley & Sons, 605 Third Ave., New York, NY 10016.

658.403   US
COMPUTER-BASED SYSTEMS IN INFORMATION MANAGEMENT. 1986. irreg. price varies. Ablex Publishing Corp., 355 Chestnut St., Norwood, NJ 07648. TEL 201-767-8450. Ed. Michael Ginzburg.

001.6 658.403   US
DATA BASE MONOGRAPH SERIES. no.6, 1978. irreg. $15 per no. Q E D Information Sciences, Inc., Box 181, 141 Lind, Wellesley, MA 02181. TEL 617-237-5656. Ed. Robert M. Curtice.

658.403 001.539   UK
DIRECTORY OF TRAINING. 1982. a. £72.50. Directory of Training Ltd., 5-9 Headstone Rd., Harrow, Middlesex HA1 1PL, England. Ed. Colin G. Steed. adv. charts. illus. index. circ. 3,000. (back issues avail.)
    Former titles: Directory of Computer Training & Directory of Management Training.

001.6 658.403   US
INTERNATIONAL CONFERENCE ON VERY LARGE DATA BASES. PROCEEDINGS. 1974? a. $35 to individuals; institutions $55. (International Conference on Very Large Data Bases) Morgan Kaufmann Publishers, 95 First St., Los Altos, CA 94022. TEL 415-941-4960.

MICROCOMPUTER INDUSTRY UPDATE; concise news capsules for managers and executives. see *COMPUTERS — Abstracting, Bibliographies, Statistics*

658.403   US
NATIONAL ONLINE MEETING. PROCEEDINGS. 1980. a. $50. Learned Information, Inc., 143 Old Marlton Pike, Medford, NJ 08055. Eds. Martha Williams, Thomas H. Hogan.
    Formerly (1980): National Online Information Meeting. Proceedings.

OFFICE AUTOMATION CONFERENCE DIGEST. see *COMPUTERS — Electronic Data Processing*

658.4031   US
PUBLISHING PROGRAM IN COMPUTER SCIENCE: DISTRIBUTED DATABASE SYSTEMS. irreg., vol.16, 1985. U M I Research Press, 300 N. Zeeb Rd., Ann Arbor, MI 48106. Ed. Harold Stone.

SYMPOSIUM ON RELIABILITY IN DISTRIBUTED SOFTWARE AND DATABASE SYSTEMS. PROCEEDINGS. see *COMPUTERS — Software*

COMPUTERS — Data Communications And Data Transmission Systems

DIRECTORY OF SPECIAL DATABASES IN ISRAEL. see *COMPUTERS — Computer Industry Directories*

651.8   US
INTERNATIONAL CONFERENCE ON COMPUTER COMMUNICATIONS. (PROCEEDINGS) 1972. irreg., 2nd Stockholm 1976; 3rd Toronto 1976; 4th Kyoto 1978; 5th Atlanta 1980. Elsevier Science Publishing Co., Inc. (New York), 52 Vanderbilt Ave., New York, NY 10017. TEL 212-916-1150.

621.387   CN
PROFESSIONAL DEVELOPMENT WEEK. 1962. a. Can.$150. Data Processing Institute, Box 2458, Station D, Ottawa, Ont. K1P 5W6, Canada. TEL 613-993-7791. Ed. J.P. Hession. circ. 1,000.

621.387   US
TOPICS IN INFORMATION SYSTEMS. 1984. irreg., latest 1986. Springer-Verlag, 175 Fifth Ave., New York, NY 10010 TEL 212-460-1500. (Also Berlin, Heidelberg, Tokyo, Vienna) (reprint service avail. from ISI)

COMPUTERS — Electronic Data Processing

see also *Business and Economics—Banking and Finance—Computer Applications*

A C M ADMINISTRATIVE DIRECTORY OF COLLEGE AND UNIVERSITY COMPUTER SCIENCE/DATA PROCESSING PROGRAMS AND COMPUTER FACILITIES. (Association for Computing Machinery, Inc.) see *COMPUTERS*

001.64   US
A D A P S O MEMBERSHIP DIRECTORY. 1963. a. $95. Association of Data Processing Service Organizations (ADAPSO), 1300 N. 17th St., Arlington, VA 22209. Ed. John Gracza. circ. 10,000 (controlled)
    Former titles: A D A P S O Membership; A D A P S O Directory; Directory of Data Processing Service Organizations (ISSN 0084-9901)

001.64 658.403   US   ISSN 0196-8696
ADVANCES IN DATA PROCESSING MANAGEMENT. irreg. Heyden & Sons, Inc., c/o John Wiley & Sons, 605 Third Ave., New York, NY 10016. TEL 215-382-6673. Indexed: Sci.Abstr.

AMERICAN BANKERS ASSOCIATION. NATIONAL OPERATIONS & AUTOMATION CONFERENCE. PROCEEDINGS. see *BUSINESS AND ECONOMICS — Banking And Finance—computer Applications*

AMERICAN BANKERS ASSOCIATION. OPERATIONS AND AUTOMATION DIVISION. RESULTS OF THE NATIONAL OPERATIONS & AUTOMATION SURVEY. see *BUSINESS AND ECONOMICS — Banking And Finance—computer Applications*

621.38 001.64   US
AUDIO-VIDEO I CS D.A.T.A. BOOK. 1981. a. $95. D.A.T.A., Inc., Box 26825, San Diego, CA 92126. TEL 619-578-7600.
    Formerly: Consumer I C's D.A.T.A. Book (ISSN 0276-5101)

001.64   SZ   ISSN 0379-0258
AUTOMATIC DATA PROCESSING INFORMATION BULLETIN. (Editions in English, French, German, Spanish) 1967. irreg. approx. 3/yr. free. International Social Security Association, Box 1, 1211 Geneva 22, Switzerland (Dist. by: ISSA Data Processing Consultative Service, c/o Office National de l'Emploi, 7 Boulevard de l'Empereur, B-1000 Brussels, Belgium) Ed. Vitezslav Velimsky. bibl. circ. 2,700. Indexed: Sci.Abstr. Comput.Cont. Soft.Abstr.Eng.

001.64   US
BUSINESS DATA PROCESSING: A WILEY SERIES. 1971. irreg., unnumbered, latest 1980. price varies. John Wiley & Sons, Inc., 605 Third Ave., New York, NY 10016. TEL 212-850-6000. Ed. Richard G. Canning.

001.64   CN   ISSN 0316-8956
CANADIAN INFORMATION PROCESSING SOCIETY. COMPUTER CENSUS. a. Can.$150. Canadian Information Processing Society, 243 College St., 5th Floor, Toronto, Ont. M5T 2Y1, Canada. adv. charts. stat.

001.6   US
D I D S DOINGS. irreg., vol.3, 1981. Decision Information Display System, Program Management Office, 722 Jackson Pl., Washington, DC 20500. TEL 202-822-8433. Ed. Eric Larson.

001.64 621.381   AT   ISSN 0314-1578
D P INDEX AND SOFTWARE REGISTER. 1977. a. Aus.$55. Peter Isaacson Publications, 45-50 Porter St., Prahran, Vic. 3181, Australia. adv.

651.8   US   ISSN 0011-6858
DATA PROCESSING DIGEST. (Editions in English and Spanish) 1955. m. $123 domestic; foreign $132. ‡ Data Processing Digest, Inc., c/o Gisela I. Wermke, Box 1249, Los Angeles, CA 90078. TEL 213-851-3156. Ed. M. Milligan. bk. rev. index. circ. 4,500. (looseleaf format; also avail. in microfilm from UMI; microfiche; reprint service avail. from UMI) Indexed: Comput.Rev. Resour.Ctr.Ind.

001.642 621.381   DK   ISSN 0108-3708
DATALOGI O. 1973. a. Koebenhavns Universitet, Datalogisk Institut, Sigurdsgade 41, 2200 Copenhagen N, Denmark. illus.

DATAPRO REPORTS ON BANKING AUTOMATION. see *BUSINESS AND ECONOMICS — Banking And Finance—computer Applications*

001.64   CN
E D P BUYER'S GUIDE. 1975. a. Can.$49. Page Publishing Co., 501 Oakdale Rd., Downsview, Ont. M3N 1W7, Canada. TEL 416-746-7360. Ed. Steve Wexler. adv. circ. 40,000.

621.381   US   ISSN 0190-3918
INTERNATIONAL CONFERENCE ON PARALLEL PROCESSING. PROCEEDINGS. 1972. a. price varies. (Institute of Electrical and Electronics Engineers, Inc.) I E E E Computer Society Press, 1730 Massachusetts Ave., N.W., Washington, DC 20036-1903 TEL 202-371-0101. (And 345 E. 47th St., New York, NY 10017)
    Formerly (until 1975): Sagamore Computer Conference on Parallel Processing. Proceedings.

001.64   SP
INTERNATIONAL COUNCIL FOR AUTOMATIC DATA PROCESSING IN GOVERNMENT ADMINISTRATION. PROCEEDINGS OF CONFERENCE. (Proceedings of 3rd to 5th Conferences published in "ICA-Information") 1968. irreg., 1972, 6th, West Germany. International Council for Automatic Data Processing in Government Administration, c/o Manuel Heredero, Servicio Central de Informatica, Paseo de Calvo Sotelo 16, Madrid 1, Spain. Ed. Ephraim Wagner.
    Formerly: Intergovernmental Council for Automatic Data Processing. Proceedings of Conference (ISSN 0085-1981)

001.64 651.8   JA
KYOTO UNIVERSITY. DATA PROCESSING CENTER. REPORT/KYOTO DAIGAKU OGATA KEISANKI SENTA EIBUN REPOTO. (Text in English) irreg. exchange basis. Kyoto University, Data Processing Center - Kyoto Daigaku Ogata Keisanki Senta, Yoshida Hon-cho, Sakyo-ku, Kyoto-shi 606, Japan.

001.64 658.403   US   ISSN 0272-4855
OFFICE AUTOMATION CONFERENCE DIGEST. 1980. a. price varies. American Federation of Information Processing Societies Press, Office Automation Conference Program Committee, 1899 Preston White Dr., Reston, VA 22091. TEL 703-620-8937. Ed.Bd.
Formerly: Office Automation Digest.

COMPUTERS — Hardware

Includes: Analog Computers, Digital Computers. Disk Drives, Input–Output Systems, Memory Structures, Modems, Monitors, Peripherals, Printers, Tape Decks, Terminals.

621.381   US   ISSN 0888-224X
ADVANCES IN V L S I AND COMPUTER SYSTEMS. 1983. irreg. $50 per issue. Computer Science Press, Inc., 1803 Research Blvd., Ste. 500, Rockville, MD 20850-3155. TEL 301-251-9050. Ed. Jean-Loup Baer. bk. rev. circ. 350. Indexed: Curr.Cont. Eng.Ind. Math.R. Sci.Abstr. Comput.& Control Abstr. Compumath. INSPEC.
Supersedes: Journal of V L S I and Computer Systems (ISSN 0733-5644) & Journal of Digital Systems (ISSN 0195-4350); Journal of Design Automation and Fault-Tolerant Computing (ISSN 0099-1708)

621.38   UR   ISSN 0135-1281
ANALOGO-DISKRETNYE PREOBRAZOVANIYA SIGNALOV. 1975. irreg. (Akademiya Nauk Latviiskoi S.S.R., Institut Elektroniki i Vychislitel'noi Tekhniki) Izdatel'stvo Zinatne, Turgeneva iela, 19, Riga, 226018, Latvian S.S.R., U.S.S.R. Ed. R. Nemirovsky.

621.381 658.8   UK
BRITAIN'S D I Y INDUSTRY. 1986. irreg. £125($150) Jordan & Sons Ltd., Jordan House, 47 Brunswick Place, London N1 6EE, England.

621.381 001.642 651.2   SA
COMPUTER USERS HANDBOOK. Variant title: South African Computer Users Handbook. 1977. a. R.225. Systems Publishers (Pty) Ltd., P.O. Box 41345, Craighall 2024, South Africa. adv.

DATA COMMUNICATIONS PRODUCT DIRECTORY. see *COMMUNICATIONS — Computer Applications*

DIRECTORY OF COMPUTER INSTALLATIONS: MID-ATLANTIC STATE. see *COMPUTERS — Computer Industry Directories*

621.381   US
INTEGRATED VOICE/DATA P B X'S. irreg., latest 2nd edt. $167. Architecture Technology Corporation, Box 24344, Minneapolis, MN 55424. TEL 612-935-2035. Ed. Harvey Freeman.

621.381 338   US
INTEL YELLOW PAGES. a. free. Intel Corporation, Literature Department, 3065 Bowers Ave., Santa Clara, CA 95051. adv.
For Intel computer users

621.381   US
INTERNATIONAL CONFERENCE ON COMPUTER WORKSTATIONS. PROCEEDINGS. 1985. biennial. price varies. (Institute of Electrical and Electronics Engineers, Inc., Computer Society) I E E E Computer Society Press, 1730 Massachusetts Ave., N.W., Washington, DC 20036-1907 TEL 202-371-0101. (And: 345 E. 47th St., New York, NY 10017) (also avail. in microfiche)

621.38   US
INTERNATIONAL DIRECTORY OF DISCONTINUED I CS & SEMICONDUCTORS D.A.T.A. BOOK. 1981. a. $75. D.A.T.A., Inc., Box 26875, San Diego, CA 92126. TEL 619-578-7600.
Formerly: Discontinued Type Locator D.A.T.A. Book (ISSN 0730-4943)

621.381   US
INTERNATIONAL SYMPOSIUM ON COMPUTER HARDWARE DESCRIPTION LANGUAGES. PROCEEDINGS. 4th, 1979. irreg., 6th, 1983. (I E E E, Computer Society) Elsevier Science Publishing Co., Inc. (New York), 52 Vanderbilt Ave., New York, NY 10017. TEL 212-916-1150.

621.381   US
INTERNATIONAL TEST CONFERENCE. PROCEEDINGS. 1972. a. price varies. (Institute of Electrical and Electronics Engineers, Inc.) I E E E Computer Society Press, 1730 Massachusetts Ave., N.W., Washington, DC 20036-1903 (And 345 E. 47th St., New York, NY 10017)
Former titles (1981-1982): International Test Conference. Digest of Papers; (1979-1980): Test Conference. Digest of Papers; (1978): Semiconductor Test Conference. Digest of Papers; (1974-1977): Semiconductor Test Symposium. Digest of Papers; (1973): Symposium on Semiconductor Memory Testing. Digest of Papers. In 1972: Testing to Integrate Semiconductor Memories into Computer Mainframes. Digest of Papers.

001.6
INTERNATIONAL ZURICH SEMINAR ON DIGITAL COMMUNICATIONS. (PROCEEDINGS) 1970. biennial. price varies. (I E E E, Switzerland Chapter on Digital Communication Systems) Institute of Electrical and Electronics Engineers, Inc., 345 E. 47th St., New York, NY 10017. TEL 212-705-7900.
Former titles (1972): International Zurich Seminar on Integrated Systems for Speech, Video and Data Communications. Proceedings; (1970): International Seminar on Digital Processing of Analog Signals (Proceedings)

KEY ABSTRACTS - COMPUTER COMMUNICATIONS AND STORAGE. see *COMPUTERS — Abstracting, Bibliographies, Statistics*

MICRO TO MAINFRAME COMMUNICATIONS. see *COMPUTERS — Microcomputers*

OPTICAL MEMORY REPORT. see *PHYSICS — Optics*

PICK RESOURCES GUIDE. see *COMPUTERS — Microcomputers*

COMPUTERS — Information Science And Information Theory

see also Computers

001.539   US
ADVANCES IN INFORMATION PROCESSING IN ORGANIZATIONS. 1984. a. $23.75 to individuals; institutions $47.50. J A I Press Inc., Box 1678, 36 Sherwood Pl., Greenwich, CT 06836. TEL 203-661-7602. Eds. Lee S. Sproull, Patrick D. Larkey.

BIBLIOGRAFIA BRASILEIRA DE DOCUMENTACAO. see *LIBRARY AND INFORMATION SCIENCES — Computer Applications*

DIRECTORY OF TRAINING. see *COMPUTERS — Data Base Management*

001.539   US   ISSN 0271-4655
I E E E INTERNATIONAL SYMPOSIUM ON INFORMATION THEORY. ABSTRACTS OF PAPERS. 1967. every 18 mos. (I E E E, Information Theory Group) Institute of Electrical and Electronics Engineers, Inc., 345 E. 47th St., New York, NY 10017 TEL 212-705-7900. (Subscr. address: 445 Hoes Lane, Piscataway, NJ 08854)

651.8   IS   ISSN 0073-7879
INFORMATION PROCESSING ASSOCIATION OF ISRAEL. NATIONAL CONFERENCE ON DATA PROCESSING. PROCEEDINGS. (Text in Hebrew and English) 1964. a. £15. Information Processing Association of Israel, Box 13009, Jerusalem, Israel.

001.539   US
INFORMATION TECHNOLOGY SERIES. 1976. irreg., latest vol.6. price varies. American Federation of Information Processing Societies, 1899 Preston White Dr., Reston, VA 22091. TEL 703-620-8919.

001.6 350   FR
INFORMATIQUE DANS LES ADMINISTRATIONS ET LES ENTREPRISES PUBLIQUES. 1975. irreg., latest 1982. price varies. (Commission Interministerielle de l'Informatique) Documentation Francaise, 29-30 Quai Voltaire, 75340 Paris, France.
Formerly: Informatique dans les Administrations Francaises.

001.539   UK   ISSN 0265-0711
OXFORD SURVEY IN INFORMATION TECHNOLOGY. 1984. a. £35($80) Oxford University Press, Walton St., Oxford OX2 6DP, England. Ed. P. Zorkoczy. bk. rev.

001.539   PL   ISSN 0208-7286
POLITECHNIKA SLASKA. ZESZYTY NAUKOWE. INFORMATYKA. (Text in Polish; summaries in English and Russian) 1980. irreg. price varies. Politechnika Slaska, W. Pstrowskiego 7, 44-100 Gliwice, Poland (Distributed by: Ars Polona-Ruch, Krakowskie Przedmiescie 7, 00-068 Warsaw, Poland) Ed. Stanislaw Kozielski. circ. 300.

001.539   US
SCIENCE AND COMPUTER LITERACY AUDIOVISUALS. 1977. irreg. $50. (National Information Center for Educational Media) Access Innovations, Inc., Box 40130, Albuquerque, NM 87196. TEL 505-265-3591. cum.index.
Supersedes (until 1987): N I C E M Index to Environmental Studies - Multimedia & Index to Ecology.

COMPUTERS — Microcomputers

see also Computers–Personal Computers

621.389   UK
AUDIO VISUAL AND MICRO-COMPUTER HANDBOOK. 1980. irreg. £12.95. Kogan Page Ltd., 120 Pentonville Rd., London N1 9JN, England. adv.
Former titles: Audio Visual Handbook & Navac Audio Visual Handbook.

BOOK OF APPLE SOFTWARE. see *COMPUTERS — Software*

BOOK OF IBM SOFTWARE. see *COMPUTERS — Software*

621.381 028.1   US
COMPUTER BOOKBASE; reference guide to microcomputer books. a. $4.95. McPheters, Wolfe & Jones, 16704 Marquardt Ave., Cerritos, CA 90701. TEL 213-926-9544. Ed. Laura Lang. adv. bk. rev. circ. 20,813.

COMPUTER CONTENTS; semi-monthly compilation of tables of contents from more than 250 of the latest computer periodicals. see *COMPUTERS — Abstracting, Bibliographies, Statistics*

COMPUTERTALK PHARMACY SYSTEMS BUYERS GUIDE. see *MEDICAL SCIENCES — Computer Applications*

621.381   US
EDUCATIONAL MICROCOMPUTING ANNUAL. 1985. a. $31. Oryx Press, 2214 N. Central at Encanto, Phoenix, AZ 85004-1483. TEL 602-254-6156. Ed. John H. Tasher. bibl. charts. illus. index.

621.381 001.642   US
INFOPRO: THE DIRECTORY; independent IBM Personal Computer hardware and software. Running title: Directory of Independent IBM Personal Computer Hardware and Software. 1983. a. $31.95. Infopro Inc., Box 22, Bensalem, PA 19020. TEL 215-750-1023.

INTEL YELLOW PAGES. see *COMPUTERS — Hardware*

INTERNATIONAL SYMPOSIUM ON MINI AND MICROCOMPUTERS. PROCEEDINGS. see *COMPUTERS — Minicomputers*

KINGDOM COMPUTER CONCEPTS'
NEWSLETTER - CATALOG. see
COMPUTERS — Personal Computers

LAW OFFICE GUIDE IN COMPUTERS (YEAR)
DIRECTORY. see *LAW — Computer Applications*

LOCALNETTER DESIGNER'S HANDBOOK; the
annual publication devoted solely to local network
equipments. see *COMPUTERS — Computer
Networks*

MICRO SOFTWARE EVALUATIONS. see
COMPUTERS — Software

821.381   US
MICRO TO MAINFRAME COMMUNICATIONS.
1984. irreg. $107. Architecture Technology
Corporation, Box 24344, Minneapolis, MN 55424.
TEL 612-935-2035.

MICROCOMPUTER INDEX. see *COMPUTERS —
Abstracting, Bibliographies, Statistics*

MICROCOMPUTER INDUSTRY UPDATE; concise
news capsules for managers and executives. see
*COMPUTERS — Abstracting, Bibliographies,
Statistics*

621.381   338   US   ISSN 0735-1925
MICROCOMPUTER MARKET PLACE. 1983. a.
$110. R.R. Bowker Company, 245 W. 17th St.,
New York, NY 10011. TEL 800-521-8110.

621.381   US
MICROELECTRONIC MANUFACTURING AND
TESTING DESK MANUAL. 1982. a. $30. Lake
Publishing Corporation, 17730 West Peterson Rd.,
Box 159, Libertyville, IL 60048. TEL 312-362-8711.
Ed. Terrence Thompson. adv. bk. rev. circ. 35,000.

MICROPROCESSOR-BASED SYSTEMS
ENGINEERING. see *ENGINEERING*

001.642   US
MICROPROGRAMMING WORKSHOP.
PROCEEDINGS. Short title: Micro. 4th, 1971. a.
price varies. ‡ (Institute of Electrical and
Electronics Engineers, Inc.) I E E E Computer
Society Press, 1730 Massachusetts Ave., N.W.,
Washington, DC 20036-1903 (And 345 E. 47th St.,
New York, NY 10017) (Co-publisher in alternate
years: Association for Computing Machinery,
Special Interest Group on Microcomputers) bibl.
charts.
    Former titles (1983): Annual Microprogramming
Workshop. Proceedings (ISSN 0194-1895); (1978-
1982): Workshop on Microprogramming.
Proceedings; (1974-1976?): Micro Proceedings
(ISSN 0361-2163); (1973): Annual Workshop on
Microprogramming. Preprints; (1972): Annual
Workshop on Microprogramming. Conference
Record. In 1969: Joint A C M/SIGMICRO-I E E
E Workshop on Microprogramming (Proceedings) :
(1968): A C M Workshop on Microprogramming
(Proceedings)

621.381   US
MODEL II - 12 - 16 NEWSLETTER. 1978. irreg.
$24 for 12 issues. H & E Computronics, Inc., 50 N.
Pascak Rd., Spring Valley, NY 10977. TEL 914-
425-1535. Ed. Andy Hofer. adv. circ. 5,000.
    Formerly: Model II - A Regular 16 Newsletter.

621.381   US
NORTHERN BYTES. 1980. irreg., vol.7, no.3, 1985.
$4 per no. Alternate Source Information Outlet, 704
N. Pennsylvania Ave., Lansing, MI 48906-5319.
TEL 517-482-8270. Ed. Jack Decker. adv. bk. rev.
circ. 2,000. (also avail. in microform)
    Formerly: 80-User Digest.
    For TRS-80 users

NOTABLE INDIVIDUALS. see *ENERGY*

P C ABSTRACTS. see *COMPUTERS — Abstracting,
Bibliographies, Statistics*

621.381   UK
P C YEAR BOOK. 1985. a. £40. V N U Business
Publications BV, 32-34 Broadwick St., London W1A
2HG, England. Ed. Chris Long. circ. 5,500.
    Formerly: Microcomputer User's Year Book.

621.381   001.642   UK
PICK RESOURCES GUIDE. 1985. a. £29.95.
A.L.L.M. Books, 21 Beechcroft Rd., Bushey, Herts.
WD2 2JU, England.

PLUS; Plus System newsletter. see *PUBLISHING
AND BOOK TRADE — Computer Applications*

RADIO - ELECTRONICS EXPERIMENTERS
HANDBOOK (YEAR) see *ELECTRICITY AND
ELECTRICAL ENGINEERING*

S. KLEIN COMPUTER GRAPHICS REVIEW. see
COMPUTERS — Computer Graphics

SIN-TIME REVIEW BUYERS GUIDE. see
COMPUTERS — Personal Computers

TANDY EDUCATIONAL SOFTWARE
SOURCEBOOK. see *COMPUTERS — Software*

COMPUTERS — Minicomputers

DIRECTORY OF COMPUTER INSTALLATIONS:
MID-ATLANTIC STATE. see *COMPUTERS —
Computer Industry Directories*

621.381   CN
INTERNATIONAL SYMPOSIUM ON MINI AND
MICROCOMPUTERS. PROCEEDINGS. 1976? a.
price varies. (International Society of Mini and
Microcomputers) Acta Press, Box 25, Calgary, Alta.
T3A 2G1, Canada. Ed. M.H. Hamza.

COMPUTERS — Personal Computers

see also Computers — Microcomputers

A I CH E APPLICATIONS SOFTWARE SURVEY
OF PERSONAL COMPUTERS. (American
Institute of Chemical Engineers) see
COMPUTERS — Software

BOOK OF APPLE SOFTWARE. see
COMPUTERS — Software

BOOK OF IBM SOFTWARE. see *COMPUTERS —
Software*

COMPUTER BOOKBASE; reference guide to
microcomputer books. see *COMPUTERS —
Microcomputers*

001.642   GW
COMPUTER KATALOG; Marktuebersicht fuer
Home und Personal-Computer. 1983. a. F. Ch. Heel
Verlag, Koenigswinterer Strasse 528-536, 5300 Bonn
3 (Oberkassel), W. Germany (B.R.D.) Ed. Klaus
Bachmann. circ. 10,000.

INFOPRO: THE DIRECTORY; independent IBM
Personal Computer hardware and software. see
COMPUTERS — Microcomputers

INTEL YELLOW PAGES. see *COMPUTERS —
Hardware*

621.381   US
KINGDOM COMPUTER CONCEPTS'
NEWSLETTER - CATALOG.* irreg., (4-6 per yr.)
$5. Palos Computer Concepts, Box 560, Palos Park,
IL 60464. bk. rev. circ. 750.
    Formerly: Kingdom Computer Concepts'
Newsletter.

LAW OFFICE GUIDE IN COMPUTERS (YEAR)
DIRECTORY. see *LAW — Computer Applications*

MICROCOMPUTER INDUSTRY UPDATE; concise
news capsules for managers and executives. see
*COMPUTERS — Abstracting, Bibliographies,
Statistics*

MICROCOMPUTER MARKET PLACE. see
COMPUTERS — Microcomputers

P C ABSTRACTS. see *COMPUTERS — Abstracting,
Bibliographies, Statistics*

PERSONAL COMPUTER - AN INDUSTRY
SOURCE BOOK. see *COMPUTERS — Computer
Industry Directories*

621.381   001.644   US
PERSONAL COMPUTER LOCAL NETWORKS
REPORT. irreg. $195. Architecture Technology
Corporation, Box 24344, Minneapolis, MN 55424.
TEL 612-935-2035. Ed. Harvey Freeman.

PLUS; Plus System newsletter. see *PUBLISHING
AND BOOK TRADE — Computer Applications*

S. KLEIN COMPUTER GRAPHICS REVIEW. see
COMPUTERS — Computer Graphics

621.381   658.8   US
SIN-TIME REVIEW BUYERS GUIDE. (Supplement
to: Sin-Times Review) a. $4.95. Box 742163,
Houston, TX 77274.
    For Timex-Sinclair users

SOFTWARE REPORTS: GUIDE TO EVALUATED
EDUCATIONAL SOFTWARE. see
COMPUTERS — Software

SOFTWAREFUEHRER FUER HOME-COMPUTER.
see *COMPUTERS — Computer Programming*

SOFTWAREFUEHRER FUER PERSONAL-
COMPUTER. see *COMPUTERS — Computer
Programming*

TANDY EDUCATIONAL SOFTWARE
SOURCEBOOK. see *COMPUTERS — Software*

COMPUTERS — Software

*see also Computers — Computer
Programming*

001.642   621.281   US   ISSN 0743-0183
A I CH E APPLICATIONS SOFTWARE SURVEY
OF PERSONAL COMPUTERS. 1984. irreg., latest
1985-86. price varies. American Institute of
Chemical Engineers, 345 E. 47th St., New York, NY
10017. TEL 212-705-7657. Ed.Bd. index.

001.642   US
ADVANCES IN SOFTWARE ENGINEERING.
1985. a. $28.75 to individuals; institutions $57.50. J
A I Press Inc., Box 1678, 36 Sherwood Pl.,
Greenwich, CT 06836-1678. TEL 203-661-7602.
Ed. Stephen S. Yau.

001.642   SZ
BASIC SOFTWARE. 1977. irreg., no. 4, 1984. price
varies. Paul Haupt AG, Falkenplatz 14, CH-3001
Berne, Switzerland.

001.642   621.381   US   ISSN 0736-2692
BOOK OF APPLE SOFTWARE. 1981. a. $24.95.
Arrays, Inc., Book Division, 6711 Valjean Ave., Van
Nuys, CA 91406. TEL 818-994-1899. Ed.Bd.

001.642   621.381   US   ISSN 0738-7172
BOOK OF IBM SOFTWARE. 1983. a. $24.95.
Arrays, Inc., Book Division, 6711 Valjean Ave., Van
Nuys, CA 91406. TEL 818-994-1899. Eds. Michael
Mellin, Mia McCroskey.

001.642   US   ISSN 0730-3157
C O M P S A C/I E E E COMPUTER SOCIETY'S.
INTERNATIONAL COMPUTER SOFTWARE &
APPLICATIONS CONFERENCE.
PROCEEDINGS. 1977. a. price varies. (Institute of
Electrical and Electronics Engineers, Inc.) I E E E
Computer Society Press, 1730 Massachusetts Ave.,
N.W., Washington, DC 20036-1903 (And 345 E.
47th St., New York, NY 10017) Indexed:
Comput.Lit.Ind.

COMPUTER USERS HANDBOOK. see
COMPUTERS — Hardware

001.642   US
CONFERENCE ON SOFTWARE
MAINTENANCE. PROCEEDINGS. 1983.
biennial. price varies. (Institute of Electrical and
Electronics Engineers, Inc., Computer Society) I E
E E Computer Society Press, 1730 Massachusetts
Ave., N.W., Washington, DC 20036-1903 TEL 202-
371-0101. (And: 345 E. 47th St., New York, NY
10017)
    Formerly (until 1983): Software Maintenance
Workshop. Record.

CONSTRUCTION COMPUTER APPLICATIONS DIRECTORY. see *BUILDING AND CONSTRUCTION*

D P INDEX AND SOFTWARE REGISTER. see *COMPUTERS — Electronic Data Processing*

DATA COMMUNICATIONS PRODUCT DIRECTORY. see *COMMUNICATIONS — Computer Applications*

DIRECTORY OF COMPUTER & SOFTWARE RETAILERS. see *COMPUTERS — Computer Industry Directories*

DIRECTORY OF COMPUTER INSTALLATIONS: MID-ATLANTIC STATE. see *COMPUTERS — Computer Industry Directories*

001.642 US
DIRECTORY OF COMPUTER SOFTWARE. a. $48. U.S. National Technical Information Service, 5285 Port Royal Rd., Springfield, VA 22161. TEL 703-487-4650.

001.642 370 US ISSN 8755-5107
EDUCATIONAL SOFTWARE SELECTOR. Abbreviated title: T E S S. 1984. a. $59.95. Educational Products Information Exchange (EPIE) Institute, Box 839, Water Mill, NY 11976. TEL 516-283-4922. Ed. Robert Haven. index. circ. 6,000. (back issues avail.)
• Also available online. Vendors: CompuServe Consumer Information Service.

FILM PROGRAMMER'S GUIDE TO 16MM RENTALS. see *MUSEUMS AND ART GALLERIES — Abstracting, Bibliographies, Statistics*

ICON NEWSLETTER. see *COMPUTERS — Computer Programming*

INFOPRO: THE DIRECTORY; independent IBM Personal Computer hardware and software. see *COMPUTERS — Microcomputers*

001.642 US ISSN 0270-5257
INTERNATIONAL CONFERENCE ON SOFTWARE ENGINEERING. PROCEEDINGS. 1975. a. (Institute of Electrical and Electronics Engineers, Inc.) I E E E Computer Society Press, 1730 Massachusetts Ave., N.W., Washington, DC 20036-1903 TEL 202-371-0101. (And 345 E. 47th St., New York, NY 10017)
Formerly: National Conference on Software Engineering. Proceedings.

001.642 US
INTERNATIONAL ENGINEERING/SCIENTIFIC SOFTWARE DIRECTORY. 1985. a. $35. Technical Database Corp., Box 720, Conroe, TX 77305. TEL 409-539-9688. Ed. Philip Flora. adv. illus. stat. tr.lit. index. circ. 3,000. (also avail. in microfilm)
Formerly: International Engineering Software Directory.

001.642 US
INTERNATIONAL MANUFACTURING SOFTWARE DIRECTORY. 1984. a. $35. Technical Database Corp., Box 720, Conroe, TX 77305. TEL 409-539-9688. Ed. Philip Flora. adv. illus. stat. tr.lit. index. circ. 3,000.

001.642 500 US
INTERNATIONAL SCIENTIFIC SOFTWARE DIRECTORY. 1984. a. $35. Technical Database Corp., Box 720, Conroe, TX 77305. TEL 409-539-9688. Ed. Philip Flora. adv. illus. stat. tr.lit. index. circ. 2,000.

001.642 US
INTERNATIONAL WORKSHOP ON SOFTWARE SPECIFICATION AND DESIGN (PROCEEDINGS) 1982. irreg. price varies. (Institute of Electrical and Electronics Engineers, Inc., Computer Society) I E E E Computer Society Press, 1730 Massachusetts Ave., N.W., Washington, DC 20036-1903 TEL 202-371-0101. (And: 345 E. 47th St., New York, NY 10017)
Former titles (until 1984): International Workshop on Models and Languages for Software Specification and Design (Proceedings); (until 1982): International Symposium on Current Issues of Requirements Engineering Environments.

KEY ABSTRACTS - SOFTWARE ENGINEERING. see *COMPUTERS — Abstracting, Bibliographies, Statistics*

LAW OFFICE GUIDE IN COMPUTERS (YEAR) DIRECTORY. see *LAW — Computer Applications*

001.642 621.381 US ISSN 8755-5794
MICRO SOFTWARE EVALUATIONS. a. $95. Meckler Publishing, 11 Ferry Lane W., Westport, CT 06880. TEL 203-226-6967. Ed. Jeanne Nolan. circ. 600.

001.642 670 US
N A S A SOFTWARE DIRECTORY. a. $20. High Tech Publishing Company, 10 Ridge Rd., Box 360, Ridge, NY 11961. TEL 516-924-6168.
• Also available online.

PERSONAL COMPUTER - AN INDUSTRY SOURCE BOOK. see *COMPUTERS — Computer Industry Directories*

001.642 US ISSN 0743-6750
PETROLEUM SOFTWARE DIRECTORY. 1984. a. $95. PennWell Publishing Co., Box 1260, Tulsa, OK 74101. TEL 918-835-3161. Ed. William R. Leek, Jr. adv. circ. 1,000.

PICK RESOURCES GUIDE. see *COMPUTERS — Microcomputers*

001.642 690 UK ISSN 0268-5124
R I B A COMPUTER SOFTWARE SELECTOR. 1985. a. £12.50. (Royal Institute of British Architects) R I B A Services Ltd., 66 Portland Place, London W1N 4AD, England. (Co-sponsor: Construction Industry Computing Association) Ed. David Clegg. adv. circ. 1,000.

SNOBOL4 INFORMATION BULLETIN. see *COMPUTERS — Computer Programming*

001.539 US
SOFTFAIR: A CONFERENCE ON SOFTWARE DEVELOPMENT TOOLS, TECHNIQUES, AND ALTERNATIVES. PROCEEDINGS. 1983. biennial. price varies. (Institute of Electrical and Electronics Engineers, Inc.) I E E E Computer Society Press, 1730 Massachusetts Ave., N.W., Washington, DC 20036-1903 (And 345 E. 47th St., New York, NY 10017) (Co-publisher: Association for Computing Machinery)

620 001.642 IE ISSN 0790-150X
SOFTWARE ABSTRACTS FOR ENGINEERS. 1984. q. £115($120) C I T I S Ltd., 2 Rosemount Terrace, Blackrock, Dublin, Ireland. TEL 353-1-885-971. Ed. D.P. Murphy. adv. index. (back issues avail.; avail. in CD-ROM)

001.642 011 US
SOFTWARE ENCYCLOPEDIA. (In 2 vols.) 1985. a. $149.95. R.R. Bowker Company, Database Publishing Group, 245 W. 17th St., New York, NY 10011. TEL 800-521-8110.
• Also available online. Vendors: DIALOG.

001.642 GW
SOFTWARE KATALOG; Marktuebersicht fuer alle IBM-kompatiblen Programme. 1984. a. F. Ch. Heel Verlag, Koenigswinterer Str. 528-536, 5300 Bonn 3 (Oberkassel), W. Germany (B.R.D.) Ed. Klaus Bachmann. circ. 10,000.

001.539 011 020 US ISSN 0740-5022
SOFTWARE PUBLISHERS' CATALOGS ANNUAL. 1983. a. $165.00. Meckler Publishing, 11 Ferry Lane West, Westport, CT 06880. TEL 203-226-6967. Ed. Nancy Jean Melin. index. circ. 250. (microfiche)

001.642 370 621.381 US
SOFTWARE REPORTS: GUIDE TO EVALUATED EDUCATIONAL SOFTWARE. 1983. a. $180 including bi-w updates. Trade Service Publications, Inc, Software Reports, 10996 Torreyana Rd., San Diego, CA 92121 TEL 619-457-5920. Ed. Bonnie J. Dudley.

001.642 UK
SOFTWARE USERS' YEAR BOOK. 1985. a. £99. V N U Business Publications BV, 32-34 Broadwick St., London W1A 2HG, England. Ed. Anne Maher. circ. 4,500.
Formerly: Microcomputer Software Directory/International Directory of Software.

SPECIALWARE DIRECTORY; a guide to software sources for special education. see *EDUCATION — Computer Applications*

621.381 US
SWIFT'S DIRECTORY OF EDUCATIONAL SOFTWARE FOR THE IBM PC. a. plus s-a. updates. $19.95. Sterling Swift Publishing Company, 7901 S. IH-35, Austin, TX 28744. TEL 512-282-6840.

001.642 658.381 US
SYMPOSIUM ON RELIABILITY IN DISTRIBUTED SOFTWARE AND DATABASE SYSTEMS. PROCEEDINGS. 1981. a. price varies. (Institute of Electrical and Electronics Engineers, Inc.) I E E E Computer Society Press, 1730 Massachusetts Ave., N.W., Washington, DC 20036 (And 345 E. 47th St., New York, NY 10017) (Co-sponsors: Association for Computing Machinery; University of Pittsburgh)

001.642 NE ISSN 0167-7888
T R W SERIES OF SOFTWARE TECHNOLOGY. 1978. irreg., vol.4, 1984. price varies. Elsevier Science Publishers B.V., Box 211, 1000 AE Amsterdam, Netherlands. Indexed: Sci.Abstr.

001.644 621.381 370 US
TANDY EDUCATIONAL SOFTWARE SOURCEBOOK. 1981. a. $13.95. Radio Shack Education Division, 1400 One Tandy Center, Ft. Worth, TX 76102. TEL 817-390-3832.
Formerly: T R S - 80 Educational Software Sourcebook.

COMPUTERS — Theory Of Computing

001.539 US
A C M SYMPOSIUM ON THE THEORY OF COMPUTING. 1969. a. price varies. Association for Computing Machinery, Special Interest Group on Automata and Compatibility Theory, 11 W. 42nd St., New York, NY 10036. bibl. charts.

COMPUTERS — Word Processing

651.8 US
KELLY - GRIMES BUYERS GUIDE FOR WORD PROCESSING. 1984. a. John Wiley & Sons, Inc., 605 Third Ave., New York, NY 10158. TEL 212-850-6779. adv. circ. 20,000.

CONSERVATION

see also Environmental Studies; Forests and Forestry; Water Resources

A.C.A. REVIEW. (Anglers Cooperative Association) see *FISH AND FISHERIES*

333.7 PL ISSN 0208-533X
ACTA UNIVERSITATIS NICOLAI COPERNICI. ZABYTKOZNAWSTWO I KONSERWATORSTWO. 1966. irreg. price varies. Uniwersytet Mikolaja Kopernika, Fosa Staromiejska 3, Torun, Poland (Dist. by Osrodek Rozpowszechniania Wydawnictw Naukowych PAN, Palac Kultury i Nauki, 00-901 Warsaw, Poland)

333.78 US ISSN 0065-5708
ALASKA. DEPARTMENT OF FISH AND GAME. ANNUAL REPORT. 1949. a. Department of Fish and Game, Box 3-2000, Juneau, AK 99802. TEL 907-465-4112.

639 US ISSN 0516-4303
ALASKA. DEPARTMENT OF FISH AND GAME. INFORMATIONAL LEAFLET. 1961. irreg. Department of Fish and Game, Box 3-2000, Juneau, AK 99802.

333.7 US ISSN 0084-0130
ALASKA. DEPARTMENT OF FISH AND GAME. WILDLIFE BOOKLET SERIES. irreg. Department of Fish and Game, Box 3-2000, Juneau, AK 99802. TEL 907-465-4112.

CONSERVATION

639.9 US ISSN 0065-9150
AMERICAN LITTORAL SOCIETY. SPECIAL PUBLICATIONS. 1962. irreg. (3-5/yr.) $20. American Littoral Society, Sandy Hook, Highlands, NJ 07732. TEL 201-291-0055. Ed. D.W. Bennett. adv. bk. rev. circ. 5,000. (also avail. in microform from UNM; reprint service avail. from UMI) Indexed: Biol.Abstr.

AQUATIC SCIENCES & FISHERIES ABSTRACTS. PART 1: BIOLOGICAL SCIENCES & LIVING RESOURCES. see *WATER RESOURCES — Abstracting, Bibliographies, Statistics*

333.78 US
ASSOCIATION OF MIDWEST FISH AND WILDLIFE AGENCIES. PROCEEDINGS. (Notes: Publisher varies according to host state.) 1934. a. Association of Midwest Fish and Wildlife Agencies, Box 30028, Lansing, MI 48909. TEL 316-672-6473.
Former titles: Association of Midwest Fish and Wildlife Commissioners. Proceedings; Association of Midwest Fish and Game Commissioners. Proceedings (ISSN 0066-9601)

ATLANTIC SALMON FEDERATION. SPECIAL PUBLICATION SERIES. see *FISH AND FISHERIES*

333.7 614.7 AT ISSN 0313-5780
AUSTRALIA. ENVIRONMENTAL STUDIES WORKING PAPERS. 1976. irreg. price varies. Board of Environmental Studies, University of Tasmania, G.P.O. Box 252C, Hobart, Tas. 7001, Australia. Ed. John Todd. circ. 100. (back issues avail.)

333.7 AT ISSN 0587-5846
AUSTRALIAN CONSERVATION FOUNDATION. ANNUAL REPORT. 1968. a. Australian Conservation Foundation, 672B Glenferrie Rd, Hawthorn, Vic. 3122, Australia. illus.

639.9 AT
AUSTRALIAN NATIONAL PARKS AND WILDLIFE SERVICE. REPORT. a. Australian Government Publishing Service, G.P.O. Box 84, Canberra, A.C.T. 2601, Australia. illus.

333.7 AT ISSN 0313-7414
AUSTRALIAN NATIONAL UNIVERSITY. CENTRE FOR RESOURCE AND ENVIRONMENTAL STUDIES. WORKING PAPERS. 1974. irreg. free. Australian National University, Centre for Resource and Environmental Studies (C.R.E.S.), Canberra, A.C.T. 2600, Australia. Ed. Gordon Sheldon. circ. 500.

333.7 GW ISSN 0525-4736
BEITRAEGE ZUR LANDESENTWICKLUNG. 1966. irreg., no. 40, 1980. price varies. (Landschaftsverband Rheinland, Referat Landschaftspflege) Rheinland-Verlag, Kennedy-Ufer 2, 5000 Cologne 21, W. Germany (B.R.D.) (Distr. by: Rudolf Habelt Verlag, Am Buchenhang 1, 5300 Bonn, W. Germany (B.R.D.))

BIRDWATCHER'S YEARBOOK AND DIARY. see *BIOLOGY — Ornithology*

639.9 ZA ISSN 0045-219X
BLACK LECHWE. 1956; N.S. 1981. irreg., 2-3/yr. K.7($9) free to members. Wildlife Conservation Society of Zambia, P.O. Box 255, Lusaka, Zambia. Eds. R. Jeffrey, R. lumbe. adv. bk. rev. circ. 3,500. Indexed: Biol.Abstr.

333.7 CN
BRITISH COLUMBIA. MINISTRY OF ENVIRONMENT AND PARKS. ANNUAL REPORT. 1964. a. free. Ministry of Environment and Parks, Informations Branch, 810 Blanshard Street, Victoria, B.C. V8V 3E1, Canada. TEL 604-387-9422. circ. 3,000.
Former titles: British Columbia. Ministry of Environment. Annual Report (ISSN 0227-7506); British Columbia. Department of Lands, Forests and Water Ressources. Water Resources Service. Report (ISSN 0068-1873)

333.7 CN ISSN 0706-4152
C C I TECHNICAL BULLETINS. (Text in English and French) 1975. irreg. free. Canadian Conservation Institute, 1030 Innes Rd., Ottawa, Ont. K1A 0M8, Canada. TEL 613-995-9832. (Affiliate: National Museums of Canada) bibl. illus. (back issues avail.)

333.7 US
CALIFORNIA. DEPARTMENT OF FISH AND GAME. FISH AND GAME CODE. a. $7.30. (Department of Fish and Game) Gould Publications, 199 State St., Binghamton, NY 13901. TEL 607-724-3000. Ed. Harold Cribbs. index. circ. 1,550. (also avail. in looseleaf format)

333.7 US
CALIFORNIA. DEPARTMENT OF FISH AND GAME. FISH AND GAME CODE. SUPPLEMENT. irreg. $7. (Department of Fish and Game) Gould Publications, 199 State St., Binghamton, NY 13901. TEL 607-724-3000. Ed. Harold Cribbs. index.

639.9 CN
CANADA. CANADIAN WILDLIFE FEDERATION. PUBLICATION LIST. a. Canadian Wildlife Federation, 1673 Carling Ave., Ottawa, Ont. K2A 1C4, Canada. TEL 613-725-2191.
Formerly: Canada. Federal-Provincial Wildlife Conference. Wildlife Management Papers.

333.91 CN
CANADA. FISHERIES AND ENVIRONMENT CANADA. REPORT OF OPERATIONS UNDER THE CANADA WATER ACT.* (Text in English and French) 1973. a. Department of Fisheries & Oceans, 200 Kent St., Ottawa, Ont. K1A 0E6, Canada. TEL 613-995-4031.

333.7 CN ISSN 0068-7693
CANADA LAND INVENTORY. REPORT. 1965. irreg. Lands Directorate, 20th Floor P.V.M., Ottawa, Ont. K1A 0E7, Canada. TEL 819-997-2320. Ed. T. Pierce. circ. 1,500.

333.7 CN ISSN 0318-2789
CANADIAN CONSERVATION DIRECTORY. 1971. irreg. Can.$12.95. Canadian Nature Federation, 75 Albert St., Suite 203, Ottawa, Ont. K1P 6G1, Canada. TEL 613-238-6154. (reprint service avail. from UMI)

590 CN ISSN 0069-0015
CANADIAN WILDLIFE SERVICE. MONOGRAPH SERIES. (Editions in English, French) 1961. irreg., no.6, 1981. price varies. Canadian Wildlife Service, Environment Canada, Ottawa, Ont. K1A 0E7, Canada TEL 613-997-1095. (Dist. by: Dept. of Supply and Services, Ottawa, Ont. K1A 0S9, Canada) Indexed: Biol.Abstr.

639.9 CN ISSN 0576-6370
CANADIAN WILDLIFE SERVICE. OCCASIONAL PAPERS. (Editions in English, French) 1966. irreg., no.58, 1986. free. ‡ Canadian Wildlife Service, Environment Canada, Ottawa, Ont. K1A 0E7, Canada. TEL 819-997-1095. circ. 2,000. Indexed: Biol.Abstr. Nutr.Abstr. Key Word Ind.Wildl.Res. Rural Recreat.Tour.Abstr. World Agri.Econ.& Rural Sociol.Abstr.

639.9 CN ISSN 0069-0023
CANADIAN WILDLIFE SERVICE. PROGRESS NOTES/SERVICE CANADIEN DE LA FAUNE. CAHIERS DE BIOLOGIE. (Editions in English, French) 1967. irreg., no.164, 1986. free. ‡ Canadian Wildlife Service, Environment Canada, Ottawa, Ont. K1A 0E7, Canada. TEL 819-997-1095. circ. 2,000. Indexed: Biol.Abstr. Key Word Ind.Wildl.Res.

333.7 574 CN ISSN 0069-0031
CANADIAN WILDLIFE SERVICE. REPORT SERIES. (Editions in English, French) 1966. irreg., no.47, 1986. price varies. ‡ Canadian Wildlife Service, Environment Canada, Ottawa, Ont. K1A 0E7, Canada TEL 613-997-1095. (Dist. by: Dept. of Supply and Services, Ottawa, Ont. K1A 0S9, Canada) circ. 2,000. Indexed: Biol.Abstr. Geo.Abstr. Key Word Ind.Wildl.Res.

333.7 SA
CAPE OF GOOD HOPE. DEPARTMENT OF NATURE CONSERVATION AND MUSEUM SERVICES. ANNUAL REPORT. (Text in Afrikaans and English) 1965. a. free. Department of Nature Conservation, Wale St., Private Bag 9086, Cape Town 8000, South Africa. charts. illus. circ. 2,000. (processed) Indexed: Biol.Abstr.
Former titles: Cape of Good Hope. Department of Nature Conservation. Annual Report; Cape of Good Hope. Department of Nature Conservation. Newsletter (ISSN 0008-5804)

CARIBBEAN RESEARCH INSTITUTE. REPORT. see *HISTORY — History Of North And South America*

333.7 US ISSN 0084-8875
COLORADO. DIVISION OF WILDLIFE. SPECIAL REPORT. 1962. irreg., no. 57, 1984. $1. ‡ Division of Wildlife, 317 W. Prospect, Ft. Collins, CO 80526. TEL 303-484-2836. circ. 1,200. (back issues avail.) Indexed: Biol.Abstr. Key Word Ind.Wildl.Res. Wild Life Rev.

333.7 639.9 US ISSN 0084-8883
COLORADO. DIVISION OF WILDLIFE. TECHNICAL PUBLICATION. 1955. irreg., no.34, 1983. $1 per issue. Division of Wildlife, 317 W. Prospect, Ft. Collins, CO 80526. TEL 303-484-2836. Ed. Nancy W. McEwen. bibl. charts. illus. stat. circ. 1,200. Indexed: Biol.Abstr. Wild Life Rev.

639.9 AT ISSN 0813-0493
COMMONWEALTH SCIENTIFIC AND INDUSTRIAL RESEARCH ORGANIZATION. DIVISION OF WILDLIFE AND RANGELANDS RESEARCH. TECHNICAL MEMORANDUM. 1969. irreg. C.S.I.R.O., Division of Wildlife and Rangelands Research, Box 84, Lyneham, A.C.T. 2602, Australia. circ. 400.
Formerly: Commonwealth Scientific and Industrial Research Organization. Division of Wildlife Research. Technical Memorandum (ISSN 0084-9073)

639.9 AT ISSN 0812-2237
COMMONWEALTH SCIENTIFIC AND INDUSTRIAL RESEARCH ORGANIZATION. DIVISION OF WILDLIFE AND RANGELANDS RESEARCH. TECHNICAL PAPER. 1958. irreg. Aus.$2 per no. C.S.I.R.O., Division of Wildlife Research, P.O. Box 84, Lyneham 2602, A.C.T., Australia. index. circ. 600. Indexed: Biol.Abstr.

333.7 CN
CONSERVATION COUNCIL OF ONTARIO. CONFERENCE PROCEEDINGS. irreg. price varies. Conservation Council of Ontario, 74 Victoria St., 202, Toronto, Ont. M5C 2A5, Canada. TEL 416-362-2218.

333.7 CN
CONSERVATION COUNCIL OF ONTARIO. REPORTS. irreg. price varies. Conservation Council of Ontario, 74 Victoria St., 202, Toronto, Ont. M5C 2A5, Canada. TEL 416-362-2218.

333.7 US ISSN 0069-911X
CONSERVATION DIRECTORY; a listing of organizations, agencies and officials concerned with natural resource use and management. 1955. a. $15. ‡ National Wildlife Federation, Inc., 1412 16th St. N.W., Washington, DC 20036. TEL 703-790-4402. Ed. Rue Gordon. circ. 8,000. (back issues avail.)

333.72 US ISSN 0094-1670
CONSERVATION IN KANSAS. 1972. a. free. State Conservation Commission, 109 S.W. Ninth St., Rm. 300, Topeka, KS 66612. TEL 913-296-3600. Ed. Lola Warner. illus. stat. circ. 600.
Continues: Kansas. State Conservation Commission. Conservation in Kansas (ISSN 0453-2384)

333.7 UK ISSN 0140-0096
CONSERVATOR. 1977. a. £25 to individuals; institutions £40; students £10. United Kingdom Institute for Conservation, Conservation Department, Tate Gallery, Millbank, London SW1P 4RG, England. Ed. Suzanne Keene. bk. rev. circ. 950. Indexed: Art & Archaeol.Tech.Abstr. Br.Archaeol.Abstr. Key to Econ.Sci.

COORDINATION DIRECTORY OF STATE AND FEDERAL WATER RESOURCE OFFICIALS IN THE MISSOURI RIVER BASIN. see *WATER RESOURCES*

333.7 FR
COUNCIL OF EUROPE. EUROPEAN INFORMATION CENTRE FOR NATURE CONSERVATION. DOCUMENTATION SERIES. 1976. irreg. free. Council of Europe, European Information Centre for Nature Conservation, B.P. 431R6, 67006 Strasbourg Cedex, France. bibl.

CONSERVATION

339.49 UK ISSN 0070-3001
DAWN SONG AND ALL DAY.* 1949. irreg. World Bird Research Station, Glanton, Northumberland, England.
   Formerly: Dawn Song.

DELAWARE. DEPARTMENT OF NATURAL RESOURCES AND ENVIRONMENTAL CONTROL. ANNUAL REPORT. see *ENVIRONMENTAL STUDIES*

639.9 US ISSN 0418-7598
DESERT BIGHORN COUNCIL. TRANSACTIONS. 1957. a. $6. Desert Bighorn Council, 1500 N. Decatur Blvd., Las Vegas, NV 89108. Ed. Paul Krausman. cum. index. circ. 300. (back issues avail.)

DIRECTORY OF CO-OPERATIVE NATURALISTS' PROJECTS IN ONTARIO. see *BIOLOGY — Ornithology*

DIRECTORY OF ENVIRONMENTAL ORGANIZATIONS. see *ENVIRONMENTAL STUDIES*

DIRECTORY OF STATE ENVIRONMENT AGENCIES. see *ENVIRONMENTAL STUDIES*

DISCOVERY (RICHMOND) see *HISTORY*

333.7 US
ECO-HUMANE LETTER. 1976. irreg. $7. International Ecology Society, 1471 Barclay St., St. Paul, MN 55106. Ed. R. J. Kramer. adv. bk. rev. circ. 3,000.
   Formerly: Eco-Letter.

333.7 EC
ECUADOR. MINISTERIO DE RECURSOS NATURALES Y ENERGETICOS. INFORME DE LABORES. a. Ministerio de Recursos Naturales y Energeticos, Oficio 609-Director de Planificacion, Quito, Ecuador. illus.

333.7 ES
EL SALVADOR. MINISTERIO DE AGRICULTURA Y GANADERIA. DIRECCION GENERAL DE RECURSOS NATURALES RENOVABLES. PLAN ANUAL OPERATIVO. a. Direccion General de Recursos Naturales Renovables, Final la Avda. Norte, Santa Tecla, El Salvador.

ENVIRONMENTAL HOTLINE. see *ENVIRONMENTAL STUDIES*

ENVIRONMENTAL POLLUTION, CITY DEVELOPMENT AND REGIONAL DEVELOPMENT INDEX. see *ENVIRONMENTAL STUDIES*

FAR SEAS FISHERIES RESEARCH LABORATORY. BULLETIN. see *FISH AND FISHERIES*

FAR SEAS FISHERIES RESEARCH LABORATORY. SERIES. see *FISH AND FISHERIES*

639.9 SA ISSN 0250-7013
FAUNA & FLORA. Afrikaans Edition (ISSN 0046-3388) (Editions in Afrikaans and English) 1950. irreg. free. ‡ Transvaal Nature Conservation Division, Private Bag X209, Pretoria, South Africa. Ed. Karin Holtshousen. illus. circ. 40,000. Indexed: Biol.Abstr. Ind.S.A.Per. Wild Life Rev. Zoo.Rec.

639.9 574 FI ISSN 0015-2447
FINNISH GAME RESEARCH/ RIISTATIETEELLISIA JULKAISUJA. (Text mainly in English) 1948. irreg. free. Finnish Game and Fisheries Research Institute, Game Division, Turunlinnantie 8, SF-00930 Helsinki, Finland. Ed. Harto Linden. circ. 650. Indexed: Biol.Abstr. Key Word Ind.Wildl.Res. Wild Life Rev. Zoo.Rec.
   Formerly (1948-1964): Papers on Game Research.

333.7 US
FOCUS (MOSCOW); on renewable natural resources. 1975. a. free. University of Idaho, Forest, Wildlife and Range Experiment Station, Moscow, ID 83843. TEL 208-885-6673. Ed. George H. Savage. circ. 1,500.

333.7 UK
FOCUS ON NATURE CONSERVATION. 1983. irreg. Nature Conservancy Council, Interpretive Services, Northminster House, Peterborough PE1 1UA, England.

FORTH NATURALIST AND HISTORIAN. see *SCIENCES: COMPREHENSIVE WORKS*

333.7 DK ISSN 0900-9825
FREDNINGSSTYRELSEN RAPPORT. irreg. (Fredningsstyrelsen) Bibliotekscentralen, Telegrafvej 5, DK-2750 Ballerup, Denmark.

FUNDACION MIGUEL LILLO. SERIE CONSERVACION DE LA NATURALEZA. see *BIOLOGY — Botany*

639.9 598.2 UK
GAME CONSERVANCY ANNUAL REVIEW. 1968. a. £3($5.19) Game Conservancy, Fordingbridge, Hants. SP6 1EF, England. Ed.Bd. adv. illus. stat. index. circ. 14,000. (back issues avail.) Indexed: Biol.Abstr.

333.7 550 UK ISSN 0260-6925
GREAT BRITAIN. INSTITUTE OF TERRESTRIAL ECOLOGY. BANGOR OCCASIONAL PAPER. 1977. irreg. Institute of Terrestrial Ecology, Bangor Research Station, Penrhos Rd., Bangor, Gwynedd LL57 2LQ, Wales.

333.7 550 UK ISSN 0308-3675
GREAT BRITAIN. INSTITUTE OF TERRESTRIAL ECOLOGY. MERLEWOOD RESEARCH AND DEVELOPMENT PAPER. 1968. irreg. free. Institute of Terrestrial Ecology, Merlewood Research Station, Grange-over-Sands, Cumbria LA11 6JU, England.

333.7 550 UK ISSN 0141-6464
GREAT BRITAIN. INSTITUTE OF TERRESTRIAL ECOLOGY. STATISTICAL CHECKLIST. 1978. irreg. £0.30. Institute of Terrestrial Ecology, Monks Wood Experimental Station, Huntingdon Cambs PE17 2LS, England.

333.7 UK ISSN 0263-8614
GREAT BRITAIN. INSTITUTE OF TERRESTRIAL ECOLOGY. SYMPOSIA. 1965. irreg. price varies. Institute of Terrestrial Ecology, Monks Wood Experimental Station, Huntingdon, Cambs PE17 2LS, England.
   Formerly (until no.7, 1975): Great Britain. Monks Wood Experimental Station. Symposia (ISSN 0077-0426)

333.7 AT ISSN 0727-0119
GREEN PAGES: DIRECTORY OF NON-GOVERNMENT ENVIRONMENTAL GROUPS IN AUSTRALIA. 1970. irreg. price varies. Australian Conservation Foundation, 672 B Glenferrie Rd., Hawthorn, Vic. 3122, Australia.
   Formerly: Australian Conservation Foundation. Conservation Directory.

333.7 634.9 US ISSN 0073-3369
HORACE M. ALBRIGHT CONSERVATION LECTURESHIP. 1961. a. free. University of California, Berkeley, Department of Forestry and Resource Management, 145 Mulford Hall, Berkeley, CA 94720. TEL 415-642-0376. Indexed: Forest.Abstr.

333.7 AT ISSN 0085-1663
HUNTER VALLEY RESEARCH FOUNDATION. MONOGRAPHS. 1959. irreg. price varies. Hunter Valley Research Foundation, Box 23, Tighes Hill, N.S.W. 2297, Australia. Indexed: Aus.Sci.Ind.

333.7 AT ISSN 0310-0111
HUNTER'S HILL TRUST JOURNAL. 1971. irreg. free. Hunter's Hill Trust, P.O. Box 85, Hunter Hill, N.S.W. 2110, Australia. bk. rev. circ. 1,000. (back issues avail.)

630 US
I C A S A L S ANNUAL REPORT. a. International Center for Arid and Semi-Arid Land Studies, Texas Tech University, Box 4620 Tech Sta., Lubbock, TX 79409-4620. Eds. Nancy M. Hood, Idris R. Traylor. illus.

333.7 SZ
I U C N ANNUAL REPORT.* (Text in English) 1970. a. International Union for Conservation of Nature and Natural Resources, Ave. du Mont-Blanc, CH-1196 Gland, Switzerland. Ed. Robert I. Standish. circ. 2,000. Indexed: Biol.Abstr.
   Formerly (until 1975/1976): I U C N Yearbook (ISSN 0074-9265)

639 US ISSN 0073-4527
IDAHO. DEPARTMENT OF FISH AND GAME. FEDERAL AID INVESTIGATION PROJECTS. PROGRESS REPORTS AND PUBLICATIONS. 1940? irreg., (approx. a.) free limited distribution. Department of Fish and Game, Box 25, Boise, ID 83707. TEL 208-334-3700. circ. controlled. (also avail. in microfiche)

333.9 RE
INFO-NATURE. 1974. irreg. 20 Fr.CFA. Societe Reunionnaise pour l'Etude et la Protection de l'Environnement, B.P. 1012, 97481 Saint Denis Cedex, Reunion. illus.

333.7 639.9 US ISSN 0161-3332
INTERNATIONAL ASSOCIATION OF FISH AND WILDLIFE AGENCIES. PROCEEDINGS OF THE CONVENTION. 1946. a. price varies. International Association of Fish and Wildlife Agencies, 1412 16th St. N.W., Washington, DC 20036. TEL 202-232-1652. Eds. Jack H. Berryman, Merle Markley. circ. 1,250. (back issues avail.)
   Formerly: Convention of the International Association of Fish and Wildlife Agencies (ISSN 0163-8653)

INTERNATIONAL CENTRE OF INSECT PHYSIOLOGY AND ECOLOGY. ANNUAL REPORT. see *BIOLOGY — Genetics*

INTERNATIONAL COMMISSION FOR THE CONSERVATION OF ATLANTIC TUNAS. REPORT. see *BIOLOGY — Zoology*

333.7 SZ ISSN 0074-9281
INTERNATIONAL UNION FOR CONSERVATION OF NATURE AND NATURAL RESOURCES. PROCEEDINGS AND PAPERS OF THE TECHNICAL MEETING.* 1949. triennial; 12th meeting with 11th general assembly, 1972, Banff, Canada. $7.50. International Union for Conservation of Nature and Natural Resources, Ave. du Mont-Blanc, CH-1196 Gland, Switzerland (Dist. in the U.S. by: Unipub, Inc., Box 433, Murray Hill Sta., New York, NY 10016) Ed. Sir Hugh Elliott. Indexed: Biol.Abstr.

333.7 SZ ISSN 0074-929X
INTERNATIONAL UNION FOR CONSERVATION OF NATURE AND NATURAL RESOURCES. PROCEEDINGS OF THE GENERAL ASSEMBLY.* 1948. triennial; 11th, Banff, Canada, 1972. International Union for Conservation of Nature and Natural Resources, Ave. du Mont-Blanc, CH-1196 Gland, Switzerland. Ed. Sir Hugh Elliott.

INTERNATIONAL WHALING COMMISSION. REPORT. see *FISH AND FISHERIES*

INTERNATIONAL WHALING COMMISSION. SPECIAL ISSUES. see *BIOLOGY*

333.7 II ISSN 0022-457X
JOURNAL OF SOIL AND WATER CONSERVATION IN INDIA. (Text in English) 1952. a. Rs.12($2) Soil Conservation Society of India, DVC Campus, Hazaribagh, Bihar, India. Ed. K.S.V. Raman. adv. charts. illus. circ. 600. (back issues avail.) Indexed: Biol.Abstr. Chem.Abstr. GeoRef.

333.9 AU ISSN 0022-7595
KAERNTNER NATURSCHUTZBLAETTER. 1962. a. S.30. Amt der Kaerntner Landesregierung, Abteilung Landesplanung, Wulfengasse 13, A-9020 Klagenfurt, Austria. Ed. Oskar Glanzer. bk. rev. charts. illus. index. circ. 8,000.

CONSERVATION

500.9　　　　　　SA　ISSN 0075-6458
KOEDOE; research journal for National Parks in the Republic of South Africa. (Text in Afrikaans and English; summaries in English) 1958. a. R.25. National Parks Board - Nasionale Parkeraad, P.O. Box 787, Pretoria 0001, South Africa. Ed. G. de Graaff. cum.index: vols. 1-25 in vol. 25(1982) circ. 1,200. Indexed: Biol.Abstr. Field Crop Abstr. Forest.Abstr. Forest Prod.Abstr. Geo.Abstr. Helminthol.Abstr. Herb.Abstr. Ind.Vet. Ind.S.A.Per. Zoo.Rec. Rev.Appl.Entomol. Soils & Fert. Vet.Bull.

500.9　　　　　　SA　ISSN 0075-6466
KOEDOE. MONOGRAPHS. 1966. irreg. R.25. National Parks Board - Nasionale Parkeraad, P.O. Box 787, Pretoria 0001, South Africa. Ed. G. de Graaff. circ. 2,000. Indexed: Biol.Abstr. Zoo.Rec.

333.7　　　　　　SA　ISSN 0075-7780
LAMMERGEYER. (Text in English) 1960. irreg. $4. Natal Parks, Game & Fish Preservation Board, P.O. Box 662, Pietermaritzburg 3200, South Africa. Ed. D.N. Johnson. circ. 700. Indexed: Biol.Abstr. Curr.Cont. Ind.S.A.Per. Rev.Appl.Entomol. Sel.Water Res.Abstr. Wild Life Rev. Vet.Bull.

LINCOLN INSTITUTE OF LAND POLICY. BASIC CONCEPT SERIES. see *HOUSING AND URBAN PLANNING*

LIVING WITH THE SHORE. see *ENVIRONMENTAL STUDIES*

LUDWIG BOLTZMANN-INSTITUT FUER UMWELTWISSENSCHAFTEN UND NATURSCHUTZ. MITTEILUNGEN. see *ENVIRONMENTAL STUDIES*

LUNDS UNIVERSITET. VAEXTEKOLOGISKA INSTITUTIONEN. MEDDELANDEN. see *BIOLOGY — Botany*

MALAWI. DEPARTMENT OF FORESTRY AND GAME. REPORT. see *FORESTS AND FORESTRY*

340　639.9　　　　US　ISSN 0196-4690
MARINE MAMMAL PROTECTION ACT OF 1972 ANNUAL REPORT. a. U.S. National Marine Fisheries Service, National Oceanic and Atmospheric Administration, Washington, DC 20235. TEL 202-655-4000.
　Formerly: Administration of the Marine Mammal Protection Act of 1972 (ISSN 0148-186X)

333.78　　　　　　US
MASSACHUSETTS. DIVISION OF FISHERIES AND WILDLIFE. ANNUAL REPORT. 1866. a. Division of Fisheries and Wildlife, 100 Cambridge St., Boston, MA 02202. TEL 617-727-3151.
　Formerly: Massachusetts. Division of Fisheries and Game. Annual Report (ISSN 0076-4957)

333.7　　　　　　US　ISSN 0090-8177
MINNESOTA. DEPARTMENT OF NATURAL RESOURCES. BIENNIAL REPORT. 1968. biennial. free. ‡ Department of Natural Resources, DNR Bldg., 500 Lafayette Rd., Box 46, St. Paul, MN 55146. TEL 612-296-6157. Ed. Gail Gendler. charts. illus. circ. 500.

639.9　　　　　　US
MINNESOTA. DIVISION OF FISH & WILDLIFE. TECHNICAL BULLETIN. 1944. irreg. free. ‡ Department of Natural Resources, Division of Fish and Wildlife, 500 Lafayette Rd., St. Paul, MN 55146. TEL 612-296-3344.
　Formerly: Minnesota. Division of Game and Fish. Technical Bulletin (ISSN 0076-9134)

MISSISSIPPI. DEPARTMENT OF WILDLIFE CONSERVATION. ANNUAL REPORT. see *FISH AND FISHERIES*

333.7　　　　　　US　ISSN 0085-3496
MISSOURI. DEPARTMENT OF CONSERVATION. ANNUAL REPORT. 1937. a. $1. Department of Conservation, Box 180, Jefferson City, MO 65102. Ed. June Hunzeker. circ. 800. (processed) Indexed: GeoRef.

MONOGRAPHS ON SOIL AND RESOURCES SURVEY. see *AGRICULTURE — Crop Production And Soil*

MONTANA FOREST AND CONSERVATION EXPERIMENT STATION. BIENNIAL REPORT. see *FORESTS AND FORESTRY*

333.7　　　　　　RM
MUZEUL DE ISTORIE AL REPUBLICII SOCIALISTE ROMANIA. CERCETARI DE CONSERVARE SI RESTAURARE A PATRIMONIULUI MUZEAL. (Text in Rumanian; summaries in English, French) 1981. irreg. Muzeul de Istorie al Republicii Socialiste Romania, Calea Victoriei 12, Bucharest, Rumania. Ed.Bd.

333.7　　　　　　UK　ISSN 0077-5916
NATIONAL TRUST FOR SCOTLAND YEARBOOK. 1931. a. membership. ‡ National Trust for Scotland, 5 Charlotte Sq., Edinburgh EH2 4DU, Scotland. Ed. P.E. Rooney. circ. 110,000.

NATURAL RESOURCES RESEARCH. see *EARTH SCIENCES*

339.49　　　　　　FR
NATURE AND ENVIRONMENT SERIES. (Editions in English and French) 1967. irreg. price varies. Council of Europe, European Information Centre for Nature Conservation, Publications Section, B.P. 431R6, 67006 Strasbourg, France (Dist. in U.S. by Manhattan Publishing Co., 225 Lafayette St., New York, N.Y. 10012)
　Formerly: Conservation of Nature and Natural Resources (ISSN 0069-9144)

333.7　　　　　　UK
NATURE CONSERVANCY COUNCIL. ANNUAL REPORT. 1975. a. Nature Conservancy Council, Interpretive Services, Northminster House, Peterborough PE1 1UA, England.

333.7　　　　　　UK　ISSN 0143-0378
NATURE CONSERVANCY COUNCIL. CHIEF SCIENTIST TEAM REPORTS. 1978. irreg. Nature Conservancy Council, Information and Library Services, Northminster House, Peterborough PE1 1UA, England.

333.7　614.7　　　　AT
NATURE CONSERVATION COUNCIL OF N.S.W. NEWSLETTER. 1972. irreg. free. Nature Conservation Council of New South Wales, 176 Cumberland St., Sydney, N.S.W., Australia. circ. 450.
　Formerly: Nature Conservation Council of N.S.W. Bulletin (ISSN 0311-0745)

639.9　333.7　　　　UK　ISSN 0143-9634
NATURE IN DEVON. 1980. a. £2. Devon Trust for Nature Conservation, 35 New Bridge St., Exeter, Devon, England. Ed. Stephen Locke. illus. charts. circ. 750. Indexed: Geo.Abstr.

333.7　　　　　　CN
NEW BRUNSWICK. FIELD SERVICES BRANCH. PROVINCIAL PARK STATISTICS. a. free. Field Services Branch, P.O. Box 12345, Fredericton, N.B. E3B 5C3, Canada. TEL 506-453-2730. illus.

333.7　　　　　　US　ISSN 0077-8362
NEW HAMPSHIRE. FISH AND GAME DEPARTMENT. BIENNIAL REPORT. 1865. biennial. free. Fish and Game Department, 34 Bridge St., Concord, NH 03301. TEL 603-271-3211. circ. 1,000.

353.9　　　　　　US
NEW YORK (STATE). DEPARTMENT OF ENVIRONMENTAL CONSERVATION. ANNUAL REPORT. Cover title: State of New York's Environment. a. Department of Environmental Conservation, 50 Wolf Rd., Albany, NY 12233. TEL 518-457-2344. illus.

333.7　　　　　　NZ　ISSN 0110-2079
NEW ZEALAND. SOIL BUREAU. SOIL SURVEY REPORTS. 1973. irreg. price varies. Soil Bureau, Private Bag, Lower Hutt, New Zealand.

712.5　　　　　　CN　ISSN 0078-0502
NIAGARA PARKS COMMISSION. ANNUAL REPORT. 1886. a. free. Niagara Parks Commission, Niagara Falls, Ont. L2E 6T2, Canada. TEL 416-356-2241. circ. 500.

333.7　　　　　　US　ISSN 0078-1355
NORTH AMERICAN WILDLIFE AND NATURAL RESOURCES CONFERENCE. TRANSACTIONS. 1915. a. $21. Wildlife Management Institute, 1101 14 St., N.W., Ste. 725, Washington, DC 20005. TEL 202-371-1808. Ed. R.E. McCabe. cum.index. circ. 1,000. (reprint service avail. from ISI) Indexed: Biol.Abstr. Forest.Abstr. Forest Prod.Abstr.
　Former titles, 1915-1936: Transactions of the American Game Conference; North American Wildlife Conference. Transactions (ISSN 0097-6830); North American Wildlife Conference. Proceedings.

333.7　　　　　　US　ISSN 0097-7268
NORTH CAL-NEVA RESOURCE CONSERVATION AND DEVELOPMENT PROJECT. ANNUAL WORK PLAN. a. North Cal-Neva Resource Conservation and Development Project, Box 888, Alturas, CA 96101. illus. Key Title: Annual Work Plan - North Cal-Neva Resource Conservation and Development Project.

639.9　　　　　　AT　ISSN 0159-8821
NORTHERN TERRITORY. CONSERVATION COMMISSION. ANNUAL REPORT. 1978. a. Conservation Commission, P.O. Box 1046, Alice Springs, N.T. 5750, Australia.
　Formerly: Northern Territory. Territory Parks and Wildlife Commission. Annual Report.

NOVA SCOTIA TRAPPERS NEWSLETTER. see *LEATHER AND FUR INDUSTRIES*

NOW AND THEN. see *LITERATURE*

339.49　　　　　　PL　ISSN 0078-3250
OCHRONA PRZYRODY. (Text in Polish; summaries in English and French) 1920. a. price varies. (Polska Akademia Nauk, Zaklad Ochrony Przyrody i Zasobow Naturalnych) Panstwowe Wydawnictwo Naukowe, Ul. Miodowa 10, 00-251 Warsaw, Poland (Dist by: Ars Polona, Krakowskie Przedmiescie 7, 00-068 Warsaw, Poland) Ed. Kazimierz Zarzycki. bibl. charts. illus. Indexed: Biol.Abstr.

333.9　　　　　　US　ISSN 0095-442X
OKLAHOMA. CONSERVATION COMMISSION. BIENNIAL REPORT. 1941. biennial. contr. free circ. Conservation Commission, 2800 Lincoln, Ste. 160, Oklahoma City, OK 73105. TEL 405-521-2384. Ed. Mason Mungle. stat. circ. 175.

OLD-HOUSE JOURNAL CATALOG. see *BUILDING AND CONSTRUCTION*

333.7　　　　　　CN　ISSN 0704-2809
ONTARIO. MINISTRY OF NATURAL RESOURCES. FOREST RESEARCH. 1952. irreg. free. Ministry of Natural Resources, 99 Wellesley St. W., Toronto, Ont. M7A 1W3, Canada. TEL 416-965-2000. circ. 800. Indexed: Forest.Abstr. Forest Prod.Abstr.
　Former titles: Ontario. Ministry of Natural Resources. Forest Research Report (ISSN 0381-3924); Ontario. Division of Forests. Research Library. Research Report (ISSN 0078-4753); Ontario. Department of Lands and Forests. Research Branch. Research Report.

ONTARIO. MINISTRY OF THE ENVIRONMENT. ANNUAL REPORT. see *ENVIRONMENTAL STUDIES*

333.7　　　　　　SA
ORANGE FREE STATE. NATURE CONSERVATION BRANCH. ANNUAL REPORT. (Text in Afrikaans and English) 1971. a. free. ‡ Nature Conservation Branch, Box 517, Bloemfontein 9300, South Africa. circ. 500.
　Formerly: Orange Free State. Nature Conservation Division. Annual Report.

574　　　　　　SA
ORANGE FREE STATE. NATURE CONSERVATION BRANCH. MISCELLANEOUS PUBLICATIONS SERIES. (Text in Afrikaans and English) 1970. irreg. free. ‡ Nature Conservation Branch, P.O. Box 517, Bloemfontein 9300, South Africa.
　Formerly: Orange Free State. Nature Conservation Division. Miscellaneous Publications Series.

CONSERVATION

333.7 SA
PELEA. (Text in Afrikaans and English) 1982. a. R.6. East Cape Game Management Association, P.O. Box 1059, Queenstown 5320, South Africa. Ed. W.S. Stretton. circ. 800. (back issues avail.) Indexed: Ind.S.A.Per.

PHILIPPINES. BUREAU OF MINES. ANNUAL REPORT. see *MINES AND MINING INDUSTRY*

PHILIPPINES. MINISTRY OF NATURAL RESOURCES. ANNUAL REPORT. see *ENVIRONMENTAL STUDIES*

333.7 614.7 PH
PHILIPPINES. MINISTRY OF NATURAL RESOURCES. PLANS AND PROGRAMS. 1976. a. Department of Natural Resources, Diliman, Quezon City, Philippines. charts. stat.

POLAR BEARS. see *BIOLOGY — Zoology*

PRAIRIE WIND. see *ENVIRONMENTAL STUDIES*

719.32 US ISSN 0270-1308
PUBLICATIONS IN ARCHAELOGY. 1951. irreg. U.S. National Park Service, Interior Bldg., Washington, DC 20240 TEL 202-343-1100. (Orders to: Supt. Doc., Washington, DC 20402) Indexed: GeoRef.
Formerly: U.S. National Park Service. Archaeological Research Series (ISSN 0083-2308)

333.7 634.9 CN
QUEBEC (PROVINCE). CONSEIL CONSULTATIF SUR LES RESERVES ECOLOGIQUES. RAPPORT ANNUEL. 1975/76. a. Ministere des Communications du Quebec, Conseil Consultatif sur les Reserves Ecologiques, 3900, rue Marly, Sainte-Foy, Que. G1X 4E4, Canada. circ. 500.
Former Titles: Quebec (Province) Ministere de l'Environment. Conseil Consultatif des Reserves Ecologoques. Rapport Annuel; Quebec (Province) Ministere des Terres et Forets. Conseil Consultatif des Reserves Ecologiques. Rapport Annuel (ISSN 0700-3749)

333.7 CN ISSN 0703-0940
QUEBEC (PROVINCE) MINISTERE DES RICHESSES NATURELLES. RAPPORT. English edition: Quebec (Province). Department of Natural Resources. Report. a. Ministere des Richesses Naturelles, Distribution et Documentation, 1620 Bd. l'Entente, Quebec G1S 4N6, Canada. illus. stat.

333.7 574 US ISSN 0079-9211
QUETICO-SUPERIOR WILDERNESS RESEARCH CENTER, ELY, MINNESOTA. ANNUAL REPORT. 1949. irreg. free. Wilderness Research Foundation, 3100 Prudential Plaza, Chicago, IL 60601. Ed. Clifford E. Ahlgren. Indexed: Biol.Abstr.

333.7 US ISSN 0079-922X
QUETICO-SUPERIOR WILDERNESS RESEARCH CENTER, ELY, MINNESOTA. TECHNICAL NOTES. 1952. irreg., 1968, no. 5. Wilderness Research Foundation, 3100 Prudential Plaza, Chicago, IL 60601. Ed. Clifford E. Ahlgren. Indexed: Biol.Abstr.

RAPTOR REPORT. see *BIOLOGY — Ornithology*

RESEARCH REPORT DIGEST. see *CONSERVATION — Abstracting, Bibliographies, Statistics*

352 AT
RIVERLANDER NOTES. 1946. irreg., approx. 4-5/yr. Aus.$6. Murray Valley Development League, Box 359, Albury 2640, Australia. Ed. Geoff Wilson. adv. bk. rev. illus. index. circ. 10,000.
Formerly: Riverlander (ISSN 0035-5682)

333.7 BL ISSN 0101-7616
ROESSLERIA. 1977. irreg., vol.6, no.1, 1984. free. Instituto de Pesquisas de Recursos Naturais Renovaveis "Ataliba Paz", Rua Goncalves Dias 570, Porto Alegre 90000, Brazil. illus. circ. 500. Indexed: Biol.Abstr.

333.7 US ISSN 0085-5898
SAN FRANCISCO BAY CONSERVATION AND DEVELOPMENT COMMISSION. ANNUAL REPORT. 1971. a. free. ‡ San Francisco Bay Conservation and Development Commission, 30 Van Ness Ave., San Francisco, CA 94102. TEL 415-557-3606. Ed. R. A. Abramson. illus. circ. 10,000.

354 CN ISSN 0318-4684
SASKATCHEWAN. PARKS AND RENEWABLE RESOURCES ANNUAL REPORT. 1929. a. free. Department of Parks and Renewable Resources, 3211 Albert St., Regina, Sask. S4S 5W6, Canada. TEL 306-787-2700. stat. circ. 1,500. (also avail. in microform from MMI)
Formerly (until 1983): Saskatchewan. Tourism and Renewable Resources Annual Report.

SAVON LUONTO. see *BIOLOGY*

SAVONIA. see *BIOLOGY*

333 AT
SCOPE. 1967. irreg. free. Department of Lands, G.P.O. Box 39, Sydney, NSW 2001, Australia. Ed. J. Markey.

333.7 UK ISSN 0080-7850
SCOTLAND. RED DEER COMMISSION. ANNUAL REPORT. 1959. a. price varies. H.M.S.O. (Scotland), 13a Castle St., Edinburgh EH2 3AR, Scotland. illus. circ. 300.

639.9 TZ
SERENGETI RESEARCH INSTITUTE. ANNUAL REPORT. 1966. a. price varies. Serengeti Research Institute, P.O. Seronera, via Arusha, Arusha, Tanzania. illus. circ. 200. Indexed: Biol.Abstr.

333.7 SA
SOUTH AFRICA. NATIONAL PARKS BOARD. ANNUAL REPORT. a. R.10. National Parks Board - Nasionale Parkeraad, Box 787, Pretoria 0001, South Africa. illus. stat.

SOUTHERN BIRDS. see *BIOLOGY — Ornithology*

SPEAK. see *SOCIOLOGY*

639.9 333.95 PL
STUDIA NATURAE. SERIA A. WYDAWNICTWA NAUKOWE. (Text in English and Polish; summaries in English) 1967. irreg., 27, 1984. price varies. (Polska Akademia Nauk, Zaklad Ochrony Przyrody, Zasobow Naturalnych) Panstwowe Wydawnictwo Naukowe, Miodowa 10, 00-251 Warsaw, Poland (Dist. by: Ars Polona, Krakowskie Przedmiescie 7, 00-068 Warsaw, Poland) Ed. K. Klimek. bibl. charts. circ. 320.
Supersedes in part: Studia Naturae (ISSN 0081-6760)

639.9 333.95 PL ISSN 0551-4193
STUDIA NATURAE. SERIA B. WYDAWNICTWA POPULARNO-NAUKOWE. (Text in English and Polish; summaries in English) 1952. irreg., vol.30, 1982. price varies. (Polska Akademia Nauk, Zaklad Ochrany Przyrody i Zasobow Naturalnych) Panstwowe Wydawnictwo Naukowe, Miodowa 10, 00-251 Warsaw, Poland (Dist. by: Ars Polona, Krakowskie Przedmiescie 7, 00-068 Warsaw, Poland) Ed. K. Zabierowski. bibl. charts. illus. circ. 1,200.
Supersedes in part: Studia Naturae (ISSN 0081-6760)

333 SW ISSN 0347-8173
SWEDEN. STATENS NATURVAARDSVERK. NATURVAARDSVERKETS AARSBOK. (Subseries of: Sweden. Statens Naturvaardsverk. Publikationer) a. Kr.43. Biblioteket - National Environment Protection Board, Smidesvagen 5, S-171 21 Solna, Sweden.

639.9 US ISSN 0070-833X
TALL TIMBERS CONFERENCE ON ECOLOGICAL ANIMAL CONTROL BY HABITAT MANAGEMENT. PROCEEDINGS. 1969. irreg. Tall Timbers Research Station, Route 1, Box 678, Tallahassee, FL 32312. TEL 904-893-4153. Ed. Roy Komarek. (reprint service avail. from UMI) Indexed: Biol.Abstr.

TALL TIMBERS RESEARCH STATION. MISCELLANEOUS PUBLICATION. see *FORESTS AND FORESTRY*

333.7 US ISSN 0363-101X
TENNESSEE VALLEY AUTHORITY. ANNUAL REPORT. 1934. a. free. Tennessee Valley Authority, Treasurer's Office, Knoxville, TN 37902. TEL 615-632-4100. circ. 300. Indexed: Soils & Fert.

333.7 US ISSN 0096-1248
TENNESSEE VALLEY AUTHORITY. DIVISION OF LAND AND FOREST RESOURCES. TECHNICAL NOTE. no.27, 1953. irreg., no. 1051, 1980. Tennessee Valley Authority, Division of Land and Forest Resources, Norris, TN 37828. TEL 615-494-7137. bibl. stat. (reprint service avail. from NTI)

U S - CANADIAN RANGE MANAGEMENT; a selected bibliography on ranges, pastures, wildlife, livestock, and ranching. see *BIBLIOGRAPHIES*

333.7 UG
UGANDA. GAME DEPARTMENT. ANNUAL REPORT. 1925. a. EAs.51. Game Department, Box 4, Entebbe, Uganda (Orders to Uganda Government Printer, Box 33, Entebbe, Uganda) Ed. J.B. Bushara. circ. 200.

333.7 UN
UNITED NATIONS. ECONOMIC AND SOCIAL COMMISSION FOR ASIA AND THE PACIFIC. DEVELOPMENT PAPERS. 1981. irreg., no.4, 1984. price varies. Economic and Social Commission for Asia and the Pacific (ESCAP), United Nations Bldg., Rajadamnern Ave., Bangkok 2, Thailand (Dist. by: United Nations Publications, Room DC2-0853 New York, NY 10017; or Distribution and Sales Section, Palais des Nations, CH-1211 Geneva 10, Switzerland) (Back issues avail.)

333.7 US
U.S. BUREAU OF RECLAMATION. ANNUAL REPORT. 1949. a. price varies. U.S. Bureau of Reclamation, Engineering and Research Center, Box 25007, Denver Federal Center, Denver, CO 80225. TEL 303-236-6741.
Former titles: U.S. Water and Power Resources Service. Annual Report; Federal Reclamation Projects: Water and Land Resource Accomplishments.

333.7 US ISSN 0092-9433
U.S. ENVIRONMENTAL PROTECTION AGENCY. CLEAN WATER; REPORT TO CONGRESS. a. U.S. Environmental Protection Agency, Water Planning Division, 401 M St. S.W, Washington, DC 20460. TEL 202-655-4000. circ. 15,000. Indexed: GeoRef.

U.S. FISH AND WILDLIFE SERVICE. RESEARCH REPORTS. see *FISH AND FISHERIES*

U.S. FISH AND WILDLIFE SERVICE. SELECTED LIST OF FEDERAL LAWS AND TREATIES RELATING TO SPORT FISH AND WILDLIFE. see *LAW*

339.49 US ISSN 0084-0165
U.S. FISH AND WILDLIFE SERVICE. WILDLIFE LEAFLETS. 1939. irreg., no. 515, 1983. U.S. Fish and Wildlife Service, Dept. of the Interior, Washington, DC 20240. TEL 202-343-4307. Indexed: Biol.Abstr.

333.7 US ISSN 0361-9737
U.S. NATIONAL PARK SERVICE. PUBLIC USE OF THE NATIONAL PARK SYSTEM; CALENDAR YEAR REPORT. 1972. a. free. National Park Service, Interior Bldg., Washington, DC 20240. TEL 202-343-1000. circ. 2,000.

333.7 US ISSN 0093-3074
U.S. NATIONAL PARK SERVICE. PUBLIC USE OF THE NATIONAL PARK SYSTEM; FISCAL YEAR REPORT. 1972/73. a. ‡ National Park Service, Interior Bldg., Washington, DC 20240. TEL 202-343-1100. illus. stat. circ. 2,000. Key Title: Public Use of the National Park System (Washington)

333.7 US ISSN 0073-4586
UNIVERSITY OF IDAHO. FOREST, WILDLIFE AND RANGE EXPERIMENT STATION, MOSCOW. STATION BULLETIN. 1965. irreg., no.38, 1985. price varies. ‡ University of Idaho, Forest, Wildlife and Range Experiment Station, Moscow, ID 83843. TEL 208-885-6673. circ. 1,000. Indexed: Biol.Abstr. Forest.Abstr.

CONSERVATION — ABSTRACTING, BIBLIOGRAPHIES, STATISTICS

333.7   US   ISSN 0073-4594
UNIVERSITY OF IDAHO. FOREST, WILDLIFE AND RANGE EXPERIMENT STATION, MOSCOW. STATION NOTE. 1965. irreg., no.39, 1983. free. ‡ University of Idaho, Forest, Wildlife and Range Experiment Station, Moscow, ID 83843. TEL 208-885-6673. circ. 1,000. Indexed: Biol.Abstr. Forest.Abstr.

UNIVERSITY OF MINNESOTA. CENTER FOR NATURAL RESOURCE POLICY AND MANAGEMENT. WORKING PAPERS. see *WATER RESOURCES*

337.7   AT   ISSN 0814-0049
UNIVERSITY OF TASMANIA. CENTER FOR ENVIRONMENTAL STUDIES. PROJECT REPORT. 1975. irreg. Aus.$5. University of Tasmania, Board of Environmental Studies, GPO Box 252C, Hobart, Tas. 7001, Australia. Ed. John Todd. circ. 50. (back issues avail.)

UNIVERSITY OF WATERLOO. DEPARTMENT OF GEOGRAPHY. PUBLICATION SERIES. see *GEOGRAPHY*

333.7 628   GW   ISSN 0300-8665
VEREIN FUER WASSER-, BODEN- UND LUFTHYGIENE. SCHRIFTENREIHE. irreg. price varies. Gustav Fischer Verlag, Wollgrasweg 49, Postfach 720143, 7000 Stuttgart 70, W. Germany (B.R.D.) Ed. F. Meinck. Indexed: Ind.Med.

339.49   GW
VEREIN ZUM SCHUTZ DER BERGWELT. JAHRBUCH. 1900. a. DM.35. Verein zum Schutz der Bergwelt e.V., Praterinsel 5, 8000 Munich 22, W. Germany (B.R.D.) TEL 089 23500. Ed. Dr. Meister. circ. controlled. Indexed: Biol.Abstr.
Formerly: Verein zum Schutze der Alpenpflanzen und Tiere. Jahrbuch (ISSN 0083-5625)

VIZGAZDALKODAS ES KORNYEZETVEDELEM. see *WATER RESOURCES*

574 333.7   ET   ISSN 0083-7059
WALIA. (Text in English) 1969. irreg. $5. ‡ Ethiopian Wildlife and Natural History Society, P.O. Box 1160, Addis Ababa, Ethiopia. Ed.Bd. adv. circ. 450. Indexed: Biol.Abstr.

639   US
WASHINGTON (STATE) GAME DEPARTMENT. MITIGATION SECTION. BULLETIN. 1974. irreg. free. Game Department, 600 N. Capitol Way, Olympia, WA 98501. TEL 206-753-5700. Ed.Bd. circ. 300.
Formerly: Washington (State) Game Department. Applied Research Section. Bulletin.

333.7   US
WESTERN ASSOCIATION OF FISH AND WILDLIFE AGENCIES. PROCEEDINGS. 1940. a. $10. Western Association of Fish and Wildlife Agencies, c/o Sandra J. Wolfe, Dept. of Fish & Game, 1416 Ninth St., Sacramento, CA 95814. TEL 916-445-9880. cum.index: 1940-1969. circ. 400. (processed) Indexed: Forest.Abstr. Forest Prod.Abstr.
Formerly: Western Association of State Game and Fish Commissioners. Proceedings (ISSN 0085-8102)

WESTERN AUSTRALIA. DEPARTMENT OF FISHERIES AND WILDLIFE. REPORT. see *FISH AND FISHERIES*

639.9   AT   ISSN 0726-0725
WESTERN AUSTRALIA. DEPARTMENT OF FISHERIES AND WILDLIFE. WILDLIFE RESEARCH BULLETIN. 1956. irreg., no. 12, 1983. free. Department of Fisheries and Wildlife, 108 Adelaide Terrace, Perth, W.A. 6000, Australia. Ed.Bd. circ. 1,000. (back issues avail.)

333.7 614.7   AT
WESTERN AUSTRALIA. ENVIRONMENTAL PROTECTION AUTHORITY. ANNUAL REPORT. 1972. a. free. ‡ Department of Conservation and Environment, 1 Mount St., Perth, W.A. 6000, Australia. (Co-sponsor: Western Australia. Environmental Protection Authority) circ. 1,000.
Incorporating: Western Australia. Conservation and Environment Council Annual Report; Formerly: Western Australia. Environmental Protection Council. Annual Report.

WESTERN AUSTRALIAN WILDLIFE AUTHORITY. ANNUAL REPORT. see *FISH AND FISHERIES*

333.7   US   ISSN 0083-8934
WESTERN LANDS AND WATERS SERIES. 1959. irreg. price varies. Arthur H. Clark Co., Box 230, Glendale, CA 91209-0230. index.

333.7 591   NZ   ISSN 0110-604X
WILDLIFE - A REVIEW. 1970. a. free. Department of Internal Affairs, Wildlife Service, Wellington, New Zealand. Ed. L. Harris. charts. illus. index. circ. 2,000. (processed) Indexed: Biol.Abstr.

333.7 799   US   ISSN 0084-0173
WILDLIFE MONOGRAPHS. 1958. irreg., no.95, 1986. included with subscr. to Journal of Wildlife Management. Wildlife Society, Inc., 5410 Grosvenor Lane, Bethesda, MD 20814. TEL 301-897-9770. Ed. Roy L. Kirkpatrick. circ. 7,000. (reprint service avail. from UMI) Indexed: Biol.Abstr. Curr.Cont. Nutr.Abstr. Geo.Abstr. Ind.Vet. Vet.Bull.

333.7   US   ISSN 0084-0564
WISCONSIN. DEPARTMENT OF NATURAL RESOURCES. TECHNICAL BULLETIN. 1950. irreg. free. Department of Natural Resources, Box 7921, Madison, WI 53707. TEL 608-266-7704. Eds. Stefanie Brouwer, Betty Les. circ. 1,500. Indexed: Biol.Abstr. Ocean.Abstr. Pollut.Abstr. Key Title: Technical Bulletin - Department of Natural Resources (Madison)

333.7   IS   ISSN 0334-0554
YEDION; rashut shamurat hateva. 1975. irreg. Nature Reserves Authority, Rehov Heleni Hamalca 13, Jerusalem, Israel. TEL 02-232926.

354.689   ZA   ISSN 0084-4586
ZAMBIA. COMMISSION FOR THE PRESERVATION OF NATURAL AND HISTORICAL MONUMENTS AND RELICS. ANNUAL REPORT. 1948. a. K.3.00. ‡ Commission for the Preservation of Natural and Historical Monuments and Relics, P.O. Box 60124, Livingstone, Zambia.

333.7   ZA
ZAMBIA. NATURAL RESOURCES DEPARTMENT. ANNUAL REPORT. 1964-1973; resumed 1976. a. 30 n. Government Printer, P.O. Box 136, Lusaka, Zambia.
Former titles: Zambia. Natural Resources Advisory Board. Annual Report; Zambia. Office of the Conservateur of Natural Resources. Annual Report; Zambia. Natural Resources Board. Annual Report (ISSN 0084-4993)

333.7   RH
ZIMBABWE. MINISTRY OF LANDS AND NATURAL RESOURCES. REPORT OF THE SECRETARY FOR LANDS AND NATURAL RESOURCES. (Subseries of: Rhodesia. Parliament. C.S.R.) 1968. a. Rhod.$1.05. ‡ Government Printer, Box 8062, Causeway, Zimbabwe. stat. circ. 400.
Supersedes in part: Rhodesia. Ministry of Mines and Lands. Report of the Secretary for Mines and Lands.

CONSERVATION — Abstracting, Bibliographies, Statistics

333.7 550   US   ISSN 0163-1438
ABSTRACT NEWSLETTER: NATURAL RESOURCES & EARTH SCIENCES. w. $89. U.S. National Technical Information Service, 5285 Port Royal Road, Springfield, VA 22161. TEL 703-487-4630. Ed. Linda J. LaGarde. abstr. index. (back issues avail.)
Former titles: Weekly Abstract Newsletter: Natural Resources and Earth Sciences; Weekly Government Abstracts. Natural Resources and Earth Sciences; Weekly Government Abstracts. Natural Resources (ISSN 0364-4979)

333.7 016   CN
QUEBEC (PROVINCE) MINISTERE DES RICHESSES NATURELLES. REPERTOIRE DES PUBLICATIONS. (Text in French) irreg. free. Ministere des Richesses Naturelles, Distribution et Documentation, 1620 Bd. l'Entente, Quebec G1S 4N6, Canada. bibl.

574.5 333.7   UK   ISSN 0143-0386
RESEARCH REPORT DIGEST. 1978. irreg. free. Nature Conservancy Council, Information and Library Services, Northminster House, Peterborough PE1 1UA, England.

639.9 016   US   ISSN 0043-5511
WILDLIFE REVIEW (FORT COLLINS); an abstracting service for wildlife management. 1935. q. free to qualified personnel. U.S. Fish and Wildlife Service (Fort Collins), 1025 Pennock Place, Fort Collins, CO 80524 TEL 303-493-8401. (Subscr. to: Goverment Printing Office, Washington, DC 20402) Ed. Terry Sexson. bk. rev. abstr. cum.ind: 1935-1951; 1952-1955; 1956-1960; 1961-1970; 1971-1975; 1976-1980. circ. 4,600. (also avail. in microform from UMI) Indexed: Biol.Dig.

CONSUMER EDUCATION AND PROTECTION

ADVANCES IN CONSUMER RESEARCH. see *BUSINESS AND ECONOMICS — Marketing And Purchasing*

640.73   US   ISSN 0275-1356
AMERICAN COUNCIL ON CONSUMER INTERESTS. PROCEEDINGS OF THE ANNUAL CONFERENCE. 1957. a. $25 to non-members; members $15. American Council on Consumer Interests, c/o Barbara Slusher, Exec. Dir., 240 Stanley Hall, University of Missouri, Columbia, MO 65211. TEL 314-882-3817. Ed. Vickie Hampton. circ. 1,200. (also avail. in microfilm) Indexed: BPIA.
Formerly: Council on Consumer Information. Proceedings of Annual Conference.

640.73 381   AT
BARGAIN SHOPPER'S GUIDE TO MELBOURNE. biennial. Aus.$4.95. Horan, Wall & Walker, P.O. Box 8, Surry Hills, NSW 2010, Australia.

640.73 381   AT
BARGAIN SHOPPERS GUIDE TO SYDNEY. biennial. Aus.$4.95. Horan, Wall and Walker, P.O. Box 8, Surry Hills, N.S.W. 2010, Australia.

640.73   BB
CARIBBEAN NEWSLETTER. 1975. a. Caribbean Consumers Documentation Centre, Gibson House, Spry Street, St. Michael, Barbados, W. Indies. Ed. Doreen Devonish. (processed)

640.73   AT
CONSUMER AFFAIRS COUNCIL. ANNUAL REPORT. 1971. a. free. Consumer Affairs Council, 25 Davey St., Hobart, Tas. 7001, Australia. Ed.Bd. stat. circ. 1,000. (back issues avail.)

640.73   US   ISSN 0193-9297
CONSUMER COMPLAINT CONTACT SYSTEM, ANNUAL REPORT. 1978. a. U.S. Consumer Product Safety Commission, Directorate for Communications, Washington, DC 20207. TEL 202-492-6550.

640.73   US   ISSN 0738-0518
CONSUMER SOURCEBOOK. 1974. irreg., 4th edt., 1983. $185. Gale Research Company, Book Tower, Detroit, MI 48226. TEL 313-961-2242. Eds. Paul Wasserman, Gita Siegman.

640.73   AT
CONSUMERS AFFAIRS COUNCIL OF TASMANIA. ANNUAL REPORT. 1971. a. free. Consumers Affairs Council of Tasmania, P.O. Box 1320N, Hobart, Tas., Australia. charts. stat. circ. 750. (back issues avail.)
Formerly: Consumers Protection Council of Tasmania. Annual Report.

641   NE   ISSN 0069-9284
CONSUMERS DIRECTORY. (Text in English) 1960. biennial. $20. International Organization of Consumers Unions, Emmastraat 9, 2595 EG The Hague, Netherlands. circ. 1,200.

640.73   US
CONSUMER'S RESOURCE HANDBOOK. 1981. a. free. U.S. Office of Consumer Affairs, Consumer Information Center, Pueblo, CO 81009. Ed. Deborah K. Tinsworth. circ. 1,000,000.

381   US   ISSN 0094-8853
COUNCIL OF BETTER BUSINESS BUREAUS. ANNUAL REPORT. 1972. a. Council of Better Business Bureaus, 1515 Wilson Blvd., Arlington, VA 22209. TEL 202-276-0100. circ. 5,000 (controlled)

640.73   US
DIRECTORY OF INFORMATION AND REFERRAL AGENCIES IN THE UNITED STATES AND CANADA. (Alliance of Information and Referral Systems) biennial. A I R S, 1100 W. 42nd St., Ste. 310, Indianapolis, IN 46208. TEL 317-923-8727.

640.73   US   ISSN 0196-8203
DISCLOSURE. 1974. irreg., (approx. 6/yr.) $15. National Training and Information Center, 954 W. Washington, Chicago, IL 60607. TEL 312-243-8580. Ed. Naomi Cohn. bk. rev. charts. stat. circ. 10,000. (tabloid format; back issues avail.)

640.73   DK   ISSN 0105-5992
ERHVERVFREMMENDE OG FORBRUGERPOLITISKE FORANSTALTNINGER. 1977. irreg. free. Industriministeriet, Biblioteket, Slotholmsgade 12, 1216 Copenhagen K, Denmark.
Formerly: Denmark. Handelsministeriet. Oversigt over Erhvervfremmende og Forbruger Politiske Foranstaltninger.

640.73   US   ISSN 0732-0485
EVERYBODY'S MONEY COMPLAINT DIRECTORY FOR CONSUMERS. 1970. a. $2.50. Credit Union National Association, Inc., Box 431, Madison, WI 53701. TEL 608-231-4000. Ed. J. Hanson.
Formerly: E M Complaint Directory for Consumers (ISSN 0363-2083)

640.73   US
FACTORY OUTLET SHOPPING GUIDE FOR NEW ENGLAND.* 1973. a. $3.95. Factory Outlet Shopping Guide Publications, 11 Tory Ln., Newtown, CT 06470. Ed. Jean D. Bird. adv. bk. rev. circ. 25,000.

640.73   DK   ISSN 0900-2049
FAMILIEN DANMARKS FORBRUGER. HAANDBOG; kend dine muligheder og rettigheder. Variant title: Forbruger. Haandbog. 1984. a. Kr.39.85. Forlag for Sicial & Sundhedssektor, Albertslund, Denmark. illus.

FEDERATION DES ENTREPRISES DE BELGIQUE. RAPPORT ANNUEL/VERBOND VAN BELGISCHE ONDERNEMINGEN. JAARLYKS VERSLAG. see *BUSINESS AND ECONOMICS — Production Of Goods And Services*

640.73   UK
FORBES HANDBOOK OF HOME ECONOMICS & CONSUMER EDUCATION. 1981. a. £7. Forbes Publications Ltd., 120 Bayswater Rd., London W2 3JH, England. Ed. Anne P. Neville. adv.

640.73   DK   ISSN 0105-9122
FORBRUGERINDEKS. 1978. a. Kr.573.75. Bibliotekscentralen, Tempovej 7-11, DK-2750 Ballerup, Denmark.

640.73   DK   ISSN 0106-4932
FORBRUGERKLAGENAEVNET. AARSBERETNING. 1975. a. free. Forbrugerklagenaevnet, Axeltorv 6/4, 1609 Copenhagen V, Denmark. circ. 3,500.

640.73 658.7   CN   ISSN 0225-4190
HANDBOOK OF CANADIAN CONSUMER MARKETS. 1979. biennial. Can.$30 to non-members; Can.$10 to students. Conference Board of Canada, 255 Smyth Road, Ottawa, Ont. K1H 8M7, Canada. TEL 613-526-3280. Ed. Carolyn R. Farquhar. charts.

640.73   GW
DER HUETTENMANN. 1935. irreg. Saarstahl Voelkingen GmbH, P.O. Box 101980, 6620 Volklingen/Saar, W. Germany (B.R.D.) circ. 20,000.

640   NE   ISSN 0538-8988
INTERNATIONAL ORGANIZATION OF CONSUMERS UNIONS. PROCEEDINGS. (Each proceeding has a distinctive title) 1960. irreg., 10th, 1981 The Hague. $20. International Organization of Consumers Unions, Emmastraat 9, 2595 EG The Hague, Netherlands. Ed.Bd. bibl.

MOTORCYCLE DEALERNEWS BUYERS GUIDE. see *SPORTS AND GAMES — Bicycles And Motorcycles*

640.73   US   ISSN 0095-5590
NEW YORK (STATE) CONSUMER PROTECTION BOARD. ANNUAL REPORT. 1976. a. free. Consumer Protection Board, Albany, NY 12210. illus. circ. 500. Key Title: Annual Report - State Consumer Protection Board.

640.73   US
OKLAHOMA. COMMISSION ON CONSUMER AFFAIRS. ANNUAL REPORT. a. Commission on Consumer Affairs, 460 Jim Thorpe Bldg., Oklahoma City, OK 73105. TEL 405-521-2011.

640.73   UK   ISSN 0144-4379
PAPER BAG. 1979. a. free. National Federation of Consumer Groups, 12 Mosley St., Newcastle upon Tyne, NE1 1DE, England. circ. 2,000.

640.73   UK   ISSN 0261-4073
PRODUCT FINDER: SWIFT-SASCO BUYERS GUIDE. 1981. a. £3. Lane Advertising, Box 2000, Gatwick Rd., Crawley, Sussex RH10 2RU, England. illus.
Formerly: Sasco Catalogue.

640.73   CN   ISSN 0319-8774
QUEBEC (PROVINCE). CONSEIL DE LA PROTECTION DU CONSOMMATEUR. RAPPORT ANNUEL.* irreg. (Conseil de la Protection du Consommateur) Editeur Officiel du Quebec, 1283 Bd. Charest Ouest, Quebec, P.Q. G1N 2C9, Canada. TEL 413-643-5895.
Formerly: Quebec (Province). Consumer Protection Council. Rapport Annuel du Conseil de la Protection du Consommateur.

381   US   ISSN 0276-6701
S.O.S. DIRECTORY.* 1979. a. $7.95. Save on Shopping Directory, 9109 San Jose Blvd., Jacksonville, FL 32217-5016. Ed. Iris Ellis. adv. bk. rev. circ. 250,000.
Formerly: Save On Shopping (ISSN 0092-8003)

SCHRIFTTUMS FUER DEN BEREICH HAUSHALT UND VERBAUCH. BIBLIOGRAPHIE. see *HOME ECONOMICS*

SPA & SAUNA BUYERS GUIDE. see *PHYSICAL FITNESS AND HYGIENE*

640.73   CN
TRUFAX DIRECTORY & CONSUMER GUIDE. 1979. a. free. Better Business Bureau of Metropolitan Toronto, Inc., 1 St. Johns Rd., 4th Floor, Toronto, ONt. M6P 4C7, Canada. TEL 416-766-5744. Ed. Susan Ostroff. adv. circ. 1,000,000.

640.73 658.8   NN
VANUATU. NATIONAL PLANNING AND STATISTICS OFFICE. CONSUMER PRICES INDEXES/INDICES DES PRIX A LA CONSOMMATION. (Text in English and French) 1976. a. free. Informations Department, Statistics Division, NP 50, Port-Vila, Vanuatu. stat. circ. 300.
Formerly: Vanuatu. Condominium Bureau of Statistics. Consumer Price Indexes/Indices des Prix a la Cosommation.

640.73   US
WORLD ALMANAC CONSUMER INFORMATION KIT (YEAR) 1982. a. World Almanac Publications (Subsidiary of: United Media Enterprises) 200 Park Ave., New York, NY 10166. TEL 212-692-3700. circ. 150,000.

CONSUMER EDUCATION AND PROTECTION — Abstracting, Bibliographies, Statistics

640.73 016   US   ISSN 0094-0534
CONSUMERS INDEX; product evaluations and information sources. 1973. q. with annual cum. $79.50 ($145 including annual) Pierian Press, Box 1808, Ann Arbor, MI 48106. TEL 313-434-5530. Ed. Karen Bell. bk. rev. (also avail. in magnetic tape)

COOPERATIVES

see *Business and Economics—Cooperatives*

CRIMINOLOGY AND LAW ENFORCEMENT

see also *Criminology and Law Enforcement—Security; Education—Special Education and Rehabilitation; Medical Sciences—Forensic Sciences*

364   US   ISSN 0270-2991
A M S STUDIES IN CRIMINAL JUSTICE. 1975. irreg., vol.3, 1980. price varies. A M S Press, Inc., 56 E. 13th St., New York, NY 10003. TEL 212-777-4700. (back issues avail.)

ADMINISTRATION OF JUVENILE JUSTICE IN CALIFORNIA. see *LAW*

353.9   US   ISSN 0095-3415
ALASKA. VIOLENT CRIMES COMPENSATION BOARD. ANNUAL REPORT. 1973. a. Violent Crimes Compensation Board, Pouch N, Juneau, AK 99811. TEL 907-465-3040. illus. Key Title: Annual Report - State of Alaska. Violent Crimes Compensation Board.

364   II   ISSN 0065-6283
ALL INDIA CRIME PREVENTION SOCIETY. ANNUAL REPORT AND AUDITED STATEMENT OF ACCOUNTS.* 1962. a. free. All India Crime Prevention Society, Pragati Ashran, Balaganj, Lucknow, India. Ed. Paripurnanand Varma. bk. rev.

364   US   ISSN 0065-7948
AMERICAN CORRECTIONAL ASSOCIATION. ANNUAL CONGRESS OF CORRECTION. PROCEEDINGS. 1870. a. $18.75 (free to qualified personnel) American Correctional Association, 4321 Hartwick Rd., L208, College Park, MD 20740. TEL 301-699-7600. circ. 2,000. (also avail. in microfiche)

365   US   ISSN 0066-0051
AMERICAN SERIES OF FOREIGN PENAL CODES. 1960. irreg., no.28, 1987. price varies. (Wayne State University Law School, Comparative Criminal Law Project) Fred B. Rothman & Co., 10368 W. Centennial Rd., Littleton, CO 80127. TEL 303-979-5657. Ed. Edward M. Wise. (back issues avail.)

364   US   ISSN 0272-3816
ANNUAL EDITIONS: CRIMINAL JUSTICE. 1976. a. $9.50. Dushkin Publishing Group, Inc., Sluice Dock, Guilford, CT 06437. TEL 203-453-4351. Ed. Ian Nielsen.
Formerly: Annual Editions: Readings in Criminal Justice.

365   KE
ANNUAL REPORT ON THE ADMINISTRATION OF PRISONS IN KENYA. (Text in English) a. Government Printing and Stationery Department, Box 30128, Nairobi, Kenya. (Co-sponsor: Ministry of Home Affairs)

364   PL   ISSN 0066-6890
ARCHIWUM KRYMINOLOGII. (Text in Polish; summaries in English) 1960. irreg., vols.11, 1984. price varies. (Polska Akademia Nauk, Instytut Nauk Prawnych) Ossolineum, Publishing House of the Polish Academy of Sciences, Rynek 9, Wroclaw, Poland. Ed. J. Jasinski.

364   US
AUDIOVISUAL MATERIALS: A LISTING OF CRIMINAL JUSTICE FILMS AND VIDEOTAPES. 1982. a. $17.50. U.S. Department of Justice, National Institute of Justice, National Criminal Justice Reference Service, Box 6000, Rockville, MD 20850. TEL 301-251-5500.

364   AT
AUSTRALIAN CRIME PREVENTION COUNCIL. NATIONAL CONFERENCE. PROCEEDINGS. 1960. biennial. price varies. Australian Crime Prevention Council, No. 1 Carmel Court, Rio Vista, Qld. 4217, Australia.

364.4   AT
AUSTRALIAN CRIME PREVENTION COUNCIL. NATIONAL NEWSLETTER. irreg. Australian Crime Prevention Council, No. 1 Carmel Court, Rio Vista, Qld. 4217, Australia. Ed. J. H. Purcell.

345.73   US   ISSN 0098-8049
B A R-B R I BAR REVIEW. CRIMINAL LAW. a. B A R-B R I Bar Review, 11801 W. Olympic Blvd., Los Angeles, CA 90064. TEL 213-477-2542. Key Title: Criminal Law.

346   US   ISSN 0098-7611
B A R-B R I BAR REVIEW. TORTS. a. B A R-B R I Bar Review, 11801 W. Olympic Blvd., Los Angeles, CA 90064. TEL 213-477-2542. Key Title: Torts.

365   GW   ISSN 0067-5237
BEITRAEGE ZUR STRAFVOLLZUGSWISSENSCHAFT. 1967. irreg., no. 15, 1976. price varies. C. F. Mueller Juristischer Verlag GmbH, Im Weiher 10, Postfach 102640, 6900 Heidelberg 1, W. Germany (B.R.D.) Eds. Th. Wuertenberger, H. Mueller-Dietz.

364   SZ   ISSN 0067-6144
BERNER KRIMINOLOGISCHE UNTERSUCHUNGEN. 1962. irreg., vol. 9, 1980. price varies. Paul Haupt AG, Falkenplatz 14, CH-3001 Berne, Switzerland.

351.74   BS   ISSN 0068-046X
BOTSWANA. COMMISSIONER OF THE POLICE. ANNUAL REPORT. 1885. a. R.1. Commissioner of the Police, c/o Assistant Commissioner, Police Headquarters, Gaborone, Botswana. circ. 250.

364   UK
CAMBRIDGE UNIVERSITY. INSTITUTE OF CRIMINOLOGY. OCCASIONAL PAPERS. 1974. irreg., no.11, 1984. price varies. Cambridge University, Institute of Criminology, 7 West Rd., Cambridge CB3 9DT, England.

354.71   CN   ISSN 0383-4379
CANADA. CORRECTIONAL INVESTIGATOR. ANNUAL REPORT. (Text in English and French) 1974. a. Supply and Services, Correctional Investigator, Box 2324, Sta. D, Ottawa, Ont. K1P 5W5, Canada. TEL 613-996-9771. illus. circ. 2,500.

364   CN   ISSN 0068-9777
CANADIAN STUDIES IN CRIMINOLOGY. 1971. irreg. (University of Toronto, Centre of Criminology) University of Toronto Press, Front Campus, Toronto, Ont. M5S 1A6, Canada. TEL 613-667-7791. Ed. G.A.B. Watson.

362.8   US
CAPITAL PUNISHMENT. (Subseries of: National Prisoner Statistics) 1971. a. free. U.S. Department of Justice, Bureau of Justice Statistics, 633 Indiana Ave., N.W., Washington, DC 20531 TEL 301-251-5500. (Orders to: Box 6000, Rockville, MD 20850) circ. 7,000.

364   343   VE
CAPITULO CRIMINOLOGICO. 1973. a. Bs.15. Universidad del Zulia, Facultad de Derecho, Apdo. 526, Maracaibo, Venezuela.

CHARTERED INSTITUTE OF PUBLIC FINANCE AND ACCOUNTANCY. ADMINISTRATION OF JUSTICE. ESTIMATES. see *CRIMINOLOGY AND LAW ENFORCEMENT — Abstracting, Bibliographies, Statistics*

363.2   US   ISSN 0091-8806
CINCINNATI. DIVISION OF POLICE. ANNUAL REPORT. At head of title, 1971-: Police Statistics of Cincinnati. a. $4. Division of Police, Dept. of Safety, Records Section, 310 Ezzard Charles DR., Cincinnati, OH 45214. stat. circ. 2,000. Key Title: Annual Report of the Division of Police (Cincinnati)

364   US   ISSN 0090-2756
CONNECTICUT. DEPARTMENT OF CORRECTION. PUBLICATIONS. 1970. irreg. Department of Corrections, Research Section, 340 Capitol Ave., Hartford, CT 06115. TEL 203-566-5710. Ed. James Harris. stat. circ. 200 (controlled) (processed)

364   US   ISSN 0732-4464
CONTRIBUTIONS TO CRIMINOLOGY AND PENOLOGY. 1983. irreg., no.2, 1984. price varies. Greenwood Press, 88 Post Rd. West, Box 5007, Westport, CT 06881. TEL 203-226-3571.

364.36   US
CRIME AND DELINQUENCY IN CALIFORNIA. 1965. a. free. Department of Justice, Bureau of Criminal Statistics and Special Services, Box 13427, Sacramento, CA 95813. TEL 916-322-3360.
Formerly: California. Bureau of Criminal Statistics. Crime and Delinquency. Incorporating: Adult Criminal Detention Reference Tables (ISSN 0092-2080); Adult Probation Program Report; Which was formerly: Adult Probation Reference Report; Adult Prosecution; Crimes and Arrests; Juvenile Probation; Reference Tables Adult and Juvenile Probation (ISSN 0094-7717)

364   US   ISSN 0146-5759
CRIME IN VIRGINIA.* a. Department of State Police, Uniform Crime Reporting Section, Box 27472, Richmond, VA 23261-7472. TEL 804-323-2031.

364   US
CRIME, LAW, AND DEVIANCE SERIES. 1979. irreg., latest 1985. price varies. Rutgers University Press, 109 Church St., New Brunswick, NJ 08901. Ed. Marlie Wasserman. adv. bk. rev.

364.9   US   ISSN 0194-0953
CRIMINAL JUSTICE HISTORY; an international annual. 1980. a. $49.50. Meckler Publishing, 11 Ferry Lane West, Westport, CT 06880. TEL 203-226-6967. Ed.Bd. Indexed: Hist.Abstr. Amer.Hist.& Life.

364   US
CRIMINAL JUSTICE INFORMATION EXCHANGE DIRECTORY. 1982. a. $5. U.S. Department of Justice, National Institute of Justice, National Criminal Justice Reference Service, Box 6000, Rockville, MD 20850. TEL 301-251-5500.

364   US   ISSN 0092-4652
CRIMINAL JUSTICE PLAN FOR NEW JERSEY. 1972. a. free. State Law Enforcement Planning Agency, CN083, Trenton, NJ 08625-0083. TEL 609-588-3920. Ed. Donald J. Apai. illus. circ. 2,000.
Continues: New Jersey Plan for Criminal Justice.

364   US   ISSN 0192-3323
CRIMINAL LAW REVIEW. 1979. a. $62.50. Clark Boardman Company, Ltd., 435 Hudson St., New York, NY 10014. TEL 212-929-7500. Ed. James G. Carr. Indexed: Crim.Just.Abstr.

CRIMINAL PROCEDURE; Canadian law and practice. see *LAW*

362.8   US   ISSN 0095-5833
CRIMINAL VICTIMIZATION IN THE UNITED STATES. (Subseries of: National Crime Survey Report) 1973. a. free. U.S. Department of Justice, Bureau of Justice Statistics, 633 Indiana Ave. N.W., 11th Fl., Washington, DC 20531 TEL 800-732-3277. (Orders to: Box 6000, Rockville, MD 20850) Marilyn Marbrook. stat. circ. 5,500. (also avail. in microfiche; back issues avail.)

364   US   ISSN 0163-9056
CRIMINOLOGY REVIEW YEARBOOK. 1979. a. $40. Sage Publications, Inc., 2111 W. Hillcrest Dr., Newbury Park, CA 91320 TEL 605-499-0721. (And Sage Publications, Ltd., 28 Banner St., London EC1Y 8QE, England) Ed.Bd.

364   UK
CROPWOOD ROUND-TABLE CONFERENCE PAPERS. 1968. irreg., no. 15, 1983. price varies. Cambridge University, Institute of Criminology, 7 West Rd., Cambridge CB3 9DT, England.

364   IT
DELITTI E DELLE PENE. (Text in English, Italian) 1983. irreg. L.36000. Edizioni Scientifiche Italiane s.p.a., Via Chiatamone, 7, Naples, Italy. Ed. Alessandro Baratta. circ. 1,500.

364   DK
DENMARK. DIREKTORATET FOR KRIMINALFORSORGEN. KRIMINALPOLITISK FORSKNINGSGRUPPE. FORSKNINGSRAPPORT. No. 18, 1981. irreg. Direktoratet for Kriminalforsorgen, Kriminalpolitisk Forskningsgruppe, Justitsministeriet, Klareboderne 1, DK-1115 Copenhagen K, Denmark. TEL 01-13 57 83. illus.

F C L ACTION. (Friends Committee on Legislation of California) see *POLITICAL SCIENCE*

364   UK   ISSN 0072-6435
GREAT BRITAIN. HOME OFFICE. RESEARCH STUDIES. irreg. H.M.S.O., P.O. Box 569, London SE1 9NH, England. (reprint service avail. from UMI)

GREAT BRITAIN. HOME OFFICE. STUDIES IN THE CAUSES OF DELINQUENCY AND THE TREATMENT OF OFFENDERS. see *CHILDREN AND YOUTH — About*

353.9   US   ISSN 0098-5708
HAWAII. CRIMINAL INJURIES COMPENSATION COMMISSION. ANNUAL REPORT. a. Criminal Injuries Compensation Commission, Box 339, Honolulu, HI 96809. TEL 808-548-6714. Key Title: Annual Report - Criminal Injuries Compensation Commission.

312.276   US   ISSN 0098-8537
HOMICIDE IN CALIFORNIA. 1963. irreg. free. Department of Justice, Bureau of Criminal Statistics and Special Services, 3301 C St, Box 13427, Sacramento, CA 95813. TEL 916-322-3360. illus. stat.

343   364.4   US
I D CHECKING GUIDE (YEAR); U. S. & Canadian edition. 1971. a. $15.95. Drivers License Guide Company, 1492 Oddstad Drive, Redwood City, CA 94063. TEL 415-369-4849. Ed. Keith Doerge.
Formerly: Drivers License Guide (ISSN 0276-1696)

364.4   301   YU
INSTITUT ZA KRIMINOLOSKA I SOCIOLOSKA ISTRAZIVANJA. ZBORNIK. (Summaries in English, French and Russian) 1972. a. $4. Institut za Kriminoloska i Socioloska Istrazivanja, Gracanicka 18, 11000 Belgrade, Yugoslavia. bk. rev.

364   NG   ISSN 0534-4816
INTER-AFRICAN CONFERENCE ON THE TREATMENT OF OFFENDERS. MEETINGS. REUNION.* 1953. irreg. (Commission for Technical Co-Operation in Africa South of the Sahara) Maison de l'Afrique, B.P. 878, Niamey, Niger.

364   US   ISSN 0538-7191
INTERNATIONAL DIRECTORY OF PRISONERS' AID AGENCIES. irreg. $1. International Prisoners' Aid Association, c/o Badr-El-Din Ali, Executive Dir., Department of Sociology, University of Louisville, Louisville, KY 40208. TEL 502-588-5555.

364   FR   ISSN 0252-063X
INTERNATIONAL EXCHANGE OF INFORMATION ON CURRENT CRIMINOLOGICAL RESEARCH PROJECTS IN MEMBER STATES. (Text in English and French) 1966. a. price varies. Council of Europe, Directorate of Legal Affairs, Division of Crime Problems, Publications Section, 67000 Strasbourg, France (Dist. in U.S. by: Manhattan Publishing Co., 80 Brook St., P.O. Box 650, Croton, NY 10520) Ed. Hans G. Nilsson. circ. 500.

364   US   ISSN 0538-8821
INTERNATIONAL NARCOTIC ENFORCEMENT OFFICERS ASSOCIATION. ANNUAL CONFERENCE REPORT.* 1965, no. 6. a. International Narcotic Enforcement Officers Association, Ste. 1310, 112 State St., Albany, NY 12207. TEL 518-463-6232.

351.74   UK   ISSN 0579-5567
INTERNATIONAL POLICE ASSOCIATION. MEETING OF THE INTERNATIONAL EXECUTIVE COUNCIL. (Text in English, French and German) 1950. a., latest edition 1976. £2. International Police Association, County Police Hqtrs., Sutton Rd., Maidstone, Kent, England. Ed. H.V.D. Hallett. index.

CRIMINOLOGY AND LAW ENFORCEMENT

351.74   UK   ISSN 0579-6881
INTERNATIONAL POLICE ASSOCIATION. TRAVEL SCHOLARSHIPS. 1970. a., latest edition 1976. £2. International Police Association, County Police Hqtrs., Sutton Rd., Maidstone, Kent., England. Ed. H.V.D. Hallett. index. circ. controlled.

364   UN   ISSN 0074-7688
INTERNATIONAL REVIEW OF CRIMINAL POLICY. (Text in English, French and Spanish) 1946. a., latest no.37, 1984. price varies. United Nations, Department of Economic and Social Affairs, Secretariat, New York, NY 10017 (Dist. by: United Nations Sales Section, Room A-3315, New York, NY; or Palais des Nations, CH-1211 Geneva 10, Switzerland) (also avail. in microform from UMI; reprint service avail. from UMI) Indexed: Excerp.Med. Leg.Per. Crim.Just.Abstr. C.L.I.

364   FR   ISSN 0539-032X
INTERNATIONAL SOCIETY OF CRIMINOLOGY. BULLETIN. irreg. International Society of Criminology, 4 rue de Mondovi, 75001 Paris, France.

364   FR
INTERNATIONAL SOCIETY OF CRIMINOLOGY. RAPPORTS QUINQUENNAUX. (Text in English and French) every 5 years. International Society of Criminology, 4 rue de Mondovi, 75001 Paris, France.

364   SW
INTERNATIONAL SYMPOSIUM ON WOUND BALLISTICS. PROCEEDINGS. (Supplement to: Acta Chirurgica Scandinavica) 3rd, 1978. irreg. $42. Almqvist & Wiksell International, Box 62, S-101 20 Stockholm, Sweden. Ed. T. Seeman. illus.

364   IS   ISSN 0075-1006
ISRAEL. CENTRAL BUREAU OF STATISTICS. CRIMINAL STATISTICS. (Subseries of its Special Series) (Text in English and Hebrew) 1948/49. irreg., latest issue, no. 758, 1982. price varies. Central Bureau of Statistics, Box 13015, Jerusalem, Israel.

364   IS   ISSN 0075-1391
ISRAEL STUDIES IN CRIMINOLOGY. (Text in English) 1970. irreg. $11. (Tel Aviv University, Institute of Criminology and Criminal Law) Bezalel Tcherikover, Pubs., Ltd., 12 Ha'sharon St., Tel Aviv, Israel. Ed. Shlomo Shoham.

364   US
JOHN JAY COLLEGE OF CRIMINAL JUSTICE. CRIMINAL JUSTICE CENTER. MONOGRAPHS. 1976. irreg., no. 13, 1981. $3. John Jay Press, 444 W. 56th St., New York, NY 10019. TEL 212-489-3515. Ed. Dorothy Bracey.

364   US   ISSN 0735-648X
JOURNAL OF CRIME & JUSTICE. 1981. a. $12 to individuals; institutions $22. (Midwestern Criminal Justice Association) Anderson Publishing Co., Pilgrimage Division, Box 1576, 646 Main St., Cincinnati, OH 45201. TEL 513-421-4142. Ed. Francis T. Cullen. adv. Indexed: Crim.Just.Abstr. CJPI.

364.6   US   ISSN 0278-1042
JOURNAL OF PROBATION AND PAROLE. 1969. a. $5. New York State Probation and Parole Officers Association, Box 114, Canal St. Sta., New York, NY 10013. Ed. Robert A. Nunz. adv. circ. 1, 200. Indexed: CJPI. Crim.Just.Abstr.
Formerly: Probation and Parole (ISSN 0079-5615)

362.8   US
JUSTICE EXPENDITURE AND EMPLOYMENT IN THE U.S. 1969. a. free. U.S. Department of Justice, Bureau of Justice Statistics, 633 Indiana Ave., N.W., Washington, DC 20531 TEL 800-732-3277. (Orders to: Box 6000, Rockville, MD 20850) circ. 6,000.
Former titles: Justice Expenditure and Employment Data in the U.S; Expenditure and Employment Data for the Criminal Justice Systems (ISSN 0149-0478)

JUSTICE IN AMERICA SERIES. see *LAW*

364   US   ISSN 0190-2555
JUVENILE AND ADULT CORRECTIONAL DEPARTMENTS, INSTITUTIONS, AGENCIES, AND PAROLING AUTHORITIES OF THE UNITED STATES AND CANADA. 1939. a. $35. American Correctional Association, 4321 Hartwick Rd., Suite L-208, College Park, MD 20740. TEL 301-699-7600. Ed. Diana Travisono. adv. circ. 14, 000.
Former titles: Directory - Juvenile and Adult Correctional Departments, Institutions, Agencies, and Paroling Authorities of the United States and Canada (ISSN 0362-9287) (1972-1973): Directory - Juvenile Adult Correctional Institutions and Agencies of the United States of America, Canada, and Great Britain (ISSN 0090-4872); Directory of Correctional Institutions and Agencies of the United States of America, Canada, and Great Britain (ISSN 0070-5373); American Correctional Association Directory: State and Federal Correctional Institutions (ISSN 0065-7956)

364.36   US
KANSAS. JUVENILE JUSTICE INFORMATION CENTER. ANNUAL REPORT. 1976. a. Bureau of Investigation, Statistical Analysis Center, 1620 S.W. Tyler St., Topeka, KS 66612-1837. TEL 913-232-6000. Ed. M. Kathleen Bledsoe. circ. 1,500.

345   DK
KRIMINALFORSORGENS AARSBERETNING. 1910. a. free. Direktoratet for Kriminalforsorgen, Justitsministeriet, Klareboderne 1, DK-1115 Copenhagen K, Denmark. bk. rev. illus. circ. 6,000.
Formerly: Denmark. Direktoratet for Kriminalforsorgen. Kriminalforsorgen (ISSN 0107-511X)

364   GW
KRIMINALITAET UND IHRE VERWALTER. 1972. irreg., no. 7, 1980. price varies. Ferdinand Enke Verlag, Postfach 1304, 7000 Stuttgart 1, W. Germany (B.R.D.) Eds. H. Peters, D. Peters.

364   GW   ISSN 0454-5265
KRIMINALWISSENSCHAFTLICHE ABHANDLUNGEN. 1967. irreg., vol. 10, 1978. price varies. Max Schmidt-Roemhild Verlag, Mengstr. 16, 2400 Luebeck 1, W. Germany (B.R.D.) Ed. Friedrich Geerds.

364   GW   ISSN 0075-7144
KRIMINOLOGIE. ABHANDLUNGEN UEBER ABWEGIGES SOZIALVERHALTEN. 1964. irreg., no.20, 1984. price varies. Ferdinand Enke Verlag, Postfach 1304, 7000 Stuttgart 1, W. Germany (B.R.D.) Ed. T. Wuertenberger.

364   GW   ISSN 0075-7136
KRIMINOLOGISCHE GEGENWARTSFRAGEN. 1953. irreg., no.17, 1986. price varies. Ferdinand Enke Verlag, Postfach 1304, 7000 Stuttgart 1, W. Germany (B.R.D.)
Formerly: Kriminalbiologische Gegenwartsfragen.

364   GW
KRIMINOLOGISCHE SCHRIFTENREIHE. 1961. irreg. price varies. (Deutsche Kriminologische Gesellschaft) Kriminalistik Verlag GmbH, Im Weiher 10, D-6900 Heidelberg 1, W. Germany (B.R.D.) Eds. Hans-Dieter Schwind, Gernot Steinhilper. adv.

364   US
LAW REPRINTS: CRIMINAL LAW SERIES. 1969. irreg. $297. Congressional Information Service, Inc., 3420 East-West Hwy., Ste. 800, Bethesda, MD 20814. TEL 800-638-8380. index.
Former titles: B N A's Law Reprints: Criminal Law Series (ISSN 0275-6986); Law Reprints: Criminal Law Series.

364   MW   ISSN 0076-308X
MALAWI. POLICE FORCE. ANNUAL REPORT. a., latest 1971/72. K.0.60. Government Printer, P.O. Box 37, Zomba, Malawi.

353.9   US   ISSN 0362-9198
MARYLAND. DIVISION OF CORRECTION. REPORT.* a. Division of Correction, 6776 Reisterstown Rd., Ste. 309, Baltimore, MD 21215-2306. Key Title: Report - Maryland Division of Correction.

363.2   MF
MAURITIUS POLICE FORCE. ANNUAL REPORT. (Text in English) a. Police Force, Police Headquarters, Line Barracks, Port Louis, Mauritius.

363.2   MF
MAURITIUS POLICE MAGAZINE. (Text in English and French) 1954. a. Rs.15. Police Force, Police Headquarters, Line Barracks, Port Louis, Mauritius. Ed. Alex Parfait. adv. circ. 5,000.

353.9   US
MICHIGAN. DEPARTMENT OF STATE POLICE. ANNUAL REPORT. 1919. a. ‡ Department of State Police, 714 S. Harrison Rd., East Lansing, MI 48823. TEL 517-332-2521. illus. circ. controlled.
Formerly: Michigan. State Police. Annual Report.

MICHIGAN YEARBOOK OF INTERNATIONAL LEGAL STUDIES. see *LAW*

353.9   US   ISSN 0094-1409
MINNESOTA. OFFICE OF OMBUDSMAN FOR CORRECTIONS. ANNUAL REPORT. 1973. a. Office of Ombudsman for Corrections, 333 Sibley St., Ste. 895, St. Paul, MN 55101. TEL 612-296-4500. Ed. John Poupart. illus. circ. 550. (also avail. in microform) Key Title: Annual Report - Ombudsman for Corrections (St. Paul)

364.6   US
N C J R S DOCUMENT RETRIEVAL INDEX. Cover title: National Institute of Justice/N C J R S Document Retrieval Index (DRI) - Cumulative. 1972. a. updates. $94 (annual supplements $27) U.S. National Institute of Justice, National Criminal Justice Reference Service, Box 6000, Department F, MD 20850. TEL 301-251-5500. (microfiche)
●Also available online.
Former titles: U.S. Department of Justice. National Institute of Justice. Document Retrieval Index; U.S. Law Enforcement Assistance Administration. Document Retrieval Index.

364.36   371.93   US   ISSN 0077-3476
NATIONAL ASSOCIATION OF TRAINING SCHOOLS AND JUVENILE AGENCIES. PROCEEDINGS. 1904. a. $3. National Association of Training Schools and Juvenile Agencies, 5256 N. Central Ave., Indianapolis, IN 46220. circ. 1,000.

365   US
NATIONAL DIRECTORY OF LAW ENFORCEMENT ADMINISTRATORS AND CORRECTIONAL INSTITUTIONS. 1964. a. $34.85. ‡ National Police Chiefs & Sheriffs Information Bureau, Box 92007, Milwaukee, WI 53202. TEL 414-272-3853. Ed. Martin E. Wyrick. circ. 7,100.
Formerly: National Directory of Law Enforcement Administrators and Correctional Agencies.

363.2   US   ISSN 0194-0813
NATIONAL EMPLOYMENT LISTING SERVICE FOR THE CRIMINAL JUSTICE SYSTEM. POLICE EMPLOYMENT GUIDE. 1978. a. $10. Sam Houston State University, National Employment Listing Service, Criminal Justice Center, Huntsville, TX 77341. TEL 409-294-1692. Ed. Laure E. Pegoda. circ. 2,000.

371.42   US   ISSN 0194-0805
NATIONAL EMPLOYMENT LISTING SERVICE FOR THE CRIMINAL JUSTICE SYSTEM. SPECIAL EDITION: EDUCATION OPPORTUNITIES. 1978. a. $7. Sam Houston State University, National Employment Listing Service, Criminal Justice Center, Huntsville, TX 77341. TEL 409-294-1692. Ed. Linda Goetsch. circ. 2,000.

365   US   ISSN 0192-8228
NATIONAL JAIL AND ADULT DETENTION DIRECTORY. triennial. $35. American Correctional Association, 4321 Hartwick Rd., Suite L-208, College Park, MD 20740. TEL 301-699-7675. Ed. Diana Travisono. adv. circ. 4,000.

364   JA   ISSN 0453-0667
NATIONAL RESEARCH INSTITUTE OF POLICE SCIENCE. ANNUAL REPORT/KAGAKU KEISATSU KENKYUSHO NENPO. (Text in Japanese) 1948. a. National Research Institute of Police Science - Kagaku Keisatsu Kenkyusho, 6 Sanban-cho, Chiyoda-ku, Tokyo 102, Japan. circ. 1, 000.

353.9   US   ISSN 0094-1247
NEBRASKA. STATE PATROL. ANNUAL REPORT. a. free. State Patrol, State House, Box 94637, Lincoln, NE 68509. TEL 402-471-4545. illus. circ. 75. Key Title: Annual Report - Nebraska State Patrol.

364 NE ISSN 0168-4280
NETHERLANDS. CENTRAAL BUREAU VOOR DE STATISTIEK. CRIMINELE STATISTIEK. CRIMINAL STATISTICS. (Text in Dutch and English) 1950/51. a. fl.17. Centraal Bureau voor de Statistiek, Prinses Beatrixlaan 428, Voorburg, Netherlands (Orders to: Staatsuitgeverij, Christoffel Plantijnstraat, The Hague, Netherlands)

365 NE ISSN 0077-6815
NETHERLANDS. CENTRAAL BUREAU VOOR DE STATISTIEK. GEVANGENISSTATISTIEK. STATISTICS OF PRISONS. (Text in Dutch and English) 1950/51. a. fl.12.10. Centraal Bureau voor de Statistiek, Prinses Beatrixlaan 428, Voorburg, Netherlands (Orders to: Staatsuitgeverij, Christoffel Plantijnstraat, The Hague, Netherlands)

364 AT ISSN 0310-3684
NEW SOUTH WALES. ATTORNEY-GENERAL. BUREAU OF CRIME STATISTICS AND RESEARCH. STATISTICAL REPORT. 1972. a. free. Attorney General's Department, Bureau of Crime Statistics and Research, Goodsell Bldg., 8-12 Chifley Square, Sydney, N.S.W. 2000, Australia.

364 AT
NEW SOUTH WALES. ATTORNEY GENERAL'S DEPARTMENT. BUREAU OF CRIME STATISTICS AND RESEARCH. RESEARCH STUDIES. 1982. irreg. Attorney General's Department, Bureau of Crime Statistics and Research, Goodsell Bldg., 8-12 Chifley Square, Sydney, N.S.W. 2001, Australia.
Formerly: New South Wales. Attorney-General Justice Department. Bureau of Crime Statistics and Research. Research Report.

NEW YORK (CITY). DEPARTMENT OF JUVENILE JUSTICE. ANNUAL REPORT. see *LAW*

364 US
NEW YORK (STATE). CRIME VICTIMS BOARD. REPORT. (Subseries of New York (State) Legislature. Legislative Document) 1967. a. Crime Victims Board, 97 Central Ave., Albany, NY 12206. Ed. Anthony Menna. circ. 500(controlled)
Formerly (until 1982): New York (State) Crime Victims Compensation Board. Report (ISSN 0077-9148)

353.9 US ISSN 0095-4047
NEW YORK (STATE). DIVISION OF CRIMINAL JUSTICE SERVICE. ANNUAL REPORT. 1973. a. Division of Criminal Justice Services, Executive Park Tower, Stuyvesant Plaza, Albany, NY 12203. Ed.Bd. circ. 200. Key Title: Annual Report - State of New York, Division of Criminal Justice Services.

364.36 UK ISSN 0261-9296
ORCHARD LODGE STUDIES OF DEVIANCY; a forum for debate regarding issues concerning troublesome adolescents. 1981. irreg. £2 per no. Orchard Lodge Regional Resource Centre, William Booth Rd., Anerly, London SE20 8BG, England. Eds. Hugh Gault, Carol Sheldrick.

362.8 US
PAROLE IN THE UNITED STATES. (Subseries of: Uniform Parole Reports) 1976. a. free. U.S. Department of Justice, Bureau of Justice Statistics, 633 Indiana Ave., N.W., Washington, DC 20531 TEL 800-732-3277. (Orders to: Box 6000, Rockville, MD 20850) circ. 5,000.

364 US ISSN 0091-4118
PENNSYLVANIA. CRIME COMMISSION. REPORT.* 1970. biennial. free. ‡ Crime Commission, Executive House, 101 S. 2nd St., Box 1167, Harrisburg, PA 17108.

364 US
PERSPECTIVES IN CRIMINAL JUSTICE. 1981. a. $22 cloth; $10.95 paper. Sage Publications, Inc., 2111 W. Hillcrest Dr., Newbury Park, CA 91320. TEL 805-499-0721. Ed. John A. Conley.

363.2 UK ISSN 0477-2008
POLICE & CONSTABULARY ALMANAC; official register. 1861. a. £16($30) Court & Judicial Publishing Co. Ltd., Box 39, Henley-on-Thames, Oxfordshire RG9 5UA, England. (Co-publisher: R. Hazell & Co.) Ed. C.G.A. Parker. adv. index.

345 US ISSN 0092-8933
POLICE AND LAW ENFORCEMENT. 1973. a. $57.50. A M S Press Inc., 56 E. 13th St., New York, NY 10003. TEL 212-777-4700. bibl. stat. (back issues avail.)

351.74 US ISSN 0079-2950
POLICE YEARBOOK. 1961. a. $8. Davis Publishing Co., 250 Potrero St., Santa Cruz, CA 95060. TEL 408-423-4968. Eds. Robert A. Davis, Sr., Robert E. Ford.
Civil Service questions

363.2 DK ISSN 0108-3376
POLITIETS AARSBERETNING. 1948. irreg. free. Rigspolitichefen, Polititorvet 14, 1588 Copenhagen V, Denmark. circ. 4,500.

363.2 DK ISSN 0107-3893
POLITIHISTORISK SELSKAB. AARSSKRIFT. 1981. a. Kr.60. Polithistorisk Selskab, Polititorvet 14, 1588 Copenhagen V, Denmark. Ed. C. Aage Redlich. illus. circ. 3,500.

365 US ISSN 0732-0965
PROBATION AND PAROLE DIRECTORY. triennial. $35. American Correctional Association, 4321 Hartwick Rd., Suite L-208, College Park, MD 20740. TEL 301-699-7600. Ed. Diana Travisono.

PROBLEMY PRAWA KARNEGO. see *LAW*

364 PL ISSN 0137-5415
PRZESTEPCZOSC NA SWIECIE. irreg., no.16, 1983. price varies. (Instytut Problematyki Przestepczosci) Panstwowe Wydawnictwo Naukowe, Miodowa 10, 00-251 Warsaw, Poland (Dist. by: Ars Polona, Krakowskie Przedmiescie 7, 00-068 Warsaw, Poland) Ed. B. Holyst. bibl.

362.7 UK
RAINER FOUNDATION. ANNUAL REPORT. 1876. a. £5. Rainer Foundation, 227-23a Todey St., 2nd Fl., London SE1 2JX, England. Ed. C. Naylor. circ. 2,000.
Continues: London Police Court Mission. Annual Report.

REGENCY INTERNATIONAL DIRECTORY; of private investigators, process servers, private detectives & debt collecting agencies. see *BUSINESS AND ECONOMICS — Trade And Industrial Directories*

365 MF
REPORT ON THE TREATMENT OF OFFENDERS IN MAURITIUS; PART 1: PRISONS SERVICE. (Text in English) a., latest 1979. Government Printing Office, Elizabeth II Ave., Port Louis, Mauritius.

364 MF
REPORT ON THE TREATMENT OF OFFENDERS IN MAURITIUS; PART 2: PROBATION SERVICE. (Text in English) a., latest 1979. Government Printing Office, Elizabeth II Ave., Port Louis, Mauritius.

364 US
RESEARCH IN CRIMINOLOGY. 1986. irreg. price varies. Springer-Verlag, 175 Fifth Ave., New York, NY 10160 TEL 212-460-1500. (Also Berlin, Heidelberg, Tokyo, Vienna) (reprint service avail. from ISI)

364 VE
REVISTA C E N I P E C. 1976. a. $9. Universidad de los Andes, Centro de Investigaciones Penales y Criminologicas, Apdo. 730, Merida 5101, Venezuela (Subscr. to: Andres Bello, Consejo de Publicaciones, Via la Parroqquia, Merida, Venezuela) Ed. Luis Gerardo Gabaldon. bk. rev. circ. 1,000.

364 NO ISSN 0085-5936
SCANDINAVIAN STUDIES IN CRIMINOLOGY. 1965. irreg. price varies. Norwegian University Press, Kolstadgt. 1, Box 2959-Toeyen, 0608 Oslo 6, Norway (U. S. address: Publications Expediting Inc., 200 Meacham Ave., Elmont, NY 11003) Ed. Nils Christie.

364 CN
SCARLET & GOLD. 1919. a. Can.$7. (Veterans of Royal Canadian Mounted Police, Vancouver Division) Scarlet & Gold Publishing Inc., 210-1089 West Broadway, Vancouver, B.C. V6H 1E5, Canada. TEL 604-253-3767. Ed. E.A. MacDonald. circ. 2,500. (back issues avail.)

345 US
SEARCH GROUP. TECHNICAL MEMORANDUM. no. 11, 1975. irreg. (3-4/yr.) Search Group, Inc., 925 Secret River Dr., Sacramento, CA 95831. TEL 916-392-2550.

345 US
SEARCH GROUP. TECHNICAL REPORT. no. 13, 1975. irreg. (1-2/yr.) Search Group, Inc., 925 Secret River Dr., Sacramento, CA 95831. TEL 916-392-2556.

364.4 UK ISSN 0307-7780
SECURITECH; the international guide to security equipment. (Text in Arabic, English, French, German, Spanish and other languages) 1972. a. £17.50. Unisaf Publications Ltd., Queensway House, 2 Queensway, Redhill, Surrey RH1 1QS, England. circ. 13,000.

365 BL
SERIE ESTUDOS PENITENCIAROS. irreg. Cortez e Moraes Ltda., Rua Ministro Godoy 1002, 05015 Sao Paulo, Brazil. bibl.

364.12 US ISSN 0038-0008
SOCIETY OF PROFESSIONAL INVESTIGATORS. BULLETIN.* 1956. a. free to qualified personnel. Society of Professional Investigators, 85-04 Queens Midtown Expy., Elmhurst, NY 11373. TEL 718-335-3257. bk. rev. circ. 1,000. (processed) Indexed: Excerp.Criminol.

362.8 US
SOURCEBOOK OF CRIMINAL JUSTICE STATISTICS. 1973. a. free. U.S. Department of Justice, Bureau of Justice Statistics, 633 Indiana Ave., N.W., Washington, DC 20531 TEL 800-732-3277. (Orders to: Box 6000, Rockville, MD 20850) circ. 9,000.

365.6 SA
SOUTH AFRICA. PRISONS DEPARTMENT. ANNUAL STATISTICS BY THE COMMISSIONER OF PRISONS/JAARLIKSE STATISTIEKE DEUR DIE KOMMISSARIS VAN GEVANGENISSE. (Report year ends June 30) (Text in Afrikaans and English) a. Government Printer, Bosman St., Private Bag X85, Pretoria 0001, South Africa.

364.4 SA ISSN 0300-1555
SOUTH AFRICA. PRISONS DEPARTMENT. REPORT OF THE COMMISSIONER OF PRISONS/VERSLAG VAN DIE KOMMISSARIS VAN GEVANGENISSE. Cover title: Prisons. (Order and language of titles varies) a. Government Printer, Bosman St., Private Bag X85, Pretoria 0001, South Africa. illus. stat.
Continues its Annual Report of the Director of Prisons.

362.8 US
STATE COURT CASELOAD STATISTICS. 1975. a. free. U.S. Department of Justice, Bureau of Justice Statistics, 633 Indiana Ave., N.W., Washington, DC 20531 TEL 800-732-3277. (Orders to: Box 6000, Rockville, MD 20850) circ. 5,000.

364 US ISSN 0090-3221
STATE OF NEBRASKA UNIFORM CRIME REPORT. Cover title: Crime in Nebraska. 1972. a. free. Commission on Law Enforcement and Criminal Justice, Box 94946, Lincoln, NE 68509. Ed. Marilyn Keelan. charts. stat. circ. 1,500.

364 US
STUDIES IN CRIME AND JUSTICE. 1972. irreg., latest 1984. price varies. University of Chicago Press, 5801 S. Ellis Ave., Chicago, IL 60637. TEL 312-962-7700. Ed.Bd. adv. bk. rev. (reprint service avail. from UMI,ISI)

SUPREME COURT HISTORICAL SOCIETY. YEARBOOK. see *LAW*

364 GW ISSN 0082-1934
TASCHENBUCH FUER KRIMINALISTEN. 1951. a. DM.17.80. Verlag Deutsche Polizeiliteratur GmbH, Forststr. 3a, 4010 Hilden, W. Germany (B.R.D.) Ed. Waldemar Burghard. adv. bk. rev. circ. 1,500.

364 US ISSN 0278-663X
TERRORISM; annual survey. 1982-1983. N.S. 1986 (Feb.) q. $45. J.L. Scherer, Ed. & Pub., 4900 18 Ave., Minneapolis, MN 55417. TEL 612-722-2947. Indexed: Crim.Just.Abstr. Lang.& Lang.Behav.Abstr. PROMT.

CRIMINOLOGY AND LAW ENFORCEMENT — ABSTRACTING, BIBLIOGRAPHIES, STATISTICS

364.6 US ISSN 0095-1900
TEXAS. DEPARTMENT OF CORRECTIONS. RESEARCH AND DEVELOPMENT DIVISION. RESEARCH REPORT. 1971. irreg., no. 27, 1975. Department of Corrections, Research and Development Division, Huntsville, TX 77348. TEL 713-295-6371. Key Title: Research Report - Texas Department of Corrections; Treatment Directorate, Research and Development Division.

364.36 US ISSN 0733-6551
TODAY'S DELINQUENT. 1982. a. $10. National Center for Juvenile Justice, 701 Forbes Ave., Pittsburgh, PA 15219. Ed. Hunter Hurst. charts. stat. circ. 6,000.

364 US ISSN 0082-7592
UNIFORM CRIME REPORTS FOR THE UNITED STATES. Cover title: Crime in the United States. a. (plus s-a update) price varies. U.S. Federal Bureau of Investigation, Ninth St. and Pennsylvania Ave., N.W., Washington, DC 20535. TEL 202-324-3000.

364 UN ISSN 0082-8025
UNITED NATIONS CONGRESS ON THE PREVENTION OF CRIME AND THE TREATMENT OF OFFENDERS. REPORT. irreg. price varies. United Nations Publications, Room DC2-853, New York, NY 10017 (Or Distribution and Sales Section, CH-1211 Geneva 10, Switzerland) (also avail. in microfiche)

364 UN
UNITED NATIONS SOCIAL DEFENCE RESEARCH INSTITUTE. PUBLICATION. 1969. irreg., latest no.28, 1986. price varies. United Nations Social Defence Research Institute - Institut de Recherche des Nations Unies sur la Defense Sociale, Via Giulia 52, 00186 Rome, Italy. circ. 1, 600.

364.164 US ISSN 0273-5032
U.S. BUREAU OF ALCOHOL, TOBACCO AND FIREARMS. EXPLOSIVES INCIDENTS; annual report. a. U.S. Bureau of Alcohol, Tobacco & Firearms, 15th & Pennsylvania Ave., N.W., Washington, DC 20224. TEL 202-566-7777.

364.1 US ISSN 0360-3245
U.S. FEDERAL BUREAU OF INVESTIGATION. BOMB SUMMARY. a. U.S. Federal Bureau of Investigation, Ninth St. and Pennsylvania Ave., N.W., Washington, DC 20535. TEL 202-324-3000. (Co-sponsor: National Bomb Data Center) Key Title: Bomb Summary.

353 US ISSN 0272-8974
U.S. URBAN INITIATIVES ANTI-CRIME PROGRAM. ANNUAL REPORT TO CONGRESS. 1980. a. U.S. Department of Housing and Urban Development, Urban Initiatives Anti-Crime Program, 451 Seventh St. S.W., Washington, DC 20410. TEL 202-655-4000. Key Title: Annual Report to Congress - Urban Initiatives Anti-Crime Program.

364 VE ISSN 0507-570X
UNIVERSIDAD CENTRAL DE VENEZUELA. INSTITUTO DE CIENCIAS PENALES Y CRIMINOLOGICAS. ANUARIO. 1967. irreg., no. 5, 1977. price varies. Universidad Central de Venezuela, Facultad de Ciencias Juridicas y Politicas, Instituto de Ciencias Penales y Criminologicas, Caracas, Venezuela. Ed. Tulio Chiossone. bk. rev. bibl. charts.

364 CN ISSN 0824-5134
UNIVERSITY OF ALBERTA. CENTRE FOR CRIMINOLOGICAL RESEARCH. DISCUSSION PAPERS. 1983. irreg. free. University of Alberta, Department of Sociology, Centre for Criminological Research, Edmonton, Alberta T6G 2H4, Canada. TEL 403-432-4659.

364 AT ISSN 0085-7033
UNIVERSITY OF SYDNEY. INSTITUTE OF CRIMINOLOGY. PROCEEDINGS. 1967. irreg. price varies. University of Sydney, Institute of Criminology, Publications Officer, 173-175 Phillip St., Sydney, N.S.W. 2000, Australia (Orders to: Government Printer. Box 75, Pyrmont, N.S.W. 2009, Australia) Ed. Gordon Hawkins. cum.index. circ. 2,00. (back issues avail.)

URBAN INSIGHTS MONOGRAPH SERIES. see HOUSING AND URBAN PLANNING

VIOLENCE AND VICTIMS. see PSYCHOLOGY

VIRGINIA. CRIMINAL JUSTICE SERVICES COMMISSION. ANNUAL REPORT. see LAW

365 800 US
VOICES FROM WITHIN. 1978. a. $2. Department of Corrections, Education Unit, Attn: Roberta Richman, Education Administrator, Box 8273, Cranston, RI 02919. TEL 401-464-2688. Ed. Tina Letcher. circ. 500.

364 US
WAYNE STATE UNIVERSITY LAW SCHOOL. COMPARATIVE CRIMINAL LAW PROJECT. MONOGRAPH SERIES. 1969. irreg., no.8, 1974. price varies. (Wayne State University Law School) Fred B. Rothman & Co., 10368 W. Centennial Rd., Littleton, CO 80127. TEL 303-979-5657. Ed. Edward M. Wise. (back issues avail.)
Formerly: New York University. Criminal Law Education and Research Center. Monograph Series (ISSN 0077-9458)

364 US
WAYNE STATE UNIVERSITY LAW SCHOOL. COMPARATIVE CRIMINAL LAW PROJECT. PUBLICATIONS SERIES. 1961. irreg., no.17, 1987. price varies. (Wayne State University Law School) Fred B. Rothman & Co., 10368 W. Centennial Rd., Littleton, CO 80127. TEL 303-979-5657. Ed. Edward M. Wise. (back issues avail.)
Formerly (until 1983): New York University. Comparative Criminal Law Project. Publications (ISSN 0077-944X)

354.941 AT
WESTERN AUSTRALIA. DEPARTMENT OF CORRECTIONS. ANNUAL REPORT. 1957. a. Aus.$2. ‡ Western Australia Government Printing Office, Station St., Wembley, W.A. 6014, Australia.
Formerly: Western Australia. Department of Prisons. Annual Report.

WILCOX REPORT NEWSLETTER. see POLITICAL SCIENCE

364 US
WISCONSIN CRIME AND ARRESTS (YEAR) 1969. a. free. Wisconsin Council on Criminal Justice, Statistical Analysis Center, 30 W. Mifflin St., Suite 1,000, Madison, WI 53702. TEL 608-266-7314. Ed. Roland Reboussin. index. circ. 500. (tabloid format)

345.54 II ISSN 0377-6719
YEARLY ALL INDIA CRIMINAL DIGEST. (Supplement to Shree Krishan Agarwal's All India Criminal Digest, 1961-1970) (Text in English) 1971. a. Rs.65. Law Book Co., Sardar Patel Marg, Box 4, Allahabad 1, India. Ed. S. K. Agarwal. circ. 2,600.

365 ZA ISSN 0084-4659
ZAMBIA. PRISONS DEPARTMENT. REPORT. 1964. a. 35 n. Government Printer, P.O. Box 136, Lusaka, Zambia.

CRIMINOLOGY AND LAW ENFORCEMENT — Abstracting, Bibliographies, Statistics

364.4 319 AT
AUSTRALIA. BUREAU OF STATISTICS. QUEENSLAND OFFICE. LAW AND ORDER, QUEENSLAND. a. Aus.$2.10. Australian Bureau of Statistics, Queensland Office, 313 Adelaide St., Brisbane, Qld. 4000, Australia.

364.9 US
CALIFORNIA. BUREAU OF CRIMINAL STATISTICS AND SPECIAL SERVICES. CRIMINAL JUSTICE PROFILE; STATEWIDE. a. Department of Justice, Division of Law Enforcement, Bureau of Criminal Statistics and Special Services, Box 13427, Sacramento, CA 95813. TEL 916-739-2222.
Formerly: California. Bureau of Criminal Statistics. Criminal Justice Profile; Statewide.

364 016 UK ISSN 0068-6883
CAMBRIDGE UNIVERSITY. INSTITUTE OF CRIMINOLOGY. BIBLIOGRAPHICAL SERIES. 1966. irreg., no. 9, 1979. price varies. Cambridge University, Institute of Criminology, 7 West Rd., Cambridge CB3 9DT, England. Indexed: Abstr.Crim. & Pen.

364.1 CN ISSN 0825-432X
CANADA. STATISTICS CANADA. HOMICIDE IN CANADA: A STATISTICAL PERSPECTIVE/ L'HOMICIDE AU CANADA: PERSPECTIVE STATISTIQUE. (Catalog 85-209) (Text in English and French) 1961. a. Can.$25($26.50) Statistics Canada, Communications Division, 3rd Floor, R.H. Coats Bldg., Ottawa, Ont. K1A 0T6, Canada TEL 613-993-7276. (Subscr. to: Publications Sales and Services, Ottawa, Ont. K1A 0T6, Canada) stat. (also avail. in microform from MML)
Former titles: Canada. Statistics Canada. Homicide Statistics/Statistique de l'Homicide (ISSN 0706-2788) & Canada. Statistics Canada. Murder Statistics/Statistique de l'Homicide (ISSN 0575-917X)

364 UK ISSN 0264-6552
CHARTERED INSTITUTE OF PUBLIC FINANCE AND ACCOUNTANCY. ADMINISTRATION OF JUSTICE. ESTIMATES. 1983. a. £11. Chartered Institute of Public Finance and Accountancy, 3 Robert St., London WC2N 6BH, England.

362.2 UK ISSN 0144-9915
CHARTERED INSTITUTE OF PUBLIC FINANCE AND ACCOUNTANCY. POLICE STATISTICS. ACTUALS. 1949. a. £10. Chartered Institute of Public Finance and Accountancy, 3 Robert St., London WC2N 6BH, England. (back issues avail.)

362.2 UK ISSN 0144-9885
CHARTERED INSTITUTE OF PUBLIC FINANCE AND ACCOUNTANCY. POLICE STATISTICS. ESTIMATES. 1974. a. £14. Chartered Institute of Public Finance and Accountancy, 3 Robert St., London WC2N 6BH, England. (back issues avail.)

CRIME AND DELINQUENCY IN CALIFORNIA. see CRIMINOLOGY AND LAW ENFORCEMENT

364 016 US ISSN 0146-9177
CRIMINAL JUSTICE ABSTRACTS. 1968. q. $100 to individuals; institutions $90. ‡ Willow Tree Press, Inc., 124 Willow Tree Rd., Monsey, NY 10952. TEL 914-354-9139. Ed. Richard Allinson. adv. abstr. bibl. cum.index. index. circ. 1,100. (also avail. in microfilm from WSH) Indexed: Leg.Per. CJPI. C.L.I.
Former titles: Abstracts on Crime and Juvenile Delinquency; Crime and Delinquency Literature (ISSN 0037-1327); Formed by the merger of: Information Review on Crime and Delinquency; Selected Highlights of Crime and Delinquency.

364 016 US ISSN 0145-5818
CRIMINAL JUSTICE PERIODICAL INDEX. 1975. 3/yr. $195. University Microfilms International, 300 N. Zeeb Road, Ann Arbor, MI 48106. TEL 313-761-4700. Ed. Jean Julvezan. bk. rev. (back issues avail.)
●Also available online. Vendors: DIALOG.

364 614.19 US
CRIMINALIST'S SOURCE BOOK. a. $20. International Reference Organization in Forensic Medicine & Sciences, c/o Wm. G. Eckert, Ed., Box 8282, Witchita, KS 67208.

364 016 NE ISSN 0166-6231
CRIMINOLOGY & PENOLOGY ABSTRACTS. 1961. bi-m. fl.580($235) (Criminologica Foundation) Kugler Publications B.V., Box 516, 1180 AM Amstelveen, Netherlands.
Former titles: Abstracts on Criminology and Penology; Excerpta Criminologica (ISSN 0001-3684)

364 314 CY ISSN 0253-8695
CYPRUS. DEPARTMENT OF STATISTICS AND RESEARCH. CRIMINAL STATISTICS. (Text in English and Greek) 1974. a. £C3. Department of Statistics and Research, Ministry of Finance, Nicosia, Cyprus.

364 314 DK ISSN 0070-3540
DENMARK. DANMARKS STATISTIK. KRIMINALSTATISTIK /CRIME STATISTICS. (Text in Danish) 1933/37. a. Kr.68.85. Danmarks Statistik, Sejrøegade 11, 2100 Copenhagen OE, Denmark.

CRIMINOLOGY AND LAW ENFORCEMENT — SECURITY

364 318   CK
ESTADISTICA DE CRIMINALIDAD. 1963. a.
Policia Nacional, Carrera 15, No. 10-41, Bogota, Colombia. illus. stat.
Formerly: Criminalidad (1963-1973)

364   FI   ISSN 0355-2160
FINLAND. TILASTOKESKUS. RIKOLLISUUS. POLIISIN TIETOON TULLUT RIKOLLISUUS/ FINLAND. STATISTIKCENTRALEN. BROTTSLIGHET. BROTTSLIGHET SOM KOMMIT TILL POLISHENS KAENNEDOM/ FINLAND. CENTRAL STATISTICAL OFFICE. CRIMINALITY. CRIMINALITY KNOWN TO THE POLICE. (Section XXIII A of Official Statistics of Finland) (Text in English, Finnish and Swedish) 1928. a. Fmk.56. Tilastokeskus, Annankatu 44, SF-00100 Helsinki 10, Finland (Subscr. to: Government Printing Centre, Box 516, SF-00100 Helsinki 10, Finland)

364   FI   ISSN 0355-2179
FINLAND. TILASTOKESKUS. RIKOLLISUUS. TUOMIOISTUINTEN TUTKIMAT RIKOKSET/ FINLAND. STATISTIKCENTRALEN. BROTTSLIGHET. VID DOMSTOLAR RANNSAKADE BROTT/FINLAND. CENTRAL STATISTICAL OFFICE. CRIMINALITY. CRIMINAL CASES TRIED BY THE COURTS. (Section XXIII B of Official Statistics of Finland) (Text in English, Finnish and Swedish) 1955. a. Fmk.52. Tilastokeskus, Annankatu 44, SF-00100 Helsinki 10, Finland (Subscr. to: Government Printing Centre, Box 516, SF-00101 Helsinki 10, Finland)

314 364   FI   ISSN 0355-2187
FINLAND. TILASTOKESKUS. TUOMIOISTUINTEN TOIMINTA/FINLAND. STATISTIKCENTRALEN. DOMSTOLARNAS VERKSAMHET/FINLAND. CENTRAL STATISTICAL OFFICE. FUNCTION OF COURTS. (Section 23 C of Official Statistics of Finland) (Text in English, Finnish and Swedish) 1929. a. Fmk.42. Tilastokeskus, Annankatu 44, SF-00100 Helsinki 10, Finland (Subscr. to: Government Printing Centre, Box 516, SF-00100 Helsinki 10, Finland)

364   GR   ISSN 0256-3665
GREECE. NATIONAL STATISTICAL SERVICE. STATISTICS ON CIVIL, CRIMINAL AND REFORMATORY JUSTICE. (Text in Greek) a., latest 1983. $5. National Statistical Service, Publications and Information Division, 14-16 Lycourgou St., 10166 Athens, Greece.

HOMICIDE IN CALIFORNIA. see
CRIMINOLOGY AND LAW ENFORCEMENT

363.2 016   UK
INTERNATIONAL BIBLIOGRAPHY OF SELECTED POLICE LITERATURE. 1968. a. £1.50. International Police Association, 1 Fox Rd., West Bridgford, Nottingham NG2 6AJ, England. Ed. H.V.D. Hallett.

365   NO   ISSN 0333-3914
NORWAY. STATISTISK SENTRALBYRAA. KRIMINALSTATISTIKK/CRIMINAL STATISTICS. (Subseries of its Norges Offisielle Statistikk) (Text in English and Norwegian) 1966. a. Kr.50. Statistisk Sentralbyraa, Box 8131-Dep., 0033 Oslo 1, Norway. circ. 1,500.

364.4   NO   ISSN 0550-0532
NORWAY. STATISTISK SENTRALBYRAA. SIVILRETTSSTATISTIKK/CIVIL JUDICIAL STATISTICS. (Subseries of its Norges Offisielle Statistikk) (Text in English and Norwegian) 1886. a. Kr.30. Statistisk Sentralbyraa, Box 8131-Dep., 0033 Oslo 1, Norway. illus. stat. circ. 1,000.

363.2 340.6 016   NE   ISSN 0166-6282
POLICE SCIENCE ABSTRACTS. 1973. bi-m. fl.415($168) (Criminologica Foundation) Kugler Publications B.V., Box 516, 1180 AM Amstelveen, Netherlands.
Formerly: Abstracts on Police Science (ISSN 0301-0112)

364   US
PROSECUTION OF FELONY ARRESTS (YEAR) a.? U.S Department of Justice, Bureau of Justice Statistics, 633 Indiana Ave., N.W., Washington, DC 20531.

364   BE   ISSN 0081-5268
STATISTIQUE CRIMINELLE DE LA BELGIQUE. (Text in Dutch and French) 1944. a. 145 Fr. Institut National de Statistique, 44 rue de Louvain, 1000 Brussels, Belgium.
Formerly (until 1944): Statistique Judiciaire de la Belgique.

364   US   ISSN 0360-9146
UNIFORM CRIME REPORT FOR THE STATE OF MICHIGAN. 1973. a. Department of State Police, 714 S. Harrison Rd., East Lansing, MI 48823. TEL 517-332-2521. illus.
Continues: Michigan Law Enforcement Officials Report on Crime.

365   US
WISCONSIN. DIVISION OF CORRECTIONS. OFFICE OF INFORMATION MANAGEMENT. ADMISSIONS TO JUVENILE INSTITUTIONS. (Subseries of its Statistical Bulletin) 1972. a. Division of Corrections, Office of Information Management, Box 7925, Madison, WI 53707. TEL 608-266-2471. stat. (processed)

365   US
WISCONSIN. DIVISION OF CORRECTIONS. OFFICE OF INFORMATION MANAGEMENT. RELEASES FROM JUVENILE INSTITUTIONS. (Statistical Bulletin C-52) 1972. a. Division of Corrections, Office of Information Management, Box 7925, Madison, WI 53707. TEL 608-266-2471. stat. (processed)
Formerly: Wisconsin. Division of Corrections. Bureau of Planning, Development and Research. Releases from Juvenile Institutions (ISSN 0362-7470)

CRIMINOLOGY AND LAW ENFORCEMENT — Security

see also *Computers—Computer Security*

ADVANCES IN COMPUTER SECURITY MANAGEMENT. see *COMPUTERS — Computer Security*

BAILRIGG PAPERS ON INTERNATIONAL SECURITY. see *POLITICAL SCIENCE — International Relations*

614.84   UK   ISSN 0268-568X
BRITISH SECURITY INDUSTRY BUYER'S GUIDE (YEAR); now including fire protection. 1986. a. £19.95. Millbank Publications, 25 Catherine St., London WC2B 5JW, England. TEL 01-379-3036. Ed. A.E. Waring. adv. illus. circ. 3,000.

364   US
CARNAHAN CONFERENCE ON SECURITY TECHNOLOGY. PROCEEDINGS. 1968. a. $22.50. (University of Kentucky, College of Engineering) O E S Publications, Office of Engineering Services, University of Kentucky, Lexington, KY 40506-0046. TEL 606-257-3343. Eds. R. William DeVere, John S. Jackson. circ. 500. (back issues avail.)
Former titles: Conference on Crime Countermeasures and Security. Proceedings (ISSN 0737-1160); Carnahan Conference on Security Technology. Proceedings (ISSN 0731-7875); Carnahan Conference on Electronic Crime Countermeasures. Proceedings.

364.5   SZ
CERBERUS SECURITY. (Editions in English, French, and German) 1975. irreg. free. Cerberus Ltd., CH-8708 Maennedorf, Switzerland. Ed. M. Kuhn. illus. circ. 9,000.

COMPENSATION IN THE SECURITY/LOSS PREVENTION FIELD. see *BUSINESS AND ECONOMICS — Labor And Industrial Relations*

621.38   US
HUTTON'S BUILDING SYSTEMS AND CONTROLS CATALOG. 1986. a. Hutton Publishing Co., Inc., 375 N. Broadway, Jericho, NY 11753. TEL 516-935-2740. circ. 13,500.

I E E E SYMPOSIUM ON SECURITY AND PRIVACY. PROCEEDINGS. see
COMPUTERS — Computer Security

INDUSTRIAL FIRE PROTECTION & SECURITY HANDBOOK. see *INDUSTRIAL HEALTH AND SAFETY*

351.7 614.84   UK   ISSN 0074-7890
INTERNATIONAL SECURITY DIRECTORY; world defense, police & fire hqs., security companies, their products and supplies. 1963. biennial. £19.85($35) Court & Judicial Publishing Co. Ltd., Box 39, Henley-on-Thames, Oxfordshire RG9 5UA, England. Ed. C.G.A. Parker. adv. index.

LOCKSMITH LEDGER/SECURITY GUIDE & DIRECTORY. see *BUILDING AND CONSTRUCTION — Hardware*

SECURITY DEALER PRODUCT DIRECTORY AND REFERENCE GUIDE. see *BUSINESS AND ECONOMICS — Trade And Industrial Directories*

364   US   ISSN 0736-0401
SECURITY LETTER SOURCE BOOK. 1983. biennial. $69.95. Security Letter, Inc., 166 E. 96th St., New York, NY 10128. TEL 212-348-1553. Ed. Robert McCrie. adv. circ. 3,000.

CROP PRODUCTION AND SOIL

see *Agriculture—Crop Production and Soil*

CRYSTALLOGRAPHY

see *Chemistry—Crystallography*

CYBERNETICS

see *Computers—Cybernetics*

CYTOLOGY AND HISTOLOGY

see *Biology—Cytology and Histology*

DAIRYING AND DAIRY PRODUCTS

see *Agriculture—Dairying and Dairy Products*

DANCE

see also *Music; Theater*

793.33   GW   ISSN 0001-0979
A D T V - NACHRICHTEN. 1950. a. membership. Allgemeiner Deutscher Tanzlehrer Verband, Oberheidter Str. 34 B, 5600 Wuppertal 12, W. Germany (B.R.D.)
Ballroom dancing

BUYERS GUIDE: FOOTNOTES. see *MUSIC*

CONTACTS & FACILITIES; in the entertainment industry. see *THEATER*

CONTRIBUTIONS TO THE STUDY OF MUSIC AND DANCE. see *MUSIC*

793.34 780 US ISSN 0070-1262
COUNTRY DANCE AND SONG. 1968. a. membership. Country Dance Society, Inc., 505 Eighth Ave., Rm. 2500, New York, NY 10018-6505. TEL 212-594-8833. Ed. David Sloane. bk. rev. circ. 1,900. (also avail. in microfilm from UMI; reprint service avail. from UMI) Indexed: Music Ind.
  Formerly: Country Dancer.

900 US
DANCE: CURRENT SELECTED RESEARCH. 1987. a. (National Dance Foundation) A M S Press, Inc., 56 E. 13th St., New York, NY 10003. TEL 212-777-4700.

793.3 US ISSN 0070-2676
DANCE DIRECTORY; programs of professional preparation in American colleges and universities. irreg., 13th edt., 1986. $9.95. American Alliance for Health, Physical Education, Recreation, and Dance, 1900 Association Dr., Reston, VA 22091. TEL 703-476-3481. circ. 2,000,000. (reprint service avail. from ISI,UMI) Indexed: ERIC.

792.8 378.0025 US ISSN 0193-1202
DANCE MAGAZINE COLLEGE GUIDE; a directory to dance in North American colleges and universities. biennial. $6. Dance Magazine, Inc., 33 W. 60 St., New York, NY 10023. TEL 212-245-9050. Ed. June L. Thomas. adv. illus.
  Formerly: Dance Magazine Directory of College and University Dance.

790 420 375.4 US
DANCE NOTATION BUREAU NEWSLETTER. 1943. irreg. (approx. 2/yr.) membership. Dance Notation Bureau, 33 W. 21 St., 3rd Fl., New York, NY 10010. TEL 212-807-7899. Ed.Bd. circ. 350. (back issues avail.)

793.32 US ISSN 0070-2692
DANCE WORLD. 1966. a., latest edition 1979. $19.95. Crown Publishers, Inc., One Park Ave., New York, NY 10016. TEL 212-532-9200. Ed. John Willis.

793.33 UK
DANCING YEAR BOOK. 1958. a. £4.50. International Dance Teachers Association Ltd, 76 Bennett Road, Brighton BN2 5JL, England. Ed. Jay Dearling. adv. bibl. index. cum.index. circ. 4,000.
  Formerly: Ballroom Dancing Year Book (ISSN 0404-6919)

793.3 US ISSN 0363-972X
DIRECTORY OF DANCE COMPANIES.* a. (National Endowment for the Arts) Charles Reinhart Management, Inc., 1697 Broadway, Ste. 1201, New York, NY 10019-5904.

EDUCATIONAL DRAMA ASSOCIATION. NEWSLETTER. see THEATER

792 780 US
ENJOYING THE ARTS. 1975. irreg. $10.97 per no. Rosen Publishing Group, 29 E. 21 St., New York, NY 10010. TEL 212-777-3017. Ed. Ruth C. Rosen. illus.
  Young adult

ESSAYS ON ASIAN THEATER, MUSIC AND DANCE. see THEATER

793.32 780 792 CN
FACILITIES DIRECTORY/REPERTOIRE DES SALLES DE SPECTACLE. (In four volumes) (Text in English and French) 1980. irreg. Can.$100 (Can.$10 for updates) Canada Council, Touring Office, Box 1047, 99 Metcalfe St., Ottawa, Ont. K1P 5V8, Canada. TEL 613-598-4342. illus.

793.3 US ISSN 0071-6294
FOCUS ON DANCE. 1960. irreg., no. 9, 1980. price varies. American Alliance for Health, Physical Education, Recreation, and Dance, 1900 Association Dr., Reston, VA 22091. TEL 703-476-3400. (reprint service avail. from ISI,UMI)

793.31 US ISSN 0163-528X
FOLK DANCE DIRECTORY. a. $0.60. Folk Dance Association, Box 500, Midwood Station, Brooklyn, NY 11230. TEL 718-434-2304.

793.31 UK
FOLK DIRECTORY. 1977? a. £3 to non-members; members £2. English Folk Dance and Song Society, Cecil Sharp House, 2 Regents Park Rd., London NW1 7AY, England.

FOLK MUSIC JOURNAL. see MUSIC

793.31 US
FORWARD AND BACK. 1979. irreg. $1 per no. Jacob Bloom, Ed. & Pub., 34 Andrew St., Newton, MA 02161. circ. 100.

793.31 IS ISSN 0334-2301
ISRAEL DANCE. 1975. a. $9.95. Israel Dance Society, Israel Dance Library, 26 Bialik St., 65241 Tel-Aviv, Israel (U.S. subscr. addr.: c/o Judith Imgber, 4209 Basswood Rd., St. Louis Park, MN 55416) Ed. Giora Manor. adv. illus. cum.index: 1975-1985. circ. 2,000.

793.3 PL ISSN 0076-2989
MALA BIBLIOTEKA BALETOWA. 1957. irreg. price varies. Polskie Wydawnictwo Muzyczne, Al. Krasinskiego 11a, 31-111 Krakow, Poland (Dist. by: Ars Polona-Ruch, Krakowskie Przedmiescie 7, 00-068 Warsaw, Poland)

792.8 UK
MOVEMENT AND DANCE. 1948. a. £7.50. Laban Guild, c/o Su Johnston, Ed., 2 Brockham Warren, Boxhill Rd., Tadworth, Surrey, England. adv. bk. rev. circ. 1,000.
  Formerly (until Jan. 1982): Laban Art of Movement Guild Magazine.

NATIONAL FOUNDATION FOR ADVANCEMENT IN THE ARTS. ANNUAL REPORT. see ART

NEW YORK CASTING/SURVIVAL GUIDE; and datebook. see THEATER

793.3 US
PERFORMING ARTS DIRECTORY; catalogue of dance artists and attractions, programs, resources and services. 1967. a. $33.50. Dance Magazine, Inc., 33 W. 60 St., New York, NY 10023. TEL 212-245-9050. Ed. Carol E. Svecz. adv. index. circ. 10,600. Indexed: Mag.Ind.
  Former titles: Dance Magazine Annual Performing Arts Directory & Dance Magazine Annual (ISSN 0070-2684)

793.31 US
U.C.L.A. JOURNAL OF DANCE ETHNOLOGY. 1977. a. $9. (Dance Ethnology Association) University of California, Los Angeles, 10487 Wellworth, Los Angeles, CA 90024. TEL 213-825-5761. Ed. Yvonne Cootz. bk. rev. circ. 250.
  Formerly (until vol.9, 1985): Association of Graduate Dance Ethnologists U.C.L.A. Journal (ISSN 0273-2068)

W.P.A.S. MUSELETTER. (Washington Performing Arts Society) see MUSIC

DANCE — Abstracting, Bibliographies, Statistics

792 016 US ISSN 0360-2737
BIBLIOGRAPHIC GUIDE TO DANCE. (Supplement to New York Public Library. Performing Arts Research Center. Dictionary Catalog of the Dance Collection) 1975. a. G.K. Hall & Co., 70 Lincoln St., Boston, MA 02111. TEL 617-423-3990.

BIBLIOGRAPHIES AND INDEXES IN THE PERFORMING ARTS. see THEATER — Abstracting, Bibliographies, Statistics

DATA BASE MANAGEMENT

see Computers—Data Base Management

DATA COMMUNICATIONS AND DATA TRANSMISSION SYSTEMS

see Computers—Data Communications and Data Transmission Systems

DEAF

see also Education—Special Education and Rehabilitation; Social Services and Welfare

A S H A REPORTS. (American Speech-Language-Hearing Association) see MEDICAL SCIENCES — Otorhinolaryngology

AMERICAN SPEECH - LANGUAGE - HEARING ASSOCIATION. DIRECTORY. see MEDICAL SCIENCES — Otorhinolaryngology

617.8 GW ISSN 0571-8678
AUDIO-TECHNIK. (Text in German; summaries in English, French and German) 1958. irreg., no.35, 1985. free. Robert Bosch GmbH, Geschaeftsbereich Elektronik, Forckenbeckstr. 9-13, 1000 Berlin 33, W. Germany (B.R.D.) Ed. Wolfram H. Siebler. circ. 5,000. Indexed: Excerp.Med.

371.912 AT ISSN 0005-0334
AUSTRALIAN TEACHER OF THE DEAF. 1956. a. Aus.$18. Australian Association of Teachers of the Deaf, 25 Marshall Ave., Kew, Vic. 3101, Australia. Ed. Edith Mayhew. adv. bk. rev. stat. cum.index. circ. 500. Indexed: Aus.Educ.Ind. DSH Abstr.
  Study and teaching

CATALOG OF CAPTIONED FILMS FOR THE DEAF. see MOTION PICTURES

362.4 US
CONNECTICUT. COMMISSION ON THE DEAF AND HEARING-IMPAIRED. ANNUAL REPORT. (Included in Connecticut Administrative Reports) 1974. a. free. Department of Administrative Services, Commission on the Deaf and Hearing-Impaired, 40 Woodland St., Hartford, CT 06105. TEL 203-566-7414. Ed. Barbara S. Brasel. circ. 5,000.
  Formerly: Connecticut. Commission to Study and Investigate the Problems of Deaf and Hearing-Impaired Persons. Annual Report (ISSN 0094-727X)

DIRECTORY OF FEDERAL AID FOR THE HANDICAPPED. see SOCIAL SERVICES AND WELFARE

DIRECTORY OF INFORMATION RESOURCES FOR THE HANDICAPPED. see EDUCATION — Special Education And Rehabilitation

371.912 DK ISSN 0105-7723
DOEVES JUL. a. Kr.20. (Danske Doeves Landsforbund) Bibliotekscentralen, Telegrafvej 5, DK-2750 Ballerup, Denmark.

GUIDE TO GRADUATE EDUCATION IN SPEECH-LANGUAGE PATHOLOGY AND AUDIOLOGY. see EDUCATION — Guides To Schools And Colleges

362.42 384.6 US
INTERNATIONAL TELEPHONE DIRECTORY OF T D D USERS. 1968. a. $10. Telecommunications for the Deaf, Inc., 814 Thayer Ave., Silver Springs, MD 20910. Ed. Alfred Sonnenstrahl. adv. bk. rev. circ. 14,000.
  Formerly: International Telephone Directory of the Deaf (ISSN 0160-7472)

155.4512 UK
NATIONAL DEAF CHILDREN'S SOCIETY. YEAR BOOK AND ANNUAL ACCOUNTS. 1948. a. National Deaf Children's Society, 45 Hereford Rd., London W2 5AH, England. Ed. Harry Cayton. adv. circ. 10,000.

NATIONAL REHABILITATION CENTER FOR THE DISABLED. RESEARCH BULLETIN. see BLIND

DENTISTRY

REHABILITATION GAZETTE; international journal of independent living for the disabled. see *EDUCATION — Special Education And Rehabilitation*

362.42   SA
SOUTH AFRICAN NATIONAL COUNCIL FOR THE DEAF. ANNUAL DIARY. 1930. a. R.16. South African National Council for the Deaf, Private Bag X4, Westhoven 2142, South Africa. Ed. H.A. Opperman. circ. 4,000.

371.9   362.42   GW
STATISTISCHE NACHRICHTEN BILDUNGS- UND SOZIALEINRICHTUNGEN FUER HOERGESCHAEDIGTE IN DER BUNDESREPUBLIK DEUTSCHLAND. 1930. triennial. DM.32. Bund Deutscher Taubstummenlehrer, Franz-Arens-Str. 1, 4300 Essen 1, W. Germany (B.R.D.) Ed.Bd.
Formerly: Statistische Nachrichten ueber Bildungs- und Sozialeinrichtungen fuer Hoergeschaedigte im Deutschsprachigen Raum.

362   IT   ISSN 0510-8292
WORLD CONGRESS OF THE DEAF. PROCEEDINGS. irreg. World Federation of the Deaf, c/o C. Magarotto, Secretary, Via Gregorio VII, N. 120, 00165 Rome, Italy.

362   IT
WORLD CONGRESS OF THE W F D. PROCEEDINGS. 1951. quadrennial, 1983, Palermo. World Federation of the Deaf, c/o C. Magarotto, Secretary, Via Gregorio VII N. 120, 00165 Rome, Italy.
Formerly: World Congress of the Deaf. Lectures and Papers (ISSN 0084-1625)

DENTISTRY

see *Medical Sciences — Dentistry*

DERMATOLOGY AND VENEREOLOGY

see *Medical Sciences — Dermatology and Venereology*

DOMESTIC COMMERCE

see *Business and Economics — Domestic Commerce*

DRUG ABUSE AND ALCOHOLISM

see also *Pharmacy and Pharmacology*

616.86   157.63   CN
ADDICTION RESEARCH FOUNDATION OF ONTARIO. ANNUAL REPORT. 1951. a. contr.free circ. Addiction Research Foundation of Ontario, 33 Russell St., Toronto, Ontario M5S 2S1, Canada. TEL 416-595-6123. circ. 4,000.
Formerly: Alcoholism and Drug Addiction Research Foundation. Annual Report (ISSN 0065-6119)

157.61   362.2   US   ISSN 0270-3106
ADVANCES IN ALCOHOL & SUBSTANCE ABUSE. 1981. q. $45 to individuals; institutions $115; libraries $175. Haworth Press, Inc., 12 W. 32nd St., New York, NY 10001 TEL 212-279-1200. (Subscr. to: 75 Griswold St., Binghamton, NY 13904) Ed. Dr. Barry Stimmel. adv. bk. rev. bibl. circ. 873. (also avail. in microfiche; back issues avail.) Indexed: Biol.Abstr. Chem.Abstr. Excerp.Med. I.P.A. Ind.Med. Psychol.Abstr. Ref.Zh. Sociol.Abstr. Adol.Ment.Hlth.Abstr. Child Devel.Abstr. CJPI. Crim.Just.Abstr. Soc.Work Res. & Abstr. Saf.Sci.Abstr.
Supersedes (1977-1981): Drug Abuse and Alcoholism Review (ISSN 0149-5968)

616.8   US   ISSN 0272-1740
ADVANCES IN SUBSTANCE ABUSE: BEHAVIORAL AND BIOLOGICAL RESEARCH; a research annual. (Supplement avail.: Control Issues in Alcohol Abuse Prevention) 1980. a. $24.75 to individuals; institutions $49.50. J A I Press Inc., Box 1678, 36 Sherwood Pl., Greenwich, CT 06836 TEL 203-661-7602. (And 3 Henrietta St., London WC2E 8LU, England) Ed. Nancy K. Mello. Indexed: Psychol.Abstr.

353.9   US   ISSN 0095-3318
ALASKA. OFFICE OF ALCOHOLISM. REPORT.* a. free. Department of Health and Social Services, Office of Alcoholism and Drug Abuse, 231 S. Franklin, Pouch H-05F, Juneau, AK 99811. TEL 907-586-6201. illus. Key Title: Report - Office of Alcoholism, Department of Health and Social Services, State of Alaska.

616.861   362.292   CN
ALBERTA. ALCOHOL AND DRUG ABUSE COMMISSION. ANNUAL REPORT. 1970. a. Alcohol and Drug Abuse Commission (AADAC), Program Resource Development, Pacific Plaza Bldg., 2nd Fl., 10909 Jasper Ave., Edmonton, Alta. T5J 3M9, Canada. TEL 403-427-7319. Ed. George Claxton. circ. 200.
Formerly: Alberta. Alcoholism and Drug Abuse Commission. Annual Report (ISSN 0319-423X)

157.61   614.19   US
ALCOHOL, DRUGS AND DRIVING: ABSTRACTS AND REVIEWS. 1985. q. free. (Anheuser-Busch Foundation) University of California, Los Angeles, Alcohol Research Center, No. 43-367 CHS, Los Angeles, CA 90024. TEL 213-825-3417. Ed. Herbert Moskowitz. bk. rev. circ. 5,500. (back issues avail.)

157.61   US
ALCOHOL RECOVERY SERVICES: DIRECTORY OF COMMUNITY RESOURCES IN CALIFORNIA. irreg. free. Department of Alcohol and Drug Programs, 111 Capitol Mall, Sacramento, CA 95814. TEL 916-323-2014. circ. 4,000.
Formerly: Alcohol Abuse and Alcoholism: A Directory of Community Services in California.

616.863   157.63   AT   ISSN 0157-8200
AUSTRALIA. NATIONAL INFORMATION SERVICE ON DRUG ABUSE. TECHNICAL INFORMATION BULLETIN. 1971. irreg. (4-6/yr.) free. (Department of Health, Information Service on Drug Abuse) Australian Government Publishing Service, P.O. Box 100, Woden, A.C.T. 2607, Australia. circ. 1,793.
Formerly: Australia. National Drug Information Service. Technical Information Bulletin (ISSN 0310-6012)

AUTUMN SCHOOL OF STUDIES ON ALCOHOL & DRUGS. PROCEEDINGS OF SEMINARS. see *CHILDREN AND YOUTH — For*

C C H R NEWSLETTER. (Citizens Committee on Human Rights) see *MEDICAL SCIENCES — Psychiatry And Neurology*

157.61   US
CALIFORNIA ALCOHOL PROGRAM: REPORT TO THE LEGISLATURE (YEAR) 1981. a. Health and Welfare Agency, Alcohol and Drug Programs, 111 Capitol Mall, Sacramento, CA 95814. TEL 916-322-2974.
Formerly: California Alcohol Program Plan (ISSN 0273-2076)

362.2   CN   ISSN 0705-5587
CANADA ADDICTIONS FOUNDATION. DIRECTORY/FONDATION CANADIENNE DES TOXICOMANIES. REPERTOIRE. (Text in English and French) 1977. irreg. Fondation Canadienne des Toxicomanies, 4254-93 St., Edmonton, Alta. T6E 5P5. TEL 403-450-2299. circ. 1,000.

616.86   YU   ISSN 0033-8567
CENTAR ZA PROUCANANJE I SUZBIJANJE ALKOHOLIZMA I DRUGIH OVISNOSTI. RADOVI. (Text in Croatian, summaries in English) 1966. irreg. price varies. Centar za Proucavanje i Suzbijanje Alkoholizma i Drugih Ovisnosti - Centre for Study and Control of Alcoholism and Other Addictions, Vinogradska 29, 41000 Zagreb, Yugoslavia. Ed. Dr. Vladimir Hudolin. adv. illus. stat. circ. 1,000.

616.86   157.6   US
COPING CATALOG; a guide to resources in the greater Washington area for alcohol and drug addiction problems. 1974. a. $16.50. Washington Area Council on Alcoholism & Drug Abuse, Inc., 1232 M St., N.W., Washington, DC 20005. TEL 202-783-1300. Ed. Joseph L. Wright. adv. index. circ. 1,000. (processed)
Formerly: Directory of Resources for Alcoholics.

COUNCIL FOR TOBACCO RESEARCH--U.S.A. REPORT. see *MEDICAL SCIENCES*

157.63   616.86   CN   ISSN 0228-863X
DIRECTORY OF ALCOHOL AND DRUG TREATMENT RESOURCES IN ONTARIO. 1981. a. Can.$20.00. Addiction Research Foundation of Ontario, 33 Russell St., Toronto, Ont. M5S 2S1, Canada. TEL 416-595-6123. Ed. Donna Heughan.

016   616.863   US   ISSN 0070-6000
DIRECTORY OF ON-GOING RESEARCH IN SMOKING AND HEALTH. 1967. biennial. free; limited distribution. U.S. Office on Smoking and Health, Technical Information Center, Park Bldg., Rm. 116, 5600 Fishers Lane, Rockville, MD 20857. TEL 301-443-1575. Ed. Donald R. Shopland. index.

360   US
DRUG ABUSE: DIRECTORY OF COMMUNITY SERVICES IN CALIFORNIA. 1974. irreg. free. Department of Alcohol and Drug Programs, 111 Capitol Mall, Sacramento, CA 95814. TEL 916-323-2014. circ. 4,000.
Formerly: Directory of Community Services for Drug Abuse in California.

ESTIMATED WORLD REQUIREMENTS OF NARCOTIC DRUGS. see *PHARMACY AND PHARMACOLOGY*

618   US   ISSN 0361-4344
F D A DRUG BULLETIN. 1970. irreg. free. U.S. Food and Drug Administration, 5600 Fisher's Lane, Rockville, MD 20857. TEL 301-443-3220. Ed. Judith Willis. (back issues avail.) Indexed: Excerp.Med. I.P.A. Ind.Med. Curr.Lit.Fam.Plan. Ind.U.S.Gov.Per. Med. Care Rev.
●Also available online.

157.63   GW
FAMILIEN-KALENDER. 1902. a. DM.4.90. Blaukreuz-Verlag Wuppertal, Freiligrathstr. 27, 5600 Wuppertal 2, W. Germany (B.R.D.) Ed. Alexander Schubert. bk. rev. circ. 35,000. (back issues avail.)

616.863   610   US   ISSN 0098-311X
HEALTH CONSEQUENCES OF SMOKING. 1964. a. free; limited distribution. U.S. Office on Smoking and Health, Technical Information Center, Park Bldg., Rm. 116, 5600 Fishers Lane, Rockville, MD 20857. TEL 301-443-1575. Ed.Bd. bibl. charts. illus. stat. index. cum.index: 1964-1982.

362.2   HK
HONG KONG NARCOTICS REPORT. 1965/66. a. free to qualified personnel. Action Committee Against Narcotics, c/o Narcotics Division, Government Secretariat, Queensway Government Offices, High Block, 66 Queensway, Hong Kong, Hong Kong. illus. circ. 10,000.
Former titles: Action Committee Against Narcotics. Annual Report; Narcotics Progress Report.

DRUG ABUSE AND ALCOHOLISM

613.81 SZ
INTERNATIONAL CONGRESS ON ALCOHOLISM AND DRUG DEPENDENCE. PROCEEDINGS. triennial, 34th, 1985, Calgary. 65 Fr. International Council on Alcohol and Drug Dependence, C.P. 189, 1001 Lausanne, Switzerland.

613.81 SZ ISSN 0074-6622
INTERNATIONAL INSTITUTE ON THE PREVENTION AND TREATMENT OF ALCOHOLISM. SELECTED PAPERS. 1964. a., 27th, 1982, Munich. price varies. International Council on Alcohol and Drug Dependence, C.P. 189, 1001 Lausanne, Switzerland. Eds. Archer Tongue & Eva Tongue. circ. 1,500.
Formerly: European Institute on the Prevention and Treatment of Alcoholism. Selected Papers.

613.81 SZ
INTERNATIONAL INSTITUTE ON THE PREVENTION AND TREATMENT OF DRUG DEPENDENCE. SELECTED PAPERS. 1970. a., 11th, 1981 Vienna. price varies. International Council on Alcohol and Drug Dependence, C.P. 189, 1001 Lausanne, Switzerland. circ. 1,000. Indexed: Chem.Abstr.

INTERNATIONAL NARCOTICS CONTROL BOARD. COMPARATIVE STATEMENT OF ESTIMATES AND STATISTICS ON NARCOTIC DRUGS FOR (YEAR) see *PHARMACY AND PHARMACOLOGY*

INTERNATIONAL NARCOTICS CONTROL BOARD. REPORT FOR (YEAR) see *PHARMACY AND PHARMACOLOGY*

INTERNATIONAL NARCOTICS CONTROL BOARD. STATISTICS ON NARCOTIC DRUGS FOR (YEAR) see *PHARMACY AND PHARMACOLOGY*

INTERNATIONAL NARCOTICS CONTROL BOARD. STATISTICS ON PSYCHOTROPIC SUBSTANCES FOR (YEAR) see *PHARMACY AND PHARMACOLOGY*

362.2 US
IOWA COMPREHENSIVE STATE PLAN FOR SUBSTANCE ABUSE (YEAR) 1973. a. Department of Public Health, Division of Substance Abuse, Lucas State Office Bldg., 321 E. 12th St., Des Moines, IA 50319. Ed. Louise Lex. circ. 1,000.
Former titles: Iowa Comprehensive State Plan for Substance Abuse Prevention: Annual Performance Report; (until 1980): Iowa Comprehensive State Plan for Drug Abuse Prevention: Annual Performance Report (ISSN 0363-4507)

616.8 GW ISSN 0170-7337
JAHRBUCH ZUR FRAGE DER SUCHTGEFAHREN. 1958. a. DM.12.80. (Deutsche Hauptstelle gegen die Suchtgefahren) Neuland-Verlagsgesellschaft mbH, Adenauerallee 45, 2000 Hamburg 1, W. Germany (B.R.D.) Ed.Bd. adv. circ. 9,000.
Formerly: Jahrbuch zur Alkohol- und Tabakfrage (ISSN 0075-2827)

616.861 US ISSN 0363-468X
JOURNAL OF STUDIES ON ALCOHOL. SUPPLEMENT. 1961. irreg., no.10, 1985. price varies. (Rutgers Center of Alcohol Studies) Alcohol Research Documentation, Inc., Box 969, Piscataway, NJ 08854. TEL 201-932-2190. Eds. Jack H. Mendelson, Nancy K. Mello. adv. index. circ. 3,000. (also avail. in microfilm from UMI) Indexed: Biol.Abstr. Bull.Signal. Chem.Abstr. Curr.Cont. Excerp.Med. Hist.Abstr. Ind.Med. P.A.I.S. Psychol.Abstr. Ref.Zh. SSCI. Sociol.Abstr. Abstr.Crim.& Pen. Crim.Just.Abstr. Occup.Saf.& Health Abstr. Psychopharmacol.Abstr. Soc.Work Res.& Abstr.
Formerly (until 1975): Quarterly Journal of Studies on Alcohol. Supplement (ISSN 0079-8312)

362.2 US ISSN 0362-7098
LOUISIANA. DIVISION OF MENTAL HEALTH. ANNUAL PERFORMANCE REPORT AND CONTINUATION OF THE STATE PLAN FOR DRUG ABUSE PREVENTION. a. Division of Mental Health, Box 42215, Baton Rouge, LA 70804. TEL 504-342-2544. Key Title: Annual Performance Report and Continuation of the State Plan for Drug Abuse Prevention.

MONITORING THE FUTURE; questionnaire responses from the nation's high school seniors. see *EDUCATION*

362.2 US
MONTANA COMPREHENSIVE CHEMICAL DEPENDENCY PLAN. 1972. a. free. Department of Institutions, 1539 11th Ave., Helena, MT 59620. TEL 406-449-3930. circ. 100.
Formerly: Montana State Plan for Alcohol Abuse and Alcoholism Prevention, Treatment and Rehabilitation (ISSN 0090-3809)
Report year ends June 30

616.861 US ISSN 0147-0515
N I A A A - R U C A S ALCOHOLISM TREATMENT SERIES. 1978. irreg. price varies. Rutgers Center of Alcohol Studies, Publications Division, New Brunswick, NJ 08903. TEL 201-932-2190. index. Indexed: Psychol.Abstr.
Formerly: N.I.A.A.A.-R.U.C.A.S. Alcoholism Treatment Monographs.

616.86 US ISSN 0094-3991
NARCOTICS AND DRUG ABUSE A-Z. (Text in English and Spanish) 1971. base vol. plus q. supplements. $54.95. Croner Publications Inc., 211-05 Jamaica Ave., Queens Village, NY 11428. TEL 718-464-0866. bibl. (looseleaf format)

616.861 616.863 US
NATIONAL DIRECTORY OF DRUG ABUSE AND ALCOHOLISM TREATMENT AND PREVENTION PROGRAMS. 1979. biennial. $16. U.S. Department of Health and Human Services, National Institute on Alcohol Abuse and Alcoholism, 5600 Fishers Ln., Rm. 14C-26, Rockville, MD 20857. (Co-sponsor: National Institute on Drug Abuse) circ. 20,000.

616.861 NO ISSN 0078-673X
NORWAY. STATENS INSTITUTT FOR ALKOHOLFORSKNING. SKRIFTER. (Text in English or Norwegian) 1962. irreg. price varies. (Statens Institutt for Alkoholforskning) Norwegian University Press, Kolstadgt. 1, Box 2959-Toeyen, 0608 Oslo 6, Norway (U.S. address: Publications Expediting Inc., 200 Meacham Ave., Elmont, NY 11003) Ed. Sverre Brun-Gulbrandsen. (back issues avail.)

616.86 CN ISSN 0707-9834
NOVA SCOTIA. COMMISSION ON DRUG DEPENDENCY. ANNUAL REPORT. 1972. a. Commission on Drug Dependency, Halifax, N. S., Canada. TEL 902-424-4270.

353.9 US
OKLAHOMA. DRUG ABUSE DIVISION. ANNUAL REPORT. Variant title: Oklahoma. Office of Drug Abuse. Annual Performance Report, Drug Abuse Treatment Programs and Continuation Plan. a. free. Department of Mental Health, Drug Abuse Division, Box 53277, Capitol Sta., Oklahoma City, OK 73152. TEL 405-521-0044. charts, stat.

616.863 UK ISSN 0334-1186
PERSPECTIVES IN DRUG ABUSE. (Text in English) 1986. a. $25. Freund Publishing House, Ltd., Suite 500, Chesham House, 150 Regent St., London W1R 5FA, England. Eds. Dr. Jordan Scher, Dr. Mark Segal. adv. circ. 1,000.

PSYCHEDELIC MONOGRAPHS AND ESSAYS. see *PSYCHOLOGY*

616.863 US
RECENT DEVELOPMENTS IN ALCOHOLISM. irreg. price varies. (American Medical Society on Alcoholism) Plenum Publishing Corp., 233 Spring St., New York, NY 10013. TEL 212-620-8047. (Co-sponsor: Research Society on Alcoholism) Ed. Marc Galanter. Indexed: Ind.Med. Psychol.Abstr. Dent.Ind.

616.8 US ISSN 0093-9714
RESEARCH ADVANCES IN ALCOHOL & DRUG PROBLEMS. 1974-1976; resumed 19?? irreg. price varies. Plenum Publishing Corp., 233 Spring St., New York, NY 10013. TEL 212-620-8047. Ed. Yedy Israel. Indexed: Biol.Abstr.

616.8 US
RUTGERS CENTER OF ALCOHOL STUDIES. MONOGRAPH. 1958. irreg., no.14, 1981. price varies. Rutgers Center of Alcohol Studies, Publications Division, New Brunswick, NJ 08903. TEL 201-932-2190. index. Indexed: Biol.Abstr.
Formerly: Rutgers University. Center of Alcohol Studies. Monograph (ISSN 0080-4983)

157.6 US ISSN 0190-5104
SAGE ANNUAL REVIEWS OF DRUG AND ALCOHOL ABUSE. 1977. irreg., vol.5, 1981. $14.95 for softcover; hardcover $29.95. Sage Publications, Inc., 2111 W. Hillcret Dr., Newbury Park, CA 91320 TEL 805-499-0721. (And Sage Publications, Ltd., 28 Banner St., London EC1Y 8QE, England) Ed. James A. Inciardi. (back issues avail.)

354 CN
SASKATCHEWAN. ALCOHOL AND DRUG ABUSE COMMISSION. ANNUAL REPORT. 1969. a. free. Saskatchewan Alcohol and Drug Abuse Commission, Prevention and Training Division, 3475 Albert St., Regina, Saskatchewan, Canada. TEL 306-787-4097. illus. stat. circ. 1,000.
Formerly: Saskatchewan. Alcoholism Commission. Annual Report (ISSN 0381-2278)

616.86 CN
SOCIETE DES ALCOOLS DU QUEBEC. RAPPORT ANNUEL. (Vols. for 1967/68-1969/70 issued by the Board under its French form of name: Regie des Alcools du Quebec) 1971. a. Societe des Alcools du Quebec, C. P. 1058, Place d'Armes, Montreal, P. Q., Canada. TEL 514-873-3131.
Formerly: Quebec (Province). Liquor Board. Rapport Annuel (ISSN 0481-2875)

157.6 DK ISSN 0109-0852
STOF; et ungdomsblad om rusmidler og meget andet. 1983. irreg. Alkohol- og Narkotikaraadet, Hovedvagtsgade 6/4, 1103 Copenhagen K, Denmark. illus.

157.63 616.863 US
U.S. NATIONAL INSTITUTE ON DRUG ABUSE. RESEARCH ISSUES. irreg. free. U.S. National Institute on Drug Abuse, Division of Research, 5600 Fishers Lane, Rockville, MD 20857. TEL 301-443-6500. Indexed: Biol.Abstr.

157.63 616.863 US
U.S. NATIONAL INSTITUTE ON DRUG ABUSE. RESEARCH MONOGRAPH SERIES. Variant title: N I D A Research Monograph. 1975. irreg., no.63, 1985. free. U.S. National Institute on Drug Abuse, 5600 Fishers Lane, Rockville, MD 20857. TEL 301-443-6500. Ed. Jack Durell, M.D. bibl. charts. circ. 3,000. (also avail. in microfiche; back issues avail.) Indexed: Chem.Abstr. Curr.Cont. Excerp.Med. Ind.Med. Psychol.Abstr. Psychopharmacol.Abstr.

178 SW ISSN 0346-3869
VERDANDISTEN. 1897. irreg. (5-12/yr.) Kr.75. (Nykterhetsorganisationen Verdandi) Verdandi, Kungsgatan 56 A, 111 22 Stockholm, Sweden. Ed. Erik Trost. adv.

178 360 US
WORLD'S WOMAN'S CHRISTIAN TEMPERANCE UNION. TRIENNIAL REPORT. 1891. triennial. $5. World's Woman's Christian Temperance Union, c/o Mrs. Edith K. Stanley, V.P., 1121 West Ninth St., Anderson, IN 46011. bk. rev. index. circ. 600.
Formerly: World's Woman's Christian Temperance Union. Convention Report (ISSN 0084-2540)

362.2 US ISSN 0273-3722
YEARBOOK OF SUBSTANCE USE AND ABUSE. (Subseries of Drug Abuse Series) 1973. irreg., vol.3, 1985. price varies. Human Sciences Press, Inc., 72 Fifth Ave., NY 10011. TEL 212-243-6000. Ed. Leon Brill. (reprint service avail. from ISI,UMI)
Formerly: Yearbook of Drug Abuse (ISSN 0090-662X)

DRUG ABUSE AND ALCOHOLISM —
Abstracting, Bibliographies, Statistics

016   616.861   CN   ISSN 0065-1885
ADDICTION RESEARCH FOUNDATION OF ONTARIO. BIBLIOGRAPHIC SERIES. 1967. irreg. price varies. Addiction Research Foundation of Ontario, 33 Russell St., Toronto, Ont. M5S 2S1, Canada. TEL 416-595-6123. Ed. R.J. Hall.

BIBLIOGRAPHY ON COLD REGIONS SCIENCE & TECHNOLOGY. see *ENGINEERING — Abstracting, Bibliographies, Statistics*

616.86   016   US   ISSN 0093-2515
DRUG ABUSE BIBLIOGRAPHY. (Supplement to: Drugs of Addiction and Non-Addiction, Their Use and Abuse. A Comprehensive Bibliography 1960-1969) 1970. a. price varies. Whitston Publishing Co. Inc., Box 958, Troy, NY 12181. TEL 518-283-4363.

616.861   016   US   ISSN 0074-204X
INTERNATIONAL BIBLIOGRAPHY OF STUDIES ON ALCOHOL. 1966. irreg. price varies. Rutgers Center of Alcohol Studies, Publications Division, New Brunswick, NJ 08903. TEL 201-932-2190. Ed. Mark Keller. index.

616.863   UK
MISUSE OF DRUGS IN THE UNITED KINGDOM. STATISTICS. a. Home Office, 50 Queen Anne's Gate, London SW1H 9AT, England.

616.861   CN   ISSN 0715-7657
STATISTICS ON ALCOHOL AND DRUG USE IN CANADA AND OTHER COUNTRIES. 1983. irreg. Can.$30.00. Addiction Research Foundation of Ontario, 33 Russell St., Toronto, Ont. M5S 2S1, Canada. TEL 416-595-6123.

EARTH SCIENCES

see also *Earth Sciences—Geology; Earth Sciences—Geophysics; Earth Sciences—Hydrology; Earth Sciences—Oceanography*

A N A R E REPORT. (Australian National Antarctic Research Expeditions) see *SCIENCES: COMPREHENSIVE WORKS*

ACTA ALBERTINA RATISBONENSIA. see *BIOLOGY*

550   577   YU
ACTA CARSOLOGICA/KRASOSLOVNI ZBORNIK. vol. 7, 1976. a. (Slovenska Akademija Znanosti in Umetnosti, Razred za Prirodoslovne Vede) Institut za Raziskovanje Krasa, Novi trg 3, Ljubljana, Yugoslavia. Ed. Svetozar Ilesic. Indexed: GeoRef.

ACTA HISTORIAE RERUM NATURALIUM NEC NON TECHNICARUM. see *HISTORY — History Of Europe*

550   US
ADVANCES IN SOIL SCIENCES. 1985. irreg., vol.6, 1987. Springer-Verlag, 175 Fifth Ave., New York, NY 10010 TEL 212-460-1500. (Also Berlin, Heidelberg, Tokyo, Vienna) (reprint service avail. from ISI)

551   UR
AKADEMIYA NAUK C.S.S.R. VOSTOCHNO-SIBIRSKII FILIAL, IRKUTSK. INSTITUT GEOKHIMII. GEOKHIMYA ENDOGENNYCH PROTSESSOV. 1977. irreg. 1.19 Rub. per issue. Institut Geokhimii, Ul. Favorskogo, 1, 664033 Irkutsk, Russian S.F.S.R., U.S.S.R. Ed. L. Tauson. circ. 700.

551   UR
AKADEMIYA NAUK C.S.S.R. VOSTOCHNO-SIBIRSKII FILIAL, IRKUTSK. INSTITUT GEOKHIMII. GEOKHIMICHESKIE METODY POISKOV, METODY ANALIZA. 1977. irreg. 1.40 Rub. per issue. Institut Geokhimii, Ul. Favorskogo, 1, 664033 Irkutsk, Russian S.F.S.R., U.S.S.R. Ed. L. Tauson. circ. 700.

550   CN
ALBERTA RESEARCH COUNCIL. EARTH SCIENCE REPORTS. 1955. irreg. price varies. Alberta Research Council, Publications Dept., P.O. Box 8330, Sta. F, Edmonton, Alta. T6H 5X2, Canada. TEL 403-450-5111. Indexed: Geo.Abstr.

550   US   ISSN 0569-2393
AMERICAN ASSOCIATION FOR THE ADVANCEMENT OF SCIENCE. COMMITTEE ON DESERT AND ARID ZONE RESEARCH. CONTRIBUTIONS. irreg. free. American Association for the Advancement of Science, Southwestern and Rocky Mountain Division, Box 3AF, Las Cruces, NM 88001. Ed. Donald D. MacPhail. Indexed: Biol.Abstr. GeoRef.

550   US   ISSN 0084-6597
ANNUAL REVIEW OF EARTH AND PLANETARY SCIENCES. 1973. a. $44. Annual Reviews Inc., 4139 El Camino Way, Palo Alto, CA 94306. TEL 415-493-4400. Ed. George W. Wetherill. bibl. cum.index. (back issues avail.; reprint service avail. from ISI) Indexed: Chem.Abstr. Curr.Cont. Sci.Cit.Ind. GeoRef. Int.Aerosp.Abstr. Ind.Sci.Rev. M.M.R.I.

500   RH   ISSN 0250-6386
ARNOLDIA ZIMBABWE. 1964. irreg. price varies. National Museums and Monuments of Zimbabwe, P.O. Box 240, Bulawayo, Zimbabwe. Ed. H.D. Jackson. illus. index. circ. 500. (looseleaf format) Indexed: Biol.Abstr. GeoRef. Rev.Appl.Entomol. Zoo.Rec.
Former titles: Arnoldia Zimbabwe Rhodesia; Arnoldia Rhodesia (ISSN 0066-7781)

550   UK   ISSN 0066-8044
ARTHUR HOLMES SOCIETY. JOURNAL. 1959-1981; resumed 1985/86. a. £1. Arthur Holmes Society, University of Durham, Department of Geological Sciences, South Road, Durham DH1 3LE, England. Eds. D. Jones, T. West. circ. 300. Indexed: GeoRef.
Until 1966: Durham University Geological Society. Journal.

551.9   CN
ASSOCIATION OF EXPLORATION GEOCHEMISTS. SPECIAL PUBLICATIONS. irreg. price varies. Association of Exploration Geochemists, Box 523, Rexdale, Ont. M9W 5L4, Canada. Indexed: GeoRef.

550   NE
ATMOSPHERIC SCIENCES LIBRARY. 1982. irreg. price varies. D. Reidel Publishing Company, Box 17, 3300 AA Dordrecht, Netherlands. Ed.Bd.

AUSTRALIA. BUREAU OF MINERAL RESOURCES. GEOLOGY AND GEOPHYSICS. AUSTRALIAN PETROLEUM ACCUMULATIONS REPORT. see *PETROLEUM AND GAS*

550   AT   ISSN 0084-7089
AUSTRALIA. BUREAU OF MINERAL RESOURCES. GEOLOGY AND GEOPHYSICS. BULLETIN. 1932. irreg. price varies. Bureau of Mineral Resources, Geology & Geophysics, Box 378, Canberra, A.C.T. 2601, Australia. Indexed: Biol.Abstr. Aus.Sci.Ind. Geo.Abstr. GeoRef.

550   AT   ISSN 0084-7100
AUSTRALIA. BUREAU OF MINERAL RESOURCES. GEOLOGY AND GEOPHYSICS. REPORTS. 1948. irreg. price varies. Bureau of Mineral Resources, Geology & Geophysics, Box 378, Canberra, A.C.T. 2601, Australia. (microfiche) Indexed: Biol.Abstr. GeoRef.

AUSTRALIA. BUREAU OF MINERAL RESOURCES. GEOLOGY AND GEOPHYSICS. RESOURCE REPORT. see *MINES AND MINING INDUSTRY*

550   AT   ISSN 0158-7285
AUSTRALIA. BUREAU OF MINERAL RESOURCES. GEOLOGY AND GEOPHYSICS. YEARBOOK. 1980. a. free. Bureau of Mineral Resources, Geology and Geophysics, G.P.O. Box 378, Canberra, A.C.T. 2601, Australia.

AUSTRALIA. BUREAU OF MINERAL RESOURCES, GEOLOGY, AND GEOPHYSICS. 1: 250000 GEOLOGICAL MAPS AND EXPLANATORY NOTES SERIES. see *EARTH SCIENCES — Geology*

550   BO   ISSN 0067-9828
BOLIVIA. SERVICIO GEOLOGICO. BOLETIN. 1961. irreg. price varies. Servicio Geologico, Casilla 2729, La Paz, Bolivia.

550   BO   ISSN 0067-9836
BOLIVIA. SERVICIO GEOLOGICO. CIRCULARE. 1964. irreg. P.2($0.20) Servicio Geologico, Casilla 2729, La Paz, Bolivia.

550   BO   ISSN 0067-9844
BOLIVIA. SERVICIO GEOLOGICO. INFORME. a. P.240($0.35) Servicio Geologico, Casilla 2729, La Paz, Bolivia.

BOLIVIA. SERVICIO GEOLOGICO. SERIE MINERALOGICA. CONTRIBUCIONE. see *MINES AND MINING INDUSTRY*

BRITISH MUSEUM (NATURAL HISTORY) BULLETIN. HISTORICAL. see *BIOLOGY*

550   US
BUFFALO SOCIETY OF NATURAL SCIENCES. BULLETIN. 1873. irreg., vol.31, 1985. price varies. Buffalo Society of Natural Sciences, Humboldt Pkwy., Buffalo, NY 14211. TEL 716-896-5200. Ed. Dr. R. Michael Gramly. charts. illus. circ. 500. (back issues avail.) Indexed: Biol.Abstr. GeoRef.

550   SZ
BULLETIN DE LA MURITHIENNE. (Text in French) 1862. a. 20 Fr. Societe Valaisanne des Science Naturelles, Case Postale 175, CH-1952 Sion, Switzerland. bk. rev. circ. 750. Indexed: Biol.Abstr.

550.5   II
BULLETIN OF EARTH SCIENCES. (Text in English) 1972. a. Rs.15($3) Indian Society of Earth Scientists, c/o Dept. of Geology, Poona University, Poona 411007, India. Ed. V.G. Phansalkar. adv. illus. circ. 300.

550   UK
CAMBRIDGE EARTH SCIENCE SERIES. irreg. price varies. Cambridge University Press, Edinburgh Bldg., Shaftesbury Rd., Cambridge CB2 2RU, England (And 32 E.57th St., New York NY 10022) Ed.Bd.

550   551.46   CN   ISSN 0706-2354
CANADA. HYDROGRAPHIC SERVICE. WATER LEVELS. VOL. 1: DAILY MEANS. (Text in English and French) 1962. a. free. Fisheries and Oceans, Scientific Information & Publications Branch, 200 Kent St., Ottawa, Ont. K1A 0E6, Canada TEL 613-990-0229. (Avail. from: Fisheries and Oceans, Hydrographic Chart Distribution Office, Box 8080, Ottawa, Ont. K1G 3H6, Canada) circ. 600.
Supersedes in part: Canada. Hydrographic Service. Water Levels (ISSN 0068-7669)

550   551.46   CN   ISSN 0706-2346
CANADA. HYDROGRAPHIC SERVICE. WATER LEVELS. VOL. 2: TIDAL HIGHS AND LOWS. 1962. a. free. Fisheries and Oceans, Scientific Information & Publications Branch, 200 Kent St., Ottawa, Ont. K1A 0E6, Canada TEL 613-990-0229. (Avail. from: Fisheries and Oceans, Hydrographic Chart Distribution Office, Box 8080, Ottawa, Ont. K1G 3H6, Canada) circ. 600.
Supersedes in part: Canada. Hydrographic Service. Water Levels (ISSN 0068-7669)

550   581   591   GW   ISSN 0176-3997
CAROLINEA; Beitraege zur Naturkundliche Forschung in Sueddeutschland. (Text in English, German; summaries in English and French) 1864. a. DM.45($15) Landessammlungen fuer Naturkunde, Erbprinzenstr. 13, Postfach 3949, 7500 Karlsruhe 1, W. Germany (B.R.D.) Ed. S. Rietschel. bk. rev. charts. illus. circ. 700. (back issues avail.) Indexed: Biol.Abstr. GeoRef.
Formerly (until 1982): Beitraege zur Naturkundlichen Forschung in Suedwestdeutschland (ISSN 0005-8122)

550   GT
COLECCION EDITORIAL UNIVERSITARIA. irreg., no. 63, 1983. Universidad de San Carlos de Guatemala, Guatemala City, C.A., Guatemala.

628 550 JA ISSN 0547-1435
COLLECTED PAPERS ON SCIENCES OF
ATMOSPHERE AND HYDROSPHERE. (Text in
English and Japanese) 1964. a. exchange basis.
Nagoya University, Water Research Institute -
Nagoya Daigaku Suishitsu Kagaku Kenkyu Shisetsu,
Furo-cho, Chikusa-ku, Nagoya 464, Japan. Indexed:
GeoRef.

COLORADO SCHOOL OF MINES.
PROFESSIONAL CONTRIBUTIONS. see *MINES
AND MINING INDUSTRY*

550 FR ISSN 0074-9427
COMMISSION FOR THE GEOLOGICAL MAP OF
THE WORLD. BULLETIN. (Text in English and
French) 1962. irreg., approx. 2 per year; latest
no.36, 1986. 125 F.($17) Commission for the
Geological Map of the World (CGMW), Maison de
la Geologie, 77 rue Claude-Bernard, 75005 Paris,
France. Ed. O. Dottin. adv. bk. rev. illus. circ. 300.
Indexed: GeoRef.

COMMONWEALTH SCIENTIFIC AND
INDUSTRIAL RESEARCH ORGANIZATION.
DIVISION OF GEOMECHANICS. TECHNICAL
REPORT. see *MINES AND MINING
INDUSTRY*

553 CY ISSN 0574-8267
CYPRUS. GEOLOGICAL SURVEY
DEPARTMENT. ANNUAL REPORT. 1956. a.
free to institutions. Geological Survey Department,
Nicosia, Cyprus. charts. illus. stat. index.
(processed) Indexed: GeoRef.

550 CY
CYPRUS. GEOLOGICAL SURVEY
DEPARTMENT. BULLETIN. 1963. irreg., no. 7,
1977. price varies. Geological Survey Department,
Nicosia, Cyprus. Indexed: GeoRef.

550 CY ISSN 0574-8259
CYPRUS. GEOLOGICAL SURVEY
DEPARTMENT. MEMOIRS. (Text and summaries
in English) 1959. irreg., latest no.8. Mils.3500.
Geological Survey Department, Nicosia, Cyprus.
charts. illus.

DECHENIANA-BEIHEFTE (BONN) see *BIOLOGY*

550 598.1 US ISSN 0191-3875
DESERT TORTOISE COUNCIL. PROCEEDINGS
OF SYMPOSIUM. 1976. a. $11. Desert Tortoise
Council, 5319 Cerritos Ave., Long Beach, CA
90805. Ed. K.A. Hashagen. circ. 600.

550 378.0025 US ISSN 0364-7811
DIRECTORY OF GEOSCIENCE DEPARTMENTS,
UNITED STATES AND CANADA. 1952. a.
$18.95. American Geological Institute, 4220 King
St., Alexandria, VA 22302-1507. TEL 800-336-
4764. Ed. Nicholas H. Claudy. adv. circ. 1,600.
(back issues avail.)

DORTMUNDER BEITRAEGE ZUR
LANDESKUNDE. see *BIOLOGY*

550 UN ISSN 0070-7910
EARTH SCIENCES SERIES. (Text in English and
French) 1969. irreg., no.18. Unesco, 7-9 Place de
Fontenoy, 75700 Paris, France (Dist. in U.S. by:
Bernan Associates-Unipub, 4611-F Assembly Dr.,
Lanham, MD 20706-4391)

550 US
ENCYCLOPEDIA OF EARTH SCIENCES SERIES.
(Each vol. has distinctive title) 1966. irreg., latest
1984. price varies. Van Nostrand Reinhold
Company, 7625 Empire Dr., Florence, KY 41042.
TEL 606-525-6600. Ed. R.W. Fairbridge. index.

550 NE
ENVIRONMENTAL FLUID MECHANICS. 1982.
irreg. price varies. D. Reidel Publishing Co., Box 17,
3300 AA Dordrecht, Netherlands (And 190 Old
Derby St., Hingham, MA 02043) Ed. G.T. Csanady.

550 GW ISSN 0170-3188
ERDWISSENSCHAFTLICHE FORSCHUNG. (Text
in English and German) irreg., vol.20, 1987. price
varies. (Akademie der Wissenschaften und der
Literatur, Mainz, Kommission fuer
Erdwissenschaftliche Forschung) Franz Steiner
Verlag Wiesbaden GmbH, Birkenwaldstr. 44,
Postfach 347, D-7000 Stuttgart 1, W. Germany
(B.R.D.) Ed. Wilhelm Lauer.

550 PO ISSN 0870-001X
ESTUDOS ENSAIOS E DOCUMENTOS. (Former
name of issuing body: Junta de Investigacoes
Cientificas Ultramar) 1950. irreg. Instituto de
Investigacao Cientifica Tropical, Rua Jau, 54, 1300
Lisbon, Portugal. circ. 2,000.

550 610 DK ISSN 0105-7502
FORSKNING I GROENLAND-TUSAAT. (Text in
Danish and Greenlandic) 1977. irreg. (2-3/yr.)
Kr.40. Commission for Scientific Research in
Greenland, Oester Voldgade 10, DK-1350
Copenhagen K, Denmark. Ed. Gregers E. Andersen.
illus. cum.index. circ. 2,000. (back issues avail.)

550 GE ISSN 0071-9404
FREIBERGER FORSCHUNGSHEFTE.
MONTANWISSENSCHAFTEN: REIHE C.
GEOWISSENSCHAFTEN. irreg. price varies.
(Bergakademie Freiberg) VEB Deutscher Verlag fuer
Grundstoffindustrie, Karl-Heine-Str. 27, DDR-7031
Leipzig, E. Germany (D.D.R.) Indexed:
Chem.Abstr.

GEOBIOS NEW REPORTS. see *BIOLOGY*

550 BL ISSN 0101-9082
GEOCIENCIAS. (Text in Portuguese; summaries in
English and Portuguese) 1982. a. $30 or exchange
basis. Universidade Estadual Paulista, Av. Vicente
Ferreira, 1278, Caixa Postal 603, 17.500 Marilia SP,
Brazil. bibl. charts. illus. circ. 1,000. Indexed:
Bull.Signal. Geo.Abstr.
  Incorporating: Noticia Geomorfologica.

550 GW ISSN 0170-3250
GEOECOLOGICAL RESEARCH. (Text in English)
irreg., vol. 4, 1983. price varies. Franz Steiner
Verlag Wiesbaden GmbH, Birkenwaldstr. 44,
Postfach 347, D-7000 Stuttgart 1, W. Germany
(B.R.D.) Ed. Ulrich Schweinfurth.

550 AT
GEOLOGICAL SOCIETY OF AUSTRALIA.
ABSTRACTS SERIES. 1980. irreg., no.18, 1986.
price varies. Geological Society of Australia, 10
Martin Pl., Sydney, N.S.W. 2000, Australia.

GEOLOGICAL SOCIETY OF CHINA.
PROCEEDINGS. see *EARTH SCIENCES —
Geology*

550 551 JA ISSN 0441-0785
GEOLOGICAL SURVEY OF HOKKAIDO.
REPORT. (Text in Japanese; summaries in English)
1950. a. exchange basis. Geological Survey of
Hokkaido, Kita 19, Nishi 12 Kita-Ku, Sapporo 060,
Japan. Ed. Sumitoshi Sakoh. circ. 800.

550 SZ ISSN 0171-1687
GEOMETHODICA. Represents: Basler
Geomethodisches Colloquium. Veroeffentlichungen/
Basel Geomethodological Meeting. Proceedings.
(Proceedings for 1st and 2nd meetings published in
Basler Afrika Bibliographien. Mitteilungen, vol. 15
(1976) and vol. 19 (1977)) (Text in German;
summaries in English, French and German) 1978. a.
30 Fr. (Vols.1-10 26 Fr. each) Basler Afrika
Bibliographien, Postfach 2037, CH-4001 Basel,
Switzerland. Ed. Hartmut Leser. illus. circ. 300.
Indexed: Geo.Abstr.

550 US ISSN 0072-1409
GEOSCIENCE INFORMATION SOCIETY.
PROCEEDINGS. (Contains papers presented at
symposium held at annual meeting) 1969. a. $35 to
non-members. ‡ Geoscience Information Society,
c/o American Geological Institute, 4220 King St.,
Alexandria, VA 22302. circ. 250. Indexed: GeoRef.

550 UK
GEOSOURCES. 1969. irreg., 3rd edt., 1979. £25($50)
Geosystems, P.O. Box 40, Didcot, Oxon OX11
9BX, England. adv.
● Also available online. Vendors: DIALOG.
  Formerly: Geoserials (ISSN 0072-1417)

550 US ISSN 0016-8556
GEOTIMES; news of the earth sciences. 1956. m.
$18. American Geological Institute, 4220 King St.,
Alexandria, VA 22302-1507. TEL 703-379-2480.
Ed. Gail Papa. adv. bk. rev. illus. index. circ. 13,
500. (also avail. in microform from UMI; reprint
service avail. from UMI) Indexed: Biol.Abstr.
Curr.Cont. C.I.J.E. Curr.Tit.Ocean. Geo.Abstr.
GeoRef. Petrol.Abstr. Risk Abstr. Sel.Water
Res.Abstr.

550 BL ISSN 0072-4998
GONDWANA NEWSLETTER. (Text in English)
1969. irreg. exchange basis. Universidade Federal do
Rio Grande do Sul, Instituto de Geociencias, Centro
de Investigacao do Gondwana, Rua Gen. Vitorino
255, 90,000 Porto Alegre, Rio Grande do Sul,
Brazil. Ed. Maria E. Pacheco. adv. bibl.

550 574 913 IT ISSN 0391-5859
GORTANIA; atti del Museo Friulano di Storia
Naturale. (Text in English, French, German, Italian;
summaries in English, French, German, Italian,
Slovenian) 1979. a. exchange. Museo Friulano di
Storia Naturale, Via Grazzano 1, I-33100 Udine,
Italy. TEL 0432 293821. Ed. Carlo Morandini. circ.
600. Indexed: Biol.Abstr.

GREAT BRITAIN. INSTITUTE OF TERRESTRIAL
ECOLOGY. BANGOR OCCASIONAL PAPER.
see *CONSERVATION*

GREAT BRITAIN. INSTITUTE OF TERRESTRIAL
ECOLOGY. MERLEWOOD RESEARCH AND
DEVELOPMENT PAPER. see *CONSERVATION*

GREAT BRITAIN. INSTITUTE OF TERRESTRIAL
ECOLOGY. STATISTICAL CHECKLIST. see
CONSERVATION

550 665.5 531.64 US
GUIDE TO U S G S GEOLOGIC AND
HYDROLOGIC MAPS. (U.S. Geological Survey)
1986. biennial. $110. Documents Index, Inc., Box
195, McLean, VA 22101. TEL 703-356-2434. Ed.
Laurie Andriot.

555.4 II
INDIAN ACADEMY OF GEOSCIENCE.
JOURNAL. (Text in English) vol. 14, 1972. a. $24.
Indian Academy of Geoscience, Osmania
University, Department of Geology, Hyderabad
500007, Andhra Pradesh, India (Subscr. to: Prints
India, 11 Darya Ganj, New Delhi 110002, India)
illus.
  Continues: Indian Geoscience Association.
Journal.

550 JA ISSN 0389-9128
INSTITUTE OF NATURE EDUCATION IN
SHIGA HEIGHTS. BULLETIN/SHIGA SHIZEN
KYOIKU KENKYU SHISETSU KENKYU
GYOSEKI. 1962. a. Shinshu University, Institute of
Nature Education in Shiga Heights, 1-Ha 7148
Shiga Kogen, Yamanouchi-machi, Shimotakai-gun,
Nagano, Japan. Ed. Kenzo Haneda. (back issues
avail.) Indexed: Biol.Abstr.

550 PO ISSN 0870-0036
INSTITUTO DE INVESTIGACAO CIENTIFICA
TROPICAL. MEMORIAS. 1943. irreg. Instituto de
Investigacao Cientifica Tropical, Rua Jau 54, 1300
Lisbon, Portugal (Subscr. to: Centro de
Documentacao e Informacao, Rua Jau 47, 1300
Lisbon, Portugal) circ. 2,000.
  Formerly: Junta de Investigacoes Cientifica do
Ultramar. Memorias.

550 RM ISSN 0020-4234
INSTITUTUL GEOLOGIE SI GEOFIZICA.
MEMOIRE. (Text in English, French, German or
Rumanian; contents page in French; summaries in
English) 1924. a. price varies. Institutul de Geologie
si Geofizica, Str. Caransebes Nr. 1, 78344
Bucharest, Rumania. bk. rev. abstr. charts. illus.
Indexed: Bull.Signal. Ref.Zh.

549 US
INTERNATIONAL GEMOLOGICAL SYMPOSIUM
PROCEEDINGS. irreg. Gemological Institute of
America, 1660 Stewart St., Santa Monica, CA
90404. Ed. Dianne M. Eash.

550 UK ISSN 0538-9984
INTERNATIONAL SERIES ON EARTH
SCIENCES. 1958. irreg., vol.36, 1981. price varies.
Pergamon Press, Ltd., Headington Hill Hall, Oxford
OX3 0BW, England (U.S. subscr. to: Maxwell
House, Fairview Park, Elmsford, NY 10523) index.
  Formerly: International Series of Monographs on
Earth Sciences.

550 540 UR
ISSLEDOVANIYA V OBLASTI KHIMII
REDKOZEMEL'NYKH ELEMENTOV. 1969.
irreg. 0.55 Rub. Saratovskii Universitet, Saratov,
Russian S.F.S.R., U.S.S.R.

EARTH SCIENCES

550   JA
JAPAN MARINE SCIENCE AND TECHNOLOGY CENTER. ANNUAL REPORT. 1972. a. free. Japan Marine Science and Technology Center, 2-15 Natsushima-cho, Yokosuka City 237, Japan. Ed.Bd. circ. 1,000.

550   JA   ISSN 0075-3343
JAPANESE ANTARCTIC RESEARCH EXPEDITION DATA REPORTS. (Text in English) 1966. irreg., no.118, 1986. exchange basis. National Institute of Polar Research - Kokuritsu Kyokuchi Kenkyujo, 9-10, Kaga 1-chome, Itabashi-ku, Tokyo 173, Japan. Ed. Tatsuro Matsuda. circ. 600. Indexed: Biol.Abstr. Curr.Antarc.Lit. GeoRef.

550   JA   ISSN 0022-0442
JOURNAL OF EARTH SCIENCES. 1953. a. exchange basis. Nagoya University, Department of Earth Sciences - Nagoya Daigaku Rigakubu Chikyu Kagaku Kyoshitsu, Faculty of Science, Chikusa-ku, Nagoya 464, Japan. Ed.Bd. circ. 376. Indexed: Biol.Abstr. Chem.Abstr. Nutr.Abstr. Br.Geol.Lit. GeoRef.

550   JA   ISSN 0449-2560
JOURNAL OF GEOSCIENCES/OSAKA-SHIRITSU DAIGAKU RIGAKUBU CHIGAKU KIYO. (Text in English) 1957. a. exchange basis. Osaka City University, Department of Geosciences - Osaka-shiritsu Daigaku Rigakubu Chigaku Kyoshitsu, Faculty of Sciences, 459 Sugimoto-cho, Sumiyoshi-ku, Osaka 558, Japan. Indexed: Biol.Abstr.

KANSAS GEOLOGICAL SURVEY. ENERGY RESOURCES SERIES. see *ENERGY*

KENSETSU KOGAKU KENKYUSHYO HOKOKU/ CONSTRUCTION ENGINEERING RESEARCH INSTITUTE FOUNDATION REPORT. see *ENGINEERING — Engineering Mechanics And Materials*

KEVO SUBARCTIC RESEARCH INSTITUTE. REPORTS. see *BIOLOGY*

KOBLENZER GEOGRAPHISCHES KOLLOQUIUM. see *GEOGRAPHY*

KONGELIGE DANSKE VIDENSKABERNES SELSKAB. BIOLOGISKE SKRIFTER. see *BIOLOGY*

550   UR
LITOLOGIYA I PALEOGEOGRAFIYA. 1972. triennial. 1 Rub. Leningradskii Universitet, Kafedra Litologii i Morskoi Geologii, Universitetskaya nab. 7/9, Leningrad B-164, Russian S.F.S.R., U.S.S.R. (Subscr. to: Mezhdunarodnaya Kniga, Moscow, G-200, Russian S.F.S.R., U.S.S.R.) Ed. N.V. Logvinenko. bibl. illus. circ. 600. Indexed: Ref.Zh. GeoRef.

550 572   US
LOUISIANA STATE UNIVERSITY. DEPARTMENT OF GEOGRAPHY & ANTHROPOLOGY. MISCELLANEOUS PUBLICATIONS. 1967. irreg., latest issue 1983. price varies. Louisiana State University, Department of Geography & Anthropology, Geology Building, Baton Rouge, LA 70803. TEL 504-388-6245. Indexed: GeoRef.
    Formerly: Louisiana State University. School of Geoscience. Miscellaneous Publications.

550   US
LOUISIANA STATE UNIVERSITY. MUSEUM OF GEOSCIENCE. PUBLICATIONS. 1971. irreg., approx. a. price varies. ‡ Louisiana State University, Museum of Geoscience, Geology Building, Baton Rouge, LA 70803. TEL 504-388-6245. illus. (back issues avail.) Indexed: GeoRef.
    Formerly: Melanges.

550   CN   ISSN 0076-1850
MCGILL UNIVERSITY, MONTREAL. AXEL HEIBERG ISLAND RESEARCH REPORTS. 1961. irreg. Can.$3 per no. McGill University, P.O. Box 6070, Montreal 101, Canada. TEL 514-392-4311. Indexed: Chem.Abstr. Arct.Bibl.

551.9 551   NE   ISSN 0076-6895
METHODS IN GEOCHEMISTRY AND GEOPHYSICS. 1964. irreg., vol.23, 1985. price varies. Elsevier Science Publishers B.V., Box 211, 1000 AE Amsterdam, Netherlands. Indexed: GeoRef.

550 574   FR   ISSN 0078-9763
MUSEE NATIONAL D'HISTOIRE NATURELLE, PARIS. MEMOIRES. NOUVELLE SERIE. SERIE C. SCIENCES DE LA TERRE. 1950. irreg. price varies. Musee National d'Histoire Naturelle, 38 rue Geoffroy Saint-Hilaire, 75005 Paris, France. Indexed: Biol.Abstr. Ocean.Abstr. Pollut.Abstr. GeoRef.

550 559   JA   ISSN 0386-5533
NATIONAL INSTITUTE OF POLAR RESEARCH. MEMOIRS. SERIES C: EARTH SCIENCES. (Text and Abstracts in English) 1964. irreg., no.16, 1984. exchange basis. National Institute of Polar Research - Kokuritsu Kyokuchi Kenkyujo, 9-10, Kaga 1-chome, Itabashi-ku, Tokyo 173, Japan. Ed. Tatsuro Matsuda. circ. 1,000. Indexed: Curr.Antarc.Lit. GeoRef.
    Supersedes: Japanese Antarctic Research Expedition, 1956-1962. Scientific Reports. Series C: Earth Sciences. (ISSN 0075-3378)

550   JA   ISSN 0386-0744
NATIONAL INSTITUTE OF POLAR RESEARCH. MEMOIRS. SPECIAL ISSUE. (Text and abstracts in English) 1967. irreg., no.43, 1986. exchange basis. National Institute of Polar Research - Kokuritsu Kyokuchi Kenkyujo, 9-10, Kaga 1-chome, Itabashi-ku, Tokyo 173, Japan. Ed. Tatsuro Matsuda. circ. 1, 000. Indexed: Geo.Abstr. GeoRef.
    Supersedes: Japanese Antarctic Research Expedition, 1956-1962. Scientific Reports. Special Issue (ISSN 0386-5452)

NATIONAL RESEARCH COUNCIL, CANADA. ASSOCIATE COMMITTEE ON GEOTECHNICAL RESEARCH. TECHNICAL MEMORANDUM. see *ENGINEERING*

NATUR UND MENSCH: JAHRESMITTEILUNGEN DER NATURHISTORISCHEN GESELLSCHAFT NUERNBERG. see *BIOLOGY*

550 333.7   UN   ISSN 0077-6092
NATURAL RESOURCES RESEARCH. (Text in English and French) 1963. irreg., vol.20, 1983. price varies. Unesco, 7-9 Place de Fontenoy, 75700 Paris, France (Dist. in U.S. by: Bernan Associates-Unipub, 4611-F Assembly Dr., Lanham, MD 20706-4391) Indexed: Biol.Abstr. Forest.Abstr. Forest Prod.Abstr. GeoRef.

NATURHISTORISCHE GESELLSCHAFT HANNOVER. BEIHEFTE ZU DEN BERICHTEN. see *BIOLOGY*

550   GW   ISSN 0365-9844
NATURHISTORISCHE GESELLSCHAFT HANNOVER. BERICHTE. (Summaries in English) 1800. a. DM.20. Naturhistorische Gesellschaft Hannover, Postfach 510153, Stilleweg 2, 3000 Hannover 51, W. Germany (B.R.D.) circ. 850. Indexed: Biol.Abstr. GeoRef.

NATURHISTORISCHE GESELLSCHAFT NUERNBERG. ABHANDLUNGEN. see *ARCHAEOLOGY*

NAUKA O ZEMI. SERIA GEOGRAPHICA. see *GEOGRAPHY*

550   AU
NEUE DENKSCHRIFTEN DES NATURHISTORISCHEN MUSEUMS IN WIEN. 1977. irreg. price varies. Verlag Ferdinand Berger und Soehne GmbH, A-3580 Horn, Austria. Eds. Ortwin Schultz, Friedrich Bachmayer. circ. 500. Indexed: Biol.Abstr. GeoRef.

550 910 551.5   US
OHIO STATE UNIVERSITY. INSTITUTE OF POLAR STUDIES. CONTRIBUTION SERIES. 1961. irreg., no. 570, 1986. free or exchange basis. Ohio State University, Institute of Polar Studies, 125 S. Oval Mall, Columbus, OH 43210. TEL 614-422-6446. (reprint service avail.)

550 910 551.5   US
OHIO STATE UNIVERSITY. INSTITUTE OF POLAR STUDIES. MISCELLANEOUS SERIES. 1958. irreg., no. 236-19864. free or exchange basis. Ohio State University, Institute of Polar Studies, 125 S. Oval Mall, Columbus, OH 43210. TEL 614-422-6531.

550 910 551.5   US   ISSN 0078-415X
OHIO STATE UNIVERSITY. INSTITUTE OF POLAR STUDIES. REPORT SERIES. 1962. irreg., no.87, 1984. price varies. ‡ Ohio State University, Institute of Polar Studies, 103 Mendenhall, 125 S. Oval Mall, Columbus, OH 43210. TEL 614-422-6531. circ. 500. Indexed: Geo.Abstr. GeoRef.

550 331   CN
ONTARIO EDUCATION RELATIONS COMMISSION. ANNUAL REPORT. (Editions in English and French) 1975. a. Education Relations Committee, 111 Ave. Rd., Suite 400, Toronto, Ont. M5R 3J8, Canada. TEL 416-922-7679. circ. 2,000. (back issues avail.)

550   US   ISSN 0079-1946
PHYSICS AND CHEMISTRY OF THE EARTH. 1956. a. $145. Pergamon Press, Inc., Journals Division, Maxwell House, Fairview Park, Elmsford, NY 10523 TEL 914-592-7700. (And Headington Hill Hall, Oxford OX3 OBW, England) Ed. J.A. Pearce. index. (also avail. in microform from MIM, UMI) Indexed: Chem.Abstr. Curr.Cont. Sci.Abstr. GeoRef.

550   PL   ISSN 0370-0836
POLITECHNIKA WROCLAWSKA. INSTYTUT GEOTECHNIKI. PRACE NAUKOWE. KONFERENCJE. (Text in Polish; summaries in English and Russian) 1972. irreg., no.19, 1985. price varies. Politechnika Wroclawska, Wybrzeze Wyspianskiego 27, 50-370 Wroclaw, Poland (Dist. by: Ars Polona-Ruch, Krakowskie Przedmiescie 7, Warsaw, Poland) Ed. Jerzy Ciekot.

550   PL   ISSN 0084-2834
POLITECHNIKA WROCLAWSKA. INSTYTUT GEOTECHNIKI. PRACE NAUKOWE. MONOGRAFIE. (Text in Polish; summaries in English, French and Russian) 1971. irreg., no.17, 1984. price varies. Politechnika Wroclawska, Wybrzeze Wyspianskiego 27, 50-370 Wroclaw, Poland (Dist. by: Ars Polona-Ruch, Krakowskie Przedmiescie 7, Warsaw, Poland) Ed. Jerzy Ciekot.

550   PL   ISSN 0084-2842
POLITECHNIKA WROCLAWSKA. INSTYTUT GEOTECHNIKI. PRACE NAUKOWE. STUDIA I MATERIALY. (Text in Polish; summaries in English, French and Russian) 1969. irreg., no.11, 1985. price varies. Politechnika Wroclawska, Wybrzeze Wyspianskiego 27, 50-370 Wroclaw, Poland (Dist. by: Ars Polona-Ruch, Krakowskie Przedmiescie 7, Warsaw, Poland) Ed. Jerzy Ciekot.

550   GW   ISSN 0341-9665
POLLICHIA. MITTEILUNGEN. (Summaries in English, French and German) 1888. a. DM.35. Pollichia Verein fuer Naturforschung und Landespflege, Hermann Schaefer Str. 17, 6702 Bad Duerkheim, W. Germany (B.R.D.) Ed. K. Stapf. (back issues avail.) Indexed: Biol.Abstr. GeoRef.

550 560   GE   ISSN 0138-3116
QUARTAERPALAEONTOLOGIE. (Text in English, French, German and Russian) 1975. irreg., vol.5, 1984. (Institut fuer Quartaerpalaeontologie) Akademie-Verlag Berlin, Leipziger Str. 3-4, 1086 Berlin, E. Germany (D.D.R.) Ed. Hans Dietrich Kahlke.

RESEARCH INSTITUTE NEDRI AS. BULLETIN. see *BIOLOGY — Botany*

550   FR   ISSN 0249-7557
REUNION ANNUELLE DES SCIENCES DE LA TERRE; resumes des communications. 1973. biennial. Societe Geologique de France, 77 rue Claude Bernard, 75005 Paris, France. illus. Indexed: GeoRef.

550   GW   ISSN 0080-2689
RHEINISCHE SCHRIFTEN. 1963. irreg. price varies. Rheinland-Verlag, Kennedy-Ufer 2, 5000 Cologne 21, W. Germany (B.R.D.) (Distr. by: Rudolf Habelt Verlag, Am Buchenhang 1, 5300 Bonn, W. Germany (B.R.D.))

SAINT MARY'S UNIVERSITY. OCCASIONAL PAPERS IN GEOGRAPHY. see *GEOGRAPHY*

550   FR
SCIENCES DE LA TERRE. LEXIQUE. (Text in English and French) 1978. a. 400 F.($420) Centre National de la Recherche Scientifique, Centre de Documentation Scientifique et Technique, 26 rue Boyer, 75971 Paris Cedex 20, France.

SCIENCES DE LA TERRE: SERIE INFORMATIQUE GEOLOGIQUE. see *EARTH SCIENCES — Geology*

620 550　　　　　SZ　ISSN 0080-9004
SERIES ON ROCK AND SOIL MECHANICS. 1971. irreg., (4-6/yr.) price varies. ‡ Trans Tech Publications, P.O. Box 266, D-3392 Clauthal-Zellerfeld, W. Germany (B.R.D.) Ed. Dr. R. H. Wohlbier. Indexed: GeoRef. Geotech.Abstr.

550 551　　　　　JA　ISSN 0385-8286
SHIMABARA EARTHQUAKE AND VOLCANO OBSERVATORY. SCIENCES REPORTS. (Text in Japanese; summaries in English) 1965. a. Shimabara Earthquake and Volcano Observatory, c/o Kyushu University, Faculty of Science, 5643-29, Shimabara 855, Japan. TEL 0957-62-6621. Kazuya Ohta. circ. 500.

550　　　　　US　ISSN 0081-0274
SMITHSONIAN CONTRIBUTIONS TO THE EARTH SCIENCES. 1969. irreg., no.26, 1984. Smithsonian Institution Press, 955 L'Enfant Plaza, Rm. 2100, Washington, DC 20560. TEL 202-287-3738. Ed. Barbara T. Spann. circ. 1,900. (reprint service avail. from UMI) Indexed: Biol.Abstr. GeoRef.

550　　　　　US　ISSN 0196-0768
SMITHSONIAN CONTRIBUTIONS TO THE MARINE SCIENCES. 1977. irreg., no.26, 1985. Smithsonian Institution Press, 955 L'Enfant Plaza, Rm. 2100, Washington, DC 20560. TEL 202-287-3738. Ed. Barbara T. Spann. abstr. bibl. charts. illus. circ. 1,800. (also avail. in microfilm; microfiche; back issues avail., reprint service avail. from UMI) Indexed: Biol.Abstr. GeoRef.

550　　　　　MX
SOCIEDAD MEXICANA DE HISTORIA NATURAL. REVISTA. (Text in Spanish; summaries in English) 1940. a. Mex.$250($25) Sociedad Mexicana de Historia Natural, Ave. Dr. Vertiz 724, Mexico City 12 D.F., Mexico. Ed. Ambrosio Gonzalez Cortes. bk. rev. circ. 1,000. (back issues avail.) Indexed: Biol.Abstr. GeoRef.

SOCIETA SARDA DI SCIENZE NATURALI. BOLLETTINO. see *BIOLOGY — Ornithology*

SOCIETE DES NATURALISTES LUXEMBOURGEOIS. BULLETIN; publication de la societe botanique/annee de la Fauna. see *BIOLOGY*

550 622　　　　　AT　ISSN 0726-1527
SOUTH AUSTRALIA. DEPARTMENT OF MINES AND ENERGY. SPECIAL PUBLICATIONS. 1982. irreg. price varies. Department of Mines and Energy, 191 Greenhill Road, Parkside, Adelaide, S.A. 5063, Australia. Ed. J. Selby. circ. 300. (back issues avail.) Indexed: GeoRef.

550 910　　　　　JA
SPELEOLOGICAL SOCIETY OF JAPAN. JOURNAL. (Text in English and Japanese) 1976. a. 3.000 Yen($21) Speleological Society of Japan, c/o Kitakyushu Museum of Natural History, 3-6-1 Nishihon-Machi, Yahata-Higashiku, Kitakyushu-Shi 805, Japan. Eds. T. Kuramoto, K. Yoshimura. circ. 250. (back issues avail.)

550　　　　　US
U S S R REPORT: EARTH SCIENCES. irreg. (approx. 10/yr.) $5 per no. U.S. Joint Publications Research Service, 1000 N. Glebe Rd., Arlington, VA 22201 TEL 703-487-4630. (Orders to: NTIS, Springfield, VA 22161)

550　　　　　US
U.S. NATIONAL AERONAUTICS AND SPACE ADMINISTRATION. EARTH RESOURCES LABORATORY. RESEARCH AND TECHNOLOGY. ANNUAL REPORT. a. U.S. National Aeronautics and Space Administration, Washington, DC 20546. TEL 202-755-2320.

550　　　　　CL　ISSN 0069-357X
UNIVERSIDAD DE CHILE. DEPARTAMENTO DE GEOLOGIA. SERIE COMMUNICACIONES. (Text in Spanish; summaries in English) 1960. a. $10. Universidad de Chile, Departamento de Geologia y Geofisica, Casilla 13518, Correo 21, Santiago, Chile. Ed. Francisco Herve. bk. rev. circ. 400.

550　　　　　UY　ISSN 0250-6521
UNIVERSIDAD DE LA REPUBLICA. FACULTAD DE HUMANIDADES Y CIENCIAS. REVISTA. SERIE CIENCIAS DE LA TIERRA. N.S. 1979. irreg. exchange basis. Universidad de la Republica, Facultad de Humanidades y Ciencias, Seccion Revista, Tristan Narvaja 1674, Montevideo, Uruguay. Dir. Beatriz Martinez Osorio.
Supersedes in part: Universidad de la Republica. Facultad de Humanidades y Ciencias. Revista.

550 520　　　　　BL
UNIVERSIDADE DE SAO PAULO. INSTITUTO DE GEOCIENCIAS. BOLETIM. (Includes some summaries in English) 1970. irreg. Universidade de Sao Paulo, Instituto de Geociencias, Cidade Universitaria "Armando de Salles Oliveira", Bloco, 19, Sao Paulo, Brazil. illus. Indexed: Geo.Abstr.
Formerly: Universidade de Sao Paulo. Instituto de Geociencias y Astronomia. Boletim. Supersedes: Mineralogia, and Geologia (issued by the university's Faculdade de Filosofia, Ciencias e Letras)

550　　　　　BL
UNIVERSIDADE FEDERAL DE PERNAMBUCO. DEPARTAMENTO DE GEOLOGIA. SERIE B. ESTUDOS E PESQUISAS. (Text in Portuguese; summaries in English, French or German) 1971. irreg. exchange basis. Universidade Federal de Pernambuco, Centro de Tecnologia, Recife, PE, Brazil. Ed. J.M. Mabesoone. circ. 1,000.
Formerly: Universidade Federal de Pernambuco. Instituto de Geociencias. Serie B: Estudos e Pesquisas (ISSN 0080-0244)

550　　　　　BL
UNIVERSIDADE FEDERAL DO RIO GRANDE DO SUL. INSTITUTO DE GEOCIENCIAS. PESQUISAS. (Text in Portuguese; summaries in English) 1972. irreg. $7. Universidade Federal do Rio Grande do Sul, Instituto de Geociencias, Rua Gen. Vitorino 255, 90.000 Porto Alegre, Rio Grande do Sul, Brazil. Indexed: Geosci.Doc.

550 560　　　　　GW　ISSN 0585-7856
UNIVERSITAET STUTTGART. INSTITUT FUER GEOLOGIE UND PALAEONTOLOGIE ARBEITEN NEUE FOLGE. (Text in German; summaries in English and French) 1954. irreg., vol.72, 1978. price varies. Universitaet Stuttgart, Institut fuer Geologie und Palaeontologie, Boeblinger Str. 72, 7000 Stuttgart 1, W. Germany (B.R.D.) Ed. K. Hinkelbein. illus. circ. 400.

UNIVERSITE DE SHERBROOKE. DEPARTMENT DE GEOGRAPHIE. BULLETIN DE RECHERCHE. see *GEOGRAPHY*

550　　　　　US　ISSN 0068-645X
UNIVERSITY OF CALIFORNIA PUBLICATIONS IN GEOLOGICAL SCIENCES. 1893. irreg. price varies. University of California Press, 2120 Berkeley Way, Berkeley, CA 94720. TEL 415-642-4247. Indexed: Biol.Abstr.

UNIVERSITY OF COLORADO. INSTITUTE OF ARCTIC AND ALPINE RESEARCH. OCCASIONAL PAPERS. see *SCIENCES: COMPREHENSIVE WORKS*

550　　　　　JA
UNIVERSITY OF TOKYO. EARTHQUAKE RESEARCH INSTITUTE. SPECIAL BULLETIN. (Text in English, Japanese) 1943. irreg. University of Tokyo, Earthquake Research Institute, 1-1-1 Yayoi, Bunkyo-ku, Tokyo 113, Japan. circ. 1,200.

550　　　　　JA　ISSN 0040-8999
UNIVERSITY OF TOKYO. FACULTY OF SCIENCE. JOURNAL. SECTION 2: GEOLOGY, MINERALOGY, GEOGRAPHY, GEOPHYSICS/ TOKYO DAIGAKU RIGAKUBU KIYO, DAI-2-RUI, CHISHITSUGAKU, KOBUTSUGAKU, CHIRIGAKU, CHIKYU BUTSURIGAKU. (Text in English) 1925. a. price Varies. University of Tokyo, Faculty of Science - Tokyo Daigaku Rigakubu, Hongo, Tokyo, Japan TEL 03-812-2111. (Order from: Maruzen Co., Ltd., 2-3-10 Nihonbashi, Chuo-ku, Tokyo 103, Japan; or their Import and Export Department, Box 5050, Tokyo International, Tokyo 100-31, Japan) Ed. Azuma Ijima. bibl. charts. illus. circ. 850. Indexed: Biol.Abstr. Chem.Abstr. Met.Abstr. GeoRef.

UNIVERSITY OF TORONTO. FACULTY OF FORESTRY. RESEARCH REPORT. see *FORESTS AND FORESTRY*

WHO'S WHO IN CIVIL ENGINEERING, EARTH SCIENCES & ENERGY. see *ENGINEERING — Civil Engineering*

550　　　　　CS
Z DEJIN GEODEZIE A KARTOGRAFIE. 1981. irreg. exchange basis. Narodni Technicke Muzeum, Kostelni 42, Prague 7, Czechoslovakia. bibl. illus.

EARTH SCIENCES — Abstracting, Bibliographies, Statistics

ABSTRACT NEWSLETTER: NATURAL RESOURCES & EARTH SCIENCES. see *CONSERVATION — Abstracting, Bibliographies, Statistics*

621.4 016　　　　　US
ABSTRACT NEWSLETTER: OCEAN TECHNOLOGY & ENGINEERING. w. $79. U.S. National Technical Information Service, 5285 Port Royal Rd., Springfield, VA 22161. TEL 703-487-4630. Ed. Linda J. LaGarde. index. (back issues avail.)
Former titles: Weekly Abstract Newsletter: Ocean Technology and Engineering; Weekly Government Abstracts. Ocean Technology and Engineering (ISSN 0364-6424)

550 910 016　　　　　BU　ISSN 0204-9406
ABSTRACTS OF BULGARIAN SCIENTIFIC LITERATURE. NAUKI ZA ZEMIATA. (Editions in English and Russian) 1958. q. 3.44 lv. Bulgarska Akademiia na Naukite, Centur za Nauchna Informaciia - Scientific Information Centre of Bulgarian Academy of Sciences, 7 Noemvri St., 1, 1040 Sofia, Bulgaria (Dist. by: RP, Klokotnic St., no.2A, Sofia 1202, Bulgaria) Ed. I. Kostov. bk. rev. abstr. index. circ. 433. (also avail. in microfiche) Indexed: Chem.Abstr.
Formerly: Abstracts of Bulgarian Scientific Literature. Geology and Geography (ISSN 0001-3498)

551.7 560 560　　　　　US　ISSN 0192-7272
AMERICAN ASSOCIATION OF STRATIGRAPHIC PALYNOLOGISTS. ABSTRACTS OF PAPERS PRESENTED AT THE ANNUAL MEETINGS. a. $2. American Association of Stratigraphic Palynologists Foundation., c/o Robert T. Clarke, Mobil R & D Corp.-D R L, Box 819047, Dallas, TX 75381. Indexed: GeoRef.

550 620 016　　　　　TH　ISSN 0301-4169
ASIAN GEOTECHNICAL ENGINEERING ABSTRACTS. (Text in English) 1973. s-a. membership. Asian Information Center for Geotechnical Engineering, c/o Asian Institute of Technology, Box 2754, Bangkok, Thailand. abstr. circ. 300(controlled) (processed)

551　　　　　PL　ISSN 0373-1987
BIBLIOGRAFIA GEOLOGICZNA POLSKI. (Text in English, Polish, Russian) 1921. a. price varies. Instytut Geologiczny, Ul. Rakowiecka 4, 00 975 Warsaw, Poland. index. circ. 400. (back issues avail.)

551.4　　　　　PL　ISSN 0239-6246
BIBLIOGRAFIA HYDROLOGII I OCEANOLOGII/ BIBLIOGRAPHY OF HYDROLOGY AND OCEANOLOGY. (Text in English, French, German, Polish and Russian) 1936. irreg. $180. Instytut Meteorologii i Gospodarki Wodnej - Institute of Meteorology and Water Management, 61 Podlesna St., 01-673 Warsaw, Poland. circ. 300.

551 016　　　　　US　ISSN 0098-2784
BIBLIOGRAPHY AND INDEX OF GEOLOGY. 1969. m. $1,155. American Geological Institute, 4220 King St., Alexandria, VA 22302-1507. TEL 703-379-2480. Ed. G.N. Rassam. index. circ. 900. (reprint service avail. from UMI)
●Also available online. Vendors: CISTI, DIALOG, Orbit Information Technologies.
Formed by the merger of: Bibliography of North American Geology; Bibliography and Index of Geology Exclusive of North America (ISSN 0006-1522)

551 016   SA   ISSN 0584-2360
BIBLIOGRAPHY AND SUBJECT INDEX OF
SOUTH AFRICAN GEOLOGY. 1957. a., latest
1983. R.2.50. Geological Survey, Private Bag X112,
Pretoria 0001, South Africa.

012 559   FJ   ISSN 0252-8398
BIBLIOGRAPHY OF THE GEOLOGY OF FIJI.
1969. irreg. price varies. Mineral Resources
Department, P.M. Bag, Suva, Fiji. Ed. Peter Rodda.
circ. 500.

557 016   US   ISSN 0067-7272
BIBLIOGRAPHY OF THE GEOLOGY OF
MISSOURI. 1956. a. price varies. Department of
Natural Resources, Division of Geology and Land
Survey, Box 250, Rolla, MO 65401. TEL 314-364-
1752.

557 016   CN   ISSN 0707-2996
CANADA. GEOLOGICAL SURVEY. INDEX OF
PUBLICATIONS OF THE GEOLOGICAL
SURVEY OF CANADA. 1900. a. price varies.
Geological Survey of Canada, 601 Booth St.,
Ottawa K1A 0E8, Canada TEL 613-995-4342.
(Dist. by: Supply and Services Canada, Ottawa,
Ont. K1A 0S9, Canada) index. cum.index: 1959-
1974; 1975-1979.

551.46 333.91 011   US   ISSN 0883-4725
CURRENT TITLES IN OCEAN, COASTAL, LAKE
& WATERWAY SCIENCES; reader's information
bulletin and service. 1986. q. $25 to individuals;
institutions $35. Coastal Education & Research
Foundation, Inc., Box 8068, Charlottesville, VA
22906. TEL 804-973-1863. Eds. Charles W. Finkl,
Rhodes W. Fairbridge. adv. abstr. bibl. illus. circ.
500. (back issues avail.)

551.3 016   UK   ISSN 0268-7917
GEOGRAPHICAL ABSTRACTS E
(SEDIMENTOLOGY) 1972. 6/yr. £43.50. Geo
Abstracts Ltd., Regency House, 34 Duke St.,
Norwich NR3 3AP, England. Ed. A. Pitty. index;
cum.index: 1972-1976. circ. 1,100. (back issues
avail.) Indexed: Petrol.Abstr.
    Formerly: Geo Abstracts E (Sedimentology)
(ISSN 0305-1935)

551 016   UK   ISSN 0268-800X
GEOLOGICAL ABSTRACTS: ECONOMIC
GEOLOGY. 1986. bi-m. £58. Geo Abstracts Ltd.,
Regency House, 34 Duke St., Norwich NR3 3AP,
England. Ed. John Barber. circ. 300.

551 016   UK   ISSN 0268-7941
GEOLOGICAL ABSTRACTS: GEOPHYSICS AND
TECTONICS. 1977. 6/yr. £58. Geo Abstracts Ltd.,
Regency House, 34 Duke St., Norwich NR3 3AP,
England. Ed. John Barber. index. circ. 400. (back
issues avail.)
    Former titles: Geophysics and Tectonics
Abstracts (ISSN 0262-0847); Geophysical Abstracts
(ISSN 0309-4332)

551 016   UK   ISSN 0268-8018
GEOLOGICAL ABSTRACTS: PALAEONTOLOGY
AND STRATIGRAPHY. 1986. bi-m. £58. Geo
Abstracts Ltd., Regency House, 34 Duke St.,
Norwich NR3 3AP, England. Ed. A. Cruikshank.
circ. 300.

551 016   UK
GEOLOGICAL ABSTRACTS: SEDIMENTARY
GEOLOGY. 1986. bi-m. £58. Geo Abstracts Ltd.,
Regency House, 34 Duke St., Norwich NR3 3AP,
England. Eds. Alistair Pitty, Keith Clayton. bk. rev.
circ. 300.
    Formerly: Geological Abstracts: Sedimentology
(ISSN 0268-8026)

551 016   US   ISSN 0016-7592
GEOLOGICAL SOCIETY OF AMERICA.
ABSTRACTS WITH PROGRAMS. 1969. a. price
varies. Geological Society of America, Marketing
Department, 3300 Penrose Pl., Box 9140, Boulder,
CO 80301. TEL 303-447-2020. Ed. F. Michael
Wahl. adv. circ. 7,000. Indexed: GeoRef.

557 016   US
GEORGIA. GEOLOGIC SURVEY. CIRCULAR 1.
LIST OF PUBLICATIONS. 14 edt., 1973. irreg.,
18th edt., 1983. free. Department of Natural
Resources, Georgia Geologic Survey, 19 Martin
Luther King Jr. Dr., S.W., Rm. 400, Atlanta, GA
30334. TEL 404-656-3214.
    Formerly: Georgia. Geological Survey. Circular 1.
List of Publications.

550 016   UK   ISSN 0016-8483
GEOSCIENCE DOCUMENTATION; a bi-monthly
journal for the study of geoscience literature. 1969.
bi-m. £50($100) Geosystems, Box 40, Didcot, Oxon
OX11 9BX, England. adv. bk. rev. abstr. bibl.
charts. illus. patents. stat. index. Indexed:
Bibl.Cart.
    ●Also available online. Vendors: DIALOG.

011 614.7   CN   ISSN 0831-5000
GEOTECHNICAL SCIENCE LABORATORIES.
PUBLICATIONS, REPORTS, AND THESES.
1972. a. free. Geotechnical Science Laboratories,
Geography Department, Carleton University,
Ottawa, Ont. K1S 5B6, Canada. TEL 613-564-2815.
index. cum.index: 1976-1984. circ. 550.

I M M ABSTRACTS; a survey of world literature on
the economic geology and mining of all minerals
(except coal), mineral processing and non-ferrous
extraction metallurgy. (Institution of Mining and
Metallurgy) see MINES AND MINING
INDUSTRY — Abstracting, Bibliographies,
Statistics

551 016   II   ISSN 0379-511X
INDIAN GEOLOGICAL INDEX. Alternate title:
I.G.I. (Text in English) 1971. a. Rs.50. D-42 Vivek
Vihar, Delhi 32, India.
    Geological literature of India

551   CN
MANITOBA ENERGY AND MINES.
BIBLIOGRAPHY SERIES. irreg. Manitoba Energy
and Mines, 555-330 Graham Ave., Winnipeg, MB
R3C 4E3, Canada. TEL 204-945-6541.
    Formerly: Manitoba. Mineral Resources Division.
Bibliography Series.

MARINE SCIENCE CONTENTS TABLES. see
BIOLOGY — Abstracting, Bibliographies, Statistics

METEOROLOGICAL AND
GEOASTROPHYSICAL ABSTRACTS. see
METEOROLOGY — Abstracting, Bibliographies,
Statistics

550   UK   ISSN 0026-4601
MINERALOGICAL ABSTRACTS; a quarterly
journal of abstracts in English, covering the world
literature of mineralogy and related subjects. 1959.
q. £105($190) Mineralogical Society, 41 Queen's
Gate, London S.W.7 5HR, England. (Co-sponsor:
Mineralogical Society of America) Ed. R.A. Howie.
bk. rev. abstr. index. circ. 1,800. Indexed:
Chem.Abstr. Anal.Abstr. Br.Ceram.Abstr.
GeoRef.

551.46 016   US   ISSN 0093-6901
OCEANIC ABSTRACTS. 1964. bi-m. $652.
Cambridge Scientific Abstracts, 5161 River Rd.,
Bethesda, MD 20816. TEL 301-951-1400. adv.
abstr. bibl. illus. index; cum.index. circ. 500. (also
avail. in microform from MIM; back issues avail.)
Indexed: Nutr.Abstr. Cal.Tiss.Abstr.
Chemorec.Abstr. Oncol.Abstr.
    ●Also available online. Vendors: DIALOG,
European Space Agency.
    Supersedes: Oceanic Index (ISSN 0029-8093) &
Oceanic Citation Index (ISSN 0029-8085)

551 016   SP
SPAIN. INSTITUTO GEOLOGICO Y MINERO.
CATALOGO DE EDICIONES.* irreg. Instituto
Geologico y Minero, Rios Rosas 23, Madrid 3,
Spain. bibl. illus.

551.44   SZ   ISSN 0253-8296
SPELEOLOGICAL ABSTRACTS/BULLETIN
BIBLIOGRAPHIQUE SPELEOLOGIQUE. (Text
in English and French) 1969. a. 20 Fr. International
Union of Speleology, c/o Jean-Claude Lalou, 97,
Route de Suisse, CH-1290 Versoix, Switzerland. Ed.
Jean-Claude Lalou. adv. bk. rev. circ. 600. Indexed:
GeoRef.
    Speleology

551 520   US
U S S R REPORT: SPACE. 1961. irreg. (approx. 8/
yr.) $5 per no. U.S. Joint Publications Research
Service, 1000 N. Glebe Rd., Arlington, VA 22201
TEL 703-487-4630. (Orders to: NTIS, Springfield,
VA 22161)
    Former titles: U S S R Report: Geophysics,
Astronomy, and Space; U S S R and Eastern
Europe Scientific Abstracts: Geophysics,
Astronomy, and Space (ISSN 0363-7220); Soviet-
Bloc Research in Geophysics, Astronomy, and
Space (ISSN 0038-5336)

551.46 016   VE   ISSN 0590-3343
UNIVERSIDAD DE ORIENTE. INSTITUTO
OCEANOGRAFICO BIBLIOTECA. BOLETIN
BIBLIOGRAFICO. 1964. a., no.11, 1974. $1.
Universidad de Oriente, Instituto Oceanografico,
Cumana, Venezuela. Ed. Mario G. Revollo. bibl.
circ. 1,000 controlled.

EARTH SCIENCES — Geology

see also Mines and Mining Industry

552   US   ISSN 0271-8510
A A P G STUDIES IN GEOLOGY SERIES. 1975.
irreg., no.22, 1986. price varies. American
Association of Petroleum Geologists, Box 979,
Tulsa, OK 74101. TEL 918-584-2555. cum.index:
1971-75, 1976-80, 1981-85. Indexed: Biol.Abstr.
Chem.Abstr. GeoRef.

549   AT   ISSN 0045-0707
A M D E L BULLETIN. 1966. a. free. Australia
Mineral Development Laboratories, Flemington St.,
Frewville, S.A. 5063, Australia. Ed. K. J. Henley.
circ. 800. Indexed: Chem.Abstr. Eng.Ind.
Mineral.Abstr.

A.P.E.A. JOURNAL. (Australian Petroleum
Exploration Association) see PETROLEUM AND
GAS

551   DK   ISSN 0105-8258
AARHUS UNIVERSITET. GEOLOGISK INSTITUT.
GEOKOMPENDIER. irreg., no.23, 1984. price
varies. Aarhus Universitet, Geologisk Institut,
Biblioteket, C.F. Mollers Alle bygn. 120, 8000
Aarhus C, Denmark. illus.

551   DK   ISSN 0105-8266
AARHUS UNIVERSITET. GEOLOGISK INSTITUT.
GEORAPPORTER. 1978. irreg., no. 5, 1978. price
varies. Aarhus University, Geologisk Institut, C.F.
Mollers Alle, Bygn. 120, DK-8000 Aarhus C,
Denmark. illus.

551 910   DK   ISSN 0105-824X
AARHUS UNIVERSITET. GEOLOGISK INSTITUT.
GEOSKRIFTER. irreg., no.23, 1985. price varies.
Aarhus Universitet, Geologisk Institut, C.F. Mollers
Alle, Bygn. 120, 8000 Aarhus C, Denmark. illus.
Indexed: Geo.Abstr.
    Formerly: Skrifter i Fysisk Geografi.

550   CU
ACADEMIA DE CIENCIAS DE CUBA.
INSTITUTO DE GEOLOGIA. RESUMENES,
COMUNICACIONES Y NOTAS DEL
CONSEJO CIENTIFICO.* irreg. Academia de
Ciencias de Cuba, Instituto de Geologia, Calfada no.
851, Esq. a Calle 4, Havana 4, Cuba. illus.
    Formerly: Academia de Ciencias de Cuba.
Instituto de Geologia. Resumenes del Consejo
Cientifico.

557   CU
ACADEMIA DE CIENCIAS DE CUBA.
INSTITUTO DE GEOLOGIA. SERIE
GEOLOGICA.* (Summaries in English) 1968.
irreg. (3-4/yr.) exchange basis. Academia de
Ciencias de Cuba, Instituto de Geologia, Calzada
no. 851, Esq. a Calle 4, Havana 4, Cuba. bibl.
charts. illus. stat. circ. controlled. Indexed:
GeoRef.

551   US
ACADEMIC PRESS GEOLOGY SERIES. 1981.
irreg., vol.3, 1985. Academic Press Inc., Orlando,
FL 32887. TEL 305-345-2000.

ACTA GEOGRAPHICA DEDRECINA. see
GEOGRAPHY

EARTH SCIENCES — GEOLOGY

550 AG ISSN 0567-7513
ACTA GEOLOGICA LILLOANA. (Text in Spanish; summaries in English, French, German, Italian) 1957. irreg., vol.16, no.2, 1981. Fundacion Miguel Lillo, Miguel Lillo 251, 4000 Tucuman, Argentina. Ed. Dr. Jose A. Haedo Rossi. bibl. charts. illus. stat. index. circ. 500. (back issues avail.) Indexed: Biol.Abstr. Bull.Signal. Ref.Zh. GeoRef.

550.1 CH ISSN 0065-1265
ACTA GEOLOGICA TAIWANICA. (Text in English) 1947. a. exchange basis. National Taiwan University, Department of Geology, Taipei, Taiwan, Republic of China. Ed. Cheng-Hong Chen. bk. rev. circ. 600. Indexed: Biol.Abstr. Chem.Abstr. GeoRef. Mineral.Abstr.

551 GW ISSN 0375-5452
ACTA HUMBOLDTIANA. SERIES GEOLOGICA, PALAEONTOLOGICA ET BIOLOGICA. (Text in French and German) irreg., vol.2, 1972. price varies. (Deutsche Ibero-Amerika-Stiftung) Franz Steiner Verlag Wiesbaden GmbH, Birkenwaldstr. 44, Postfach 347, D-7000 Stuttgart 1, W. Germany (B.R.D.) Ed. Wolfgang Haberland. Indexed: GeoRef.

ACTA NATURALIA ISLANDICA. see
BIOLOGY — Botany

551 NE
ADVANCES IN EARTH AND PLANETARY SCIENCES; a series of conference proceedings volumes. 1977. irreg. price varies. D. Reidel Publishing Co., Box 17, 3300 AA Dordrecht, Netherlands (And 190 Old Derby St., Hingham, MA 02043) Ed. T. Rikitake. Indexed: Chem.Abstr.

ADVANCES IN GEOPHYSICAL DATA PROCESSING; a research annual. see
COMPUTERS

551.9 US ISSN 0722-3269
ADVANCES IN PHYSICAL GEOCHEMISTRY. 1981. irreg., vol.6, 1986. Springer-Verlag, 175 Fifth Ave., New York, NY 10010 TEL 212-460-1500. (Also Berlin, Heidelberg, Tokyo and Vienna) Ed. S. Saxena. (reprint service avail. from ISI) Indexed: Chem.Abstr.

551 PL
AKADEMIA GORNICZO-HUTNICZA IM. STANISTAWA STASZICA. ZESZYTY NAUKOWE. GEOLOGIA. (Text in English and Polish; summaries in English, Polish, Russian) 1956. irreg., no. 34, 1986. price varies. (Akademia Gorniczo-Hutnicza im. Stanislawa Staszica) Wydawnictwo A G H, Manifestu Lipcowego 16, 31-109 Krakow, Poland (Dist. by: Ars Polona, Krakowskie Przedmiescie 7, 00-068 Warsaw, Poland) Ed. Z. Kleczek. illus. circ. 300.

551 UR
AKADEMIYA NAUK S.S.S.R. SIBIRSKOE OTDELENIE. VOSTOCHNO-SIBIRSKII FILIAL. INSTITUT GEOKHIMII. EZHEGODNIK.* (Text in Russian; summaries in English) 1969. irreg. 1 Rub. Akademiya Nauk S.S.S.R., Vostochno-Sibirskii Filial, Institut Geokhimii, Ul. Favorskogo, 1, 664033 Irkutsk, Russian S.F.S.R., U.S.S.R. Ed. L.V. Tauson. bibl.

557 US ISSN 0065-5635
ALABAMA GEOLOGICAL SOCIETY. GUIDEBOOK FOR THE ANNUAL FIELD TRIP. (Title varies: vol.1, Field Trip Guidebook) 1964. a. (two books appeared in 1964) price varies. Alabama Geological Society, Box 6184, University, AL 35486. TEL 205-349-2852. circ. 100-150. Indexed: GeoRef.

551 US
ALASKA. DIVISION OF GEOLOGICAL AND GEOPHYSICAL SURVEYS. GEOLOGIC/PROFESSIONAL REPORT. 1969. irreg. price varies. Department of Natural Resources, Division of Geological and Geophysical Surveys, 794 University Ave., Basement, Fairbanks, AK 99709. TEL 907-474-7147.
Formerly: Alaska. Division of Geological and Geophysical Surveys. Laboratory Report (ISSN 0065-5775)

557 US ISSN 0065-5759
ALASKA. DIVISION OF GEOLOGICAL AND GEOPHYSICAL SURVEYS. INFORMATION CIRCULAR. irreg. free. Department of Natural Resources, Division of Geological and Geophysical Surveys, 794 University Ave., Basement, Fairbanks, AK 99709. TEL 907-474-7147.

551 US
ALASKA. DIVISION OF GEOLOGICAL AND GEOPHYSICAL SURVEYS. REPORT OF INVESTIGATIONS. irreg. price varies. Department of Natural Resources, Division of Geological and Geophysical Surveys, 794 University Ave., Basement, Fairbanks, AK 99709. TEL 907-474-7147.
Former titles: Alaska. Division of Geological and Geophysical Surveys. Open-File Report; Alaska. Division of Geological and Geophysical Surveys. Laboratory Note (ISSN 0065-5767)

551 US ISSN 0360-3881
ALASKA. DIVISION OF GEOLOGICAL AND GEOPHYSICAL SURVEYS. SPECIAL REPORT. 1967. irreg. price varies. Department of Natural Resources, Division of Geological and Geophysical Surveys, 794 University Ave., Basement, Fairbanks, AK 99709. TEL 907-474-7147. Indexed: Chem.Abstr. GeoRef.

550 CN ISSN 0034-5172
ALBERTA RESEARCH COUNCIL. BULLETINS. 1958. irreg. price varies. Alberta Research Council, Publications Dept., P.O. Box 8330, Sta. F, Edmonton, Alta. T6H 5X2, Canada. TEL 403-450-4111. bibl. charts. illus. stat. Indexed: Geo.Abstr. GeoRef.

ALTENBURGER NATURWISSENSCHAFTLICHE FORSCHUNGEN. see *BIOLOGY*

551 665.5 US ISSN 0065-731X
AMERICAN ASSOCIATION OF PETROLEUM GEOLOGISTS. MEMOIR. 1962. irreg., no.42, 1986. price varies. American Association of Petroleum Geologists, Box 979, Tulsa, OK 74101. TEL 918-584-2555. cum.index: 1956-65, 1966-70, 1971-75, 1976-80, 1981-85. Indexed: Biol.Abstr. GeoRef.

551 US ISSN 0160-8843
AMERICAN ASSOCIATION OF STRATIGRAPHIC PALYNOLOGISTS. CONTRIBUTIONS SERIES. irreg. price varies. American Association of Stratigraphic Palynologists Foundation, c/o Robert T. Clarke, Mobil R & D Corp.-D R L, Box 819047, Dallas, TX 75381. Indexed: Biol.Abstr. GeoRef.

ANDRIAS. see *BIOLOGY — Botany*

550 AO ISSN 0003-3456
ANGOLA. DIRECCAO PROVINCIAL DOS SERVICOS DE GEOLOGIA E MINAS. BOLETIM. (Text in English, French and Portuguese) 1960. irreg. Esc.50. Direccao Provincial dos Servicos de Geologia e Minas, C. P. 1260-C, Luanda, Angola. (Co-sponsor: Instituto Nacional de Geologia) charts. illus. maps. stat. Indexed: GeoRef.

550.1 FI ISSN 0066-197X
ANNALES ACADEMIAE SCIENTIARUM FENNICAE. SERIES A, III: GEOLOGICA-GEOGRAPHICA. (Text in English, French and German) 1941. irreg. price varies. Suomalainen Tiedeakatemia - Academia Scientiarum Fennica, Snellmaninnk, 9-11, 00170 Helsinki, Finland. Ed. Toive Aartolahti. circ. 600. (also avail. in microform; back issues avail.) Indexed: Biol.Abstr. Bull.Signal. Psychol.Abstr. Ref.Zh. Doc.Geogr. Geo.Abstr. GeoRef.

ANNALES UNIVERSITATIS MARIAE CURIE-SKLODOWSKA. SECTIO B. GEOGRAPHIA, GEOLOGIA, MINERALOGIA ET PETROGRAPHIA. see *GEOGRAPHY*

551.31 UK ISSN 0260-3055
ANNALS OF GLACIOLOGY. 1980. a. price varies. International Glaciological Society, Cambridge CB2 1ER, England. illus. circ. 800. Indexed: Chem.Abstr. Geo.Abstr.

556 016 ZA ISSN 0066-2410
ANNOTATED BIBLIOGRAPHY AND INDEX OF THE GEOLOGY OF ZAMBIA. 1959. irreg., latest issue 1980. price varies. Geological Survey, P.O. Box R.W. 50135, Lusaka, Zambia.

ANUARIO DE LA MINERIA DE CHILE. see
MINES AND MINING INDUSTRY

ANUARIOS DE GEOMAGNETISMO (YEAR) see
EARTH SCIENCES — Geophysics

558 622 AG ISSN 0066-7145
ARGENTINA. SERVICIO NACIONAL MINERO GEOLOGICO. ANALES. 1904; N.S. 1947. irreg., no.17, 1976. price varies. Servicio Nacional Minero Geologico, Biblioteca, Avenida Santa Fe 1548, Buenos Aires, Argentina.
Formerly: Argentine Republic. Direccion Nacional de Geologia y Mineria. Anales.

558 622 AG ISSN 0066-7153
ARGENTINA. SERVICIO NACIONAL MINERO GEOLOGICO. BOLETIN. 1914; N.S. 1932. irreg. price varies. Servicio Nacional Minero Geologico, Biblioteca, Av. Santa Fe 1548, Buenos Aires, Argentina. Indexed: GeoRef.
Formerly: Argentine Republic. Direccion Nacional de Geologia y Mineria. Boletin.

551 AG
ARGENTINA. SERVICIO NACIONAL MINERO GEOLOGICO. INFORMES TECNICOS. 1957. irreg. Servicio Nacional Minero Geologico, Biblioteca, Av. Santa Fe 1548, Buenos Aires, Argentina.

553 AG ISSN 0066-717X
ARGENTINA. SERVICIO NACIONAL MINERO GEOLOGICO. REVISTA. 1965. irreg. free. Servicio Nacional Minero Geologico, Julio a Roca 651, 9 Piso, Buenos Aires, Argentina. Indexed: GeoRef.
Formerly: Argentina. Instituto Nacional de Geologia y Mineria. Revista.

ARIZONA. OIL AND GAS CONSERVATION COMMISSION. REPORT OF INVESTIGATION. see *PETROLEUM AND GAS*

557 US ISSN 0066-7412
ARIZONA GEOLOGICAL SOCIETY DIGEST. 1958. irreg. price varies. Arizona Geological Society, P.O. Box 4503, University Station, Tucson, AZ 85717. Ed. Judith P. Jenney. adv. circ. 1,000. Indexed: GeoRef.

557 US
ARKANSAS. GEOLOGICAL COMMISSION. INFORMATION CIRCULARS. 1956. irreg., no.23, 1975. price varies. Geological Commission, Vardelle Parham Geology Center, 3815 West Roosevelt Rd., Little Rock, AR 72204. TEL 501-663-9714. illus. (back issues avail.)

557 US
ARKANSAS. GEOLOGICAL COMMISSION. MISCELLANEOUS PUBLICATIONS. 1940. irreg., latest 1975. price varies. (Geological Commission) Vardell Parham Geology Center, 3815 West Roosevelt Rd., Little Rock, AR 72204. illus. circ. 1, 000. (back issues avail.)

551 US
ASSOCIATION OF ENGINEERING GEOLOGISTS. SPECIAL PUBLICATIONS. irreg. price varies. Association of Engineering Geologists, c/o Patricia S. Osiecki, Exec. Dir., 3479 Rambow Dr., Palo Alto, CA 94306. TEL 415-494-6785.

ASSOCIATION OF ISLAND MARINE LABORATORIES OF THE CARIBBEAN. PROCEEDINGS. see *BIOLOGY*

ATLANTIC SUMMARY REPORT/INDEX. see
PETROLEUM AND GAS

526 AT
AUSTRALIA. BUREAU OF MINERAL RESOURCES, GEOLOGY, AND GEOPHYSICS. 1: 250000 GEOLOGICAL MAPS AND EXPLANATORY NOTES SERIES. irreg. Aus.$8 per sheet. Bureau of Mineral Resources, Geology, and Geophysics, Box 378, Canberra, A.C.T. 2601, Australia.
Cartography

EARTH SCIENCES — GEOLOGY

AUSTRALIAN INSTITUTE OF PETROLEUM. ANNUAL REPORT. see *PETROLEUM AND GAS*

551   AT   ISSN 0084-750X
AUSTRALIAN NATIONAL UNIVERSITY, CANBERRA. GEOLOGY DEPARTMENT. PUBLICATION. 1962. irreg. price varies. Australian National University, Geology Department, Box 4, Canberra, A.C.T. 2600, Australia. circ. 500.

796.525   AT
AUSTRALIAN SPELEO ABSTRACTS. 1970. irreg. price varies. Sydney Speleological Society, P.O. Box 198, Broadway, N.S.W. 2007, Australia. Ed. Gregory J. Middleton. index; cum.index. circ. 125. *Speleology*

550.5   AT   ISSN 0572-5860
BAAS BECKING GEOBIOLOGICAL LABORATORY. ANNUAL REPORT. 1967. a. free. Baas Becking Geobiological Laboratory, c/o Bureau of Mineral Resources, P.O. Box 378, Canberra City A.C.T., 2601, Australia. Ed. M.R. Walter. illus. circ. 600. Indexed: GeoRef.

BADISCHER LANDESVEREIN FUER NATURKUNDE UND NATURSCHUTZ, FREIBURG. MITTEILUNGEN. NEUE FOLGE. see *BIOLOGY*

554   UR   ISSN 0067-3064
BALTICA. (International Yearbook for Quaternary Geology and Palaeogeography, Coastal Morphology and Shore Processes, Marine Geology and Recent Tectonics of the Baltic Sea Area) (Text in English, French, German and Russian; summaries in English, German and Russian) 1963. biennial. price varies. Akademiya Nauk Litovskoi S.S.R., Lenino Prospektas 3, Vilnius, Lithuanian S.S.R., U.S.S.R. Ed. Vytautas Gudelis. Indexed: Geo.Abstr. GeoRef.

BAYERISCHE STAATSSAMMLUNG FUER PALAEONTOLOGIE UND HISTORISCHE GEOLOGIE. MITTEILUNGEN. see *PALEONTOLOGY*

BEITRAEGE ZUR NATURKUNDE IN OSTHESSEN. see *BIOLOGY*

538.7   BE   ISSN 0524-7764
BELGIUM. INSTITUT ROYAL METEOROLOGIQUE. ANNUAIRE: MAGNETISME TERRESTRE/JAARBOEK: AARDMAGNETISME. (Text in Dutch and French) a. 500 Fr. Institut Royal Meteorologique, 3 av. Circulaire, 1180 Brussels, Belgium. circ. 150.

551   US
BENCHMARK PAPERS IN GEOLOGY. (Each vol. has distinctive title) 1972. irreg., vol.90 , 1985. price varies. Van Nostrand Reinhold Company, 7625 Empire Dr., Florence, KY 41042. TEL 606-525-6600. Ed. R.W. Fairbridge. illus. index.

551   US
BENCHMARK PAPERS IN SOIL SCIENCE. 1982. irreg., vol.4, 1984. price varies. Van Nostrand Reinhold Company, 7625 Empire Dr., Florence, KY 41042. TEL 606-525-6600. Ed. C. W. Finkl. illus. index.

BIBLIOGRAFIA GEOLOGICZNA POLSKI. see *EARTH SCIENCES — Abstracting, Bibliographies, Statistics*

BIBLIOGRAPHY OF THE GEOLOGY OF FIJI. see *EARTH SCIENCES — Abstracting, Bibliographies, Statistics*

550   PL   ISSN 0067-9003
BIULETYN GEOLOGICZNY. (Text in Polish; summaries in English) 1961. irreg. price varies. (Uniwersytet Warszawski, Wydzial Geologii) Wydawnictwa Uniwersytetu Warszawskiego, Ul. Obozna 8, 00-927 Warsaw, Poland (Distr. by: CHZ ARS Polona, Krakowskie Przedmiescie 7, 00-068 Warsaw, Poland) Ed. Barbara Grabowska-Olszewska. circ. 500. Indexed: GeoRef.

551   UK   ISSN 0260-714X
BLACK COUNTRY GEOLOGIST. 1981. a. Black Country Geological Society, c/o Hon. Sec., 16 St. Nicholas Gardens, Kings Norton, Birmingham B38 8TW, England. illus.

558   CK   ISSN 0120-1425
BOLETIN GEOLOGICO. (Text in Spanish; summaries in English) 1953. irreg., latest vol.27, 1984. $20. Instituto Nacional de Investigaciones Geologico Mineras, Diagonal 53 No. 34-53, Apdo. Aereo 4865, Bogota D.E., Colombia. Indexed: Chem.Abstr. GeoRef.

354   BS
BOTSWANA. GEOLOGICAL SURVEY DEPARTMENT. ANNUAL REPORTS. 1953. a. $3. Geological Survey Department, Gaborone, Botswana. illus. circ. 300.
    Formerly: Botswana. Geological Survey and Mines Department. Annual Reports.

BRAGANTIA. see *AGRICULTURE*

622 557   CN   ISSN 0068-144X
BRITISH COLUMBIA. MINISTRY OF ENERGY, MINES AND PETROLEUM RESOURCES. BULLETIN. 1940; N.S. 19?? irreg. price varies. Ministry of Energy, Mines and Petroleum Resources, Parliament Bldgs, Victoria, B.C. V8V 1X4, Canada. TEL 604-387-5178. Indexed: Eng.Ind. GeoRef.

551.4   UK   ISSN 0306-3380
BRITISH GEOMORPHOLOGICAL RESEARCH GROUP. TECHNICAL BULLETIN. irreg. (2-3/yr.) price varies. Geo Books, Regency House, 34 Duke St., Norwich NR3 3AP, England. (back issues avail.) Indexed: Geo.Abstr. GeoRef.

551   UK   ISSN 0007-1471
BRITISH MUSEUM (NATURAL HISTORY) BULLETIN. GEOLOGY. 1949. a. £117. British Museum (Natural History), Cromwell Rd., London SW7 5BD, England. bibl. illus, stat. index. circ. 750. Indexed: Biol.Abstr. Chem.Abstr. Br.Geol.Lit. GeoRef. Petrol.Abstr.
    Incorporating: British Museum (Natural History) Bulletin. Mineralogy (ISSN 0007-148X)

554   UK
BRITISH REGIONAL GEOLOGY. 1935. irreg. price varies. British Geological Survey, Keyworth, Nottingham NG12 5GG, England (Avail. from H.M.S.O., c/o Liaison Officer, Nine Elms, London SW8 5DR, England) illus. circ. 15,000.

551 560   PL
BUDOWA GEOLOGICZNA POLSKI. (Text in English, Polish; summaries in English, Russian) 1968. irreg. price varies. Instytut Geologiczny, Ul. Rakowiecka 4, 00-975 Warsaw, Poland. bibl. circ. 1, 500. Indexed: Bull.Signal. Ref.Zh.

551   FR   ISSN 0008-0241
CAHIERS GEOLOGIQUES. (Summaries in English and French) 1950. irreg. (1-2/yr.), latest no.105, 1985. 170 F. 144 F. for institutions. Association des Amis et Ancien Eleves du Laboratoire de Geologie, I, Faculte des Science, Tour 14-15-16, 9 Quai St. Bernard, 4 Etage, 75005 Paris, France. Ed. J.P. Michel. adv. bk. rev. abstr. bibl. illus. stat. index. circ. 1,000. Indexed: Biol.Abstr. Chem.Abstr. GeoRef.

551   US   ISSN 0008-1000
CALIFORNIA. DIVISION OF MINES AND GEOLOGY. BULLETIN. 1888. irreg. (2-3/yr.) Division of Mines and Geology, 1416 Ninth St., Room 1341, Sacramento, CA 95814. TEL 916-445-1825. index. Indexed: GeoRef.

551 622   US
CALIFORNIA. DIVISION OF MINES AND GEOLOGY. SPECIAL PUBLICATION. 1962. irreg. price varies. Department of Conservation, Division of Mines and Geology, 1516 Ninth St., 4th Fl., Sacramento, CA 95814. Ed.Bd. circ. 2,200.

551 622   US   ISSN 0527-0014
CALIFORNIA. DIVISION OF MINES AND GEOLOGY. SPECIAL REPORT. irreg. Division of Mines and Geology, 1416 Ninth St., Rm. 1341, Sacramento, CA 95814. TEL 916-445-1825.

551 520   US   ISSN 0045-3943
CALIFORNIA INSTITUTE OF TECHNOLOGY. DIVISION OF GEOLOGICAL AND PLANETARY SCIENCES. REPORT ON GEOLOGICAL AND PLANETARY SCIENCES FOR THE YEAR. 1971-1973; resumed 1978. a. California Institute of Technology, Division of Geological and Planetary Sciences, Pasadena, CA 91125. Ed. Paul Hawley. circ. 1,600. Indexed: GeoRef.

551   UK
CAMBRIDGE PLANETARY SCIENCE SERIES. 1981. irreg., no.5, 1985. $59.50 for latest vol. Cambridge University Press, Edinburgh Bldg., Shaftesbury Rd., Cambridge CB2 2RU, England (And 32 E. 57th St., New York, NY 10022)

557   CN   ISSN 0068-7626
CANADA. GEOLOGICAL SURVEY. BULLETIN. (Text in English and French) 1945. irreg. price varies. Geological Survey of Canada, 601 Booth St., Ottawa, Ont. K1A 0E8, Canada TEL 613-995-4342. (Dist. by: Supply and Services Canada, Ottawa, Ont. K1A 0S9, Canada) index. cum.index: 1845-1969. circ. 1,500. Indexed: Biol.Abstr. GeoRef. Petrol.Abstr.

557   CN
CANADA. GEOLOGICAL SURVEY. ECONOMIC GEOLOGY REPORT. 1909. irreg. Geological Survey of Canada, 601 Booth St., Ottawa, Ont. K1A 0E8, Canada. TEL 613-995-4342. bibl. illus. Indexed: GeoRef.

557   CN   ISSN 0068-7634
CANADA. GEOLOGICAL SURVEY. MEMOIR. (Text in English and French) 1910. irreg. price varies. Geological Survey of Canada, 601 Booth St., Ottawa, Canada TEL 613-995-4342. (Dist. by: Supply and Services Canada, Ottawa, Ont. K1A 0S9, Canada) index. cum.index: 1945-1969. circ. 1, 500. Indexed: Petrol.Abstr.

557   CN   ISSN 0068-7642
CANADA. GEOLOGICAL SURVEY. MISCELLANEOUS REPORT. 1960. irreg. price varies. Geological Survey of Canada, 601 Booth St., Ottawa, Canada TEL 613-995-4342. (Dist. by: Supply and Services Canada, Ottawa, Ont. K1A 0S9, Canada) circ. 2,000. Indexed: GeoRef.

557   CN   ISSN 0068-7650
CANADA. GEOLOGICAL SURVEY. PAPER. (Text in English and French) 1935. irreg. price varies. Geological Survey of Canada, 601 Booth St., Ottawa, Canada TEL 613-995-4343. (Dist. by: Supply and Services Canada, Ottawa, Ont. K1A 0S9, Canada) bibl. index. cum.index. circ. 1,500. Indexed: Biol.Abstr. Petrol.Abstr.

552   CN
CANADA. INDIAN AND NORTHERN AFFAIRS CANADA. SCHEDULE OF WELLS. 1960. a. price varies. (Indian and Northern Affairs Canada) Canadian Government Publishing Centre, Supply and Services Canada, Hull, PQ K1A 0S9, Canada. TEL 613-997-0380. bibl. stat. index. cum.index. circ. 2,000.
    Formerly: Canada. Department of Indian and Northern Affairs. Schedule of Wells, Oil and Gas North of 60.

551   CL   ISSN 0716-0194
CARTA GEOLOGICA DE CHILE. (Text in Spanish; summaries in English) 1959. irreg. $8 (or exchange basis) Servicio Nacional de Geologia y Mineria, Casilla 10465, Santiago, Chile. Eds. John Davidson, Sergio Rivano. circ. 1,000.

558   BL
CARTA GEOLOGICA DO BRASIL AO MILIONESIMO. 1974. irreg. Cr.$100. Departamento Nacional da Producao Mineral, Setor Autarcuia Norte, Quadra 1, Bloco B, Brasilia, D.F., Brazil. charts.

551   US
CASEBOOKS IN EARTH SCIENCES. 1984. irreg., latest 1985. price varies. Springer-Verlag, 175 Fifth Ave., New York, NY 10010 TEL 212-460-1500. (Also Berlin, Heidelberg, Tokyo, Vienna) (reprint service avail. from ISI)

551.44   UK   ISSN 0263-760X
CAVE SCIENCE: TRANSACTIONS OF THE
BRITISH CAVE RESEARCH ASSOCIATION.
1974. irreg. (3/yr.) £16 to non-members. British
Cave Research Association, c/o Bryan Ellis, 20
Woodland Ave., Westonzoyland, Bridgwater,
Somerset TA7 0LQ, England. Ed. T.D. Ford. adv.
index. circ. 1,400. Indexed: Br.Archaeol.Abstr.
Geo.Abstr. GeoRef.
    Former titles: British Cave Research Association.
Transactions (ISSN 0305-859X); Cave Research
Group of Great Britain. Transactions (ISSN 0069-
1305); Cave Science; British Hypogean Fauna and
Biological Records.
    Speleology

551.4   FR   ISSN 0068-4791
CENTRE DE GEOMORPHOLOGIE, CAEN.
BULLETIN. 1967. irreg. by exchange. Centre
National de la Recherche Scientifique, Centre de
Geomorphologie, Rue des Tilleuls, 14000 Caen,
France. Indexed: GeoRef.

CENTRO DE EDAFOLOGIA Y BIOLOGIA
APLICADA. ANUARIO. see *AGRICULTURE —
Agricultural Economics*

796.525   UK   ISSN 0309-409X
CHELSEA SPELAEOLOGICAL SOCIETY.
RECORDS. irreg. ‡ Chelsea Spelaeological Society,
Chelsea Community Centre, Worlds End Estate,
Kings Rd., London, England. Ed. Harry Pearman.
circ. 250. (processed) Indexed: GeoRef.

550   GE   ISSN 0009-2819
CHEMIE DER ERDE/GEOCHEMISTRY;
JOURNAL FOR CHEMICAL PROBLEMS OF
THE GEO-SCIENCES AND
EXTRATERRESTRIAL MINERALOGY;
Zeitschrift fuer chemische Mineralogie,
Petrographie, Bodenkunde, Geochemie und
Meteoritenkunde. (Text and summaries in English
and German) 1914. irreg.(4-8/yr.) M.112 per vol.
VEB Gustav Fischer Verlag, Villengang 2, Postfach
176, 6900 Jena, E. Germany (D.D.R.) Ed. K.
Heide. bk. rev. bibl. charts. illus. index. (reprint
service avail. from ISI) Indexed: Chem.Abstr.
Econ.Geol. GeoRef. Mineral.Abstr.

550   CL   ISSN 0020-3939
CHILE. SERVICIO NACIONAL DE GEOLOGIA Y
MINERIA. BOLETIN. (Text in Spanish; summaries
in English) 1958. irreg. $8 or exchange basis.
Servicio Nacional de Geologia y Mineria, Casilla de
Correo 10465, Santiago, Chile. Eds. John Davidson,
Sergio Rivano. charts. illus. circ. 1,000. Indexed:
GeoRef.
    Formerly: Instituto de Investigaciones Geologicas.
Boletin.

551   CH
CHINA, REPUBLIC. CENTRAL GEOLOGICAL
SURVEY. BULLETIN. (Text in Chinese and
English) 1981. irreg. NT.$400($10) Ministry of
Economic Affairs, Central Geological Survey, 2
Lane 109, Huahsin St., Chungho, Taipei, Taiwan,
Republic of China (Subscr. to: Central Geological
Survey, Ministry of Economic Affairs, P.O. Box
968, Taipei, Taiwan, Republic of China) Ed. Tieh-
Kiang Hsu. circ. 750.
    Supersedes: China, Republic. Geological Survey
of Taiwan. Bulletin.

552 551.3   JA   ISSN 0385-8545
CHISHITSUGAKU RONSHU/GEOLOGICAL
SOCIETY OF JAPAN. MEMOIRS. 1968. irreg.
3.000 Yen. Geological Society of Japan, 10-4,
Kajicho 1 Chome, Chiyoda-Ku, Tokyo 101, Japan.
circ. 1,250. (back issues avail.)

558   CK
COLOMBIA. MINISTERIO DE MINAS Y
ENERGIA. MEMORIA AL CONGRESO DE LA
REPUBLICA. 1940. a. Ministerio de Minas y
Energia, Oficina de Planeacion-Investigaciones
Economicas, Bogota, Colombia. circ. 1,500.
    Continues: Colombia. Ministerio de Minas y
Petroleos. Informe.

551   US
CONTRIBUTION TO PRECAMBRIAN
GEOLOGY. 1969. irreg., no.16, 1987. Department
of Natural Resources, Division of Geology and
Land Survey, Box 250, Rolla, MO 65401. TEL 314-
364-1752. bibl. charts. illus. circ. 1,500.

069   US
CONTRIBUTIONS IN BIOLOGY AND
GEOLOGY. 1974. irreg.,(approx. 12/yr.)
Milwaukee Public Museum, 800 W. Wells St.,
Milwaukee, WI 53233. TEL 414-278-2787. Ed.
Mary M. Garity. circ. 1,500. Indexed: Georef.

551   II
CONTRIBUTIONS TO HIMALAYAN GEOLOGY.
(Text in English) 1979. irreg. price varies.
Hindustan Publishing Corp., 6 U.B. Jawahar Nagar,
Delhi 110007, India. Ed. V.J. Gupta.

551.3   GW   ISSN 0343-4125
CONTRIBUTIONS TO SEDIMENTOLOGY. (Text
in English and German) 1973. irreg. (1-2/yr.) price
varies. E. Schweizerbart'sche Verlagsbuchhandlung,
Johannesstr. 3A, 7000 Stuttgart 1, W. Germany
(B.R.D.) Ed.Bd. Indexed: GeoRef. Petrol.Abstr.

557 551   US   ISSN 0092-9565
CURRENT GEOLOGICAL AND GEOPHYSICAL
STUDIES IN MONTANA. (Subseries of: Montana.
State Bureau of Mines and Geology. Special
Publications) 1969. a. ‡ Bureau of Mines and
Geology, Montana College of Mineral Science and
Technology, Room 203-B, Main Hall, Butte, MT
59701. TEL 406-496-4180. Comp. Richard B. Berg.
stat. circ. 700.

551.3 551 624   II   ISSN 0253-5122
CURRENT PRACTICES IN GEOTECHNICAL
ENGINEERING. 1984. a. $50. Geo-Environ
Academia, A-42 Shastri Nagar, Jodhpur 342 002,
India. (Co-sponsor: International Book Traders
(Delhi)) Eds. Alan Simgh, M.L. Ohri.

554   DK   ISSN 0011-6114
DANMARKS GEOLOGISKE UNDERSOEGELSE/
GEOLOGICAL SURVEY OF DENMARK. (Text
in Danish and English) 1890. irreg. (3-5/yr.) price
varies. (Danmarks Geologiske Undersoegelse) C. A.
Reitzels Forlag, Norregade 20, DK-1165
Copenhagen K, Denmark. Indexed: GeoRef.

554   DK   ISSN 0105-063X
DANMARKS GEOLOGISKE UNDERSOEGELSE.
AARBOG/GEOLOGICAL SURVEY OF
DENMARK. YEARBOOK. Spine title: R G U
Aarbog. 1973. a. Kr.329.40. C.A. Reitzels Forlag,
Norregade 29, 1165 Copenhagen K, Denmark. illus.

551   DK
DANMARKS GEOLOGISKE UNDERSOEGELSE.
SERIE A/GEOLOGICAL SURVEY OF
DENMARK. SERIES A. 1976. irreg. price varies.
Denmarks Geologiske Undersoegelse, 31 Thoravej,
DK-2400 Copenhagen, Denmark. Indexed:
Biol.Abstr.

551   DK   ISSN 0420-1132
DANSK GEOLOGISK FORENING. AARSSKRIFT.
(Text in Danish; abstracts in English) 1893. a.
membership. Dansk Geologisk Forening -
Geological Society of Denmark, Oester Voldgade
10, 1350 Copenhagen K, Denmark. Ed. Steen
Sjoerring. bk. rev. illus. circ. 850.

557   US   ISSN 0070-3273
DELAWARE GEOLOGICAL SURVEY
BULLETINS. 1953. irreg., no.17, 1985. ‡
Geological Survey, University of Delaware, Newark,
DE 19716. TEL 302-451-2833. Indexed:
Abstr.N.Amer.Geol. GeoRef.

557   US   ISSN 0011-7749
DELAWARE GEOLOGICAL SURVEY REPORTS
OF INVESTIGATIONS. 1957. irreg., no.39, 1985.
‡ Geological Survey, Univ. of Delaware, Newark,
DE 19716. TEL 302-451-2833. Indexed:
Chem.Abstr. Abstr.N.Amer.Geol. GeoRef.

551   NE
DEVELOPMENTS IN EARTH AND PLANETARY
SCIENCES; a series of monographs. 1980. irreg.
price varies. D. Reidel Publishing Co., Box 17, 3300
AA Dordrecht, Netherlands (And 190 Old Derby
St., Hingham, MA 02043) Ed. T. Rikitake.

551   NE
DEVELOPMENTS IN ECONOMIC GEOLOGY.
1975. irreg.,vol.19, 1985. price varies. Elsevier
Science Publishers B.V., Box 211, 1000 AE
Amsterdam, Netherlands. Indexed: GeoRef.

551   NE
DEVELOPMENTS IN GEOCHEMISTRY. 1978.
irreg., vol.3, 1984. price varies. Elsevier Science
Publishers B.V., Box 211, 1000 AE Amsterdam,
Netherlands.

551.8   NE   ISSN 0419-0254
DEVELOPMENTS IN GEOTECTONICS. 1965.
irreg.,vol.20, 1983. price varies. Elsevier Science
Publishers B.V., Box 211, 1000 AE Amsterdam,
Netherlands. Indexed: GeoRef.

551   NE
DEVELOPMENTS IN MINERAL PROCESSING.
1977. irreg., vol.6, 1985. price varies. Elsevier
Science Publishers B.V., Box 211, 1000 AE
Amsterdam, Netherlands.

552   NE
DEVELOPMENTS IN PETROLOGY. 1971. irreg.,
vol.11, 1984. price varies. Elsevier Science
Publishers B.V., Box 211, 1000 AE Amsterdam,
Netherlands.

551   NE
DEVELOPMENTS IN PRECAMBRIAN
GEOLOGY. 1978. irreg., vol.7, 1983. price varies.
Elsevier Science Publishers B.V., Box 211, 1000 AE
Amsterdam, Netherlands. Indexed: Chem.Abstr.

551.3   NE   ISSN 0070-4571
DEVELOPMENTS IN SEDIMENTOLOGY. 1964.
irreg.,vol.40, 1985. price varies. Elsevier Science
Publishers B.V., Box 211, 1000 AE Amsterdam,
Netherlands. Indexed: Chem.Abstr. GeoRef.

551 540 560   MY   ISSN 0126-9046
DISTRICT MEMOIR. (Text in English) 1937. irreg.
M.30. Geological Survey Malaysia, P.O. Box 1015,
Ipoh, Perak, Malaysia. (back issues avail.) Indexed:
Biol.Abstr.

DIVREI HA-AKADEMIA HA-LEUMIT HA-
YISRAELIT LEMADAIM-HA-HATIVA LE-
MADAEI HA-TEVA. see *PHYSICS*

551 560   JA   ISSN 0422-7727
EHIME UNIVERSITY. MEMOIRS. SERIE:
NATURAL SCIENCE. (Text in English and
Japanese; summaries in English) 1950. a. Seki
Yoshiten Publishing Co., 7-7-1 Minato-machi,
Matsuyama City, Ehime 790, Japan. Ed. Shuichiro
Maeda. circ. 400.

ENTWICKLUNGSLAENDER-STUDIEN;
Verzeichnis entwicklungslaenderbezogener
Forschungsarbeiten. see *BUSINESS AND
ECONOMICS — International Development And
Assistance*

ERLANGER BAUSTEINE ZUR FRAENKISCHEN
HEIMATFORSCHUNG. see *HISTORY*

557 622   CN
EXPLORATION IN BRITISH COLUMBIA. 1969. a.
Can.$20. Ministry of Energy, Mines and Petroleum
Resources, Publications Distribution Section, 522
Michigan St., Victoria, B.C. V8V 1X4, Canada. TEL
604-387-5178.
    Former titles: Geology, Exploration, and Mining
in British Columbia (ISSN 0085-1027); Lode Metals
in British Columbia.

551   US
EXPLORATION OF THE DEEP CONTINENTAL
CRUST. 1986. irreg. price varies. Springer-Verlag,
175 Fifth Ave., New York, NY 10160 TEL 212-
460-1500. (Also Berlin, Heidelberg, Tokyo, Vienna)
(reprint service avail. from ISI)

551   US   ISSN 0096-2651
FIELDIANA: GEOLOGY. 1895. irreg. price varies.
Field Museum of Natural History, Division of
Publications, Roosevelt Rd. at Lake Shore Dr.,
Chicago, IL 60605-2496. TEL 312-922-9410. Ed.
Dr. Timothy Plowman. bibl. charts. illus. circ. 450.
(back issues avail.; reprint service avail. from UMI)
Indexed: Biol.Abstr. Chem.Abstr. GeoRef.

559   FJ   ISSN 0379-1580
FIJI. MINERAL RESOURCES DEPARTMENT.
BULLETIN. (Text in English) 1976. irreg. price
varies. Mineral Resources Department, P.M. Bag,
Suva, Fiji. Ed. Peter Rodda. Indexed: GeoRef.
    Former titles: Fiji. Mineral Resources Division.
Bulletin (ISSN 0250-7242); Until 1972: Fiji.
Geological Survey. Bulletin (ISSN 0015-0924)

EARTH SCIENCES — GEOLOGY

559   FJ   ISSN 0250-7277
FIJI. MINERAL RESOURCES DEPARTMENT.
GEOTHERMAL REPORT. (Text in English) 1980. irreg. price varies. Mineral Resources Department, P.M. Bag, Suva, Fiji. Ed. Peter Rodda.

551   FJ   ISSN 0252-2497
FIJI. MINERAL RESOURCES DEPARTMENT.
MEMOIR. (Text in English) 1980. irreg. price varies. ‡ Mineral Resources Department, P.M. Bag, Suva, Fiji. Ed. Peter Rodda. Indexed: GeoRef.
Former titles: Fiji Mineral Resources Division. Memoir (ISSN 0250-7269); Until 1972: Fiji. Geological Survey. Memoir (ISSN 0430-3938)

557   US   ISSN 0085-0608
FLORIDA. BUREAU OF GEOLOGY.
GEOLOGICAL BULLETINS. (Former issuing body: Florida Geological Survey) 1908. irreg., latest, no.58. price varies. ‡ Department of Natural Resources, Division of Resource Management, Bureau of Geology, 903 W. Tennessee St., Tallahassee, FL 32304. TEL 904-488-9380. circ. 500. Indexed: GeoRef.

557   US   ISSN 0085-0616
FLORIDA. BUREAU OF GEOLOGY.
INFORMATION CIRCULARS. (Former issuing body: Florida Geological Survey) 1948. irreg., latest, no.101. price varies. ‡ Department of Natural Resources, Division of Resource Management, Bureau of Geology, 903 W. Tennessee St., Tallahassee, FL 32304. TEL 904-488-9380. circ. 500.

557   US   ISSN 0085-0624
FLORIDA. BUREAU OF GEOLOGY. MAP SERIES. (Former issuing body: Florida Geolgical Survey) 1952. irreg., latest, no.110. price varies. ‡ Department of Natural Resources, Division of Resource Management, Bureau of Geology, 903 W. Tennessee St., Tallahassee, FL 32304. TEL 906-488-9380. circ. 500. Indexed: GeoRef.

557   US   ISSN 0096-0489
FLORIDA. BUREAU OF GEOLOGY. REPORT OF INVESTIGATIONS. (Former issuing body: Florida Geological Survey) 1934. irreg., latest no.95. price varies. ‡ Department of Natural Resources, Division of Resource Management, Bureau of Geology, 903 W. Tennessee St., Tallahassee, FL 32304. TEL 904-488-9380. circ. 500. Indexed: GeoRef.
Formerly: Florida. Geological Survey. Report of Investigations.

557   US   ISSN 0085-0640
FLORIDA. BUREAU OF GEOLOGY. SPECIAL PUBLICATIONS. (Former issuing body: Florida Geological Survey) 1956. irreg., latest no.28. price varies. ‡ Department of Natural Resources, Division of Resource Management, Bureau of Geology, 903 W. Tennessee St., Tallahassee, FL 32304. TEL 904-488-9380. circ. 500. Indexed: GeoRef.

550   CS
FOLIA FACULTATIS SCIENTIARUM NATURALIUM UNIVERSITATIS PURKYNIANAE BRUNENSIS: GEOLOGIA. irreg. (7-12/yr.) price varies. Universita J. E. Purkyne, Prirodovedecka Fakulta, Kotlarska 2, 611 37 Brno, Czechoslovakia. Indexed: GeoRef.

FOLIA GEOGRAPHICA. GEOGRAPHICA-PHYSICA. see *GEOGRAPHY*

554   GW   ISSN 0071-8009
FORTSCHRITTE IN DER GEOLOGIE VON RHEINLAND UND WESTFALEN. (Text in German; summaries in English and French) 1958. irreg., no.33, 1985. price varies. Geologisches Landesamt Nordrhein-Westfalen, De Greiff-Str. 195, 4150 Krefeld 1, W. Germany (B.R.D.) Ed. Hanns D. Hilden. circ. 900. Indexed: Biol.Abstr. Fuel & Energy Abstr. Petrol.Abstr.

551   FR   ISSN 0221-2536
FRANCE. BUREAU DE RECHERCHES GEOLOGIQUES ET MINIERES. DOCUMENTS. (Text in French) 1973; N.S. 1979. irreg. (10-15/yr.) price varies. Bureau de Recherches Geologiques et Minieres, Division Edition et Vente, BP 6009, 45060 Orleans Cedex, France. Ed. C. Cavelier. Indexed: Bull.Signal. Chem.Abstr. Ocean.Abstr. Ref.Zh. Geo.Abstr.

551 622   FR   ISSN 0245-9345
FRANCE. BUREAU DE RECHERCHES GEOLOGIQUES ET MINIERES. MANUELS ET METHODES. 1980. irreg. (2-3/yr.) price varies. Bureau de Recherches Geologiques et Minieres, Division Edition et Vente, B.P. 6009, 45060 Orleans Cedex, France. Ed. C. Cavelier. Indexed: Bull.Signal. Chem.Abstr. Ref.Zh. Geo.Abstr.

554 622   FR   ISSN 0071-8246
FRANCE. BUREAU DE RECHERCHES GEOLOGIQUES ET MINIERES. MEMOIRES. (Text in French; summaries in English, French and German) 1960. irreg., no.126, 1984. price varies. Bureau de Recherches Geologiques et Minieres, Division Edition et Vente, B.P. 6009, 45060 Orleans Cedex, France. Ed. C. Cavelier. Indexed: Bull.Signal. Chem.Abstr. Ref.Zh. Sci.Abstr. Geo.Abstr. GeoRef.

554   FR
FRANCE. BUREAU DE RECHERCHES GEOLOGIQUES ET MINIERES. RESUME DES PRINCIPAUX RESULTATS SCIENTIFIQUES ET TECHNIQUES. a. free. Bureau de Recherches Geologiques et Minieres, Division Edition et Vente, Boite Postale 6009, 45060 Orleans Cedex, France. illus.

FUNDACION MIGUEL LILLO. MISCELANEA. see *BIOLOGY — Botany*

551   NE
G U A PAPERS OF GEOLOGY. (Text in English) 1972. irreg. Stichting G U A Papers of Geology, c/o Geologisch Instituut, Nieuwe Prinsengracht 130, Amsterdam, Netherlands. Ed.Bd.

GANBAN RIKIGAKU NI KANSURI SHINPOJUMU RONBUNSHU/PROCEEDINGS OF THE SYMPOSIUM ON ROCK MECHANICS. see *ENGINEERING — Civil Engineering*

551   GW
GEO KATALOG. BAND 2.
GEOWISSENSCHAFTEN. 1976. base vol. with 2-3 updates/yr. DM.295. Internationales Landkartenhaus Geo Center, Schockenriedstr. 40a, 7000 Stuttgart 80, W. Germany (B.R.D.) Eds. S. Bischoff, F. Grupp. circ. 1,500.
Formerly: Geo Katalog. Band 2. International.

551   II   ISSN 0368-2323
GEOCHEMICAL SOCIETY OF INDIA. JOURNAL. (Text in English) 1965. a. Rs.35($8) Geochemical Society of India, Patna 5, India. Ed. R.C. Sinha. bk. rev. bibl. charts. illus. Indexed: Chem.Abstr.

GEOGRAFIJA IR GEOLOGIJA. see *GEOGRAPHY*

551.9   UR   ISSN 0130-1128
GEOKHIMIYA I RUDOOBRAZOVANIE; respublikanskii mezhvedomstvennyi sbornik nauchnykh trudov. (Text in Russian) 1972. a. (Akademiya Nauk Ukrainskoi S.S.R., Institut Geokhimii i Fiziki Mineralov) Izdatel'stvo Naukova Dumka, c/o Yu.A. Khramov, Dir, Ul. Repina, 3, Kiev 252 601, Ukrainian S.S.R., U.S.S.R. (Subscr. to: Mezhdunarodnaya Kniga, Moscow, G-200, Russian S.F.S.R., U.S.S.R.) Ed. N.P. Semenenko. Indexed: Chem.Abstr.

559.4   AT   ISSN 0079-8800
GEOLGICAL SURVEY OF QUEENSLAND PUBLICATIONS. 1879. irreg. exchange basis. Department of Mines, 61 Mary St., Brisbane, Qld. 4000, Australia. TEL 07-224-2302. cum.index. circ. 400. (back issues avail.) Indexed: AESIS. GeoRef.

551 624   IT   ISSN 0435-3870
GEOLOGIA APPLICATA E IDROGEOLOGIA. (Text and summaries in English, Italian) 1986. a. Istituto di Geologia Applicata e Geotecnica, Universita di Bari, Facolta di Ingegneria, Via re David 200, 70125 Bari, Italy. TEL 080 242362. (Co-sponsor: Italian National Research Council (C.N.R.)) charts. illus. circ. 1,000. (back issues avail.)

558   CK   ISSN 0072-0992
GEOLOGIA COLOMBIANA. (Text in Spanish; summaries in English, French, German and Italian) 1962. irreg. exchange basis. ‡ Universidad Nacional de Colombia, Departamento de Geociencias, Apdo. Aereo 14490, Bogota, D.E., Colombia. Ed.Bd. bk. rev. circ. 5,000. Indexed: GeoRef.

554   GW   ISSN 0016-755X
GEOLOGICA BAVARICA. 1949. irreg. price varies. Bayerisches Geologisches Landesamt, Hessstr. 128, 8000 Munich 40, W. Germany (B.R.D.) Ed. K. Schwerd. charts. illus. maps. circ. 800. Indexed: Biol.Abstr. Chem.Abstr. GeoRef.

551 560   GW   ISSN 0072-1018
GEOLOGICA ET PALAEONTOLOGICA. (Text in English and German) 1967. a. price varies. N.G. Elwert Verlag, Reitgasse 7/9, Postfach 1128, 3550 Marburg, W. Germany (B.R.D.) Eds. M. Lindstroem, W. Schmidt. circ. 500. Indexed: GeoRef.

554   NE   ISSN 0072-1026
GEOLOGICA ULTRAIECTINA. (Text in English) 1957. irreg., no.23, 1980. price varies. Rijksuniversiteit te Utrecht, Instituut voor Aardwetenschappen, Budapestlaan 4, Box 80021, 3508 TA Utrecht, Netherlands. Indexed: GeoRef.

557   CN   ISSN 0072-1042
GEOLOGICAL ASSOCIATION OF CANADA. SPECIAL PAPER. 1956. irreg. price varies. Geological Association of Canada, 111 Peter St. Suite 509, Toronto, Ont. M5V 2H1, Canada. Indexed: Biol.Abstr. Geo.Abstr. GeoRef.

551   UN   ISSN 0302-069X
GEOLOGICAL CORRELATION; report of the international geological correlation programme. (Text in English and French) 1973. a. free to qualified personnel. Unesco, International Union of Geological Sciences, 7 place de Fontenoy, 75007 Paris, France. Ed. D.F. Merriam. (back issues avail.)

551   UK   ISSN 0435-3951
GEOLOGICAL JOURNAL - SPECIAL ISSUES. 1965. irreg. price varies. John Wiley & Sons Ltd., Baffins Lane, Chichester, Sussex P019 1UD, England. Ed. P.J. Brenchley. bk. rev. circ. 850. (reprint service avail. from UMI,ISI)

551   US
GEOLOGICAL MAP SERIES. 1962. irreg., latest GMS-42, 1986. price varies. Department of Geology and Mineral Industries, 910 State Office Bldg., Portland, OR 97201. TEL 503-229-5580.

550 553   II   ISSN 0016-7576
GEOLOGICAL, MINING AND METALLURGICAL SOCIETY OF INDIA. BULLETIN. (Text in English) 1936. irreg. price varies. Geological, Mining and Metallurgical Society of India, Geology Department, University of Calcutta, 35 B.C. Rd., Calcutta 700019, India. Ed. Supriya Sengupta, Sanjib C. Sarkar. charts. illus. maps. circ. 300.

551   US   ISSN 0277-5816
GEOLOGICAL SOCIETY OF AMERICA. MEMBERSHIP DIRECTORY. a. Geological Society of America, Marketing Department, 3300 Penrose Pl., Box 9140, Boulder, CO 80301. TEL 303-447-8850. circ. 3,300.
Formerly: Geological Society of America. Yearbook (ISSN 0095-3547)

551 560   US   ISSN 0072-1069
GEOLOGICAL SOCIETY OF AMERICA. MEMOIRS. (Each vol. has distinctive title) 1934. irreg., no.165, 1986. price varies. Geological Society of America, Marketing Department, 3300 Penrose Pl., Box 9140, Boulder, CO 80301. TEL 303-447-8850. index. (reprint service avail. from UMI) Indexed: Biol.Abstr. Chem.Abstr. GeoRef. Petrol.Abstr.

551   US   ISSN 0091-5041
GEOLOGICAL SOCIETY OF AMERICA. MEMORIALS. 1973. a. price varies. Geological Society of America, Marketing Department, 3300 Penrose Pl., Box 9140, Boulder, CO 80301. TEL 303-447-8850. bibl. illus. Indexed: GeoRef. Key Title: Memorials - Geological Society of America.

551 560   US   ISSN 0072-1077
GEOLOGICAL SOCIETY OF AMERICA. SPECIAL PAPERS. (Each vol. has distinctive title) 1934. irreg., no.208, 1986. price varies. Geological Society of America, Marketing Department, 3300 Penrose Pl., Box 9140, Boulder, CO 80301. TEL 303-447-8850. index. (reprint service avail. from UMI) Indexed: Biol.Abstr. Chem.Abstr. Geo.Abstr. Petrol.Abstr.

GEOLOGICAL SOCIETY OF AUSTRALIA.
ABSTRACTS SERIES. see EARTH SCIENCES

559.4   AT   ISSN 0072-1085
GEOLOGICAL SOCIETY OF AUSTRALIA.
SPECIAL PUBLICATION. 1967. irreg., no.12,
1986. price varies. Geological Society of Australia,
10 Martin Pl., Sydney, N.S.W. 2000, Australia.
Indexed: GeoRef.

555   CH
GEOLOGICAL SOCIETY OF CHINA. MEMOIRS.
(Text in English) irreg, no.2, 1977. $21. Geological
Society of China, Box 3317, Taipei, Taiwan,
Republic of China. circ. 420. Indexed: Geo.Abstr.

551 550   CH
GEOLOGICAL SOCIETY OF CHINA.
PROCEEDINGS. (Text in English) 1958. a. $14.
Geological Society of China, P.O. Box 3317, Taipei,
Taiwan, Republic of China. Ed. J.C. Chen. (back
issues avail.) Indexed: Biol.Abstr.

551   UA   ISSN 0446-4648
GEOLOGICAL SOCIETY OF EGYPT. ANNUAL
MEETING. ABSTRACTS OF PAPERS.
(Summaries in English) 1963. a. free. National
Information and Documentation Centre (NIDOC),
Tahrir St., Dokki, Awqaf P.O., Cairo, Egypt. Ed.
E.M. el-Shazly.

551   IQ   ISSN 0533-8301
GEOLOGICAL SOCIETY OF IRAQ. JOURNAL.
(Text in Arabic and English) 1968. a. $15. ‡
Geological Society of Iraq, P.O. Box 547, Baghdad,
Iraq. Ed. N. Al-Ansari. bk. rev. charts. illus. circ.
500.

551   JM   ISSN 0435-401X
GEOLOGICAL SOCIETY OF JAMAICA
JOURNAL. 1958. a. (plus special issues)
Jam.$2.50($10) Geological Society of Jamaica,
University of the West Indies, Geology Department,
Mona, Kingston 7, Jamaica. Ed. T. Jackson. adv. bk.
rev. charts. illus. circ. 1,000. Indexed: Biol.Abstr.
Met.Abstr. GeoRef. World Alum.Abstr.

555   MY   ISSN 0126-6187
GEOLOGICAL SOCIETY OF MALAYSIA.
BULLETIN. (Text in English) 1968. irreg., no.19,
1986. price varies. Geological Society of Malaysia,
c/o Department of Geology, University of Malaya,
59100 Kuala Lumpur, Malaysia. Ed. G.H. Teh. circ.
700. (back issues avail.) Indexed: Biol.Abstr.

556   SA
GEOLOGICAL SOCIETY OF SOUTH AFRICA.
SPECIAL PUBLICATION. 1970. irreg., latest
issue, 1976. price varies. Geological Society of
South Africa, P.O. Box 61019, Marshalltown,
Transvaal, South Africa. circ. 2,000. Indexed:
Geo.Abstr. GeoRef.

557   US   ISSN 0364-6017
GEOLOGICAL SURVEY CIRCULAR. 1933. irreg.
free. U.S. Geological Survey, 12201 Sunrise Valley
Dr., Reston, VA 22092 TEL 703-860-7000. (Orders
to: 604 S. Pickett St., Alexandria, VA 22304)
Indexed: Geo.Abstr.
  Formerly: U.S. Geological Survey. Circular (ISSN
0083-1107)

GEOLOGICAL SURVEY OF HOKKAIDO.
REPORT. see EARTH SCIENCES

554   IE   ISSN 0085-0985
GEOLOGICAL SURVEY OF IRELAND.
BULLETIN. 1970. irreg., vol.3, pt.4, 1986. £5.50.
Geological Survey of Ireland, Department of
Energy, Beggars Bush, Haddington Rd., Dublin 4,
Ireland. cum.index. circ. 650. Indexed: Br.Geol.Lit.
Geo.Abstr.

554   IE   ISSN 0790-0260
GEOLOGICAL SURVEY OF IRELAND. GUIDE
SERIES. 1976. irreg. price varies. Geological Survey
of Ireland, Department of Energy, Beggars Bush,
Haddington Rd., Dublin 4, Ireland.

554   IE   ISSN 0085-0993
GEOLOGICAL SURVEY OF IRELAND.
INFORMATION CIRCULARS. 1970. irreg. price
varies. Geological Survey of Ireland, Department of
Energy, Beggars Bush, Haddington Rd., Dublin 4,
Ireland. circ. 500.

554   IE   ISSN 0790-0279
GEOLOGICAL SURVEY OF IRELAND. REPORT
SERIES. irreg. price varies. Geological Survey of
Ireland, Department of Energy, Beggars Bush,
Haddington Rd., Dublin 4, Ireland. Indexed:
Geo.Abstr.

554   IE   ISSN 0085-1019
GEOLOGICAL SURVEY OF IRELAND. SPECIAL
PAPERS. 1971. irreg. price varies. Geological
Survey of Ireland, Department of Energy, Beggars
Bush, Haddington Rd., Dublin 4, Ireland. circ. 600.
Indexed: Geo.Abstr.

559.4   AT
GEOLOGICAL SURVEY OF SOUTH AUSTRALIA.
BULLETIN. 1912. irreg. price varies. Department
of Mines and Energy, P.O. Box 151, Eastwood, S.A.
5063, Australia. Ed. J. Selby. circ. 1,000.

551   AT   ISSN 0572-0125
GEOLOGICAL SURVEY OF SOUTH AUSTRALIA.
EXPLANATORY NOTES. 1972. irreg. price
varies. Department of Mines and Energy, P.O. Box
151, Eastwood, S. A. 5063, Australia. Indexed:
Eng.Ind. AESIS. GeoRef.

551   AT   ISSN 0016-7681
GEOLOGICAL SURVEY OF SOUTH AUSTRALIA.
REPORT OF INVESTIGATIONS. 1954. irreg.
price varies. Department of Mines and Energy, P.O.
Box 151, Eastwood, S. A. 5063, Australia. Indexed:
Eng.Ind. GeoRef.

556   SX
GEOLOGICAL SURVEY OF SOUTH WEST
AFRICA/NAMIBIA. MEMOIRS. (Text in English;
summaries in Afrikaans) 1965. irreg., no.8, 1983.
Department of Economic Affairs, Geological Survey
Windhoek, P.O. Box 2168, Windhoek, Namibia.
circ. 1,500.
  Formerly: South West Africa Series. Memoirs.

550   YU   ISSN 0016-7789
GEOLOGIJA; razprave in poročila. (Text in English,
French, German, Serbocroatian and Slovenian)
1953. biennial. 400 din.($14) Geoloski Zavod -
Geological Survey, Parmova Ul. 33, 1000 Ljubljana,
Yugoslavia. (Co-sponsor: Slovensko Geolosko
Drustvo) Ed. Stefan Kolenko. bk. rev. charts. illus.
index. circ. 1,000. Indexed: Chem.Abstr.

551 560   GW   ISSN 0341-4043
GEOLOGISCHE ABHANDLUNGEN HESSEN.
1976. a. price varies. Hessisches Landesamt fuer
Bodenforschung, Leberberg 9, 6200 Wiesbaden, W.
Germany (B.R.D.) (Subscr. to: Hessisches
Landesamt fuer Bodenforschung, Vertriebsstelle,
Hasengartenstr. 26, 6200 Wiesbaden, W. Germany
(B.R.D.)) (back issues avail.)

551   AU   ISSN 0378-0864
GEOLOGISCHE BUNDESANSTALT, VIENNA.
ABHANDLUNGEN. (Text mainly in German;
occasionally in other languages) 1852. irreg. price
varies. Geologische Bundesanstalt, Rasumofskygasse
23, Postfach 154, A-1031 Vienna, Austria. Ed.
Albert Daurer. circ. 1,250. (also avail. in microfilm)
Indexed: Ref.Zh.

551 560   AU   ISSN 0016-7800
GEOLOGISCHE BUNDESANSTALT, VIENNA.
JAHRBUCH. (Text and summaries in English and
German) 1850. a. price varies. Geologische
Bundesanstalt, Rasumofskygasse 23, Postfach 154,
1031 Vienna, Austria. Ed. Albert Daurer. (also
avail. in microfilm) Indexed: Biol.Abstr. GeoRef.

554 560   GW   ISSN 0341-6399
GEOLOGISCHES JAHRBUCH. REIHE A:
ALLGEMEINE UND REGIONALE GEOLOGIE
B.R. DEUTSCHLAND UND
NACHBARGEBIETE, TEKTONIK,
STRATIGRAPHIE, PALAEONTOLOGIE. (Text
in German; summaries in English, French, Italian,
Russian and Spanish) 1972. irreg. price varies.
(Bundesanstalt fuer Geowissenschaften und
Rohstoffe) E. Schweizerbart'sche
Verlagsbuchhandlung, Johannesstr. 3A, 7000
Stuttgart 1, W. Germany (B.R.D.) illus. Indexed:
Chem.Abstr. Petrol.Abstr.
  Supersedes in part: Geologisches Jahrbuch (ISSN
0016-7851); Beihefte zum Geologischen Jahrbuch
(ISSN 0005-8017)

554   GW   ISSN 0341-6402
GEOLOGISCHES JAHRBUCH. REIHE B:
REGIONALE GEOLOGIE AUSLAND. (Text in
German; summaries in English, French, German
and Russian) 1972. irreg. price varies.
(Bundesanstalt fuer Geowissenschaften und
Rohstoffe) E. Schweizerbart'sche
Verlagsbuchhandlung, Johannesstr. 3A, 7000
Stuttgart 1, W. Germany (B.R.D.) illus. Indexed:
Chem.Abstr. Petrol.Abstr.
  Supersedes in part: Geologisches Jahrbuch (ISSN
0016-7851); Beihefte zum Geologischen Jahrbuch
(ISSN 0005-8017)

551   GW   ISSN 0341-6410
GEOLOGISCHES JAHRBUCH. REIHE C:
HYDROGEOLOGIE. INGENIEURGEOLOGIE.
(Text in German; summaries in English, French,
German and Russian) 1972. irreg. price varies.
(Bundesanstalt fuer Geowissenschaften und
Rohstoffe) E. Schweizerbart'sche
Verlagsbuchhandlung, Johannesstr. 3A, 7000
Stuttgart 1, W. Germany (B.R.D.) illus. Indexed:
Chem.Abstr. Petrol.Abstr.
  Supersedes in part: Geologisches Jahrbuch (ISSN
0016-7851); Beihefte zum Geologischen Jahrbuch
(ISSN 0005-8017)

551 549   GW   ISSN 0341-6429
GEOLOGISCHES JAHRBUCH. REIHE D:
MINERALOGIE. PETROGRAPHIE,
GEOCHEMIE, LAGERSTAETTENKUNDE.
(Text in German, summaries in English, French,
German and Russian) 1972. irreg. price varies.
(Bundesanstalt fuer Geowissenschaften und
Rohstoffe) E. Schweizerbart'sche
Verlagsbuchhandlung, Johannesstr. 3A, 7000
Stuttgart 1, W. Germany (B.R.D.) illus. Indexed:
Chem.Abstr. Petrol.Abstr.
  Supersedes in part: Geologisches Jahrbuch (ISSN
0016-7851); Beihefte zum Geologischen Jahrbuch
(ISSN 0005-8017)

551   GW   ISSN 0341-6437
GEOLOGISCHES JAHRBUCH. REIHE E:
GEOPHYSIK. (Text in English and German,
summaries in English, French, German, Russian)
1972. irreg. price varies. (Bundesanstalt fuer
Geowissenschaften und Rohstoffe) E.
Schweizerbart'sche Verlagsbuchhandlung,
Johannesstr. 3A, 7000 Stuttgart 1, W. Germany
(B.R.D.) illus. Indexed: Biol.Abstr. Petrol.Abstr.

551   GW   ISSN 0341-6445
GEOLOGISCHES JAHRBUCH. REIHE F:
BODENKUNDE. (Text in English and German;
summaries in English, French, German, Russian)
1973. irreg. price varies. (Bundesanstalt fuer
Geowissenschaften und Rohstoffe) E.
Schweizerbart'sche Verlagsbuchhandlung,
Johannesstr. 3A, 7000 Stuttgart 1, W. Germany
(B.R.D.) Indexed: Chem.Abstr.

551 560   GW   ISSN 0341-4027
GEOLOGISCHES JAHRBUCH HESSEN. 1976. a.
price varies. Hessisches Landesamt fuer
Bodenforschung, Leberberg 9, 6200 Wiesbaden, W.
Germany (B.R.D.) (Subscr. to: Hessisches
Landesamt fuer Bodenforschung, Vertriebsstelle,
Hasengartenstr. 26, 6200 Wiesbaden, W. Germany
(B.R.D.)) Ed.Bd. (back issues avail.)

551   UK   ISSN 0260-0463
GEOLOGIST'S DIRECTORY. 1980. biennial. £12.50.
Institution of Geologists, Burlington House,
Piccadilly, London W1V 9AG, England. circ. 2,000.

551   UK
GEOLOGISTS' YEAR BOOK. 1977. a. Dolphin
Press, Link House, West St., Poole, Dorset BH15
1LL, England.

551   GW   ISSN 0720-8863
GEOLOGY OF PETROLEUM. (Text in English)
1981. irreg., latest no.7, 1983. price varies.
Ferdinand Enke Verlag, Postfach 1304, D 7000
Stuttgart 1, W. Germany (B.R.D.) Ed. H.
Beckmann.

550   YU   ISSN 0016-7924
GEOLOSKI VJESNIK. (Text in Serbo-Croatian) 1959.
irreg. (Hrvatsko Geolosko Drustvo) Institut za
Geoloska Istrazivanja u Zagrebu, Sachsova 2,
Zagreb, Yugoslavia. Ed. Josip Ogulinec. Indexed:
Biol.Abstr. Chem.Abstr.

EARTH SCIENCES — GEOLOGY

555   PK   ISSN 0435-4311
GEONEWS. (Text in English) 1968. irreg., vol. 2, 1972. Geological Survey of Pakistan, c/o Chief Librarian, Box 15, Quetta, Pakistan.

GEOOEKODYNAMIK. see *GEOGRAPHY*

557   US
GEORGIA. GEOLOGIC SURVEY. BULLETIN. 1894. irreg. price varies. ‡ Department of Natural Resources, Georgia Geologic Survey, 19 Martin Luther King Jr. Dr., S.W., Rm. 400, Atlanta, GA 30334. TEL 404-656-3214. Ed. L. Stoutenburg.

557   US
GEORGIA. GEOLOGIC SURVEY. GEOLOGIC GUIDE. 1977. irreg. price varies. Department of Natural Resources, Georgia Geologic Survey, 19 Martin Luther King Jr. Dr., S.W., Rm. 400, Atlanta, GA 30334. TEL 404-656-3214.

551   US
GEORGIA. GEOLOGIC SURVEY. GEOLOGIC REPORT. 1971. irreg. price varies. Department of Natural Resources, Georgia Geologic Survey, Georgia Geologic Survey, 19 Martin Luther King Jr. Dr., S.W., Rm. 400, Atlanta, GA 30334. TEL 404-656-3214.

557   US
GEORGIA. GEOLOGIC SURVEY. GUIDEBOOK. 1962. irreg. price varies. Department of Natural Resources, Georgia Geologic Survey, 19 Martin Luther King Jr. Dr., S.W., Rm. 400, Atlanta, GA 30334. TEL 404-656-3214.

557   US
GEORGIA. GEOLOGIC SURVEY. OPEN FILE REPORT. 1979. irreg. price varies. Department of Natural Resources, Georgia Geologic Survey, 19 Martin Luther King Jr. Dr., S.W., Rm. 400, Atlanta, GA 30334. TEL 404-656-3214.

557   US
GEORGIA. GEOLOGIC SURVEY. SPECIAL PUBLICATION. 1963. irreg. price varies. Department of Natural Resources, Georgia Geologic Survey, 19 Martin Luther King Jr. Dr., S.W., Rm. 400, Atlanta, GA 30334. TEL 404-656-4214.

551   VE   ISSN 0435-5601
GEOS. (Text in Spanish; summaries in English) 1959. a. Bs.60($12) Universidad Central de Venezuela, Escuela de Geologia, Faculdade Ingenieria, Caracas 1051, Venezuela. Ed. Franco Urbani. circ. 1,000. (back issues avail.) Indexed: Bull.Signal. GeoRef.

557   US   ISSN 0164-2049
GEOSCIENCE WISCONSIN. 1977. irreg., no.9, 1984. price varies. Geological and Natural History Survey, University of Wisconsin, 3817 Mineral Point Rd., Madison, WI 53705. TEL 608-262-1705.

557   CN   ISSN 0707-2422
GEOSCIENCES IN CANADA. (Subseries of: Canada. Geological Survey. Paper) 1976. a. price varies. Geological Survey of Canada, 601 Booth St., Ottawa, Canada (Dist. by: Supply and Services Canada, Hull, Que. K1A 0S9) illus. circ. 1,200. Indexed: GeoRef.
Formerly: Aspects of the Geosciences in Canada (ISSN 0707-2430)

551   YU
GEOTEHNIKA; informativno glasilo radne zajednice Geotehnika. 1965. irreg. Geotehnika, Kupska 2, Zagreb, Yugoslavia. Ed. Zvonko Jelic. Indexed: Chem.Abstr.

551   US   ISSN 0094-9779
GEOTHERMAL WORLD DIRECTORY. 1972. a. $55. ‡ Geothermal World Publishers, 17304 Village, No. 17, Camarillo, CA 93010-7406. adv. bk. rev. bibl. charts. illus. tr.lit. circ. 8,000.

551   551.4   560   AU
GESELLSCHAFT DER GEOLOGIE- UND BERGBAUSTUDENTEN. MITTEILUNGEN. 1949. a. S.404($20) Gesellschaft der Geologie- und Bergbaustudenten, Universitaetsstrasse 7/III, A-1010 Vienna, Austria. Eds. Richard Lein, Hartwig Frimmel. circ. 450. (back issues avail.)

551.31   US   ISSN 0149-1776
GLACIOLOGICAL DATA. 1977. irreg. exchange basis. World Data Center A for Glaciology (Snow and Ice), CIRES, Campus Box 449, University of Colorado, Boulder, CO 80309. TEL 303-497-5311. Eds. R.G. Barry, Ann M. Brennan. bk. rev. index. circ. 1,100. (back issues avail.)
●Also available online. Vendors: Orbit Information Technologies.
Supersedes the quarterly issued from 1960-1976: Glaciological Notes (ISSN 0017-0712)
Glaciology

551 910   NE
GLACIOLOGY AND QUATERNARY GEOLOGY. 1985. irreg. price varies. D. Reidel Publishing Company, Box 17, 3300 AA Dordrecht, Netherlands.

551   GW   ISSN 0163-3171
GLOBAL TECTONICS AND METALLOGENY. (Text in English) 1978. irreg. DM.112($45.90) to institutions, individuals DM 31, ($12.70) E. Schweizerbart'sche Verlagsbuchhandlung, Johannesstr. 3A, 7000 Stuttgart 1, W. Germany (B.R.D.) Ed. Jan Kutina.

551   UK
GREAT BRITAIN. BRITISH GEOLOGICAL SURVEY. ANNUAL REPORT. 1965. biennial, latest 1984/85. price varies. British Geological Survey, Keyworth, Nottingham NG12 5GG, England (Avail. from H.M.S.O., c/o Liaison Officer, Nine Elms, London SW8 5DR, England) illus. circ. 1,000.
Former titles (until Jan.1984): Great Britain. Institute of Geological Sciences. Annual Report (ISSN 0073-9308); Great Britain. Geological Survey. Summary of Progress.

551 557   UK
GREAT BRITAIN. BRITISH GEOLOGICAL SURVEY. CLASSICAL AREAS OF BRITISH GEOLOGY. 1968. irreg. British Geological Survey, Keyworth, Nottingham NG12 5GG, England. circ. 2,500.
Formerly (until Jan. 1984): Great Britain. Institute of Geological Sciences. Classical Areas of British Geology.

554 560   UK
GREAT BRITAIN. BRITISH GEOLOGICAL SURVEY. MEMOIRS. 1846. irreg. price varies. British Geological Survey, Keyworth, Nottingham NG12 5GG, England (Avail. from H.M.S.O., c/o Liaison Officer, Nine Elms, London SW8 5DR, England) illus. circ. 2,000.
Formerly (until Jan. 1984): Great Britain. Institute of Geological Sciences. Memoirs of the Geological Survey of Great Britain (ISSN 0072-6494)

553 622   UK
GREAT BRITAIN. BRITISH GEOLOGICAL SURVEY. MINERAL ASSESSMENT REPORT. irreg. price varies. British Geological Survey, Keyworth, Nottingham NG12 5GG, England (Avail. from H.M.S.O., c/o Liaison Officer, Nine Elms, London SW8 5DR, England) illus. circ. 500.
Formerly (until Jan. 1984): Great Britain. Institute of Geological Sciences. Mineral Assessment Report (ISSN 0308-5333)

551   UK
GREAT BRITAIN. BRITISH GEOLOGICAL SURVEY. OVERSEAS GEOLOGY AND MINERAL RESOURCES. 1950. irreg. price varies. British Geological Survey, Keyworth, Nottingham NG12 5GG, England (Avail. from H.M.S.O., c/o Liaison Officer, Nine Elms, London SW8 5DR, England) illus. circ. 1,000. Indexed: GeoRef.
Formerly (until Jan. 1984): Great Britain. Institute of Geological Sciences. Overseas Geology and Mineral Resources (ISSN 0073-9332)

551   UK
GREAT BRITAIN. BRITISH GEOLOGICAL SURVEY. OVERSEAS MEMOIRS. 1976. irreg. price varies. British Geological Survey, Keyworth, Nottingham NG12 5GG, England (Avail. from H.M.S.O., c/o Liaison Officer, Nine Elms, London SW8 5DR, England) illus. circ. 1,000.
Formerly (until Jan. 1984): Great Britain. Institute of Geological Sciences. Overseas Memoirs (ISSN 0308-5325)

551   UK
GREAT BRITAIN. BRITISH GEOLOGICAL SURVEY. REPORT. 1969. irreg. price varies. British Geological Survey, Keyworth, Nottingham RG12 5GG, England (Avail. from H.M.S.O., c/o Liaison Officer, Nine Elms, London SW8 5DR, England) circ. 1,000.
Formerly (until Jan. 1984): Great Britain. Institute of Geological Sciences. Report (ISSN 0073-9359)

551   DK   ISSN 0105-3507
GROENLANDS GEOLOGISKE UNDERSOEGELSE. BULLETIN/GEOLOGICAL SURVEY OF GREENLAND. BULLETIN. (Nos.1-114 also published in Meddelelser Om Groenland) (Text mainly in English) 1948. irreg. price varies. Groenlands Geologiske Undersoegelse, Oester Voldgade 10, DK-1350 Copenhagen K, Denmark.

551   DK   ISSN 0418-6559
GROENLANDS GEOLOGISKE UNDERSOEGELSE. RAPPORT/GEOLOGICAL SURVEY OF GREENLAND. REPORT. (Text mainly in English) 1964. irreg. (6-10/yr.) price varies. Groenlands Geologiske Undersoegelse, Oester Voldgade 10, DK-1350 Copenhagen K, Denmark. bibl. charts. illus. Indexed: Geo.Abstr. Petrol.Abstr.

551 910   IT
GROTTE D'ITALIA. 1927. a. Societa Speleologica Italiana, Via Zamboni, 67, I-40127 Bologna, Italy. Ed. Paolo Forti. circ. 1,000.

796.525   VE   ISSN 0583-774X
GUACHARO; boletin de divulgacion espeleologica. (Text in Spanish; summaries in English) 1968. a. Bs.50($2) Sociedad Venezolana de Espeleologia, Apdo. 47334, Caracas 1041A, Venezuela. Ed. F. Urbani. circ. 500. (back issues avail.) Indexed: Speleol.Abstr.
Speleology

557   GY
GUYANA. GEOLOGY & MINES COMMISSION. ANNUAL REPORT. a. $5. Geology and Mines Commission, P.O. Box 1028, Georgetown, Guyana.
Formerly: Guyana. Geological Survey Department. Annual Reports (ISSN 0072-9108)

557   GY
GUYANA. GEOLOGY & MINES COMMISSION. MINERAL RESOURCES PAMPHLET. 1953. irreg., no.15, 1980. Geology & Mines Commission, P.O. Box 1028, Georgetown, Guyana.
Formerly: Guyana. Geological Survey Department. Mineral Resources Pamphlet (ISSN 0072-9124)

551   NE
HANDBOOK OF EXPLORATION GEOCHEMISTRY. 1981. irreg., vol.3, 1983. price varies. Elsevier Science Publishers B.V., Box 211, 1000 AE Amsterdam, Netherlands. Ed. G.J.S. Govett.

551.7   GW   ISSN 0073-0130
HANDBUCH DER STRATIGRAPHISCHEN GEOLOGIE. 1959. irreg. price varies. Ferdinand Enke Verlag, Postfach 1304, 7000 Stuttgart 1, W. Germany (B.R.D.) Ed. G. Luettig.

555   II   ISSN 0379-5101
HIMALAYAN GEOLOGY. (Text in English) 1971. a. price varies. Hindustan Publishing Corp., 6-U.B. Jawahar Nagar, Delhi 110007, India. Indexed: Chem.Abstr.

555   JA   ISSN 0073-2303
HIROSHIMA UNIVERSITY. DEPARTMENT OF GEOLOGY. GEOLOGICAL REPORT. (Text in Japanese; summaries in English) 1951. irreg., no. 23, 1980. not for sale. Hiroshima University, Department of Geology and Mineralogy, 1-89 1-chome Higashisenda-cho, Hiroshima 730, Japan. Indexed: Biol.Abstr.

551 549   JA   ISSN 0075-4374
HIROSHIMA UNIVERSITY. JOURNAL OF SCIENCE. SERIES C. GEOLOGY AND MINERALOGY. (Text in English, French and German) 1951. irreg., vol. 8, no.2, 1983. not for sale. Hiroshima University, Department of Geology and Mineralogy, 1-89 1-chome Higashisenda-cho, Hiroshima 730, Japan. title index. Indexed: Biol.Abstr. Met.Abstr.

IDAHO. GEOLOGICAL SURVEY. BULLETIN. see *MINES AND MINING INDUSTRY*

IDAHO. GEOLOGICAL SURVEY. INFORMATION CIRCULAR. see *MINES AND MINING INDUSTRY*

551   US
IDAHO. GEOLOGICAL SURVEY. TECHNICAL REPORT. 1978. irreg. (6-10/yr.) Idaho Geological Survey, Morrill Hall, Rm. 332, University of Idaho, Moscow, ID 83843.
    Formerly (1978-1984): Idaho. Geological Survey. Open-File Report.

558   BL   ISSN 0073-4713
IHERINGIA. SERIE GEOLOGIA. (Text in English, French, German, Italian, Latin, Portuguese and Spanish) 1967. irreg., no.10, 1985. price varies. Fundacao Zoobotanica do Rio Grande do Sul, Museu de Ciencias Naturais, Caixa Postal 1188, 90.000 Porto Alegre, Rio Grande do Sul, Brazil. Ed. Arno A. Lise. bibl. illus. circ. 600. Indexed: Biol.Abstr. GeoRef.

557   US   ISSN 0073-5051
ILLINOIS. STATE GEOLOGICAL SURVEY. BULLETINS. 1906. irreg., no.95, 1975. price varies. ‡ State Geological Survey, Natural Resources Bldg., 615 E. Peabody Dr., Champaign, IL 61820. TEL 217-344-1481. abstr. bibl. charts. illus. maps. circ. 2,500. Indexed: Biol.Abstr. Bibl.& Ind.Geo. GeoRef.

557   US   ISSN 0073-506X
ILLINOIS. STATE GEOLOGICAL SURVEY. CIRCULARS. 1932. irreg., no.537, 1986. price varies. ‡ State Geological Survey, Natural Resources Bldg., 615 E. Peabody Dr., Champaign, IL 61820. TEL 217-344-1481. abstr. bibl. charts. illus. maps. stat. Indexed: Biol.Abstr. Geo.Abstr. GeoRef.

557   US   ISSN 0073-5078
ILLINOIS. STATE GEOLOGICAL SURVEY. EDUCATIONAL SERIES. 1931. irreg., no.12, 1980. $1 per no. ‡ State Geological Survey, Natural Resources Bldg., 615 E. Peabody Dr., Champaign, IL 61820. TEL 217-344-1481. charts. illus. stat. circ. 28,000. Indexed: GeoRef.

557   US   ISSN 0073-5086
ILLINOIS. STATE GEOLOGICAL SURVEY. ENVIRONMENTAL GEOLOGY NOTES. 1965. irreg., no.115, 1986. $1.25 per no. ‡ State Geological Survey, Natural Resources Bldg., 615 E. Peabody Dr., Champaign, IL 61820. TEL 217-344-1481. abstr. bibl. charts. illus. stat. Indexed: Biol.Abstr. Bibl.&Ind.Geol. GeoRef.

557   US   ISSN 0073-5094
ILLINOIS. STATE GEOLOGICAL SURVEY. GUIDEBOOK SERIES. 1950. irreg., no.19, 1985. $1.25 per no. ‡ State Geological Survey, Natural Resources Bldg., 615 E. Peabody Dr., Champaign, IL 61820. TEL 217-344-1481. abstr. bibl. charts. illus. stat. circ. 2,000. Indexed: Biol.Abstr. GeoRef.

ILLINOIS MINERALS NOTES. see *MINES AND MINING INDUSTRY*

ILLINOIS PETROLEUM. see *PETROLEUM AND GAS*

551.3   II
INDIAN STRATIGRAPHY. (Text in English) 1973. irreg. price varies. Hindustan Publishing Corp., 6-U.B. Jawahar Nagar, Delhi 110007, India.

353.9   US   ISSN 0362-3513
INDIANA. GEOLOGICAL SURVEY. ANNUAL REPORT OF THE STATE GEOLOGIST. a. Geological Survey, Department of Natural Resources, Indianapolis, IN 46204. TEL 317-232-3140. Indexed: GeoRef.

INSTITUT FRANCAIS D'ETUDES ANDINES. TRAVAUX. see *ANTHROPOLOGY*

551.3   BE   ISSN 0374-6291
INSTITUT ROYAL DES SCIENCES NATURELLES DE BELGIQUE. BULLETIN. SERIE SCIENCES DE LA TERRE. (Text in English, French and German) 1930. irreg. (5-10/yr.) 900 Fr.($18) Koninklijk Belgisch Instituut voor Natuurwetenschappen - Institut Royal des Sciences Naturelles de Belgique, Vautierstraat 29, 1040 Brussels, Belgium. abstr. bibl. charts. illus. cum.index. (back issues avail.) Indexed: Biol.Abstr. Bull.Signal. Ref.Zh. Zoo.Rec.

553   GT   ISSN 0073-9936
INSTITUTO CENTRO AMERICANO DE INVESTIGACION Y TECNOLOGIA INDUSTRIAL. PUBLICACIONES GEOLOGICAS. (Text in English or Spanish) 1966. irreg.; no.5, 1977. price varies. Instituto Centro Americano de Investigacion y Tecnologia Industrial, Avenida la Reforma 4-47, Zona 10, Apdo. Postal 1552, Guatemala, Guatemala. Ed. Dr. Gabriel Dengo. circ. 1,000. (back issues avail.)

558   CK
INSTITUTO NACIONAL DE INVESTIGACIONES GEOLOGICO MINERAS. INFORME ANUAL DE ACTIVIDADES. a., latest 1981. Instituto Nacional de Investigaciones Geologico Mineras, Diagonal 53 No.34-53, Apdo. Aereo 4865, Bogota D.E., Colombia.

558   CK
INSTITUTO NACIONAL DE INVESTIGACIONES GEOLOGICO MINERAS. PUBLICACIONES GEOLOGICAS ESPECIALES DEL INGEOMINAS. (Text in English or Spanish) 1978. irreg., latest no.18, 1986. Instituto Nacional de Investigaciones Geologico Mineras, Diagonal 53 No. 34-53, Apdo. Aereo 4865, Bogota D.E., Colombia.

550   RM
INSTITUTUL DE GEOLOGIE SI GEOFIZICA. ANUARUL. (Text in English, French and Rumanian; summaries in English) 1908. a. price varies. Institutul de Geologie si Geofizica, Str. Caransebes, Nr. 1, 78344 Bucharest, Rumania. Indexed: Bull.Signal. Ref.Zh.

550   RM
INSTITUTUL DE GEOLOGIE SI GEOFIZICA. STUDII TEHNICE SI ECONOMICE. (Text in English, French and Rumanian; summaries in English, French and German) 1933. irreg. price varies. Institutul de Geologie si Geofizica, Str. Caransebes, Nr. 1, 78344 Bucharest, Rumania. Indexed: Chem.Abstr. Ref.Zh.

551   PL   ISSN 0138-0389
INSTYTUT GEOLOGICZNY. BIULETYN. GEOLOGY OF POLAND. (Text in English; summaries in Polish) 1979. irreg., approx. a. (Instytut Geologiczny) Przedsiebiorstwo Panstwowe Wydawnictwa Geologiczne, Ul. Rakowiecka 4, 00-975 Warsaw, Poland (Dist. by: Ars Polona-Ruch, Krakowskie Przedmiescie 7, Warsaw, Poland) Ed. Wladyslaw Pozaryski. circ. 400. Indexed: Chem.Abst. Geo.Abstr.

551 560   PL   ISSN 0208-645X
INSTYTUT GEOLOGICZNY. PRACE. (Text in English, French, Polish; summaries in English, Russian) 1921. irreg., (2-4/yr.) circ. varies. Instytut Geologiczny, Ul. Rakowiecka 4, 00-975 Warsaw, Poland. abstr. bibl. charts. illus. circ. 400. (back issues avail.) Indexed: Bull.Signal. Ref.Zh.

551   US   ISSN 0740-5162
INTERNATIONAL COAL TESTING CONFERENCE; proceedings of the conference. 1981. a. $100. Standard Laboratories, Inc., 3322 Pennsylvania Ave., Charleston, WV 25304. TEL 304-343-5173. Ed. Lee Rigsby. (back issues avail.)

INTERNATIONAL OIL AND GAS DEVELOPMENT YEARBOOK. see *PETROLEUM AND GAS*

INTERNATIONAL OIL SCOUTS ASSOCIATION DIRECTORY. see *BUSINESS AND ECONOMICS — Trade And Industrial Directories*

551.3   GW   ISSN 0074-7904
INTERNATIONAL SEDIMENTOLOGICAL CONGRESS. GUIDEBOOK. (Represents International Sedimentological Congress. Proceedings) 1946. quadrennial, 1971, 8th, Heidelberg. DM.48. Institut fuer Sediment Forschung, Postfach 103020, 6900 Heidelberg, W. Germany (B.R.D.)
    Proceedings published in host country

INTERNATIONAL SOCIETY FOR ROCK MECHANICS. CONGRESS. PROCEEDINGS. see *ENGINEERING — Civil Engineering*

551   SZ   ISSN 0074-932X
INTERNATIONAL UNION FOR QUATERNARY RESEARCH. CONGRESS PROCEEDINGS. (Text and summaries in English, French, German and Russian) 1936. quadrennial, 1982, 11th, Moscow. free. International Union of Quaternary Research, c/o Dr. Chistian Schluchter, Institute of Foundation Engineering, ETH - Honggerberg, CH-8093 Zurich, Switzerland. circ. 3,000.

557   US
IOWA GEOLOGICAL SURVEY BUREAU. REPORTS OF INVESTIGATIONS. 1964. irreg., approx. biennial. price varies. Geological Survey Bureau, 123 North Capitol St., Iowa City, IA 52242. TEL 319-338-1173. Ed. Donald Koch.
    Formerly: Iowa Geological Survey. Reports of Investigations.

555   IR   ISSN 0075-0484
IRAN. GEOLOGICAL SURVEY. REPORT. 1964. irreg., no.24, 1972. price varies. ‡ Geological Survey, Box 1555, Teheran, Iran. circ. 2,000.

555   IS   ISSN 0075-1200
ISRAEL. GEOLOGICAL SURVEY. BULLETIN. (Text in English; summaries in Hebrew) 1956. irreg., no.79, 1986. $15 per no. ‡ Geological Survey Library, 30 Malkhe Israel St., Jerusalem, Israel. Ed.Bd. circ. 1,200. Indexed: Biol.Abstr.

555   IS   ISSN 0333-6425
ISRAEL. GEOLOGICAL SURVEY. CURRENT RESEARCH. (Text in English) 1975. a. free. Geological Survey, 30 Malkhe Israel Street, Jerusalem 95 501, Israel.

551 549   UR   ISSN 0202-7348
ITOGI NAUKI I TEKHNIKI: GEOKHIMIYA - MINERALOGIYA - PETROGRAFIYA. irreg., latest vol.14, 1985. price varies. Vsesoyuznyi Institut Nauchno-Tekhnicheskoi Informatsii (VINITI), Baltiiskaya ul. 14, Moscow A-219, Russian S.F.S.R., U.S.S.R. (Subscr. to: Mezhdunarodnaya Kniga, Dimitrova ul. 39, 113095 Moscow, Russian S.F.S.R., U.S.S.R.)

552   UR   ISSN 0302-542X
ITOGI NAUKI I TEKHNIKI: MESTOROZHDENIYA GORYUCHIKH POLEZNYKH ISKOPAEMYKH. irreg., latest vol.15, 1987. price varies. Vsesoyuznyi Institut Nauchno-Tekhnicheskoi Informatsii (VINITI), Baltiiskaya ul. 14, Moscow A-219, Russian S.F.S.R., U.S.S.R. (Subscr. to: Mezhdunarodnaya Kniga, Dimitrova ul. 39, 113095 Moscow, Russian S.F.S.R., U.S.S.R.) Indexed: Chem.Abstr.

551   UR   ISSN 0202-7372
ITOGI NAUKI I TEKHNIKI: OBSHCHAYA GEOLOGIYA. irreg., vol.23, 1987. price varies. Vsesoyuznyi Institut Nauchno-Tekhnicheskoi Informatsii (VINITI), Baltiiskaya ul. 14, Moscow A-219, Russian S.F.S.R., U.S.S.R. Indexed: Chem.Abstr.

IVORY COAST. DIRECTION DES MINES ET DE LA GEOLOGIE. RAPPORT PROVISOIRE SUR LES ACTIVITIES DU SECTEUR. see *MINES AND MINING INDUSTRY*

551   GE   ISSN 0448-1518
JAHRBUCH FUER GEOLOGIE. irreg. price varies. (Zentrales Geologisches Institut) Akademie-Verlag, Leipziger Strasse 3-4, 1086 Berlin, E. Germany (D.D.R.)

EARTH SCIENCES — GEOLOGY

551   US   ISSN 0075-3890
JOHNS HOPKINS UNIVERSITY STUDIES IN GEOLOGY. 1922. irreg., no.21, 1973. price varies. ‡ (Johns Hopkins University, Department of Earth and Planetary Sciences) Johns Hopkins University Press, 701 W. 40th St., Ste. 275, Baltimore, MD 21211. TEL 301-338-6900. (reprint service avail. from UMI) Indexed: GeoRef.

551   551.31   551.4   IC   ISSN 0449-0576
JOKULL. (Text in English and Icelandic) 1951. a. $23. Joklarannsoknafelag Islands - Iceland Glaciological Society, National Energy Authority, Grensasvegur 9, 108 Reykjavik, Iceland (Subscr. to: Box 5128 Reykjavik, Iceland) (Co-sponsor: Jarofradafelag Islands - Geoscience Society of Iceland) Ed. O.G. Flovenz. circ. 1,100. Indexed: Geo.Abstr.

551   574   YU   ISSN 0351-3297
JUGOSLAVENSKE AKADEMIJE ZNANOSTI I UMJETNOSTI. RAZRED ZA PRIRODNE ZNANOSTI. RAD. (Text and summaries in Croatian, English, French and German) 1866. a. 30 din. Jugoslavenska Akademija Znanosti i Umjetnosti, Razred za Prirodne Znanosti - Yugoslav Academy of Sciences and Arts, Brace Kavurica 1, 41000 Zagreb, Yugoslavia. Indexed: Biol.Abstr.

557   US
KANSAS GEOLOGICAL SURVEY. BULLETIN. 1913. irreg., no.225, 1982. $7.50 per no. Geological Survey, 1930 Constant Ave., Campus West, University of Kansas, Lawrence, KS 66046. TEL 913-864-3965. illus. maps.

557   US
KANSAS GEOLOGICAL SURVEY. CHEMICAL QUALITY SERIES. 1975. irreg., no. 11, 1986. price varies. Geological Survey, 1930 Constant Ave., Campus West, University of Kansas, Lawrence, KS 66046. TEL 913-864-3965. Indexed: GeoRef.

557   US
KANSAS GEOLOGICAL SURVEY. EDUCATIONAL SERIES. 1973. irreg., no.5, 1978. price varies. Geological Survey, 1930 Constant Ave., Campus West, University of Kansas, Lawrence, KS 66046. TEL 913-864-3965. Indexed: GeoRef.

557   US
KANSAS GEOLOGICAL SURVEY. GEOLOGY SERIES. 1975. irreg., no 2, 1976. $5 per no. Geological Survey, 1930 Constant Ave., Campus West, University of Kansas, Lawrence, KS 66046. TEL 913-864-3965. Indexed: GeoRef.

557   US   ISSN 0075-4935
KANSAS GEOLOGICAL SURVEY. SHORT PAPERS IN RESEARCH. (Included with Bulletins) 1967. a. ‡ Geological Survey, University of Kansas, 1930 Constant Ave., Campus West, Lawrence, KS 66044. TEL 913-864-3965. Ed. Gary Alan Waldron.

557   US
KANSAS GEOLOGICAL SURVEY. SUBSURFACE GEOLOGY SERIES. 1974. irreg., no.7, 1985. price varies. Geological Survey, 1930 Constant Ave., Campus West, University of Kansas, Lawrence, KS 66046. TEL 913-864-3965. Indexed: GeoRef.

557   US   ISSN 0075-5575
KENTUCKY GEOLOGICAL SURVEY. GUIDEBOOK TO GEOLOGICAL FIELD TRIPS. 1952. irreg. price varies. Kentucky Geological Survey, 311 Breckinridge Hall, University of Kentucky, Lexington, KY 40506-0056. TEL 606-257-5863. Ed. Donald W. Hutcheson.

551   US
KENTUCKY GEOLOGICAL SURVEY. SERIES 11. ANNUAL REPORT. 1979. a. Kentucky Geological Survey, 311 Breckinridge Hall, University of Kentucky, Lexington, KY 40506-0056. TEL 606-257-5863. Ed. Donald W. Hutcheson.
    Formerly: Kentucky Geological Survey. Annual Report (ISSN 0731-2784)

557   US   ISSN 0075-5559
KENTUCKY GEOLOGICAL SURVEY. SERIES 11. BULLETIN. 1879. irreg., no.1, 1982. price varies. Kentucky Geological Survey, 311 Breckinridge Hall, University of Kentucky, Lexington, KY 40506-0056. TEL 606-257-5863. Ed. Donald W. Hutcheson.

557   US   ISSN 0075-5567
KENTUCKY GEOLOGICAL SURVEY. SERIES 11. COUNTY REPORT. 1912. irreg., no.2, 1982. price varies. Kentucky Geological Survey, 311 Breckinridge Hall, University of Kentucky, Lexington, KY 40506-0056. TEL 606-257-5863. Ed. Donald W. Hutcheson.

557   US   ISSN 0075-5583
KENTUCKY GEOLOGICAL SURVEY. SERIES 11. INFORMATION CIRCULAR. 1951. irreg., no.18, 1986. price varies. Kentucky Geological Survey, 311 Breckinridge Hall, University of Kentucky, Lexington, KY 40506-0056. TEL 606-257-5863. Ed. Donald W. Hutcheson.

557   US   ISSN 0075-5591
KENTUCKY GEOLOGICAL SURVEY. SERIES 11. REPORT OF INVESTIGATIONS. 1949. irreg., no.3, 1985. price varies. Kentucky Geological Survey, 311 Breckinridge Hall, University of Kentucky, Lexington, KY 40506-0056. TEL 606-257-5863. Ed. Donald W. Hutcheson.

557   US   ISSN 0075-5605
KENTUCKY GEOLOGICAL SURVEY. SERIES 11. REPRINTS. 1925. irreg., no.23, 1986. price varies. Kentucky Geological Survey, 311 Breckinridge Hall, University of Kentucky, Lexington, KY 40506-0056. TEL 606-257-5863. Ed. Donald W. Hutcheson.

557   US   ISSN 0075-5613
KENTUCKY GEOLOGICAL SURVEY. SERIES 11. SPECIAL PUBLICATION. Issued also in this series: Kentucky Oil and Gas Association. Technical Sessions. Proceedings. 1953. irreg., no.12, 1985. price varies. Kentucky Geological Survey, 311 Breckinridge Hall, University of Kentucky, Lexington, KY 40506-0056. TEL 606-257-5863. Ed. Donald W. Hutcheson.

557   US   ISSN 0075-5621
KENTUCKY GEOLOGICAL SURVEY. SERIES 11. THESIS SERIES. 1966. irreg., no.3, 1985. price varies. Kentucky Geological Survey, 311 Breckinridge Hall, University of Kentucky, Lexington, KY 40506-0056. TEL 606-257-5863. Ed. Donald W. Hutcheson.

551.44   SP
KOBIE. (Text in Basque and Spanish; summaries in English and French) 1969. a. 700 ptas. (Grupo Espeleologico Vizcaino) Diputacion de Vizcaya, c/o Sr. Ugalde, Biblioteca Provincial, Astarloa St., Bilbao, Spain.
Speleology

551   DK
KOEBENHAVNS UNIVERSITET. GEOLOGISK CENTRALINSTITUT. AARSBERETNING. 1970. a. contr. free circ. Koebenhavns Universitet, Geologisk Centralinstitut, Oester Voldgade 10, 1350 Copenhagen K, Denmark. circ. 525(controlled)

551   622   NE   ISSN 0075-6741
KONINKLIJK NEDERLANDS GEOLOGISCH MIJNBOUWKUNDIG GENOOTSCHAP. VERHANDELINGEN. (Before 1969 published in 2 series: Geologische Serie, and Mijnbouwkundige Serie) (Text in English) 1912. irreg., no. 32, 1980. price varies. (Koninklijk Nederlands Geologisch Mijnbouwkundig Genootschap - Royal Geological and Mining Society of the Netherlands) Martinus Nijhoff Publishers, Postbus 163, 3300 AD Dordrecht, Netherlands. circ. 2,250.

796.525   PL   ISSN 0137-5482
KRAS I SPELEOLOGIA. (Text and summaries in English, French and Polish) 1977. irreg. Uniwersytet Slaski w Katowicach, Ul. Bankowa 14, 40-007 Katowice, Poland.
Speleology

552   CS
KRYSTALINIKUM; contributions to the geology and petrology of crystalline complexes. (Text in English) vol. 11, 1975. a. price varies. Academia, Publishing House of the Czechoslovak Academy of Sciences, Vodickova 40, 112 29 Prague 1, Czechoslovakia (Dist. in Western Countries: E. Schweiserbart'sche Verlagsbuchhandlung, Johannesstr. 3A, 7000 Stuttgart 1, W. Germany (B.R.D.)) bibl. charts. illus. Indexed: Chem.Abstr. Br.Geol.Lit.

555   JA
KUMAMOTO UNIVERSITY. DEPARTMENT OF GEOLOGY. JOURNAL. (Text in English) 1952. irreg. on exchange basis. Kumamoto University, Department of Geology - Kumamoto Daigaku Rigakubu Chigaku Kyoshitsu, Faculty of Science, 2-39-1 Kurokami, Kumamoto 860, Japan.

551   560   665.5   JA   ISSN 0385-8278
KYUSHU UNIVERSITY. DEPARTMENT OF GEOLOGY. SCIENCE REPORTS/KYUSHU DAIGAKU RIGAKUBU KENKYU HOKOKU CHISHITSUGAKU. (Text in Japanese; summaries in English) 1941. irreg. exchange basis only. Kyushu University 33, Department of Geology, 6-10-1 Hakozaki, Higashi-ku, Fukuoka 812, Japan. Ed.Bd. circ. 650. Indexed: Chem.Abstr. Geo.Abstr. GeoRef.

555   JA   ISSN 0023-6179
KYUSHU UNIVERSITY. FACULTY OF SCIENCE. MEMOIRS. SERIES D: GEOLOGY/KYUSHU DAIGAKU RIGAKUBU KIYO, D, CHISHITSUGAKU. (Text in English, French and German) 1940. a. exchange basis. Kyushu University, Faculty of Science, Department of Geology - Kyushu Daigaku Rigakubu, 6-10-1 Hakozaki, Higashi-ku, Fukuoka 812, Japan. circ. 1, 050. Indexed: Biol.Abstr. Chem.Abstr. Geo.Abstr. GeoRef.

LANDESMUSEUM JOANNEUM. ABTEILUNG FUER GEOLOGIE, PALAEONTOLOGIE UND BERGBAU. MITTEILUNGEN. see *PALEONTOLOGY*

551.44   AU
LANDESVEREIN FUER HOEHLENKUNDE IN DER STEIERMARK. MITTEILUNGEN. 1972. a. S.100. Landesverein fuer Hoehlenkunde in der Steiermark, Brandhofgasse 18, A-8010 Graz, Austria. Ed. Mag. Volker Weissensteiner. adv. bk. rev. bibl. illus. circ. 300.
Speleology

554   UR   ISSN 0459-0805
LENINGRADSKII UNIVERSITET. UCHENYE ZAPISKI. SERIYA GEOLOGICHESKIKH NAUK. 1950. irreg. 1 Rub. Leningradskii Universitet, Geologicheskii Fakultet, Universitetskaya nab. 7/9, Leningrad B-164, Russian S.F.S.R., U.S.S.R. illus. Indexed: GeoRef.

557   US   ISSN 0459-8474
LOUISIANA. GEOLOGICAL SURVEY. WATER RESOURCES BULLETIN. 1960. irreg., no.20, 1975. $3 per no. Geological Survey, Box 66492, Baton Rouge, LA 70896. TEL 504-342-6754. illus. (back issues avail.) Indexed: GeoRef.

538.7   SW   ISSN 0076-1354
LOVOE GEOMAGNETIC OBSERVATORY YEARBOOK. (Text in English) 1930. a. Kr.25. Sveriges Geologiska Undersoekning - Geological Survey of Sweden, Box 670, S-751 28 Uppsala, Sweden.

556   MG
MADAGASCAR. SERVICE GEOLOGIQUE. RAPPORT D'ACTIVITE: GEOLOGIE. (Text in French) 1975. a. FMG.2000. Service Geologique de Madagascar, B.P. 322, Antananarivo, Malagasy Republic.

551   US
MAINE GEOLOGIST. 1973. irreg., approx. 4/yr. $7. Geological Society of Maine, Inc., c/o Robert G. Gerber, Inc., 17 West St., Freeport, ME 04032. TEL 207-865-6138. Ed. Robert Johnston. circ. 250. (tabloid format)

556   MW   ISSN 0076-311X
MALAWI. GEOLOGICAL SURVEY DEPARTMENT. ANNUAL REPORT. 1923. a. price varies. Geological Survey Department, Box 27, Zomba, Malawi. TEL 522-166.

559   MY   ISSN 0127-0559
MALAYSIA. GEOLOGICAL SURVEY. ANNUAL REPORT. (Text in English) 1949. a. M.$20. Geological Survey, c/o Library, Kuching, Sarawak, Malaysia. S. Senathi Rajah. circ. 500. Indexed: Biol.Abstr.

557 CN
MANITOBA ENERGY AND MINES. ECONOMIC
GEOLOGY PAPER SERIES. 1979. irreg. price
varies. Manitoba Energy and mines, 555-330
Graham Ave., Winnipeg, MB R3C 4E3, Canada.
TEL 204-945-6541.
Formerly: Manitoba. Mineral Resources Division.
Economic Geology Paper Series.

557 CN
MANITOBA ENERGY AND MINES.
EDUCATIONAL SERIES. 1976. irreg. price varies.
Manitoba Energy and Mines, 555-330 Graham
Ave., Winnipeg, MB R3C 4E3, Canada. TEL 204-
945-6541.
Formerly: Manitoba. Mineral Resources Division.
Educational Series.

551 CN
MANITOBA ENERGY AND MINES.
GEOLOGICAL PAPER. 1968. irreg. price varies.
Manitoba Energy and Mines, 555-330 Graham
Ave., Winnipeg, MB R3C 4E3, Canada. TEL 204-
945-6541. Indexed: GeoRef.
Formerly: Manitoba. Mineral Resources Division.
Geological Paper (ISSN 0076-387X)

557 CN
MANITOBA ENERGY AND MINES.
GEOLOGICAL REPORT. 1937. irreg. price varies.
Manitoba Energy and Mines, 555-330 Graham
Ave., Winnipeg, MB R3C 4E3, Canada. TEL 204-
945-6541.
Former Titles: Manitoba. Mineral Resources
Division. Geological Report; Manitoba. Mines
Branch. Publication (ISSN 0085-3070)

557 CN
MANITOBA ENERGY AND MINES. OPEN FILE
REPORT SERIES. 1976. irreg. price varies.
Manitoba Energy and Mines, 555-330 Graham
Ave., Winnipeg, MB R3C 4E3, Canada. TEL 204-
945-6541.
Formerly: Manitoba. Mineral Resources Division.
Open File Report Series.

557 CN
MANITOBA ENERGY AND MINES. REPORT OF
FIELD ACTIVITIES. 1968. a. price varies.
Manitoba Energy and Mines, 555-330 Graham
Ave., Winnipeg, MB R3C 4E3, Canada. TEL 204-
945-6541.
Former Titles: Manitoba. Mineral Resources
Division. Report of Field Activities; Manitoba.
Mines Branch. Summary of Geological Field Work.

MARSCHENRAT ZUR FOERDERUNG DER
FORSCHUNG IM KUESTENGEBIET DER
NORDSEE. NACHRICHTEN. see SCIENCES:
COMPREHENSIVE WORKS

557 US ISSN 0076-4779
MARYLAND. GEOLOGICAL SURVEY.
BULLETIN. 1944. irreg., no.32, 1977. price varies.
Maryland Geological Survey, 2300 St. Paul St.,
Baltimore, MD 21218. TEL 301-554-5500. index.
Indexed: Chem.Abstr. GeoRef.

557 US ISSN 0076-4787
MARYLAND. GEOLOGICAL SURVEY.
EDUCATIONAL SERIES. 1964. irreg., no.5, 1980.
price varies. Maryland Geological Survey, 2300 St.
Paul St., Baltimore, MD 21218. TEL 301-554-5500.
Indexed: GeoRef.

557 US ISSN 0076-4795
MARYLAND. GEOLOGICAL SURVEY.
INFORMATION CIRCULAR. 1963. irreg., no.43,
1986. price varies. Maryland Geological Survey,
2300 St. Paul St., Baltimore, MD 21218. TEL 301-
554-5500.

557 US ISSN 0076-4809
MARYLAND. GEOLOGICAL SURVEY. REPORT
OF INVESTIGATIONS. 1965. irreg., no.46, 1986.
price varies. Maryland Geological Survey, 2300 St.
Paul St., Blatimore, MD 21218. TEL 301-554-5500.
Indexed: GeoRef.

551 NE
MATERIALS SCIENCE OF MINERALS AND
ROCKS. 1983. irreg. price varies. D. Reidel
Publishing Co., Box 17, 3300 AA Dordrecht,
Netherlands (And 190 Old Derby St., Hingham,
MA 02043) Ed. I. Sunagawa.

551 581 DK ISSN 0106-1046
MEDDELELSER OM GROENLAND,
GEOSCIENCE. (Text mainly in English,
occasionally in Danish, French or German) 1979.
irreg. (Kommissionen for Videnskabelige
Undersoegelser i Groenland, GL - Commission for
Scientific Research in Greenland) Nyt Nordisk
Forlag - Arnold Busck A-S, Koebmagergade 49,
DK-1150 Copenhagen K, Denmark. Ed. T.C.R.
Pulvertaft. charts. illus. maps. Indexed: Biol.Abstr.
Chem.Abstr. GeoRef.
Formerly: Greenland Biosciences; Supersedes in
part (1878-1979): Meddelelser om Groenland (ISSN
0025-6676)

554 BE
MEMOIRES POUR SERVIR A L'EXPLICATION
DES CARTES GEOLOGIQUES ET MINIERES
DE LA BELGIQUE. (Text in Dutch, English,
French and German) 1955. irreg. Ministry of
Economical Affairs, Service Geologique de Belgique,
13, rue Jenner, 1040 Brussels, Belgium. Ed.Bd.
charts. circ. 500.

551 IT
MEMORIE DI SCIENZE GEOLOGICHE. (Text in
English, French, German, Italian; summaries in
English and Italian) 1912. a. L.70000. Universita di
Padova, Istituto di Geologia Paleontologia e
Geologia Applicata, Via Giotto 1, 35100 Padua,
Italy. Ed.Bd. Indexed: Biol.Abstr.

551 GW ISSN 0076-7689
MEYNIANA; Veroeffentlichungen aus dem
Geologischen Institut der Universitaet Kiel. 1952. a.
price varies. Universitaet Kiel, Geologisch-
Palaeontologisches Institut, Olshausenstr. 40, D-
2300 Kiel, W. Germany (B.R.D.) (Co-sponsor:
Museum der Universitaet Kiel) Ed. Werner Prange.
circ. 300. (back issues avail.) Indexed: Biol.Abstr.
Geo.Abstr. GeoRef.

557 US ISSN 0543-8497
MICHIGAN. GEOLOGICAL SURVEY DIVISION.
BULLETIN. 1964. irreg., no.6, 1976. Department of
Natural Resources, Geological Survey Division, Box
30028, Lansing, MI 48909. TEL 517-373-1256. Ed.
I.V. Kuehner. illus. maps. Indexed: GeoRef.

557 US
MICHIGAN. GEOLOGICAL SURVEY DIVISION.
REPORT OF INVESTIGATION. 1963. irreg.,
no.17, 1979. price varies. Department of Natural
Resources, Geological Survey Division, Box 30028,
Lansing, MI 48909. TEL 517-373-1256. Ed. I.V.
Kuehner. illus. maps. Indexed: GeoRef.
Formerly: Michigan. Department of
Conservation. Geological Survey Division. Progress
Report (ISSN 0096-5022)

551 549 US ISSN 0343-2181
MINERALS AND ROCKS; monograph series of
theoretical and experimental studies. 1968. irreg.,
vol.18, 1985. price varies. Springer-Verlag, 175 Fifth
Ave., New York, NY 10010 TEL 212-460-1500.
(Also Berlin, Heidelberg, Tokyo and Vienna) Ed.
P.J. Wyllie. (reprint service avail. from ISI) Indexed:
GeoRef.
Former titles: Mineralogie und Petrographie in
Einzel Darstellungen; Minerals, Rocks and
Inorganic Materials (ISSN 0076-8944)

550 VE ISSN 0006-6281
MINISTERIO DE ENERGIA Y MINAS. BOLETIN
DE GEOLOGIA. (Summaries in English and
Spanish) 1951. irreg. price varies. Ministerio de
Energia y Minas, Direccion de Geologia, Torre
Norte, Centro Simon Bolivar, Piso 19, Caracas,
Venezuela. Ed.Bd. Indexed: Biol.Abstr.

557 US ISSN 0544-3105
MINNESOTA. GEOLOGICAL SURVEY.
INFORMATION CIRCULARS. 1962. irreg., no.22,
1985. price varies. Geological Survey, 2642
University Ave., St. Paul, MN 55114-1057. TEL
612-373-3372. (back issues avail.)

557 US ISSN 0076-9177
MINNESOTA. GEOLOGICAL SURVEY. REPORT
OF INVESTIGATIONS. 1963. irreg., vol.33, 1985.
price varies. Geological Survey, 2642 University
Ave., St. Paul, MN 55114-1057. TEL 612-373-3372.
Ed. N.H. Balaban. circ. 400. (back issues avail.)
Indexed: GeoRef.

551.44 US ISSN 0026-671X
MISSOURI SPELEOLOGY. 1959. irreg. $12 per vol.
Missouri Speleological Survey, Inc., c/o Alberta
Zumwalt, Circ.Mgr., Rt. 1, Lohman, MO 65053.
TEL 314-782-3560. Ed. Jim Vandike. bk. rev.
charts. illus. circ. 275. (back issues avail.) Indexed:
GeoRef.

551 560 US ISSN 0077-085X
MONOGRAPHS IN GEOLOGY AND
PALEONTOLOGY. 1967. irreg. price varies.
Princeton University Press, Princeton, NJ 08540.
TEL 609-896-2111. (reprint service avail. from
UMI)

557 US ISSN 0077-1090
MONTANA. BUREAU OF MINES AND
GEOLOGY. BULLETIN. 1919. irreg., B123, 1985.
price varies. Bureau of Mines and Geology,
Montana College of Mineral Science and
Technology, Butte, MT 59701. TEL 406-496-4180.
Indexed: GeoRef.
Incorporating (after 1959): Montana. Bureau of
Mines and Geology. Ground Water Reports (ISSN
0077-1112)

557 622 US ISSN 0077-1120
MONTANA. BUREAU OF MINES AND
GEOLOGY. MEMOIR. 1928. irreg., M58, 1985.
Bureau of Mines and Geology, Montana College of
Mineral Science and Technology, Butte, MT 59701.
TEL 406-496-4180. Indexed: GeoRef.

557 US ISSN 0077-1139
MONTANA. BUREAU OF MINES AND
GEOLOGY. SPECIAL PUBLICATIONS.
(Continues numbering of Miscellaneous
Contributions, 1932-1957) 1957. irreg., SP 93, 1985.
price varies. Bureau of Mines and Geology,
Montana College of Mineral Science and
Technology, Butte, MT 59701. TEL 406-496-4180.

557 US ISSN 0163-2825
MOUNTAIN STATE GEOLOGY. 1961. a. free.
Geological and Economic Survey, Box 879,
Morgantown, WV 26507-0879. circ. 5,000. (back
issues avail.) Indexed: GeoRef.
Formerly: West Virginia Geological Survey
Newsletter (ISSN 0083-8470)

500.9 915 FR
MUSEE NATIONAL D'HISTOIRE NATURELLE,
PARIS. NOTES ET MEMOIRES SUR LE
MOYEN-ORIENT. 1933. irreg. price varies.
Museum National d'Histoire Naturelle, 38 rue
Geoffroy Saint-Hilaire, 75005 Paris, France. Dir.
Louis Dubertret. illus.
Formerly (vol. 1-5): Musee National d'Histoire
Naturelle, Paris. Notes et Memoires de la Section
d'Etudes Geologiques de Haut-Commissariat
Francais en Syrie et au Liban.

551 BE
MUSEE ROYAL DE L'AFRIQUE CENTRALE.
ANNALES. SERIE IN 8. SCIENCES
GEOLOGIQUES/KONINKLIJK MUSEUM
VOOR MIDDEN-AFRIKA. ANNALEN. REEKS
IN 8. GEOLOGISCHE WETENSCHAPPEN.
1948. irreg., no.90, 1985. price varies. Musee Royal
de l'Afrique Centrale, 13 Steenweg op Leuven, B-
1980 Tervuren, Belgium. charts. illus. Indexed:
Biol.Abstr.

551 BE
MUSEE ROYAL DE L'AFRIQUE CENTRALE.
DEPARTEMENT DE GEOLOGIE ET DE
MINERALOGIE. RAPPORT ANNUEL. 1957. a.
650 Fr. Musee Royal de l'Afrique Centrale,
Departement de Geologie et de Mineralogie, 13
Steenweg op Leuven, B-1980 Tervuren, Belgium.
Ed. J. Klerkx. charts. circ. 1,000. Indexed:
Biol.Abstr. Chem.Abstr. GeoRef.

EARTH SCIENCES — GEOLOGY

550 AG ISSN 0027-3880
MUSEO ARGENTINO DE CIENCIAS NATURALES "BERNARDINO RIVADAVIA." INSTITUTO NACIONAL DE INVESTIGACION DE LAS CIENCIAS NATURALES. REVISTA. GEOLOGIA. 1949. irreg., latest vol.8, no.4, 1980. free. Museo Argentino de Ciencias Naturales "Bernardino Rivadavia", Instituto Nacional de Investigacion de las Ciencias Naturales, Avda. Angel Gallardo 470, Casilla de Correo 220-Sucursal 5, Buenos Aires, Argentina. illus.
Supersedes: Museo Argentino de Ciencias Naturales "Bernardino Rivadavia." Instituto Nacional de Investigacion de las Ciencias Naturales. Revista y Communicaciones; Formerly: Buenos Aires. Museo Argentino de Ciencias Naturales Bernardino Rivadavia. Instituto Nacional de Investigacion de las Ciencias Naturales. Revista. Ciencias Geologicas.

500.907 AG
MUSEO MUNICIPAL DE HISTORIA NATURAL DE SAN RAFAEL. INSTITUTO DE CIENCIAS NATURALES. NOTAS. 1957. irreg. $2 per no. Museo Municipal de Historia Natural, Parque Mariano Moreno, 5600 San Rafael, Argentina. Ed. Humberto A. Lagiglia. circ. 1,000.
Formerly: Museo de Historia Natural de San Rafael. Instituto de Ciencias Naturales. Notas.

550 BL ISSN 0080-3200
MUSEU NACIONAL, RIO DE JANEIRO. BOLETIM. NOVA SERIE. GEOLOGIE. 1943. irreg. exchange only. Museu Nacional, Quinta da Boa Vista, Rio de Janeiro, GB 08, Brazil. Indexed: Biol.Abstr.

551 BL ISSN 0077-2224
MUSEU PARAENSE EMILIO GOELDI. BOLETIM. NOVA SERIE: GEOLOGIA. 1957. irreg., no.27, 1982. Conselho Nacional de Desenvolvimento Cientifico e Tecnologico, Museu Paraense Emilio Goeldi, Caixa Postal 399, Belem, Para, Brazil. circ. 1,000. Indexed: Biol.Abstr. GeoRef.

550 PL ISSN 0032-6275
MUZEUM ZIEMI. PRACE. (Text in English or Polish) 1958. irreg. Polska Akademia Nauk, Muzeum Ziemi, Al. na Skarpie 20-26, 00-488 Warsaw, Poland. Ed. Antoni Laszkiewicz. Indexed: Chem.Abstr.

554 NO ISSN 0332-5768
N G U BULLETIN. (Text in English) 1890. irreg. price varies. (Norges Geologiske Undersoekelse - Geological Survey of Norway) Norwegian University Press, Kolstadgt. 1, Box 2959-Toeyen, 0608 Oslo 6, Norway (U.S. address: Publications Expediting Inc., 200 Meacham Ave., Elmont, NY 11003) Ed. David Roberts. bibl. charts. illus. Indexed: Biol.Abstr. Chem.Abstr. Br.Geol.Lit. Geo.Abstr. GeoRef. Key Title: Bulletin - Norges Geologiske Undersokelse.

351 NO ISSN 0377-8894
N G U SKRIFTER. (Text in Norwegian; summaries in English) irreg. price varies. (Norges Geologiske Undersoekelse - Geological Survey of Norway) Norwegian University Press, Kolstadgt. 1, Box 2959-Toeyen, 0608 Oslo 6, Norway (U.S. distribution address: Publications Expediting Inc., 200 Meacham Ave., Elmont NY 11003) Ed. David Roberts. Indexed: Br.Geol.Lit. Geo.Abstr.

553.53 US ISSN 0077-5673
N S G A CIRCULAR. 1928. irreg., no. 120, 1973. price varies. National Sand and Gravel Association, 900 Spring St., Silver Spring, MD 20910. TEL 301-587-1400. Ed. R.D. Gaynor. circ. 1,000.

551.44 AT
NARGUN. 1967. 10/yr. Aus.$12. Victorian Speleological Association Inc., G.P.O. Box 5425cc, Melbourne, Vic.3001, Australia. Ed. S. White. adv. bk. rev. circ. 170. Indexed: Aus.Speleo.Abstr.

559 JA ISSN 0386-5517
NATIONAL INSTITUTE OF POLAR RESEARCH. MEMOIRS. SERIES A: AERONOMY. (Text and abstracts in English) 1963. irreg., no. 18, 1981. exchange basis. National Institute of Polar Research - Kokuritsu Kyokuchi Kenkyujo, 9-10, Kaga 1-chome, Itabashi-ku, Tokyo 173, Japan. Ed. Tatsuro Matsuda. circ. 1,000. Indexed: Curr.Antarc.Lit. Int.Aerosp.Abstr.

NATUR UND MENSCH: JAHRESMITTEILUNGEN DER NATURHISTORISCHEN GESELLSCHAFT NUERNBERG. see *BIOLOGY*

NATURHISTORISCHES MUSEUM BASEL. VEROEFFENTLICHUNGEN. see *ANTHROPOLOGY*

NATURWISSENSCHAFTLICHER VEREIN WUPPERTAL. JAHRESBERICHTE. see *BIOLOGY — Botany*

526 UR
NAUCHNO-ISSLEDOVATEL'SKII INSTITUT PRIKLADNOI GEODEZII. TRUDY. 1976. irreg. 0.80 Rub. per issue. Izdatel'stvo Tsniigaik, Ul. Onezhskaya, 26, Moscow A-Y13, Russian S.F.S.R., U.S.S.R. Ed. V. Chernikov. abstr. charts. circ. 500.

554 BU ISSN 0204-5109
NEFTENA I VUGLISTNA GEOLOGIIA/ PETROLEUM AND COAL GEOLOGY. (Text in Bulgarian or Russian; summaries in English, French and German) 1975. irreg. 1.15 lv. per no. (Bulgarska Akademiia na Naukite) Publishing House of the Bulgarian Academy of Sciences, Acad. G. Bonchev St., Bldg. 6, 1113 Sofia, Bulgaria (Dist. by: Hemus, 6, Rouski Blvd., 1000 Sofia, Bulgaria) illus. circ. 420. Indexed: Chem.Abstr. Geo.Abstr. GeoRef.
Formerly: Bulgarska Akademiia na Naukite. Geologicheski Institut. Izvestiia. Seriie Neftena i Vuglishtna Geologiia.

554 NE ISSN 0077-7617
NETHERLANDS. RIJKS GEOLOGISCHE DIENST. JAARVERSLAG/NETHERLANDS GEOLOGICAL SURVEY. ANNUAL REPORT. (Text in Dutch; summaries in English) free. a. free. Rijks Geologische Dienst, Postbus 157, 2000 AD Haarlem, Netherlands. TEL 023-319362. Indexed: GeoRef.

551 560 GW ISSN 0077-7749
NEUES JAHRBUCH FUER GEOLOGIE UND PALAEONTOLOGIE. ABHANDLUNGEN. 1807. irreg., (3 nos./vol., 2-3 vols./yr.) price varies. E. Schweizerbart'sche Verlagsbuchhandlung, Johannesstr. 3A, 7000 Stuttgart 1, W. Germany (B.R.D.) Ed.Bd. adv. index. Indexed: Biol.Abstr. Chem.Abstr. Petrol.Abstr.
Supersedes in part and continues volume numbering of: Neues Jahrbuch fuer Mineralogie, Geologie und Palaeontologie. Abhandlungen.

557 622 US
NEVADA. BUREAU OF MINES AND GEOLOGY. BULLETIN. 1904. irreg. no.33, 1978. price varies. Bureau of Mines and Geology, University of Nevada, Reno, NV 89557-0088. TEL 702-784-6691. Indexed: GeoRef.

557 622 US ISSN 0095-5264
NEVADA. BUREAU OF MINES AND GEOLOGY. REPORT. 1962. irreg., no.33, 1977. Bureau of Mines and Geology, University of Nevada, Reno, NV 89557-0088. illus. Indexed: GeoRef. Key Title: Report - Nevada Bureau of Mines and Geology. Continues: Nevada. Bureau of Mines. Report.

NEW CALEDONIA. SERVICE DES MINES ET DE L'ENERGY. RAPPORT ANNUEL. see *MINES AND MINING INDUSTRY*

557 US
NEW JERSEY. BUREAU OF GEOLOGY AND TOPOGRAPHY. GEOLOGIC REPORT SERIES. 1959. irreg., no.14, 1982. price varies. Geological Survey, CN-029, Trenton, NJ 08625. Ed. David P. Harper. circ. 500. Indexed: GeoRef.

557 US
NEW JERSEY GEOLOGICAL SURVEY. BULLETIN. 1910. irreg. price varies. Geological Survey, CN-029, Trenton, NJ 08625. Ed. David P. Harper. circ. 500. Indexed: GeoRef.
Formerly: New Jersey. Bureau of Geology and Topography. Bulletin.

557 US ISSN 0077-8567
NEW MEXICO GEOLOGICAL SOCIETY. GUIDEBOOK, FIELD CONFERENCE. 1950. irreg. price varies. New Mexico Geological Society, Inc., Campus Station, Socorro, NM 87801. Ed. Jivi Zidek. circ. 1,500. Indexed: GeoRef.

559.4 AT ISSN 0155-5561
NEW SOUTH WALES. GEOLOGICAL SURVEY. BULLETIN. 1922. irreg., no.31, 1984. price varies. Department of Mineral Resources, G.P.O. Box 5288, Sydney, N.S.W. 2001, Australia. Ed. H. Basden. index. circ. 400. Indexed: GeoRef.

559.4 AT ISSN 0077-8710
NEW SOUTH WALES. GEOLOGICAL SURVEY. MEMOIRS: GEOLOGY. 1887. irreg., no. 11, 1971. price varies. Department of Mineral Resources, Box 5288, Sydney, N.S.W. 2001, Australia. Ed. H. Basden. index. circ. 400. Indexed: GeoRef.

551 549 AT ISSN 0727-9418
NEW SOUTH WALES. GEOLOGICAL SURVEY. MINE DATA SHEETS AND METALLOGENIC STUDY. 1972. irreg. price varies. Department of Mineral Resources, G.P.O. Box 5288, Sydney, N.S.W. 2001, Australia. Ed. H. Basden. circ. 400.

NEW SOUTH WALES. GEOLOGICAL SURVEY. MINERAL INDUSTRY SERIES. see *MINES AND MINING INDUSTRY*

NEW SOUTH WALES. GEOLOGICAL SURVEY. MINERAL RESOURCES SERIES. see *MINES AND MINING INDUSTRY*

559.4 AT ISSN 0155-3372
NEW SOUTH WALES. GEOLOGICAL SURVEY. RECORDS. 1889. irreg., no.22, 1986. price varies. Department of Mineral Resources, G.P.O. Box 5288, Sydney, N.S.W. 2001, Australia. Ed. H. Basden. circ. 400. Indexed: GeoRef.

559 NZ ISSN 0077-9628
NEW ZEALAND. DEPARTMENT OF SCIENTIFIC AND INDUSTRIAL RESEARCH. GEOLOGICAL SURVEY. BULLETIN. 1906. irreg., no.98, 1986. price varies. Department of Scientific and Industrial Research, Science Information Publishing Centre, Box 9741, Wellington, New Zealand. Ed. I. Mackenzie. bibl. charts. illus. circ. 800. (back issues avail.)

557 CN ISSN 0078-0308
NEWFOUNDLAND. MINERAL DEVELOPMENT DIVISION. GEOLOGICAL SURVEY. BULLETIN. 1934. irreg., no.38, 1969. price varies. Mineral Development Division, P.O. Box 4750, 95 Bonaventure Ave., St. John's, Newfoundland, Canada. TEL 709-576-3159.

557 CN ISSN 0078-0383
NEWFOUNDLAND. MINES BRANCH. GEOLOGICAL SURVEY OF NEWFOUNDLAND. REPORT SERIES. 1953. irreg. price varies. Mineral Development Division, P.O. Box 4750, 95 Bonaventure Ave., St. John's, Newfoundland, Canada. TEL 709-576-3159.

NIGERIAN MINING AND GEOSCIENCES SOCIETY. JOURNAL. see *MINES AND MINING INDUSTRY*

555 549 JA ISSN 0369-3627
NIIGATA UNIVERSITY. FACULTY OF SCIENCE. SCIENCE REPORTS. SERIES E: GEOLOGY AND MINERALOGY. (Text in English) 1967. a. exchange basis. Niigata University, Faculty of Science - Niigata Daigaku Rigakubu, 8050 Igarashi Nino-cho, Niigata-shi 950-21, Japan. Indexed: Biol.Abstr.

551 NO ISSN 0333-4112
NORGES GEOLOGISKE UNDERSOEKELSE. ARSMELDING. 1922. a. free. Norges Geologiske Undersoekelse - Geological Survey of Norway, Leiv Erikssons vei 39, Trondheim 7000, Norway. Ed. Jan Hoest. illus. circ. 3,000.

551 NO ISSN 0085-4271
NORSK POLARINSTITUTT. AARBOK. (Text in English and Norwegian; summaries in English and Russian) 1960. a, latest 1977 (pub. 1978) price varies. Norsk Polarinstitutt, Postboks 158, 1330 Oslo Lufthavn, Norway. Ed. Tore Gjelsvik. Indexed: Biol.Abstr. Geo.Abstr. GeoRef.

551 NO
NORSK POLARINSTITUTT. MEDDELELSER. 1926. irreg., no.106, 1976. Norsk Polarinstitutt, Postboks 158, 1330 Oslo Lufthavn, Norway. Indexed: Biol.Abstr. GeoRef.
Formerly: Norges Svalbard- og Ishavs-Undersoekelser.

551 NO ISSN 0474-8042
NORSK POLARINSTITUTT. POLARHAANDBOK.
Short title: Polarhaandbok. 1964. irreg., latest 1979.
Norsk Polarinstitutt, Postboks 158, 1330 Oslo
Lufthavn, Norway. Indexed: Biol.Abstr. GeoRef.

551 NO
NORSK POLARINSTITUTT. SKRIFTER. 1929.
irreg., latest no.169, 1978 (not pub. consecutively)
Norsk Polarinstitutt, Postboks 158, 1330 Oslo
Lufthavn, Norway. Indexed: Biol.Abstr.
Br.Geol.Lit. Geo.Abstr. GeoRef.
Former titles: Norges Svalbard- og Ishavs-
Undersoekelser. Skrifter; Skrifter om Svalbard og
Ishavet; Skrifter om Svalbard og Nordishavet;
Norske Statsunder Stoettede
Spitsbergenekspedisjoner. Resultater.

557 US ISSN 0546-5001
NORTH DAKOTA. GEOLOGICAL SURVEY.
BULLETIN. 1920. irreg., no.80, 1985. free.
Geological Survey, University Station, Grand Forks,
ND 58202-8156. TEL 701-777-2231. (back issues
avail.) Indexed: GeoRef.

557 US ISSN 0091-9004
NORTH DAKOTA. GEOLOGICAL SURVEY.
EDUCATIONAL SERIES. 1972. irreg., no.16,
1983. price varies. Geological Survey, University
Sta., Grand Forks, ND 58202-8156. TEL 701-777-
2231. (Co-sponsor: North Dakota Department of
Public Instruction) illus. (back issues avail.) Indexed:
GeoRef. Key Title: Educational Series - North
Dakota Geological Survey.

557 US ISSN 0078-1576
NORTH DAKOTA. GEOLOGICAL SURVEY.
MISCELLANEOUS SERIES. 1957. irreg., no.65,
1984. price varies. Geological Survey, University
Sta., Grand Forks, ND 58202-8156. TEL 701-777-
2231. (back issues avail.) Indexed: GeoRef.

551 US
NORTH DAKOTA. GEOLOGICAL SURVEY.
REPORT OF INVESTIGATION. 1949. irreg., no.
86, 1986. price varies. North Dakota Geological
Survey, University Sta., Grand Forks, ND 58202-
8156. TEL 701-777-2231. Ed. John P. Bluemle. circ.
1,500. (back issues avail.)

557 US
NORTHWEST GEOLOGY. 1972. a. $2. ‡ University
of Montana, Department of Geology, Missoula, MT
59812. TEL 406-243-0211. Ed. Sheila Fountain.
bibl. charts. illus. circ. 400. (back issues avail.)
Indexed: GeoRef.

O.R.S.T.O.M. RESUMES DES TRAVAUX.
OCEANOGRAPHIE. (Office de la Recherche
Scientifique et Technique Outre-Mer) see *EARTH
SCIENCES — Oceanography*

554 GW ISSN 0078-2939
OBERRHEINISCHE GEOLOGISCHE
ABHANDLUNGEN. 1929. a. price varies. Verlag
C. F. Mueller GmbH (Karlsruhe), Rheinstr. 122,
Postfach 210949, 7500 Karlsruhe 21, W. Germany
(B.R.D.) Ed. H. Illies. circ. 450. Indexed: GeoRef.

551 GW ISSN 0078-2947
OBERRHEINISCHER GEOLOGISCHER VEREIN.
JAHRESBERICHTE UND MITTEILUNGEN.
1911. a. price varies. E. Schweizerbart'sche
Verlagsbuchhandlung, Johannesstr. 3a, 7000
Stuttgart 1, W. Germany (B.R.D.) Ed. K.
Hinkelbein. Indexed: GeoRef.

551 560 AU ISSN 0251-7493
OESTERREICHISCHE GEOLOGISCHE
GESELLSCHAFT. MITTEILUNGEN. (Summaries
in English or French) 1908. a. S.300.($16)
Oesterreichische Geologische Gesellschaft,
Universitaet Str. 7, A-1010 Vienna, Austria. Eds.
Alexander and Edith Tollmann. adv. bk. rev. circ. 1,
300. Indexed: Biol.Abstr.
Continues: Geologische Gesellschaft, Vienna.
Mitteilungen (ISSN 0016-7843)

557 US
OHIO. DIVISION OF GEOLOGICAL SURVEY.
BULLETIN. 1903. irreg., no.68, 1982. price varies.
Department of Natural Resources, Division of
Geological Survey, Fountain Sq, Bldg. B, Columbus,
OH 43224. TEL 614-265-6605. illus. (back issues
avail.) Indexed: GeoRef.

557 US ISSN 0472-6685
OHIO. DIVISION OF GEOLOGICAL SURVEY.
EDUCATIONAL LEAFLET. 1956. irreg. no.13,
1982. free. Department of Natural Resources,
Division of Geological Survey, Fountain Sq., Bldg.
B, Columbus, OH 43224. TEL 614-265-6605. (back
issues avail.)

557 US
OHIO. DIVISION OF GEOLOGICAL SURVEY.
GEOLOGICAL NOTE. 1975. irreg., no. 6, 1979.
price varies. Department of Natural Resources,
Division of Geological Survey, Fountain Sq., Bldg.
B, Columbus, OH 43224. TEL 614-265-6605. illus.
(back issues avail.)

557 US ISSN 0097-9473
OHIO. DIVISION OF GEOLOGICAL SURVEY.
GUIDEBOOK. 1973. irreg., no.4, 1975. price
varies. Department of Natural Resources, Division
of Geological Survey, Fountain Sq., Columbus, OH
43224. TEL 614-265-6605. illus. (back issues avail.)
Key Title: Guidebook - State of Ohio, Department
of Natural Resources, Division of Geological
Survey.

557 US
OHIO. DIVISION OF GEOLOGICAL SURVEY.
INFORMATION CIRCULAR. 1946. irreg., no.51,
1981. price varies. Department of Natural
Resources, Division of Geological Survey, Fountain
Sq., Bldg. B, Columbus, OH 43224. TEL 614-265-
6605. illus. (back issues avail.)

557 US ISSN 0361-0519
OHIO. DIVISION OF GEOLOGICAL SURVEY.
MISCELLANEOUS REPORT. 1974. irreg.
Department of Natural Resources, Division of
Geological Survey, Fountain Sq., Bldg. B,
Columbus, OH 43224. TEL 614-265-6605. (back
issues avail.) Indexed: Chem.Abstr. Key Title:
Miscellaneous Report - State of Ohio, Department
of Natural Resources, Division of Geological
Survey.

557 US
OHIO. DIVISION OF GEOLOGICAL SURVEY.
REPORT OF INVESTIGATIONS. 1947. irreg.,
no.131, 1986. price varies. Department of Natural
Resources, Division of Geological Survey, Fountain
Sq., Bldg. B, Columbus, OH 43224. TEL 614-265-
6605. illus. (back issues avail.) Indexed: GeoRef.

557 US ISSN 0078-4389
OKLAHOMA. GEOLOGICAL SURVEY.
BULLETIN. 1908. irreg., no.139, 1985. price varies.
Geological Survey, University of Oklahoma, 830
Van Vleet Oval, Room 163, Norman, OK 73019.
TEL 405-325-3031. bibl. charts. illus. index. circ.
500. (also avail. in microfilm; back issues avail.)
Indexed: Chem.Abstr. GeoRef. Petrol.Abstr.

557 US ISSN 0078-4397
OKLAHOMA. GEOLOGICAL SURVEY.
CIRCULAR. 1908. irreg., no.86, 1983. price varies.
Geological Survey, University of Oklahoma, 830
Van Vleet Oval, Rm. 163, Norman, OK 73019. TEL
405-325-3031. bibl. charts. illus. stat. index. circ.
500. (microfilm; back issues avail.) Indexed:
Biol.Abstr. Chem.Abstr. Petrol.Abstr. Geo.Abstr.
GeoRef.

557 US ISSN 0160-8746
OKLAHOMA. GEOLOGICAL SURVEY.
EDUCATIONAL PUBLICATION. 1971. irreg.
price varies. Oklahoma Geological Survey,
University of Oklahoma, 830 Van Vleet Oval, Room
163, Norman, OK 73019. TEL 405-321-3031. Ed.
Larry N. Stout. circ. 1,200. (reprint service avail.
from UMI)

557 US ISSN 0078-4400
OKLAHOMA. GEOLOGICAL SURVEY.
GUIDEBOOK. 1953. irreg., no.22, 1982. price
varies. Geological Survey, University of Oklahoma,
830 Van Vleet Oval, Rm. 163, Norman, OK 73019.
TEL 405-325-3031. circ. 500. (reprint service avail.
from UMI)

557 US ISSN 0275-0929
OKLAHOMA. GEOLOGICAL SURVEY. SPECIAL
PUBLICATION SERIES. irreg., latest issue, no.85-
3. Geological Survey, University of Oklahoma, 830
Van Vleet Oval, Rm.163, Norman, OK 73019. TEL
405-325-3031. Ed. Connie Smith. (reprint service
avail. from UMI)

ONTARIO. GEOLOGICAL SURVEY. ANNUAL
REPORT OF THE REGIONAL AND RESIDENT
GEOLOGISTS. see *MINES AND MINING
INDUSTRY*

ONTARIO. GEOLOGICAL SURVEY.
GEOLOGICAL REPORT. see *MINES AND
MINING INDUSTRY*

557 622 CN
ONTARIO. GEOLOGICAL SURVEY. GUIDE
BOOKS. 1968. irreg., (approx. 1-2/yr.). price varies.
Geological Survey, 77 Grenville St., Rm. 719,
Toronto, Ont. M7A 1W4, Canada TEL 416-965-
2000. (Ministry of Natural Resources, Public
Service Center Room 1640, Whitney Block, Queen's
Park, Toronto, Ont. M7A 1W3 Canada) (also avail.
in microfiche)
Formerly: Ontario. Division of Mines. Guide
Books.

ONTARIO INSTITUTE OF PEDOLOGY.
DEPARTMENT OF LAND RESOURCE
SCIENCE. PROGRESS REPORT. see
AGRICULTURE — Crop Production And Soil

OPERA LILLOANA. see *BIOLOGY — Botany*

551 US
OREGON. SPECIAL PAPERS. 1978. irreg., latest
1984. price varies. Department of Geology and
Mineral Industries, 910 State Office Bldg., Portland,
OR 97201. TEL 503-229-5580.

557 622 US ISSN 0078-5709
OREGON. STATE DEPARTMENT OF GEOLOGY
AND MINERAL INDUSTRIES. BULLETIN.
1938. irreg., no.102, 1981. price varies. Department
of Geology and Mineral Industries, 910 State Office
Building, Portland, OR 97201. TEL 503-229-5580.

OREGON. STATE DEPARTMENT OF GEOLOGY
AND MINERAL INDUSTRIES. OIL AND GAS
INVESTIGATIONS. see *PETROLEUM AND
GAS*

555 PK ISSN 0078-8163
PAKISTAN. GEOLOGICAL SURVEY. RECORDS.
(Text in English) 1949. irreg. price varies. ‡
Geological Survey of Pakistan, c/o Chief Librarian,
Box 15, Quetta, Pakistan. circ. 1,500.

554 560 UK
PALAEONTOGRAPHICAL SOCIETY.
MONOGRAPHS (LONDON) (Text in English;
summaries in French, German, Russian) 1848. a.
£17 to individuals; institutions £30.
Palaeontographical Society, c/o Secretary, British
Geological Survey, Keyworth, Nottingham NG12
5GG, England. Ed. P.D. Lane. circ. 750. (also avail.
in microfiche; back issues avail.) Indexed:
Biol.Abstr.

PALEOBIOS. see *PALEONTOLOGY*

561 560 US ISSN 0191-6122
PALYNOLOGY. 1977. a. $18. American Association
of Stratigraphic Palynologists Foundation, c/o
Robert T. Clarke, Mobil R & D Corp.-D R L, Box
819047, Dallas, TX 75381. Ed. Douglas J. Nichols.
circ. 950. Indexed: Biol.Abstr. Ocean.Abstr.
Pollut.Abstr. Br.Geol.Lit. Geo.Abstr. GeoRef.
Petrol.Abstr.
Supersedes (as of 1977): Geoscience and Man
(ISSN 0072-1395); Incorporating (1970-1976):
American Association of Stratigraphic Palynologists.
Proceedings of the Annual Meeting (ISSN 0270-
1316)

PETROLEUM GEOLOGY OF TAIWAN/T'AIWAN
SHIH YU TI CHIH. see *PETROLEUM AND GAS*

550 PL ISSN 0079-3396
POLSKA AKADEMIA NAUK. ODDZIAL W
KRAKOWIE. KOMISJA NAUK
MINERALOGICZNYCH. PRACE
MINERALOGICZNE. (Text in English or Polish;
summaries in English or Russian) 1965. irreg.,
no.77, 1986. price varies. Ossolineum, Publishing
House of the Polish Academy of Sciences, Rynek 9,
50-106 Wroclaw, Poland (Dist. by: Ars Polona -
Ruch, Krakowskie Przedmiescie 7, Warsaw, Poland)
Ed. Andrzej Bolewski. Indexed: Chem.Abstr.

EARTH SCIENCES — GEOLOGY

551   PO   ISSN 0037-2730
PORTUGAL. SERVICOS GEOLOGICOS.
COMUNICACOES. (Text and summaries in English, French, Portuguese) 1887. irreg. (1-2/yr.) Servicos Geologicos, Rua Academia das Ciencias 19-2, Lisbon 2, Portugal. circ. 2,000. Indexed: Biol.Abstr. GeoRef.

550 910   PL   ISSN 0137-9771
POZNANSKIE TOWARZYSTWO PRZYJACIOL NAUK. KOMISJA GEOGRAFICZNO-GEOLOGICZNA. PRACE. (Text in Polish; summaries in English) 1936. irreg., vol.20, 1980. price varies. Panstwowe Wydawnictwo Naukowe, Miodowa 10, 00-251 Warsaw, Poland (Dist. by: Ars Polona, Krakowskie Przedmiescie 7, 00-068 Warsaw, Poland) Ed. Andrzej Karczewski. bibl. circ. 400.

550   PL   ISSN 0079-3361
PRACE GEOLOGICZNE. (Text in Polish; summaries in English and Russian) 1960. irreg., no.131, 1986. price varies. (Polska Akademia Nauk, Oddzial w Krakowie, Komisja Nauk Geologicznych) Ossolineum, Publishing House of the Polish Academy of Sciences, Rynek 9, Wroclaw, Poland (Dist. by: Ars Polona-Ruch, Krakowskie Przedmiescie 7, Warsaw, Poland) index. Indexed: GeoRef.

549 550 560   YU   ISSN 0367-4983
PRIRODNJACKI MUZEJ U BEOGRADU. GLASNIK. SERIJA A: MINEROLOGIJA, GEOLOGIJA, PALEONTOLOGIJA. 1948. irreg. Prirodnjacki Muzej u Beogradu, Njegoseva 51, Belgrade, Yugoslavia. Ed. Zivomir Vasic. Indexed: GeoRef.

551   UK   ISSN 0141-3376
PROSPECTING IN AREAS OF GLACIATED TERRAIN. 1973. biennial. £24($60) Institution of Mining and Metallurgy, 44 Portland Place, London W1N 4BR, England. circ. 700.

551   NE
QUANTITATIVE GEOLOGY AND GEOSTATISTICS. 1985. irreg. price varies. D. Reidel Publishing Company, Box 17, 3300 AA Dordrecht, Netherlands.

551   UK   ISSN 0261-9784
QUATERNARY STUDIES. 1981. biennial. £3. City of London Polytechnic, Geography Section, Calcutta House, Old Castle St., London E1 7NT, England. Ed.Bd. illus. charts. circ. 300. Indexed: Br.Archaeol.Abstr. Geo.Abstr.

796.525   AT   ISSN 0155-2880
QUAVER; notes from M.U.C.G. 1977. a. Aus.$1. Macquarie University Caving Group, c/o Macquarie University Sports Association, Macquerie University, N.S.W. 2109, Australia. Ed. David Hamilton. circ. 100.

557   CN   ISSN 0079-8738
QUEBEC (PROVINCE) DEPARTMENT OF NATURAL RESOURCES. GEOLOGICAL REPORTS. (Text in English and French) 1930. irreg. price varies. ‡ Ministere des Richesses Naturelles, Distribution et Documentation, 1620 Bd. de l'Entente, Quebec G1S 4N6, Canada. Ed. R. Gagnon. circ. 800. (also avail. in microfiche)

557   CN   ISSN 0079-8746
QUEBEC (PROVINCE) MINISTERE DES RICHESSES NATURELLES. TRAVAUX SUR LE TERRAIN. 1927. a. price varies. Ministere des Richesses Naturelles, Distribution et Documentation, 1620 Bd. de l'Entente, Quebec G1S 4N6, Canada.

551   SW   ISSN 0348-7377
QUFO. (Text in Swedish) 1979. irreg., no.3, 1985. price varies. Societas Upsaliensis pro Geologia Quaternaria, Department of Quaternary Geology, Box 555, S-751 22 Uppsala, Sweden. Ed. L.K Koeningsson.

551   DK   ISSN 0109-7466
RAASTOFPRODUKTIONEN, HAVOMRAADET; produktionsmaengden fra samtlige optagningslokaliteter samt udloesningssteder og maengder. 1982. a. free. Danmarks Geologiske Undersoegelse, Kvartergeologisk Afdeling, Copenhagen, Denmark.
Formerly: Raastofproduktionsopgoerelse fra Havbunden.

551   DK   ISSN 0109-7474
RAASTOFPRODUKTIONEN, LANDOMRAADET. HANDELSVARER OG ANVENDELSE, GRAVFORHOLD, AREALFORHOLD. 1982. a. free. Danmarks Geologiske Undersoegelse, Kvartergeologisk Afdeling, Copenhagen, Denmark.
Formerly: Raastofproduktionsopgoerelse (ISSN 0109-503X)

551   DK   ISSN 0109-7458
RAASTOFPRODUKTIONEN, LANDOMRAADET. PRODUKTIONSMAENGDEN AF GEOLOGISKE RAASTOFFER FORDELT PAA ANTSKOMMUNER OG KOMMUNER. 1982. a. free. Danmarks Geologiske Undersoegelse, Kvartergeologisk Afdeling, Copenhagen, Denmark.
Formerly: Raastofproduktionsopgoerelse fra Landomraadet.

REAL SOCIEDAD ESPANOLA DE HISTORIA NATURAL. BOLETIN DE GEOLOGIA Y BIOLOGIA. see *BIOLOGY*

551   II
RECENT RESEARCHES IN GEOLOGY. (Text in English) 1973. irreg. price varies. Hindustan Publishing Corp., 6-U.B. Jawahar Nagar, Delhi 110007, India. Indexed: GeoRef.

558   CL   ISSN 0716-0208
REVISTA GEOLOGICA DE CHILE. (Text in Spanish or English; summaries in English or Spanish) 1974. irreg. $8 (or exchange basis) Servicio Nacional de Geologia y Mineria, Casilla 10465, Santiago, Chile. Ed. Ernesto Perez. circ. 1,000. Indexed: Chem.Abstr. GeoRef.

551   RM   ISSN 0556-8102
REVUE ROUMAINE DE GEOLOGIE, GEOPHYSIQUE ET GEOGRAPHIE. GEOLOGIE. (Text in English, French, German and Russian) 1957. a. $32. (Academia Republicii Socialiste Romania) Editura Academiei Republicii Socialiste Romania, Calea Victoriei 125, 79717 Bucharest, Rumania (Subscr. to: ROMPRESFILATELIA, Calea Grivitei 64-66, P.O. Box 12-201, 78104 Bucharest, Rumania) Ed. Dan Giusca. bk. rev. charts. illus. index. Indexed: Chem.Abstr. Geotimes. GeoRef.
Supersedes in part: Revue de Geologie et de Geographie.

554   NE
RIJKS GEOLOGISCHE DIENST. MEDEDELINGEN. (Text in Dutch, English) 1946. irreg., (1-3/yr.) Rijks Geologische Dienst, Postbus 157, 2000 AD Haarlem, Netherlands (Subscr. to: Staatsuitgeverij, Postbus 20014, 2500 EA The Hague, Netherlands) Ed. H.W.J. van Amerom.

ROYAL IRISH ACADEMY. PROCEEDINGS. SECTION B: BIOLOGICAL, GEOLOGICAL AND CHEMICAL SCIENCES. see *BIOLOGY*

550   CS   ISSN 0036-5270
SBORNIK GEOLOGICKYCH VED: ANTROPOZOIKUM/JOURNAL OF GEOLOGICAL SCIENCES: ANTHROPOZOIC. (Text and summaries in Czech, English, French and German) 1951. irreg. Ustredni Ustav Geologicky, Malostranske nam. 19, 118 21 Prague 1, Czechoslovakia (Subscr. to: Artia, Ve Smeckach 30, 111 27 Prague 1, Czechoslovakia) Ed. Jaroslav Tyracek. charts. illus. circ. 600. (back issues avail.) Indexed: Bull.Signal. Chem.Abstr. Ref.Zh. GeoRef.

551   CS   ISSN 0581-9172
SBORNIK GEOLOGICKYCH VED: GEOLOGIE/ JOURNAL OF GEOLOGICAL SCIENCES: GEOLOGY. (Text in Czech, English or German; summaries also in French and Russian) 1921. irreg., (1-3/yr.) Ustredni Ustav Geologicky, Malostranske nam. 19, 118 21 Prague 1, Czechoslovakia (Subscr. to: Artia, Ve Smeckach 30, 111 27 Prague 1, Czechoslovakia) Ed. Zdenek Kukal. charts. illus. maps. circ. 850. Indexed: Bull.Signal. Chem.Abstr. Ref.Zh. GeoRef.

551   CS   ISSN 0581-9180
SBORNIK GEOLOGICKYCH VED: LOZISKOVA GEOLOGIE, MINERALOGIE/JOURNAL OF GEOLOGICAL SCIENCES: ECONOMIC GEOLOGY, MINERALOGY. (Text in Czech, English or German; summaries also in French and Russian) 1963. irreg. Ustredni Ustav Geologicky, Malostranske nam. 19, 118 21 Prague 1, Czechoslovakia (Subscr. to: Artia, Ve Smeckach 30, 111 27 Prague 1, Czechoslovakia) Ed. Joel Pokorny. charts. illus. circ. 600. (back issues avail.) Indexed: Bull.Signal. Chem.Abstr. Ref.Zh. GeoRef.

550   CS   ISSN 0036-5300
SBORNIK GEOLOGICKYCH VED: TECHNOLOGIE, GEOCHEMIE/JOURNAL OF GEOLOGICAL SCIENCES: TECHNOLOGY, GEOCHEMISTRY. (Text in Czech, English or German; summaries in Czech and Russian) 1962. irreg. Ustredni Ustav Geologicky, Malostranske nam. 19, 118 21 Prague 1, Czechoslovakia (Subscr. to: Artia, Ve Smeckach 30, 111 27 Prague 1, Czechoslovakia) (Co-sponsor: Ustav Nerostnych Surovin, Kutna Hora) Ed. Jiri Vtelensky. charts. illus. circ. 600. (back issues avail.) Indexed: Bull.Signal. Chem.Abstr. Ref.Zh. GeoRef.

551   GE   ISSN 0323-8946
SCHRIFTENREIHE FUER GEOLOGISCHE WISSENSCHAFTEN. (Text in English and German; summaries in English, German and Russian) 1974. irreg., vol.24, 1985. price varies. (Vorstand der Gesellschaft fuer Geologische Wissenschaften der D.D.R.) Akademie-Verlag, Leipziger Str. 3-4, 1086 Berlin, E. Germany (D.D.R.) Ed.Bd. Indexed: GeoRef.

551.23   JA   ISSN 0030-2821
SCIENCE OF HOT SPRINGS/ONSEN KAGAKU. (Text in Japanese and European languages; summaries in Japanese and English) 1941. irreg., (3-4/yr.) 4000 Yen. Balneological Society of Japan - Nippon Onsen Kagakukai, c/o Tokyo-toritsu Daigaku Rigakubu Kagaku Kyoshitsu, 2-1 Fukazawa, Setagaya-ku, Tokyo 158, Japan. Ed. Kimio Noguchi. circ. 500.

551 550   FR   ISSN 0335-9255
SCIENCES DE LA TERRE: SERIE INFORMATIQUE GEOLOGIQUE. Cover title: Sciences de la Terre: Informatique Geologique. (Text in English and French) vol. 15, 1980. irreg. price varies. Fondation Scientifique de la Geologie et des ses Applications, 94 Ave. de Lattre, 54000 Nancy, France (Subscribe to: Sciences de la Terre, rue Doyen Roubault, B.P. 40-54501 Vandoeuvre, France.) Ed. J.M. Royer. play rev. circ. 400. (back issues avail.) Indexed: Chem.Abstr. GeoRef.

554   FR   ISSN 0302-2684
SCIENCES GEOLOGIQUES - MEMOIRES. 1929. irreg., 3-4/yr. price varies. Universite Louis Pasteur de Strasbourg, Institut de Geologie, Bibliotheque, 1 rue Blessig, 67084 Strasbourg Cedex, France. Ed. Yves Tardy. adv. bk. rev. circ. 1,000. Indexed: Chem.Abstr. Geo.Abstr. GeoRef.
Formerly: Service de la Carte Geologique d'Alsace et de Lorraine. Memoires (ISSN 0080-9020)

550   CS
SCRIPTA FACULTATIS SCIENTIARUM NATURALIUM UNIVERSITATIS PURKYNIANAE BRUNENSIS: GEOLOGIA. (Text in English, French, German and Russian) 1971. irreg., (1-2/yr.) 13 Kcs. per no. Universita J. E. Purkyne, Prirodovedecka Fakulta, Kotlarska 2, 611 37 Brno, Czechoslovakia. illus.

551   NE   ISSN 0375-7587
SCRIPTA GEOLOGICA. (Text in English; occasionally in French, German or Spanish) 1971. irreg. price varies. Rijksmuseum van Geologie en Mineralogie - Netherlands National Museum of Geology and Mineralogy, Hooglandse Kerkgracht 17, 2312 HS Leiden, Netherlands. Ed.Bd. bibl. charts. illus. circ. 350. Indexed: GeoRef. Mineral.Abstr.

551.3   CN   ISSN 0080-8482
SEDIMENT DATA FOR SELECTED CANADIAN RIVERS. 1965. a. free. Inland Waters Directorate, Environment Canada, Ottawa, Ont. K1A OE7, Canada. TEL 613-997-2540. (also avail. in microfiche) Indexed: Eng.Ind. GeoRef.

551 BL
SEMINARIO BRASILEIRO SOBRE TECNICAS EXPLORATORIAS EM GEOLOGIA. ANAIS. 1976. irreg. Departamento Nacional da Producao Mineral, Av. Pasteur 404, Rio de Janeiro, Brazil.

SHIMABARA EARTHQUAKE AND VOLCANO OBSERVATORY. SCIENCES REPORTS. see *EARTH SCIENCES*

550 CS ISSN 0036-1372
SLOVENSKA AKADEMIA VIED. GEOLOGICKY USTAV D. STURA: ZBORNIK: ZAPADNE KARPATY. (Text in English, German or Slovak; summaries in English or German) irreg., (1-2/yr.) 44 Kcs.($3.50) per no. Veda, Publishing House of the Slovak Academy of Sciences, Klemensova 19, 814 30 Bratislava, Czechoslovakia (Subscr. to: Geologicky Ustav D. Stura, Mlynska Dolina 1, 817 04 Bratislava, Czechoslovakia) Ed. Ondrej Samuel. charts. illus. index. Indexed: Chem.Abstr.
Supersedes: Slovenska Akademia Vied. Geologicky Ustav D. Stura. Geologicke Prace.

558 PE ISSN 0079-1091
SOCIEDAD GEOLOGICA DEL PERU. BOLETIN. (Text in Spanish; summaries in English and French) 1925. irreg. S.5000($8.50) Sociedad Geologica del Peru, Apartado 2559, Lima, Peru. Ed. C. Canepa. adv. bk. rev. cum.index: vols.1-18 (1925-45); vols.19-27 (1946-55) circ. 1,000. Indexed: Biol.Abstr. GeoRef.

796.525 VE ISSN 0583-7731
SOCIEDAD VENEZOLANA DE ESPELEOLOGIA. BOLETIN. (Text in Spanish; summaries in English) 1967. a. Bs.100($5) Sociedad Venezolana de Espeleologia, Apdo. 47334, Caracas 1041A, Venezuela. Ed. M.A. Perera. circ. 1,000. (back issues avail.) Indexed: Biol.Abstr. GeoRef. Speleol.Abstr.
Speleology

SOCIETAT D'HISTORIA NATURAL DE BALEARES. BOLETIN. see *BIOLOGY*

554 FR ISSN 0249-7549
SOCIETE GEOLOGIQUE DE FRANCE. MEMOIRES. irreg. (1-4/yr.) price varies. Societe Geologique de France, 77, rue Claude-Bernard, 75005 Paris, France. Indexed: Biol.Abstr. Br.Geol.Lit. GeoRef.

551 BU
SOFIISKI UNIVERSITET. GEOLOGO-GEOGRAFSKI FAKULTET. GEOLOGIIA. GODISHNIK. (Summaries in English, French and German) 1905. irreg. 2.74 lv. per issue. Sofiiski Universitet, Geologo-Geografski Fakultet, 15, Rouski Blvd., 1000 Sofia, Bulgaria. Ed. N. Nikolova. circ. 580. Indexed: Geo.Abstr.

SOUTH AFRICA. DEPARTMENT OF MINERAL AND ENERGY AFFAIRS. ANNUAL REPORT. see *MINES AND MINING INDUSTRY*

551 SA ISSN 0584-2352
SOUTH AFRICA. GEOLOGICAL SURVEY. ANNALS. 1962. a., latest vol.19, 1985. R.2.50. Geological Survey, Private Bag X112, Pretoria 0001, South Africa. Indexed: GeoRef. Ind.S.A.Per.

551 SA
SOUTH AFRICA. GEOLOGICAL SURVEY. BULLETIN. 1934. irreg., latest no.78. R.2.50. Geological Survey, Private Bag X112, Pretoria 0001, South Africa. Indexed: GeoRef.

550 SA ISSN 0560-9208
SOUTH AFRICA. GEOLOGICAL SURVEY. HANDBOOK. 1959. irreg., latest no.8. price varies. Geological Survey, Private Bag X112, Pretoria 0001, South Africa. Indexed: GeoRef.

551 SA
SOUTH AFRICA. GEOLOGICAL SURVEY. MEMOIRS. 1905. irreg., latest no.71. R.2.50. Geological Survey, Private Bag X112, Pretoria 0001, South Africa. Indexed: GeoRef.

551 SA
SOUTH AFRICA. GEOLOGICAL SURVEY. SEISMOLOGIC SERIES. 1972. irreg., latest no.18. R.2.50. Geological Survey, Private Bag X112, Pretoria 0001, South Africa. Indexed: GeoRef.

551 SA
SOUTH AFRICA. GEOLOGICAL SURVEY. SPECIAL PUBLICATIONS. 1910. irreg., latest no.20. R.2.50 price varies. Geological Survey, Private Bag X112, Pretoria 0001, South Africa. Indexed: GeoRef.

551 AT ISSN 0159-7043
SOUTH AUSTRALIA. DEPARTMENT OF MINES AND ENERGY. ANNUAL REPORT. 1912. a. avail. on exchange basis, free in Australia. Department of Mines and Energy, P.O. Box 151, Eastwood, S. A. 5063, Australia. Indexed: Eng.Ind. GeoRef.

557 US ISSN 0085-6479
SOUTH DAKOTA GEOLOGICAL SURVEY. BULLETIN. 1894. irreg., no.28, 1980. price varies. Geological Survey, Science Center University, Vermillion, SD 57069. circ. controlled. Indexed: GeoRef.

557 US ISSN 0085-6487
SOUTH DAKOTA GEOLOGICAL SURVEY. CIRCULAR. 1917. irreg., no.43, 1976. price varies. Geological Survey, Science Center University, Vermillion, SD 57069. circ. controlled. Indexed: GeoRef.

557 US ISSN 0085-6495
SOUTH DAKOTA GEOLOGICAL SURVEY. REPORTS OF INVESTIGATION. 1929. irreg., no.111, 1974; no 113 in prep. price varies. Geological Survey, Science Center University, Vermillion, SD 57069. circ. controlled. Indexed: Biol.Abstr. GeoRef.

557 US ISSN 0038-3678
SOUTHEASTERN GEOLOGY. 1959. irreg. $11. Duke University, Geology Department, Old Chemistry Bldg., Durham, NC 27706. TEL 919-684-5321. Ed. S. Duncan Heron, Jr. charts. illus. circ. 675. (also avail. in microform from UMI; reprint service avail. from UMI) Indexed: Biol.Abstr. Chem.Abstr. Abstr.N.Amer.Geol. GeoRef. Mineral.Abstr. Petrol.Abstr.

551.44 AT ISSN 0157-8464
SOUTHERN CAVER. 1967. irreg. Aus.$8. Southern Caving Society, Box 121, Moonah, Tas. 7009, Australia. Ed. Steve Harris. adv. bk. rev. circ. 60. Indexed: Geo.Abstr.
Speleology

551 SP
SPAIN. INSTITUTO GEOLOGICO Y MINERO. INFORMES.* irreg. 300 ptas. Instituto Geologico y Minero, Rios Rosas 23, Madrid 3, Spain.

551 US ISSN 0081-4350
STANFORD UNIVERSITY. PUBLICATIONS. GEOLOGICAL SCIENCES. irreg., vol.20, 1986. price varies. Stanford University, School of Earth Sciences, Stanford, CA 94305. TEL 415-723-2544. Indexed: Biol.Abstr. GeoRef.

551 US ISSN 0039-0089
STATE GEOLOGISTS JOURNAL. 1949. a. $5. (Association of American State Geologists) Virginia Division of Mineral Resources, c/o Robert C. Milici, Box 3667, Charlottsville, VA 22903. TEL 804-293-5121. circ. 200. Indexed: GeoRef.

551 SW ISSN 0345-0074
STRIAE; a monograph series for quaternary studies. (Text in English, French and German) 1975. irreg., no.23, 1985. price varies. Societas Upsaliensis pro Geologia Quaternaria, Department of Quaternary Geology, Box 555, S-751 22 Uppsala, Sweden. Ed. Lars-Koenig Koenigsson. Indexed: GeoRef. Geo.Abstr.

551 SW ISSN 0348-4386
STRIOLAE. (Text in English, French and German) 1979. irreg., no.21, 1985. price varies. Societas Upsaliensis pro Geologia Quaternaria, Department of Quaternary Geology, Box 555, S-751 22 Uppsala, Sweden. Indexed: Geo.Abstr.

550 PL ISSN 0081-6426
STUDIA GEOLOGICA POLONICA. (Text in English and Polish) 1958. irreg. price varies. (Polska Akademia Nauk, Oddzial w Krakowie, Komisja Nauk Geologicznych) Wydawnictwa Geologiczne, Rakowiecka 4, 00-975 Warsaw, Poland (Dist. by Ars Polona-Ruch, Krakowskie Przedmiescie 7, Warsaw, Poland) Indexed: Biol.Abstr. Geo.Abstr. Petrol.Abstr.

STUDIA I MATERIALY DO DZIEJOW ZUP SOLNYCH W POLSCE. see *ARCHAEOLOGY*

STUDIA SOCIETATIS SCIENTIARUM TORUNENSIS. SECTIO C (GEOGRAFIA ET GEOLOGIA) see *GEOGRAPHY*

550 910 RM ISSN 0039-341X
STUDIA UNIVERSITATIS "BABES-BOLYAI". GEOLOGIA. GEOGRAPHIA. (Text in Rumanian; summaries in English, French, German and Russian) 1958. a. exchange basis. Universitatea "Babes-Bolyai", Biblioteca Centrala Universitara, Str.Clinicilor. Nr. 2, Cluj-Napoca, Rumania. charts. illus. maps. index. Indexed: Biol.Abstr. Chem.Abstr. GeoRef.

551.44 UK ISSN 0585-718X
STUDIES IN SPELEOLOGY. 1964. a. £12 to non-members. William Pengelly Cave Studies Trust Ltd., 107 Andover Rd., Newbury, Berks. RG14 6JH, England. Ed. R.G. Cooper. adv. bk. rev. index. circ. 600. Indexed: Biol.Abstr. Br.Archaeol.Abstr. GeoRef.

551 RM
STUDII SI CERCETARI DE GEOLOGIE, GEOFIZICA SI GEOGRAPHIE. GEOLOGIE/ STUDIES AND RESEARCH IN GEOLOGY, GEOPHYSICS AND GEOGRAPHY. GEOLOGY. vol. 25, 1980. a. 60 lei($32) (Academia Republicii Socialiste Romania) Editura Academiei Republicii Socialiste Rumania, Calea Victoriei 125, 79717 Bucharest, Rumania (Subscr. to: ROMPRESFILATELIA, Calea Grivitei 64-66, P.O. Box 12-201, 78104 Bucharest, Rumania) Ed. Dan Giusca.

556 622 SQ ISSN 0081-9999
SWAZILAND. GEOLOGICAL SURVEY AND MINES DEPARTMENT. ANNUAL REPORT. 1947. a. ‡ Geological Survey and Mines Department, P.O. Box 9, Mbabane, Swaziland. Ed. Aminah Mohammed. circ. 500. Indexed: GeoRef.

556 622 SQ ISSN 0082-0008
SWAZILAND. GEOLOGICAL SURVEY AND MINES DEPARTMENT. BULLETIN. 1961. a. price varies. ‡ Geological Survey and Mines Department, P.O. Box 9, Mbabane, Swaziland. Ed. Aminah Mohammed. circ. 500. Indexed: GeoRef.

538.7 SW ISSN 0075-403X
SWEDEN. SVERIGES GEOLOGISKA UNDERSOEKNING. JORDMAGNETISKA PUBLIKATIONER/GEOMAGNETIC PUBLICATIONS. (Text in English) 1919; N.S. 1981. irreg. Kr.50. Sveriges Geologiska Undersoekning - Geological Survey of Sweden, Box 670, S-751 28 Uppsala, Sweden.

554 SW ISSN 0082-0024
SWEDEN. SVERIGES GEOLOGISKA UNDERSOEKNING. SERIE C. AVHANDLINGAR OCH UPPSATSER/ MEMOIRS AND NOTICES. (Text in Swedish, English and German; summaries in English) 1868. irreg., no.777, 1981. price varies. Sveriges Geologiska Undersoekning - Geological Survey of Sweden, Box 670, S-751 28 Uppsala, Sweden. cum.index: 1858-1958.

554 SW ISSN 0082-0016
SWEDEN. SVERIGES GEOLOGISKA UNDERSOEKNING. SERIE CA. AVHANDLINGAR OCH UPPSATSER I KVARTO/NOTICES IN QUARTO AND FOLIO. 1900. irreg., no.50, 1980. price varies. Sveriges Geologiska Undersoekning - Geological Survey of Sweden, Box 670, S-751 28 Uppsala, Sweden.

551.44 AT
SYDNEY SPELEOLOGICAL SOCIETY. OCCASIONAL PAPER. 1965. irreg. price varies. ‡ Sydney Speleological Society, P.O. Box 198, Broadway, Sydney, N.S.W. 2007, Australia. Ed. Ross Ellis. circ. 2,600. Indexed: Aus.Speleo Abstr. GeoRef.
Formerly: Sydney Speleological Society. Communications (ISSN 0085-7017)

559.4 AT ISSN 0082-2043
TASMANIA. DEPARTMENT OF MINES. GEOLOGICAL SURVEY BULLETINS. 1907. irreg., no.62, 1986. price varies. Department of Mines, Geological Survey of Tasmania, Box 56, Rosny Park, Tasmania, Australia 7018. Ed. E.L. Martin. circ. 300. Indexed: GeoRef.

EARTH SCIENCES — GEOLOGY

551 560 NE
TERTIARY RESEARCH SPECIAL PAPERS. irreg. (1-2/yr.) (Tertiary Research Group, UK) E.J. Brill, P.O. Box 9000, 2300 PA Leiden, Netherlands. Indexed: Biol.Abstr. GeoRef.
Formerly: Tertiary Research Group. Special Papers (ISSN 0308-7506)

THALASSAS; revista de ciencias del mar. see BIOLOGY

551 560 JA ISSN 0082-4658
TOHOKU UNIVERSITY. INSTITUTE OF GEOLOGY AND PALEONTOLOGY. CONTRIBUTIONS/TOHOKU DAIGAKU RIGAKUBU CHISHITSUGAKU KOSEIBUTSUGAKU KYOSHITSU KENKYU HOBUN HOKOKU. (Text in Japanese; summaries in English) 1921. irreg., no.87, 1985. available on exchange. Tohoku University, Institute of Geology and Paleontology - Tohoku Daigaku Rigakubu Chishitsugaku Koseibutsugaku Kyoshitsu, Aobayama, Sendai 980, Japan. Ed.Bd. circ. 750. Indexed: Biol.Abstr. GeoRef.

551 560 JA ISSN 0082-464X
TOHOKU UNIVERSITY. INSTITUTE OF GEOLOGY AND PALEONTOLOGY. SCIENCE REPORTS. SECOND SERIES. (Text and summaries in English) 1912. irreg., vol. 57, no.1, 1986. exhange. Tohoku University, Institute of Geology and Paleontology - Tohoku Daigaku Rigakubu Chishitsugaku Koseibutsugaku Kyoshitsu, Aobayama, Sendai 980, Japan. Ed.Bd. circ. 750.

551 574 US
TOPICS IN GEOBIOLOGY. a. price varies. Plenum Publishing Corp., 233 Spring St., New York, NY 10013. TEL 212-620-8047. Ed. Francis G. Stehli.

551 SP ISSN 0474-9588
TRABAJOS DE GEOLOGIA. 1967. a. price varies. Universidad de Oviedo, Facultad de Geologia, 33005 Oviedo, Spain (Subscr. to: Servicio de Publicaciones, Un. de Oviedo, Calle Arias de Velasco s/n, 33005 Oviedo, Spain) Ed. Maria Martinez Chacon. abstr. illus. circ. 1,000. Indexed: Biol.Abstr. Bull.Sign. Georef. Zool.Rec.

TRAPANANDA. see HISTORY — History Of North And South America

TURUN YLIOPISTO. JULKAISUJA. SARJA A. II. BIOLOGICA- GEOGRAPHICA- GEOLOGICA. see BIOLOGY

556 UG ISSN 0082-7215
UGANDA. GEOLOGICAL SURVEY AND MINES DEPARTMENT. ANNUAL REPORT. a., latest 1973. price varies. Geological Survey and Mines Department, P.O. Box 9, Entebbe, Uganda.

557 US ISSN 0083-1093
U.S. GEOLOGICAL SURVEY. BULLETIN. 1883. irreg. U.S. Geological Survey, 12201 Sunrise Valley Dr., Reston, VA 22092 TEL 703-860-7000. (Orders to: 604 S. Pickett St., Alexandria, VA 22304) Indexed: Geo.Abstr.

557 US
U.S. GEOLOGICAL SURVEY. PROFESSIONAL PAPERS. no. 845, 1974. irreg., no. 1200, 1982. U.S. Geological Survey, 12201 Sunrise Valley Drive, Reston, VA 22092 TEL 703-860-7000. (Orders to: 604 S. Pickett St., Alexandria, VA 22304) Indexed: Bibl.Cart. Geo.Abstr.

557 US ISSN 0162-9484
U.S. GEOLOGICAL SURVEY. YEARBOOK. a. U.S. Geological Survey, 2201 Sunrise Valley Dr., Reston, VA 22092 TEL 703-860-7000. (Orders to: 604 S. Pickett St., Alexandria, VA 22304) Indexed: GeoRef.
Formerly: U.S. Geological Survey. Annual Report (ISSN 0147-8478)

551 669 MX
UNIVERSIDAD AUTONOMA DE SAN LUIS POTOSI. INSTITUTO DE GEOLOGIA Y METALURGIA. FOLLETO TECNICO. irreg., no.104, 1985. Universidad Autonoma de San Luis Potosi, Instituto de Geologia y Metalurgia, Av. Dr. Manuel Nava 5, San Luis Potosi S.L.P., Mexico. Indexed: Chem.Abstr.

550 CK ISSN 0120-0283
UNIVERSIDAD INDUSTRIAL DE SANTANDER. BOLETIN DE GEOLOGIA. (Text in Spanish, occasionally in English and French) 1958. irreg. $3 or exchange basis. Universidad Industrial de Santander, Biblioteca, Apdo. Aereo 678, Bucaramanga, Santander, Colombia. abstr. charts. illus. circ. 1,200. Indexed: Biol.Abstr. Chem.Abstr.

UNIVERSIDAD NACIONAL DE ROSARIO. FACULTAD DE CIENCIAS, INGENIERIA Y ARQUITECTURA. INSTITUTO DE FISIOGRAFIA Y GEOLOGIA. PUBLICACIONES. see GEOGRAPHY

558 BL
UNIVERSIDADE DE SAO PAULO. INSTITUTO DE GEOGRAFIA, SEDIMENTOLOGIA E PEDOLOGIA. (Summaries in English and French) 1971. irreg., (approx. 2-3/yr.) Universidade de Sao Paulo, Instituto de Geografia, Sedimentologia e Pedologia, Cidade Universitaria, C.P. 20715, 05508 Sao Paulo-SP, Brazil. Ed. Lylian Coltrinari. circ. 400.

551 560 IT
UNIVERSITA DEGLI STUDI DI FERRARA. ISTITUTO DI GEOLOGIA. ANNALI. SEZIONE 9. SCIENZE GEOLOGICHE. (Text in Engish, French or Italian) 1951. irreg., vol. 5, no.13, 1978. exchange basis. Universita degli Studi di Ferrara, Istuto di Geologia, C.So Ercole 1 d'Este 32, Ferrara, Italy. index. circ. 450.
Formerly: Universite degli Studi di Ferrara. Istituto di Geologia, Paleontologia e Paleontologia Umana. Annali. Sezione 9. Scienze Geologiche (ISSN 0071-4550)

554 560 IT
UNIVERSITA DEGLI STUDI DI FERRARA. ISTITUTO DI GEOLOGIA. PUBBLICAZIONI. (Text in English, French or Italian) 1950. a. available on exchange. Universita degli Studi di Ferrara, Istituto di Geologia, C.So Ercole 1 d' Este, 32, Ferrara, Italy. index. circ. 450.
Formerly: Universite degli Studi di Ferrara. Istituto di Geologia, Paleontologia e Paleontologia Umana. Pubblicazioni (ISSN 0071-4577)

554 IT
UNIVERSITA DEGLI STUDI DI NAPOLI. ISTITUTO DI GEOLOGIA APPLICATA. MEMORIE E NOTE. 1948. irreg. free. Universita degli Studi di Napoli, Istituto di Geologia Applicata, Naples, Italy. illus.

554 560 GW ISSN 0072-1115
UNIVERSITAET HAMBURG. GEOLOGISCH-PALAEONTOLOGISCHES INSTITUT. MITTEILUNGEN. (Text in German and English) 1948. a. DM.20($5) Universitaet Hamburg, Geologisch-Palaeontologisches Institut, Bundesstr. 55, 2000 Hamburg 13, W. Germany (B.R.D.) Ed. Gero Hillmer. Indexed: Biol.Abstr.

554 AU
UNIVERSITAET INNSBRUCK. ALPENKUNDLICHE STUDIEN. (Subseries of: Universitaet Innsbruck. Veroeffentlichungen) 1968. irreg., vol. 10, 1972. price varies. Oesterreichische Kommissionsbuchhandlung, Maximilianstrasse 17, A-6020 Innsbruck, Austria. Ed. Franz Fliri.

551 GW
UNIVERSITAET KIEL. GEOLOGISCH-PALAEONTOLOGISCHES INSTITUT. BERICHTE. 1983. irreg., vol.16, 1986. price varies. Universitaet Kiel, Geologisch-Palaeontologisches Institut, Olshausenstr. 40, D-2300 Kiel, W. Germany (B.R.D.)

554 GW ISSN 0069-5874
UNIVERSITAET ZU KOELN. GEOLOGISCHES INSTITUT. SONDERVEROEFFENTLICHUNGEN. (Text in German; summaries in English) 1956. irreg., 1986, no.51. price varies. Universitaet zu Koeln, Geologisches Institut, Zuelpicher Str. 49, 5000 Cologne 41, W. Germany (B.R.D.) Ed. E. Kempf.

550 RM ISSN 0379-7902
UNIVERSITATEA "AL. I. CUZA" DIN IASI. ANALELE STIINTIFICE. GEOLOGIE-GEOGRAFIE. (Text in Rumanian, English, French, Russian) 1955. a. 35 lei. Universitatea "Al. I. Cuza" din Iasi, Calea 23 August Nr. 11, Jassy, Rumania (Subscr. to: ILEXIM, Str. 13 Decembrie Nr.3, P.O. Box 136-137, Bucharest, Rumania) Eds. V. Erhan, I. Donisa. circ. 350.
Formed by the merger of: Universitatea "Al. I. Cuza" din Iasi. Analele Stiintifice. Sectiunea 2b: Geologie (ISSN 0075-3521); Universitatea "Al. I. Cuza" din Iasi. Analele Stiintifice. Sectiunea 2c: Geografie.

551 TU ISSN 0253-1216
UNIVERSITE D'ANKARA. FACULTE DES SCIENCES. COMMUNICATIONS. SERIE C1. GEOLOGIE. (Text in English, French and German) 1947. a. exchange basis. University of Ankara, Faculty of Sciences, Besevler, Ankara, Turkey. circ. 250. (back issues avail.) Indexed: Biol.Abstr.

554 549 FR ISSN 0069-4711
UNIVERSITE DE CLERMONT-FERRAND II. ANNALES SCIENTIFIQUES. SERIE GEOLOGIE ET MINERALOGIE. 1959. irreg. price varies. Universite de Clermont-Ferrand II, Unite d'Enseignement et de Recherche de Sciences Exactes et Naturelles, B.P. 45, 63170 Aubiere, France. circ. 250. (back issues avail.)

557 CN
UNIVERSITY OF BRITISH COLUMBIA. DEPARTMENT OF GEOLOGICAL SCIENCES. REPORT. 1962. irreg., no.18, 1987. Can.$3 per no. or on exchange basis. ‡ University of British Columbia, Department of Geological Sciences, Vancouver, B.C. V6T 2B4, Canada. TEL 604-228-2211. Ed. W.R. Danner. circ. 400.
Formerly: University of British Columbia. Department of Geology. Report (ISSN 0068-1733)

556 SA ISSN 0250-216X
UNIVERSITY OF CAPE TOWN. DEPARTMENT OF GEOLOGY. PRECAMBRIAN RESEARCH UNIT. ANNUAL REPORT. 1963. a. University of Cape Town, Department of Geology. Precambrian Research Unit, Rondebosch 7700, South Africa. Ed. P. Joubert. circ. 400.

556 SA
UNIVERSITY OF CAPE TOWN. DEPARTMENT OF GEOLOGY. PRECAMBRIAN RESEARCH UNIT. BULLETIN. 1965. irreg., no.33, 1984. exchange basis only. University of Cape Town, Department of Geology. Precambrian Research Unit, Rondebosch 7700, South Africa. bibl. charts. circ. 375.

551 US
UNIVERSITY OF TEXAS AT AUSTIN. BUREAU OF ECONOMIC GEOLOGY. SPECIAL PUBLICATIONS. irreg. $12.50. University of Texas at Austin, Bureau of Economic Geology, University Sta., Box X, Austin, TX 78713.

553 557 US ISSN 0082-3287
UNIVERSITY OF TEXAS, AUSTIN. BUREAU OF ECONOMIC GEOLOGY. ANNUAL REPORT. 1960. a. free. University of Texas at Austin, Bureau of Economic Geology, University Station, Box X, Austin, TX 78713. TEL 512-471-1534. (reprint service avail. from UMI) Indexed: GeoRef.

557 US ISSN 0082-3309
UNIVERSITY OF TEXAS, AUSTIN. BUREAU OF ECONOMIC GEOLOGY. GEOLOGICAL CIRCULAR. 1965. irreg., no.85-5. price varies. University of Texas at Austin, Bureau of Economic Geology, University Station, Box X, Austin, TX 78713. TEL 512-471-7721. (reprint service avail. from UMI)

557 US ISSN 0363-4132
UNIVERSITY OF TEXAS, AUSTIN. BUREAU OF ECONOMIC GEOLOGY. GUIDEBOOK. 1958. irreg, no.21, 1984. price varies. University of Texas at Austin, Bureau of Economic Geology, University Station, Box X, Austin, TX 78713. TEL 512-471-7721. (reprint service avail. from UMI)
Formerly: University of Texas. Bureau of Economic Geology. Guidebook (ISSN 0082-3295)

553 US ISSN 0082-3333
UNIVERSITY OF TEXAS, AUSTIN. BUREAU OF ECONOMIC GEOLOGY. MINERAL RESOURCE CIRCULARS. 1930. irreg., no.77, 1985. price varies. University of Texas at Austin, Bureau of Economic Geology, University Station, Box X, Austin, TX 78713. TEL 512-471-7721. (back issues avail.; reprint service avail. from UMI) Indexed: Geo.Abstr.

557 US ISSN 0082-335X
UNIVERSITY OF TEXAS, AUSTIN. BUREAU OF ECONOMIC GEOLOGY. REPORT OF INVESTIGATIONS. 1946. irreg., no.148, 1985. price varies. University of Texas at Austin, Bureau of Economic Geology, University Station, Box X, Austin, TX 78713. TEL 512-471-7721. (reprint service avail. from UMI) Indexed: Geo.Abstr.

550 PK
UNIVERSITY OF THE PUNJAB. INSTITUTE OF GEOLOGY. GEOLOGICAL BULLETIN. (Text in English) 1961. irreg., no. 19, 1984. Rs.50. University of the Punjab, Institute of Geology, New Campus, Lahore, Pakistan. Ed. F.A. Shams. bk. rev. circ. controlled. (back issues avail.) Indexed: Biol.Abstr. Mineral.Abstr.

559.8 597 551.9 NZ ISSN 0110-2192
UNIVERSITY OF WAIKATO. ANTARCTIC RESEARCH UNIT. REPORT. 1972. a. free. University of Waikato, Private Bag, Hamilton, New Zealand. circ. 350. Indexed: Chem.Abstr. GeoRef.

550 PL ISSN 0083-4238
UNIWERSYTET IM. ADAMA MICKIEWICZA W POZNANIU. WYDZIAL BIOLOGII I NAUK OF ZIEMI. PRACE. SERIA GEOLOGIA. 1961. irreg. price varies. Adam Mickiewicz University Press, Marchlewskiego 128, 61-874 Poznan, Poland.

796.525 PL ISSN 0208-5534
UNIWERSYTET SLASKI W KATOWICACH. GEOLOGY. (Text in Polish; summaries in English, Russian) 1977. irreg. price varies. Uniwersytet Slaski w Katowicach, Ul. Bankowa 14, 40-007 Katowice, Poland.

551 SW
UPPSALA UNIVERSITET. GEOLOGICAL INSTITUTION. BULLETIN. (Subseries of Acta Universitatis Upsaliensis) (Text in English) N.S. 1970. irreg. price varies. Almqvist & Wiksell International, Box 62, S-101 20 Stockholm, Sweden. Eds. Bengt Collini, Richard A. Reyment. bibl. charts. illus. Indexed: Biol.Abstr.

557 553 US ISSN 0098-4825
UTAH GEOLOGICAL AND MINERAL SURVEY. BULLETIN. no. 35, 1948. irreg., no. 118, 1982. price varies. Geological and Mineral Survey, 606 Black Hawk Way, Salt Lake City, UT 84108. TEL 801-581-6831. illus. Indexed: Chem.Abstr. GeoRef. Key Title: Bulletin - Utah Geological and Mineral Survey.

557 553 US
UTAH GEOLOGICAL AND MINERAL SURVEY. SPECIAL STUDIES. 1962. irreg., no.55, 1981. price varies. Geological and Mineral Survey, 606 Black Hawk Way, Salt Lake City, UT 84108. TEL 801-581-6831. Indexed: GeoRef.

557 US ISSN 0083-484X
UTAH GEOLOGICAL ASSOCIATION. ANNUAL GUIDEBOOK. (Not published 1978) 1971. a. price varies. Utah Geological Association, Box 11334, Salt Lake City, UT 84147 TEL 801-531-2331. (Dist. by: Utah Geological and Mineral Survey, 606 Black Hawk Way, Salt Lake City, UT 84108) Ed. Richard S. Kopp. adv. circ. 850.

559 NN
VANUATU. GEOLOGICAL SURVEY. ANNUAL REPORTS. 1964. a. price varies. Vanuatu Geological Survey, G. P. O., Port Vila, Vanuatu. Indexed: Geo.Abstr. GeoRef.
Former titles: New Hebrides. Condominium Geological Survey. Annual Reports & New Hebrides. Anglo-French Condominium Geological Survey. Annual Reports (ISSN 0077-8435).

559 NN ISSN 0077-8443
VANUATU. GEOLOGICAL SURVEY. REPORTS. (Numbering of reports has been discontinued) 1966. irreg. price varies. Vanuatu Geological Survey, G. P. O., Port Vila, Vanuatu.
Formerly: New Hebrides. Condominium Geological Survey. Report.

557 US ISSN 0083-5757
VERMONT. GEOLOGICAL SURVEY. BULLETIN. 1950-1969 (no.31); resumed 1984. irreg., no. 32, 1984. Geological Survey, Montpelier, VT 05602 TEL 802-828-3261. (Order from: Vermont Dept. of Libraries, 111 State St., Montpelier, VT 05602) Indexed: Biol.Abstr. GeoRef.

559.4 AT ISSN 0085-7750
VICTORIA, AUSTRALIA. GEOLOGICAL SURVEY. BULLETIN. 1903. irreg. price varies. ‡ Geological Survey of Victoria, Department of Industry, Technology and Resources, P.O. Box 173, East Melbourne, Vic. 3002, Australia. circ. 750. Indexed: GeoRef.

559.4 AT ISSN 0085-7769
VICTORIA, AUSTRALIA. GEOLOGICAL SURVEY. MEMOIRS. 1903. irreg. price varies. ‡ Geological Survey of Victoria, Dept. of Industry, Technology & Resources, P.O. Box 173, East Melbourne, Vic. 3002, Australia. circ. 750. Indexed: Biol.Abstr. GeoRef.

559.4 AT ISSN 0810-6959
VICTORIA, AUSTRALIA. GEOLOGICAL SURVEY. REPORTS. 1968. irreg. price varies. Geological Survey of Victoria, Dept. of Industry, Technology & Resources, P.O. Box 173, East Melbourne, Vic. 3002, Australia.

VIRGINIA. DIVISION OF MINERAL RESOURCES. REPORTS. see *MINES AND MINING INDUSTRY*

557 US ISSN 0507-1259
VIRGINIA POLYTECHNIC INSTITUTE AND STATE UNIVERSITY. DEPARTMENT OF GEOLOGICAL SCIENCES. GEOLOGICAL GUIDEBOOKS. 1961. irreg., no.9, 1973. price varies. Virginia Polytechnic Institute and State University, Department of Geological Sciences, 4044 Derring Hall, Blacksburg, VA 24061. TEL 703-961-6521. circ. controlled. (back issues avail.) Indexed: GeoRef.
Continues: Virginia Polytechnic Institute, Blacksburg. Engineering Extension Division. Geological Guidebook.

551 552 IC ISSN 0376-2599
VISINDAFELAG ISLENDINGA RIT. (Text in English) 1923. irreg. price varies. Societas Scientiarum Islandica, University of Iceland, Haskolabokasafn - University Library, 101 Reykjavik, Iceland (Subscr. to: Bokaverslun Sigfusar Eymundssonar, Austurstraeti 18, 101 Reykjavik, Iceland) Indexed: Biol.Abstr.

526 BU ISSN 0324-1114
VISSHA GEODEZIIA. (Text in various languages) 1975. irreg. 1.10 lv. per no. (Bulgarska Akademiia na Naukite) Publishing House of the Bulgarian Academy of Sciences, Acad. G. Boncev St., Bldg. 6, 1113 Sofia, Bulgaria. circ. 480.

551 US
WASHINGTON. DEPARTMENT OF NATURAL RESOURCES. REPORT OF INVESTIGATIONS. 1926. irreg. price varies. Geology and Earth Resources Division, Olympia, WA 98504. Ed. Katherine Reed.

557 622 US
WASHINGTON (STATE). DIVISION OF GEOLOGY AND EARTH RESOURCES. BULLETIN. 1910. irreg., no.76, 1983. price varies. Department of Natural Resources, Division of Geology and Earth Resources, Olympia, WA 98504. TEL 206-459-6372. (back issues avail.)

WASHINGTON (STATE). DIVISION OF GEOLOGY AND EARTH RESOURCES. INFORMATION CIRCULAR. see *MINES AND MINING INDUSTRY*

551.44 UK ISSN 0083-811X
WESSEX CAVE CLUB OCCASIONAL PUBLICATION. 1967. irreg. (approx. 1/yr.) price varies. ‡ Wessex Cave Club, Priddy, Wells, Somerset BA5 3AX, England. bk. rev. index. circ. 300. Indexed: GeoRef.
Speleology

557 US
WEST TEXAS GEOLOGICAL SOCIETY. FIELDTRIP GUIDEBOOK. a. West Texas Geological Society, Box 1595, Midland, TX 79702. TEL 915-683-1573.

557 US
WEST TEXAS GEOLOGICAL SOCIETY. PUBLICATIONS. 1939. a. West Texas Geological Society, Box 1595, Midland, TX 79702. TEL 915-683-1573. adv. Indexed: GeoRef.

551 US
WEST VIRGINIA. GEOLOGICAL AND ECONOMIC SURVEY. ANNUAL REPORT. 1987. a. free. Geological and Economic Survey, Box 879, Morgantown, WV 26507-0879. Ed. Fred Schroyer. circ. 500.

557 US
WEST VIRGINIA REPORTS OF GEOLOGIC INVESTIGATIONS. 1947. irreg. ‡ Geological and Economic Survey, Box 879, Morgantown, WV 26507-0879.
Former titles: West Virginia Geologic Investigations; West Virginia Geological Survey. Reports of Investigations (ISSN 0083-8543)

557 551.48 US
WEST VIRGINIA RIVER BASIN BULLETINS. 1968. irreg. ‡ Geological and Economic Survey, Box 879, Morgantown, WV 26507-0879.
Formerly: West Virginia Geological Survey. River Basin Bulletins (ISSN 0083-856X)

559.4 AT ISSN 0085-8137
WESTERN AUSTRALIA. GEOLOGICAL SURVEY. BULLETIN. 1896. irreg. price varies. Geological Survey of Western Australia, Rm. 501, 66 Adelaide Tce., Perth, W.A. 6000, Australia. (also avail. in microfiche; back issues avail.) Indexed: GeoRef.

559.4 AT ISSN 0085-8145
WESTERN AUSTRALIA. GEOLOGICAL SURVEY. REPORT. 1969. irreg. price varies. Geological Survey of Western Australia, 66 Adelaide Tce., Perth, W.A. 6000, Australia. Indexed: GeoRef.

557 US
WISCONSIN. GEOLOGICAL AND NATURAL HISTORY SURVEY. BULLETIN. 1898. irreg., no. 89, 1982. price varies. Geological and Natural History Survey, University of Wisconsin, 3817 Mineral Point Rd., Madison, WI 53705. TEL 608-262-1705. Indexed: Biol.Abstr.

551 US
WISCONSIN. GEOLOGICAL AND NATURAL HISTORY SURVEY. FIELD TRIP GUIDE BOOKS. 1978. irreg., no. 11, 1984. price varies. Geological and Natural History Survey, University of Wisconsin, 3817 Mineral Point Rd., Madison, WI 53705. TEL 608-262-1705.

557 US
WISCONSIN. GEOLOGICAL AND NATURAL HISTORY SURVEY. GEOSCIENCE EDUCATIONAL SERIES. 1977 no. 2, 1961. irreg., no. 27, 1983. $4. Geological and Natural History Survey, University of Wisconsin, 3817 Mineral Point Rd., Madison, WI 53705. TEL 608-262-1705.
Supersedes (1953-1976?): Wisconsin. Geological and Natural History Survey. Geoscience Information Series.

557 US ISSN 0512-0640
WISCONSIN. GEOLOGICAL AND NATURAL HISTORY SURVEY. INFORMATION CIRCULARS. 1955. irreg., no.45, 1983. price varies. Geological and Natural History Survey, University of Wisconsin, 3817 Mineral Point Rd., Madison, WI 53705-4096. TEL 608-262-1705.

EARTH SCIENCES — GEOPHYSICS

557 US
WISCONSIN. GEOLOGICAL AND NATURAL HISTORY SURVEY. PROGRAMS AND ACTIVITIES. 1854. biennial. free. Geological and Natural History Survey, 3817 Mineral Point Rd., Madison, WI 53705.
Former titles, until 1984: Wisconsin. Geological and Natural History Survey. Biennial Report; 1854-1880: Wisconsin Geological Survey. Annual Report.

557 US ISSN 0512-0659
WISCONSIN. GEOLOGICAL AND NATURAL HISTORY SURVEY. SPECIAL REPORT. 1967. irreg., no. 7, 1981. price varies. Geological and Natural History Survey, University of Wisconsin, 3817 Mineral Point Rd., Madison, WI 53705. TEL 608-262-1705.

557 US
WYOMING. GEOLOGICAL SURVEY. BULLETIN. 1911. irreg., no.66, 1986. price varies. Geological Survey of Wyoming, Box 3008, University Sta., Laramie, WY 82071. TEL 307-766-2286. Indexed: GeoRef.

557 US
WYOMING. GEOLOGICAL SURVEY. PUBLIC INFORMATION CIRCULARS. 1976. irreg., no.26, 1986. price varies. Geological Survey of Wyoming, Box 3008, University Sta., Laramie, WY 82071.

557 US
WYOMING. GEOLOGICAL SURVEY. REPORT OF INVESTIGATIONS. 1934. irreg., no.36, 1986. price varies. Geological Survey of Wyoming, Box 3008, University Sta., Laramie, WY 82071. TEL 307-766-2286.

551 US ISSN 0096-9842
WYOMING MINERAL YEARBOOK. 1971. a. free. Economic Development and Stabilization Board, Mineral Division, Herschler Bldg., Cheyenne, WY 82002. TEL 307-777-7284. Eds. John T. Goodier, Dale Hoffman. circ. 1,000.

556 ZA ISSN 0084-473X
ZAMBIA. GEOLOGICAL SURVEY. ANNUAL REPORTS. 1951. a. K.4. Geological Survey, P.O. Box R.W. 50135, Lusaka, Zambia (Avail. from: Government Printer, Box 30136, Lusaka, Zambia) Indexed: GeoRef.

556 ZA ISSN 0084-4748
ZAMBIA. GEOLOGICAL SURVEY. ECONOMIC REPORTS. 1964. irreg. price varies. Geological Survey, P.O. Box R.W. 50135, Lusaka, Zambia. Indexed: GeoRef.

556 ZA ISSN 0084-4756
ZAMBIA. GEOLOGICAL SURVEY. OCCASIONAL PAPERS. irreg., latest no.121. price varies. ‡ Geological Survey, P.O. Box R.W. 50135, Lusaka, Zambia. Indexed: GeoRef.

556 ZA ISSN 0084-4764
ZAMBIA. GEOLOGICAL SURVEY. REPORTS. 1954. irreg., latest no.69. price varies. Geological Survey, P.O. Box R.W. 50135, Lusaka, Zambia. Indexed: GeoRef.
Accounts of regional mapping

556 ZA
ZAMBIA. GEOLOGICAL SURVEY. TECHNICAL REPORTS. irreg., latest no.101. price varies. Geological Survey, Box R.W. 50135, Lusaka, Zambia. Indexed: GeoRef.

ZIMBABWE. MINISTRY OF ENERGY AND WATER RESOURCES AND DEVELOPMENT. HYDROLOGICAL SUMMARIES. see *ENGINEERING — Hydraulic Engineering*

ZITTELIANA; Abhandlungen der Bayerischen Staatssammlung fuer Palaeontologie und historische Geologie. see *PALEONTOLOGY*

EARTH SCIENCES — Geophysics

551 UR ISSN 0065-0080
A.I. VOEIKOV MAIN GEOPHYSICAL OBSERVATORY, LENINGRAD. DATA OF MEASUREMENTS OF ELECTRIC FIELD STRENGTH OF THE ATMOSPHERE AT VARIOUS ALTITUDES BY THE RESULTS OF SOUNDINGS. (Text and tables in English and Russian) irreg. Glavnaya Geofizicheskaya Observatoriya im. A.I. Voeikova, Karbysheva, 7, Leningrad K-18, Russian S.F.S.R., U.S.S.R.

551 UR ISSN 0065-0099
A.I. VOEIKOV MAIN GEOPHYSICAL OBSERVATORY, LENINGRAD. RESULTS OF GROUND OBSERVATIONS OF ATMOSPHERIC ELECTRICITY. ADDITIONAL ISSUE. (Text and tables in English and Russian) a. Glavnaya Geofizicheskaya Observatoriya im. A.I. Voeikova, Karbysheva, 7, Leningrad K-18, Russian S.F.S.R., U.S.S.R.

551 SW ISSN 0072-4815
ACTA REGIAE SOCIETATIS SCIENTIARUM ET LITTERARUM GOTHOBURGENSIS. GEOPHYSICA. (Text in various languages) 1968. irreg., latest no.2, 1969. price varies; also exchange basis. Kungliga Vetenskaps- och Vitterhets-Samhaellet i Goeteborg, c/o Goeteborgs Universitetsbibliotek, P.O. Box 5096, S-402 22 Goeteborg, Sweden (Dist. in U.S., Canada and Mexico by: Humanities Press, Inc., 171 First Ave., Atlantic Highlands, NJ 07716)
Supersedes in part: Goeteborgs Kungliga Vetenskaps- och Vitterhets-Samhaelle. Handlingar.

551 US ISSN 0065-2687
ADVANCES IN GEOPHYSICS. 1952. irreg., vol.29, 1986. Academic Press, Inc., Orlando, FL 32887. TEL 305-345-2000. Ed. Barry Saltzman. index. Indexed: Fuel & Energy Abstr. Petrol.Abstr.

ALASKA. DIVISION OF GEOLOGICAL AND GEOPHYSICAL SURVEYS. GEOLOGIC/PROFESSIONAL REPORT. see *EARTH SCIENCES — Geology*

ALASKA. DIVISION OF GEOLOGICAL AND GEOPHYSICAL SURVEYS. INFORMATION CIRCULAR. see *EARTH SCIENCES — Geology*

ALASKA. DIVISION OF GEOLOGICAL AND GEOPHYSICAL SURVEYS. REPORT OF INVESTIGATIONS. see *EARTH SCIENCES — Geology*

ALASKA. DIVISION OF GEOLOGICAL AND GEOPHYSICAL SURVEYS. SPECIAL REPORT. see *EARTH SCIENCES — Geology*

551 US
AMERICAN GEOPHYSICAL UNION. GEOPHYSICAL MONOGRAPH BOOK SERIES. 1956. irreg. price varies. American Geophysical Union, 2000 Florida Ave. N.W., Washington, DC 20009. TEL 202-462-6903. Ed.Bd. (reprint service avail. from ISI) Indexed: GeoRef.
Formerly: American Geophysical Union. Geophysical Monograph (ISSN 0065-8448)

538.7 SP
ANUARIOS DE GEOMAGNETISMO (YEAR) 1962. a. free to geophysical centers. Instituto Geografico Nacional, Seccion de Geomagnetismo, General Ibanez de Ibero, 3, Apdo. 3007, 28003 Madrid, Spain. Ed.Bd. circ. 250(controlled)
Former titles (until 1983): Anuario de Geomagnetismo - Observatorios de San Pablo (Toledo) y Almeria; (until 1981): Anuario de Geomagnetismo - Centro Geogisico de Canarias; (until 1975): Anuarios del Servicio de Geomagnetismo y Aeronomia.

551 559.8 AT
AUSTRALIAN ACADEMY OF SCIENCE. NATIONAL COMMITTEE FOR ANTARCTIC RESEARCH. AUSTRALIAN ANTARCTIC AND SUB-ANTARCTIC RESEARCH PROGRAMMES. 1976. a. Australian Academy of Science, National Committee for Antarctic Research, P.O. Box 65, Belconnen, ACT 2617, Australia. circ. 250.

AUSTRIA. ZENTRALANSTALT FUER METEOROLOGIE UND GEODYNAMIK. JAHRBUCH. see *METEOROLOGY*

BELGIUM. INSTITUT ROYAL METEOROLOGIQUE. PUBLICATIONS. see *METEOROLOGY*

551 PL ISSN 0067-9038
BIULETYN PERYGLACJALNY. (Text in English) 1954. irreg., no.31, 1986. price varies. (Lodzkie Towarzystwo Naukowe) Ossolineum, Publishing House of the Polish Academy of Sciences, Rynek 9, Wroclaw, Poland (Dist. by: Ars Polona - Ruch, Krakowskie Przedmiescie 7, Warsaw, Poland) (Co-sponsor: Polska Akademia Nauk) Ed. A. Dylikowa. Indexed: Br.Geol.Lit. GeoRef. Soils & Fert.

551 DK ISSN 0109-2170
BRORFELDE, MAGNETIC RESULTS. 1983. a. free. Danske Meteorologiske Institut, Geofysisk Afdeling, Copenhagen, Denmark. illus. circ. 300.

551.21 JA ISSN 0525-1524
BULLETIN OF VOLCANIC ERUPTIONS. (Issued with "Bulletin Volcanologique," published by the co-sponsor) (Text in English) 1961. a., no.22, 1984. 7.500 Yen. Volcanological Society of Japan - Nihon Kazan Gakkai, c/o Earthquake Research Institute, University of Tokyo, 1-1-1 Yayoi, Bunkyo-ku, Tokyo 113, Japan. (Co-sponsor: International Association of Volcanology and Chemistry of the Earth's Interior) Eds. Yoshio Katsui, Shigeo Aramaki. adv. bk. rev. Indexed: GeoRef.

551.22 CN
CANADA. EARTH PHYSICS BRANCH. GEODYNAMIC SERIES. 1974. a. Earth Physics Branch, 1 Observatory Cresc., Ottawa, Ont. K1A 0Y3, Canada. TEL 613-995-5558.

651.22 CN ISSN 0704-3015
CANADA. EARTH PHYSICS BRANCH. GEOMAGNETIC SERIES. 1975. a. Earth Physics Branch, 1 Observatory Cresc., Ottawa, Ont. K1A 0Y3, Canada. TEL 613-995-5558. Indexed: Sci.Abstr.

551.22 CN
CANADA. EARTH PHYSICS BRANCH. GEOTHERMAL SERIES. 1974. a. Earth Physics Branch, 1 Observatory Cresc., Ottawa, Ont. K1A 0Y3, Canada. TEL 613-995-5558.

551.22 CN
CANADA. EARTH PHYSICS BRANCH. GRAVITY MAP SERIES. 1961. a. Earth Physics Branch, 1 Observatory Cresc., Ottawa, Ont. K1A 0Y3, Canada. TEL 613-995-5558.

551.22 CN ISSN 0084-8387
CANADA. EARTH PHYSICS BRANCH. SEISMOLOGICAL SERIES. 1954. a. Earth Physics Branch, 1 Observatory Cresc., Ottawa, Ont., Canada. TEL 613-995-5558. (processed)
Formerly: Ottawa. Dominion Observatory. Seismological Series.
Seismology

551.22 CN ISSN 0225-6002
CANADIAN EARTHQUAKES/TREMBLEMENTS DE TERRE CANADIENS. (Text in English and French) 1960. a. Earth Physics Branch, 1 Observatory Cresc., Ottawa, Ont. K1A 0Y3, Canada. TEL 613-995-5558. abstr. charts.

551 SZ
CONTRIBUTIONS TO CURRENT RESEARCH IN GEOPHYSICS. 1975. irreg. price varies. Birkhaeuser Verlag, P.O. Box 133, CH-4010 Basel, Switzerland. Indexed: GeoRef.

551 US
CRUSTAL AND UPPER MANTLE STRUCTURE IN EUROPE. MONOGRAPHS. 1976. irreg. (European Seismological Commission) Springer Verlag, 175 Fifth Ave., New York, NY 10010 TEL 212-460-1500. (Also Berlin, Heidelberg, Vienna) (reprint service avail. from ISI)

CURRENT GEOLOGICAL AND GEOPHYSICAL STUDIES IN MONTANA. see *EARTH SCIENCES — Geology*

CURRENT PRACTICES IN GEOTECHNICAL ENGINEERING. see *EARTH SCIENCES — Geology*

EARTH SCIENCES — GEOPHYSICS

551   DK   ISSN 0109-1085
D S S -NYT. (Text in Danish and English) 1983. irreg., (1-2/yr.) Kr.100. Danish Speleological Society - Dansk Grotteforening, c/o Conrad Aub-Robinson, Geologisk Institut, Bygn. 520, Ny Munkegade, 8000 Aarhus C, Denmark. Ed. Conrad Aub-Robinson. bk. rev. illus. circ. 100. Indexed: Geo.Abstr.

551 510   NE
DEVELOPMENTS IN GEOMATHEMATICS. 1974. irreg., vol. 4, 1982. price varies. Elsevier Science Publishers B.V., Box 211, 1000 AE Amsterdam, Netherlands. Indexed: GeoRef.

551   NE   ISSN 0070-458X
DEVELOPMENTS IN SOLID EARTH GEOPHYSICS. 1964. irreg., vol.15, 1983. price varies. Elsevier Science Publishers B.V., Box 211, 1000 AE Amsterdam, Netherlands. Indexed: GeoRef.

551   IE   ISSN 0070-7422
DUBLIN INSTITUTE FOR ADVANCED STUDIES. SCHOOL OF COSMIC PHYSICS. GEOPHYSICAL BULLETIN. 1950. irreg., no. 33, 1975. price varies. Dublin Institute for Advanced Studies, 10 Burlington Rd., Dublin 4, Ireland. Indexed: GeoRef.
    Issued also as: Dublin Institute for Advanced Studies. Communications. Series D.

551.22   US
EARTHQUAKE HISTORY OF THE UNITED STATES. 1928. irreg., approx. every 5 yrs. $10. U.S. National Geophysical Data Center, 325 Broadway, Boulder, CO 80303. TEL 303-497-6215. Ed.Bd. stat. (also avail. in microfiche from NTI)
Seismology

551   HU   ISSN 0524-8655
EOTVOS LORAND GEOPHYSICAL INSTITUTE OF HUNGARY. ANNUAL REPORT/MAGYAR ALLAMI EOTVOS LORAND GEOFIZIKAI INTEZET EVI JELENTESE. (Text in English, Hungarian and Russian) 1966. a. Eotvos Lorand Geophysical Institute of Hungary, Columbus u. 17-23, 1145 Budapest 14, Hungary. Ed. Eva Kilenyi. charts. illus. maps. circ. 1,400.

551   UK   ISSN 0531-2728
EUROPEAN ASSOCIATION OF EXPLORATION GEOPHYSICISTS. CONSTITUTION AND BY-LAWS, MEMBERSHIP LIST. 1953. a. fl.24. (European Association of Exploration Geophysicists, NE) Blackwell Scientific Publications, Osney Mead, Oxford 0X2 0EL, England. Ed. E. van der Gaag. circ. 3,800. Indexed: GeoRef.

551.22   UK   ISSN 0144-2376
FELT AND DAMAGING EARTHQUAKES. 1976. a. £5. International Seismological Centre, Newbury, Berks. RG13 1LZ, England. Indexed: Abstr.J.Earthq.Eng.

551   GE   ISSN 0138-4600
FORSCHUNGSBEREICHS FUER GEO- UND KOSMOWISSENSCHAFTEN. VEROEFFENTLICHEN. (Text in English and German) 1973. irreg., vol.12, 1985. (Akademie der Wissenschaften der DDR) Akademie-Verlag Berlin, Leipziger Str. 3-4, 1086 Berlin, E. Germany (D.D.R.)

910   DK   ISSN 0105-9696
GEODAETISK INSTITUT. MEDDELELSE. (Text and summaries in Danish, English) 1928. irreg., latest no.56. Geodaetisk Institut - Geodetic Institute, Gamlehave Alle 22, DK-2920 Charlottenlund, Denmark.

551   YU   ISSN 0352-3659
GEOFIZIKA. 1923. a. avail. on exchange only. (Sveuciliste u Zagrebu, Prirodoslovno-Matematicki Fakultet) Geofizicki Zavod, Horvatovac bb, p.p. 224, 41000 Zagreb, Yugoslavia. Ed. Inga Lisac.
    Formerly: Radovi.

GEOLOGICAL SOCIETY OF CHINA. PROCEEDINGS. see *EARTH SCIENCES — Geology*

GEOLOGISCHE ABHANDLUNGEN HESSEN. see *EARTH SCIENCES — Geology*

GEOLOGISCHES JAHRBUCH HESSEN. see *EARTH SCIENCES — Geology*

551   NO   ISSN 0072-1174
GEOPHYSICA NORVEGICA. (Text in English) 1934. irreg. price varies. Norwegian University Press, Kolstadgt. 1, Box 2959-Toeyen, 0608 Oslo 6, Norway (U.S. address: Publications Expediting Inc., 200 Meacham Ave., Elmont, NY 11003) Ed. J.A. Holtet. (back issues avail.) Indexed: Chem.Abstr. Meteor.& Geoastrophys.Abstr. Sci.Abstr. Int.Aerosp.Abstr.

551   US
GEOPHYSICAL DIRECTORY. 1946. a. $25. ‡ Geophysical Directory, Inc., 2200 Welch Ave., Box 13508, Houston, TX 77219. TEL 713-529-8789. Ed. Claudia La Calli. adv. circ. 9,500.

GEOPHYSICS AND ASTROPHYSICS MONOGRAPHS; a series of graduate-level textbooks and monographs on plasma astrophysics and geophysics, including magnetospheric, solar, and stellar physics. see *ASTRONOMY*

551   GE   ISSN 0138-2357
GEOPHYSIK UND GEOLOGIE; Geophysikalische Veroeffentlichungen der Karl-Marx-Universitaet Leipzig. Dritte Serie. 1974. irreg. price varies. (Karl-Marx-Universitaet) Akademie-Verlag, Leipziger Str. 3-4, 1086 Berlin, E. Germany (D.D.R.) Ed. R. Lauterbach. Indexed: Chem.Abstr.
    Formerly: Leipzig. Universitaet. Geophysikalisches Institut. Veroeffentlichungen. Zweite Serie (ISSN 0016-8041)

551   DK   ISSN 0069-987X
GEOTEKNISK INSTITUT, COPENHAGEN. BULLETIN. (Text in English; some earlier issues in Danish) 1956. irreg., latest no.36, 1985. price varies. Geoteknisk Institut - Danish Geotechnical Institute, 1 Maglebjergvej, DK-2800 Lyngby, Denmark. Indexed: Geotech.Abstr.

551   US   ISSN 0149-8991
GEOTHERMAL RESOURCES COUNCIL. SPECIAL REPORT. no.3, 1973. irreg., no.13, 1983. price varies. Geothermal Resources Council, Box 1350, Davis, CA 95617. TEL 916-758-2360.

551   US   ISSN 0193-5933
GEOTHERMAL RESOURCES COUNCIL. TRANSACTIONS. 1977. a. $33. Geothermal Resources Council, Box 1350, Davis, CA 95617. TEL 916-758-2360.

551   DK   ISSN 0109-4300
GODHAVN MAGNETIC RESULTS. 1983. a. free. Dansk Meteorologisk Institut, Geofysisk Afdeling, Copenhagen, Denmark. illus. circ. 250.
    Formerly: Godhavn Geophysical Observatory. Magnetic Results.

538.7   UK
GREAT BRITAIN. BRITISH GEOLOGICAL SURVEY. GEOMAGNETIC BULLETIN. 1969. irreg. price varies. British Geological Survey, Keyworth, Nottingham NG12 5GG, England (Avail. from H.M.S.O., c/o Liaison Officer, Nine Elms, London SW8 5DR, England) circ. 600.
    Formerly (until Jan. 1984): Great Britain. Institute of Geological Sciences. Geomagnetic Bulletin (ISSN 0073-9316)

551.22   UK
GREAT BRITAIN. BRITISH GEOLOGICAL SURVEY. SEISMOLOGICAL BULLETINS. 1972. irreg. price varies. British Geological Survey, Keyworth, Nottingham NG12 5GG, England (Avail. from H.M.S.O., c/o Liaison Officer, Nine Elms, London SW8 5DR, England) circ. 500.
    Formerly (until Jan. 1984): Great Britain. Institute of Geological Sciences. Seismological Bulletins (ISSN 0308-5082)
Seismology

551   UK   ISSN 0072-6613
GREAT BRITAIN. METEOROLOGICAL OFFICE. GEOPHYSICAL MEMOIRS. 1912. irreg. price varies. H.M.S.O., Box 569, London SE1 9NH, England. (reprint service avail. from UMI)

551   US
HAWAII INSTITUTE OF GEOPHYSICS. TECHNICAL REPORTS AND SPECIAL PUBLICATIONS. irreg. Hawaii Institute of Geophysics, 2525 Correa Rd., Honolulu, HI 96822. TEL 808-948-7059.
    Formerly: Hawaii Institute of Geophysics. Technical Reports, Data Reports and Special Publications.

551   US
HAWAII INSTITUTE OF GEOPHYSICS. YEARBOOK. a. Hawaii Institute of Geophysics, 2525 Correa Rd., Honolulu, HI 96822. TEL 808-948-7059.
    Formerly: Hawaii Institute of Geophysics. Contributions (ISSN 0073-1234)

551   JA   ISSN 0441-067X
HOKKAIDO UNIVERSITY. FACULTY OF SCIENCE. JOURNAL. SERIES 7: GEOPHYSICS. (Text in English) 1957. irreg. exchange basis. Hokkaido University, Faculty of Science - Hokkaido Daigaku Rigakubu, Nishi-8-chome, Kita-10-jo, Kita-ku, Sapporo 060, Japan. Ed. K. Kikuchi. circ. 400. (back issues avail.) Indexed: Geo.Abstr.

HVAR OBSERVATORY BULLETIN. see *ASTRONOMY*

538.7   UK   ISSN 0536-1095
I A G A NEWS. 1963. a. free. International Association of Geomagnetism and Aeronomy - Association Internationale de Geomagnetisme et d'Aeronomie, c/o Prof. M. Gadsden, Ed., Natural Philosophy Dept., Aberdeen University, Aberdeen AB9 2UE, Scotland. circ. 2,400.

551   II
INDIAN GEOPHYSICAL UNION BULLETIN. 1964. a. Indian Geophysical Union, Hyderabad 7, India. Ed.Bd. bibl. charts.

551.44   RM   ISSN 0065-0498
INSTITUT DE SPEOLOGIE EMIL RACOVITZA. TRAVAUX. (Text in English, French, German) 1962. a. 60 lei($40) Editura Academiei Republicii Socialiste Rumania, Calea Victoriei 125, 79717 Bucharest, Rumania (Subscr. to: Rompresfilatelia, Calea Grivitei 64-66, P.O. Box 12-201, 78104 Bucharest, Rumania) Ed. T. Orghidan. bk. rev. circ. 450. Indexed: Biol.Abstr. Ref.Zh. Zoo.Rec.
    Formerly: Academia Republicii Socialiste Rumania. Institutul de Speologie Emil Racovitza. Travaux.

INSTITUTE FOR PETROLEUM RESEARCH AND GEOPHYSICS, HOLON, ISRAEL. REPORT. see *PETROLEUM AND GAS*

551   JA
INSTITUTE OF GEOSCIENCE. ANNUAL REPORT. (Text in English) no.3, 1976. a. University of Tsukuba, Institute of Geoscience, Ibaraki-Prefecture 300-31, Japan. Ed.Bd. Indexed: Geo.Abstr. GeoRef.

551   SP   ISSN 0080-5955
INSTITUTO Y OBSERVATORIO DE MARINA. OBSERVACIONES METEOROLOGICAS, MAGNETICAS Y SISMICAS. ANALES. 1870. a. 500 ptas. Instituto y Observatorio de Marina, Seccion de Geofisica, San Fernando (Cadiz), Spain. circ. 400.

526 551   BE   ISSN 0542-6766
INTERNATIONAL ASSOCIATION OF GEODESY. COMMISSION PERMANENTE DES MAREES TERRESTRES. MAREES TERRESTRES BULLETIN D'INFORMATION. 1957. irreg., 2-3/yr. 800 Fr.($18) International Association of Geodesy, Commission Permanente des Marees Terrestres, c/o Observatoire Royal de Belgique, 3 Avenue Circulaire, 1180 Brussels, Belgium. Ed. P. Melchior.

551   US   ISSN 0074-6142
INTERNATIONAL GEOPHYSICS SERIES. 1959. irreg., vol.34, 1986. Academic Press Inc., Orlando, FL 32887. TEL 305-345-2000. Ed. J. Van Mieghem.

551.22 624.151   JA   ISSN 0074-655X
INTERNATIONAL INSTITUTE OF SEISMOLOGY AND EARTHQUAKE ENGINEERING. BULLETIN. 1964. a. International Institute of Seismology and Earthquake Engineering - Kensetsu-sho Kenchiku Kenkyusho Kokusai Jishin Kogakubu, Building Research Institute-Ministry of Construction, 1 Tatehara, Oho-machi, Tsukuba-gun, Ibaraki Prefecture 305, Japan. Ed. Sadaiku Hattori. circ. 820. Indexed: Abstr.J.Earth.Eng. Geo.Abstr.

EARTH SCIENCES — GEOPHYSICS

551.22　　　　　JA
INTERNATIONAL INSTITUTE OF SEISMOLOGY AND EARTHQUAKE ENGINEERING. INDIVIDUAL STUDIES BY PARTICIPANTS AT I I S E E. 1965. a. International Institute of Seismology and Earthquake Engineering - Kensetsusho Kenchiku Kenkyusho Kokusai Jishin Kogakubu, Building Research Institute-Ministry of Construction, 1 Tatehara, Oho-machi, Tsukuba-gun, Ibaraki Prefecture 305, Japan. Ed. Sadaiku Hattori. circ. 560. Indexed: Abstr.J.Earthq.Eng.
   Formerly: International Institute of Seismology and Earthquake Engineering. Report of Individual Study by Participants to I S E E (ISSN 0074-6606)

551.22　　　　JA　　ISSN 0074-6614
INTERNATIONAL INSTITUTE OF SEISMOLOGY AND EARTHQUAKE ENGINEERING. YEAR BOOK. 1964. biennial. International Institute of Seismology and Earthquake Engineering - Kensetsusho Kenchiku Kenkyusho Kokusai Jishin Kogakubu, Building Research Institute-Ministry of Construction, 1 Tatehare, Oho-machi, Tsukuba-gun, Ibaraki Prefecture 305, Japan. Ed. Sadaiku Hattori. circ. controlled. Indexed: Geo.Abstr.

551　　　　　NE　　ISSN 0538-9771
INTERNATIONAL SEDIMENTARY PETROGRAPHICAL SERIES. 1955. irreg., no. 16, 1977. price varies. E. J. Brill, P.O. Box 9000, 2300 PA Leiden, Netherlands. Ed.Bd. (back issues avail.)

INTERNATIONAL UNION OF GEODESY AND GEOPHYSICS. MONOGRAPH. see *GEOGRAPHY*

INTERNATIONAL UNION OF GEODESY AND GEOPHYSICS. PROCEEDINGS OF THE GENERAL ASSEMBLY. see *GEOGRAPHY*

538　　　　　UR　　ISSN 0202-7275
ITOGI NAUKI I TEKHNIKI: GEOMAGNETIZM I VYSOKIE SLOI ATMOSFERY. irreg., latest vol.8, 1986. price varies. Vsesoyuznyi Institut Nauchno-Tekhnicheskoi Informatsii (VINITI), Ul. Baltiiskaya, 14, Moscow A-219, Russian S.F.S.R., U.S.S.R. illus.

551　　　　　JA
JAPAN METEOROLOGICAL AGENCY. REPORT OF GEOMAGNETIC AND GEOELECTRIC OBSERVATIONS. a. Japan Meteorological Agency, Kakioka Magnetic Observatory, Kakioka 595, Yasato-Machi, Niibari-Gun, Ibaraki, Japan.

551　　　　　JA
JAPAN METEOROLOGICAL AGENCY. REPORT OF MAGNETIC PULSATIONS. a. Japan Meteorological Agency, Kakioka Magnetic Observatory, Kakioka 595, Yasato-Machi, Niibari-Gun, Ibaraki, Japan.

JOKULL. see *EARTH SCIENCES — Geology*

551　　　　　SW　　ISSN 0283-1686
KIRUNA GEOPHYSICAL INSTITUTE. ANNUAL REPORT. 1985. a. price varies. Kiruna Geophysical Institute, P.O. Box 704, S-981 27 Kiruna, Sweden. Eds. Lars Eliasson, Ingrid Sandahl. circ. 380.

551　　　　　SW　　ISSN 0349-2656
KIRUNA GEOPHYSICAL INSTITUTE. PREPRINT. Short title: K G I Preprint. (Text and summaries in English) 1969. irreg. price varies; free to qualified institutions and libraries. Kiruna Geophysical Institute, P.O. Box 704, S-91827 Kiruna, Sweden. charts. circ. 375. (back issues avail.)

551　　　　　SW　　ISSN 0283-1694
KIRUNA GEOPHYSICAL INSTITUTE. SCIENTIFIC REPORT. Short title: K G I Scientific Report. (Text in English) 1973. irreg. price varies; free to qualified institutions, libraries and personnel. Kiruna Geophysical Institute, Box 704, S-98127 Kiruna, Sweden. charts. circ. 300. (back issues avail.)
   Formerly: Kiruna Geophysical Institute. Report (ISSN 0347-6405)

551　　　　　SW　　ISSN 0349-2664
KIRUNA GEOPHYSICAL INSTITUTE. SOFTWARE REPORT. Short title: K G I Software Report. (Text in English) 1977. irreg. price varies; free to qualified institutions, libraries and personnel. Kiruna Geophysical Institute, Box 704, S-98127 Kiruna, Sweden. (back issues avail.)

551　　　　　SW　　ISSN 0349-2672
KIRUNA GEOPHYSICAL INSTITUTE. TECHNICAL REPORT. Short title: K G I Technical Report. (Text and summaries in English and Swedish) 1969. irreg. price varies; free to qualified institutions, libraries and personnel. Kiruna Geophysical Institute, Box 704, S-98127 Kiruna, Sweden. (back issues avail.)

551　　　　　US　　ISSN 0075-790X
LANDOLT-BOERNSTEIN, ZAHLENWERTE UND FUNKTIONEN AUS NATURWISSENSCHAFTEN UND TECHNIK. NEUE SERIE. GROUP 5: GEOPHYSICS. 1981. irreg., vol.4A, 1986. Springer-Verlag, 175 Fifth Ave., New York, NY 10010 TEL 212-460-1500. (Also Berlin, Heidelberg, Tokyo and Vienna) (reprint service avail. from ISI)

M E R I T NEWSLETTER. (Monitored Earth Rotation and Intercompared Techniques) see *ASTRONOMY*

551.4　　　　UR　　ISSN 0130-3686
MATERIALY GLYATSIOLOGICHESKIKH ISSLEDOVANII/DATA OF GLACIOLOGICAL STUDIES. (Text in Russian; abstracts in English) 1961. irreg., (3-4 vols./yr.) exchange basis. Akademiya Nauk S.S.S.R., Mezhduvedomstvennyi Geofizicheskii Komitet - Academy of Sciences of the U.S.S.R., Soviet Geophysical Committee, Molodezhnaya ul., 3, Moscow, Russian S.F.S.R., U.S.S.R. (Co-sponsor: Institute of Geography of the Academy of Sciences of the U.S.S.R.) Eds. G.A. Avsyuk, V.M. Kotlyakov. circ. 950.

MEMORIE DI SCIENZE GEOLOGICHE. see *EARTH SCIENCES — Geology*

551　　　　　GW　　ISSN 0543-5927
"METEOR" FORSCHUNGSERGEBNISSE. REIHE C. GEOLOGIE UND GEOPHYSIK. (Text in German; summaries in English) 1968. irreg. price varies. (Deutsche Forschungsgemeinschaft) Gebrueder Borntraeger Verlagsbuchhandlung, Johannesstr. 3A, 7000 Stuttgart 1, W. Germany (B.R.D.) Eds. M. Sarnthein, H.J. Duerbaum. charts. illus. Indexed: Chem.Abstr. GeoRef.

METHODS IN GEOCHEMISTRY AND GEOPHYSICS. see *EARTH SCIENCES*

551.5　520　　　　MZ
MOZAMBIQUE. SERVICO METEOROLOGICO. INFORMACOES DE CARACTER ASTRONOMICO. 1955. a. free. Servico Meteorologico, C.P. 256, Maputo, Mozambique. stat.

551　　　　　II　　ISSN 0073-4144
NATIONAL GEOPHYSICAL RESEARCH INSTITUTE. PUBLICATIONS. 1963. a. price varies. National Geophysical Research Institute, Uppal Rd., Hyderabad 500007, India. (Affiliate: Council of Scientific and Industrial Research) bk. rev.

551.22　　　　JA
NATIONAL RESEARCH CENTER FOR DISASTER PREVENTION. SEISMOLOGICAL BULLETIN. (Text in English) 1970. irreg. on exchange basis. National Research Center for Disaster Prevention - Kokuritsu Bosai Kagaku Gijutsu Senta, 3-chome, Tennodai, Sakura-mura, Ibaraki-ken 305, Japan. circ. 200.
   Seismology

551　　　　　NZ　　ISSN 0110-6112
NEW ZEALAND. DEPARTMENT OF SCIENTIFIC AND INDUSTRIAL RESEARCH. GEOPHYSICS DIVISION. REPORT. 1952. irreg. NZ.$10. Department of Scientific and Industrial Research, Geophysics Division, P.O. Box 1320, Wellington, New Zealand. circ. 200. Indexed: GeoRef.

551　　　　　NZ　　ISSN 0110-7089
NEW ZEALAND. DEPARTMENT OF SCIENTIFIC AND INDUSTRIAL RESEARCH. GEOPHYSICS DIVISION. TECHNICAL NOTE. 1952. irreg. NZ.$10. Department of Scientific and Industrial Research, Geophysics Division, P.O. Box 1320, Wellington, New Zealand. circ. 100. Indexed: GeoRef.

551　　　　　NO　　ISSN 0078-1193
NORGES GEOTEKNISKE INSTITUTT. PUBLIKASJON/NORWEGIAN GEOTECHNICAL INSTITUTE. PUBLICATIONS. (Text in English; occassionally French, German and Norwegian) 1953. irreg., (4-6/yr.), latest no.164, 1986. price varies. Norges Geotekniske Institutt - Norwegian Geotechnical Institute, Box 40 Taasen, 0801 Oslo 8, Norway. Ed. Finn A. Joerstad. cum.index: no. 1-30. circ. 1,000. Indexed: Geo.Abstr. GeoRef. Geotech.Abstr. HRIS.

OBSERVATORIO NACIONAL RIO DE JANEIRO. PUBLICACOES. see *ASTRONOMY*

551.05　　　　BO
PAN AMERICAN INSTITUTE OF GEOGRAPHY AND HISTORY. COMMISSION ON GEOPHYSICS. BOLETIN. irreg. Instituto Panamericano de Geografia e Historia, Casilla 6003, La Paz, Bolivia.

551　　　　　PL　　ISSN 0137-2440
POLISH ACADEMY OF SCIENCES. INSTITUTE OF GEOPHYSICS. SERIES A. PHYSICS OF THE EARTH'S INTERIOR. (Text in English and Polish; summaries in English) 1963. irreg. price varies. Panstwowe Wydawnictwo Naukowe, Ul. Miodowa 10, 00-251 Warsaw, Poland (Dist. by: Ars Polona, Krakowskie Przedmiescie 7, 00-068 Warsaw, Poland) Ed. Roman Teisseyre. Indexed: GeoRef.
   Supersedes in part: Polska Akademia Nauk. Instytut Geofizyki. Materialy i Prace (ISSN 0079-3574)

551　　　　　PL　　ISSN 0209-0406
POLISH ACADEMY OF SCIENCES. INSTITUTE OF GEOPHYSICS. SERIES B. SEISMOLOGY. (Text in English, French, Polish; summaries in English) irreg. price varies. Panstwowe Wydawnictwo Naukowe, Miodowa 10, 00-251 Warsaw, Poland (Dist. by: Ars Polona, Krakowskie Przedmiescie 7, 00-068 Warsaw, Poland)
   Supersedes in part: Polska Akademia Nauk. Instytut Geofizyki. Materialy i Prace (ISSN 0079-3574)

551　　　　　PL　　ISSN 0208-8525
POLISH ACADEMY OF SCIENCES. INSTITUTE OF GEOPHYSICS. SERIES C. GEOMAGNETISM. (Text in English, French, Polish; summaries in English) irreg. price varies. Panstwowe Wydawnictwo Naukowe, Miodowa 10, 00-251 Warsaw, Poland (Dist. by: Ars Polona, Krakowskie Przedmiescie 7, 00-068 Warsaw, Poland)
   Supersedes in part: Polska Akademia Nauk. Instytut Geofizyki. Materialy i Prace (ISSN 0079-3574)

551　　　　　PL　　ISSN 0138-0125
POLISH ACADEMY OF SCIENCES. INSTITUTE OF GEOPHYSICS. SERIES D. PHYSICS OF THE ATMOSPHERE. (Text in English, French, Polish; summaries in English) irreg. price varies. Panstwowe Wydawnictwo Naukowe, Miodowa 10, 00-251 Warsaw, Poland (Dist. by: Ars Polona, Krakowskie Przedmiescie 7, 00-068 Warsaw, Poland)
   Supersedes in part: Polska Akademia Nauk. Instytut Geofizyki. Materialy i Prace (ISSN 0079-3574)

551　　　　　PL　　ISSN 0138-0214
POLISH ACADEMY OF SCIENCES. INSTITUTE OF GEOPHYSICS. SERIES F. PLANETARY GEODESY. (Text in English, French, Polish; summaries in English) irreg. price varies. Panstwowe Wydawnictwo Naukowe, Miodowa 10, 00-251 Warsaw, Poland (Dist. by: Ars Polona, Krakowskie Przedmiescie 7, 00-068 Warsaw, Poland)
   Supersedes in part: Polska Akademia Nauk. Instytut Geofizyki. Materialy i Prace (ISSN 0079-3574)

551　　　　　PL　　ISSN 0208-8061
POLISH ACADEMY OF SCIENCES. INSTITUTE OF GEOPHYSICS. SERIES G. NUMERICAL METHODS IN GEOPHYSICS. (Text in English, French, Polish; summaries in English) irreg. price varies. Panstwowe Wydawnictwo Naukowe, Miodowa 10, 00-251 Warsaw, Poland (Dist. by: Ars Polona, Krakowskie Przedmiescie 7, 00-068 Warsaw, Poland)
   Supersedes in part: Polska Akademia Nauk. Instytut Geofizyki. Materialy i Prace (ISSN 0079-3574)

EARTH SCIENCES — GEOPHYSICS

551   PL   ISSN 0138-015X
POLISH ACADEMY OF SCIENCES. INSTITUTE OF GEOPHYSICS. SERIES M. MISCELLANEA. (Text in English, French, Polish; summaries in English) irreg. price varies. Panstwowe Wydawnictwo Naukowe, Miodowa 10, 00-251 Warsaw, Poland (Dist. by: Ars Polona, Krakowskie Przedmiescie 7, 00-058 Warsaw, Poland)
    Supersedes in part: Polska Akademia Nauk. Instytut Geofizyki. Materialy i Prace (ISSN 0079-3574)

551   UR
PRIKLADNAYA GEOFIZIKA. vol.85, 1977. irreg. 1.00 Rub. per no. (Vsesoyuznyi Nauchno-Issledovatel'skii Institut Geofizicheskikh Metodov Razvedki) Izdatel'stvo Nedra, Tret'yakovskii Proezd 1/19, Moscow K-12, Russian S.F.S.R., U.S.S.R. Ed. M. Polshkov. abstr. circ. 25,000. Indexed: Chem.Abstr. Sci.Abstr. GeoRef.

551.22   FI   ISSN 0079-774X
PUBLICATIONS IN SEISMOLOGY.* (Text in English; occasionally in Finnish) 1960. irreg. exchange basis. Helsingin Yliopisto, Seismologian Laitos - University of Helsinki, Institute of Seismology, Et. Hesperiankatu 4, Helsinki 10, Finland. Ed. Ekjo Vesanen.

551   RM   ISSN 0556-8110
REVUE ROUMAINE DE GEOLOGIE, GEOPHYSIQUE ET GEOGRAPHIE. GEOPHYSIQUE. (Text in English, French, German and Russian) 1957. a. 60 lei($32) (Academia Republicii Socialiste Romania) Editura Academiei Republicii Socialiste Rumania, Calea Victoriei 125, 79717 Bucharest, Rumania (Subscr. to: ROMPRESFILATELIA, Export-Import Press, Calea Grivitei 64-66, P.O. Box 12-201, 78104 Bucharest, Rumania) Ed. Sabba Stefanescu. bk. rev. charts. illus. index. Indexed: GeoRef.
    Supersedes in part: Revue de Geologie et de Geographie.

551.4   UR   ISSN 0568-6245
REZUL'TATY ISSLEDOVANII PO MEZHDUNARODNYM GEOFIZICHESKIM PROEKTAM. GLYATSIOLOGICHESKIE ISSLEDOVANIYA/RESULTS OF RESEARCHES ON THE INTERNATIONAL GEOPHYSICAL PROJECTS. GLACIOLOGICLA RESEARCHES. 1959. irreg. exchange basis. Akademiya Nauk S.S.S.R., Mezhduvedomstvennyi Geofizicheskii Komitet - Academy of Sciences of the U.S.S.R., Soviet Geophysical Committee, Molodezhnaya ul., 3, Moscow, Russian S.F.S.R., U.S.S.R. Eds. G.A. Avsyuk, V.M. Kotlyakov. adv. circ. 1,000. (also avail. in microfilm) Indexed: Ref.Zh.

RIJKSUNIVERSITEIT TE GENT. STERRENKUNDIG OBSERVATORIUM. MEDEDELINGEN: METEOROLOGIE EN GEOFYSICA. see *METEOROLOGY*

552.06 551   JA   ISSN 0385-2520
ROCK MAGNETISM AND PALEOGEOPHYSICS. (Text in English) 1973. a. controlled free circ. Rock Magnetism and Paleogeophysics Research Group in Japan, c/o Tokyo Institute of Technology, Department of Applied Physics, Ookayama 2-12-1, Meguro-ku, Tokyo 152, Japan. Ed. Masaru Kono. circ. 500. Indexed: GeoRef.

551 538.7   PL   ISSN 0082-0458
ROCZNIK MAGNETYCZNY/ANNUAIRE MAGNETIQUE. (Text in French and Polish; summaries in French) 1949. irreg., vol.42, 1971. price varies. (Polska Akademia Nauk, Instytut Geofizyki) Panstwowe Wydawnictwo Naukowe, Miodowa 10, Warsaw, Poland (Dist. by Ars Polona-Ruch, Krakowskie Przedmiescie 7, Warsaw, Poland) Ed. Roman Teisseyre.

526   YU
SAVEZ GEODETSKIH INZENJERA I GEOMETARA HRVATSKE. GEODET. (Text in Serbo-Croatian) 1958. irreg. (2-3/yr.) free to members. (Savez Geodetskih Inzenjera i Geometara SR Hrvatske) Savez Drustava Geodeta sr Hrvatske, Berislaviceva 6, Zagreb, Yugoslavia. Ed. Miljenko Solaric.
    Formerly: Savez Geodetskih Inzenjera i Geometara Hrvatske. Obavijesti (ISSN 0029-7461)

551   CS   ISSN 0036-5319
SBORNIK GEOLOGICKYCH VED: UZITA GEOFYZIKA/JOURNAL OF GEOLOGICAL SCIENCES: APPLIED GEOPHYSICS. (Text in Czech, English, German and Russian) 1963. irreg. Ustredni Ustav Geologicky, Malostranske nam. 19, 118 21 Prague 1, Czechoslovakia (Subscr. to: Artia, Ve Smeckach 30, 111 27 Prague 1, Czechoslovakia) (Co-sponsor: Geofyzika, n.p. Brno) Ed. Karel Cidlinsky. charts. illus. circ. 600. (back issues avail.) Indexed: Bull.Signal. Ref.Zh. GeoRef.

551   NE
SEISMOLOGY AND EXPLORATION GEOPHYSICS. 1985. irreg. price varies. D. Reidel Publishing Company, Box 17, 3300 AA Dordrecht, Netherlands.

551   CS
SLOVAK SEISMOGRAPHIC STATIONS: BRATISLAVA, SROBAROVA, HURBANOVO AND SKALNATE PLESO. BULLETIN. (Text and summaries in English) 1972. a. 17($2.85) (Slovenska Akademia Vied, Geofyzikalny Ustav) Veda, Publishing House of the Slovak Academy of Sciences, Klemensova 19, 814 30 Bratislava, Czechoslovakia (Subscr. to: Slovart, Gottwaldovo nam. 6, 817 64 Bratislava, Czechoslovakia) Ed. Klara Mrazova. abstr. circ. 500. (tabloid format)

551   CS   ISSN 0586-4607
SLOVENSKA AKADEMIA VIED. GEOFYZIKALNY USTAV. CONTRIBUTIONS. (Text and summaries in English and Russian) 1971. irreg. price varies. Veda, Publishing House of the Slovak Academy of Sciences, Klemensova 19, 814 30 Bratislava, Czechoslovakia (Subscr. to: Slovart, Gottwaldovo nam. 6, 817 64 Bratislava, Czechoslovakia) Ed. Petronela Ochabova. circ. 500. Indexed: Sci.Abstr. GeoRef.

622.15   US
SOCIETY OF EXPLORATION GEOPHYSICISTS. SPECIAL PUBLICATIONS (SYMPOSIA) SERIES. 1947. irreg. price varies. Society of Exploration Geophysicists, Box 702740, Tulsa, OK 74170-2740. TEL 918-493-3516. adv. bk. rev. circ. 19,000. (also avail. in microform)

538.767   JA   ISSN 0386-5444
SOLAR TERRESTRIAL ENVIRONMENTAL RESEARCH IN JAPAN. (Text in English) 1949. irreg. (3-4/yr.) University of Tokyo, Institute of Space and Aeronautical Science, 4-6-1 Komaba, Meguro-ku, Tokyo 153, Japan. Ed.Bd. abstr. circ. 1, 200. (also avail. in microfilm) Indexed: Appl.Mech.Rev. Chem.Abstr. Sci.Abstr.
    Supersedes (1959-1976): Report of Ionosphere and Space Research in Japan (ISSN 0034-4672); Formerly (until 1959): Report of Ionosphere Research in Japan.

551.22   US
SOVIET SEISMOLOGICAL RESEARCH. (Includes 2 subseries: Computational Seismology & Seismic Instruments) 1979. irreg. approx. 1/yr. $80 per subseries. Allerton Press, Inc., 150 Fifth Ave., New York, NY 10011. TEL 212-924-3950.
Seismology

551   SW   ISSN 0348-0755
STATENS GEOTEKNISKA INSTITUT. RAPPORT/ SWEDISH GEOTECHNICAL INSTITUTE. REPORT. (Text in English or Swedish) 1977. irreg. price varies. Statens Geotekniska Institut - Swedish Geotechnical Institute, 581 01 Linkoeping, Sweden. circ. 1,000. Indexed: GeoRef. Geotech.Abstr.
    Supersedes: Statens Geotekniska Institut. Meddelanden & Statens Geotekniska Institut. Saertryck och Preliminaera Rapporter (ISSN 0562-0953) & Statens Geotekniska Institut. Proceedings (ISSN 0081-5705)

551.4   PL   ISSN 0081-6434
STUDIA GEOMORPHOLOGICA CARPATHO-BALCANICA. (Text in English) 1967. a. price varies. (Polska Akademia Nauk, Oddzial w Krakowie, Komisja Nauk Geograficznych) Ossolineum, Publishing House of the Polish Academy of Sciences, Rynek 9, Wroclaw, Poland (Dist. by: Ars Polona-Ruch, Krakowskie Przedmiescie 7, Warsaw, Poland) Ed. Leszek Starkel. Indexed: Geo.Abstr. GeoRef.

551   RM
STUDII SI CERCETARI DE GEOLOGIE, GEOFIZICA SI GEOGRAPHIE. GEOFIZICA. vol.18, 1980. a. $32. (Academia Republicii Socialiste Romania) Editura Academiei Republicii Socialiste Rumania, Calea Victoriei 125, 79717 Bucharest, Rumania (Subscr. to: ROMPRESFILATELIA, Export-Import Presa, Calea Grivitei 64-66, P.O. Box 12-201, 78104 Bucharest, Rumania) Ed. Sabba Stefanescu. Indexed: GeoRef.

526   FI   ISSN 0085-6932
SUOMEN GEODEETTISEN LAITOKSEN. JULKAISUJA/FINNISH GEODETIC INSTITUTE. PUBLICATIONS/FINNISCHE GEODAETISCHE INSTITUT. VEROEFFENTLICHUNGEN. (Text and summaries in English, French or German) 1923. irreg., no.102, 1984. price varies. Suomen Geodeettinen Laitos - Finnish Geodetic Institute, Ilmalankatu 1 A, SF-00240 Helsinki 24, Finland. circ. 800.

551   FI   ISSN 0355-1962
SUOMEN GEODEETTISEN LAITOKSEN. TIEDONANTOJA/FINNISH GEODETIC INSTITUTE. REPORTS. (Text in English) 1973. irreg. price varies. Suomen Geodeettinen Laitos - Finnish Geodetic Institute, Ilmalankatu 1 A, 00240 Helsinki 24, Finland.

551   NE   ISSN 0257-4284
TIDAL GRAVITY CORRECTIONS. 1970. a. fl.40. European Association of Exploration Geophysicists, Wassenaarseweg 22, 2596 CH The Hague, Netherlands. Ed. E. van der Gaag. circ. 200.

551   JA   ISSN 0040-8794
TOHOKU GEOPHYSICAL JOURNAL; Science Reports of Tohoku University. Fifth Series. (Text in English) 1949. irreg. (3-4/yr.) exchange basis. Tohoku University, Faculty of Science, Geophysical Institute, Aramaki Aza Aoba, Sendai 980, Japan. Ed. Prof. Akira Takagi. bibl. charts. illus. index. circ. 600. Indexed: Chem.Abstr. Sci.Abstr. GeoRef.
    Formerly: Tohoku University. Science Reports. Series 5: Geophysics.

551.22   UN   ISSN 0082-7479
UNESCO EARTHQUAKE STUDY MISSIONS. (Text in English and French) irreg. price varies. Unesco, 7-9 Place de Fontenoy, 75700 Paris, France (Dist. in U.S. by: Bernan Associates-Unipub, 4611-F Assembly Dr., Lanham, MD 20706-4391)
Seismology

UNITED KINGDOM RESEARCH ON GEODESY. see *GEOGRAPHY*

U.S. AIR FORCE GEOPHYSICS LABORATORY. A F G L (SERIES) see *MILITARY*

551.22   US   ISSN 0091-1429
UNITED STATES EARTHQUAKES. 1928. a. price varies. U.S. National Earthquake Information Center, Denver, CO 80225 (Subscr. to: U.S. Geological Survey, Open-File Services Section, Box 25425, Federal Center, Denver, CO 80225) Ed. Carl W. Stover. illus. (also avail. in microfilm) Indexed: GeoRef.
Seismology

551   MX   ISSN 0076-7204
UNIVERSIDAD NACIONAL AUTONOMA DE MEXICO. INSTITUTO DE GEOFISICA. MONOGRAFIAS. 1959; suspended 1963; resumed 1981. irreg. Universidad Nacional Autonoma de Mexico, Instituto de Geofisica, Circuito Exterior, Ciudad Universitaria, Mexico 20, D.F., Mexico. Ed. Francisco Graffe.

551   GW   ISSN 0343-7493
UNIVERSITAET MUENCHEN. GEOPHYSIKALISCHES OBSERVATORIUM, FUERSTENFELDBRUCK. VEROEFFENTLICHUNGEN. SERIE A. 1959. a. exchange basis. Universitaet Muenchen, Geophysikalisches Observatorium, Ludwigshoehe 8, 8080 Fuerstenfeldbruck, W. Germany (B.R.D.)

551   GW   ISSN 0077-2100
UNIVERSITAET MUENCHEN. GEOPHYSIKALISCHES OBSERVATORIUM, FUERSTENFELDBRUCK. VEROEFFENTLICHUNGEN. SERIE B. 1960. irreg., no.8, 1985. exchange basis. Universitaet Muenchen, Geophysikalisches Observatorium, Ludwigshoehe 8, 8080 Fuerstenfeldbruck, W. Germany (B.R.D.)

551 551.5   GW   ISSN 0069-5882
UNIVERSITAET ZU KOELN. INSTITUT FUER GEOPHYSIK UND METEOROLOGIE. MITTEILUNGEN. (Text in English and German) 1965. irreg., no.22, 1975. Universitaet zu Koeln, Institut fuer Geophysik und Meteorologie, Albertus Magnus Platz, 5000 Cologne, W. Germany (B.R.D.)

551   US   ISSN 0041-9362
UNIVERSITY OF ALASKA. GEOPHYSICAL INSTITUTE. REPORT SERIES. 1948. irreg. free. Geophysical Institute, University of Alaska, Fairbanks, AK 99701. TEL 907-474-7503.

551 520   CN   ISSN 0068-1725
UNIVERSITY OF BRITISH COLUMBIA. DEPARTMENT OF GEOPHYSICS AND ASTRONOMY. ANNUAL REPORT. 1958. a. free. ‡ University of British Columbia, Department of Geophysics and Astronomy, 2075 Wesbrook Mall, Vancouver, B.C. V6T 1W5, Canada. TEL 604-228-2267. Ed. T.K. Menon. circ. 700.

551.22   US   ISSN 0092-4288
UNIVERSITY OF NEVADA. SEISMOLOGICAL LABORATORY. BULLETIN. 1970. irreg., latest 1982 (for 1980) ‡ University of Nevada, Seismological Laboratory, Reno, NV 89507. TEL 702-784-4975. Ed. G.M. Smith. illus. circ. 100. Indexed: GeoRef. Key Title: Bulletin of the Seismological Laboratory (Reno)
Seismology

EARTH SCIENCES — Hydrology

551.48 370   PL
ACTA UNIVERSITATIS LODZIENSIS: FOLIA LIMNOLOGICA. (Text in Polish; summaries in various languages) irreg. Uniwersytet Lodzki, Drukarnia Wojskowa, Ul. Gdanska 130, Lodz, Poland (Dist. by: Ars Polona-Ruch, Krakowskie Przedmiescie 7, Warsaw, Poland)

551.4   US   ISSN 0065-2768
ADVANCES IN HYDROSCIENCE. 1964. irreg., vol.14, 1986. Academic Press, Inc., Orlando, FL 32887. TEL 305-345-2000. Ed. Ven Te Chow. index. Indexed: Biol.Abstr. GeoRef. Geotech.Abstr.
Formerly: Methods in Hydroscience (ISSN 0076-6909)

AKITA PREFECTURAL COLLEGE OF AGRICULTURE. BULLETIN. see *BIOLOGY — Botany*

ALBERTA RESEARCH COUNCIL. RIVER ENGINEERING AND SURFACE HYDROLOGY REPORTS. see *ENGINEERING — Civil Engineering*

ALGOLOGICAL STUDIES; Archiv fuer Hydrobiologie, Supplementbaende. see *BIOLOGY*

070 551.4   FR   ISSN 0373-3629
ANNALES HYDROGRAPHIQUES. 1848. irreg. (1-2/yr.) price varies. Service Hydrographique et Oceanographique de la Marine, 3 av. Octave Greard, 75200 Paris Naval, France (Subscr. address: EPSHOM, B.P. 426, 29275 Brest Cedex, France) charts. illus. index. cum.index. circ. 400. Indexed: Chem.Abstr.

551.4   UN
ANUARIO HIDROLOGICO DEL ISTMO CENTROAMERICANO. 1966/67. a. free. United Nations Central American Hydrometeorological Project, Regional Committee for Water Resources, Apdo. 4328, Managua, Nicaragua. Ed. Eduardo Basso. circ. 300. (back issues avail.)

ARCHIVO DI OCEANOGRAFIA E LIMNOLOGIA. see *EARTH SCIENCES — Oceanography*

551.4   AT
AUSTRALIA. AUSTRALIAN WATER RESOURCES COUNCIL. CONFERENCE SERIES. 1979. irreg., no.12, 1986. Department of Resources and Energy, G.P.O. Box 858, Canberra, A.C.T. 2601, Australia. Indexed: Biol.Abstr. Chem.Abstr.

551.4   AT   ISSN 0067-219X
AUSTRALIA. AUSTRALIAN WATER RESOURCES COUNCIL. HYDROLOGICAL SERIES. 1966. irreg. price varies. Australian Government Publishing Service, G.P.O. Box 84, Canberra, A.C.T. 2601, Australia. Indexed: Sel.Water Res.Abstr. GeoRef.

551.4   AT   ISSN 0725-2293
AUSTRALIA. AUSTRALIAN WATER RESOURCES COUNCIL. OCCASIONAL PAPERS SERIES. 1982. irreg. Department of Resources and Energy, Australian Water Resouces Council, G.P.O. Box 858, Canberra, A.C.T. 2601, Australia. Ed.Bd.

551.4   AT
AUSTRALIA. AUSTRALIAN WATER RESOURCES COUNCIL. TECHNICAL PAPER. irreg., no.87, 1986. Department of Resources and Energy, Australian Water Resources Council, G.P.O. Box 858, Canberra, A.C.T. 2601, Australia. Ed.Bd. Indexed: Biol.Abstr. Geo.Abstr. GeoRef.

551.4   AT   ISSN 0728-9502
AUSTRALIA. AUSTRALIAN WATER RESOURCES COUNCIL. WATER MANAGEMENT SERIES. 1982. irreg. Department of Resources and Energy, Australian Water Resources Council, G.P.O. Box 858, Canberra, A.C.T. 2601, Australia. Ed.Bd. charts.

551.4   PL   ISSN 0239-622X
BIBLIOGRAFIA GOSPODARKI I INZYNIERII WODNEJ/BIBLIOGRAPHY OF WATER MANAGEMENT AND ENGINEERING. (Text in English, French, German, Polish and Russian) 1977. irreg. $180. Instytut Meteorologii i Gospodarki Wodnej - Institute of Meteorology and Water Management, 61 Podlesna St., 01-673 Warsaw, Poland. circ. 270.

551.48   GW   ISSN 0067-8643
DIE BINNENGEWAESSER; Einzeldarstellungen aus der Limnologie und ihren Grenzgebieten. (Text in English and German) 1926. irreg., vol.16, 1984. price varies. E. Schweizerbart'sche Verlagsbuchhandlung, Johannesstr. 3A, 7000 Stuttgart 1, W. Germany (B.R.D.) Eds. H.J. Elster, W. Ohle. Indexed: Biol.Abstr. Ber.Biochem.Biol.

551.48   CR   ISSN 0067-9747
BOLETIN HIDROLOGICO. 1958. a. limited distribution. Instituto Costarricense de Electricidad, Apto. 10032, San Jose, Costa Rica. charts. illus. stat. index. circ. controlled.

551.4   US
CALIFORNIA WATER RESOURCES CENTER. REPORT. no.61, 1984. a. California Water Resources Center, University of California, 2102 Wickson Hall, Davis, CA 95616. TEL 916-752-1544. illus. circ. 265.
Formerly: California Water Resources Center. Annual Report (ISSN 0575-4968)

551.4   CN
CANADA. INLAND WATERS DIRECTORATE. WATER RESOURCES RESEARCH SUPPORT PROGRAM /PROGRAMME DE SUBVENTION A LA RECHERCHE SUR LES RESOURCES EN EAU. (Text in English and French) irreg. Inland Waters Directorate, Environment Canada, Ottawa, Ont. K1A 0E7, Canada. TEL 613-997-2540. Indexed: Geo.Abstr. GeoRef.

553.79   US   ISSN 0094-9671
CONFERENCE ON GROUND WATER. PROCEEDINGS. biennial. $5. University of California, Davis, Water Resources Center, Davis, CA 95616. TEL 916-752-1544. (Co-sponsor: California Department of Water Resources) Key Title: Proceedings - Conference on Ground Water.

551.48   US   ISSN 0589-400X
CONNECTICUT WATER RESOURCES BULLETIN. irreg. Department of Environmental Protection, Hartford, CT 06106. TEL 203-566-5599. illus. Indexed: Biol.Abstr. GeoRef.

DEUTSCHES GEWAESSERKUNDLICHES JAHRBUCH. DONAUGEBIET. see *WATER RESOURCES*

DEUTSCHES GEWAESSERKUNDLICHES JAHRBUCH. KUESTENGEBIET DER NORD-UND OSTSEE. see *WATER RESOURCES*

DEUTSCHES GEWAESSERKUNDLICHES JAHRBUCH. RHEINGEBIET TEIL 2: MAIN. see *WATER RESOURCES*

DEVELOPMENTS IN HYDROBIOLOGY. see *BIOLOGY*

551.48   NE
DEVELOPMENTS IN WATER SCIENCE. 1974. irreg., vol.24, 1985. price varies. Elsevier Science Publishers B.V., Box 211, 1000 AE Amsterdam, Netherlands.

DIRECTORY OF U K FLUID POWER DISTRIBUTORS. see *BUSINESS AND ECONOMICS — Trade And Industrial Directories*

551.48   EC
ECUADOR. INSTITUTO NACIONAL DE METEOROLOGIA E HIDROLOGIA. ANUARIO HIDROLOGICO. 1963. a. available on exchange. Instituto Nacional de Meteorologia e Hidrologia, Daniel Hidalgo 132 y 10 de Agosto, Quito, Ecuador. index.
Supersedes: Ecuador. Servicio Nacional de Meteorologia e Hidrologia. Anuario Hidrologico (ISSN 0070-8933)

551.4   SZ
EIDGENOESSISCHE TECHNISCHE HOCHSCHULE ZUERICH. VERSUCHSANSTALT FUER WASSERBAU, HYDROLOGIE UND GLAZIOLOGIE. JAHRESBERICHT. 1971. a. free. Eidgenoessische Technische Hochschule Zurich, Versuchsanstalt fuer Wasserbau, Hydrologie und Glaziologie, ETH-Zentrum, CH-8092 Zurich, Switzerland. Ed. D. Vischer. illus.

551.4 627   SZ
EIDGENOESSISCHE TECHNISCHE HOCHSCHULE ZUERICH. VERSUCHSANSTALT FUER WASSERBAU, HYDROLOGIE UND GLAZIOLOGIE. MITTEILUNGEN. (Text in English and German) 1971. a. free. Eidgenoessische Technische Hochschule Zurich, Versuchsanstalt fuer Wasserbau, Hydrologie und Glaziologie, ETH-Zentrum, CH-8092 Zurich, Switzerland. Ed. D. Vischer. illus.

551.48   GW   ISSN 0071-1128
ERGEBNISSE DER LIMNOLOGIE/ADVANCES IN LIMNOLOGY. (Supplement to Archiv fuer Hydrobiologie) (Text in English and German) 1964. irreg., no.23, 1986. price varies. (Internationale Vereinigung fuer Theoretische und Angewandte Limnologie) E. Schweizerbart'sche Verlagsbuchhandlung, Johannesstr. 3A, 7000 Stuttgart 1, W. Germany (B.R.D.) Eds. H.J. Elster, W. Ohle. adv. Indexed: Biol.Abstr. Chem.Abstr. Sel.Water Res.Abstr.

551.48   DK
FOLIO LIMNOLOGICA SCANDINAVICA. (Text in English) 1943. irreg., no.18, 1982. Koebenhavns Universitet, Freshwater Biological Laboratory, 51 Helsingoersgade, DK-3400 Hilleroed, Denmark. Ed.Bd.

GEOLOGIA APPLICATA E IDROGEOLOGIA. see *EARTH SCIENCES — Geology*

GEOLOGISCHES JAHRBUCH. REIHE C: HYDROGEOLOGIE. INGENIEURGEOLOGIE. see *EARTH SCIENCES — Geology*

GEOOEKODYNAMIK. see *GEOGRAPHY*

GESELLSCHAFT DER GEOLOGIE- UND BERGBAUSTUDENTEN. MITTEILUNGEN. see *EARTH SCIENCES — Geology*

551.4   DK   ISSN 0109-2073
GROENLANDS GEOLOGISKE UNDERSOEGELSE. GLETSCHER-HYDROLOGISKE MEDDELELSER. 1981. irreg. price varies. Groenlands Geologiske Undersoegelse, Oester Voldgade 10, DK-1350 Copenhagen K, Denmark. illus.

EARTH SCIENCES — HYDROLOGY

GROTTE D'ITALIA. see *EARTH SCIENCES — Geology*

551.49   US   ISSN 0468-5067
GROUNDWATER BULLETIN. 1945. irreg. free. Department of Natural Resources and Community Development, Groundwater Section, Box 27687, Raleigh, NC 27611. TEL 919-733-3221. illus.
  Continues: North Carolina. Division of Ground Water. Ground Water Bulletin.

551.48   IS   ISSN 0073-4217
HYDROLOGICAL YEARBOOK OF ISRAEL/ SHENATON HIDROLOGI LE-YISRAEL. (Text in English and Hebrew) 1946/47. a. $5. Ministry of Agriculture Water Commission, Hydrological Service, Box 6381, Jerusalem 91063, Israel. Ed. S. Polak. circ. 150.

551.4   621.3   US
I E E E WORKING CONFERENCE ON CURRENT MEASUREMENT. PROCEEDINGS. 1978. irreg., 2nd, 1982. (I E E E, Oceanic Engineering Society) Institute of Electrical and Electronics Engineers, Inc., 345 E. 47th St., New York, NY 10017 (Subscr. address: 445 Hoes Ln., Piscataway, NJ 08854)

INDEX DE REFERENCES: INVENTAIRE DES STATIONS HYDROMETRIQUES. see *WATER RESOURCES*

INSTITUT FUER WASSERWIRTSCHAFT, HYDROLOGIE UND LANDWIRTSCHAFTLICHEN WASSERBAU. see *WATER RESOURCES*

551.48   SW   ISSN 0082-0032
INSTITUTE OF FRESHWATER RESEARCH, DROTTNINGHOLM. REPORT. (Text in English) 1933. irreg., no.62, 1986. exchange basis. Institute of Freshwater Research, S-170 11 Drottningholm, Sweden. Ed. Lennart Nyman. circ. 1,800. Indexed: Biol.Abstr. Geo.Abstr.

551.4   FR   ISSN 0579-6733
INTERNATIONAL ASSOCIATION OF HYDROGEOLOGISTS. MEMOIRES. irreg. International Association of Hydrogeologists, 6-8 rue Chasseloup Laubat, 75737 Paris Cedex 15, France.

551.48   GW   ISSN 0538-4680
INTERNATIONAL ASSOCIATION OF THEORETICAL AND APPLIED LIMNOLOGY. COMMUNICATIONS. (Text in English and German) 1953. irreg. (approx. 1/yr.) price varies. ‡ (International Association of Theoretical and Applied Limnology) E. Schweizerbart'sche Verlagsbuchhandlung, Johannesstr. 3A, D-7000 Stuttgart 1, W. Germany (B.R.D.) Ed. V. Sladecek. circ. 4,000 (approx.) Indexed: Biol.Abstr.

551.48   GW   ISSN 0368-0770
INTERNATIONAL ASSOCIATION OF THEORETICAL AND APPLIED LIMNOLOGY. PROCEEDINGS/INTERNATIONALE VEREINIGUNG FUER THEORETISCHE UND ANGEWANDTE LIMNOLOGIE. VERHANDLUNGEN. (Text in English, French and German) 1922. triennial. E. Schweizerbart'sche Verlagsbuchhandlung, Johannesstr. 3, 7000 Stuttgart 1, W. Germany (B.R.D.) Ed. V. Sladecek. index. Indexed: Biol.Abstr. Chem.Abstr. Excerp.Med.

INTERNATIONAL HYDROGRAPHIC CONFERENCE. REPORTS OF PROCEEDINGS. see *EARTH SCIENCES — Oceanography*

INTERNATIONAL HYDROGRAPHIC ORGANIZATION. YEARBOOK. see *EARTH SCIENCES — Oceanography*

551.4   GW   ISSN 0344-5259
INTERNATIONALE HYDROLOGISCHES PROGRAMM: OPERATIONELLES HYDROLOGISCHES PROGRAMM: JAHRBUCH BUNDESREPUBLIK DEUTSCHLAND UND BERLIN (WEST)/INTERNATIONAL HYDROLOGICAL PROGRAMME: OPERATIONAL HYDROLOGICAL PROGRAMME: YEARBOOK FEDERAL REPUBLIC OF GERMANY AND BERLIN (WEST) (Text in English and German) 1965. a. on exchange basis. Bundesanstalt fuer Gewaesserkunde, Kaisern-Augusta-Anlagen 15-17, D-5400 Koblenz, W. Germany (B.R.D.)
  Formerly: Internationale Hydrologische Dekade: Yearbook of the Federal Republic of Germany (ISSN 0538-7779)

551.4   AT
INVENTORY OF WATER RESOURCES RESEARCH IN AUSTRALIA. 1965. irreg. (Australian Water Resources Council) Australian Government Publishing Service, G.P.O. Box 84, Canberra, A.C.T. 2601, Australia.

551.4   UR   ISSN 0202-7356
ITOGI NAUKI I TEKHNIKI: GIDROGEOLOGIYA. INZHENERNAYA GEOLOGIYA. irreg., latest vol.10, 1985. price varies. Vsesoyuznyi Institut Nauchno-Tekhnicheskoi Informatsii (VINITI), Baltiiskaya ul. 14, Moscow A-219, Russian S.F.S.R., U.S.S.R. (Subscr. to: Mezhdunarodnaya Kniga, Dimitrova ul. 39, 113095 Moscow, Russian S.F.S.R., U.S.S.R.) Indexed: GeoRef.

551.4   JA   ISSN 0021-4485
JAPAN. MARITIME SAFETY AGENCY. HYDROGRAPHIC DEPARTMENT. HYDROGRAPHIC BULLETIN/SUIRO YOHO. (Text in Japanese) 1922. a. 1700 Yen. Maritime Safety Agency, Hydrographic Department - Kaijo Hoan-cho Suiro-bu, 5-3-1 Tsukiji, Chuo-ku, Tokyo 104, Japan. Ed. Daitaro Shoji.

551.4   JA
JAPAN. MARITIME SAFETY AGENCY. HYDROGRAPHIC DEPARTMENT. REPORT OF HYDROGRAPHIC RESEARCH. no.14, 1979. irreg. Maritime Safety Agency, Hydrographic Department, 5-3-1 Tsukiji, Chuo-ku, Tokyo 104, Japan.

JOKULL. see *EARTH SCIENCES — Geology*

551.48   614.7   US   ISSN 0270-5060
JOURNAL OF FRESHWATER ECOLOGY. vol.3, 1986. irreg. $35. Oikos Publishers, Inc., Box 2558, La Crosse, WI 54602-2558. TEL 608-526-9477. Ed. Joseph A. Kawatski. Indexed: Biol.Abstr. Chem.Abstr. Curr.Cont.

551.48   US
KANSAS GEOLOGICAL SURVEY. BASIC DATA SERIES. GROUND-WATER RELEASES. 1973. irreg, no.7, 1980. $5. Geological Survey, 1930 Constant Ave., Campus West, University of Kansas, Lawrence, KS 66046. TEL 913-864-3965.

551.48   US
KANSAS GEOLOGICAL SURVEY. GROUND WATER SERIES. 1974. irreg., no. 8, 1985. price varies. Geological Survey, 1930 Constant Ave., Campus West, University of Kansas, Lawrence, KS 66046-2598.

551.4   LO
LESOTHO. MINISTRY OF WATER, ENERGY AND MINING. HYDROLOGICAL YEARBOOK. (Text in English) 1970. quinquennial. $5. Ministry of Water, Energy and Mining, Water Affairs Department, P.O. Box MS772, Maseru 100, Lesotho. (back issues avail.)

551.48   GE   ISSN 0075-9511
LIMNOLOGICA. 1962. irreg., vol.16, 1985. price varies. (Akademie der Wissenschaften des DDR, Zentralinstitut fuer Mikrobiologie und Experimentelle Therapie) Akademie-Verlag, Leipziger Str. 3-4, 108 Berlin, E. Germany (D.D.R.) Ed. J. Casper. Indexed: Biol.Abstr. Chem.Abstr. Excerp.Med. GeoRef. Sel.Water Res.Abstr.

LIST OF HYDROBIOLOGICAL PAPERS OF BRITISH FRESH WATERS. see *ENVIRONMENTAL STUDIES*

LOUISIANA WATER RESOURCES RESEARCH INSTITUTE. ANNUAL REPORT. see *WATER RESOURCES*

551.4   PL   ISSN 0239-6238
MATERIALY BADAWCZE. SERIA: GOSPODARKA WODNA I OCHRONA WOD/ RESEARCH PAPERS SERIES: WATER MANAGEMENT AND WATER PROTECTION. (Text in Polish; summaries in English and Russian) 1973. irreg. $273. Instytut Meteorologii i Gospodarki Wodnej - Institute of Meteorology and Water Management, 61 Podlesna St., 01-673 Warsaw, Poland. circ. 350.

551.4   PL
MATERIALY BADAWCZE. SERIA: HYDROLOGIA I OCEANOLOGIA/RESEARCH PAPERS SERIES: HYDROLOGY AND OCEANOLOGY. (Text in Polish; summaries in English and Russian) 1977. irreg. $273. Instytut Meteorologii i Gospodarki Wodnej - Institute of Meteorology and Water Management, 61 Podlesna St., 01-673 Warsaw, Poland. circ. 350.

MEMORIE DI SCIENZE GEOLOGICHE. see *EARTH SCIENCES — Geology*

MISSOURI. DIVISION OF GEOLOGICAL SURVEY AND WATER RESOURCES. WATER RESOURCES REPORT. see *WATER RESOURCES*

551.4   DK   ISSN 0900-0267
N H P RAPPORT. 1981. irreg. price varies. Nordisk Hydrologisk Forening, c/o Miljoestyrelsen, Vandressource Kontoret, Strandgade 29, 1401 Copenhagen K, Denmark. illus.

551.48   US
NEW MEXICO. BUREAU OF MINES AND MINERAL RESOURCES. HYDROLOGIC REPORT. 1971. irreg., no.6, 1982. price varies. Bureau of Mines and Mineral Resources, Socorro, NM 87801. illus. (also avail. in microfiche) Indexed: GeoRef.
  Supersedes: Ground-Water Reports (1948-1970)

551   NO
NORSK INSTITUTT FOR VANNFORSKNING. AARBOK. 1958/67. a. free. Norsk Institutt for Vannforskning - Norwegian Institute for Water Research, Postboks 333, Blindern, Oslo 3, Norway. Ed. illus.

551   NO
NORSK INSTITUTT FOR VANNFORSKNING. TEMARAPPORT. irreg., latest no.5, 1981. Norsk Institutt for Vannforskning - Norwegian Institute for Water Research, Postboks 333, Blindern, Oslo 3, Norway. charts. illus.

OCCASIONAL PAPERS IN MARITIME AFFAIRS; Australia's offshore maritime interests. see *ENVIRONMENTAL STUDIES*

551.48   CN   ISSN 0475-0942
ONTARIO. MINISTRY OF THE ENVIRONMENT. WATER RESOURCES BRANCH. WATER RESOURCES REPORT. irreg. Ministry of the Environment, Water Resources Branch, 135 St. Clair Ave. W., Toronto, Ont. M4V 1P5, Canada. TEL 416-965-6141.

551.48   UN
OPERATIONAL HYDROLOGY REPORTS. irreg. price varies. World Meteorological Organization, 41 Av. Giuseppe Motta, CH-1211 Geneva 20, Switzerland (Dist. in U.S. by: American Meteorological Society, 45 Beacon St., Boston, MA 02108)

551.4   US
PROCEEDINGS OF THE ARIZONA SECTION, AMERICAN WATER RESOURCES ASSOCIATION AND THE HYDROLOGY SECTION, ARIZONA-NEVADA ACADEMY OF SCIENCE. 1971. a. $14. American Water Resources Association, Arizona Section, Office of Arid Lands Studies, 845 N. Park Ave., Tucson, AZ 85719. Ed.Bd. charts. illus. stat. (back issues avail.)

551.4 623.82 UK
PROGRESS IN UNDERWATER SCIENCE.
(Contains papers submitted at annual and regional symposia of the Underwater Association) vol.5, 1979(N.S.) a. £5. Underwater Association, c/o Erika Charlier, Dunmoine, Salen, Isle of Mull, Scotland. Eds. K. Hiscock, A.D. Baume. circ. 500. Indexed: Biol.Abstr.

551.4 CS ISSN 0036-5289
SBORNIK GEOLOGICKYCH VED:
HYDROGEOLOGIE, INZENYRSKA GEOLOGIE/JOURNAL OF GEOLOGICAL SCIENCES: HYDROGEOLOGY, ENGINEERING GEOLOGY. (Text and summaries in Czech, English, French, German, Russian) 1964. irreg. Ustredni Ustav Geologicky, Malostranske nam. 19, 118 21 Prague 1, Czechoslovakia (Subscr. to: Artia, Ve Smeckach 30, 111 27 Prague 1, Czechoslovakia) Ed. Jan Jetel. charts. illus. circ. 600. (back issues avail.) Indexed: Bull.Signal. Ref.Zh. GeoRef.

SCHRIFTENREIHE DES BAYER.
LANDESAMTES FUER WASSERWIRTSCHAFT. see WATER RESOURCES

551.48 CN
SELECTED STREAMFLOW DATA FOR ONTARIO. 1969. a. Ministry of the Environment, Water Resources Branch, 135 St. Clair Avenue West, Toronto, Ontario M4V 1P5, Canada. TEL 416-965-6141.

SOVIET HYDROLOGY: SELECTED PAPERS. see WATER RESOURCES

551.4 CE
SRI LANKA. IRRIGATION DEPARTMENT. HYDROLOGY DIVISION. HYDROLOGICAL ANNUAL. a. Irrigation Department, Hydrology Division, Bauddhaloka Mawatha, Colombo 7, Sri Lanka. illus.

551.48 US ISSN 0376-4826
STEIRISCHE BEITRAEGE ZUR HYDROGEOLOGIE. a. $30. Springer-Verlag, 175 Fifth Ave., New York, NY 10010 TEL 212-460-1500. (Also Berlin, Heidelberg, Tokyo and Vienna) Ed. Josef Zoetl. (reprint service avail. from ISI) Indexed: GeoRef.

551.48 UN ISSN 0081-7449
STUDIES AND REPORTS IN HYDROLOGY SERIES. (Text in English and French) 1969. irreg., no.41, 1984. Unesco, 7-9 Place de Fontenoy, 75700 Paris, France (Dist. in U.S. by: Bernan Associates-Unipub, 4611-F Assembly Dr., Lanham, MD 20706-4391) Indexed: GeoRef.

627 RM
STUDII DE HIDRAULICA. (Text in Rumanian; summaries in English and French) a. Academia de Stiinte Agricole si Silvice, Institutul de Cercetari Pentru Imbunatatiri Funciare, B-dul Marasti Nr. 61, Bucharest, Rumania (Subscr. to: ILEXIM, Str. 13 Decembrie Nr. 3, P.O. Box 136-137, Bucharest, Rumania)

SYMPOSIUM ON SURFACE MINING, HYDROLOGY, SEDIMENTOLOGY AND RECLAMATION. PROCEEDINGS. see MINES AND MINING INDUSTRY

551.48 UN ISSN 0082-2310
TECHNICAL PAPERS IN HYDROLOGY SERIES. 1970. irreg., no.26, 1983. Unesco, 7-9 Place de Fontenoy, 75700 Paris, France (Dist. in U.S. by: Bernan Associates-Unipub, 4611-F Assembly Dr., Lanham, MD 20706-4391)

553.7 US ISSN 0092-332X
U.S. GEOLOGICAL SURVEY. WATER RESOURCES INVESTIGATIONS. no.121, 1978. irreg., no. 4061, 1983. U.S. Geological Survey, 12201 Sunrise Valley Dr., Reston, VA 22092 TEL 703-860-7000. (Most reports avail. only in microfiche from: NTIS, 5285 Port Royal Rd., Springfield, VA 22161) Indexed: Pollut.Abstr. Geo.Abstr. GeoRef. Key Title: Water-Resources Investigations.

333.91 US ISSN 0083-1131
U.S. GEOLOGICAL SURVEY. WATER SUPPLY PAPERS. 1896. irreg. U.S. Geological Survey, 12201 Sunrise Valley Dr., Reston, VA 22092 TEL 703-860-7000. (Orders to: 604 S. Pickett St., Alexandria, VA 22304) Indexed: Geo.Abstr.

551.4 MX
UNIVERSIDAD NACIONAL AUTONOMA DE MEXICO. INSTITUTO DE GEOFISICA. DATOS GEOFISICOS A TABLAS DE PREDICCION DE MAREAS, PUERTOS DEL GOLFO DE MEXICO Y MAR CARIBE. 1963. a. $20. Universidad Nacional Autonoma de Mexico, Instituto de Geofisica, Circuito Exterior, Ciudad Universitaria, Mexico 20, D.F., Mexico. Ed. Francisco Graffe.

551.4 MX
UNIVERSIDAD NACIONAL AUTONOMA DE MEXICO. INSTITUTO DE GEOFISICA. DATOS GEOFISICOS A TABLAS DE PREDICCION DE MAREAS, PUERTOS DEL OCEANO PACIFICO. 1963. a. $20. Universidad Nacional Autonoma de Mexico, Instituto de Geofisica, Circuito Exterior, Ciudad Universitaria, Mexico 20, D.F., Mexico. Ed. Francisco Graffe.

574 BL
UNIVERSIDADE FEDERAL DO RIO GRANDE DO NORTE. CENTRO DE BIOCIENCIAS. DEPARTAMENTO DE OCEANOGRAFIA E LIMNOLOGIA. BOLETIM. 1964. irreg. exchange basis. Universidade do Rio Grande do Norte, Departamento de Oceanografia e Limnologia, Av. Hermes da Fonseca 780, Natal, Rio Grande, Brazil. Ed. Prof. Sebastiao Monte. circ. 1,000. Indexed: Biol.Abstr.
Formerly: Universidade Federal do Rio Grande do Norte. Instituto de Biologia Marinha. Boletim (ISSN 0041-8927)

551.4 SZ
UNIVERSITE DE NEUCHATEL. CENTRE D'HYDROGEOLOGIE. BULLETIN. (Text in French and German) 1976. a. 20 Fr. (Universite de Neuchatel, Centre d'Hydrogeologie) Editions Peter Lang SA, 15 Jupiterstr., CH Berne, Switzerland. adv. circ. 500.

WATER RESOURCES SUMMARY. see WATER RESOURCES

WEST VIRGINIA RIVER BASIN BULLETINS. see EARTH SCIENCES — Geology

551.4 US
WESTERN SNOW CONFERENCE. PROCEEDINGS. 1948. a. $20. Western Snow Conference, Box 14884, Spokane, WA 99214. TEL 509-928-4787. Ed. Bernard A. Shafer. circ. 800.

EARTH SCIENCES — Oceanography

551.46 AT
A I M S MONOGRAPH SERIES. 1976. irreg. price varies. Australian Institute of Marine Science, Townsville, Queensland 4810, Australia. Indexed: Biol.Abstr.

551.46 CU
ACADEMIA DE CIENCIAS DE CUBA. INSTITUTO DE OCEANOLOGIA. REPORTE DE INVESTIGACION. (Text in Spanish; summaries in English) irreg. Academia de Ciencias de Cuba, Instituto de Oceanologia, Avda. 1ra. no. 18406, Playa, Havana, Cuba. Dir. Guillermo Garcia Montero. illus.
Supersedes (after no.187): Academia de Ciencias de Cuba. Instituto de Oceanologia. Informes Cientificos Tecnicos.

550 CU
ACADEMIA DE CIENCIAS DE CUBA. INSTITUTO DE OCEANOLOGIA. TABLAS DE MAREAS. Cover title: Tablas de Mareas: Costas de Cuba. a. Academia de Ciencias de Cuba, Instituto de Oceanologia, Avda. 1ra. no. 18406, Havana, Cuba. illus.

551.46 YU ISSN 0001-5113
ACTA ADRIATICA. 1932. a. exchange basis. Institut za Oceanografiju i Ribarstvo - Institute of Oceanography and Fisheries, Mose Pijade 63, Box 114, 58001 Split, Yugoslavia. Ed. Mira Zore Armanda. circ. 400. Indexed: Biol.Abstr. Chem.Abstr. Ocean.Abstr. Pollut.Abstr. GeoRef.

551.4 CH
ACTA OCEANOGRAPHICA TAIWANICA. (Text in English; summaries in Chinese and English) 1971. a. $20. National Taiwan University, Institute of Oceanography, Box 23-13, Taipei, Taiwan, Republic of China. Ed.Bd. bk. rev. circ. 600-1,000. Indexed: Chem.Abstr. Ocean.Abstr. Pollut.Abstr. Deep Sea Res.& Oceanogr.Abstr. GeoRef.

551.46 PL ISSN 0208-5348
ACTA UNIVERSITATIS NICOLAI COPERNICI. PRACE LIMNOLOGICZNE. 1965. irreg. price varies. Uniwersytet Mikolaja Kopernika, Fosa Staromiejska 3, Torun, Poland (Dist. by Osrodek Rozpowszechniania Wydawnictw Naukowych PAN, Palac Kultury i Nauki, 00-901 Warsaw, Poland) Indexed: Biol.Abstr.

ADVANCES IN FISHERIES OCEANOGRAPHY. see BIOLOGY — Zoology

ADVANCES IN MARINE BIOLOGY. see BIOLOGY

551.46 UY
ALMANAQUE. a. Servicio de Oceanografia e Hidrografia, Capurro 980, Casilla de Correo 1381, Montevideo, Uruguay.

551.46 II ISSN 0066-1686
ANDHRA UNIVERSITY MEMOIRS IN OCEANOGRAPHY. (Text in English) 1954. irreg. price varies. Andhra University Press and Publications, Waltair, Visakhapatnam 530003, Andhra Pradesh, India. Ed. E.C. la Fond.

551.46 FR ISSN 0180-989X
ANNUAIRE DES MAREES POUR L'AN. TOME 1. PORTS DE FRANCE. 1958. a. price varies. Service Hydrographique et Oceanographique de la Marine, 3 av. Octave Greard, 75200 Paris Naval, France (Subscr. address: EPSHOM., B.P. 426, 29275 Brest Cedex, France) index. circ. 10,000. (tabloid format)

551.46 FR ISSN 0180-9962
ANNUAIRE DES MAREES POUR L'AN. TOME 2. PORTS D'OUTRE MER. 1958. a. price varies. Service Hydrographique et Oceanographique de la Marine, 3 av. Octave Greard, 75200 Paris Naval, France (Subscr. address: E.P.S.H.O.M., B.P. 426, 29275 Brest Cedex, France)

ARCHAEONAUTICA. see ARCHAEOLOGY

551.46 551.48 IT ISSN 0066-667X
ARCHIVO DI OCEANOGRAFIA E LIMNOLOGIA. (Text in Italian or congress languages; summaries in English and Italian) 1941. irreg., vol.19, no.2. L.5000 per no. Istituto di Biologia del Mare, Riva 7 Martiri 1364-A, 30122 Venice, Italy. Ed. B. Battaglia. bk. rev. circ. 500. Indexed: Biol.Abstr. Ocean.Abstr. Pollut.Abstr.

551.4 AG ISSN 0004-1076
ARGENTINA. SERVICIO DE HIDROGRAFIA NAVAL. BOLETIN. 1964. irreg.; latest, vol.13, nos.1/2, 1976. exchange basis. Servicio de Hidrografia Naval, Montes de Oca 2124, Codigo Postal 1271, Buenos Aires, Argentina. bk. rev. circ. 300. Indexed: GeoRef.

551.46 AT
AUSTRALIAN INSTITUTE OF MARINE SCIENCE. YEARLY REPORT. 1972. a. Australian Institute of Marine Science, Private Mail Bag No. 3, Townsville M.C., Queensland 4810, Australia. charts. illus. circ. 2,000.

551.46 CN ISSN 0229-8910
BEDFORD INSTITUTE OF OCEANOGRAPHY REVIEW. (Editions in English and French) 1968. a. free. Department of Fisheries and Oceans, Bedford Institute of Oceanography, Dartmouth, N.S. B2Y 4A2, Canada. TEL 902-426-5947. Ed. M.P. Latremouille. circ. 5,000(controlled) Indexed: Aqua.Sci.& Fish.Abstr. GeoRef.
Formerly: Bedford Institute of Oceanography. Biennial Review (ISSN 0067-480X)

551.46 GE ISSN 0067-5148
BEITRAEGE ZUR MEERESKUNDE. 1961. irreg., no.54, 1986. price varies. (Akademie der Wissenschaften der DDR, Institut fuer Meereskunde, Warnemuende) Akademie-Verlag, Leipziger Strasse 3-4, 1086 Berlin, E. Germany (D.D.R.) Ed. K. Voigt. Indexed: Ocean.Abstr. Pollut.Abstr. GeoRef.

551.46 614.7   BM
BERMUDA. BIOLOGICAL STATION FOR
RESEARCH. SPECIAL PUBLICATIONS. 1969.
irreg., vol.27, 1984. price varies. Biological Station
for Research, Inc., Ferry Reach 1-15, Bermuda. circ.
250. (back issues avail.) Indexed: Biol.Abstr.
GeoRef.

551.46   US
C G O U TECHNICAL REPORT. 1964. irreg. U.S.
Coast Guard, Oceanographic Unit, 400 Seventh St.,
S.W., Washington, DC 20590 TEL 703-426-2158.
(Order from: N T I S, Springfield, VA 22151) circ.
300.

CANADA. HYDROGRAPHIC SERVICE. WATER
LEVELS. VOL. 1: DAILY MEANS. see *EARTH
SCIENCES*

CANADA. HYDROGRAPHIC SERVICE. WATER
LEVELS. VOL. 2: TIDAL HIGHS AND LOWS.
see *EARTH SCIENCES*

CANADIAN INDUSTRY REPORT OF FISHERIES
AND AQUATIC SCIENCES. see *FISH AND
FISHERIES*

CANADIAN MANUSCRIPT REPORT OF
FISHERIES AND AQUATIC SCIENCES. see
ENVIRONMENTAL STUDIES

623.894   CN   ISSN 0068-9882
CANADIAN TIDE AND CURRENT TABLES.
1967. a. Can.$0.50. Department of Fisheries and
Oceans, Canadian Hydrographic Service, P.O. Box
8080, 1675 Russell Rd., Ottawa, Ont. K1G 3H6,
Canada. TEL 613-995-3065.

CENTRAL MARINE FISHERIES RESEARCH
INSTITUTE. BULLETIN. see *FISH AND
FISHERIES*

551.46   JA
CHOI NENPO/YEARBOOK OF TIDAL
RECORDS. (Text in Japanese) 1966. a.
Geographical Survey Institute, Kitazato-1, Yatabe-
Machi, Tsukuba-Gun, Ibaraki-Ken 305, Japan. circ.
400.

551.46   CL
CIENCIA Y TECNOLOGIA DEL MAR. (Text in
Spanish; summaries in English) a. Comite
Oceanografico Nacional, Errauriz 232, Casilla 324,
Valparaiso, Chile. Indexed: GeoRef.

COASTAL ENGINEERING RESEARCH
COUNCIL. PROCEEDINGS. see
ENGINEERING — Civil Engineering

551.46   FR   ISSN 0761-392X
COMITES FRANCAIS DE GEODESIE ET
GEOPHYSIQUE. ANNALES. (Text in English or
French) 1934. irreg. price varies. International
Association for the Physical Sciences of the Ocean,
I U G G Publications Office, 39 rue Gay Lussac,
Paris, France. Ed. Dr. E.L. LaFond. circ. 600. (back
issues avail.)
 Former titles: International Association for the
Physical Science of the Ocean. Proces-Verbaux;
International Association for the Physical Science of
Oceanography. Proces-Verbaux.

COMMONWEALTH SCIENTIFIC AND
INDUSTRIAL RESEARCH ORGANIZATION.
MARINE LABORATORIES. REPORT. see *FISH
AND FISHERIES*

COMMONWEALTH SCIENTIFIC AND
INDUSTRIAL RESEARCH ORGANIZATION.
MARINE LABORATORIES. RESEARCH
REPORT. see *FISH AND FISHERIES*

551.2 551   UK   ISSN 0069-9691
CONTRIBUTIONS TO MARINE SCIENCE. 1957.
a. exchange basis. University College of North
Wales., Marine Science Laboratories, Menai Bridge,
Anglesey, Wales. circ. 140. Indexed: Curr.Cont.

551.46   DK   ISSN 0070-2668
DANA-REPORT. (Carlsberg Foundation's
oceanographical expedition round the world 1928-30
and previous Dana expeditions) (Text in English;
occasionally French or German) 1934. irreg. price
varies. (Carlsberg Foundation) Scandinavian Science
Press Ltd., Langasen 4, Ganlose, 2760 Malov,
Denmark. Ed. E. Bertelsen. cum.index: 1934-1969.
Indexed: Biol.Abstr.

551.46   IS   ISSN 0070-3095
DEAD SEA WORKS, BEERSHEBA, ISRAEL.
REPORT OF THE DIRECTORS. (English
translation of Hebrew text) 1963/64. a. ‡ Dead Sea
Works, Ltd., Beersheba, Israel. circ. 1,000.

551.46   GW   ISSN 0070-4164
DEUTSCHE HYDROGRAPHISCHE
ZEITSCHRIFT. ERGAENZUNGSHEFT. REIHE
A. 1952. irreg., no.15, 1978. Deutsches
Hydrographisches Institut, Bernhard-Nocht-Str. 78,
2000 Hamburg 4, W. Germany (B.R.D.) Eds. G.
Heise, D. Voppel.

551.46   GW   ISSN 0070-4172
DEUTSCHE HYDROGRAPHISCHE
ZEITSCHRIFT. ERGAENZUNGSHEFT. REIHE
B. 1956. irreg., no.15, 1980. Deutsches
Hydrographisches Institut, Bernhard-Nocht-Str. 78,
2000 Hamburg 4, W. Germany (B.R.D.) Eds. G.
Heise, D. Voppel.

551.46   GW   ISSN 0070-4458
DEUTSCHES HYDROGRAPHISCHES INSTITUT.
JAHRESBERICHT. 1947. a. DM.9.50. Deutsches
Hydrographisches Institut, Bernhard-Nocht-Str. 78,
2000 Hamburg 4, W. Germany (B.R.D.) circ. 2,200.
Indexed: GeoRef.

551.46   UK   ISSN 0070-6698
DISCOVERY REPORTS. 1929. irreg. price varies.
Institute of Oceanographic Sciences, Wormley,
Godalming, Surrey GU8 5UB, England. Ed. M.V.
Angel. Indexed: Biol.Abstr. Aqua.Sci.& Fish.Abstr.
Geo.Abstr.

551.46   AT   ISSN 0729-0403
EBB AND FLOW. 1982. irreg. Great Barrier Reef
Marine Park Authority, P.O. Box 1379, Townsville
Qld. 4810, Australia. circ. 10,000. (tabloid format)

551.46   NE   ISSN 0078-3226
ELSEVIER OCEANOGRAPHY SERIES. 1964.
irreg., vol.40, 1985. price varies. Elsevier Science
Publishers B.V., Box 211, 1000 AE Amsterdam,
Netherlands. Indexed: Biol.Abstr. Chem.Abstr.
Math.R. GeoRef.

EPIMENIDES/EPIMENIS. see *ASTRONOMY*

551.4   CL   ISSN 0071-173X
ESTUDIOS OCEANOLOGICOS. 1965-1966;
resumed 1983. irreg., latest vol.5, 1986. $10.
Universidad de Antofagasta, Instituto de
Investigaciones Oceanologicas, Casilla 1240,
Antofagasta, Chile. Ed. Oscar Zuniga Romero. circ.
600.

551.4   FI   ISSN 0357-1076
FINNISH MARINE RESEARCH. (Text mainly in
English) 1920. irreg., no.252, 1985. price varies.
Finnish institute of Marine Research, Box 33, SF-
00931 Helsinki 93, Finland (Orders to: Government
Printing Centre, Box 516, SF-00101 Helsinki 10,
Finland) Ed. Aarno Voipio. circ. 800. (back issues
avail.) Indexed: Biol.Abstr. Chem.Abstr.
Ocean.Abstr. Ref.Zh. Aqua.Sci.& Fish.Abstr.
Pollut.Abstr.
 Formerly (until 1978): Finland.
Merentutkimuslaitoksen. Julkaisu (ISSN 0025-9985)

FLINDERS INSTITUTE FOR ATMOSPHERIC
AND MARINE SCIENCES. COMPUTING
REPORTS. see *METEOROLOGY*

551.5   AT
FLINDERS INSTITUTE FOR ATMOSPHERIC
AND MARINE SCIENCES. CRUISE REPORTS.
1972. irreg., no.7, 1978. Flinders Institute for
Atmospheric and Marine Sciences, Bedford Park,
S.A. 5042, Australia. Ed. Peter Schwerdtfeger. circ.
150.

FLINDERS INSTITUTE FOR ATMOSPHERIC
AND MARINE SCIENCES. RESEARCH
REPORTS. see *METEOROLOGY*

FLINDERS INSTITUTE FOR ATMOSPHERIC
AND MARINE SCIENCES. TECHNICAL
REPORTS. see *METEOROLOGY*

551.46   FR   ISSN 0761-3962
FRANCE. I.F.RE.MER. CENTRE DE BREST.
COLLOQUES. ACTES. 1971. irreg. Institut
Francais de Recherche pour l'Exploitation de la Mer
(IFREMER), Centre de Brest, Service
Documentation et Publications, B.P. 337, 29273
Brest Cedex, France. Ed. Raoul Piboubes. Indexed:
Biol.Abstr. Bull.Signal. Chem.Abstr. Ocean.Abstr.
Poll.Abstr. Bibl.Geogr.Int. GeoRef.
Ocean.Abstr.Bibl.
 Formerly: France. Centre National pour
l'Exploitation des Oceans. Colloques. Actes (ISSN
0335-8259)

551.46 347.75   FR   ISSN 0761-3938
FRANCE. I.F.RE.MER. CENTRE DE BREST.
PUBLICATIONS. SERIE: RAPPORTS
ECONOMIQUES ET JURIDIQUES. 1973. irreg.,
latest no.11, 1982. Institut Francais de Recherche
pour l'Exploitation de la Mer (IFREMER), Centre
de Brest, B.P. 337, 29273 Brest Cedex, France. Ed.
Raoul Piboubes. Indexed: Biol.Abstr. Bull.Signal.
Chem.Abstr. Ocean.Abstr. Poll.Abstr.
Bibl.Geogr.Int. GeoRef. Ocean.Abstr.Bibl.
Zoo.Rec.
 Formerly: France. Centre National pour
l'Exploitation des Oceans. Publications. Serie:
Rapports Economiques et Juridiques (ISSN 0339-
2910)

551.46   FR   ISSN 0761-3970
FRANCE. I.F.RE.MER. CENTRE DE BREST.
PUBLICATIONS. SERIE: RAPPORTS
SCIENTIFIQUES ET TECHNIQUES. 1971. irreg.,
latest no.55, 1982. Institut Francais de Rechercher
pour l'Exploitation de la Mer (IFREMER), Service
de la Documentation et des Publications, B.P. 337,
29273 Brest Cedex, France. Ed. Raoul Piboubes.
Indexed: Biol.Abstr. Bull.Signal. Chem.Abstr.
Ocean.Abstr. Poll.Abstr. Bibl.Geogr.Int. GeoRef.
Ocean.Abstr.Bibl. Zoo.Rec.
 Formerly: France. Centre National pour
l'Exploitation des Oceans. Publications. Serie:
Rapports Scientifiques et Techniques (ISSN 0339-
2899)

551.46   FR   ISSN 0761-3989
FRANCE. I.F.RE.MER. CENTRE DE BREST.
PUBLICATIONS. SERIE: RESULTATS DES
CAMPAGNES A LA MER. 1971. irreg., latest
no.29, 1982. Institut Francais de Recherche pour
l'Exploitation de la Mer (IFREMER), Centre de
Brest, B.P. 337, 29273 Brest Cedex, France. Ed.
Raoul Piboubes. charts. stat. Indexed: Biol.Abstr.
Bull.Signal. Chem.Abstr. Ocean.Abstr. Poll.Abstr.
Bibl.Geogr.Int. GeoRef. Ocean Abstr.Bibl.
Zoo.Rec.
 Formerly: France. Centre National pour
l'Exploitation des Oceans. Publications. Serie:
Resultats des Campagnes a la Mer (ISSN 0339-
2902)

551.4   GW   ISSN 0084-9774
GEZEITENTAFELN. 1879. a. DM.30. Deutsches
Hydrographisches Institut, Bernhard-Nocht-Str. 78,
2000 Hamburg 4, W. Germany (B.R.D.) circ. 6,300.
(tabloid format)

551.46   SW
GOETEBORGS UNIVERSITET.
OCEANOGRAFISKA INSTITUTIONEN.
REPORTS. (Text in English) 1969. irreg., no.42,
1982. free. Goeteborgs Universitet, Oceanografiska
Institutionen, Box 4038, 400 40 Goeteborg, Sweden.
circ. 100.
 Supersedes (1930-1964, no.31): Oceanografiska
Institutet, Goeteborg. Meddelanden (ISSN 0072-
5072)

551.46   AT   ISSN 0705-8764
GREAT BARRIER REEF MARINE PARK
AUTHORITY BULLETIN. 1980. irreg. free. Great
Barrier Reef Marine Park Authority, Box 1379,
Townsville, Qld. 4810, Australia. circ. 1,500.

551.46   AT   ISSN 0156-5842
GREAT BARRIER REEF MARINE PARK
AUTHORITY WORKSHOP SERIES. 1978. irreg.
free. Great Barrier Reef Marine Park Authority,
Box 1379, Townsville, Qld. 4810, Australia. circ. 1,
500.

EARTH SCIENCES — OCEANOGRAPHY

551.46 639.2 JA ISSN 0439-3511
HOKKAIDO UNIVERSITY. FACULTY OF FISHERIES. DATA RECORD OF OCEANOGRAPHIC OBSERVATIONS AND EXPLORATORY FISHING/KAIYO CHOSA GYOGYO SHIKEN YOHO. (Text in Japanese and European languages) 1957. a. exchange basis. Hokkaido University, Faculty of Fisheries, 3-1-1 Minato-machi, Hakodate, Hokkaido 041, Japan. circ. 600.

551.46 JA
HOKKAIDO UNIVERSITY. INSTITUTE OF ALGOLOGICAL RESEARCH. SCIENTIFIC PAPERS/HOKKAIDO DAIGAKU RIGAKUBU KAISO KENKYUSHO OBUN HOKOKU. (Text in English) 1935. irrege. exchange basis. Hokkaido University, Institute of Algological Research, Bokoi, Muroran, Hokkaido 051, Japan. Indexed: Biol.Abstr.

551.46 DK ISSN 0106-6935
I C E S OCEANOGRAPHIC DATA LISTS AND INVENTORIES. (Text in English) 1971. irreg., no.68, 1986. price varies. International Council for the Exploration of the Sea, Palaegade 2, DK-1261 Copenhagen K, Denmark (Subscr. to: C. A. Reitzels Boghandel, Noerregade 20, DK-1165 Copenhagen K, Denmark) circ. 300. (Back issues avail.)
Supersedes: I C E S Oceanographic Data Lists (ISSN 0074-4328) & International Council for the Exploration of the Sea. Bulletin Hydrographique.

551.46 MC ISSN 0304-5722
INSTITUT OCEANOGRAPHIQUE. BULLETIN. (Text in English or French) 1904. irreg., no.1436, 1986. price varies. Musee Oceanographique, Service des Publications, Avenue Saint-Martin, Monaco-Ville, MC 98000, Monaco. illus. (back issues avail.) Indexed: Biol.Abstr. Ref.Zh.

551.46 MC ISSN 0304-5714
INSTITUT OCEANOGRAPHIQUE. MEMOIRES. (Text in English and French) 1970. irreg., latest no.14, 1983. price varies. Musee Oceanographique, Service des Publications, Ave. Saint-Martin, Monaco-Ville, MC 98000, Monaco. Ed. Jacqueline Carpine-Lancre. illus. circ. 850. (back issues avail.) Indexed: Biol.Abstr. Ref.Zh.

551.46 JA ISSN 0386-1198
INSTITUTE FOR SEA TRAINING. JOURNAL. (Text in Japanese, summaries in English) 1951. irreg. free. Ministry of Transport, Institute for Sea Training, 2-1-3 Kasumigaseki, Chiyoda-ku, Tokyo 100, Japan. Ed.Bd. circ. 300.

551.46 UK ISSN 0309-4472
INSTITUTE OF OCEANOGRAPHIC SCIENCES. ANNUAL REPORT. 1973. a. £5. Institute of Oceanographic Sciences, Wormley, Godalming, Surrey GU8 5UB, England. Indexed: Biol.Abstr. Ocean.Abstr. GeoRef.

551.46 UK ISSN 0309-7463
INSTITUTE OF OCEANOGRAPHIC SCIENCES. COLLECTED REPRINTS. 1953. a. available on exchange. ‡ Institute of Oceanographic Sciences, Wormley, Godalming, Surrey GU8 5UB, England.
Formerly: Wormley, England (Surrey) National Institute of Oceanography. Collected Reprints (ISSN 0084-2605)

551.46 SP ISSN 0074-0195
INSTITUTO ESPANOL DE OCEANOGRAFIA. BOLETIN. (Text in Spanish; summaries in English and French) 1948. irreg., no.171, 1969. Instituto Espanol de Oceanografia, Alcala 27, Madrid 14, Spain. Indexed: Biol.Abstr. Helminthol.Abstr.

551.46 SP ISSN 0074-0209
INSTITUTO ESPANOL DE OCEANOGRAFIA. TRABAJOS. (Text in Spanish; summaries in French) 1929. irreg. Instituto Espanol de Oceanografia, Alcala 27, Madrid 14, Spain.

551 AG ISSN 0325-6790
INSTITUTO NACIONAL DE INVESTIGACION Y DESARROLLO PESQUERO. SERIE CONTRIBUCIONES. (Text in English or Spanish; summaries in English, French and Spanish) 1961. irreg. available on exchange. ‡ Instituto Nacional de Investigacion y Desarrollo Pesquero, Casilla de Correo 175, 7600 Mar del Plata, Argentina. index. Indexed: Ocean.Abstr. Aqua.Sci.& Fish.Abstr.
Formerly: Instituto de Biologia Marina. Serie Contribuciones (ISSN 0076-4302)

551.46 IT ISSN 0082-6456
INSTITUTO SPERIMENTALE TALASSOGRAFICO, TRIESTE. PUBBLICAZIONE. 1919. irreg., no.528, 1976. price varies. Istituto Sperimentale Talassografico, c/o Consiglio Nazionalle delle Ricerche, Servizio Pubblicazioni, Piazzale Aldo Moro 7, I-00100 Rome, Italy. Indexed: Ocean.Abstr. Pollut.Abstr.

551.46 UN ISSN 0074-1175
INTERGOVERNMENTAL OCEANOGRAPHIC COMMISSION. TECHNICAL SERIES. (Text in English, French, Russian and Spanish) 1965. irreg., no.27, 1984. price varies. Unesco, 7-9 Place de Fontenoy, 75700 Paris, France (Dist. in U.S. by: Bernan Associates-Unipub, 4611-F Assembly Dr., Lanham, MD 20706-4391) Indexed: Biol.Abstr. Ocean.Abstr.

INTERNATIONAL ASSOCIATION OF THEORETICAL AND APPLIED LIMNOLOGY. PROCEEDINGS/INTERNATIONALE VEREINIGUNG FUER THEORETISCHE UND ANGEWANDTE LIMNOLOGIE. VERHANDLUNGEN. see EARTH SCIENCES — Hydrology

551.46 639.3 DK ISSN 0373-2045
INTERNATIONAL COUNCIL FOR THE EXPLORATION OF THE SEA. BULLETIN STATISTIQUE. (Text in English) 1906. a. price varies. International Council for the Exploration of the Sea, Palaegade 2, DK-1261 Copenhagen K, Denmark (Subscr. to: C.A. Reitzels Boghandel, Noerregade 20, DK-1165, Copenhagen K, Denmark) stat. circ. 450. (back issues avail.)

551.46 639.3 DK ISSN 0105-3213
INTERNATIONAL COUNCIL FOR THE EXPLORATION OF THE SEA. COOPERATIVE RESEARCH REPORTS. (Series A and B merged into one series in 1972) (Text in English and French) 1962. irreg., no.139, 1986. price varies. International Council for the Exploration of the Sea, Palaegade 2, DK-1261 Copenhagen K, Denmark (Subscr. to: C.A. Reitzels Boghandel, Noerregade 20, DK-1165, Copenhagen K, Denmark) circ. 400. (Back issues avail.) Indexed: Biol.Abstr.

551.46 639.3 DK ISSN 0020-6466
INTERNATIONAL COUNCIL FOR THE EXPLORATION OF THE SEA. JOURNAL DU CONSEIL. (Text and summaries in English or French) 1926. irreg., vol.42, 1986. Kr.150. International Council for the Exploration of the Sea, Palaegade 2-4, DK-1261 Copenhagen K, Denmark (Subscr. to: C.A. Reitzels Boghandel, Noerrgade 20, DK-1165, Copenhagen K, Denmark) Ed. R.J.H. Beverton. bk. rev. cum.index (vols. 1-25) circ. 1,200. (Back issues avail.) Indexed: Chem.Abstr. Biol.Abstr. Ocean.Abstr. Pollut.Abstr.

551.46 639.3 DK ISSN 0074-4336
INTERNATIONAL COUNCIL FOR THE EXPLORATION OF THE SEA. RAPPORTS ET PROCES-VERBAUX DES REUNIONS. (Text in English or French) 1903. irreg., no.186, 1986. price varies. International Council for the Exploration of the Sea, Palaegade 2, DK-1261 Copenhagen K, Denmark (Subscr. to: C.A. Reitzels Boghandel, Noerregade 20, DK-1165, Copenhagen K, Denmark) circ. 500(approx.) (back issues avail.) Indexed: Biol.Abstr. Nutr.Abstr. Ocean.Abstr.

INTERNATIONAL DIRECTORY OF MARINE SCIENTISTS. see BIOLOGY

551.48 MC ISSN 0074-6274
INTERNATIONAL HYDROGRAPHIC CONFERENCE. REPORTS OF PROCEEDINGS. (Editions in English and French) 1919. quinquennial, 12th, 1982, Monte Carlo. 75 F. International Hydrographic Organization, 7 av. President J. F. Kennedy, Monte Carlo MC 98000, Monaco. (reprint service avail. from ISI,UMI)

551.46 MC
INTERNATIONAL HYDROGRAPHIC ORGANIZATION. YEARBOOK. (Text in English and French) 1928. a. 55 F. International Hydrographic Organization, 7 av. President J.F. Kennedy, Monte Carlo MC 98000, Monaco. circ. 400. (reprint service avail. from ISI, UMI)
Formerly: International Hydrographic Bureau. Yearbook (ISSN 0074-6282)

551.46 MM
INTERNATIONAL OCEAN INSTITUTE. OCCASIONAL PAPERS. Short title: I O I Occasional Papers. 1973. irreg., no. 8, 1981. price varies. International Ocean Institute, P.O. Box 524, Valletta, Malta. circ. 200. Indexed: Chem.Abstr. Ocean.Abstr.
Formerly: University of Malta. International Ocean Institute. Occasional Papers.

551.46 MM
INTERNATIONAL OCEAN INSTITUTE. PACEM IN MARIBUS. PROCEEDINGS. 1971. a? price varies. International Ocean Institute, Box 524, Valletta, Malta. circ. 200.

551.46 UN ISSN 0538-8880
INTERNATIONAL OCEANOGRAPHIC TABLES. (Prepared under the supervision of the Joint Panel on Oceanographic Tables and Standards. Published in cooperation with the National Institute of Oceanography, Great Britain) (Text in English, French, Russian and Spanish) 1966. a? Unesco Press, 7 Place de Fontenoy, F-75700 Paris, France (Dist. in U.S. by: Bernan Associates-Unipub, 4611-F Assembly Dr., Lanham, MD 20706-4391)

551.46 US
INTERNATIONAL OFFSHORE EXPLORATION CONFERENCE;* O E C O N Middle East. 1968. irreg., 1st, Athens, 1968. $17.50. Offshore Exploration Conference, 840 van Camp St, Long Beach, CA 90802.

INTERNATIONAL SEAWEED SYMPOSIUM. PROCEEDINGS. see BIOLOGY — Botany

551.4 IS ISSN 0304-7423
ISRAEL OCEANOGRAPHIC AND LIMNOLOGICAL RESEARCH. BIENNIAL REPORT. (Text and summaries in English) 1971. biennial. free. Israel Oceanographic and Limnological Research Ltd., Tel Shikmona, Box 8030, Haifa 31080, Israel. Ed.Bd. bibl. charts. illus. stats. circ. 500. Indexed: Aqua.Sci.& Fish.Abstr.
Former titles: Israel Oceanographic and Limnological Research. Triennial Report; (1982-83): Israel Oceanographic and Limnological Research. Biennial Report.

ISTITUTO RICERCHE PESCA MARITTIMA. QUADERNI. see FISH AND FISHERIES

551.46 US ISSN 0075-3858
JOHNS HOPKINS OCEANOGRAPHIC STUDIES. 1962. irreg., no.6, 1977. price varies. Johns Hopkins University Press, 701 W. 40th St., Ste. 275, Baltimore, MD 21211. TEL 301-338-6900. (reprint service avail. from UMI) Indexed: Biol.Abstr. GeoRef.

551 JA ISSN 0368-5969
KOBE KAIYO KISHODAI IHO/KOBE MARINE OBSERVATORY. BULLETIN. (Text in Japanese; summaries in English) 1925. irreg. Kobe Marine Observatory, 7-14-1, Nakayamate-dori, Chuo-ku, Kobe-shi 650, Japan. Ed.Bd. circ. 400.

551.4 623 333.7 GW ISSN 0452-7739
DIE KUESTE; Archiv fuer Forschung und Technik an der Nord- und Ostsee. 1952. irreg. (1-2/yr.) price varies. Kuratorium fuer Forschung im Kuesteningenieurwesen) Westholsteinische Verlagsanstalt Boyens und Co., Am Wulf-Isebrand-Platz, Postfach 1880, 2240 Heide, W. Germany (B.R.D.) Ed. Harald Goehren. illus. Indexed: GeoRef.

551.46 US ISSN 0724-5890
LECTURE NOTES ON COASTAL AND ESTUARINE STUDIES. 1980. irreg., vol.19, 1986. price varies. Springer-Verlag, 175 Fifth Ave., New York, NY 10010 TEL 212-460-1500. (Also Berlin, Heidelberg, Tokyo and Vienna) Ed.Bd. (reprint service avail. from ISI)

LIVING WITH THE SHORE. see ENVIRONMENTAL STUDIES

551.46 US
LOUISIANA COASTAL LAW REPORT; coastal zone management and other coastal issues. 1971. irreg. (3-4/yr.) free. Louisiana State University, Sea Grant Legal Program, 170 Law Center, Baton Rouge, LA 70803. TEL 504-388-1558. Ed. Michael W. Wascom. bibl. circ. 6,000.

EARTH SCIENCES — OCEANOGRAPHY

551.46   CN
MCGILL UNIVERSITY, MONTREAL. MARINE SCIENCES CENTRE. MANUSCRIPT REPORT. 1966. irreg. Can.$3 per no. ‡ McGill University, Box 6070, Station A, Montreal H3C 3G1, Canada. TEL 514-392-4311. circ. controlled. Indexed: Biol.Abstr. Ocean.Abstr. GeoRef.

551.4   IO   ISSN 0079-0435
MARINE RESEARCH IN INDONESIA. (Text in English and German) 1956. irreg. $3. Centre for Oceanological Research and Development - Pusat Penelitian den Pengembangan Oseanologi, Jalan Pasir Putih No.1, Ancol Timur Box 580, Jakarta 11001, Indonesia. Ed. Aprilani Soegiarto. circ. 500. Indexed: Biol.Abstr.

551.46   GW   ISSN 0341-6836
MEERESFORSCHUNG/REPORTS ON MARINE RESEARCH. N.S. 1925. irreg. (4-5/yr.) $161 for at most 24 booklets of 16 pages (approx.) Verlag Paul Parey (Hamburg), Spitalerstr. 12, Postfach 10 63 04, 2000 Hamburg 1, W. Germany (B.R.D.) Eds. G. Hempel, D. Sahrhage. bk. rev. charts. index. circ. 500. (reprint service avail. from ISI; back issues avail.) Indexed: Biol.Abstr. Chem.Abstr. Curr.Cont. Nutr.Abstr. A.S.C.A. Geo.Abstr. GeoRef. Helminthol.Abstr. Ind.Sci.Rev. Sci.Cit.Ind.
Former title: Deutsche Wissenschaftliche Kommission fuer Meeresforschung. Berichte (ISSN 0012-0987)

551.46   FI   ISSN 0356-0023
MERI. (Text in English, Finnish and Swedish; summaries in English) 1975. irreg. (1-2/yr.) Fmk.10. Finnish Institute of Marine Research, Box 33, SF-00931 Helsinki 93, Finland (Subscr. to: Government Printing Centre, Box 516, SF-00101 Helsinki, Finland) Ed. Aarno Voipio. circ. 300. (back issues avail.)

"METEOR" FORSCHUNGSERGEBNISSE. REIHE C. GEOLOGIE UND GEOPHYSIK. see *EARTH SCIENCES — Geophysics*

551.46   MX
MEXICO. DIRECCION GENERAL DE OCEANOGRAFIA. CALENDARIO GRAFICO DE MAREAS. 1971. a. $8. Universidad Nacional Autonoma de Mexico, Instituto de Geofisica, Circuito Exterior, Ciudad Universitaria, Mexico 20, D.F., Mexico.

333.9   US   ISSN 0095-6783
MISSISSIPPI MARINE RESOURCES COUNCIL. ANNUAL REPORT. a. free. Mississippi Marine Resources Council, Box 959, Long Beach, MS 39560. TEL 601-864-4602. illus. Key Title: Annual Report - Mississippi Marine Resources Council.

551.46   UN   ISSN 0077-104X
MONOGRAPHS ON OCEANOGRAPHIC METHODOLOGY. 1966. irreg., no.10. Unesco, 7-9 Place de Fontenoy, 75700 Paris, France (Dist. in U.S. by: Bernan Associates-Unipub, 4611-F Assembly Dr., Lanham, MD 20706-4391) Indexed: Biol.Abstr.

551.46   UR   ISSN 0076-4477
MORSKAYA GEOLOGIYA I GEOFIZIKA/ MARINE GEOLOGY AND GEOPHYSICS. (Text in Russian; summaries in English) 1970. biennial. $1. Vsesoyuznyi Issledovatel'skii Institut Morskoi Geologii i Geofiziki, Ul. Lacpliesa, 13, Riga, Latvian S.S.R., U.S.S.R. Ed. K. Springis.

551.46   NZ   ISSN 0112-0395
N Z O I HYDROLOGY STATION DATA. 1978. irreg. price varies. New Zealand Oceanographic Institute, P.O. Box 12-346, Wellington North, New Zealand. Ed. D.P. Gordon.

551.46   NZ   ISSN 0510-0054
N Z O I MISCELLANEOUS PUBLICATIONS. 1958. irreg. price varies. New Zealand Oceanographic Institute, P.O. Box 12-346, Wellington North, New Zealand. Ed. D.P. Gordon. Indexed: Ocean.Abstr.

551.46   NZ   ISSN 0110-5205
N Z O I OCEANOGRAPHIC FIELD REPORT. 1974. irreg. price varies. New Zealand Oceanographic Institute, P.O. Box 12-346, Wellington North, New Zealand. Ed. D.P. Gordon. circ. 64.

551.46   NZ   ISSN 0111-1302
N Z O I OCEANOGRAPHIC SUMMARY. 1973. irreg. price varies. New Zealand Oceanographic Institute, P.O. Box 12-346, Wellington North, New Zealand. Ed. D.P. Gordon. Indexed: GeoRef.

551.46   NZ   ISSN 0110-618X
N Z O I RECORDS. 1972. irreg. price varies. New Zealand Oceanographic Institute, P.O. Box 12-346, Wellington North, New Zealand. Ed. D.P. Gordon. Indexed: Biol.Abstr. Pollut.Abstr. GeoRef.

551.468   JA
NATIONAL INSTITUTE OF POLAR RESEARCH. MEMOIRS. SERIES D: OCEANOGRAPHY. (Text and abstracts in English) 1964. irreg. exchange basis. National Institute of Polar Research - Kokuritsu Kyokuchi Kenkyujo, 9-10, Kaga 1-chome, Itabashi-ku, Tokyo 173, Japan. Ed. Tatsuro Matsuda. circ. 1,000. Indexed: Curr.Antarc.Lit.
Supersedes: Japanese Antarctic Research Expedition, 1956-1962. Scientific Reports. Series D: Oceanography (ISSN 0075-3386)

NEW ZEALAND MARINE SCIENCES NEWSLETTER. see *BIOLOGY*

551.46   NZ   ISSN 0083-789X
NEW ZEALAND OCEANOGRAPHIC INSTITUTE. COLLECTED REPRINTS. 1952. a. exchange basis. New Zealand Oceanographic Institute, P.O. Box 12-346, Wellington North, New Zealand. Ed. D.P. Gordon. index. Indexed: Ocean.Abstr. Pollut.Abstr. GeoRef.

551.46   NZ   ISSN 0083-7903
NEW ZEALAND OCEANOGRAPHIC INSTITUTE. MEMOIR. 1955. irreg. price varies. New Zealand Oceanographic Institute, P.O. Box 12-346, Wellington North, New Zealand. Ed. G. Stephenson. index. Indexed: Chem.Abstr. Ocean.Abstr. GeoRef.

551.46   NL
O.R.S.T.O.M. RESUMES DES TRAVAUX. OCEANOGRAPHIE. (Text in French; summaries in English) 1969. irreg., vol.11, 1986. avail. on exchange. Office de la Recherche Scientifique et Technique Outre-Mer, Centre O.R.S.T.O.M., B.P. A5, Noumea, New Caledonia. Ed. Rene Grandperrin. circ. 270.
Formerly: O.R.S.T.O.M. Recueils des Travaux. Oceanographie (ISSN 0078-2130)

623   US
OCEAN ENGINEERING: A WILEY SERIES. 1973. irreg., latest 1984. John Wiley & Sons, Inc., 605 Third Ave., New York, NY 10016. TEL 212-850-6000. Ed. M.E. McCormick.

551.46 333.91
OCEAN SCIENCE, RESOURCES AND TECHNOLOGY. 1980. irreg., latest vol.2, 1986. Academic Press Inc., Orlando, FL 32887. TEL 305-345-2000. Eds. D.S. Cronan, H. Herman.

551.46 333.9   US   ISSN 0191-8575
OCEAN YEARBOOK. 1978. every 18 mos. (International Ocean Institute, MM) University of Chicago Press, 5801 S. Ellis Ave, Chicago, IL 60637 TEL 312-962-7600. (Orders to: Box 37005, Chicago IL 60637) Eds. Elisabeth Mann Borgese, Norton M. Ginsburg. bibl. index. (also avail. in microform from UMI; reprint service avail. from UMI,ISI) Indexed: Biol.Abstr. GeoRef. Mar.Aff.Bibl.

551.46   SA   ISSN 0078-320X
OCEANOGRAPHIC RESEARCH INSTITUTE, DURBAN. INVESTIGATIONAL REPORT. 1961. irreg., no.61, 1985. price varies, free to qualified personnel. ‡ Oceanographic Research Institute, Durban, Box 10712, Marine Parade 4056, Durban, South Africa. (Co-sponsor: South African Association for Marine Biological Research) Ed. A.J. Freitas. circ. 400 (controlled) (back issues avail.) Indexed: Biol.Abstr. Ocean.Abstr. Aqua.Sci.& Fish.Abstr. Zoo.Rec.

551.46   JA
OCEANOGRAPHICAL MAGAZINE/KISCHO-CHO OBUN KAIYO HOKOKU. (Text in English) 1949. a. exchange basis. Japan Meteorological Agency, 3-4 Otemachi, 1-chome, Chiyoda-ku, Tokyo 100, Japan.

551.46 574.92   UK   ISSN 0078-3218
OCEANOGRAPHY AND MARINE BIOLOGY: AN ANNUAL REVIEW. 1963. a. £52. Aberdeen University Press, Farmers Hall, Aberdeen AB9 2XT, Scotland. Ed. Margaret Barnes. Indexed: Biol.Abstr. Chem.Abstr. Geo.Abstr. Helminthol.Abstr.

551.46   PL   ISSN 0078-3234
OCEANOLOGIA. (Text in English and Polish) 1971. irreg., no.20, 1985. price varies. (Polska Akademia Nauk, Komitet Badan Morza) Ossolineum, Publishing House of the Polish Academy of Sciences, Rynek 9, 50-106 Wroclaw, Poland (Dist. by: Ars Polona-Ruch, Krakowskie Przedmiescie 7, Warsaw, Poland) Ed. J. Dera. (reprint service avail. from UMI) Indexed: Pollut.Abstr. Curr.Tit.Ocean. GeoRef.

551.4   BU   ISSN 0324-0878
OKEANOLOGIIA. 1975. irreg. 1.36 lv. per no. (Bulgarska Akademiia na Naukite) Publishing House of the Bulgarian Academy of Sciences, Acad. G. Bonchev St., Bldg. 6, 1113 Sofia, Bulgaria. circ. 580. Indexed: Chem.Abstr. Ocean.Abstr.

551.46   US
PACIFIC RIM RESEARCH SERIES. vol.2, 1977. irreg. price varies. D. C. Heath & Company, 125 Spring St., Lexington, MA 02173. TEL 617-862-6650. index.

PUBLICATIONS ON OCEAN DEVELOPMENT; a series of studies on the international, legal, institutional and policy aspects of the ocean development. see *LAW — International Law*

551.46   US
RADIONAVIGATION JOURNAL. 1975. a. Wild Goose Association, Box 556, Bedford, MA 01730.

551.46 597   CL   ISSN 0716-1069
REVISTA INVESTIGACIONES MARINAS. 1970. a. $12. (Universidad Catolica de Valparaiso, Escuela de Ciencias del Mar) Ediciones Universitarias de Valparaiso, Casilla 1415, Valparaiso, Chile. Indexed: Biol.Abstr.

551.46   US
SCRIPPS INSTITUTION OF OCEANOGRAPHY. ANNUAL REPORT. (Report year ends June 30) a. Scripps Institution of Oceanography, Technical Publications, University of California, San Diego, La Jolla, CA 92093. TEL 619-534-2309. illus.
Former titles: Scripps Institution of Oceanography (Year) (ISSN 0194-2816); S I O: A Report on the Work and Programs of Scripps Institution of Oceanography (ISSN 0091-1518)

551.46   US   ISSN 0080-8318
SCRIPPS INSTITUTION OF OCEANOGRAPHY. BULLETIN. 1927. irreg. price varies. University of California Press, 2120 Berkeley Way, Berkeley, CA 94720. TEL 415-642-4247. Indexed: Biol.Abstr.

551.46   US
SCRIPPS INSTITUTION OF OCEANOGRAPHY. CONTRIBUTIONS. NEW SERIES. 1930. a. avail. only on exchange with libraries and scientific institutions. Scripps Institution of Oceanography, Technical Publications, University of California, San Diego, La Jolla, CA 92093. TEL 619-534-2309.
Formerly: Scripps Institution of Oceanography. Contributions (ISSN 0080-8326)

551.46   US   ISSN 0080-8334
SCRIPPS INSTITUTION OF OCEANOGRAPHY. DEEP SEA DRILLING PROJECT. INITIAL REPORTS. irreg. Scripps Institution of Oceanography, Technical Publications, University of California, San Diego, La Jolla, CA 92093 TEL 619-534-3504. (Dist. by: Supt. of Documents, Washington, DC 20402)

SEA TECHNOLOGY BUYERS GUIDE/ DIRECTORY. see *ENGINEERING*

SEARS FOUNDATION FOR MARINE RESEARCH. MEMOIRS. see *BIOLOGY*

551.46 574.92   GW   ISSN 0080-889X
SENCKENBERGIANA MARITIMA. ZEITSCHRIFT FUER MEERESGEOLOGIE UND MEERESBIOLOGIE. irreg. price varies. (Senckenbergische Naturforschende Gesellschaft) Verlag Dr. Waldemar Kramer, Bornheimer Landwehr 57a, Postfach 600445, 6000 Frankfurt 60, W. Germany (B.R.D.) Eds. G. Hertweck, S. Little-Gadow. Indexed: Biol.Abstr. Ocean.Abstr. Pollut.Abstr. Geo.Abstr. GeoRef.

551.46 574   SG   ISSN 0850-1602
SENEGAL. CENTRE DE RECHERCHE OCEANOGRAPHIQUE. DOCUMENT SCIENTIFIQUE. (Text in French) 1966. irreg. 50.000 F. Centre de Recherche Oceanographique de Dakar-Thiaroye, B.P. 2241, Dakar, Senegal. (back issues avail.)

SHIMA MARINELAND. SCIENCE REPORT. see *BIOLOGY*

SNOWY MOUNTAINS ENGINEERING CORPORATION. ANNUAL REPORT. see *ENGINEERING*

551.46   UK
SOUTH WALES PORTS TIDES TABLES. a. £0.50. Associated British Ports, South Wales Group Office, Pierhead Bldng., Bute Docks, Cardiff CF1 5TH, Wales. circ. 5,000.

551.46   UK
SOUTHAMPTON (PORT OF), TIDE TABLES. 1927. a. Association British Ports (Southampton), Dock House, Canute Rd., Southampton SO9 1PZ, England. circ. 6,000.

551.46   PL   ISSN 0208-421X
STUDIA I MATERIALY OCEANOLOGICZNE. (Summaries in English) no.29, 1980. irreg., no.49, 1986. price varies. Ossolineum, Publishing House of the Polish Academy of Sciences, Rynek 9, Wroclaw, Poland (Dist. by: Ars Polona-Ruch, Krakowskie Przedmiescie 7, Warsaw, Poland) Ed. Stanislaw Szymborski. Indexed: GeoRef.

551.46   US   ISSN 0081-8720
STUDIES IN TROPICAL OCEANOGRAPHY. 1963. irreg., no.12, 1974. price varies. Rosenstiel School of Marine and Atmospheric Science, University of Miami, 4600 Rickenbacker Causeway, Miami, FL 33149. TEL 305-361-4190. Ed. William Richards. Indexed: Biol.Abstr. Zoo.Rec.

551.4 574.92   FR   ISSN 0040-4012
TETHYS. 1969. irreg. (1-2/yr.) $45. Universite d'Aix-Marseille, Station Marine d'Endoume, Rue de la Batterie des Lions, 13007 Marseille, France. Ed. J.M. Peres. charts. illus. circ. 400. Indexed: Biol.Abstr. Bull.Signal. Chem.Abstr. Nutr.Abstr. Ocean.Abstr. Pollut.Abstr. Ref.Zh. Aqua.Sci.& Fish.Abstr. Mar.Sci.Cont.Tab. Geo.Abstr. Helminthol.Abstr. Sel.Water Res.Abstr.

551.46   US   ISSN 0069-9640
TEXAS A & M UNIVERSITY. COLLEGE OF GEOSCIENCES. CONTRIBUTIONS IN OCEANOGRAPHY. 1950. irreg. price varies or exchange basis. Texas A & M University, Department of Oceanography, College Station, TX 77843. TEL 409-845-7327. Comp. Gloria Guffy. abstr. circ. controlled. Indexed: GeoRef.

THALASSAS; revista de ciencias del mar. see *BIOLOGY*

551.461   DK   ISSN 0106-8342
TIDEVANDSTABELLER FOR FAEROERNE. 1977. a. Kr.30.50. Farvandsdirektoratet, Nautisk Afdelning, Esplanaden 19, 1263 Copenhagen K, Denmark.

551.461   DK   ISSN 0107-0398
TIDEVANDSTABELLER FOR GROENLAND. (Text in Danish and English) 1966. a. Kr.39.75. Farvandsdirektoratet, Nautisk Afdeling, Esplanaden 19, 1263 Copenhagen K, Denmark. circ. 600.

551   US
TOPICS IN ATMOSPHERIC AND OCEANOGRAPHIC SCIENCES. 1982. irreg., latest 1986. Springer-Verlag, 175 Fifth Ave., New York, NY 10010 TEL 212-460-1500. (Also Berlin, Heidelberg, Tokyo and Vienna) Eds. M. Ghil, J. Suenderman.

551.46 639.3   TI   ISSN 0579-7926
TUNISIA. INSTITUT NATIONAL SCIENTIFIQUE ET TECHNIQUE D'OCEANOGRAPHIE ET DE PECHE. BULLETIN. (Text in French; summaries in Arabic, English, and French) 1966 N.S. irreg. Institut National Scientifique et Technique d'Oceanographie et de Peche, Salammbo, Tunisia. circ. 1,150. Indexed: Bull.Signal.

551.4 574.92   UN   ISSN 0503-4299
UNESCO TECHNICAL PAPERS IN MARINE SCIENCE. 1965. irreg. Unesco, 7-9 Place de Fontenoy, F-75700 Paris, France. Indexed: Biol.Abstr. Ocean.Abstr.

551.46   US   ISSN 0082-9625
U.S. COAST GUARD. OCEANOGRAPHIC REPORTS (CG-373 SERIES) 1962. irreg., no.71, 1976. price varies. U.S. Coast Guard, Oceanographic Unit, 2100 Second St., S.W., Washington, DC 20593 TEL 202-426-1830. (Avail. from: NTIS, Springfield, VA 22151) circ. 500. (also avail. in microfiche) Indexed: Ocean.Abstr. Pollut.Abstr. Geo.Abstr.

551.46   US
U.S. NATIONAL OCEAN SERVICE HYDROGRAPHIC CONFERENCE. ANNUAL MEETING. PROCEEDINGS. 7th, 1980. a. U.S. National Ocean Service, Rockville, MD 20850. TEL 301-655-4000.
Formerly: U.S. National Ocean Survey Hydrographic Conference. Annual Meeting. Proceedings (ISSN 0276-4849)

551.46   US
U.S. NATIONAL OCEANIC AND ATMOSPHERIC ADMINISTRATION. ENGINEERING SUPPORT OFFICE. TECHNICAL MEMORANDUM. 1969. irreg. free. ‡ U.S. National Oceanic and Atmospheric Administration, Engineering Support Office, Rockville, MD 20852. TEL 301-655-4000. circ. 3,000. Indexed: Ocean.Abstr. Pollut.Abstr. Geo.Abstr.
Former titles: U.S. National Oceanic and Atmospheric Administration. Test and Evaluation Office. Technical Memorandum; U.S. National Oceanographic Instrumentation Center. Technical Memorandum.

U.S. NATIONAL OCEANIC AND ATMOSPHERIC ADMINISTRATION. MANNED UNDERSEA SCIENCE AND TECHNOLOGY PROGRAM; REPORT. see *ENGINEERING*

551.46   US
U.S. NATIONAL OCEANIC AND ATMOSPHERIC ADMINISTRATION. TECHNICAL BULLETIN. 1964. irreg. free. ‡ U.S. National Oceanic and Atmospheric Administration, Engineering Support Office, Rockville, MD 20852. TEL 301-655-4000. circ. 3,000.
Former titles: U.S. National Oceanic and Atmospheric Administration. Test and Evaluation Laboratory. Technical Bulletin; U.S. National Oceanographic Instrumentation Center. Technical Bulletin.

551.46   US   ISSN 0091-9500
U.S. NATIONAL OCEANOGRAPHIC DATA CENTER. KEY TO OCEANOGRAPHIC RECORDS DOCUMENTATION. 1973. irreg., no.15, 1984. U.S. National Oceanographic Data Center, N O A A, Universal S. Bldg., Rm. 415, E-OC21, Washington, DC 20235. TEL 202-673-5561. Ed. Richard Abram.

551.46 574.92   CK
UNIVERSIDAD DE BOGOTA JORGE TADEO LOZANO. MUSEO DEL MAR. BOLETIN. (Text in Spanish; summaries in English) 1970. a. price varies. Universidad de Bogota Jorge Tadeo Lozano, Museo del Mar, Calle 23 No. 4-47, Bogota, Colombia. Ed. Jorge Barreto Soulier. bibl. illus. circ. 1,200(controlled) (cards)
Marine biology

551.46   VE   ISSN 0590-3351
UNIVERSIDAD DE ORIENTE. INSTITUTO OCEANOGRAFICO. CUADERNOS OCEANOGRAFICOS. irreg. Bol.$12($3) Universidad de Oriente, Instituto Oceanografico, Biblioteca, Cumana, Venezuela. Indexed: Biol.Abstr.

551.46   BL   ISSN 0373-5524
UNIVERSIDADE DE SAO PAULO. INSTITUTO OCEANOGRAFICO. BOLETIM. (Text in various languages; summaries in English) 1950. biennial. $17 or exchange basis. Universidade de Sao Paulo, Instituto Oceanografico, Cidade Universitaria, Butanta, 05508 Sao Paulo, SP, Brazil. circ. 650. Indexed: Biol.Abstr. Ocean.Abstr. Aqua.Sci.& Fish.Abstr. Deep Sea Res.& Oceanogr.Abstr. Zoo.Rec.

550   BL   ISSN 0100-5146
UNIVERSIDADE DE SAO PAULO. INSTITUTO OCEANOGRAFICO. PUBLICACAO ESPECIAL. (Multilingual text; summaries in English) 1972. irreg., no.4, 1977. price varies; avail. on exchange. Universidade de Sao Paulo, Instituto Oceanografico, Cidade Universitaria, Butanta, 05508 Sao Paulo, SP, Brazil. circ. 650.

551   BL   ISSN 0100-5197
UNIVERSIDADE DE SAO PAULO. INSTITUTO OCEANOGRAFICO. RELATORIO DE CRUZEIROS. (Text in various languages; summaries in English) 1976. irreg., no.6, 1985. price varies; avail. on exchange. Universidade de Sao Paulo, Instituto Oceanografico, Cidade Universitaria, Butanta, 05508 Sao Paulo, S.P., Brazil. Ed. W. Besuard. circ. 650.

551   BL   ISSN 0100-5243
UNIVERSIDADE DE SAO PAULO. INSTITUTO OCEANOGRAFICO. RELATORIO INTERNO. (Text in various languages; summaries in English) 1974. irreg., no.14, 1985. price varies; exchange basis. Universidade de Sao Paulo, Instituto Oceanografico, Cidade Universitaria, Butanta, 05508 Sao Paulo, S.P., Brazil. circ. 200.

551.46   GW
UNIVERSITAET HAMBURG. INSTITUT FUER MEERSKUNDE. MITTEILUNGEN. 1962. a. avail. on exchange basis. Universitaet Hamburg, Institut fuer Meerskunde, Edmund Siemers Allee 1, 2000 Hamburg 13, W. Germany (B.R.D.) Ed. Jurgen Sundermann. illus.

551.46   US
UNIVERSITY OF CALIFORNIA, SANTA CRUZ. INSTITUTE FOR MARINE SCIENCES. SPECIAL PUBLICATION. 1974. irreg., no.9, 1978. price varies. University of California, Santa Cruz, Institute for Marine Studies, Santa Cruz, CA 95064. TEL 408-429-2464. circ. 500.
Former titles: University of California, Santa Cruz. Center for Marine Studies. Special Publication; University of California, Santa Cruz. Coastal Marine Laboratory. Special Publication.

551.46   II
UNIVERSITY OF COCHIN. DEPARTMENT OF MARINE SCIENCES. BULLETIN. (Text in English) 1963. irreg. Rs.20 per no. University of Cochin, Department of Marine Sciences, Foreshore Rd., Ernakulam, Cochin 16, Kerala, India. Ed. C.V. Kurian. (back issues avail.) Indexed: Georef.
Formerly: University of Cochin. Department of Marine Biology and Oceanography. Bulletin.

551.46 574.92   US
UNIVERSITY OF RHODE ISLAND. GRADUATE SCHOOL OF OCEANOGRAPHY. COLLECTED REPRINTS. 1958. irreg., vol.13, 1976. ‡ University of Rhode Island, Graduate School of Oceanography, Kingston, RI 02881. TEL 401-792-1000. circ. 350.
Formerly (vols. 1-6): University of Rhode Island. Narragansett Marine Laboratory. Collected Reprints (ISSN 0077-281X)

551.46 574.92   US
UNIVERSITY OF RHODE ISLAND. GRADUATE SCHOOL OF OCEANOGRAPHY. MARINE TECHNICAL REPORTS. 1950. irreg., latest issue no.35. not avail. for distribution. University of Rhode Island, Graduate School of Oceanography, Kingston, RI 02881. TEL 401-792-1000.
Formerly: Narragansett Marine Laboratory. Technical Reports (ISSN 0077-2836)

551.46   US
UNIVERSITY OF SOUTH CAROLINA. BELLE W. BARUCH LIBRARY IN MARINE SCIENCE AND COASTAL RESEARCH. COLLECTED PAPERS. 1973. irreg. (approx. 2/yr.) $39.95. University of South Carolina Press, Columbia, SC 29208. TEL 803-777-5243. charts. illus.

551.46   PL   ISSN 0302-3125
UNIWERSYTET GDANSKI. WYDZIAL BIOLOGII,
I NAUK O ZIEMI. ZESZYTY NAUKOWE.
OCEANOGRAFIA. (Text in Polish; summaries in
Polish and Russian) 1973. irreg. price varies.
Uniwersytet Gdanski, Ul. Armii Czerwonej 110, 81-
824 Sopot, Poland. Ed. Krystyna Wiktor.

551.46   US
VIRGINIA INSTITUTE OF MARINE SCIENCE.
CONTRIBUTIONS. 1940. irreg., latest 1979.
exchange basis. Virginia Institute of Marine Science,
Library, Gloucester Point, VA 23062. TEL 804-642-
7116.

551.46   US
VIRGINIA INSTITUTE OF MARINE SCIENCE,
GLOUCESTER POINT. SPECIAL REPORT IN
APPLIED MARINE SCIENCE AND OCEAN
ENGINEERING. 1955. irreg., no.282, 1986. price
varies. Virginia Institute of Marine Science,
Gloucester Point, VA 23062. TEL 804-642-7116.
(also avail. in microfiche) Indexed: Ocean.Abstr.

551.46   UR
VSESOYUZNYI NAUCHNO-ISSLEDOVATEL'SKII
INSTITUT MORSKOGO RYBNOGO
KHOZYAISTVA I OKEANOGRAFII (V N I R O)
. TRUDY. vol.117, 1976. irreg. price varies.
Ul.Verkhnyaya Krasnosel'skaya, 17, Moscow
107140, Russian S.F.S.R., U.S.S.R. Ed. K.
Yablonskaya. circ. 500. Indexed: Biol.Abstr.
Chem.Abstr. Geo.Abstr. GeoRef.
Helminthol.Abstr.

551.46   US
WILD GOOSE ASSOCIATION. ANNUAL
TECHNICAL SYMPOSIUM PROCEEDINGS.
1975. a. Wild Goose Association, Box 556, Bedford,
MA 01730.

621.381 551.46   US
WORKING SYMPOSIUM ON OCEANOGRAPHIC
DATA SYSTEMS. PROCEEDINGS. 1975. irreg.,
no.3, 1983. price varies. (Institute of Electrical and
Electronics Engineers, Inc.) I E E E Computer
Society Press, 1730 Massachusetts Ave., N.W.,
Washington, DC 20036-1903 (And 345 E. 47th St.,
New York, NY 10017) (Co-sponsor: Woods Hole
Oceanographic Institution)
  Formerly: Working Conference on Oceanographic
Laboratory Systems. Proceedings.

551.46   US
WORLD AQUACULTURE SOCIETY. JOURNAL.
irreg. (2-4/yr.) World Aquaculture Society, 341
Pleasant Hall, Baton Rouge, LA 70803. TEL 504-
388-3137.

551.46   US
WORLD AQUACULTURE SOCIETY.
PROCEEDINGS. irreg., latest vol.11. price varies.
World Aquaculture Society, 341 Pleasant Hall,
Baton Rouge, LA 70803. TEL 504-388-3137.

551.46   US
WORLD AQUACULTURE SOCIETY. SPECIAL
PUBLICATIONS. irreg. $25. World Aquaculture
Society, 341 Pleasant Hall, Baton Rouge, LA 70803.
TEL 504-388-3137.

551.46   UN   ISSN 0084-2001
WORLD METEOROLOGICAL ORGANIZATION.
REPORTS ON MARINE SCIENCE AFFAIRS.
1970. irreg. price varies. World Meteorological
Organization, 41 Av. Giuseppe Motta, 1211 Geneva
20, Switzerland (Dist. in U.S. by: American
Meteorological Society, 45 Beacon St., Boston, MA
02108) Indexed: Biol.Abstr.

ECONOMIC SITUATION AND CONDITIONS

see Business and Economics—Economic
Situation and Conditions

ECONOMIC SYSTEMS AND THEORIES, ECONOMIC HISTORY

see Business and Economics—Economic
Systems and Theories, Economic History

ECONOMICS

see Business and Economics

EDUCATION

see also Education—Adult Education;
Education—Computer Applications;
Education—Guides to Schools and
Colleges; Education—Higher Education;
Education—International Education
Programs; Education—School
Organization and Administration;
Education—Special Education and
Rehabilitation; Education—Teaching
Methods and Curriculum

370   AT
A C S S O POLICY (YEAR) a. Aus.$6. Australian
Council of State School Organisations, Hughes
Primary School, Kent St., Hughes, A.C.T. 2605,
Australia.

A F T ISSUES BULLETIN. (American Federation of
Teachers) see LABOR UNIONS

370   US   ISSN 0882-438X
A M S STUDIES IN EDUCATION. 1974. irreg.,
no.6, 1986. price varies. A M S Press, Inc., 56 E.
13th ST., New York, NY 10003. TEL 212-777-
4700. (back issues avail.)

A P U PRESS ALASKANA BOOK SERIES. (Alaska
Pacific University Press) see HISTORY — History
Of North And South America

370   UK
A R E L S - F E L C O BROCHURE. a. free.
Association of Recognised English Language
Schools, Federation of English Language Course
Organisations, 125 High Holborn, London WC1,
England. adv. circ. 80,000.
  Former titles: A R E L S Brochure & A R E L S
Handbook.

371   AT
A T F ANNUAL REPORT. 1943. a. Aus.$10.
Australian Teachers' Federation, P.O. Box 415,
Carlton South, Vic. 3053, Australia. adv. circ.
controlled. (processed)
  Formerly: A T F Monthly Report (ISSN 0001-
2726)

370   SW   ISSN 0065-0196
AARSBOK FOER SKOLAN. 1964. a. price varies.
Sveriges Laerarfoerbund, Box 12239, S-102 26
Stockholm 12, Sweden. Ed. Anders Ternstroem.
circ. 12,000.
  Supersedes (1920-1963): Folkskolans Aarsbok.

ABHANDLUNGEN ZUR PHILOSOPHIE,
PSYCHOLOGIE UND PAEDAGOGIK. see
PHILOSOPHY

ACTA COLLOQUII DIDACTICI CLASSICI;
didactica classica gandensia. see LINGUISTICS

370   HU   ISSN 0567-7912
ACTA PAEDAGOGICA DEBRECINA. (Summaries
in German and Russian) 1962. irreg., vol.86, 1984.
Kossuth Lajos Tudomanyegyetem,
Nevelestudomanyi Tanszek, Egyetem Ter 1, 4010
Debrecen, Hungary. bibl.

ACTA UNIVERSITATIS LODZIENSIS: FOLIA
ARCHAEOLOGICA. see ARCHAEOLOGY

ACTA UNIVERSITATIS LODZIENSIS: FOLIA
BIOCHIMICA ET BIOPHYSICA. see
BIOLOGY — Biological Chemistry

ACTA UNIVERSITATIS LODZIENSIS: FOLIA
BOTANICA. see BIOLOGY — Botany

ACTA UNIVERSITATIS LODZIENSIS: FOLIA
CHIMICA. see CHEMISTRY

ACTA UNIVERSITATIS LODZIENSIS: FOLIA
ETHNOGRAPHICA. see ANTHROPOLOGY

ACTA UNIVERSITATIS LODZIENSIS: FOLIA
GEOGRAPHICA. see GEOGRAPHY

ACTA UNIVERSITATIS LODZIENSIS: FOLIA
HISTORICA. see HISTORY

ACTA UNIVERSITATIS LODZIENSIS: FOLIA
IURIDICA. see LAW

ACTA UNIVERSITATIS LODZIENSIS: FOLIA
LIMNOLOGICA. see EARTH SCIENCES —
Hydrology

ACTA UNIVERSITATIS LODZIENSIS: FOLIA
LINGUISTICA. see LINGUISTICS

ACTA UNIVERSITATIS LODZIENSIS: FOLIA
LITTERARIA. see LITERATURE

ACTA UNIVERSITATIS LODZIENSIS: FOLIA
MATHEMATICA. see MATHEMATICS

ACTA UNIVERSITATIS LODZIENSIS: FOLIA
OECONOMICA. see BUSINESS AND
ECONOMICS

ACTA UNIVERSITATIS LODZIENSIS: FOLIA
PAEDAGOGICA ET PSYCHOLOGICA. see
PSYCHOLOGY

ACTA UNIVERSITATIS LODZIENSIS: FOLIA
PHILOSOPHICA. see PHILOSOPHY

ACTA UNIVERSITATIS LODZIENSIS: FOLIA
PHYSICA. see PHYSICS

ACTA UNIVERSITATIS LODZIENSIS: FOLIA
SCIENTIARUM ARTIUM ET LIBRORUM
POLITOLOGIA. see HUMANITIES:
COMPREHENSIVE WORKS

ACTA UNIVERSITATIS LODZIENSIS: FOLIA
SOCIOLOGICA. see SOCIOLOGY

ACTA UNIVERSITATIS LODZIENSIS: FOLIA
ZOOLOGICA ET ANTHROPOLOGICA. see
BIOLOGY — Zoology

301   PL   ISSN 0208-5267
ACTA UNIVERSITATIS NICOLAI COPERNICI.
SOCJOLOGIA WYCHOWANIA. (Text in Polish;
summaries in English) 1976. irreg. price varies.
Uniwersytet Mikolaja Kopernika, Fosa Staromiejska
3, Torun, Poland (Dist. by Osrodek
Rozpowszechniania Wydawnictw Naukowych PAN,
Palac Kultury i Nauki, 00-901 Warsaw, Poland)
  Formerly: Uniwersytet Mikolaja Kopernika,
Torun. Nauki Humanistyczno-Spoleczne. Socjologia.

ACTA UNIVERSITATIS SZEGEDIENSIS DE
ATTILA JOZSEF NOMINATAE. ACTA
BIBLIOTHECARIA. see LIBRARY AND
INFORMATION SCIENCES

ACTA UNIVERSITATIS SZEGEDIENSIS DE
ATTILA JOZSEF NOMINATAE. SECTIO
PAEDAGOGICA ET PSYCHOLOGICA. see
PSYCHOLOGY

370   PL   ISSN 0137-1096
ACTA UNIVERSITATIS WRATISLAVIENSIS.
PRACE PEDAGOGICZNE. (Subseries of Acta
Universitatis Wratislaviensis) (Summaries in English,
French and Russian) 1973. irreg. price varies.
(Uniwersytet Wroclawski) Biuro Wydawnictw i
Bibliotek PAN, P.O. Box 24, 00-901 Warsaw,
Poland (Dist. by: Ars Polona, Krakowskie
Przedmiescie 7, 00-068 Warsaw, Poland) circ. 600.
Indexed: Geo.Abstr. Rural Recreat.Tour.Abstr.
World Agri.Econ.& Rural Sociol.Abstr.
  Supersedes in part: Uniwersytet Wroclawski.
Prace Pedagogiczne i Psychologia.

370   ET   ISSN 0072-9388
ADDIS ABABA UNIVERSITY. UNIVERSITY
TESTING CENTER. TECHNICAL REPORT.*
(Name of issuing body varies: Haile Sellassie I
University, University of Addis Ababa, National
University) (Text in English) 1967. irreg., no.5,
1971. free. Addis Ababa University, University
Testing Center, Box 1176, Addis Ababa, Ethiopia.

372.21   US   ISSN 0270-4021
ADVANCES IN EARLY EDUCATION AND DAY
CARE; a research annual. 1980. a. $23.75 to
individuals; institutions $47.50. J A I Press Inc.,
Box 1678, 36 Sherwood Pl., Greenwich, CT 06836.
TEL 203-661-7602. Ed. Sally J. Kilmer. Indexed:
Psychol.Abstr.

EDUCATION

370　　　　　　　　US
ADVANCES IN READING/LANGUAGE
RESEARCH. 1982. a. $23.75 to individuals;
institutions $47.50. J A I Press Inc., Box 1678, 36
Sherwood Pl., Greenwich, CT 06836. TEL 203-661-
7602. Ed. Barbara A. Hutson. Indexed:
Psychol.Abstr.

ADVANCES IN TEST ANXIETY RESEARCH. see
PSYCHOLOGY

ADVENTURES IN WESTERN NEW YORK
HISTORY. see *HISTORY — History Of North
And South America*

370　　　　　NR　ISSN 0065-4752
AHMADU BELLO UNIVERSITY. INSTITUTE OF
EDUCATION. PAPER.* irreg. Ahmadu Bello
University, Institute of Education, Zaria, Nigeria.

AISTHESIS; revista chilena de investigaciones
esteticas. see *PHILOSOPHY*

370　　　　　DK　ISSN 0109-3762
AKSEL. 1982. irreg. (4-6/yr.) free. Amtskommunernes
Speciallaererforening, Noerregade 48, 7400 Herning,
Denmark. Ed. Preben Eriksen. bk. rev. illus. circ.
450.

ALBARREGAS. see *HUMANITIES:
COMPREHENSIVE WORKS*

371.1　　　　　CN　ISSN 0706-9839
ALBERTA TEACHERS' ASSOCIATION.
MEMBERS' HANDBOOK. a. Can.$7. Alberta
Teachers' Association, Barnett House, 11010-142
St., Edmonton, Alta. T5N 2R1, Canada. TEL 403-
453-2411. circ. 6,300.

370　　　　　IS　ISSN 0334-5084
ALIM. 1980. a. Jewish Agency, Department of Child
and Youth Immigration, P.O. Box 92, Jerusalem,
Israel. TEL 02-233241.

377.9　　　　　US　ISSN 0002-6093
ALLIANCE REVIEW.* vol.25, 1973. irreg.
membership. American Friends of the Alliance
Israelite Universelle Inc., 135 William St., New
York, NY 10038. TEL 212-349-0537. Ed. Saadiah
Cherniak. illus.
　Religious

370　　　　　IS　ISSN 0334-5076
ALON LAMORAH LESIFRUT. 1972. a. Atlas Ltd.,
49 Chelnov St., Tel Aviv, Israel.

AMERICAN ARTIST DIRECTORY OF ART
SCHOOLS & WORKSHOPS. see *ART*

370　　　　　US　ISSN 0084-6333
AMERICAN COUNCIL ON INDUSTRIAL ARTS
TEACHER EDUCATION. YEARBOOK. 1952. a.
$15. (American Council on Industrial Arts Teacher
Education) MacMillan-McKnight Publishing Co.,
809 W. Detweiller, Peoria, IL 61615-2190 TEL 319-
273-2311. (Address of Council: c/o Illinois State
University, Department of Industrial Technology,
210 Turner Hall, IL 61761) circ. 1,500. (also avail.
in microform from UMI; reprint service avail. from
UMI) Indexed: Educ.Ind.
　Formerly: American Industrial Arts Association.
Yearbook (ISSN 0065-8634)

AMERICAN FEDERATION OF TEACHERS.
CONVENTION PROCEEDINGS (ABRIDGED)
see *LABOR UNIONS*

370　　　　　US
AMERICAN STATISTICAL ASSOCIATION.
SECTION ON STATISTICAL EDUCATION.
PROCEEDINGS. 4th edt., 1982. a. $13 to non-
members; members $8. American Statistical
Association, 808 15th St., N.W., Washington, DC
20005.

370　　　　　DK　ISSN 0900-3096
AMTSKOMMUNALE ENKELTFAGSKURSER.
1984. a. free. Undervisningsministeriet, Direktoratet
for Folkeoplysning, Copenhagen, Denmark (Subscr.
to: Undervisningsministeriet Tekstbehandlingsenhed,
Frederiksholms Kanal 25 F, 1220 Copenhagen K,
Denmark) circ. 1,500.

ANNUAIRE DES COMMUNAUTES D'ENFANTS.
see *CHILDREN AND YOUTH — About*

372　　　　　US
ANNUAL EDITIONS: EARLY CHILDHOOD
EDUCATION. 1977. a. Dushkin Publishing Group,
Inc., Sluice Duck, Guilford, CT 06437. TEL 203-
453-4351. Ed. Ian Nielsen.

370　　　　　US
ANNUAL EDITIONS: EDUCATION. 1973. a.
Dushkin Publishing Group, Inc., Sluice Dock,
Guilford, CT 06437. TEL 203-453-4351. Ed. Ian
Nielsen.

ANNUAL EDITIONS: EDUCATIONAL
PSYCHOLOGY. see *PSYCHOLOGY*

370　　　　　US　ISSN 0095-5787
ANNUAL EDITIONS: READINGS IN
EDUCATION. Short title: Readings in Education.
a. $9.50. Dushkin Publishing Group, Inc., Sluice
Dock, Box 426, Guilford, CT 06437. TEL 203-453-
4351. illus.

370　　　　　US　ISSN 0085-4077
ANNUAL EDUCATIONAL SUMMARY, NEW
YORK STATE. 1904. a. free. Education
Department, Information Center on Education,
Albany, NY 12234. charts. stat. circ. controlled.
(processed; back issues avail.)

ANNUAL REPORT OF EDUCATIONAL
PSYCHOLOGY IN JAPAN/KYOIKU
SHINRIGAKU NEMPO. see *PSYCHOLOGY*

574.92　　　　　US　ISSN 0270-1480
ANNUAL STUDENT SYMPOSIUM ON MARINE
AFFAIRS. PROCEEDINGS. 1976. a. free to
qualified personnel. Hawaiian Academy of Science,
Box 19073, Honolulu, HI 96819. Ed. Sister Edna L.
Demanche, SS.CC. circ. 200.

370　　　　　GW　ISSN 0066-569X
ARBEITEN ZUR PAEDAGOGIK. 1963. irreg.,
vol.24, 1984. price varies. Calwer Verlag,
Scharnhauser Str.44, 7000 Stuttgart 70, W.
Germany (B.R.D.) Eds. Otto Duerr, Helmut Frik.

370　060　　　　PL　ISSN 0066-6831
ARCHIWUM DZIEJOW OSWIATY. (Text in Polish)
1959. irreg., vol.10, 1981. price varies. (Polska
Akademia Nauk, Instytut Historii Nauki, Oswiaty i
Techniki) Ossolineum, Publishing House of the
Polish Academy of Sciences, Rynek 9, Wroclaw,
Poland (Dist. by Ars Polona-Ruch, Krakowskie
Przedmiescie 7, Warsaw, Poland) circ. 1,000.

370　　　　　AG　ISSN 0066-7021
ARGENTINA. DEPARTAMENTO DE
ESTADISTICA EDUCATIVA. BOLETIN
INFORMATIVO. 1965. a. free. Ministerio de
Cultura y Educacion, Departamento de Estadistica
Educativa, Avda. Eduardo Madero 235, 1 Piso,
Buenos Aires, Argentina.

379　　　　　US　ISSN 0095-5310
ARIZONA. DEPARTMENT OF EDUCATION.
ANNUAL REPORT OF THE
SUPERINTENDENT OF PUBLIC
INSTRUCTION. a. $9.80. Department of
Education, Superintendent of Public Instruction,
Central Distribution Center, 1535 W. Jefferson,
Phoenix, AZ 85007. TEL 602-255-5393. illus. stat.
Key Title: Annual Report of the Superintendent of
Public Instruction.

371.9　　　　　US
ARIZONA STATE PLAN FOR THE EDUCATION
OF MIGRATORY CHILDREN. Cover title:
Education for Migrant Children; Arizona State Plan.
1967. irreg., latest 1985/1986. free. Department of
Education, 1535 W. Jefferson, Phoenix, AZ 85007.
TEL 602-255-5393. illus. stat.

370　　　　　DK　ISSN 0106-7478
ASKOV LAERLINGE. 1904. a. Kr.50. Askov
Hoejskoles Elevforening, Maltvej 1, 6600 Vejen,
Denmark. illus.

370　　　　　UK　ISSN 0066-8672
ASPECTS OF EDUCATION. 1964. irreg. (approx. 2/
yr.) price varies. University of Hull, Institute of
Education, 173, Cottingham Rd., Hull HU5 2EH,
England. Ed. V.A. McClelland. bk. rev. circ. 500.
(back issues avail.) Indexed: Curr.Cont. SSCI.
Br.Educ.Ind.

370　　　　　CN　ISSN 0228-7730
ASSOCIATION DES COLLEGES DU QUEBEC
ANNUAIRE. 1968. a. free. (Association des
Colleges du Quebec) Centre d'Animation de
Developpement et de Recherche en Education
(C.A.D.R.E.), 1940 est. Blvd. Henri-Bourassa,
Montreal, Que. H2B 1S2, Canada. TEL 514-381-
8891. adv. circ. 8,500.

373　　　　　CN　ISSN 0066-8990
ASSOCIATION DES INSTITUTIONS
D'ENSEIGNEMENT SECONDAIRE.
ANNUAIRE. 1968. a. free. (Association des
Institutions d'Enseignement Secondaire) Centre
d'Animation de Developpement et de Recherche en
Education (C.A.D.R.E.), 1940 Est Blvd. Henri-
Bourassa, Montreal, Que. H2B 1S2, Canada. TEL
514-381-8891. adv. circ. 8,500.
　Formerly: Annuaire des Institutions
d'Enseignement Secondaire (ISSN 0084-6511)

ASSOCIATION OF SURGEONS OF EAST
AFRICA. PROCEEDINGS. see *MEDICAL
SCIENCES — Surgery*

370　　　　　IO
ATMA JAYA RESEARCH CENTRE. EDUCATION
DEVELOPMENT RESEARCH REPORT/PUSAT
PENELITIAN ATMA JAYA. STUDI TENTANG
PENGEMBANGAN PENDIDIKAN. 1980. irreg.
Atma Jaya Research Centre - Pusat Penelitian Atma
Jaya, Jalan Jenderal Sudirman 49a, Box 2639/JKT,
Jakarta 10001, Indonesia.

370　　　　　PE
AULA ABIERTA. 1976. irreg. Instituto Nacional de
Investigacion y Desarrollo de la Educacion, Centro
Nacional de Documentacion e Informacion
Educacional, Van de Velde 160, San Borja, Lima
100, Peru. bibl. charts. illus.

372　373　　　　AT
AUSTRALIA. BUREAU OF STATISTICS.
VICTORIAN OFFICE. NATIONAL SCHOOLS
STATISTICS, VICTORIA. 1967. a. Aus.$1.80.
Australian Bureau of Statistics, Victorian Office,
Box 2796Y, G.P.O. Melbourne, Victoria 3001,
Australia. circ. 3,000.
　Formerly: Australia. Bureau of Statistics.
Victorian Office. Primary and Secondary Education,
Victoria (ISSN 0067-1150)

370　　　　　AT
AUSTRALIA. EDUCATION RESEARCH AND
DEVELOPMENT COMMITTEE. ANNUAL
REPORT. 1970/71. a. price varies. Australian
Government Publishing Service, G.P.O. Box 84,
Canberra, A.C.T. 2601, Australia.
　Formerly: Australia. Advisory Committee on
Research and Development in Education. Annual
Report.

370　　　　　AT
AUSTRALIAN COUNCIL FOR EDUCATIONAL
RESEARCH. ANNUAL REPORT. a. membership.
Australian Council for Educational Research, Box
210, Hawthorn, Vic. 3122, Australia.

370　　　　　AT　ISSN 0067-1835
AUSTRALIAN COUNCIL FOR EDUCATIONAL
RESEARCH. OCCASIONAL PAPERS. irreg.
Australian Council for Educational Research, Box
210, Hawthorn, Victoria 3122, Australia. circ. 500.

370　　　　　AT
AUSTRALIAN COUNCIL FOR EDUCATIONAL
RESEARCH. RESEARCH SERIES. irreg.
Australian Council for Educational Research, Box
210, Hawthorn, Vic.3122, Australia.

372.21　　　　　AT
AUSTRALIAN EARLY CHILDHOOD
ASSOCIATION. VICTORIAN BRANCH.
NEWSLETTER. 1960. a. free. Chevron Advertising
& Publishing Agency Pty. Ltd., Acton House,
Edinburgh Ave., Canberra City, ACT 2601,
Australia. Ed. Lee Tregloan. adv. bk. rev. circ. 1,
500. Indexed: Aus.Educ.Ind.
　Formerly: Australian Pre-School Association.
Victoria Branch. Newsletter.

EDUCATION

370　　　　　　　　AT
AUSTRALIAN RESEARCH GRANTS SCHEME. REPORT ON GRANTS APPROVED. a. price varies. Australian Government Publishing Service, G.P.O. Box 84, Canberra, A.C.T. 2601, Australia. stat. (back issues avail.)
Formerly: Australian Research Grants Committee. Report.

AUSTRALIAN TEACHER OF THE DEAF. see *DEAF*

370　　　　　　　　BF
BAHAMAS. MINISTRY OF EDUCATION AND CULTURE. ANNUAL REPORT. a. Ministry of Education and Culture, N 7147, Nassau, Bahamas. illus.

370　　　　　　　　US
BALDWIN LECTURES. 1957. a. $1.50. Northeast Missouri State University, Office of the President, Kirksville, MO 63501. TEL 816-785-4000. circ. 200.
Formerly: Baldwin Lectures in Teacher Education (ISSN 0067-303X)

370　150　　　　　　US
BASIC CONCEPTS IN EDUCATIONAL PSYCHOLOGY SERIES. irreg. price varies. Brooks-Cole Publishing Co., 555 Abrego St., Monterey, CA 93940. TEL 408-373-0728.

BASIC CONCEPTS IN PSYCHOLOGY SERIES. see *PSYCHOLOGY*

379　　　　　　GW　ISSN 0005-7207
BAYERISCHES STAATSMINISTERIUM FUER UNTERRICHT UND KULTUS. AMTSBLATT. 1865. irreg. DM.86.50 for Teil I, DM. 68 for Teil II. (Staatsministerium fuer Unterricht und Kultus) Kommunalschriften-Verlag J. Jehle, Kirschstr. 12, 8000 Munich 50, W. Germany (B.R.D.) Ed.Bd. index. circ. 10,000. (tabloid format)

370　　　　　　BE　ISSN 0067-5598
BELGIUM. MINISTERE DE L'EDUCATION NATIONALE ET DE LA CULTURE FRANCAISE. RAPPORT ANNUEL.* a. Ministere de l'Education Nationale et de la Culture Francaise, Cite Administrative de l'Etat, Bd. Pacheco, 1010 Brussels, Belgium.

BIBLIOGRAPHIE PAEDAGOGIK/ EDUCATIONAL BIBLIOGRAPHY. see *BIBLIOGRAPHIES*

370　　　　　　　　BL
BIBLIOTECA DE EDUCACAO. 1982. irreg., vol.2, 1982. Edicoes Graal Ltda., Rua Hermenegildo de Barros, 31-A, Gloria 20240, Rio de Janeiro, Brazil.

BOOKS FOR SECONDARY SCHOOL LIBRARIES. see *LIBRARY AND INFORMATION SCIENCES*

BRAZIL. MINISTERIO DA EDUCACAO E CULTURA. SERVICO DE ESTATISTICA DA EDUCACAO E CULTURA. SINOPSE ESTATISTICA DA EDUCACAO BASICA. see *EDUCATION — Abstracting, Bibliographies, Statistics*

379.70　　　　　CN　ISSN 0709-8383
BRITISH COLUMBIA. MINISTRY OF EDUCATION. ANNUAL REPORT. 1978. a. Ministry of Education, Parliament Bldgs., Victoria, B.C. V8V 2M4, Canada. TEL 604-387-4611. circ. 3, 000.

371.4　　　　　　CN　ISSN 0705-8802
BRITISH COLUMBIA SCHOOL COUNSELLORS' ASSOCIATION. NEWSLETTER. 1956. irreg. Can.$30 to non-members. B.C. Teachers' Federation, 2235 Burrard St., Vancouver, B. C. V6J 3H9, Canada. TEL 604-731-8121. circ. 525.
Formerly: British Columbia Counsellors' Association. Newsletter (ISSN 0045-2947)

371　　　　　　CN　ISSN 0005-2965
BRITISH COLUMBIA TEACHERS' FEDERATION. NEWSLETTER. 1960. irreg. (approx. 13/yr) B.C. Teachers' Federation, 105-2235 Burrard St., Vancouver, B.C. V6J 3H9, Canada. TEL 604-731-8121. Ed. Clive Cocking. circ. 41,000.

370　　　　　　UK　ISSN 0141-5972
BRITISH QUALIFICATIONS. 1970. a. £22. Kogan Page Ltd., 120 Pentonville Rd., London N1 9JN, England. adv.

BUSINESS EDUCATION FILMS CATALOG. see *BUSINESS AND ECONOMICS*

371.2　　　　　　CN　ISSN 0068-8657
C E A HANDBOOK/KI-ES-KI. (Text in English or French) 1949. a. Canadian Education Association, 252 Bloor St. W., Ste. 8-200, Toronto, Ont. M5S 1V5, Canada. TEL 416-924-7721. Ed. H. Goldsborough. circ. 2,500.
Formerly: Directory of Administrative Officials in Public Education - Canada.

C G R B BULLETIN. (Citizens' Governmental Research Bureau) see *PUBLIC ADMINISTRATION — Municipal Government*

370　　　　　　II　ISSN 0007-8425
C.I.E. NEWSLETTER.* no.48, 1967. irreg. (3-4/yr.) Central Institute of Education, Patel Mar, University Campus, Delhi 1100016, India. Ed. Dr. R.S. Vashishj. bk. rev.

371.42　　　　　UY　ISSN 0577-2931
C I N T E R F O R ESTUDIOS Y MONOGRAFIAS. 1967. irreg. price varies. Centro Interamericano de Investigacion y Documentacion Sobre Formacion Profesional, Avda. Uruguay 1238, Casilla de Correo 1761, Montevideo, Uruguay. Indexed: CIRF Abstr.

370　　　　　　　AG
CALENDARIO ESCOLAR. a. Ministerio de Educacao y Justicia, Secretaria de Educacion, Directorio 1801, Buenos Aires, Argentina. circ. 20, 000.

370　　　　　　UK　ISSN 0068-6816
CAMBRIDGE TEXTS AND STUDIES IN THE HISTORY OF EDUCATION. 1966. irreg., no.14, 1973. $25.95 for latest vol. Cambridge University Press, Edinburgh Bldg., Shaftesbury Rd., Cambridge CB2 2RU, England (And 32 E. 57 St., New York, NY 10022) Ed.Bd.

CANADIAN NURSES ASSOCIATION. ENTRANCE REQUIREMENTS FOR DIPLOMA SCHOOLS OF NURSING AND SCHOOLS OF PRACTICAL NURSING. see *MEDICAL SCIENCES — Nurses And Nursing*

CANADIAN NURSES ASSOCIATION. NURSING PROGRAMS AND ENTRANCE REQUIREMENTS AT CANADIAN UNIVERSITIES. see *MEDICAL SCIENCES — Nurses And Nursing*

704　　　　　　CN　ISSN 0384-1839
CANADIAN REVIEW OF ART EDUCATION RESEARCH. (Text in English and French) 1977. a. Can.$55 (combined subscription) Canadian Society for Education Through Art, 3186 Newbound Court, Malton, Ont. L4T 1R9, Canada. circ. 700.

704　　　　　　CN　ISSN 0068-9645
CANADIAN SOCIETY FOR EDUCATION THROUGH ART. ANNUAL JOURNAL. a. Can.$55 (combined subscription) ‡ Canadian Society for Education Through Art, 3186 Newbound Court, Malton, Ont. L4T 1R9, Canada. bk. rev. circ. 700.

371　　　　　　US　ISSN 0069-0651
CARNEGIE FOUNDATION FOR THE ADVANCEMENT OF TEACHING. ANNUAL REPORT. 1906. a. free. ‡ Carnegie Foundation for the Advancement of Teaching, 5 Ivy Ln., Princeton, NJ 08540. TEL 609-452-1780. Ed. V.A. Stadtman. circ. 1,700.

370　　　　　　　US
CASE STUDIES IN EDUCATION AND CULTURE. irreg. price varies. Holt, Rinehart and Winston, Inc., 383 Madison Ave., New York, NY 10017. TEL 212-688-9100.

CATALOGO DE PUBLICACIONES LATINOAMERICANAS SOBRE FORMACION PROFESIONAL. see *OCCUPATIONS AND CAREERS — Abstracting, Bibliographies, Statistics*

CATHOLIC EDUCATION. see *RELIGIONS AND THEOLOGY — Roman Catholic*

370　　　　　　　CJ
CAYMAN ISLANDS. EDUCATION DEPARTMENT. REPORT OF THE CHIEF EDUCATION OFFICER. a. Education Department, Grand Cayman, Cayman Islands, B.W.I. illus.

340　370　　　　US　ISSN 0276-203X
CENTER FOR LAW AND EDUCATION. NEWSNOTES. 1979. irreg. free. Center for Law and Education, Inc., Larsen Hall, 14 Appian Way, Cambridge, MA 02138. TEL 617-495-4666. (reprint service avail. form UMI) Indexed: Rehabil.Lit.

370　　　　　　FR　ISSN 0069-2069
CENTRE REGIONAL DE DOCUMENTATION PEDAGOGIQUE DE TOULOUSE. ANNALES;* dossier d'information et de Perfectionnement (Francais-Mathematiques) (Supplements its Bulletin Regional d'Informations Universitaires) 1970. irreg. price varies. Centre Regional de Documentation Pedagogique de Toulouse, 3 rue Roquelaine, 31000 Toulouse, France.

371.42　016　　　　UY
CENTRO INTERAMERICANO DE INVESTIGACION Y DOCUMENTACION SOBRE FORMACION PROFESIONAL. SERIE BIBLIOGRAFICA. 1968. irreg. Centro Interamericano de Investigacion y Documentacion Sobre Formacion Profesional, Avda. Uruguay 1238, Casilla de Correo 1761, Montevideo, Uruguay. bk. rev. abstr. bibl.

370　　　　　　　US
CHILD AND FAMILY POLICY. 1981. irreg. price varies. Ablex Publishing Corp., 355 Chestnut St., Norwood, NJ 07648. TEL 201-767-8450. Eds. James J. Gallagher, Ron Haskins.

155.4　　　　　　US
CHILD STUDY JOURNAL MONOGRAPH. 1980. irreg. price varies. State University of New York, College at Buffalo, Bacon Hall 312J, 1300 Elmwood Ave., Buffalo, NY 14222. TEL 716-878-5302. (reprint service avail. from UMI) Indexed: Child Devel.Abstr. Lang.& Lang.Behav.Abstr.

CHILDREN'S BOOKS OF THE YEAR (YEAR) see *CHILDREN AND YOUTH — For*

370　　　　　　　UK
CITY OF LONDON SCHOOL CHRONICLE. a. £1.25. City of London School, Victoria Embankment, London EC4Y 0DL, England. circ. 1, 000.

370　　　　　　　US
COGNITION AND LITERACY. 1986. irreg. price varies. Ablex Publishing Corporation, 355 Chestnut St., Norwood, NJ 07648. TEL 201-767-8450. Ed. Judith Orasanu.

370　　　　　　BL　ISSN 0080-3103
COLEGIO MILITAR DO RIO DE JANEIRO. REVISTA DIDACTICA.* 1902. a. free. Colegio Militar do Rio de Janeiro, Rua Sao Francisco Xavier 267 - ZC-11, ZC-11 Rio de Janeiro, Brazil.

378.1　370　　　　CN　ISSN 0706-5000
COLLEGE MEDIA DIRECTOR NEWSLETTER. 1977. irreg. (3-4/yr.) Can.$10. Media Directors Association, c/o David Bennett, Ed., Durham College, Oshawa, Ont. L1H 7L7, Canada. TEL 416-576-0210. (Co-sponsors: Ontario Colleges of Applied Arts & Technology) bk. rev. circ. 200.

370　　　　　　　CK
COLOMBIA. MINISTERIO DE EDUCACION NACIONAL. EDUCACION PARA DESARROLLO. irreg. Ministerio de Educacion Nacional, Division de Educacion de Adultos, Bogota, Colombia.

370　　　　　　UK　ISSN 0010-1842
COLSTONIAN. 1894. a. £2. Colston's School, Stapleton, Bristol, England. Ed. B.D. Miller. adv. illus. circ. 1,000.

370　　　　　　　SP
COMISION MIXTA DE COORDINACION ESTADISTICA DE BARCELONA. ESTADISTICAS DE ENSENANZA DE LA PROVINCIA DE BARCELONA. (Subseries of: Comision Mixta de Coordinacion Estadistica de Barcelona. Serie Estadistica) 1970/71. a? $3. Comision Mixta de Coordinacion Estadistica, Urgel 187, Barcelona 11, Spain. circ. 1,000.

331.2   AT
COMMONWEALTH TEACHING SERVICE. ANNUAL REPORT. (Subseries of: Australia. Parliament. Parliamentary Papers) 1972. a. price varies. Australian Government Publishing Service, G.P.O. Box 84, Canberra, A.C.T. 2601, Australia. illus.

370   BE   ISSN 0588-9049
COMPARATIVE EDUCATION SOCIETY IN EUROPE. PROCEEDINGS OF THE GENERAL MEETING. (Text in English and French) 1963. biennial. Comparative Education Society in Europe, c/o Henk Van daele, 51 rue de la Concorde, 1050 Brussels, Belgium.

379   US   ISSN 0363-650X
CONNECTICUT. ADVISORY COUNCIL ON VOCATIONAL AND CAREER EDUCATION. VOCATIONAL EDUCATION EVALUATION REPORT. 1969. a. $10. Advisory Council on Vocational and Career Education., 61 Woodland St., Hartford, CT 06105. TEL 203-566-4035. Ed. Richard G. Rausch. circ. 1,000. (also avail. in microfiche) Key Title: Vocational Education Evaluation Report.

370 340   US
CONNECTICUT EDUCATION ASSOCIATION. LEGISLATIVE BULLETIN. irreg. Connecticut Education Association, 21 Oak St., Hartford, CT 06106. TEL 203-525-5641. Ed. Eugene Scalise.

379   US   ISSN 0095-5329
CONSOLIDATED REPORT ON ELEMENTARY AND SECONDARY EDUCATION IN COLORADO. a. $4. Department of Education, State Office Bldg., 201 E. Colfax Ave., Denver, CO 80203. TEL 303-866-2212. illus. stat.

370   US   ISSN 0196-707X
CONTRIBUTIONS TO THE STUDY OF EDUCATION. 1981. irreg., no.8, 1983. price varies. Greenwood Press, Box 5006, 88 Post Rd. West, Westport, CT 06881. TEL 203-226-3571.

371.42   US   ISSN 0069-9810
COOPERATIVE EDUCATION ASSOCIATION MEMBERSHIP DIRECTORY. 1965. a. $10. Cooperative Education Association, 655 15th St., N.W., Ste. 300, Washington, DC 20005-5701. circ. 3,000.

370   ZA
COPPERBELT EDUCATION. (Text in English) irreg. (1-2/yr.) Box 1552, Ndola, Zambia. illus.

370   US
CORRESPONDENCE EDUCATIONAL DIRECTORY. 1976. quadrennial. $46.50. Racz Publishing Company, Branch Office, Box 287, Oxnard, CA 93032. TEL 805-642-1186. Ed. Jeanette G. Racz. adv. bk. rev. circ. 10,000.

370   US   ISSN 0070-069X
COUNCIL FOR BASIC EDUCATION. OCCASIONAL PAPERS. 1961. irreg., latest no.33. $2 per no. Council for Basic Education, 725 15th St., N.W., Washington, DC 20005. TEL 202-347-4171. circ. 10,000.

371.4   US   ISSN 0271-5368
COUNSELOR PREPARATION (YEAR); programs, personnel, trends. 1971. triennial, 6th edt., 1986. $29.95. Accelerated Development Inc., 3400 Kilgore Ave., Muncie, IN 47304. Eds. Joseph W. Hollis, Richard A. Wantz. circ. 800.
Formerly: Counselor Education Directory: Personnel and Programs (ISSN 0190-2199)

370   VE   ISSN 0070-1718
CUADERNOS DE PEDAGOGIA.* 1966. irreg. Bs.2($0.45) Universidad del Zulia, Facultad de Humanidades y Educacion, Apartado de Correos 415, Maracaibo, Venezuela.

372.21   US   ISSN 0363-8332
CURRENT TOPICS IN EARLY CHILDHOOD EDUCATION. 1977. a. price varies. Ablex Publishing Corp., 355 Chestnut St., Norwood, NJ 07640. TEL 201-767-8450. Ed. Lillian G. Katz.

370   US   ISSN 0094-1050
CURRICULUM IMPROVEMENT. 1950. a. $15. Professors of Curriculum, c/o Arizona State University, Education B Bldg., Rm. 412, Tempe, AZ 85281. TEL 602-965-9011. Ed. James J. Jelinek. illus. circ. 2,000. (reprint service avail. from UMI) Indexed: ERIC.
Former titles: Philosophy of Education; Far Western Philosophy of Education Society. Proceedings (ISSN 0430-0661)

370   CN
CYCLOPEDIA. 1981. a. free contr. circ. Student Enterprises & Assistance League, Box 250, Station P., Toronto, Ont. M5S 2T9, Canada. illus. circ. 25, 000.

370   DK   ISSN 0900-5781
DANMARKS LAERERHOEJSKOLE. INSTITUT FOR INFORMATIK. ARBEJDSPAPIR. 1984. irreg. free. Danmarks Laererhoejskole, Institut for Informatik, Emdrupvej 115B, 2400 Copenhagen NV, Denmark. circ. 500.

370 150   DK   ISSN 0107-1637
DANMARKS LAERERHOESKOLE. INSTITUT FOR PAEDAGOGIK OG PSYKOLOGI. TESTSAMLING. 1978. a. free. Danmarks Laererhoejskole, Institut for Paedagogik og Psykologi, Copenhagen, Denmark.

370   SP   ISSN 0070-2897
DATOS Y CIFRAS DE LA ENSENANZA EN ESPANA. 1978. irreg. Ministerio de Educacion, Secretaria General Tecnica, Servicio de Publicaciones, Madrid 3, Spain.

370   US   ISSN 0091-6188
DELAWARE. DEPARTMENT OF PUBLIC INSTRUCTION. EDUCATIONAL PERSONNEL DIRECTORY. 1921. a. contr. free circ. Department of Public Instruction, Division of Planning, Research & Evaluation, Townsend Building, Dover, DE 19901. Ed. Wilmer E. Wise. circ. 3,500.

370   US   ISSN 0362-8787
DELAWARE. STATE BOARD OF EDUCATION. REPORT OF EDUCATIONAL STATISTICS. 1921. a. State Board of Education, Townsend Building, Box 1402, Dover, DE 19901. TEL 302-736-4629. circ. 300. Key Title: Report of Educational Statistics.

370   DK   ISSN 0107-4652
DENMARK. STATENS PAEDAGOGISKE FORSOEGSCENTER. ARBEJDSBESKRIVELSE. 1980. a. free. Statens Paedagogiske Forsoegscenter, Ungdomsbyens Skole, Islevgaard Alle 5, 2610 Roedovre, Denmark. illus.
Formerly: Denmark. Statens Paedagogiske Forsoegscenter. Projektbeskrivelser.

370   DK   ISSN 0107-5152
DENMARK. STATENS UDDANNELSESSTOETTE. REGELSAMLING FOR STOETTEAARET. 1970. a. free. Statens Uddannelsesstoette, Danasvej 30, 1910 Frederiksberg C, Denmark. circ. 6,000.

370   PK   ISSN 0080-1321
DEVELOPMENT OF EDUCATION IN PAKISTAN. (Text in English) 1965. a. Ministry of Education, Documentation Section, Curriculum Wing, Sector H-9, P.O. Shaigan, Industrial Area, Islamabad, Pakistan.
Title varies: Report on the Progress of Education in Pakistan.

370   BL   ISSN 0101-059X
DIDATICA; serie educacao. (Text in Portuguese; summaries in English and Portuguese) 1964-1977; resumed 1979. a. $30 or exchange basis. Universidade Estadual Paulista, Av. Vicente Ferreira 1278, Caixa Postal 603, 17.500 Marilia, SP, Brazil. bibl. charts. circ. 1,000. Indexed: Psychol.Abstr.

371   US   ISSN 0362-5710
DIRECTORY OF DELAWARE SCHOOLS. a. $5. Department of Public Instruction, Townsend Building, Federal St. at Loockerman St., Dover, DE 19901 (Orders to: Public Information Office, Dept. of Public Instruction, Box 1402, Dover, DE 19901)

DIRECTORY OF DEVELOPMENT AND TRAINING INSTITUTES IN AFRICA. see BUSINESS AND ECONOMICS — International Development And Assistance

370   CN   ISSN 0070-5454
DIRECTORY OF EDUCATION STUDIES IN CANADA/ANNUAIRE D'ETUDES EN EDUCATION AU CANADA. (Text in English or French) 1968. a. Can.$30. Canadian Education Association, 252 Bloor St. W., Ste. 8-200, Toronto, Ont. M5S 1V5, Canada. TEL 416-924-7721. Ed. Maureen Davis. circ. 400.

374   US   ISSN 0084-991X
DIRECTORY OF EDUCATIONAL INSTITUTIONS IN NEW MEXICO; approved for the education of veterans, war orphans and other eligible persons. (Subseries of its Bulletin) 1966. a. free. Department of Education, Veterans Approval Division, Box 4277, Santa Fe, NM 87501. Dir. Rudy Silva.

DIRECTORY OF MUSIC FACULTIES IN COLLEGES & UNIVERSITIES U S AND CANADA. see MUSIC

370 371.9   AT
DIRECTORY OF RESEARCH AND DEVELOPMENTAL PROJECTS. 1978. a. free. Melbourne College of Advanced Education, 757 Swanston St, Carlton, VIC 3053, Australia. Ed. Rosalind Hurworth. circ. 500. (back issues avail.)

370   UK
DIRECTORY OF TRAINER SUPPORT SERVICES. 1985. a. £13.50. (Institute for Training and Development) Kogan Page Ltd., 120 Pentonville Rd., London N1 9JN, England. Ed. Barry Williamson.

371   US   ISSN 0277-2736
DISCUSSIONS ON TEACHING. 1971. irreg. price varies. ‡ American Historical Association, 400 A St. S.E., Washington, DC 20003. TEL 202-544-2422. bibl. charts. illus.

370   US   ISSN 0077-9210
DISTRIBUTION OF HIGH SCHOOL GRADUATES AND COLLEGE GOING RATE, NEW YORK STATE. 1967. a. free. ‡ Education Department, Information Center on Education, Albany, NY 12234. circ. controlled.

370   YU   ISSN 0012-5636
DOSTIGNUCA;* casopis za skolstvo, prosvjetu i kultura. (Text in Serbo-Croatian) 1965. irreg. 5 din.per no. Pedagoska Akademija u Gospicu, Marka Oreskovica 24/2, Gospic, Yugoslavia. Ed. Zlata Derossi.

970.1   US   ISSN 0070-7171
DOWNDRAFT. 1967. irreg. U.S. Bureau of Indian Affairs, 1951 Constitution Ave., N.W., Washington, DC 20245. TEL 202-346-1100.
American Indian interests

370   GW   ISSN 0070-7767
DURCH STIPENDIEN STUDIEREN. 1964. a. DM.18. Verein Freunde und Foerderer der Deutschen Studentenschaft e.V., Untere Hausbreite 11, 8000 Munich 45, W. Germany (B.R.D.) Ed. Gundolf Seidenspinner. adv.

370 362.7 917.306   US   ISSN 0889-8022
E R I C/C U E TRENDS AND ISSUES. 1985. irreg. (Institute for Urban and Minority Education) E R I C Clearinghouse on Urban Education, Box 40, Teachers College, Columbia University, New York, NY 10027. TEL 212-678-3433. Ed. Erwin Flaxman. bibl. stat. (also avail. in microfiche; back issues avail.) Indexed: Res.Educ.

370   US   ISSN 0889-8030
E R I C/C U E URBAN DIVERSITY SERIES. 1972. irreg., no.94, 1986. price varies. E R I C Clearinghouse on Urban Education, Box 40, Teachers College, Columbia University, New York, NY 10027. TEL 212-678-3433. Ed. Erwin Flaxman. bibl. stat. circ. 1,000. (also avail. in microfilm; back issues avail.) Indexed: ERIC. Res.Educ.

370   US
E R I C CLEARINGHOUSE ON TEACHER EDUCATION. CURRENT ISSUES PUBLICATIONS. irreg. (4-5/yr.) E R I C Clearinghouse on Teacher Education, One Dupont Circle, Ste. 610, Washington, DC 20036. TEL 202-293-2450. (also avail. in microfiche; reprint service avail. from UMI,EDR)
Formerly: E R I C Clearinghouse on Teacher Education. Special Current Issues Publications.

370 US
E R I C CLEARINGHOUSE ON TESTS, MEASUREMENT, AND EVALUATION. T M E REPORT SERIES. 1979. irreg., approx. 3/yr. price varies. E R I C Clearinghouse, Tests, Measurement, & Evaluation - Educational Resources Information Center, Educational Testing Service, Princeton, NJ 08541. TEL 609-734-5181. Ed. Betsy Smith. circ. 500. (also avail. in microfiche; back issues avail.) Indexed: ERIC. Res.Educ.

370 362.7 917.306 US ISSN 0889-8049
E R I C CLEARINGHOUSE ON URBAN EDUCATION. DIGEST. 1980. irreg. (Institute for Urban and Minority Education) E R I C Clearinghouse on Urban Education, Box 40, Teachers College, Columbia University, New York, NY 10027. TEL 212-678-3433. Ed. Erwin Flaxman. bibl. (also avail. in microfiche; back issues avail.) Indexed: Res.Educ.

370 PE
EDUCACION; revista del maestro peruano. 1970. irreg. Instituto Nacional de Investigacion y Desarrollo de la Educacion, Centro Nacional de Documentacion e Informacion Educacional, Van de Velde 160, San Borja, Lima 100, Peru. Ed. Raul Vargas Vega. bibl. charts. illus.

370 GT
EDUCACION Y PLANEAMIENTO.* 1970. irreg. Oficina de Planeamiento Integral de la Educacion, 4A. Avenida 8-56, Zona 1, Guatemala, Guatemala.

370.193 CN
EDUCATION ADVISORY. 1975. irreg. (approx. 2/yr) Can.$3. 2267 Kings Ave., West Vancouver, B.C. V7V 2C1, Canada. Ed. Tunya Audain. bk. rev. circ. 3,000.

370 371.42 SA
EDUCATION & CAREERS IN SOUTH AFRICA. (Text in Afrikaans and English) a. R.45. Erudita Publications (Pty) Ltd., Cnr. 11th Ave. & Main Rd., P.O. Box 29159, Melville, Johannesburg 2109, South Africa. adv.

370 FR
EDUCATION AND CULTURE. SECTION 1: CULTURAL DEVELOPMENT. 1979. irreg. Council of Europe, Council for Cultural Co-Operation, Publications Section, Strasbourg, France (Dist. in U.S. by Manhattan Publishing Co., Box 650, Croton-on-Hudson, N.Y. 10520)

370 FR
EDUCATION AND CULTURE. SECTION 2: HIGHER EDUCATION AND RESEARCH. 1979. irreg. Council of Europe, Council for Cultural Co-Operation, Publications Section, Strasbourg, France (Dist. in U.S. by Manhattan Publishing Co, Box 650, Croton-on-Hudson, NY 10520)

EDUCATION AND TRAINING IN INDEXING AND ABSTRACTING. see LIBRARY AND INFORMATION SCIENCES

370 US
EDUCATION AROUND THE WORLD. 1958. irreg. U.S. Department of Education, Washington, DC 20202 (Subscr. to: Supt. of Documents, Washington, DC 20402) Indexed: P.A.I.S. Ind.U.S.Gov.Per.

370.58 UK ISSN 0070-9131
EDUCATION AUTHORITIES' DIRECTORY AND ANNUAL. 1902. a. £33. School Government Publishing Co. Ltd., Darby House, Bletchingley Rd., Merstham, Redhill RH1 3DN, England. Ed. McCormack. circ. 8,000.

375 US ISSN 0424-5407
EDUCATION DEVELOPMENT CENTER. ANNUAL REPORT. 1967. a. Education Development Center, Inc., 55 Chapel St., Newton, MA 02160. TEL 617-969-7100. illus. circ. 6,500.

370 US ISSN 0273-4346
EDUCATION DIRECTORY. LOCAL EDUCATION AGENCIES. irreg. $15.50. U.S. National Center for Education Statistics, U.S. Department of Education, 400 Maryland Ave., S.W., Washington, DC 20202 TEL 201-655-4000. (Orders to: National Technical Information Service, 8285 Port Royal Rd., Springfield, VA 22161)
 Formerly: Education Directory. Public Schools Systems (ISSN 0083-2677)

370 AT ISSN 0729-8528
EDUCATION GUIDELINES. 1979. 3/yr. (plus a. cumulation) Aus.$12. Bibliographic Services, Box 2, Mount Waverley, Vic. 3149, Australia. Ed. K.S. Darling. circ. 500. (also avail. in microfiche)

370 UN
EDUCATION IN ASIA AND THE PACIFIC: REVIEWS, REPORTS AND NOTES. (Nos. 1-3 issued as: Unesco Regional Office for Education in Asia. Bulletin. Supplement) (Text in English) 1972. a. price varies. (Library and Documentation Service) Unesco, Principal Regional Office for Education in Asia and the Pacific, G.P.O. Box 1425, Bangkok 10501, Thailand (Dist. in U.S. by: Bernan Associates-UNIPUB, 4611-F Assembly Dr., Lanham, MD 20706-4391) bk. rev. abstr. bibl. circ. 2,650. Indexed: ERIC.
 Former titles: Education in Asia and Oceania: Reviews, Reports and Notes; Education in Asia: Reviews, Reports and Notes.

370 FR
EDUCATION IN EUROPE. CULTURAL DEVELOPMENT. 1974. irreg. price varies. Council of Europe, Council for Cultural Co-Operation, Publications Section, Strasbourg, France (Dist. in U.S. by Manhattan Publishing Co., Box 650, Croton-on-Hudson, N.Y. 10520)

370 II
EDUCATION IN INDIA. (Issued in 2 Vols.) (Text in English) 1950. irreg. price varies. Ministry of Education and Social Welfare, Department of Education, Shastri Bhavan, New Delhi 110001, India (Orders to: Controller of Publications, Government of India, Civil Lines, Delhi 110054, India)

370 JA ISSN 0070-9220
EDUCATION IN JAPAN; A GRAPHIC PRESENTATION. (Text in English) 1954. irreg., 8th edt., 1971. 1400 Yen. Ministry of Education, 3-2-2 Kasumigaseki, Chiyoda-ku, Tokyo 100, Japan (Subscr. to Government Publications Service Center, 1-2-1 Kasumigaseki, Chiyoda-ku, Tokyo 100, Japan)

370 UK ISSN 0424-5512
EDUCATION IN THE NORTH. 1965. a. £1.70. Aberdeen College of Education, Hilton Place, Aberdeen AB9 1FA, Scotland. Ed.Bd. adv. bk. rev. circ. 2,000. Indexed: Br.Educ.Ind. High.Educ.Curr.Aware.Bull.

370 UK ISSN 0261-8966
EDUCATION IN THE ROYAL COUNTY OF BERKSHIRE. 1981. irreg. (Berkshire Education Department) Coles & Sons, 223 Southampton St., Reading RG1 2RB, England. illus.

370 340 US ISSN 0276-718X
EDUCATION LAW BULLETIN. 1975. irreg. $24 for 3 nos. Center for Law and Education, Inc., Larsen Hall, 14 Appian Way, Cambridge, MA 02138. TEL 617-495-4666. Ed. Robert Pressman. circ. 1,800. (also avail. in microform from UMI; reprint service avail. from UMI)

EDUCATION NEWS FROM METROLOGIC. see INSTRUMENTS

370 UK
EDUCATION STATISTICS FOR THE UNITED KINGDOM. a. price varies. H.M.S.O., Box 569, London SE1 9NH, England. (Co-sponsor: Department of Education and Science)

370 UK ISSN 0143-5469
EDUCATION YEAR BOOK. 1939. a. £27. (Society of Education Officers) Councils and Education Press (Subsidiary of: Longman Group Ltd.) Westgate House, The High, Harlow, Essex CM20 1NE, England. Ed. Susan Higgins. adv.
 Formerly: Education Committees Year Book (ISSN 0070-9158)

EDUCATIONAL AND PSYCHOLOGICAL INTERACTIONS. see PSYCHOLOGY

EDUCATIONAL DRAMA ASSOCIATION. NEWSLETTER. see THEATER

370 JA
EDUCATIONAL STANDARDS IN JAPAN. (Text in English) 1959. irreg. Ministry of Education, 3-2-2 Kasumigaseki, Chiyoda-ku, Tokyo 100, Japan. illus. stat.

370 FR
EDUCATIONAL STATISTICS IN O E C D COUNTRIES. (Text in English and French) 1974. irreg. price varies. Organisation for Economic Cooperation and Development, Rue Andre-Pascal, 75775 Paris 16, France (U.S. orders to: O.E.C.D. Publications and Information Center, 1750 Pennsylvania Ave. N.W., Washington, D.C. 20006) (also avail. in microfiche)
 Formerly: Educational Statistics Yearbook.

370 PK
EDUCATIONAL STATISTICS OF PUNJAB. (Text in English) a. Bureau of Education, Lahore, Punjab, Pakistan. stat.

370 UN ISSN 0070-9344
EDUCATIONAL STUDIES AND DOCUMENTS. (Text in English, French or Spanish) 1953. irreg., no.49, 1984. price varies. Unesco, 7-9 Place de Fontenoy, 75700 Paris, France (Dist. in U.S. by: Bernan Associates-Unipub, 4611-F Assembly Dr., Lanham, MD 20706-4391) Indexed: Rural Recreat.Tour.Abstr. World Agri.Econ.& Rural Sociol.Abstr.

370 US ISSN 0091-8989
EDUCATIONAL TESTING SERVICE ANNUAL REPORT. 1949. a. free. ‡ Educational Testing Service, Princeton, NJ 08541-0001. TEL 609-921-9000. Ed. Peter B. Mann. illus. circ. 65,000. Key Title: Annual Report - Educational Testing Service.

370 DK ISSN 0108-8262
EFTERSKOLER. FORTEGNELSE. 1971. a. free. Undervisnungsministeriet, Direktoratet for Folkeoplysning, Frie Grundskoler, Copenhagen, Denmark.

ELEMENTARY SCHOOL LIBRARY COLLECTION. see LIBRARY AND INFORMATION SCIENCES

372 RM
ENSEIGNEMENT ET LA PEDAGOGIE EN ROUMANIE. (Summaries in French) 1978. a. 60 lei exchange basis to foreign subscribers. Biblioteca Centrala Pedagogica, Str. Zalomit Nr. 12, Bucharest 70714, Rumania. Ed. Alfred Lauterman. bk. rev. index. circ. 2,000.

378.666 IV
ENSEIGNEMENT SUPERIEUR EN COTE-D'IVOIRE. a. Universite Nationale de Cote d'Ivoire, B.P. 859, Abidjan-08, Ivory Coast.

370 SZ ISSN 0071-125X
ERZIEHUNG UND UNTERRICHT. 1967. irreg., no.34, 1986. price varies. Paul Haupt AG, Falkenplatz 14, CH-3001 Berne, Switzerland. Ed.Bd. (reprint service avail. from UMI)

370 GE ISSN 0075-2622
ERZIEHUNGS- UND SCHULGESCHICHTE JAHRBUCH. 1961. irreg. price varies. (Akademie der Paedagogischen Wissenschaften der DDR) Verlag Volk und Wissen, Berlin, E. Germany (D.D.R.)

370 UK
ESSEX EDUCATION. 1947. irreg. £1. (Essex County Council) Essex Education Committee, County Hall, Chelmsford Essex, England. Ed. M. Rees. adv. bk. rev. cum.index. circ. 8,150.

370 US
EVALUATION COMMENT; the journal of educational evaluation. 1968. a. free. University of California, Los Angeles, Center for the Study of Evaluation, 145 Moore Hall, Graduate School of Education, 405 Hilgard Ave., Los Angeles, CA 90024. TEL 213-825-4711. Ed.Bd. circ. 10,000.

370 US ISSN 0071-3481
EXPLORATIONS IN EDUCATION. 1963. a. free. South Carolina State College, Orangeburg, SC 29115. TEL 803-356-7000. Ed. Ernest W. Boston.

371 US
FACT BOOK. 1967. a. free. Department of Education, 200 W. Baltimore St., Baltimore, MD 21201. TEL 301-659-2000. charts. circ. 8,500.
 Former titles: Facts About Maryland Public Education (ISSN 0092-461X) & Facts About Maryland Schools.

414　EDUCATION

370　　　　　FJ
FIJI. MINISTRY OF EDUCATION. REPORT.
(Subseries of: Fiji. Parliament. Parliamentary Paper) a. Ministry of Education, Suva, Fiji.
Formerly (until 1977): Fiji. Ministry of Education, Youth and Sport. Report.

FILM AUSTRALIA CATALOGUE. see MOTION PICTURES

FINE. see ART

FINLAND. TILASTOKESKUS. AMMATILLISET OPPILAITOKSET/FINLAND. STATISTIKCENTRALEN. YRKESUTBILDNINGSANSTALTERNA/ FINLAND. CENTRAL STATISTICAL OFFICE. VOCATIONAL EDUCATION. see BUSINESS AND ECONOMICS — Abstracting, Bibliographies, Statistics

371　　　　　US
FLORIDA. DEPARTMENT OF EDUCATION. PROFESSIONAL PRACTICES COUNCIL. REPORT. 1969/70. a. free. Department of Education, Professional Practices Council, Tallahassee, FL 32304. TEL 904-488-2481. Ed. Hugh Ingram. circ. 300.

370　　　　　DK　ISSN 0108-7746
FOCUS PAA UNDERVISNING. 1982. irreg. free. Arbejderbevaegelsens Skolekontaktudvalg, Teglvaerksgade 27, 2100 Copenhagen OE, Denmark. Ed. Erick Hein. bk. rev. illus. circ. 10,000.

FORD FOUNDATION ANNUAL REPORT. see SOCIAL SCIENCES: COMPREHENSIVE WORKS

FORENINGEN AF FILMLAERERE I GYMNASIET. MEDDELELSER. see MOTION PICTURES

370　　　　　DK　ISSN 0109-1425
FORTVIVL. 1980. irreg. (5-6/yr.) membership. Invandrerlaererforeningen, Christianborggade 1/st, 1558 Copenhagen V, Denmark. illus.

370　335　　　GW　ISSN 0067-589X
FREIE UNIVERSITAET BERLIN. OSTEUROPA-INSTITUT. ERZIEHUNGSWISSENSCHAFTLICHE VEROEFFENTLICHUNGEN. 1964. irreg., vol.17, 1985. price varies. (Freie Universitaet Berlin, Osteuropa-Institut) Verlag Otto Harrassowitz, Taunusstr. 14, Postfach 2929, 6200 Wiesbaden, W. Germany (B.R.D.) Ed. Oskar Anweiler, Siegfried Baske. circ. 500.

370　　　　　US　ISSN 0016-1004
FREMONT SCHOOLS. 1964. irreg. (3-4/yr.) free. Fremont Unified School District, 4210 Technology Dr., Fremont, CA 94538. TEL 415-657-2350. Ed. Wess Peterson. circ. 55,000.

370　　　　　DK　ISSN 0108-4259
FRISKOLER OG PRIVATE GRUNDSKOLER; noegletal og finansieringskilder. 1980. a. free. Undervisningsministeriet, Oekonomisk-Statistiske Konsulent, Vester Voldgade 104, 1552 Copenhagen V., Denmark. illus.

G L V MITTEILUNGEN. (Graphische Lehr- und Versuchsanstalt) see PRINTING

370　　　　　US
G P N EDUCATIONAL MEDIA. CROSSOVER. 1985. biennial. Great Plains National Instructional Television Library, Box 80669, Lincoln, NE 68501 TEL 800-228-4630. Eds. Richard L. Spence, Thomas Henderson. circ. 10,000.
Superseded in part: Great Plains National Instructional Television Library. Recorded Visual Instruction (ISSN 0740-2732)

374　　　　　II　ISSN 0072-0720
GENERAL EDUCATION READING MATERIAL SERIES.* (Text in English and Hindi) 1959. irreg. price varies. Aligarh Muslim University, Aligarh, Uttar Pradesh, India.

370　　　　　UK　ISSN 0142-2154
GENERAL TEACHING COUNCIL FOR SCOTLAND. BULLETIN. 1976. irreg. General Teaching Council for Scotland, 5 Royal Terrace, Edinburgh EH2 4DF, Scotland. circ. 85,000.

370　　　　　GH
GHANA. MINISTRY OF EDUCATION. EDUCATIONAL STATISTICS. a. NC.2. Ministry of Education, Box M 45, Accra, Ghana. charts. stat.

370　　　　　SW　ISSN 0436-1121
GOETEBORG STUDIES IN EDUCATIONAL SCIENCES. (Subseries of Acta Universitatis Gothoburgensis) (Text in English and Swedish) 1966. irreg., no.57, 1986. price varies; also exchange basis. Acta Universitatis Gothoburgensis, Box 5096, S-402 22 Goeteborg, Sweden (Dist. in U.S., Canada, and Mexico by: Humanities Press, Inc., 171 First Ave., Atlantic Highlands, NJ 07716) Ed.Bd.

370　　　　　UK
GREAT BRITAIN. DEPARTMENT OF EDUCATION AND SCIENCE. ANNUAL REPORT. a. price varies. (Department of Education and Science) H.M.S.O., Box 569, London SE1 9NH, England.
Formerly: Education and Science (ISSN 0070-9115)

370　　　　　UK　ISSN 0072-5897
GREAT BRITAIN. DEPARTMENT OF EDUCATION AND SCIENCE. EDUCATION SURVEYS. 1967. irreg. price varies. (Department of Education and Science) H.M.S.O., Box 569, London SE1 9NH, England.

370　　　　　UK　ISSN 0072-5900
GREAT BRITAIN. DEPARTMENT OF EDUCATION AND SCIENCE. STATISTICS OF EDUCATION. 1961. a. in 6 pts. price varies. (Department of Education and Science) H.M.S.O., Box 569, London SE1 9NH, England.

373　　　　　UK　ISSN 0072-7121
GREAT BRITAIN. SCHOOLS COUNCIL PUBLICATIONS. EXAMINATIONS BULLETINS. 1963. irreg. price varies. ‡ Methuen Educational, 11 New Fetter Lane, London EC4P 4EE, England.

370　　　　　UK　ISSN 0072-713X
GREAT BRITAIN. SCHOOLS COUNCIL PUBLICATIONS. WORKING PAPERS. 1965. irreg. price varies. ‡ Methuen Educational, 11 New Fetter Lane, London EC4P 4EE, England.

370　　　　　US　ISSN 0271-9509
GREENWOOD ENCYCLOPEDIA OF AMERICAN INSTITUTIONS. 1977. irreg. price varies. Greenwood Press, Box 5007, 88 Post Rd. West, Westport, CT 06881. TEL 203-226-3571.

370　　　　　IS
HACHEINUCH VE SIVEVO. a. College of Education, Kibbutz Seminar, Tel Aviv, Israel. Ed. Mordechai Segel.

HANDELSHOEJSKOLEN I KOEBENHAVN. CENTER FOR UDDANNELSES FORSKNING. ARBEJDSNOTE. see BUSINESS AND ECONOMICS

370.25　　　　　US　ISSN 0092-1777
HAWAII. DEPARTMENT OF EDUCATION. EDUCATIONAL DIRECTORY: STATE & DISTRICT OFFICE. 1924. a. $1.50. Department of Education, Box 2360, Honolulu, HI 96804. Ed. Kathleen Jones. illus.

371.2　　　　　US
HAWAII. DEPARTMENT OF EDUCATION. OFFICE OF BUSINESS SERVICES. PUBLIC AND PRIVATE SCHOOL ENROLLMENT. 1970? a. Department of Education, Office of Business Services, Box 2360, Honolulu, HI 96804. Ed. Dr. Linda Wheeler. circ. 550.
Formerly: Hawaii. Department of Education. Office of Research and Planning. Information Systems Branch. Public and Private School Enrollment.

370　　　　　US　ISSN 0018-148X
HIGH POINTS; in the New York City public schools. 1919. irreg. free to N.Y. City public school personnel. Board of Education, 110 Livingston St., Brooklyn, NY 11201. bk. rev. bibl. Indexed: Educ.Ind.

370　　　　　PK
HIGH SCHOOLS STATISTICS IN PUNJAB. 1973/74. irreg. Bureau of Education, Lahore, Punjab, Pakistan.

HISTORISCHE UND PAEDAGOGISCHE STUDIEN. see HISTORY

370　　　　　HO
HONDURAS. UNIVERSIDAD NACIONAL AUTONOMA. REVISTA DE LA UNIVERSIDAD; publicacion cientifico y cultural. irreg., no.19, 1982. Universidad Nacional Autonoma, Tegucigalpa, Honduras.

370　410　　　GW　ISSN 0073-3792
HUEBER HOCHSCHULREIHE. 1971. irreg., vol.35, 1975. price varies. Max Hueber Verlag, Max-Hueber-Str.4, 8045 Ismaning, W. Germany (B.R.D.)

370　150　　　US
HYMAN BLUMBERG SYMPOSIUM SERIES. 1973. irreg., no.6, 1977. price varies. Johns Hopkins University Press, 701 W. 40th St., Ste. 275, Baltimore, MD 21211. TEL 301-338-6900. (reprint service avail. from UMI)

I A S L CONFERENCE PROCEEDINGS. (International Association of School Librarianship) see LIBRARY AND INFORMATION SCIENCES

370　　　　　US　ISSN 0073-8697
I D E A MONOGRAPHS. 1967. irreg. price varies. Institute for Development of Educational Activities, Inc., 259 Regency Ridge, Dayton, OH 45459. TEL 513-434-6969.

370　　　　　US　ISSN 0073-8700
I D E A OCCASIONAL PAPERS. 1967. irreg. price varies. Institute for Development of Educational Activities, Inc., 259 Regency Ridge, Dayton, OH 45459. TEL 513-434-6969.

370　　　　　US
I N E T UP-DATE. a. Michigan State University, International Network in Education and Development (INET), College of Education, 237 Erickson Hall, E. Lansing, MI 48824. Ed.Bd. circ. 6,000.
Formerly: N F E Exchange (Non-Formal Education)

370　　　　　SP　ISSN 0536-2512
IBERO-AMERICAN BUREAU OF EDUCATION. INFORMATION AND PUBLICATIONS DEPARTMENT SERIES V: TECHNICAL SEMINARS AND MEETINGS.* 1964. irreg.? Ibero-American Bureau of Education, Avenida de los Reyes Catolicos, Ciudad Universitaria, Madrid 3, Spain.

370　　　　　CN
IBIDEM: GLENDON COLLEGE STUDENT HANDBOOK. a. Glendon College, Student Union, 2275 Bayview Ave., Toronto, Ont. M4N 3M6, Canada. TEL 416-487-6720. adv. circ. 1,000.

371.9　　　　　US　ISSN 0093-7223
IDAHO. STATE SUPERINTENDENT OF PUBLIC INSTRUCTION. ANNUAL REPORT. STATE OF IDAHO JOHNSON-O'MALLEY PROGRAM. Cover title: Indian Education Annual Report. 1966. irreg. State Department of Education, Adult Education, Boise, ID 83720. TEL 208-334-3300. circ. 200. Key Title: Annual Report: State of Idaho Johnson-O'Malley Program.

370　　　　　US　ISSN 0073-4497
IDAHO EDUCATION ASSOCIATION. PROCEEDINGS. a. membership. Idaho Education Association, 620 N. Sixth St., Box 2638, Boise, ID 83702. TEL 208-344-1341.

379　　　　　US　ISSN 0147-2860
ILLINOIS. STATE BOARD OF EDUCATION. ANNUAL REPORT. a. State Board of Education, 100 N. First St., Springfield, IL 62706. TEL 217-782-4648. Ed. Lee Milner. illus. stat.
Supersedes: Illinois. Department of Public Instruction. Annual State of Education Message (ISSN 0098-0269)

EDUCATION

370   II
INDIA. MINISTRY OF EDUCATION AND SOCIAL WELFARE. DEPARTMENT OF EDUCATION. REPORT. 1948/49. a. free. Ministry of Education and Social Welfare, Department of Education, Shastri Bhavan, New Delhi 110001, India (Avail. from: Assistant Educational Adviser (Publications), Ministry of Human Resource Development, Department of Education, EX AFO Hutments, Dr. Rajendra Prasad Road, New Delhi 110001) circ. 3,500.
    Formerly: India. Ministry of Education and Social Welfare. Department of Education. Report (ISSN 0073-6201)

370   II   ISSN 0579-6105
INDIA. MINISTRY OF EDUCATION AND SOCIAL WELFARE. PROVISIONAL STATISTICS OF EDUCATION IN THE STATES. (Text in English) 1954. a. controlled free circ. Ministry of Education and Social Welfare, Department of Education, Shastri Bhavan, New Delhi 110001, India.

INDIAN MUSIC JOURNAL; devoted to general reader and student. see *MUSIC*

INDIANA DIRECTORY OF MUSIC TEACHERS. see *MUSIC*

370   US
INFORMATION ON EDUCATION. 1971/72. a. Department of Education, Office of Administrative Services, Frankfort, KY 40601. TEL 502-564-3930. stat. circ. 1,000.
    Formerly: Summary of Kentucky Education Statistics (ISSN 0362-6679)

370   US   ISSN 0073-800X
INGLIS LECTURE. 1926. a., latest ed. 1965. price varies. Harvard University Press, 79 Garden St., Cambridge, MA 02138. TEL 617-495-2600.

370   CN   ISSN 0073-8123
INSIGHTS. 1964. irreg. (2-4/yr.) membership. John Dewey Society, c/o John M. Novak, Graduate Student Education, Brock University, St. Catherine, Ontario, Canada (Subscr. to: Robert C. Morris, Sec-Treas., Department of Curriculum & Instruction, Northern Illinois University, Dekalb, IL 60115) Ed. James C. Carper. circ. 400.

370   FR
INSTITUT COLLEGIAL EUROPEEN. ACTES DES COLLOQUES DE LOCHES. 1963. a. 75 F. Institut Collegial Europeen, 4 rue des Princes, 92100 Boulogne-sur-Seine, France. Ed. Gilbert Gadoffre. circ. 300.
    Formerly: Institute Collegial Europeen. Bulletin (ISSN 0073-8174)

INSTITUT FUER DEN WISSENSCHAFTLICHEN FILM. PUBLIKATIONEN ZU WISSENSCHAFTLICHEN FILMEN. SEKTION GESCHICHTE, PUBLIZISTIK. see *MOTION PICTURES*

INSTITUTUL PEDAGOGIC ORADEA. LUCRARI STIINTIFICE: SERIA PEDAGOGIE, PSIHOLOGIE, METODICA. see *PSYCHOLOGY*

370 500   US   ISSN 0074-0829
INTER-AMERICAN COUNCIL FOR EDUCATION, SCIENCE, AND CULTURE. FINAL REPORT. (Text in English, French, Portuguese and Spanish) a. $4. Organization of American States, Department of Publications, Washington, DC 20006. TEL 703-941-1617. circ. 2,000.

341.1   US   ISSN 0020-5273
INTERCOM (NEW YORK) 1959. irreg. price varies. Global Perspectives in Education, Inc., 45 John St., Ste. 1200, New York, NY 10038. TEL 212-732-8606. Ed. Del Franz. bk. rev. bibl. charts. (also avail. in microform from UMI; reprint service avail. from UMI) Indexed: P.A.I.S. C.I.J.E.

370   FR
INTERNATIONAL ASSOCIATION FOR EDUCATIONAL AND VOCATIONAL INFORMATION. STUDIES AND REPORTS. irreg. International Association for Educational and Vocational Information, 20 rue de l'Estrapade, 75005 Paris, France.

370   SZ   ISSN 0074-1973
INTERNATIONAL BACCALAUREATE OFFICE. ANNUAL BULLETIN. (Editions in English, French, Spanish) 1968. a. 10 Fr. International Baccalaureate Office - Office du Baccalaureat International, Route des Morillons 15, Grand Saconnex, Geneva, Switzerland (Order in the U.S. from: International Baccalaureate North America, 200 Madison Ave., New York, NY 10016) Ed. Roger M. Peel. circ. 5,000 (approx.)
    Before 1972: International Baccalaureate Office. Semi-Annual Bulletin.

370   JA
INTERNATIONAL CHRISTIAN UNIVERSITY. INSTITUTE FOR EDUCATIONAL RESEARCH AND SERVICE. EDUCATIONAL STUDIES/ KOKUSAI KIRISUTOKYO DAIGAKU, KYOIKU KENKYU. (Text in English and Japanese) vol.22, 1979. a. $5. International Christian University, Institute for Educational Research and Service, 3-10 Osawa, Mitaka, Tokyo 181, Japan. Ed. Masatake Muraki. circ. 500. (back issues avail.)

370   UN
INTERNATIONAL CONFERENCE ON EDUCATION. FINAL REPORT/CONFERENCE INTERNATIONAL DE L'EDUCATION. RAPPORT FINAL. (Editions in Arabic, Chinese, English, French, Russian, and Spanish) 1934, 3rd (none 1940-45, 1969) a. until 33rd, 1971; thereafter biennial. free. Unesco, International Bureau of Education, Case Postale 199, CH-1211 Geneva 20, Switzerland. (also avail. in microfiche)
    Former titles: International Conference on Education. Proceedings (ISSN 0074-3275); Before no.32, 1970: International Conference on Public Education. Proceedings.

371.9
INTERNATIONAL CONFERENCE ON PIAGETIAN THEORY AND THE HELPING PROFESSIONS. PROCEEDINGS. 8th, 1978. a. price varies. (Childrens Hospital of Los Angeles, University Affiliated Program) University of Southern California Press, c/o Bookstore, Mail Order Dept., University Park, Los Angeles, CA 90007. TEL 213-743-5371.

370   II
INTERNATIONAL JOURNAL OF EDUCATIONAL SCIENCES. (Text in English) 1984. a. Institute for Studies in Psychological Testing, 17 Karanpur, Dehradun 248001, India. Ed. Sr. S.P. Kulshaestha. circ. 1,000. (back issues avail.)

370   US   ISSN 0278-2731
INTERNATIONAL RESEARCH CENTERS DIRECTORY. 1982. irreg., latest 3rd edt. $330. Gale Research Company, Book Tower, Detroit, MI 48226. TEL 313-961-2242. Eds. Kay Gill, Darren Smith.

370   UN
INTERNATIONAL STUDIES IN EDUCATION. (Text in English & French) 1961. irreg., no.37, 1980. price varies. Unesco Institute for Education - Unesco Institut fuer Paedagogik, c/o Head of the Publications Unit, Feldbrunnenstr. 58, D-2000 Hamburg 13, W. Germany (B.R.D.) (Dist. by: Swets & Zeitlinger B.V., Heerweg 347B, Lisse, Netherlands)

370   UN   ISSN 0047-1240
INTERNATIONAL UNDERSTANDING AT SCHOOL. (Editions in English, French, Spanish) 1961. irreg. free. Unesco, Department of Curriculum, Structure and Methods of Education, 7-9 Place de Fontenoy, 75700 Paris, France. (also avail. in microform from UMI; reprint service avail. from UMI) Indexed: C.I.J.E.

371.7 614.8   BE   ISSN 0074-9524
INTERNATIONAL UNION OF SCHOOL AND UNIVERSITY HEALTH AND MEDICINE. CONGRESS REPORTS.* quadrennial, 1975, 7th, Mexico City. International Union of School and University Health and Medicine, c/o Dr. Guy Roggen, Pres., Serv. Medical de l'ULB, Ave. Paul Heger 28, B-1050 Brussels, Belgium.

920 370   UK
INTERNATIONAL WHO'S WHO IN EDUCATION. 1974. irreg. price varies. Melrose Press Ltd., 3 Regal Lane, Soham, Ely, Cambridgeshire CB7 5BA, England.

379   US   ISSN 0091-8962
IOWA. DEPARTMENT OF PUBLIC INSTRUCTION. SUMMARY OF FEDERAL PROGRAMS. 1971. a. free. Department of Public Instruction, Grimes State Office Bldg, Des Moines, IA 50319. TEL 515-281-3191. Ed. Earl Linden. circ. 600.

370   IE
IRISH COUNTRYWOMEN'S ASSOCIATION: AN GRIANAN PROGRAMME. 1954. a. 70p. per issue. Irish Countrywomen's Association, An Grianan, Termonfechine, Co. Louth, Ireland. circ. 5,000.

370   IS
ISRAEL. CENTRAL BUREAU OF STATISTICS. STUDENTS IN UNIVERSITIES. (Subseries of its Special Series) 1964/65. irreg. price varies. Central Bureau of Statistics, Box 13015, Jerusalem, Israel.
    Formerly: Israel. Central Bureau of Statistics. Students in Academic Institutions (ISSN 0075-1081)

370   CN   ISSN 0704-6936
ISSUES, EVENTS & IDEAS. 1976. irreg. (4-5/yr.) included in subscription to 'Early Childhood Education' Alberta Teachers' Association, Early Childhood Education Council, 11010 142nd St., Edmonton, Alta. T5N 2R1, Canada. Ed. Theresa Pond. circ. 2,242. Indexed: Can.Educ.Ind.

370 410   US
ITALICA. 1924. a. $25. American Association of Teachers of Italian, 4 Oakmount Rd., Welland, Ont. L3C 4X8, Canada. TEL 416-732-2149. Ed. Robert J. Rodini. adv. bk. rev. circ. 1,500.
    Formerly: American Association of Teachers of Italian. Directory.

370   US   ISSN 0098-7549
IT'S HAPPENING. 1974. irreg. membership. National Association for Creative Children and Adults, 8080 Springvalley Dr., Cincinnati, OH 45236. TEL 513-631-1777. Ed. Ann F. Isaacs. adv. circ. 2,000. (reprint service avail. from UMI)

370   JA   ISSN 0289-405X
JAPAN COMPARATIVE EDUCATION SOCIETY. BULLETIN. 1975. a. 1500 Yen($10) Japan Comparative Education Society. Bulletin, c/o National Institute for Education Research, 6-5-22, Shimomeguro, Meguro-Ku, Tokyo 153, Japan. circ. 700. (back issues avail.)

370   MY
JOURNAL OF EDUCATIONAL RESEARCH/ JURNAL PENDIDIKAN. (Text mainly in English) 1970. a. National University of Malaysia, Box 1124, Jalan Pantai Baru, Kuala Lumpur 22-12, Malaysia.

370   US   ISSN 0022-3336
JOURNAL OF OUTDOOR EDUCATION. 1966. 1/yr. free. Northern Illinois University, Department of Outdoor Teacher Education, Taft Field Campus, Box 299, Oregon, IL 61061. TEL 815-732-2111. Ed. Robert L. Vogl. bk. rev. circ. 2,500(controlled) (also avail. in microform from UMI; reprint service avail. from UMI) Indexed: Educ.Ind. C.I.J.E.

370   DK   ISSN 0107-8887
JULEHILSEN. 1962. a. Elevforeningen for Hoven Ungdomsskole, 6880 Tarm, Denmark. illus.

370   LB
JULIUS C. STEVENS ANNUAL LECTURES IN EDUCATION. irreg. University of Liberia, William V.S. Tubman Teachers College, Monrovia, Liberia.

150 300 370   FI   ISSN 0075-4625
JYVASKYLA STUDIES IN EDUCATION, PSYCHOLOGY AND SOCIAL RESEARCH. (Text in English or Finnish; summaries in English) 1962. irreg. price varies. Jyvaskylan Yliopisto - University of Jyvaskyla, Seminaarinkatu 15, 40100 Jyvaskyla 10, Finland. Ed. Mikko Korkiakangas. circ. 450. Indexed: Psychol.Abstr.

370   JA
KANAZAWA UNIVERSITY. FACULTY OF EDUCATION. BULLETIN: HUMANITIES, SOCIAL AND EDUCATIONAL SCIENCES. (Text in Japanese; summaries and some articles in English) irreg. Kanazawa University, Faculty of Education - Kanazawa Daigaku Kyoikugabuku, 1-1 Marunouchi, Kanazawa 920, Japan.

EDUCATION

374.8   SZ   ISSN 0254-1270
KARGER CONTINUING EDUCATION SERIES. (Text in English) 1982. irreg. S. Karger AG, Allschwilerstr. 10, P.O. Box, CH-4009 Basel, Switzerland.

KATALOG FOR SKOLEBIBLIOTEKER. EMNEKATALOG. see *BIBLIOGRAPHIES*

KATALOG FOR SKOLEBIBLIOTEKER. TITELKATALOG. see *BIBLIOGRAPHIES*

370   KE   ISSN 0075-5869
KENYA. MINISTRY OF EDUCATION. ANNUAL REPORT. a, latest 1977. EAs.12. Government Printing and Stationery Department, Box 30128, Nairobi, Kenya.

370   KE
KENYA INSTITUTE OF EDUCATION. ANNUAL REPORT. (Text in English) a. Kenya Institute of Education, Box 30231, Nairobi, Kenya. Ed. W. Muya. circ. 200.

KETTERING REPORT. see *POLITICAL SCIENCE*

KOBLENZER GEOGRAPHISCHES KOLLOQUIUM. see *GEOGRAPHY*

370   DK   ISSN 0109-7679
LANDSCENTRALEN FOR UNDERVISNINGSMIDLER. TEKNISK INFORMATION. 1984. irreg. free. Landscentralen for Undervisningsmidler, Teknisk Afdelning - National Institute of Educational Media, Oernevej 30, 2400 Copenhagen N, Denmark. Ed. K.E. Hauberg-Tychsen. bk. rev. illus. circ. 1,300.

LEHRBUECHER UND MONOGRAPHIEN ZUR DIDAKTIK DER MATHEMATIK. see *MATHEMATICS*

370   GW
LEHRERINNEN- UND LEHRERKALENDER. 1977. a. DM.12. Anabas-Verlag Guenter Kaempf KG, Unterer Hardthof 25, D-6300 Giessen, W. Germany (B.R.D.) adv. bk. rev. circ. 20,000.

370   IT   ISSN 0075-8760
LEONARDO; almanacco di educazione popolare. 1952. a. L.1000. Ente Nazionale per le Biblioteche Popolari e Scholastiche, Via Michele Mercati, 4, 00197 Rome, Italy. Indexed: Curr.Cont. Arts & Hum.Cit.Ind. Artbibl. RILA.

370   LO
LESOTHO. MINISTRY OF EDUCATION, SPORTS AND CULTURE. ANNUAL REPORT OF THE PERMANENT SECRETARY. 1966. a. Ministry of Education, Sports and Culture, Box 47, Maseru, Lesotho.
Formerly: Lesotho. Ministry of Education and Culture. Annual Report of the Permanent Secretary.

370   SP   ISSN 0075-9201
LIBROS Y MATERIAL DE ENSENANZA. 1958. a. free. Instituto Nacional del Libro Espanol, Comision Asesora de Editores de Libros de Ensenanza, Santiago Rusinol, 8, Madrid-3, Spain. Ed. Ramon Grimaldo Huete. adv. bk. rev. circ. 10,000.

370   UN
LIFELONG EDUCATION NETWORK. 1980. irreg. DM.6. Unesco Institute for Education, Feldbrunnenstr. 58, D 2000 Hamburg 13, W. Germany (B.R.D.) (Dist. in U.S.A. by: Bernan Associates-Unipub, 4611-F Assembly Dr., Lanham, MD 20706-4391)

374.012   CN   ISSN 0700-5369
LITERACY/ALPHABETISATION. (Text in English and French) vol.2, 1976. irreg., approx. 3/yr. Can.$20. Movement for Canadian Literacy, P.O. Box 6366, Sta. A, St. John, New Brunswick E2L 4R8, Canada. Ed. Joan Mansfield. bk. rev. circ. 500. (back issues avail.)

370   US
LOUISIANA PHILOSOPHY OF EDUCATION JOURNAL. vol.5, 1979. a. $14. Louisiana Philosophy of Education Society, c/o Joe L. Green, Chairman, Department of Education, Louisiana State University in Shreveport, 8515 Youree Dr., Shreveport, LA 71115. TEL 318-797-5032. Ed. Richard J. Elliott.

MACQUARIE UNIVERSITY FRENCH MONOGRAPHS. see *LINGUISTICS*

370   NZ   ISSN 0076-4280
MAORI EDUCATION FOUNDATION. ANNUAL REPORT. 1962. a. free. Maori Education Foundation, Box 3745, Wellington, New Zealand.

370   MY   ISSN 0126-5024
MASALAH PENDIDIKAN; bulletin on current issues in education. (Text in English and Malay) 1965. a. M.$12. University of Malaya, Faculty of Education - Universiti Malaya. Fakulti Pendidikan, Lembah Pantai, 59100 Kuala Lumpur, Malaysia. Ed. Rahimah Bte. Hj. Ahmad. circ. 300.

370 016   US   ISSN 0076-5112
MASTER'S THESES IN EDUCATION. 1951. a. $30. Research Publications, Box 92, Cedar Falls, IA 50613. TEL 319-273-6412. Ed. H.M. Silvey.

370   GW   ISSN 0173-3842
MATERIALIEN AUS DER BILDUNGSFORSCHUNG. 1972. irreg., vol.28, 1986. price varies. Max-Planck-Institut fuer Bildungsforschung - Max-Planck-Institute for Human Development and Education, Lentzeallee 94, 1000 Berlin 33, W. Germany (B.R.D.)

370 510 301   NE
MATHEMATICS EDUCATION LIBRARY. 1983. irreg., latest vols.3-4, 1986. price varies. D. Reidel Publishing Company, Box 17, 3300 AA Dordrecht, Netherlands (And 190 Derby St., Hingham, MA 02043) Ed. A. Bishop. bibl. illus. (back issues avail.)

370   MF
MAURITIUS INSTITUTE OF EDUCATION. ANNUAL REPORT. a. Mauritius Institute of Education, Reduit, Mauritius.

370   MF
MAURITIUS INSTITUTE OF EDUCATION. JOURNAL. (Text in English) 1977. a. Mauritius Institute of Education, Reduit, Mauritius.

370   GW   ISSN 0076-5627
MAX-PLANCK-INSTITUT FUER BILDUNGSFORSCHUNG, BERLIN. STUDIEN UND BERICHTE. (Text usually in German; summaries in English) 1965. irreg., vol.42, 1982. price varies. Max-Planck-Institut fuer Bildungsforschung - Max-Planck-Institute for Human Development and Education, Lentzeallee 94, 1000 Berlin 33, W. Germany (B.R.D.) (And: Klett-Cotta, D-7000 Stuttgart 1, W. Germany (B.R.D.))

370   AT   ISSN 0076-6275
MELBOURNE STUDIES IN EDUCATION. 1957. a. Aus.$29. (University of Melbourne, School of Education) Melbourne University Press, Box 278, Carlton South, Vic. 3053, Australia (Dist. by: International Specialized Book Services, Inc., P.O. Box 1632, Beaverton, OR 97075-3640) Ed. Imelda Palmer. circ. 2,000. Indexed: Aus.P.A.I.S.

370   GO
MESSAGE; bulletin de liaison des enseignants gabonais. irreg. 600 Fr.CFA. Direction de l'Enseignement du Premier Degre, B.P. 221, Libreville, Gabon.
Formerly: Tam-Tam.

370   MX
MEXICO. SECRETARIA DE EDUCACION PUBLICA. INFORME DE LABORES. irreg. Secretaria de Educacion Publica, Mexico D.F., Mexico.

370   US
MICHIGAN STATE UNIVERSITY. INTERNATIONAL NETWORKS IN EDUCATION AND DEVELOPMENT. PUBLICATIONS. 1962. irreg. Michigan State University, International Networks in Education and Development (INET), College of Education, 237 Erickson Hall, E. Lansing, MI 48824-1034. TEL 517-335-5522.
Formerly: Michigan State University. Institute for International Studies in Education. Publications.

370   UK
MIDDLE EAST EDUCATION & TRAINING BUYERS GUIDE. (Editions in Arabic, English) 1982. a. $60. International Business Publications Ltd., Queensway House, 2 Queensway, Redhill, Surrey RH1 1QS, England. Ed. Geoff Napier. adv.

370   PK
MIDDLE SCHOOLS STATISTICS IN PUNJAB. 1973/74. irreg. Bureau of Education, Lahore, Punjab, Pakistan.

370   US   ISSN 0092-2986
MIDWEST HISTORY OF EDUCATION SOCIETY. JOURNAL. 1972. a. $4. University of Northern Iowa, College of Education, Education Center 513, Cedar Falls, IA 50613. TEL 319-273-2609. Ed. Edward Rutkowski. circ. 100. Key Title: Journal of the Midwest History of Education Society.

370   IS
MISIFRUT HA-HINUKH: EDUCATIONAL ISSUES; translations from the educational literature. 1969. irreg. (approx. 3/yr.) Hebrew University of Jerusalem, School of Education, Jerusalem, Israel. circ. 1,500.

373 157.61   US   ISSN 0190-9185
MONITORING THE FUTURE; questionnaire responses from the nation's high school seniors. 1975. a. $40. Institute for Social Research, University of Michigan, Box 1248, Ann Arbor, MI 48106. TEL 313-764-8271.
Secondary

370   UN   ISSN 0077-1007
MONOGRAPHS ON EDUCATION. (Text in English, French and Spanish) 1962. irreg., vol.10, 1979. price varies. Unesco, 7-9 Place de Fontenoy, 75700 Paris, France (Dist. in U.S. by: Bernan Associates-Unipub, 4611-F Assembly Dr., Lanham, MD 20706-4391)

370   GE   ISSN 0077-1481
MONUMENTA PAEDAGOGICA. 1946. irreg. price varies. (Akademie der Wissenschaften der DDR) Verlag Volk und Wissen, Berlin, E. Germany (D.D.R.)

370   CN   ISSN 0829-9137
MULTICULTURAL EDUCATION; council newsletter. 1973. irreg. (3-4/yr.) Alberta Teachers' Association, Multicultural Education Council, 11010 142nd St., Edmonton, Alta. T5N 2R1, Canada. Ed. Dean Wood. bk. rev. circ. 420.
Formerly: Intercultural Education Council. Newsletter (ISSN 0708-9619)

370   PH   ISSN 0115-8473
N F E/W I D EXCHANGE - ASIA. OCCASIONAL PAPER. (Text in English) 1981. irreg. exchange basis. University of the Philippines at Los Banos, College of Agriculture, Department of Agricultural Education, Laguna 3720, Philippines. Ed. Dr. Priscilla A. Juliano. circ. 800. (back issues avail.)

370 371.3   UK   ISSN 0262-8163
N I C E R BULLETIN. 1969. a. free. Northern Ireland Council for Educational Research, Queen's University of Belfast, 52 Malone Road, Belfast BT9 5BS, N. Ireland. Ed. Dr. J.A. Wilson. bk. rev. stat. circ. 4,000. (back issues avail.)

370   US
N S C T E MONOGRAPHS. (National Society of College Teachers of Education) a. price varies. Society of Professors of Education, c/o Martha Tevis, School of Education, Pan American University, Edinburg, TX 78539.

370   CN   ISSN 0027-7037
N T A JOURNAL. vol.69, 1980. irreg. $7.50 (Includes NTA Bulletin) Newfoundland Teachers Association, 3 Kenmount Rd., St. John's, Nfld. A1B 1W1, Canada. TEL 709-726-3223. Ed. Myrle I. Vokey. adv. bk. rev. charts. illus. circ. 8,500. Indexed: Can.Ind.

370   NZ   ISSN 0111-2821
N Z C E R NEWSLETTER. 1965. irreg. free. New Zealand Council for Educational Research, Box 3237, Wellington, New Zealand. Ed.Bd. bibl. illus. circ. 5,000. (also avail. in microfilm from UMI)

370   NZ   ISSN 0111-395X
NAT ED NEWSLETTER. 1974. every 2 to 3 weeks during school term. NZ.$11. New Zealand Educational Institute, Box 466, Wellington 1, New Zealand. Ed. Cathy Jackson. circ. 9,200.

EDUCATION 417

371 US ISSN 0550-7421
NATIONAL ASSOCIATION OF INDEPENDENT SCHOOLS. ANNUAL REPORT. 1963. a. National Association of Independent Schools, 18 Tremont St., Boston, MA 02108. TEL 617-723-6900. stat. (reprint service avail. from UMI) Key Title: Annual Report - National Association of Independent Schools.

NATIONAL COUNCIL OF TEACHERS OF MATHEMATICS. PROFESSIONAL REFERENCE SERIES. see *MATHEMATICS*

NATIONAL COUNCIL OF TEACHERS OF MATHEMATICS. YEARBOOK. see *MATHEMATICS*

370 US
NATIONAL EDUCATION ASSOCIATION OF THE UNITED STATES. PROCEEDINGS OF THE REPRESENTATIVE ASSEMBLY. 1860. a. $8. ‡ National Education Association of the United States, 1201 16th St., N.W., Washington, DC 20036 TEL 203-934-2669. (Order from: N E A Professional Library, Box 509, West Haven CT 06516) index.
  Former titles: National Education Association of the United States. Proceedings of the Annual Meeting (ISSN 0190-7662); National Education Association of the United States. Addresses and Proceedings (ISSN 0077-4243)

370 JA ISSN 0085-378X
NATIONAL INSTITUTE FOR EDUCATIONAL RESEARCH. RESEARCH BULLETIN. (Text in English) 1959. irreg. free. National Institute for Educational Research, Planning Section, 6-5-22 Shimomeguro, Meguro-ku, Tokyo 153, Japan. Ed. Bd. charts. illus. stat. circ. controlled. (tabloid format) Indexed: Psychol.Abstr.

370 US ISSN 0077-5762
NATIONAL SOCIETY FOR THE STUDY OF EDUCATION. YEARBOOK. 1902. a. in 2 pts. price varies. National Society for the Study of Education, University of Chicago, Judd Hall, Chicago, IL 60637 TEL 312-702-1582. (Dist. by: Univ. of Chicago Press, 5835 Kimbark Ave., Chicago, IL 60637) Ed. Kenneth J. Rehage. circ. 2,700. Indexed: Educ.Ind.

370 CH
NATIONAL TAIWAN NORMAL UNIVERSITY. GRADUATE INSTITUTE OF EDUCATION. BULLETIN. (Text in Chinese and English) vol.17, 1975. a. $9. National Taiwan Normal University, Graduate Institute of Education, East Ho-Ping Road, Taipei, Taiwan, Republic of China.

372 NE ISSN 0168-4809
NEDERLANDSE JEUGD EN HAAR ONDERWIJS/NETHERLANDS YOUTH AND ITS EDUCATION. (Text in Dutch and English) 1947. a. fl.20.75. Centraal Bureau voor de Statistiek, Prinses Beatrixlaan 428, Voorburg, Netherlands (Orders to: Staatsuitgeverij, Christoffel Plantijnstraat, The Hague, Netherlands)

370 US ISSN 0548-1384
NEED A LIFT? 1951. a. $1 per no. ‡ American Legion, Need a Lift, Box 1050, Indianapolis, IN 46206. TEL 317-635-8411. Ed. Lee A. Hardy. adv. circ. 120,000.

NEPAL. DEPARTMENT OF AGRICULTURAL EDUCATION AND RESEARCH. ANNUAL REPORT. see *AGRICULTURE*

370 NE ISSN 0168-5708
NETHERLANDS. CENTRAAL BUREAU VOOR DE STATISTIEK. STATISTIEK VAN HET BEROEPSONDERWIJS: BEROEPSBEGELEIDEND ONDERWIJS LEERLINGWEZEN. a. fl.8.40. Centraal Bureau voor de Statistiek, Prinses Beatrixlaan 428, Voorburg, Netherlands (Orders to: Staatsuitgeverij, Christoffel Plantijnstraat, The Hague, Netherlands) stat.

370 NE ISSN 0168-5600
NETHERLANDS. CENTRAAL BUREAU VOOR DE STATISTIEK. STATISTIEK VAN HET BEROEPSONDERWIJS: SOCIAAL-PEDAGOGISCH ONDERWIJS. (Text in Dutch and English) 1968/69. a. fl.12.10. Centraal Bureau voor de Statistiek, Prinses Beatrixlaan 428, Voorburg, Netherlands (Orders to: Staatsuitgeverij, Christoffel Plantijnstraat, The Hague, Netherlands)
  Formerly: Netherlands. Centraal Bureau voor de Statistiek. Statistiek van het Sociaal-Pedagogisch Onderwijs. Statistics on Socio-Pedagogic Training (ISSN 0077-7374)

370 NE
NETHERLANDS. MINISTERIE VAN ONDERWIJS EN WETENSCHAPPEN. ONDERWIJSVERSLAG. 1973. a. price varies. Staatsuitgeverij, Chr. Plantijnstraat, The Hague, Netherlands. (Prepared by: Ministerie van Onderwijs en Wetenschappen) circ. 1,000.

NEUE WEGE; Kulturzeitschrift junger Menschen. see *CHILDREN AND YOUTH — For*

NEW HAMPSHIRE QUARTER NOTES. see *MUSIC*

371.2 US ISSN 0362-5958
NEW JERSEY. DEPARTMENT OF EDUCATION. EDUCATIONAL ASSESSMENT PROGRAM STATE REPORT. 1972. a. Department of Education, Division of Operations Research and Evaluation, 225 W. State St., Trenton, NJ 08625. TEL 609-292-4040. Ed. Carl Johnson. Key Title: Educational Assessment Program State Report.

NEW JERSEY JOURNAL OF SCHOOL PSYCHOLOGY. see *PSYCHOLOGY*

370 US
NEW SCHOOLS EXCHANGE. DIRECTORY AND RESOURCE GUIDE. 1969. a. $5. New Schools Exchange, Pettigrew, AR 72752. Ed. Grace Dailey-Harwood. adv. bk. rev. bibl. film rev. cum.index. circ. 3,000. (back issues avail.)

370 PK ISSN 0077-8826
NEW TEACHER. (Text in English, Urdu and Pashto) 1952. a. Rs.8. University of Peshawar, College of Education, Peshawar, Pakistan. Ed.Bd.

370 379 NZ ISSN 0077-958X
NEW ZEALAND. CENTRAL ADVISORY COMMITTEE ON THE APPOINTMENTS AND PROMOTION OF PRIMARY TEACHERS. REPORT TO THE MINISTER OF EDUCATION. 1961. quinquennial. free. ‡ (Central Advisory Committee) Government Printing Office, c/o Department of Education, Private Bag, Government Buildings, Wellington, New Zealand. circ. controlled.

NIHON KYOIKUHO GAKKAI NEMPO. see *LAW*

370 US ISSN 0077-9253
NONPUBLIC SCHOOL ENROLLMENT AND STAFF, NEW YORK STATE. 1966. a. free. ‡ Education Department, Information Center on Education, Albany, NY 12234. charts. stat. circ. controlled. (back issues avail.)
  Formerly: Survey of Nonpublic Schools in New York State.

NORTHWEST ASSOCIATION OF SCHOOLS AND COLLEGES. PROCEEDINGS. see *EDUCATION — Higher Education*

370 GW
NUMERUS CLAUSUS - FINESSEN. 1973. a. DM.18. Verein Freunde und Foerderer der Deutschen Studentenschaft e.V., Untere Hausbreite 11, 8000 Munich 45, W. Germany (B.R.D.) Ed. Gundolf Seidenspinner. adv.
  Former titles: Numerus Clausus - Alternativen; Numerus Clausus - Ersatzstudiengaenge.

370 DK ISSN 0900-162X
OM FORSOEGSARBEJDET. 1984. a. Statens Paedagogiske Forsoegscenter, Islevgaard Alle 5, 2610 Roedovre, Denmark.

370 CN ISSN 0317-6436
ONTARIO. MINISTRY OF EDUCATION. REPORT. a. Ministry of Education, Toronto, Ont. M7A 1L2, Canada. TEL 416-965-2054.

370.25 CN ISSN 0316-8549
ONTARIO DIRECTORY OF EDUCATION. a. Can.$6 per no. Ministry of Education, Toronto, Ont. M7A 1L2, Canada TEL 416-965-2054. (Orders to: Publications Services, Ministry of Government Services, 880 Bay St., Toronto, Ont. M7A 1N8, Canada)

370 AT
OPEN BOOK. 1972. irreg. Aus.$5. 21 Smith St., Thornbury, Vic. 3071, Australia. Ed.Bd.

370 DK ISSN 0109-1255
OPGAVESAET TIL DANSK SKRIFTLIG FREMSTILLING, FOLKESKOLENS AFGANGSPROEVE; dagproeve aftenproeve, ekstraordinaere proevetermin. 1983. a. Kr.10. Dansklaererforeningen-Folkeskolefraktionen, Noerre Soegade 49C, 1370 Copenhagen K, Denmark. circ. 20,000.
  Formerly: Opgavesaet til Dansk Skr. Fremstilling, Folkeskolens Udvidede Afgangsproeve (ISSN 0109-1247)

370 DK ISSN 0106-7125
ORIENTING OM SKOLEAARET. (Subseries of: Denmark. Folkeskolens Forsoegsraad. Publikation) 1978. a. free. Folkeskolens Forsoegsraad, c/o Undervisningsministeriets Tekstbehandlingsenhed, Frederiksholms Kanal 25 F, 1220 Copenhagen K, Denmark.

372 AU
P A - KONTAKTE. (Text in German) 1972. irreg. free. International Institute for Children's Literature and Reading Research, Mayerhofgasse 6, A-1040 Vienna, Austria. Ed. Lucia Binder. bk. rev. bibl.

370 BE ISSN 0079-0370
PAEDAGOGICA BELGICA ACADEMICA; periodical survey of the Belgian University Studies in Education. (Text in Dutch, English, and French; summaries in Dutch or French) 1951. a. 350 Fr. Rijksuniversiteit te Gent, Seminaries voor Historische en voor Vergelijkende Pedagogiek, A. Baertsoenkaai 3, B-9000 Ghent, Belgium. Ed. H. Van daele. circ. 400.

370 US
PAIDEIA. 1972. a. $5. State University of New York at Buffalo, Department of Foundational Studies, 1300 Elmwood Ave., Buffalo, NY 14222. TEL 716-831-2000. Ed. Albert Grande. adv. bk. rev. (back issues avail.) Indexed: M.L.A.

370 PL ISSN 0137-3943
PAIDEIA; miedzynarodowy rocznik pedagogiczny. (Text in English, French and German) a. price varies. (Polska Akademia Nauk, Komitet Nauk Pedagogicznych) Ossolineum, Publishing House of the Polish Academy of Sciences, Rynek 9, Wroclaw, Poland (Dist. by: Ars Polona-Ruch, Krakowskie Przedmiescie 7, Warsaw, Poland) Ed. B. Suchodolski.

370 PK ISSN 0078-7914
PAKISTAN. CENTRAL BUREAU OF EDUCATION. EDUCATIONAL STATISTICS BULLETIN SERIES. (Text in English) 1966. irreg. Central Bureau of Education, Sector H-9, Cultural Area, Islamabad, Pakistan.

370 PK ISSN 0078-8287
PAKISTAN. MINISTRY OF EDUCATION. YEARBOOK. (Text in English) a. Ministry of Education, Documentation Section, Curriculum Wing, Sector H-9, P.O. Shaigan, Industrial Area, Islamabad, Pakistan.
  Formerly: Pakistan. Central Bureau of Education. Yearbook (ISSN 0078-7922)

372.21 US
PARENT COOPERATIVE PRESCHOOLS INTERNATIONAL. DIRECTORY. 1969. a. membership. Parent Cooperative Preschools International, Box 90410, Indianapolis, IN 46290-0410. Ed. Sita Likuski. adv. bk. rev. circ. 6,500.

370 PL ISSN 0208-5526
PEDAGOGIKA PRACY KULTURALNO-OSWIATOWEJ. (Text in Polish; summaries in English and Russian) 1976. irreg. price varies. Uniwersytet Slaski w Katowicach, Ul. Bankowa 14, 40-007 Katowice, Poland.

370　　　　　　　SW　ISSN 0281-6776
PEDAGOGISKA RAPPORTER/EDUCATIONAL
REPORTS. (Text in English or Swedish) 1969 N.S.
1984. irreg. free. Umeaa Universitet, Pedagogiska
Institutionen, S-901 87 Umeaa, Sweden. Ed. Jarl
Backman. circ. 200.
　　Formerly: Pedagogiska Rapporter Umeaa (ISSN
0348-9388)

370　　　　　　　US　ISSN 0079-0451
PENN STATE STUDIES. irreg. price varies.
Pennsylvania State University Press, 215 Wagner
Bldg., University Park, PA 16802. TEL 814-865-
1327. (reprint service avail. from UMI)

370　　　　　　　US　ISSN 0085-4824
PENNSYLVANIA. OFFICE OF THE BUDGET.
PROGRAM BUDGET. Cover title: Commonwealth
of Pennsylvania. Executive Budget. (In 2 volumes)
1927. a. free. Office of the Budget, Main Capitol
Bldg., Harrisburg, PA 17120. TEL 717-787-8767.
circ. 1,400.

370　　　　　　　US　ISSN 0079-0508
PENNSYLVANIA SCHOOL STUDY COUNCIL.
REPORTS. 1947. irreg. (20-25/yr.) price varies
(free to members) Pennsylvania School Study
Council, 246 Chambers Bldg., Pennsylvania State
University, University Park, PA 16802. TEL 814-
865-0321. Ed. Paul V. Bredeson. bk. rev. circ. 250.

370　　　　　　　PE
PERU. MINISTERIO DE EDUCACION PUBLICA.
OFICINA SECTORIAL DE PLANIFICACION.
PLAN BIENAL. irreg. Ministerio de Educacion
Publica, Oficina Sectorial de Planificacion, Lima,
Peru. illus.

PHILIPPINE NORMAL COLLEGE. LANGUAGE
STUDY CENTER. OCCASIONAL PAPER. see
LINGUISTICS

370　378　　　　　PH
PHILIPPINES. MINISTRY OF EDUCATION &
CULTURE. NATIONAL SCHOLARSHIP
CENTER. DIRECTORY OF ALUMNI. 1978.
irreg. free. Ministry of Education & Culture,
National Scholarship Center, Arroceros St., Manila
2801, Philippines. Ed. Ms. Milagros R. Bersamin.
circ. 800.

370　378　　　　　PH　ISSN 0115-4249
PHILIPPINES. MINISTRY OF EDUCATION,
CULTURE AND SPORTS. NATIONAL
SCHOLARSHIP CENTER. ANNUAL REPORT.
a. Ministry of Education, Culture and Sports,
National Scholarship Center, Arroceros St., Manila
2801, Philippines. charts. illus. circ. 1,000.

370　　　　　　　US　ISSN 0160-7561
PHILOSOPHICAL STUDIES IN EDUCATION;
proceedings of the annual meeting of the Ohio
Valley Philosophy of Education Society. 1968. a.
$2.50 (institutions $5) ‡ Ohio Valley Philosophy of
Education Society, c/o Dennis Senchuk, Ed.,
Indiana University, Department of Philosophy and
History of Education, Bloomington, IN 47401. TEL
813-332-0211. circ. 220. (also avail. in microfilm
from UMI; microfiche from EDR; reprint service
avail. from UMI) Indexed: Phil.Ind.
　　Formerly: Ohio Valley Philosophy of Education
Society. Proceedings of the Annual Meeting (ISSN
0078-4044)

370　　　　　　　US　ISSN 0079-1733
PHILOSOPHY OF EDUCATION SOCIETY.
PROCEEDINGS OF THE ANNUAL
MEETINGS. (Proceedings from 1st-13th meetings
not published) 1958, 14th meeting proceedings. a.
$25. Philosophy of Education Society, c/o Prof.
Thomas Nelson, Ed., Illinois State Univ., Normal,
IL 61761. TEL 309-438-5422. circ. 1,200. Indexed:
SSCI. Phil.Ind. Res.Educ.

PLANBOOK FOR LEADERS OF CHILDREN. see
RELIGIONS AND THEOLOGY — Protestant

372.21　　　　　US　ISSN 0032-1443
PLAY SCHOOLS NEWSLETTER. 1969. a. free
contr.circ. Play Schools Association, 19 W. 44th St.,
New York, NY 10036. TEL 212-921-2940. Ed.
Joseph Corrado. bk. rev. illus. circ. 2,500.

370　　　　　　　PL　ISSN 0079-3418
POLSKA AKADEMIA NAUK. ODDZIAL W
KRAKOWIE. KOMISJA NAUK
PEDAGOGICZNYCH. ROCZNIK. (Text in
Polish; summaries in English, French, German,
Russian) 1961. a. price varies. Ossolineum,
Publishing House of the Polish Academy of
Sciences, Rynek 9, 50-106 Wroclaw, Poland (Dist.
by: Ars Polona-Ruch, Krakowskie Przedmiescie 7,
Warsaw, Poland) Ed. Kamila Arozowska.

370　　　　　　　PL　ISSN 0079-340X
POLSKA AKADEMIA NAUK. ODDZIAL W
KRAKOWIE. KOMISJA NAUK
PEDAGOGICZNYCH. PRACE. (Text in Polish;
summaries in English and Russian) 1958. irreg.,
no.19, 1980. price varies. Ossolineum, Publishing
House of the Polish Academy of Sciences, Rynek 9,
50-106 Wroclaw, Poland (Dist. by: Ars Polona-
Ruch, Krakowskie Przedmiescie 7, Warsaw, Poland)

370　　　　　　　PO
PORTUGAL. INSTITUTO NACIONAL DE
ESTATISTICA. ESTATISTICAS DE
EDUCACAO. CONTINENTE, ACORES E
MADEIRA. (Text in French and Portuguese) 1940.
a. Esc.500. Instituto Nacional de Estatistica, Av.
Antonio Jose de Almeida, 1078 Lisbon Codex,
Portugal (Orders to: Imprensa Nacional, Casa da
Moeda, Direccao Comercial, rua D. Francisco
Manuel de Melo 5, 1000 Lisbon, Portugal)
　　Formerly: Portugal. Instituto Nacional de
Estatistica. Estatisticas de Educacao (ISSN 0079-
4155)

370　　　　　　　RM
PROBLEME DE PEDAGOGIE
CONTEMPORANA. 1970. biennial. 20 lei
(exchange basis to foreign subscribers) Biblioteca
Centrala Pedagogica, Str. Zalomit Nr. 12, Bucharest
70714, Rumania. Ed. Alfred Lauterman. index. circ.
5,000.
　　Supersedes: Buletin de Informare Pedagogica
(ISSN 0007-3792)

379.73　　　　　　US
PROGRESS OF EDUCATION IN THE UNITED
STATES OF AMERICA. (Editions in Arabic,
Chinese, English, French, Japanese, Russian and
Spanish) biennial. price varies; single copies free.
U.S. Department of Education, Washington, DC
20202. TEL 202-655-4000.
　　Formerly: Progress of Public Education in the
United States (ISSN 0079-6891)

370　　　　　　　US
PROJECTIONS OF EDUCATION STATISTICS.
1964. biennial. U.S. National Center for Education
Statistics, 400 Maryland Ave., S.W., Washington,
DC 20202. Ed. Debra E. Gerald. charts. stat.

PROLOGUE (MEDFORD) see *THEATER*

PSYCHOLOGIA A SKOLA. see *PSYCHOLOGY*

378.1　　　　　　US
PUBLIC SCHOOL ENROLLMENT AND STAFF,
NEW YORK STATE. 1961. a. free. ‡ Education
Department, Information Center on Education,
Albany, NY 12234. charts. stat. circ. controlled.
(back issues avail.)
　　Formerly: New York (State) Education
Department. Survey of Enrollment, Staff and School
Housing.

370　　　　　　　US　ISSN 0077-9229
PUBLIC SCHOOL PROFESSIONAL PERSONNEL
REPORT, NEW YORK STATE. 1967. a. free. ‡
Education Department, Information Center on
Education, Albany, NY 12234. charts. illus. circ.
controlled. (back issues avail.)
　　Formerly: New York (State) Education
Department. Public School Professional Personnel
Report (ISSN 0077-9245)

372　　　　　　　AT　ISSN 0310-4079
QUEENSLAND. DEPARTMENT OF
EDUCATION. RESEARCH AND
CURRICULUM BRANCH. CURRICULUM
PAPER. 1973. irreg. free. Department of Education,
Research and Curriculum Branch, Box 33, North
Quay, Qld. 4001, Australia. Ed. J. Fitzgerald. circ.
1,500.

370　　　　　　　AT
QUEENSLAND. DEPARTMENT OF
EDUCATION. RESEARCH BRANCH.
RESEARCH SERIES. 1975. irreg. Department of
Education, Research Branch, Box 33, North Quay,
Qld. 4000, Australia.

507　　　　　　　MY　ISSN 0377-3450
R E C S A M ANNUAL REPORT. (Text in English)
1972. a. free. Southeast Asian Ministers of
Education Organisation, Regional Centre for
Education in Science and Mathematics, Glugor,
Penang, Malaysia. illus. circ. 150.

371　　　　　　　US　ISSN 0085-4093
RACIAL/ETHNIC DISTRIBUTION OF PUBLIC
SCHOOL STUDENTS AND STAFF, NEW
YORK STATE. 1968. a. free. ‡ Education
Department, Information Center on Education,
Albany, NY 12234. charts. stat. circ. controlled.
(back issues avail.)

370　　　　　　　SA
RANDSE AFRIKAANSE UNIVERSITEIT.
JAARBOEK. 1968. a. free. Rand Afrikaans
University, Box 524, Johannesburg 2000, South
Africa. circ. controlled. (processed)

370　　　　　　　SA
RANDSE AFRIKAANSE UNIVERSITEIT. OP EN
OM DIE KAMPUS. 1968. a. free. Rand Afrikaans
University, Box 524, Johannesburg 2000, South
Africa. adv. circ. controlled. (processed)

370　　　　　　　SA
RANDSE AFRIKAANSE UNIVERSITEIT.
PROSPEKTUS. 1968. a. free. Rand Afrikaans
University, Box 524, Johannesburg 2000, South
Africa. circ. controlled. (processed)

REPERTORIO DE SERVICIOS DE
DOCUMENTACION E INFORMACION
EDUCATIVA IBEROAMERICANOS. see
LIBRARY AND INFORMATION SCIENCES

370　　　　　　　UK
REPORTS ON EDUCATION. irreg. (4-6/yr.) free.
H.M.S.O., Box 569, London SE1 9NH, England.
(Co-sponsor: Department of Education and Science)

370　　　　　　　CN　ISSN 0080-1437
REQUIREMENTS FOR TEACHING
CERTIFICATES IN CANADA. 1971. every 5
years. Can.$6. Canadian Education Association, 252
Bloor St. W. Ste. 8-200, Toronto, Ont. M5S 1V5,
Canada. TEL 416-924-7721. Ed. Harriett
Goldsborough. circ. 1,400.

370　　　　　　　CN
RESEARCH AND STUDIES. (Published in sections:
Science, Engineering, Arts, Social Sciences) 1970.
biennial. Carleton University, Faculty of Graduate
Studies and Research, Office of Research
Administration, Ottawa, Ont. K15 5B6. TEL 613-
564-5552. Ed. Anne Burgess.

370　378　　　　　AT　ISSN 0155-6223
RESEARCH DEVELOPMENT IN HIGHER
EDUCATION. PUBLICATIONS. 1979. a.
Aus.$20($22) Higher Education Research and
Development Society of Australasia, c/o T.E.R.C.,
University of New South Wales, Kensington,
N.S.W. 2033, Australia. circ. 400. (back issues
avail.)

370.19　　　　　US　ISSN 0197-5080
RESEARCH IN SOCIOLOGY OF EDUCATION
AND SOCIALIZATION; a research annual. 1980.
a. $23.75 to individuals; institutions $47.50. J A I
Press Inc., Box 1285, 36 Sherwood Pl., Greenwich,
CT 06836. TEL 203-661-7602. Ed. Alan C.
Kerkhoff. Indexed: Lang.& Lang.Behav.Abstr.

370　371.3　　　　CN
RESOURCE BOOK/RESSOURCES. 1958. a.
Maclean Hunter Ltd., Business Publication Division,
777 Bay St., Toronto, Ont. M5W 1A7, Canada.
TEL 416-596-5029. Ed. Clive Hobson. circ. 275,
000.

370　　　　　　　US　ISSN 0197-9973
RESOURCES IN EDUCATION ANNUAL
CUMULATION. 1979. a. $237. Oryx Press, 2214
N. Central at Encanto, Phoenix, AZ 85004-1483.
TEL 602-254-6156. Ed.Bd. index. circ. 1,000. (back
issues avail.)

REVIEW OF CHILD DEVELOPMENT
RESEARCH. see *CHILDREN AND YOUTH —
About*

370　　　　　　　　II
REVIEW OF EDUCATION IN INDIA. 1950. a.
Ministry of Education and Social Welfare,
Department of Education, Shastri Bhavan, New
Delhi 110001, India (Avail. from: Assistant
Educational Adviser (Publications), Ministry of
Human Resource Development, Department of
Education Ex. AFO Hutments, Dr.Rajendra Prasad
Road, New Delhi 110001.)

370　　　　　BL　　ISSN 0482-5527
REVISTA DE EDUCACAO E CULTURA.* 1960. a.
Secretaria de Estado de Educacao de Cultura, Rua
Ulhoa Cintra s/n, Recife-Pernambuco, Brazil.

370　　　　　　　　IT
RICERCHE DI SOCIOLOGIA
DELL'EDUCAZIONE E PEDAGOGIA
COMPARATA. 1974. irreg. (Universita degli Studi
di Messina, Istituto di Pedagogia) Peloritana
Editrice, Messina, Italy. Dir. Giuseppe Catalfamo.
Educational sociology & comparative teaching

370　　　　　PL　　ISSN 0137-9585
ROCZNIK PEDAGOGICZNY. irreg., vol.9, 1984.
price varies. (Polska Akademia Nauk, Komitet Nauk
Pedagogicznych) Ossolineum, Publishing House of
the Polish Academy of Sciences, Rynek 9, Wroclaw,
Poland (Dist. by: Ars Polona-Ruch, Krakowskie
Przedmiescie 7, Warsaw, Poland) Ed. H.
Muszynski.

370　　　　　PL　　ISSN 0080-4754
ROZPRAWY Z DZIEJOW OSWIATY. (Text in
Polish; summaries in English or Russian) 1958. a.
price varies. (Polska Akademia Nauk, Instytut
Historii Nauki, Oswiaty i Techniki, Pracownia
Dziejow Oswiaty) Ossolineum, Publishing House of
the Polish Academy of Sciences, Rynek 9, Wroclaw,
Poland (Dist. by: Ars Polona-Ruch, Krakowskie
Przedmiescie 7, Warsaw, Poland) Ed. Jozef Miaso.
bk. rev. circ. 600.
History

370　　　　　UK　　ISSN 0140-4776
RURAL EXTENSION, EDUCATION AND
TRAINING ABSTRACTS. 1978. bi-m. £50($88)
C.A.B. International, Farnham House, Farnham
Royal, Slough SL2 3BN, England (U.S. subscr. to:
C.A.B. International, North American Office, 845
N. Park Ave., Tucson, AR 85719) circ. 400. (also
avail. in microfiche; back issues avail.)
●Also available online. Vendors: BRS, CISTI,
DIMDI, DIALOG, European Space Agency.

RUTGERS PROFESSIONAL PSYCHOLOGY
REVIEW. see *PSYCHOLOGY*

370　　　　　DK　　ISSN 0108-3856
S L F INFORMATION; for laerere ved boernehave,
fritidspaedagog- og socialpaedagogishe seminarier.
1979. irreg. (6-8/yr.) Kr.100 to non-members.
Seminarielaererforeningen, Schleppegrellsgade 10,
2200 Copenhagen N, Denmark.
Formerly: B F L Information.

370　　　　　US　　ISSN 0882-1100
S P E MONOGRAPH SERIES. irreg. Society of
Professors of Education, c/o Martha Tevis, School
of Education, Pan American University, Edinburg,
TX 78539. TEL 512-381-3436.
Formerly: National Society of College Teachers
of Education. Monographs.

370　　　　　DK　　ISSN 0108-7665
SAMTIDSORIENTERING. (Subseries of: Fagkatalog
for Laerere) 1983. biennial. Kr.38.50.
Bibliotekscentralen, Tempovej 7-11, DK-2750
Ballerup, Denmark.

379　　　　　BL
SAO PAULO, BRAZIL (STATE). SECRETARIA DA
EDUCACAO. ATIVIDADES DESENVOLVIDAS.
1973. irreg. Secretaria da Educacao, Sao Paulo,
Brazil.

370　　　　　GW
SCHECKHEFT STADIUM. 1980. a. DM.25. Verein
Freunde und Foerderer der Deutschen
Studentenschaft, Untere Hausbreite 11, 8000
Munich 45, W. Germany (B.R.D.) Ed. Gundolf
Seidenspinner. adv. bk. rev. circ. 100.

370　　　　　UK　　ISSN 0306-1736
SCHOLARSHIPS GUIDE FOR
COMMONWEALTH POSTGRADUATE
STUDENTS. 1972. biennial. £14.90. Association of
Commonwealth Universities, John Foster House, 36
Gordon Square, London WC1H OPF, England.

370　　　　　CN　　ISSN 0382-7879
SCHOOL CALENDAR/CALENDRIER SCOLAIRE;
opening and closing dates, number of working days
and prescribed holidays in Canada. (Text in English
and French) 1969. a. Can.$4. Canadian Education
Association - Association Canadienne d'Education,
252 Bloor St. W., Ste. 8-200, Toronto, Ont. M5S
1V5, Canada. TEL 416-924-7771. Ed. H.
Goldsborough. circ. 600. Indexed: Can.Educ.Ind.

370　500　　　　ZA
SCIENCE EDUCATION IN ZAMBIA. vol.8, 1977.
a. membership. ‡ Zambia Association of Science
Education, Box R.W. 335, Lusaka, Zambia. (Co-
sponsor: Zambia Agriculture Education Association)
Ed. W.M. Gleeson. adv. bk. rev. illus. circ. 700.
Formerly: Z.A.S.E. Bulletin.

370　　　　　　　　II
SELECTIONS FROM EDUCATIONAL RECORDS
OF THE GOVERNMENT OF INDIA. (Text in
English) 1976. irreg. Jawaharlal Nehru University,
Zakir Husain Centre for Educational Studies, New
Delhi 110 067, India. Ed. Joseph Bara. bibl. circ.
100.

370　　　　　　　　AG
SERIE LEGISLACION EDUCATIVA
ARGENTINA. no.23, 1980. irreg. (Ministerio de
Educacion y Justicia) Centro Nacional de
Documentacion e Informacion Educativa, Paraguay
1657-ler. piso, 1062-Capital Federal, Argentina.

370　　　　　　　　US
SERIE MONOGRAFIAS Y ESTUDIOS DE LA
EDUCACION. (Published by host country) (Text
in Spanish) 1974. irreg. Organization of American
States, 1889 F St. N.W., Washington, DC 20006-
4499. TEL 703-789-3319. circ. 2,000. (back issues
avail.)

370　　　　　SL　　ISSN 0080-9551
SIERRA LEONE. MINISTRY OF EDUCATION.
REPORT. 1961/62. a. Ministry of Education,
Freetown, Sierra Leone. circ. 1,200.

370　　　　　PK　　ISSN 0560-0871
SIND UNIVERSITY JOURNAL OF EDUCATION.
(Text in English) vol.16, 1971. a. Rs.5($1.50)
(University of Sind, Institute of Education &
Research) Sind University Press, Jamshoro,
Hyderabad 6, Pakistan. Ed. N.A. Baloch. bk. rev.
bibl. circ. 1,000.

SISTEMA DE INDICADORES SOCIO-
ECONOMICOS Y EDUCATIVOS DE LA O E I.
(Organizacion de Estados Iberoamericanos (OEI))
see *SOCIAL SCIENCES: COMPREHENSIVE
WORKS*

SKOLE & LANDBRUG. see *AGRICULTURE*

370　　　　　DK　　ISSN 0900-2006
SKOLE OG EDB. 1985. a. Kr.135. Munksgaard,
Noerre Soegade 35, 1370 Copenhagen K, Denmark.
illus.

SKOLEMUSIKHAANDBOGEN. see *MUSIC*

370　　　　　NO　　ISSN 0080-9950
SKOLENS AARBOK. 1965. a. Kr.155. Forlaget
Tanum-Norli A-S, Kr. Augustsgt. 7 A, Oslo 1,
Norway. Ed. Einar Ness. circ. 2,700.

370　　　　　DK　　ISSN 0107-3028
SKOLESTART. 1978. a. Kr.24. Ole Camaae,
Lerbjergstien 18, 3460 Birkenroed, Denmark. TEL
02 27 62 82. illus.

370　　　　　　　　CH
SOCIAL EDUCATION YEARLY.* (Text in Chinese)
a. Social Education Society of China, c/o Social
Education Dept, Ministry of Education, Chungshan
S. Rd., Taipei, Taiwan, Republic of China. Ed.
Shing Chou Wang. abstr. charts. stat. index.
cum.index. (processed)

370　　　　　SP　　ISSN 0213-3636
SOCIEDAD DE ESTUDIOS VASCOS.
CUADERNOS DE SECCION. EDUCACION.
1985. irreg. (Sociedad de Estudios Vascos) Eusko
Ikaskuntza, S.A., Churruca, 7 - 2, 20004 Donostia,
Spain.

370　　　　　US　　ISSN 0081-0916
SOCIETE DES PROFESSEURS FRANCAIS EN
AMERIQUE. BULLETIN ANNUEL. 1930. a.
membership. Societe des Professeurs Francais et
Francophones en Amerique, 22 E. 60th St., New
York, NY 10022. TEL 212-355-6100. Ed. Jean
Collignon. bk. rev. circ. 1,000. Indexed: M.L.A.

370　741　　　UK　　ISSN 0037-9743
SOCIETY FOR ITALIC HANDWRITING.
JOURNAL. 1952. a. £8($12) Society for Italic
Handwriting, c/o Eric Vickers, 4/75 Torrington
Park, London N12 9PN, England. Ed. Dr. A.S.
Osley. adv. bk. rev. charts. illus. circ. 1,400.
Indexed: RILA.

370　　　　　US　　ISSN 0882-7141
SOCIETY OF PROFESSORS OF EDUCATION.
OCCASIONAL PAPERS. 1974. irreg. price varies.
Society of Professors of Education, c/o Martha
Tevis, School of Education, Pan American
University, Edinburg, TX 78539. circ. controlled.
Formerly: National Society of College Teachers
of Education. Occasional Papers.

370　　　　　　　　SA
SOUTH AFRICA. DEPARTMENT OF
EDUCATION AND TRAINING. ANNUAL
REPORT. 1963. a. price varies. Department of
Education and Training, Private Bag X212, Pretoria
0001, South Africa (Orders to: Government Printer,
Bosman St., Private Bag X85, Pretoria 0001, South
Africa)
Formerly: South Africa. Department of Bantu
Education. Annual Report (ISSN 0081-2188)

370　　　　　　　　SA
SOUTH AFRICA. DEPARTMENT OF NATIONAL
EDUCATION. JAARVERSLAG/ANNUAL
REPORT. (Text in Afrikaans and English) a.
Government Printer, Bosman St., Private Bag X85,
Pretoria 0001, South Africa. illus. stat.

370　　　　　US　　ISSN 0081-3060
SOUTHERN REGIONAL EDUCATION BOARD.
ANNUAL REPORT. a. free. Southern Regional
Education Board, 1340 Spring St., N.W., Atlanta,
GA 30309. TEL 404-875-9211. Ed. Margaret
Sullivan. circ. 2,200.

370　500　　　　SP
SPAIN. MINISTERO DE EDUCACION. GUIA.
irreg. Ministerio de Educacion, Servicio de
Publicaciones, Madrid, Spain.
Formerly: Spain. Ministerio de Educacion y
Ciencia. Guia.

370　　　　　　　　BF
SPOTLIGHT. 1976. irreg. $1 per no. Ministry of
Education and Culture, Box N 7147, Nassau,
Bahamas.

379.544　　　　　　II
STATE INSTITUTE OF EDUCATION,
RAJASTHAN. ANNUAL REPORT. (Text in
English) a. State Institute of Education, Udaipur,
Rajasthan, India.

STATISTICAL REPORTS OF CHANGWAT. see
GEOGRAPHY

371　　　　　　　　SO
STATISTICS OF EDUCATION IN SOMALIA.*
irreg. Ministry of Education, Department of
Planning, Mogadishu, Somalia. illus. stat.

370　　　　　UK　　ISSN 0144-0764
STIRLING TECHNICAL REPORTS IN
EDUCATION. 1980. irreg. University of Stirling,
Department of Education, Stirling FK9 4LA,
Scotland.

370　　　　　　　　US
STOPOUT: WORKING WAYS TO LEARN. 1978.
irreg. $8.95. Garrett Park Press, Box 190F, Garrett
Park, MD 20896. TEL 301-946-2553. Ed. Joyce
Slayton Mitchell.

EDUCATION

370   UK
STUDENTS REPRESENTATIVE COUNCIL. HANDBOOK. 1972. a. £0.50. Students Representative Council, John McIntyre Bldg., The University, Glasgow G12 8QQ, Scotland. Eds. Murdo Morrisson, Maureen M. Alpine. adv. circ. 7,000.

370   IT   ISSN 0392-2146
STUDI SULL'EDUCAZIONE. 1981. irreg., no.14, 1986. price varies. Liguori Editore s.r.l., Via Mezzocannone 19, 80134 Naples, Italy. Eds. Raffaele Laporta, Paolo Orefice.

370   PL   ISSN 0081-6795
STUDIA PEDAGOGICZNE. 1954. irreg., vol.49, 1985. price varies. (Polska Akademia Nauk, Komitet Nauk Pedagogicznych) Ossolineum, Publishing House of the Polish Academy of Sciences, Rynek 9, 50-106 Wroclaw, Poland (Dist. by: Ars Polona-Ruch, Krakowskie Przedmiescie 7, Warsaw, Poland)

370.15   SW
STUDIA PSYCHOLOGICA ET PAEDAGOGICA. (Text in English or Swedish; summaries in English) 1946. irreg., no.80, 1985. price varies. (University of Lund) Liber Forlag, S-205 10, Malmo, Sweden. (Co-sponsor: Malmoe Institute of Education) Ed. Aake Bjerstedt.

370   GW
DER STUDIENBEGINN. 1968. a. DM.10. Verein Freunde und Foerderer der Deutschen Studentenschaft e.V., Untere Hausbreite 11, 8000 Munich 45, W. Germany (B.R.D.) Ed. Gundolf Seidenspinner. adv.

STUDIENREIHE PAEDAGOGISCHE PSYCHOLOGIE. see *PSYCHOLOGY*

370.15   SW
STUDIES IN EDUCATION AND PSYCHOLOGY. (Text in English) 1977. irreg., no.20, 1985. price varies. (Stockholm University, Institute of Education) Almqvist & Wiksell International, Box 1034, S-171 21 Solna, Sweden. Ed.Bd.

370   375   II   ISSN 0254-0185
STUDIES IN EDUCATION AND TEACHING TECHNIQUES. 1979. irreg. Bahri Publications Pvt. Ltd., 57 Santnagar (East of Kailash), Box 7023, New Delhi 110065, India. Ed. Ujjal Singh Bahri.

STUDIES IN LANGUAGE DISABILITY AND REMEDIATION. see *LINGUISTICS*

370   150   FR
STUDIES IN THE LEARNING SCIENCES. (Editions in English and French) 1973. irreg. price varies. Organization for Economic Cooperation and Development, Centre for Educational Research and Innovation, 2 rue Andre Pascal, 75775 Paris Cedex 16, France (U.S. orders to: O.E.C.D. Publications and Information Center, 1750 Pennsylvania Ave., N.W., Washington DC 20006)

379   US   ISSN 0094-8268
SUMMARY OF EXPENDITURE DATA FOR MICHIGAN PUBLIC SCHOOLS. a. free. Department of Education, Box 30009, Lansing, MI 48909. TEL 517-373-0424. charts. stat.

331.1   US   ISSN 0094-2308
SUPPLY AND DEMAND: EDUCATIONAL PERSONNEL IN DELAWARE. Variant title: Educational Personnel in Delaware. a. Department of Public Instruction, Dover, DE 19901. TEL 302-736-4583. illus.
    Continues: Delaware. Department of Public Instruction. Teacher Supply and Demand.

370   SW
SWEDEN. STATISTISKA CENTRALBYRAAN. UTBILDNINGSSTATISTISK AARSBOK/ SWEDISH EDUCATIONAL STATISTICS YEARBOOK. a. Kr.110. Statistiska Centralbyraan, Distribution, S-701 89 Oerebro, Sweden.

370   620   US   ISSN 0082-1217
SYSTEMS ENGINEERING OF EDUCATION SERIES. 1965. irreg. (1-2/yr.) price varies. Education and Training Consultants Co. (ETC), Box 2085, Sedona, AZ 86336-2085. TEL 602-282-3009. Ed. Leonard C. Silvern. circ. 2,000. Indexed: ERIC.

370   HU   ISSN 0082-1632
TANULMANYOK A NEVELESTUDOMANY KOREBOL. (Text in Hungarian; summaries in English and Russian) 1958. irreg. price varies. (Magyar Tudomanyos Akademia) Akademiai Kiado, Publishing House of the Hungarian Academy of Sciences, Box 24, H-1363 Budapest, Hungary.

370   910.09   US
TEACHERS' GUIDE TO OVERSEAS TEACHING; a complete and comprehensive guide of English-language schools and colleges overseas. 1977. irreg. $19.95. Friends of World Teaching, Box 1049, San Diego, CA 92112-1049. TEL 619-274-5282. Ed. Louis A. Bajkai. adv. bk. rev. circ. 5,000.

371   AT
TEACHERS GUILD OF NEW SOUTH WALES. PROCEEDINGS. 1923. a. Aus.$2. Teachers' Guild of New South Wales, Assembly Hall, 44 Margaret St., Sydney, N.S.W. 2000, Australia. Ed. T. Gayzer. adv. bk. rev. circ. 800. Indexed: Aus.Educ.Ind.
    Formerly: Australian Teacher (ISSN 0045-091X)

370   UK   ISSN 0268-6732
TEACHERS OF HISTORY IN THE UNIVERSITIES AND POLYTECHNICS OF THE UNITED KINGDOM. a. £2.50. University of London, Institute of Historical Research, Senate House, London WC1E 7HU, England. circ. 350. (processed)
    Formerly: Teachers of History in the Universities of the United Kingdom (ISSN 0085-7114)

TECHNICAL, TRADE & BUSINESS SCHOOL DATA HANDBOOK. see *TECHNOLOGY: COMPREHENSIVE WORKS*

TEST - INFO. see *COLLEGE AND ALUMNI*

372   US
TEXAS CHILD MIGRANT PROGRAM. ANNUAL REPORT. Variant title: Texas Migrant Program. Annual Report. 1966. a. free. Texas Education Agency, Division of Evaluation, 1701 N. Congress, Austin, TX 78711. TEL 512-463-9524. charts. stat. circ. 2,000.

370   940.1   US   ISSN 0082-3732
TEXTS AND STUDIES IN THE HISTORY OF MEDIAEVAL EDUCATION. (Text in English and French; footnotes in Latin, German, French) 1953. irreg., no.16, 1979. price varies. ‡ University of Notre Dame Press, Notre Dame, IN 46556. TEL 219-239-6346. Ed. Astrik L. Gabriel.

370   020   US
THESAURUS OF E R I C DESCRIPTORS. (Educational Resources Information Center) 1980. a. $65. Oryx Press, 2214 N. Central at Encanto, Phoenix, AZ 85004-1483. TEL 602-254-6156. Ed.Bd. index. circ. 6,000. (back issues avail.)

TIDSSKRIFTINDEKS FOR SKOLEBIBLIOTEKER. see *BIBLIOGRAPHIES*

370   US   ISSN 0737-1888
TODAY'S EDUCATION ANNUAL. 1913. a. membership. National Education Association of the United States, 1201 16th St., N.W., Washington, DC 20036. TEL 202-822-7200. Ed. William Fischer. adv. bk. rev. illus. index. circ. 1,800,000. (also avail. in microform from BLH,UMI) Indexed: Educ.Ind. Psychol.Abstr. R.G. Abr.R.G. Bus.Ind. C.I.J.E. Mag.Ind. PMR. Tr.& Indus.Ind.
    Former titles: Today's Education. General Edition (ISSN 0272-3573); Supersedes in part: Today's Education (ISSN 0040-8484); Which was formerly: N E A Journal.

378   US   ISSN 0194-0988
TRANSFER CREDIT PRACTICES OF DESIGNATED EDUCATIONAL INSTITUTIONS. biennial. $10. American Association of Collegiate Registrars and Admissions Officers, One Dupont Circle, N.W., Ste. 330, Washington, DC 20036. TEL 202-293-9161. (reprint service avail. from UMI)
    Formerly: Report of Credit Given by Educational Institutions (ISSN 0569-2482)

370   UK   ISSN 0260-1729
TRENT PAPERS IN EDUCATION. 1980. irreg. £1. Trent Polytechnic, Centre for Educational Research, Clifton Hall, Clifton NG11 8NJ, England. Ed. Michael Bassey. circ. 100.

370   TU
TURKEY. DEVLET ISTATISTIK ENSTITUSU. MILLI EGITIM ISTATISTIKLERI: OGRETIM YILI BASI. (Subseries of its Yayin) 1970/71. a., latest 1972/74. free or on exchange basis. State Institute of Statistics, Necatibey Caddesi 114, Ankara, Turkey. stat.

370   UN
U I E CASE STUDIES. (Text in English, French and Spanish) irreg., no.7, 1986. price varies. Unesco Institute for Education, Feldbrunnenstr. 58, D 2000 Hamburg 13, W. Germany (B.R.D.) (Dist. in U.S.A. by: Bernan Associates-Unipub, 4611-F Assembly Dr., Lanham, MD 20706-4391)

370   UN
U I E MONOGRAPHS. (Text in English, French, Spanish) 1973. irreg., no.11, 1985. DM.12. Unesco Institute for Education, Felbrunnenstr. 58, D-2000 Hamburg 13, W. Germany (B.R.D.) (Dist. in U.S. by: Bernan Associates-Unipub, 4611-F Assembly Dr., Lanham, MD 20706-4391)

370   DK   ISSN 0107-3435
UDDANNELSESNOEGLEN. 1974. a. Kr.130. Noegleforlaget, Haslevej 12-14, 6000 Kolding, Denmark. illus.
    Formerly: Uddannelsesvejviser.

370   DK
UDDANNELSHISTORIE. SELSKABET FOR DANSK SKOLEHISTORIE. AARBOG. 1967. a. Kr.150. Selskabet for Dansk Skolehistorie, Lersoe Parkalle 101, DK-2100 Copenhagen OE, Denmark. Ed. Soren Ehlers. bk. rev. circ. 1,000.
    Formerly: Dansk Skolehistorie. Aarbog (ISSN 0065-0145)

370   DK   ISSN 0108-7886
UDVIKLINGSTENDENSERNE PAA DE LANGVARIGT UDDANNEDES ARBEJDSMARKED. 1980. a. free. Undervisningsministeriet, Oekonomisk-Statistik Kontor, Copenhagen, Denmark (Orders to: Undervisningsministeriets Tekstbehandlingsenhed, Frederiksholms Kanal 25, 1220 Copenhagen K, Denmark)

370   UN
UNESCO. REGIONAL OFFICE FOR EDUCATION IN ASIA AND THE PACIFIC. BULLETIN. (Text in English) 1966. a. price varies. Unesco, Principal Regional Office for Education in Asia and the Pacific, G.P.O. Box 1425, Bangkok 10501, Thailand (Dist. in U.S. by: Bernan Associates-UNIPUB, 4611-F, Assembly Drive, Lanham, MD 20706) circ. 3,200. Indexed: ERIC.
    Former titles: Unesco. Regional Office for Education in Asia and Oceania. Bulletin; Unesco. Regional Office for Education in Asia. Bulletin. (ISSN 0503-4450)

370   DK   ISSN 0108-2426
UNGDOMSSKOLEN I TAL.* 1981. a. free. Undervisningsministeriet, Frederiksholms Kanal 21-25, 1220 Copenhagen K, Denmark.

370   DK   ISSN 0900-1395
UNGDOMSUDDANNELSER. 1985. a. Kr.125. Ole Camaae, Lerbjergstien 18, 3460 Birkeroed, Denmark. illus.

UNION NATIONALE DE L'ENSEIGNEMENT AGRICOLE PRIVE. ANNUAIRE. see *AGRICULTURE*

370   UN
UNITED NATIONS INSTITUTE FOR NAMIBIA. PROSPECTUS. a. United Nations Institute for Namibia, Publications Section, Box 33811, Lusaka, Zambia. TEL 216468. Ed. N.K. Duggal.

370.6   II
UNITED SCHOOLS ORGANISATION OF INDIA. ANNUAL REPORT. (Text in English) 19th edt., 1969. a. United Schools Organisation of India, U S O House, 6 Special Institutional Area, New Delhi 110 067, India. illus.

EDUCATION

379   US   ISSN 0149-2497
U.S. NATIONAL CENTER FOR EDUCATION STATISTICS. REVENUES AND EXPENDITURES FOR PUBLIC ELEMENTARY AND SECONDARY EDUCATION. (Report year ends June 30) U.S. National Center for Education Statistics, U.S. Department of Education, 400 Maryland Ave., S.W., Washington, DC 20201 TEL 202-655-4000. (Orders to: Supt. of Documents, Washington DC 20402)
    Formerly: U.S. National Center for Education Statistics. Expenditures and Revenues for Public Elementary and Secondary Education (ISSN 0090-7618)

372 373   US
U.S. NATIONAL CENTER FOR EDUCATION STATISTICS. STATISTICS OF PUBLIC ELEMENTARY AND SECONDARY SCHOOL SYSTEMS. 1954. a. U.S. National Center for Education Statistics, U.S. Department of Education, 400 Maryland Ave., S.W., Washington, DC 20202 TEL 202-655-4000. (Orders to: Supt. of Documents, Washington, DC 20402)
    Formerly: U.S. National Center for Education Statistics. Statistics of Public Elementary and Secondary Day Schools.

370 100   SP
UNIVERSIDAD DE MURCIA. ANALES DE FILOSOFIA Y CIENCIAS DE LA EDUCACION. vol.34, 1980. irreg. ($600) Universidad de Murcia, Secretariado de Publicaciones e Intercambio Cientifico, Santo Cristo, 1, 30001 Murcia, Spain. TEL 968 24 92 00.

370   SP   ISSN 0212-8322
UNIVERSIDAD DE MURCIA. ANALES DE PEDAGOGIA. 1983. a. ($1000) Universidad de Murcia, Secretariado de Publicaciones e Intercambio Cientifico, Santo Cristo, 1, 30001 Murcia, Spain. TEL 968 24 92 00.

370   SP
UNIVERSIDAD DE NAVARRA. FACULTAD DE CIENCIAS DE LA EDUCACION. COLECCION. 1969. irreg., no.29, 1984. price varies. Ediciones Universidad de Navarra, S.A., Apdo. 396, 31080 Pamplona, Spain.
    Formerly: Universidad de Navarra. Instituto de Ciencias de la Educacion. Coleccion I C E (ISSN 0078-8686)

370   BL   ISSN 0085-0284
UNIVERSIDADE FEDERAL DO ESPIRITO SANTO. COMISSAO DE PLANEJAMENTO. DOCUMENTARIO ESTATISTICO SOBRE A SITUACAO EDUCACIONAL.* irreg. Universidade Federal do Espirito Santo, Sub-Reitoria de Planejamento e Desenvolvimento, Vitoria, Espirito Santo, Brazil.

370   BL   ISSN 0085-0292
UNIVERSIDADE FEDERAL DO ESPIRITO SANTO. COMISSAO DE PLANEJAMENTO. DOCUMENTARIO ESTATISTICO SOBRE A SITUACAO EDUCACIONAL. SUPPLEMENTO.* irreg. Universidade Federal do Espirito Santo, Sub Reitoria de Planejamento e Desenvolvimento, Vitoria, Espirito Santo, Brazil.

370   IT   ISSN 0082-6480
UNIVERSITA DEGLI STUDI DI TRIESTE. ISTITUTO DI PEDAGOGIA. QUADERNI. 1966. irreg. price varies. (Universita degli Studi di Trieste) Casa Editrice Felice le Monnier, Via A. Meucci 2, Casella Postale 202, 50100 Florence, Italy.

370   FR
UNIVERSITE DE BRETAGNE OCCIDENTALE. GUIDE DE L'ETUDIANT. 1971. a. free. Universite de Brest (Brestagne Occidentale), Rue de Archives, 29269 Brest, France. circ. controlled. (processed)

370   NO   ISSN 0800-6113
UNIVERSITET I OSLO. PEDAGOGISK FORSKNINGSINSTITUTT. RAPPORT. a. price varies. Universitet i Oslo, Pedagogisk Forskningsinstitutt, Postboks 1092, Blindern, Oslo 3, Norway.

370   MY
UNIVERSITI KEBANGSAAN MALAYSIA. LAPURAU TAHUNAN/ANNUAL REPORT. (Text in English & Malay) 1971. a. free. National University of Malaysia - Universiti Kebangsaan Malaysia, Bangi, Kajang, Selangor, Malaysia. stat.

370   II   ISSN 0084-621X
UNIVERSITY OF ALLAHABAD. EDUCATION DEPARTMENT. RESEARCHES AND STUDIES. 1950. a. exchange basis. University of Allahabad, Education Department, Allahabad 211002, Uttar Pradesh, India. Ed. R.S. Asthana. bk. rev. circ. controlled.

371.42   PH   ISSN 0070-8259
UNIVERSITY OF EASTERN PHILIPPINES. RESEARCH CENTER. REPORT. 1965. irreg. $2. University of Eastern Philippines, Research Center, University Town, Northern Samar, Philippines. Ed. Andres F. Celestino. circ. 3,000. (processed)

370   FI   ISSN 0073-179X
UNIVERSITY OF HELSINKI. DEPARTMENT OF EDUCATION. RESEARCH BULLETIN. (Text in English, French or German) 1957. irreg., no.63, 1984. exchange basis. Helsingin Yliopisto, Kasvatustieteen Laitos, Fabianinkatu 28, SF-00100 Helsinki 10, Finland. circ. 325. (also avail. in microfiche) Indexed: Psychol.Abstr. ERIC.

370   NR
UNIVERSITY OF IBADAN. INSTITUTE OF EDUCATION. ANNUAL REPORT. a. University of Ibadan, Institute of Education, Ibadan, Nigeria.

370   NR   ISSN 0073-4314
UNIVERSITY OF IBADAN. INSTITUTE OF EDUCATION. OCCASIONAL PUBLICATIONS. irreg. price varies. University of Ibadan, Institute of Education, Ibadan, Nigeria.

370   UK   ISSN 0075-854X
UNIVERSITY OF LEEDS. INSTITUTE OF EDUCATION. PAPERS. 1955. irreg. price varies. ‡ University of Leeds, Institute of Education, Leeds, LS2 9JT, England.

370   US
UNIVERSITY OF MINNESOTA. CENTER FOR RESEARCH IN HUMAN LEARNING. REPORT AND FELLOWSHIP OFFERINGS. a. University of Minnesota, Center for Research in Human Learning, 205 Elliott Hall, Minneapolis, MN 55455. TEL 612-373-2851.
    Formerly: University of Minnesota. Center for Research in Human Learning. Report (ISSN 0076-9282)

UNIVERZITA J.E. PURKYNE. FILOZOFICKA FAKULTA. SBORNIK PRACI. I: RADA PEDAGOGICKA - PSYCHOLOGICKA. see *PSYCHOLOGY*

370   CS   ISSN 0083-4165
UNIVERZITA KOMENSKEHO. FILOZOFICKA FAKULTA. ZBORNIK: PAEDAGOGICA. (Text in Slovak; summaries in English, German, Russian) 1968. a. exchange basis. Univerzita Komenskeho, Filozoficka Fakulta, Gondova 2, 806 01 Bratislava, Czechoslovakia. Ed. Jozef Matej. circ. 700.

370 150   PL   ISSN 0072-047X
UNIWERSYTET GDANSKI. WYDZIAL HUMANISTYCZNY. ZESZYTY NAUKOWE. PEDAGOGIKA, HISTORIA WYCHOWANIA. 1966. irreg. price varies. Uniwersytet Gdanski, Ul. Czerwonej Armii 110, 81-824 Sopot, Poland (Dist. by: Ars Polona-Ruch, Krakowskie Przedmiescie 7, Warsaw, Poland)

UNIWERSYTET JAGIELLONSKI. ZESZYTY NAUKOWE. PRACE PSYCHOLOGICZNO-PEDAGOGICZNE. see *PSYCHOLOGY*

370   PL   ISSN 0208-5429
UNIWERSYTET SLASKI W KATOWICACH. PRACE PEDAGOGICZNE. (Text in Polish; summaries in English and Russian) 1972. irreg. price varies. Uniwersytet Slaski w Katowicach, Ul. Bankowa 14, 40-007 Katowice, Poland. charts.

370   GW
DER UNTERMIETER. 1966. irreg. DM.5. Verein Freunde und Foerderer der Deutschen Studentenschaft e.V., Untere Hausbreite 11, 8000 Munich 45, W. Germany (B.R.D.) Ed. Peter Gantzer. adv.

370   SW   ISSN 0347-1314
UPPSALA STUDIES IN EDUCATION. (Subseries of Acta Universitatis Upsaliensis) (Text in English and Swedish; summaries in English) 1976. irreg. price varies. (Uppsala Universitet, Pedagogiska Institutionen - University of Uppsala, Department of Education) Almqvist & Wiksell International, Box 62, S-101 20 Stockholm, Sweden. Ed.Bd. index. circ. 750. Indexed: Psychol.Abstr.
    Supersedes: Studia Scientiae Paedagogicae Upsaliensia (ISSN 0081-6892)

373   AT
V C A B HANDBOOK. 1979. a. Aus.$7. Victorian Curriculum and Assessment Board, 582 St. Kilda Rd., Melbourne, Vic. 3004, Australia. Ed. Murray Paterson. adv. circ. 5,000.
    Formerly: V I S E Handbook (ISSN 0156-1987)

370   VE
VENEZUELA. DEPARTAMENTO DE INVESTIGACIONES EDUCACIONALES. SECCION DE ESTADISTICA. ESTADISTICAS EDUCACIONALES.* 1971. a. Ministerio de Educacion, Departamento de Investigaciones Educacionales, Seccion de Estadistica, Caracas, Venezuela. illus. stat.

370   US
VERMONT EDUCATION DIRECTORY. a. free. Department of Education, State Office Building, Montpelier, VT 05602. TEL 802-828-3121. Ed. Lesley Bean. circ. 6,000.

370   AT
VICTORIA. CLASSIFIED ROLL OF POSTPRIMARY STATE SCHOOL TEACHERS. triennial. Ministry of Education, Materials Production, G.P.O. Box 4367, Melbourne, Vic. 3001, Australia. Ed. G.T. Alves. circ. 2,500.
    Formerly: Classified Roll of the State School Teachers in the Secondary Schools Division.

370   NZ   ISSN 0083-6036
VICTORIA UNIVERSITY OF WELLINGTON. AWARDS HANDBOOK. 1969. a. free. Victoria University of Wellington, Administration Office, Private Bag, Wellington, New Zealand. circ. 1,450.

VIDEO OUT DISTRIBUTION CATALOGUE. see *ART*

370   US   ISSN 0083-6354
VIRGINIA EDUCATIONAL DIRECTORY. a. $3. Department of Education, Box 6-Q, Richmond, VA 23216. TEL 804-225-2020.

W C O T P REPORT. (World Confederation of Organizations of the Teaching Profession) see *EDUCATION — School Organization And Administration*

370   US
WASHINGTON EDUCATION DIRECTORY. 1972/73. a. $11 prepaid; $12 invoiced. (Superintendent of Public Instruction) Barbara Krohn and Associates, 835 Securities Bldg., Seattle, WA 98101. Ed. N.G. Slauson. circ. 8,500.

370   UK   ISSN 0083-7946
WELSH STUDIES IN EDUCATION SERIES. 1968. irreg. price varies. (University College of Wales, Aberystwyth, Faculty of Education) University of Wales Press, 6 Gwennyth St., Cathays, Cardiff CF2 4YD, Wales. Ed. Prof. Jac L. Williams.

370   US   ISSN 0085-8099
WEST VIRGINIA EDUCATION DIRECTORY. 1934. a. free. ‡ Department of Education, Capitol Complex, Bldg. B-204, Charleston, WV 25305. TEL 304-348-3667. Ed. Elnora Pepper. circ. 5,000.

370   UK   ISSN 0140-6728
WESTMINSTER STUDIES IN EDUCATION. 1978. a. $80. Carfax Publishing Co., P.O. Box 25, Abingdon, Oxfordshire OX14 3UE, England (U.S. distr.: 85 Ash St., Hopkinton, MA 01748) Ed. Glynn Phillips. bk. rev. illus. stat. circ. 700. (also avail. in microfiche; back issues avail.) Indexed: High.Educ.Curr.Aware.Bull. Res.High.Educ.Abstr.

371.33   US   ISSN 0361-2120
WISCONSIN. EDUCATIONAL COMMUNICATIONS BOARD. BIENNIAL REPORT.* biennial. Educational Communications Board, 3319 W. Beltline Hwy., Madison, WI 53713. Key Title: Biennial Report-Educational Communications Board.

422   EDUCATION — ABSTRACTING, BIBLIOGRAPHIES, STATISTICS

WISCONSIN COUNCIL OF TEACHERS OF ENGLISH. SERVICE BULLETIN SERIES. see *LITERATURE*

370   CN
WOMEN'S NETWORK/RESEAU FEMMES. irreg. (approx. 4/yr.) Federation Nationale des Enseignants et des Enseignantes du Quebec, 1601 rue de Lorimer, Montreal, Que. H2K 4M5, Canada. TEL 514-598-2241. circ. controlled.
    Former titles: Info-F N E E Q; (until 1983): Nouveau Pouvoir.

370   BE
WORLD ASSOCIATION FOR EDUCATIONAL RESEARCH. CONGRESS REPORTS. 1953. quadrennial, 9th, 1985, Madrid, published in 1985. 1200 Fr. World Association for Educational Research, Henri Dunantlaan 1, B-9000 Ghent, Belgium (Orders from: Prof. A De la Orden; Calle General Yague 11,8,E, Madrid 20, Spain) Ed. M.L. van Herreweghe.
    Formerly: International Association for the Advancement of Educational Research. Congress Reports (ISSN 0074-154X)

370 331.88   GE   ISSN 0020-8884
WORLD FEDERATION OF TEACHERS' UNIONS. INFORMATION LETTER. 1969. irreg. free. World Federation of Teachers' Unions, W.-Wolff-Str. 21, 1110 Berlin, E. Germany (D.D.R.) (FISE, Wilhelm-Wolf-Str. 21, 1110 Berlin, DDR) bk. rev. circ. 1,500.

370   UK   ISSN 0084-2508
WORLD YEARBOOK OF EDUCATION. (Each vol. has distinctive subtitle) 1968. a. £19($35) Kogan Page Ltd., 120 Pentonville Rd., London N1 9JN, England (Dist. by: Nichols Publishing Company, Box 96, New York, NY 10025) Ed. John Twinning. Indexed: High.Educ.Curr.Aware.Bull.

370   US
WYOMING. DEPARTMENT OF EDUCATION. EDUCATION DIRECTORY. a. $3. Department of Education, Hathaway Bldg, Cheyenne, WY 82002. TEL 307-777-6203.

YEARBOOK OF SCHOOL LAW. see *LAW*

370   JA   ISSN 0513-5656
YOKOHAMA NATIONAL UNIVERSITY. EDUCATIONAL SCIENCES/YOKOHAMA KOKURITU DAIGAKU KYOIKU KIYO. (Text in English and Japanese) 1962. irreg. Yokohama National University, Faculty of Education - Yokohama Kokuritsu Daigaku Kyoikugakubu, 156 Tokiwadai, Hodogaya-ku, Yokohama 240, Japan. cum.index nos. 11-15, 1971-1975.

YOUTH PLANBOOK. see *RELIGIONS AND THEOLOGY — Protestant*

370   ZA   ISSN 0084-487X
ZAMBIA. MINISTRY OF EDUCATION. ANNUAL REPORT. 1964. a. Ministry of Education, Box 50093, Lusaka, Zambia (Orders to: Government Printer, Box 30136, Lusaka, Zambia)

370   ZA   ISSN 0084-5086
ZAMBIA. TEACHING SERVICE COMMISSION. ANNUAL REPORT. a. 5 n. Government Printer, Box 136, Lusaka, Zambia.

370   ZA
ZAMBIA EDUCATIONAL JOURNAL. 1971. a. $13. University of Zambia, School of Education, Department of Education, Box 32379, Lusaka, Zambia. Ed. P.M. Haamujompa. bk. rev. charts. illus.
    Formerly: Educational Front.

370   YU   ISSN 0514-6151
ZBORNIK ZA ISTORIJU SKOLSTVA I PROSVETE. (Text in Serbo-Croatian, Slovenian; summaries in English, French, German) 1968. a. 250 din.($5) Pedgoski Muzej, Uzun Mirkova 14, 11000 Belgrade, Yugoslavia. Ed. Dragutin Frankovic. bk. rev. circ. 800. (back issues avail.)

370   GW   ISSN 0174-0830
ZEITSCHRIFT FUER BERUFS UND WIRTSCHAFTSPAEDAGOGIK. BEIHEFTE. irreg., vol.6, 1986. price varies. Franz Steiner Verlag Wiesbaden GmbH, Birkenwaldstr. 44, Postfach 347, D-7000 Stuttgart 1, W. Germany (B.R.D.) Ed.Bd.

370   RH   ISSN 0080-2859
ZIMBABWE. MINISTRY OF EDUCATION. AFRICAN EDUCATION REPORT. a. Rhod.$1.05. Government Printer, Box 8062, Causeway, Zimbabwe.

370   GW
ZULASSUNGSARBEIT. 1972. irreg. DM.10. Verein Freunde und Foerderer der Deutschen Studentenschaft e.V., Untere Hausbreite 11, 8000 Munich 45, W. Germany (B.R.D.) Ed. Gundolf Seidenspinner. adv.

370   GW
ZUSAMMENSTELLUNG STUDIENEINFUEHRENDER SCHRIFTEN. 1974. irreg. DM.2. Verein Freunde und Foerderer der Deutschen Studentenschaft e.V., Untere Hausbreite 11, 8000 Munich 45, W. Germany (B.R.D.) adv. bk. rev.

EDUCATION — Abstracting, Bibliographies, Statistics

A.A.T.E. GUIDE TO ENGLISH BOOKS. (Australian Association for the Teaching of English) see *LITERATURE — Abstracting, Bibliographies, Statistics*

100 370 016   BU
ABSTRACTS OF BULGARIAN SCIENTIFIC LITERATURE. PHILOSOPHY, SOCIOLOGY, SCIENCE OF SCIENCES, PSYCHOLOGY AND PEDAGOGICS. (Editions in English and Russian) 1958. q. 3.44 lv.($8) (Bulgarska Akademiia na Naukite) Publishing House of the Bulgarian Academy of Sciences, 7 Noemvri St. 1, 1040 Sofia, Bulgaria (Dist. by: Hemus, 6, Rouski Blvd., 1000 Sofia, Bulgaria) Ed.Bd. abstr. author index. circ. 390 (English edt.)
    Continues: Abstracts of Bulgarian Scientific Literature. Philosophy, Psychology and Pedagogics (ISSN 0001-3528)

016 370   US
AMERICAN DISSERTATIONS ON FOREIGN EDUCATION; a bibliography with abstracts. irreg. price varies. Whitston Publishing Co. Inc., Box 958, Troy, NY 12181. TEL 518-283-4363. Ed. Franklin Parker.

370   DK   ISSN 0106-8172
ANMELDELSER I PAEDAGOGISKE TIDSSKRIFTER. 1971. irreg. Kr.769.98. Bibliotekscentralen, Tempovej 7-11, 2750 Ballerup, Denmark.

ANNUAL REPORT ON DENTAL AUXILIARY EDUCATION. see *MEDICAL SCIENCES — Abstracting, Bibliographies, Statistics*

ANNUAL REPORT ON DENTAL EDUCATION. see *MEDICAL SCIENCES — Abstracting, Bibliographies, Statistics*

370   IT   ISSN 0390-6582
ANNUARIO STATISTICO DELL'ISTRUZIONE-TOMO 1. a. Istituto Centrale di Statistica, Via Cesare Balbo 16, 00100 Rome, Italy.

370   IT   ISSN 0390-6590
ANNUARIO STATISTICO DELL'ISTRUZIONE-TOMO 2. a. L.8500. Istituto Centrale di Statistica, Via Ceasre Balbo 16, 00100 Rome, Italy.

370.982 318   AG
ARGENTINA. MINISTERIO DE CULTURA Y EDUCACION. ESTADISTICAS DE LA EDUCACION. 1974. a. Ministerio de Cultura y Educacion, Departamento de Estadistica Educativa, Avenida E. Madero 235, Buenos Aires, Argentina. illus. stat.
    Formerly: Estadistica Educativa.

370 016   US
AUDIOCASSETTE FINDER. 1971. irreg. $75. (National Information Center for Educational Media) Access Innovations, Inc., Box 40130, Albuquerque, NM 87196. TEL 505-265-3591. abstr. cum.index 1971-1986. (back issues avail.)
●Also available online.
    Formerly (until 1986): N I C E M Index to Educational Audio Tapes.

379.121   AT
AUSTRALIA. BUREAU OF STATISTICS. EXPENDITURE ON EDUCATION, AUSTRALIA. a. free. Australian Bureau of Statistics, Box 10, Belconnen, A.C.T. 2616, Australia. stat. circ. 1,000.

370 319.4   AT
AUSTRALIA. BUREAU OF STATISTICS. NEW SOUTH WALES OFFICE. TERTIARY EDUCATION, NEW SOUTH WALES. 1972. a. free. Australian Bureau of Statistics, N.S.W. Office, St. Andrews House, Sydney Square, George St., Sydney, N.S.W. 2000, Australia. charts, stat.

372.21   AU
AUSTRIA. STATISTISCHES ZENTRALAMT. KINDERGAERTEN (KINDERTAGSHEIME) (Subseries of its Beitraege zur Oesterreichschen Statistik) a. 520. Oesterreichisches Statistisches Zentralamt, Hintere Zollamtsstr. 2b, 1033 Vienna, Austria.

370 012   UN   ISSN 0211-8335
B I B E ANNUAL SUMMARY. (International Bulletin of Bibliography on Education) (Text in English, French, German, Italian, Portuguese and Spanish) 1981. a. $85. Unesco, B I B E Project, Apartado 52, San Lorenzo del Escorial, Madrid, Spain.

370 016   TH   ISSN 0067-3498
BANGKOK, THAILAND. COLLEGE OF EDUCATION. THESIS ABSTRACT SERIES.* (Editions in English and Thai) 1967/69. a. $1. Suan Sunautha Teacher College, Samsen, Bangkok 4, Thailand.

370   BE
BELGIUM. MINISTERE DE L'EDUCATION NATIONALE ET DE LA CULTURE FRANCAISE. ANNUAIRE STATISTIQUE DE L'ENSEIGNEMENT. (Text in Dutch and French) 1957. a. 90 Fr. Ministere de l'Education Nationale et de la Culture Francaise, Cite Administrative de l'Etat, Bd. Pacheco, 1010 Brussels, Belgium.
    Formerly: Belgium. Institut National de Statistique. Annuaire Statistique de l'Enseignement (ISSN 0067-5423)

371.9   FI   ISSN 0357-2498
BIBLIOGRAFIA ERITYSIRYHMIEN LIIKUNNAN TUTKIMUKSESTA/BIBLIOGRAPHY ON RESEARCH IN PHYSICAL EDUCATION AND SPORT FOR THE HANDICAPPED. (Text in English and Finnish) 1975. irreg. Liikunnan ja Kansanterveyden Edistaemisaeaetion Tutkmuslaitos - Research Institute of Physical Culture and Health, Uimahalli, Yliopiston Alue, 40100-Jyvaeskylae 10, Finland. bibl. circ. 500.

370 011   US
BIBLIOGRAPHIC GUIDE TO EDUCATION. 1975. a. price varies. G.K. Hall & Co., 70 Lincoln St., Boston, MA 02111. TEL 617-423-3990. bibl.

370 016   GE   ISSN 0067-6969
BIBLIOGRAPHIE DER PAEDAGOGISCHEN VEROEFFENTLICHUNGEN IN DER DEUTSCHEN DEMOKRATISCHEN REPUBLIK. a. price varies. Akademie der Paedagogischen Wissenschaften der DDR, Zentralstelle fuer Paedagogische Information und Dokumentation, Otto-Grotewohl-Str. 11, 108 Berlin, E. Germany (D.D.R.) Ed. Rosemarie Kohls.

370   US   ISSN 0742-6917
BIBLIOGRAPHIES AND INDEXES IN EDUCATION. 1984. irreg. price varies. Greenwood Press, 88 Post Rd. W., Box 5007, Westport, CT 06881. TEL 203-226-3571.

370 370.15 300 020   AT   ISSN 0811-0174
BIBLIOGRAPHY OF EDUCATION THESES IN AUSTRALIA. 1982. a. Aus.$18. Australian Council for Educational Research, Radford House, Box 210, Hawthorn, Vic. 3122, Australia. Eds. Elizabeth Oley, Julie Badger. bibl. circ. 350. (back issues avail.)
●Also available online. Vendors: AUSINET.

EDUCATION — ABSTRACTING, BIBLIOGRAPHIES, STATISTICS

370 314   GW
BILDUNG IM ZAHLENSPIEGEL. 1974. a. DM.16.50. (Bundesministerium fuer Bildung und Wissenschaft) W. Kohlhammer-Verlag GmbH, Abt. Veroeffentlichungen des Statistischen Bundesamtes, Philipp-Reis-Str. 3, Postfach 421120, 6500 Mainz 42, W. Germany (B.R.D.) (Co-sponsor: Statistisches Bundesamt) stat.

BRAILLE BOOKS (LARGE PRINT EDITION) see *BLIND — Abstracting, Bibliographies, Statistics*

370   BL
BRAZIL. MINISTERIO DA EDUCACAO E CULTURA. SERVICO DE ESTATISTICA DA EDUCACAO E CULTURA. SINOPSE ESTATISTICA DA EDUCACAO BASICA. 1983. a. Ministerio da Educacao e Cultura, Servico de Estatistica da Educacao e Cultura, Via N2-Anexo 2 do MEC Terreo, CEP 70047 Brasilia, DF, Brazil. circ. 3,000. (back issues avail.)

378   BL
BRAZIL. MINISTERIO DA EDUCACAO E CULTURA. SERVICO DE ESTATISTICA DA EDUCACAO E CULTURA. SINOPSE ESTATISTICA DO ENSINO SUPERIOR. 1954. a. Ministerio da Educacao e Cultura, Servico de Estatistica da Educacao e Cultura, Via N2 Anexo 2 do MEC, 70047 Brasilia DF, Brazil.

372   BL
BRAZIL. MINISTERIO DA EDUCACAO. SERVICO DE ESTATISTICA DA EDUCACAO E CULTURA. SINOPSE ESTATISTICA DA EDUCACAO PRE-ESCOLAR. 1984. a. Ministerio da Educacao e Cultura, Servico de Estatistica da Educacao e Cultura, Via N2 Anexo 22 do MEC, 70047 Brasilia DF, Brazil.
Supersedes (1968-1973): Brazil. Servico de Estatistica da Educacao e Cultura. Sinopse Estatistica do Ensino Primario.

BRITISH CATALOGUE OF AUDIO-VISUAL MATERIALS. see *SOUND RECORDING AND REPRODUCTION — Abstracting, Bibliographies, Statistics*

370 016   UK   ISSN 0007-0637
BRITISH EDUCATION INDEX.* 1961. a. (plus 3 quarterly issues) £42. University of Leeds, Education Library, c/o J.R.V. Johnston, Leeds LS2 9JT, England. circ. 1,000.

375 650 016   US   ISSN 0068-4414
BUSINESS EDUCATION INDEX. 1941. a. $12. Delta Pi Epsilon Graduate Business Education Society, National Office, Gustavus Adolphus College, St. Peter, MN 56082. TEL 507-931-8000. Ed. Rose McCauley. circ. 11,000. (also avail. in microform from UMI; reprint service avail. from UMI)

370   CN   ISSN 0706-3679
CANADA. STATISTICS CANADA. EDUCATION IN CANADA/EDUCATION AU CANADA. (Catalogue 81-229) (Text in English and French) 1973. a. Can.$40($41.50) Statistics Canada, Communications Division, 3rd Floor, R.H. Coats Bldg., Ottawa, Ont. K1A 0T6, Canada TEL 613-993-7276. (Subscr. to: Publications Sales and Services, Ottawa, Ont. K1A 0T6, Canada) (also avail. in microform from MML)

371.2   CN   ISSN 0704-6596
CANADA. STATISTICS CANADA. ELEMENTARY-SECONDARY SCHOOL ENROLLMENT/EFFECTIFS DES ECOLES PRIMAIRES ET SECONDAIRES. (Catalog 81-210) (Text in English and French) 1960/61. a. Can.$20($21) Statistics Canada, Communications Division, 3rd Floor, R.H. Coats Bldg., Ottawa, Ont. K1A 0T6, Canada TEL 613-993-7276. (Subscr. to: Publications Sales and Services, Ottawa, Ont. K1A 0T6, Canada) (also avail. in microform from MML)

378   CN   ISSN 0382-0920
CANADA. STATISTICS CANADA. ENROLLMENT IN COMMUNITY COLLEGES/ EFFECTIFS DES COLLEGES COMMUNAUTAIRES. (Catalogue 81-222) (Text in English and French) 1969. a. Can.$20($21) Statistics Canada, Communications Division, 3rd Floor, R.H. Coats Bldg., Ottawa, Ont. K1A 0T6, Canada TEL 613-993-7276. (Subscr. to: Publications Sales and Services, Ottawa, Ont. K1A 0T6, Canada) (also avail. in microform from MML)

310 370   CN   ISSN 0703-9328
CANADA. STATISTICS CANADA. FINANCIAL STATISTICS OF EDUCATION/STATISTIQUES FINANCIERES DE L'EDUCATION. (Catalog 81-208) (Text in English and French) 1954. a. Can.$35($36) Statistics Canada, Communications Division, 3rd Floor, R.H. Coats Bldg., Ottawa, Ont. K1A 0T6, Canada TEL 613-993-7276. (Subscr. to: Publications Sales and Services, Ottawa, Ont. K1A 0T6, Canada) (also avail. in microform from MML)

338.2   CN   ISSN 0318-3874
CANADA. STATISTICS CANADA. SALARIES AND QUALIFICATIONS OF TEACHERS IN PUBLIC, ELEMENTARY AND SECONDARY SCHOOLS/TRAITEMENTS ET QUALIFICATIONS DES ENSEIGNANTS DES ECOLES PUBLIQUES, PRIMAIRES ET SECONDAIRES. (Catalogue 81-202) (Text in English and French) 1936. a. Can.$20($21) Statistics Canada, Communications Division, 3rd Floor, R.H. Coats Bldg., Ottawa, Ont. K1A 0T6, Canada TEL 613-993-7276. (Subscr. to: Publications Sales and Services, Ottawa, Ont. K1A 0T6, Canada) (also avail. in microform from MML)

CANADIAN EDUCATION INDEX/REPERTOIRE CANADIEN SUR L'EDUCATION. see *ABSTRACTING AND INDEXING SERVICES*

370 016   CN
CANADIAN TEACHERS' FEDERATION. BIBLIOGRAPHIES IN EDUCATION. 1969. irreg. price varies. Canadian Teachers' Federation, 110 Argyle Ave., Ottawa, Ont. K2P 1B4, Canada. TEL 613-232-1505. circ. 750. (also avail. in microform from UMI; reprint service avail. from UMI) Indexed: Can.Educ.Ind.

310 370   UK   ISSN 0307-0514
CHARTERED INSTITUTE OF PUBLIC FINANCE AND ACCOUNTANCY. EDUCATION ESTIMATES STATISTICS. 1974. a. £14. Chartered Institute of Public Finance and Accountancy, 3 Robert St., London WC2N 6BH, England. (back issues avail.)

310 370   UK   ISSN 0309-5614
CHARTERED INSTITUTE OF PUBLIC FINANCE AND ACCOUNTANCY. EDUCATION STATISTICS. ACTUALS. 1948-49. a. £14. Chartered Institute of Public Finance and Accountancy, 3 Robert St., London WC2N 6BH, England. stat. (back issues avail.)

370   UK   ISSN 0264-7125
CHARTERED INSTITUTE OF PUBLIC FINANCE AND ACCOUNTANCY. EDUCATION STATISTICS. UNIT COSTS. 1980. a. £8. Chartered Institute of Public Finance and Accountancy, 3 Robert St, London WC2N 6BH, England.

370   UK   ISSN 0266-2949
CHARTERED INSTITUTE OF PUBLIC FINANCE AND ACCOUNTANCY. SCHOOL MEALS STATISTICS. 1984. a. £8. Chartered Institute of Public Finance and Accountancy, 3 Robert St., London WC2N 6BH, England.

370 016   CL
CHILE. CENTRO DE DOCUMENTACION PEDAGOGICA. BIBLIOGRAFIA DE LA EDUCACION CHILENA. 1974. irreg. Centro de Documentacion Pedagogica, Morande 322, Santiago, Chile. Ed. Maria Cornejo Acosta. bibl.

378 011   US
CLARK UNIVERSITY BULLETIN (WORCESTER, MASS.) 1929 N.S. 1953. biennial. free. Clark University, Graduate School, 950 Main St., Worcester, MA 01610. TEL 617-793-7676. Ed. Melanie Lajoie. circ. 400. (also avail. in microform) Indexed: D.A.
Formerly: Clark University (Worcester, Mass.) Dissertations and Theses (ISSN 0578-4247)

370   US   ISSN 0098-4752
CONDITION OF EDUCATION; a statistical report on the condition of American education. 1975. a. price varies. U.S. National Center for Education Statistics, U.S. Department of Education, 400 Maryland Ave. S.W., Washington, DC 20202 TEL 202-655-4000. (Orders to: Supt. of Documents, Washington, DC 20402) stat.

370   UK   ISSN 0265-9220
CONTENTS PAGES IN EDUCATION. 1986. m. $205. Carfax Publishing Co., P.O. Box 25, Abingdon, Oxfordshire OX14 3UF, England (U.S. distr. addr.: 85 Ash St., Hopkinton, MA 01748) Ed. Mark Higgins. index. (also avail. in microfiche; back issues avail.)

378.1   CN   ISSN 0382-912X
COUNCIL OF ONTARIO UNIVERSITIES. RESEARCH DIVISION. APPLICATION STATISTICS. 1973. a. Council of Ontario Universities, Research Division, 130 St. George St., Suite 8039, Toronto, Ont. M5S 2T4, Canada. TEL 416-979-2165. (reprint service avail from MML)

CURRENT CONTENTS/SOCIAL & BEHAVIORAL SCIENCES. see *SOCIOLOGY — Abstracting, Bibliographies, Statistics*

370 016   US   ISSN 0011-3565
CURRENT INDEX TO JOURNALS IN EDUCATION. 1969. m. $207 (s-a. cums. $198) (Educational Resources Information Center) Oryx Press, 2214 N. Central Ave., Phoenix, AZ 85004-1483. TEL 602-254-6156.
●Also available online. Vendors: BRS, CISTI, DIALOG, Orbit Information Technologies.

378   DK
DENMARK. UNDERVISNINGSMINISTERIET. OEKONOMISK-STATISTISKE KONSULENT. STATISTIK DE VIDEREGAENDE UDDANNELSER. irreg. price varies. Undervisningsministeriet, Oekonomisk-Statistiske Konsulent, Copenhagen, Denmark.

370 016   CH   ISSN 0419-3733
DIRECTORY OF THE CULTURAL ORGANIZATIONS OF THE REPUBLIC OF CHINA. (In four parts; Learned Societies, Universities and Colleges, Libraries and Social Educational Centers) 5th edt., 1978. every 2-3/yrs. $8. National Central Library, Bureau of International Exchange of Publications, 43 Nan-Hai Rd., Taipei 107, Taiwan, Republic of China. Ed. Teresa Wang Chang. circ. 1,000.

378 011   KE
EDUCATION IN KENYA; index of articles on education. 1977. a. $16. Kenyatta University College Library, Box 43844, Nairobi, Kenya. Ed. J.M. Murage. circ. 200.

370 016   US   ISSN 0013-1385
EDUCATION INDEX; an author-subject index to educational publications in the English language. 1929. m. (Sep.-Jun.) plus q. and a. cumulations. service basis. ‡ H.W. Wilson Co., 950 University Ave., Bronx, NY 10452. TEL 212-588-8400. Ed. Mary Louise Hewitt. (avail. on CD-ROM)
●Also available online. Vendors: Wilsonline.

370   US
EDUCATION STATISTICS, NEW YORK STATE; prepared especially for members of the Legislature. 1968. a. free. ‡ Education Department, Information Center on Education, Albany, NY 12234. charts. stat. circ. controlled. (back issues avail.)

370   TZ   ISSN 0856-0005
EDUCATIONAL ABSTRACTS FOR TANZANIA. 1983. a. Library Services Board, National Documentation Centre, P.O. Box 9283, Dar es Salaan, Tanzania. Ed. E.A. Mwinymvua. circ. 1,000.

371 016   US   ISSN 0013-1601
EDUCATIONAL ADMINISTRATION ABSTRACTS. 1966. q. $45 to individuals; institutions $110. (University Council for Educational Administration) Sage Publications, Inc., 2111 W. Hillcrest Dr., Newbury Park, CA 91320. TEL 805-499-0721. (Co-sponsor: Washington State University) Ed. Donald Reed. adv. abstr. index. (also avail. in microform from UMI; back issues avail.; reprint service avail. from UMI,ISI) Formerly: Educational Abstracts.

371.33 016   US
EDUCATIONAL FILM AND VIDEO (YEAR); a rental catalog. 1950. triennial (with yearly supplements) free. University of Michigan, Media Resources Center, 400 Fourth St., Ann Arbor, MI 48103. TEL 313-764-5360. Ed. Ann M. Sprunger. adv. circ. 20,000.
Formerly: Educational Films.

EDUCATION — ABSTRACTING, BIBLIOGRAPHIES, STATISTICS

371.3 011 UK ISSN 0266-3368
EDUCATIONAL TECHNOLOGY ABSTRACTS.
1985. q. $120. Carfax Publishing Co., P.O. Box 25, Abingdon, Oxfordshire OX14 3UE, England (U.S. distr.: 85 Ash St., Hopkinton, MA 01748) Ed. Keith Roach. adv. bk. rev. index. (also avail. in microfiche; back issues avail.)

016 370 US ISSN 0000-0825
EL HI TEXTBOOKS AND SERIALS IN PRINT; including related teaching materials. 1969. a. $85. R.R. Bowker Company, Database Publishing Group, 245 W. 17th St., New York, NY 10011. TEL 800-521-8110.
Former titles: Textbooks in Print & El Hi Textbooks in Print (ISSN 0070-9565)

370 318 MX
ESTADISTICA BASICA DEL SISTEMA EDUCATIVO NACIONAL. 1975. irreg. Secretaria de Educacion Publica, Mexico, D. F., Mexico.

370 310 PN ISSN 0378-4967
ESTADISTICA PANAMENA. SITUACION CULTURAL. SECCION 511. EDUCACION. 1967. a. Bl.0.75. Direccion de Estadistica y Censo, Contraloria General, Apartado 5213, Panama 5, Panama. circ. 1,100.

370 016 US
FILM & VIDEO FINDER. 1971. a. $295. (National Information Center for Educational Media) Access Innovations, Inc., Box 40130, Albuquerque, NM 87196. TEL 505-265-3591. (also avail. in microfiche; avail. on CD ROM)
●Also available online.
Formed by the merger of (1967-1987): N I C E M Index to 16mm Educational Films; (1971-1987): N I C E M Index to Educational Video Tapes.

314 378 FI ISSN 0355-2225
FINLAND. TILASTOKESKUS. KORKEAKOULUT/FINLAND. STATISTIKCENTRALEN. HOEGSKOLORA/FINLAND. CENTRAL STATISTICAL OFFICE. HIGHER EDUCATION. (Section 37 of Official Statistics of Finland) (Text in English, Finnish and Swedish) 1969. a. Fmk.70. Tilastokeskus, Annankatu 44, SF-00100 Helsinki 10, Finland (Subscr. to: Government Printing Centre, Box 516, SF-00100 Helsinki 10, Finland)

314 373 FI ISSN 0355-2446
FINLAND. TILASTOKESKUS. YLEISSIVISTAVAT OPPILAITOKSET/FINLAND. STATISTIKCENTRALEN. ALLMAENBILDANDE LAEROANSTALTER/FINLAND. CENTRAL STATISTICAL OFFICE. GENERAL EDUCATION. (Section 10 A of Official Statistics of Finland) (Text in Finnish, Swedish and English) 1973. a. Fmk.11. Tilastokeskus, Annankatu 44, SF-00100 Helsinki 10, Finland (Subscr. to: Government Printing Centre, Box 516, SF-00100 Helsinki 10, Finland)
Formed by the merger of: Finland. Tilastokeskus. Kansanopetus & Finland. Tilastokeskus. Oppikoulut.

FOR YOUNGER READERS, BRAILLE AND TALKING BOOKS (LARGE PRINT EDITION) see BLIND — Abstracting, Bibliographies, Statistics

016 370 DK ISSN 0107-1491
FORLAGSSERIEKATALOG FOR BOERNE- OG SKOLEBIBLIOTEKER. 1980. a. Kr.129.20. Bibliotekscentralen, Tempovej 7-11, DK-2750 Ballerup, Denmark.
Formerly: Forlagsseriekatalog.

370 FR
FRANCE. INSTITUT NATIONAL DE LA STATISTIQUE ET DES ETUDES ECONOMIQUES. L'ENSEIGNEMENT DANS LES DEPARTMENTS D'OUTRE-MER. irreg. Institut National de la Statistique et des Etudes Economiques, 97487 St. Denis, France.

370.967 GO
GABON. MINISTERE DE L'EDUCATION NATIONALE. ANNUAIRE STATISTIQUE DE L'ENSEIGNEMENT. a. Ministere de l'Education Nationale, Service des Statistiques Scolaires et de l'Emploi, B.P. 334, Libreville, Gabon. illus.
Formerly: Statistiques de l'Enseignement au Gabon.

370 GM
GAMBIA. CENTRAL STATISTICS DEPARTMENT. EDUCATION STATISTICS. a. d.10. Central Statistics Department, Wellington St., Banjul, Gambia. stat.
Former titles: Gambia. Education Department. Education Statistics; Gambia. Education Department. Annual Report and Statistics.

370 317 US ISSN 0094-1557
GEORGIA. DEPARTMENT OF EDUCATION. STATISTICAL REPORT. a. Department of Education, Atlanta, GA 30334. TEL 404-656-2534. stat. Key Title: Statistical Report - Georgia Department of Education.

370 314 GW ISSN 0072-1778
GERMANY (FEDERAL REPUBLIC, 1949-). STATISTISCHES BUNDESAMT. FACHSERIE 11: BILDUNG UND KULTUR. (Consists of several subseries) 1960. a. price varies. W. Kohlhammer-Verlag GmbH, Abt. Veroeffentlichungen des Statistischen Bundesamtes, Philipp-Reis-Str. 3, Postfach 421120, 6500 Mainz 42, W. Germany (B.R.D.)

370 US
GUIDE TO AMERICAN EDUCATIONAL DIRECTORIES. triennial. $55. Todd Publications, Box 92, Lenox Hill Sta., New York, NY 10021. Ed. Barry Klein.

370 016 II ISSN 0019-4697
INDIAN EDUCATION ABSTRACTS. 1955. q. Rs.15.60($5.62) Ministry of Education and Social Welfare, Department of Education, Shastri Bhavan, New Dehli 110001, India. abstr. bibl. index. circ. controlled.

378 310 IS
ISRAEL. CENTRAL BUREAU OF STATISTICS. INPUTS IN RESEARCH AND DEVELOPMENT IN ACADEMIC INSTITUTIONS. (Text in English and Hebrew) 1970. irreg. price varies. Central Bureau of Statistics, P.O.B. 13015, Jerusalem, Israel. (Co-sponsor: National Council for Research and Development) charts. stat.

372 IS ISSN 0075-1065
ISRAEL. CENTRAL BUREAU OF STATISTICS. SCHOOLS AND KINDERGARTENS. (Subseries of its Special Series) (Text in English and Hebrew) 1954. irreg., latest issue, no.701, 1982. $5.50. Central Bureau of Statistics, Box 13015, Jerusalem, Israel.

310 IS ISSN 0333-600X
ISRAEL. CENTRAL BUREAU OF STATISTICS. STAFF IN UNIVERSITIES. (Text in English, Hebrew) 1981. biennial. Central Bureau of Statistics, Hakirya, Romema, 91130 Jerusalem, Israel. Ed. Ms. Lifshitz. (back issues avail.)

378 016 GE ISSN 0323-455X
JAHRESVERZEICHNIS DER HOCHSCHULSCHRIFTEN DER DDR, DER BRD UND WESTBERLINS. 1884. irreg. price varies. VEB Bibliographisches Institut, Gerichtsweg 26, 7010 Leipzig, E. Germany (D.D.R.)
Formerly: Jahresverzeichnis der Deutschen Hochschulschriften (ISSN 0075-2940)

370.196 016 US ISSN 0094-2383
JOURNAL OF ABSTRACTS IN INTERNATIONAL EDUCATION. 1970. s-a. $4. (University of Toledo, College of Education) University of Toledo Press, Toledo, OH 43606 TEL 419-372-7334. (Subscr. address: c/o Malcolm Campbell, Bowling Green State University, Bowling Green, OH 43403) (Co-sponsors: Bowling Green State University, University of Portland) Ed.Bd. adv. bk. rev. abstr. circ. 250.

378.1 US
KENTUCKY. COUNCIL ON HIGHER EDUCATION. ORIGIN OF KENTUCKY COLLEGE & UNIVERSITY ENROLLMENTS. 1968. a. free. Council on Higher Education, 1050 US 127 Bypass, Frankfort, KY 40601. TEL 502-564-7980. Dir. Sue D. McDade. charts. illus. stat. circ. 500. (also avail. in microfiche)
Formerly: Kentucky. Council on Public Higher Education. Origin of Enrollments, Accredited Colleges and Universities (ISSN 0098-9770)

370 315 KO
KOREA (REPUBLIC). MINISTRY OF EDUCATION. BASIC STATISTICS OF EDUCATION. a. Ministry of Education, Seoul, S. Korea. charts. stat.

370 315 KO
KOREA (REPUBLIC). MINISTRY OF EDUCATION. EDUCATIONAL DEVELOPMENT IN KOREA; a graphic presentation. a. Ministry of Education, Seoul, S. Korea. charts. illus.

016 DK ISSN 0106-7737
LANDSCENTRALEN FOR UNDERVISNINGSMIDLER. BAANDCENTRALEN. BAANDKATALOG. 1978. a. Kr.21. Landscentralen for Undervisningsmidler, Baandcentralen, Oernevej 30, 2400 Copenhagen NV, Denmark.
Formerly: Landscentralen for Undervisningsmidler. Baandcentralen. Katalog.

400 370 016 UK ISSN 0261-4448
LANGUAGE TEACHING. 1968. q. $35.50 to individuals; institutions $68. Cambridge University Press, Edinburgh Bldg., Shaftesbury Rd., Cambridge CB2 2RU, England (and 32 E. 57th St., New York, N.Y. 10022) Ed. Valerie Kinsella. adv. abstr. bibl. index. cum.index. circ. 2,200.
Former titles (until 1982): Language Teaching and Linguistics Abstracts (ISSN 0306-6304); (until 1975): Language-Teaching Abstracts (ISSN 0023-8279); English Teaching Abstracts.

370 016 KO
LIST OF THESES FOR THE DOCTOR'S AND MASTER'S DEGREE IN KOREA/HANKUK BAKSA MIT SEUKSA HAK WEE LONMUN CHONG MOKROK. (Text in Korean) 1969. a. free. National Assembly, Library, Processing & Reference Bureau, Yoido-Dong 1, Yeongdeungpo-gu, Seoul, S. Korea. circ. 700.

371 MM ISSN 0076-3489
MALTA. CENTRAL OFFICE OF STATISTICS. EDUCATION STATISTICS. a. Central Office of Statistics, Auberge d'Italie, Valletta, Malta (Subscr. to: Information Division, Auberge de Castille, Valletta, Malta)

378 016 US
MISSISSIPPI STATE UNIVERSITY ABSTRACTS OF THESES AND DISSERTATIONS. 1953. biennial. free. Mississippi State University, Graduate School, c/o Mitchell Memorial Library, Box 5408, Mississippi State, MS 39762. TEL 601-325-3060. Ed. George R. Lewis. circ. controlled.
Formerly: Mississippi State University Abstracts of Theses (ISSN 0540-3847)

370 016 UK ISSN 0260-9770
MULTICULTURAL EDUCATION ABSTRACTS. 1982. q. $120. Carfax Publishing Co., P.O. Box 25, Abingdon, Oxfordshire OX14 3UE, England (U.S. distr.: 85 Ash St., Hopkinton, MA 01748) Ed. Derek Cherrington. adv. bk. rev. cum.index. (also avail. in microfiche; back issues avail.)

N I C E M INDEX TO PRODUCERS AND DISTRIBUTORS. (National Information Center for Educational Media) see MOTION PICTURES — Abstracting, Bibliographies, Statistics

370 016 US
N I C E M INDEX TO 35MM EDUCATIONAL FILMSTRIPS. vol.6, 1976. irreg. $200. (National Information Center for Educational Media) Access Innovations, Inc., Box 40130, Albuquerque, NM 87196. TEL 505-265-3591. (avail. on CD ROM)
●Also available online.

EDUCATION — ABSTRACTING, BIBLIOGRAPHIES, STATISTICS

371 379   NE   ISSN 0168-5244
NETHERLANDS. CENTRAAL BUREAU VOOR DE STATISTIEK. PER LEERLING BESCHIKBAAR GESTELDE BEDRAGEN VOOR HET LAGER ONDERWIJS. AMOUNTS PER PUPIL PROVIDED FOR PRIMARY EDUCATION. (Text in Dutch and English) 1949. a. fl.9.50. Centraal Bureau voor de Statistiek, Prinses Beatrixlaan 428, Voorburg, Netherlands (Orders to: Staatsuitgeverij, Christoffel Plantijnstraat, The Hague, Netherlands)
    Formerly: Netherlands. Centraal Bureau voor de Statistiek. Statistiek van de Gemeentewege per Leerling Beschikbaar Gestelde Bedragenter Bestrijding van de Materiele Exploitatiekosten der Lagere Scholen. Statistics of the Amounts per Pupil Provided by the Municipality to Meet the Material Cost of Elementary Education (ISSN 0077-7226)

371.3 314   NE   ISSN 0168-423X
NETHERLANDS. CENTRAAL BUREAU VOOR DE STATISTIEK. STATISTIEK VAN DE VOORLICHTING BIJ SCHOLEN EN BEROEPSKEUZE. STATISTICS OF VOCATIONAL GUIDANCE. 1946. a. fl.8.40. Centraal Bureau voor de Statistiek, Prinses Beatrixlaan 428, Voorburg, Netherlands (Orders to: Staatsuitgeverij, Christoffel Plantijnstraat, The Hague, Netherlands)
    Formerly: Netherlands. Centraal Bureau voor de Statistiek. Statistiek van de Voorlichting Bij Beroepskeuze. Statistics of Vocational Guidance and Selection of Personnel (ISSN 0077-7218)

378   NE
NETHERLANDS. CENTRAAL BUREAU VOOR DE STATISTIEK. STATISTIEK VAN HET BEROEPSONDERWIJS: OPLEIDINGSSCHOLEN KLEUTERLEIDSTERS EN PEDAGOGISCHE ACADEMIES. (Text in Dutch and English) 1943/44. a. fl.9.40. Centraal Bureau voor de Statistiek, Prinses Beatrixlaan 428, Voorburg, Netherlands (Orders to: Staatsuitgeverij, Christoffel Plantijnstraat, The Hague, Netherlands)
    Formerly: Netherlands. Centraal Bureau voor de Statistiek. Statistiek van het Kweekschoolonderwijs. Statistics on Teacher Training Colleges (ISSN 0077-7323)

375 314   NE   ISSN 0168-5457
NETHERLANDS. CENTRAAL BUREAU VOOR DE STATISTIEK. STATISTIEK VAN HET BEROEPSONDERWIJS: TECHNISCH EN NAUTISCH ONDERWIJS. STATISTICS ON VOCATIONAL TRAINING. (Text in Dutch and English) 1968/69. a. price varies. Centraal Bureau voor de Statistiek, Prinses Beatrixlaan 428, Voorburg, Netherlands (Orders to: Staatsuitgeverij, Christoffel Plantijnstraat, The Hague, Netherlands)
    Formerly: Netherlands. Centraal Bureau voor de Statistiek. Statistiek van het Beroepsonderwijs (ISSN 0077-7285)

375 314   NE
NETHERLANDS. CENTRAAL BUREAU VOOR DE STATISTIEK. STATISTIEK VAN HET HOGER BEROEPSONDERWIJS: AGRARISCH ONDERWIJS. (Text in Dutch and English) 1940/41. a. fl.8.65. Centraal Bureau voor de Statistiek, Prinses Beatrixlaan 428, Voorburg, Netherlands (Orders to: Staatsuitgeverij, Christoffel Plantijnstraat, The Hague, Netherlands)
    Former titles: Netherlands. Centraal Bureau voor de Statistiek. Statistiek van het Beroepsonderwijs: Landbouwonderwijs; Netherlands. Centraal Bureau voor de Statistiek. Statistiek van het Land- en Tuinbouwonderwijs. Statistics Concerning Agricultural and Horticultural Education (ISSN 0077-7331); Netherlands. Centraal Bureau voor de Statistiek. Statistiek van het Beroepsonderwijs: Agrarisch Onderwijs (ISSN 0169-1007)

373   NE   ISSN 0168-485X
NETHERLANDS. CENTRAAL BUREAU VOOR DE STATISTIEK. VOORTGEZET ONDERWIJS REGIONAAL BEZIEN. 1949. a. fl.20.45. Centraal Bureau voor de Statistiek, Prinses Beatrixlaan 428, Voorburg, Netherlands (Orders to: Staatsuitgeverij, Christoffel Plantijnstraat, The Hague, Netherlands) circ. 500.

379   US
NORTH DAKOTA. DEPARTMENT OF PUBLIC INSTRUCTION. BIENNIAL REPORT OF THE SUPERINTENDENT OF PUBLIC INSTRUCTION. 1888. biennial. Department of Public Instruction, Bismarck, ND 58505. TEL 701-224-2260. Ed. Joe Linnertz. circ. 5,000.

371   NO   ISSN 0800-2169
NORWAY. STATISTISK SENTRALBYRAA. UTDANNINGSSTATISTIKK: EDUCATIONAL STATISTICS. (Subseries of its Norges Offiseille Statistikk) (Text in Norwegian and English) 1952/53. a. Kr.30. Statistisk Sentralbyraa, Box 8131-Dep., 0033 Oslo 1, Norway. circ. 1,800.

370 016   US   ISSN 0029-3962
NOTES AND ABSTRACTS IN AMERICAN AND INTERNATIONAL EDUCATION. 1963. irreg. (1-2/yr.), no.65, 1985. $5. (University of Michigan, Associates in the Social Foundations of Education) Prakken Publications, Inc., 416 Longshore Dr., Box 8623, Ann Arbor, MI 48107. TEL 313-769-1211. Eds. Claude A. Eggertsen, Alan H. Jones. bk. rev. abstr. bibl. circ. 350. (back issues avail.)

378 314   AU   ISSN 0067-2343
OESTERREICHISCHE HOCHSCHULSTATISTIK. (Subseries of: Beitraege zur Oesterreichischen Statistik) 1965/66. a. S.140. ‡ Oesterreichisches Statistisches Zentralamt, Hintere Zollamsstr. 2b, 1033 Vienna, Austria. circ. 1,000.

378.771   US   ISSN 0094-6109
OHIO HIGHER EDUCATION. BASIC DATA SERIES. 1970. biennial, latest 1983. free. Board of Regents, 30 E. Broad St., Columbus, OH 43215. TEL 614-466-6000. Ed. Rosemary Jones. illus. circ. 500. Indexed: ERIC.

370 318   PN
PANAMA. DIRECCION NACIONAL DE PLANEAMIENTO Y REFORMA EDUCATIVA. DEPARTAMENTO DE ESTADISTICA. SERIE: ANALISIS ESTADISTICO. irreg. Direccion Nacional de Planeamiento y Reforma Educativa, Departamento de Estadistica, Panama, Panama.

370 314   PL   ISSN 0079-2799
POLAND. GLOWNY URZAD STATYSTYCZNY. ROCZNIK STATYSTYCZNY SZKOLNICTWA. YEARBOOK OF EDUCATION STATISTICS. (Subseries of its: Statystyka Polski) 1967. a. Glowny Urzad Statystyczny, Al. Niepodleglosci 208, 00-925 Warsaw, Poland.

QUALITY CONTROL AND APPLIED STATISTICS; abstract service. see *ABSTRACTING AND INDEXING SERVICES*

370 016   UK   ISSN 0080-1674
RESEARCH IN THE HISTORY OF EDUCATION: A LIST OF THESES FOR HIGHER DEGREES IN THE UNIVERSITIES OF ENGLAND AND WALES. (1969 Ed. includes Ireland) 1969. a. £1.85. History of Education Society, c/o Mrs. B. Starkey, 4 Marydene Dr., Evington, Leicester LE5 6HD, England. Ed. V.F. Gilbert. circ. 250.

378 016   UK   ISSN 0034-5326
RESEARCH INTO HIGHER EDUCATION ABSTRACTS. 1966. 3/yr. $120. (Society for Research into Higher Education) Carfax Publishing Co., P.O. Box 25, Abingdon, Oxfordshire OX14 3UE, England (U.S. distr.: 85 Ash St., Hopkinton, MA 01748) Ed. Gareth Williams. adv. bk. rev. cum.index. circ. 1,200. (also avail. in microfiche; back issues avail.)

370 016   US   ISSN 0098-0897
RESOURCES IN EDUCATION. Short title: R I E. Cumulated as: Resources in Education. Annual Cumulation (ISSN 0197-9973) 1966. m. $56. (U.S. Department of Education, Office of Educational Research and Improvement) Educational Resources Information Center, E R I C Processing and Reference Facility, 4833 Rugby Ave., Ste. 301, Bethesda, MD 20814 TEL 301-656-9723. (Subscr. to Supt. of Documents, U.S. Government Printing Office, Washington, DC 20402) Ed. Carolyn Weller. abstr. bibl. cum.index s-a. circ. 4,000. (also avail. in microform from UMI; reprint service avail. from UMI)
    ●Also available online. Vendors: BRS, CISTI, DIALOG, Orbit Information Technologies.
    Formerly (until 1975): Research in Education (ISSN 0034-5229)

370   US
RHODE ISLAND. DEPARTMENT OF EDUCATION. (YEAR) STATISTICAL TABLES. 1932. a. free. Department of Education, 22 Hayes St., Providence, RI 02908. TEL 401-277-2842. Ed. Donley R. Taft. stat. circ. controlled. (tabloid format)

370   RW
RWANDA. MINISTERE DE L'ENSEIGNEMEMT PRIMAIRE ET SECONDAIRE. DIRECTION DE LA PLANIFICATION. STATISTIQUE DE L'ENSEIGNEMENT. 1966. a. 10 F. Ministere de l'Enseignement Primaire et Secondaire, Direction de la Planification, B.P. 622, Kigali, Rwanda. circ. 150.
    Formerly: Rwanda. Ministere de l'Education Nationale. Direction de la Planification, Statistique et Information. Statistique de l'Enseignement.

SAUDI ARABIA. MINISTRY OF EDUCATION. ANNUAL STATISTICAL REPORT. see *EDUCATION — International Education Programs*

370.196   SU
SAUDI ARABIA. MINISTRY OF EDUCATION. EDUCATIONAL ABSTRACTS. (Text in Arabic) s-a. Ministry of Education, Center for Statistical Data, Box 2871, Riyadh, Saudi Arabia.

370.953   SU
SAUDI ARABIA. MINISTRY OF EDUCATION. EDUCATIONAL STATISTICS. (Text in Arabic and English) irreg. Ministry of Education, Statistics, Research and Education Documents Unit, Statistics Section, Box 2871, Riyadh, Saudi Arabia. illus.

370 016   UK   ISSN 0261-2755
SCHOOL ORGANISATION & MANAGEMENT ABSTRACTS. 1982. q. $120. Carfax Publishing Co., P.O. Box 25, Abingdon, Oxfordshire OX14 3UE, England (U.S. distr.: 85 Ash St., Hopkinton, MA 01748) Ed. David Smetherham. cum.index. (also avail. in microfiche; back issues avail.)

032 370   AT   ISSN 0311-2373
SERIALS IN EDUCATION IN AUSTRALIAN LIBRARIES: A UNION LIST. 1972. irreg. Australian Council for Educational Research, Box 210, Hawthorn, Vic. 3122, Australia. Eds. Margaret A. Findlay, Elspeth Miller.

370 016   UK   ISSN 0038-0415
SOCIOLOGY OF EDUCATION ABSTRACTS. 1965. q. $180. Carfax Publishing Co., P.O. Box 25, Abingdon, Oxfordshire OX14 3UE, England (U.S. distr.: 85 Ash St., Hopkinton, MA 01748) Ed. Dr. Roger Dale. cum.index. circ. 1,450. (also avail. in microfiche; back issues avail.) Indexed: E.I.

370   SA
SOUTH AFRICA. CENTRAL STATISTICAL SERVICE. EDUCATION: ASIAN. (Report No. 21-03) a. Central Statistical Service, Private Bag X44, Pretoria 0001, South Africa (Orders to: Government Printer, Bosman St., Private Bag X85, Pretoria 0001, South Africa)
    Former titles: South Africa. Department of Statistics. Education: Asian; South Africa. Department of Statistics. Education: Coloureds and Asians.

370   SA
SOUTH AFRICA. CENTRAL STATISTICAL SERVICE. EDUCATION: WHITES. (Report No. 21-02) a. Central Statistical Service, Private Bag X44, Pretoria 0001, South Africa (Orders to: Government Printer, Bosman St., Private Bag X85, Pretoria 0001, South Africa)
    Formerly: South Africa. Department of Statistics. Education: Whites.

613.7 016   UK
SPORTS DOCUMENTATION CENTRE. SERIAL. (Text in English and other languages) 1974. a. free. Sports Documentation Centre, Main Library, Box 363, University of Birmingham, Birmingham B15 2TT, England. Ed.Bd. circ. 333.
    Formerly: Sports Documentation Centre. List of Periodical and Abstracting and Indexing Journal Holdings.
Physical education

370 016   US   ISSN 0039-0046
STATE EDUCATION JOURNAL INDEX; an annotated index to materials in the field of education. 1962. s-a. $75. State Education Journal Index Publications, Box 244, Westminster, CO 80030. TEL 303-494-8073. Ed. Dr. L. Stanley Ratliff. bk. rev. bibl. circ. 500.

370 312   CY   ISSN 0253-8733
STATISTICS OF EDUCATION IN CYPRUS. (Text in English) 1969. a. cyprus pounds 4. Ministry of Finance, Department of Statistics and Research, Nicosia, Cyprus.

370 UK ISSN 0262-8317
STATISTICS OF EDUCATION IN WALES. 1975. a.
£4. Welsh Office, Economic & Statistical Services
Division, New Crown Bldg., Cathays Park, Cardiff
CF1 3NQ, Wales. Ed. E. Swires-Hennessy. stat.
circ. 700.

370 316 SQ
SWAZILAND. CENTRAL STATISTICAL OFFICE.
EDUCATION STATISTICS. 1968. a. free. Central
Statistical Office, Box 456, Mbabane, Swaziland.

370 SW ISSN 0082-0342
SWEDEN. STATISTISKA CENTRALBYRAAN.
STATISTISKA MEDDELANDEN. SUBGROUP U
(EDUCATION AND RESEARCH) (Text in
Swedish; table heads and summaries in English)
1963 N.S. irreg. Kr.500. Statistiska Centralbyraan,
Distribution, S-701 89 Oerebro, Sweden. circ. 2,000.

370 SZ
SWITZERLAND. BUNDESAMT FUER STATISTIK.
SCHUELERSTATISTIK/STATISTIQUE DES
ELEVES. (Text in French and German) 1976. a.
Bundesamt fuer Statistik, Hallwylstrasse 15, 3003
Berne, Switzerland.

TALKING BOOKS, ADULT (LARGE PRINT
EDITION) see *BLIND — Abstracting,
Bibliographies, Statistics*

600 378 016 UK ISSN 0040-0920
TECHNICAL EDUCATION ABSTRACTS. 1961. q.
$120. Carfax Publishing Co., P.O. Box 25,
Abingdon, Oxfordshire OX14 3UE, England (U.S.
distr.: 85 Ash St., Hopkinton, MA 01748) Ed. Dr.
Roger Dale. cum.index. circ. 1,200. (also avail. in
microfiche; back issues avail.)

370 UN
UNESCO. REGIONAL OFFICE FOR
EDUCATION IN ASIA AND THE PACIFIC.
ABSTRACT BIBLIOGRAPHY SERIES ON
POPULATION EDUCATION. (Text in English) a.
Unesco, Principal Regional Office for Education in
Asia and the Pacific, Population Education
Programme Service, G.P.O. Box 1425, Bangkok
10501, Thailand.

370 US
U.S. NATIONAL CENTER FOR EDUCATION
STATISTICS. DIGEST OF EDUCATION
STATISTICS. 1962. a. U.S. National Center for
Education Statistics, U.S. Department of Education,
400 Maryland Ave., S.W., Washington, DC 20202
TEL 202-655-4000. (Orders to: Supt. of Documents,
Washington, DC 20402)
Formerly: U.S. National Center for Education
Statistics. Digest of Educational Statistics (ISSN
0083-2634)

378 016 YU
UNIVERZITET U SARAJEVU. DOKTORSKE
DISERTACIJE. REZIMEI. (Supplement to:
Univerzitet u Sarajevu. Bilten) 1969. a. Univerzitet
u Sarajevu, Vojvode Stepe obala 7/111, 71000
Sarajevo, Yugoslavia. illus.

378 016 US
VANDERBILT UNIVERSITY. ABSTRACTS OF
THESES. 1950. irreg. Vanderbilt University,
Publications Office, 117 Alumni Hall, Nashville, TN
37240. TEL 615-322-6096. circ. 800.

013 US ISSN 0083-6451
VIRGINIA MILITARY INSTITUTE, LEXINGTON.
PUBLICATIONS, THESES, AND
DISSERTATIONS OF THE STAFF AND
FACULTY. 1963/64. irreg., 9th 1983. free. Virginia
Military Institute, Preston Library, Lexington, VA
24450. TEL 703-463-6201. Dir. Gen. Sam S.
Walker. circ. 500.

082 KO
YONSEI UNIVERSITY. GRADUATE SCHOOL.
ABSTRACTS OF FACULTY RESEARCH
REPORTS. (Text in English) 1972. a. Yonsei
University, Graduate School, Seoul, S. Korea.

371.0025 NZ ISSN 0111-0489
YOUTH STUDIES IN NEW ZEALAND; a
bibliography 1960-1983. 1984. a. NZ.$9.95 per no.
Ministry of Recreation and Sport, Department of
Internal Affairs, Private Bag, Wellington, New
Zealand. Ed. Ray Jones. circ. 100.

370 314 YU
YUGOSLAVIA. SAVEZNI ZAVOD ZA
STATISTIKU. OSNOVNA I SREDNJE. (Subseries
of its Statisticki Bilten) irreg. 30 din.($1.11) Savezni
Zavod za Statistiku, Kneza Milosa 20, Belgrade,
Yugoslavia. circ. 1,000.

370 314 YU ISSN 0513-0832
YUGOSLAVIA. SAVEZNI ZAVOD ZA
STATISTIKU. UCENICI U PRIVREDI. (Subseries
of its Statisticki Bilten) irreg. 20 din.($1.11) Savezni
Zavod za Statistiku, Kneza Milosa 20, Belgrade,
Yugoslavia. circ. 1,000.

EDUCATION — Adult Education

374 US
ADULT & COMMUNITY EDUCATION
ORGANIZATIONS & LEADERS DIRECTORY.
1977. a. $40. Today Publications and News Service,
Inc., 621 National Press Building, Washington, DC
20045. TEL 202-638-0348. Ed. Lester A. Barrer.

374 KE
AFRICAN ADULT EDUCATION ASSOCIATION.
JOURNAL. (Text in English; summaries in French)
1979. irreg. $6.50 to non-members; $4. to members.
African Adult Education Association, Box 50768,
Nairobi, Kenya. Ed. Paul Wangoola. circ. 500. (back
issues avail.)

374 US
ALASKA ADULT EDUCATION. a. Department of
Education, Pouch G, Juneau, AK 99811. TEL 907-
465-2800.

374 BG ISSN 0070-8135
BANGLADESH. EDUCATION DIRECTORATE.
REPORT ON PILOT PROJECT ON ADULT
EDUCATION. Bengali; edition: Barshika Bibarani
Bayaska Siksha Parikshya Prakalpa Bangladesh.
(Text in English) 1964. a. Tk.2 per no. Education
Directorate, Adult Education Branch, B E E R I,
Dhanmond, Dacca 5, Bangladesh. circ. 500.
Supersedes: East Pakistan. Education Directorate.
Adult Education Branch. Report on Pilot Project on
Adult Education.

C C E T S W REPORTING. (Central Council for
Education and Training in Social Work) see
SOCIOLOGY

374 II
C I I L ADULT LITERACY SERIES. (Text in
English) 1976. irreg., latest 1979. Central Institute
of Indian Languages, Manasagangotri, Mysore
570006, India. bibl.

374.4 CN
CANADIAN UNIVERSITY DISTANCE
EDUCATION DIRECTORY. 1957/58. a. Can.$15
to non-members. Association of Universities and
Colleges of Canada (A U C C) - Association des
Universites et Colleges du Canada, 151 Slater,
Ottawa, Ont. K1P 5N1, Canada. circ. 1,000.
Former titles (until 1984): Directory of
University Correspondence Courses (ISSN 0708-
2193) & Canadian Correspondence Courses for
University Credit (ISSN 0068-855X)

374 AT ISSN 0310-1649
CANBERRA PAPERS IN CONTINUING
EDUCATION. 1972; N.S. 1974. irreg., latest no.5,
1985. price varies. Australian National University,
Centre for Continuing Education, c/o The Director,
Box 4, Canberra, A.C.T. 2600, Australia.

374.013 UY
CATALOGO DE PUBLICACIONES DIDACTICAS
LATINOAMERICANAS DE FORMACION
PROFESIONAL. 1976. irreg. price varies. Centro
Interamericano de Investigacion y Documentacion
Sobre Formacion Profesional, Avda. Uruguay 1238,
Casilla de Correo 1761, Montevideo, Uruguay.
Supersedes (1969-1976): Catalogo de Manuales
Latinoamericanos.

374.013 UY
CENTRO INTERAMERICANO DE
INVESTIGACION Y DOCUMENTACION
SOBRE FORMACION PROFESIONAL.
INFORMES. 1964. irreg. price varies. Centro
Interamericano de Investigacion y Documentacion
Sobre Formacion Profesional, Avda. Uruguay 1238,
Casilla de Correo 1761, Montevideo, Uruguay.

374.013 UY
COLECCIONES BASICAS C I N T E R F O R.
(Text in Spanish and Portuguese) 1970. irreg. price
varies. Centro Interamericano de Investigacion y
Documentacion Sobre Formacion Profesional, Avda.
Uruguay 1238, Casilla de Correo 1761, Montevideo,
Uruguay. Indexed: CIRF Abstr.

028 US
COLLEGE AND ADULT READING. 1962. irreg.,
vol.12, 1984. North Central Reading Association,
Rm. 14 Morehouse Hall, Drake University, Des
Moines, IA 50311. Ed. Joseph Fisher. bk. rev. circ.
1,000.
Former titles: N C R A Yearbook; College and
Adult Reading (ISSN 0069-553X)

374 301 BO
CUADERNOS C I P C A (SERIE POPULAR) 1974.
irreg. price varies. Centro de Investigacion y
Promocion del Campesinado, Casilla 5854, La Paz,
Bolivia.
Study and teaching

374 PE
CUADERNOS DE CAPACITACION. 1979. irreg.
$40 includes subscr. to: Testimonios (en Historieta),
Cuadernos de Estudio and Cuadernos Populares.
Comision Evangelica Latinoamericana de Educacion
Cristiana, Av. General Garzon 2267, Lima 11, Peru.

374 MX
CUADERNOS DEL C R E F A L. 1976. irreg.
Centro Regional de Educacion de Adultos y
Alfabetizacion Funcional para America Latina,
Quinta Erendira, 61600 Patzcuaro, Michoacan,
Mexico. circ. 2,500. Indexed: Rural
Recreat.Tour.Abstr. World Agri.Econ. & Rural
Sociol.Abstr.

374 PE
CUADERNOS POPULARES. 1977. irreg. $40
(includes subscr. to Testimonios (en Historieta),
Cuadernos de Capacitation, and Cuadernos de
Estudios) Comision Evangelica Latinoamericana de
Educacion Cristiana, Av. General Garzon 2267,
Lima 11, Peru.

374 DK
DANISH FOLK HIGH SCHOOL TODAY. 1981. a.
free. Hoejskolernes Sekretariat, Farvergade 27/
opg.G, 1463 Copenhagen K, Denmark. Ed. Arne
Andresen. illus. circ. 8,000.

374 GW
DEUTSCHER FACHHOCHSCHULFUEHRER.
1954. irreg., latest, 23nd edition. DM.48.40. V D E-
Verlag GmbH, Bismarckstr. 33, 1000 Berlin 12, W.
Germany (B.R.D.) adv. bk. rev.

FORSCHUNGSDOKUMENTATION ZUR
ARBEITSMARKT- UND BERUFSFORSCHUNG.
see *BUSINESS AND ECONOMICS — Labor And
Industrial Relations*

374 UK ISSN 0260-3306
GREAT BRITAIN. ADVISORY COUNCIL FOR
ADULT AND CONTINUING EDUCATION.
ANNUAL REPORT. 1979. a. 2.50. H.M.S.O., P.O.
Box 569, London SE1 9NH, England. (reprint
service avail. from UMI)

GUIDE TO COLLEGE COURSES IN FILM AND
TELEVISION. see *MOTION PICTURES*

HANDBOOK OF TRADE AND TECHNICAL
CAREERS AND TRAINING. see
EDUCATION — Guides To Schools And Colleges

374 CN ISSN 0705-1166
I N D E C COMMUNICATOR. (Supplement
included: News and Notes) 1962. a. Can.$15.
Alberta Teachers' Association, Industrial Education
Council, 11010 142nd St., Edmonton, Alta. T5N
2R1, Canada. Ed. Norman Mathew. bk. rev. circ.
600.

379 US ISSN 0091-5882
IDAHO. STATE BOARD FOR VOCATIONAL
EDUCATION. ANNUAL DESCRIPTIVE
REPORT OF PROGRAM ACTIVITIES FOR
VOCATIONAL EDUCATION. 1963. a. State
Board for Vocational Education, 650 W. State St.,
Boise, ID 83720. TEL 208-334-3210. Key Title:
Annual Descriptive Report of Program Activities for
Vocational Education.

374   TZ   ISSN 0856-1109
JOURNAL OF ADULT EDUCATION. (Text in English) 1975. a. $12. Institute of Adult Education, Box 20679, Dar es Salaam, Tanzania. Ed. Lawrence Kagaruki. adv. bk. rev. circ. 1,500.
    Formerly (until 1977): Fikara.

374   CN   ISSN 0381-1387
LEARNING. 1976. irreg. Can.$18. Canadian Association for Adult Education, 29 Prince Arthur Ave., Toronto, Ont. M5R 1B2, Canada. TEL 416-964-0559. Ed.Bd. bk. rev. tr.lit. circ. 1,500. Indexed: C.I.J.E. CMI.

374   US
LEARNING INDEPENDENTLY; a directory of self-instruction resources. 1979. irreg. $200. Gale Research Company, Book Tower, Detroit, MI 48226. TEL 313-961-2242. Ed. Paul Wasserman.

374.013   DK   ISSN 0109-9299
LEDER. KURSUSKATALOG. a. Kr.32. (Administrationsdepartmentet) Bibliotekscentralen, Telegrafvej 5, DK-2750 Ballerup, Denmark.

379   US   ISSN 0094-1506
MICHIGAN STATE PLAN FOR VOCATIONAL EDUCATION. a. Department of Education, Division of Vocational Education, Box 30009, Lansing, MI 48909. TEL 517-373-3373. illus.

374   US
MICHIGAN STATE UNIVERSITY. COOPERATIVE EXTENSION SERVICE. ANNUAL REPORT. 1915. a. free. Michigan State University, Cooperative Extension Service, East Lansing, MI 48824. TEL 517-355-1855.

374   US
MYRIN INSTITUTE FOR ADULT EDUCATION PROCEEDINGS. 1954. irreg. $2 per no. Myrin Institute for Adult Education, 136 E. 64th St., New York, NY 10021. TEL 212-758-6475. Ed.Bd. bk. rev. bibl. circ. 2,000.

NARA WOMEN'S UNIVERSITY. HEALTH ADMINISTRATION CENTER. ARCHIVES OF HEALTH CARE/NARA JOSHIDAIGAKU HOKEN SENTA NENPO. see *PUBLIC HEALTH AND SAFETY*

379   US
NEVADA STATE PLAN FOR OCCUPATIONAL EDUCATION. a. free. State Board for Vocational Education, 400 W. King St., Carson City, NV 89710. TEL 702-885-3144. illus. circ. 350.
    Former titles: Nevada. State Board for Vocational Education. Annual Program Plan for Vocational Education & Nevada State Plan for Vocational Education (ISSN 0094-1123); Nevada State Plan for Career Education.

374   US
OFF CAMPUS STUDY PROGRAMS: U S AND ABROAD. 1983. a. $9.95. Association of Collegiate Schools of Architecture, Inc., 1735 New York Ave., N. W., Washington, DC 20006. Ed. Richard E. McCommons. circ. 1,500.

379   US   ISSN 0091-5114
PENNSYLVANIA STATE PLAN FOR THE ADMINISTRATION OF VOCATIONAL - TECHNICAL EDUCATION PROGRAMS. Cover title: Vocational - Technical Education Programs. a. free. Department of Education, Bureau of Vocational and Adult Education, 333 Market St., Harrisburg, PA 17126. TEL 717-787-8804. stat. circ. controlled; for official use only.

020   US   ISSN 0032-0382
PIVOT. 1969. irreg. free. ‡ Free Library of Philadelphia, Reader Development Program, Logan Square, Philadelphia, PA 19103. TEL 215-686-5346. Ed. Melissa Buckingham. bk. rev. abstr. bibl. circ. 1,000. (processed)

374   US
RESOURCES FOR EDUCATORS OF ADULTS. Variant title: International Handbook of Resources for the Educators of Adults. no.4, 1976. irreg. $20. Syracuse University, Publications in Continuing Education, 224 Huntington Hall, Syracuse, NY 13210. TEL 315-423-1870. Ed. Alexander N. Charters. circ. 1,000. (looseleaf format)

374.0   MX
REVISTA INTERAMERICANA DE EDUCACION DE ADULTOS. 1978. a. (Organization of American States) Centro Regional de Educacion de Adultos y Alfabetizacion Funcional para America Latina, Quinta Erendira, 61600 Patzcuaro, Michoacan, Mexico. circ. 3,000. (back issues avail.)

374   UK
SCOTTISH HANDBOOK OF ADULT AND CONTINUING EDUCATION. 1965. irreg. £3.25($7) Scottish Institute of Adult & Continuing Education, 30 Rutland Square, Edinburgh EH1 2BW, Scotland. Ed.Bd. adv. bibl. stat. circ. 2,000.
    Former titles: Handbook of Adult Education in Scotland; Yearbook of Adult Education in Scotland.

374.013   DK   ISSN 0107-4733
SPECIALARBEJDERKURSER. 1973. a. Direktoratet for Arbejdsmarkedsuddannelserne, Noerre Voldgade 16, 1358 Copenhagen K, Denmark. illus.
    Formerly: Specialarbejdkurser paa Specialarbejderskolerne.

374   CE
SRI LANKA FOUNDATION INSTITUTE. NEWS. (Text in English, Sinhalese, or Tamil) irreg. Rs.3. Sri Lanka Foundation Institute, 100 Independence Square, Colombo 8, Sri Lanka. Indexed: Sri Lanka Sci.Ind.

374   UK
STUDIES IN THE EDUCATION OF ADULTS. 1969. a. £16 for two issues. National Institute of Adult Continuing Education, 19B De Montfort St., Leicester LE1 7GE, England. Ed. Stuart Marriott. adv. bk. rev. bibl. illus. index. circ. 750. Indexed: Educ.Ind. C.I.J.E. High.Educ.Curr.Aware.Bull.
    Formerly: Studies in Adult Education (ISSN 0039-3525)

374   US
SYRACUSE UNIVERSITY PUBLICATIONS IN CONTINUING EDUCATION. LANDMARK AND NEW HORIZONS SERIES. 1971. irreg. Syracuse University, Publications in Continuing Education, Syracuse, NY 13210. TEL 315-423-3421.

374   US
SYRACUSE UNIVERSITY PUBLICATIONS IN CONTINUING EDUCATION. NOTES AND ESSAYS. no.72, 1972. irreg. price varies. Syracuse University, Publications in Continuing Education, 224 Huntington Hall, 150 Marshall St., Syracuse, NY 13210. TEL 315-423-1870. bibl. illus.

374   US   ISSN 0082-1179
SYRACUSE UNIVERSITY PUBLICATIONS IN CONTINUING EDUCATION. OCCASIONAL PAPERS. irreg., no.46, 1976. Syracuse University, Publications in Continuing Education, 224 Huntington Hall, Syracuse, NY 13210. TEL 315-423-3421.

378 630   UN   ISSN 0251-1495
TRAINING FOR AGRICULTURE AND RURAL DEVELOPMENT. French edition: Formation pour l'Agriculture et le Developpement Rural. Spanish edition: Adiestramento para el Desarrollo Agropecuario y Rural. 1967. a. $9. Food and Agriculture Organization of the United Nations, Agricultural Education and Training Service, Distribution and Sales Section, Via delle Terme di Caracalla, 00100 Rome, Italy (Dist. in U.S. by: Bernan Associates-Unipub, 4611-F Assembly Drive, Lanham, MD 20706-4391)
    Former titles: Training for Agriculture; From 1971-72: Extension; Until 1971: Agricultural Education and Training.

374.8   UN
U I E STUDIES ON POST-LITERACY AND CONTINUING EDUCATION. (Text in English, French and Spanish) 1984. irreg. DM.24. Unesco Institute for Education, Feldbrunnenstr. 58, D 2000 Hamburg 13, W. Germany (B.R.D.)

374   CN
UNIVERSITY OF BRITISH COLUMBIA. CENTER FOR CONTINUING EDUCATION. MONOGRAPHS ON COMPARATIVE AND AREA STUDIES IN ADULT EDUCATION. 1977. irreg. price varies. University of British Columbia, Center for Continuing Education, Vancouver, B.C. V6T 2A4, Canada. TEL 604-222-5281. (Co-sponsor: International Council for Adult Education) circ. 500.

374.8   CN   ISSN 0068-1695
UNIVERSITY OF BRITISH COLUMBIA. CENTER FOR CONTINUING EDUCATION. OCCASIONAL PAPERS IN CONTINUING EDUCATION. 1968. irreg. price varies. ‡ University of British Columbia, Center for Continuing Education, Vancouver, B.C. V6T 2A4, Canada. TEL 604-222-5281. Ed. J. Kulich. circ. 300. Indexed: Can.Ind. ERIC.

374.8   NR   ISSN 0075-7667
UNIVERSITY OF LAGOS. CONTINUING EDUCATION CENTRE. OCCASIONAL PAPERS. 1970. irreg., no.2, 1971. price varies. (University of Lagos, Continuing Education Centre) Lagos University Press, P.O. Box 132, Akoka, Yaba, Lagos, Nigeria. Ed. E.A. Tugbiyele.

374.9   ZA
UNIVERSITY OF ZAMBIA. CENTRE FOR CONTINUING EDUCATION. REPORT OF THE ANNUAL RESIDENT TUTORS' CONFERENCE. 1975. a, 8th, 1976. free. University of Zambia, Centre for Continuing Education, Box 516, Lusaka, Zambia. circ. 1,000.
    Formerly: University of Zambia. Centre for Continuing Education. Report of the Annual Staff Conference.

374.013   HK
VOCATIONAL TRAINING COUNCIL. ANNUAL REPORT. a. Vocational Training Council, 15/Fl., Harbour Centre, 25 Harbour Rd., Wanchai, Hong Kong.

374   US   ISSN 0084-2486
WORLDWIDE REGISTER OF ADULT EDUCATION; directory of home study schools. 1960. irreg., latest 1973 (with 1980 supp.) $8.95. ‡ Aurea Publications, Box 176, Allenhurst, NJ 07711. TEL 201-531-4535. Ed. Alex Sandri-White.

374   UK
YEARBOOK OF ADULT CONTINUING EDUCATION. 1961. a. £3.50. National Institute of Adult Continuing Education, 19B De Montfort St., Leicester LE1 7GE, England. Ed. A.K. Stock. bk. rev. index. circ. 2,000. (also avail. in microfiche)
    Formerly: Yearbook of Adult Education (ISSN 0084-3601)

EDUCATION — Computer Applications

see also *Computers—Computer Assisted Instruction*

ASSOCIATION FOR EDUCATIONAL DATA SYSTEMS. ANNUAL CONVENTION PROCEEDINGS. see *COMPUTERS — Computer Assisted Instruction*

370   US
COLLEGE AND UNIVERSITY COMPUTER DIRECTORY: FACILITIES AND PERSONNEL.* 1984. a. $49.50. Frederick F. Hafner, Inc., 2946 Sleepy Hollow Rd., Falls Church, VA 22044. adv. circ. 35,000.

370   US
COMPUTER STUDIES: COMPUTERS IN EDUCATION. 1985. a. $8.95. Dushkin Publishing Group, Inc., Sluice Dock, Guilford, CT 06437. TEL 203-453-4351. Ed. Steven Taffee.

370 510   US   ISSN 0888-2193
COMPUTERS AND MATH SERIES. 1984. irreg. Computer Science Press, Inc., 1803 Research Blvd., Ste. 500, Rockville, MD 20850. TEL 301-251-9050. Ed. Marvin Marcus. (back issues avail.)

370   US   ISSN 0888-2177
COMPUTERS IN EDUCATION SERIES. 1982. irreg. Computer Science Press, Inc., 1803 Research Blvd., Ste. 500, Rockville, MD 20850. TEL 301-251-9050. Eds. Rachelle S. Heller, C. Diane Martin. (back issues avail.)

EDUCATIONAL SOFTWARE SELECTOR. see *COMPUTERS — Software*

HANDS ON! see *EDUCATION — Higher Education*

428   EDUCATION — GUIDES TO SCHOOLS AND COLLEGES

SOFTWARE REPORTS: GUIDE TO EVALUATED EDUCATIONAL SOFTWARE. see *COMPUTERS — Software*

370   US
SPECIALWARE DIRECTORY; a guide to software sources for special education. irreg., 2nd edt. 1985. $19.50. (Linc Associates, Inc.) Oryx Press, 2214 N. Central at Encanto, Phoenix, AZ 85004-1482.

TANDY EDUCATIONAL SOFTWARE SOURCEBOOK. see *COMPUTERS — Software*

EDUCATION — Guides To Schools And Colleges

378.025   US   ISSN 0270-1715
ACCREDITED INSTITUTIONS OF POSTSECONDARY EDUCATION. 1964. a. $22.50. American Council on Education, One Dupont Circle, N.W., Washington, DC 20036 (Dist. by: Macmillan Publishing Company, 866 Third Ave., New York, NY 10022). circ. 8,000.
   Former titles: Accredited Institutions of Postsecondary Education and Programs; Accredited Institutions of Postsecondary Education and Programs (ISSN 0361-9362); Accredited Institutions of Post Secondary Education; Accredited Institutions of Higher Education (ISSN 0065-0862)

ACCREDITED JOURNALISM AND MASS COMMUNICATION EDUCATION. see *JOURNALISM*

ADMISSION REQUIREMENTS OF U S AND CANADIAN DENTAL SCHOOLS. see *MEDICAL SCIENCES — Dentistry*

371.0025   UK
AFTER SCHOOL; a guide to post school opportunities. a. £16.95. Kogan Page Ltd., 120 Pentonville Rd., London N1 9JN, England. Ed. Felicity Taylor.
   Formerly: How to Find Out About Further Education and Training.

610 378.0025   US   ISSN 0194-3766
ALLIED HEALTH EDUCATION DIRECTORY. 1968. a. $25.95. American Medical Association, 535 N. Dearborn St., Chicago, IL 60610. TEL 312-645-5000. Ed. John T. Boberg.
   Formerly: Allied Medical Education Directory (ISSN 0163-2590)

370   US   ISSN 0516-9313
AMERICAN ASSOCIATION OF COLLEGES FOR TEACHER EDUCATION. DIRECTORY. a. $8. American Association of Colleges for Teacher Education, 1 Du Pont Circle, N.W., Washington, DC 20036. TEL 202-293-2450.

660 540 016   US   ISSN 0193-5011
AMERICAN CHEMICAL SOCIETY. DIRECTORY OF GRADUATE RESEARCH. 1955. biennial. $46. American Chemical Society, Committee on Professional Training, 1155 16th St., N.W., Washington, DC 20036. TEL 202-872-8065. (back issues avail.)
   ●Also available online.

370.025 378   US   ISSN 0066-0922
AMERICAN UNIVERSITIES AND COLLEGES. 1928. quadrennial. $99.50. (American Council on Education) Walter De Gruyter, Inc., 200 Sawmill River Rd., Hawthorne, NY 10532. TEL 914-747-0110. Ed.Bd.

ASSOCIATION OF THEOLOGICAL SCHOOLS IN THE UNITED STATES AND CANADA. DIRECTORY. see *RELIGIONS AND THEOLOGY*

378.0025   US
BARRON'S PROFILES OF AMERICAN COLLEGES. VOL. 1: DESCRIPTIONS OF THE COLLEGES. 14th edt., 1984. biennial, 14th edt., 1984. $28.95 hardbound; $12.95 paper. Barron's Educational Series, Inc., 113 Crossways Park Dr., Woodbury, NY 11797. TEL 516-921-8750.

378.0025   US   ISSN 0533-1072
BARRON'S PROFILES OF AMERICAN COLLEGES. VOL. 2: INDEX TO MAJOR AREAS OF STUDY. 1973. biennial, 14th edt., 1984. $19.95 hardbound; $10.95 paperback. Barron's Educational Series, Inc., 113 Crossways Park Drive, Woodbury, NY 11797. TEL 516-921-8750.

BRICKER'S INTERNATIONAL DIRECTORY OF UNIVERSITY EXECUTIVE PROGRAMS. see *BUSINESS AND ECONOMICS — Management*

378.0025   UK
BRITISH UNIVERSITIES' GUIDE TO GRADUATE STUDIES. 1973. a. £20. Association of Commonwealth Universities, John Foster House, 36 Gordon Sq., London WC1H 0PF, England.
   Former titles: Postgraduate Courses in United Kingdom Universities (ISSN 0263-6182) & Schedule of Postgraduate Courses in United Kingdom Universities (ISSN 0306-1728)

371.0025   US   ISSN 0162-9646
C I C'S STATE SCHOOL DIRECTORIES. (Curriculum Information Center) (Published by state in 51 vols.) 1976. a. $795 per set; price varies per vol. Market Data Retrieval, 16 Progress Dr., Shelton, CT 06484. TEL 203-926-4800. (looseleaf format)
   Continues: School Universe Data Book (ISSN 0146-4329)

371.0025 384.5   US   ISSN 0742-3632
C I N C O M: COURSES IN COMMUNICATIONS. 1983. a. (updated 6/yr.) $25. Communications Institute, Communications Library, 1535 Francisco St., Lockbox 5891, San Francisco, CA 94101-5891. TEL 415-626-5050. bk. rev. circ. 1,200. (looseleaf format; back issues avail.)

371.0025   US   ISSN 0098-5147
CALIFORNIA PRIVATE SCHOOL DIRECTORY. 1969. a. $9. Department of Education, Bureau of Publications, State Education Bldg., 721 Capitol Mall, Sacramento, CA 95814. TEL 916-445-7608. Ed. Theodore R. Smith. index. circ. 3,000. (back issues avail.)
   Formerly: Directory of Private Elementary Schools and High Schools in California.

370.025   US   ISSN 0068-5771
CALIFORNIA PUBLIC SCHOOL DIRECTORY. 1928. a. $14. Department of Education, Bureau of Publications, 721 Capitol Mall, Sacramento, CA 95814-4785. TEL 916-445-7608. Ed. Theodore R. Smith. index. circ. 10,000.
   Before 1970: Directory of Administrative and Supervisory Personnel of California Public Schools.

378.0025   US   ISSN 0191-3670
CHRONICLE FOUR-YEAR COLLEGE DATABOOK. 1974. a. $20.90. Chronicle Guidance Publications, Inc., Box 1190, Moravia, NY 13118. TEL 315-497-0330.
   Formerly: Guide to Four-Year College Databook (ISSN 0361-8927); Supersedes in part: Chronicle College Chart (ISSN 0163-9242)

378.0025   US   ISSN 0191-3662
CHRONICLE TWO-YEAR COLLEGE DATABOOK. 1974. a. $18.65. Chronicle Guidance Publications, Inc., Box 1190, Moravia, NY 13118. TEL 315-497-0330.
   Formerly (until 1978): Chronicle Guide to Two-Year College Majors and Careers; Guide to Two-Year College Majors and Careers (ISSN 0362-420X); Supersedes in part: Chronicle College Charts (ISSN 0590-630X)

378.0025   US   ISSN 0276-0371
CHRONICLE VOCATIONAL SCHOOL MANUAL. 1979. a. $18.15. Chronicle Guidance Publications, Inc., Box 1190, Moravia, NY 13118. TEL 315-497-0330.
   Formerly: Chronicle Annual Vocational School Manual (ISSN 0163-4100)

370.025   US   ISSN 0069-5572
COLLEGE BLUE BOOK. (5-vol. set) 1923. biennial. $175. Macmillan Publishing Company, 866 Third Ave., New York, NY 10022.

378   US   ISSN 0069-5688
COLLEGE FACTS CHART. 1952. a. $3. ‡ National Beta Club, Box 730, Spartanburg, SC 29304. TEL 803-583-4553. Ed. Jean H. Byrum. circ. 15,000.

378.0025   US
COLLEGE TRANSFER GUIDE. a. $5. Catholic News Publishing Co., Inc., 210 N. Ave., New Rochelle, NY 10801. TEL 914-632-7771. Ed. V.L. Ridder, Jr. adv.

378.0025   US
COLLEGES AND UNIVERSITIES GRANTING DEGREES IN MICROBIOLOGY. 1973. irreg. (every 3-5 yrs.), latest issue 1980. $5. American Society for Microbiology, 1913 I St., N.W., Washington, DC 20006. TEL 202-833-9680. circ. 2,000.

378.025   US
COMMUNITY, TECHNICAL, AND JUNIOR COLLEGE DIRECTORY: A STATISTICAL ANALYSIS. 1950. a. $25. American Association of Community and Junior Colleges, One Dupont Circle, N.W., Washington, DC 20036. TEL 202-293-7050. Ed. James R. Mahoney. circ. 5,000. (also avail. in microfiche) Indexed: ERIC.
   Former titles: Community, Technical, and Junior College Directory & Community and Junior College Directory; Junior College Directory (ISSN 0075-4552)

378.0025   US
COMPARATIVE GUIDE TO AMERICAN COLLEGES; for students, parents and counselors. Harper & Row, Publishers, Inc., 10 E. 53 St., New York, NY 10022. TEL 212-593-7000.

COMPENDIUM OF ADVANCED COURSES IN COLLEGES OF FURTHER & HIGHER EDUCATION. see *EDUCATION — Higher Education*

371.0025 378.0025   US
COMPENDIUM OF TEXAS COLLEGES & FINANCIAL AID CALENDAR FOR HIGH SCHOOL SENIORS.* 1965. a. free. Minnie Stevens Piper Foundation, 800 NW Loop 410, No. 530, San Antonio, TX 78216-5616. circ. 30,000.

DANCE MAGAZINE COLLEGE GUIDE; a directory to dance in North American colleges and universities. see *DANCE*

371.0025   DK   ISSN 0108-3082
DANMARKS FOLKEHOEJSKOLER. 1950. a. free. Hoejskolernes Sekretariat, Vartov, Farvergade 27/opg.G, 1463 Copenhagen K, Denmark. Ed. Arne Andresen. illus. circ. 170,000.
   Formerly: Danmarks Hoejskoler.

370.025   GW
DEUTSCHER HOCHSCHULFUEHRER. 1925. a. DM.39. Verlag Dr. Josef Raabe KG, Ahrstr. 46, 5300 Bonn 2, W. Germany (B.R.D.) adv. circ. 5,000.

370   CL   ISSN 0120-5056
DIRECTORIO DE LA EDUCACION SUPERIOR EN COLOMBIA. 1977. a. Col.500($10) Instituto Colombiano para el Fomento de la Educacion Superior, Calle 17 N. 3-40, Apdo. Aereo 6319, Bogota, D.E., Colombia. (Co-sponsor: Division de Recursos Bibliograficos) circ. 5,000. (also avail. in microfiche)

378   US
DIRECTORY: A GUIDE TO COLLEGES, VOCATIONAL-TECHNICAL SCHOOLS & SPECIAL PURPOSE INSTITUTIONS. 1966. biennial. free. Georgia Student Finance Commission, 2082 E. Exchange Pl., Ste. 200, Tucker, GA 30084. Ed. Deborah R. Howell. circ. 5,000.
   Former titles: Directory: a Guide to Colleges, Vocational-Technical and Diploma Schools of Nursing & Directory of Educational Opportunities in Georgia (ISSN 0419-2559)

370.025   US
DIRECTORY OF ACCREDITED HOME STUDY SCHOOLS. 1953. a. free. National Home Study Council, 1601 18 St. N.W., Washington, DC 20009. TEL 202-234-5100. circ. 60,000.
   Formerly: Directory of Accredited Private Home Study Schools (ISSN 0070-5055)

DIRECTORY OF AVIATION AND SPACE EDUCATION. see *AERONAUTICS AND SPACE FLIGHT*

DIRECTORY OF BANKERS SCHOOLS. see *BUSINESS AND ECONOMICS — Banking And Finance*

EDUCATION — GUIDES TO SCHOOLS AND COLLEGES

378.0025 616.8 US
DIRECTORY OF BEHAVIORAL GRADUATE STUDY. 1980. biennial. $12. Association for Advancement of Behavior Therapy, 15 W. 36th St., New York, NY 10018. TEL 212-279-7970. circ. 1,000.

378.025 US
DIRECTORY OF COLLEGE FACILITIES AND SERVICES FOR THE DISABLED. 1983. irreg., 2nd edt. 1986. $95. Oryx Press, 2214 N. Central at Encanto, Phoenix, AZ 85004. Ed. Carol H. Thomas.

378.025 US
DIRECTORY OF COMMUNITY, JUNIOR, AND TECHNICAL COLLEGES. 1986. a. $35. American Association of Community and Junior Colleges, One Dupont Circle, N.W., Washington, DC 20036 (Order from: AACJC Publications, 80 S. Early St., Alexandria, VA 22304)
    Formerly: Who's Who in American Community, Technical, and Junior Colleges.

371.0025 296 US
DIRECTORY OF DAY SCHOOLS IN THE UNITED STATES AND CANADA. biennial. $7. Torah Umesorah, National Society for Hebrew Day Schools, 160 Broadway, New York, NY 10038. TEL 212-227-1000. Ed. Rabbi Yaakov Fruchter. circ. 2,500.
    Formerly: Directory of Day Schools in the United States, Canada and Latin America.

DIRECTORY OF EDUCATIONAL INSTITUTIONS. see BUSINESS AND ECONOMICS

DIRECTORY OF GEOSCIENCE DEPARTMENTS, UNITED STATES AND CANADA. see EARTH SCIENCES

DIRECTORY OF GRADUATE PROGRAMS IN THE COMMUNICATION ARTS AND SCIENCES. see EDUCATION — Higher Education

DIRECTORY OF MEDICAL SCHOOLS WORLDWIDE (YEAR) see MEDICAL SCIENCES

371.0025 US
DIRECTORY OF MINORITY FOUR YEAR TEACHER PREPARATORY INSTITUTIONS. irreg. $10. Association for School, College and University Staffing, 301 S. Swift Rd., Addison, IL 60101-1499. TEL 312-495-4707.

659.1 US
DIRECTORY OF MODEL-TALENT AGENCIES AND SCHOOLS USA AND INTERNATIONAL. 1970. biennial. $25. Peter Glenn Publications, Inc., 17 E. 48th St., New York, NY 10017. TEL 212-688-6215. Ed. Peter Glenn. circ. 1,000.
    Formerly: Models Mart Directory of Modeling Schools and Agencies USA and Canada.

371.0025 US
DIRECTORY OF PUBLIC SCHOOLS IN THE U S. a. $60 to non-members. Association for School, College and University Staffing, 301 S. Swift Rd., Addison, IL 60101-1499. TEL 312-495-4707. circ. 1,000.

370 US
DIRECTORY OF PUBLIC VOCATIONAL TECHNICAL SCHOOLS AND INSTITUTES. 1982. biennial. $65. Minnesota Scholarly Press, Box 224, Mankato, MN 56001. TEL 507-387-4964. Ed. Marliss Johnston.

DIRECTORY OF RELIGIOUS BROADCASTING. see COMMUNICATIONS — Radio And Television

DIRECTORY OF SERVICES AND FACILITIES FOR THE LEARNING DISABLED. see EDUCATION — Special Education And Rehabilitation

371 378.0025 371 US ISSN 0093-9501
DIRECTORY OF SPECIAL PROGRAMS FOR MINORITY GROUP MEMBERS; CAREER INFORMATION SERVICES, EMPLOYMENT SKILLS, BANKS, FINANCIAL AID SOURCES. 1974. irreg., latest 4th edt. $25. Garrett Park Press, Box 190F, Garrett Park, MD 20896. TEL 301-946-2553. Ed. Willis L. Johnson. bibl.

378.0025 JA
DIRECTORY OF UNIVERSITY PROFESSORS AND RESEARCHERS IN JAPAN. a. 19000 Yen. Japan Society for the Promotion of Science, 5-3-1 Kojimachi, Chiyoda-ku, Tokyo, Japan.

378.0025 300.7 UK
E S R C STUDENTSHIP HANDBOOK; postgraduate studentships in the social sciences. 1970. a. free. Economic and Social Research Council, 160 Gt. Portland St., London W1N 6BA, England.
    Former titles (until Jan. 1984): S S R C Studentship Handbook; Social Science Research Council (Gt. Brit.) Postgraduate Studentships in the Social Sciences.

370.025 US
EDUCATION DIRECTORY. (SCHOOL YEAR): COLLEGES AND UNIVERSITIES. 1967. a. price varies. U.S. National Center for Education Statistics, U.S. Department of Education, 400 Maryland Ave., Washington, DC 20202 TEL 202-655-4000. (Orders to: Supt. of Documents, Washington, DC 20402)
    Formerly: Directory of U.S. Institutions of Higher Education (ISSN 0070-654X)

EDUCATION FOR BUSINESS AND MANAGEMENT IN THE REGION. see EDUCATION — Higher Education

374 US
EDUCATIONAL OPPORTUNITIES OF GREATER BOSTON. 1923. a. $7.95 (summer supplement $2) Educational Exchange of Greater Boston, 1430 Mass Ave., Cambridge, MA 02138. TEL 617-876-3080. Ed. Zelda Lions. circ. 3,500.

374 UK
FLOODLIGHT;* I L E A guide to evening classes. 1945. a. 30p. Inner London Education Authority, County Hall, Rm 77, London SE1 7PB, England. Ed. Ted Enever. adv. circ. 125,000.

370.025 US
FLORIDA EDUCATION DIRECTORY. a. Department of Education, Knott Building, Tallahassee, FL 32302. TEL 904-488-3284.

371.0025 DK ISSN 0107-4504
FOLKEHOEJSKOLER.* 1971. a. free. Undervisningsministeriet, Frederiksholms Kanal 21-25, Copenhagen K, Denmark.

371.025 DK ISSN 0106-2530
FOLKESKOLEN I DE ENKELTE KOMMUNER. 1979. a. Kr.100. Undervisningsministeriet, Oekonomisk-Statistiske Konsulent, Vester Voldgade 104, 1552 Copenhagen V., Denmark.

378.002 US
GRADUATE SCHOOL GUIDE. a. $5. Catholic News Publishing Co., Inc., 210 N. Ave., New Rochelle, NY 10801. TEL 914-632-7771. Ed. Victor L. Ridder, Jr. adv. stat. circ. 35,000.

GRADUATE STUDY IN PSYCHOLOGY AND ASSOCIATED FIELDS. see PSYCHOLOGY

377 SP ISSN 0211-4410
GUIA DE CENTROS EDUCATIVOS CATOLICOS. 1970. a. 5000 ptas. Federacion Espanola de Religiosos de la Ensenanza (F.E.R.E.), Servicio Estadistico, Conde de Penalver, 45, 28006 Madrid, Spain. adv. stat.
    Formerly: Guia de Centros Docentes de la Iglesia.

371.9 US
GUIDE TO C O P A RECOGNIZED ACCREDITING BODIES. 1980. biennial. $10.45. Council on Postsecondary Accreditation, One Dupont Circle, N.W., Ste. 305, Washington, DC 20036. TEL 202-452-1433. Ed. Janet D. Froom. circ. 200.
    Formerly: Guide to Recognized Accrediting Agencies (ISSN 0196-4402)

GUIDE TO DEPARTMENTS OF GEOGRAPHY IN THE UNITED STATES AND CANADA. see GEOGRAPHY

378.0025 975 US
GUIDE TO DEPARTMENTS OF HISTORY (YEAR); colleges, universities, and research institutions in the United States and Canada. 1975. a. $25 to non-members; members $20. American Historical Association, 400 A St., S.E., Washington, DC 20003. TEL 202-544-2422. Ed. Maureen Vincent-Morgan. stat. index. circ. 2,000.

370.025 378 US ISSN 0737-3163
GUIDE TO FOUR-YEAR COLLEGES (YEAR) 1970. a. $14.95. Peterson's Guides, Inc., 166 Bunn Dr., Box 2123, Princeton, NJ 08543-2123. TEL 609-924-5338. Ed. Andrea E. Lehman. circ. 40,000. (also avail. in microform).
    Supersedes in part: Peterson's Annual Guide to Undergraduate Study (ISSN 0147-8451); Formerly: Annual Guide to Undergraduate Study (ISSN 0091-0465)

371.002 371.912 US
GUIDE TO GRADUATE EDUCATION IN SPEECH-LANGUAGE PATHOLOGY AND AUDIOLOGY. 1982. biennial. price varies. American Speech-Language-Hearing Association, 10801 Rockville Pike, Rockville, MD 20852. circ. 5,000.

378.025 US ISSN 0072-8500
GUIDE TO GRADUATE STUDY IN BOTANY FOR THE UNITED STATES AND CANADA. 1966. irreg., latest 1983. $5. Botanical Society of America Inc., c/o Dept. of Biology, Indiana University, Bloomington, IN 47405.

378.025 US ISSN 0091-9632
GUIDE TO GRADUATE STUDY IN POLITICAL SCIENCE. 1972. triennial. $15 for members; $20 for non-members. American Political Science Association, 1527 New Hampshire Ave. N.W., Washington, DC 20036. TEL 202-483-2512. circ. 2,500.

371.0025 420 375.4 UK
GUIDE TO PRIVATE ENGLISH LANGUAGE SCHOOLS IN THE U.K. FOR OVERSEAS STUDENTS. 1985. a. £15.95. Magna Graecia's Publishers, Office 8, Groundfloor, 38 Mount Pleasant, London WC1X 0AP, England. Ed. Luigi Gigliotti. circ. 60,000.

370.025 US ISSN 0072-8705
GUIDE TO SUMMER CAMPS AND SUMMER SCHOOLS. 1936. biennial. $23 for cloth; paper $18. Porter Sargent Publishers, Inc., 11 Beacon St., Boston, MA 02108. TEL 617-523-1670. Ed. Ann C. Himebaugh. adv. illus. stat. index. circ. 4,500. (back issues avail.)

378 UK
HANDBOOK OF DEGREE AND ADVANCED COURSES IN INSTITUTES/COLLEGES OF HIGHER EDUCATION, COLLEGES OF EDUCATION, POLYTECHNICS, UNIVERSITY DEPARTMENTS OF EDUCATION.* 1954. a. £8.50. (National Association of Teachers in Further and Higher Education in England and Wales) Lund Humphries, Ely House, Dover St., London N1 6AJ, England. Ed. Jonathan R. Garnett.

371.0025 US ISSN 0072-9884
HANDBOOK OF PRIVATE SCHOOLS; an annual descriptive survey of independent education. 1914. a. $45. Porter Sargent Publishers, Inc., 11 Beacon St., Boston, MA 02018. TEL 617-523-1670. Ed.Bd. charts. illus. stat. index. circ. 6,000. (back issues avail.)

371.0025 US ISSN 0278-4920
HANDBOOK OF TRADE AND TECHNICAL CAREERS AND TRAINING. 1966. a. free. National Association of Trade and Technical Schools, 2251 Wisconsin Ave., N.W., Ste. 200, Washington, DC 20007. TEL 202-333-1021. Ed.Bd. circ. 440,000.

371.002 US
IDAHO EDUCATIONAL DIRECTORY. 1919. a. $3. Department of Education, Division of Finance and Administration, Len B. Jordan Bldg., Boise, ID 83720. TEL 208-334-3328. circ. 5,000.

EDUCATION — GUIDES TO SCHOOLS AND COLLEGES

373 370.025   US   ISSN 0073-5779
INDEPENDENT SCHOOLS ASSOCIATION OF THE SOUTHWEST. MEMBERSHIP LIST. 1966. a. free. Independent Schools Association of the Southwest, Box 52297, Tulsa, OK 74152. TEL 918-749-5927. Ed. Richard W. Ekdahl. circ. 500.
List of schools accredited by the Association

370.025 374.4   US   ISSN 0733-6020
INDEPENDENT STUDY CATALOG: N U C E A'S GUIDE TO INDEPENDENT STUDY THROUGH CORRESPONDENCE INSTRUCTION. 1964. biennial. $8.95. (National University Continuing Education Association) Peterson's Guides, Box 2123, Princeton, NJ 08543-2123. TEL 609-924-5338.
Former titles: Guide to Independent Study Through Correspondence Instruction (ISSN 0149-1083) & Guide to Correspondence Studies in Colleges and Universities (ISSN 0072-8322)

371.002   US
INDIANA SCHOOL DIRECTORY. a. $2. Department of Education, 227 State House, Indianapolis, IN 46204. TEL 317-232-6610.

INTERNATIONAL DIRECTORY OF CENTERS FOR ASIAN STUDIES. see *ORIENTAL STUDIES*

370.025   IE   ISSN 0075-0662
IRELAND DEPARTMENT OF EDUCATION. LIOSTA DE IAR-BHUNSCOILEANNA AITHEANTA. LIST OF RECOGNISED POST-PRIMARY SCHOOLS. 1968. a. £1. Government Publications Sales Office, Sun Alliance House, Molesworth St., Dublin 2, Ireland.

371.0025 850   UK
ITALIAN PRIVATE ENGLISH LANGUAGE SCHOOLS & ITALIAN LANGUAGE SCHOOLS FOR OVERSEAS & ITALY. 1986. a. £15.95. Magna Graecia's Publishers, Office 8, Groundfloor, 38 Mount Pleasant, London WC1X 0AP, England. Ed. Luigi Gigliotti. circ. 55,000.

JOURNALISM AND MASS COMMUNICATION DIRECTORY. see *JOURNALISM*

JOURNALISM CAREER AND SCHOLARSHIP GUIDE; information on journalism career scholarships available for the study of journalism and directory of college journalism programs. see *JOURNALISM*

370   US   ISSN 0091-0775
KENTUCKY SCHOOL DIRECTORY. 1975/76. a. $6. ‡ Department of Education, Capital Plaza Tower, Frankfort, KY 40601. TEL 502-564-4770. Ed. Rick McComb. stat. circ. controlled. (processed)

378.002   JA   ISSN 0389-4088
KOCHI GAKUEN COLLEGE. BULLETIN. (Text in English or Japanese; summaries in English) 1970. a. Kochi Gakuen College, 292 Asahitenjin-Cho, Kochi-Shi 780, Japan. Ed. Isao Yoshimura. circ. 500. (back issues avail.)

LONDON AND SOUTH EASTERN REGIONAL ADVISORY COUNCIL FOR FURTHER EDUCATION. BULLETIN OF SPECIAL COURSES. see *EDUCATION — Higher Education*

LONDON AND SOUTH EASTERN REGIONAL ADVISORY COUNCIL FOR FURTHER EDUCATION. INDEX OF COURSES. see *EDUCATION — Higher Education*

378   AT   ISSN 0812-230X
MELBOURNE COLLEGE OF ADVANCED EDUCATION. HANDBOOK. a. Aus.$3. Melbourne College of Advanced Education, Institute of Early Childhood Development, 737 Swanston Str., Carlton, Victoria 3053, Australia. circ. 3,000. (also avail. in microfiche; back issues avail.)

378.774   US
MICHIGAN POSTSECONDARY ADMISSIONS & FINANCIAL ASSISTANCE HANDBOOK. a. Department of Education, Box 30008, Lansing, MI 48909. TEL 517-373-0457. illus.
Formerly: Michigan. Department of Education. College Admissions and Financial Assistance Handbook (ISSN 0094-3754)

370   US   ISSN 0092-7899
MISSISSIPPI EDUCATIONAL DIRECTORY. 1977. a. $5. Department of Education, c/o Management Information System, Box 771, Jackson, MS 39205. TEL 601-359-3519. Ed. Jack Lynch. circ. 2,000.
Formerly: Educational Directory of Mississippi Schools (ISSN 0363-874X)

377.82   US   ISSN 0147-8044
N C E A GANLEY'S CATHOLIC SCHOOLS IN AMERICA.* 1974. a. $33. (National Catholic Educational Association) Fisher Publishing Company, Box 1073, Montrose, CO 81402. Ed. Mary Mahar. circ. 500.
Former titles: Ganley's Catholic Schools in America - Elementary/Secondary; Catholic Schools in the United States (ISSN 0091-9527)

371.0025 700   US
NATIONAL ASSOCIATION OF SCHOOLS OF ART AND DESIGN. DIRECTORY. 1977. a. $5. National Association of Schools of Art and Design, 11250 Roger Beacon Dr., No. 5, Reston, VA 22090. TEL 703-437-0700. Ed. Carol P. Moynahan. circ. 1,000.
Formerly: National Association of Schools of Art. Directory.

378.002   US
NATIONAL DIRECTORY OF CATHOLIC HIGHER EDUCATION. a. $10. Catholic News Publishing Co., Inc., 210 N. Ave., New Rochelle, NY 10801. TEL 914-632-1220. Ed. Victor L. Ridder. adv.

NATIONAL DIRECTORY OF EDUCATIONAL PROGRAMS IN GERONTOLOGY. see *GERONTOLOGY AND GERIATRICS*

NATIONAL UNIVERSITY CONTINUING EDUCATION ASSOCIATION. DIRECTORY. see *EDUCATION — Higher Education*

NETHERLANDS. CENTRAAL BUREAU VOOR DE STATISTIEK. STATISTIEK VAN HET BEROEPSONDERWIJS: KUNSTONDERWIJS. ART COLLEGES. see *EDUCATION — Higher Education*

371.002   US   ISSN 0731-8650
OCCUPATIONAL PROGRAMS IN CALIFORNIA PUBLIC COMMUNITY COLLEGES. a. Leo A. Meyer Associates, Inc., 23850 Clawiter Rd., Ste. 1, Hayward, CA 94545. TEL 415-785-1091.

370.025   US   ISSN 0078-5679
OREGON SCHOOL DIRECTORY. a. $5. Department of Education, 700 Pringle Parkway, S.E., Salem, OR 97310. TEL 503-378-3569. Ed. Sharon Case. circ. 8,500. (also avail. in microfiche)
Formerly (1972-1973): Oregon School-Community College Directory.

370.025   US   ISSN 0079-0230
PATTERSON'S AMERICAN EDUCATION. 1904. a. $47.50. Educational Directories Inc., P.O. Box 199, Mount Prospect, IL 60056. TEL 312-392-1811. Ed. Douglas Moody. index. circ. 5,000.
Formerly: Patterson's American Educational Directory (ISSN 0163-2728)

371.0025   US   ISSN 0553-4054
PATTERSON'S SCHOOLS CLASSIFIED. (Also incl. in Patterson's American Education) 1952. a. $8. Educational Directories Inc., Box 199, Mount Prospect, IL 60056. TEL 312-392-1811. Ed. Douglas Moody. circ. 10,000. (processed)

370.025   US
PETERSON'S GRADUATE AND PROFESSIONAL PROGRAMS: AN OVERVIEW. 1966. a. $17.95. Peterson's Guides, Box 2123, Princeton, NJ 08543-2123. TEL 609-924-5338. Ed. Amy J. Goldstein. circ. 11,000. (also avail. in microform)
Formerly: Peterson's Guides. Annual Guides to Graduate Study. Book 1: Graduate and Professional Programs: An Overview; Supersedes: Peterson's Guides. Annual Guides to Graduate Study. Book 1: Accredited Institutions Offering Graduate Work-An Overview.

370.025 570   US
PETERSON'S GRADUATE PROGRAMS IN THE BIOLOGICAL, AGRICULTURAL AND HEALTH SCIENCES. 1966. a. $19.95. Peterson's Guides, Box 2123, Princeton, NJ 08543-2123. TEL 609-924-5338. Ed. Amy J. Goldstein. circ. 5,500. (also avail. in microform)
Formerly: Peterson's Guides. Annual Guides to Graduate Study. Book 3: Biological, Agricultural and Health Sciences.

370.025 650   US
PETERSON'S GRADUATE PROGRAMS IN THE HUMANITIES AND SOCIAL SCIENCES. 1966. a. $27.95. Peterson's Guides, Box 2123, Princeton, NJ 08543-2123. TEL 609-924-5338. Ed. Amy J. Goldstein. circ. 6,000. (also avail. in microform)
Formerly: Peterson's Guides. Annual Guides to Graduate Study. Book 2: Humanities and Social Sciences.

370.025 500   US
PETERSON'S GRADUATE PROGRAMS IN THE PHYSICAL SCIENCES AND MATHEMATICS (YEAR) 1966. a. $24.95. Peterson's Guides, Box 2123, Princeton, NJ 08543-2123. TEL 609-924-5338. Ed. Amy S. Goldstein. circ. 4,500.
Former titles: Peterson's Annual Guides/Graduate Study. Graduate Programs in the Physical Science and Mathematics. (ISSN 0163-6111); Peterson's Guides. Annual Guide to Graduate Study. Book 4: Physical Sciences and Mathematics; Supersedes: Peterson's Guides. Annual Guides to Graduate Study. Book 4: Physical Sciences.

378.0025   US
PETERSON'S GUIDE TO INDEPENDENT SECONDARY SCHOOLS. 1980. a. $15.95. Peterson's Guides, Box 2123, Princeton, NJ 08543-2123. TEL 609-924-5338. Ed. Christopher Billy. circ. 12,000. (also avail. in microform)
Formerly: Peterson's Annual Guide to Independent Secondary Schools (ISSN 0196-7495)

378.002   US   ISSN 0737-3171
PETERSON'S GUIDE TO TWO-YEAR COLLEGES (YEAR) 1960. a. $10.95. Peterson's Guides, Inc., 166 Bunn Dr., Box 2123, Princeton, NJ 08543-2123. TEL 609-924-5338. Ed. Andrea E. Lehman. circ. 20,000. (also avail. in microfiche)
Supersedes in part: Peterson's Annual Guide to Undergraduate Study (ISSN 0147-8451)

370.025 620   US
PETERSON'S GUIDES. ANNUAL GUIDES TO GRADUATE STUDY. BOOK 5: ENGINEERING AND APPLIED SCIENCES. 1966. a. $26.95. Peterson's Guides, Box 2123, Princeton, NJ 08540. TEL 609-924-5338. Ed. Diane Conley. circ. 5,500. (also avail. in microform)

POSTGRADUATE STUDY AT THE UNIVERSITY OF LIVERPOOL. see *EDUCATION — Higher Education*

370.025   US   ISSN 0079-5399
PRIVATE INDEPENDENT SCHOOLS; the Bunting and Lyon Blue Book. 1943. a. $49. Bunting and Lyon, Inc., 238 N. Main St., Wallingford, CT 06492. TEL 203-269-3333. Ed.Bd. adv. circ. 4,000.

371.002   US   ISSN 0885-1603
PRIVATE SCHOOLS OF THE UNITED STATES. 1985. a. $75. (Curriculum Information Center) Market Data Retrieval, 16 Progress Dr., Shelton, CT 06484. TEL 203-226-8941.

378.0025   US   ISSN 0097-5206
RANDAX EDUCATION GUIDE; to colleges seeking students. 1971. a. $9.95. Education Guide, Inc., Box 421, Randolph, MA 02368. TEL 617-961-2217. Ed. Stephen E. Marshall. adv. bk. rev. circ. 20,000.

370   US
SCHOOL GUIDE. 1935. a. $5. Catholic News Publishing Co., Inc., 210 North Ave., New Rochelle, NY 10801. TEL 914-632-7771. Ed. Victor L. Ridder, Jr. adv. stat. circ. 230,000.

SCHOOLS AND COLLEGES WELCOME. see *TRAVEL AND TOURISM*

SCHOOLS IN THE UNITED STATES AND CANADA OFFERING GRADUATE EDUCATION IN PHARMACOLOGY. see *PHARMACY AND PHARMACOLOGY*

370.025 UK ISSN 0080-6919
SCHOOLS OF ENGLAND, WALES, SCOTLAND AND IRELAND. (Includes: Continental Tutors and Special Training Sections) 1910. a. price varies. J. Burrow & Co. Ltd., Publicity House, Streatham Hill, London SW2 4TR, England. adv.

378.0025 SP
SERIE GUIAS DE LOS ESTUDIOS UNIVERSITARIOS. 1977. irreg., no.13, 1984. (Universidad de Navarra, Instituto de Ciencias de la Educacion) Ediciones Universidad de Navarra, S.A., Apdo. 396, 31080 Pamplona, Spain.

375 US
SPECIALIZED STUDY OPTIONS U.S.A. (In 2 vols.: vol.1, Technical Education; vol.2, Professional Development) 1984. biennial. $19.95 per volume. Institute of International Education, 809 U.N. Plaza, New York, NY 10017. TEL 212-883-8200. Ed. Edrice Howard. index. circ. 5,000. (back issues avail.)

STATE-APPROVED SCHOOLS OF NURSING - L.P.N./L.V.N. see *MEDICAL SCIENCES — Nurses And Nursing*

STATE-APPROVED SCHOOLS OF NURSING - R.N. see *MEDICAL SCIENCES — Nurses And Nursing*

STUDENT GUIDE TO GRADUATE LAW STUDY PROGRAMS. see *LAW*

378.0025 JA ISSN 0385-1478
STUDIES IN INFORMATION AND BEHAVIORAL SCIENCES; memoirs of the Faculty of Integrated Arts and Sciences III. (Text in English and Japanese) 1975. a. exchange only. Hiroshima University, Faculty of Integrated Arts and Sciences III, 1-1-89 Higashi-Sendamashi, Naka-ku, Hiroshima, 730, Japan. circ. 200. (back issues avail.)

SURVEY OF ARTS ADMINISTRATION TRAINING. see *ART*

371 US ISSN 0363-4566
TEXAS SCHOOL DIRECTORY. 1915. a. $5. Texas Education Agency, Publications Distribution, 1701 N. Congress Ave., Austin, TX 78701. Ed. Caron Edge. circ. 10,000.
 Former titles: Public School Directory of the State of Texas & Texas Public School Directory.

371.002 DK ISSN 0107-1629
UDDANNELSE INSTITUTIONER OVER GRUNDSKOLENIVEAU. 1979. a. Kr.85. Undervisningministeriet, Oekonomisk-Statistike Konsulent, Copenhagen, Denmark (Orders to: Danske Boghendleres Kommissionsanstalt, Siljangade 6, 2300 Copenhagen S, Denmark)

378.025 IT
UNIVERSITA DEGLI STUDI IN ITALIA. ANNUARIO. 1981. biennial. L.50000. (Istituto Nazionale dell'Informazione) Editoriale Italiana, Via Vigliena 10, 00192 Rome, Italy. Ed. Franco Rivara. adv. circ. 50,000.

UNIVERSITY OF LIVERPOOL PROSPECTUS. see *EDUCATION — Higher Education*

371 US
UTAH PUBLIC SCHOOL DIRECTORY. a. $2. State Board of Education, 250 East 5th South, Salt Lake City, UT 84111. TEL 801-533-5431. circ. 2,000.

371.0025 016 US
VOCATIONAL AND TECHNICAL AUDIOVISUALS: A TEACHER'S SOURCEBOOK. 1972. irreg. $50. (National Information Center for Educational Media) Access Innovations, Inc., Box 40130, Albuqerque, NM 87196. TEL 505-265-3591. abstr. bibl. cum.index: 1934-1975.
 Formerly (until 1986): N I C E M Index to Vocational and Technical Education-Multimedia.

370 US
WESTERN ASSOCIATION OF SCHOOLS AND COLLEGES DIRECTORY. 1962. a. free. Western Association of Schools and Colleges, Box 9990 Mills College, Oakland, CA 94613. Ed. Delsie Austinson. circ. 3,600.

378.0025 659.1 US
WHERE SHALL I GO TO COLLEGE TO STUDY ADVERTISING? 1965. a. $2. Advertising Education Publications, 3429 55th St., Lubbock, TX 79413. Ed. Billy I. Ross. circ. 5,000.

378 US
WHERE THE COLLEGES RANK. irreg., latest 1973. $2. College-Rater, Inc., 2121 South 12th St., Allentown, PA 18103.

378.025 UK
WHICH DEGREE. 1963. a. £23.50. V N U Business Publications BV, 53-55 Frith St., London W1A 2HG, England (Dist. in U.S. by Barnes & Noble, Inc., 105 Fifth Ave., New York, NY 10003) Ed. Iris Rosier.
 Formerly: Which University (ISSN 0083-923X)

370.025 UK
WHICH SCHOOL? 1924. a. £8.50. Truman and Knightley Educational Trust, 76-78 Notting Hill Gate, London, W11 3LJ, England. Ed. Marie O'Riordan. adv. circ. 2,800.
 Former titles: Schools (ISSN 0080-6897); (until 1982): Directory of Catholic Schools and Colleges (ISSN 0070-5233)

371.0025 US ISSN 0148-5059
WISCONSIN PUBLIC SCHOOL DIRECTORY. a. $3. Department of Public Instruction, 125 S. Webster St., Madison, WI 53707-7841. TEL 608-266-1098. Ed. David R. Jamieson.

370.025 378 UK ISSN 0084-1889
WORLD LIST OF UNIVERSITIES, OTHER INSTITUTIONS OF HIGHER EDUCATION AND UNIVERSITY ORGANIZATIONS. 1952. biennial. £35. ‡ (International Association of Universities) Globe Book Services Ltd., Brunel Rd., Houndmills, Basingstoke, Hants. RG21 2XS, England. Eds. H.M.R. Keyes, D.J. Aitken. index.

370.025 UK ISSN 0084-2117
WORLD OF LEARNING. 1947. a. $190. Europa Publications, Ltd., 18 Bedford Squ., London WC1B 3JN, England.
 Guide and directory of learned societies, research institutes, libraries, museums and universities

378.0025 FI ISSN 0355-1784
YLIOPPILASAINEITA. 1948. a. Fmk.20. Suomalaisen Kirjallisuuden Seura, PL 259, Hallitusakatu 1, P.O. Box 259, 00170 Finland 17, Finland. circ. 20,000.

EDUCATION — Higher Education

see also College and Alumni

A A M C DIRECTORY OF AMERICAN MEDICAL EDUCATION. (Association of American Medical Colleges) see *EDUCATION — School Organization And Administration*

378 US ISSN 0065-7344
A A S C U STUDIES. 1970. irreg. price varies. American Association of State Colleges and Universities, One Dupont Circle, N.W., Suite 700, Washington, DC 20036. TEL 202-293-7070.

378 US ISSN 0065-7832
A C T MONOGRAPH SERIES. 1967. irreg., no.15, 1974. $3 price varies. American College Testing Program, Box 168, Iowa City, IA 52243. TEL 319-337-1000. (also avail. in microfiche from EDR) Indexed: Coll.Stud.Pers.Abstr. Eric.

378 US ISSN 0569-3993
A C T RESEARCH REPORT. 1965. irreg., no.84, 1984. free. American College Testing Program, P. O. Box 168, Iowa City, IA 52243. TEL 319-337-1000. circ. 3,354. (also avail. in microfiche) Indexed: Col.Stud.Pers.Abstr. ERIC. Psychol.Abstr.
 Formerly: A C T Research Service Report (ISSN 0065-7840)

378 US
A C T SPECIAL REPORT SERIES. 1971. irreg., no.31, 1982. price varies. American College Testing Program, Box 168, Iowa City, IA 52243. TEL 319-337-1000. Indexed: Col.Stud.Pers.Abstr. ERIC.

378 959 TH ISSN 0066-9695
A S A I H L. SEMINAR REPORTS. 1963. irreg. $6. Association of Southeast Asian Institutions of Higher Learning, Ratasastra Building, Chulalongkorn University, Henri Dunant Rd., Bangkok 10500, Thailand. circ. 1,000.

A S I L S INTERNATIONAL LAW JOURNAL. (Association of Student International Law Societies) see *LAW*

A T M OCCASIONAL PAPERS. (Association of Teachers of Management) see *BUSINESS AND ECONOMICS — Management*

378 FI ISSN 0355-5798
AABO AKADEMI. AARSSKRIFT. 1917. a. Aabo Akademi, Domkyrkotorget 3, 20500 Aabo, Finland.

378 CN ISSN 0711-7051
ACADEMIC AND ADMINISTRATIVE OFFICERS AT CANADIAN UNIVERSITIES/DIRIGEANTS ET ADMINISTRATEURS DES UNIVERSITES CANADIENNES. (Text in English and French) a. Can.$8.00($9.00) Association of Universities and Colleges of Canada, 151 Slater St., Ottawa, Ont. K1P 5N1, Canada. TEL 613-563-1236.

378 SZ
ACADEMICA HELVETICA. 1976. irreg., no.6/2, 1984. price varies. Paul Haupt AG, Falkenplatz 14, CH-3001 Berne, Switzerland.

060 IT
ACCADEMIA NAZIONALE DI SAN LUCA. ANNUARIO. a. Accademia Nazionale di San Luca, Piazza dell'Accademia di San Luca 77, Rome, Italy.

378.761 US
ALABAMA. COMMISSION ON HIGHER EDUCATION. ANNUAL REPORT. 1973. a. free. Commission on Higher Education, One Court Sq., Ste. 221, Montgomery, AL 36197-0001. TEL 205-269-2700. Ed. Joseph T. Sutton. illus.
 Formerly (until 1978): Alabama. Commission on Higher Education. Biennial Report to the Governor and the Legislature (ISSN 0095-1285)

378 UK
ALTERNATIVES TO "A" LEVEL. biennial. 75p. London and South Eastern Regional Advisory Council for Further Education, Tavistock House South, Tavistock Square, London WC1H 9LR, England.

AMERICAN ASSEMBLY OF COLLEGIATE SCHOOLS OF BUSINESS. MEMBERSHIP DIRECTORY. see *BUSINESS AND ECONOMICS*

AMERICAN ASSOCIATION OF COLLEGES FOR TEACHER EDUCATION. DIRECTORY. see *EDUCATION — Guides To Schools And Colleges*

AMERICAN ASSOCIATION OF ENGINEERING SOCIETIES. ENGINEERING MANPOWER COMMISSION. SALARIES OF ENGINEERS IN EDUCATION. see *ENGINEERING*

378 US
AMERICAN ASSOCIATION OF STATE COLLEGES AND UNIVERSITIES. PROCEEDINGS. a. $6. American Association of State Colleges and Universities, 1 Du Pont Circle, N.W., Washington, DC 20036. TEL 202-293-7070.

378 US ISSN 0517-0680
AMERICAN COLLEGE TESTING PROGRAM. ANNUAL REPORT. 1959/60. a. free. American College Testing Program, 2201 N. Dodge St., Box 168, Iowa City, IA 52243. TEL 319-337-1000.

378.1 US ISSN 0065-7905
AMERICAN CONFERENCE OF ACADEMIC DEANS. PROCEEDINGS. 1946. a. $5. American Conference of Academic Deans, c/o Shelagh Casey, 1818 R St., N.W., Washington, DC 20009. TEL 202-387-3760. Ed. Albert Hamilton. circ. 750. (also avail. in microfilm from UMI,UNM)

EDUCATION — HIGHER EDUCATION

378.242 US ISSN 0065-809X
AMERICAN DOCTORAL DISSERTATIONS. 1956. a. $40. (Association of Research Libraries) University Microfilms International, 300 N. Zeeb Rd., Ann Arbor, MI 48106. TEL 313-761-4700. Ed. Patricia M. Colling. author index. circ. 1,000. (also avail. in microfiche)
Complete listing of all doctoral dissertations accepted by American and Canadian universities

378 FR ISSN 0066-2771
ANNUAIRE DES CHERCHEURS FRANCAIS DU FONDS DE BOURSES DE RECHERCHE SCIENTIFIQUE ET TECHNIQUE DE L'ORGANISATION DU TRAITE DE L'ATLANTIQUE NORD. 1959. irreg. (North Atlantic Treaty Organization, Commission Francaise d'Attribution des Bourses de Recherche Scientifique) Conservatoire National des Arts et Metiers, 292 rue Saint-Martin, 75141 Paris Cedex 03, France. circ. 2,000.

378 FR ISSN 0066-281X
ANNUAIRE DES DOCTEURS (LETTRES) DE L'UNIVERSITE DE PARIS ET AUTRES UNIVERSITES FRANCAISES;* bibliographie analytique des theses. 1967. a. Association Internationale des Docteurs (Lettres) de l'Universite de Paris, 29 rue d'Ulm, 75005 Paris, France.

378 US ISSN 0882-7133
ANNUAL DEGARMO LECTURES. 1975. a. price varies. Society of Professors of Education, c/o Martha Tevis, School of Education, Pan American University, Edinburg, TX 78539. TEL 512-381-3436.
Formerly: DeGarmo Lectures.

378 379 US ISSN 0066-4049
ANNUAL REGISTER OF GRANT SUPPORT: A DIRECTORY OF FUNDING SOURES. 1967. a. $69.50. National Register Publishing Co., Inc. (Subsidiary of: Standard Rate and Data Service) 3400 Glenview Rd., Wilmette, IL 60091. TEL 312-441-2210. index.
Formerly: Grant Data Quarterly.

APPROVED COURSES FOR ACCOUNTANCY EDUCATION. see *BUSINESS AND ECONOMICS — Accounting*

378 700 UK
ART AND DESIGN IN THE REGION. biennial. 60p. London and South Eastern Regional Advisory Council for Further Education, Tavistock House South, Tavistock Square, London WC1H 9LR, England.

378.3 US
A'S & B'S: YOUR GUIDE TO ACADEMIC SCHOLARSHIP. 1978. a. $5. Octameron Associates, Inc., Box 3437, Alexandria, VA 22302. TEL 703-823-1882.
Former titles: A's and B's of Academic Scholarships (ISSN 0277-1470); A's and B's of Merit Scholarships (ISSN 0162-9883)

ASSOCIATE DEGREE EDUCATION FOR NURSING. see *MEDICAL SCIENCES — Nurses And Nursing*

378 US
ASSOCIATED WESTERN UNIVERSITIES. PROGRAM REPORT. biennial. Associated Western Universities, Inc., 142 E. 200 So., Ste. 200, Salt Lake City, UT 84111-1519. TEL 801-364-5659.
Former titles: Associated Western Universities. Biennial Report; Associated Western Universities. Annual Report (ISSN 0066-877X); Associated Western Universities. Report.

378.15 US
ASSOCIATION FOR CONTINUING HIGHER EDUCATION. PROCEEDINGS. 1939. a. $5. Association for Continuing Higher Education, c/o Dr. Roger H. Sublett, Exec. V.P., 1800 Lincoln Ave., Evansville, IN 47722. TEL 812-479-2472. circ. 700.
Formerly: Association of University Evening Colleges. Proceedings (ISSN 0066-9741)

ASSOCIATION FOR PROFESSIONAL EDUCATION FOR MINISTRY. REPORT OF THE BIENNIAL MEETING. see *RELIGIONS AND THEOLOGY*

ASSOCIATION OF AFRICAN UNIVERSITIES. NEW ACQUISITIONS LIST. see *LIBRARY AND INFORMATION SCIENCES*

378 GH
ASSOCIATION OF AFRICAN UNIVERSITIES. REPORT OF THE GENERAL CONFERENCE. 1967. irreg., 6th, 1984. Association of African Universities, Box 5744, Accra, Ghana.

378 US
ASSOCIATION OF COLLEGE UNIONS-INTERNATIONAL. DIRECTORY. a. $30 to non-members; members $15. Association of College Unions-International, 400 E. 7th St., Bloomington, IN 47405. TEL 812-332-8017.

378 US ISSN 0147-1120
ASSOCIATION OF COLLEGE UNIONS-INTERNATIONAL. PROCEEDINGS OF THE ANNUAL CONFERENCE. a. $20 to non-members; members $10. Association of College Unions-International, 400 E. 7th St., Bloomington, IN 47405. TEL 812-332-8017. (also avail. in microfiche)

378 UK
ASSOCIATION OF COLLEGES FOR FURTHER AND HIGHER EDUCATION. HANDBOOK. 1894. biennial. £1.50. Association of Colleges for Further and Higher Education, Doncaster Metropolitan Institute of Higher Education, High Melton, Doncaster DN5 4SZ, England. circ. 1,500.

378 UK ISSN 0307-2274
ASSOCIATION OF COMMONWEALTH UNIVERSITIES. ANNUAL REPORT OF THE COUNCIL TOGETHER WITH THE ACCOUNTS OF THE ASSOCIATION. 1964. a. free. Association of Commonwealth Universities, John Foster House, 36 Gordon Square, London WC1H 0PF, England.
Formerly: Association of Commonwealth Universities. Report of the Council Together with the Accounts of the Association (ISSN 0571-6241)

378 TH ISSN 0066-9687
ASSOCIATION OF SOUTHEAST ASIAN INSTITUTIONS OF HIGHER LEARNING. HANDBOOK: SOUTHEAST ASIAN INSTITUTIONS OF HIGHER LEARNING. (Text in English) 1966. triennial. $28. Association of Southeast Asian Institutions of Higher Learning, Ratasastra Building, Chulalongkorn University, Henri Dunant Rd., Bangkok 10500, Thailand. circ. 1,000.

378 US ISSN 0066-975X
ASSOCIATION OF UNIVERSITY SUMMER SESSIONS. SUMMARY REPORT. 1919. a. membership. Association of University Summer Sessions, Office of Summer Sessions, Indiana University, Bloomington, IN 47405. TEL 821-332-0211. Ed. Leslie J. Coyne. circ. 110.
Formerly: Association of Summer Session Deans and Directors. Summary of Reports.

378 AU
AUSTRIA. BUNDESMINISTERIUM FUER WISSENSCHAFT UND FORSCHUNG. HOCHSCHULBERICHT. triennial. free. Bundesministerium fuer Wissenschaft und Forschung, Minoritenplatz 5, 1010 Vienna, Austria. stat.

378 UK ISSN 0144-4611
AWARDS FOR COMMONWEALTH UNIVERSITY ACADEMIC STAFF. 1971. biennial. £14.90. Association of Commonwealth Universities, John Foster House, 36 Gordon Sq., London WC1H 0PF, England.
Formerly: Awards for Commonwealth University Staff (ISSN 0305-8697)

BACCALAUREATE EDUCATION IN NURSING: KEY TO A PROFESSIONAL CAREER IN NURSING. see *MEDICAL SCIENCES — Nurses And Nursing*

378 US
BALANCE WHEEL FOR ACCREDITATION. 1975. a. Council on Postsecondary Accreditation, One Dupont Circle, N.W., Ste. 305, Washington, DC 20036. TEL 202-452-1433. Ed. J.D. Froom. bibl. circ. 6,000.

378 330 US
BARRON'S GUIDE TO GRADUATE BUSINESS SCHOOLS. a. $12.95. Barron's Educational Series, Inc., 113 Crossways Park Dr., Woodbury, NY 11797.
Formerly: Barron's Guide to Graduate Business Schools: Eastern Edition.

378 BE
BELGIUM. MINISTERE DES AFFAIRES ETRANGERES. REPERTOIRE DES THESES DE DOCTORAT/BELGIUM. MINISTERIE VAN BUITENLANDSE ZAKEN. REPERTORIUM VAN DE DOCTORALE PROEFSCHRIFTEN. (Text in Dutch, English, French, German, Italian and Spanish) 1972. a. free. Ministere des Affaires Etrangeres, 2 rue des Quatre Bras, 1000 Brussels, Belgium.

378 BL
BRAZIL. DEPARTAMENTO DE ASSUNTOS UNIVERSITARIOS. COORDENACAO DE AVALIACAO E CONTROLE. ATIVIDADES DAS INSTITUICOES FEDERAIS DE ENSINO SUPERIOR. a. Ministerio da Educacao e Cultura, Departamento de Assuntos Universitaries, Coordenacao de Avaliacao e Controle, Esplanada dos Ministerios, Bloco H 7. andar, Brasilia, Brazil. charts. stat.

378 BL
BRAZIL. DEPARTAMENTO DE ASSUNTOS UNIVERSITARIOS. COORDENACAO DE AVAILIACAO E CONTROLE. CATALOGO GERAL DAS INSTITUICOES DE ENSINO SUPERIOR. 1973. irreg. Ministerio da Educacao e Cultura, Departamento de Assuntos Universitarios, Coordenacao de Avaliacao e Controle, Esplanada dos Ministerios, Bloco - H 7. andar, Brasilia, Brazil. stat.

378 CN
BUSINESS RESOURCES TOURISM/HOSPITALITY/RECREATION. biennial. free. Tourism Canada, 4E - 235 Queen St., Ottawa, Ont. K1A 0H6, Canada. TEL 613-995-5771.
Supersedes in part: Resources for Tourism/Hospitality/Recreation.

C A L I C O. MONOGRAPH SERIES. (Computer Assisted Language & Instruction Consortium) see *COMPUTERS — Computer Assisted Instruction*

378 US
CALIFORNIA COMMUNITY COLLEGES. MASTER PLAN AND INVENTORY OF PROGRAMS. 1972. a. free. Community Colleges, Chancellor's Office, 1107 Ninth St., Sacramento, CA 95814. TEL 916-322-4656. Ed. Norma Morris. charts. stat. circ. 1,200.

378 UK
CAMBRIDGE UNIVERSITY HANDBOOK. a. $13.95. Cambridge University Press, The Edinburgh Bldg., Shaftesbury Road, Cambridge, CB2 2RU, England.

378 UK
CAMBRIDGE UNIVERSITY REPORTER. 1870. irreg. 20p. per no. Cambridge University Press, The Edinburgh Bldg., Shaftesbury Rd., Cambridge, CB2 2RU, England.

378 CN ISSN 0711-8635
CANADIAN DIRECTORY OF AWARDS FOR GRADUATE STUDY/REPERTOIRE CANADIEN DES BOURSES D'ETUDES SUPERIEURES. (Text in English and French) biennial. Can.$11($12) Association of Universities and Colleges of Canada, 151 Slater St., Ottawa, Ont. K1P 5N1, Canada. TEL 613-563-1236.

378 US
CAPE OF GOOD HOPE IMVO/NEWS. 1986. a. $4 to non-members. Cape of Good Hope Foundation, 425 Ninita Parkway, Pasadena, CA 91106. Ed. Dorothy Raymond.

378 US ISSN 0069-0783
CARSON-NEWMAN COLLEGE, JEFFERSON CITY, TENNESSEE. FACULTY STUDIES. 1965. a. free; limited distribution. ‡ Carson-Newman College, Jefferson City, TN 37760. TEL 615-475-9061. Ed. Robert M. Shurden. circ. 600.

EDUCATION — HIGHER EDUCATION

378 BL
CATALOGO DE PESQUISAS CONCLUIDAS E EM DESENVOLVIMENTO. 1975. irreg. (Universidade Federal de Pernambuco) Editora Universitaria, Recife, Brazil.

378 BL
CATALOGO DOS CURSOS DE POS-GRADUACAO NO BRASIL. 1975. irreg. Ministerio da Educacao e Cultura, Departamento de Assuntos Universitarios, Coordenacao do Aperfeicoamento de Pessoal de Nivel Superior, Brasilia, Brazil.

378 IE ISSN 0069-1399
CELTICA. 1946. irreg., vol.10, 1974. price varies. Dublin Institute for Advanced Studies, 10 Burlington Rd., Dublin, 4, Ireland. Ed.Bd. bk. rev. circ. 212. Indexed: M.L.A. Br.Archaeol.Abstr. Ind.Bk.Rev.Hum.

378 CF
CENTRE D'ENSEIGNEMENT SUPERIEUR DE BRAZZAVILLE. ANNALES. 1965. a. Centre d'Enseignement Superieur de Brazzaville, B.P. 69, Brazzaville, Congo.

378 UK
CHELTENHAM LADIES COLLEGE MAGAZINE. 1880. a. 75p. Magazine Treasurer, Ladies Colllege, Cheltenham, England.

CHEMICAL ENGINEERING FACULTIES. see
ENGINEERING — Chemical Engineering

378 UK
CHRIST'S COLLEGE MAGAZINE. 1886. a. membership. Christ's College, Cambridge, England. adv. bk. rev.

378.3 US ISSN 0190-339X
CHRONICLE STUDENT AID ANNUAL. 1955. a. $21.95. Chronicle Guidance Publications, Inc., Box 1190, Moravia, NY 13118. TEL 315-497-0330. circ. 10,000.
Former titles: Student Aid Annual (ISSN 0585-4555); Student Aid Manual (ISSN 0145-8043)
Alphabetical listing of scholarship titles

378 CN
CLAN MACDONALD ANNUAL. a. McGill University, MacDonald Campus, Students Council, Box 98, MacDonald College, Quebec, Que. H0A 1C0, Canada. TEL 514-392-4311. Ed. Elizabeth Koessler. adv.

378 331.8 US ISSN 0738-1913
COLLECTIVE BARGAINING IN HIGHER EDUCATION AND THE PROFESSIONS. ANNUAL BIBLIOGRAPHY. 1973. a. $20. National Center for the Study of Collective Bargaining in Higher Education and the Professions, Bernard M. Baruch College, City University of New York, 17 Lexington Ave., Box 322, New York, NY 10010. TEL 212-725-3390. Ed. Joel M. Douglas. circ. 1,000.

378.1 US
COLLEGE ADMISSIONS DATA HANDBOOK. Spine title: College Admissions Data. 1960. a. (in 4 vols.) $135. Orchard House, Inc., Balls Hill Rd., Concord, MA 01742. TEL 617-369-0467. Ed. Louis Mazzari. circ. 7,500.
Formerly: College Admissions Data Service.

378 US ISSN 0195-3990
COLLEGE AND UNIVERSITY ADMINISTRATORS DIRECTORY; guide to officers, deans, managers, and other administrative personnel in American colleges and universities. 1980. irreg., latest 1980. $150. Gale Research Company, Book Tower, Detroit, MI 48226. TEL 313-961-2242.

378 US ISSN 0147-5894
COLLEGE AND UNIVERSITY ADMISSIONS AND ENROLLMENT, NEW YORK STATE. 1948. a. free. ‡ Education Department, Information Center on Education, Albany, NY 12234. charts. stats. circ. controlled. (back issues avail.)
Formerly: College and University Enrollment in New York State (ISSN 0077-9180)

378 US ISSN 0077-9172
COLLEGE AND UNIVERSITY DEGREES CONFERRED, NEW YORK STATE. 1950. a. free. Education Department, Information Center on Education, Albany, NY 12234. charts. stats. circ. controlled. (back issues avail.)

378 US ISSN 0093-3414
COLLEGE AND UNIVERSITY EMPLOYEES, NEW YORK STATE. 1960. a. Education Department, Information Center on Education, Albany, NY 12234. charts. stats. circ. 1,000. (back issues avail.)
Formerly: New York (State). Education Department. Employees in Colleges and Universities.

378 FR ISSN 0069-5580
COLLEGE DE FRANCE. ANNUAIRE; Resume des Cours et Travaux. 1901. a. 90 F. College de France, 11 place Marcelin Berthelot, 75231 Paris Cedex 05, France (Order from: C I D, 131 bd. St. Michel, 75005 Paris, France) Ed.Bd.

378 US
COLLEGE GRANTS FROM UNCLE SAM. 1981. a. $3. Octameron Associates, Inc., Box 3437, Alexandria, VA 22302. TEL 703-823-1882.
Supersedes (1979-1980): Am I Eligible? The Easy Way to Calculate the B E O G Index.

COLLEGE - INDUSTRY EDUCATION CONFERENCE. PROCEEDINGS. see
ENGINEERING

378 US
COLLEGE LOANS FROM UNCLE SAM. 1981. a. $3. Octameron Associates, Inc., Box 3437, Alexandria, VA 22302. TEL 703-823-1882.
Formerly (1979-1980): Quick Help from the Governor; a Directory of State Financial Aid Agencies.

360 US
COLLEGES AND UNIVERSITIES WITH ACCREDITED UNDERGRADUATE SOCIAL WORK PROGRAMS. a. $2. Council on Social Work Education, 1744 R St., N.W., Washington, DC 20009.

378 US
COMMITTEE ON INSTITUTIONAL COOPERATION. BIENNIAL REPORT. 1979-1981. biennial. free. ‡ Committee on Institutional Cooperation, 302 E. John St., Ste. 1705, Champaign, IL 61820. TEL 217-333-8475. Ed. Eric Weir. circ. controlled.
Formerly: Committee on Institutional Cooperation. Annual Report (ISSN 0069-6854)

378 UK ISSN 0069-7745
COMMONWEALTH UNIVERSITIES YEARBOOK. 1914. a. $185. Association of Commonwealth Universities, John Foster House, 36 Gordon Sq., London WC1H 0PF, England (Dist. in U.S. by: Gale Research Co., Detroit, Mich. 48226) Ed. T. Craig. index.

378 UK
COMPENDIUM OF ADVANCED COURSES IN COLLEGES OF FURTHER & HIGHER EDUCATION. a. £3.25. London and South Eastern Regional Advisory Council for Further Education, Tavistock House South, Tavistock Square, London WC1H 9LR, England.

378 UK ISSN 0571-625X
COMPENDIUM OF UNIVERSITY ENTRANCE REQUIREMENTS FOR FIRST DEGREE COURSES IN THE UNITED KINGDOM. 1963. a. £10.71. Association of Commonwealth Universities, John Foster House, 36 Gordon Square, London WC1 H OPF, England (Avail. only from: Sheed and Ward Ltd., 2 Creechurch Lane, London EC3A 5AQ, England) circ. 15,000.

378 II
CONFERENCE OF VICE-CHANCELLORS. PROCEEDINGS. 1961. irreg. University Grants Commission, 35 Ferozeshah Rd., 110 001 New Delhi, India. TEL 386 365. Ed. V. Appa Rao. circ. 6,000.

378.54 II
CONFERENCE OF VICE-CHANCELLORS. REPORT. (Text in English) University Grants Commission, 35 Ferozeshah Rd., New Delhi 110001, India.

378 SZ
CONFERENCE UNIVERSITAIRE SUISSE. RAPPORT ANNUEL. German edition: Schweizerische Hochschulkonferenz. Jahresbericht. 1969. a. free. Conference Universitaire Suisse - Schweizerische Hochschulkonferenz, Wildhainweg 21, CH-3012 Berne, Switzerland. circ. 600 (German edt.); 300 (French edt.)

378 VE
CONSEJO NACIONAL DE INVESTIGACIONES CIENTIFICAS Y TECNOLOGICAS. DEPARTAMENTO DE EDUCACION. DIRECTORIO NACIONAL DE CURSOS DE POSTGRADO. irreg. Consejo Nacional de Investigaciones Cientificas y Tecnologicas, Departamento de Educacion, Apartado 70617 Los Ruices, Caracas, Venezuela.

378 IT
CONSORZIO UNIVERSITARIO. PUBBLICAZIONI. SEZIONE MISCELLANEA. 1975. irreg. exchange. Universita degli Studi di Udine, Biblioteca Centrale, Udine, Italy.

378.1 US
COUNCIL FOR ADVANCEMENT AND SUPPORT OF EDUCATION. MEMBERSHIP DIRECTORY. 1974. a. $75. Council for Advancement and Support of Education, 11 Dupont Circle, Suite 400, Washington, DC 20036. TEL 202-328-5900. Ed. Claudia Perry.
Formerly: Council for Advancement and Support of Education. Directory; Supersedes in part: American College Public Relations Association. Directory (ISSN 0065-7816)

378.15 US ISSN 0070-1076
COUNCIL OF GRADUATE SCHOOLS IN THE UNITED STATES. PROCEEDINGS OF THE ANNUAL MEETING. 1961. a. price varies. Council of Graduate Schools in the U.S., One Dupont Circle, Suite 430, Washington, DC 20036. TEL 202-223-3791. Ed. E. Khalil. circ. 750. Indexed: ERIC.

378 CN
COUNCIL OF ONTARIO UNIVERSITIES QUADRENNIAL REVIEW. 1975. quadrennial. free. Council of Ontario Universities, Suite 8039, 130 St. George Street, Toronto, Ontario M5S 2T4, Canada. TEL 416-979-2165. Ed. Willliam Sayres. circ. 15,000. (reprint service avail. from UMI)
Former titles: Council of Ontario Universities Triennial Review (ISSN 0315-9590); Council of Ontario Universities Biennial Review (ISSN 0084-8972); Council of Ontario Universities. Annual Review (ISSN 0315-9000)

378 060 VE ISSN 0070-170X
CUADERNOS DE ORIENTACION.* 1966. irreg. Universidad del Zulia, Facultad de Humanidades y Educacion, Apartado de Correos 415, Maracaibo, Venezuela.

378 US ISSN 0070-1971
CURRENT ISSUES IN HIGHER EDUCATION. (Issues 1981 and before are based on presentations at annual National Conference on Higher Education) 1946. irreg. price varies. American Association for Higher Education, One Dupont Circle, Suite 600, Washington, DC 20036. TEL 202-293-6440. index. circ. 6,000. (also avail. in microform from UMI) Indexed: Educ.Ind. CERDIC.

CURRICULA IN THE ATMOSPHERIC, OCEANIC AND RELATED SCIENCES. see
METEOROLOGY

378 US
D.H.E. DATA BRIEFS. 1973-1976; resumed 1981. irreg. Department of Higher Education, 225 West State St., Box 1293, Trenton, NJ 08625. TEL 609-292-4390. charts. stat.

378 US
D.H.E. RESEARCH NOTE. 1975. irreg. Department of Higher Education, 225 West State St., Box 1293, Trenton, NJ 08625. TEL 609-292-4390. charts. stat.

378 US
DANFORTH FOUNDATION. ANNUAL REPORT. 1927. a. Danforth Foundation, 231 South Bemiston Ave., St. Louis, MO 63105-1903. TEL 314-862-6200.

EDUCATION — HIGHER EDUCATION

378 070   DK   ISSN 0108-285X
DANMARKS JOURNALISTHOEJSKOLES
AARSKRIFT. 1967. a. Danmarks
Journalisthoejskole, Olof Palmes Alle 11, 8200
Aarhus N, Denmark. Ed. Thorkild Behrens. illus.
circ. 1,400.
    Formerly: D J H.

378   US   ISSN 0098-5279
DATA BOOK ON ILLINOIS HIGHER
EDUCATION. a. Board of Higher Education, 4 W.
Old Capitol Sq., 500 Reisch Bldg., Springfield, IL
62701. TEL 217-782-2551.

378   US   ISSN 0092-3761
DATA ON IOWA'S AREA SCHOOLS. a.
Department of Public Instruction, Grimes State
Building, Des Moines, IA 50319. TEL 515-281-
3191. illus, stat. Indexed: ERIC. Key Title: Data on
Iowa's Area Schools and Public Junior College.

378.41   UK
DEGREE COURSE OFFERS. 1971. a. £9.95.
(Midland Bank Plc) Trotman and Co. Ltd., 12-14
Hill Rise, Richmond Hill, Richmond, Surrey TW10
6UA, England. Ed. Brian Heap. adv. circ. 17,000.

378   GH
DIRECTORY OF AFRICAN UNIVERSITIES.
biennial. $15 per copy. Association of African
Universities, Box 5744, Accra, Ghana.

378   CN   ISSN 0706-2338
DIRECTORY OF CANADIAN UNIVERSITIES/
REPERTOIRE DES UNIVERSITES
CANADIENNES. (Text in English and French)
1956. biennial. Can.$12.50($15) ‡ Association of
Universities and Colleges of Canada, 151 Slater St.,
Ottawa, Ontario K1P 5N1, Canada. TEL 613-563-
1236. circ. 6,000.
    Former titles: Directory of Canadian Universities
and Colleges; Universities and Colleges of Canada
(ISSN 0083-3932)

378   US   ISSN 0084-988X
DIRECTORY OF COLLEGE STORES. 1956. irreg.
$50. B. Klein Publications, Box 8503, Coral Springs,
FL 33065. TEL 305-752-1708.

378   CN   ISSN 0705-8160
DIRECTORY OF COURSES/TOURISM/
HOSPITALITY/RECREATION. 1976. biennial.
free. Tourism Canada, 235 Queen Canada, 4th Fl.
East, Ottawa, Ont. K1A 0H6, Canada. TEL 613-
995-5771.

617.6 378   US
DIRECTORY OF DENTAL EDUCATORS. 1966.
biennial. price varies. American Association of
Dental Schools, 1625 Massachusetts Ave., N.W.,
Washington, DC 20036. TEL 202-667-9433.
(reprint service avail. from UMI)
    Former titles: Directory of Dental and Allied
Dental Educators (ISSN 0271-8677); Directory of
Dental Educators (ISSN 0090-0141); until 1971-
1972: Directory of Dental Educators in the United
States and Canada.

378 331.8   US   ISSN 0276-7805
DIRECTORY OF FACULTY CONTRACTS AND
BARGAINING AGENTS IN INSTITUTIONS OF
HIGHER EDUCATION. 1975. a. $20. National
Center for the Study of Collective Bargaining in
Higher Education and the Professions, Bernard M.
Baruch College, City University of New York, 17
Lexington Ave., Box 322, New York, NY 10010.
TEL 212-725-3390. Ed. Joel M. Douglas.

378   UK   ISSN 0266-8467
DIRECTORY OF FIRST DEGREE AND
DIPLOMA OF HIGHER EDUCATION
COURSES. a. free. Council for National Academic
Awards, 344-354 Gray's Inn Rd., London WC1X
8BP, England. circ. 30,000.

378.3   II   ISSN 0084-9936
DIRECTORY OF FULBRIGHT ALUMNI. (Text in
English) 1969. triennial. free. United States
Educational Foundation in India, Fulbright House,
12 Hailey Rd., New Delhi 110001, India. Ed. Dr.
P.D. Sayal. cum.index 1950-70. circ. controlled.

378   UK
DIRECTORY OF FURTHER EDUCATION. 1962.
a. £48.25 hardcover; £39.95 paperback. Hobsons
Ltd., Bateman St., Cambridge CB2 1LZ, England.
circ. 2,700.

370   US   ISSN 0732-2755
DIRECTORY OF GRADUATE PROGRAMS IN
THE COMMUNICATION ARTS AND
SCIENCES. 1967. every 5 yrs. $12.50. Speech
Communication Association, 5105 Backlick Rd.,
No. E, Annandale, VA 22003. TEL 703-750-0533.
Ed. Robert N. Hall. circ. 1,000.
    Formerly: Directory of Graduate Programs in the
Speech Communication Arts and Sciences (ISSN
0070-5616)

378.774   US
DIRECTORY OF MICHIGAN INSTITUTIONS OF
HIGHER EDUCATION. a. Department of
Education, Box 30008, Lansing, MI 48909. TEL
517-373-3360.

378 530   US
DIRECTORY OF PHYSICS & ASTRONOMY
STAFF (YEAR) 1959. biennial. $30. American
Institute of Physics, 335 E. 45th St., New York, NY
10017. TEL 516-349-7800. Ed. Dion W.J. Shea.
stat. circ. 4,000.
    Former titles: Directory of Physics & Astronomy
Staff Members (ISSN 0361-2228) & Directory of
Physics and Astronomy Facilities in North
American Colleges and Universities (ISSN 0419-
3253)

378   UK   ISSN 0266-8459
DIRECTORY OF POSTGRADUATE AND POST-
EXPERIENCE COURSES. a. free. Council for
National Academic Awards, 344/354 Gray's Inn
Rd., London WC1X 8BP, England. circ. 10,000.
    Formerly: Directory of Postgraduate and Post-
Graduate Experience Courses.

378   US
DIRECTORY OF PROFESSIONAL PERSONNEL:
STATE HIGHER EDUCATION AGENCIES
AND BOARDS. a. $10. State Higher Education
Executive Officers, 310 Lincoln Tower, 1860
Lincoln St., Denver, CO 80295. TEL 303-830-3686.

378   US   ISSN 0146-7336
DIRECTORY OF RESEARCH GRANTS. 1975. a.
$74.50. Oryx Press, 2214 N. Central at Encanto,
Ste. 103, Phoenix, AZ 85004. TEL 602-254-6156.

378 610   US
DIRECTORY OF RESIDENCY TRAINING
ACCREDITED BY THE ACCREDITATION
COUNCIL FOR GRADUATE MEDICAL
EDUCATION. 1914. a. American Medical
Association, 535 N. Dearborn St., Chicago, IL
60611. TEL 312-645-5000. Ed. Anne Crowley.
(reprint service avail. from UMI)
    Former titles: American Medical Association.
Directory of Residency Training Programs;
American Medical Association. Directory of
Accredited Residencies (ISSN 0164-1670);
American Medical Association. Directory of
Approved Residencies (ISSN 0097-899X); until
1975: American Medical Association. Directory of
Approved Internships and Residencies (ISSN 0419-
2141)

378   IT
DOC ITALIA. 1972. biennial. L.130000. (Istituto
Nazionale Informazione) Editoriale Italiana, Via
Vigliena, 10, Rome, Italy. illus. circ. 5,000.
    Formerly: Doc; Documentazione (ISSN 0391-
5018)

DOKUMENTATION
SPRACHWISSENSCHAFTLICHE
FORSCHUNGSVORHABEN. see *LINGUISTICS*

DOKUMENTE ZUM HOCHSCHULSPORT. see
SPORTS AND GAMES

378   US   ISSN 0277-6987
DON'T MISS OUT; the ambitious student's guide to
scholarships and loans. 1976. a. $5. Octameron
Associates, Inc., Box 3437, Alexandria, VA 22302.
TEL 703-823-1882. Eds. Robert Leider, Anna
Leider. bibl. illus. stat. circ. 300,000. (back issues
avail.)

378   US
E R I C CLEARINGHOUSE FOR JUNIOR
COLLEGES. HORIZONS ISSUES.
MONOGRAPH SERIES. 1968. a. $5. E R I C
Clearinghouse for Junior Colleges, 8118 Math
Sciences Bldg., University of California, Los
Angeles, CA 90024. TEL 213-825-3931. circ. 2,000.

378   US   ISSN 0531-9315
E R I C CLEARINGHOUSE FOR JUNIOR
COLLEGES. TOPICAL PAPER SERIES. 1968.
irreg. (1-2/yr.) free. E R I C Clearinghouse for
Junior Colleges, 8118 Math Sciences Bldg.,
University of California, Los Angeles, CA 90024.
TEL 213-825-4321. Dir. Arthur M. Cohen. bibl.
charts. stat. circ. 2,000. (also avail. in microfiche)
Indexed: Res.Educ.

378   US   ISSN 0277-7002
EARN & LEARN: COOPERATIVE EDUCATION
OPPORTUNITIES OFFERED BY THE
FEDERAL GOVERNMENT. 1979. a. $3.50.
Octameron Associates, Inc., Box 3437, Alexandria,
VA 22302. TEL 703-836-1019. circ. 20,000.
    Formerly: Federal Government and Cooperative
Education (ISSN 0270-434X)

378 323   SA   ISSN 0070-8976
EDGAR BROOKES ACADEMIC AND HUMAN
FREEDOM LECTURE. 1965. a. University of
Natal, Students Representative Council, Box 375,
Pietermaritzburg, South Africa. circ. 1,000.

378   UK
EDUCATION FOR BUSINESS AND
MANAGEMENT IN THE REGION. biennial.
£1.40. London and South Eastern Regional
Advisory Council for Further Education, Tavistock
House South, Tavistock Square, London WC1H
9LR, England.

EDUCATION FOR NURSING: THE DIPLOMA
WAY. see *MEDICAL SCIENCES — Nurses And
Nursing*

378 690   UK
EDUCATION FOR THE CONSTRUCTION
INDUSTRY IN THE REGION. biennial. £1.
London and South Eastern Regional Advisory
Council for Further Education, Tavistock House
South, Tavistock Square, London WC1H 9LR,
England.

378   FR   ISSN 0070-9182
EDUCATION IN EUROPE. SECTION 1: HIGHER
EDUCATION AND RESEARCH. 1963. irreg.
price varies. Council of Europe, Council for Cultural
Co-Operation, Publications Section, Strasbourg,
France (Dist. in U.S. by Manhattan Publishing Co.,
P.O. Box 650, Croton-on-Hudson, N.Y. 10520)

EDUCATION IN KENYA; index of articles on
education. see *EDUCATION — Abstracting,
Bibliographies, Statistics*

ENGINEERING COLLEGE RESEARCH AND
GRADUATE STUDY. see *ENGINEERING*

378 620   UK
ENGINEERING EDUCATION IN THE REGION.
biennial. £1.25. London and South Eastern Regional
Advisory Council for Further Education, Tavistock
House South, Tavistock Square, London WC1H
9LR, England.

378   US   ISSN 0071-1187
ERNEST BLOCH LECTURES. 1969. irreg. price
varies. University of California Press, 2120 Berkeley
Way, Berkeley, CA 94720. TEL 415-642-4247.

370.7   CL   ISSN 0716-050X
ESTUDIOS PEDAGOGICOS. (Abstracts in English
and Spanish) 1976. a. Esc.450($5) Universidad
Austral de Chile, Facultad de Filosofia y
Humanidades, Casilla 567, Valdivia, Chile. Ed. Rene
Novoa J. abstr. bibl. charts. stat. circ. 650.

378.761   US
FACT BOOK. HIGHER EDUCATION IN
ALABAMA. 1972. a. Commission on Higher
Education, Montgomery, AL 36104. TEL 205-269-
2700. illus.
    Formerly: Fact Book. Alabama Institutions of
Higher Education, Universities and Colleges (ISSN
0095-0637)

EDUCATION — HIGHER EDUCATION

378.73   US
FACT BOOK FOR HIGHER EDUCATION. 1958. biennial. $36. (American Council on Education) Macmillan Publishing Company, 866 Third Ave., New York, NY 10022. Ed. Cecilia Ottinger. stat. cum.index.
    Former titles: Fact Book for Academic Administrators (ISSN 0198-8425); Fact Book for Academic Administration; Until 1980: Fact Book on Higher Education (ISSN 0363-6720); F B; A Fact Book on Higher Education (ISSN 0014-6501)

378   US   ISSN 0191-1643
FACT BOOK ON HIGHER EDUCATION IN THE SOUTH. 1965. biennial. price varies. Southern Regional Education Board, 1340 Spring St., N.W., Atlanta, GA 30309. TEL 404-875-9211.

378   UK   ISSN 0260-0749
FINANCIAL AID FOR FIRST DEGREE STUDY AT COMMONWEALTH UNIVERSITIES. 1973. biennial. £3.95. Association of Commonwealth Universities, John Foster House, 36 Gordon Square, London WC1H OPF, England.

378.3   US   ISSN 0085-0543
FINANCIAL AIDS TO ILLINOIS STUDENTS. 1968. biennial. State Board of Education, 100 N. First St., Springfield, IL 62777. TEL 217-782-7913.

020 378.3   US   ISSN 0569-6275
FINANCIAL ASSISTANCE FOR LIBRARY EDUCATION. a. free. American Library Association, Standing Committee on Library Education, 50 E. Huron St., Chicago, IL 60611. TEL 312-944-6780.

378   US
FINANCING HIGHER EDUCATION. 1959. irreg. free. Southern Regional Education Board, 1340 Spring St., N.W., Atlanta, GA 30309. TEL 404-875-9211. charts. stat.

371   US   ISSN 0071-5999
FLORIDA REQUIREMENTS FOR TEACHER CERTIFICATION. 1923. irreg. free. Department of Education, Knott Bldg., Tallahassee, FL 32304. TEL 904-488-1234. Ed. Ralph D. Turlington.

016.05   US   ISSN 0428-6766
FLORIDA STATE UNIVERSITY. PUBLICATIONS OF THE FACULTY. Running title: F S U Faculty Publications. 1954. irreg. Florida State University, Office of the Dean, Graduate Studies & Research, Tallahassee, FL 32306. TEL 904-644-2428. Ed. Clifton Paisley. circ. 2,500. Key Title: Publications of the Faculty - Research Council, Florida State University.
    Continues: Florida State University. Publications of the Faculty and Theses Directed.

378   UK
FOOD TECHNOLOGY AND CATERING IN THE REGION. biennial. £1. London and South Eastern Regional Advisory Council for Further Education, Tavistock House South, Tavistock Square, London WC1H 9LR, England.

378   US
FOR GRADUATES ONLY. 1979. a. Senior Publications, Ltd., 339 N. Main St., New City, NY 10956. TEL 914-638-0333. Ed. Gerald Greyson. circ. 100,000.

378   AU   ISSN 0429-1573
FORSCHUNGEN ZUR INNSBRUCKER UNIVERSITAETSGESCHICHTE. (Subseries of: Universitaet Innsbruck. Veroeffentlichungen) 1962. irreg., vol.10, 1971. price varies. (Universitaet Innsbruck) Oesterreichische Kommissionsbuchhandlung, Maximilianstrasse 17, A-6020 Innsbruck, Austria. Ed. Franz Huter.

378   US
G P N EDUCATIONAL MEDIA. COLLEGE-ADULT. 1985. biennial. Great Plains National Instructional Television Library, Box 80669, Lincoln, NE 68501 TEL 800-228-4630. Eds. Richard L. Spence, Thomas Henderson. circ. 8,500.
    Superseded in part: Great Plains National Instructional Television Library. Recorded Visual Instruction (ISSN 0740-2732)

378   GE
GERMANY (DEMOCRATIC REPUBLIC, 1949-). MINISTERIUM FUER HOCH- UND FACHSCHULWESEN. VERFUEGUNGEN UND MITTEILUNGEN.* irreg. M.0.90. Ministerium fuer Hoch- und Fachschulwesen, Rechtsabteilung, Marx-Engels-Platz 2, Berlin 102, E. Germany (D.D.R.)

378   GH
GHANA. NATIONAL COUNCIL FOR HIGHER EDUCATION. ANNUAL REPORT. a. National Council for Higher Education, Accra, Ghana.

001.3 378   GW   ISSN 0085-1108
GOETTINGER UNIVERSITAETSREDEN. 1941. irreg. price varies. Vandenhoeck und Ruprecht, Theaterstr. 13, Postfach 37 53, 3400 Goettingen, W. Germany (B.R.D.)

378   US   ISSN 0072-4904
GOING-TO-COLLEGE HANDBOOK. 1946. a. $2. Outlook Publishers, Inc., 512 E. Main St., Richmond, VA 23219. TEL 804-649-1371. Ed. Aubrey N. Brown, Jr. adv. bk. rev. circ. 40,000.

378 507   US   ISSN 0072-5250
GRADUATE FELLOWSHIP AWARDS ANNOUNCED BY NATIONAL SCIENCE FOUNDATION. a. free. U.S. National Science Foundation, 1800 G St., N.W., Washington, DC 20550 TEL 202-655-4000. (Orders to: Supt. Doc., Washington, DC 20402)

GRADUATE PROGRAMS: PHYSICS, ASTRONOMY, AND RELATED FIELDS. see PHYSICS

GRADUATE SCHOOL JOURNAL. see EDUCATION — School Organization And Administration

378   UK
GRADUATE STUDIES. 1972. a. £54.80. Hobsons Ltd., Bateman St., Cambridge CB2 1LZ, England. Ed. Jenny Knight. adv. circ. 2,000.

378   UK   ISSN 0144-462X
GRANTS FOR STUDY VISITS BY UNIVERSITY ADMINISTRATORS AND LIBRARIANS. 1979. biennial. £4.20. Association of Commonwealth Universities, John Foster House, 36 Gordon Square, London WC1H 0PF, England.

378   UK
GRANTS REGISTER (UK) 1968. biennial. Macmillan Publishers Ltd., Brunel Rd., Houndmills, Basingstoke, Hants, England (And St. Martins Press, 175 Fifth Ave., New York, NY 10010)

GREAT BRITAIN. ECONOMIC & SOCIAL RESEARCH COUNCIL. BURSARY HANDBOOK. see SOCIAL SCIENCES: COMPREHENSIVE WORKS

GREAT BRITAIN. ECONOMIC & SOCIAL RESEARCH COUNCIL. STUDENTSHIP HANDBOOK. see SOCIAL SCIENCES: COMPREHENSIVE WORKS

378   UK   ISSN 0072-7237
GREAT BRITAIN. UNIVERSITY GRANTS COMMITTEE. ANNUAL SURVEY. 1964/65. a. £1. University Grants Committee, 14 Park Crescent, London W1N 4DH, England (Avail. from H.M.S.O., c/o Liaison Officer, Atlantic House, Holborn Viaduct, London EC1P 1BN, England)

301.07   CN   ISSN 0316-1854
GUIDE TO DEPARTMENTS OF SOCIOLOGY, ANTHROPOLOGY AND ARCHAEOLOGY IN UNIVERSITIES AND MUSEUMS IN CANADA/ ANNUAIRE DES DEPARTEMENTS DE SOCIOLOGIE, D'ANTHROPOLOGIE ET D'ARCHEOLOGIE DES UNIVERSITIES ET DES MUSEES DU CANADA. 1974. irreg. Can.$5 to non-members. Canadian Sociology and Anthropology Association, Concordia University, 1455 Bd. de Maisonneuve W., Montreal, Que. H3G 1M8, Canada. TEL 514-848-8780. Ed. Kathleen Herman.
    Formerly: Guide to Departments of Sociology and Anthropology in Canadian Universities (ISSN 0315-0895)

GUIDE TO GRADUATE DEPARTMENTS OF SOCIOLOGY. see SOCIOLOGY

378   UK   ISSN 0265-2730
GUIDE TO POSTGRADUATE DEGREES, DIPLOMAS AND COURSES IN MEDICINE. 1975. a. £6. Council for Postgraduate Medical Education in England & Wales, 7 Marylebone Rd., London NW1 5HH, England.
    Formerly: Summary of Postgraduate Diplomas and Courses in Medicine (ISSN 0302-3494)

378   US
HANDBOOK FOR RECRUITING MINORITY COLLEGE STUDENTS. 1973. biennial. $15. Council on Career Development for Minorities, Inc., 1341 W. Mockingbird Ln., Ste. 412E, Dallas, TX 75247. TEL 214-631-3677. Ed. Andre G. Beaumont. circ. 2,500.
    Former titles: Handbook for Recruiting at Minority Colleges (ISSN 0163-2795); (until 1979): Handbook for Recruiting at the Historically Black Colleges (ISSN 0146-5104)

HANDBOOK OF DEGREE AND ADVANCED COURSES IN INSTITUTES/COLLEGES OF HIGHER EDUCATION, COLLEGES OF EDUCATION, POLYTECHNICS, UNIVERSITY DEPARTMENTS OF EDUCATION. see EDUCATION — Guides To Schools And Colleges

378   AU
HANDBUCH DER ALLGEMEINBILDENDEN HOEHEREN SCHULEN OESTERREICHS. 1954. biennial. S.150($10) Gewerkschaft der Oeffentlich Bediensteten, Bundessektion Hoehere Schule, Lackierergasse 7, A-1090 Vienna, Austria. Ed. Herbert Kreuzer. adv.

HANDELSHOEJSKOLEN I KOEBENHAVN. H A-CENTER. RAPPORT. see BUSINESS AND ECONOMICS

378 001.6   US   ISSN 0743-0221
HANDS ON! 1977. irreg. $10 contribution. Technical Education Research Centers (TERC), 1696 Massachusetts Ave., Cambridge, MA 02138. TEL 617-547-3890. Ed. Peggy Kapisovsky. bk. rev. circ. 10,000. Indexed: Sci.Abstr.

378   FI
HELSINGIN KAUPPAKORKEAKOULU. JULKAISUSARJA A. VAEITOESKIRJOJA. (Text in English and Finnish) irreg. Helsinki School of Economics, Runeberginkatu 22-24, 00100 Helsinki 10, Finland.

378 011 310   US   ISSN 0748-4364
HIGHER EDUCATION ABSTRACTS; abstracts of periodical literature, monographs and conference papers on college students, faculty and administration. 1965. q. $45 to individuals; institutions $80. Claremont Graduate School, Claremont, CA 91711. TEL 714-621-8000. Ed. Bonny M. McLaughlin. bk. rev. abstr. index. circ. 1,600. (also avail. in microform from UMI; back issues avail.)
    Formerly (until fall, 1984): College Student Personnel Abstracts (ISSN 0010-1168)

378   UK   ISSN 0306-1744
HIGHER EDUCATION IN THE UNITED KINGDOM. 1936. biennial. £7.50. Longman Group Ltd., Fourth Ave., Harlow, Essex CM19 5AA, England. adv.

378 323.42   US
HIGHER EDUCATION OPPORTUNITIES FOR MINORITIES AND WOMEN: ANNOTATED SELECTIONS. a. free. U.S. Department of Education, Washington, DC 20202.

378   US
HISTORY OF HIGHER EDUCATION ANNUAL. 1981. a. $10. University of Rochester, Latimore Hall, Rochester, NY 14627. Ed. Harold S. Wechsler. adv. bk. rev. circ. 200.

378 942   UK   ISSN 0144-5138
HISTORY OF UNIVERSITIES. (Text in English, French, German, Italian and Spanish) 1981. a. £24($48) Oxford University Press, Walton St., Oxford OX2 6DP, England. Ed. Charles Schmitt. adv. bk. rev. index. circ. 500. Indexed: Hist.Abstr. Amer.Hist.& Life. Rel.Ind.One.

HOME ECONOMICS IN INSTITUTIONS GRANTING BACHELORS OR HIGHER DEGREES. see HOME ECONOMICS

EDUCATION — HIGHER EDUCATION

378 NO ISSN 0333-3620
I A S P NEWSLETTER. (Text in English) 1982. irreg. (5-6/yr.) free. (International Association of Scholarly Publishers) Norwegian University Press, Box 2959, Toyen, 0608 Oslo 6, Norway. Ed. E. Aslaksen.

I C T C REVIEW. (International Co-operative Training Centre) see *BUSINESS AND ECONOMICS — Cooperatives*

378 CN ISSN 0382-0769
I D E E S. (Innovations, Demarches, Experiences dans l'Enseignement Superieur) 1975-1980, N.S. 198? irreg. Association des Universites Partiellement Ou Entierement de Langue Francaise, Universite de Montreal, B.P. 6128, Montreal, Que. H3C 3J7, Canada. TEL 514-343-6630. circ. 700.

378 068 II
I I A S OCCASIONAL PAPERS. (Text in English) 1974. irreg. price varies. Indian Institute of Advanced Study, Rashtrapati Nivas, Summer Hill, Simla 171005, India.

378.773 US ISSN 0094-8322
ILLINOIS. BOARD OF HIGHER EDUCATION. DIRECTORY OF HIGHER EDUCATION. a. Board of Higher Education, 4 W. Old Capitol Sq., 500 Reisch Bldg., Springfield, IL 62701. TEL 217-782-2551. Key Title: Directory of Higher Education.

378.1 US ISSN 0362-5524
ILLINOIS. BOARD OF HIGHER EDUCATION. STATEWIDE SPACE SURVEY. 1962. biennial. Board of Higher Education, 500 Reisch Bldg., 4 W. Old Capitol Sq., Springfield, IL 62701. TEL 217-782-2551. Key Title: Statewide Space Survey.

378.1 US
ILLINOIS COMMUNITY COLLEGE BOARD. BIENNIAL REPORT. 1967? biennial. Community College Board, 509 S. 6th St., Rm. 400, Springfield, IL 62701. TEL 217-785-0123. Ed. James M. Howard. stat.
Supersedes: Illinois. Junior College Board. Annual Report (ISSN 0092-7783)

378.73 US ISSN 0734-6735
INDEPENDENT HIGHER EDUCATION.* a. National Institute of Independent Colleges and Universities, 122 C St., N.W., Ste. 750, Washington, DC 20001.
Formerly: Private Higher Education (ISSN 0364-3735)

378 IO
INDONESIA. DIRECTORATE GENERAL OF HIGHER EDUCATION. ANNUAL REPORT/ INDONESIA. DIREKTORAT JENDERAL PENDIDIKAN TINGGI. LAPORAN TAHUNAN. (Text in Indonesian) 1975. a. Directorate General of Higher Education, Jakarta, Indonesia. circ. 500.

378 AU ISSN 0020-0077
INFORMATION FUER AUSLAENDISCHE STUDIENBEWERBER AN OESTERREICHISCHEN HOCHSCHULEN/ INFORMATION FOR FOREIGN STUDENTS INTENDING TO STUDY AT AN AUSTRIAN INSTITUTION OF HIGHER LEARNING; fuer auslaendische Studienbewerber an oesterreichischen Universitaeten und Kunsthochschulen. 1961/1962. irreg. ‡ Oesterreichischer Auslandsstudentendienst, Dr. Karl Lueger-Ring 1, A-1010 Vienna, Austria. Eds. Elisabeth Elser, Ludwig Koller. circ. 12,500.

378 PL ISSN 0239-9253
INFORMATOR DLA KANDYDATON NA STUDIA PODYPLOMOWE I DOKTORANCKIE. 1971/72. a. price varies. (Ministerstwo Nauki, Szkolnictwa Wyzszego i Techniki) Panstwowe Wydawnictwo Naukowe, Miodowa 10, 00-251 Warsaw, Poland (Dist. by: Ars Polona, Krakowskie Przedmiescie 7, 00-068 Warsaw, Poland) Ed. K. Dolinski. circ. 3,900.

378.1 US ISSN 0363-2601
INNOVATIVE GRADUATE PROGRAMS DIRECTORY. 1975. irreg., 1986 edt. in prep. $8. Empire State College, Learning Resources Center, Saratoga Springs, NY 12866. TEL 518-587-2100. Ed. Allyn Van Deusen. circ. 10,000.

378 AU
INNSBRUCKER UNIVERSITAETSREDEN. (Subseries of: Universitaet Innsbruck. Veroeffentlichungen) 1969. irreg., vol.8, 1974. price varies. (Universitaet Innsbruck) Oesterreichische Kommissionsbuchhandlung, Maximilianstrasse 17, A-6020 Innsbruck, Austria.

INSTEAD. see *EDUCATION — School Organization And Administration*

378 EI
INSTITUT DE LA COMMUNAUTE EUROPEENNE POUR LES ETUDES UNIVERSITAIRES. RECHERCHE. RESEARCH. no.8, 1974. irreg. European Community Institute for University Studies - Institut de la Communaute Europeenne pour les Etudes Universitaires, 200 rue de la Loi, B-1040 Brussels, Belgium.

378 UK
INTERNATIONAL ASSOCIATION OF UNIVERSITIES. PAPERS & REPORTS. a. $25. (FR) Carfax Publishing Co., c/o Sue Dommet, P.O. Box 25, Abingdon, Oxfordshire OX14 3UE, England (U.S. distr.: 85 Ash St., Hopkinton, MA 01748) (also avail. in microfiche; back issues avail.)

378 FR ISSN 0579-3866
INTERNATIONAL FEDERATION OF CATHOLIC UNIVERSITIES. GENERAL ASSEMBLY. (REPORT) 1963. irreg. $10. International Federation of Catholic Universities(IFCU), Secretariat Permanent, 78 A rue de Sevres, 75341 Paris Cedex 07, France. circ. 500.

378 UK ISSN 0074-6215
INTERNATIONAL HANDBOOK OF UNIVERSITIES AND OTHER INSTITUTIONS OF HIGHER EDUCATION. Title varies: International Handbook of Universities. (Text in English) 1959. triennial, 8th ed., 1980. £45. ‡ (International Association of Universities) Macmillan Press Ltd., 4 Little Essex St., London WC2R 3LF, England. Eds. H. M. R. Keyes, D. J. Aitken. index.

371.8 CS
INTERNATIONAL UNION OF STUDENTS. CONGRESS AND EXECUTIVE COMMITTEE MEETINGS RESOLUTIONS. (Editions in Arabic, English, French, Spanish) a. price varies. International Union of Students, 17th November St., 110 01 Prague 1, Czechoslovakia.
Formerly: International Union of Students. Congress Resolutions (ISSN 0074-9532)

378 IS
ISRAEL INSTITUTE OF TECHNOLOGY-TECHNION. ABSTRACTS OF RESEARCH THESES. (Text in English) a. free. Israel Institute of Technology-Technion, Graduate School, Kiryat Hatechnion, Haifa 32 000, Israel. Ed. Lea Carmon.

378 US
ISSUES IN HIGHER EDUCATION. 1970. irreg. free. Southern Regional Education Board, 1340 Spring St., N.W., Atlanta, GA 30309. TEL 404-875-9211.
Supersedes in part: Southern Regional Education Board. State and Local Revenue Potential (ISSN 0090-8649)

378 GW ISSN 0342-6300
JAHRBUCH DEUTSCH ALS FREMDSPRACHE. 1975. a. price varies. Max Hueber Verlag, Max-Hueber-Str. 4, 8045 Ismaning, W. Germany (B.R.D.) Ed. Alois Wierlacher. circ. 1,500. (back issues avail.; reprint service avail. from UMI)

JOURNAL OF FINANCIAL EDUCATION. see *BUSINESS AND ECONOMICS — Banking And Finance*

JOURNAL OF MARKETING FOR HIGHER EDUCATION. see *BUSINESS AND ECONOMICS — Marketing And Purchasing*

378 US
JUNIOR COLLEGE RESOURCE REVIEW. 1978. irreg. (1-2/yr.) E R I C Clearinghouse for Junior Colleges, 8118 Math Sciences Bldg., University of California, Los Angeles, CA 90024. TEL 213-825-4321. Dir. Arthur M. Cohen. circ. 1,800.
Supersedes: Junior College Research Review (ISSN 0022-6548)

378 340 CN
JUSTICE INSTITUTE OF BRITISH COLUMBIA. ANNUAL REPORT. (Text in English) 1979. a. Justice Institute of British Columbia, 4180 W. 4th Ave., Vancouver, B.C. V6R 4J5, Canada. Ed. Genie Mac Murtery. (back issues avail.)

378 KE
KENYATTA UNIVERSITY COLLEGE. BUREAU OF EDUCATIONAL RESEARCH. RESEARCH PROJECTS. 1973. a. Kenyatta University College, Bureau of Educational Research, Box 43844, Nairobi, Kenya. bk. rev. stat. circ. 200.
Formerly: University of Kenya. Bureau of Educational Research. Research Projects.

378 KE
KENYATTA UNIVERSITY COLLEGE. DIRECTORY OF RESEARCH. 1975. a. supplements to base vol. free. Kenyatta University College Library, Box 43844, Nairobi, Kenya. Ed. J.M. Ng'Ang'A. circ. 200.

378 SI ISSN 0047-3383
KESATUAN BULLETIN. vol.10, 1975. irreg. free. ‡ Kesatuan Akademis Universiti Singapura, Singapore, Singapore. Ed. Tham Seong Chee. adv. bk. rev. charts. circ. 1,000.

378 US
LINZER UNIVERSITAETSSCHRIFTEN. 1969. irreg. price varies. Springer-Verlag, 175 Fifth Ave., New York, NY 10010 TEL 212-460-1500. (Also Berlin, Heidelberg, Tokyo and Vienna) (reprint service avail. from ISI)
Formerly: Linzer Hochschulschriften (ISSN 0075-9724)

378 FR ISSN 0457-9976
LISTE DES SOCIETES SAVANTES ET LITTERAIRES. 1975. irreg., latest 1985. Ministere de l'Education Nationale, Comite des Travaux Historiques et Scientifique, 3-5 bd. Pasteur, 75015 Paris, France. circ. 1,000.

378 UK
LONDON AND SOUTH EASTERN REGIONAL ADVISORY COUNCIL FOR FURTHER EDUCATION. BULLETIN OF SPECIAL COURSES. a. £1.50. London and South Eastern Regional Advisory Council for Further Education, Tavistock House South, Tavistock Square, London WC1H 9LR, England.
Formerly: London and Home Counties Regional Advisory Council for Technological Education. Bulletin of Special Courses.

378 UK
LONDON AND SOUTH EASTERN REGIONAL ADVISORY COUNCIL FOR FURTHER EDUCATION. INDEX OF COURSES. 1965. a. £1.75. London and South Eastern Regional Advisory Council for Further Education, Tavistock House South, Tavistock Square, London WC1H 9LR, England. Ed. R. Eberhard. circ. 1,700.
Formerly: London and Home Counties Regional Advisory Council for Technological Education. Index of Courses.

370.73 UG
MAKERERE UNIVERSITY. FACULTY OF EDUCATION. HANDBOOK. Added title: Teacher Education in Uganda. a. Makerere University, Faculty of Education, Box 7062, Kampala, Uganda. illus.

MANCHESTER TRAINING HANDBOOKS. see *BUSINESS AND ECONOMICS — Management*

378 MY
MARA INSTITUTE OF TECHNOLOGY. ANNUAL REPORT/INSTITUT TEKNOLOGI MARA. LAPORAN TAHUNAN. (Text in Malay) a. Mara Institute of Technology, Shah Alam, Selangor, Malaysia.

MASTER'S EDUCATION: ROUTE TO OPPORTUNITIES IN CONTEMPORARY NURSING. see *MEDICAL SCIENCES — Nurses And Nursing*

MASTER'S THESES IN THE ARTS AND SOCIAL SCIENCES. see *ART*

EDUCATION — HIGHER EDUCATION 437

378 610.7   US   ISSN 0066-9423
MEDICAL SCHOOL ADMISSION REQUIREMENTS, UNITED STATES AND CANADA. 1950. a. $7.50. ‡ Association of American Medical Colleges, One Dupont Circle, N.W., Washington, DC 20036. TEL 202-828-0400.
    Formerly, until 1964: Admission Requirements of American Medical Colleges, Including Canada (ISSN 0271-6518)

MELBOURNE COLLEGE OF ADVANCED EDUCATION. HANDBOOK. see
EDUCATION — Guides To Schools And Colleges

378   US
MIDDLE STATES ASSOCIATION OF COLLEGES AND SCHOOLS. PROCEEDINGS OF THE ANNUAL CONVENTION. 1888. a. $5. Middle States Association of Colleges and Secondary Schools, 3624 Market St., Philadelphia, PA 19104. Ed. Cecile C. Betit. circ. 3,000. (also avail. in microfilm from UMI; reprint service avail. from UMI)
    Formerly: Middle States Association of Colleges and Secondary Schools. Proceedings (ISSN 0076-8561)

378   US
MIDWESTERN ASSOCIATION OF GRADUATE SCHOOLS. PROCEEDINGS OF THE ANNUAL MEETING. 1949. a. $20. Midwestern Association of Graduate Schools, Kansas State University, Graduate School, Fairchild 102, Manhattan, KS 66506. TEL 913-532-6191. Ed. R.F. Kruh. circ. 200.
    Supersedes: Midwest Conference on Graduate Study and Research. Proceedings.

MINORITY STUDENT OPPORTUNITIES IN UNITED STATES MEDICAL SCHOOLS. see
MEDICAL SCIENCES

370 338   US
N A B T E REVIEW. 1973. a. $5. ‡ (National Association for Business Teacher Education) National Business Education Association, 1914 Association Drive, Reston, VA 22091. TEL 703-860-8300. bibl. circ. 1,200.

378.1   US   ISSN 0090-3965
NATIONAL ASSOCIATION OF COLLEGE ADMISSIONS COUNSELORS. MEMBERSHIP DIRECTORY. a. $20 to non-members; members $10. National Association of College Admissions Counselors, 9933 Lawler Ave., Ste. 500, Skokie, IL 60077. TEL 312-676-0500. Key Title: Membership Directory - National Association of College Admissions Counselors.
    Continues: Association of College Admissions Counselors. Membership Directory.

378.1   US   ISSN 0077-3425
NATIONAL ASSOCIATION OF STATE UNIVERSITIES AND LAND-GRANT COLLEGES. APPROPRIATIONS OF STATE TAX FUNDS FOR HIGHER EDUCATION. a. $3.50 to non-members; free to members. National Association of State Universities and Land-Grant Colleges, One Dupont Circle, N.W., Ste. 710, Washington, DC 20036. TEL 202-293-7120.

378.15 379   US   ISSN 0077-3433
NATIONAL ASSOCIATION OF STATE UNIVERSITIES AND LAND-GRANT COLLEGES. PROCEEDINGS. 1887. a. free. National Association of State Universities and Land-Grant Colleges, One Dupont Circle, Ste. 710, Washington, DC 20036. TEL 202-293-7120. Ed. C.K. Arnold. circ. 1,000.

378 331   US   ISSN 0742-3667
NATIONAL CENTER FOR THE STUDY OF COLLECTIVE BARGAINING IN HIGHER EDUCATION AND THE PROFESSIONS. ANNUAL CONFERENCE PROCEEDINGS. 1973. a. $15. City University of New York, Bernard M. Baruch College, 17 Lexington Ave., Box 322, New York, NY 10010. TEL 212-725-3000. Ed. Joel M. Douglas. bibl. circ. 1,000. Indexed: ERIC.
    Formerly: National Center for the Study of Collective Bargaining in Higher Education. Annual Conference Proceedings (ISSN 0095-9294)

507.2   LE
NATIONAL COUNCIL FOR SCIENTIFIC RESEARCH. ANNUAL REPORT. French edition: Conseil National de la Recherche Scientifique. Rapport Annuel. (Editions in Arabic, English and French) a., latest 1974. free to institutions. National Council for Scientific Research, Box 8281, Beirut, Lebanon.

378   US   ISSN 0191-8133
NATIONAL DEAN'S LIST. (Notes: In 2 vols., by region) 1978. a. $32.50. Educational Communications, Inc., 721 N. McKinley, Lake Forest, IL 60045. TEL 312-295-6650.

NATIONAL DIRECTORY OF EDUCATIONAL PROGRAMS IN GERONTOLOGY. see
GERONTOLOGY AND GERIATRICS

378   US
NATIONAL UNIVERSITY CONTINUING EDUCATION ASSOCIATION. DIRECTORY. 1974. a. $10. National University Continuing Education Association, 1 Dupont Circle N.W., Ste. 420, Washington, DC 20036. TEL 202-659-3130.
    Former titles: National University Continuing Education Association. Handbook and Directory; National University Extension Association. Handbook and Directory (ISSN 0097-0255)

378 500   CN
NATURAL SCIENCES AND ENGINEERING RESEARCH COUNCIL OF CANADA. LIST OF SCHOLARSHIPS AND GRANTS IN AID OF RESEARCH/CONSEIL DE RECHERCHES EN SCIENCES NATURELLES ET EN GENIE DU CANADA. LISTE DES BOURSES ET SUBVENTIONS DE RECHERCHE. (Text and summaries in English and French) 1978. a. Natural Sciences & Engineering Research Council of Canada, 200 Kent St., Ottawa, Ont. K1A 1H5, Canada. TEL 613-995-5992. stat. circ. 2,200. Indexed: BMT. Petrol.Abstr.
    Former titles: National Research Council of Canada. Annual Report on Scholarships and Grants in Aid of Research (ISSN 0316-4047); National Research Council of Canada. Annual Report on Support of University Research.

378 500   CN
NATURAL SCIENCES AND ENGINEERING RESEARCH COUNCIL OF CANADA. REPORT OF THE PRESIDENT/CONSEIL DE RECHERCHES EN SCIENCES NATURELLES ET EN GENIE DU CANADA. RAPPORT DU PRESIDENT. (Text and summaries in English and French) 1978. a. Natural Sciences & Engineering Research Council of Canada, 200 Kent St., Ottawa, Ont. K1A 1H5, Canada. TEL 613-995-5992. circ. 4,000.

378   NE   ISSN 0168-5503
NETHERLANDS. CENTRAAL BUREAU VOOR DE STATISTIEK. STATISTIEK VAN HET BEROEPSONDERWIJS: KUNSTONDERWIJS. ART COLLEGES. (Text in Dutch and English) 1966/67. a. fl.9.50. Centraal Bureau voor de Statistiek, Prinses Beatrixlaan 428, Voorburg, Netherlands (Orders to: Staatsuitgeverij, Christoffel Plantijnstraat, The Hague, Netherlands)
    Formerly: Netherlands. Centraal Bureau voor de Statistiek. Statistiek van het Kunstonderwijs. Statistics on Art Colleges (ISSN 0077-7307)

378   NE   ISSN 0168-5058
NETHERLANDS. CENTRAAL BUREAU VOOR DE STATISTIEK. STATISTIEK VAN HET WETENSCHAPPELIJK ONDERWIJS. STATISTICS OF UNIVERSITY EDUCATION. (Text in Dutch and English) 1937/38. a. fl.18.90. Centraal Bureau voor de Statistiek, Prinses Beatrixlaan 428, Voorburg, Netherlands (Orders to: Staatsuitgeverij, Christoffel Plantijnstraat, The Hague, Netherlands)

327   NE
NETHERLANDS UNIVERSITIES FOUNDATION FOR INTERNATIONAL COOPERATION. A PORTRAIT. (Text in English) biennial. Netherlands Universities Foundation for International Cooperation, Badhuisweg 251, Box 90734, 2509 LS The Hague, Netherlands.
    Formerly: Netherlands Universities Foundation for International Cooperation. Annual Report.

378   US
NEW ENGLAND BOARD OF HIGHER EDUCATION. NEW ENGLAND REGIONAL STUDENT PROGRAM: ENROLLMENT REPORT. 1968. a. free. New England Board of Higher Education, 45 Temple Pl., Boston, MA 02111. Ed. Virginia Quinn.

378   US
NEW ENGLAND BOARD OF HIGHER EDUCATION. NEW ENGLAND REGIONAL STUDENT PROGRAM: GRADUATE LEVEL. 1955. a. free. ‡ New England Board of Higher Education, 45 Temple Pl., Boston, MA 02111. circ. 13,000.

378   US
NEW ENGLAND BOARD OF HIGHER EDUCATION. NEW ENGLAND REGIONAL STUDENT PROGRAM: UNDERGRADUATE LEVEL. 1955. a. free. ‡ New England Board of Higher Education, 45 Temple Pl., Boston, MA 02111. circ. 13,000.

378   US
NEW JERSEY. DEPARTMENT OF HIGHER EDUCATION. RESEARCH REPORT. 1976. irreg. Department of Higher Education, 225 West State St., Box 1293, Trenton, NJ 08625. TEL 609-292-4390. charts. stat.

378   AT
NEW SOUTH WALES. HIGHER EDUCATION BOARD. ANNUAL REPORT. 1977. a. free. Higher Education Board, 13th Floor, 189 Kent St., Sydney, N.S.W. 2000, Australia. circ. 600.

378   US
NEW YORK STATE. EDUCATION DEPARTMENT. COLLEGE AND UNIVERSITY ENROLLMENT. 1960. biennial. Education Department, Washington Ave., Albany, NY 12234. stat. charts. circ. 500. (back issues avail.)

378 658.15   US
NEW YORK STATE. EDUCATION DEPARTMENT. COLLEGE AND UNIVERSITY REVENUES AND EXPENDITURES. 1960. a. Education Department, Washington Ave., Albany, NY 12234. charts. stat. circ. 500.

378.669   NR
NIGERIA. NATIONAL UNIVERSITIES COMMISSION. ANNUAL REPORT. a. National Universities Commission, P.M.B. 12694, Lagos, Nigeria.

378.1   US
NORTH CAROLINA STATE UNIVERSITY. CHANCELLOR'S ANNUAL REPORT. 1958. a. free. North Carolina State University, Development Board, 12 Holladay Hall, Raleigh, NC 27650. TEL 919-737-2846. Ed. Rudolph Pate. circ. 2,500.
    Incorporates (1958-1984): North Carolina State University. Development Board. Report; Whose former titles were: North Carolina State University. Development Council. Report. (ISSN 0078-1428); North Carolina University. State College of Agriculture and Engineering, Raleigh. Development Council. Report.

378   US
NORTHWEST ASSOCIATION OF SCHOOLS AND COLLEGES. PROCEEDINGS. Variant name of organization: Northwest Association of Secondary and Higher Schools. 1926. a. $5. Northwest Association of Schools and Colleges, 3700-B University Way N.E., Seattle, WA 98105. TEL 206-543-0195. Ed. James F. Bemis. circ. controlled.

378   US
OAK RIDGE ASSOCIATED UNIVERSITIES. ANNUAL REPORT. 1947. a. free. ‡ Oak Ridge Associated Universities, Inc., Office of Information Services, Box 117, Oak Ridge, TN 37831-0117. TEL 615-576-3000. Ed. John M. Haffey, Jr. circ. 3,000.
    Formerly: Oak Ridge Associated Universities. Report (ISSN 0078-2904)

371.4   US   ISSN 0360-5434
OCCUPATIONAL EDUCATION. (Included in 5-vol. College Blue Book series) 1972. biennial. $44. Macmillan Publishing Company, 866 Third Ave., New York, NY 10022.
    Formerly: Blue Book of Occupational Education (ISSN 0067-9275)

EDUCATION — HIGHER EDUCATION

378   DK   ISSN 0107-1742
ODENSE UNIVERSITETSBIBLIOTEK. SPECIALER OG PRISOPGAVER. 1980. a. free. Odense Universitetsbibliotek - Odense University Library, Campusvej 55, 5230 Odense M, Denmark. Ed. Inga Mollerup.

OESTERREICHISCHER KRANKENPFLEGERVERBAND. FORTBILDUNGSPROGRAMM. see *MEDICAL SCIENCES — Nurses And Nursing*

OFFICIAL GUIDE FOR G M A T REVIEW. (Graduate Management Admission Test) see *BUSINESS AND ECONOMICS — Management*

OFFICIAL GUIDE TO M B A PROGRAMS. see *BUSINESS AND ECONOMICS — Management*

378   UK
ORATORY SCHOOL MAGAZINE. 1891. a. Oratory School, Woodcote, Near Reading, England. Ed. I.C. McLean. adv. circ. 2,000.

378   US
OXFORD UNIVERSITY ALMANACK. a. price varies. Oxford University Press, 200 Madison Ave., New York, NY 10016 TEL 212-679-7300. (And Ely House, 37 Dover St., London W1X 4AH, England)

378   US
OXFORD UNIVERSITY CALENDAR. a. price varies. Oxford University Press, 200 Madison Ave., New York, NY 10016 TEL 212-679-7300. (And Ely House, 37 Dover St., London W1X 4AH, England)

378   UK
OXFORD UNIVERSITY LIST OF RESIDENT MEMBERS. 1928. a. £4.25. Oxford University Press, 116 High St., Oxford OX1 4BZ, England.

370.7   PH
PHILIPPINE NORMAL COLLEGE RESEARCH SERIES. 1976. irreg., no.3, 1977. price varies. Philippine Normal College, Manila 2801, Philippines. charts. circ. 500.

378   530   US   ISSN 0569-5716
PHYSICS MANPOWER - EDUCATION AND EMPLOYMENT STATISTICS. 1964. irreg. free. American Institute of Physics, 335 E. 45th St., New York, NY 10017. TEL 212-661-9404. Ed. Susanne D. Ellis. circ. 1,000.

378   371   UK   ISSN 0268-0645
POSTGRADUATE STUDY AT THE UNIVERSITY OF LIVERPOOL. 1985. irreg. free. University of Liverpool, Editorial & Publishing Office, P.O. Box 147, Liverpool L69 3BX, England. Ed. M.S. Harrington. circ. 20,000.

378   US
POSTSECONDARY EDUCATION IN CALIFORNIA: INFORMATION DIGEST. 1977. a. Postsecondary Education Commission, 1020 12th St., Sacramento, CA 95814. TEL 916-445-3427. Ed. Murray J. Haberman. circ. 2,000.

378   SA
POTCHEFSTROOM UNIVERSITY FOR CHRISTIAN HIGHER EDUCATION. WETENSKAPLIKE BYDRAES. REEKS H: INOUGURELE REDES. (Text in Afrikaans; sometimes in English) irreg. free. Potchefstroom University for Christian Higher Education, Potchefstroom, South Africa.

378   HO
PRESENCIA UNIVERSITARIA. 1964. irreg. (Universidad Nacional Autonoma de Honduras) Editorial Universitaria, Ciudad Universitaria, Tegucigalpa, Honduras. illus.

378   UK
PRIOR PARK MAGAZINE. a. £3. Prior Park College, Bath, Avon, England. Ed. Anna G. Rhodes. adv. circ. 500.

378   UK
QUEEN MARY COLLEGE STUDENTS UNION HANDBOOK. 1958. a. free. University of London, Queen Mary College Students Union, 432 Bancroft Rd., London E1 4DH, England. Ed. Keith Garwood. adv. circ. 3,500.

378   GW
R I A S-FUNKUNIVERSITAET, BERLIN. SCHRIFTENREIHE. FORSCHUNG UND INFORMATION. 1967. irreg. DM.24.80. Colloquium Verlag, Unter den Eichen 93, 1000 Berlin 45, W. Germany (B.R.D.) Ed. Ruprecht Kurzrock. circ. 3,000.
Formerly: R I A S-Funkuniversitaet, Berlin. Forschung und Information (ISSN 0067-5997)

378   US   ISSN 0034-3390
REGIONAL SPOTLIGHT; news of education in the South. 1974. irreg. free. Southern Regional Education Board, 1340 Spring St., N.W., Atlanta, GA 30309. TEL 404-875-9211. Ed. Margaret Sullivan. circ. 8,500.

RESEARCH DEVELOPMENT IN HIGHER EDUCATION. PUBLICATIONS. see *EDUCATION*

RESEARCH FIELDS IN PHYSICS AT UNITED KINGDOM UNIVERSITIES AND POLYTECHNICS. see *PHYSICS*

378   UK
RESEARCH OPPORTUNITIES IN COMMONWEALTH DEVELOPING COUNTRIES. REGISTER. 1976. irreg. £14.95. Association of Commonwealth Universities, John Foster House, 36 Gordon Square, London WC1H OPF, England.
Formerly: Research Strengths of Universities in the Developing Countries of the Commonwealth.

378   BL
REVISTA UNIMAR. (Summaries in English, Portuguese) 1974. a. exchange basis. Universidade Estadual de Maringa, Caixa Postal 331, 87.100 Maringa-PR, Brazil. Ed. Erivelto Goulart. abstr. bibl. illus.

378   NE
RIJKSUNIVERSITEIT UTRECHT. JAARVERSLAG. 1815. a. fl.10. Rijksuniversiteit te Utrecht, Heidelberglaan 8, 3584 CS Utrecht, Netherlands. circ. 1,000. (back issues avail.)

378   UK
ST. AUGUSTINE'S MAGAZINE. 1886. a. £3. St. Augustine's Abbey, Westgate-on-Sea, Kent, England. Ed. K. Koherty. circ. 400.

378   UK
ST. EDWARD'S COLLEGE MAGAZINE. 1908. a. £2.50. St. Edward's College, Sandfield Park, Liverpool L12 1LF, England. Ed.Bd. adv. circ. 1, 000.

378   AU   ISSN 0080-5734
SALZBURGER UNIVERSITAETSREDEN. 1966. irreg., no.76, 1985. price varies. (Universitaet Salzburg) Universitaetsverlag Anton Pustet, Bergstr. 12, Postschliessfach 144, A-5021 Salzburg, Austria.

378   GW   ISSN 0344-0591
SAMMLUNG GROOS. 1977. irreg. price varies. Julius Groos Verlag, Hertzstr. 6, Postfach 102423, D-6900 Heidelberg, W. Germany (B.R.D.) circ. 500. (back issues avail.)

SCHOOLS AND COLLEGES WELCOME. see *TRAVEL AND TOURISM*

360   US
SCHOOLS OF SOCIAL WORK WITH ACCREDITED MASTER'S DEGREE PROGRAMS. a. $1. Council on Social Work Education, 111 Eighth Ave., Ste. 501, New York, NY 10011. TEL 212-242-3800. circ. 10,000.
Formerly: Graduate Professional Schools of Social Work in Canada and the U.S.A.

378   UK
SCIENCE EDUCATION IN THE REGION. 1965. biennial. £1. London and South Eastern Regional Advisory Council for Further Education, Tavistock House South, Tavistock Square, London WC1H 9LR, England. Ed. D.T.M. Bennett. circ. 1,500.

378   DK   ISSN 0106-9551
SEMINARIEHAANDBOGEN. 1981. a. Kr.6.10. Laererstuderendes Landsrad, Valdemarsvej 19A, 1665 Copenhagen V, Denmark. illus.
Formerly: Seminariekalenderen.

378   UK
SHEFFIELD UNIVERSITY ANNUAL REPORT. 1906. a. free. Sheffield University, Sheffield S10 2TN, England. circ. 10,000.

378   UK   ISSN 0307-6202
SHEFFIELD UNIVERSITY CALENDAR. 1905. a. £8. Sheffield University, Sheffield S10 2TN, England. circ. 1,100.

378   UK
SHEFFIELD UNIVERSITY UNDEGRADUATE PROSPECTUS. a. free. Sheffield University, Sheffield S10 2TN, England. circ. 50,000.
Formerly: Sheffield University General Prospectus.

378   II   ISSN 0080-9322
SHRI CHHATRAPATI SHIVAJI UNIVERSITY. REPORT. (Text in English) 1963/64. a. Shri Chhatrapati Shivaji University, Kolhapur, India. circ. 218.

378   SA   ISSN 0081-220X
SOUTH AFRICA. DEPARTMENT OF HIGHER EDUCATION. ANNUAL REPORT. (Text in Afrikaans and English) 1910. a. Government Printer, Bosman St., Private Bag X85, Pretoria 0001, South Africa.

378   379   US
SOUTHERN HIGHER EDUCATION LEGISLATIVE REPORT. 1961. irreg. price varies. Southern Regional Education Board, 1340 Spring St., N.W., Atlanta, GA 30309. TEL 404-875-9211.
Formerly (1962-1976): Southern Regional Education Board. State Legislation Affecting Higher Education in the South (ISSN 0081-3087)

378   808.5   US   ISSN 0190-2075
SPEECH COMMUNICATION DIRECTORY. 1935. a. $15. Speech Communication Association, 5105 Backlick Rd., No. E, Annandale, VA 22003. TEL 703-750-0533. Ed. Robert N. Hall. circ. 1,500.
Former titles: Speech Communication Directory of S C A and the Regional Speech Communication Organizations; Speech Communication Association. Directory (ISSN 0081-3648); Speech Association of America. Directory.

378   US   ISSN 0081-4644
STATISTICAL ABSTRACT OF HIGHER EDUCATION IN NORTH CAROLINA. 1968. a. free. ‡ University of North Carolina, Box 2688, Chapel Hill, NC 27514. TEL 919-962-6981. Ed. Linda F. Balfour. circ. 2,500. (also avail. in microfiche) Indexed: ERIC.

378   US
STUDENT WORK STUDY TRAVEL CATALOG.* 1974. a. free. Council on International Educational Exchange, 356 W. 34th St., New York, NY 10001. Ed. Gillian Batchelder. adv. circ. 500,000.

378   SZ
STUDENTEN AN DER SCHWIEZ. HOCHSCHULEN/ETUDIANTS DES HAUTES ECOLES SUISSES. (Text in French and German) 1970. a. 14 Fr. Bundesamt fuer Statistik, Hallwylstrasse 15, CH-3003 Berne, Switzerland.
Former titles (until 1980): Statistik des Hochschulwesens in der Schwiez; Studierenden an den Schweizerischen Hochschulen.

378   DK   ISSN 0108-1101
STUDENTERAVISEN. 1970. irreg. free. Danmarks Konservative Studerende, Sct. Peders Straede 26A, 1453 Copenhagen K, Denmark. illus.

378   DK   ISSN 0108-1020
STUDENTERHAANDBOGEN. Vol.73, 1981. a. Kr.90. Koebenhavns Universitet, Studenterraadet, Krystalgade 16, 1172 Copenhagen K, Denmark. adv. illus.

STUDIENFUEHRER MATHEMATIK. see *MATHEMATICS*

370   150   GW   ISSN 0081-7392
STUDIENHEFTE PSYCHOLOGIE IN ERZIEHUNG UND UNTERRICHT. 1964. irreg. price varies. Ernst Reinhardt, GmbH und Co., Verlag, Kemnatenstr. 46, 8000 Munich 19, W. Germany (B.R.D) Ed.Bd.
Formerly: Studienhefte der Paedagogischen Hochschule.

EDUCATION — HIGHER EDUCATION

STUDIENSTIFTUNG. JAHRESBERICHT. see
SOCIAL SERVICES AND WELFARE

378   CN   ISSN 0081-7988
STUDIES IN HIGHER EDUCATION IN
CANADA. 1960. irreg. price varies. (National
Conference of Canadian Universities and Colleges
Committee) University of Toronto Press, Front
Campus, Toronto, Ont. M5S 1A6, Canada. TEL
613-667-7791.

370   SW   ISSN 0283-7692
STUDIES OF HIGHER EDUCATION AND
RESEARCH. (Text in English) 1983. irreg. Kr.65.
National Board of Universities and Colleges, R & D
Unit, Box 45501, S-104 30 Stockholm, Sweden. Ed.
Eskil Bjorklund. circ. 400. Indexed: Hist.Abstr.
ERIC. Int.Polit.Sci.Abstr. Phil.Ind.
Res.High.Educ.Abstr. Sociol.Educ.Abstr.
    Former Titles: Swedish Research on Higher
Education (ISSN 0281-3408); R & D for Higher
Education (ISSN 0347-4976); Which Supersedes
(1971-1976): Educational Development (ISSN 0346-
6175); Sweden. Universitetskanslersaembetet. (ISSN
0082-0377)

360   US
SUMMARY INFORMATION ON MASTER OF
SOCIAL WORK PROGRAMS. a. $6.95. Council
on Social Work Education, 111 Eighth Ave., Ste.
501, New York, NY 10011. TEL 212-242-3800.
Dir. Arthur J. Katz.

378   SW
SWEDEN. UNIVERSITETS- OCH
HOEGSKOLEAMBETET.
ANSLAGSFRAMSTAELLNING FOER
BUDGETAARET. (Subseries of its Skriftserie)
1965. a. Kr.25 per no. Universitetskanslersaembetet
- Office of the Chancellor of the Swedish
Universities, S-162 89, Stockholm, Sweden. illus.
stat. circ. 5,500.
    Formerly (until 1976): Sweden.
Universitetskanslersaembetet. Hoegre Utbildning och
Forskning.

378   PH
TARLAC COLLEGE OF TECHNOLOGY.
ANNUAL REPORT OF THE PRESIDENT. 1966.
a. Tarlac College of Technology, Tarlac, Philippines.
Ed. Lita Nicdao. circ. 105. (back issues avail.)

378   UK
TEARS; higher education. 1950. irreg. Exeter
University, Teaching Service Centre, Streatham
Court, Rennes Drive, Exeter, Devon, England.

371.42   US
TECHNICIAN EDUCATION DIRECTORY. 1963.
biennial. $45. Prakken Publications, Inc., 416
Longshore Dr., Box 8623, Ann Arbor, MI 48107.
TEL 313-769-1211. Ed. ALan H. Jones. adv. circ.
2,000. (back issues avail.)
    Formerly (until 1986): Technician Education
Yearbook (ISSN 0082-2353)

378   GW
TECHNISCHE UNIVERSITAET
BRAUNSCHWEIG. BERICHTSBAND.
FORSCHUNG. every 5 years. Technische
Universitaet Braunschweig, Pockelsstr. 14, Postfach
3329, 3300 Braunschweig, W. Germany (B.R.D.)

378   IS
TEL-AVIV UNIVERSITY. PH.D. DEGREES AND
ABSTRACTS. (Text in English and Hebrew) 1972.
irreg. Tel-Aviv University, Tel-Aviv, Israel.

378   US
TENNESSEE. HIGHER EDUCATION
COMMISSION. BIENNIAL REPORT. 1970.
biennial. free. Higher Education Commission, Union
Bldg., Suite 300, Nashville, TN 37219. TEL 615-
741-3605. Ed. Matte Campbell. circ. 1,000.

378   US
TEXAS. COORDINATING BOARD. TEXAS
COLLEGE AND UNIVERSITY SYSTEM. C B
ANNUAL REPORT AND STATISTICAL
SUPPLEMENT. 1965. a. free; selective distribution.
Texas College and University System, Coordinating
Board, Capitol Sta., Box 12788, Austin, TX 78711.
TEL 512-462-6403. Ed. Janice Monger. circ. 2,000
(controlled)
    Formerly: Texas. Coordinating Board. Texas
College and University System. C B Annual Report
(ISSN 0082-2981)

378   US   ISSN 0082-299X
TEXAS. COORDINATING BOARD. TEXAS
COLLEGE AND UNIVERSITY SYSTEM. C B
POLICY PAPER. 1968. irreg., no. 9, 1970. free;
selective distribution. Texas College and University
System, Coordinating Board, Capitol Sta., Box
12788, Austin, TX 78711. TEL 512-462-6403. Ed.
Janis Monger. circ. 2,000 (controlled)

378   US   ISSN 0082-3007
TEXAS. COORDINATING BOARD. TEXAS
COLLEGE AND UNIVERSITY SYSTEM. C B
STUDY PAPER. 1968. irreg., no.30, 1983. free;
selective distribution. Texas College and University
System, Coordinating Board, Capitol Sta., Box
12788, Austin, TX 78711. TEL 512-462-6403. Ed.
Janice Monger. circ. 2,000 (controlled)

TEXAS TECH UNIVERSITY. GRADUATE
STUDIES. see *HUMANITIES:
COMPREHENSIVE WORKS*

378   US   ISSN 0748-8475
THOUGHT & ACTION. 1984. biennial. membership.
National Education Association of the United
States, 1201 16th St., N.W., Washington, DC
20036. TEL 202-822-7200. circ. 88,000.
    Supersedes: Today's Education: Higher Education
Edition.

378   JA   ISSN 0082-4844
TOKYO UNIVERSITY OF FOREIGN STUDIES.
SUMMARY. 1954/55. a. exchange basis. Tokyo
University of Foreign Studies - Tokyo Gaikogu
Daigaku, 4-51-21 Nishigahara, Kitaku, Tokyo,
Japan. circ. 1,000.

378   CN   ISSN 0712-7456
TRAINING RESOURCES TOURISM/
HOSPITALITY/RECREATION. 1979. biennial.
free. Tourism Canada, 4E - 235 Queen St., Ottawa,
Ont. K1A 0H6, Canada. TEL 613-995-5771.
    Supersedes in part: Resources for Tourism/
Hospitality/Recreation.

378   AT   ISSN 0156-1006
U N E CONVOCATION BULLETIN & ALUMNI
NEWS. 1957. a. to graduates only. University of
New England, Armidale, N.S.W. 2351, Australia.
Ed. S. Bearman. bk. rev. circ. 14,000.
    Former titles: U N E Bulletin; University of New
England. Bulletin (ISSN 0084-6740)

378   US   ISSN 0565-744X
U.S. NATIONAL CENTER FOR EDUCATION
STATISTICS. EARNED DEGREES
CONFERRED. 1948. a. U.S. National Center for
Education Statistics, U.S. Department of Education,
400 Maryland Ave., S.W., Washington, DC 20202
TEL 202-655-4000. (Orders to: National Technical
Information Service, U.S. Dept. of Commerce, 8285
Port Royal Rd., Springfield, VA 22161) Indexed:
Educ.Ind. R.G.

378   US
U.S. NATIONAL CENTER FOR EDUCATION
STATISTICS. FALL ENROLLMENT IN
HIGHER EDUCATION. 1947. a. price varies. U.S.
National Center for Education Statistics, U.S.
Department of Education, 400 Maryland Ave.,
S.W., Washington, DC 20202 TEL 202-655-4000.
(Orders to: Supt. of Documents, Washington, DC
20402)
    Formerly: Opening Fall Enrollment in Higher
Education (ISSN 0083-2758)

378   US   ISSN 0095-6716
U.S. NATIONAL CENTER FOR EDUCATION
STATISTICS. FINANCIAL STATISTICS OF
INSTITUTIONS OF HIGHER EDUCATION. a.
price varies. U.S. National Center for Education
Statistics, U.S. Department of Education, 400
Maryland Ave., S.W., Washington, DC 20202 TEL
202-655-4000. (Orders to: Supt. of Documents,
Washington DC 20402)

378   US
U.S. NATIONAL CENTER FOR EDUCATION
STATISTICS. LIBRARY STATISTICS OF
COLLEGES AND UNIVERSITIES. irreg. U.S.
National Center for Education Statistics, U.S.
Department of Education, 400 Maryland Ave.,
S.W., Washington, DC 20202 TEL 202-655-4000.
(Orders to: National Technical Information Service,
U.S. Dept. of Commerce, 8285 Port Royal Rd.,
Springfield, VA 22161)

507   US   ISSN 0094-7881
U.S. NATIONAL SCIENCE FOUNDATION.
GRADUATE SCIENCE EDUCATION
STUDENT SUPPORT AND POSTDOCTORALS.
(Subseries of NSF's Surveys of Science Resources
Series) a. U.S. National Science Foundation, 1800 G
St. N.W., Washington, DC 20550 TEL 202-655-
4000. (Orders to: Supt. of Documents, Washington,
DC 20402) Key Title: Graduate Science Education
Student Support and Postdoctorals.

378   DR
UNIVERSIDAD AUTONOME DE SANTO
DOMINGO. COMISION PARA EL
DESARROLLO Y REFORMA
UNIVERSITARIOS.* irreg. Universidad Autonoma
de Santo Domingo, Comision para el Desarrollo y
Reforma Universitarios, Ciudad Universitaria, Apdo.
1355, Santo Domingo, Dominican Republic.

378   BO
UNIVERSIDAD BOLIVIANA GABRIEL RENE
MORENO. REVISTA. vol.18, 1974. irreg.
Universidad Boliviana Gabriel Rene Moreno, Santa
Cruz de la Sierra, Bolivia. illus.
    Formerly: Universidad Mayor Gabriel Rene
Moreno. Revista.

378   BO
UNIVERSIDAD BOLIVIANA JUAN MISAEL
SARACHO. INFORME DE LABORES. irreg.
Universidad Boliviana Juan Misael Saracho, Av. Las
Americas, Casilla 51, Tarija, Bolivia. charts. illus.
stat.

378   VE   ISSN 0083-5439
UNIVERSIDAD CENTRAL DE VENEZUELA.
CONSEJO DE DESARROLLO CIENTIFICO Y
HUMANISTICO. BIBLIOGRAFIA DE
HUMANIDADES Y CIENCIAS SOCIALES Y
BIBLIOGRAFIA DE CIENCIA Y TECNOLOGIA
DEL PROFESORADO. (Title varies slightly:
Catalogo de la Investigacion Universitaria) 1963.
triennial. Universidad Central de Venezuela,
Consejo de Desarrollo Cientifico y Humanistico,
Ciudad Universitaria, Caracas, Venezuela. circ. 1,
000.
    Formerly: Universidad Central de Venezuela.
Consejo de Desarrollo Cientifico y Humanistico.
Catalogo.

378   CK
UNIVERSIDAD DE MEDELLIN. REVISTA. 1975.
irreg. Universidad de Medellin, Apdo. Aereo 1983,
Medellin, Colombia. illus.

378.46   SP   ISSN 0080-6145
UNIVERSIDAD INTERNACIONAL MENENDEZ
PELAYO. PUBLICACIONES. 1947. biennial,
no.43, 1974. Universidad Internacional Menendez
Pelayo, Palacio de la Magdalena, Santander, Spain.
circ. 1,000.

505   PE
UNIVERSIDAD NACIONAL DEL CENTRO DEL
PERU. ANALES CIENTIFICOS. 1971. a. price
varies. Universidad Nacional del Centro del Peru,
Departamento de Publicaciones e Impresiones, c/o
Secretaria de Publicaciones, Calle Real 160,
Huancayo, Peru. illus. circ. 1,000.

378 060   VE   ISSN 0076-4337
UNIVERSIDAD NACIONAL DEL ZULIA.
FACULTAD DE HUMANIDADES Y
EDUCACION. ARTES Y LETRAS.* 1966. irreg.
price varies. Universidad del Zulia, Facultad de
Humanidades y Educacion, Apartado de Correos
415, Maracaibo, Venezuela.

378 060   VE   ISSN 0076-4353
UNIVERSIDAD NACIONAL DEL ZULIA.
FACULTAD DE HUMANIDADES Y
EDUCACION. FUERA DE SERIE.* 1962. irreg.
price varies. Universidad del Zulia, Facultad de
Humanidades y Educacion, Apartado de Correos
415, Maracaibo, Venezuela.

378 060   VE   ISSN 0076-4361
UNIVERSIDAD NACIONAL DEL ZULIA.
FACULTAD DE HUMANIDADES Y
EDUCACION. MANUALES DE LA ESCUELA
DE EDUCACION.* 1965. irreg. Bs.7.($1.60)
Universidad del Zulia, Facultad de Humanidades y
Educacion, Apartado de Correos 415, Maracaibo,
Venezuela.

440   EDUCATION — HIGHER EDUCATION

378 060   VE   ISSN 0076-437X
UNIVERSIDAD NACIONAL DEL ZULIA. FACULTAD DE HUMANIDADES Y EDUCACION. MONOGRAFIAS Y ENSAYOS.* 1963. irreg. price varies. Universidad del Zulia, Facultad de Humanidades y Educacion, Apartado de Correos 415, Maracaibo, Venezuela.

UNIVERSIDAD TECNOLOGICA DEL CHOCO. REVISTA. see *TECHNOLOGY: COMPREHENSIVE WORKS*

378   BL
UNIVERSIDADE ESTADUAL PAULISTA. DEPARTAMENTO DE EDUCACAO. BOLETIM. irreg. $20 per no. Universidade Estadual Paulista, Departamento de Educacao, Rua Roberto Simonsen 305, C.P. 957, Presidente Prudente, Brazil. illus.

800   BL
UNIVERSIDADE FEDERAL DE GOIAS. PUBLICACAO. 1975. irreg., no.74, 1983. Universidade Federal de Goias, Av. Universitaria 1533, Caixa Postal 131, 74000 Goiania, Goias, Brazil. Ed.Bd. adv. circ. 1,000.

378   BL
UNIVERSIDADE FEDERAL DE PERNAMBUCO. JORNAL. 1967. irreg. Universidade Federal de Pernambuco, Recife, Pernambaco, Brazil. (microfilm)

378   BL
UNIVERSIDADE FEDERAL DE PERNAMBUCO. RELATORIO DES ATTIVIDADES UNIVERSITARIAS. a. Universidade Federal de Pernambuco, Biblioteca Central, Cidade Universitaria, Recife, Pernambuco, Brazil. (also avail. in microfilm)

378   BL
UNIVERSIDADE FEDERAL DO PARA. RELATORIO ANUAL. a. Universidade Federal do Para, Belem, Para, Brazil.

378   IT
UNIVERSITA DEGLI STUDI DI MILANO. ANNUARIO. 1924. a. ‡ Universita degli Studi di Milano, Via Festa del Perdono 7, 20122 Milan, Italy. circ. 1,000.

378   IT   ISSN 0078-7752
UNIVERSITA DEGLI STUDI DI PADOVA. ISTITUTO PER LA STORIA. CONTRIBUTI. 1964. irreg., no.11, 1979. price varies. Editrice Antenore, Via G. Rusca 15, 35100 Padua, Italy.

378   IT   ISSN 0078-7760
UNIVERSITA DEGLI STUDI DI PADOVA. ISTITUTO PER LA STORIA. QUADERNI. 1968. irreg., no.16, 1983. price varies. Editrice Antenore, Via G. Rusca 15, 35100 Padua, Italy.

378   GW   ISSN 0070-7457
UNIVERSITAET DUESSELDORF. JAHRBUCH. 1969. a. DM.34. Triltsch Druck und Verlag GmbH und Co. KG, Herzstr. 53, 4000 Duesseldorf, W. Germany (B.R.D.) Ed. Hans Schadewaldt. adv.

378   GW   ISSN 0436-1202
UNIVERSITAET GOETTINGEN. JAHRESBERICHT. 1966/67. irreg. Universitaet Goettingen, Wilhelmsplatz 1, 3400 Goettingen, W. Germany (B.R.D.) stat.

378   GW   ISSN 0069-5890
UNIVERSITAET ZU KOELN. JAHRBUCH. 1966. a. DM.8. (Freunde und Foerderer der Universitaet zu Koeln) Drei Kronen Druck, Reifferscheidt GmbH und Co. KG, Rondorfer Str. 224, 5030 Huerth, W. Germany (B.R.D.) Ed. Wolfgang Mathias. adv. circ. 8,000.

054   CF   ISSN 0302-4814
UNIVERSITE DE BRAZZAVILLE. ANNALES. (Text in French; summaries in English) a. Universite de Brazzaville, B.P. 69, Brazzaville, Congo. illus. Indexed: Biol.Abstr. M.L.A.

378   SZ
UNIVERSITE DE GENEVE. DEPARTEMENT D'HISTOIRE ECONOMIQUE. BULLETIN. (Text in French) 1970. a. free. Universite de Geneve, Departement d'Histoire Economique, 1211 Geneva 4, Switzerland. Ed. A.M. Piuz. circ. 350.

378.494   SZ
UNIVERSITE DE NEUCHATEL. ANNALES. 1969/70. a. 15 Fr. Universite de Neuchatel, Av. du Premier Mars 26, 2000 Neuchatel, Switzerland. illus.

378.714   CN
UNIVERSITE DU QUEBEC (PROVINCE). RAPPORT ANNUEL. 1970. a. free. Universite du Quebec, 2875 Bd. Laurier, Ste. Foy, Que G1V 2M3, Canada. TEL 418-657-3551. circ. 3,500.

378   UK
UNIVERSITY BRISTOL CALENDAR. 1910. biennial. University of Bristol, Senate of House, Bristol BS8 1TH, England.

378   UK
UNIVERSITY COLLEGE LONDON CALENDAR. a. £6. University College London, Gower St., London WC1E 6BT, England. circ. 1,300.

378   NR
UNIVERSITY EDUCATION IN NIGERIA. 1984. irreg. free. National Universities Commission, P.M.B. 12694, Lagos, Nigeria. Ed. Chinelo 'Amaka Chizea.

378.794   US
UNIVERSITY OF CALIFORNIA, BERKELEY. CAMPUS STATISTICS. 1966/67. irreg., latest 1986. free. University of California, Berkeley, Office of Institutional Research, Office of Student Research, Berkeley, CA 94720. TEL 415-642-5743. Ed. Adell Ziegler. circ. 500. Indexed: ERIC.
Formerly: University of California, Berkeley. Office of Institutional Research. Campus Statistics (ISSN 0092-0290)

378   SA
UNIVERSITY OF CAPE TOWN. RESEARCH REPORT. 1976. a. free. University of Cape Town, Rondebosch 7700, South Africa. (back issues avail.)

378   US   ISSN 0362-4706
UNIVERSITY OF CHICAGO RECORD. 1967. irreg. (1-2/yr.) free. University of Chicago, 5801 S. Ellis Avenue, Rm. 200, Chicago, IL 60637. TEL 312-962-8352. Ed. Colleen King. charts. circ. 9,000.

378   US   ISSN 0070-3044
UNIVERSITY OF DAYTON. SCHOOL OF EDUCATION. ABSTRACTS OF RESEARCH PROJECTS. 1968. a. free. University of Dayton, School of Education, Dayton, OH 45469. TEL 513-229-3146. Ed. Louis J. Faerber. index.
Projects completed by candidates for the M.S.

378   UK
UNIVERSITY OF DUNDEE STUDENTS ASSOCIATION HANDBOOK. 1968. a. free to new students. University of Dundee, Students Association, Airlie Pl., Dundee DD1 4HN, Scotland. adv. circ. 3,000.

378   UK
UNIVERSITY OF DURHAM CALENDAR. 1837. a. £10. University of Durham, Registrar & Secretary, University Office, Old Shire Hall, Durham DH1 3HP, England.

378.669   NR
UNIVERSITY OF IBADAN. STUDENT AFFAIRS OFFICE. STUDENT HANDBOOK OF INFORMATION ON UNIVERSITY POLICIES AND PRACTICES. irreg. University of Ibadan, Student Affairs Office, Ibadan, Nigeria. illus.

378.549   II
UNIVERSITY OF KASHMIR. ANNUAL REPORT. (Text in English) a. University of Kashmir, Hazratbal, Srinagar 190006, India.

378.1   UK   ISSN 0041-9737
UNIVERSITY OF LEEDS REVIEW. 1948. a. £3.55. University of Leeds, Leeds LS2 9JT, England. Ed. F.A. Felsenstein. circ. 1,400. Indexed: M.L.A.

378   UK   ISSN 0305-9227
UNIVERSITY OF LIVERPOOL CALENDAR. 1881. a. £12. University of Liverpool, Registrar, P.O. Box 147, Liverpool L69 3BX, England. Ed. M.S. Harrington. circ. 1,000. (also avail. in microfiche)

378 371   UK   ISSN 0268-2362
UNIVERSITY OF LIVERPOOL PROSPECTUS. 1984. a. free. University of Liverpool, Editorial & Publishing Office, P.O. Box 147, Liverpool L69 3BX, England. Ed. M.S. Harrington. circ. 45,000.

378   II   ISSN 0076-2210
UNIVERSITY OF MADRAS. ENDOWMENT LECTURES.* a. University of Madras, Chepauk, Triplicane, Madras 600005, Tamil Nadu, India.

378.1   MW
UNIVERSITY OF MALAWI. CENTRE FOR EXTENSION STUDIES. ANNUAL REPORT. a. University of Malawi, Centre for Extension Studies, Box 86, Zomba, Malawi.

658.15   MM
UNIVERSITY OF MALTA. ANNUAL REPORT. a. University of Malta, Msida, Malta. Ed. Lawrence Ellul. circ. 1,000.

378   MF
UNIVERSITY OF MAURITIUS. ANNUAL REPORT. 1968/1969. a. University of Mauritius, Reduit, Mauritius. stat. circ. 450. (back issues avail.)

378   AT   ISSN 0375-4588
UNIVERSITY OF NEW ENGLAND. ANNUAL REPORT. 1968. a. University of New England, Information Office, Armidale, N.S.W. 2351, Australia. Ed. Sally Bearman. stats. circ. 250. (back issues avail.) Indexed: Biol.Abstr.

013.379   AT   ISSN 0548-6831
UNIVERSITY OF NEW SOUTH WALES, KENSINGTON. RESEARCH AND PUBLICATIONS. (Title Varies Slightly) a. University of New South Wales, Kensington, New South Wales, Australia.

378.669   NR
UNIVERSITY OF NIGERIA. ANNUAL REPORT. a. University of Nigeria, Nsukka, Nigeria.

378   IO
UNIVERSITY OF NORTH SUMATRA. BULLETIN/MAJALAH UNIVERSITAS SUMATERA UTARA. (Text in Indonesian) 1975. irreg.? University of North Sumatra, Jl. Universitas No. 9, Biro Rektor, Kampus, Medan, Indonesia.

378   AT   ISSN 0157-1133
UNIVERSITY OF QUEENSLAND. HIGHER DEGREE HANDBOOK. 1976. a. Aus.$10. University of Queensland, Registrar, St. Lucia, Qld. 4067, Australia (Subscr. to: University Bookshop, P.O. Box 86, St. Lucia, Qld. 4067, Australia) circ. 1, 400. (also avail. in microfiche)
Formerly: University of Queensland. Combined Higher Degree Handbook.

378   AT   ISSN 0157-1079
UNIVERSITY OF QUEENSLAND. UNDERGRADUATE DEGREE HANDBOOK. a. Aus.$10. University of Queensland, Registrar, St. Lucia, Qld. 4067, Australia (Subscr. to: University Bookshop, P.O. Box 86, St. Lucia, Qld. 4067, Australia) circ. 10,000. (also avail. in microfiche)
Formerly: University of Queensland. Combined Faculty Directory.

378   UK   ISSN 0305-5574
UNIVERSITY OF STRATHCLYDE. ANNUAL REPORT. 1982. a. free. University of Strathclyde, McCance Building, 16 Richmond St., Glasgow G1 1XQ, Scotland. circ. 25,000. (back issues avail.) Indexed: Biol.Abstr.

378   US
UNIVERSITY OF THE WEST INDIES. VICE-CHANCELLOR'S REPORT. a. free. University of the West Indies, Vice Chancellor's Office, Mona, Kingston 7, Jamaica, W. Indies. stat.

378   ZA
UNIVERSITY OF ZAMBIA. SCHOOL OF HUMANITIES AND SOCIAL SCIENCES. ANNUAL REPORT. a. School of Humanities and Social Sciences, Box 2379, Lusaka, Zambia.

378   US
VERMONT ACADEMY OF ARTS AND SCIENCES. STUDENT SYMPOSIUM AND ANNUAL CONFERENCE. OCCASIONAL PAPERS. 1985. irreg. (approx. a.) $2.50. Vermont Academy of Arts and Sciences, Box 723, Middletown Springs, VT 05757. TEL 802-235-2302.

378.776   US   ISSN 0095-5744
VIKING. 1904. a. $5. St. Olaf College, Northfield, MN 55057. TEL 507-663-3276. Ed. Julia A. Blount. adv. illus. circ. 2,500. Key Title: Viking (Northfield)

371.42   US   ISSN 0083-6575
VIRGINIA'S SUPPLY OF PUBLIC SCHOOL INSTRUCTIONAL PERSONNEL. 1968. a. free. Department of Education, Division of Teacher Education, Box 6-Q, Richmond, VA 32316. TEL 804-225-2097. circ. 5,000.

378   US
WASHINGTON. COUNCIL FOR POSTSECONDARY EDUCATION. REPORT. 1972. irreg. Council for Postsecondary Education, 908 East Fifth Ave., Olympia, WA 98504. TEL 206-753-2210.

378.1   US   ISSN 0511-6848
WESTERN ASSOCIATION OF GRADUATE SCHOOLS. PROCEEDINGS OF THE ANNUAL MEETING. 19th, 1977, Albuquerque. a. $6. Western Association of Graduate Schools, c/o Charlene Kanzlarich, Central Washington University, Graduate Studies & Research, Ellensburg, WA 98926. TEL 509-963-3101. Ed. Dale R. Comstock. circ. 500.

607   AT
WESTERN AUSTRALIA. TECHNICAL EDUCATION DIVISION. HANDBOOK. 1948. a. free. ‡ Education Department, Technical Education Division, 151 Royal St., East Perth W.A. 6000, Australia. circ. 2,500.

WHO'S WHO AMONG STUDENTS IN AMERICAN JUNIOR COLLEGES. see *BIOGRAPHY*

WHO'S WHO AMONG STUDENTS IN AMERICAN UNIVERSITIES AND COLLEGES. see *BIOGRAPHY*

378   GW
WO GEHT'S LANG; Tips und Infos fuer Studenten. 1976. a. free. Technische Universitaet Berlin, Allgemeine Studienberatung, Strasse des 17. Juni 135, 1000 Berlin 12, W. Germany (B.R.D.) circ. 13,000.
Former titles: Information nicht nuer fuer Studieanfaenger; until 1982: Informationen fuer Studienanfaenger.

378.3   US   ISSN 0084-1137
WOODROW WILSON NATIONAL FELLOWSHIP FOUNDATION. NEWSLETTER. 1963. irreg. (approx. 3/yr.) free. Woodrow Wilson National Fellowship Foundation, Box 642, Princeton, NJ 08540. TEL 609-924-4666. Ed. Carolyn Q. Wilson.

378.3   US   ISSN 0084-1145
WOODROW WILSON NATIONAL FELLOWSHIP FOUNDATION. REPORT. 1958. irreg., latest issue, 1980. free. Woodrow Wilson National Fellowship Foundation, Box 642, Princeton, NJ 08540. TEL 609-924-4666.

378   US   ISSN 0084-344X
YALE SCENE; UNIVERSITY SERIES. 1967. irreg., no.3, 1974. price varies. Yale University Press, 92A Yale Sta., New Haven, CT 06520. TEL 203-432-0940.

EDUCATION — International Education Programs

371.39 378.35   US
ACADEMIC YEAR ABROAD. Alternate title: Learning Traveler. Vol. 1. 1964. a. $16.95. ‡ Institute of International Education, 809 United Nations Plaza, New York, NY 10017. TEL 212-984-5412. Ed. Edrice Howard. index.
Supersedes in part: Learning Traveler. U S College-Sponsored Programs Abroad: Academic Year; Former titles: U S College-Sponsored Programs Abroad. Academic Year (ISSN 0082-8602); United States Academic Programs Abroad.

378   CN   ISSN 0821-1272
C U S O JOURNAL. 1983. a. free. C U S O, 135 Rideau St., Ottawa, Ont. K1N 9K7, Canada. Ed. Leslie Cole. circ. 10,000.

370.196   CN
CANADIAN BUREAU FOR INTERNATIONAL EDUCATION. ANNUAL REPORT. (Text in English and French) 1971. a. Canadian Bureau for International Education, 85 Albert St., Ste. 1400, Ottawa, Ont. K1P 6A4, Canada. TEL 613-237-4820.

370.196   US
DIRECTORY OF AMERICAN FULBRIGHT SCHOLARS; university lecturing, advanced research abroad. a. free. Council for International Exchange of Scholars, 11 Dupont Circle, N.W., Ste. 300, Washington, DC 20036. TEL 202-939-5401. circ. 100,000.
Formerly: American Fulbright Scholars.

378.35   PK   ISSN 0070-606X
DIRECTORY OF PAKISTANI SCHOLARS ABROAD. (Text in English) 1965. a. Ministry of Education, Documentation Section, Curriculum Wing, Sector H-9, P.O. Shaigan, Industrial Area, Islamabad, Pakistan.

378.35   US
DIRECTORY OF VISITING FULBRIGHT SCHOLARS AND OCCASIONAL LECTURERS. a. free. Council for International Exchange of Scholars, 11 Dupont Circle, Ste. 300, Washington, DC 20036. TEL 202-939-5401. (Affiliate: American Council of Learned Societies)
Former titles: Directory of Visiting Fulbright Scholars and Occasional Lecturer Program; Directory of Visiting Fulbright Scholars in the United States (ISSN 0098-1508); Directory of Visiting Lecturers and Research Scholars in the United States Under the Mutual Educational Exchange Program (the Fulbright-Hays Act); Directory of Visiting Scholars in the United States Awarded Grants Under the Mutual Educational and Cultural Exchange Act (the Fulbright-Hays Act) (ISSN 0070-6582)

370.196   BE
E F I L DOCUMENTATION.* irreg., no.3, 1979. European Federation for Intercultural Learning, 18 Av. des Ombrages, B-1200 Brussels, Belgium.

370.196   KO
EDUCATION IN KOREA. 1978. a. free. National Institute of Education, 25, Samcheong-Dong, Jongro-Gu, Seoul, S. Korea. circ. 3,000.

EMPLOIS D'ETE EN FRANCE. see *OCCUPATIONS AND CAREERS*

371.39   US
EXPERIMENT IN INTERNATIONAL LIVING. ANNUAL REPORT. 1960. a. free. ‡ Experiment in International Living, U S Office, Brattleboro, VT 05301. TEL 802-257-7751. Ed. David J. Corey. circ. 11,000.
Formerly: Experiment in International Living. President's Report (ISSN 0071-3376)

370.196   US
FULBRIGHT SCHOLAR PROGRAM: FACULTY GRANTS, RESEARCH AND LECTURING AWARDS. a. free. Council for International Exchange of Scholars, 11 Dupont Circle, N.W., Ste. 300, Washington, DC 20036. TEL 202-939-5401. circ. 100,000.
Former titles: Fulbright Scholar Program: Research Awards and Lectureships; Fulbright Awards Abroad.

370   UN   ISSN 0071-9862
FUNDAMENTALS OF EDUCATIONAL PLANNING. (English and French editions) 1966. irreg., no.36, 1987. price varies. ‡ International Institute for Educational Planning, 7-9 rue Eugene Delacroix, 75116 Paris, France (Dist. in U.S. by: Bernan Associates-Unipub, 4611-F Assembly Dr., Lanham, MD 20706-4391) Indexed: ERIC. Rural Recreat.Tour.Abstr. World Agri.Econ.& Rural Sociol.Abstr.

378.3   US
GRANTS REGISTER. 1969. biennial. $37.50. St. Martins Press, 175 Fifth Avenue, New York, NY 10010. Ed. Norman Frankel.

370   UN   ISSN 0074-6401
I I E P OCCASIONAL PAPERS. (Some titles in English; others in French) 1968. irreg., no.72, 1986. price varies. ‡ International Institute for Educational Planning, 7-9 rue Eugene Delacroix, 75116 Paris, France. Indexed: ERIC. Rural Recreat.Tour.Abstr. World Agri.Econ. & Rural Sociol.Abstr.

370.196   UN
I I E P RESEARCH REPORTS. (Text in English and French) 1975. irreg., no.59, 1986. price varies. International Institute for Educational Planning, 7-9 rue Eugene-Delacroix, 75116 Paris, France. Indexed: ERIC. Rural Recreat.Tour.Abstr. World Agri.Econ & Rural Sociol.Abstr.

370.196 338.91   UN
I I E P SEMINAR PAPERS. (Text in English and French) 1975. irreg., no.45, 1986. price varies. International Institute for Educational Planning, 7-9 rue Eugene Delacroix, 75116 Paris, France. Indexed: ERIC.

940   US   ISSN 0073-926X
INSTITUTE OF EUROPEAN STUDIES. ANNOUNCEMENTS. (Text in English; some parts in French, German and Spanish) 1962. a. free. Institute of European Studies, 223 W. Ohio, Chicago, IL 60610. Ed. Karen Hoover. index.

370.196   US   ISSN 0073-9278
INSTITUTE OF EUROPEAN STUDIES. PAPERS AND ADDRESSES OF THE ANNUAL CONFERENCE AND ACADEMIC COUNCIL. 1966. irreg. (approx. 1/yr.) free. Institute of European Studies, 223 W. Ohio, Chicago, IL 60610. TEL 312-944-1750. Ed. Michael Steinberg.

370   NG   ISSN 0534-4727
INTER-AFRICAN CONFERENCE ON INDUSTRIAL COMMERCIAL AND AGRICULTURAL EDUCATION MEETING.* 1954. irreg. (Commission for Technical Co-Operation in Africa South of the Sahara) Maison de l'Afrique, B.P. 878, Niamey, Niger.

378.3   GR   ISSN 0538-4427
INTERNATIONAL ASSOCIATION FOR THE EXCHANGE OF STUDENTS FOR TECHNICAL EXPERIENCE. ANNUAL REPORT. Short title: I A E S T E Annual Report. 1948. a. International Association for the Exchange of Students for Technical Experience, c/o National Technical University, 42 Patission Str., Athens, Greece. circ. 7,000.

370.196   US
INTERNATIONAL FOUNDATION DIRECTORY. 1974. irreg., 4th edt., 1986. $95. Gale Research Company, Book Tower, Detroit, MI 48226. TEL 313-961-2242. Ed. H.V. Hodson.

371.3   US   ISSN 0736-4660
N A F S A DIRECTORY. 1950. biennial. $25 to members; non-members $30. National Association for Foreign Student Affairs, Publications Order Desk, 1860 19th St., N.W., Washington, DC 20009. TEL 202-462-4811. Ed. Carole Fenn. adv. index. circ. 5,000.

370.196   AU
OESTERREICHISCHER AUSLANDSSTUDENTENDIENST. RECHENSCHAFTSBERICHT. 1961. a. S.200. ‡ Oesterreichischer Auslandsstudentendienst, Dr.-Karl-Lueger-Ring 1, A-1010 Vienna, Austria. illus. stat. circ. 350.

378.3   US   ISSN 0078-5172
OPEN DOORS; report on international exchange. 1955. a. $29.95. ‡ Institute of International Education, 809 United Nations Plaza, New York, NY 10017. TEL 212-984-5412.

370.196   SU
PROGRESS OF EDUCATION IN SAUDI ARABIA; a statistical review. (Text in English) irreg. Ministry of Education, Center for Statistical Data, Box 2871, Riyadh, Saudi Arabia.

370.196   SU
SAUDI ARABIA. MINISTRY OF EDUCATION. ANNUAL STATISTICAL REPORT. (Text in Arabic) a. Ministry of Education, Center for Statistical Data, Box 2871, Riyadh, Saudi Arabia.

EDUCATION — SCHOOL ORGANIZATION AND ADMINISTRATION

371.39　　　　US　ISSN 0080-6900
SCHOOLS ABROAD. Variant title: Schools Abroad of Interest to Americans. 1959. irreg., 6th edt., 1985/86. $29. Porter Sargent Publishers, Inc., 11 Beacon St., Boston, MA 02108. TEL 617-523-1670. index.

SCHOOLS AND COLLEGES WELCOME. see *TRAVEL AND TOURISM*

370.196　371.3　　　UN
STUDIES IN MATHEMATICS EDUCATION/ ETUDES SUR L'ENSEIGNEMENT DES MATHEMATIQUES/ESTUDIOS EN EDUCACION MATEMATICA. (Editions in English, French, Spanish) 1980. irreg. 24 F.($8) Unesco, 7 Place de Fontenoy, 75700 Paris, France (Dist. in the U.S. by: Bernan Associates-Unipub, 4611-F Assembly Dr., Lanham, MD 20706-4391) Ed. Robert Morris. circ. 1,500. (also avail. in microfiche; back issues avail.)

378.391　　　　UN　ISSN 0081-895X
STUDY ABROAD/ETUDES A L'ETRANGER/ ESTUDIOS EN EL EXTRANJERO; international scholarships and courses. (Text in English, French and Spanish) 1949. biennial. Unesco, 7-9 Place de Fontenoy, 75700 Paris, France (Dist. in U.S. by: Bernan Associates-Unipub, 4611-F Assembly Dr., Lanham, MD 20706-4391)

870.196　　　　US
STUDY IN THE UNITED KINGDOM. a. $12.95. Institute of International Education, 809 United Nations Plaza, New York, NY 10017. TEL 212-984-5412. Ed. Edrice Howard. adv. circ. 5,000.

UNESCO. RECORDS OF THE GENERAL CONFERENCE. RESOLUTIONS. see *POLITICAL SCIENCE — International Relations*

UNESCO. REPORT OF THE DIRECTOR-GENERAL ON THE ACTIVITIES OF THE ORGANIZATION. see *POLITICAL SCIENCE — International Relations*

371.142　　　　US
U.S. DEPARTMENT OF EDUCATION. OPPORTUNITIES FOR TEACHERS ABROAD. a. price varies; $0.55 for 1977/78 edt. U.S. Department of Education, Washington, DC 20202 TEL 202-655-4000. (Orders to: Supt. of Documents, Washington, DC 20402)
　Formerly: Opportunities Abroad for Teachers (ISSN 0078-5458)

371.39　　　　US
VACATION STUDY ABROAD. Alternate title: Learning Traveler. Vol.2. 1947. a. $16.95. ‡ Institute of International Education, 809 United Nations Plaza, New York, NY 10017. TEL 212-984-5412. Ed. Edrice Howard.
　Supersedes in part: Learning Traveler. Vacation Study Abroad (ISSN 0271-1702); Formerly: Summer Study Abroad (ISSN 0081-9379)
　University-level

060　　　　US　ISSN 0092-4261
WOODROW WILSON INTERNATIONAL CENTER FOR SCHOLARS. ANNUAL REPORT. 1970. a. free. ‡ Woodrow Wilson International Center for Scholars, Smithsonian Institution Building, Washington, DC 20560. TEL 202-357-2018. illus. circ. 5,000. Key Title: Annual Report - Woodrow Wilson International Center for Scholars.

EDUCATION — School Organization And Administration

371.2　610　378　US　ISSN 0360-7437
A A M C DIRECTORY OF AMERICAN MEDICAL EDUCATION. a. $8.50. Association of American Medical Colleges, One DuPont Circle, N.W., Washington, DC 20036. TEL 202-828-0400.

379.15　　　　CN　ISSN 0703-766X
A G M REPORTER. 1976. a. free. British Columbia School Trustees Association, 1155 West 8th Ave, Vancouver, B.C. V6H 1C5, Canada. TEL 604-734-2721.
　Formerly: B C S T A Convention Reporter (ISSN 0319-0684)

371　　　　US
A S C U S ANNUAL - A JOB SEARCH HANDBOOK FOR EDUCATORS. 1966. a. $6 to non-members. Association for School, College and University Staffing, 301 S. Swift Rd., Addison, IL 60101-1499. TEL 312-495-4707. circ. 110,000.
　Formerly (until 1980): A S C U S Annual - Teaching Opportunities for You (ISSN 0066-9156)

371　　　　US　ISSN 0066-9164
A S C U S DIRECTORY OF MEMBERSHIP AND SUBJECT FIELD INDEX. a. $20 to non-members. Association for School, College and University Staffing, 301 S. Swift Rd., Addison, IL 60101-1499. TEL 312-495-4707. circ. 2,000. (back issues avail.)

371.2　　　　DK　ISSN 0106-0465
AARBOG FOR FOLKESKOLEN. 1978. a. Kr.168.03. (Danmarks Laererforening) Dafolo Forlag, Frederikshavn, Denmark. adv. bk. rev.

371.2　　　　US
ACADEMIC COLLECTIVE BARGAINING INFORMATION SERVICE. MONOGRAPHS. irreg., latest no.7. Academic Collective Bargaining Information Service, 724 Ninth St., N.W., Ste. 210, Washington, DC 20001. TEL 202-727-2903.

371.2　　　　US
ACADEMIC COLLECTIVE BARGAINING INFORMATION SERVICE. RESEARCH SUMMARY. 1975. irreg., latest no.6. Academic Collective Bargaining Information Service, 724 Ninth St., N.W., Ste. 210, Washington, DC 20001. TEL 202-727-2903.

371.2　　　　US
ACADEMIC COLLECTIVE BARGAINING INFORMATION SERVICE. SPECIAL REPORTS. irreg., latest no.35. Academic Collective Bargaining Information Service, 724 Ninth St., N.W., Ste. 210, Washington, DC 20001. TEL 202-727-2903.

378.3　　　　US　ISSN 0094-2227
AMERICAN COLLEGE TESTING PROGRAM. HANDBOOK FOR FINANCIAL AID ADMINISTRATORS. Spine title: A C T Handbook for Financial Aid Administrators. a. free. American College Testing Program, Box 168, Iowa City, IA 52243. TEL 319-337-1000. stat.

371.2　　　　US　ISSN 0740-4565
AMERICAN UNIVERSITY STUDIES. SERIES 14. EDUCATION. 1984. irreg. Peter Lang Publishing, Inc., 62 W. 45th St., New York, NY 10036. TEL 212-302-6740. Ed. Jay Wilson.

371　379　　　US　ISSN 0077-9342
ANALYSIS OF SCHOOL FINANCES, NEW YORK STATE SCHOOL DISTRICTS. a. free. Education Department, Educational Research Services Unit, University of the State of New York, Education Bldg. Annex - Rm. 367, Albany, NY 12234. TEL 518-474-5213. (Co-sponsor: University of the State of New York)

371　379　　　US　ISSN 0066-8753
ASSOCIATED PUBLIC SCHOOLS SYSTEMS. YEARBOOK. 1951. a. $5. (Associated Public School Systems) Columbia University, Teachers College, 525 W. 120 St., New York, NY 10027. TEL 212-280-1754. circ. 1,000.

371.8　　　　GW　ISSN 0076-1745
ASTA-PRESS. 1971. irreg. (Technische Universitaet Muenchen, Studentenvertretung) Asta-Presse, Tsingtauerstr. 66a, D-8000 Munich 82, W. Germany (B.R.D.) Ed. Heino Jahn. adv. circ. 10,000.
　Formerly: M S Z: Muenchener Studentenzeitung.

371　　　　US
BEST OF E R I C (EDUCATIONAL MANAGEMENT) 1974. 7/yr. free. E R I C Clearinghouse on Educational Management, University of Oregon, Eugene, OR 97403. TEL 503-686-5043. Ed. Stuart C. Smith. circ. 21,000. (tabloid format; also avail. in microfiche from EDR)

371　　　　AG　ISSN 0067-7922
BIBLIOTHECA DEL PLANEAMIENTO EDUCATIVO.* 1961. irreg. Ministerio de Cultura y Educacion, Departamento de Documentacion Informacion Educativa, Parera 55, Buenos Aires, Argentina.

370　　　　GW　ISSN 0006-9582
BREMER SCHULBLATT. 1954. irreg. price varies. Senator fuer Bildung Wissenschaft und Kunst, Rembertiring 8-12, 2800 Bremen, W. Germany (B.R.D.) abstr. cum.index. circ. 860. (looseleaf format)

371.2　　　　CN　ISSN 0381-5978
BRITISH COLUMBIA SCHOOL TRUSTEES ASSOCIATION. NEWSLETTER. 1967. irreg. British Columbia School Trustees Association, 1155 West 8th Ave., Vancouver 6, B.C., Canada.

353.9　　　　US　ISSN 0090-5593
CALIFORNIA. TEACHERS RETIREMENT BOARD. STATE TEACHER'S RETIREMENT SYSTEM; ANNUAL REPORT TO THE GOVERNOR AND THE LEGISLATURE. (Report Year Ends June 30.) 1963. a. $5. Teachers Retirement Board, Box 15275-C, Sacramento, CA 95851. TEL 916-383-0181. Ed. Larry D. Kurmel. circ. 1,500. Key Title: Annual Report to the Governor and Legislature - Teacher's Retirement Board.

371.2　658.15　　　US
CITIZEN'S GUIDE TO SCHOOL DISTRICT BUDGETING. a. $25. Washington Research Council, 906 S. Columbia, Ste. 350, Olympia, WA 98501. TEL 206-357-6643.

658.15　　　　US
COSTS AT U S EDUCATIONAL INSTITUTIONS. a. $29.95. Institute of International Education, 809 United Nations Plaza, New York, NY 10017. TEL 212-984-5412.

371.2　　　　US
DIRECTORY OF MONTANA SCHOOLS. 1980. a. $3. Office of Public Instruction, State Capital, Helena, MT 59620. TEL 406-444-3095. Ed. Marilyn Miller.

371.0025　　　　US
DIRECTORY OF NONPUBLIC SCHOOLS AND ADMINISTRATORS, NEW YORK STATE. a. Education Department, Information Center on Education, Albany, NY 12234. circ. controlled.

371　　　　US
DIRECTORY OF ORGANIZATIONS AND RESEARCHERS IN EDUCATIONAL MANAGEMENT. 1968. irreg. (approx. biennial) 7th edt., 1984. $7.95. ‡ E R I C Clearinghouse on Educational Management, University of Oregon, Eugene, OR 97403. TEL 503-686-5043. Ed. Stuart C. Smith. subject index. circ. 1,500. (also avail. in microfiche from EDR)
　Former titles: Directory of Organizations and Personnel in Educational Management (ISSN 0070-6035); Directory of Organizations and Personnel in Educational Administration.

378.1　　　　US
DIRECTORY OF PUBLIC SCHOOLS AND ADMINISTRATORS, NEW YORK STATE. 1977. a. $1.50. Education Department, Information Center on Education, Albany, NY 12234. charts. stat. (back issues avail.)
　Formerly: Directory of New York State Public Schools and Administrators.

371.2　　　　UK　ISSN 0140-0428
EDUCATIONAL ADMINISTRATION AND HISTORY MONOGRAPHS. 1973. irreg., no.16, 1986. price varies. University of Leeds, Museum of the History of Education, Parkinson Court, Leeds LS2 9JT, England. Eds. P.H. Gosden, W.B. Stephens.

EDUCATIONAL BUILDING DIGEST. see *BUILDING AND CONSTRUCTION*

371　　　　US
GEORGIA CONGRESS OF PARENTS AND TEACHERS. ANNUAL LEADERSHIP TRAINING CONFERENCE. WORKSHOP FOR P T A LEADERS. a., 61st edt., 1983. $3. University of Georgia, Center for Continuing Education, Athens, GA 30602. TEL 404-542-1725. circ. 700.
　Formerly: Georgia Congress of Parents and Teachers. Annual Summer Institute. Handbook for P T A Leaders (ISSN 0072-1220)

EDUCATION — SCHOOL ORGANIZATION AND ADMINISTRATION

371.2 301 378 350   PH   ISSN 0115-3110
GRADUATE SCHOOL JOURNAL. (Text in English) 1976. a. P.20($3) Catanduanes State Colleges Graduate School, Virac, Catanduanes, Philippines. Ed. Rosario T. Azanza. bk. rev. circ. 1,000. (back issues avail.)

371.6   UK   ISSN 0260-0471
GREAT BRITAIN. DEPARTMENT OF EDUCATION AND SCIENCE. ARCHITECTS AND BUILDING BRANCH. BROADSHEETS. 1980. irreg. free. Department of Education and Science, Architects and Building Branch, Elizabeth House, York Rd., London SE1 7PH, England. Ed. J.M. Brown. circ. 2,000.

379   UK   ISSN 0144-8048
GREAT BRITAIN. DEPARTMENT OF EDUCATION AND SCIENCE. ASSESSMENT OF PERFORMANCE UNITS. SUMMARIES OF REPORTS. irreg. (6-10/yr.) price varies. H M S O, P.O. Box 276, London SW8 5DT, England. (Co-sponsor: Department of Education and Science)

371.6   UK   ISSN 0072-5870
GREAT BRITAIN. DEPARTMENT OF EDUCATION AND SCIENCE. BUILDING BULLETINS. 1955-64, no.1-23; 1964 N.S. irreg. price varies. H.M.S.O., P.O. Box 569, London SE1 9NH, England. (Co-sponsor: Department of Education and Science)

371   US   ISSN 0072-8101
GUIDE FOR PLANNING EDUCATIONAL FACILITIES. 1949. triennial. $25. Council of Educational Facility Planners, 1060 Carmack Rd., Ste. 160, Columbus, OH 43210. TEL 614-292-1521. index.
Formerly: Guide for Planning School Plants.

379   US
GUIDE TO FEDERAL FUNDING FOR EDUCATION. 1975. a. (plus q. supplements) $134.95. Education Funding Research Council, 1611 N. Kent St., Ste. 508, Arlington, VA 22209. TEL 703-528-1082. Ed. Charles J. Edwards.
Former titles: Federal Funding Guide for Education; Guide to Federal Funding for Education (ISSN 0275-8393); Federal Funding Guide for Elementary and Secondary Education (ISSN 0095-3342)

370   US
GUIDE TO THE EVALUATION OF EDUCATIONAL EXPERIENCES IN THE ARMED SERVICES. (3-vol. set) 1946. biennial. $50. American Council on Education, Center for Adult Learning and Educational Credentials, One Dupont Circle, Washington, DC 20036. TEL 202-939-9470. circ. 20,000.

371   GW
HESSISCHER KULTURMINISTER. BILDUNGSPOLITISCHE INFORMATIONEN. 1969. irreg. free. Kultusministerium, Luisenplatz 10, 6200 Wiesbaden, W. Germany (B.R.D.) circ. 50, 000.

371   UK
INDEPENDENT SCHOOLS YEARBOOK: BOYS SCHOOLS. 1890. a. £12. A. & C. Black (Publishers) Ltd., 35 Bedford Row, London WC1R 4JH, England. Ed. J.F. Burnet. adv. index.
Formerly (until 1986): Public and Preparatory Schools. Yearbook (ISSN 0079-7537)

371   UK
INDEPENDENT SCHOOLS YEARBOOK: GIRLS SCHOOLS. 1906. a. £7.95. A. & C. Black (Publishers) Ltd., 35 Bedford Row, London WC1R 4JH, England. Ed. J.F. Burnet. adv. index.
Formerly (until 1986): Girls School Year Book (ISSN 0072-4564)

379   II
INDIA. DEPARTMENT OF CULTURE. DEMANDS FOR GRANTS/SAMSKRITI VIBHAGA KI ANUDANOM KI MANGEM. (Text in Hindi and English) 1971/72. a. Government of India Press, General Manager, Minto Rd., New Delhi, India.

370 378   AT   ISSN 0313-3249
INSTEAD. 1970. irreg. free. Western Australian Institute of Educational Administration, c/o Head Office, Ministry of Education, Royal St., East Perth, W.A. 6000, Australia. Ed. C.W. Rielly. circ. 750. (back issues avail)

378.3   US
IOWA. COLLEGE AID COMMISSION. BIENNIUM REPORT. 1967. biennial. $20. College Aid Commission, 201 Jewett Bldg., Des Moines, IA 50309. TEL 515-281-3501. Ed. James E. Shay. stat. circ. 1,000.
Former titles (until 1978): Iowa. Higher Education Facilities Commission. Biennium Report; State of Iowa Scholarships, Tuition Grants. Biennium Report (ISSN 0091-3588)

371   DK   ISSN 0108-836X
L U INFORMATION. 1978. irreg. Kr.12.20 per no. Landsforeningen af Ungdomsskoledere, Vesterbrogade 14 A/2, 1620 Copenhagen, Denmark.

371   US   ISSN 0076-9460
MISSISSIPPI CONGRESS OF PARENTS AND TEACHERS. PROCEEDINGS. a. Mississippi Congress of Parents and Teachers, 414 North St., Box 1946, Jackson, MS 39215. TEL 601-352-7383. circ. controlled.

371   US   ISSN 0076-9479
MISSISSIPPI CONGRESS OF PARENTS AND TEACHERS. YEARBOOK. a. ‡ Mississippi Congress of Parents and Teachers, 414 N. St., Box 1946, Jackson, MS 39215. TEL 601-352-7383. circ. controlled.

371   US   ISSN 0077-4472
NATIONAL FACULTY DIRECTORY. 1971. a. $480 for 3 vols. Gale Research Company, Book Tower, Detroit, MI 48226. TEL 313-961-2242.

370   US
NATIONAL GUIDE TO EDUCATIONAL CREDIT FOR TRAINING PROGRAMS. 1976. a. $35. (American Council on Education, Office on Educational Credit) Macmillan Publishing Co., Inc., 866 Third Ave., New York, NY 10022. TEL 202-833-4700. Ed. Sylvia Galloway. adv. circ. 3,000. (also avail. in microfiche) Indexed: ERIC.
Formerly: National Guide to Credit Recommendations for Noncollegiate Courses.

371 379   NE   ISSN 0168-7905
NETHERLANDS. CENTRAAL BUREAU VOOR DE STATISTIEK. STATISTIEK VAN DE UITGAVEN DER OVERHEID VOOR ONDERWIJS. STATISTICS OF THE EXPENDITURE OF THE STATE, THE PROVINCES AND THE MUNICIPALITIES ON EDUCATION. (Text in Dutch and English) 1964. a. fl.13.30. Centraal Bureau voor de Statistiek, Prinses Beatrixlaan 428, Voorburg, Netherlands (Orders to: Staatsuitgeverij, Christoffel Plantijnstraat, The Hague, Netherlands)

371 373   NE   ISSN 0168-5856
NETHERLANDS. CENTRAAL BUREAU VOOR DE STATISTIEK. STATISTIEK VAN HET W V O, H A V O EN M A V O: INSTROOM, DOORSTROOM EN UITSTROOM VAN LEERLINGEN. (Text in Dutch and English) 1950/54. a. fl.10.55. Centraal Bureau voor de Statistiek, Prinses Beatrixlaan 428, Voorburg, Netherlands (Orders to: Staatsuitgeverij, Christoffel Plantijnstraat, The Hague, Netherlands)
Formerly: Netherlands. Centraal Bureau voor de Statistiek. Statistiek van het Voorbereidend Hoger en Middelbaar Onderwijs: Leraren. Statistics of Secondary Education: Teachers (ISSN 0077-7404)

NEW YORK STATE. EDUCATION DEPARTMENT. COLLEGE AND UNIVERSITY REVENUES AND EXPENDITURES. see *EDUCATION — Higher Education*

371.2   US
NEW YORK STATE. EDUCATION DEPARTMENT. RACIAL-ETHNIC DISTRIBUTION OF PUBLIC SCHOOL STUDENTS AND STAFF. 1967. a. Education Department, Washington Ave., Albany, NY 12234. stat. charts. circ. 1,500. (back issues avail.)

379   US   ISSN 0079-2071
PILOT STUDIES APPROVED FOR STATE AID IN PUBLIC SCHOOL SYSTEMS IN VIRGINIA. 1964. a. ‡ Department of Education, Division of Educational Research, Box 6-Q, Richmond, VA 23216. TEL 804-225-2103. Ed. Dr. Mary F. Lovern.

379   US
PLAN REVIEW PROCESS FOR CONSOLIDATED PROGRAM SCHOOLS.* a. State Department of Education, Superintendent of Public Instruction, 721 Capitol Mall, Sacramento, CA 95814.

658.15   CN
QUEBEC (PROVINCE). DIRECTION GENERALE DES RESSOURCES MATERIELLES ET FINANCIERES. REGLES BUDGETAIRES DES COMMISSION SCOLAIRES ET DES COMISSIONS REGIONALES. 1965. a. Direction Generale des Ressources Materielles et Financieres, Service General des Communications, 1035 rue de la Chevrotiere, Quebec, P.Q. G1R 5A5, Canada. TEL 418-643-7095.
Former titles: Quebec (Province). Ministere de l'Education. Regles Budgetaires des Commissions Scolaires et des Commissions Regionales; Quebec (Province). Ministere de l'Education. Direction du Financement. Regles Budgetaires des Commissions Scolaires et des Commissions Regionales.

371.2   AT
QUEENSLAND. DEPARTMENT OF EDUCATION. INFORMATION AND PUBLICATIONS BRANCH. DOCUMENT. 1973. irreg. Department of Education, Information and Publications Branch, P.O. Box 33, North Quay, Qld. 4000, Australia. Ed. J.L. Finger.
Formerly: Queensland. Department of Education. Research and Curriculum Branch. Document (ISSN 0310-4087)

371 372   US   ISSN 0080-1429
REQUIREMENTS FOR CERTIFICATION OF TEACHERS, COUNSELORS, LIBRARIANS, ADMINISTRATORS FOR ELEMENTARY SCHOOLS, SECONDARY SCHOOLS, JUNIOR COLLEGES. 1935. a. price varies. University of Chicago Press, 5801 S. Ellis Ave., Chicago, IL 60637. TEL 312-962-7700. Ed. Mary P. Burks. (reprint service avail. from UMI,ISI)

371.2   IS   ISSN 0334-4770
STUDIES IN EDUCATIONAL ADMINISTRATION AND ORGANIZATION. (Text in Hebrew; summaries in English) 1973. a. Haifa University, School of Education, Center for Educational Administration, Hacarmel, Haifa 31 999, Israel. Ed. Dr. Lya Kremer-Hayon.

371.2 331.1   US
TEACHER SUPPLY/DEMAND. a. $10. Association for School, College and University Staffing, 302 S. Swift Rd., Addison, IL 60101. TEL 312-495-4707.

370   SA
U.T.S.A. ANNUAL. (Text in English, occasionally in Afrikaans) 1979. a. free. Union of Teachers' Associations of South Africa, Private Bag X12, Kasselsvlei 7533, South Africa. Ed. Randall van den Heever. adv. bk. rev. circ. 20,000.

379 500   US
U.S. NATIONAL SCIENCE FOUNDATION. GUIDE TO PROGRAMS. 1966. a. $3.50. U.S. National Science Foundation, 1800 G. St. N.W., Washington, DC 20550 TEL 202-357-9494. (Orders to: Supt. of Documents, Washington, DC 20402) circ. 35,000.

378   BL
UNIVERSIDADE FEDERAL DE PERNAMBUCO. ANUARIO ESTATISTICO. (Includes University Master Plan) 1972. a. (with supplement) free. Universidade Federal de Pernambuco, Assessoria da Area de Informacao, Cidade Universitaria, Av. Prof. Morais Rego, Recife, Pernambuco, Brazil. stat.

371   US
UNIVERSITY OF OREGON. CENTER FOR EDUCATIONAL POLICY AND MANAGEMENT. MONOGRAPHS. irreg., latest 1980. University of Oregon, Center for Educational Policy and Management, 235 Education Bldg., Eugene, OR 97401. TEL 503-686-5173.
Formerly: University of Oregon. Center for the Advanced Study of Educationl Administration. Monographs (ISSN 0078-6004)

379.792　　　US　ISSN 0094-8314
UTAH. STATE OFFICE OF EDUCATION. ANNUAL REPORT OF THE STATE SUPERINTENDENT OF PUBLIC INSTRUCTION. At head of title: Utah Public School System. a. State Office of Education, Publications Secretary, 250 East 5th South, Salt Lake City, UT 84111. TEL 801-533-5431. illus. Key Title: Annual Report of the State Superintendent of Public Instruction Utah Public School System.

371.2　　　US　ISSN 0093-0040
UTAH. STATE OFFICE OF EDUCATION. OPINIONS OF THE UTAH STATE SUPERINTENDENT OF PUBLIC INSTRUCTION. 1963. irreg., latest issue 1972. State Board of Education, 250 East 5th South, Salt Lake City, UT 84111. TEL 801-533-5431. Key Title: Opinions of the Utah State Superintendent of Public Instruction.

371 370　　　SZ
W C O T P REPORT. (Editions in English, French and Spanish) 1952. biennial. 8 Fr.($4) ‡ World Confederation of Organizations of the Teaching Profession, 5 Avenue du Moulin, 1110 Morges, Switzerland. Ed. Lona Towsley. circ. 1,400(combined)
　Formerly: W C O T P Annual Report (ISSN 0084-1528)

371　　　AT　ISSN 0811-1154
WESTERN AUSTRALIA. EDUCATION DEPARTMENT. SCHOOLS & STAFFING. a. Aus.$10. Superintendent Publications, 151 Royal St., East Perth, W.A. 6000, Australia. circ. 5,500.

EDUCATION — Special Education And Rehabilitation

see also Blind; Criminology and Law Enforcement; Deaf; Social Services and Welfare

A S H A REPORTS. (American Speech-Language-Hearing Association) see *MEDICAL SCIENCES — Otorhinolaryngology*

ADVANCES IN LEARNING AND BEHAVIORAL DISABILITIES. see *CHILDREN AND YOUTH — About*

371.9　　　US　ISSN 0270-4013
ADVANCES IN SPECIAL EDUCATION; a research annual. 1980. a. $23.75 to individuals; institutions $47.50. J A I Press Inc., 36 Sherwood Pl., Box 1678, Greenwich, CT 06836. TEL 203-661-7602. Ed. Barbara K. Keogh. Indexed: Psychol.Abstr.

618　　　IS
AKIM REVIEW. (Text in English) 1951. a. free. Akim-Israel Association for Rehabilitation of the Mentally Handicapped, 69 Herzlia Rd., Neot Afeka, Tel Aviv 69410, Israel. Ed. Binyamin Hoffman. illus.
　Formerly: Tidings.

371.9　　　CN　ISSN 0315-3509
ALBERTA TEACHERS' ASSOCIATION. SPECIAL EDUCATION COUNCIL. NEWSLETTER. 1971. irreg. (3-4/yr.) (included in subscr. to T A S A) Alberta Teachers' Association, Special Education Council, 11010 142nd St., Edmonton, Alta. T5N 2R1, Canada. Ed. Ken O'Sullivan. circ. 909. Indexed: Can.Educ.Ind.

371.9　　　US
AMERICAN PRINTING HOUSE FOR THE BLIND, LOUISVILLE, KENTUCKY. DEPARTMENT OF EDUCATIONAL RESEARCH. REPORT OF RESEARCH AND DEVELOPMENT ACTIVITIES. 1958. a. free. American Printing House for the Blind, Department of Educational Research, Box 6085, Louisville, KY 40206. TEL 502-895-2405. Ed. June E. Morris. circ. 1,000.
　Formerly: American Printing House for the Blind, Louisville, Kentucky. Department of Educational Research. Annual Report (ISSN 0065-9800)

AMERICAN SPEECH - LANGUAGE - HEARING ASSOCIATION. DIRECTORY. see *MEDICAL SCIENCES — Otorhinolaryngology*

371.9　　　US　ISSN 0474-7534
ANNALS OF DYSLEXIA; an interdisciplinary journal of specific language disability. 1951. a. price varies. Orton Dyslexia Society, 724 York Rd., Baltimore, MD 21204. TEL 301-296-0232. Ed. Rosemary Bowler. circ. 7,500. (also avail. in microform from UMI; reprint service avail. from UMI) Indexed: Educ.Ind.　DSH Abstr. Psychol.Abstr.　SSCI.　C.I.J.E.　Child Devel.Abstr. Except.Child.Educ.Abstr.　Lang.& Lang.Behav.Abstr.
　Former Titles: Orton Society. Bulletin. (ISSN 0078-6624); Orton Society. Monograph.

371.9　　　US　ISSN 0198-7518
ANNUAL EDITIONS: EDUCATING EXCEPTIONAL CHILDREN. 1979. a. $9.95. Dushkin Publishing Group, Inc., Sluice Dock, Guilford, CT 06437. TEL 203-453-4351. Ed. Ian Nielsen. Key Title: Educating Exceptional Children.

371.9　　　CN
B C JOURNAL OF SPECIAL EDUCATION. vol.3, 1979. a. Can.$20 to non-members. Special Education Association, Dept. of Special Education, University of British Columbia, 2075 Wesbrook Mall, Vancouver, B.C. V6T 1W5, Canada. TEL 604-228-6361. Ed. Marg Csapo. adv. bk. rev. circ. 1,500. Indexed: C.I.J.E.　Can.Educ.Ind.　ERIC. Except.Child Educ.Abstr.　Educ.Admin.Abstr.

371　　　GW　ISSN 0171-9718
BEHINDERTENHILFE DURCH ERZIEHUNG, UNTERRICHT UND THERAPIE. 1977. irreg., no.13, 1983. price varies. Ernst Reinhardt, GmbH und Co., Verlag, Kemnatenstr. 46, 8000 Munich 19, W. Germany (B.R.D.) Ed. Otto Speck.

BIBLIOGRAFIA ERITYSIRYHMIEN LIIKUNNAN TUTKIMUKSESTA/BIBLIOGRAPHY ON RESEARCH IN PHYSICAL EDUCATION AND SPORT FOR THE HANDICAPPED. see *EDUCATION — Abstracting, Bibliographies, Statistics*

371.9　　　GW
BUNDESARBEITSGEMEINSCHAFT HILFE FUER BEHINDERTE. JAHRESPIEGEL. a. free. (Bundesarbeitsgemeinschaft Hilfe fuer Behinderte e.V.) Verlag fuer Medizin Dr. Ewald Fischer GmbH, Fritz-Frey-Str. 21, Postfach 10 57 67, D-6900 Heidelberg 1, W. Germany (B.R.D.)

371.9　　　US
CONTEMPORARY PERSPECTIVES IN REHABILITATION. 1986. irreg. price varies. F A Davis Co., 1915 Arch St., Philadelphia, PA 19103. TEL 800-523-4049. Ed. Steven L. Wolf.

CONTRIBUTIONS TO RESIDENTIAL TREATMENT. see *PSYCHOLOGY*

371.9　　　AT　ISSN 0310-5709
DEVELOPING EDUCATION. 1973. irreg. free. Department of Education, P.M.B. 25, Winnellie N.T. 5789, Australia. bk. rev. circ. 3,000. Indexed: Aus.Educ.Ind.
　Supersedes: Special Schools Bulletin (ISSN 0048-0800)

371.9 136.7　　　US　ISSN 0070-5012
DIRECTORY FOR EXCEPTIONAL CHILDREN; a listing of educational and training facilities. 1950. biennial. $45. Porter Sargent Publishers, Inc., 11 Beacon St., Boston, MA 02108. TEL 617-523-1670. index. index. circ. 6,000. (back issues avail.)

DIRECTORY OF COLLEGE FACILITIES AND SERVICES FOR THE DISABLED. see *EDUCATION — Guides To Schools And Colleges*

DIRECTORY OF FEDERAL AID FOR THE HANDICAPPED. see *SOCIAL SERVICES AND WELFARE*

371.9　　　US
DIRECTORY OF INFORMATION RESOURCES FOR THE HANDICAPPED. irreg. Ready Reference Press, Box 5169, Santa Monica, CA 90405.

DIRECTORY OF RESEARCH AND DEVELOPMENTAL PROJECTS. see *EDUCATION*

371.9　　　US
DIRECTORY OF SERVICES AND FACILITIES FOR THE LEARNING DISABLED. 1968. biennial. free. Academic Therapy Publications, 20 Commercial Blvd., Novato, CA 94947. TEL 415-883-3314. Ed. Betty Lou Kratoville. adv. circ. 40,000.
　Former titles: Directory of Educational Facilities for the Learning Disabled (ISSN 0093-7703); Directory of Facilities for the Learning Disabled (ISSN 0092-3257)

371.9　　　NZ
DIRECTORY OF SPECIAL EDUCATION AND GUIDANCE SERVICES IN NEW ZEALAND. 1960. a. free. Department of Education, Education Services, Wellington, New Zealand. circ. 500.

362.8　　　EI
EUROPEAN SOCIAL FUND. ANNUAL REPORT ON THE ACTIVITIES OF THE NEW EUROPEAN SOCIAL FUND. 1972. a. Office for Official Publications of the European Communities, P.O. Box 1003, L-2985 Luxembourg, Luxembourg (Dist. in the U.S. by: European Community Information Service, 2100 M St., NW, Suite 707, Washington, DC 20037) stat.

371.9　　　AT　ISSN 0156-6555
EXCEPTIONAL CHILD; the Australian journal on the education of backward children. 1954. a. Aus.$36($33) (Fred and Eleanor Schonell Educational Research Centre) University of Queensland Press, Box 42, St. Lucia, Qld. 4067, Australia. Ed.Bd. adv. bk. rev. bibl. charts. circ. 1,400. Indexed: Curr.Cont.　Psychol.Abstr.　SSCI. C.I.J.E.　Except.Child.Educ.Abstr.
　Formerly: Slow Learning Child (ISSN 0037-704X)

371.9 362.4　　　US
HANDICAPPED FUNDING DIRECTORY; a guide to sources of funding in the United States for handicapped programs & services. 1978. biennial. $25.50. Research Grant Guides, Box 357, Oceanside, NY 11572. TEL 213-306-2931. Ed. Richard M. Eckstein. (back issues avail.)

371.9　　　US　ISSN 0275-4819
HOW TO GET HELP FOR KIDS; reference guide to services for handicapped children. 1980. irreg. $29.95. Gaylord Professional Publications, Box 4901, Syracuse, NY 13221. TEL 315-457-5070. (Co-sponsor: Neal-Schuman) Ed. B. Zang.

371.9 410　　　US
HUMAN COMMUNICATION AND ITS DISORDERS. 1987. irreg. price varies. Ablex Publishing Corporation, 355 Chestnut St., Norwood, NJ 07648. TEL 201-767-8450. Ed. Harris Winitz.

371.9　　　GW
I C E V H EDUCATOR. 1952. quinquennial, 1967, 5th, U.S. $5. International Council for Education of the Visually Handicapped, Postfach 364, D-6140 Besheim 1, W. Germany (B.R.D.) Ed. W. Stein. circ. 1,000.
　Formerly: International Conference of Educators of Blind Youth. Proceedings (ISSN 0074-2937)

379.155　　　US
INDIANA STATE PLAN FOR VOCATION-TECHNICAL EDUCATION. (FISCAL YEAR) 1978. a. State Board of Vocational and Technical Education, c/o Linda Piper, 401 Illinois Bldg., 17 W. Market St., Indianapolis, IN 46204. TEL 317-232-1810. stat. circ. 1,000.
　Formerly: Indiana State Plan for Vocational Education.

INSTITUTO INTERAMERICANO DEL NINO. EDUCACION ESPECIAL. INFORMES TECNICOS. see *SOCIAL SERVICES AND WELFARE*

371.9　　　FR　ISSN 0074-1787
INTERNATIONAL ASSOCIATION OF WORKERS FOR MALADJUSTED CHILDREN. CONGRESS REPORTS. (Text in English and French) 1955. irreg., 10th, 1982, Copenhagen. $6. International Association of Workers for Maladjusted Children, 66 Chaussee d'Antin, Paris 9e, France.

INTERNATIONAL CONFERENCE ON PIAGETIAN THEORY AND THE HELPING PROFESSIONS. PROCEEDINGS. see *EDUCATION*

EDUCATION — SPECIAL EDUCATION AND REHABILITATION

370 US
INTERNATIONAL INTERDISCIPLINARY SEMINAR ON PIAGETIAN THEORY AND ITS IMPLICATIONS FOR THE HELPING PROFESSIONS. PROCEEDINGS; emphasis: the handicapped child. 1970. a. $12. Children's Hospital of Los Angeles, University Affilitated Program, Piaget Conference Committee, Box 54700, Los Angeles, CA 90054. TEL 213-660-2450. (Co-sponsor: University of Southern California, School of Education) Ed. James F. Magary. bibl. circ. 4,000. (back issues avail.) Indexed: P.A.I.S. Psychol.Abstr. SSCI. A.B.C.Pol.Sci. Can.Ind. Rehabil.Lit.

INTERNATIONAL REVIEW OF RESEARCH IN MENTAL RETARDATION. see *MEDICAL SCIENCES — Psychiatry And Neurology*

331.8 IS ISSN 0075-1383
ISRAEL SOCIETY FOR REHABILITATION OF THE DISABLED. ANNUAL. (Added title page in Hebrew: Shenaton) (Text in English and Hebrew) 1964. a. free. ‡ Israel Society for Rehabilitation of the Disabled, 10 Ibn Gvirol St., Tel Aviv, Israel. Ed. E. Chigier. adv. circ. 850.

JAHRBUCH FUER BLINDENFREUNDE. see *BLIND*

371.9 FR ISSN 0075-4420
JOURNEE DE REEDUCATION. a. Expansion Scientifique, 15 rue St. Benoit, 75278 Paris Cedex 06, France. Eds. Prof. DeSeze, Prof. Debeyre J. Samuel.

371.9 KO
KOREA SOCIAL WORK COLLEGE. RESEARCH INSTITUTE FOR SPECIAL EDUCATION. JOURNAL/KWANG-EUNG YEO. (Text in Korean) vol.6, 1978. a. Korea Social Work College, Research Institute for Special Education, 2288 Daemyung-dong Nam Gu, Daegu 634-00, S.Korea.

379 US ISSN 0093-9137
MICHIGAN. ADVISORY COUNCIL FOR VOCATIONAL EDUCATION. ANNUAL REPORT. 1970. a. Advisory Council for Vocational Education, Box 30008, Lansing, MI 48909. TEL 517-373-3373. circ. 2,000. Key Title: Annual Report of the Michigan State Advisory Council for Vocational Education.

420 US
MICHIGAN ASSOCIATION OF SPEECH COMMUNICATION JOURNAL. 1964. a. $3.50. Michigan Association of Speech Communication, Herrick Center, Albion College, Albion, MI 49224. TEL 517-629-5511. Ed. Jim Gilchrist. circ. 250. (back issues avail.)
Formerly (until 1984): Michigan Speech Association Journal.

371.9 NE ISSN 0076-9916
MODERN APPROACHES TO THE DIAGNOSIS AND INSTRUCTION OF MULTI-HANDICAPPED CHILDREN. 1971. irreg., vol.18, 1985. price varies. Swets Publishing Service (Subsidiary of: Swets en Zeitlinger B.V.) Heereweg 347, 2161 CA Lisse, Netherlands (Dist. in the U.S. and Canada by: Hogrefe International, Inc., 525 Eglinton Ave. East, Toronto, Ont., M4P 1N5)

NATIONAL ASSOCIATION OF TRAINING SCHOOLS AND JUVENILE AGENCIES. PROCEEDINGS. see *CRIMINOLOGY AND LAW ENFORCEMENT*

371.9 UK
NATIONAL COUNCIL FOR SPECIAL EDUCATION. OCCASIONAL PUBLICATIONS. 1983. irreg. £1 per issue. National Council for Special Education, 1 Wood St., Stratford-upon-Avon, Warwickshire CV37 6JE, England. Ed. Richard Rose.

371.9 JA ISSN 0387-3528
NATIONAL INSTITUTE OF SPECIAL EDUCATION. BULLETIN/KOKURITSU TOKUSHU KYOIKU SOGO KENKYUJO KENKYU KIYO. (Text in Japanese; summaries in English) 1974. a. free. National Institute of Special Education - Kokuritsu Tokushu Kyoiku Sogo Kenkyusho, 2360 Nobi, Yokosuka 239, Japan. Ed.Bd. circ. 1,480.

NATIONAL REHABILITATION CENTER FOR THE DISABLED. RESEARCH BULLETIN. see *BLIND*

NATIONAL RESEARCH COUNCIL, CANADA. DIVISION OF ELECTRICAL ENGINEERING. BULLETIN/CONSEIL NATIONAL DE RECHERCHES DU CANADA. DIVISION DE GENIE ELECTRIQUE. BULLETIN. see *ENGINEERING*

362.8 US ISSN 0093-7843
NORTH DAKOTA STATE PLAN FOR REHABILITATION FACILITIES AND WORKSHOPS; annual modification. a. free. Division of Vocational Rehabilitation, State Capitol Bldg., Bismarck, ND 58505. TEL 701-224-2907. stat.

371.9 SZ
O R T YEARBOOK. (Organization for Rehabilitation Through Training) 1971. a. World O R T Union, 1, rue de Varembe, 1211 Geneva 20, Switzerland. charts. illus. stat. circ. 10,000.

PSYCSCAN: LEARNING AND COMMUNICATION DISORDERS AND MENTAL RETARDATION. see *PSYCHOLOGY — Abstracting, Bibliographies, Statistics*

371.9 US ISSN 0270-1448
READINGS ON EQUAL EDUCATION. 1970. a. $47.50. A M S Press, Inc., 56 E. 13th St., New York, NY 10003. TEL 212-777-4700. bibl. charts. stat. (back issues avail.)
Formerly: Educating the Disadvantaged (ISSN 0531-8327)

371.9 GW ISSN 0080-0708
REHABILITATION DER ENTWICKLUNGSGEHEMMTEN. 1961. irreg., no.9, 1978. price varies. Ernst Reinhardt, GmbH und Co., Verlag, Kemnatenstr. 46, 8000 Munich 19, W. Germany (B.R.D.) Ed. Gerhard Heese.
Rehabilitation

371.9 US ISSN 0361-4166
REHABILITATION GAZETTE; international journal of independent living for the disabled. (Editions in English, French, German, Japanese, Portuguese and Spanish) 1958. biennial. $15 to individuals; institutions $20. Gazette International Networking Institute, 4502 Maryland Ave., St. Louis, MO 63108. TEL 314-361-0475. Eds. Gini Laurie, Judith Raymond. adv. abstr. illus. circ. 7,000. (also avail. in microform; talking book; back issues avail.) Indexed: Excerp.Med. Except.Child.Educ.Abstr. Rehabil.Lit.
Formerly: Toomey J Gazette (ISSN 0495-8667)

338 II ISSN 0080-0724
REHABILITATION INDUSTRIES CORPORATION. ANNUAL REPORT.* (Report year ends Mar. 31) (Text in English) 1959/60. a. Rehabilitation Industries Corporation Ltd., 25 Free School St., Calcutta 16, India.

371.9 US
REHABILITATION INTERNATIONAL. WORLD CONGRESS. PROCEEDINGS. 1921. quadrennial. $30. Rehabilitation International, 25 E. 21st St., 4th Fl., New York, NY 10010. TEL 212-420-1500. circ. 3,000.

SERIES IN CLINICAL AND COMMUNITY PSYCHOLOGY. see *PSYCHOLOGY*

SPEECH COMMUNICATION DIRECTORY. see *EDUCATION — Higher Education*

371.9 CN ISSN 0315-1808
T A S A. 1971. a. Can.$20. Alberta Teachers' Association, Special Education Council, 11010 142nd St., Edmonton, Alta. T5N 2R1, Canada. Ed. Doug Anderson. circ. 909. Indexed: Can.Educ.Ind.

373.2 US ISSN 0093-9889
TENNESSEE. STATE BOARD FOR VOCATIONAL EDUCATION. INFORMATION SERIES. irreg. State Board for Vocational Education, Nashville, TN 37219. TEL 615-741-3446. Key Title: Information Series - Tennessee State Board of Vocational Education.

THEIR WORLD. see *CHILDREN AND YOUTH — About*

371.9 JA
TOKYO METROPOLITAN GOVERNMENT. FUCHU REHABILITATION SCHOOL. ANNUAL REPORT. (Text in Japanese) 1971. a. free. Tokyo Metropolitan Government, Fuchu Rehabilitation School, 9-2, 2-chome, Musashidai, Fuchu-shi 183, Japan. circ. 300.

371.9 US ISSN 0070-6736
U S C ANNUAL DISTINGUISHED LECTURE SERIES MONOGRAPHS IN SPECIAL EDUCATION AND REHABILITATION. 1962. a. price varies. (University of Southern California, School of Education) University of Southern California Press, c/o Bookstore, University Park, Los Angeles, CA 90007. TEL 213-743-5371. Ed. James F. Magary. circ. 3,000. Indexed: ERIC. Except.Child Educ.Abstr. Rehabil.Lit.

371.9 DK ISSN 0107-377X
UNDERVISNINGSMATERIALER TIL BEGYNDER- OG SPECIALUNDERVISNING. 1980. a. free. Special Paedagogisk Forlag, Herning, Denmark. illus.
Formerly: Test- og Undervisningsmaterialer.

371.9 US
U.S. DEPARTMENT OF HEALTH AND HUMAN SERVICES. ANNUAL REPORT TO THE CONGRESS OF THE UNITED STATES ON SERVICES PROVIDED TO HANDICAPPED CHILDREN IN PROJECT HEAD START. At head of title: Head Start Services to Handicapped Children. 1973. a. U.S. Administration for Children, Youth and Families, 330 Independence Ave., S.W., Washington, DC 20201. TEL 202-755-7762. circ. 10,000. Key Title: Annual Report of the U.S. Department of Health and Human Services to the Congress of the United States on Services Provided to Handicapped Children in Project Head Start.
Formerly: U.S. Department of Health, Education and Welfare. Annual Report to the Congress of the United States on Services to Handicapped Children in Project Head Start (ISSN 0093-3430)

371.9 CS ISSN 0083-4211
UNIVERZITA KOMENSKEHO. ODDELENIE LIECEBNEJ A SPECIALNEJ PEDAGOGIKY. ZBORNIK: PAEDAGOGICA SPECIALIS.* (Text in Slovak; summaries in English, German and Russian) 1970. irreg. exchange basis. Univerzita Komenskeho, Oddelenie Liecebnej a Specialnej Pedagogiky, Safarikova nam.6, 885 45 Bratislava, Czechoslovakia. Ed. Juraj Brtka.

362.8 US
WASHINGTON (STATE). VOCATIONAL REHABILITATION SERVICES DIVISION. STATE FACILITIES DEVELOPMENT PLAN. 1969. irreg. free. Department of Social and Health Services, Division of Vocational Rehabilitation, OB 2, Olympia, WA 98504. TEL 206-753-0291. circ. 1,000.
Formerly: Washington (State). Vocational Rehabilitation Services Division. State Facilities Plan (ISSN 0092-5543)

371.9 371.3 UK ISSN 0144-5359
WESSEX STUDIES IN SPECIAL EDUCATION. 1981. biennial. £3.20. King Alfred's College, Winchester SO22 4NR, England. Ed. Robin Jackson. bk. rev. circ. 400. (looseleaf format; also avail. in microfiche) Indexed: Br.Educ.Ind. Except.Child.Educ.Abstr.

378.1 US ISSN 0148-6381
WHO'S WHO AMONG VOCATIONAL AND TECHNICAL STUDENTS IN AMERICA. 1975. a. $23.80. Randall Publishing Co., Box 2029, Tuscaloosa, AL 35401. TEL 205-349-2990.
Formerly: Who's Who Among Students in American Vocational and Technical Schools (ISSN 0360-5248)

371.9 155.4 US
WORLD COUNCIL FOR GIFTED AND TALENTED CHILDREN. YEARBOOK. 1981. biennial. $15. Trillium Press, Inc., Box 209, Monroe, NY 10950. TEL 914-783-2999. (back issues avail.)

YEAR BOOK OF REHABILITATION. see *MEDICAL SCIENCES*

EDUCATION — Teaching Methods And Curriculum

see also specific subjects

610.7 US ISSN 0092-0371
A A M C CURRICULUM DIRECTORY. 1972. a. $7.50. Association of American Medical Colleges, One Dupont Circle, N.W., Washington, DC 20036. TEL 202-828-0400.

375 US ISSN 0147-1236
A C T F L FOREIGN LANGUAGE EDUCATION SERIES. 1969. a. $14.60 to non-members; members $10.95. (American Council on the Teaching of Foreign Languages) National Textbook Co., 4255 W. Touhy Ave., Lincolnwood, IL 60646. TEL 312-679-5500.
Former titles: A C T F L Review of Foreign Languages Education (ISSN 0091-2476); A C T F L Annual Review of Foreign Language Education (ISSN 0068-1180); Britannica Review of Foreign Language Education.

A T S S BULLETIN. (Association of Teachers of Social Studies in the City of New York) see *SOCIAL SCIENCES: COMPREHENSIVE WORKS*

371.33 JA ISSN 0065-0102
A V E IN JAPAN. (Text in English) 1963. a. 1.000 Yen. Japan Audio-Visual Education Association, 1-17-1 Toranomon, Minato-ku, Tokyo 105, Japan. Ed. Kenji Fujii. circ. 2,000.

613.7 370.15 US ISSN 0890-4073
ADVANCES IN HEALTH EDUCATION. 1987. a. $47.50. A M S Press, Inc., 56 E. 13th St., New York, NY 10003. TEL 212-777-4700. Ed. James H. Humphrey. index. (back issues avail.)

371.3 US ISSN 0748-0067
ADVANCES IN TEACHER EDUCATION. 1984. a. price varies. Ablex Publishing Corp., 355 Chestnut St., Norwood, NJ 07648. TEL 201-767-8450. Eds. Lilian Katz, James Raths.

ADVANCES IN THE PSYCHOLOGY OF HUMAN INTELLIGENCE. see *PSYCHOLOGY*

371.3 CN ISSN 0380-1306
ALBERTA LEARNING RESOURCES JOURNAL. 1975. irreg. (1-2/yr.) Can.$30. Alberta Teachers' Association, Learning Resources Council, Barnett House, 11010 142nd St., Edmonton, Alta. T5N 2R1, Canada. TEL 403-453-2411. Ed. Christine Spring-Gifford. bk. rev. circ. 593.
Former titles: Alberta Teachers' Association. Audio-Visual Council. Newsletter (ISSN 0380-8513); Alberta Teachers' Association. School Library Council. Newsletter (ISSN 0380-8505)

ALBERTA SCIENCE EDUCATION JOURNAL. see *SCIENCES: COMPREHENSIVE WORKS*

ALBERTA TEACHERS' ASSOCIATION. MATH MONOGRAPH. see *MATHEMATICS*

AMERICAN LANGUAGE JOURNAL; a journal for intensive English studies. see *LINGUISTICS*

ANNUAL REPORT ON ADVANCED DENTAL EDUCATION. see *MEDICAL SCIENCES — Dentistry*

379 US
ARIZONA. STATE ADVISORY COUNCIL FOR VOCATIONAL TECHNICAL EDUCATION. ANNUAL REPORT. 1970. a. free. Advisory Council for Vocational Education, 4725 N. 19th Ave., Suite 2, Phoenix, AZ 85015. TEL 602-255-5040. Ed. Pat Sperling. circ. 2,500.
Formerly: Arizona. State Advisory Council for Vocational Education. Annual Report (ISSN 0091-8792)

371.3 UK ISSN 0141-5956
ASPECTS OF EDUCATIONAL TECHNOLOGY. 1975. a. £19.95. Kogan Page Ltd., 120 Pentonville Rd., London N1 9JN, England. Ed.Bd. Indexed: High.Educ.Curr.Aware.Bull.

375 US
ASSOCIATION FOR EDUCATIONAL COMMUNICATIONS AND TECHNOLOGY. MEMBERSHIP DIRECTORY AND HUMAN RESOURCES. a. $35 to non-members. Association for Educational Communications and Technology, 1126 16th St. N.W., Washington, DC 20036. TEL 202-466-4780. Ed. Leslie Hayward. adv. circ. 5,800. (reprint service avail. from UMI)
Former titles: Association for Educational Communications and Technology. Directory of Human Resources; Formerly: Association for Educational Communications and Technology. Membership Directory and Data Book.

375 016.3 US
ASSOCIATION FOR SUPERVISION AND CURRICULUM DEVELOPMENT. CURRICULUM MATERIALS DIGEST. a. $8. Association for Supervision and Curriculum Development, 125 N. West St., Alexandria, VA 22314. TEL 703-549-9110. (also avail. in microform)
Formerly: Association for Supervision and Curriculum Development. Curriculum Materials (ISSN 0084-6864)

375 960 NR
ASSOCIATION OF HISTORY TEACHERS IN NIGERIA. 1971. a. S.10. Educational Research Institute, Box 277, Ibadan, Nigeria. Ed. Od Olusola Akintay.

371.3 IO
ATMA JAYA RESEARCH CENTRE. ANNUAL REPORT. (Text in English) 1973. a. Atma Jaya Research Centre - Pusat Penelitian Atma Jaya, Jalan Jenderal Sudirman 49a, Box 2639, Jakarta 10001, Indonesia. illus. (also avail. in microfiche)

371.3 US
AUDIO VIDEO MARKET PLACE; a multimedia guide. 1969. a. since 1976; previously biennial. $65. R.R. Bowker Company, Database Publishing Group, 245 W. 17th St., New York, NY 10011. TEL 800-521-8110.
Formerly (until 1984): Audiovisual Market Place (ISSN 0067-0553)

375.38 AT ISSN 0084-6961
AUSTRALASIAN COMMERCIAL TEACHERS' ASSOCIATION. JOURNAL.* 1968. a. $1. Australasian Commercial Teachers' Association, 20 Napoleon St., Roseberry, N.S.W. 2018, Australia.

507 375 AT ISSN 0157-244X
AUSTRALIAN SCIENCE EDUCATION RESEARCH ASSOCIATION. RESEARCH IN SCIENCE EDUCATION. 1971. a. Aus.$14. Australian Science Education Research Association, c/o Richard T. White, Faculty of Education, Monash University, Melbourne, 3168, Australia. Ed. Richard P. Tisher. adv. circ. 300. (also avail. in microfiche) Indexed: Aus.Educ.Ind. Aus.Educ.Ind. ERIC.

371.33 AT
AUSTRALIAN SOCIETY FOR EDUCATION IN FILM AND TELEVISION. PRESIDENT'S NEWSLETTER. 1971. irreg. Australian Society for Education in Film and Television, G.P.O. Box 252c, Hobart, Tas. 7001, Australia.

371.3 AU
AUSTRIA. BUNDESMINISTERIUM FUER UNTERRICHT UND KUNST. SCHRIFTENREIHE. 1971. irreg. price varies. Manzsche Verlags- und Universitaetsbuchhandlung, Kohlmarkt 16, A-1014 Vienna, Austria.

507 CN ISSN 0381-6036
B.C. SCIENCE TEACHER. 1959. irreg. Can.$30 to non-members. (B.C. Science Teachers' Association) B.C. Teachers' Federation, 2235 Burrard St., Vancouver, B.C. V6J 3H9, Canada. TEL 604-731-8121. adv. bk. rev. charts. illus. circ. 600. Indexed: Can.Educ.Ind.
Former titles: S T A News (ISSN 0048-9719); British Columbia Science Teachers' Association. Newsletter.

BALAI PENDIDIKAN DAN LATIHAN TENAGA SOCIAL. LAPORAN. see *SOCIAL SERVICES AND WELFARE*

370.1 707 CN ISSN 0316-1544
BRITISH COLUMBIA ART TEACHERS' ASSOCIATION. JOURNAL. 1960. irreg. Can.$37 to non-members. (B.C. Art Teachers' Association) B.C. Teachers' Federation, 2235 Burrard St., Vancouver, B. C. V6J 3H9, Canada. TEL 604-731-8121. adv. circ. 375. Indexed: Can.Educ.Ind.
Formerly: British Columbia Art Teachers' Association. Newsletter (ISSN 0045-2904)

420 820 CN ISSN 0316-0173
BRITISH COLUMBIA ENGLISH TEACHERS' ASSOCIATION. JOURNAL. (Supplement avail: Update) 1960. a. Can.$35 to non-members. (B.C. English Teachers' Association) B.C. Teachers' Federation, 2235 Burrard St., Vancouver, B. C. V6J 3H9, Canada. TEL 604-731-8121. adv. bk. rev. circ. 450. Indexed: Can.Educ.Ind.
Formerly (1966-1971): British Columbia English Teacher (ISSN 0045-2955)

C A L I C O. MONOGRAPH SERIES. (Computer Assisted Language & Instruction Consortium) see *COMPUTERS — Computer Assisted Instruction*

371.3 US
C S E MONOGRAPH SERIES IN EVALUATION. 1973. a. University of California, Los Angeles, Center for the Study of Evaluation, 405 Hilgard Ave., 145 Moore Hall, Los Angeles, CA 90024. TEL 213-825-4711. Indexed: ERIC.

CANADIAN UNIVERSITY MUSIC REVIEW/REVUE DE MUSIQUE DES UNIVERSITES CANADIENNES. see *MUSIC*

CENTRAL STATES CONFERENCE ON THE TEACHING OF FOREIGN LANGUAGES. EDUCATION SERIES. see *LINGUISTICS*

375 FR ISSN 0069-2050
CENTRE REGIONAL DE RECHERCHE ET DE DOCUMENTATION PEDAGOGIQUES DE LYON. ANNALES. 1970. irreg. price varies depending on series. Centre Regional de Recherche et de Documentation Pedagogiques de Lyon, 47-49 rue Philippe-De-Lassalle, 69 Lyon (4e), France.

370 510 FR ISSN 0395-7837
CHANTIERS DE PEDAGOGIE MATHEMATIQUE. 1970. irreg. Association des Professeurs de Mathematiques de l'Enseignement Public, Regionale Parisienne, c/o Institut National de Recherche et de Documentation Pedagogiques, 29 rue d'Ulm, 75230 Paris Cedex 05, France.

CHUCHOTERIES. see *LINGUISTICS*

375 US
CLAREMONT READING CONFERENCE. YEARBOOK. 1932. a. $15. (Claremont Reading Conference) Claremont Graduate School, Center for Development Studies, Harper 200, Claremont, CA 91711-6160. Ed. Malcolm P. Douglass. circ. 1,200. (also avail. in microfilm from UMI; reprint service avail. from UMI,EDR) Indexed: Educ.Ind. ERIC.

COLLEGE MEDIA DIRECTOR NEWSLETTER. see *EDUCATION*

371.3 UK
CREATIVE ARTS & CRAFTS HANDBOOK. biennial. £4.95. Educational Institute of Design Craft & Technology, c/o P.E. Dawson, Ed., 52 Locarno Ave., Gillingham, Kent ME8 6ES, England (Subscr. addr.: c/o F.R. Willmore, 38 Hall Close, Whissendine, Oakham, Rutland, Leics., England)

375 780 US ISSN 0070-198X
CURRENT ISSUES IN MUSIC EDUCATION. 1963. irreg., no.5, 1970. price varies. ‡ Ohio State University, School of Music, Div. of Music Education, Columbus, OH 43210. TEL 615-422-6511.

375 300 US ISSN 0747-4857
DATA BOOK OF SOCIAL STUDIES MATERIALS AND RESOURCES. 1971. a. $10. Social Science Education Consortium, Inc., 855 Broadway, Boulder, CO 80302. TEL 303-492-8154. bk. rev. circ. 500. (also avail. in microform from EDR)
Former titles: Social Studies Materials and Resources Data Book. Annual; (until vol.4, 1979): Social Studies Curriculum Materials Data Book Supplement.

EDUCATION — TEACHING METHODS AND CURRICULUM

650   US   ISSN 0416-9336
DELTA PI EPSILON. RESEARCH BULLETIN. 1962. irreg. price varies. Delta Pi Epsilon Graduate Business Education Society, National Office, Gustavus Adolphus College, St. Peter, MN 56082. TEL 507-931-8000. circ. 10,000. (reprint service avail. from UMI) Indexed: Bus.Educ.Ind.

430.07 378   AU   ISSN 0012-1398
DEUTSCHKURSE/GERMAN LANGUAGE COURSES. 1961/1962. a. ‡ Oesterreichischer Auslandsstudentendienst, Dr. Karl Lueger-Ring 1, A-1010 Vienna, Austria. Ed. Ludwig Koller. adv. circ. 10,000.

371.3   UK
DEVELOPING HORIZONS IN SPECIAL EDUCATION SERIES. 1982. irreg. £1 per no. National Council for Special Education, 1 Wood St., Stratford-upon-Avon, Warwickshire CV37 6JE, England. Ed. Richard Rose.

DIALOGUES ET CULTURES. see *LINGUISTICS*

371.3   US   ISSN 0070-4881
DIMENSION: LANGUAGES; proceedings of the Southern Conference on Language Teaching. 1966. a. $4. Southern Conference on Language Teaching, c/o James S. Gates, Exec.Sec., Spelman College, Atlanta, GA 30314. TEL 404-681-3643.

DIRECTORY OF RESEARCH AND DEVELOPMENTAL PROJECTS. see *EDUCATION*

371.3   UK   ISSN 0266-9544
E.I.D.C.T.- C.D.T. YEAR BOOK. 1984. biennial. £4.95. Educational Institute of Design Craft & Technology, c/o P.E. Dawson, 52 Locarno Ave., Gillingham, Kent. ME8 6ES, England. Ed. F.R. Willmore. adv. circ. 2,000.
  Incorporating: Craft Buyer's Guide; Formerly: E.I.D.C.T. Year Book.

371.3   BB
EASTERN CARIBBEAN STANDING CONFERENCE ON TEACHER EDUCATION. REPORT. 1957. biennial. bds. 8. University of the West Indies, Faculty of Education, Research & Development Section, Cave Hill, Barbados, W. Indies. Ed. R.M. Nicholson. circ. 800.
  Formerly: Conference on Teacher Education in the Eastern Caribbean. Report (ISSN 0069-8695)

ECHANGE. see *LINGUISTICS*

EDUCATIONAL FILM/VIDEO LOCATOR. see *MOTION PICTURES — Abstracting, Bibliographies, Statistics*

371.33   US   ISSN 8755-2094
EDUCATIONAL MEDIA AND TECHNOLOGY YEARBOOK. 1973. a. $47.50 to non-members; members $38. (Association for Educational Communications and Technology) Libraries Unlimited, Inc., Box 263, Littleton, CO 80160. TEL 303-770-1220. Ed. Elwood E. Miller.
  Formerly (until 1985): Educational Media Yearbook (ISSN 0000-037X)

375   US
EDUCATIONAL MEDIA CATALOGS ON MICROFICHE. 1975. s-a. $87.50. Olympic Media Information, 550 First St., Hoboken, NJ 07030. TEL 201-963-1600. Ed. Walter J. Carroll. index. circ. 1,000. (also avail. in microfiche)

371.3   US   ISSN 0070-9387
EDUCATORS GRADE GUIDE TO FREE TEACHING AIDS. 1955. a. $43.50. Educators Progress Service, Inc., Randolph, WI 53956. TEL 414-326-3126. Ed. Kathleen S. Nehmer. index. (also avail. in looseleaf format)

371.3   US   ISSN 0160-1296
EDUCATORS GUIDE TO FREE AUDIO AND VIDEO MATERIALS. 1954. a. $20.25. Educators Progress Service, Inc., Randolph, WI 53956. TEL 414-326-3126. Eds. James L. Berger, Walter A. Wittich.
  Formerly: Educators Guide to Free Tapes, Scripts, and Transcriptions (ISSN 0070-9441)

371.3   US   ISSN 0070-9395
EDUCATORS GUIDE TO FREE FILMS. 1941. a. $27. Educators Progress Service, Inc., Randolph, WI 53956. TEL 414-326-3126. Eds. John Diffor, Elaine Diffor. index.

371.3   US   ISSN 0070-9409
EDUCATORS GUIDE TO FREE FILMSTRIPS. 1949. a. $19. Educators Progress Service, Inc., Randolph, WI 53956. TEL 414-326-3126. Eds. John Diffor, Elaine Diffor. index.

371.42   US   ISSN 0070-9417
EDUCATORS GUIDE TO FREE GUIDANCE MATERIALS. 1962. a. $24.25. Educators Progress Service, Inc., Randolph, WI 53956. TEL 414-326-3126. Eds. Mary Horkheimer Saterstrom, Gail F. Farwell.

371.3   US   ISSN 0424-6241
EDUCATORS GUIDE TO FREE HEALTH, PHYSICAL EDUCATION & RECREATION MATERIALS. 1968. a. $25.75. Educators Progress Service, Inc., Randolph, WI 53956. TEL 414-326-3126. Ed. Patricia Horkheimer.

371.3   US   ISSN 0070-9425
EDUCATORS GUIDE TO FREE SCIENCE MATERIALS. 1960. a. $24.75. Educators Progress Service, Inc., Randolph, WI 53956. TEL 414-326-3126. Eds. Mary Horkheimer Saterstrom, John W. Renner. index.

371.3   US   ISSN 0070-9433
EDUCATORS GUIDE TO FREE SOCIAL STUDIES MATERIALS. 1961. a. $26.50. Educators Progress Service, Inc., Randolph, WI 53956. TEL 414-326-3126. Eds. Steven A. Suttles, Sharon F. Suttles.

371.3   US
EDUCATORS INDEX OF FREE MATERIALS. 1934. a. $45.50. Educators Progress Service, Inc., Randolph, WI 53956. TEL 414-326-3126. Ed. Mary P. Parent. (looseleaf format)

375   US   ISSN 0070-9980
ELEMENTARY TEACHERS GUIDE TO FREE CURRICULUM MATERIALS. 1944. a. $22.75. Educators Progress Service, Inc., Randolph, WI 53956. TEL 414-326-3126. Ed. Kathleen S. Nehmer.

371.3 407   US   ISSN 0071-0601
ENGLISH LANGUAGE AND ORIENTATION PROGRAMS IN THE UNITED STATES; including a list of programs for training teachers of English as a second language. 1960. irreg. $8.95. ‡ Institute of International Education, 809 United Nations Plaza, New York, NY 10017. TEL 212-984-5412.

373   IR
ENGLISH LANGUAGE TEACHERS ASSOCIATION. REVIEW/ANJOMAN-E DABIRAN-E ZABANHA-YE KHAREJI. NASHRIYEH. (Text in Persian, English) 1972. irreg. free. English Language Teachers Association, Box 33-59, Tajrish, Teheran, Iran. Ed. Gholam Hoseyn Kehtari.

371.3   US
FEATURE FILMS ON 8MM, 16MM AND VIDEOTAPE; a directory of feature films on 16 mm and videotape available for rental, sale and lease. Variant title: Feature Films Available for Rental, Sale and Lease. 1967. irreg., 8th edt., 1985. $75. R.R. Bowker Company, 245 W. 17th St., New York, NY 10011. TEL 800-521-8110.
  Formerly: Feature Films on 8mm and 16mm (ISSN 0071-4100)

375   AT   ISSN 0310-6020
FILTER: A PAPER FOR SECONDARY SCIENCE TEACHERS. 1973. irreg. Aus.$6. Education Department, Curriculum Branch, 151 Royal St., East Perth, W.A. 6000, Australia. bk. rev. circ. 2, 300. Indexed: Aus.Educ.Ind.

613   JA
FUKUI UNIVERSITY. FACULTY OF EDUCATION. MEMOIRS. SERIES 6: PHYSICAL EDUCATION. (Text in Japanese) a. Fukui University, Faculty of Education, 9-1, 3-chome, Bunkyo, Fukui 910, Japan.

371   US
G P N EDUCATIONAL MEDIA. ELEMENTARY-SECONDARY. 1967. a. free. ‡ Great Plains National Instructional Television Library, P.O. Box 80669, Lincoln, NE 68501. TEL 402-472-2007. (Affiliate: University of Nebraska) Eds. Richard L. Spence, Thomas Henderson. circ. 12,000.
  Superseded in part: Great Plains National Instructional Television Library. Recorded Visual Instruction (ISSN 0740-2732); (until 1973): Catalog of Recorded Instruction for Television.

910   AT   ISSN 0085-0969
GEOGRAPHICAL EDUCATION. 1969. a. Aus.$8. Australian Geography Teachers' Association, c/o John Fien, Brisbane CAE, Kelvin Grove, Qld. 4059, Australia (Subscr. to: Business Manager, Brisbane CAE, Mt.Gravatt Campus, Qld. 4122, Australia) adv. bk. rev. circ. 3,000. Indexed: ERIC. Aus.Educ.Ind. Aus.P.A.I.S. Geo.Abstr.

375   GW
GERMANY (FEDERAL REPUBLIC, 1949-). BUNDESANSTALT FUER ARBEIT. FOERDERUNG DER BERUFLICHEN BILDUNG; ERGEBNISSE DER TEILNEHMERSTATISTIK. (Supplement to the Amtliche Nachrichten der Bundesanstalt fuer Arbeit) 1970. a. DM.9. ‡ Bundesanstalt fuer Arbeit, Regensburger Strasse 104, 8500 Nuernberg 1, W. Germany (B.R.D.)

370   SW   ISSN 0348-2219
GOETEBORGS UNIVERSITET. INSTITUTIONEN FOER PRAKTISK PEDAGOGIK. RAPPORT. 1966. irreg., no.91, 1979. free. Goeteborgs Universitet, Institutionen foer Praktisk Pedagogisk, Box 1010, S-431 26 Moelndal, Sweden. Ed. K.G. Stukat.
  Former titles: Laerarhoegskolan i Moelndal. Pedagogiska Institutionen. Rapport; Laerarhoegskolan i Goeteborg. Pedagogiska Institutionen. Rapport (ISSN 0534-042X)

375   UK   ISSN 0072-7113
GREAT BRITAIN. SCHOOLS COUNCIL PUBLICATIONS. CURRICULUM BULLETINS. 1965. irreg. price varies. ‡ Methuen Educational, 11 New Fetter Lane, London EC4P 4EE, England.

371.3   UK   ISSN 0072-8918
GUIDELINES FOR TEACHERS. 1971. irreg. price varies. National Council for Special Education, 1 Wood St., Stratford-Upon-Avon, Warwickshire CV37 6JE, England.

371.3   UK   ISSN 0073-1714
HELPS FOR STUDENTS OF HISTORY. 1950. irreg. Historical Association, 59a Kennington Park Rd., London SE11 4JH, England. (reprint service avail. from UMI)

HISTORIE OG SAMTIDSORIENTERING. see *HISTORY*

372.83   CN   ISSN 0315-8527
HORIZON. 1961. irreg. Can.$25 to non-members. ‡ (B.C. Social Studies Teachers Association) B.C. Teachers' Federation, 2235 Burrard St., Vancouver, B.C. V6J 2H9, Canada. TEL 604-731-8121. bk. rev. circ. 500. Indexed: CMI. Can.Educ.Ind.
  Formerly: British Columbia Social Studies Teachers' Association. Newsletter (ISSN 0045-3048)

371.33   US
I C I A MEMBERSHIP DIRECTORY. 1947. a. $15. ‡ International Communications Industries Association, Inc., 3150 Spring St., Fairfax, VA 22031. TEL 703-273-7200. Ed. Bobbie Hunt. circ. 10,000.
  Former titles: N A V A/I C I A Membership Directory (National Audio-Visual Association); N A V A Membership Directory.

ILLINOIS SPEECH AND THEATRE ASSOCIATION. JOURNAL. see *THEATER*

379   US
INDIANA. COUNCIL ON VOCATIONAL EDUCATION. ANNUAL REPORT. 1970. a. State Council for Vocational Technical Education, 524 Illinois Bldg., 17 W. Market, Indianapolis, IN 46204. TEL 317-232-1981. Ed. Walter Penrod. illus.
  Formerly: Indiana. State University Council for Vocational Technical Education. Annual Report (ISSN 0091-8970)

EDUCATION — TEACHING METHODS AND CURRICULUM

371.26 US
INDIANA STUDIES IN HIGHER EDUCATION. 1961. irreg. $1. Indiana University, Bureau of Evaluative Studies and Testing, Bloomington, IN 47401. TEL 812-332-0211. Ed. Clinton I. Chase. circ. 200.
Formerly: Indiana Studies in Prediction (ISSN 0073-6945)

371.3 UK ISSN 0307-9732
INTERNATIONAL YEARBOOK OF EDUCATIONAL & INSTRUCTIONAL TECHNOLOGY. 1976. biennial. £21. Kogan Page Ltd., 120 Pentonville Rd., London N1 9JN, England (Dist. by: Nichols Publishing Company, Box 96, New York, NY 10024) Ed. C.W. Osborne.

371.3 407 US
IOWA ENGLISH BULLETIN. 1956. a. $3. Iowa Council of Teachers of English, English Department, Drake University, Des Moines, IA 50311. Ed. Sally Barr Reagan. adv. bk. rev. circ. 700. Indexed: M.L.A. Abstr.Engl.Stud.
Former titles: Iowa English Bulletin--Yearbook; Iowa English Yearbook (ISSN 0075-0352)

371.3 US
IOWA MIDDLE LEVEL EDUCATORS BULLETIN. a. $2 to non-members. (Iowa Association for Middle Level Educators) University of Northern Iowa, College of Education, Cedar Falls, IA 50614. TEL 319-273-2167. Ed. Mary Nan Aldrige.

371 IS
ISRAEL. MINISTRY OF EDUCATION AND CULTURE. DEPARTMENT OF EDUCATIONAL TECHNOLOGY. BULLETIN/ALON LE-TEKHNOLOGYAH BE-KHINUKH. (Text in Hebrew) irreg. Ministry of Education and Culture, Department of Educational Technology, Jerusalem, Israel.

ISTITUTO CAMPANO PER LA STORIA DELLA RESISTENZA. BOLLETTINO. see HISTORY

IWATE UNIVERSITY. FACULTY OF EDUCATION. ANNUAL REPORT. see LITERATURE

JOURNAL OF AGRONOMIC EDUCATION. see AGRICULTURE — Crop Production And Soil

371.3 US
JOURNAL OF CLINICAL READING: RESEARCH AND PROGRAMS. 1984. biennial. $10. (College Reading Association, Clinical Division) Cleveland State University, Rhodes Tower, 1333, E. 22nd St., Cleveland, OH 44115. TEL 216-687-4604. Ed. Lillian R. Hinds. bk. rev. bibl. stat. circ. 100. (back issues avail.)

371.3 360 US ISSN 0884-1233
JOURNAL OF TEACHING IN SOCIAL WORK; innovations in instruction, training and educational practice. 1987. biennial. $20 to individuals; institutions $28; libraries $32. Haworth Press, Inc., 28 E. 22nd St., New York, NY 10010-6194. Eds. Florence Vigilante, Harold Lewis. (also avail. in microfiche)

KODALY INSTITUTE OF CANADA. MONOGRAPH; a selected bibliography of the Kodaly concept of music education. see MUSIC — Abstracting, Bibliographies, Statistics

371.3 JA
KYOKA KYOIKU KENKYU.* 1968. a. Kanazawa University, Faculty of Education - Kanazawa Daigaku Kyoikugakubu, 1-1 Marunouchi, Kanazawa 920, Japan. illus. Indexed: Lang.& Lang.Behav.Abstr.

371.3 US
LANGUAGE AND LEARNING FOR HUMAN SERVICE PROFESSIONS. 1984. irreg. price varies. Ablex Publishing Corp., 355 Chestnut St., Norwood, NJ 07648. TEL 201-767-8450. Ed. Cynthia Wallat.

371.3 CN ISSN 0380-8491
LEARNING RESOURCES COUNCIL NEWSLETTER. 1975. irreg. (3-4/yr.) included in subscr. to Alberta Learning Resources Journal. Alberta Teachers' Association, Learning Resources Council, Barnett House, 11010 142nd St., Edmonton, Alba. T5N 2R1, Canada. TEL 403-453-2411. Ed. Judy Abel. circ. 593.

LINGUISTIQUE ET ENSEIGNEMENT. see LINGUISTICS

420 PH ISSN 0047-5289
M S T ENGLISH QUARTERLY. 1950. a. price varies. D C S Manila Teachers of Secondary English, Office of the Supervisors of Secondary English, Manila Science High School, Taft Ave., Manila, Philippines. Ed.Bd. bk. rev. circ. 700. Indexed: Ind.Phil.Per.

MENTAL MEASUREMENTS YEARBOOK. see PSYCHOLOGY

MISSOURI JOURNAL OF RESEARCH IN MUSIC EDUCATION. see MUSIC

510 AT
MOBIUS. 1967. a. Aus.$5. ‡ Mathematical Association of South Australia, 163a Greenhill Rd., Parkside, S.A. 5066, Australia. circ. 500. Indexed: Aus.Educ.Ind. CINAHL.
Formerly: Mathematical Association of South Australia. S.A. Mathematics Teacher (ISSN 0047-6242)

MODERN ENGLISH JOURNAL/EIGO KYOIKU JAANARU. see LINGUISTICS

371.3 PL ISSN 0077-0558
MONOGRAFIE Z DZIEJOW OSWIATY. (Text in Polish; summaries in English, French or Russian) 1957. irreg., vol.30, 1985. price varies. (Polska Akademia Nauk, Instytut Historii Nauki, Oswiaty i Techniki, Pracownia Dziejow Oswiaty) Ossolineum, Publishing House of the Polish Academy of Sciences, Rynek 9, 50-106 Wroclaw, Poland (Dist. by: Ars Polona-Ruch, Krakowskie Przedmiescie 7, Warsaw, Poland) Ed. Jozef Miaso.

MUZYKAL'NOE VOSPITANIE V SHKOLE. see MUSIC

613.7 US ISSN 0276-461X
N A P E H E PROCEEDINGS. 1979. a. $18. ‡ (National Association for Physical Education in Higher Education) Human Kinetics Publishers, Inc., Box 5076, Champaign, IL 61820. TEL 217-351-5076. circ. 710. (back issues avail.)
Former titles: National Association for Physical Education for College Women; (until 1978): N C P E A M Proceedings (National College Physical Education Association for Men)

375 700 US ISSN 0077-3174
NATIONAL ART EDUCATION ASSOCIATION. RESEARCH MONOGRAPH. 1965. irreg., no.5, 1972. $2. National Art Education Association, 1916 Association Dr., Reston, VA 22091. TEL 703-860-8000. Ed. Thomas A. Hatfield.

370 US
NATIONAL ASSESSMENT OF EDUCATIONAL PROGRESS. ASSESSMENT REPORTS. 1970. irreg. (approx. 10-25/yr.) price varies. (Educational Testing Service) National Assessment of Educational Progress, CN 6710, Princeton, NJ 08541-6710 (Subscr. to: Supt. of Documents, Govt. Printing Office, Washington, DC 20402) bibl. charts. stat. circ. 10,000. (also avail. in microfiche from EDR) Indexed: ERIC.
Formerly: Education Commission of the States. National Assessment of Educational Progress. Assessment Reports.

NATIONAL ASSOCIATION OF SCHOOLS OF MUSIC. DIRECTORY. see MUSIC

NATIONAL ASSOCIATION OF SCHOOLS OF MUSIC. HANDBOOK. see MUSIC

650 338 US ISSN 0547-4728
NATIONAL BUSINESS EDUCATION YEARBOOK. 1963. a. $8. ‡ National Business Education Association, 1914 Association Drive, Reston, VA 22091. TEL 703-860-8300. Ed. Eddie L. Green. bibl. circ. 18,000. (also avail. in microform from UMI; reprint service avail. from UMI)

371.3 US
NATIONAL CENTER FOR AUDIO TAPES ARCHIVE. CATALOG. 1966. triennial. $4.50. National Center for Audio Tapes, University of Colorado, Campus Box 379, Boulder, CO 80309. TEL 303-492-7341. Ed. Richard Borkowski. subject index. circ. 10,000.
Formerly: National Center for Audio Tapes. Catalog (ISSN 0077-3719); Supersedes: National Tape Recording Catalog.

910 US
NATIONAL COUNCIL FOR GEOGRAPHIC EDUCATION. TOPICS IN GEOGRAPHY. irreg., no.8, 1986. price varies. National Council for Geographic Education, c/o James W. Vining, Exec. Dir., Western Illinois University, Macomb, IL 61455. TEL 309-298-2470.

371.3 UK
NATIONAL COUNCIL FOR SPECIAL EDUCATION. CONFERENCE REPORTS. irreg. price varies. National Council for Special Education, 1 Wood St., Stratford-upon-Avon, Warwickshire CV37 6JE, England.

371.3 UK ISSN 0077-5940
NATIONAL UNION OF TEACHERS. ANNUAL REPORT. 1871. a. £1. National Union of Teachers, Hamilton House, Mabledon Place, London, WC1H 9BD, England.

371.3 PL ISSN 0077-653X
NEODIDAGMATA. (Text in Polish, occasionally in English, French or German; summaries in English, French and Russian) 1970. irreg. price varies. Adam Mickiewicz University Press, Marchlewskiego 128, 61-874 Poznan, Poland. Ed. Leon Leja. Indexed: Psychol.Abstr.

375 NE ISSN 0168-5406
NETHERLANDS. CENTRAAL BUREAU VOOR DE STATISTIEK. STATISTIEK VAN HET BEROEPSONDERWIJS: HUISHOUD- EN NIJVERHEIDSONDERWIJS. (Text in Dutch and English) 1946/47. a. fl.9.45. Centraal Bureau voor de Statistiek, Prinses Beatrixlaan 428, Voorburg, Netherlands (Orders to: Staatsuitgeverij, Christoffel Plantijnstraat, The Hague, Netherlands)
Formerly: Netherlands. Centraal Bureau voor de Statistiek. Statistiek van het Nijverheidsonderwijs (ISSN 0077-734X)

375 NE ISSN 0168-4906
NETHERLANDS. CENTRAAL BUREAU VOOR DE STATISTIEK. STATISTIEK VAN HET ERKENDE SCHRIFTELIJK ONDERWIJS. STATISTICS ON CORRESPONDENCE COURSES. (Text in Dutch and English) 1947. a. fl.7.65. Centraal Bureau voor de Statistiek, Prinses Beatrixlaan 428, Voorburg, Netherlands (Orders to: Staatsuitgeverij, Christoffel Plantijnstraat, The Hague, Netherlands)
Formerly: Netherlands. Centraal Bureau voor de Statistiek. Statistiek van het Schriftelijk Onderwijs. Statistics on Correspondence Courses (ISSN 0077-7366)

371.3 GW ISSN 0723-3280
NEUE DIDAKTISCHE MODELLE. 1972. irreg. DM.14.80. Colloquium Verlag, Unter den Eichen 93, 1000 Berlin 45, W. Germany (B.R.D.) Eds. W. Northemann, Hans-Fred Rathenow. circ. 3,000.

NEW TEACHER. see EDUCATION

371 500 UN
NEW TRENDS IN INTEGRATED SCIENCE TEACHING. (Text in English) 1971. irreg. price varies. Unesco, 7-9 Place de Fontenoy, 75700 Paris, France (Dist. in U.S. by: Bernan Associates-Unipub, 4611-F Assembly Dr., Lahham, MD 20706-4391) Ed. P.E. Richmond.

NEW YORK STATE ENGLISH COUNCIL. MONOGRAPH SERIES. see LITERATURE

379.155 US ISSN 0094-8306
NORTH DAKOTA. STATE ADVISORY COUNCIL FOR VOCATIONAL EDUCATION. ANNUAL EVALUATION REPORT.* a. State Advisory Council for Vocational Education, Liberty Memorial Bldg., 3rd Fl., State Capitol Grounds, Bismarck, ND 58505. illus. Key Title: Annual Evaluation Report - North Dakota State Advisory Council for Vocational Education.

EDUCATION — TEACHING METHODS AND CURRICULUM

371.3   US   ISSN 0733-1169
NORTHEAST CONFERENCE ON THE TEACHING OF FOREIGN LANGUAGES. NORTHEAST CONFERENCE REPORTS. 1954. a. $6. Northeast Conference on the Teaching of Foreign languages, Inc., Box 623, Middlebury, VT 05753. TEL 802-388-4017. adv. cum.index: 1954-1975. circ. 5,000. Indexed: C.I.J.E. Key Title: Northeast Conference Reports.
    Former titles: N E C Reports (ISSN 0733-1177); Northeast Conference on the Teaching of Foreign Languages. Reports of the Working Committees (ISSN 0078-1665)

371.3   US
PAPERS AND RECORDINGS IN EDUCATION. 1971. a. $5 paper; recording $10. Arizona State University, College of Education, Tempe, AZ 85287. TEL 602-965-3306. Ed. James John Jelinek. circ. 1,000. (looseleaf format; also avail. in audio cassette; back issues avail.) Indexed: ERIC.

PAPERS IN JAPANESE LINGUISTICS. see *LINGUISTICS*

371.3   UK
PERSPECTIVES ON ACADEMIC GAMING & SIMULATION. irreg. £14.95. (Society for Academic Gaming and Simulation in Education and Training) Kogan Page Ltd., 120 Pentonville Rd., London N1 9JN, England. Ed. Fred Percival. (also avail. in microform from UMI; reprint service avail. from UMI) Indexed: C.I.J.E.
    Formerly: Simulation/Games for Learning (ISSN 0142-9361)

371.7   US   ISSN 0079-189X
PHYSICAL EDUCATION AROUND THE WORLD. MONOGRAPH. 1966. irreg., no.7, 1976. $3. Phi Epsilon Kappa Fraternity, 9030 Log Run Drive N., Indianapolis, IN 46234. TEL 317-299-4004. Ed. William Johnson. (reprint service avail. from UMI)

PHYSICAL EDUCATION INDEX. see *PHYSICAL FITNESS AND HYGIENE — Abstracting, Bibliographies, Statistics*

POLITISCHE BILDUNG. see *POLITICAL SCIENCE*

371.3 600   II   ISSN 0032-6690
PRAJNAN. (Text in English) 1967. a. price varies. Technical Teachers' Training Institute, Block FC, Sector III, Calcutta 700 064, India. Ed. K.M. Ghosh. bk. rev. abstr. bibl. charts. illus. stat. circ. 500.
    Study and teaching

613.7   CN   ISSN 0048-5381
PRO MOTION. 1960. irreg. Can.$15 to non-members. (B.C. Physical Education Teachers' Association) B.C. Teachers' Federation, 2235 Burrard St., Vancouver, B.C. V6J 3H9, Canada. TEL 604-731-8121. circ. 275. Indexed: Can.Educ.Ind. Sportsearch.

375   AT
QUEENSLAND. DEPARTMENT OF EDUCATION. INFORMATION AND PUBLICATIONS BRANCH. INFORMATION STATEMENT. irreg. Department of Education, Information and Publications Branch, P.O. Box 33, North Quay, Qld. 4000, Australia. Ed. J. L. Finger.
    Formerly: Queensland. Department of Education. Research and Curriculum Branch. Information Statement (ISSN 0310-5121)

375   AT
QUEENSLAND. DEPARTMENT OF EDUCATION. RESEARCH BRANCH. REPORTING RESEARCH. 1971. irreg. Department of Education, Research Branch, P.O. Box 33, North Quay, Qld. 4000, Australia. Ed. E. Cassin.
    Formerly: Queensland. Department of Education. Research and Curriculum Branch. Reporting Research (ISSN 0310-4095)

R E C S A M ANNUAL REPORT. (Regional Centre for Education in Science and Mathematics) see *EDUCATION*

028   II   ISSN 0377-3426
READING JOURNAL. (Text in English and Hindi) 1973. a. Rs.3($0.50) Indian Reading Association, J-15 Haus Khas Enclave, Mehrauli Road, New Delhi 16, India. Ed. K. Bose. bk. rev.

428.4   US   ISSN 0191-0914
READING RESEARCH. ADVANCES IN THEORY AND PRACTICE. 1979. irreg., vol.5, 1985. $55. Academic Press, Inc., Orlando, FL 32887. TEL 305-345-2000.

REHOVOT. see *SCIENCES: COMPREHENSIVE WORKS*

RESOURCE BOOK/RESSOURCES. see *EDUCATION*

370.78   US   ISSN 0091-732X
REVIEW OF RESEARCH IN EDUCATION. 1973. a. $23 to individuals; institutions $29. American Educational Research Association, 1230 17th St., N.W., Washington, DC 20036. TEL 202-223-9485. Ed. Ernst Rothkopf. index. circ. 4,000. Indexed: SSCI.

SBORNIK STATEI PO FRANTSUZSKOI LINGVISTIKE I METODIKE PREPODAVANIYA INOSTRANNOGO YAZIKA V V U ZE. see *LINGUISTICS*

371.3   GW
SCHULFERNSEHEN. 1973. irreg. price varies. (Landesbildstelle Berlin, Zentrum fuer Audiovisuelle Medien) Colloquium Verlag, Unter den Eichen 93, 1000 Berlin 45, W. Germany (B.R.D.) circ. 300.

SCIENCE NOTES AND NEWS. see *SCIENCES: COMPREHENSIVE WORKS*

650.07 370   UK
SCOTTISH VOCATIONAL EDUCATION COUNCIL. HANDBOOK. 1978. a. free. Scottish Vocational Education Council, 38 Queen St., Glasgow G1 3DY, Scotland. Ed. Joe McLaughlin. Indexed: Lang. & Lang.Behav.Abstr.
    Formerly: Scottish Business Education Council. Business Education Guide (ISSN 0144-0101)

371.33 300   US
SOCIAL STUDIES AUDIOVISUALS: A TEACHER'S SOURCEBOOK. 1972. irreg. $50. (National Information Center for Educational Media) Access Innovations, Inc., Box 40130, Albuquerque, NM 87196. TEL 505-265-3591. cum.index. circ. controlled.
    Formerly (until 1987): N I C E M Index to Psychology-Multimedia.

370   MY   ISSN 0126-8155
SOUTHEAST ASIAN-MINISTERS OF EDUCATION ORGANISATION. REGIONAL CENTRE FOR EDUCATION IN SCIENCE AND MATHEMATICS. GOVERNING BOARD MEETING. FINAL REPORT. (Text in English) a. free. Southeast Asian Ministers of Education Organisation, Regional Centre for Education in Science and Mathematics, Glugor, Penang, Malaysia. circ. 150.

STADION; Internationale Zeitschrift fuer Geschichte des Sports und der Koerperkultur. see *SPORTS AND GAMES*

371.3   US
STUDENT ACCELERATION IN FLORIDA PUBLIC EDUCATION. 1975. a. Department of Education, Knott Building, Tallahassee, FL 32301. TEL 904-487-1630.

375   TZ
STUDIES IN CURRICULUM DEVELOPMENT. irreg. price varies. ‡ University of Dar es Salaam, Institute of Education, Box 35094, Dar es Salaam, Tanzania. Ed. A.A. Lema. adv. bk. rev. bibl.

STUDIES IN EDUCATION AND TEACHING TECHNIQUES. see *EDUCATION*

STUDIES IN MATHEMATICS EDUCATION/ ETUDES SUR L'ENSEIGNEMENT DES MATHEMATIQUES/ESTUDIOS EN EDUCACION MATEMATICA. see *EDUCATION — International Education Programs*

371.3   UK   ISSN 0073-2605
TEACHING OF HISTORY. 1961. irreg. Historical Association, 59a Kennington Park Rd., London SE11 4JH, England. (reprint service avail. from UMI)

TESTS IN PRINT. see *PSYCHOLOGY*

UCITELSKE VZDELANI. see *HISTORY — History Of Europe*

370   UN   ISSN 0502-9554
UNESCO SOURCE BOOKS ON CURRICULA AND METHODS. irreg. price varies. Unesco, 7 Place de Fontenoy, F-75700 Paris, France (Dist. in U.S. by: Bernan Associates-Unipub, 4611-F Assembly Dr., Lanham, MD 20706-4391)

UNITED NATIONS ECONOMIC AND SOCIAL COMMISSION FOR ASIA AND THE PACIFIC. SOCIAL DEVELOPMENT DIVISION. SOCIAL WORK EDUCATION AND DEVELOPMENT. see *SOCIAL SERVICES AND WELFARE*

370   CK   ISSN 0120-2839
UNIVERSIDAD PEDAGOGICA NACIONAL. CENTRO DE INVESTIGACIONES. BOLETIN INFORMATIVO. 1981. biennial. Universidad Pedagogica Nacional, Centro de Investigaciones, Av. 46 Nr. 15-99, Bogota, Colombia. circ. 1,500.

UNIVERSITE DE LA REUNION. CAHIER. see *LINGUISTICS*

371.3   FR   ISSN 0077-2712
UNIVERSITE DE NANCY II. CENTRE DE RECHERCHES ET D'APPLICATIONS PEDAGOGIQUES EN LANGUES. MELANGES. Spine title: Melanges CRAPEL. (Text in French; occasionally in English) 1970. a. 120 F. individuals; institutions 240 F (for 3 years) Universite de Nancy II, Centre de Recherches et d'Applications Pedagogiques en Langues, B.P. 33-97, 54015 Nancy, France. Ed. C. Heddesheimer. circ. 1,000. Indexed: Lang.& Lang.Behav.Abstr.

910 375   US   ISSN 0435-5113
UNIVERSITY OF GEORGIA. GEOGRAPHY CURRICULUM PROJECT PUBLICATIONS. 1968. irreg. price varies. University of Georgia, Geography Curriculum Project, 107 Dudley Hall, Athens, GA 30602. TEL 404-542-2856. Ed. Marion J. Rice. (also avail. in microfiche) Indexed: ERIC.

371.33   US   ISSN 0076-9274
UNIVERSITY OF MINNESOTA. AUDIO-VISUAL LIBRARY SERVICE. EDUCATIONAL RESOURCES BULLETIN. 1932. irreg. $6 per issue. University of Minnesota, Audio Visual Library Service, 3300 University Ave. S.E., Minneapolis, MN 55414. TEL 612-373-3810. Ed. W.D. Philipson. circ. 25,000.

UNIWERSYTET GDANSKI. WYDZIAL HUMANYSTYCZNY. ZESZYTY NAUKOWE. STUDIUM PRAKTYCZNEJ NAUKI JEZYKOW OBCYCH. see *LINGUISTICS*

UNIWERSYTET GDANSKI. WYDZIAL MATEMATYKI, FIZYKI I CHEMII. ZESZYTY NAUKOWE. PROBLEMY DYDAKTYKI FIZYKI. see *PHYSICS*

375   AT   ISSN 0085-7726
VICTORIA, AUSTRALIA. EDUCATION DEPARTMENT. CURRICULUM AND RESEARCH BRANCH. RESEARCH REPORTS. 1967. irreg. contr. free circ. Department of Education, Curriculum & Research Branch, 234 Queensberry St., Carlton, Vic. 3053, Australia. circ. 300. Indexed: Aus.Educ.Ind.

VOCATIONAL AND TECHNICAL AUDIOVISUALS: A TEACHER'S SOURCEBOOK. (National Information Center for Educational Media) see *EDUCATION — Guides To Schools And Colleges*

WESSEX STUDIES IN SPECIAL EDUCATION. see *EDUCATION — Special Education And Rehabilitation*

371.3   US   ISSN 0083-9116
WHAT RESEARCH SAYS TO THE TEACHER SERIES. 1953. irreg. price varies. ‡ National Education Association of the United States, 1201 16th St., N.W., Washington, DC 20036 TEL 203-934-2669. (Order from: N E A Professional Library, Box 509, West Haven, CT 06516)

371.3 PL
WYZSZA SZKOLA PEDAGOGICZNA, OPOLE. ZESZYTY NAUKOWE. SERIA A. DYDAKTYKA. 1969. irreg., vol.13, 1980. price varies; avail. on exchange basis. Wyzsza Szkola Pedagogiczna, Opole, Oleska 48, 45-052 Opole, Poland (Dist. by: Ars Polona-Ruch, Krakowskie Przedmiescie 7, Warsaw, Poland)

371.3 PL
WYZSZA SZKOLA PEDAGOGICZNA, OPOLE. ZESZYTY NAUKOWE. SERIA A. PEDAGOGIKA. (Text in Polish; summaries in English) 1956. irreg., vol.13, 1983. price varies; avail. on exchange basis. Wyzsza Szkola Pedagogiczna, Opole, Oleska 48, 45-052 Opole, Poland (Dist. by: Ars Polona-Ruch, Krakowskie Przedmiescie 7, Warsaw, Poland)

ELECTRICITY AND ELECTRICAL ENGINEERING

see also Communications — Radio and Television

621.3 UK
A S P E C T. (Anti-Static Proposals & Electro-Conductive Technologies) 1979. irreg. Hunter Bureau of Communications, Drayton House, Gordon St., London WC1, England.

621.38 DK
AALBORG UNIVERSITETSCENTER. INSTITUT FOR ELEKTRONISKE SYSTEMER. RAPPORT. 1977. irreg. Aalborg Universitetscenter, Institut for Elektroniske Systemer, Aalborg, Denmark. Ed. Martin Ranssen. illus.

621.38 FR ISSN 0001-558X
ACTA ELECTRONICA. (Text in French; summaries in English) 1956. a. 120 F. Laboratoires d'Electronique et de Physique Appliquee (LEP), 3 av. Descartes, 94451 Limeil-Brevannes, France. Ed. A. Mircea-Roussel. charts. illus. index. circ. 1,800. Indexed: Bull.Signal. Chem.Abstr. Curr.Cont. Eng.Ind. Sci.Abstr. Elec.Eng.Abstr. ASCA. Solid.St.Abstr.
Electronics

621.3 FI ISSN 0001-6845
ACTA POLYTECHNICA SCANDINAVICA. ELECTRICAL ENGINEERING SERIES. (Text and summaries in English) irreg. (2-3/yr.) Fmk.130. Teknillisten Tieteiden Akatemia - Finnish Academy of Technical Sciences, Kansakoulukatu 10 A, SF-00100 Helsinki 10, Finland. Ed. Seppo Halme. index. cum.index: 1958-1985. circ. 250. (also avail. in microfilm from UMI; back issues avail.; reprint service avail. from UMI) Indexed: Chem.Abstr. Curr.Cont. Eng.Abstr. Excerp.Med. Math.R. Sci.Abstr. ASCA. Int.Aerosp.Abstr.

537.5 621.38 US ISSN 0065-2539
ADVANCES IN ELECTRONICS AND ELECTRON PHYSICS. 1948. irreg., vol.68, 1986. Academic Press, Inc., Orlando, FL 32887. TEL 305-345-2000. Ed. Claire Marton. Indexed: Chem.Abstr. Sci.Cit.Ind. Ind.Sci.Rev. Mass Spectr.Bull.

621.38 US ISSN 0094-7032
ADVANCES IN IMAGE PICKUP AND DISPLAY. 1974. irreg., vol.6, 1983. Academic Press, Inc., Orlando, FL 32887. TEL 305-345-2000. Ed. B. Kazani. illus.

ADVANCES IN MAGNETIC RESONANCE. see *PHYSICS*

537.5 US ISSN 0065-2946
ADVANCES IN MICROWAVES. 1966. irreg., vol.8, 1974. Academic Press, Inc., Orlando, FL 32887. TEL 305-345-2000. Ed. Leo Young. index.

621.3 PL ISSN 0454-4773
AKADEMIA GORNICZO-HUTNICZA IM. STANISLAWA STASZICA. ZESZYTY NAUKOWE. AUTOMATYKA. (Text in Polish and English; summaries in English, Polish, Russian) 1966. irreg., no.38, 1985. price varies. (Akademia Gorniczo-Hutnicza im. Stanislawa Staszica) Wydawnictwo A G H, Manifestu Lipcowego 16, 31-109 Krakow, Poland (Dist. by: Ars Polona, Krakowskie Przedmiescie 7, 00-068 Warsaw, Polnd) Ed. Z. Kleczek. illus. circ. 300.

621.3 PL ISSN 0239-5312
AKADEMIA GORNICZO-HUTNICZA IM. STANISLAWA STASZICA. ZESZYTY NAUKOWE. ELEKTROTECHNIKA. (Text in English and Polish; summaries in English, Polish, Russian) 1982. irreg., no.11, 1986. price varies. (Akademia Gorniczo-Hutnicza im. Stanislawa Staszica) Wydawnictwo A G H, Manifestu Lipcowego 16, 31-109 Krakow, Poland (Dist. by: Ars Polona, Krakowskie Przedmiescie 7, 00-068 Warsaw. Poland) Ed. Z. Kleczek. illus. circ. 300.

ALBERTA ELECTRIC INDUSTRY, ANNUAL STATISTICS. see *ENERGY*

621.3 US
AMERICAN CONTROL CONFERENCE. CONFERENCE PROCEEDINGS. 1961. a. price varies. American Automatic Control Council, c/o William E. Miller, Secr., 1051 Camino Velasquez, Green Valley, AZ 85614 (Orders to I E E E Service Center, 445 Hoes Lane, Piscataway, NJ 08854) (Co-sponsors: Instrument Society of America; American Society of Mechanical Engineers; American Institute of Chemical Engineers) circ. 1, 500. (reprint service avail. from UMI,ISI)
Former titles: American Control Conference. Conference Records & Joint Automatic Control Conference. Record (ISSN 0075-3939)

621.38 US
AMERICAN ELECTRONICS ASSOCIATION DIRECTORY. 1949. a. price varies. American Electronics Association, 5201 Great America Parkway, Santa Clara, CA 95054. Ed. Barbara Myers. adv. circ. 12,000.
Formerly (until 1977): W E M A Directory (ISSN 0509-5190)

621.32 FR ISSN 0066-264X
ANNUAIRE DE L'ECLAIRAGE. a. Association Francaise de l'Eclairage, 52 Bd. Malesherbes, 75008 Paris, France. adv. bk. rev. circ. 4,000.

621.3 US
ANNUAL ALLERTON CONFERENCE ON COMMUNICATION, CONTROL AND COMPUTING. 1963. a. $35. University of Illinois at Urbana-Champaign, Coordinated Science Laboratory, Department of Electrical and Computer Engineering, Urbana, IL 61801. TEL 217-333-1000. Eds. M.C. Loui, J.V. Medanic. circ. 2,000.
Formerly: Annual Allerton Conference on Circuit and System Theory.

ANNUAL BOOK OF A S T M STANDARDS. VOLUME 02.03. ELECTRICAL CONDUCTORS. see *ENGINEERING — Engineering Mechanics And Materials*

ANNUAL BOOK OF A S T M STANDARDS. VOLUME 10.01. ELECTRICAL INSULATION, COMPOSITES, AND COATINGS--SOLIDS. see *ENGINEERING — Engineering Mechanics And Materials*

ANNUAL BOOK OF A S T M STANDARDS. VOLUME 10.03. ELECTRICAL INSULATING LIQUIDS AND GASES; ELECTRICAL PROECTIVE EQUIPMENT. see *ENGINEERING — Engineering Mechanics And Materials*

ANNUAL BOOK OF A S T M STANDARDS. VOLUME 10.04. ELECTRONICS (1) see *ENGINEERING — Engineering Mechanics And Materials*

ANNUAL BOOK OF A S T M STANDARDS. VOLUME 10.05. ELECTRONICS (2) see *ENGINEERING — Engineering Mechanics And Materials*

621.38 IT
ANNUARIO DI ELETTRONICA. 1978. a. L.30000 per vol. Edizioni di Protezione Civile, Monte delle Gioie 1, 00199 Rome, Italy. Ed. Pier Roberto Pais. adv. circ. 10,000.
Formerly: Elettronica.

621.3 US
ANTENNAS AND PROPAGATION. Represents: I E E E Antennas and Propagation Society. International Symposium Digest. a. price varies. (I E E E, Antennas and Propagation Society) Institute of Electrical and Electronics Engineers, Inc., 345 E. 47th St., New York, NY 10017 TEL 212-705-7900. (Subscr. to: IEEE Service Center, 445 Hoes Lane, Piscataway, NJ 08854) charts. illus. stat. (also avail. in microfiche)

621.38 US ISSN 0066-5533
APPLIED SOLID STATE SCIENCE; advances in materials and device research. 1969. irreg., vol.6, 1977. Academic Press, Inc., Orlando, FL 32887. TEL 305-345-2000. Ed. R. Wolfe.
Electronics

621.3 AG
ARGENTINA. DIRECCION GENERAL DE EVALUACION ENERGETICA. ANUARIO DE COMBUSTIBLES. 1961. a. free. Direccion General de Evaluacion Energetica, Departamento de Informacion e Investigacion Aplicada, Av. Julio A. Roca 651, Piso 7, Sector 22, C.P. 1322 Buenos Aires, Argentina. circ. 500.
Former titles: Argentina. Direccion General de Coordinacion e Informacion Energetica. Anuario de Combustibles & Argentina. Direccion General de Planificacion y Control Energetico. Anuario Estadistico. Combustibles; Argentina. Direccion Nacional de Energia y Combustibles. Departamento de Estadistica. Anuario Estadistico Combustibles; Argentina. Oficina Sectorial de Desarrollo de Energia. Anuarios Estadisticos: Combustible. (ISSN 0066-7277)

621.3 AG
ARGENTINA. DIRECCION GENERAL DE EVALUACION ENERGETICA. ANUARIO DE ENERGIA ELECTRICA. 1961. a. free. Direccion General de Evaluacion Energetica, Av. Julio A. Roca 651, Piso 7, Sector 22, C.P. 1322 Buenos Aires, Argentina.
Former titles: Argentina. Direccion General de Coordinacion e Informacion Energetica. Anuario Energia Electrica & Argentina. Oficina Sectorial de Desarrollo de Energia. Anuarios Estadisticos. Energia Electrica (ISSN 0066-7285)

621.3 UK
ASIAN ELECTRICITY CATALOGUE. 1984. a. Standard Catalogue Information Services Ltd., Medway Wharf Rd., Tonbridge, Kent TN9 1QR, England. circ. 6,500.

621.3 SA
ASSOCIATION OF MUNICIPAL ELECTRICITY UNDERTAKINGS OF SOUTH AFRICA. PROCEEDINGS OF CONVENTION. (Text in Afrikaans and English) a. Association of Municipal Electricity Undertakings of South Africa, 613 Volkskas Bldg., 76 Market St., Johannesburg 2001, South Africa. Ed. Bennie van der Walt. adv.

537 621.3 IT ISSN 0066-9822
ASSOCIAZIONE ELETTROTECNICA ED ELETTRONICA ITALIANA. RENDICONTI DELLA RIUNIONE ANNUALE. 1922. a. price varies. Associazione Elettrotecnica ed Elettronica Italiana, Viale Monza, 259, 20126 Milan, Italy. circ. 1,200. Indexed: Chem.Abstr.

621.38 AT ISSN 0159-2947
AUSTRALIAN ELECTRONICS DIRECTORY. a. Aus.$72. Technical Indexes Pty. Ltd., 4 Kembla St., East Cheltenham, Vic. 3192, Australia (Subscr. to: Technical Indexes Pty. Ltd., P.O. Box 98, Cheltenham, Vic. 3192, Australia) Ed. Ross MacKay. adv. circ. 5,000.

621.3 US
AUTOTESTCON/I E E E INTERNATIONAL AUTOMATIC TESTING CONFERENCE. 1965. a. price varies. (I E E E, Aerospace and Electronic Systems Society) Institute of Electrical and Electronics Engineers, Inc., 345 E. 47th St., New York, NY 10017 TEL 212-705-7900. (Subscr. address: IEEE Service Center, 445 Hoes Lane, Piscataway, NJ 08854)
  Formerly: Automatic Support Systems Symposium for Advanced Maintainability. Proceedings (ISSN 0067-2491)

621.35 US
BATTERY REPLACEMENT DATA BOOK. 1972. a. $4. Battery Council International, 111 E. Wacker Dr., Chicago, IL 60601. TEL 312-644-6610. illus. circ. 350,000.

621.38 UK ISSN 0265-0959
BENN ELECTRONICS EXECUTIVE. 1983. irreg. Benn Electronics Publications Ltd., Chiltern House, 146 Midland Rd., Luton LU2 0BL, England. TEL 0582 421981. Ed. Philip Rathkey. circ. 5,000.

621.3 YU ISSN 0351-2177
BEOGRADSKI UNIVERZITET. ELEKTROTEHNICKI FAKULTET. PUBLIKACIJE. SERIJA: ELEKTRONIKA, TELEKOMUNIKACIJE, AUTOMATIKA. (Text in English) no.53/58, 1970. irreg. free or exchange basis. Univerzitet u Beogradu, Elektrotehnicki Fakultet, Studentski trg 1, Belgrade, Yugoslavia. Ed. Milic Stojic. bk. rev. illus. circ. 1,000. Indexed: Ref.Zh. Elec. & Electron.Abstr.
  Continues: Belgrade. Univerzitet. Elektrotehnicki Fakultet. Publikacije. Serija: Telekomunikacije i Elektronika (ISSN 0409-0179)

BERGER BUILDING & DESIGN COST FILE. UNIT PRICES. VOL. 2: MECHANICAL AND ELECTRICAL TRADES. see *BUILDING AND CONSTRUCTION*

BERNARDS AND BABANI PRESS RADIO & ELECTRONICS & COMPUTER BOOKS. see *COMMUNICATIONS — Radio And Television*

BRENNSTOFFSTATISTIK DER WAERMEKRAFTWERKE FUER DIE OEFFENTLICHE ELEKTRIZITAETSVERSORGUNG IN OESTERREICH. see *PUBLIC ADMINISTRATION*

BRITAIN'S TOP 500 ELECTRONIC COMPANIES. see *BUSINESS AND ECONOMICS — Trade And Industrial Directories*

BRITISH GAS PLC. MONITOR. see *ENERGY*

621.38 US
BROWN BOVERI SYMPOSIA. PROCEEDINGS. 1969. irreg. Plenum Publishing Corp., 233 Spring St., New York, NY 10013. TEL 212-620-8047.

621.3 UK ISSN 0305-7194
C E G B RESEARCH. 1974. irreg. (approx. 2/yr.) free to qualified personnel. Central Electricity Generating Board, Technology Planning and Research Division, Courtenay House, 18 Warwick Lane, London EC4P 4EB, England. Eds. D.J. Littler, T.E.L. Langford. circ. 12,500. (back issues avail.) Indexed: Met.Abstr. Sci.Abstr. Br.Ceram.Abstr. Fluidex. World Alum.Abstr.

338.4 CN ISSN 0833-2002
CANADA. STATISTICS CANADA. COMMUNICATIONS AND ENERGY WIRE AND CABLE INDUSTRY/INDUSTRIE DES FILS ET CABLES ELECTRIQUES ET DE COMMUNICATIONS. (Catalogue 43-209) (Text in English and French) a. Can.$20($21) Statistics Canada, Communications Division, 3rd Floor, R.H. Coats Bldg., Ottawa, Ont. K1A 0T6, Canada TEL 613-993-7276. (Subscr. to: Publications Sales and Services, Ottawa, Ont. K1A 0T6, Canada) (also avail. in microform from MML)
  Formerly: Canada. Statistics Canada. Manufacturers of Electric Wire and Cable/Fabricants de Fils et de Cables Electriques (ISSN 0527-5504)

621.3 CN ISSN 0576-5161
CANADIAN ELECTRICAL ASSOCIATION. ENGINEERING AND OPERATING DIVISION. TRANSACTIONS. 1962. a. Can.$75. Canadian Electrical Association - Association Canadienne de l'Electricite, 1 Westmount Sq, Suite 580, Montreal, Que. H3Z 2P9, Canada. TEL 514-937-6181.

621.38 CN
CANADIAN ELECTRONICS ENGINEERING COMPONENTS AND EQUIPMENT DIRECTORY. 1957. a. Can.$12. Maclean-Hunter Ltd., Business Publication Division, Maclean-Hunter Bldg., 777 Bay St., Toronto, Ont. M5W 1A7, Canada. TEL 416-596-5731. Ed. Peter Thorneg.
  Former titles: Canadian Electronics Engineering Annual Buyers' Guide and Catalog Directory (ISSN 0075-5990); Key to Electronics Engineering Purchasing in Canada.

CANADIAN HARDWARE, ELECTRICAL & BUILDING SUPPLY DIRECTORY. see *BUSINESS AND ECONOMICS — Trade And Industrial Directories*

CANADIAN NATIONAL ENERGY FORUM PROCEEDINGS. see *ENERGY*

621.3 US
CAPACITORS D.A.T.A. BOOK. (Subseries of: D.A.T.A. Book Electronic Information Series) a. $75. D.A.T.A., Inc. (Subsidiary of: International Thomson Organization) 9889 Willow Creek Rd., Box 26875, San Diego, CA 26875. TEL 619-578-7600. Ed. Steven d'Adolf.

338.4 RH ISSN 0069-147X
CENTRAL AFRICAN POWER CORPORATION. ANNUAL REPORT AND ACCOUNTS. 1956. a. ‡ Central African Power Corporation, Box 630, Club Chambers, Baker Ave., Salisbury, Zimbabwe. index.

621.38 629.286 FR
CHAMBRE SYNDICALE NATIONALE DES ELECTRICIENS ET SPECIALISTES DE L'AUTOMOBILE. ANNUAIRE. 1948. a. 119.60 F. Electricite Automobile, 59 rue du Faubourg Poissonniere, 75009 Paris, France. Ed. Pierre Carrette. circ. 3,000.

683.8 621.9 CH
CHINA, REPUBLIC. MACHINERY AND ELECTRICAL APPARATUS INDUSTRY YEARBOOK/CHUNG-HUA MIN KUO CHI CHI YU TIEN KUNG CHI TSAI NIEN CHIEN. (Text in Chinese and English) a. World Enterprise, 247 San Ming Road, Tai - Chung, Taiwan, Republic of China.

621.3 US ISSN 0278-7024
CLEVELAND ELECTRICAL/ELECTRONICS CONFERENCE AND EXPOSITION. CONFERENCE RECORD. Short title: C E C O N. 1978. a. price varies. Institute of Electrical and Electronics Engineers, Inc., 345 E. 47th St., New York, NY 10017 TEL 212-705-7900. (Subscr. address: 445 Hoes Lane, Piscataway, NJ 08854)

621.3 SA
COLIMPEX ELECTRICAL EXECUPAD. (Text in Afrikaans and English) a. free to qualified personnel. Colimpex Africa (Pty) Ltd., Box 889, Wendywood 2144, South Africa. adv.

621.3 UY
COMISION DE INTEGRACION ELECTRICA REGIONAL. DIRECTORIO DEL SECTOR ELECTRICO. 1968. irreg., no.6, 1978. price varies. Comision de Integracion Electrica Regional, Bulevar Artigas 996, Montevideo, Uruguay.

537 665.5 BE
COMITE DE CONTROLE DE L'ELECTRICITE ET DU GAZ. RAPPORT ANNUEL. 1956. a. free. Comite de Controle de l'Electricite et du Gaz - Controle Comite voor de l'Electriceit en het Gas, Boulevard du Regent 8, 1000 Brussels, Belgium. Ed.Bd. charts. illus. circ. 5,500.

COMITE INTERNATIONAL DES POIDS ET MESURES. COMITE CONSULTATIF D'ELECTRICITE. (RAPPORT ET ANNEXES) see *METROLOGY AND STANDARDIZATION*

621.3 US
COMMUNICATOR (INDIANAPOLIS); a TV technicians newsletter. 1958. irreg. ‡ R C A Corporation, Technical Services Training, 600 North Sherman Drive, Indianapolis, IN 46201. TEL 317-267-5000. Ed. C.W. Mitchell. illus. circ. 15,000. (looseleaf format)
  Supersedes: R C A Plain Talk and Technical Tips (ISSN 0048-6582)

621.3 BL
COMPANHIA DE ELETRICIDADE DE BRASILIA. RELATORIO DE ADMINISTRACAO. 1968. a. free. Companhia de Eletricidade de Brasilia, Quadra 04-Bloco A, Lotes 106 e 136, Brasilia-DF, Brazil. charts. illus. circ. 3,000. (back issues avail.)
  Formerly: Companhia de Eletricidade de Brasilia. Relatorio de Atividades.

621.31 BL
COMPANHIA PAULISTA DE FORCA E LUZ. BOLETIM ESTATISTICO; acompanhamento do mercado de energia eletrica. 1970. irreg. free. Companhia Paulista de Forca e Luz, Assessoria de Planejamento e Gestao Empresarial, Rodovia Campinas/Mogiv-Mirim, km 2,5, Caixa Postal 1808, Campinas, Brazil. charts. circ. 40.

621.3 US
COMPARISON OF (YEARS) PRODUCTION EXPENSES FOR SELECTED STEAM ELECTRIC PLANTS. 1985. a. $225. Utility Data Institute, Inc., 1700 K St., N.W., Ste. 400, Washington, DC 20006. TEL 212-466-3660. (avail. on P C diskettes)

621.319 621 US ISSN 0084-9162
CONFERENCE ON ELECTRICAL INSULATION AND DIELECTRIC PHENOMENA. ANNUAL REPORT. (Formerly issued by: U.S. National Research Council) 1928? a. price varies. (I E E E, Electrical Insulation Society) Institute of Electrical and Electronics Engineers, Inc., 345 E. 47th St., New York, NY 10017 (Subscr. address: 445 Hoes Lane, Piscataway, NJ 08854) Indexed: Chem.Abstr.
  Formerly (until 1966): Conference on Electrical Insulation. Annual Report.

621.366 US
CONFERENCE ON LASERS AND ELECTRO-OPTICS (PUBLICATIONS) Short title: C L E O. a. price varies. Optical Society of America, Inc., 1816 Jefferson Pl., N.W., Washington, DC 20036. TEL 202-223-8130. (Co-sponsors: Institute of Electrical and Electronics Engineers Lasers and Electro-Optics Society)
  Formed by the 1981 merger of: I E E E/O S A Conference on Laser Engineering and Applications. Digest of Technical Papers (ISSN 0099-121X) & Conference on Laser and Electro-Optical Systems (CLEOS); Formerly: Conference on Laser Engineering and Applications (ISSN 0069-858X); Supersedes: Electron, Ion and Laser Beam Technology Conference. Record (ISSN 0070-9808)

537 US
CONFERENCE ON PRECISION ELECTROMAGNETIC MEASUREMENTS. DIGEST. Short title: C P E M Digest. (Earlier abstracts and papers 1958-1962 published in IRE Transactions on Instrumentation, and in IEEE Transactions on Instrumentation and Measurement) 1966. biennial. (I E E E, Group on Instrumentation and Measurement) Institute of Electrical and Electronics Engineers, Inc., 345 E. 47th St., New York, NY 10017 (Subscr. address: 445 Hoes Lane, Piscataway, NJ 08854) (Co-sponsors: U.S. National Bureau of Standards; International Scientific Radio Union)
  Former titles (until 1964): International Conference on Precision Electromagnetic Measurements; 1960: Conference on Standards and Electronic Measurements (Proceedings); 1958: Conference on Electronic Standards and Measurement (Proceedings)

621.3 US
CONSTRUCTION COSTS: U S STEAM ELECTRICAL PLANTS, 1970-1985. 1982. a. $150. Utility Data Institute, 1700 K St., N.W., Ste. 400, Washington, DC 20006. TEL 202-466-3660. stat. index. (magnetic tape)

621.32 BL
CONSUMO INDUSTRIAL DE ENERGIA ELETRICA DO ESTADO DA BAHIA. 1975. a. free. Secretaria das Minas e Energia, Coordenacao de Energia, Av. Centro Administrativo da Bahia, Av. Luiz Viana Filho, Salvador - Bahia, Brazil. stat.

621.3 US
CONVENTION OF ELECTRICAL AND ELECTRONICS ENGINEERS IN ISRAEL. PROCEEDINGS. 5th, 1965. biennial. Institute of Electrical and Electronics Engineers, Inc., 345 E. 47th St., New York, NY 10017 TEL 212-705-7900. (Subscr. address: 445 Hoes Lane, Piscataway, NJ 08854) (also avail. in microfiche)
Formerly: National Convention of Electrical and Electronics Engineers in Israel. Proceedings.

CONVERGENCE: INTERNATIONAL COLLOQUIUM ON AUTOMOTIVE ELECTRONIC TECHNOLOGY. PROCEEDINGS. see *TRANSPORTATION — Automobiles*

621.3 US ISSN 0070-0002
CORNELL BIENNIAL ELECTRICAL ENGINEERING CONFERENCE. 1967. biennial. price varies. (Institute of Electrical and Electronics Engineers, Inc.) Cornell University, School of Electrical Engineering, Phillips Hall, Ithaca, NY 14853. Ed. Michael G. Adlerstein. Indexed: GeoRef.

D A N T E C INFORMATION. see *METROLOGY AND STANDARDIZATION*

621.3 DK ISSN 0107-4466
D E K HAANDBOG. 1955. a. free. Dansk Elektroteknisk Komite, Strandgade 36, DK-1401 Copenhagen K, Denmark. circ. 350.

621.3 DK ISSN 0106-4711
DANSK ELFORSYNING. (Summaries in English) 1976. a. Kr.37. Danske Elvaerkers Forening Forlag - Association of Danish Electric Utilities, Rosenoerns Allee 9, DK-1970 Frederiksberg C, Denmark. illus. circ. 6,000.
Formerly: Dansk Elvaerksstatistik (ISSN 0070-2803)

621.38 355 670 US
DEFENSE ELECTRONICS. MARKETING DIRECTORY AND BUYERS GUIDE. 1984. a. E W Communications, Inc., 1170 E. Meadows Dr., Palo Alto, CA 94303. TEL 415-494-2800. adv. circ. 40,000. (reprint service avail.)

621.38 BE
DESIGN ENGINEERS MASTER. 1977. a. Pan European Publishing Co., Rue Verte 216, 1210 Brussels, Belgium. circ. 24,753.

621.38 US ISSN 0271-0803
DIODE D.A.T.A. BOOK. a. $95. D.A.T.A., Inc. (Subsidiary of: International Thomson Organization) 9889 Willow Creek Rd., Box 26875, San Diego, CA 92126. TEL 619-578-7600. Ed. Steven d'Adolf. adv.
Former titles: Semiconductor Diode D.A.T.A. Book (ISSN 0091-9675); Semiconductor Diode & S C R D.A.T.A. Book (ISSN 0037-1904)
Electronics

621.38 US
DIODE DISCONTINUED DEVICES D.A.T.A. BOOK. 1975. a. $65. D.A.T.A., Inc. (Subsidiary of: International Thomson Organization) 9889 Willow Creek Rd., Box 26875, San Diego, CA 92126. TEL 619-578-7600. Ed. Steve d'Adolf. (also avail. in microfilm; magnetic tape)
Former titles: Discontinued Diodes D.A.T.A. Book (ISSN 0270-9465); D.A.T.A. Book of Discontinued Semiconductor Diodes (ISSN 0148-7604)
Electronics

623.043 US
DIRECTORY OF DEFENSE ELECTRONIC PRODUCTS AND SERVICES: UNITED STATES SUPPLIERS. 1975. a. $85. Frost and Sullivan, Inc., 106 Fulton St., New York, NY 10038. TEL 212-354-2424. adv. illus. circ. 5,000.

621.31 665.5 US ISSN 0092-4970
DIRECTORY OF ELECTRIC LIGHT AND POWER COMPANIES. 1972. a. $25. Midwest Oil Register, Inc., Box 700597, Tulsa, OK 74170. TEL 918-742-9925. Ed. Ross G. Sloan.

537.5 NZ
DIRECTORY OF ELECTRONICS & INSTRUMENTATION. 1973. a. NZ.$10. Associated Group Media Ltd., Box 28349, Auckland 5, New Zealand.

621.3 JA
E B G. (Electronics Buyers Guide) 1968. a. $46. Dempa Publications Inc., 1-11-15 Higashi Gotanda, Shinagawa-ku, Tokyo 141, Japan (U.S. address: 380 Madison Ave., New York, NY 10017) adv.

621.3 UK
E C A YEAR BOOK DESK DIARY. 1918. a. £5. Electrical Contractors' Association, 34 Palace Court, London W2 4HY, England. adv. circ. 4,000.
Formerly: Electrical Contractors' Year Book (ISSN 0070-9654)

338.4 US ISSN 0093-3236
E C & M'S ELECTRICAL PRODUCTS YEARBOOK. (Electrical Construction and Maintenance) a. $6 (free to qualified personnel) McGraw Hill Information Systems Co., 1221 Avenue of the Americas, New York, NY 10020. TEL 212-512-4685. Ed. Al Berutti. adv. illus. circ. 101,000 (controlled) Key Title: Electrical Products Yearbook.

E E M. (Electronic Engineers Master) see *BUSINESS AND ECONOMICS — Trade And Industrial Directories*

621.38 CN
E P & T'S ELECTROSOURCE PRODUCT REFERENCE GUIDE & TELEPHONE DIRECTORY. 1984. a. Can.$30($40) Lakeview Publications Inc., 1200 Aerowood Dr., 27, Mississauga, Ont. L4W 2S7, Canada. TEL 416-624-8100. Ed. E. David Kerfoot. adv. circ. 19,200.

621.31 338.4 US
EDISON ELECTRIC INSTITUTE. STATISTICAL YEARBOOK OF THE ELECTRIC UTILITY INDUSTRY. 1928. a. $27.50. Edison Electric Institute, Statistical Committee, 1111 19th St. N.W., Washington, DC 20036. TEL 202-828-7400. Ed. J. David Bailey. charts. stat. circ. 3,200. Indexed: Fuel & Energy Abstr.

621.38 691 US ISSN 0745-4309
ELECTRI-ONICS DESK MANUAL; for the electrical/electronic industries. 1961. a. $30. Lake Publishing Corporation, 17730 W. Peterson Rd., Box 159, Libertyville, IL 60048. TEL 312-362-8711. Ed. William Davenport. adv. circ. 46,000. (also avail. in microform) Indexed: Chem.Abstr. Eng.Ind.
Former titles: Insulation/Circuits Desk Manual; Insulation/Circuits Directory/Encyclopedia (ISSN 0074-0659); Insulation Directory /Encylopedia.

621.3 US
ELECTRIC POWER ANNUAL REPORT. 1949. a. $10. Edison Electric Institute, Electric Power Survey Committee, 1111 19th St. N.W., Washington, DC 20036. TEL 202-828-7400. Ed. Carl Tobie. charts. illus. stat. circ. 3,000.
Incorporating (as of 1982): Year-End Summary of the Electric Power Situation in the United States (ISSN 0424-480X); Former titles: Annual Electric Power Survey (ISSN 0190-5600) Electric Power Survey (ISSN 0190-5619); Semi-Annual Electric Power Survey (ISSN 0190-5589)

621.3 UN ISSN 0252-4406
ELECTRIC POWER IN ASIA AND THE PACIFIC. 1971. biennial, latest 1981-82. price varies. United Nations Economic and Social Commission for Asia and the Pacific, United Nations Bldg., Rajadamnern Ave., Bangkok 2, Thailand (Dist. by: United Nations Publications, Romm DC2-0853, New York, NY 10017; or Distribution and Sales Section, Palais des Nations, D-CH-1211 Geneva 10, Switzerland)

ELECTRIC POWER IN CANADA. see *ENERGY*

ELECTRIC POWER INDUSTRY ABSTRACTS. see *ELECTRICITY AND ELECTRICAL ENGINEERING — Abstracting, Bibliographies, Statistics*

621.313 US
ELECTRIC UTILITY GENERATION PLANBOOK. Variant title: Power's Electric Utility Generation Planbook. 1972. a. $10. McGraw-Hill Publications Co., 1221 Avenue of Americas, New York, NY 10020. Ed. Bob Schwieger. adv. charts. illus. stat. circ. 17,000. (reprint service avail. from UMI)

621.3 UK ISSN 0070-9638
ELECTRICAL AND ELECTRONIC TRADER YEAR BOOK. 1965. biennial. £10. Consumer Industries Press, Quadrant House, The Quadrant, Sutton, Surrey SM2 5AS, England. Ed. A. Ord-Home. adv. bk. rev.
Formerly: Wireless and Electrical Trader Year Book.

621.3 CN
ELECTRICAL BLUE BOOK. 1979. a. Can.$25. Kerrwil Publications Ltd., 501 Oakdale Rd., Downsview, Ont. M3N 1W7, Canada. TEL 416-746-7360. circ. 24,000.

621.38 US
ELECTRICAL/ELECTRONICS INSULATION CONFERENCE. PROCEEDINGS. Short title: E I C. 1958. biennial. price varies. (I E E E, Electrical Insulation Society) Institute of Electrical and Electronics Engineers, Inc., TEL 212-705-7900. (Subscr. to: 445 Hoes Lane, Piscataway, NJ 08854) (Co-sponsor: National Electrical Manufacturers Association)
Former titles (1965-1973): Electrical Insulation Conference. Proceedings; (1962-1963): Electrical Insulation Conference: Materials and Applications. Technical Papers; (1958-1960): National Conference on the Application of Electrical Insulation. Technical Papers.

621.31 US ISSN 0070-9697
ELECTRICAL/ELECTRONICS INSULATION CONFERENCE. RECORD. 1958. biennial. price varies. National Electrical Manufacturers Association, 2101 L St. N.W., Washington, DC 20037. TEL 202-457-8400. (Co-Sponsor: Institute of Electrical and Electronic Engineers) Indexed: Chem.Abstr.
Formerly: Electrical Insulation Technical Conference. Record.

621.3 US ISSN 0070-9689
ELECTRICAL EQUIPMENT REPRESENTATIVES ASSOCIATION. DIRECTORY. 1951. a. free. ‡ Electrical Equipment Representatives Association, 1308 Pennsylvania Ave., Kansas City, MO 64105. Ed. John S. McDermott. index. circ. 1,800.

621.3 918 US
ELECTRICAL MACHINERY: LATIN AMERICAN INDUSTRIAL REPORT. 1985. a. $235 per country report. Aurora International, Box 9099, Bridgeport, CT 06601-2099. TEL 203-368-0579. Ed. Andres C. Aquino.

621.3 US ISSN 0070-9719
ELECTRICAL PROCESS HEATING IN INDUSTRY. TECHNICAL CONFERENCE. RECORD. Variant title: Conference on Electric Process Heating in Industry. Conference Record. biennial, latest 1977. price varies. (I E E E, Industry Applications Society) Institute of Electrical and Electronics Engineers, Inc., 345 E. 47th St., New York, NY 10017 TEL 212-705-7900. (Subscr. address: 445 Hoes Lane, Piscataway, NJ 08854)

621.3 US
ELECTRICAL WORLD DIRECTORY OF ELECTRIC UTILITIES. 1892? a. $245. McGraw-Hill Publications Co., 1221 Ave. of the Americas, New York, NY 10020. Ed. Eileen Macdonald. stat.

621.3 KO
ELECTRICAL YEARBOOK/UNKI YONKAM. 1965. a. Korean Electrical Association, 11-4 Supyo-dong, Chung-ku, Seoul 100, S. Korea. Ed. Lee-Yong Hee. adv. circ. 4,000.

338 537 FR ISSN 0070-9735
ELECTRICITE DE FRANCE. RAPPORT D'ACTIVITE. 1950. a. Electricite de France, Service de l'Information et des Relations Publiques, 2 rue Louis Murat, 75384 Paris Cedex 08, France.

338 537 FR ISSN 0070-9751
ELECTRICITE DE FRANCE. STATISTIQUES DE LA PRODUCTION ET DE LA CONSOMMATION. 1950. a. Electricite de France, Direction de la Production et du Transport, Departement Statistiques, 6 rue de Messine, 75008 Paris, France. circ. controlled.

621.3 UK ISSN 0261-2127
ELECTRICITY CONSUMERS COUNCIL. ANNUAL REPORT. 1979. a. Electricity Consumers Council, Brook House, 2-16 Torrington Place, London WC1E 7LL, England.

ELECTRICITY COUNCIL ABSTRACTS BULLETIN. see *ENERGY — Abstracting, Bibliographies, Statistics*

537.5   UK   ISSN 0070-976X
ELECTRICITY SUPPLY HANDBOOK. 1948. a. £10. Electrical Electronic Press, Quadrant House, The Quadrant, Sutton, Surrey SM2 5AS, England. Ed. Alan Jack. adv. circ. 7,000.

621.3   SI
ELECTRO. (Text Mainly in English; occasionally in Chinese) 1973. biennial. free contr. circ. Electrical & Electronic Engineering Society, Ngee Ann Technical College, 535, Clementi Road, Singapore 21, Singapore. illus.

621.3   FR
ELECTRO. ANNUAIRE; electricite, electronique, electromenager. a. 55 F. Societe Nouvelle d'Editions Publicitaires, 16, Av. de Verdun, 75010 Paris, France. adv. illus. index.

621.3   US
ELECTROMECHANICAL BENCH REFERENCE. 1974. a. included in subscr. to monthly Electrical Apparatus. Barks Publications, Inc., 400 N. Michigan Ave., Chicago, IL 60611-4198. TEL 312-321-9440. Ed. Elsie Dickson. adv. bk. rev. circ. 15, 000.

621.38   US   ISSN 0569-5503
ELECTRONIC COMPONENTS CONFERENCE. PROCEEDINGS. a., latest 1986. price varies. (I E E E, Components, Hybrids, and Manufacturing Technology Society) Institute of Electrical and Electronics Engineers, Inc., 345 E. 47th St., New York, NY 10017 TEL 212-705-7900. (Subscr. address: 445 Hoes Lane, Piscataway, NJ 08854) Indexed: Chem.Abstr.
    Formerly (until 1958): Electronic Components Symposium. Proceedings.

621.38   US   ISSN 0145-0085
ELECTRONIC CONNECTOR STUDY GROUP. ANNUAL CONNECTOR SYMPOSIUM. PROCEEDINGS. 1968. a. $35. Electronic Connector Study Group, Inc., Box 167, Fort Washington, PA 19034. TEL 215-825-3840. charts. illus. circ. 1,500. (also avail. in microfilm)
    Electronics

ELECTRONIC DESIGN'S GOLD BOOK. see *BUSINESS AND ECONOMICS — Trade And Industrial Directories*

621.38   338.4   UK   ISSN 0070-9859
ELECTRONIC ENGINEERING ASSOCIATION. ANNUAL REPORT. a. free. Electronic Engineering Association, Leicester House, 8 Leicester St., London, WC2H 7BN, England.

ELECTRONIC ENGINEERING INDEX. see *ELECTRICITY AND ELECTRICAL ENGINEERING — Abstracting, Bibliographies, Statistics*

ELECTRONIC INDUSTRIES ASSOCIATION. TRADE DIRECTORY AND MEMBERSHIP LIST. see *BUSINESS AND ECONOMICS — Trade And Industrial Directories*

ELECTRONIC INDUSTRY TELEPHONE DIRECTORY. see *BUSINESS AND ECONOMICS — Trade And Industrial Directories*

621.38   658   US   ISSN 0070-9867
ELECTRONIC MARKET DATA BOOK. 1951. a. $80. Electronic Industries Association, 2001 Eye St. N.W., Washington, DC 20006. TEL 202-457-4955. cum.index.
    Formerly: Electronic Industries Review; Supersedes: Electronic Industries Yearbook.

621.38   338   US   ISSN 0070-9875
ELECTRONIC NEWS FINANCIAL FACT BOOK AND DIRECTORY. 1962. a. $125. Fairchild Books (Subsidiary of: Fairchild Publications Inc.) 7 E. 12th St., New York, NY 10003. TEL 212-741-4280. Ed. Robert Benjamin. circ. 2,000. (back issues avail.)

ELECTRONIC REPRESENTATIVES DIRECTORY. see *BUSINESS AND ECONOMICS — Trade And Industrial Directories*

621.3   US
ELECTRONICOM. CONFERENCE PROCEEDINGS. 3rd, 1958. biennial. price varies. (I E E E, Canadian Region) Institute of Electrical and Electronics Engineers, Inc., 345 E. 47th St., New York, NY 10017 TEL 212-705-7900. (Subscr. to: 445 Hoes Lane, Piscataway, NJ 08865)
    Former titles (until 1983): International Electrical, Electronics Donference and Exposition. Proceedings; (1973-1981): International Electrical, Electronics Conference and Exposition. Conference Digest; (until 1971): International Electrical, Electronics Conference. Conference Digest; (1967-1969): International Electronics Conference. Pre-Conference Digest; (1963-1965): Canadian Electronics Conference. I E E E Pre-Conference Digest. 1958: Canadian Convention (Proceedings)

621.38   670   US   ISSN 0090-5291
ELECTRONICS BUYERS' GUIDE. 1945. a. $40. McGraw-Hill Information Systems Co., 1221 Ave. of the Americas, New York, NY 10020. TEL 212-512-4685. Ed. Regina Hera. adv. stat. circ. 38, 000(controlled) (also avail. in microfilm)

621   US
ELECTRONICS: LATIN AMERICAN INDUSTRIAL REPORT. (Avail. for each of 22 Latin American countries) 1985. a. $435 per country report per industry covered. Aurora International, Box 9099, Bridgeport, CT 06601-2099. TEL 203-368-0579. Ed. Andres C. Aquino.

621.389   UK   ISSN 0261-2666
ELECTROSONIC WORLD. 1980. irreg., latest 1984. free. Electrosonic Limited, 815 Woolwich Rd., London SE7 8LT, England. Ed. R.S. Simpson. illus. circ. 80,000.

621.3   GW
ELEKTRO-INDUSTRIE; Elektronik und Ihre Helfer. 1952. a. DM.38. Industrieschau-Verlagsgesellschaft, Berliner Allee 8, 6100 Darmstadt, W. Germany (B.R.D.) adv. charts. illus. circ. 7,000.

537.5   GW   ISSN 0070-9956
ELEKTRO-JAHR; eine Neuheiten-Dokumentation der Elektro-Industrie. 1957. a. DM.24.80. Vogel-Verlag KG, Max-Planck-Str. 7/9, Postfach 6740, 8700 Wuerzburg 1, W. Germany (B.R.D.) Ed. Ernst Pohl. adv. circ. 17,000. Indexed: Sci.Abstr.

621.38   DK   ISSN 0108-8149
ELEKTRONIK INDKOEBSBOGEN. 1979. a. Kr.225.70. Teknisk Forlag A-S, Skelbaekgade 4, 1717 Copenhagen V, Denmark. illus.

621.3   DK
ELEKTRONIK NYTS LEVERANDOERREGISTER. a. Thomson Communications (Scandinavia) A-S, Struenseegade 7-9, DK-2200 Copenhagen N, Denmark. adv. circ. 10,572.

621.3   DK
ELEKTRONIKINDUSTRIENS INDKOEBSBOG. 1974. a. Kr.170. Teknisk Forlag A-S, Skelbaeksgade 4, DK-1717 Copenhagen V, Denmark. adv. circ. 3, 000.

537   UR
ELEKTRONY V POLUPROVODNIKAKH/ ELECTRONS IN SEMICONDUCTORS. (Text in Russian; summaries in English and Lithuanian) 1978. irreg. price varies. (Akademiya Nauk Litovskoi S.S.R., Institute of Semiconductor Physics) Izdatel'stvo Mokslas, Zvaigzdziu 23, Vilnius 232050, Lithuanian S.S.R., U.S.S.R. Ed. Y. Pozela. circ. 2,000.

621   UR
ELEKTROTECHNIKA IR MECHANIKA. (Text in Lithuanian or Russian; summaries in the other language) 1963. irreg. Kaunas Polytechnic Institute, Editing and Publishing Group - Kauno Politechninis Institutas, K. Donelaicio 73, 233006 Kaunas, Lithuanian S.S.R., U.S.S.R. Ed. J. Gecevicius. illus.
    Formerly: Mechanika.

537   UR
ELEKTROVYMIRIUVALNA TEKHNIKA. (Subseries of: Kharkivskyi Politekhnichnyi Instytut. Vestnik) 1973. irreg. 0.53 Rub. Kharkivskyi Politekhnichnyi Instytut, Ul. Frunze, 21, Kharkov, Ukrainian S.S.R., U.S.S.R. illus.

537   CL
EMPRESA NACIONAL DE ELECTRICIDAD. MEMORIA. 1944. a. free. Empresa Nacional de Electricidad, S.A., Santa Rosa 76, Casilla 1392, Santiago, Chile. circ. 3,000.

621.3   HO
EMPRESA NACIONAL DE ENERGIA ELECTRICA. DATOS ESTADISTICOS. 1960. a. free. Empresa Nacional de Energia Electrica, Departamento de Planificacion Economica, Tegucigalpa, Honduras. adv. stat. circ. 180. (also avail. in microform)

621.32   IV
ENERGIE ELECTRIQUE DE LA COTE D'IVOIRE. RAPPORT ANNUEL. Variant title: Energie Electrique de la Cote d'Ivoire. Compte Rendu de Gestion. a. free. Energie Electrique de la Cote d'Ivoire, B.P. 04.1245.04, Abidjan, Ivory Coast.

ENERGY. see *ENERGY*

621.3   GW
EUROPEAN ELECTRICAL & ELECTRONIC ENGINEERING. (Text in Chinese) a. DM.25. Deutscher Fachverlag GmbH, Schumannstr. 27, Postfach 100606, D-6000 Frankfurt, W. Germany (B.R.D.)

621.3   UK
EUROPEAN MICROWAVE CONFERENCE PROCEEDINGS. 1974. a. price varies. Microwave Exhibitions & Publishers Ltd., 90 Calverley Rd., Tunbridge Wells, Kent TN1 2UN, England.

EUROPEAN ORGANISATION FOR CIVIL AVIATION ELECTRONICS. GENERAL ASSEMBLY. ANNUAL REPORT. see *AERONAUTICS AND SPACE FLIGHT*

621.3   BE
FEDERATION PROFESSIONNELLE DES PRODUCTEURS ET DISTRIBUTEURS D'ELECTRICITE DE BELGIQUE. REPERTOIRE DES CENTRALES ELECTRIQUES/ REPERTORIUM VAN DE ELEKTRISCHE CENTRALES. (Editions in Dutch, French) 1959. a. 200 Fr. Federation Professionnelle des Producteurs et Distributeurs d'Electricite de Belgique, Avenue de Tervueren 34, B.P. 38, 1040 Brussels, Belgium.
    Formerly: Federation Professionnelle des Producteurs et Distributeurs d'Electricite de Belgique. Repertoire des Enterprises de Production d'Electricite/Repertorium des Ondernemingen van Electriciteitscoorbrenging (ISSN 0071-4461)

338.4   621.31   BE   ISSN 0071-4488
FEDERATION PROFESSIONNELLE DES PRODUCTEURS ET DISTRIBUTEURS D'ELECTRICITE DE BELGIQUE. SECTEURS DE DISTRIBUTION. (Text in Dutch and French) 1959. a. 200 Fr. Federation Professionnelle des Producteurs et Distributeurs d'Electricite de Belgique (F.P.E.), Avenue de Tervueren 34, B.P. 38, 1040 Brussels, Belgium. Ed. Lestienne. circ. 800.

621.3   FR
FRANCE. ACTIVITES INTERNATIONALES. RAPPORT ANNUEL D'ACTIVITE-ELECTRICITE DE FRANCE. a. Electricite de France, 68 rue du Faubourg St. Honore, 75008 Paris, France. illus.
    Formerly: France. Direction des Affaires Exterieures et de la Cooperation. Rapport d'Activite-Electricite de France.

621.38   534   US
FREQUENCY CONTROL SYMPOSIUM. Variant titles: Symposium on Frequency Control. Proceedings. Also: Frequency Symposium. 10th, 1956. a. price varies. (I E E E, Sonics and Ultrasonics Group) Institute of Electrical and Electronics Engineers, Inc., 345 E. 47th St., New York, NY 10017 TEL 212-705-7900. (Subscr to: 445 Hoes Lane, Piscataway, NJ 08865; 1956-1977 avail. from NTIS, Sills Bldg., 5285 Port Royal Rd., Springfield, VA 22161; 1978-1981 avail. from Electronic Industries Association, 2001 Eye St., Washington, DC 20006; 1982 avail. from Systematics General Corp., Brinley Plaza, Rte. 38, Wall Township, NJ 07719) (Co-sponsor: U.S. Army Electronics Research and Development Command, Electronics Technology and Devices Laboratory) Indexed: Chem.Abstr.
    Formerly: Annual Frequency Control Symposium.

ELECTRICITY AND ELECTRICAL ENGINEERING

621.3　　　　　US　ISSN 0190-5848
FRONTIERS IN EDUCATION CONFERENCE.
PROCEEDINGS. 1971. a. price varies. (I E E E,
Education Society) Institute of Electrical and
Electronics Engineers, Inc., 345 E. 47th St., New
York, NY 10017 TEL 212-705-7900. (Subscr.
address: 445 Hoes Lane, Piscataway, NJ 08854)
　　　Formerly: Conference on Frontiers in Education.
Digest (ISSN 0069-8547)

537　　　　　JA　ISSN 0429-8357
FUJIKURA TECHNICAL REVIEW. (Text in
English) 1969. a. free. Fujikura Cable Works Co.,
Ltd. - Fujikura Densen K.K., 1-5-1 Kiba, Koto-ku,
Tokyo 135, Japan. charts. illus. Indexed:
Chem.Abstr. Sci.Abstr. JCT.

621.3　　　　　JA　ISSN 0429-9159
FURUKAWA REVIEW. (Text in English and
Japanese) 1947. s-a. free. Furukawa Electric Co.,
Ltd., 6-1 Marunouchi 2-chome, Chiyoda-ku, Tokyo
100, Japan. circ. 3,500. (back issues avail.) Indexed:
Chem.Abstr. Sci.Abstr.

621.3　　　　　US
GA AS I C SYMPOSIUM. (Symposia prior to 1982
not published) 4th, 1982. a. (I E E E, Electron
Devices Society) Institute of Electrical and
Electronics Engineers, Inc., 345 E. 47th St., New
York, NY 10017. (Co-sponsor: I E E E Microwave
Theory and Techniques Society)

621.3　　　　　UK　ISSN 0307-1146
GREAT BRITAIN. ELECTRICITY COUNCIL.
ANNUAL REPORT AND ACCOUNTS. 1958/59.
a. £2.50. Electricity Council, 30 Millbank St.,
London SW1P 4RD, England. illus. circ. 10,000.

338.4　　　　　FR
GROUPEMENT DES INDUSTRIES
ELECTRONIQUES. RAPPORT D'ACTIVITES.
1971. a. free. Groupement des Industries
Electroniques, 11 rue Hamelin, 75783 Paris 16,
France. stat. circ. 200.
　　　Formerly: Electronique Francaise.

338.4　　　　　FR
GROUPEMENT DES INDUSTRIES
ELECTRONIQUES. STATISTIQUES
ANNUELLES. a. free. Groupement des Industries
Electroniques, 11 rue Hamelin, 75783 Paris 16,
France. stat.
　　　Formerly: Industrie Electronique Francaise.

621.3　　　　　IT
GUIDA POLLINI: INDUSTRIA
ELETTROTECNICA ED ELETTRONICA. 1931.
a. L.3500. Casa Editrice Guida Pollini, Viale
Campania 33, 20133 Milan, Italy. adv. circ. 2,500.

621.38　　　　　II
GUIDE TO ELECTRONICS INDUSTRY IN
INDIA. (Text in English) no.2, 1974. irreg.
Rs.50($10) per no. Statistics Investigations Bureau,
4-A Naaz Bldg., Lamington Rd., Bombay 400004,
India. Ed. S. Swarn. illus.
　　　Continues: Guide to Radio Electronics &
Components Trade and Industry in India (ISSN
0533-540X)

621.38　537.5　　US　ISSN 0072-9795
HANDBOOK OF ELECTRONIC MATERIALS.
1971. irreg., vol.9, 1972. price varies. Plenum
Publishing Corp., I.F.I.--Plenum Data Co., 233
Spring St., New York, NY 10013. TEL 212-741-
6680.
　　　Electronics

HOBSON'S ENGINEERING CASEBOOK. see
ENGINEERING — Civil Engineering

621.3　　　　　JA　ISSN 0439-3465
HOKKAIDO UNIVERSITY. RESEARCH
INSTITUTE OF APPLIED ELECTRICITY.
MONOGRAPH SERIES. (Text in English) 1950. a.
exchange basis. Hokkaido University, Research
Institute of Applied Electricity - Hokkaido Daigaku
Oyo Denki Kenkyusho, Nishi-6-chome, Kita-12-jo,
Kita-ku, Sapporo 060, Japan. Indexed: Biol.Abstr.

621.3　　　　　US
HOLM CONFERENCE ON ELECTRICAL
CONTACTS (PROCEEDINGS) 1953. a. price
varies. (I E E E Components, Hybrids and
Manufacturing Technology Society) Institute of
Electrical and Electronics Engineers, 345 E. 47th
St., New York, NY 10017-2394. TEL 212-705-
7900.

621.38　　　　　UK　ISSN 0073-4136
HYBRID MICROELECTRONICS SYMPOSIUM.
(PAPERS)* Variant title: Symposium on Hybrid
Microelectronics. irreg., 3rd, 1968. price varies.
International Society for Hybrid Microelectronics,
c/o David Boswell, 20 Hale Lane, London NW 7,
England.

537　　　　　US
I C MASTER. Variant title: I C Update Master. 1975.
a. $140. Hearst Business Communications, 645
Stewart Ave., Garden City, NY 11530. TEL 516-
222-2500. Ed. Dave Howell. adv. illus. circ. 60,000.

621.3　　　　　UK　ISSN 0537-9989
I E E CONFERENCE PUBLICATION SERIES.
1962. irreg. Institution of Electrical Engineers,
Savoy Place, London WC2R 0BL, England (Orders
to: Box 26, Hitchin, Herts. SG5 1SA, England)
Indexed: Chem.Abstr. Math.R.

537　　　　　US
I E E E APPLIED POWER ELECTRONICS
CONFERENCE AND EXPOSITION.
CONFERENCE PROCEEDINGS. Short title: A P
E C. 1986. a. price varies. (I E E E, Power
Electronics Council) Institute of Electrical and
Electronics Engineers, Inc., 345 E. 47th St., New
York, NY 10017-2394 TEL 212-705-7900. (Subscr.
to: I E E E Service Center, 445 Hoes Lane,
Piscataway, NJ 08854-4150) (microfiche)

I E E E CONFERENCE ON HUMAN FACTORS
AND NUCLEAR SAFETY. CONFERENCE
RECORD. see PHYSICS — Nuclear Energy

621.38　　　　　US
I E E E CUSTOM INTEGRATED CIRCUITS
CONFERENCE. PROCEEDINGS. 1979. a. (I E E
E, Electron Devices Society) Institute of Electrical
and Electronics Engineers, Inc., 345 E. 47th St.,
New York, NY 10017 (Subscr. address: 445 Hoes
Lane, Piscataway, NJ 08854) (Co-sponsor: I E E E
Rochester Section)
　　　Formerly (until 1984): Custom Integrated
Circuits Conference. Proceedings.

620.7　621.38　629.1　US
I E E E/E A S C O N. ELECTRONICS AND
AEROSPACE CONFERENCE. (RECORD) a.
price varies. (I E E E, Aerospace and Electronics
Systems Society) Institute of Electrical and
Electronics Engineers, Inc., 345 E. 47th St., New
York, NY 10017 TEL 212-705-7900. (Subscr.
address: 445 Hoes Lane, Piscataway, NJ 08854)
illus.
　　　Former titles: E A S C O N. Electronics and
Aerospace Conference and Exposition. (Record);
(1982): E A S C O N. Annual Electronics and
Aerospace Systems Conference. (Record); (1974-
1981): E A S C O N. Electronics and Aerospace
Systems Convention. Record (ISSN 0531-6863)
1968-1974: E A S C O N. Electronics and
Aerospace Systems Convention. Record; 1967:
Aerospace and Electronic Systems Conference.
Record; 1966): Aerospace Systems Convention.
Record.

621.3　　　　　US　ISSN 0748-9196
I E E E ELECTROTECHNOLOGY REVIEW. 1984.
irreg. $5 price varies. Institute of Electrical and
Electronics Engineers, Inc., 345 E. 47th St., New
York, NY 10017 TEL 212-705-7900. (Subscr. to:
IEEE Service Center, 445, Hoes Lane, Piscataway,
NJ 08854)

621.3　　　　　US
I E E E INTERNATIONAL CONFERENCE ON
ACOUSTICS, SPEECH AND SIGNAL
PROCESSING. PROCEEDINGS. 1976. a. price
varies. (I E E E, Acoustics, Speech, and Signal
Processing Society) Institute of Electrical and
Electronics Engineers, Inc., 345 E. 47th St., New
York, NY 10017 TEL 212-705-7900. (Subscr.
address: 445 Hoes Lane, Piscataway, NJ 08854)
　　　Formerly: I E E E International Conference on
Acoustics, Speech and Signal Processing. Record.

621.38　　　　　US
I E E E INTERNATIONAL CONFERENCE ON
CONSUMER ELECTRONICS. DIGEST OF
TECHNICAL PAPERS. Short title: I C C E. 1982.
a. (I E E E, Consumer Electronics Society) Institute
of Electrical and Electronics Engineers, Inc., 345 E.
47th St., New York, NY 10017 (Subscr. address:
445 Hoes Lane, Piscataway, NJ 08854)

621.3　　　　　US　ISSN 0730-9244
I E E E INTERNATIONAL CONFERENCE ON
PLASMA SCIENCE. I E E E CONFERENCE
RECORD-ABSTRACTS. Variant title, 1974-1976:
International Conference on Plasma Science.
Conference Record Abstracts. 1974. a. price varies.
(I E E E, Nuclear and Plasma Sciences Society)
Institute of Electrical and Electronics Engineers,
Inc., 345 E. 47th St., New York, NY 10017 TEL
212-705-7900. (Subscr. address: 445 Hoes Lane,
Piscataway, NJ 08854)

683.83　　　　　US
I E E E INTERNATIONAL ELECTRONIC
MANUFACTURING TECHNOLOGY
SYMPOSIUM. Short title: I E M T. Variant title: I
E E E/C H M T International Electronic
Manufacturing Technology Symposium. 1984. a.
price varies. (I E E E, Components, Hybrids and
Manufacturing Technology Society) Institute of
Electrical and Electronics Engineers, Inc., 345 E.
47th St., New York, NY 10017-2394 TEL 212-705-
7900. (Subscr. to: I E E E Service Center, 445 Hoes
Lane, Piscataway, NJ 08854-4150)

621.38　　　　　US　ISSN 0193-6530
I E E E INTERNATIONAL SOLID STATE
CIRCUITS CONFERENCE. DIGEST OF
TECHNICAL PAPERS. 1958. a. price varies. (I E
E E, Solid-State Circuits Society) Institute of
Electrical and Electronics Engineers, Inc., 345 E.
47th St., New York, NY 10017 TEL 212-706-7900.
(Subscr. address: 445 Hoes Lane, Piscataway, NJ
08854)
　　　Supersedes: International Solid State Circuits
Conference. Digest (ISSN 0074-8587); Solid-State
Circuits Conference. Digest of Technical Papers
(ISSN 0277-7983)

621.38　　　　　US　ISSN 0277-674X
I E E E INTERNATIONAL SYMPOSIUM ON
CIRCUITS AND SYSTEMS. PROCEEDINGS.
Variant title: International Symposium on Circuits
and Systems. a. price varies. (I E E E, Circuits and
Systems Society) Institute of Electrical and
Electronics Engineers, Inc., 345 E. 47th St., New
York, NY 10017 TEL 212-705-7900. (Subscr.
address: 445 Hoes Lane, Piscataway, NJ 08854)
　　　Supersedes: I E E E International Symposium on
Circuit Theory. Symposium Digest. Summaries of
Papers (ISSN 0579-4234)

621.3　　　　　US
I E E E INTERNATIONAL SYMPOSIUM ON
ELECTRICAL INSULATION. I E E E
CONFERENCE RECORD. biennial. (I E E E,
Dielectrics and Electrical Insulation Society)
Institute of Electrical and Electronics Engineers,
Inc., 345 E. 47th St., New York, NY 10017 TEL
212-705-7900. (Subscr. address: 445 Hoes Lane,
Piscataway, NJ 08854) charts. Indexed:
Chem.Abstr.

621.38　　　　　US
I E E E INTERNATIONAL SYMPOSIUM ON
ELECTROMAGNETIC COMPATIBILITY.
(RECORD) a. price varies. (I E E E,
Electromagnetic Compatibility Society) Institute of
Electrical and Electronics Engineers, Inc., 345 E.
47th St., New York, NY 10017 TEL 212-705-7900.
(Subscr. address: 445 Hoes Lane, Piscataway, NJ
08854)
　　　Former titles (until 1977): I E E E International
Symposium on Electromagnetic Compatibility.
Symposium Record (ISSN 0190-1494); (1971-1974):
I E E E International Electromagnetic Compatibility
Symposium. Record (ISSN 0074-8811); (1967-1970):
I E E E Electromagnetic Compatibility
Symposium. Record. (ISSN 0531-6847); (1964-
1966): National Symposium Electromagnetic
Compatibility. Symposium Digest (ISSN 0730-1723)
1960-1963: National Symposium on Radio
Frequency Interference. Symposium Digest.

621.38　　　　　US　ISSN 0149-645X
I E E E/M T T - S INTERNATIONAL
MICROWAVE SYMPOSIUM. DIGEST. a. price
varies. (I E E E, Microwave Theory and Techniques
Society) Institute of Electrical and Electronics
Engineers, Inc., 345 E. 47th St., New York, NY
10017 TEL 212-705-7900. (Subscr. address: 445
Hoes Lane, Piscataway, NJ 08854)
　　　Former titles: I E E E/M T T - S International
Microwave Symposium. Digest of Technical Papers
& International Microwave Symposium Digest
(ISSN 0074-7009)

ELECTRICITY AND ELECTRICAL ENGINEERING

621.3 US
I E E E MICROWAVE AND MILLIMETER-WAVE MONOLITHIC CIRCUITS SYMPOSIUM. DIGEST OF PAPERS. 1982. a. (I E E E, Microwave Theory and Techniques Society) Institute of Electrical and Electronics Engineers, Inc., 345 E. 47th St., New York, NY 10017 TEL 212-705-7900. (Subscr. address: 445 Hoes Lane, Piscataway, NJ 08854) (Co-sponsor: I E E E Electron Devices Society)

621.3 US
I E E E MILITARY COMMUNICATIONS CONFERENCE. CONFERENCE RECORD. Short title: M I L C O M. Variant title, 1983: I E E E Military Communications Conference. Proceedings. 1982. (I E E E, Communications Society) Institute of Electrical and Electronics Engineers, Inc., 345 E. 47th St., New York, NY 10017 TEL 212-705-7900. (Subscr. address: 445 Hoes Lane, Piscataway, NJ 08854)

621.38 US
I E E E NATIONAL RADAR CONFERENCE. PROCEEDINGS. 1984. biennial. price varies. (I E E E, Aerospace and Electronic Systems Society) Institute of Electrical and Electronics Engineers, Inc., 345 E. 47th St., New York, NY 10017 TEL 212-705-7900. (Subscr. address: 445 Hoes Lane, Piscataway, NJ 08854)

621.3 US ISSN 0160-8371
I E E E PHOTOVOLTAIC SPECIALISTS CONFERENCE. CONFERENCE RECORD. a. price varies. (I E E E, Electron Devices Society) Institute of Electrical and Electronics Engineers, Inc., 345 E. 47th St., New York, NY 10017 TEL 212-705-7900. (Subscr. address: 445 Hoes Lane, Piscataway, NJ 08854) Indexed: Chem.Abstr.

621.3 621.38 US
I E E E POSITION LOCATION AND NAVIGATION SYMPOSIUM. RECORD. Short title: P L A N S. 1976. biennial. price varies. (I E E E, Aerospace and Electronic Systems Society) Institute of Electrical and Electronics Engineers, Inc., 345 E. 47th St., New York, NY 10017 TEL 212-705-7900. (Subscr. address: 445 Hoes Lane, Piscataway, NJ 08854)

621.3 US
I E E E POWER ENGINEERING SOCIETY. SUMMER MEETING. PREPRINTS. a. $6 each to non-members. (I E E E, Power Engineering Society) Institute of Electrical and Electronics Engineers, Inc., 345 E. 47th St., New York, NY 10017 TEL 212-705-7900. (Subscr. address: 445 Hoes Lane, Piscataway, NJ 08854)

621.3 US
I E E E POWER ENGINEERING SOCIETY. WINTER MEETING. PREPRINTS. a. $6 each to non-members. (I E E E, Power Engineering Society) Institute of Electrical and Electronics Engineers, Inc., 345 E. 47th St., New York, NY 10017 TEL 212-705-7900. (Subscr. address: 445 Hoes Lane, Piscataway, NJ 08854)

621.3 US ISSN 0073-9197
I E E E REGION 5 CONFERENCE. RECORD. a. price varies. Institute of Electrical and Electronics Engineers, Inc., 345 E. 47th St., New York, NY 10017 TEL 212-705-7900. (Subscr. address: 445 Hoes Lane, Piscataway, NJ 08854)
Former titles: S W I E E C O Record of Technical Papers; Institute of Electrical and Electronics Engineers. Southwestern I E E E Conference and Exhibition. Record.

621.3 US
I E E E SOUTHEASTCON (REGION 3 CONFERENCE) RECORD. a. price varies. Institute of Electrical and Electronics Engineers, Inc., 345 E. 47th St., New York, NY 10017 TEL 212-705-7900. (Subscr. address: 445 Hoes Lane, Piscataway, NJ 08854)

621.3 US ISSN 0362-4536
I E E E STUDENT PAPERS. 1975. a. only avail. on request. Institute of Electrical and Electronics Engineers, Inc., IEEE Service Center, 345 E. 47th St., New York, NY 10017 TEL 212-705-7900. (Subscr. address: I E E E Student Services, 445 Hoes Lane, Piscataway, NJ 08854) illus.

I E E E WORKING CONFERENCE ON CURRENT MEASUREMENT. PROCEEDINGS. see EARTH SCIENCES — Hydrology

621.32 US ISSN 0073-5469
I E S LIGHTING HANDBOOK. 1949. irreg., latest 1984. $350 for 2 vols. set. Illuminating Engineering Society, 345 E. 47th St., New York, NY 10017. TEL 212-705-7926. Eds. J.E. Kaufman, Jack F. Christensen. circ. 20,000.

621.3 US ISSN 0190-0943
I T E M. (Interference Technology Engineers Master) 1971. a. $40. R & B Enterprises (Subsidiary of: Robar Industries, Inc.) 20 Clipper Rd., West Conshohocken, PA 19428. TEL 215-825-1960. Ed. Sanford Z. Meschkow. adv. bibl. charts. illus. tr.lit. index. circ. 27,000(controlled) (record)

338.7 II ISSN 0377-7340
INDIAN ELECTRONICS DIRECTORY. (Text in English) 1974. biennial. Rs.60($25) Electronic Component Industries Association, 408 Sahyog, 58 Nehru Place, New Delhi 110019, India. adv. circ. 1, 000.

621.3 IO
INDONESIA. DEPARTMENT OF PUBLIC WORKS AND ELECTRIC POWER. ADMINISTRATION BUREAU. ANNUAL REPORT/INDONESIA. DEPARTEMEN PEKERJAAN UMUM DAN TENAGA LISTRIK. BIRO UMUM. LAPORAN TAHUNAN. (Text in Indonesian) a. Department of Public Works and Electric Power, Administration Bureau, Jl. K. H. Hasjim Asjhari 6-12, Jakarta, Indonesia.

683.83 DK
INDRETNINGSHAANDBOGEN; idebog for indretning af virksomheder, institutioner og offentligt miljoe. 1980. a. Kr.59. Signum Kommunikation, Holte Stationsvej 6, 2840 Holte, Denmark. illus.

621.3 US
INDUSTRIAL AND COMMERCIAL POWER SYSTEMS TECHNICAL CONFERENCE. 1964. a. (I E E E, Industry Applications Society) Institute of Electrical and Electronics Engineers, Inc., 345 E. 47th St., New York, NY 10017 TEL 212-705-7900. (Subscr. address: 445 Hoes Lane, Piscataway, NJ 08854)
Formerly (until 1972): Industrial and Commercial Power Systems and Electrical Space Heating and Air Conditioning Joint Technical Conference. Record (ISSN 0073-733X)

001.3 US ISSN 0197-2618
INDUSTRY APPLICATIONS SOCIETY. I E E E - I A S ANNUAL MEETING. CONFERENCE RECORD. a. (I E E E, Industry Applications Society) Institute of Electrical and Electronics Engineers, Inc., 345 E. 47th St., New York, NY 10017. TEL 212-705-7900. Key Title: Conference Record, Industry Applications Society, I E E E - I A S Annual Meeting.
Formerly (1980): I A S Annual Meeting. Conference Record (ISSN 0160-8592)

537 380 CR ISSN 0074-0047
INFORME DE OPERACION DE LAS PRINCIPALES EMPRESAS PRODUCTORAS Y DISTRIBUIDORAS DE ENERGIA ELECTRICA DE COSTA RICA. 1958. a. free; limited distribution. Instituto Costarricense de Electricidad, Direccion de Planificacion Electrica, P.O. Box 10032, San Jose, Costa Rica. charts. stat. index. circ. controlled.

INSPEC MATTERS. see SCIENCES: COMPREHENSIVE WORKS — Computer Applications

INSPEC THESAURUS. see SCIENCES: COMPREHENSIVE WORKS — Computer Applications

621.3 DK
INSTALLATIONS NYTS LEVERANDOERREGISTER. a. Thomson Communications (Scandinavia) A-S, Struenseegade 7-9, DK-2200 Copenhagen N, Denmark. adv. circ. 7,807.

621.3 MX
INSTITUTO DE INVESTIGACIONES ELECTRICAS. INFORME ANUAL. 1978. a. free. Instituto de Investigaciones Electricas, Interior Internado Palmira, Apartado Postal 475, Cuernavaca, Mor., 62000 Mexico. circ. 3,000.

INSTITUTO NACIONAL DE ASTROFISICA, OPTICA Y ELECTRONICA. BOLETIN. see ASTRONOMY

621.3 PL ISSN 0032-6216
INSTYTUT ELEKTROTECHNIKI. PRACE. (Text in Polish; summaries in English, French and Russian) 1951. irreg. $3.60 per no. Instytut Elektrotechniki - Electrotechnical Research Institute, Ul. Pozaryskiego 28, 04-703 Warsaw, Poland (Dist. by: Ars Polona-Ruch, Krakowskie Przedmiescie 7, 00-068 Warsaw, Poland) Ed. Wiestaw Seruga. circ. 450. Indexed: Chem.Abstr. Sci.Abstr.

621.3 US
INTERFACE & MEMORY DISCONTINUED DEVICES D.A.T.A. BOOK. (Subseries of: D.A.T.A. Book Electronic Information Series) a. $65. D.A.T.A., Inc. (Subsidiary of: International Thomson Organization) 9889 Willow Creek Rd., Box 26875, San Diego, CA 92126. TEL 619-578-7600.

621.32 HU ISSN 0074-2724
INTERNATIONAL COMMISSION ON ILLUMINATION. PROCEEDINGS. 1900. quadrennial; 20th, 1983, Amsterdam. (Commission Internationale de l'Eclairage, FR - International Commission on Illumination) Orszagos Muszaki Informacios Kozpont es Konyvtar (O.M.I.K.K.), Muzeum u. 17, 1428 Budapest, Hungary (U.S. subscr. addr.: c/o Dr. K.D. Mielenz, Secy., U.S. National Committee CIE, B-306 Metrology Bldg., National Bureau of Standards, Washington DC 20234) bk. rev.

INTERNATIONAL COMMUNICATIONS AND ENERGY CONFERENCE (PROCEEDINGS)/ CONFERENCE INTERNATIONALE SUR LES COMMUNICATIONS ET L'ENERGIE (PROCEEDINGS) see COMMUNICATIONS

621.3 US
INTERNATIONAL CONFERENCE ON CONDUCTION AND BREAKDOWN IN DIELECTRIC LIQUIDS. CONFERENCE RECORD. Short title: I C D L. 3rd, 1968. triennial. price varies. (I E E E, Dielectrics and Electrical Insulation Society) Institute of Electrical and Electronics Engineers, Inc., 345 E. 47th St., New York, NY 10017 TEL 212-705-7900. (Subscr. address: 445 Hoes Lane, Piscataway, NJ 08854)

621.3 US
INTERNATIONAL CONFERENCE ON CONDUCTION AND BREAKDOWN IN SOLID DIELECTRICS. PROCEEDINGS. Short title: I C S D. 1983. triennial. price varies. (I E E E, Electrical Insulation Society) Institute of Electrical and Electronics Engineers, Inc., 345 E. 47th St., New York, NY 10017 TEL 212-705-7900. (Subscr. addr.: 445 Hoes Lane, Piscataway, NJ 08854)

621.3 US
INTERNATIONAL CONFERENCE ON INFRARED AND MILLIMETER WAVES. CONFERENCE DIGEST. (Published by other organizations when held outside of U.S.) 1974. a. price varies. (I E E E, Microwave Theory and Techniques Society) Institute of Electrical and Electronics Engineers, Inc., 345 E. 47th St., New York, NY 10017 TEL 212-705-7900. (Subscr. address: 445 Hoes Lane, Piscataway, NJ 08854) Ed. Kenneth J. Button.
Former titles: International Conference on Infrared and Millimeter Waves and Their Applications. Conference Digest; International Conference on Submillimeter Waves and Their Applications. Conference Digest.

621.31 FR ISSN 0074-3151
INTERNATIONAL CONFERENCE ON LARGE HIGH VOLTAGE ELECTRIC SYSTEMS. PROCEEDINGS. (Text in French and English) 1921. biennial. price varies. International Conference on Large High Voltage Electric Systems, 112 bd. Haussmann, 75008 Paris, France.
Formerly: International Conference on Large High Tension Electric Systems. Proceedings.

621 US
INTERNATIONAL CONFERENCE ON THERMOELECTRIC ENERGY CONVERSION. PROCEEDINGS. 1976. biennial. University of Texas at Arlington, International Conference on Thermoelectric Energy Conversion, Arlington, TX 76019. Indexed: Chem.Abstr.

ELECTRICITY AND ELECTRICAL ENGINEERING

621.3 US
INTERNATIONAL CONFERENCE ON TRANSMISSION AND DISTRIBUTION CONSTRUCTION AND LIVE-LINE MAINTENANCE. CONFERENCE PAPERS. 1977. triennial. price varies. (I E E E, Power Engineering Society, Engineering in the Safety, Maintenance and Operation of Lines Subcommittee of T & D) Institute of Electrical and Electronics Engineers, Inc., 345 E. 47th St., New York, NY 10017 TEL 212-705-7900. (Subscr. address: 445 Hoes Lane, Piscataway, NJ 08854)
Formerly (until 1983): International Conference on Live-Line Maintenance. Conference Papers.

621.3 US
INTERNATIONAL DISPLAY RESEARCH CONFERENCE. CONFERENCE RECORD. (Publication rotates among Europe, U.S., and Japan; and title alternates with rotation: Eurodisplay. Japan Display.) 1970. a. (I E E E, Electron Devices Society) Institute of Electrical and Electronics Engineers, Inc., 345 E. 47th St., New York, NY 10017 (Subscr. address: 445 Hoes Lane, Piscataway, NJ 08854)
Former titles, 1981: International Display Research Conference. Proceedings; 1978-1981: Biennial Display Research Conference. Conference Record; I E E E Conference on Display Devices. Conference Record.

621.38 US ISSN 0163-1918
INTERNATIONAL ELECTRON DEVICES MEETING. I E D M TECHNICAL DIGEST. a. (I E E E, Electron Devices Society) Institute of Electrical and Electronics Engineers, Inc., 345 E. 47th St., New York, NY 10017 TEL 212-705-7900. (Subscr. address: 445 Hoes Lane, Piscataway, NJ 08854)
Formerly (until 1973): International Electron Devices Meeting. Abstracts (ISSN 0074-4670)
Electronics

621.38 US
INTERNATIONAL ELECTRONICS PACKAGING SOCIETY. (PUBLICATION) 1981. a. $95. International Electronics Packaging Society, Box 333, Glen Ellyn, IL 60137. TEL 312-260-1044. circ. 300.

621.3 SZ
INTERNATIONAL ELECTROTECHNICAL COMMISSION. REPERTOIRE/ INTERNATIONAL ELECTROTECHNICAL COMMISSION. DIRECTORY. (Text in English and French) a. 15 Fr. International Electrotechnical Commission, 3 rue de Varembe, 1211 Geneva 20, Switzerland (Dist. in the U.S. by: American National Standards Institute, 1430 Broadway, New York, NY 10018)

621.3 SZ ISSN 0074-4697
INTERNATIONAL ELECTROTECHNICAL COMMISSION. YEARBOOK/ANNUAIRE. (Text in English and French) 1961. a. 48 Fr. International Electrotechnical Commission, 3 rue de Varembe, 1211 Geneva 20, Switzerland (Dist. in the U.S. by: American National Standards Institute, 1430 Broadway, New York, NY 10018)
Formerly: International Electrotechnical Commission. Central Office Report (ISSN 0534-9907)

621.3 621.38 US
INTERNATIONAL GEOSCIENCE AND REMOTE SENSING SYMPOSIUM DIGEST. Short title: I G A R S S. 1981. a. price varies. (I E E E, Geoscience and Remote Sensing Society) Institute of Electrical and Electronics Engineers, Inc., 345 E. 47th St., New York, NY 10017 TEL 212-705-7900. (Subscr. address: 445 Hoes Lane, Piscataway, NJ 08854)

621.3 US
INTERNATIONAL I E E E V L S I MUTILEVEL INTERCONNECTION CONFERENCE. PROCEEDINGS. Short title: V - M I C Conference. 1984. a. price varies. (I E E E, Electron Devices Society) Institute of Electrical and Electronics Engineers, Inc., 345 E. 47th St., New York, NY 10017-2394 TEL 212-705-7900. (Subscr. to: IEEE Service Center, 445 Hoes Lane, Piscataway, NJ 08854-4150) (Co-sponsor: I E E E Components, Hybrids, and Manufacturing Technology Society)

621.3 US ISSN 0538-9275
INTERNATIONAL QUANTUM ELECTRONICS CONFERENCE. DIGEST OF TECHNICAL PAPERS. 1959. biennial. Optical Society of America, Inc., 1816 Jefferson Pl., N.W., Washington, DC 20036. TEL 202-223-8130. (Co-sponsors: American Physical Society; Institute of Electrical and Electronics Engineers Lasers and Electro-Optics Society)

INTERNATIONAL RADAR CONFERENCE. RECORD. see *COMMUNICATIONS*

621.3 UK ISSN 0074-803X
INTERNATIONAL SERIES OF MONOGRAPHS IN ELECTRICAL ENGINEERING. irreg. price varies. Pergamon Press, Ltd., Headington Hill Hall, Oxford OX3 0BW, England (U.S. subscr. to: Maxwell House, Fairview Park, Elmsford, NY 10523)

621.319 US
INTERNATIONAL SYMPOSIUM ON DISCHARGES AND ELECTRICAL INSULATION. Short title: Discharges and Electrical Insulation in Vacuum. (Published by host organization when held outside U.S.) 1964. biennial. price varies. (I E E E, Dielectrics and Electrical Insulation Society) Institute of Electrical and Electronics Engineers, Inc., 345 E. 47th St., New York, NY 10017-2394 TEL 212-705-7900. (Subscr. to: I E E E Service Center, 445 Hoes Lane, Piscataway, NJ 10017-2394)
Formerly: International Symposium on Insulation of High Voltages in Vacuum.

621.3 US
INTERNATIONAL SYMPOSIUM ON SUBSCRIBER LOOP AND SERVICES. PROCEEDINGS. Short title: I S S L S. (Published by other organizations when held outside of U.S.) biennial. Institute of Electrical and Electronics Engineers, Inc., 345 E. 47th St., New York, NY 10017 (Subscr. address: 445 Hoes Lane, Piscataway, NJ 08854)

INTERNATIONAL SYMPOSIUM ON WIND ENERGY SYSTEMS. PROCEEDINGS. see *ENERGY*

338.39 621.31 FR ISSN 0074-9486
INTERNATIONAL UNION OF PRODUCERS AND DISTRIBUTORS OF ELECTRICAL ENERGY. (CONGRESS PROCEEDINGS) triennial, 1976 Vienna; 1979, Warsaw; 1982, Brussels; 1985, Athens. International Union of Producers and Distributors of Electrical Energy, 39 ave. de Friedland, 75008 Paris, France.

683.83 UR ISSN 0202-8301
ITOGI NAUKI I TEKHNIKI: ELEKTRICHESKIE APPARATY. irreg., latest vol.4, 1986. 3.30 Rub. Vsesoyuznyi Institut Nauchno-Tekhnicheskoi Informatsii (VINITI), Baltiiskaya ul. 14, Moscow A-219, Russian S.F.S.R., U.S.S.R. (Subscr. to: Mezhdunarodnaya Kniga, Dimitrova ul. 39, 113095 Moscow, Russian S.F.S.R., U.S.S.R.)

621.31 UR
ITOGI NAUKI I TEKHNIKI: ELEKTRICHESKIE STANTSII I SETI. irreg., latest vol.18, 1987. price varies. Vsesoyuznyi Institut Nauchno-Tekhnicheskoi Informatsii (VINITI), Baltiiskaya ul. 14, Moscow A-219, Russian S.F.S.R., U.S.S.R. (Subscr. to: Mezhdunarodnaya Kniga, Dimitrova ul. 39, 113095 Moscow, Russian S.F.S.R., U.S.S.R.)
Formerly: Itogi Nauki i Tekhniki: Elektricheskie Stantsii, Seti i Sistemy (ISSN 0202-8328)

621.38 UR
ITOGI NAUKI I TEKHNIKI: ELEKTRONIKA. irreg., latest vol.19, 1987. price varies. Vsesoyuznyi Institut Nauchno-Tekhnicheskoi Informatsii (VINITI), Baltiiskaya ul. 14, Moscow A-219, Russian S.F.S.R., U.S.S.R. (Subscr. to: Mezdunarodnaya Kniga, Dimitrova ul. 39, 113095 Moscow, Russian S.F.S.R., U.S.S.R.)

621.3 GW
JAHRBUCH ELEKTROTECHNIK. 1982. a. DM.45. V D E - Verlag GmbH, Bismarckstr. 33, 1000 Berlin 12, W. Germany (B.R.D.) Ed. A. Gruetz.

621.3 GW ISSN 0344-6581
JAHRBUCH FUER DAS ELEKTROHANDWERK. 1955. a. DM.11.80. Huethig & Pflaum Verlag, Lazarettstr. 4, 8000 Munich, W. Germany (B.R.D.) (Subscr. addr.: Im Weiher 10, 6900 Heidelberg 1, W. Germany) circ. 30,000.

621.3 GW
JAHRBUCH FUER ELEKTROMASCHINENBAU UND ELEKTRONIK. 1960. a. DM.11.80. Huethig & Pflaum Verlag, Lazarettstr. 4, 8000 Munich 19, W. Germany (B.R.D.) (Subscr. addr.: Im Weiher 10, 6900 Heidelberg 1, W. Germany (B.R.D.)) Ed. W. Seher. circ. 6,000.

621.38 380.3 JA ISSN 0167-5036
JAPAN ANNUAL REVIEWS IN ELECTRONICS, COMPUTERS & TELECOMMUNICATIONS. AMORPHOUS SEMICONDUCTOR TECHNOLOGIES & DEVICES. 1982. a. 16000 Yen. Ohmsha, Ltd., 3-1 Kanda Nishiki-cho, Chiyoda-ku, Tokyo 101, Japan. Ed. Y. Hamakawa. circ. 1,500. Indexed: Chem.Abstr. Compumath.

338.4 US
JAPAN ELECTRONICS ALMANAC. (Text in English) a. $35. Dempa Publications, Inc, 400 Madison Ave., New York, NY 10017. TEL 212-752-3003. Ed. Hideo Hirayama. adv.
Former titles: Japan's Electronics Almanac and Leading Firms & Japan Fact Book.

JAPAN ELECTRONICS BUYERS' GUIDE. see *BUSINESS AND ECONOMICS — Trade And Industrial Directories*

621.3 UR
KHAR'KOVSKII GOSUDARSTVENNYI UNIVERSITET. RADIOFIZIKA I ELEKTRONIKA. (Subseries of its: Visnyk) 1972. irreg. 2.20 Rub. (Khar'kovskii Gosudarstvennyi Universitet) Izdatel'stvo Vysshaya Shkola, Khar'kovskoe Otdelenie, Ul. Universitetskaya 16, 310003 Kharkov, Ukrainian S.S.R., U.S.S.R. Ed. L. Stepin. illus. circ. 1,000.

621.38 YU ISSN 0350-5537
KONCAR STRUCNE INFORMACIJE. (Text in Croatian; summaries in English, French and Russian) 1954. irreg. free. S O U R Rade Koncar, O O U R Elektrotehnicki Institut, Bastijanova ul. bb, 41001 Zagreb, Yugoslavia. Ed. Nenad Marinovic. bk. rev. bibl. charts. illus. circ. 2,500(controlled) Indexed: Sci.Abstr.
Formerly (until 1977): Informacije Rade Koncar (ISSN 0033-7536)

621.3 SZ ISSN 0023-7949
LANDIS UND GYR MITTEILUNGEN. English edition.: Landis & Gyr Review (ISSN 0304-5803); French edition: Revue Landis et Gyr. (Text and summaries in English, French and German) 1953. irreg. free. ‡ L G Z Landis und Gyr Zug AG, CH-6301 Zug, Switzerland. Ed. U. Hofmann. charts. illus. circ. 4,500(English edt.); 4,500(French edt.); 7,300(German edt.) Indexed: Sci.Abstr.

621.366 US
LASER APPLICATIONS. 1971. irreg. vol.5, 1984. Academic Press, Inc, Orlando, FL 32887. TEL 305-345-2000. Ed. Monte Ross. Indexed: Chem.Abstr.

621.3 UK ISSN 0023-6381
LAURENCE SCOTT ENGINEERING BULLETIN. (Summaries in English, French and German) 1949. irreg., (2-3/yr.) free. ‡ Laurence, Scott & Electromotors Ltd., Norwich NR1 1JD, England. Ed. K.K. Schwarz. charts. illus. cum.index: vols. 1-13 (1949-1976) circ. 8,500. Indexed: Sci.Abstr.

621.3 US
LINEAR DISCONTINUED DEVICES D.A.T.A. BOOK. (Subseries of: D.A.T.A. Book Electronic Information Series) a. $65. D.A.T.A., Inc. (Subsidiary of: International Thomson Organization) 9889 Willow Creek Rd., Box 26875, San Diego, CA 92126. TEL 619-578-7600.

621.38 338.4 UK ISSN 0264-0724
MACKINTOSH YEARBOOK OF INTERNATIONAL ELECTRONICS DATA. 1983. a. $875. Benn Electronics Publications Ltd., P.O. Box 28, Luton, Beds. LU2 0ED, England. TEL 0582 421981. adv. charts. illus. stat.

ELECTRICITY AND ELECTRICAL ENGINEERING

621.3   UR
MAGNITNOIMPUL'SNAYA OBRABOTKA METALLOV. (Subseries of: Kharkivskyi Politeknichnyi Instytut. Vestnik) 1971. irreg. 0.55 Rub. Kharkivskyi Politekhnichnyi Instytut, Ul. Frunze, 21, Kharkov, Ukrainian S.S.R., U.S.S.R. illus.

021.38   UR
MAGNITO-POLUPROVODNIKOVYE I ELEKTROMASHINNYE ELEMENTY AVTOMATIKI. 1974. irreg. 0.52 Rub. Ryazanskii Radiotekhnicheskii Institut, Ul. Gagarina 59/1, 390024 Ryazan, Russian S.F.S.R., U.S.S.R.

537.5   US   ISSN 0163-9218
MASSACHUSETTS INSTITUTE OF TECHNOLOGY. RESEARCH LABORATORY OF ELECTRONICS. R L E PROGRESS REPORT. 1946. a. free. ‡ Massachusetts Institute of Technology, Research Laboratory of Electronics, Cambridge, MA 02139. TEL 617-253-2511. Ed. Janet E. Moore. circ. 1,000.
    Formerly: Massachusetts Institute of Technology. Research Laboratory of Electronics. Quarterly Progress Report (ISSN 0025-4827)

354   MF
MAURITIUS. CENTRAL ELECTRICITY BOARD. ANNUAL REPORT. a. Central Electricity Board, Curepipe, Mauritius. illus.

MECHANICAL COST DATA. see *BUILDING AND CONSTRUCTION*

621.3   US
MEDITERRANEAN ELECTROTECHNICAL CONFERENCE. Short title: M E L E C O N. 1981. biennial. Institute of Electrical and Electronics Engineers, Inc., 345 E. 47th St., New York, NY 10017.

MERSEYSIDE AND NORTH WALES ELECTRICITY BOARD. REPORT AND ACCOUNTS. see *ENERGY*

621.38   US   ISSN 0271-0773
MICROWAVE D.A.T.A. BOOK. 1958. a. $95. D.A.T.A., Inc. (Subsidiary of: International Thomson Organization) 9889 Willow Creek Rd., Box 26875, San Diego, CA 92126. TEL 619-578-7600. adv.
    Former titles (1978-1979): Microwave Tube D.A.T.A. Book (ISSN 0026-2900); Microwave Tubes (ISSN 0164-0135)

621.38   US   ISSN 0278-5676
MICROWAVE DISCONTINUED DEVICES D.A.T.A. BOOK. 1980. a. $65. D.A.T.A., Inc. (Subsidiary of: International Thomson Organization) 9889 Willow Creek Rd., Box 26875, San Diego, CA 92126. TEL 619-578-7600.

621.38   US
MICROWAVE POWER SYMPOSIUM. PROCEEDINGS. no.8, 1973. a. International Microwave Power Institute, 13542 Union Village Cir., Clifton, VA 22024-2305. TEL 703-830-5588.

621.3   US
MICROWAVE SYSTEM DESIGNER'S HANDBOOK. 1983. a. $14.95. E W Communications, Inc., 1170 E. Meadow Dr., Palo Alto, CA 94303. TEL 415-494-2800. circ. 40,000.

621.38   US
MICROWAVES PRODUCT DATA DIRECTORY. 1973. a. $20. Hayden Publishing Co., Inc., 10 Mulholland Dr., Hasbrouck Heights, NJ 07604. TEL 201-288-7520. adv. illus. circ. 40,259.

621.3   UK
MIDDLE EAST ELECTRICITY CATALOGUE. 1983. a. £15. Standard Catalogue Information Services Ltd., Medway Wharf Rd., Tonbridge, Kent TN9 1QR, England. circ. 8,500.

MILITARY MICROWAVES (YEAR). PROCEEDINGS OF CONFERENCE. see *MILITARY*

621.3   JA
MITSUBISHI CABLE INDUSTRIES REVIEW. (Text in Japanese; summaries in English) 1951. a. free. Mitsubishi Cable Industries, Ltd., Patent & Technology Administration Department, Umeda Bldg., 1-12-17, Umeda Kita-ku, Osaka 530, Japan. Ed.Bd. charts. illus. cum.index. circ. 6,500. Indexed: Chem.Abstr. Met.Abstr. Sci.Abstr. JCT. World Alum.Abstr.
    Formerly: Dainichi-Nippon Cables Review (ISSN 0011-5541)

621.3   540   US
MODELING AND SIMULATION ON MICROCOMPUTERS. 1982. a. $24. Society for Computer Simulation, Box 17900, San Diego, CA 92117. TEL 619-277-3888. Ed. Rosemary Whiteside. circ. 500. (back issues avail.)

621.3   US
MODULES/HYBRIDS D.A.T.A. BOOK. (Subseries of: D.A.T.A. Book Electronic Information Series) a. $95. D.A.T.A., Inc. (Subsidiary of: International Thomson Organization) 9889 Willow Creek Rd., Box 26875, San Diego, CA 92126. TEL 619-578-7600.

621.3   621.38   US
MONOGRAPHS IN ELECTRICAL AND ELECTRONIC ENGINEERING. irreg. price varies. Oxford University Press, 200 Madison Ave., New York, NY 10016 TEL 212-679-7300. (And Ely House, 37 Dover St., London W1X 4AH, England) Eds. P. Hammond, D. Walsh.

621.3   US
MONTECH CONFERENCES. (Topics vary per conference) 1986. a. price varies. (I E E E, Montreal Section) Institute of Electrical and Electronics Engineers, Inc., 345 E. 47th St., New York, NY 10017-2394 TEL 212-705-7900. (Subscr. to: I E E E Service Center, 445 Hoes Lane, Piscataway, NJ 08854-4150)

621.3   CN
N.B. POWER NEWS. 1953. irreg. (8-10/yr.) free. ‡ New Brunswick Electric Power Commission, 515 King St., Fredericton, N.B. E3B 4X1, Canada. TEL 506-458-3099. Ed. Jerome Peterson. charts. illus. circ. 3,500.
    Formerly: Current Events (Fredericton) (ISSN 0011-3468)
    Organization news

N E I S S DATA HIGHLIGHTS. (National Electronic Injury Surveillance System) see *PUBLIC HEALTH AND SAFETY*

537.5   621.38   US
NATIONAL COMMUNICATIONS FORUM. PROCEEDINGS. 1944. a. $85. (National Engineering Consortium) Professional Education International, Inc., 505 N. Lake Shore Dr., Ste. 4808, Chicago, IL 60611. TEL 312-828-0491. charts. index. cum.index every 5 years. circ. 4,000. (reprint service avail. from UMI)
    Former titles: National Electronics Conference National Communications Forum. Proceedings; (until 1979): National Electronics Conference. Proceedings (ISSN 0077-4413)

621.38   UK   ISSN 0305-2257
NATIONAL ELECTRONICS REVIEW; technical articles & a survey of progress in electronics over the previous year. vol.6, 1970. a. £5. National Electronics Council, Rm. 212, Savoy Hill House, Savoy Hall, London WC2R 0BU, England. Ed.Bd. adv. bibl. charts. illus. circ. 18,500. Indexed: Sci.Abstr.
    Formerly: National Electronics Council. Review (ISSN 0047-8857)

621.3   II
NATIONAL HYDRO ELECTRIC POWER CORPORATION. ANNUAL REPORT. (Text in English) 1976. a. National Hydro Electric Power Corporation Ltd., Manjusha, 57 Nehru Place, New Delhi 110019, India.

621.38   US   ISSN 0077-5401
NATIONAL RELAY CONFERENCE. PROCEEDINGS;* Relay Conference Papers. 1952. a. $22. (National Association of Relay Manufacturers) New Forums Press Inc., Box 876, Stillwater, OK 74074 (Address of Association: Box 1505, Elkhart, IN 46515) Ed. A.C. Johnson. circ. 700. (also avail. in microfilm; back issues avail.)

621.3   UK
NEW ELECTRONICS' DISTRIBUTOR PRODUCT FINDER AND GUIDE.* 1977. a. £8.50. International Thompson Publishing, Elm House, Elm St., London WC1X 0B, England. Ed. Kim Bachmann.

621.3   US   ISSN 0548-4456
NEW ENGLAND ELECTRICAL BLUE BOOK. 1957. a. $27.50. Trade Register & Data, 13 Main St., Hingham, MA 02043. TEL 617-749-0716. Ed. Donna Maligno. adv. circ. 8,900.

621.38   NZ
NEW ZEALAND ELECTRONICS REVIEW. 1967. a. NZ.$3. (National Electronics Development Association) Associated Group Media Ltd., P.O. Box 9092, Wellington, New Zealand. Ed. J. Holdem. adv. circ. 9,500. Indexed: Sci.Abstr.

621.3   NR
NIGERIA. NATIONAL ELECTRIC POWER AUTHORITY. ANNUAL REPORT AND ACCOUNTS. 1972. a. National Electric Power Authority, Electricity Headquarters, 24-25 Marina, Lagos, Nigeria. Ed.Bd. charts. illus. stat. circ. 5, 000.

621.3   US
NORTH AMERICAN ELECTRIC RELIABILITY COUNCIL. ANNUAL REPORT. 1969. a. North American Electric Reliability Council, 101 College Rd. East, Research Park, Princeton, NJ 08540. TEL 609-452-8060. circ. 5,000.

621.3   US
NORTHEAST BIOENGINEERING CONFERENCE. PROCEEDINGS. (Conferences prior to 1982 published by Pergamon Press) 1973. a. (no 1983 or 1984 meetings) Institute of Electrical and Electronics Engineers, Inc., 345 E. 47th St., New York, NY 10017 (Subscr. address: 445 Hoes Lane, Piscataway, NJ 08854)
    Former titles, 1979: New England (Northeast) Bioengineering Conference. Proceedings; 1973-1978: New England Bioengineering Conference. Proceedings.

621.3   US
NORTHWEST ELECTRIC UTILITY DIRECTORY. 1948. a. $10. Northwest Public Power Association, 9817 N.E., 54th St., Box 4576, Vancouver, WA 98662. TEL 206-254-0109. Ed. Rick Kellogg. adv. circ. 5,000.

621.312   CN   ISSN 0078-2459
NOVA SCOTIA POWER CORPORATION. ANNUAL REPORT. 1913. a. free. ‡ Nova Scotia Power Corporation, P.O. Box 910, Halifax, N.S. B3J 2W5, Canada. TEL 902-424-6230. circ. 4,500.

621.3   UR
NOVYE ISSLEDOVANIYA V GORNOI ELEKTROMEKHANIKE. (Subseries of: Gornyi Institut, Leningrad. Nauchnye Trudy) irreg. 0.45 Rub. Leningradskii Gornyi Institut, Leningrad, Russian S.F.S.R., U.S.S.R. illus.

621.3   AU
OESTERREICHISCHES STATISTISCHES ZENTRALAMT. WIRTSCHAFTSSTATISTIK DER ELEKTRIZITATSVERSORGUNGSUNTERN EN. 1975. a. S.80. Oesterreichisches Statistisches Zentralamt, Hintere Zollamtstr. 2b, 1033 Vienna, Austria. Ed.Bd. circ. 300.

621.3   US   ISSN 0078-3706
OFF-SHORE TECHNOLOGY CONFERENCE. RECORD.* a. Offshore Technology Conference, Program Department, Box 833836, Richardson, TX 75083-3836.

363.6   CN   ISSN 0382-2834
ONTARIO HYDRO. STATISTICAL YEARBOOK. 1971. a. ‡ Ontario Hydro, 700 University Ave., Toronto, Ont. M5G 1X6, Canada. TEL 416-592-5111. Ed. K.B. Wilson. stat. circ. 1,500.

621.31   CN   ISSN 0227-9916
ONTARIO HYDRO RESEARCH REVIEW. 1980. irreg. free to qualified personnel. Ontario Hydro, Research Division, 800 Kipling Ave., Toronto, Ont. M8Z 5S4, Canada. TEL 416-231-4111. Ed. G.R. Floyd. circ. 4,500.

ELECTRICITY AND ELECTRICAL ENGINEERING

621.38   US   ISSN 0164-002X
OPTOELECTRONICS D.A.T.A. BOOK. 1975. a.
$95. D.A.T.A., Inc. (Subsidiary of: International
Thomson Organization) 9889 Willow Creek Rd.,
Box 26875, San Diego, CA 92126. TEL 619-578-7600.

621.38   US
OPTOELECTRONICS DISCONTINUED DEVICES
D.A.T.A. BOOK. 1978. a. $65. D.A.T.A., Inc.
(Subsidiary of: International Thomson Organization)
9889 Willow Creek Rd., Box 26875, San Diego, CA
92126. TEL 619-578-7600.
   Formerly: Discontinued Optoelectronics
D.A.T.A. Book (ISSN 0732-4235)

621.3   US
P C E A ANNUAL ENGINEERING &
OPERATING CONFERENCE. (Each paper
published separately) a. $5 per paper. Pacific Coast
Electrical Association, Inc., 1545 Wilshire Blvd.,
Los Angeles, CA 90017. TEL 213-483-3891. Ed.
W.E. Vaughn, Jr. tr.lit.

536   US
PHYSICS OF QUANTUM ELECTRONICS;
proceedings of summer schools. 1974. irreg., vol.7,
1980. price varies. Addison-Wesley Publishing Co.,
Advanced Book Program, Reading, MA 01867.
TEL 617-944-3700. Ed.Bd. illus. bibl. Indexed:
Chem.Abstr. Sci.Abstr. Nucl.Sci.Abstr.

629   PL   ISSN 0137-6977
POLITECHNIKA CZESTOCHOWSKA. ZESZYTY
NAUKOWE. NAUKI TECHNICZNE.
ELEKTROTECHNIKA. (Text in Polish; summaries
in English and Russian) 1969. irreg. Politechnika
Czestochowska, Ul. Deglera 31, 42-200
Czestochowa, Poland (Dist. by: Ars Polona-Ruch,
Krakowskie Przedmiescie 7, Warsaw, Poland) Ed.
Pawel Rolicz.

621.38   PL
POLITECHNIKA GDANSKA. RAPORT.
WYDZIAL ELEKTRONIKI. 1982. a. price varies.
Politechnika Gdanska, Ul. Majakowskiego 11/12,
80-952 Gdansk 6, Poland.

621.3   PL
POLITECHNIKA GDANSKA. RAPORT.
WYDZIAL ELEKTRYCZNY. 1982. a. Politechnika
Gdanska, Ul. Majakowskiego 11/12, 80-952 Gdansk
6, Poland.

621.38   PL   ISSN 0418-3614
POLITECHNIKA GDANSKA. ZESZYTY
NAUKOWE. ELEKTRONIKA. (Text in Polish;
summaries in English and Russian) 1956. irreg. price
varies. Politechnika Gdanska, Majakowskiego 11/12,
81-952 Gdansk 6, Poland (Dist. by: Osrodek
Rozpowszechniania Wydawnctw Naukowych Pan,
Palac Kultury i Nauki, 00-901 Warsaw, Poland)

621   PL
POLITECHNIKA GDANSKA. ZESZYTY
NAUKOWE. ELEKTRYKA. (Text in Polish;
summaries in English and Russian) 1955. irreg. price
varies. Politechnika Gdanska, Majakowskiego 11/12,
81-952 Gdansk 6, Poland (Dist. by: Osrodek
Rozpowszechniania Wydawnictw Naukowych Pan,
Palac Kultury i Nauki, 00-901 Warsaw, Poland)

621.3   PL   ISSN 0459-682X
POLITECHNIKA LODZKA. ZESZYTY
NAUKOWE. ELEKTRYKA. (Text in Polish;
summaries in English and Russian) 1955. irreg. price
varies. Politechnika Lodzka, Ul. Zwirki 36, 90-924
Lodz, Poland (Dist. by: Ars Polona-Ruch,
Krakowskie Przedmiescie 7, Warsaw, Poland) Ed.
Andrzej Czajkowski. circ. 383. Indexed:
Chem.Abstr. Comput.& Contr.Abstr. Elec.&
Electron.Abstr. Phys.Abstr. Sci.Abstr.

621.3   PL   ISSN 0079-4503
POLITECHNIKA POZNANSKA. ZESZYTY
NAUKOWE. ELEKTRYKA. (Text in Polish;
summaries in English and Russian) 1959. irreg. price
varies. Politechnika Poznanska, Pl. Curie-
Sklodowskiej 5, Poznan, Poland. Ed. Aleksander
Kordus. circ. 150.

537 621.3   PL   ISSN 0072-4688
POLITECHNIKA SLASKA. ZESZYTY NAUKOWE.
ELEKTRYKA. (Text in Polish: summaries in
English and Russian) 1954. irreg. price varies.
Politechnika Slaska, W. Pstrowskiego 7, 44-100
Gliwice, Poland (Dist. by: Ars Polona, Krakowskie
Przedmiescie 7, 00-068 Warsaw, Poland) Ed. Zofia
Cichowska. circ. 280.

621.3   PL   ISSN 0324-9778
POLITECHNIKA WROCLAWSKA. INSTYTUT
ENERGOELEKTRYKI. PRACE NAUKOWE.
KONFERENCJE. (Text in Polish and English)
1973. irreg., no.22, 1985. price varies. Politechnika
Wroclawska, Wybrzeze Wyspianskiego 27, 50-370
Wroclaw, Poland (Dist. by: Ars Polona-Ruch,
Krakowskie Przedmiescie 7, Warsaw, Poland) Ed.
Jerzy Ciekot. circ. 480.

621.3   PL   ISSN 0324-976X
POLITECHNIKA WROCLAWSKA. INSTYTUT
ENERGOELEKTRYKI. PRACE NAUKOWE.
MONOGRAFIE. (Text in Polish; summaries in
English, French and Russian) 1972. irreg., no.16,
1986. price varies. Politechnika Wroclawska,
Wybrzeze Wyspianskiego 27, 50-370 Wroclaw,
Poland (Dist. by: Ars Polona-Ruch, Krakowskie
Przedmiescie 7, Warsaw, Poland) Ed. Jerzy Ciekot.

621.3   PL   ISSN 0084-2826
POLITECHNIKA WROCLAWSKA. INSTYTUT
ENERGOELEKTRYKI. PRACE NAUKOWE.
STUDIA I MATERIALY. (Text in Polish;
summaries in English, French, German, Russian)
1969. irreg., no.30, 1979. Politechnika Wroclawska,
Ul. Wybrzeze Wyspianskiego 27, 50-370 Wroclaw,
Poland (Dist. by: Ars Polona-Ruch, Krakowskie
Przedmiescie 7, Warsaw, Poland) Ed. Marian Kloza.

621.3 389   PL   ISSN 0324-9557
POLITECHNIKA WROCLAWSKA. INSTYTUT
METROLOGII ELEKTRYCZNEJ. PRACE
NAUKOWE. KONFERENCJE. (Text in Polish and
English) 1973. irreg., no.12, 1986. price varies.
Politechnika Wroclawska, Wybrzeze Wyspianskiego
27, 50-370 Wroclaw, Poland (Dist. by : Ars Polona-
Ruch, Krakowskie Przedmiescie 7, Warsaw, Poland)
Ed. Jerzy Ciekot. circ. 480. Indexed: Sci.Abstr.

621.3 389   PL   ISSN 0324-9549
POLITECHNIKA WROCLAWSKA. INSTYTUT
METROLOGII ELEKTRYCZNEJ. PRACE
NAUKOWE. MONOGRAFIE. (Text in Polish;
summaries in English and Russian) 1974. irreg.,
no.6, 1985. price varies. Politechnika Wroclawska,
Wybrzeze Wyspianskiego 27, 50-370 Wroclaw,
Poland (Dist. by: Ars Polona-Ruch, Krakowskie
Przedmiescie 7, Warsaw, Poland) Ed. Jerzy Ciekot.
circ. 375.

621.3 389   PL   ISSN 0084-2958
POLITECHNIKA WROCLAWSKA. INSTYTUT
METROLOGII ELEKTRYCZNEJ. PRACE
NAUKOWE. STUDIA I MATERIALY. (Text in
Polish; summaries in English, Russian) 1970. irreg.,
no.8, 1982. price varies. Politechnika Wroclawska,
Wybrzeze Wyspianskiego 27, 50-370 Wroclaw,
Poland (Dist. by: Ars Polona-Ruch, Krakowskie
Przedmiescie 7, Warsaw, Poland) Ed. Marian Kloza.
Indexed: Chem.Abstr.

621   PL   ISSN 0324-9441
POLITECHNIKA WROCLAWSKA. INSTYTUT
PODSTAW ELEKTROTECHNIKI I
ELEKTROTECHNOLOGII. PRACE NAUKOWE.
KONFERENCJE. (Text in Polish; summaries in
English and Russian) 1975. irreg., no.5, 1986. price
varies. Politechnika Wroclawska, Wybrzeze
Wyspianskiego 27, 50-370 Wroclaw, Poland (Dist.
by: Ars Polona-Ruch, Krakowskie Przedmiescie 7,
Warsaw, Poland) Ed. Jery Ciekot.

621   PL   ISSN 0324-945X
POLITECHNIKA WROCLAWSKA. INSTYTUT
PODSTAW ELEKTROTECHNIKI I
ELEKTROTECHNOLOGII. PRACE NAUKOWE.
MONOGRAFIE. (Text in Polish; summaries in
English and Russian) 1972. irreg., no.9, 1986. price
varies. Politechnika Wroclawska, Wybrzeze
Wyspianskiego 27, 50-370 Wroclaw, Poland (Dist.
by: Ars Polona-Ruch, Krakowskie Przedmiescie 7,
Warsaw, Poland) Ed. Jerzy Ciekot. circ. 250.

621.3   PL   ISSN 0370-0852
POLITECHNIKA WROCLAWSKA. INSTYTUT
PODSTAW ELEKTROTECHNIKI I
ELEKTROTECHNOLOGII. PRACE NAUKOWE.
STUDIA I MATERIALY. (Text in Polish;
summaries in English and Russian) 1970. irreg.,
no.8, 1980. price varies. Politechnika Wroclawska,
Wybrzeze Wyspianskiego 27, 50-370 Wroclaw,
Poland (Dist. by: Ars Polona-Ruch, Krakowskie
Przedmiescie 7, Warsaw, Poland) Ed. Marian Kloza.
circ. 250. Indexed: Chem.Abstr.

621.3   PL
POLITECHNIKA WROCLAWSKA. INSTYTUT
PODSTAW ELEKTROTECHNIKI I
ELEKTROTECHNOLOGII. PRACE NAUKOWE.
WSPOLPRACA. (Text in Polish; summaries in
English and Russian) 1977. irreg., no.2, 1985. price
varies. Politechnika Wroclawska, Wybrzeze
Wyspianskiego 27, 50-370 Wroclaw, Poland. Ed.
Jery Ciekot. circ. 250.

621.38   PL   ISSN 0370-0887
POLITECHNIKA WROCLAWSKA. INSTYTUT
TECHNOLOGII ELEKTRONOWEJ. PRACE
NAUKOWE. KONFERENCJE. (Text in Polish;
summaries in English, French and Russian) 1973.
irreg., no.7, 1986. price varies. Politechnika
Wroclawska, Wybrzeze Wyspianskiego 27, 50-370
Wroclaw, Poland (Dist. by: Ars Polona-Ruch,
Krakowskie Przedmiescie 7, Warsaw, Poland) Ed.
Jerzy Ciekot.

621.38   PL   ISSN 0084-280X
POLITECHNIKA WROCLAWSKA. INSTYTUT
TECHNOLOGII ELEKTRONOWEJ. PRACE
NAUKOWE. MONOGRAFIE. (Text in Polish;
summaries in English, Russian) 1970. irreg., no.12,
1984. price varies. Politechnika Wroclawska,
Wybrzeze Wyspianskiego 27, 50-370 Wroclaw,
Poland (Dist. by: Ars Polona-Ruch, Krakowskie
Przedmiescie 7, Warsaw, Poland) Ed. Jerzy Ciekot.
Indexed: Sci.Abstr.

621.3 530   PL   ISSN 0084-2885
POLITECHNIKA WROCLAWSKA. INSTYTUT
TECHNOLOGII ELEKTRONOWEJ. PRACE
NAUKOWE. STUDIA I MATERIALY. (Text in
Polish; summaries in English, Russian) 1970. irreg.,
no.14, 1984. price varies. Politechnika Wroclawska,
Wybrzeze Wyspianskiego 27, 50-370 Wroclaw,
Poland (Dist. by: Ars Polona-Ruch, Krakowskie
Przedmiescie 7, Warsaw, Poland) Ed. Jerzy Ciekot.
Indexed: Chem.Abstr.

621.38 534   PL   ISSN 0324-9344
POLITECHNIKA WROCLAWSKA. INSTYTUT
TELEKOMUNIKACJI I AKUSTYKI. PRACE
NAUKOWE. KONFERENCJE. (Text in Polish;
summaries in English and Russian) 1973. irreg.,
no.18, 1986. price varies. Politechnika Wroclawska,
Wybrzeze Wyspianskiego 27, 50-370 Wroclaw,
Poland (Dist. by: Ars Polona-Ruch, Krakowskie
Przedmiescie 7, Warsaw, Poland) Ed. Jerzy Ciekot.

621.38 534   PL   ISSN 0324-9328
POLITECHNIKA WROCLAWSKA. INSTYTUT
TELEKOMUNIKACJI I AKUSTYKI. PRACE
NAUKOWE. MONOGRAFIE. (Text in Polish;
summaries in English and Russian) 1969. irreg.,
no.25, 1986. price varies. Politechnika Wroclawska,
Wybrzeze Wyspianskiego 27, 50-370 Wroclaw,
Poland (Dist. by: Ars Polona-Ruch, Krakowskie
Przedmiescie 7, Warsaw, Poland) Ed. Jeny Ciekot.

621.38 534   PL   ISSN 0324-9336
POLITECHNIKA WROCLAWSKA. INSTYTUT
TELEKOMUNIKACJI I AKUSTYKI. PRACE
NAUKOWE. STUDIA I MATERIALY. (Text in
Polish; summaries in English and Russian) 1971.
irreg., no.12, 1980. price varies. Politechnika
Wroclawska, Wybrzeze Wyspianskiego 27, 50-370
Wroclaw, Poland (Dist. by: Ars Polona-Ruch,
Krakowskie Przedmiescie 7, Warsaw, Poland) Ed.
Marian Kloza.

621.3   PL   ISSN 0324-931X
POLITECHNIKA WROCLAWSKA. INSTYTUT
UKLADOW ELEKTROMASZYNOWYCH.
PRACE NAUKOWE. KONFERENCJE. (Text in
Polish: summaries in English and Russian) 1973.
irreg., no.9, 1982. price varies. Politechnika
Wroclawska, Wybrzeze Wyspianskiego 27, 50-370
Wroclaw, Poland (Dist. by: Ars Polona-Ruch,
Krakowskie Przedmiescie 7, Warsaw, Poland) Ed.
Jeny Ciekot.

ELECTRICITY AND ELECTRICAL ENGINEERING

621.3   PL   ISSN 0137-6284
POLITECHNIKA WROCLAWSKA. INSTYTUT UKLADOW ELEKTROMASZYNOWYCH. PRACE NAUKOWE. MONOGRAFIE. (Text in Polish; summaries in English and Russian) 1969. irreg., no.8, 1986. price varies. Politechnika Wroclawska, Ul. Wybrzeze Wyspianskiego 27, 50-370 Wroclaw, Poland (Dist. by: Ars Polona-Ruch, Krakowskie Przedmiescie 7, Warsaw, Poland) Ed. Jeny Ciekot. Indexed: Sci.Abstr.

621.3   PL   ISSN 0084-294X
POLITECHNIKA WROCLAWSKA. INSTYTUT UKLADOW ELEKTROMASZYNOWYCH. PRACE NAUKOWE. STUDIA I MATERIALY. (Text in Polish; summaries in English and Russian) 1969. irreg., no.16, 1981. price varies. Politechnika Wroclawska, Ul. Wybrzeze Wyspianskiego 27, 50-370 Wroclaw, Poland (Dist. by: Ars Polona-Ruch, Krakowskie Przedmiescie 7, Warsaw, Poland) Ed. Jeny Ciekot.

621.38   537   UR
POLUTEHNILINE INSTITUUT TALLINN. AVTOMATIZIROVANNYE MHD-I LINEINYE ELEKTROPRIVODY I IKH ELEMENTY. (Subseries of its Toimetised) (Text in Russian; summaries in English or German) irreg. price varies. Polutehniline Instituut Tallinn, Ehitajate tee 5, Tallinn, Estonian S.S.R., U.S.S.R.

621.3   UR   ISSN 0320-3336
POLUTEHNILINE INSTITUUT TALLINN. ISSLEDOVANIE ELEKTROMAGNITNYKH I ELEKTROMASHINNYKH USTROISTV UPRAVLENIYA I KONTROLYA SPETSIAL'NOGO NAZNACHENIYA. (Subseries of its Toimetised) (Text in Russian; summaries in English or German) irreg. price varies. Polutehniline Instituut Tallinn, Ehitajate tee 5, Tallinn, Estonian S.S.R., U.S.S.R.

683.88   621.3   UR
POLUTEHNILINE INSTITUUT TALLINN. ISSLEDOVANIE RABOTY PAROGENERATOROV ELEKTROSTANTSII. (Subseries of its Toimetised) (Text in Russian; summaries in English or German) irreg. price varies. Polutehniline Instituut Tallinn, Ehitajate tee 5, Tallinn, Estonian S.S.R., U.S.S.R.

537.5   DK
POLYTEKNISKE LAEREANSTALT, DANMARKS TEKNISKE HOEJSKOLE. LABORATORIET FOR ELEKTRONIK. BERETNING. 1970-1982. a. free. Polytekniske Laereanstalt, Danmarks Tekniske Hoejskole, Laboratoriet for Elektronik - Technical University of Denmark, Electronics Laboratory, Bygning 344, DK-2800 Lyngby, Denmark. Ed. Peter W. Becker. circ. 400.

537   PL   ISSN 0079-4260
POSTEPY NAPEDU ELEKTRYCZNEGO. 1960. irreg. price varies. (Polska Akademia Nauk, Komitet Elektrotechniki) Panstwowe Wydawnictwo Naukowe, Miodowa 10, 00-251 Warsaw, Poland (Dist. by: Ars Polona, Krakowskie Przedmiescie 7, 00-068 Warsaw, Poland)

621.3   US
POWER DIRECTORY. a. $90 to individuals; members $72. Edison Electric Institute, 1111 19th St., N.W., Washington, DC 20036.

621.3   US
POWER MODULATOR SYMPOSIUM. I E E E CONFERENCE RECORD. biennial. price varies. (I E E E, Electron Devices Society) Institute of Electrical and Electronics Engineers, Inc., 345 E. 47th St., New York, NY 10017 TEL 212-705-7900. (Subscr. to 445 Hoes Lane, Piscataway, NJ 08854)
    Former titles: Power Modulator Conference. I E E E Conference Record; (1978-1980): Pulse Power Modulator Symposium. I E E E Conference Record; (1973-1976): Modulator Symposium. (Record)

621.38   US   ISSN 0164-0038
POWER SEMICONDUCTORS D.A.T.A. BOOK. 1974. a. $100. D.A.T.A., Inc. (Subsidiary of: International Thomson Organization) Box 26875, San Diego, CA 92126. TEL 619-578-7600. adv. illus.
    Formerly: Power Semiconductors (ISSN 0095-4225)

621.35   621.38   US   ISSN 0079-4457
POWER SOURCES SYMPOSIUM. PROCEEDINGS. 1956. biennial. $60. ‡ Electrochemical Society, Inc., 10 S. Main St., Pennington, NJ 08534-2896. TEL 609-737-1902. circ. 700. Indexed: Chem.Abstr.

621.38   NP
POWER STATISTICS JOURNAL OF NEPAL.* (Text in English) 1970/71. irreg. Department of Electricity, Katmandu, Nepal. illus. stat.

621.3   US
POWER SUPPLIES D.A.T.A. BOOK. (Subseries of: D.A.T.A. Book Electronic Information Series) a. $95. D.A.T.A., Inc. (Subsidiary of: International Thomson Organization) 9889 Creek Rd., Box 26875, San Diego, CA 92126. TEL 619-578-7600.

621.3   US
PRODUCTION COSTS: OPERATING STEAM ELECTRIC PLANTS. 1983. a. $150. Utility Data Institute, 1700 K St., N.W., Ste. 400, Washington, DC 20006. TEL 202-466-3660. stat. index. (also avail. in magnetic tape; back issues avail.)

PROFESSIONAL ELECTRONICS YEARBOOK. see BUSINESS AND ECONOMICS — Trade And Industrial Directories

537   NZ
PROFILE NEW ZEALAND/THE ELECTRICAL INDUSTRY. a. NZ.$10. Associated Group Media Ltd., Private Bag Newmarket, Auckland, New Zealand.

537.5   US   ISSN 0079-6727
PROGRESS IN QUANTUM ELECTRONICS. 1969. 4/yr. $135 (annual bound volume $126) Pergamon Press, Inc., Journals Division, Maxwell House, Fairview Park, Elmsford, NY 10523 TEL 914-592-7700. (And: Headington Hill Hall, Oxford OX3 0BW, England) Ed. Stig Stenholm. (also avail. in microform from MIM,UMI) Indexed: Chem.Abstr. Sci.Abstr. Phys.Ber.

621.3   US   ISSN 0033-4537
PURDUE UNIVERSITY. SCHOOL OF ELECTRICAL ENGINEERING. ANNUAL RESEARCH SUMMARY. 1964. a. free to qualified personnel. Purdue University, School of Electrical Engineering, West Lafayette, IN 47907. TEL 317-494-3536. Ed. K.S. Fu. abstr. circ. 750. (processed)

621.3   CN   ISSN 0075-6091
QUEEN'S UNIVERSITY AT KINGSTON. DEPARTMENT OF ELECTRICAL ENGINEERING. RESEARCH REPORT. 1962. irreg. free. ‡ Queen's University, Department of Electrical Engineering, Kingston, Ont. K7L 3N6, Canada. TEL 613-547-6935. Ed. Dr. P.H. Wittke. circ. 50. (back issues avail.)

621.381   US
RADIO - ELECTRONICS EXPERIMENTERS HANDBOOK (YEAR) 1983. a. $2.95. Gernsback Publications, Inc., 500 Bi-Country Rd., Farmingdale, NY 11735. Ed. Art Kleiman. adv. illus. circ. 125, 000. Indexed: Sci.Abstr.
    Formerly (until 1987): Radio - Electronics Annual.

683.88   UK
REGULATIONS FOR THE ELECTRICAL EQUIPMENT OF BUILDINGS. 1966. irreg., 15th ed., 1981. £18. Institution of Electrical Engineers, Savoy Place, London WC2H 0BL, England.

621.3   US   ISSN 0149-144X
RELIABILITY AND MAINTAINABILITY SYMPOSIUM. PROCEEDINGS. 1954. a. price varies. (I E E E, Reliability Society) Institute of Electrical and Electronics Engineers, Inc., 345 E. 47th St., New York, NY 10017 TEL 212-705-7900. (Subscr. address: 445 Hoes Lane, Piscataway, NJ 08854) (Co-Sponsor: American Society for Quality Control)
    Former titles: Reliability and Maintainability Conference. Record & Symposium on Reliability. Proceedings (ISSN 0082-092X)

621.3   614.7   JA   ISSN 0911-6923
RESEARCH INSTITUTE OF INDUSTRIAL SAFETY. RESEARCH REPORT. (Text in Japanese; summaries in English) 1968. a. Research Institute of Industrial Safety, 35-1, 5-Chome, Shiba, Minato-ku, Tokyo 108, Japan. circ. 450. (back issues avail.)

621.3   620   JA   ISSN 0911-8063
RESEARCH INSTITUTE OF INDUSTRIAL SAFETY. TECHNICAL RECOMMENDATION. (Text in Japanese) 1970. irreg. Research Institute of Industrial Safety, 35-1, 5-Chome, Shiba, Minato-Ku, Tokyo 108, Japan. circ. 450. (back issues avail.)

ROBOTRON TECHNISCHE MITTEILUNGEN. see COMPUTERS — Artificial Intelligence

621.31   US
RURAL ELECTRIC POWER CONFERENCE. PAPERS PRESENTED. 1977. a. (I E E E, Industry Applications Society, Rural Electric Power Committee) Institute of Electrical and Electronics Engineers, Inc., 345 E. 47th St., New York, NY 10017 TEL 212-705-7900. (Subscr. address: 445 Hoes Lane, Piscataway, NJ 08854)

621.38   629   FR
S P E R ANNUAIRE. 1962. a. free. Syndicat des Industries de Materiel Professionnel Electronique et Radioelectrique, 11 rue Hamelin, 75783 Paris Cedex 16, France. Ed.Bd. circ. 2,000.
    Formerly: Syndicat des Industries de Material Professionnel Electronique et Radioelectrique. Annuaire (ISSN 0082-1020)

621.31   MY   ISSN 0127-144X
SARAWAK ELECTRICITY SUPPLY CORPORATION. ANNUAL REPORT. (Text in English) 1957. a. M.10. Sarawak Electricity Supply Corporation - Perbadanan Pembekalan Letrik Sarawak, Box 149, Kuching, Sarawak, Malaysia. stat. circ. 850.

621.3   MX
SECTOR ELECTRICO EN MEXICO. 1981. a. price varies. Instituto Nacional de Estadistica, Geografia e Informatica, Secretaria de Programacion y Presupuesto, Patriotismo 711 Torre "A" P.H., Col. San Juan Mixcoac, Deleg. Benito Juarez, 03910 Mexico, D.F., Mexico TEL 598-99-05. (Subscr. to: Rio Rhin No. 56, Col. Cuauhtemoc, 06500 Mexico, D.F., Mexico)

621.3   UK
SEMICONDUCTOR EVALUATION TECHNIQUES. 1985. irreg. $190. Benn Electronics Publications Ltd., 146 Midland Rd., Luton LU2 0BL, England. TEL 0582 421981. Eds. D.A. Taylor, R.J. Garner.

621.3   US
SEMICONDUCTOR INDUSTRY ASSOCIATION. YEARBOOK AND DIRECTORY. 1981. a. $60. Semiconductor Industry Association, 10201 Torre Ave., Ste. 275, Cupertino, CA 95014. TEL 408-973-9973. Ed. Sheila M. Sandow.

621.3   US
SEMICONDUCTOR INTERNATIONAL MASTER BUYING GUIDE. a. included in subscr. to: Semiconductor International. Cahners Publishing Co., Inc., Electronics Group (Des Plaines), Division of Reed Publishing USA, Box 5080, 1350 E. Touhy Ave., Des Plaines, IL 60018. TEL 312-635-8800. Ed. Donald E. Swanson. adv. tr.lit. circ. 36,000. (reprint service avail.)

621.3   JA
SHIKOKU ELECTRIC POWER CO., INC. ANNUAL REPORT. a. Shikoku Electric Power Co., Inc., 2-5 Marunouchi, Takamatsu, Kagawa 760, Japan.

621.3   US
SLIG BUYERS' GUIDE. 1969. biennial. $8. Independent Battery Manufacturers Association, Inc., 100 Larchwood Dr., Largo, FL 33540. TEL 813-586-1408. Ed. Celwyn E. Hopkins. adv. circ. 6,000.

621.38   US
SOLID STATE PROCESSING AND PRODUCTION BUYERS GUIDE AND DIRECTORY. a. Technical Publishing Co. (New York) (Subsidiary of: Dun & Bradstreet Corporation) 14 Vanderventer Ave., Port Washington, NY 11050. TEL 516-883-6200. Ed. Samuel L. Marshall.

621.3   UK   ISSN 0305-4543
SPON'S MECHANICAL & ELECTRICAL SERVICES PRICE BOOK. 1968. a. £28.95. E. & F.N. Spon Ltd., 11 New Fetter Lane, London EC4P 4EE, England. Ed.Bd. adv. circ. 5,000.

621.3 530   US   ISSN 0172-5734
SPRINGER SERIES IN ELECTROPHYSICS. 1977.
irreg., vol.21, 1985. price varies. Springer-Verlag,
175 Fifth Ave., New York, NY 10010 TEL 212-
460-1500. (Also Berlin, Heidelberg, Tokyo and
Vienna) Ed.Bd. (reprint service avail. from ISI)
Indexed: Chem.Abstr.

621.3   US
SPRINGER TEXTS IN ELECTRICAL
ENGINEERING. 1982. irreg., latest 1984.
Springer-Verlag, 175 Fifth Ave., New York, NY
10010 TEL 212-460-1500. (Also Berlin, Heidelberg,
Tokyo and Vienna) Indexed: Math.R.

621.3   NE
STUDIES IN ELECTRICAL AND ELECTRONIC
ENGINEERING. 1978. irreg., vol.19, 1985. price
varies. Elsevier Science Publishers B.V., Box 211,
1000 AE Amsterdam, Netherlands. Indexed:
Chem.Abstr.

621.3   US
SWEET'S ELECTRICAL ENGINEERING AND
RETROFIT FILE. a. free to qualified personnel.
Sweet's Catalog Files (Subsidiary of: McGraw-Hill
Information Systems Co.) 1221 Ave. of the
Americas, New York, NY 10020. TEL 212-512-
4303. circ. 13,000.

621.38   US   ISSN 0272-5428
SYMPOSIUM ON FOUNDATIONS OF
COMPUTER SCIENCE. PROCEEDINGS. 1960.
a. price varies. (Institute of Electrical and
Electronics Engineers, Inc.) I E E E Computer
Society Press, 1730 Massachusetts Ave., N.W.,
Washington, DC 20036 TEL 202-371-0101. (And
345 E. 47th St., New York, NY 10017)
  Former titles (1966-1974): Annual Symposium on
Switching and Automata Theory. Proceedings (ISSN
0272-4847); Symposium on Switching and
Automata Theory; Switching and Automata Theory
Conference. Record (ISSN 0082-0490); (1960-1965) :
Symposium on Switching Circuit Theory and
Logical Design.

621.3   US
SYMPOSIUM ON FUSION ENGINEERING.
PROCEEDINGS. 1965. biennial. price varies.
Institute of Electrical and Electronics Engineers,
Inc., 345 E. 47th St., New York, NY 10017 TEL
212-705-7900. (Subscr. address: 445 Hoes Lane,
Piscataway, NJ 08854) Indexed: Chem.Abstr.
  Formerly (until 1983): Symposium on
Engineering Problems of Fusion Research.
Proceedings (ISSN 0145-5958)

621.38   HU
SYMPOSIUM ON RELIABILITY IN
ELECTRONICS. (Text in English and Russian)
1962. quinquennial, latest 6th, Budapest, Hungary,
1985. $38. Orszagos Muszaki Informacios Kozpont
es Konyvtar (O.M.I.K.K.) - National Technical
Information Centre and Library, Muzeum u.17, Box
12, 1428 Budapest, Hungary. (Co-sponsor: Scientific
Society for Telecommunication) Ed. Merey.

621.3 331.8   FR
SYNDICAT GENERAL DE LA CONSTRUCTION
ELECTRIQUE. ANNUAIRE. a. 530 Fr.
(Federation des Industries Electriques et
Electroniques, Syndicat General de la Construction
Electrique) Union Francaise d'Annuaires
Professionnels, 13 av. Vladimir Komarov, B.P. 36,
78192 Trappes Cedex, France.

537   GE
TECHNISCHE HOCHSCHULE KARL-MARX-
STADT. WISSENSCHAFTLICHE
SCHRIFTENREIHE. 1977. irreg. Technische
Hochschule Karl-Marx-Stadt, Sektion Physik-
Elektronische Bauelemente, P.F. 964, 90 Karl-Marx-
Stadt, E. Germany (D.D.R.) Ed.Bd. Indexed:
Chem.Abstr.

537.5   JA
TECHNOPOLIS. a. Tokuma Shoku, 4-10-1, Shinbashi,
Minato-Ku, Tokyo 105, Japan. circ. 180,000.

TEKNOLOGI. see *TECHNOLOGY:
COMPREHENSIVE WORKS*

363.6 380   US   ISSN 0730-4889
TENNESSEE VALLEY AUTHORITY. POWER
PROGRAM SUMMARY. 1980. a. free. Tennessee
Valley Authority, Office of Power, 6N31 A
Missionary Ridge Pl., Chattanooga, TN 37402-2801.
TEL 615-751-2864. Ed. Judith Elb. circ. 12,000.
Indexed: Amer.Stat.Ind.
  Formed by the merger of (1960-1980): Tennessee
Valley Authority. Power Annual Report (ISSN
0082-2795); (1963-1980): Tennessee Valley
Authority. Operations: Municipal and Cooperative
Distributors of T.V.A. Power (ISSN 0362-3432)

621.3   US   ISSN 0082-2809
TENNESSEE VALLEY AUTHORITY.
TECHNICAL MONOGRAPHS. 1934. irreg. price
varies. Tennessee Valley Authority, Treasurer's
Office, Knoxville, TN 37902. TEL 615-632-8143.
circ. 600.

621.3   US   ISSN 0082-2817
TENNESSEE VALLEY AUTHORITY.
TECHNICAL REPORTS. 1940. irreg. price varies.
Tennessee Valley Authority, Treasurer's Office,
Knoxville, TN 37902. TEL 615-632-8143. circ. 2,
000.

537.5   US
TEXAS ANNUAL OF ELECTRONICS
RESEARCH. 1964/65. a. $6 per no. University of
Texas at Austin, Electronics Research Center,
Austin, TX 78712. TEL 512-471-3954. Ed. Edward
J. Powers. abstr. bibl. illus.
  Formerly: Texas Biannual of Electronics Research
(ISSN 0563-2625)

621.38   US   ISSN 0732-6092
THYRISTOR D.A.T.A. BOOK. (Subseries of:
D.A.T.A. Reference Standards for Industry) 1973. a.
$95. D.A.T.A., Inc. (Subsidiary of: International
Thomson Organization) 9889 Willow Creek Rd.,
Box 26876, San Diego, CA 92126. TEL 619-578-
7600. adv. illus.

621.38   US
THYRISTOR DISCONTINUED DEVICES D.A.T.A.
BOOK. 1969. a. $65. D.A.T.A., Inc. (Subsidiary of:
International Thomson Organization) 9889 Willow
Creek Rd., Box 26875, San Diego, CA 92126. TEL
619-578-7600. Ed. Steven d'Adolf.
  Former titles: Discontinued Thyristors D.A.T.A.
Book (ISSN 0730-4838); D.A.T.A. Book of
Discontinued Thyristors (ISSN 0092-508X)

621.3   JA
TOHOKU ELECTRIC POWER CO., INC.
ANNUAL REPORT. Tohoku Electric Power Co.,
Inc., 7-1, 3-chome, Ichibancho, Sendai 980, Japan.

TOKYO DENKI UNIVERSITY. FACULTY OF
ENGINEERING. GENERAL EDUCATION.
RESEARCH REPORTS. see *ENGINEERING*

TOKYO DENKI UNIVERSITY. FACULTY OF
ENGINEERING. RESEARCH REPORTS. see
ENGINEERING

TRACTEBEL. ANNUAL REPORT. see
ENGINEERING

621.38   US   ISSN 0732-6203
TRANSISTOR D.A.T.A. BOOK. 1956. a. $95.
D.A.T.A., Inc. (Subsidiary of: International
Thomson Organization) 9889 Willow Creek Rd.,
Box 26875, San Diego, CA 92126. TEL 619-578-
7600. adv.

621.38   US   ISSN 0730-4846
TRANSISTOR DISCONTINUED DEVICES
D.A.T.A. BOOK. 1965. a. $65. D.A.T.A., Inc.
(Subsidiary of: International Thomson Organization)
9889 Willow Creek Rd., Box 26875, San Diego, CA
92126. TEL 619-578-7600.
  Former titles: Discontinued Transistors D.A.T.A.
Book (ISSN 0271-0722) & D.A.T.A. Book of
Discontinued Transistors (ISSN 0070-2498)

621.3   US
TRANSMISSION AND DISTRIBUTION
SPECIFIERS & BUYERS GUIDE. 1965. a. $10.
Cleworth Publishing Co. (Subsidiary of: Andrews
Communications, Inc.) One River Rd., Cos Cob, CT
06807. TEL 203-661-5000. Ed. Elgin G. Enabnit,
Jr. adv. circ. 33,000. (also avail. in microfilm from
UMI; reprint service avail. from UMI)

354   TU
TURKISH ELECTRICITY AUTHORITY. ANNUAL
REPORT. (Text in English) a. Turkish Electricity
Authority - Turkiye Elektrik Kurumu, Necatibey
Caddesi No. 36, Ankara, Turkey. charts. illus. stat.

621.3   US
U S NUCLEAR PLANT STATISTICS. 1985. a. $95.
Utility Data Institute, Inc., 1700 K St., N.W., Ste.
400, Washington, DC 20006. TEL 202-466-3660.

U.S. NATIONAL BUREAU OF STANDARDS.
SEMICONDUCTOR MEASUREMENT
TECHNOLOGY. see *METROLOGY AND
STANDARDIZATION*

621.393   US   ISSN 0083-3177
U.S. RURAL ELECTRIFICATION
ADMINISTRATION. ANNUAL STATISTICAL
REPORT. RURAL ELECTRIFICATION
BORROWERS. a. free. U.S. Rural Electrification
Administration, U.S. Dept. of Agriculture,
Washington, DC 20250. TEL 202-857-9583.

621.393   US   ISSN 0083-3185
U.S. RURAL ELECTRIFICATION
ADMINISTRATION. ANNUAL STATISTICAL
REPORT. RURAL TELEPHONE PROGRAM.
1958. a. ‡ U.S. Rural Electrification Administration,
Dept. of Agriculture, Washington, DC 20250. TEL
202-857-9583.

621.393   US   ISSN 0083-3193
U.S. RURAL ELECTRIFICATION
ADMINISTRATION. REPORT OF THE
ADMINISTRATOR OF THE RURAL
ELECTRIFICATION ADMINISTRATION. 1936.
a. free. U.S. Rural Electrification Administration,
Department of Agriculture, Washington, DC 20250.
TEL 202-857-9583.

621.3   AG   ISSN 0082-6693
UNIVERSIDAD NACIONAL DE TUCUMAN.
INSTITUTO DE INGENIERIA ELECTRICA.
REVISTA. 1963. irreg. $1.50. Universidad Nacional
de Tucuman, Instituto de Ingenieria Electrica, Avda.
Independencia 1700, San Miguel de Tucuman,
Argentina. Ed. Herberto Carlos Buhler. bk. rev.
index. circ. 1,500.

621.3   US
UNIVERSITY/GOVERNMENT/INDUSTRY
MICROELECTRONICS SYMPOSIUM.
PROCEEDINGS. 1975. biennial. Institute of
Electrical and Electronics Engineers, Inc., 345 E.
47th St., New York, NY 10017 TEL 212-705-7900.
(Subscr. address: 445 Hoes Lane, Piscataway, NJ
08854)

621.3   US   ISSN 0568-0581
UNIVERSITY OF ILLINOIS AT URBANA-
CHAMPAIGN. DEPARTMENT OF
ELECTRICAL ENGINEERING. AERONOMY
LABORATORY. AERONOMY REPORT. 1963.
irreg. free. University of Illinois at Urbana-
Champaign, Department of Electrical Engineering,
Aeronomy Laboratory, Urbana, IL 61801. TEL 217-
333-1000. Ed. Belva Edwards. circ. controlled.

621.3   AT   ISSN 0085-3259
UNIVERSITY OF MELBOURNE. DEPARTMENT
OF ELECTRICAL ENGINEERING. RESEARCH
REPORT. 1966. irreg. free. University of
Melbourne, Department of Electrical and Electronic
Engineering, Parkville, Vic. 3052, Australia. Ed.
John C. McCutchan. circ. 100.

621.3   AT
UNIVERSITY OF NEWCASTLE. DEPARTMENT
OF ELECTRICAL AND COMPUTER
ENGINEERING. TECHNICAL REPORT EE.
1967. irreg. contr. free circ. ‡ University of
Newcastle, Department of Electrical and Computer
Engineering, Shortland, N.S.W. 2308, Australia.
circ. 800.
  Formerly: University of Newcastle. Department
of Electrical Engineering. Technical Report EE
(ISSN 0085-4158)

621.3 621.38   JA   ISSN 0563-7929
UNIVERSITY OF TOKYO. ELECTRICAL AND
ELECTRONIC ENGINEERING DEPARTMENT.
BULLETIN. (Text in Japanese) 1952. a. University
of Tokyo, Electrical and Electronic Engineering
Department, 7-3-1, Hongo, Bunkyo-Ku, Tokyo 113,
Japan. Ed. T. Oda. circ. 1,000.

ELECTRICITY AND ELECTRICAL ENGINEERING — ABSTRACTING, BIBLIOGRAPHIES, STATISTICS 461

621.3   CN   ISSN 0082-514X
UNIVERSITY OF TORONTO. DEPARTMENT OF ELECTRICAL ENGINEERING. RESEARCH REPORT.* 1954. irreg. University of Toronto, Department of Electrical Engineering, Toronto, Ont., Canada.

621.3   GW   ISSN 0505-2904
V D E W DIE OEFFENTLICHE ELEKTRIZITAETSVERSORGUNG. 1953. a. DM.13.50. Vereinigung Deutscher Elektrizitaetswerke e.V., Stresemannallee 23, 6000 Frankfurt, W. Germany (B.R.D.) charts. stat. index. circ. controlled.
  Formerly: V D E W Arbeitsbericht.

537   UR
VOPROSY ELEKTRONIKI TVERDOGO TELA. vol.7, 1978. irreg. 1.80 Rub. per no. Leningradskii Universitet, Universitetskaya Nab. 7/9, Leningrad B-164, Russian S.F.S.R., U.S.S.R. abstr. bibl. circ. 1,500.

WHO'S WHO IN ELECTRONICS. see BUSINESS AND ECONOMICS — Trade And Industrial Directories

WHO'S WHO IN ELECTRONICS & COMPUTER SCIENCE. see BUSINESS AND ECONOMICS — Trade And Industrial Directories

621.3   NE
WIE LEVERT. a. Kluwer Technische Tijdschriften B.V., Postbus 23, 7400 GA Deventer, Netherlands. adv. circ. 2,750.
  Formerly: Wie Levert Elektro.

621.3   US
WINTER SIMULATION CONFERENCE. PROCEEDINGS. (Earlier papers published in: IEEE Transactions on Systems Science and Cybernetics) 2nd, 1968. a. $75. Society for Computer Simulation, Box 17900, San Diego, CA 92117. circ. 1,050.
  Former titles (1968-1970): Conference on the Applications of Simulation; 1967: Conference on the Applications of GPSS.

Z V E I ELEKTRO-EINKAUFSFUEHRER. see ENGINEERING — Computer Applications

354   ZA
ZAMBIA ELECTRICITY SUPPLY CORPORATION. ANNUAL REPORT. a., latest 1973/74. free. Zambia Electricity Supply Corporation, Box 3304, Lusaka, Zambia. stat.

621.3 531.64 620   GW
300-MW-THTR-KERNKRAFTWERK HAMM-UENTROP, PROJEKTINFORMATION. (Text in English, German) 1971. irreg. Consortium THTR, Gottlieb-Daimler-Str. 8, 6800 Mannheim 1, W. Germany (B.R.D.) circ. 10,000.

ELECTRICITY AND ELECTRICAL ENGINEERING — Abstracting, Bibliographies, Statistics

621.3 016   US   ISSN 0163-1462
ABSTRACT NEWSLETTER: ELECTROTECHNOLOGY. w. $79. U.S. National Technical Information Service, 5285 Port Royal Rd., Springfield, VA 22161. TEL 703-487-4630. Ed. Linda J. LaGarde. index. (back issues avail.)
  Former titles: Weekly Abstract Newsletter: Electrotechnology; Weekly Government Abstracts. Electrotechnology.

ABSTRACTS ON SCIENCE AND TECHNOLOGY IN JAPAN: ELECTRONICS AND COMMUNICATION. see COMMUNICATIONS — Abstracting, Bibliographies, Statistics

621.3 314   UN   ISSN 0066-3816
ANNUAL BULLETIN OF ELECTRIC ENERGY STATISTICS FOR EUROPE. (Text in English, French and Russian) 1956 (covering 1955) a., latest vol.29, 1983. price varies. Economic Commission for Europe (ECE), Palais des Nations, 1211 Geneva, Switzerland (Or United Nations Publications, Rm. DC2-853, New York, NY 10017)

621.3 539.7   UK   ISSN 0267-0372
C E G B ABSTRACTS. 1948. m. £50. Central Electricity Generating Board, 15 Newgate St., London EC1A 7AU, England. Ed. D.C. Levitt. circ. 500. Indexed: Fluidex.
  Formerly (until 1984): C E G B Digest.

CANADA. STATISTICS CANADA. COMMUNICATIONS AND ENERGY WIRE AND CABLE INDUSTRY/INDUSTRIE DES FILS ET CABLES ELECTRIQUES ET DE COMMUNICATIONS. see ELECTRICITY AND ELECTRICAL ENGINEERING

338.4 621.31   CN   ISSN 0380-951X
CANADA. STATISTICS CANADA. ELECTRIC POWER STATISTICS VOLUME 1: ANNUAL ELECTRIC POWER SURVEY OF CAPABILITY AND LOAD/STATISTIQUE DE L'ENERGIE ELECTRIQUE. VOLUME 1: ENQUETE ANNUELLE SUR LA PUISSANCE MAXIMALE ET SUR LA CHARGE DES RESEAUX. (Catalog 57-204) 1955. a. Can.$20($21) Statistics Canada, Communications Division, 3rd Floor, R.H. Coats Bldg., Ottawa, Ont. K1A 0T6, Canada TEL 613-993-7276. (Subscr. to: Publications Sales and Services, Ottawa, Ont. K1A 0T6, Canada) (also avail. in microform from MML)

621.3 690   CN   ISSN 0702-8083
CANADA. STATISTICS CANADA. ELECTRICAL CONTRACTING INDUSTRY/ENTREPRENEURS D'INSTALLATIONS ELECTRIQUES. (Catalogue 64-205) (Text in English and French) 1969. a. Can.$15($16) Statistics Canada, Communications Division, 3rd Floor, R.H. Coats Bldg., Ottawa, Ont. K1A 0T6, Canada TEL 613-993-7276. (Subscr. to: Publications Sales and Services, Ottawa, Ont. K1A 0T6, Canada) (also avail. in microform from MML)

621.3   US
ELECTRIC POWER INDUSTRY ABSTRACTS. Short title: E P I A. 1975. bi-m. Edison Electric Institute, c/o Utility Data Institute, 2011 I St., N.W., Ste. 700, Washington, DC 20006. Indexed: Pollut.Abstr.
  •Also available online. Vendors: Orbit Information Technologies.
  Former titles: Inforum: Energy-Environment Information System; Inforum: Environmental Report Data System (ISSN 0360-4985)

621.3 016   UK   ISSN 0036-8105
ELECTRICAL & ELECTRONICS ABSTRACTS. Alternative title: INSPEC, Section B. 1898. m. $1335. INSPEC, I.E.E., Station House, Nightingale Rd., Hitchin, Herts. SG5 1RJ, England (U.S. address: 445 Hoes Lane, Piscataway, NJ 08854) abstr. bibl. index. cum.index every 4 years. (also avail. in microform from MIM) Indexed: Chem.Abstr. Ergon.Abstr.
  •Also available online. Vendors: BRS, CEDOCAR, CISTI, Data-Star, DIALOG, European Space Agency, JICST, Orbit Information Technologies, STN International, University of Tsukuba.

621.38   UK   ISSN 0308-8375
ELECTRONIC ENGINEERING INDEX. 1965. 3/yr. Technical Indexes Ltd., Willoughby Rd., Bracknell, Berks RG12 4DW, England. Ed. Michael Ford. circ. 10,678.
  Formerly: Electronic Product Data.

ELECTRONICS AND COMMUNICATIONS ABSTRACTS. see COMMUNICATIONS — Abstracting, Bibliographies, Statistics

ELECTRONICS AND COMMUNICATIONS ABSTRACTS JOURNAL; an abstract journal involving the theory, design and application of electronic devices and systems. see COMMUNICATIONS — Abstracting, Bibliographies, Statistics

621.38 016   HU   ISSN 0231-0783
ELEKTROTECHNIKAI SZAKIRODALMI TAJEKOZTATO/ELECTRICAL ENGINEERING ABSTRACTS. 1949. m. 3900 Ft. Orszagos Muszaki Informacios Kozpont es Konyvtar (O.M.I.K.K.) - National Technical Information Centre and Library, Muzeum u. 17, Box 12, 1428 Budapest, Hungary (Subscr. to: Kultura, Box 149, H-1389 Budapest, Hungary) Ed. E. Vajda. abstr. index. circ. 520.
  Supersedes (as of 1982): Muszaki Lapszemle. Elektrotechnika/Technical Abstracts. Electrical Engineering (ISSN 0133-0373); Formerly: Muszaki Lapszemle. Elektrotechnika, Hiradastechnika (ISSN 0027-4968).

FINANCIAL STATISTICS OF SELECTED ELECTRIC UTILITIES. see ENERGY — Abstracting, Bibliographies, Statistics

621.3 016   SZ
I E C CATALOGUE OF PUBLICATIONS. (Text in English and French) 1960. a. with supplements twice per year. 12 Fr. International Electrotechnical Commission, 3 rue de Varembe, 1211 Geneva 20, Switzerland (Dist. in the U.S. by: American National Standards Institute, 1430 Broadway, New York, NY 10018) adv. index.

016 621.3   UK   ISSN 0950-477X
KEY ABSTRACTS - ARTIFICIAL INTELLIGENCE. 1975. m. $110 to non-members. INSPEC, I.E.E., Station House, Nightingale Rd., Hitchin, Herts. SG5 1RJ, England (U.S. distr. addr.: 445 Hoes Lane, Piscataway, NJ 08854) index.
  Formerly (until 1987): Key Abstracts - Systems Theory (ISSN 0306-5553)

621.38   UK   ISSN 0306-557X
KEY ABSTRACTS - ELECTRONIC CIRCUITS. 1975. m. $110 to non-members. INSPEC, I.E.E., Station House, Nightingale Rd., Hitchin, Herts. SG5 1RJ, England (U.S. addr.: 445 Hoes Lane, Piscataway, NJ 08854) Indexed: Agri.Eng.Abstr.

621.31 016   UK   ISSN 0950-4834
KEY ABSTRACTS - POWER SYSTEMS & APPLICATIONS. 1975. m. $110 to non-members. INSPEC, I.E.E., Station House, Nightingale Rd., Hitchin, Herts. SG5 1RJ, England (U.S. addr.: 445 Hoes Lane, Piscataway, NJ 08854) index.
  Formerly (until 1987): Key Abstracts - Power Transmission and Distribution (ISSN 0306-5561)

016 621.3   UK   ISSN 0950-4842
KEY ABSTRACTS - ROBOTICS & CONTROL. 1975. m. $110 to non-members. INSPEC, I.E.E., Station House, Nightingale Rd., Hitchin, Herts. SG5 1RJ, England (U.S. distr. addr.: 445 Hoes Lane, Piscataway, NJ 08854) index.
  Formerly (until 1987): Key Abstracts - Industrial Power and Control Systems (ISSN 0306-5596)

621.38 016   UK   ISSN 0950-4850
KEY ABSTRACTS - SEMICONDUCTOR DEVICES. 1975. m. $110 to non-members. INSPEC, I.E.E., Station House, Hitchin, Herts. SG5 1RJ, England (U.S. addr.: 445 Hoes Lane, Piscataway, NJ 08854) index.
  Formerly (until 1987): Key Abstracts - Solid State Devices (ISSN 0306-5537)

338.4 621.38   UK   ISSN 0306-5774
MACKINTOSH YEARBOOK OF WEST EUROPEAN ELECTRONICS DATA. 1973. a. $550. Benn Electronics Publications Ltd., Box 28, Luton, Beds. LU2 0ED, England. TEL 0582 421981. adv. illus. stat. circ. 450. (back issues avail.)

621.3 016   FR
P A S C A L EXPLORE. PART 20: ELECTRONIQUE ET TELECOMMUNICATIONS. 1985. 10/yr. 850 F. Centre National de la Recherche Scientifique, Centre de Documentation Scientifique et Technique, Service des Abonnements, 26 rue Boyer, 75971 Paris 20, France. abstr. index; cum.index. (also avail. in microform from MIM)
  Supersedes (1961-1984): Bulletin Signaletique. Part 145: Electronique; Bulletin Signaletique. Part 145: Eldoc-Electronique (ISSN 0240-8554); Bulletin Signaletique. Part 145: Electronique (ISSN 0301-3316); Which superseded in part: Bulletin Signaletique. Part 140: Electricite-Electronique (ISSN 0007-5353)

ELECTROCHEMISTRY

621.3 016   FR
P A S C A L FOLIO. PART 21: ELECTROTECHNIQUE. 1961. 10/yr. 570 F. Centre National de la Recherche Scientifique, Centre de Documentation Scientifique et Technique, Service des Abonnements, 26 rue Boyer, 75971 Paris 20, France. abstr. index; cum.index. (also avail. in microform from MIM)
    Supersedes (1961-1984): Bulletin Signaletique. Part 140: Electrotechnique (1983); Bulletin Signaletique. Part 140: Eldoc-Electrotechnique. (ISSN 0240-8562); Bulletin Signaletique. Part 140: Electrotechnique (ISSN 0301-3308); Which supersedes in part: Bulletin Signaletique. Part 140: Electricite-Electronique (ISSN 0007-5353)

621.38 016   UR   ISSN 0206-5452
REFERATIVNYI ZHURNAL. ELEKTRONIKA. 1963. m. 124 Rub. (148 Rub. including index) Vsesoyuznyi Institut Nauchno-Tekhnicheskoi Informatsii (VINITI), Baltiiskaya ul., 14, Moscow A-219, Russian S.F.S.R., U.S.S.R (Subscr. to: Mezhdunarodnaya Kniga, Dimitrova ul. 39, 113095 Moscow, Russian S.F.S.R., U.S.S.R.)
    Formerly: Referativnyi Zhurnal. Elektronika i ee Primenenie (ISSN 0486-2287)

621.3 016   UR   ISSN 0134-7772
REFERATIVNYI ZHURNAL. ELEKTROSVYAZ' 1967. m. 50 Rub. (64 Rub. including index) Vsesoyuznyi Institut Nauchno-Tekhnicheskoi Informatsii (VINITI), Baltiiskaya ul., 14, Moscow A-219, Russian S.F.S.R., U.S.S.R. (Subscr. to: Mezhdunarodnaya Kniga, Dimitrova ul. 39, 113095 Moscow, Russian S.F.S.R., U.S.S.R.)

621.38 016   UR
REFERATIVNYI ZHURNAL. ELEKTROTEKHNIKA. m. 180.80 Rub. (206 Rub. including index) Vsesoyuznyi Institut Nauchno-Tekhnicheskoi Informatsii (VINITI), Baltiiskaya ul., 14, Moscow A-219, Russian S.F.S.R., U.S.S.R. (Subscr. to: Mezhdunarodnaya Kniga, Dimitrova ul. 39, 113095 Moscow, Russian S.F.S.R., U.S.S.R.) Indexed: Agri.Eng.Abstr.
    Former titles: Referativnyi Zhurnal. Elektrotekhnika i Elektroenergetika (ISSN 0203-5189); Until Dec. 1980: Referativny Zhurnal. Elektrotekhnika i Energetika (ISSN 0034-2327)

338.4   US
STATISTICS FOR ELECTRIC UTILITIES IN PENNSYLVANIA. a. free. Department of Commerce, Bureau of Policy, Planning, & Systems Development, 474 Forum Bldg., Harrisburg, PA 17120. TEL 717-787-7532. illus.

621.381   US
U S S R REPORT: ELECTRONICS AND ELECTRICAL ENGINEERING. 1973. irreg., approx. 10/yr. $5 per no. U.S. Joint Publications Research Service, 1000 N. Glebe Rd., Arlington, VA 22201 TEL 703-841-1050. (Orders to: NTIS, Springfield, VA 22161)
    Formerly: U S S R and Eastern Europe Scientific Abstracts: Electronics and Electrical Engineering; Which was formed by the merger of: U S S R Scientific Abstracts: Electronics and Electrical Engineering; East European Scientific Abstracts: Electronics and Electrical Engineering.

ELECTROCHEMISTRY

see *Chemistry — Electrochemistry*

ELECTRONIC DATA PROCESSING

see *Computers — Electronic Data Processing*

ENCYCLOPEDIAS AND GENERAL ALMANACS

035   IT
ALMANACCO REPUBBLICANO. a. L.3000. Edizioni della Voce s.r.l., Via Tomacelli 146, 00186 Rome, Italy. Ed. Giuseppe Ciranna. adv. illus. circ. 15,000.

031 920   CN   ISSN 0065-650X
ALMANACH DU PEUPLE. 1869. a. Can.$4.95. Le Groupe Polygone Editeurs Inc., 11440 Albert-Hudon, Montreal, Que. H1G 3J9, Canada. TEL 514-327-4464. adv. bk. rev. circ. 133,000.

ALMANAKH GOMONU UKRAINY. see *ETHNIC INTERESTS*

ALMANAQUE NAUTICO REDUCIDO PARA USO CON MAQUINAS DE CALCULAR. see *ASTRONOMY*

036   PR
ALMANAQUE PUERTORRIQUENO (YEAR) 1978. a. (1984 edt. not published) $4 per no. Editorial Edil, Inc., Box 23088, U P R Station, Rio Piedras, PR 00931. Ed. Jose A. Toro Sugrones. circ. 3,000.

032   UK
ALTERNATIVE ENGLAND AND WALES. 1970. biennial (with quarterly supplements) £2.50. 65 Edith Grove, London SW10, England. Ed. Nicholas Saunders. bk. rev. charts. illus. index. circ. 30,000. (back issues avail.)
    Formerly: Alternative London.

030   US   ISSN 0196-0180
AMERICANA ANNUAL. 1923. a. $19.50. Grolier Incorporated, Sherman Turnpike, Danbury, CT 06816. TEL 203-797-3500.

036.9   BL
ANUARIO DELTA LAROUSSE. (Covers the events of the previous year) 1972. a. $13. Editora Delta S.A., Avda. Almirante Barroso 63-26, 20036 Rio de Janeiro, Brazil. Ed. Paulo Geiger. illus.

007   US   ISSN 0196-6316
AWARDS, HONORS AND PRIZES. (Vol.1, U.S. and Canada; Vol.2, International and Foreign) 1969. irreg., 6th edt., 1985. vol.1, $145; vol.2, $170. Gale Research Company, Book Tower, Detroit, MI 48226. TEL 313-961-2242. Ed. Gita Siegman. index.

031   US   ISSN 0068-1156
BRITANNICA BOOK OF THE YEAR. Variant Title: World Data Annual. 1938. a. $28.90. Encyclopaedia Britannica, Inc., 310 S. Michigan Ave., Chicago, IL 60604. TEL 312-347-7000. Ed. Daphne Daume. index.

CALIFORNIA HANDBOOK; a comprehensive guide to sources of current information and action. see *PUBLIC ADMINISTRATION*

CARITAS-KALENDER. see *RELIGIONS AND THEOLOGY*

CATHOLIC DIRECTORY (SAN FRANCISCO); Marin, San Francisco and San Mateo Counties. see *RELIGIONS AND THEOLOGY — Roman Catholic*

030   US   ISSN 0577-5728
CHASES' CALENDAR OF ANNUAL EVENTS; special days, weeks and months in the year. 1958. a. $14.95. Contemporary Books, Inc., 180 N. Michigan Ave., Chicago, IL 60601. TEL 313-234-5451. Eds. William D. Chase, Helen M. Chase. index. circ. 30,000.

031   US   ISSN 0069-5793
COLLIER'S YEARBOOK. (Supplement to: Collier's Encyclopedia and Merit Students Encyclopedia) 1939. a. $18.95 to libraries. Macmillan Educational Company, 866 Third Ave., New York, NY 10022. Ed. Robert Famighetti. index.

031   US
COMPTON'S YEARBOOK. 1958. a. $21.85 to individuals; institutions $21.20. Compton's Learning Co. (Subsidiary of: Encyclopaedia Britannica, Inc.) 310 S. Michigan Ave., Chicago, IL 60604. TEL 312-347-7000. Ed. Dale Good. adv. index.
    Formerly: Compton Yearbook (ISSN 0069-8091)

032   CN   ISSN 0315-7083
CORPUS ALMANAC & CANADIAN SOURCEBOOK. 1966. a. Can.$129. Corpus Information Services (Subsidiary of: Southam Communications Ltd.) 1450 Don Mills Rd., Don Mills, Ont. M3B 2X7, Canada. TEL 416-445-6641. Ed. Gordon Sova. bibl. charts. illus. index. circ. 4, 500. (back issues avail.)

030   UK   ISSN 0301-7761
DAILY MAIL YEAR BOOK. a. Associated Newspapers Group Ltd., Carmelite House, Carmelite St., London EC4Y 0JA, England. (back issues avail.)

DICTIONNAIRE DES COMMUNES (LAVAUZELLE ET CIE) see *PUBLIC ADMINISTRATION*

030   FR   ISSN 0073-4640
DICTIONNAIRES DU SAVOIR MODERNE; les idees, les oeuvres, les hommes. 1969. irreg. price varies. (Centre d'Etudes et de Promotion de la Lecture) Editions Denoel, 19 rue de l'Universite, Paris 7e, France.

032   CN   ISSN 0316-0734
DIRECTORY OF ASSOCIATIONS IN CANADA. 1973. a. Can.$125. Micromedia Limited, 158 Pearl St., Toronto, Ont. M5H 1L3, Canada. TEL 416-593-5211. Ed. Liba Berry. circ. 1,800.
    ●Also available online. Vendors: CISTI.

011   UK   ISSN 0070-5152
DIRECTORY OF BRITISH ASSOCIATIONS. 1965. biennial, latest no.8, 1985. £59($140) ‡ C.B.D. Research Ltd., 15 Wickham Rd., Beckenham, Kent BR3 2JS, England (Dist. in U.S. by: Gale Research Co., Penobscot Bldg., Detroit, MI 48226) Eds. G.P. Henderson, S.P.A. Henderson. index. circ. 6,000.

035   IT
DIZIONARIO ENCICLOPEDICO D'INFORMAZIONI. 1977. a. L.7000. Rusconi Editori Associati S.p.A., Via Vitruvio 43, 20124 Milan, Italy.

030 366   US   ISSN 0071-0202
ENCYCLOPEDIA OF ASSOCIATIONS. (In 3 vols: Vol.1, National Organizations of the U.S., Vol.2, Geographic-Executive Index; Vol.3, New Associations and Projects) 1956. a. vol.1, $212; vol.2, $200; vol.3, $210; vol.4, $185. Gale Research Company, Book Tower, Detroit, MI 48226. TEL 313-961-2242. Ed. Katherine Gruber.
    ●Also available online. Vendors: DIALOG.
    Formerly: Encyclopedia of American Associations (ISSN 0190-3071)

ENCYCLOPEDIA OF ECONOMICS. see *BUSINESS AND ECONOMICS — Management*

031   US   ISSN 0196-0172
ENCYCLOPEDIA YEAR BOOK. 1947. a. $18.45. Grolier Incorporated, Sherman Turnpike, Danbury, CT 06816. TEL 203-797-3500. Eds. James E. Churchill, Jr. charts. illus. stat. index.

940   UK   ISSN 0071-2302
EUROPA YEAR BOOK; a world survey. 1926. a. $265 for 2 vols. Europa Publications Ltd., 18 Bedford Sq., London WC1B 3JN, England.

030   US
FORD ALMANAC; for farm and home. 1954. a. $1.25. Almanac Co., Box 589, Woodstock, IL 60098. TEL 815-338-2053. Ed. Cliff Granschow. adv. illus. circ. 100,000.

030   UK   ISSN 0071-8084
FOULSHAM'S ORIGINAL OLD MOORE'S ALMANACK. 1867. a. 40p. W. Foulsham & Co. Ltd., Yeovil Road, Slough, Bucks., England.

030   IE   ISSN 0072-0887
GENUINE IRISH OLD MOORE'S ALMANAC. 1764. a. 76p. per copy. John Arigho & Sons (1964) Ltd., 16 Knocklyon Park, Temleogue, Dublin 16, Ireland. Ed. K. Ryan. adv. index. circ. 90,000.

032   MW
GUIDE TO PROFESSIONAL BODIES IN MALAWI. a. Centraf Associates Ltd., Box 3046, Chichiri, Blantyre 3, Malawi.

001.9 US
GUINNESS BOOK OF WORLD RECORDS.
(Editions in 25 other languages) 1955. a. $14.95. ‡
Sterling Publishing Co., Inc., Two Park Ave., New
York, NY 10016. TEL 212-532-7160. Ed. David A.
Boehm. bk. rev. illus. circ. 450,000.
Formerly: Guinness Book of Records (ISSN
0300-1679)

032 II ISSN 0073-4284
I N F A PRESS AND ADVERTISERS YEAR
BOOK. (Text in English) 1962. a. $25. (India News
and Feature Alliance) I N F A Publications, Jeevan
Deep Bldg., Parliament St., New Delhi 110001,
India. adv. circ. 3,000.

050 PL
INFORMATOR ROBOTNICZY. 1973. a. 50 Zl.
Panstwowe Wydawnictwo Naukowe, Ul. Miodowa
10, 00-251 Warsaw, Poland. illus.
Continues: Kalendarz Robotniczy.

035 IT
ISTITUTO DELLA ENCICLOPEDIA ITALIANA.
ANNUARIO. 1972. a. L.18000. Istituto della
Enciclopedia Italiana, Piazza Paganica 4, 00186
Rome, Italy.

035 IT
ISTITUTO DELLA ENCICLOPEDIA ITALIANA.
BIBLIOTHECA BIOGRAPHICA. irreg. price
varies. Istituto della Enciclopedia Italiana, Piazza
Paganica 4, 00186 Rome, Italy.

630 133.5 US
J. GRUBER'S HAGERS-TOWN TOWN AND
COUNTRY ALMANACK. 1797. a. $1.45. Gruber
Almanack Company, 111 W. Washington St., Box
609, Hagerstown, MD 21741-0609. TEL 301-733-
2530. Ed. Charles W. Fisher. circ. 175,000.

034 FR ISSN 0449-4733
JOURNAL DE L'ANNEE. 1966. a. Larousse, 17 rue
de Montparnasse, 75280 Paris Cedex 06, France.
illus.

089 HU ISSN 0133-9214
LUDAS MATYI EVKONYVE. 1970. a. $1.90.
Hirlapkiado Vallalat, Blaha Lujza ter 3, 1959
Budapest 8, Hungary (Subscr. to: Kultura, Box 149,
H-1389 Budapest, Hungary) Ed. Jozsef Arkus. adv.
illus. circ. 350,000.

017 US ISSN 0094-1484
MAGYAR EVKONYV. (Text in Hungarian) a. $5.
(Amerikai Magyar Szo) Hungarian Word, Inc., 130
E. 16th St., New York, NY 10003. TEL 212-254-
0397. illus. circ. 2,000.
Former titles: Magyar Naptar; Magyar Evkonyv.

039 YU ISSN 0541-9344
MAGYAR SZO NAPTARA. (Text in Hungarian)
1969. a. 58 din. Forum, Novi Sad, Vojvode Misica
1, Novi Sad, Yugoslavia. illus.

030 JA
MAINICHI DAILY NEWS. (Text in English) 1972.
a. 3200 Yen($17.50) Mainichi Newspapers, 1-1
Hitotsubashi, 1-Chome, Chiyoda-ku, Tokyo 100,
Japan. adv. charts. stat.
Formerly: Japan Almanach.

033 DK ISSN 0109-3347
MUNKSGAARDS SOCIAL AARBOG. (Text in
Danish, Norwegian and Swedish) 1984. a. Kr.115.
Munksgaard, Noerre Soegade 35, 1370 Copenhagen
K, Denmark.

030 US ISSN 0196-0148
NEW BOOK OF KNOWLEDGE ANNUAL; the
young people's book of the year. 1940. a. $16.95.
Grolier Incorporated, Sherman Turnpike, Danbury,
CT 06816. TEL 203-797-3500. Ed. Fern Mamberg.
(back issues avail.)

031 631 US ISSN 0078-4516
OLD FARMER'S ALMANAC. 1792. a. $2.25.
Yankee Publishing, Inc., Dublin, NH 03444. TEL
603-563-8111. Ed. Judson D. Hale, Sr. adv. circ. 3,
500,000. (reprint service avail. from UMI)

032 UK ISSN 0079-0362
PEARS CYCLOPAEDIA. 1897. a. £9.95. Pelham
Books Ltd., 27 Wrights Lane, London W8 5TZ,
England. Ed. Dr. Chris Cook. circ. 100,000.

032 UK
PEARS JUNIOR ENCYCLOPAEDIA. 1961. a.
£7.95. Pelham Books Ltd., 27 Wrights Lane,
London W8 5TZ, England. Ed. Edward Blishen.

948 038 NE ISSN 0079-8223
PYTTERSEN'S NEDERLANDSE ALMANAK;
jaarlijks verschijnend handboek van personen en
instellingen in Nederland en de Nederlandse
Antillen. (Text in Dutch; table of contents in
English) 1901. a. fl.125. Van Loghum Slaterns bv
Deventer, Deventer, Netherlands. Ed. J. Hanssen.
index. circ. 5,000.

031.02 US ISSN 0079-9831
READER'S DIGEST ALMANAC AND
YEARBOOK. 1966. a. $5.95. Readers Digest
Association, Inc., Pleasantville, NY 10570. TEL
914-769-7000. Ed. David C. Whitney. bk. rev.

REFERENCE ENCYCLOPEDIA OF THE
AMERICAN INDIAN. see *ETHNIC INTERESTS*

500 US ISSN 0080-7621
SCIENCE YEAR. 1965. a. price varies. World Book,
Inc., 510 Merchandise Mart Plaza, Chicago, IL
60654. TEL 312-245-3456. Ed. A. Richard Harmet.
cum.index.

309.23 UV
SECRETARIAT PERMANENT DES
ORGANISATIONS NON
GOUVERNEMENTALES. RAPPORT
D'ACTIVITIES. 1976. a. Secretariat Permanent des
Organisations Non Gouvernementales, B.P. 131,
Ouagadougou, Burkina Faso.

030 369 US ISSN 0080-8512
SEEKER'S GUIDE; a directory of unusual
organizations. 1961. irreg., latest edt., 1970. $5.60. ‡
Aurea Publications, Box 176, Allenhurst, NJ 07711.
TEL 201-531-4535. Ed. Alex Sandri White.

030 UK ISSN 0083-7067
WALKER'S OLD MOORE'S ALMANACK. 1844. a.
5p. W. Walker & Sons (Otley) Ltd., Victoria Works,
Otley, England.

032 UK ISSN 0083-9256
WHITAKER'S ALMANACK. 1869. a. £13.95. J.
Whitaker & Sons Ltd., 12 Dyott St., London WC1A
1DF, England (Dist. in U.S. by: Gale Research Co.,
Book Tower, Detroit, MI 48226)

031 US ISSN 0084-1382
WORLD ALMANAC AND BOOK OF FACTS.
1868. a. $5.95 paperback; $12.95 hardcover. Pharos
Books, 200 Park Ave., New York, NY 10166. TEL
212-692-3824. Ed. Mark S. Hoffman. index. circ. 1,
800,000. (also avail. in microform from BLH)
Formerly: World Almanac and Encyclopedia.

031 US ISSN 0084-1439
WORLD BOOK YEAR BOOK. (Supplement To:
World Book Encyclopedia) 1962. a. World Book,
Inc., 510 Merchandise Mart Plaza, Chicago, IL
60654. TEL 312-245-3456. Ed. A. Richard Harmet.
cum.index.

ENCYCLOPEDIAS AND GENERAL ALMANACS — Abstracting, Bibliographies, Statistics

314 NE ISSN 0303-6448
STATISTICAL YEARBOOK OF THE
NETHERLANDS. 1942. a. fl.88.50. Centraal
Bureau voor de Statistiek, Prinses Beatrixlaan 428,
Voorburg, Netherlands (Orders to: Staatsuitgeverij,
Christoffel Plantijnstraat, The Hague, Netherlands)

ENDOCRINOLOGY

see *Medical Sciences — Endocrinology*

ENERGY

Here are entered serials covering the economic, social and technical aspects of many types of energy sources.

see also Earth Sciences — Geology; Earth Sciences — Geophysics; Electricity and Electrical Engineering; Mines and Mining Industry; Petroleum and Gas; Physics — Nuclear Energy

539 665.5 AT ISSN 0157-6224
A A E C NUCLEAR NEWS. irreg. Australian
Atomic Energy Commission, Menai, N.S.W. 2234,
Australia. Ed. G. Carrard. illus.

531.64 621.48 SW
A E. no. 511, 1975. irreg. A B Atomenergi, Fack, S-
611 01 Nykoeping 1, Sweden.

A E C L REPORT SERIES. (Atomic Energy of
Canada Ltd.) see *PHYSICS — Nuclear Energy*

621.47 US ISSN 0731-8618
ADVANCES IN SOLAR ENERGY. AN ANNUAL
REVIEW OF RESEARCH AND
DEVELOPMENT. 1982. a. $95. (American Solar
Energy Society, Inc.) Plenum Publishing
Corporation, 233 Spring St., New York, NY 10013.
Eds. K.W. Boer, J. Duffie. Indexed: Biol.Abstr.

330 531.64 US ISSN 0192-558X
ADVANCES IN THE ECONOMICS OF ENERGY
AND RESOURCES. 1979. a. $23.75 to individuals;
institutions $47.50. J A I Press Inc., Box 1678, 36
Sherwood Pl., Greenwich, CT 06836. TEL 203-661-
7602. Ed. John R. Moroney. stat.

333.7 363.6 CN ISSN 0706-1420
ALBERTA ELECTRIC INDUSTRY, ANNUAL
STATISTICS. 1972. a. Can.$15. Energy Resources
Conservation Board, 640 5th Ave. S.W., Calgary,
Alta. T2P 3G4, Canada. TEL 403-297-8311. illus.
stat. Indexed: CS Ind.
Formerly (until 1979): Alberta Electric Industry,
Cumulative Annual Statistics.

ALBERTA'S RESERVE OF GAS: COMPLETE
LISTING. see *PETROLEUM AND GAS*

600 US ISSN 0097-2126
AMERICAN POWER CONFERENCE.
PROCEEDINGS. 1952. a. price varies. American
Power Conference, Illinois Institute of Technology,
Chicago, IL 60616. Ed. Patricia Dawkins. index.
cum.index: 1938-1963. circ. 3,400. Indexed:
Chem.Abstr.

531.64 US
AMERICAN SOLAR ENERGY SOCIETY.
ANNUAL MEETING. (Last meeting 1984,
Anaheim, California) 1976. a. American Solar
Energy Society, Inc., 2030 17th St., Boulder, CO
80302. TEL 303-443-3130. Eds. Gregory E. Franta,
Keith W. Haggard. Indexed: Eng.Ind. Energy
Info.Abstr.
Former titles: Progress in Solar Energy (ISSN
0731-860X); Supersedes (as of July, 1982):
International Solar Energy Society. American
Section. Annual Meeting. Proceedings (ISSN 0146-
4566)

621.47 US
AMERICAN SOLAR ENERGY SOCIETY.
PASSIVE CONFERENCE. ANNUAL MEETING.
vol.7, 1982. a. American Solar Energy Society, Inc.,
2030 17th St., Boulder, CO 80302-5404. Ed. John
W. Hayes. Indexed: Eng.Ind. Energy Info.Abstr.
Former titles: Progress in Passive Solar Energy
Systems (ISSN 0731-8626); Incorporates and
continues numbering of: National Passive Solar
Conference. Proceedings. (ISSN 0161-7443)

621.47 US
AMERICAN SOLAR ENERGY SOCIETY.
RESEARCH REPORTS. a. (American Solar
Energy Society, Inc.) Plenum Publishing
Corporation, 233 Spring St., New York, NY 10013.
Indexed: Eng.Ind. Energy Info.Abstr.

ANNUAL BOOK OF A S T M STANDARDS.
VOLUME 12.02. NUCLEAR (2), SOLAR, AND
GEOTHERMAL ENERGY. see
ENGINEERING — *Engineering Mechanics And Materials*

ENERGY

346.730   US   ISSN 0273-7000
ANNUAL ENERGY LITIGATION INSTITUTE. EFFECTIVE STRATEGIES AND TECHNIQUES.* a. Law & Business, Inc., 855 Valley Rd., Clifton, NJ 07013. TEL 201-472-7400.

531.6   US   ISSN 0362-1626
ANNUAL REVIEW OF ENERGY. 1976. a. $56. Annual Reviews Inc., 4139 El Camino Way, Box 10139, Palo Alto, CA 94306. TEL 415-493-4400. Ed. Jack M. Hollander. bibl. index. cum.index every 5 yrs. (back issues avail.; reprint service avail. from ISI) Indexed: Chem.Abstr. Curr.Cont. Sci.Cit.Ind. GeoRef. Ind.Sci.Rev.

621.47   US
ANNUAL SOLAR HEATING AND COOLING RESEARCH AND DEVELOPMENT BRANCH CONTRACTORS' MEETING. PROCEEDINGS. 3rd, 1979. a. U.S. Department of Energy, Solar Buildings Technical Division, 100 Independence Ave., S.W., Washington, DC 20585. TEL 202-586-8110. Ed. David M. Pellish.

ARAB SCHOOL ON SCIENCE AND TECHNOLOGY. PROCEEDINGS. see *ENGINEERING*

ATOMIC ENERGY OF CANADA. ANNUAL REPORT. see *PHYSICS — Nuclear Energy*

ATOMIC ENERGY POCKETBOOK. see *PHYSICS — Nuclear Energy*

531.64   380.1   AT
AUSTRALASIAN SOLAR INDEX AND BUYERS GUIDE. 1979. a. Aus.$25. Australian Syndicators Pty Ltd., Box 45, South Yarra, Vic. 3141, Australia.

AUSTRALIA. ENVIRONMENTAL STUDIES WORKING PAPERS. see *CONSERVATION*

531.64   BL   ISSN 0101-6636
BALANCO ENERGETICO NACIONAL. 1976. a. Ministerio das Minas e Energia, Esplanada dos Ministerios, Bloco J, 70056 Brasilia DF, Brazil. stat. circ. 8,000.

621.3   DK   ISSN 0109-4149
BEFOLKNINGENS ENERGISPAREBESTRAEBELSER. 1974. a. free. (Scantest, Institut for Scandinavisk Media og Markedsanalyse) Energi-Spareudvalget, Pilestraede 35/1, 1112 Copenhagen, Denmark.

500   US
BENCHMARK PAPERS ON ENERGY. (Each vol. has distinctive title) 1973. irreg., vol.10, 1983. price varies. Van Nostrand Reinhold Company, 7625 Empire Dr., Florence, KY 41042. TEL 606-525-6600. Eds. R. B. Lindsay, M. E. Hawley. illus. index.

531   BL
BOLETIM DE INDICADORES ENERGETICOS. 1984. irreg. free. Companhia Paulista de Forca e Luz, Assessoria de Pesquisa e Desenvolvimento, Caixa Postal 1808, 13100 Campinas, Brazil.

531.64   621.3   CN
BRITISH COLUMBIA. UTILITIES COMMISSION. ANNUAL REPORT. 1973. a. free. Utilities Commission, Fourth floor, 800 Smithe St., Vancouver, B.C. V6Z 2E1, Canada. TEL 604-660-4700. stat. circ. 2,000.
Formerly (until 1980): British Columbia. Energy Commission. Annual Report (ISSN 0703-086X); Supersedes: British Columbia Energy Board. Annual Report (ISSN 0524-5672)

531.64   621.3   UK
BRITISH GAS PLC. MONITOR. 1985. a. free. British Gas Plc., Research & Development Division, 152 Grosvenor Rd., London SW1V 3JL, England. Ed. J.S. Carmichael. charts. illus. patents. circ. 20, 000.
Formerly: British Gas Corporation. Monitor (ISSN 0268-3296)

C S I CONGRESSIONAL RECORD ABSTRACTS: ENERGY EDITION. see *PUBLIC ADMINISTRATION — Abstracting, Bibliographies, Statistics*

531.64   US
CALIFORNIA. STATE ENERGY COMMISSION. BIENNIAL REPORT. 1977. biennial. free. Energy Commission, 1516 Ninth St., Sacramento, CA 95814. TEL 916-324-3009.

537   CN   ISSN 0068-7901
CANADA. NATIONAL ENERGY BOARD. ANNUAL REPORT. a. National Energy Board, Ottawa, Ont. K1A 0E5, Canada. TEL 613-998-7192.

537   CN
CANADA. NATIONAL ENERGY BOARD. REASONS FOR DECISION. irreg. National Energy Board, 473 Albert St., Ottawa, Ont. K1A 0E5, Canada. TEL 613-998-7192.

338.2   CN   ISSN 0315-8233
CANADIAN GAS ASSOCIATION. MEMBERSHIP DIRECTORY. a. membership only. Canadian Gas Association, 55 Scarsdale Rd., Don Mills, Ont., Canada. TEL 416-447-6465. circ. controlled.

665.5   CN   ISSN 0068-8800
CANADIAN GAS ASSOCIATION. STATISTICAL SUMMARY OF THE CANADIAN GAS INDUSTRY. 1961. a. Can.$1. ‡ Canadian Gas Association, 55 Scarsdale Rd., Don Mills, Ont., Canada. TEL 416-447-6465.

665.5   CN
CANADIAN GAS ASSOCIATION DIRECTORY; utilities, transmission & production companies. 1966. a. Can.$8. Canadian Gas Association, 55 Scarsdale Rd., Don Mills, Ont. M3B 2R3, Canada. TEL 416-447-6465.
Former titles: Canadian Gas Utilities Directory (ISSN 0576-5269); Directory of Gas Utilities (ISSN 0315-8349)

333.8   CN   ISSN 0316-3547
CANADIAN GAS FACTS. a. Canadian Gas Association, 55 Scarsdale Road, Don Mills, Ont. M3B 2R3, Canada. TEL 416-447-6465.

531.64   621.3   665.5   CN
CANADIAN NATIONAL ENERGY FORUM PROCEEDINGS. 1974. irreg. price varies. World Energy Conference, Canadian National Committee, Suite 305, 130 Albert St., Ottawa, Ont. K1P 5G4, Canada.

CATALYST FOR ENVIRONMENT/ENERGY. see *ENVIRONMENTAL STUDIES*

CONSTRUCTION COSTS: U S STEAM ELECTRICAL PLANTS, 1970-1985. see *ELECTRICITY AND ELECTRICAL ENGINEERING*

621.3   DK   ISSN 0108-4011
DENMARK. ENERGIMINISTERIET. ENERGIFORSKNINGSPROGRAM; program for udbygning af Dansk energiforskning og udvikling. 1980. a. free. Energiministeriet, Slotholmsgade 1, DK-1216 Copenhagen K, Denmark. circ. 2,000.

DENMARK. FORSOEGSANSLAEG RISOE. RISOE-R. see *PHYSICS — Nuclear Energy*

531.64   UK   ISSN 0141-5689
DEPARTMENT OF ENERGY. PUBLICATIONS IN PRINT. 1977. a. free. Department of Energy, Library, Room 1020, Thames House South, Millbank, London SW1P 4QJ, England.

333.8   UK   ISSN 0307-0603
DIGEST OF UNITED KINGDOM ENERGY STATISTICS. 1974. a. Department of Energy, Thames House South, Millbank, London SW1P 4QJ, England (Avail. from H.M.S.O., P.O. Box 276, London SW8 5DT, England) illus.
Formerly: Great Britain. Department of Trade and Industry. Digest of Energy Statistics.

665.5   CN
DIRECTORY OF CERTIFIED APPLIANCES AND ACCESSORIES. a. Can.$18.50 (yearly revision service Can.$55) Canadian Gas Association, 55 Scarsdale Rd., Don Mills, Ont. M3B 2R3, Canada. TEL 416-447-6465.

531.64   620   IT
E N I ANNUAL REPORT. a. Ente Nazionale Idrocarburi, Piazzale Enrico Mattei 1, 00144 Rome, Italy. illus.

531.6   US
EARTHMIND NEWSLETTER. 1975. a. $2. 1728 Carver St., Redondo Beach, CA 90278-2820. Ed. Michael Hackleman. bk. rev. circ. 500.

621.3   CN   ISSN 0070-962X
ELECTRIC POWER IN CANADA. French Edition (ISSN 0821-8218) (Text and summaries in English and French) 1979. a. free. Department of Energy, Mines and Resources, Energy Sector, 580 Booth St., Ottawa, Ont. K1A 0E4, Canada. TEL 613-995-3065. Ed. C. Zwicker. circ. 7,500.

551.64   US
ELECTRIC RATE BOOK. 1986. a. $595. Casazza, Schultz and Associates, Inc., 1901 N. Fort Myer Dr., Ste. 503, Arlington, VA 22209. TEL 703-841-9644. Ed. Elizabeth A. Casazza. circ. 200.

531.64   DK
ENERGI NYT.* irreg., (approx. 4-6/yr.) Dansk Energi Information, Gl. Mont 4, 1147 Copenhagen K, Denmark. Ed. Ole Bischoff Kristensen. adv. circ. 74,000.

531.64   NE
ENERGIEONDERZOEK CENTRUM NEDERLAND. JAARVERSLAG. 1955. a. Energieonderzoek Centrum Nederland, Scheveningseweg 112, The Hague, Netherlands. circ. 2,000.

531.64   621.3   FI   ISSN 0782-2952
ENERGY. (Editions in English and Russian) 1985. a. Fmk.20($4) Finnish Energy Economy Association, Satamakatu 4, 00160 Helsinki, Finland. Ed. Avomaa Pentti. circ. 5,000. (back issues avail.)

531.64   US
ENERGY BALANCES OF O.E.C.D. COUNTRIES. (Text in English and French) 1976. a. $20. Organization for Economic Cooperation and Development, International Energy Agency, 1750 Pennsylvania Ave., N.W., Washington, DC 20006. (also avail. in microfilm)

531.64   GW   ISSN 0342-5665
ENERGY DEVELOPMENTS; journal of energy engineering. (Text in English) 1977. a. DM.30. Technischer Verlag Resch KG, Geigerstr. 13, 8032 Graefelfing, W. Germany (B.R.D.) (U.S. subscr. to: Lynn Western Inc., Box 2549, Rancho Palos Verdes, CA 90274) Ed. Jan Muehlstein. adv. charts. illus. patents. Indexed: Excerp.Med. Chi.Abstr.

531.64   SW   ISSN 0281-8515
ENERGY, ENVIRONMENT AND DEVELOPMENT IN AFRICA. (Text in English) 1984. irreg. Kr.75. Scandinavian Institute of African Studies and the Beijer Institute - Nordiska Afrikainstitutet, P.O. Box 1703, S-751 47 Uppsala, Sweden. Eds. Phil O'Keefe & Gordon T. Goodman. circ. 2,000.

531.64   DK   ISSN 0901-3768
ENERGY IN DENMARK; a report on energy planning. 1983. a. free. (Minstry of Energy) Bibliotekscentralen, Telegrafvej 5, DK-2750 Ballerup, Denmark.

531.64   UK
ENERGY INDUSTRIES COUNCIL CATALOGUE. biennial. £36. C.H.W. Roles & Associates Ltd., Rawplug House, London Rd., Kingston upon Thames, Surrey KT2 6NH, England. adv. circ. 5, 000.

531   US
ENERGY: LATIN AMERICAN INDUSTRIAL REPORT. (Avail. for each of 22 Latin American countries) 1985. a. $435 per country report per industry covered. Aurora International, Box 9099, Bridgeport, CT 06601-2099. TEL 203-368-0579. Ed. Andres C. Aquino.

531.64   US   ISSN 0882-3537
ENERGY POLICY STUDIES. a. $19.95. (Eds. John Byrne, Daniel Rich) Transaction Books, Rutgers University, New Brunswick, NJ 08903.

531.64   NE
ENERGY RESEARCH. 1980. irreg., no.6, 1984. price varies. Elsevier Science Publishers B.V., Box 211, 1000 AE Amsterdam, Netherlands. bibl.

621.3 UN
ENERGY STATISTICS YEARBOOK. (Text in English and French) 1952. a. $45. United Nations, Department of Economic and Social Affairs, Secretariat, New York, NY 10017 (Dist. by: United Nations Sales Section, Room A-3315, New York, NY; or Palais des Nations, CH-1211 Geneva 10, Switzerland)
  Former titles (until 1981): Yearbook of World Energy Statistics; (until 1978): World Energy Supplies (ISSN 0084-1749)

621.042 US ISSN 0161-6048
ENERGY TECHNOLOGY CONFERENCE. PROCEEDINGS. 1974. a. $69. Government Institutes, Inc., 966 Hungerford Dr., No. 24, Rockville, MD 20850. TEL 301-251-9250. Ed. Richard F. Hill. Indexed: Chem.Abstr. GeoRef. Key Title: Energy Technology.

531.6 DK ISSN 0900-419X
ENERGYLAB NEWSLETTER. 1985. irreg.,(approx. 3/4 yr.) free. Energy Research Laboratory, Niels Bohr Alle 25, 5230 Odense M, Denmark. illus.

ENVIRONMENTAL BIOLOGY. see ENVIRONMENTAL STUDIES

539.7 531.64 US
ENVIRONMENTAL COALITION ON NUCLEAR POWER NEWSLETTER. 1970. irreg. $6. Environmental Coalition on Nuclear Power, 433 Orlando Ave., State College, PA 16803. Ed. J.H. Johnsrud. bk. rev. illus. circ. 600.

500 600 US
EXXON BACKGROUND SERIES. 1971. irreg., latest Dec., 1984. free. Exxon Corporation, 1251 Ave. of the Americas, New York, NY 10020. TEL 212-333-6197. Ed. Werner Renberg.

531.64 665.5 338.91 AU
FACTS & FIGURES; a comparative statistical analysis. (Text in English) 1979. a. free. Organization of the Petroleum Exporting Countries, Obere Donaustrasse 93, A-1020 Vienna, Austria. Ed.Bd. bk. rev. circ. 10,000.

FINANCIAL POST SURVEY OF MINES AND ENERGY RESOURCES. see MINES AND MINING INDUSTRY

531.64 011 FI ISSN 0358-2019
FINLAND. TILASTOKESKUS. ENERGIATILASTOT/FINLAND. STATISTIKCENTRALEN. ENERGISTATISTIK. (Text in English, Finnish, Swedish) 1982. a. Fmk.20. Tilastokeskus, Annankatu 44, SF-00100 Helsinki 10, Finland.

531.6 DK
FORSKNINGSCENTER RISOE. AARSBERETNING/RISOE ANNUAL REPORT. (Text in Danish; summaries in English) 1977. a. free. Forskningscenter Risoe, Roskilde, Denmark.
  Former Titles: Forsoegsanlaeg Risoe. Aarsberetning (ISSN 0106-2557) & Beretning om Atomenergikommissionens Virksomhed.

531.6 DK
FORSKNINGSCENTER RISOE. ENERGI SYSTEMS GRUPPEN. ANNUAL PROGRESS REPORT. 1980. a. Kr.24.40. Forskningscenter Risoe, Roskilde, Denmark.
  Formerly: Forsoegsanlaeg Risoe. (ISSN 0107-9077)

FRANCE. COMMISSARIAT A L'ENERGIE ATOMIQUE. ANNUAL REPORT. see PHYSICS — Nuclear Energy

550 622 GE ISSN 0071-9390
FREIBERGER FORSCHUNGSHEFTE. MONTANWISSENSCHAFTEN: REIHE A. BERGBAU UND GEOTECHNIK, ARBEITSSCHUTZ UND SICHERHEITSTECHNIK, GRUNDSTOFF-VERFAHRENSTECHNIK, MASCHINEN- UND ENERGIETECHNIK. irreg. price varies. (Bergakademie Freiberg) VEB Deutscher Verlag fuer Grundstoffindustrie, Karl-Heine-Str. 27, DDR-7031 Leipzig, E. Germany (D.D.R.) Indexed: Chem.Abstr. Geotech.Abstr.

333 AG
FUNDACION BARILOCHE. INSTITUTO DE ECONOMIA DE LA ENERGIA. PUBLICACIONES. irreg. price varies. Fundacion Bariloche, Instituto de Economia de la Energia, Casilla de Correo 138, 8400 San Carlos de Bariloche - Rio Negro, Argentina.
  Supersedes in part: Fundacion Bariloche. Departamento de Recursos Naturales y Energia. Publicaciones; Formerly: Fundacion Bariloche. Programa de Recursos Naturales y Energia. Publicaciones (ISSN 0071-9846)

531.64 US
FUSION-FISSION ENERGY SYSTEMS REVIEW MEETING. PROCEEDINGS. 1978. irreg. $11.75. U.S. Department of Energy, Office of Fusion Energy, 1000 Independence Ave., S.W., Washington, DC 20585 TEL 202-252-5000. (Orders to: NTIS, Springfield, VA 22161) Ed. S. Locke Bogart. charts. illus. (also avail. in microfiche)

531.6 US
GAS CALORIMETER WORKSHOP. PROCEEDINGS. 1982. irreg. Fermi National Accelerator Laboratory, Batavia, IL 60510.
  (until 1985): Gas Sampling Calorimeter Workshop II; Former titles (until 1982): Gas Calorimeter Workshop.

GEOTHERMAL WORLD DIRECTORY. see EARTH SCIENCES — Geology

GREAT BRITAIN. DEPARTMENT OF ENERGY. DEVELOPMENT OF THE OIL AND GAS RESOURCES OF THE UNITED KINGDOM. see PETROLEUM AND GAS

GUIDE TO U S G S GEOLOGIC AND HYDROLOGIC MAPS. see EARTH SCIENCES

621.3 UK
HANDBOOK OF POWER DRIVES. 1977. irreg. £78. Trade & Technical Press Ltd., Crown House, Morden, Surrey, SM4 5EW, England.

531.64 DK
HANDELSMINISTERIETS ENERGIFORSKNINGSPROGRAM. 1978. a. Energistyrelsen, Strandgade 29, DK-1401 Copenhagen K, Denmark.

HARBINGER FILE; a descriptive directory of organizations concerned with environmental issues in California. see ENVIRONMENTAL STUDIES

HUTTON'S BUILDING SYSTEMS AND CONTROLS CATALOG. see CRIMINOLOGY AND LAW ENFORCEMENT — Security

363.6 II
INDIA. DEPARTMENT OF POWER. REPORT. (Text in English) 1975. a. Department of Power, Ministry of Energy, New Delhi, India.

531.64 665.5 UK
INSTITUTE OF ENERGY. REPORT AND ACCOUNTS. 1980. irreg. Institute of Energy, 18 Devonshire St., Portland Place, London W1N 2AU, England.

531.64 UK
INTERNATIONAL BUSINESS OPPORTUNITIES. OIL & GAS IN AFRICA. 1984. irreg. £90($180) I.C. Publications Ltd., P.O. Box 261, Carlton House, 69 Gt. Queen St., London WC2B 5BN, England.

531.64 UK
INTERNATIONAL BUSINESS OPPORTUNITIES. OIL & GAS IN THE MIDDLE EAST. 1984. irreg. £90($180) I.C. Publications Ltd., P.O. Box 261, Carlton House, 69 Gt. Queen St., London WC2B 5BN, England.

INTERNATIONAL COMMUNICATIONS AND ENERGY CONFERENCE (PROCEEDINGS)/ CONFERENCE INTERNATIONALE SUR LES COMMUNICATIONS ET L'ENERGIE (PROCEEDINGS) see COMMUNICATIONS

531.64 UN
INTERNATIONAL DIRECTORY OF NEW AND RENEWABLE ENERGY; information sources and research centres. 1982. irreg. Unesco, 7-9 Place de Fontenoy, 75700 Paris, France.

539.7 US ISSN 0742-5821
INTERNATIONAL DIRECTORY OF NUCLEAR UTILITIES. 1983. a. $195. Lotte, Ltd., Box 237, Contract Sta. 27, Lakewood, CO 80215. TEL 303-232-3026. Ed. Joseph H. Bach. adv. circ. 400.

531.64 US
INTERNATIONAL ENERGY ANNUAL. 1976. a. $4.75 per vol. U.S. Energy Information Administration, 1000 Independence Ave., Washington, DC 20585 TEL 202-252-8800. (Subscr. to Supt. of Documents, Washington, DC 20402) charts. Indexed: PROMT.

INTERNATIONAL GAS RESEARCH CONFERENCE. PROCEEDINGS. see PETROLEUM AND GAS

531.64 US
INTERNATIONAL POWER SYSTEMS. a. $15. (American Business Press, Inc.) McGraw-Hill Publications Co., 1221 Ave. of the Americas, New York, NY 10020. TEL 212-512-4724. Ed. Thomas C. Elliott.

INTERNATIONAL SYMPOSIUM ON WAVE AND TIDAL ENERGY. PROCEEDINGS. see WATER RESOURCES

621.3 UK
INTERNATIONAL SYMPOSIUM ON WIND ENERGY SYSTEMS. PROCEEDINGS. 1977. irreg., 4th, 1982. price varies. B H R A Fluid Engineering, Cranfield, Bedford MK43 0AJ, England (Dist. in U.S. by: Learned Information Inc., 143 Old Marlton Pike, Medford, NJ 08055)

531.64 UK
INTERNATIONAL WHO'S WHO IN ENERGY AND NUCLEAR SCIENCES. 1983. irreg. £90. Longman Group Ltd., Fourth Ave., Harlow, Essex CM19 5AA, England (Dist. in U.S. and Canada by: Gale Research Co. Ltd., Book Tower, Detroit, MI 48226)

INTERSOCIETY ENERGY CONVERSION CONFERENCE. PROCEEDINGS. see PHYSICS — Nuclear Energy

338 IT ISSN 0075-1650
ITALY. DIREZIONE GENERALE DELLE FONTI DI ENERGIA E DELLE INDUSTRIE DI BASE. BILANCI ENERGETICI. a. Direzione Generale delle Fonti di Energia, Rome, Italy.

JAARBOEK VAN DE OPENBARE GASVOORZIENING. see PETROLEUM AND GAS

551 US
KANSAS GEOLOGICAL SURVEY. ENERGY RESOURCES SERIES. 1973. irreg., no.25, 1985. price varies. Geological Survey, 1930 Constant Ave., Campus West, University of Kansas, Lawrence, KS 66046. TEL 913-864-3965.

KYOTO UNIVERSITY. RESEARCH REACTOR INSTITUTE. ANNUAL REPORTS. see CHEMISTRY — Inorganic Chemistry

531.64 UK ISSN 0269-4999
LONDON ENERGY GROUP DATA BOOK AND DIARY. 1986. a. £4.60($9) Ambient Press Ltd., P.O. Box 25, Lutterworth, Leics LE17 4FF, England. Ed. Jack Peach. circ. 20,000.

531.64 333.9 TZ
MAJI REVIEW. (Text in English) 1974. irreg., approx. a. Ministry of Water, Energy and Minerals, Research and Training Division, Box 35066, Dar es Salaam, Tanzania. illus. Indexed: GeoRef.

531.64 670 UK ISSN 0268-2311
MAJOR ENERGY COMPANIES OF EUROPE. 1985. a. £55($88) Graham & Trotman Ltd., Sterling House, 66 Wilton Rd., London SW1V 1DE, England (Distr. in U.S. and Canada by: Graham & Trotman Inc., 13 Park Ave., Gaithersburg, MD 20877) Ed. Ruth Whiteside.

531.64 622 CN
MANITOBA. ENERGY AND MINES. ANNUAL REPORT SERIES. 1980. a. Manitoba Energy and Mines, 555-330 Graham Ave., Winnipeg, MB R3C 4E3, Canada. TEL 204-945-6541. circ. 1,000.
  Formerly: Manitoba. Mineral Resources Division. Annual Report Series.

ENERGY

621.3   UK
MERSEYSIDE AND NORTH WALES
ELECTRICITY BOARD. REPORT AND
ACCOUNTS. a. Merseyside and North Wales
Electricity Board, Sealand Road, Chester, CH1
4LR, England.

621.3   GW   ISSN 0580-3403
MUSTERANLAGEN DER
ENERGIEWIRTSCHAFT. 1966. irreg. price varies.
Energiewirtschaft und Technik Verlagsgesellschaft
mbH, Wendelsteinstr. 8, Postfach 1229, 8032
Graefelfing, W. Germany (B.R.D.) Ed. Edmund
Graefen. bk. rev.

621.3   622.338   US   ISSN 0470-3219
NATIONAL STRIPPER WELL SURVEY. a.
Interstate Oil Compact Commission, Box 53127,
Oklahoma City, OK 73152. TEL 405-525-3556.

531.64   665.7   US
NATURAL GAS ANNUAL. a. $9.50. U.S. Energy
Information Administration, Forrestal Bldg.,
Washington, DC 20585. TEL 202-252-8800.
    Supersedes (after 1979): Natural Gas Production
and Consumption (ISSN 0732-6629)

531.64   340   US
NEW INITIATIVES IN ENERGY LEGISLATION;
a state by state guide. irreg. Energy Project,
Conference on Alternative State and Local Policies,
2000 Florida Ave., N.W., Washington, DC 20009.

531.64   AT   ISSN 0158-0809
NEW SOUTH WALES. ENERGY AUTHORITY.
ANNUAL REPORT. 1977. a. Energy Authority,
Pearl House, 1 Castlereagh St., Sydney, N.S.W.
2000, Australia. circ. 1,500.

NIHON UNIVERSITY. ATOMIC ENERGY
RESEARCH INSTITUTE. ANNUAL REPORT.
see *PHYSICS — Nuclear Energy*

531.64   CN
NORTHERN CANADA POWER COMMISSION.
ANNUAL REPORT/COMMISSION D'ENERGIE
DU NORD CANADIEN. REVUE ANNUELLE.
(Text in English and French) 1969. a. Northern
Canada Power Commission, Box 5700, rue L,
Edmonton, Alta. T6C 4J8, Canada. TEL 403-465-
3377. charts. illus.
    Former titles: Northern Canada Power
Commission. Annual Review (ISSN 0704-1551) &
Commission d'Energie du Nord Canadien. Revue de
l'Exploitation (ISSN 0704-1543)

NORTHROP UNIVERSITY LAW JOURNAL OF
AEROSPACE, BUSINESS AND TAXATION. see
AERONAUTICS AND SPACE FLIGHT

NORTHWEST ELECTRIC UTILITY DIRECTORY.
see *ELECTRICITY AND ELECTRICAL
ENGINEERING*

531.64   621.381   US
NOTABLE INDIVIDUALS. 1982. a. $70 per no.
Harpska Publishing Co., Box 3214, Thousand Oaks,
CA 91359. TEL 805-498-9700.

NUCLEAR ALMANAC/GENSHIRYOKU
NENKAN. see *PHYSICS — Nuclear Energy*

NUCLEAR POWER PLANTS IN THE WORLD/
GENSHIRYOKU HATSUDENSYO. see
PHYSICS — Nuclear Energy

531.64   614.8   US
NUCLEAR POWER SAFETY REPORT. 1979. a. $5
to individuals; institutions $10. Public Citizen's
Critical Mass Energy Project, 215 Pennsylvania
Ave., S.E., Washington, DC 20003. TEL 202-546-
4996. Ed. Ken Bossong. circ. 2,000.

531.64   US   ISSN 0364-6866
NUCLEAR REACTORS BUILT, BEING BUILT, OR
PLANNED IN THE UNITED STATES. a? $10
per no. U.S. Department of Energy, Office of
Scientific and Technical Information, Box 62, Oak
Ridge, TN 37831 (Subscr. to: NTIS, U.S.
Department of Commerce, Springfield, VA 22161)

O E C S ENERGY BULLETIN. (Organisation of
Eastern Caribbean States) see *STATISTICS*

531.64   US   ISSN 0271-2946
OCEAN THERMAL ENERGY CONVERSION
WORKSHOP. WORKSHOP PROCEEDINGS.
2nd, 1974. irreg. $30. (University of Miami,
Department for Renewable Energy) U.S.
Department of Energy, 1000 Independence Ave.,
S.W., Washington, DC 20585. TEL 202-586-5630.
(also avail. in microfiche)

OIL AND ARAB COOPERATION. ANNUAL
REVIEW. see *PETROLEUM AND GAS*

621.3   CN
ONTARIO ENERGY BOARD. ANNUAL REPORT.
1962. a. Can.$2. Ontario Energy Board, 14 Carlton
St., 9th floor, Toronto, Ont. M5B 1J2, Canada. TEL
416-598-4000. circ. 500.

531.64   FR
ORGANIZATION FOR ECONOMIC
COOPERATION AND DEVELOPMENT.
INTERNATIONAL ENERGY AGENCY.
ANNUAL REPORT ON ENERGY RESEARCH,
DEVELOPMENT AND DEMONSTRATION. a.
$35. Organization for Economic Cooperation and
Development, International Energy Agency, 1750
Pennsylvania Ave., N.W., Washington, DC 20006.

ORGANIZATION FOR ECONOMIC
COOPERATION AND DEVELOPMENT.
NUCLEAR ENERGY AGENCY. ACTIVITY
REPORT. see *PHYSICS — Nuclear Energy*

ORGANIZATION FOR ECONOMIC
COOPERATION AND DEVELOPMENT.
NUCLEAR ENERGY AGENCY. SUMMARY OF
NUCLEAR POWER AND FUEL CYCLE DATA
IN O E C D MEMBER COUNTRIES. see
PHYSICS — Nuclear Energy

ORGANIZATION OF ARAB PETROLEUM
EXPORTING COUNTRIES. ANNUAL ENERGY
REPORT. see *PETROLEUM AND GAS*

531.64   US
PETROLEUM SITUATION. 1950. irreg. free. Chase
Manhattan Bank, Energy Economics Division, One
Chase Manhattan Plaza, New York, NY 10015.
TEL 212-552-4168. Ed. David Behling. Indexed:
PROMT.
    Incorporating: Energy Report from Chase.

531.6   614.7   CN   ISSN 0708-918X
PLANETARY ASSOCIATION FOR CLEAN
ENERGY. NEWSLETTER. (Text in English) 1979.
irreg., (4-6/yr.) Can.$25($30) Planetary Association
for Clean Energy, Inc., 191 Promenade du Portage
600, Hull, Ont. J8X 2K6, Canada. TEL 613-236-
6265. Ed. Monique Michaud Michrowski. adv. bk.
rev. circ. 2,600. (back issues avail.)

621   PL   ISSN 0372-9796
POLITECHNIKA SLASKA. ZESZYTY NAUKOWE.
ENERGETYKA. (Text in Polish; summaries in
English and Russian) 1957. irreg. price varies.
Politechnika Slaska, W. Pstrowskiego 7, 44-100
Gliwice, Poland (Dist. by: Ars Polona, Krakowskie
Przedmiescie 7, 00-068 Warsaw, Poland) Ed.
Gerard Kosman. circ. 250. Indexed: Chem.Abstr.

531.64   UR
POLUTEHNILINE INSTITUUT TALLINN.
METODY STOKHASTICHESKOGO
UPRAVLENIYA REZHIMAMI
ENERGETICHESKIH SISTEM. (Subseries of its
Toimetised) (Text in Russian; summaries in English
or German) irreg. price varies. Polutehniline
Instituut Tallinn, Ehitajate tee 5, Tallinn, Estonian
S.S.R., U.S.S.R.
    Formerly: Polutehniline Instituut Tallinn. Metody
Upravleniya Rezhimami Energeticheskih Sistem.

621.3   537   UR
POLUTEHNILINE INSTITUUT TALLINN.
RASCHET ELEKTROMAGNITNYKH I
TEPLOVYKH REZHIMOV
MAGNITOGIDRODINAMICHESKIKH I
LINEINYKH ELEKTRODVIGATELEI. (Subseries
of Its Toimetised) (Text in Russian; summaries in
English or German) irreg. price varies. Polutehniline
Instituut Tallinn, Ehitajate tee 5, Tallinn, Estonian
S.S.R., U.S.S.R.

531.64   PO   ISSN 0377-2233
PORTUGAL. ESTATISTICAS DA ENERGIA:
CONTINENTE, ACORES E MADEIRA. (Text in
French and Portuguese) 1969. a. Esc.525. Instituto
Nacional de Estatistica, Servicos Centrais, Av.
Antonio Jose de Almeida, 1078 Lisbon Codex,
Portugal (Orders to: Imprensa Nacional, Casa da
Moeda, Direccao Comercial, rua D. Francisco
Manuel de Melo 5, 1000 Lisbon, Portugal)
    Formerly: Estatisticas da Energia: Continente e
Ilhas Adjacentes.

531.64   US
POWER AUTHORITY OF THE STATE OF NEW
YORK. ANNUAL REPORT. 1931. a. free. Power
Authority, 10 Columbus Circle, New York, NY
10019. TEL 212-397-6200. Ed. Susan Gessner. circ.
12,000.

PRODUCTION COSTS: OPERATING STEAM
ELECTRIC PLANTS. see *ELECTRICITY AND
ELECTRICAL ENGINEERING*

531.64   IT
PRODUZIONE E CONSUMO DI ENERGIA
ELETTRICA IN ITALIA. a. free. Ente Nazionale
per l'Energia Elettrica, Direzione della
Programmazione, Via Marini 3, 00198 Rome, Italy.

531.4   CN
QUEBEC (PROVINCE) DIRECTION GENERALE
DE L'ENERGIE. RAPPORT ANNUEL-
ENERGIE QUEBEC.* a. Editeur Officiel du
Quebec, 1283 Bd. Charest Ouest, Quebec, P.Q.
G1N 2C9, Canada. TEL 413-643-3895. illus.

531   644   UK   ISSN 0268-330X
R & D DIGEST. 1977. a. free. British Gas Plc.,
Research & Development Division, 152 Grosvenor
Rd., London SW1V 3JL, England. Ed. B. Bellwood.
charts. illus. circ. 10,000. (back issues avail.)

RADIOACTIVE REPORTER. see
ENVIRONMENTAL STUDIES

531.64   US
RELIABILITY REVIEW. 1970. a. North American
Electric Realiability Council, 101 College Rd., E.,
Research Park, Princeton, NJ 08540. TEL 609-452-
8060. circ. 6,000.
    Formerly (until 1985): Overall Reliability and
Adequacy of the North American Bulk Powder
Systems. Annual Review.

531.64   US
RENEWABLE ENERGY MANUFACTURERS
LISTS: BIOMASS FUELS. a. $4. Synerjy, Box
4790, Grand Central Sta., New York, NY 10017.

531.64   US
RENEWABLE ENERGY MANUFACTURERS
LISTS: HEAT CONSERVATION. a. $5. Synerjy,
Box 4790, Grand Central Sta., New York, NY
10017.
    Formerly: Renewable Energy Manufacturers
Lists: Heat Conversion.

531.64   US
RENEWABLE ENERGY MANUFACTURERS
LISTS: SOLAR ENERGY. a. $6. Synerjy, Box
4790, Grand Central Sta., New York, NY 10017.

531.64   US
RENEWABLE ENERGY MANUFACTURERS
LISTS: WIND AND HYDRO POWER. a. $4.
Synerjy, Box 4790, Grand Central Sta., New York,
NY 10017.

333.7   622   CN   ISSN 0380-4275
RESERVES OF COAL, PROVINCE OF ALBERTA.
1972. a. Can.$25. Energy Resources Conservation
Board, 640 5th Ave. S.W., Calgary, Alta. T2P 3G4,
Canada. TEL 403-297-8311. illus. Indexed: CS Ind.

333.7   622.338   CN   ISSN 0380-4305
SCHEDULE OF WELLS DRILLED FOR OIL AND
GAS IN ALBERTA. 1938. a. Can.$500. Energy
Resources Conservation Board, 640 5th Ave. S.W.,
Calgary, Alta. T2P 3G4, Canada. TEL 403-297-
8311. (also avail. in microfiche; back issues avail)

333.8   GW
SCHRIFTENREIHE AKTUELLE FRAGEN DER
ENERGIEWIRTSCHAFT. irreg., no. 9, 1976. price
varies. R. Oldenbourg Verlag GmbH, Rosenheimer
Str. 145, 8000 Munich 80, W. Germany (B.R.D.)

ENERGY

621.47 338 US ISSN 0197-2030
SOLAR COLLECTOR MANUFACTURING
ACTIVITY. a. $2.75. U.S. Energy Information
Administration, Forrestal Bldg., Washington, DC
20585. TEL 202-252-8800.
 Formerly: Solar Collector Manufacturing Activity
and Applications in the Residential Sector.

621.47 NE
SOLAR ENERGY RESEARCH AND
DEVELOPMENT IN THE EUROPEAN
COMMUNITY. SERIES. A. SOLAR ENERGY
APPLICATIONS TO DWELLINGS. 1982. irreg.
price varies. (Commission of the European
Communities, Directorate-General Information
Marketing and Innovation, EI) D. Reidel
Publishing Co., Box 17, 3300 AA Dordrecht,
Netherlands (And 190 Old Derby St., Hingham,
MA 02043)

621.47 NE
SOLAR ENERGY RESEARCH AND
DEVELOPMENT IN THE EUROPEAN
COMMUNITY. SERIES B: THERMO-
MECHANICAL SOLAR POWER PLANTS. 1983.
irreg. price varies. (Commission of the European
Communities, Directorate-General Information
Marketing and Innovation, EI) D. Reidel
Publishing Co., Box 17, 3300 AA Dordrecht,
Netherlands (And 190 Old Derby St., Hingham,
MA 02043)

621.47 NE
SOLAR ENERGY RESEARCH AND
DEVELOPMENT IN THE EUROPEAN
COMMUNITY. SERIES C. PHOTOVOLTAIC
POWER GENERATION. 1982. irreg. price varies.
(Commission of the European Communities,
Directorate-General Information Marketing and
Innovation, EI) D. Reidel Publishing Co., Box 17,
3300 AA Dordrecht, Netherlands (And 190 Old
Derby St., Hingham, MA 02043)

621.47 NE
SOLAR ENERGY RESEARCH AND
DEVELOPMENT IN THE EUROPEAN
COMMUNITY. SERIES D. PHOTOCHEMICAL,
PHOTOELECTROCHEMICAL AND
PHOTOBIOLOGICAL PROCESSES. 1982. irreg.
price varies. (Commission of the European
Communities, Directorate-General Information
Marketing and Innovation, EI) D. Reidel
Publishing Co., Box 17, 3300 AA Dordrecht,
Netherlands (And 190 Old Derby St., Hingham,
MA 02043) Indexed: Chem.Abstr.

621.47 NE
SOLAR ENERGY RESEARCH AND
DEVELOPMENT IN THE EUROPEAN
COMMUNITY. SERIES E. ENERGY FROM
BIOMASS. 1981. irreg. price varies. (Commission
of the European Communities, Directorate-General
Information Marketing and Innovation, EI) D.
Reidel Publishing Co., Box 17, 3300 AA Dordrecht,
Netherlands (And 190 Old Derby St., Hingham,
MA 02043)

621.47 NE
SOLAR ENERGY RESEARCH AND
DEVELOPMENT IN THE EUROPEAN
COMMUNITY. SERIES F. SOLAR RADIATION
DATA. 1982. irreg. price varies. (Commission of
the European Communities, Directorate-General
Information Marketing and Innovation, EI) D.
Reidel Publishing Co., Box 17, 3300 AA Dordrecht,
Netherlands (And 190 Old Derby St., Hingham,
MA 02043)

621.47 NE
SOLAR ENERGY RESEARCH AND
DEVELOPMENT IN THE EUROPEAN
COMMUNITY. SERIES G. WIND ENERGY.
1983. irreg. price varies. (Commission of the
European Communities, Directorate-General
Information Marketing and Innovation, EI) D.
Reidel Publishing Co., Box 17, 3300 AA Dordrecht,
Netherlands (And 190 Old Derby St., Hingham,
MA 02043)

621.47 NE
SOLAR ENERGY RESEARCH AND
DEVELOPMENT IN THE EUROPEAN
COMMUNITY. SERIES H. SOLAR ENERGY IN
AGRICULTURE AND INDUSTRY. irreg. price
varies. (Commission of the European Communities,
Directorate-General Information Marketing and
Innovation, EI) D. Reidel Publishing Co., Box 17,
3300 AA Dordrecht, Netherlands (And 190 Old
Derby St., Hingham, MA 02043)

621.47 US
SOLAR ENERGY RESEARCH AND
DEVELOPMENT REPORTS. irreg. U.S.
Department of Energy, 1000 Independence Ave.,
S.W., Washington, DC 20585. TEL 202-586-1539.

621.47 US
SOLAR ENGINEERING. a. American Society of
Mechanical Engineers, Solar Energy Division, 345
E. 47th St., New York, NY 10017. Ed. W.D.
Turner.

531.64 330.9 314 EI
STATISTICAL OFFICE OF THE EUROPEAN
COMMUNITIES. GAS PRICES. (Text in English
and French) 1971. a. Statistical Office of the
European Communities, B.P. 1903, L-2920
Luxembourg, Luxembourg. Ed.Bd. circ. 2,000. (back
issues avail.)

STRATHCLYDE OIL REGISTER. see BUSINESS
AND ECONOMICS — Trade And Industrial
Directories

531.64 US
TOPICS IN ENERGY. 1982. irreg., vol.3, 1984.
Springer-Verlag, 175 Fifth Ave., New York, NY
10010 TEL 212-460-1500. (Also Berlin, Heidelberg,
Tokyo and Vienna)

531.64 UN
UNITED NATIONS. ECONOMIC COMMISSION
FOR ASIA AND THE PACIFIC. ENERGY
RESOURCES DEVELOPMENT SERIES. 1954.
irreg., no.27, 1984. price varies. Economic
Commission for Asia and the Pacific (ESCAP),
United Nations Bldg., Rajadamnern Ave., Bangkok
2, Thailand (Dist. by: United Nations Publications,
Room DC2-0853, New York, NY 10017; or
Distribution and Sales Section, Palais des Nations,
CH-1211 Geneva 10, Switzerland)

531.64 US ISSN 0161-1674
U.S. DEPARTMENT OF ENERGY. OFFICE OF
STATE AND LOCAL PROGRAMS. ANNUAL
REPORT TO THE PRESIDENT AND THE
CONGRESS ON THE STATE ENERGY
CONSERVATION PROGRAM. a. U.S.
Department of Energy, Office of State and Local
Programs, Washington, DC 20461. TEL 202-252-
5000. Key Title: Annual Report to the President
and the Congress on the State Energy Conservation
Program.

351.64 US ISSN 0161-5807
U.S. ENERGY INFORMATION
ADMINISTRATION. ANNUAL REPORT TO
CONGRESS. a. free. U.S. Energy Information
Administration, Forrestal Bldg., Washington, DC
20585. TEL 202-252-8800.

531.64 UY
URUGUAY. UNIDAD ASESORA DE
PROMOCION INDUSTRIAL. MEMORIA DE
ACTIVIDADES. 1980. a. Ministerio de Industria y
Energia, Montevideo, Uruguay.

531.64 DK ISSN 0108-4615
VARMEFORSYNINGSPLANLAEGNING:
STATUS. 1981. a. free. Energistyrelsen,
Landemaerket II, 1119 Copenhagen K, Denmark.
illus.

354.941 AT
WESTERN AUSTRALIA. STATE ENERGY
COMMISSION. ANNUAL REPORT. 1976. a.
State Energy Commission, Perth, W.A., Australia.
Ed. John Terrell. illus. circ. 6,000.

WHO'S WHO IN CIVIL ENGINEERING, EARTH
SCIENCES & ENERGY. see ENGINEERING —
Civil Engineering

531.64 GW ISSN 0720-3926
WIND-ENERGIE. 1970. a. DM.28($12) Wind-
Energie, Sekretariat, Gielsdorfer Str. 16, 5300 Bonn,
W. Germany (B.R.D.) Ed. Walter Schonball. adv.
bk. rev. circ. 1,200.

WIND ENERGY ABSTRACTS; the international
wind power abstracts journal. see ENERGY —
Abstracting, Bibliographies, Statistics

620 US ISSN 0891-639X
WIND ENERGY AND DIESEL INSTALLATIONS
INTERNATIONAL (YEAR) 1986. a. $65.
Windbooks, Inc., Box 4008, St. Johnsbury, VT
05819. TEL 802-748-2425. Ed. Farrell Smith Seiler.
adv. bibl. charts. illus. stat. tr.lit. circ. 635.

531.64
WIND ENERGY WORKSHOP. PROCEEDINGS.
3rd, 1978. biennial. U.S. Department of Energy,
Division of Solar Technology, Washington, DC
20545 TEL 202-252-5000. (Order from: Supt. of
Documents, Washington DC 20402)

WOODHEAT. see HEATING, PLUMBING AND
REFRIGERATION

531.64 640 US
WOODHEAT. 1984. a. $6. Energy Publications, Inc.,
Box 2008, Laconia, NH 03247. TEL 603-528-4285.
Ed. Jason Perry. adv. tr.lit. circ. 175,000. (reprint
service avail.)
 Formerly: Home Energy.

531.64 UK ISSN 0261-7633
WORLD ENERGY BUSINESS CENTRE
REFERENCE BOOK AND BUYERS' GUIDE.
1982. a. Sterling Publications Ltd., 86-88 Edgware
Rd., London W2 2YW, England.

531.64 FR
WORLD ENERGY CONFERENCE. DIRECTORY
OF ENERGY INFORMATION CENTRES IN
THE WORLD. (Text in English & French) 1976.
triennial, latest 3rd, 1983. $44. Institut Francais de
l'Energie, 3 rue Henri Heine, 75016 Paris, France.

363.6 FR ISSN 0084-1722
WORLD ENERGY CONFERENCE. PLENARY
CONFERENCES. TRANSACTIONS. triennial,
12th, 1983, New Delhi; 13th, 1986, Cannes. $155.
French National Committee of the W E C, 89 blvd.
Haussmann, 75008 Paris, France.

621.3 UK ISSN 0084-1730
WORLD ENERGY CONFERENCE. SURVEY OF
ENERGY RESOURCES. 1962. every 6 years
(updated statistical tables every 3 years) £25. Alan
Armstrong and Associates Ltd., 72 Park Rd.,
London NW1 4SH, England.

531.64 UK
WORLD ENERGY CONFERENCE. TECHNICAL
DATA ON FUEL. irreg., latest edt. 7th. Scottish
Academic Press Ltd., 33 Montgomery St.,
Edinburgh EH7 5JX, England. Eds. J.W. Rose, J.R.
Cooper.

531.64 UK
WORLD ENERGY DIRECTORY. 1981. irreg., 2nd
edt., 1985. £120. Longman Group Ltd., Fourth
Ave., Harlow, Essex CM19 5AA, England (Dist. in
U.S. and Canada by: Gale Research Co. Ltd., Book
Tower, Detroit, MI 48226)

531.64 US
WORLD ENERGY SURVEY. 1979. irreg., latest
1981. $5. (Rockefeller Foundation) World Priorities,
Inc., Box 25140, Washington, DC 20007. TEL 202-
965-1661. Ed. Ruth Leger Sivard. circ. 10,000.
 Formerly: Wilderness Energy Survey.

531.64 665.5 US ISSN 0731-2369
WORLDWIDE SYNTHETIC FUELS AND
ALTERNATE ENERGY DIRECTORY. 1982. a.
$50. PennWell Publishing Co., Box 1260, Tulsa, OK
74101 (Subscr. to: PennWell Directories, Box
21278, Tulsa, OK 74121) Ed. Robert M. Wilkerson.
adv.

300-MW-THTR-KERNKRAFTWERK HAMM-
UENTROP, PROJEKTINFORMATION. see
ELECTRICITY AND ELECTRICAL
ENGINEERING

ENERGY — Abstracting, Bibliographies, Statistics

531.64   TH
A I T REPORTS AND PUBLICATIONS ON RENEWABLE ENERGY RESOURCES. ABSTRACTS. (Text in English) 1979. a. $40 membership; $75 to institutions. Asian Institute of Technology, Renewable Energy Resources Information Center, G.P.O. Box 2754, Bangkok 10501, Thailand. Ed. H.A. Vespry. adv. cum.index. circ. 600. (back issues avail.) Indexed: Geotech.Abstr.

621 016   US   ISSN 0148-446X
ABSTRACT NEWSLETTER: ENERGY. w. $109. U.S. National Technical Information Service, 5285 Port Royal Rd., Springfield, VA 22161. TEL 703-487-4630. Ed. Linda J. LaGarde. index. (back issues avail.)
  Former titles: Weekly Abstract Newsletter: Energy; Weekly Government Abstracts. Energy.

531.64   JA   ISSN 0287-5012
ABSTRACTS ON SCIENCE AND TECHNOLOGY IN JAPAN: RENEWABLE ENERGY. (Text in English) 1981. q. 14,000 Yen. Japan Information Center of Science and Technology - Nihon Kagaku Gijutsu Joho Senta, 5-2, Nagata-cho, 2-Chome, Chiyoda-Ku, Tokyo 100, Japan. circ. 1,000.

ANNUAL BULLETIN OF ELECTRIC ENERGY STATISTICS FOR EUROPE. see *ELECTRICITY AND ELECTRICAL ENGINEERING — Abstracting, Bibliographies, Statistics*

338 314   UN
ANNUAL BULLETIN OF GENERAL ENERGY STATISTICS FOR EUROPE. (Text in English, French and Russian) 1970 (covering 1967 & 1968) a., latest vol.16, 1983. price varies. Economic Commission for Europe (ECE), Palais des Nations, 1211 Geneva 10, Switzerland (Or United Nations Publications, Rm. DC2-853, New York, NY 10017)

531.64 310   BL
ANUARIO ESTATISTICO DE ENERGIA ELECTRICA. 1970. a. Cr.$5000. Companhia Energetica de Sao Paulo, Divisao de Estudos do Mercado de Energia Eletrica, Av. Angelica, 2565, 15 Andar, 01227 Sao Paulo, Brazil. circ. 1,000.

ATOMIC ENERGY OF CANADA. LIST OF PUBLICATIONS. see *PHYSICS — Abstracting, Bibliographies, Statistics*

531.64   AT   ISSN 0727-2596
AUSTRALIAN ENERGY STATISTICS. 1981. a. Aus.$4.10. Australian Government Publishing Service, G.P.O. Box 84, Canberra, A.C.T. 2601, Australia.

531.64   BL
BIBLIOGRAFIA BRASILEIRA DE ENERGIA NUCLEAR. 1981. a. Cr.$25000($45) Comissao Nacional de Energia Nuclear, Centro de Informacoes Nucleares, Rio de Janeiro, Brazil. circ. 500.

531.64 639.9 016   AT   ISSN 0816-1070
C R R E R I S RENEWABLE ENERGY INDEX. 1981. q. Aus.$50. C.S.I.R.O., Editorial and Publications Service, 314 Albert St., East Melbourne, Victoria 3002, Australia. bibl. index. circ. 600. (back issues avail.)
  Formerly: Commonwealth Regional Renewable Energy Resources Index (ISSN 0159-6845); Supersedes: Australian Renewable Energy Resources Index (ISSN 0155-9443)

CANADA. STATISTICS CANADA. ELECTRIC POWER STATISTICS VOLUME 1: ANNUAL ELECTRIC POWER SURVEY OF CAPABILITY AND LOAD/STATISTIQUE DE L'ENERGIE ELECTRIQUE. VOLUME 1: ENQUETE ANNUELLE SUR LA PUISSANCE MAXIMALE ET SUR LA CHARGE DES RESEAUX. see *ELECTRICITY AND ELECTRICAL ENGINEERING — Abstracting, Bibliographies, Statistics*

318   BL
COMPANHIA PARANAENSE DE ENERGIA. INFORME ESTATISTICO ANUAL. 1971. a. free. Companhia Paranaense de Energia, Sup. de Planejamento e Estudos, Rua Voluntarios da Patria, 233 10 Andar, 80000 Curitiba, Parana, Brazil. stat. charts. circ. 1,500. (back issues avail.)

CURRENT BIBLIOGRAPHIES ON SCIENCE AND TECHNOLOGY: METALLURGY, NATURAL RESOURCES & ENERGY. see *METALLURGY — Abstracting, Bibliographies, Statistics*

621.3   UK   ISSN 0269-7513
ELECTRICITY COUNCIL ABSTRACTS BULLETIN. 1977. m. free. Electricity Council, Intelligence Branch, 30 Millbank, London SW1P 4RD, England. Ed. A. Goldfinch. circ. controlled.
  Incorporating (as of 1985): Economics, Management and Marketing & Management Aspects of Computers; Electricity Utilisation and Energy Abstracts; Electrical Distribution and Installations.

620 016   US   ISSN 0093-8408
ENERGY ABSTRACTS. 1974. m. $470 domestic; foreign $520. Engineering Information, Inc., 345 E. 47th St., New York, NY 10017. TEL 212-705-7600.
  Incorporates: Energy Conversion Abstracts (ISSN 0093-8416)

531.6 016   US   ISSN 0098-5104
ENERGY ABSTRACTS FOR POLICY ANALYSIS. 1975. m. $72. U.S. Department of Energy, Office of Scientific and Technical Information, Box 62, Oak Ridge, TN 37831 TEL 615-576-1155. (Subscr. to: Supt. of Documents, Washington, DC 20402) Ed. M. Catherine Grissom. abstr. index. (back issues avail.) Indexed: Petrol.Abstr.

614.7 016   US   ISSN 0094-6281
ENERGY INDEX. 1973. a. $285. E I C Intelligence, Inc., 48 W. 38 St., New York, NY 10018. TEL 212-944-8500. Ed. Marc Sherman. abstr. charts. stat. index. (magnetic tape; back issues avail.) Indexed: GeoRef.

620 016   US   ISSN 0147-6521
ENERGY INFORMATION ABSTRACTS. 1976. 10/yr. $800. E I C Intelligence, Inc., 48 W. 38 St., New York, NY 10018. TEL 212-944-8500.
●Also available online. Vendors: DIALOG, European Space Agency, Orbit Information Technologies.

531.64   US
ENERGY INFORMATION INDEX/ABSTRACTS ANNUAL. 1975. a. $525. E I C Intelligence, Inc., 48 W. 38th St., New York, NY 10018. TEL 800-223-6275. Ed. Marc Sherman. (back issues avail.)
  Formerly: Energy Information Abstracts Annual (ISSN 0147-6521)

531.6 016   US   ISSN 0160-3604
ENERGY RESEARCH ABSTRACTS. 1976. s-m. $146. U.S. Department of Energy, Office of Scientific and Technical Information, Box 62, Oak Ridge, TN 37831 TEL 615-576-1155. (Subscr. to: Supt. of Documents, Washington DC 20402) index. cum.index. (also avail. in microform from MIM, UMI; reprint service avail. from UMI) Indexed: Chem.Abstr. Anal.Abstr. Petrol.Abstr.
  Formerly: E R D A Energy Research Abstracts (ISSN 0360-3571)

318.1   BL   ISSN 0512-350X
ESTATISTICA BRASILEIRA DE ENERGIA/BRAZILIAN ENERGY STATISTICS. (Text in Portuguese and English; summaries in English) 1965. a. free controlled circulation. World Energy Conference, Comite Nacional Brasileiro, Av. Presidente Vargas, 642, Rio de Janeiro, Brazil. Eds. Antonio Carlos Holtz, Jose L. Alqueres. charts. stat. circ. 1,000. (back issues avail.)

621.31 310   US
FINANCIAL STATISTICS OF SELECTED ELECTRIC UTILITIES. 1938. a. $23. U.S. Energy Information Administration, Forrestal Bldg., Washington, DC 20585 TEL 202-252-8800. (Orders to: Supt. of Documents, Washington, DC 20402) (also avail. in microfiche from NTI)
  Former titles: Statistics of Privately Owned Electric Utilities in the United States (ISSN 0161-9004) & Statistics of Electric Utilities in the United States. Classes A and B Privately Owned Companies (ISSN 0083-0828)

FINLAND. TILASTOKESKUS. ENERGIATILASTOT/FINLAND. STATISTIKCENTRALEN. ENERGISTATISTIK. see *ENERGY*

338 314   GW
GERMANY (FEDERAL REPUBLIC, 1949-). STATISTISCHES BUNDESAMT. FACHSERIE 19, UMWELTSCHUTZ, REIHE 2: WASSERVERSORGUNG UND ABWASSERBESEITIGUNG. (Consists of several subseries) irreg. price varies. W. Kohlhammer-Verlag GmbH, Abt. Veroeffentlichungen des Statistischen Bundesamtes, Philipp-Reis-Str. 3, Postfach 421120, 6500 Mainz 42, W. Germany (B.R.D.)

531.64   JA
HOKURIKU NO DENKI TO KOGYO/ELECTRICITY AND INDUSTRY IN HOKURIKI. (Text in Japanese) 1955. a. Hokuriku Denki Kyokai, Toyama Bldg., 5-13 Sakurabashi Douri, Toyama City 930, Japan. Ed.Bd. circ. 180.

378   NO
NORWAY. STATISTISK SENTRALBYRAA. ELEKTRISITESSTATISTIKK/ELECTRICITY STATISTICS. (Subseries of its Norges Offisielle Statistikk) 1937. a. Kr.45. Statistisk Sentralbyraa, Box 8131 Dep., 0033 Oslo 1, Norway. circ. 1,400.

621   FR
ORGANIZATION FOR ECONOMIC COOPERATION AND DEVELOPMENT. ENERGY STATISTICS. (Text in English and French) 1965. a. price varies. Organization for Economic Cooperation and Development, 2 rue Andre-Pascal, 75775 Paris Cedex 16, France (U.S. orders to: O.E.C.D. Pubications and Information Center, 1750 Pennsylvania Ave., N.W., Washington, D.C. 20006) (also avail. in microfiche)
  Formerly: Organization for Economic Cooperation and Development. Statistics of Energy.

REFERATIVNYI ZHURNAL. ELEKTROTEKHNIKA. see *ELECTRICITY AND ELECTRICAL ENGINEERING — Abstracting, Bibliographies, Statistics*

531.64   UR   ISSN 0203-5308
REFERATIVNYI ZHURNAL. ENERGETIKA. 1955. m. 173 Rub. (196.80 Rub. with index) Vsesoyuznyi Institut Nauchno-Tekhnicheskoi Informatsii (VINITI), Baltiiskaya ul. 14, Moscow A-219, Russian S.F.S.R., U.S.S.R. (Subscr. to: Mezhdunarodnaya Kniga, Dimitrova ul. 39, 113095 Moscow, Russian S.F.S.R., U.S.S.R.)

531.64 016   UR   ISSN 0203-6436
REFERATIVNYI ZHURNAL. TEPLO I MASSOBMEN. 1976. m. 33 Rub. (35.20 Rub. with index) Vsesoyuznyi Institut Nauchno-Tekhnicheskoi Informatsii (VINITI), Baltiiskaya ul. 14, Moscow A-219, Russian S.F.S.R., U.S.S.R. (Subscr. to: Mezhdunarodnaya Kniga, Dimitrova ul. 39, 113095 Moscow, Russian S.F.S.R., U.S.S.R.)

621.47   US
SOLAR BIBLIOGRAPHY. 1976. irreg. U.S. Department of Housing and Urban Development, Office of Policy Development and Research, 451 Seventh St., S.W., Washington, DC 20410 (Orders to: Supt. of Documents, Washington, DC 20402)

621   US
SOLAR ENERGY INDEX. 1980. biennial. (Arizona State University) Pergamon Press, Maxwell House, Fairview Park, Elmsford, NY 10523. TEL 914-592-7700. Ed. Geroge Machovec. (also avail. in microfilm)

531.6 310   SA
SOUTH AFRICA. CENTRAL STATISTICAL SERVICE. CENSUS OF ELECTRICITY, GAS AND STEAM. (Report No. 15-01) 1963. a. Central Statistical Service, Private Bag X44, Pretoria 0001, South Africa (Orders to: Government Printer, Bosman St., Private Bag X85, Pretoria 0001, South Africa)
  Formerly: South Africa. Department of Statistics. Census of Electricity, Gas and Steam (ISSN 0301-8105)

ENGINEERING 469

330   EI   ISSN 0081-489X
STATISTICAL OFFICE OF THE EUROPEAN COMMUNITIES. ENERGY STATISTICS. YEARBOOK. (Text in Dutch, English, French, German, Italian) a. $28.50. Rue Alcide de Gasperi, B.P. 1907, Luxembourg, Luxembourg (Dist. in the U.S. by: European Community Information Service, 2100 M St., NW, Suite 707, Washington, DC 20037)

310   621.3   FR
STATISTIQUES DE L'INDUSTRIE GAZIERE. a. Ministere de la Recherche et de l'Industrie, Direction du Gaz, de l'Electricite et du Charbon, 101 rue de Grenelle, 75007 Paris, France.

310   380.5   US
U.S. DEPARTMENT OF TRANSPORTATION. NATIONAL TRANSPORTATION STATISTICS. ANNUAL; a supplement to the summary of national transportation statistics. a. U.S. Department of Transportation, Statistical Information Reporting Branch, Office of the Assistant Secretary for Policy, Plans, and International Affairs, Washington, DC 20590 TEL 202-655-4000. (Orders to Supt. of Documents, Washington, DC 20402) illus.
Formed by the 1977 merger of: U.S. Department of Transportation. Energy Statistics & U.S. Department of Transportation. Summary of National Transportation Statistics (ISSN 0360-8980)

318   531.64   VE
VENEZUELA. MINISTERIO DE ENERGIA Y MINAS. APENDICE ESTADISTICO. (Supplement to: Venezuela. Ministerio de Energia y Minas. Memoria) a. Ministerio de Energia y Minas, Oficina de Estudios Economicos Energeticos, Caracas, Venezuela. charts.

318   531.64   VE
VENEZUELA. MINISTERIO DE ENERGIA Y MINAS. MEMORIA. a. Ministerio de Energia y Minas, Oficina de Estudios Economicos Energeticos, Torre Norte, Centro Simon Bolivar, Caracas, Venezuela (Subscr. to: Ministerio de Energia y Minas, Biblioteca, Torre Oeste, Parque Central Piso 2, Caracas-Venezuela)

620   US   ISSN 0277-2140
WIND ENERGY ABSTRACTS; the international wind power abstracts journal. 1983. m. $145. WindBooks, Box 4008, St. Johnsbury, VT 05819-4008. TEL 802-748-2425. Ed. Farrell Smith Seiler. adv. bk. rev. circ. 1,250. (looseleaf format; back issues avail.)

620   016   UK   ISSN 0263-0915
WIND ENGINEERING ABSTRACTS. 1982. 4/yr. £60($100) Multi-Science Publishing Co. Ltd., 107 High St., Brentwood, Essex CM14 4RX, England. index.

ENGINEERING

see also Engineering – Chemical Engineering; Engineering – Civil Engineering; Engineering – Computer Applications; Engineering – Engineering Mechanics and Materials; Engineering – Hydraulic Engineering; Engineering – Mechanical Engineering; Electricity and Electrical Engineering

A E. see ENERGY

620   US   ISSN 0164-0917
A E E DIRECTORY OF ENERGY PROFESSIONALS. biennial. (Association of Energy Engineers) Fairmont Press, Box 14227, Atlanta, GA 30324. TEL 404-447-5314.

620   690   US
A E M S SEMINAR (PAPERS) 1970. a. $20. American Engineering Model Society, Box 2066, Aiken, SC 29802. TEL 803-649-6710. circ. 750. (reprint service avail. from ISI)

620   US
A S A E MONOGRAPH SERIES. 1971. irreg. American Society of Agricultural Engineers, 2950 Niles Rd., St. Joseph, MI 49085. TEL 616-429-0300. Ed. James Basselman.

620   DK
AARET RUNDT. a. Teknisk Forlag A-S, Skelbaekgade 4, 1717 Copenhagen V, Denmark. adv. circ. 53,400.

671.7   US   ISSN 0363-8065
ABRASIVE ENGINEERING SOCIETY. ABRASIVE USAGE CONFERENCE. PROCEEDINGS. Variant title: Annual International Technical Conference and Exhibit. 1962. a. price varies. Abrasive Engineering Society, 1700 Painters Run Rd., Pittsburgh, PA 15243. index.
Formerly: American Society for Abrasive Methods. Technical Conference. Proceedings (ISSN 0066-006X)

660.63   US   ISSN 0065-2210
ADVANCES IN BIOCHEMICAL ENGINEERING. 1972. irreg., vol.33, 1986. Springer-Verlag, 175 Fifth Ave., New York, NY 10010 TEL 212-460-1500. (Also Berlin, Heidelberg, Tokyo and Vienna) Eds. T.K Ghose, A. Fiechter. (reprint service avail. from ISI) Indexed: Chem.Abstr. Ind.Med. Biotech.Abstr. Food Sci.& Tech.Abstr.

ADVANCES IN BIOENGINEERING. see BIOLOGY

ADVANCES IN CRYOGENIC ENGINEERING. see PHYSICS — Heat

ADVANCES IN NUCLEAR SCIENCE AND TECHNOLOGY. see PHYSICS — Nuclear Energy

ALLIANCE FOR ENGINEERING IN MEDICINE AND BIOLOGY. PROCEEDINGS OF THE ANNUAL CONFERENCE. see MEDICAL SCIENCES

AMERICAN ACADEMY OF ENVIRONMENTAL ENGINEERS. CONSULTANT DIRECTORY. see ENVIRONMENTAL STUDIES

AMERICAN ACADEMY OF ENVIRONMENTAL ENGINEERS. ROSTER. see ENVIRONMENTAL STUDIES

650   657   US   ISSN 0065-7158
AMERICAN ASSOCIATION OF COST ENGINEERS. TRANSACTIONS OF THE ANNUAL MEETING. 1967. a. $45 to non-members; members $32.50. American Association of Cost Engineers, 308 Monongahela Bldg, Morgantown, WV 26505. TEL 304-296-8444. Eds. Betsy Humphreys, Betty Wiley. circ. 1,500. (also avail. in microform from UMI; reprint service avail. from UMI)

620   US   ISSN 0071-0393
AMERICAN ASSOCIATION OF ENGINEERING SOCIETIES. ENGINEERING MANPOWER COMMISSION. ENGINEERING AND TECHNOLOGY DEGREES. (Former name of organization: Engineers Joint Council) a. $200 (or Part 1, $75; Part 2, $100; Part 3 $75) American Association of Engineering Societies, Engineering Manpower Commission, 415 2 St. N.E., Ste. 200, Washington, DC 20002-4994.

331.7   620   US   ISSN 0071-0407
AMERICAN ASSOCIATION OF ENGINEERING SOCIETIES. ENGINEERING MANPOWER COMMISSION. ENGINEERING AND TECHNOLOGY ENROLLMENTS. Variant title: Engineering Enrollment Data. (Former name of organization: Engineers Joint Council) a. $200 (or $100 each part) American Association of Engineering Societies, Engineering Manpower Commission, 415 2 St. N.E., Ste. 200, Washington, DC 20002-4994.

331.7   620   US   ISSN 0071-0415
AMERICAN ASSOCIATION OF ENGINEERING SOCIETIES. ENGINEERING MANPOWER COMMISSION. ENGINEERS' SALARIES: SPECIAL INDUSTRY REPORT. (Former name of organization: Engineers Joint Council) a. $225. American Association of Engineering Societies, Engineering Manpower Commission, 415 2 St. N.E., Ste. 200, Washington, DC 20002-4994.

331.7   620   US   ISSN 0071-0423
AMERICAN ASSOCIATION OF ENGINEERING SOCIETIES. ENGINEERING MANPOWER COMMISSION. PROFESSIONAL INCOME OF ENGINEERS. (Former name of organization: Engineers Joint Council) 1953. a. $75. American Association of Engineering Societies, Engineering Manpower Commission, 415 2 St. N.E., Ste. 200, Washington, DC 20002-4994.

620   US
AMERICAN ASSOCIATION OF ENGINEERING SOCIETIES. ENGINEERING MANPOWER COMMISSION. SALARIES OF ENGINEERS IN EDUCATION. 1972. biennial. $80. American Association of Engineering Societies, Engineering Manpower Commission, 415 2 St. N.E., Ste 200, Washington, DC 20002-4994. Ed. Patrick J. Sheridan.

620   US   ISSN 0190-1052
AMERICAN SOCIETY FOR ENGINEERING EDUCATION. ANNUAL CONFERENCE PROCEEDINGS. a. $55 to non-members; members $45. American Society for Engineering Education, 11 Dupont Circle, N.W., Suite 200, Washington, DC 20036. TEL 202-293-7080.

AMERICAN SOCIETY FOR PHOTOGRAMMETRY AND REMOTE SENSING. TECHNICAL PAPERS FROM THE ANNUAL MEETING. see GEOGRAPHY

620.86   US
AMERICAN SOCIETY OF SAFETY ENGINEERS. PROCEEDINGS. PROFESSIONAL CONFERENCE. a. $10 to members; non-members $12. American Society of Safety Engineers, 1800 E. Oakton St., Des Plaines, IL 60018-2187. TEL 312-692-4121.

620   SP
ANALES DE LA UNIVERSIDAD HISPALENSE. SERIE: INGENIERIA. irreg. price varies. Universidad de Sevilla, San Fernando 4, Seville, Spain.

ANALYTICAL CALORIMETRY. see PHYSICS — Heat

ANNUAIRE DE L'ACTIVITE NUCLEAIRE FRANCAISE. see PHYSICS — Nuclear Energy

ANNUAL BOOK OF A S T M STANDARDS. VOLUME 12.01. NUCLEAR ENERGY (1) see ENGINEERING — Engineering Mechanics And Materials

ANNUAL CONFERENCE ON ACTIVATED SLUDGE PROCESS CONTROL. PROCEEDINGS. see PUBLIC HEALTH AND SAFETY

ANNUAL REVIEW OF BIOPHYSICS AND BIOPHYSICAL CHEMISTRY. see BIOLOGY — Biophysics

APPLIED PHYSICS AND ENGINEERING. see PHYSICS

620   US   ISSN 0275-939X
APPLIED RESEARCH SUMMARY OF AWARDS. 1979. a. U.S. National Science Foundation, 1800 G St., N.W., Washington, DC 20550. TEL 202-655-4000.

620   531.624   US   ISSN 0730-7845
ARAB SCHOOL ON SCIENCE AND TECHNOLOGY. PROCEEDINGS. 1983. irreg, latest 1984. price varies. (Arab School on Science and Technology, SY) Hemisphere Publishing Corporation, 79 Madison Ave., New York, NY 10016. bibl. charts. illus. index. (back issues avail.)

621.9   US
ASSEMBLY TECHNOLOGY BUYER'S GUIDE. 1962. a. Hitchcock Publishing Co., Hitchcock Bldg., Wheaton, IL 60188. TEL 312-665-1000. Ed. Walter Maczka. adv. circ. 40,000. (reprint service avail. from UMI)
Former titles: Assembly Engineering Master Catalog (ISSN 0066-8702) & Assembly Directory and Handbook (ISSN 0066-8699)

ENGINEERING

620 IV
ASSOCIATION DES INGENIEURS ET TECHNICIENS AFRICAINS DE COTE D'IVOIRE. ANNUAIRE.* a. Association des Ingenieurs et Techniciens Africains de Cote d'Ivoire, Autoroute de Port-Bouet, Boite Postale 794, Abidjan, Ivory Coast.

ASSOCIATION FOR INTEGRATED MANUFACTURING TECHNOLOGY. PROCEEDINGS. see *TECHNOLOGY: COMPREHENSIVE WORKS*

620 FR ISSN 0066-9237
ASSOCIATION FRANCAISE DES INGENIEURS ET CHEFS D'ENTRETIEN. ANNUAIRE.* a. Entreprise Moderne d'Edition, 17 rue Vieta, 75017 Paris, France (Subscr. Address: 9 rue du Roussillon-Zone Industrielle, 91220 Bretigny-sur-Orge, France)

620.2 II
ASSOCIATION OF INDIAN ENGINEERING INDUSTRY. HANDBOOK OF STATISTICS. (Text in English) 1963. a. price varies. Association of Indian Engineering Industry, Secretary, 172 Jorbaugh, New Delhi 110003, India. Ed. Tarun Das. adv. circ. 1,000.
Continues: Indian Engineering Association. Handbook of Statistics (ISSN 0073-6333)

620 AT ISSN 0084-6996
AUSTRALASIAN SOCIETY OF ENGINEERS. ENGINEERS HANDBOOK.* 1954/55. a. contr. free circ. Australasian Society of Engineers, 422-424 Kent St., Sydney, N.S.W. 2000, Australia.

AUSTRALIA. ATOMIC ENERGY COMMISSION. RESEARCH ESTABLISHMENT. A A E C/E. see *PHYSICS — Nuclear Energy*

AUSTRALIA. ATOMIC ENERGY COMMISSION. RESEARCH ESTABLISHMENT. A A E C/M. see *PHYSICS — Nuclear Energy*

AUSTRALIA. NATIONAL CAPITAL DEVELOPMENT COMMISSION. TECHNICAL PAPERS. see *HOUSING AND URBAN PLANNING*

620 AT ISSN 0159-2955
AUSTRALIAN ENGINEERING DIRECTORY. a. Aus.$72. Technical Indexes Pty. Ltd., 4 Kembla St., East Cheltenham, Vic. 3192, Australia (Subscr. to: Technical Indexes Pty. Ltd., P.O. Box 98, Cheltenham, Vic. 3192, Australia) Ed. Ross Mackay. circ. 5,000.

620 UK ISSN 0067-5709
B E M A ENGINEERING DIRECTORY. 1937. a. £8 for non-members. Bristol and West of England Engineering Manufacturers Association Ltd., BEMA House, 4 Broad Plain, Bristol BS2 0NG, England. Ed. W.A.J. Williams. adv. circ. 2,500.

620 BG ISSN 0070-8186
BANGLADESH UNIVERSITY OF ENGINEERING AND TECHNOLOGY, DACCA. TECHNICAL JOURNAL.* (Text in English) 1962. a. Bangladesh University of Engineering and Technology, Ramna, Dacca 2, Bangladesh.
Supersedes: Technical Journal of the University of Dacca's Ahsanullah Engineering College.

620 US
BIOMEDICAL ENGINEERING AND INSTRUMENTATION SERIES. 1976. irreg., vol.8, 1981. price varies. Marcel Dekker, Inc., 270 Madison Ave., New York, NY 10016.

620 TU
BOGAZICI UNIVERSITY JOURNAL: ENGINEERING. (Text in English or Turkish) 1973. a. $10. Bogazici Universitesi, Box 2, Istanbul, Turkey.

620 BL ISSN 0067-9607
BOLETIM DE ENGENHARIA DE PRODUCAO.* 1962. irreg. Universidade de Sao Paulo, Departamento de Engenharia de Electricidade, Cidade Universitaria, "Armando de Salles Oliveira", C.P.8191, Sao Paulo, Brazil.

620 CL
BOLETIN INGENIERIA COMERCIAL. 1975. irreg. free. Universidad Catolica de Valparaiso, Escuela de Ingenieria Comercial, Pilcomayo 478, Cerro Concepcion, Valparaiso, Chile. adv. circ. 300.

620 US
BOLTON LANDING CONFERENCE. PROCEEDINGS. 3rd, 1970. irreg., 4th, 1975. $32. Claitors Publishing Division, 3165 S. Arcadian, Box 3333, Baton Rouge, LA 80821. TEL 504-344-0476. Ed.Bd. illus.

620 US ISSN 0068-1008
BRIGHAM YOUNG UNIVERSITY. COLLEGE OF ENGINEERING SCIENCES AND TECHNOLOGY. ANNUAL ENGINEERING SYMPOSIUM. ABSTRACTS. 1960. a. price varies. Brigham Young University Press, 205 University Press Bldg., Provo, UT 84602. circ. 500.

620 US
CALIFORNIA INSTITUTE OF TECHNOLOGY. DIVISION OF ENGINEERING AND APPLIED SCIENCE. RESEARCH REPORT. 1953/54. biennial. free. California Institute of Technology, Division of Engineering and Applied Science, Mail Code 104-44, Pasadena, CA 91125. circ. 2,500.
Former titles: California Institute of Technology. Division of Engineering and Applied Science. Annual Report; California Institute of Technology. Division of Engineering and Applied Science. Report of Research and Other Activities (ISSN 0068-5658)

620 621.9 CN ISSN 0068-8665
CANADIAN ENGINEERING & INDUSTRIAL YEAR BOOK. 1945. a. Can.$35($50) Lloyd Publications of Canada, Box 262, West Hill, Ont. M1E 4R5, Canada. TEL 416-686-2131. Ed. J. Lloyd. adv. index. circ. 9,500.
Formerly: Canadian Engineering and Machinery Year Book.

620 690 US
CATALOG OF MODEL SERVICES AND SUPPLIES. 1975. irreg. $5. American Engineering Model Society, Box 2066, Aiken, SC 29802. TEL 803-649-6710. Ed. R.J. Hale. circ. 500. (reprint service avail. from ISI)

620 US
CENTER FOR HIGH ENERGY FORMING. INTERNATIONAL CONFERENCE. PROCEEDINGS.* irreg. $25. Denver Research Institute, Box 10127, Denver, CO 80210.

620 JA ISSN 0009-6202
CHUBU INSTITUTE OF TECHNOLOGY. MEMOIRS/CHUBU KOGYO DAIGAKU. KIYO. (Text in English or Japanese; summaries mainly in English, occasionally in French or German) 1965. irreg., (1-2/yr.) exchange basis to libraries. Chubu Institute of Technology - Chubu Kogyo Daigaku, Kasugai, Nagoya-Sub. 487, Japan. Ed.Bd. bibl. charts. illus. circ. 1,000. Indexed: Appl.Mech.Rev. Chem.Abstr. Sci.Abstr. Jap.Period.Ind. Nucl.Sci.Abstr.
Formerly: Chubu Institute of Technology. Bulletin.

620 SP
COLECCION INGENIERIA. 1982. irreg., no.1, 1982. price varies. (Universidad de Navarra, Escuela Tecnica Superior de Ingenieros Industriales) Ediciones Universidad de Navarra, S.A., Plaza de los Sauces 1 y 2, Baranain, Pamplona, Spain.

620 SP
COLECCION TEMAS BASICOS DE INGENIERIA. irreg. Editorial Gustavo Gili, S.A., Rosellon 87-89, Barcelona 15, Spain.

620 VE
COLEGIO DE INGENIEROS DE VENEZUELA. DIRECTORIO.* a. Colegio de Ingenieros de Venezuela, Apdo 2006, Bosque Los Caobos, Caracas 101, Venezuela. adv.

620 378 US
COLLEGE - INDUSTRY EDUCATION CONFERENCE. PROCEEDINGS. 1967. a. $30. ‡ American Society for Engineering Education, College Industry Education Conference, 11 Dupont Circle, Suite 200, Washington, DC 20036. TEL 202-293-7080. Eds. Joseph M. Biedenbach, Lawrence P. Grayson. circ. 1,000.
Supersedes (as of 1976): Industry - Engineering Education Series (ISSN 0073-7801) & Continuing Engineering Studies Series (ISSN 0069-956X)

620 II
COLLEGE OF ENGINEERING, TRIVANDRUM. MAGAZINE. (Text in English or Malayalam) 1942. a. Rs.10. College of Engineering, Trivandrum 16, Kerala, India. adv. illus.

620 US
COMMUNICATIONS AND CONTROL ENGINEERING SERIES. 1982. irreg., latest 1986. Springer-Verlag, 175 Fifth Ave., New York, NY 10010 TEL 212-460-1500. (And Berlin, Heidelberg, Tokyo and Vienna) Ed.Bd.

CONFERENCE ON REMOTE SYSTEMS TECHNOLOGY. PROCEEDINGS. see *PHYSICS — Nuclear Energy*

620 CN ISSN 0317-6525
CONSULTING ENGINEERS-CANADA-INGENIEURS-CONSEILS. (Text in English, French) 1958. a. $60. ‡ Association of Consulting Engineers of Canada, 130 Albert St., St. 616, Ottawa K1P 5G4, Canada. TEL 613-236-0569. Ed. H.R. Pinault. circ. 2,500.
Formerly: Association of Consulting Engineers of Canada. Specialization Typical Projects (ISSN 0084-6899)

620 657 US
COST ENGINEERS' NOTEBOOK. 1956. irreg. $42. American Association of Cost Engineers, 308 Monogahela Bldg., Morgantown, WV 26505-5468. TEL 304-296-8444. Ed. Tracy A. Novak. circ. 6,000. (back issues avail.)

620 UK
COUNCIL OF ENGINEERING INSTITUTIONS DIARY. a. Welbecson Ltd., 3 Thomas St., Hull HU9 1EJ, England.

620 338 658 NZ ISSN 0111-8587
D S I R INDUSTRIAL INFORMATION SERIES. 1982. irreg. price varies. (Department of Scientific and Industrial Research) Science Information Publishing Center, P.O. Box 9741, Wellington, New Zealand. charts. illus. (back issues avail.)

620 DK ISSN 0900-3045
DANSK INGENIOERFORENING. MEDLEMSFORTEGNELSE. 1977. biennial. Kr.103.70. Dansk Ingenioerforening, Vester Farimagsgade 29-31, 1606 Copenhagen V, Denmark (Subscr. to: Teknisk Forlag A-S, Skelbaekgade 4, 1717 Copenhagen V, Denmark)

DENMARK. FORSOEGSANSLAEG RISOE. RISOE-R. see *PHYSICS — Nuclear Energy*

620 US
DIRECTORY OF CONSULTING ENGINEERING SERVICES IN NORTH CAROLINA. biennial. $15. North Carolina State University, School of Engineering, Industrial Extension Service, Box 7902, Raleigh, NC 27695-7902. TEL 919-737-2358. Ed. Paul Cowgill.

620 US
DIRECTORY OF ENGINEERING/ARCHITECTURAL MINORITY AND WOMEN OWNED FIRMS. irreg. $20. American Consulting Engineers Council, 1015 15th St., N.W., Ste. 802, Washington, DC 20005. TEL 202-347-7474. Ed. Terry Griffith.

620 US ISSN 0070-5470
DIRECTORY OF ENGINEERING SOCIETIES AND RELATED ORGANIZATIONS. 1956. biennial. $100. American Association of Engineering Societies, 415 2nd St. N.E., Ste. 200, Washington, DC 20002-4994. TEL 202-546-2237. Ed. Gordon Davis. index.

620 US ISSN 0420-2155
DIRECTORY OF ENGINEERS AND LAND SURVEYORS REGISTERED IN SOUTH CAROLINA. (Continues the Board's Roster of Registered Professional Engineers and Land Surveyors) 1923. a. $10. ‡ Board of Registration for Professional Engineers and Land Surveyors, Drawer 50408, 2221 Devine St., Ste. 404, Columbia, SC 29250.

DIRECTORY OF INDIAN ENGINEERING EXPORTERS. see *BUSINESS AND ECONOMICS — Trade And Industrial Directories*

ENGINEERING

658.5   IS
DIRECTORY OF INDUSTRIAL LABORATORIES IN ISRAEL. (Text in English and Hebrew) irreg., 4th ed., 1984. $40. National Center of Scientific of Technological Information, Box 20215, Tel Aviv, Israel. Ed. G. Gilat.

DIRECTORY OF THE SCIENTISTS, TECHNOLOGISTS, AND ENGINEERS OF THE P C S I R. (Pakistan Council of Scientific and Industrial Research) see *SCIENCES: COMPREHENSIVE WORKS*

E N I ANNUAL REPORT. (Ente Nazionale Idrocarburi) see *ENERGY*

620   US   ISSN 0098-6305
E N R DIRECTORY OF DESIGN FIRMS. 1974. biennial. $32.50. McGraw-Hill Information Systems Co., 1221 Ave. of the Americas, New York, NY 10020. TEL 212-512-4634. Ed. James H. Webber. illus. circ. 11,000.

621.3   UR
ELEKTROENERGETIKA I AVTOMATIZATSIYA ENERGOUSTANOVOK. (Subseries of: Kharkivskyi Politekhnichnyi Instytut. Vestnik) 1971. irreg. 0.67 Rub. Kharkivskyi Politekhnichnyi Instytut, Ul. Frunze, 21, Kharkov, Ukrainian S.S.R., U.S.S.R. illus.

620   GW
ELSNERS HANDBUCH FUER STAEDTISCHES INGENIEURWESEN. 1973. a. DM.28.40. Otto Elsner Verlagsgesellschaft, Schoefferstr. 15, 6100 Darmstadt, W. Germany (B.R.D.) Ed. Otto Sill. circ. 3,500.
Formerly: Elsners Handbuch fuer Staedtischen Ingenieurbau.

620   UK   ISSN 0071-0288
ENGINEER BUYERS GUIDE. 1897. a. £24. Morgan-Grampian Book Publishing Co. Ltd., 30 Calderwood St., London SE18 6QH, England. Ed. Phil Brown. adv. circ. 4,000.

ENGINEERING APPLICATION SOFTWARE D.A.T.A. BOOK. see *ENGINEERING — Computer Applications*

620.7   370.58   US
ENGINEERING COLLEGE RESEARCH AND GRADUATE STUDY. (Supplement to Engineering Education) 1967. a. $19. American Society for Engineering Education, 11 Dupont Circle, N.W., Suite 200, Washington, DC 20036. TEL 202-293-7080. Ed. Patricia W. Samaras. adv. index. circ. 12,500. (also avail. in microfiche; microfilm) Indexed: Curr.Cont. Eng.Ind.
Formerly: Directory of Engineering College Research and Graduate Study (ISSN 0070-5462)

ENGINEERING COMMITTEE ON OCEANIC RESOURCES. PROCEEDINGS OF THE GENERAL ASSEMBLY. see *WATER RESOURCES*

ENGINEERING EDUCATION IN THE REGION. see *EDUCATION — Higher Education*

620   UK   ISSN 0141-7592
ENGINEERING EMPLOYERS' FEDERATION DIRECTORY. a. £38. Guardian Communications Ltd., Albany House, Hurst St., Birmingham B5 4BD, England.

620   US
ENGINEERING FOUNDATION ANNUAL REPORT. 1914. a. free. Engineering Foundation, United Engineering Center, 345 E. 47th St., New York, NY 10017. TEL 212-705-7835. circ. 300.

620   UK   ISSN 0071-0342
ENGINEERING INDUSTRIES ASSOCIATION. CLASSIFIED DIRECTORY AND BUYERS GUIDE. 1949. biennial. Northern Advertising Agency Ltd., 16 Dartmouth St., London SW1H 9BL, England. Ed. Eric Ford. adv. circ. 45,000.

620   UK
ENGINEERING INDUSTRIES ASSOCIATION. DIARY. a. Northern Advertising Agency Ltd., 16 Dartmouth St., London SW1H 9BL, England.

620   SI   ISSN 0129-6531
ENGINEERING JOURNAL OF SINGAPORE. 1973. a. S.5($5) ‡ University of Singapore, Faculty of Engineering, Kent Ridge, Singapore 0511, Singapore. Ed.Bd. circ. 1,000. Indexed: Chem.Abstr. Eng.Ind.
Formerly: University of Singapore. Faculty of Engineering. Journal.

620   US   ISSN 0013-8037
ENGINEERING MANPOWER BULLETIN. (Formerly published by Engineers Joint Council, Engineering Manpower Commission) 1965. irreg., (approx. 5/yr.) $50. ‡ American Association of Engineering Societies, 415 2nd St., N.E., Ste. 200, Washington, DC 20002-4994. TEL 202-546-2237. Ed. R.A. Ellis. charts. stat. circ. 500.

620   US
ENGINEERING NOW. 1976. a. Virginia Polytechnic Institute and State University, College of Engineering, 333 Norris Hall, Blacksburg, VA 24061. TEL 703-961-6641. Ed. Lynn A. Nystrom. circ. 15,000.

658   US
ENGINEERING RESEARCH CENTRES. 1984. irreg. $300. Gale Research Company, Book Tower, Detroit, MI 38226. Ed.Bd.

620   II
ENGINEERING TIMES ANNUAL DIRECTORY. (Text in English) 14th edt., 1974/75. a. Engineering Times Publications Pvt. Ltd., Wachel Molla Mansion, 8 Lenin Sarani, Calcutta 700013, India.
Continues: Indian Engineering & Industries Register.

620   US
EQUIPMENT SHOW DAILY. 1985. a. (in 3 eds.) free to convention attendees. Harcourt Brace Jovanovich, Inc., 7500 Old Oak Blvd., Cleveland, OH 44130 TEL 216-243-8100. (Subscr. address: 1 E. First St., Duluth, MN 55802) Ed. Vernon E. Henry. circ. 10,390.

F I D I C INTERNATIONAL DIRECTORY OF CONSULTING ENGINEERS. see *BUSINESS AND ECONOMICS — Trade And Industrial Directories*

FRANCE. COMMISSARIAT A L'ENERGIE ATOMIQUE. ANNUAL REPORT. see *PHYSICS — Nuclear Energy*

FRANCE. SERVICE D'ETUDE DES STRATEGIES ET DES STATISTIQUES INDUSTRIELLES. SOCIETES D'ETUDES ET DE CONSEILS, INGENIEURS-CONSEILS. see *BUSINESS AND ECONOMICS*

620   FR   ISSN 0245-0283
FRENCH ENGINEERING CATALOG. (Text in Arabic, English, French and Spanish) 1977. a. 200 Fr. Documentations Industrielles et Techniques, 11 Rue de Madrid, 75008 Paris, France. adv. circ. 6,000.

620   SA   ISSN 0071-979X
FULCRUM. a. free. University of the Witwatersrand, Johannesburg, Student Engineers Council, South West Engineering Block, Room B1, 1 Jan Smuts Ave., Johannesburg 2001, South Africa. Ed. P. Harrod. adv. circ. 3,000.

620   NE
FUNDAMENTAL STUDIES IN ENGINEERING. 1978. irreg., vol.6, 1985. price varies. Elsevier Science Publishers B.V., Box 211, 1000 AE Amsterdam, Netherlands.

620.005   GY
G.A.P.E. 1968. irreg. $10. Guyana Association of Professional Engineers, Georgetown, Guyana. Ed. Melvyn B. Sankie. illus. circ. 300.

620   FR   ISSN 0072-0844
GENIE INDUSTRIEL; CATALOGUE DE L'INGENIERIE. (Text mainly in French; one section in English, Arabic, French and Spanish) 1960. a. 580 F. Documentations Industrielles et Techniques, 11 rue de Madrid, 75 Paris 8, France. Ed. Gaston Berard. circ. controlled.

621.48   GW
GESELLSCHAFT FUER REAKTORSICHERHEIT. JAHRESBERICHT. 1977. a. Gesellschaft fuer Reaktorsicherheit, Schwertnergasse 1, 5000 Cologne 1, W. Germany (B.R.D.) illus.
Formerly: Institut fuer Reaktorsicherheit der Technischen Ueberwachungs-Vereine. Taetigkeitsbericht.

620   BL
GRANDES VULTOS DA ENGENHARIA BRASILEIRA. 1975. a. $12. Clube de Engenharia, Av. Rio Branco 124, Rio de Janeiro, Gb, Brazil.

HACETTEPE FEN VE MUHENDISLIK BILIMLERI DERGISI. see *SCIENCES: COMPREHENSIVE WORKS*

620   JA   ISSN 0073-2311
HIROSHIMA UNIVERSITY. FACULTY OF ENGINEERING. MEMOIRS. (Text in English, French and German) 1957. a. Hiroshima University, Faculty of Engineering - Hiroshima Daigaku Kogakubu, Saijo-cho, Higashi-Hiroshima 724, Japan. Ed. Akiharu Kanamaru. circ. 750. Indexed: Chem.Abstr. Math.R. Sci.Abstr. P.

620   JA
HOKKAIDO UNIVERSITY. FACULTY OF ENGINEERING. MEMOIRS. (Text in European languages) 1927. a. exchange basis. Hokkaido University, Faculty of Engineering, Nishi-8-chome, Kita-13-jo, Kita-ku, Sapporo 060, Japan. Ed. T. Sato. Indexed: Chem.Abstr. Met.Abstr. Sci.Abstr. Int.Aerosp.Abstr. Rev.Appl.Entomol. World Alum.Abstr.

HUMAN FACTORS SOCIETY ANNUAL MEETING. PROCEEDINGS. see *PSYCHOLOGY*

I A T U L QUARTERLY. (International Association of Technological Universities Libraries) see *LIBRARY AND INFORMATION SCIENCES*

620   681   US
I & C S BUYERS' GUIDE. 1935. a. $45 to non-qualified; free to qualified individuals. Chilton Company, Chilton Way, Radnor, PA 19089. TEL 215-964-4418. Ed. Pat O'Donnell. adv. circ. 85,000. (also avail. in microform from UMI) Indexed: A.S.& T.Ind.
Formerly: Instruments and Control Systems Buyers' Guide.

620   FR   ISSN 0066-8982
I C A M ANNUAIRE. (Institut Catholique d'Arts et Metiers de Lille) 1970. a. price varies. Association des Ingenieurs I C A M, 15 rue de Madrid, 75008 Paris, France. adv.

620   US
I E E E PULSED POWER CONFERENCE. DIGEST OF TECHNICAL PAPERS. 1976. biennial. Institute of Electrical and Electronics Engineers, Inc., 345 E. 47th St., New York, NY 10017 TEL 212-705-7900. (Subscr. to: 445 Hoes Lane, Piscataway, NJ 08854) Ed. A.H. Guenther. (reprint service avail. from ISI)
Former titles (1979-1981): I E E E International Pulsed Power Conference. Digest of Technical Papers; Until 1979: I E E E International Pulsed Power Conference. Proceedings.

620   US
I P A - FORSCHUNG UND PRAXIS. (Text in German) vol.38, 1980. irreg., vol.79, 1984. (Fraunhofer-Institute fuer Produktionstechnik und Automatisierung, GW) Springer-Verlag, 175 Fifth Ave., New York, NY 10010. TEL 212-460-1500. Ed. H.J. Warnecke.

INDEX AND DIRECTORY OF U.S. INDUSTRY STANDARDS. see *METROLOGY AND STANDARDIZATION*

620   II   ISSN 0073-6554
INDIAN JOURNAL OF ENGINEERS. ANNUAL FOUNDRY NUMBER. (Text in English) 1960. a. Rs.25 in India; Rs.40 elsewhere. Technical and General Press, Engineers' Bureau, c/o Jyotsnmay Guha Thakurta, 21B Lansdowne Terrace, Calcutta 26, India. Ed. A.K. Bose.

620   UK
INDUSTRIAL FASTENERS HANDBOOK. vol.2, 1980. irreg. £82. Trade & Technical Press Ltd., Crown House, Morden, Surrey SM4 5EW, England.

ENGINEERING

620 US ISSN 0173-0274
INGENIEURWISSENSCHAFTLICHE BIBLIOTHEK/ENGINEERING SCIENCE LIBRARY. (Text in German) 1964. irreg., latest 1977. price varies. Springer-Verlag, 175 Fifth Ave., New York, NY 10010 TEL 212-460-1500. (Also Berlin, Heidelberg, Tokyo and Vienna) (reprint service avail. from ISI)

620 DK ISSN 0109-9639
INGENIOER. a. free. (Tekniske Hoejskole) Bibliotekscentralen, Telegrafvej 5, DK-2750 Ballerup, Denmark.

INSTITUTE OF ENVIRONMENTAL SCIENCES. ANNUAL MEETING. PROCEEDINGS. see ENVIRONMENTAL STUDIES

INSTITUTE OF ENVIRONMENTAL SCIENCES. TUTORIAL SERIES. see ENVIRONMENTAL STUDIES

INSTITUTE OF NUCLEAR MATERIALS MANAGEMENT. PROCEEDINGS OF ANNUAL MEETING. see PHYSICS — Nuclear Energy

620 UK ISSN 0261-7641
INSTITUTION OF ENGINEERING DESIGNERS OFFICIAL REFERENCE BOOK AND BUYERS GUIDE. a. £27.50. Sterling Publications Ltd., 86-88 Edgware Rd., London, W2 2YW, England. adv.

620 BG ISSN 0073-9219
INSTITUTION OF ENGINEERS. YEAR BOOK.* (Text in English) a. Institution of Engineers, Ramna, Dacca 2, Bangladesh.

620 AT ISSN 0812-3314
INSTITUTION OF ENGINEERS, AUSTRALIA. TRANSACTIONS. MULTI-DISCIPLINARY ENGINEERING. 1983. irreg. Aus.$23 to non-members. (Institution of Engineers, Australia) Miadna Pty. Ltd., P.O. Box 588, Crows Nest, N.S.W. 2065, Australia. Ed. W. Rourke. illus. index. circ. 2,000. Indexed: Excerp.Med. Sci.Abstr.
Institution of Engineers, Australia. General Engineering Transactions.

620 IE
INSTITUTION OF ENGINEERS OF IRELAND. REGISTER OF CHARTERED ENGINEERS AND MEMBERS. 1960. a. £6. Irish Engineering Publications Ltd., 22 Clyde Road, Ballsbridge, Dublin, 4, Ireland. adv. circ. 6,000.
Formerly: Directory of Engineers (ISSN 0070-5489)

620 IE ISSN 0073-9790
INSTITUTION OF ENGINEERS OF IRELAND. TRANSACTIONS. 1835. a. £3. Irish Engineering Publications Ltd., 22 Clyde Road, Ballsbridge, Dublin, 4, Ireland. circ. 6,000.

620 CE
INSTITUTION OF ENGINEERS, SRI LANKA. TRANSACTIONS. 1906. a. Institution of Engineers, Sri Lanka, 120/15 Wijerama Mawatha, Colombo 7, Sri Lanka. adv. illus. circ. 3,000.

620 CE
INSTITUTION OF ENGINEERS, SRI LANKA. YEAR BOOK. 1973. a. Institution of Engineers, Sri Lanka, 120/15 Wijerama Mawatha, Colombo 7, Sri Lanka.

629.8 PL ISSN 0084-2788
INSTYTUT AUTOMATYKI SYSTEMOW ENERGETYCZNYCH. PRACE. 1964. irreg., no.40, 1986. 200 Zl. Instytut Automatyki Systemow Energetycznych, Wystawowa 1, 51-618 Wroclaw, Poland. Ed.Bd. circ. 200.

INTERNATIONAL ATOMIC ENERGY AGENCY. ANNUAL REPORT. see PHYSICS — Nuclear Energy

INTERNATIONAL ATOMIC ENERGY AGENCY. NUCLEAR POWER REACTORS IN THE WORLD. see PHYSICS — Nuclear Energy

INTERNATIONAL ATOMIC ENERGY AGENCY. PANEL PROCEEDINGS SERIES. see PHYSICS — Nuclear Energy

INTERNATIONAL ATOMIC ENERGY AGENCY. PROCEEDINGS SERIES. see PHYSICS — Nuclear Energy

INTERNATIONAL ATOMIC ENERGY AGENCY. TECHNICAL DIRECTORIES. see PHYSICS — Nuclear Energy

INTERNATIONAL ATOMIC ENERGY AGENCY. TECHNICAL REPORT SERIES. see PHYSICS — Nuclear Energy

620 US ISSN 0272-880X
INTERNATIONAL CENTRE FOR HEAT AND MASS TRANSFER. PROCEEDINGS. 1972. irreg., no.20, 1985. price varies. Hemisphere Publishing Corporation, 79 Madison Ave., New York, NY 10016. Ed. Z.P. Zaric. bibl. charts. illus. index. (back issues avail.) Indexed: Chem.Abstr.

620 UK
INTERNATIONAL CONFERENCE ON THE PROTECTION OF PIPES. PROCEEDINGS. 1975. irreg., 6th, 1985. price varies. B H R A Fluid Engineering, Cranfield, Bedford MK43 0AJ, England (Dist. in U.S. by: Learned Information Inc., 143 Old Marlton Pike, Medford, NJ 08055)

620 US ISSN 0074-5774
INTERNATIONAL ENGINEERING DIRECTORY. 1965. biennial. $20. American Consulting Engineers Council, 1015 15th St., N.W., Washington, DC 20005. TEL 202-347-7474. Ed. Lillian Semples. circ. 5,000.

620 US
INTERNATIONAL HEAT TRANSFER CONFERENCE. irreg., 8th, 1986. Hemisphere Publishing Corporation, 79 Madison Ave., New York, NY 10016. Ed.Bd.

620 US ISSN 0736-1831
INTERNATIONAL INDUSTRIAL SENSOR DIRECTORY. 1983. a. $45. Technical Database Corp., Box 720, Conroe, TX 77305. TEL 409-539-9688. adv. tr.lit. index. circ. 5,000.
Formerly: Industrial Sensor Directory.

620 536 US ISSN 0741-5877
INTERNATIONAL SERIES IN HEAT AND MASS TRANSFER. 1984. irreg. price varies. Hemisphere Publishing Corporation, 79 Madison Ave., New York, NY 10016. Eds. A.E. Bergles, U. Grigull. bibl. charts. illus. index. (back issues avail.)

621 PL
INTERNATIONAL SYMPOSIUM ON SWITCHING ARC PHENOMENA. PROCEEDINGS. (Text in English, German, Russian; summaries in English) irreg., 2nd, 1973. price varies. Politechnika Lodzka, Ul. Zwirki 36, 90-924 Lodz, Poland. (Co-sponsor: Stowarzyszenie Elektrykow Polskich) illus.

620 US
INTERNATIONAL UNION OF THEORETICAL AND APPLIED MECHANICS. SYMPOSIA. 1956. irreg., latest 1986. Springer-Verlag, 175 Fifth Ave., New York, NY 10010. TEL 212-460-1500. (reprint service avail. from ISI)

620 US ISSN 0075-0433
IOWA STATE UNIVERSITY. ENGINEERING RESEARCH INSTITUTE. ENGINEERING RESEARCH REPORT. 1949/50. irreg. price varies. Iowa State University, Engineering Research Institute, Ames, IA 50011. TEL 515-294-2336. Indexed: Geotech.Abstr.

620 UR
ISSLEDOVANIE, KONSTRUIROVANIE I RASCHET REZBOVYKH SOEDINENII. 1973. irreg. 0.50 Rub. per no. (Ulyanovskii Politekhnicheskii Institut) Privolzhskoe Knizhnoe Izdatel'stvo, Ul. Goncharova, 52, Ulyanovsk, Russian S.F.S.R., U.S.S.R.

620 JA ISSN 0085-2325
IWATE UNIVERSITY. FACULTY OF ENGINEERING. TECHNOLOGY REPORTS/ IWATE DAIGAKU KOGAKUBU KENKYU HOKOKU. (Text in English) 1965. a. free. Iwate University, Faculty of Engineering - Iwate Daigaku Kogakubu, 4-3-5 Ueda, Morioka 020, Iwate, Japan. Ed. Sadamasa Murai. Indexed: Appl.Mech.Rev. Sci.Abstr. GeoRef. JCT.

JAPAN ATOMIC ENERGY COMMISSION. ANNUAL REPORT/GENSHIRYOKU NENPO. see PHYSICS — Nuclear Energy

620 620.11 JA ISSN 0285-3833
JAPAN ELECTRONIC MATERIALS SOCIETY. BULLETIN. 1968. a. 33.000 Yen($180) Nihon Denshi Zairyo Gijutsu Kyokai, 1-38 Yoyogi, Shibuya-ku, Tokyo 151, Japan. Ed. Teruo Sakamoto.

621.8 JA ISSN 0389-5483
JAPAN SOCIETY OF LUBRICATION ENGINEERS. JOURNAL. INTERNATIONAL EDITION. (Text in English) 1980. a. $20. Japan Society of Lubrication Engineers, No. 407-2 Kikai Shinko Bldg., 5-8 Shiba Koen 3-chome, Minato-Ku, Tokyo 105, Japan (Subscr. to: Maruzen Co., Ltd., Export Department, P.O. Box 5050, Tokyo International 100-31, Japan) Ed. N. Ishihara. Indexed: API Abstr. Fluidex.

621 UR
KAZANSKII UNIVERSITET. SBORNIK ASPIRANTSKIKH RABOT: TEORIYA PLASTIN I OBOLOCHEK. 1971. irreg. 0.67 Rub. Kazanskii Universitet, Ul. Lenina, 4/5, Kazan, Russian S.F.S.R., U.S.S.R. illus. Indexed: Math.R.

620 US
KELLOGGRAM. irreg. free. Pullman Kellogg, Three Greenway Plaza East, Houston, TX 77046. TEL 713-961-8600. charts. illus.
Supersedes: Kellogg World (ISSN 0453-4867)

620 UK ISSN 0075-5400
KEMPE'S ENGINEERS YEAR-BOOK. 1894. a. £45. Morgan-Grampian Book Publishing Co. Ltd., 30 Calderwood St., London SE18 6QH, England. Ed. Carill Sharpe. adv. bibl. illus. index. circ. 5,000.

KERNFORSCHUNGSZENTRUM KARLSRUHE. ERGEBNISBERICHT UEBER FORSCHUNG UND ENTWICKLUNG. see PHYSICS — Nuclear Energy

KOBE UNIVERSITY OF MERCANTILE MARINE. REVIEW. PART 2. MARITIME STUDIES, AND SCIENCE AND ENGINEERING. see SCIENCES: COMPREHENSIVE WORKS

KOCHI UNIVERSITY. FACULTY OF AGRICULTURE. MEMOIRS. see AGRICULTURE

DIE KUESTE; Archiv fuer Forschung und Technik an der Nord- und Ostsee. see EARTH SCIENCES — Oceanography

620 JA ISSN 0023-5334
KUMAMOTO UNIVERSITY. FACULTY OF ENGINEERING. MEMOIRS/KUMAMOTO DAIGAKU KOGAKUBU KIYO. (Text in English) 1954. irreg. free. Kumamoto University, Faculty of Engineering, 2-39-1 Kurokami, Kumamoto 860, Japan. bibl. charts. illus. Indexed: Met.Abstr. Sci.Abstr. JCT. World Alum.Abstr.

620 JA ISSN 0023-5296
KUMAMOTO UNIVERSITY. FACULTY OF ENGINEERING. TECHNICAL REPORTS/ KUMAMOTO DAIGAKU KOGAKUBU KENKYU HOKOKU. 1952. irreg. free. Kumamoto University, Faculty of Engineering, 2-39-1 Kurokami, Kumamoto 860, Japan. Indexed: Chem.Abstr. Sci.Abstr. JCT.

620 JA ISSN 0369-0512
KYUSHU INSTITUTE OF TECHNOLOGY. MEMOIRS: ENGINEERING. (Text in English) 1971. a. exchange basis. Kyushu Institute of Technology - Kyushu Kogyo Daigaku, 1-1 Sensui-cho, Tobata, Kitakyushu 804, Japan. Indexed: Chem.Abstr. Sci.Abstr. JCT.

620 US ISSN 0176-5035
LECTURE NOTES IN ENGINEERING. 1983. irreg., vol.24, 1986. price varies. Springer-Verlag, 175 Fifth Ave., New York, NY 10010. Eds. C.A. Brebbia, S.A. Orszag.

620 500 US
LOS ANGELES COUNCIL OF ENGINEERS & SCIENTISTS. PROCEEDINGS SERIES.* 1975. irreg. $25. Los Angeles Council of Engineers & Scientists, 1661 Mohawk St., Los Angeles, CA 90026. Indexed: Chem.Abstr.

620　　　　　　　　　GW
M.A.N. FORSCHEN, PLANEN, BAUEN. English edition: M.A.N. Research, Engineering, Manufacturing. (Editions also in Chinese, French and Spanish) 1970. a. free. Maschinenfabrik Augsburg-Nuernberg AG, Stadtbachstr. 1, 8900 Augsburg, W. Germany (B.R.D.) Ed.Bd. illus. circ. 40,000(comb.) Indexed: Sci.Abstr.

MANITOBA CONSTRUCTION INDUSTRY DIRECTORY. PURCHASING GUIDE. see BUILDING AND CONSTRUCTION

MATERIALS RESEARCH AND ENGINEERING/ REINE UND ANGEWANDTE METALLKUNDE. see METALLURGY

620.11　　　　　　　　NE
MATERIALS SCIENCE MONOGRAPHS. 1978. irreg., vol.31, 1986. price varies. Elsevier Science Publishers B.V., Box 211, 1000 AE Amsterdam, Netherlands. Ed. C. Laird. adv. Indexed: Chem.Abstr.

MATHEMATICS IN SCIENCE AND ENGINEERING; series of monographs and textbooks. see MATHEMATICS

620　　　　　　　US　　ISSN 0748-7002
MEANS ELECTRICAL COST DATA. 1977. a. $46.95. R.S. Means Company, Inc., 100 Construction Plaza, Kingston, MA 02364-0800. Ed. Albert Sauerbier. bk. rev. circ. 10,000. (back issues avail.)
 Supersedes in part: Means Mechanical and Electrical Cost Data.

621　　　　　　　SW　　ISSN 0025-6609
MECMAN - TECHNIQUE. (Editions in Danish, English, Finnish, French, Italian, German, Hungarian, Japanese, Norwegian, and Swedish) 1965. irreg. free. A B Mecman, Box 32 035, S-126 11 Stockholm 32, Sweden. Ed. Carl Eric Beckman. charts. illus. circ. 100,000.
 Formerly: Mecman - Teknik.

380.1　　　　　　AT　　ISSN 0314-1586
METAL & ENGINEERING INDUSTRY YEAR BOOK. 1975. a. Aus.$65. (Metal & Engineering Industry Association) Peter Isaacson Publications, 45-50 Porter St., Prahran, Vic. 3181, Australia. adv. circ. 8,000.
 Formerly: Metal and Engineering Industry Handbook (ISSN 0156-370X)

620　621.381　　　　　　NE
MICROPROCESSOR-BASED SYSTEMS ENGINEERING. 1983. irreg., latest no.3, 1985. price varies. D. Reidel Publishing Company, Box 17, 3300 AA Dordrecht, Netherlands. Ed. S.G. Tzafestas.

620　　　　　　　JA　　ISSN 0540-4924
MIYAZAKI UNIVERSITY. FACULTY OF ENGINEERING. MEMOIRS/MIYAZAKI DAIGAKU KOGAKUBU KIYO. (Text in English) 1956. irreg. exchange basis. Miyazaki University, Faculty of Engineering - Miyazaki Daigaku Kogakubu, 1-1-1 Kirishima, Miyazaki 880, Japan. circ. 450. Indexed: Math.R.

620　530　　　　　　　　US
MONOGRAPHS IN PHYSICAL MEASUREMENT. 1978. irreg., latest vol.2, 1983. Academic Press Inc., Orlando, FL 32887. TEL 305-345-2000. Ed. A.H. Cook.

600　　　　　　　　　US
MONOGRAPHS ON CRYOGENICS. irreg. price varies. Oxford University Press, 200 Madison Ave., New York, NY 10016 TEL 212-679-7300. (And Ely House, 37 Dover St., London W1X 4AH, England) Ed. R.G. Scurlock.

620　　　　　　　US　　ISSN 0276-1459
MULTIPHASE SCIENCE AND TECHNOLOGY; an international series of books. 1982. irreg. price varies. Hemisphere Publishing Corporation, 79 Madison Ave., New York, NY 10016. Ed.Bd. bibl. charts. illus. index. (back issues avail.)

620　　　　　　　US　　ISSN 0077-4081
NATIONAL COUNCIL OF ENGINEERING EXAMINERS. PROCEEDINGS. a. National Council of Engineering Examiners, Box 1686, Clemson, SC 29633. TEL 803-654-6824.

620　　　　　　　　　US
NATIONAL DIRECTORY OF SAFETY CONSULTANTS. 1974. a. $25. American Society of Safety Engineers, 1800 E. Oakton St., Des Plaines, IL 60018-2187. TEL 312-692-4121. Ed. Dwight B. Esau. circ. 1,000.

NATIONAL INDUSTRIAL RESEARCH INSTITUTE. REPORT. see TECHNOLOGY: COMPREHENSIVE WORKS

620　　　　　　　CN　　ISSN 0077-5428
NATIONAL RESEARCH COUNCIL, CANADA. ASSOCIATE COMMITTEE ON GEOTECHNICAL RESEARCH. TECHNICAL MEMORANDUM. 1945. irreg. price varies. National Research Council of Canada, Associate Committee on Geotechnical Research, Ottawa, Ont. K1A OR6, Canada. TEL 613-993-9546. (back issues avail.) Indexed: Eng.Ind. Arct.Bibl.

620　610　371.9　　　CN　　ISSN 0706-568X
NATIONAL RESEARCH COUNCIL, CANADA. DIVISION OF ELECTRICAL ENGINEERING. BULLETIN/CONSEIL NATIONAL DE RECHERCHES DU CANADA. DIVISION DE GENIE ELECTRIQUE. BULLETIN. (Text in English and French) 1975. a. free. National Research Council of Canada, Division of Electrical Engineering, Rm. 301, Ottawa, Ont., K1A OR8, Canada. TEL 613-993-1880. Ed. E.M. Kidd. circ. 900. (also avail. in microfilm; back issues avail.)

620　　　　　　　US　　ISSN 0028-5900
NEW JERSEY PROFESSIONAL ENGINEER. 1939. a. $5. New Jersey Society of Professional Engineers, 407 W. State St., Trenton, NJ 08618. Ed. Joseph A. Simonetta. adv. charts. illus. stat. circ. 11,000.
 Formerly: Who's Who of Engineering in New Jersey.

620　600　　　　　UK　　ISSN 0372-0187
NEWCOMEN SOCIETY FOR THE STUDY OF THE HISTORY OF ENGINEERING AND TECHNOLOGY. TRANSACTIONS. 1922. a. £10. Newcomen Society for the Study of the History of Engineering and Technology, Science Museum, South Kensington, London SW7 2DD, England. Ed. J.G.B. Hills. bibl. charts. illus. (also avail. in microfilm) Indexed: Br.Hum.Ind.

NIHON UNIVERSITY. ATOMIC ENERGY RESEARCH INSTITUTE. ANNUAL REPORT. see PHYSICS — Nuclear Energy

658.5　670　　　　　　　US
NORTH AMERICAN MANUFACTURING RESEARCH CONFERENCE. PROCEEDINGS. (Includes: C I R P Review) 1972. a. $70. Society of Manufacturing Engineers, One S M E Dr., Box 930, Dearborn, MI 48121. TEL 313-271-1500. Ed. David Dornfeld. circ. 600. (also avail. in microform from UMI; reprint service avail. from UMI)
 Former titles: North American Manufacturing Research Conference (Publication) & Manufacturing Engineering. Engineering Transactions (ISSN 0363-700X) & S M E Transactions & North American Metalworking Research Conference. Proceedings (ISSN 0146-132X)

NUCLEAR SCIENCE TECHNOLOGY MONOGRAPH SERIES. see PHYSICS — Nuclear Energy

OCEAN ENGINEERING: A WILEY SERIES. see EARTH SCIENCES — Oceanography

620.41　　　　　　US　　ISSN 0197-7385
OCEANS. CONFERENCE RECORD. a. (I E E E, Oceanic Engineering Society) Institute of Electrical and Electronics Engineers, Inc., 345 E. 47th St., New York, NY 10017 TEL 212-705-7900. (Subscr. address: 445 Hoes Lane, Piscataway, NJ 08854)
 Former titles: I E E E International Conference on Engineering in the Ocean Environment. Record; International Conference on Engineering in the Ocean Environment. Digest (ISSN 0074-3062)

OPPORTUNITIES IN SCIENCE AND ENGINEERING. see OCCUPATIONS AND CAREERS

OPTICAL PHYSICS AND ENGINEERING. see PHYSICS — Optics

ORGANIZATION FOR ECONOMIC COOPERATION AND DEVELOPMENT. NUCLEAR ENERGY AGENCY. ACTIVITY REPORT. see PHYSICS — Nuclear Energy

ORGANIZATION FOR ECONOMIC COOPERATION AND DEVELOPMENT. NUCLEAR ENERGY AGENCY. SUMMARY OF NUCLEAR POWER AND FUEL CYCLE DATA IN O E C D MEMBER COUNTRIES. see PHYSICS — Nuclear Energy

620　　　　　　　JA　　ISSN 0078-6659
OSAKA CITY UNIVERSITY. FACULTY OF ENGINEERING. MEMOIRS/OSAKA-SHIRITSU DAIGAKU KOGAKUBU OBUN KIYO. (Text and summaries in English) 1959. a. free. Osaka City University, Faculty of Engineering - Osaka-shiritsu Daigaku Kogakubu, 3-138 Sugimoto 3-chome, Sumiyoshi-ku, Osaka 558, Japan. Ed.Bd. circ. 2,000. Indexed: Chem.Abstr. Met.Abstr. Sci.Abstr. JCT. World Alum.Abstr.

620　　　　　　　　　CN
P E M SOURCEBOOK. (Plant Engineering & Maintenance) a. Can.$12. Clifford Elliot & Associates Ltd., P.O. Box 247, 277 Lakeshore Rd. E. Oakville, Ont. L6J 6L9, Canada. Ed. Lee Scott. circ. 17,200.

620　　　　　　　UY　　ISSN 0078-8791
PAN AMERICAN FEDERATION OF ENGINEERING SOCIETIES. BULLETIN.* (Running title: U P A D I Bulletin) (Text in English, Portuguese and Spanish) 1951. a. Pan American Federation of Engineering Societies, c/o Maria L. Pinero, Secr., Daig Norte 777, 8 piso, Oficina 826, 1364 Buenos Aires, Argentina.

620　　　　　　　UK　　ISSN 0079-0869
PERGAMON UNIFIED ENGINEERING SERIES. irreg., vol. 22, 1980. price varies. Pergamon Press, Ltd., Headington Hill Hall, Oxford OX3 0BW, England (U.S. subscr. to: Maxwell House, Fairview Park, Elmsford, NY 10523) Eds. J. P. Hartnett, T. F. Irvine, Jr.

620　　　　　　　　　UK
PERSPECTIVES IN STRUCTURAL SCIENCE. (Text in English) 1984. a. $40. Freund Publishing House, Ltd., Suite 500, Chesham House, 150 Regent St., London W1R 5FA, England. Ed. Frank Herbstein. circ. 1,000.

620　　　　　　　US　　ISSN 0730-0980
PETERSON'S GUIDE TO ENGINEERING, SCIENCE AND COMPUTER JOBS (YEAR) 1980. a. $17.95. Peterson's Guides, 166 Bunn Dr., Box 2123, Princeton, NJ 08543-2123. TEL 609-924-5338. Ed. Chritopher Billy. adv. illus. circ. 25,000. (also avail. in microform)
 Formerly: Peterson's Annual Guide to Careers and Employment for Engineers, Computer Scientists and Physical Scientists (ISSN 0190-4213)

PETERSON'S GUIDES. ANNUAL GUIDES TO GRADUATE STUDY. BOOK 5: ENGINEERING AND APPLIED SCIENCES. see EDUCATION — Guides To Schools And Colleges

PION APPLIED PHYSICS SERIES. see PHYSICS

658.5　　　　　　US　　ISSN 0554-2693
PLANT ENGINEERING DIRECTORY & SPECIFICATIONS CATALOG. 1965. a. $35. Technical Publishing Co. (Barrington), 1301 So. Grove Ave., Barrington, IL 60010. TEL 312-381-1840. Ed. Leo F. Spector. adv. charts. illus. circ. controlled.

620　　　　　　　PL　　ISSN 0079-323X
POLISH ACADEMY OF SCIENCES. INSTITUTE OF FUNDAMENTAL TECHNOLOGICAL RESEARCH. SCIENTIFIC ACTIVITIES. (Text in English) 1962. a. price varies. (Polska Akademia Nauk, Instytut Podstawowych Problemow Techniki) Panstwowe Wydawnictwo Naukowe, Miodowa 10, 00-251 Warsaw, Poland. Ed. Z. Mroz. bibl. illus. circ. 630.

620　　　　　　　PL　　ISSN 0574-9069
POLITECHNIKA CZESTOCHOWSKA. ZESZYTY NAUKOWE. NAUKI PODSTAWOWE. (Text in Polish; summaries in English and Russian) 1960. irreg. Politechnika Czestochowska, Ul. Deglera 31, 42-200 Czestochowa, Poland (Dist. by: Ars Polona-Ruch, Krakowskie Przedmiescie 7, Warsaw, Poland) Ed. Boleslaw Wyslocki. Indexed: Chem.Abstr.

628 PL ISSN 0324-9719
POLITECHNIKA WROCLAWSKA. INSTYTUT INZYNIERII OCHRONY SRODOWISKA. PRACE NAUKOWE. KONFERENCJE. 1972. irreg., no.11, 1985. price varies. Politechnika Wroclawska, Wybrzeze Wyspianskiego 27, 50-370 Wroclaw, Poland (Dist. by: Ars Polona-Ruch, Krakowskie Przedmiescie 7, Warsaw, Poland) Ed. Jerzy Ciekot.

628 PL ISSN 0084-2877
POLITECHNIKA WROCLAWSKA. INSTYTUT INZYNIERII OCHRONY SRODOWISKA. PRACE NAUKOWE. STUDIA I MATERIALY. (Text in Polish; summaries in English, French, German and Russian) 1969. irreg., no. 21, 1986. price varies. Politechnika Wroclawska, Wybrzeze Wyspianskiego 27, 50-370 Wroclaw, Poland (Dist. by: Ars Polona-Ruch, Krakowskie Przedmiescie 7, Warsaw, Poland) Ed. Jery Ciekot. Indexed: Chem.Abstr.

620 PL ISSN 0239-3433
POLITECHNIKA WROCLAWSKA. INSTYTUT STEROWANIA I TECHNIKI SYSTEMOW. PRACE NAUKOWE. KONFERENCJE. 1983. irreg., no.2, 1986. price varies. Politechnika Wroclawska, Wybrzeze Wyspianskiego 27, 50-370 Wroclaw, Poland. Ed. Jerzy Ciekot.

620 PL ISSN 0209-2573
POLITECHNIKA WROCLAWSKA. INSTYTUT STEROWANIA I TECHNIKI SYSTEMOW. PRACE NAUKOWE. MONOGRAFIE. 1983. irreg., no.2, 1987. price varies. Politechnika Wroclawska, Wybrzeze Wyspianskiego 27, 50-370 Wroclaw, Poland. Ed. Jerzy Ciekot.

620 EC ISSN 0032-3055
POLITECNICA; revista de informacion tecnico - cientifica. (Text in Spanish; summaries in English) 1967. irreg. (3-4/yr.) $20. Escuela Politecnica Nacional, Isabel la Catolica y Veintimilla, Apdo. 2759, Quito, Ecuador. Ed.Bd. bibl. charts. illus. Indexed: Biol.Abstr. Chem.Abstr. GeoRef.

POLSKA AKADEMIA NAUK. INSTYTUT PODSTAW INZYNIERII SRODOWISKA. PRACE I STUDIA. see ENVIRONMENTAL STUDIES

620 SW
POWER SYSTEMS COMPUTATION CONFERENCE. P S C C PROCEEDINGS. 1968. triennial, 5th, 1975, Cambridge; next conference, 6th, 1978, Darmstadt. $35. Kungliga Tekniska Hoegskolan, Power Systems Research Group - Royal Institute of Technology, 100 44 Stockholm 70, Sweden. Ed. J.A. Bubenko.

620 SA ISSN 0555-6945
PULSE. vol. 22, 1975. a. membership. University of Natal, Students Engineering Society, King George IV Ave., Durban 4001, South Africa. Ed. V.N. Hatley.

PURE AND APPLIED PHYSICS; a series of monographs and textbooks. see PHYSICS

620 US
QUALITY AND RELIABILITY. 1985. irreg., vol.7, 1986. price varies. Marcel Dekker, Inc., 270 Madison Ave., New York, NY 10016. TEL 212-696-9000. Ed. Edward G. Schilling.

620 US ISSN 0033-6327
QUEST (PULLMAN); seeking for knowledge. 1964. irreg. free. Washington State University, Engineering Publications, Pullman, WA 99164-2712. TEL 509-335-5095. Ed. David C. Flaherty. circ. 10,000. Indexed: Ocean.Abstr. Pollut.Abstr.
Formerly: Washington State University. College of Engineering. Annual Report (ISSN 0083-7512)

RADIONAVIGATION JOURNAL. see EARTH SCIENCES — Oceanography

683.83 US
RECIPROCATING PUMP SPECIFICATIONS.* a. Gordon Reference Book Group (Subsidiary of: Gordon Publications, Inc.) Box 1952, Dover, NJ 07801. adv. circ. 1,076.

RESEARCH INSTITUTE OF INDUSTRIAL SAFETY. TECHNICAL RECOMMENDATION. see ELECTRICITY AND ELECTRICAL ENGINEERING

RIKKYO UNIVERSITY. INSTITUTE FOR ATOMIC ENERGY. REPORT. see PHYSICS — Nuclear Energy

RIVER AND FLOOD CONTROL ABSTRACTS. see ENGINEERING — Hydraulic Engineering

ROZPRAWY HYDROTECHNICZNE/ HYDROTECHNICAL TRANSACTIONS. see WATER RESOURCES

620 US ISSN 0080-4975
RUTGERS UNIVERSITY. BUREAU OF ENGINEERING RESEARCH. ANNUAL REPORT. 1927. a. free. ‡ Rutgers University, College of Engineering, Bureau of Engineering Research, New Brunswick, NJ 08903. TEL 201-932-7625. Ed. R. C. Ahlert. index. circ. 500.

S F S CATALOGUE; catalogue of Finnish national standards. (Suomen Standardisoimisliitto) see METROLOGY AND STANDARDIZATION

S H E. (Subject Headings for Engineering) see LIBRARY AND INFORMATION SCIENCES

621.38 US ISSN 0097-966X
S I D INTERNATIONAL SYMPOSIUM. DIGEST OF TECHNICAL PAPERS. 1970. a. $50 to non-members; members $40. Society for Information Display, 8055 W. Manchester Ave., No. 615, Playa Del Rey, CA 90293. circ. 2,000. Key Title: Digest of Technical Papers.
Formerly: Symposium on Information Display. Digest of Technical Papers (ISSN 0082-0830)

620 510 530 JA ISSN 0385-6186
SAGA UNIVERSITY. FACULTY OF SCIENCE AND ENGINEERING. REPORTS. (Text in English, Japanese; summaries in English) 1973. a. Saga University, Faculty of Science and Engineering, 1 Honjo-machi, Saga 840, Japan. Ed. Hirishi Takata. circ. 400. (back issues avail.) Indexed: JCT.

SASKATCHEWAN CONSTRUCTION INDUSTRY DIRECTORY. PURCHASING GUIDE. see BUILDING AND CONSTRUCTION

623 US
SEA TECHNOLOGY BUYERS GUIDE/ DIRECTORY. 1967. a. $20.50. Compass Publications, Inc. (Arlington), 1117 N. 19th St., Ste. 1000, Arlington, VA 22209. TEL 703-524-3136. Ed. David M. Graham. adv. circ. 10,000. (reprint service avail. from UMI)
Formerly: Sea Technology Handbook and Directory.

SENDAI NATIONAL COLLEGE OF TECHNOLOGY. RESEARCH REPORTS. see SOCIAL SCIENCES: COMPREHENSIVE WORKS

620 SZ
SERIES ON BULK MATERIALS HANDLING. 1975. irreg., 3-5/yr. price varies. Trans Tech Publications, P.O. Box 266, D-3392 Clauthal-Zellerfeld, W. Germany (B.R.D.) Ed. R.H. Wohlbier. adv. circ. 6,500.
Formerly: Series on Bulk Materials Engineering.

620 JA
SHINSHU UNIVERSITY. FACULTY OF TEXTILE SCIENCE AND TECHNOLOGY. JOURNAL. SERIES B: ENGINEERING. (Text in European languages) 1952. irreg. exchange basis. Shinshu University, Faculty of Textile Science and Technology - Shinshu Daigaku Sen'i Gakubu, 3-15-1 Tokida, Ueda, Nagano 386, Japan.

620 SI
SINGAPORE POLYTECHNIC ENGINEERING SOCIETY. JOURNAL. 1963. a. free. ‡ Singapore Polytechnic Engineering Society, c/o Singapore Polytechnic Students Union, 9 Prince Edward Rd., Singapore, Singapore. adv. illus. circ. 3,000.

328.94 338.7 AT
SNOWY MOUNTAINS ENGINEERING CORPORATION. ANNUAL REPORT. a. price varies. Australian Government Publishing Service, G.P.O. Box 84, Canberra, A.C.T. 2601, Australia. illus.

620 PE
SOCIEDAD DE INGENIEROS. INFORMACIONES Y MEMORIAS. 1975. irreg. Sociedad de Ingenieros, Avda. Nicolas de Pierola 788, Lima, Peru.

SOUTH AFRICAN MINING AND ENGINEERING YEARBOOK. see MINES AND MINING INDUSTRY

620 UK ISSN 0038-3570
SOUTH WALES INSTITUTE OF ENGINEERS. PROCEEDINGS. 1857. a. £1. South Wales Institute of Engineers, Coal House, Ty Glas Ave., Llanishen, Cardiff CF4 5YS, Wales. Ed. T.H. Rhodes. adv. charts. illus. index. circ. 650. Indexed: Chem.Abstr. Eng.Ind. Met.Abstr. GeoRef. World Alum.Abstr.

SYMPOSIUM ON WIND EFFECTS ON STRUCTURES IN JAPAN. PROCEEDINGS. see METEOROLOGY

SYSTEMS ENGINEERING OF EDUCATION SERIES. see EDUCATION

620.1 SW
T L I - INGENJOEREN. 1949. irreg., 4-6/yr. Kr.25($3) Ingenjoersfoerbundet T L I, Norrlandsgatan 31-33, 5 tr, S-11143 Stockholm, Sweden. Ed. Tomas Pira. adv. pat. tr.lit. circ. 5,000. (tabloid format)
Formerly: Gymnasieingenjoeren (ISSN 0017-5919)

620 GE ISSN 0372-7610
TECHNISCHE HOCHSCHULE KARL-MARX-STADT. WISSENSCHAFTLICHE ZEITSCHRIFT. 1958/59. a. M.73.20. Technische Hochschule Karl-Marx-Stadt, Bibliothek, Postfach 964, 901 Karl-Marx-Stadt, E. Germany (D.D.R.) Ed. Christine Haeckel. charts. index. circ. 1,100. Indexed: Chem.Abstr. Math.R. Met.Abstr. World Text.Abstr.
Formerly: Hochschule fuer Maschinenbau Karl-Marx-Stadt. Wissenschaftliche Zeitschrift.

620 NE
TECHNISCHE HOGESCHOOL TE DELFT. BIBLIOTHEEK. LIJST VAN LOPENDE TIJDSCHRIFTABONNEMENTEN. 1967. a. fl.4. ‡ Technische Hogeschool te Delft, Bibliotheek, P.O.B. 98, 2600 MG Delft, Netherlands. index. circ. 1,000.

620 AU ISSN 0259-0697
TECHNISCHE UNIVERSITAET WIEN. DISSERTATIONEN. 1968. irreg., no.44, 1986. price varies. Verband der Wissenschaftlichen Gesellschaften Oesterreichs, Lindengasse 37, A-1070 Vienna, Austria.
Formerly: Technische Hochschule Wien. Dissertationen.

620 DK
TEKNISK NYTS LEVERANDOERREGISTER. a. Thomson Communications (Scandinavia) A-S, Struenseegade 7-9, DK-2200 Copenhagen N, Denmark. adv. circ. 18,605.

620 JA ISSN 0285-3817
TOHOKU INSTITUTE OF TECHNOLOGY. MEMOIRS. SERIES 1: SCIENCE AND ENGINEERING. (Text in English or Japanese; summaries in English) 1981. a. exchange bases only. Tohoku Institute of Technology, 35-1 Yagiyama-Kasumicho, Sendai 982, Japan. Ed. Kazuo Kusano. circ. 730. (back issues avail.)
Supersedes (in 1981): Tohoku Institute of Technology. Bulletin. Section B. Sciences and Technology.

620 CN ISSN 0049-4038
TOIKE OIKE. 1911. irreg., 5-7/yr. Can.$2. University of Toronto Engineering Society, Sandford Fleming Bldg, Rm SF B670, 10 King's College Rd., Toronto, Ont. M5S 1A4, Canada. Ed. Jeremy Bateson. adv. circ. 20,000. (tabloid format)

620 621 JA ISSN 0288-5530
TOKYO DENKI UNIVERSITY. FACULTY OF ENGINEERING. GENERAL EDUCATION. RESEARCH REPORTS. (Text in Japanese; summaries in English and Japanese) 1982. a. members only. Tokyo Denki University, Faculty of Engineering, 2-2, Kanda nishiki-Cho, Chiyoda-Ku, Tokyo 101, Japan. (back issues avail.)

620 621　　　　　JA　ISSN 0389-617X
TOKYO DENKI UNIVERSITY. FACULTY OF ENGINEERING. RESEARCH REPORTS. (Text in Japanese; summaries in English and Japanese) 1951. a. members only. Tokyo Denki University, Faculty of Engineering, 2-2, Kanda Nishiki-Cho, Chiyoda-Ku, Tokyo 101, Japan. (back issues avail.) Indexed: JCT.

TOPICS IN APPLIED PHYSICS. see *PHYSICS*

620　　　　　US
TOPICS IN BOUNDARY ELEMENTS RESEARCH. 1984. irreg., vol.2, 1985. Springer-Verlag, 175 Fifth Ave., New York, NY 10010 TEL 212-460-1500. (Also Berlin, Heidelberg, Tokyo, Vienna) (reprint service avail. from ISI)

621.3　　　　　BE
TRACTEBEL. ANNUAL REPORT. (Text in English) 1896. a. free. Tractebel s.a., Services Relations Exterieures, 1 place du Trone, 1000 Brussels, Belgium. Ed. Adrian de Schietere. charts. illus. circ. 10,000.
　Formerly: Tractionel. Annual Report (ISSN 0770-9595)

TRANSLATION SERIES IN MATHEMATICS AND ENGINEERING. see *MATHEMATICS*

TUNNELLING DIRECTORY; an international yearbook of consultants and companies in sub-surface construction. see *ENGINEERING — Civil Engineering*

ULTRASONICS SYMPOSIUM. PROCEEDINGS. see *PHYSICS — Sound*

UNITED KINGDOM ATOMIC ENERGY AUTHORITY. ANNUAL REPORT. see *PHYSICS — Nuclear Energy*

620　　　　　US　ISSN 0083-0313
U.S. ARMY. CORPS OF ENGINEERS. TECHNICAL REPORTS, T R (SERIES)* irreg. U.S. Army, Corps of Engineers, Publications Office, Washington, DC 20310 TEL 202-272-6001. (Order from: National Technical Information Service, 5285 Port Royal Rd., Springfield, VA 22151)

623　　　　　US　ISSN 0092-8917
U.S. NATIONAL OCEANIC AND ATMOSPHERIC ADMINISTRATION. MANNED UNDERSEA SCIENCE AND TECHNOLOGY PROGRAM; REPORT. 1971/72. a. $1. U.S. National Oceanic and Atmospheric Administration, 6010 Executive Blvd., Rockville, MD 20852 TEL 301-655-4000. (Orders to: NTIS, 5285 Port Royal Rd., Springfield, VA 22161) Ed. Kurt Stehling. illus. circ. 1,000. (also avail. in microfiche) Key Title: Manned Undersea Science and Technology Program.

526.9　　　　　UY
UNIVERSIDAD DE LA REPUBLICA. FACULTAD DE INGENIERIA. BOLETIN. (Text in Spanish; summaries in English and Spanish) 1935. irreg. Urg.$60($5) per no. Universidad de la Republica, Facultad de Ingeniera, Casilla de Correo 30, Montevideo, Uruguay. Ed. Prof. Enrique M. Cabana. bk. rev. charts. illus. index. circ. 400. Indexed: Chem.Abstr. Eng.Ind. Sci.Abstr. GeoRef.
　Formerly: Universidad de la Republica. Facultad de Ingenieria y Agrimensura. Boletin (ISSN 0027-013X)

620 610 001.3　　CK　ISSN 0120-0852
UNIVERSIDAD INDUSTRIAL DE SANTANDER. REVISTA - INVESTIGACIONES. (Summaries in English, French, German and Spanish) 1959. irreg. P.100($2.) per no. or exchange basis. Universidad Industrial de Santander, Apdo. Aereo 678, Bucaramanga, Santander, Colombia. adv. bk. rev. bibl. charts. illus. stat. cum.index every 5 yrs. circ. 1,200. Indexed: Met.Abstr.
　Supersedes in part (since 1969): Universidad Industrial de Santander. Revista (ISSN 0041-8587)

UNIVERSITEXTS. see *MATHEMATICS*

620　　　　　US
UNIVERSITY OF ARIZONA. COLLEGE OF ENGINEERING. E E S SERIES REPORT. (Engineering Experiment Station) no. 51, 1981. irreg. University of Arizona, College of Engineering, Tucson, AZ 85721. TEL 602-621-2361.

620　　　　　US　ISSN 0073-5272
UNIVERSITY OF ILLINOIS AT URBANA - CHAMPAIGN. ENGINEERING EXPERIMENT STATION. BULLETIN. 1904. irreg., no. 505, 1970. price varies. University of Illinois at Urbana - Champaign, Engineering Publications Office, 112 Engineering Hall, 1308 W. Green St., Urbana, IL 61801. TEL 217-333-1510. (back issues avail.) Indexed: Geotech.Abstr.

620　　　　　US　ISSN 0073-5280
UNIVERSITY OF ILLINOIS AT URBANA - CHAMPAIGN. ENGINEERING EXPERIMENT STATION. SUMMARY OF ENGINEERING RESEARCH. 1958. a. free. University of Illinois at Urbana - Champaign, College of Engineering, 112 Engineering Hall, 1308 W. Green St., Urbana, IL 61801. TEL 217-333-1510. Ed. Ann R. Sapoznik. (back issues avail.)

620　　　　　MY
UNIVERSITY OF MALAYA. FACULTY OF ENGINEERING. JOURNAL/UNIVERSITI MALAYA. FAKULTI KEJURUTERAAN. JERNAL. 1958. a. free. University of Malaya, Faculty of Engineering, Lembah Pantai, Kuala Lumpur 22-11, Malaysia. adv. illus. Indexed: Geotech.Abstr.
　Formerly: University of Malaya. Department of Engineering. Journal.

620　　　　　JA　ISSN 0040-8883
UNIVERSITY OF TOKUSHIMA. FACULTY OF ENGINEERING. BULLETIN. (Text in English) 1964. a. free. University of Tokushima, Faculty of Engineering - Tokushima Daigaku Kogakubu, 2-1 Minami Josanjima-cho, Tokushima 770, Japan. Ed. Kazumi Nishioka. charts. circ. 600. Indexed: Sci.Abstr.

620　　　　　US
UNIVERSITY SERIES IN MODERN ENGINEERING. 1983. irreg., latest 1984. (Optimization Software Inc., New York) Springer-Verlag, 175 Fifth Ave., New York, NY 10010 TEL 212-460-1500. (Also Berlin, Heidelberg, Tokyo, Vienna) (reprint service avail. from ISI)

620　　　　　PL　ISSN 0208-5402
UNIWERSYTET SLASKI W KATOWICACH. PRACE WYDZIALU TECHNIKI. (Text in Polish; summaries in English and Russian) 1969. irreg. price varies. Uniwersytet Slaski w Katowicach, Ul. Bankowa 14, 40-007 Katowice, Poland.

620　　　　　GW　ISSN 0083-5560
V D I - BERICHTE. 1954. irreg., 20-30/yr. price varies. (Verein Deutscher Ingenieure) V D I-Verlag GmbH, Graf Recke Str. 84, Postfach 1139, 4000 Duesseldorf 1, W. Germany (B.R.D.) (Subscr. to: V D I Verlag, Box 1831, Birmingham AL 35201 U.S.A.) circ. 500. Indexed: Chem.Abstr. Eng.Ind. Int.Aerosp.Abstr.

624 552　　　　UR
VOPROSY TEORII RAZRABOTKI MESTOROZHDENII POLEZNYKH ISKOPAEMYKH. a. 0.85 Rub. Akademiya Nauk S.S.S.R., Institut Fiziki Zemli, B. Gruzinskaya ul. 10, Moscow, Russian S.F.S.R., U.S.S.R.

621　　　　　CS
VYSOKA SKOLA BANSKA. SBORNIK VEDECKYCH PRACI: RADA STROJNI. (Text in Czech; summaries also in English, German and Russian) 1967. irreg., vol. 20, 1974. 25 Kcs.($1) per issue. Statni Pedagogicke Nakladatelstvi, Ostrovni 30, 113 01 Prague 1, Czechoslovakia. Ed. L. Kuchar. charts. illus. index. circ. 600. Indexed: Met.Abstr. Nutr.Abstr.

620　　　　　US
W B K FORSCHUNGSBERICHTE. (Text in German) 1980. irreg., vol.6, 1982. (Univeritaet Karlsruhe, Institut fuer Werkzeugmaschinen und Betriebstechnik, GW) Springer-Verlag, 175 Fifth Ave., New York, NY 10010 TEL 212-460-1500. (Also Berlin; Heidelberg) Ed. H. Victor. (reprint service avail. from ISI)
　Formerly: W B K.

620　　　　　US
W F T - WERKSTOFF-FORSCHUNG UND - TECHNIK. 1984. irreg., vol.2, 1984. Springer-Verlag, 175 Fifth Ave., New York, NY 10010 TEL 212-460-1500. (Also Berlin, Heidelberg, Tokyo, Vienna) (reprint service avail. from ISI)

WASEDA UNIVERSITY. SCHOOL OF SCIENCE AND ENGINEERING. MEMOIRS/WASEDA DAIGAKU RIKOGAKUBU KIYO. see *SCIENCES: COMPREHENSIVE WORKS*

WASEDA UNIVERSITY. SCIENCE AND ENGINEERING RESEARCH LABORATORY. REPORT. see *SCIENCES: COMPREHENSIVE WORKS*

620　　　　　US　ISSN 0149-7537
WHO'S WHO IN ENGINEERING. 1970. biennial. $200. American Association of Engineering Societies, 415 2nd St., N.E., Ste. 200, Washington, DC 20002-4994. TEL 202-546-2237. Ed. Gordon Davis.
　Formerly: Engineers of Distinction (ISSN 0149-7545)

WILD GOOSE ASSOCIATION. ANNUAL TECHNICAL SYMPOSIUM PROCEEDINGS. see *EARTH SCIENCES — Oceanography*

620.7　　　　　US　ISSN 0084-019X
WILEY SERIES ON SYSTEMS ENGINEERING AND ANALYSIS. 1980. irreg., unnumbered, latest 1983. price varies. John Wiley & Sons, Inc., 605 Third Ave., New York, NY 10016. TEL 212-850-6000. Ed. H. Chestnut.

620 338　　　　US
WIRE JOURNAL INTERNATIONAL DIRECTORY/CATALOG. 1969. a. $50 to non-members. (Wire Association International) Wire Journal, Inc., 1570 Boston Post Rd., Guilford, CT 06437. TEL 415-453-2777. adv. abstr. tr.lit. index. circ. 12,000.
　Formerly: Wire Journal Directory/Catalog (ISSN 0512-5405)

620 500　　　　US
WOMEN AND MINORITIES IN SCIENCE AND ENGINEERING. 1982. biennial. National Science Foundation, 1800 G St. N.W., Rm. 533, Washington, DC 20550. TEL 202-634-4622.

620　　　　　PL　ISSN 0324-8992
WYZSZA SZKOLA PEDAGOGICZNA, OPOLE. ZESZYTY NAUKOWE. SERIA A. NAUKI TECHNICZNE. (Text in Polish; summaries in English and Russian) 1975. irreg., vol. 8, 1982. price varies; avail. on exchange basis. Wyzsza Szkola Pedagogiczna, Opole, Oleska 48, 45-052 Opole, Poland (Dist. by: Ars Polona-Ruch, Krakowskie Przedmiescie 7, Warsaw, Poland) Ed. Jozef Pietrzykowski.

620　　　　　JA　ISSN 0513-2592
YOKOHAMA NATIONAL UNIVERSITY. FACULTY OF ENGINEERING. BULLETIN/ YOKOHAMA KOKURITSU DAIGAKU KOGAKUBU KIYO. (Text in English and European languages) 1951. a. exchange basis. Yokohama National University, Faculty of Engineering - Yokohama Kokuritsu Daigaku Kogakubu, 156 Tokiwadai Hodogaya-ku, Yokohama 240, Japan. circ. 800. Indexed: Chem.Abstr. Met.Abstr. Sci.Abstr. World Alum.Abstr.

300-MW-THTR-KERNKRAFTWERK HAMM-UENTROP, PROJEKTINFORMATION. see *ELECTRICITY AND ELECTRICAL ENGINEERING*

ENGINEERING — Abstracting, Bibliographies, Statistics

624.173 016　　US　ISSN 0363-5732
ABSTRACT JOURNAL IN EARTHQUAKE ENGINEERING. 1972. a. $80. University of California, Berkeley, Earthquake Engineering Research Center, 1301 S. 46 St., Richmond, CA 94804. TEL 415-231-9413. Ed. Ruth C. Denton. index. circ. 500. (back issues avail.) Indexed: Bibl.Seismol. GeoRef.

ENGINEERING — ABSTRACTING, BIBLIOGRAPHIES, STATISTICS

624 016　　　　　US　ISSN 0163-1454
ABSTRACT NEWSLETTER: CIVIL
ENGINEERING. w. $89. U.S. National Technical
Information Service, 5285 Port Royal Rd.,
Springfield, VA 22161. TEL 703-487-4630. Ed.
Linda J. LaGarde. abstr. index.
　　Former titles: Weekly Abstract Newsletter: Civil
Engineering; Weekly Government Abstracts. Civil
Engineering; Weekly Government Abstracts. Civil
and Structural Engineering (ISSN 0145-0344)

620.1 016　　　　　US
ABSTRACT NEWSLETTER: MATERIALS
SCIENCES. w. $89. U.S. National Technical
Information Service, 5285 Port Royal Rd.,
Springfield, VA 22161. TEL 703-487-4630. Ed.
Linda J. LaGarde. index. (back issues avail.)
Indexed: Met.Abstr.
　　Former titles: Weekly Abstract Newsletter:
Materials Sciences; Weekly Government Abstracts.
Materials Sciences (ISSN 0364-4928)

ABSTRACT NEWSLETTER: OCEAN
TECHNOLOGY & ENGINEERING. see *EARTH
SCIENCES — Abstracting, Bibliographies,
Statistics*

AGRICULTURAL ENGINEERING ABSTRACTS.
see *AGRICULTURE — Abstracting,
Bibliographies, Statistics*

669.141　　　　　US
AMERICAN IRON AND STEEL INSTITUTE.
ANNUAL STATISTICAL REPORT. a. price
varies. American Iron and Steel Institute, 1000 16
St., N.W., Washington, DC 20036. TEL 202-452-
7100.

624　　　　　US　ISSN 0066-0604
AMERICAN SOCIETY OF CIVIL ENGINEERS.
TRANSACTIONS. 1867. a. $60. American Society
of Civil Engineers, 345 E. 47th St., New York, NY
10017. TEL 212-705-7538. Ed. Melanie G.
Edwards. circ. 9,000. (also avail. in microform;
reprint service avail. from UMI) Indexed: GeoRef.

600 016 500　　　US　ISSN 0003-6986
APPLIED SCIENCE AND TECHNOLOGY
INDEX; a cumulative subject index to English
language periodicals in the fields of aeronautics and
space science, automation, chemistry, construction,
earth sciences, electricity and electronics, etc. 1958.
m. (except July) service basis. H.W. Wilson Co.,
950 University Ave., Bronx, NY 10452. TEL 212-
588-8400. Ed. Rose Mankofsky. circ. 3,916. (avail.
on CD-ROM) Indexed: Abstr.Bull.Inst.Pap.Chem.
●Also available online. Vendors: Wilsonline.

ASIAN GEOTECHNICAL ENGINEERING
ABSTRACTS. see *EARTH SCIENCES —
Abstracting, Bibliographies, Statistics*

AUSTRALIAN ROAD INDEX. see
*TRANSPORTATION — Abstracting,
Bibliographies, Statistics*

624 388 015　　　AT　ISSN 0705-9213
AUSTRALIAN ROAD RESEARCH IN PROGRESS.
1980. a. Aus.$33. Australian Road Research Board,
Box 156 (Bag 4), Nunawading, Vic. 3131, Australia.
●Also available online. Vendors: AUSINET.

621.4 016　　　UK　ISSN 0001-3447
B I C E R I ABSTRACTS FROM TECHNICAL
AND PATENT PUBLICATIONS. 1949. w. £85.
British Internal Combustion Engine Research
Institute Ltd., 111/112 Buckingham Ave., Slough,
Berks. SL1 4PH, England. Ed. A.E. Russell. bk. rev.
pat. circ. 100. (processed) Indexed: Nutr.Abstr.

620 016　　　　BL　ISSN 0100-0705
BIBLIOGRAFIA BRASILEIRA DE ENGENHARIA.
1972. a. Cr.$600($25) Instituto Brasileiro de
Informacao em Ciencia e Tecnologia, SCRN
7081709 Blocob loja 18E 30, 70740 Brasilia DF,
Brazil. circ. 500.

624 016　　　　　PO
BIBLIOGRAFIA PORTUGUESA DE
ENGENHARIA CIVIL. (Text in Portuguese and
English) 1963. a. no subscr. avail. Laboratorio
Nacional de Engenharia Civil, Avenida do Brasil,
101, 1799 Lisbon Codex, Portugal. bk. rev. circ.
750.
　　Formerly: Bibliografia Portuguesa de Construcao
Civil (ISSN 0067-6756)

624 551.4 551　　　US
BIBLIOGRAPHY ON COLD REGIONS SCIENCE
& TECHNOLOGY. 1951. a. $30.50. U.S. Army,
Cold Regions Research and Engineering Laboratory,
72 Lyme Rd., Hanover, NH 03755. TEL 603-646-
4221. Ed. Geza Thuronyi. bibl. index. cum.index.
(also avail. in microfiche; back issues avail.)
●Also available online. Vendors: Orbit Information
Technologies.

620 016　　　　US　ISSN 0736-6213
BIOENGINEERING ABSTRACTS. 1974. m. $70
domestic; foreign $75. Engineering Information,
Inc., 345 E. 47th St., New York, NY 10017 TEL
212-705-7600. (U.K. subscr. to: Thompson, Henry
Ltd., London Road, Sunningdale, Berks. SL5 OEP,
England)

625.7 016　　　　II　ISSN 0045-6055
C R R I ROAD ABSTRACTS. 1961. a. free contr.
circ. Central Road Research Institute, P.O. Central
Road Research Institute, New Delhi 110020, India.
(Affiliate: Council of Scientific and Industrial
Research) abstr. circ. controlled. Indexed:
Chem.Abstr. Eng.Ind.

624 625　　　　　CN　ISSN 0706-2451
CANADA. STATISTICS CANADA. HIGHWAY,
ROAD, STREET AND BRIDGE
CONTRACTING INDUSTRY/
ENTREPRENEURS DE GRANDE ROUTE,
CHEMIN, RUE ET PONT. (Catalogue 64-206)
(Text in English and French) 1970. a. Can.$15($16)
Statistics Canada, Communications Division, 3rd
Floor, R.H. Coats Bldg., Ottawa, Ont. K1A 0T6,
Canada TEL 613-993-7276. (Subscr. to: Publications
Sales and Services, Ottawa, Ont. K1A 0T6, Canada)
(also avail. in microform from MML)

690　　　　　　CN　ISSN 0576-0097
CANADA. STATISTICS CANADA.
MECHANICAL CONTRACTING INDUSTRY/
LES ENTREPRENEURS D'INSTALLATIONS
MECANIQUES. (Catalogue 64-204) (Text in
English and French) 1967. a. Can.$15($16)
Statistics Canada, Communications Division, 3rd
Floor, R.H. Coats Bldg., Ottawa, Ont. K1A 0T6,
Canada TEL 613-993-7276. (Subscr. to: Publications
Sales and Services, Ottawa, Ont. K1A 0T6, Canada)
(also avail. in microform from MML)

660 540 016　　　UK　ISSN 0262-6438
CHEMICAL ENGINEERING ABSTRACTS. 1982.
m. £185($359) Royal Society of Chemistry,
Information Services, University of Nottingham,
Nottingham NG7 2RD, England (Subscr. to:
Distribution Centre, Blackhorse Rd., Letchworth,
Herts SE16 1HN, England) Ed. J.F. Taylor.
●Also available online. Vendors: Data-Star,
European Space Agency, Orbit Information
Technologies, Pergamon Infoline.

627 016　　　　UK　ISSN 0305-9456
CIVIL ENGINEERING HYDRAULICS
ABSTRACTS. 1968. m. £100. B H R A Fluid
Engineering, Cranfield, Bedford MK43 0AJ,
England (Dist. in U.S. by: Learned Information Inc.,
143 Old Marlton Pike, Medford, NJ 08055) bk. rev.
abstr. index. cum.index.
●Also available online. Vendors: European Space
Agency.

620 615　　　　　UK
CONTAMINATION CONTROL ABSTRACTS.
1986. q. £50($80) Particle Science and Technology
Information Service, Dept. of Chemical Engineering,
University of Technology, Loughborough, Leics.
LE11 3TU, England. TEL 0509-222528. Ed. R.W.
Newbold.

DEPARTMENT OF ENERGY. PUBLICATIONS IN
PRINT. see *ENERGY*

620.1　　　　　GW　ISSN 0340-3475
DOKUMENTATION TRIBOLOGIE/
DOCUMENTATION TRIBOLOGY. (Text in
English, and German) 1967. a. price varies.
Bundesanstalt fuer Materialpruefung, Unter den
Eichen 87, D-1000 Berlin 45, W. Germany (B.R.D.)
(Co-sponsor: Gesellschaft fuer Tribologie) Ed.
Harald Tischer. index. circ. 500. (back issues from
no. 5/1968 avail.)
●Also available online. Vendors: INKA.
　　Formerly: Dokumentation Verschleiss, Reibung
und Schmierung (ISSN 0070-7023)

ENERGY ABSTRACTS. see *ENERGY —
Abstracting, Bibliographies, Statistics*

011 620　　　　　US
ENGINEERED MATERIALS ABSTRACTS. 1986.
m. $775 ($635. with subscr. to Metals Abstracts)
American Society for Metals, Metals Park, OH
44073. TEL 216-338-5151. abstr.

620　　　　　US　ISSN 0360-8557
ENGINEERING INDEX ANNUAL. 1884. a. $840
domestic; foreign $900. Engineering Information,
Inc., 345 E. 47 St., New York, NY 10017 TEL 212-
705-7600. (U.K. subscr. to: Thompson, Henry Ltd.,
London Road, Sunningdale, Berks SL5 OEP,
England) (also avail. in microfilm; magnetic tape;
back issues avail.)

621 011　　　　　US
ENGINEERING INDEX CUMULATIVE INDEX.
1979. irreg., no.3, 1985. $1500. Engineering
Information, Inc., 345 E. 47th St., New York, NY
10017. TEL 212-705-7600.

620 016　　　　US　ISSN 0162-3036
ENGINEERING INDEX MONTHLY AND
AUTHOR INDEX; abstracting and indexing
services covering sources of the world's engineering
literature. m. $1420 domestic; foreign $1530.
Engineering Information, Inc., 345 E. 47th St., New
York, NY 10017 TEL 212-705-7600. (U.K. subscr.
to: Thompson, Henry Ltd., London Road,
Sunningdale, Berks. SL5 OEP, England)
●Also available online. Vendors: BRS, CEDOCAR,
CISTI, Data-Star, DIALOG, European Space
Agency, INKA, NERAC, Inc., Orbit Information
Technologies, Pergamon Infoline, STN
International.
　　Formerly: Engineering Index (ISSN 0013-7960)

620 016　　　　　UK
ENGINEERING SCIENCES DATA UNIT INDEX.
1966. a. Engineering Sciences Data Unit Ltd., 251-
259 Regent St., London W1R 7AD, England. Ed.
J.A. Shaw. cum.index 1943-1979. circ. 4,000.
Indexed: Chem.Abstr.
　　Formerly: Engineering Sciences Data Index
(ISSN 0071-0377)

620 016　　　　UK　ISSN 0046-2446
ERGONOMICS ABSTRACTS. 1968. q. £270.
(Ergonomics Information Analysis Centre) Taylor &
Francis Ltd., Rankine Rd., Basingstoke, Hants
RG24 0PR, England. Ed. C. Stapleton. adv. bk. rev.
(also avail. in microform from MIM) Indexed:
Agri.Eng.Abstr. Sportsearch. World Text.Abstr.

621 016　　　　UK　ISSN 0305-9235
FLUID FLOW MEASUREMENT ABSTRACTS.
1974. bi-m. £99($163) B H R A Fluid Engineering,
Cranfield, Bedford MK43 OAJ, England (Dist. in
U.S. by: Learned Indormation Inc., 143 Old
Marlton Pike, Medford, NJ 08055) Ed.Bd. bk. rev.
abstr. index. cum.index.
●Also available online. Vendors: European Space
Agency.

620.106 016　　　UK　ISSN 0015-4644
FLUID POWER ABSTRACTS. 1970. bi-m. £99($163)
B H R A Fluid Engineering, Cranfield, Bedford
MK43 0AJ, England (Dist. in U.S. by: Learned
Information Inc., 143 Old Marlton Pike, Medford,
NJ 08055) bk. rev. abstr. pat. index. cum.index.

621.2 016　　　　UK　ISSN 0015-4660
FLUID SEALING ABSTRACTS. 1970. q. £93($142)
B H R A Fluid Engineering, Cranfield, Bedford
MK43 0AJ, England (Dist. in U.S. by: Learned
Information Inc., 143 Old Marlton Pike, Medford,
NJ 08055) bk. rev. abstr. pat. index. cum.index.
●Also available online. Vendors: European Space
Agency.

FUEL AND ENERGY ABSTRACTS; a summary of
world literature on all technical and scientific
aspects of fuel and power. see *PETROLEUM AND
GAS — Abstracting, Bibliographies, Statistics*

624.15 016　　　GW　ISSN 0016-8491
GEOTECHNICAL ABSTRACTS. 1970. m. DM.430.
Deutsche Gesellschaft fuer Erd- und Grundbau e.V.,
Kronprinzenstr. 35a, 43 Essen, W. Germany
(B.R.D.) (Co-sponsor: International Society for Soil
Mechanics and Foundation Engineering) Eds. H.
Kuehn, R. Floss. index.

H R I S ABSTRACTS. (Highway Research
Information Service) see *TRANSPORTATION —
Abstracting, Bibliographies, Statistics*

INDIAN LITERATURE IN ENVIRONMENTAL ENGINEERING; a bibliographic review. see ENVIRONMENTAL STUDIES — Abstracting, Bibliographies, Statistics

620 016   UK   ISSN 0019-7823
INDUSTRIAL AERODYNAMICS ABSTRACTS. 1970. bi-m. £99($163) B H R A Fluid Engineering, Cranfield, Bedford MK43 0AJ, England (Dist. in U.S. by: Learned Information Inc., 143 Old Marlton Pike, Medford, NJ 08055) bk. rev. abstr. index. cum.index.
●Also available online. Vendors: European Space Agency.

624   IE
INTERNATIONAL BIBLIOGRAPHY OF STRUCTURAL ENGINEERING. 1986. irreg. £65($95) C I T I S Ltd., 2 Rosemount Terrace, Blackrock, Dublin, Ireland. TEL 353-1-885-971. Ed. Donald P. Murphy. bk. rev. index.

624 016   IE   ISSN 0332-4095
INTERNATIONAL CIVIL ENGINEERING ABSTRACTS. (Also avail. on CD-ROM) 1974. m.(except Jan. & Aug.) £210($415) C I T I S Ltd., 2 Rosemount Terrace, Blackrock, Dublin, Ireland. TEL 353-1-885-971. Ed. Donal P. Murphy. adv. bk. rev. index. (back issues avail.)
Former titles (until 1982): I C E Abstracts (ISSN 0305-2176); Until 1975: European Civil Engineering Abstracts (ISSN 0046-273X)

662 011   UK   ISSN 0266-2922
INTERNATIONAL POWDER & BULK SOLIDS ABSTRACTS. 1984. 3/yr. (in 1 vol.) £80($168) Childwall University Press Ltd., Box 78, London NW11 0PG, England.

662 011   UK   ISSN 0266-2930
INTERNATIONAL PROCESS TECHNOLOGY ABSTRACTS. 1984. 3/yr. (in 1 vol.) £80($168) Childwall University Press Ltd., Box 78, London NW11 0PG, England.

624   IE   ISSN 0790-5750
INTERNATIONAL STRUCTURAL ENGINEERING ABSTRACTS. 1986. q. £80($120) C I T I S Ltd., 2 Rosemount Terrace, Blackrock, Dublin, Ireland. TEL 353-1-885-971. Ed. Donald P. Murphy. (back issues avail.; avail. in CD-ROM)

690 016   II   ISSN 0027-6138
N B O ABSTRACTS. 1956. m. exchange basis. ‡ National Buildings Organisation, G Wing, Nirman Bhavan, Maulana Azad Rd., New Delhi 11, India. Ed. S. Protar. bk. rev. film rev. stat. cum.index. circ. 500. (processed)

016 620   US   ISSN 0085-4581
P I E. (Publications Indexed for Engineering) a. $35. Engineering Information, Inc., 345 E. 47th St., New York, NY 10017. TEL 212-705-7600.

540 016   US   ISSN 0161-8032
PREDICASTS OVERVIEW OF MARKETS AND TECHNOLOGIES. 1977. m. $850. Predicasts, Inc., 200 University Circle Research Center, 11001 Cedar Ave., Cleveland, OH 44106. TEL 216-795-3000. abstr. charts. stat. q. and a. cum.indexes. Key Title: P R O M T. Predicasts Overview of Markets and Technologies.
Formed by the merger of: Chemical Market Abstracts (ISSN 0009-2606) & Equipment Market Abstracts (ISSN 0098-4779); Which was formerly titled: Electronics Market Abstracts; Electronics and Equipment Market Abstracts (ISSN 0095-7275)

660   UK
PROCESS ENGINEERING INDEX. 1965. s-a. Technical Indexes Ltd., Willoughby Rd., Bracknell, Berks. RG12 4DW, England. Ed. N. Saksena. charts. circ. 3,466.
Former titles: Chemical Engineering Index (ISSN 0308-8391); Chemical Product Data.

526.9 016   UK
R I C S LIBRARY INFORMATION SERVICE ABSTRACTS AND REVIEWS. 1965. m. £100 to non-members. Royal Institution of Chartered Surveyors, 12 Great George St., Parliament Square, London SW1P 3AD, England. Ed. Pauline Lane-Gilbert. stat. cum.index: 1965-1969, 1970-1974. circ. 1,300. (reprint service avail. from UMI)
Formerly: R I C S Abstracts and Reviews (ISSN 0033-6939)

621 016   UK   ISSN 0038-1063
SOLID-LIQUID FLOW ABSTRACTS. 1970. q. £93($142) B H R A Fluid Engineering, Cranfield, Bedford MK43 0AJ, England (Dist. in U.S. by: Learned Information Inc., 143 Old Marlton Pike, Medford, NJ 08055) abstr. bibl. index.

TECHNICAL EDUCATION ABSTRACTS. see EDUCATION — Abstracting, Bibliographies, Statistics

660.2 016   UK   ISSN 0040-5787
THEORETICAL CHEMICAL ENGINEERING ABSTRACTS. 1964. bi-m. Box 146, Liverpool L69 2BL, England. Ed. A.J. Wilson. bk. rev. abstr. index. Indexed: Fluidex.

621.8 016   UK   ISSN 0041-2694
TRIBOS - TRIBOLOGY ABSTRACTS. 1968. bi-m. £99($163) B H R A Fluid Engineering, Cranfield, Bedford MK43 0AJ, England (Dist. in U.S. by: Learned Information Inc., 143 Old Marlton Pike, Medford, NJ 08055) bk. rev. abstr. index. cum.index. Indexed: Br.Ceram.Abstr.
●Also available online. Vendors: European Space Agency.
Formerly: Tribos.

620   US
U S S R REPORT: ENGINEERING AND EQUIPMENT. 1973. irreg., (approx. 10/yr.) $5 per no. U.S. Joint Publications Research Service, 1000 N. Glebe Rd., Arlington, VA 22201 TEL 703-487-4630. (Orders to: NTIS, Springfield, VA 22161) Indexed: Petrol.Abstr.
Formerly: U S S R and Eastern Europe Scientific Abstracts: Engineering and Equipment; Which was formed by the merger of: U S S R Scientific Abstracts: Engineering and Equipment; East European Scientific Abstracts: Engineering and Equipment.

620.11 669   US
U S S R REPORT: MATERIALS SCIENCE AND METALLURGY. 1973. irreg., (approx. 20/yr.) $5. U.S. Joint Publications Research Service, 1000 N. Glebe Rd., Arlington, VA 22201 TEL 703-487-4630. (Orders to: NTIS, Springfield, VA 22161)
Formerly: U S S R and Eastern Europe Scientific Abstracts: Materials Science and Metallurgy; Which was formed by the merger of: U S S R Scientific Abstracts: Materials Science and Metallurgy; East European Scientific Abstracts: Materials Science and Metallurgy.

VACUUM; the international journal and abstracting service for vacuum science and technology. see PHYSICS — Abstracting, Bibliographies, Statistics

011 621.9   GW   ISSN 0724-1976
VEREIN DEUTSCHER INGENIEURE. INFORMATIONSDIENST. INSTANDHALTUNG. 1983. q. DM.195. Verein Deutsche Ingenieure, Graf-Recke-Str. 84, 4000 Duesseldorf 1, W. Germany (B.R.D.) Ed. G. Gentzsch. bk. rev. abstr. charts. illus. (back issues avail.)

ENGINEERING — Chemical Engineering

see also Plastics

660.2 542   US   ISSN 0569-5473
A I CH E EQUIPMENT TESTING PROCEDURES. 1952. irreg. price varies. American Institute of Chemical Engineers, Equipment Testing Procedures Committee, 345 E. 47th St., New York, NY 10017. TEL 212-705-7657. Ed.Bd. (also avail. in microform from ISI; back issues avail.) Indexed: Eng.Ind.

660   US   ISSN 0270-7632
A I CH E M I MODULAR INSTRUCTION. SERIES C: TRANSPORT. 1980. irreg.,(approx. 1/yr) $30 to non-members; members $15. American Institute of Chemical Engineers, 345 E. 47th St., New York, NY 10017. TEL 212-705-7657. bibl. charts. (back issues avail.) Indexed: Eng.Ind.
Study and teaching

660   US   ISSN 0890-0582
A I CH E M I MODULAR INSTRUCTION. SERIES G: DESIGN OF EQUIPMENT. 1985. irreg.,(approx. 1/yr.) $30 to non-members; members $15. American Institute of Chemical Engineers, 345 E. 47th St., New York, NY 10017. TEL 212-705-7657. bibl. charts. (back issues avail.) Indexed: Eng.Ind.

660   US   ISSN 0065-8804
A I CH E MONOGRAPH SERIES. 1951. irreg., latest vol.82. American Institute of Chemical Engineers, 345 E. 47th St., New York, NY 10017. TEL 212-705-7657.

660   US   ISSN 0065-8812
A I CH E SYMPOSIUM SERIES. 1951. a. vol.83, 1987. American Institute of Chemical Engineers, 345 E. 47th St., New York, NY 10017. TEL 212-705-7657. (back issues avail.) Indexed: Biol.Abstr. Chem.Abstr. Eng.Ind. API Abstr. Dairy Sci.Abstr. Forest.Abstr. GeoRef. Sel.Water Res.Abstr.
Supersedes: Chemical Engineering Progress Symposium Series (ISSN 0069-2948)

660   US   ISSN 0569-5457
A I CH E WORKSHOP SERIES. 1967. irreg., latest 1979. price varies. American Institute of Chemical Engineers, 345 E. 47th St., New York, NY 10017. TEL 212-705-7657. bibl. charts. (back issues avail.) Indexed: Eng.Ind.

660   US
ADDITIVES FOR PLASTICS D.A.T.A. BOOK. 1987. biennial. $125. D.A.T.A., Inc. (Subsidiary of: International Thomson Organization) 9889 Willow Creek Rd., Box 26875, San Diego, CA 92131. TEL 619-578-7600. Ed. Steven d'Adolf.

661   US   ISSN 0001-821X
ADHESIVES AGE. 1958. m. (plus annual Directory) $27. Communication Channels, Inc., 6255 Barfield Rd., Atlanta, GA 30328. TEL 404-256-9800. Ed. Ann Barker. adv. bk. rev. charts. illus. patents. tr.lit. index. circ. 23,200. (also avail. in microform from UMI) Indexed: A.S.& T.Ind. Chem.Abstr. Curr.Cont. Eng.Ind. Excerp.Med. Sci.Cit.Ind. Abstr.Bull.Inst.Pap.Chem. Art & Archaeol.Tech.Abstr. Curr.Pack.Abstr. Fluidex. ISMEC. Int.Sci.Rev. Int.Aerosp.Abstr. PROMT. Text.Tech.Dig.

668   US
ADHESIVES AGE DIRECTORY. 1968. a. $34.95. Communication Channels, Inc., 6255 Barfield Rd., Atlanta, GA 30328. TEL 404-256-9800. Ed. Barbara Kalinsky.
Formerly: Adhesives Red Book (ISSN 0065-1931)

660.2   US   ISSN 0065-2377
ADVANCES IN CHEMICAL ENGINEERING. 1956. irreg., vol.12, 1983. Academic Press, Inc., Orlando, FL 32887. TEL 305-345-2000. Eds. Thomas B. Drew, John W. Hoopes, Jr. index.

ADVANCES IN DRYING. see ENGINEERING — Mechanical Engineering

ADVANCES IN ELECTROCHEMISTRY AND ELECTROCHEMICAL ENGINEERING. see CHEMISTRY — Electrochemistry

ADVANCES IN POLYMER SCIENCE/ FORTSCHRITTE DER HOCHPOLYMEREN-FORSCHUNG. see CHEMISTRY — Organic Chemistry

661   US   ISSN 0271-2334
ADVANCES IN TRANSPORT PROCESSES. 1980. irreg. price varies. John Wiley & Sons, Inc., 605 Third Ave., New York, NY 10158. TEL 212-850-6000. Ed. Arun S. Mujumdar. Indexed: Chem.Abstr.

ADVANCES IN URETHANE SCIENCE AND TECHNOLOGY. see CHEMISTRY — Organic Chemistry

661   US   ISSN 0149-3701
AMMONIA PLANT SAFETY AND RELATED FACILITIES; a C E P technical manual. 1959. a. price varies. American Institute of Chemical Engineers, 345 E. 47th St., New York, NY 10017. TEL 212-705-7657. (back issues avail.) Indexed: Chem.Abstr.
Formerly: Chemical Engineering Progress. Safety in Air and Ammonia Plants (ISSN 0069-293X)

ENGINEERING — CHEMICAL ENGINEERING

ANNUAL BOOK OF A S T M STANDARDS. VOLUME 06.03. PAINT - FATTY OILS AND ACIDS, SOLVENTS, MISCELLANEOUS; AROMATIC HYDROCARBONS. see
ENGINEERING — Engineering Mechanics And Materials

ANNUAL BOOK OF A S T M STANDARDS. VOLUME 15.05. ENGINE COOLANTS; HALOGENATED ORGANIC SOLVENTS; INDUSTRIAL CHEMICALS. see
ENGINEERING — Engineering Mechanics And Materials

660   AT
APPLIED CHEMICAL NEWS. 1964. a. free. Applied Chemicals Pty. Ltd., Domville Ave., Hawthorn, Vic. 3122, Australia. Ed. Marcus May. circ. 12,000.

668.4   US   ISSN 0066-5517
APPLIED POLYMER SYMPOSIUM. PAPERS. 1965. irreg., no.36, 1981. price varies. (Brooklyn Polytechnic Institute) John Wiley & Sons, Inc., 605 Third Ave., New York, NY 10016. TEL 718-850-6000. (also avail. in microfilm)

660   665.5   AT
AUSTRALIAN CONFERENCE ON CHEMICAL ENGINEERING. PROCEEDINGS. 1973. a. price varies. Institution of Chemical Engineers in Australia, Box 9, Killara, N.S.W. 2071, Australia. circ. 2,500. (back issues avail.)

BIOTECHNOLOGY AND GENETIC ENGINEERING REVIEWS. see *BIOLOGY*

660   670   US   ISSN 0746-9012
C P I PURCHASING CHEMICALS DIRECTORY. 1984. a. $35 (included in subscr. to CPI Purchasing magazine) Cahners Publishing Co., Inc., Manufacturing Group, Division of Reed Publishing USA, 275 Washington St., Newton, MA 02158. TEL 617-964-3030. adv. circ. 20,000.

661   US   ISSN 0276-8429
CHEMICAL ENGINEERING CATALOG. 1915. a. $40. Penton Publishing, Reinhold Division, 600 Summer St., Box 1361, Stamford, CT 06904. TEL 203-348-7531. adv. tr.lit. circ. 35,000. (also avail. in microfilm; reprint service avail. from UMI)

660   US   ISSN 0272-4057
CHEMICAL ENGINEERING EQUIPMENT BUYER'S GUIDE. a. McGraw-Hill Publications Co., 1221 Ave. of the Americas, New York, NY 10020.
Formerly: Chemical Engineering. Equipment Buyer's Guide Issue (ISSN 0094-9841)

660.2   378   US
CHEMICAL ENGINEERING FACULTIES. a. price varies. American Institute of Chemical Engineers, Chemical Engineering Education Projects Committee, 345 E. 47th St., New York, NY 10017. TEL 212-705-7657. Ed. Keith P. Johnston.
Formerly: Chemical Engineering Faculties of Canada and the United States.

660   NE
CHEMICAL ENGINEERING MONOGRAPHS. 1975. irreg., vol.23, 1985. price varies. Elsevier Science Publishers B.V., Box 211, 1000 AE Amsterdam, Netherlands. Ed. S.W. Churchill. Indexed: Chem.Abstr.

338.4   II   ISSN 0304-1166
CHEMICAL INDIA ANNUAL. (Text in English) a. Rs.5. c/o S.K. Bhanot, 640 Double Storey, New Rajinder Nagar, New Delhi, India. illus.

660   US
CHEMICAL INDUSTRIES SERIES. 1979. irreg., vol.27, 1986. price varies. Marcel Dekker, Inc., 270 Madison Ave., New York, NY 10016.

660   UK   ISSN 0069-2980
CHEMICAL INDUSTRY DIRECTORY. 1923. a. £60. Benn Business Information Services Ltd., P.O. Box 20, Sovereign Way, Tonbridge, Kent TN9 1RQ, England. adv. index. circ. 2,200.

660
CHEMICAL PLANT CONTRACTOR PROFILES. 1977. a. £80. Chemical Intelligence Services, 39A Bowling Green Lane, London EC1R 0BJ, England.

660   FR   ISSN 0430-2222
CONGRESS F A T I P E C. Variant title: Federation d'Associations de Techniciens des Industries des Peintures, Vernis, Emaux et Encres d'Imprimerie de l'Europe Continentale. Congress Proceedings. 1951. biennial. Federation d'Associations de Techniciens des Industries des Peintures, Vernis, Emaux et Encres d'Imprimerie de l'Europe Continentale, Maison de la Chimie, 28 rue Saint Dominique, 75007 Paris, France.
17th Lugano, Switzerland. 1984; 19th Venice, Italy. 1986.

660   US
CORROSION DATABASE. 1984. irreg. price varies. Marcel Dekker, Inc., 270 Madison Ave., New York, NY 10016. TEL 212-696-9000. Ed. Philip Schweitzer.

660   US
DIRECTORY OF CHEMICAL ENGINEERING CONSULTANTS. 1978. irreg. $7.50. American Institute of Chemical Engineers, 345 E. 47th St., New York, NY 10017. TEL 212-705-7657. Ed. Mary Pat Healy. index.

660.28   CN   ISSN 0070-525X
DIRECTORY OF CHEMICAL ENGINEERING RESEARCH IN CANADIAN UNIVERSITIES.* (Text in English and French) 1961. biennial. Can.$12 to non-members. Canadian Society for Chemical Engineering, 151 Slater St., Ste. 906, Ottawa, Ont., K1P 5H3, Canada. TEL 613-233-5623. Ed. A. Rollin. circ. 400.

661   UK   ISSN 0140-2129
EUROPEAN CONFERENCE ON MIXING AND CENTRIFUGAL SEPARATION. PROCEEDINGS. 1975. irreg., 5th, 1985. price varies. B H R A Fluid Engineering, Cranfield, Bedford MK43 0AJ, England (Dist. in U.S. by: Learned Information Inc., 143 Old Marlton Pike, Medford, NJ 08055) Indexed: Chem.Abstr.

660   380.1   BE   ISSN 0425-9076
FEDERATION DES INDUSTRIES CHIMIQUES DE BELGIQUE. ANNUAIRE. (Text in English, Flemish, French, German) irreg., latest edt., 1985. 1500 Fr. Federation des Industries Chimiques de Belgique, Square Marie Louise 49, B-1040 Brussels, Belgium. adv. circ. 4,500.

660.28   330.9   BE   ISSN 0085-0489
FEDERATION DES INDUSTRIES CHIMIQUES DE BELGIQUE. RAPPORT ANNUEL. (Text in Flemish and French) 1928. a. free. Federation des Industries Chimiques de Belgique, 49 Square Marie-Louise, B-1040 Brussels, Belgium. Ed. Paul-F. Smets.

662   SW   ISSN 0348-6613
FOEREDRAG VID PYROTEKNIKDAGEN. (Text in English and Swedish) 1969. biennial. price varies. Svenska Nationalkommitten foer Mekanik, Sektionen foer Detonik och Foerbraenning, Box 608, S-551 18 Joenkoeping, Sweden. Ed. J. Hansson. illus. Indexed: Chem.Abstr.
Explosives

GLASNIK HEMICARA I TEHNOLOGA BOSNE I HERCEGOVINE. see *CHEMISTRY*

661   MX
GUIA DE LA INDUSTRIA QUIMICA; productos quimicos. 1956. a. Mex.$450($50) Editorial Cosmos, Espana 396, Granjas Estrella, 09880 Mexico, DF, Mexico. Ed. Catalina Ramirez de Arrellano. adv.
Formerly: Petro Quimica.

660   II
GUIDE TO INDIAN CHEMICAL PLANTS AND EQUIPMENT. Bound with: Indian Chemical Directory (ISSN 0073-6295) (Text in English) 1966. irreg. $60 for Indian Chemical Directory. Technical Press Publications, 5/1 Convent St., Colaba, Bombay 400039, India. TEL 2021446. Ed. J.P. de Sousa. adv. circ. 9,000.
Formerly: Catalogue of Indian Chemical Plants (ISSN 0069-1151)

660   540   II   ISSN 0073-6295
INDIAN CHEMICAL DIRECTORY. (Text in English) 1955. irreg., latest 12th edt., 1987. $60. Technical Press Publications, 5/1 Convent St., Colaba, Bombay 2021446, India. TEL 2021446. Ed. J.P. de Sousa. adv. circ. 9,000.

660   MX
INDUSTRIA QUIMICA EN MEXICO. 1981. a. price varies. Instituto Nacional de Estadistica, Geografia e Informatica, Secretaria de Programacion y Presupuesto, Patriotismo 711 Torre "A" P.H., Col. San Juan Mixcoac, Deleg. Benito Juarez, 03910 Mexico, D.F., Mexico TEL 598-99-05. (Subscr. to: Rio Rhin No. 56, Col. Cuauhtemoc, 06500 Mexico, D.F., Mexico)

628.96   US   ISSN 8756-1530
INSECTICIDE PRODUCT GUIDE. 1982. a. $28. Meister Publishing Co., 37841 Euclid Ave., Willoughby, OH 44094. TEL 216-942-2000. Ed. Charlotte Sine. adv. circ. 7,680.

500   662   UK
INSTITUTE OF ENERGY. SYMPOSIUM SERIES. 1975. irreg. £7. Institute of Energy, 18 Devonshire St., London W1N 2AU, England. Indexed: Chem.Abstr.
Formerly: Institute of Fuel. Symposium Series.

INSTRUMENTATION IN THE CHEMICAL AND PETROLEUM INDUSTRIES. see
INSTRUMENTS

INTERNATIONAL CONGRESS OF PURE AND APPLIED CHEMISTRY. (LECTURES) see
CHEMISTRY

INTERNATIONAL POWDER & BULK SOLIDS ABSTRACTS. see *ENGINEERING — Abstracting, Bibliographies, Statistics*

INTERNATIONAL PROCESS TECHNOLOGY ABSTRACTS. see *ENGINEERING — Abstracting, Bibliographies, Statistics*

660.2   US   ISSN 0071-3112
INTERNATIONAL SYMPOSIUM ON CHEMICAL REACTION ENGINEERING. PROCEEDINGS. (First and Second published by Pergamon Press in Chemical Engineering Science; Third and Fourth in supplement to Chemical Engineering Science; Fifth by Elsevier; Sixth by the Federation itself) 1976. irreg., 8th, 1984, Edinburgh. University of Deleware, Department of Chemical Engineering, c/o Prof. K.B. Bischoff, Newark, DE 19716.
Formerly: European Symposium on Chemical Reaction Engineering. Proceedings.

660   UR   ISSN 0202-8069
ITOGI NAUKI I TEKHNIKI: KHIMIYA I TEKHNOLOGIYA VYSOKOMOLEKULYARNYKH SOEDINENII. vol.23, 1987. irreg. price varies. Vsesoyuznyi Institut Nauchno-Tekhnicheskoi Informatsii (VINITI), Baltiiskaya ul. 14, Moscow A-219, Russian S.F.S.R. (Subscr. to: Mezhdunarodnaya Kniga, Dimitrova ul. 39, 113095 Moscow, Russian S.F.S.R., U.S.S.R.) Indexed: Chem.Abstr.

660   UR   ISSN 0202-8018
ITOGI NAUKI I TEKHNIKI: PROTSESSY I APPARATY KHIMICHESKOI TEKHNOLOGII. vol.15, 1987. irreg. price varies. Vsesoyuznyi Institut Nauchno-Tekhnicheskoi Informatsii (VINITI), Baltiiskaya ul. 14, Moscow A-219, Russian S.F.S.R., U.S.S.R. (Subscr. to: Mezhdunarodnaya Kniga, Dimitrova ul. 39, 113095 Moscow, Russian S.F.S.R., U.S.S.R.) Indexed: Chem.Abstr.

660   JA   ISSN 0075-319X
JAPAN CHEMICAL ANNUAL. (Text in English) a. 5400 Yen($27) Chemical Daily Co., Ltd. - Kagaku Kogyo Nipposha, 3-19-16 Shibaura, Minato-ku, Tokyo 108, Japan. Ed. Shozo Tanaka.

660   JA   ISSN 0075-3203
JAPAN CHEMICAL DIRECTORY. (Text in English) 1963. a. 26200 Yen($135) Chemical Daily Co., Ltd. - Kagaku Kogyo Nipposha, 3-16-8 Nihonbashi Hamacho, Cho-ku, Tokyo 108, Japan.

668.4   US   ISSN 0570-4898
JOURNAL OF APPLIED POLYMER SCIENCE. SYMPOSIA. Short title: Applied Polymer Symposia. 1965. irreg., no.36, 1981. price varies. John Wiley & Sons, Inc., 605 Third Ave., New York, NY 10016. TEL 212-850-6000. Indexed: Chem.Abstr. ASCA. Abstr.Bull.Inst.Pap.Chem. Art & Archaeol.Tech.Abstr. Ind.Sci.Rev. World Text.Abstr.

660   CC
JOURNAL OF CHEMICAL INDUSTRY AND ENGINEERING CHINA; selected papers. 1982. irreg. (Chemical Industry and Engineering Society of China) Chemical Industry Press, P.O. Box 1423, Beijing, People's Republic of China (U.S. distr. addr.: American Institute of Chemical Engineers, 345 E. 47th St., New York, NY 10017) Ed. Su Yuanfu. bibl. charts. index. (back issues avail.) Indexed: Chem.Abstr. Eng.Ind.

660   UK   ISSN 0260-6275
JOURNAL OF SEPARATION PROCESS TECHNOLOGY. 1979. a. £50($105) Childwall University Press Ltd., Box 78, London NW11 0PG, England. Ed. Dr. David Reay. Indexed: Chem.Abstr. Excerp.Med.

628.96   UR   ISSN 0206-3441
KHEMORETSEPTSIYA NASEKOMYKH/INSECT CHEMORECEPTION. (Text in Russian; summaries in English) 1975. biennial. price varies. (Akademiya Nauk Litovskoi S.S.R., Institute of Zoology and Parasitology) Izdatel'stvo Mokslas, Zvaigzdziu 23, Vilnius 232050, Lithuanian S.S.R., U.S.S.R. Ed. A. Skirkevicius.

665   US   ISSN 0077-4022
NATIONAL COTTONSEED PRODUCTS ASSOCIATION. TRADING RULES. 1897. a. $10 to non-members. National Cottonseed Products Association, Box 12023, Memphis, TN 38112. TEL 901-324-4417. Ed. Lewis C. Williamson. circ. 1,000.

662   NO
NORWAY. DIREKTORATET FOR BRANN OG EKSPLOSJONSVERN. AARSBERETNING. 1915. a. Direktoratet for Brann og Eksplosjonvern, Postboks 355, 3101 Toensberg, Norway. illus. circ. 2,500.
     Former titles: Norway. Statens Sprengstoffinspeksjon. Aarsberetning; Norway. Sprengstoffinspeksjonen. Aarsberetning.

NOVYE ISSLEDOVANIYA V KHIMII, METALLURGII I OBOGASHCHENII. see *METALLURGY*

P N C REVIEW. (Power Reactor and Nuclear Fuel Development Corporation) see *PHYSICS — Nuclear Energy*

660 655   US   ISSN 0090-3507
PETROLEUM AND CHEMICAL INDUSTRY CONFERENCE. RECORD OF CONFERENCE PAPERS. a. (I E E E, Industry Applications Society) Institute of Electrical and Electronics Engineers, Inc., 345 E. 47th St., New York, NY 10017 TEL 212-705-7900. (Subscr. address: 445 Hoes Lane, Piscataway, NJ 08854)
     Former titles: Petroleum Industry Conference. Record; Petroleum and Chemical Industry Technical Conference. Record (ISSN 0079-1288)

668.4   SI
PLASTICHEM. 1969. a. free to qualified personnel. Singapore Polytechnic Polymer Society, Dover Rd., Singapore 5, Singapore. Ed. Tang Sook Mui. adv. circ. 1,000 (controlled) Indexed: Chem.Abstr.
     Formerly: Polymer Journal.

660.2   PL   ISSN 0137-2602
POLITECHNIKA LODZKA. ZESZYTY NAUKOWE. INZYNIERIA CHEMICZNA. (Text in Polish; summaries in English and Russian) 1973. irreg. price varies. Politechnika Lodzka, Ul. Zwirki 36, 90-924 Lodz, Poland (Dist. by: Ars Polona-Ruch, Krakowskie Przedmiescie 7, Warsaw, Poland) Ed. Stanislaw Michalowski. circ. 250.

665   PL   ISSN 0324-9867
POLITECHNIKA WROCLAWSKA. INSTYTUT CHEMII I TECHNOLOGII NAFTY I WEGLA. PRACE NAUKOWE. KONFERENCJE. (Text in Polish and English) 1975. irreg., no.5, 1985. price varies. Politechnika Wroclawska, Wybrzeze Wyspianskiego 27, 50-370 Wroclaw, Poland (Dist. by: Ars Polona-Ruch, Krakowskie Przedmiescie 7, Warsaw, Poland) Ed. Jerzy Ciekot. circ. 375.

665   PL   ISSN 0324-9859
POLITECHNIKA WROCLAWSKA. INSTYTUT CHEMII I TECHNOLOGII NAFTY I WEGLA. PRACE NAUKOWE. MONOGRAFIE. (Text in Polish; summaries in English, French and Russian) 1972. irreg., no.17, 1986. price varies. Politechnika Wroclawska, Wybrzeze Wyspianskiego 27, 50-370 Wroclaw, Poland (Dist. by: Ars Polona-Ruch, Krakowskie Przedmiescie 7, Warsaw, Poland) Ed. Jery Ciekot. Indexed: Chem.Abstr.

665   PL   ISSN 0084-2818
POLITECHNIKA WROCLAWSKA. INSTYTUT CHEMII I TECHNOLOGII NAFTY I WEGLA. PRACE NAUKOWE. STUDIA I MATERIALY. (Text in Polish; summaries in English, Russian) 1969. irreg., no.20, 1981. price varies. Politechnika Wroclawska, Wybrzeze Wyspianskiego 27, 50-370 Wroclaw, Poland (Dist. by: Ars Polona-Ruch, Krakowskie Przedmiescie 7, Warsaw, Poland) Ed. Marian Kloza.

660 697   PL
POLITECHNIKA WROCLAWSKA. INSTYTUT INZYNIERII CHEMICZNEJ I URZADZEN CIEPLNYCH. PRACE NAUKOWE. KONFERENCJE. (Text in Polish; summaries in English, French and Russian) 1972. irreg., no.10, 1987. price varies. Politechnika Wroclawska, Wybrzeze Wyspianskiego 27, 50-370 Wroclaw, Poland (Dist. by: Ars Polona-Ruch, Krakowskie Przedmiescie 7, Warsaw, Poland) Ed. Jerzy Ciekot.

660 697   PL   ISSN 0084-2850
POLITECHNIKA WROCLAWSKA. INSTYTUT INZYNIERII CHEMICZNEJ I URZADZEN CIEPLNYCH. PRACE NAUKOWE. MONOGRAFIE. (Text in Polish; summaries in English, French and Russian) 1970. irreg., no.27, 1987. price varies. Politechnika Wroclawska, Wybrzeze Wyspianskiego 27, 50-370 Wroclaw, Poland (Dist. by: Ars Polona-Ruch, Krakowskie Przedmiescie 7, Warsaw, Poland) Ed. Jerzy Ciekot.

660 697   PL   ISSN 0324-9751
POLITECHNIKA WROCLAWSKA. INSTYTUT INZYNIERII CHEMICZNEJ I URZADZEN CIEPLNYCH. PRACE NAUKOWE. STUDIA I MATERIALY. (Text in Polish: Summaries in English and Russian) 1970. irreg., no. 13, 1976. price varies. Politechnika Wroclawska, Wybrzeze Wyspianskiego 27, 50-370 Wroclaw, Poland (Dist. by: Ars Polona-Ruch, Krakowskie Przedmiescie 7, Warsaw Poland) Ed. Marian Kloza. Indexed: Chem.Abstr.

660   PL   ISSN 0084-2893
POLITECHNIKA WROCLAWSKA. INSTYTUT TECHNOLOGII NIEORGANICZNEJ I NAWOZOW MINERALNYCH. PRACE NAUKOWE. KONFERENCJE. 1972. irreg., no.16, 1986. price varies. Politechnika Wroclawska, Wybrzeze Wyspianskiego 27, 50-370 Wroclaw, Poland (Dist. by: Ars Polona-Ruch, Krakowskie Przedmiescie 7, Warsaw, Poland) Ed. Jerzy Ciekot.

660   PL   ISSN 0084-2907
POLITECHNIKA WROCLAWSKA. INSTYTUT TECHNOLOGII NIEORGANICZNEJ I NAWOZOW MINERALNYCH. PRACE NAUKOWE. MONOGRAFIE. (Text in Polish; summaries in English, Russian) 1971. irreg., no.11, 1986. price varies. Politechnika Wroclawska, Wydawnictwo, Wybrzeze Wyspianskiego 27, 50-370 Wroclaw, Poland. Ed. Jerzy Ciekot.

660   PL   ISSN 0084-2915
POLITECHNIKA WROCLAWSKA. INSTYTUT TECHNOLOGII NIEORGANICZNEJ I NAWOZOW MINERALNYCH. PRACE NAUKOWE. STUDIA I MATERIALY. (Text in Polish; summaries in English and Russian) 1970. irreg., no.5, 1978. price varies. Politechnika Wroclawska, Wybrzeze Wyspianskiego 27, 50-370 Wroclaw, Poland (Dist. by: Ars Polona-Ruch, Krakowskie Przedmiescie 7, Warsaw, Poland) Ed. Marian Kloza. Indexed: Chem.Abstr.

668.4   PL   ISSN 0137-1398
POLITECHNIKA WROCLAWSKA. INSTYTUT TECHNOLOGII ORGANICZNEJ I TWORZYW SZTUCZNYCH. PRACE NAUKOWE. KONFERENCJE. (Text in Polish; summaries in English and Russian) 1972. irreg., no.15, 1986. price varies. Politechnika Wroclawska, Wybrzeze Wyspianskiego 27, 50-370 Wroclaw, Poland (Dist. by: Ars Polona-Ruch, Krakowskie Przedmiescie 7, Warsaw, Poland) Ed. Jerzy Ciekot.

668.4   PL
POLITECHNIKA WROCLAWSKA. INSTYTUT TECHNOLOGII ORGANICZNEJ I TWORZYW SZTUCZNYCH. PRACE NAUKOWE. MONOGRAFIE. (Text in Polish; summaries in English and Russian) 1971. irreg., no.9, 1986. price varies. Politechnika Wroclawska, Wybrzeze Wyspianskiego 27, 50-370 Wroclaw, Poland (Dist. by: Ars Polona-Ruch, Krakowskie Przedmiescie 7, Warsaw, Poland) Ed. Jerzy Ciekot.

661 660.284   UR
POLUTEHNILINE INSTITUUT TALLINN. INZHENERNAYA ENZIMOLOGIYA. (Subseries of Its Toimetised) (Text in Russian; summaries in English or German) irreg. price varies. Polutehniline Instituut Tallinn, Ehitajate tee 5, Tallinn, Estonian S.S.R., U.S.S.R.
     Formerly: Polutehniline Instituut Tallinn. Poluchenie i Svoistva Immobilizovannykh Fermentov.

661 660   UR   ISSN 0320-3468
POLUTEHNILINE INSTITUUT TALLINN. SINTEZ I PRIMENENIE POLIKONDENSATSIONNYKH KLEEV. (Subseries of Its Toimetised) (Text in Russian; summaries in English or German) irreg. price varies. Polutehniline Instituut Tallinn, Ehitajate tee 5, Tallinn, Estonian S.S.R., U.S.S.R.

660 691   UR   ISSN 0203-9710
POLUTEHNILINE INSTITUUT TALLINN. TEORIYA I TEKHNOLOGIYA POLUCHENIYA STROITEL'NYKH MATERIALOV IZ ZOL TVERDYKH TOPLIV. (Subseries of Its Toimetised) (Text in Russian; summaries in English or German) irreg. price varies. Polutehniline Instituut Tallinn, Ehitajate tee 5, Tallinn, Estonian S.S.R., U.S.S.R.

660   US
POWDER/BULK SOLIDS' DIRECTALOG. 1985. a. included in subscription to Powder/Bulk Solids' Magazine. Machalek Publishing Co., 15 S. Ninth St., Minneapolis, MN 55402. TEL 612-370-0413. Ed. Rob Machalek. adv. circ. 20,000.

662 380.1   UK   ISSN 0143-1455
PROCESS ENGINEERING DIRECTORY. 1978. a. £35. Morgan-Grampian Book Publishing Co. Ltd., 30 Calderwood St., Woolwich, London SE18 6QH, England. Ed. Phil Brown. adv. circ. 1,000.

660   US
PROCESS EQUIPMENT SERIES. 1979. irreg. Technomic Publishing Co., Inc., 851 New Holland Ave., Box 3535, PA 17604. TEL 717-291-5609. Eds. Paul N. Cheremisinoff, Mahesh V. Bhatia. charts.

660   MX
PRODUCCION QUIMICA MEXICANA. 1963. a. Mex.$850($35) Editorial Cosmos, Espana 396, Col. Granjas Estrella, 09880 Mexico, DF, Mexico. Ed. Cesar Macazaga. adv. index. cum.index. circ. 5,000.

662.8   US   ISSN 0192-6551
PROGRESS IN BIOMASS CONVERSION. 1979. a., vol.5, 1984. $49. Academic Press, Inc., Orlando, FL 32887. TEL 305-345-2000. Eds. K.V. Sarkanen, D.A. Tillman. Indexed: Chem.Abstr.

PROGRESS IN POLYMER SCIENCE. see *CHEMISTRY — Organic Chemistry*

660   UK   ISSN 0456-4804
RAMSAY SOCIETY OF CHEMICAL ENGINEERS. JOURNAL. 1934. a. £2.50. ‡ Ramsay Society of Chemical Engineers, Dept. of Chemical and Biochemical Engineering, University College London, Torrington Place, London WC1E 7JE, England. Ed. A. Mole. adv. illus. circ. 500. (tabloid format)

660   IT
REPERTORIO CHIMICO ITALIANO; industriale e commerciale. biennial. Edizioni Ragno, Via Crescenzio 43, 00193 Rome, Italy (Distr. by: Edizioni Ragno, Via Crescenzio 43, 00193 Rome, Italy)

660   CK   ISSN 0120-100X
REVISTA ION. (Text in Spanish; summaries in English) 1953. a. Col.$120($3) per no. or exchange basis. Universidad Industrial de Santander, Centro de Estudios de Ingenieria Quimica, Apdo. Aereo 678, Bucaramanga, Colombia. adv. bk. rev. bibl. charts. illus. circ. 600.

SERIES IN THERMAL AND FLUIDS
ENGINEERING. see *ENGINEERING —
Mechanical Engineering*

660 677 JA ISSN 0559-8621
SHINSHU UNIVERSITY. FACULTY OF TEXTILE
SCIENCE AND TECHNOLOGY. JOURNAL.
SERIES C: CHEMISTRY. (Text in English) 1951.
irreg. exchange basis. Shinshu University, Faculty of
Textile Science and Technology - Shinshu Daigaku
Sen'i Gakubu, 3-15-1 Tokida, Ueda, Nagano 386,
Japan.

660 SA
SOUTH AFRICAN CHEMICALS
MANUFACTURED & IMPORTED. a. R.25.
African Business Publications (Pty) Ltd., P.O. Box
2901, Johannesburg 2001, South Africa. Ed.
Graham Hulley, Jean Hey. adv.

333.7 665 UK
SYMPOSIUM ON FLAMES AND INDUSTRY.
PROCEEDINGS. no.4, 1972. irreg. £15($37.50)
Institute of Fuel, British Flame Research
Committee, 18 Devonshire St., London W1N 2AU,
England.

660 US ISSN 0082-1144
SYNTHETIC ORGANIC CHEMICALS, UNITED
STATES PRODUCTION AND SALES. 1918. a.
price varies. U.S. International Trade Commission,
701 E St., N.W., Washington, DC 20436 TEL 202-
523-0161. (Orders to: Supt. of Documents,
Washington, DC 20402)

660 AG ISSN 0376-0456
UNIVERSIDAD NACIONAL DEL LITORAL.
FACULTAD DE INGENIERIA QUIMICA.
REVISTA. irreg. Universidad Nacional del Litoral,
Facultad de Ingenieria Quimica, Santiago del Estero
2829, 3000 Santa Fe, Argentina. Ed. Jorge Douglas
Maldonado. charts. Indexed: Chem.Abstr.

VEGYIPARI SZAKIRODALMI TAJEKOZTATO/
CHEMICAL ENGINEERING ABSTRACTS. see
*CHEMISTRY — Abstracting, Bibliographies,
Statistics*

ENGINEERING — Civil Engineering

*see also Building and Construction;
Transportation — Roads and Traffic*

A R T B A OFFICIALS AND ENGINEERS
DIRECTORY, TRANSPORTATION AGENCY
PERSONNEL. (American Road and Transportation
Builders Association) see *TRANSPORTATION —
Roads And Traffic*

624 US
A S C E ANNUAL COMBINED INDEX. a. $20.
American Society of Civil Engineers, 345 E. 47th
St., New York, NY 10017-2398. TEL 212-705-
7538. Ed. Melanie Edwards. cum.index. circ. 4,000.
(also avail. in microfilm; microfiche; magnetic tape;
back issues avail.)

690 FI ISSN 0355-2705
ACTA POLYTECHNICA SCANDINAVICA. CIVIL
ENGINEERING AND BUILDING
CONSTRUCTION SERIES. (Text in English)
irreg., 2-3/yr. Fmk.130. Teknillisten Tieteiden
Akatemia - Finnish Academy of Technical Sciences,
Kansakoulukatu 10 A, SF-00100 Helsinki 10,
Finland. Ed. Jussi Hyyppa. index. cum.index (1958-
1985) circ. 250. (also avail. in microfilm from UMI;
back issues avail.; reprint service avail. from UMI)
Indexed: Curr.Cont. Sci.Cit.Ind. ASCA. GeoRef.

627.1 551.44 CN
ALBERTA RESEARCH COUNCIL. RIVER
ENGINEERING AND SURFACE HYDROLOGY
REPORTS. irreg. price varies. Alberta Research
Council, Publications Dept., P.O. Box 8330, Sta. F,
Edmonton, Alta. T6H 5X2, Canada. TEL 403-450-
5111.
Formerly: Alberta Research. Highways and River
Engineering Reports (ISSN 0080-1550)

624 US ISSN 0065-9932
AMERICAN PUBLIC WORKS ASSOCIATION.
RESEARCH FOUNDATION. SPECIAL
REPORTS. irreg. latest 1986. free. American Public
Works Association, 1313 E. 60th St., Chicago, IL
60637.

627 US
AMERICAN SOCIETY OF CIVIL ENGINEERS.
OFFICIAL REGISTER. a. American Society of
Civil Engineers, 345 E. 47th St., New York, NY
10017. TEL 212-705-7275. Ed. Phyllis Lanz.

ANNUAIRE BATIMENT ET TRAVAUX PUBLICS.
see *BUILDING AND CONSTRUCTION*

625.8 US ISSN 0066-9466
ASSOCIATION OF ASPHALT PAVING
TECHNOLOGISTS. PROCEEDINGS. Variant
title, vol.49 (1980): Asphalt Paving Technology.
1928. a. $50. Association of Asphalt Paving
Technologists, 134 CME Bldg., 500 Pillsbury Dr.,
S.E., University of Minnesota, Minneapolis, MN
55455-0220. TEL 612-625-8062. Ed. E.L. Skok, Jr.
cum.index through vol.54. (also avail. in microform
from UMI; reprint service avail. from UMI)
Indexed: Chem.Abstr.
Roads and streets

625.72 CN ISSN 0700-5989
ASSOCIATION OF ONTARIO LAND
SURVEYORS. ANNUAL REPORT. a. Can.$20.
Association of Ontario Land Surveyors, 1043
McNicoll Ave, Scarborough, Ont. M1W 3W6,
Canada. TEL 416-491-9020.
Surveying

AUSTRALIAN ROAD RESEARCH BOARD.
PROCEEDINGS. see *TRANSPORTATION —
Roads And Traffic*

B S HANDBOOK 3. SUMMARIES OF BRITISH
STANDARDS FOR BUILDING. see *BUILDING
AND CONSTRUCTION*

624 BF
BAHAMAS. MINISTRY OF WORKS AND
UTILITIES. ANNUAL REPORT. 1965. a. $2.
Ministry of Works and Utilities, P.O. Box N8156,
Nassau, Bahamas (Orders to: Government
Publications Office, Bank Lane, Nassau, Bahamas)
charts. illus. stat. circ. 100(approx.)
Formerly: Bahamas. Ministry of Works. Annual
Report (ISSN 0376-5490)

624.183 GW ISSN 0067-6365
BETON- UND FERTIGTEIL-JAHRBUCH. 1951. a.
DM.27. Bauverlag GmbH, P.O. Box 1460, 6200
Wiesbaden, W. Germany (B.R.D.)
Formerly: Betonstein-Jahrbuch.

BUILDING SOCIETIES WHO'S WHO. see
*BUSINESS AND ECONOMICS — Trade And
Industrial Directories*

624 690 UK ISSN 0305-4047
C I R I A ANNUAL REPORT. 1964. a. free.
Construction Industry Research and Information
Association, 6 Storey's Gate, London SW1P 3AU,
England.
Formerly: C I R I A. Bulletin (ISSN 0069-9209)

624 690 UK ISSN 0305-408X
C I R I A REPORT. 1965. irreg., (approx. 6/yr.) price
varies per no. Construction Industry Research and
Information Association, 6 Storey's Gate, London
SW1P 3AU, England. circ. 500(controlled) Indexed:
GeoRef. Geotech.Abstr. HRIS.

624 690 UK ISSN 0305-1781
C I R I A TECHNICAL NOTE. 1968. irreg., (approx.
6/yr.) price varies. Construction Industry Research
and Information Association, 6 Storey's Gate,
London SW1P 3AU, England.

624.176 CN
CANADIAN CONFERENCE ON EARTHQUAKE
ENGINEERING. PROCEEDINGS. 1971.
quadrennial. price varies. University of British
Columbia, Department of Civil Engineering,
Vancouver, B.C. V6T 1W5, Canada. TEL 604-228-
2637. Ed. S. Cherry. charts, illus. circ. 1,000.

624 CN ISSN 0318-0522
CANADIAN STRUCTURAL ENGINEERING
CONFERENCE. PROCEEDINGS. 1968. biennial.
Can.$80. Canadian Steel Construction Council, 201
Consumers Rd., Suite 300, Toronto, Ont. M2J 4G8,
Canada. TEL 416-491-9898. circ. 400. Indexed:
Eng.Ind.

628 BL
CATALOGO BRASILEIRO DE ENGENHARIA
SANITARIA E AMBIENTAL. 1975. a. $20. A B
E S, Av. Beira-Mar, 216-13 andar, 20021 Rio de
Janeiro, RJ, Brazil. Ed. Tania Bitencourt. adv. circ.
14,000.

624 UK
CHARTERED INSTITUTE OF BUILDING DIARY.
a. Welbecson Ltd., 3 Thomas St., Hull, Humberside
HU9 1EJ, England.

624 SA
CIVIL ENGINEERING ADVISORY COUNCIL.
ANNUAL REPORT/SIVIELE
INGENIEURSWESE-ADVIESRAAD.
JAARVERSLAG. (Text in English, Afrikaans)
1983. a. free. Department of Transport, Civil
Engineering Advisory Council, P.O. Box 415,
Pretoria 0001, South Africa. circ. 1,000.

624 JA ISSN 0578-3747
CIVIL ENGINEERING IN JAPAN. (Text English)
1961. a. 4.500 Yen($36) Doboku Gakkai - Japan
Society of Civil Engineers, Mubanchi, Shinjuku 1-
Chome, Shinjuku-ku, Tokyo, 160, Japan TEL 03-
272-7211. (Subscr. to: Mazuren Co., Ltd., P.O. Box
5050, Tokyo International 100-31, Japan) adv. circ.
1,300. (back issues avail.)

624 US
CIVIL ENGINEERING SERIES. 1979. irreg., vol.6,
1983. Marcel Dekker, Inc., 270 Madison Ave., New
York, NY 10016.

624 AT ISSN 0156-2126
CIVIL ENGINEERING WORKING PAPERS. 1978.
irreg. price varies. Monash University, Wellington
Rd., Clayton, Vic. 3168, Australia. TEL 03-565-
4000. (back issues avail.)

627 JA ISSN 0578-5634
COASTAL ENGINEERING IN JAPAN. (Text in
English) 1958. irreg. price varies. Japan Society of
Civil Engineers - Doboku Gakkai, 1-chome,
Yotsuya, Shinjuku-ku, Tokyo 160, Japan TEL 03-
373-7211. (Subscr. to: Maruzen Co., Ltd., Deport
Dept., P.O. Box 5050, Tokyo International, 100-31
Tokyo, Japan) Indexed: Ocean.Abstr. Pollut.Abstr.
Fluidex.

620 US
COASTAL ENGINEERING RESEARCH
COUNCIL. PROCEEDINGS. 1954. biennial. price
varies. American Society of Civil Engineers, 345 E.
47th St., New York, NY 10017. Ed. Billy L. Edge.
circ. 1,000. (back issues avail.; reprint service avail.
from UMI) Indexed: GeoRef.

COMMONWEALTH SCIENTIFIC AND
INDUSTRIAL RESEARCH ORGANIZATION.
DIVISION OF GEOMECHANICS. TECHNICAL
REPORT. see *MINES AND MINING
INDUSTRY*

526.9 625.72 SA
CONFERENCE OF SOUTH AFRICAN
SURVEYORS. PROCEEDINGS/KONFERENSIE
VAN SUID-AFRIKAANSE OPMETERS.
VERRIGTINGE. irreg. R.10.50. South African
Council for Surveyors, Registrar, Box 62041,
Marshalltown 2107, South Africa.
Formerly: National Conference of South African
Surveyors. Proceedings.
Surveying

624 US ISSN 0271-2067
COST DATA FOR LANDSCAPE
CONSTRUCTION. 1980. a. $32. Kerr Associates,
Inc., 1942 Irving Ave., S., Minneapolis, MN 55403.
TEL 612-374-5438. Ed. Kathleen W. Kerr.

CURRENT PRACTICES IN GEOTECHNICAL
ENGINEERING. see *EARTH SCIENCES —
Geology*

624.176 NE
DELFT SOIL. 1980. irreg. free. Delft Geotechnics,
Postbus 69, 2600 AB Delft, Netherlands. circ. 2,
300.

ENGINEERING — CIVIL ENGINEERING

624 621.381 JA
DENSANKI RIYO NI KANSURU SHINPOJUMU KOENGAIYO/PROCEEDINGS OF THE SYMPOSIUM OF COMPUTER RESEARCH. (Text in Japanese; summaries in English) 1976. a. price varies. Doboku Gakkai, Doboku Joho Shisutemu Iinkai - Japan Society of Civil Engineers, Mubanchi, Yotsuya 1-Chome, Shinjuku-Ku, Tokyo, 160, Japan (Subscr. to: JSCE or Mazuren Co., Ltd., P.O. Box 5050, Tokyo International 100-31, Japan) circ. 350. (back issues avail.)

624.151 NE
DEVELOPMENTS IN GEOTECHNICAL ENGINEERING. 1972. irreg., vol.39, 1985. price varies. Elsevier Science Publishers B.V., Box 211, 1000 AE Amsterdam, Netherlands. Indexed: Geotech.Abstr.

624 UK ISSN 0260-5007
DIRECTORY OF LAND AND HYDROGRAPHIC SURVEY SERVICES IN THE UNITED KINGDOM. 1979. a. Royal Institution of Chartered Surveyors, 12 Great George St., Parliament Square, London SW1P 3AD, England. charts.

624 JA
DOBOKU GAKKAI NENJI KOENKAI KOEN GAIYOSHU/JAPAN SOCIETY OF CIVIL ENGINEERS. PROCEEDINGS OF THE ANNUAL CONFERENCE. 1937. a. Doboku Gakkai - Japan Society of Civil Engineers, Mubanchi, Yotsua 1-Chome, Shinjuku-Ku, Tokyo, 160, Japan TEL 03-272-7211. (Subscr.to: Mazuren Co., Ltd., P.O. Box 5050, Tokyo International 100-31, Japan) circ. 4,850.

624 JA
DOBOKU KEIKAKUGAKU SHINPOJUMU/ SYMPOSIUM ON CIVIL ENGINEERING PLANNING. PROCEEDINGS. 1967. a. price varies. Doboku Gakkai - Japan Society of Civil Engineers, Yotsuya 1-Chome, Shinjuku-Ku, Tokyo, 160, Japan TEL 03-272-7211. (Subscr. to: Maruzen Co., ltd., P.O. Box 5050, Tokyo International 100-31, Japan) (back issues avail.)

DODGE HEAVY CONSTRUCTION COST DATA. see BUILDING AND CONSTRUCTION

624 US ISSN 0271-0323
E E R C REPORTS. a. $300 per annual series ($200 to educational institutions) University of California, Berkeley, Earthquake Engineering Research Center, 1301 S. 46th St., Richmond, CA 94804 TEL 415-231-9576. (Single copies from: NTIS, Springfield, VA 22161)

ECONOMIE FRANCAISE EN PERSPECTIVES SECTORIELLES: FILIERE BATIMENT, GENIE CIVIL, MATERIAUX DE CONSTRUCTION. see BUILDING AND CONSTRUCTION

625.7 GW
ELSNERS HANDBUCH FUER STRASSENWESEN. 1937. a. DM.28.40. Otto Elsner Verlagsgesellschaft, Schoefferstr. 15, 6100 Darmstadt, W. Germany (B.R.D.) Ed. E.W. Goerner. adv. circ. 12,500.
Formerly: Elsner; Handbuch fuer Strassenbau und Strassenverkehrstechnik (ISSN 0071-0067)
Roads and streets

624.151 US ISSN 0071-0318
ENGINEERING GEOLOGY AND SOILS ENGINEERING SYMPOSIUM. PROCEEDINGS. Variant title: Annual Symposium on Engineering Geology and Soils Engineering. Proceedings. 1963. a. $9.50. Engineering Geology & Soils Engineering Symposium, Box 7129, Boise, ID 83707. TEL 208-334-5253. circ. 325. Indexed: HRIS.
Formerly: Engineering Geology Symposium. Proceedings.

624.151 US ISSN 0071-0326
ENGINEERING GEOLOGY CASE HISTORIES. (Each vol. has distinctive title) 1957. irreg., no.10, 1974. price varies. Geological Society of America, Marketing Department, 3300 Penrose Pl., Box 9140, Boulder, CO 80301. TEL 303-447-8850. Indexed: GeoRef. Geotech.Abstr.

ENTREPRISE EUROPEENNE. see BUILDING AND CONSTRUCTION

624 FR
ENTRETIEN ET TRAVAUX NEUFS.* irreg. 127 F. Entreprise Moderne d'Edition, 17 rue Vieta, 75017 Paris, France (Subscr. address: 9 rue du Roussillon-Zone Industrielle, 91220 Bretigny-sur-Orge, France)

625.7 FR
EUROPEAN SYMPOSIUM ON CONCRETE PAVEMENTS. REPORTS. 1969. irreg., 5th, Aachen (Germany), 1986. 1250 F. Cembureau, 2 rue Saint Charles, 75740 Paris Cedex 15, France. circ. 1,140.
Roads and streets

625.7 016 GW ISSN 0340-3998
FORSCHUNG IM STRASSENWESEN. 1972. irreg. DM.50. ‡ Forschungsgesellschaft fuer Strassen-und Verkehrswesen, Alfred-Schuette-Allee 10, 5000 Cologne 21, W. Germany (B.R.D.) Ed. Herbert Kuehn. bibl. circ. 3,000.
Roads and streets

624 GW ISSN 0341-5872
FORSCHUNGSARBEITEN AUS DEM STRASSENWESEN. SCHRIFTENREIHE. 1952. irreg. price varies. (Forschungsgesellschaft fuer Strassen und Verkehrswesen) Kirschbaum Verlag, Siegriedstr. 28, Postfach 210 209, D-5300 Bonn 2, W. Germany (B.R.D.)

625.8 GW
FORSCHUNGSGESELLSCHAFT FUER STRASSEN-UND VERKEHRSWESEN. ARBEITSGRUPPE ASPHALT-UND TEERSTRASSEN. SCHRIFTENREIHE. 1948. irreg. price varies. (Forschungsgesellschaft fuer Strassen-und Verkehrswesen) Kirschbaum Verlag, Siegfriedstr. 28, Postfach 210209, D-5300 Bonn 2, W. Germany (B.R.D.)
Formerly: Forschungsgesellschaft fuer das Strassenwesen. Arbeitsgruppe Asphalt-und Teerstrassen. Schriftenreihe (ISSN 0426-9918)
Roads and streets

625.8 GW
FORSCHUNGSGESELLSCHAFT FUER STRASSEN-UND VERKEHRSWESEN. ARBEITSGRUPPE BETONSTRASSEN. SCHRIFTENREIHE. 1950. irreg. price varies. (Forschungsgesellschaft fuer Strassen-und Verkehrswesen) Kirschbaum Verlag, Siegfriedstr. 28, Postfach 210209, D-5300 Bonn 2, W. Germany (B.R.D.)
Formerly: Forschungsgesellschaft fuer das Strassenwesen. Arbeitsgruppe Betonstrassen. Schriftenreihe (ISSN 0429-1816)
Roads and streets

624 US ISSN 0015-8933
FOUNDATION FACTS. 1965. irreg. free. (International Society for Soil Mechanics and Foundation Engineering) Raymond International Builders, Inc., Box 22718, Houston, TX 77227. TEL 713-961-4521. Ed. Frank M. Fuller. charts. illus. circ. 18,000. Indexed: Eng.Ind. Geo.Tech.Abstr.

624 388.31 FR ISSN 0222-8394
FRANCE. LABORATOIRE CENTRAL DES PONTS ET CHAUSSEES. RAPPORT DE RECHERCHE. (Text in French) 1969. irreg. free. Laboratoire Central des Ponts et Chaussees, 58 Bd. Lefebvre, 75732 Paris cedex 15, France. (back issues avail.)

624 FR ISSN 0085-2643
FRANCE. LABORATOIRES DES PONTS ET CHAUSEES. RAPPORT DE RECHERCHE. (Summaries in English, French, German, Russian, Spanish) 1969. irreg., latest no.139, 1986. free. Laboratoire Central des Ponts et Chaussees, 58 bd. Lefebvre, 75732 Paris cedex 15, France.

624 551 JA
GANBAN RIKIGAKU NI KANSURI SHINPOJUMU RONBUNSHU/PROCEEDINGS OF THE SYMPOSIUM ON ROCK MECHANICS. (Text in Japanese; summaries in English) a. price varies. Doboku Gakkai - Japan Society of Civil Engineers, Committee on Rock Mechanics, Mubanchi, Yotsuya 1-Chome, Shinjuku-Ku, Tokyo, 160 TEL 03-272-7211. (Subscr. to: Mazuren Co., Ltd., P.O. Box 5050, Tokyo International 100-31, Japan) circ. 500. (back issues avail.)

GEOLOGIA APPLICATA E IDROGEOLOGIA. see EARTH SCIENCES — Geology

625.7 GW
GERMANY (FEDERAL REPUBLIC, 1949-). BUNDESANSTALT FUER STRASSENWESEN, ERFAHRUNGSAUSTAUCH UEBER ERDARBEITEN IM STRASSENBAU. 1972. a. free. Bundesanstalt fuer Strassenwesen, Brueerstr. 53, 5060 Bergisch-Gladbach, W. Germany (B.R.D.)
Roads and streets

624 UK ISSN 0072-6850
GREAT BRITAIN. DEPARTMENT OF THE ENVIRONMENT. ENGINEERING SPECIFICATIONS. irreg. price varies. H.M.S.O., Box 569, London SE1 9NH, England.

624 JA
GYOKO KENSETSU GIJUTSU KENKYU HAPPYOKAI KOENSHU/PROCEEDINGS OF FISHING PORT ENGINEERING. 1956. a. 3.700 Yen($20) Fisheries Agency, 2-1,1-Chome, Kasumigaseki, Cyiyoda-Ku, Tokyo 100, Japan.

624 US ISSN 0340-4838
HAFENBAUTECHNISCHE GESELLSCHAFT. JAHRBUCH. vol.39, 1983. irreg. price varies. Springer-Verlag, 175 Fifth Ave., New York, NY 10010 TEL 212-460-1500. (Also Berlin, Heidelberg, Tokyo and Vienna) (reprint service avail. from ISI)

671 NE
HANDBOOK OF POWDER TECHNOLOGY. 1980. irreg. price varies. Elsevier Science Publishers B.V., Box 211, 1000 AE Amsterdam, Netherlands. Eds. J.C. Williams, T. Allen.

624 JA
HASHI/BRIDGES IN JAPAN. (Text in English and Japanese) 1967. a. price varies. Doboku Gakkai - Japan Society of Civil Engineers, Mubanchi, Yotsuya 1-Chome, Shinjuku-Ku, Tokyo, 160, Japan TEL 03-272-7211. (Subscr. to: Maruzen Co., Ltd., P.O. Box 5050, Tokyo International 100-31, Japan) circ. 800. (back issues avail.)

625.7 US ISSN 0073-2176
HIGHWAY PLANNING NOTES. 1962. irreg. U.S. Federal Highway Administration, Management Systems Branch, 400 Seventh St., S.W., Washington, DC 20591. TEL 202-426-0632. (newsletter format)
Roads and streets

625.7 II
HIGHWAY RESEARCH RECORD; general report on road research work done in India during (year) (Text in English) 1974. a. $1. Indian Roads Congress, Highway Research Board, Jamnagar House, Shahjahan Rd., New Delhi 110011, India. TEL 381649. circ. 6,000.

624 621 UK
HOBSON'S ENGINEERING CASEBOOK. 1979. a. £8. (Careers Research and Advisory Centre) Hobsons Ltd., Bateman St., Cambridge, England. Eds. Sean Gallagher, Bill Jolly. adv. circ. 20,000.

624 SZ
I A B S E CONGRESS REPORT. (Text in English, French or German; summaries in English, French and German) 1932. quadrennial, 12th, 1984, Vancouver B.C. price varies. International Association for Bridge and Structural Engineering, ETH-Hoenggerberg, CH-8093 Zurich, Switzerland.
Formerly: International Association for Bridge and Structural Engineering. Final Report (of Congress) (ISSN 0074-1418)

624 SZ
I A B S E REPORT. (Text in English, French and German) 1964. irreg., no.51, 1986. price varies. International Association for Bridge and Structural Engineering, ETH-Hoenggerberg, CH-8093 Zurich, Switzerland.
Formerly: International Association for Bridge and Structural Engineering. Reports of the Working Commissions (ISSN 0074-1442)

624 UK
I C E LIST OF MEMBERS. biennial. £80($120) (Institution of Civil Engineers) Thomas Telford, Ltd., 1-7 Great George St., Westminster, London SW1P 3AA, England (Dist. in U.S. by: American Society of Civil Engineers, 345 E. 47th St., New York, NY 10017) adv.
Formerly: I C E Yearbook (ISSN 0308-4159)

ENGINEERING — CIVIL ENGINEERING

624   US   ISSN 0172-8008
INGENIEURBAUTEN. (Text in German) 1971. irreg., vol.8, 1976. price varies. Springer-Verlag, 175 Fifth Ave., New York, NY 10010 TEL 212-460-1500. (Also Berlin, Heidelberg, Tokyo and Vienna) Eds. K. Sattler, P. Stein. (reprint service avail. from ISI)

624   UK
INSTITUTION OF STRUCTURAL ENGINEERS. SESSIONAL YEARBOOK AND DIRECTORY OF MEMBERS. 1910. a. £20. Institution of Structural Engineers, 11 Upper Belgrave St., London SW1X 8BH, England. adv. circ. 2,000.
Formerly: Institution of Structural Engineers. Yearbook (ISSN 0073-9847)

624.2   US
INTERNATIONAL BRIDGE CONFERENCE. PROCEEDINGS. 1984. a. $40 domestic; foreign $45. Engineers' Society of Western Pennsylvania, 530 Wm. Penn Place, Pittsburgh, PA 15219. TEL 412-261-0710. circ. 1,500.

627.8   FR   ISSN 0534-8293
INTERNATIONAL COMMISSION ON LARGE DAMS. BULLETIN. no.57, 1986. irreg. price varies. International Commission on Large Dams, 151 bd. Haussmann, 75008 Paris, France (Dist. in US: USCOLD, P.O. Box 15103, Denver, CO 80215)

627.8   US   ISSN 0074-4115
INTERNATIONAL COMMISSION ON LARGE DAMS. TRANSACTIONS. triennial since 1961; 1982, 15th, Lausanne. U.S. Committee on Large Dams, Box 15103, Denver, CO 80215. TEL 303-236-6960.

624   UK   ISSN 0074-6045
INTERNATIONAL FEDERATION OF PRESTRESSING. CONGRESS PROCEEDINGS. 1952. quadrennial, 9th, 1982, Stockholm. price varies. International Federation of Prestressing - Federation Internationale de la Precontrainte, Wexham Springs, Slough SL3 6PL, England. circ. 2,000.

INTERNATIONAL INSTITUTE OF SEISMOLOGY AND EARTHQUAKE ENGINEERING. BULLETIN. see *EARTH SCIENCES — Geophysics*

INTERNATIONAL INSTITUTE OF SEISMOLOGY AND EARTHQUAKE ENGINEERING. INDIVIDUAL STUDIES BY PARTICIPANTS AT I I S E E. see *EARTH SCIENCES — Geophysics*

INTERNATIONAL INSTITUTE OF SEISMOLOGY AND EARTHQUAKE ENGINEERING. YEAR BOOK. see *EARTH SCIENCES — Geophysics*

INTERNATIONAL ROAD CONGRESSES. PROCEEDINGS. see *TRANSPORTATION — Roads And Traffic*

624.151   PO   ISSN 0074-848X
INTERNATIONAL SOCIETY FOR ROCK MECHANICS. CONGRESS. PROCEEDINGS. (Proceedings published in host country) (Text in English, French and German) 1966. irreg., (approx. every 4/yrs.), next 1987 in Canada. price varies. International Society for Rock Mechanics, c/o Laboratorio Nacional de Engenharia Civil, 101 Avenida do Brasil, P-1799 Lisbon Codex, Portugal. Indexed: GeoRef.

624   MX   ISSN 0074-3313
INTERNATIONAL SOCIETY FOR SOIL MECHANICS AND FOUNDATION ENGINEERING. PROCEEDINGS. (Text in English or French) 1936. quadrennial; 7th, 1969. $50. Sociedad Mexicana de Mecanica de Suelos - Mexican Society for Soil Mechanics, Valle de Bravo No. 19, Col. Vergel de Coyoacan, Tlalpan, 14340 Mexico, D.F., Mexico.

625.732   US   ISSN 0074-8498
INTERNATIONAL SOCIETY FOR TERRAIN-VEHICLE SYSTEMS. PROCEEDINGS OF INTERNATIONAL CONFERENCE. 1961. irreg., 8th, Cambridge, England, 1984. $75. (International Society for Terrain-Vehicle Systems) Pergamon Press, Maxwell House, Fairview Park, Elmsford, NY 10523. Ed. J.R. Radforth. bk. rev. circ. 500. Indexed: Eng.Ind.
Roads and streets

624 380.5   UK
INTERNATIONAL SYMPOSIUM ON THE AERODYNAMICS AND VENTILATION OF VEHICLE TUNNELS. PROCEEDINGS. irreg., 5th, 1985. price varies. B H R A Fluid Engineering, Cranfield, Bedford MK43 0AJ, England (Dist. in U.S. by: Learned Information Inc., 143 Old Marlton Pike, Medford, NJ 08055)

625.7 388.314   UR   ISSN 0202-7844
ITOGI NAUKI I TEKHNIKI: AVTOMOBIL'NYI I GORODSKOI TRANSPORT. irreg., latest vol.11, 1986. price varies. Vsesoyuznyi Institut Nauchno-Tekhnicheskoi Informatsii (VINITI), Baltiiskaya ul. 14, Moscow A-219, Russian S.F.S.R. (Subscr. to: Mezhdunarodnaya Kniga, Dimitrova ul. 39, 113095 Moscow, Russian S.F.S.R., U.S.S.R.)

624   FR   ISSN 0021-5554
JAUNE ET LA ROUGE. 1948. irreg., 10-11/yr. (plus special nos.) 100 F. (special nos. not included in subscr.) Ecole Polytechnique (Ax), Societe Amicale des Anciens Eleves, 5 rue Descartes, 75005 Paris, France. adv. bk. rev. circ. 12,500.

624   GE
JOURNAL FOR PHOTOGRAMMETRISTS & SURVEYORS. (Text in English) 1955. irreg. free. Jenoptik Jena GmbH, Carl-Zeiss-Str. 1, 69 Jena, E. Germany (D.D.R.) Ed. H. Schoeler. adv. bk. rev. abstr. illus. circ. 3,000. (also avail. in microfiche)
Formerly: Vermessungs-Informationen.

624   US   ISSN 0733-9402
JOURNAL OF ENERGY ENGINEERING. Short title: Energy. 1956. irreg., (2-3/yr.) $46 to non-members. American Society of Civil Engineers, 345 E. 47th St., New York, NY 10017. TEL 212-705-7275. circ. 3,300. (also avail. in microform from UMI; reprint service avail. from UMI) Indexed: A.S.& T.Ind. Chem.Abstr. Curr.Cont. Excerp.Med. Sci.Cit.Ind. Fluidex. GeoRef. Geotech.Abstr. Ind.Sci.Rev. Intl.Abstr.Oper.Res. Sel.Water Res.Abstr.
Former titles (1979-1983): American Society of Civil Engineers. Energy Division. Journal (ISSN 0190-8294); (until 1979): American Society of Civil Engineers. Power Division. Journal (ISSN 0569-8030)

625.72   US   ISSN 0733-9453
JOURNAL OF SURVEYING ENGINEERING. 1956. irreg., (2-3/yr.) $36 to non-members. American Society of Civil Engineers, 345 E. 47th St., New York, NY 10017. TEL 212-705-7275. circ. 3,500. (also avail. in microform from UMI; reprint service avail. from UMI) Indexed: A.S.& T.Ind. Curr.Cont. Eng.Ind. Fluidex. HRIS. Ind.Sci.Rev.
Former titles: Journal of Surveying and Mapping; (until 1982): American Society of Civil Engineers. Surveying and Mapping Division. Journal (ISSN 0569-8073)
Surveying

JOURNAL OF URBAN PLANNING AND DEVELOPMENT. see *HOUSING AND URBAN PLANNING*

K B S-RAPPORTER. see *HOUSING AND URBAN PLANNING*

K B S TEKNISKA FOERESKRIFTER/K B S TECHNICAL REGULATIONS; krav och raad/requirements and recommendations. see *HOUSING AND URBAN PLANNING*

624   JA
KAIGAN KOGAKU KOENKAI RONBUNSHU/PROCEEDINGS OF THE JAPANESE CONFERENCE ON COASTAL ENGINEERING. (Text in Japanese) 1954. a. price Varies. Doboku Gakkai - Japan Society of Civil Engineers, Committee on Coastal Engineering, Mubanchi, Yotsuya 1-Chome, Shinjuku-Ku, Tokyo, 160, Japan TEL 03-272-7211. (Subscr. to: Mazuren Co., Ltd., P.O. Box 5050, Tokyo International 100-31, Japan) adv. circ. 1,000. (back issues avail.)

624   JA
KAIYO KAIHATSU RONBUNSHU/PROCEEDINGS OF THE OCEAN DEVELOPMENT SYMPOSIUM. (Text in Japanese) 1970. a. price varies. Dobuku Gakkai - Japan Society of Civil Engineers, Committee on Ocean Development, Mubanchi, Yotsuya 1-Chome, Shinjuku-Ku, Tokyo, 160, Japan TEL 03-272-7211. (Subscr. to: JSCE or Maruzen Co., Ltd., P.O. Box 5050, Tokyo International 100-31, Japan) circ. 250. (back issues avail.)

624 614.7   JA
KANKYO MONDAI SHINPOJUMU KOEN RONBUNSHU/PROCEEDINGS OF THE SYMPOSIUM ON ENVIRONMENTAL PROBLEMS. (Text in Japanese; summaries in English) 1973. a. price varies. Doboku Gakkai - Japan Society of Civil Engineers, Committee on Environmental Problems, Mubanchi, Yotsuya 1-Chome, Shinjuku-Ku, Tokyo, 160, Japan TEL 03-272-7211. (Subscr. to: Mazuren Co., Ltd., P.O. Box 5050, Tokyo International 100-31, Japan) circ. 350. (back issues avail.)

624   JA   ISSN 0075-7365
KYOTO UNIVERSITY. RESEARCH ACTIVITIES IN CIVIL ENGINEERING AND RELATED FIELDS. (Text in English) 1963. triennial. free. Kyoto University, Department of Civil Engineering, Sakyo-ku, Kyoto 606, Japan.

354   LB
LIBERIA. MINISTRY OF LANDS, MINES AND ENERGY. ANNUAL REPORT. 1961. a. Ministry of Lands, Mines and Energy, Monrovia, Liberia. circ. 600.
Formerly: Liberia. Ministry of Lands and Mines. Annual Report (ISSN 0304-7296)

MADISON WASTE CONFERENCE. ANNUAL PROCEEDINGS; municipal and industrial waste. see *ENVIRONMENTAL STUDIES*

624   GW   ISSN 0340-983X
MATERIALIENSAMMLUNG STAEDTEBAU. 1972. irreg. price varies. Ferd. Duemmlers Verlag, Postfach 1480 Kaiserstr. 31-37, D-5300 Bonn 1, W. Germany (B.R.D.)

624   BE   ISSN 0025-9195
MEMOIRES C.E.R.E.S. N.S. 1961. irreg. price varies. Universite de Liege, Centre d'Etudes, de Recherches et d'Essais Scientifiques du Genie Civil, 6 Quai Banning, 4000 Liege, Belgium. adv. bk. rev. abstr. bibl. stat. index. circ. 550. (also avail. in microform) Indexed: Appl.Mech.Rev.

624   MX   ISSN 0185-402X
MEXICAN SOCIETY FOR SOIL MECHANICS MEETING. PROCEEDINGS. (Text in Spanish) 1970. biennial, 12th, 1984. price varies. Sociedad Mexicana de Mecanica de Suelos - Mexican Society for Soil Mechanics, Valle de Bravo 19, Col. Vergel de Coyoacan, Tlalpan, 14340 Mexico, D.F., Mexico.

557   US   ISSN 0076-9606
MISSOURI. DIVISION OF GEOLOGICAL SURVEY AND WATER RESOURCES. ENGINEERING GEOLOGY SERIES. 1968. irreg., no.7, 1983. price varies. Department of Natural Resources, Division of Geology and Land Survey, Box 250, Rolla, MO 65401. TEL 314-364-1752.

624 631   MX   ISSN 0185-4011
NABOR CARRILLO LECTURE SERIES. PROCEEDINGS. (Text in English and Spanish) 1972. biennial, 7th 1984. price varies. Sociedad Mexicana de Mecanica de Suelos - Mexican Society for Soil Mechanics, Valle de Bravo 19, Col. Vergel de Coyoacan, 14340 Mexico. Indexed: GeoRef.

NATIONAL COOPERATIVE HIGHWAY RESEARCH PROGRAM REPORTS. see *TRANSPORTATION — Roads And Traffic*

NATIONAL COOPERATIVE HIGHWAY RESEARCH PROGRAM SYNTHESIS OF HIGHWAY PRACTICE. see *TRANSPORTATION — Roads And Traffic*

NATIONAL INSTITUTE FOR TRANSPORT AND ROAD RESEARCH. ANNUAL REPORT/NASIONALE INSTITUUT VIR VERVOER- EN PADNAVORSING. JAARVERSLAG. see *TRANSPORTATION — Roads And Traffic*

ENGINEERING — CIVIL ENGINEERING

388   US
NEBRASKA. DEPARTMENT OF ROADS. CHALLENGE OF THE 80'S; one and six-year program. 1970. a. Department of Roads, So. Jct. N-2 & U.S. 77, Box 94759, Lincoln, NE 68509. TEL 402-471-4512. Ed. Larry Shafer. charts. illus. stat. circ. controlled. (processed)
   Formerly: Focus on Nebraska Highways.

NETHERLANDS. RIJKSCOMMISSIE VOOR GEODESIE. PUBLICATIONS ON GEODESY. NEW SERIES. see *GEOGRAPHY*

625.8   US
PAVING AND TRANSPORTATION CONFERENCE. PROCEEDINGS. 1962. a. $15. University of New Mexico, Department of Civil Engineering, Albuquerque, NM 87131. TEL 505-277-2722. Ed. John B. Carney. circ. 200. (back issues avail.)
   Formerly: Paving Conference. Proceedings. (ISSN 0079-0273)
   Roads and streets

624   PL
POLITECHNIKA GDANSKA. RAPORT. WYDZIAL BUDOWNICTWA LADOWEGO. 1982. a. price varies. Politechnika Gdanska, Ul. Majakowskiego 11/12, 80-952 Gdansk 6, Poland.

624   690   PL   ISSN 0373-8671
POLITECHNIKA GDANSKA. ZESZYTY NAUKOWE. BUDOWNICTWO LADOWE. (Text in Polish; summaries in English and Russian) 1956. irreg. price varies. Politechnika Gdanska, Majakowskiego 11/12, 81-952 Gdansk 6, Poland (Dist. by: Osrodek Rozpowszechniania Wydawnictw Naukowych Pan, Palac Kulturi Nauki, 00-901 Warsaw, Poland)

624   PL   ISSN 0454-4862
POLITECHNIKA KRAKOWSKA. ZESZYTY NAUKOWE. BUDOWNICTWO LADOWE. (Text in Polish; summaries in English, French, German and Russian) 1957. irreg. price varies. Politechnika Krakowska, Ul. Warszawska 24, 31-155 Krakow, Poland (Dist. by: Ars Polona-Ruch, Krakowskie Przedmiescie 7, 00-068 Warsaw, Poland) bibl. charts. illus. circ. 200.

624   PL   ISSN 0076-0323
POLITECHNIKA LODZKA. ZESZYTY NAUKOWE. BUDOWNICTWO. (Text in Polish; summaries in English and Russian) 1967. irreg. price varies. Politechnika Lodzka, Ul. Zwirki 36, 90-924 Lodz, Poland (Dist by: Ars Polona-Ruch, Krakowskie Przedmiescie 7, Warsaw, Poland) Ed. Stefan Przewlocki. circ. 223.

624   PL
POLITECHNIKA POZNANSKA. ZESZYTY NAUKOWE. BUDOWNICTWO LADOWE. (Text in Polish; summaries in English and Russian) 1956. irreg. price varies. Politechnika Poznanska, Pl. Curie Sklodowskiej 5, Poznan, Poland. Ed. Boleslaw Nowakowski. circ. 150.
   Former titles: Politechnika Poznanska. Zeszyty Naukowe. Budownictwo; Politechnika Poznanska. Zeszyty Naukowe. Budownictwo Ladowe (ISSN 0079-449X)

624   PL   ISSN 0434-0779
POLITECHNIKA SLASKA. ZESZYTY NAUKOWE. BUDOWNICTWO. (Text in Polish; summaries in English and Russian) 1956. irreg. price varies. Politechnika Slaska, W. Pstrowskiego 7, 44-100 Gliwice, Poland (Dist. by: Ars Polona, Krakowskie Przedmiescie 7, 00-068 Warsaw, Poland) Ed. Zdzislaw Trojan. circ. 265.

624   PL   ISSN 0324-9743
POLITECHNIKA WROCLAWSKA. INSTYTUT INZYNIERII LADOWEJ. PRACE NAUKOWE. KONFERENCJE. (Text in Polish; summaries in English) 1973. irreg., no.12, 1986. price varies. Politechnika Wroclawska, Wybrzeze Wyspianskiego 27, 50-370 Wroclaw, Poland (Dist. by: Ars Polona-Ruch, Krakowskie Przedmiescie 7, Warsaw, Poland) Ed. Jerzy Ciekot. illus.

624   PL   ISSN 0324-9727
POLITECHNIKA WROCLAWSKA. INSTYTUT INZYNIERII LADOWEJ. PRACE NAUKOWE. MONOGRAFIE. (Text in Polish; summaries in English and Russian) 1972. irreg., no.11, 1986. price varies. Politechnika Wroclawska, Wybrzeze Wyspianskiego 27, 50-370 Wroclaw, Poland (Dist. by: Ars Polona-Ruch, Krakowskie Przedmiescie 7, Warsaw, Poland) Ed. Jerzy Ciekot.

624   PL   ISSN 0370-0844
POLITECHNIKA WROCLAWSKA. INSTYTUT INZYNIERII LADOWEJ. PRACE NAUKOWE. STUDIA I MATERIALY. (Text in Polish; summaries in English and Russian) 1970. irreg., no.10, 1973. price varies. Politechnika Wroclawska, Wybrzeze Wyspianskiego 27, 50-370 Wroclaw, Poland (Dist. by: Ars Polona-Ruch, Krakowskie Przedmiescie 7, Warsaw, Poland) Ed. Marian Kloza.

624   690   UR   ISSN 0203-9745
POLUTEHNILINE INSTITUUT TALLINN. OPTIMAL'NYE SISTEMY I ALGORITMY. (Subseries of Its Toimetised) (Text in Russian; summaries in English or German) irreg. price varies. Polutehniline Instituut Tallinn, Ehitajate tee 5, Tallinn, Estonian S.S.R., U.S.S.R.

PORT AND HARBOUR RESEARCH INSTITUTE. GUIDE/KOWAN GIJUTSU KENKYUSHO. GUIDE. see *TRANSPORTATION — Ships And Shipping*

624   US   ISSN 0079-8096
PURDUE UNIVERSITY. CIVIL ENGINEERING REPRINTS. 1940. irreg., no.306, 1978. single copies free. Purdue University, School of Civil Engineering, West Lafayette, IN 47907. TEL 317-494-5600. circ. 300. (back issues avail.) Indexed: Trans.Res.Abstr.

625.7   US   ISSN 0079-810X
PURDUE UNIVERSITY. ENGINEERING EXPERIMENT STATION. JOINT HIGHWAY RESEARCH PROJECT. RESEARCH REPORTS. (Issues not numbered consecutively) 1937. irreg., no.24, 1978. $5. Purdue University, School of Civil Engineering, Joint Highway Research Project, West Lafayette, IN 47907. TEL 317-494-5600. (Co-sponsor: Indiana State Highway Commission) circ. 100.
   Roads and streets

624   SP
RELACION DE INGENIEROS DE CAMINOS, CANALES Y PUERTOS. irreg., latest 1984. price varies. Colegio de Ingenieros de Caminos, Canales y Puertos, Almagro, 42, 28010 Madrid, Spain. illus.

624.151   US   ISSN 0080-2018
REVIEWS IN ENGINEERING GEOLOGY. 1961. irreg., vol.6, 1984. price varies. Geological Society of America, Marketing Department, 3300 Penrose Pl., Box 9140, Boulder, CO 80301. TEL 303-447-8850. index. (reprint service avail. from UMI) Indexed: GeoRef.

624   SP
REVISTA A T E M C O P. ESPECIAL ALQUILADORES. 1976. a. $10. Asociacion Espanola de Tecnicos de Maquinaria para la Construccion y Obras Publicas, c/o D. Fernando Garcia-Lopez Sahuquillo, C-Cruz del Sur 3, 28007 Madrid, Spain. illus.

625.7   US   ISSN 0080-3278
ROAD BUILDER'S CLINIC. PROCEEDINGS. 1950. a. $18. ‡ Washington State University, Conferences and Institutes, College of Enginnering and Architecture, Pullman, WA 99164. TEL 509-335-4677. (Co-sponsor: University of Idaho, College of Engineering)
   Roads and streets

SAO PAULO, BRAZIL (STATE). DEPARTAMENTO DE EDIFICIOS E OBRAS PUBLICAS. RELATORIO DE ATIVIDADES. see *PUBLIC ADMINISTRATION*

SCOTTISH BUILDING & CIVIL ENGINEERING YEAR BOOK. see *BUILDING AND CONSTRUCTION*

SERIES ON ROCK AND SOIL MECHANICS. see *EARTH SCIENCES*

624   FR
SOCIETE DES INGENIEURS ET SCIENTIFIQUES DE FRANCE. ANNUAIRE. 1883. a. price varies. Societe des Ingenieurs et Scientifiques de France, 19 rue Blanche, 75009 Paris, France.
   Formerly: Societe des Ingenieurs Civils de France. Annuaire (ISSN 0081-0886)

625.72   SA
SOUTH AFRICA. DEPARTMENT OF PUBLIC WORK AND LAND AFFAIRS. DIRECTORATE OF SURVEYS AND MAPPING. ANNUAL REPORT OF THE CHIEF DIRECTOR. 1973/74. a. Department of Public Work and Land Affairs, Directorate of Surveys and Mapping, Rhodes Ave., Mowbray 7705, South Africa. circ. 400.
   Former titles (until 1984): South Africa. Department of Community Development. Division of Surveys and Mapping. Annual Report of the Chief Director; South Africa. Division of Surveys. Report of the Director-General of Surveys.
   Surveying

624   UK   ISSN 0265-1025
SPON'S CIVIL ENGINEERING PRICE BOOK. 1984. biennial. £20. E. & F.N. Spon Ltd., 11 New Fetter Ln., London EC4P 4EE, England.

711.7   624   US
STANDARD SPECIFICATIONS FOR HIGHWAY BRIDGES. 1983. a. $25. American Association of State Highway and Transportation Officials, 444 N. Capitol St., N.W., Ste. 225, Washington, DC 20001. TEL 202-624-5800.

625   SZ
STRUCTURAL ENGINEERING DOCUMENTS. (Text in English, French and German) 1982. irreg. price varies. International Association for Bridge and Structural Engineering, ETA- Hoenggerberg, CH-8093 Zurich, Switzerland.
   Bridges

620   PL   ISSN 0137-5393
STUDIA Z ZAKRESU INZYNIERII. (Text in Polish; summaries in English, Russian) 1958. irreg., vol.22, 1983. price varies. (Polska Akademia Nauk, Komitet Inzynierii Ladowej i Wodnej) Panstwowe Wydawnictwo Naukowe, Miodowa 10, 00-251 Warsaw, Poland (Dist. by: Ars Polona, Krakowskie Przedmiescie 7, 00-068 Warsaw, Poland) bibl.
   Formerly: Studia z Zakresu Budownictwa (ISSN 0081-7139)

SWEDEN. STATENS RAAD FOER BYGGNADSFORSKNING. DOCUMENT. see *BUILDING AND CONSTRUCTION*

SWEDEN. STATENS RAAD FOER BYGGNADSFORSKNING. RAPPORT. see *BUILDING AND CONSTRUCTION*

SWEDEN. STATENS RAAD FOER BYGGNADSFORSKNING. VERKSAMHETSPLAN. see *BUILDING AND CONSTRUCTION*

624   US
SWEET'S CATALOG FILE FOR THE CIVIL ENGINEERING & RETROFIT MARKET. 1976. a. free to qualified personnel. Sweet's Catalog Files (Subsidiary of: McGraw-Hill Information Systems Co.) 1221 Ave. of the Americas, New York, NY 10020. TEL 212-512-3957. charts. illus. tr.lit. index. circ. 13,000.
   Formerly: Sweet's Civil Engineering and Retrofit File.

TABLEAU DE BORD DU BATIMENT, GENIE CIVIL ET MATERIAUX DE CONSTRUCTION. see *BUILDING AND CONSTRUCTION*

THOM'S DUBLIN & COUNTY STREET DIRECTORY. see *GEOGRAPHY*

TRANSPORT AND ROAD RESEARCH LABORATORY. RESEARCH REPORTS. see *TRANSPORTATION — Roads And Traffic*

TRANSPORTATION RESEARCH BOARD SPECIAL REPORT. see *TRANSPORTATION — Roads And Traffic*

TRANSPORTATION RESEARCH RECORD. see *TRANSPORTATION — Roads And Traffic*

484   ENGINEERING — COMPUTER APPLICATIONS

624   UK
TUNNELLING DIRECTORY; an international yearbook of consultants and companies in sub-surface construction. 1980. a. £20($40) Morgan-Grampian (Construction Press) Ltd., Morgan-Grampian House, 30 Calderwood St., London SE18 6QH, England. Ed. Anna Way.

624   US
U.S. BUREAU OF RECLAMATION. ENGINEERING AND RESEARCH CENTER. TECHNICAL RECORDS OF DESIGN AND CONSTRUCTION. irreg. price varies. U.S. Bureau of Reclamation, Engineering and Research Center, Box 25007, Denver Federal Center, Denver, CO 80225. TEL 303-236-6741. (back issues avail.)
Former titles: U.S. Water and Power Resources Service. Engineering and Research Center. Technical Records of Design and Construction; U.S. Bureau of Reclamation. Engineering and Research Center. Technical Records of Design and Construction.

625.7   US   ISSN 0073-2184
U.S. FEDERAL HIGHWAY ADMINISTRATION. HIGHWAY PLANNING TECHNICAL REPORTS. 1963. irreg. free. ‡ U.S. Federal Highway Administration, Dept. of Transportation, 400 Seventh St., S.W., Washington, DC 20590 TEL 202-426-0632. (Subscr. to: Supt. of Documents, Government Printing Office, Washington, DC 20402)
Roads and streets

624.151   US
U.S. GEOLOGICAL SURVEY. STRON MOTION PROGRAM. REPORT. 1974. a. free. U.S. Geological Survey, 345 Middlefield Rd., Mail Stop 977, Menlo Park, CA 94025 (Requests to: U.S. Geological Survey, Branch of Distribution, 604 S. Pickett St., Alexandria, VA 22304) Ed.Bd. charts. stat. circ. 4,000.
Formerly (until 1980): U.S. Geological Survey. Seismic Engineering Branch. Seismic Engineering Program Report.
Seismology

624.176   CN   ISSN 0068-1709
UNIVERSITY OF BRITISH COLUMBIA. DEPARTMENT OF CIVIL ENGINEERING. SOIL MECHANICS SERIES. 1966. irreg., latest no.105. Can.$5 per no. ‡ University of British Columbia, Department of Civil Engineering, Vancouver, B.C. V6T 1W5, Canada. TEL 604-228-2637.

624   CN
UNIVERSITY OF BRITISH COLUMBIA. DEPARTMENT OF CIVIL ENGINEERING. STRUCTURAL RESEARCH SERIES. 1970. irreg. price varies. University of British Columbia, Department of Civil Engineering, Vancouver, B.C. V6T 1W5, Canada. TEL 604-228-2637.

624   CN
UNIVERSITY OF BRITISH COLUMBIA. DEPARTMENT OF CIVIL ENGINEERING. TRANSPORTATION RESEARCH SERIES. 1972. irreg. Can.$10. University of British Columbia, Department of Civil Engineering, Vancouver, B.C. V6T 1W5, Canada. TEL 604-228-2637.

624   CN
UNIVERSITY OF BRITISH COLUMBIA. DEPARTMENT OF CIVIL ENGINEERING. WATER RESOURCES RESEARCH SERIES. 1969. irreg. Can.$5. University of British Columbia, Department of Civil Engineering, Vancouver, B.C. V6T 1W5, Canada. TEL 604-228-2637.

624   CN
UNIVERSITY OF CALGARY. DEPARTMENT OF CIVIL ENGINEERING RESEARCH REPORT. 1971. irreg., (approx. 25/yr.) free. University of Calgary, Department of Civil Engineering, Calgary T2N 1N4, Alta, Canada. TEL 403-284-7578.

624   US   ISSN 0442-1744
UNIVERSITY OF ILLINOIS AT URBANA-CHAMPAIGN. CIVIL ENGINEERING STUDIES. HYDRAULIC ENGINEERING RESEARCH SERIES. 1951. irreg., no.38, 1985. price varies. University of Illinois at Urbana-Champaign, Department of Civil Engineering, B106 Newmark Civil Engineering Lab, 208 N. Romine St., Urbana, IL 61801. TEL 217-333-1516. (also avail. in microform from NTI)

624   US   ISSN 0578-3755
UNIVERSITY OF ILLINOIS AT URBANA-CHAMPAIGN. CIVIL ENGINEERING STUDIES. PHOTOGRAMMETRY SERIES. 1963. irreg., no.43, 1976. price varies. University of Illinois at Urbana-Champaign, Department of Civil Engineering, B106 Newmark Civil Engineering Lab., 208 N. Romine St., Urbana, IL 61801. TEL 217-333-1516. (also avail. in microform from NTI)

624.1   US   ISSN 0069-4274
UNIVERSITY OF ILLINOIS AT URBANA-CHAMPAIGN. CIVIL ENGINEERING STUDIES. STRUCTURAL RESEARCH SERIES. 1950. irreg., no.520, 1985. University of Illinois at Urbana-Champaign, Department of Civil Engineering, Newmark Civil Engineering Lab, 208 N. Romine St., Urbana, IL 61801. TEL 217-333-1516. (also avail. in microform from NTI)

624   US   ISSN 0197-9191
UNIVERSITY OF ILLINOIS AT URBANA-CHAMPAIGN. CIVIL ENGINEERING STUDIES. TRANSPORTATION ENGINEERING SERIES. 1972. irreg., no.42, 1985. price varies. University of Illinois at Urbana-Champaign, Department of Civil Engineering, B106 Newmark Civil Engineering Lab., 208 N. Romine St., Urbana, IL 61801. TEL 217-333-1516. (also avail. in microform from NTI)

624   AT   ISSN 0085-3240
UNIVERSITY OF MELBOURNE. DEPARTMENT OF CIVIL ENGINEERING. RESEARCH REPORT. 1962. irreg. price varies. ‡ University of Melbourne, Department of Civil Engineering, Parkville, Vic. 3052, Australia.

624   AT   ISSN 0077-8796
UNIVERSITY OF NEW SOUTH WALES. SCHOOL OF CIVIL ENGINEERING. U N I C I V REPORTS. SERIES I. 1963. irreg. Aus.$50. University of New South Wales, P.O. Box 1, Kensington, N.S.W. 2033, Australia. circ. 220.

624   AT   ISSN 0077-880X
UNIVERSITY OF NEW SOUTH WALES. SCHOOL OF CIVIL ENGINEERING. U N I C I V REPORTS. SERIES R. 1963. irreg. Aus.$30 combined subscription for Series I & R; free to qualified libraries. University of New South Wales, School of Civil Engineering, P.O. Box 1, Kensington, N.S.W. 2033, Australia. Ed.Bd. circ. 220.

VIRGINIA HIGHWAY AND TRANSPORTATION CONFERENCE. PROCEEDINGS. see TRANSPORTATION — Roads And Traffic

625.7   US   ISSN 0161-6730
VIRGINIA ROAD BUILDER. 1945. a. membership. (Virginia Road and Transportation Builders Association) V R B A Publishing Co., Inc., 30 LaBrook Dr., Richmond, VA 23225. TEL 804-276-3393. Ed. William H. Craig, Jr. adv. bk. rev. circ. controlled.
Roads and streets

624   918   US
WATER & WASTE TREATMENT: LATIN AMERICAN INDUSTRIAL REPORT. 1985. a. $235 per country report. Aurora International, Box 9099, Bridgeport, CT 06601-2099. TEL 203-368-0579. Ed. Andres C. Aquino.

625.7   US   ISSN 0083-8918
WESTERN HIGHWAY INSTITUTE. RESEARCH COMMITTEE. REPORT.* 1969. irreg. price varies. Western Highway Institute, 1200 Bay Hill Dr., San Bruno, CA 94066.
Roads and streets

624 550 531.64   US   ISSN 0888-5966
WHO'S WHO IN CIVIL ENGINEERING, EARTH SCIENCES & ENERGY. 1979. biennial. $545. Research Publications, Inc. (Woodbridge), 12 Lunar Dr., Drawer AB, Woodbridge, CT 06525.

625.7 388.314   US
WORLD SURVEY OF CURRENT RESEARCH AND DEVELOPMENT ON ROADS AND ROAD TRANSPORT (YEAR) 1965. a. (Federal Highway Administration) International Road Federation, 525 School St., S.W., Washington, DC 20024. abstr. index. circ. 4,000. (also avail. in microform from NTI)

624   GW   ISSN 0514-2938
ZEMENT-TASCHENBUCH. 1950. biennial. DM.28. (Verein Deutscher Zementwerke e.V.) Bauverlag GmbH, Wittelsbacherstr. 10, 6200 Wiesbaden, W. Germany (B.R.D.) adv. index. circ. 50,000.

624   GW   ISSN 0084-5485
ZIEGELEITECHNISCHES JAHRBUCH. 1950. a. DM.45. Bauverlag GmbH, Wittelsbacherstr. 10, 6200 Wiesbaden, W. Germany (B.R.D.)

ENGINEERING — Computer Applications

620   US
A A C C NEWSLETTER. irreg. American Automatic Control Council, 1051 Camino Velasquez, Green Valley, AZ 85614. TEL 602-625-0401. (Co-sponsors: American Institute of Aeronautics and Astronautics (AIAA) ; American Institute of Chemical Engineers (AIChE); American Society of Mechanical Engineers (ASME); Association of Iron and Steel Engineers (AISE); Institute of Electrical and Electronic Engineers (IEEE); Instrument Society of America (ISA); Society for Computer Simulation (SCS)) Ed. Hiro Mukai.

620 610   US   ISSN 0888-2215
ADVANCES IN BIOMEDICAL COMPUTING SERIES. 1987. irreg. Computer Science Press, Inc., 1803 Research Blvd., Ste. 500, Rockville, MD 20850. TEL 301-251-9050. Ed. Jack Cohen. (back issues avail.)

620 380.3   US   ISSN 0888-2207
ADVANCES IN SATELLITE COMMUNICATIONS SERIES. 1987. irreg. Computer Science Press, Inc., 1803 Research Blvd., Ste. 500, Rockville, MD 20850. TEL 301-251-9050. Ed. William W. Wu. (back issues avail.)

620   AT   ISSN 0084-7496
AUSTRALIAN NATIONAL UNIVERSITY, CANBERRA. DEPARTMENT OF ENGINEERING PHYSICS. PUBLICATION EP-RR. 1959. irreg. Australian National University, Research School of Physical Sciences, Dept. of Engineering Physics, G.P.O. Box 4, Canberra, A.C.T. 2601, Australia. Ed. Prof. S. Kaneff.

621.3 001.6   US
BENCHMARK PAPERS IN ELECTRICAL ENGINEERING & COMPUTER SCIENCE. (Each vol. has distinctive title) 1973. irreg., vol.31, 1985. price varies. Van Nostrand Reinhold Company, 7625 Empire Dr., Florence, KY 41042. TEL 606-525-6600. Ed. John B. Thomas. illus. index.

621.381   NE
COMPUTER-AIDED DESIGN OF ELECTRONIC CIRCUITS. 1978. irreg., vol.2, 1980. price varies. Elsevier Science Publishers B.V., Box 211, 1000 AE Amsterdam, Netherlands. Ed. R. Spence.

620   US   ISSN 0888-2088
COMPUTER SOFTWARE ENGINEERING SERIES. 1978. irreg. Computer Science Press, Inc., 1803 Research Blvd., Ste. 500, Rockville, MD 20850. TEL 301-251-9050. Ed. Arthur D. Friedman. (back issues avail.)

620   US   ISSN 0888-2118
DIGITAL SYSTEM DESIGN SERIES. 1975. irreg. price varies. Computer Science Press, Inc., 1803 Research Blvd., Ste. 500, Rockville, MD 20850. TEL 301-251-9050. Ed. Arthur D. Friedman. (back issues avail.)

620 380.3   US
ELECTRICAL ENGINEERING, TELECOMMUNICATIONS AND SIGNAL PROCESSING. 1981. irreg. Computer Science Press, Inc., 1803 Research Blvd., Ste. 500, Rockville, MD 20850. TEL 301-251-9050. Ed. Raymond L. Pickholtz. (back issues avail.)
Formerly: Electrical Engineering Communications and Signal Processing (ISSN 0888-2134)

620 US
ENGINEERING APPLICATION SOFTWARE
D.A.T.A. BOOK. (Subseries of: D.A.T.A. Book Electronic Information Series) a. $125. D.A.T.A., Inc. (Subsidiary of: International Thomson Organization) 9889 Willow Creek Rd., Box 26875, San Diego, CA 92126. TEL 619-578-7600. Ed. Steven d'Adolf.
Formerly: Microprocessor Technical Software D.A.T.A. Book.

INTERNATIONAL C A D/C A M INDUSTRY DIRECTORY. see COMPUTERS — Computer Graphics

KEY ABSTRACTS - COMPUTING IN ELECTRONICS & POWER. see COMPUTERS — Abstracting, Bibliographies, Statistics

620 510 US ISSN 0888-2096
PRINCIPLES OF COMPUTER SCIENCE SERIES. 1981. irreg. Computer Science Press, Inc., 1803 Research Blvd., Ste. 500, Rockville, MD 20850. TEL 301-251-9050. Eds. Alfred V. Aho, Jeffrey D. Ullman. (back issues avail.)

SOFTWARE ABSTRACTS FOR ENGINEERS. see COMPUTERS — Software

620 621.3 GW
Z V E I ELEKTRO-EINKAUFSFUEHRER. English edition: Z V E I Electro Buyers' Guide. French edition: Z V E I Guide de l'Equipement Electrique. Spanish edition: Z V E I Guia de Equipos Electricos. (Editions in English, French, German, Spanish) 1950. a. DM.88 per no. Verlag W. Sachon, Schloss Mindelburg, 8949 Mindelheim, W. Germany (B.R.D.) circ. 15,000.

ENGINEERING — Engineering Mechanics And Materials

620.1 US ISSN 0066-0515
A S T M PROCEEDINGS. 1898. a. $29.50 to non-members. American Society for Testing and Materials, 1916 Race St., Philadelphia, PA 19103. TEL 215-299-5400. Ed. R. Storer. circ. 2,000. (also avail. in microform from UMI) Indexed: Appl.Mech.Rev. Ceram.Abstr. BMT. Geotech.Abstr.

620.1 US ISSN 0568-0204
ADVANCEMENT IN TEST MEASUREMENT. PROCEEDINGS. a. Instrument Society of America, 67 Alexander Dr., Research Triangle Park, NC 27709. TEL 919-549-8411.
Supersedes in part: I S A Aerospace Instrumentation Symposium. Proceedings (ISSN 0536-2008)

ADVANCES IN APPLIED MECHANICS. see PHYSICS — Mechanics

620.112 US ISSN 0065-2474
ADVANCES IN CORROSION SCIENCE AND TECHNOLOGY. 1970. irreg. price varies. Plenum Publishing Corp., 233 Spring St., New York, NY 10013. TEL 212-620-8047. Eds. M.G. Fontana, R.W. Staehle.

ADVANCES IN X-RAY ANALYSIS. see TECHNOLOGY: COMPREHENSIVE WORKS

620.1 690 US ISSN 0066-0523
AMERICAN SOCIETY FOR TESTING AND MATERIALS. COMPILATION OF A S T M STANDARDS IN BUILDING CODES. (In 2 vols.) 1952. irreg., 23rd edt. 1986. $195 to non-members. American Society for Testing and Materials, 1916 Race St., Philadelphia, PA 19103. TEL 215-299-5400. Ed. R. Storer. circ. 2,000. Indexed: GeoRef.

620.1 US ISSN 0066-0531
AMERICAN SOCIETY FOR TESTING AND MATERIALS. DATA SERIES PUBLICATIONS. 1964. irreg., no.63, 1985. American Society for Testing and Materials, 1916 Race St., Philadelphia, PA 19103. TEL 215-299-5400.

620.1 US ISSN 0066-054X
AMERICAN SOCIETY FOR TESTING AND MATERIALS. FIVE-YEAR INDEX TO A S T M TECHNICAL PAPERS AND REPORTS. (Supplements the A.S.T.M. 50-Year Index) 1950. quinquennial. $20 to non-members. American Society for Testing and Materials, 1916 Race St., Philadelphia, PA 19103. TEL 215-299-5400. circ. 2,000.

620.1 US ISSN 0066-0558
AMERICAN SOCIETY FOR TESTING AND MATERIALS. SPECIAL TECHNICAL PUBLICATIONS. 1911. a., no.900, 1986. American Society for Testing and Materials, 1916 Race St., Philadelphia, PA 19103. TEL 215-299-5400. Indexed: Biol.Abstr. Pollut.Abstr. Geotech.Abstr. HRIS.

620.1 US ISSN 0066-0493
ANNUAL BOOK OF A S T M STANDARDS. VOLUME 00.01. INDEX; subject and alphanumeric. (Vol. numbering revised 1986; formerly Part 48) a. $33 to non-members; members $29.70. American Society for Testing and Materials, 1916 Race St., Philadelphia, PA 19103. TEL 215-299-5400.

620.1 US ISSN 0066-0183
ANNUAL BOOK OF A S T M STANDARDS. VOLUME 01.01. STEEL-PIPING, TUBING, FITTINGS. (Vol. numbering revised 1986; formerly Part 1) 1898. a. $74 to non-members; members $66.60. American Society for Testing and Materials, 1916 Race St., Philadelphia, PA 19103. TEL 215-299-5400. Ed. R. Storer. (also avail. in microfiche) Indexed: Art & Archaeol.Tech.Abstr.

620.1 669 US
ANNUAL BOOK OF A S T M STANDARDS. VOLUME 01.02. FERROUS CASTINGS, FERRO ALLOYS; SHIPBUILDING. a. $75 to non-members; members $67.50. American Society for Testing and Materials, 1916 Race St., Philadelphia, PA 19103. TEL 215-299-5400. (also avail. in microfiche)
Formerly (until 1986): Annual Book of A S T M Standards. Part 2. Ferrous Castings, Ferro Alloys (ISSN 0066-0191)

620.1 US
ANNUAL BOOK OF A S T M STANDARDS. VOLUME 01.03. STEEL PLATE, SHEET, STRIP WIRE. a. $51 to non-members; members $51.30. American Society for Testing and Materials, 1916 Race St., Philadelphia, PA 19103. TEL 215-299-5400. (also avail. in microfiche)
Former titles (until 1986): Annual Book of A S T M Standards. Part 3. Steel Plate, Sheet, Strip and Wire; Metallic Coated Products; Fences; (until 1982): Annual Book of A S T M Standards. Part 3. Steel Plate, Sheet, Strip and Wire; Metallic Coated Products; Annual Book of A S T M Standards. Part 3. Steel Strip, Bar, Rod, Wire, Chain, and Spring; Wrought Iron; Metallic Coated Products; Ferrous Surgical Implants (ISSN 0066-0205)

620.1 US
ANNUAL BOOK OF A S T M STANDARDS. VOLUME 01.04. STEEL-STRUCTURAL, REINFORCING, PRESSURE VESSEL; RAILWAY. a. $65 to non-members; members $58.50. American Society for Testing and Materials, 1916 Race St., Philadelphia, PA 19103. TEL 215-299-5400.
Former titles (until 1986): Annual Book of A S T M Standards. Part 4. Structural Steel; Concrete Reinforcing Steel; Pressure Vessel Plate and Forgings; Steel Rails, Wheels, and Tires; Steel Fasteners; Annual Book of A S T M Standards. Part 4. Structural Steel; Concrete Reinforcing Steel; Pressure Vessel Plate; Steel Rails; Wheels, and Tires; Bearing Steel; Steel Forgings (ISSN 0066-0213)

620.1 US
ANNUAL BOOK OF A S T M STANDARDS. VOLUME 01.05. STEEL-BARS, BEARINGS, FORGINGS, CHAIN, SPRINGS. a. $70 to non-members; members $63.00. American Society for Testing and Materials, 1916 Race St., Philadelphia, PA 19103. TEL 215-299-5400. (also avail. in microfiche)
Formerly (until 1986): Annual Book of A S T M Standards. Part 5. Steel Bars, Chain, and Springs; Bearing Steel; Steel Forgings.

620 669.1 US
ANNUAL BOOK OF A S T M STANDARDS. VOLUME 01.06. COATED STEEL PRODUCTS. 1986. a. $54 to non-members; members $48.60. American Society for Testing and Materials, 1916 Race St., Philadelphia, PA 19103. TEL 215-299-5400. (also avail. in microfiche)
Supersedes in part: Annual Book of A S T M Standards. Part 3. Steel Plate, Sheet, Strip and Wire; Metallic Coated Products; Fences.

620.1 US
ANNUAL BOOK OF A S T M STANDARDS. VOLUME 02.01. COPPER AND COPPER ALLOYS. a. $79 to non-members; members $71.10. American Society for Testing and Materials, 1916 Race St., Philadelphia, PA 19103. TEL 215-299-5400. (also avail. in microfiche)
Formerly (until 1986): Annual Book of A S T M Standards. Part 6. Copper and Copper Alloys (Including Electrical Conductors) (ISSN 0066-0221)

620.1 US
ANNUAL BOOK OF A S T M STANDARDS. VOLUME 02.02. DIE-CAST METALS; ALUMINUM AND MAGNESIUM ALLOYS. a. $77 to non-members; members $69.30. American Society for Testing and Materials, 1916 Race St., Philadelphia, PA 19103. TEL 215-299-5400. (also avail. in microfiche)
Former titles: Annual Book of A S T M Standards. Volume 02.02. Die-Cast; Light Metals and Alloys; (until 1986): Annual Book of A S T M Standards. Part 7. Die-Cast Metals; Light Metals and Alloys (Including Electrical Conductors) (ISSN 0066-023X)

620 621.3 US
ANNUAL BOOK OF A S T M STANDARDS. VOLUME 02.03. ELECTRICAL CONDUCTORS. 1986. a. $51 to non-members; members $45.90. American Society for Testing and Materials, 1916 Race St., Philadelphia, PA 19103. TEL 215-299-5400. (also avail. in microfiche)
Supersedes in part: Annual Book of A S T M Standards. Part 6. Copper and Copper Alloys (Including Electrical Conductors) & Annual Book of A S T M Standards. Part 7. Die-Cast Metals; Light Metals and Alloys (Including Electrical Conductors)

620.1 US
ANNUAL BOOK OF A S T M STANDARDS. VOLUME 02.04. NONFERROUS METALS-NICKEL, LEAD, TIN ALLOYS, PRECIOUS, PRIMARY, REACTIVE METALS. (Vol. numbering revised 1986; formerly Part 8.) a. $69 to non-members; members $62.10. American Society for Testing and Materials, 1916 Race St., Philadelphia, PA 19103. TEL 215-299-5400. (also avail. in microfiche)
Former titles: Annual Book of A S T M Standards. Volume 02.04. Nonferrous Metals - Nickel, Lead, and Tin Alloys, Precious Metals, Primary Metals; Reactive Metals; Annual Book of A S T M Standards. Part 7. Nonferrous Metals and Alloys (Including Corrosion Tests); Electrodeposited Metallic Coatings; Metal Powders; Surgical Implants. (ISSN 0066-0248)

620.1 US
ANNUAL BOOK OF A S T M STANDARDS. VOLUME 02.05. METALLIC AND INORGANIC COATINGS; METAL POWDERS, SINTERED P/M STRUCTURAL PARTS. (Vol. numbering revised 1986; formerly Part 9) a. $69 to non-members; members $62.10. American Society for Testing and Materials, 1916 Race St., Philadelphia, PA 19103. TEL 215-299-5400. (also avail. in microfiche)
Formerly: Annual Book of A S T M Standards. Part 9. Electrodeposited Metallic Coatings; Metal Powders, Sintered P/M Structural Parts.

620.1 669 US
ANNUAL BOOK OF A S T M STANDARDS. VOLUME 03.01. METALS-MECHANICAL TESTING; ELEVATED AND LOW-TEMPERATURE TESTS METALLOGRAPHY. a. $75 to non-members; members $67.50. American Society for Testing and Materials, 1916 Race St., Philadelphia, PA 19103. TEL 215-299-5400. (also avail. in microfiche)
  Former titles: Annual Book of A S T M Standards. Volume 03.01. Mechanical Testing; Elevated and Low-Temperature Tests; (until 1986): Annual Book of A S T M Standards. Part 10. Metals--Mechanical, Fracture, and Corrosion Testing; Fatigue; Erosion; Effect of Temperature; Annual Book of A S T M Standards. Part 31. Metals--Physical, Mechanical, Nondestructive, and Corrosion Tests, Metallography, Fatigue, Effect of Temperature. (ISSN 0066-0477)

620 669 US
ANNUAL BOOK OF A S T M STANDARDS. VOLUME 03.02. WEAR AND EROSION; METAL CORROSION. 1986. a. $48 to non-members; members $43.20. American Society for Testing and Materials, 1916 Race St., Philadelphia, PA 19103. TEL 215-299-5400. (also avail. in microfiche)
  Supersedes in part: Annual Book of A S T M Standards. Part 10. Metals--Mechanical, Fracture and Corrosion Testing; Fatigue; Erosion; Effect of Temperature.

620.1 US
ANNUAL BOOK OF A S T M STANDARDS. VOLUME 03.03. NONDESTRUCTIVE TESTS. (Vol.numbering revised 1986; formerly Part 11) a. $57 to non-members; members $51.30. American Society for Testing and Materials, 1916 Race St., Philadelphia, PA 19103. TEL 215-299-5400. (also avail. in microfiche)
  Formerly: Annual Book of A S T M Standards. Volume 03.03. Metallography; Nondestructive Testing.

620.1 US
ANNUAL BOOK OF A S T M STANDARDS. VOLUME 03.04. MAGNETIC PROPERTIES; METALLIC MATERIALS FOR THERMOSTATS, ELECTRICAL RESISTANCE, HEATING, CONTACTS. a. $51 to non-members; members $45.90. American Society for Testing and Materials, 1916 Race St., Philadelphia, PA 19103. TEL 215-299-5400. (also avail. in microfiche)
  Former titles: Annual Book of A S T M Standards. Volume 03.04. Magnetic Properties; Magnetic Materials; Metallic Materials for Thermostats, Electrical Resistance, Heating, and Contacts; (until 1986): Annual Book of A S T M Standards. Part 44. Magnetic Properties and Magnetic Materials ; Metallic Materials for Thermostats and for Electrical Resistance, Heating, and Contacts; Temperature Measurement; Illuminating Standards; Annual Book of A S T M Standards. Part 8. Magnetic Properties; Metallic Materials for Thermostats and Contacts; Materials for Electron Devices and Microelectronics (ISSN 0066-0507)

620.1 542 US ISSN 0066-0485
ANNUAL BOOK OF A S T M STANDARDS. VOLUME 03.05. CHEMICAL ANALYSIS OF METALS; METAL BEARING ORES. (Vol. numbering revised 1986; formerly Part 12) a. $70 to non-members; members $63. American Society for Testing and Materials, 1916 Race St., Philadelphia, PA 19103. TEL 215-299-5400. (also avail. in microfiche)
  Formerly: Annual Book of A S T M Standards. Volume 03.05. Chemical Analysis of Metals; Sampling and Analysis of Metal Bearing Ores.

620 US
ANNUAL BOOK OF A S T M STANDARDS. VOLUME 03.06. EMISSION SPECTROSCOPY; SURFACE ANALYSIS. 1986. a. $49 to non-members; members $44.10. American Society for Testing and Materials, 1916 Race St., Philadelphia, PA 19103. TEL 215-299-5400. (also avail. in microfiche)
  Supersedes in part: Annual Book of A S T M Standards. Part 42. Emission, Molecular, and Mass Spectroscopy; Chromatography; Resinography; Microscopy; Computerized Systems.

620.1 690 US
ANNUAL BOOK OF A S T M STANDARDS. VOLUME 04.01. CEMENT; LIME; GYPSUM. (Vol. numbering revised 1986; formerly Part 13) a. $56 to non-members; members $50.40. American Society for Testing and Materials, 1916 Race St., Philadelphia, PA 19103. TEL 215-299-5400. (also avail. in microfiche)
  Former titles: Annual Book of A S T M Standards. Volume 04.01. Cement; Lime; Gypsum (Including Manual of Cement Testing); Annual Book of A S T M Standards. Part 13. Cement; Lime; Ceilings and Walls (Including Manual of Cement Testing); Annual Book of A S T M Standards. Part 9. Cement; Lime; Gypsum (ISSN 0066-0256)

620.1 690 US
ANNUAL BOOK OF A S T M STANDARDS. VOLUME 04.02. CONCRETE AND MINERAL AGGREGATES (INCLUDING MANUAL OF AGGREGATE AND CONCRETE TESTING) (Vol. numbering revised 1986; formerly Part 14) a. $67 to non-members; members $60.30. American Society for Testing and Materials, 1916 Race St., Philadelphia, PA 19103. TEL 215-299-5400. (also avail. in microfiche)
  Former titles: Annual Book of A S T M Standards. Volume 04.02. Concrete and Mineral Aggregates (Including Manual of Aggregate and Concrete Testing); Annual Book of A S T M Standards. Part 14. Concrete and Mineral Aggregates (Including Manual of Concrete Testing) (ISSN 0066-0264)

620.1 US
ANNUAL BOOK OF A S T M STANDARDS. VOLUME 04.03. ROAD AND PAVING MATERIALS; TRAVELED SURFACE CHARACTERISTICS. a. $62 to non-members; members $55.80. American Society for Testing and Materials, 1916 Race St., Philadelphia, PA 19103. TEL 215-299-5400. (also avail. in microfiche)
  Former titles (until 1986): Annual Book of A S T M Standards. Part 15. Road and Paving Materials; Bituminous Materials for Highway Construction, Waterproofing and Roofing, and Pipe; Traveled Surface Characteristics; Annual Book of A S T M Standards. Part 15. Road and Paving Materials; Bituminous Materials for Highway Construction, Waterproofing and Roofing, and Pipe; Skid Resistance; Annual Book of A S T M Standards. Part 11. Bituminous Materials for Highway Construction, Waterproofing and Roofing: Soil and Rock; Skid Resistance (ISSN 0066-0272)

620 US
ANNUAL BOOK OF A S T M STANDARDS. VOLUME 04.04. ROOFING, WATERPROOFING, AND BITUMINOUS MATERIALS. 1986. a. $45 to non-members; members $40.50. American Society for Testing and Materials, 1916 Race St., Philadelphia, PA 19103. TEL 215-299-5400. (also avail. in microfiche)
  Supersedes in part: Annual Book of A S T M Standards. Part 15. Road and Paving Materials; Bituminous Materials for Highway Construction, Waterproofing and Roofing, and Pipe; Traveled Survace Characteristics.

620.1 691 US
ANNUAL BOOK OF A S T M STANDARDS. VOLUME 04.05. CHEMICAL-RESISTANT MATERIALS; VITRIFIED CLAY, CONCRETE; MASONRY; MORTARS; FIBER-CEMENT PRODUCTS. a. $63 to non-members; members $56.70. American Society for Testing and Materials, 1916 Race St., Philadelphia, PA 19103. TEL 215-299-5400. (also avail. in microfiche)
  Former titles: Annual Book of A S T M Standards. Volume 04.05. Chemical-Resistant Nonmetallic Materials; Vitrified Clay, Concrete Pipe and Tile; Masonary Mortars and Units; Fiber-Cement Products, Precast Concrete Products; (until 1986): Annual Book of A S T M Standards. Part 16. Chemical Resistant Nonmetallic Materials; Vitrified Clay, and Concrete Pipe and Tile; Masonary Mortars and Units; Fiber-Cement Products; Annual Book of A S T M Standards. Part 16. Chemical-Resistant Nonmetallic Materials. Vitrified Clay and Concrete Pipe and Tile; Masonry Mortars and Units; Asbestos-Cement Products; Annual Book of A S T M Standards. Part 12. Chemical-Resistant Nonmetallic Materials; Clay and Concrete Pipe and Tile; Masonry Mortars and Units; Asbestos-Cement Products; Natural Building Stones (ISSN 0066-0280)

620.1 US
ANNUAL BOOK OF A S T M STANDARDS. VOLUME 04.06. THERMAL INSULATION; ENVIRONMENTAL ACOUSTICS. a. $73 to non-members; members $65.70. American Society for Testing and Materials, 1916 Race St., Philadelphia, PA 19103. TEL 215-299-5400. (also avail. in microfiche)
  Former titles (until 1986): Annual Book of A S T M Standards. Part 18. Thermal Insulation; Building Seals and Sealants; Fire Tests; Building Construction; Environmental Acoustics; Annual Book of A S T M Standards. Part 18. Thermal and Cryogenic Insulating Materials; Building Seals and Sealants; Fire Tests; Building Constructions; Environmental Acoustics (ISSN 0066-0302)

620 US
ANNUAL BOOK OF A S T M STANDARDS. VOLUME 04.07. BUILDING SEALS AND SEALANTS; FIRE STANDARDS; BUILDING CONSTRUCTIONS. 1986. a. $84 to non-members; members $75.60. American Society for Testing and Materials, 1916 Race St., Philadelphia, PA 19103. TEL 215-299-5400. (also avail. in microfiche)
  Supersedes in part: Annual Book of A S T M Standards. Part 18. Thermal Insulation; Building Seals and Sealants; Fire Tests; Building Constructions; Environmental Acoustics.

620.1 US
ANNUAL BOOK OF A S T M STANDARDS. VOLUME 04.08. SOIL AND ROCK; BUILDING STONES. a. $78 to non-members; members $70.20. American Society for Testing and Materials, 1916 Race St., Philadelphia, PA 19103. TEL 215-299-5400. (also avail. in microfiche)
  Former titles (until 1986): Annual Book of A S T M Standards. Part 19. Natural Building Stones; Soil and Rock; Annual Book of A S T M Standards. Part 19. Natural Building Stones; Soil and Rock; Peats, Mosses and Humus.

620.1 US
ANNUAL BOOK OF A S T M STANDARDS. VOLUME 04.09. WOOD. a. $55 to non-members; members $49.50. American Society for Testing and Materials, 1916 Race St., Philadelphia, PA 19103. TEL 215-299-5400. (also avail. in microfiche)
  Former titles (until 1986): Annual Book of A S T M Standards. Part 22. Wood; Adhesives (ISSN 0066-0329); Annual Book of A S T M Standards. Part 16. Structural Sandwich Constructions; Wood; Adhesives.

620.1 665.5 US
ANNUAL BOOK OF A S T M STANDARDS. VOLUME 05.01. PETROLEUM PRODUCTS AND LUBRICANTS (1) a. $88 to non-members; members $79.20. American Society for Testing and Materials, 1916 Race St., Philadelphia, PA 19103. TEL 215-299-5400. (also avail. in microfiche)
  Former titles: Annual Book of A S T M Standards. Volume 05.01. Petroleum Products and Lubricants (1); D 56 to D 1947; (until 1986): Annual Book of A S T M Standards. Part 23. Petroleum Products and Lubricants (1): D 56 to D 1660; Annual Book of A S T M Standards. Part 17. Petroleum Products - Fuels; Solvents; Burner Fuel Oils; Lubricating Greases; Hydraulic Fluids (ISSN 0066-0337)

620.1 665.5 US
ANNUAL BOOK OF A S T M STANDARDS. VOLUME 05.02. PETROLEUM PRODUCTS AND LUBRICANTS (2) a. $88 to non-members; members $79.20. American Society for Testing and Materials, 1916 Race St., Philadelphia, PA 19103. TEL 215-299-5400. (also avail. in microfiche)
  Former titles: Annual Book of A S T M Standards. Volume 05.02. Petroleum Products and Lubricants (2); D 1949 to D 3601; (until 1986): Annual Book of A S T M Standards. Part 24. Petroleum Products and Lubricants (2); D 1661 to D 2896; Annual Book of A S T M Standards. Part 18. Petroleum Products - Measurement and Sampling; Liquefied Petroleum Gases; Light Hydrocarbons; Plant Spray Oils; Aerospace Materials; Sulfonates; Crude Petroleum; Petroleum; Wax; Graphite (ISSN 0066-0345)

ENGINEERING — ENGINEERING MECHANICS AND MATERIALS

620.1 665.5 629.3   US
ANNUAL BOOK OF A S T M STANDARDS. VOLUME 05.03. PETROLEUM PRODUCTS AND LUBRICANTS (3); CATALYSTS. a. $85 to non-members; members $76.50. American Society for Testing and Materials, 1916 Race St., Philadelphia, PA 19103. TEL 215-299-5400. (also avail. in microfiche)
   Former titles: Annual Book of A S T M Standards. Volume 05.03. Petroleum Products and Lubricants (3); D 3602 to Latest; Catalysts; (until 1986): Annual Book of A S T M Standards. Part 25. Petroleum Products and Lubricants (3); Aerospace Materials; Catalysts; Annual Book of A S T M Standards. Part 25. Petroleum Products and Lubricants (3); Aerospace Materials.

620.1   US
ANNUAL BOOK OF A S T M STANDARDS. VOLUME 05.04. TEST METHODS FOR RATING MOTOR, DIESEL, AND AVIATION FUELS. (Vol. numbering revised 1986; formerly Part 47) a. $49 to non-members; members $44.10. American Society for Testing and Materials, 1916 Race St., Philadelphia, PA 19103. TEL 215-299-5400. (also avail. in microfiche)

620.1   US
ANNUAL BOOK OF A S T M STANDARDS. VOLUME 05.05. GASEOUS FUELS; COAL AND COKE. a. $49 to non-members; members $44.10. American Society for Testing and Materials, 1916 Race St., Philadelphia, PA 19103. TEL 215-299-5400. (also avail. in microfiche)
   Former titles (until 1986): Annual Book of A S T M Standards. Part 26. Gaseous Fuels; Coal and Coke; Atmospheric Analysis; Annual Book of A S T M Standards. Part 26. Gaseous Fuels; Coal and Coke (ISSN 0066-0353)

620.1 667.4   US   ISSN 0066-037X
ANNUAL BOOK OF A S T M STANDARDS. VOLUME 06.01. PAINT - TESTS FOR FORMULATED PRODUCTS AND APPLIED COATINGS. (Vol. numbering revised 1986; formerly Part 27) a. $84 to non-members; members $75.60. American Society for Testing and Materials, 1916 Race St., Philadelphia, PA 19103. TEL 215-299-5400. (also avail. in microfiche)

620.1 667.4   US
ANNUAL BOOK OF A S T M STANDARDS. VOLUME 06.02. PAINT - PIGMENTS, RESINS AND POLYMERS. (Vol. numbering revised 1986; formerly Part 28) a. $52 to non-members; members $46.80. American Society for Testing and Materials, 1916 Race St., Philadelphia, PA 19103. TEL 215-299-5400. (also avail. in microfiche)

620.1   US
ANNUAL BOOK OF A S T M STANDARDS. VOLUME 06.03. PAINT - FATTY OILS AND ACIDS, SOLVENTS, MISCELLANEOUS; AROMATIC HYDROCARBONS. (Vol. numbering revised 1986; formerly Part 29) a. $74 to non-members; members $66.60. American Society for Testing and Materials, 1916 Race St., Philadelphia, PA 19103. TEL 215-299-5400.
   Former titles: Annual Book of A S T M Standards. Volume 06.03. Paint - Fatty Oils and Acids, Solvents, Miscellaneous; Aromatic Hydrocarbons (Includes Naval Stores) & Annual Book of A S T M Standards. Part 20. Paint, Varnish, Lacquer, and Related Products - Materials Specifications and Tests; Naval Stores; Industrial Aromatic Hydrocarbons and Related Chemicals (ISSN 0066-0361)

620.1 677   US   ISSN 0066-040X
ANNUAL BOOK OF A S T M STANDARDS. VOLUME 07.01. TEXTILES--YARN, FABRICS, AND GENERAL TEST METHODS. (MF) a. $83 to non-members; members $74.70. American Society for Testing and Materials, 1916 Race St., Philadelphia, PA 19103. TEL 215-299-5400.

620.1 677   US
ANNUAL BOOK OF A S T M STANDARDS. VOLUME 07.02. TEXTILES--FIBERS, ZIPPERS. (Vol. numbering revised 1986; formerly Part 33) a. $66 to non-members; members $59.40. American Society for Testing and Materials, 1916 Race St., Philadelphia, PA 19103. TEL 215-299-5400. (also avail. in microfiche)
   Formerly: Annual Book of A S T M Standards. Part 33. Textiles--Fibers, Zippers; High Modulus Fibers (ISSN 0066-0418)

620.1 668.4   US
ANNUAL BOOK OF A S T M STANDARDS. VOLUME 08.01. PLASTICS (1): C 177 TO D 1600. a. $55 to non-members; members $49.50. American Society for Testing and Materials, 1916 Race St., Philadelphia, PA 19103. TEL 215-299-5400.
   Supersedes in part (after 1986): Annual Book of A S T M Standards. Part 35. Plastics--General Test Methods; Nomenclature (ISSN 0066-0434)

620.1 668.4   US
ANNUAL BOOK OF A S T M STANDARDS. VOLUME 08.02. PLASTICS (2): D 1601 TO D 3099. a. $61 to non-members; members $54.90. American Society for Testing and Materials, 1916 Race St., Philadelphia, PA 19103. TEL 215-299-5400.
   Supersedes in part: Annual Book of A S T M Standards. Part 36. Plastics--Materials, Film, Reinforced and Cellular Plastics; High Modulus Fibers and Their Composites; Formerly: Annual Book of A S T M Standards. Part 26. Plastics--Specifications; Methods of Testing Pipe, Film, Reinforced and Cellular Plastics (ISSN 0066-0426)

620   US
ANNUAL BOOK OF A S T M STANDARDS. VOLUME 08.03. PLASTICS (3): D 3100 TO LATEST. 1986. a. $71 to non-members; members $63.90. American Society for Testing and Materials, 1916 Race St., Philadelphia, PA 19103. TEL 215-299-5400. (also avail. in microfiche)

620.1 668.4 690   US
ANNUAL BOOK OF A S T M STANDARDS. VOLUME 08.04. PLASTIC PIPE AND BUILDING PRODUCTS. (Vol. numbering revised; formerly Part 34) a. $92 to non-members; members $82.80. American Society for Testing and Materials, 1916 Race St., Philadelphia, PA 19103. TEL 215-299-5400. (also avail. in microfiche)
   Formerly: Annual Book of A S T M Standards. Part 34. Plastic Pipe.

620.1 678.2   US
ANNUAL BOOK OF A S T M STANDARDS. VOLUME 09.01. RUBBER, NATURAL AND SYNTHETIC--GENERAL TEST METHODS; CARBON BLACK. (Vol. numbering revised 1986; formerly Part 37.) a. $73 to non-members; members $65.70. American Society for Testing and Materials, 1916 Race St., Philadelphia, PA 19103. TEL 215-299-5400. (also avail. in microfiche)

620.1 678.2   US
ANNUAL BOOK OF A S T M STANDARDS. VOLUME 09.02. RUBBER PRODUCTS, INDUSTRIAL--SPECIFICATIONS AND RELATED TEST METHODS; GASKETS; TIRES. (Vol. numbering revised 1986; formerly Part 38) a. $66 to non-members; members $59.40. American Society for Testing and Materials, 1916 Race St., Philadelphia, PA 19103. TEL 215-299-5400. (also avail. in microfiche)
   Formerly: Annual Book of A S T M Standards. Part 28. Rubber; Carbon Black; Gaskets (ISSN 0066-0442)

620.1   US
ANNUAL BOOK OF A S T M STANDARDS. VOLUME 10.01. ELECTRICAL INSULATION, COMPOSITES, AND COATINGS--SOLIDS. a. $54 to non-members; members $48.60. American Society for Testing and Materials, 1916 Race St., Philadelphia, PA 19103. TEL 215-299-5400. (also avail. in microfiche)
   Former titles: Annual Book of A S T M Standards. Volume 10.01. Electrical Insulation--Soils (1); Supersedes in part: Annual Book of A S T M Standards. Part 39. Electrical Insulation--Test Methods; Solids and Solidifying Fluids; Annual Book of A S T M Standards. Part 39. Electrical Insulating Materials--Test Methods (ISSN 0066-0450)

620   US
ANNUAL BOOK OF A S T M STANDARDS. VOLUME 10.02. ELECTRICAL INSULATION; WIRE AND CABLE, HEATINGS AND ELECTRICAL TESTS--SOLIDS (2) 1986. a. $51 to non-members; members $45.90. American Society for Testing and Materials, 1916 Race St., Philadelphia, PA 19103. TEL 215-299-5400. (also avail. in microfiche)
   Formerly: Annual Book of A S T M Standards. Volume 10.02. Electrical Insulation--Solids (2); Supersedes in part: Annual Book of A S T M Standards. Part 39. Electrical Insulation--Test Methods; Solids and Solidifying Fluids.

620.1   US
ANNUAL BOOK OF A S T M STANDARDS. VOLUME 10.03. ELECTRICAL INSULATING LIQUIDS AND GASES; ELECTRICAL PROECTIVE EQUIPMENT. a. $53 to non-members; members $47.70. American Society for Testing and Materials, 1916 Race St., Philadelphia, PA 19103. TEL 215-299-5400. (also avail. in microfiche)
   Former titles (until 1986): Annual Book of A S T M Standards. Part 40. Electrical Insulation--Specifications: Solids, Liquids, and Gases; Test Methods: Liquids and Gases; Protective Equipment; Annual Book of A ST M Standards. Part 40. Electrical Insulation--Specifications: Solids, Liquids, and Gases; Test Methods: Liquids and Gases.

620.1 621.38
ANNUAL BOOK OF A S T M STANDARDS. VOLUME 10.04. ELECTRONICS (1) (Vol. numbering revised 1986; formerly Part 43) a. $68 to non-members; members $61.20. American Society for Testing and Materials, 1916 Race St., Philadelphia, PA 19103. TEL 215-299-5400. (also avail. in microfiche)

620   US
ANNUAL BOOK OF A S T M STANDARDS. VOLUME 10.05. ELECTRONICS (2) 1986. a. $55 to non-members; members $49.50. American Society for Testing and Materials, 1916 Race St., Philadelphia, PA 19103. TEL 215-299-5400. (also avail. in microfiche)
   Supersedes in part: Annual Book of A S T M Standards. Part 43. Electronics.

620.1   US
ANNUAL BOOK OF A S T M STANDARDS. VOLUME 11.01. WATER (1) a. $58 to non-members; members $52.20. American Society for Testing and Materials, 1916 Race St., Philadelphia, PA 19103. TEL 215-299-5400. (also avail. in microfiche)
   Supersedes in part (as of 1986): Annual Book of A S T M Standards. Part 31. Water; Formerly: Annual Book of A S T M Standards. Part 23. Water; Atmospheric Analysis (ISSN 0066-0396)

620   US
ANNUAL BOOK OF A S T M STANDARDS. VOLUME 11.02. WATER (2) 1986. a. $83 to non-members; members $74.70. American Society for Testing and Materials, 1916 Race St., Philadelphia, PA 19103. TEL 215-299-5499. (also avail. in microfiche)
   Supersedes in part: Annual Book of A S T M Standards. Part 31. Water.

620   US
ANNUAL BOOK OF A S T M STANDARDS. VOLUME 11.03. ATMOSPHERIC ANALYSIS; OCCUPATIONAL HEALTH AND SAFETY. 1986. a. $54 to non-members; members $48.60. American Society for Testing and Materials, 1900 Race St., Philadelphia, PA 19103. TEL 215-299-5400. (also avail. in microfiche)
   Supersedes in part: Annual Book of A S T M Standards. Part 26. Gaseous Fuels; Coal and Coke; Atmospheric Analysis.

620   US
ANNUAL BOOK OF A S T M STANDARDS. VOLUME 11.04. PESTICIDES; RESOURCE RECOVERY; HAZARDOUS SUBSTANCES AND OIL SPILL RESPONSE; WASTE DISPOSAL; BIOLOGICAL EFFECTS. 1986. a. $74 to non-members; members $66.60. American Society for Testing and Materials, 1916 Race St., Philadelphia, PA 19103. TEL 215-299-5400.

620.1 621.48   US
ANNUAL BOOK OF A S T M STANDARDS. VOLUME 12.01. NUCLEAR ENERGY (1) a. $74 to non-members; members $66.60. American Society for Testing and Materials, 1916 Race St., PA 19103. TEL 215-299-5400.
Supersedes in part (as of 1986): Annual Book of A S T M Standards. Part 45. Nuclear Standards.

620 531.6   US
ANNUAL BOOK OF A S T M STANDARDS. VOLUME 12.02. NUCLEAR (2), SOLAR, AND GEOTHERMAL ENERGY. 1986. a. $74 to non-members; members $66.60. American Society for Testing and Materials, 1916 Race St., Philadelphia, PA 19103. TEL 215-299-5400. (also avail. in microfiche)
Supersedes in part: Annual Book of A S T M Standards. Part 45. Nuclear Standards.

620 610   US
ANNUAL BOOK OF A S T M STANDARDS. VOLUME 13.01. MEDICAL DEVICES. 1986. a. $50 to non-members; members $45. American Society for Testing and Materials, 1916 Race St., Philadelphia, PA 19103. TEL 215-299-5400. (also avail. in microfiche)

620.1 542   US
ANNUAL BOOK OF A S T M STANDARDS. VOLUME 14.01. ANALYTICAL METHODS - SPECTROSCOPY; CHROMATOGRAPHY; TEMPERATURE MEASUREMENT; COMPUTERIZED SYSTEMS. a. $69 to non-members; members $62.10. American Society for Testing and Materials, 1916 Race St., Philadelphia, PA 19103. TEL 215-299-5400. (also avail. in microfiche)
Former titles: Annual Book of A S T M Standards. Volume 14.01. Molecular Mass Spectroscopy; Chromatography; Resinography; Temperature Measurement; Microscopy; Computerized Systems; (until 1986): Annual Book of A S T M Standards. Part 42. Emission, Molecular, and Mass Spectroscopy; Chromatography; Resinography; Microscopy; Computerized Systems; Annual Book of A S T M Standards. Part 42. Emission, Molecular, and Mass Spectroscopy; Chromatography; Resinography; Microscopy.

620.1   US
ANNUAL BOOK OF A S T M STANDARDS. VOLUME 14.02. GENERAL TEST METHODS, NONMETAL; LABORATORY APPARATUS; STATISTICAL METHODS; APPEARANCE OF MATERIALS; DURABILITY OF NONMETALLIC MATERIALS. a. $88 to non-members; members $79.20. American Society for Testing and Materials, 1916 Race St., Philadelphia, PA 19103. TEL 215-299-5400. (also avail. in microfiche)
Former titles (until 1986): Annual Book of A S T M Standards. Part 41. General Test Methods, Nonmetal; Statistical Methods; Space Simulation; Particle Size Measurement; Laboratory Apparatus; Durability of Nonmetallic Materials; Metric Practice; Solar Energy Conversion; Annual Book of A S T M Standards. Part 41. General Test Methods, Nonmetal; Statistical Methods; Space Simulation; Particle Size Measurement; General Laboratory Apparatus; Durability of Nonmetallic Materials; Metric Practice; Annual Book of A S T M Standards. Part 41. General Test Methods (Nonmetal); Statistical Methods; Space Simulation; Particle Size Measurement; Deterioration of Nonmetallic Materials (ISSN 0066-0469)

620.1   US
ANNUAL BOOK OF A S T M STANDARDS. VOLUME 15.01. REFRACTORIES, MANUFACTURED CARBON AND GRAPHITE PRODUCTS; ACTIVATED CARBON. a. $43 to non-members; members $38.70. American Society for Testing and Materials, 1916 Race St., Philadelphia, PA 19103. TEL 215-299-5400. (also avail. in microfiche)
Formerly (until 1986): Annual Book of A S T M Standards. Part 17. Refractories, Glass and Other Ceramic Materials; Manufactured Carbon and Graphite Products (ISSN 0066-0299)

620   US
ANNUAL BOOK OF A S T M STANDARDS. VOLUME 15.02. GLASS; CERAMIC WHITEWARES. 1986. a. $45 to non-members; members $40.50. American Society for Testing and Materials, 1916 Race St., Philadelphia, PA 19103. TEL 215-299-5400. (also avail. in microfiche)
Supersedes in part: Annual Book of A S T M Standards. Part 17. Refractories, Glass and Other Ceramic Materials; Manufactured Carbon and Graphite Products (ISSN 0066-0299)

620   US
ANNUAL BOOK OF A S T M STANDARDS. VOLUME 15.03. SPACE SIMULATION; AEROSPACE MATERIALS; HIGH MODULUS FIBERS AND THEIR COMPOSITES. 1986. a. $59 to non-members; members $53.10. American Society for Testing and Materials, 1916 Race St., Philadelphia, PA 19103. TEL 215-299-5400. (also avail. in microfiche)
Supersedes in part: Annual Book of A S T M Standards. Part 41. General Test Methods, Nonmetal; Statistical Methods; Space Simulation; Particle Size Measurement; Laboratory Apparatus; Durability of Nonmetallic Materials; Metric Practice; Solar Energy Conversion.

620.1   US
ANNUAL BOOK OF A S T M STANDARDS. VOLUME 15.04. SOAPS; POLISHES; CELLULOSE; LEATHER; RESILIENT FLOOR COVERING. a. $64 to non-members; members $57.60. American Society for Testing and Materials, 1916 Race St., Philadelphia, PA 19103. TEL 215-299-5400. (also avail. in microfiche)
Formerly (until 1986): Annual Book of A S T M Standards. Part 21. Cellulose; Leather; Flexible Barrier Materials; Supersedes in part: Annual Book of A S T M Standards. Part 30. Soap; Engine Collants; Polishes; Halogenated Organic Solvents; Activated Carbon.

620.1   US
ANNUAL BOOK OF A S T M STANDARDS. VOLUME 15.05. ENGINE COOLANTS; HALOGENATED ORGANIC SOLVENTS; INDUSTRIAL CHEMICALS. a. $55 to non-members; members $49.50. American Society for Testing and Materials, 1916 Race St., Philadelphia, PA 19103. TEL 215-299-5400. (also avail. in microfiche)
Formerly (until 1986): Annual Book of A S T M Standards. Part 30. Soap; Engine Coolants; Polishes; Halogenated Organic Solvents; Activated Carbon (ISSN 0066-0388)

620   US
ANNUAL BOOK OF A S T M STANDARDS. VOLUME 15.06. ADHESIVES. 1986. a. $44 to non-members; members $39.60. American Society for Testing and Materials, 1916 Race St., Philadelphia, PA 19103. TEL 215-299-5400. (also avail. in microfiche)
Supersedes in part: Annual Book of A S T M Standards. Part 22. Wood; Adhesives (ISSN 0066-0329)

620.1   US
ANNUAL BOOK OF A S T M STANDARDS. VOLUME 15.07. END USE PRODUCTS. a. $69 to non-members; members $62.10. American Society for Testing and Materials, 1916 Race St., Philadelphia, PA 19103. TEL 215-299-5400. (also avail. in microfiche)
Formerly (until 1986): Annual Book of A S T M Standards. Part 46. End Use and Consumer Products.

620   US
ANNUAL BOOK OF A S T M STANDARDS. VOLUME 15.08. FASTENERS. 1986. a. $50 to non-members; members $45. American Society for Testing and Materials, 1916 Race St., Philadelphia, PA 19103. TEL 215-299-5400. (also avail. in microfiche)
Supersedes in part: Annual Book of A S T M Standards. Part 4. Structural Steel; Concrete Reinforcing Steel; Pressure Vessel Plate and Forgings; Steel Rails, Wheels and Tires; Steel Fasteners.

620.1   US
ANNUAL BOOK OF A S T M STANDARDS. VOLUME 15.09. PAPER; PACKAGING; FLEXIBLE BARRIER MATERIALS; BUSINESS COPY PRODUCTS. a. $86 to non-members; members $77.40. American Society for Testing and Materials, 1916 Race St., Philadelphia, PA 19103. TEL 215-299-5400. (also avail. in microfiche)
Former titles (until 1986): Annual Book of A S T M Standards. Part 20. Paper; Packaging; Business Copy Products; Annual Book of A S T M Standards. Part 15. Paper; Packaging; Cellulose; Casein; Flexible Barrier Materials; Carbon Paper; Leather (ISSN 0066-0310)

620.11   UN   ISSN 0255-9293
ANNUAL REVIEW OF ENGINEERING INDUSTRIES AND AUTOMATION. (Text in English, French and Russian) 1979. a. $27. (Economic Commission for Europe (ECE), Working Party on Engineering Industries and Automation) United Nations Publications, Room DC2-0853, New York, NY 10017 (Or: Distribution and Sales Section, Palais des Nations, 1211 Geneva 10, Switzerland) charts. stats. circ. 300. (also avail. in microfiche; back issues avail.)

620.1   BE   ISSN 0066-8796
ASSOCIATION BELGE POUR L'ETUDE, L'ESSAI ET L'EMPLOI DES MATERIAUX. PUBLICATION A.B.E.M. (Text in Dutch, English, French; summaries in Dutch, French) 1927. irreg. price varies. Association Belge pour l'Etude, l'Essai et l'Emploi des Materiaux, 2 De Croylaan, 3030 Heverlee, Belgium.

620.1   BE   ISSN 0066-8818
ASSOCIATION BELGE POUR L'ETUDE, L'ESSAI ET L'EMPLOI DES MATERIAUX. PROCES VERBAL DE L'ASSEMBLEE GENERALE ORDINAIRE. (Subseries of its publication A.B.E.M.) (Text in Dutch, French) 1931. a. price varies. Association Belge pour l'Etude, l'Essai et l'Emploi des Materiaux, 2 De Croylaan, 3030 Heverlee, Belgium.

620.1   FR   ISSN 0066-9792
ASSOCIATION SCIENTIFIQUE DE LA PRECONTRAINTE. SESSIONS D'ETUDES. 1956. irreg. Association Scientifique de la Precontrainte, 1, Place Genevieres, 59000 Lille, France.

620.11   AT
AUSTRALIAN ENGINEERING CASE STUDIES. 1983. a. Aus.$6.95. Hobsons Press Australia Pty Ltd, 491 Kent St., Sydney, N.S.W. 2000, Australia. Ed. Luke Roberts. circ. 6,500. (back issues avail.)

620.1   PL   ISSN 0067-7701
BIBLIOTEKA MECHANIKI STOSOWANEJ. (Text in Polish; summaries in English) 1956. irreg. price varies. (Polska Akademia Nauk, Instytut Podstawowych Problemow Techniki) Panstwowe Wydawnictwo Naukowe, Miodowa 10, 00-251 Warsaw, Poland (Dist. by: Ars Polona, Krakowskie Przedmiescie 7, 00-068 Warsaw, Poland) Ed. H. Zorski. Indexed: Math.R.

621.8   US   ISSN 0360-2877
CONCRETE PIPE INDUSTRY STATISTICS. 1974. biennial. $425. American Concrete Pipe Association, 8320 Old Courthouse Rd., Vienna, VA 22180. TEL 703-821-1990. illus.

620.1   DK   ISSN 0108-0768
DANMARKS TEKNISKE HOEJSKOLE. AFDELINGEN FOR BAERENDE KONSTRUKTIONER. SERIE R. (Text in Danish and English) 1967. irreg., (5-8/yr); latest no.215, 1986. Kr.130. Danmarks Tekniske Hoejskole, Afdelingen for Baerende Konstruktioner - Technical University of Denmark, Structural Research Laboratory, Bygning 118, DK-2800 Lyngby, Denmark. Ed. P. Lange-Hansen. charts. illus. circ. 300. Indexed: Appl.Mech.Rev. Eng.Ind.

620.11   SZ
EIDGENOESSISCHE TECHNISCHE HOCHSCHULE ZUERICH. INSTITUT FUER BAUSTATIK UND KONSTRUKTION. ALLGEMEINE BERICHTE. (Text in English and German; summaries in English, French, and German) no.88, 1978. irreg. price varies. (Swiss Federal Institute of Technology, Institute of Structural Engineering) Birkhaeuser Verlag, P.O. Box 133, CH-4010 Basel, Switzerland. bibl.

ENGINEERING — ENGINEERING MECHANICS AND MATERIALS

620.111   SZ
EIDGENOESSISCHE TECHNISCHE HOCHSCHULE ZUERICH. INSTITUT FUER BAUSTATIK UND KONSTRUKTION. VERSUCHSBERICHTE. (Text in English and German; summaries in English, French and German) irreg. price varies. (Swiss Federal Institute of Technology, Institute of Structural Engineering) Birkhaeuser Verlag, P.O. Box 133, CH-4010 Basel, Switzerland.

ELECTRICITY SUPPLY HANDBOOK. see *ELECTRICITY AND ELECTRICAL ENGINEERING*

620.1   US   ISSN 0071-4046
FASTENER STANDARDS. 1941. irreg., 5th edt., 1970. $40. Industrial Fasteners Institute, 1505 E. Ohio Bldg., 1717 E. Ninth St., Cleveland, OH 44114. TEL 216-241-1482. Ed. Richard B. Belford. index. circ. 20,000.

620.1   US   ISSN 0428-7738
FLUID POWER HANDBOOK & DIRECTORY. 1956. biennial. $40. Penton Publishing, 1100 Superior Ave., Cleveland, OH 44114. TEL 216-696-7000. Ed. Tobi Goldoftas. adv. charts. illus. stat. tr.lit. circ. 36,000. (also avail. in microform; reprint service avail. from UMI)

620.1   US   ISSN 0891-4052
FUNDAMENTALS OF TEST MEASUREMENT. a. Instrument Society of America, 67 Alexander Dr., Box 12777, Research Triangel Park, NC 27709. TEL 919-549-8411.

620.1   GW   ISSN 0341-0528
GERMANY (FEDERAL REPUBLIC, 1949-). BUNDESANSTALT FUER MATERIALPRUEFUNG. JAHRESBERICHT. 1957. a. DM.10. ‡ Bundesanstalt fuer Materialpruefung, Unter den Eichen 87, 1000 Berlin 45, W. Germany (B.R.D.) illus. index. circ. 1,500.

629   US
GUIDE TO ENGINEERED MATERIALS. 1986. a. $44. American Society for Metals International, Metals Park, OH 44073. TEL 216-338-5151. Ed. John C. Bittence. adv. bk. rev. index. circ. 53,000.

HANDBOOK OF ELECTRONIC MATERIALS. see *ELECTRICITY AND ELECTRICAL ENGINEERING*

I E E E INTERNATIONAL ELECTRONIC MANUFACTURING TECHNOLOGY SYMPOSIUM. see *ELECTRICITY AND ELECTRICAL ENGINEERING*

671.5   621.9   PL   ISSN 0020-4528
INSTYTUT OBROBKI SKRAWANIEM. ZESZYTY NAUKOWE. (Subseries of its "Prace") (Text in Polish; summaries in English, French, German, Russian) 1959. irreg. Instytut Obrobki Skrawaniem - Institute of Metal Cutting, Ul. Wroclawska 37a, 30-011 Krakow, Poland. Ed. J. Kaczmarek. bibl. charts. illus. circ. 260. (also avail. in microfilm) Indexed: Ref.Zh.

620   US   ISSN 0074-3437
INTERNATIONAL CONGRESS FOR STEREOLOGY. PROCEEDINGS. 1963. quadriennial. price varies. International Society for Stereology, c/o Dr. Anna Mary Carpenter, N W C Med Ed., 3400 Broadway, Glen Park, IN 46408. TEL 219-980-6517. circ. 400.

531   620.1   US   ISSN 0071-3422
INTERNATIONAL CONGRESS ON EXPERIMENTAL MECHANICS. PROCEEDINGS. 1980. quadrennial. $90. Society for Experimental Mechanics, 7 School St., Bethel, CT 06801. TEL 203-790-6373.

620.1   US
INTERNATIONAL S A M P E TECHNICAL CONFERENCE SERIES. N S T C PREPRINT SERIES. (Fall conferences) 1969. a. price varies. Society for the Advancement of Material and Process Engineering, Box 2459, Covina, CA 91722. TEL 818-331-0616. Ed. Marge Smith. Indexed: Chem.Abstr.
   Former titles: National S A M P E Technical Conference Series. N S T C Preprint Series (ISSN 0081-1556); Society of Aerospace Material and Process Engineers. National S A M P E Technical Conference. N S T C Preprint Series.

620.1   JA   ISSN 0368-3141
JAPAN CONGRESS ON MATERIALS RESEARCH. PROCEEDINGS/ZAIRYO KENKYU RENGO KOENKAI RONBUNSHU. (Text in English) 1957. a. price varies. Society of Materials Science, Japan - Nihon Zairyo Gakkai, 1-101 Yoshida Izumidono-cho, Sakyo-ku, Kyoto 606, Japan. (Co-sponsor: Science Council of Japan) adv. Indexed: Chem.Abstr.

JAPAN ELECTRONIC MATERIALS SOCIETY. BULLETIN. see *ENGINEERING*

620.11   550   614.7   JA   ISSN 0453-5146
KENSETSU KOGAKU KENKYUSHO HOKOKU/ CONSTRUCTION ENGINEERING RESEARCH INSTITUTE FOUNDATION REPORT. (Text and summaries in Japanese) 1960. a. free. Construction Engineering Research Institute Foundation, 3-10, 1-chome, Tsurukabuto, Nada-ku, Kobe 657, Japan. circ. 500.

551   JA
KYUSHU UNIVERSITY. RESEARCH INSTITUTE FOR APPLIED MECHANICS. ABSTRACTS OF PAPERS. (Text in English and Japanese) 1974. a. on exchange basis. Kyushu University, Research Institute for Applied Mechanics - Kyushu Daigaku Oyorikigaku Kenkyusho, 87, Hakozaki, Higashi-ku, Fukuoka 812, Japan. Ed.Bd. circ. 600. Indexed: Int.Aerosp.Abstr.

620.1   US
LAWRENCE BERKELEY LABORATORY. MATERIALS AND MOLECULAR RESEARCH DIVISION. ANNUAL REPORT. a. University of California, Berkeley, Lawrence Berkeley Laboratory, Berkeley, CA 94720 TEL 415-422-1100. (Order from: National Technical Information Service, 5285 Port Royal Rd., Springfield, VA 22151) illus.
   Formerly: Lawrence Berkeley Laboratory. Inorganic Materials Research Division. Annual Report (ISSN 0092-6248)

620.1   CN   ISSN 0076-2059
MCMASTER UNIVERSITY, HAMILTON, ONTARIO. INSTITUTE FOR MATERIALS RESEARCH. ANNUAL REPORT. 1967. a. free. ‡ McMaster University, Institute for Materials Research, 1280 Main St., W., Hamilton, Ont. L8S 4M1, Canada. TEL 416-525-9140. circ. 750.

620   BU   ISSN 0204-7535
MATERIALOZNANIE I TEKHNOLOGIIA. 1975. irreg. 1.20 lv. per no. (Bulgarska Akademiia na Naukite) Publishing House of the Bulgarian Academy of Sciences, Acad. G. Bonchev St., Bldg. 6, 1113 Sofia, Bulgaria. circ. 470. Indexed: Chem.Abstr. Met.Abstr. World Alum.Abstr.

620.11   IE
MATERIALS HANDLING YEARBOOK (DUBLIN) 1981. a. Irish Trade & Technical Publications Ltd., 5-7 Main St., Blackrock, Co. Dublin, Ireland. illus.

620.1   UK
MATERIALS RESEARCH CENTRES; a world directory of organizations and programmes in materials science. 1983. irreg. £110. Longman Group Ltd., Fourth Ave., Harlow, Essex CM19 5AA, England (Dist. in U.S. & Canada by: Gale Research Co. Ltd., Book Tower, Detroit, MI 48226)

620.1   US   ISSN 0079-8126
MATERIALS RESEARCH IN SCIENCE AND ENGINEERING AT PURDUE UNIVERSITY. PROGRESS REPORT. 1962. a. free. Purdue University, Materials Research Business Office, Physics Bldg., West Lafayette, IN 47907. TEL 317-494-4571. Ed. A.I. Schindler. circ. 200.
   Continues: Materials Research in Science and Engineering at Purdue University. Annual Report.

620.1   US   ISSN 0076-5201
MATERIALS SCIENCE RESEARCH. 1963. irreg. price varies. Plenum Publishing Corp., 233 Spring St., New York, NY 10013. TEL 212-620-8047. Ed.Bd.

620.1   US
METRIC FASTENER STANDARDS. 1976. irreg., 2nd edt., 1983. $60. Industrial Fasteners Institute, 1505 E. Ohio Bldg., 1717 E. Ninth St., Cleveland, OH 44114. TEL 216-241-1482.

620.1   US   ISSN 0077-0000
MODERN MATERIALS. ADVANCES IN DEVELOPMENT AND APPLICATIONS. 1958. irreg., vol.7, 1970. Academic Press, Inc, Orlando, FL 32887. TEL 305-345-2000. Ed. B.W. Gonser. index.

620.1   AT
N.A.T.A. ANNUAL DIRECTORY. 1968. a. Aus.$85. National Association of Testing Authorities, 688 Pacific Highway, Chatswood, N.S.W. 2067, Australia. Ed. I.R. Wables. circ. 800. (also avail. in microfiche)
   Absorbed: N A T A Register of Laboratories. Quarterly Amendment Sheets; Formerly: N.A.T.A. Directory; Continues: N.A.T.A. Index.

620   US
NORTHWESTERN UNIVERSITY. MATERIALS RESEARCH CENTER. ANNUAL TECHNICAL REPORT. 1961. a. free. ‡ (National Science Foundation) Northwestern University, Materials Research Center, 2145 Sheridan Rd., Evanston, IL 60201. TEL 312-491-3606. circ. controlled. (processed)

620.1   US   ISSN 0079-6425
PROGRESS IN MATERIALS SCIENCE. 1949. irreg., (approx. 4/yr.) $165 (annual bound volume $156) Pergamon Press, Inc., Journals Division, Maxwell House, Fairview Park, Elmsford, NY 10523 TEL 914-592-7700. (And: Headington Hill Hall, Oxford OX3 0BW, England) Ed. T.B. Massalski. index. (also avail. in microform from MIM,UMI) Indexed: Chem.Abstr. Curr.Cont. Eng.Ind. Met.Abstr. Sci.Abstr. GeoRef. Int.Aerosp.Abstr. Phys.Ber. World Alum.Abstr.

620.1   389
S E M PROCEEDINGS. 1943. a. $70. Society for Experimental Mechanics, 7 School St., Bethel, CT 06801. TEL 203-790-6373. illus. index. cum.index: vols.1-35. Indexed: Chem.Abstr. Eng.Ind. Met.Abstr.
   Incorporating: S E S A Proceedings (Society for Experimental Stress Analysis) (ISSN 0036-1313)

620.1   US   ISSN 0080-7559
SCIENCE OF ADVANCED MATERIAL AND PROCESS ENGINEERING SERIES. (Spring Symposia) 1959. a. price varies. Society for the Advancement of Material and Process Engineering, Box 2459, Covina, CA 91722. TEL 818-331-0616. Ed. Marge Smith. Indexed: Chem.Abstr.

STANDARD SPECIFICATIONS FOR TRANSPORTATION MATERIALS AND METHODS OF SAMPLING AND TESTING. see *METROLOGY AND STANDARDIZATION*

620.1   US   ISSN 0081-430X
STANDARDS ENGINEERING SOCIETY. PROCEEDINGS OF ANNUAL MEETING. 1951. a. $35 to non-members; members $25. Standards Engineering Society, 6700 Penn Ave. S., Minneapolis, MN 55423. Ed. Raymond E. Monahan. index. circ. 1,000.

530   620.1   US
SYMPOSIUM ON NONDESTRUCTIVE EVALUATION. PROCEEDINGS. 1962. biennial. price varies. Southwest Research Institute, Nondestructive Testing Information Analysis Center, 6220 Culebra Rd., Drawer 28510, San Antonio, TX 78284. TEL 512-522-2362. circ. 500. Indexed: Chem.Abstr.
   Formerly: Symposium on Physics and Nondestructive Testing, San Antonio. Proceedings (ISSN 0082-0903)

620.1   530   US   ISSN 0073-5264
T & A M REPORT. 1946. irreg., no.437, 1979. controlled circ. University of Illinois at Urbana-Champaign, Department of Theoretical and Applied Mechanics, 216 Talbot Laboratory, Urbana, IL 61801. TEL 217-333-1000. circ. 120.

620.11   DK
TRAEKONSTRUKTIONER. 1985. a. Kr.43. Bibliotekscentralen, Telegrafvej 5, DK-2750 Ballerup, Denmark.

620.1   US
TREATISE ON MATERIALS SCIENCE & TECHNOLOGY. 1972. irreg. approx. 1/yr., vol.26, 1985. $69.50. Academic Press, Inc., Orlando, FL 32887. TEL 305-345-2000. Ed. H. Herman. Indexed: Chem.Abstr.

669 GW
UNIVERSITAET HANNOVER. INSTITUT FUER STAHLBAU. SCHRIFTENREIHE. 1960. irreg. price varies. Universitaet Hannover, Institut fuer Stahlbau, Callinstr. 32, 3000 Hannover 1, W. Germany (B.R.D.)
Formerly: Technische Universitaet Hannover. Lehrstuhl fuer Stahlbau. Schriftenreihe (ISSN 0073-0289)

624.17 GW
UNIVERSITAET HANNOVER. INSTITUT FUER STATIK. MITTEILUNGEN. 1959. irreg., no.31, 1986. price varies. Universitaet Hannover, Institut fuer Statik, Callinstrasse 32, II, 3000 Hannover 1, W. Germany (B.R.D.) Ed. H. Rothert. circ. 150.
Formerly: Technische Universitaet Hannover. Institut fuer Statik. Mitteilungen (ISSN 0073-0300)

620.1 CN ISSN 0317-7130
UNIVERSITY OF WATERLOO. SOLID MECHANICS DIVISION. PAPERS. 1969. irreg. free. University of Waterloo, Solid Mechanics Division, Waterloo, Ont. N2L 3G1, Canada. TEL 519-885-1211.

620.1 CN ISSN 0317-7114
UNIVERSITY OF WATERLOO. SOLID MECHANICS DIVISION. REPORTS. 1969. irreg. free. University of Waterloo, Solid Mechanics Division, Waterloo, Ont. N2L 3G1, Canada. TEL 519-885-1211.
Formerly: University of Waterloo. Solid Mechanics Division. Technical Notes.

620.1 CN ISSN 0318-3122
UNIVERSITY OF WATERLOO. SOLID MECHANICS DIVISION. STUDIES SERIES. 1969. irreg. price varies. University of Waterloo, Solid Mechanics Division, Waterloo, Ont. N2L 3G1, Canada. TEL 519-885-1211.

ENGINEERING — Hydraulic Engineering

627 NZ ISSN 0571-9291
AUSTRALASIAN CONFERENCE ON HYDRAULICS AND FLUID MECHANICS. PROCEEDINGS. 1962. triennial; 6th, 1977, Adelaide; 7th, 1981, Brisbane; 8th, 1983, Univ. of Newcastle. price varies. University of Auckland, Faculty of Engineering, Auckland, New Zealand (Proceedings published by host) circ. 300. Indexed: GeoRef.
1st Perth, Univ. of Western Australia, 1962; 2nd Auckland, Univ. of Auckland, 1965; 3rd Sydney, Institution of Engineers, 1968; 4th Melbourne, Monash Univ., 1971; 5th Christchurch, N.Z., 1974, 9th Auckland. N.Z., 1986.

627 UK
B.H.R.A. FLUID ENGINEERING SERIES. irreg. price varies. B H R A Fluid Engineering, Cranfield, Bedford MK43 0AJ, England (Dist in U.S. by: Learned Information Inc., 143 Old Marlton Pike, Medford, NJ 08055)

627 UK ISSN 0306-6916
BRITISH HYDROMECHANICS RESEARCH ASSOCIATION. PROCEEDINGS OF HYDROTRANSPORT. irreg., 10th, 1986. £55. B H R A Fluid Engineering, Cranfield, Bedford MK43 0AJ, England (Dist. in U.S. by: Learned Information Inc., 143 Old Marlton Pike, Medford, NJ 08055)

627 UK ISSN 0140-1785
BRITISH HYDROMECHANICS RESEARCH ASSOCIATION. PROCEEDINGS OF PNEUMOTRANSPORT. 1972. irreg., 5th, 1980. price varies. B H R A Fluid Engineering, Cranfield, Bedford MK43 0AJ, England (Dist. in U.S. by: Learned Information Inc., 143 Old Marlton Pike, Medford, NJ 08055)

620.106 UK ISSN 0140-2145
BRITISH PUMP MANUFACTURERS ASSOCIATION. TECHNICAL CONFERENCE PROCEEDINGS. irreg., 10th, 1987. £48. B H R A Fluid Engineering, Cranfield, Bedford MK43 0AJ, England (Dist. in U.S. by: Learned Information Inc., 143 Old Marlton Pike, Medford, NJ 08055)

D N O C S - FINS E ATIVIDADES. (Departamento Nacional de Obras Contra as Secas) see *AGRICULTURE — Crop Production And Soil*

EIDGENOESSISCHE TECHNISCHE HOCHSCHULE ZUERICH. VERSUCHSANSTALT FUER WASSERBAU, HYDROLOGIE UND GLAZIOLOGIE. JAHRESBERICHT. see *EARTH SCIENCES — Hydrology*

EIDGENOESSISCHE TECHNISCHE HOCHSCHULE ZUERICH. VERSUCHSANSTALT FUER WASSERBAU, HYDROLOGIE UND GLAZIOLOGIE. MITTEILUNGEN. see *EARTH SCIENCES — Hydrology*

620 US
FLUID POWER AND CONTROL SERIES. 1984. irreg. vol.6, 1986. Marcel Dekker, Inc., 270 Madison Ave., New York, NY 10016. TEL 212-696-9000. Eds. Z.L. Lansky, F. Yeaple.

627 US
FLUID POWER STANDARDS. quinquennial. National Fluid Power Association, 3333 N. Mayfair Rd., Milwaukee, WI 53222. TEL 414-778-3344. (also avail. in microfilm; back issues avail.) Indexed: PROMT.

627 UK ISSN 0140-2099
FLUID POWER SYMPOSIUM. PROCEEDINGS. 1969. irreg., 6th, 1981. price varies. B H R A Fluid Engineering, Cranfield, Bedford MK43 0AJ, England (Dist. in U.S. by: Learned Information Inc., 143 Old Marlton Pike, Medford, NJ 08055)

627 UK
HYDRAULIC HANDBOOK. vol.8, 1979. irreg. £78. Trade & Technical Press Ltd., Crown House, Mordon, Surrey, SM4 5EW, England.

627 GW ISSN 0073-7755
INDUSTRIEABWAESSER. 1958. a. DM.7. Deutscher Kommunal-Verlag GmbH, Roseggerstr. 5a, 4000 Duesseldorf 30, W. Germany (B.R.D.) Indexed: Chem.Abstr.

627 UR
INSTITUT VODNOGO TRANSPORTA, LENINGRAD. GIDROTEKHNICHESKAYA LABORATORIYA. MATERIALY. (Subseries of: Institut Vodnogo Transporta, Leningrad. Trudy) irreg. 0.85 Rub. Izdatel'stvo Transport, Leningradskoe Otdelenie, Ul. Dekabristov, 33, 190121 Leningrad, Russian S.F.S.R., U.S.S.R. illus.

627 NE ISSN 0074-1477
INTERNATIONAL ASSOCIATION FOR HYDRAULIC RESEARCH. CONGRESS PROCEEDINGS. 1935. biennial, 21st, 1985, Melbourne. $200 for 5-6 issues. International Association for Hydraulic Research, Rotterdamseweg 185, P.O. Box 177, 2600 MH Delft, Netherlands.
Proceedings published in host country

627.52 II ISSN 0074-2732
INTERNATIONAL COMMISSION ON IRRIGATION AND DRAINAGE. CONGRESS REPORTS. 1951. triennial since 1984, 12th Fort Collins, U.S.A. price varies. International Commission on Irrigation and Drainage - Commission Internationale des Irrigations et du Drainage, 48 Nyaya Marg, Chanakyapuri, New Delhi 1100021, India. (back issues avail.)

627 UK ISSN 0140-1769
INTERNATIONAL SYMPOSIUM ON DREDGING TECHNOLOGY. PROCEEDINGS. 1976. irreg., 4th, 1983. price varies. B H R A Fluid Engineering, Cranfield, Bedford MK43 0AJ, England (Dist. in U.S. by: Learned Information Inc., 143 Old Marlton Pike, Medford, NJ 08055) Indexed: GeoRef.

INTERNATIONAL SYMPOSIUM ON JET CUTTING TECHNOLOGY. PROCEEDINGS. see *ENGINEERING — Mechanical Engineering*

INTERNATIONAL WATER CONFERENCE. PROCEEDINGS. see *WATER RESOURCES*

627 PL ISSN 0239-6254
MATERIALY BADAWCZE. SERIA: INZYNIERIA WODNA/RESEARCH PAPERS SERIES: WATER ENGINEERING. (Text in Polish; summaries in English and Russian) 1979. irreg. $273. Instytut Meteorologii i Gospodarki Wodnej - Institute of Meteorology and Water Management, 61 Podlesna St., 01-673 Warsaw, Poland. circ. 150.

627 US
N F P A DIRECTORY AND MEMBER GUIDE. 1955. a. $150. National Fluid Power Association, 3333 N. Mayfair Rd., Milwaukee, WI 53222. TEL 414-778-3344. circ. 2,000.
Formerly: N F P A Directory.

627 011 US ISSN 0160-8428
NATIONAL CONFERENCE ON FLUID POWER. PROCEEDINGS. 1947. a. $48. (National Conference on Fluid Power) Manufacturing Productivity Center, 10 W. 35th St., Chicago, IL 60616. TEL 312-567-4414. Ed. Keith E. McKee. circ. 600.
Formerly: National Conference on Industrial Hydraulics.

NAVAL ARCHITECTURE AND OCEAN ENGINEERING. see *BUILDING AND CONSTRUCTION — Hardware*

627 NO
NORWEGIAN HYDROTECHNICAL LABORATORY. BULLETIN. (Text in English) 1959. a. free. Norwegian Hydrotechnical Laboratory, Klaebuveien 153, N-7034 Trondheim-NTH, Norway. circ. 1,200.
Formerly: Universitet i Trondheim. Norges Tekniske Hoegskole. Vassdrags-og Havnelaboratoriet. Meddlelelse (ISSN 0082-6618)

620 665.5 US
OILS, LUBRICANTS, AND PETROLEUM PRODUCTS. 1985. irreg. price varies. Marcel Dekker, Inc., 270 Madison Ave., New York, NY 10016. TEL 212-696-9000.

627.8 US ISSN 0078-4508
OKLAHOMA. GRAND RIVER DAM AUTHORITY. ANNUAL REPORT. 1967. a. free. Grand River Dam Authority, Box 409, Vinita, OK 74301. TEL 918-256-5545.

621.3 PK ISSN 0083-8349
PAKISTAN. WATER AND POWER DEVELOPMENT AUTHORITY. REPORT. (Text in English) 1958/59. a. Rs.120. Water and Power Development Authority, WAPDA House, Shara-e-Quaid-e-Azam, Lahore, Pakistan. circ. 1,000.

627 UR
POLIMERY V MELIORATSII I VODNOM KHOZYAISTVE. 1974. irreg. 0.44 Rub. Latviiskii Nauchno-Issledovatel'skii Institut Gidrotekhniki i Melioratsii - Latvijas Hidrotehnikas Un Melioracijas Zinatniski Petnieciskais Instituts, Ul. Revoliutsiias, 43, Elgava, Latvian S.S.R., U.S.S.R. illus.

627 PL
POLITECHNIKA GDANSKA. INSTYTUT HYDROTECHNIKI. RAPORT. 1982. a. price varies. Politechnika Gdanska, Ul. Majakowskiego 11/12, 80-592 Gdansk 6, Poland.

627 PL ISSN 0373-8663
POLITECHNIKA GDANSKA. ZESZYTY NAUKOWE. BUDOWNICTWO WODNE. (Text in Polish; summaries in English and Russian) 1956. irreg. price varies. Politechnika Gdanska, Majakowskiego 11/12, 81-952 Gdansk 6, Poland (Dist. by: Osrodek Rozpowszechniania Wydawnictw Naukowych Pan, Palac Kultury i Nauki, 00-901 Warsaw, Poland)

PROJECT SKYWATER. ANNUAL REPORT. see *WATER RESOURCES*

620 UK ISSN 0266-9870
RIVER AND FLOOD CONTROL ABSTRACTS. 1985. q. £93($142) B H R A Fluid Engineering, Cranfield, Bredford MK43 0AJ, England. Eds. K. Rolfe, T. Abbott. (back issues avail.)

621.2 UK
SYMPOSIUM ON JET PUMPS & EJECTORS AND GAS LIFT TECHNIQUES. PROCEEDINGS. irreg., 2nd 1975 Cambridge. price varies. B H R A Fluid Engineering, Cranfield, Bedford MK43 0AJ, England (Dist. in U.S. by: Learned Information Inc., 143 Old Marlton Pike, Medford, NJ 08055)

627 II ISSN 0080-4045
U.P. IRRIGATION RESEARCH INSTITUTE. GENERAL ANNUAL REPORT.* (Uttar Pradesh) (Issued in its Technical Memorandum Series) a. U. P. Irrigation Research Institute, Roorkee, Uttar Pradesh, India.

627 II ISSN 0080-4053
U.P. IRRIGATION RESEARCH INSTITUTE. TECHNICAL MEMORANDUM.* (Uttar Pradesh) (Text in English) irreg. U.P. Irrigation Research Institute, Roorkee, Uttar Pradesh, India.

627 US
U.S. WATER AND POWER RESOURCES SERVICE. ENGINEERING MONOGRAPH. no.6, 1950. irreg. U.S. Water and Power Resources, Engineering and Research Center, Box 25007, Denver Federal Center, Denver, CO 80225. TEL 303-234-3815. Indexed: Geotech.Abstr.
Formerly: U.S. Bureau of Reclamation. Engineering Monograph.
Land reclamation

VODNI PROBLEMI. see *WATER RESOURCES*

VON KARMAN INSTITUTE FOR FLUID DYNAMICS. LECTURE SERIES. see *AERONAUTICS AND SPACE FLIGHT*

627 UK
WATER SERVICES YEAR BOOK. 1929. a. £25. Industrial & Marine Publications Ltd., Queensway House, 2 Queensway, Redhill, Surrey RH 1 1QS, England. Ed. Derek Eddowes. adv.
Former titles: Water Services Handbook (ISSN 0307-1782); Water Engineer's Handbook (ISSN 0083-7644)

627 RH
ZIMBABWE. MINISTRY OF ENERGY AND WATER RESOURCES AND DEVELOPMENT. HYDROLOGICAL SUMMARIES. 1965. quinquennial, latest 1979-80. $3. Ministry of Energy and Water Resources and Development, c/o Chief Hydrological Engineer, P.O. Box 8132, Causeway, Harare, Zimbabwe.
Former titles: Zimbabwe. Ministry of Water Resources and Development. Hydrological Summaries (ISSN 0080-2832); Zimbabwe. Division of Water Development. Hydrological Summaries.

ENGINEERING — Mechanical Engineering

see also Machinery

620.1 690 PL ISSN 0860-2956
ACTA ACADEMIAE AGRICULTURAE AC TECHNICAE OLSTENENSIS. AEDIFICATIO ET MECHANICA/MECHANICS AND BUILDING ENGINEERING. (Subseries of its: Zeszyty Naukowe) (Text in Polish; summaries in English and Russian) 1974. irreg. price varies. Akademia Rolniczo-Techniczna, Blok 21, 10-718 Olsztyn-Kortowo, Poland (Distr. by: Ars Polona-Ruch, Krakowskie Przedmiescie 7, 00-901 Warsaw, Poland) illus.
Formerly: Mechanika i Budownictwo Ladowe (ISSN 0324-9182)

621 FI ISSN 0001-687X
ACTA POLYTECHNICA SCANDINAVICA. MECHANICAL ENGINEERING SERIES. (Text and summaries in English) irreg. (2-3/yr.) Fmk.130. Teknillisten Tieteiden Akatemia - Finnish Academy of Technical Sciences, Kansakoulukatu 10 A, SF-00100 Helsinki 10, Finland. Ed. Matti Ranta. index. cum.index: 1958-1985. circ. 250. (also avail. in microfilm from UMI; back issues avail.; reprint service avail. from UMI) Indexed: Appl.Mech.Rev. Curr.Cont. Sci.Abstr. ASCA. ISMEC. Int.Aerosp.Abstr.

621 UK
ADVANCED MANUFACTURING TECHNOLOGY. 1985. irreg. £95($150) Jordan & Sons Ltd., Jordan House, 47 Brunswick Place, London N1 6EE, England.

621 660 US ISSN 0272-4790
ADVANCES IN DRYING. 1980. irreg., vol.4, 1985. price varies. Hemisphere Publishing Corporation, 79 Madison Ave., New York, NY 10016. Ed. A.S. Mujumdar. bibl. charts. illus. index. (back issues avail.) Indexed: Chem.Abstr.

621 PL ISSN 0239-5320
AKADEMIA GORNICZO-HUTNICZA IM. STANISLAWA STASZICA. ZESZYTY NAUKOWE. MECHANIKA. (Text in English or Polish; summaries in English, Polish, Russian) 1982. irreg., no.10, 1987. price varies. (Akademia Gorniczo-Hutnicza im. Stanislawa Staszica) Wydawnictwo A G H, Manifestu Lipcowego 16, 31-109 Krakow, Poland (Dist. by: Ars Polona, Krakowskie Przedmiescie 7, 00-068 Warsaw, Poland) Ed. Z. Kleczek. illus. circ. 300.

621 PL ISSN 0137-1800
AKADEMIA ROLNICZA, POZNAN. ROCZNIKI. MECHANICZNA TECHNOLOGIA DREWNA. (Text in Polish; summaries in English and Russian) 1974. irreg. price varies. Akademia Rolnicza, Poznan, Ul. Wojska Polskiego 28, 60-637 Poznan, Poland. Indexed: Bibl.Agri.

621 US
APPLIED MECHANISMS CONFERENCE PROCEEDINGS. 1969. biennial? price varies. Oklahoma State University, College of Engineering, Engineering Extension, 512 Engineering North, Stillwater, OK 74078. TEL 405-624-5146.

AUSTRALIAN GAS INDUSTRY DIRECTORY. see *PETROLEUM AND GAS*

621 DK ISSN 0900-8659
BIL TESTEN. 1985. a. Kr.85. Bibliotekscentralen, Telegrafvej 5, DK-2750 Ballerup, Denmark.

621 AT
BOYCE'S SERVICE STATION MANUAL. 1985. a. Aus.$60($70) David Boyce Publishing and Associates, 44 Regent Street, Redfern, N.S.W. 2016, Australia. circ. 2,500.

BRITISH PUMP MANUFACTURERS ASSOCIATION. TECHNICAL CONFERENCE PROCEEDINGS. see *ENGINEERING — Hydraulic Engineering*

621 GW ISSN 0011-815X
DEMAG KURIER. 1958. irreg., (5-6/yr) free. Mannesmann Demag AG, Wolfgang-Reuter-Platz, 4100 Duisburg, W. Germany (B.R.D.) Ed. E. Schmacke. charts. illus. stat. circ. 35,000. (tabloid format) Indexed: C.I.S. Abstr.

621 US ISSN 0070-4822
DIESEL AND GAS TURBINE WORLD WIDE CATALOG. 1935. a. $75. Diesel & Gas Turbine Publications, 13555 Bishop's Ct., Brookfield, WI 53005. TEL 414-784-9177. adv. circ. 14,359. (also avail. in microform from UMI)

ELEKTROTEHNIKA IR MECHANIKA. see *ELECTRICITY AND ELECTRICAL ENGINEERING*

HEALTH CARE INSTRUMENTATION; the information journal of current medical technology. see *INSTRUMENTS*

621 US
HEAT PUMP TECHNOLOGY CONFERENCE PROCEEDINGS. 1975. irreg. $25. Oklahoma State University, College of Engineering, Engineering Extension, 512 Engineering North, Stillwater, OK 74078. TEL 405-624-5146.

621 US ISSN 0730-3173
HEMISPHERE ENGINEERING PAPERBACK. 1981. irreg. price varies. Hemisphere Publishing Corporation, 79 Madison Ave., New York, NY 10016. bibl. charts. illus. index. (back issues avail.)

HOBSON'S ENGINEERING CASEBOOK. see *ENGINEERING — Civil Engineering*

629.8 US
I F A C SYMPOSIUM ON MULTIVARIABLE TECHNICAL CONTROL SYSTEMS. PROCEEDINGS. 1968. irreg. (International Federation of Automatic Control) Pergamon Journals, Inc., Maxwell House, Fairview Park, Elmsford, NY 10523. Ed. Janos J. Gertler. bibl.

621 US
INTERNATIONAL CENTRE FOR MECHANICAL SCIENCES (CISM). COURSES AND LECTURES. (Text mainly in English) 1969. irreg., vol.289, 1985. price varies. Springer-Verlag, 175 Fifth Ave., New York, NY 10010 TEL 212-460-1500. (Also Berlin, Heidelberg, Tokyo and Vienna) (reprint service avail. from ISI)

621 532 UK ISSN 0074-3089
INTERNATIONAL CONFERENCE ON FLUID SEALING. PROCEEDINGS. 1961. irreg., 10th. 1984. price varies. B H R A Fluid Engineering, Cranfield, Bedford MK 43 0AJ, England (Dist. in U.S. by: Learned Information Inc., 143 Old Marlton Pike, Medford, NJ 08055)

621 UK ISSN 0140-2080
INTERNATIONAL CONFERENCE ON PRESSURE SURGES. PROCEEDINGS. 1973. irreg., 5th, 1986. price varies. B H R A Fluid Engineering, Cranfield, Bedford MK43 0AJ, England (Dist. in U.S. by: Learned Information Inc., 143 Old Marlton Pike, Medford, NJ 08055)

621.4 FR ISSN 0074-4077
INTERNATIONAL CONGRESS ON COMBUSTION ENGINES. PROCEEDINGS. 1951. biennial. price varies. International Council on Combustion Engines - Conseil International des Machines a Combustion (CIMAC), 10 av. Hoche, 75382 Paris Cedex 08, France (Proceedings of 14th Congress avail. from: P. Tuunanen, Federation of Metal and Engineering Industries, Etelaranta 10, SF 00130 Helsinki 13, Finland)

621 UK
INTERNATIONAL GAS BEARING SYMPOSIUM. PROCEEDINGS. irreg., 8th, 1981. price varies. B H R A Fluid Engineering, Cranfield, Bedford MK43 0AJ, England (Dist in U.S. by: Learned Information Inc., 143 Old Marlton Pike, Medford, NJ 08055)

621 UK ISSN 0306-2732
INTERNATIONAL SYMPOSIUM ON JET CUTTING TECHNOLOGY. PROCEEDINGS. 1972. irreg., 8th, 1986. price varies. B H R A Fluid Engineering, Cranfield, Bedford MK43 0AJ, England (Dist. in U.S. by: Learned Information Inc., 143 Old Marlton Pike, Medford, NJ 08055)

621 UR ISSN 0202-7542
ITOGI NAUKI I TEKHNIKI: DVIGATELI VNUTRENNEGO SGORANIYA. vol.4, 1985. irreg. price varies. Vsesoyuznyi Institut Nauchno-Tekhnicheskoi Informatsii (VINITI), Baltiiskaya ul. 14, Moscow A-219, Russian S.F.S.R., U.S.S.R. (Subscr. to: Mezhdunarodnaya Kniga, Dimitrova ul. 39, 113095 Moscow, Russian S.F.S.R., U.S.S.R.)
Internal combustion engines

621 UR ISSN 0202-781X
ITOGI NAUKI I TEKHNIKI: MEKHANIKA ZHIDKOSTI I GAZA. vol.21, 1987. irreg. price varies. Vsesoyuznyi Institut Nauchno-Tekhnicheskoi Informatsii (VINITI), Baltiiskaya ul. 14, Moscow A-219, Russian S.F.S.R., U.S.S.R. (Subscr. to: Mezhdunarodnaya Kniga, Dimitrova ul. 39, 113095 Moscow, Russian S.F.S.R., U.S.S.R.) Indexed: Chem.Abstr.

621 UR ISSN 0202-7917
ITOGI NAUKI I TEKHNIKI: TRUBOPROVODNYI TRANSPORT. vol.11, 1986. irreg. price varies. Vsesoyuznyi Institut Nauchno-Tekhnicheskoi Informatsii (VINITI), Baltiiskaya ul. 14, Moscow A-219, Russian S.F.S.R., U.S.S.R. (Subscr. to: Mezhdunarodnaya Kniga, Dimitrova ul. 39, 113095 Moscow, Russian S.F.S.R., U.S.S.R.)

ENGINEERING — MECHANICAL ENGINEERING

621 GW
JAHRBUCH SCHLEIFFEN, HONEN, LAEPPEN UND POLIEREN, VERFAHREN UND MASCHINEN. 1932. a. DM.72. Vulkan- Verlag Dr. W. Classen, Hollestr. 1G, Postfach 103962, 4300 Essen, W. Germany (B.R.D.) Ed. E. Salje. adv. circ. 2,500.
Former titles: Jahrbuch der Schleiff-, Hon-, Laepp- und Poliertechnik (ISSN 0075-2398); Jahrbuch der Schleif- und Poliertechnik und der Oberflaechenbehandlung.

621 US ISSN 0146-4140
JOURNAL OF BALLISTICS;* a communication journal. 1976. irreg., vol.8, no.4, 1985. $105. Douglas Documentation Systems, Inc., c/o City Wide Press, Inc., 2198 Horning Rd., Philadelphia, PA 19116. Eds. Bruce W. Brodman, Michael P. Devine. adv. bk. rev. charts. illus. circ. 200. (back issues avail.) Indexed: Chem.Abstr.

621 CN ISSN 0076-1966
MCGILL UNIVERSITY, MONTREAL. MECHANICAL ENGINEERING RESEARCH LABORATORIES. REPORT. 1962. irreg. McGill University, Mechanical Engineering Department, 817 Sherbrooke St. W., Montreal, Que. H3A 2K6, Canada. TEL 514-392-4311.

621 CN ISSN 0076-1974
MCGILL UNIVERSITY, MONTREAL. MECHANICAL ENGINEERING RESEARCH LABORATORIES. TECHNICAL NOTE. 1962. irreg. free when avail. McGill University, Mechanical Engineering Department, 817 Sherbrooke St. W., Montreal, Que. H3A 2K6, Canada. TEL 514-392-4311.

621 UR
MEKHANICHESKAYA TEKHNOLOGIYA/ MECHANINE TECHNOLOGIJA. (Text in Lithuanian or Russian) irreg. Kaunas Politechnic Institute, Editing and Publishing Group - Kauno Politechninis Institutas, K. Donelaicio 73, 233006 Kaunas, Lithuanian S.S.R., U.S.S.R. Ed. J. Gecevicius. illus.

NATIONAL CONFERENCE ON FLUID POWER. PROCEEDINGS. see ENGINEERING — Hydraulic Engineering

621 CN ISSN 0077-555X
NATIONAL RESEARCH COUNCIL, CANADA. NATIONAL AERONAUTICAL ESTABLISHMENT. MECHANICAL ENGINEERING REPORTS. 1947. irreg. free. National Research Council of Canada, N A E Publications Section, Ottawa, Ont. K1A OR6, Canada. TEL 613-993-2413. circ. 1,200. Indexed: Chem.Abstr.

NUMERICAL FLUID MECHANICS AND HEAT TRANSFER REVIEW. see PHYSICS

620 US
PNEUMATIC PACKAGING. 1935. irreg. Pneumatic Scale Corporation, 65 Newport Ave., Quincy, MA 02171. TEL 617-328-6100. Ed. Donald R. McKay. circ. 12,500.

629 PL ISSN 0137-6969
POLITECHNIKA CZESTOCHOWSKA. ZESZYTY NAUKOWE. NAUKI TECHNICZNE. MECHANIKA. (Text in Polish; summaries in English and Russian) 1969. irreg. Politechnika Czestochowska, Ul. Deglera 31, 42-200 Czestochowa, Poland (Dist. by: Ars Polona-Ruch, Krakowskie Przedmiescie 7, Warsaw, Poland) Ed. Ryszard Parkitny. Indexed: Chem.Abstr.

621 PL
POLITECHNIKA GDANSKA. INSTYTUT ORGANIZACJI I PROJEKTOWANIA. RAPORT. 1982. a. price varies. Politechnika Gdanska, Ul. Majakowskiego 11/12, 80-592 Gdansk 6, Poland.

621 PL
POLITECHNIKA GDANSKA. RAPORT. WYDZIAL BUDOWY MASZYN. 1982. a. price varies. Politechnika Gdanska, Ul. Majakowskiego 11/12, 80-952 Gdansk 6, Poland.

621 PL
POLITECHNIKA GDANSKA. RAPORT. WYDZIAL MECHANICZNY TECHNOLOGICZNY. 1982. a. price varies. Politechnika Gdanska, Ul. Majakowskiego 11/12, 80-952 Gdansk 6, Poland.

621 PL ISSN 0072-0380
POLITECHNIKA GDANSKA. ZESZYTY NAUKOWE. MECHANIKA. (Text in Polish; summaries in English and Russian) 1955. irreg. price varies. Politechnika Gdanska, Majakowskiego 11/12, 81-952 Gdansk 6, Poland (Dist. by: Osrodek Rozpowszechniania Wydawnictw Naukowych Pan, Palac Kultury i Nauki, 00-901 Warsaw, Poland)

621.8 PL ISSN 0137-2661
POLITECHNIKA LODZKA. ZESZYTY NAUKOWE. CIEPLNE MASZYNY PRZEPLYWOWE. (Text in various languages; summaries in English and Russian) irreg. price varies. Politechnika Lodzka, Ul. Zwirki 36, 90-924 Lodz, Poland (Dist. by: Ars Polona-Ruch, Krakowskie Przedmiescie 7, Warsaw, Poland) Ed. Ryszard Przybylski. circ. 183.

621 PL ISSN 0458-1563
POLITECHNIKA LODZKA. ZESZYTY NAUKOWE. MECHANIKA. (Text in Polish; summaries in English and Russian) 1954. irreg. price varies. Politechnika Lodzka, Ul. Zwirki 36, 90-924 Lodz, Poland (Dist. by: Ars Polona-Ruch, Krakowskie Przedmiescie 7, Warsaw, Poland) Ed. Zdzislaw Orzechowski. circ. 583. Indexed: Chem.Abstr. Met.Abstr.

620 PL ISSN 0434-0817
POLITECHNIKA SLASKA. ZESZYTY NAUKOWE. MECHANIKA. (Text in Polish; summaries in English and Russian) 1955. irreg. price varies. Politechnika Slaska, W. Pstrowskiego 7, 44-100 Gliwice, Poland (Dist. by: Ars Polona, Krakowskie Przedmiescie 7, 00-068 Warsaw, Poland) Ed. Jozef Wojnarowski.

621 PL ISSN 0324-9573
POLITECHNIKA WROCLAWSKA. INSTYTUT MATERIALOZNAWSTWA I MECHANIKI TECHNICZNEJ. PRACE NAUKOWE. KONFERENCJE. (Text in Polish; summaries in English and Russian) 1974. irreg., no.2, 1973. Politechnika Wroclawska, Wybrzeze Wyspianskiego 27, 50-370 Wroclaw, Poland (Dist. by: Ars Polona-Ruch, Krakowskie Przedmiescie 7, Warsaw, Poland) Ed. Marian Kloza. illus.

621 PL ISSN 0324-9379
POLITECHNIKA WROCLAWSKA. INSTYTUT TECHNOLOGII BUDOWY MASZYN. PRACE NAUKOWE. KONFERENCJE. (Text in Polish; summaries in English and Russian) 1975. irreg., no.10, 1986. price varies. Politechnika Wroclawska, Wybrzeze Wyspianskiego 27, 50-370 Wroclaw, Poland (Dist. by: Ars Polona-Ruch, Krakowskie Przedmiescie 7, Warsaw, Poland) Ed. Jerzy Ciekot.

621 PL ISSN 0324-9352
POLITECHNIKA WROCLAWSKA. INSTYTUT TECHNOLOGII BUDOWY MASZYN. PRACE NAUKOWE. MONOGRAFIE. (Text in Polish; summaries in English and Russian) 1972. irreg., no.6, 1987. price varies. Politechnika Wroclawska, Wybrzeze Wyspianskiego 27, 50-370 Wroclaw, Poland (Dist. by: Ars Polona-Ruch, Krakowskie Przedmiescie 7, Warsaw, Poland) Ed. Jerzy Ciekot.

621 PL ISSN 0324-9360
POLITECHNIKA WROCLAWSKA. INSTYTUT TECHNOLOGII BUDOWY MASZYN. PRACE NAUKOWE. STUDIA I MATERIALY. (Text in Polish; summaries in English and Russian) 1970. irreg., no.16, 1980. price varies. Politechnika Wroclawska, Wybrzeze Wyspianskiego 27, 50-370 Wroclaw, Poland (Dist. by: Ars Polona-Ruch, Krakowskie Przedmiescie 7, Warsaw, Poland) Ed. Marian Kloza. Indexed: Chem.Abstr.

621 PL ISSN 0079-3205
POLSKA AKADEMIA NAUK. INSTYTUT MASZYN PRZEPLYWOWYCH. PRACE/POLISH ACADEMY OF SCIENCES. INSTITUTE OF FLUID-FLOW MACHINERY. TRANSACTIONS. (Text in Polish; summaries in English and Russian) 1960. irreg., vol.87, 1984. price varies. Panstwowe Wydawnictwo Naukowe, Ul. Miodowa 10, 00-257 Warsaw, Poland (Dist. by: Ars Polona, Krakowskie Przedmiescie 7, 00-068 Warsaw, Poland) Ed. Kazimierz Steller. bibl, charts, illus.

621 UR ISSN 0136-3549
POLUTEHNILINE INSTITUUT TALLINN. AVTOMATIZATSIYA TEKHNOLOGICHESKOGO PROYEKTIROVANIYA PROTSESSOV MEKHANICHESKOI OBRABOTKI. (Subseries of: Its Toimetised) (Text in Russian; summaries in English or German) irreg. price varies. Polutehniline Instituut Tallinn, Ehitajate tee 5, Tallinn, Estonian S.S.R., U.S.S.R.

621 UR ISSN 0320-3352
POLUTEHNILINE INSTITUUT TALLINN. ISSLEDOVANIE DVUMERNOGO VOZMUSHCHENNOGO POLYA NAPRYAZHENIYA. (Subseries of: its Toimetised) (Text in Russian; summaries in English or German) irreg. price varies. Polutehniline Instituut Tallinn, Ehitajate tee 5, Tallinn, Estonian S.S.R., U.S.S.R.

621 UR ISSN 0320-3344
POLUTEHNILINE INSTITUUT TALLINN. TRENIE I IZNOS V MASHINAKH. (Subseries of: Its Toimetised) (Text in Russian; summaries in English or German) irreg. price varies. Polutehniline Instituut Tallinn, Ehitajate tee 5, Tallinn, Estonian S.S.R., U.S.S.R.

621.31 US
POWER TRANSMISSION DESIGN HANDBOOK. 1961/62. biennial. $25. Penton Publishing, 1100 Superior Ave., Cleveland, OH 44114. TEL 216-696-7000. Ed. Phil Kingsley. adv. circ. 52,000. (reprint service avail. from UMI)
Formerly: Power Transmission and Bearing Handbook (ISSN 0554-890X)

621 338.91 GW
PROGRESS & ENGINEERING. DEVELOPING COUNTRIES EDITION. (Editions in English and French) 1921. a. Vogel-Verlag KG, Box 6740, 8700 Wuerzburg, W. Germany (B.R.D.) Ed. Arnold Metzner. adv. circ. 18,000.

PUBLICATIONS OF THE TECHNICAL UNIVERSITY FOR HEAVY INDUSTRY. SERIES C, MACHINERY. see MACHINERY

621.6 UK
PUMPING MANUAL. vol.6, 1979. irreg. £48. Trade & Technical Press Ltd., Crown House, Morden, Surrey SM4 5EW, England.

621 629.1 UK ISSN 0432-2924
R E M E JOURNAL. 1952. a. £1.75. Royal Electrical & Mechanical Engineers, Isaac Newton Rd., Arborfield, Reading, Berks. RG2 9LN, England. Ed. I.G. Swan. adv. bk. rev. circ. 3,000. Indexed: Sci.Abstr.

621 US ISSN 0272-4804
SERIES IN COMPUTATIONAL METHODS IN MECHANICS AND THERMAL SCIENCES. 1980. irreg., unnumbered, latest 1985. price varies. Hemisphere Publishing Corporation, 79 Madison Ave., New York, NY 10016. Eds. W.J. Minkowycz, E.M. Sparrow. bibl. charts. illus. index. (back issues avail.)

627 US ISSN 0146-0854
SERIES IN THERMAL AND FLUIDS ENGINEERING. 1976. irreg., unnumbered, latest 1980. Hemisphere Publishing Corporation, 79 Madison Ave., New York, NY 10016. (back issues avail.) Indexed: Chem.Abstr. Eng.Ind.

621 US ISSN 0146-2059
STRUCTURAL MECHANICS SOFTWARE SERIES. 1977. irreg., vol.5, 1985. $30. (University of Virginia, Department of Engineering Science and Systems) University Press of Virginia, Box 3608 University Sta., Charlottesville, VA 22903. TEL 804-924-3468. Eds. Nicholas Perrone, Walter Pilkey. index. circ. 1,500.

621 NE
STUDIES IN MECHANICAL ENGINEERING. 1980. irreg., vol.4, 1985. price varies. Elsevier Science Publishers B.V., Box 211, 1000 AE Amsterdam, Netherlands.

623.82 YU ISSN 0350-3097
SVEUCILISTE U ZAGREBU. FAKULTET STROJARSTVA I BRODOGRADNJE. ZBORNIK RADOVA. (Summaries in English or German) 1970. a. free. Sveuciliste u Zagrebu, Fakultet Strojarstva i Brodogradnje, Djure Salaja 5, Zagreb, Yugoslavia. Ed. Zora Smolcic-Zerdik. illus.

621 US
SWEET'S MECHANICAL ENGINEERING AND RETROFIT FILE. a. free to qualified personnel. Sweet's Catalog Files (Subsidiary of: McGraw-Hill Information Systems Co.) 1221 Ave. of the Americas, New York, NY 10020. circ. 13,000.

621 GW ISSN 0170-303X
TECHNIQUE DU ROULEMENT. English edition: Ball and Roller Bearing Engineering (ISSN 0522-0629); German edition: Waelzlagertechnik (ISSN 0511-0653); Italian edition: Cuscinetti Volventi (ISSN 0170-3048); Spanish edition: Tecnica de los Rodamientos (ISSN 0170-3056) (Text in French) 1962. irreg. (1-3/yr.) FAG Kugelfischer Georg Schaefer KGaA, Postfach 1260, 8720 Schweinfurt 1, W. Germany (B.R.D.)

TECHNISCHE MITTEILUNGEN KRUPP. see *METALLURGY*

621 GW ISSN 0170-3056
TECNICA DE LOS RODAMIENTOS. English edition: Ball and Roller Bearing Engineering (ISSN 0522-0629); French edition: Technique du Roulement (ISSN 0170-303X); German edition: Waelzlagertechnik (ISSN 0511-0653); Italian edition: Cuscinetti Volventi (ISSN 0170-3048) (Text in Spanish) 1962. irreg. (1-3/yr.) FAG Kugelfischer Georg Schaefer KGaA, Postfach 1260, 8720 Schweinfurt 1, W. Germany (B.R.D.)

TOKYO DENKI UNIVERSITY. FACULTY OF ENGINEERING. GENERAL EDUCATION. RESEARCH REPORTS. see *ENGINEERING*

TOKYO DENKI UNIVERSITY. FACULTY OF ENGINEERING. RESEARCH REPORTS. see *ENGINEERING*

621 IT
TRASMISSIONI DI POTENZA; guida Italiana dei fornitori. 1960. a. L.60000. Tecniche Nuove s.r.l., Via Moscova 46/9a, 20121 Milan, Italy. circ. 8,000.

621.89 NE
TRIBOLOGY SERIES. 1978. irreg., vol.9, 1985. Elsevier Science Publishers B.V., Box 211, 1000 AE Amsterdam, Netherlands. charts. Indexed: Chem.Abstr.

621.4 US ISSN 0748-0903
TURBOMACHINERY INTERNATIONAL HANDBOOK. 1963. a. $45. Turbomachinery International Publications (Subsidiary of: Business Journals, Inc.) Box 5550, Norwalk, CT 06856. TEL 203-853-6015. Ed. Frances Lyon. adv. (reprint service avail. from UMI)
Former titles: Turbomachinery Catalog and Workbook; Sawyer's Gas Turbine Catalog; Gas Turbine Catalog (ISSN 0072-0267)

621.9 US
U S MACHINE TOOL DIRECTORY. a. free. National Machine Tool Builders' Association, 7901 Westpark Dr., McLean, VA 22102. TEL 703-893-2900. circ. 30,000.
Formerly: Directory of Machine Tools and Related Products (ISSN 0070-5772)

UNIVERSITAET STUTTGART. INSTITUT FUER STEUERUNGSTECHNIK DER WERKZEUGMASCHINEN UND FERTIGUNGSEINRICHTUNGEN. I S W BERICHTE. see *MACHINERY*

621.8 RM
UNIVERSITATEA DIN BRASOV. BULETINUL. SERIA A. MECANICA APLICATA-CONSTRUCTII DE MASINI. (Text in Romanian; summaries in English, French, German) vol.14, 1972. a. price varies. Universitatea din Brasov, Bd. Gh. Gheorghiu-Dej, Nr. 29, Brasov, Rumania. bibl. illus. Indexed: Sci.Abstr.

621 CN ISSN 0082-5182
UNIVERSITY OF TORONTO. DEPARTMENT OF MECHANICAL ENGINEERING. TECHNICAL PUBLICATION SERIES. 1962. irreg. University of Toronto, Department of Mechanical Engineering, Toronto, Ont., Canada. TEL 613-978-7198. circ. 100.

621 SA
UNIVERSITY OF WITWATERSRAND, JOHANNESBURG. SCHOOL OF MECHANICAL ENGINEERING. RESEARCH REPORTS. 1957. irreg. free. University of the Witwatersrand, Johannesburg, School of Mechanical Engineering, Jan Smuts Ave., Johannesburg, South Africa. Eds. H.H. Jawurek, C.J. Rallis. circ. 250. (also avail. in microfiche)

629.2 UK
VEHICLE BUILDERS & REPAIRERS ASSOCIATION. DIRECTORY OF MEMBERS & BUYERS GUIDE. a. £12($18) (Vehicle Builders & Repairers Association) V B R A Publications Ltd., Belmont House, 102 Finkle Lane, Gildersome, Leeds LS27 7TW, England. Ed. Paul Rouse. adv. circ. 6,800.
Former titles: Vehicle Builders and Repairers Association. Yearbook (ISSN 0083-5331); Vehicle Builders and Repairers Association. Directory.

VEREIN DEUTSCHER INGENIEURE. INFORMATIONSDIENST. INSTANDHALTUNG. see *ENGINEERING — Abstracting, Bibliographies, Statistics*

620.1 UR
VOPROSY INZHENERNOI GEOLOGII I GRUNTOVEDENIYA; proceedings of the seminar of the chair of the theory of elasticity under the guidance A.A. Ilushin. 1963. biennial. 4.20 Rub. Moskovskii Universitet, Kafedra Gruntovedeniya i Inzhenernoi Geologii, Leninskie Gory, Moscow V-234, Russian S.F.S.R., U.S.S.R. Ed. P.U. Ogibalov.

621 GW ISSN 0171-5038
W E M A BEZUGSQUELLENVERZEICHNIS. (Text in German; index in English, French) 1950. irreg. Wirtschaftsverband Eisen-Maschinen-und Apparatebau e. V.(WEMA), Karolingerplatz 10-11, 1000 Berlin 19, W. Germany (B.R.D.) circ. 3,000.

621 GW ISSN 0511-0653
WAELZLAGERTECHNIK. English edition: Ball and Roller Bearing Engineering (ISSN 0522-0629); French Edition: Technique du Roulement (ISSN 0170-303X); Italian edition: Cuscinetti Volventi (ISSN 0170-3048); Spanish edition: Tecnica de los Rodamientos (ISSN 0170-3056) 1962. irreg. (1-3/yr.) free. FAG Kugelfischer Georg Schaefer KG2A, Postfach 1260, D-8720 Schweinfurt 1, W. Germany (B.R.D.) circ. 90,000.

621 GW ISSN 0083-9299
WER BAUT MASCHINEN. English edition: Who Makes Machinery (ISSN 0171-1148); French edition: Qui Construit des Machines (ISSN 0171-1156); Spanish edition: Quien Construye Maquinas (ISSN 0171-1164) 1928. a. DM.25. (Verband Deutscher Maschinen und Anlagenbau e.V.) Verlag Hoppenstedt und Co., Havelstr. 9, Postfach 4006, 6100 Darmstadt, W. Germany (B.R.D.) adv.

621 530 US ISSN 0888-594X
WHO'S WHO IN MECHANICAL ENGINEERING & MATERIALS SCIENCE. 1979. biennial. $545. Research Publications, Inc. (Woodbridge), 12 Lunar Dr., Drawer AB, Woodbridge, CT 06525. TEL 203-297-2600.

ENTOMOLOGY

see *Biology—Entomology*

ENVIRONMENTAL STUDIES

see also *Biology; Conservation; Public Health and Safety; Water Resources*

363.6 US
A P C A GOVERNMENT AGENCIES DIRECTORY. 1970. a. $3 to members; $4 non-members. A P C A, The Association Dedicated to Air Pollution Control and Hazardous Waste Management, Box 2861, Pittsburgh, PA 15230. TEL 412-621-1090. Ed. H.M. Englund. (reprint service avail. from UMI)
Former titles: Directory of Governmental Air Pollution Agencies & A.P.C.A. Directory and Resource Book (ISSN 0094-9191); Supersedes: A P C A Directory.

614.7 US
ACID RAIN ANNUAL INDEX. a. E I C Intelligence, Inc., 48 W. 38th St., New York, NY 10018. TEL 212-944-8500.

574.5 US ISSN 0065-2504
ADVANCES IN ECOLOGICAL RESEARCH. 1962. irreg., vol.15, 1986. Academic Press Inc., Orlando, FL 32887. TEL 305-345-2000. Eds. A. MacFadyen, E.D. Ford. Indexed: Biol.Abstr. Biol.& Agr.Ind. Sci.Cit.Ind. Field Crop Abstr. Forest.Abstr. Forest Prod.Abstr. Herb.Abstr. Ind.Sci.Rev. Plant Breed.Abstr. Sel.Water Res.Abstr.

ADVANCES IN ENVIRONMENTAL PSYCHOLOGY. see *PSYCHOLOGY*

600 US ISSN 0141-8106
ADVANCES IN ENVIRONMENTAL SCIENCE AND ENGINEERING. vol.5, 1986. irreg. price varies. Gordon and Breach Science Publishers, 50 W. 23rd St., New York, NY 10010. TEL 212-206-8900. Eds. J.R. Pfafflin, E.N. Ziegler. Indexed: Chem.Abstr.

614.7 US ISSN 0065-2563
ADVANCES IN ENVIRONMENTAL SCIENCE AND TECHNOLOGY. 1969. irreg., vol.19, 1987. price varies. John Wiley & Sons, Inc., 605 Third Ave., New York, NY 10016. TEL 212-850-6000. Ed. Jerome O. Nriagu. Indexed: Biol.Abstr.
Formerly: Advances in Environmental Sciences (ISSN 0095-4535)

ADVANCES IN RISK ANALYSIS. see *PUBLIC HEALTH AND SAFETY*

AEROSPACE TESTING SEMINAR. PROCEEDINGS. see *AERONAUTICS AND SPACE FLIGHT*

301.31 SG
AFRICAN ENVIRONMENT; environmental studies and regional planning bulletin. (Text in English and French) 1974. irreg. 60.000 Fr.CFA. E N D A Publications, Box 3370, Dakar, Senegal. Ed.Bd. bk. rev. circ. 2,200. Indexed: Curr.Cont.Africa. Geo.Abstr. Rural Recreat.Tour.Abstr. Soils & Fert. World Agri.Econ.& Rural Sociol.Abstr.
Supersedes: Environment in Africa.

301.31 SG
AFRICAN ENVIRONMENT. OCCASIONAL PAPERS/ETUDES ET RECHERCHES. (Text in English or French) irreg. 10.00 Fr.CFA for 10 nos. E N D A Publications, Box 3370, Dakar, Senegal.

614.7 UK ISSN 0309-345X
AFRICAN ENVIRONMENT SPECIAL REPORTS.* 1974. irreg. International African Institute, Lionel Robbins Bldg., 10 Portugal St., London WC2A 2HD, England. bk. rev. bibl.

614.7 US
AIR QUALITY DATA FOR ARIZONA. 1972. a. Department of Health Services, Bureau of Air Quality Control, 1740 W. Adams St., Phoenix, AZ 85007. TEL 602-255-1142. Ed. James L. Guyton. illus. circ. controlled.
Former titles: Air Pollution Effects Surveillance Network Data Report (ISSN 0092-1009); Air Quality Monitoring Network Data.

354 CN ISSN 0383-3739
ALBERTA. DEPARTMENT OF THE ENVIRONMENT. ANNUAL REPORT. a. Department of the Environment, 9820 106th St., Edmonton, Alta. T5K 2J6, Canada. TEL 403-427-6267.

ENVIRONMENTAL STUDIES

333.7   CN   ISSN 0707-2783
ALBERTA. FISH AND WILDLIFE DIVISION. FISHERIES POLLUTION REPORT. 1978. irreg. Fish and Wildlife Division, Lethbridge, Alta., Canada. bibl. charts. illus.
Formerly: Alberta. Fish and Wildlife Division. Pollution Report (ISSN 0707-2791)

614.7   620   US
AMERICAN ACADEMY OF ENVIRONMENTAL ENGINEERS. CONSULTANT DIRECTORY. 1985. a. free. American Academy of Environmental Engineers, 93 Main St., Box 269, Annapolis, MD 21404.

614.7   620   US   ISSN 0065-6860
AMERICAN ACADEMY OF ENVIRONMENTAL ENGINEERS. ROSTER. 1956. a. $50. American Academy of Environmental Engineers, Box 269, Annapolis, MD 21404. bk. rev.

614.7   CN   ISSN 0707-5723
ANALYSIS. 1977. irreg. Ministry of the Environment, Laboratory Services Branch, Box 213, Rexdale, Ont. M9W 5L1, Canada. TEL 416-965-7117. illus. Indexed: Curr.Cont.

ANNUAL BOOK OF A S T M STANDARDS. VOLUME 11.01. WATER (1) see
ENGINEERING — Engineering Mechanics And Materials

614.7   US   ISSN 0272-9008
ANNUAL EDITIONS: ENVIRONMENT. 1979. a. $9.50. Dushkin Publishing Group, Inc., Sluice Dock, Guilford, CT 06437. TEL 203-453-4351. Ed. Ian Nielsen.
Formerly: Readings in Environment (ISSN 0196-4542)

574.5   US   ISSN 0066-4162
ANNUAL REVIEW OF ECOLOGY AND SYSTEMATICS. 1970. a. $31. Annual Reviews Inc., 4139 El Camino Way, Palo Alto, CA 94306. TEL 415-493-4400. Ed. Richard F. Johnston. bibl. index. cum.index. (back issues avail., reprint service avail. from ISI) Indexed: Biol.Abstr. Biol.& Agr.Ind. Chem.Abstr. Curr.Cont. Field Crop Abstr. Forest.Abstr. Forest Prod.Abstr. Geo.Abstr. Helminthol.Abstr. Herb.Abstr. Ind.Sci.Rev. M.M.R.I. Plant Breed.Abstr. Rev.Appl.Entomol. Soils & Fert.

614.7   352.7   340   IT
ANNUARIO EUROPEO DELL'AMBIENTE. English edition: European Environmental Yearbook. (Text in Italian) 1984. biennial. L.100000. (Istituto di Studi e Documentazione per il Territorio - Institute for Environmental Documentation) DocTer Edizioni Srl, Foro Bonaparte 12, 20121 Milan, Italy TEL 01-937-3660. (Distr. by: DocTer International U.K. Ltd., 22 South Audley St., London W1, England) (Co-sponsor: Commission of the European Communities (EEC)) Eds. Achille Cutrera, Valerio Onida. adv. bk. rev. bibl. circ. 4,500. (back issues avail.)

363.6   US
ARIZONA. COMMISSION ON THE ARIZONA ENVIRONMENT. ANNUAL REPORT. 1965. a. Commission on the Arizona Environment, 1645 W. Jefferson, Ste. 416, Phoenix, AZ 85007. TEL 602-255-2102. illus. circ. 1,000.
Former titles: Arizona. Governor's Commission on Arizona Environment. Annual Report & Arizona. Governor's Commission on Arizona Environment. Biennial Report; Arizona. Governor's Commission on Arizona Environment. Annual Report (ISSN 0097-9953)

ARIZONA RADIATION REVIEW. see PHYSICS — Nuclear Energy

AUSTRALIA. ENVIRONMENTAL STUDIES WORKING PAPERS. see CONSERVATION

AUSTRALIA. NATIONAL CAPITAL DEVELOPMENT COMMISSION. TECHNICAL PAPERS. see HOUSING AND URBAN PLANNING

153   AT   ISSN 0726-6987
AUSTRALIAN WASTE DISPOSAL CATALOGUE. 1979. a. Aus.$4.50. Editorial and Publishing Consultants Pty. Ltd., 29 First Ave., Klemzig SA 5087, Australia. Ed. Frank H. Schmidt. adv. circ. 2, 000.

BEITRAEGE ZUR GEOGRAPHIE. see GEOGRAPHY

614.7   GW   ISSN 0340-9716
BEITRAEGE ZUR UMWELTGESTALTUNG. REIHE A. irreg. price varies. Erich Schmidt Verlag GmbH (Berlin), Genthiner Str. 30G, 1000 Berlin 30, W. Germany (B.R.D.)

614.7   GW   ISSN 0340-949X
BEITRAEGE ZUR UMWELTGESTALTUNG. REIHE B. irreg. price varies. Erich Schmidt Verlag GmbH (Berlin), Genthiner Str. 30G, 1000 Berlin 30, W. Germany(B.R.D.)

BERMUDA. BIOLOGICAL STATION FOR RESEARCH. SPECIAL PUBLICATIONS. see EARTH SCIENCES — Oceanography

BIOTRONICS. see BIOLOGY

614.7   SA
BONTEBOK. (Text in Afrikaans and English) 1981. irreg. Cape Department of Nature and Environmental Conservation, Private Bag 9086, Capetown 8000, South Africa. circ. 1,000. (back issues avail.)

614.7   BS
BOTSWANA. DEPARTMENT OF MINES. AIR POLLUTION CONTROL. ANNUAL REPORT. a. Department of Mines, Private Bag 0049, Gaborone, Botswana.

BRITISH COLUMBIA. MINISTRY OF THE ENVIRONMENT. NORTHEAST COAL STUDY PRELIMINARY ENVIRONMENTAL REPORT. see MINES AND MINING INDUSTRY

628.53   US   ISSN 0068-5496
CALIFORNIA. AIR RESOURCES BOARD. ANNUAL REPORT. a. free. Air Resources Board, Box 2815, Sacramento, CA 95812. TEL 916-322-2990.

614.7   US
CALIFORNIA. AIR RESOURCES BOARD. FACT SHEETS. 1972. irreg. free. Air Resources Board, Information Office, Box 2815, Sacramento, CA 95812. TEL 916-322-2990.

614.7   US
CALIFORNIA AIR BASINS. 1969. irreg. free. Air Resources Board, Box 2815, Sacramento, CA 95812. TEL 916-322-2990. charts. illus. stat. (processed)

301.31   US   ISSN 0148-0324
CALIFORNIA ENVIRONMENTAL DIRECTORY; a guide to organizations and resources. 1973. irreg., 3rd edt., 1980. $18.50. California Institute of Public Affairs, Box 10, Claremont, CA 91711. TEL 714-624-5212. (Affiliate: Claremont Colleges) illus. index. circ. 1,000(approx.)
Formerly: California Enviromental Yearbook and Directory (ISSN 0092-1343)

CANADA. AGRICULTURE CANADA. ANNUAL REPORT OF PRAIRIE FARM REHABILITATION ADMINISTRATION/ RAPPORT ANNUAL: RETABLISSEMENT AGRICOLE DES PRAIRIES. see
AGRICULTURE — Crop Production And Soil

363.6   CN
CANADA. ENVIRONMENT CANADA. CONSERVATION AND PROTECTION SERVICE. ANNUAL SUMMARY: NATIONAL AIR POLLUTION SURVEILLANCE. (Subseries of: Canada. Environment Canada. Surveillance Report - Environmental Protection Directorate) (Text in English and French) 1970. a. free. Environment Canada, Ottawa, Ont. K1A 0E7, Canada. TEL 613-997-3405. Ed. V. Jones. illus. circ. 600. (also avail. in microfiche)
Former titles: Canada. Environment Canada. Environment Protection Service. Annual Summary: National Air Pollution Surveillance (ISSN 0381-2995); Canada. Air Pollution Control Directorate. Annual Summary: National Air Pollution Surveillance.

363.6   CN
CANADA. FISHERIES AND ENVIRONMENT CANADA. OCCASIONAL PAPER.* (Text in English and French) 1975. irreg. Department of Fisheries & Oceans, 200 Kent St., Ottawa, Ont. K1A 0E6, Canada. TEL 613-995-4031.

550   CN
CANADIAN ENVIRONMENTAL ADVISORY COUNCIL. ANNUAL REVIEW. a. free. Canadian Environmental Advisory Council, Ottawa, Ont. K1A OH3, Canada. TEL 819-997-2395.

550   CN
CANADIAN ENVIRONMENTAL ADVISORY COUNCIL. REPORTS. irreg. free. Canadian Environmental Advisory Council, Ottawa K1A 0H3, Canada. TEL 819-997-2395.

CANADIAN ENVIRONMENTAL LAW. see LAW

614.7   551.46   CN   ISSN 0706-6473
CANADIAN MANUSCRIPT REPORT OF FISHERIES AND AQUATIC SCIENCES. French edition (ISSN 0706-6589) 1925. irreg. price varies. Department of Fisheries and Oceans, 1202-200 Kent St., Ottawa, Ont. K1A 0E6, Canada. TEL 613-998-4931. (also avail. in microfilm from MML) Incorporating: Canada. Marine Environmental Data Service. Manuscript Report Series.

CAPE OF GOOD HOPE. DEPARTMENT OF NATURE CONSERVATION AND MUSEUM SERVICES. ANNUAL REPORT. see CONSERVATION

333.7   US   ISSN 0194-1445
CATALYST FOR ENVIRONMENT/ENERGY. 1970. irreg. $16 for 4 nos. Catalyst for Environment, Energy, 274 Madison Ave., New York, NY 10016. TEL 212-685-8310. Ed. Laura E. Freed. adv. bk. rev. illus. circ. 30,000. (also avail. in microform from UMI) Indexed: Ocean.Abstr. Pollut.Abstr.
Formerly (until vol.6, 1979): Catalyst for Environmental Quality (ISSN 0008-7688)

CHALMERS UNIVERSITY OF TECHNOLOGY. DEPARTMENT OF SANITARY ENGINEERING; Current reports on research in water supply and sewage disposal. see WATER RESOURCES

CHELMER WORKING PAPERS IN ENVIRONMENTAL PLANNING. see SOCIAL SCIENCES: COMPREHENSIVE WORKS

CHEMICAL INDUSTRY INSTITUTE OF TOXICOLOGY SERIES. see INDUSTRIAL HEALTH AND SAFETY

540   350   US   ISSN 0148-7973
CHEMICAL REGULATION REPORTER; a weekly review of activity affecting chemical users and manufacturers. 1977. w. plus irreg. supplements. $996. The Bureau of National Affairs, Inc., 1231 25th St., N.W., Washington, DC 20037. TEL 202-452-4200. Ed. Hazel B. Becker. index. (looseleaf format)
●Also available online. Vendors: Mead Data Central, WESTLAW.

614.7   US
CHESAPEAKE BAY FOUNDATION. ANNUAL REPORT. a. Chesapeake Bay Foundation, 162 Prince George St., Annapolis, MD 21401. TEL 301-268-8816.
Formerly: Chesapeake Bay Journal.

CIVIC TRUST AWARDS. see ARCHITECTURE

614.71   UK   ISSN 0301-9039
CLEAN AIR CONFERENCE (GT. BRIT.) a. £9.80. National Society for Clean Air, 136 North St., Brighton, Sussex BN1 1RG, England.

COMPANHIA ESTADUAL DE TECNOLOGIA DE SANEAMENTO BASICO E DE DEFESA DO MEIO AMBIENTE. DIRECTORIA RELATORIA ANUAL. see PUBLIC HEALTH AND SAFETY

CONFERENCE ON SPACE SIMULATION. PROCEEDINGS. see AERONAUTICS AND SPACE FLIGHT

363.6   US   ISSN 0095-4624
CONNECTICUT. COUNCIL ON ENVIRONMENTAL QUALITY. ANNUAL REPORT. 1973. a. Council on Environmental Quality, State Office Bldg., Hartford, CT 06106. TEL 203-566-3510. circ. 800. Key Title: Annual Report - State of Connecticut, Council on Environmental Quality.

ENVIRONMENTAL STUDIES

614 US
CRITICAL ISSUES. (Topics vary per issue) 1986. irreg. price varies. Heritage Foundation, 214 Massachusetts Ave., N.E., Washington, DC 20002. TEL 202-546-4400.

614.7 333.91 II
CURRENT PRACTICES IN ENVIRONMENTAL SCIENCE AND ENGINEERING. 1984. irreg? $50. Geo-Environ Academia, A-42 Shastri Nagar, Jodhpur 342 003, India. (Co-sponsor: International Book Traders (Delhi)) Eds. Alam Singh, U.S. Sharma.
  Formerly: Current Practices in Environmental Engineering (ISSN 0253-5114)

CURRENT TOPICS IN ENVIRONMENTAL AND TOXICOLOGICAL CHEMISTRY. see *CHEMISTRY*

747 UK ISSN 0306-6185
D I A YEARBOOK - DESIGN ACTION. 1916. a. £5. Design and Industries Association, 17 Lawn Crescent, Kew Gardens, Surrey TW9 3NR, England. Ed. Raymond Plummer. adv. bk. rev. circ. 2,000.
  Formerly: Design and Industries Association. Year Book and Membership List (ISSN 0070-3834)

614.7 DK ISSN 0109-4033
D M V NYT. 1973. irreg., (4-6/yr.) Kr.30. Dansk Miljoevaern, Slagelsegade 6, 2100 Copenhagen OE, Denmark.

DANSKE HEDESELSKAB. FORSOEGSVIRKSOMHEDEN. BERETNING. see *FORESTS AND FORESTRY*

333.7 US ISSN 0084-9642
DELAWARE. DEPARTMENT OF NATURAL RESOURCES AND ENVIRONMENTAL CONTROL. ANNUAL REPORT. 1970. a. free. Department of Natural Resources and Environmental Control, Box 1401, Dover, DE 19903. TEL 302-736-4403. circ. 100.

DEMOKRATIE- UND ARBEITERGESCHICHTE. see *HISTORY — History Of Europe*

614.7 DK ISSN 0900-3738
DENMARK. BETAENKNING FRA MILJOESTYRELSEN. 1985. irreg. price varies. Miljoestyrelsen - National Agency of Environmental Protection, Strandgade 29, DK-1401 Copenhagen K, Denmark.

614.7 340 DK ISSN 0900-2758
DENMARK. LOVINFORMATION FRA MILJOESTYRELSEN. 1985. irreg. price varies. Miljoestyrelsen - National Agency of Environmental Protection, Strandgade 29, DK-1401 Copenhagen K, Denmark.

614.7 DK ISSN 0108-7487
DENMARK. MILJOEKREDITRAADET. BERETNING. 1977. a. free. Miljoekreditraadet, Miljoestyrelsen, Strandgade 29, 1401 Copenhagen K, Denmark. circ. 1,000.

614.7 DK ISSN 0107-7430
DENMARK. MILJOESTYRELSEN. HAVFORURENINGSLABORATORIUM. REPORT OF THE MARINE POLLUTION LABORATORY. no.5, 1983. irreg. free. Miljoestyrelsen, Havforureningslaboratorium, Charlottenlund, Denmark. Ed. Kurt Jensen. illus.

614.7 DK
DENMARK. MILJOESTYRELSEN KEMIKALIEKONTROL. AARSBERETNING. (Text in Danish) 1971. a. Miljoestyrelsen Kemikaliekontrol - State Chemical Supervision Service, Moerkhoej Bygade 26, DK-2860 Soeborg, Denmark. TEL 45-1-697088. (back issues avail.)

614.7 DK ISSN 0105-5836
DENMARK. NYT FRA MILJOESTYRELSEN. 1974. irreg. Miloestyrelsen - National Agency of Environmental Protection, Strandgade 29, DK-1401 Copenhagen K, Denmark.

614.7 DK ISSN 0107-2722
DENMARK. ORIENTERING FRA MILJOESTYRELSEN. 1985. irreg. price varies. Mijoestyrelsen - National Agency of Environmental Protection, Strandgade 29, DK-1401 Copenhagen K, Denmark.

614.7 DK ISSN 0900-6788
DENMARK. REDEGOERELSE FRA MILJOESTYRELSEN. 1985. irreg. price varies. Miloestyrelsen - National Agency of Environmental Protection, Strandgade 29, DK-1401 Copenhagen K, Denmark.

614.7 DK
DENMARK. VEJLEDNING FRA MIJOESTYRELSEN. 1974. irreg. price varies. Miloestyrelsen - National Agency of Environmental Protection, Strandgade 29, DK-1401 Copenhagen K, Denmark.

614.7 333.7 US
DIRECTORY OF ENVIRONMENTAL ORGANIZATIONS. 1975. a. $25. Educational Communications, Inc., Ecology Center of Southern California, Box 35473, Los Angeles, CA 90035. TEL 213-559-9160. Ed. Nancy Pearlman. adv. circ. 100.

614.7 CN
DIRECTORY OF HAZARDOUS WASTE SERVICES. 1985. a. Can.$65.95. Corpus Information Services, Division of Southam Communications Ltd., 1450 Don Mills Road, Don Mills, Ont. M3B 2X7, Canada. TEL 416-445-6641. Eds. William M. Glenn, Deborah Orchard. adv. circ. 1,200.

614.7 US
DIRECTORY OF NATIONAL ENVIRONMENTAL ORGANIZATIONS. 1984. irreg., latest 1986. $27.50. U S Environmental Directories, Inc., Box 65156, St. Paul, MN 55165. Eds. John C. Brainard, Roger N. McGrath.

DIRECTORY OF OFFICIAL ARCHITECTURE AND PLANNING. see *ARCHITECTURE*

614 US
DIRECTORY OF STATE ENVIRONMENT AGENCIES. 1983. irreg. $22.50. Environmental Law Institute, 1616 P St., N.W., Ste. 200, Washington, DC 20036. TEL 202-328-5150. Eds. T. Henderson, A. Spector.

614.7 US
DISCUSSIONS IN ENVIRONMENTAL HEALTH PLANNING. 1977? irreg., latest 1982. Cornell University, City and Regional Planning Publications, 106 W. Sibley Hall, Ithaca, NY 14853. (Co-sponsor: Cornell University Department of City and Regional Planning, Environmental Health Training Program) (reprint service avail. from UMI)

620.8 US
DISTRICT OF COLUMBIA. AIR MONITORING SECTION. ANNUAL REPORT ON THE QUALITY OF THE AIR IN WASHINGTON, D.C. 1974. a. Department of Consumer and Regulatory Affairs, Air Monitoring Section, 5010 Overlook Ave., S.W., Washington, DC 20032. TEL 202-767-7370. circ. 200.
  Formerly: District of Columbia. Air Monitoring Division. Annual Report on the Quality of the Air in Washington, D.C.

614 CL
DOCUMENTOS TALLER MULTIDISCIPLINARIO DEL MEDIO AMBIENTE. 1978. a. free. Universidad Catolica de Valparaiso, Vicerrectoria Academica Direccion General de Investigacion, Casilla 4059, Valparaiso, Chile. Ed.Bd. abstr. circ. 1, 000.

DUKE PRESS GLOBAL ISSUES SERIES. see *POLITICAL SCIENCE*

614.7 US ISSN 0276-9956
ENFO. 1971. irreg., 6 or more/yr. $15 to individuals; institutions $25. Florida Conservation Foundation, Environmental Information Center, 1203 Orange Ave., Winter Park, FL 32789. TEL 305-644-5377. Eds. William R. Barada, Gerald Grow. bk. rev. circ. 1,200.

614.7 US ISSN 0270-0751
ENVIROLINE USER'S MANUAL. a. $45. E I C Intelligence, Inc., 48 W. 38th St., New York, NY 10018.

614.7 TR
ENVIRON; patterns of progress in the Caribbean. 1977. a. $6.50. Key Caribbean, 1 El Socorro Extension Rd., Kirpalani's Complex, San Juan, Trinidad, W.I. (Subscr. to: P.O. Box 21, Port of Spain, Trinidad, W.I.) Ed. Roy Boyke. circ. 5,000. (back issues avail)

614.7 917.9 US
ENVIRONMENTAL ASSESSMENT OF THE ALASKAN CONTINENTAL SHELF. ANNUAL REPORTS SUMMARY. a. U.S. National Oceanic and Atmospheric Administration, Environmental Research Laboratories, 6010 Executive Blvd., Rockville, MD 20852. TEL 301-655-4000. (Co-sponsor: U.S. Bureau of Land Management)

614.7 574.5 US
ENVIRONMENTAL BIOLOGY. 1972. irreg. $3 per issue. Cornell University, Department of Entomology, Ithaca, NY 14853. TEL 607-256-2212. Ed. David Pimentel. (back issues avail.) Indexed: Biol.Abstr.

ENVIRONMENTAL CHEMISTRY. see *CHEMISTRY*

301.31 US ISSN 0091-9837
ENVIRONMENTAL DEFENSE FUND. ANNUAL REPORT. a. membership. Environmental Defense Fund, 257 Park Ave. S., New York, NY 10010. TEL 212-505-2100.

614.7 US
ENVIRONMENTAL DESIGN SERIES. 1982. irreg., vol.6, 1984. price varies. Van Nostrand Reinhold Company, 7625 Empire Dr., Florence, KY 41042. TEL 606-525-6600. Ed. R.P. Dober. illus. index.

614.7 UK
ENVIRONMENTAL DIRECTORY. 1968. irreg. £2.50. Civic Trust, 17 Carlton House Terrace, London SW1Y 5AW, England. Ed. Saskia Hallam.

614.7 333.7 US
ENVIRONMENTAL HOTLINE. 1969. irreg. $20. Ohio Environmental Council, Inc., 150 North High St., Ste. 300, Columbus, OH 43215-3094. TEL 614-224-4900. Ed. Steve Sedam. circ. 400. (tabloid format; back issues avail.)

614.7 AT
ENVIRONMENTAL LAW REFORM GROUP. PUBLICATION. no.2, 1972. irreg. Environmental Law Reform Group, c/o Dr. R. J. K. Chapman, Dept. of Political Science, University of Tasmania, Box 252c, Hobart, Tas. 7001, Australia. circ. 500.

614.7 333.7 JA ISSN 0912-1722
ENVIRONMENTAL POLLUTION, CITY DEVELOPMENT AND REGIONAL DEVELOPMENT INDEX. 1971. a. 1.000 Yen. Japan Economic Research Institute, 2-39, Akasaka 5-Chome, Minato-Ku, Tokyo 107, Japan. Ed. Hiromichi Nosaka. circ. 1,100.

363.6 US ISSN 0509-769X
ENVIRONMENTAL RADIATION SURVEILLANCE IN WASHINGTON STATE. ANNUAL REPORT. 1961. a. Department of Social and Health Services, Health Division, Radiation Control Section, MS.LF-13, Olympia, WA 98504. TEL 206-753-3468. Ed. Robert Mooney. illus. circ. 500.

614.7 JA
ENVIRONMENTAL RESEARCH IN JAPAN. (Text in English) 1975. a. free. Environment Agency, 1-2-2 Kasumigaseki, Chiyoda-Ku, Tokyo 100, Japan. index. (back issues avail.)

614.7 628.5 US ISSN 0194-0287
ENVIRONMENTAL SCIENCE AND TECHNOLOGY: A WILEY-INTERSCIENCE SERIES OF TEXTS AND MONOGRAPHS. 1982. irreg., unnumbered, latest 1987. price varies. John Wiley & Sons, Inc., 605 Third Ave., New York, NY 10016. TEL 212-850-6000. Ed. R.L. Metcalf.

614.7 340 US ISSN 0736-573X
ENVIRONMENTAL STATUTES. 1979. a. $38.95. Government Institutes, Inc., 966 Hungerford Dr., No. 24, Rockville, MD 20850. bk. rev. Indexed: Chem.Abstr.

ENVIRONMENTAL STUDIES

614.7   CN
ENVIRONNEMENT. 1973. irreg. Can.$10 to individuals; institutions Can.$15. Societe pour Vaincre la Pollution, B.P. 65, Place d'Armes, Montreal, Que. H27 3E9, Canada. TEL 514-844-5477. Ed. Claudine Leonard. adv. circ. 5,000.
     Formerly: Bulletin - S V P (ISSN 0382-5302); Supersedes: Societe pour Vaincre la Pollution. Bulletin de Liaison (ISSN 0382-5310)

614.71   FR   ISSN 0071-1942
ETUDES DE POLLUTION ATMOSPHERIQUE A PARIS ET DANS LES DEPARTMENTS PERIPHERIQUES. 1964. a. free. Prefecture de Police, Laboratoire Central, 39 bis rue de Dantzig, 75015 Paris, France. bk. rev. Indexed: Bull.Signal.

614.7   CN   ISSN 0069-0007
FEDERAL-PROVINCIAL WILDLIFE CONFERENCE. TRANSACTIONS. (Editions in English, French) 1922. a. free. Canadian Wildlife Service, Environment Canada, Ottawa, Ont. K1A 0E7, Canada. circ. 800. Indexed: Biol.Abstr.

614.7   UK   ISSN 0428-304X
FIELD STUDIES. 1959. a. £10.50 to non-members. Field Studies Council, 62 Wilson St., London EC2A 2BU, England. Ed. J.H. Crothers. bk. rev. bibl. cum.index every 4 yrs. circ. 2,000. Indexed: Biol.Abstr. Br.Geol.Lit. Br.Archaeol.Abstr. Geo.Abstr. GeoRef. Soils & Fert. Zoo.Rec.

614.7   UK
FIELD STUDIES COUNCIL. OCCASIONAL PUBLICATIONS. irreg. price varies. Field Studies Council, 62 Wilson St., London EC2A 2BU, England.

FOREST PEST MANAGEMENT INSTITUTE PROGRAM REVIEW. see *BIOLOGY*

FORTH NATURALIST AND HISTORIAN. see *SCIENCES: COMPREHENSIVE WORKS*

363.6   FR
FRANCE. MINISTERE DE LA CULTURE ET DE L'ENVIRONNEMENT. BILAN D'ACTIVITE DES AGENCES FINANCIERES DE BASSIN. irreg. Ministere de la Culture et de l'Environnement, Service de l'Information des Relations et de l'Action Educative, 3 rue de Valois, 75042 Paris, France. illus.

FREEDOM OF INFORMATION FACT SHEETS. see *LAW*

FUKUOKA-KEN EISEI KOGAI SENTA NENPO/ FUKUOKA ENVIRONMENTAL RESEARCH CENTER. ANNUAL REPORT. see *PUBLIC HEALTH AND SAFETY*

614.7   AG
FUNDACION BARILOCHE. GRUPO DE ANALISIS DE SISTEMAS ECOLOGICOS. PUBLICACIONES. irreg. price varies. Fundacion Bariloche, Grupo de Analisis de Sistemas Ecologicos, Casilla de Correo 138, 8400 San Carlos de Bariloche - Rio Negro, Argentina. Indexed: GeoRef.
     Supersedes in part: Fundacion Bariloche. Departamento de Recursos Naturales y Energia. Publicaciones.

614.7   NE
FUNDAMENTAL ASPECTS OF POLLUTION CONTROL AND ENVIRONMENTAL SCIENCE. 1977. irreg., vol.7, 1985. price varies. Elsevier Science Publishers B.V., Box 211, 1000 AE Amsterdam, Netherlands. Indexed: GeoRef.

GEOECOLOGICAL RESEARCH. see *EARTH SCIENCES*

628.44   US
GEORGIA. GEOLOGIC SURVEY. CIRCULAR 5. MONITORING WELL CONSTRUCTION FOR HAZARDOUS-WASTE SITES IN GEORGIA. 1981. irreg. $1. Department of Natural Resources, Georgia Geologic Survey, 19 Martin Luther King Jr. Dr., S.W., Rm. 400, Atlanta, GA 30334. TEL 404-656-3214.

GEOTECHNICAL SCIENCE LABORATORIES. PUBLICATIONS, REPORTS, AND THESES. see *EARTH SCIENCES — Abstracting, Bibliographies, Statistics*

614.7   UK
GOLDEN LIST OF BEACHES; indicates which beaches are likely to be polluted and which are believed to be free from sewage pollution. 1960. quinquennial. £5. Coastal Anti-Pollution League, Alverstoke, 94 Greenway Lane, Bath, Avon, England. Ed. J. Wakefield. circ. 2,000.

301.31   UK
GREAT BRITAIN. DEPARTMENT OF THE ENVIRONMENT. REPORT ON RESEARCH AND DEVELOPMENT. 1973. a. price varies. ‡ H.M.S.O., Box 569, London SE1 9NH, England.

GREAT BRITAIN. MINISTRY OF AGRICULTURE, FISHERIES AND FOOD. DIRECTORATE OF FISHERIES RESEARCH. FISHERIES RESEARCH TECHNICAL REPORT. see *FISH AND FISHERIES*

GREAT BRITAIN. MINISTRY OF AGRICULTURE, FISHERIES AND FOOD. DIRECTORATE OF FISHERIES RESEARCH. REPORT OF THE DIRECTOR OF FISHERIES RESEARCH. see *FISH AND FISHERIES*

614.7   UK   ISSN 0072-7008
GREAT BRITAIN. NATURAL ENVIRONMENT RESEARCH COUNCIL. REPORT. 1965/66. a. £5. Natural Environment Research Council, Polaris House, North Star Ave., Swindon, Wiltshire SN2 1EU, England. circ. 4,000.

628.5   UK   ISSN 0141-3279
GREAT BRITAIN. WARREN SPRING LABORATORY. ANNUAL REVIEW. a. free. Warren Spring Laboratory, Gunnels Wood Rd., Stevenage, Herts. SG1 2BX, England.

628.5   UK
GREAT BRITAIN. WARREN SPRING LABORATORY. U K SMOKE AND SULPHUR DIOXIDE MONITORING NETWORKS. a. price varies. Warren Spring Laboratory, Gunnels Wood Rd., Stevenage, Herts. SG1 2BX, England.
     Formerly: Great Britain. Warren Spring Laboratory. Investigation of Air Pollution: National Survey, Smoke and Sulphur Dioxide (ISSN 0585-2730)

GREEN PAGES: DIRECTORY OF NON-GOVERNMENT ENVIRONMENTAL GROUPS IN AUSTRALIA. see *CONSERVATION*

HANDBOOK OF ENVIRONMENTAL CHEMISTRY. see *CHEMISTRY*

531.64   614.7   US
HARBINGER FILE; a descriptive directory of organizations concerned with environmental issues in California. 1979. biennial. $16.50. Harbinger Communications, Box 624, Santa Cruz, CA 95061. TEL 408-429-8727. Ed. Bill Leland. (back issues avail.)

614.7   CN
HAZARDOUS WASTE MANAGEMENT HANDBOOK. 1982. a. Can.$177. Corpus Information Services, Division of Southam Communications Ltd., 1450 Don Mills Rd., Don Mills, Ont. M3B 2X7, Canada. TEL 416-445-6641. Eds. William M. Glenn, Deborah Orchard. circ. 1,000.

HESSE. MINISTER FUER LANDESENTWICKLUNG, UMWELT, LANDWIRTSCHAFT UND FORSTEN. MITTEILUNGEN. LAND UND UMWELT. see *FOOD AND FOOD INDUSTRIES — Grocery Trade*

614.7   JA
HOKKAIDO RESEARCH INSTITUTE FOR ENVIRONMENTAL POLLUTION. REPORT/ HOKKAIDO KOGAI BOSHI KENKYUJO HO. (Text in Japanese; summaries in English or Japanese.) 1975. irreg. Hokkaido Research Institute for Environmental Pollution - Hokkaido Kogai Boshi Kenkyujo., Nishi 12-chome, Kita 19-Jo, Kita-ku, Sapporo 060, Japan. Ed. K. Nakamura. illus.

614.7   UK
I C C E T ANNUAL REPORT. 1978. a. free. Imperial College of Science and Technology, University of London, Centre for Environmental Technology, 48 Prince's Gardens, London SW7 2PE, England. Ed. D.S. Paterson. circ. 300.

614.7   UK   ISSN 0260-4833
I E S PROCEEDINGS. 1980. irreg. £1.50 per issue to non-members. Institution of Environmental Sciences, 14 Princes Gate, London SW7 1PU, England. Ed. John F. Potter. circ. 700.

I L Z R O ANNUAL REVIEW. (International Lead Zinc Research Organization, Inc.) see *METALLURGY*

614.7   US
I L Z R O ENVIRONMENTAL HEALTH RESEARCH DIGEST. (Editions in French and Japanese) 1981. a. free. International Lead Zinc Research Organization, Inc., 292 Madison Ave., New York, NY 10017. TEL 212-532-2373. Ed. A. L. Ponikvar. bibl. charts. illus. patents. stat. circ. 3,500.

614.7   NE
I M G-T N O RESEARCH INSTITUTE FOR ENVIRONMENTAL HYGIENE. ANNUAL REPORT. (Annual report in Dutch; biennial report in English) 1942. a. free. I M G-T N O Research Institute for Environmental Hygiene, Box 214, Schoemakerstraat 97, 2600 AE Delft, Netherlands. bibl. charts. illus. circ. 1,300.
     Formerly: IG-TNO Research Institute for Environmental Hygiene. Annual Report.

614.7   US
ILLINOIS. DIVISION OF AIR POLLUTION CONTROL. ANNUAL AIR QUALITY REPORT. 1968. a. free. Environmental Protection Agency, Division of Air Pollution Control, Ambient Air Monitoring Section, 2200 Churchill Rd., Springfield, IL 62706. circ. 1,500.
     Former titles (until 1975): Illinois Air Quality Report (ISSN 0360-9162); Incorporating: Illinois. Division of Air Pollution Control. Semi-Annual Report; Until 1974: Illinois Air Sampling Network Report (ISSN 0092-3281)

333.7   US   ISSN 0094-5749
INDIANA. ENVIRONMENTAL MANAGEMENT BOARD. ANNUAL REPORT. 1973. a. free. Environmental Management Board, 1330 W. Michigan St., Indianapolis, IN 46206. TEL 317-633-8404.

614.76   628.168   US   ISSN 0073-7682
INDUSTRIAL WASTE CONFERENCE, PURDUE UNIVERSITY, LAFAYETTE, INDIANA. PROCEEDINGS. 1944. a. $69.95. Purdue University, School of Civil Engineering, West Lafayette, IN 47907 TEL 617-933-8260. (Distr. by: Butterworth Publishers, 10 Tower Office Park, Woburn, MA 01801) Ed. John M. Bell. Indexed: Biol.Abstr. Chem.Abstr. Abstr.Bull.Inst.Pap.Chem.

614.7   AT
INFORMATION ON ENVIRONMENTAL POLLUTION IN FOREIGN COUNTRIES. a. Tokyo Metropolitan Research Institute for Environmental Protection, 7-5, Shinsuna 1-Chome, Koto-Ku, Tokyo 136, Japan.

614.7   338.91   KE
INFOTERRA INTERNATIONAL; directory of sources for environmental information. (Text and summaries in English, French, Russian and Spanish) 1977. biennial. $200. United Nations Environment Programme, Infoterra Programme Activity, P.O. Box 30552, Nairobi, Kenya. circ. 200.

INSTITUT ROYAL DES SCIENCES NATURELLES DE BELGIQUE. BULLETIN. SERIE BIOLOGIE. see *BIOLOGY*

574.5   US   ISSN 0073-9227
INSTITUTE OF ENVIRONMENTAL SCIENCES. ANNUAL MEETING. PROCEEDINGS. 1960. a. $40. Institute of Environmental Sciences, 940 E. Northwest Hwy., Mt. Prospect, IL 60056. TEL 312-255-1561. (also avail. in microfilm from UMI; reprint service avail. from UMI) Indexed: Biol.Abstr. Chem.Abstr.
Ecology

574.5   US   ISSN 0073-9251
INSTITUTE OF ENVIRONMENTAL SCIENCES. TUTORIAL SERIES. irreg. price varies. Institute of Environmental Sciences, 940 E. Northwest Hwy., St. Prospect, IL 60056. TEL 312-255-1561.
Ecology

INSTITUUT VOOR CULTUURTECHNIEK EN WATERHUISHOUDING. JAARVERSLAG. see *AGRICULTURE — Crop Production And Soil*

INSTITUUT VOOR CULTUURTECHNIEK EN WATERHUISHOUDING. MEDEDELING. NIEUWE SERIE. see *AGRICULTURE — Crop Production And Soil*

INSTITUUT VOOR CULTUURTECHNIEK EN WATERHUISHOUDING. TECHNICAL BULLETINS. NEW SERIES. see *AGRICULTURE — Crop Production And Soil*

614.71   US   ISSN 0085-2090
INTERNATIONAL CLEAN AIR CONGRESS. PROCEEDINGS. 1966, 1st, London. irreg., 1970, 2nd, Washington, D.C. International Union of Air Pollution Prevention Associations, c/o Air Pollution Control Association, 4400 Fifth Ave., Pittsburgh, PA 15213. Ed. Harold M. Englund.
   Proceedings published in host country

614.7   US
INTERNATIONAL CONFERENCE ON THE ENVIRONMENTAL IMPACT OF AEROSPACE OPERATIONS IN THE HIGH ATMOSPHERE. (PROCEEDINGS) 1973. irreg., 9th, 1983, Omaha. $20. American Meteorological Society, 45 Beacon St., Boston, MA 02108. TEL 617-227-2425. (Co-sponsor: American Institute of Aeronautics and Astronautics)

INTERSTATE COMMISSION ON THE POTOMAC RIVER BASIN. PROCEEDINGS. see *WATER RESOURCES*

628.168   US
INTERSTATE COMMISSION ON THE POTOMAC RIVER BASIN. TECHNICAL REPORTS. 1977. irreg. Interstate Commission on the Potomac River Basin, 6110 Executive Blvd., Ste. 300, Rockville, MD 20852. TEL 301-984-1908.
   Supersedes: Interstate Commission on the Potomac River Basin. Technical Bulletin (ISSN 0074-9966)

628   IS   ISSN 0334-3162
ISRAEL. ENVIRONMENTAL PROTECTION SERVICE. EKHUT HA-SVIVAH BE-YISRAEL. LUAKH SHNATI. (Text in Hebrew) 1973. a. free. Environmental Protection Service, Ministry of the Interior, Box 6158, Jerusalem 91061, Israel. Ed. Tamar Ben-Yeshaiya. circ. 2,500.
   Formerly: Israel. Environment Protection Agency. Ekhut ha-Svivah be-Yisrael. Luakh Shnati.

614.7   UR   ISSN 0202-7321
ITOGI NAUKI I TEKHNIKI: OKHRANA PRIRODY I VOSPROIZVODSTVO PRIRODNYKH RESURSOV. irreg., vol.18, 1987. price varies. Vsesoyuznyi Institut Nauchno-Tekhnicheskoi Informatsii (VINITI), Baltiiskaya ul. 14, Moscow A-219, Russian S.F.S.R., U.S.S.R. (Subscr. to: Mezhdunarodnaya Kniga, Dimitrova ul. 39, 113095 Moscow, Russian S.F.S.R., U.S.S.R.)

JOURNAL OF FRESHWATER ECOLOGY. see *EARTH SCIENCES — Hydrology*

JOURNAL OF HIMALAYAN STUDIES AND REGIONAL DEVELOPMENT. see *ANTHROPOLOGY*

KANKYO MONDAI SHINPOJUMU KOEN RONBUNSHU/PROCEEDINGS OF THE SYMPOSIUM ON ENVIRONMENTAL PROBLEMS. see *ENGINEERING — Civil Engineering*

KENSETSU KOGAKU KENKYUSHYO HOKOKU/CONSTRUCTION ENGINEERING RESEARCH INSTITUTE FOUNDATION REPORT. see *ENGINEERING — Engineering Mechanics And Materials*

614.7   II
KERALA (INDIA). BOARD FOR PREVENTION AND CONTROL OF WATER POLLUTION. ANNUAL REPORT. (Text in English) a. Board for Prevention and Control of Water Pollution, Trivandrum 685001, India. stat.

KEVO SUBARCTIC RESEARCH INSTITUTE. REPORTS. see *BIOLOGY*

614.7   JA
KOGAI CHOSA HOKOKUSHO/REPORT OF ENVIRONMENTAL POLLUTION IN MEGURO WARD. 1971. a. free. Meguro Ward Office, Environmental Pollution Department, 4-5, 2-Chome, Chuo-Chyou, Meguro-ku, Tokyo 152, Japan.

DIE KUESTE; Archiv fuer Forschung und Technik an der Nord- und Ostsee. see *EARTH SCIENCES — Oceanography*

340 574.5   US   ISSN 0192-8309
LAND USE & ENVIRONMENT LAW REVIEW. 1970. a. $68.50. Clark Boardman Company, Ltd., 435 Hudson St., New York, NY 10014. Ed. Frederic Strom. index. Indexed: Leg.Per. C.L.I. GeoRef. L.R.I.
   Formerly: Environment Law Review (ISSN 0071-0830)

614.7 551.48   UK
LIST OF HYDROBIOLOGICAL PAPERS OF BRITISH FRESH WATERS. 1976. a. £6. Freshwater Biological Association, Ferry House, Ambleside, Cumbria LA22, England.

614.7   GW   ISSN 0340-4900
LITERATURBERICHTE UEBER WASSER, ABWASSER, LUFT UND FESTE ABFALLSTOFFE. irreg. DM.378 per vol. (6 issues) Gustav Fischer Verlag, Wollgrasweg 49, Postfach 720143, 7000 Stuttgart 70, W. Germany (B.R.D.)

614.7 351.46 333.7   US
LIVING WITH THE SHORE. 1983. irreg. price varies. Duke University Press, 6697 College Sta., Durham, NC 27708. TEL 919-684-2173. Eds. Orrin H. Pilkey, Jr., William J. Neal.

333.9   AU
LUDWIG BOLTZMANN-INSTITUT FUER UMWELTWISSENSCHAFTEN UND NATURSCHUTZ. MITTEILUNGEN. 1975. irreg. Ludwig Boltzmann-Institut fuer Umweltwissenschaften und Naturschutz, Oesterreichischen Akademie der Wissenschaften, Heinrichstr. 5, A-8010 Graz, Austria.

614.7   GW   ISSN 0460-2374
LUFTVERUNREINIGUNG. 1973. a. DM.7. Deutscher Kommunal-Verlag GmbH, Roseggerstr. 5a, 4000 Duesseldorf 30, W. Germany (B.R.D.) Ed. H.J. Schumacher. adv. bk. rev. charts. illus.

614.7   DK   ISSN 0106-343X
M S T LUFT. A. no.62, 1982. irreg. free. Miljoestyrelsen, Luftforureningslaboratorium - National Agency of Environmental Protection, Air Pollution Laboratory, Forsoeganlaeg Risoe, 4000 Roskilde, Denmark. Ed. Jes Fenger. illus. circ. 100.

628.44 624   US
MADISON WASTE CONFERENCE. ANNUAL PROCEEDINGS; municipal and industrial waste. 1978. a. $30. University of Wisconsin-Extension, Department of Engineering Professional Development, 432 N. Lake St., Madison, WI 53706. TEL 608-262-0493. Ed. Philip R. O'Leary. cum.index: 1982-1984. circ. 500. Indexed: Chem.Abstr. Environ.Abstr. Water Resour.Abstr.
   Formerly: Annual Madison Conference of Applied Research and Practice on Municipal and Industrial Waste.

MAINE AGRICULTURAL EXPERIMENT STATION. ANNUAL REPORT. see *AGRICULTURE*

614.7 301.3   US   ISSN 0025-1550
MAN - ENVIRONMENT SYSTEMS. 1969. bi-m. $25 to individuals; libraries $37.50; students $15. Association for the Study of Man-Environment Relations, Box 57, Orangeburg, NY 10962. TEL 914-634-8221. Ed. Aristide H. Esser. adv. bk. rev. bibl. index. circ. 600. (looseleaf format; also avail. in microform from UMI; back issues avail.) Indexed: Psychol.Abstr. Sociol.Abstr. Environ.Per.Bibl. Geo.Abstr. Lang.& Lang.Behav.Abstr. Psycscan. Sage Urb.Stud.Abstr.

354   CN   ISSN 0380-9803
MANITOBA. ENVIRONMENTAL COUNCIL. ANNUAL REPORT. 1973. a. free. Environmental Council, Box 139, 139 Tuxedo Ave., Winnipeg, Man. R3N 0H6, Canada. TEL 204-944-7100. illus. circ. 900. (also avail. in microfiche from MML)

354   CN   ISSN 0380-979X
MANITOBA. ENVIRONMENTAL COUNCIL. STUDIES. 1973. irreg. free. Environmental Council, Box 139, 139 Tuxedo Ave., Winnipeg, Man. R3N 0H6, Canada. TEL 204-944-7100. illus. circ. 1,000. (also avail. in microform from MML)

354   CN   ISSN 0711-8422
MANITOBA. ENVIRONMENTAL COUNCIL. TOPICS. 1982. irreg. free. Environmental Council, Box 139, 139 Tuxedo Ave., Winnipeg, Man. RN3 0H6, Canada. TEL 204-944-7100.

363.6   US
MARYLAND AIR MANAGEMENT ADMINISTRATION. DATA REPORT. Cover title: Maryland Air Quality Data Report. 1971. a. free. Air Management Administration, Division of Air Quality Planning, 201 W. Preston St., Baltimore, MD 21201. illus. circ. 400.
   Former titles: Maryland Air Quality Programs. Data Report; Maryland Air Quality Programs; Maryland. Bureau of Air Quality and Noise Control. Data Report; Maryland. Bureau of Air Quality Control. State-Local Cooperative Air Sampling Program Yearly Data Report. (ISSN 0094-4629)

MEDDELELSER OM GROENLAND, BIOSCIENCE. see *BIOLOGY*

301.3   CL
MEDIO AMBIENTE. (Text in Spanish; summaries in English) 1975. irreg. $10. Universidad Austral de Chile, Instituto de Ecologia y Evolucion, Facultad de Ciencias, Casilla 567, Valdivia, Chile. Ed. Eduardo del Solar Osses. circ. 1,000.
   ●Also available online.

614.7   SP
MEDIO AMBIENTE EN ESPANA. vol.2, 1978. irreg. 1400 ptas. Ministerio de Obras Publicas y Urbanismo, Secretaria General Tecnica, Servicio de Publicaciones, Avda. del Generalisimo 3, Madrid 3, Spain (Subscr. to: Caja Postal de Ahorros de Madrid, Oficina 2088, Clave 9002)

614.7   JA
MEGURO-KU NO KOGAI/ENVIRONMENTAL POLLUTION IN MEGURO WARD. (Text and summaries in Japanese) 1971. a. free. Meguro Ward Office, Environmental Pollution Department, 4-5, 2-chome, Chuo-Chiyou, Meguro-ku, Tokyo 152, Japan.

614.7   NE
MENS EN MILIEU. no.2, 1979. irreg. price varies. Van Gorcum, Box 43, 9400 AA Assen, Netherlands. Ed. Bd.

628   US   ISSN 0544-0327
MID-ATLANTIC INDUSTRIAL WASTE CONFERENCE PROCEEDINGS. 1968. irreg., 8th, 1976. $10. University of Delaware, Department of Civil Engineering, John M. Clayton Hall, Newark, DE 19711. TEL 302-738-2442. Ed. Richard I. Dick.

614   JA
MIE PREFECTURE. ENVIRONMENTAL SCIENCE INSTITUTE. ANNUAL REPORT/MIE-KEN KOGAI SENTA NEMPO. (Text in Japanese) 1973. a. Environmental Science Institute, 8-ban 12-jo Shinjo 4-chome, Yokkaichi, Japan.

614.7   DK   ISSN 0105-3094
MILJOE-PROJEKTER. 1975. irreg., no.41, 1981. price varies. Miljoestyrelsen, Strandgade 29, 1401 Copenhagen K, Denmark (Orders to: Danske Boghendleres Kommissionsanstalt, Siljangade 6, 2300 Copenhagen S, Denmark)

614.7   DK   ISSN 0108-8203
MILJOEUNDERSOEGELSER VED IVIGTUT. (Text in Danish; summaries in English or Eskimo) 1982. irreg. price varies. Groenlands Geologiske Undersoegelse, Oester Voldgade 10, DK-1350 Copenhagen K, Denmark. (Co-sponsor: Groenlands Fiskeriundersoegelser)

614.7   DK   ISSN 0107-8550
MILJOEVAERN. Short title: M V. 1978. irreg., approx. 2-3/yr. free. Kongelige Veterinaer- og Landbohoejshole, Miljoevaernscentret, Bulowsvej 13, 1870 Frederiksberg C, Denmark. Ed. Boerge Bundgaard. bk. rev. illus.

ENVIRONMENTAL STUDIES

301.31 US
MINNESOTA. GOVERNOR. GOVERNOR'S REPORT ON ENVIRONMENTAL QUALITY.* 1974. a. Department of Energy Planning and Development, Environmental Quality Board, Capitol Square Building, 550 Cedar St., St. Paul, MN 55101. TEL 612-296-2007. bibl.
Formerly (until 1980): Minnesota. Governor. Annual Report on the Quality of the Environment (ISSN 0094-1697)

614.7 US
N A T O ADVANCED STUDY INSTITUTE SERIES G: ECOLOGICAL SCIENCES. 1983. irreg., vol.12, 1986. Springer-Verlag, 175 Fifth Ave., New York, NY 10010 (Also Berlin, Heidelberg, Tokyo and Vienna)

614.7 US
N E I W P C C ANNUAL REPORT. a. New England Interstate Water Pollution Control Commission, 85 Merrimack St., 3rd Fl., Boston, MA 02114-2519. TEL 617-367-8522. illus.

614.71 628.53 UK ISSN 0140-6795
N.S.C.A. REFERENCE BOOK; comprehensive guide to all aspects of air pollution control. 1978. irreg. National Society for Clean Air, 136 North Brighton, Sussex BN1 1RG, England. Ed. J. Dunmore. adv. index.
Former titles: N.S.C.A. Yearbook; Clean Air Year Book (ISSN 0069-4606)

NAGOYA UNIVERSITY. RESEARCH INSTITUTE OF ENVIRONMENTAL MEDICINE. ANNUAL REPORT/NAGOYA DAIGAKU KANKYO IGAKU KENKYUSHO NENPO. see *MEDICAL SCIENCES*

614.7 US
NATIONAL AIR QUALITY AND EMISSIONS TRENDS REPORT. Variant title: Ambient Assessment Air Portion. 1973. a. price varies. U.S. Environmental Protection Agency, Office of Air Quality Planning and Standards, Air Pollution Technical Information Center, Research Triangle Park, NC 27711 TEL 919-541-5558. (Orders to: NTIS, Springfield, VA 22161) Ed. William F. Hunt. charts. stat. circ. 5,000. (also avail. in microfiche from NTI) Indexed: Air Pollut.Abstr.
Until 1977: National Air Monitoring Program Air Quality and Emissions Trends. Report (ISSN 0092-9670)

614.7 US
NATIONAL COUNCIL OF THE PAPER INDUSTRY FOR AIR AND STREAM IMPROVEMENT. TECHNICAL BULLETIN. irreg. $330. National Council of the Paper Industry for Air and Stream Improvement, Inc., 260 Madison Ave., New York, NY 10016. TEL 212-532-9000. (back issues avail.) Indexed: Abstr.Bull.Inst.Pap.Chem.
Formed by the merger of: Stream Improvement Technical Bulletin (ISSN 0360-8751); Atmospheric Quality Improvement Technical Bulletin (ISSN 0360-8778); Which was formerly: Atmospheric Pollution Technical Bulletin.

301.31 CN ISSN 0316-0114
NATIONAL RESEARCH COUNCIL, CANADA. ASSOCIATE COMMITTEE ON SCIENTIFIC CRITERIA FOR ENVIRONMENTAL QUALITY. STATUS REPORT/CONSEIL NATIONAL DE RECHERCHES, CANADA. COMITE ASSOCIE SUR LES CRITERES SCIENTIFIQUES. RAPPORT D'ACTIVITE. (Text in English and French) 1972. irreg. National Research Council of Canada, Associate Committee on Scientific Criteria for Environmental Quality, Ottawa, Ont., Canada. TEL 613-993-9101. illus. Indexed: Biol.Abstr. Chem.Abstr. Ind.Med. Ocean.Abstr. Pollut.Abstr.

614.7 SP
NATURALIA HISPANICA. (Text in Spanish; summaries in English, French, German) 1974. irreg. avail. on exchange basis. Instituto Nacional para la Conservacion de la Naturaleza, Gran via San Francisco 35, Madrid 5, Spain. Ed. P. Ceballos. charts. illus. circ. 1,000. (back issues avail.) Indexed: Biol.Abstr. Chem.Abstr. Curr.Cont. Aqua.Sci. & Fish.Abstr. Wild Life Rev. Zoo.Rec.

574.5 US ISSN 8756-3592
NATURALIST. irreg. $25 per 6 issues. De Young Press, Spencer, IA 51301-7252.

NATURE CONSERVATION COUNCIL OF N.S.W. NEWSLETTER. see *CONSERVATION*

353.9 US ISSN 0092-3311
NEW JERSEY. DEPARTMENT OF ENVIRONMENTAL PROTECTION. ANNUAL REPORT. 1971/72. a. free. Department of Environmental Protection, John Fitch Plaza, Trenton, NJ 08625. TEL 609-292-2885. illus. circ. 5,000. Key Title: Annual Report - Department of Environmental Protection (Trenton)

614.71 US ISSN 0077-8451
NEW JERSEY CLEAN AIR COUNCIL. REPORT. a. Department of Environmental Protection, New Jersey Clean Air Council, 401 E. State St., Trenton, NJ 08625. TEL 609-292-2885.

614.7 US
NEW YORK STATE ENVIRONMENTAL FACILITIES CORPORATION. INDUSTRIAL MATERIALS RECYCLING ACT. ANNUAL REPORT. 1982. a. free. New York State Environmental Facilities Corporation, 50 Wolf Rd., Albany, NY 12205. Ed.Bd. circ. 2,000.

614 NZ ISSN 0110-9944
NEW ZEALAND. DEPARTMENT OF HEALTH. ENVIRONMENTAL RADIOACTIVITY ANNUAL REPORT. 1961. a. NZ.$2.75. New Zealand. Department of Health, National Radiation Laboratory, P.O. Box 25-099, Christchurch, New Zealand. Ed. K.M. Matthews. circ. 300. (back issues avail.) Indexed: Biol.Abstr.

614.7 JA
NEWS OF SHINOBAZU. (Text in Japanese) 1976. irreg. 1.000 Yen. Society of Natural Observation in Shinobazu, 1-59, Ueno-Park, Taito-Ku, Tokyo, Japan. Ed. Kiyoshi Ogawa. circ. 250.

614.7 JA
NIIGATA-SHI NI OKERU KOGAI/ ENVIRONMENTAL POLLUTION IN NIIGATA CITY. a. free. Niigata-Shi, 866, Rokuban-Cho, Nishibori-Dori, Niigata-Shi 951, Japan.

614.7 IT ISSN 0546-2347
NOISE AND SMOG NEWS. (Text in English, Italian) 1952. a. N.A.N.S., Belvedere Golfo Paradiso 21, 16036 Recco, Genoa, Italy. adv. circ. 18,595.
Formerly: Audiotecnica News.

NORSK VILTFORSKNING. MEDDELESER. see *BIOLOGY*

628.5 BE ISSN 0377-7669
NORTH ATLANTIC TREATY ORGANIZATION. EXPERT PANEL ON AIR POLLUTION MODELING. PROCEEDINGS. (Subseries of: Air Pollution) a. North Atlantic Treaty Organization, Committee on the Challenges of Modern Society, 1110 Brussels, Belgium.

NORTHROP UNIVERSITY LAW JOURNAL OF AEROSPACE, BUSINESS AND TAXATION. see *AERONAUTICS AND SPACE FLIGHT*

354 CN ISSN 0317-3526
NOVA SCOTIA. ENVIRONMENTAL CONTROL COUNCIL. ANNUAL REPORT. 1973. a. Environmental Control Council, Box 2107, Halifax, N.S. B3J 3B7, Canada. TEL 902-424-5300.

614.7 387 639.2 551.4 AT
OCCASIONAL PAPERS IN MARITIME AFFAIRS; Australia's offshore maritime interests. 1985. a. Aus.$15. Australian Centre for Maritime Studies, P.O. Box E20, Queen Victoria Terrace, Canberra, ACT, Australia. Eds. M. Ward, S. Bateman. circ. 500. (back issues avail.)

614.7 340 CN
OCEAN DUMPING CONTROL ACT ANNUAL REPORT. (Text in English and French) 1985. a. free. Environment Canada, Environmental Protection Service, Ottawa, Ont. K1A 1C8, Canada. Ed.Bd. index. circ. 1,250. (also avail. in microfiche)

ONE WORLD. see *PETS*

354 CN
ONTARIO. MINISTRY OF THE ENVIRONMENT. ANNUAL REPORT. 1973. a. Can.$5. Ministry of the Environment, 135 St. Clair Ave. W., Toronto, Ont. M4V 1P5, Canada TEL 416-965-7117. (Subscr. to: Ontario Goverment Bookstore, 880 Bay St., Toronto, Ont. M7A 1N8, Canada) charts. illus.

628.44 CN ISSN 0078-4893
ONTARIO. MINISTRY OF THE ENVIRONMENT. INDUSTRIAL WASTE CONFERENCE. PROCEEDINGS. 1954. a. free contr. circ. ‡ Ministry of the Environment, Water Resources Branch, 135 St. Clair Ave., Toronto, Ont. M4V 1P5, Canada. TEL 416-965-6141. Ed. M.F. Cheetham.

614.7 CN ISSN 0078-5148
ONTARIO. MINISTRY OF THE ENVIRONMENT. POLLUTION CONTROL BRANCH. RESEARCH PUBLICATION. 1959. irreg. free. Ministry of the Environment, Pollution Control Branch, 135 St. Clair Ave., Toronto, Ont. M4V 1P5, Canada. TEL 416-965-6971. circ. 300. Indexed: Pollut.Abstr. GeoRef.

301.31 US ISSN 0092-7937
PENNSYLVANIA. CITIZENS ADVISORY COUNCIL TO THE DEPARTMENT OF ENVIRONMENTAL RESOURCES. ANNUAL REPORT. 1971/72. a. free. Citizens Advisory Council to the Pennsylvania Department of Environmental Resources, Box 2357, 816 Executive House, Harrisburg, PA 17120. Ed. Mark M. McClellan. stat. circ. 2,500. Key Title: Annual Report - Citizens Advisory Council (Harrisburg)

PHILADELPHIA HERPETOLOGICAL SOCIETY. BULLETIN. see *BIOLOGY — Zoology*

614.7 333.7 PH
PHILIPPINES. MINISTRY OF NATURAL RESOURCES. ANNUAL REPORT. a. Department of Natural Resources, Diliman, Quezon City, Philippines.

PHILIPPINES. MINISTRY OF NATURAL RESOURCES. PLANS AND PROGRAMS. see *CONSERVATION*

614.7 620 PL ISSN 0208-4112
POLSKA AKADEMIA NAUK. INSTYTUT PODSTAW INZYNIERII SRODOWISKA. PRACE I STUDIA. irreg., no.29, 1985. price varies. Ossolineum, Publishing House of the Polish Academy of Sciences, Rynek 9, Wroclaw, Poland (Dist. by: Ars Polona-Ruch, Krakowskie Przedmiescie 7, Warsaw, Poland) Ed. Stefan Jarzebski. Indexed: Pollut.Abstr.
Supersedes (as of 1971): Polska Akademia Nauk. Centrum Badan Naukowych w Wojewodztwie Katowikim. Prace i Studia (ISSN 0079-3582)

POTOMAC RIVER BASIN WATER QUALITY REPORTS. see *WATER RESOURCES*

614.7 UK ISSN 0262-4540
PRACTICAL ALTERNATIVES; a magazine of ways of saving resources in everyday life. 1981. irreg. £25 per 6 issues. (Life Style 2000 Ltd.) David Stephens, Ed. & Pub., Victoria House, Bridge St., Rhayader, Powys LD6 5AG, England. TEL 0597- 810929. Ed. David Stephens. circ. 2,000.
Incorporating: Ecological Life Style. Newsletter & Environmental Building Developments Ltd. News.

614.7 US
PRAIRIE WIND. 1971. irreg. free. Institute for Ecological Studies, University of North Dakota, Box 8278, University Station, Grand Forks, ND 58202. TEL 701-777-2851. Ed. Rodney D. Sayler. bk. rev. circ. 1,000. (looseleaf format; back issues avail.)
Formerly (until 1982): Contact.

628 CN
PRINCE EDWARD ISLAND. DEPARTMENT OF COMMUNITY AND CULTURAL AFFAIRS. ANNUAL REPORT. 1970. a. Department of Community Affairs, Box 2000, Charlottetown, Prince Edward Island, Canada. TEL 902-892-3561. Ed.Bd. circ. 150.
Former titles: Prince Edward Island. Department of Community Affairs. Annual Report (ISSN 0701-6956); (until 1980): Prince Edward Island. Department of the Environment Annual Report (ISSN 0085-5138); Prince Edward Island. Water Authority. Annual Report.

ENVIRONMENTAL STUDIES

614.7　　　　　　UR　ISSN 0135-2253
PROBLEMY KONTROLYA I ZASHCHITA ATMOSFERY OT ZAGRYAZNENIYA; respublikanskii mezhvedomstvennyi sbornik nauchnykh trudov. (Text in Russian) 1974. a. (Akademiya Nauk Ukrainskoi S.S.R, Institut Tekhnicheskoi Teplofiziki) Izdatel'stvo Naukova Dumka, c/o Yu.A. Khramov, Dir, Ul. Repina, 3, Kiev 252 601, Ukrainian S.S.R., U.S.S.R. (Subscr. to: Mezhdunarodnaya Kniga, Moscow, G-200, Russian S.F.S.R., U.S.S.R.) Ed. A.N. Shcherban' Indexed: Chem.Abstr. Int.Aerosp.Abstr.

628.71　　　　　　US
PURDUE AIR QUALITY CONFERENCE. PROCEEDINGS. 1961. a. Purdue University, School of Civil Engineering, W. Lafayette, IN 47907. TEL 317-494-5600. (Co-sponsor: Indiana State Board of Health) Ed. Dr. Robert B. Jacko.

614.7　581　　　　US
PYMATUNING SYMPOSIA IN ECOLOGY. 1956. irreg., no.6, 1982. price varies. University of Pittsburgh, Pymatuning Laboratory of Ecology, RR 1, Box 7, Linesville, PA 16424. TEL 814-683-5813. Ed. Richard T. Hartman. (back issues avail.)

614.7　　　　　　CN
QUEBEC (PROVINCE). CONSEIL CONSULTATIF DE L'ENVIRONNEMENT. RAPPORT ANNUEL.* a. Editeur Officiel du Quebec, 1283 Bd. Charest Ouest, Quebec, P.Q. G1N 2C9, Canada. TEL 413-643-3895.
　　Formerly: Quebec (Province). Advisory Council of the Environment. Annual Report.

QUEBEC (PROVINCE) MINISTERE DES RICHESSES NATURELLES. RAPPORT. see CONSERVATION

354　　　　　　AT
QUEENSLAND. AIR POLLUTION COUNCIL. ANNUAL REPORT. a. Queensland. Government Printer, Brisbane, Australia. illus.

614.7　531.64　　US
RADIOACTIVE REPORTER. irreg. $8. Keystone Alliance, 1006 S. 46th St., Philadelphia, PA 19143. TEL 215-387-5254. Ed. Pat Gourley.

614.7　　　　DK　ISSN 0107-7090
RECIPIENTUNDERSOEGELSE VED MARMORILIK. (Text in Danish; summaries in English, Greenlandic) 1974. irreg. price varies. Groenlands Geologiske Undersoegelse, Oester Voldgade 10, DK-1350 Copenhagen K, Denmark. (Co-sponsor: Groenlands Fiskeriundersoegsler)

614.7　　　　　　US
RENE DUBOS CENTER FOR HUMAN ENVIRONMENTS. NEWSLETTER. irreg. Rene Dubos Center for Human Environment, Inc., 100 E. 85th St., New York, NY 10028. TEL 212-249-7745.

RESEARCH INSTITUTE OF INDUSTRIAL SAFETY. RESEARCH REPORT. see ELECTRICITY AND ELECTRICAL ENGINEERING

614.7　574　　UK　ISSN 0271-6194
RESOURCE AND ENVIRONMENTAL SCIENCE SERIES. 1977. irreg. price varies. Edward Arnold (Publishers) Ltd., 41 Bedford Square, London WC1B 3DQ, England.

614.7　　　　　　MX
REUNION NACIONAL SOBRE PROBLEMAS DE CONTAMINACION AMBIENTAL. MEMORIA. 1973. irreg. Secretaria de Salud, Av. Dr. Francisco de P. Miranda 177, Col. Merced Gomez, Deleg. Alvaro Obregon, C.P. 01600, Mexico, D.F., Mexico. illus.

614.7　398　　　　US
ROBIN. 1984. irreg. $10. Yankee Permaculture, Box 202, Orange, MA 01364. TEL 617-544-7810. Ed. Dan Hemenway. bk. rev. circ. 50. (back issues avail.)

550　　　　　　BL
SAO PAULO, BRAZIL (STATE). SUPERINTENDENCIA DE SANEAMENTO AMBIENTAL. RELATORIO ANUAL DE ATIVIDADES. a. Superintendencia de Saneamento Ambiental, Secretaria de Estado da Saude, Sao Paulo, Brazil.

354　　　　CN　ISSN 0317-4611
SASKATCHEWAN. DEPARTMENT OF THE ENVIRONMENT. ANNUAL REPORT. 1973. a. free. Department of the Environment, Information & Communications Branch, 3085 Albert St., Regina, Sask. S4S 0B1, Canada. TEL 306-787-6113. illus. stat. circ. 400.

614.7　　　　　　GW
SCHRIFTENREIHE LUFTREINHALTUNG. ceased 1980. irreg. (last vol. 18) price varies. (Landesamt fuer Umweltschutz) R. Oldenbourg Verlag GmbH, Rosenheimer Str. 145, 8000 Munich 80, W. Germany (B.R.D.)

614.7　　　　　　SI
SINGAPORE. MINISTRY OF THE ENVIRONMENT. ANNUAL REPORT. (Text in English) 1972. a. Ministry of the Environment, Princess House, Alexandra Rd., Singapore 3, Singapore. illus. circ. controlled.

SKENECTADA. see BIOLOGY

SOVIET HYDROLOGY: SELECTED PAPERS. see WATER RESOURCES

SPAIN. INSTITUTO NACIONAL DE INVESTIGACIONES AGRARIAS. COMUNICACIONES. SERIE: RECURSOS NATURALES. see FORESTS AND FORESTRY

614.7　　　　　　SP
SPAIN. INSTITUTO NACIONAL PARA LA CONSERVACION DE LA NATURALEZA. MONOGRAFIAS. 1974. irreg. avail. on exchange basis. Instituto Nacional para la Conservacion de la Naturaleza, Gran via San Francisco 35, Madrid 5, Spain. bibl. charts. illus. circ. 1,000. (back issues avail.) Indexed: Biol.Abstr. Chem.Abstr. Curr.Cont. Aqua.Sci. & Fish.Abstr. Wild Life Rev. Zoo.Rec.

SPORTS TURF RESEARCH INSTITUTE. JOURNAL. see AGRICULTURE — Crop Production And Soil

614.7　　　　US　ISSN 0172-6161
SPRINGER SERIES ON ENVIRONMENTAL MANAGEMENT. 1979. irreg., latest 1986. price varies. Springer-Verlag, 175 Fifth Ave., New York, NY 10010 TEL 212-460-1500. (Also Berlin, Heidelberg, Tokyo and Vienna) Ed. Dr. Robert DeSanto. (reprint service avail. from ISI)

STANFORD ENVIRONMENTAL LAW JOURNAL. see LAW

353.00　　　US　ISSN 0275-2271
STATE/E P A AGREEMENTS. ANNUAL REPORT. a. U.S. Environmental Protection Agency, Program Evaluation Division, 401 M St., N.W., Washington, DC 20460. TEL 202-655-4000.

614.7　　　　　　US
STATE OF THE ENVIRONMENT (YEAR) 1982. irreg., (approx. biennial); latest 1984. $15. Conservation Foundation, 1255 23rd St., N.W., Washington, DC 20037. TEL 202-293-4800.
　　Formerly: State of the Environment.

614.7　　　　　　US
STATE OF VIRGINIA'S ENVIRONMENT: BIENNIAL REPORT. 1973. biennial. Council on the Environment, 903 9th St., Office Bldg., Richmond, VA 23219. TEL 804-786-4500.
　　Formerly: State of Virginia's Environment: Annual Report.

614.7　　　　　　JA
STATISTICAL TABLES OF PUBLIC NUISANCE, TOKYO. 1970. biennial. 520 Yen. Tokyo Metropolitan Research Institute for Environmental Protection, 7-5, Shinsuna 1-Chome, Koto-Ku, Tokyo 136, Japan.

614.7　　　　　　NE
STUDIES IN ENVIRONMENTAL SCIENCE. 1978. irreg., vol.25, 1984. price varies. Elsevier Science Publishers B.V., Box 211, 1000 AE Amsterdam, Netherlands. Indexed: Chem.Abstr.

614.7　　　　SW　ISSN 0346-6868
SWEDISH NATURAL SCIENCE RESEARCH COUNCIL. ECOLOGICAL BULLETINS. (Text in English) 1968. irreg., latest no.36 1984. price varies. Publishing House of the Swedish Research Councils, Ecological Research Committee, Box 6710, S-113 85 Stockholm, Sweden. Ed. Pehr H. Enckell. circ. 1,500. (back issues avail.) Indexed: Biol.Abstr. Geo.Abstr. GeoRef.

614.7　　　　　　NE
T N O RESEARCH INSTITUTE FOR ENVIRONMENTAL HYGIENE. ANNUAL REPORT. (Text in English) a. T N O Research Institute for Environmental Hygiene, Box 214, 2600 AE Delft, Netherlands. circ. 1,000. Indexed: Excerp.Med.

628.168　　　　　AT
TASMANIA. HOBART REGIONAL WATER BOARD. REPORT. 1963. a. free. ‡ Hobart Regional Water Board, G.P.O. Box 179, Hobart, Tasmania, Australia.
　　Formerly: Tasmania. Metropolitan Water Board. Report. (ISSN 0082-2094)

614.7　　　　　　US
TECHNICAL ASSOCIATION OF THE PULP AND PAPER INDUSTRY. ENVIRONMENTAL CONFERENCE PROCEEDINGS. a. $69.95 to non-members; members $46.87. Technical Association of the Pulp and Paper Industry, Inc., Technology Park/Atlanta, Box 105113, Atlanta, GA 30348. TEL 404-446-1400.

614　　　　US　ISSN 0361-5162
TRACE SUBSTANCES IN ENVIRONMENTAL HEALTH. 1967. a. price varies. ‡ University of Missouri-Columbia, Environmental Trace Substances Research Center, Extension Division, Columbia, MO 65211. TEL 314-882-2121. Ed. Delbert D. Hemphill. index. circ. 2,000. Indexed: Biol.Abstr. Chem.Abstr. Nutr.Abstr. Pollut.Abstr. GeoRef.
　　Formerly: Conference on Trace Substances in Environmental Health. Proceedings (ISSN 0069-8741)

614.7　　　　　　UN
U N E P INFORMATION. (Text in English) 1975. irreg., no.86, 1983. United Nations Environment Programme, Information Service, Box 30552, Nairobi, Kenya.

614.7　　　　　　UN
UNITED NATIONS ENVIRONMENT PROGRAMME. EVALUATION REPORT (YEAR) a. United Nations Environment Programme, P.O. Box 30552, Nairobi, Kenya.

614.7　　　　　　UN
UNITED NATIONS ENVIRONMENT PROGRAMME. FEATURE. Variant title: U N E P Feature. (Text in English) 1976. irreg. United Nations Environment Programme, Information Service, Box 30552, Nairobi, Kenya.

614.7　　　　　　UN
UNITED NATIONS ENVIRONMENT PROGRAMME. GOVERNING COUNCIL. REPORT ON THE WORK OF ITS SESSION. (Text in English) a. United Nations Environment Programme, Information Service, Nairobi, Kenya.

614.7　　　　　　UN
UNITED NATIONS ENVIRONMENT PROGRAMME. THE STATE OF THE ENVIRONMENT; REPORT OF THE EXECUTIVE DIRECTOR. (Text in English) a. United Nations Environment Programme, Information Service, Box 30552, Nairobi, Kenya.

614.7　　　　US　ISSN 0092-0320
U.S. COAST GUARD. POLLUTING INCIDENTS IN AND AROUND U.S. WATERS. a. free contr. circ. U.S. Coast Guard, 2100 Second St., S.W., Washington, DC 20593. TEL 202-426-1830.

614.7　　　　　　US
U.S. DEPARTMENT OF HOUSING AND URBAN DEVELOPMENT. INTERIM GUIDE FOR ENVIRONMENT ASSESSMENT. irreg. $22. U.S. Department of Housing and Urban Development, Washington, DC 20410 TEL 202-655-4000. (Subscr. to: Supt. of Documents, Washington, DC 20402)

614.7   US
U.S. ENVIRONMENTAL PROTECTION
  AGENCY. OFFICE OF RESEARCH AND
  DEVELOPMENT. PROGRAM GUIDE. 1977? a.
  Environmental Protection Agency, Office of
  Research and Development, Washington, DC
  20460. TEL 513-569-7562. circ. 12,000. (also avail.
  in microfilm; reprint service avail.)

333.9   US   ISSN 0098-4922
U.S. NATIONAL OCEANIC AND ATMOSPHERIC
  ADMINISTRATION. REPORT TO THE
  CONGRESS ON OCEAN POLLUTION,
  OVERFISHING, AND OFFSHORE
  DEVELOPMENT. 1973. a. $1.45. U.S. National
  Oceanic and Atmospheric Administration, 6010
  Executive Blvd., Rockville, MD 20852 TEL 301-
  655-4000. (Orders to: NTIS, 5285 Port Royal Rd.,
  Springfield, VA 22161) Key Title: Report to
  the Congress on Ocean Pollution, Overfishing, and
  Offshore Development.
    Formerly: U.S. National Oceanic and
  Atmospheric Administration. Report to the
  Congress on Ocean Dumping and Other Man-
  Induced Changes to Ocean Ecosystems (ISSN 0094-
  5196)

UNIVERSIDAD DE MURCIA. ANALES DE
  BIOLOGIA. SECCION BIOLOGIA
  AMBIENTAL. see BIOLOGY

UNIVERSITY OF CALGARY.
  ARCHAEOLOGICAL ASSOCIATION.
  ARCHAEOLOGICAL CONFERENCE.
  PROCEEDINGS. see ARCHAEOLOGY

614 301.32   TZ   ISSN 0084-960X
UNIVERSITY OF DAR ES SALAAM. BUREAU OF
  RESOURCE ASSESSMENT AND LAND USE
  PLANNING. ANNUAL REPORT. 1968. a. free.
  University of Dar es Salaam, Bureau of Resource
  Assessment and Land Use Planning, Box 35097,
  Dar es Salaam, Tanzania. Ed. Adolfo Mascarenhas.
  circ. 250.

614 301.32   TZ   ISSN 0084-9626
UNIVERSITY OF DAR ES SALAAM. BUREAU OF
  RESOURCE ASSESSMENT AND LAND USE
  PLANNING. RESEARCH PAPER. 1968. irreg.,
  no.60, 1979. $50. University of Dar es Salaam,
  Bureau of Resource Assessment and Land Use
  Planning, Box 35097, Dar es Salaam, Tanzania. Ed.
  Adolfo Mascarenhas. circ. 200.

614 301.32   TZ   ISSN 0084-9634
UNIVERSITY OF DAR ES SALAAM. BUREAU OF
  RESOURCE ASSESSMENT AND LAND USE
  PLANNING. RESEARCH REPORT. 1969. irreg.,
  no.39, 1979 (N.S.) price varies. University of Dar es
  Salaam, Bureau of Resource Assessment and Land
  Use Planning, Box 35097, Dar es Salaam, Tanzania.
  Ed. Adolfo Mascarenhas. circ. 200. Indexed:
  Geo.Abstr.

574.5   US   ISSN 0094-9205
UNIVERSITY OF GEORGIA. INSTITUTE OF
  ECOLOGY. ANNUAL REPORT. Cover title:
  Ecology. 1972. a. free. University of Georgia,
  Institute of Ecology, Athens, GA 30602. TEL 404-
  542-2968. Ed. Barbara Smalley. bibl. circ. 1,200.
  Key Title: Annual Report - University of Georgia,
  Institute of Ecology.

614.7   AT
UNIVERSITY OF NEWCASTLE. BOARD OF
  ENVIRONMENTAL STUDIES. RESEARCH
  PAPERS. 1973. a. free. University of Newcastle,
  Board of Environmental Studies, Newcastle, N.S.W.,
  Australia. Ed.Bd. bibl. charts. circ. 200.

614.7   US
UNIVERSITY OF NORTH DAKOTA. INSTITUTE
  FOR ECOLOGICAL STUDIES. RESEARCH
  REPORT. 1971. irreg., no.30, 1981. price varies.
  Institute for Ecological Studies, University of North
  Dakota, Box 8278, University Station, Grand Forks,
  ND 58202. TEL 701-777-2851. Ed. Dr. R.D.
  Sayler. circ. 200. Indexed: Wild Life Rev.

614.7   US   ISSN 0079-8207
UNIVERSITY OF PITTSBURGH. PYMATUNING
  LABORATORY OF ECOLOGY. SPECIAL
  PUBLICATION. 1956. irreg., no.5, 1978. price
  varies. University of Pittsburgh, Pymatuning
  Laboratory of Ecology, R.D. 1, Box 7, PA 16424.
  TEL 412-624-4141. Ed. R.T. Hartman. index. circ.
  1,000.

614.7   AT   ISSN 0810-4395
UNIVERSITY OF TASMANIA.
  ENVIRONMENTAL STUDIES. OCCASIONAL
  PAPER. 1976. irreg. Aus.$15. University of
  Tasmania, Board of Environmental Studies, GPO
  Box 252C, Hobart 7001, Australia. Ed. John Todd.
  circ. 50. (back issues avail.) Indexed: Biol.Abstr.

333.77   CN
UNIVERSITY OF WATERLOO. DEPARTMENT
  OF GEOLOGY. WORKING PAPERS SERIES.
  1977. irreg. University of Waterloo, Department of
  Geology, Waterloo, Ont. N2L 3G1, Canada. TEL
  519-885-1211.

614.7 627   US   ISSN 0093-6332
VANDERBILT UNIVERSITY. DEPARTMENT OF
  ENVIRONMENTAL AND WATER
  RESOURCES ENGINEERING. TECHNICAL
  REPORTS. 1962. irreg., no.43, 1984. price varies.
  Vanderbilt University, Department of Civil &
  Environmental Engineering, Box 6304, Sta. B,
  Nashville, TN 37235. TEL 615-322-2720. Ed.
  Edward L. Thackston. circ. 100.

VEREIN FUER WASSER-, BODEN- UND
  LUFTHYGIENE. SCHRIFTENREIHE. see
  CONSERVATION

VIRGINIA. STATE WATER CONTROL BOARD.
  ANNUAL REPORT. see WATER RESOURCES

614.7   US
WATCH IT. 1969. irreg. free to members. Wilderness
  Watch, Inc., Box 3184, Green Bay, WI 54303. Ed.
  Jerry Gandt.

614.7   US
WATER POLLUTION: A SERIES OF
  MONOGRAPHS. 1974. irreg., no.7, 1983.
  Academic Press, Inc., Orlando, FL 32887. TEL
  305-345-2000. Eds. K.S. Speigler, J. Bregman.

WATER QUALITY DATA FOR ONTARIO
  STREAMS & LAKES. see WATER RESOURCES

363.6   US   ISSN 0097-7519
WATER QUALITY MONITORING DATA FOR
  GEORGIA STREAMS. a. Department of Natural
  Resources, Environmental Protection Division,
  Water Quality Control Section, 148 International
  Blvd., Ste. 350, Atlanta, GA 30303. TEL 404-656-
  4708. Indexed: GeoRef.

628.168   UK
WATER RESEARCH CENTRE. ANNUAL
  REVIEW. 1974. a. Water Research Centre, P.O.
  Box 16, Henley Rd., Medmenham, Marlow, Bucks
  SL7 2HD, England. circ. 5,000.
    Formerly: Water Research Centre. Annual Report
  (ISSN 0143-2443); Formed by the merger: Water
  Research Association. Report; Water Pollution
  Research.

WESTERN AUSTRALIA. DEPARTMENT OF
  FISHERIES AND WILDLIFE. FISHERIES
  RESEARCH BULLETIN. see FISH AND
  FISHERIES

WESTERN AUSTRALIA. ENVIRONMENTAL
  PROTECTION AUTHORITY. ANNUAL
  REPORT. see CONSERVATION

614.7 628.44   CN
WESTERN CANADA WATER AND WASTE
  WATER ASSOCIATION. BULLETIN. 1949; N.S.
  1983. a. Can.$20 price varies. Western Canada
  Water and Waste Water Association, P.O. Box
  6168, Postal Station A, Calgary, Alta. T2H 2L4,
  Canada. Ed. A. Stephen. adv. bk. rev. circ. 3,000.
    Former titles: Western Canada Water and Sewage
  Conference. Bulletin; Western Canada Water and
  Sewage Conference. Papers Presented at Annual
  Convention (ISSN 0083-8799)

WESTERN GEOGRAPHICAL SERIES. see
  GEOGRAPHY

614.7   US   ISSN 0362-5354
WISCONSIN. DEPARTMENT OF NATURAL
  RESOURCES. ANNUAL WATER QUALITY
  REPORT TO CONGRESS. biennial. Department of
  Natural Resources, Box 7921, Madison, WI 53707.
  TEL 608-267-7610. illus. Key Title: Annual Water
  Quality Report to Congress.

614.7   US   ISSN 0749-1069
WORLD ENVIRONMENT HANDBOOK; a
  directory of government natural resource
  management agencies and non-governmental
  environment organizations in 145 countries. 1983.
  irreg., 2nd edt., 1985. $33. World Environment
  Center, Inc., 605 3rd Ave., 17th Fl., New York, NY
  10158. TEL 212-986-7200. Ed.Bd.

551.5 614.7   UN
WORLD METEOROLOGICAL ORGANIZATION.
  SPECIAL ENVIRONMENTAL REPORTS.
  (Subseries of: World Meteorological Organization.
  W M O (Publications)) irreg. World Meteorological
  Organization, 41 Av. Giuseppe Motta, CH-1211
  Geneva 20, Switzerland (Dist. in U.S. by: American
  Meteorological Society, 45 Beacon St., Boston, MA
  02108) illus. Indexed: Biol.Abstr.

614.7   US
WORLD WASTES EQUIPMENT CATALOG. 1963.
  a. $21.95. Communication Channels, Inc., 6255
  Barfield Rd., Atlanta, GA 30328. TEL 404-256-
  9800. Ed. Bill Wolpin. adv. circ. 27,100. (also avail.
  in microform from UMI) Indexed: Eng.Ind.
    Formerly: Sanitation Industry Yearbook (ISSN
  0080-6021)

300   US
WORLDWATCH PAPERS. 1975. irreg., no.74, 1986.
  $25. Worldwatch Institute, 1776 Massachusetts
  Ave., N.W., Washington, DC 20036. TEL 202-452-
  1999. Ed. Robin Bell. circ. 5,000. (also avail. in
  microfiche; back issues avail.) Indexed: Biol.Abstr.
  Forest.Abstr. Forest Prod.Abstr. Geo.Abstr.
  Popul.Ind. Rural Recreat.Tour.Abstr. World
  Agri.Econ. & Rural Sociol.Abstr.

353.9   US   ISSN 0099-1279
WYOMING. DEPARTMENT OF
  ENVIRONMENTAL QUALITY. ANNUAL
  REPORT. 1974. a. Department of Environmental
  Quality, Cheyenne, WY 82002. TEL 307-777-7937.
  Key Title: Annual Report of the Department of
  Environmental Quality.

333.9   US   ISSN 0098-0846
WYOMING. WATER QUALITY DIVISION.
  WYOMING STATE PLAN. a. Department of
  Environmental Quality, Water Quality Division,
  Cheyenne, WY 82002. TEL 307-777-7937. Key
  Title: Wyoming State Plan.

614.7 643   JA
YAMAGUCHI-KEN KOGAI SENTA NENPO/
  YAMAGUCHI PREFECTURAL
  ENVIRONMENTAL POLLUTION RESEARCH
  CENTER. ANNUAL REPORT. (Text in Japanese)
  1974. a. Yamaguchi Prefectural Environmental
  Pollution Research Center, 535 Hiruta Asada,
  Yamaguchi-Shi 753, Japan. circ. 500.

628   GW   ISSN 0173-6507
ZAHLENTAFELN DER PHYSIKALISCH-
  CHEMISCHEN UNTERSUCHUNGEN DES
  RHEINWASSERS/TABLEAUX NUMERIQUES
  DES ANALYSES PHYSICO-CHIMIQUES DES
  EAUX DU RHIN. (Text in French, German) 1963.
  a. free. International Commission for the Protection
  of the Rhine Against Pollution - Internationale
  Kommission zum Schutze des Rheins gegen
  Verunreinigung, Mainzer Str. 37A, Postfach 309,
  5400 Koblenz, W. Germany (B.R.D.) Ed.Bd. circ. 1,
  200.
    Formerly (until 1978): Zahlentafeln der
  Physikalisch-Chemischen Untersuchungen des
  Rheins sowie der Mosel (ISSN 0539-1539)

ENVIRONMENTAL STUDIES —
Abstracting, Bibliographies, Statistics

614.7 016   BE   ISSN 0379-1815
BELGIAN ENVIRONMENTAL RESEARCH
  INDEX. 1969. a. 250 Fr. Centre National de
  Documentation Scientifique et Technique - National
  Center for Scientific and Technical Documentation,
  4 Bd. de l'Empereur, B-1000 Brussels, Belgium. Ed.
  L. Dooms. Indexed: Pollut.Abstr.

614.7 DK ISSN 0109-7695
DENMARK. MILJOEMINISTERIET.
MILJOEMINISTERIET
PUBLIKATIONSREGISTER; oversigt over
publikationer. (Suppl. to: Miljoeministeriet
Lovregister) 1983. a. free. Miljoeministeriet,
Slotsholmsgade 12, 1216 Copenhagen K, Denmark.
Ed. Birgitte Pedersen. circ. 100.

614.7 US ISSN 0190-0250
E I S CUMULATIVE.* (Environmental Impact
Statement) 1977. a. price varies, includes 3 vols.
(1970-1976) Cambridge Scientific Abstracts, 5160
River Rd., Bethesda, MD 20816.
●Also available online. Vendors: DIALOG.

ECOLOGY ABSTRACTS. see *WATER
RESOURCES — Abstracting, Bibliographies,
Statistics*

ENERGY INDEX. see *ENERGY — Abstracting,
Bibliographies, Statistics*

614.7 016 US ISSN 0090-791X
ENVIRONMENT INDEX; a guide to the key
environmental literature of the year. 1970. a. $295.
E I C Intelligence, Inc., 48 W. 38th St., New York,
NY 10018. TEL 212-944-8500.

614.7 016 NE ISSN 0300-5194
EXCERPTA MEDICA. SECTION 46:
ENVIRONMENTAL HEALTH AND
POLLUTION CONTROL. 1971. 10/yr. $102.
Elsevier Science Publishers B.V., Box 211, 1000 AE
Amsterdam, Netherlands. Ed.Bd. adv. bk. rev.
index. cum.index. Indexed: Excerp.Med.
●Also available online. Vendors: BRS, DIALOG.
Formerly: Excerpta Medica. Section 46:
Environmental Health (ISSN 0046-2268)

628.44 FI
FINLAND. TILASTOKESKUS. TILASTOLLISIA
TIEDONANTOJA. YMPARISTOTILASTO/
FINLAND. STATISTIKCENTRALEN.
STATISTIKA MEDDELANDEN.
MILJOESTATISTIK/FINLAND. CENTRAL
STATISTICAL OFFICE. STATISTICAL
SURVEYS. ENVIRONMENTAL STATISTICS.
(Text in English, Finnish, and Swedish) 1977. irreg.,
latest 1980. Fmk.45. Tilastokeskus, Annankatu 44,
SF-00100 Helsinki 10, Finland (Subscr. to:
Government Printing Cetnre, Box 516, SF-00101
Helsinki 10, Finland)

301.31 016 UK ISSN 0141-2604
GREAT BRITAIN. DEPARTMENTS OF THE
ENVIRONMENT AND TRANSPORT. LIBRARY
SERVICES. ANNUAL LIST OF PUBLICATIONS.
1971. a. price varies. Department of the
Environment, 2 Marsham Street, Room P3/178,
London SW1P 3EB, England. (Co-sponsor:
Department of Transport) Ed. J. Stannard. bibl. circ.
3,000. (also avail. in microfiche)
Formerly: Great Britain. Department of the
Environment. Library Services. D.O.E. Annual List
of Publications.

340 333.7 016 GW
I C E L REFERENCES; to publications concerning
legal, administrative and policy aspects of
environmental conservation. (Text in various
languages) 1970. irreg. (16-20/yr.) $20.
International Council on Environmental Law, 214
Adenauerallee, 5300 Bonn, W. Germany (B. R. D.)
Ed. Ms. G. Julemont. circ. 300(controlled) (cards)

614.7 016 II
INDIAN LITERATURE IN ENVIRONMENTAL
ENGINEERING; a bibliographic review. (Text in
English) 1971. a. Rs.80($5) National Environmental
Engineering Research Institute, Documentation and
Library Services, Nehru Marg, Nagpur 440020,
India. (Affiliate: Council of Scientific and Industrial
Research) Ed.Bd. author and geographical indexes.
(processed)

333.7 CN
ONTARIO. MINISTRY OF NATURAL
RESOURCES. STATISTICS. a. Ministry of Natural
Resources, Parliament Bldgs., Whitney Block,
Toronto, Ont. M7A 1W3, Canada. TEL 416-965-
2000.

614.7 UR ISSN 0234-7059
REFERATIVNYI ZHURNAL. ENVIRONMENT
MANAGEMENT ABSTRACTS. (English edition)
1987. m. Vsesoyuznyi Institut Nauchno-
Tekhnicheskoi Informatsii (VINITI), Baltiiskaya ul.
14, A-219 Moscow, Russian S.F.S.R., U.S.S.R.

150 011 CN ISSN 0824-3336
RISK ABSTRACTS; a quarterly journal of abstracts,
reviews and references. 1984. q. Can.$40($30) to
individuals; institutions Can.$80 ($65) University of
Waterloo, Institute for Risk Research, Waterloo
N2L 3G1, Canada. TEL 519-885-1211. Ed. N.C.
Lind. bk. rev. abstr. bibl. index. circ. 500.

614.7 US
U.S. ENVIRONMENTAL PROTECTION
AGENCY. JOURNAL HOLDINGS REPORT.
1971. a. U.S. Environmental Protection Agency,
Information Management and Services Division, 401
M St., S.W., Rm. 2003, PM-211D, Washington, DC
20460 TEL 703-487-4630. (Orders to: National
Technical Information Service, 5285 Port Royal
Rd., Springfield, VA 22161) circ. 250.

URBAN ABSTRACTS. see *PUBLIC
ADMINISTRATION — Abstracting,
Bibliographies, Statistics*

016 614.7 US
WATER POLLUTION CONTROL FEDERATION
CONFERENCE. ABSTRACTS OF TECHNICAL
PAPERS.* 46th, 1973. a. Water Pollution Control
Federation, 601 Wythe St., Alexandria, VA 22314-
1994. Indexed: Biol.Abstr.

ETHNIC INTERESTS

917.306 US ISSN 0889-9487
A A A S S DIRECTORY OF PROGRAMS. 1987/89.
triennial. $11.75 to members; non-members $26.75.
American Association for the Advancement of
Slavic Studies, Stanford University, 128 Encina
Commons, Stanford, CA 94305. TEL 415-723-9668.

960 US
A S A PAPERS. 1960? a. African Studies Association,
U C L A, 255 Kinsey Hall, 405 Hilgard Ave., Los
Angeles, CA 90024. TEL 213-206-8011.

AFRICAN - AMERICAN HERITAGE SERIES. see
*HISTORY — History Of North And South
America*

960 US
AFRICAN STUDIES. 1985. irreg. $39.95 per no.
Edwin Mellen Press, Box 450, Lewiston, NY 14092.

910.03 US
AFRO-AMERICAN AFFAIRS. 1981. a. $6. Jackson
& Edwards, Inc., Box 16606, Philadelphia, PA
19139. TEL 215-476-3455. Ed. John Jackson. circ.
5,000.

AFRO-AMERICAN CULTURE AND SOCIETY
MONOGRAPH SERIES. see *SOCIAL
SCIENCES: COMPREHENSIVE WORKS*

947 US ISSN 0516-3145
AKADEMISKA DZIVE/ACADEMIC LIFE. (Text in
Latvian; summaries in English) 1958. a. $5.
Association of Latvian Academic Societies, One
Vincent Ave. S., Minneapolis, MN 55405. Ed.Bd.
bk. rev. illus. circ. 1,100. Indexed: Hist.Abstr.
M.L.A. Amer.Hist.& Life.

057.91 CN ISSN 0441-1196
ALMANAKH GOMONU UKRAINY. 1956
(Suspended during 1974) a. Homin Ukrainy
Publishing Co., 140 Bathurst St., Toronto, Ont.
M5V 2R3, Canada. TEL 416-368-3443. illus.

970.1 US ISSN 0193-8207
AMERICAN INDIAN LIBRARIES NEWSLETTER.
1976. irreg. $5 to individuals; institutions $7.
American Library Association, Office for Library
Outreach Services, 50 E. Huron St., Chicago, IL
60611. TEL 312-944-6780. Ed. Thomas Blumer.
circ. 1,500.
American Indian interests

AMERICAN INDIAN TREATIES PUBLICATIONS
SERIES. see *LAW*

917.306 US
AMERICAN ITALIAN HISTORICAL
ASSOCIATION. PROCEEDINGS. (Each vol. has
distinctive title.) 1968. a. $9.95 or membership.
American Italian Historical Association, 209 Flagg
Pl., Staten Island, NY 10304. TEL 212-667-6628.
circ. 450.
Italian interests

AMERICAN JEWISH ALTERNATIVES TO
ZIONISM. REPORT. see *POLITICAL
SCIENCE — International Relations*

296 US
AMERICAN O R T FEDERATION. YEARBOOK.
1952. a. free. American O R T Federation, 817
Broadway, New York, NY 10003. TEL 212-677-
4400. Ed. Avi Feinglass. stat. index. circ. 18,000.
(back issues avail.)

947 US
AMERICAN ROMANIAN ACADEMY OF ARTS
AND SCIENCES. PUBLICATIONS. irreg. vol.4,
1984. A R A Publication, 4310 Finley Ave., Los
Angeles, CA 90027. TEL 213-666-8379.

917.106 800 700 US ISSN 0747-9301
AMERICAN SOCIETY FOR ARMENIAN
STUDIES. JOURNAL. Short title: J S A S. 1984. a.
American Society for Armenian Studies, University
of California, Los Angeles, Dept. of Near Eastern
Languages and Cultures, Los Angeles, CA 90024.
TEL 213-825-1307. Ed. Avedis K. Sanjian. adv. bk.
rev. charts. illus.

296 AG
ANALES DE LA COMUNIDAD ISRAELITA DE
BUENOS AIRES. Cover title: Pinkes Fun der
Kehile in Buenos Ayres. (Text in English and
Spanish) 1953/54. a. membership. Asociacion
Mutual Israelita Argentina, Kultur Departament bay
der Kehile in Buenos Aires, Pasteur 633, Buenos
Aires, Argentina.
Jewish interests

956 US ISSN 0742-9576
ARAB AMERICAN ALMANAC. 1974. irreg., latest
1984. $9.95 per no. News Circle Publishing Co.,
Box 3684, Glendale, CA 91201. TEL 818-240-1918.
Ed. Joseph R. Haiek. adv. circ. 15,000.

971.3 AT
ARCHIVS; Raksti par latviskam problemam. (Text and
summaries in Latvian) 1960. a. Aus.$9. World
Federation of Free Latvians, Karla Zarina fonds, 3
Dickens St., Elwood 3184, Australia. Ed. Edgars
Dunsdorfs. circ. 2,300. (back issues avail.) Indexed:
M.L.A.

915 US
ASIAN STUDIES CENTER BACKGROUNDER.
Short title: Backgrounder. (Topics vary; Updates and
Issue Bulletins avail.) irreg., no. 544. Heritage
Foundation, 214 Massachusetts Ave., N.E.,
Washington, DC 20002. TEL 202-546-4400. (also
avail. in looseleaf format)

ASIATIC SOCIETY. ANNUAL REPORT. see
GENERAL INTEREST PERIODICALS — India

301 AT
ASPECTS OF FRANCE. biennial. Aus.$3. Courrier
Australien, 396 Kent St., Sydney, N.S.W. 3000,
Australia. Ed. J.P. Sourdin. circ. 15,000.

ASSOCIATION OF JEWISH SPONSORED
CAMPS. CAMP DIRECTORY. see *SPORTS AND
GAMES — Outdoor Life*

919.4 052 AT
AUSTRALIA. DEPARTMENT OF ABORIGINAL
AFFAIRS. REPORT. 1975. a. price varies.
Australian Government Publishing Service, G.P.O.
Box 84, Canberra, A.C.T. 2601, Australia. illus.
Native Australian interests

914.406 AT
AUSZTRALIAI MAGYAR UJSAF. HUNGARIAN
WEEKLY. 1950. irreg. Aus.$0.20. c/o F. Antal,
Ed., P.O. Box 66, Fitzroy, Vic. 3065, Australia.
Hungarian interests

910.03 SA
B L A C. (Text in Afrikaans and English) irreg. Black
Literature and Arts Congress, 1 Long St., Mowbray,
South Africa.

ETHNIC INTERESTS

BAYAVAYA USKALOS; Byelorussian literary magazine. see LITERATURE

BAYERISCHES JAHRBUCH FUER VOLKSKUNDE. see FOLKLORE

BEBOP DRAWING CLUB BOOK. see ART

BELARUSKI INSTYTUT NAVUKI MACTATSTVA. ZAPISY/BYELORUSSIAN INSTITUTE OF ARTS AND SCIENCES. ANNALS. see HISTORY — History Of Europe

910.03 US ISSN 0732-7269
BLACK CAUCUS JOURNAL. 1968. a. $5. Howard University, Institute for Urban Affairs and Research, 2900 Van Ness St., N.W., Washington, DC 20008. TEL 202-686-6770. Ed. Lawrence E. Gary. bk. rev. circ. 4,000. (back issues avail.)
Black interests

BLACK ELECTED OFFICIALS; a national roster. see PUBLIC ADMINISTRATION

BLACK JACK. see LITERATURE

910.03 US
BLACK MESSIAH.* 1981. irreg. $12. Vagabond Press, Box 395, Ellensburg, WA 98926-0395. Ed. John Bennett.

910.03 286 US
BLACK MINISTRIES. a. Episcopal Commission for Black Ministries, Executive Council, 815 Second Ave., New York, NY 10017. TEL 212-867-8400.

910.03 US
BLACK PAGES PAMPHLET SERIES. 1973. irreg. $1.50 per copy. Institute of Positive Education, 7524 S. Cottage Grove Ave., Chicago, IL 60619. TEL 312-651-0700. Ed. Haki Madhubuti. bibl. illus. circ. 5,000.

910.03 US
BLACK RESOURCE GUIDE. 1981. a. $30. Black Resource Guide Inc., 501 Oneida Pl., N.W., Washington, DC 20011. Ed. Ben Johnson. bk. rev. circ. 7,000.

960 SA
BLACK REVIEW. irreg. Black Community Programmes, 86 Beatrice St., Durban, South Africa.
Black interests

301.45 US
BLACK STUDIES SERIES. 1972. irreg., latest 1978. $13.50. Edward-Lynne Jones & Associates, Inc., 5517 17th Ave. N.E., Seattle, WA 98105. TEL 206-543-4242. Ed. E.L. Jones. (reprint service avail. from UMI) Indexed: M.L.A.

910.03 US
BLACKS IN THE NEW WORLD. irreg. University of Illinois Press, 54 E. Gregory Dr., Champaign, IL 61820. TEL 217-333-0950. (reprint service avail. from UMI)
Black interests

BOLLETTINO DELL'ATLANTE LINGUISTICO ITALIANO. see LINGUISTICS

BRAVO; the poet's magazine. see LITERATURE — Poetry

296 US
BROWN UNIVERSITY. PROGRAM IN JUDAIC STUDIES. ANNUAL REPORT. 1983. a. free. Brown University, Program in Judaic Studies, 163 George St., Providence, RI 02912-1826. TEL 401-863-3900. Eds. Ernest S. Frerichs, Jacob Neusner. circ. 2,500.

C A A S SPECIAL PUBLICATION SERIES. (Center for Afro-American Studies) see SOCIAL SCIENCES: COMPREHENSIVE WORKS

296 CN ISSN 0576-5528
CANADIAN JEWISH ARCHIVES (NEW SERIES) 1955; N.S 1974. irreg. price varies. Canadian Jewish Congress, 1590 Dr. Penfield Ave., Montreal, Que. H3G 1C5, Canada. TEL 514-931-7531. Ed. David Rome. circ. 500. (back issues avail.)

296 CN ISSN 0824-8907
CANADIAN JEWISH CONGRESS. NATIONAL ARCHIVES NEWSLETTER. (Text in English and French) 1984. s-a. free. Canadian Jewish Congress, 1590 Dr. Penfield Ave., Montreal, Que. H3G 1C5, Canada. TEL 514-931-7531. bibl.

917.306 327 US
CANADO-AMERICAIN. 1900. a. $10 to non-members. ‡ Association Canado-Americaine, 52 Concord St., Box 989, Manchester, NH 03105. TEL 603-625-8577. Ed. Julien Olivier. adv. bk. rev. illus. circ. 22,000.

CENTER FOR HOLOCAUST STUDIES NEWSLETTER. see HISTORY — History Of Europe

CHARIOTEER; an annual review of modern Greek culture. see LITERATURE — Poetry

CHICANO LAW REVIEW. see LAW

917.306 US ISSN 0891-6985
CHICANO PERIODICAL INDEX. 1981. a. $90. University of California, Berkeley, Chicano Studies Library, 3404 Dwinelle Hall, Berkeley, CA 94720. TEL 415-642-3859. Ed. Lillian Castillo-Speed. circ. 500. (back issues avail.)

917.306 US
CHINESE CULTURE ASSOCIATION, MAGAZINE. (Text in Chinese) 1966. a. $5. Chinese Culture Association, Box 1272, Palo Alto, CA 94301. Ed. P.F. Tao. adv. bk. rev. circ. 2,500.

917.306 US
CHINESE HISTORICAL SOCIETY OF AMERICA. ANNIVERSARY BULLETIN. a. $1. Chinese Historical Society of America, 17 Adler Place, off 1140 Grant Ave., San Francisco, CA 94133. TEL 415-391-1188. Ed. Annie Soo.

CHRONICLE OF THE CATHOLIC CHURCH IN LITHUANIA. see RELIGIONS AND THEOLOGY — Roman Catholic

296 IS
CHRONIKA. (Text in Greek) 1984. a. Center for Research on Saloniki Jewry, Rehov Levinsky 68, Tel Aviv, Israel.

972 860 CR
COLECCION MIGUEL SALGUERO. irreg, no.4, 1981. Editorial Universidad Estatal a Distancia, San Jose, Costa Rica.

296 FR
COLLECTION FRANCO-JUDAICA. a. price varies. (Commission Francaise des Archives Juives) Editions Edouart Privat, 14, rue des Arts, 31000 Toulouse, France. Ed. Bernhard Blumenkranz. Indexed: Bull.Signal.

296 US ISSN 0160-7057
CONFERENCE OF PRESIDENTS OF MAJOR AMERICAN JEWISH ORGANIZATIONS. ANNUAL REPORT. 1965. a. free. Conference of Presidents of Major American Jewish Organizations, 515 Park Ave., New York, NY 10022. TEL 212-752-1616. Ed. Richard Cohen. illus.
Former titles: Conference of Presidents of Major American Jewish Organizations. Report; Conference of Presidents of Major American Jewish Organizations. Annual Report (ISSN 0160-7049)

296 US ISSN 0147-1694
CONTEMPORARY JEWRY; a journal of sociological inquiry. 1974. a. $19.95. (Association for the Sociological Study of Jewry) Transaction Periodicals Consortium, Rutgers University, New Brunswick, NJ 08903. TEL 201-932-2280. Ed. Arnold Dashefsky. circ. 1,500. (also avail. in microform from UMI; reprint service avail. from UMI)
Jewish interests

CONTRIBUTION TO THE STUDY OF WORLD HISTORY. see HISTORY

917 US ISSN 0196-7088
CONTRIBUTIONS IN ETHNIC STUDIES. 1980. irreg. price varies. Greenwood Press, Box 5007, 88 Post Rd. West, Westport, CT 06881. TEL 203-226-3571. Ed. Leonard W. Doob.

CORNISH BIOLOGICAL RECORDS. see BIOLOGY

910.03 398 US
CRITICAL STUDIES ON BLACK LIFE AND CULTURE. irreg., vol.24, 1982. Garland Publishing, Inc., 136 Madison Ave., New York, NY 10016.

296 AG
CUADERNOS DE ESTUDIOS JUDIOS. 1973. irreg. Arg.$1.50. Comite Judio Americano, Oficina Sudamericana, Bartolome Mitre 1943, 1-B, Buenos Aires, Argentina. Eds. Natalio Mazar, Santiago E. Kovadloft.
Jewish interests

CULTURES DU CANADA FRANCAIS. see HISTORY — History Of North And South America

970.1 US ISSN 0740-3984
D.C. DIRECTORY. 1979. a. $25. Phelps-Stokes Fund, American Indian Program, 1228 M St., N.W., Washington, DC 20005. TEL 202-638-7066. Ed. Rose Robinson. circ. 1,000.

DEMOKRATIE- UND ARBEITERGESCHICHTE. see HISTORY — History Of Europe

DIOZESE GURK. JAHRBUCH/KRSKE SKOFIJE. ZBORNIK. see RELIGIONS AND THEOLOGY — Roman Catholic

960
DIRECTORY OF AFRIKANAMERICAN RESEARCH CENTERS. biennial. $10. Afram Associates, Inc., U B A Building, 68-72 E. 131 St., Harlem, NY 10037.

DIRECTORY OF DAY SCHOOLS IN THE UNITED STATES AND CANADA. see EDUCATION — Guides To Schools And Colleges

296 US
DIRECTORY OF JEWISH COMMUNITY CENTERS. a. Jewish Welfare Board, 15 E. 26 St., New York, NY 10010. TEL 212-532-4949.

DIRECTORY OF JEWISH RESIDENT SUMMER CAMPS. see SPORTS AND GAMES — Outdoor Life

DIRECTORY OF SPECIAL PROGRAMS FOR MINORITY GROUP MEMBERS; CAREER INFORMATION SERVICES, EMPLOYMENT SKILLS, BANKS, FINANCIAL AID SOURCES. see EDUCATION — Guides To Schools And Colleges

323.4 US
DOCUMENTS OF UKRAINIAN SAMVYDAV. (Text in English) 1975. irreg., no.8, 1981. price varies per no. Smoloskyp Publishers, Box 561, Ellicott City, MD 21043. TEL 301-461-1764. Ed. Bohdan Yasen. circ. 3,000.

DOWNDRAFT. see EDUCATION

E R I C/C U E TRENDS AND ISSUES. see EDUCATION

E R I C CLEARINGHOUSE ON URBAN EDUCATION. DIGEST. see EDUCATION

296 001.3 IS
EAST AND MAGHREB. (Text in Hebrew; summaries in English) a. Bar Ilan Universtiy Press, Ramat Gan 52 100, Israel.

296 US ISSN 0743-7757
ECHAD; a whole global anthology series. 1978. irreg., vol.4, 1982. price varies. Micah Publications, 255 Humphrey St., Marblehead, MA 01945. TEL 617-631-7601. Ed. Roberta Kalechofsky. circ. 1,000.

ECONOMIC IMPACT OF THE NEGRO TRAVELER. see TRAVEL AND TOURISM

296 350 US
ETHICS AND PUBLIC POLICY CENTER. NEWSLETTER. no.17, 1986. irreg. membership. Ethics and Public Policy Center, 1030 Fifteenth St., N.W., Ste. 300, Washington, DC 20005. TEL 202-682-1200.

ETHNIC AMERICAN VOLUNTARY ORGANIZATIONS. see SOCIAL SERVICES AND WELFARE

ETHNIC INTERESTS 503

971.004   CN
ETHNIC DIRECTORY OF CANADA. 1976. irreg. Can.$15. Western Publishers, Box 30193, Sta. "B", Calgary, Alta., Canada. Ed. Vladimir Markotic.

917.306   US   ISSN 0738-1719
ETHNIC INFORMATION SOURCES OF THE U.S. 1976. irreg., 2nd edt., 1983. $165. Gale Research Company, Book Tower, Detroit, MI 48226. TEL 313-961-2242. Eds. Paul Wasserman, Alice Kennington.

910.03   US   ISSN 0736-6086
ETHNIC RACIAL BROTHERHOOD. Abbreviated title: E R B. 1980. irreg., no.153, 1985. free. Black Employees of the Library of Congress, 6100 East View, Kenwood Park, Washington, DC 20817 TEL 301-229-6366. (And: 1412 Arcadia Ave., Capitol Heights, MD 20743) (Co-sponsor: Ethnic Employees of the Library of Congress) Eds. George E. Perry, Howard R.L. Cook. index. (back issues avail.)
     Former titles: Racial Ethnic Brotherhood (ISSN 0731-1133); Ethnic Racial Brotherhood (ISSN 0270-9937)

910.306   US   ISSN 0735-6471
ETHNIC RACIAL REVIEW. Abbreviated title: E R R. 1975. irreg., no.109, 1985. free. Black Employees of the Library of Congress, 6100 East View, Kenwood Park, Washington, DC 20817 TEL 301-229-6366. (And: 1412 Arcadia Ave., Capitol Heights, MD 20743) (Co-sponsor: Ethnic Employees of the Library of Congress) Eds. George E. Perry, Howard R.L. Cook. cum.index 1975-1981. (back issues avail.)

917.306   US
ETHNIC REVIEW. irreg. Hungarian Freedom Fighters (Guardian) World Federation, Inc., Box 441, Gracie Sta., New York, NY 10028.

572   PL   ISSN 0137-4079
ETHNOLOGIA POLONA. (Text in English) vol.2, 1976. a. price varies. (Polska Akademia Nauk, Instytut Historii Kultury Materialnej) Ossolineum Publishing House of the Polish Academy of Sciences, Rynek 9, Wroclaw, Poland. Ed. Maria Frankowska. bk. rev. bibl. illus. circ. 450.

390 955   IR
ETNOLOGIE ET TRADITIONS POPULAIRES DE L'IRAN/MARDON SENSAI VA FARHANGE-E AMME-E IRAN.* (Text in Persian, French, English) 1974. irreg. price varies. Ministry of Culture and Arts, Centre for Iranian Anthropology, Ostad Nejato Uahi St., Teheran 15, Iran. Dir. Mahmood Khaliqi.

910.03   US   ISSN 0733-3323
EXPLORATIONS IN SIGHTS AND SOUNDS. (Supplement to: Exploration in Ethnic Studies) 1981. a. $25. National Association for Ethnic Studies, Inc., c/o Charles C. Irby, Ed., 1861 Rosemount Ave., Claremont, CA 91711-2635. TEL 714-625-8070. adv. bk. rev. circ. 350. (back issues avail.)

910.03   US
FACTS ABOUT BLACKS. a. $3.50. Jeffries and Associates, Inc., 3540 Wilshire Blvd., Los Angeles, CA 90010. TEL 213-388-9638.

914.8   DK   ISSN 0107-6183
FACTSHEET DENMARK. French edition: Documentation Danoise (ISSN 0107-6205); German edition: Daenische Themen (ISSN 0107-6191) 1981. irreg. free. Udenrigsministeriet, Asiatisk Plads 2, DK-1448 Copenhagen K, Denmark. Eds. Preben Hansen, Flemming Andre Larsen. illus.

FLOWER OF THE FOREST BLACK GENEALOGICAL JOURNAL. see GENEALOGY AND HERALDRY

FORD FOUNDATION ANNUAL REPORT. see SOCIAL SCIENCES: COMPREHENSIVE WORKS

296 809   GW   ISSN 0342-0078
FRANKFURTER JUDAISTISCHE BEITRAEGE. 1973. a. price varies. Gesellschaft zur Foerderung Judaistischer Studien e.V., Postfach 970134, 6000 Frankfurt am Main 97, W. Germany (B.R.D.) index. circ. 250.
     Jewish interests

DE FRANSE NEDERLANDEN/PAYS-BAS FRANCAIS. see SCIENCES: COMPREHENSIVE WORKS

917.309   US
FURDEK. vol.24, 1961. a. First Catholic Slovak Union, 3289 E. 55th St., Cleveland, OH 44127. TEL 216-341-3355. Ed. Joseph C. Krajsa. bibl. index.
     Slovak-American interests

296   IS   ISSN 0334-4258
GAL-ED; on the history of the Jews in Poland. (Text in Hebrew; summaries in English) 1973. irreg., vol.9, 1986. $20. Tel Aviv University, Diaspora Research Institute, c/o Publication Department, Tel-Aviv, Israel. Ed. Moshe Mishkinsky. Indexed: Hist.Abstr. Amer.Hist.& Life.
     Jewish interests

917.1   CN   ISSN 0316-8603
GERMAN-CANADIAN YEARBOOK/ DEUTSCHKANADISCHES JAHRBUCH. (Text in English and German) 1973. a. Can.$16. Historical Society of Mecklenburg Upper Canada, Box 193, Station K, Toronto, Ont. M6M 2X9, Canada. Eds. Gerhard Friesen, Karin Guerttler. bk. rev. illus. circ. 2,000. Indexed: M.L.A. Amer.Bibl.Slavic & E.Eur.Stud.
     German-Canadian interests

GLENBOW-ALBERTA INSTITUTE. OCCASIONAL PAPER. see HISTORY — History Of North And South America

059.8 281.9   UK   ISSN 0265-6922
GREEK ORTHODOX CALENDAR. 1983. a. £5. Kyriakos H. Metaxas, Ed. & Pub., 55 Westbourne Grove, London W2 4UA, England. adv. circ. 12,000.

GREENWOOD ENCYCLOPEDIA OF BLACK MUSIC. see MUSIC

910.03   US
GUIDE TO AFRO-AMERICAN RESOURCES. 1973. biennial. $50. Black Resources Information Coordinating Services, Inc., 614 Howard Ave., Box 6353, Tallahassee, FL 32304. Ed. Emily A. Copeland.
     Formerly: Guide to Minority Resources.
     Black interests

914   BE
GUIDE TOURISTIQUE EUROPEEN POUR ISRAELITES/EUROPEAN TRAVEL GUIDE FOR JEWS. (Text in English and French) 1961. a. 250 Fr. Belgisch Israelitisch Weekblad, Pelikaanstraat 104-108, Antwerp, Belgium. (Co-sponsor: Belgian National Tourist Office) adv. illus.

296   US
HARVARD JUDAIC MONOGRAPHS. 1975. irreg., no.5, 1985. price varies. Center for Jewish Studies, Cambridge, MA 02138 (Distr. by: Harvard University Press, 79 Garden St., Cambridge, MA 02138)

917.306   US   ISSN 0362-8078
HARVARD UKRAINIAN RESEARCH INSTITUTE. MINUTES OF THE SEMINAR IN UKRAINIAN STUDIES. a. $3 to individuals; institutions $5. (Harvard University, Ukrainian Research Institute) Harvard Ukrainian Research Institute, 1581-1583 Massachusetts Ave., Cambridge, MA 02138. circ. 300. (back issues avail.)

296 956.94   US   ISSN 0360-9049
HEBREW UNION COLLEGE ANNUAL. (Text in English, French, German and Hebrew) 1924. a. $20. Hebrew Union College-Jewish Institute of Religion, 3101 Clifton Ave., Cincinnati, OH 45220 TEL 513-221-1875. (Distr. by: Ktav Publishing House, Inc., 900 Jefferson St., Hoboken, NJ 07030) Eds. Sheldon H. Blank, Herbert H. Paper. cum.index 1924-1982 in 1982 vol. circ. 2,500. (also avail. in microfilm; back issues avail.) Indexed: Hist.Abstr. Old Test.Abstr. Amer.Hist.& Life. CERDIC. New Test.Abstr. Rel.Ind.One. Rel.& Theol.Abstr.
     Supersedes: Journal of Jewish Lore and Philosophy (ISSN 0190-4361)

296   US   ISSN 0275-9993
HEBREW UNION COLLEGE ANNUAL SUPPLEMENTS. 1976. irreg. Hebrew Union College-Jewish Institute of Religion, 3101 Clifton Ave., Cincinnati, OH 45220 TEL 513-221-1875. (Dist. by: Ktav Publishing House, Inc., 900 Jefferson St., Hoboken, NJ 07030) Eds. Sheldon H. Blank, Herbert H. Paper. Indexed: Old Test.Abstr.

HOLOCAUST STUDIES ANNUAL. see HISTORY — History Of Europe

296   UK
I C J C NEWSLETTER. 1970. irreg. £8($20) International Council of Jews from Czechoslovakia, 31 Craven St., London WC2N 5NP, England. Ed. K. Baum. bk. rev. bibl. circ. 2,500.
     Jewish interests

296 323.4   UK   ISSN 0257-6406
I J A. RESEARCH REPORTS. 1968. irreg., approx. 20/yr. £25($90) Institute of Jewish Affairs, 11 Hertford St., London W1Y 7DX, England. (Co-sponsor: World Jewish Congress) Ed. A. Lerman. abstr. circ. 1,500. Indexed: HR Rep.

I W G I A DOCUMENTS; documentation of oppression of ethnic groups in various countries. (International Work Group for Indigenous Affairs) see ANTHROPOLOGY

I W G I A NEWSLETTER. (International Work Group for Indigenous Affairs) see ANTHROPOLOGY

IDAHO. STATE SUPERINTENDENT OF PUBLIC INSTRUCTION. ANNUAL REPORT. STATE OF IDAHO JOHNSON-O'MALLEY PROGRAM. see EDUCATION

IMMIGRANT COMMUNITIES & ETHNIC MINORITIES IN THE UNITED STATES & CANADA. see POPULATION STUDIES

INDEX TO REPRODUCTIONS IN ART PERIODICALS. see ABSTRACTING AND INDEXING SERVICES

INDIAN BOOK REVIEW DIGEST. see PUBLISHING AND BOOK TRADE

INDIAN HISTORY AND CULTURE. SERIES. see HISTORY — History Of Asia

296   IS
INDIAN JEWRY. 1985. a. P.O. Box 781, Haifa, Israel. Ed. Ben-Eliah.

914.106   UK
INSTITUTE OF CORNISH STUDIES. SPECIAL BIBLIOGRAPHY. no.2, 1973. irreg. price varies. Institute of Cornish Studies, Trevenson House, Pool, Redruth, Cornwall TR15 3RE, England. Ed. Charles Thomas. circ. 300.

910.03   US
INSTITUTE OF THE BLACK WORLD. BLACK PAPER. vol.2, 1970. irreg. $3. Institute of the Black World, Distribution Department, 87 Chestnut St. S.W., Atlanta, GA 30314. TEL 404-523-7805.
     Black interests

910.03   US
INSTITUTE OF THE BLACK WORLD. OCCASIONAL PAPER SERIES. irreg. Institute of the Black World, 87 Chestnut St. S.W., Atlanta, GA 30314. TEL 404-523-7805.

301.1   US
INSTITUTE ON PLURALISM AND GROUP IDENTITY. WORKING PAPER SERIES. no.17, 1976. irreg. $1.25 per no. Institute on Pluralism and Group Identity, 165 E. 56th St., New York, NY 10022. (Affiliate: American Jewish Committee)

914.467   SP   ISSN 0211-2329
INSTITUTO DE ESTUDIOS GERUNDENSES. ANALES. (Text in Spanish and Catalan) 1946. a. 500 ptas.($10) Instituto de Estudios Gerundenses, Forca 27, Gerona, Spain. bk. rev. (back issues avail.) Indexed: Hist.Abstr. Amer.Hist.& Life.

914.467   SP   ISSN 0211-2477
INSTITUTO DE ESTUDIOS GERUNDENSES. SERIE MONOGRAFICA. 1947. irreg. price varies. Instituto de Estudios Gerundenses, Forca 27, Gerona, Spain.

ETHNIC INTERESTS

914.106 058.7   SW   ISSN 0280-8773
INVANDRARFRAAGOR. AARSBOK. 1983. a. price varies. Immigrant Institutet, Kvarngatan 16, S-502 44 Boras, Sweden. Ed. Miguel Benito. adv.

052   UK   ISSN 0260-650X
IRISH IN BRITAIN DIRECTORY. 1979. irreg. £1. Brent Irish Advisory Service, 76 Salusbury Rd., London, NW6 6NY, England. Ed. Donal Mac Craith. adv. circ. 5,000.

296   GW
ISRAELITISCHE KULTUSGEMEINDE FUERTH. a. Israelitische Kultusgemeinde Fuerth, Blumenstr. 31, 8510 Fuerth, W. Germany (B.R.D.) circ. 5,000.

839.5 395   IT
ISTITUTO UNIVERSITARIO ORIENTALE. ANNALI; studi Nederlandesi, studi Nordici. (Text in English, French and Italian) 1975. a. Istituto Universitario Orientale, Piazza San Giovanni, Maggiore 30, 80134 Naples, Italy. Ed. Ludovica Koch. circ. 600.

917.306   US   ISSN 0579-2290
ITTIHAD. 1963. a. $7 to students; others $12; institutions $20. Islamic Society of North America, Box 38, Plainfield, IN 46168. TEL 317-839-8197. adv. bk. rev. circ. 8,000. (also avail. in microfiche)

296   IS   ISSN 0334-4096
JERUSALEM LETTER. (Text in English) 1977. irreg. Jerusalem Center for Public Affairs, 21 Arlozorov St., Jerusalem 92 181, Israel.

917.309   US   ISSN 0085-2368
JEWISH BOSTON; guide to Jewish life in the greater Boston Jewish community with a Massachusetts supplement. 1969. biennial? $2.50. Jewish Boston, Inc., 233 Bay State Road, Boston, MA 02215. Eds. Morey Schapira, Chaim Casper. adv. bk. rev. illus. circ. 10,000.
Formerly: Jewish Boston and New England Jewry.

296   US   ISSN 0191-3034
JEWISH CIVILIZATION: ESSAYS AND STUDIES. 1980. a. price varies. Reconstructionist Press, Church Rd. and Greenwood Ave., Wyncote, PA 19095. TEL 215-576-0800. Ed. Ronald A. Brauner. circ. 1,000. Indexed: Ind.Jew.Per.

296   US
JEWISH COMMUNITY HANDBOOK. a. Wisconsin Jewish Chronicle, 1360 N. Prospect Ave., Milwaukee, WI 53202.

296   US
JEWISH HERITAGE LIBRARIES. ETHNIC STUDIES INSTITUTE. YEAR END REPORT. a. Queens College of the City University of New York, Ethnic Studies Project, 65-30 Kissena Blvd., Flushing, NY 11367. TEL 718-520-7000.

296   US
JEWISH HISTORICAL SOCIETY OF NEW YORK. PUBLICATIONS. 1976. irreg., no.4, 1987. Jewish Historical Society of New York, 8 W. 70th St., New York, NY 10023. TEL 212-873-0300.

917.1 296   CN   ISSN 0317-1655
JEWISH HISTORICAL SOCIETY OF WESTERN CANADA. ANNUAL PUBLICATION. (Text in English; summaries in Yiddish) 1970. a. Jewish Historical Society of Western Canada, 365 Hargrave St., Rm. 406, Winnipeg, Man. R3B 2K3, Canada. TEL 204-942-4822.

JEWISH LANGUAGE REVIEW. see *LINGUISTICS*

JEWISH LAW ANNUAL SUPPLEMENTS. see *LAW*

JEWISH PROCLAIMER. see *RELIGIONS AND THEOLOGY — Judaic*

296   US
JEWISH STUDIES. 1986. irreg., vol.2 $39.95 no per. Edwin Mellen Press, Box 450, Lewiston, NY 14092.

296   DK   ISSN 0107-7333
JOEDISK PLEVY. 1981. irreg. free for members of Det Moesaiske Troessamfund. Dan Melchior, Enighedsvej 10, 2920 Charlottenlund, Denmark. illus.

572   CL
JUDAICA IBEROAMERICANA. 1973. irreg., latest no.6, 1985. Universidad de Chile, Centro de Estudios de Cultura Judaica, Miguel Claro 182, Casilla 13583, Santiago, Chile. circ. 1,000. (back issues avail.)

917.106   CN
KALENDAR-AL'MANAKH NOVOHO SHLIAKHU/NEW PATHWAY ALMANAC. (Text in Ukrainian) 1986. a. Can.$10($10) (Ukrainian National Federation of Canada) New Pathway, 295 College St., Toronto, Ont. M5T 1S2, Canada. TEL 416-925-6764. Ed. Wasyl Veryha. adv. circ. 1,500.

KELTICA; the Inter-Celtic journal. see *HISTORY — History Of Europe*

KISWAHILI. see *LINGUISTICS*

296   US
KOSHER DIRECTORY.* a. Union of Orthodox Jewish Congregations of America, Kashruth Division, 70 W. 36th St., 9th Fl., New York, NY 10018-8002. Ed. Goldie Feinberg. adv.

055.1   IT
LADINIA; sfoi cultural dai Ladins dles Dolomites. (Text in German, Italian, Ladin) 1977. a. L.20000. Istitut Ladin "Micura de Ru", 39030 San Martino in Badia, Italy. (back issues avail.)

LATIN AMERICAN JEWISH STUDIES NEWSLETTER. see *GEOGRAPHY*

917.306   US   ISSN 0093-8920
LATVIJA SODIEN. 1972. a. $10 per no. World Federation of Free Latvians, 400 Hurley Ave., Box 4016, Rockville, MD 20850. TEL 301-340-7646. Ed. Dr. I. Spilners. bk. rev. illus. circ. 2,000.

LATVJU MAKSLA. see *ART*

LAW & INEQUALITY; a journal of theory and practice. see *LAW*

960   UK
LIBRARY OF PEASANT STUDIES. 1975. irreg., vol.4, 1977. price varies. Frank Cass & Co. Ltd., Gainsborough House, 11 Gainsborough Rd., London E11 1RS, England (Dist. by: International Scholarly Book Services, 10300 S.W. Allen Blvd., Beaverton, OR 97005) bibl. index.

971.004   CN   ISSN 0317-6983
MALTESE DIRECTORY: CANADA, UNITED STATES. 1954. irreg. free. Malta Service Bureau, Box 826 Station B, Ottawa, Ont. K1P 5P9, Canada. Ed. George Bonavia. bk. rev. circ. 1,000.

377   IS   ISSN 0543-1786
MA'YANOT. 1952. irreg., latest issue no.4. price varies. World Zionist Organization, P.O. Box 92, Jerusalem, Israel.

970.1   US
MEETING GROUND. 1973. a. free. Newberry Library, D'Arcy McNickle Center for the History of the American Indian, 60 W. Walton St., Chicago, IL 60610. TEL 312-943-9090. Ed. Colin Calloway. bk. rev. circ. 2,500.

917.206   US
MEXICAN AMERICAN MONOGRAPH SERIES. 1975. irreg. price varies. University of Texas at Austin, Center for Mexican American Studies, Austin, TX 78712. TEL 512-471-3434. Ed.Bd. circ. 1,000.

296   IS   ISSN 0334-4150
MICHAEL; on the history of the Jews in the Diaspora. (Text in English, French, German, Hebrew and Italian) 1972. irreg., vol.10,1985. $25 per vol. Tel-Aviv University, Diaspora Research Institute, Sales Division, Tel Aviv, Israel. Ed.Bd. Indexed: Hist.Abstr. Ind.Heb.Per. Amer.Hist.& Life.

917.306   US
MINORITY ORGANIZATIONS: A NATIONAL DIRECTORY. 1978. irreg., latest 2nd edt. $30. Garrett Park Press, Box 190F, Garrett Park, MD 20896. TEL 301-946-2553. Ed. Katherine W. Cole.

914.706   US   ISSN 0110-0068
MIORITA; a journal of romanian studies. 1973. irreg., approx. 1/yr. $6 to individuals; institutions $8. New Zealand Romanian Cultural Association, Department of Foreign Languages, Literature and Linguistics, c/o Charles M. Carlton, Dewey 482, University of Rochester, Rochester, NY 14627. TEL 716-275-4258. Eds. C.M. Carlton, N. Simms. bk. rev. circ. 150 (controlled) Indexed: M.L.A.

296   IS   ISSN 0542-9943
MISHUA. 1973. a. Yad Lechavrei Hatnvot Hatzioniot Beshoah Ubemeri, 48 King George St., Tel Aviv, Israel.

MUZEUM ARCHEOLOGICZNE I ETNOGRAFICZNE, LODZ. PRACE I MATERIALY. SERIA ETNOGRAFICZNA. see *ANTHROPOLOGY*

NARODNA UMJETNOST. see *FOLKLORE*

917.306   US
NATIONAL DIRECTORY OF LATIN AMERICANISTS. 1965. irreg., latest 1985. $34. U.S. Library of Congress, Hispanic Division, Washington, DC 20540 TEL 202-287-5400. (Subscr. to: Supt. of Documents, Washington, DC 20402) Ed. Inge Maria Harman.

NATIONAL INDIAN COUNCIL ON AGING. see *GERONTOLOGY AND GERIATRICS*

970   US   ISSN 0196-4240
NATIVE SELF-SUFFICIENCY. 1978. irreg. (4-5/yr.) $6 to individuals; institutions $15. Seventh Generation Fund, Box 10, Forestville, CA 95436. TEL 707-887-1559. Ed. Victoria Bomberry. bk. rev. illus. circ. 2,000. (tabloid format; back issues avail.) Indexed: Alt.Press Ind.
American Indian interests

NATURHISTORISCHE GESELLSCHAFT NUERNBERG. ABHANDLUNGEN. see *ARCHAEOLOGY*

908   US
NAUKOVE TOVARYSTVO IMENI SHEVCHENKA. UKRAINS'KYI ARKHIV/ UKRAINIAN ARCHIVES. (Text in Ukrainian; summaries in English) no.16, 1960. irreg. price varies. Shevchenko Scientific Society, 63 Fourth Ave., New York.

917.306   US
NAUKOVE TOVARYSTVO IMENI SHEVCHENKA. ZAPYSKY. MITTEILUNGEN/ MEMOIRS. (Text in Ukrainian; summaries in English) 1893. irreg. price varies. Shevchenko Scientific Society, 63 Fourth Ave., New York, NY 10003. TEL 202-254-5130.

296   CN   ISSN 0705-7822
NAYER DOR/NEW GENERATION; magazine en Yiddish pour les jeunes et les adultes. (Text in Yiddish; summaries in English) 1978. irreg. Can.$2 per no. David Botwinik, Ed.& Pub., 5775 Wentworth, Cote St. Luc, Montreal, Que. H4W 2S3, Canada. circ. 1,000.
Jewish interests

353.9   US   ISSN 0360-683X
NEBRASKA. INDIAN COMMISSION. REPORT.* 1972. irreg. Indian Commission, Box 19153, Denver, CO 80219-0153. TEL 402-471-2757. illus. circ. 100. Key Title: Report of the Nebraska Indian Commission.

910.03   US
NEW ENGLAND JOURNAL OF BLACK STUDIES. 1981. a. $15. (National Council for Black Studies, New England Regional Conference) University of Rhode Island, African and Afro-American Studies Program, c/o Melvin K. Hendrix, Ed., Box GE, Hampshire College, Amherst, MA 01002. adv. bk. rev.

960   US
NORTHEAST AFRICAN MONOGRAPH SERIES. irreg., no.10, 1981. price varies. Michigan State University, African Studies Center, Committee on Northeast African Studies, 100 Center for International Programs, East Lansing, MI 48824. TEL 517-353-1700.
Formerly: Ethiopian Monograph Series.

390 YU
NOVA DUMKA. 1971. irreg. Sojuz Rusinoh i Ukraincoh Gorvatskej, Pionirske Naselene 10, Vukovar, Yugoslavia. Ed. Vladd Kostelnik.

O'CASEY ANNUAL. see *LITERATURE*

OKYEAME; Ghana's literary magazine. see *LITERATURE*

296 US
OSCAR ISRAELOWITZ'S GUIDE TO JEWISH NEW YORK CITY. 1983. a. $8.50. Oscar Israelowitz, Pub., Box 228, Brooklyn, NY 11229. adv. bibl. circ. 5,000.

971.3 CN ISSN 0315-0771
OTTAWA ETHNIC GROUPS DIRECTORY. 1971. a. free to qualified personnel. Ottawa-Carleton Immigrant Services Organization, 425 Gloucester St., Ottawa, Ont. K1R 5E9, Canada. TEL 613-238-4256. Ed. G. Bonavia. circ. 1,000.

OVERTURE; a Black theatre annual. see *THEATER*

914.706 US
P A C NEWSLETTER. 1945. irreg. Polish American Congress Charitable Foundation, Inc., 1200 N. Ashland Ave., Chicago, IL 60622. TEL 312-252-5838. Ed. Kazimierz Lukomski. circ. 10,000. (back issues avail.)

LA PALABRA. see *LITERATURE*

970.1 US
PAN-AMERICAN INDIAN ASSOCIATION NEWS. 1984. irreg. $12. (Pan-American Indian Association & Adopted Tribal Peoples) Chief Piercing Eyes, Ed.& Pub., Box 244, Nocatee, FL 33864-0244. TEL 813-494-6930. adv. bk. rev. circ. 3,000.
Formerly (until May 1985): Tribal Advisor.

PILIPINAS; an interdisciplinary scholarly journal of Philippine studies. see *HISTORY — History Of Asia*

296 UK ISSN 0268-1056
POLIN; a journal of Polish-Jewish studies. 1986. a. £33.50($49.50) Basil Blackwell Ltd., 108 Cowley Rd., Oxford OX4 1JF, England. Ed. Antony Polonsky. adv. bk. rev. (also avail. in microform)

PROSPECTS; annual journal of American cultural studies. see *HISTORY — History Of North And South America*

READINGS IN LONG ISLAND ARCHAEOLOGY AND ETHNOHISTORY. see *HISTORY — History Of North And South America*

970.1 US
REFERENCE ENCYCLOPEDIA OF THE AMERICAN INDIAN. triennial. $90 per set. Todd Publications, Box 92, Lenox Hill Sta., New York, NY 10021. Ed. Barry Klein.

917.309 US ISSN 0034-3269
DER REGGEBOGE. 1967. irreg. membership. ‡ Pennsylvania German Society, Box 97, Bindsboro, PA 19508. Ed. Frederick S. Weiser. bk. rev. illus. circ. 2,000.
Pennsylvania German interests

960 US ISSN 0360-7410
RENAISSANCE TWO; JOURNAL OF AFRO-AMERICAN STUDIES. 1972. a. $3.50. Yale University, Afro-American Cultural Center, 211 Park St., New Haven, CT 06520. TEL 203-436-8700. adv. bk. rev. illus. circ. 10,000. Key Title: Renaissance 2.
African studies

970.1 US
RENEGADE. 1968. irreg. $5. Survival of American Indians Association, Box 719, Tacoma, WA 98401. TEL 206-456-2567. Ed. H.L. Adams. illus. stat. circ. 8,000. (looseleaf format)

052 930.1 UK
REVIEW OF SCOTTISH CULTURE. Cover title: R O S C. 1984. a. £6. (National Museum of Scotland) John Donald Publishers Ltd., 138 St. Stephen St., Edinburgh EH3 5AA, Scotland. Ed. Alexander Fenton. bk. rev. circ. 1,000. (back issues avail.)

296 US ISSN 0556-8609
RHODE ISLAND JEWISH HISTORICAL NOTES. 1954. a. $10. ‡ Rhode Island Jewish Historical Association, 130 Sessions St., Providence, RI 02906. TEL 401-331-1360. Ed. Michael Fink. bk. rev. bibl. charts. illus. stat. cum.index every 4 yrs. circ. 550. (processed) Indexed: Hist.Abstr. Amer.Hist. & Life.

353.9 US ISSN 0093-9951
ROSTER OF BLACK ELECTED OFFICIALS IN THE SOUTH.* irreg. Voter Education Project Inc., 604 Beckwith St., S.W., Atlanta, GA 30314-4113.

ROYAL ONTARIO MUSEUM. ETHNOGRAPHY MONOGRAPH. see *ANTHROPOLOGY*

947 US
RUSSIAN ARCHIVAL SERIES. 1982. irreg. $36 per issue. (Columbia University, Harriman Institute) Oriental Research Partners, Box 158, Newtonville, MA 02160.

917.106 971 CN
SCANDINAVIAN HERITAGE. 1983. irreg. (1-2/yr.) Can.$12.50 per issue. Dundurn Press Ltd., Box 245, Station F, Toronto, Ont. M4Y 2L5, Canada. Ed. J.K. Howard. index.

917.306 US ISSN 0273-0693
SCOTIA; American-Canadian journal of Scottish studies. 1977. a. $7.50. Old Dominion University, Institute on Scottish Studies, Arts and Letters Building, Norfolk, VA 23508. TEL 804-440-3179. Ed. Charles H. Haws. adv. bk. rev. circ. 250.
Supersedes (1973-1976): Conference on Scottish Studies. Proceedings.

SEMANA INTERNACIONAL DE ANTROPOLOGIA VASCA. ACTAS. see *ANTHROPOLOGY*

892.49 956.94 US
SEPHARDIC SCHOLAR. 1973. a. $10. (American Society of Sephardic Studies) Yeshiva University, Sephardic Studies Program, 500 W. 185 St., New York, NY 10033. TEL 212-960-5277. Ed. R. Dalven. bk. rev. circ. 5,000.
Formerly: American Society of Sephardic Studies Series.

918.8 GE
SERBSKA PRATYJA. (Text in Serbian) 1971. a. VEB Domowina Verlag, Tuchmacherstr. 27, 86 Bautzen, E. Germany (D.D.R.) illus.

SERIE DE VOCABULARIOS Y DICCIONARIOS INDIGENAS "MARIANO SILVA Y ACEVES". see *LINGUISTICS*

917.2 810 US ISSN 0190-3640
SEZ; a multi-racial journal of poetry & people's culture. (Text in English and Spanish) 1978. irreg. $7 to individuals; institutions $8.50. Shadow Press, U.S.A., Box 8803, Minneapolis, MN 55408. TEL 612-822-3488. Ed. Jim Dochniak. adv. bk. rev. bibl. illus. circ. 1,500. (back issues avail.)

296 IS
SHVUT; Jewish problems in the USSR and Eastern Europe. (Text in Hebrew; summaries in English) 1973. a. $6. ‡ Tel-Aviv University, Diaspora Research Institute, Sales Division, Tel Aviv, Israel. Ed. M. Minc. bk. rev. circ. 1,500. Indexed: Ind.Heb.Per.

296 US
SIMON WIESENTHAL CENTER ANNUAL. 1984. a. $30. Kraus International Publications (Subsidiary of: Kraus-Thomson Organization Ltd.) One Water St., White Plains, NY 10601. TEL 914-761-9600. Eds. Henry Freidlander, Sybil Milton.
Jewish interests

917.309 US ISSN 0037-6914
SLOVAK PRESS DIGEST. 1968. irreg. free. ‡ Slovak-American Cultural Center, Box 291, New York, NY 10008. TEL 914-428-0703. Ed. Jozef Ihnat. bk. rev. abstr. bibl. stat. tr.lit. circ. 500. (looseleaf format)

943.7 US ISSN 0583-5623
SLOVAKIA. 1951. a. $6 softbound; hardbound $8. Slovak League of America, 700 Penfield Ave., Havertown, PA 19083. Ed. Mark Stolarik. bk. rev. bibl. circ. 1,500. (also avail. in microform from UMI; reprint service avail. from UMI) Indexed: M.L.A. Amer.Bibl.Slavic & E.Eur.Stud.

SLOVANSKE STUDIE. see *HISTORY — History Of Europe*

SOCIEDAD DE ESTUDIOS VASCOS. CUADERNOS DE SECCION. ANTROPOLOGIA-ETNOGRAFIA. see *ANTHROPOLOGY*

SPIEGEL LECTURES IN EUROPEAN JEWISH HISTORY. see *HISTORY — History Of Europe*

910.03 US
STATUS OF BLACK NEW YORK REPORT. a. New York Urban League, 218 W. 40th St., New York, NY 10018. TEL 212-730-5200.

970.1 342 CN ISSN 0226-3491
STUDIES IN ABORIGINAL RIGHTS. 1980. irreg., latest no.9, 1986. price varies. University of Saskatchewan, Native Law Centre, Saskatoon, Sask. S7N 0W0, Canada. TEL 306-966-6189. Ed. Zandra MacEachern.

STUDIES IN AMERICAN JEWISH LITERATURE. see *LITERATURE*

301.45 US
STUDIES IN AMERICAN NEGRO LIFE.* irreg., latest no.35, 1975. price varies. Atheneum Publishers, 115 Fifth Ave., New York, NY 10003. Ed. August Meier.

STUDIES IN BLACK AMERICAN LITERATURE. see *LITERATURE*

296 US ISSN 0740-8625
STUDIES IN CONTEMPORARY JEWRY.* 1984. a. (Institute of Contemporary Jewry) Oxford University, 200 Madison Ave., New York, NY 10016. TEL 212-679-7300. Ed.Bd. bk. rev. bibl. (back issues avail.)

917.306 940 US
STUDIES IN GERMAN THOUGHT AND HISTORY. vol.3, 1987. irreg. $39.95 per no. Edwin Mellen Press, Box 450, Lewiston, NY 14092.

296 309 US ISSN 0734-4937
STUDIES OF ISRAELI SOCIETY. 1981. irreg. $29.95 cloth; paper $14.95. (Israel Sociological Society) Transaction Books, Rutgers University, New Brunswick, NJ 08903. Ed. Ernest Krausz.

970.1 US
SUN TRACKS; an American Indian literary series. 1971. irreg., no.14, 1986. price varies. (University of Arizona, Department of English) University of Arizona Press, 1615 E. Speedway, Tucson, AZ 85721. TEL 602-621-1441. Ed. Larry Evers. circ. 2,000.

TALLADEGAN. see *COLLEGE AND ALUMNI*

THEATA. see *ANTHROPOLOGY*

TIKUFAT HASHOAH. see *HISTORY — History Of Europe*

TOLEDOT; the journal of Jewish genealogy. see *GENEALOGY AND HERALDRY*

TRY US; national minority business directory. see *BUSINESS AND ECONOMICS*

053.1 GW
TUDUV-STUDIE. REIHE KULTURWISSENSCHAFTEN. 1974. irreg. price varies. Tuduv Verlagsgesellschaft mbH, Gabelsbergerstr. 15, 8000 Munich 2, W. Germany (B.R.D.)

947 US ISSN 0503-1001
UKRAINIAN ACADEMY OF ARTS AND SCIENCES IN THE U S. ANNALS. 1951. irreg., approx. a. $20 per no. Ukrainian Academy of Arts and Sciences in the U S, Inc., c/o Dr. William Omelchenko, 206 W. 100th St., New York, NY 10025. TEL 212-222-1866. bk. rev. circ. 1,000. Indexed: Biol.Abstr. Hist.Abstr. Amer.Bibl.Slavic & E.Eur.Stud. Amer.Hist.& Life.

UKRAINIAN ART DIGEST/NOTATKZ Z MISTETSTBA. see *ART*

UNIVERSITE DE BORDEAUX II. CAHIERS ETHNOLOGIQUES. see *SOCIOLOGY*

UNIVERSITY OF ABERDEEN. AFRICAN STUDIES GROUP. BULLETIN. see *HISTORY — History Of Africa*

UNIVERSITY OF ABERDEEN. AFRICAN STUDIES GROUP. OCCASIONAL PUBLICATIONS. see *HISTORY — History Of Africa*

UNIVERSITY OF NEW MEXICO. LATIN AMERICAN INSTITUTE. RESEARCH PAPER SERIES. see *SOCIAL SCIENCES: COMPREHENSIVE WORKS*

943   GW
VEREIN FUER NIEDERSAECHSISCHES VOLKSTUM. BREMER HEIMATBUND. MITTEILUNGEN. 1925. irreg. membership. Verein fuer Niedersaechsisches Volkstum, Erlanstr. 76, 2800 Bremen 1, W. Germany (B.R.D.) Eds. Karl Dillschneider, Wilhelm Klooke. adv. bk. rev. circ. 1, 000.
 Formerly: Verein fuer Niedersaechsisches Volkstum. Mitteilungen.

057.9   CN
VILNE SLOVO ANNUAL. (Text in Ukrainian) 1961. biennial. $5.50. Toronto Free Press Publications Ltd., 196 Bathurst St., Toronto, Ont. M5T 2R8, Canada. TEL 416-368-7282. Ed. Dr. Stephen Rosocha. adv. abstr. bibl. charts. illus. stat. circ. 5,000(controlled)

296   CN   ISSN 0704-5352
VOIX SEPHARADE. 17. bi-m. Can.$20.
Communaute Sepharade du Quebec, 4735 Chemin de la Cote Ste Catherine, Montreal, Que. H3W 1M1, Canada. adv. bk. rev. circ. 7,000.

948.406   US   ISSN 0742-7018
W I T S. (Wisconsin Introduction to Scandinavia) 1982. irreg. $2.50 per no. University of Wisconsin, Department of Scandinavian Studies, 1306 Van Hise Hall, Madison, WI 53706. TEL 608-262-2090. Eds. Harald S. Naess, Niels Ingwersen. circ. 100. (back issues avail.)

WHO'S WHO IN AMERICAN JEWRY (LOS ANGELES) see *BIOGRAPHY*

WILCOX REPORT NEWSLETTER. see *POLITICAL SCIENCE*

970.1   US
WILDFIRE; a "plus" network magazine. 1966. q. $5. Bear Tribe Medicine Society, Box 9167, Spokane, WA 99209. TEL 509-258-7755. Ed. Matthew Ryan. adv. bk. rev. circ. 10,000. (also avail. in microfilm from MCA; back issues avail.)
 Formerly (until 1984): Many Smokes (ISSN 0025-2670)

941.5   US   ISSN 0732-2674
WORKING PAPERS IN IRISH STUDIES. 1983. irreg., approx. 6/yr. $12. Northeastern University, Irish Studies Program, 118 Cushing Hall, 360 Huntington Ave., Boston, MA 02115. TEL 617-437-2907. Ed. James E. Doan. index. circ. 60. (back issues avail.)

296   US
WORKING PAPERS IN YIDDISH AND EAST EUROPEAN JEWISH STUDIES/IN GANG FUN ARBET: YIDISH UN MIZRAKH EYROPEISHE YIDISHE SHTUDIES. (Text in various languages) 1974. irreg. $12 to institutions. YIVO Institute for Jewish Research, Max Weinreich Center for Advanced Jewish Studies, 1048 Fifth Ave., New York, NY 10028. TEL 212-535-6700. Ed. Joan Bratkowsky. circ. 125. Indexed: M.L.A.

296   IS   ISSN 0334-5904
YEARBOOK FOR JEWISH COMMUNITIES AND ORGANIZATIONS. (Text in English) 1970. a. P.O. Box 5086, Ramat Gan 52 150, Israel. Ed. Zvi Porath-Noy.

296   US
YESHIVA UNIVERSITY SEPHARDIC BULLETIN. 1973. a. free. Yeshiva University, Sephardic Studies Program, 500 W. 185th St., New York, NY 10033. TEL 212-960-5277. Ed. Rabbi M. Mitchell Serels. circ. 24,000.

YIDDISH LITERARY AND LINGUISTIC PERIODICALS AND MISCELLANIES; a selective annotated bibliography. see *LINGUISTICS*

296   IS
ZION. (Text in Russian) irreg. Israel Public Council for Soviet Jewry, Rehov Bak 1, Tel-Aviv, Israel. TEL 03-338267. Ed. Rafael Nudelman.
 Jewish interests

ETHNIC INTERESTS — Abstracting, Bibliographies, Statistics

970.1   US
AMERICAN INDIAN BIBLIOGRAPHIC SERIES. 1977. a. University of California, Los Angeles, American Indian Studies Center, 405 Hilgard Ave., 3220 Campbell Hall, Los Angeles, CA 90024. Eds. G. Edward Evans, Jeffrey Clark. circ. 500.

910.03 016   US   ISSN 0360-2710
BIBLIOGRAPHIC GUIDE TO BLACK STUDIES. 1975. a. G. K. Hall & Co., 70 Lincoln St., Boston, MA 02111. TEL 617-423-3990.

016   US
BURT FRANKLIN ETHNIC BIBLIOGRAPHICAL GUIDES. vol.2, 1977. irreg. price varies. Burt Franklin & Co., Inc., 235 E. 44th St., New York, NY 10017. TEL 212-687-5250. Eds. Francesco Cordasco, William W. Brickman.

980.2   US
HISPANIC FOCUS. 1982. irreg. free. U.S. Library of Congress, Hispanic Division, Washington, DC 20540. TEL 202-287-5400. circ. 1,000.

029   US   ISSN 0161-8245
INDEX TO PERIODICAL ARTICLES BY AND ABOUT BLACKS. 1960. a. $79.50. (Central State University, Hallie Q. Brown Memorial Library) G. K. Hall & Co., 70 Lincoln St., Boston, MA 02111. TEL 617-423-3990. (Co-sponsor: Schomburg Collection of Negro Literature and History)
 Former titles: Index to Periodical Articles by and About Negroes (ISSN 0073-5973) & Index to Selected Periodicals.

016 910.03   US
MINORITY INFORMATION TRADE ANNUAL; publishers and producers lists of Afro-American material. 1977. a? $35. Black Resources Information Coordinating Services, Inc., 614 Howard Ave., Box 6353, Tallahassee, FL 32304. Ed. Emily A. Copeland.

016.342   US
NATIONAL INDIAN LAW LIBRARY. CATALOGUE; an index to Indian legal materials and resources. 1973/74. every 5 yrs. $75. ‡ National Indian Law Library, Native American Rights Fund, 1506 Broadway, Boulder, CO 80302-6296. TEL 303-447-8760. bibl. circ. 1,000.
 Formerly: Native American Rights Fund. Catalogue (ISSN 0092-3419)

970.1 016   US
NATIVE AMERICAN BIBLIOGRAPHY SERIES. 1980. irreg., approx. 3/yr. price varies. Scarecrow Press, Inc., Box 4167, Metuchen, NJ 08840. TEL 201-548-8600. Ed. Jack W. Marken.

EXPERIMENTAL MEDICINE, LABORATORY TECHNIQUE

see *Medical Sciences—Experimental Medicine, Laboratory Technique*

FASHIONS

see *Clothing Trade—Fashions*

FEED, FLOUR AND GRAIN

see *Agriculture—Feed, Flour and Grain*

FIRE PREVENTION

614.84   US
ANNUAL CONFERENCE ON FIRE RESEARCH. a. National Bureau of Standards, Center for Fire Research, Bldg. 224, Rm. A252, Washington, DC 20234 TEL 301-921-3249. Ed. S. Cherry. (back issues avail.)

352.3   UK
ASSOCIATED SOCIETY OF LOCOMOTIVE ENGINEERS AND FIREMEN. ANNUAL REPORT AND BALANCE SHEET. 1880. a. £1. Associated Society of Locomotive Engineers and Firemen, 9 Arkwright Rd., Hampstead, London NW3 6AB, England.

614.84   AT
AUSTRALIAN FIRE PROTECTION ASSOCIATION. CONFERENCE PAPERS. 1966. biennial. Aus.$35. Australian Fire Protection Association Pty Ltd., 2 Arden St., North Melbourne, Vic. 3051, Australia. Ed. E. Bennet.

344.73   US
B O C A BASIC-NATIONAL FIRE PREVENTION CODE. 1975. triennial. Building Officials and Code Administrators International, 4051 W. Flossmoor Rd., Country Club Hills, IL 60477-5795.
 Formerly: B.O.C.A. Basic Fire Prevention Code.

628.92   UK
BRITAIN'S FIRE PROTECTION INDUSTRY. 1985. irreg. £95($150) Jordan & Sons Ltd., Jordan House, 47 Brunswick Place, London N1 6EE, England.

BRITISH SECURITY INDUSTRY BUYER'S GUIDE (YEAR); now including fire protection. see *CRIMINOLOGY AND LAW ENFORCEMENT — Security*

628.92 164.84   GW   ISSN 0071-4674
FEUERWEHR-JAHRBUCH; ein Jahresbericht ueber das Feuerwehrwesen in der Bundesrepublik Deutschland. 1964. a. DM.10. Deutscher Feuerwehrverband, Koblenzer str. 133, D-5300 Bonn 2, W. Germany (B.R.D.) adv. circ. 5,000.
 Formerly: Freiwilliger Feuerwehren.

614.84   CN   ISSN 0071-5395
FIRE PREVENTION NEWS.* a. Joint Fire Prevention Publicity Committee Inc., 7 Liverpool Ct., No.1590, Ottawa, Ont. K1B 4L2, Canada. (Co-sponsors: Canadian Association of Fire Chiefs; Association of Fire Commissioners and Fire Marshalls)

614.84   UK   ISSN 0071-5409
FIRE PROTECTION DIRECTORY. 1940. a. £15. Benn Publications Ltd., 25 New Street Square, London EC4A 3JA, England. Ed. J.L. Eades. adv. index.

614.84   US   ISSN 0071-5417
FIRE PROTECTION HANDBOOK. 1896. quinquennial. $60 to non-members; members $54. National Fire Protection Association, c/o Joseph Scaramozza, Batterymarch Park, Quincy, MA 02269. TEL 617-770-3000. Ed. Gordon P. McKinnon. (reprint service avail. from UMI)

614.84   US   ISSN 0361-8382
FIRE PROTECTION REFERENCE DIRECTORY. 1975. a. National Fire Protection Association, c/o Joseph Scaramozza, Batterymarch Park, Quincy, MA 02269. TEL 617-770-3000. adv. index. circ. 75, 000. (reprint service avail. from UMI)

352.3   US   ISSN 0071-5468
FIRE YEARBOOK. 1961. a. $15. Davis Publishing Co., 2015 McFarland Blvd., E., Tuscaloosa, AL 35405. TEL 205-759-1508. Ed. W.W. Smith.
 Civil Service questions

628.92   US
FIREHOUSE MAGAZINE BUYERS GUIDE. 1981. a. $21. Firehouse Communications, Inc., 33 Irving Pl., New York, NY 10003 TEL 212-475-5400.

614.84　　　UK　ISSN 0307-2118
FITECH; the international equipment guide for the emergency services. (Text in Arabic, English, French, German, Spanish) 1971. a. £15. Unisaf Publications Ltd., Queensway House, 2 Queensway, Redhill, Surrey RH1 1QS, England. circ. controlled.

614.84　690　　　UK
GREAT BRITAIN. BUILDING RESEARCH ESTABLISHMENT. REPORTS. 1961. irreg. Building Research Establishment, Garston, Watford WD2 7JR, England.
　Supersedes: Great Britain. Department of the Environment. Fire Research Station. Fire Notes (ISSN 0071-5379) & Great Britain. Department of the Environment. Fire Research Station. Technical Papers (ISSN 0071-545X)

614.84　　　FR　ISSN 0337-5781
GUIDE DU FEU. 1962. a. 162 F. France-Selection, 9-13 rue du Departement, 75925 Paris Cedex 19, France. adv. bk. rev.
　Formerly: Guide du Feu et de la Protection Civile (ISSN 0072-8047)

INSULATION HANDBOOK. see *BUILDING AND CONSTRUCTION*

614.84　　　MF
MAURITIUS. GOVERNMENT FIRE SERVICES. ANNUAL REPORT. (Text in English) a. Government Printing Office, Elizabeth II Ave., Port Louis, Mauritius.

352.3　　　UK
N A F O YEARBOOK. 1971. a. membership. National Association of Fire Officers, 10 Cuthbert Rd., Croydon, CR0 3RB, England. Ed. R. Rhythian. adv. circ. 8,000.

614.84　　　US　ISSN 0077-4545
NATIONAL FIRE PROTECTION ASSOCIATION. NATIONAL FIRE CODES. 1938. a. $210 to non-members; members $189. National Fire Protection Association, Attn.: Joseph Scaramozza, Batterymarch Park, Quincy, MA 02269. TEL 617-770-3000. (also avail. in microform; reprint service avail. from UMI) Key Title: National Fire Codes.
　All codes, standards, recommended practices, and manuals by technical committees of the NFPA.

614.84　　　US
NATIONAL FIRE PROTECTION ASSOCIATION. NATIONAL FIRE CODES. SUPPLEMENT. 1951. a. $55 to non-members; members $49.50. National Fire Protection Association, Attn.: Joseph Scaramozza, Batterymarch Park, Quincy, MA 02269. TEL 617-770-3000. index. (also avail. in microfiche; reprint service avail. from UMI)
　All codes, standards, recommended practices, and manuals by technical committees of the N F P A.

614.84　　　NE　ISSN 0077-6955
NETHERLANDS. CENTRAAL BUREAU VOOR DE STATISTIEK. STATISTIEK DER BRANDEN. FIRE STATISTICS. (Text in Dutch and English) 1950. a. fl.20.75. Centraal Bureau voor de Statistiek, Prinses Beatrixlaan 428, Voorburg, Netherlands (Orders to: Staatsuitgeverij, Christoffel Plantijnstraat, The Hague, Netherlands)

614.84　　　CN　ISSN 0085-4395
NOVA SCOTIA. FIRE MARSHAL. ANNUAL REPORT. a. Department of Labour, Box 697, Halifax, Nova Scotia, Canada. TEL 902-424-4125.

614.84　　　JA
OKINAWA PREFECTURE. ANNUAL REPORT OF FIRE AND DISASTER PREVENTION. 1973. a. Okinawa-ken, 2-32, 1-chome, Izumizaki, Naha-shi 900, Japan. circ. 450.

352.3　350　　　JA
SAIGAI NO JITTAI TO SHOBO NO GENKYO/ ANNUAL REPORT OF FIRE AND DISASTER PREVENTION. (Text and summaries in Japanese) 1967. a. free. Fire and Disaster Prevention, Section of General Affair Department of Miyagi Prefecture, 8-1, 3 Chome, Honcho, Sendai City 980, Japan. circ. 400.

FIRE PREVENTION — Abstracting, Bibliographies, Statistics

363.3　　　UK　ISSN 0309-622X
CHARTERED INSTITUTE OF PUBLIC FINANCE AND ACCOUNTANCY. FIRE SERVICE STATISTICS. ACTUALS. 1948. a. £10. Chartered Institute of Public Finance and Accountancy, 3 Robert St., London WC2N 6BH, England. stat. (back issues avail.)

310　　　UK　ISSN 0307-0573
CHARTERED INSTITUTE OF PUBLIC FINANCE AND ACCOUNTANCY. FIRE SERVICE STATISTICS. ESTIMATES. 1974. a. £10. Chartered Institute of Public Finance and Accountancy, 3 Robert St., London WC2N 6BH, England. (back issues avail.)

614.84　　　US
FIRE RESEARCH PUBLICATIONS. 1972. a. price varies. (U.S. National Bureau of Standards) U.S. National Technical Information Service, 5285 Port Royal Rd., Springfield, VA 22161. TEL 703-487-4600. Ed. Nora H. Jason. (also avail. in microfiche)

FISH AND FISHERIES

see also Biology—Zoology

799.1　　　UK　ISSN 0044-8257
A.C.A. REVIEW. 1948. a. membership. Anglers Cooperative Association, Midland Bank Chambers, Westgate, Grantham, Lincs. NG31 6LE, England. Ed. Ken Sutton. adv. bk. rev. circ. 10,000. Indexed: Sportsearch.

639.9　　　US　ISSN 0095-4632
A.D.F.& G. TECHNICAL DATA REPORT. irreg. Department of Fish and Game, Box 3-2000, Juneau, AK 99802. TEL 907-465-4210. illus.

639　　　NO
AARSBERETNING VEDKOMMENDE NORGES FISKERIER. 1894. a. price varies. Fiskeridirektoratet - Directorate of Fisheries, Box 185, 5001 Bergen, Norway. Indexed: Biol.Abstr.

ACTA ACADEMIAE AGRICULTURAE AC TECHNICAE OLSTENENSIS. PROTECTIO AQUARUM ET PISCATORIA/WATER CONSERVATION AND INLAND FISHERIES. see *WATER RESOURCES*

ACTA ADRIATICA. see *EARTH SCIENCES — Oceanography*

AGRICULTURA, LA PESCA Y LA ALIMENTACION ESPANOLAS. see *AGRICULTURE*

639.2　630　　　SP
AGRICULTURA Y LA PESCA ESPANOLAS. 1980. a. 1300 ptas. Ministerio de Agricultura, Pesca y Alimentacion, Secretaria General Tecnica, Paseo de Infanta Isabel, 1, 28014 Madrid, Spain.

639.2　664　　　PL
AKADEMIA ROLNICZA W SZCZECINIE. ZESZYTY NAUKOWE. RYBACTWO MORSKIE I TECHNOLOGIA ZYWNOSCI. 1966. irreg., no. 108, 1984. price varies. Akademia Rolnicza, Janosika 8, 71-424 Szczecin, Poland. Ed. Prof. Mieczyslaw Jasnowski. bk. rev. Indexed: Chem.Abstr. Nutr.Abstr. Field Crop Abstr.

ALABAMA MARINE RESOURCES BULLETIN. see *BIOLOGY*

338.4　　　US
ALASKA. DEPARTMENT OF FISH AND GAME. COMMERCIAL OPERATORS. Title varies: Alaska Fisheries Commercial Operators. 1961. a. Department of Fish and Game, Juneau, AK 99802. TEL 907-465-4210. illus.

ALBERTA. FISH AND WILDLIFE DIVISION. FISHERIES POLLUTION REPORT. see *ENVIRONMENTAL STUDIES*

639.2　　　US　ISSN 0097-0638
AMERICAN FISHERIES SOCIETY. SPECIAL PUBLICATION. 1948. irreg., no.14, 1984. price varies. American Fisheries Society, 5410 Grosvenor Lane, Ste. 110, Bethesda, MD 20814. TEL 301-897-8616. Ed. Robert L. Kendall. (back issues avail.) Indexed: Biol.Abstr. Chem.Abstr. Curr.Cont. Ocean.Abstr. Pollut.Abstr.

639.2　　　US　ISSN 0362-1715
AMERICAN FISHERIES SOCIETY MONOGRAPH. 1976. irreg., no.3, 1982. price varies. American Fisheries Society, 5410 Grosvenor Lane, Suite 110, Bethesda, MD 20814. TEL 301-897-8616. Ed. Robert L. Kendall. (back issues avail.)

639　　　FR　ISSN 0066-2623
ANNUAIRE DE L'ARMEMENT A LA PECHE; guide de la peche professionelle francaise. 1956. a. 335 F. Editions Maritimes, 190 Boulevard Haussmann, 75008 Paris, France. index.

639　　　FR　ISSN 0066-2542
ANNUAIRE DE LA MAREE; guide de la commercialisation des produits de la mer. 1930. a. 385 F. Editions Maritimes, 190, Boulevard Haussmann, Paris 75008, France. index.

639.3　　　CH　ISSN 0254-6493
AQUICULTURE. (Text in Chinese or English) 1970. irreg. exchange basis. Taiwan Fisheries Research Institute, Tungkang Marine Laboratory, Tungkang, Pingtung, Taiwan, Republic of China. Ed. I-Chiu Liao. adv. bk. rev.

639.2　　　GW　ISSN 0003-9063
ARCHIV FUER FISCHEREIWISSENSCHAFT. 1949. irreg., vol.37, 1986. price varies. Bundesforschungsanstalt fuer Fischerei, Palmaille 9, 2000 Hamburg 50, W. Germany (B.R.D.) Eds. Klaus Tiews, Dietrich Sahrhage. adv. bk. rev. charts. illus. maps. Indexed: Biol.Abstr. Chem.Abstr. Curr.Cont. Excerp.Med. Sci.Cit.Ind. Aquz.Sci.& Fish.Abstr. Food Sci.& Tech.Abstr. Helminthol.Abstr. Sel.Water Res.Abstr.

639.2　333.7　　　CN
ATLANTIC SALMON FEDERATION. SPECIAL PUBLICATION SERIES. 1971. irreg. (1-2/yr.) price varies. Atlantic Salmon Federation, P.O. Box 4295, St. Andrews, New Brunswick E0G 2X0, Canada. TEL 506-529-8889. Ed. John M. Anderson. circ. 300. (back issues avail.) Indexed: Biol.Abstr. Ocean.Abstr.
　Formerly: International Atlantic Salmon Foundation. Special Publication Series.

639.2　　　AT　ISSN 0705-2146
AUSTRALIA. BUREAU OF STATISTICS. WESTERN AUSTRALIAN OFFICE. FISHERIES. 1968/69. a. free. Australian Bureau of Statistics, Western Australian Office, 1-3 St. George's Tce., Perth 6000, W.A., Australia. circ. 500. (processed) Indexed: Nutr.Abstr. Forest.Abstr.

639.2　　　AT　ISSN 0157-9630
AUSTRALIA. DEPARTMENT OF PRIMARY INDUSTRY. AUSTRALIAN FISHING INDUSTRY DIRECTORY. 1985. biennial. free. Department of Primary Industry, Australian Fisheries Service, Edmund Barton Bldg., Broughton St., Barton, A.C.T. 2600, Australia.

350　639.2　　　AT　ISSN 0311-8959
AUSTRALIA. DEPARTMENT OF PRIMARY INDUSTRY. FISHING INDUSTRY RESEARCH COMMITTEE. ANNUAL REPORT. 1970. a. free. Department of Primary Industry, Australian Fisheries Service, Edmund Barton Bldg., Broughton St., Barton, A.C.T. 2600, Australia.

350　639.2　　　AT　ISSN 0067-1436
AUSTRALIA. DEPARTMENT OF PRIMARY INDUSTRY. OPERATION OF THE FISHING INDUSTRY, A.C.T. ANNUAL REPORT. 1957. a. free. Department of Primary Industry, Australian Fisheries Service, Edmund Barton Bldg., Broughton St., Barton, A.C.T. 2600, Australia.

328.94　639　　　AT
AUSTRALIA. FISHING INDUSTRY RESEARCH COMMITTEE. ANNUAL REPORT. 1970. a. price varies. Australian Government Publishing Service, G.P.O. Box 84, Canberra, A.C.T. 2601, Australia. illus.

639.2 AT
AUSTRALIA. PROFESSIONAL FISHERMAN'S FISHING VESSEL YEARBOOK. 1980. a. $10. Baird Publications Pty. Ltd., 427 Chapel St., South Yarra, Vic. 3141, Australia. Ed. Neil Baird. adv. bk. rev. circ. 6,000. (back issues avail)

639.3 BE ISSN 0303-9072
BELGIUM. RIJKSSTATION VOOR ZEEVISSERIJ. MEDEDELINGEN. 1969. irreg. free. Rijksstation voor Zeevisserij, Ankerstraat 1, B-8400 Oostende, Belgium. Ed. P. Hovart. circ. 500. (back issues avail.) Indexed: Biol.& Agr.Ind.

BERMUDA. DEPARTMENT OF AGRICULTURE AND FISHERIES. REPORT FOR THE YEAR. see *AGRICULTURE*

639 IE ISSN 0068-0265
BORD IASCAIGH MHARA. TUARASCAIL AGUS CUNTAISI/IRISH SEA FISHERIES BOARD. ANNUAL REPORT. (Text in English and Gaelic) 1953. a. contr. free circ. to libraries & institutions. Irish Sea Fisheries Board, P.O. Box 12, Crofton Rd., Dun Laoghaire, Co. Dublin, Ireland. TEL 841544. Ed. Sean Freeman. circ. 3,500.

BURKINA FASO. DIRECTION DES EAUX ET FORETS ET DE LA CONSERVATION DES SOLS. RAPPORT ANNUEL. see *FORESTS AND FORESTRY*

639.2 UN
C I F A TECHNICAL PAPERS. 1972. irreg., no.15, 1986. Food and Agriculture Organization of the United Nations, Committee for Inland Fisheries of Africa, Distribution and Sales Section, Via delle Terme di Caracalla, I-00100 Rome, Italy. Ed. J.J. Kambona. (also avail. in microfiche) Indexed: Biol.Abstr.

639 CN ISSN 0711-0782
CANADA. DEPARTMENT OF FISHERIES AND OCEANS. ANNUAL REPORT. 1931. a. Department of Fisheries and Oceans, Ottawa, Ont. K1A 0E6, Canada. TEL 613-993-0999. circ. 700.
Supersedes in part: Canada. Fisheries and Environment Canada. Annual Report (ISSN 0068-7375)

388.3 CN
CANADA. FISHERIES AND OCEANS. PACIFIC REGION. ANNUAL SUMMARY OF BRITISH COLUMBIA CATCH STATISTICS. 1951. a. Fisheries and Oceans, Economics and Statistics Branch, 1090 West Pender St., Vancouver, B.C. V6E 2P1, Canada. TEL 604-666-1985.

639 574.92 CN ISSN 0706-6503
CANADIAN BULLETIN OF FISHERIES AND AQUATIC SCIENCES. French edition (ISSN 0706-6511) (Editions in English or French) 1918. irreg., no.212, 1984. price varies. Department of Fisheries and Oceans, Scientific Information and Publications Branch, 200 Kent St., Ottawa, Ont. K1A 0E6, Canada. TEL 613-990-0229. Ed. J. Watson. circ. 10,000. Indexed: Biol.Abstr. Chem.Abstr. Ocean.Abstr. Aqua.Sci.& Fish.Abstr. Arct.Bibl. Food Sci.& Tech.Abstr. Helminthol.Abstr.
Formerly: Canada. Fisheries Research Board. Bulletin (ISSN 0068-7537)

639.2 551.46 CN ISSN 0704-3694
CANADIAN INDUSTRY REPORT OF FISHERIES AND AQUATIC SCIENCES. French edition: Rapport Canadien a l'Industrie sur les Sciences Halieutiques et Aquatiques (ISSN 0704-3708) (Editions in English and/or French) 1966. irreg. price varies. Department of Fisheries and Oceans, Scientific Information and Publications Branch, 200 Kent St., Ottawa, Ont. K1A 0E6, Canada. circ. 250. (also avail. in microfiche from MML) Indexed: Biol.Abstr. Aqua.Sci.& Fish.Abstr.

639.2 CN ISSN 0706-6481
CANADIAN SPECIAL PUBLICATION OF FISHERIES AND AQUATIC SCIENCES. French edition: Publication Speciale Canadienne des Sciences Halieutiques et Aquatiques (ISSN 0706-649X) (Editions in English or French) 1929. irreg., no.73, 1984. price varies. Fisheries and Oceans, Scientific Information and Publications Branch, 200 Kent St., Ottawa, Ont. K1A 0E6, Canada. TEL 613-990-0229. Ed. J. Watson. circ. 8,500. Indexed: Biol.Abstr. Chem.Abstr. Aqua.Sci.& Fish.Abstr.
Formerly: Canada. Fisheries Research Board. Miscellaneous Special Publication Series.

639 574.92 CN ISSN 0706-6457
CANADIAN TECHNICAL REPORT OF FISHERIES AND AQUATIC SCIENCES. French edition: Rapport Technique Canadien des Sciences Halieutiques et Aquatiques (ISSN 0706-6570) (Editions in English and/or French) 1967. irreg. price varies. Fisheries and Oceans, 200 Kent St., Ottawa, Ont. K1A 0E6, Canada. TEL 613-990-0229. circ. 350. Indexed: Biol.Abstr. Chem.Abstr. Aqua.Sci.& Fish.Abstr. GeoRef.
Formerly: Canada. Fisheries and Marine Service. Technical Report Series (ISSN 0068-7553)

639.3 CN
CARTES DE PECHES DE CHALUTIERS QUEBECOIS. CAHIER SPECIAL D'INFORMATION. no.1, Apr. 1977. a. Ministere de l'Agriculture, des Pecheries et de l'Alimentation, Bureaux des echanges, C.P. 340, Grande-Riviere, Cte de Gaspe, Que. G0C 1V0, Canada. TEL 418-385-2251.

639.2 II
CENTRAL INLAND FISHERIES RESEARCH INSTITUTE. ANNUAL REPORT. (Text in English) 1967. a. exchange basis. Central Inland Fisheries Research Institute, Barrackpore 743101, West Bengal, India. charts. stat. Indexed: Biol.Abstr.
Formerly: Central Inland Fisheries Research Institute. Technical Progress Report.

639.2 II ISSN 0008-9427
CENTRAL INLAND FISHERIES RESEARCH INSTITUTE. BULLETIN. 1963. irreg. exchange basis. Central Inland Fisheries Research Institute, Barrackpore 743101, West Bengal, India. abstr. bibl. circ. 132. (processed) Indexed: Biol.Abstr. Sci.Cit.Ind. Helminthol.Abstr.

597 551.46 II ISSN 0577-084X
CENTRAL MARINE FISHERIES RESEARCH INSTITUTE. BULLETIN. (Text in English) 1968. a. price varies. Central Marine Fisheries Research Institute, P.B. No.1912, Cochin 682018, India. Ed. E.G. Silas. circ. 2,000. (looseleaf format) Indexed: Biol.Abstr.

CENTRO DE PESQUISAS DO CACAU. INFORME TECNICO. see *AGRICULTURE*

639 591 CL
CHILE. SERVICIO NACIONAL DE PESCA. ANUARIO ESTADISTICO DE PESCA. 1944. a. exchange basis. Servicio Nacional de Pesca, Casilla 4088, Santiago, Chile. circ. controlled. (also avail. in microform)
Former titles: Chile. Servicio Agricola y Ganadero. Division Proteccion Pesquera. Anuario Estadistico (ISSN 0069-3537) & Chile. Direccion de Agricultura y Pesquera. Departamento Estadistica. Anuario Estadistico de Pesca.

639 AT ISSN 0157-8081
COMMONWEALTH SCIENTIFIC AND INDUSTRIAL RESEARCH ORGANIZATION. MARINE LABORATORIES. FISHERY SITUATION REPORT. 1979. irreg. C.S.I.R.O. Laboratories, G.P.O. Box 1538, Hobart, Tas. 7001, Australia.

639 AT ISSN 0726-4283
COMMONWEALTH SCIENTIFIC AND INDUSTRIAL RESEARCH ORGANIZATION. MARINE LABORATORIES. MICROFICHE REPORT. 1978. irreg. free. C.S.I.R.O. Laboratories, G.P.O. Box 1538, Hobart, Tas. 1538, Australia.

639 551.46 AT ISSN 0725-4598
COMMONWEALTH SCIENTIFIC AND INDUSTRIAL RESEARCH ORGANIZATION. MARINE LABORATORIES. REPORT. 1956. irreg. free. C.S.I.R.O. Marine Laboratories, G.P.O. Box 1538, Hobart, Tas. 7001, Australia. circ. 600. Indexed: Biol.Abstr. Ocean.Abstr.
Supersedes: Commonwealth Scientific and Industrial Research Organization. Division of Fisheries and Oceanography. Annual Report (ISSN 0069-7370)

639 551.46 AT ISSN 0726-4291
COMMONWEALTH SCIENTIFIC AND INDUSTRIAL RESEARCH ORGANIZATION. MARINE LABORATORIES. RESEARCH REPORT. 1960/61. biennial. free. C.S.I.R.O. Marine Laboratories, G.P.O. Box 1538, Hobart, Tas. 7001, Australia. circ. 1,000. Indexed: Biol.Abstr.
Supersedes: Commonwealth Scientific Industrial Research Organization. Division of Fisheries and Oceanography. Report (ISSN 0069-7397)

354.564 CY
CYPRUS. DEPARTMENT OF FISHERIES. ANNUAL REPORT ON THE DEPARTMENT OF FISHERIES AND THE CYPRUS FISHERIES. (Text in English) 1963. a. free. Department of Fisheries, Nicosia, Cyprus. circ. 1,000.
Supersedes: Cyprus. Department of Fisheries. Annual Report of the Cyprus Fisheries.

639 DK ISSN 0106-553X
DANA; a journal of fisheries and marine research. (Text in English) 1904; N.S. 1980. irreg. price varies. Danmarks Fiskeri- og Havundersoegelser - Danish Institute for Fisheries and Marine Research, Charlottenlund Castle, 2920 Charlottenlund, Denmark. Ed. E. Hoffmann. index. cum.index: 1904-1983. Indexed: Biol.Abstr. Curr.Cont. Ref.Zh. Sci.Cit.Ind. Aqua.Sci.& Fish.Abstr.
Formerly: Denmark. Danmarks Fiskeri- og Havundersoegelser. Meddelelser fra (ISSN 0070-3435)

639.2 DK ISSN 0109-4432
DANMARKS FISKERI OG HAVUNDERSOEGELSER. RAPPORT. 1985. a. (Danmarks Fiskeri og Havundersoegelser) Bibliotekscentralen, Telegrafvej 5, DK-2750 Ballerup, Denmark.

639 574.92 DK ISSN 0070-3605
DENMARK. FISKERIMINISTERIET. FORSOEGSLABORATORIUM. AARSBERETNING/ANNUAL REPORT. (Triennial Reports Available in English) 1952. a. free. Fiskeriministeriet, Forsoegslaboratorium - Ministry of Fisheries, Technological Laboratory, Polytekniske Laereanstalt, Danmarks Tekniske Hoejskole, Building 221, 2800 Lyngby, Denmark. circ. 2,000. Indexed: Chem.Abstr. Aqua.Sci.& Fish.Abstr. Food Sci.& Tech.Abstr.

639 UK
DEPARTMENT OF AGRICULTURE AND FISHERIES FOR SCOTLAND. FRESHWATER FISHERIES LABORATORY. TRIENNIAL REVIEW OF RESEARCH. 1977. triennial. free. Department of Agriculture and Fisheries, Freshwater Fisheries Laboratory, Faskally, Pitlochry, Perthshire PH16 5LB, Scotland. circ. 1, 250. (also avail. in microfiche) Indexed: Aqua.Sci.& Fish.Abstr.
Former titles: Scotland Department of Agriculture and Fisheries. Freshwater Fisheries Laboratory Pitlochry. Triennial Review of Research; Scotland. Department of Agriculture and Fisheries. Freshwater Fisheries Triennial Review of Research; Scotland. Department of Agriculture and Fisheries. Freshwater Fisheries Triennial (ISSN 0140-5004)

DEVELOPMENTS IN AQUACULTURE AND FISHERIES SCIENCE. see *BIOLOGY — Zoology*

639.2 UN ISSN 0429-9329
F A O FISHERIES CIRCULARS. irreg., no.792, 1985. price varies. Food and Agriculture Organization of the United Nations, Distribution and Sales Section, Via delle Terme di Caracalla, I-00100 Rome, Italy (Dist. in U.S. by: Bernan Associates-Unipub, 4611-F Assembly Drive, Lanham, MD 20706-4391) Indexed: Biol.Abstr. Ocean.Abstr.

639.2 UN ISSN 0429-9337
F A O FISHERIES REPORTS. irreg., no.351, 1986. price varies. Food and Agriculture Organization of the United Nations, Distribution and Sales Section, Via delle Terme di Caracalla, I-00100 Rome, Italy (Dist. in U.S. by: Bernan Associates-Unipub, 4611-F Assembly Drive, Lanham, MD 20706-4391) Indexed: Biol.Abstr. Ocean.Abstr.
Incorporates: Indian Ocean Fishery Commission. Report of the Session; (as from 1975): C I F A Reports.

FISH AND FISHERIES

639   UN
F A O FISHERIES SERIES. (Text in English, French and Spanish) irreg., no.24, 1983. price varies. Food and Agriculture Organization of the United Nations, Distribution and Sales Section, Via delle Terme di Caracalla, 00100 Rome, Italy (Dist. in U.S. by: Bernan Associates-Unipub, 4611-F Assembly Drive, Lanham, MD 20706-4391) Ed. Chris A. Theodore. Indexed: Nutr.Abstr.
    Formerly: F A O Fisheries Studies (ISSN 0071-7037)

639   UN
F A O FISHERIES SYNOPSIS. 1962. irreg. Food and Agriculture Organization of the United Nations, Via delle Terme di Caracalla, 00100 Rome, Italy.
    Formerly: Fisheries Biology Synopsis.

639   UN   ISSN 0429-9345
F A O FISHERIES TECHNICAL PAPER. 1960. irreg., no.270, 1985. Food and Agriculture Organization of the United Nations, Distribution and Sales Section, Via delle Terme di Caracalla, 00100 Rome, Italy (Dist. in U.S. by: Bernan Associates-Unipub, 4611-F Assembly Drive, Lanham, MD 20706-4391) Indexed: Biol.Abstr. Excerp.Med. Nutr.Abstr. Ocean.Abstr. Food Sci.& Tech.Abstr.

639   UN   ISSN 0071-7061
F A O MANUALS IN FISHERIES SCIENCE. (Text in English, French and Spanish) 1965. irreg., no.5, 1972. price varies. Food and Agriculture Organization of the United Nations, Distribution and Sales Section, Via delle Terme di Caracalla, 00100 Rome, Italy (Dist. in U.S. by: Bernan Associates-Unipub, 4611-F Assembly Drive, Lanham, MD 20706-4391)

639.2   AT
F R V KAPALA CRUISE REPORT. 1971. irreg. free. Department of Agriculture, Fisheries Research Vessel, P.O. Box K220, Haymarket, N.S.W. 2000, Australia. circ. 800.

639.7 597 333.91   JA   ISSN 0386-7285
FAR SEAS FISHERIES RESEARCH LABORATORY. BULLETIN. (Text in English and Japanese) 1969. a. Fisheries Agency, Far Seas Fisheries Research Laboratory, 5-7-1 Orido, Shimizu 424, Japan. Indexed: Biol.Abstr. Helminthol.Abstr.

639.3 597   JA
FAR SEAS FISHERIES RESEARCH LABORATORY. SERIES. (Text in English and Japanese) a. Fisheries Agency, Far Seas Fisheries Research Laboratory, 5-7-1 Orido, Shimizu 424, Japan. Indexed: Biol.Abstr.

639   FI   ISSN 0301-908X
FINNISH FISHERIES RESEARCH. (Text and summaries in English) 1972. a. exchange basis. Finnish Game and Finish Research Institute, Fisheries Division, P.O. Box 193, SF-00131 Helsinki 13, Finland. Ed. Pekka Tuunainen. circ. 1,000. Indexed: Biol.Abstr. Aqua.Sci.& Fish.Abstr. Sport Fish.Abstr.

639.2   AT
FISH AND WILDLIFE GAZETTE. 1962. irreg. New South Wales Institute of Freshwater Fishermen, P.O. Box 195, Lindfield, NSW 2070, Australia. Ed. R.B. Hungerford. circ. controlled.

639   US   ISSN 0071-5492
FISH DISEASE LEAFLETS. 1966. irreg., no.66, 1983. U.S. Fish and Wildlife Service, Dept. of the Interior, Washington, DC 20240. TEL 202-653-7501. (looseleaf format)

639.3   NZ
FISHDEX. 1980. irreg. free. Ministry of Agriculture and Fisheries, Information Services, Private Bag, Wellington, New Zealand. Ed. B. Greenfield. illus.

FISHERIES AND WILDLIFE RESEARCH. see SPORTS AND GAMES — Outdoor Life

591 236   IE   ISSN 0332-4338
FISHERIES BULLETIN. 1981. irreg. free. Department of Fisheries and Forestry, Library, Abbotstown, Castleknock, Dublin 15, Ireland. bk. rev. circ. 400. Indexed: Biol.Abstr.

639   UK   ISSN 0080-1283
FISHERIES OF SCOTLAND REPORT. 1882. a. price varies. H.M.S.O. (Scotland), 13a Castle St., Edinburgh EH2 3AR, Scotland.

338.3   US
FISHERIES OF THE UNITED STATES. 1942. a. U.S. National Marine Fisheries Service, National Oceanic and Atmospheric Administration, Washington, DC 20235 TEL 202-655-4000. (Orders to: Supt. of Documents, Government Printing Office, Washington, DC 20402) stat. circ. 1,700. (also avail. in microfiche) Indexed: Amer.Stat.Ind. C.I.S.Ind.
    Formerly: Fishery Statistics of the United States (ISSN 0071-5603); Which supersedes: U.S. Bureau of Commercial Fisheries. United States Fisheries.

639   ZA   ISSN 0084-4713
FISHERIES RESEARCH BULLETIN OF ZAMBIA. (Text in English) 1962/63. irreg. Central Fisheries Research Institute, Box 100, Chilanga, Zambia. Indexed: Biol.Abstr.

639 338.1   JA   ISSN 0071-5581
FISHERIES STATISTICS OF JAPAN. (Text in English) 1963. a. Ministry of Agriculture and Forestry, Statistics Bureau - Norin-sho Norin Keizai-Kyoku Tokei Joho-bu, 11-14 2-Chome, Meguro-Ku, Tokyo 153, Japan (Orders to: Government Publications Service Center, 1-2-1 Kasumigaseki, Chiyoda-Ku, Tokyo 100, Japan) cum.index: 1963-67.

639.2   IO
FISHERMAN UNION OF INDONESIA. CENTRAL GOVERNING BOARD. ANNUAL REPORT/HIMPUNAN NELAYAN SELURAH INDONESIA. DEWAN PIMPANAN PUSAT. LAPORAN KEGIATAN. (Text in Indonesian) 1980. a. $5. Fisherman Union of Indonesia, Central Governing Board, Jalan Juanda no. 2, Jakarta, Indonesia. Ed. E.Q. Djatikusumo. adv. bk. rev. circ. 5,000.

639   US
FISHING: LATIN AMERICAN INDUSTRIAL REPORT. (Avail. for each of 22 Latin American countries) 1985. a. $435 per country report per industry covered. Aurora International, Box 9099, Bridgeport, CT 06601-2099. TEL 203-368-0579. Ed. Andres C. Aquino.

639 574.92   DK   ISSN 0105-9211
FISK OG HAV. 1904; N.S. 1972. irreg. price varies. Danmarks Fiskeri- og Havundersoegelser - Danish Institute for Fisheries and Marine Research, Charlottenlund Castle, DK-2920 Charlottenlund, Denmark. Ed. Erik Hoffmann. cum.index: 1904-52.
    Formerly: Denmark. Danmarks Fiskeri- og Havundersoegelser. Skrifter fra.

639   NO   ISSN 0071-5638
FISKEN OG HAVET. (Reports published from 1960 to 1976 in Fiskets Gang.) (Text in Norwegian; summaries in English) 1959. irreg. Fiskeridirektoratet, Havforskningsinstituttet - Directorate of Fisheries, Institute of Marine Research, Box 1870-72, N-5011 Bergen-Nordnes, Norway. Ed. Erling Bratberg. Indexed: Biol.Abstr. Ocean.Abstr. Pollut.Abstr. Aqua.Sci. & Fish.Abstr.

639.2   DK   ISSN 0900-9787
FISKERIAARBOGEN. 1986. a. Kr.122. Danske Fiskerflaade, Fiskeriministeriet, Copenhagen, Denmark.

639.2   DK   ISSN 0108-8629
FISKERIET VED GROENLAND & GROENLANDS FISKERIUNDERSOEGELSERS AKTIVITET. Eskimo edition: Kalaallit Nunaata Imartaant Aalisarneq Aalisarnikkullu Mississuisut. Suliarisimasaat. 1982. a. free. Groenlands Fiskeri og Miljoeundersoegelser, Tagensvej 135/1, 2200 Copenhagen N, Denmark. Ed. Finn O. Kapel. illus. circ. 500.
    Formerly: Fiskeri and Fiskeriundersoegelser ved Groenland.

FOCUS ON RENEWABLE NATURAL RESOURCES. see FORESTS AND FORESTRY

639   UN
FOOD AND AGRICULTURE ORGANIZATION OF THE UNITED NATIONS. EUROPEAN INLAND FISHERIES ADVISORY COMMISSION. OCCASIONAL PAPERS. (Editions in English and French) 1968. irreg. free. Food and Agriculture Organization of the United Nations, European Inland Fisheries Advisory Commission, Secretariat, Via delle Terme di Caracalla, I-00100 Rome, Italy. circ. 2,000. (also avail. in microfiche; back issues avail.)

639   UN
FOOD AND AGRICULTURE ORGANIZATION OF THE UNITED NATIONS. EUROPEAN INLAND FISHERIES ADVISORY COMMISSION. TECHNICAL PAPERS. (Editions in English and French) 1964. irreg. free. Food and Agriculture Organization of the United Nations, European Inland Fisheries Advisory Committee, Secretariat, Via delle Terme di Caracalla, I-00100 Rome, Italy. circ. 2,000. (also avail. in microfiche; back issues avail.)

639   UN   ISSN 0072-0747
GENERAL FISHERIES COUNCIL FOR THE MEDITERRANEAN. PROCEEDINGS AND TECHNICAL PAPERS. DEBATS ET DOCUMENTS TECHNIQUES. (Text in English and French) 1952. irreg., no.17, 1984. Food and Agriculture Organization of the United Nations, Distribution and Sales Section, Via delle Terme di Caracalla, 00100 Rome, Italy (Dist. in U.S. by: Bernan Associates-Unipub, 4611-F Assembly Drive, Lanham, MD 20706-4391)

639   UN   ISSN 0072-0755
GENERAL FISHERIES COUNCIL FOR THE MEDITERRANEAN. REPORTS OF THE SESSIONS. 1968. irreg., no.17, 1984. price varies. Food and Agriculture Organization of the United Nations, Distribution and Sales Section, Via delle Terme di Caracalla, 00100 Rome, Italy (Dist. in U.S. by: Bernan Associates-Unipub, 4611-F Assembly Drive, Lanham, MD 20706-4391) Indexed: Biol.Abstr. Ocean.Abstr. Aqua.Sci.& Fish.Abstr.

639   UN   ISSN 0433-3519
GENERAL FISHERIES COUNCIL FOR THE MEDITERRANEAN. STUDIES AND REVIEWS. 1957. irreg., no.61, 1984. price varies. Food and Agriculture Organization of the United Nations, Distribution & Sales Section, Via delle Terme di Caracalla, I-00100 Rome, Italy (Dist. in U.S. by: Bernan Associates-Unipub, 4611-F Assembly Drive, Lanham, MD 20706-4391) Indexed: Biol.Abstr.

639.22   UK   ISSN 0308-0935
GREAT BRITAIN. MINISTRY OF AGRICULTURE, FISHERIES AND FOOD. DIRECTORATE OF FISHERIES RESEARCH. FISHING PROSPECTS. 1969. a. free. Ministry of Agriculture, Fisheries and Food, Directorate of Fisheries Research, Marine Laboratory, P.O. Box 101, Victoria Rd., Aberdeen AB9 8DB, Scotland. Indexed: Aqua.Sci.& Fish Abstr.
    Formerly: Fish Stock Record (ISSN 0264-1240)

639.22 614.7   UK   ISSN 0308-5589
GREAT BRITAIN. MINISTRY OF AGRICULTURE, FISHERIES AND FOOD. DIRECTORATE OF FISHERIES RESEARCH. FISHERIES RESEARCH TECHNICAL REPORT. 1971. irreg. free. Ministry of Agriculture, Fisheries and Food, Directorate of Fisheries Research, Lowestoft, Suffolk NR33 0HT, England. Indexed: Chem.Abstr. Aqua.Sci.& Fish Abstr.

639.22   UK   ISSN 0143-8018
GREAT BRITAIN. MINISTRY OF AGRICULTURE, FISHERIES AND FOOD. DIRECTORATE OF FISHERIES RESEARCH. LABORATORY LEAFLET. irreg., no.49, 1979. free. Ministry of Agriculture, Fisheries and Food, Directorate of Fisheries Research, Lowestoft, Suffolk NR33 0HT, England. Indexed: Biol.Abstr. Nutr.Abstr.

639.22 614.7   UK   ISSN 0308-5570
GREAT BRITAIN. MINISTRY OF AGRICULTURE, FISHERIES AND FOOD. DIRECTORATE OF FISHERIES RESEARCH. REPORT OF THE DIRECTOR OF FISHERIES RESEARCH. biennial. free. Ministry of Agriculture, Fisheries and Food, Directorate of Fisheries Research, Lowestoft, Suffolk NR33 0HT, England.

FISH AND FISHERIES

639   UK
GREAT BRITAIN. SEA FISH INDUSTRY AUTHORITY. ANNUAL REPORT AND ACCOUNTS. 1951/52. a. price varies. Sea Fish Industry Authority, Sea Fisheries House, 10 Young St., Edinburgh EH2 4JQ, Scotland (Avail. from H.M.S.O., c/o Liaison Officer, Atlantic House, Holborn Viaduct, London EC1P 1BN, England) circ. 1,200.
    Former titles (since 1981): Great Britain. Herring Industry Board. Annual Report (ISSN 0072-6419); Great Gritain. White Fish Authority. Annual Report and Accounts (ISSN 0072-7261)

639   US   ISSN 0072-7296
GREAT LAKES FISHERY COMMISSION (UNITED STATES AND CANADA) ANNUAL REPORT. 1956. a. free. Great Lakes Fishery Commission, 1451 Green Rd., Ann Arbor, MI 48105. TEL 313-662-3209. circ. 500. Indexed: Biol.Abstr.

639   US   ISSN 0072-730X
GREAT LAKES FISHERY COMMISSION (UNITED STATES AND CANADA) TECHNICAL REPORT SERIES. 1961. irreg., no.47, 1985. free. Great Lakes Fishery Commission, 1451 Green Rd., Ann Arbor, MI 48105. TEL 313-662-3209. circ. 500. Indexed: Biol.Abstr.

639   US   ISSN 0072-9019
GULF AND CARIBBEAN FISHERIES INSTITUTE. ANNUAL PROCEEDINGS. 1948. a. $30. University of Miami, Gulf and Caribbean Fisheries Institute, Inc., 4600 Rickenbacker Causeway, Miami, FL 33149. Ed. Frank Williams. cum.index: 1948-64. circ. 1,000. Indexed: Biol.Abstr.

639.3   SW   ISSN 0374-8030
HAVSFISKELABORATORIET. MEDDELANDE. (Text in English or Swedish) 1962. irreg. free. National Board of Fisheries, Institute of Marine Research, Box 4, 453 00 Lysekil, Sweden. Ed. Bernt I. Dybern. circ. 450. Indexed: Biol.Abstr.

HOKKAIDO UNIVERSITY. FACULTY OF FISHERIES. DATA RECORD OF OCEANOGRAPHIC OBSERVATIONS AND EXPLORATORY FISHING/KAIYO CHOSA GYOGYO SHIKEN YOHO. see *EARTH SCIENCES — Oceanography*

639.2 597   PH   ISSN 0115-4435
I C L A R M CONFERENCE PROCEEDINGS. (Text in English) 1979. irreg. price varies. International Center for Living Aquatic Resources Management, MCC P.O. Box 1501, Makati, Metro Manila, Philippines. abstr. bibl. illus. index. circ. 1, 200. (back issues avail.) Indexed: Curr.Cont.

639.2   PH   ISSN 0115-4389
I C L A R M STUDIES AND REVIEWS. (Text in English) 1979. irreg. price varies. International Center for Living Aquatic Resources Management, MCC P.O. Box 1501, Makati, Metro Manila, Philippines.

639.2   PH   ISSN 0115-5547
I C L A R M TECHNICAL REPORTS. (Text in English) 1981. irreg. price varies. International Center for Living Aquatic Resources Management, MCC P.O. Box 1501, Makati, Metro Manila, Philippines.

639.2   PH   ISSN 0115-4141
I C L A R M TRANSLATIONS. (Text in English) irreg. price varies. International Center for Living Aquatic Resources Management, MCC P.O. Box 150, Makati, Metro Manila, Philippines.

369.2   UN
I P F C PROCEEDINGS. 1949. biennial. free. Indo-Pacific Fishery Commission, c/o Secretary, F A O Regional Office for Asia and the Pacific, Maliwan Mansion, Phra Atit Rd., Bangkok 10200, Thailand. circ. 1,000. Indexed: Biol.Abstr.
    Formerly (until 1976): Indo-Pacific Fisheries Council. Proceedings.

IDAHO. DEPARTMENT OF FISH AND GAME. FEDERAL AID INVESTIGATION PROJECTS. PROGRESS REPORTS AND PUBLICATIONS. see *CONSERVATION*

597   II   ISSN 0537-2003
INDIAN JOURNAL OF FISHERIES. (Text in English) 1954. a. $7. Central Marine Fisheries Research Institute, P.O. 1912, Cochin 682018, India. circ. 700. (looseleaf format) Indexed: Biol.Abstr. Chem.Abstr. Nutr.Abstr. Pollut.Abstr. Helminthol.Abstr.

639   UN   ISSN 0537-3654
INDO-PACIFIC FISHERIES COUNCIL. REGIONAL STUDIES. 1965. irreg. Food and Agriculture Organization of the United Nations, Regional Office for Asia and the Far East, Maliwan Mansion, Phra Atit Road, Bangkok 2, Thailand. Indexed: Biol.Abstr.

639   MR   ISSN 0069-0821
INSTITUT DES PECHES MARITIMES. BULLETIN. (Text in French) 1953. irreg., no.17, Jul. 1969. Institut des Peches Maritimes, Rue de Tiznit, Casablanca, Morocco. (Affiliate: Office National des Peches) Indexed: Biol.Abstr.

639   BL   ISSN 0046-9939
INSTITUTO DE PESCA, SAO PAULO. BOLETIM. (Text in Portuguese; summaries in English) 1971. irreg. free. Instituto de Pesca, Av. Francisco Matarazzo, 455, 05001 Sao Paulo, S.P., Brazil. Ed. Dr. Newton Castagnolli. adv. circ. 1,000. Indexed: Nutr.Abstr.

630   BL
INSTITUTO DE PESCA, SAO PAULO. BOLETIM. SERIE DE DIVULGACAO. 1972. irreg. free. Instituto de Pesca, Av. Francisco Matarazzo, 455, 05001 Sao Paulo, S.P., Brazil. Ed. Dr. Newton Castagnolli. circ. 1,000. Indexed: Nutr.Abstr.

639.1 639.2   PE   ISSN 0378-7699
INSTITUTO DEL MAR DEL PERU. BOLETIN. (Text in Spanish; summaries in English) 1963. irreg. (4-5/yr.) $40. Instituto del Mar del Peru, Centro de Informacion, Apdo. 22, Callao, Peru. Indexed: Biol.Abstr.

639.2 639.3   PE   ISSN 0378-7702
INSTITUTO DEL MAR DEL PERU. INFORME. (Text in Spanish; summaries in English) 1962. irreg. (4-5/yr.) $40. Instituto del Mar del Peru, Centro de Informacion, Apdo. 22, Callao, Peru. bibl. charts. illus. stat. Indexed: Biol.Abstr.

639.2   AG   ISSN 0325-6987
INSTITUTO NACIONAL DE INVESTIGACION Y DESARROLLO PESQUERO. MEMORIA. a. Instituto Nacional de Investigacion y Desarrollo Pesquero, Casilla de Correo 175, 7600 Mar del Plata, Argentina.

639   US   ISSN 0074-1000
INTER-AMERICAN TROPICAL TUNA COMMISSION. ANNUAL REPORT/COMISION INTER-AMERICANA DEL ATUN TROPICAL. (Text in English and Spanish) 1951. a. price varies. Inter-American Tropical Tuna Commission, c/o Scripps Institution of Oceanography, La Jolla, CA 92093. TEL 619-453-2820. Ed. William H. Bayliff. circ. 1,200.

639   US   ISSN 0074-0993
INTER-AMERICAN TROPICAL TUNA COMMISSION. BULLETIN/COMISION INTERAMERICANA DEL ATUN TROPICAL. BOLETIN. (Text in English and Spanish) 1954. irreg., vol.18, no.6, 1986. price varies. Inter-American Tropical Tuna Commission, c/o Scripps Institution of Oceanography, La Jolla, CA 92093. TEL 619-453-2820. Ed. William H. Bayliff. circ. 1, 000. Indexed: Biol.Abstr.

639   US   ISSN 0538-3609
INTER-AMERICAN TROPICAL TUNA COMMISSION. DATA REPORT. 1966. irreg., no.7, 1984. price varies. Inter-American Tropical Tuna Commission, c/o Scripps Institution of Oceanography, La Jolla, CA 92093. TEL 619-453-2820. Ed. William H. Bayliffon. circ. 500 (approx.)

639   US
INTER-AMERICAN TROPICAL TUNA COMMISSION. SPECIAL REPORT. 1975. irreg., no. 5, 1985. price varies. Inter-American Tropical Tuna Commission, c/o Scripps Institution of Oceanography, La Jolla, CA 92093. TEL 619-453-2820. Ed. William H. Bayliff. circ. 500. Indexed: Biol.Abstr.

639.2   SP
INTERNATIONAL COMMISSION FOR THE CONSERVATION OF ATLANTIC TUNAS. COLLECTIVE VOLUME OF SCIENTIFIC PAPERS. (Text in English, French and Spanish) 1973. irreg. International Commission for the Conservation of Atlantic Tunas, Principe de Vergara 17, 28001 Madrid, Spain. Ed. P.M. Miyake. circ. controlled.

639.2   SP
INTERNATIONAL COMMISSION FOR THE CONSERVATION OF ATLANTIC TUNAS. NEWSLETTER. (Editions in English, French and Spanish) 1971. irreg. (3-4/yr.). International Commission for the Conservation of Atlantic Tunas, Principe de Vergara 17, 28001 Madrid, Spain. Ed. P.M. Miyake.

INTERNATIONAL COUNCIL FOR THE EXPLORATION OF THE SEA. ANNALES BIOLOGIQUES. see *BIOLOGY*

INTERNATIONAL COUNCIL FOR THE EXPLORATION OF THE SEA. BULLETIN STATISTIQUE. see *EARTH SCIENCES — Oceanography*

INTERNATIONAL COUNCIL FOR THE EXPLORATION OF THE SEA. COOPERATIVE RESEARCH REPORTS. see *EARTH SCIENCES — Oceanography*

INTERNATIONAL COUNCIL FOR THE EXPLORATION OF THE SEA. JOURNAL DU CONSEIL. see *EARTH SCIENCES — Oceanography*

INTERNATIONAL COUNCIL FOR THE EXPLORATION OF THE SEA. RAPPORTS ET PROCES-VERBAUX DES REUNIONS. see *EARTH SCIENCES — Oceanography*

639   US   ISSN 0074-7238
INTERNATIONAL PACIFIC HALIBUT COMMISSION (U.S. AND CANADA). ANNUAL REPORT. 1969. a. free. International Pacific Halibut Commission, Box 95009, Seattle, WA 98145-2009. circ. 2,000. (back issues avail.) Indexed: Biol.Abstr. Ocean.Abstr.

639   US   ISSN 0074-7246
INTERNATIONAL PACIFIC HALIBUT COMMISSION (U.S. AND CANADA). SCIENTIFIC REPORTS. no.62, 1976. irreg. free. International Pacific Halibut Commission, Box 95009, Seattle, WA 98145-2009. circ. 1,500. Indexed: Biol.Abstr. Ocean.Abstr.

639   US   ISSN 0579-3920
INTERNATIONAL PACIFIC HALIBUT COMMISSION (U.S. AND CANADA). TECHNICAL REPORTS. 1969. irreg., no.20, 1982. free. International Pacific Halibut Commission, Box 95009, Seattle, WA 98145-2009. circ. 3,000. (back issues avail.) Indexed: Biol.Abstr. Ocean.Abstr.
    Formerly: International Pacific Halibut Commission. Report (ISSN 0096-1221)

639.28 591   UK   ISSN 0074-9591
INTERNATIONAL WHALING COMMISSION. REPORT. 1950. a. price varies. International Whaling Commission, The Red House, Station Rd., Histon, Cambridge CB4 4NP, England. Ed. G.P. Donovan. illus. stat. circ. 500. (back issues avail.) Indexed: Biol.Abstr. Zoo.Rec.

639.2 574   IE
IRISH FISHERIES INVESTIGATIONS. SERIES A: FRESHWATER. 1967. irreg. Department of Fisheries and Forestry, Library, Fisheries Research Centre, Abbotstown, Castleknock, Dublin 15, Ireland. circ. 550. (back issues avail.) Indexed: Biol.Abstr.

639.2 574.92   IE
IRISH FISHERIES INVESTIGATIONS. SERIES B: MARINE. 1967. irreg. Department of Fisheries and Forestry, Library, Fisheries Research Centre, Abbotstown, Castleknock, Dublin 15, Ireland. circ. 550. (back issues avail.) Indexed: Biol.Abstr.

FISH AND FISHERIES

639　　　　　　　IS　ISSN 0075-1189
ISRAEL. MINISTRY OF AGRICULTURE. DEPARTMENT OF FISHERIES. ISRAEL FISHERIES IN FIGURES/DAYIG BE-YISRAEL BE-MISPARIM. (Text in Hebrew and English) 1964. a. Ministry of Agriculture, Dept. of Fisheries, P.O. Box 7011, Haleirya, Tel-Aviv 61070, Israel. circ. 500.

639.3　551.46　　IT　ISSN 0393-3571
ISTITUTO RICERCHE PESCA MARITTIMA. QUADERNI. (Summaries in English, French, Italian) 1970. irreg. avail. only on exchange basis. Laboratorio di Tecnologia della Pesca, Molo Mandracchio, 60100 Ancona, Italy. Ed. C. Froglia. circ. 500.
　　Formerly: Laboratorio di Tecnologia della Pesca. Quaderni.

639　　　　　　　GW　ISSN 0075-2851
JAHRESBERICHT UEBER DIE DEUTSCHE FISCHWIRTSCHAFT. 1949. a. DM.48. Bundesministerium fuer Ernaehrung, Landwirtschaft und Forsten, 5300 Bonn, W. Germany (B.R.D.)

639　　　　　　　TH　ISSN 0125-7978
KASETSART UNIVERSITY, BANGKOK, THAILAND. FACULTY OF FISHERIES. NOTES. (Text in English) 1965. irreg. exchange basis. Kasetsart University, Faculty of Fisheries, Bangkok 10900, Thailand. circ. 500.

639　　　　　　　KE
KENYA FISHERIES REPORTS. irreg. Ministry of Tourism and Wildlife, Box 30027, Nairobi, Kenya.

597　574.5　574.92　KU　ISSN 0250-362X
KUWAIT BULLETIN OF MARINE SCIENCE. (Text and summaries in Arabic and English) 1979. irreg. free. Kuwait Institute for Scientific Research, Mariculture and Fisheries Department, Library, P.O. Box 1638, Salmiya, Kuwait. Ed. M.S. Abdulla. charts. illus. stats. cum.index. circ. 700. (back issues avail.) Indexed: Biol.Abstr. Aqua.Sci.& Fish.Abstr.

639.2　591　　JA　ISSN 0453-0314
KYUSHU UNIVERSITY. CONTRIBUTIONS FROM THE DEPARTMENT OF FISHERIES AND THE FISHERY RESEARCH LABORATORY/ KYUSHU DAIGAKU NOGAKUBU SUISANGAKKA GYOSEKISHU. (Text in English and Japanese) 1959. a. exchange basis. Kyushu University, Department of Fisheries - Kyushu Daigaku Nogakubu Suisan Gakka, 3575-1 Hakozaki, Higashi-ku, Fukuoka 812, Japan.

639　　　　　　　US
MAINE. DEPARTMENT OF MARINE RESOURCES. FISHERIES CIRCULARS. 1947. irreg., no.30, 1977. Department of Marine Resources, State House Annex, Augusta, ME 04330. TEL 207-289-2291.
　　Incorporating: Maine. Department of Sea and Shore Fisheries. General Bulletin (ISSN 0076-2636)

639.2　　　　　　US
MAINE. DEPARTMENT OF MARINE RESOURCES. FISHERY BULLETIN. vol.74, 1976. irreg. free. Department of Marine Resources, State House Annex, Augusta, ME 04330. TEL 207-289-2291.

639.2　　　　　　US
MAINE. DEPARTMENT OF MARINE RESOURCES. RESEARCH BULLETIN. 1949. irreg. free. Department of Marine Resources, State House Annex, Augusta, ME 04330. TEL 207-289-2291.

639.2　　　　　　MW
MALAWI. FISHERIES DEPARTMENT. FISHERIES BULLETIN. 1971. irreg. Fisheries Department, Ministry of Agriculture and Natural Resources, Capital City, Box 30134, Lilongwe 3, Malawi. illus.

639.2　　　　　　MY　ISSN 0126-8856
MALAYSIA. MINISTRY OF AGRICULTURE. FISHERIES DIVISION. ANNUAL FISHERIES STATISTICS/MALAYSIA. KEMENTERIAN PERTANIAN. BAHAGIAN PERIKANAN. PERANGKAAN TAHUNAN PERIKANAN. (Text in English and Malay) 1954. a. M.$10. Ministry of Agriculture, Department of Fisheries, Jalan Mahameru, 50628 Kuala Lumpur, Malaysia. Ed. Sani B. Mohd Isa. illus. circ. 500.

MALAYSIA. MINISTRY OF AGRICULTURE. TECHNICAL AND GENERAL BULLETINS. see *AGRICULTURE*

639.2　　　　　　US　ISSN 0161-522X
MARINE RECREATIONAL FISHERIES. 1976. a. $15. Sport Fishing Institute, 1010 Massachusetts Ave., N.W., Ste. 100, Washington, DC 20001. TEL 202-898-0770. Ed. Henry Clepper. circ. 1,500. (back issues avail.)

639　　　　　　　LY
MARINE RESEARCH CENTRE. BULLETIN. 1980. a. Marine Research Centre, P.O. Box 315, Tripoli, Libya.

639.2　　　　　　DK
MEDDELELSER FRA FERSKVANDSFISKERILABORATORIET. 1979. irreg. free. Danmarks Fiskeri- og Havundersoegelser, Ferskvandsfiskerilaboratoriet, Lysbrogade 52, DK-8600 Silkeborg, Denmark. Ed. J. Dahl. circ. 300. Indexed: Geo.Abstr.
　　Formerly: Danmarks Fiskeri- og Havunersoegelser. Ferskvandsfiskerilaboratoriet. Meddelelser. (ISSN 0108-4844)

639　　　　　　　US　ISSN 0076-7905
MICHIGAN. DEPARTMENT OF NATURAL RESOURCES. INSTITUTE FOR FISHERIES RESEARCH. MISCELLANEOUS PUBLICATION. 1944. irreg. Department of Natural Resources, Institute for Fisheries Research, Univ. Museums Annex, Ann Arbor, MI 48109. TEL 313-662-3209.

639　　　　　　　JA
MIE UNIVERSITY. FACULTY OF FISHERIES. JOURNAL. (Text in Japanese and English; summaries in English) 1950. a. exchange basis. Mie University, Faculty of Fisheries - Mie Daigaku Suisan Gakubu, 2-80 Edobashi, Tsu-shi 514, Japan. circ. controlled. Indexed: Biol.Abstr. Nutr.Abstr. Vet.Bull.
　　Formerly: Mie Prefectural University. Faculty of Fisheries. Bulletin (ISSN 0539-998X)

639　　　　　　　US　ISSN 0076-9150
MINNESOTA FISHERIES INVESTIGATIONS. 1958. irreg. free to qualified personnel. ‡ Department of Natural Resources, Division of Fish and Wildlife, 500 Lafayette Rd., St. Paul, MN 55146. TEL 612-296-3325. Ed. P.J. Wingate. Indexed: Biol.Abstr.
　　Formerly: Minnesota Fish and Game Investigations. Fish Series.

353.9　　　　　　US　ISSN 0733-2017
MISSISSIPPI. DEPARTMENT OF WILDLIFE CONSERVATION. ANNUAL REPORT. a. Department of Wildlife Conservation, Box 451, Jackson, MS 39205. TEL 601-961-5310.
　　Former titles: Mississippi. Department of Wildlife Conservation. Annual Report to the Regular Session of the Mississippi Legislature (ISSN 0731-4221); Mississippi. State Game and Fish Commission. Annual Report to the Regular Session of the Mississippi Legislature (ISSN 0098-7840)

639　　　　　　　CN　ISSN 0704-4798
N A F O ANNUAL REPORT. 1951. a. price varies. Northwest Atlantic Fisheries Organization, P.O. Box 638, Dartmouth, N.S. B2Y 3Y9, Canada. TEL 902-469-9105. Ed. J.C.E. Cardoso. Indexed: Biol.Abstr.
　　Former titles (until vol.29, 1980): International Commission for the Northwest Atlantic Fisheries. Annual Report (ISSN 0303-4151); International Commission for the Northwest Atlantic Fisheries. Annual Proceedings (ISSN 0074-2627)

639　　　　　　　CN　ISSN 0250-7811
N A F O LIST OF FISHING VESSELS. 1980. triennial. price varies. Northwest Atlantic Fisheries Organization, P.O. Box 638, Dartmouth, N.S. B2Y 3Y9, Canada. TEL 902-469-9105. circ. controlled.
　　Formerly (until 1980): International Commission for the Northwest Atlantic Fisheries. List of Fishing Vessels (ISSN 0074-2635)

639　　　　　　　CN　ISSN 0250-6416
N A F O SCIENTIFIC COUNCIL MEETING REPORTS. 1980. a. price variesribution. Northwest Atlantic Fisheries Organization, P.O. Box 638, Dartmouth, N.S. B2Y 3Y9, Canada. TEL 902-469-9105. Ed. V.M. Hodder. Indexed: Biol.Abstr.
　　Formerly (until Dec. 1980): International Commission for the Northwest Atlantic Fisheries. Redbook (ISSN 0074-2643)

639　　　　　　　CN　ISSN 0250-6432
N A F O SCIENTIFIC COUNCIL STUDIES. 1980. irreg. price varies. Northwest Atlantic Fisheries Organization, P.O. Box 638, Dartmouth, N.S. B2Y 3Y9, Canada. TEL 902-469-9105. Ed. V.M. Hodder. Indexed: Biol.Abstr.
　　Formerly (until 1980): International Commission for the Northwest Atlantic Fisheries. Selected Papers (ISSN 0380-4933)

639　　　　　　　CN　ISSN 0250-6394
N A F O STATISTICAL BULLETIN. 1952. a. price varies. Northwest Atlantic Fisheries Organization, P.O. Box 638, Dartmouth, Nova Scotia, B2Y 3Y9, Canada. TEL 902-469-9105. Ed. V.M. Hodder. Indexed: Biol.Abstr. CS Ind.
　　Formerly (until vol.28, 1980): International Commission for the Northwest Atlantic Fisheries. Statistical Bulletin (ISSN 0074-266X)

NATIONAL FISHERIES UNIVERSITY OF PUSAN. INSTITUTE OF MARINE SCIENCES. CONTRIBUTIONS. see *BIOLOGY*

639.3　　　　　　CH
NATIONAL TAIWAN UNIVERSITY. INSTITUTE OF FISHERY BIOLOGY. REPORT. (Text and summaries in Chinese or English) 1956. irreg., approx. biennial. exchange basis. National Taiwan University, Institute of Fishery Biology, Taipei, Taiwan 107, Republic of China. (back issues avail) Indexed: Biol.Abstr.

353.9　　　　　　US　ISSN 0092-1696
NEBRASKA. FISHERIES PRODUCTION DIVISION. ANNUAL REPORT. 1971. a. Game and Parks Commission, Fisheries Division, Box 30370, Lincoln, NE 68503. TEL 702-464-0641. illus.

639　　　　　　　NE　ISSN 0168-4167
NETHERLANDS. CENTRAAL BUREAU VOOR DE STATISTIEK. STATISTIEK VAN DE VISSERIJ. STATISTICS OF FISHERIES. (Text in Dutch and English) 1950. a. fl.8.40. Centraal Bureau voor de Statistiek, Prinses Beatrixlaan 428, Voorburg, Netherlands (Orders to: Staatsuitgeverij, Christoffel Plantijnstraat, The Hague, Netherlands)

639　　　　　　　CN　ISSN 0077-8036
NEW BRUNSWICK DEPARTMENT OF FISHERIES. ANNUAL REPORT. (Text in English and French) 1964. a. free. Department of Fisheries, Box 6000, Fredericton, N.B. E3B 5H1, Canada. TEL 506-453-2251.

NEW HAMPSHIRE. FISH AND GAME DEPARTMENT. GAME MANAGEMENT AND RESEARCH DIVISION. BIOLOGICAL SURVEY BULLETIN. see *BIOLOGY*

NEW HAMPSHIRE. FISH AND GAME DEPARTMENT. GAME MANAGEMENT AND RESEARCH DIVISION. TECHNICAL CIRCULAR SERIES. see *BIOLOGY*

NEW SOUTH WALES. DEPARTMENT OF AGRICULTURE. ANNUAL REPORT. see *AGRICULTURE*

639.2　　　　　　AT　ISSN 0814-0545
NEW SOUTH WALES. DEPARTMENT OF AGRICULTURE. FISHERIES BULLETIN. 1984. irreg. price varies. Department of Agriculture, P.O. Box K220, Haymarket, N.S.W. 2000, Australia. Ed. A.S. Mitchell. circ. 750.

639　　　　　　　AT
NEW SOUTH WALES. STATE FISHERIES. KAPALA CRUISE REPORT. 1970. irreg., no.76, 1982. free. Department of Agriculture, Division of Fisheries, 211 Kent St., Sydney, N.S.W. 2000, Australia. Eds. T. Gorman, K. Graham. circ. 800. (back issues avail.)

FISH AND FISHERIES

639.3   NZ   ISSN 0110-1749
NEW ZEALAND. MINISTRY OF AGRICULTURE AND FISHERIES. FISHERIES RESEARCH DIVISION. BULLETIN. irreg. Ministry of Agriculture and Fisheries, Fisheries Research Centre, P.O. Box 297, Wellington, New Zealand. Eds. R.M. Ogilvie, G.G. Baird. illus. (back issues avail.) Indexed: Biol.Abstr.

639.3   NZ   ISSN 0110-4519
NEW ZEALAND. MINISTRY OF AGRICULTURE AND FISHERIES. FISHERIES RESEARCH DIVISION: INFORMATION LEAFLET. irreg. free. Ministry of Agriculture and Fisheries, Fisheries Research Centre, P.O. Box 297, Wellington, New Zealand.

639.2   NZ   ISSN 0110-1765
NEW ZEALAND. MINISTRY OF AGRICULTURE AND FISHERIES. FISHERIES RESEARCH DIVISION. OCCASIONAL PUBLICATION. 1967. irreg. Ministry of Agriculture and Fisheries, Fisheries Research Centre, P.O. Box 297, Wellington, New Zealand.

639.2   NZ
NEW ZEALAND. MINISTRY OF AGRICULTURE AND FISHERIES. FISHERIES TECHNICAL REPORT. 1974, no.157. irreg. free. ‡ Ministry of Agriculture and Fisheries, Private Bag, Wellington, New Zealand. bibl. illus. circ. 600. Indexed: Biol.Abstr.

NEW ZEALAND MARINE SCIENCES NEWSLETTER. see *BIOLOGY*

639.2   NR
NIGERIA. FEDERAL DEPARTMENT OF FISHERIES. FEDERAL FISHERIES OCCASIONAL PAPER. (Continues occasional paper issued by the Dept. of Fisheries Research of Nigeria) 1969. irreg., latest issue 1974. price varies. Federal Department of Fisheries, P.M.B. 12529, Lagos, Nigeria. Indexed: Biol.Abstr.

639.2   799.1   NO
NORSK FISKARALMANAKK. 1903. a. Kr.138. (Selskabet for de Norske Fiskeriers Fremme) A-S Nordanger Forlag, Postboks 731, N-5001 Bergen, Norway. adv. circ. 7,000.

639   US   ISSN 0094-128X
NORTHEAST PACIFIC PINK AND CHUM SALMON WORKSHOP. PROCEEDINGS. quadrennial. Department of Fish and Game, Box 3-2000, Juneau, AK 99801. TEL 907-465-4293. illus. Key Title: Proceedings of the Northeast Pacific Pink Salmon Workshop.

639   NO
NORWAY. FISKERIDIREKTORATET. FISKEFLAATEN. (Subseries of Aarsberetning Vedkommende Norges Fiskerier) 1952. a. price varies. Fiskeridirektoratet - Directorate of Fisheries, Box 185, 5001 Bergen, Norway.

639   574.92   NO   ISSN 0015-3117
NORWAY. FISKERIDIREKTORATET. SKRIFTER. SERIE HAVUNDERSOEKELSER. (Text in English and Norwegian; summaries in English) 1900. irreg., vol.18, no.4, 1986. price varies. Fiskeridirektoratet, Havforskningsinstituttet - Directorate of Fisheries, Institute of Marine Research, Box 1870-72, N-5011 Bergen-Nordnes, Norway. Ed. Erling Bratberg. Indexed: Biol.Abstr. Ocean.Abstr. Aqua.Sci.& Fish.Abstr. B.R.I.
Report on Norwegian fishery & marine investigations

OCCASIONAL PAPERS IN MARITIME AFFAIRS; Australia's offshore maritime interests. see *ENVIRONMENTAL STUDIES*

639   CN   ISSN 0827-570X
OKAY ANGLERS FISHING DIRECTORY & ATLAS; B.C. lakes & streams. 1984. a. Can.$8.95. Hoshi Enterprises, 753 Kinnear Ave., Kelowna, B.C. V1Y 5B2, Canada. TEL 604-763-4425. Ed. Bill Hoshizaki. adv. circ. 10,000.

639   US   ISSN 0078-7574
PACIFIC MARINE FISHERIES COMMISSION. ANNUAL REPORT. 1949. a. free. Pacific Marine Fisheries Commission, 305 State Office Bldg., 1400 S.W. Fifth Ave., Portland, OR 97201. TEL 503-229-5840. Ed. Russell G. Porter. circ. 1,050. Indexed: Biol.Abstr. Ocean.Abstr.

639   US   ISSN 0078-7582
PACIFIC MARINE FISHERIES COMMISSION. BULLETIN. 1948. irreg., no.8, 1972. free. Pacific Marine Fisheries Commission, 305 State Office Bldg., 1400 S.W. Fifth Ave., Portland, OR 97201. TEL 503-229-5840. Ed. Larry Six. Indexed: Biol.Abstr.

639.2   PP
PAPUA NEW GUINEA. DEPARTMENT OF PRIMARY INDUSTRY, FISHERIES RESEARCH & SURVEYS BRANCH. ANNUAL REPORT. (Text and summaries in English) 1970. a. free to institutions. Department of Primary Industry, Fisheries Research & Surveys Branch, P.O. Box 417, Konedobu, Papua New Guinea. Ed. David Coates. circ. 500. Indexed: Biol.Abstr.

639   PO
PORTUGAL. INSTITUTO NACIONAL DE ESTATISTICA. ESTATISTICAS DA PESCA/ STATISTIQUES DE LA PECHE. CONTINENTE, ACORES E MADEIRA. (Text and summaries in French and Portuguese) 1969. a. Esc.300. Instituto Nacional de Estatistica, Av. Antonio Jose de Almeida, 1078 Lisbon Codex, Portugal (Orders to: Imprensa Nacional, Casa da Moeda, Direccao Comercial, rua D. Francisco Manuel de Melo 5, 1000 Lisbon, Portugal) stat. (processed)
Formerly: Portugal. Instituto Nacional de Estatistica. Estatisticas da Pesca/Statistiques de la Peche.

PORTUGAL. INSTITUTO NACIONAL DE INVESTIGACAO DAS PESCAS. BOLETIM. see *BIOLOGY — Zoology*

639.2   US   ISSN 0197-4106
PROPAGATION & DISTRIBUTION OF FISHES FROM NATIONAL FISH HATCHERIES FOR THE FISCAL YEAR. (Subseries of Fish Distribution Report) 1872. a. free. U.S. Fish & Wildlife Service, Division of Fish Hatcheries, Dept. of the Interior, Washington, DC 20240. TEL 202-653-7581. stat. circ. 1,275.

639.2   GW   ISSN 0438-4555
PROTOKOLLE ZUR FISCHEREITECHNIK. (Text and summaries in English and German) 1962. irreg. (1-3/yr.) price varies. Bundesforschungsanstalt fuer Fischerei, Institut fuer Fangtechnik, Palmaille 9, D-2000 Hamburg 50, W. Germany (B.R.D.) Ed. Dr. Steinberg. stat. circ. 400(controlled) Indexed: Biol.Abstr. Aqua.Sci.& Fish Abstr.

574   PR
PUERTO RICO. DEPARTMENT OF AGRICULTURE. AGRICULTURAL AND FISHERIES CONTRIBUTIONS/PUERTO RICO. DEPARTAMENTO DE AGRICULTURA. CONTRIBUCIONES AGROPECUARIAS Y PESQUERAS. (Text and summaries in Spanish and English) 1969. irreg. free. Commercial Fisheries Laboratory, Box 3665, Mayaguez, PR 00708. abstr. bibl. charts. illus. stat. index.

639.2   IC
RANNSOKNASTOFNUN FISKIDNADARINS. ARSSKYRSLA. (Summaries in English) 1968. a. exchange basis. Icelandic Fisheries Laboratories, P.O. Box 1390, 121 Reykjavik, Iceland. Ed. Pall Olafsson. circ. 1,600. (back issues avail.) Indexed: Biol.Abstr.

639   US   ISSN 0083-7555
RESEARCH IN FISHERIES. (Represents the College's Annual Report) 1958. biennial. free. ‡ University of Washington, College of Fisheries, Seattle, WA 98105. TEL 206-543-6605. index. circ. 2,000. Indexed: Biol.Abstr.

338.3   FR   ISSN 0078-6241
REVIEW OF FISHERIES IN O.E.C.D. MEMBER COUNTRIES. 1967. a. $22. Organization for Economic Cooperation and Development, 2 rue Andre-Pascal, 75775 Paris 16, France (U.S. subscr. to: O.E.C.D. Publications and Information Center, 1750 Pennsylvania Ave., N. W., Washington, D. C. 20006) (also avail. in microfiche)

639   CU
REVISTA CUBANA DE INVESTIGACIONES PESQUERAS. BOLETINES BIBLIOGRAFICOS. 1953. irreg. exchange basis. Centro de Investigaciones Pesqueras, Av. Primera y 26, Miramar, Playa, Havana, Cuba. Ed. Raul Valdes Alonso. circ. 900. Indexed: Biol.Abstr.
Former titles: Revista Cubana de Investigaciones Pesqueras (ISSN 0138-8452); (until vol.2, no.3, 1977): Centro de Investigaciones Pesqueras. Revista de Investigaciones; Supersedes (after 1975): Centro de Investigaciones Pesqueras. Contribuciones (ISSN 0067-4656)

639.2   FI   ISSN 0355-0648
RIISTA- JA KALATALOUDEN TUTKIMUSLAITOS. KALANTUTKIMUSOSASTO. TIEDONANTOJA. (Text in Finnish; tables in English) 1971. irreg. exchange basis. Finnish Game and Fisheries Research Institute, Fisheries Division, Box 193, SF-00131 Helsinki 13, Finland. Ed. Eero Aro. stat. circ. 1,200 (controlled) (back issues avail.) Indexed: Biol.Abstr.

639.3   IC   ISSN 0484-9019
RIT FISKIDEILDAR/MARINE RESEARCH INSTITUTE. JOURNAL. (Text in English and German; summaries in English and Icelandic) 1940. irreg. exchange basis. Marine Research Institute - Hafrannsoknastofnunin, Skulagata 4, P.O. Box 1390, 121 Reykjavik, Iceland. Ed. Unnsteinn Stefansson. circ. 400. (back issues avail.) Indexed: Biol.Abstr.

639   PL   ISSN 0080-3723
ROCZNIKI NAUK ROLNICZYCH. SERIA H. RYBACTWO. (Text in Polish; summaries in English and Russian) 1903. irreg., vol.100, 1984. price varies. (Polska Akademia Nauk, Komitet Nauk Zootechnicznych) Panstwowe Wydawnictwo Naukowe, Ul. Miodowa 10, 00-251 Warsaw, Poland (Dist. by: Ars Polona, Krakowskie Przedmiescie 7, 00-068 Warsaw, Poland) Ed. J. Szczerbowski. illus. circ. 360. Indexed: Excerp.Med. Nutr.Abstr. Ind.Vet. Vet.Bull.

RURAL INDUSTRY DIRECTORY. see *AGRICULTURE*

SAINT MARY'S UNIVERSITY. STUDIES IN MARINE AND COASTAL GEOGRAPHY. see *GEOGRAPHY*

639   UK   ISSN 0140-5012
SCOTLAND. DEPARTMENT OF AGRICULTURE AND FISHERIES. MARINE LABORATORY. TRIENNIAL REVIEW OF RESEARCH. 1968. triennial, latest 1982/1984. Department of Agriculture and Fisheries, Marine Laboratory, P.O. Box 101, Victoria Rd., Aberdeen AB9 8DB, Scotland.
Formerly (until 1972): Scotland. Directorate of Fisheries Research. Annual Report (ISSN 0072-6141)

639   UK   ISSN 0559-1791
SCOTTISH FISHERIES BULLETIN. 1952. irreg. (1-2/yr.) free. Department of Agriculture and Fisheries, Marine Laboratory, P.O. Box 101, Victoria Rd., Aberdeen AB9 8DB, Scotland. charts. illus. Indexed: Biol.Abstr. Aqua Sci.& Fish Abstr.

639   UK   ISSN 0309-9105
SCOTTISH FISHERIES INFORMATION PAMPHLETS. 1977 N.S. irreg., no.11, 1984. Department of Agriculture and Fisheries, Marine Laboratory, P.O. Box 101, Victoria Rd., Aberdeen AB9 8DB, Scotland. Indexed: Nutr.Abstr. Ocean.Abstr. Aqua Sci.& Fish Abstr.

639   UK   ISSN 0308-8022
SCOTTISH FISHERIES RESEARCH REPORTS. 1975. irreg., no.36, 1986. Department of Agriculture and Fisheries, Marine Laboratory, P.O. Box 101, Victoria Rd., Aberdeen AB9 8DB, Scotland. charts. Indexed: Biol.Abstr. Nutr.Abstr. Ocean.Abstr. Aqua Sci.& Fish Abstr.

639   UK   ISSN 0080-8202
SCOTTISH SEA FISHERIES STATISTICAL TABLES. 1939. a. price varies. H.M.S.O. (Scotland), 13a Castle St., Edinburgh EH2 3AR, Scotland.

FISH AND FISHERIES

639.2   CL
SERIE INVESTIGACION PESQUERA. (Text in Spanish; summaries in English) 1965. irreg., no.31, 1984. $5. ‡ Instituto de Fomento Pesquero, Seccion Edicion y Publicaciones, Jose Domingo Canas 2277, Casilla 1287, Santiago, Chile. abstr. bibl. charts. stat. circ. 600. (processed) Indexed: Biol.Abstr.
    Formerly: Instituto de Fomento Pesquero. Boletin Cientifico (ISSN 0020-3882)

SHIMA MARINELAND. SCIENCE REPORT. see *BIOLOGY*

639   SA
SOUTH AFRICA. SEA FISHERIES RESEARCH INSTITUTE. INVESTIGATIONAL REPORT. (Text in Afrikaans and English) 1934. irreg., no.127, 1984. exchange basis. Sea Fisheries Research Institute, Private Bag X2, Rogge Bay 8012, Cape Town, South Africa. Eds. H. Boonstra, A. Payne. circ. 1,500. Indexed: Biol.Abstr. Ocean.Abstr. GeoRef.
    Former titles: South Africa. Sea Fisheries Branch. Investigational Report; South Africa. Sea Fisheries Institute. Investigational Report (ISSN 0081-2234)

639   SA
SOUTH AFRICA. SEA FISHERIES RESEARCH INSTITUTE. MARINE DEVELOPMENT BRANCH. ANNUAL REPORT. (Text in Afrikaans and English) 1921. a. exchange basis. ‡ Sea Fisheries Research Institute, Private Bag X2, Rogge Bay 8012, Cape Town, South Africa. circ. 2,000. Indexed: Biol.Abstr.
    Formerly (until 1982): South Africa. Sea Fisheries Institute. Annual Report; South Africa. Sea Fisheries Branch. Annual Report; South Africa. Division of Sea Fisheries. Annual Report (ISSN 0081-2218)

639.2   SA   ISSN 0080-5076
SOUTH AFRICAN FISHING INDUSTRY HANDBOOK AND BUYER'S GUIDE. Variant title: S.A. Fishing Industry Handbook and Buyer's Guide. 1951. biennial. R.45. Thomson Publications S.A. (Pty) Ltd., Thomson House, Cnr. Will Scarlet & H.F. Verwoerd Dr., Randburg, P.O. Box 56182, Pinegowrie 2123, South Africa. Ed. Heinz Engelhardt. adv.

639   SA
SOUTH AFRICAN JOURNAL OF MARINE SCIENCE. (Text in Afrikaans and English) 1935. irreg., no.2, 1984. exchange basis. Sea Fisheries Research Institute, Private Bag X2, Rogge Bay 8012, Cape Town, South Africa. Eds. H. Boonstra, A. Payne. circ. 1,600. Indexed: Biol.Abstr. Ocean.Abstr. Ind.S.A.Per.
    Former titles (until 1983): South Africa. Sea Fisheries Institute. Fisheries Bulletin; South Africa. Sea Fisheries Branch. Fisheries Bulletin; South Africa. Division of Sea Fisheries. Fisheries Bulletin.

639.2   338.1   NL   ISSN 0081-2811
SOUTH PACIFIC COMMISSION. HANDBOOK. (Text in English or French) 1968. irreg., no.20, 1980. price varies. South Pacific Commission, B.P. D5, Noumea, Cedex, New Caledonia.

639.2   338.1   NL   ISSN 0081-282X
SOUTH PACIFIC COMMISSION. INFORMATION CIRCULAR. (Text in English or French) 1968. irreg., no.85, 1980. free. South Pacific Commission, B.P. D5, Noumea, Cedex, New Caledonia.

639.2   338.1   NL   ISSN 0081-2838
SOUTH PACIFIC COMMISSION. INFORMATION DOCUMENT. (Text in English or French) 1967. irreg., no.48, 1979. free. South Pacific Commission, B.P. D5, Noumea, Cedex, New Caledonia.

639.2   338.1   NL
SOUTH PACIFIC COMMISSION. OCCASIONAL PAPER. 1977. irreg., no.17, 1980. South Pacific Commission, B.P. D5, Noumea, Cedex, New Caledonia. bibl.

639.2   338.1   NL   ISSN 0081-2846
SOUTH PACIFIC COMMISSION. REPORT OF S P C FISHERIES TECHNICAL MEETINGS. (Text in English or French) irreg. free. South Pacific Commission, B.P. D5, Noumea, Cedex, New Caledonia.

639.2   SP
SPAIN. DIRECCION GENERAL DE PESCA MARITIMA. PUBLICACIONES TECNICAS. irreg. Direccion General de Pesca Maritima, Madrid, Spain. illus.

639   SP   ISSN 0081-3362
SPAIN. INSTITUTO NACIONAL DE ESTADISTICA. INDUSTRIAS DERIVADAS DE LA PESCA. a. Instituto Nacional de Estadistica, P de la Castellana, 183, Madrid 16, Spain.

SPORTFISKAREN. see *SPORTS AND GAMES — Outdoor Life*

639   FI   ISSN 0085-6940
SUOMEN KALATALOUS. (Text in Finnish; summaries in Swedish and English) 1912. irreg., vol.51, 1983. exchange basis only. Finnish Game and Fisheries Research Institute, Fisheries Division, Box 193, SF-00131 Helsinki 13, Finland. Ed. Kai Westman. circ. 1,300. Indexed: Biol.Abstr.

639   CH   ISSN 0082-1489
TAIWAN. FISHERIES RESEARCH INSTITUTE, KEELUNG. BULLETIN. (Text mainly in Chinese; occasionally in English) 1953. irreg., no.28, 1977. not for sale. Taiwan Fisheries Research Institute, 199 Hou-Ih Rd., Keelung, Taiwan, Republic of China.

639   574   CH   ISSN 0082-1497
TAIWAN. FISHERIES RESEARCH INSTITUTE, KEELUNG. LABORATORY OF FISHERY BIOLOGY. REPORT. (Text in English) 1951. irreg., no.28, 1976. not for sale. Taiwan Fisheries Research Institute, 199 Hon-Ih Rd., Keelung, Taiwan, Republic of China. Indexed: Biol.Abstr.

639   JA   ISSN 0910-2078
TANSUIGYO; freshwater fish. 1975. a. 4000 Yen($20) Tansuigyo Hogo Kyokai, 2/38 Nichome Dojima, Kitaku, Osaka, Japan. Ed. Eizo Kimura. circ. 2,000.

338   500   JA   ISSN 0563-8372
TOKYO UNIVERSITY OF FISHERIES. REPORT/ TOKYO SUISAN DAIGAKU RONSHU. (Text mainly in Japanese; summaries in English) 1966. a. Tokyo University of Fisheries - Tokyo Suisan Daigaku, 4-5-7 Konan, Minato-ku, Tokyo 108, Japan. Ed. Yutaka Uno. illus.

639   919.9   551.4   JA   ISSN 0388-0966
TOKYO UNIVERSITY OF FISHERIES. TRANSACTIONS. (Text in English or Japanese; summaries in English) 1974. irreg. Tokyo University of Fisheries - Tokyo Suisan Daigaku, 4-5-7 Konan, Minato-ku, Tokyo 108, Japan. TEL 03-471-1251. Ed. Yutaka Uno. Indexed: Biol.Abstr. Vet.Bull.

639   JA   ISSN 0082-4836
TOKYO UNIVERSITY OF FISHERIES JOURNAL. SPECIAL EDITION /TOKYO SUISAN DAIGAKU TOKUBETU KENKYU HONOKU. (Text in English or Japanese) 1958. irreg. exchange basis. Tokyo University of Fisheries - Tokyo Suisan Daiguku, 4-5-7 Minato-Ku, Tokyo 108, Japan. Ed. Toyoo Takahashi. charts. illus.

639   607   UK   ISSN 0082-5352
TORRY RESEARCH STATION, ABERDEEN, SCOTLAND. ANNUAL REPORT. 1958. a. free. Torry Research Station, P.O. Box 31, 135 Abbey Rd., Aberdeen, Scotland. Ed. J.J. Connell. circ. 3, 000. Indexed: Biol.Abstr.

639   CN   ISSN 0082-609X
TRAVAUX SUR LES PECHERIES DU QUEBEC. (Text in French and English) 1964. irreg., no.45, 1976. available on exchange. ‡ Ministere de l'Agriculture, Pecheries et Alimentation, C.P. 340, Grand-Riviere, Cte de Gaspe, Que. G0C 1V0, Canada. TEL 418-643-3846. circ. 1,300. Indexed: Biol.Abstr. Ocean.Ind.

TUNISIA. INSTITUT NATIONAL SCIENTIFIQUE ET TECHNIQUE D'OCEANOGRAPHIE ET DE PECHE. BULLETIN. see *EARTH SCIENCES — Oceanography*

639.21   UG
UGANDA FRESHWATER FISHERIES RESEARCH ORGANIZATION. ANNUAL REPORT. 1948. a. $10. Uganda Freshwater Fisheries Research Organization, P.O. Box 343 (Nile Crescent), Jinja, Uganda. circ. 1,000. Indexed: Biol.Abstr.
    Formerly: East African Freshwater Fisheries Research Organization. Annual Report (ISSN 0070-7953)

639   BE
UITKOMSTEN VAN DE BELGISCHE ZEEVISSERIJ. 1957. a. free. Dienst voor de Zeevisserij, Administratief Centrum, Vrijhavenstr. 5, 8400 Oostende, Belgium. Ed.Bd. stat. circ. 200.

639   US   ISSN 0565-0704
U.S. FISH AND WILDLIFE SERVICE. INVESTIGATIONS IN FISH CONTROL. no.25, 1969. irreg., no.91, 1982. U.S. Fish and Wildlife Service, U.S. Dept. of the Interior, Washington, DC 20242. TEL 202-653-7501. Indexed: Biol.Abstr. Chem.Abstr. Pollut.Abstr. Key Title: Investigations in Fish Control.

639   US   ISSN 0083-0941
U.S. FISH AND WILDLIFE SERVICE. RESEARCH REPORTS. 1941. irreg., no.80, 1980. U.S. Fish and Wildlife Service., Department of the Interior, Washington, DC 20240 TEL 303-226-9403. (Orders to: Supt. Doc., Washington, DC 20402) Indexed: Biol.Abstr. Weed Abstr.

639   US   ISSN 0094-7008
U.S. NATIONAL MARINE FISHERIES SERVICE. GRANT-IN-AID FOR FISHERIES: PROGRAM ACTIVITIES. a. $5. U.S. National Marine Fisheries Service, 3300 Whitehaven St. N.W., Washington, DC 20235. TEL 202-655-4000.

639.2   US
U.S. NATIONAL MARINE FISHERIES SERVICE. IMPORTS AND EXPORTS OF FISHERY PRODUCTS. ANNUAL SUMMARY. a. U.S. National Marine Fisheries Service, Statistics and Market News Division, National Oceanic and Atmospheric Administration, Washington, DC 20235. TEL 202-655-4000.

639   US
U.S. NATIONAL MARINE FISHERIES SERVICE. TECHNICAL REPORT. 1940. irreg. price varies. U.S. National Marine Fisheries Service, Scientific Publications Office, 7600 Sandpoint Way NE, Bin C15700, Seattle, WA 98115. Ed. Bd. index. circ. 2, 000. (also avail. in microfiche from NTI) Indexed: Biol.Abstr. Ocean.Abstr.
    Former titles: U.S. National Marine Fisheries Service. Special Scientific Report: Fisheries; U.S Bureau of Commercial Fisheries. Special Scientific Report (ISSN 0082-8904)

639.2   US   ISSN 0085-7939
UNIVERSITY OF WASHINGTON PUBLICATIONS IN FISHERIES. 1962. N.S. irreg., vol.6, 1975. price varies. (University of Washington, College of Fisheries) University of Washington Press, Seattle, WA 98105. TEL 206-543-4050. Indexed: Biol.Abstr.

639.2   NE
VISSERIJ IN CIJFERS. (Text in Dutch; summaries in English) 1962. a. price varies. Landbouw-Economisch Instituut, Conradkade 175, 2517 CL The Hague, Netherlands. Ed. M.N. de Groot.

639   US   ISSN 0083-7474
WASHINGTON (STATE) DEPARTMENT OF FISHERIES. TECHNICAL REPORT. 1970. irreg. (5-7/yr.), no.90, 1986. free. Department of Fisheries, 115 G.A. Bldg., AX-11, Olympia, WA 98504. TEL 206-753-6720. (back issues avail.) Indexed: Biol.Abstr.

639.34   CN   ISSN 0383-2031
WATERS. 1976. irreg. membership. Vancouver Public Aquarium Association, Box 3232, Vancouver, B.C. V6B 3X8, Canada. TEL 604-685-3364. Ed. S.J. Proctor. illus. circ. 17,000.

WER UND WAS IN DER DEUTSCHEN FLEISCH- FISCH- UND FEINKOST-INDUSTRIE. see *AGRICULTURE — Poultry And Livestock*

639.2 614.7   AT   ISSN 0155-9435
WESTERN AUSTRALIA. DEPARTMENT OF
FISHERIES AND WILDLIFE. FISHERIES
RESEARCH BULLETIN. 1941. irreg., no.27, 1982.
free. Fisheries Department, Extension and Publicity
Office, 108 Adelaide Terrace, Perth, W.A. 6000,
Australia. Ed. M.L. Taylor. circ. 1,000. (back issues
avail.) Indexed: Biol.Abstr.
 Formerly part of: Western Australia. Fisheries
and Fauna Department. Bulletin (ISSN 0083-8683)

639.2 639.9   AT   ISSN 0726-0733
WESTERN AUSTRALIA. DEPARTMENT OF
FISHERIES AND WILDLIFE. REPORT. 1964.
irreg., no.59, 1983. free. Department of Fisheries &
Wildlife, 108 Adelaide Terrace, Perth, W.A. 6000,
Australia. circ. 1,000. Indexed: Biol.Abstr.

639.9   AT
WESTERN AUSTRALIAN WILDLIFE
AUTHORITY. ANNUAL REPORT. a. Department
of Fisheries and Wildlife, 108 Adelaide Terrace,
Perth, W.A. 6000, Australia. illus.

639.2   US   ISSN 0270-160X
WHO'S WHO IN THE FISH INDUSTRY. 1980. a.
$95. Urner Barry Publications, Inc., Box 389, Toms
River, NJ 08754. TEL 201-240-5330. Ed. Paul B.
Brown. adv. circ. 2,000.

597   US   ISSN 0194-3340
WORLD RECORD GAME FISHES. 1946. a. $9.75.
‡ International Game Fish Association, 3000 E. Las
Olas Blvd., Fort Lauderdale, FL 33316-1616. TEL
305-467-0161. Ed. Ray Crawford. adv. illus. stat.
circ. 25,000.
 Formerly: World Record Marine Fishes (ISSN
0084-2214)

639.2   UN   ISSN 0084-375X
YEARBOOK OF FISHERY STATISTICS. (Text in
English, French, and Spanish) 1947. a. free. Food
and Agriculture Organization of the United Nations,
Distribution and Sales Section, Via delle Terme di
Caracalla, Rome, Italy (Dist. in U.S. by: Bernan
Associates-Unipub, 4611-F Assembly Drive,
Lanham, MD 20706-4391) circ. 4,000. Indexed: EC
Ind.

639   ZA   ISSN 0514-8731
ZAMBIA. CENTRAL STATISTICAL OFFICE.
FISHERIES STATISTICS (NATURAL WATERS)
1965. a. K.3. Central Statistical Office, P.O. Box
31908, Lusaka, Zambia.

639.2   ZA
ZAMBIA. DEPARTMENT OF FISHERIES.
ANNUAL REPORT. (Text in English) a.
Government Printer, Box 30136, Lusaka, Zambia.
 Supersedes in part (since 1974): Zambia.
Department of Wildlife, Fisheries and National
Parks. Annual Report.

FISH AND FISHERIES — Abstracting, Bibliographies, Statistics

318 639.2   CL
AGRICULTURA Y PESCA. 1911/12. a. $9. Instituto
Nacional de Estadisticas, Av. Bulnes 418, Casilla
4908, Correo 3-Santiago, Chile. stat. (processed)
 Formerly: Agricultura e Industrias Agropecuarias
y Pesca.

AQUATIC SCIENCES & FISHERIES ABSTRACTS.
PART 1: BIOLOGICAL SCIENCES & LIVING
RESOURCES. see *WATER RESOURCES —
Abstracting, Bibliographies, Statistics*

AQUATIC SCIENCES & FISHERIES ABSTRACTS.
PART 2: OCEAN TECHNOLOGY, POLICY
AND NON-LIVING RESOURCES. see *WATER
RESOURCES — Abstracting, Bibliographies,
Statistics*

354.71 310   CN
CANADA. FISHERIES AND OCEANS.
COMMUNICATIONS DIRECTORATE.
STATISTICS ON SALES OF SPORT FISHING
LICENCES IN CANADA. (Text in English and
French) 1971. a. free. Fisheries and Oceans,
Communications Directorate, 200 Kent St., 14th
floor, Ottawa, Ont. K1A 0E6, Canada. TEL 613-
995-2041. circ. 500.
 Formerly: Canada. Fisheries and Marine Service.
Recreational Fisheries Branch. Statistics on Sales of
Sport Fishing Licences in Canada.

639.2 664.94   CN   ISSN 0527-5172
CANADA. STATISTICS CANADA. FISH
PRODUCTS INDUSTRY/INDUSTRIE DE LA
TRANSFORMATION DU POISSON. (Catalogue
32-216) (Text in English, French) 1949. a.
Can.$20($21) Statistics Canada, Communications
Division, 3rd Floor, R.H. Coats Bldg., Ottawa, Ont.
K1A 0T6, Canada TEL 613-993-7276. (Subscr. to:
Publications Sales and Services, Ottawa, Ont. K1A
0T6, Canada) (also avail. in microform from MML)

639   CN
CANADIAN FISHERIES. STATISTICAL
HIGHLIGHTS. 1984. a. Department of Fisheries &
Oceans, Scientific Information and Publications
Branch, 200 Kent St., Ottawa, Ont. circ. 2,400.

639.2 310   US   ISSN 0162-6108
FROZEN FISHERY PRODUCTS. ANNUAL
SUMMARY. a. U.S. National Marine Fisheries
Service, National Oceanic and Atmospheric
Administration, Washington, DC 20235. TEL 301-
655-4000.

639 338.2   GW   ISSN 0072-3673
GERMANY (FEDERAL REPUBLIC, 1949-).
STATISTISCHES BUNDESAMT. FACHSERIE 3,
LAND- UND FORSTWIRTSCHAFT,
FISCHEREI; REIHE 4.5: FISCHEREI. (Includes
subseries: Hochsee- und Kuestenfischerei;
Bodenseefischerei) m. (plus a.) DM.38.40. W.
Kohlhammer-Verlag GmbH, Abt.
Veroeffentlichungen des Statistischen Bundesamtes,
Philipp-Reis-Str. 3, Postfach 421120, 6500 Mainz
42, W. Germany (B.R.D.)

639.2   GR   ISSN 0256-3584
GREECE. NATIONAL STATISTICAL SERVICE.
RESULTS OF SEA FISHERY SURVEY BY
MOTOR VESSELS. (Text in English and Greek)
1964. a. $3. National Statistical Service, Publications
and Information Division, 14-16 Lycourgou St.,
10166 Athens, Greece.

597   PH   ISSN 0115-5997
I C L A R M BIBLIOGRAPHIES. 1980. irreg. price
varies. International Center for Living Aquatic
Resources Management, MCC P.O. Box 1501,
Makati, Metro Manila, Philippines.

639 016   II
INDIAN FISHERIES ABSTRACTS. 1962. q.
exchange basis. Central Inland Fisheries Research
Institute, Barrackpore 743101, West Bengal, India.
Ed.Bd. cum.index. circ. 210. (processed)
 Formerly: Bibliography of Indian Fisheries (ISSN
0006-1557)

338.476   CK
INSTITUTO DE DESARROLLO DE LOS
RECURSOS NATURALES RENOVABLES.
OFICINA DE PLANEACION. ESTADISTICAS
PESQUERAS. a. Instituto de Desarrollo de los
Recursos Naturales Renovables, Oficina de
Planeacion, Bogota, Colombia.

639.2 310   SP
INTERNATIONAL COMMISSION FOR THE
CONSERVATION OF ATLANTIC TUNAS.
STATISTICAL BULLETIN. (Text in English,
French and Spanish) 1971. a. International
Commission for the Conservation of Atlantic Tunas,
Principe de Vergara 17, 28001 Madrid, Spain. Ed.
P.M. Miyake. circ. controlled.

MARINE SCIENCE CONTENTS TABLES. see
BIOLOGY — Abstracting, Bibliographies, Statistics

639.3 310   NO
NORWAY. STATISTISK SENTRALBYRAA.
FISKERISTATISTIKK/FISHERY STATISTICS.
(Text in English and Norwegian) 1868. biennial.
Kr.50. Statistisk Sentralbyra - Central Bureau of
Statistics, Box 8131 Dep, N-Oslo 1, Norway. circ.
1,600. Indexed: Biol.Abstr.

QUEBEC. BUREAU DE STATISTIQUE.
STATISTIQUES DE L'AGRICULTURE, DES
PECHES ET DE L'ALIMENTATION, EDITION
(YEAR) see *AGRICULTURE — Abstracting,
Bibliographies, Statistics*

639 338   SP
SPAIN. DIRECCION GENERAL DE PESCA
MARITIMA. ANUARIO DE PESCA
MARITIMA. 1973. a. Direccion General de Pesca
Maritma, Madrid, Spain.
 Formed by the merger of: Spain. Direccion
General de Pesca Maritima. Estadistica de Pesca &
Spain. Direccion General de Pesca Maritima. Flota
Pesquera Espanola.

639 016   US   ISSN 0038-786X
SPORT FISHERY ABSTRACTS; an abstracting
service for fishery research and management. 1955.
q. U.S. Fish and Wildlife Service, Washington, DC
20240 TEL 303-226-9403. (Editorial address:
Aylesworth Hall, CSU, Fort Collins, CO 80523) Ed.
Roger Schoumacher.

FLORIST TRADE

see *Gardening and Horticulture — Florist Trade*

FOLKLORE

398   SW   ISSN 0065-0897
ACTA ACADEMIAE REGIAE GUSTAVI
ADOLPHI. (Text in English, German and
Scandinavian languages; summaries in English)
1933. irreg., no.56, 1983. price varies. Kungliga
Gustav Adolfs Akademien, Klostergatan 2, S-753 21
Uppsala, Sweden (Subscr.to: Almqvist & Wiksell
International, P.O. Box 45150, S-104 30 Stockholm,
Sweden) Ed. Lennart Elmevik.

301.2 398 943   CS
ACTA ETHNOLOGICA SLOVACA. 1974. irreg.
price varies. (Slovenska Akademia Vied,
Narodopisny Ustav) Veda, Publishing House of the
Slovak Academy of Sciences, Klemensova 19, 814
30 Bratislava, Czechoslovakia (Exchange to:
Oddelenie Vymeny Publikacii, Ustredna Kniznica
Sav, Klemensova 19, 814 67 Bratislava)

398 949.5   GR
AKADEMIA ATHENON. KENTRON EREUNES
TES HELLENIKES LAOGRAPHIAS. EPETERIS.
(Text in Greek; summaries in French) 1939. irreg.
Academy of Athens, Kentron Laographias, Leoforos
Sygrou 129, 117 45 Athens, Greece. TEL 93.44-
811. Ed. Anna Papamichael-Koutroubas. bibl.
cum.index. circ. 500. (back issues avail.) Indexed:
Hist.Abstr. M.L.A. Amer.Hist. & Life.
 Formerly: Laographikon Archeion. Epeteris.

ALTERNATE CELEBRATIONS CATALOGUE. see
*BUSINESS AND ECONOMICS — Trade And
Industrial Directories*

398   GW
ALTES HANDWERK. 1972. irreg., no.54, 1985. price
varies. (Gesellschaft fuer Volkskunde, Basel,
Abteilung Film, SZ) Dr. Rudolf Habelt GmbH, Am
Buchenhang 1, 5300 Bonn 1, W. Germany (B.R.D.)
Ed. Paul Hugger.

398   US
AMERICAN MATERIAL CULTURE AND
FOLKLIFE. irreg., vol.4, 1986. U M I Research
Press, 300 N. Zeeb Rd., Ann Arbor, MI 48106. Ed.
Simon Bronner.

ANUARIO DE EUSKO-FOLKLORE; etnografia y
paletnografia. see *ANTHROPOLOGY*

398   RM
ANUARUL DE FOLCLOR. (Text in Rumanian;
summaries in English, French, German) 1980. a. 70
lei. University of Cluj-Napoca, Department of
Ethnology, Sectorul de Etnologie si Sociologie, Str.
Republicii 9, Rumania. Ed. Ion Talos. bk. rev. abstr.
bibl. charts. illus. stats. circ. 1,000. (back issues
avail.)

APPELTJES VAN HET MEETJESLAND. see
HISTORY — History Of Europe

ARCHIV FUER VOELKERKUNDE. see
ANTHROPOLOGY

ARCHIVIO PER L'ALTO ADIGE; rivista di studi
alpini. see LINGUISTICS

ARCHIVOS DE HISTORIA ANDINA. see
HISTORY — History Of North And South
America

ARSTRYCK. see ARCHAEOLOGY

398   HU   ISSN 0139-4649
ARTES POPULARES. a. Lorand Eotvos University,
Department of Folklore, Egyetem-ter 1-3, P.O.B.
109, 1364 Budapest, V, Hungary. Eds. Luiz Boglar,
Geza Kezdi Nagy.

398   SW   ISSN 0066-8176
ARV/JOURNAL OF SCANDINAVIAN
FOLKLORE; journal of Scandinavian folklore/
tidskrift foer nordisk folkminnesforskning. (Text in
English and German; summaries in English) 1945.
a. Kr.55. (Kungliga Gustav Adolfs Akademien -
Royal Gustavus Adolphus Academy) Almqvist &
Wiksell International, Box 62, S-101 20 Stockholm,
Sweden. Ed. Dag Stromback. bk. rev. circ. 500.
Indexed: Hist.Abstr. M.L.A. Amer.Hist.& Life.

ATLAS POLSKICH STROJOW LUDOWYCH. see
ANTHROPOLOGY

398 398   IT   ISSN 0067-9860
B R A D S. (Bollettino del Repertorio e dell'Atlante
Demologico Sardo) (Summaries in English and
German) 1966. irreg., latest no.12-13, 1986. L.5000
or exchange. Universita degli Studi di Cagliari,
Cattedra di Storia delle Tradizioni Popolari,
Cagliari, Italy (Dist. by: Libreria CUEC, Via Is
Mirrionis 1, I-09100 Cagliari, Italy) Ed. Enrica
Delitala. bk. rev. circ. 500.

398 745   GW   ISSN 0067-4591
BAUERNHAEUSER DER SCHWEIZ. 1965. irreg.,
no.12, 1985. price varies. Dr. Rudolf Habelt GmbH,
Am Buchenhang 1, 5300 Bonn 1, W. Germany
(B.R.D.)

398   GW   ISSN 0067-4729
BAYERISCHES JAHRBUCH FUER
VOLKSKUNDE. 1950. a. price varies. (Bayerische
Akademie der Wissenschaften, Institut fuer
Volkskunde) Karl Hart, 8712 Volkach, W. Germany
(B.R.D) Ed. T. Gebhard. bk. rev. circ. 800.

398 301.2   BL
BIBLIOGRAFICA FOLCLORICA. 1977. a.
Cr.$1000. (Fundacao Nacional de Arte) Instituto
Nacional do Folclore, Rua do Catete, 179, 22220
Rio de Janeiro, RJ, Brazil (Subscr. to: Fundacao
Nacional de Arte, Rua Araujo Porto Alegre-80,
20030 Rio de Janeiro-RJ, Brazil) bk. rev. circ. 2,
000.

398   BL
BOLETIM ALAGOANO DE FOLCLORE. 1977.
irreg. Comissao Alagoana de Folclore, Av. Tomas
Espindola 489, Farol, Maceio, Brazil. illus.

398   II
C I I L FOLKLORE SERIES. (Text in English) 1975.
irreg., latest 1977. Central Institute of Indian
Languages, Manasagangotri, Mysore 570006, India.
bibl.

398   BL   ISSN 0575-0075
CADERNOS DE FOLCLORE. 1975. irreg.
(Fundacao Nacional de Arte) Instituto Nacional do
Folclore, Rua do Catete, 179, 22220 Rio de Janeiro,
RJ, Brazil (Subscr. to: Fundacao Nacional de Arte,
Rua Araujo Porto Alegre-80, 20030 Rio de Janeiro-
RJ, Brazil) circ. 2,000.

398 780   CN   ISSN 0708-4226
CANADA'S ATLANTIC FOLKLORE AND
FOLKLIFE SERIES. no.5, 1979. a. Breakwater
Books Ltd., P.O. Box 2188, St. John's,
Newfoundland A1C 6E6, Canada. TEL 709-722-
6680.

CANU GWERIN/FOLK SONG. see MUSIC

200 900   US   ISSN 0528-1458
CARL NEWELL JACKSON LECTURES. irreg. price
varies. Harvard University Press, 79 Garden St.,
Cambridge, MA 02138. TEL 617-495-2600.

CHIAKA CHRONIKA. see HISTORY — History Of
Europe

398   BL
COLECAO ARQUIVOS DE FOLCLORE. 1969.
irreg. Centro de Estudios Sociologicos de Juiz de
Fora, Rua Halfeld 805-Sala 403, Caixa Postal 298,
Juiz de Fora, Brazil.

398   BL
COLECAO CULTURA BRASILEIRA. 1983. irreg.
Editora Codecri, Ltda., Rua Saint Roman, 142,
Copacabana 22071, Rio de Janeiro, Brazil.

COMUNIDADES Y CULTURAS PERUANAS. see
ANTHROPOLOGY

COUNTRY DANCE AND SONG. see DANCE

COW NECK PENINSULA HISTORICAL
JOURNAL. see HISTORY — History Of North
And South America

CRITICAL STUDIES ON BLACK LIFE AND
CULTURE. see ETHNIC INTERESTS

398   PE
CUADERNOS DEL TALLER DE FOLKLORE.
1977. irreg. Universidad Nacional Federico Villareal,
Direccion Universitaria de Proyeccion Social, Apdo.
1408, Lima, Peru. Ed. Francisco E. Iriarte Brenner.
circ. 1,000.

398   CN   ISSN 0701-0184
CULTURE & TRADITION. (Text in English and
French) 1976. a. Can.$6. Memorial University of
Newfoundland, St. John's, Nfld. A1C 5S7, Canada.
TEL 709-737-8402. (Co-sponsor: Laval University)
Ed.Bd. bk. rev. illus. circ. 300. Indexed: M.L.A.

DATOS ETNO-LINGUISTICOS. see LINGUISTICS

398   GW
DEUTSCHE GESELLSCHAFT FUER
VOLKSKUNDE. D G V INFORMATIONEN.
1970. irreg. membership. Deutsche Gesellschaft fuer
Volkskunde e.V., Universitaet Regensburg, Postfach
397, D-8400 Regensburg, W. Germany (B.R.D.) Ed.
Konrad Koestlin. bk. rev. circ. 900. Indexed: Dairy
Sci.Abstr.
   Continues Its Mitteilungen.

EDICIONES DEL PUEBLO. see LITERATURE

398   MX   ISSN 0071-1683
ESTUDIOS DE FOLKLORE. 1961. irreg., latest issue
1971. price varies. ‡ Universidad Nacional
Autonoma de Mexico, Instituto de Investigaciones
Esteticas, Ciudad Universitaria, Mexico 20, D.F.,
Mexico.

398   PY
ESTUDIOS FOLKLORICOS PARAGUAYOS. 1978.
irreg. Casilla Postal 611, Asuncion, Paraguay.

398   PL   ISSN 0209-2077
ETNOGRAFIA. (Text in Polish; summaries in various
languages) 1961. irreg. price varies. Adam
Mickiewicz University Press, Marchlewskiego 128,
61-874 Poznan, Poland.
   Formerly: Uniwersytet im. Adama Mickiewicza w
Poznaniu. Wydzial Filozoficzno-Historyczny. Seria
Etnografia.

ETNOLOGIE ET TRADITIONS POPULAIRES DE
L'IRAN/MARDON SENSAI VA FARHANGE-E
AMME-E IRAN. see ETHNIC INTERESTS

EULENSPIEGEL-JAHRBUCH. see LITERATURE

EUROPAEISCHE VOLKSMUSIKINSTRUMENTE.
HANDBUCH. see MUSIC

398   FI   ISSN 0014-5815
F F COMMUNICATIONS. (Folklore Fellows) (Text
mainly in English; occasionally in French and
German) 1910. irreg., 2-5/yr. price varies.
Suomalainen Tiedeakatemia - Academia Scientiarum
Fennica, Snellmanninkatu 9-11, 00170 Helsinki,
Finland. Ed. Lauri Honko. cum.index. circ. 550.
(back issues avail.; reprint service avail. from UMI)
Indexed: Bull.Signal. Curr.Cont. M.L.A. Ref.Zh.
Abstr.Folk.Stud. Arts & Hum.Cit.Ind.

FEDERATION ARCHEOLOGIQUE ET
HISTORIQUE DE BELGIQUE. ANNALES/
FEDERATIE VAN NEDERLANDSTALIGE
VERENIDENIS VOOR OUDHEIDKUNDE EN
GESCHIEDENIS VAN BELGISCHE.
JAARBOEKEN. see HISTORY — History Of
Europe

398 914.603   SP
FLAMENCO; boletin de informacion. vol.5, 1975.
irreg. (2-3/yr.) contribution. Tertulia Flamenca de
Ceuta, P.O. Box 344, Ceuta, Spain. adv. bk. rev.
illus.

398   US
FOLKLIFE ANNUAL. 1985. a. $16. U.S. Library of
Congress, American Folklife Center, Washington,
DC 20540 TEL 202-783-3238. (Subscr. to: Supt. of
Documents, Government Printing Office,
Washington, DC 20402) Eds. Alan Jabbour, James
Hardin. illus. (back issues avail.)

398   SW   ISSN 0071-6766
FOLKLIVSSKILDRINGAR OCH
BYGDESSTUDIER. 1934. irreg., no.11, 1985. price
varies. Kungliga Gustav Adolfs Akademien,
Klostergatan 2, S-753 21 Uppsala, Sweden (Subscr.
to: Almqvist & Wiksell International, P.O. Box
45150, S-104 30 Stockholm, Sweden) Ed. Lennart
Elmevik.

398   UR
FOL'KLOR URALA. vol.2, 1976. irreg. 0.65 Rub. per
issue. Ural'skii Gosudarstvennyi Universitet, Pr.
Lenina 51, Sverdlovsk, Russian S.F.S.R., U.S.S.R.
circ. 600.

398   US   ISSN 0162-6280
FOLKLORE AND MYTHOLOGY STUDIES. 1977.
a. $3. University of California, Los Angeles,
Folklore Graduate Students' Association, Los
Angeles, CA 90024. TEL 213-825-4321.

398   BE
FOLKLORE DU MONDE. 1969. irreg., no.2, 1975.
Librairie-Editions Thanh-Long, 34 rue Dekens, 1040
Brussels, Belgium.

398   US   ISSN 0071-6804
FOLKTALES OF THE WORLD. 1963. irreg. ,no.13,
1980. price varies. University of Chicago Press,
5801 S. Ellis Ave., Chicago, IL 60637. TEL 312-
962-7700. Ed. Richard M. Dorson. (reprint service
avail. from UMI,ISI)

FORSCHUNGEN ZUR RECHTSARCHAEOLOGIE
UND RECHTLICHEN VOLKSKUNDE. see LAW

398   US
GARLAND FOLKLORE CASEBOOKS. 1981. irreg.
Garland Publishing, Inc., 136 Madison Ave., 2nd
Fl., New York, NY 10016.

GESCHICHTSBLAETTER FUER WALDECK. see
HISTORY — History Of Europe

GYPSY LORE SOCIETY. NORTH AMERICAN
CHAPTER. PUBLICATIONS. see
ANTHROPOLOGY

HARVEST BOOK SERIES. see SOCIOLOGY

398   IS   ISSN 0075-3661
HEBREW UNIVERSITY OF JERUSALEM.
FOLKLORE RESEARCH CENTER. STUDIES.
(Text in Hebrew and English) 1970. irreg., vol. 5,
1975. Magnes Press, Hebrew University of
Jerusalem, Jerusalem, Israel. Eds. Dov Noy, I. Ben-
Ami. Indexed: Ind.Heb.Per.

HEIMATBRIEF DER STADT GERMERSHEIM. see
HISTORY — History Of Europe

HOUTLAND. see HISTORY — History Of Europe

IMMENSTAADER HEIMATBLAETTER. see
HISTORY — History Of Europe

398   AU
INSTITUT FUER GEGENWARTSVOLKSKUNDE.
MITTEILUNGEN. (Issues also published in other
series of the Akademie) 1973. irreg. price varies.
Verlag der Oesterreichischen Akademie der
Wissenschaften, Dr. Ignaz Seipel-Platz 2, A-1010
Vienna, Austria. (Affiliate: Oesterreichische
Akademie der Wissenschaften)

FOLKLORE

INSTITUTO INTERAMERICANO DE ETNOMUSICOLOGIA Y FOLKLORE. REVISTA. see *MUSIC*

398   AG
INSTITUTO NACIONAL DE INVESTIGACIONES FOLKLORICAS. CUADERNOS. 1960. a. Instituto Nacional de Investigaciones Folkloricas, Sanchez de Bustamente 2663, Buenos Aires, Argentina. bibl.

JAHRBUCH FUER MUSIKALISCHE VOLKS- UND VOELKERKUNDE. see *MUSIC*

398   301.2   GW   ISSN 0075-2738
JAHRBUCH FUER OSTDEUTSCHE VOLKSKUNDE. 1962. a. price varies. (Deutsche Gesellschaft fuer Volkskunde e.V., Kommission fuer Ostdeutsche Volkskunde) N.G. Elwert Verlag, Reitgasse 7/9, Postfach 1128, 3550 Marburg, W. Germany (B.R.D.) Ed. Ulrich Tolksdorf. circ. 1,000.

396   GE   ISSN 0138-4503
JAHRBUCH FUER VOLKSKUNDE UND KULTURGESCHICHTE. NEUE FOLGE. 1974. a. M.30. Akademie-Verlag, Leipziger Str. 3-4, 1086 Berlin, E. Germany (D.D.R.) Ed.Bd. adv. bk. rev. bibl. illus. stat. index. Indexed: Hist.Abstr. Amer.Hist.& Life.
 Formerly (1955-1973): Jahrbuch fuer Volkskunde und Kulturgeschichte (ISSN 0012-1312)
 Ethnography

398   AU   ISSN 0022-7560
KAERNTNER HEIMATLEBEN. 1959. irreg. price varies. Landesmuseum fuer Kaernten, Museumgasse 2, A-9010 Klagenfurt, Austria. circ. 600.

KINAADMAN/WISDOM; a journal of the Southern Philippines. see *HISTORY — History Of Asia*

398   FR   ISSN 0075-7160
KRYPTADIA: JOURNAL OF EROTIC FOLKLORE. (Text in English) 1883. irreg., approx. a. $15. ‡ La Cle des Champs, Valbonne (Alpes-Maritimes), France. Ed. G. Legman.

L C FOLK ARCHIVE FINDING AID. (U.S. Library of Congress) see *LIBRARY AND INFORMATION SCIENCES*

390   IT   ISSN 0075-8019
LARES. BIBLIOTECA. 1957. irreg., no.47, 1983. price varies. Casa Editrice Leo S. Olschki, Casella Postale 66, 50100 Florence, Italy. Ed. G.B. Bronzini. adv. bk. rev. circ. 1,000.

390   572   PL   ISSN 0076-0382
LODZKIE STUDIA ETNOGRAFICZNE. (Text in Polish; summaries in English) 1959. a. price varies. (Polskie Towarzystwo Ludoznawcze, Oddzial w Lodzi) Panstwowe Wydawnictwo Naukowe, Ul. Miodowa 10, 00-251 Warsaw, Poland (Dist. by: Ars Polona, Krakowskie Przedmiescie 7, 00-068 Warsaw, Poland) Ed. Jadwiga Kucharska. bibl. illus. circ. 750.

390   US   ISSN 0459-8962
LOUISIANA FOLKLORE MISCELLANY.* 1958. irreg., vol.5, 1981. $7. Louisiana Folklore Society, c/o Department of Anthropology & Geography, University of New Orleans, New Orleans, LA 70148.

MAKEDONIKA. see *HISTORY — History Of Europe*

MEXICO. DEPARTAMENTO DE INVESTIGACION DE LAS TRADICIONES POPULARES. BOLETIN. see *ANTHROPOLOGY*

398   959   PH   ISSN 0115-6853
MINDANAO ART & CULTURE. (Text in English) 1979. irreg. Mindanao State University, University Research Center, P.O. Box 5594, Iligan City 8801, Philippines. Ed. Raymond Llorca.

398   US   ISSN 0731-2946
MISSOURI FOLKLORE SOCIETY. JOURNAL. 1979. a. $10. Missouri Folklore Society, Box 1757, Columbia, MO 65205. Ed. Donald M. Lance. bk. rev. circ. 300. Indexed: M.L.A.

398   BO
MUSEO NACIONAL DE ETNOGRAFIA Y FOLKLORE. AVANCES DE INVESTIGACION. 1982. irreg. $10. Museo Nacional de Etnografia y Folklore, Calle Ingavi 916, Casilla 5817, La Paz, Bolivia. Ed.Bd. circ. 500.

MUZYKAL'NAYA FOL'KLORISTIKA. see *MUSIC*

NAPRSTKOVO MUZEUM ASIJSKYCH, AFRICKYCH A AMERICKYCH KULTUR. ANNALS. see *ANTHROPOLOGY*

398   YU   ISSN 0547-2504
NARODNA UMJETNOST. (Text and summaries in English, German, Serbocroatian) 1962. a. 4,000 din.($10) Zavod za Istrazivanje Folklora Instituta za Filologiju i Folkloristiku, Ul. Socijalisticke Revolucije 17/4, 41000 Zagreb, Yugoslavia. TEL 041-440-880. Ed. Zorica Rajkvic. bk. rev. circ. 600. Indexed: Bull.Signal.

NEPRAJZI KOZLEMENYEK. see *ANTHROPOLOGY*

398   US   ISSN 0887-8048
NEW JERSEY FOLKLIFE; a statewide publication. 1977. a. $12.50 to individuals; institutions $15; students $8.50. New Jersey Folklore Society, c/o American Studies Dept., Douglass College, Rutgers, the State University, New Brunswick, NJ 08903. TEL 201-932-9174. Ed. Angus K. Gillespie. adv. bk. rev. circ. 300.
 Formerly: New Jersey Folklore.

390   DK   ISSN 0008-1345
NORD NYTT; Nordic periodical for folklife studies. (Text in English, Danish, Norwegian and Swedish) 1963. irreg. (8-10/yr.) price varies. N E F A-Norden, Institut for Europaeisk Folkelivsforskning, Brede Alle 69, DK-2800 Lyngby, Denmark (Subscr. to: Museumstjenesten, Lysgaard, DK-8800 Viborg, Denmark) Ed. Joergen Burchardt. adv. bk. rev. bibl. illus. index. circ. 1,500.
 Ethnology

398   FI
NORDIC INSTITUTE OF FOLKLORE. PUBLICATIONS. 1972. irreg. Nordic Institute of Folklore, Henrinkatu 3, SF-20300 Turku 30, Finland. circ. 300.

398   US   ISSN 0078-1681
NORTHEAST FOLKLORE. (Text in English; occasionally in French) 1958. a. $5. Northeast Folklore Society, South Stevens Hall, University of Maine, Orono, ME 04469. TEL 207-581-1891. Ed. Edward D. Ives. circ. 400.

398   AU
OESTERREICHISCHE VOLKSKUNDLICHE BIBLIOGRAPHIE. 1966. irreg., no.15/16, 1984. price varies. Verband der Wissenschaftlichen Gesellschaften Oesterreichs, Verein fuer Volkskunde, Lindengasse 37, A-1070 Vienna, Austria. Ed. Klaus Beitl.

398   AU
OESTERREICHISCHES MUSEUM FUER VOLKSKUNDE: VEROEFFENTLICHUNGEN. 1952. irreg. price varies. Verlag Ferdinand Berger und Soehne OHG, Wiener Str. 21-23, A-3580 Horn, Austria. circ. 1,000.

OLD TIME MUSIC. see *MUSIC*

PIONEER AMERICA SOCIETY. TRANSACTIONS. see *HISTORY — History Of North And South America*

QUELLENWERKE ZUR ALTEN GESCHICHTE AMERIKAS. see *HISTORY — History Of North And South America*

398   AU
RAABSER MAERCHEN-REIHE. 1974. irreg., vol.7, 1986. Oesterreichisches Museum fuer Volkskunde, Laudongasse 15-19, A-1080 Vienna, Austria. Ed. Klaus Beitl. circ. 1,000.

398   YU   ISSN 0034-0251
RAZPRAVE IN GRADIVO/TREATISES AND DOCUMENTS. (Text mainly in Slovene; summaries and abstracts in English) 1960. a. $5. Institut za Narodnostna Vprasanja - Institute for Ethnic Studies, Cankarjeva 5, 61000 Ljubljana, Yugoslavia. TEL 061-210-879. Ed. Silvo Devetak. adv. circ. 800. Indexed: Hist.Abstr.

398   GW   ISSN 0080-2697
RHEINISCHES JAHRBUCH FUER VOLKSKUNDE. 1950. a. price varies. (Rheinische Vereinigung fuer Volkskunde) Ferdinand Duemmlers Verlag, Kaiserstr. 31-37, D-5300 Bonn 1, W. Germany (B.R.D.) Ed. H.L. Cox. bk. rev. Indexed: M.L.A.

ROBIN. see *ENVIRONMENTAL STUDIES*

398   PL   ISSN 0080-3561
ROCZNIK SADECKI. (Text in Polish; summaries in English, French, and Russian) 1938. a. 100 Zl. Polskie Towarzystwo Historyczne, Oddzial w Nowym Saczu, Rynek Ratusz, Nowy Sacz, Poland. Ed. Kazimierz Zajac. bk. rev. circ. 1,500.

398   SW   ISSN 0586-5360
SAGA OCH SED. (Text in English, German and Scandinavian Languages; summaries in English) 1932. a. Kr.90. Kungliga Gustav Adolfs Akademien, Klostergatan 2, S-753 21 Uppsala, Sweden (Order from: Almqvist & Wiksell, Box 45150, S-104 30 Stockholm, Sweden) Ed. Lennart Elmevik. circ. 500. (back issues avail.) Indexed: M.L.A.

SAGA OF THE SANPITCH. see *HISTORY — History Of North And South America*

398   GW   ISSN 0080-732X
SCHWEIZERISCHE GESELLSCHAFT FUER VOLKSKUNDE. SCHRIFTEN. 1902. irreg., no.70, 1985. price varies. (SZ) Dr. Rudolf Habelt GmbH, Am Buchenhang 1, 5300 Bonn 1, W. Germany (B.R.D.)

SCOTTISH STUDIES. see *HISTORY — History Of Europe*

SERIE DE VOCABULARIOS Y DICCIONARIOS INDIGENAS "MARIANO SILVA Y ACEVES". see *LINGUISTICS*

398   BL
SERIE THESAURUS-FOLCLORE.* 1976. irreg. Thesaurus Editora, SIG-Quadra 8-Lote 2356, 70160 Brasilia, Brazil. TEL 061-225-3011.

398   US
SMITHSONIAN FOLKLIFE STUDIES. irreg., no.4, 1985. Smithsonian Institution Press, 955 L'Enfant Plaza, Rm. 2100, Washington, DC 20560. TEL 202-287-3738. Ed. Barbara T. Spann. bibl. charts. illus. cum.index: 1978-1983. circ. 2,000. (back issues avail.)
 Formerly: Smithsonian Folklore Studies.

398   SP   ISSN 0212-7547
SOCIEDAD DE ESTUDIOS VASCOS. CUADERNOS DE SECCION. FOLKLORE. 1983. irreg. (Sociedad de Estudios Vascos) Eusko Ikaskuntza, S.A., Churruca, 7 - 2, 20004 Donostia, Spain.

390   IT   ISSN 0081-5837
STORIA, COSTUMI E TRADIZIONI. 1962. irreg., vol.15, 1981. price varies. ALFA Edizioni, Via Santo Stefano 13, I-40125 Bologna, Italy. Ed. Andrea Emiliani. circ. 4,000.

398   GW
STUDIES IN FOLKLORE. 1973. irreg. price varies. Walter de Gruyter & Co., Mouton Publishers, Postfach 110240, D-1000 Berlin 11, W. Germany (B.R.D.) (U.S. addr.: Mouton Publishers, division of Walter de Gruyter, Inc., 200 Saw Mill River Road, Hawthorne, NY 10532)

398   US
STUDIES IN U S HISTORY AND CULTURE. irreg., vol.39, 1984. U M I Research Press, 300 N. Zeeb Rd., Ann Arbor, MI 48106. Ed. Robert Berkhofer.

SUEDOSTDEUTSCHES ARCHIV. see *HISTORY — History Of Europe*

398   US   ISSN 0082-3023
TEXAS FOLKLORE SOCIETY. PUBLICATIONS. 1916. a. price varies. (Texas Folklore Society) Southern Methodist University Press, Box 13007 SFA Sta., Nacogdoches, TX 75962. TEL 409-569-4407. Ed. Francis E. Abernethy. index. circ. 2,000.

THEATA. see *ANTHROPOLOGY*

390 YU
TRADITIONES. (Text in Slovenian; summaries in English, French, German and Italian) 1972. irreg. price varies. Slovenska Akademija Znanosti in Umetnosti, Razred za Filoloske in Literarne Vede, Novi Trg 5/1, Ljubljana, Yugoslavia (Dist. by: Trubarjew Antikwariat, Mestni Trg 25, 61000 Ljubljana) Ed. Milko Maticetov. bk. rev. illus. bibl. circ. 1,000. Indexed: M.L.A.

398 TR
TRINIDAD CARNIVAL; the world's most colourful festival. 1973. a. $12. Key Caribbean Publications Ltd., Corner Park St. & Ariapita Ave., Port-of-Spain, Trinidad. Ed. Roy Boyke. adv. circ. 20,000.

398 GW ISSN 0068-0893
UEBERSEE-MUSEUM, BREMEN. VEROEFFENTLICHUNGEN. REIHE B: VOELKERKUNDE. 1950. irreg., vol.3, 1973. price varies. Uebersee-Museum, Bremen, Bahnhofsplatz 13, 2800 Bremen, W. Germany (B.R.D.)

UJ MAGYAR NEPKOLTESI GYUJTEMENY. see LITERATURE — Poetry

398 UK ISSN 0082-7347
ULSTER FOLKLIFE. 1955. a. £5. Ulster Folk and Transport Museum, Cultra Manor, Holywood, County Down BT18 0EU, N. Ireland. Ed. Jonathan Bell. bk. rev. circ. 750. Indexed: Curr.Cont. M.L.A. Arts & Hum.Cit.Ind. Br.Archaeol.Abstr.

398 780 CK ISSN 0067-9534
UNIVERSIDAD NACIONAL DE COLOMBIA. CENTRO DE ESTUDIOS FOLKLORICOS. MONOGRAFIAS. irreg., latest issue 1973. $40 free. Universidad Nacional de Colombia, Facultad de Artes, Conservatorio de Musica, Bogota, Colombia. Ed. Guillermo Abadia Morales. circ. 2, 000.

UNIVERSIDADE DE SAO PAULO. INSTITUTO DE ESTUDOS BRASILEIROS. PUBLICACOES. see GEOGRAPHY

UNIVERSIDADE DE SAO PAULO. INSTITUTO DE ESTUDOS BRASILEIROS. REVISTA. see GEOGRAPHY

398 IT ISSN 0069-1186
UNIVERSITA DEGLI STUDI DI CATANIA. ISTITUTO DI STORIA DELLE TRADIZIONI POPOLARI. STUDI E TESTI. 1964. irreg., no.2, 1964. price varies. Casa Editrice Leo S. Olschki, Casella Postale 66, 50100 Florence, Italy. Ed. Sebastiano Lo Nigro. circ. 1,000.

398 CN ISSN 0085-5243
UNIVERSITE LAVAL. ARCHIVES DE FOLKLORE. (Text and summaries in French) 1946. irreg., no.4, 1972. price varies. Presses de l'Universite Laval, C.P. 2447, Quebec G1K 7R4, Canada. TEL 418-656-2590. Ed. Luc Lacourciere. bibl. circ. processed. Indexed: M.L.A.

398 US
UNIVERSITY FOLKLORE ASSOCIATION. FOLKLORE PAPERS. 1969. a. free on exchange. (University Folklore Association) University of Texas at Austin, Center for Intercultural Studies in Folklore and Ethnomusicology, S.S.B. 3106, Austin, TX 78712. TEL 512-471-1288. bk. rev. circ. 500.
Formerly: Folklore Annual (ISSN 0071-6782)

398 US ISSN 0068-6247
UNIVERSITY OF CALIFORNIA, LOS ANGELES. CENTER FOR THE STUDY OF COMPARATIVE FOLKLORE AND MYTHOLOGY. PUBLICATIONS. irreg. University of California Press, 2120 Berkeley Way, Berkeley, CA 94720. TEL 415-642-4247.

398 US
UNIVERSITY OF CALIFORNIA PUBLICATIONS. FOLKLORE & MYTHOLOGY STUDIES. 1953. irreg. price varies. University of California Press, 2120 Berkeley Way, Berkeley, CA 94720. TEL 415-642-4247.
Formerly: University of California Publications. Folklore Studies (ISSN 0068-6360)

UNIVERZITA KOMENSKEHO. FILOZOFICKA FAKULTA. ZBORNIK: ETHNOLOGIA SLAVICA; an international review of Slavic ethnology. see ANTHROPOLOGY

398 AU
VEREIN FUER VOLKSKUNDE IN WIEN. SONDERSCHRIFTEN. 1955. irreg., vol.3, 1978. Verein fuer Volkskunde, Laudongasse 19, A-1080 Vienna, Austria. Ed. Klaus Beitl. bk. rev. circ. 600.

VEREIN OBERPFAELZISCHES BAUERNMUSEUM. MITTEILUNGEN. see AGRICULTURE

398 909 GE ISSN 0138-3167
VEROEFFENTLICHUNGEN ZUR VOLKSKUNDE UND KULTURGESCHICHTE. 1950. irreg., vol.71, 1982. price varies. Akademie-Verlag, Leipziger Str. 3-4, 1086 Berlin, E. Germany (D.D.R.) Ed.Bd. Indexed: M.L.A. RILM.
Continues: Akademie der Wissenschaften, Berlin. Volkskundliche Veroeffentlichungen (ISSN 0065-5228)

390 GW
VOLKSKUENDLICHEN KOMMISSION FUER WESTFALEN. SCHRIFTEN. 1937. irreg. price varies. Aschendorffsche Verlagsbuchhandlung, Soester Str. 13, 4400 Muenster, W. Germany (B.R.D.)
Former titles: Landschaftsverband Westfalen-Lippe (ISSN 0170-8090); Landschaftsverband Westfalen-Lippe. Volkskundliche Kommission. Schriften (ISSN 0075-7942)

390 AU
VOLKSKUNDLICHE STUDIEN. (Subseries of: Universitaet Innsbruck. Veroeffentlichungen) 1970. irreg. price varies. (Universitaet Innsbruck) Oesterreichische Kommissionsbuchhandlung, Maximilianstrasse 17, A-6020 Innsbruck, Austria. Ed. Karl Ilg.

398 GE ISSN 0232-3702
VOLKSMAERCHEN. 1964. irreg., vol.15, 1984. (Akademie der Wissenschaften der DDR) Akademie-Verlag Berlin, Leipziger Str. 3-4, 1086 Berlin, E. Germany (D.D.R.)

398 GW ISSN 0083-6877
VOLKSTUM DER SCHWEIZ. 1941. irreg., no.12, 1979. price varies. Dr. Rudolf Habelt GmbH, Am Buchenhang 1, 5300 Bonn 1, W. Germany (B.R.D.)

WESTFAELISCHE FORSCHUNGEN. see HISTORY — History Of Europe

390 AU ISSN 0084-0068
WIENER VOELKERKUNDLICHE MITTEILUNGEN. 1953. a. S.150($7) (Oesterreichische Ethnologische Gesellschaft) Museum fuer Voelkerkunde, Neue Hofburg, A-1014 Vienna, Austria. Ed.Bd. adv. bk. rev. circ. 500. Indexed: E.I.

YEARBOOK FOR TRADITIONAL MUSIC. see MUSIC

398 IS
YEDA-AM. (Text in Hebrew; summaries in English) 1948. biennial. $5. Israeli Society for Folklore and Ethnology, P.O. Box 314, Tel Aviv, Israel. Eds. Itzchak Ganuz, Issachar Ben-Ami. bk. rev. circ. 800. Indexed: Ind.Heb.Per.

398 301.32 YU ISSN 0581-751X
ZEMALJSKI MUZEJ BOSNE I HERCEGOVINE. GLASNIK. ETNOLOGIJA. (Vols. for 1965-66, 1969-70 issued in combined form) (Summaries in French or German, 1965-68) 1974. a. Zemaljski Muzej Bosne i Hercegovine, Vojvode Putnika 7, Sarajevo, Yugoslavia. Ed. Vlajko Palavestra. illus.
Continues the publication with the same title issued by the museum under its earlier name: Zemaljski Muzej u Sarajevu.

FOLKLORE — Abstracting, Bibliographies, Statistics

BIBLIOGRAPHIE ZUR SYMBOLIK, IKONOGRAPHIE UND MYTHOLOGIE. see ANTHROPOLOGY — Abstracting, Bibliographies, Statistics

INTERNATIONAL ARTHURIAN SOCIETY. BIBLIOGRAPHICAL BULLETIN/SOCIETE INTERNATIONALE ARTHURIENNE. BULLETIN BIBLIOGRAPHIQUE. see LITERATURE — Abstracting, Bibliographies, Statistics

390 016 GW ISSN 0074-9737
INTERNATIONALE VOLKSKUNDLICHE BIBLIOGRAPHIE/INTERNATIONAL FOLKLORE BIBLIOGRAPHY/BIBLIOGRAPHIE INTERNATIONALE D'ETHNOLOGIE. (Entries in various languages) 1954. irreg., 1986. price varies. Dr. Rudolf Habelt GmbH, Am Buchenhang 1, 5300 Bonn 1, W. Germany (B.R.D.) Eds. Rolf W. Bredrich, James R. Dow.

M L A DIRECTORY OF PERIODICALS; a guide to journals and series in languages and literatures. (Modern Language Association of America) see LITERATURE — Abstracting, Bibliographies, Statistics

FOOD AND FOOD INDUSTRIES

see also Food and Food Industries—Bakers and Confectioners; Food and Food Industries—Grocery Trade; Agriculture; Fish and Fisheries; Home Economics; Hotels and Restaurants; Nutrition and Dietetics

664 VE ISSN 0084-683X
A T A V E BOLETIN INFORMATIVO.* irreg. free. Asociacion de Tecnicos Azucareros de Venezuela, Estacion Experimental de Occidente, Yarituguce, Yaracuy, Venezuela.

664 PL ISSN 0860-2859
ACTA ACADEMIAE AGRICULTURAE AC TECHNICAE OLSTENENSIS. TECHNOLOGIA ALIMENTORUM/FOOD TECHNOLOGY. (Subseries of Its: Zeszyty Naukowe) (Text in Polish; summaries in English and Russian) 1956. irreg. price varies. Akademia Rolniczo-Techniczna, Blok 21, 10-718 Olsztyn-Kortowo, Poland (Dist. by: Ars Polona-Ruch, Krakowskie Przedmiescie 7, 00-901 Warsaw, Poland) illus.
Formerly: Technologia Zywnosci (ISSN 0324-9212)

664 US ISSN 0065-2628
ADVANCES IN FOOD RESEARCH. 1948. irreg., vol.30, 1986. Academic Press, Inc., Orlando, FL 32887. TEL 305-345-2000. Eds. E.M. Mrak, George F. Stewart. index. Indexed: Biol.Abstr. Biol.& Agr.Ind. Chem.Abstr. Ind.Med. Nutr.Abstr. Abstr.Hyg. Dairy Sci.Abstr. Food Sci.& Tech.Abstr. Trop.Dis.Bull.

664 PL
AKADEMIA ROLNICZA, POZNAN. ROCZNIKI. TECHNOLOGIA ZYWNOSCI. (Text in Polish; summaries in English and Russian) 1960. irreg. price varies. Akademia Rolnicza, Poznan, Ul. Wojska Polskiego 28, 60-637 Poznan, Poland. Indexed: Bibl.Agri.
Formerly: Akademia Rolnicza, Poznan. Rocznik. Technologia Rolno-Spozywcza (ISSN 0137-1762)

AKADEMIA ROLNICZA W SZCZECINIE. ZESZYTY NAUKOWE. RYBACTWO MORSKIE I TECHNOLOGIA ZYWNOSCI. see FISH AND FISHERIES

664 MX
ALIMENTARIA. 1963. a. Mex.$2000($25) Litoimpresores, S.A., Espana 396, 09880 Mexico, D.F., Mexico. Ed. Cesar Macazaga. adv.

664.7 US ISSN 0065-7107
AMERICAN ASSOCIATION OF CEREAL CHEMISTS. MONOGRAPH SERIES. irreg., latest no.7, 1986. American Association of Cereal Chemists, Inc., 3340 Pilot Knob Road, St. Paul, MN 55121. TEL 800-328-7560. (also avail. in microfilm from UMI) Indexed: Biol.Abstr.

FOOD AND FOOD INDUSTRIES

664　　　　　　　US　ISSN 0361-0888
AMERICAN FROZEN FOOD INSTITUTE.
MEMBERSHIP DIRECTORY AND BUYERS'
GUIDE. 1943. a. $100. American Frozen Food
Institute, 1764 Old Meadow Lane, Ste.350,
McLean, VA 22102. TEL 703-821-0770. Ed. Scott
Ramminger. adv. circ. 3,000 (controlled)
　　Formerly: American Frozen Food Institute.
Membership Directory (ISSN 0084-635X)

636　　　　　　　US
AMERICAN MEAT SCIENCE ASSOCIATION.
RECIPROCAL MEAT CONFERENCE.
PROCEEDINGS. 1948. a. $20. National Live Stock
and Meat Board, 444 N. Michigan Ave., Chicago,
IL 60611. TEL 312-467-5520. Ed. H. Kenneth
Johnson. circ. 650. (reprint service avail. from UMI)
Indexed: Chem.Abstr.

664.028　　　　　　　FR
ANNUAIRE INTERPROFESSIONNEL DE LA
SURGELATION ET DE LA CONGELATION. a.
390 F. Editions Fructidor, 14 Blvd. Montmartre,
75009 Paris, France.

664　　　　　　　FR　ISSN 0245-1301
ANNUAIRE NATIONAL DE LA CONSERVE.
1952. a. 530 F. Editions Comindus, 1 rue
Descombes, 75017 Paris, France.
　　Formerly: Annuaire National des Industries de la
Conserve (ISSN 0084-652X)

ASSOCIATION EURATOM-ITAL. ANNUAL
REPORT. see *AGRICULTURE*

641.38　　　　　　　AT　ISSN 0067-1894
AUSTRALIAN HONEY BOARD. ANNUAL
REPORT. 1963/64. a. free. Australian Honey
Board, 647 George St., Sydney, N.S.W., Australia.
Indexed: Apic.Abstr.
　　Honey

AUSTRALIAN MEAT RESEARCH COMMITTEE.
ANNUAL REPORT. see *AGRICULTURE —
Poultry And Livestock*

664.1　　　　　　　AT　ISSN 0726-0822
AUSTRALIAN SOCIETY OF SUGAR CANE
TECHNOLOGISTS. PROCEEDINGS. 1930. a.
Aus.$35. Australian Society of Sugar Cane
Technologists, c/o Sugar Research Institute, P.O.
Box 5611, MacKay Mail Center, Qld. 4741,
Australia. Ed. B.T. Egan. cum.index every 5 years.
circ. 1,000. Indexed: Biol.Abstr. Chem.Abstr.
Hort.Abstr. Rev.Plant Path. Soils & Fert.
　　Formerly (until April 1978): Queensland Society
of Sugar Cane Technologists. Proceedings (ISSN
0079-8851)

664.1　　　　　　　AT　ISSN 0067-2173
AUSTRALIAN SUGAR YEAR BOOK. 1941. a.
Aus.$29. Publishing & Marketing Australia, 480 St.
Kilda Rd., Melbourne, Vic. 3000, Australia. adv.
circ. 3,000.
　　Sugar

664.1　　　　　　　BG
BANGLADESH SUGAR MILLS CORPORATION.
ANNUAL REPORT. (Text in English) a. Tk.20.
Bangladesh Sugar Mills Corporation, Shilpa Bhaban,
Motijheel Commercial Area, Dacca 2, Bangladesh.
stat.

BEVERAGE AND FOOD WORLD. see
BEVERAGES

664 607　　　　　　　UK　ISSN 0067-8651
BINSTED'S DIRECTORY OF FOOD TRADE
MARKS AND BRAND NAMES. 1959. a. £42.
Food Trade Press Ltd., 29 High St., Green Street
Green, Orpington, Kent BR6 6LS, England. Ed.
Adrian Binsted. adv. circ. 2,500.

664.028　　　　　　　UK
BRITISH FROZEN FOOD FEDERATION. YEAR
BOOK. 1968. a. £22. British Frozen Food
Federation, Honeypot Lane, Colsterworth,
Grantham, Lincolnshire NG33 5LX, England. adv.
circ. 1,000.

664　　　　　　　BL　ISSN 0101-630X
C T A A. BOLETIM DE PESQUISA. (Text in
Portuguese; summaries in English) 1970. irreg.
Centro Nacional de Pesquisa de Tecnologia
Agroindustrial de Alimentos, Av. das Americas,
29501 Guaratiba, 23020 Rio de Janeiro, R.J., Brazil.
TEL 021-3101353. circ. 1,000. (tabloid format; back
issues avail.) Indexed: Chem.Abstr.

664　　　　　　　CN　ISSN 0068-7308
CANADA. AGRICULTURE CANADA. FOOD
RESEARCH INSTITUTE, OTTAWA.
RESEARCH REPORT. 1962/64. irreg. free.
Agriculture Canada, Food Research Institute,
Ottawa, Canada. TEL 613-995-5362. circ. 200.

CANADIAN FOOD AND PACKAGING
DIRECTORY. see *BUSINESS AND
ECONOMICS — Trade And Industrial Directories*

664.1　338.1　　　　　CN　ISSN 0068-8770
CANADIAN FRUIT WHOLESALERS'
ASSOCIATION. YEARBOOK. 1925. a. Can.$40.
Canadian Fruit Wholesalers Association, 3
Amberwood Crescent, Nepean, Ont. K2E 7L1,
Canada. TEL 613-226-4187. Ed. H.R. Taylor. adv.
circ. 1,200.

664　　　　　　　UK　ISSN 0268-5663
CATERING MANAGER'S BUYER'S GUIDE
(YEAR) 1986. a. £19.95. Millbank Publications, 25
Catherine St., London WC2B 5JW, England. TEL
01-379-3036. Ed. K.J. Allen. adv. illus. circ. 3,000.

663.92　　　　　　　GH　ISSN 0300-1385
COCOA RESEARCH INSTITUTE. ANNUAL
REPORT. 1962. a. NC.8. Cocoa Research Institute,
Box 8, Tafo, Ghana. Indexed: Biol.Abstr.
Hort.Abstr. Rev.Appl.Entomol. Rev.Plant Path.

663.93　　　　　　　KE
COFFEE BOARD OF KENYA. ANNUAL
REPORT, BALANCE SHEET AND ACCOUNTS.
(Text in English and Swahili) a. Coffee Board of
Kenya, Coffee Plaza, Haile Selassie Ave., Box
30566, Nairobi, Kenya.
　　Coffee

663.93　　　　　　　UK　ISSN 0264-5378
COFFEE INTERNATIONAL DIRECTORY. 1981.
a. $80. International Trade Publications Ltd., Coffee
& Cocoa International, Queensway House, 2
Queensway, Redhill, Surrey RH1 1QS, England. Ed.
Freda Troughton. adv. circ. 2,000.

COMMENTS FROM C A S T. (Council for
Agricultural Sciences and Technology) see
AGRICULTURE

664　　　　　　　AT　ISSN 0069-7419
COMMONWEALTH SCIENTIFIC AND
INDUSTRIAL RESEARCH ORGANIZATION.
DIVISION OF FOOD RESEARCH. REPORT OF
RESEARCH. (Before 1969 entitled Annual Report)
1959/60. a. Aus.$2. ‡ C.S.I.R.O., Division of Food
Research, P.O. Box 52, North Ryde, N.S.W. 2113,
Australia. circ. 1,700. Indexed: Biol.Abstr.
Chem.Abstr. Hort.Abstr.

664　　　　　　　AT　ISSN 0069-7427
COMMONWEALTH SCIENTIFIC AND
INDUSTRIAL RESEARCH ORGANIZATION.
DIVISION OF FOOD RESEARCH. TECHNICAL
PAPER. 1956. irreg. Aus.$2.50. ‡ C.S.I.R.O.,
Division of Food Research, P.O. Box 52, North
Ryde, N.S.W. 2113, Australia. circ. 500. Indexed:
Biol.Abstr. Chem.Abstr. Nutr.Abstr.

COST OF PICKING AND HAULING FLORIDA
CITRUS FRUITS. see *AGRICULTURE —
Agricultural Economics*

664　　　　　　　DK　ISSN 0107-0517
DENMARK. STATENS
LEVNEDSMIDDELINSTITUT. PUBLIKATION.
No.56, 1981. irreg. Miljoeministeriet,
Levnedsmiddelstyrelsen, Moerkhoej Bygade 19, DK-
2860 Soeborg, Denmark.

338.1　　　　　　　US
DIRECTORY OF CONVENIENCE STORES. 1978.
a. $140. Progressive Grocer Co. (Subsidiary of:
Maclean Hunter Media) 1351 Washington Blvd.,
Stamford, CT 06902. TEL 203-325-3500. Ed.
Maribeth McMahon.
　　Former titles: Directory of Convenience Store
Companies and Profile of the Industry & Directory
of Convenience Store Companies (ISSN 0278-9698)

642.5　338　　　　　CN
DIRECTORY OF RESTAURANT & FAST FOOD
CHAINS IN CANADA. 1980. a. Can.$125.
Maclean Hunter Ltd., Business Publications
Division, 777 Bay St., Toronto, Ont. M5W 1A7,
Canada. Ed. Maureen Cavanaugh.

DIRECTORY OF THE CANNING, FREEZING,
PRESERVING INDUSTRIES. see *BUSINESS
AND ECONOMICS — Trade And Industrial
Directories*

F D A CLINICAL EXPERIENCE ABSTRACTS.
(U.S. Food and Drug Administration) see
PHARMACY AND PHARMACOLOGY

664 615　　　　　　　US
F D A COMPLIANCE POLICY GUIDES.
MANUAL. base vol. plus 12 updates. $165. (U.S.
Food and Drug Administration) U.S. National
Technical Information Service, 5285 Port Royal
Rd., Springfield, VA 22161. TEL 703-487-4600.
　　Formerly: F D A Compliance Policy Guide.

633　　　　　　　CK
FEDERACION NACIONAL DE CAFETEROS DE
COLOMBIA. INFORME DE LABORES DE LOS
COMITES DEPARTAMENTALES DE
CAFETEROS. irreg. Federacion Nacional de
Cafeteros de Colombia, Av. Jimenez 7-65, Bogota,
Colombia. illus.
　　Coffee trade

664.028　　　　　　　FR
FEDERATION INTERPROFESSIONNELLE DE
LA CONGELATION ULTRA-RAPIDE.
RAPPORT STATISTIQUE ANNUEL. a. 420 F.
Ficur, 3 rue de Logelbach, 75347 Paris Cedex 17,
France.

664 658.8　　　　　　GW　ISSN 0014-9691
FEINKOST-REVUE. 1967. a. DM.94.80. Deutsche
Fachverlag GmbH, Schuemannstr. 27, 6000
Frankfurt 1, W. Germany(B.R.D.) Ed. Axel Bohl.
adv. bk. rev. bibl. charts. illus. circ. 6,500.

633.6　　　　　　　FJ
FIJI SUGAR YEAR BOOK. (Text in English, Fijian
and Hindi) 1979. a. Fiji Sugar Industry, Box 644,
Suva, Fiji. Ed. D.V. Tarte. charts. illus. stat. tr.lit.
circ. 5,000.

664.7　　　　　　　UK　ISSN 0071-6243
FLOUR MILLING AND BAKING RESEARCH
ASSOCIATION. ANNUAL REPORT AND
ACCOUNTS. 1968. a. membership. Flour Milling
and Baking Research Association, Chorleywood,
Rickmansworth, Herts. WD3 5SH, England. circ. 1,
750.
　　Issued formerly under name of one of its partent
organizations: British Baking Industries Research
Association. Annual Report.

664.06 340　　　　　　UK
FOOD ADDITIVES - DESCRIPTIONS,
FUNCTIONS AND U.K. LEGISLATIONS. 1976.
irreg. £30 to members, non-members £90. British
Food Manufacturing Industries Research
Associations, Randalls Rd., Leatherhead, Surrey,
KT22 7RY, England.

664 663　　　　　　　UK
FOOD AND DRINK TRADE HANDBOOK. 1970.
a. £5.50. National Food and Drink Federation, 60
Church Crescent, London N20 OJP, England. Ed.
L.E. Reeves-Smith.

664　　　　　　　UK　ISSN 0071-7177
FOOD INDUSTRIES MANUAL. 1928. irreg., 21th
edt., 1984. £90. Leonard Hill Blackie Publishing
Group, Western Cleddens Rd., Bishopbriggs,
Glasgow G64 2NZ, Scotland (Dist. in U.S. and
Canada by: Kapitan Szabo Publishers, 1740 Lanier
Place N.W. Washington DC 20009) Ed. M.
Ranken. adv. index. circ. 1,500.

664　　　　　　　SA
FOOD INDUSTRIES YEARBOOK AND BUYERS'
GUIDE. 1952. biennial. R.45($36) Thomson
Publications S.A. (Pty) Ltd., Thomson House, Cnr.
Will Scarlet & Hendrik Verwoerd Dr., Randburg,
P.O. Box 56182, Pinegowrie 2123, South Africa.
adv.
　　Former titles: Food Industries Yearbook and
Buyers' Directory; Food Industries of S.A. Buyers'
Guide (ISSN 0071-7185); Food Industries of South
Africa Manual and Buyer's Guide.

664　　　　　　　UK　ISSN 0264-4037
FOOD INDUSTRY DIRECTORY. 1954. biennial.
£23. Newman Books Ltd., 48 Poland St., London
W1V 4PP, England. adv.
　　Former titles: Food Processing Industry
Directory; Food Processing and Packaging
Directory (ISSN 0071-7207)

FOOD AND FOOD INDUSTRIES 519

FOOD INDUSTRY DIRECTORY. see *BUSINESS AND ECONOMICS — Trade And Industrial Directories*

664   UN
FOOD IRRADIATION NEWSLETTER. (Text in English) 1977. irreg. free. International Atomic Energy Agency, Wagramer Strasse 5, Box 100, A-1400 Vienna, Austria. (Co-sponsor: Food and Agriculture Organization) 500.

664   US
FOOD: LATIN AMERICAN INDUSTRIAL REPORT. (Avail. for each of 22 Latin American countries) 1985. a. $435 per country report per industry covered. Aurora International, Box 9099, Bridgeport, CT 06601-2099. TEL 203-368-0579. Ed. Andres C. Aquino.

664 340   UK
FOOD LEGISLATION SURVEYS. irreg. British Food Manufacturing Industries Research Association, Randalls Rd., Leatherhead, Surrey, KT22 7RY, England. TEL 0372-376761.

664 621.9   UK
FOOD MANUFACTURE INGREDIENT AND MACHINERY SURVEY. (Supplement avail.) 1966. a. £16. Morgan-Grampian (Publishers) Ltd., 30 Calderwood St., Woolwich, London SE18 6QH, England. Ed. Hugh Darrington. adv. circ. 1,500.

664 658.8   UK
FOOD PROCESSING. 1984. irreg. £95($150) Jordan & Sons Ltd., Jordan House, 47 Brunswick Place, London N1 6EE, England. Indexed: Curr.Pack.Abstr.

FOOD RESEARCH INSTITUTE STUDIES. see *AGRICULTURE — Agricultural Economics*

664   US   ISSN 0071-7223
FOOD SCIENCE SERIES. 1971. irreg., vol.21, 1986. price varies. Marcel Dekker, Inc., 270 Madison Ave., New York, NY 10016. TEL 212-696-9000. Ed. O. Fennema. Indexed: Biol.Abstr.

664   US
FOOD SERVICE RESEARCH ABSTRACTS. 1971. a. $7.50. Society for the Advancement of Food Service Research, 304 W. Liberty St., Ste. 301, Louisville, KY 40202. TEL 813-465-7090. Ed. Helen M. Spencer. circ. 250. (back issues avail.)

664   UK   ISSN 0309-0264
FOOD TRADES DIRECTORY & FOOD BUYER'S YEARBOOK. 1958. biennial. £57. Newman Books Ltd., 48 Poland St., London W1V 4PP, England. Ed Karen Rasmussen. adv.

664   CN
FOODBORNE AND WATERBORNE DISEASE IN CANADA. a. Can.$12.50. (Health and Welfare Canada, Health Protection Branch) Polyscience Publications Inc., 555 Legendre E, Suite 24, Montreal, Que. H2M 1G2, Canada.

664   US
FOODSERVICE INFORMATION ABSTRACTS. bi-w. $35 to members; non-members $70. National Restaurant Association, 311 First St., N.W., Washington, DC 20001. TEL 202-638-6100. Ed. Ann Walker Smalley. circ. 300. (back issues avail.)

664 658.8   US
FRESH PRODUCE FOODSERVICE DIRECTORY. 1985. a. $15 per no. Vance Publishing Corporation (Kansas City), Box 2939, Shawnee Mission, KS 66201. TEL 913-451-2200. Ed. Carol Holstead. adv. circ. 28,277(controlled)

664.028 641   UK
FROZEN AND CHILLED FOODS YEAR BOOK. 1957. a. £12. Retail Journals Ltd., Queensway House, 2 Queensway, Redhill, Surrey RH1 1QS, England. circ. 2,500.
    Formerly: Frozen Foods Year Book (ISSN 0071-9692)

664.028   DK
FROZEN FOODS IN DENMARK. 1963. a. free. Dybfrostraadet - Frozen Food Institute, Kastelvej 11, 2100 Copenhagen OE, Denmark. stat. circ. 115.

664   GW   ISSN 0341-0498
GRUNDLAGEN UND FORTSCHRITTE DER LEBENSMITTELUNTERSUCHUNG UND LEBENSMITTELTECHNOLOGIE. 1953. irreg. price varies. Verlag Paul Parey (Berlin), Lindenstr. 44-47, 1000 Berlin 61, W. Germany (B.R.D.) Ed. Friedrich Kiermeier. bibl. illus. index. Indexed: Biol.Abstr. Food Sci.& Tech.Abstr.
    Formerly: Grundlagen und Fortschritte der Lebensmitteluntersuchung (ISSN 0432-7454)

664   MX
GUIA DE LA INDUSTRIA: ALIMENTARIA. 1963. a. 2000($25) Editorial Cosmos, Espana No. 396, Mexico 09880, DF, Mexico. Dir. Cesar Macazaga Orodono. adv. circ. 5,000.

GUIDE TO THE FOOD REGULATIONS IN THE U.K. see *LAW*

664   NE
HANDBOOK OF AROMA RESEARCH. 1982. irreg., latest vol.2, 1983. fl.196($70) price varies. D. Reidel Publishing Company, Postbus 17, 3300 AA Dordrecht, Netherlands. Ed. Michael Ruse. adv. bk. rev. circ. 500.

641.5   US   ISSN 0278-906X
HANDBOOK OF FOOD PREPARATION. irreg., 8th, 1980. $6. American Home Economics Association, 2010 Massachusetts Ave., N.W., Washington, DC 20036. TEL 202-862-8300.

HOKKAIDO EIYO SYOKURYO GAKKAISHI/ HOKKAIDO SOCIETY OF FOOD AND NUTRITION. JOURNAL. see *AGRICULTURE — Dairying And Dairy Products*

664   UK   ISSN 0142-1824
HOTEL, RESTAURANT AND CATERING SUPPLIES. 1964. a. £30. Sell's Publications Ltd., 55 High St., Epsom, Surrey KT19 8DW, England. adv. bk. rev. circ. 5,000.
    Former titles: Sell's Hotel, Restaurant and Canteen Supplies (ISSN 0073-3504); Hotel, Restaurant and Canteen Supplies.

I D HANDBOOK OF FOODSERVICE DISTRIBUTION. (Institutional Distribution) see *BUSINESS AND ECONOMICS — Trade And Industrial Directories*

I F T BASIC SYMPOSIUM SERIES. (Institute of Food Technologists) see *NUTRITION AND DIETETICS*

642.5   US
INSITE (YEAR) 1980. a. $35 to non-members. National Association of Concessionaires, 35 E. Wacker Dr., Ste. 1849, Chicago, IL 60601. TEL 312-236-3858. Ed. Mandy Pava. adv. charts. stat. circ. 3,500.

664.9   UK
INSTITUTE OF FOOD RESEARCH - BRISTOL. LABORATORY BIENNIAL REPORT. 1977. biennial. Institute of Food Research - Bristol, Langford, Bristol BS18 7DY, England. illus. Indexed: Biol.Abstr. Anim.Breed.Abstr.
    Former titles: Food Research Institute Bristol. Biennial Report & Meat Research Institute. Biennial Report.
    Meat

664 641   BL   ISSN 0100-350X
INSTITUTO DE TECNOLOGIA DE ALIMENTOS. COLETANEA. 1965. a. $12. Instituto de Tecnologia de Alimentos, Caixa Postal 139, Campinas SP, Brazil. circ. 500. Indexed: Biol.Abstr. Nutr.Abstr. Food Sci.& Tech.Abstr. Hort.Abstr.

664 658.8   BL   ISSN 0100-4964
INSTITUTO DE TECNOLOGIA DE ALIMENTOS. ESTUDOS ECONOMICOS. ALIMENTOS PROCESSADOS. 1975. irreg. $6. Instituto de Tecnologia de Alimentos, Caixa Postal 139, Campinas, S.P., Brazil.

INSTITUTO SUPERIOR DE AGRONOMIA. ANAIS. see *AGRICULTURE*

INSTRUMENTATION IN THE FOOD INDUSTRY. see *INSTRUMENTS*

664   AU   ISSN 0074-1450
INTERNATIONAL ASSOCIATION FOR CEREAL CHEMISTRY. WORKING AND DISCUSSION MEETINGS REPORTS. 1958. biennial; 10th, Vienna, 1978. International Association for Cereal Chemistry, Schmidgasse 3-7, A-2320 Schwechat, Austria.

664.1   UK
INTERNATIONAL COMMISSION FOR UNIFORM METHODS OF SUGAR ANALYSIS. REPORT OF THE PROCEEDINGS OF THE SESSION. 1936. irreg., 18th, 1982, Dublin (published in 1983) (International Commission for Uniform Methods of Sugar Analysis) I C U M S A Publications, c/o British Sugar plc, Research Laboratories, Colney, Norwich, Norfolk NR4 7UB, England. circ. 1,000.
    Sugar

664.1   BE   ISSN 0074-2708
INTERNATIONAL COMMISSION OF SUGAR TECHNOLOGY. PROCEEDINGS OF THE GENERAL ASSEMBLY. (Text in English, French and German) 1953. quadriennial, 17th, 1983, Copenhagen. 1800 Fr. International Commission of Sugar Technology - Commission Internationale Technique de Sucrerie, c/o R. Pieck, General Secretary-Treasurer, 1 Aandorenstraat, B-3300 Tienen, Belgium. circ. 800. Indexed: Chem.Abstr. Sugar Ind.Abstr.
    Sugar

641 664   US   ISSN 0074-3666
INTERNATIONAL CONGRESS OF FOOD SCIENCE AND TECHNOLOGY. PROCEEDINGS. 1962. quadriennial; 1978, 5th, Kyoto, Japan. price varies. ‡ International Union of Food Science and Technology, c/o C. L. Wiley, Institute of Food Technologists, 221 N. La Salle St., Chicago, IL 60601 (For 5th Congress inquire: Prof. Hisateru Mitsuda, 64 Takanawate-Cho, Kamigamo, Kita-Ku, Kyoto, 603, Japan) circ. 3,000.

664   IO   ISSN 0074-3968
INTERNATIONAL CONGRESS OF SUGARCANE TECHNOLOGISTS. PROCEEDINGS. 1965. triennial, 1986, 19th, Indonesia. $110. International Society of Sugarcane Technologists, Box 86 JKWB, Jakarta 10270, Indonesia. Ed. John Clayton. circ. 3,000.

663   FR
INTERNATIONAL FEDERATION OF FRUIT JUICE PRODUCERS. RAPPORT ANNUEL D'ACTIVITE. (Text in English and French) 1958. a. 25 F. International Federation of Fruit Juice Producers, 10 rue de Liege, 75009 Paris, 75009 Paris.
    Formerly: International Federation of Fruit Juice Producers. Proceedings. Berichte. Rapports (ISSN 0535-0182)

664 670   US
INTERNATIONAL FOOD DIRECTORY. 1982. a. $75. Supermarket Productions, Ltd., Box 6124, San Rafael, CA 94903. TEL 415-479-0211. Ed. Gabriel M. Lubitz. adv. bk. rev. circ. 30,000.

INTERNATIONAL SUGAR ORGANIZATION. ANNUAL REPORT. see *AGRICULTURE — Crop Production And Soil*

664.1   UK
INTERNATIONAL SUGAR ORGANIZATION. SUGAR YEAR BOOK. a. £10. International Sugar Organization, 28 Haymarket, London SW1Y 4SP, England.

INTERNATIONAL UNION OF FOOD AND ALLIED WORKERS' ASSOCIATIONS. MEETING OF THE EXECUTIVE COMMITTEE. I. DOCUMENTS OF THE SECRETARIAT. II. SUMMARY REPORT. see *LABOR UNIONS*

338.4   JA
JAPAN SUGAR YEARBOOK. (Text in English) 1958. a. free. Mitsui & Co., Ltd., C.P.O. Box 822, Tokyo 100-91, Japan. adv. charts. illus. stat. circ. 600.

JOINT F A O/W H O CODEX ALIMENTARIUS COMMISSION. REPORT OF THE SESSION. see *PUBLIC HEALTH AND SAFETY*

FOOD AND FOOD INDUSTRIES

663.94   KE
KENYA TEA DEVELOPMENT AUTHORITY. ANNUAL REPORT AND ACCOUNTS. (Text in English) a. Kenya Tea Development Authority, Box 30213, Nairobi, Kenya.
Tea

KOMPASS PROFESSIONNELS. see *BUSINESS AND ECONOMICS — Trade And Industrial Directories*

664   US
LATIN AMERICAN INTERNATIONAL FOOD INDUSTRY DIRECTORY. (Text in English, Portuguese, Spanish) 1985. a. $150 per m. Aurora International, Box 9099, Bridgeport, CT 06601-2099. TEL 203-368-0579. Ed. Andres C. Aquino.

664.1   MF
MAURITIUS SUGAR INDUSTRY RESEARCH INSTITUTE. ADVISORY BULLETIN. 1981. irreg. Mauritius Sugar Industry Research Institute, Reduit, Mauritius.
Sugar

664.1   MF
MAURITIUS SUGAR INDUSTRY RESEARCH INSTITUTE. ANNUAL REPORT. (Text in English) 1953. a., latest 1984. Mauritius Sugar Industry Research Institute, Reduit, Mauritius. circ. 1,000. Indexed: Biol.Abstr. Field Crop Abstr. Herb.Abstr. Hort.Abstr. Rev.Appl.Entomol. Rev.Plant Path. Weed Abstr.
Sugar

664.1   MF
MAURITIUS SUGAR INDUSTRY RESEARCH INSTITUTE. OCCASIONAL PAPER. 1958. irreg., latest 1984. price varies. Mauritius Sugar Industry Research Institute, Reduit, Mauritius. circ. 500. (back issues avail.) Indexed: Biol.Abstr.
Sugar

664   US   ISSN 0090-5631
MEAT SCIENCE INSTITUTE. PROCEEDINGS. 1972. a. $10 price varies. (National Meat Association) University of Georgia, Center for Continuing Education, Athens, GA 30602. TEL 404-542-1725. Ed. John A. Carpenter.

636   UK
MEAT TRADE YEARBOOK & DIARY. 1959. a. $18. Wheatland Journals Ltd., Penn House, Penn Place, Rickmansworth, Herts. WD3 1SN, England. Ed. Joan Barraclough. adv. circ. 4,500.
Former titles: Meat Trade Yearbook (ISSN 0082-7967); United Kingdom Meat Trade Annual.

664.9 331.88   AT   ISSN 0310-6721
MEATWORKER. 1971. irreg. Australasian Meat Industry Employees Union, Queensland Branch, Room 47 Trades Hall, Brisbane, Qld. 4000, Australia. Ed. R. Anear. (newspaper)

664.8 658.8   US
MICHIGAN STATE HORTICULTURAL SOCIETY. ANNUAL REPORT. 1870. a. $10. Michigan State Horticultural Society, Michigan State University, A388D Plant and Soil Science Bldg., East Lansing, MI 48824. TEL 517-355-5194. Ed. Jerome Hull, Jr. circ. 2,300. (back issues avail.)

MOVEMENT OF CALIFORNIA FRUITS AND VEGETABLES BY RAIL, TRUCK, AND AIR. see *TRANSPORTATION*

642.5   US
N A C U F S JOURNAL. 1968. a. membership. National Association of College-University Food Services, c/o Clark Dehaven, Seven Olds Hall, Michigan State University, East Lansing, MI 48824. TEL 517-355-1855. Ed. Frances Cloyd. bibl. circ. 1, 600.
Supersedes: N A C I F S Technical Bulletin (ISSN 0027-5751)

664 630   JA   ISSN 0301-9780
NATIONAL FOOD RESEARCH INSTITUTE. REPORT. irreg. National Food Research Institute, Ministry of Agriculture and Forestry and Fisheries, 2-1-2, Kannondai, Yatabe-Cho, Tsukuba-Gun, Ibaraki-Ken 350, Japan.

664.02 338.47   US
NATIONAL FROZEN FOOD ASSOCIATION DIRECTORY. 1948. a. $50. National Frozen Food Association, Inc., 604 W. Derry Rd., Hershey, PA 17033. TEL 717-534-1601. Ed. Dick Fralick. adv. index. circ. 3,500.
Formerly (until 1985): Frozen Food Factbook and Directory (ISSN 0071-9684)

NATIONAL RESEARCH INSTITUTE OF VEGETABLES, ORNAMENTAL PLANTS AND TEA. BULLETIN. see *AGRICULTURE*

664   NE
NETHERLANDS. MINISTERIE VAN WELZIJN, VOLKSGEZONDHEID EN CULTUUR. VERSLAG LEVENSMIDDELEN EN KEURING VAN WAREN. (Subseries of: Netherlands. Ministerie van Welzijn, Volksgezondheid en Cultuur. Verslagen, Adviezen, Rapporten) 1973. irreg. fl.42.50. Ministerie van Welzijn, Volksgezondheid en Cultuur - Ministry of Health and Culture, Leidschendam, Netherlands. circ. 800.
Formerly: Netherlands. Ministerie van Volksgezondheid en Milieuhygiene. Verslag Levensmiddelen en Keuring van Waren.

NUTRITION SOCIETY OF INDIA. PROCEEDINGS. see *NUTRITION AND DIETETICS*

664   UK
PERISHERS ANNUAL. a. World Distributors Ltd., Box 111, 12 Lever St., Manchester M6O 1TS, England.

PESTICIDRESTER I DANSKE LEVNEDSMIDLER/PESTICIDE RESIDUES IN DANISH FOOD. see *AGRICULTURE — Crop Production And Soil*

664   PL   ISSN 0528-9254
POLITECHNIKA LODZKA. ZESZYTY NAUKOWE. TECHNOLOGIA I. CHEMIA SPOZYWCZA. (Text in Polish; summaries in English and Russian) 1955. irreg. price varies. Politechnika Lodzka, Ul. Zwirki 36, 90-924 Lodz, Poland (Dist. by: Ars Polona-Ruch, Krakowskie Przedmiescie 7, Warsaw, Poland) Ed. Anna Nowakowska-Waszczuk. circ. 983. Indexed: Chem.Abstr.

664   UR   ISSN 0203-9788
POLUTEHNILINE INSTITUUT TALLINN. VOPROSY POVYSHENIYA KACHESTVA PISHCHEVYKH PRODUKTOV. (Subseries of Its Toimetised) (Text in Russian; summaries in English or German) irreg. price varies. Polutehniline Instituut Tallinn, Ehitajate tee 5, Tallinn, Estonian S.S.R., U.S.S.R.

664 668.8   US
PRODUCE MARKETING ALMANAC. 1976. a. $35. Produce Marketing Association, 700 Barksdale Plaza, Newark, DE 19711. TEL 302-738-7100. Ed. Nancy Tucker. adv. circ. 4,000.
Formerly: Produce Marketing Association Almanac; Supersedes (1968-1976): Produce Marketing Association. Yearbook (ISSN 0079-5860) ; Which was formerly titled: Produce Packaging and Marketing Association. Yearbook.

338.1   US   ISSN 0079-6921
PROGRESSIVE GROCER'S MARKETING GUIDEBOOK. 1967. a. $240. Progressive Grocer Co. (Subsidiary of: Maclean Hunter Media) 1351 Washington Blvd., Stamford, CT 06902. TEL 203-325-3500. Ed. Donna Wetmore. adv. index. (back issues avail.)

PURE-PAK NEWS. see *PACKAGING*

664   FR
REPERTOIRE DES CENTRES DE RECHERCHE ALIMENTAIRE. irreg. 315 F. Societe d'Edition et de Promotion Agro-Alimentaires, Industrielles et Commerciales, B.P. 551, 42 rue du Louvre, 75027 Paris Cedex 01, France.

664 663.19   US
S I C 2038 PROCESS/QUALITY CONTROL INSTRUMENTATION BUYERS GUIDE. 1983. a. S I C Publishing Co., 401 Christopher Ave., Ste. 11, Gaithersburg, MD 20879. TEL 301-963-8070. adv. circ. 10,000.

664   US
S I C 2087/AROMA BUYERS GUIDE. 1982. a. $65. S I C Publishing Co., 401 Christopher Ave., Ste. 11, Gaithersburg, MD 20879. TEL 301-963-8070. adv. circ. 5,000.

664   SW
S I K ANNUAL REPORT. (Text in English and Swedish) 1951. a. Svenska Livsmedelsinstitutet - Swedish Food Institute, Box 5401, S-402 29 Goeteborg, Sweden. circ. 2,000. Indexed: Dairy Sci.Abstr.
Formerly: Swedish Food Institute. Annual Report.

664.028   SW
S I K INFORMATION. (Text in English) 1972. irreg. free. Svenska Livsmedelsinstitutet - Swedish Food Institute, Box 5401, S-402 29 Goeteborg, Sweden. circ. 700.

664 658.8   US
S N DISTRIBUTION STUDY OF GROCERY STORE SALES. 1978. a. $45. Fairchild Books, 7 E. 12th St., New York, NY 10003. TEL 212-741-4280. circ. 1,500. (back issues avail.)

SAMMLUNG LEBENSMITTELRECHTLICHER ENTSCHEIDUNGEN. see *LAW*

664   SP
SERIE DE COCINA POR LUIS RIPOLI. (Subject varies with each issue) irreg. price varies. Luis Ripoll Ed. & Pub., Calatrava 34, 07001 Palma de Mallorca, Spain.

642   US   ISSN 0081-1483
SOCIETY FOR THE ADVANCEMENT OF FOOD SERVICE RESEARCH. PROCEEDINGS. 1959. a. $25 price may vary. Society for the Advancement of Food Service Research, 304 W. Liberty St., Ste. 301, Louisville, KY 40202. TEL 813-465-7090. Ed. Charles E. Eshbach.

634   NE
SPRENGER INSTITUUT. COMMUNICATIONS. (Text in Dutch; summaries in English, French and German) vol.35, 1976. irreg. price varies. Sprenger Instituut, Postbus 17, 6700 AA Wageningen, Netherlands. (back issues avail.)

634 664   NE   ISSN 0081-3850
SPRENGER INSTITUUT. JAARVERSLAG/ANNUAL REPORT. (Text in Dutch and English) 1956. a. price varies. ‡ Sprenger Instituut, Postbus 17, 6700 AA Wageningen, Netherlands. Indexed: Food Sci.& Tech.Abstr. Hort.Abstr.

634   NE
SPRENGER INSTITUUT. RAPPORTEN. irreg. price varies. Sprenger Instituut, Postbus 17, 6700 AA Wageningen, Netherlands. (back issues avail.)

664   US
STOKELY-VAN CAMP ANNUAL SYMPOSIUM. PROCEEDINGS. 1979. a. University of Tennessee, Department of Nutrition and Food Sciences, 229 Home Economics Bldg., Knoxville, TN 37916. TEL 615-974-5445. circ. 900.

664.005   SJ
SUDAN JOURNAL OF FOOD SCIENCE AND TECHNOLOGY. (Text in English) 1968. a. $10. Food Research Centre, P.O. Box 213, Khartoum North, Sudan. illus. Indexed: Biol.Abstr. Chem.Abstr. Dairy Sci.Abstr.

664   GW   ISSN 0081-9174
SUESSWAREN JAHRBUCH; Wer und Was in der deutschen Suesswarenindustrie. 1949. a. DM.109.50. B. Behr's Verlag GmbH, Averhoffstr. 10, 2000 Hamburg 76, W. Germany (B.R.D.)

664   TR   ISSN 0302-4555
SUGAR TECHNOLOGISTS' ASSOCIATION OF TRINIDAD AND TOBAGO. PROCEEDINGS. 1967. a. free. ‡ Sugar Technologists' Association of Trindad & Tobago, 80 Abercromby St., Box 230, Port of Spain, Trinidad. Ed. M.Y. Khan. circ. controlled. (processed)

664.1   US   ISSN 0081-9212
SUGAR Y AZUCAR YEARBOOK. (Text in English and Spanish) a. $38.75. Ruspam Communications, Inc., 2050 Center Ave., Ft. Lee, NJ 07024. TEL 201-461-8660.
Sugar

338.1 CH ISSN 0492-1712
TAIWAN SUGAR. irreg. $5. Good Earth Press, Box 697, Taipei, Taiwan, Republic of China. illus. Indexed: Hort.Abstr. Plant Breed.Abstr.

663.94 MW ISSN 0258-4476
TEA RESEARCH FOUNDATION OF CENTRAL AFRICA. ANNUAL REPORT. 1966. a. K.30($24) Tea Research Foundation of Central Africa, Box 51, Mulanje, Malawi. Ed. W.J. Grice. circ. 200. Indexed: Hort.Abstr.
Tea

663.94 KE
TEA RESEARCH FOUNDATION OF KENYA. ANNUAL REPORT. 1950. a. EAs.70. Tea Research Foundation of Kenya, P.O. Box 820, Kericho, Kenya. Ed. C.O. Othieno. circ. 400. Indexed: Weed Abstr.
Former titles: Tea Research Foundation. Annual Report; Tea Research Institute of East Africa. Annual Report.
Tea

TROPICAL DEVELOPMENT & RESEARCH INSTITUTE. CROP AND PRODUCT SERIES. see AGRICULTURE — Crop Production And Soil

664 US
UNITED STATES. FOOD SAFETY AND INSPECTION SERVICE. PROGRAM PLAN. a. U.S. Department of Agriculture, Food Safety and Inspection Service, Washington, DC 20250.

UNIVERSITY OF READING. DEPARTMENT OF AGRICULTURAL ECONOMICS & MANAGEMENT. FOOD ECONOMICS STUDIES. see AGRICULTURE — Agricultural Economics

664 641.1 PL ISSN 0208-5755
WARSAW AGRICULTURAL UNIVERSITY. S G G W-A R. ANNALS. FOOD TECHNOLOGY AND NUTRITION. (Szkola Glowna Gospodarstwa Wiejskiego - Akademia Rolnicza, Warsaw) (Text mainly in English; occasionally in French, German or Russian; summaries in Polish) 1957. irreg. $6 per no. Warsaw Agricultural University Press, Ul. Nowoursynowska 166, 02-766 Warsaw, Poland (Dist. by: Ars Polona-Ruch, Krakowskie Przedmiescie 7, 00-680 Warsaw, Poland) Ed. S. Zmarlick.

WEST AFRICA RICE DEVELOPMENT ASSOCIATION. OCCASIONAL PAPER. see AGRICULTURE

641.345 634 AT ISSN 0312-8997
WEST AUSTRALIAN NUT AND TREE CROP ASSOCIATION YEARBOOK. 1975. a. Aus.$30. West Australian Nut & Tree Crop Association (Inc.), Box 565, Subiaco, WA 6008, Australia. Ed. David Turner. adv. bk. rev. circ. 500. Indexed: Biol.Abstr. Hort.Abstr.
Formerly: West Australian Nutgrowing Society Yearbook.

338.1 UN ISSN 0084-179X
WORLD FOOD PROBLEMS. (Text in English, French, and Spanish) 1956. irreg., no.14, 1971. price varies. Food and Agriculture Organization of the United Nations, Distribution and Sales Section, Via delle Terme di Caracalla, Rome, Italy (Dist. in U.S. by: Bernan Associates-Unipub, 4611-F Assembly Drive, Lanham, MD 20706-4391)

664 US
WORLD FOOD PRODUCTION CONFERENCE SUMMARY REPORT. 9th, 1973. a. available on request. International Minerals and Chemicals Corporation, 421 E. Hawley St., Mundlein, IL 60060. TEL 312-566-2600. Ed. Norman S. Youngsteadt.
Incorporating: Latin American Food Production Conference Summary Report.

664 UN
WORLD FOOD REPORT. a. Food and Agriculture Organization of the United Nations, Via delle Terme di Caracalla, 00100 Rome, Italy.

WORLD GASTRONOMY. see BEVERAGES

641 ZA ISSN 0084-4969
ZAMBIA. NATIONAL FOOD AND NUTRITION COMMISSION. ANNUAL REPORT. (Text in English) 1968. a. free. ‡ National Food and Nutrition Commission, Box 32669, Lusaka, Zambia. circ. 2,000.

664 GW ISSN 0084-5736
ZUCKERWIRTSCHAFTLICHES TASCHENBUCH/ SUGAR ECONOMY/ECONOMIE SUCRIERE. 1954. a. DM.33. Verlag Dr. Albert Bartens, Lueckhoffstr. 16, 1000 Berlin 38, W. Germany (B.R.D.) adv. circ. 2,200.

FOOD AND FOOD INDUSTRIES — Abstracting, Bibliographies, Statistics

ABSTRACT NEWSLETTER: AGRICULTURE & FOOD. see AGRICULTURE — Abstracting, Bibliographies, Statistics

664 016 UK ISSN 0001-3439
ABSTRACTS FROM CURRENT SCIENTIFIC AND TECHNICAL LITERATURE. 1947. m. £80 to individuals; institutions £100. British Food Manufacturing Industries Research Association, Randalls Road, Leatherhead, Surrey, England. Ed. A. Pernet. abstr. pat. index. circ. 1,000(approx.)

ABSTRACTS ON TROPICAL AGRICULTURE. see AGRICULTURE — Abstracting, Bibliographies, Statistics

664 US ISSN 0276-3109
BIOSIS/CAS SELECTS: BIOCHEMISTRY OF FERMENTED FOODS. 1981. bi-w. $105. BioSciences Information Service (BIOSIS), 2100 Arch St., Philadelphia, PA 19103-1399. TEL 215-587-4800. (Co-publisher: Chemical Abstracts Service) (reprint service avail.)

664 658.8 CN ISSN 0316-9537
BLUE BOOK OF FOOD STORE OPERATORS & WHOLESALERS. a. Can.$16.50. Sanford Evans Communications Ltd., 1077 St. James St., Box 6900, Winnipeg, Man. R3C 3B1, Canada. TEL 204-775-0201. Ed. Gary Henry. circ. 1,000.

338.4 CN ISSN 0384-2843
CANADA. STATISTICS CANADA. CANE AND BEET SUGAR PROCESSORS/TRAITEMENT DU SUCRE DE CANNE ET DE BETTERAVES. (Catalogue 32-222) (Text in English and French) 1918. a. Can.$20($21) Statistics Canada, Communications Division, 3rd Floor, R.H. Coats Bldg., Ottawa, Ont. K1A 0T6, Canada TEL 613-993-7276. (Subscr. to: Publications Sales and Services, Ottawa, Ont. K1A 0T6, Canada) (also avail. in microform from MML)

CANADA. STATISTICS CANADA. FISH PRODUCTS INDUSTRY/INDUSTRIE DE LA TRANSFORMATION DU POISSON. see FISH AND FISHERIES — Abstracting, Bibliographies, Statistics

338.4 CN ISSN 0700-0324
CANADA. STATISTICS CANADA. FLOUR AND BREAKFAST CEREAL PRODUCTS INDUSTRY/MEUNERIE ET FABRICATION DE CEREALES DE TABLE. (Catalogue 32-228) (Text in English and French) 1970. a. Can.$20($21) Statistics Canada, Communications Division, 3rd Floor, R.H. Coats Bldg., Ottawa, Ont. K1A 0T6, Canada TEL 613-993-7276. (Subscr. to: Publications Sales and Services, Ottawa, Ont. K1A 0T6, Canada) (also avail. in microform from MML)

664 CN ISSN 0384-4420
CANADA. STATISTICS CANADA. FRUIT AND VEGETABLE PROCESSING INDUSTRIES/ PREPARATION DE FRUITS ET DE LEGUMES. (Catalogue 32-218) (Text in English and French) 1918. a. Can.$20($21) Statistics Canada, Communications Division, 3rd Floor, R.H. Coats Bldg., Ottawa, Ont. K1A 0T6, Canada TEL 613-993-7276. (Subscr. to: Publications Sales and Services, Ottawa, Ont. K1A 0T6, Canada) (also avail. in microform from MML)

664 CN ISSN 0384-3696
CANADA. STATISTICS CANADA. MISCELLANEOUS FOOD PROCESSORS/ TRAITMENT DES PRODUITS ALIMENTAIRES DIVERS. (Catalogue 32-224) (Text in English and French) 1918. a. Can.$20($21) Statistics Canada, Communications Division, 3rd Floor, R.H. Coats Bldg., Ottawa, Ont. K1A 0T6, Canada TEL 613-993-7276. (Subscr. to: Publications Sales and Services, Ottawa, Ont. K1A 0T6, Canada) (also avail. in microform from MML)

338.4 CN ISSN 0527-6403
CANADA. STATISTICS CANADA. VEGETABLE OIL MILLS/MOULINS A HUILE VEGETALE. (Catalogue 32-223) (Text in English and French) 1918. a. Can.$20($21) Statistics Canada, Communications Division, 3rd Floor, R.H. Coats Bldg., Ottawa, Ont. K1A 0T6, Canada TEL 613-993-7276. (Subscr. to: Publications Sales and Services, Ottawa, Ont. K1A 0T6, Canada) (also avail. in microform from MML)

664 310 US ISSN 0145-5168
CURRENT INDUSTRIAL REPORTS: FATS AND OILS. OILSEED CRUSHINGS. (Series M-20-J) m. (plus a. issue) $37. U.S. Bureau of the Census, Customer Services Dept., Washington, DC 20233 TEL 301-763-1584. (Subscr. to: Supt. of Documents, Washington, DC 20402) (also avail. in microfiche) Indexed: Chem.Abstr. Key Title: Fats and Oils. Oilseed Crushings.

664 310 US ISSN 0145-5176
CURRENT INDUSTRIAL REPORTS: FATS AND OILS. PRODUCTION, CONSUMPTION, AND FACTORY AND WAREHOUSE STOCKS. (Series M-20-K) m. (plus a. issue) $37. U.S. Bureau of the Census, Customer Services Dept., Washington, DC 20233 TEL 301-763-4100. (Subscr. to: Supt. of Documents, Washington, DC 20402) Indexed: Chem.Abstr. Key Title: Fats and Oils. Production, Consumption, and Factory and Warehouse Stocks.

664.752 664.7 016 UK ISSN 0430-7941
FLOUR MILLING AND BAKING RESEARCH ASSOCIATION ABSTRACTS. 1948. bi-m. £118 to non-members. Flour Milling and Baking Research Association, Chorleywood, Rickmansworth, Herts WD3 5SH, England. Ed. C.R.H. Parsons. bk. rev. abstr. pat. tr.lit. index. circ. 1,500.
Former titles: British Baking Industries Research Association. Abstracts (ISSN 0300-421X); Baking Research Association. Abstracts (ISSN 0005-4143)

664 310 FR
FOOD CONSUMPTION STATISTICS IN THE O.E.C.D. COUNTRIES. (Text in English and French) irreg. price varies. Organisation for Economic Cooperation and Development, 2 rue Andre Pascal, 75775 Paris 16, France (U.S. orders to: O.E.C.D. Publications and Information Center, 1750 Pennsylvania Ave. N.W., Washington, D.C. 20006) (also avail. in microfiche)
Formerly: Food Consumption in the O.E.C.D. (ISSN 0474-537X)

664 016 UK ISSN 0015-6574
FOOD SCIENCE AND TECHNOLOGY ABSTRACTS. (Former name of issuing body: Commonwealth Agricultural Bureaux) 1969. m. £437($926) ‡ C.A.B. International, International Food Information Service, Farnham House, Farnham Royal, Slough SL2 3BN, England (U.S. subscr. to: C.A.B. International, North American Office, 845 N. Park Ave., Tucson, AR 85719) bk. rev. index. circ. 1,250. (also avail. in microfiche; back issues avail.)
●Also available online. Vendors: BRS, CISTI, DIMDI, Data-Star, DIALOG, European Space Agency, JICST, Orbit Information Technologies.

FOODSERVICE INFORMATION ABSTRACTS. see FOOD AND FOOD INDUSTRIES

664 NE ISSN 0168-5287
NETHERLANDS. CENTRAAL BUREAU VOOR DE STATISTIEK. PRODUKTIESTATISTIEKEN: SUIKERFABRIEKEN. a. fl.7.10. Centraal Bureau voor de Statistiek, Prinses Beatrixlaan 428, Voorburg, Netherlands (Orders to: Staatsuitgeverij, Christoffel Plantijnstraat, The Hague, Netherlands)

FOOD AND FOOD INDUSTRIES — BAKERS AND CONFECTIONERS

664 016   UR   ISSN 0034-2521
REFERATIVNYI ZHURNAL. OBORUDOVANIE PISHCHEVOI PROMYSHLENNOSTI. 1956. m. 51.20 Rub. (52 Rub. including index) Vsesoyuznyi Institut Nauchno-Teknicheskoi Informatsii (VINITI), Baltiiskaya ul., 14, Moscow A-219, Russian S.F.S.R., U.S.S.R (Subscr. to: Mezhdunarodnaya Kniga, Dimitrova ul. 39, 113095 Moscow, Russian S.F.S.R., U.S.S.R.)

658.8 016   US
REFERENCE POINT: FOOD INDUSTRY ABSTRACTS. 1971. m. $70 to non-members. Food Marketing Institute, 1750 K St., N.W., Washington, DC 20006. TEL 202-452-8444. Ed. Barbara L. McBride. abstr. bibl. cum.index. circ. 300.
    Former titles: F M I Monthly Index Service (ISSN 0270-0352) & S M I Monthly Index Service (Super Market Institute)

664.1 016   UK
TATE AND LYLE'S SUGAR INDUSTRY ABSTRACTS. 1948. bi-m. $185. Tate & Lyle Group Research & Development, P.O. Box 68, Reading RG6 2BX, England. TEL 0734-861361. Ed. Margaret E. Cope. adv. bk. rev. abstr. pat. index. (back issues avail.)
    Formerly: Sugar Industry Abstracts (ISSN 0250-2887)

FOOD AND FOOD INDUSTRIES — Bakers And Confectioners

664.752   US   ISSN 0066-0582
AMERICAN SOCIETY OF BAKERY ENGINEERS. PROCEEDINGS OF THE ANNUAL MEETING. 1925. a. free to members. American Society of Bakery Engineers, 2 N. Riverside Plaza, Rm. 1921, Chicago, IL 60606. TEL 312-332-2246. Ed. Robert A. Fischer. index. cum.index every 10 yrs. circ. 3,000.

664.15   FR
ANNUAIRE SUCRIER. a. 460 F. Societe d'Edition et de Promotion Agro-Alimentaires, Industrielles et Commerciales, B.P. 551, 42 rue du Louvre, 75027 Paris Cedex 01, France.

664.752   US
BAKERY PRODUCTION AND MARKETING RED BOOK. 1976. a. $105. Gorman Publishing Co., President's Plaza III, 8750 W. Bryn Mawr Ave., Chicago, IL 60631. TEL 312-693-3200. Ed. Edward Lee. adv. circ. 26,183.

664.752   UK
BRITISH BAKER DIRECTORY AND BUYERS GUIDE. a. £7.95 per issue. Maclaren Publishers Ltd., Maclaren House, 19 Scarbrook Rd., Croydon CR9 1QH, England. circ. 10,291.

CANDY BUYERS DIRECTORY. see *BUSINESS AND ECONOMICS — Trade And Industrial Directories*

664.15   US
CANDY INDUSTRY BUYING GUIDE. 1945. a. $25. Harcourt Brace Jovanovich, Inc., 7500 Old Oak Blvd., Cleveland, OH 44130 TEL 216-243-8100. (Subscr. to: 1 E. First St., Duluth, MN 55802) Ed. Patricia L. Magee-Nemetz. adv. circ. 3,976.

664.15   UK
CONFECTIONERY BUYER'S GUIDE. 1971. a. £10. J.G. Kennedy & Co. Ltd., 22 Methuen Park, London N10 2JS, England. Ed. Margaret Lang. circ. 5,000.

664.752   US
INDEPENDENT (WASHINGTON) 1978. a. free. Independent Bakers Association, 1701 K St., N.W., Ste. 1004, Washington, DC 20006. TEL 202-223-2325. Ed. Robert N. Pyle. circ. 3,000. (back issues avail.)

664.752   US
INDEPENDENT BAKERS ASSOCIATION NEWSLETTER. a. membership. Independent Bakers Association, 1701 K St., N.W., Ste. 1004, Box 3731, Washington, DC 20007. TEL 202-223-2325. Ed. Robert N. Pyle. circ. 300.

664.15   BE
INTERNATIONAL OFFICE OF COCOA AND CHOCOLATE AND THE INTERNATIONAL SUGAR CONFECTIONARY MANUFACTURERS' ASSOCIATION. ANNUAL STATISTICAL BULLETIN. Short title: I O C C/I S C M A a. $25. International Office of Cocoa and Chocolate, Av. de Cortenbergh 172, B-1040 Brussels, Belgium. (Co-sponsor; International Sugar Confectionary Manufacturers' Association)
    Formerly: International Office of Cocoa and Chocolate and the International Sugar Confectionary Manufacturers' Association. Periodic Bulletin (ISSN 0444-0978)

663   BE   ISSN 0535-1626
INTERNATIONAL OFFICE OF COCOA AND CHOCOLATE AND THE INTERNATIONAL SUGAR CONFECTIONARY MANUFACTURERS' ASSOCIATION. REPORT OF THE GENERAL ASSEMBLY. biennial, latest 1987, Berlin. $20. International Office of Cocoa and Chocolate, Av. de Cortenbergh 172, 1040 Brussels, Belgium. (Co-sponsor: International Sugar Confectionary Manufacturers' Association)

664.752   UK
MASTER BAKER'S HANDBOOK AND BUYER'S GUIDE. a. £12.50($16) Turret-Wheatland Ltd., 12 Greycaine Rd., Watford, Herts WD2 4JP, England. Ed. Marjorie Voss.

664.752   MX
PAN DIRECTORIO DE PROVEEDORES/BREAD CATERERS' DIRECTORY. 1967. a. $20. Bravo Grupo Editorial, S.A., Jose Maria Bustillos 49, Colonia Algarin, Mexico 8, DF, Mexico. Ed. Lazaro Bravo Bernabe. adv. circ. 10,000.

664   UK   ISSN 0080-7974
SCOTTISH BAKERS' YEAR BOOK. 1894. a. membership. ‡ Scottish Association of Master Bakers, Atholl House, 4 Torphichen St., Edinburgh EH3 8JQ, Scotland. Ed. J.D. Copeman. adv. bk. rev. circ. 1,100.

664.752   AT
SOUTH AUSTRALIAN BAKER AND PASTRYCOOK. 1969. biennial. (Baking Trade Federation of Australia, South Australian Branch) Percival Publishing Co. Pty. Ltd., 17 Currie St., Adelaide, S.A. 5000, Australia. Ed. James Fryer.

UNITED STATES TOBACCO AND CANDY JOURNAL SUPPLIER DIRECTORY. see *TOBACCO*

FOOD AND FOOD INDUSTRIES — Grocery Trade

A L A WORLDWIDE DIRECTORY AND FACT BOOK. (American Logistics Association) see *MILITARY*

658.8   UK
BRITAIN'S GROCERY RETAILERS. 1985. biennial. £95. Jordan & Sons Ltd., 47 Brunswick Place, London N1 6EE, England.

658.8   US
BUYERS GUIDE FOR FRESH PRODUCE. 1974. a. $3.75. Produce Marketing Association, 700 Barksdale Plaza, Newark, DE 19711. TEL 302-738-7100. Ed. Steve Ahlberg.
    Formerly: Food Service Directory and Buyers Guide for Fresh Produce.

658.8   US   ISSN 0084-9294
CONVENIENCE STORE INDUSTRY REPORT. 1970. a. $30. ‡ B M T Publications, Inc., 254 W. 31st St., New York, NY 10001. TEL 212-594-4120. Ed. Denise Melinsky. adv.

658.8   US
CORNELL REPORT ON PRODUCTIVITY IN GROCERY DISTRIBUTION CENTERS. a. $75. (New York State College of Agriculture and Life Sciences) Cornell University, Department of Agricultural Economics, Ithaca, NY 14853. TEL 607-256-4595. stat. (looseleaf format; back issues avail.)

658.86   US   ISSN 0271-7662
DIRECTORY OF FOOD SERVICE DISTRIBUTORS. 1973. a. $179. Chain Store Guide (Subsidiary of: Lebhar-Friedman, Inc.) 425 Park Ave., New York, NY 10022. TEL 212-371-9400. (also avail. in magnetic tape)
    Formerly: Chain Store Guide Directory: Food Service Distributors (ISSN 0091-9152)

DIRECTORY OF SUPERMARKET, GROCERY & CONVENIENCE STORE CHAINS. see *BUSINESS AND ECONOMICS — Trade And Industrial Directories*

658.878   US
F M I ANNUAL FINANCIAL REVIEW. 1973. a. $15 to non-members; members $7.50. Food Marketing Institute, 1750 K St., N.W., Washington, DC 20006. TEL 202-452-8444. Ed. Judith Kozacik.

664 658.8   US   ISSN 0732-233X
FACTS ABOUT STORE DEVELOPMENT. 1953. a. $20 to non-members; members $10. Food Marketing Institute, 1750 K St., N.W., Washington, DC 20006. TEL 202-452-8444. Ed. Judith Kozacik.
    Formerly: Facts About New Supermarkets (ISSN 0081-9522)

658.8   US   ISSN 0894-184X
FOOD MARKETERS' HANDBOOK. Variant title: Thomas Grocery Register's Food Marketers' Handbook. (Supplement to 3-vol. Thomas Grocery Register) 1983. a. $8.95. Thomas Publishing Co., One Penn Plaza, New York, NY 10019. TEL 215-695-0500. charts. stat. circ. 5,000.

664 658.8   US   ISSN 0190-3349
FOOD MARKETING INDUSTRY SPEAKS. 1949. a. $15. Food Marketing Institute, 1750 K St., N.W., Washington, DC 20006. TEL 202-452-8444. Ed. Judith Kozacik.
    Formerly: Supermarket Industry Speaks (ISSN 0081-9530)

FRESH PRODUCE FOODSERVICE DIRECTORY. see *FOOD AND FOOD INDUSTRIES*

658.8   UK
GROCER MARKETING DIRECTORY. 1954. a. £7. William Reed Ltd., 5 Southwark St., London SE1 1RQ, England. Ed. Margaret Beddall. circ. 5,000.
    Former titles: Grocer Directory; Grocer Directory of Multiples and Co-Operatives (ISSN 0072-7695)

658.8 380   FR
GUIDOR. (Guide Annuaire Officiel du Complexe de Rungis) a. Compagnie de Documentation, 17 rue de Paradis, 75010 Paris, France. charts.

658.86 630 634.9 614.7   GW
HESSE. MINISTER FUER LANDESENTWICKLUNG, UMWELT, LANDWIRTSCHAFT UND FORSTEN. MITTEILUNGEN. LAND UND UMWELT. 1981. irreg., approx. 6/yr. free. Minister fuer Landesentwicklung, Umwelt, Landwirtschaft und Forsten, Postfach 3127, 6200 Wiesbaden, W. Germany (B.R.D.) Ed. Gerd Kallweit. Indexed: Nutr.Abstr.

658.86   GW
HESSE. MINISTER FUER LANDWIRTSCHAFT, FORSTEN. ERNTEN, MAERKTE, PREISEN. 1954. a. free. Minister fuer Landeswirtschaft und Forsten, Postfach 3127, 6200 Wiesbaden, W. Germany (B.R.D.) circ. 3,500.
    Former titles: Hesse. Minister fuer Landesentwicklung, Umwelt, Landwirtschaft und Forsten. Ernten, Maerkte, Preise; Hesse. Ministerium fuer Landwirtschaft und Umwelt. Ernten, Maerkte, Preise. Jahresbericht.

INSTITUTO DE TECNOLOGIA DE ALIMENTOS. ESTUDOS ECONOMICOS. ALIMENTOS PROCESSADOS. see *FOOD AND FOOD INDUSTRIES*

658.8   US
KANSAS CITY GROCER ANNUAL FOOD INDUSTRY DIRECTORY.* 1957. a. $1.50. Retail Grocers Association, 2809 W. 47th St., Mission, KS 66205. adv. circ. 2,400.

OPERATING RESULTS OF INDEPENDENT SUPERMARKETS. see *BUSINESS AND ECONOMICS — Small Business*

S N DISTRIBUTION STUDY OF GROCERY STORE SALES. see *FOOD AND FOOD INDUSTRIES*

SUDAN JOURNAL OF FOOD SCIENCE AND TECHNOLOGY. see *FOOD AND FOOD INDUSTRIES*

658.8　　　　　　　　SA
SUGAR MILLING RESEARCH INSTITUTE. ANNUAL REPORT. (Text in English) 1950. a. free. Sugar Milling Research Institute, University of Natal, King George V Ave., 4001 Durban, South Africa. Ed. M.J. Kort. illus. circ. 400. Indexed: Sugar Ind.Abstr.

338.4　　　　　US　ISSN 0082-4151
THOMAS GROCERY REGISTER. (3-vol. set) 1898. a. $99. Thomas Publishing Co., One Penn Plaza, 250 W. 34th St., New York, NY 10119. TEL 212-695-0500. Ed. John Kovac. adv. bk. rev. circ. 5,300.

658.8　　　　　US　ISSN 0278-6346
TRENDS: CONSUMER ATTITUDES AND THE SUPERMARKET UPDATE. 1974. a. $30 to non-members; members $15. Food Marketing Institute, Research Division, 1750 K St., N.W., Washington, DC 20006. TEL 202-452-8444. circ. 4,000.
　　Formerly: Supermarket Trends (ISSN 0163-4488)

FORENSIC SCIENCES

see *Medical Sciences — Forensic Sciences*

FORESTS AND FORESTRY

see also *Forests and Forestry — Lumber and Wood; Conservation*

ACADEMIA DE STIINTE AGRICOLE SI SILVICE. BULETIN. see *AGRICULTURE*

634.9　　　　　IT　ISSN 0515-2178
ACCADEMIA ITALIANA DI SCIENZE FORESTALI. ANNALI. 1953. a. L.30000. Accademia Italiana di Scienza Forestali, Piazza Edison II, 50133 Florence, Italy. Dir. Mario Cantiani. circ. 400. Indexed: Biol.Abstr. Forest.Abstr. Forest Prod.Abstr. Soils & Fert.

634.9　　　　　PL　ISSN 0065-0927
ACTA AGRARIA ET SILVESTRIA. SERIES SILVESTRIS. (Text in Polish; summaries in English and Russian) 1961. a. price varies. (Polska Akademia Nauk, Oddzial w Krakowie, Komisja Nauk Rolniczych i Lesnych) Ossolineum, Publishing House of the Polish Academy of Sciences, Rynek 9, Wroclaw, Poland (Dist. by Ars Polona-Ruch, Krakowskie Przedmiescie 7, Warsaw, Poland) Ed. Jerzy Fabijanowski. bibl. charts. illus. Indexed: Biol.Abstr. Excerp.Med. Nutr.Abstr. Forest.Abstr. Forest Prod.Abstr. Plant Breed Abstr.

634.9　　　　　CS　ISSN 0231-5335
ACTA DENDROBIOLOGICA. (Text in Slovak; summaries in English, German and Russian) a. Veda, Publishing House of the Slovak Academy of Sciences, Klemensova 19, 895 30 Bratislava, Czechoslovakia. Indexed: Biol.Abstr. Forest.Abstr. Forest Prod.Abstr.

634.9　　　　　CS
ACTA FACULTATIS FORESTALIS, ZVOLEN/ VYSOKA SKOLA LESNICKA A DREVARSKA VO ZVOLENE. LESNICKA FAKULTA. ZBORNIK VEDECKYCH PRAC. (Text mainly in Slovak; occasionally in English, German, Russian; summaries in English, German, Russian) 1957. a. exchange basis. Vysoka Skola Lesnicka a Drevarska vo Zvolene, Lesnicka Fakulta - College of Forestry and Wood Technology, Zvolen, Marxova 24, 960 53 Zvolen, Czechoslovakia. Ed. Stefan Smelko. charts. illus. circ. 300. Indexed: Forest.Abstr. Forest Prod.Abstr. Helminthol.Abstr. Rev.Appl.Entomol. Soils & Fert.

634.9　　　　　FI　ISSN 0001-5636
ACTA FORESTALIA FENNICA. (Text in English, Finnish or German) 1913. irreg. (2-6/yr.) Fmk.60 per no. Suomen Metsatieteellinen Seura - Society of Forestry in Finland, Unioninkatu 40 B, SF-00170 Helsinki 17, Finland (Subscr. to: Academic Bookstore, Keskuskatu 1, SF-00100 Helsinki 10, Finland) Ed. Seppo Oja. illus. cum.index: 1913-1972; 1973-1984) circ. 1,100. Indexed: Agrindex. Biol.Abstr. Curr.Adv.Plant Sci. Forest.Abstr. Abstr.Bull.Inst.Pap.Chem. Forest Prod.Abstr. Rev.Plant Path. Soils & Fert.

634.9　674　　　　　PL　ISSN 0137-172X
AKADEMIA ROLNICZA, POZNAN. ROCZNIKI. LESNICTWO. (Text in Polish; summaries in English and Russian) 1957. irreg. price varies. Akademia Rolnicza, Poznan, Ul. Wojska Polskiego 28, 60-637 Poznan, Poland. Indexed: Bibl.Agri. Forest.Abstr.

ALABAMA AGRICULTURAL EXPERIMENT STATION. RESEARCH REPORT SERIES. see *AGRICULTURE*

634.9　　　　　YU　ISSN 0351-2045
ANNALES FORESTALES/ANALI ZA SUMARSTVO. (Text and summaries in Croatian, English, French and German) vol.6, 1974. a. price varies. Jugoslavenska Akademija Znanosti i Umjetnosti, Razred za Prirodne Znanosti, Brace Kavurica 1, 41000 Zagreb, Yugoslavia. Ed. Mirko Vidakovic. circ. 800. Indexed: Biol.Abstr. Forest.Abstr. Foerst Prod.Abstr.

ARANETA RESEARCH JOURNAL. see *AGRICULTURE*

634.9　　　　　GW　ISSN 0003-7796
ARBEITSTECHNISCHE MERKHEFTE DER WALDARBEIT. 1950. irreg. (3-4/yr.) price varies. Wirtschafts- und Forstverlag Euting KG, Tannenstr. 1, 5451 Strassenhaus, W. Germany (B.R.D.) adv. charts. illus.

634.9　　　　　AG　ISSN 0570-8834
ARGENTINA. INSTITUTO FORESTAL NACIONAL. ANUARIO DE ESTADISTICA FORESTAL. irreg., latest issue 1980. exchange. Instituto Forestal Nacional, Pueyrredon 2446, Buenos Aires, Argentina. Ed.Bd. charts. stat.

634.9　　　　　US　ISSN 0066-7404
ARIZONA FORESTRY NOTES. 1966. irreg., no.21, 1984. free. Northern Arizona University, School of Forestry, Box 4098, Flagstaff, AZ 86011. TEL 602-523-3031. Ed. Alan S. White. charts. stat. circ. 800. Indexed: Biol.Abstr.

634.9　　　　　AT　ISSN 0314-1438
AUSTRALIAN FOREST RESOURCES. 1975. a. free to government agencies. Bureau of Agricultural Economics, G.P.O. Box 1563, Canberra, A.C.T. 2601, Australia (Subscr. to: Australian Government Publishing Service, Sales & Dist. Sect., P. O. Box 84, Canberra, A.C.T. 2600, Australia) bk. rev. circ. 700(controlled) Indexed: Forest.Abstr.
　　Former titles: Forest Resources; Commonwealth Scientific and Industrial Research Organization. Division of Forest Research. Forest Resources Newsletter; Australia. Forestry and Timber Bureau. Forest Resources Newsletter (ISSN 0067-1460)

634.9　　　　　GW　ISSN 0067-4710
BAYERISCHES FORSTDIENST-TASCHENBUCH. 1966. a. DM.77.80. (Bund Deutscher Forstmaenner, Landesverband Bayern e.V.) Walhalla-und Praetoria-Verlag, Dolomitenstr. 1, Postfach 301, 8400 Regensburg 1, W. Germany (B.R.D.) Ed. Klaus Baer.

634.9　　　　　NE
BEDRIJFSUITKOMSTEN IN DE NEDERLANDSE PARTICULIERE BOSBOUW. 1974. a. price varies. Landbouw-Economisch Instituut, Conradkade 175, 2517 CL The Hague, Netherlands. Ed. M.N. de Groot.

BIOLOGISCHE BUNDESANSTALT FUER LAND- UND FORSTWIRTSCHAFT, BERLIN-DAHLEM. MITTEILUNGEN. (Biologische Bundesanstalt fuer Land- und Forstwirtschaft in Berlin-Dahlem) see *AGRICULTURE*

BIOTECHNOLOGY IN AGRICULUTURE AND FORESTRY. see *AGRICULTURE*

634.9　　　　　CN
BRITISH COLUMBIA. MINISTRY OF FORESTS AND LANDS. ANNUAL REPORT. 1912. a. Ministry of Forests & Lands, Public Affairs Branch, 1450 Government St., Victoria, B.C. V8W 3E7, Canada. TEL 604-387-5985. illus. index. Indexed: Biol.Abstr.
　　Formerly: British Columbia. Forest Service. Annual Report (ISSN 0068-1490)

634.9　　　　　CN　ISSN 0226-9368
BRITISH COLUMBIA. MINISTRY OF FORESTS AND LANDS. RESEARCH NOTES. 1938; N.S. irreg., no.54, 1970. free. Ministry of Forests and Lands, Research Branch, 1450 Government St., Victoria, B.C. V8W 3E7, Canada. TEL 604-387-3468. Ed. Tim Mock. circ. 300. Indexed: Forest.Abstr. Forest Prod.Abstr.
　　Former titles: British Columbia. Ministry of Forests. Research Notes; British Columbia. Forest Service. Research Notes (ISSN 0068-1520)

634.9　　　　　CN
BRITISH COLUMBIA. MINISTRY OF FORESTS AND LANDS. RESEARCH REVIEW. 1957. a. Ministry of Forests & Lands, Public Affairs Branch, 1450 Government St., Victoria, B.C. V8W 3E7, Canada. TEL 604-387-5985. index. Indexed: Biol.Abstr.
　　Formerly: British Columbia. Forest Service. Research Review (ISSN 0068-1539)

BUNDESFORSCHUNGSANSTALT FUER FORST- UND HOLZWIRTSCHAFT, HAMBURG. MITTEILUNGEN. see *FORESTS AND FORESTRY — Lumber and Wood*

354　　　　　UV
BURKINA FASO. DIRECTION DES EAUX ET FORETS ET DE LA CONSERVATION DES SOLS. RAPPORT ANNUEL. a. Direction des Eaux et Forets et de la Conservation des Sols, Ouagadougou, Burkina Faso. stat.
　　Formerly: Upper Volta. Direction des Eaux et Forets et de la Conservation des Sols. Rapport Annuel.

634.9　　　　　US
CALIFORNIA FORESTRY NOTE. 1960. irreg., no.97, 1986. free. Department of Forestry, 1416 Ninth St., Sacramento, CA 95814. TEL 916-445-5571. Ed. Clifford E. Fago. cum.index: 1960-71. circ. 1,500. Indexed: Forest.Abstr. Forest Prod.Abstr.
　　Formerly: California. Department of Forestry. State Forest Notes (ISSN 0068-5577)

634.96　　　　　CN
CANADA. CANADIAN FORESTRY SERVICE. INSECT AND DISEASE CONDITIONS IN CANADA. French edition (ISSN 0226-9767) (Editions in English and French) 1980. a. free. Canadian Forestry Service, Ottawa, Ont. K1A 1G5, Canada. TEL 819-997-9390.
　　Formerly: Canada. Environment Canada. Insect and Disease Conditions in Canada (ISSN 0226-9759); Supersedes: Canada. Department of the Environment. Forest Insect and Disease Survey. Annual Report (ISSN 0068-7588)

634.9　595　　　　　CN　ISSN 0834-406X
CANADA. CANADIAN FORESTRY SERVICE-MARITIMES, FREDERICTON, NEW BRUNSWICK. INFORMATION REPORT M-X. French Edition (ISSN 0833-1162) (Editions in English, French) 1966. irreg. (10-12/yr.) free. Canadian Forestry Service-Maritimes, P.O. Box 4000, Fredericton, N.B. E3B 5P7, Canada. TEL 506-452-3500. Ed. M.D. Cameron. circ. 500-1,000. (also avail. in microform from MML) Indexed: Biol.Abstr. Forest.Abstr. Forest Prod.Abstr.
　　Formerly: Canada. Maritimes Forest Research Centre, Fredericton, New Brunswick. Information Report M-X (ISSN 0704-769X)

634.9　　　　　CN　ISSN 0714-1181
CANADA. NORTHERN FORESTRY CENTRE. FOREST MANAGEMENT NOTE. 1980. irreg. (7/yr.) free. Northern Forestry Centre, 5320-122 St., Edmonton, Alta. T6H 3S5, Canada. TEL 403-435-7210. Ed. J. Samoil. circ. 1,000. (back issues avail.) Indexed: Forest.Abstr.

FORESTS AND FORESTRY

634.9 CN ISSN 0709-9959
CANADA. NORTHERN FORESTRY CENTRE.
FORESTRY REPORT. 1971. irreg. (1-2/yr.) free.
Northern Forestry Centre, 5320-122 St., Edmonton,
Alta. T6H 3S5, Canada. TEL 403-435-7210. Ed. J.
Samoil. circ. 3,000. (back issues avail.) Indexed:
Chem.Abstr.
  Formerly: Canadian Forestry Service. Prairies
Region. Forestry Report.

634.9 CN ISSN 0704-7673
CANADA. NORTHERN FORESTRY CENTRE.
INFORMATION REPORT. 1971. irreg. (10/yr.)
free. Northern Forestry Centre, 5320-122 St.,
Edmonton, Alta. T6H 3S5, Canada. TEL 403-435-
7210. Ed. J. Samoil. bibl. charts. illus. stat. circ. 1,
100. (back issues avail.) Indexed: Chem.Abstr.
Forest.Abstr. Forest Prod.Abstr.
  Formerly: Canadian Forestry Service.
Department of Fisheries & Forestry. Prairies Region.
Information Report.

634.9 CN
CANADA. PACIFIC FOREST RESEARCH
CENTRE. INFORMATION REPORT. (Text in
English and French) 1971. irreg. free. Pacific Forest
Research Centre, 506 West Burnside Rd., Victoria,
B.C. V8Z 1M5, Canada. TEL 604-387-5985. abstr.
bibl. charts. illus.

634.9 CN ISSN 0228-0736
CANADA. PETAWAWA NATIONAL FORESTRY
INSTITUTE. INFORMATION REPORT/
CANADA. INSTITUT FORESTIER NATIONAL
DE PETAWAWA. RAPPORT
D'INFORMATION. (Editions in English and
French) 1979. irreg. free. Petawawa National
Forestry Insititute., Chalk River, Ont. K0J 1J0,
Canada. Ed. Asoka C. Yapa. circ. 500. (also avail.
in microform from MML) Indexed: Forest.Abstr.
Forest Prod.Abstr.

634.9 CN ISSN 0710-4251
CANADA. PETAWAWA NATIONAL FORESTRY
INSTITUTE. PROGRAM REVIEW. French
edition: Institut Forestier National de Petawawa.
Revue de Programme (ISSN 0710-426X) (Editions
in English and French) 1981. a. free. Petawawa
National Forestry Insititute, Chalk River, Ont. K0J
1J0, Canada. Ed.Bd. charts. stat. circ. 1,
500(combined)
  Supersedes: Canada. Forest Management
Institute. Program Review (ISSN 0071-7495)

634.9 CN
CANADIAN FOREST FIRE WEATHER INDEX.
irreg. free. Pacific Research Centre, 506
West Burnside Rd., Victoria, B.C. V8Z 1M5,
Canada. (back issues avail.)

634.9 CN ISSN 0068-8991
CANADIAN INSTITUTE OF FORESTRY.
ANNUAL REPORT. Included in: Forestry
Chronicle (ISSN 0015-7546) a. Canadian Institute
of Forestry, 1005-151 Slater St., Ottawa, Ont. K1P
5H3, Canada. TEL 613-234-2242. adv. bk. rev. circ.
3,000.

634.9 574.5 BE
CENTRE D'ECOLOGIE FORESTIERE ET
RURALE. COMMUNICATIONS. (Text in French;
summaries in German and English) 1943; N.S.
no.41, 1983. irreg. price varies. Centre d'Ecologie
Forestiere et Rurale, Passage des Deportes no.2,
5800 Gembloux, Belgium. circ. 200. Indexed:
Forest.Abstr. Herb.Abstr.
  Formerly: Centre de Cartographie
Phytosociologique. Communications (ISSN 0069-
1747)

634.9 BE
CENTRE D'ECOLOGIE FORESTIERE ET
RURALE. NOTES TECHNIQUES. A:
FORESTIERES. 1968. irreg., no.48, 1984. price
varies. Centre d'Ecologie Forestiere et Rurale,
Passage des Deportes no.2, 5800 Gembloux,
Belgium. Indexed: Forest.Abstr. Forest Prod.Abstr.
  Supersedes in part: Centre d'Ecologie Forestiere.
Notes Techniques (ISSN 0069-1801)

634.9 BE
CENTRE D'ECOLOGIE FORESTIERE ET
RURALE. NOTES TECHNIQUES. B:
HERBAGERES. 1968. irreg., no.10, 1978. price
varies. Centre d'Ecologie Forestiere et Rurale,
Passage des Deportes no.2, 5800 Gembloux,
Belgium. Indexed: Forest.Abstr. Herb.Abstr.
  Supersedes in part: Centre d'Ecologie Forestiere.
Notes Techniques (ISSN 0069-1801)

634.9 CM
CENTRE TECHNIQUE FORESTIERE TROPICAL
DU CAMEROUN. RAPPORT ANNUEL. a. free.
Centre Technique Forestier Tropical du Cameroun,
B.P. 832, Douala, Cameroon.

634.9 US
CLEMSON UNIVERSITY. DEPARTMENT OF
FORESTRY. FOREST RESEARCH SERIES.
irreg., no.47, 1985. Clemson University, Department
of Forestry, Clemson, SC 29634-1003. TEL 803-
656-3302. Indexed: Biol.Abstr.

634.9 US ISSN 0093-0083
CLEMSON UNIVERSITY. DEPARTMENT OF
FORESTRY. FORESTRY BULLETIN. 1967.
irreg., no.50, 1986. free. Clemson University,
Department of Forestry, Clemson, SC 29634-1003.
TEL 803-656-3302. charts. illus. stat. circ.
500(controlled) (back issues avail.) Indexed:
Biol.Abstr. Forest.Abstr.

634.9 US
CLEMSON UNIVERSITY. DEPARTMENT OF
FORESTRY. TECHNICAL PAPER. irreg., no.16,
1985. Clemson University, Department of Forestry,
Clemson, SC 29634-1003. TEL 803-656-3302.
Indexed: Biol.Abstr. Forest.Abstr. Forest
Prod.Abstr.

338.4 US ISSN 0362-191X
COMMODITY DRAIN REPORT OF FLORIDA'S
PRIMARY FOREST INDUSTRIES. 1960. a. free.
Department of Agriculture and Consumer Services,
Division of Forestry, 3125 Conner Blvd.,
Tallahassee, FL 32301. TEL 904-488-6358. Ed.
Leon Irvin. stat. circ. 1,200.

CONSTRUCTION EQUIPMENT BUYERS GUIDE.
see BUILDING AND CONSTRUCTION

634.9 CU ISSN 0138-7782
CUBA. CENTRO DE INFORMACION Y
DOCUMENTACION AGROPECUARIO.
BOLETIN DE RESENAS. SERIE: FORESTALES.
(Abstracts in English) 1981. irreg. exchange basis.
Centro de Informacion y Documentacion
Agropecuario, Gaveta Postal 4149, Havana 4, Cuba
(Dist. by: Ediciones Cubanas, Obispo No. 461,
Aptdo. 605, Havana, Cuba) Indexed: Agrindex.
  Formerly: Centro de Informacion y Divulgacion
Agropecuario. Boletin de Resenas. Serie: Forestales.

634.96 DK ISSN 0415-3944
DANISH PLANT PROTECTION SERVICE.
ANNUAL REPORT. (Text in Danish; summaries
in English) 1950. a. free. Statens Plantetilsyn,
Gersonsvej 13, DK-2900 Hellerup, Denmark. Ed.
Lars Hendriksen. circ. 400.

634.9 DK ISSN 0106-0031
DANSKE HEDESELSKAB.
FORSOEGSVIRKSOMHEDEN. BERETNING.
(Text in Danish; summaries in English and German)
irreg. price varies. Danske Hedeselskab,
Forsoegsvirksomheden, Postbox 110, 8800 Viborg,
Denmark. illus.

634.9 DK ISSN 0109-5234
DANSKE STATSSKOVES UDBYTTE AF VED OG
PENGE. 1982. a. free to libraries. Skovstyrelsen,
Strandvejen 863, 2930 Klampenborg, Denmark.
  Formerly: Oversigt over de Danske Statsskoves
Udbytte af Ved og Penge for Finansaaret.

DEUTSCHE DENDROLOGISCHE
GESELLSCHAFT. MITTEILUNGEN. see
BIOLOGY — Botany

634.96 GW
DEUTSCHER FORSTVEREIN. JAHRESBERICHT.
1950. biennial. DM.15. Deutscher Forstverein,
Emmeramsplatz 5, 8400 Regensburg, W. Germany
(B.R.D.) adv. illus. circ. 6,000.

630 634.9 NE
DEVELOPMENTS IN AGRICULTURAL AND
MANAGED FOREST ECOLOGY. 1975. irreg.,
vol.15, 1985. price varies. Elsevier Science
Publishers B.V., Box 211, 1000 AE Amsterdam,
Netherlands.

634.9 SZ
EIDGENOESSISCHE ANSTALT FUER DAS
FORSTLICHE VERSUCHSWESEN. BERICHTE.
(Text in German; summaries in English, French and
Italian) 1968. irreg. price varies. Eidgenoessische
Anstalt fuer das Forstliche Versuchswesen, CH-8903
Birmensdorf, Switzerland. Ed. W. Bosshard.
cum.index. (back issues avail.) Indexed: Biol.Abstr.
Geo.Abstr.

634.9 SZ
EIDGENOESSISCHE ANSTALT FUER DAS
FORSTLICHE VERSUCHSWESEN.
JAHRESBERICHT. (Text in German) 1946. a. free.
Eidgenoessische Anstalt fuer das Forstliche
Versuchswesen, CH-8903 Birmendsdorf,
Switzerland. Ed. W. Bosshard. bk. rev.

634.9 676 UN
F A O FORESTRY STUDIES. 1950. irreg. Food and
Agriculture Organization of the United Nations,
Distribution and Sales Section, Via delle Terme di
Caracalla, 00100 Rome, Italy (Dist. in U.S. by:
Bernan Associates-Unipub, 4611-F Assembly Drive,
Lanham, MD 20706-4391)
  Formerly: F A O Forestry and Forest Products
Studies (ISSN 0532-0283)

634.9 US
F W S SERIES. 1972. irreg. Virginia Polytechnic
Institute and State University, School of Forestry
and Wildlife Resources, Blacksburg, VA 24061. TEL
703-961-5481. circ. 500. (back issues avail.)

FACULTAD NACIONAL DE AGRONOMIA
MEDELLIN. see AGRICULTURE

FOCUS (MOSCOW); on renewable natural resources.
see CONSERVATION

634.9 639.2 591 US
FOCUS ON RENEWABLE NATURAL
RESOURCES. 1974. a. free. University of Idaho,
College of Forestry, Forest, Wildlife and Range
Experiment Sta., Moscow, ID 83843. TEL 208-885-
6674. Ed. George Savage. circ. 3,000.

582.16 634.9 635.977 CS
FOLIA DENDROLOGICA. irreg., vol.3, 1977. price
varies. (Slovenska Akademia Vied, Ustav
Dendrobiologie) Veda, Publishing House of the
Slovak Academy of Sciences, Klemensova 19, 814
30 Bratislava, Czechoslovakia (Subscr. to: Slovart,
Gottwaldovo nam. 6, 817 64 Bratislava) (Co-
sponsor: Arboretum Mlynany) Ed. Frantisek Bencat.
Indexed: Biol.Abstr. Chem.Abstr. Forest.Abstr.
Forest Prod.Abstr. Hort.Abstr.

634.9 PL ISSN 0071-6677
FOLIA FORESTALIA POLONICA. SERIES A.
LESNICTWO. (Text in Polish; summaries in
English, German or Russian) 1958. a. price varies.
(Polska Akademia Nauk, Komitet Nauk Lesnych)
Panstwowe Wydawnictwo Naukowe, Miodowa 10,
00-251 Warsaw, Poland (Dist. by: Ars Polona,
Krakowskie Przedmiescie 7, 00-068 Warsaw,
Poland) Ed. Wieslaw Grochowski. circ. 720.
Indexed: Biol.Abstr. Abstr.Bull.Inst.Pap.Chem.
Forest.Abstr. Forest Prod.Abstr.

FOLIA VENATORIA; pol'ovnicky zbornik. see
VETERINARY SCIENCE

634.9 674 AT ISSN 0015-7392
FOREST AND TIMBER. 1963. a. free. Forestry
Commission, 95-99 York St., Sydney, N.S.W. 2000,
Australia. Ed. Robert West. bk. rev. charts. illus.
stat. circ. 10,000. Indexed: Biol.Abstr. Aus.Sci.Ind.
Forest.Abstr. Forest Prod.Abstr.

634.9 US ISSN 0071-7452
FOREST FARMER. MANUAL EDITION. 1950.
biennial. $15. Forest Farmers Association, Box
95385, Atlanta, GA 30329. TEL 404-325-2954. Ed.
Tom Wiseman. adv. index. circ. 4,000.

FORESTS AND FORESTRY

634.9 US ISSN 0015-7449
FOREST LOG. 1930. a. free. ‡ State Department of Forestry, 2600 State St., Salem, OR 97310. TEL 503-378-2562. Ed. Shawn Morford. circ. 6,000.
Includes: Oregon. Department of Forestry. Biennial Report of the State Forester (ISSN 0090-6409)

634.9 595.7 CN ISSN 0704-772X
FOREST PEST MANAGEMENT INSTITUTE. INFORMATION REPORT SERIES. French edition (ISSN 0827-1119) (Text in English and French) 1977. irreg. free. Canadian Forestry Service, Forest Pest Management Institute, P.O. Box 490, 1219 Queen St. E., Sault Ste. Marie, Ontario P6A 5M7, Canada. TEL 705-949-9461. Ed. K. Jamieson.

634.96 595.7 CN ISSN 0826-0532
FOREST PEST MANAGEMENT INSTITUTE. TECHNICAL NOTE SERIES. (Text in English and French) 1984. irreg. free. Canadian Forestry Service, Forest Pest Management Institute, P.O. Box 490, 1219 Queen St. E., Sault Ste. Marie, Ontario, P6A 5M7, Canada. TEL 705-949-9461. Ed. K. JAmieson.

FOREST PEST MANAGEMENT INSTITUTE PROGRAM REVIEW. see *BIOLOGY*

634.9 IO
FOREST RESEARCH BULLETIN. (Text in Indonesian; summaries in English) 1948. irreg. Pusat Penelitian dan Pengembangen Hutan, Jalan Gunung Batu, PO Box 66, Bogor, Indonesia. Ed. K. Soemarna. circ. 500. (back issues avail.) Indexed: Biol.Abstr. VITIS.
Former titles: Forest Research Institute. Report; Buletin Penelitian Hutan (ISSN 0216-4760); Pusat Penelitian dan Pengembangan Hutan. Laporan/ Forest Research and Development Centre. Report.

634.9 MY ISSN 0126-8198
FOREST RESEARCH INSTITUTE: RESEARCH PAMPHLET. 1953. irreg., latest no.100, 1986. M.$3($1.50) Forest Research Institute Malaysia - Institut Penyelidikan Perhutan Malaysia, Peninsular Malaysia, Kepong, 52109 Kuala Lumpur, Malaysia. bk. rev. circ. 300. (back issues avail.) Indexed: Biol.Abstr.

634.9 US ISSN 0071-7568
FOREST SCIENCE MONOGRAPHS. 1959. irreg., no.23, 1980. included in subscription to Forest Science. ‡ Society of American Foresters, 5400 Grosvenor Ln., Bethesda, MD 20814. TEL 301-897-8720. Ed. Harold Burkhardt. bk. rev. circ. 1,567. Indexed: Biol.Abstr. Biol. & Agri.Ind. Chem.Abstr. Abstr.Bull.Inst.Pap.Chem. Forest.Abstr. Forest Prod.Abstr. Geo.Abstr. Soils & Fert.

634.9 DK ISSN 0105-4120
FOREST TREE IMPROVEMENT. 1969. irreg. price varies. (Royal Agricultural University) DSR Booksellers, Thorvaldsensvej 40, DK-1871 Frederiksberg C, Denmark. illus. Indexed: Forest.Abstr. Forest Prod.Abstr.

634.9 US
FOREST WORLD. 1972. q. $15. World Forestry Center, 4033 S.W. Canyon Rd., Portland, OR 97221. TEL 503-228-1367. Ed. Sue Fisher. adv. bk. rev. circ. 5,000.
Formerly (until 1984): Western Forestry Center. Annual Report.

634 US
FORESTRY: LATIN AMERICAN INDUSTRIAL REPORT. (Avail. for each of 22 Latin American countries) 1985. a. $435 per country report per industry covered. Aurora International, Box 9099, Bridgeport, CT 06601-2099. TEL 203-368-0579. Ed. Andres C. Aquino.

634.9 AT
FORESTRY LOG. 1968. a. Aus.$5. Australian National University, Forestry Department, Forestry Students Society, Canberra, A.C.T. 2600, Australia. Ed. John Kelley. adv. circ. 600.

634.9 UN ISSN 0532-0747
FORESTRY NEWSLETTER OF THE ASIA-PACIFIC REGION. irreg. Food and Agriculture Organization of the United Nations, Regional Office for Asia and the Far East, Maliwan Mansion, Phra Atit Road, Bangkok 2, Thailand.

634.9 MW
FORESTRY RESEARCH INSTITUTE OF MALAWI. RESEARCH RECORD. (Text in English) 1967. irreg. (Forestry Research Institute) Government Printing Office, Box 37, Zomba, Malawi. circ. 200. (back issues avail.) Indexed: Forest.Abstr.

FORSCHUNGSSTELLE FUER JAGDKUNDE UND WILDSCHADENVERHUETUNG. SCHRIFTENREIHE. see *SPORTS AND GAMES — Outdoor Life*

634.9 DK ISSN 0367-2174
FORSTLIGE FORSOEGSVAESEN I DANMARK. (Text in Danish; summaries in English) 1905. irreg. Kr.100 per vol. (4-5 parts) Statens Forstlige Forsoegsvaesen - Danish Forest Experiment Station, Springforbivej 4, DK-2930 Klampenborg, Denmark. Ed. Erik Holmsgaard. charts. illus. circ. 800. Indexed: Biol.Abstr. Forest.Abstr. Forest Prod.Abstr. Soils & Fert.

634.9 GW ISSN 0071-772X
FORSTWISSENSCHAFTLICHE FORSCHUNGEN; Beihefte zum Forstwissenschaftlichen Centralblatt. 1952. irreg., no.38, 1983. price varies. (Forstliche Forschungsanstalt Muenchen) Verlag Paul Parey (Hamburg), Spitalerstr. 12, 2000 Hamburg 1, W. Germany (B.R.D.) Ed. U. Ammer. (reprint service avail. from ISI) Indexed: Biol.Abstr.

338.4 634.9 FR
FRANCE. DIRECTION DES FORETS. PRODUCTION DE LA BRANCHE EXPLOITATION FORESTIERE ET PRODUCTION DES BRANCHES SCIENCE ET CARBONISATION EN FORET. a. free. Direction des Forets, 1 Ave. de Lowendal, 75007 Paris, France.

333.7 634.9 FR
FRANCE. DIRECTION DES FORETS. RAPPORT SUR LE FONDS FORESTIER NATIONAL; rapport au Comite de Controle pour l'annee. 1948. a. free. Direction des Forets, 1 av. de Lowendal, 75007 Paris, France. stat.

634.9 FR ISSN 0761-3067
GAUSSENIA; Travaux du Laboratoire Forestier de Toulouse. (Text in French; summaries in various languages) 1984. a. 20 F. Universite Paul Sabatier, Laboratoire Botanique et Forestier, 31062 Toulouse, France. Ed. G. Durrieu. bk. rev. circ. 250.

634.9 CN ISSN 0072-9140
H.R. MACMILLAN LECTURESHIP IN FORESTRY. 1950. a. free. University of British Columbia, Faculty of Forestry, 270-2357 Main Mall, Vancouver, B.C. V6T 1W5, Canada. TEL 604-228-2211. Indexed: Forest.Abstr.

HESSE. MINISTER FUER LANDESENTWICKLUNG, UMWELT, LANDWIRTSCHAFT UND FORSTEN. MITTEILUNGEN. LAND UND UMWELT. see *FOOD AND FOOD INDUSTRIES — Grocery Trade*

HORACE M. ALBRIGHT CONSERVATION LECTURESHIP. see *CONSERVATION*

634.9 II ISSN 0073-635X
INDIAN FOREST BULLETIN (NEW SERIES) (Text in English) 1911. irreg., no.276, 1979. price varies. ‡ Forest Research Institute & Colleges, P.O. New Forest, Dehra Dun, India. circ. 500. Indexed: Biol.Abstr. Forest.Abstr. Forest Prod.Abstr. Indian Sci.Abstr. Rev.Appl.Entomol. Rev.Plant Path.

634.9 II ISSN 0073-6368
INDIAN FOREST LEAFLETS (NEW SERIES) (Text in English) 1941. irreg., no.197, 1982. price varies. ‡ Forest Research Institute & Colleges, P.O. New Forest, Dehra Dun, India. circ. 500. Indexed: Biol.Abstr. Forest.Abstr. Forest Prod.Abstr. Indian Sci.Abstr.

634.9 II
INDIAN FOREST RECORDS (NEW SERIES) FOREST MANAGEMENT AND MENSURATION. (Text in English) 1976. irreg., vol. 3, no.5, 1979. price varies. Forest Research Institute and Colleges, P.O. New Forest, Dehra Dun, India. circ. 500. Indexed: Biol. Abstr. Forest. Abstr. Indian Sci. Abstr.

634.9 II ISSN 0073-6406
INDIAN FOREST RECORDS (NEW SERIES) FOREST PATHOLOGY. (Text in English) 1950. irreg., vol.2, no.11, 1973. price varies. Forest Research Institute & Colleges, P.O. New Forest, Dehra Dun, India. circ. 500. Indexed: Biol.Abstr. Forest.Abstr. Indian Sci.Abstr.
Formerly: Indian Forest Records (New Series) Mycology.

634.9 II ISSN 0073-6422
INDIAN FOREST RECORDS (NEW SERIES) SILVICULTURE. (Text in English) 1936. irreg., vol.13, no.1, 1974. price varies. ‡ Forest Research Institute & Colleges, P.O. New Forest, Dehra Dun, India. circ. 500. Indexed: Biol.Abstr. Forest.Abstr. Indian Sci.Abstr.

634.9 II ISSN 0073-6430
INDIAN FOREST RECORDS (NEW SERIES) STATISTICAL. (Text in English) 1960. irreg., vol.3, no.1, 1983. price varies. ‡ Forest Research Institute & Colleges, P.O. New Forest, Dehra Dun, India. circ. 500. Indexed: Biol.Abstr. Forest.Abstr. Indian Sci.Abstr.

634.9 IO
INDONESIAN STATISTICS ON TRADE OF FOREST PRODUCTS. 1971. a. Rps.1500($4) Directorate General of Forestry, Forest Product Marketing Development Project, Jl. Salemba Raya 16, Jakarta, Indonesia.
Formerly (1971-1975): Forest Products Trade Statistics of Indonesia (ISSN 0302-203X)

634.9 KO ISSN 0073-9294
INSTITUTE OF FOREST GENETICS, SUWON, KOREA. RESEARCH REPORT. (Text in English, Korean) 1959. a. free. Institute of Forest Genetics, Breeding Section, Director, Suwon, S. Korea. Dir. Sang Yung Shim. circ. 1,500. Indexed: Biol.Abstr. Forest.Abstr. Forest Prod.Abstr.

634.9 BL ISSN 0100-3151
INSTITUTO FLORESTAL. BOLETIM TECNICO. 1972. irreg. $10. Instituto Florestal, C.P. 1322, Sao Paulo 01000, Brazil. stat. circ. 500. Indexed: Biol.Abstr. Forest Prod.Abstr.

INSTITUTO NACIONAL DE INVESTIGACIONES FORESTALES. BOLETIN DIVULGATIVO. see *BIOLOGY — Entomology*

INSTITUTO NACIONAL DE INVESTIGACIONES FORESTALES. BOLETIN TECNICO. see *BIOLOGY — Entomology*

634.9 MX
INSTITUTO NACIONAL DE INVESTIGACIONES FORESTALES. CATALOGO. 1981. irreg. price varies. Instituto Nacional de Investigaciones Forestales Y Agropecuarias, Documentacion Cientifica y Tecnologica, Av. Progreso No. 5, Col. Coyoacan, Delegacion Coyoacan, 04110 Mexico, D.F., Mexico. TEL 658-43-33.

INSTITUTO NACIONAL DE INVESTIGACIONES FORESTALES. PUBLICACION ESPECIAL. see *BIOLOGY — Entomology*

634.9 NG ISSN 0534-4824
INTER-AFRICAN FORESTRY CONFERENCE. CONFERENCE FORESTIERE INTERAFRICAINE (COMMUNICATIONS)* (Text in English and French) 1951. irreg. Maison de l'Afrique, B.P. 878, Niamey, Niger.

634.9 KE
INTERNATIONAL COUNCIL FOR RESEARCH IN AGROFORESTRY. ANNUAL REPORT. (Text in English) 1979. a. International Council for Research in Agroforestry, Box 30677, Nairobi, Kenya. Ed. Richard C. Ntiru. circ. 2,000.

634.9 AU ISSN 0074-9400
INTERNATIONAL UNION OF FORESTRY RESEARCH ORGANIZATIONS. CONGRESS PROCEEDINGS/RAPPORTS DU CONGRES/ KONGRESSBERICHTE. 1893. quinquennial, 18th, 1986, Yugoslavia. price varies. International Union of Forestry Research Organizations, A-1131 Vienna, Austria. circ. 5,000.

FORESTS AND FORESTRY

634.9   IT
ISTITUTO SPERIMENTALE PER LA SELVICOLTURA. ANNALI. (Summaries in English and French) 1970. a. price varies. Istituto Sperimentale per la Selvicoltura, Viale S. Margherita 80-82, 52100 Arezzo, Italy. circ. 1,200. (back issues avail.) Indexed: Biol.Abstr. Forest.Abstr.

634.9   IT   ISSN 0075-1707
ITALY. ISTITUTO CENTRALE DI STATISTICA. ANNUARIO DI STATISTICA FORESTALE. a. L.6000. Istituto Centrale di Statistica, Via Cesare Balbo 16, 00100 Rome, Italy. circ. 1,050.

634.9   JA
JAPAN. FORESTRY AND FOREST PRODUCTS RESEARCH INSTITUTE. ANNUAL REPORT/ NORINSHO RINGYO SHIKENJO NENPO. (Text in Japanese) 1963. a. Forestry and Forest Products Research Institute, Box 2, Ushiku, Ibaraki 300-12, Japan.
    Formerly: Japan. Government Forest Experiment Station, Tokyo. Annual Report (ISSN 0557-0352)

634.9   JA
JAPAN. FORESTRY AND FOREST PRODUCTS RESEARCH INSTITUTE. BULLETIN. irreg. (8-10/yr.) Forestry and Forest Products Research Institute, Box 2, Ushiku, Ibaraki 300-12, Japan. Indexed: Forest.Abstr. Rev.Plant Path.

634.9   JA   ISSN 0557-0395
JAPAN. GOVERNMENT FOREST EXPERIMENT STATION. KYUSHU BRANCH. ANNUAL REPORT/RINGYO SHIKENJO KYUSHU SHIJO NENPO. (Text in Japanese) 1960. a. Government Forest Experiment Station, Kyushu Branch - Rin'yacho Ringyo Shikenjo Kyushu Shijo, 4-11-16 Kurokami, Kumamoto 860, Japan.

JAPAN. MINISTRY OF AGRICULTURE AND FORESTRY. ANNUAL REPORT/NORIN-SHO NENPO. see *AGRICULTURE*

JARDIM BOTANICO DO RIO DE JANEIRO. ARQUIVOS. see *BIOLOGY — Botany*

630   634.9   NO   ISSN 0075-7853
LANDBRUKETS AARBOK. JORDBRUK, HAGEBRUK, SKOGBRUK. 1962. a. Kr.148. Forlaget Tanum-Norli A-S, Kr. Augustsgt. 7A, Oslo 1, Norway. Ed. A. Bruaset. circ. 3,800.
    Incorporating: Landbrukets Aarbok. Skogbruk (ISSN 0075-7861)

LESNICKE DREVARSKE A POL'OVNICKE MUZEUM. see *HISTORY — History Of Europe*

634.9   US
LOUISIANA STATE UNIVERSITY. SCHOOL OF FORESTRY, WILDLIFE, AND FISHERIES. ANNUAL FORESTRY SYMPOSIUM. PROCEEDINGS. 1952. a. $12.50. Louisiana State University, School of Forestry, Wildlife, and Fisheries, Baton Rouge, LA 70803. TEL 504-338-4131. circ. 750. Indexed: Biol.Abstr. Forest.Abstr.
    Formerly: Louisiana State University. School of Forestry and Wildlife Management. Annual Forestry Symposium. Proceedings. (ISSN 0076-1095)

634.9   MW   ISSN 0076-3071
MALAWI. DEPARTMENT OF FORESTRY AND GAME. REPORT. irreg. (approx. a.) Government Printer, Box 37, Zomba, Malawi. cum.index: 1960-65.

634.9   MF
MAURITIUS. FORESTRY SERVICE. ANNUAL REPORT. (Text in English) 1900. a. rs. 10.00. Ministry of Agriculture, Fisheries, and Natural Resources, Forestry Service, Botanical Gardens St., Curepipe, Mauritius.
    Formerly (until 1968): Mauritius. Forest Department. Annual Report.

634.9   FI   ISSN 0356-343X
METSATILASTOLLINEN VUOSIKIRJA/ YEARBOOK OF FOREST STATISTICS. (Subseries of Folia Forestalia. Section XVII A of Official Statistics of Finland) (Text in English and Finnish) 1969. a. Metsantutkimuslaitos - Finnish Forest Research Institute, Unioninkatu 40 A, SF-00170 Helsinki 17, Finland. Ed. Matti Uusitalo. charts. stat. circ. 4,400.

MINNESOTA AGRICULTURAL EXPERIMENT STATION. STATION BULLETIN. see *AGRICULTURE*

634.96   US
MONTANA FOREST AND CONSERVATION EXPERIMENT STATION. BIENNIAL REPORT. biennial. (Montana Forest and Conservation Experiment Station) University of Montana, School of Forestry, Missoula, MT 59812.

634.9   US   ISSN 0077-2046
MULTILINGUAL FORESTRY TERMINOLOGY SERIES. 1971. irreg. $15. ‡ Society of American Foresters, 5400 Grosvenor Ln., Bethesda, MD 20814. TEL 301-897-8720.

634.9   AT   ISSN 0085-3984
NEW SOUTH WALES. FORESTRY COMMISSION. RESEARCH NOTES. 1958. irreg. price varies. Forestry Commission, 95-99 York St., Sydney, N.S.W. 2000, Australia. circ. 500. Indexed: Aus.Sci.Ind. Forest.Abstr. Soils & Fert.

634.9   NZ
NEW ZEALAND. DIRECTOR-GENERAL OF FORESTS. REPORT. (Text and summaries in English) 1919. a. NZ.$3.85($1) New Zealand Forest Service, Private Bag, Wellington, New Zealand. circ. 2,000. Indexed: Biol.Abstr.

634.9   NZ   ISSN 0111-8129
NEW ZEALAND. F R I BULLETIN. 1982. irreg. price varies. Forest Research Institute, Private Bag, Rotorua, New Zealand. charts. illus. circ. 500.

634.9   NZ   ISSN 0077-9997
NEW ZEALAND. FOREST RESEARCH INSTITUTE. REPORT. 1952. a. free. Forest Research Institute, Private Bag, Rotorua, New Zealand. charts. illus. circ. 3,000. (back issues avail.) Indexed: Biol.Abstr. Forest.Abstr. Rev.Appl.Entomol. Rev.Plant Path. Weed Abstr.

634.9   NO   ISSN 0332-5709
NORSK INSTITUTT FOR SKOGFORSKNING. MEDDELELSER/NORWEGIAN FOREST RESEARCH INSTITUTE. REPORTS. (Text in English; summaries in Norwegian) 1920. irreg. Kr.60. Norsk Institutt for Skogforskning, Box 61, 1432 As-NLH, Norway. circ. 1,000. (back issues avail.) Indexed: Biol.Abstr. Forest.Abstr. Forest Prod.Abstr. Rev.Plant Path. Soils & Fert.
    Formerly (1920-1974): Norske Skogforsoksvesen. Meddelelser.

634.9   NO   ISSN 0333-001X
NORSK INSTITUTT FOR SKOGFORSKNING. RAPPORT/NORWEGIAN FOREST RESEARCH INSTITUT. RESEARCH PAPER. (Text in Norwegian; summaries in English) 1980. irreg. Kr.50. Norwegian Forest Research Institute, Postboks 61, 1432 Aas-NLH, Norway. (back issues avail.) Indexed: Biol.Abstr.

634.9   US   ISSN 0090-0664
NORTH CAROLINA STATE UNIVERSITY. SCHOOL OF FOREST RESOURCES. TECHNICAL REPORT. 1950. irreg. (3-4/yr.) exchange basis. North Carolina State University, School of Forest Resources, Raleigh, NC 27695. TEL 919-737-2883. circ. 160(controlled) Indexed: Forest.Abstr. Forest Prod.Abstr.

634.9   UK
O F I OCCASIONAL PAPERS. 1978. irreg. price varies. Oxford Forestry Institute, Department of Plant Sciences, University of Oxford, South Parks Rd., Oxford OX1 3RB, England. circ. 375. (also avail. in microform; back issues avail.) Indexed: Biol.Abstr. Forest.Abstr.
    Formerly (until Oct., 1985): C F I Occasional Papers (ISSN 0141-8181)

OHIO STATE UNIVERSITY. AGRICULTURAL RESEARCH AND DEVELOPMENT CENTER. SPECIAL CIRCULAR. see *AGRICULTURE*

634.9   CN
ORDRE DES INGENIEURS FORESTIERS DU QUEBEC. CONGRES ANNUEL. TEXTE DES CONFERENCES.* 1928. a. free. Ordre Professionnelle des Ingenieurs Forestiers du Quebec, 2022 rue Lavoisier, Bur. 165, Ste. Foy, Que. G1N 4L5, Canada. TEL 418-683-2379. circ. 1,200.
    Formerly: Corporation des Ingenieurs Forestiers du Quebec. Congres Annuel. Texte des Conferences (ISSN 0070-0304)

634.9   US
OREGON STATE UNIVERSITY. FOREST RESEARCH LABORATORY. BIENNIAL REPORT. 1958. a. free. Oregon State University, Forest Research Laboratory, Corvallis, OR 97331. TEL 503-753-9166. Ed. Ralph E. McNees. index. Indexed: Biol.Abstr.
    Formerly: Oregon State University. Forest Research Laboratory. Annual Report (ISSN 0078-5865)

634.9   US   ISSN 0078-5903
OREGON STATE UNIVERSITY. FOREST RESEARCH LABORATORY. RESEARCH BULLETIN. 1949. irreg., no.49, 1985. free. Oregon State University, Forest Research Laboratory, Corvallis, OR 97331. TEL 503-753-9166. Ed. Ralph E. McNees. circ. 2,000. (reprint service avail. from UMI) Indexed: Biol.Abstr. Forest.Abstr. Forest Prod.Abstr.

634.9   US   ISSN 0078-5911
OREGON STATE UNIVERSITY. FOREST RESEARCH LABORATORY. RESEARCH NOTE. 1949. irreg., no.78, 1985. free. Oregon State University, Forest Research Laboratory, Corvallis, OR 97331. TEL 503-753-9166. Ed. Ralph E. McNees. (reprint service avail. from UMI) Indexed: Biol.Abstr. Forest.Abstr. Forest Prod.Abstr.

634.9   US   ISSN 0078-592X
OREGON STATE UNIVERSITY. FOREST RESEARCH LABORATORY. RESEARCH PAPER. 1965. irreg., no.47, 1984. free. Oregon State University, Forest Research Laboratory, Corvallis, OR 97331. TEL 503-753-9166. Ed. Ralph E. McNees. circ. 2,000. (also avail. in microform from UMI; reprint service avail. from UMI) Indexed: Chem.Abstr. Forest.Abstr. Soils & Fert.

634.96   CN
PACIFIC FOREST RESEARCH CENTRE. PEST LEAFLET. no.68, 1981. irreg. free. Pacific Forest Reseach Centre, 506 West Burnside Rd., Victoria, B.C. V8Z 1M5, Canada. Ed. Alister McEwan. (back issues avail.) Indexed: Forest.Abstr.

634.9   CN
PACIFIC FOREST RESEARCH CENTRE. PEST REPORT. irreg. free. Pacific Forest Research Centre, 506 West Burnside Rd., Victoria, B.C. V8Z 1M5, Canada.

634.92   PK   ISSN 0078-8147
PAKISTAN FOREST INSTITUTE, PESHAWAR. ANNUAL PROGRESS REPORT. (Text in English) 1950. a. Pakistan Forest Institute, Peshawar, Pakistan. circ. 500. Indexed: Biol.Abstr. Chem.Abstr. Forest. Abstr.

POZNANSKIE TOWARZYSTWO PRZYJACIOL NAUK. KOMISJA NAUK ROLNICZYCH I KOMISJA NAUK LESNYCH. PRACE. see *AGRICULTURE*

QUEBEC (PROVINCE). CONSEIL CONSULTATIF SUR LES RESERVES ECOLOGIQUES. RAPPORT ANNUEL. see *CONSERVATION*

634.9   CN
QUEBEC (PROVINCE) MINISTERE DE L'ENERGIE ET DES RESSOURCES. DIRECTION DE LA RECHERCHE ET DU DEVELOPPEMENT. GUIDE. (Text in French; summaries in English and French) 1970. irreg. free. Ministere de l'Energie et des Ressources, Direction de la Recherche du Developpement, 2700 rue Einstein, Sainte-Foy, Que. G1P 3W8, Canada. TEL 418-643-7994. circ. 900.
    Former titles: Quebec (Province) Ministere de l'Energie et des Ressources. Service de la Recherche Appliquee. Guide; Quebec (Province) Ministere de l'Energie et des Resources. Services de la Recherche (Terres et Forest). Guide; Quebec (Province) Ministere de l'Energie et des Ressources. Service de la Recherche Forestiere. Guide.

FORESTS AND FORESTRY

634.9   CN
QUEBEC (PROVINCE) MINISTERE DE L'ENERGIE ET DES RESSOURCES. DIRECTION DE LA RECHERCHE ET DU DEVELOPPEMENT. MEMOIRE. (Text in French; summaries in English and French) 1970. irreg. free. Ministere de l'Energie et des Ressources, Direction de la Recherche et du Developpement, 2700 rue Einstein, Sainte-Foy, Que. G1P 3W8, Canada. TEL 418-643-7994. Ed. Fabien Caron. circ. 900. (back issues avail.) Indexed: Forest.Abstr.
    Former titles: Quebec (Province) Ministere de l'Energie et des Ressources. Service de la Recherche (Appliquee). Memoire; Quebec (Province) Ministere de l'Energie et des Ressources. Service de la Recherche (Terres et Forets). Memoire; Quebec (Province) Ministere de l'Energie et des Ressources. Service de la Recherche Forestiere. Memoire; Quebec (Province) Ministere de l'Energie et des Ressources. Service de la Recherche. Memoire.

634.9   CN
QUEBEC (PROVINCE) MINISTERE DE L'ENERGIE ET DES RESSOURCES. DIRECTION DE LA RECHERCHE ET DU DEVELOPPEMENT. NOTE DE RECHERCHE FORESTIERE. (Text in French; summaries in English and French) 1972. irreg. free. Ministere de l'Energie et des Ressources, Direction de la Recherche et du Development, 2700 rue Einstein, Sainte-Foy, Que. G1P 3W8, Canada. TEL 418-643-7994. Ed. Fabien Caron. charts. illus. circ. 900.
    Former titles: Quebec (Province) Ministere de l'Energie et des Ressources. Service de la Recherche (Appliquee). Note; Quebec (Province) Ministere de l'Energie et des Ressources. Service de la Recherche (Terres et Forets). Note; Quebec (Province) Ministere de l'Energie et des Ressources. Service de la Recherche Forestiere. Note.

634.9   AT   ISSN 0480-9653
QUEENSLAND. DEPARTMENT OF FORESTRY. ANNUAL REPORT. 1958. a. Department of Forestry, Box 5, Brisbane, Qld. 4000, Australia. illus.

634.9   AT   ISSN 0157-809X
QUEENSLAND. DEPARTMENT OF FORESTRY. RESEARCH PAPER. 1971. irreg. Department of Forestry, Box 5, Brisbane, Qld. 4000, Australia. Indexed: Biol.Abstr. Aus.Sci.Ind. Forest.Abstr. Forest Prod.Abstr. Soils & Fert.

634.8   AT   ISSN 0155-9664
QUEENSLAND. DEPARTMENT OF FORESTRY. TECHNICAL PAPER. 1974. irreg. Queensland Department of Forestry, G.P.O. Box 944, Brisbane 4001, Queensland, Australia. Ed. A.M. Said. circ. 350. Indexed: Biol.Abstr.

333.7   II   ISSN 0377-3302
RAJASTHAN FOREST STATISTICS. (Text in English) irreg. Forest Department, Jaipur, Rajasthan, India.

674.9   US
RENEWABLE MATERIALS INSTITUTE SERIES. irreg. Syracuse University Press, 1600 Jamesville Ave., Syracuse, NY 13244. TEL 315-423-2596.

634.9   UK
RESEARCH AND DEVELOPMENT PAPER. 1951. irreg. price varies. Forestry Commission, 231 Corstorphine Rd., Edinburgh EH12 7AT, Scotland (Subscr. to: Forest Research Station, Publications, Alice Holt Lodge, Wrecclesham, Farnham, Surrey GU10 4LH, England) Ed. E.J. Parker. circ. 1, 000(controlled) Indexed: Biol.Abstr. Forest.Abstr.

634.9   AT   ISSN 0481-3219
RESEARCH NOTE. 1954. irreg. Department of Forestry, G.P.O. Box 944, Brisbane 4001, Queensland, Australia (Subscr. to: Division of Technical Services, P.O. Box 5, Roma St., Brisbane 4000, Australia) Indexed: Biol.Abstr.

RURAL INDUSTRY DIRECTORY. see *AGRICULTURE*

634.9   RW
RWANDA. PROJET PILOTE FORESTIER. RAPPORT ANNUEL. (Text in French) 1972. a. free. Project Pilote Forestier, B.P. 1, Kibuye, Rwanda.

634.9   US   ISSN 0080-5092
S.J. HALL LECTURESHIP IN INDUSTRIAL FORESTRY. 1969. a. free. University of California, Berkeley, Department of Forestry and Resource Management, 145 Mulford Hall, Berkeley, CA 94720. TEL 415-642-0376.

634.9   MY   ISSN 0080-5211
SABAH. FOREST DEPARTMENT. ANNUAL REPORT. (Text in English) 1963. a. M.$6. Forest Department, Sandakan, Sabah, Malaysia. circ. controlled.

634.9   SZ
SCHWEIZERISCHER FORSTVEREIN. ZEITSCHRIFT. BEIHEFTE. irreg. price varies. Schweizerischer Forstverein, ETH-Zentrum, Schmelzbergstr. 25, 8092 Zurich, Switzerland.

634.9   674   KO
SEOUL NATIONAL UNIVERSITY FORESTS. RESEARCH BULLETIN. (Text in English and Korean) 1962. a. 10,000 Won($13) Seoul National University Forests, Seoul National University, Suwon 170, Korea. Ed. Don K. Lee. Index. circ. 500. (also avail. in talking book) Indexed: Forest.Abstr.
    Formerly: Seoul National University Forests. Bulletin.

634.9   CL
SERIE INFORMATICA E INFORME TECNICO. 1962. a. exchange. Instituto Forestal, Of. del Jefe Biblioteca, Huerfanos 554-Casilla 3085, Santiago, Chile. circ. (controlled)

634.9   BL   ISSN 0583-3132
SILVICULTURA EM SAO PAULO. 1962. irreg. $15. Instituto Florestal, C.P. 1322, Sao Paulo 01000, Brazil. circ. 900. Indexed: Biol.Abstr. Forest.Abstr. Forest Prod.Abstr.

634.9   AT
SOUTH AUSTRALIA. DEPARTMENT OF WOODS AND FORESTS. BULLETIN. 1928. irreg. price varies. Woods and Forests Department, 135 Waymouth St., Adelaide, South Australia, Australia. Indexed: Aus.Sci.Ind. Forest Abstr.

634.9   614.7   SP   ISSN 0210-3338
SPAIN. INSTITUTO NACIONAL DE INVESTIGACIONES AGRARIAS. COMUNICACIONES. SERIE: RECURSOS NATURALES. 1974. irreg. 175 ptas. Instituto Nacional de Investigaciones Agrarias, Jose Abascal 56, 28003 Madrid, Spain. bibl. charts. illus. Indexed: Biol.Abstr. Forest.Abstr. Hort.Abstr. Plant Breed.Abstr. Soils & Fert.

634.9   US
SPRINGER SERIES IN WOOD SCIENCE. 1983. irreg., latest 1986. Springer-Verlag, 175 Fifth Ave., New York, NY 10010 (Also Berlin, Heidelberg, Tokyo and Vienna) Ed. T.E. Timell.

634.9   US   ISSN 0082-318X
STEPHEN F. AUSTIN STATE UNIVERSITY. SCHOOL OF FORESTRY. BULLETIN. 1957. irreg., no.25, 1972. price varies. Stephen F. Austin State University, School of Forestry, Nacogdoches, TX 75961. TEL 409-569-3304. Indexed: Biol.Abstr.

634.9   SW   ISSN 0039-3150
STUDIA FORESTALIA SUECICA. (Text & summaries in English) 1963. irreg., no.167, 1985. price varies. Swedish University of Agricultural Sciences, Research Information Centre, Box 7077, S-750 07 Uppsala, Sweden (Subscr.to: The Almqvist & Wiksell Periodical Company, P.O. Box 45150, S-10430 Stockholm, Sweden) Ed. Goeran Grant. charts. circ. 1,200. Indexed: Biol.Abstr. Chem.Abstr. Excerp.Med. Abstr.Bull.Inst.Pap.Chem. Forest.Abstr. Forest Prod.Abstr. Rev.Appl.Entomol. Rev.Plant Path. Soils & Fert.

634.9   SJ
SUDAN SILVA. (Text in English) no.13, 1962. a. Sudan Forestry Society, Box 658, Khartoum, Sudan. (Co-sponsor: National Council for Research) Indexed: Forest.Abstr. Forest Prod.Abstr. Soils & Fert.

634.9   674   SW   ISSN 0348-4599
SVERIGES LANTBRUKSUNIVERSITET. INSTITUTIONEN FOER VIRKESLAERA. RAPPORTER. (Text in Swedish; summaries in English) 1955. irreg., no.136, 1982. free. Sveriges Lantbruksuniversitet, Institutionen foer Virkeslaera - Swedish University of Agricultural Sciences, Department of Forest Products, Box 7008, S-750 07 Uppsala, Sweden. Indexed: Forest.Abstr. Forest Prod.Abstr.
    Formerly (until 1977): Kungliga Skogshoegskolan. Institutionen foer Virkeslaera. Rapporter (ISSN 0082-0040)

634.9   674   SW
SVERIGES LANTBRUKSUNIVERSITET. INSTITUTIONEN FOER VIRKESLAERA. UPPSATSER. (Text in English and Swedish) 1954. irreg., no.118, 1982. free. Sveriges Lantbruksuniversitet, Institutionen foer Virkeslaera - Swedish University of Agricultural Sciences, Department of Forestry Products, Box 7008, S-750-07 Uppsala, Sweden.
    Formerly (until 1977): Kungliga Skogshoegskolan. Institutionen foer Virkeslaera. Uppsatser (ISSN 0082-0059)

634.9   SZ
SWITZERLAND. EIDGENOESSISCHE ANSTALT FUER DAS FORSTLICHE VERSUCHSWESEN. MITTEILUNGEN. (Text in German; Summaries in English, French, German and Italian) 1891. irreg. (approx. 4/yr.) price varies. ‡ (Eidgenoessische Anstalt fuer das Forstliche Versuchswesen - Swiss Federal Institute of Forestry Research) F. Fluck-Wirth Buchhandlung, CH-9053 Teufen, Switzerland. Ed. Walter Bosshard. bk. rev. charts. illus. stats. index. cum.index. circ. 750. (back issues avail.) Indexed: GeoRef.
    Formerly: Switzerland. Schweizerische Anstalt fuer das Forstliche Versuchswesen. Mitteilungen (ISSN 0080-7257)

634.94   US
TALL TIMBERS ECOLOGY AND MANAGEMENT CONFERENCE. PROCEEDINGS. 1969. a. price varies. Tall Timbers Research Station, Route 1, Box 678, Tallahassee, FL 32312. TEL 904-893-4153. Ed. Roy Komarek. (reprint service avail. from UMI) Indexed: Biol.Abstr. Excerp.Med. Forest.Abstr. Forest Prod.Abstr.
    Formerly: Tall Timbers Fire Ecology Conference. Proceedings (ISSN 0082-1527)

634.9   US   ISSN 0496-7631
TALL TIMBERS RESEARCH STATION. BULLETIN. 1962. irreg. price varies. Tall Timbers Research Station, Rte 1, Box 678, Tallahassee, FL 32512. TEL 904-893-4153.

634.9   US   ISSN 0496-764X
TALL TIMBERS RESEARCH STATION. MISCELLANEOUS PUBLICATION. 1961. irreg., vol.7, 1981. price varies. Tall Timbers Research Station, Route 1, Box 678, Tallahassee, FL 32312. TEL 904-893-4153. Ed. Ev Komarck. (back issues avail.)

634.928   US   ISSN 0082-3031
TEXAS. FOREST SERVICE. COOPERATIVE FOREST TREE IMPROVEMENT PROGRAM. PROGRESS REPORT. 1953. a. (Texas Forest Service) Texas A & M University, College Sta., TX 77843. TEL 409-845-1325. Ed. J.P. van Buijtenen.
Forest genetics research project

634.9   US   ISSN 0082-304X
TEXAS FORESTRY PAPERS. 1970. irreg., no.16, 1972. Stephen F. Austin State University, School of Forestry, Nacogdoches, TX 75961. TEL 409-569-3304. Indexed: Biol.Abstr. Forest.Abstr. Forest Prod.Abstr.

634   336.2   US   ISSN 0563-5446
TIMBER TAX JOURNAL.* 1967. a. $35. Forest Industries Committee on Timber Valuation and Taxation, c/o International Specialized Book Services, Inc., Box 1632, Beaverton, OR 97075 TEL 202-223-2314. (Distr. by: International Specialized Book Services, Inc., Box 1632, Beaverton, OR 97075) Ed. William K. Condrell. charts. stat. cum.index. circ. 1,200.

FORESTS AND FORESTRY

634.9 JA ISSN 0082-4720
TOKYO METROPOLITAN AGRICULTURAL EXPERIMENT STATION, ITSUKAICHI OFFICE. FORESTRY EXPERIMENTAL BULLETIN/RINGYO SHIKEN KENKYU HOKOKU. (Text and summaries in English, French, German and Japanese) 1904. irreg. (8-10 vols. per year) exchange basis. Tokyo Metropolitan Agricultural Experiment Station, Itsukaichi Office - Tokyo-to Nogyo Shikenjo Itsukaichi Bunjo, 853 Tokura, Itsukaichi-machi, Nishitama-gun, Tokyo 190-01, Japan.

634.9 JA
TOTTORI UNIVERSTY FORESTS. RESEARCH BULLETIN/TOTTORI DAIGAKU NOGAKUBU FUZOKU ENSHURIN HOKOKU. (Text in Japanese; summaries in English) 1958. biennial. Tottori University Forests - Tottori Daigaku Nogakubu Fuzoku Enshurin, 1-1 Koyama-cho, Tottori 680, Japan. Ed.Tetuzo Kurimura. Indexed: Biol.Abstr. Forest.Abstr. Forest Prod.Abstr. Plant Breed.Abstr.
  Formerly: Tottori University Forests. Bulletin (ISSN 0082-5379)

634.9 UG ISSN 0082-7177
UGANDA. FORESTRY DEPARTMENT. ANNUAL REPORT. 1904. a. EAs.100. Forestry Department, Box 31, Entebbe, Uganda. cum.index. Indexed: Forest.Abstr.

634.9 UG ISSN 0082-7193
UGANDA. FORESTRY DEPARTMENT. TECHNICAL NOTES. 1953. irreg., latest no.222, 1979. free. Forestry Department, Box 31, Entebbe, Uganda. cum.index: 1953-79. Indexed: Biol.Abstr. Forest.Abstr.

634.9 US ISSN 0092-9654
U.S. FOREST SERVICE. GENERAL TECHNICAL REPORT INT. 1966. irreg. free. U.S. Department of Agriculture, Intermountain Research Station, 324 25th St., Ogden, UT 84401. TEL 801-625-5437. bibl. (also avail. in microfiche) Indexed: Biol.Abstr. Forest.Abstr. Forest Prod.Abstr.

634.9 US ISSN 0083-2480
U.S. FOREST SERVICE. GENERAL TECHNICAL REPORT NE. 1927. a. U.S. Forest Service, Northeastern Forest Experiment Sta., 370 Reed Rd., Broomall, PA 19008. TEL 215-461-3102. Indexed: Biol.Abstr. Forest.Abstr. Forest Prod.Abstr. Rev.Plant Path.

634.9 US ISSN 0196-2094
U.S. FOREST SERVICE. PACIFIC SOUTHWEST FOREST AND RANGE EXPERIMENT STATION. GENERAL TECHNICAL REPORT P S W. 1972. irreg. price varies. U.S. Forest Service, Pacific Southwest Forest and Range Experiment Station, 1960 Addison St., Berkeley, CA 94701. (also avail. in microfiche) Indexed: Biol.Abstr. Forest.Abstr. Forest Prod.Abstr. Soils & Fert. Key Title: General Technical Report P S W.
  Formerly: U.S. Forest Service. General Technical Report PSW (ISSN 0092-9662)

634.9 US
U.S. FOREST SERVICE. RESEARCH NOTE INT. irreg. U.S. Forest Service, Intermountain Research Station, 324 25th St., Ogden, UT 84401. TEL 801-625-5137. Indexed: Biol.Abstr. Excerp.Med.

634.9 US ISSN 0502-4994
U.S. FOREST SERVICE. RESEARCH NOTE RM. 1963. irreg., no.456, 1985. free. U.S. Forest Service, Rocky Mountain Forest and Range Experiment Sta., 240 W. Prospect, Fort Collins, CO 80526. TEL 303-224-1719. Indexed: Biol.Abstr. Excerp.Med. Pollut.Abstr. Forest.Abstr. Forest PRod.Abstr.

634.9 US
U.S. FOREST SERVICE. RESEARCH PAPER INT. irreg. U.S. Forest Service, Intermountain Research Station, 324 25th St., Ogden, UT 84401. TEL 801-625-5137. Indexed: Biol.Abstr.

634.9 US ISSN 0502-5001
U.S. FOREST SERVICE. RESEARCH PAPER RM. 1963. irreg., no.261, 1975. free. U.S. Forest Service, Rocky Mountain Forest and Range Experiment Sta., 240 W. Prospect, Fort Collins, CO 80526. TEL 303-224-1719. Indexed: Biol.Abstr. Forest.Abstr. Forest Prod.Abstr.

634 US
U.S. FOREST SERVICE. RESOURCE BULLETIN INT. irreg., no.30, 1983. U.S. Forest Service, Intermountain Research Station, 324 25th St., Ogden, UT 84401. TEL 801-625-5137. Indexed: Biol.Abstr.

634.9 US
U.S. FOREST SERVICE. RESOURCE BULLETIN PNW. 1963. irreg. free. ‡ U.S. Forest Service, Pacific Northwest Forest and Range Experiment Sta., Box 3890, Portland, OR 97208. TEL 503-231-6756. Indexed: Biol.Abstr. Forest.Abstr. Soils & Fert.

634.9 PR
U.S. INSTITUTE OF TROPICAL FORESTRY. ANNUAL LETTER. (Text in English and Spanish) 1939. a. free. U.S. Institute of Tropical Forestry, Southern Forest Experiment Sta., U S D A Forest Service, Call Box 25000, Rio Piedras, PR 00928-2500. Dir. Ariel E. Lugo. circ. 2,500.

UNIVERSITAET FUER BODENKULTUR IN WIEN. DISSERTATIONEN. see *AGRICULTURE*

634.9 RM
UNIVERSITATEA DIN BRASOV. BULETINUL. SERIA B. ECONOMIA FORESTIERA. (Text in Rumanian; summaries in English, French, German) 1956. a. price varies. Universitatea din Brasov, Bd. Gh. Gheorghiu-Dej, Nr. 29, Brasov, Rumania. Ed. Darie Parascan. bibl. illus. Indexed: Forest.Abstr. Forest Prod.Abstr.

634.9 UK ISSN 0065-0277
UNIVERSITY OF ABERDEEN. DEPARTMENT OF FORESTRY. ECONOMIC SURVEY OF PRIVATE FORESTRY. 1952; N.S. 1963. a. £2.50. University of Aberdeen, Department of Forestry, St. Machar Dr., Old Aberdeen AB9 2UU, Scotland. circ. 250. Indexed: Forest.Abstr. Forest Prod.Abstr.

634.9 CN ISSN 0084-8069
UNIVERSITY OF BRITISH COLUMBIA. RESEARCH FOREST ANNUAL REPORT. 1962. a. Can.$5. University of British Columbia, Faculty of Forestry, 270-2357 Main Mall, Vancouver, B.C. V6T 1W5, Canada. TEL 604-228-2211. Indexed: Biol.Abstr. Forest.Abstr.

UNIVERSITY OF DAR ES SALAAM. FACULTY OF AGRICULTURE, FORESTRY AND VETERINARY SCIENCE. ANNUAL RECORD OF RESEARCH. see *AGRICULTURE*

634.9 575.1 US
UNIVERSITY OF FLORIDA. SCHOOL OF FOREST RESOURCES & CONSERVATION. COOPERATIVE FOREST GENETICS RESEARCH PROGRAM. PROGRESS REPORT. (Subseries of its Research Report) 1957. irreg., no.36, 1985. free. University of Florida, School of Forest Resources & Conservation, Gainesville, FL 32601. TEL 904-392-1792. Ed. R.E. Goddard. circ. 300.
  Formerly: University of Florida. School of Forestry. Cooperative Forest Genetics Research Program. Progress Report (ISSN 0071-6146)

UNIVERSITY OF IDAHO. FOREST, WILDLIFE AND RANGE EXPERIMENT STATION, MOSCOW. STATION BULLETIN. see *CONSERVATION*

UNIVERSITY OF IDAHO. FOREST, WILDLIFE AND RANGE EXPERIMENT STATION, MOSCOW. STATION NOTE. see *CONSERVATION*

UNIVERSITY OF MINNESOTA. CENTER FOR NATURAL RESOURCE POLICY AND MANAGEMENT. WORKING PAPERS. see *WATER RESOURCES*

634.9 US ISSN 0077-1155
UNIVERSITY OF MONTANA. FOREST AND CONSERVATION EXPERIMENT STATION, MISSOULA. BULLETIN. 1949. irreg., no. 47, 1982. price varies. University of Montana, School of Forestry, Montana Forest and Conservation Experiment Sta., Missoula, MT 59812. TEL 406-243-6655. Ed. Jennifer O'Loughlin.

634.9 US ISSN 0077-1163
UNIVERSITY OF MONTANA. FOREST AND CONSERVATION EXPERIMENT STATION, MISSOULA. RESEARCH NOTES. 1964. irreg., no.22, 1985. free. University of Montana, School of Forestry, Montana Forest and Conservation Experiment Sta., Missoula, MT 59812. TEL 406-243-6655. Ed. Jennifer O'Loughlin.

634.9 550 574 CN
UNIVERSITY OF TORONTO. FACULTY OF FORESTRY. RESEARCH REPORT. 1980. a. free. University of Toronto, Faculty of Forestry, 203 College St., Toronto, Ont. M5S 1A1, Canada. TEL 416-978-6184. Ed. Irene Jardine. circ. 1,500.

DIE VEGETATION UNGARISCHER LANDSCHAFTEN. see *BIOLOGY — Botany*

634.9 AT
VICTORIA, AUSTRALIA. DEPARTMENT OF CONSERVATION, FORESTS AND LANDS. BULLETIN. 1937. irreg. free. Department of Conservation, Forests and Lands, 240 Victoria Parade, East Melbourne, Vic. 3002, Australia. Ed. David Meagher. Indexed: Biol.Abstr. Aus.Sci.Ind. Forest.Abstr. Forest Prod.Abstr.
  Formerly: Victoria, Australia. Forest Commission. Bulletin (ISSN 0085-7742)

634.9 574 CS
VYSKUMNY USTAV LESNEHO HOSPODARSTVA VO ZVOLENE. LESNICKE STUDIE. (Text in Slovak; summaries in English, German, Russian) 1960. irreg. price varies. (Vyskumny Ustav Lesneho Hospodarstva vo Zvolene) Priroda, Krizkova 9, 815 34 Bratislava, Czechoslovakia. charts. illus. index. Indexed: Biol.Abstr.

WASHINGTON (STATE). DEPARTMENT OF REVENUE. FOREST TAX SECTION. FOREST TAX ANNUAL REPORT. see *BUSINESS AND ECONOMICS — Public Finance, Taxation*

WEST VIRGINIA. AGRICULTURAL AND FORESTRY EXPERIMENT STATION. BULLETIN. see *AGRICULTURE*

634.9 US ISSN 0197-1387
WEST VIRGINIA FORESTRY NOTES. 1973. irreg., (approx. 1/yr.) West Virginia University, Agricultural and Forestry Experiment Station, Morgantown, WV 26506. TEL 304-293-3411. Eds. John Luchok, Harry V. Wiant, Jr. circ. 2,500.

634.9 US
WESTERN FORESTRY CONFERENCE. PROCEEDINGS. 1930. a. $5 (individual papers avail. and priced separately) Western Forestry and Conservation Association, 4033 S.W. Canyon Rd., Portland, OR 97221. circ. 600.
  Former titles: Western Forestry Conference. Executive Summaries of Proceedings; Supersedes (as of 1977): Western Forestry Conference. Proceedings; Western Forest Fire Committee. Proceedings (ISSN 0511-750X); Western Forest Pest Committee. Proceedings (ISSN 0511-7518); Western Reforestation Coordinating Committee. Proceedings (ISSN 0511-7526) Western Stand Management Committee. Proceedings.

634.9 US ISSN 0511-9723
WILLIAM L. HUTCHESON MEMORIAL FOREST. BULLETIN. irreg. price varies. Rutgers University, Department of Biological Sciences, New Brunswick, NJ 08903. TEL 201-932-2075. (Co-Sponsor: William H. Hutcheson Memorial Forest Committee) Eds. Dr. Charles Leck, Dr. Helen F. Buell.

639.9 UG
WOODSMAN NEWSLETTER. 1962. a. free. Forestry Department, Box 31, Entebbe, Uganda. Indexed: Forest.Abstr.
  Formerly: Woodsman.

634.9 SP ISSN 0084-1811
WORLD FORESTRY CONGRESS. PROCEEDINGS.* (Text in English, French and Spanish) irreg., 1966, 6th, Madrid. Direccion General de Montes, Ministerio de Agricultura, Paseo de Infanta Isabel, Madrid, Spain. Indexed: Forest.Abstr. Forest Prod.Abstr.
  Proceedings published in host country

634.9 US ISSN 0361-4425
YALE UNIVERSITY. SCHOOL OF FORESTRY. BULLETIN. 1912. irreg. Yale University, School of Forestry, New Haven, CT 06511. TEL 203-436-0440. Indexed: Biol.Abstr. Forest.Abstr. Forest Prod.Abstr.

634.9 US
YANKEE WOODLOT. 1942. irreg. free. University of Maine at Orono, Cooperative Extension Service, 107 Nutting Hall, Orono, ME 04473. TEL 207-581-3188. (Co-sponsor: United States Department of Agriculture) Ed. Bud Blumenstock. bk. rev. circ. 4, 500.
Formerly: Maine Cooperative Extension Service. Forestry Facts.

634.9 ZA ISSN 0084-4616
ZAMBIA. DEPARTMENT OF FORESTRY. REPORT. 1964. a. 25 n. Government Printer, Box 136, Lusaka, Zambia.

634.9 CS
ZBORNIK VEDECKYCH PRAC DREVARSKEJ FAKULTY VYSOKEJ SKOLY LESNICKEJ A DREVARSEJ VO ZVOLENE. (Text in Slovak; a part of science articles and summaries in English, German, Russian) 1957. a. exchange basis. Vysoka Skola Lesnicka a Drevarska vo Zvolene, Drevarska Fakulta - College of Forestry and Wood Technology, Zvolen, Marxova 24, 960-53 Zvolen, Czechoslovakia (Subscr. to: Ustredna Lesnicka a Drevarska Kniznica SSR pri VSLD vo Zvolene (Central Library of Forestry and Wood Technology at the University College), Marxova 20, 961 02 Zvolen, Czechoslovakia) Ed. Imrich Melcer. illus. circ. 300.

FORESTS AND FORESTRY — Abstracting, Bibliographies, Statistics

ABSTRACTS OF BULGARIAN SCIENTIFIC LITERATURE. AGRICULTURE AND FORESTRY. VETERINARY MEDICINE. see AGRICULTURE — Abstracting, Bibliographies, Statistics

634.9 016 UK
C.A.B. INTERNATIONAL. FORESTRY BUREAU. ANNOTATED BIBLIOGRAPHIES. (Former name of issuing body: Commonwealth Agricultural Bureaux) 1966. irreg. price varies. C.A.B. International, Forestry Bureau, Farnham House, Farnham Royal, Slough SL2 3BN, England. Ed. W. Finlayson. Indexed: Forest.Abstr.
Formerly: Commonwealth Forestry Bureau Annotated Bibliographies (ISSN 0069-7052)

634.9 CN ISSN 0384-4633
CANADA. STATISTICS CANADA. PULP AND PAPER MILLS/USINES DE PATES ET PAPIERS. (Catalogue 36-204) (Text in English and French) 1917. a. Can.$20($21) Statistics Canada, Communications Division, 3rd Floor, R.H. Coats Bldg., Ottawa, Ont. K1A 0T6, Canada TEL 613-993-7276. (Subscr. to: Publications Sales and Services, Ottawa, Ont. K1A 0T6, Canada) (also avail. in microform from MML)

338.4 CN ISSN 0828-9867
CANADA. STATISTICS CANADA. SAWMILL, PLANING MILL AND SHINGLE MILL PRODUCTS INDUSTRIES/INDUSTRIES DES PRODUITS DE SCIERIES ET D'ATALIERS DE RABOTAGE. (Catalogue 35-204) (Text in English and French) 1917. a. Can.$20($21) Statistics Canada, Communications Division, 3rd Floor, R.H. Coats Bldg., Ottawa, Ont. K1 A0T6, Canada TEL 613-993-7276. (Subscr. to: Publications Sales and Services, Ottawa, Ont. K1A 0T6, Canada) stat. (also avail. in microform from MML)
Formerly: Canada. Statistics Canada. Sawmills and Planing Mills and Shingle Mills/Scieries et Ateliers de Rabotage et Usines de Bardeaux (ISSN 0318-7128)

634.9 016 UK ISSN 0140-4784
FOREST PRODUCTS ABSTRACTS. (Former name of issuing body: Commonwealth Agricultural Bureaux) 1978. m. £104($182) to non-members. C.A.B. International, Forestry Bureau, Farnham House, Farnham Royal, Slough SL2 3BN, England (U.S. subscr. to: C.A.B. International, North American Office, 845 N. Park Ave., Tucson, AR 85719) (also avail. in microfiche; back issues avail.) Indexed: Abstr.Bull.Inst.Pap.Chem. Forest.Abstr.
●Also available online. Vendors: BRS, CISTI, DIMDI, DIALOG, European Space Agency.

634.9 016 UK ISSN 0015-7538
FORESTRY ABSTRACTS; compiled from world literature. 1939. m. £216($374) to non-members. C.A.B. International, Forestry Bureau, Farnham House, Farnham Royal, Slough SL2 3BN, England. abstr. index; cum.index: v.1-5. circ. 1,200. (also avail. in microfiche; back issues avail.) Indexed: Chem.Abstr. Abstr.Bull.Inst.Pap.Chem. Field Crop Abstr. Rev.Appl.Entomol. Rural Recreat.Tour.Abstr. Weed Abstr. World Agri.Econ.& Rural Sociol.Abstr.
●Also available online. Vendors: BRS, CISTI, DIMDI, DIALOG, European Space Agency.

634.9 016 UK ISSN 0071-7584
FORESTRY ABSTRACTS. LEADING ARTICLE REPRINT SERIES. 1942. irreg. price varies. C.A.B. International, Forestry Bureau, Farnham House, Farnham Royal, Slough SL2 3BN, England. Indexed: Forest.Abstr.
●Also available online. Vendors: BRS, CISTI, DIMDI, DIALOG, European Space Agency.

634.9 314 GW ISSN 0084-7690
FORSTSTATISTISCHES JAHRBUCH. 1953. a. DM.35. Ministerium fuer Ernaehrung, Landwirtschaft, Umwelt und Forsten, Marienstr. 41, 7000 Stuttgart 1, W. Germany (B.R.D.)

634.9 NO ISSN 0468-8155
NORWAY. STATISTISK SENTRALBYRAA. SKOGSTATSTIKK/FORESTRY STATISTICS. (Subseries of its Norges Offisielle Statistikk) 1952. a. Kr.45. Statistisk Sentralbyraa, Box 8131 Dep., 0033 Oslo 1, Norway. circ. 1,300.

634.9 314 PL
POLAND. GLOWNY URZAD STATYSTYCZNY. ROCZNIK STATYSTYCZNY LESNICTWA I GOSPODARKI DREWNEM. (Issued in its Seria Roczniki Branzowe. Branch Yearbooks) irreg., latest 1979. Glowny Urzad Statystyczny, Al. Niepodleglosci 208, 00-925 Warsaw, Poland.
Formerly: Poland. Glowny Urzad Statystyczny. Rocznik Statystyczny Lesnictwa (ISSN 0079-2721)

674 US ISSN 0485-9960
RANDOM LENGTHS YEARBOOK. 1965. a. $24.75. Random Lengths Publications, Inc., Box 867, Eugene, OR 97440-0867. TEL 503-686-9925. Ed. Terri L. Richards. charts. stat.

674 310 SQ
SWAZILAND. CENTRAL STATISTICAL OFFICE. TIMBER STATISTICS. 1970. a. free. Central Statistical Office, Box 456, Mbabane, Swaziland. charts. stat.
Formerly: Swaziland. Central Statistical Office. Commercial Timber Plantation and Wood Products Statistics.

634.9 016 US
U.S. FOREST SERVICE. NORTH CENTRAL FOREST EXPERIMENT STATION. LIST OF PUBLICATIONS. 1966. a. contr. free. ‡ U.S. Forest Service, North Central Forest Experiment Sta., 1992 Folwell Ave., St.Paul, MN 55108. TEL 612-642-5233. Ed. Robert D. Wray. circ. 1,500.
Formerly: U.S. Forest Service. North Central Forest Experiment Station, St. Paul, Minnesota. Annual Report (ISSN 0083-2472)

634.961 310 US
WASHINGTON (STATE). DEPARTMENT OF NATURAL RESOURCES. ANNUAL FIRE STATISTICS. a. Department of Natural Resources, Olympia, WA 98504. TEL 206-753-5327.

674 310 US ISSN 0195-931X
WESTERN WOOD PRODUCTS ASSOCIATION. STATISTICAL YEARBOOK. 1968. a. $12.50. Western Wood Products Association, 1500 Yeon Bldg., Portland, OR 97204. TEL 503-224-3930. (back issues avail.)
Formerly: Statistical Supplement to Facts.

FORESTS AND FORESTRY — Lumber And Wood

see also Paper and Pulp

674 CN ISSN 0065-0013
A B C BRITISH COLUMBIA LUMBER TRADE DIRECTORY AND YEAR BOOK. 1916. biennial. Can.$33. Progress Publishing Co. Ltd., C-310 Marine Bldg., 355 Burrard St., Vancouver, B.C. V6C 2G6, Canada. TEL 604-685-4385.

674 634.9 PL
AKADEMIA ROLNICZA, POZNAN. ROCZNIKI. CHEMICZNA TECHNOLOGIA DREWNA. (Text in Polish; summaries in English and Russian) 1961. irreg. price varies. Akademia Rolnicza, Poznan, Ul. Wojska Polskiego 28, 60-637 Poznan, Poland. circ. 1,960. Indexed: Bibl.Agri. Forest.Abstr.
Formerly: Akademia Rolnicza, Poznan. Rocznik. Technologia Drewna (ISSN 0137-1797)

674 US
AMERICAN WOOD PRESERVERS' ASSOCIATION. PROCEEDINGS. 1905. a. $50 paper; $55 clothbound. American Wood Preservers Association, Box 849, Stevensville, MD 21666. Ed. Pauline D. Paul. adv. circ. 2,000. Indexed: Chem.Abstr. Forest.Abstr. Forest Prod.Abstr.

ANNUAL BOOK OF A S T M STANDARDS. VOLUME 04.09. WOOD. see ENGINEERING — Engineering Mechanics And Materials

674 AT
AUSTRALIAN FOREST INDUSTRIES DIRECTORY. biennial. Australian Forest Industries Journal Pty Ltd., 243 Elizabeth St., Sydney NSW 2000, Australia.

674 BG
BANGLADESH FOREST INDUSTRIES DEVELOPMENT CORPORATION. ANNUAL REPORT. (Text in English) a. Bangladesh Forest Industries Development Corporation, 186 Circular Rd., Motijheel, Dacca 2, Bangladesh.

634.9 674 GW ISSN 0007-5892
BUNDESFORSCHUNGSANSTALT FUER FORST- UND HOLZWIRTSCHAFT, HAMBURG. MITTEILUNGEN. 1947. irreg., no.151, 1986. price varies. Kommissionverlag Max Wiedebusch, Dammtorstr. 20, 2000 Hamburg 36, W. Germany (B.R.D.) bk. rev. Indexed: Abstr.Bull.Inst.Pap.Chem. Geo.Abstr.

674 US ISSN 0008-1094
CALIFORNIA FORESTRY AND FOREST PRODUCTS; technical notes. 1957. irreg., latest, no.60, 1985. free or on exchange basis. University of California, Berkeley, Department of Forestry and Resource Management, 47th St. & Hoffman Blvd., Richmond, CA 94804. TEL 415-231-4561. Ed.Bd. charts. illus. stat. circ. 775. Indexed: Chem.Abstr. Forest.Abstr.

674 FR ISSN 0008-9885
CENTRE TECHNIQUE DU BOIS ET DE L'AMEUBLEMENT. CAHIERS. 1954. irreg. price varies with issue. ‡ Centre Technique du Bois et de l'Ameublement, 10 av. de St Mande, 75012 Paris, France. charts. illus. circ. 4,000. Indexed: Forest.Abstr. Forest Prod.Abstr.

DIRECTORY OF THE FOREST PRODUCTS INDUSTRY. see BUSINESS AND ECONOMICS — Trade And Industrial Directories

F A O FORESTRY STUDIES. (Food and Agriculture Organization of the United Nations) see FORESTS AND FORESTRY

674.8 PL ISSN 0071-6685
FOLIA FORESTALIA POLONICA. SERIES B. DRZEWNICTWO. (Text in Polish; summaries in English and Russian) 1959. irreg., no.15, 1984. price varies. (Polska Akademia Nauk, Komitet Technologii Drewna) Panstwowe Wydawnictwo Naukowe, Miodowa 10, 00-251 Warsaw, Poland (Dist. by: Ars Polona, Krakowskie Przedmiescie 7, 00-068 Warsaw, Poland) Ed. M. Lawniczak. circ. 610. Indexed: Biol.Abstr. Abstr.Bull.Inst.Pap.Chem. Forest.Abstr. Forest Prod.Abstr.

FOREST AND TIMBER. see FORESTS AND FORESTRY

FORESTS AND FORESTRY — LUMBER AND WOOD

674 GH ISSN 0586-8440
FOREST PRODUCTS RESEARCH INSTITUTE. ANNUAL REPORT. a. Ghana Forestry Commission, Forest Products Research, University P.O. Box 63, Accra, Ghana. Ed. F.W. Addo-Ashong. bibl. Indexed: Biol.Abstr.
Formerly: Council for Scientific and Industrial Research, Ghana. Forest Product Research Institute. Annual Report.

674 CN ISSN 0824-2119
FORINTEK CANADA CORP., WESTERN LABORATORY. SPECIAL PUBLICATIONS. 1979. irreg. membership. Forintek Canada Corp., Western Laboratory, 6620 Northwest Marine Drive, Vancouver, B.C. V6T 1X2, Canada. TEL 604-224-3221. circ. 1,100. (also avail. in microfiche from MML) Indexed: Forest.Abstr.

GREAT BRITAIN. BUILDING RESEARCH ESTABLISHMENT. REPORTS. see *FIRE PREVENTION*

674 SW ISSN 0072-9922
HANDBOOK OF THE NORTHERN WOOD INDUSTRIES. (Text in English) 1887. biennial. Kr.280. AB Svensk Traevarutidning, Observatoriegatan 17, S-113 29 Stockholm, Sweden. Ed. Rune Lindqvist. adv. index. circ. 3,500.

674 GW ISSN 0518-0147
HANDBUCH HOLZ. 1950. a. DM.15. Wirtschafts- und Forstverlag Euting KG, Tannenstr. 1, 5451 Strassenhaus, W. Germany (B.R.D.)

674 GW ISSN 0018-3865
DIE HOLZSCHWELLE. 1907. a. DM.40. Studiengesellschaft fuer Holzschwellenoberbau e.V., Ritterstr. 14, D-6500 Mainz 1, W. Germany (B.R.D.) Ed. Herbert Zimmermann. adv. bk. rev. charts. illus. stat. circ. 2,000.

674 NE
HOUTADRESBOEK. 1979. a. fl.66.50 free with subscr. to Houtwereld. Nijgh Periodieken B.V., Postbox 122, 3100 AC Schiedam, Netherlands. adv. circ. 2,500.

674 382 US
IMPORTING WOOD PURCHASING GUIDE. 3rd edt., 1976. a. $50. International Wood Trade Publications, Inc., 1235 Sycamore View, Box 34908, Memphis, TN 38134. TEL 901-372-8280.
Formerly: Import/Export Wood Purchasing Guide.

674 II ISSN 0073-6384
INDIAN FOREST RECORDS (NEW SERIES) COMPOSITE WOOD. (Text in English) 1952. irreg., 1964, vol.1, no.2. price varies. ‡ Forest Research Institute & Colleges, P. O. New Forest, Dehra Dun, India. circ. 500. Indexed: Biol.Abstr. Forest.Abstr. Indian Sci.Abstr.

674 II ISSN 0073-6414
INDIAN FOREST RECORDS (NEW SERIES) LOGGING. (Text in English) 1966. irreg., 1972, vol.1, no.3. price varies. ‡ Forest Research Institute & Colleges, P.O. New Forest, Dehra Dun, India. circ. 500. Indexed: Biol.Abstr. Forest.Abstr. Indian Sci.Abstr.

674 II ISSN 0073-6449
INDIAN FOREST RECORDS (NEW SERIES) TIMBER MECHANICS. (Text in English) 1952. irreg., vol.4, no.1, 1981. price varies. ‡ Forest Research Institute & Colleges, P.O. New Forest, Dehra Dun, India. circ. 500. Indexed: Biol.Abstr. Forest.Abstr. Indian Sci.Abstr.

674 II ISSN 0442-6827
INDIAN FOREST RECORDS WOOD ANATOMY. (Text and summaries in English) 1950. irreg. price varies. Forest Research Institute & Colleges, P.O. New Forest, Dehra Dun 248 006, India. circ. 500. Indexed: Biol.Abstr. Forest.Abstr. Indian Sci.Abstr.
Formerly: Indian Forest Records Wood Technology.

674 MX
INSTITUTO NACIONAL DE INVESTIGACIONES SOBRE RECURSOS BIOTICOS. NOTA TECNICA. 1982. irreg. $10. Instituto Nacional de Investigaciones sobre Recursos Bioticos, Apdo. Postal 63, 91000 Xalapa, Veracruz, Mexico. bibl. charts. illus. circ. 2,500. (back issues avail.) Indexed: Forest.Abstr. Forest Prod.Abstr.

674 US ISSN 0076-1109
L S U WOOD UTILIZATION NOTES. 1960. irreg., no. 39, 1986. free. ‡ Louisiana State University, School of Forestry, Wildlife, and Fisheries, Baton Rouge, LA 70803. TEL 504-388-4131. Ed. Peter J. Fogg. circ. 350.

674 690 MX
MADERA Y SU USO EN LA CONSTRUCCION. 1976. irreg., vol.11 in prep. $10. Instituto Nacional de Investigaciones sobre Recursos Bioticos, Apdo. Postal 63, 91000 Xalapa, Veracruz, Mexico. bibl. charts. illus. circ. 2,500. (back issues avail.)

674 380.1 MY ISSN 0126-6330
MALAYSIA. DIRECTORY OF TIMBER TRADE. (Text in English) 1970. biennial. M.$20. Malaysian Timber Industry Board - Lembaga Perindustrian Kayu Malaysia, P.O. Box 10887, 50728 Kuala Lumpur, Malaysia. Ed. Baharuddin Hj. Ghazali. circ. 5,000.

674 US ISSN 0076-9509
MISSISSIPPI STATE UNIVERSITY. FOREST PRODUCTS UTILIZATION LABORATORY. INFORMATION SERIES. 1965. irreg. Mississippi State University, Forest Products Utilization Laboratory, Drawer F P, Mississippi State, MS 39762. TEL 601-325-2116.

674 US ISSN 0026-640X
MISSISSIPPI STATE UNIVERSITY. FOREST PRODUCTS UTILIZATION LABORATORY. RESEARCH REPORT. 1966. irreg. free. Mississippi State University, Forest Products Utilization Laboratory, Drawer F P, Mississippi State, MS 39762. TEL 601-325-2116.

674 US
NATIONAL HARDWOOD LUMBER ASSOCIATION YEARBOOK. 1912. a. $30. ‡ National Hardwood Lumber Association, Box 34518, Memphis, TN 38184-0518. Ed. S.C. White. adv. circ. 2,000.

674 PL ISSN 0079-4724
POZNANSKIE TOWARZYSTWO PRZYJACIOL NAUK. KOMISJA TECHNOLOGII DREWNA. PRACE. (Text in Polish; summaries in English) 1968. a. price varies. (Poznanskie Towarzystwo Przyjaciol Nauk) Panstwowe Wydawnictwo Naukowe, Ul. Miodowa 10, Warsaw, Poland (Dist. by Ars Polona-Ruch, Krakowskie Przedmiescie 7, Warsaw, Poland) Ed. Jerzy Wislocki. Indexed: Biol.Abstr.

SEOUL NATIONAL UNIVERSITY FORESTS. RESEARCH BULLETIN. see *FORESTS AND FORESTRY*

674 387 UK ISSN 0080-9284
SHIPPING MARKS ON TIMBER. 1894. triennial. £18. Benn Publications Ltd., 25 New Street Sq., London EC4A 3JA, England. Ed. John Topham. adv. index. circ. 2,500.

674 NO
SKOGBRUKETS OG SKOGINDUSTRIENES FORSKNINGSRAAD. AARBOK. no.28, 1975. a. Skogbrukets og Skogindustrienes Forskningsraad, Box 250, Vinderen, Oslo 3, Norway.
Continues: Skogbrukets og Skogindustrienes Forsknings-Forening. Arbok.

674 676.12 SW ISSN 0039-6796
SVENSK TRAEVARU- OCH PAPERSMASSETIDNING/SWEDISH TIMBER AND WOOD PULP JOURNAL. (Text in English and Swedish) 1885. m. Kr.235. AB Svensk Traevarutidning, Observatoriegatan 17, S-113 29 Stockholm, Sweden. Ed. Jan Westlin. adv. illus. mkt. stat. circ. 2,250. Indexed: Key to Econ.Sci. PROMT.
Formerly: Svensk Travarutidning.

674 SW ISSN 0346-7090
SVENSKA TRAESKYDDSINSTITUTET. MEDDELANDEN/SWEDISH WOOD PRESERVATION INSTITUTE. REPORTS. (Text in English and Swedish) 1952. irreg., no.158, 1986. $60. Svenska Traeskyddsinstitutet - Swedish Wood Preservation Institute, Box 5607, S-114 86 Stockholm, Sweden. Ed. Joeran Jermer. circ. 1,000.

674 US ISSN 0082-089X
SYMPOSIUM ON PARTICLEBOARD. PROCEEDINGS. 1967. a. $50. Washington State University, Wood Materials Laboratory, Pullman, WA 99164-1806. TEL 509-335-2262. Ed. Tom Maloney.

674 US
SYRACUSE WOOD SCIENCE SERIES. irreg. Syracuse University Press, 1600 Jamesville Ave., Syracuse, NY 13244. TEL 315-423-2596. Ed. Wilfred A. Cote.

TIMBER TRADES DIRECTORY. see *BUSINESS AND ECONOMICS — Trade And Industrial Directories*

674 UK ISSN 0082-4364
TIMBER TRADES JOURNAL. ANNUAL SPECIAL ISSUE. 1879. a. £12. Benn Publications Ltd., Sovereign Way, Tonbridge, Kent TN9 1RW, England. adv. circ. 7,000.

TRAE NYTS LEVERANDOERREGISTER. see *BUILDING AND CONSTRUCTION — Carpentry And Woodwork*

674 UG
UGANDA. FORESTRY DEPARTMENT. TIMBER LEAFLET. 1953. irreg., latest no.53, 1972. free. Forestry Department, Box 31, Entebbe, Uganda. cum.index: 1953-72.

674 CN ISSN 0079-8355
UNIVERSITE LAVAL. DEPARTEMENT D'EXPLOITATION ET UTILISATION DES BOIS. NOTE DE RECHERCHES. (Text in French) 1967. irreg. free. Universite Laval, Departement Sciences du Bois, Quebec, P.Q. G1K 7P4, Canada. TEL 418-656-2131. Ed. Dr. Marcel Goulet. circ. 1,000. Indexed: Forest.Abstr.

674 CN ISSN 0079-8363
UNIVERSITE LAVAL. DEPARTEMENT D'EXPLOITATION ET UTILISATION DES BOIS. NOTE TECHNIQUE. (Text in English and French) 1967. irreg. free. ‡ Universite Laval, Departement Sciences du Bois, Quebec, P.Q. G1K 7P4, Canada. TEL 418-656-2131. circ. 1,000. Indexed: Forest.Abstr.

674.1 690 US
VIRGINIA POLYTECHNIC INSTITUTE AND STATE UNIVERSITY. PALLET AND CONTAINER RESEARCH LABORATORY. SPECIAL REPORT. 1949. irreg. price varies. Virginia Polytechnic Institute and State University, Pallet and Container Research Laboratory, Attn.: M.S. White, Ed., Blacksburg, VA 24061. TEL 703-961-7134. circ. 1,000.
Formerly: Virginia Polytechnic Institute and State University. Wood Research and Wood Construction Laboratory. Special Report (ISSN 0083-6508)

674 PL ISSN 0208-5704
WARSAW AGRICULTURAL UNIVERSITY. S G G W-A R. ANNALS. FORESTRY AND WOOD TECHNOLOGY. (Szkola Glowna Gospodarstwa Wiejskiego-Akademia Rolnicza) (Text mainly in English; occasionally in French, German or Russian; summaries in Polish) 1957. irreg., no.12, 1980. $6 per no. Warsaw Agricultural University Press, Ul. Nowoursynowska 166, 02-766 Warsaw, Poland (Dist. by: Ars Polona-Ruch, Krakowskie Przedmiescie 7, 00-680 Warsaw, Poland) Eds. T. Dudzinska, J. Olszewski. illus.
Formerly (until 1980): Akademia Rolnicza, Warsaw. Zeszyty Naukowe. Technologia Drewna.

674 US
WESTERN DRY KILN ASOCIATION. PROCEEDINGS. 1948. a. membership. West Coast Dry Kiln Association, Oregon State University, College of Forestry, Corvallis, OR 97331. TEL 503-753-9166. Ed. Charles J. Kozlik. circ. 700. Indexed: Forest.Abstr. Forest Prod.Abstr.
Formerly: Western Dry Kiln Clubs. Proceedings.

674 CN
WESTERN RETAIL LUMBERMEN'S DIRECTORY. a. Can.$40. (Western Retail Lumbermen's Association) Naylor Communications Ltd., 124 W. 8th St., North Vancouver, B.C. V7M 3H2, Canada (Subscr. addr.: 100 Sutherland Ave., Winnipeg, Man. R2W 3C7, Canada) circ. 850.

WESTERN WOOD PRODUCTS ASSOCIATION. STATISTICAL YEARBOOK. see *FORESTS AND FORESTRY — Abstracting, Bibliographies, Statistics*

WHERE TO BUY HARDWOOD PLYWOOD AND VENEER. see *BUILDING AND CONSTRUCTION — Carpentry And Woodwork*

674 634.98 JA ISSN 0083-9272
WHITE PAPER ON JAPAN'S FOREST INDUSTRIES. Title varies: Directory of Asian Forest Products. (English edition) 1965. decennial. $90. Japan Lumber Journal, Inc., C.P.O. Box 1945, Tokyo 100-91, Japan. Ed. Satoshi Ogawa.

674 US
WOOD & WOOD PRODUCTS REFERENCE BUYING GUIDE. 1963. a. $2.50. Vance Publishing Corporation, 400 Knightsbridge Parkway, Lincolnshire, IL 60069. Ed. Harry Urban. circ. 38, 000. (also avail. in microform from UMI)
Formerly: Wood & Wood Products Reference Data/Buying Guide (ISSN 0084-1080)

338.1 US
WOOD INDUSTRIES OF NEW MEXICO. 1973. irreg. free. State Forestry Division, Box 2167, Santa Fe, NM 87504-2167. TEL 505-827-5830. Ed. David D. Brown. circ. 300.
Formerly: New Mexico Forest Products Directory (ISSN 0094-2782)

674 JA ISSN 0049-7916
WOOD RESEARCH/MOKUZAI KENKYU. (Text in English) 1949. irreg. (1-2/yr.) exchange basis. Wood Research Institute, Kyoto University, Gokansho, Uji, Kyoto 611, Japan. Ed.Bd. charts. stat. circ. 800. Indexed: Biol.Abstr. Chem.Abstr. Abstr.Bull.Inst.Pap.Chem. Forest.Abstr. Forest Prod.Abstr.

674 UN ISSN 0084-3768
YEARBOOK OF FOREST PRODUCTS. (Text in English, French and Spanish) 1947. a. price varies. Food and Agriculture Organization of the United Nations, Distribution and Sales Section, Via delle Terme di Caracalla, Rome, Italy (Dist. in U.S. by: Bernan Associates-Unipub, 4611-F Assembly Drive, Lanham, MD 20706-4391) Indexed: Forest.Abstr. Forest Prod.Abstr.

FUNERALS

A M A PRODUCT DIRECTORY. (American Monument Association) see *MINES AND MINING INDUSTRY*

614.6 US ISSN 0065-7565
AMERICAN BLUE BOOK OF FUNERAL DIRECTORS. 1932. biennial. $50. Kates-Boylston Publications, Inc., 1501 Broadway, New York, NY 10036. TEL 212-398-9266.

614.6 US
AMERICAN CEMETERY ASSOCIATION. MEMBERSHIP DIRECTORY. 1961. a. $45. American Cemetery Association, 3 Skyline Pl., Ste. 1111, 5201 Leesburg Pike, Falls Church, VA 22041. Ed. Kathleen Loomis. adv. circ. 3,000.
Formerly: International Cemetery Directory (ISSN 0074-2155)

614.6 UK ISSN 0143-3164
DIRECTORY OF CREMATORIA. 1969. a. £11.50. Cremation Society of Great Britain, 2nd Fl., Brecon House, 16/16a Albion Place, Maidstone, Kent ME14 5DZ, England. Ed. R.N. Arber. adv. circ. 350.
Former titles: Handbook and Directory of Crematoria (ISSN 0305-9537); Directory of Crematoria in the British Isles & Overseas Cremation Societies.
Cremation

MARKERS. see *ART*

614.6 DK ISSN 0108-2302
VORE KIRKEGAARDE; aarsskrift. 1923. a. Kr.70. Foreningen for Kirkegaardskultur, Eksp. Kirkevaenget 8, 2500 Valby, Denmark. illus.

381 US ISSN 0098-3322
YELLOW BOOK OF FUNERAL DIRECTORS & SERVICES. Cover title: National Yellow Book of Funeral Directors and Suppliers. 1974. a. $35 to non-advertisers. Nomis Publications Inc., Box 5122, Youngstown, OH 44514. TEL 216-788-9603. Ed. Chester E. Simon. adv. illus. circ. 23,000.

FURNITURE AND HOUSE FURNISHINGS

see *Interior Design and Decoration — Furniture and House Furnishings*

GARDENING AND HORTICULTURE

see also *Gardening and Horticulture — Florist Trade; Agriculture — Crop Production and Soil; Biology — Botany*

635 UK
A.G.S. GUIDES. irreg. price varies. (Alpine Garden Society) A.G.S. Publications Ltd., c/o D.K. Haselgrove, 282/286 Hoe St., Walthamstow, London E17 9QD, England. Ed. R.C. Elliott. illus. cum.index. circ. 9,500. (back issues avail.)

634 SA
A P G A ANNUAL/A P K V JAARBLAD. (Text in Afrikaans and English) a. Apricot, Peach and Pear Growers' Association, P.O. Box 414, Paarl 7620, Cape Province, South Africa. Ed. J.F. van den Berg. adv. circ. 2,000.

635 580.7 RM ISSN 0068-3329
ACTA BOTANICA HORTI BUCURESTIENSIS. (Text and summaries in English, French, German, and Rumanian) 1958. a. available on exchange. Universitatea Bucuresti, Gradina Botanica, Soseaua Cotroceni Nr. 32, 76258 Bucharest, Rumania. Indexed: Biol.Abstr.

635 NE ISSN 0567-7572
ACTA HORTICULTURAE. 1963. irreg., latest no. 182. price varies. International Society for Horticultural Science, De Dreyen 6, 6703 BC Wageningen, Netherlands. Indexed: Biol.Abstr. Chem.Abstr. Nutr.Abstr. Field Crop Abstr. Food Sci.& Tech.Abstr. Helminthol.Abstr. Hort.Abstr. Plant Breed.Abstr. Rev.Plant Path. Rural Recreat.Tour.Abstr. World Agri.Econ.& Rural Sociol.Abstr.

ADELAIDE BOTANIC GARDENS. JOURNAL. see *BIOLOGY — Botany*

635 PL ISSN 0137-1738
AKADEMIA ROLNICZA, POZNAN. ROCZNIKI. OGRODNICTWO. (Text in Polish; summaries in English and Russian) 1959. irreg. price varies. Akademia Rolnicza, Poznan, Ul. Wojska Polskiego 28, 60-637 Poznan, Poland. Indexed: Bibl.Agri.

ALABAMA AGRICULTURAL EXPERIMENT STATION. RESEARCH REPORT SERIES. see *AGRICULTURE*

ALLERTONIA; a series of occasional papers. see *BIOLOGY — Botany*

AMERICAN ASSOCIATION OF NURSERYMEN DIRECTORY FOR THE NURSERY INDUSTRY AND RELATED ASSOCIATIONS. see *AGRICULTURE*

635.9 US ISSN 0065-762X
AMERICAN CAMELLIA YEARBOOK. 1946. a. $7.50. American Camellia Society, Box 1217, Fort Valley, GA 31030. TEL 912-967-2358. Ed. Ann B. Brown. index. cum.index from 1946. circ. 5,200. Indexed: Hort.Abstr.
Camellias

635.9 US ISSN 0066-0000
AMERICAN ROSE ANNUAL. 1916. a. $9.50. American Rose Society, Inc., Box 30,000, Shreveport, LA 71130. Ed. Harold S. Goldstein. index. cum.index: 1916-41.
Roses

635 MX ISSN 0066-0116
AMERICAN SOCIETY FOR HORTICULTURAL SCIENCE. TROPICAL REGION. PROCEEDINGS OF THE ANNUAL MEETING.* (Text and summaries in English and Spanish) 1957. a. $5. American Society for Horticultural Science, 701 N. St. Asaph St., Alexandria, VA 22314. TEL 703-836-4606. Ed. Dr. C.E. Fernandez. index. cum.index: vols.1-12, 1957-68. cum.index. circ. 700. Indexed: Hort.Abstr. Trop.Abstr. Weed Abstr.
Formerly: American Society for Horticultural Science. Caribbean Region. Proceedings of the Annual Meeting.

635 FR
ANNUAIRE FEDERAL DE L'HORTICULTURE ET DES PEPINIERES. 1973. triennial, latest 1985. Federation Nationale des Producteurs de l'Horticulture et des Pepinieres, 19 bd. Magenta, 75010 Paris, France. adv. bk. rev. cum.index. circ. 6,000.
Formerly: Annuaire Professionnel de l'Horticulture et des Pepinieres (ISSN 0517-9130)

635 621.9 FR ISSN 0224-2478
ANNUAIRE REPERTOIRE DE LA MOTOCULTURE DE PLAISANCE JARDINAGE. 1979. biennial. 120 F. Societe SERS, Groupe SLOCAM, 83 rue de Villiers, 92200 Neuilly-sur-Seine, France. Ed. A. Magarian. adv. circ. 2,000.

BAILEYA; a journal of horticultural taxonomy. see *BIOLOGY — Botany*

635 BE ISSN 0303-903X
BELGIUM. RIJKSSTATION VOOR SIERPLANTENTEELT. MEDEDELINGEN. (Text in Dutch; summaries in English, French, and German) 1961. irreg. (1-3/yr.) 250 Fr. Rijksstation voor Sierplantenteelt, Caritasstraat 21, B-9230 Melle, Belgium. circ. 400. Indexed: Biol. & Agr.Ind. Hort.Abstr.

635 GW ISSN 0303-1241
BETRIEBS- UND MARKTWIRTSCHAFT IM GARTENBAU. 1974. irreg. price varies. Verlag Paul Parey (Berlin), Lindenstr. 44-47, 1000 Berlin 61, W. Germany (B.R.D.) bibl. illus. index. Indexed: Rural Recreat.Tour.Abstr. World Agri.Econ. & Rural Sociol.Abstr.

BETTER HOMES AND GARDENS HOME PLAN IDEAS. see *HOME ECONOMICS*

635 PL ISSN 0509-6839
BIULETYN WARZYWNICZY. (Supplement to: Bibliografia Publikacji Pracownikow Instytutu Warzywnictwa) (Text in Polish; summaries in English and Russian) 1953. irreg., no.27, 1984. 700 Zl. Instytut Warzywnictwa - Research Institute of Vegetable Crops, Ul. 22 Lipca 1/3, 96-100 Skierniewice, Poland. Ed. J. Skierkowski. charts. illus. cum.index. circ. 600. (tabloid format; also avail. in cards) Indexed: Biol.Abstr. Ref.Zh. Field Crop Abstr. Herb.Abstr. Hort.Abstr. Plant Breed.Abstr. Soils & Fert. Weed Abstr.

634 CN
BRITISH COLUMBIA FRUIT GROWERS ASSOCIATION. HORTICULTURAL FORUM PROCEEDINGS. 1969. a. British Columbia Fruit Growers Association, 1473 Water St., Kelowna, B.C. V1Y 7N6, Canada.
Formerly: British Columbia Fruit Growers Association. Horticultural Conference Proceedings (ISSN 0068-1555)

634 CN ISSN 0068-1563
BRITISH COLUMBIA FRUIT GROWERS ASSOCIATION. MINUTES OF THE PROCEEDINGS OF THE ANNUAL CONVENTION. 1890. a. British Columbia Fruit Growers Association, 1473 Water St., Kelowna, B.C. W1Y 7N6, Canada.

GARDENING AND HORTICULTURE

635 US
BROWN THUMBER'S HANDBOOK OF HOUSE PLANTS. 1977. a. $2. Snibbe Books, 1115 Ponce de Leon, Clearwater, FL 33516. TEL 813-586-1779. Ed. Gil Whitton. circ. 200,000.

635 630 SI
BULLETIN OF AGRI-HORTICULTURE. (Text in English and Chinese) 1965. irreg. Tri-Products Private Ltd., 33-A Phillip St., Singapore 0104, Singapore. Ed. Low Siew Liap. adv. circ. 5,000.

635.933 US ISSN 0008-204X
CAMELLIA JOURNAL. 1946. 4/yr. (plus Yearbook) $15.00. American Camellia Society, Box 1217, Fort Valley, GA 31030. TEL 912-967-2358. Ed. Ann B. Brown. adv. bk. rev. index. cum.index. circ. 5,000. Indexed: Hort.Abstr.
Camellias

635.9 CN ISSN 0319-1915
CANADIAN GLADIOLUS SOCIETY. ANNUAL. 1921. a. Can.$8. Canadian Gladiolus Society, 1274 129 A St., Ocean Park, B.C. V4A 3Y4, Canada. Ed. Grant Wilson. adv.
Gladiolus and Dahlias

635 CN ISSN 0828-8259
CANADIAN HISTORICAL HORTICULTURE/ HISTOIRE DE L'HORTICULTURE AU CANADA. (Text in English, French) 1985. irreg. Can.$14 per vol. to individuals; institutions Can.$18. Royal Botanical Gardens, P.O. Box 399, Hamilton, Ont. L8N 3H8, Canada. TEL 416-527-1158. Ed. Ina Vrugtman.

635 CN ISSN 0068-8908
CANADIAN HORTICULTURAL COUNCIL. ANNUAL MEETING REPORTS. 1922. a. Can.$40. Canadian Horticultural Council, 3 Amberwood Crescent, Nepean, Ont. K2E 7L1, Canada. TEL 613-226-4187.

635 CN ISSN 0068-8916
CANADIAN HORTICULTURAL COUNCIL. COMMITTEE ON HORTICULTURAL RESEARCH. ANNUAL REPORTS. 1963. a. Can.$40. Canadian Horticultural Council, 3 Amberwood Crescent, Nepean, Ont. K2E 7L1, Canada. TEL 613-226-4187. Eds. C.J. Bishop, D. Dempster.

635 CN
CANADIAN SOCIETY FOR HORTICULTURAL SCIENCE. NEWSLETTER. 1956. a. membership. Canadian Society for Horticultural Science, c/o T.H. Haliburton, Box 550, Nova Scotia Agricultural College, Plant Science Department, Truro, N.S. B2N 5E3, Canada. circ. 250.
Formerly: Canadian Society for Horticultutral Science. Journal (ISSN 0315-6877)

635 JA ISSN 0069-3227
CHIBA UNIVERSITY. FACULTY OF HORTICULTURE. TECHNICAL BULLETIN/ CHIBA DAIGAKU ENGEIGAKUBU GAKUJUTSU HOKOKU. (Text in Japanese; summaries and tables of contents in English) 1953. a. Chiba University, Faculty of Horticulture - Chiba Daigaku Engeigakubu, 648 Matsudo, Matsudo-shi, Chiba 271, Japan. circ. 750. Indexed: Biol.Abstr. Field Crop Abstr. Helminthol.Abstr. Herb.Abstr. Rev.Plant Path. Soils & Fert.

635.9 UK
CLASSIFIED DIRECTORY OF DAHLIAS AND GUIDE TO JUDGING. 1946. biennial. £1. National Dahlia Society, 26 Burns Rd., Lillington, Leamington Spa, Warwickshire, England. Ed. Philip Damp. adv. circ. 4,000.

COMMENTS FROM C A S T. (Council for Agricultural Sciences and Technology) see *AGRICULTURE*

635 AT ISSN 0069-7435
COMMONWEALTH SCIENTIFIC AND INDUSTRIAL RESEARCH ORGANISATION. DIVISION OF HORTICULTURAL RESEARCH. REPORT. 1962/63. biennial. free. ‡ C.S.I.R.O., Division of Horticultural Research, Box 350, G.P.O., Adelaide, S.A. 5001, Australia. Ed. R.A. Wren. circ. 3,000. Indexed: Biol.Abstr. Field Crop Abstr. Hort.Abstr. Herb.Abstr.

634 US
CORNELL RECOMMENDATIONS FOR COMMERCIAL TREE-FRUIT PRODUCTION. 1950. a. $2.50. ‡ New York State College of Agriculture and Life Sciences, Cornell University, Ithaca, NY 14853. circ. 4,000.
Formerly: Tree Fruit Production Recommendations (ISSN 0070-0118)

CRUCIFERAE NEWSLETTER. see *AGRICULTURE*

635 UK
DAFFODIL SOCIETY. JOURNAL. 1960. a. £1. ‡ Daffodil Society, c/o D.J. Pearce, 1, Noak's Cross, Cottages, Great Braxted, Witham, Essex, England. adv. stat. circ. controlled.
Daffodils

635.9 UK ISSN 0070-2544
DAFFODILS. 1913. a. £2.75. Royal Horticultural Society, Vincent Sq., London SW1P 2PE, England. (Co-sponsor: Daffodil Society) Ed. Elspeth Napier. circ. 1,000. Indexed: Rev.Plant Path.
Formerly: Daffodil and Tulip Year Book.
Daffodils

DAILY PLANET ALMANAC. see *ASTROLOGY*

635 UK
DELPHINIUM SOCIETY YEARBOOK. 1929. a. £1($2) ‡ Delphinium Society, 11 Long Grove, Seer Green, Beaconsfield, Bucks HP9 2YN, England. Ed. C.R. Edwards. adv. bk. rev. circ. 2,500.

635.9 US ISSN 0418-2057
DWARF IRIS SOCIETY PORTFOLIO.* 1952. a. $2. ‡ American Iris Society, Dwarf Iris Society, 6518 Beachy Ave., Wichita, KS 67206. TEL 316-686-8734. illus. circ. 300. (processed)

EAST MALLING RESEARCH STATION. ANNUAL REPORT. see *AGRICULTURE — Crop Production And Soil*

635 UK ISSN 0260-8081
FAIRFIELD EXPERIMENTAL HORTICULTURE STATION. SUMMARY ANNUAL REVIEW. 1980. a. Fairfield Experimental Horticulture Station, Greenhalgh, Kirkham, Lancs. PR4 3HH, England. illus.

FARMING UNCLE; periodical for natural people and mother nature lovers. see *AGRICULTURE*

635 UK
FINANCIAL RESULTS OF HORTICULTURAL HOLDINGS. a. University of Reading, Department of Agricultural Economics & Management, 4 Earley Gate, Whiteknights Rd., Reading RG5 3RG, England. Ed. J. Rendell. circ. 500. (back issues avail.)

FOLIA DENDROLOGICA. see *FORESTS AND FORESTRY*

635 DK ISSN 0106-2573
FORSKNINGSLABORATORIET FOR FRUGT OG GROENTINDUSTRI. AARSBERETNING. (Text in Danish) 1970. a. exchange basis. Ministry of Agriculture, Institut of Pomology, Kirstinebjergvej 12, DK-5792 Aarslev, Denmark. circ. 500.

635 UK ISSN 0071-9730
FUCHSIA ANNUAL. 1938. a. £1.75. British Fuchsia Society, 29 Princes Crescent, Dollar, Clackmannanshire, Scotland. Ed. G. Bartlett. adv. bk. rev. circ. 5,000.

635 GW ISSN 0301-2719
GAERTNERISCHE BERUFSPRAXIS. (Series A: Produktionsgartenbau; Series B: Landschafts- und Sportplatzbau) 1937. irreg. price varies. Verlag Paul Parey (Berlin), Lindenstr. 44-47, 1000 Berlin 61, W. Germany (B.R.D.) bibl. illus. index.

635 CN
GARDEN FAX. 1976. irreg. Department of Agriculture, Printmedia Branch, 7000 113th St., Edmonton, Alta. T6H 5T6, Canada. TEL 403-427-2121. illus. circ. controlled.

635.9 UK ISSN 0307-1243
GARDEN HISTORY. 1973. irreg. $30. Garden History Society, 5 The Knoll, Hereford HR1 1RU, England. Ed. Brent Elliott. bibl. illus. circ. 1,700. Indexed: Br.Tech.Ind. RILA.

635 US ISSN 0195-1386
GARDEN SUPPLY RETAILER GREEN BOOK. 1950. a. $10. ‡ Miller Publishing Co., 2501 Wayzata Blvd., Box 67, Minneapolis, MN 55440. TEL 612-374-5200. adv. bk. rev. index. circ. 43, 453(controlled) (also avail. in microfilm from UMI; reprint service avail. from UMI)
Formerly: Home & Garden Supply Merchandiser Green Book.

635 US ISSN 0270-3041
GARDENING. 1979. a. Conde Nast Publications, 350 Madison Ave., New York, NY 10017. TEL 212-880-8800.
Former titles (until 1981): House and Garden Gardening Guide (ISSN 0270-9899); Gardens (ISSN 0147-8591)

635 UK ISSN 0261-7951
GARDENING HANDBOOK. 1981. a. £5.95. Beacon Publications PLC, York House, Newton Close, Park Farm, Wellingborough, Northamptonshire NN8 3UW, England.

790 UK
GARDENS IN ENGLAND AND WALES. 1927. a. price varies. National Gardens Scheme Charitable Trust, 57 Lower Belgrave St., London SW1W 0LR, England. adv. index. circ. 100,000.
Former titles (until 1983): Gardens Open to the Public in England and Wales (ISSN 0141-2361); (until 1979): Gardens of England and Wales Open to the Public (ISSN 0072-0186)

635 UK ISSN 0436-0524
GLASSHOUSE CROPS RESEARCH INSTITUTE. ANNUAL REPORT. 1957. a. £5. Glasshouse Crops Research Institute, Worthing Rd., Littlehampton, West Sussex BN17 6LP, England. Eds. J.N. Davies, C.R. Worthing. index. circ. 1,350. Indexed: Biol.Abstr. Hort.Abstr.

635 IS
GREEN PAGES. a. Green Pages Ltd., P.O. Box 6092, Tel Aviv, Israel. TEL 03-263378.

712 DK ISSN 0108-4755
GROENT MILJOE. 1983. irreg. (approx 6/yr) Landsforeningen Danske Anlaegsgartnermestre, Linde Alle 16, 2720 Vanloese, Denmark. adv. bk. rev. circ. 6,000.
Formerly: Anlaegsgartneren.

635 GW ISSN 0072-7717
DER GROSSE GARTENKATALOG. 1970. a. DM.24.80. Fachschriften-Verlag GmbH, Hoehenstr. 17, Postfach 1329, 7012 Fellbach, W. Germany (B.R.D.)

635.9 UK
GROW DAHLIAS WITH US. 1976. irreg. £1. National Dahlia Society, 26 Burns Rd., Lillington, Leamington Spa, Warwickshire, England. Ed. Philip Damp.

635 UK ISSN 0440-5757
HEATHER SOCIETY. YEARBOOK. 1963. a. membership. Heather Society, 7 Rossley Close, Highcliffe, Christchurch, Dorset BH23 4RR, England. Ed. A.W. Jones. adv. bk. rev. bibl. illus. cum.index: 1963-1972. circ. 1,500.

635 US
HERBARIST. 1935. a. $5. Herb Society of America, Inc., 2 Independence Court, Concord, MA 01742. TEL 617-371-1486. Ed. Jeanne Bird. adv. bk. rev. illus. cum.index: 1934-1981. circ. 3,000. (back issues avail.)

635 AT
HORTICULTURAL GUIDE TO AUSTRALIAN PLANTS. 1975. a. Aus.$6. Society for Growing Australian Plants, Queensland Region, Box 809, Fortitude Valley, Qld. 4006, Australia.

635 NE ISSN 0441-7461
HORTICULTURAL RESEARCH INTERNATIONAL; directory of horticultural research institutes and their activities in 63 countries. irreg., latest 1986. fl.300. International Society for Horticultural Science, Distributor, Pudoc, Box 4, 6700 AA Wageningen, Netherlands.

635 US ISSN 0163-7851
HORTICULTURAL REVIEWS. 1979. a. $54.
(American Society for Horticultural Science) A V I
Publishing Company, 250 Post Rd. East, Box 831,
Westport, CT 06881. TEL 203-226-0738. Ed. Jules
Janick. Indexed: Biol.Abstr. Chem.Abstr.
Hort.Abstr. Rev.Plant Path. Soils & Fert.

635 ET
HORTICULTURAL SOCIETY OF ETHIOPIA.
BULLETIN. (Text in English) irreg. Horticultural
Society of Ethiopia, Box 1261, Addis Ababa,
Ethiopia.

635 382 UK ISSN 0264-1291
HORTICULTURAL TRADES ASSOCIATION
MEMBERS' REFERENCE BOOK. 1983. a.
Sterling Publications Ltd., 86-88 Edgware Rd.,
London, W2 2YW, England. adv. circ. 7,000.

635 II
INDIAN JOURNAL OF MUSHROOMS. 1973. a.
Rs.50($10) Indian Mushroom Growers Association,
Mushroom Research Laboratory, College of
Agriculture, Solan 173213, India. Ed. Dr. P.K. Seth.
circ. 300. (back issues avail.) Indexed: Rev.Plant
Path.

INSTITUTUL AGRONOMIC CLUJ-NAPOCA.
BULETINUL. SERIA AGRICULTURA. see
AGRICULTURE

635 RM ISSN 0379-8372
INSTITUTUL AGRONOMIC ION IONESCU DE
LA BRAD. LUCRARI STIINTIFICE. SERIA
HORTICULTURA. 1957. a. Institutul Agronomic
"Ion Ionescu de la Brad", Aleea M. Sadoveanu, nr.
3, Jassy, Rumania. Indexed: Biol.Abstr.
Chem.Abstr. Field Crop Abstr. Herb.Abstr.
Hort.Abstr. Plant Breed.Abstr.
  Supersedes in part: Institutul Agronomic Ion
Ionescu de la Brad. Lucrari Stiintifice. Seria
Agronomie-Horticultura (ISSN 0075-3505)

634 PL ISSN 0208-5925
INSTYTUT SADOWNICTWA I KWIACIARSTWA
W SKIERNIEWICACH. PRACE. SERIA B:
ROSLINY OZDOBNE. 1975. irreg. 450 Zl.($10)
Research Institute of Pomology and Floriculture -
Instytut Sadownictwa i Kwiaciarstwa, Ul.
Pomologiczna 18, 96-100 Skierniewice, Poland.

635 NE ISSN 0074-6231
INTERNATIONAL HORTICULTURAL
CONGRESS. PROCEEDINGS. 1899. quadrennial;
21st, 1982, Hamburg, West Germany. fl.70.
International Society for Horticultural Science, c/o
H.H. van der Borg, De Dreyen 6, 6703 BC
Wageningen, Netherlands. Indexed: Biol.Abstr.
Weed Abstr.
  Proceedings published by organizing committee

581 US
INTERNATIONAL PLANT PROPAGATORS'
SOCIETY. COMBINED PROCEEDINGS OF
ANNUAL MEETINGS. 1950. a. price varies.
International Plant Propagators' Society, Center for
Urban Horticulture, University of Washington, GF-
15, Seattle, WA 98195. TEL 209-543-8602. Ed.
Hudson T. Hartmann.

635 UK ISSN 0075-0700
IRIS YEAR BOOK. 1924. a. price varies. British Iris
Society, Haygarth, Cleeton St. Mary, Cleobury
Mortimer, Kidderminster DY14 0QU, England. Ed.
Mrs. J. Hewitt. adv. bk. rev. circ. 1,000.
  Irises

635 IS
ISRAEL INSTITUTE OF HORTICULTURE.
SCIENTIFIC ACTIVITIES. triennial. $6.
Agricultural Research Organization (Subsidiary of:
Scientific Publications) Volcani Centre, P.O. Box 6,
Bet-Dagan, Israel. Indexed: Biol.Abstr.

635.9 UK
JANUARY BULLETIN. a. £7($9) National Dahlia
Society, 26 Burns Rd., Lillington, Leamington Spa,
Warwickshire, England.

JARDIM BOTANICO DO RIO DE JANEIRO.
ARQUIVOS. see *BIOLOGY — Botany*

635.9 CN ISSN 0319-3098
JARDIN BOTANIQUE DE MONTREAL.
ANNUELLES ET LEGUMES: RESULTATS DES
CULTURES D'ESSAI. (Text in French) 1969. a.
free to botanical and horticultural institutions. Jardin
Botanique de Montreal, 4101 est, rue Sherbrooke,
Montreal, Que. H1X 2B2. TEL 514-872-1422. illus.
circ. 600.
  Formerly: Jardin Botanique de Montreal.
Annuelle (ISSN 0319-3101)

635 JA ISSN 0374-8731
KANAGAWA HORTICULTURAL EXPERIMENT
STATION. BULLETIN. (Text in Japanese;
summaries in English) 1952. a. free. Prefectural
Horticultural Experiment Sta., 1217 Ninomiya,
Ninomiya-machi, Kanagawa, Japan. Indexed:
Biol.Abstr. Hort.Abstr. Plant Brred.Abstr.

635.9 647 US ISSN 0023-9402
LAWN CARE. 1928. a. free. O. M. Scott & Sons
Company, Marysville, OH 43041. TEL 513-644-
0011. Ed. David J. Slaybaugh. charts. illus. circ. 2,
100,000.

635 330 US
LAWN CARE INDUSTRY SHOW EXTRA. a. free
to convention attendees. Harcourt Brace
Jovanovich, Inc., 7500 Old Oak Blvd., Cleveland,
OH 44130 TEL 216-243-8100. (Subscr. address: 1
E. First St., Duluth, MN 55802) Ed. Elliot Maras.
circ. 1,705.

635 NZ ISSN 0069-3820
LINCOLN COLLEGE. DEPARTMENT OF
HORTICULTURE. BULLETIN. 1967. irreg. price
varies. Lincoln College, Department of Horticulture,
Canterbury, New Zealand. circ. 2,750. Indexed:
Bibl.Agri. Hort.Abstr. Rural Recreat.Tour.Abstr.
World Agri.Econ. & Rural Sociol.Abstr.

LLEWELLYN'S MOON SIGN BOOK; gardening
guide and lunar almanac. see *ASTROLOGY*

LONGWOOD PROGRAM SEMINARS. see
BIOLOGY — Botany

635 UK
N.C.S. YEARBOOK. 1930. a. membership. National
Chrysanthemum Society, 2 Lucas House, Craven
Rd., Rugby, Warwickshire, England. Ed. H. Randall.
adv. circ. 6,000.
  Chrysanthemums

N T C WORKSHOP REPORT SERIES. (National
Turfgrass Council) see *BIOLOGY — Botany*

635 UK ISSN 0027-8726
NATIONAL AURICULA & PRIMULA SOCIETY
(NORTHERN) YEAR BOOK. 1872. a. $15. ‡
National Auricula & Primula Society, c/o J.J.
Wemyss-Cooke, Ed., Elphinhurst, 28 Millers Lane,
Atherton, Lancs. M29 9BW, England. adv. bk. rev.
illus. index. cum.index covering 3 yrs. circ. 500.
(back issues avail.)

635 UK ISSN 0077-4189
NATIONAL DAHLIA SOCIETY ANNUAL. a.
£7($9) ‡ National Dahlia Society, 26 Burns Rd.,
Lillington, Leamington Spa, England. Ed. Philip
Damp. adv. bk. rev. circ. 5,500.
  Dahlias

635 US
NATIONAL GARDENING SURVEY (YEAR); An
exclusive market research report for the lawn and
garden industry. 1977. a. $250. National Gardening
Association, 180 Flynn Ave., Burlington, VT 05401.
TEL 802-863-1308. Ed. Bruce W. Butterfield. circ.
500. (back issues avail.)
  Formerly: G F A/Gallup National Gardening
Survey (Year)

635 US ISSN 0077-5088
NATIONAL JUNIOR HORTICULTURAL
ASSOCIATION. NEWSLETTER. 1940. irreg. free.
National Junior Horticultural Association, 1847
Hess Lake Dr., Newago, MI 49337. TEL 616-652-
3270. Ed. Jan Hoffman. bk. rev. circ. 6,000.

635 016 US
NORTH AMERICAN HORTICULTURE: A
REFERENCE GUIDE. irreg. $45. American
Horticultural Society, Box 0105, Mount Vernon, VA
22121. TEL 703-768-5700.
  Formerly: Directory of American Horticulture
(ISSN 0417-5522)

635 UK
NORTHERN IRELAND. HORTICULTURAL
CENTRE. ANNUAL REPORT. 1950. a. free.
Department of Agriculture, Horticultural Centre,
Loughgall, Co. Armagh, N. Ireland. charts. illus.
circ. 900. (back issues avail.)

635 US
NORTHERN NUT GROWERS ASSOCIATION.
ANNUAL REPORT. 1911. a. $15 membership.
Northern Nut Growers Association, 13 Broken
Arrow Rd., Hamden, CT 06518. TEL 203-288-
1026. Ed. Dr. Jerry A. Payne. circ. 2,000. Indexed:
Hort.Abstr.

635 DK ISSN 0109-4262
ORGANISATIONER OG TAL I GARTNERIET.
(Supplement to: Gartner-Tidende) 1983. a. (included
in subscr. to: Gartner-Tidende) Dansk
Erhvervsgartnerforening, Postboks 3073, 1508
Copenhagen V, Denmark.
  Formerly: D E G.

635 UK ISSN 0267-1891
PELARGONIUM NEWS. 1967. 3/yr. (plus annual
year book) £3. British Pelargonium and Geranium
Society, 66 Sundridge Ave., Chislehurst, Kent BR7
5LU, England. Ed. Leslie A. Cross. adv. bk. rev.
illus. circ. 1,800.

635.9 US ISSN 0031-448X
PENNSYLVANIA FLOWER GROWERS.
BULLETIN. 1950. irreg. (approx. 8/yr.)
membership (non-members $20.) (Pennsylvania
Flower Growers) King Printing, 740 S. Atherton St.,
State College, PA 16801. Ed. Jay Holcomb. adv. bk.
rev. illus. index. cum.index for bulletins 1-150
published in 1963. circ. 650. (looseleaf format)
Indexed: Hort.Abstr. Soils & Fert.

PLANT PROTECTION SOCIETY OF THE
REPUBLIC OF CHINA. ANNUAL REPORT. see
AGRICULTURE — Crop Production And Soil

635 NE
PRODUKTSCHAP VOOR SIERGEWASSEN.
JAARVERSLAG/STATISTIEK. 1947. a. ‡
Produktschap voor Siergewassen, Bezuidenhoutse
Weg 153, Postbus 930 99, 2509 AB The Hague,
Netherlands. circ. 1,500.
  Formed by the merger of: Produktschap voor
Siergewassen. Jaarverslag (ISSN 0077-7609) &
Produktschap voor Siergewassen. Statistiek (ISSN
0556-543X)

635 UK ISSN 0080-441X
R.H.S. GARDENER'S DIARY. 1912. a. £2.65. Royal
Horticultural Society, Vincent Sq., London SW1P
2PE, England. circ. 66,000.

635.9 UK ISSN 0080-2891
RHODODENDRONS, WITH MAGNOLIAS AND
CAMELLIAS. 1946. a. £3.50. Royal Horticultural
Society, Vincent Sq., London SW1P 2PE, England.
Ed. Elspeth Napier. index. circ. 1,250.
  Formerly: Rhododendron and Camellia Yearbook.

635 US ISSN 0485-2044
RIO GRANDE VALLEY HORTICULTURAL
SOCIETY. JOURNAL. 1946. a. $10. Rio Grande
Valley Horticultural Society, Box 107, Weslaco, TX
78596. TEL 512-968-5000. Ed. Robert Leyden.
charts. illus. stat. index. cum.index: v.25, 1946-
1971. circ. 400. (back issues avail.) Indexed:
Biol.Abstr. Chem.Abstr. Nutr.Abstr. Hort.Abstr.
Soils & Fert.

580.744 CN ISSN 0072-9647
ROYAL BOTANICAL GARDENS, HAMILTON,
ONT. SPECIAL BULLETIN. 1947. a. free. Royal
Botanical Gardens, Box 399, Hamilton, Ont. L8N
3H8, Canada. TEL 416-527-1158. Ed. Hugh
Pearson. circ. 3,000. (back issues avail.)

ROYAL BOTANICAL GARDENS, HAMILTON,
ONT. TECHNICAL BULLETIN. see
BIOLOGY — Botany

635 NZ ISSN 0110-5760
ROYAL NEW ZEALAND INSTITUTE OF
HORTICULTURE. ANNUAL JOURNAL. 1973. a.
NZ.$8. Royal New Zealand Institute of
Horticulture, Box 12, Lincoln College, Canterbury,
New Zealand. Ed. Mike Oates. bk. rev. illus. circ.
500. Indexed: Hort.Abstr. Soils & Fert.
  Supersedes: Royal New Zealand Institute of
Horticulture. Journal (ISSN 0557-6601)

635 UK ISSN 0080-7737
SCIENTIFIC HORTICULTURE. 1932. a. £1.
(Horticultural Education Association) The
Canterbury Printers Ltd., 11 Best Ln., Canterbury,
Kent, England. Ed. Dr. W.M. Dullforce. bk. rev.
circ. 1,300. Indexed: Biol.Abstr. Excerp.Med.
ASCA. Field Crop Abstr. Helminthol.Abstr.
Herb.Abstr. Hort.Abstr. Plant Breed.Abstr.
Rev.Plant Path. Soils & Fert. VITIS.

635 JA ISSN 0037-4407
SHUBYO TO ENGEI. (Text in Japanese) 1947. a.
free. Tokita Seed Co. Ltd., 1069 Nakagawa, Omiya,
Saitama, Japan. Ed. Tsutomu Tokita. bk. rev. mkt.

635 US
SOCIETY FOR LOUISIANA IRISES. SPECIAL
PUBLICATIONS. 1952. irreg. $7.50. Society for
Louisiana Irises, Box 4-0175, U.S.L., Lafayette, LA
70504. TEL 318-235-8700. Ed. Marie Caillet. illus.
circ. 250.
  Irises

635 GW
TECHNISCHE UNIVERSITAET MUENCHEN.
INSTITUT FUER WIRTSCHAFTSLEHRE DES
GARTENBAUES. FORSCHUNGSBERICHTE
ZUR OEKONOMIE IN GARTENBAU. 1968.
irreg. Technische Universitaet Muenchen, Institut
fuer Wirtschaftslehre des Gartenbaues,
Weihenstephan, 8000 Munich, W. Germany
(B.R.D.)

635 US ISSN 0073-3075
U.S. DEPARTMENT OF AGRICULTURE. HOME
AND GARDEN BULLETIN. 1950. irreg. U.S.
Department of Agriculture, Washington, DC 20250.
TEL 202-655-4000. Indexed: Biol.Abstr.
Nutr.Abstr. Forest.Abstr.

635 CN ISSN 0042-3092
VEGETABLES NEWSLETTER. 1967. irreg.
Department of Agriculture & Rural Development,
Horticulture Division, Plant Industry Branch,
Fredericton, N.B., Canada. TEL 506-453-2666. Ed.
T.J. Johnson. bk. rev. circ. 200.

635 PL ISSN 0208-5747
WARSAW AGRICULTURAL UNIVERSITY. S G G
W-A R. ANNALS. HORTICULTURE. (Szkola
Glowna Gospodarstwa Wiejskiego-Akademia
Rolnicza) (Text mainly in English; occasionally in
French, German or Russian; summaries in Polish)
1957. irreg. $6 per no. Warsaw Agricultural
University Press, Ul. Nowoursynowska 166, 02-766
Warsaw, Poland (Dist. by: Ars Polona-Ruch,
Krakowskie Przedmiescie 7, 00-680 Warsaw,
Poland) Ed. J.R. Starck. Indexed: Hort.Abstr.
Weed Abstr.
  Formerly (until 1980): Akademia Rolnicza,
Warsaw. Zeszyty Naukowe. Ogrodnictwo (ISSN
0083-7288)

WEED CONTROL MANUAL AND HERBICIDE
GUIDE. see *AGRICULTURE — Crop Production
And Soil*

635 796.352 US
WEEDS TREES & TURF GOLF DAILY. a. Harcourt
Brace Jovanovich, Inc., 7500 Old Oak Blvd.,
Cleveland, OH 44130 TEL 216-243-8100. (Subscr.
address: 1 E. First St., Duluth, MN 55802) Ed.
Gerald Roche. circ. 5,732.

635 CN ISSN 0083-8810
WESTERN CANADIAN SOCIETY FOR
HORTICULTURE . REPORT OF
PROCEEDINGS OF ANNUAL MEETING. 1943.
a. Can.$30. ‡ Western Canadian Society for
Horticulture Inc., Plant Science Dept., University of
Manitoba, Winnipeg, Man. R3T 2N2, Canada. TEL
204-474-6095. circ. 300.

635 AT ISSN 0085-8382
YOUR AUSTRALIAN GARDEN. 1965. irreg.
Aus.$2.50 per no. ‡ David G. Stead Memorial
Wildlife Research Foundation of Australia, Box
4840, Sydney, N.S.W. 2001, Australia. Ed. Thistle
Y. Stead. bk. rev. circ. 3,000.

634 RH
ZIMBABWE. CENTRAL STATISTICAL OFFICE.
CENSUS OF REGISTERED DECIDUOUS
FRUIT GROWERS. a. Z.$20($.28) Central
Statistical Office, Box 8063, Causeway, Zimbabwe.
circ. 600. (looseleaf format; back issues avail.)

GARDENING AND HORTICULTURE — Abstracting, Bibliographies, Statistics

634 016 GW ISSN 0302-4601
AKTUELLE LITERATURINFORMATIONEN AUS
DEM OBSTBAU. (Text in German and English)
1972. irreg. free. Technische Universitaet Berlin,
Universitaetsbibliothek, Str. des 17. Juni 135, 1000
Berlin 12 (Charlottenburg), W. Germany (B.R.D.)
Ed. Gudrun Weiland. circ. 350. Indexed: VITIS.

338.1 635 CN ISSN 0318-5184
CANADA. STATISTICS CANADA. SURVEY OF
CANADIAN NURSERY TRADES INDUSTRY/
ENQUETE SUR L'INDUSTRIE DES
PEPINIERES CANADIENNES. (Catalogue 22-
203) (Text in English and French) 1919. a.
Can.$20($21) Statistics Canada, Communications
Division, 3rd Floor, R.H. Coats Bldg., Ottawa, Ont.
K1A 0T6, Canada TEL 613-993-7276. (Subscr. to:
Publications Sales and Services, Ottawa, Ont. K1A
0T6, Canada) (also avail. in microform from MML)

635 US
FARM AND GARDEN PERIODICALS ON
MICROFILM. 1978. a. Bell & Howell Microphoto,
Old Mansfield Rd., Wooster, OH 44691.

GERMANY (FEDERAL REPUBLIC, 1949-).
STATISTISCHES BUNDESAMT. FACHSERIE 3,
LAND- UND FORTWIRTSCHAFT, FISCHEREI;
REIHE 3: BODENNUETZUENG UND
PFLANZLICHE ERZEUGUNG. see
*AGRICULTURE — Abstracting, Bibliographies,
Statistics*

635 016 UK ISSN 0018-5280
HORTICULTURAL ABSTRACTS; compiled from
world literature and temperate and tropical fruits,
vegetables, ornaments, plantation crops. 1931. m.
£277($484) to non-members. C.A.B. International,
Bureau of Horticulture and Plantation Crops,
Farnham House, Farnham Royal, Slough SL2 3BN,
England. adv. bk. rev. abstr. index. cum.index:
vol.1-30 (1931-1960) (in 5 vols.) circ. 1,650. (also
avail. in microfiche; back issues avail.) Indexed:
Biol.Abstr. Nutr.Abstr. Forest.Abstr. Forest
Prod.Abstr. Helminthol.Abstr. Rev.Appl.Entomol.
VITIS.
●Also available online. Vendors: BRS, CISTI,
DIMDI, DIALOG, European Space Agency.

635 310 NE
LANDBOUW-ECONOMISCH INSTITUUT.
TUINBOUWCIJFERS. a. price varies. Landbouw-
Economisch Instituut, Conradkade 175, 2517 CL
The Hague, Netherlands.

631.53 016 UK ISSN 0032-0803
PLANT BREEDING ABSTRACTS. 1930. m.
£293($525) to non-members. C.A.B. International,
Bureau of Plant Breeding and Genetics, Farnham
House, Farnham Royal, Slough SL2 3BN, England
(U.S. subscr. to: C.A.B. International, North
American Office, 845 N. Park Ave., Tucson, AR
85719) adv. bk. rev. abstr. index. circ. 1,600.
Indexed: Biol.Abstr. Anim.Breed.Abstr.
Apic.Abstr. Field Crop Abstr. Forest.Abstr.
Helminthol.Abstr. Herb.Abstr. Rural
Recreat.Tour.Abstr. Rev.Plant Path. World
Agri.Econ. & Rural Sociol.Abstr.
●Also available online. Vendors: BRS, CISTI,
DIMDI, DIALOG, European Space Agency.

GARDENING AND HORTICULTURE — Florist Trade

EDGAR BROOKES ACADEMIC AND HUMAN
FREEDOM LECTURE. see *EDUCATION —
Higher Education*

635.9 US
FLORAL MARKETING DIRECTORY AND
BUYER'S GUIDE. 1975. a. $20. Produce
Marketing Association, 700 Barksdale Plaza,
Newark, DE 19711. TEL 302-738-7100. Ed. James
Johnson.

367 UK
GLADIOLUS ANNUAL. 1926. a. £4 to non-
members. British Gladiolus Society, 10 Sandbach
Rd., Thurlwood, Rode Heath, Stoke-on-Trent ST7
3RN, England. Ed. M.P. Jones. adv. circ. 500.
Indexed: Hort.Abstr.

635.9 UK
HARDY PLANT DIRECTORY. 1978. biennial. £3.
Hardy Plant Society, Nottingham Branch, The
Willows, 5 Rockley Ave., Radcliffe-on-Trent,
Nottingham NG12 2AR, England. Ed. Joan D.
Grout. index. circ. 3,000. (looseleaf format)

745.92 JA
TOKYO NO IKEBANA. (Text in Japanese) a. Tokyo-
to Kado Kyokai, c/o Shinkosha Bldg., 2-1-8 Koraku,
Bunkyo-ku, Tokyo, Japan. illus.
  Flower arrangement

WHO'S WHO IN FLORICULTURE. see
BIOGRAPHY

GASTROENTEROLOGY

see *Medical Sciences—Gastroenterology*

GENEALOGY AND HERALDRY

929 US
A F R A MEMBER DIRECTORY AND
ANCESTRAL SURNAME REGISTRY. 1984. a.
$3.95. American Family Records Association, 311
E. 12th St., Kansas City, MO 64106. TEL 816-453-
1294. Ed. Kermit B. Karns. circ. 300.

929.6 US ISSN 0892-4201
A M S STUDIES IN THE EMBLEM. 1987. irreg.
price varies. (Abrahams Magazine Service) A M S
Press, Inc., 56 E. 13th St., New York, NY 10003.
TEL 212-777-4700. Eds. Peter M. Daly, Daniel S.
Russell.

929 GT ISSN 0065-0463
ACADEMIA GUATEMALTECA DE ESTUDIOS
GENEALOGICOS, HERALDICOS E
HISTORICOS. REVISTA. (Text in Spanish) 1967.
irreg., no.9, 1987. price varies. Academia
Guatemalteca de Estudios Genealogicos, Heraldicos
e Historicos, 12 Calle 11-51, Zona 1, Guatemala
City, Guatemala. Ed. Ramiro Ordonez Jonama. circ.
400.

929 GW ISSN 0170-2653
AHNENLISTEN KARTEI. irreg. Verlag Degener,
Nuerenberger Str. 27, Postfach 1340, 8530
Neustadt-Aisch, W. Germany (B.R.D.)

929 CN
ALBERTA GENEALOGICAL SOCIETY.
ANCESTOR INDEX. 1975. a. Alberta
Genealogical Society, Box 12015, Edmonton, Alta.
T5J 3L2, Canada. Ed. J. Nuthack. circ. 200.
  Formerly: Alberta Genealogical Society.
Surnames Register (ISSN 0704-9145)

929 CN
AMIS DE L'HISTOIRE DE LA PERADE.
COLLECTION "NOS VIEILLES FAMILLES".
(Text in French) no.2, 1973. irreg. Can.$3.90. Amis
de l'Histoire de la Perade, Case Postale 157, Sainte-
Anne de la Perade, Que. G0X 2J0, Canada. illus.
circ. 1,000.

929 FR ISSN 0066-2569
ANNUAIRE DE LA NOBLESSE DE FRANCE ET
D'EUROPE. 1843. a. Nobiliaire, 120 Av. du Roule,
92200 Neuilly sur Seine, France. Eds. M. Martin, J.
Koenig.

ARCHAEOLOGIA. see *ARCHAEOLOGY*

ARMAS E TROFEUS; revista de historia, heraldica,
genealogia e arte. see *HISTORY — History Of
Europe*

GENEALOGY AND HERALDRY

929   US
ASHLEYS ADDENDA ANNUAL.* 1970. a. $5. Ashleys of America, Inc., 69 Knott Ave., Sandwich, MA 02563-1970. Ed. Robert E. Ashley. bk. rev. circ. 250.
     Former titles: Ashleys of America; Ashleys of America Quarterly (ISSN 0096-1469)

929   UK   ISSN 0261-8850
ASPECTS OF EDENBRIDGE. 1980. irreg. £0.95 per no. Edenbridge and District Historical Society, c/o J. Willsmer, Little Hatch, Crouch House Rd., Edenbridge TN8 5EL, England. illus. charts.

929   US
ASSOCIATION OF PROFESSIONAL GENEALOGISTS. LIST OF PROFESSIONAL GENEALOGISTS AND RELATED SERVICES. 1979. a. $4 to non-members. Association of Professional Genealogists, Box 11601, Salt Lake City, UT 84147. Ed. Johni Cerny. adv. circ. 600.
     Formerly: Directory of Professional Genealogists and Related Services (ISSN 0272-3387)

929   US
AUGUSTAN SOCIETY NEWSLETTER. irreg. membership. Augustan Society, Inc., Box P, Torrance, CA 90507. TEL 213-320-7766. Ed. Rodney Hartwell.

929   US
BARKER-JOSLYN FAMILY TREE CLIMBER. irreg. Jonathan Bacon, Ed. & Pub., 9615 England, Overland Park, KS 66212. TEL 913-383-9116. circ. 150.

929   US
BARRETT BRANCHES. 1982. irreg. $6 per no. McNeill Enterprises, c/o Ruby Simonson McNeill, Ed., N. 4015 Marguerite Rd., Spokane, WA 99212-1818. TEL 509-922-4521. adv. bk. rev. circ. 75. (back issues avail.)

929   US
BATEMAN DATUM. 1980. a. $3. Bateman Family Association, Box 211, Lebo Rt., West Plains, MO 65775. Ed. Mary Jo Burroughs. bk. rev. circ. 50.

929   US
BE-NE-LUX GENEALOGIST. 1977. irreg. $10. Augustan Society, Inc., Box P, Torrance, CA 90507. TEL 213-320-7766. bibl.

929   GW   ISSN 0067-5261
BEITRAEGE ZUR WESTFAELISCHEN FAMILIENFORSCHUNG. irreg. price varies. (Westfaelische Gesellschaft fuer Genealogie und Familienforschung) Aschendorffsche Verlagsbuchhandlung, Soester Str. 13, 4400 Muenster, W. Germany (B.R.D.) Ed. Werner Frese. bk. rev.

929   CN   ISSN 0707-820X
BLACKWELL NEWSLETTER. 1979. a. Can.$8.50($8.50) Cluny Press, P.O. Box 2207, Kingston, Ont. K7L 5J9, Canada. Ed. John D. Blackwell. adv. bk. rev. circ. 150. (back issues avail.)

929   US   ISSN 0733-6764
BORGO FAMILY HISTORIES. 1983. a. $19.95 (hardcover); $9.95 (paperback) per no. Borgo Press, Box 2845, San Bernardino, CA 92406. TEL 714-884-5813.

929   US
BRINGIN' HOME THE BACON. 1981. irreg. Jonathan Bacon Ed. & Pub., 9615 England, Overhead Park, KS 66212. TEL 913-383-9116. Ed. Jonathan Bacon. circ. 150.

928   UK
BURKE'S FAMILY INDEX. 1976. irreg. £8.50. Burke's Peerage Ltd., 56 Walton St., London SW1 1RB, England (Dist. in U.S. by: British Book Centre, Fairview Park, Elmsford, NY 10523) Ed. Hugh Montgomery-Massingberd.

929   UK
BURKE'S IRISH FAMILY RECORDS. 1976. irreg. £38($110) Burke's Peerage Ltd., 56 Walton St., London SW3 1RB, England (Dist. in U.S. by: British Book Centre, Fairview Park, Elmsford, N.Y. 10523) illus.

929   UK
BURKE'S ROYAL FAMILIES OF THE WORLD. VOL. 1; EUROPE AND LATIN AMERICA. 1977. irreg. £26. Burke's Peerage Ltd., 56 Walton St., London SW3 1RB, England.

929   UK
BURKE'S ROYAL FAMILIES OF THE WORLD. VOL. 2: AFRICA & THE MIDDLE EAST. 1979. irreg. £45. Burke's Peerage Ltd., 1 Hay Hill, London, W1X 7LF, England. Ed. H. Montgomery-Massingberd.

929   US   ISSN 0743-4235
BUTSON FAMILY NEWSLETTER. 1979. a. $5. c/o W. Wesley Johnston, Ed., 3140 Montevideo Dr., San Ramon, CA 94583-2630. TEL 415-829-2471. charts. circ. 300.

929   US
CAIN CONNECTIONS. 1982. irreg., vol.6, 1983. $6 per no. McNeill Enterprises, N. 4015 Marguerite Rd., Spokane, WA 99212. Ed. Ruby Simonson McNeill. circ. 50. (back issues avail.)

929   UK   ISSN 0260-8391
CARAHER FAMILY HISTORY SOCIETY. JOURNAL. (1985 issue title: Catalogue of Genealogical Research Sources, Ireland) 1980. a. £3.25. Caraher Family History Society, 71 King St., Crieff, Perthshire PH7 3HB, Scotland. Ed. Doreen Caraher-Manning. bk. rev. bibl. illus. index. circ. 150.

929   NE
CENTRAAL BUREAU VOOR GENEALOGIE. JAARBOEK. 1947. a. fl.45. Centraal Bureau voor Genealogie, Prins Willem-Alexanderhof 22, Postbus 11755, 2502 AT The Hague, Netherlands. illus. index. circ. 6,600.

929   AG
CENTRO DE ESTUDIOS GENEALOGICOS DE CORDOBA. BOLETIN. 1972. a. $7.50 per no. Centro de Estudios Genealogicos de Cordoba, Pasaje Arturo M. Bas 330, 5000 Cordoba, Argentina. Ed. Alejandro Moyano Aliaga. bk. rev. circ. 300.

929   US   ISSN 0197-0798
CHRISTIAN FAMILY CHRONICLES. 1979. irreg. $7.50. Agnes B. Pearlman, Ed. & Pub., 2001 N. Westwood Ave., Santa Ana, CA 92706. bk. rev. circ. X.

929   US
CURRENT GENEALOGICAL PUBLICATIONS. 1984. irreg. Claudette Maerz, Pub., Box 37010, Bloomington, MN 55431.

929   US
CURTIS LEGACY. 1983. a. National Association of the Curtis Family of America, 1661 Shadybrook Dr., Fullerton, CA 92631. TEL 714-870-9583. Ed. Paul Curtis. circ. 200.

929   920   UK
DEBRETT'S HANDBOOK.* Australian edition: Debrett's Handbook of Australia and New Zealand (ISSN 0728-8697) 1982. biennial. £39.95. Debrett's Peerage Ltd., 73-77 Britannia Rd., Fulham, London SW6 2JR, England. Ed. Lucinda de Laroque. circ. 6,000. (back issues avail.)

929   UK
DEBRETT'S PEERAGE & BARONETAGE.* 1976. irreg. £45. Debrett's Peerage Ltd., 73/77 Britannia Rd., Fulham, London SW6 2JR, England. Eds. Charles Kidd, David Williamson. adv.

929   US
DESCENDANTS OF JAMES BINGHAM OF COUNTY DOWN, NORTHERN IRELAND. NEWSLETTER. 1980. a. free. James Barry Bingham, Ed. & Pub., 2226 Kehrsglen Ct., Chesterfield, MO 63017. circ. 500. (looseleaf format)

929   US
DILLINGHAM FAMILY GENEALOGY EXCHANGE BULLETIN. 1981. a. $15. Margaret W. Haile, Ed. & Pub., 3053 Via Serena No. B, Laguna Hills, CA 92653-2717. Ed. Mrs. Margaret W. Haile. circ. 65.

929   US
DIRECTORY OF FAMILY 'ONE-NAME' PERIODICALS. 1983. a. $5. Summit Publications, Box 222, Munroe Falls, OH 44262. Ed. J. Konrad. circ. 1,000.

929   US
DIRECTORY OF GENEALOGICAL PERIODICALS. 1981. biennial. $5. Summit Publications, Box 222, Munroe Falls, OH 44262. Ed. J. Konrad. circ. 1,000.

929   US
EAST ASIAN GENEALOGIST. irreg. $10. Augustan Society, Inc., Box P, Torrance, CA 90507. TEL 213-320-7766.

929   US
EASTERN EUROPEAN GENEALOGIST. 1977. a. $10. Augustan Society, Inc., Box P, Torrance, CA 90507. TEL 213-320-7766. Ed. Rodney Hartwell.

929   GW   ISSN 0427-9522
FAMILIENGESCHICHTLICHE BLAETTER. 1903. irreg. Verein zur Foerderung der Zentralstelle fuer Deutsche Personen- und Familiengeschichte E.V., Archivstr. 12-14, D-1000 Berlin 33, W. Germany (B.R.D.) Ed. Rolf Koehler.
     Formerly: Verein zur Erhaltung der Zentralstelle fuer Deutsche Personen-und Familiengeschichte, Rundschrieben. Mitteilungen.

929   GW   ISSN 0430-0440
FAMILIENKUNDLICHES JAHRBUCH SCHLESWIG-HOLSTEIN. 1962. a. membership. Schleswig-Holsteinische Gesellschaft fuer Familienforschung und Wappenkunde e.V., Gartenstr. 12, D-2300 Kiel, W. Germany (B.R.D.) Ed. Friedrich Schmidt-Sibeth. circ. 550. (back issues avail.)

929   GW   ISSN 0014-7176
FAMILIENVERBAND AVENARIUS. FAMILIENZEITSCHRIFT. 1961. irreg. DM.25. Familienverband Avenarius e.V., Eschersheimer Landstr. 460, 6000 Frankfurt/Main 50, W. Germany (B.R.D.) Ed. Gert Avenarius. charts. illus. stat. circ. 200. (tabloid format)

929   US
FAMILY ASSOCIATIONS, SOCIETIES & REUNIONS. 1981. a. $6. Summit Publications, Box 222, Munroe Falls, OH 44262. Ed. J. Konrad.

929   CN   ISSN 0227-0994
FAMILY GENEALOGIES. 1981. irreg. Can.$5 per no. Highland Heritage, RR 1, Lancaster, Ont. K0C 1N0, Canada. Ed. 613-347-2363. circ. 325.

929   GW
FAMILY NOTES: A JOURNAL OF THE HUECK FAMILIES. 1968. a. $10 to libraries. ‡ Hueck Family Association, 4030 Ratingen-Hosel, Am Rennbaum 14, Germany (B.R.D.) Ed. Edward Hueck. circ. 200.

929   AT   ISSN 0157-8804
FITZHARDINGE'S NOBILIARY; information concerning the gentry and nobility. 1980. quadrennial. $38. C.D. FitzHardinge-Bailey, 15 Dutton St., Bankstown, NSW 2200, Australia. Ed. Charles Bailey. adv. bk. rev. circ. 2,000. (back issues avail.)

929   US
FLOWER OF THE FOREST BLACK GENEALOGICAL JOURNAL. 1982. a. $5. Mullac Publishing, 822 Bonaparte Ave., Baltimore, MD 21218. TEL 301-235-6697. Ed. Agnes Kane Callum. adv. bk. rev. circ. 300. (back issues avail.)

929   US   ISSN 0071-7738
FORT BELKNAP GENEALOGICAL ASSOCIATION. BULLETIN. 1962. a. $2. ‡ Fort Belknap Genealogical Association, Murray Rte., Graham, TX 76046. TEL 817-549-1856. Ed. Barbara Ledbetter. circ. 100.

929   US   ISSN 0887-6320
FRARY FAMILY JOURNAL. 1970. a. membership. Frary Family Association, 12 Lohmann Place, Dumont, NJ 07628. Ed. Grace L. Frary. circ. 1,000.

GENEALOGY AND HERALDRY

929 US
FREELAND AND ALLIED FAMILIES. 1971. a. $3.50 per issue. Freeland Family Association, 220 4 St., Del Mar, CA 92014. TEL 619-755-1284. Ed. Bernard French Freeland. bibl. charts. illus. circ. 300.
Formerly: Freeland Quarterly and Allied Families.

929 US
FREEMAN FOOTNOTES. 1983. irreg. $6 per no. McNeill Enterprises, N. 4015 Marguerite Rd., Spokane, WA 99212. Ed. Ruby Simonson McNeill. (back issues avail.)

929 US
FRENCH GENEALOGIST. 1977. irreg. $10. Augustan Society, Inc., Box P, Torrance, CA 90507. TEL 213-320-7766. Ed. Baron Roland De Vigier.

929 US
FRITTS/FRITZ FAMILY NEWSLETTER. 1981. a. $2. Fritts Cousins, c/o Gregory & Patti Fritts, Eds., 2838 Meadowwood Dr., Toledo, OH 43606. TEL 419-535-8675. circ. 1,200.

929 NE
FRYSKE NAMMEN. (Text in Frisian) 1978. a. Fryske Akademy, Doelestrjitte 8, 8911 DX Ljouwert/Leeuwarden, Netherlands. Ed.Bd.

929 AT
GENEALOGICAL RESEARCH DIRECTORY. 1981. a. Aus.$19.25. c/o K. Johnson, 17 Mitchell St., North Sydney, NSW 2060, Australia (U.S. subscr. to: N. Schreiner Yantis, 6818 Lois Dr., Springfield, VA 22150, U.S.A.) Eds. K.A. Johnson, M.R. Sainty. adv. bk. rev. circ. 10,000. (back issues avail.)

929 GW ISSN 0085-0934
GENEALOGISCHES HANDBUCH DES BAYERISCHEN ADELS. 1950. biennial. DM.96. (Vereinigung des Adels in Bayern) Verlag Degener und Co., Nuernberger Str. 27, Postfach 1340, 8530 Neustadt /Aisch, W. Germany (B.R.D.)

929 GW ISSN 0514-3292
GENEALOGISCHES JAHRBUCH. 1961. a. (Zentralstelle fuer Personen und Familiengeschichte) Verlag Degener, Nuernberger Str. 27, Postfach 1340, 8530 Neustadt-Aisch, W. Germany (B.R.D.)

929 NE
GENEALOGYSK JIERBOEKJE. (Text in Dutch and Frisian) 1951. a. Fryske Akademy, Doelestrjitte 8, 8911 DX Ljouwert/Leeuwarden, Netherlands. TEL 058-131414.

929 US
GEST-GUEST QUARTERLY. 1982. irreg. (approx. 3/yr.) $9 (for 2 yrs.) 2503 Blue Willow, Houston, TX 77042. Ed. Henry G. Guest, Jr. circ. 200.

929 UK ISSN 0141-8009
GLASGOW & WEST OF SCOTLAND FAMILY HISTORY SOCIETY. NEWSLETTER. 1978. irreg. membership. Glasgow & West of Scotland Family History Society, 5 Laburnum Grove, Kirkintilloch, Glasgow G66 4DF, Scotland. Ed. Hazel M. Wright. adv. bk. rev. circ. 600(controlled)

GREENBRIER HISTORICAL SOCIETY. JOURNAL. see *HISTORY — History Of North And South America*

929 US
GRISWOLD FAMILY OF ENGLAND & AMERICA. 1983. irreg., vol.7, 1983. $45. Griswold Family Association, Inc., c/o Esther L. French, RD Box 139, Chatham, NY 12037. Eds. Charles and Edna Townsend.

929 UK ISSN 0262-4672
GWENT FAMILY HISTORY SOCIETY. JOURNAL. 1981. irreg. membership. Gwent Family History Society, c/o Bernard W.W. Short, 18 Greenway Drive, Griffithstown, Pontypool, Gwent NP4 5AZ, Wales. Ed. W.M. Thomas. adv. bk. rev. circ. 450.

929 AU ISSN 0073-1897
HERALDISCH-GENEALOGISCHE GESELLSCHAFT ADLER. JAHRBUCH. 1874. irreg., 3rd series, vol.11, 1982/83. S.430. Heraldisch-Genealogische Gesellschaft Adler, Haarhof 4a, A-1010 Vienna, Austria.

929 DK ISSN 0109-3061
HERALDISKE STUDIER. 1985. a. Kr.75. (Societas Heraldica Scandinavica) Bibliotekscentralen, Telegrafvej 5, DK-2750 Ballerup, Denmark.

929 CN ISSN 0707-2554
HIGHLAND HERITAGE. 1979. irreg. R.R. 1, Lancaster, Ont. K0C 1N0, Canada. Ed. Alex W. Fraser. adv.

929 CN ISSN 0828-4466
HILBORN'S FAMILY NEWSLETTER DIRECTORY. 1980. irreg. Can.$9.95($9.95) Hilborn Media, 42 Sources Blvd. No. 29, Pointe Claire, Quebec H9S 2H9, Canada. TEL 514-695-2515. Ed. Robin R. Hilborn. bk. rev. illus. circ. 200.
Formerly: Family Newsletter Directory (ISSN 0227-5317)

HISTORISCHER VEREIN DES KANTONS BERN. ARCHIV. see *HISTORY — History Of Europe*

929 US
HOUSER HUNTERS: FAMILY OF CHARLES FRANKLIN HOUSER. 1982. a. free. Houser Enterprises, 6412 N. University Dr., Ste. 312, Lauderdale, FL 33321-4019. TEL 305-721-0045. Ed. E.A. Houser, Jr. circ. 100. (back issues avail.)

HUGUENOT SOCIETY OF LONDON. PROCEEDINGS. see *HISTORY — History Of Europe*

HUGUENOT SOCIETY OF LONDON. QUARTO SERIES. see *HISTORY — History Of Europe*

929 UK
I'ANSON TIMES. 1976. irreg. membership. c/o Thomas Henry Wolstencroft, 29 Meadowfield, Whaley Bridge, Stockport, Cheshire (England)

929 US
IN SEARCH OF THE GUIBORD-CHOPP FAMILY. irreg. Jonathan Bacon, Ed. & Pub., 9615 England, Overland Park, KS 66212. TEL 913-383-9116. circ. 150.

929 US ISSN 0090-905X
IOWA GENEALOGICAL SOCIETY. SURNAME INDEX. 1973. irreg. price varies. Iowa Genealogical Society, Box 7735, Des Moines, IA 50322. TEL 515-276-0287. illus. circ. 1,200.

929 US ISSN 0272-1015
IRISH-AMERICAN GENEALOGIST. 1974. a. $10. Augustan Society Inc., Box P, Torrance, CA 90507. TEL 213-320-7766. illus. Indexed: Geneal.Per.Ind.
Formerly: Irish Genealogical Helper (ISSN 0360-4519)

929 US
ITALIAN GENEALOGIST. 1977. a. $10. Augustan Society, Inc., Box P, Torrance, CA 90507. TEL 213-320-7766. Rev. L.W. Casati III.

929 DK ISSN 0105-8647
JEG ARBEJDER MED; Dansk Slaegtsforskerfortegnelse. 1978. a. Kr.20. Dansk Historisk Haandbogsforlag, Klintevej 25, DK-2800 Lyngby, Denmark. Eds. Henning Jensen, Ebba Thorkelin. adv. bk. rev. circ. 2,400.

929 US
JOURNAL OF ANCIENT AND MEDIEVAL STUDIES. 1982. a. $25. Octavian Society, 1617 W. 261 St., Harbor City, CA 90710. TEL 213-326-8603. Ed. Sir Rodney Hartwell. bk. rev. circ. 200.
Formerly: Societas Gaius Julius Caesar Octavianus. Newsletter.

929 NE
KONINKLIJK NEDERLANDSCH GENOOTSCHAP VOOR GESLACHT- EN WAPENKUNDE. WERKEN UITGEGEVEN. 1974. a. price varies. (Koninklijk Nederlandsch Genootschap voor Geslacht- en Wapenkunde) Walburg Pers, Zaadmarkt 84a-86, Box 222, 7200 AE Zutphen, Netherlands. TEL 05750-10522.

929 DK ISSN 0108-5190
KONTAKT;* blade af slaegtens historie. 1977. irreg. (1-2/yr.) membership. Kaerbyholmslaegten, Hejrevej 38, 2400 Copenhagen NV, Denmark. illus.

LEICESTERSHIRE HISTORIAN. see *HISTORY*

929 US
LIPSCOMB NEWSLETTER. 1981. a. $5. Phillip Heritage House, 605 Benton Ave., Missoula, MT 59801. TEL 406-543-3495.

929 US
LITTELL'S LIVING AGE. 1972. a. $7.50. Littell Families of America, Inc., 1219 Katcalani Ave., Sebring, FL 33870. Ed. N.K. Littell. bk. rev. circ. 500.

929 US
MCNEILL MEMORANDA. 1983. irreg. $6 per no. McNeill Enterprises, N. 4015 Marguerite Rd., Spokane, WA 99212. TEL 509-922-4521. Ed. Ruby Simonson McNeill. bk. rev. circ. 50. (back issues avail.)

929 US ISSN 0732-3395
MEYER'S DIRECTORY OF GENEALOGICAL SOCIETIES IN THE U S A & CANADA. 1976. biennial. $19. Libra Publications, 5179 Perry Rd., Mt. Airy, MD 21771. TEL 301-875-2824. Ed. Mary K. Meyer. adv. circ. 1,500.
Formerly: Directory of Genealogical Societies in the U S A & Canada.

929 CN
MISSISQUOI HISTORICAL SOCIETY REPORTS. (Text in English and French) 1960. a. Can.$15. Missisquoi Historical Society, 2 River St., Stanbridge East, PQ J0J 2H0, Canada. TEL 514-248-3153. Ed. Paige A. Knight. circ. 750.

929 UK
MOOT: THIRKILL - THRELKELD FAMILY NEWSLETTER. 1973. irreg., (approx. a.) latest 1985. $6 per issue. c/o Eunice Wilson, Ed., 143 Harbord St., London SW6 6PN, England. bk. rev.
Formerly: Moot.

929 US
N S U LIBRARY. GENEALOGY SERIES. 1979. irreg. $15. Nicholls State University, Library, Box 2028, Thibodaux, LA 70310.

929 NE
NEDERLAND'S ADELSBOEK. a. Centraal Bureau voor Genealogie, Prins Willem-Alexanderhof 22, P.O. Box 11755, 2502 AT The Hague, Netherlands. illus. index.

929 NE
NEDERLAND'S PATRICIAAT. 1910. a. Centraal Bureau voor Genealogie, Prins Willem Alexanderhof 22, Postbus 11755, 2502 AT The Hague, Netherlands. illus. cum.index.

929 NE
NEDERLANDS REPERTORIUM VAN FAMILIENAMEN. 1963. a. price varies. (Koninklijke Nederlandse Academie van Wetenschappen) Walburg Pers, Zaadmarkt 84a-86, Box 222, 7200 AE Zutphen, Netherlands. TEL 05750-10522.

929 UK ISSN 0260-695X
NEWTH-NUTH FAMILY HISTORY SOCIETY. NEWSLETTER. 1979. irreg., (approx. a.) membership. Newth-Nuth Family History Society, c/o Mrs. Janet D. Nuth, Ed., 27 Charville Lane, Hayes, Middlesex, England.
Formerly (until 1980): Newth Nuth News.

929 NE
NIET ZO BENAUWD. (Summaries in English) 1959. a. fl.10($5) ‡ Stichting Familieclub Johannes van der Linden - Foundation Family Club Johannes van der Linden, c/o M.E. Leegwater-van der Linden, Salomeschouw 61, 2726 JP Zoetermeer, Netherlands. Ed. M.E. Leegwater-van der Linden. adv. illus. circ. 150 (controlled) (processed)

929 NR
NIGERIAN NAMES. 1972. irreg. Daystar Press, Box 1261, Ibadan, Nigeria.

929 DK
NORDISK FLAGGSKRIFT. no.2, 1976. irreg. C. F. Pederson, Listedvej 84, Kastrup, Denmark.

929 UK
NORTH WEST SOCIETIES. COMBINED
REGISTER OF MEMBERS' INTERESTS. 1977.
irreg., (approx. every 2-3 yrs.) £0.60 to non-
members. Lancashire Family History and Heraldry
Society, c/o A.A. Todd, 78 Albert St., Ramsbottom,
Bury, Lancs BL0 9EL, England. (Co-sponsors:
Family History Society of Cheshire; North Cheshire
Family History Society; Liverpool Family History
Society) bk. rev. circ. 2,000.
 Formerly (until 1981): Inquisition (ISSN 0144-
7211)

929 US ISSN 0882-1933
OLSCHWANGER JOURNAL. 1983. a. $15. Anna
Olswanger, Ed.& Pub., 177 North Highland, Rm.
909, Memphis, TN 38111. TEL 901-327-4341. circ.
250.

929 US ISSN 0890-2364
OSWALD OUTLINES. 1984. irreg. $6. Family Quest,
2204 W. Houston, Spokane, WA 99208. TEL 509-
326-2089. Ed. Donna Potter Phillips. bk. rev. circ.
25. (looseleaf format; back issues avail.)

PANORAMA. see HISTORY — History Of Europe

929 BE
PARCHEMIN. RECUEIL GENEALOGIQUE ET
HERALDIQUE. 1952. a. price varies. Office
Genealogique et Heraldique de Belgique, c/o
Musees Royaux d'Art et d'Histoire, Parc du
Cinquantenaire 10, B-1040 Brussels, Belgium. Ed.
Patrick d'Hose. charts. illus. index. cum.index:
1952-1960; 1961-1973; 1973-1980. circ. 1,000.
Indexed: Numis.Llt.

929 US
PETER WILLCOCKS SOCIETY. JOURNAL. 1973.
a. $25. Laird Wilcox, Box 2047, Olathe, KS 66061.
circ. 50. (looseleaf format; also avail. in microfilm)

929 US ISSN 0734-2055
RAINEY TIMES. 1981. a. $16. Rt. 4, Box 62 St.,
Sulphur Springs, TX 75482. TEL 214-885-3523. Ed.
Marynell Bryant. adv. index. circ. 300. (back issues
avail.)

929.6 US
ROLL OF ARMS. 1928. irreg. $12.50. New England
Historic Genealogical Society, Committee on
Heraldry, 101 Newbury St., Boston, MA 02116.
illus.

929 UK
RUVIGNY'S TITLED NOBILITY OF EUROPE.
1910. irreg. £45. Burke's Peerage Ltd., 1 Hay Hill,
London W1X 7LF, England.

929 SZ
SCHWEIZER FAMILIENFORSCHER. (Text in
French and German) 1934. irreg. (Schweizerischen
Gesellschaft fuer Familienforschung) H.G. Kutter,
Feldeggstr. 58, 8008 Zurich, Switzerland. bk. rev.

929 UK ISSN 0141-6405
SCOLTOCK FAMILY BULLETIN. 1971. irreg.
(approx. 6/yr.) £2($4) J.K. Scoltock, Ed. & Pub., 43
Peacroft Lane, Hilton, Derby, England. circ. 100.

929 US ISSN 0271-5031
SCOTTISH-AMERICAN GENEALOGIST. a. $10.
Augustan Society Inc., Box P, Torrance, CA 90507.
TEL 213-320-7766. Ed. Scott R. Macmillan. illus.
Indexed: Geneal.Per.Ind.
 Formerly: Scottish Genealogical Helper (ISSN
0360-4500)

929 US ISSN 8755-0547
SHERBONDY BEACON. 1984. a. membership.
Sherbondy Family Association, 6509 W. 102nd St.,
Overland Park, KS 66212-1723. Ed. Jeffrey D.
Sherbondy. circ. 100. (back issues avail.)

929 US
SIMONSON MISCELLANEOUS RESEARCH
DATA. 1978. irreg. price varies. McNeill
Enterprises, N. 4015 Marguerite Rd., Spokane, WA
99212. Ruby Simonson McNeill. circ. 50. (back
issues avail.)

929 DK ISSN 0108-3880
SLAEGTEN FISKER; aarsskrift. 1973. a. membership.
(Slaegten Fisker Forening) Anders Fisker,
Moellegaardsvej 15, Resenbro, 8600 Silkeborg,
Denmark. illus.

929 DK ISSN 0107-1971
SLAEGTSBLADET. 1929. irreg. membership.
Slaegtsforeningen Muenster-Mynster, c/o Karl Erik
Mynster, Arnegaards Alle 4, 2840 Holte, Denmark.
Ed. Karl Erik Mynster. circ. 90.

929 FI
SLAEKT OCH BYGD. (Text in Swedish) 1957. a.
Slaektforskarforeningen i Jakobstad,
Pedersesplanaden 7B, 68600 Jakobstad, Finland.
circ. 500.

929 970 US
SONS AND DAUGHTERS OF THE SODDIES.
REPORTS;* sod houses and dugouts in North
America. 1955. irreg. (1-2/yr.) $2 (2 yrs) Sod House
Society of America, Sod House Survey, Colby, KS
67701. TEL 913-462-2021. illus. stat. tr.lit. circ.
10,000. (processed)

929 US
SPANISH-AMERICAN GENEALOGIST. a. $10.
Augustan Society Inc., Box P, Torrance, CA 90507.
TEL 213-320-7766. Eds. Rudecinda Lo Buglio,
Rodney Hartwell. illus. Indexed: Geneal.Per.Ind.
 Formerly: Spanish Genealogical Helper.

929 US
STAFFORD DATA. 1982. irreg. $6 per no. McNeill
Enterprises, N. 4015 Marguerite Rd., Spokane, WA
99212. Ed. Ruby Simonson McNeill. circ. 50. (back
issues avail.)

929 UK ISSN 0143-8859
STRAYS. 1979. irreg. Cumbria Family History
Society, c/o Mrs. M.M. Russell, 32 Granada Rd.,
Denton, Manchester M38 2LJ, England.

929 301 SW ISSN 0280-8633
STUDIA ANTHROPONYMICA SCANDINAVICA;
tidskrift foer nordisk personnamnsforskning. (Text in
English, German, Scandinavian languages) 1983. a.
Kr.65. (Studia Anthroponymica Scandinavica)
Almqvist & Wiksell International, Sankt
Johannesgatan 11, S-752 21 Uppsala, Sweden
(Subscr. to: Almqvist & Wiksell International, Box
451 50, S-104 30 Stockholm) Eds. Thorsten
Andersson, Lena Peterson. bk. rev. charts. illus.
circ. 400. (back issues avail.)

929 UK
SUSSEX GENEALOGICAL CENTRE.
OCCASIONAL PAPERS. 1979. irreg. £4. Sussex
Genealogical Centre, 105 Springett Ave., Ringmer,
Lewes, East Sussex BN8 5QS, England. adv. bk.
rev. circ. 1,000.

929 UK
TABARD. 1977. irreg. Bath Heraldic Society, 5
Bloomfield Ave., Bath BA2 3AB, England.

929 US
TALBOTT TREE. 1982. irreg. $6 per no. McNeill
Enterprises, c/o Ruby Simonson McNeill, Ed., N.
4015 Marguerite Rd., Spokane, WA 99212-1818.
TEL 509-922-4521. bk. rev. circ. 80. (back issues
avail.)

929 296 US ISSN 0146-9568
TOLEDOT; the journal of Jewish genealogy. 1977.
irreg. $10. Toledot Press, 155 E. 93rd St., Ste. 3C,
New York, NY 10128. TEL 212-427-5395. Ed.
Steven W. Siegel. adv. bk. rev. circ. 1,200. Indexed:
Amer.Bibl.Slavic & E.Eur.Stud. Geneal. Per. Ind.

929.2 US ISSN 0098-8960
UPSHAW FAMILY JOURNAL. 1974. irreg., vol.8,
no.2, 1981. $10. Upshaw Family Association of
America, c/o Ted O. Brooke, Ed., 79 Wagonwheel
Ct., N.E., Marietta, GA 30067. bk. rev. index. circ.
60. (back issues avail.)

929 GW
WESTDEUTSCHE GESELLSCHAFT FUER
FAMILIEKUNDE. MITTEILUNGEN. 1913. irreg.
(Westdeutsche Gesellschaft fuer Familiekunde)
Degener Verlag, Postfach 1340, 8530 Neustadt-
Aisch, W. Germany (B.R.D.)

WHITE COUNTY HERITAGE. see HISTORY —
History Of North And South America

929 US
WIGFIELD NEWSLETTER. 1971. a. $5. Phillip
Heritage House, 605 Benton Ave., Missoula, MT
59801. TEL 406-543-3495. abstr. bibl. charts.
illus. stats. tr.lit. (looseleaf format; back issues
avail.)

929 US
WILEY WORLD. 1985. a. $6 per no. McNeill
Enterprises, N. 4015 Marguerite Rd., Spokane, WA
99212-1818. Ed. Ruby Simonson McNeill. bk. rev.
(back issues avail.)

929 UK
YORKSHIRE ARCHAEOLOGICAL SOCIETY
PARISH REGISTER SERIES. 1899. a. £10.
Yorkshire Archaeological Society, Claremont, 23
Clarendon Rd., Leeds LS2 9NZ, England. Ed.
J.T.M. Nussey. index. circ. 300.

GENEALOGY AND HERALDRY —
Abstracting, Bibliographies, Statistics

929 US
GENEALOGICAL ABSTRACTS; the genealogical
serial published for H.O.T.9 Clearinghouse. 1983.
irreg. $9.90 per vol. Barbara G. Holley, Ed.& Pub.,
Box 3014, Silver City, NM 88062. adv. bk. rev.
circ. 150.
 Formerly: Genealogical Abstracter.

929 US
GENEALOGICAL PERIODICAL ANNUAL
INDEX; key to the genealogical literature. 1962. a.
$17.50. Heritage Books, Inc., 3602 Maureen Ln.,
Bowie, MD 20715. TEL 301-464-1159. Ed. Laird
C. Towle. circ. 1,000. (back issues avail.)

GENERAL INTEREST
PERIODICALS — Africa

see also General Interest
 Periodicals—Libya; General Interest
 Periodicals—Sudan; General Interest
 Periodicals—Tanzania; General Interest
 Periodicals—Zambia

BIBLIOGRAPHIE DES TRAVAUX EN LANGUE
FRANCAISE SUR L'AFRIQUE AU SUD DU
SAHARA, SCIENCES HUMAINES ET
SOCIALES. see SOCIAL SCIENCES:
COMPREHENSIVE WORKS — Abstracting,
Bibliographies, Statistics

960 PL
INFORMATORY REGIONALNE. 1968. irreg.
Uniwersytet Warszawski, Instytut Geograffi Krajow
Rozwijajacych sie, Al. Zwirki i Wigury 93, 00-089
Warsaw, Poland. Ed. Zygmunt Komorowski.

960 PL
PRZEGLAD INFORMACJI; AFRYKA, AZJA,
AMERYKA LACINSKA. 1972. irreg. 80 Zl.
Uniwersytet Warszawski, Instytut Krajow
Rozwijajacychsie, Al. Zwirki i Wigury 93, 02-089
Warsaw, Poland (Dist. by: Ars Polona-Ruch,
Krakowskie Przedmiescie 7, Warsaw, Poland) Ed.
Magdalena Kenig. bk. rev. circ. 500. Indexed:
Curr.Cont.Africa.
 Formerly: Przeglad Informacji o Afryce.

GENERAL INTEREST
PERIODICALS — Argentina

056.1 AG
BIBLIOTECA CULTURA POPULAR. 1984. irreg.
Ediciones del Sol, S.A., Alsina 1290, 1 piso, 1088
Buenos Aires, Argentina.

056.1 AG
CUADERNOS DE MAIPU; informar para servir.
1985. irreg. Centro de Estudios de Relaciones
Internacionales y de Estrategia Nacional, Maipu
889, Segundo Poso, 1006 Buenos Aires, Argentina.
Ed. Antonio Rodriguez Villar.

GENERAL INTEREST
PERIODICALS — Australasia

see also General Interest
 Periodicals—Australia

GENERAL INTEREST PERIODICALS — Australia

CHALLENGE (PETERSHAM NORTH) see
POLITICAL SCIENCE

052   AT   ISSN 0726-4690
THIS IS NEWCASTLE AND THE HUNTER REGION. 1960. a. Newcastle City Council, Hunter Valley Research Foundation, P.O. Box 23, Tighes Hill, N.S.W. 2297, Australia. charts. illus. stats.

GENERAL INTEREST PERIODICALS — Bangladesh

051   BG
DHAKA BISVABIDYALAYA PATRIKA. Added title: Dacca Visva Vidyalaya Patrika. (Text in Bengali) 1973. a. University of Dacca, Ramna, Dacca 2, Bangladesh.

GENERAL INTEREST PERIODICALS — Brazil

918   BL
ALMANAQUE ABRIL. 1975. a. price varies. Editora Abril S A, Av. Otaviano Alves de Lima 4,400, Sao Paulo, Brazil. Ed. Victor Civita. adv. film rev. charts. illus. circ. 163,700.

056.9   BL
ALMANAQUE BRAZIL. 1975. a. per no. Editora Abril Ltda., R. Geraldo Flausino Gomes 61, 10 andar, Sao Paulo, Brazil. Victor Civita. adv. charts. illus. circ. 118,000.

056.9   BL
QUEM E QUEM NA ECONOMIA BRASILEIRA. 1967. a. $16. Editora Visao Ltda., Rua Afonso Celso, 243, CEP 04119 - Sao Paulo, Brazil. Ed. Henry Maksoud. adv. circ. 140,000.

GENERAL INTEREST PERIODICALS — Bulgaria

059.918   BU
SHUMEN. PEDAGOGICHESKI INSTITUT. GODISHNIK. (Text in Bulgarian) irreg., vol.5, 1981. 1.12 lv. (Pedagogicheski Institut, Prirodomatematicheski Fakultet) Hemus Foreign Trade Co., 6 Ruski Blvd., Sofia, Bulgaria (Subscr. addr.: Pedagogicheski Institut, 9700 Shumen, Bulgaria) Ed.Bd.

GENERAL INTEREST PERIODICALS — Canada

CANADIAN MAGAZINE INDEX. see
ABSTRACTING AND INDEXING SERVICES

051   CN
NEXT YEAR COUNTRY NEWS. 1979. irreg. (4-8/yr) Can.$5 (subscr. includes Next Year Country Journal) Next Year Country Magazine Inc., Box 3446, Regina, Sask., Canada. Ed. Sheila Kuziak. bk. rev. (tabloid format)
 Supersedes in part: Next Year Country (ISSN 0315-758X)

GENERAL INTEREST PERIODICALS — Central America

see also *General Interest Periodicals–Cuba; General Interest Periodicals–Guatemala*

056.1   HO
HONDURAS AL DIA; boletin internacional. (Text in English and Spanish) 1978. irreg. free. Junta Militar de Gobierno, Secretaria de Prensa, Apdo. Postal 403, Tegucigalpa, D.C., Honduras. Ed.Bd.

056.1   CR
PENSAMIENTO COSTARRICENSE. 1977. irreg. free (not for international distribution) Ministerio de Cultura, Juventud y Deportes, Dept. de Publicaciones, Apdo. 10227, San Jose, Costa Rica.

GENERAL INTEREST PERIODICALS — Cuba

056.1   CU
ACTUALIDAD CULTURAL. irreg. Ministerio de Cultura, 4 No. 251 esq. a 11, Vedado, Havana, Cuba.

056.1   CU
COMICOS. irreg. Union de Periodistas y Escritores de Cuba, 23 esq. a I, Plaza, Habana 4, Havana, Cuba.

GENERAL INTEREST PERIODICALS — Denmark

052   DK   ISSN 0011-6084
DANISH JOURNAL. French edition: Revue Danoise (ISSN 0035-0982); German edition: Daenische Rundschau (ISSN 0414-9262); Spanish edition: Informaciones Danesas (ISSN 0107-1335) 1920. irreg. Udenrigsministeriet - Ministry of Foreign Affairs, Asiatisk Plads 2, DK-1448 Copenhagen K, Denmark. Eds. Preben Hansen, Flemming Andre Larsen. illus. Indexed: Key to Econ.Sci.
 Formerly: Danish Foreign Office Journal.

058   DK   ISSN 0106-5726
DANSK NATUR-DANSK SKOLE. 1961. a. Kr.50. Landsforeningen Dansk Natur-Dansk Skole, Gaerdebred 20, 2300 Copenhagen S, Denmark. Ed. Henner Bahnson. illus.

058   DK   ISSN 0107-4393
DANSKERNE; meninger, holdninger, vaner. (Text in Danish and English) 1978. irreg., latest Vol.3,1985. Kr.610. Observa, Staktoften 20, 2950 Vedbaek, Denmark. Ed. joergen Skalberg.

058   DK   ISSN 0109-6702
FEATURE FRA DANMARK. French Edition: En Bref du Danemark (ISSN 0109-6737); English Edition: News Feature from Denmark (ISSN 0109-6710); Spanish Edition: Notas Breves Danesas (ISSN 0109-6745) 1984. irreg. free. Udenrigsministeriet, Press og Kulturafdelningen, Copenhagen, Denmark.

058   DK   ISSN 0107-9840
GRENZLAND; Informationen und Hinweise zu aktuellen Fragen des Grenzlandes aus der Sicht der deutschen Volksgruppe. 1980. irreg. (Bund Deutscher Nordschleswiger) Deutsches Generalsekretariat, Vestergade 30, 6200 Apenrade, Denmark. illus.

058   DK   ISSN 0108-8653
HEDNOS DANESES. irreg., vol.16 1983. free. Udenrigsministeriet - Real Ministerio de Relaciones Exteriores de Dinamarca, Asiatisk Plads 2, 1448 Copenhagen K, Denmark. illus.

058   DK   ISSN 0107-2188
NORDSCHLESWIG; Berichte-Daten-Meinungen. 1978. a. Kr.30. (Bund Deutscher Nordschleswiger) Deutsches Generalsekretariat, Vestergade 30, 6200 Apenrade, Denmark. Ed.Bd. illus.

GENERAL INTEREST PERIODICALS — Germany, West

053.1   GW
FORSCHUNGSBERICHTE DES LANDES NORDRHEIN-WESTFALEN. irreg. price varies. Westdeutscher Verlag GmbH, Postfach 300320, 5090 Leverkusen 3, W. Germany (B.R.D.) Indexed: Met.Abstr.

053.1   GW
GEROLDSECKER LAND; Jahrbuch einer Landschaft. 1958. a. DM.17.80. Landkreis Ortenau, Badstr. 20, 7600 Offenburg, W. Germany (B.R.D.) circ. 4,000.

053.1   GW
JAHRESRING. 1954. a. DM.32. (Kulturkreis Im Bund der Deutschen Industrie) Deutsche Verlags-Anstalt, Postfach 209, 7000 Stuttgart 1, W. Germany (B.R.D.) bk. rev. circ. 4,000. (back issues avail.) Indexed: M.L.A.

053.1   GW
WALLDUERNER HEIMATBLAETTER. 1968. a. DM.2.50. Heimat- und Museumsverein e.V., Hauptstr., 6968 Wallduern, W. Germany (B.R.D.)

791   GW   ISSN 0037-461X
7 TAGE. a. DM.104. Klambt-Verlag GmbH, Im Neudeck 1, Postfach 1545 A, 6720 Speyer, W. Germany (B.R.D.) Ed. Herbert Hofner, Angelika Haug. circ. 299,466.

GENERAL INTEREST PERIODICALS — Great Britain

052   UK
BLACK COUNTRY BUGLE ANNUAL. 1973. a. £7. Mercia Publicity, 68 Brettell Lane, Amblecote, Nr. Stourbridge, West Midlands DLY8 48P, England. Ed. H. Taylor. adv. circ. 25,000.

942   UK
CAMBRIDGE TOWN, GOWN & COUNTY SERIES. 1976. irreg. price varies. Oleander Press, 17 Stansgate Ave., Cambridge CB2 2QZ, England (U.S. address: 210 Fifth Ave., New York, N.Y. 10010) Eds. Audrey Ward, Philip Ward. circ. 2,500.

052   UK
HOUSE AND GARDEN. REAL-LIFE KITCHEN GUIDE. 1979. a. £2. Conde Nast Publications Ltd., Vogue House, Hanover Sq., London W1R 0AD, England. Ed. Barbara Tims. adv.

052   UK   ISSN 0141-3511
LEICESTER LITERARY & PHILOSOPHICAL SOCIETY. TRANSACTIONS. 1879. a. £2($3) Leicester Literary & Philosophical Society, c/o Leicestershire Museums, 96 New Walk, Leicester, England. Ed. T.D. Ford. circ. 300. (back issues avail.)

051   UK
SOLENT GUIDES. 1977. a. free. Spotlight Magazine Group, 16a Marine Parade West, Lee on Solent, Hants., England. Ed. Jean Harvey. adv.

052   UK
SUBJECT INDEX TO WELSH PERIODICALS. (Text in English, Welsh) 1978. irreg. National Library of Wales, Aberstwyth, Dyfed, Wales.

052   UK   ISSN 0306-1108
UNIVERSITY OF SUSSEX. CENTRE FOR CONTINUING EDUCATION. OCCASIONAL PAPER. 1975. irreg., no.27, 1987. price varies. University of Sussex, Centre for Continuing Education, Falmer, Brighton, Sussex BN1 9RG, England. Ed. Fred Gray. circ. 1,000. Indexed: Geo.Abstr.

GENERAL INTEREST PERIODICALS — Greenland

059   GL   ISSN 0107-9948
GREENLAND NEWSLETTER. 1982. irreg. free. Greenland Home Rule Information Service, Tusarliivik, P.O. Box 1020, 3900 Nuuk, Greenland. illus.

GENERAL INTEREST PERIODICALS — Guatemala

056.1 972   GT
REVISTA 13 GRAFICO. a. free. Ministerio de Educacion, Centro Nacional de Libros de Texto y Material Didactico (CENALTEX), 35 Calle Final, Zona 11, Finca Las Charcas, Guatemala. Ed. Adolfo Lopez Alfaro. circ. 4,000.

GENERAL INTEREST PERIODICALS — India

068 II ISSN 0403-4457
ASIATIC SOCIETY. ANNUAL REPORT. (Text in English) a. Asiatic Society, 1 Park St., Calcutta 16, India.

059 II
MADHYA PRADESH VIKAS VARSHIKI. (Text in Hindi) 1973/74. a. Rs.38.50. c/o Kamla Kundra, E-32, 45 Bungalows, Bhopal 462003, India. Ed. Prakash Kundra. adv. circ. 1,500.
Former titles: Madhya Pradesh Yearbook; Madhya Pradesh Varshiki.

052 II
OH CALCUTTA. (Text in English) 1971. a., from 1984. $8. Aditi Nath Roy, Ed. & Pub., 49-11-A Hindusthan Park, Calcutta 700029, India. Ed. A.N. Roy. adv. bk. rev. film rev. charts. illus. circ. 25,000.
Calcutta and Eastern India

052 II
RABINDRA BHARATI JOURNAL. (Text in English) 1968. irreg., latest issue, 1973. Rs.2. Rabindra Bharati University, 6/4 Dwarkanath Tagore Ln., Calcutta 700007, India. Ed. Ramendranath Mullick. circ. 500.
Essays and poems

052 II
SEVARTHAM; Indian culture in a christian context. (Text in English, Hindi; summaries in English) 1976. a. Rs.25. St. Albert's College, P.O. Box 5, Ranchi 834001, India. Ed. J. Feys. bk. rev. cum.index. circ. 550. (back issues avail.)

GENERAL INTEREST PERIODICALS — Indonesia

HARVARD-YENCHING LIBRARY BIBLIOGRAPHICAL SERIES. see *BIBLIOGRAPHIES*

GENERAL INTEREST PERIODICALS — Israel

059.92 IS
DAPAI TAMAR. irreg. Regional Council Tamar, D.N. Dead Sea 86 910, Israel. TEL 057-84184.

059.92 IS
DAYAN CENTER FOR MIDDLE EASTERN AND AFRICAN STUDIES. BULLETIN. (Text in English) irreg. free. Dayan Center for Middle Eastern and African Studies, P.O. Box 39012, Tel Aviv 69 978, Israel.

059.92 IS
NEGEV; journal of Ben Gurion University of the Negev. (Text in English) irreg. Ben Gurion University, Department of Public Affairs, P.O. Box 653, Beersheva 84 120, Israel. TEL 057-39943.

059.92 IS
TEL AVIV-YAFO. CENTER FOR ECONOMIC AND SOCIAL RESEARCH. YEARBOOK. (Text in English and Hebrew) 1961. a. Center for Economic and Social Research, Tel Aviv-Jaffa Municipality, Malkhei Israel Square, Tel Aviv, Israel. illus.
Former titles: Tel Aviv-Yafo. Department of Research and Statistics; Tel Aviv Yearbook.

296 059 IS
WORLD ZIONIST PRESS SERVICE. (Text in English) irreg. (4-8/w.) World Zionist Organization, P.O.B. 92, Jerusalem, Israel. Ed. June Spitzer.
Formerly: World Zionist Organization Press Service.

GENERAL INTEREST PERIODICALS — Italy

055.1 IT
ARCHIVIO STORICO PER LE PROVINCE PARMENSI. 1890. a. L.40800. Deputazione Storia Patria, Borgo Schizzati, 3, 43100 Parma, Italy. Ed. Giuseppina Allegri Tassoni.

055.1 IT ISSN 0392-9884
CIRCOLO CULTURALE B.G. DUNS SCOTO DI ROCCARAINOLA. ATTI. (Summaries occasionally in English) 1975. irreg. free. Scuola Tipo-litografica "Istituto Anselmi", Via Roma, I-80034 Marigliano, Italy.

055.1 IT
FONDAZIONE LUIGI EINAUDI, ANNALI. (Text in English, French, Italian) a. Fondazione Luigi Einaudi, Via Principe Amedeo 34, 10123 Turin, Italy. TEL (11) 83 56 56. circ. 1,200.

055.1 YU ISSN 0543-1077
ISELJENICKI KALENDAR. (Text in Croatian, English, Spanish) 1954. a. 800 din.($5) Matica Iseljenika Hrvatske, Trnjanska bb, 41000 Zagreb, Yugoslavia. Ed. Ivo Smoljan. circ. 5,500. (back issues avail.)

055.1 IT
LECCIO - LITERARY REVIEW. 1953. irreg. Mario Cesare Guidi, Ed. & Pub., Via di Cammori 54, 50145 Florence, Italy. adv. circ. 1,500. (reprint service avail. from UMI,ISI)
Formerly: Leccio - Press Agency.

055.1 IT
SOCIETA SAVONESE DI STORIA PATRIA. ATTI E MEMORIE. 1888. a. L.20000. Societa Savonese di Storia Patria, Piazza della Maddalena 14, 17100 Savona, Italy. index. circ. 1,000.

065 IT ISSN 0393-6368
UNIVERSITA E ISTITUTI DI STUDIO E RICERCA IN ITALIA. ANNUARIO DEA. 1983. a. $40. DEA Editrice, Via Lima, 28, I-00198 Rome, Italy.

GENERAL INTEREST PERIODICALS — Japan

952 JA
CHANGING JAPAN. 1973. irreg. price varies. International Society for Educational Information, Inc., Koryo Bldg., 18 Wakaba 1-chome, Shinjuku-ku, Tokyo 160, Japan. illus. (back issues avail.)

051 DK ISSN 0107-752X
NIPPON NYT. 1979. irreg. (3-5/yr.) Skandinavisk Japan Samlerforening, Postboks 1463, 2000 Copenhagen F, Denmark. illus.

GENERAL INTEREST PERIODICALS — Libya

320.9 ZR
CAHIERS ZAIROIS DE LA RECHERCHE ET DU DEVELOPPEMENT. 1967. irreg. $8.00. Office National de la Recherche et du Developpement, B.P. 16706, Kinshasa, Zaire. bk. rev. illus. circ. 2,000.
Continues: Cahiers Congolais de la Recherche et du Developpement.

GENERAL INTEREST PERIODICALS — Pakistan

059.914 PK
PAKISTAN YEAR BOOK. (Text in English) 1973. biennial. $25. East-West Publishing Company, 22 Corner Chambers, I.I. Chundrigar Road, Karachi 0102, Pakistan. Ed. Rafique Akhtar.

GENERAL INTEREST PERIODICALS — Peru

056.1 PE ISSN 0567-753X
ACTA HEREDIANA. 1968. a. Universidad Peruana Cayetano Heredia, Direccion de Biblioteca Publicaciones y Museos, Avda. Honorio Delgado 932, Apdo. 2563, Lima 100, Peru.

ORGANIZATION FOR ECONOMIC COOPERATION AND DEVELOPMENT. CATALOGUE OF PUBLICATIONS. see *BIBLIOGRAPHIES*

GENERAL INTEREST PERIODICALS — Poland

057.85 PL ISSN 0039-3355
STUDIA SLASKIE/SILESIAN STUDIES. (Text in Polish; summaries in English, German, Russian) 1958. irreg. 150 Zl. Instytut Slaski w Opolu, Ul. Piastowska 17, 45-082 Opole, Poland. bk. rev. circ. 600. (back issues avail.)

GENERAL INTEREST PERIODICALS — Puerto Rico

051 US ISSN 0033-4049
PUERTO RICO LIVING. 1963. a. $3.50. Northeast Outdoors, Inc., Box 2180, Waterbury, CT 06722-2180. TEL 203-755-0158. Ed. Barbara Dimando. circ. 12,000.

GENERAL INTEREST PERIODICALS — Scandinavia

see *General Interest Periodicals — Denmark; General Interest Periodicals — Sweden*

GENERAL INTEREST PERIODICALS — Singapore

052 SI ISSN 0129-766X
SINGAPORE. (Text in English) 1964. a. S.19.95($15) M P H Magazines Ltd., 601 Sims Drive 03-01/03, Pan-I Warehouse Complex, Singapore 0617. Ed. K.I. Sudderuddin. circ. 16,000. (back issues avail.)

GENERAL INTEREST PERIODICALS — South America

see also *General Interest Periodicals — Argentina; General Interest Periodicals — Brazil; General Interest Periodicals — Peru; General Interest Periodicals — Uruguay; General Interest Periodicals — Venezuela*

GENERAL INTEREST PERIODICALS — Sudan

915.6 059 SJ
NILE MIRROR. (Text in English) irreg. Ministry of Southern Affairs, Khartoum, Sudan.

GENERAL INTEREST PERIODICALS — Sweden

058.7   SW
CURRENT SWEDEN. 1970. irreg. (10-15/yr.) free. Svenska Institutet - Swedish Institute, Box 7434, S-103 91 Stockholm, Sweden (U.S. dist: Swedish Information Service, 825 Third Ave., New York, NY 10022) Ed. Gabrielle Sjoestedt. index. circ. 4,500(English edt.);2,000(French edt.); 2,500(German edt.);2,000(Spanish edt.) (processed) Indexed: Biol.Dig.
    Incorporates (1973-1978): Environment Planning and Conservation in Sweden.

INVANDRARFRAAGOR. AARSBOK. see *ETHNIC INTERESTS*

GENERAL INTEREST PERIODICALS — Tanzania

967.8   TZ   ISSN 0039-9485
TANZANIA NOTES & RECORDS. 1936. a. $18 individuals; institutions $22. Tanzania Society, c/o Mrs. Carol Sharp, Ex. Sec., Box 511, Dar es Salam, Tanzania. Ed. I.N. Kimambo. adv. bk. rev. bibl. charts. illus. index. circ. 1,200. Indexed: Curr.Cont.Africa.
    Formerly: Tanganyika Notes and Records.

GENERAL INTEREST PERIODICALS — U S S R

057.1   UR
ESTONIAN PANORAMA. (Text in English) 1983. a. Izdatel'stvo Perioodika, Tallinn, Estonian S.S.R., U.S.S.R.

GENERAL INTEREST PERIODICALS — United States

979   US   ISSN 0191-328X
ALASKA TODAY. 1973. a. University of Alaska, Department of Journalism and Broadcasting, Fairbanks, AK 99775-0940. TEL 907-474-7761. adv. bk. rev. circ. 6,000.

051   US
ALTERNATIVE AMERICA. 1974. a. $19.95. Box 1067, Harvard Sq., Cambridge, MA 02238-1067. TEL 617-876-2789. Ed. Richard Gardner. bk. rev. circ. 1,500.
    Formerly: Resources (Cambridge)

051   US
AMERICAN PUBLIC OPINION DATA. a. Opinion Research Service, Box 70205, Louisville, KY 40270. TEL 502-456-5320.

051   US
CONVERSATIONS WITH. 1977. irreg. $46 per vol. Gale Research Company, Book Tower, Detroit, MI 48226. TEL 313-962-2242. Ed.Bd. illus.

051   US
DOOR COUNTY ALMANAK. 1982. a. $5.95 per no. Dragonsbreath Press, 10905 Bay Shore Dr., Sister Bay, WI 54234. TEL 414-854-2742. Ed. Fred Johnson. adv. bk. rev. circ. 4,000.
    Local interests

051   011   US
FANATIC READER. bi-m. $30. 9513 S.W. Barbur Blvd., Ste. 162, Portland, OR 97219. Ed. Jim Burnett.

973   US   ISSN 0017-3673
GREAT PLAINS JOURNAL. 1961. a. $7.50 includes s-a. newsletter. (Institute of the Great Plains) Museum of the Great Plains, Box 68, Lawton, OK 73502. TEL 405-353-5675. Ed. Steve Wilson. adv. bk. rev. bibl. circ. 1,000. (tabloid format; also avail. in microform from UMI; reprint service avail. from UMI) Indexed: Hist.Abstr. Amer.Hist.& Life. Geo.Abstr.

974.7   US
NEW YORK GOOD NEWS; a journal for optimists. 1966. irreg. price varies. ‡ Arete Activities, Inc., 101 St. Marks Pl., New York, NY 10009. TEL 212-777-7856. Ed. Stephen Kraus. adv. bk. rev.
    Formerly: Good News (ISSN 0017-2138)

051   US   ISSN 0737-3813
NEWSBANK (NEW CANAAN) 1970. m. (q. and a. cums.) price varies. NewsBank, Inc., 58 Pine St., New Canaan, CT 06840. Ed. Jessica Milstead. index. (paper index; articles on microfiche)
    Formerly: NewsBank Library.

SPECTRUM; a guide to the independent press and informative organizations. see *LIBRARY AND INFORMATION SCIENCES*

051   US   ISSN 0884-9064
WASHINGTON'S ALMANAC.* 1985. a. Evergreen Publishing Co., 901 Lenora St., Seattle, WA 98121. Ed. Knute Berger.

WESTERN NEW YORK INDEX. see *ABSTRACTING AND INDEXING SERVICES*

GENERAL INTEREST PERIODICALS — Uruguay

056.1   UY
CRITICA; revista sociocultural. 1985. irreg. Ministerio de Educacion y Cultura, Calle Pando 2975, Montevideo, Uruguay. Ed. Roberto Genta Dorado.

GENERAL INTEREST PERIODICALS — Venezuela

056.1   VE
CARACAS. (Text in English and Spanish) 1980. a. $3. Elaboraciones Venezuela, Apdo. del Este 60182, Caracas, Venezuela. Ed. Lynn Grossberg. adv. illus. circ. 8,000.

GENERAL INTEREST PERIODICALS — Vietnam

059.959 028.5   VN   ISSN 0049-6375
VIETNAM YOUTH. French edition: Jeunesse du Vietnam. irreg. (Vietnam Youth Federation) Vietnam National Union of Students, 64 Ba Trieu St., Hanoi, Vietnam. illus.

GENERAL INTEREST PERIODICALS — West Indies

052   BB
CHALLENGES IN THE NEW CARIBBEAN. Also called: Issues in the New Caribbean. irreg. Cedar Press, P.O. Box 616, Bridgetown, Barbados, W. Indies. (Affiliate: Caribbean Conference of Churches)

GENERAL INTEREST PERIODICALS — Yugoslavia

057.8   YU   ISSN 0019-1523
IDRIJSKI RAZGLEDI. (Text in Slovenian) 1956. a. 600 din.($1.70) Mestni Muzej v Idrii, Idrija, Yugoslavia. Ed. Jurij Bavdaz. circ. 1,000.

057.8   YU   ISSN 0350-8498
ZBORNIK OBCINE GROSUPLJE. (Text in Slovenian; summaries in English, German) 1969. biennial. 250 din. O.K. S.Z.D.L. Grosuplje, P.O. Box 11, Grosuplje, Yugoslavia. Ed. France Adamic. adv. bk. rev. circ. 1,000. (back issues avail.)

GENERAL INTEREST PERIODICALS — Zambia

052   ZA
VOICE OF S O M A F C O. (Text in English) 1983. irreg. on exchange basis. Solomon Mahlangu Freedom College, c/o African National Congress, P.O. Box 31791, Lusaka, Zambia. circ. 1,000.

GENETICS

see *Biology — Genetics*

GEOGRAPHY

see also *History; Travel and Tourism*

A L P R NEWS. (Association for Arid Lands Studies) see *AGRICULTURE*

910   DK   ISSN 0106-9047
AARHUS UNIVERSITET. GEOGRAFISK INSTITUT. NOTAT. 1979. irreg.,latest no.58,1986. price varies. Aarhus Universitet, Geografisk Institut, DK-8000 Aarhus C, Denmark. Ed. Adrian Randall. circ. 200. (back issues avail)

AARHUS UNIVERSITET. GEOLOGISK INSTITUT. GEOSKRIFTER. see *EARTH SCIENCES — Geology*

917.2 986   GT   ISSN 0252-337X
ACADEMIA DE GEOGRAFIA E HISTORIA DE GUATEMALA. ANALES. 1924. a. Q.10.00($10) Academia de Geografia e Historia de Guatemala, 3a. Avenida 8-35, Zona 1, Guatemala City, Guatemala. Eds. Jorge Luis Arriola, Flavio Rojas Lima. index. circ. 1,000. (back issues avail.)

551   HU   ISSN 0567-7475
ACTA GEOGRAPHICA DEDRECINA. (Text in English, French, German, Hungarian, Russian) 1962. irreg., vol.22, 1984. Kossuth Lajos Tudomanyegyetem, Egyetem Ter 1, H-4010 Debrecen, Hungary. Ed. Z. Borsy. Indexed: Geo.Abstr. GeoRef.

910   PL   ISSN 0065-1249
ACTA GEOGRAPHICA LODZIENSIA. (Text in Polish; summaries in English and French) 1947. irreg., no.54, 1986. price varies. Ossolineum, Publishing House of the Polish Academy of Sciences, Rynek 9, Wroclaw, Poland (Dist. by: Ars Polona - Ruch, Krakowskie Przedmiescie 7, Warsaw, Poland) Ed. Halina Klatkowa. Indexed: Gero.Abstr. GeoRef.

949.3   BE   ISSN 0065-1257
ACTA GEOGRAPHICA LOVANIENSIA. 1961. irreg., latest no. 16. price varies. Universite Catholique de Louvain, Institut de Geographie, Batiment Mercator, 1348 Louvain-la-Neuve, Belgium. Eds. Th. Brulard, M. Goosens. circ. 250. Indexed: GeoRef. Geo.Abstr.

ACTA HUMBOLDTIANA. see *ANTHROPOLOGY*

ACTA PHYTOGEOGRAPHICA SUECICA. see *BIOLOGY — Botany*

910 370   PL   ISSN 0208-6123
ACTA UNIVERSITATIS LODZIENSIS: FOLIA GEOGRAPHICA. (Text in Polish; summaries in various languages) 1955; N.S. 1982. irreg. Uniwersytet Lodzki, Drukarnia Wojskowa, Ul. Gdanska 130, Lodz, Poland (Dist. by: Ars Polona-Ruch, Krakowskie Przedmiescie 7, Warsaw, Poland)
    Supersedes in part: Uniwersytet Lodzki. Zeszyty Naukowe. Seria 2: Nauki Matematyczno-Przyrodnicze.

GEOGRAPHY

910   PL   ISSN 0208-5291
ACTA UNIVERSITATIS NICOLAI COPERNICI. GEOGRAFIA. 1963. irreg. price varies. Uniwersytet Mikolaja Kopernika, Fosa Staromiejska 3, Torun, Poland (Dist. by Osrodek Rozpowszchniania Wydwnictw Naukowych PAN, Palac Kultury i Nauki, 00-901 Warsaw, Poland) Indexed: Biol.Abstr. Geo.Abstr. GeoRef.

910   940   SW   ISSN 0349-0564
ACTA WEXIONENSIA. SERIE 1: HISTORY & GEOGRAPHY. 1979. irreg. Hoegskolan i Vaexjoe, Box 5053, S-350 05 Vaexjoe, Sweden. circ. 600. (back issues avail.)

AFRICA SOUTH OF THE SAHARA. see *HISTORY — History Of Africa*

910   NR   ISSN 0065-4698
AHMADU BELLO UNIVERSITY. DEPARTMENT OF GEOGRAPHY. OCCASIONAL PAPER. 1965. irreg, no.9, 1985. Ahmadu Bello University, Department of Geography, Zaria, Nigeria. Ed. Robert J. Hyde. adv. circ. 350.

526.1   GE
AKADEMIE DER WISSENSCHAFTEN DER DDR. ZENTRALINSTITUT FUER PHYSIK DER ERDE. VEROEFFENTLICHUNGEN. 1949. irreg. exchange basis. Akademie der Wissenschaften der DDR, Zentralinstitut fuer Physik der Erde, Telegrafenberg A17, 45 Potsdam, E. Germany (D.D.R.) Ed. H. Kautzleben. Indexed: Math.R. GeoRef.
    Formerly (1949-1969): Akademie der Wissenschaften der DDR. Geodaetisches Institut. Veroeffentlichungen (ISSN 0065-5015)

910   CN   ISSN 0065-6097
ALBERTAN GEOGRAPHER. 1965. a. Can.$1.50. University of Alberta, Department of Geography, Edmonton, Alta. T6G 2H4, Canada. TEL 403-432-3329. circ. 300. Indexed: GeoRef.

915   HK   ISSN 0072-4939
ALL-ASIA GUIDE. 1961. biennial (14th ed.) HK.$100($12.95) Far Eastern Economic Review Ltd., Box 160, Hong Kong, Hong Kong.
    Formerly: Golden Guide to South and East Asia.

914   UK   ISSN 0065-6569
ALPINE JOURNAL. 1863. a. £15. Alpine Club, 74 S. Audley St., London W1Y 5FF, England. Ed. John Fairley. adv. bk. rev. index. circ. 2,500. Indexed: Br.Hum.Ind. GeoRef. Sportsearch.

526   US   ISSN 0277-2876
AMERICAN CONGRESS ON SURVEYING AND MAPPING. TECHNICAL PAPERS. 1968. irreg. (approx. 2/yr.) $30. American Congress on Surveying and Mapping, 210 Little Falls St., Church, VA 22046. TEL 703-241-2446. index. (also avail. in microfilm from UMI; reprint service avail. from UMI) Indexed: Bibl.Cart. GeoRef.
    Formerly: American Congress on Surveying and Mapping. Proceedings of Annual Meeting (ISSN 0161-0945); Incorporating: American Congress on Surveying and Mapping. Papers from the Annual Meetings (ISSN 0065-7913)

526.982   US
AMERICAN SOCIETY FOR PHOTOGRAMMETRY AND REMOTE SENSING. TECHNICAL PAPERS FROM THE ANNUAL MEETING. a. $75 to non-members; members $45. American Society for Photogrammetry and Remote Sensing, 210 Little Falls St., Falls Church, VA 22046. TEL 703-534-6617. index. Indexed: GeoRef.
    Formerly: American Society of Photogrammetry. Technical Papers from the Annual Meeting (ISSN 0277-2094)
    Photogrammetry

526.9   US
AMERICAN SOCIETY FOR PHOTOGRAMMETRY AND REMOTE SENSING FALL CONVENTION. TECHNICAL PAPERS. (Vol. for 1982 and 1983 published jointly with American Congress on Surveying and Mapping) a. $30 to non-members; members $20. American Society for Photogrammetry and Remote Sensing, 210 Little Falls St., Falls Church, VA 22046. TEL 703-534-6617. Indexed: Bibl.Cart.
    Former titles: American Society of Photogrammetry Fall Convention. Technical Papers (ISSN 0271-4043); (until 1983): American Society of Photogrammetry Fall Convention. Proceedings (ISSN 0196-674X)

910   MX
ANALES DE GEOGRAFIA. 1975. a. Universidad Nacional Autonoma de Mexico, Facultad de Filosofia y Letras, Villa Obregon, Ciudad Universitaria, 04510 Mexico 20, D.F., Mexico. illus.
    Formerly: Instituto de Geografia. Annales.

910   551   PL   ISSN 0137-1983
ANNALES UNIVERSITATIS MARIAE CURIE-SKLODOWSKA. SECTIO B. GEOGRAPHIA, GEOLOGIA, MINERALOGIA ET PETROGRAPHIA. (Text in English or Polish; summaries in English, French, Russian) 1946. a. price varies. Uniwersytet Marii Curie-Sklodowskiej, Plac Marii Curie-Sklodowskiej 5, 20-031 Lublin, Poland. Ed. E. Michna. circ. 900. Indexed: Biol.Abstr. Chem.Abstr. Doc.Geogr. Geo.Abstr. Soils & Fert.

914.4   FR
ANNUAIRE DES NOTABLES REGIONAUX. 1975. a. Editions Dany Thibaud, 52 rue Labrouste, 75015 Paris, France.

ANNUAIRE DES PAYS DE L'OCEAN INDIEN. see *SOCIAL SCIENCES: COMPREHENSIVE WORKS*

910   US
ANNUAL EDITIONS: GLOBAL ISSUES. 1985. a. Dushkin Publishing Group, Inc., Sluice Dock, Guilford, CT 06437. TEL 203-453-4351. Ed. Ian Nielsen.

919   US   ISSN 0066-4626
ANTARCTIC BIBLIOGRAPHY. 1965. every 18 mos. price varies. U.S. National Science Foundation, Office of Polar Programs, 1800 G St., N.W., Washington, DC 20550. TEL 202-655-4000. Ed. Geza T. Thuronyi. circ. 1,500.
    •Also available online. Vendors: Orbit Information Technologies.

919.9   US
ANTARCTIC RESEARCH BOOK SERIES. 1964. irreg. price varies. American Geophysical Union, 2000 Florida Ave. N.W., Washington, DC 20009. TEL 202-462-6903. Ed.Bd. (reprint service avail. from ISI) Indexed: Biol.Abstr.
    Formerly: Antarctic Research Series (ISSN 0066-4634)

919.8   AG   ISSN 0302-5691
ANTARTIDA. 1971. a. Direccion Nacional del Antartico, Cerrito 1248, Buenos Aires 1010, Argentina. Ed. Juan Alberto Nadaud. charts. illus. Indexed: GeoRef.

917.203   MX
ANUARIO BAJA CALIFORNIA Y SUS HOMBRES. 1975. a. Mex.$500. Publicidad Hernandez Tirado, S.A., Madero y Calle I, No. 134, Apdo. Postal 500, Mexicali, B.C., Mexico. Ed. Humberto Hernandez Tirado. adv. circ. 3,000.

917.2   310   MX
ANUARIO DE ESTADISTICAS ESTATALES. 1984. a. $13. Instituto Nacional de Estadistica, Geografia e Informatica, Secretaria de Programacion y Presupuesto, Patriotismo 711 Torre "A" P.H., Col. San Juan Mixcoac, Deleg. Benito Juarez, 03910 Mexico, D.F., Mexico TEL 598-99-05. (Subscr. to: Rio Rhin No. 56, Col. Cuauhtemoc, 06500 Mexico, D.F., Mexico)

ANUARIO GEOGRAFICO DEL PERU. see *HISTORY — History Of North And South America*

910   US   ISSN 0192-8996
APPLIED GEOGRAPHY CONFERENCES. 1977. a. $10 to individuals; libraries $15. State University of New York at Binghamton, Geography Department, Binghamton, NY 13901. TEL 607-777-2755. Ed. John W. Frazier. charts. illus. stat. circ. 300. (back issues avail.) Indexed: Geo.Abstr.

914.3   GW   ISSN 0373-7187
ARBEITEN ZUR RHEINISCHEN LANDESKUNDE. 1950. irreg. price varies. (Universitaet Bonn, Geographisches Institut) Ferd. Duemmlers Verlag, Postfach 1480-Kaiserstr. 31-37, D-5300 Bonn 1, W. Germany (B.R.D.) Indexed: GeoRef.

910   US
ASSOCIATION OF AMERICAN GEOGRAPHERS. DIRECTORY. 1956. irreg., latest 1982. $8. Association of American Geographers, 1710 16th St., N.W., Washington, DC 20009. TEL 202-234-1450.
    Formerly: Association of American Geographers. Handbook-Directory (ISSN 0571-5962)

910   JA   ISSN 0066-958X
ASSOCIATION OF JAPANESE GEOGRAPHERS. SPECIAL PUBLICATION. (Text in English) 1966. irreg., no.4, 1980. price varies. Association of Japanese Geographers - Nippon Chiri Gakkai, c/o Japan Academic Societies Centre, 2-4-16 Yayoi, Bunkyo-ku, Tokyo 113, Japan. index.

910   US   ISSN 0066-9628
ASSOCIATION OF PACIFIC COAST GEOGRAPHERS. YEARBOOK. 1935. a. $7. Oregon State University Press, 101 Waldo Hall, Corvallis, OR 97331. TEL 503-754-3166. Ed. James Scott. abstr. bibl. charts. illus. cum.index: vols. 27, 35 and 40. circ. 800. (also avail. in microform from UMI; back issues avail.; reprint service avail. from UMI) Indexed: GeoRef.

910   HU   ISSN 0324-5268
ATTILA JOZSEF UNIVERSITY. ACTA GEOGRAPHICA. (Text in English, German and Russian) 1955. a. exchange basis. Attila Jozsef University, c/o E. Szabo, Exchange Librarian, Dugonics ter 13, P.O.B. 393, Szeged H-6701, Hungary (Subscr. to: Kultura, Box 149, H-1389 Budapest, Hungary) Eds. Laszlo Jakucs, Gyula Krajko. charts. illus. circ. 300.

AUSTRALIA. BUREAU OF MINERAL RESOURCES, GEOLOGY, AND GEOPHYSICS. PUBLICATIONS. see *BIBLIOGRAPHIES*

AUSTRALIAN MAPS. see *BIBLIOGRAPHIES*

910   US   ISSN 0501-9966
BACKGROUND NOTES ON THE COUNTRIES OF THE WORLD. irreg. $32. U.S. Department of State, Office of Public Communication, Bureau of Public Affairs, 2201 C St., N.W., Washington, DC 20520 TEL 202-783-3238. (Subscr. to: Supt. of Documents, Washington, DC 20402) Indexed: Ind.U.S.Gov.Per.

910   PL   ISSN 0067-2807
BADANIA FIZJOGRAFICZNE NAD POLSKA ZACHODNIA. SERIA A. GEOGRAFIA FIZYCZNA. (Text in Polish; summaries in English, French or German) 1948. irreg., vol.34, 1982. price varies. (Poznanskie Towarzystwo Przyjaciol Nauk) Panstwowe Wydawnictwo Naukowe, Ul. Miodowa 10, 00-251 Warsaw, Poland (Dist. by: Ars Polona Krakowskie Przedmiescie 7, 00-068 Warsaw, Poland) illus. Indexed: Geo.Abstr. GeoRef.

BAETICA; estudios de arte, geografia e historia. see *ART*

910   SZ   ISSN 0067-4486
BASLER BEITRAEGE ZUR GEOGRAPHIE. (Text in German; summaries in English or French) 1968. irreg. Verlag Wepf und Co., Eisengasse 5, CH-4001 Basel, Switzerland.

910   GE   ISSN 0138-4422
BEITRAEGE ZUR GEOGRAPHIE. 1951. irreg., vol.32, 1985. price varies. (Akademie der Wissenschaften der DDR, Institut fuer Geographie und Geooekologie) Akademie-Verlag, Leipziger Str. 3-4, 1086 Berlin, E. Germany (D.D.R.)
    Formerly (until 1979): Akademie der Wissenschaften der DDR. Institut fuer Geographie und Geooekologie. Wissenschaftliche Veroeffentlichungen.

GEOGRAPHY

915   BG
BHUGOLA SAMAYIKI. (Text in Bengali) 1974. a. Tk.10. Bangladesh National Geographical Association, c/o Dept. of Geography, Dacca College, Dhanmondi, Dacca 2, Bangladesh.

910   UK   ISSN 0067-9232
BLOOMSBURY GEOGRAPHER. 1968. a. £1. University College London, Department of Geography, 26 Bedford Way, London WC1H 0AP, England. Ed. Elizabeth Chubb. adv. bk. rev. circ. 550. (back issues avail.)

910   BL   ISSN 0006-6079
BOLETIM PAULISTA DE GEOGRAFIA. 1941. irreg. (2-3/yr.) $20 (for 4 nos.) Associacao dos Geografos Brasileiros, Secao Regional de Sao Paulo, C.P. 8. 105, 01000 Sao Paulo, Brazil. Ed. Manuel F. G. Serbra. bk. rev. bibl. charts. illus. circ. 2,000. Indexed: Hist.Abstr. GeoRef. Geo.Abstr.

910   GW   ISSN 0373-0468
BONNER GEOGRAPHISCHE ABHANDLUNGEN. 1948. irreg. price varies. Ferd. Duemmlers Verlag, Postfach 1480-Kaiserstr. 31-37, D-5300 Bonn 1, W. Germany (B.R.D.) Ed.Bd. Indexed: Bibl.Cart. Forest.Abstr. GeoRef. Geo.Abstr. Rural Recreat.Tour.Abstr. Soils & Fert. World Agri.Econ. & Rural Sociol.Abstr.

910   GW   ISSN 0524-2444
BRAUNSCHWEIGER GEOGRAPHISCHE STUDIEN. 1964. irreg. price varies. Verlag Erich Goltze GmbH und Co. KG, Stresemannstr. 28, 3400 Goettingen, W. Germany (B.R.D.) Ed. Arno Beuermann. Indexed: Geo.Abstr.

910   GW   ISSN 0720-9738
BREMER BEITRAEGE ZUR GEOGRAPHIE UND RAUMPLANUNG. 1978. irreg. price varies. Universitaet Bremen, Drueckschriftenlager, Postfach 330440, D-2800 Bremen 33, W. Germany (B.R.D.) Indexed: Geo.Abstr.

912   US   ISSN 0068-1148
BRITANNICA ATLAS. (Text in English, French, German, Portuguese, and Spanish) 1969. biennial. $89.50. Encyclopaedia Britannica, Inc., 310 S. Michigan Ave., Chicago, IL 60604. TEL 312-347-7000. Ed. William A. Cleveland. index.

910   CN   ISSN 0068-1571
BRITISH COLUMBIA GEOGRAPHICAL SERIES: OCCASIONAL PAPERS IN GEOGRAPHY. 1960. irreg., latest no.36, 1983. price varies. (Canadian Association of Geographers, Western Division) Tantalus Research Ltd., Box 34248, 2405 Pine St., Vancouver, B.C. V6J 4N8, Canada. Ed. W.G. Hardwick. circ. 400.

910   301.3   UK   ISSN 0306-6142
C A T M O G. (Concepts and Techniques in Modern Geography) 1975. irreg. (approx. 5/yr) price varies. Geo Books, Regency House, 34 Duke St., Norwich NR3 3AP, England. (back issues avail.)

910   FR   ISSN 0526-8133
CAHIERS DES EXPLORATEURS. 1957. a. membership only. Societe des Explorateurs et des Voyageurs Francais, 184 bd. St. Germain, 75006 Paris, France.

917.9   US   ISSN 0883-6264
CALIFORNIA FACTS. 1985. triennial. $47.50. Clements Research, Inc., 16850 Dallas Pkwy., Dallas, TX 75248. TEL 214-931-8827.

910   UK   ISSN 0068-6654
CAMBRIDGE GEOGRAPHICAL STUDIES. 1969. irreg., no.17, 1983. $49.50 for latest vol. Cambridge University Press, Edinburgh Bldg., Shaftesbury Rd., Cambridge CB2 2RU, England (and 32 E. 57 St., New York, N.Y. 10022) Ed.Bd. index.

910   UK
CAMBRIDGE STUDIES IN HISTORICAL GEOGRAPHY. 1982. irreg. price varies. Cambridge University Press, Edinburgh Bldg., Shaftesbury Rd., Cambridge CB2 2RU, England (And 32 E. 57th St., New York, NY 10022)

916.7   CM   ISSN 0301-7753
CAMEROON YEAR BOOK. (Text in English) 1973. a. 300 Fr.CFA. United Publishers, Box 200, Victoria, Cameroon. Ed. Jennie Gwellem. adv. illus. stat. circ. 10,000.

910   CN   ISSN 0707-3844
CANADIAN ASSOCIATION OF GEOGRAPHERS. DIRECTORY. (Text in English and French) 1964. a. Can.$10. Canadian Association of Geographers, McGill University, 805 Sherbrooke St. W., Montreal, Que. H3A 2K6, Canada. TEL 514-392-4311. Ed. Wm. Barr. circ. 1,400.
   Formerly: Canadian Association of Geographers. Newsletter (ISSN 0068-8312)

910   JM   ISSN 0252-9939
CARIBBEAN GEOGRAPHY; a journal of geography for the region. 1983. a. Jam.$17.50($7) Longman Jamaica Ltd., 95 Newport Blvd., Newport West, P.O. Box 489, Kingston 10, Jamaica. Eds. David Barker, Mike Morrissey. adv. bk. rev. abstr. bibl. charts. illus. pat. stat. tr.lit. cum.index. circ. 300. (back issues avail.) Indexed: Geo.Abstr.

CENTRE EUROPEEN D'ETUDES BURGONDO-MEDIANES. PUBLICATION. see *HISTORY — History Of Europe*

CENTRE FOR URBAN AND COMMUNITY STUDIES. BIBLIOGRAPHIC SERIES. see *HOUSING AND URBAN PLANNING*

526.982   CK   ISSN 0120-2499
CENTRO INTERAMERICANO DE FOTOINTERPRETACION. REVISTA. Short title: Revista C I A F. 1972. a. $20. Centro Interamericano de Fotointerpretacion, Carrera 30 No. 47a-57, Apdo. Aereo 53754, Bogota, Colombia. Ed. Jonas Cirilo Leon Perez. adv. bk. rev. illus. circ. 1,000.

910   CS
CESKOSLOVENSKY KRAS. 1948. a. Academia, Publishing House of the Czechoslovak Academy of Sciences, Vodickova 40, 11229 Prague 1, Czechoslovakia. bk. rev. bibl. circ. 500. (back issues avail.)

910   GW   ISSN 0588-3253
COLLOQUIUM GEOGRAPHICUM. 1952. irreg. price varies. (Geographisches Institut) Ferd. Duemmlers Verlag, Postfach 1480, Kaiserstr. 31-37, D-5300 Bonn, W. Germany (B.R.D.) Indexed: GeoRef.

910   FR   ISSN 0071-8424
COMITE DES TRAVAUX HISTORIQUES ET SCIENTIFIQUES. SECTION DE GEOGRAPHIE. ACTES DU CONGRES NATIONAL DES SOCIETES SAVANTES. 1960 (congress of 1959) a. price varies. Ministere de l'Education Nationale, Comite des Travaux Historiques et Scientifiques, 3-5 bd. Pasteur, 75015 Paris, France. circ. 600.

910   UK   ISSN 0069-7109
COMMONWEALTH INSTITUTE, LONDON. ANNUAL REPORT. 1926. a. free. ‡ Commonwealth Institute, Kensington High St., London W.8, England. index. circ. controlled.

CONFERENCE OF SOUTH AFRICAN SURVEYORS. PROCEEDINGS/KONFERENSIE VAN SUID-AFRIKAANSE OPMETERS. VERRIGTINGE. see *ENGINEERING — Civil Engineering*

338   FR   ISSN 0396-2024
CONNAISSANCE DE L'OUEST. 1971. irreg. Association pour le Developpment Industriel de l'Ouest Atlantique, Immeuble Neptune, 44000 Nantes, France.

COSTA RICA. ARCHIVO NACIONAL. REVISTA. see *HISTORY*

910   SP   ISSN 0210-5462
CUADERNOS GEOGRAFICOS. (Includes: monographic supplements) (Text in Spanish; summaries in English, French) 1971. a. price varies. Universidad de Granada, Secretariado de Publicaciones, Antiguo Colegio Maximo de Cartujo, Granada, Spain. Ed. Victoriano Olmedo.

910   DK   ISSN 0105-4856
DANMARKS LAERERHOEJSKOLE. GEOGRAFISK INSTITUT. SKRIFTER. irreg. (Laererhoejskole, Geografisk Institut) Biblioteksentralen, Telegrafvej 5, DK-2750 Ballerup, Denmark.

526.982   DK   ISSN 0105-5194
DANMARKS TEKNISKE HOEJSKOLE. INSTITUTTET FOR LANDMAALING OG FOTOGRAMMETRI. MEDDELELSE. 1941. irreg., no.12, 1982. price varies. Danmarks Tekniske Hoejskole, Instituttet for Landmaaling og Fotogrammetri, Landmaalervej 7, 2800 Lyngby, Denmark. illus. circ. 300. Indexed: Geo.Abstr

526   GW   ISSN 0065-5309
DEUTSCHE GEODAETISCHE KOMMISSION. VEROEFFENTLICHUNGEN: REIHE A. THEORETISCHE GEODAESIE. 1951. irreg. price varies. Deutsche Geodaetische Kommission, Marstallplatz 8, D-8000 Munich 22, W. Germany (B.R.D.) Indexed: GeoRef.

526   GW   ISSN 0065-5317
DEUTSCHE GEODAETISCHE KOMMISSION. VEROEFFENTLICHUNGEN: REIHE B. ANGEWANDTE GEODAESIE. 1952. irreg. price varies. Deutsche Geodaetische Kommission, Marstallplatz 8, D-8000 Munich 22, W. Germany (B.R.D.) Indexed: GeoRef.

526   GW   ISSN 0065-5325
DEUTSCHE GEODAETISCHE KOMMISSION. VEROEFFENTLICHUNGEN: REIHE C. DISSERTATIONEN. 1952. irreg. price varies. Deutsche Geodaetische Kommission, Marstallplatz 8, D-8000 Munich 22, W. Germany (B.R.D.) Indexed: Geo.Abstr. GeoRef.

526   GW   ISSN 0065-5333
DEUTSCHE GEODAETISCHE KOMMISSION. VEROEFFENTLICHUNGEN: REIHE D. TAFELWERKE. 1956. irreg. price varies. Deutsche Geodaetische Kommission, Marstallplatz 8, 8000 Munich 22, W. Germany (B.R.D.)

526   GW   ISSN 0065-5341
DEUTSCHE GEODAETISCHE KOMMISSION. VEROEFFENTLICHUNGEN: REIHE E. GESCHICHTE UND ENTWICKLUNG DER GEODAESIE. 1961. irreg. price varies. Deutsche Geodaetische Kommission, Marstallplatz 8, D-8000 Munich 22, W. Germany (B.R.D.) Indexed: GeoRef.

912   CN   ISSN 0070-5217
DIRECTORY OF CANADIAN MAP COLLECTIONS. (Text in English and French) 1969. irreg (5th edt. 1986) Association of Canadian Map Libraries, c/o National Map Collection, Public Archives of Canada, 395 Wellington St., Ottawa, Ont. K1A 0N3, Canada. TEL 613-995-5138. Ed. Lorraine Dubreuil.

DOCUMENTOS DE GEOHISTORIA REGIONAL. see *HISTORY — History Of North And South America*

DOCUMENTS DE CARTOGRAPHIE ECOLOGIQUE. see *BIOLOGY*

910   UK
DRUMLIN. 1955. a. 70p. University of Glasgow Geographical Society, c/o Department of Geography, University of Glasgow, Glasgow G12 8QQ, Scotland. Ed. Paul Clark. adv. bk. rev. circ. 300.

916.76   UG   ISSN 0070-7961
EAST AFRICAN GEOGRAPHICAL REVIEW. 1963. a. $12.50. Uganda Geographical Association, Makerere University, Box 7062, Kampala, Uganda. Ed. J.B. Kabera. adv. bk. rev. circ. 1,000. Indexed: Curr.Cont.Africa. Field Crop Abstr. Herb.Abstr. Rural Recreat.Tour.Abstr. World Agri.Econ.& Rural Sociol.Abstr.

917   US   ISSN 0070-8127
EAST LAKES GEOGRAPHER. 1964. a. $4. (Association of American Geographers, East Lakes Division) Western Michigan University, Department of Geography, Kalamazoo, MI 49008. TEL 616-383-1839. (Co-sponsor: Association of American Geographers, East Lakes Division) Ed. David G. Dickason. circ. 500. (back issues avail.) Indexed: Geo.Abstr.

910   US
ENCYCLOPEDIA OF GEOGRAPHIC INFORMATION SOURCES. (Companion to Encyclopedia of Business Information Sources) irreg., 4th edt., 1986. $210. Gale Research Company, Book Tower, Detroit, MI 48226. TEL 313-961-2242. Ed. Jennifer Mossman.

ENVIRONMENTAL ASSESSMENT OF THE ALASKAN CONTINENTAL SHELF. ANNUAL REPORTS SUMMARY. see *ENVIRONMENTAL STUDIES*

910　　　　　　　GW　ISSN 0425-1741
ERDKUNDLICHES WISSEN; Schriftenfolge fuer Forschung und Praxis. (Supplement to Geographische Zeitschrift) 1952. irreg., vol.85, 1987. price varies. Franz Steiner Verlag Wiesbaden GmbH, Birkenwaldstr. 44, Postfach 347, D-7000 Stuttgart 1, W. Germany (B.R.D.) Eds. Emil Meynen, Ernst Plewe.

ERETZ-ISRAEL. ARCHAEOLOGICAL, HISTORICAL AND GEOGRAPHICAL STUDIES. see *ARCHAEOLOGY*

910　　　　　　　PO
ESTUDOS PARA O PLANEAMENTO REGIONAL E URBANO. 1976. irreg., latest no.24. Universidade de Liboa, Centro de Estudos Geograficos, Lisbon, Portugal. circ. 500.

EXPLORE MINNESOTA MINNETOURS. see *TRAVEL AND TOURISM*

910　　　　　　　DK　ISSN 0108-996X
FACTS OM DANMARK. 1984. irreg. free. Udenrigsministeriet, Asiatisk Plads 2, 1448 Copenhagen K, Denmark. illus.

FAR EAST AND AUSTRALASIA. see *HISTORY — History Of Australasia And Other Areas*

910　　　　　　　SW　ISSN 0349-0823
FAUNA NORRLANDICA. 1978. irreg. free. University of Umeo, Department of Ecological Zoology, c/o Prof. Karl Muller, S-90187 Umea, Sweden.

912　　　　　　　GW　ISSN 0176-1633
FERNERKUNDUNG IN RAUMORDUNG UND STADTEBAU. 1952. irreg., vol.16, 1984. price varies. Bundesforschungsanstalt fuer Landeskunde und Raumordnung, Am Michaelshof 8, Postfach 200130, 5300 Bonn 2, W. Germany(B.R.D.) circ. 800. Indexed: Geo.Abstr.
　Formerly: Landeskundliche Luftbildauswertung im Mitteileuropaeischen Raum (ISSN 0457-0715)

FLAMENCO; boletin de informacion. see *FOLKLORE*

917.59　　　　　　US　ISSN 0739-0041
FLORIDA GEOGRAPHER. 1967. a. $7. ‡ Florida Society of Geographers, Florida Atlantic University, Department of Geography, Boca Raton, FL 33431. TEL 305-393-3250. Ed. David Lee. bk. rev. circ. 300.

910　　　　　　　HU　ISSN 0428-819X
FOLDRAJZI MONOGRAFIAK. (Text in Hungarian; occasional summaries in French, German or Russian) 1955. irreg. price varies. (Magyar Tudomanyos Akademia) Akademiai Kiado, Publishing House of the Hungarian Academy of Sciences, Box 24, H-1363 Budapest, Hungary.

910　　　　　　　HU　ISSN 0071-6650
FOLDRAJZI TANULMANYOK. 1964. irreg., vol.19, 1984. price varies. (Magyar Tudomanyos Akademia) Akademiai Kiado, Publishing House of the Hungarian Academy of Sciences, Box 24, H-1363 Budapest, Hungary.

910　　　　　　　PL　ISSN 0071-6707
FOLIA GEOGRAPHICA. GEOGRAPHICA-OECONOMICA. (Text in Polish; summaries in English) 1968. a. price varies. (Polska Akademia Nauk, Oddziai w Krakowie, Komisja Nauk Geograficznych) Ossolineum, Publishing House of the Polish Academy of Sciences, Rynek 9, Wroclaw, Poland. Ed. B. Kortus. Indexed: Geo.Abstr.

910　　　　　　　PL　ISSN 0071-6715
FOLIA GEOGRAPHICA. GEOGRAPHICA-PHYSICA. (Text in Polish; summaries in English) 1967. a. price varies. (Polska Akademia Nauk, Oddzial w Krakowie, Komisja Nauk Geograficznych) Ossolineum, Publishing House of the Polish Academy of Sciences, Rynek 9, Wroclaw, Poland. Ed. T. Zietara. circ. 600. Indexed: Geo.Abstr. GeoRef.

914　　　　　　　DK　ISSN 0071-6693
FOLIA GEOGRAPHICA DANICA. (Text in Danish and English; summaries in English and Danish) 1940. irreg., (approx. 1/yr.) price varies. Kongelige Danske Geografiske Selskab - Royal Danish Geographical Society, Oester Voldgade 10, DK-1350 Copenhagen K, Denmark (Subscr. to: C. A. Reitzels Forlag, Noerregade 20, DK-1165 Copenhagen K, Denmark) Ed. Dr. N. Kingo Jacobsen. abstr. bibl. charts. illus. (reprint service avail. from UMI) Indexed: Geo.Abstr. GeoRef.

526.982　　　　　　SW　ISSN 0071-8068
FOTOGRAMMETRISKA MEDDELANDEN/PHOTOGRAMMETRIC NOTES. (Text in English, German, Swedish; summaries in English) 1944. irreg. Kr.150. Kungliga Tekniska Hoegskolan, Institutionen foer Fotogrammetri - Royal Institute of Technology, Department of Photogrammetry, S-100 44 Stockholm, Sweden. Ed. Kennert Torlegaard. cum.index: 1944-69. circ. 300.
　Photogrammetry

526.982　　　　　　PL　ISSN 0071-8076
FOTOINTERPRETACJA W GEOGRAFII. (Text in English, Polish; summaries in English, French, Polish) 1964. irreg. price varies. Uniwersytet Slaski w Katowicach, Ul. Bankowa 14, 40-007 Katowice, Poland.
　Photogrammetry

914　　　　　　　GW　ISSN 0071-8173
FRAENKISCHE GEOGRAPHISCHE GESELLSCHAFT. MITTEILUNGEN. 1954. irreg. price varies. Fraenkische Geographische Gesellschaft, Kochstr. 4, D-8520 Erlangen, W. Germany (B.R.D.) Ed. Eugen Wirth. adv. bk. rev. circ. 1,000. Indexed: GeoRef.

910　　　　　　　FR　ISSN 0071-8432
FRANCE. COMITE DES TRAVAUX HISTORIQUES ET SCIENTIFIQUES. SECTION DE GEOGRAPHIE. BULLETIN. 1913. irreg., vol.83, 1978. price varies. Ministere de l'Education Nationale, Comite des Travaux Historiques et Scientifiques, 3-5 bd. Pasteur, 75015 Paris, France. cum.index: 1886-1916. circ. 650. (back issues avail.)

526.8 910　　　　　　FR　ISSN 0071-8262
FRANCE. SERVICE DE DOCUMENTATION ET DE CARTOGRAPHIE GEOGRAPHIQUES. MEMOIRES ET DOCUMENTS. N.S. 1966. irreg. price varies. Editions du C N R S, 295 rue St. Jacques, 75005 Paris, France.

910　　　　　　　GW　ISSN 0071-9447
FREIBURGER GEOGRAPHISCHE HEFTE. 1963. irreg., vol.23, 1984. price varies. Universitaet Freiburg, Institut fuer Physische Geographie, Werderring 4, 7800 Freiburg, W. Germany (B.R.D.) Ed. W. Weischet. circ. 500. Indexed: GeoRef.

910　　　　　　　SP
FUENTES CARTOGRAFICAS ESPANOLAS. irreg. (3-4/yr) 200 ptas. per no. Instituto de Geografia Aplicada, Serrano 115, Madrid-6, Spain. circ. 1,500. (tabloid format)

GALLIA PREHISTOIRE. SUPPLEMENT. see *ARCHAEOLOGY*

917.1　　　　　　　CN　ISSN 0576-1999
GAZETTEER OF CANADA. (Text in English; some issues have text in English and French) 1952. irreg., latest 1987. price varies. Surveys and Mapping Branch, Permanent Committee on Geographical Names, c/o Dept. of Energy, Mines and Resources, 615 Booth St., Ottawa, Ont. K1A 0E9, Canada TEL 613-995-3065. (Orders to: Canadian Government Publishing Centre, Department of Supply and Services, Hull, Que. K1A 0S9, Canada) maps. circ. 1,500.

910　　　　　　　GW
GEO KATALOG (YEAR). VOLUME 1. TOURISTISCHE VEROEFFENTLICHUNGEN. 1972. a. DM.135. GeoCenter Verlagsvertrieb GmbH, Neumarkterstr. 18, D-8000 Munich 80, W. Germany (B.R.D.) TEL 089/43189613. adv. circ. 2, 500.
　Formerly: Geo Katalog. Band 1. Touristische Veroeffentlichungen.

910　　　　　　　DK　ISSN 0108-7657
GEOGRAFI. (Subseries of: Fagkatalog for Laerere) 1983. biennial. Kr.64.75. Bibliotekscentralen, Tempovej 7-11, DK-2750 Ballerup, Denmark.

910　　　　　　　PL　ISSN 0554-8128
GEOGRAFIA. (Text in Polish; summaries in English and German) 1957. irreg. Adam Mickiewicz University Press, Marchlewsiego 128, 61-874 Poznan, Poland. (also avail. in microfilm) Indexed: Geo.Abstr.
　Formerly: Uniwersytet im. Adama Mickiewicza w Poznaniu. Wydzial Biologii i Nauk o Ziemi. Zeszyty Naukowe. Geografia.

910 301　　　　　　BL　ISSN 0533-9286
GEOGRAFIA URBANA. irreg. Universidade de Sao Paulo, Instituto de Geografia, Edificio de Geografia e Historia, Cidade Universitaria, C.P. 20.7015, 01000 Sao Paulo, Brazil.

900　　　　　　　AG
GEOGRAFICA. 1972. a., no.3, 1974. $4. ‡ Universidad Nacional del Nordeste, Instituto de Geografia, Las Heras, 727, Resistencia, Argentina. Ed.Bd. illus. circ. 1,000.

910 550　　　　　　UR　ISSN 0202-327X
GEOGRAFIJA IR GEOLOGIJA. (Proceedings of the Lithuanian High Schools: Lietuvos T.S.R. Aukstuju Mokyklu Mokslo Darbai) (Text in Lithuanian; summaries in German and Russian) 1961. irreg. $2. Vilniusskii Gosudarstvennyi Universitet, Vilnius 31, Lithuanian S.S.R., U.S.S.R. Ed. A. Basalykas. Indexed: Ref.Zh.

910　　　　　　　UR　ISSN 0072-0917
GEOGRAFINIS METRASTIS/GEOGRAPHICAL ANNUAL. (Text in Lithuanian; summaries in English, German and Russian) 1958. irreg. price varies. Akademiya Nauk Litovskoi S.S.R., Lenino Prospektas 3, Vilnius, Lithuanian S.S.R., U.S.S.R. Ed. K. Bieliukas.

910　　　　　　　UK　ISSN 0308-6992
GEOGRAPHERS; biobibliographical studies. 1977. a. price varies. (International Geographical Union, Working Group on the History of Geographical Thought) Mansell Publishing Ltd., 6 All Saints St., London N1 9RL, England (Dist. in U.S. by: H.W. Wilson Co., 950 University Ave., Bronx, NY 10452) Ed. T.W. Freeman. index.

910　　　　　　　PL　ISSN 0208-5054
GEOGRAPHIA; studia et dissertationes. (Text in Polish; summaries in English and Russian) 1976. irreg. price varies. Uniwersytet Slaski w Katowicach, Ul. Bankowa 14, 40-007 Katowice, Poland.

910 610　　　　　　HU　ISSN 0300-807X
GEOGRAPHIA MEDICA; international journal on geography of health/journal international de la geographie de la sante. 1970. a. $10. (Hungarian Academy of Sciences, Institute of Geography) Hungarian Geographical Society, Medico-Geographical Section, c/o Illes Desi, Ed., Institute of Hygiene and Epidemiology, Univ. Med. School Szeged, H-6720 Szeged, Hungary. (Co-sponsor: International Geographical Union, Working Group on Geography of Health) Ed. Illes Desi. adv. bk. rev. Indexed: Biol.Abstr. Excerp.Med. Ind.Med. Geo.Abstr.
　Formerly: Geographia Medica Hungarica (ISSN 0435-3730)

910　　　　　　　PL　ISSN 0016-7282
GEOGRAPHIA POLONICA. (Text in English and French) 1964. irreg., vol.50, 1984. price varies. (Polska Akademia Nauk, Institute of Geography and Spatial Organization) Panstwowe Wydawnictwo Naukowe, Miodowa 10, 00-251 Warsaw, Poland (Dist. by: Ars Polona, Krakowskie Przedmiescie 7, 00-068 Warsaw, Poland) Ed. J. Kostrowicki. bibl. charts. illus. Indexed: Chem.Abstr. Geo.Abstr.

910　　　　　　　MY
GEOGRAPHICA. (Text in English) 1965. a. M.$5. University of Malaya, Department of Geography, 59100 Kuala Lumpur, Malaysia, Malaysia. Dir. S.H. Khoo. adv. bk. rev. bibl. charts. illus. circ. 1,000.

GEOGRAPHICAL EDUCATION. see *EDUCATION — Teaching Methods And Curriculum*

914.2　　　　　　　UK　ISSN 0078-2084
GEOGRAPHICAL FIELD GROUP (NOTTINGHAM). REGIONAL STUDIES. 1957. irreg., no.24, 1985. irreg. price varies. Geographical Field Group, c/o Dept. of Geography, University of Nottingham, Notts NG7 2RD, England. circ. 500.

GEOGRAPHY

910   NP
GEOGRAPHICAL JOURNAL OF NEPAL. 1978. a. Rs.30($61) Tribhuvan University, Geography Instruction Committee, Kirtipur, Nepal. Ed. Bal Kumar K.C. bk. rev. circ. 500.

910   II   ISSN 0072-0925
GEOGRAPHICAL OBSERVER. (Text in English and Hindi) 1965. a. $15 plus postage. Meerut College Geographical Society, c/o Department of Geography, Meerut College, Meerut 250 001, Uttar Pradesh, India. Ed. N.P. Saxena. bk. rev. circ. 300. Indexed: Doc.Geogr. Geo.Abstr.

910   UK   ISSN 0305-5914
GEOGRAPHICAL PAPERS. 1970. irreg. University of Reading, Department of Geography, White Knights, Reading RG6 2AB, England. adv. Indexed: Geo.Abstr.

001.6   CH
GEOGRAPHICAL SOCIETY OF CHINA. BULLETIN. 1973. a. $10. Geographical Society of China, c/o Department of Geography, National Taiwan, Taipei, Taiwan (R.O.C.) abstr. circ. 1,000.

914   CY
GEOGRAPHIKA CHRONIKA/GEOGRAPHICAL CHRONICLES. (Text in English or Greek) 1971. a. $10. Cyprus Geographical Association - Geographikos Homilos Kyprou, P.O. Box 3656, Nicosia, Cyprus. Ed. P. Argyrides. illus. circ. 1,000.

910   GW   ISSN 0374-9061
GEOGRAPHISCHE GESELLSCHAFT IN HAMBURG. MITTEILUNGEN. irreg., vol.76, 1986. price varies. Franz Steiner Verlag Wiesbaden GmbH, Birkenwaldstr. 44, Postfach 347, D-7000 Stuttgart 1, W. Germany (B.R.D.) Ed. Albert Kolb. Indexed: Biol.Abstr. GeoRef.

910   GW   ISSN 0072-0941
GEOGRAPHISCHE GESELLSCHAFT, MUNICH. MITTEILUNGEN. 1900. a. DM.50. Geographische Gesellschaft e.V., Muenchen, Heinrich Voglstr. 7, 8000 Munich 71, W. Germany (B.R.D.) Ed. Heinz G. Zimpel. bk. rev. circ. 700. Indexed: Bibl.Cart. GeoRef.

910   SZ
GEOGRAPHISCHE GESELLSCHAFT VON BERN. JAHRBUCH. (Text in French and German) 1878. irreg. (2-3/yr.) price varies. (Stadt und Universitaetsbibliothek) Geographische Gesellschaft von Bern, Muenstergasse 61, Postfach 58, 3000 Bern 7, Switzerland. Ed.Bd.

910   GW   ISSN 0723-175X
GEOGRAPHISCHE HOCHSCHULMANUSKRIPTE. 1973. irreg. price varies. Gesellschaft zur Foerderung Regionalwissenschaftlicher Erkenntnisse e.V., Postfach 1940, 2900 Oldenburg, W. Germany (B.R.D.) Indexed: Geo.Abstr.

910   GW   ISSN 0723-1679
GEOGRAPHISCHE HOCHSCHULMANUSKRIPTE. DISKUSSIONSPAPIERE. 1981. irreg. price varies. Gesellschaft zur Foerderung Regionalwissenschaftlicher Erkenntnisse e.V., Postfach 1940, 2900 Oldenburg, W. Germany (B.R.D.)

910   GE   ISSN 0072-095X
GEOGRAPHISCHES JAHRBUCH. a. VEB Hermann Haack, Geographisch-Kartographische Anstalt Gotha, Justus-Perthes-Str. 3-9, 5800 Gotha, E. Germany (D.D.R.) Indexed: Bibl.Cart.

910   GW   ISSN 0072-0968
GEOGRAPHISCHES TASCHENBUCH. 1949. irreg. price varies. Franz Steiner Verlag Wiesbaden GmbH, Birkenwaldstr. 44, Postfach 347, D-7000 Stuttgart 1, W. Germany (B.R.D.) Eds. Eckhart Ehlers, Emil Meynen. Indexed: Bibl.Cart.

914   UK
GEOGRAPHY OF THE BRITISH ISLES SERIES. irreg. price varies. Cambridge University Press, Edinburgh Bld., Shaftesbury Rd., Cambridge CB2 2RU, England (And 32 E. 57th St., New York NY 10022) Ed. A.V. Hardy.

910   HU   ISSN 0303-6634
GEOGRAPHY OF WORLD AGRICULTURE. (Text in English) 1972. irreg., vol.12, 1983. price varies. (Magyar Tudomanyos Akademia) Akademiai Kiado, Publishing House of the Hungarian Academy of Sciences, Box 24, H-1363 Budapest, Hungary.

910   US
GEOGRAPHY RESEARCH FORUM. (Text in English) 1979. a. $19.95. (Ben Gurion University of the Negev, Department of Geography) Transaction Books, c/o Alicja Garbie, Mkt. Dir., Rutgers University, New Brunswick, NJ 08903. TEL 201-932-2280. Ed. E. Stern. bk. rev.
Formerly: Geographical Research Forum (ISSN 0333-5275)

910   551   551.4   GW   ISSN 0720-454X
GEOOEKODYNAMIK. (Text in English, German; summaries in English, French, German, Italian) 1980. irreg. (2-4/yr.) DM.117($70) Verein fuer Erdkunde in Darmstadt e.V., Mainstr. 50, 614 Bensheim 1, W. Germany (B.R.D.) (Subscr. to: Geooekoverlag, Lessingstr. 19, W. Germany (B.R.D.)) Ed. O. Seuffert. adv. bk. rev. index. circ. 1,000. (back issues avail.) Indexed: Geo.Abstr.

916   GH   ISSN 0016-9536
GHANA GEOGRAPHICAL ASSOCIATION. BULLETIN. 1957. a. membership. Ghana Geographical Association, University of Ghana, Department of Geography, Legon, Accra, Ghana. Ed. E. Ardayfio-Schandorf. adv. bk. rev. circ. 500.

GLACIOLOGY AND QUATERNARY GEOLOGY. see *EARTH SCIENCES — Geology*

526   AT   ISSN 0311-3930
GLOBE. 1974. irreg. Aus.$25. Australian Map Circle, P.O. Box E133, Queen Victoria Terrace A.C.T. 2600, Australia. Ed. Glenys Faragher. bk. rev. circ. 250. (also avail. in microfiche) Indexed: Aus.P.A.I.S. Bibl.Cart.

526   AU   ISSN 0436-0664
GLOBUSFREUND. (Text in English, French and German) 1952. irreg., 1-3/yr. membership. Internationale Coronelli-Gesellschaft fuer Globen- und Instrumentenkunde, Dominikanerbastei 21/28, A-1010 Vienna, Austria. Ed. Rudolf Schmidt. bk. rev. charts. illus. stat. index. circ. 300. Indexed: Bibl.Cart.

GREENER PASTURES GAZETTE; the newsletter dedicated to the search for countryside Edens where the good life still exists. see *REAL ESTATE*

GROTTE D'ITALIA. see *EARTH SCIENCES — Geology*

910   US
GUIDE TO DEPARTMENTS OF GEOGRAPHY IN THE UNITED STATES AND CANADA. a. $15. Association of American Geographers, 1710 16th St., N.W., Washington, DC 20009. TEL 202-234-1450. Ed. Barbara Zimman. (reprint service avail. from UMI)
Formerly: Guide to Graduate Departments of Geography in the United States and Canada (ISSN 0072-8497)

526   US   ISSN 0073-0610
HARVARD PAPERS IN THEORETICAL GEOGRAPHY. 1967. irreg., no.57, 1972. price varies. Harvard University, Laboratory for Computer Graphics and Spatial Analysis, Graduate School of Design, 520 Gund Hall, 48 Quincy St., Cambridge, MA 02138. TEL 617-495-1000. circ. 500.

910   NP
HIMALAYAN REVIEW. (Text in English) 1968. a. Rs.20($5) Nepal Geographical Society, Tribhuvan University, Dept. of Geography, Kirtipur, Kathmandu, Nepal. Ed. Mangal S. Manandhar. adv. bk. rev. bibl. circ. 1,000.

911   UK   ISSN 0143-683X
HISTORICAL GEOGRAPHY RESEARCH SERIES. 1979. irreg. Geo Books, Regency House, 34 Duke St., Norwich NR3 3AP, England. Indexed: Br.Archaeol.Abstr. Geo.Abstr.

910   IS   ISSN 0334-3774
HORIZONS; studies in geography. (Text in Hebrew; summaries in English) irreg. Haifa University, Department of Geography, Hacarmel, Haifa 31 999, Israel. Ed. Dr. Micha Klein.

914.3   GW   ISSN 0441-5302
HYDRONYMIA GERMANIAE. irreg., vol.14, 1987. price varies. (Akademie der Wissenschaften und Literatur, Mainz) Franz Steiner Verlag Wiesbaden GmbH, Birkenwaldstr. 44, Postfach 347, D-7000 Stuttgart 1, W. Germany (B.R.D.) Ed. Wolfgang P. Schmid.

I C A S A L S ANNUAL REPORT. (International Center for Arid and Semi-Arid Land Studies) see *CONSERVATION*

910   UK   ISSN 0253-4894
I C M E NEWS. 1981. a. free. (International Committee for Museums of Ethnography) Commonwealth Institute, Kensington High St., London W8 6NQ, England.

914   NE
I D G-BULLETIN. (Editions in English, Dutch, French, German, Spanish) 1976. a. free. Information and Documentation Centre for the Geography of the Netherlands - Informatie- en Documentatie Centrum voor de Geographie van Nederland, Postbus 80115, 3508 TC Utrecht, Netherlands. (Co-Sponsor: Ministry of Foreign Affairs) Ed. Henk Meyer. adv. (also avail. in microfilm) Indexed: ERIC. Geo.Abstr.

910   MY   ISSN 0126-7000
ILMU ALAM. (Text and summaries in English and Malay) 1972. a. M.$9($4) National University of Malaysia, Department of Geography - Universiti Kebangsaan Malaysia, Bangi, Selangor, Malaysia. Ed. Abd. Hamid Abdullah. bk. rev. circ. 400. Indexed: Geo.Abstr.

910   UK   ISSN 0308-5694
IMAGO MVNDI; a review of early cartography. (Text and summaries in English) 1935. a. $40. (International Society for the History of Cartography, PO) Imago Mundi Ltd., Geography Department, King's College, London WC2R 2LS, England. Ed. E.M.J. Campbell. adv. bk. rev. charts. illus. circ. 700. Indexed: Bibl.Cart. Geo.Abstr.

917.3   557   US   ISSN 0073-6937
INDIANA STATE UNIVERSITY. DEPARTMENT OF GEOGRAPHY AND GEOLOGY. PROFESSIONAL PAPER. 1968. a. price varies. Indiana State University, Department of Geography and Geology, Terre Haute, IN 47809. TEL 812-232-6311. Eds. Dr. Akhtar H. Siddiqi, Dr. Alan Swenson. abstr. bibl. charts. circ. 1,000. Indexed: Geo.Abstr. GeoRef.

910   US   ISSN 0073-6953
INDIANA UNIVERSITY. DEPARTMENT OF GEOGRAPHY. GEOGRAPHIC MONOGRAPH SERIES. 1966. irreg., vol.7, 1984. Indiana University, Department of Geography, Kirkwood Hall 208, Bloomington, IN 47451. TEL 812-335-1153.

910   US   ISSN 0073-6961
INDIANA UNIVERSITY. DEPARTMENT OF GEOGRAPHY. OCCASIONAL PUBLICATION. 1964. irreg., vol.7, 1981. price varies. Indiana University, Department of Geography, Kirkwood Hall 208, Bloomington, IN 47451. TEL 812-335-1153.

INFORME DEMOGRAFICO. see *POPULATION STUDIES*

526   GW   ISSN 0071-9196
INSTITUT FUER ANGEWANDTE GEODAESIE. MITTEILUNGEN. 1952. irreg. price varies. Institut fuer Angewandte Geodaesie, Richard-Strauss-Allee 11, D-6000 Frankfurt 70, W. Germany (B.R.D.) (Subscr. to: Institut fuer Angewandte Geodaesie, Aussenstelle Berlin, Stauffenbergstr. 13, D-1000 Berlin 30, W. Germany (B.R.D.)) circ. 600.

916.75   526.8   ZR   ISSN 0443-3173
INSTITUT GEOGRAPHIQUE DU ZAIRE. RAPPORT ANNUEL. 1953. a. Institut Geographique du Zaire, B.P. 3086, Kinshasa, Zaire. illus.
Continues: Institut Geographique du Congo. Rapport.

GEOGRAPHY

526 PO ISSN 0870-015X
INSTITUTO DE INVESTIGACAO CIENTIFICA TROPICAL. CENTRO DE ESTUDOS DE HISTORIA E CARTOGRAFIA ANTIGA. SERIE DE MEMORIAS. 1963. irreg. Instituto de Investigacao Cientifica Tropical, Centro de Estudos de Historia e Cartografia Antiga, Rua Jau 54, 1300 Lisbon, Portugal. circ. 2,000.
Formerly: Estudos de Cartografia Antiga.

INSTITUTO DE INVESTIGACAO CIENTIFICA TROPICAL. CENTRO DE ESTUDOS DE HISTORIA E CARTOGRAFIA ANTIGA. SERIE SEPARATAS. see HISTORY

918.602 CK
INSTITUTO GEOGRAFICO AGUSTIN CODAZZI. INFORME DE LABORES. a. Instituto Geografico Agustin Codazzi, Carrera 30 No. 48-51, Apdo. Aero 6721, Bogota, Colombia. illus.

INSTITUTO HISTORICO E GEOGRAFICO DO ESPIRITO SANTO. REVISTA. see HISTORY

914 RM
INSTITUTUL PEDAGOGIC ORADEA. LUCRARI STIINTIFICE: SERIA GEOGRAFIE. (Continues in part its Lucrari Stiintifice: Seria A and Seria B (1969-70), and its Lucrari Stiintifice (1967-68)) (Text in Rumanian, occasionally in English or French; summaries in English, French, German, or Rumanian) 1967. a. Institutul Pedagogic Oradea, Calea Armatei Rosii Nr. 5, Oradea, Rumania.

526 GR ISSN 0081-0312
INTERNATIONAL ASSOCIATION OF GEODESY. CENTRAL BUREAU FOR SATELLITE GEODESY. INFORMATION BULLETIN. 1966. irreg. International Association of Geodesy, Central Bureau for Satellite Geodesy, National Technical University, K. Zographou 9, Athens 624, Greece.

INTERNATIONAL ASSOCIATION OF GEODESY. COMMISSION PERMANENTE DES MAREES TERRESTRES. MAREES TERRESTRES BULLETIN D'INFORMATION. see EARTH SCIENCES — Geophysics

910 341 US ISSN 0502-0034
INTERNATIONAL BOUNDARY STUDY. 1961. irreg., no.173, 1984. free. U.S. Department of State, Office of the Geographer, c/o Bureau of Intelligence and Research, 2201 C St.N.W., Washington, DC 20520. TEL 202-632-2022.

526 UK ISSN 0307-6113
INTERNATIONAL DIRECTORY OF CURRENT RESEARCH IN THE HISTORY OF CARTOGRAPHY AND IN CARTO-BIBLIOGRAPHY. 1974. biennial. £3. Geo Books, Regency House, 34 Duke St., Norwich NR3 3AP, England. Ed. Elzabeth Clutton. circ. 200.
Cartography

910 UR ISSN 0074-6134
INTERNATIONAL GEOGRAPHICAL UNION. PAPERS. 1968. quadrennial; 23rd, Moscow 1976. ‡ International Geographical Union, Soviet Organizing Committee, c/o Yuri Badenkov, Deputy Dir., Staromonetnyi Per. 29, Moscow 109017, Russian S.F.S.R., U.S.S.R. circ. 2,000.
Formerly: International Geographical Union. Report of Congress.

956.1 US ISSN 0272-7919
INTERNATIONAL JOURNAL OF TURKISH STUDIES. 1979/80. irreg. $20 individuals; institutions $25. University of Wisconsin, 4255 Humanities Bldg., Madison, WI 53706. Ed. Kemal H. Karpat. adv. bk. rev. circ. 700. (back issues avail.) Indexed: Amer.Bibl.Slavic & E.Eur.Stud.

INTERNATIONAL STRAITS OF THE WORLD. see POLITICAL SCIENCE — International Relations

526 US
INTERNATIONAL SYMPOSIUM ON COMPUTER-ASSISTED CARTOGRAPHY. PROCEEDINGS. irreg. $35 to non-members; members $25. American Society for Photogrammetry and Remote Sensing, 210 Little Falls St., Falls Church, VA 22046. TEL 703-534-6617. (Co-publisher: American Congress on Surveying and Mapping)
Formerly: International Symposium on Cartography and Computing. Proceedings (ISSN 0270-5133)

526 551 CN ISSN 0539-1016
INTERNATIONAL UNION OF GEODESY AND GEOPHYSICS. MONOGRAPH.* (Text in English and French) irreg. International Union of Geodesy and Geophysics, University of Toronto, Geophysics Laboratory, Toronto 5, Canada.

INTERNATIONAL UNION OF GEODESY AND GEOPHYSICS. MONOGRAPH. see GEOGRAPHY

526 551 FR ISSN 0074-9419
INTERNATIONAL UNION OF GEODESY AND GEOPHYSICS. PROCEEDINGS OF THE GENERAL ASSEMBLY. (Text in English and French) 1921. quadrennial. $20. International Union of Geodesy and Geophysics, Publications Office, 39 ter rue Gay Lussac, 75005 Paris, France. circ. 3, 500.

526.8 GW ISSN 0341-0986
INTERNATIONALES JAHRBUCH FUER KARTOGRAPHIE. (Text in English, French, German) 1961. a. price varies. (International Cartographic Association) Kirschbaum Verlag, Siegfriedstr. 28, Postfach 210209, 5300 Bonn 2, W. Germany (B.R.D.) Ed. K.H. Meine. adv. bk. rev. illus. circ. 2,000. Indexed: Bibl.Cart.

910.5 SA
ISIZWE. 1974. a. R.2. University of Natal, Students Geographical Society, Durban, South Africa. illus.

526.8 IS
ISRAEL. DEPARTMENT OF SURVEYS. CARTOGRAPHIC PAPERS. (Text in Hebrew; with English abstracts) 1965. irreg. price varies. Department of Surveys, P.O.B. 14171, Tel-Aviv 61141, Israel.

526.8 IS ISSN 0075-1138
ISRAEL. DEPARTMENT OF SURVEYS. GEODETIC PAPERS. (Text in Hebrew; summaries in English) 1965. irreg. price varies. Department of Surveys, P.O.B. 14171, Tel Aviv 61141, Israel.

526.8 IS
ISRAEL. DEPARTMENT OF SURVEYS. PHOTOGRAMMETRIC PAPERS. (Text in Hebrew; with English Abstract) 1976. irreg. price varies. Department of Surveys, P.O.B. 14171, Tel-Aviv 61141, Israel.

526.982 UR ISSN 0202-0726
ITOGI NAUKI I TEKHNIKI: GEODEZIYA I AEROS'EMKA. irreg., latest vol.25, 1987. price varies. Vsesoyuznyi Institut Nauchno-Tekhnicheskoi Informatsii (VINITI), Baltiiskaya ul. 14, Moscow A-219, Russian S.F.S.R., U.S.S.R. (Subscr. to: Mezhdunarodnaya Kniga, Dimitrova ul. 39, 113095 Moscow, Russian S.F.S.R., U.S.S.R.) Indexed: Int.Aerosp.Abstr.
Geodesy and aerial photography

910 UR ISSN 0202-7208
ITOGI NAUKI I TEKHNIKI: GEOGRAFIYA ZARUBEZHNYKH STRAN. irreg., latest vol.13, 1985. price varies. Vsesoyuznyi Institut Nauchno-Tekhnicheskoi Informatsii (VINITI), Baltiiskaya ul. 14, Moscow A-219, Russian S.F.S.R., U.S.S.R. (Subscr. to: Mezhdunarodnaya Kniga, Dimitrova ul. 39, 113095 Moscow, Russian S.F.S.R., U.S.S.R.)

526 UR ISSN 0202-7240
ITOGI NAUKI I TEKHNIKI: KARTOGRAFIYA. irreg., vol.12, 1986. price varies. Vsesoyuznyi Institut Nauchno-Tekhnicheskoi Informatsii (VINITI), Baltiiskaya ul. 14, Moscow A-219, Russian S.F.S.R., U.S.S.R. (Subscr. to: Mezhdunarodnaya Kniga, Dimitrova ul. 39, 113095 Moscow, Russian S.F.S.R., U.S.S.R.) Indexed: Bibl.Cart. Geo.Abstr.

917.29 JM
JAMAICAN GEOGRAPHICAL SOCIETY NEWSLETTER. 1967-1979; resumed 1981. a. $1.30. Jamaican Geographical Society, c/o Geography Dept., University of the West Indies, Kingston 7, Jamaica. Ed. M. Morrissey. bk. rev. bibl. circ. 200.
Former titles: Jamaica Geographical Society Proceedings; (until 1979): Jamaica Geographical Society Newsletter.

910 AT
JAMES COOK UNIVERSITY OF NORTH QUEENSLAND. DEPARTMENT OF GEOGRAPHY. MONOGRAPH SERIES. 1970. irreg. (approx. 2/yr.) price varies. James Cook University, Department of Geography, Douglas Townsville, Queensland 4811, Australia, Australia. Ed. David Hopley. circ. 300. Indexed: Geo.Abstr. GeoRef.

914.3 GW ISSN 0075-4528
JUGENDHERBERGS-VERZEICHNIS. 1920. a. DM.6. Hauptverband fuer Jugendwandern und Jugendherbergeu e.V., Postfach 220, 4930 Detmold 1, W. Germany (B.R.D.) Ed. Bert Pichel. adv. circ. 80,000.

526 US
K G S - N C I C NEWSLETTER. (Kentucky Geological Survey) irreg., no.15, 1987. U.S. National Cartographic Information Center, 311 Breckinridge Hall, University of Kentucky, Lexington, KY 40506-0056. TEL 606-257-3196.

526 UR
KARTOGRAFICHESKAYA LETOPIS' 1931. a. Izdatel'stvo Kniga, Ul. Nezhdanovoi, 8-10, Moscow K-9, Russian S.F.S.R., U.S.S.R. bibl. circ. 1,200.

KEVO SUBARCTIC RESEARCH INSTITUTE. REPORTS. see BIOLOGY

910 550 320 GW
KOBLENZER GEOGRAPHISCHES KOLLOQUIUM. 1979. a. DM.5. Seminar fuer Geographie der Erziehungswissenschaft. Hochschule Koblenz, Rheinau 3-4, Gebaeude F10, D-5400 Koblenz, W. Germany (B.R.D.) Ed. Heinz Fischer, Richard Graafen. bk. rev. bibl. (back issues avail.)

910 DK ISSN 0106-3618
KOEBENHAVNS UNIVERSITET. GEOGRAFISK CENTRALINSTITUT. LABORATORIUM FOR GEOMORFOLOGI. 1972. irreg. price varies. Koebenhavns Universitet, Geografisk Centralinstitut, Laboratorium for Geomorfologi, Oester Voldgade 10, DK-1350 Copenhagen K, Denmark. illus.

909.09 NE
KONINKLIJK INSTITUUT VOOR DE TROPEN. SURVEY. biennial. Koninklijk Instituut voor de Tropen - Royal Tropical Institute, Mauritskade 63, 1092 AD Amsterdam, Netherlands. illus.
Formerly: Koninklijk Instituut voor de Tropen. Annual Report.

914 DK ISSN 0106-2956
KRIGSPLAN. no.11, 1982. irreg. price varies. Krigsplangruppen, c/o Geografisk Institut, Vennelyst Boulevard, 8000 Aarhus C, Denmark.

910 DK ISSN 0108-3945
KULTURGEOGRAFISKE HAEFTERS SKRIFTSERIE. 1981. irreg., no.13,1985. Kr.120. Kulturgeografiske Haefter, Oestervoldgade 10, 1350 Copenhagen K, Denmark.

900 910 GW
LAENDERMONOGRAPHIEN. 1969. irreg. price varies. (Institut fuer Auslandsbeziehungen, Stuttgart) K. Thienemanns Verlag, Blumenstr. 36, 7000 Stuttgart 1, W. Germany (B.R.D.) circ. 4,000.

296 US ISSN 0738-1379
LATIN AMERICAN JEWISH STUDIES NEWSLETTER. 1980. irreg. (2-3/yr.) $15 to individuals; institutions $25. Latin American Jewish Studies Association, 2104 Georgetown Blvd., Ann Arbor, MI 48105. TEL 313-996-2880. Ed. Judith Laikin Elkin. adv. bk. rev. bibl. circ. 500. (looseleaf format; back issues avail)

914.503 IT
LIGURIA TERRITORIO E CIVILTA. no.4, 1977. irreg. Sagep Editrice S.p.A., Piazza della Vittoria 14, 16121 Genoa, Italy. Ed. Gaspare De Fiore.

910 UK ISSN 0076-0641
LONDON SCHOOL OF ECONOMICS AND POLITICAL SCIENCE. DEPARTMENT OF GEOGRAPHY. GEOGRAPHICAL PAPERS. 1964. irreg., latest no.7. price varies. London School of Economics & Political Science, Dept. of Geography, Houghton St., Aldwych, London WC2A 2AE, England. Indexed: Geo.Abstr.

GEOGRAPHY

910.02 910 SW ISSN 0076-146X
LUND STUDIES IN GEOGRAPHY. SERIES A. PHYSICAL GEOGRAPHY. (Text in English and German) 1950. irreg., no.60, 1983. price varies. (Lunds Universitet, Department of Geography) Liber Forlag, S-205 10, Malmo, Sweden. index. cum.index: 1950-54, 1956-58, 1960-66. Indexed: GeoRef.

LUND STUDIES IN GEOGRAPHY. SERIES B. HUMAN GEOGRAPHY. see *BIOLOGY*

910 526 SW ISSN 0076-1486
LUND STUDIES IN GEOGRAPHY. SERIES C. GENERAL AND MATHEMATICAL GEOGRAPHY. (Text in English) 1962. irreg., no.13, 1985. price varies. (Lunds Universitet, Department of Geography) LIber Forlag, S-205 10, Malmo, Sweden. index. cum.index: 1962-65.

917.1 CN ISSN 0076-1982
MCGILL SUB-ARCTIC RESEARCH PAPERS. 1956. irreg. Can.$3 per no. McGill University, Box 6070, Montreal, Que. 101, Canada TEL 514-392-4311. (Dist. by McGill Sub-Arctic Research Laboratory, Box 790, Schefferville, Que. Canada) circ. 500. Indexed: Geo.Abstr.

910 CN
MCGILL UNIVERSITY SAVANNA RESEARCH PROJECT - SAVANNA RESEARCH SERIES. 1964. irreg. Can.$100. McGill University, Department of Geography, 805 Sherbrooke St. West, Montreal, Que. H3A 2K6, Canada. TEL 514-392-5495. Ed. Dr. Theo L. Hills.
Formerly: Publications in Tropical Geography Savanna Research Series (ISSN 0079-7758)

914 HU ISSN 0076-2512
MAGYARORSZAG TAJFOLDRAJZA. 1967. irreg., vol.4, 1981. price varies. (Magyar Tudomanyos Akademia) Akademiai Kiado, Publishing House of the Hungarian Academy of Sciences, P.O. Box 24, H-1363 Budapest, Hungary.

910 UG ISSN 0075-4722
MAKERERE UNIVERSITY. DEPARTMENT OF GEOGRAPHY. OCCASIONAL PAPER. 1967. irreg., no.71, 1977. price varies. Makerere University, Department of Geography, Box 7062, Kampala, Uganda. adv. bk. rev. Indexed: GeoRef.

910 MW
MALAWIAN GEOGRAPHER. (Text in English) 1968. a. $4. Geography Teacher's Association, c/o Chancellor College, Box 280, Zomba, Malawi. Eds. E.D. Kadzombe, D.D. Chimrenje. adv. bk. rev. circ. 300. Indexed: GeoRef.

917.1 CN
MANITOBA GEOGRAPHICAL STUDIES. 1973. irreg. (2-3/yr.) price varies. University of Manitoba, Department of Geography, Winnipeg, Manitoba, Canada. TEL 204-474-9256. Ed. D. Todd. circ. 750.

MARSCHENRAT ZUR FOERDERUNG DER FORSCHUNG IM KUESTENGEBIET DER NORDSEE. NACHRICHTEN. see *SCIENCES: COMPREHENSIVE WORKS*

910 UK ISSN 0140-7961
MATTER OF DEGREE; a guide to geography courses in the United Kingdom. 1971. a. £2. Geo Books, Regency House, 34 Duke St., Norwich NR3 3AP, England. circ. 2,000.

910.9 500 CN
MAWDSLEY MEMOIRS. 1973. irreg. price varies. University of Saskatchewan, Extension Division, Saskatoon, Sask. S7N 0W0, Canada. TEL 306-966-5696. bibl. Indexed: Biol.Abstr.

910 IE
MAYNOOTH OCCASIONAL PAPERS. 1978. irreg. £5($5) per issue. St. Patrick's College, Department of Geography, Maynooth, Co. Kildare, Ireland. Ed. Dennis G. Pringle. circ. 200. (back issues avail.)

915 IS
MERHAVIM; collection of geographical research about Israel and the Middle East. (Text in Hebrew; summaries in English) 1974. irreg. Tel Aviv University, Department of Geography, Tel Aviv, Israel. illus.

MIDDLE EAST AND NORTH AFRICA; survey and directory of lands of Middle East and North Africa. see *HISTORY — History Of The Near East*

910 AT ISSN 0313-8410
MONASH UNIVERSITY. PUBLICATIONS IN GEOGRAPHY. 1972. irreg. Aus.$4 per no. Monash University, Department of Geography, Clayton, Australia. Ed. David Mercer. bibl. illus. index. circ. 100.

910 GW
MUENCHENER GEOGRAPHISCHE ABHANDLUNGEN. 1970. irreg., 3-4/yr. price varies. (Universitaet Muenchen, Institut fuer Geographie) Nelles Verlag, Schleissheimer Str. 371b, 8000 Munich 45, W. Germany (B.R.D.) circ. 600. Indexed: GeoRef.

910.1 GW ISSN 0077-1902
MUENCHENER STUDIEN ZUR SOZIAL- UND WIRTSCHAFTSGEOGRAPHIE. (Text in German; summaries in English, French and Russian) 1966. irreg. price varies. (Universitaet Muenchen, Wirtschaftsgeographisches Institut) Verlag Michael Lassleben, Lange Gasse 19, Postfach 20, 8411 Kallmuenz, W. Germany (B.R.D.) Indexed: Rural Recreat.Tour.Abstr. World Agri.Econ.& Rural Sociol.Abstr.

MUSEE NATIONAL D'HISTOIRE NATURELLE, PARIS. NOTES ET MEMOIRES SUR LE MOYEN-ORIENT. see *EARTH SCIENCES — Geology*

MUSEUM OF ANTIQUITIES OF TEL-AVIV-YAFO. PUBLICATIONS. see *ARCHAEOLOGY*

526 GW ISSN 0469-4236
NACHRICHTEN AUS DEM KARTEN- UND VERMESSUNGSWESEN. REIHE I: ORIGINALBEITRAEGE. 1956. irreg. price varies. Institut fuer Angewandte Geodaesie, Richard-Strauss-Allee 11, D-6000 Frankfurt 70, W. Germany (B.R.D.) bk. rev. circ. 550. Indexed: Bibl.Cart. Geo.Abstr. GeoRef.
Supersedes in part: Nachrichten aus dem Karten-und Vermessungswesen (ISSN 0071-920X)

526 GW ISSN 0469-4244
NACHRICHTEN AUS DEM KARTEN- UND VERMESSUNGSWESEN. REIHE II: UEBERSETZUNGEN. 1957. irreg. price varies. Institut fuer Angewandte Geodaesie, Richard-Strauss-Allee 11, D-6000 Frankfurt 70, W. Germany (B.R.D.) bk. rev. circ. 550. Indexed: Geo.Abstr. GeoRef.

914 SW ISSN 0077-2704
NAMN OCH BYGD; journal for Nordic place-name research. (Text in English, German and Scandinavian Languages; summaries in English) 1913. a. Kr.65($12) Kungliga Gustav Adolfs Akademien - Royal Gustavus Adolphus Academy, St. Johannesgatan 11, S-75221 Uppsala, Sweden (Subscr. to: Almqvist & Wiksell International, P.O. Box 638, S-101 28 Stockholm, Sweden) Ed. Thorsten Andersson. bk. rev. circ. 500.

910 US
NATIONAL COUNCIL FOR GEOGRAPHIC EDUCATION. PACESETTER SERIES. 1970. a. price varies. National Council for Geographic Education, c/o James W. Vining, Exec. Dir., Western Illinois University, Macomb, IL 61455. TEL 309-298-2470. Ed. Basheer Nijim. Indexed: Educ.Ind.
Formerly: National Council for Geographic Education. Yearbook (ISSN 0077-4030)

NATIONAL COUNCIL FOR GEOGRAPHIC EDUCATION. TOPICS IN GEOGRAPHY. see *EDUCATION — Teaching Methods And Curriculum*

910 II ISSN 0470-0929
NATIONAL GEOGRAPHER. (Text in English) 1958. a. $15. Allahabad Geographical Society, University of Allahabad, Department of Geography, Allahabad 211002, Uttar Pradesh, India. Ed. R.C. Tiwayi. bk. rev. illus. circ. 450. Indexed: Rural Recreat.Tour.Abstr. World Agri.Econ.& Rural Sociol.Abstr.

910 US ISSN 0077-4618
NATIONAL GEOGRAPHIC BOOKS (SERIES) Also known as: National Geographic Society. Special Publications Series. 1966. irreg. (approx. 4/yr) National Geographic Society, 17th & M Sts., N.W., Washington, DC 20036. TEL 202-857-7000.

508.98 US ISSN 0361-2279
NATIONAL RESEARCH COUNCIL. COMMITTEE ON POLAR RESEARCH. REPORT ON UNITED STATES ANTARCTIC RESEARCH ACTIVITIES. Added title: Polar Research. 1974. a. free. (National Research Council, Polar Research Board) National Academy Press, National Academy of Sciences, 2101 Constitution Ave., Washington, DC 20418. TEL 202-334-2000. illus. Key Title: Report on United States Antarctic Research Activities.

910 CH
NATIONAL TAIWAN UNIVERSITY. DEPARTMENT OF GEOGRAPHY. SCIENCE REPORTS. (Text and summaries in English or Chinese) 1962. irreg. free. National Taiwan University, Department of Geography, National Taiwan University, Taipei, Taiwan (R.O.C.) (Subscr. to: National Taiwan University Library, Serials Section, Taipei, Taiwan, Republic of China) Dir. Chang-Yi Chang. circ. 500. Indexed: GEo.Abstr.

910 US ISSN 0082-5166
NATURAL HAZARD RESEARCH WORKING PAPERS. 1968. irreg., no.54, 1985. $3. (Natural Hazards Research and Applications Information Center) University of Colorado, Institute of Behavioral Science, Campus Box 482, Boulder, CO 80309. TEL 303-492-6818. Eds. Sarah Nathe, David Butler. circ. 130. Indexed: Geo.Abstr.

910 CS
NAUKA O ZEMI. SERIA GEOGRAPHICA. (Text in Slovak; summaries in English and Russian) 1966. irreg. (Slovenska Akademia Vied) Veda, Publishing House of the Slovak Academy of Sciences, Klemensova 19, 814 30 Bratislava, Czechoslovakia (Subscr. to: Slovart, Gottwaldovo nam. 6, 817 64 Bratislava, Czechoslovakia) Indexed: GeoRef.

778 NE ISSN 0169-4839
NEDERLANDSE GEOGRAFISCHE STUDIES/ NETHERLANDS GEOGRAPHICAL STUDIES (NGS) (Text mainly in Dutch, occasionally in English) 1985. irreg. (approx. 20/yr.) Koninklijk Nederlands Aardrijkskundig Genootschap, Weterigschans 12, 1017 SG Amsterdam, Netherlands. Ed. Johan G. Borchert. Indexed: Geo.Abstr.

526 624 NE ISSN 0077-7625
NETHERLANDS. RIJKSCOMMISSIE VOOR GEODESIE. PUBLICATIONS ON GEODESY. NEW SERIES. (Text usually in English) 1961. irreg. price varies. ‡ Rijkscommissie voor Geodesie - Netherlands Geodetic Commission, Thijsseweg 11, Delft, Netherlands. circ. 700.

917.4 US ISSN 0888-4285
NEW YORK FACTS. 1986. triennial. Clements Research, Inc., 16850 Dallas Pkwy., Dallas, TX 75248. TEL 214-931-8827.

919.31 NZ ISSN 0078-0022
NEW ZEALAND GEOGRAPHICAL SOCIETY. MISCELLANEOUS SERIES. 1950. irreg., no.8, 1983. price varies. New Zealand Geographical Society Inc., Dept. of Geography, University of Canterbury, Private Bag, Christchurch, New Zealand.

919.31 NZ ISSN 0078-0030
NEW ZEALAND GEOGRAPHY CONFERENCE PROCEEDINGS SERIES. 1955. biennial, no.12, 1983. ‡ New Zealand Geographical Society Inc., Dept. of Geography, University of Canterbury, Private Bag, Christchurch, New Zealand. circ. 950. Indexed: Excerp.Med. GeoRef.

NORSK POLARINSTITUTT. AARBOK. see *EARTH SCIENCES — Geology*

NORSK POLARINSTITUTT. MEDDELELSER. see *EARTH SCIENCES — Geology*

NORSK POLARINSTITUTT. POLARHAANDBOK. see *EARTH SCIENCES — Geology*

NORSK POLARINSTITUTT. SKRIFTER. see *EARTH SCIENCES — Geology*

NORTH SHORE DINING GUIDE. see *TRAVEL AND TOURISM*

917.7 US
NORTH SHORE NEWCOMERS' GUIDE. 1983. a. $1.50 per no. P B Communications, Inc., 874 Green Bay Rd., Winnetka, IL 60093. TEL 312-441-7892. Ed. Asher J. Birnbaum. adv. illus. circ. 50,000.

NORTH STAFFORDSHIRE JOURNAL OF FIELD STUDIES. see HISTORY — History Of Europe

917 US
NORTHERN ARIZONA SCENE; a pictorial and prose profile of Arizona's northlands. 1976. a. $2. Halamar, Inc., 9800 Flint Rock Rd., Manassas, VA 22111. Ed. Hal Sundstrom. illus. circ. 50,000.

910 GW ISSN 0546-9112
NUERNBERGER WIRTSCHAFTS-UND SOZIALGEOGRAPHISCHE ARBEITEN. (Text in German; summaries in English) 1957. irreg., vol.38, 1985. price varies. Gesellschaft fuer Regionalforschung und angewandte Geographie e.V., Wirtschafts- und Sozialgeographisches Institut, Lange Gasse 20, 8500 Nuernberg, West Germany (B.R.D.) Eds. Ernst Weigt, Wigand Ritter. circ. 700.

910 UK ISSN 0078-3056
OCCASIONAL PAPERS IN GEOGRAPHY. 1965. irreg. price varies. Hull University Press, Hull HU6 7RX, England. Ed. R.C. Ward. Indexed: SSCI.

OCCASIONAL PAPERS ON RELIGION IN EASTERN EUROPE. see RELIGIONS AND THEOLOGY

910 US ISSN 0094-9043
OHIO GEOGRAPHERS: RECENT RESEARCH THEMES. (Supplement avail.) 1973. a. $8. Miami University, Department of Geography, 218 Shideler Hall, Oxford, OH 45056. TEL 513-529-5010. Eds. Carville Earle, Jerry Green. bk. rev. circ. 100(controlled) (also avail. in microform from UMI) Indexed: ERIC. Geo.Abstr.

OHIO STATE UNIVERSITY. INSTITUTE OF POLAR STUDIES. MISCELLANEOUS SERIES. see EARTH SCIENCES

OHIO STATE UNIVERSITY. INSTITUTE OF POLAR STUDIES. REPORT SERIES. see EARTH SCIENCES

917.6 US
OKLAHOMA LAKE LIVING. 1979. a. $2 per no. Oklahoma Lake Living Magazine, Box 1781, Muskogee, OK 74401. adv. circ. 50,000.

910 GW ISSN 0030-4395
ORBIS GEOGRAPHICUS; world directory of geography. (Text in German, English, French) 1952. irreg. price varies. (International Geographical Union) Franz Steiner Verlag Wiesbaden GmbH, Birkenwaldstr. 44, Postfach 347, D-7000 Stuttgart 1, W. Germany (B.R.D.) Ed. E. Meynen.

ORIGINAL NEW ENGLAND GUIDE. see TRAVEL AND TOURISM

910 NZ ISSN 0078-690X
OTAGO GEOGRAPHER. 1968. irreg. NZ.$1. University of Otago, Geography Students Assn., c/o Geography Dept., Box 56, Dunedin, New Zealand. Ed. G.O. Crombie. circ. 200.

526.8 AT ISSN 0311-9319
OVERSEAS MAP ACQUISITIONS. 1975. a. National Library of Australia, Sales and Subscription Section, Parkes, ACT 2600, Australia. circ. 550.

526 MX
PAN AMERICAN INSTITUTE OF GEOGRAPHY AND HISTORY. GUIDES FOR INVESTIGATORS. irreg. price varies. Instituto Panamericano de Geografia e Historia, Ex-Arzobispado 29, Col. Observatorio, Deleg. Miguel Hidalgo, 11860 Mexico, D.F., Mexico.
Cartography

910 US
PERSPECTIVES IN GEOGRAPHY. 1971. irreg. price varies. Northern Illinois University Press, Dekalb, IL 60115. TEL 815-753-1826.

PILIPINAS; an interdisciplinary scholarly journal of Philippine studies. see HISTORY — History Of Asia

POLAR RESEARCH. see SCIENCES: COMPREHENSIVE WORKS

POLITICAL HANDBOOK OF THE WORLD. see POLITICAL SCIENCE

910 PL ISSN 0373-6547
POLSKA AKADEMIA NAUK. INSTYTUT GEOGRAFII I PRZESTRZENNEGO ZAGOSPODAROWANIA. PRACE GEOGRAFICZNE. (Text in Polish; summaries in English and Russian) 1954. irreg., no.145, 1983. price varies. Ossolineum, Publishing House of the Polish Academy of Sciences, Rynek 9, Wroclaw, Poland. Ed. M. Kielczewska-Zaleska. Indexed: GeoRef.
Formerly: Polska Akademia Nauk. Instytut Geografii. Prace Geograficzne (ISSN 0554-5749)

526 PL ISSN 0079-3299
POLSKA AKADEMIA NAUK. ODDZIAL W KRAKOWIE. KOMISJA GORNICZO-GEODEZYJNA. PRACE: GEODEZJA. (Text in Polish; summaries in English and Russian) 1964. irreg., no.32, 1986. price varies. Ossolineum, Publishing House of the Polish Academy of Sciences, Rynek 9, Wroclaw, Poland (Dist. by: Ars Polona-Ruch, Krakowskie Przedmiescie 7, Warsaw, Poland) Ed. Jozef Jachimski.

910.02 PL ISSN 0137-2939
POLSKA AKADEMIA NAUK. ODDZIAL W KRAKOWIE. OSRODEK DOKUMENTACJI FIZJOGRAFICZNEJ. STUDIA. 1972. a. price varies. Ossolineum, Publishing House of the Polish Academy of Sciences, Rynek 9, Wroclaw, Poland, Dist. by: Ars Polona-Ruch, Krakowskie Przedmiescie 7, Warsaw, Poland. Ed. Antoni Kleczkowski.

914.7 PL ISSN 0208-4082
POMORSKIE MONOGRAFIE TOPONOMASTYCZNE. (Text in Polish; summaries in English and Russian) irreg., vol.7, 1986. price varies. (Gdanskie Towarzystwo Naukowe) Ossolineum, Publishing House of the Polish Academy of Sciences, Rynek 9, Wroclaw, Poland (Dist. by: Ars Polona-Ruch, Krakowskie Przedmiescie 7, Warsaw, Poland) Ed. H. Gornowicz. circ. 950.

POZNANSKIE TOWARZYSTWO PRZYJACIOL NAUK. KOMISJA GEOGRAFICZNO-GEOLOGICZNA. PRACE. see EARTH SCIENCES — Geology

910 PL ISSN 0208-4589
PRACE I STUDIA GEOGRAFICZNE. (Text in Polish; summaries in English) 1979. irreg., vol.8, 1985. price varies. (Uniwersytet Warszawski, Wydzial Geografii i Studiow Regionalnych) Wydawnictwa Uniwersytetu Warszawskiego, Ul. Obozna 8, 00-927 Warsaw, Poland (Dist. by: CHZ ARS Polona, Krakowskie Przedmiescie 7, 00-068 Warsaw, Poland) circ. 500.

910 PL ISSN 0137-477X
QUAESTIONES GEOGRAPHICAE. (Text in English) 1974. a. price varies. Adam Mickiewicz University Press, Marchlewskiego 128, 61-874 Poznan, Poland. Ed. Stefan Kozarski. circ. 1,000. (also avail. in microfilm) Indexed: Geo.Abstr. GeoRef.

910 UK
QUEEN MARY COLLEGE. DEPARTMENT OF GEOGRAPHY AND EARTH SCIENCE. OCCASIONAL PAPERS. 1974. irreg. price varies. Queen Mary College, Department of Geography and Earth Science, Mile End Rd., London E1 4NS, England. Ed. John Eyles. circ. 600. Indexed: Geo.Abstr.
Formerly: Queen Mary College. Department of Geography. Occasional Papers (ISSN 0306-2740)

RAND MCNALLY COMMERCIAL ATLAS AND MARKETING GUIDE. see BUSINESS AND ECONOMICS — Marketing And Purchasing

910 US
RAND MCNALLY GOODE'S WORLD ATLAS. 1922. quadrennial. Rand McNally & Co., Box 7600, Chicago, IL 60680. TEL 312-673-9100. Ed. Edward B. Espenshade, Jr.

526 FR ISSN 0180-9970
RECUEIL DES CORRECTIONS DE CARTES (YEAR) 1978. a. price varies. Service Hydrographique et Oceanographique de la Marine, 3 av. Octave Gerard, 75200 Paris Naval, France (Subscr. address: E.P.S.H.O.M., B.P. 426, 29275 Brest Cedex, France)
Cartography

910 CN ISSN 0228-5851
REGINA GEOGRAPHICAL STUDIES. 1977. irreg. price varies. University of Regina, Department of Geography, Regina, Sask. S4S 0A2, Canada. TEL 306-584-4222. Indexed: Geo.Abstr.

910 FR
REPERTOIRE DES GEOGRAPHES FRANCAIS. 1969. quadrennial. 150 F. Centre National de la Recherche Scientifique, Laboratoire "Intergeo", 191 rue Saint-Jacques, 75005 Paris, France.
Formerly (until 1978): Annuaire des Geographes de la France et de l'Afrique Francophone (ISSN 0066-2844)

RESEARCH; contributions to interdisciplinary anthropology. see ANTHROPOLOGY

910 US
RESEARCH IN CONTEMPORARY AND APPLIED GEOGRAPHY; a discussion series. 1977. a. $12. State University of New York at Binghamton, Department of Geography, Binghamton, NY 13901. TEL 607-777-2755. Ed. John Frazier. circ. 100. Indexed: Geo.Abstr.

910 AT
RESEARCH PAPERS IN GEOGRAPHY. 1975. irreg. price varies. University of Newcastle, Department of Geography, Newcastle, N.S.W. 2308, Australia. Ed. D.N. Parkes. circ. 100. Indexed: Geo.Abstr.

914.38 PL
RESULTS OF INVESTIGATIONS OF THE POLISH SCIENTIFIC SPITSBERGEN EXPEDITIONS. (Subseries of its: Acta Universitatis Wratislaviensis) 1975. irreg. price varies. Wydawnictwa Universytetu Wroclawskiego, Ul. Kuznicza 34, 50-138 Wroclaw, Poland.

910 BL ISSN 0101-9457
REVISTA DE GEOGRAFIA. (Text in Portuguese; summaries in English and Portuguese) 1982. a. $30. Universidade Estadual Paulista, Av. Vicente Ferreira, 1278, Caixa Postal 603, 17.500 Marilia SP, Brazil. Ed.Bd. adv. bk. rev. circ. 1,000. Indexed: Ref.Zh. Ecol.Abstr. Geo.Abstr. Geophys.Abstr. Mineral.Abstr.

910 CL ISSN 0034-9577
REVISTA GEOGRAFICA DE VALPARAISO. 1967. a. $10. (Universidad Catolica de Valparaiso, Instituto de Geografia) Ediciones Universitarias de Valparaiso, Casilla 1415, Valparaiso, Chile. Ed. Rodolfo Allesh L. charts. illus. circ. 300.

910 BE ISSN 0770-0717
REVUE BELGE DE GEOGRAPHIE. 1876. irreg. (3-7/yr.) 1200 Fr. for non-members. Societe Royale Belge de Geographie, Bld. du Triomphe, CP 246, 1050 Brussels, Belgium. Ed. Christian Vandermotten. bk. rev. charts. illus. circ. 800. Indexed: Bibl.Cart. Geo.Abstr. GeoRef.
Formerly: Bulletin de Societe Royale Belge de Geographie.

551 RM ISSN 0556-8099
REVUE ROUMAINE DE GEOLOGIE, GEOPHYSIQUE ET GEOGRAPHIE. GEOGRAPHIE. (Text in English, French, German and Russian) 1957. a. $32. (Academia Republicii Socialiste Romania) Editura Academiei Republicii Socialiste Rumania, Calea Victoriei 125, 79717 Bucharest, Rumania (Subscr. to: ROMPRESFILATELIA, Calea Grivitei 64-66, P.O. Box 12-201, 78104 Bucharest, Rumania) Ed. Virgil Ianovici. bk. rev. charts. illus. index. Indexed: Chem.Abstr. Bibl.Cart. GeoRef.
Supersedes in part: Revue de Geologie et de Geographie.

910   IT   ISSN 0035-6697
RIVISTA GEOGRAFICA ITALIANA. (Summaries in English) 1893. irreg. (Societa di Studi Geografici di Firenze) Pagini Arti Grafiche ed Editore, Via A. Gherardesca, 56014 Ospedaletto PI, Italy, Italy. Dir. Berardo Cori. adv. bk. rev. bibl. charts. illus. index. Indexed: Bibl.Cart. Rural Recreat.Tour.Abstr. World Agri.Econ. & Rural Sociol.Abstr.

910   DK   ISSN 0106-3545
ROSKILDE UNIVERSITETSCENTER. DEPARTMENT OF GEOGRAPHY, SOCIAL ECONOMICS AND COMPUTER SCIENCE. KOMPENDIUM. 1977. irreg. free. Roskilde Universitetscenter, Department of geography, Social Economics and computer Science, Postboks 260, DK-4000 Roskilde, Denmark.

910   DK   ISSN 0106-2778
ROSKILDE UNIVERSITETSCENTER. DEPARTMENT OF GEOGRAPHY, SOCIAL ECONOMICS AND COMPUTER SCIENCE. MEDDELELSER. no.13, 1984. irreg. free. Roskilde Universitetscenter, Department of Geography, Social Economics and Computer Science, Postboks 260, 4000 Roskilde, Denmark. illus.

910   DK   ISSN 0106-3537
ROSKILDE UNIVERSITETSCENTER. DEPARTMENT OF GEOGRAPHY, SOCIAL ECONOMICS AND COMPUTER SCIENCE. RESEARCH REPORTS. no.17, 1981. irreg. price varies. Roskilde Universitetscenter, Department of Geography, Social Economics and Computer Science, Postboks 260, DK-4000 Roskilde, Denmark.

910   DK   ISSN 0106-5920
ROSKILDE UNIVERSITETSCENTER. DEPARTMENT OF GEOGRAPHY, SOCIAL ECONOMICS AND COMPUTER SCIENCE. WORKING PAPERS. no.24, 1981. irreg. free. Roskilde Universitetscenter, Department of Geography Social, Economics and Computer Science, Postbox 260, DK-4000 Roskilde, Denmark. illus.

S W L. (Shortwave Listener) see *CLUBS*

910   CN   ISSN 0226-2169
LE SAGAMIEN. 1980. irreg(vol. 5,1985) Can.$2. Universitaire du Quebec a Chichoutimi, Laboratoire de Geographie, 555 Blvd. de l'Universite, Chicoutimi, Que. G7H 2B1, Canada. TEL 418-545-5330. Ed. Prof. Majella-J. Gauthier. circ. 250. (also avail. in microfilm)

910 630   CN   ISSN 0831-8093
SAINT MARY'S UNIVERSITY. ATLANTIC REGION GEOGRAPHICAL STUDIES. (Text in English) 1977. irreg. price varies. Saint Mary's University, Department of Geography, Halifax, N.S. B3H 3C3, Canada. TEL 902-429-9780. Ed. Douglas Day. circ. 200. (back issues avail.)

910 550   CN   ISSN 0831-8107
SAINT MARY'S UNIVERSITY. OCCASIONAL PAPERS IN GEOGRAPHY. (Text in English) 1977. irreg. price varies. Saint Mary's University, Department of Geography, Halifax, N.S. B3H 3C3, Canada. TEL 902-429-9780. Ed. Hugh Millward. circ. 200. (back issues avail.)

910 624   CN   ISSN 0832-6266
SAINT MARY'S UNIVERSITY. STUDIES IN MARINE AND COASTAL GEOGRAPHY. (Text in English and French) 1982. a. price varies. Saint Mary's University, Department of Geography, Halifax, N.S. B3H 3C3, Canada. TEL 902-429-9780. Ed. Peter Ricketts. circ. 200. (back issues avail.)

910   AU
SALZBURGER EXKURSIONSBERICHTE; Salburger beitraege zur Geography des Mediteranean Raumes. (Text in English; summaries in English and Greek) 1968. a. price varies. Universitaet Salzburg, Institut fuer Geographie, Hellbrunnerstrasse 34, A-5020 Salzburg, Austria. Ed.Bd. circ. 350. (back issues avail.)

910   AU
SALZBURGER GEOGRAPHISCHE ARBEITEN. (Text in German; summaries in English) 1969. a. Universitaet Salzburg, Institut fuer Geographie, Hellbrunnerstr. 36, A-5020 Salzburg, Austria. Ed.Bd.

910   UK   ISSN 0277-044X
SCRIPTA SERIES IN GEOGRAPHY. 1980. irreg. price varies. Edward Arnold (Publishers) Ltd., 41 Bedford Sq., London WC1B 3DQ, England.

916.64   SL   ISSN 0583-239X
SIERRA LEONE GEOGRAPHICAL JOURNAL. Title varies, no.1-10: Sierra Leone Geographical Association. Bulletin. 1967. a. Le.2.50($3) Sierra Leone Geographical Association, c/o Fourah Bay College Bookshop, Freetown, Sierra Leone. Ed.Bd. adv. bk. rev. charts.

910   AG
SOCIEDAD ARGENTINA DE ESTUDIOS GEOGRAFICOS. CONTRIBUCIONES CIENTIFICAS. 1984. a. Sociedad Argentina de Estudios Geograficos - GAEA, Santa Fe 1145, 1059 Buenos Aires, Argentina. TEL 393-5682. circ. 1, 000.

910   AG   ISSN 0325-2698
SOCIEDAD ARGENTINA DE ESTUDIOS GEOGRAFICOS BOLETIN. 1931. irreg. free. Sociedad Argentina de Estudios Geograficos, Av. Santa Fe 1145, 1059 Buenos Aires, Argentina. TEL 393-5682. Ed. Susana I. Curto de Casas. bk. rev. circ. controlled. (looseleaf format)

SOCIEDAD DE ESTUDIOS VASCOS. CUADERNOS DE SECCION. HISTORIA-GEOGRAFIA. see *HISTORY*

914   FR   ISSN 0081-0789
SOCIETE DE GEOGRAPHIE DE MARSEILLE. BULLETIN. 1877. triennial. 35 F. Societe de Geographie de Marseille, 2 rue Beauvau, 13001 Marseille, France. circ. 350. Indexed: Geo.Abstr.

910   FR   ISSN 0081-086X
SOCIETE DES EXPLORATEURS ET DES VOYAGEURS FRANCAIS. ANNUAIRE GENERAL. 1962. irreg. membership. Societe des Explorateurs et des Voyageurs Francais, 184 bd. St. Germain, 75006 Paris, France. bk. rev. circ. 3,000.

910   BE   ISSN 0770-7576
SOCIETE GEOGRAPHIQUE DE LIEGE. BULLETIN. (Text in French, summaries in French and English) 1965. a. 500 Fr. Societe Geographique de Liege, 7, Place du Vingt-Aout, B-4000 Liege, Belgium. Ed. F. Dussart. bk. rev. circ. 1,000. Indexed: Geo.Abstr.
    Supersedes: Universite de Liege. Seminaire de Geographie. Travaux; Travaux Geographigues de Liege.

910   BU   ISSN 0324-0525
SOFIISKI UNIVERSITET. GEOLOGO-GEOGRAFSKI FAKULTET. GEOGRAFIIA. GODISNIK. (Text in Bulgarian and Russian; summaries in English, French, German) 1905. irreg., vol.71, 1978. price varies. Publishing House of the Bulgarian Academy of Sciences, Acad. G. Bonchev St., Bldg. 6, 1113 Sofia, Bulgaria. circ. 550. Indexed: Chem.Abstr. Geo.Abstr.

910   AT   ISSN 0811-6504
SOUTH AUSTRALIAN GEOGRAPHICAL PAPERS. 1886. a. membership. Royal Geographical Society of Australasia, South Australian Branch, Box 419, Adelaide, S.A. 5001, Australia. Ed. Peter Smailes. bk. rev. cum. index: vols. 1-40. circ. 450. Indexed: Aus.Sci.Ind. Aus.P.A.I.S. Geo.Abstr.
    Formerly: Royal Geographical Society of Australasia. South Australian Branch. Proceedings (ISSN 0085-5790)

910   US   ISSN 0073-4950
SOUTHERN ILLINOIS UNIVERSITY, CARBONDALE. DEPARTMENT OF GEOGRAPHY. DISCUSSION PAPER. 1969. irreg., no.6, 1979. ‡ Southern Illinois University, Carbondale, Department of Geography, Carbondale, IL 62901. TEL 618-536-3375.

910   US   ISSN 0073-4969
SOUTHERN ILLINOIS UNIVERSITY, CARBONDALE. OCCASIONAL PAPER SERIES IN GEOGRAPHY. 1963. irreg. price varies. ‡ Southern Illinois University, Carbondale, Department of Geography, Carbondale, IL 62901. TEL 618-536-3375. Indexed: Geo.Abstr.

SPELEOLOGICAL SOCIETY OF JAPAN. JOURNAL. see *EARTH SCIENCES*

526.3   UK   ISSN 0081-4377
STAR ALMANAC FOR LAND SURVEYORS. 1951. a. £2.50. H.M.S.O., Box 569, London SE1 9NH, England. (Co-sponsor: H.M. Nautical Almanac Office)

910 312 370 380.5   TH
STATISTICAL REPORTS OF CHANGWAT. (Text in English, Thai) 1964. a. price varies. National Statistical Office, Statistical Reports Division, Larn Luang Road, Bangkok 10100, Thailand. circ. 500.

914.38   PL   ISSN 0081-640X
STUDIA GEOGRAFICZNE. (Issued as a subseries of its Acta Universitatis Wratislaviensis) (Text in Polish; summaries in English, French) 1975. irreg. price varies. Wydawnictwo Uniwersytetu Wroclawskiego, Ul. Kuznicza no.34, 50-138 Wroclaw, Poland (Dist. by: Ars Polona, Krakowskie Przedmiescie 7, 00-068 Warsaw, Poland) Ed. H. Migaczowa. charts. illus. circ. 480. Indexed: Geo.Abstr.

910 550   PL   ISSN 0082-5549
STUDIA SOCIETATIS SCIENTIARUM TORUNENSIS. SECTIO C (GEOGRAFIA ET GEOLOGIA) (Text in Polish; summaries in English) 1953. irreg., vol.9, no.4, 1982. price varies. (Towarzystwo Naukowe w Toruniu) Panstwowe Wydawnictwo Naukowe, Miodowa 10, 00-251 Warsaw, Poland (Dist. by: Ars Polona, Krakowskie Przedmiescie 7, 00-068 Warsaw, Poland) Ed. Rajmund Galon. charts. illus. circ. 680. Indexed: Biol.Abstr.

STUDIA UNIVERSITATIS "BABES-BOLYAI". GEOLOGIA. GEOGRAPHIA. see *EARTH SCIENCES — Geology*

910   US
STUDIES IN GEOGRAPHY. 1970. irreg., no.18, 1983. price varies. University of North Carolina at Chapel Hill, Department of Geography, 203 Saunders Hall, Chapel Hill, NC 27514. TEL 919-962-8902. Ed. John D. Eyre. circ. 400.

910   HU   ISSN 0081-7961
STUDIES IN GEOGRAPHY IN HUNGARY. (Text in English) 1964. irreg., vol.19, 1986. price varies. (Magyar Tudomanyos Akademia) Akademiai Kiado, Publishing House of the Hungarian Academy of Sciences, P.O. Box 24, H-1363 Budapest, Hungary.

915.69   IS   ISSN 0081-8585
STUDIES IN THE GEOGRAPHY OF ISRAEL/MEHKARIM BE-GE'OGRAFYAH SHEL ERETS-YISRAEL. (Text in Hebrew; table of contents and summaries in English) vol.11, 1977. irreg., latest vol.12, 1986. Israel Exploration Society, Box 7041, Jerusalem, Israel. (Co-publisher: Hebrew University of Jerusalem, Department of Geography) circ. 1, 500.

910   RM   ISSN 0039-3967
STUDII SI CERCETARI DE GEOLOGIE, GEOFIZICA SI GEOGRAFIE. GEOGRAFIE. (Summaries in English, French, German, Russian and Spanish) 1954. a. 60 lei($32) Editura Academiei Republicii Socialiste Rumania, Calea Victoriei 125, 79717 Bucharest, Rumania (Subscr. to: ROMPRESFILATELIA, Calea Grivitei 64-66, P.O. Box 12-201, 78104 Bucharest, Rumania) Ed. V. Janovici. bk. rev. charts. illus. index. circ. 900. Indexed: Appl.Mech.Rev. Chem.Abstr. Doc.Geogr. Geo.Abstr. Geotimes. Geo.Abstr. GeoRef.
    Formerly: Probleme de Geografie.

910   GW   ISSN 0343-7906
STUTTGARTER GEOGRAPHISCHE STUDIEN. 1924. irreg., 1-3/yr. price varies. Universitaet Stuttgart, Geographisches Institut, Silcherstr. 9, 7000 Stuttgart 1, W. Germany (B.R.D.) Eds. W. Meckelein, Ch. Borcherdt, R. Hahn. charts. illus. stat. circ. 500. Indexed: Geo.Abstr. GeoRef.

526.982   SR
SURINAM. CENTRAAL BUREAU LUCHTKARTERING. JAARVERSLAG. (Text in Dutch) irreg. Centraal Bureau Luchtkartering, Paramaribo, Surinam.

GEOGRAPHY

910   SW   ISSN 0081-9808
SVENSK GEOGRAFISK AARSBOK/SWEDISH GEOGRAPHICAL YEARBOOK. (Text in Swedish; summaries in English,) 1925. a. Kr.70. Sydsvenska Geografiska Saellskapet, Department of Geography, Lunds Universitet, Soelvegatan 13, S-223 62 Lund, Sweden. Ed.Bd. bk. rev. cum.index 1925-34, 1935-50, 1951-84. circ. 1,000. Indexed: Field Crop Abstr. GeoRef. Herb.Abstr. Hort.Abstr.

910   UK   ISSN 0081-9980
SWANSEA GEOGRAPHER. 1959. a. £3. University College of Swansea, Department of Geography, Singleton Park, Swansea, Glam. SA2 8PP, Wales. Ed.Bd. circ. 200(controlled) Indexed: Geo.Abstr.

917.6   US   ISSN 0748-7789
TEXAS FACTS; a comprehensive look at Texas today, county by county. 1984. triennial. $47.50. Clements Research, Inc., 16850 A Dallas Pkwy., Dallas, TX 75248. TEL 214-931-9956. Ed. John Clements.

THAMES BOOK. see *TRAVEL AND TOURISM*

914.1   625.7   IE
THOM'S DUBLIN & COUNTY STREET DIRECTORY. 1851. a. $60. Thom's Directories Ltd., 38 Merrion Sq., Dublin 2, Ireland. Ed. J.L. Wootton.

910   JA   ISSN 0386-8710
TOKYO METROPOLITAN UNIVERSITY. DEPARTMENT OF GEOGRAPHY. GEOGRAPHICAL REPORTS/TOKYO-TORITSU DAIGAKU CHIRIGAKU HOKOKU. (Text in European languages) 1966. a. price varies. Tokyo Metropolitan University, Department of Geography - Tokyo-Toritsu Daigaku Rigakubu Chirigaku Kyoshitsu, 2-1-1 Fukazawa, Setagaya-ku, Tokyo 158, Japan. Ed.Bd. bibl. charts. illus. circ. 1,000. Indexed: Geo.Abstr. GeoRef.

TRAPANANDA. see *HISTORY — History Of North And South America*

916   FR   ISSN 0336-5522
TRAVAUX ET DOCUMENTS DE GEOGRAPHIE TROPICALE. 1971. irreg. price varies. Centre d'Etudes de Geographie Tropicale, Domaine Universitaire, Esplanade des Antilles, 33405 Talence Cedex, France. Ed. Pierre Usselmann. circ. 400. (also avail. in microfiche) Indexed: GeoRef.

526.3   UR
TSENTRAL'NYI NAUCHNO-ISSLEDOVATEL'SKII INSTITUT GEODEZII, AEROS"EMKI I KARTOGRAFII. TRUDY. vol.218, 1977. irreg. Tsentral'nyi Nauchno-Issledovatel'skii Institut Geodezii, Aeros"emki i Kartografii, Ul. Onezhskaya 26, Moscow 125413, Russian S.F.S.R., U.S.S.R. circ. 500.

910   GW   ISSN 0564-4232
TUEBINGER GEOGRAPHISCHE STUDIEN. 1958. irreg. (approx. 5/yr.) price varies. Universitaet Tuebingen, Geographisches Institut, Hoelderlinstr. 12, 7400 Tuebingen, W. Germany (B.R.D.) Ed.Bd. bibl. charts. illus. stat. circ. 500. Indexed: GeoRef.

TURUN YLIOPISTO. JULKAISUJA. SARJA A. II. BIOLOGICA- GEOGRAPHICA- GEOLOGICA. see *BIOLOGY*

910   GW
UEBERSEE-MUSEUM, BREMEN. VEROEFFENTLICHUNGEN. REIHE C: GEOGRAPHIE. N.S. 1977. irreg., vol.3, 1985. price varies. Uebersee-Museum, Bremen, Bahnhofsplatz 13, 2800 Bremen, W. Germany (B.R.D.)
    Former titles: Deutsche Geographische Blaetter; Uebersee-Museum, Bremen. Veroeffentlichungen. Reihe C: Geographie (ISSN 0341-9258)

526   551   UK
UNITED KINGDOM RESEARCH ON GEODESY. 1963. quadrennial. £3.50. (Royal Society's National Committee for Geodesy and Geophysics) Surveyors Publications, 12 Great George St., London SW1P 3AD, England. Ed. P.J. Carmody. circ. 600.
    Formerly: United Kingdom Geodesy Report.

910   UN
UNITED NATIONS CONFERENCE ON THE STANDARDIZATION OF GEOGRAPHICAL NAMES. REPORT OF THE CONFERENCE. 1974. irreg., latest no.4. $10. (United Nations Economic and Social Council) United Nations Publications, Room DC2-0853, New York, NY 10017 (Or Distribution and Sales Section, Palais des Nations, CH-1211 Geneva 10, Switzerland)

910   UN
UNITED NATIONS CONFERENCE ON THE STANDARDIZATION OF GEOGRAPHICAL NAMES. TECHNICAL PAPERS. 1974. irreg. price varies. (United Nations Economic and Social Council) United Nations Publications, Room DC2-0853, New York, NY 10017 (Or Distribution and Sales Section, Palais des Nations, CH-1211 Geneva 10, Switzerland)

526.8   UN
UNITED NATIONS REGIONAL CARTOGRAPHIC CONFERENCE FOR ASIA AND THE PACIFIC. REPORT OF THE CONFERENCE. 1955. irreg., latest vol.10, 1983. $6. United Nations Publications, Room DC2-0853, New York, NY 10017 (Or Distribution and Sales Section, Palais des Nations, CH-1211 Geneva 10, Switzerland) (also avail. in microfiche) Indexed: GeoRef.
    Formerly: United Nations Regional Cartographic Conference for Asia and the Far East. Proceedings of the Conference and Technical Papers (ISSN 0082-836X)

910   UN
UNITED NATIONS REGIONAL CARTOGRAPHIC CONFERENCE FOR ASIA AND THE PACIFIC. TECHNICAL PAPERS. irreg., latest 1983. price varies. (United Nations Economic and Social Council) United Nations Publications, Room DC2-0853, New York, NY 10017 (Or Distribution and Sales Sections, Palais des Nations, CH-1211 Geneva 10, Switzerland)

910   UN
UNITED NATIONS REGIONAL CARTOGRAPHIC CONFERENCE FOR THE AMERICAS. REPORT OF THE CONFERENCE. irreg. price varies. (United Nations Social and Economic Council) United Nations Publications, Room DC2-0853, New York, NY 10017 (Or Distribution and Sales Section, Palais des Nations, CH-1211 Geneva 10, Switzerland)

910   UN
UNITED NATIONS REGIONAL CARTOGRAPHIC CONFERENCE FOR THE AMERICAS. TECHNICAL PAPERS. irreg., latest vol.2, 1982. price varies. (United Nations Economic and Social Council) United Nations Publications, Room DC2-0853, New York, NY 10017 (Or Distribution and Sales Section, Palais des Nations, CH-1211 Geneva 10, Switzerland)

910   US   ISSN 0083-016X
U.S. DEPARTMENT OF STATE. OFFICE OF THE GEOGRAPHER. GEOGRAPHIC NOTES. (G E Series) 1964. irreg., no.198, 1984. free. U.S. Department of State, Office of the Geographer, c/o Bureau of Intelligence and Research, 2201 C St., N.W., Washington, DC 20520. TEL 202-632-2022. circ. 800.

526   US   ISSN 0364-7064
U.S. NATIONAL CARTOGRAPHIC INFORMATION CENTER. NEWSLETTER. 1975. irreg. free. U.S. Geological Survey, U.S. National Cartographic Information Center, 12201 Sunrise Valley Dr., Reston, VA 22092. TEL 703-860-6045. Ed. Pat Creech. bk. rev. bibl. circ. 7,000.

918.7   VE   ISSN 0076-6569
UNIVERSIDAD DE LOS ANDES. INSTITUTO DE GEOGRAFIA Y CONSERVACION DE RECURSOS NATURALES. CUADERNOS GEOGRAFICOS. 1961. irreg. price varies. Universidad de Los Andes, Instituto de Geografia y Conservacion de Recursos Naturales, Via los Chorras de Milla, Codigo Postal 5101, Merida, Venezuela. circ. 2,000.

910   SP   ISSN 0210-492X
UNIVERSIDAD DE MURCIA. DIDACTICA GEOGRAFICA. 1972. irreg., vol.14, 1986. ($1000) Universidad de Murcia, Secretariado de Publicaciones e Intercambio Cientifico, Santo Cristo, 1, 30001 Murcia, Spain. TEL 968 24 92 00.

910   SP   ISSN 0213-1781
UNIVERSIDAD DE MURCIA. PAPELES DE GEOGRAFIA. 1968. irreg., vol.10, 1985. ($1000) Universidad de Murcia, Secretariado de Publicaciones e Intercambio Cientifico, Santo Cristo, 1, 30001 Murcia, Spain. TEL 968 24 92 00.
    Formerly (1968-1978): Universidad de Murcia. Departamento de Geografia. Papeles.

910   MX   ISSN 0185-1322
UNIVERSIDAD NACIONAL AUTONOMA DE MEXICO. ANUARIO DE GEOGRAFIA. 1961. a. Mex.$25($2.50) Universidad Nacional Autonoma de Mexico, Colegio de Geografia, Ciudad Universitaria, C.P. 04510, Mexico 20, D.F., Mexico. Eds. Raquel Guzman Villanueva, Dolores Riquelme de Rejon. bk. rev. circ. 1,500. Indexed: Hisp.Amer.Per.Ind.
    Formerly: Universidad Nacional Autonoma de Mexico. Instituto de Geografia. Anuario de Geografia.

917.2   MX   ISSN 0185-1977
UNIVERSIDAD NACIONAL AUTONOMA DE MEXICO. INSTITUTO DE GEOGRAFIA. BOLETIN. 1969. a. $10. Universidad Nacional Autonoma de Mexico, Instituto de Geografia, Ciudad Universitaria, 04510 Mexico, D.F., Mexico.

910   AG   ISSN 0041-8684
UNIVERSIDAD NACIONAL DE ROSARIO. FACULTAD DE CIENCIAS, INGENIERIA Y ARQUITECTURA. INSTITUTO DE FISIOGRAFIA Y GEOLOGIA. PUBLICACIONES. (Text in Spanish; summaries in English, French) 1937. a. exchange basis. Universidad Nacional de Rosario, Avenida Pellegrini 250, Rosario, Argentina. Dir. Pierina Pasotti. charts. illus. bibl.

910   301   398   572   BL
UNIVERSIDADE DE SAO PAULO. INSTITUTO DE ESTUDOS BRASILEIROS. PUBLICACOES. 1965. irreg. Universidade de Sao Paulo, Instituto de Estudos Brasileiros, Caixa Postal 11.154, 01000 Sao Paulo, Brazil. Ed. Myriam Ellis.

910   301   398   572   BL   ISSN 0020-3874
UNIVERSIDADE DE SAO PAULO. INSTITUTO DE ESTUDOS BRASILEIROS. REVISTA. 1966. a. Cr.$500. ‡ Universidade de Sao Paulo, Instituto de Estudos Brasileiros, Caixa Postal 11 154, 01000 Sao Paulo, Brazil. Ed. Myriam Ellis. bk. rev. bibl. charts. illus. circ. 2,000. Indexed: Hist.Abstr.

910   BL
UNIVERSIDADE DE SAO PAULO. MUSEU PAULISTA. COLECAO. SERIE DE GEOGRAFIA. irreg. Universidade de Sao Paulo, Museu Paulista, Caixa Postal 42503, Parque da Independencia, 04263 Sao Paulo SP, Brazil.
    Supersedes in part (since 1975): Museu Paulista. Colecao (ISSN 0080-6382)

910   BL
UNIVERSIDADE ESTADUAL PAULISTA. DEPARTAMENTO DE GEOGRAFIA. BOLETIM. no.6, 1974. a. Universidade Estadual Paulista, Departamento de Geografia, Rua Roberto Simonsen 305, C.P. 957, Presidente Prudente, Brazil.

910   GW   ISSN 0720-9746
UNIVERSITAET BREMEN - SCHWERPUNKT GEOGRAPHIE. MATERIALIEN UND MANUSKRIPTE. 1979. irreg. price varies. Universitaet Bremen, Drueckschriftenlager, Postfach 330440, D-2800 Bremen 33, W. Germany (B.R.D.)

910   GW   ISSN 0563-1491
UNIVERSITAET DES SAARLANDES. GEOGRAPHISCHES INSTITUT. ARBEITEN. (Text in German; summaries in English, French and Spanish) 1956. irreg., vol.34, 1984. price varies. Universitaet des Saarlandes, Geographisches Institut, 6600 Saarbruecken 11, W. Germany (B.R.D.) Ed.Bd. bibl. charts. illus. circ. 1,000.

910   GW   ISSN 0723-9874
UNIVERSITAET KIEL. GEOGRAPHISCHES INSTITUT. SCHRIFTEN. 1932. irreg. price varies. Universitaet Kiel, Geographisches Institut, Neue Universitaet, Olshausenstr. 40-60, 2300 Kiel, W. Germany (B.R.D.) Ed.Bd. bk. rev. circ. 500. Indexed: Geo.Abstr.

GEOGRAPHY

910.1   GW   ISSN 0077-2127
UNIVERSITAET MUENCHEN.
WIRTSCHAFTSGEOGRAPHISCHES INSTITUT.
"W G I"-BERICHTE ZUR
REGIONALFORSCHUNG. (Text in German; summaries in English) 1970. irreg., no.14, 1974. price varies. Nelles Verlag, Schleissheimer Str. 371b, 8000 Munich 45, W. Germany (B.R.D.)

910 550   CN   ISSN 0710-0868
UNIVERSITE DE SHERBROOKE. DEPARTMENT DE GEOGRAPHIE. BULLETIN DE RECHERCHE. (Text in French; summaries in English, French) 1972. irreg. (approx. 6/yr.) Universite de Sherbrooke, Department de Geographie, Faculte des Lettres et Sciences Humaines, Local A4-161, Sherbrooke, Que. J1K 2R1, Canada. TEL 819-821-7210. Ed. Roger Nadeau. (back issues avail.) Indexed: Geo.Abstr.

910   CN
UNIVERSITE LAVAL. DEPARTEMENT DE GEOGRAPHIE. TRAVAUX. 1970. irreg. (approx. biennial) Presses de l'Universite Laval, B.P. 2447, Quebec G1K 7R4, Canada. TEL 418-656-2590. bibl. charts. illus. stat. circ. 1,500.

900   IV
UNIVERSITE NATIONALE DE COTE D'IVOIRE. ANNALES. SERIE G: GEOGRAPHIE. 1969. irreg., vol.8, 1979. price varies. Universite Nationale de Cote d'Ivoire, Tropical Geography Institute, B.P. 859, Abidjan 08, Ivory Coast. Ed. Bd. bibl. charts. illus. Indexed: Geo.Abstr.
    Formerly: Universite d'Abidjan. Annales. Serie G: Geographie.

910   NE   ISSN 0066-1317
UNIVERSITEIT VAN AMSTERDAM. FYSISCH GEOGRAFISCH EN BODEMKUNDIG LABORATORIUM. PUBLIKATIES. (Text in English and German; summaries in English, Dutch, French and German) no.31, 1980. irreg. price varies. Universiteit van Amsterdam, Fysisch Geografish en Bodemkundig Laboratorium, Dapperstraat 115, 1093 BS Amsterdam, Netherlands. Indexed: Geo.Abstr. GeoRef.

910   NR   ISSN 0083-3975
UNIVERSITY GEOGRAPHER. 1956. a. Ibadan University Geographical Society, Ibadan, Nigeria.

910   CN
UNIVERSITY OF ALBERTA. STUDIES IN GEOGRAPHY. MONOGRAPHS. irreg. price varies. University of Alberta, Department of Geography, Edmonton, Alta. T6G 2H4, Canada. TEL 403-432-4783.

910   NZ   ISSN 0112-1545
UNIVERSITY OF AUCKLAND. DEPARTMENT OF GEOGRAPHY. OCCASIONAL PUBLICATION. 1961. irreg., no.16, 1985. price varies. University of Auckland, Department of Geography, Private Bag, Auckland, New Zealand. Ed. Dr. Warwick Neville. circ. 300.
    Formerly: University of Auckland. Department of Geography. Occasional Papers.

910   US   ISSN 0068-6441
UNIVERSITY OF CALIFORNIA PUBLICATIONS IN GEOGRAPHY. 1913. irreg. price varies. University of California Press, 2120 Berkeley Way, Berkeley, CA 94720. TEL 415-642-4247.

910   US   ISSN 0069-3340
UNIVERSITY OF CHICAGO. DEPARTMENT OF GEOGRAPHY. RESEARCH PAPERS. 1947. irreg., no.220, 1986. $10 per no. University of Chicago, Department of Geography, 5828 S. University Ave., Chicago, IL 60637. TEL 312-962-8314. Ed. Bernard Lalor. circ. 600. (also avail. in microform from UMI) Indexed: Geo.Abstr.

UNIVERSITY OF COLORADO. INSTITUTE OF ARCTIC AND ALPINE RESEARCH. OCCASIONAL PAPERS. see *SCIENCES: COMPREHENSIVE WORKS*

UNIVERSITY OF GEORGIA. GEOGRAPHY CURRICULUM PROJECT PUBLICATIONS. see *EDUCATION — Teaching Methods And Curriculum*

312   UK   ISSN 0441-4004
UNIVERSITY OF HULL. DEPARTMENT OF GEOGRAPHY. MISCELLANEOUS SERIES IN GEOGRAPHY. 1965. irreg. (approx. 2/yr.), latest no.31. price varies. University of Hull, Department of Geography, Hull, Yorkshire HU6 7RX, England. Ed. R.C. Ward. bibl. charts. illus. circ. 400. Indexed: Geo.Abstr.

910   UK   ISSN 0309-2178
UNIVERSITY OF LONDON KING'S COLLEGE. DEPARTMENT OF GEOGRAPHY. OCCASIONAL PAPER. 1973. irreg. £2. University of London King's College, Department of Geography, Strand, London WC2R 2LS, England. Ed. A.M. Warnes. circ. 250.

910   AT   ISSN 0066-7706
UNIVERSITY OF NEW ENGLAND. DEPARTMENT OF GEOGRAPHY. MONOGRAPH SERIES IN GEOGRAPHY. 1963. irreg., no.2, 1966. Aus.$3($4.25) University of New England, Department of Geography, Armidale, N.S.W. 2351, Australia. Ed. M.J. Cooper. Indexed: Nutr.Abstr. Nutr.Abstr.& Rev.

910   AT
UNIVERSITY OF NEW ENGLAND. DEPARTMENT OF GEOGRAPHY. STUDIES IN APPLIED GEOGRAPHICAL RESEARCH. 1977. irreg. price varies. University of New England, Department of Geography, Armidale, N.S.W. 2351, Australia. Ed. M.J. Cooper.

910 325   UK   ISSN 0078-026X
UNIVERSITY OF NEWCASTLE-UPON-TYNE. DEPARTMENT OF GEOGRAPHY. RESEARCH SERIES. 1954. irreg. price varies. University of Newcastle-Upon-Tyne, Department of Geography, Newcastle-Upon-Tyne NE1 7RU, England. Ed. J.D. Momsen. circ. 750. Indexed: Geo.Abstr. GeoRef.

910   CN
UNIVERSITY OF OTTAWA. DEPARTMENT OF GEOGRAPHY. NOTES DE RECHERCHE/RESEARCH NOTES. (Text in English or French) 1971. irreg. price varies. University of Ottawa, Department of Geography, Ottawa, Ont. K1N 6N5, Canada. TEL 613-564-2395. Indexed: Geo.Abstr. GeoRef.
    Formerly: University of Ottawa. Department of Geography and Regional Planning. Notes de Recherches/Research Notes.

910   UK   ISSN 0305-8190
UNIVERSITY OF OXFORD. SCHOOL OF GEOGRAPHY. RESEARCH PAPERS. 1972. irreg. £2.25 per no. University of Oxford, School of Geography, Mansfield Rd., Oxford OX1 3TB, England. Ed.Bd. charts. circ. 500. Indexed: Geo.Abstr.

910   PP
UNIVERSITY OF PAPUA NEW GUINEA. DEPARTMENT OF GEOGRAPHY. OCCASIONAL PAPERS IN GEOGRAPHY. 1970. irreg. (2-3/yr.) price varies. ‡ University of Papua New Guinea, Department of Geography, Box 320, University P.O., Papua New Guinea. Ed.Bd. bibl. charts. illus. circ. 500.

910   JA   ISSN 0082-478X
UNIVERSITY OF TOKYO. DEPARTMENT OF GEOGRAPHY. BULLETIN. (Text mainly in English) 1969. a. available on exchange. University of Tokyo, Department of Geography - Tokyo Daigaku Chirigaku Kyoshitsu, 7-3-1 Hongo, Bunkyo-ku, Tokyo 113, Japan. Ed. Yukata Sakaguchi. bibl. charts. circ. 800. Indexed: Geo.Abstr. GeoRef.

910   CN   ISSN 0317-9893
UNIVERSITY OF TORONTO. DEPARTMENT OF GEOGRAPHY. DISCUSSION PAPER SERIES. 1970. irreg., no.33, 1986. price varies. University of Toronto, Department of Geography, Toronto, Ont. M5S 1A1, Canada. TEL 416-978-3376. Ed. J. Britton.

910   CN   ISSN 0082-5174
UNIVERSITY OF TORONTO. DEPARTMENT OF GEOGRAPHY. RESEARCH PUBLICATIONS. 1968. irreg. price varies. University of Toronto Press, Front Campus, Toronto, Ont. M5S 1A6, Canada TEL 613-667-7791. (and 33 E. Tupper St., Buffalo, N.Y. 14203) Ed. Ian Burton.

910   CN
UNIVERSITY OF WATERLOO. DEPARTMENT OF GEOGRAPHY. OCCASIONAL PAPERS. 1984. irreg. (1-2/yr.) price varies. University of Waterloo, Department of Geography, Waterloo, Ont. N2L 3G1, Canada. TEL 519-885-1211. Ed. Chris Bryant.

910 333.7   CN
UNIVERSITY OF WATERLOO. DEPARTMENT OF GEOGRAPHY. PUBLICATION SERIES. 1971. irreg., (approx. 2/yr.) price varies. University of Waterloo, Department of Geography, Waterloo, Ont. N2L 3G1, Canada. TEL 519-885-1211. Ed. Prof. Chris Bryant.

914.38   PL
UNIWERSYTET GDANSKI. WYDZIAL BIOLOGII, GEOGRAFII I OCEANOLOGII. ZESZYTY NAUKOWE. GEOGRAFIA. (Text in Polish; summaries in English) 1970. irreg. price varies. Uniwersytet Gdanski, Wydzial Biologii, Geografii i Oceanologii, Ul. Czerwonej Armii 110, 81-824 Sopot, Poland (Dist. by Ars Polona-Ruch, Krakowskie Przedmiescie 7, Warsaw, Poland) Ed. Jerzy Szukalski. bk. rev. circ. 300.
    Formerly: Uniwersytet Gdanski. Wydzial Biologii i Nauk o Ziemi. Zeszyty Naukowe. Geografia (ISSN 0208-4937)

910   PL   ISSN 0083-4343
UNIWERSYTET JAGIELLONSKI. ZESZYTY NAUKOWE. PRACE GEOGRAFICZNE. (Text in Polish, summaries in English) 1960. irreg. price varies. ‡ (Instytut Geografii) Panstwowe Wydawnictwo Naukowe, Miodowa 10, 00-251 Warsaw, Poland (Dist. by: Ars Polona, Krakowskie Przedmiescie 7, 00-068 Warsaw, Poland) Ed. M. Hess. circ. 570. (also avail. in microfilm) Indexed: Ref.Zh. Geo.Abstr.

910.02   PL
UNIWERSYTET WROCLAWSKI. INSTYTUT GEOGRAFICZNY. PRACE. SERIA A: GEOGRAFIA FIZYCZNA. (Subseries of: Acta Universitatis Wratislaviensis) 1975. irreg. price varies. Wydawnictwa Uniwersytetu Wroclawskiego, Ul. Kuznicza no.34, 50-138 Wroclaw, Poland. Indexed: GeoRef.

910   PL
UNIWERSYTET WROCLAWSKI. INSTYTUT GEOGRAFICZNY. PRACE. SERIA B: GEOGRAFIA SPOLECZNA I EKONOMICZNA. (Subseries of: Acta Universitatis Wratislaviensis) 1975. irreg. price varies. Wydawnictwa Uniwersytetu Wroclawskiego, Ul. Kuznicza no.34, 50-138 Wroclaw, Poland.

910   BG
UPOKUL. (Text in Bengali and English) 1972. irreg. Dacca University Geography Association, Ramna, Dacca 2, Bangladesh. adv. illus.

914.8   DK   ISSN 0109-2472
VADEHAVSRAPPORT. 1982. irreg. free. Koebenhavns Universitet, Geografisk Institut, Oester Volgade 10, 1350 Copenhagen K, Denmark. Eds. Margot Jespersen, Erik Rasmussen. circ. 125.

910   GW   ISSN 0083-5684
VERHANDLUNGEN DES DEUTSCHEN GEOGRAPHENTAGES. 1881. biennial. price varies. (Zentralverband der Deutschen Geographen) Franz Steiner Verlag Wiesbaden GmbH, Birkenwaldstr. 44, Postfach 347, D-7000 Stuttgart 1, W. Germany (B.R.D.) cum.index: 1881-1963.

915   UR
VOPROSY GEOGRAFII. vol.103, 1977. irreg. 1.25 Rub. per no. Izdatel'stvo Mysl', Leninskii Prospekt 15, 117071 Moscow B-71, Russian S.F.S.R., U.S.S.R. Ed. S. Kovalev. bibl. circ. 9,800. Indexed: GeoRef.

WERTE UNSERER HEIMAT; Ergebnisse der heimatkundlichen Bestandsaufnahme in der DDR. see *HISTORY — History Of Europe*

910   AT   ISSN 0313-8860
WESTERN GEOGRAPHER. 1972. a. Aus.$5. Geographical Association of Western Australia, Box 152, Nedlands, W.A. 6009, Australia. G. Gentilli. circ. 200.

910   CN   ISSN 0315-2022
WESTERN GEOGRAPHICAL SERIES. 1970. irreg.
(1-2/yr.) Can.$10 per vol. University of Victoria,
Department of Geography, Victoria, B.C. V8W 2Y2,
Canada. TEL 604-721-7331. Ed. Harold D. Foster.
circ. 1,000. (tabloid format) Indexed: Geo.Abstr.

910   AU   ISSN 0083-9957
WIENER GEOGRAPHISCHE SCHRIFTEN.
(Summaries in English) 1957. irreg., no.48, 1976.
price varies. (Geographisches Institut der
Hochschule fuer Welthandel) Verlag Ferdinand Hirt
GmbH, Widerhofergasse 8, Postfach 39, A-1094
Vienna, Austria. Ed. Leopold Scheidl.

581   GW   ISSN 0084-0912
WISSENSCHAFTLICHE ALPENVEREINSHEFTE.
1897. irreg. Deutscher Alpenverein, Praterinsel 5,
8000 Munich 22, W. Germany (B.R.D.) (Co-
sponsor: Oesterreichischer Alpenverein)

526   UN   ISSN 0084-1471
WORLD CARTOGRAPHY. 1951. irreg., latest
vol.18. $8.50. United Nations Publications, Rm.
DC2-853, New York, NY 10017 (Or Distribution
and Sales Section, CH-1211 Geneva 10,
Switzerland) (also avail. in microfiche) Indexed:
Bibl.Cart.

WORLD LITHUANIAN ROMAN CATHOLIC
DIRECTORY. see *RELIGIONS AND
THEOLOGY* — Roman Catholic

910   GW   ISSN 0510-9833
WUERZBURGER GEOGRAPHISCHE ARBEITEN.
1953. irreg., (approx. 3-4/yr.) price varies.
Universitaet Wuerzburg, Geographisches Institut,
Am Hubland, 8700 Wuerzburg, W. Germany
(B.R.D.) (Co-sponsor: Geographische Gesellschaft,
Wuerzburg) Ed.Bd. illus. circ. 625. (tabloid format)
Indexed: Geo.Abstr. GeoRef.
   Supersedes: Fraenkische Studien.

910   GW   ISSN 0931-8623
WUERZBURGER GEOGRAPHISCHE
MANUSKRIPT. 1975. irreg. (3-4/yr.) price varies.
Universitaet Wuerzburg, Geographisches Institut,
Am Hubland, D-8700 Wuerzburg, W. Germany
(B.R.D.) TEL (0931)8885555.

YUKON BIBLIOGRAPHY UPDATE. see
BIBLIOGRAPHIES

910   ZA   ISSN 0250-8109
Z G A OCCASIONAL STUDIES. Variant title: Z G
A Occasional Studies and Special Publications.
1968. irreg., no.13, 1984. price varies. Zambia
Geographical Association, Box 50287, Lusaka,
Zambia. Ed. G.J. Williams. charts. circ. 500. (back
issues avail.) Indexed: Geo.Abstr.

910   ZA   ISSN 0250-8117
Z G A SCHOOL SUPPLEMENT. 1973. a. K.2.50.
Zambia Geographical Association, Box 50287,
Lusaka, Zambia. bk. rev. charts. circ. 400. (tabloid
format)

526.9   ZA   ISSN 0084-5078
ZAMBIA. SURVEY DEPARTMENT. REPORT. a.
20 n. Government Printer, P.O. Box 136, Lusaka,
Zambia.

910   ZA
ZAMBIA GEOGRAPHICAL ASSOCIATION.
OCCASIONAL NEWSLETTER. 1977. irreg. free
to members; individual non-members $12;
institutional non-members $15. Zambia
Geographical Association, P. O. Box 50287, Lusaka,
Zambia. circ. 200. (looseleaf format)

968.94   ZA   ISSN 0250-8133
ZAMBIA GEOGRAPHICAL ASSOCIATION.
REGIONAL HANDBOOK. Cover title: Z G A
Regional Handbook. irreg., no.8, 1980. Zambia
Geographical Association, Box 50287, Lusaka,
Zambia. illus. (back issues avail.)
   Formerly: Zambia Geographical Association.
Conference Handbook.

910   ZA   ISSN 0250-5657
ZAMBIAN GEOGRAPHICAL JOURNAL. (Text
and summaries in English) 1967. a. K.8($15)
Zambia Geographical Association, Box 50287,
Lusaka, Zambia. Ed. G.J. Williams. bk. rev. bibl,
charts. circ. 500. (tabloid format; back issues avail.)
Indexed: Biol.Abstr. Curr.Cont.Africa. Geo.Abstr.
   Formerly: Z G A Magazine.

GEOGRAPHY — Abstracting, Bibliographies, Statistics

ABSTRACTS OF BULGARIAN SCIENTIFIC
LITERATURE. NAUKI ZA ZEMIATA. see
*EARTH SCIENCES — Abstracting, Bibliographies,
Statistics*

526 016   GW   ISSN 0340-0409
BIBLIOGRAPHIA CARTOGRAPHICA; international
documentation of cartographical literature. 1957. a.
DM.58. (Staatsbibliothek Preussischer Kulturbesitz)
K.G. Saur Inc., Poessenbacherstr. 12B, Postfach
711009, D-8000 Munich 71, W. Germany (B.R.D.)
(Co-sponsor: Deutsche Gesellschaft fuer
Kartographie e.V.) Ed. Lothar Zoegner. (4eprint
service avail. from UMI, ISI)
   Formerly: Bibliotheca Cartographica.

551 910   US
BIBLIOGRAPHIC GUIDE TO MAPS AND
ATLASES. 1979. a. price varies. G. K. Hall & Co.,
70 Lincoln St., Boston, MA 02111. TEL 617-423-
3990. bibl. circ. 250. (back issues avail.)

526 011   FR   ISSN 0150-5998
BIBLIOGRAPHIE DE LA FRANCE.
SUPPLEMENT 4: ATLAS, CARTES ET PLANS.
a. Editions du Cercle de la Librairie, 35 rue
Gregoire de Tours, 75279 Paris Cedex 06, France.

910 016   UK   ISSN 0268-7879
GEOGRAPHICAL ABSTRACTS A (LANDFORMS
AND THE QUATERNARY) 1960. 6/yr. Geo
Abstracts Ltd., Regency House, 34 Duke St.,
Norwich NR3 3AP, England. Ed. K.M. Clayton.
adv. bk. rev. index. cum.index: 1960-1965, 1966-
1970, 1971-1975. circ. 1,350. (back issues avail.)
   Formerly (until 1985): Geo Abstracts A
(Landforms and the Quaternary) (ISSN 0305-1897)

526 016   UK   ISSN 0268-7887
GEOGRAPHICAL ABSTRACTS B
(CLIMATOLOGY AND HYDROLOGY) 1966. 6/
yr. £43.50. Geo Abstracts Ltd., Regency House, 34
Duke St., Norwich NR3 3AP, England. Eds. D.
Tout, L. Musk. index. cum.index: 1966-1970, 1971-
1975. circ. 1,100. (back issues avail.) Indexed: Field
Crop Abstr. Forest.Abstr. Forest Prod.Abstr.
Herb.Abstr.
   Former titles: Geo Abstracts B (Climatology and
Hydrology) (ISSN 0305-1900); Geographical
Abstracts B (Biogeography, Climatology and
Cartography) (ISSN 0016-7339)

526 016   UK   ISSN 0268-7895
GEOGRAPHICAL ABSTRACTS C (ECONOMIC
GEOGRAPHY) 1966. 6/yr. £43.50. Geo Abstracts
Ltd., Regency House, 34 Duke St., Norwich NR3
3AP, England. Ed. J. D'Arth. index. cum.index:
1966-1970, 1971-1975. circ. 1,100. (back issues
avail.) Indexed: Field Crop Abstr. Forest.Abstr.
Forest Prod.Abstr. Herb.Abstr. Popul.Ind.
   Formerly: Geo Abstracts C (Economic
Geography) (ISSN 0305-1919)

526 016   UK   ISSN 0268-7909
GEOGRAPHICAL ABSTRACTS D (SOCIAL &
HISTORICAL GEOGRAPHY) 1966. 6/yr. £43.50.
Geo Abstracts Ltd., Regency House, 34 Duke St.,
Norwich NR3 3AP, England. Ed. G. Sheail. index.
cum.index: 1966-1970, 1971-1975. circ. 1,100. (back
issues avail.) Indexed: Br.Archaeol.Abstr.
Popul.Ind.
   Formerly: Geo Abstracts D (Social and Historical
Geography) (ISSN 0305-1927)

526 016   UK   ISSN 0268-7933
GEOGRAPHICAL ABSTRACTS G (REMOTE
SENSING PHOTOGRAMMETRY AND
CARTOGRAPHY) 1974. 6/yr. £43.50. Geo
Abstracts Ltd., Regency House, 34 Duke St.,
Norwich NR3 3AP, England. Eds. M. Blakemore,
D. Fairbairn. index. cum.index: 1974-1978. circ.
950. (back issues avail.) Indexed: Forest.Abstr.
Forest Prod.Abstr. Petrol.Abstr.
   Formerly: Geo Abstracts G (Remote Sensing
Photogrammetry and Cartogrpaphy) (ISSN 0305-
1951)

910   II   ISSN 0250-9687
I C S S R JOURNAL OF ABSTRACTS AND
REVIEWS: GEOGRAPHY. (Text in English) 1975.
s-a. Rs.15($4) to individuals; institutions Rs. 20.
Indian Council of Social Science Research, 35
Ferozshah Rd, New Delhi 110001, India (Subscr.
address: Concept Publishing Co., H-13, Bali Nagar,
New Delhi 110015 India) Ed. Moonis Raza. adv.
bk. rev. circ. 500. (back issues avail.)

526 016   GR
INTERNATIONAL ASSOCIATION OF GEODESY.
CENTRAL BUREAU FOR SATELLITE
GEODESY. BIBLIOGRAPHY. 1965. irreg. free.
International Association of Geodesy, Central
Bureau for Satellite Geodesy, National Technical
University, K. Zographou 9, Athens 624, Greece.
   Formerly: Bibliography on Satellite Geodesy and
Related Subjects (ISSN 0067-7353)

910 016   UK   ISSN 0262-0855
INTERNATIONAL DEVELOPMENT ABSTRACTS.
1982. 6/yr. £56. Geo Abstracts Ltd., Regency
House, 34 Duke St., Norwich NR3 3AP, England.
Ed. P. Creese. adv.

011   ZA   ISSN 0250-8125
Z G A BIBLIOGRAPHIC SERIES. 1974. irreg., no.4,
1982. price varies. Zambia Geographical
Association, Box 50287, Lusaka, Zambia. Ed. G.J.
Williams. (back issues avail.) Indexed: Geo.Abstr.

GEOLOGY

see *Earth Sciences — Geology*

GEOPHYSICS

see *Earth Sciences — Geophysics*

GERONTOLOGY AND GERIATRICS

301.435 618.97   US   ISSN 0065-2709
ADVANCES IN GERONTOLOGICAL
RESEARCH. 1964. irreg., vol.4, 1972. Academic
Press, Inc., Orlando, FL 32887. TEL 305-345-2000.
Ed. B. Strehler. index. Indexed: Biol.Abstr.

ADVANCES IN MOTOR DEVELOPMENT
RESEARCH. see *PHYSICAL FITNESS AND
HYGIENE*

612.67 616.8   US
ADVANCES IN NEUROGERONTOLOGY. 1980.
irreg. Praeger Publishers (Subsidiary of: Greenwood
Press, Inc.) 521 Fifth Ave., New York, NY 10175.
TEL 212-599-8400. Eds. Gabe J. Maletta, Francis J.
Pirozzolo. (back issues avail.) Indexed: Chem.Abstr.

612.67   US   ISSN 0361-0179
AGING (NEW YORK) 1975. irreg., vol.10, 1979.
price varies. Raven Press, 1185 Ave. of the
Americas, New York, NY 10036. TEL 212-575-
0335. Indexed: Biol.Abstr. Chem.Abstr. Curr.Cont.
Sci.Cit.Ind.

305.2   US   ISSN 0272-3808
ANNUAL EDITIONS: AGING. 1978. a. Dushkin
Publishing Group, Inc., Sluice Dock, Guilford, CT
06437. TEL 203-453-4351. Ed. Ian Nielsen. index.
(back issues avail.) Indexed: Bk.Rev.Ind.
   Formerly: Annual Editions. Focus: Aging (ISSN
0162-3621)

ANNUAL REPORT OF ADVOCACY FOR
NURSING HOME REFORM. see *HOSPITALS*

362.5   US   ISSN 0198-8794
ANNUAL REVIEW OF GERONTOLOGY &
GERIATRICS. 1980. a. price varies. Springer
Publishing Company, 536 Broadway, New York,
NY 10012. TEL 212-431-4370. Ed. Carl Eisdorfer.
circ. 420.

552   GERONTOLOGY AND GERIATRICS — ABSTRACTING, BIBLIOGRAPHIES, STATISTICS

301.435   DK
COMPREHENSIVE GERONTOLOGY. SERIE C: INTERDISCIPLINARY TOPICS. (Text in English) 1987. a. Kr.824 for the 3 series. MunKsgaard, Noerre Soegade 35, DK-1370 Copenhagen K, Denmark. Ed. Andrus Viidik.

353.9   US   ISSN 0090-6077
CONNECTICUT. DEPARTMENT ON AGING. REPORT TO THE GOVERNOR AND GENERAL ASSEMBLY. (Report year ends June 30) 1969. a. Department on Aging, 175 Main St., Hartford, CT 06106-1818. Ed. Robert Kapan. circ. 500.

612.6
CONTEMPORARY GERIATRIC MEDICINE. irreg. price varies. Plenum Publishing Corp., 233 Spring St., New York, NY 10013. TEL 212-620-8047. Ed. Steven R. Gambert.

301.435   US   ISSN 0732-085X
CONTRIBUTIONS TO THE STUDY OF AGING. 1982. irreg. price varies. Greenwood Press (Subsidiary of: Congressional Information Service, Inc.) Box 5007, 88 Post Rd. West, Westport, CT 06881. TEL 203-226-3571. index.

DIRECTORY OF FEDERAL AID FOR THE AGING. see SOCIAL SERVICES AND WELFARE

612.67   US   ISSN 0271-955X
FRONTIERS IN AGING SERIES. 1980. irreg., vol.4, 1984. price varies. Human Sciences Press, Inc., 72 Fifth Ave., New York, NY 10011-8004. TEL 212-243-6000. Ed. Gari Lesnoff-Caravaglia.

612.67   SP   ISSN 0212-9744
GERIATRIKA; revista iberoamericana de geriatria y gerontologia. no.4, 1986. Alpe Editores, S.A., Arzobispo Morcillo, 24, 28029-Madrid, Spain. TEL 733 88 11/92.

301.435   US
GERONTOLOGICAL SOCIETY. MONOGRAPHS.* irreg., vol.7, 1982. 1411 K St., N.W., Ste. 300, Washington, DC 20005. TEL 202-466-6752.

610   SZ   ISSN 0074-1132
INTERDISCIPLINARY TOPICS IN GERONTOLOGY. (Text in English) 1968. irreg. (approx. 1/yr.) price varies. S. Karger AG, Allschwilerstrasse 10, P.O. Box, CH-4009 Basel, Switzerland. Ed. H.P. von Hahn. (reprint service avail. from ISI) Indexed: Biol.Abstr. Chem.Abstr. Curr.Cont. Ind.Med.

301.45 612.67 618.97   IT   ISSN 0074-1620
INTERNATIONAL ASSOCIATION OF GERONTOLOGY. EUROPEAN CLINICAL SECTION PROCEEDINGS.* irreg., 1965, 4th, San Remo, Italy. Foreign Relations Secretary of the 4th Congress, Societa Italiana di Gerontologia e Geriatria, Via Malcontenti 12, Florence, Italy (Inquire: Prof. B. Steinmann. Medizinische Abteilung CL. Laury Haus, Berne 3008, Berne, Switzerland)
  Proceedings published in host country; 1971, Berne

301   US   ISSN 0884-8688
JOURNAL OF AGING AND JUDAISM. 1986. biennial. $19 to individuals; institutions $40. Human Sciences Press, Inc., 72 Fifth Ave., New York, NY 10011. TEL 212-243-6000. Ed. Rabbi Kerry M. Olitzky.

362.6   US
LIFECARE INDUSTRY. 1981. a. $35. Laventhol & Horwath, 1845 Walnut St., Philadelphia, PA 19103. TEL 215-299-1600. charts. circ. 10,000.

612.67   US   ISSN 0275-360X
MODERN AGING RESEARCH. 1980. irreg., vol.8, 1986. price varies. Alan R. Liss, Inc., 41 E. 11th St., New York, NY 10003. TEL 212-475-7700. Eds. Richard C. Adelman, Jay Roberts. Indexed: Biol.Abstr. Chem.Abstr.
●Also available online.

362.6   UK   ISSN 0309-0078
NATIONAL ASSOCIATION OF PENSION FUNDS. ANNUAL SURVEY. 1975. a. £40 to non-members; members £18. National Association of Pension Funds, 12-18 Grosvenor Gardens, London SW1W 0DH, England. Ed. Basil Lofthouse.

362.6   UK
NATIONAL ASSOCIATION OF PENSION FUNDS. YEAR BOOK. 1979. a. £30 to non-members; members £20. National Association of Pension Funds, 12-18 Grosvenor Gardens, London SW1W 0DH, England. Ed. Nick Jager. circ. 4,000.

362.6   378.0025   US   ISSN 0148-4508
NATIONAL DIRECTORY OF EDUCATIONAL PROGRAMS IN GERONTOLOGY. 1976. biennial. $31. Association for Gerontology in Higher Education, 600 Maryland Ave., S.W., W. Wing, Ste. 204, Washington, DC 20024. TEL 202-484-7505. Ed. Ellen N. Sullivan. circ. 1,000. (back issues avail.)

301.435   US
NATIONAL INDIAN COUNCIL ON AGING. 1976. biennial. National Indian Council on Aging, Box 2088, Albuquerque, NM 87103.

353.9   US
OHIO. DEPARTMENT OF AGING. ANNUAL REPORT. 1973. a. (Department of Aging) National Graphics, 50 W. Broad St., 9th Fl., Columbus, OH 43215. TEL 614-466-5500. circ. 1,000.
  Formerly: Ohio. Commission on Aging. Annual Report (ISSN 0363-9207)

362.6   UK
OLD AGE: A REGISTER OF SOCIAL RESEARCH. 1955. biennial. Centre for Policy on Ageing, 25/31 Ironmonger Row, London EC1V 3QP, England. Ed. Hilary Todd.

PENNSYLVANIA. ADMINISTRATION ON AGING. STATE PLAN ON AGING. see SOCIAL SERVICES AND WELFARE

155.67   UK   ISSN 0267-0348
SELECTED BIBLIOGRAPHIES ON AGEING. 1984. irreg. Centre for Policy on Ageing, 25/31 Ironmonger Row, London EC1V 3QP, England. Ed. Gillian Crosby.

362.6   US
SENIORS IN SACRAMENTO. 1972. irreg. (10-12/yr.) $10 to individuals; institutions $15. California Rural Legal Assistance Foundation, Senior Citizens Program, 1900 K St., Sacramento, CA 95814. TEL 916-447-1835. Ed. Emma Gunterman. circ. 800.

618.97   SZ
TEACHING AND TRAINING IN GERIATRIC MEDICINE. (Text in English) 1987. irreg. price varies. S. Karger AG, Allschwillerstrasse 10, P.O. Box, CH-4009 Basel, Switzerland. Ed. W. Meier-Ruge.

301.435   US
UNIVERSITY OF FLORIDA. CENTER FOR GERONTOLOGICAL STUDIES. RESEARCH SERIES. irreg. (University of Florida, Center for Gerontological Studies) University Presses of Florida, 15 N.W. 15th St., Gainesville, FL 32603. TEL 904-392-1351. Ed. Gordon F. Streib. Indexed: Biol.Abstr.

618.97   301.435   US   ISSN 0071-6103
UNIVERSITY OF FLORIDA. CENTER FOR GERONTOLOGY. STUDIES AND PROGRAMS. 1951. irreg. price varies. University Presses of Florida, 15 N.W. 15th St., Gainesville, FL 32603. TEL 904-392-1351. Ed. Carter C. Osterbind.

362.6   US   ISSN 0083-8438
WEST VIRGINIA. COMMISSION ON AGING. ANNUAL PROGRESS REPORT. 1961. a. controlled free circ. Commission on Aging, State Capitol, Charleston, WV 25305. TEL 304-348-3317. Ed. Donna S. Hawkins. circ. 500.

360   US   ISSN 0731-6526
WOODALL'S RETIREMENT DIRECTORY. 1976. a. $10.95. Woodall Publishing Co., 500 Hyacinth Pl., Highland Park, IL 60035. TEL 312-433-4550. adv. circ. 50,000.
  Former titles: Woodall's Florida and Southern States Retirement and Resort Communities Directory (ISSN 0163-4313); Woodall's Retirement and Resort Communities Directory; Woodall's Mobile Home Park Directory (ISSN 0094-1891); Woodall's Mobile-Modular Living (ISSN 0084-1102); Incorporating: Woodall's Directory of Mobile Home Communities (ISSN 0093-7274)

612.67   618.97   JA
YOKUFUKAI GERIATRIC JOURNAL/ YOKUFUKAI CHOSA KENKYU KIYO. (Text in Japanese; summaries in English) 1930. a. free. Yokufukai Geriatric Hospital - Yokufukai Byoin, 1-12-1 Nishi Takaido, Suginami-ku, Tokyo 168, Japan. Indexed: Biol.Abstr. Chem.Abstr. Excerp.Med.
  Formerly: Acta Gerontologica Japonica (ISSN 0001-5768)

618.97   362.6   GE   ISSN 0084-5272
ZEITSCHRIFT FUER ALTERNSFORSCHUNG. SUPPLEMENTBAENDE. 1970. irreg. price varies. VEB Verlag Volk und Gesundheit, Neue Gruenstr. 18, 1020 Berlin, E. Germany (D.D.R.) (reprint service avail. from ISI)

612.67   360   GW   ISSN 0721-1872
ZEITSCHRIFTENBIBLIOGRAPHIE GERONTOLOGIE. 1977. a. DM.10. Deutsches Zentrum fuer Altersfragen e.V., Manfred von Richthofen Strasse 2, 1000 Berlin 42, W. Germany (B.R.D.) Ed.Bd. circ. 500. (back issues avail.)

GERONTOLOGY AND GERIATRICS — Abstracting, Bibliographies, Statistics

301.435   US   ISSN 0743-7560
BIBLIOGRAPHIES AND INDEXES IN GERONTOLOGY. 1985. irreg. price varies. Greenwood Press, 88 Post Rd. W., Box 5007, Westport, CT 06881. TEL 203-226-3571.

612.67   016   US   ISSN 0011-3662
CURRENT LITERATURE ON AGING. 1957. q. $24 to non-members. National Council on the Aging, 600 Maryland Ave., S.W., West Wing 100, Washington, DC 20024. TEL 202-479-1200. Ed. Carol E. Forney. index. circ. 5,000. (processed)

618.97   016   NE   ISSN 0014-424X
EXCERPTA MEDICA. SECTION 20: GERONTOLOGY AND GERIATRICS. 1958. 10/yr. fl.575($102) Elsevier Science Publishers B.V., Box 211, 1000 AE Amsterdam, Netherlands. adv. bk. rev. abstr. index. cum.index. Indexed: Excerp.Med.
●Also available online. Vendors: BRS, DIALOG.

612.67   016   US
GERONTOLOGICAL ABSTRACTS. vol.5, 1978. bi-m. $90 to individuals; institutions $130. University Information Services, Inc., Box 1048, Ann Arbor, MI 48106. TEL 313-764-1817. Ed. Seong S. Han.

301.435   016   US   ISSN 0882-3405
INDEX TO PERIODICAL LITERATURE ON AGING. 1982. biennial. $150. Lorraine Publications, 9000 E. Jefferson, Ste. 7-5, Detroit, MI 48214. TEL 313-822-7834. Ed. Jean Owens. bk. rev. circ. 1,200.
  Former titles: Areco's Index to Periodical Literature on Aging; (as of 1983): Areco's Quarterly Index to Periodical Literature on Aging (ISSN 0734-5569)

GIFTWARE AND TOYS

658.72   790.13   UK
B T H A BUYERS GUIDE. 1984. a. British Toy & Hobby Manufacturers Association, 80 Camberwell Rd., London, SE5 OEG, England. Ed. Gordon Webb. adv.

CANADIAN JEWELLERY & GIFTWARE DIRECTORY. see BUSINESS AND ECONOMICS — Trade And Industrial Directories

688   US   ISSN 0072-4505
GIFT AND DECORATIVE ACCESSORIES BUYERS DIRECTORY. 1917. a. incl. in subscr. to Gifts and Decorative Accessories. Geyer-McAllister Publications, Inc., 51 Madison Ave., New York, NY 10010. TEL 212-689-4411. Ed. Phyllis Sweed. adv. circ. 34,300.

GIFT AND TABLEWARE REPORTER. GIFT GUIDE; a buyers' guide. see BUSINESS AND ECONOMICS — Trade And Industrial Directories

HEATING, PLUMBING AND REFRIGERATION

658.8   HK
HONG KONG TOYS. (Text in English) 1970. a. $12 per issue; free to qualified personnel. Hong Kong Trade Development Council, Great Eagle Centre, 31st fl., 23 Harbour Rd., Hong Kong. Ed. Saul Lockhart. adv. illus. stat. circ. 35,000(controlled)

688   CN   ISSN 0713-4118
JEUX ET JOUETS. (Text in French) 1981. a. Can.$6.95. Centrale des Bibliotheques, 1685 rue Fleury est, Montreal, Que. H2C 1T1, Canada. circ. 1,500. (back issues avail.)
    Formerly: Choix Jeunesse: Jeux et Jouets.

688   FR   ISSN 0075-4056
JOUETS ET JEUX. (Text in French; summaries in German, Italian, English, Spanish) 1950. a. 135 F. Creations, Editions et Productions Publicitaires, 1 Place d'Estienne d'Orves, 75009 Paris, France. Ed. Georges Prieux. adv. circ. 8,500.

658.72   643   640   US
NATIONWIDE DIRECTORY OF GIFT, HOUSEWARES & HOME TEXTILE BUYERS. a., with 2 supplements. $95. Salesman's Guide, Inc., 1140 Broadway, New York, NY 10001. TEL 212-684-2985.
    Formerly: Nationwide Directory of Gift and Housewares Buyers.

688.72   US   ISSN 0079-2349
PLAYTHINGS DIRECTORY. 1903. a. $20. Geyer-McAllister Publications, Inc., 51 Madison Ave., New York, NY 10010. TEL 212-689-4411. Ed. Frank Reysen, Jr. adv. circ. 14,201.

688   CN   ISSN 0317-9443
TOY AND DECORATION FAIR DIRECTORY. (Text in English and French) 1941. a. Can.$10. Canadian Toy Manufacturers Association, Box 294, Kleinburg, Ont. LOJ 1CO, Canada. TEL 416-851-1118. Ed. Henry Wittenberg. adv. circ. 3,500.
    Formerly: Canadian Toy Fair. Trade Show Directory (ISSN 0068-9890)

TOY TRADER DAILY NEWS (EARLS COURT) see BUSINESS AND ECONOMICS — Domestic Commerce

TOY TRADER DAILY NEWS (HARROGATE) see BUSINESS AND ECONOMICS — Domestic Commerce

688   UK   ISSN 0082-5611
TOY TRADER YEAR BOOK. 1953. a. Wheatland Journals Ltd., Penn House, Penn Place, Rickmansworth, Herts. WD3 1SN, England. Ed. Chris Darby. adv. circ. 2,500.
    Incorporating: Pram and Nursery Trader Year Book (ISSN 0306-6541)

688   UK
TOYS & GAMES TRADER YEARBOOK.* 1920. a. £2.50. Wheatland Journal Ltd., Penn House, Penn Place, Rickmansworth, Herts. WD3 1SN, England. tr.mkt. index.
    Formerly: Games and Toys Yearbook (ISSN 0072-0135)

745.5   US
WOMAN'S DAY BEST IDEAS FOR CHRISTMAS. a. $2.50. C B S Publications, Woman's Day, 1515 Broadway, New York, NY 10036. TEL 212-719-6812. Ed. Ellen Parlapiano. adv. charts. illus. tr.lit. (back issues avail.)
    Formerly: Woman's Day Gifts You Can Make for Christmas (ISSN 0092-3850)

GROCERY TRADE

see Food and Food Industries — Grocery Trade

GUIDES TO SCHOOLS AND COLLEGES

see Education — Guides to Schools and Colleges

HARDWARE

see Building and Construction — Hardware

HARDWARE (COMPUTER)

see Computers — Hardware

HEAT

see Physics — Heat

HEATING, PLUMBING AND REFRIGERATION

697   BE
A B C. (Annuaire Belge de Chauffage et Climatisation) (Text in Flemish and French) 1970. biennial. 800 Fr. Editions Coppieters S.P.R.L., 393 Bd. de Smet de Naeyer, B-1090, Brussels, Belgium. adv. bk. rev. circ. 4,000.

697   US
A S H R A E HANDBOOK. (In 4 vols.: Fundamentals, Refrigeration Systems/Applications, Equipment, HVAC Systems/Applications) 1922. a. $100. American Society of Heating, Refrigerating and Air-Conditioning Engineers Inc., 1791 Tullie Circle, N.E., Atlanta, GA 30329. TEL 404-636-8400. index. circ. 60,000. (reprint service avail.) Indexed: Eng.Ind.
    Former titles: A S H R A E Handbook & Product Specification File; A S H R A E Handbook and Product Directory (ISSN 0066-0620); A S H R A E Handbook of Fundamentals; Supersedes in part: A S H R A E Guide and Data Book. Fundamentals and Equipment.

697   US   ISSN 0002-418X
ALABAMA CONTRACTOR. 1954. a. membership. Associated Plumbing, Heating & Cooling Contractors of Alabama, Inc., 972 Montclair Rd., Ste. D, Birmingham, AL 35213. TEL 205-956-6769. Ed. Sally Clow. adv. circ. 1,200.

343   US
B O C A BASIC-NATIONAL PLUMBING CODE. triennial. $26. Building Officials and Code Administrators International, 4051 West Flossmoor Rd., Country Club Hills, IL 60477-5795. illus.
    Formerly: B O C A Basic Plumbing Code (ISSN 0098-1702)

697   UK   ISSN 0305-5973
B S R I A APPLICATION GUIDES. 1959. irreg. price varies; free to members. Building Services Research and Information Association, Old Bracknell Ln. West, Bracknell, Berks. RG12 4AH, England. bk. rev. circ. 1,500.
    Formerly: Heating and Ventilating Research Association. Laboratory Reports (ISSN 0438-8887)

697   UK   ISSN 0309-0248
B S R I A TECHNICAL NOTES. 1959. irreg. price varies. Building Services Research and Information Association, Old Bracknell Lane West, Bracknell,

697   FR   ISSN 0153-999X
CATALOGUE NATIONAL DU GENIE CLIMATIQUE-CHAUFFAGE ET CONDITIONNEMENT D'AIR/NATIONAL CATALOGUE OF HEATING AND AIR CONDITIONING/NAZIONALER KATALOG DER HEIZUNG UND KLIMATISIERUNG. 1952. a. 65 F. Editions du Cartel, 51 rue Vivienne, 75002 Paris, France. Ed. A.L. Savu. adv. circ. 12,000.
    Former titles (1966-1973): Catalogue National du Chauffage et du Conditionnement d'Air; (1952-1966: Annuaire-Guide du Chauffage et du Conditionnement d'Air.

697   UK
COMBINED HEAT AND POWER ASSOCIATION. HANDBOOK. 1984. a. £10. Combined Heat and Power Publications Ltd., Bedford House, Stafford Rd., Caterham, Surrey CR3 6JA, England.
    Formerly: District Heating Association. Handbook.

621.56   US   ISSN 0070-6167
DIRECTORY OF PUBLIC REFRIGERATED WAREHOUSES. 1930. a. $150 to all others (free to qualified personnel) International Association of Refrigerated Warehouses, 7315 Wisconsin Ave., Ste. 1200N, Bethesda, MD 20814. TEL 301-652-5674. Dir. J. William Hudson. adv. circ. 6,000.

H M T: THE SCIENCE AND APPLICATION OF HEAT MASS TRANSFER; reports, reviews & computer programs. see PHYSICS — Heat

697   UK
H V A C RED BOOK OF HEATING, VENTILATING AND AIR CONDITIONING EQUIPMENT. 1971. biennial. £22.50. Heating and Ventilating Publications (Developments) Ltd., Faversham House, 111 St. James's Rd., Croydon, Surrey CR9 2TH, England. adv. circ. 2,500.
    Formerly (until 1979): Air Conditioning, Ventilating and Heating Equipment (ISSN 0065-4809)

696   CN   ISSN 0382-6996
HEATING, PLUMBING, AIR CONDITIONING BUYERS' GUIDE. a. Can.$15. Southam Communications Ltd., 1450 Don Mills Rd., Don Mills, Ont. M3B 2X7, Canada. TEL 416-445-6641. Ed. Ron Shuker. adv. circ. 14,893.

697   UK   ISSN 0306-3585
HEATING, VENTILATING AND AIR CONDITIONING YEAR BOOK. 1968. a. £28($42) ‡ Heating and Ventilating Contractors', 2 Engel Park, London NW7 2HD, W. Sussex BN17 5DE, England. (Co-sponsors: H E V A C Association; Chartered Institution of Building Services Engineers Research and Information Association) Ed. Donald Edwards. adv. circ. 5,000.
    Formerly: Heating and Ventilating Year Book (ISSN 0073-1552)

600   US
HUTTON'S PLUMBING-HEATING-COOLING CATALOG. 1970. a. Hutton Publishing Co., Inc., 375 N. Broadway, Jericho, NY 11753. TEL 516-935-2740. circ. 14,407.

696   US
I C B O PLUMBING CODE. triennial. $26 to members; non-members $34. International Conference of Building Officials, 5360 S. Workman Mill Rd., Whittier, CA 90601. TEL 213-699-0541.

636   637   US
I M A C A DIRECTORY. 1987. a. $10. ‡ International Mobile Air Conditioning Association, 3003 LBJ Freeway, Ste. 219, Dallas, TX 75234. Ed. Paul M. Allen. adv. bk. rev. charts. illus. pat. stat. tr.lit. circ. 10,000.
    Supersedes (as of 1981): International Buyer's Guide of Mobile Air Conditioning; As of 1977: Mobile Air Conditioning.

697   331.8   US   ISSN 0569-4043
INDUSTRIAL VENTILATION; A MANUAL OF RECOMMENDED PRACTICE. 1951. biennial. price varies. American Conference of Governmental Industrial Hygienists, Inc., 6500 Glenway Ave., Bldg. D-7, Cincinnati, OH 45211. TEL 513-661-7881. circ. 25,000.

HEATING, PLUMBING AND REFRIGERATION — ABSTRACTING, BIBLIOGRAPHIES, STATISTICS

621.56   UK
INSTITUTE OF REFRIGERATION.
PROCEEDINGS. 1899. a. £12. Institute of Refrigeration, 76 Mill Lane, Carshalton, Surrey SM5 2JR, England. circ. 2,500.

697   US   ISSN 0074-4638
INTERNATIONAL DISTRICT HEATING ASSOCIATION. PROCEEDINGS. 1909. a. $75 free to members. ‡ International District Heating Association, 1101 Conneticut Ave., Washington, DC 20036. TEL 202-429-5111. circ. 500. Indexed: Therm.Abstr.

621.56   FR   ISSN 0074-6541
INTERNATIONAL INSTITUTE OF REFRIGERATION. PROCEEDINGS OF COMMISSION MEETINGS. 1952. irreg. price varies. International Institute of Refrigeration - Institut International du Froid, 177 bd. Malesherbes, 75017 Paris, France. circ. 2,000.

697 621.56   UK   ISSN 0538-9895
INTERNATIONAL SERIES ON HEATING, VENTILATION AND REFRIGERATION. 1966. irreg., vol.15, 1981. price varies. Pergamon Press, Ltd., Headington Hill Hall, Oxford OX3 0BW, England (U.S. subscr. to: Maxwell House, Fairview Park, Elmsford, NY 10523) index.
   Formerly: International Series of Monographs on Heating, Ventilation and Refrigeration.

696 697   UK   ISSN 0141-0288
NATIONAL ASSOCIATION OF PLUMBING, HEATING AND MECHANICAL SERVICES CONTRACTORS YEARBOOK. a. £7.50. Sterling Publications Ltd., 86-88 Edgware Rd., London W2 2YW, England.

697   UR
POLUTEHNILINE INSTITUUT TALLINN. PROBLEMY RABOTY KOTELNYKH USTANOVOK TEPLOVYKH ELEKTROSTANTSII. (Subseries of Its Toimetised) (Text in Russian; summaries in English or German) irreg. price varies. Polutehniline Instituut Tallinn, Ehitajate tee 5, Tallinn, Estonian S.S.R., U.S.S.R.
   Formerly: Polutehniline Instituut Tallinn. Problemy Raboty Kotelnykh Ustanovok.

697 621.56   UK   ISSN 0305-0777
REFRIGERATION AND AIR CONDITIONING YEAR BOOK. 1898. a. price varies. E M A P Maclaren Publishers Ltd., P.O. Box 109, Maclaren House, Scarbrook Rd., Croydon CR9 1QH, Surrey, England. Ed. Terry O'Gordon. adv. bk. rev. index. circ. 5,200. (also avail. in microfilm)
   Formerly: Refrigeration and Air Conditioning Directory (ISSN 0080-0503)

SOLAR COLLECTOR MANUFACTURING ACTIVITY. see *ENERGY*

697   DK
VARME OG SANITETS NYT. LEVERANDOERREGISTER. Variant title: Varme og Sanitets Nyt's Leverandoerregister. 1976. a. free to libraries. Thomson Communications (Scandinavia) A-S, Struenseegade 7-9, DK-2200 Copenhagen N, Denmark. illus. circ. 13,630.

697   US
WOODHEAT. 1978. a. $6. Salls-Wright Publishing Group, Box 2008, Laconia, NH 03247. TEL 608-528-4285. Ed. Jason Perry. adv. bk. rev. charts. illus. stat. tr.lit. index. circ. 175,000. (back issues avail.)
   Former titles: Woodstove, Wood, Coal and Solar Equipment Directory (ISSN 0744-0820); Woodstove, Coalstove, Fireplace & Equipment Directory (ISSN 0271-5090)

HEATING, PLUMBING AND REFRIGERATION — Abstracting, Bibliographies, Statistics

697 016   UK   ISSN 0140-4237
INTERNATIONAL BUILDING SERVICES ABSTRACTS. 1966. bi-m. £77. Building Services Research and Information Association, Old Bracknell Lane West, Bracknell, Berks RG12 4AH, England. Ed. M. McCarthy. index. circ. 700. Indexed: Agri.Eng.Abstr.
   ●Also available online. Vendors: European Space Agency, Pergamon Infoline.

   Former titles (until 1978): Thermal Abstracts (ISSN 0040-599X); H.V.R.A. Library Bulletin.

621.9 016   UR   ISSN 0370-8098
REFERATIVNYI ZHURNAL. KHIMICHESKOE, NEFTEPERERABATYVAYUSCHCHEE I POLIMERNOE MASHINOSTROENIE. 1962. m. 57.20 Rub. 61 Rub. including index. Vsesoyuznyi Institut Nauchno-Tekhnicheskoi Informatsii (VINITI), Baltiiskaya ul., 14, Moscow A-219, Russian S.F.S.R., U.S.S.R (Subscr. to: Mezhdunarodnaya Kniga, Dimitrova ul. 39, 113095 Moscow, Russian S.F.S.R., U.S.S.R.) Indexed: Chem.Abstr.
   Formerly: Referativnyi Zhurnal. Khimicheskoe i Kholodil'noe Mashinostroenie (ISSN 0034-2416)

HEMATOLOGY

see *Medical Sciences—Hematology*

HIGHER EDUCATION

see *Education—Higher Education*

HISTORY

see also *History—History of Africa; History—History of Asia; History—History of Australasia and Other Areas; History—History of Europe; History—History of North and South America; History—History of the Near East; Anthropology; Archaeology; Folklore*

also specific subjects

900   US   ISSN 0270-6253
A M S STUDIES IN SOCIAL HISTORY. 1976. irreg., no.6, 1986. price varies. A M S Press, Inc., 56 E. 13th St., New York, NY 10003. TEL 212-777-4700. (back issues avail.)

900 800   US   ISSN 0270-6261
A M S STUDIES IN THE MIDDLE AGES. 1978. irreg., no.11, 1986. price varies. A M S Press Inc., 56 E. 13th St., New York, NY 10003. TEL 212-777-4700. (back issues avail.) Indexed: M.L.A.

987   AG   ISSN 0001-382X
ACADEMIA NACIONAL DE LA HISTORIA. BOLETIN. 1912. irreg., latest no.52. no subscriptions avail. Academia Nacional de la Historia, Balcarce 139, Buenos Aires, Argentina. bk. rev. index. circ. 3,000. Indexed: Hist.Abstr. Amer.Hist.& Life.

900   CH
ACADEMIA SINICA. INSTITUTE OF MODERN HISTORY. BULLETIN/CHUNG YANG YEN CHIU YUAN. CHIU TAI SHIH YEN CHIU SO CHI K'AN. (Text in Chinese) 1969. a. $3. Academia Sinica, Institute of Modern History, Nankang, Taipei, Taiwan, Republic of China. Ed. Lu Pao-ch'ien. bk. rev. circ. 1,500. Indexed: Hist.Abstr. Amer.Hist.& Life.

ACADEMIE DES INSCRIPTIONS ET BELLES-LETTRES. ETUDES ET COMMENTAIRES. see *LINGUISTICS*

ACADEMIE INTERNATIONALE D'HISTOIRE DES SCIENCES. COLLECTION DES TRAVAUX. see *SCIENCES: COMPREHENSIVE WORKS*

900   US   ISSN 0361-7491
ACTA (ALBANY) 1974. a. $15. State University of New York Press, State University Plaza, Albany, NY 12246. TEL 518-472-5025. circ. 250.

907   US   ISSN 0361-7491
ACTA (BINGHAMTON) 1974. a. $15. (State University of New York at Binghamton, Center for Medieval and Early Renaissance Studies) State University of New York Press, State University Plaza, Albany, NY 12246. TEL 518-472-5025. Dir. Paul E. Szarmach. circ. 300. (back issues avail.; reprint service avail. from ISI) Indexed: M.L.A. RILA.

900   GW   ISSN 0567-7599
ACTA HUMBOLDTIANA. SERIES HISTORICA. 1966. irreg. price varies. (Deutsche Ibero-Amerika-Stiftung) Franz Steiner Verlag Wiesbaden GmbH, Birkenwaldstr. 44, Postfach 347, D-7000 Stuttgart 1, W. Germany (B.R.D.) Ed. Wolfgang Haberland.

ACTA REGIAE SOCIETATITIS HUMANIORUM LITTERATUM LUNDENSIS. see *ARCHAEOLOGY*

900 370   PL
ACTA UNIVERSITATIS LODZIENSIS: FOLIA HISTORICA. (Text in Polish; summaries in various languages) irreg. Uniwersytet Lodzki, Drukarnia Wojskowa, Ul. Gdanska 130, Lodz, Poland (Dist. by: Ars Polona-Ruch, Krakowskie Przedmiescie 7, Warsaw, Poland)

960 950   BL   ISSN 0002-0591
AFRO-ASIA. (Text in Portuguese; summaries in English and French) 1965. irreg. $3 exchange. Universidade Federal da Bahia, Centro de Estudos Afro-Orientais, C.P. 1163, 40.000 Salvador, Bahia, Brazil. Ed. Leovigildo Filgueiras. bk. rev. bibl. charts. illus. circ. 1,000. Indexed: Hist.Abstr. Amer.Hist.& Life.

990   US   ISSN 0884-5816
AGE OF JOHNSON. 1987. a. $50. A M S Press, Inc., 56 E. 13th St., New York, NY 10003. TEL 212-777-4700. Ed. Paul J. Korshin. index. circ. 550.

AKADEMIE DER WISSENSCHAFTEN, GOETTINGEN. NACHRICHTEN 1. PHILOLOGISCH-HISTORISCHE KLASSE. see *LINGUISTICS*

900 658   AT
ALCAN FACTS - AUSTRALIA (YEAR) 1968. biennial. free. Alcan Australia Ltd., G.P.O. Box 4130, Sydney, N.S.W. 2001, Australia. Ed. A.A. Smith. circ. 5,000.

900   US   ISSN 0065-8561
AMERICAN HISTORICAL ASSOCIATION. ANNUAL REPORT. a. American Historical Association, 400 A St. S.E., Washington, DC 20003. TEL 202-544-2422. (also avail. in microform from UMI)

900 500 100   US   ISSN 0065-9738
AMERICAN PHILOSOPHICAL SOCIETY. MEMOIRS. 1935. irreg., vol.164, 1985. price varies. American Philosophical Society, 104 S. Fifth St, Philadelphia, PA 19106. TEL 215-627-0706. Ed. Herman H. Goldstine. index to each vol. (reprint service avail. from UMI,ISI) Indexed: Biol.Abstr. Math.R. GeoRef.

900 500 100   US   ISSN 0065-9746
AMERICAN PHILOSOPHICAL SOCIETY. TRANSACTIONS. 1769. 1 vol./yr. containing 1-7 parts published irregularly. $65. American Philosophical Society, 104 S. Fifth St, Philadelphia, PA 19106. TEL 215-627-0706. Ed. Herman H. Goldstine. index in some volumes; cum.index: 1769-1960. (reprint service avail. from UMI,ISI) Indexed: Biol.Abstr. Math.R. SSCI. GeoRef.

AMERICAN UNIVERSITY STUDIES. SERIES 7. THEOLOGY AND RELIGION. see *RELIGIONS AND THEOLOGY*

900   US   ISSN 0740-0462
AMERICAN UNIVERSITY STUDIES. SERIES 9. HISTORY. 1984. irreg. Peter Lang Publishing, Inc., 62 W. 45th St., New York, NY 10036. TEL 212-302-6740. Ed. Jay Wilson.

ANCIENT GREEK CITIES REPORT. see *HOUSING AND URBAN PLANNING*

930 BE ISSN 0066-1619
ANCIENT SOCIETY. (Text in Dutch, English, French, German, Italian) 1970. a. price varies. Katholieke Universiteit te Leuven, Afdeling Oude Geschiedenis, Blijde Inkomststraat 21, B-3000 Leuven, Belgium. Ed. H. Verdin. circ. 500. (back issues avail.) Indexed: Br.Archaeol.Abstr. Numis.Lit.

ANGLO-AMERICAN FORUM. see *LITERATURE*

900 PL
ANNALES UNIVERSITATIS MARIAE CURIE-SKLODOWSKA. SECTIO F. HISTORIA. (Text in English, French or Polish; summaries in English, French, German and Russian) 1946. a. price varies. Uniwersytet Marii Curie-Sklodowskiej, Plac Marii Curie-Sklodowskiej 5, 20-031 Lublin, Poland. Ed. Wieslaw Sladkowski. circ. 550. Indexed: Hist.Abstr. Amer.Hist.& Life.
 Formerly (until 1983): Annales Universitatis Mariae Curie-Sklodowska. Sectio F. Humaniora (ISSN 0137-2033)

900 US
ANNUAL EDITIONS: WESTERN CIVILIZATION. (In 2 vols.) 1981. irreg., latest vol.2. Dushkin Publishing Group, Inc., Sluice Dock, Guilford, CT 06437. TEL 203-453-4351. Ed. Ian Nielsen.

ANNUAL REGISTER. see *POLITICAL SCIENCE — International Relations*

913 100 400 IT ISSN 0066-4766
ANTICHITA CLASSICA E CRISTIANA. 1965. irreg., latest no.27. price varies. Paideia Editrice, Via Corsica 130, 25125 Brescia, Italy.

930 GW ISSN 0066-4839
ANTIQUITAS. REIHE 1. ABHANDLUNGEN ZUR ALTEN GESCHICHTE. (Text in English, French, German and Italian) 1955. irreg., no.35, 1986. price varies. Dr. Rudolf Habelt GmbH, Am Buchenhang 1, 5300 Bonn 1, W. Germany (B.R.D.) Ed.Bd.

930 GW ISSN 0066-4847
ANTIQUITAS. REIHE 2. ABHANDLUNGEN AUS DEM GEBIETE DER VOR- UND FRUEHGESCHICHTE. 1955. irreg., no.12, 1982. price varies. Dr. Rudolf Habelt GmbH, Am Buchenhang 1, 5300 Bonn 1, W. Germany (B.R.D.) Ed.Bd.

930 913 GW ISSN 0066-4855
ANTIQUITAS. REIHE 3. ABHANDLUNGEN ZUR VOR- UND FRUEHGESCHICHTE, ZUR KLASSISCHEN UND PROVINZIAL-ROEMISCHEN ARCHAEOLOGIE UND ZUR GESCHICHTE DES ALTERTUMS. (Text in German and French) 1960. irreg., no.28, 1986. price varies. Dr. Rudolf Habelt GmbH, Am Buchenhang 1, 5300 Bonn 1, W. Germany (B. R. D.) Ed.Bd.

930 GW ISSN 0066-4863
ANTIQUITAS. REIHE 4. BEITRAEGE ZUR HISTORIA-AUGUSTA-FORSCHUNG. (Text in German, English, French, Italian) 1963. irreg., vol.17, 1985. price varies. Dr. Rudolf Habelt GmbH, Am Buchenhang 1, 5300 Bonn 1, W. Germany (B.R.D.) Ed. A. Alfoeldi.

909 SP ISSN 0210-9603
ANUARIO DE HISTORIA MODERNA Y CONTEMPORANEA. 1974. a. price varies. Universidad de Granada, Secretariato de Publicaciones, Antiguo Colegio Maximo de Cartujo, Granada, Spain. Ed. Octavio Ruiz Manjon.

913 931 GE ISSN 0066-6459
ARCHIV FUER PAPYRUSFORSCHUNG UND VERWANDTE GEBIETE. 1901. a. M.65. (Staatliche Museen zu Berlin) BSB B.G. Teubner Verlagsgesellschaft, Sternwartenstrasse 8, 7010 Leipzig, E. Germany (D.D.R.) Ed.Bd. adv. bk. rev.

ARCHIV FUER SCHLESISCHE KIRCHENGESCHICHTE. see *RELIGIONS AND THEOLOGY*

900 GW ISSN 0003-9497
ARCHIVALISCHE ZEITSCHRIFT. 1950. a. price varies. (Hauptstaatsarchiv) Boehlau Verlag GmbH, Niehler Str. 272-274, 5000 Cologne 60, W. Germany (B.R.D.) bk. rev. circ. 700. Indexed: Hist.Abstr. Amer.Hist.& Life.
Archives

900 913 UR
ARKHEOGRAFICHESKII EZHEGODNIK. 1957. a. Izdatel'stvo Nauka, Profsoyuznaya 90, Moscow B-485, Russian S.F.S.R., U.S.S.R. Ed. S.O. Shmidt. bibl. index. circ. 1,500.

ARKIV, SAMHAELLE OCH FORSKNING. see *LIBRARY AND INFORMATION SCIENCES*

900 UK
ASSOCIATION OF CONTEMPORARY HISTORIANS. BULLETIN. 1969. irreg. £1.50($5) Association of Contemporary Historians, c/o Secretary, Prof. D.C. Watt, London School of Economics, Aldwych, London WC2A 2AE, England. Ed. Dr. Neville Waites. circ. 125.

914.6 SP
ASTURIENSIA MEDIEVALIA. (Subseries of Dept's Publicaciones) 1972. a. 2.500 ptas.($30) per no. Universidad de Oviedo, Departamento de Historia Medieval, Avenida del Cristo, s/n, 33006, Oviedo, Spain. illus.

901 US ISSN 0067-0588
AUGUSTANA HISTORICAL SOCIETY, ROCK ISLAND, ILLINOIS. PUBLICATIONS. 1930. irreg., no.32, 1984. price varies. Augustana Historical Society, c/o Augustana College, Rock Island, IL 61201. TEL 309-794-7000. Ed. Ross Paulson. bk. rev. circ. 1,000. (reprint service avail. from UMI)

900 SZ
BASLER BEITRAEGE ZUR GESCHICHTSWISSENSCHAFT. 1938. irreg. price varies. Helbing und Lichtenhahn Verlag AG, Freie Strasse 82, CH-4051 Basel, Switzerland (Subscr. to: Sauerlaender AG, Postfach, CH-5001 Aarau, Switzerland)

BAUERNHAEUSER AUS MITTELEUROPA; Aufmasse und Publikationen von Gerhard Eitzen. see *ARCHITECTURE*

900 GW
BAYERISCHE AKADEMIE DER WISSENSCHAFTEN. HISTORISCHE KOMMISSION. SCHRIFTENREIHE. 1957. irreg. Vandenhoeck & Ruprecht, Robert-Bosch-Breite 6, Postfach 3753, D-3400 Goettingen, W. Germany (B.R.D.)

940 GW
BEITRAEGE ZUR SOZIAL- UND WIRTSCHAFTSGESCHICHTE. 1970. a. price varies. Verlag Walter G. Muehlau, Holtenauer Str. 116, 2300 Kiel, W. Germany (B.R.D.) Ed. Wilhelm Koppe.

901 GW ISSN 0723-3299
BEITRAEGE ZUR ZEITGESCHICHTE. 1980. irreg. DM.14.80. Colloquium Verlag, Unter den Eichen 93, 1000 Berlin 45, W. Germany (B.R.D.) Ed. Peter Haungs, Eckhard Jesse. circ. 5,000.

900 AU
BEZIRKSHAUPTMANNSCHAFT AMSTETTEN. HEIMATKUNDLICHE BEILAGE ZUM AMSTBLATT. 1972. irreg. Bezirkshauptmannschaft Amstetten, Preinsbacherstr. 11, 3302 Amstetten, Austria.

900 AU
BEZIRKSHAUPTMANNSCHAFT MELK. HEIMATKUNDLICHE BEILAGE ZUM AMTSBLATT. 1975. irreg. Bezirkshauptmannschaft Melk, Abt-Karl-Str. 23, 3390 Melk, Austria.

900 AU
BEZIRKSHAUPTMANNSCHAFT TULLN. HEIMATKUNDLICHES BEIBLATT ZUM AMTSBLATT. 1974. irreg. Bezirkshauptmannschaft Tulln, Hauptplatz 33, 3430 Tulln, Austria.

BIBLIOTECA DE MENENDEZ PELAYO. BOLETIN. see *LIBRARY AND INFORMATION SCIENCES*

900 SW
BIBLIOTECA HISTORICA LUNDENSIS. (Text in Swedish; summaries in English or German) 1955. irreg., no.60, 1985. price varies. Liber Forlag, S-205 10, Malmo, Sweden. Eds. Birgitta Oden, Goeran Rystad.

BIBLIOTEKA POLONIJNA/POLONIA LIBRARY. see *POLITICAL SCIENCE*

930 GW ISSN 0067-8201
BIBLIOTHEK DER KLASSISCHEN ALTERTUMSWISSENSCHAFTEN. NEUE FOLGE. 1963. irreg. price varies. Carl Winter Universitaetsverlag, Lutherstr. 59, 6900 Heidelberg, W. Germany (B.R.D.)

909 016 GW ISSN 0081-900X
BIBLIOTHEK FUER ZEITGESCHICHTE, STUTTGART. SCHRIFTEN.* 1962. irreg. price varies. Bernard und Graefe Verlag, Karl-Mand-Str. 2, Postfach 2060, 5400 Koblenz, W. Germany (B.R.D.)

900 FR
BIBLIOTHEQUE HISTORIQUE. 1976. irreg. Editions Payot, 106 Bd. Saint-Germain, 76006 Paris, France.

900 BE
BIJDRAGEN TOT DE GESCHIEDENIS VAN DE STAD DEINZE EN VAN HET LAND AAN LEIE EN SCHELDE. (Text in Dutch) 1934. a. 500 F. Kunst en Oudheidkundige Kringe-Deinze, Kapelstraat 104, 9800 Deize, Belgium. circ. 250.

900 UY
BOLETIN HISTORICO DEL EJERCITO. 1929. irreg., latest no. 270, 1984. free. Departmento de Estudios Historicos del Estado Mayor del Ejercito, Garibaldi 2313, Montevideo, Uruguay.
 Former titles: Boletin Historico.

900 800 011 320 US ISSN 0270-3653
BORGO REFERENCE LIBRARY. 1981. irreg., approx. 5/yr. price varies. Borgo Press, Box 2845, San Bernardino, CA 92406. TEL 714-884-5813.

900 800 UK ISSN 0260-8952
BRADFORD CENTER OCCASIONAL PAPERS. 1979. a. (University of Leeds, Department of Adult and Continuing Education) Bradford Centre, 10 Mornington Villas, Bradford, West Yorkshire BD8 7MB, England. Ed. J.A. Jowitt. circ. 500. (back issues avail.)

930 NE ISSN 0165-9367
BULLETIN ANTIEKE BESCHAVING. Short title: Babesch. 1926. a. $73. Stichting Bulletin Antieke Beschaving, Postbus 9515, 2300 RA Leiden, Netherlands. adv. bk. rev.
 Supersedes: Vereniging tot Bevordering der Kennis van de Antieke Beschaving. Bulletin.

BULLETIN OF MEDIEVAL CANON LAW. NEW SERIES. see *LAW*

900 AU
BURGEN UND SCHLOESSER IN OESTERREICH. 1965. a. Oesterreichischer Burgenverein, Plankengasse 7, 1010 Vienna, Austria.

BURT FRANKLIN ART HISTORY AND ART REFERENCE SERIES. see *ART*

900 300 330 US ISSN 0068-4317
BURT FRANKLIN ESSAYS IN HISTORY, ECONOMICS, AND SOCIAL SCIENCES. (Text in various languages) 1962; N.S. 1972. irreg. price varies. Lenox Hill Publishing and Distributing Corporation, 235 E. 44th St., New York, NY 10017. (back issues avail.)

900 US ISSN 0068-4341
BURT FRANKLIN RESEARCH AND SOURCE WORKS SERIES. (Text in various languages) 1960; N.S. 1972. irreg. price varies. Lenox Hill Publishing and Distributing Corporation, 235 E. 44th St., New York, NY 10017.

900 323.4 FR ISSN 0182-2705
CAHIERS DE L'AVENIR DE LA BRETAGNE. 1975. a. 100 F.($16) 21, place Duguesclin, 22000 Saint-Brieuc, Brittany, France. Ed. Yann Fouere. bk. rev. circ. 2,500.

900 001.3 300 UK
CAMBRIDGE COMMONWEALTH SERIES. irreg. price varies. Cambridge University Press, Edinburgh Bldg., Shaftesbury Rd., Cambridge CB2 2RU, England (And 32 E. 57th St., New York NY 10022) Ed. E.T. Stokes.

909 UK ISSN 0084-8336
CAMBRIDGE STUDIES IN EARLY MODERN
HISTORY. 1970. irreg. price varies. Cambridge
University Press, Edinburgh Bldg., Shaftesbury Rd.,
Cambridge CB2 2RU, England (And 32 E. 57th St.,
New York, N.Y. 10022) Eds. J.H. Elliot, H.G.
Koenigsberger.

CAMBRIDGE UNIVERSITY LIBRARY.
HISTORICAL BIBLIOGRAPHY SERIES. see
BIBLIOGRAPHIES

900 CN ISSN 0316-1900
CANADA. NATIONAL MUSEUM OF MAN.
MERCURY SERIES. HISTORY DIVISION.
PAPERS/CANADA. MUSEE NATIONAL DE
L'HOMME. COLLECTION MERCURE.
DIVISION DE L'HISTOIRE. DOSSIERS. (Text in
English or French) 1972. irreg., no.39, 1986. free.
(National Museum of Man, History Division)
National Museums of Canada, Ottawa, Ontario
K1A 0M8, Canada. TEL 613-992-3497.

013 900 CN
CANADA. REGISTER OF POST GRADUATE
DISSERTATIONS IN PROGRESS IN HISTORY
AND RELATED SUBJECTS. 1966. a. Can.$4.
Canadian Historical Association, 395 Wellington St.,
Ottawa, Ont. K1A 0N3, Canada. TEL 613-233-
7885. Ed. C. Gaffield. circ. 800.
   Formerly: Canada. Public Archives. Register of
Post Graduate Dissertations in Progress in History
and Related Subjects (ISSN 0068-8088)

971 CN ISSN 0068-8878
CANADIAN HISTORICAL ASSOCIATION.
HISTORICAL PAPERS; a selection from the
papers presented at the annual meeting. (Text in
English and French) 1923. a. $10. ‡ Canadian
Historical Association, 395 Wellington St., Ottawa,
Ont. K1A 0N3, Canada. TEL 613-233-7885. Eds.
D. Johnson, L Ouellette. cum.index: 1922-1959.
circ. 3,000. Indexed: CMI.

900 CN
CANADIAN WAR MUSEUM. HISTORICAL
PUBLICATIONS. (Text in English and French)
1968. irreg., no.16, 1981. price varies. (National
Museum of Man) National Museums of Canada,
Ottawa, Ont. K1A 0M8, Canada. TEL 613-992-
3497.

900 US ISSN 0069-1461
CENTERS OF CIVILIZATION SERIES. 1958. irreg.
price varies. University of Oklahoma Press, 1005
Asp Ave., Norman, OK 73019. TEL 405-325-5111.
Indexed: M.L.A.

900 IT
CENTRO DI RICERCA E DI STUDIO SUL
MOVIMENTO DEI DISCIPLINATI.
QUADERNI. 1965. irreg., no.21, 1981. Centro di
Documentazione Sul Movimento dei Disciplinati,
Casella Postale 73, Perugia 06100, Italy. Ed. Ugolini
Nicolini. adv. bk. rev. bibl. illus.
   Formerly: Centro di Documentazione Sul
Movimento dei Disciplinati. Quaderni (ISSN 0009-
0026)

900 UK ISSN 0069-2263
CEREDIGION. 1950. a. £5. Ceredigion Antiquarian
Society, Dolau Gwyn, Dole, Bow St., Dyfed, Wales.
Ed. Geraint H. Jenkins. bk. rev. circ. 800. Indexed:
Br.Hum.Ind. Br.Archaeol.Abstr.

900 CN ISSN 0069-2646
CHAMPLAIN SOCIETY, TORONTO. REPORT.
1906. a. membership. Champlain Society, Royal
York Hotel, 100 Front St. W., Toronto, Ont., M5J
1E3, Canada. TEL 416-363-8310.

978 US ISSN 0162-217X
CHARLES REDD MONOGRAPHS IN WESTERN
HISTORY. 1972. irreg. (1-2/yr.) price varies.
(Charles Redd Center for Western Studies)
Signature Press, 350 S. 400 E., No. G-4, Salt Lake
City, UT 84111-2905. Eds. Thomas Alexander,
Leonard J. Arrington. circ. 2,000.

500 610 US ISSN 0073-2745
CHICAGO HISTORY OF SCIENCE AND
MEDICINE. 1971. irreg., vol.4, 1981. price varies.
University of Chicago Press, 5801 S. Ellis Ave.,
Chicago, IL 60637. TEL 312-962-7600. Ed. Allen
G. Debus. (reprint service avail. from UMI,ISI)

CHIROPRACTIC HISTORY. see MEDICAL
SCIENCES — Chiropractics, Homeopathy,
Osteopathy

900 309 US
CIVILIZATION AND SOCIETY: STUDIES IN
SOCIAL, ECONOMIC AND CULTURAL
HISTORY. irreg., latest 1987. D.C. Heath &
Company, 125 Spring St., Lexington, MA 02173.
TEL 617-862-6650.

CLAIRLIEU: TIJDSCHRIFT GEWIJD AAN DE
GESCHIEDENIS DER KRUISHEREN. see
RELIGIONS AND THEOLOGY

CLASSICAL ASSOCIATION. PROCEEDINGS. see
LITERATURE

900 US
CLIO HISTORICAL PERIODICALS DIRECTORY.
1982. irreg., no.5, 1986. A B C-Clio, 2040 Alameda
Padre Serra, Box 4397, Santa Barbara, CA 93140-
4397. TEL 805-963-4221. Ed.Bd.
   Formerly: Clio Periodicals Directory.

900 SP ISSN 0077-2054
COLECCION MUNDO ANTIGUO. 1962. irreg.,
no.6, 1983. price varies. (Universidad de Navarra,
Departamento de Historia Antigua) Ediciones
Universidad de Navarra, S.A., Apdo. 396, 31080
Pamplona, Spain.

940 FR ISSN 0069-5343
COLLECTION D'HISTOIRE CONTEMPORAINE.
1969. irreg. price varies. ‡ Librarie A. Hatier, 8 rue
d'Assas, 75278 Paris, France. bk. rev.

COMITATUS; A JOURNAL OF MEDIEVAL AND
RENAISSANCE STUDIES. see LITERATURE

900 BE ISSN 0774-8396
COMMISSION ROYALE DE TOPONYMIE ET DE
DIALECTOLOGIE. BULLETIN/KONINKLIJKE
COMMISSIE VOOR TOPONYMIE EN
DIALECTOLOGIE. HANDELINGEN. (Editions
in Dutch and French) 1927. a. 600 Fr. Commission
Royale de Toponymie et de Dialectologie -
Koninklijke Commissie voor Toponymie en
Dialectologie, c/o Frans Debrabandere, Keizer
Karelstraat 83, 8000 Bruges, Belgium. circ. 500.
   Formerly: Commission Nationale Belge de
Folklore. Annuaire.

930 340 BE
COMMISSION ROYALE DES ANCIENNES LOIS
ET ORDONNANCES DE BELGIQUE.
BULLETIN/KONINKLIJKE COMMISSIE VOOR
DE UITGAVE DER OUDE WETTEN EN
VERORDENINGEN VAN BELGIE.
HANDELINGEN. (Editions in Flemish and
French) 1848. irreg., vol.31, 1986. Commission
Royale des Anciennes Lois et Ordonnances de
Belgique - Koninklijke Commissie voor de Uitgave
der Oude Wetten en Verordeningen van Belgie,
Ministere de la Justice, Place Poelaert, 1000
Brussels, Belgium. Ed. P.H. Godding. circ. 500.
   Formerly: Commission des Anciennes Lois et
Ordonnances de Belgique. Proces-Verbaux.

900 FR
CONFLUENTS. no.2, 1976. irreg. Societe d'Edition
les Belles Lettres, 95 Bd. Raspail, 75006 Paris,
France. illus. Indexed: M.L.A.

900 800 IT
CONTEMPORANEA; studi e testi. irreg. Angelo
Longo Editore, Via Paolo Costa 33, P.O. Box 431,
48100 Ravenna, Italy.

909 917.306 US ISSN 0885-9159
CONTRIBUTION TO THE STUDY OF WORLD
HISTORY. irreg. Greenwood Press, Inc., 88 Post
Rd., W., Box 5007, Westport, CT 06881. TEL 203-
226-3571.

CORPUS VITREARUM MEDII AEVI. see ART

972.86 CR ISSN 0034-9003
COSTA RICA. ARCHIVO NACIONAL. REVISTA.
1936. irreg., latest 1979. free. Archivo Nacional,
Apartado 10217, San Jose, Costa Rica. Ed. Luz
Alba Chacon Leon. charts. illus. index. circ. 2,100.

CRITICAL REVIEW. see LITERATURE

900 UK
CYFRES LLYGAD Y FFYNNON. (Text in Welsh)
1972. irreg. price varies. (Welsh Joint Education
Committee) University of Wales Press, 6 Gwennyth
St., Cathays, Cardiff CF2 4YD, Wales. Ed. Hugh
Thomas.

DANCE: CURRENT SELECTED RESEARCH. see
DANCE

900 IS ISSN 0333-5151
DAPIM LICHEKER TIKUFAT HASHOAH. 1979.
irreg. University for Holocaust Studies, Hacarmel,
Haifa 31 999, Israel. TEL 04-667045.

900 NE
DAT WAS DE TOESTAND IN DE WERELD.
1973. a. B.V. Uitgeversmaatschappij Annoventura,
Box 152, Amsterdam, Netherlands. illus.
   Supersedes: Toestand in de Wereld.

930 FR
DIALOGUES D'HISTOIRE ANCIENNE. (Subseries
of Besancon, France. Universite. Annales
Litteraires) 1969. a. price varies. (Universite de
Besancon, Centre de Recherches d'Histoire
Ancienne) Societe d'Edition les Belles Lettres, 95
Boulevard Raspail, 75006 Paris, France.

909 PK ISSN 0070-4873
DIGEST OF WORLD EVENTS. (Text in English)
1957. a. Rs.3.25. Modern Book Depot, Sialkot
Cantt, Pakistan. Ed. Qayyum Wazirabadi. circ. 1,
000.

900 711.5 US ISSN 0300-7316
DISCOVERY (RICHMOND) 1969. a. membership. ‡
Association for the Preservation of Virginia
Antiquities, 2300 E. Grace St., Richmond, VA
23223-7152. TEL 804-648-1889. Ed. Catherine A.
Long. illus. circ. 6,100.

900 100 800 IS ISSN 0334-2816
DIVREI HA-AKADEMIA HA-LEUMIT HA-
YISRAELIT LEMADAIM. 1964. irreg. $3 per no.
Israel Academy of Sciences and Humanities, 43
Jabotinski St., P.O.B. 4040, 91040 Jerusalem, Israel.
circ. 900. (back issues avail.) Indexed: Ind.Heb.Per.

901 US
DOCUMENTARY REFERENCE COLLECTIONS.
1971. irreg. price varies. Greenwood Press, 88 Post
Rd. W., Box 5007, Westport, CT 06881. TEL 203-
226-3571.

900 IT
DOCUMENTI E TESTIMONIANZE DI STORIA
CONTEMPORANEA. 1976. irreg. Editrice la
Scuola S.p.A., Via Cadorna 11, 25186 Brescia, Italy.

900 US ISSN 0749-4831
DOCUMENTS IN IMPERIAL HISTORY. 1985.
irreg. price varies. Greenwood Press, 88 Post Rd.
W., Box 5007, Westport, CT 06881. TEL 203-226-
3571.

900 US
DOCUMENTS OF MODERN HISTORY. irreg. price
varies. Saint Martins Press, 175 Fifth Ave., New
York, NY 10010.

DOCUMENTS OF REVOLUTION. see POLITICAL
SCIENCE

DRESS. see CLOTHING TRADE — Fashions

900 US ISSN 0070-7562
DUMBARTON OAKS TEXTS. (English translation of
original Greek) 1968. irreg. price varies.
(Dumbarton Oaks Center for Byzantine Studies) J.
J. Augustin, Inc., Locust Valley, NY 11560. TEL
506-676-1510.

930 AT ISSN 0085-0187
EDUBBA; studies ancient history. 1967. a. price
varies. University of Sydney, Department of
History, Ancient History Society, Sydney, N.S.W.
2006, Australia. Ed.Bd. bk. rev. circ. 500.

EDUCATIONAL ADMINISTRATION AND
HISTORY MONOGRAPHS. see EDUCATION —
School Organization And Administration

900 320 UK ISSN 0262-7612
ENLIGHTENMENT AND DISSENT. 1982. a. £4.50
to individuals; £12 to institutions. c/o M.
Fitzpatrick, Dept. of History, University College of
Wales, Dyfed SY23 3DY, Wales. Eds. Martin
Fitzpatrick, D.O. Thomas. adv. bk. rev. circ. 250.
Formerly: Price-Priestley Newsletter.

900 GW ISSN 0071-0989
EPIGRAPHISCHE STUDIEN. 1967. irreg., vol.12,
1981. Rheinland-Verlag, Kennedy-Ufer 2, 5000
Cologne 21, W. Germany (B.R.D.) (Distr. by:
Rudolf Habelt Verlag, Am Buchenhang 1, 5300
Bonn, W. Germany (B.R.D.)) Indexed:
Br.Archaeol.Abstr.

EPOCHE; journal of the history of religions at
U.C.L.A. see RELIGIONS AND THEOLOGY

900 NE
ERFDEEL VAN DE KLASSIEKE ROMEINSE
JURISTEN. 1982. a. fl.30. Walburg Pers, Zaadmarkt
84a-86, Box 222, 7200 AE Zutphen, Netherlands.
TEL 05750-10522. (Co-sponsor: Universiteit van de
Nederlandse Antillen)

900 011 581 551 GW
ERLANGER BAUSTEINE ZUR FRAENKISCHEN
HEIMATFORSCHUNG. 1954. a. DM.25
membership. Heimatverein Erlangen und
Umgebung, Marktplatz 1, D-8520 Erlangen, W.
Germany (B.R.D.) Ed.Bd. bk. rev. (back issues
avail.)

900 HU ISSN 0071-1233
ERTEKEZESEK A TORTENETI TUDOMANYOK
KOREBOL. 1857. irreg., vol.106, 1985. price varies.
(Magyar Tudomanyos Akademia) Akademiai Kiado,
Publishing House of the Hungarian Academy of
Sciences, P.O. Box 24, H-1363 Budapest, Hungary.

900 US ISSN 0071-1411
ESSAYS IN HISTORY. 1954. a. $5. University of
Virginia, Corcoran Department of History, VA
22903. TEL 804-924-4784. Ed. Scott Burnet.
cum.index: vols.1-20. circ. 250. (also avail. in
microform from UMI; reprint service avail. from
UMI; back issues avail.)

ESSAYS IN PUBLIC WORKS HISTORY. see
PUBLIC ADMINISTRATION

ESTUDOS ITALIANOS EM PORTUGAL. see ART

900 HU ISSN 0071-2108
ETUDES HISTORIQUES. (Text in English, French,
German and Russian) 1960. quinquennial. (Magyar
Tudomanyos Akademia) Akademiai Kiado,
Publishing House of the Hungarian Academy of
Sciences, P.O. Box 24, H-1363 Budapest, Hungary.
Indexed: Hist.Abstr. Amer.Hist.& Life.
Represents: International Congress of Historical
Sciences. Proceedings.

025 946.9 PO ISSN 0430-4497
FILMOTECA ULTRAMARINA PORTUGUESA.
BOLETIM. 1954. irreg., no.47, 1986. Instituto de
Investigacao Cientifica Tropical, Centro de Estudos
de Historia Cartografia Antiga, Rua Jau 54, 1300
Lisbon, Portugal. bibl. circ. 1,000.

900 US
FLORIDA STATE MUSEUM. BULLETIN.
BIOLOGICAL SCIENCES. 1956. irreg. price
varies. Florida State Museum, University of Florida,
Museum Rd., Gainesville, FL 32611. TEL 904-392-
1721. Ed. Oliver L. Austin, Jr. cum.index. circ. 700.
Indexed: Biol.Abstr. GeoRef.
Formerly: Florida State Museum. Bulletin.
Biological Series (ISSN 0071-6154)

320 SA
FOCUS ON POLITICS. irreg., no.2, 1976. L.3.
University of the Orange Free State, Institute for
Contemporary History - Universiteit van die Oranje-
Vrystaat, Instituut vir Eietydse Geskiedenis, Box
2320, Bloemfontein 9300, South Africa. Ed.Bd.

943.6 AU
FORSCHUNGEN UND BEITRAEGE ZUR
WIENER STADTGESCHICHTE. 1978. irreg., 2-3/
yr. price varies. Verein fuer Geschichte der Stadt
Wien, Rathaus, A-1082 Vienna, Austria. Ed. Felix
Czeike. circ. 2,100.

930 GW ISSN 0071-7665
FORSCHUNGEN ZUR ANTIKEN SKLAVEREI.
1967. irreg., vol.19, 1987. price varies. (Akademie
der Wissenschaften und der Literatur, Mainz,
Kommission fuer Geschichte des Altertums) Franz
Steiner Verlag Wiesbaden GmbH, Birkenwaldstr. 44,
Postfach 347, D-7000 Stuttgart 1, W. Germany
(B.R.D.) Eds. Joseph Vogt, Heinz Bellen.

FORT; the international journal of military
architecture and fortification. see HISTORY —
History Of Europe

FORVM. see POLITICAL SCIENCE

901 GW
FRANZ DELITZSCH-VORLESUNGEN. NEUE
FOLGE. 1978. irreg. price varies. Verlag Lambert
Schneider, Hausackerweg 16, D-6900 Heidelberg,
W. Germany (B.R.D.)

930 GW
FREUNDE DER BAYERISCHEN VOR- UND
FRUEHGESCHICHTE. MITTEILUNGEN. 1976.
irreg. membership. Freunde der Bayerische vor- und
Fruegeschichte, Von-der-Tann-Str. 2, W. Germany
(B.R.D.) circ. 600.

900 UK ISSN 0533-9685
GREAT BRITAIN. ROYAL COMMISSION ON
HISTORICAL MANUSCRIPTS. SECRETARY'S
REPORT TO THE COMMISSIONERS. 1968/69.
a. price varies. H.M.S.O., P.O. Box 569, London
SE1 9NH, England.

909 031 US ISSN 0072-7288
GREAT IDEAS TODAY. 1961. a. $21.95.
Encyclopaedia Britannica, Inc., 310 S. Michigan
Ave, Chicago, IL 60604. TEL 312-347-7000. Ed.
John Van Doren.

GYPSY LORE SOCIETY. NORTH AMERICAN
CHAPTER. PUBLICATIONS. see
ANTHROPOLOGY

930 GW ISSN 0072-9175
HABELTS DISSERTATIONSDRUCKE. REIHE
ALTE GESCHICHTE. 1963. irreg., no.22, 1986.
price varies. Dr. Rudolf Habelt GmbH, Am
Buchenhang 1, 5300 Bonn 1, W. Germany (B.R.D.)
Eds. H. Schmitt, J. Straub.

930 GW ISSN 0072-9213
HABELTS DISSERTATIONSDRUCKE. REIHE
MITTELALTERLICHE GESCHICHTE. 1965.
irreg., no.2, 1981. price varies. Dr. Rudolf Habelt
GmbH, Am Buchenhang 1, 5300 Bonn 1, W.
Germany (B.R.D.)

900 GW ISSN 0072-9558
HAMBURGER HISTORISCHE STUDIEN. 1969.
irreg., no.11, 1982. price varies. Verlag Helmut
Buske, Schlueterstr. 14, 2000 Hamburg 13, W.
Germany (B.R.D.)

943 GW ISSN 0073-0149
HANDBUCH DER SUDETENDEUTSCHEN
KULTURGESCHICHTE. 1961. irreg., vol.6, 1973.
price varies. (Collegium Carolinum) Verlag Robert
Lerche, Waltherstr. 27, 8000 Munich 15, W.
Germany (B.R.D.)

900 US ISSN 0073-0521
HARVARD HISTORICAL MONOGRAPHS. 1932.
irreg., no.73, 1984. price varies. (Harvard
University, Department of History) Harvard
University Press, 79 Garden St., Cambridge, MA
02138. TEL 617-495-2600.

900 US ISSN 0073-053X
HARVARD HISTORICAL STUDIES. 1886. irreg.,
no.104, 1985. price varies. (Harvard University,
Department of History) Harvard University Press,
79 Garden St., Cambridge, MA 02138. TEL 617-
495-2600.

HARVEST BOOK SERIES. see SOCIOLOGY

930 GW ISSN 0930-1208
HEIDELBERGER ALTHISTORISCHE
BEITRAEGE UND EPIGRAPHISCHE
STUDIEN. irreg., vol.3, 1987. price varies. Franz
Steiner Verlag Wiesbaden GmbH, Birkenwaldstr. 44,
Postfach 347, 7000 Stuttgart 1, W. Germany
(B.R.D.) Ed. Geza Alfoldy.

900 GW
HEIMATBUCH DES KREISES VIERSEN. 1950. a.
DM.7.50. Kreisverwaltung Viersen, Kulturamt,
Thomasstr. 20, 4152 Kempen 1, W. Germany
(B.R.D.) circ. 16,000. (back issues avail.)

090 SZ ISSN 0073-2419
HISTOIRE ET CIVILISATION DU LIVRE. 1966.
irreg., no.17, 1986. price varies. (Ecole Pratique des
Hautes Etudes, Centre de Recherches d'Histoire et
de Philologie, FR) Librarie Droz, 11, rue Massot,
1211 Geneva 12, Switzerland. circ. 1,000.

900 BL ISSN 0101-9074
HISTORIA. (Text in Portuguese; summaries in English
and Portuguese) 1969-1977 (vol.9); resumed 1982.
a. or exchange basis. Universidade Estadual Paulista,
Av. Vicente Ferreira, 1278, Caixa Postal 603,
17.500 Marilia SP, Brazil. bk. rev. circ. 1,000.
Indexed: Hist.Abstr. Amer.Hist.& Life.
Formed by the merger of: Anais de Historia &
Estudos Historicos.

900 GW ISSN 0341-0056
HISTORIA. EINZELSCHRIFTEN. (Supplement to
Historia) (Text in English, French, and German)
irreg., vol.48, 1986. price varies. Franz Steiner
Verlag Wiesbaden GmbH, Birkenwaldstr. 44,
Postfach 347, D-7000 Stuttgart 1, W. Germany
(B.R.D.) Ed.Bd.

HISTORIA HOSPITALIUM. see HOSPITALS

900 PL ISSN 0137-3277
HISTORIA I WSPOLCZESNOSC. (Text in Polish;
summaries in English, Russian) 1977. irreg. price
varies. Uniwersytet Slaski w Katowicach, Ul.
Bankowa 14, 40-007 Katowice, Poland.

909 SP
HISTORIA UNIVERSAL. 1979. irreg., no.14, 1984. 5,
000 ptas. (Universidad de Navarra, Facultad de
Filosofia y Letras) Ediciones Universidad de
Navarra, S.A., Apdo. 396, 31080 Pamplona, Spain.

900 FI ISSN 0359-3223
HISTORIALLINEN KIRJASTO. 1929. irreg., no.20,
1982. Historian Ystavain Liitto - Society of the
Friends of History, Vuorikatu 6 A, 00100 Helsinki,
Finland.

900 FI ISSN 0439-2183
HISTORIAN AITTA. 1929. irreg., latest no.19, 1982.
Historian Ystavain Liitto - Society of the Friends of
History, Vuorikatu 6 A, 00100 Helsinki, Finland.
Indexed: Hist.Abstr. Amer.Hist.& Life.

900 UK
HISTORICAL ASSOCIATION, LONDON.
GENERAL SERIES. irreg. Historical Association,
59a Kennington Park Rd., London SE11 4JH,
England. (reprint service avail.) Indexed:
Br.Archaeol.Abstr.

900 284 US ISSN 0270-4919
HISTORICAL INTELLIGENCER. 1980. a. $4.
United Church of Christ, Historical Council, 105
Madison Ave., New York, NY 10016. Ed. Harold
F. Worthley. circ. 1,000.

900 SI
HISTORICAL MISCELLANY. (Text in Chinese and
English) 1967. a. S.$2($1) (Historical Society of
Nanyang University) Nanyang University, Jurong
Road, Singapore 22, Singapore.

901 UK ISSN 0073-2621
HISTORICAL PROBLEMS: STUDIES AND
DOCUMENTS. 1968. irreg. price varies. George
Allen & Unwin (Publishers) Ltd., 40 Museum St.,
London WC1, England (U.S. addr.: Allen & Unwin
Inc., 8 Winchester Place, Winchester, MA 01890)

900 UK ISSN 0268-6716
HISTORICAL RESEARCH FOR HIGHER
DEGREES IN THE UNITED KINGDOM. PART
1: THESES COMPLETED. 1967. a. £2. University
of London, Institute of Historical Research, Senate
House, London WC1E 7HU, England. Ed. Joyce
M. Horn. circ. 750.
Formerly: Historical Research for University
Degrees in the United Kingdom. Part 1: Theses
Completed (ISSN 0308-7417)

HISTORY

900 UK ISSN 0268-6724
HISTORICAL RESEARCH FOR HIGHER DEGREES IN THE UNITED KINGDOM. PART 2: THESES IN PROGRESS. 1967. a. £3. University of London, Institute of Historical Research, Senate House, London WC1E 7HU, England. Ed. Joyce M. Horn. circ. 750.
Formerly: Historical Research for University Degrees in the United Kingdom. Part 2: Theses in Progress (ISSN 0308-7425)

900 DK ISSN 0108-1934
HISTORIE (BALLERUP); fagkatalog for laerere. 1982. biennial. Kr.80.50. Bibliotekscentralen, Tempovej 7-11, DK-2750 Ballerup, Denmark. Indexed: Hist.Abstr. Amer.Hist.& Life.

907 DK
HISTORIE OG SAMTIDSORIENTERING. irreg., 5-8/yr. Dansk Historielaererforening, Noerrebakken 26, 2820 Gentofte, Denmark. Ed. Heino Doeygaard. adv. circ. 3,800.

900 GW ISSN 0440-9558
HISTORISCHE FORSCHUNGEN. (Text in English, French, and German) irreg., vol.12, 1987. price varies. (Akademie der Wissenschaften und der Literatur, Mainz, Historische Kommission) Franz Steiner Verlag Wiesbaden GmbH, Birkenwaldstr. 44, Postfach 347, D-7000 Stuttgart 1, W. Germany (B.R.D.) Ed.Bd.

930 GW ISSN 0930-6404
HISTORISCHE GRUNDWISSENSCHAFTEN IN EINZELDARSTELLUNGEN. irreg., vol.2, 1986. Franz Steiner Verlag Wiesbaden GmbH, Birkenwaldstr. 44, Postfach 347, 7000 Stuttgart 1, W. Germany (B.R.D.) Eds. Thomas Frenz, Peter-Johannes Schuler.

900 GW ISSN 0067-5857
HISTORISCHE KOMMISSION ZU BERLIN. EINZELVEROEFFENTLICHUNGEN. 1968. irreg. price varies. Colloquium Verlag, Unter den Eichen 93, 1000 Berlin 45, W. Germany (B.R.D.) circ. 1,000.

907 GW ISSN 0723-3264
HISTORISCHE UND PAEDAGOGISCHE STUDIEN. 1971. irreg. price varies. Colloquium Verlag, Unter den Eichen 93, 1000 Berlin 45, W. Germany (B.R.D.) Ed. Otto Buesch, Gerd Heinrich. circ. 1,000.

900 UK ISSN 0144-2791
HISTORY JOURNAL. 1980. a. £1. Middlesex Polytechnic, School of History, All Saints, White Hart Lane, London N17, England. Ed. Dr. Norman Levy. bk. rev. circ. 200. Indexed: Curr.Cont.

907 UK
HISTORY TEACHING REVIEW. 1969. a. £8. Scottish Association of Teachers of History, 8 Angle Park Crescent, Kirriemuir, Angus DD8 4TJ, Scotland (Subscr. to: Eastwood High School, Newton Mearns, Glasgow, Scotland) Ed. Eric Summers. adv. bk. rev. circ. 400. (back issues avail.)

900 FR ISSN 0073-3202
HOMMES ET LA TERRE. 1956. irreg., no.19, 1986. price varies. Editions de l' Ecole des Hautes Etudes en Sciences Sociales, 131 bd. Saint Michel, 75005 Paris, France.

900 GE
ILLUSTRIERTE HISTORISCHE HEFTE. 1976. irreg. M.7. (Zentralinstitut fuer Geschichte der Akademie der Wissenschaften der DDR) VEB Deutscher Verlag der Wissenschaften, Postfach 1216, 1080 Berlin, E. Germany (D.D.R.)

INSTITUT FUER DEN WISSENSCHAFTLICHEN FILM. PUBLIKATIONEN ZU WISSENSCHAFTLICHEN FILMEN. SEKTION GESCHICHTE, PUBLIZISTIK. see *MOTION PICTURES*

900 GW ISSN 0170-365X
INSTITUT FUER EUROPAEISCHE GESCHICHTE, MAINZ. VEROEFFENTLICHUNGEN. ABTEILUNG UNIVERSALGESCHICHTE. BEIHEFTE. (Text in English, French, and German) irreg., vol.21, 1987. price varies. Franz Steiner Verlag Wiesbaden GmbH, Birkenwaldstr. 44, Postfach 347, D-7000 Stuttgart 1, W. Germany (B.R.D.) Ed. K.O. von Aretin.

930 PO
INSTITUTO DE INVESTIGACAO CIENTIFICA TROPICAL. CENTRO DE ESTUDOS DE HISTORIA E CARTOGRAFIA ANTIGA. SERIE SEPARATAS. 1961. irreg. Instituto de Investigacao Cientifica Tropical, Centro de Estudos de Historia e Cartografia Antiga, Rua Jau 54, 1300 Lisbon, Portugal. circ. 500.

900 910 BL
INSTITUTO HISTORICO E GEOGRAFICO DO ESPIRITO SANTO. REVISTA. (Text in Portuguese) 1917. a. $3. Instituo Historico e Geografico do Espirito Santo, Rua Avenida Republica, 374, Vitoria, Espirito Santo, Brazil. Ed. E.E. Santos Zamprogno. circ. 1,000. (back issues avail.)

940 RM
INSTITUTUL PEDAGOGIC ORADEA. LUCRARI STIINTIFICE: SERIA ISTORIE. (Continues in part its Lucrari Stiintifice: Seria Istorie, Stiinte Sociale, Pedagogie (1971-72), its Lucrari Stiintifice: Seria A and Seria B (1969-70), and its Lucrari Stiintifice (1967-68)) (Text in Rumanian, occasionally in English or French; summaries in English, French, German or Rumanian) a. Institutul Pedagogic Oradea, Calea Armatei Rosii Nr. 5, Oradea, Rumania.

900 FR ISSN 0074-2783
INTERNATIONAL COMMITTEE FOR HISTORICAL SCIENCE. BULLETIN D'INFORMATION. 1953. irreg., no.11, May 1980. International Committee for Historical Science, c/o Michel Francois, Sec. Gen, 270 Bd. Raspail, 75014 Paris, France (Subscr. to: Jean-Charles Biaudet, la Folie, CH 1605 Chexbres, Switzerland)

900 001.3 300 JA ISSN 0538-6012
INTERNATIONAL CONFERENCE OF ORIENTALISTS IN JAPAN. TRANSACTIONS. (Text in English) 1957. a. 2000 Yen($13) Toho Gakkai Institute of Eastern Culture, 4-1, Nishi-Kanda 2-chome, Chiyoda-ku, Tokyo 101, Japan. Ed.Bd. (back issues avail.) Indexed: M.L.A.

INTERVENTI CLASSENSI. see *LITERATURE*

942 500.9 UK
ISLE OF MAN NATURAL HISTORY AND ANTIQUARIAN SOCIETY. PROCEEDINGS. 1888. biennial. £2. ‡ Isle of Man Natural History and Antiquarian Society, c/o Manx Museum, Douglas, Isle of Man. Ed. R.A. Curphey. index. cum.index. circ. 300. Indexed: Br.Archaeol.Abstr.

900 375 IT
ISTITUTO CAMPANO PER LA STORIA DELLA RESISTENZA. BOLLETTINO. 1977. irreg. (1-2/yr.) free. Istituto Campano per la Storia della Resistenza, Via Carlo Poerio 89/a, 80121 Naples, Italy. TEL 39 81 403880. Ed. Luciano Scateni. bibl. circ. 1,500. (back issues avail.)
Study and teaching

900 UR
ISTORICHESKIE ZAPISKI. vol.97, 1976. irreg. price varies. (Akademiya Nauk S.S.S.R., Institut Istorii S.S.S.R.) Izdatel'stvo Nauka, Podsosenskii Per., 21, Moscow K-62, Russian S.F.S.R., U.S.S.R. (Subscr. to: Mezhdunarodnaya Kniga, Moscow, G-200, Russian S.F.S.R., U.S.S.R.) Ed. A.M. Samsonov. circ. 2,050. Indexed: Hist.Abstr. Amer.Hist.& Life.

900 RM ISSN 0075-1626
ISTORIE SI CIVILIZATIE. 1970. irreg., vol.9, 1978. (Academia Republicii Socialiste Romania) Editura Academiei Republicii Socialiste Rumania, Calea Victoriei 125, 79717 Bucharest, Rumania (Subscr. to: ARTEXIM, Str. Piata Scinteii 1, P.O. Box 33-16, 70055 Bucharest, Rumania)

900 UR ISSN 0135-2202
ISTORYCHNI DOSLIDZHENNYA. ISTORIYA ZARUBIZHNYKH KRAYIN; respublikanskyj mizhvidomchyj zbirnik naukovykh prac. (Text in Ukrainian; summaries in Russian) 1974. a. (Akademiya Nauk Ukrainskoi S.S.R., Institut Istorii) Izdatel'stvo Naukova Dumka, c/o Yu.A. Khramov, Dir, Ul. Repina, 3, Kiev 252 601, Ukrainian S.S.R., U.S.S.R. (Subscr. to: Mezhdunarodnaya Kniga, Moscow, G-200, Russian S.F.S.R., U.S.S.R.) Ed. Yu.Yu. Kondufor.

900 UR ISSN 0135-2210
ISTORYCHNI DOSLIDZHENNYA. VITCHYZNYANA ISTORIYA; respublikanskyj mizhvidomchyj zbirnik naukovykh prac. (Text in Ukrainian; summaries in Russian) 1974. a. (Akademiya Nauk Ukrainskoi S.S.R., Institut Istorii) Izdatel'stvo Naukova Dumka, c/o Yu.A. Khramov, Dir, Ul. Repina, 3, Kiev 252 601, Ukrainian S.S.R., U.S.S.R. (Subscr. to: Mezhdunarodnaya Kniga, Moscow, G-200, Russian S.F.S.R., U.S.S.R.) Ed. Yu.Yu. Kondufor.

902 GW ISSN 0075-2835
JAHRESBERICHT DER BAYERISCHEN BODENDENKMALPFLEGE. 1960. a. price varies. (Landesamt fuer Denkmalpflege) Dr. Rudolf Habelt GmbH, Am Buchenhang 1, 5300 Bonn 1, W. Germany (B.R.D.)

900 US ISSN 0075-3610
JEROME LECTURES. 1933. irreg. University of Michigan Press, Box 1104, 839 Greene St., Ann Arbor, MI 48106. TEL 313-764-4392.

900 US ISSN 0075-3874
JOHNS HOPKINS SYMPOSIA IN COMPARATIVE HISTORY. 1970. irreg. price varies. Johns Hopkins University Press, 701 W. 40th St., Ste. 275, Baltimore, MD 21211. TEL 301-338-6900. (reprint service avail. from UMI)

900 320 US ISSN 0075-3904
JOHNS HOPKINS UNIVERSITY STUDIES IN HISTORICAL AND POLITICAL SCIENCE. 1882. irreg. price varies. Johns Hopkins University Press, 701 W. 40th St., Ste. 275, Baltimore, MD 21211. TEL 301-338-6900. (also avail. in microform from UMI; reprint service avail. from UMI)

KAERNTNER MUSEUMSSCHRIFTEN. see *ART*

900 491 PL
KATOLICKI UNIWERSYTET LUBELSKI WYDZIAL HISTORYCZNO-FILOLOGICZNY. ROZPRAWY. (Text in Polish; summaries in German) 1947. irreg. price varies. Katolicki Uniwersytet Lubelski, Towarzystwo Naukowe, Chopina 29, 20-023 Lublin, Poland. index. circ. 450.

900 SA ISSN 0023-2084
KLEIO. (Text in Afrikaans, Dutch and English) 1969. a. R.4. University of South Africa, Department of History, Box 392, Pretoria 0001, South Africa. Ed. J.P. Brits. adv. bk. rev. bibl. illus. cum.index: vols.1-4 in vol.6, no.2, 1974. circ. 2,700. (back issues avail.) Indexed: Hist.Abstr. Amer.Hist. & Life. Ind.S.A.Per.

KOKALOS. see *ARCHAEOLOGY*

900 II
KOODAL HISTORICAL SERIES. (Text in English) irreg. Koodal Publishers, 217-A South Masi St., Madurai 625001, Tamilnadu, India. Ed. N. Subrahmanian. bibl.

900 GW
KRITISCHE STUDIEN ZUR GESCHICHTSWISSENSCHAFT. 1972. irreg. price varies. Vandenhoeck und Ruprecht, Theaterstr. 13, Postfach 37 53, 3400 Goettingen, W. Germany (B.R.D.)

300 900 GW
KULTUR UND GESELLSCHAFT; Neue historische Forschungen. 1976. irreg. price varies. Friedrich Frommann Verlag Guenther Holzboog GmbH and Co., Postfach 500460, Koenig-Karl-Str. 27, 7000 Stuttgart 50, W. Germany (B.R.D.) Ed. R. van Duelmen. bibl.

KUNSTHISTORISCHES INSTITUT IN FLORENZ. MITTEILUNGEN. see *ART*

LAENDERMONOGRAPHIEN. see *GEOGRAPHY*

900 US ISSN 0075-7772
LAMAR LECTURE SERIES. 1958. a. price varies. (Eugenia Dorothy Blount Lamar Lectures at Mercer University, Macon, Georgia) University of Georgia Press, Athens, GA 30602. (reprint service avail. from UMI)

LANDESMUSEUM FUER KAERNTEN. BUCHREIHE. see *ART*

930   GE   ISSN 0232-5446
LANDESMUSEUM FUER VORGESCHICHTE, DRESDEN. KLEINE SCHRIFTEN. 1980. irreg., vol.5, 1986. price varies. (Landesmuseum fuer Vorgeschichte) VEB Deutscher Verlag der Wissenschaften, Postfach 1216, DDR-1080 Berlin, E. Germany (D.D.R.)

900   IT
LATOMISTICA. (Text in English and Italian) irreg. Angelo Longo Editore, Via Paolo Costa 33, P.O. Box 431, 48100 Ravenna, Italy. Ed. Giordano Gamberini.

LECCIONES DE HISTORIA JURIDICA. see *LAW*

LEEDS PHILOSOPHICAL AND LITERARY SOCIETY. PROCEEDINGS. LITERARY AND HISTORICAL SECTION. see *LITERATURE*

942 929   UK   ISSN 0024-0664
LEICESTERSHIRE HISTORIAN. 1967. a. £1.50. Leicestershire Local History Council, c/o Mrs. J. M. Mason, Ramses, Walton, Lutterworth, Leics. LE17 5RP, England. Ed. J. Goodacre. bk. rev. bibl. circ. 500. Indexed: Br.Hum.Ind. Br.Archaeol.Abstr.
Local

900   NE   ISSN 0458-998X
LEIDSE HISTORISCHE REEKS. 1953. irreg., vol.21, 1977. price varies. c/o Martinus Nijhoff, Box 33, 2300 AA Leiden, Netherlands.

900   SZ
LINET DE LA QUATRIEME SECTION, ECOLE PRATIQUE HAUTES ETUDES. 1880. irreg., no.2, 1985. price varies. (FR) Librarie Droz, 11 rue Massot, 1211 Geneva 12, Switzerland. Indexed: Numis.Lit.
    Formerly (until 1979): Ecole Pratique des Hautes Etudes. Quatrieme Section. Historiques et Philologiques. Annuaire (ISSN 0078-964X)

LINGUARUM MINORUM DOCUMENTA HISTORIOGRAPHICA. see *LINGUISTICS*

LITTERAE NUMISMATICAE VINDOBONENSES. see *NUMISMATICS*

900   SW   ISSN 0076-1494
LUND STUDIES IN INTERNATIONAL HISTORY. (Text in English and German) 1970. irreg. price varies. (University of Lund) Liber International, S-205 10 Malmoe, Sweden. Eds. Goeran Rystad, Sven Taegil. index. circ. 850.

MAGILL'S LITERARY ANNUAL: HISTORY AND BIOGRAPHY. see *LITERATURE*

900   II   ISSN 0464-5030
MAHARAJA SAYAJIRAO UNIVERSITY OF BARODA. DEPARTMENT OF HISTORY SERIES. 1958. irreg. price varies. Maharaja Sayajirao University of Baroda, Department of History, Baroda 390002, Gujarat, India. Ed. Satish C. Misra. circ. 500.

900   US
MAKING OF THE TWENTIETH CENTURY. irreg. St. Martin's Press, 175 Fifth Ave., New York, NY 10010.

900   IT
MATERIALI DI STORIA URBANA. 1978. irreg. Officina Edizioni, Passeggiata di Ripetta 25, 00186 Rome, Italy.

900   PL
MATERIALY HISTORYCZNO-METODYCZNE. 1966. irreg. price varies. Politechnika Poznanska, Pl. Curie Sklodowskiej 5, Poznan, Poland.
    Formerly: Politechnika Poznanska. Materialy Historyczno-Metodyczne. Studia Filozoficzne (ISSN 0079-4481)

900   GW
MAX-PLANCK-INSTITUT FUER GESCHICHTE. VEROEFFENTLICHUNGEN. 1958. irreg. (Max-Planck-Institut fuer Geschichte) Vandenhoeck & Ruprecht, Verlagsbuchhandlung, Robert-Bosch-Breite 6, Postfach 3753, D-3400 Goettingen, W. Germany (B.R.D.) Ed.Bd.

900   SP   ISSN 0210-2943
MEMORIAS DE HISTORIA ANTIGUA. 1978. a. Universidad de Oviedo, Instituto de Historia Antigua, Facultad de Geografia e Historia, Oviedo, Spain (Subscr. to: Servicio de Publicaciones, Un. de Oviedo, Calle Arias de Velasco s/n, 30005 Oviedo, Spain) Ed. Narciso Santos Yanguas.

MEMORIE DOMENICANE. see *RELIGIONS AND THEOLOGY*

940   GW   ISSN 0340-8140
MENDELSSOHN STUDIEN; Beitraege zur neueren deutschen Kultur- und Wirtschaftsgeschichte. (Text in English and German) 1972. irreg., vol.6, 1986. price varies. (Mendelssohn-Gesellschaft e.V.) Duncker und Humblot GmbH, Dietrich-Schaefer-Weg 9, Postfach 410329, 1000 Berlin 41, W. Germany (B.R.D.) Eds. Cecile Lowenthal-Hensel, Rudolf Elvers. Indexed: RILM.

900   BU
METODOLOGICHESKI I ISTORIOGRAFSKI PROBLEMI NA ISTORICHESKATA NAUKA. (Summaries in English, French, German and Russian) 1973. irreg. 4.31 lv. (Bulgarska Akademiia na Naukite, Institut za Istoriia) Publishing House of the Bulgarian Academy of Sciences, Acad. G. Bonchev St., Bldg. 6, 1113 Sofia, Bulgaria (Dist. by: Hemus, 6, Rouski Blvd., 1000 Sofia, Bulgaria) circ. 570.

900   IS   ISSN 0334-0740
METOV TIBERIA. 1983. irreg. Bar Ilan University, Faculty for Israel History, Center for Research on Tiberias, Ramat Gan, Israel.

MISCELLANEA MEDIAEVALIA. see *PHILOSOPHY*

330.1   FR   ISSN 0077-0434
MONNAIES, PRIX, CONJONCTURE. 1952. irreg., no.11, 1973. price varies. Editions de l' Ecole des Hautes Etudes en Sciences Sociales, 131 bd. Saint-Michel, 75005 Paris, France.

930   GW   ISSN 0077-2003
MUENSTERSCHE BEITRAEGE ZUR VOR- UND FRUEHGESCHICHTE. 1964. irreg. price varies. (Universitaet Muenster) Verlag August Lax, Postfach 10 08 65, 3200 Hildesheim, W. Germany (B.R.D.) Eds. K Tackenberg, K.J. Narr.
    Formerly: Muenstersche Beitraege zur Vorgeschichtsforschung.

913 069   GE   ISSN 0079-4376
MUSEUM FUER UR- UND FRUEHGESCHICHTE DER BEZIRKE POTSDAM, FRANKFURT/ODER UND COTTBUS. VEROEFFENTLICHUNGEN. 1962. a. price varies. (Museum fuer Ur- und Fruehgeschichte, Potsdam) VEB Deutscher Verlag der Wissenschaften, Postfach 1216, 1080 Berlin, E. Germany (D.D.R.) Ed. Bernhard Gramsch.

NARODNI TECHNICKE MUZEUM. ROZPRAVY. see *TECHNOLOGY: COMPREHENSIVE WORKS*

943   GW
NEUZEIT IM AUFBAU; Darstellung und Dokumentation. 1977. irreg. price varies. Friedrich Frommann Verlag Guenther Holzboog GmbH und Co., Postfach 500460, Koenig-Karl-Str. 27, 7000 Stuttgart 50, W. Germany (B.R.D.) Ed.Bd.

900   US
NEW PERSPECTIVES IN HISTORY. irreg. price varies. Houghton Mifflin Co., One Beacon St., Boston, MA 02107. TEL 617-725-5000.

900   GW
NIEDERSAECHSISCHE ARCHIVVERWALTUNG. VEROEFFENTLICHUNGEN. 1953. irreg. Vandenhoeck & Ruprecht, Robert-Bosch-Breite 6, Postfach 3753, D-3400 Goettingen, W. Germany (B.R.D.)

900   NO   ISSN 0029-2311
NORSKE VIDENSKAPS-AKADEMI. HISTORISK-FILOSOFISK KLASSE. AVHANDLINGER TWO. (Text in several languages) 1925. irreg. price varies. (Norwegian Academy of Sciences and Letters) Norwegian University Press, Kolstadgt. 1, Box 2959-Toeyen, 0608 Oslo 6, Norway (U.S. address: Publications Expediting Inc., 200 Meacham Ave., Elmont, NY 11003) bibl. circ. 775.

900   GW   ISSN 0078-2742
NUNTIATURBERICHTE AUS DEUTSCHLAND NEBST ERGAENZENDEN AKTENSTUECKEN. (Text in German and Latin) 1959. irreg. price varies. (Deutsches Historisches Institut in Rom, IT) Max Niemeyer Verlag, Pfrondorfer Str.4, 7400 Tuebingen, W. Germany (B.R.D.) (back issues avail.)

NUOVA UNIVERSALE STUDIUM. see *LITERATURE*

900   UR
OCHERKI PO ISTORII ESTESTVOZNANIYA I TEKHNIKI; respublikanskii mezhvedomstvennyi sbornik nauchnykh trudov. 1962. a. (Akademiya Nauk Ukrainskoi S.S.R, Otdel Istorii Estestvoznaniya (C.I.N.P.I.N.T.) Izdatel'stvo Naukova Dumka, c/o Yu.A. Khramov, Dir, Ul. Repina, 3, Kiev 252 601, Ukrainian S.S.R., U.S.S.R. (Subscr. to: Mezhdunarodnaya Kniga, Moscow, G-200, Russian S.F.S.R., U.S.S.R.)
    Formerly (until 1987): Naryzy z Istoriyi Pryrodoznavstva i Tekhniky (ISSN 0320-0647)

900   US   ISSN 0094-0798
ORAL HISTORY REVIEW. (Contains selections from its Proceedings) 1973. a. $12. Oral History Association, Box 13734, North Texas State University, Denton, TX 76203. TEL 817-387-1021. Ed. Arthur A. Hansen. circ. 1,700. (back issues avail.) Indexed: Hum.Ind. Amer.Bibl.Slavic & E.Eur.Stud.
    Formerly (1966-72): National Colloquium on Oral History. Proceedings (ISSN 0077-3832)

900   GW
ORDEN POUR LE MERITE FUER WISSENSCHAFTEN UND KUENSTE. REDEN UND GEDENKWORTE. 1955. a. DM.32. Verlag Lambert Schneider, Hausackerweg 16, D-6900 Heidelberg, W. Germany (B.R.D.)

OSIRIS; a research journal devoted to the history of science and its cultural influences. see *SCIENCES: COMPREHENSIVE WORKS*

930   IT
PAPYROLOGICA FLORENTINA. 1976. irreg. Edizioni Gonnelli, Florence, Italy. illus.

900   GW
PAPYROLOGISCHE TEXTE UND ABHANDLUNGEN. 1968. irreg., no.37, 1986. price varies. Dr. Rudolf Habelt GmbH, Am Buchenhang 1, 5300 Bonn 1, W. Germany (B.R.D.) Ed.Bd.

PARERGON. see *LITERATURE*

940   AG   ISSN 0325-2280
PATRISTICA ET MEDIAEVALIA. 1975. a. $12. Universidad de Buenos Aires, Centro de Estudios de Filosofia Medieval, 25 de Mayo 217, Piso 2, 1002 Buenos Aires, Argentina. Ed. Carlos Francisco Bertelloni. adv. bk. rev. circ. 1,000. (back issues avail.)

900   BL   ISSN 0553-8491
PESQUISAS: PUBLICACOES DE HISTORIA. (Numbering is in continuation of articles published in Pesquisas) no. 12, 1960. irreg. price varies or exchange basis. (Universidade do Vale do Rio dos Sinos, Instituto Anchietano de Pesquisas) Unisinos, Av. Unisinos, 950, 93000 Sao Leopoldo RS, Brazil. Supersedes in part: Pesquisas.

900   GR
PETALON; sylloge historikou hylikou peri tes nesiou Androu. 1977. biennial. $5. D.I. Polemis, Apatouria, Andros, Greece.

800 900   PL   ISSN 0079-337X
POLSKA AKADEMIA NAUK. ODDZIAL W KRAKOWIE. KOMISJA HISTORYCZNOLITERACKA. ROCZNIK. (Text in Polish; summaries in English, French, German, Russian) 1963. a. price varies. Ossolineum, Publishing House of the Polish Academy of Sciences, Rynek 9, 50-106 Wroclaw, Poland (Dist. by: Ars Polona-Ruch, Krakowskie Przedmiescie 7, Warsaw, Poland) Ed. Marian Stepien. circ. 580.

900 PL
POLSKA AKADEMIA NAUK. ODDZIAL W KRAKOWIE. KOMISJA NAUK HISTORYCZNYCH. MATERIALY. (Text in Polish and Latin) 1958. irreg., no.29, 1984. price varies. Ossolineum, Publishing House of the Polish Academy of Sciences, Rynek 9, 50-106 Wroclaw, Poland (Dist. by: Ars Polona-Ruch, Krakowskie Przedmiescie 7, Warsaw, Poland)

PORTS O'CALL. see *COMMUNICATIONS — Telephone And Telegraph*

PROBLEMS OF THE CONTEMPORARY WORLD/PROBLEMES DU MONDE CONTEMPORAIN/PROBLEMAS DEL MUNDO CONTEMPORANEO. see *SOCIAL SCIENCES: COMPREHENSIVE WORKS*

PUBLICATIONS OF THE NEW SOCIETY OF LETTERS AT LUND. see *ART*

900 UY ISSN 0079-8061
PUPILA: LIBROS DE NUESTRO TIEMPO.* irreg. Editorial Arca, Colonia 1263, Montevideo, Uruguay.

QUADERNI FIORENTINI PER LA STORIA DEL PENSIERO GIURIDICO MODERNO. see *LAW*

900 GW ISSN 0079-9068
QUELLEN UND FORSCHUNGEN AUS ITALIENISCHEN ARCHIVEN UND BIBLIOTHEKEN. (Text in German, Greek, Italian, Latin) a. price varies. (Deutsches Historisches Institut in Rom, IT) Max Niemeyer Verlag, Pfrondorfer Str. 4, 7400 Tuebingen, W. Germany (B.R.D.) (back issues avail.)

REAL SOCIEDAD ARQUEOLOGICA. BOLETIN ARQUEOLOGICO. see *ARCHAEOLOGY*

900 FR ISSN 0249-5619
RECHERCHES D'HISTOIRE ET DE SCIENCES SOCIALES/STUDIES IN HISTORY AND THE SOCIAL SCIENCES. 1980. irreg., latest 1986. Editions de l' Ecole des Hautes Etudes en Sciences Sociales, 131 bd. Saint-Michel, 75005 Paris, France.

909 342 GW ISSN 0486-1493
RECHT UND GESCHICHTE. irreg., vol.7, 1977. price varies. (Universitaet Mainz, Institut fuer Rechts- und Verfassungsgeschichte) Franz Steiner Verlag Wiesbaden GmbH, Birlenwaldstr. 44, Postfach 347, D-7000 Stuttgart 1, W. Germany (B.R.D.) Ed. Johannes Baermann.

900 US ISSN 0080-0287
RECORDS OF CIVILIZATION. SOURCES AND STUDIES. 1915. irreg., latest no.96. price varies. Columbia University Press, 562 W. 113th St., New York, NY 10025. TEL 212-678-6777.

900 US
REFERENCE GUIDES TO STATE HISTORY AND RESEARCH. 1982. irreg. price varies. Greenwood Press, 88 Post Rd. W., Box 5007, Westport, CT 06881. TEL 203-226-3571.

900 UK ISSN 0080-0554
REGESTA REGUM SCOTTORUM. (Text in Latin; commentary and introduction in English) 1960. irreg. price varies. Edinburgh University Press, George Sq., Edinburgh EH8 9LF, Scotland. Ed. W.S. Barrow.

RESEARCH; contributions to interdisciplinary anthropology. see *ANTHROPOLOGY*

900 CK
REVISTA DE HISTORIA. 1977. irreg. Libreria y Editorial America Latina, Avda Caracas 55-16, Apdo. Aeroe 53613, Bogota 2, Colombia.

RHODE ISLAND JEWISH HISTORICAL NOTES. see *ETHNIC INTERESTS*

907 US
RICHARD B. RUSSELL LECTURE SERIES. 1983. a. price varies. University of Georgia Press, Athens, GA 30602. TEL 404-542-2830.

RIVISTA DI STORIA E LETTERATURA RELIGIOSA. BIBLIOTECA; studi e testi. see *RELIGIONS AND THEOLOGY*

900 US
ROCKEFELLER ARCHIVE CENTER. NEWSLETTER. 1982. a. Rockefeller University, Rockefeller Archive Center, Pocantico Hills, North Tarrytown, NY 10591. circ. 4,000.

930 GW
ROEMER PELIZAEUS MUSEUM. ZEITSCHRIFT DES MUSEUMS ZU HILDESHEIM. irreg. Roemer und Pelizaeus Museum, Am Steine 1-2, 3200 Hildesheim, W. Germany (B.R.D.)

900 069 GW ISSN 0076-275X
ROEMISCH-GERMANISCHES ZENTRALMUSEUM, MAINZ. KATALOGE VOR- UND FRUEHGESCHICHTLICHER ALTERTUEMER. 1909. irreg., no.24, 1985. price varies. Dr. Rudolf Habelt GmbH, Am Buchenhang 1, 5300 Bonn 1, W. Germany (B.R.D.)

900 AT ISSN 0085-5804
ROYAL HISTORICAL SOCIETY OF QUEENSLAND. JOURNAL. 1914. a. Aus.$10. Royal Historical Society of Queensland, Box 57, Brisbane North Quay 4000, Australia. Ed. John D. Kerr. circ. 600. Indexed: Aus.P.A.I.S.

900 700 CN ISSN 0316-1269
ROYAL ONTARIO MUSEUM. HISTORY, TECHNOLOGY AND ART MONOGRAPHS. 1973. irreg. price varies. Royal Ontario Museum, Publication Services, 100 Queen's Park, Toronto, Ont. M5S 2C6, Canada. TEL 416-586-5581.

ROYAL SOCIETY OF TASMANIA, HOBART. PAPERS AND PROCEEDINGS. see *SCIENCES: COMPREHENSIVE WORKS*

RUSKIN COLLEGE, OXFORD. LIBRARY. OCCASIONAL PUBLICATION. see *BUSINESS AND ECONOMICS — Labor And Industrial Relations*

930 GW ISSN 0080-5181
SAARBRUECKER BEITRAEGE ZUR ALTERTUMSKUNDE. 1964. irreg., no.44, 1986. price varies. Dr. Rudolf Habelt GmbH, Am Buchenhang 1, 5300 Bonn 1, W. Germany (B.R.D.) Eds. R. Hachmann, W. Schmitthenner. Indexed: Br.Archaeol.Abstr.

SAECHSISCHE AKADEMIE DER WISSENSCHAFTEN, LEIPZIG. PHILOLOGISCH-HISTORISCHE KLASSE. ABHANDLUNGEN. see *LINGUISTICS*

SAECHSISCHE AKADEMIE DER WISSENSCHAFTEN, LEIPZIG. PHILOLOGISCH-HISTORISCHE KLASSE. SITZUNGSBERICHTE. see *LINGUISTICS*

930 001.3 GW ISSN 0343-2009
SAECULA SPIRITALIA. (Text in English, French, German, Italian, Latin) 1979. irreg., vol.19, 1987. price varies. Verlag Valentin Koerner, H-Sielcken-Str. 36, Postfach 304, D-7570 Baden-Baden 1, W. Germany(B.R.D.) Ed. Dieter Wuttke.

900 GW ISSN 0080-5319
SAECULUM; Jahrbuch fuer Universalgeschichte. 1950. a. DM.68. Karl Alber GmbH, Hermann-Herder-Str. 4, 7800 Freiburg, W. Germany (B.R.D.) Ed. Oskar Koehler. Indexed: Curr.Cont. Arts & Hum.Cit.Ind.

SALZBURGER BEITRAEGE ZUR PARACELSUSFORSCHUNG. see *PHILOSOPHY*

900 320 US
SCHOULER LECTURES IN HISTORY AND POLITICAL SCIENCE. irreg. price varies. Johns Hopkins University Press, 701 W. 40th St., Ste. 275, Baltimore, MD 21211. TEL 301-338-6900. (reprint service avail. from UMI)

SCHRIFTEN AUS DEM FINNLAND-INSTITUT KOELN. see *LITERATURE*

SCHRIFTEN UND QUELLEN DER ALTEN WELT. see *ARCHAEOLOGY*

900 930 GE ISSN 0138-3361
SCHRIFTEN ZUR UR- UND FRUEHGESCHICHTE. 1953. irreg., vol.41, 1985. price varies. (Akademie der Wissenschaften der DDR, Zentralinstitut fuer Alte Geschichte und Archaeologie) Akademie-Verlag, Leipziger Str. 3-4, 1086 Berlin, E. Germany (D.D.R.)
Continues: Akademie der Wissenschaften, Berlin. Sektion fuer Vor- und Fruehgeschichte. Schriften (ISSN 0065-5198)

SELDEN SOCIETY, LONDON. HANDBOOK: PUBLICATIONS, LIST OF MEMBERS AND RULES. see *LAW*

SELDEN SOCIETY, LONDON. LECTURES. see *LAW*

SELDEN SOCIETY, LONDON. MAIN (ANNUAL) SERIES. see *LAW*

SELDEN SOCIETY, LONDON. SUPPLEMENTARY SERIES. see *LAW*

SIKELIKA. SERIE ARCHEOLOGICA. see *ARCHAEOLOGY*

930 913 IT ISSN 0392-0917
SIKELIKA. SERIE STORICA. 1958. irreg., vol.7, 1981. price varies. (Centro Siciliano di Studi Storico-Archeologici "Biagio Pace") Giorgio Bretschneider, Via Crecenzo 43, 00193 Rome, Italy. (back issues avail.)

900 CS
SLOVENSKEHO NARODNEHO MUZEA. FONTES HISTORICKEHO. 1966. irreg. price varies. (Slovenske Narodne Muzeum) Osveta, Ul. Osloboditelov 21, 036 54 Martin, Czechoslovakia. Ed. Alojz Habovstiak. charts. illus. maps. circ. 800.
Supersedes in part: Fontes.

900 US ISSN 0081-0193
SMITH COLLEGE STUDIES IN HISTORY. 1915. irreg., vol.49, 1982. price varies. (Smith College, History Department) Smith College Library, Northampton, MA 01063. TEL 413-584-2700. (reprint service avail. from UMI)

900 600 US ISSN 0081-0258
SMITHSONIAN STUDIES IN HISTORY AND TECHNOLOGY. 1969. irreg., no.47, 1986. Smithsonian Institution Press, 955 L'Enfant Plaza, Rm. 2100, Washington, DC 20560. TEL 202-287-3738. Ed. Barbara T. Spann. circ. 1,400. (reprint service avail. from UMI)

900 910 SP
SOCIEDAD DE ESTUDIOS VASCOS. CUADERNOS DE SECCION. HISTORIA-GEOGRAFIA. 1983. irreg. (Sociedad de Estudios Vascos) Eusko Ikaskuntza, S.A., Churruca, 7 - 2, 20004 Donostia, Spain.

900 IT ISSN 0085-6231
SOCIETA STORICA VALTELLINESE. BOLLETTINO. 1921. a. L.15000($8) Societa Storica Valtellinese, c/o Renzo Sertoli Salis, Via Gorizia 29, Sondrio, Italy. bk. rev.

SOCIETE D'HISTOIRE ET D'ARCHAEOLOGIE DE GENEVE. BULLETIN. see *ARCHAEOLOGY*

900 FR ISSN 0081-0975
SOCIETE D'HISTOIRE MODERNE. ANNUAIRE. 1957. irreg., latest 1977. $10. Societe d'Histoire Moderne, 47 bd. Bessieres, 75017 Paris, France.

526.8 SZ ISSN 0078-9518
SOCIETE DE L'ECOLE DES CHARTES. MEMOIRES ET DOCUMENTS. 1896. irreg., no.29, 1985. price varies. Librarie Droz, 11 rue Massot, 1211 Geneva 12, Switzerland. circ. 1,000.

930 FR ISSN 0294-5495
SOCIETE SPELEOLOGIQUE ET PREHISTORIQUE DE BORDEAUX. MEMOIRE. 1975. irreg. 50 F. Societe Speleologique et Prehistorique de Bordeaux, Hotel des Societes Savantes, 1 place Bardinaux, Bordeaux, France. illus. circ. 500.

900   BU   ISSN 0204-4005
SOFIISKI UNIVERSITET. ISTORICHESKI
FAKULTET. GODISHNIK/UNIVERSITE DE
SOFIA. FACULTE D'HISTOIRE. ANNUAIRE.
(Text in Bulgarian) irreg., vol.71, 1977. 4.93 lv.
Sofiiski Universitet, Istoricheski Fakultet, Sofia,
Bulgaria. Ed.Bd. circ. 550. Indexed: Hist.Abstr.
Amer.Hist.& Life.

SOUTH STAFFORDSHIRE ARCHAEOLOGICAL
AND HISTORICAL SOCIETY.
TRANSACTIONS. see *ARCHAEOLOGY*

SOUTH EAST ASIAN MONOGRAPH SERIES. see
POLITICAL SCIENCE

900   CN
STATE AND ECONOMIC LIFE SERIES. 1979.
irreg. price varies. University of Toronto Press,
Front Campus, Toronto, Ont. M5S 1A6, Canada.
TEL 613-667-7791. Eds. Mel Watkins, Leo Panitch.

901 320   US   ISSN 0270-5338
STOKVIS STUDIES IN HISTORICAL
CHRONOLOGY & THOUGHT. 1982. irreg.,
approx. 3/yr. $17.95 (hardcover); $8.95 (paperback)
per no. Borgo Press, Box 2845, San Bernardino, CA
92406. TEL 714-884-5813.

STUDI GENUENSI. see *ARCHAEOLOGY*

STUDI URBINATI. SERIE B: LETTERATURA,
STORIA, FILOSOFIA. see *LITERATURE*

901   GW
STUDIA DELITZSCHIANA. NEUE FOLGE. 1980.
irreg. price varies. Verlag Lambert Schneider,
Hausackerweg 16, D-6900 Heidelberg, W. Germany
(B.R.D.)

900 340   VC
STUDIA ET DOCUMENTA HISTORIAE ET
IURIS. 1935. a. $95. Pontificia Universita
Lateranense, Pontificio Istituto Utriusque Iuris,
Piazza S. Giovanni in Laterano 4, 00120 Vatican
City. Ed. Gabrio Lombardi. bk. rev. bibl. index.
(tabloid format)

930   NE
STUDIA GAIANA. 1948. irreg., vol.6, 1981. price
varies. E.J. Brill, P.O. Box 9000, 2300 PA Leiden,
Netherlands. Ed.Bd.

900   HU   ISSN 0076-2458
STUDIA HISTORICA ACADEMIAE
SCIENTIARUM HUNGARICAE. (Text in
English, French, German, Russian) 1951. irreg.,
vol.187, 1986. price varies. (Magyar Tudomanyos
Akademia) Akademiai Kiado, Publishing House of
the Hungarian Academy of Sciences, P.O. Box 24,
H-1363 Budapest, Hungary.

900   RM   ISSN 0039-3428
STUDIA UNIVERSITATIS "BABES-BOLYAI".
HISTORIA. (Text in Rumanian; summaries in
English, French, German, Italian or Russian) 1956.
a. exchange basis. Universitatea Babes-Bolyai,
Biblioteca Centrala Universitara, Str. Clinicilor Nr.
2, Cluj-Napoca, Rumania. bk. rev. charts. illus.
index. Indexed: Numis.Lit.

950 325   GE   ISSN 0138-5550
STUDIEN UEBER ASIEN, AFRIKA UND
LATEINAMERIKA. 1972. irreg., vol.37, 1983.
price varies. (Zentraler Rat fuer Asien-, Afrika- und
Lateinamerikawissenschaften in der DDR)
Akademie-Verlag, Leipziger Str. 3-4, 1086 Berlin, E.
Germany (D.D.R.) Ed. Lothar Rathmann.
   Formerly: Studien zur Geschichte Asiens, Afrikas
und Lateinamerikas. (ISSN 0081-7287)

900   GW   ISSN 0081-7309
STUDIEN ZUR GESCHICHTE DES
NEUNZEHNTEN JAHRHUNDERTS. irreg. price
varies. R. Oldenbourg Verlag GmbH, Rosenheimer
Str. 145, 8000 Munich 80, W. Germany (B.R.D.)

900   GW
STUDIEN ZUR MODERNEN GESCHICHTE.
irreg., vol.31, 1985. price varies. Steiner Verlag,
Birkenwaldstr. 44, D-7000 Stuttgart, W. Germany
(B.R.D.)

930   GW   ISSN 0081-7546
STUDIES IN ANCIENT HISTORY. irreg. price
varies. Walter de Gruyter & Co., Mouton
Publishers, Postfach 110240, D-1000 Berlin 11, W.
Germany (B.R.D.) (U.S. addr: Mouton Publishers,
division of Walter de Gruyter, Inc., 200 Saw Mill
River Road, Hawthorne, NY 10532)

930   US
STUDIES IN CHRISTIAN ANTIQUITY. irreg.,
vol.21. 1981. price varies. Catholic University of
America Press, 620 Michigan Ave. N.E.,
Washington, DC 20064. TEL 202-635-5052.
(reprint service avail. from UMI)

STUDIES IN EIGHTEENTH CENTURY
CULTURE; American Society for Eighteenth
Century Studies. Proceedings of the Annual
Meeting. see *HUMANITIES: COMPREHENSIVE
WORKS*

STUDIES IN JUDAICA & THE HOLOCAUST. see
RELIGIONS AND THEOLOGY — Judaic

900 800   US   ISSN 0085-6878
STUDIES IN MEDIEVAL CULTURE. 1964. irreg.
price varies. ‡ Medieval Institute Publications,
Western Michigan University, Kalamazoo, MI
49008. TEL 616-383-4980. charts. illus. stat. circ.
1,000. (tabloid format) Indexed: M.L.A.
Rel.Ind.Two.

900   UK
STUDIES IN THE EARLY HISTORY OF BRITAIN.
1960. irreg. Leicester University Press, Fielding
Johnson Bldg., University of Leicester, University
Rd., Leicester, England. Ed. Nicholas Brooks.
   Formerly: Studies in Early English History (ISSN
0081-7821)

STUDIES IN THE HISTORY AND
INTERPRETATION OF MUSIC. see *MUSIC*

STUDIES IN THE HISTORY OF PHILOSOPHY.
see *PHILOSOPHY*

STUDII SI CERCETARI DE ISTORIA ARTEI.
SERIA ARTA PLASTICA. see *ART*

900 800   US   ISSN 8756-5382
SUN DANCE REPRINTS. irreg., latest no. 7. Borgo
Press, Box 2845, San Bernardino, CA 92406. TEL
714-884-5813.

SURMACH. see *MILITARY*

839.7 920   FI   ISSN 0039-6842
SVENSKA LITTERATURSAELLSKAPET I
FINLAND. SKRIFTER. (Text mainly in Swedish;
occasionally in other languages) 1886. irreg. (4-8/
yr.) price varies. Svenska Litteratursaellskapet i
Finland, Snellmansg. 9-11, 00170 Helsinki 17,
Finland.

900   GE   ISSN 0082-1950
TASCHENBUCH GESCHICHTE. 1969. irreg. price
varies. VEB Deutscher Verlag der Wissenschaften,
Postfach 1216, 1080 Berlin, E. Germany (D.D.R.)

TEACHING OF HISTORY. see *EDUCATION —
Teaching Methods And Curriculum*

900   US   ISSN 0082-2884
TERRAE INCOGNITAE; the journal for the history
of discoveries. (Text in English) 1969. a. $23.
(Society for the History of Discoveries) Wayne
State University Press, 5959 Woodward Ave.,
Detroit, MI 48202. TEL 313-577-4603. Ed. David
Buisseret. adv. bk. rev. bibl. charts. illus.
cum.index. circ. 1,000. (back issues avail.) Indexed:
Geo.Abstr.

TESTIMONIA SICILIAE ANTIQUA. see
ARCHAEOLOGY

930   US   ISSN 0082-3759
TEXTS FROM CUNEIFORM SOURCES. 1966.
irreg. price varies. J. J. Augustin, Inc., Locust
Valley, NY 11560. TEL 516-676-1510. Ed. A. Leo
Oppenheimer. index.
   *Up-to-date editions of Akkadian, Sumerian,
Hittite and other sources written in Cuneiform*

900   UK   ISSN 0265-4601
THOMAS CALLANDER MEMORIAL LECTURES.
1981. irreg. University of Aberdeen, Regent Walk,
Aberdeen AB9 1FX, Scotland.

900   UK   ISSN 0082-4232
THORESBY SOCIETY, LEEDS, ENGLAND.
PUBLICATIONS. 1891. a. price varies. ‡ Thoresby
Society, Claremont, 23 Clarendon Rd., Leeds LS2
9NZ, England. Eds. W.B. Stephens, P.S. Kirby. circ.
530. (back issues avail.) Indexed: Br.Hum.Ind.
Br.Archaeol.Abstr.

TOOLS AND TILLAGE; a journal on the history of
the implements of cultivation and other agricultural
processes. see *AGRICULTURE*

TOWARZYSTWO NAUKOWE W TORUNIU.
FONTES. see *HISTORY — History Of Europe*

TRANSPORT HISTORY. see *TRANSPORTATION*

900   SZ   ISSN 0082-6073
TRAVAUX D'HISTOIRE ETHICO-POLITIQUE.
1963. irreg., no.46, 1986. price varies. Librarie
Droz, 11, rue Massot, 1211 Geneva 12, Switzerland.
Ed. Alain Dufour. circ. 1,000.

900   GW
TUDUV-STUDIE. REIHE
GESCHICHTSWISSENSCHAFTEN. 1986. irreg.
price varies. Tuduv Verlagsgesellschaft mbH,
Gabelsbergerstrasse 15, 8000 Munich 2, W.
Germany (B.R.D.)

901   US   ISSN 0276-864X
U C L A HISTORICAL JOURNAL. 1980. a. $5 to
individuals; institutions $7. University of California,
Los Angeles, Graduate Students Association, Dept.
of History, Los Angeles, CA 90024. TEL 213-825-
4601. adv. bk. rev. circ. 800. Indexed: Hist.Abstr.
Amer.Hist. & Life.

973 952 327   US   ISSN 0748-2809
U S - JAPAN RELATIONS. a. $14.95. Transaction
Books, Rutgers University, New Brunswick, NJ
08903. Ed. Richard B. Finn.

930   GW   ISSN 0170-348X
UEBERSETZUNGEN AUSLAENDISCHER
ARBEITEN ZUR ANTIKEN SKLAVEREI. 1966.
irreg., vol.3, 1972. price varies. (Akademie der
Wissenschaften und der Literatur, Mainz,
Kommission fuer Geschichte des Altertums) Franz
Steiner Verlag Wiesbaden GmbH, Birkenwaldstr. 44,
Postfach 347, D-7000 Stuttgart 1, W. Germany
(B.R.D.) Eds. Herbert Braeuer, Joseph Vogt.

900   US   ISSN 0083-1611
U.S. LIBRARY OF CONGRESS. MANUSCRIPT
DIVISION. REGISTERS OF PAPERS. 1958. irreg.
free to libraries. ‡ U.S. Library of Congress,
Washington, DC 20540. TEL 202-287-5000. circ.
500.

UNIVERS HISTORIQUE. see *SCIENCES:
COMPREHENSIVE WORKS*

900   BL   ISSN 0070-1815
UNIVERSIDADE DO PARANA.
DEPARTAMENTO DE HISTORIA. BOLETIM.
Title varies: Historia Moderna e Contemporanea.
1962. irreg., no.29, 1984. available on exchange.
Universidade Federal do Parana, Departamento de
Historia, Rua General Carneiro, 460-6 andar, 80.060
Curitiba, Parana, Brazil. charts. illus. stat. circ.
500.

909   IT   ISSN 0068-4805
UNIVERSITA DEGLI STUDI DI CAGLIARI.
ISTITUTO DI STORIA MEDIOEVALE.
PUBLICAZIONI. 1961. irreg., no.25, 1977. price
varies. (Universita degli Studi di Cagliari, Istituto di
Storia Medioevale) Casa Editrice Dott. Antonio
Milani, Via Jappelli 5, 35100 Padua, Italy. circ. 800.

930   IT
UNIVERSITA DEGLI STUDI DI GENOVA.
FONDAZIONE NOBILE AGOSTINO POGGI
(PUBBLICAZIONE) 1940. irreg., no.14, 1979. Casa
Editrice Dott. A. Giuffre, Via B. Arsizio 40, 20151
Milan, Italy.
   Roman empire

UNIVERSITA DEGLI STUDI DI MACERATA.
FACOLTA DI LETTERE E FILOSOFIA.
ANNALI. see *ARCHAEOLOGY*

562 HISTORY — ABSTRACTING, BIBLIOGRAPHIES, STATISTICS

900   IT   ISSN 0078-7744
UNIVERSITA DEGLI STUDI DI PADOVA ISTITUTO DI STORIA ANTICA. PUBBLICAZIONI. 1953. irreg., no.15, 1984. price varies. Erma di "Bretschneider", Via Cassiodoro, 19, 00193 Rome, Italy.

090 950   GW   ISSN 0072-4491
UNIVERSITAETSBIBLIOTHEK GIESSEN. KURZBERICHTE AUS DEN PAPYRUS-SAMMLUNGEN. (Text in various languages) 1956. irreg., no.42, 1986. price varies. Universitaetsbibliothek Giessen, Otto-Behaghel-Str. 8, Giessen, W. Germany (B.R.D.) TEL (0641) 702 2331. Ed. B. Dugall. circ. 500.

900   RM   ISSN 0041-9125
UNIVERSITATEA "AL. I. CUZA" DIN IASI. ANALELE STIINTIFICE. SECTIUNEA 3A: ISTORIE. (Text in English, French, German, Italian, Rumanian or Russian) 1955. a. 35 lei. Universitatea "Al. I. Cuza" din Iasi, Calea 23 August Nr. 11, Jassy, Rumania (Subscr. to: ILEXIM, Str. 13 Decembrie Nr. 3, P.O. Box 136-137, Bucharest, Rumania) Ed. Gh. Platon. bk. rev. abstr. charts. illus. circ. 300.

900   CN
UNIVERSITE LAVAL. LES CAHIERS D'HISTOIRE. 1959. irreg. Presses de l'Universite Laval, Quebec, Que. G1K 7R4, Canada. TEL 418-656-2590.
   Formerly: Universite Laval. Institut d'Histoire. Cahiers (ISSN 0079-8398)

900   US   ISSN 0068-6239
UNIVERSITY OF CALIFORNIA, LOS ANGELES. CENTER FOR MEDIEVAL AND RENAISSANCE STUDIES. CONTRIBUTIONS. irreg. price varies. University of California Press, 2120 Berkeley Way, Berkeley, CA 94720. TEL 415-642-4247.

900   US   ISSN 0068-6220
UNIVERSITY OF CALIFORNIA, LOS ANGELES. CENTER FOR MEDIEVAL AND RENAISSANCE STUDIES. PUBLICATIONS. irreg. price varies. University of California Press, 2120 Berkeley Way, Berkeley, CA 94720. TEL 415-642-4247.

907   CN
UNIVERSITY OF OTTAWA. CAHIERS D'HISTOIRE. (Text in French) 1968. irreg. University of Ottawa Press, 608 Cumberland, Ottawa, Ont. K1N 6N5, Canada. TEL 613-564-2270.

909   CN
UNIVERSITY OF OTTAWA. MEDIEVAL TEXTS AND STUDIES/UNIVERSITE D'OTTAWA. PUBLICATIONS MEDIEVALES. (Text in English and French) 1973. irreg. University of Ottawa Press, 603 Cumberland, Ottawa, Ont. K1N 6N5, Canada. TEL 613-564-2270. Ed. Pierre Kunstmann.

UNIVERSITY OF WARWICK LIBRARY. OCCASIONAL PUBLICATIONS. see LIBRARY AND INFORMATION SCIENCES

900   CS   ISSN 0083-4122
UNIVERZITA KOMENSKEHO. FILOZOFICKA FAKULTA. ZBORNIK: HISTORICA. (Text in Slovak; summaries in German and Russian) 1958. irreg. exchange basis. (Univerzita Komenskeho, Filozoficka Fakulta) Slovenske Pedagogicke Nakladatelstvo, Sasinkova 5, 818 06 Bratislava, Czechoslovakia. Ed. Branislav Varsik. bk. rev. circ. 700.

UNIWERSYTET GDANSKI. WYDZIAL HUMANISTYCZNY. ZESZYTY NAUKOWE. PRACE HISTORYCZNO-LITERACKIE. see LITERATURE

VERDI. see MUSIC

VEREENIGING NEDERLANDSCH HISTORISCH SCHEEPVAART MUSEUM TE AMSTERDAM. JAARVERSLAG. see TRANSPORTATION — Ships And Shipping

900   NE
VEREENIGING TOT UITGAAF DER BRONNEN VAN HET OU-VADERLANDSCHE RECHT. WERKEN. a. 1968. price varies. De Walburg Pers, Zaadmarkt 84a-86, Box 222, 7200 AE Zutphen, Netherlands. TEL 05750-10522.

900   US   ISSN 0083-5897
VIATOR; Medieval and Renaissance Studies. (Contributions in English and other major modern languages) 1970. a. $40. (University of California, Los Angeles, Center for Medieval and Renaissance Studies) University of California Press, Journals Division, 2120 Berkeley Way, Berkeley, CA 94720. TEL 415-642-4191. Ed.Bd. illus. (back issues avail.) Indexed: M.L.A. Amer.Bibl.Slavic & E.Eur.Stud. Br.Archaeol.Abstr. Geo.Abstr. RILA.

VIERTELJAHRSCHRIFT FUER SOZIAL- UND WIRTSCHAFTSGESCHICHTE. BEIHEFTE. see SOCIAL SCIENCES: COMPREHENSIVE WORKS

VRIJE FRIES. see LINGUISTICS

040   US
WALKER - AMES LECTURES. 1958. irreg., latest 1978. price varies. University of Washington Press, Seattle, WA 98105. TEL 206-543-4050.

930   GW   ISSN 0340-6229
DIE WELT DES ORIENTS; wissenschaftliche Beitraege zur Kunde des Morgenlandes. 1947. irreg. DM.64. Verlag Vandenhoeck und Ruprecht, Theaterstr. 13, Postfach 77, 3400 Goettingen, W. Germany (B.R.D.) Eds. Wolfgang Roellig, Wolfram von Soden. adv. bk. rev.

900   SZ
WELTRUNDSCHAU. 1956. a. 86 Fr. Weltrundschau Verlag AG, Oberneuhofstrasse 1, Postfach 427, 6340 Baar, Switzerland. circ. 100,000.

900 913 700   US
WILBOUR MONOGRAPHS. 1968. irreg., no.7, 1974. Brooklyn Museum, Department of Egyptian and Classical Art, The Gallery Shop, Eastern Pkwy., Brooklyn, NY 11238. TEL 718-638-5000. circ. 1,000.

900   GW
WOLFENBUETTELER STUDIEN ZUR AUFKLAERUNG. SCHRIFTENREIHE. 1974. irreg. price varies. Verlag Lambert Schneider, Hausackerweg 16, D-6900 Heidelberg, W. Germany (B.R.D.) Indexed: M.L.A.

WOMAN IN HISTORY. see WOMEN'S INTERESTS

900   US   ISSN 0084-3350
YALE HISTORICAL PUBLICATIONS (MISCELLANY) 1914. irreg., no.129, 1983. price varies. Yale University Press, 92A Yale Sta., New Haven, CT 06520. TEL 203-432-0940.

900   UN   ISSN 0084-4322
YOUR UNITED NATIONS; official guidebook. 1952. irreg. $9.95. United Nations Publications, Room DC2-853, New York, NY 10017 (Or Distribution and Sales Section, CH-1211 Geneva 10, Switzerland) (also avail. in microfiche)

900 913   GE   ISSN 0138-3914
ZENTRALINSTITUTS FUER ALTE GESCHICHTE UND ARCHAEOLOGIE. VEROEFFENTLICHEN. 1973. irreg., vol.15, 1986. (Akademie der Wissenschaften der DDR) Akademie-Verlag Berlin, Leipziger Str. 3-4, 1086 Berlin, E. Germany (D.D.R.)

901   GW   ISSN 0514-8294
ZUR POLITIK UND ZEITGESCHICHTE. 1961. irreg. price varies. (Landeszentrale fuer politische Bildung, Berlin) Colloquium Verlag, Unter den Eichen 93, 1000 Berlin 45, W. Germany (B.R.D.) circ. 3,000.

HISTORY — Abstracting, Bibliographies, Statistics

960 016   US
AFRICA SOUTH OF THE SAHARA: INDEX TO PERIODICAL LITERATURE. SUPPLEMENTS. 1973. irreg., latest, 1973. price varies. G. K. Hall and Co., 70 Lincoln Street, Boston, MA 02111. TEL 617-423-3990.

016 960   US
AFRICAN BIBLIOGRAPHY SERIES. 1971. irreg. Africana Publishing Co. (Subsidiary of: Holmes & Meier Publishers, Inc.) 30 Irving Pl., New York, NY 10003. TEL 212-254-4100. (back issues avail.)

016   US   ISSN 0749-2308
AFRICAN SPECIAL BIBLIOGRAPHIC SERIES. 1985. irreg. price varies. Greenwood Press, 88 Post Rd. W., Box 5007, Westport, CT 06881. TEL 203-226-3571.
   Supersedes: African Bibliographic Center, Washington D.C. Special Bibliographic Series (ISSN 0065-3934)

970 011   US   ISSN 0002-7065
AMERICA: HISTORY AND LIFE. PART A: ARTICLE ABSTRACTS AND CITATION. 1964. 3/yr. price varies. A B C-Clio, 2040 Alameda Padre Serra, Box 4397, Santa Barbara, CA 93140-4397. TEL 805-963-4221. Ed. Pamela R. Byrne. index.
   ●Also available online. Vendors: DIALOG.

970 016   US   ISSN 0097-6172
AMERICA: HISTORY AND LIFE. PART B: INDEX TO BOOK REVIEWS. 2/yr. A B C-Clio, 2040 Alameda Padre Serra, Box 4397, Santa Barbara, CA 93140-4397. TEL 805-963-4221. Ed. Pamela R. Byrne. index. cum.index.
   ●Also available online. Vendors: DIALOG.

970 016   US   ISSN 0363-1249
AMERICA: HISTORY AND LIFE. PART C: AMERICAN HISTORY BIBLIOGRAPHY. a. A B C-Clio, 2040 Alameda Padre Serra, Box 4397, Santa Barbara, CA 93140-4397. TEL 805-963-4221. Ed. Pamela R. Byrne. index.
   ●Also available online. Vendors: DIALOG.

970 011   US
AMERICA: HISTORY AND LIFE. PART D: ANNUAL INDEX. a. A B C-Clio, 2040 Alameda Padre Serra, Box 4397, Santa Barbara, CA 93140-4397. TEL 805-963-4221. Ed. Pamela Byrne.

016 940   US   ISSN 0094-3770
AMERICAN BIBLIOGRAPHY OF SLAVIC AND EAST EUROPEAN STUDIES. 1956. a. $55 to non-members; members $40. American Association for the Advancement of Slavic Studies, 128 Encina Commons, Stanford University, Stanford, CA 94305-6029. TEL 415-723-9668. Ed. Roberta Goldblatt. bibl.
   Formerly: American Bibliography of Russian and East European Studies.

973 015   US
AMERICAN HERITAGE CUMULATIVE INDEX. a. $50. American Heritage Inc., 60 Fifth Ave., New York, NY 10011. TEL 212-205-5500.
   Formerly: American Heritage Index.

011   US
AMERICAN HISTORY; a bibliographic review. 1985. a. $49.50. Meckler Publishing, 11 Ferry Lane W., Westport, CT 06880. Ed. Carol Bondhus Fitzgerald.

900   DK
ANNUAL BIBLIOGRAPHY OF THE HISTORY OF NATURAL HISTORY. 1985. a. £8. British Museum (Natural History), Cromwell Rd., London SW7 5BD, England. circ. 500. (back issues avail.)

011 962   NE
ANNUAL EGYPTOLOGICAL BIBLIOGRAPHY/ BIBLIOGRAPHIE EGYPTOLOGIQUE ANNUELLE/JAEHRLICHE AEGYPTOLOGISCHE BIBLIOGRAPHIE. Short title: AEB. (Text in English, French, German) 1947. a. £18.75($50) International Association of Egyptologists (IAE), c/o L.M.J. Zonhoven, Ed., Instituut voor Egyptologie, P.O. Box 9515, 2300 RA Leiden, Netherlands. bk. rev. index. circ. 500. (back issues avail.)

011   MX   ISSN 0185-1578
BIBLIOGRAFIA HISTORICA MEXICANA. 1967. irreg. (Centro de Estudios Historicos) Colegio de Mexico, A.C., Camino al Ajusco 20, 10740 Mexico D.F., Mexico. circ. 1,500. (reprint service avail. from Swets & Zeitlinger)

HISTORY — ABSTRACTING, BIBLIOGRAPHIES, STATISTICS

016 943.8   PL   ISSN 0067-6721
BIBLIOGRAFIA HISTORII POLSKIEJ. 1962. irreg., latest 1985. (Polska Akademia Nauk, Instytut Historii) Ossolineum, Publishing House of the Polish Academy of Sciences, Rynek 9, Wroclaw, Poland (Dist. by Ars Polona-Ruch, Krakowskie Przedmiescie 7, Warsaw, Poland) Ed. W. Bienkowski. circ. 1,500.

016 943.8   PL   ISSN 0409-3453
BIBLIOGRAFIA POMORZA ZACHODNIEGO. (Text in Polish; summaries in English and Russian) 1963. irreg. 500 Zl. Wojewodzka i Miejska Biblioteka Publiczna-Biblioteka Glowna im. S. Staszica, Podgorna 15, 70-952 Szczecin, Poland. Ed. Stanislaw Krzywicki.

970 016   US   ISSN 0147-6491
BIBLIOGRAPHIC GUIDE TO NORTH AMERICAN HISTORY. a. G.K. Hall & Co., 70 Lincoln St., Boston, MA 02111. TEL 617-423-3990.

960 016   FR
BIBLIOGRAPHIE ANALYTIQUE DE L'AFRIQUE ANTIQUE. 1969. irreg. Diffusion de Boccard, 11 rue de Medicis, Paris 6e, France (U.S. subscr. to: Institute for the Arts, Rice University, Box 1892, Houston TX 77001) Eds. Jehan Desanges, Serge Lancel.

944   FR   ISSN 0067-6918
BIBLIOGRAPHIE ANNUELLE DE L'HISTOIRE DE FRANCE. 1955. a. price varies. Editions du C N R S, 295 rue St. Jacques, 75005 Paris, France.

949.35 016   LU   ISSN 0067-7043
BIBLIOGRAPHIE D'HISTOIRE LUXEMBOURGEOISE. 1964. a. 150 Fr. Bibliotheque Nationale, 37 Boulevard F.-D. Roosevelt, 2450 Luxembourg. circ. 500.

949.4   SZ   ISSN 0250-5673
BIBLIOGRAPHIE DER BERNER GESCHICHTE/ BIBLIOGRAPHIE DE L'HISTOIRE BERNOISE. (Text in French & German) 1975. a. 6 Fr. Burgerbibliothek Bern - Bibliotheque de la Bourgeoisie de Berne, Muenstergasse 63, CH 3000 Berne 7, Switzerland. Ed. Bd. circ. 1,500.

BIBLIOGRAPHIE GESCHICHTE DER TECHNIK. see *TECHNOLOGY: COMPREHENSIVE WORKS — Abstracting, Bibliographies, Statistics*

960 016   BE
BIBLIOGRAPHIES ANALYTIQUES SUR L'AFRIQUE CENTRALE. 1977. irreg. 1000 Fr. per copy. Centre d'Etudes et de Documentation Africaines, 7 Place Royale, 1000 Brussels, Belgium. Ed. Edwine Simons. abstr. index. circ. 300.

960   US   ISSN 0742-6925
BIBLIOGRAPHIES AND INDEXES IN AFRO-AMERICAN AND AFRICAN STUDIES. 1984. irreg., latest no.4, 1985. price varies. Greenwood Press, 88 Post Rd. W., Box 5007, Westport, CT 06881. TEL 203-226-3571.

970   US   ISSN 0742-6828
BIBLIOGRAPHIES AND INDEXES IN AMERICAN HISTORY. 1984. irreg. price varies. Greenwood Press, 88 Post Road W., Box 5007, Westport, CT 06881. TEL 203-226-3571.

900   US   ISSN 0742-6852
BIBLIOGRAPHIES AND INDEXES IN WORLD HISTORY. 1984. irreg. price varies. Greenwood Press, 88 Post Rd. W., Box 5007, Westport, CT 06881. TEL 203-226-3571.

950 016   US   ISSN 0067-7159
BIBLIOGRAPHY OF ASIAN STUDIES. 1954. a. $55. Association for Asian Studies, Inc., 1 Lane Hall, University of Michigan, Ann Arbor, MI 48109. TEL 313-665-2490. Ed. Estrella Bryant. circ. 3,000. (also avail. in microform from UMI; back issues avail.; reprint service avail. from UMI) Indexed: E.I.

BIBLIOGRAPHY OF MARITIME AND NAVAL HISTORY PERIODICAL ARTICLES. see *TRANSPORTATION — Abstracting, Bibliographies, Statistics*

948 448   DK   ISSN 0067-7213
BIBLIOGRAPHY OF OLD NORSE-ICELANDIC STUDIES. (Text in several languages) 1964. a. price varies. Kongelige Bibliotek, 8 Christians Brygge, DK-1219 Copenhagen K, Denmark. Ed. Hans Bekker-Nielsen. circ. 600.

900 016   GW   ISSN 0081-8992
BIBLIOTHEK FUER ZEITGESCHICHTE, STUTTGART. JAHRESBIBLIOGRAPHIE;* Neue Folge der Buecherschau der Weltkriegsbuecherei. 1961. irreg. price varies. (Bibliothek fuer Zeitgeschichte, Stuttgart) Bernard and Graefe Verlag, Karl-Mand-Str. 2, Postfach 2060, 5400 Koblenz, W. Germany (B.R.D.)

960 016   BE   ISSN 0067-5601
BIBLIOTHEQUE AFRICAINE. CATALOGUE DES ACQUISITIONS. CATOLOGUS VAN DE AANWINSTEN. 1949. a. Bibliotheque Africaine, Place Royale, 7, B-1000 Brussels, Belgium. circ. 400.

BOOKS ABOUT SINGAPORE. see *TRAVEL AND TOURISM — Abstracting, Bibliographies, Statistics*

940 001.3   US
CLIO BIBLIOGRAPHY SERIES. 1972. irreg., no.22, 1985. A B C-Clio, 2040 Alameda Padre Serra, Box 4397, Santa Barbara, CA 93140-4397. TEL 805-963-4221. Ed. Pamela R. Byrne.

900   US
COMPUBIBS. 1984. irreg. price varies. Vantage Information Consultants, Inc., Box 22684, Lexington, KY 40522. Ed. Charlotte L. Levy. abstr. (back issues avail.)

948.9   DK   ISSN 0107-0436
DANSK HISTORISK AARSBIBLIOGRAFI. 1967. irreg. Dansk Historisk Faellesforening, Rigsarkivet, Rigsdagsgaarden 9, DK-1218 Copenhagen K, Denmark.

960 016   NE   ISSN 0166-2694
DOCUMENTATIEBLAD: THE ABSTRACTS JOURNAL OF THE AFRICAN STUDIES CENTRE LEIDEN. (Text in Dutch, English, French, German) 1968. q. fl.20. Afrika-Studiecentrum, Stationsplein 10, 2312 AK Leiden, Netherlands. Ed.Bd. abstr. circ. 550. (processed)
Supersedes (1968-1980): Afrika Studiecentrum. Documentatieblad (ISSN 0002-0419)

960 016   II   ISSN 0418-582X
DOCUMENTATION LIST: AFRICA. (Text in English) 1962. a. avail. on exchange basis. University of Delhi, Department of African Studies, Delhi 110 007, India. subject index. circ. 300.

E I. (Excerpta Indonesica) see *ANTHROPOLOGY — Abstracting, Bibliographies, Statistics*

EAST EUROPE IN GERMAN BOOKS; a bulletin listing new books on East Europe published in the German language. see *TRAVEL AND TOURISM — Abstracting, Bibliographies, Statistics*

950 016   FR   ISSN 0140-492X
EUROPEAN BIBLIOGRAPHY OF SOVIET, EAST EUROPEAN AND SLAVONIC STUDIES/ BIBLIOGRAPHIE EUROPEENE DES TRAVAUX SUR L'URSS ET L'EUROPE DE L'EST/EUROPAISCHE BIBLIOGRAPHIE DER SOWJET- UND OESTEUROPASTUDIEN. (Text in English, French and German) 1975. a. $12. (International Committee for Soviet and East European Studies, Ecoles des Hautes Etudes en Sciences Sociales) Institut d'Etude Slaves, 9 rue Michelet, 75006 Paris, France. Ed. Marguerite Aymard. bk. rev. circ. 500.
Supersedes: Soviet, East European and Slavonic Studies in Western Europe.

900   US   ISSN 0196-0040
FACTS ON FILE. YEARBOOK. 1941. a. $95. Facts on File, Inc., 460 Park Ave. South, New York, NY 10016. TEL 212-683-2244. 5-year cum.index. (back issues avail.)

940 016   GW   ISSN 0067-5881
FREIE UNIVERSITAET BERLIN. OSTEUROPA-INSTITUT. BIBLIOGRAPHISCHE MITTEILUNGEN. 1959. irreg., vol.24, 1987. price varies. (Freie Universitaet Berlin, Osteuropa Institut) Verlag Otto Harrassowitz, Taunustr. 14, Postfach 2929, 6200 Wiesbaden, W. Germany (B.R.D.) circ. 500.

016   US   ISSN 0191-9199
FRENCH 17; an annual descriptive bibliography of French seventeenth century studies. 1953. a. $4.50. (Modern Language Association of America, Seventeenth Century French Division) Colorado State University, Department of Foreign Languages, Fort Collins, CO 80523. Ed. J.D. Vedvik. bk. rev. circ. 400.
Former titles: Bibliography of French 17th Century Studies; French 3.

090 942   UK
GREAT BRITAIN. ROYAL COMMISSION ON HISTORICAL MANUSCRIPTS. ACCESSIONS TO REPOSITORIES AND REPORTS ADDED TO THE NATIONAL REGISTER OF ARCHIVES. a. price varies. H.M.S.O., P.O. Box 569, London SE1 9NH, England.

942 090 015   UK   ISSN 0072-7083
GREAT BRITAIN. ROYAL COMMISSION ON HISTORICAL MANUSCRIPTS. COMMISSIONERS' REPORTS TO THE CROWN. 1870. irreg. price varies. H.M.S.O., P.O. Box 569, London SE1 9NH, England.

090 942 015   UK   ISSN 0072-7091
GREAT BRITAIN. ROYAL COMMISSION ON HISTORICAL MANUSCRIPTS. JOINT PUBLICATION. 1962. irreg. price varies. H.M.S.O., P.O. Box 569, London SE1 9NH, England.

985   PE
GUIAS BIBLIOGRAFICAS. (Text in Castellano) 1971. irreg. price varies. (Instituto de Estudios Peruanos) I E P Ediciones, Horacio Urteaga 694 (Campe de Marte), Lima 11, Peru. (back issues avail.)

090 994 016   AT
GUIDE TO COLLECTIONS OF MANUSCRIPTS RELATING TO AUSTRALIA. 1964. irreg. price varies. National Library of Australia, Sales and Subscription Section, Canberra, A.C.T. 2600, Australia. (looseleaf format)
Formerly: Guide to Manuscripts Relating to Australia.

016 960   SZ
GUIDE TO THE SOURCES OF THE HISTORY OF THE NATIONS. B: AFRICA. (Text in English, French and German) irreg. price varies. Inter-Documentation Company, Poststrasse 14, Zug, Switzerland.

980   US   ISSN 0361-5502
HISPANIC AMERICAN PERIODICALS INDEX. 1978. a. $235. University of California, Los Angeles, Latin American Center, 405 Hilgard Ave., Los Angeles, CA 90024. TEL 213-825-6634. Ed. Barbara G. Valk.

900 016   US   ISSN 0363-2717
HISTORICAL ABSTRACTS. PART A: MODERN HISTORY ABSTRACTS, 1450-1914. 1955. q. service basis. A B C-Clio, 2040 Alameda Padre Serra, Box 4397, Santa Barbara, CA 93140-4397. TEL 805-963-4221. Ed. Pamela R. Byrne. index. cum.index every 5 yrs.
●Also available online. Vendors: DIALOG.
Supersedes in part: Historical Abstracts (ISSN 0018-2435)

900 016   US   ISSN 0363-2725
HISTORICAL ABSTRACTS. PART B: TWENTIETH CENTURY ABSTRACTS, 1914 TO THE PRESENT. 1955. q. service basis. ‡ A B C-Clio, 2040 Alameda Padre Serra, Box 4397, Santa Barbara, CA 93140-4397. TEL 805-963-4221. Ed. Pamela R. Byrne. index. cum.index every 5 yrs.
●Also available online. Vendors: DIALOG.
Supersedes in part: Historical Abstracts (ISSN 0018-2435)

960 016   ZA
HISTORY IN ZAMBIA.* 1970. a., latest no.12, 1980. $5. Historical Association of Zambia, c/o University of Zambia, Box 31338, Lusaka, Zambia. Eds. Kusum Datta, Martin Kaniki. adv. bk. rev. bibl. circ. 350.

564   HISTORY — HISTORY OF AFRICA

954 016   II
INDIA AND WORLD AFFAIRS: AN ANNUAL BIBLIOGRAPHY. (Part 1: India's Foreign Policy and Relations with Other Countries of the World; Part 2: Indian Opinions on World Events) (Text in English) 1958. a. (Jawaharlal Nehru University, School of International Studies) Vikas Publishing House Pvt. Ltd., Vikas House, 20/4 Industrial Area, Sahibabad, Distt. Ghaziabad U.P., India.

900   US   ISSN 0074-2015
INTERNATIONAL BIBLIOGRAPHY OF HISTORICAL SCIENCES. (Text in French and English) 1947. a. price varies. (International Committee of Historical Sciences) K.G. Saur, Inc., 175 Fifth Ave., New York, NY 10010. Eds. Jean Glenisson, Michel Keil.

016 980   UK   ISSN 0085-2694
LATIN AMERICAN STUDIES IN THE UNIVERSITIES OF THE UNITED KINGDOM. 1967. irreg. free. University of London, Institute of Latin American Studies, 31 Tavistock Sq., London WC1H 9HA, England. Ed. D.F. Rodger.

016 980 300   UK   ISSN 0085-2708
LATIN AMERICAN STUDIES IN THE UNIVERSITIES OF THE UNITED KINGDOM. STAFF RESEARCH IN PROGRESS OR RECENTLY COMPLETED IN THE HUMANITIES AND THE SOCIAL SCIENCES. 1969. irreg. free. ‡ University of London, Institute of Latin American Studies, 31 Tavistock Sq., London WC1H 9HA, England. Ed. D.F. Rodger.

015   MY   ISSN 0126-5210
MALAYSIAN NATIONAL BIBLIOGRAPHY/ BIBLIOGRAFI NEGARA MALAYSIA. (Text in English and Malay) 1967. q. (plus annual cumulation) M.100. National Library, Bibliography and Indexing Division - Perpustakaan Negara Malaysia, 3rd Floor, Wisma Sachdev, Jalan Raja Laut, 50572 Kuala Lumpur, Malaysia (Orders to: University of Malaya Cooperative Bookshop Ltd, Library Building, University of Malaya, 59700 Kuala Lumpur, Malaysia) Ed. Norpisah Mohd. Noor. circ. 200.

940 016   UK   ISSN 0077-0280
MONARCHIST BOOK REVIEW; an annotated list of new and reprinted books dealing with various aspects of monarchy. 1968. a. 30p.($0.75) Monarchist Press Association, 2 Sutherland Rd., West Ealing London W13 0DX, England. Ed. James Page. circ. 600.

016   US
NEW MEXICO. STATE RECORDS CENTER & ARCHIVES. ANNUAL PUBLICATIONS LIST. 1969. irreg. $10. ‡ State Records Center and Archives, State Rules and Publications Division, 404 Montezuma, Santa Fe, NM 87503. TEL 505-827-8860. circ. 30. (also avail. in microfiche)
  Supersedes in part: New Mexico. State Records Center and Archives. Publications and Rules Filed; Formerly: New Mexico. State Records Center and Archives. Publications Filed (ISSN 0090-0931)

990   US   ISSN 0085-459X
PACIFIC ISLANDS STUDIES AND NOTES. 1971. irreg. free to selected libraries. ‡ N.L.H. Krauss, Ed. & Pub., 2437 Parker Place, Honolulu, HI 96822. circ. 500.

319 993.1   NZ   ISSN 0079-2411
POCKET DIGEST OF NEW ZEALAND STATISTICS. 1927. a. NZ.$6.54. Department of Statistics, Private Bag, Wellington, New Zealand (Subscr. to: Government Printing Office, Publications, Private Bag, Wellington, New Zealand) circ. 9,700.

950 011   UK   ISSN 0308-7395
QUARTERLY INDEX ISLAMICUS; current books, articles, and papers on Islamic Studies. (Text in all languages) 1977. q. £40($70) to institutions; individuals £20($35) (University of London, School of Oriental and African Studies) Mansell Publishing Ltd., 6 All Saints St., London N1 9RL, England (Distr. by: Carfax Publishing Co., P.O. Box 25, Abingdon, Oxfordshire OX14 3UE, England) Ed. J.D. Pearson. index.

015 948   SW   ISSN 0347-4585
R A-NYTT. (Four Series: Enskilda Arkiv, Riksarkivets Myndighetsservice, Forskarservice and Folkroerelsearkiven) 1969. irreg. (3-4/yr.) free. Riksarkivet - National Swedish Record Office, Box 12541, 102 29 Stockholm, Sweden. cum.index.

900   US   ISSN 0885-7555
REFERENCE GUIDES TO ARCHIVES AND MANUSCRIPT COLLECTIONS ON IMMIGRANT CULTURE. 1986. irreg. price varies. Greenwood Press, Box 5007, 88 Post Rd. W., Westport, CT 06881. TEL 203-226-3571.

016 949.2   NE
REPERTORIUM VAN BOEKEN EN TIJDSCHRIFTARTIKELEN BETREFFENDE DE GESCHIEDENIS VAN NEDERLAND. 1941. irreg. Uitgeverij S.M. Ontwikkeling, Box 33, 2300 AA Leiden, Netherlands.

951 016   FR   ISSN 0080-2484
REVUE BIBLIOGRAPHIQUE DE SINOLOGIE. (Text in Chinese and French) 1955; N.S. 1984. a. price varies. Editions de l' Ecole des Hautes Etudes en Sciences Sociales, FR , 131 bd. St. Michel, 75005 Paris, France. Eds. Michel Cartier, Danielle Ellisseeff. adv. bk. rev. circ. 400.

942 015   UK   ISSN 0308-4558
ROYAL HISTORICAL SOCIETY. ANNUAL BIBLIOGRAPHY OF BRITISH AND IRISH HISTORY. (Text in English, French, German, Italian, Russian, Spanish) 1976. a. £32.50. Harvester Press Ltd., 16 Ship St., Brighton, Sussex BN1 1AD, England. TEL (0273) 28320. Ed. D. Palliser. circ. 2, 000.
  Incorporating (as of 1975): Writings on British History (ISSN 0084-2753)

948.9   DK   ISSN 0105-9475
SELECT BIBLIOGRAPHY OF DANISH WORKS ON THE HISTORY OF TOWNS PUBLISHED. (Forms also part of: Byhistoriske Hjaelpemidler) 1973. irreg. free. Dansk Komite for Byhistorie, c/o Poul Stroemstad, Nationalmuseet i Brede, 2800 Lyngby, Denmark. Ed.Bd. circ. 100.

200 016   US
SIXTEENTH CENTURY BIBLIOGRAPHY. 1975. irreg., vol.25, 1985. $7.50. Center for Reformation Research, 6477 San Bonita Ave., St. Louis, MO 63105. TEL 314-727-6655. Ed. William Maltby. circ. 300. (also avail. in microfilm from UMI; reprint service avail. from UMI) Indexed: CERDIC.
  Formerly: Foundation for Reformation Research. Bulletin of the Library (ISSN 0015-8941)

011 960   SA
SOUTH AFRICA. OFFICE OF THE DIRECTOR OF ARCHIVES AND THE STATE HERALD. ANNUAL REPORT/SOUTH AFRICA. KANTOOR VAN DIE DIREKTEUR VAN ARGIEWE EN DIE STAATSHERALDIKUS. JAARVERSLAG. 1965. a. R.4.40. Office of the Director of Archives, Government Archives Service, Private Bag X236, I N A Building, Pretoria 0001, South Africa. bibl. circ. 150.
  Formerly: South Africa. Office of the Director of Archives. Annual Report of the Director of Archives/South Africa. Kantoor van die Direkteur van Argiewe. Jaarverslag van die Direkteur van Argiewe.

968 312   SA   ISSN 0302-0681
SOUTH AFRICA. OFFICIAL YEARBOOK OF THE REPUBLIC OF SOUTH AFRICA. 1979. a. Chris van Lensburg Publications, Box 29159, Melville, 2109 Johannesburg, South Africa. Ed. Bettie van Wyk.

318   US   ISSN 0081-4687
STATISTICAL ABSTRACT OF LATIN AMERICA. 1956. a. (plus supplements) price varies. University of California, Los Angeles, Latin American Center, Los Angeles, CA 90024. TEL 213-825-6634. Ed. James W. Wilkie.

947.1   FI   ISSN 0081-9417
SUOMEN HISTORIALLINEN SEURA. KASIKIRJOJA. (Text in Finnish) 1925. irreg., no.10, 1985. price varies. Suomen Historiallinen Seura - Finnish Historical Society, Vuorikatu 6 A 4, 00100 Helsinki 10, Finland. circ. 350.

SWEDEN. STATISTISKA CENTRALBYRAAN. STATISTISKA MEDDELANDEN. SUBGROUP BE (POPULATION) see POPULATION STUDIES — Abstracting, Bibliographies, Statistics

012 943   GE   ISSN 0232-3907
THURINGEN-BIBLIOGRAPHIE; Regionalbibliographie fuer die Bezirke Erfurt, Gera und Suhl. 1972. a. M.28.50($19.88) Universitaetsbibliothek der Friedrich-Schiller-Universitaet Jena, Goetheallee 6, 6900 Jena, E. Germany (D.D.R.)

940 016   CN   ISSN 0082-5042
TORONTO MEDIEVAL BIBLIOGRAPHIES. 1967. irreg. price varies. (University of Toronto, Centre for Medieval Studies) University of Toronto Press, Front Campus, Toronto, Ont. M5S 1A6, Canada. TEL 613-667-7791. Ed. J. Leyerle.

973 016   US
WRITINGS ON AMERICAN HISTORY; a subject bibliography of articles. 1962. a. $45. (American Historical Association) Kraus International Publications (Subsidiary of: Kraus-Thomson Organization Ltd.) One Water St., White Plains, NY 10601. TEL 914-761-9600. Ed. Cecelia J. Dadian. (back issues avail.)

HISTORY — History Of Africa

962   SX
A.D.K. BOOKLET: FACTS AND FIGURES/A.D.K. SCHRIFTENREIHE: DATEN AND FAKTEN. (Text in English and German) 1978. irreg. R.2.50. Afrikaans Duitse Kultuurunie (S W A), Box 2185, 9100 Windhoek, South West Africa. Ed. Erno Gauerke. circ. 124,000 (combined edts.) (back issues avail.)

960   BL   ISSN 0100-8153
AFRICA. (Text in English, French, Spanish and Portugese) 1978. a. Cr.$5200($10) Universidade de Sao Paulo, Centro de Estudos Africanos, Faculdade de Filosofia, Letras, Ciencias Humanas, Caixa Postal 8105, Cidade Universitaria, 05508 Sao Paulo, Brazil. TEL 210 9416. Ed. Fernando A.A. Mourao. adv. bk. rev. circ. 1,500. (back issues avail.)

330 960   US   ISSN 0065-3845
AFRICA CONTEMPORARY RECORD. ANNUAL SURVEY AND DOCUMENTS. 1968/69. a. $275. Africana Publishing Co. (Subsidiary of: Holmes & Meier Publishers, Inc.) 30 Irving Pl., New York, NY 10003 TEL 212-254-4100. (U.K. address: 1-3 Winton Close, Letchworth, Hertfords, SG61 1BA, England) Ed. Colin Legum. adv. circ. 3,000. (back issues avail.) Indexed: Curr.Cont.Africa.

960 309   US
AFRICA IN THE MODERN WORLD. irreg. price varies. Cornell University Press, 124 Roberts Place, Ithaca, NY 14850. TEL 607-257-7000.

960   SA
AFRICA INSTITUTE. OCCASIONAL PUBLICATIONS. Variant title: Africa Institute of South Africa. Occasional Papers. 1968. irreg., no.50, 1982. price varies. Africa Institute of South Africa, Box 630, Pretoria 0001, South Africa. (reprint service avail. from UMI)
  Supersedes: Africa Institute. Special Publications (ISSN 0065-3888)

960   KE
AFRICA INTERNATIONAL. 1974. irreg. Kenya Literature Bureau, Box 30022, Nairobi, Kenya.

968 330.1   SA   ISSN 0250-0116
AFRICA SEMINAR: COLLECTED PAPERS. 1978. irreg. R.3.50. University of Cape Town, Center for African Studies, Rondebosch 7700, South Africa (Subscr. to: Publications, Gifts & Exchanges, University of Cape Town Libraries, Rondebosch 77001, South Africa) circ. 300. (back issues avail.)

960   US   ISSN 0065-3896
AFRICA SOUTH OF THE SAHARA. 1971. a. $145. Europa Publications Ltd., 18 Bedford Sq., London WC1B 3JN, England.

AFRICAN ARCHAEOLOGICAL REVIEW. see ARCHAEOLOGY

HISTORY — HISTORY OF AFRICA

960 US
AFRICAN DOCUMENTS SERIES. 1969. irreg., no. 5, 1984. Boston University, African Studies Center, 270 Bay State Rd., Boston, MA 02215. TEL 617-353-3673.

960 NR ISSN 0568-1332
AFRICAN HISTORIAN. 1963. a. (University of Ife, Historical Society) African Education Press, P.M.B. 5617, Ibadan, Nigeria.

960 US
AFRICAN HISTORICAL DICTIONARIES. 1974. irreg., no.40, 1987. price varies. Scarecrow Press, Inc., 52 Liberty Street, Box 4167, Metuchen, NJ 08840. TEL 201-548-8600. Ed. J. Woronoff.

AFRICAN RESEARCH STUDIES. see *SOCIAL SCIENCES: COMPREHENSIVE WORKS*

960 CH
AFRICAN STUDIES. (Text in Chinese & English) no.2, 1973. a. free on exchange. National Chengchi University, Program of African Studies, Social Sciences Materials Center, Taipei, Taiwan 116, Republic of China. Ed.Bd.

960 UK ISSN 0065-406X
AFRICAN STUDIES SERIES. 1971. irreg., no.40, 1983. $49.50 cloth. Cambridge University Press, Edinburgh Bldg., Shaftesbury Rd., Cambridge CB2 2RU, England (And 32 E. 57th St., New York, NY 10022) Ed.Bd. Indexed: A.B.C.Pol.Sci.

968 SA
AFRICANA SOCIETY OF PRETORIA. JOURNAL. (Text in Afrikaans and English) 1975. irreg. R.5. Africana Society of Pretoria, Box 3239, Pretoria 0001, South Africa. Ed. W.J. Punt. adv. bk. rev. bibl. illus. circ. 150. (back issues avail.) Indexed: Ind.S.A.Per.

968.005 SA
AFRICANA SOCIETY OF PRETORIA. YEARBOOK/AFRICANA VERENIGING VAN PRETORIA. JAARBOEK. (Text in Afrikaans and English) 1975. a. R.20 to institutions. Africana Society of Pretoria, Box 3239, Pretoria 0001, South Africa. Ed. W.J. Punt. adv. bk. rev. circ. 250.

950 960 UA ISSN 0065-4191
AFRO-ASIAN PEOPLES' CONFERENCE. PROCEEDINGS. (Text in Arabic, English and French) 1957. irreg., 1972, 5th, Cairo, Egypt. Afro-Asian Peoples' Solidarity Organization, 89 Abdel Aziz al- Saoud St., Manial, Cairo, Egypt.

950 960 UA ISSN 0078-6233
AFRO-ASIAN PEOPLES' SOLIDARITY ORGANIZATION. COUNCIL. DOCUMENTS OF THE SESSION. (Subseries of Afro-Asian Publications) irreg, 13th, 1981, Dem. Rep. of Yemen. Afro- Asian Peoples' Solidarity Organization, 89, Abdel Aziz al Saoud St., Manial, Cairo, Egypt.

961 UA ISSN 0515-6327
AFRO-ASIAN PUBLICATIONS. irreg. Afro-Asian Peoples' Solidarity Organization, 89 Abdel Aziz al Saoud, 89 Abdel Aziz al-Saoud St., Cairo, Egypt.

966.9 NR
AHMADU BELLO UNIVERSITY. NORTHERN HISTORY RESEARCH SCHEME. INTERIM REPORT. 1966. irreg., latest 1981. £N3. Ahmadu Bello University, Northern History Research Scheme, Zaria, Nigeria. circ. 2,000.
Formerly: Ahmadu Bello University. Northern History Research Scheme. Papers (ISSN 0065-4760)

960 913 FR ISSN 0066-4871
ANTIQUITES AFRICAINES. 1967. a. price varies. Editions du C N R S, 295 rue St. Jacques, 75005 Paris, France. Indexed: Numis.Lit.

960 MZ
ANUARIO DO ESTADO DE MOCAMBIQUE; informacoes oficias, comerciais, geograficas e historicas. irreg. A.W. Bayly & Ca., Lda., Av. 25 de Setembro 195-197, C.P. 185, Maputo, Mozambique.
Formerly: Anuario da Provincia de Mocambique (ISSN 0570-4022)

ASIAN AND AFRICAN STUDIES. see *ORIENTAL STUDIES*

ASIEN - AFRIKA - LATEINAMERIKA. JAHRBUCH; Bilanz und Chronik. see *HISTORY — History Of Asia*

ASSOCIATION OF HISTORY TEACHERS IN NIGERIA. see *EDUCATION — Teaching Methods And Curriculum*

967 913 KE ISSN 0067-270X
AZANIA. 1966. a. $25. British Institute in Eastern Africa, P.O. Box 30710, Nairobi, Kenya. Ed. J.E.G. Sutton. index. cum.index: 1966-68; 1979-83. (back issues avail.)

960 SZ ISSN 0170-5091
BASLER AFRIKA BIBLIOGRAPHIEN. MITTEILUNGEN/BASEL AFRICA BIBLIOGRAPHY. COMMUNICATIONS. 1972. irreg. (1-3/yr.), vol.30, 1985. price varies. Basler Afrika Bibliographien, Postfach 2037, CH-4001 Basel, Switzerland. Ed. Bd. adv. bk. rev. bibl. Indexed: CERDIC.

962 GW ISSN 0170-3218
BEITRAEGE ZUR AEGYPTISCHEN BAUFORSCHUNG UND ALTERTUMSKUNDE. (Text in French and German) 1932. irreg. price varies. (Schweizerisches Institut fuer Aegyptische Bauforschung und Altertumskunde in Kairo) Franz Steiner Verlag Wiesbaden GmbH, Birkenwaldstr. 44, Postfach 347, D-7000 Stuttgart 1, W. Germany (B.R.D.)

960 SZ ISSN 0171-1660
BEITRAEGE ZUR AFRIKAKUNDE. 1978. irreg. price varies. Basler Afrika Bibliographien, Postfach 2037, CH-4001 Basel, Switzerland. circ. 300.

BOSTON UNIVERSITY PAPERS ON AFRICA. see *SOCIAL SCIENCES: COMPREHENSIVE WORKS*

968.1 BS ISSN 0525-5090
BOTSWANA NOTES AND RECORDS. 1969. a. $18. Botswana Society, Box 71, Gaborone, Botswana. Ed. Doreen Nteta. adv. bk. rev. circ. 1, 000. Indexed: Hist.Abstr. M.L.A. Key Word Ind.Wildl.Res. Amer.Hist.& Life. Field Crop Abstr. Herb.Abstr. Ind.S.A.Per. Rural Recreat.Tour.Abstr. World Agri.Econ.& Rural Sociol.Abstr.

967.6 KE ISSN 0068-2152
BRITISH INSTITUTE IN EASTERN AFRICA. ANNUAL REPORT. 1962. a. membership. British Institute in Eastern Africa, Box 30710, Nairobi, Kenya.
Formerly: British Institute of History and Archaeology in East Africa. Report.

960 KE
BRITISH INSTITUTE IN EASTERN AFRICA. MEMOIRS. 1966. irreg., no.9, 1984. price varies. British Institute in Eastern Africa, Box 30710, Nairobi, Kenya. Ed. J.E.G. Sutton. bk. rev. circ. 500.

968 UK
C S A S OCCASIONAL PAPERS. 1986. irreg. £1 per vol. University of York, Centre for Southern African Studies, Heslington, York YO1 5DD, England. Eds. Anne V. Akeroyd, Landeg White.

960 UK ISSN 0069-0899
CASS LIBRARY OF AFRICAN STUDIES. GENERAL STUDIES. 1962. irreg, no.137, 1973. price varies. Frank Cass & Co. Ltd., Gainsborough House, 11 Gainsborough Rd., London E11 1RS, England (Dist. in U.S. by: Biblio Distribution Center, 81 Adams Drive, Totowa, N.J. 07512)

960 916 UK ISSN 0069-0902
CASS LIBRARY OF AFRICAN STUDIES. RESEARCHES AND TRAVELS. 1968. irreg., no.25, 1973. price varies. Frank Cass & Co. Ltd., Gainsborough House, 11 Gainsborough Rd., London E11 1RS, England (Dist. in U.S. by: Biblio Distribution Center, 81 Adams Drive, Totowa, N.J. 07512)

960 916 UK ISSN 0069-0910
CASS LIBRARY OF AFRICAN STUDIES. SOUTH AFRICAN STUDIES. 1968. irreg., no.6, 1970. price varies. Frank Cass & Co. Ltd., Gainsborough House, 11 Gainsborough Rd., London E11 1RS, England (Dist. in U.S. by: Biblio Distribution Center, 81 Adams Drive, Totowa, N.J. 07512)

960 916 UK ISSN 0069-0929
CASS LIBRARY OF AFRICAN STUDIES. TRAVELS AND NARRATIVES. 1964. irreg., no.40, 1968. price varies. Frank Cass & Co. Ltd., Gainsborough House, 11 Gainsborough Rd., London E11 1RS, England (Dist. in U.S. by: Biblio Distribution Center, 81 Adams Drive, Totowa, N.J. 07512)

CENTRE D'ETUDES ETHNOLOGIQUES. PUBLICATIONS. SERIE 2: MEMOIRES ET MONOGRAPHIES. see *ANTHROPOLOGY*

CENTRE D'ETUDES ETHNOLOGIQUES BANDUNDU. PUBLICATIONS. see *ANTHROPOLOGY*

960 GW
CHANGE AND CONTINUITY IN AFRICA. irreg. price varies. (Afrika-Studiecentrum, Leiden) Walter de Gruyter & Co., Mouton Publishers, Postfach 110240, D-1000 Berlin 11, W. Germany (B.R.D.) (U.S. addr.: Mouton Publishers, division of Walter de Gruyter, Inc., 200 Saw Mill River Road, Hawthorne, NY 10532)

960 AO
COLECCAO N'GOLA. a. price varies. Livrangol Editores, Ave. dos Restauradores 21-1, Luanda, Angola. illus.

960 KE ISSN 0069-9330
CONTEMPORARY AFRICAN MONOGRAPHS. 1965. irreg. (East African Institute of Social and Cultural Affairs) East African Publishing House, Box 30571, Lusaka Close, off Lusaka Rd., Nairobi, Kenya. circ. 3,000.

CONTRIBUTIONS A LA CONNAISSANCE DES ELITES AFRICAINES. see *BIOGRAPHY*

960 361 US ISSN 0069-9624
CONTRIBUTIONS IN AFRO-AMERICAN AND AFRICAN STUDIES. 1970. irreg., no.71, 1983. price varies. Greenwood Press, 88 Post Rd. W., Box 5007, Westport, CT 06881. TEL 203-226-3571. Ed. John W. Blassingame, Henry Louis Gates, Jr. Indexed: Rel.Ind.Two.

960 RH ISSN 0250-2992
COOKEIA. (Text in English) irreg. National Museums and Monuments, P.O. Box 8540, Causeway, Zimbabwe. circ. 350.

960 SG
COTE D'IVOIRE EN CHIFFRES. a. 10000 Fr.CFA. Societe Africaine d'Edition, 16 bis, rue de Thiong, Dakar, Senegal (And 32 rue de l'Echiquier, Paris, France)

960 CM
CULTURE CAMEROUNAISE/CAMEROONIAN CULTURE. 1969. irreg, vol.2, 1971. Direction des Affaires Culturelle, Ministere de l'Education, de la Culture et de la Formation Professionelle, Yaounde, Cameroon. illus. (processed)

960 SW ISSN 0280-2171
CURRENT AFRICAN ISSUES. 1981. irreg. Kr.20 per no. Nordiska Afrikainstitutet - Scandinavian Institute of African Studies, Box 1703, S-751 47 Uppsala, Sweden. circ. 500.

DICTIONNAIRE DE BIOGRAPHIE MAURICIENNE/DICTIONARY OF MAURITIAN BIOGRAPHY. see *BIOGRAPHY*

960 GH ISSN 0013-712X
ENCYCLOPAEDIA AFRICANA. INFORMATION REPORT. 1962. irreg., no.18, 1979. free. Encyclopaedia Africana Project, Box 2797, Accra, Ghana.

967.5 BE ISSN 0772-6112
ENQUETES ET DOCUMENTS D'HISTOIRE AFRICAINE. 1975. irreg. 350 Fr. per no. Universite Catholique de Louvain, Centre d'Histoire de l'Afrique, 1 Place Blaise Pascal, 1348 Louvain-la-Neuve, Belgium. Ed. J.L. Vellut. circ. 300.

HISTORY — HISTORY OF AFRICA

960   ZR   ISSN 0071-1993
ETUDES D'HISTOIRE AFRICAINE/STUDIES IN AFRICAN HISTORY. 1970. a. price varies. Universite Nationale du Zaire, Lubumbashi, Department d'Histoire, B.P. 1825, Lubumbashi, Zaire. (Co-sponsor: Musee Royale de l'Afrique Centrale, Belgium) Ed. Dr. J.L. Vellut. adv. bk. rev. circ. 1,000. Indexed: Hist.Abstr. Amer.Hist.& Life. Curr.Cont.Africa.

ETUDES SENEGALAISES. see *SOCIOLOGY*

969   RE
FONDATION POUR LA RECHERCHE ET LE DEVELOPPEMENT DANS L'OCEAN INDIEN. DOCUMENTS ET RECHERCHES. 1975. irreg. 118 Fr.CFA. Fondation pour la Recherche et le Developpement dans l'Ocean Indien, Bibliotheque Departementale, Rue Roland Garros, St. Denis, Reunion.

962 961   FR
HABITATS ET SOCIETES URBAINES EN EGYPTE ET AU SOUDAN. 1973. a. (Universite de Lille III, Institut de Papyrologie et d'Egyptologie) Presses Universitaires de Lille, Rue du Barreau, B.P. 199, 59654 Villeneuve d'Ascq Cedex, France. Ed. Dominique Valbelle. illus.
Formerly: Etudes sur l'Egypte et le Soudan Anciens (ISSN 0153-5021)

960   RH
HERITAGE. 1981. a. Z.$3($8.90) History Society of Zimbabwe, Box 8268, Causeway, Harare, Zimbabwe. Ed. R. Cherey Smith. adv. bk. rev. bibl. charts. illus. index. cum.index: 1956-1973. circ. 1,000. Indexed: Hist.Abstr. Amer.Hist.& Life. Ind.S.A.Per.
Supersedes (1956-1980): Rhodesiana (ISSN 0556-9605)

960   KE
HISTORICAL ASSOCIATION OF KENYA. PAMPHLET. 1977. irreg. Kenya Literature Bureau, Box 30022, Nairobi, Kenya.

960   KE   ISSN 0440-9264
HISTORICAL ASSOCIATION OF TANZANIA. PAPERS. irreg. East African Publishing House, Box 30571, Lusaka Close, off Lusaka Rd., Nairobi, Kenya. bibl.

960   RH
HISTORICAL ASSOCIATION OF ZIMBABWE. LOCAL SERIES PAMPHLETS. 1959. a. Historical Association of Zimbabwe, c/o Z.I.P, Box 2054, Harare, Zimbabwe.
Formerly: Central Africa Historical Association. Local Series Pamphlets (ISSN 0577-036X)

960   US   ISSN 0361-5413
HISTORY IN AFRICA; an annual journal of method. 1974. a. $20. African Studies Association, c/o Memorial Library, University of Wisconsin, Madison, WI 53706 TEL 608-262-6397. (Subscr. to African Studies Association, 255 Kinsey Hall, UCLA, Los Angeles, CA 90024) Ed. David Henige. bk. rev. bibl. circ. 400. Indexed: Curr.Cont. Hist.Abstr. Arts & Hum.Cit.Ind. Amer.Hist.& Life. Curr.Cont.Africa. Hist.Abstr.

960   MW
HISTORY IN MALAWI. 1971. irreg. price varies. Chancellor College, Department of History, Box 280, Zomba, Malawi. bibl. circ. 6,200. (processed; back issues avail.)

960   US
INDIANA UNIVERSITY PUBLICATIONS. AFRICAN SERIES. Series completed with vol. 8, 1978. irreg. price varies. (Indiana University) Humanities Press, Inc., 171 First Ave., Atlantic Highlands, NJ 07716. Ed. Carleton T. Hodge.

960   SG   ISSN 0070-2617
INSTITUT FONDAMENTAL D'AFRIQUE NOIRE. CATALOGUES ET DOCUMENTS. 1947. irreg., no.22, 1972. price varies. Institut Fondamental d'Afrique Noire, Boite Postale 206, Dakar, Senegal.

960   SG   ISSN 0070-2625
INSTITUT FONDAMENTAL D'AFRIQUE NOIRE. INITIATIONS ET ETUDES AFRICAINES. Short title: Initiations et Etudes Africaines. 1955. irreg., no.31, 1974. price varies. Institut Fondamental d'Afrique Noire, Boite Postale 206, Dakar, Senegal.

960   SG   ISSN 0070-2633
INSTITUT FONDAMENTAL D'AFRIQUE NOIRE. MEMOIRES. 1939. irreg., no.89, 1975. price varies. Institut Fondamental d'Afrique Noire, Boite Postale 206, Dakar, Senegal.

963   ET   ISSN 0074-2945
INTERNATIONAL CONFERENCE OF ETHIOPIAN STUDIES. PROCEEDINGS.* (Text in English, French, Italian, Amharic) irreg., 1966, 3rd. Institute of Ethiopian Studies, Haile Sellassie I University, Addis Ababa, Ethiopia.

960   BE
INVENTAIRE DES ARCHIVES HISTORIQUES/ INVENTARIS VAN HET HISTORISCH ARCHIEF. 1961. irreg., no.7, 1977. price varies. Musee Royal de l'Afrique Centrale, 13 Steenweg op Leuven, B-1980 Tervuren, Belgium. illus.

955   IR   ISSN 0075-0476
IRAN ALMANAC AND BOOK OF FACTS. (Text in English) 1961. a. $25. Echo Publications, Av. Shiras, Kuche Khalhali No. 4, P.O. Box 2008, Teheran, Iran. adv.

960   JA   ISSN 0065-4140
JOURNAL OF AFRICAN STUDIES/AFURIKA KENKYU. 1964. irreg. 600 Yen. Japan Association of Africanists - Nihon Afrika Gakkai, c/o University of Tokyo, Dept. of Geography, Hongo, Bunkyo-ku, Tokyo 113, Japan. Ed. Shoji Hasegawa.

960   KE
KENYA. MINISTRY OF INFORMATION AND BROADCASTING. ANNUAL REPORT. 1963. a. Ministry of Information and Broadcasting, Box 30025, Nairobi, Kenya (Orders to: Government Printing and Stationery Department, Box 30128, Nairobi, Kenya)
Former titles: Kenya. Ministry of Information, Broadcasting and Tourism. Annual Report; Kenya. Ministry of Information. Annual Report (ISSN 0075-5885)

967.6   KE
KENYA NATIONAL ACADEMY FOR ADVANCEMENT OF ARTS AND SCIENCES. RESEARCH INFORMATION CIRCULARS. 1968. a., no. 9, 1978. EAs.40($5) Kenya National Academy for Advancement of Arts and Sciences, Box 47288, Nairobi, Kenya.
Formerly: East African Research Information Centre. E A R I C Information Circular (ISSN 0070-8011)

967.62 500.9   KE
KENYA PAST AND PRESENT. 1971. a., latest no.18, 1986. $20. Kenya Museum Society, c/o Kenya National Museums, P.O. Box 40658, Nairobi, Kenya. adv. illus. circ. 2,000. Indexed: Curr.Cont.Africa.

960   KE
KENYA REGIONAL STUDIES. irreg., no.2, 1975. Kenya Literature Bureau, Box 30022, Nairobi, Kenya.

960   KE   ISSN 0378-2158
KENYA UHURU YEARBOOK. (Supplements avail.) 1973. a. EAs.180($25) Newspread International, Box 46854, Nairobi, Kenya. Ed. Kul Bhushan. adv. bk. rev. circ. 5,000.

960   NR   ISSN 0075-7640
LAGOS NOTES AND RECORDS; a journal of African studies. 1967. irreg., vol. 5, 1974. (University of Lagos, School of African Studies) Lagos University Press, P.O. Box 132, Akoka, Yaba, Lagos, Nigeria.

MCGILL UNIVERSITY, MONTREAL. CENTRE FOR DEVELOPING-AREA STUDIES. BIBLIOGRAPHY SERIES. see *BIBLIOGRAPHIES*

968.97   MW
MALAWI YEARBOOK. 1969. a. K.2.40. Department of Information and Tourism, P.O. Box 494, Blantyre, Malawi. Ed. Phylis Kubwalo. adv. bk. rev. illus. circ. 2,500.
Former titles (until 1977): Malawi. Department of Information. Year in Review; until 1975: Malawi Year Book (ISSN 0076-3012)

960   US
MONOGRAPHS IN INTERNATIONAL STUDIES: AFRICA SERIES. 1968. irreg. price varies. Ohio University, Center for International Studies, Burson House, 56 E. Union St., Athens, OH 45701 TEL 614-594-5511. (Orders to: Ohio Univ. Press, Scott Quad., Athens, OH 45701) Ed. Cosmo Pieterse. bibl. charts. illus. circ. 500. (back issues avail.) Indexed: M.L.A. SSCI.
Formerly: Papers in International Studies: Africa Series (ISSN 0078-9100)

960   BE
MUSEE ROYAL DE L'AFRIQUE CENTRALE. ANNALES. SERIE IN 8. SCIENCES HISTORIQUES/KONINKLIJK MUSEUM VOOR MIDDEN-AFRIKA. ANNALEN. REEKS IN 8. HISTORISCHE WETENSCHAPPEN. 1964. irreg., latest no.7, 1985. Musee Royal de l'Afrique Centrale, 13 Steenweg op Leuven, B-1980 Tervuren., Belgium. charts. illus.

MUSEUM FUER VOELKERKUNDE, BERLIN. VEROEFFENTLICHUNGEN. NEUE FOLGE. ABTEILUNG: AFRIKA. see *ANTHROPOLOGY*

960   SA   ISSN 0085-3674
NATALIA. 1971. a. R.10. Natal Society, Box 415, Pietermaritzburg, Natal, South Africa. Ed. T.B. Frost. adv. bk. rev. bibl. illus. circ. 500. (tabloid format) Indexed: Ind.S.A.Per.

NATIONAL ARCHIVES OF ZAMBIA. ANNUAL REPORT. see *LIBRARY AND INFORMATION SCIENCES*

960 350   ZA
NATIONAL ARCHIVES OF ZAMBIA. CALENDARS OF THE DISTRICT NOTEBOOKS. (Issued in 4 vols.: Copperbelt, Luapula, Norther, Western Provinces) irreg. 1 n. National Archives, Box RW 50010, Ridgeway, Lusaka, Zambia. Ed. P.M. Mukula.

960   ZA
NATIONAL ARCHIVES OF ZAMBIA. INFORMATION. 1981. irreg. 1 n. National Archives, Box RW 50010, Ridgeway, Lusaka, Zambia. Ed. P.M. Mukula.

960   ZA
NATIONAL ARCHIVES OF ZAMBIA. NATIONAL ARCHIVES OCCASIONAL PAPER. no.2, 1973. irreg. 1 n. ‡ National Archives, Box RW 50010, Ridgeway, Lusaka, Zambia. Ed. Robin Palmer. bibl. circ. 500(approx.)

968   NE   ISSN 0077-6416
NEDERLANDS-ZUIDAFRIKAANSE VERENIGING. JAARVERSLAG. 1882. a. membership. Nederlands-Zuidafrikaanse Vereniging, Keizersgracht 141, Amsterdam C, Netherlands. circ. 1,000.

NORTHEAST AFRICAN MONOGRAPH SERIES. see *ETHNIC INTERESTS*

960 383   GH   ISSN 0072-9825
OFFICIAL HANDBOOK OF GHANA.* a. Information Services Department, P.O. Box 745, Accra, Ghana.

960 301.2   KE
PEOPLES OF EAST AFRICA. irreg. East African Publishing House, Box 30571, Lusaka Close, off Lusaka Rd., Nairobi, Kenya. bibl. illus.

PERSPECTIVES ON SOUTHERN AFRICA. see *POLITICAL SCIENCE*

962   GW   ISSN 0481-0023
QUELLEN ZUR GESCHICHTE DES ISLAMISCHEN AEGYPTENS. 1978. irreg., vol.3, 1986. price varies. (Deutsches Archaeologisches Institut, Cairo, UA) Franz Steiner Verlag Wiesbaden GmbH, Birkenwaldstr. 44, Postfach 347, D-7000 Stuttgart 1, W. Germany (B.R.D.)

960   AE   ISSN 0556-7343
REVUE D'HISTOIRE ET DE CIVILISATION DU MAGHREB.* (Text in French and Arabic) irreg. (3-4/yr.) Societe Historique Algerienne, c/o Universite d'Alger, Faculte des Lettres, Algier, Algeria. Ed. M. Kaddache.

SAGE SERIES ON AFRICAN MODERNIZATION AND DEVELOPMENT. see *BUSINESS AND ECONOMICS — International Development And Assistance*

960   SW   ISSN 0549-6330
SCANDINAVIAN INSTITUTE OF AFRICAN STUDIES. NEWSLETTER. (Text in English) 1963. a. free. Nordiska Afrikainstitutet - Scandinavian Institute of African Studies, Box 1703, S-751 47 Uppsala, Sweden. circ. 2,000. (back issues avail.)

960   SW   ISSN 0080-6714
SCANDINAVIAN INSTITUTE OF AFRICAN STUDIES. RESEARCH REPORT. (Text in English) 1967. irreg., no.58, 1981. price varies. Nordiska Afrikainstitutet - Scandinavian Institute of African Studies, Box 1703, S-751 47 Uppsala, Sweden. circ. 1,000. Indexed: Geo.Abstr. Rural Recreat.Tour.Abstr. World Agri.Econ.& Rural Sociol.Abstr.

960   SW   ISSN 0281-0018
SCANDINAVIAN INSTITUTE OF AFRICAN STUDIES. SEMINAR PROCEEDINGS. 1964. irreg. price varies. Nordiska Afrikainstitutet - Scandinavian Institute of African Studies, Box 1703, S-751 47 Uppsala, Sweden (Dist. by: Almqvist & Wiksell International, 26 Gamla Brogatan, Box 62, 101 20 Stockholm, Sweden) circ. 1,500.
Formerly: Scandinavian Institute of African Studies. Annual Seminar Proceedings (ISSN 0080-6706)

960   SG
SENEGAL EN CHIFFRES. a. 12500 Fr.CFA. Societe Africaine d'Edition, B.P. 1877, Dakar, Senegal (And 32 rue de l'Echiquier, Paris, France)

SHILOACH CENTER FOR MIDDLE EASTERN & AFRICAN STUDIES. MONOGRAPH SERIES. see *HISTORY — History Of The Near East*

SOCIAAL-HISTORISCHE STUDIEN. see *SOCIAL SCIENCES: COMPREHENSIVE WORKS*

SOUTH AFRICAN BIOGRAPHICAL AND HISTORICAL STUDIES. see *BIOGRAPHY*

960   SA
SOUTH AFRICAN HISTORICAL JOURNAL. (Text in Afrikaans and English; summaries in English) 1969. a. R.15. South African Historical Society, University of Cape Town, Department of History, Rondebosch 7700, South Africa. Ed. B.A. le Cordeur. adv. bk. rev. bibl. index. circ. 500. Indexed: Hist.Abstr. Curr.Cont.Africa. Ind.S.A.Per.

968   SA
STUDIES IN THE HISTORY OF CAPE TOWN. (Text in English) 1979. a. R.3.50. University of Cape Town, Centre for African Studies, Private Bag, Rondebosch, Cape Town 7700, South Africa. Ed. C.C. Saunders. circ. 280. (back issues avail.)

STUDIES IN ZAMBIAN SOCIETY. see *SOCIOLOGY*

961   IE   ISSN 0143-6554
SUDAN TEXTS BULLETIN. 1979. a. £2. University of Ulster, Coleraine BT52 1SA, N. Ireland. Eds. Ali Osman, Robin Thelwall. bk. rev. circ. 130.

960 410   GW   ISSN 0720-0986
SUGIA; Sprache und Geschichte in Afrika. (Text in English, French, German) 1979. a. price varies. Helmut Buske Verlag, Schlueterstr. 14, Postfach 13 22 55, D-2000 Hamburg 13, W. Germany (B.R.D.) Ed.Bd. bk. rev. bibl. charts. illus. circ. 400. (back issues avail.)

968 301.2   SA
SUID-AFRIKAANSE KULTUURHISTORIESE MUSEUM. BULLETIN/SOUTH AFRICAN CULTURAL HISTORY MUSEUM. BULLETIN. (Text in Afrikaans and English) 1980. a. R.3. Suid-Afrikaanse Kultuurhistoriese Museum - South African Cultural History Museum, Box 645, Kaapstad 8000, South Africa. Eds. L. Meltzer, M. Olivier, A. Roux. adv. bk. rev. circ. 500. Indexed: Ind.S.A.Per. Ind.S.A.Per.

968.3   SQ
SWAZILAND NATIONAL MUSEUM. YEARBOOK. a., latest 1976. Swaziland National Centre, Box 100, Lobamba, Swaziland. illus.
Formerly (until Aug. 1976): Swaziland National Centre. Yearbook.

SYRACUSE UNIVERSITY. FOREIGN AND COMPARATIVE STUDIES. AFRICAN SERIES. see *SOCIAL SCIENCES: COMPREHENSIVE WORKS*

969.1   MG
TANTARA. 1973. FMG.400. Societe d'Histoire de Madagascar, B.P. 3384, Antananarivo, Malagasy Republic.

960   TZ
TANZANIAN STUDIES. irreg. Tanzania Publishing House, Box 2138, Dar es Salaam, Tanzania.

968   SA
TOPOSCOPE. (Text in English) 1970. a. $0.90. ‡ Lower Albany Historical Society, 24 Colgate St., Port Alfred 6170, South Africa. Ed. A.S. Basson. bk. rev. circ. 250.

960   LB
TORCH. no.9, 1976. irreg. Torch Services, Box 1394, Monrovia, Liberia. Ed. Bill Frank Enoanyi. adv. illus.

960   KE
TRANSAFRICA HISTORICAL PAPERS. 960. irreg. Transafrica Publishers Ltd., Box 42990, Nairobi, Kenya.

960   GW   ISSN 0344-4317
UEBERSEE-MUSEUM, BREMEN. VEROEFFENTLICHUNGEN. REIHE F: BREMER AFRIKA-ARCHIV. Short title: B A A. 1977. irreg., vol.19, 1984. price varies. Uebersee-Museum, Bremen, Bahnhofsplatz 13, 2800 Bremen, W. Germany(B.R.D.)

967.61   UG   ISSN 0041-574X
UGANDA JOURNAL. 1934. irreg. S.500($20) membership. Uganda Society, Box 4980, Kampala, Uganda. Ed.Bd. adv. bk. rev. bibl. index. circ. 450. Indexed: Biol.Abstr.

960   US   ISSN 0083-0003
U.S. DEPARTMENT OF STATE. AFRICAN SERIES. (Subseries of its Departmental Series) 1960. irreg. price varies. U.S. Department of State, Bureau of Public Affairs, 2201 C St. N.W., Washington, DC 20520 TEL 202-632-1394. (Orders to Supt. of Documents, Washington, DC 20402)

960   UK   ISSN 0001-3196
UNIVERSITY OF ABERDEEN. AFRICAN STUDIES GROUP. BULLETIN. 1967. irreg. (1-2/yr.) exchange basis. University of Aberdeen, African Studies Group, Kings College, Aberdeen AB9 2UB, Scotland. Ed. J.C. Stone. bk. rev. circ. 350. (processed)
African studies

960   UK
UNIVERSITY OF ABERDEEN. AFRICAN STUDIES GROUP. OCCASIONAL PUBLICATIONS. irreg. price varies. University of Aberdeen, African Studies Group, Kings College, Aberdeen AB9 2UB, Scotland.

960   SA
UNIVERSITY OF CAPE TOWN. CENTRE FOR AFRICAN STUDIES. COMMUNICATIONS. 1979. irreg., latest no.9, 1984. R.2.75 per no. University of Cape Town, Centre for African Studies, Rondebosch 7700, South Africa.

960 330.9   KE   ISSN 0547-1788
UNIVERSITY OF NAIROBI. INSTITUTE FOR DEVELOPMENT STUDIES. DISCUSSION PAPERS. 1965. irreg., no.266, 1978. price varies. University of Nairobi, Institute for Development Studies, Box 30197, Nairobi, Kenya. Indexed: Rural Recreat.Tour.Abstr. World Agri.Econ.& Rural Sociol.Abstr.

960 330.9   KE
UNIVERSITY OF NAIROBI. INSTITUTE FOR DEVELOPMENT STUDIES. WORKING PAPERS. irreg., no.353, 1979. University of Nairobi, Institute for Development Studies, Box 30197, Nairobi, Kenya. Indexed: Rural Recreat.Tour.Abstr. World Agri.Econ. & Rural Sociol.Abstr.

968   SA
UNIVERSITY OF THE ORANGE FREE STATE. INSTITUTE FOR CONTEMPORARY HISTORY. ANNUAL REPORT. a. University of the Orange Free State, Institute for Contemporary History - Universiteit van die Oranje-Vrystaat, Instituut vir Eietydse Geskiedenis, Box 2320, Bloemfontein 9300, South Africa.

960   SA
UNIVERSITY OF THE WITWATERSRAND, JOHANNESBURG. AFRICAN STUDIES INSTITUTE. SEMINAR PAPERS. 1979. irreg., (10-12/yr.) R.30. University of Witwatersrand, Johannesburg, African Studies Institute, 1 Jan Smuts Ave., Johannesburg 2001, South Africa. TEL 011-716-2414. circ. 90.

968   UK
UNIVERSITY OF YORK. CENTRE FOR SOUTHERN AFRICAN STUDIES. COLLECTED PAPERS. 1974. irreg., vol.5, 1980. £1 per vol. University of York, Centre for Southern African Studies, Heslington, York YO1 5DD, England. Eds. Anne V. Akeroyd, Christopher R. Hill.

320   GW   ISSN 0341-275X
VEREINIGUNG VON AFRIKANISTEN IN DEUTSCHLAND. SCHRIFTEN. 1969. irreg., vol.10, 1986. price varies. Verlag Helmut Buske, Schlueterstr. 14, 2000 Hamburg 13, W. Germany (B.R.D.)

916.605   NR   ISSN 0083-8144
WEST AFRICA ANNUAL. (Text in English) 1963. a. $25. John West Publications Ltd., John West House, Plot A, Block 2, Acme Rd. OGBA, P.M.B. 21001, Ikeja, Lagos, Nigeria (Dist. in U.S. by: International Publications Service, 114 E. 32nd St., New York, NY 10016) Ed. L.K. Jakende. adv. bk. rev. circ. 5, 000.

WORKING PAPERS IN AFRICAN STUDIES. see *SOCIAL SCIENCES: COMPREHENSIVE WORKS*

960   US   ISSN 0084-2281
WORLD TODAY SERIES: AFRICA. 1966. a. $5.50. Stryker-Post Publications, 888 Seventeenth St., N.W., Washington, DC 20006. TEL 202-342-6055. Ed. Pierre Etienne Dostert. circ. 12,500.

960   ZA   ISSN 0084-4810
ZAMBIA. INFORMATION SERVICES. ANNUAL REPORT.* 1964. a. Information Services, Box RW 50090, Lusaka, Zambia (Orders to: Director, Box 30136, Lusaka, Zambia)

968.94   ZA   ISSN 0084-5124
ZAMBIAN PAPERS. 1938. a. price varies. University of Zambia, Box 32379, Lusaka, Zambia. Eds. M.E. Kashoki, Q.N. Parsons. circ. 1,000.
Supersedes: Rhodes-Livingstone Papers.

968.9 069   RH   ISSN 0301-4347
ZIMBABWE. NATIONAL ARCHIVES. ANNUAL REPORT. 1971. a. free. ‡ National Archives, Private Bag 7729, Causeway, Harare, Zimbabwe. circ. 350.

968.9 069   RH   ISSN 0035-4716
ZIMBABWE. NATIONAL ARCHIVES. OCCASIONAL PAPERS. 1963. irreg. Z.$0.75. ‡ National Archives, Private Bag 7729, Causeway, Harare, Zimbabwe. circ. 750.
Formerly: Southern Rhodesia. National Archives. Occasional Papers.

960   RH   ISSN 0250-3018
ZIMBABWEA. (Text in English) irreg. National Museums and Monuments, P.O. Box 8540, Causeway, Zimbabwe. circ. 350.

968   RH
ZIMBABWEAN HISTORY. (Text in English) 1970. a. $8 to individuals; institutions $10. Historical Association of Zimbabwe, P.O. Box MP 167, Harare, Zimbabwe. Ed. R.D. Roberts. bibl. circ. 1, 000. Indexed: Curr.Cont.Africa. Ind.S.A.Per.
Former titles: Rhodesian History; Journal of Rhodesian History (ISSN 0075-434X)

HISTORY — History Of Asia

see also Oriental Studies

950   US   ISSN 0748-5476
A M S ASIAN STUDIES. 1976. irreg. price varies. A M S Press, Inc., 56 E. 13th St., New York, NY 10003. TEL 212-777-4700. (back issues avail.)

A S A I H L. SEMINAR REPORTS. (Association of Southeast Asian Institutions of Higher Learning) see EDUCATION — Higher Education

958.1   AF   ISSN 0304-6133
AFGHANISTAN REPUBLIC ANNUAL. (Text in English) a. Ministry of Information and Culture, Kabul, Afghanistan. illus.

AFRO-ASIAN PEOPLES' CONFERENCE. PROCEEDINGS. see HISTORY — History Of Africa

AFRO-ASIAN PEOPLES' SOLIDARITY ORGANIZATION. COUNCIL. DOCUMENTS OF THE SESSION. see HISTORY — History Of Africa

959   II   ISSN 0065-6259
ALIGARH MUSLIM UNIVERSITY, ALIGARH, INDIA. DEPARTMENT OF HISTORY. PUBLICATION.* (Text in English) 1963. irreg. price varies. Aligarh Muslim University, Department of History, Aligarh 202002, Uttar Pradesh, India.

954   GW   ISSN 0170-3242
ALT- UND NEU-INDISCHE STUDIEN. irreg., vol.30, 1986. price varies. (Universitaet Hamburg, Seminar fuer Kultur und Geschichte Indiens) Franz Steiner Verlag Wiesbaden GmbH, Birkenwaldstr. 44, Postfach 347, D-7000 Stuttgart 1, W. Germany (B.R.D.) Ed.Bd. Indexed: Rel.Ind.Two.

954   US
AMERICAN INSTITUTE OF INDIAN STUDIES. BIENNIAL REPORT. biennial. American Institute of Indian Studies, Foster Hall, University of Chicago, Chicago, IL 60637. TEL 312-947-1000.
Formerly: A I I S Annual Report (ISSN 0360-3687)

996.1 913   NE   ISSN 0066-1554
ANATOLICA. 1967. a. price varies. Nederlands Instituut voor het Nabije Oosten, Witte Singel 24, Box 9515, 2300 RA Leiden, Netherlands. Ed.Bd. bk. rev. circ. 500. Indexed: M.L.A.

954   II
ANDHRA HISTORICAL RESEARCH SOCIETY. JOURNAL. (Text in English) 1926. a. Department of Archaeology and Museums, Hyderabad 500001, Andhra Pradesh, India (Or: Publications Bureau, Directorate of Government Printing, Chanchalguda, Hyderabad, India) Indexed: Numis.Lit.

ANDHRA PRADESH, INDIA. DEPARTMENT OF ARCHAEOLOGY AND MUSEUMS. EPIGRAPHY SERIES. see ARCHAEOLOGY

ANDHRA PRADESH, INDIA. DEPARTMENT OF ARCHAEOLOGY AND MUSEUMS. MUSEUM SERIES. see NUMISMATICS

ARIZONA STATE UNIVERSITY. CENTER FOR ASIAN STUDIES. MONOGRAPH SERIES. see LITERATURE

950   US
ASIA FOUNDATION. ANNUAL REPORT. 1968. a. free. Asia Foundation, Box 3223, San Francisco, CA 94119. TEL 415-982-4640. Ed. Renata Seidel. illus. circ. 5,000.
Former titles: Asia Foundation. President's Review and Annual Report (ISSN 0732-3085); Asia Foundation. President's Review (ISSN 0587-3606)

950.06   US   ISSN 0098-1214
ASIA SOCIETY. ANNUAL REPORT. a. Asia Society, 725 Park Ave., New York, NY 10021. TEL 212-288-6400. illus. Key Title: Annual Report - Asia Society.

ASIAN AND AFRICAN STUDIES. see ORIENTAL STUDIES

950   JA   ISSN 0454-2150
ASIAN CULTURAL STUDIES. (Text in English or Japanese) 1960. irreg. International Christian University, Institute of Asian Cultural Studies - Kokusai Kirisutokyo Daigaku, 3-10-2 Osawa, Mitaka Tokyo 181, Japan. (Co-sponsor: Institute of Asian Cultural Studies) Ed. Masayoshi Uozumi. bk. rev. illus.

951   CH   ISSN 0571-2939
ASIAN PEOPLES' ANTI-COMMUNIST LEAGUE. CHARTS ABOUT CHINESE COMMUNISTS ON THE MAINLAND. 1955. irreg. $3. World Anti-Communist League, Asian People's Anti-Communist League - China Chapter, 1 Tsingtao East Rd., Taipei, Taiwan, Republic of China.

ASIAN STUDIES ASSOCIATION OF AUSTRALIA. CONFERENCE PAPERS. see ORIENTAL STUDIES

950   US   ISSN 0066-8486
ASIAN STUDIES AT HAWAII MONOGRAPH SERIES. 1965. irreg., no.32, 1985. price varies. (University of Hawaii, Center for Asian and Pacific Studies) University of Hawaii Press, 2840 Kolowalu St., Honolulu, HI 96822. TEL 808-948-8697. Ed. Brian McKnight. (reprint service avail. from UMI, ISI)

950   CN
ASIAN STUDIES MONOGRAPHS SERIES. 1981. irreg. price varies. University of British Columbia Press, 303-6344 Memorial Rd., Vancouver, B.C. V6T 1W5, Canada. TEL 604-228-3259.

959   SZ
ASIAN STUDIES SERIES. (Text in English and French) 1979. irreg. price varies. Universite de Geneve, Institut Universitaire de Hautes Etudes Internationales, Centre Asiatique - University of Geneva, Graduate Institute of International Studies, Asian Centre, Case Postale 53, 1211 Geneva 21, Switzerland. Ed.Bd. circ. 400.
Supersedes (1973-1977, vol.2, no.6-7-8): Centre de Documentation et de Recherche sur l'Asie. Etudes et Documents.

950 960 980   GE   ISSN 0232-8410
ASIEN - AFRIKA - LATEINAMERIKA. JAHRBUCH; Bilanz und Chronik. 1969. a. price varies. (Zentraler Rat fuer Asien-, Afrika- und Lateinamerikawissenschaften in der DDR) VEB Deutscher Verlag der Wissenschaften, Johannes-Dieckmann-Str. 10, Postfach 1216, 1080 Berlin, E. Germany (D.D.R.) Ed. L. Rathmann. bk. rev. Indexed: E.I.
Formerly: Asien - Afrika - Lateinamerika (ISSN 0066-8508)

950   US
ASSOCIATION FOR ASIAN STUDIES. MONOGRAPHS, OCCASIONAL PAPERS AND REFERENCE SERIES. 1951. irreg. price varies. Association for Asian Studies, Inc., University of Michigan, 1 Lane Hall, Ann Arbor, MI 48109. Ed.Bd. (back issues avail.)
Formerly: Association for Asian Studies. Enduring Scholarship. Reference Series.

950   US
ASSOCIATION FOR ASIAN STUDIES. SOUTHEAST CONFERENCE. ANNALS. 1979. a. $6 per vol. Association for Asian Studies, Southeast Region, c/o University of South Carolina, Dept. of Religious Studies, Columbia, SC 29208 TEL 919-684-5073. (Subscr. to: Avinash C. Maheshwary, South Asia Collection, Duke University Library, Durham, NC 27706) Ed. Hal W. French. circ. 200.

954.9   BG
BANGLADESH ITIHAS SAMITI. JOURNAL/ ITIHASA SAMITI PATRIKA. (Text in Bengali or English) no.2, 1973. a. Tk.15. Bangladesh Itihas Samiti, c/o Dept. of History, University of Dacca, Dacca 2, Bangladesh. Ed. Syed Anwar Husain. bk. rev. circ. 1,000.

BEIHEFTE ZUR WIENER ZEITSCHRIFT FUER DIE KUNDE DES MORGENLANDES. see ORIENTAL STUDIES

BEITRAEGE ZUR JAPANOLOGIE. see ORIENTAL STUDIES

950   GW   ISSN 0170-3137
BEITRAEGE ZUR SUEDASIENFORSCHUNG. 1974. irreg. vol.110, 1986. price varies. (Universitaet Heidelberg, Suedasien-Institut) Franz Steiner Verlag Wiesbaden GmbH, Birkenwaldstr. 44, Postfach 347, D-7000 Stuttgart 1, W. Germany (B.R.D.)

952 890 299.56 709   JA   ISSN 0524-0654
BOOKS AND ARTICLES ON ORIENTAL SUBJECTS PUBLISHED IN JAPAN. (Text in English, Japanese) 1956. a. 4500 Yen($25) Toho Gakkai, 2-4-1 Nishi-Kanda, Chiyoda-ku, Tokyo 101, Japan. Ed.Bd. (back issues avail.)

951.5   SK   ISSN 0007-5159
BULLETIN OF TIBETOLOGY.* 1964. irreg. (3-4/yr.) Rs.15. Sikkim Research Institute of Tibetology and Other Studies, Gangtok 737 101, Sikkim. Ed.Bd. Indexed: Hist.Abstr. Amer.Hist.& Life.

954   UK   ISSN 0575-6863
CAMBRIDGE SOUTH ASIAN STUDIES. 1966. irreg., no.29, 1985. $59.50 for latest vol. Cambridge University Press, Edinburgh Bldg., Shaftesbury Rd., Cambridge CB2 2RU, England (and 32 E. 57 St., New York NY 10022) index.

951   UK
CAMBRIDGE STUDIES IN CHINESE HISTORY, LITERATURE AND INSTITUTIONS. 1970. irreg. price varies. Cambridge University Press, Edinburgh Bldg., Shaftesbury Rd., Cambridge CB2 2RU, England (And 32 E. 57th St., New York, NY 10022) Eds. P. Hanan, D. Twitchett.

950 930   UK   ISSN 0068-6891
CAMBRIDGE UNIVERSITY. ORIENTAL PUBLICATIONS. 1956. irreg., no.35, 1985. price varies. (Cambridge University, Faculty of Oriental Languages) Cambridge University Press, Edinburgh Bldg., Shaftesbury Rd., Cambridge CB2 2RU, England (and 32 E. 57 St., New York, NY 10022) index.

951   US
CENTRAL ASIA BOOK SERIES. 1986. irreg. price varies. Duke University Press, 6697 College Sta., Durham, NC 27708. TEL 919-684-2173.

959   UK   ISSN 0269-1760
CENTRE FOR SOUTH-EAST ASIAN STUDIES. BIBLIOGRAPHY AND LITERATURE SERIES. irreg., latest no.3. price varies. Centre for South-East Asian Studies, University of Hull, Cottingham Rd., Hull HU6 7RX, England. Ed. V.T. King.

959   UK   ISSN 0269-1779
CENTRE FOR SOUTH-EAST ASIAN STUDIES. OCCASIONAL PAPERS. 1980. irreg.(approx. 2/yr.) price varies. Centre for South-East Asian Studies, University of Hull, Cottingham Rd., Hull HU6 7RX, England. Ed. V.T. King. circ. 250. (looseleaf format; back issues avail.)

950   MX   ISSN 0066-8249
CENTRO DE ESTUDIOS ORIENTALES. ANUARIO. 1968. a. price varies. Universidad Nacional Autonoma de Mexico, Facultad de Filosofia y Letras, Ciudad Universitaria, Mexico 20, D.F., Mexico. Ed. Lothar Knauth.

958   CE   ISSN 0577-4691
CEYLON HISTORICAL JOURNAL.* (Text in English) 1951. irreg. Tisara Prakaskayo Ltd, 137 Dutugemunu St., Dehiwala, Sri Lanka.

CHINA FACTS AND FIGURES ANNUAL. see POLITICAL SCIENCE

CHINESE HISTORICAL SOCIETY OF AMERICA. ANNIVERSARY BULLETIN. see ETHNIC INTERESTS

CHINESE SCIENCE. see SCIENCES: COMPREHENSIVE WORKS

HISTORY — HISTORY OF ASIA

952　　　　　　IT　　ISSN 0529-7451
CINA. (Includes: Supplements) 1956. irreg., vol.20, 1984. $30. (Istituto Italiano per Il Medio ed Estremo Oriente) Herder Editrice e Libreria S.r.L., Piazza Montecitorio 120, 00186 Rome, Italy. Ed. Lionello Lanciotti.

950　　　　　　IT　　ISSN 0069-4312
CIVILTA ASIATICHE. 1960. irreg., vol.5, 1963. price varies. (Fondazione Giorgio Cini, Centro di Cultura e Civilta) Casa Editrice Leo S. Olschki, 50100 Florence, Italy. circ. 500.

COLUMBIA UNIVERSITY. EAST ASIAN INSTITUTE. STUDIES. see *ORIENTAL STUDIES*

959　　　　　　AT
CONTEMPORARY CHINA PAPERS. 1971. irreg. price varies. (Contemporary China Centre) Australian National University, Research School of Pacific Studies, Box 4, Canberra A.C.T. 2600, Australia. Ed. John Fincher. bibl.

951　　　　　　HK　　ISSN 0069-9535
CONTINENTAL RESEARCH SERIES. (Text in English) 1970. irreg. Continental Research Institute, G.P.O. Box 5699, Hong Kong, Hong Kong.

DECCAN COLLEGE. POSTGRADUATE & RESEARCH INSTITUTE. BULLETIN. see *SOCIAL SCIENCES: COMPREHENSIVE WORKS*

DHANIRAM BHALLA GRANTHAMALA. see *ORIENTAL STUDIES*

954　　　　　　II
DIGEST OF INDOLOGICAL STUDIES. (Text in English) 1963. a. Rs.30. Kurukshetra University, Registrar, Kurukshetra, Haryana, India. Ed. Gopika Mohan Bhattacharya. index.

DIRECTORY OF EAST ASIAN COLLECTIONS IN NORTH AMERICAN LIBRARIES. see *LIBRARY AND INFORMATION SCIENCES*

951　　　　　　US　　ISSN 0362-5028
EARLY CHINA. 1975. a. $10. (Society for the Study of Early China) University of California, Berkeley, Institute of East Asian Studies, 223 Fulton St., Berkeley, CA 94720. TEL 714-833-5011. Ed. Nancy Thompson Price. adv. bk. rev. abstr. bibl. charts. illus. circ. 350(controlled) Indexed: Curr.Cont. Arts & Hum.Cit.Ind.
Supersedes: Society for the Study of Pre-Han China. Newsletter (ISSN 0361-9613)

EAST ASIAN HISTORICAL MONOGRAPHS. see *ORIENTAL STUDIES*

950　　　　　　US
EAST ASIAN SOCIAL SCIENCE MONOGRAPHS. irreg. price varies. Oxford University Press, 200 Madison Ave., New York, NY 10016 TEL 212-679-7300. (And Ely House, 37 Dover St., London W1X 4AH, England)

ERETZ-ISRAEL. ARCHAEOLOGICAL, HISTORICAL AND GEOGRAPHICAL STUDIES. see *ARCHAEOLOGY*

950　　　　　　II　　ISSN 0072-0348
GAZETEER OF INDIA. (3 volume series,; Vol.1: Land and People; Vol.2: History and Culture; Vol.3: Economic Structure and Activities) (Text in English) 1965. irreg. price varies per vol. India Ministry of Education and Social Welfare., Ministry of Information and Broadcasting, Publications Division, Patiala House, Tilak Marg, New Delhi 110001, India (U.S. subscr.: M/S Inter Culture Association, Thompson, CT 06277) Ed. P. N. Chopra. circ. 5,000 (per vol.)

GAZI HUSREVBEGOVA BIBLIOTEKA. ANALI. see *ORIENTAL STUDIES*

952　　　　　　IT
GIAPPONE. 1963. a. $30. (Japanese Institute of Culture) Herder Editrice e Libreria s.r.l., Piazza di Montecitorio 120, 00186 Rome, Italy. Ed. Adolfo Tamburello.

GOETTINGER ORIENTFORSCHUNGEN. REIHE I: SYRIACA. see *ORIENTAL STUDIES*

GOETTINGER ORIENTFORSCHUNGEN. REIHE IV: AEGYPTEN. see *ORIENTAL STUDIES*

951　　　　　　US
HARVARD CONTEMPORARY CHINA SERIES. 1985. irreg., nos.3-4, 1987. $14. Harvard University, Council on East Asian Studies, Cambridge, MA 02138 (Dist. by: Harvard University Press, 79 Garden St., Cambridge, MA 02138)

950　　　　　　US　　ISSN 0073-0483
HARVARD EAST ASIAN MONOGRAPHS. irreg., no.119, 1985. price varies. Harvard University, Council on East Asian Studies, Cambridge, MA 02138 (Distr. by: Harvard University Press, 79 Garden St., Cambridge, MA 02138) Indexed: M.L.A.

950　　　　　　US　　ISSN 0073-0491
HARVARD EAST ASIAN SERIES. (Title varies nos.1-10, 1959-61 Harvard East Asian Studies) 1959. irreg., vol.101, 1986. price varies. (Harvard University, East Asian Research Center) Harvard University Press, 79 Garden St., Cambridge, MA 02138. TEL 617-495-2600. Ed. John K. Fairbank.

959　　　　　　US
HARVARD STUDIES IN AMERICAN-EAST ASIAN RELATIONS. 1972. irreg., no.10, 1985. price varies. Harvard University, Council on East Asian Studies, Cambridge., MA 02138 (Distr. by: Harvard University Press, 79 Garden St., Cambridge, MA 02138)

951　　　　　　US　　ISSN 0073-084X
HARVARD-YENCHING INSTITUTE. MONOGRAPH SERIES. irreg., vol.24, 1985. Harvard University, Council on East Asian Studies, Cambridge, MA 02138 (Distr. by: Harvard University Press, 79 Garden St., Cambridge, MA 02138)

951　　　　　　US　　ISSN 0073-0858
HARVARD-YENCHING INSTITUTE. STUDIES. 1950. irreg., no.29, 1972. price varies. Harvard University Press, 79 Garden St., Cambridge, MA 02138. TEL 617-495-2600.

354.9　　　　　PK
HISTORICAL STUDIES (PAKISTAN) SERIES. 1976. irreg. price varies. National Commission on Historical and Cultural Research, Islamabad, Pakistan.

954　　　　　　SZ
HULL MONOGRAPHS ON SOUTH-EAST ASIA. irreg., no.4, 1971. price varies. Interdocumentation Company, Poststrasse 14, Zug, Switzerland.

954　　　　　　II　　ISSN 0304-7032
INDIAN COUNCIL OF HISTORICAL RESEARCH. ANNUAL REPORT. (Text in English) 1972/73. a. Indian Council of Historical Research, 35 Ferozeshah Rd., New Delhi 110001, India. Key Title: Annual Report - Indian Council of Historical Research.

954　　　　　　II
INDIAN HISTORY AND CULTURE. SERIES. 1984. irreg. Bahri Publications Pvt. Ltd., 57 Sant Nagar (East of Kailash), P.O. Box 7023, New Delhi 110 065, India. Ed. Ujjal Singh Bahri.

INDIAN YEARBOOK OF INTERNATIONAL AFFAIRS. see *POLITICAL SCIENCE — International Relations*

915.95　　　　　MY
INFORMATION MALAYSIA. 1963. a. M.$15. Berita Publishing Sdn. Bhd., 22 Jalan Liku, 59100 Kuala Lumpur, Malaysia (Dist. in U.S. by International Publications Service, 303 Park Ave. South, New York, N.Y. 10010)
Incorporating: Malaysia Year Book (ISSN 0076-339X)

954　　　　　　KO
INQUIRY INTO THE FUTURE. (Text in English or Korean) 1970. a. $5. (Korean Society for Future Studies) Seoul National University Press, Graduate School of Environmental Studies, Rm. 13-211, Seoul National University, Seoul 151, S. Korea. Ed. An-Jae Kim. bk. rev. circ. 200.

954 891.2　　　　II　　ISSN 0073-8352
INSTITUT FRANCAIS D'INDOLOGIE. PUBLICATIONS. 1956. irreg., no.73, 1986. price varies. Institut Francais d'Indologie, B.P. No. 33, Pondicherry 605001, India (Distributor (outside India): Librairie Adrien Maisonneuve, 11 rue Saint Sulpice, 75006 Paris, France) bk. rev. circ. 1,000. Indexed: Bull.Sig.

935 913　　　　NE　　ISSN 0073-8549
INSTITUT HISTORIQUE ET ARCHEOLOGIQUE NEERLANDAIS DE ISTAMBOUL. PUBLICATIONS. (Text in English, French and German) 1956. irreg., 1985, vol.55. price varies. (TU - Netherlands Institute for the Near East) Nederlands Instituut voor Het Nabije Oosten, Witte Singel 24, Box 9515, 2300 RA Leiden, Netherlands. Ed.Bd.

950　　　　　　FR
INSTITUT NATIONAL DES LANGUES ET CIVILISATIONS ORIENTALES. LIVRET DE L'ETUDIANT. 1970. a. 30 F. Universite Paris III - Universite Sorbonne Nouvelle, Institut National des Langues et Civilisations Orientales (INALCO), 4 rue de Lille, 75007 Paris, France. adv. circ. 4,000.

956.94　　　　　LE
INSTITUTE FOR PALESTINE STUDIES. ARABIC ANNUAL DOCUMENTARY SERIES. Variant title: Palestine Documents. (Text in Arabic) 1965. a. $40. Institute for Palestine Studies, Box 11-7164, Beirut, Lebanon (U.S. subscr. to: Georgetown Station, P.O. Box 25301, Washington, D.C. 20007) index.

956.94　　　　　LE　　ISSN 0073-8808
INSTITUTE FOR PALESTINE STUDIES. INTERNATIONAL ANNUAL DOCUMENTARY SERIES. Variant title: International Documents on Palestine. (Text in English) 1967. a. $30. Institute for Palestine Studies, Box 11-7164, Beirut, Lebanon (U.S. subscr. to: Georgetown Station, P.O.Box 25301, Washington, DC 20007)
Formerly: United Nations Annual Documentary Series.

956　　　　　　LE　　ISSN 0073-8816
INSTITUTE FOR PALESTINE STUDIES. MONOGRAPH SERIES. (Text mainly in Arabic; occasionally in English or French) 1966. irreg., no.76, 1986. price varies. Institute for Palestine Studies, Box 11-7164, Beirut, Lebanon (U.S. subscr. to: Georgetown Station, P.O.Box 25301, Washington, DC 20007)

954　　　　　　II
INSTITUTE FOR REWRITING INDIAN HISTORY. ANNUAL REPORT AND GENERAL MEETING INVITATION. (Text in English) 1965. a. $3. Institute for Rewriting Indian History, N-128 Greater Kailash I, New Delhi 110048, India. Ed. P.N. Oak. adv. bk. rev. circ. 2,000.

959　　　　　　SI
INSTITUTE OF SOUTHEAST ASIAN STUDIES. ANNUAL REPORT. (Text in English) 1969. a. free. Institute of Southeast Asian Studies, Heng Mui Keng Terrace, Pasir Panjang, Singapore 0511, Singapore.

959　　　　　　SI
INSTITUTE OF SOUTHEAST ASIAN STUDIES. CURRENT ISSUES SEMINAR SERIES. (Text in English) 1973. irreg., no. 12, 1981. price varies. Institute of Southeast Asian Studies, Heng Mui Keng Terrace, Pasir Panjang, Singapore 0511, Singapore.

959　　　　　　SI
INSTITUTE OF SOUTHEAST ASIAN STUDIES. LOCAL HISTORY AND MEMOIRS. (Text in English) 1973. irreg., no.3, 1983. price varies. Institute of Southeast Asian Studies, Heng Mui Keng Terrace, Pasir Panjang, Singapore 0511, Singapore.
Formerly: Institute of Southeast Asian Studies. Oral History Programmes.

959　　　　　　SI　　ISSN 0073-9731
INSTITUTE OF SOUTHEAST ASIAN STUDIES. OCCASIONAL PAPER. (Text in English) 1970. irreg., no.80, 1987. price varies. Institute of Southeast Asian Studies, Heng Mui Keng Terrace, Pasir Panjang, Singapore 0511, Singapore. Indexed: Bibl.Asian Stud. Geo.Abstr.

HISTORY — HISTORY OF ASIA

959   SI   ISSN 0129-8828
INSTITUTE OF SOUTHEAST ASIAN STUDIES. RESEARCH NOTES AND DISCUSSION SERIES. (Text in English) 1976. irreg., no.62, 1987. price varies. Institute of Southeast Asian Studies, Heng Mui Keng Terrace, Pasir Panjang, Singapore 0511, Singapore.

954   II   ISSN 0074-123X
INTERNATIONAL ACADEMY OF INDIAN CULTURE. SATAPITAKA SERIES. (Text in English) 1957. a. price varies. International Academy of Indian Culture, J-22 Hauzkhas Enclave, New Delhi 110016, India. Ed. Lokesh Chandra. circ. 100.
    Formerly: International Academy of Indian Culture. Report.

956   UK   ISSN 0075-093X
ISLAMIC SURVEYS. 1962. irreg., no.1976. price varies. Edinburgh University Press, 22 George Square, Edinburgh EH8 9LF, Scotland. Ed. Carole Hillenbrand. circ. 4,000.

915.69   IS   ISSN 0075-1413
ISRAEL YEARBOOK. 1950/51. a. $30. Israel Yearbook Publications Ltd., 13 Blum St., P.O. Box 17130, Tel Aviv 61 171, Israel (Dist. in U.S. by International Publications Service, 303 Park Ave. So., New York, N.Y. 10010) Ed.Bd. adv.

952   IT   ISSN 0080-3928
ISTITUTO GIAPPONESE DI CULTURA, ROME. NOTIZIARIO. 1965. a. free. (Kokusai Koryu Kikin) Istituto Giapponese di Cultura in Roma, Via Antonio Gramsci 74, 00197 Roma, Italy. circ. 2,500.

959   MY
JEBAT. 1971/72. a. M.10. National University of Malaysia, Historical Society - Universiti Kebangsaan Malaysia, Persatuan Sejarah, c/o Jabatan Sejarah, Bangi, Kajang, Selangor, Malaysia. Ed.Bd. bk. rev. bibl. illus. circ. 2,000. Indexed: E.I.

954   II   ISSN 0075-4110
JOURNAL OF ANCIENT INDIAN HISTORY. 1967/68. a. Rs.30($6) University of Calcutta, Centre of Advanced Study in Ancient Indian History and Culture, 51-2 Hazra Rd., Calcutta 19, India. Ed. D.C. Sircar. Indexed: Numis.Lit.

JOURNAL OF POLITICAL SCIENCE. see POLITICAL SCIENCE

950 913   GE   ISSN 0075-532X
KEILSCHRIFTURKUNDEN AUS BOGHAZKOEI. 1953. irreg., vol.55, 1985. price varies. (Akademie der Wissenschaften der DDR, Zentralinstitut fuer alte Geschichte und Archaeologie) Akademie-Verlag, Leipziger Str. 3-4, 1086 Berlin, E. Germany (D.D.R.)

959 398   PH   ISSN 0115-6012
KINAADMAN/WISDOM; a journal of the Southern Philippines. 1979. a. P.35($9.50) Xavier University, Cagayan de Oro 8401, Philippines (Dist. in the U.S. by: Cellar Book Shop, 18090 Wyoming, Detroit, MI 48221) Ed. Miguel A. Bernad. bk. rev. bibl. circ. 800. Indexed: Ind.Phil.Per.

951.9   US   ISSN 0145-840X
KOREAN STUDIES. 1977. a. $13.50 per vol. (University of Hawaii, Center for Korean Studies) University of Hawaii Press, 2840 Kolowalu St., Honolulu, HI 96822. TEL 808-948-8697. Ed. Forrest R. Pitts. bk. rev. (reprint service avail. from UMI,ISI) Indexed: Hist.Abstr. Amer.Hist.& Life.

950 490   HU   ISSN 0075-6911
KOROSI CSOMA KISKONYVTAR. 1966. irreg., vol.19, 1985. price varies. (Magyar Tudomanyos Akademia) Akademiai Kiado, Publishing House of the Hungarian Academy of Sciences, Box 24, H-1363 Budapest, Hungary.

930 950   FR
KTEMA; civilisations de l 'Orient, de la Grece et de Rome Antiques. 1976. a. 50 F. Universite de Strasbourg II, Groupe de Recherche d'Histoire Romaine, Association pour l'Etude et la Civilisation Romaine (AECR), Box 350R9, 67009 Strasbourg, France. Eds. Edmond Frezouls, Edmond Levy.

950   PH   ISSN 0459-4835
LIPUNAN JOURNAL. (Text in English and Filipino) 1965. a. $6. University of the Philippines, Asian Center, Diliman, Quezon City 3004, Philippines. bibl. Indexed: Ind.Phil.Per.

954   II   ISSN 0076-2547
MAHARASHTRA ARCHIVES BULLETIN. (Text in English and Marathi) 1962. irreg. price varies. Department of Archives, Governmental Printing and Stationery, Charni Road Gardens, Bombay 400004, Maharashtra, India. Ed. Shri V. G. Khobrekar.

954   II   ISSN 0076-2571
MAHRATTA. (Text in English) 1881. a. Kesari-Mahratta Trust Publication, The Kesari and the Mahratta Office, 568 Narayan, Poona 2, India. Ed. J.S. Tilak.

915.95   MY   ISSN 0301-7095
MALAYSIA IN BRIEF. (Text in English) irreg. Ministry of Foreign Affairs - Kementerian Luar Negeri, Jalan Wisma Putra, Kuala Lumpur, Malaysia. illus. circ. 60,000.

959.5   MY   ISSN 0076-3373
MALAYSIA OFFICIAL YEAR BOOK. (Text in English and Malay) a. $11.50. Government Printer, Jalan Chan Sow Ling, Kuala Lumpur, Malaysia. (Prepared by: Federal Department of Information)

329.9   MY   ISSN 0542-397X
MALAYSIAN CHINESE ASSOCIATION. ANNUAL REPORT. (Text in English) 1963. a. Malaysian Chinese Association, 67, Jln. Ampang, 5th Fl., Kuala Lampur, Malaysia.

950   US   ISSN 0146-6798
MATERIALS AND STUDIES FOR KASSITE HISTORY. 1977. irreg. price varies. University of Chicago, Oriental Institute, 1155 E. 58th St., Chicago, IL 60637. TEL 312-962-9508.

959.7   BE
MESSAGE D'EXTREME-ORIENT. 1971. irreg., no.2, 1977. Librairie-Editions Thanh-Long, 34 rue Dekens, 1040 Brussels, Belgium.

951   US
MICHIGAN MONOGRAPHS IN CHINESE STUDIES. 1968. irreg. (3-4/yr.), no.40, 1980. University of Michigan, Center for Chinese Studies, 104 Lane Hall, Ann Arbor, MI 48109. TEL 313-764-1817. (back issues avail.)
    Incorporating (1970-1979, no.6): Michigan Abstracts of Chinese and Japanese Works on Chinese History (ISSN 0076-7808); Former titles: Michigan Papers in Chinese Studies (ISSN 0076-8065); University of Michigan. Center for Chinese Studies. Occasional Papers.

959   US
MICHIGAN PAPERS ON SOUTH AND SOUTHEAST ASIA. 1970. irreg., no.27, 1985. price varies per vol. University of Michigan, Center for South and Southeast Asian Studies, 130 Lane Hall, Ann Arbor, MI 48109. TEL 313-764-0352. Ed. Janet M. Opdyke. adv. bk. rev.

950   US   ISSN 0076-812X
MICHIGAN STATE UNIVERSITY. ASIAN STUDIES CENTER. OCCASIONAL PAPERS: EAST ASIA SERIES. 1969. irreg., no 9, 1985. Michigan State University, Asian Studies Center, 109 International Center, East Lansing, MI 48824. TEL 517-353-1680. (also avail. in microform from UMI; reprint service avail. from UMI)

950   US   ISSN 0076-8138
MICHIGAN STATE UNIVERSITY. ASIAN STUDIES CENTER. OCCASIONAL PAPERS: SOUTH ASIA SERIES. 1965. irreg., no.36, 1986. Michigan State University, Asian Studies Center, 109 International Center, E. Lansing, MI 48824. TEL 517-353-1680. (also avail. in microform from UMI; reprint service avail. from UMI)

MINDANAO ART & CULTURE. see FOLKLORE

950   CN
MODERN EAST ASIAN STUDIES. 1980. irreg. price varies. University of Toronto Press, Front Campus, Toronto, Ont. M5S 1A6, Canada TEL 613-667-7791. (U.S. address: 33 E. Tupper St., Buffalo, NY 14203)

956   US   ISSN 0077-0027
MODERN MIDDLE EAST SERIES. 1970. irreg., no.4, 1979. Columbia University Press, 562 W. 113th St., New York, NY 10025. TEL 212-678-6777.

959 320   AT
MONASH PAPERS ON SOUTHEAST ASIA. 1972. irreg. price varies. Monash University, Centre of Southeast Asian Studies, Clayton, Victoria 3168, Australia. Ed. David P. Chandler. circ. 300.

951   US   ISSN 0077-0396
MONGOLIA SOCIETY. OCCASIONAL PAPERS. 1964. irreg., no.12, 1986. price varies. Mongolia Society, Inc., 321-322 Goodbody Hall, Indiana University, Bloomington, IN 47405. TEL 812-335-4078. Ed. John R. Krveger. circ. 400.

950   US
MONGOLIA SOCIETY. SPECIAL PAPERS. (Text in Mongolian) 1964. irreg., no.9, 1986. price varies. Mongolia Society, Inc., 321-322 Goodbody Hall, Indiana University, Bloommeton, IN 47405. TEL 812-335-4078. Ed. John Krveger.

951   US
MONGOLIA SOCIETY NEWSLETTER. NEW SERIES. 1950. irreg. Mongolia Society, Inc., 321-322 Goodbody Hall, Indiana University, Bloomington, IN 47405. TEL 812-335-4078. Ed. Ruth I. Meserve.

959   US
MONOGRAPHS IN INTERNATIONAL STUDIES: SOUTHEAST ASIA SERIES. 1968. irreg. price varies. Ohio University, Center for International Studies, Burson House, 56 E. Union St., Athens, OH 45701 TEL 614-594-5511. (Orders to: Ohio Univ. Press, Scott Quad., Athens, OH 45701) Ed. James L. Cobban. bibl. charts. illus. circ. 700. (back issues avail.) Indexed: M.L.A. SSCI.
    Formerly: Papers in International Studies: Southeast Asia Series (ISSN 0078-9119)

MUQARNAS; an annual on Islamic art and architecture. see ART

025.17   MY   ISSN 0076-3381
NATIONAL ARCHIVES OF MALAYSIA. ANNUAL REPORT/ARKIB NEGARA MALAYSIA. LAPORAN TAHUNAN. (Text in Malay and English) 1963. a. M.$3. National Archives, Jalan Duta, Kuala Lumpur 50568, Malaysia, Malaysia.
    Supersedes: Malaya (Federation) Public Records Office and National Archives. Report.

NATIONAL INSTITUTE OF COMPILATION AND TRANSLATION. COLLECTED PAPERS ON HISTORY AND ART OF CHINA. see ART

NEUINDISCHE STUDIEN. see LINGUISTICS

949   US   ISSN 0199-9796
NEW BOOKS ON ASIA ANNOUNCED FOR PUBLICATION IN THE SOVIET UNION. a. University of Illinois, Urbana, Center for Asian Studies, 1208 W. California, Urbana, IL 61801. TEL 217-333-1000.

950   II   ISSN 0078-0855
NITYANAND UNIVERSAL SERIES. (Text in Hindi and Sanskrit) 1960. irreg., vol.11, 1976. price varies. Vishveshvaranand Vedic Research Institute, P. O. Sadhu Ashram, Hoshiarpur 146021, Punjab, India. Ed. S. Bhaskaran Nair.

959   US
NORTHERN ILLINOIS UNIVERSITY. CENTER FOR SOUTHEAST ASIAN STUDIES. OCCASIONAL PAPERS SERIES. 1974. irreg., no.12, 1986. price varies. Northern Illinois University, Center for Southeast Asian Studies, DeKalb, IL 60115 TEL 815-753-1771. (Dist. by Cellar Bookshop, 18090 Wyoming, Detroit MI 48221) Ed. Ronald Provencher. circ. 450.

959   US   ISSN 0073-4934
NORTHERN ILLINOIS UNIVERSITY. CENTER FOR SOUTHEAST ASIAN STUDIES. SPECIAL REPORT SERIES. 1969. irreg., no.24, 1986. price varies. Northern Illinois University, Center for Southeast Asian Studies, De Kalb, IL 60115 TEL 815-753-1771. (Dist. by Cellar Bookshop, 18090 Wyoming, Detroit, MI 48221) Ed. Ronald Provencher. adv. circ. 450.

HISTORY — HISTORY OF ASIA

OCCASIONAL PAPERS/REPRINT SERIES IN CONTEMPORARY ASIAN STUDIES. see *LAW*

950 US ISSN 0146-678X
ORIENTAL INSTITUTE COMMUNICATIONS. 1922. irreg., vol. 23, 1978. price varies. University of Chicago, Oriental Institute, 1155 E. 58th St., Chicago, IL 60637. TEL 312-962-9508.

950 JA ISSN 0082-562X
ORIENTAL LIBRARY. RESEARCH DEPARTMENT. MEMOIRS/ZAIDAN HOJIN TOYO BUNKO. (Text in English) 1926. a. 4500 Yen($18) Oriental Library - Toyo Bunko, 2-28-21 Honkomagome, Bunkyo-ku, Tokyo 113, Japan. Ed. Kazuo Enoki. circ. 500.

950 935 IS ISSN 0078-6543
ORIENTAL NOTES AND STUDIES. 1949. irreg. price varies. Israel Oriental Society, Hebrew University, Jerusalem, Israel. Ed. Alton Layish. bk. rev. circ. 1,500.

950 PK ISSN 0078-8481
PAKISTAN. SURVEY OF PAKISTAN. GENERAL REPORT. (Text in English) a. Survey of Pakistan, Office of the Director Map Publication, Post Box 10, Rawalpindi, Pakistan. circ. controlled.

954.7 PK ISSN 0078-8171
PAKISTAN HISTORICAL SOCIETY. MEMOIR. (Text in English) 1953. a. Rs.100. Pakistan Historical Society, 30 New Karachi Co-operative Housing Society, Karachi 5, Pakistan. adv. circ. 1, 000. (back issues avail.)

954.7 PK ISSN 0078-818X
PAKISTAN HISTORICAL SOCIETY. PROCEEDINGS OF THE PAKISTAN HISTORY CONFERENCE. (Text in English) 1953. a. Rs.100. Pakistan Historical Society, 30 New Karachi Co-operative Housing Society, Karachi 5, Pakistan. adv. bk. rev. circ. 1,000. (back issues avail.)

930 NE ISSN 0079-0893
PERSICA. (Text in English, French and German) 1963. a. fl.125. Genootschap Nederland-Iran - Netherlands-Iranian Society, c/o K. B. Kremer, Ed., Rozemarijntuin 47, Leiderdorp, Netherlands. adv. bk. rev. circ. 1,000. (back issues avail.)

950 US
PERSPECTIVES IN ASIAN HISTORY.* 1976. irreg. price varies. Porcupine Press, Inc., 310 S. Juniper St., Philadelphia, PA 19107-5818.

PHILIPPINES CHINESE HISTORICAL ASSOCIATION. ANNALS. see *POLITICAL SCIENCE — International Relations*

959.9 915.06 US
PILIPINAS; an interdisciplinary scholarly journal of Philippine studies. 1980. irreg., no.5, 1985. $6 to individuals; institutions $12. Association for Asian Studies, Southeast Asia Council, Philippine Studies Group, c/o Carl Lande, Ed., Department of Political Science, University of Kansas, Lawrence, KS 66045 TEL 716-381-5554. (Subscr. to: Mrs. Elizabeth H. Flory, Bus. Mgr., 36 Dogwood Glen, Rochester, NY 14625-1899) adv. bk. rev. circ. 150. Indexed: HR Rep.
Formerly (until 1983): Filipinas.

956 490 GW ISSN 0079-7707
PUBLICATIONS IN NEAR AND MIDDLE EAST STUDIES. SERIES A. irreg. price varies. (Columbia University, Department of Middle East Languages and Cultures, US) Walter de Gruyter & Co., Mouton Publishers, Postfach 110240, D-1000 Berlin 11, W. Germany (B.R.D.) (U.S. addr.: Mouton Publishers, division of Walter de Gruyter, Inc., 200 Saw Mill River Road, Hawthorne, NY 10532) (Co-sponsor: Middle East Institute)

PUBLICATIONS IN NEAR AND MIDDLE EAST STUDIES. SERIES B. see *LINGUISTICS*

PUNJAB UNIVERSITY INDOLOGICAL SERIES. see *ORIENTAL STUDIES*

PURUSHARTHA. see *SOCIAL SCIENCES: COMPREHENSIVE WORKS*

954 II ISSN 0079-9572
RAJASTHAN YEAR BOOK AND WHO'S WHO. (Text in English) 1962. a. Rs.60. Samriddhi Publications, C-5 Bapunagar, Jaipur 302 015, India. Ed. Milap Chand Dandia. adv. circ. 2,000.

950 GW ISSN 0340-6687
RUHR-UNIVERSITAET BOCHUM. OSTASIEN INSTITUT. VEROEFFENTLICHUNGEN. irreg., vol.36, 1986. price varies. Verlag Otto Harrassowitz, Taunusstr. 14, Postfach 2929, 6200 Wiesbaden 1, W. Germany (B.R.D.) Ed. Rudolf Herzer.

958 NE ISSN 0080-4916
RUSSIAN SERIES ON SOCIAL HISTORY. 1970. irreg. price varies. (International Institute for Social History) D. Reidel Publishing Co., Postbus 17, 3300 AA Dordrecht, Netherlands (And 190 Old Derby St., Hingham, MA 02043) Ed. Boris Sapir.

958 II ISSN 0080-6137
SANTAKUTI VEDIC RESEARCH SERIES. (Text in English and Sanskrit) 1935. irreg., no.24, 1972. price varies. Vishveshvaranand Vedic Research Institute, P. O. Sadhu Ashram, Hoshiarpur 146021, Punjab, India. Ed. Vishva Bandhu.

950 II ISSN 0080-6471
SARVADANAND UNIVERSAL SERIES. (Text in English, Hindi and Sanskrit) 1950. irreg., vol.67, 1976. price varies. Vishvshvaranand Vedic Research Institute, P. O. Sadhu Ashram, Hoshiarpur 146021, Punjab, India. Ed. S. Bhaskaran Nair.

950 US
SCHOOL OF INTERNATIONAL STUDIES. PUBLICATIONS ON ASIA. Title varies: Studies on Asia. 1952. irreg., no.36, 1983. price varies. (University of Washington, School of International Studies) University of Washington Press, Seattle, WA 98105. TEL 206-543-4050.
Formerly: Publications on Asia (ISSN 0079-7782)

950 GE ISSN 0080-6994
SCHRIFTEN ZUR GESCHICHTE UND KULTUR DES ALTEN ORIENTS. 1971. irreg., vol.17, 1984. price varies. (Akademie der Wissenschaften der D.D.R., Zentralinstitut fuer Alte Geschichte und Archaeologie) Akademie-Verlag, Leipziger Str. 3-4, 1086 Berlin, E. Germany (D.D.R.)

954 890 II ISSN 0254-0215
SERIES IN SIKH HISTORY AND CULTURE. 1979. irreg. price varies. Bahri Publications Pvt.Ltd., 57 Santnagar (East of Kailash), Box 7023, New Delhi 110065, India. Ed. Ujjal Singh Bahri.

959.5 SI ISSN 0080-9691
SINGAPORE FACTS AND PICTURES. (Text in English) 1961. a. S.$2.50($4) Ministry of Communications & Information, Information Division, 4th Storey, Govt. Offices, St. Andrew's Road, Singapore 0617, Singapore. Ed. Ng Poey Siong. circ. 50,000. (back issues avail.)

951 NE
SINICA LEIDENSIA. 1938. irreg., vol.17, 1985. price varies. E.J. Brill, P.O. Box 9000, 2300 PA Leiden, Netherlands.

SINOLOGICA COLONIENSIA; Ostasiatische Beitraege der Universitaet zu Koeln. see *ORIENTAL STUDIES*

SLAVISTIC PRINTING AND REPRINTINGS. see *LITERATURE*

954 572 301 AT ISSN 0085-6401
SOUTH ASIA: JOURNAL OF SOUTH ASIAN STUDIES. 1971. a. Aus.$30($16) South Asian Studies Association, c/o Department of History, University of New England, Armidale, N.S.W. 2351, Australia. Ed. S. Arasaratnam. adv. bk. rev. circ. 450. (back issues avail.) Indexed: Aus.P.A.I.S.

SOUTH ASIAN STUDIES. see *ORIENTAL STUDIES*

991 SI ISSN 0081-2897
SOUTH SEAS SOCIETY. MONOGRAPH. (Text in Chinese and English) 1959. irreg., no. 24, 1982. price varies. ‡ South Seas Society, P. O. Box 709, Singapore, Singapore. Ed. Gwee Yee Hean. circ. 1, 000.

959 UK
SOUTHEAST ASIAN AFFAIRS. (Text in English) 1974. a. £29.50($41.50) (Institute of Southeast Asian Studies) Gower Publishing Co. Ltd., Gower House, Croft Rd., Aldershot, Hants GU11 3HR, England (U.S. address: Heinemann Educational Books Inc, 4 Front St., Exeter, NH 03833) Ed.Bd. circ. 2,000.

950 MY ISSN 0085-6509
SOUTHEAST ASIAN ARCHIVES. (Text in English) 1968. a. M.15. Southeast Asian Regional Branch, International Council on Archives, c/o National Archives of Malaysia, Jalan Duta, Kuala Lumpur, Malaysia. Ed. Hassan Mohd. adv. bk. rev. Indexed: E.I.

959 SI
SOUTHEAST ASIAN PERSPECTIVE SERIES. (Text in English) 1973. irreg., no. 4, 1978. price varies. Institute of Southeast Asian Studies, Heng Mui Keng Terrace, Pasir Panjang, Singapore 0511, Singapore.

950 490 II ISSN 0081-3907
SRI VENKATESWARA UNIVERSITY. ORIENTAL JOURNAL. (Text in English, Hindi, Sanskrit, Tamil and Telugu) 1958. a. (issued in 2 pts.) Rs.15($4) Sri Venkateswara University, Oriental Research Institute, Tirupati 517502, District Chittoor, India. Ed. S. Sankaranarayanan. bk. rev. cum.index: vols.1-10 (1958-67)

959 808 US
STONE LION REVIEW. 1978/79. a. $4. Harvard-Yenching Institute, Harvard University, 2 Divinity Ave., Cambridge, MA 02138. Ed. Elise DeVido. adv. bk. rev. circ. 400.

STUDI CLASSICI E ORIENTALI. see *CLASSICAL STUDIES*

956 410 GW ISSN 0341-4191
STUDIEN ZUR INDOLOGIE UND IRANISTIK. (Text in English, French and German) 1975. a. DM.30. Dr. Inge Wezler Verlag fuer Orientalistische Fachpublikationen, Bernhard-Ihnen-Str. 18, D-2057 Reinbek, W. Germany (B.R.D.) Ed.Bd. circ. 225.

952 GW ISSN 0585-6094
STUDIEN ZUR JAPANOLOGIE. 1959. irreg., vol.15, 1982. price varies. Verlag Otto Harrassowitz, Taunusstr. 14, Postfach 2929, 6200 Wiesbaden 1, W. Germany (B.R.D.) Ed. Horst Hammitzsch.

931 US ISSN 0081-7554
STUDIES IN ANCIENT ORIENTAL CIVILIZATION. 1931. irreg., no.42, 1985. price varies. University of Chicago, Oriental Institute, 1155 E. 58th St., Chicago, IL 60637. TEL 312-962-9508.

930 390 US ISSN 0081-8321
STUDIES IN ORIENTAL CULTURE. 1967. irreg., no. 14, latest. Columbia University Press, 562 W. 113th St., New York, NY 10025. TEL 212-678-6777.

954 II
STUDIES IN RAJPUT HISTORY AND CULTURE SERIES. 1976. irreg. Rs.50. Bharatiya Publishing House, 42-43 U. B. Jawahar Nagar, Delhi 110007, India. bibl. circ. 1,100.

STUDIES OF CLASSICAL INDIA. see *PHILOSOPHY*

STUDIES ON SOUTHEAST ASIA. see *ORIENTAL STUDIES*

SUI YUAN WEN HSIEN. see *ORIENTAL STUDIES*

900 II
SWARBICA JOURNAL. (Text in English) 1978. a. Rs.15. International Council of Archives, South and West Asian Regional Branch, c/o National Archives of India, Janpath, New Delhi 110001, India.

959.3 TH
THAILAND NATIONAL DIRECTORY.* a. Advance Media Co., Ltd., U Chuliang Bldg., 968 Rama IV Rd., Bangkok, Thailand.

TIBET SOCIETY. JOURNAL. see *ORIENTAL STUDIES*

954 II ISSN 0082-4445
TIMES OF INDIA DIRECTORY AND YEARBOOK INCLUDING WHO'S WHO. (Text in English) a. $25. Bennett, Coleman & Co., Ltd. (Bombay), Times Bldg., Dr. D.N. Rd., Bombay 400001, India (U.S. subscr.: M/s. Kalpana, 42-75 Main St., Flushing, NY 11355) Ed. Girilal Jain. index.

572 HISTORY — HISTORY OF AUSTRALASIA AND OTHER AREAS

950   CN   ISSN 0082-5123
TORONTO SEMITIC TEXTS AND STUDIES. 1971. irreg. price varies. University of Toronto Press, Front Campus, Toronto, Ont. M5S 1A6, Canada. TEL 613-667-7791.

959   SI   ISSN 0082-6316
TRENDS IN SOUTHEAST ASIA. (Text in English) 1971. irreg., no.9, 1986. price varies. Institute of Southeast Asian Studies, Heng Mui Keng Terrace, Pasir Panjang, Singapore 0511, Singapore. Indexed: Bibl.Asian Stud.

950 956   US
U.S. DEPARTMENT OF STATE. NEAR EAST AND SOUTH ASIAN SERIES. 1948. irreg. price varies. U.S. Department of State, Bureau of Public Affairs, Washington, DC 20250 TEL 202-655-4000. (Orders to Supt. of Documents, Washington, DC 20402)
   Supersedes: U.S. Department of State. Near and Middle Eastern Series (ISSN 0083-0151)

950   GW   ISSN 0440-601X
UNIVERSITAET HEIDELBERG. SUEDASIEN-INSTITUT. SCHRIFTENREIHE. (Text in English and German) irreg., vol.30, 1983. price varies. Franz Steiner Verlag Wiesbaden GmbH, Birkenwaldstr. 44, Postfach 347, D-7000 Stuttgart 1, W. Germany (B.R.D.)

UNIVERSITAET ZU KOELN. KUNSTHISTORISCHES INSTITUT. ABTEILUNG ASIEN. PUBLIKATIONEN. see *ART*

950   BE   ISSN 0076-1265
UNIVERSITE CATHOLIQUE DE LOUVAIN. INSTITUT ORIENTALISTE. PUBLICATIONS. Short title: P.I.O.L. Variant title: Institute Orientaliste de Louvain. Publications. 1970. irreg., no.34, 1986. price varies. Universite Catholique de Louvain, Institut Orientaliste, College Erasme, Place Blaise Pascal 1, B-1348 Louvain-la-Neuve, Belgium. adv. Indexed: Rel.Ind.Two.
   Supersedes (1932-1968): Bibliotheque du Museon.

954   II   ISSN 0068-5380
UNIVERSITY OF CALCUTTA. CENTRE OF ADVANCED STUDY IN ANCIENT INDIAN HISTORY AND CULTURE. LECTURES. 1965. irreg. price varies. University of Calcutta, Centre of Advanced Study in Ancient Indian History and Culture, 51-2 Hazra Rd., Calcutta 19, West Bengal, India.

954   II   ISSN 0068-5399
UNIVERSITY OF CALCUTTA. CENTRE OF ADVANCED STUDY IN ANCIENT INDIAN HISTORY AND CULTURE. PROCEEDINGS OF SEMINARS. 1966, vol. 2. irreg., 1973, vol. 11. price varies. University of Calcutta, Centre of Advanced Study in Ancient Indian History and Culture, 51-2 Hazra Rd., Calcutta 19, West Bengal, India.

950   US   ISSN 0068-600X
UNIVERSITY OF CALIFORNIA. CENTER FOR SOUTH AND SOUTHEAST ASIA STUDIES. OCCASIONAL PAPERS. 1969. irreg., no. 11, 1973. University Press of America, 4720 Boston Way, Lanham, MD 20706. TEL 301-459-3366.

950   US   ISSN 0068-6018
UNIVERSITY OF CALIFORNIA. CENTER FOR SOUTH AND SOUTHEAST ASIA STUDIES. RESEARCH MONOGRAPH SERIES. 1970. irreg., latest no.28, 1985. University Press of America, 4720 Boston Way, Lanham, MD 20706. TEL 301-459-3366. bibl. index.

956   US   ISSN 0068-6514
UNIVERSITY OF CALIFORNIA PUBLICATIONS. NEAR EASTERN STUDIES. irreg. price varies. University of California Press, 2120 Berkeley Way, Berkeley, CA 94720. TEL 415-642-4247.

950   US   ISSN 0069-3367
UNIVERSITY OF CHICAGO ORIENTAL INSTITUTE. PUBLICATIONS. 1924. irreg., vol.105, 1983. price varies. University of Chicago, Oriental Institute, 1155 E. 58th St., Chicago, IL 60637. TEL 312-962-9508. (also avail. in microfiche)

950 100   US   ISSN 0070-8070
UNIVERSITY OF KANSAS. CENTER FOR EAST ASIAN STUDIES. INTERNATIONAL STUDIES: EAST ASIAN SERIES. REFERENCE SERIES. 1967. irreg., no.2, 1975. price varies. University of Kansas, Center for East Asian Studies, 105 Lippincott Hall, Lawrence, KS 66045. TEL 913-864-3849.

950 100   US   ISSN 0070-8062
UNIVERSITY OF KANSAS. CENTER FOR EAST ASIAN STUDIES. INTERNATIONAL STUDIES: EAST ASIAN SERIES. RESEARCH SERIES. 1967. irreg., no.11, 1984. price varies. University of Kansas, Center for East Asian Studies, 105 Lippincott Hall, Lawrence, KS 66044. TEL 913-864-3849.

950   II   ISSN 0076-2229
UNIVERSITY OF MADRAS. HISTORICAL SERIES.* 1919. irreg. University of Madras, Chepauk, Triplicane, Madras 600005, Tamil Nadu, India.

951   SI   ISSN 0080-9667
UNIVERSITY OF SINGAPORE. CHINESE SOCIETY. JOURNAL.* (Text in Chinese and English) 1961. a. M.$2. University of Singapore, Chinese Society, c/o Dept. of Chinese Studies, Cluny Rd., Singapore 10, Singapore.

950   SI   ISSN 0217-913X
UNIVERSITY OF SINGAPORE. HISTORY SOCIETY. JOURNAL. 1963. a. S.$1.50. National University of Singapore, History Dept., History Society, Kent Ridge, Singapore 0511, Singapore. Ed. Ronald Hee. adv. cum index. circ. controlled. Indexed: Hist.Abstr. Amer.Hist.& Life.

950   PH   ISSN 0079-9238
UNIVERSITY OF THE PHILIPPINES. ASIAN CENTER. MONOGRAPH SERIES. (Text in English) 1965. irreg. price varies. ‡ University of the Philippines, Asian Center, Diliman, Quezon City 3004, Philippines. circ. 500.

950   PK   ISSN 0079-8029
UNIVERSITY OF THE PUNJAB. ARABIC AND PERSIAN SOCIETY. JOURNAL.* (Text in English, Arabic or Persian) a. University of the Punjab, Arabic and Persian Society, Lahore, Pakistan.

959.7   VN   ISSN 0085-7823
VIETNAMESE STUDIES.* vol. 8, 1972. irreg. Vietnamese Studies, Xunhasaba 32, Hai Ba Trung, Socialist Republic of Vietnam, Vietnam. Ed. Nguyen Khac Vien. illus.

VISHVA VICHARAMALA. see *ORIENTAL STUDIES*

954   II   ISSN 0083-6613
VISHVESHVARANAND INDOLOGICAL PAPER SERIES. (Text in English, Hindi and Sanskrit) 1950. irreg., no. 325, 1977. price varies. Vishvshvaranand Vedic Research Institute, P. O. Sadhu Ashram, Hoshiarpur 146021, Punjab, India. Ed. S. Bhaskaran Nair.

VISHVESHVARANAND INDOLOGICAL SERIES. see *LINGUISTICS*

VISHVESHVARANAND VEDIC RESEARCH INSTITUTE. RESEARCH AND GENERAL PUBLICATIONS. see *ORIENTAL STUDIES*

954   NP
VOICE OF HISTORY. (Text in English or Nepali) 1975. a. Rs.10.50. (Tribhuvan University History Association) Tribhuvan University, Kirtipur, Nepal. Ed. K.B. Thape. adv. bk. rev. bibl.

956.1 330 950   NE   ISSN 0075-2118
VOORAZIATISCH-EGYPTISCH GENOOTSCHAP "EX ORIENTE LUX". JAARBERICHT; annuaire de la Societe Orientale Neerlandaise "Ex Oriente Lux". Short title: Jaarbericht "Ex Oriente Lux". 1933. biennial. fl.60($30) Vooraziatysch-Egyptisch Genootschap "Ex Oriente Lux" - Societe Orientale Neerlandaise "Ex Oriente Lux", Postbus 9515, 2300 RA Leiden, Netherlands. Ed. K. R. Veenhof. circ. 800.

935 330 950   NE
VOORAZIATISCH-EGYPTISCH GENOOTSCHAP "EX ORIENTE LUX". MEDEDELINGEN EN VERHANDLINGEN. (Text in English, French, German, Dutch) no. 5, 1943. irreg. price varies. Vooraziatisch-Egyptisch Genootschap "Ex Oriente Lux", Postbus 9515, 2300 RA Leiden, Netherlands. Ed. K.R. Veenhof.
   Formerly: Mededelingen "Ex Oriente Lux" (ISSN 0081-1211)

WIENER ZEITSCHRIFT FUER DIE KUNDE SUEDASIENS UND ARCHIV FUER INDISCHE PHILOSPHIE. see *PHILOSOPHY*

951   US   ISSN 0084-053X
WISCONSIN CHINA SERIES. (Text in English and Chinese) 1966. irreg., latest, no. 3. $3. University of Wisconsin-Madison, Department of East Asian Languages and Literature, 1212 Van Hise Hall, Madison, WI 53706. TEL 608-262-2291. Ed. Tse-tsung Chow.

959   US
WISCONSIN PAPERS ON SOUTHEAST ASIA. 1979. irreg. $3. University of Wisconsin-Madison, Center for Southeast Asian Studies, Madison, WI 53706. Ed. Daniel Doeppers.

950 980   US
WORLD TODAY SERIES: EAST ASIA AND THE WESTERN PACIFIC. 1968. a. $5.50. Stryker-Post Publications, 888 17th St., N.W., Washington, DC 20006. TEL 202-342-6055. Ed. Harold C. Hinton. circ. 12,500.
   Formerly: World Today Series: Far East and Southwest Pacific (ISSN 0084-229X)

950   US   ISSN 0084-2311
WORLD TODAY SERIES: MIDDLE EAST AND SOUTH ASIA. 1967. a. $5.50. Stryker-Post Publications, 888 Seventeenth St., N.W., Washington, DC 20006. TEL 202-342-6055. Ed. Ray L. Cleveland. circ. 12,500.

959   US   ISSN 0084-3466
YALE SOUTHEAST ASIA STUDIES. 1965. irreg., no.8, 1978. price varies. Yale University Press, 92A Yale Sta., New Haven, CT 06520. TEL 203-432-0940.

950   GW   ISSN 0514-857X
ZENTRALASIATISCHE STUDIEN. 1967. a. price varies. (Seminar fuer Sprach- und Kulturwissenschaft Zentralasiens) Verlag Otto Harrassowitz, Taunusstr. 14, Postfach 2929, 6200 Wiesbaden 1, W. Germany (B.R.D.) Eds. Walther Heissig, Michael Weiers. adv. bk. rev. circ. 380. (back issues avail.)

HISTORY — History Of Australasia And Other Areas

ABORIGINAL HISTORY. see *ANTHROPOLOGY*

994   AT   ISSN 0084-6732
ARMIDALE AND DISTRICT HISTORICAL SOCIETY. JOURNAL AND PROCEEDINGS. 1961. a. membership. Armidale and District Historical Society, c/o Secretary, P.O. Box 692, Armidale, N.S.W. 2350, Australia. Ed.Bd. bk. rev. circ. 400. Indexed: Hist.Abstr. Amer.Hist. & Life.

994   AT   ISSN 0082-2116
AUSTRALIA. BUREAU OF STATISTICS. TASMANIAN OFFICE. TASMANIAN YEAR BOOK. 1967. a. Aus.$20.75. Australian Bureau of Statistics, Tasmanian Office, Box 66A, G.P.O., Hobart, Tasmania 7001, Australia. Ed. D. Maclaine. index. circ. 2,700.

AUSTRALIA. BUREAU OF STATISTICS. VICTORIAN OFFICE. NATIONAL SCHOOLS STATISTICS, VICTORIA. see *EDUCATION*

309.1   AT
AUSTRALIA. DEPARTMENT OF HOME AFFAIRS. NORFOLK ISLAND ANNUAL REPORT. a. price varies. Australian Government Publishing Service, G.P.O. Box 84, Canberra, 2600 A.C.T., Australia. illus. stat.
   Formerly: Australia. Department of Territory of Norfolk Island. Report (ISSN 0572-0494)

HISTORY — HISTORY OF EUROPE

994   AT   ISSN 0067-1495
AUSTRALIA HANDBOOK. 1969. a. price varies. Australian Government Publishing Service, Sales and Distribution Branch, G.P.O. Box 84, Canberra, A.C.T. 2601, Australia.

994   AT   ISSN 0084-7259
AUSTRALIAN CATHOLIC HISTORICAL SOCIETY. JOURNAL. 1954. a. Aus.$3. Australian Catholic Historical Society, 154 Elizabeth St., Sydney, N.S.W. 2000, Australia. Ed. A. Cahill. adv. bk. rev. circ. 300. Indexed: Hist.Abstr. Amer.Hist.& Life. Aus.P.A.I.S.

990   AT   ISSN 0728-8433
AUSTRALIAN CULTURAL HISTORY. 1982. a. Aus.$10($7) Australian National University, Research School of Social Sciences, History of Ideas Unit, G.P.O. Box 4, Canberra, A.C.T. 2601, Australia. Ed. S.L. Goldberg. circ. 500. (back issues avail.)

994   NE   ISSN 0067-7876
BIBLIOTHECA AUSTRALIANA. 1967. irreg., vol. 76, 1976. price varies. Nico Isreal Publishing Co., Keizersgracht 489, 1017 DM Amsterdam, Netherlands. circ. 500.

990   AT   ISSN 0310-1584
CABBAGES AND KINGS. 1973. a. South Australian College of Advanced Education, Department of History and Australian Studies, 15 Lorne Ave., Magill, SA 5072, Australia. Ed. Elizabeth Milburn. circ. 50.

COLLECTION OF AUSTRALIAN STAMPS. see *PHILATELY*

994   AT   ISSN 0080-4738
EARLY DAYS. 1926. a. Aus.$10. ‡ Royal Western Australian Historical Society, 49 Broadway, Nedlands, 6009 WA, Australia. Ed. Ray Oldham. circ. 1,500. Indexed: Aus. P.A.I.S.
Formerly: Royal Western Australian Historical Society. Journal and Proceedings.

950 999   UK   ISSN 0071-3791
FAR EAST AND AUSTRALASIA. 1969. a. $155. Europa Publications Ltd., 18 Bedford Sq., London WC1B 3JN, England.

990 320   AT   ISSN 0726-7215
FLINDERS JOURNAL OF HISTORY AND POLITICS. 1969. irreg. Aus.$4 to individuals; students Aus.$0.80. Flinders University of South Australia, History and Politics Society, School of Social Sciences, Bedford Park, S. A. 5042, Australia. Ed.Bd. adv. bk. rev. circ. 400. Indexed: Hist.Abstr. Amer.Hist.& Life. Aus.P.A.I.S.

990   US
HAWAIIAN HISTORICAL SOCIETY. ANNUAL REPORT. 1893. a. membership only. Hawaiian Historical Society, 560 Kawaiahao St., Honolulu, HI 96813. TEL 808-537-6271. (back issues avail.) Indexed: Hist.Abstr. Amer.Hist.& Life.

990   US   ISSN 0440-5145
HAWAIIAN JOURNAL OF HISTORY; devoted to the history of Hawaii, Polynesia and the Pacific area. 1967. a. $10. Hawaiian Historical Society, 560 Kawaiahao St., Honolulu, HI 96813. TEL 808-537-6271. illus. circ. 1,000(controlled) Indexed: Hist.Abstr. Amer.Hist.& Life.

990   AT   ISSN 0311-8924
HISTORICAL JOURNAL. 1975. irreg. Wollongong University, Historical Society, Box 1144, Wollongong, N.S.W. 2500, Australia. Ed. C.J. Krawczyk. circ. 1,000. Indexed: Br.Hum.Ind. Curr.Cont. Hum.Ind. Arts & Hum.Cit.Ind. CERDIC. Rel.Ind.One.

HOCKEN LECTURE. see *ANTHROPOLOGY*

991.4   PH   ISSN 0019-2538
ILOCOS REVIEW. 1969. a. P.60($5) Immaculate Conception School of Theology, Archdiocesan Major Seminary, Vigan, Ilocos Sur 0401, Philippines. bk. rev. bibl. charts. illus. index. circ. 300. Indexed: Ind.Phil.Per.

999   CL   ISSN 0073-9871
INSTITUTO ANTARTICO CHILENO. CONTRIBUTION. SERIE CIENTIFICA. (Text in Spanish; summaries in English) 1964; N.S. 1969. irreg., no. 26, 1980. available on exchange. Instituto Antartico Chileno, Luis Thayer Ojeda 814, Casilla 16521, Correo 9, Santiago, Chile. Ed. Patricio Eberhard. circ. 600.
Supersedes: Instituto Antartico Chileno. Publicacion.

990   AT   ISSN 0814-5296
MANSFIELD HISTORICAL SOCIETY'S MAGAZINE. 1983. a. Aus.$5. Mansfield Historical Society, P.O. Box 309, Mansfield, VIC 3722, Australia. Ed. Mark Klingsporn. adv. bk. rev. illus. circ. 400. (back issues avail.)

994   AT   ISSN 0076-6232
MELBOURNE HISTORICAL JOURNAL. 1961. a. Aus.$3 to individuals; Aus.$4.50 to institutions. Melbourne Historical Journal Society, Dept. of History, University of Melbourne, Parkville, Vic. 3052, Australia. Ed.Bd. adv. bk. rev. circ. 500. Indexed: Hist.Abstr. Amer.Hist.& Life.

MUSEUM FUER VOELKERKUNDE, BERLIN. VEROEFFENTLICHUNGEN. NEUE FOLGE. ABTEILUNG: SUEDSEE. see *ANTHROPOLOGY*

994   AT
NATIONAL TRUST OF AUSTRALIA (W.A.) ANNUAL REPORT. 1958. a. free. National Trust of Australia (W.A.), 14 Havelock St., West Perth, W.A. 6005, Australia. adv. bk. rev. circ. 2,000.

919.31   NZ   ISSN 0078-0170
NEW ZEALAND OFFICIAL YEAR-BOOK. 1892. a. NZ.$39.60. Department of Statistics, Private Bag, Wellington, New Zealand (Subscr. to: Government Printing Office, Publications, Private Bag, Wellington, New Zealand) circ. 8,500.

994.42   AT   ISSN 0078-0243
NEWCASTLE HISTORY MONOGRAPHS. 1966. irreg., no.12, 1986. price varies. Newcastle Region Public Library, P.O. Box 489, Newcastle N. S. W. 2300, Australia. Ed.Bd. circ. 1,000. (back issues avail.)

993   NZ
OHINEMURI; regional history journal. 1964. a. NZ.$2. Paeroa and District Historical Society, c/o Mrs M. Townshend, Hon. Treas., 16 Taylor's Ave., Paeroa, New Zealand. Ed. Gary Staples. illus.

990   AT   ISSN 0078-7523
PACIFIC ISLANDS YEAR BOOK. 1930. irreg., 15th ed., 1984. Aus.$35. Pacific Publications (Australia) Pty. Ltd., G.P.O. Box 3408, Sydney, N.S.W. 2001, Australia. Ed. Russell Hunter. adv.
Formerly: Pacific Islands Year Book and Who's Who.

994   AT   ISSN 0085-4670
PAPERS ON THE HISTORY OF BOURKE. 1966. irreg., latest vol.10, 1985. Aus.$15 per no. Bourke Historical Society, Bourke, N.S.W. 2840, Australia. Ed. W.J. Cameron. circ. 200.

993.5   BP
SOLOMON ISLANDS RESEARCH REGISTER. 1972. a. University of the South Pacific, Solomon Islands Centre, Box 460, Honiara, British Solomon Islands. circ. 2,000.

990   AT
TIDE OF TIME. 1968. a. Aus.$2. Inverell and District Historical Society, P.O. Box 396, Inverell, NSW 2360, Australia. Ed. P.N. Whish.

990   GW   ISSN 0342-6610
UEBERSEE-MUSEUM BREMEN. VEROEFFENTLICHUNGEN. REIHE G: BREMER SUEDPAZIFIK-ARCHIV. 1977. irreg., vol. 2, 1978. price varies. Uebersee-Museum, Bremen, Bahnhofsplatz 13, 2800 Bremen, W. Germany(B.R.D.)

994   NZ   ISSN 0067-0480
UNIVERSITY OF AUCKLAND HISTORICAL SOCIETY. ANNUAL. 1967. a. NZ.$2.50. University of Auckland, Department of History, Private Bag, Auckland, New Zealand.
Student contributions

994   AT   ISSN 0085-7858
WAGGA WAGGA AND DISTRICT HISTORICAL SOCIETY. JOURNAL. 1968. a. $5 per no. Wagga Wagga & District Historical Society, Box 90, Wagga Wagga, N.S.W. 2650, Australia. Ed. Alan Ives. adv. bk. rev. circ. 1,000.

994   PP   ISSN 0085-7866
WAIGANI SEMINAR. PAPERS. 1969. irreg. price varies. University of Papua New Guinea, Box 320, University, Papua New Guinea. charts. illus. index. circ. 1,000.

994 330   AT   ISSN 0083-8756
WESTERN AUSTRALIAN POCKET YEARBOOK. 1919. a. Aus.$2.40. Australian Bureau of Statistics, Western Australian Office, 1-3 St. George's Terrace, Perth, W.A. 6000, Australia. circ. 3,000.

994 330   AT   ISSN 0083-8772
WESTERN AUSTRALIAN YEARBOOK. NEW SERIES. Title varies: Official Year Book of Western Australia. 1957. a. Aus.$22.75. Australian Bureau of Statistics, Western Australian Office, 1-3 St. George's Terrace, Perth, W.A. 6000, Australia. circ. 2,650.

993   NZ   ISSN 0110-4004
WHAKATANE & DISTRICT HISTORICAL SOCIETY. MONOGRAPHS. no 4, 1977. irreg. Whakatane & District Historical Society, Box 203, Whakatane, New Zealand. circ. 400.

HISTORY — History Of Europe

see also Classical Studies

948 630   NE   ISSN 0511-0726
A A G BIJDRAGEN. (Text in Dutch; summaries in English) 1958. irreg. exchange basis. Landbouwhogeschool, Afdeling Agrarische Geschiedenis - Agricultural University, Wageningen, Department of Rural History, Hollandseweg 1, Wageningen, Netherlands. circ. 1,100. Indexed: Hist.Abstr. Amer.Hist.& Life.

943   GW   ISSN 0065-0137
AACHENER GESCHICHTSVEREIN. ZEITSCHRIFT. 1879. a. membership. Aachener Geschichtsverein e.V., Fischmarkt 3, 5100 Aachen, W. Germany (B.R.D.) Dir. Herbert Lepper. bk. rev. index. circ. 1,500.

948   FI
AALANDSK ODLING. 1938. a. Aalands Folkminnesforbund, Aalands Museum, 22100 Mariehamn, Finland. cum.index: 1938-64.

948   DK   ISSN 0107-5055
AALBORG STIFTSBOG. 1959. a. Kr.40. Aalborg Stifts Landemode, Eksp. Bispekontoret, Adelgade 10, 9000 Aalborg, Denmark. illus. circ. 2,500.

948 331   DK   ISSN 0106-5912
AARBOG FOR ARBEJDERBEVAEGELSENS HISTORIE. 1972. a. Kr.175. Selskabet til Forskning i Arbejderbevaegelsens Historie, Rejsbygade 1, 1759 Copenhagen, Denmark. bk. rev. illus. circ. 1,100. Indexed: Hist.Abstr. Amer.Hist.& Life.

948   DK   ISSN 0106-2220
AARBOG FOR SVENDBORG E OMEGNS MUSEUM. 1979. a. Kr.75. Museumforeningen for Svendborg and Omegns Museum, Grubbmoellevej 13, 5700 Svendborg, Denmark. Ed. Henrik M. Jansen. illus. circ. 1,300.

948.1   NO   ISSN 0572-4562
AARBOK FOR HADELAND. 1968. a. Kr.75($8) Aarbok for Hadeland, c/o Lisbeth Noetnes, 2740 Roa, Norway. bibl. illus. circ. 3,000. (also avail. in talking book)

948.1   NO   ISSN 0587-4076
AARBOK FOR TELEMARK. 1955. a. Kr.60. Telemark Maallag, 3841 Flatdal, Norway. Ed. Dag Aanderaa. adv.

947   DK   ISSN 0105-4112
AARHUS UNIVERSITET. SLAVISK INSTITUT. ARBEJDSPAPIRER. 1976. irreg. price varies. Aarhus Universitet, Slavisk Institut, Ny Munkegade, 8000 Aarhus C, Denmark. circ. 100.

HISTORY — HISTORY OF EUROPE

940   FI   ISSN 0355-1644
AARNI. 1886. irreg. Kuopian Islaenmaallinen Seura, Kauppakatu 23, 70100 Kuopia 10, Finland.

948.9   DK   ISSN 0108-2787
AARSSKRIFT FOR SOTTRUP SOGN. 1982. a. membership. Lokalhistortisk Forening for Sottrup Sogn, c/o Olav Bonefeld, V. Snogbaek 33, 6400 Soenderborg, Denmark. illus.

942   UK
ABERTAY HISTORICAL SOCIETY. SERIES OF MONOGRAPHS; dealing with Dundee and Tayside history. 1953. a. price varies. Abertay Historical Society, c/o Dept. of History, The University, Dundee DD1 4HN, Scotland. Ed. Dr. Christopher Whatley. bk. rev. circ. 4,000.

330 940   GE   ISSN 0065-0358
ABHANDLUNGEN ZUR HANDELS- UND SOZIALGESCHICHTE. 1958. irreg., vol.25, 1986. price varies. (Historiker-Gesellschaft der DDR, Hansische Arbeitsgemeinschaft) Hermann Boehlaus Nachfolger, Meyerstr. 50a, 53 Weimar, E. Germany (D.D.R.)

940   PO
ACADEMIA PORTUGUESA DA HISTORIA. ANAIS. 1940. a. price varies. Academia Portuguesa da Historia, Palacio da Rosa, Largo da Rosa 5, Lisbon 1100, Portugal. circ. 550. Indexed: Hist.Abstr. Amer.Hist.& Life.

940   IT
ACADEMIE DE FRANCE A ROME. CORRESPONDANCE DES DIRECTEURS. NOUVELLE SERIE. (Text in French) 1979. a. price varies. Edizioni dell' Elefante, Piazza de Caprettari 70, 00186 Rome, Italy. Ed. Georges Brunel. circ. 1,000.

937.5   IT   ISSN 0065-0730
ACCADEMIA ETRUSCA DI CORTONA. ANNUARIO. 1935. a. price varies. Casa Editrice Leo S. Olschki, Casella Postale 66, 50100 Florence, Italy. circ. 500.

940   GW   ISSN 0567-7289
ACTA BALTICA. 1961. a. price varies. Institutum Balticum, Haus der Begegnung, Bischof-Kaller-Str. 3, 6240 Koenigstein, W. Germany (B.R.D.) bk. rev. index. circ. 1,000. Indexed: Hist.Abstr. M.L.A. Amer.Hist.& Life.

947 301   PL   ISSN 0065-1044
ACTA BALTICO - SLAVICA. (Text mainly in Polish; summaries in English and German) a. price varies. (Polska Akademia Nauk, Instytut Slowianoznawstwa) Ossolineum, Publishing House of the Polish Academy of Sciences, Rynek 9, Wroclaw, Poland (Dist. by: Ars Polona-Ruch, Krakowskie Przedmiescie 7, Warsaw, Poland) Ed. Jan Safarewicz. Indexed: M.L.A. Numis.Lit.

940   CS   ISSN 0231-5955
ACTA COMENIANA. ARCHIV PRO BADANI O ZIVOTE A DILE JANA AMOSE KOMENSKEHO. (Text in English, French, German and Russian) 1910. irreg. (Academia Nakladatelstvi C S A V) Arti, Vodickova 40, 112 29 Prague 1, Czechoslovakia. Ed. Marta Beckova. circ. 700. Indexed: Hist.Abstr. Amer.Hist.& Life.
Formerly: Archiv pro Badani o Zivote a Dile Jana Amose Komenskeho.

940 550   CS   ISSN 0231-6005
ACTA HISTORIAE RERUM NATURALIUM NEC NON TECHNICARUM. (Text in English, French, German and Russian) 1965. irreg. avail. on exchange basis only. Ustav Ceskoslovenskych a Svetovych Dejin CSAV, Vysehradska 49, 128 26 Prague 2, Czechoslovakia. Ed. Jan Janko. Indexed: Bull.Signal. Math.R.

949.8   IT   ISSN 0065-1303
ACTA HISTORICA. (Contributions in Italian, English, French and German) 1959. irreg. price varies. Societa Accademica Romena, Foro Traiano 1a, 00187 Rome, Italy.

949.7   YU
ACTA HISTORICA NOVA. (Text in Italian; summaries in Serbo-Croatian and Slovene) 1981. irreg. 500 din.($8) Centro di Ricerche Storiche, Piazza Matteotti 13, Rovigno-Rovinj, Yugoslavia. index. circ. 2,000. (back issues avail.)

940   PL
ACTA MEDIAEVALIA. (Text in Latin or Polish; summaries in French) 1973. irreg. price varies. Katolicki Uniwersytet Lubelski, Towarzystwo Naukowe, Chopina 29, 20-023 Lublin, Poland.

940   GW   ISSN 0065-146X
ACTA PACIS WESTPHALICAE. 1962. irreg. price varies. (Rheinisch-Westfaelische Akademie der Wissenschaften) Aschendorffsche Verlagsbuchhandlung, Soester Str. 13, 4400 Muenster, W. Germany (B.R.D.) (Co-sponsor: Vereinigung zur Erforschung der Neueren Geschichte e.V.) Ed. Konrad Repgen.

ACTA PRAEHISTORICA ET ARCHAEOLOGICA. see *ARCHAEOLOGY*

940 980   HU   ISSN 0324-6965
ACTA UNIVERSITATIS DE ATTILA JOZSEF NOMINATAE. ACTA HISTORICA. (Text in Hungarian and Spanish) 1957. irreg., 2-3/yr. exchange basis. Attila Jozsef University, c/o E. Szabo, Exchange Librarian, Dugonics ter 13, P.O.B. 393, Szeged H-6701, Hungary (Subscr. to: Kultura, Box 149, H-1389 Budapest, Hungary) Ed.Bd. circ. 400. Indexed: Hist.Abstr. Amer.Hist.& Life.
Incorporating: Studia Latino-Americana.

943.9   HU   ISSN 0418-4556
ACTA UNIVERSITATIS DEBRECENIENSIS DE LUDOVICO KOSSUTH NOMINATEA. SERIES HISTORICA. EGYETEMES TORTENETI TANULMANYOK. (Summaries in English and Russian) 1966. irreg., vol.16, 1983. Kossuth Lajos Tudomanyegyetem, Egyetemes Torteneti Tanszek, Egyetem Ter 1, 4010 Debrecen, Hungary. Eds. Orosz Istvan, Tokody Gyula. bibl.

943.8   HU   ISSN 0324-5454
ACTA UNIVERSITATIS DEBRECENIENSIS DE LUDOVICO KOSSUTH NOMINATEA. SERIES HISTORICA. MAGYAR TORTENETI TANULMANYOK. (Summaries in English and Russian) 1967. irreg., vol. 16, 1983. Kossuth Lajos Tudomanyegyetem, Magyar Toerteneti Tanszek, Egyetem Ter 1, 4010 Debrecen, Hungary. bibl.

943.8   PL   ISSN 0137-5830
ACTA UNIVERSITATIS NICOLAI COPERNICI. HISTORIA. 1965. irreg. price varies. Uniwersytet Mikolaja Kopernika, Fosa Staromiejska 3, Torun, Poland (Dist. by Osrodek Rozpowszechniania Wydanictw Naukowych PAN, Palac Kultury i Nauki, 00-901 Warsaw, Poland)
Formerly: Uniwersytet Mikolaja Kopernika, Torun. Nauki Humanistyczno-Spoleczne. Historia (ISSN 0083-4491)

948.5   SW   ISSN 0065-1702
ACTA VISBYENSIA; Visby-symposiet foer historiska vetenskaper. (Text in English and German) 1963. irreg. Kr.86($6) Gotlands Fornsal, 208383, S-62102 Visby, Sweden. (Co-sponsor: Swedish Council for Research in the Humanities and Social Sciences) Ed. Sven-Olof Lindquist. circ. 1,500.

ACTA WEXIONENSIA. SERIE 1: HISTORY & GEOGRAPHY. see *GEOGRAPHY*

948.9   DK   ISSN 0065-3667
AELDRE DANSKE TINGBOEGER. 1954. irreg. price varies. Landbohistorisk Selskab, H. C. Andersens Boulevard 38, DK-1553 Copenhagen K, Denmark.

380 332   FR   ISSN 0065-3799
AFFAIRES ET GENS D'AFFAIRES. 1952. irreg., no.36, 1973. price varies. Editions de l' Ecole des Hautes Etudes en Sciences Sociales, 131 bd. Saint Michel, 75005 Paris, France.

AGRIKULTURA. see *AGRICULTURE*

AKADEMIA ATHENON. KENTRON EREUNES TES HELLENIKES LAOGRAPHIAS. EPETERIS. see *FOLKLORE*

949.5   GR
AKADEMIA ATHENON. PRAGMATEIAI. (Text in English, French, German and Greek) 1935. irreg. Akademia Athenon, Odos Panapistemiou 28, Athens 143, Greece. cum.index: vols.1-20, 1969.

949.5   GR
AKADEMIA ATHENON. PRAKTIKA. 1926. a. Akademia Athenon, Odos Panapistemiou 28, Athens 143, Greece. cum.index: vols.1-30, 1926-1955; 1956-1969. Indexed: Math.R.

940   GE   ISSN 0138-3566
AKADEMIE DER WISSENSCHAFTEN DER DDR. ZENTRALINSTITUT FUER GESCHICHTE. SCHRIFTEN. (Vol. 1-37, 1957-1972: under Subtitle: Reihe 1: Allgemeine und Deutsche Geschichte) 1957. irreg., vol.65, 1986. price varies. Akademie-Verlag, Leipziger Str. 3-4, 1086 Berlin, E. Germany (D.D.R.)

949   YU   ISSN 0350-0020
AKADEMIJA NAUKA I UMJETNOSTI BOSNE I HERCEGOVINE. CENTAR ZA BALKANOLOSKA ISPITIVANJA. GODISNJAK. vol. 3, 1965. a. 1330 din. Akademija Nauka i Umjetnosti Bosne i Hercegovine, Centar za Balkanoloska Ispitivanja, 71000 Sarajevo, Yugoslavia. Ed. Alojz Benac. circ. 800. Indexed: M.L.A.

949 891 491   YU
AKADEMIJA NAUKA I UMJETNOSTI BOSNE I HERCEGOVINE. ODELJENJE ISTORIJSKO FILOLOSKIH NAUK. DJELA. 1954. irreg. price varies. Akademija Nauka i Umjetnosti Bosne i Hercegovine, Odjeljenje Istorijsko Filoloskih Nauk, Ul. 6. novembra br. 7, P.O. Box ol-54, 7100 Sarajevo, Yugoslavia. Ed. Borivoj Covic. circ. 800.

AKADEMISKA DZIVE/ACADEMIC LIFE. see *ETHNIC INTERESTS*

946   SP
AKAL UNIVERSITARIA. SERIE HISTORIA CONTEMPORANEA. irreg., no. 43, 1983. Akal Editor, Paseo de Sta. Maria de la Cabeza, 132, Madrid 26, Spain. Ed. Ramon Akal Gonzalez.

949   NE
ALKMAARSE HISTORISCHE REEKS. 1977. a. fl.33.50. Walburg Pers, Zaadmarkt 84-86, Box 222, 7200 AE Zutphen, Netherlands. Ed. E. H. Cordfunke. illus.

948 913   DK   ISSN 0108-9846
ALLE TIDERS ODSHERREDS. 1968. a. price varies. Odsherreds Museum, Kirkestraede 9a, DK-4500 Nykoebing Sjaelland, Denmark. Ed. Ole Strandgaard. adv. circ. 2,000.
Formerly (until 1984): Ting og Sager fra Odsherred.

940   GW
ALLENSBACHER ALMANACH. 1950. a. free. Allensbacher Arbeitsgemeinschaft e. V., Kappelerberg-Str. 29, 7753 Allensbach, W. Germany (B.R.D.) Ed. Stefan Egenhofer. bk. rev. illus.

948.9   DK   ISSN 0108-7142
ALLESOE, BROBY, NAESBY LOKALARKIV. 1982. a. membership. Naesby Skole, Skolevej 9, 5270 Odense N, Denmark.

340   GW
ALLGAEUER GESCHICHTSFREUND. 1888. a. DM.20. Heimatverein Kempten (Allgaeu), Braut- und Bahrweg 14, 8960 Kempten, W. Germany (B.R.D.) Ed. Wolfgang Haberl. bk. rev. illus. index. circ. 1,200.

943   GW
ALSTERVEREIN JAHRBUCH. 1901. a. Alsterverein Vereinigung fuer Heimatkunde und Heimatpflege, 65 Wellingsbuettler Weg 79g, 2000 Hamburg 65, W. Germany (B.R.D.) adv. bk. rev. circ. 700.

940   GE   ISSN 0065-6585
ALT-THUERINGEN. 1953/54. irreg. (every 1-2 yrs.), vol.21, 1985. price varies. (Museum fuer Ur- und Fruehgeschichte Thueringens) Hermann Boehlaus Nachfolger, Meyerstr. 50a, 53 Weimar, E. Germany (D.D.R.) Ed. Guenter Behm-Blancke. Indexed: Br.Archaeol.Abstr.
Formerly: Museum fuer Ur- und Fruehgeschichte Thueringens. Jahreschrift.

HISTORY — HISTORY OF EUROPE

943　　　　　GW　ISSN 0342-8699
ALTFRAENKISCHE BILDER UND
WAPPENKALENDER. 1895. a. (Freunde
Mainfraenkischer Kunst und Geschichte,
Gesellschaft Mainfraenkischer Kunst und
Geschichte) Verlag Stuertz, Beethovenstr. 5, 8700
Wuerzburg, W. Germany (B.R.D.) Ed.Bd.
　　Formerly (1895-196?): Altfraenkische Bilder.

AMSTERDAMER BEITRAEGE ZUR NEUEREN
GERMANISTIK. see LITERATURE

949.5　　　　　GR
ANAGNOSTIKA HETAIREIA KERKYRAS.
DELTION. 1964. a. Dr.500. Anagnostika Hetaireia
Kerkyras, Corfu, Greece. bibl. circ. 600.
　　Formerly: Deltion Pneumatikes kai Kallitechnikes
Drasteriotetos.

ANALECTA CARTUSIANA; review for Carthusian
history and spirituality. see RELIGIONS AND
THEOLOGY

930　　　　　IT　ISSN 0066-1392
ANALECTA ROMANA INSTITUTI DANICI. (Text
in English, French, Italian) 1960. irreg., no.12, 1983.
price varies. Erma di "Bretschneider", Via
Cassiodoro 19, 00193 Rome, Italy. (back issues
avail.) Indexed: RILA.

930　　　　　IT　ISSN 0066-1406
ANALECTA ROMANA INSTITUTI DANICI.
SUPPLEMENTUM. (Text in English, French,
Italian) 1960. irreg., no.11, 1983. price varies. Erma
di "Bretschneider", Via Cassiodoro 19, 00193 Rome,
Italy. (back issues avail.)

942　　　　　UK　ISSN 0072-5625
ANCIENT MONUMENTS BOARD FOR
ENGLAND. ANNUAL REPORT. 1954. a. price
varies. H.M.S.O., Box 569, London SE1 9NH,
England. (Co-sponsor: Department of the
Environment) Ed. A.F.W. Swift. illus. circ. 1,100.
Indexed: Br.Archaeol.Abstr.

948　　　　　IC
ANDVARI; Nyr Flokkur. 1874. a. Bokautgafa
Menningarsjods og Pjodvinafelagsins, Skalholtsstigur
7, Reykjavik, Iceland. cum.index: 1874-1975.

940　　　　　UK　ISSN 0144-5863
ANGLO-CATALAN SOCIETY. OCCASIONAL
PUBLICATIONS. 1980. a. price varies. Anglo-
Catalan Society, c/o Dr. Alan Yates, Ed.,
Department of Hispanic Studies, University of
Sheffield, Sheffield S10 2TN, England. circ. 800.

940　　　　　US
ANGLO-NORMAN STUDIES.* 1980. a. price varies.
Boydell & Brewer, Box 2069, Wolfeboro, NH
03894-2069.
　　Formerly: Battle Conference on Anglo-Norman
Studies III.

943.8　　　　　PL　ISSN 0066-2224
ANNALES SILESIAE. (Text in English, French,
German and Polish) 1960. a. price varies.
(Wroclawskie Towarzystwo Naukowe) Ossolineum,
Publishing House of the Polish Academy of
Sciences, Rynek 9, 50-106 Wroclaw, Poland (Dist.
by Ars Polona-Ruch, Krakowskie Przedmiescie 7,
Warsaw, Poland) Ed. J. Trzynadlowski.

943　　　　　IT　ISSN 0066-4642
ANTEMURALE; annual periodical devoted to the
history of Central and Eastern Europe. 1954. a.
price varies. Institutum Historicum Polonicum
Romae - Polish Historical Institute, Via Virginio
Orsini 19, 00192 Rome, Italy. cum. index. Indexed:
Numis.Lit.

946　　　　　SP　ISSN 0066-5061
ANUARIO DE ESTUDIOS MEDIEVALES. (Text in
Romance languages; summaries in English and
French) 1964. a. 2300 ptas. Consejo Superior de
Investigaciones Cientificas (C.S.I.C), Vitnuvio, 8,
Apdo. 14.458, 28046 Madrid, Spain. Ed. Emilio
Saez. adv. bk. rev. indexes. circ. 1,000. Indexed:
Hist.Abstr. Amer.Hist.& Life.

940　341　　　　SP　ISSN 0304-4319
ANUARIO DE HISTORIA DEL DERECHO
ESPANOL. 1924. a. 6000 ptas. Instituto Nacional
de Estudios Juridicos, Duque de Medinaceli St., No.
8, Madrid, Spain. bk. rev. bibl. index. Indexed:
Hist.Abstr. Amer.Hist.& Life.

943　709　　　　GW　ISSN 0341-8383
ANZEIGER DES GERMANISCHEN
NATIONALMUSEUMS. 1832. a. DM.65.
Germanisches Nationalmuseum, Nuernberg,
Postfach 9580, D-8500 Nuernberg 11, W. Germany
(B.R.D.) Eds. G. Bott. circ. 600. (back issues avail.)
Indexed: RILA.

949　398　　　　BE
APPELTJES VAN HET MEETJESLAND. (Text in
Dutch) 1950. a. 500 Fr. Heemkundig Genootschap
van het Meetjesland, Gentstraat 13, B-9971
Kaprijke (Lembeke), Belgium. bk. rev. circ. 550.

949　　　　　RM
APULUM. At head of title: Acta Musei Apulensis.
(Text in English, French, German, Italian,
Romanian; summaries in English, French, German,
Italian) 1939. a. Muzeul de Istorie si Arheologie
Alba Julia, Str. Mihai Vieazul nr. 12-14, Alba Julia,
Rumania. illus. Indexed: Numis.Lit.

943　296　　　　GW　ISSN 0341-8340
ARBEITSINFORMATIONEN UEBER
STUDIENPROJEKTE AUF DEM GEBIET DER
GESCHICHTE DES DEUTSCHEN JUDENTUMS
UND DES ANTISEMITISMUS. 1963. irreg.
DM.5. Germania Judaica, Koelner Bibliothek zur
Geschichte des Deutschen Judentums, Josef-
Haubrich-Hof 1, 5000 Cologne, W. Germany
(B.R.D.) circ. 1,500.

943　　　　　GE　ISSN 0302-6329
ARBEITSKREIS ZWEITER WELTKRIEG.
BULLETIN. 1963. irreg. Akademie der
Wissenschaften der D D R, Zentralinstitut fuer
Geschichte, Clara-Zetkin-Str. 26, 108 Berlin, E.
Germany (D.D.R.)

ARBETARROERELSENS AARSBOK. see
BUSINESS AND ECONOMICS — Labor And
Industrial Relations

948　　　　　DK
ARBOGEN FOR SKJERN. 1942. a. $4. J.
Strandbygaards Bogtrykkeri, 6900 Skjern, Denmark.
adv. circ. 800.

943　　　　　GW　ISSN 0341-1222
ARCHAEOLOGISCHE AUSGRABUNGEN;
Bodendenkmalpflege in den Regierungs Bezirken
Stuttgart und Tuebingen. 1974. a. DM.30.
Gesellschaft fuer Vor-und Fruegeschichte in
Wuerttemberg und Hohenzollern, 7000 Stuttgart, W.
Germany (B.R.D.) Ed. D. Planck. Indexed:
Br.Archaeol.Abstr.

940　　　　　PL　ISSN 0066-6041
ARCHEION. (Text in Polish; summaries in English,
French and Russian) 1927. irreg., vol.77, 1984. price
varies. (Naczelna Dyrekcja Archiwow
Panstwowych) Panstwowe Wydawnictwo Naukowe,
Ul. Miodowa 10, 00-251 Warsaw, Poland (Dist. by:
Ars Polona, Krakowskie Przedmiescie 7, 00-068
Warsaw, Poland) Ed. Czeslaw Biernat. cum.index:
vols.1-50 (issued in 1969) circ. 820. Indexed:
Hist.Abstr. Amer.Hist.& Life.

949.5　913　　　　GR
ARCHEION EUVOIKON MELETON. 1936. irreg.
Dr.1000. Hetaireia Euvoikon Spoudon, Odos
Harilaou Trikoupi 60, 106 180 Athens, Greece. bk.
rev. bibl. cum.index: vols. 1-20, 1976. circ. 1,500.
Indexed: Hist.Abstr. M.L.A. Amer.Hist.& Life.

949.5　913　　　　GR
ARCHEION PONTOU. (Text in English, French,
German and Greek) 1928. a. Epitrope Pontiakon
Meleton, Odos Kolokotrone 25, Athens 125,
Greece. bk. rev. bibl. cum.index: vols.1-24. Indexed:
RILA.

949.5　913　　　　GR
ARCHEION THESSALIKON MELETON. 1972.
irreg. Hetaireia Thessalikon Ereunon, Odos Lasonos
73, Volos, Greece. bibl.

ARCHEOLOGICKE VYSKUMY A NALEZY NA
SLOVENSKU. see ARCHAEOLOGY

943　　　　　GW　ISSN 0587-5277
ARCHIV DER DEUTSCHEN
JUGENDBEWEGUNG. JAHRBUCH. 1969. a.
Archiv der deutschen Jugendbewegung, Burg
Ludwigstein, 3430 Witzenhausen 1, W. Germany
(B.R.D.) Ed. Winfried Mogge. illus.

940　　　　　GW　ISSN 0066-6297
ARCHIV FUER DIPLOMATIK,
SCHRIFTGESCHICHTE, SIEGEL- UND
WAPPENKUNDE. 1955. a. price varies. Boehlau
Verlag GmbH, Niehler Str. 272-274, 5000 Cologne
60, W. Germany (B.R.D.) Ed. W. Heinemeyer.

943　　　　　GW　ISSN 0341-8324
ARCHIV FUER FRANKFURTS GESCHICHTE
UND KUNST. 1837. irreg. (Frankurter Verein fuer
Geschichte und Landeskunde) Buechhaendler
Vereinigung, Gr. Hirschgraben 17-21, 6000
Frankfurt 1, W. Germany (B.R.D.) Ed. W. Kloetzer.

943　　　　　GW　ISSN 0066-6335
ARCHIV FUER GESCHICHTE VON
OBERFRANKEN. 1827. a. price varies.
Historischer Verein fuer Oberfranken, Ludwigstr.
21, Neues Schloss, 8580 Bayreuth, W. Germany
(B.R.D.) Ed. Erwin Herrmann. bk. rev.

943　　　　　GW　ISSN 0066-636X
ARCHIV FUER HESSISCHE GESCHICHTE UND
ALTERTUMSKUNDE. 1835. a. DM.40 for
members. Historischer Verein fuer Hessen,
Staatsarchiv, Schloss, 6100 Darmstadt, W. Germany
(B.R.D.) bk. rev. circ. 900.

940　　　　　GW　ISSN 0066-6505
ARCHIV FUER SOZIALGESCHICHTE. 1960. a.
DM.140. (Friedrich-Ebert Stiftung) Verlag Neue
Gesellschaft GmbH, Godesberger Allee 143, 5300
Bonn 2, W. Germany (B.R.D.) (Co-sponsor: Institut
fuer Sozialgeschichte) bk. rev. circ. 1,500. Indexed:
Hist.Abstr. Amer.Hist.& Life.

900　　　　　AU　ISSN 0003-9462
ARCHIV FUER VATERLAENDISCHE
GESCHICHTE UND TOPOGRAPHIE. 1849.
irreg. price varies. Geschichtsverein fuer Kaernten,
Museumgasse 2, A-9020 Klagenfurt, Austria. Ed.
Wilhelm Neumann. bk. rev.

940　　　　　US
ARCHIVE FOR REFORMATION HISTORY/
ARCHIV FUER
REFORMATIONSGESCHICHTE. 1909. a. $26
($43 in combination with Literature Review)
American Society for Reformation Research, 6477
San Bonita, St. Louis, MO 63105. Ed. Miriam J.
Chrisman. bk. rev. bibl. circ. 500. Indexed:
Curr.Cont. Rel.Ind.One.

940　　　　　NE　ISSN 0066-6548
ARCHIVES BAKOUNINE/BAKUNIN-ARCHIV.
1961. irreg. price varies. (International Institute for
Social History) E. J. Brill, P.O. Box 9000, 2300 PA
Leiden, Netherlands. Ed. Arthur Lehning.

020　949　　　　BE　ISSN 0003-9748
ARCHIVES ET BIBLIOTHEQUES DE BELGIQUE/
ARCHIEF- EN BIBLIOTHEEKWEZEN IN
BELGIE. (Includes irregular special issues) (Text in
Dutch, English, French, German, Italian, Latin and
Spanish) 1963. irreg. (2-4/yr.) 950 Fr.($30)
Association des Archivistes et Bibliothecaires de
Belgique, 4 Bd. de l'Empereur, 1000 Brussels,
Belgium. Ed.Bd. adv. bk. rev. bibl. charts. illus.
index. cum.index: vols.1-25. Indexed: Hist.Abstr.
Lib.Lit. Lib.Sci.Abstr. Amer.Hist.& Life.
　　Formerly: Archives, Bibliotheques et Musees de
Belgique.
　　Archives

945　　　　　IT　ISSN 0066-6718
ARCHIVIO STORICO ITALIANO. BIBLIOTECA.
1949. irreg., vol. 23, 1983. price varies. Casa
Editrice Leo S. Olschki, Casella Postale 66, 50100
Florence, Italy. circ. 1,000.

945　　　　　IT　ISSN 0004-0347
ARCHIVIO STORICO LODIGIANO. 1881. a.
L.15000. Comune di Lodi, Biblioteca Comunale
Laudense, Corso Umberto 63, 20075 Lodi, Milan,
Italy. Ed. Luigi Samarati. bk. rev. index. circ. 500.
　　Local

945　　　　　IT
ARCHIVIO STORICO SARDO. (Text in Italian,
Spanish) 1905. a. Deputazione di Storia Patria per la
Sardegna, Via Cadello 11, 09100 Cagliari, Italy.

941.5　　　　　IE　ISSN 0044-8745
ARCHIVIUM HIBERNICUM; Irish historical records.
1912. a. £7. Catholic Record Society of Ireland, c/o
St. Patrick's College, Maynooth, Co. Kildare,
Ireland. Ed. Dr. Donal A. Kerr. index. circ. 400.
Indexed: Hist.Abstr. Amer.Hist.& Life.

HISTORY — HISTORY OF EUROPE

940 IT
ARCHIVUM FRATRUM PRAEDICATORUM.
1931. Text in English, French, German and Italian.
Istituto Storico Domenicano, Largo Angelicum 1,
00184 Rome, Italy (Subscr. to: Piazza Pietro d'Illiria
1, 00153 Rome, Italy) Ed. P.P. Domenicani.

943.7 330 CS
ARCHIVUM TREBONENSE. 1971. irreg. Statni
Oblastni Archiv v Treboni, 379 01 Treboni,
Czechoslovakia.

948 709 DK
ARET FORTALT I BILLEDER.* 1942. a.
Illustrationsforlaget, c/o Carlsen if, Kobmadergade
9, 1001 Copenhagen K, Denmark.

949.8 571 RM ISSN 0066-7358
ARHEOLOGIA MOLDOVEI/ARCHEOLOGIE DE
LA MOLDAVIE. (Text in Rumanian; summaries in
French) 1961. irreg., vol.9, 1980. (Academia de
Stiinte Sociale si Politice) Editura Academiei
Republicii Socialiste Rumania, Calea Victoriei 125,
79717 Bucharest, Rumania (Subscr. to: ARTEXIM,
Export-Import Presa, Piata Scinteii nr.1, P.O. Box
33-16, 70055 Bucharest, Rumania) (Co-sponsor:
Institutul de Istorie si Arheologie A.D. Xenopol)
Indexed: Numis.Lit.

949 YU
ARHIVSKI VJESNIK. (Text in Croatian; summaries
in French, German, English, Italian) 1899. a. 200
din. Arhiv Hrvatske, Marulicev trg 21, 41000
Zagreb, Yugoslavia. Ed. Bernard Stulli. bk. rev. illus.
circ. 700. Indexed: Hist.Abstr. Amer.Hist.& Life.

948 DK
ARHUS STIFTS ARBOEGER. 1908. a. Historisk
Samfund for Arhus Stift, Carit Etlars Vej 60, 8230
Abyhoej, Denmark.

949.5 GR
ARISTOTELION PANEPISTEMION
THESSALONIKES. PHILOSOPHIKE SCHOLE.
EPISTEMONIKE EPETERIS. (Text in English,
French, German and Greek) 1927. a. Philosophike
Schole Aristotelion Panepistemion Thessaloniki,
University Campus, Salonika, Greece. illus. Indexed:
M.L.A.

ARISTOTELION PANEPISTEMION
THESSALONIKES. THEOLOGIKE SCHOLE.
EPISTEMONIKE EPETERIS. see *RELIGIONS
AND THEOLOGY*

ARMAMENTARIA. see *MILITARY*

940 BE
ARMARIUM CODICUM INSIGNIUM. 1980. irreg.
N.V. Brepols I.G.P., Rue Baron Francois du Four 8,
B-2300 Turnhout, Belgium. Ed.Bd.

940 PO
ARMAS E TROFEUS; revista de historia, heraldica,
genealogia e arte. 1959. irreg. (approx. 1/yr.)
Esc.1000 per no. (Instituto Portugues de Heraldica)
Livraria Ferin, Rua Nova de Almada 70, 1200
Lisbon, Portugal. Ed. Manuel A. Norton. bk. rev.
bibl. charts. illus. circ. 500.

947 US
ARMENIAN TEXTS AND STUDIES. irreg.
(University of Pennsylvania) Scholars Press, Box
1608, Decatur, GA 30031-1608. Ed. Michael E.
Stone.

ARS SUECICA. see *ART*

948 DK ISSN 0108-0075
ARUSIA. HISTORISKE SKRIFTER. 1985. irreg.
Kr.195. Bibliotekscentralen, Telegrafvej 5, DK-2750
Ballerup, Denmark. Ed. Aage Andersen.

948 DK ISSN 0105-0192
ARV OG EJE; sommerglaeder. 1950. a. Kr.250.
Dansk Kulturhistorisk Museumsforening, Nr.
Madsbadvej 6, DK-7884 Fur, Denmark. circ. 1,500.
Indexed: Hist.Abstr. Amer.Hist.& Life.
Formerly (1950-1955): Dansk Museer.

948 FI ISSN 0358-3414
ARX TAVASTICA. 1967. irreg. Hameenlinnan
Historiallinen Seura, Hameenlinnan Museo,
Lukiokatu 6, 13100 Hameenlinna 10, Finland.
Seppo Myllyniemi. circ. 500.

943 US
ASSOCIATION FOR THE ADVANCEMENT OF
POLISH STUDIES. BULLETIN. vol. 3, 1978. irreg.
Association for the Advancement of Polish Studies,
Alliance College, Cambridge Springs, PA 16403.
TEL 814-398-4611.

940 SZ ISSN 0571-6322
ASSOCIATION OF INSTITUTES FOR
EUROPEAN STUDIES. ANNUAIRE.* 1957. a.
Association of Institutes for European Studies,
European Cultural Centre, 122 rue de Lausanne,
Geneva, Switzerland.

378 940 SZ ISSN 0571-6330
ASSOCIATION OF INSTITUTES FOR
EUROPEAN STUDIES. YEAR-BOOK.* a.
Association of Institutes for European Studies,
European Cultural Centre, 122 rue de Lausanne,
Geneva, Switzerland.

945 IT
ASSOCIAZIONE NAZIONALE PER LA TUTELA
DEL PATRIMONIO STORICO ARTISTICO E
NATURALE DELLA NAZIONE. ATTI DI
CONVEGNI. irreg., no.13, 1975. price varies.
Associazione Nazionale per la Tutela del Patrimonio
Storico Artistico e Naturale della Nazione, Corso
Vittorio Emanuele 287, 00186 Rome, Italy.

945 IT
ASSOCIAZIONE NAZIONALE PER LA TUTELA
DEL PATRIMONIO STORICO ARTISTICO E
NATURALE DELLA NAZIONE. DOCUMENTI.
irreg. L.2000. Associazione Nazionale per la Tutela
del Patrimonio Storico Artistico e Naturale della
Nazione, Corso Vittorio Emanuele 287, 00186
Rome, Italy.

945 IT
ASSOCIAZIONE NAZIONALE PER LA TUTELA
DEL PATRIMONIO STORICO ARTISTICO E
NATURALE DELLA NAZIONE. QUADERNI.
irreg. L.2000. Associazione Nazionale per la Tutela
del Patrimonio Storico Artistico e Naturale della
Nazione, Corso Vittorio Emanuele 287, 00186
Rome, Italy.

945 IT
ASSOCIAZIONE NAZIONALE PER LA TUTELA
DEL PATRIMONIO STORICO ARTISTICO E
NATURALE DELLA NAZIONE. STUDI. 1962.
irreg., no.143, 1976. L.1000. Associazione Nazionale
per la Tutela del Patrimonio Storico Artistico e
Naturale della Nazione, Corso Vittorio Emanuele
287, 00186 Rome, Italy.

949.5 GR
ATHENA. (Text in English and Greek) 1889. a.
Athenais Epistimonike Hetaireia, Odos Eressou 74,
Athens 148, Greece. bk. rev. bibl. Indexed:
Hist.Abstr. Amer.Hist.& Life.

949.5 GR
ATHENS. ETHNIKON KAI KAPODISTRIAKON
PANEPISTEMION. PHILOSOPHIKE SCHOLE.
EPISTEMONIKE EPETERIS. (Text in English,
French, German, Greek and Italian) 1935. a.
Panepistemion Athenon, Philosophike Schole, Odos
Panepistemiou, 143 Athens, Greece. illus.

945 700 IT
ATTI E MEMORIE DELLA DEPUTAZIONE DI
STORIA PATRIA PER LE ANTICHE
PROVINCIE. 1862. a. L.30000($20) Deputazione
di Storia Patria per le Antiche Provincie Modenesi,
Via Pomposa 1, 41100 Modena, Italy. Ed. Aedes
Muratoriana. bk. rev. circ. 800. (back issues avail.)
Indexed: Hist.Abstr. M.L.A. Amer.Hist.& Life.
Numis.Lit.

940 AT ISSN 0812-9428
AUSTRALASIAN AND PACIFIC SOCIETY FOR
EIGHTEENTH-CENTURY STUDIES.
NEWSLETTER. 1971. irreg. Aus.$10.60
(membership); students Aus.$3.50; institutions Aus.
$10. Australasian and Pacific Society for
Eighteenth-Century Studies, Dept. of English,
Monash University, Clayton, Victoria 3168,
Australia. Eds. C.T. Probyn, L. Borland. bk. rev.
circ. 120.

943.6 US ISSN 0067-2378
AUSTRIAN HISTORY YEARBOOK. 1965. a. price
varies. University of Minnesota, Center for Austrian
Studies, Minneapolis, MN 55455. TEL 612-624-
9811. (Co-sponsor: Conference Group for Central
European History) Ed. William E. Wright. bk. rev.
circ. 950. Indexed: Hist.Abstr. Amer.Hist.& Life.
Supersedes: Austrian History Newsletter.

946 860 SP
AWRAQ YADIDA. (Text in Arabic, English, French,
and Spanish; summaries in Arabic) 1978. a. 1000
ptas.($20) Instituto Hispano-Arabe de Cultura,
Paseo de Juan XXIII, 5, 28040 Madrid, Spain. Ed.
Ines Arguelles. bk. rev. bibl. charts. illus. circ. 2,
000. (back issues avail.)
Formerly: Awrag (ISSN 0210-0045)

940 UK
AXBRIDGE ARCHAEOLOGICAL AND LOCAL
HISTORY SOCIETY. JOURNAL. 1970. irreg. £4.
Axbridge Archaeological and Local History Society,
King John's Hunting Lodge Museum, The Square,
Axbridge, Somerset, England. illus. circ. 250.

940 PL ISSN 0067-2793
BADANIA Z DZIEJOW SPOLECZNYCH I
GOSPODARCZYCH. (Text in Polish; summaries in
English, French or German) irreg., vol.58, 1981.
price varies. (Poznanskie Towarzystwo Przyjaciol
Nauk) Panstwowe Wydawnictwo Naukowe,
Miodowa 10, 00-251 Warsaw, Poland (Dist. by: Ars
Polona, Krakowskie Przedmiescie 7, 00-068
Warsaw, Poland)

940 GW
BADISCHE BIOGRAPHIEN NEUE FOLGE. 1981.
irreg. price varies. Kommission fuer Geschichtliche
Landeskunde in Baden-Wuerttemberg, Eugen-Str. 7,
7000 Stuttgart 1, W. Germany (B.R.D.) circ. 1,000.

943 GW ISSN 0522-0033
DER BAER VON BERLIN. 1951. irreg. DM.24.80.
Westkreuz Druckerei und Verlag, Rehagener Str. 30,
1000 Berlin 49, W. Germany (B.R.D.)

BAETICA; estudios de arte, geografia e historia. see
ART

949 YU
BALCANICA. vol.5, 1974. a. Srpska Akademija
Nauka i Umetnosti, Koordinacioni Medjuakademski
Odbor za Balkanologiju, Belgrade, Yugoslavia. (Co-
sponsor: Srpska Akademija Nauka i Umetnosti.
Balkanoloski Institut) Ed. Mehmed Begovic.
Indexed: M.L.A.

949.5 GR
BALKANIKA SYMMEIKTA. 1981. a. Institute for
Balkan Studies, Odos Tsimiski 45, 54110
Thessaloniki, Greece.

949.6 UR
BALKANSKIE ISSLEDOVANIYA. 1974. irreg. price
varies. (Akademiya Nauk S.S.S.R., Institut
Slavyanovedeniya i Balkanistiki) Izdatel'stvo Nauka,
Podsosenskii Per., 21, Moscow K-62, Russian
S.F.S.R., U.S.S.R. (Subscr. to: Mezhdunarodnaya
Kniga, Moscow, G-200, Russian S.F.S.R., U.S.S.R.)
Ed. G.L. Arsh. circ. 1,700.

947.4 929 GW ISSN 0005-4534
BALTISCHE HEFTE. 1954. a. DM.14.80. Harro V.
Hirschheydt, Postfach 281769, 3000 Hannover-
Doehren, W. Germany (B.R.D.) adv. bk. rev. bibl.
illus. index. circ. 1,100. Indexed: Hist.Abstr.
M.L.A. Amer.Hist.& Life.

940 GW ISSN 0067-3099
BALTISCHE STUDIEN.* 1835. a. DM.21.
(Gesellschaft fuer Pommersche Geschichte,
Altertumskunde und Kunst) Christoph von der
Ropp, Johnsallee 18, 2000 Hamburg 20, W.
Germany (B.R.D.) Ed.Bd. bk. rev. circ. 1,000.

940 SZ ISSN 0067-4540
BASLER ZEITSCHRIFT FUER GESCHICHTE
UND ALTERTUMSKUNDE. (Text in French and
German) 1902. a. 75 Fr. Historische und
Antiquarische Gesellschaft zu Basel,
Universitaetsbibliothek, Schoenbeinstr. 18-20, CH-
4056 Basel, Switzerland. Eds. A. Staehelin, Martin
Steinmann. circ. 1,200.

943 GW
BAVARIA. 1970. irreg. Wolfgang Vogelgesang, 8000
Munich, W. Germany (B.R.D.)

940 GW ISSN 0341-3918
BAYERISCHE VORGESCHICHTSBLAETTER.
(Text in German, English, French) 1921. a. price
varies. (Bayerische Akademie der Wissenschaften,
Kommission fuer Bayerische Landesgeschichte) C.
H. Beck'sche Verlagsbuchhandlung, Wilhelmstr. 9,
8000 Munich 40, W. Germany (B.R.D.) Ed. H.J.
Kellner. bk. rev. bibl. illus. circ. 600. Indexed:
Numis.Lit.

942 UK ISSN 0067-4826
BEDFORDSHIRE HISTORICAL RECORD
SOCIETY. PUBLICATIONS. 1913. a. £6 to
individuals; institutions £10. Bedfordshire Historical
Record Society, County Record Office, County
Hall, Bedford MK42 9AP, England. Ed. C.J.
Pickford. circ. 500. Indexed: Br.Hum.Ind.
Br.Archaeol.Abstr.

947 BE ISSN 0373-1537
BEDI KARTLISA; revue de kartvelologie; etudes
georgiennes et caucasiennes. (Text in French) a.
1200 Fr. Editions Peeters s.p.r.l., Bondgenotenlaan
153, B-3000 Louvain, Belgium.

274.3 GW ISSN 0408-8344
BEITRAEGE ZUR GESCHICHTE DER
REICHSKIRCHE IN DER NEUZEIT. irreg., vol.
10, 1981. price varies. Franz Steiner Verlag
Wiesbaden GmbH, Birkenwaldstr. 44, Postfach 347,
D-7000 Stuttgart 1, W. Germany (B.R.D.) Ed.
Rudolf Reinhardt.

940 GE ISSN 0522-6562
BEITRAEGE ZUR GESCHICHTE DER
UNIVERSITAET ERFURT (1392-1816) 1956.
irreg., vol.21, 1986. price varies. (Medizinische
Akademie Erfurt) Johann Ambrosius Barth Verlag,
Salomonstr. 18b, DDR-7010 Leipzig, E. Germany
(D.D.R.) (Orders to: Buchexport, Leninstr. 16,
DDR-7010 Leipzig, E. Germany (D.D.R.))

943.08 GW ISSN 0408-8379
BEITRAEGE ZUR GESCHICHTE DER
UNIVERSITAET MAINZ. irreg., vol. 13, 1983.
price varies. (Universitaet Mainz) Franz Steiner
Verlag Wiesbaden GmbH, Birkenwaldstr. 44,
Postfach 347, D-7000 Stuttgart 1, W. Germany
(B.R.D.) Ed.Bd.

943 GW ISSN 0078-2785
BEITRAEGE ZUR GESCHICHTE UND KULTUR
DER STADT NUERNBERG. (Sub-series:
Nuernberg-Bibliographie) 1959. irreg., vol. 22, 1981.
price varies. Stadtbibliothek, Egidien-Platz 23, 8500
Nuernberg 2, W. Germany (B.R.D.) Eds. R.
Fritzsch, G. Thomann.

940 GW
BEITRAEGE ZUR HEIMATKUNDE DER STADT
SCHWELM UND IHRER UMGEBUNG. 1951. a.
price varies. Verein fuer Heimatkunde Schwelm,
Haus Martfeld, Hauptstr. 150, 5830 Schwelm, W.
Germany (B.R.D.) Ed. Guenther Voigt.

940 GW ISSN 0522-6848
BEITRAEGE ZUR KOLONIAL UND
UEBERSEEGESCHICHTE. irreg., vol.36, 1986.
price varies. Franz Steiner Verlag Wiesbaden
GmbH, Birkenwaldstr. 44, Postfach 347, D-7000
Stuttgart 1, W. Germany (B.R.D.) Ed. Rudolf von
Albertini.

943 GW ISSN 0067-5164
BEITRAEGE ZUR OBERPFALZFORSCHUNG.
1965. irreg. price varies. Verlag Michael Lassleben,
Lange Gasse 19, Postfach 20, 8411 Kallmuenz, W.
Germany (B.R.D.) Ed. Heinz K. Rademacher.

943 GW
BEITRAEGE ZUR SUEDOSTEUROPA-
FORSCHUNG. irreg. (Arbeitskreis Suedosteuropa-
Forschung) Verlag Dr. Rudolf Trofenik, Elisabethstr.
18, 8000 Munich 40, W. Germany (B.R.D.)

940 GW ISSN 0723-5453
BEITRAEGE ZUR WIRTSCHAFTS UND
SOZIALGESCHICHTE. irreg., vol.33, 1986. price
varies. Franz Steiner Verlag Wiesbaden GmbH,
Birkenwaldstr. 44, Postfach 347, D-7000 Stuttgart 1,
W. Germany (B.R.D.) Ed.Bd.

947 917.306 US ISSN 0510-3746
BELARUSKI INSTYTUT NAVUKI MACTATSTVA.
ZAPISY/BYELORUSSIAN INSTITUTE OF ARTS
AND SCIENCES. ANNALS. (Text in
Byelorussian; summaries in English) 1952. a. $20
per no. (Byelorussian Institute of Arts and Sciences,
Inc.) Byelorussian Press, 230 Springfield Ave.,
Rutherford, NJ 07070. Ed. Dr. Vitaut Kipel. adv.
bk. rev. bibl. illus. stat. circ. 1,000. (also avail. in
microfilm; back issues avail.)

943 GW ISSN 0067-5792
BERGISCHER GESCHICHTSVEREIN.
ZEITSCHRIFT. 1863. irreg. DM.18. Bergischer
Geschichtsverein e. V., Friedrich-Engels-Allee 89-
91, 5600 Wuppertal 2, W. Germany (B.R.D.) Eds.
Wolfgang Koellmann, Juergen Reulecke. bk. rev.
circ. 3,000.

943 GW ISSN 0344-4910
BERLIN; Chronik. 1945. biennial. Verlag Spitzing,
Friedrichstr. 210, 1000 Berlin 61, W. Germany
(B.R.D.)

949.50 930 GE ISSN 0067-6055
BERLINER BYZANTINISTISCHE ARBEITEN.
(Text in German; occasionally in Greek) 1956.
irreg., no.53, 1985. price varies. (Akademie der
Wissenschaften der DDR, Zentralinstitut fuer Alte
Geschichte und Archaeologie) Akademie-Verlag,
Leipziger Strasse 3-4, 1086 Berlin, E. Germany
(D.D.R.) (Co-sponsor: Martin-Luther-Universitaet,
Halle/Wittenberg) Indexed: M.L.A.

943 GW
BERLINER HISTORISCHE KOMMISSION.
VEROEFFENTLICHUNGEN. 1960. irreg., vol.57,
1984. price varies. Walter de Gruyter und Co.,
Genthiner Str. 13, 1000 Berlin 30, W. Germany
(B.R.D.) (U.S. addr.: Walter de Gruyter, Inc., 200
Saw Mill Rd., Hawthorne, N.Y. 10532) adv.

943 GW ISSN 0067-611X
BERLINISCHE REMINISZENZEN. 1963. irreg., no.
56, 1985. price varies. Haude und Spenersche
Verlagsbuchhandlung GmbH, Potsdamer Str. 199,
1000 Berlin 30, W. Germany (B.R.D.)

943.8 PL ISSN 0067-6470
BIALOSTOCKIE TOWARZYSTWO NAUKOWE.
PRACE.* 1963. irreg. Bialostockie Towarzystwo
Naukowe, Dom Technika, Sklodowskiej - Curie 2,
15-097 Bialystok, Poland (Dist by Ars Polona-Ruch,
Krakowskie Przedmiescie 7, Warsaw, Poland)

949.4 016 SZ ISSN 0067-6772
BIBLIOGRAFIA TICINESE.* 1960. a. price varies.
Biblioteca Cantonale Lugano, Viale Carlo Cattaneo,
CH-6900 Lugano, Switzerland. index.

940 015.47 US ISSN 0162-5322
BIBLIOGRAPHIC GUIDE TO SOVIET AND
EUROPEAN STUDIES. (Text in Bulgarian, Czech,
English, Latvian, Polish, Russian, Slovak and
Ukranian) 1978. a. price varies. G. K. Hall & Co.,
70 Lincoln St., Boston, MA 02111. TEL 617-423-
3990.

BIBLIOGRAPHIE LUXEMBOURGEOISE. see
BIBLIOGRAPHIES

BIBLIOLOGIA. see PUBLISHING AND BOOK
TRADE

945 IT ISSN 0067-7442
BIBLIOTECA DI STORIA TOSCANA MODERNA
E CONTEMPORANEA STUDI E DOCUMENTI.
1965. irreg., vol.32, 1985. price varies. (Unione
Regionale delle Provincie Toscane, Florence) Casa
Editrice Leo S. Olschki, Casella Postale 66, 50100
Florence, Italy. circ. 1,000.

949.8 RM ISSN 0067-7493
BIBLIOTECA ISTORICA. 1957. irreg., vol.68, 1985.
(Academia de Stiinte Sociale si Politice, Institutul
de Istorie "N. Iorga") Editura Academiei Republicii
Socialiste Rumania, Calea Victoriei 125, 71021
Bucharest, Rumania (Subscr. to: ARTEXIM,
Export-Import Presa, Str. Piata Scinteii nr.1, P.O.
Box 33-16, 70055 Bucharest, Rumania)

945 940.27 IT
BIBLIOTECA NAPOLETANA DI STORIA E
ARTE. 1976. irreg. price varies. Congedo Editore,
Galatina, Italy. Dir. Franco Strazzullo.

946 SP ISSN 0405-9212
BIBLIOTECA PROMOCION DEL PUEBLO.* 1965.
irreg. no. 100, 1977. Zero S.A., Lerida 82, Madrid
20, Spain (Dist. by: ZYX S.A., Lerida 80, Madrid
20, Spain)

945 IT ISSN 0392-0550
BIBLIOTECA STATALE E LIBRERIA CIVICA DI
CREMONA. ANNALI. 1948. a. price varies.
Biblioteca Statale e Libreria Civica di Cremona, Via
Ugolani Dati 4, Cremona, Italy. Ed. Goffredo Dotti.
circ. 1,780.

945 IT
BIBLIOTECA STORICA TOSCANA. SERIE I. 1923.
irreg., no.22, 1986. price varies. (Deputazione
Toscana di Storia Patria) Casa Editrice Leo S.
Olschki, Casella Postale 66, 50100 Florence, Italy.
circ. 1,000.
Formerly (until 1977): Biblioteca Storica Toscana
(ISSN 0067-7523)

945 IT
BIBLIOTECA STORICA TOSCANA. SERIE II.
1977. irreg., vol. 7, 1984. (Societa Toscana della
Storia del Risorgimento) Casa Editrice Leo S.
Olschki, Casella Postale 66, 0100 Florence, Italy.

BIBLIOTEKA KRAKOWSKA. see ART

949.8 RM ISSN 0067-799X
BIBLIOTHECA HISTORICA ROMANIAE.
MONOGRAPHIES. (Text in English, French,
German, Russian) 1963. irreg., vol.23, 1980.
(Academia Republicii Socialiste Romania) Editura
Academiei Republicii Socialiste Rumania, Calea
Victoriei 125, 79717 Bucharest, Rumania (Subscr.
to: ARTEXIM, Export-Import Presa, Str. Piata
Scinteii nr.1, P.O. Box 33-16, 70055 Bucharest,
Rumania) (Co-sponsor: Academia de Stiinte Sociale
si Politice) Eds. St. Pascu, St. Stefanescu.

949.8 RM ISSN 0067-7981
BIBLIOTHECA HISTORICA ROMANIAE.
STUDIES. (Text in English, French, German,
Russian) 1963. irreg., vol.67, 1984. (Academia
Republicii Socialiste Romania) Editura Academiei
Republicii Socialiste Rumania, Calea Victoriei 125,
79717 Bucharest, Rumania (Subscr. to: ARTEXIM,
Export-Import Presa, Str. Piata Scinteii nr.1, P.O.
Box 33-16, 70055 Bucharest, Rumania) (Co-sponsor:
Academia de Stiinte Sociale si Politice) Eds. St.
Pascu, St. Stefanescu.

940 PL ISSN 0067-8031
BIBLIOTHECA LATINA MEDII ET RECENTIORI
AEVI. (Text in Latin) 1960. irreg., vol.23, 1986.
price varies. (Polska Akademia Nauk, Komitet Nauk
o Kulturze Antycznej) Ossolineum, Publishing
House of the Polish Academy of Sciences, Rynek 9,
50-106 Wroclaw, Poland (Dist. by Ars Polona-Ruch,
Krakowskie Przedmiescie 7, Warsaw, Poland) Ed.
M. Cytowska.

940 SZ ISSN 0067-8406
BIBLIOTHEQUE HISTORIQUE VAUDOISE. 1940.
irreg., no. 58, 1977. price varies. Petit-Chene 18,
1002 Lausanne, Switzerland. Ed. Colin Martin.
cum.index (1940-present) in each vol. Indexed:
Numis.Lit.

948 069 SZ
BIBLIOTHEQUES ET MUSEES. 1948. a. free.
Affaires Culturelles, CH-2001 Neuchatel,
Switzerland.

BIJDRAGE TOT DE GESCHIEDENIS VAN HET
ZEEWEZEN. see MILITARY

949.2 NE ISSN 0067-8554
BIJDRAGEN TOT DE GESCHIEDENIS VAN
ARNHEM. 1966. irreg., no.5, 1981. price varies.
Gemeentearchief - Arnhem Municipal Archives,
Koningstraat 32 II, 6811 D G Arnhem,
Netherlands. circ. 1,000.

940.27 BE
BIJDRAGEN TOT DE GESCHIEDENIS VAN DE
TWEEDE WERELDOORLOG. (Text in Flemish;
French language edition avail.) 1970. irreg.
Navorsings-en Studiecentrum voor de Geschiedenis
van de Tweede Wereldoorlog, Leuvenseplein 4, P.
B. 19, 1000 Brussels, Belgium. Indexed: Hist.Abstr.
Amer.Hist.& Life.

HISTORY — HISTORY OF EUROPE

940 069   GE
BILDUNG IM GESCHICHTSMUSEUM. no. 10, 1974. a. Museum fuer Geschichte der Stadt Dresden, Ernst--Thaelmann--Str. 2, 801 Dresden, E. Germany (D.D.R.) bibl. illus.

948.9   DK   ISSN 0107-072X
BJERG-POSTEN. MEDLEMSBLAD. 1977. a. Kr.30 to members. Lokalhistorisk Forening i Frejlev-Noerholm- Soendenholm Sogne, Restrup Kaervej 16, DK-9240 Nibe, Denmark. Ed. Arne Fristrup. illus. circ. 400.

943   GW   ISSN 0006-4408
BLAETTER FUER DEUTSCHE LANDESGESCHICHTE. 1852. a. DM.140. Gesamtverein der deutschen Geschichts- und Altertumsvereine, c/o Nordrhein-Westfaelisches Hauptstaatsarchiv, Mauerstr. 55, D-4 Duesseldorf 30, W. Germany (B.R.D.) Ed. Dr. Wilhelm Janssen. bk. rev. circ. 800. Indexed: Hist.Abstr. Amer.Hist.& Life. Bibl.Cart. Numis.Lit.

BLAETTER FUER WUERTTEMBERGISCHE KIRCHENGESCHICHTE. see *RELIGIONS AND THEOLOGY*

948   DK   ISSN 0107-6094
BLICHEREGNENS MUSEUMSFORENING. AARSSKRIFT. 1980. a. Kr.50. Blicheregnens Museumsforening, Blichersvej 30, Thorning, 8620 Kjellerup, Denmark. Eds. Anton Lauritzen and Gudmund Lund. illus.

BOARD OF CELTIC STUDIES. BULLETIN. see *LITERATURE*

940   GW   ISSN 0523-8587
BOHEMIA: ZEITSCHRIFT FUER GESCHICHTE UND KULTUR DER BOHEMISCHEN LAENDER. 1960. biennial. DM.68. (Collegium Carolinum) R. Oldenbourg Verlag GmbH, Rosenheimer Str. 145, 8000 Munich 80, W. Germany (B.R.D.) Eds. Ferdinand Seibt, Hans Lemberg. Indexed: Hist.Abstr. Amer.Hist.& Life. Supersedes: Verein fuer Geschichte der Deutschen in den Sudentenlaendern. Jahrbuch; Formerly: Collegium Carolinum. Bohemia-Jahrbuch.

943   GW   ISSN 0068-0052
BONNER GESCHICHTSBLAETTER. 1937. a. DM.50. Bonner Heimat- und Geschichtsverein, Berliner Platz 2, 5300 Bonn 1, W. Germany (B.R.D.) (Co-sponsor: Stadtarchiv Bonn) Ed. Manfred van Rey. circ. 1,500.

948   DK   ISSN 0084-7976
BORNHOLMSKE SAMLINGER. 1906. irreg. Kr.75. Bornholms Historiske Samfund, Stenbrudsvej 5 A, DK 3730 Nexo, Denmark. Ed. Olaf Hansen. bk. rev. circ. 600. Indexed: Numis.Lit.

942   UK   ISSN 0084-7984
BOROUGH OF TWICKENHAM LOCAL HISTORY SOCIETY. PAPERS. 1965. irreg. price varies. Twickenham Local History Society, 59 Park House Gardens, Twickenham, Middlesex TW1 2DF, England. Ed. A.C.B. Urwin. circ. 1,500.

942.8   UK   ISSN 0305-9898
BORTHWICK INSTITUTE BULLETIN. 1975. a. £1. Borthwick Institute of Historical Research, University of York, York, England. Ed. Dr. D.M. Smith. circ. 400.

948   FI
BOTHNIA. 1922. irreg. Svenska Osterbottningar Hembygdsforening i Helsingfors, Hagsluttningen 2 M 162, 02100 Esbo 10, Finland.

914.221   UK   ISSN 0520-6790
BOURNE SOCIETY LOCAL HISTORY RECORDS. 1962. a. £2. Bourne Society, c/o 17 Manor Ave., Caterham, Surrey CR3 6AP, England. Ed. T.J. Boyle. adv. bibl. charts. illus. index. circ. 4,000. Indexed: Br.Archaeol.Abstr.

946.9   PO   ISSN 0006-8640
BRACARA AUGUSTA; revista cultural de Regionalismo e historia. 1949. irreg. price varies. (Camara Municipal de Braga) Livraria Cruz, Rua D. Diogo de Sousa 129-133, Braga, Portugal. Ed.Bd. bibl. illus. index.
Local

943.7   CS
BRATISLAVA. ROCENKA. 1965. irreg. Vydavatel'stvo Obzor, Ceskoslovenskej Armady 29, 893 36 Bratislava, Czechoslovakia (Subscr. to: Slovart, Gottwaldovo Nam 6, Bratislava 805 32, Czechoslovakia)

943 615.19   GW
BRAUNSCHWEIGER VEROEFFENTLICHUNGEN ZUR GESCHICHTE DER PHARMAZIE. 1957. irreg. Deutscher Apotheker Verlag, Postfach 40, 7000 Stuttgart 1, W. Germany (B.R.D.) illus. Formerly: Brunswick. Technische Universitaet Carolo-Wilhelmina. Pharmaziegeschichtliches Seminar. Veroeffentlichung.

943   GW   ISSN 0068-0745
BRAUNSCHWEIGISCHES JAHRBUCH. 1902. a. DM.32. Braunschweiger Geschichtsverein, Schriftleitung, Forstweg 2, 3340 Wolfenbuettel, W. Germany (B.R.D.) Ed. G. Scheel. circ. 1,300. Indexed: Bibl.Cart.

941   IE   ISSN 0068-0877
BREIFNE; journal of Cumann Seanchais Bhreifne. (Text in English and Irish) 1958. a. £5($12) Breifne Historical Society, St. Patrick's College, Cavan, Co.Cavan, Ireland. Ed. Daniel Gallogly. bk. rev. circ. 800.

940   GW   ISSN 0341-9622
BREMISCHES JAHRBUCH. 1863. a. price varies. Staatsarchiv Bremen, Am Staatsarchiv 1, 2800 Bremen 1, W. Germany (B.R.D.) (Co-sponsor: Historische Gesellschaft Bremen) Ed. Wilhelm Luehrs. bk. rev. illus. circ. 1,500. Indexed: Bibl.Cart.

940   UK   ISSN 0144-672X
BRENTFORD AND CHISWICK LOCAL HISTORY SOCIETY. JOURNAL. 1980. irreg., latest vol.3, 1985. price varies. Brentford and Chiswick Local History Society, c/o James Wisdom, Valerie Bott, Eds., 25 Hartington Rd., Chiswick, London W4 3TL, England. bk. rev. circ. 500.

BRISTOL AND GLOUCESTERSHIRE ARCHAEOLOGICAL SOCIETY, BRISTOL, ENGLAND. TRANSACTIONS. see *ARCHAEOLOGY*

942   UK   ISSN 0068-1075
BRITAIN: AN OFFICIAL HANDBOOK. a. £12.95. Central Office of Information, Overseas Publications and Foreign Languages, Hercules Rd., London SE1 7DU, England (Avail. from: Bernan Associates, Inc., 9730-E George Palmer Highway, Lanham, MD 20706, U.S.A. or Government Bookshop, 49 High Holborn, London WC1V 6HB, England) illus.

940   NE
BRITAIN AND THE NETHERLANDS. 1960. a. fl.39.50. Walburg Pers, Zaadmarkt 84a-86, Box 222, 7200 AE Zutphen, Netherlands. TEL 05750-10522.

941   UK
BRITAIN IN BRIEF. a. H.M.S.O., Box 569, London SE1 9NH, England.

940   UK   ISSN 0068-113X
BRITANNIA. (Includes annual survey of Romano-British excavations) 1970. a. membership. Society for the Promotion of Roman Studies, 31-34 Gordon Sq., London WC1H 0PP, England. Ed. M. Todd. adv. bk. rev. circ. 1,800. Indexed: Numis.Lit.
Devoted to Romano-British and connected studies

942 942   UK
BRITISH ACADEMY. PROCEEDINGS. 1903. a. Oxford University Press, Walton St., Oxford OX2 6DP, England. cum.index: vols.1-63. Indexed: Br.Hum.Ind. Br.Archaeol.Abstr. RILA.

BRITISH SCHOOL AT ROME. PAPERS. ARCHAEOLOGY. see *ARCHAEOLOGY*

948   FI   ISSN 0302-2447
BUDKAVLEN. (Text in English, German and Swedish) 1922. a. Fmk.40. Aabo Akademi, Etnologiska och Folkloristiska Institutionen, Budkavlen, 20500 Aabo 50, Finland. Ed. Nils Storaa. bk. rev. cum. index 1922-55. circ. 300.

949.75   BL   ISSN 0007-3946
BULGARIAN REVIEW. (Text in English) 1961. a. $30. Bulgarian Free Center, Caixa Postal 14590-ZC-95, 22412 Rio de Janeiro, Brazil. bk. rev. circ. 1,000. Indexed: Hist.Abstr. Amer.Hist.& Life.

949   BU   ISSN 0323-9985
BULGARSKA AKADEMIIA NA NAUKITE. INSTITUT ZA ISTORIIA. IZVESTIIA. (Summaries in various languages) 1951. irreg. 2.41 lv. Publishing House of the Bulgarian Academy of Sciences, Acad. G. Bonchev St., Bldg. 6, 1113 Sofia, Bulgaria (Dist. by: Hemus, 6, Rouski Blvd., 1000 Sofia, Bulgaria) Ed. D. Kosev. circ. 778.

944   FR   ISSN 0766-4516
BULLETIN D'HISTOIRE DE LA REVOLUTION FRANCAISE. 1961. biennial. price varies. Ministere de l'Education Nationale, Commission d'Histoire de la Revolution Francaise, 3/5 bd. Pasteur, 75015 Paris, France. bk. rev. cum.index. circ. 650. Indexed: Hist.Abstr. Amer.Hist.& Life. Formerly: Bulletin d'Histoire Economique et Sociale de la Revolution Francaise (ISSN 0068-4058)

940   AU   ISSN 0007-621X
BURGENLAENDISCHE FORSCHUNGEN. 1947. irreg. (2-3/yr.) Amt der Burgenlaendischen Landesregierung, Landesarchiv, Freiheitsplatz 1, A-7001 Eisenstadt, Austria. Ed. Dr. August Ernst. bk. rev. circ. 1,000.

BUZETSKI ZBORNIK. see *ARCHAEOLOGY*

948   NO   ISSN 0084-8212
BY OG BYGD; Norsk Folkemuseums aarbok. (Text in Norwegian; summaries in English and German) 1943. a. price varies. Norsk Folkemuseum, Bygdoey, Oslo 2, Norway. Indexed: Hist.Abstr. Amer.Hist.& Life. Br.Archaeol.Abstr.

943.8   PL   ISSN 0068-4589
BYDGOSKIE TOWARZYSTWO NAUKOWE. WYDZIAL NAUK HUMANISTYCZNYCH. PRACE. SERIA C (HISTORIA I ARCHEOLOGIA) 1963. irreg. price varies. Bydgoskie Towarzystwo Naukowe, Jezuicka 4, Bydgoszcz, Poland (Dist. by Ars Polona-Ruch, Krakowskie Przedmiescie 7, Warsaw, Poland)

948 914   DK   ISSN 0105-6433
BYHORNET; nyt fra Egnsmuseet i Pederstrup. 1972. a. Ballerup og Omegns Historiske Forening, Egnsmuseet Lindbjerggard, Pederstrupvej 51, 2750 Ballerup, Denmark. Eds. Bent Schnoeder, Henrik Mogensen. circ. 300.

949   NE   ISSN 0525-4507
BYZANTINA NEERLANDICA. 1969. irreg., vol. 9, 1986. price varies. E. J. Brill, P.O. Box 9000, 2300 PA Leiden, Netherlands. Ed.Bd.

947   BU   ISSN 0068-4686
BYZANTINOBULGARICA. (Text in English, French, German and Russian) 1962. irreg. (Bulgarska Akademiya na Naukite) Publishing House of the Bulgarian Academy of Sciences, Ul. Akad. G. Bonchev, Bldg. 6, 1113 Sofia, Bulgaria. Indexed: Numis.Lit. RILA.

943.7   CS   ISSN 0303-2221
C S S R. KRONIKA VNITROPOLITICKYCH UDALOSTI. 1970. a. Svaboda, Revolucni 15, 113 03 Prague, Czechoslovakia.

940.27   BE   ISSN 0771-6435
CAHIERS D'HISTOIRE DE SECONDE GUERRE MONDIALE. 1970. irreg. Ministere de l'Education Nationale, Centre de Recherches et d'Etudes de la Seconde Guerre Mondiale, Place de Louvain 4, 1000 Brussels, Belgium. bk. rev. circ. 2,000. Indexed: Hist.Abstr. Amer.Hist.& Life.

949   NE
CAHIERS SOCIALE GESCHIEDENIS. 1982. irreg. price varies. Uitgeverij Martinus Nijhoff, Morssingel 9-13, 2312 AZ Leiden, Netherlands.

942 913   UK
CAMBRIDGE ANTIQUARIAN SOCIETY. PROCEEDINGS. 1840. a. £6 to individuals; institutions £10. Cambridge Antiquarian Society, Museum of Archaeology and Anthropology, Downing St., Cambridge CB2 3DZ, Cambridgeshire, England. Ed. M.D. Craster. bk. rev. cum.index. circ. 550. Indexed: Br.Hum.Ind. Br.Archaeol.Abstr. Numis.Lit. RILA.

HISTORY — HISTORY OF EUROPE

942 UK
CAMBRIDGE STUDIES IN MEDIEVAL LIFE
AND THOUGHT. FOURTH SERIES. 1969. irreg.,
no.6, 1987. $49.50 for latest vol. Cambridge
University Press, Edinburgh Bldg., Shaftesbury Rd.,
Cambridge CB2 2RU, England (and 32 E. 57 St.,
New York, NY 10022) Ed. Walter Ullmann. index.
Indexed: M.L.A.
  Formerly: Cambridge Studies in Medieval Life
and Thought. Third Series (ISSN 0068-6786)

942 UK ISSN 0068-6905
CAMDEN FOURTH SERIES. 1838, Fourth Series
1964. a. membership. Royal Historical Society,
University College London, Gower St., London
WC1E 6BT, England.

940 UK ISSN 0305-4756
CAMDEN HISTORY REVIEW. 1973. a. £1 per no.
Camden History Society, Swiss Cottage Library,
Avenue Rd., London N.W. 3, England. Ed. John
Gage. bk. rev. bibl. cum.index. circ. 3,000. Indexed:
Br.Tech.Ind.
  Regional English history

CANADIAN PAPERS IN RURAL HISTORY. see
HISTORY — *History Of North And South
America*

942 IE ISSN 0332-4117
CATHAIR NA MART. 1981. irreg. £3.50. Westport
Historical Society, c/o Carrowholly Lodge,
Westport, Co. Mayo, Ireland. Ed. Jarlath Duffy.
adv. illus. circ. 1,000.

940.53 US ISSN 0737-8092
CENTER FOR HOLOCAUST STUDIES
NEWSLETTER. 1976. irreg., vol.2, 1983. per no.
Center for Holocaust Studies, Documentation &
Research, 1609 Ave. J, Brooklyn, NY 11230. TEL
718-338-6494. Ed. Bonnie Gurewitsch. bk. rev. film
rev. play rev. bibl. circ. 2,000.

940 BE ISSN 0076-1192
CENTRE BELGE D'HISTOIRE RURALE.
PUBLICATIONS/BELGISCH CENTRUM VOOR
LANDELIJKE GESCHIEDENIS. PUBLIKATIES.
(Text in French, Dutch, English) 1963. irreg., no.86,
1985. price varies. Centre Belge d'Histoire Rurale, 1
Place Blaise Pascal, 1348 Louvain-La-Neuve,
Belgium.

920 BE
CENTRE D'HISTOIRE ET D'ART DE LA
THUDINIE. PUBLICATIONS. 1977. irreg. (1-2/
yr.) 150 Fr. Centre d'Histoire et d'Art de la
Thudinie, 7 rue Louis Cambier, Bte. 14, 6530
Thuin, Belgium. illus.

940 956 FR
CENTRE DE RECHERCHE D'HISTOIRE ET
CIVILISATION DE BYZANCE. TRAVAUX ET
MEMOIRES. irreg. (Centre de Recherche
d'Histoire et Civilisation de Byzance) Diffusion de
Boccard, 11 rue de Medicis, 75006 Paris, France.

940.53 BE
CENTRE DE RECHERCHES ET D'ETUDES
HISTORIQUES DE LA SECONDE GUERRE
MONDIALE. BULLETIN. 1969. a. Ministere de
l'Education National, Centre de Recherches et
d'Etudes Historiques de la Seconde Guerre
Mondiale, Pl. de Louvain 4, 1000 Brussels, Belgium.
bk. rev. circ. 5,000. Indexed: Hist.Abstr.
Amer.Hist.& Life.

940 SZ ISSN 0069-1895
CENTRE EUROPEEN D'ETUDES BURGONDO-
MEDIANES. PUBLICATION. (Text in French and
German) 1953. a. 20 Fr. Centre Europeen d'Etudes
Burgondo-Medianes, Birfelderstr. 4, CH-4132
Muttenz, Switzerland. cum.index: 1959-1969.

CENTRE INTERNATIONAL DE
DOCUMENTATION OCCITANE. SERIE
BIBLIOGRAPHIQUE. see *BIBLIOGRAPHIES*

944 FR ISSN 0398-3765
CENTRE INTERNATIONAL DE
DOCUMENTATION OCCITANE. SERIE
ETUDES. 1978. irreg. price varies. Centre
International de Documentation Occitane, Beziers,
France. Ed. F. Pic.

943 BE ISSN 0577-179X
CENTRE INTERUNIVERSITAIRE D'HISTOIRE
CONTEMPORAINE. CAHIERS/
INTERUNIVERSITAIR CENTRUM VOOR
HEDENDAAGSE GESCHIEDENIS.
MEDEDELINGEN. (Text in Dutch and French)
irreg., latest no.97, 1985. Editions Nauwelaerts, 148
Mechelstraat, 3000 Louvain, Belgium. Ed.Bd. bk.
rev. bibl.

949.7 YU ISSN 0352-1427
CENTRO DI RICERCHE STORICHE, ROVIGNO.
ATTI. (Text in Italian; summaries in Croatian,
Slovenian) 1970. a. 2000 din.($35) Centro di
Ricerche Storiche, Piazza Matteotti 13, Rovigno-
Rovinj, Yugoslavia. index. (looseleaf format)

949.7 YU ISSN 0350-6746
CENTRO DI RICERCHE STORICHE, ROVIGNO.
QUADERNI. (Text in Italian; summaries in
Croatian, Slovenian) 1971. irreg. 2000 din.($35)
Centro di Ricerche Storiche, Piazza Matteotti 13,
Rovigno-Rovinj, Yugoslavia. index. (looseleaf
format)

949.3 BE
CERCLE D'HISTOIRE ET D'ARCHEOLOGIE DE
SAINT-GHISLAIN ET DE LA REGION.
ANALES. a. Cercle d'Histoire et d'Archeologie de
Saint-Ghislain et de la Region, Saint-Ghislain,
Belgium. adv.
  Supersedes: Cercle d'Histoire et d'Archeologie de
Saint-Ghislain et de la Region. Miettes d'Histoire.

949 913 BE
CERCLE HISTORIQUE ET FOLKLORIQUE DE
BRAINE-LE-CHATEAU DE TUBIZE ET DES
REGIONS VOISINES. ANNALES. 1972. a.
Entente Culturelle Taille d'Aulme, Musee de la
Porte, Ave. Bel-air 46, 1440 Braine le Chateau,
Belgium.

949 724 BE
CERCLE HUTOIS DES SCIENCES ET BEAUX-
ARTS. ANNALES. 1875. a. Cercle Hutois des
Sciences et Beaux-Arts, Ancien Couvent des Freres
Mineurs, Rue Vankeerberghen 20, 5200 Huy,
Belgium.

943.7 CS ISSN 0323-1313
CESKOSLOVENSKA AKADEMIE VED.
ARCHIVNI ZPRAVY. 1970. a. Ceskoslovenska
Akademie Ved., Ustredni Archiv, Karlova 2, 110 00
Prague 1, Czechoslovakia. Ed. Lubos Novy. bk. rev.
circ. 500.

943.7 CS
CESKOSLOVENSKO-SOVETSKE VZTAHY. 1972.
a. Univerzita Karlova, Ovocny Trh 5, Prague 1,
Czechoslovakia (Subscr. to: Artia, Ve Smeckach 30,
111 27 Prague 1, Czechoslovakia)

942 UK ISSN 0080-0880
CHETHAM SOCIETY PUBLICATIONS-REMAINS,
HISTORICAL AND LITERARY, CONNECTED
WITH THE PALATINE COUNTRIES OF
LANCASTER AND CHESTER. 1843. a.
membership. ‡ (Chetham Society) Manchester
University Press, Oxford Rd., Manchester M13
9PL, England.

940 913 398 400 GR
CHIAKA CHRONIKA. (Text in English, Greek;
summaries in English, French) 1911. a. Dr.650($7)
S. Fassoulakis Ed. & Pub., 47 Righa Pheraiou St.,
161 22 Kaisariani, Greece. bk. rev. bibl. charts.
illus. circ. 1,000. (back issues avail.) Indexed:
M.L.A.

940 AU
CHORHERRENSTIFT KLOSTERNEUBURG.
JAHRBUCH. 1961. a. DM.66. Hermann Boehlaus
Nachf., c/o Dr. Karl Lueger, Ring 12, A-1010
Vienna, Austria. circ. 200.

946 SP
CHRONICA NOVA. 1968. irreg. price varies.
Universidad de Granada, Secretariado de
Publicaciones, Antiguo Colegio Maximo de Cartujo,
Granada, Spain. Ed. Pedro Gan Jiminez.

CIRENCESTER EXCAVATIONS. see
ARCHAEOLOGY

CIVILTA VENEZIANA. FONTI E TESTI. SERIE
PRIMA: FONTI E TESTI PER LA STORIA
DELL'ARTE VENETA. see *ART*

945 IT ISSN 0069-4347
CIVILTA VENEZIANA. FONTI E TESTI. SERIE
TERZA. 1962. irreg., no.4, 1982. price varies.
(Fondazione Giorgio Cini) Casa Editrice Leo S.
Olschki, Casella Postale 66, 50100 Florence, Italy.
circ. 500.

945 IT ISSN 0069-4371
CIVILTA VENEZIANA. SAGGI. 1955. irreg., vol.34,
1985. price varies. (Fondazione Giorgio Cini) Casa
Editrice Leo S. Olschki, Casella Postale 66, 50100
Florence, Italy. circ. 1,000.

945 IT ISSN 0069-438X
CIVILTA VENEZIANA. STUDI. 1953. irreg., vol.40,
1985. price varies. (Fondazione Giorgio Cini) Casa
Editrice Leo S. Olschki, Casella Postale 66, 50100
Florence, Italy. circ. 1,000.

CLASSICS OF BRITISH HISTORICAL
LITERATURE. see *LITERATURE*

949 PO ISSN 0870-4104
CLIO (LISBON) (Text in French and Portuguese)
1979. a. price varies. Universidade de Lisboa,
Centro de Historia, Cidade Universitaria, 1699
Lisbon Codex, Portugal. (Co-sponsor: Instituto
Nacional de Investigacao Cientifica) bk. rev.
circ. 1,000.

940 GW ISSN 0084-8808
COBURGER LANDESSTIFTUNG. JAHRBUCH.
1956. a. DM.34 u.S. price varies. Coburger
Landesstiftung, Schloss Ehrenburg, 8630 Coburg, W.
Germany (B.R.D.) Ed. Georg Aumann. bk. rev. bibl.
illus. index. circ. 600. (back issues avail.) Indexed:
Numis.Lit. RILA.

940 PO
COLECCAO ARQUIVOS. no. 4, 1982. irreg. Assirio
e Alvim, Cooperativa Editora e Livreira, SCARL,
Rua Passos Manuel, 67-B, 1100 Lisbon, Portugal.
Ed. Manuel Herminio Monteiro. circ. 3,000.

946 SP
COLECCION ARAGON. no. 10, 1977. irreg. Libreria
General, Independencia 22, Zaragoza 1, Spain.

940 SP
COLECCION CORRESPONDENCIA
DIPLOMATICA DE LOS NUNCIOS EN
ESPANA. 1976. irreg., no.2, 1982. price varies.
(Universidad de Navarra, Facultad de Filosofia y
Letras) Ediciones Universidad de Navarra, S.A.,
Apdo. 396, 31080 Pamplona, Spain.

946 SP ISSN 0069-5106
COLECCION HISTORICA. 1958. irreg., no.43, 1986.
price varies. (Universidad de Navarra, Facultad de
Filosofia y Letras) Ediciones Universidad de
Navarra, S.A., Apdo. 396, 31080 Pamplona, Spain.

940 IT
COLLANA DI DOCUMENTI IN MEMORIA DEL
CONTE GIUSEPPE MATARAZZO DI LICOSA.
1982. irreg., no.2, 1984. price varies. Liguori Editore
s.r.l., Via Mezzocannone 19, 80134 Milan, Italy. Ed.
Franco Strazzullo.

940 IT ISSN 0391-3279
COLLANA DI STORIA MODERNA E
CONTEMPORANEA. 1978. irreg., no.12, 1986.
price varies. Liguori Editore s.r.l., Via
Mezzocannone 19, 80134 Naples, Italy. TEL 081/
20 6077. Ed. Aurelio Lepre.

940 IT
COLLANA DI STUDI IN MEMORIA DEL CONTE
GIUSEPPE MATARAZZO DI LICOSA. 1979.
irreg., no.4, 1983. price varies. Liguori Editore s.r.l.,
Via Mezzocannone 19, 80134 Milan, Italy. TEL
081/20 6077. Ed. Franco Strazzullo.

940 GW ISSN 0530-9794
COLLEGIUM CAROLINUM.
VEROEFFENTLICHUNGEN. vol.30, 1977. irreg.
price varies. R. Oldenbourg Verlag GmbH,
Rosenheimer Str. 145, 8000 Munich 80, W.
Germany (B.R.D.).

943 947 US
COLUMBIA UNIVERSITY. INSTITUTE ON EAST
CENTRAL EUROPE. EAST CENTRAL
EUROPEAN STUDIES. irreg., latest 1968. price
varies. Columbia University Press, 562 W. 113th St.,
New York, NY 10025. TEL 212-678-6777.

HISTORY — HISTORY OF EUROPE

947   US   ISSN 0588-5477
COLUMBIA UNIVERSITY. RUSSIAN INSTITUTE. STUDIES. 1953. irreg. price varies. Columbia University, Russian Institute, 420 W. 118th St., New York, NY 10027. TEL 212-280-4623.

944   FR
COMITE DES TRAVAUX HISTORIQUES ET SCIENTIFIQUES. SECTION DE PHILOLOGIE ET HISTOIRE. ACTES DU CONGRES NATIONAL DES SOCIETES SAVANTES. (Text in French) 1970. a. price varies. Comite des Travaux Historiques et Scientifiques, 3-5 bd. Pasteur, 75015 Paris, France.

943 830   GW   ISSN 0588-6414
COMMENTATIONES BALTICAE. 1954. irreg. Univeristaet Bonn, Baltisches Forschungsinstitut, Lennestr. 1, D-5300 Bonn 1, W. Germany (B.R.D.) (Co-sponsor: Deutschen Forschungsgemeinschaft)

940   NE
COMPARATIVE STUDIES IN OVERSEAS HISTORY. (Text in English) 1978. irreg. price varies. (Leiden Centre for the History of European Expansion) Kluwer Academic Publishers Group, Distribution Center, Box 322, 3300 AH Dordrecht, Netherlands (U.S. address: Kluwer Academic Publishers Group, 190 Old Derby St., Hingham MA 02043) Ed. H. L. Wesseling.

CONFERENCE ON EDITORIAL PROBLEMS: UNIVERSITY OF TORONTO. see *LITERATURE*

949.3   BE   ISSN 0010-602X
CONNAITRE LA WALLONIE/TO KNOW WALLONY. Alternate title: Institut Jules Destree. Collection: Connaitre la Wallonie. 1960. irreg., no. 22. price varies. Institut Jules Destree, Rue du Chateau 3, 6100 Mont-sur-Marchienne Charleroi, Belgium.

948   DK   ISSN 0105-7669
CONTACT WITH DENMARK. French edition: Contact avec le Danemark (ISSN 0105-7677); German edition: Kontakt mit Daenemark (ISSN 0105-7634); Flemish edition: Kontakt met Denemarken (ISSN 0105-7642); Italian edition: Contatti con la Danimarca (ISSN 0106-0287) 1970. irreg. Kr.20. Danske Selskab - Danish Cultural Institute, 2 Kultorvet, DK-1175 Copenhagen K, Denmark. illus.

941   IE   ISSN 0010-8731
CORK HISTORICAL AND ARCHAEOLOGICAL SOCIETY. JOURNAL. 1892. a. £10($22) Cork Historical and Archaeological Society, Dromainn, Crosshaven, Co. Cork, Ireland. Ed. Diarmuid O. Murchadha. bk. rev. charts. illus. index. circ. 500. Indexed: Hist.Abstr. Amer.Hist.& Life. Br.Archaeol.Abstr.

CORPUS VITREARUM MEDII AEVI. see *ART*

COSTUME. see *CLOTHING TRADE — Fashions*

270 940   UK   ISSN 0070-1394
COURTENAY LIBRARY OF REFORMATION CLASSICS. 1963. irreg., no.15, 1984. price varies. Sutton Courtenay Press, c/o Appleford, Abingdon, Oxford OX14 4PB, England. Ed. G.E. Duffield.

230 940   UK
COURTENAY REFORMATION FACSIMILES. 1973. irreg. price varies. Sutton Courtenay Press, c/o Appleford, Abingdon, Oxford OX14 4PB, England. Ed. G.E. Duffield.
    Formerly: Courtenay Facsimiles.

230 940   UK   ISSN 0070-1408
COURTENAY STUDIES IN REFORMATION THEOLOGY. 1966. irreg., no.5, 1984. price varies. Sutton Courtenay Press, c/o Appleford, Abingdon, Oxford OX 14 4PB, England. Ed. G.E. Duffield.

942   UK
COVENTRY EVENING TELEGRAPH YEAR BOOK & WHO'S WHO. 1966. a. £7.95. Coventry Newspapers Ltd., Corporation St., Coventry CV1 1FP, England. TEL 0203 633633. Ed. K.A. Burgess. adv. stat. index. circ. 900.

940   BE
CREDIT COMMUNAL DE BELGIQUE. ACTES DES COLLOQUES INTERNATIONAUX. COLLECTION HISTOIRE. SERIES IN 8. 1964. biennial. Credit Communal de Belgique, 44 bd. Pacheco, Brussels, Belgium.

940   UK   ISSN 0307-5583
CROMWELLIANA. 1968/69. a. membership. Cromwell Association, c/o Dept. of History & Archaeology, University of Exeter, Queen's Bldg., Queen's Drive, Exeter EX4 4QH, England. Ed. Prof. Ivan Roots. bk. rev. circ. 400.

940   SP
CUADERNOS DE ESTUDIOS MEDIEVALES. (Text in Spanish and French; summaries in English and French) 1973. a. Universidad de Granada, Departamento de Historia Medieval, Secretariado de Publicaciones, Hospital Real, Granada, Spain. Ed. Cristobal Torres. index. circ. 875. Indexed: Hist.Abstr. Amer.Hist.& Life.

940   SP
CUADERNOS DE TRABAJO DE HISTORIA. 1973. irreg., no. 8, 1978. price varies. (Universidad de Navarra, Departamento de Historia Medieval) Ediciones Universidad de Navarra, S.A., Apdo. 396, 31080 Pamplona, Spain.

946   SP
CUADERNOS SIMANCAS DE INVESTIGACIONES HISTORICAS: MONOGRAFIAS. irreg., no. 6, 1982. Universidad de Valladolid, Secretariado de Publicaciones, Valladolid, Spain.

940 100   PO   ISSN 0870-4546
CULTURA, HISTORIA Y FILOSOFIA. 1982. a. Esc.650. (Instituto Nacional de Investigacao Cientifica) Universidade Nova de Lisboa, Centro de Historia da Cultura, Av. de Berna 24, 1000 Lisbon, Portugal. Ed. Jose S. da Silva Diaz. bk. rev.

945   IT
CULTURA SARDA. 1975. irreg. Libreria Dessi Editrice, Sassari, Italy.

CURLEY'S STREETS & TRADES DIRECTORIES OF WEMBLEY, MIDDLESEX & SELBY, YORKSHIRE. see *BUSINESS AND ECONOMICS — Trade And Industrial Directories*

940   PL   ISSN 0070-2471
CZASOPISMO PRAWNO-HISTORYCZNE. (Text in Polish; summaries in French) 1948. irreg., vol.36, 1984. price varies. (Polska Akademia Nauk, Instytut Historii, Komisja Historii Panstwa i Prawa) Panstwowe Wydawnictwo Naukowe, Ul. Miodowa 10, 00-251 Warsaw, Poland (Dist. by: Ars Polona, Krakowskie Przedmiescie 7, 00-068 Warsaw, Poland) Ed. Henryk Olszewski. bk. rev. bibl. charts. circ. 370. Indexed: Hist.Abstr. Amer.Hist.& Life.

948.9   DK   ISSN 0070-2846
DANSKE MAGAZIN. (In 8 series; series 1-6 out of print) 1745. a. Kr.50. Kobenhavns Universitet, Historisk Institut, Njalsgade 102, 2300 Copenhagen 8, Denmark. Ed. Kai Hoerby. index. circ. 300. Indexed: Hist.Abstr. Amer.Hist.& Life.

948   DK
DANSKE STUDIER. 1904. a. Akademisk Forlag, Store Kannikestraede 8, P.O. Box 54, 1002 Copenhagen, Denmark. Indexed: M.L.A.

943   GW
DARMSTAEDTER ARCHIVSCHRIFTEN. 1975. irreg., no.7, 1984. price varies. Historischer Verein fuer Hessen, Staatsarchiv, Schloss, 6100 Darmstadt, W. Germany (B.R.D.) (Co-sponsors: Hessisches Staatsarchiv; Stadtarchiv Darmstadt)

940   NE
DAVIS MEDIEVAL TEXTS AND STUDIES. 1978. irreg., vol. 5, 1986. price varies. E.J. Brill, P.O. Box 9000, 2300 PA Leiden, Netherlands. Ed.Bd.

Z DEJIN HUTNICTVI. see *METALLURGY*

943.7   CS
Z DEJIN VIED A TECHNIKY NA SLOVENSKU. 1962. irreg. Veda Vydavatel'stvo Slovenskej Akademie Vied, Klemensova 19, 895 30 Bratislava, Czechoslovakia (Subscr. to: Slovart, Gottwaldovo Nam. 6, 805 32 Bratislava, Czechoslovakia) bk. rev. bibl.

943.7   CS   ISSN 0232-0150
DEJINY SOCIALISTICKEHO CESKOSLOVENSKA; studie a materialy. (Text in Czech) 1978. irreg. exchange basis only. Ustav Ceskoslovenskych a Svetovych Dejin CSAV, Vysehradska 49, 128 26 Prague 2, Czechoslovakia. Ed. Vaclav Pesa.

940 331.8 614.7   GW
DEMOKRATIE- UND ARBEITERGESCHICHTE. 1980. biennial. (Franz Mehring Gesellschaft, Stuttgart) Drumlin Verlag GmbH, D-7987 Weingarten, W. Germany (B.R.D.) Ed.Bd. circ. 2, 500. (back issues avail.)

945   IT   ISSN 0300-4422
DEPUTAZIONE DI STORIA PATRIA PER L'UMBRIA. BOLLETTINO. 1895. a. Deputazione di Storia Patria per l'Umbria, Palazzo dei Priori, C.P. 130, 06100 Perugia, Italy. Ed. Giovanni Antonelli. bk. rev. bibl. circ. 500. Indexed: Hist.Abstr. Amer.Hist.& Life. RILA.

943 430   GE   ISSN 0070-3893
DEUTSCH-SLAWISCHE FORSCHUNGEN ZUR NAMENKUNDE UND SIEDLUNGSGESCHICHTE. irreg., vol.35, 1984. price varies. (Saechsische Akademie der Wissenschaften, Leipzig, Historische Kommission) Akademie-Verlag, Leipziger Str. 3-4, 1086 Berlin, E. Germany (D.D.R.) Indexed: M.L.A.

943   GW
DEUTSCHE ANNALEN. 1972. a. DM.29.80. Druffel-Verlag, Assenbucher Str. 28, 8137 Berg-Leoni, W. Germany (B.R.D.) Ed. Gert Sudholt. illus. circ. 11,500.

943   GW   ISSN 0070-4016
DEUTSCHE GAUE; Zeitschrift fuer Heimatforschung Landes- und Volkskunde. 1899. irreg. (Wilhelm-Heinrich-Riehl-Doktor-Christian-Frank-Gedaechtnisstiftung, Kaufbeuren) Verlag Deutsche Gaue, Kaufbeuren, W. Germany (B.R.D.)

940   GE   ISSN 0075-286X
DEUTSCHE GESCHICHTE. JAHRESBERICHTE. 1952. a. price varies. (Akademie der Wissenschaften der DDR, Zentralinstitut fuer Geschichte, Abteilung Information und Dokumentation) Akademie-Verlag, Leipziger Str. 3-4, 1086 Berlin, E. Germany (D.D.R.)

943   GW   ISSN 0170-3080
DEUTSCHE HANDELSAKTEN DES MITTELALTERS UND DER NEUZEIT. irreg., vol.17, 1987. price varies. (Bayerische Akademie der Wissenschaften, Historische Kommission) Franz Steiner Verlag Wiesbaden GmbH, Birkenwaldstr. 44, Postfach 347, D-7000 Stuttgart 1, W. Germany (B.R.D.) Ed.Bd.

940 270   GW   ISSN 0344-2934
DEUTSCHER HUGENOTTEN-VEREIN E.V. GESCHICHTSBLAETTER. 1890. irreg. price varies. Deutscher Hugenotten-Verein E.V., Postfach 35, D 3305 Sickte, W. Germany (B.R.D.), W. Germany (B.R.D.) Ed. Helmut Kimmel. circ. 1,000.

940   GW   ISSN 0340-8396
DEUTSCHES MITTELALTER, KRITISCHE STUDIENTEXTE DER MONUMENTA GERMANIAE HISTORICA. (Text in German and Latin) 1937. irreg. price varies. Anton Hiersemann Verlag, Rosenbergstr. 113, Postfach 723, 7000 Stuttgart 1, W. Germany (B.R.D.)

948.9   DK   ISSN 0070-4938
DIPLOMATARIUM DANICUM. Danish edition: Danmarks Riges Breve (ISSN 0070-2773) (Text generally in Latin) 1938. irreg. Kr.183. Danske Sprog- og Litteraturselskab - Danish Society of Language and Literature, Frederiksholms Kanal 18 A, 1220 Copenhagen K, Denmark (Subscr. to: C.A. Reitzel Publishers, 20 Noerregade, DK-1165 Copenhagen K, Denmark) Ed. Herluf Nielsen. circ. 600.

949.8   RM   ISSN 0070-6825
DOCUMENTA ROMANIAE HISTORICA. SERIE A: LA MOLDAVIE. 1969. irreg., vol.3, 1980. (Academia de Stiinte Sociale si Politice) Editura Academiei Republicii Socialiste Rumania, Calea Victoriei 125, 71021 Bucharest, Rumania (Subscr. to: ARTEXIM, Export-Import Presa, Piata Scinteii nr.1, P.O. Box 33-16, 70055 Bucharest, Rumania)

HISTORY — HISTORY OF EUROPE

949.8   RM   ISSN 0070-6833
DOCUMENTA ROMANIAE HISTORICA. SERIE B: LA VALACHIE. 1966. irreg., vol.6, 1985. (Academia de Stiinte Sociale si Politice) Editura Academiei Republicii Socialiste Rumania, Calea Victoriei 125, 79717 Bucharest, Rumania (Subscr. to: ARTEXIM, Str. Piata Scinteii 1, P.O. Box 33-16, 70055 Bucharest, Rumania)

900 500   BE
DOCUMENTS HISTORIQUES DES SCIENCES. (Editions in Flemish and French) 1966. irreg. Comite Belge d'Histoire des Sciences, Centrale Bibliotheek der Univ., Rozier 9, 9000 Ghent, Belgium.

940   UK
DOCUMENTS OF MEDIEVAL HISTORY. no. 2, 1975. irreg. price varies. Edward Arnold (Publishers) Ltd., 441 Bedford Sq., London WC1B 3DQ, England. Eds. G.W.S. Barrow, Edward Miller.

943.6   AU
DOEBLINGER MUSEUMSBLAETTER. 1964. irreg. Museumsverein Doebling, Doeblinger Haupstr. 96, 1190 Vienna, Austria.
Formerly: Doeblinger Heimatmuseum.

DOKUMENTE ZUR DEUTSCHLANDPOLITIK. see *POLITICAL SCIENCE*

DOKUMENTE ZUR DEUTSCHLANDPOLITIK. BEIHEFTE. see *POLITICAL SCIENCE*

943   GW   ISSN 0070-7074
DONAUSCHWAEBISCHES SCHRIFTTUM. 1953. irreg., no. 17, 1972. price varies. Landsmannschaft der Donauschwaben, Goldmuehlestr. 30, 7032 Sindelfingen, W. Germany (B.R.D.) adv. bk. rev. circ. 1,000.

949.2 286   NE
DOOPSGEZINDE BIJDRAGEN. 1975. a. Doopsgezinde Historische Kring, Singel 425, 1000 Amsterdam, Netherlands. bk. rev. bibl. Indexed: CERDIC.

DREVNEISHIE GOSUDARSTVA NA TERRITORII S.S.S.R/ANCIENT STATES IN THE TERRITORY OF THE U.S.S.R; materialy i issledovaniya. see *ARCHAEOLOGY*

949 497   YU   ISSN 0419-7925
DUBROVACKI HORIZONTI. 1970. a. 90 din. Drustvo Dubrovcana i Prijatelja Dubrovacke Starine, Szabova 21/III ulaz, Zagreb, Yugoslavia. Ed. Josip Lucic. circ. 1,800.

943   GW   ISSN 0342-0019
DUESSELDORFER JAHRBUCH. 1886. irreg. Verlag Droste GmbH, Postfach 1135, 4000 Duesseldorf 1, W. Germany (B.R.D.) bk. rev.
Formerly (1886-1912): Beitraege zur Geschichte des Niederheins. Jahrbuch des Duesseldorfer Geschichtsvereins.

940   US
DUKE MONOGRAPHS IN MEDIEVAL AND RENAISSANCE STUDIES. 1974. irreg. Duke University Press, 6697 College Sta., Durham, NC 27708.

DUKHOVNA AKADEMIYA SV. KLIMENT OKHRIDSKI. GODISHNIK. see *RELIGIONS AND THEOLOGY*

DURHAM ARCHAEOLOGICAL JOURNAL. see *ARCHAEOLOGY*

DUTCH ARCHAEOLOGICAL AND HISTORICAL SOCIETY. STUDIES. see *ARCHAEOLOGY*

943.8   PL   ISSN 0419-8816
DZIEJE LUBLINA. 1965. irreg. price varies. Wydawnictwo Lubelskie, Okopowa 7, Lublin, Poland.

943.8   PL   ISSN 0070-7791
DZIEJE POLSKIEJ GRANICY ZACHODNIEJ. 1961. irreg. Instytut Zachodni, Stary Rynek 78/79, 61-772 Poznan, Poland (Dist. by Ars Polona-Ruch, Krakowskie Przedmiescie 7, Warsaw, Poland) circ. 1,500.

EALING MISCELLANY. see *LIBRARY AND INFORMATION SCIENCES*

942   UK   ISSN 0070-8208
EAST YORKSHIRE LOCAL HISTORY SERIES. 1952. irreg. membership. East Yorkshire Local History Society, Beverley Library, Champney Rd., Beverley, North Humberside HU17 9BQ, England. Ed. D.M. Woodward. circ. 350.

EASTERN EUROPEAN GENEALOGIST. see *GENEALOGY AND HERALDRY*

940   FR
ECOLE FRANCAISE DE ROME. MELANGES: MOYEN AGES, TEMPS MODERNE. (In two vols.) a. Diffusion de Boccard, 11 rue de Medicis, 75006 Paris, France. Indexed: Hist.Abstr. Amer.Hist.& Life. Numis.Lit.

940 869   FR
ECOLE PRATIQUE DES HAUTES ETUDES. CENTRE DE RECHERCHES SUR LE PORTUGAL DE LA RENAISSANCE. SERIES TEXTES. (Text in French) 1979. irreg. price varies. (Ecole Pratique des Hautes Etudes, Centre de Recherches sur le Poturgal de la Renaissance) Librarie Touzot, 38 rue Saint Sulpice, 75278 Paris Cedex 06, France.

ECONOMISCH- EN SOCIAAL-HISTORISCH JAARBOEK. see *BUSINESS AND ECONOMICS — Economic Systems And Theories, Economic History*

948.9   DK   ISSN 0109-0194
EGNSHISTORISK FORENING I GRUNDSOE. AARSSKRIFT. 1972. a. Kr.50. Egnshistorisk Forening i Grundsoe, Moellevej 24, 4040 Jyllinge, Denmark. illus.

943   GW   ISSN 0723-0877
EINHORN-JAHRBUCH. 1974. a. DM.20. Einhorn-Verlag GmbH, Sebaldstr. 9-11, D 7070 Schwaebisch Gmuend, W. Germany (B.R.D.) Ed. Eduard Dietenberger. circ. 2,500.

943   GW   ISSN 0420-8870
EINST UND JETZT. a. (Verein fuer Corpsstudentische Geschichtsforschung) Aller Druckerei, Verden, W. Germany (B.R.D.) illus.

947 913   CS   ISSN 0046-1628
EIRENE. (Text in English, French, German and Russian) 1960. irreg. Academia Nakladatelstvi C S A V, Vodickova 40, 112 29 Prague 1, Czechoslovakia (Subscr. to: John /Benjamins B.V., P.O. Box 52519, 1007 HA Amsterdam, Holland) Indexed: Bull.Signal.

943.8   IT   ISSN 0070-9972
ELEMENTA AD FONTIUM EDITIONES; unpublished sources to mediaeval and modern European history, 14th-17th centuries. (Text in English, Italian, Latin, Spanish and Swedish) 1960. irreg., vol.58, 1984. price varies. Institutum Historicum Polonicum Romae - Polish Historical Institute, Via Virginio Orsini 19, 00192 Rome, Italy. cum. index.

942   US   ISSN 0085-0225
ELIZABETHAN CLUB SERIES. 1960. irreg., no.7, 1982. price varies. Yale University Press, 92A Yale Sta., New Haven, CT 06520. TEL 203-432-0940.

942   US   ISSN 0071-058X
ENGLISH HISTORICAL DOCUMENTS. irreg., vol. 12, 1977. price varies. Oxford University Press, 200 Madison Ave., New York, NY 10016 TEL 212-679-7300. (and Ely House, 37 Dover St., London W1X 4AH, England) Ed. David C. Douglas.

942   US   ISSN 0071-0628
ENGLISH MONARCH SERIES. 1964. irreg. price varies. University of California Press, 2120 Berkeley Way, Berkeley, CA 94720. TEL 415-642-4247.

948   DK
ERHVERVSHISTORISK ARBOG. 1949. a. Kr.80. Erhvervsarkivet, Vester Alle 12, DK-8000 Aarhus C, Denmark. cum.index: 1949-58; 1959-68; 1969-80. circ. 400. Indexed: Hist.Abstr. Amer.Hist.& Life.

946   SP
ESPANA - SUS MONUMENTOS Y ARTES; SU NATURALEZA E HISTORIA. 1977. a. Ediciones el Albir, Calle de los Angeles 8, Barcelona 1, Spain. Local

946   SP
ESTUDIOS HISTORICOS Y DOCUMENTOS DE LOS ARCHIVOS DE PROTOCOLOS. (Text and summaries in Catalan and Spanish) 1948. a. 2500 ptas.($24) (Colegio Notarial de Barcelona) Ediciones el Albir, Calle de los Angeles 8, Barcelona 1, Spain.

943.7   CS
ETHNOLOGIA SLAVICA. (Text in English, French, German and Russian) 1970. a. Slovenske Pedagogicke Nakladatel'stvo, Sasinkova 5, 891 12 Bratislava, Czechoslovakia (Subscr. to: Slovart Gottwaldovo Nam 6, 805 32 Bratislava, Czechoslovakia) bk. rev. Indexed: M.L.A.

ETUDES DE PHILOLOGIE ET D'HISTOIRE. see *LITERATURE*

947   BU   ISSN 0525-0846
ETUDES HISTORIQUES. (Text in English, French, German and Russian) 1960. irreg. (Bulgarska Akademiya na Naukite) Publishing House of the Bulgarian Academy of Sciences, Ul. Akad. G. Bonchev, Bldg. 6, 1113 Sofia, Bulgaria (Subscr. to: Hemus Foreign Trade Co., 6 Ruski Blvd., 1000 Sofia, Bulgaria)

944   FR
ETUDES SAVOISIENNES. no. 2, 1975. irreg. 100 F. University de Savoie, Institut d'Edutes Savoisiennes. Departement d'Histoire, B.P. 143, 73000 Chambery, France. (Co-sponsor: Societe Savoisienne d'Histoire et d'Archeologie) Dir. Jacques Lovie. bibl. illus.

940   NE
EUROPE IN THE MIDDLE AGES; selected studies. (Text in English) 1977. irreg., vol.17, 1980. price varies. Elsevier Science Publishers B.V., Box 211, Amsterdam, Netherlands. Ed. Richard Vaughan.

940 709   US   ISSN 0098-2474
EXPLORATIONS IN RENAISSANCE CULTURE. 1974. a. $5. (University of Southwestern Louisiana, Department of English) South-Central Renaissance Conference, USL Station, Box 44612, Lafayette, LA 70504. TEL 318-231-6857. Ed. Albert W. Fields. charts. illus. stat. circ. 500. (back issues avail.) Indexed: M.L.A.

948   DK   ISSN 0106-8822
FAABORG-AARBOGEN. Cover title: Faaborg-Bogen. vol. 5, 1979. a. Kr.70. (Faaborg Lokalhistorisk Selskab) Edvard Andersen, Oesterbro 42, 5600 Faaborg, Denmark. (Co-sponsor: Byhistorisk Vennekreds) Ed. Edvard Andersen. illus.
Formerly: Arkiver: Folkemindesamlinger og Museer i Faaborg Kommune.

948   FI   ISSN 0356-5629
FARAVID. 1977. a. $16. Pohjois-Suomen Historiallinen Yhdistys, Oulun Yliopisto, Historian Laitos, Postilokero 191, 90101 Oulu, Finland. Ed. Kyoesti Julku. circ. 700.

940   PL   ISSN 0071-4038
FASCICULI HISTORICI. (Text in English, French, German and Russian) 1968. irreg., vol. 12, 1984. price varies. (Uniwersytet Warszawski, Instytut Historyczny) Wydawnictwa Uniwersytetu Warszawskiego, Ul. Obozna 8, 00-927 Warsaw, Poland (Dist. by: CHZ ARS Polona, Krakowskie Przedmiescie 7, Warsaw, Poland) circ. 500. Indexed: Hist.Abstr. Amer.Hist.& Life.

940 940 398 913   BE
FEDERATION ARCHEOLOGIQUE ET HISTORIQUE DE BELGIQUE. ANNALES/FEDERATIE VAN NEDERLANDSTALIGE VERENIDENIS VOOR OUDHEIDKUNDE EN GESCHIEDENIS VAN BELGISCHE. JAARBOEKEN. (Text in Dutch and French) 1886. irreg. 1500 Fr. Federatie van Nederlandstalige Verenigingen voor Oudheidkunde en Geschiedenis van Belgie, Leopoldlei 34, 2070 Antwerp, Belgium. adv.

FIGURA. NOVA SERIES; Uppsala studies in the history of art. see *ART*

949   BE   ISSN 0069-5386
FIGURES DE WALLONIE. Alternate title: Institut Jules Destree. Collection: Figures de Wallonie. irreg., no. 19. price varies. Institut Jules Destree, Rue du Chateau 3, 6100 Mont-sur Marchienne Charleroi, Belgium.

HISTORY — HISTORY OF EUROPE

947.1   FI   ISSN 0356-827X
FINLAND; books and publications in politics, political history and international relations. (Text in English) 1965. a. $1. University of Turku, Department of Political History, SF-20500 Turku 50, Finland. Ed. Tapani Paavonen. bk. rev. circ. 3,000.

948 410   FI   ISSN 0355-1253
FINNISCH-UGRISCHE FORSCHUNGEN; Zeitschrift fuer Finnisch-Ugrische Sprach und Volkskunde. (Text in English, French and German) 1902. irreg. Fmk.100. Suomalais-Ugrilainen Seura, Snellmaninkatu 9-11, 00170 Helsinki 17, Finland (Subscr. to: Castrenianum, Fabianinkatu 33, 00170 Helsinki, Finland) bk. rev. index. circ. 350. (back issues avail.) Indexed: M.L.A.

322 323   GE
FIRST HAND INFORMATION. (Text in English) irreg. Panorama DDR - Auslandspresseagentur GmbH, Wilhelm Pieck Str. 49, 1054 Berlin, E. Germany (D.D.R.) illus.

942   UK   ISSN 0140-8429
FLINTSHIRE HISTORICAL SOCIETY. PUBLICATIONS, JOURNAL AND RECORD SERIES. 1911. biennial. membership. ‡ Flintshire Historical Society, 50, Hafod Park, Mold, Clwyd CH7 1QW, Wales. Ed. Prof. J. Gwynn Williams. bk. rev. circ. 750. Indexed: Br.Archaeol.Abstr.

947 300   US
FLORIDA STATE UNIVERSITY. CENTER FOR YUGOSLAV-AMERICAN STUDIES, RESEARCH, AND EXCHANGES. PROCEEDINGS AND REPORTS OF SEMINARS AND RESEARCH. 1967. a. $4. Florida State University, Center for Yugoslav-American Studies, Research, and Exchanges, 930 W. Park Ave., Tallahassee, FL 32306. TEL 904-644-5465. Ed. George Macesich. adv. bk. rev. circ. 650. Indexed: Amer.Bibl.Slavic & E.Eur.Stud.
     Formerly: Florida State University. Slavic Papers (ISSN 0430-7291)

940   HU   ISSN 0133-6622
FOLIA HISTORICA. 1972. a. exchange basis. Magyar Nemzeti Muzeum, Muzeum-krt. 14-16, 1370 Budapest 8, Hungary. Ed. Ferenc Fulep. illus. circ. 700. Indexed: Art & Archaeol.Tech.Abstr.

943.7   CS   ISSN 0231-7494
FOLIA HISTORICA BOHEMICA. (Text in Czech, English, German, Russian) 1979. irreg. (1-2/yr.) exchange basis only. Ustav Ceskoslovenskych a Svetovych Dejin CSAV, Vysehradska 49, 128 26 Prague 2, Czechoslovakia. Ed. Josef Zemlicka. bk. rev. bibl.

948.9   DK   ISSN 0109-8365
FOLK FORTAELLER. 1978. a. Kr.10. (Boldrup Museumsforening) Kirsten Riis Nielsen, Vestermarksvej 5, 9610 Noerager, Denmark. illus.

948.9   DK   ISSN 0109-2766
FOLK OG LIV PAA ROENDEEGNEN-. DENGANG. 1979. a. Kr.60. Si-Mi Tryk, Ravnevej 5, 8410 Roende, Denmark. Ed. Vilfred Friborg Hansen. adv. illus. circ. 900. Indexed: Hist.Abstr.

948.9   DK   ISSN 0900-002X
FOLK OG MINDER FRA KOEBENHAVN. 1984. a. Kr.70. Dansk Bladsforlag A-S, Fredensborg, Denmark (Orders to: Danske Boghendleres Kommissionsanstalt, Siljangade 6, 2300 Copenhagen S, Denmark)

948   DK
FOLK OG MINDER FRA NORDSJAELLAND.* vol. 31, 1976. a. Kr.55. Dansk Bladforlag ApS, Hellerupvej 78, 2900 Hellerup, Denmark.
     Formerly: Jul i Nordsjaelland.

948.9   DK   ISSN 0900-3037
FOLKESAGN I TEKST OG BILLED FRA NOERREHERRED. 1983. a. Kr.28. Forlag i Stalden, Nyboelle Strand, 4913 Horslunde, Denmark. Ed. Grethe Bull Sarning. illus. circ. 300.

FONTES ARCHAEOLOGICI POSNANIENSES/ ANNALES MUSEI ARCHAEOLOGICI POSNANIENSIS. see *ARCHAEOLOGY*

943   AU
FONTES RERUM AUSTRIACARUM. REIHE 1. SCRIPTORES. (Text in German and Latin) 1855. irreg. price varies. (Oesterreichische Akademie der Wissenschaften, Historische Kommission) Verlag der Oesterreichischen Akademie der Wissenschaften, Dr. Ignaz Seipel-Platz 2, A-1010 Vienna, Austria.

943   AU
FONTES RERUM AUSTRIACARUM. REIHE 2. DIPLOMATARIA ET ACTA. (Text in German and Latin) 1849. irreg. price varies. (Oesterreichische Akademie der Wissenschaften, Historische Kommission) Verlag der Oesterreichischen Akademie der Wissenschaften, Dr. Ignaz Seipel-Platz 2, A-1010 Vienna, Austria.

943 340   AU   ISSN 0071-6898
FONTES RERUM AUSTRIACARUM. REIHE 3. FONTES JURIS. (Text in German and Latin) 1953. irreg. price varies. Verlag Herman Boehlaus Nachf., c/o Dr. Karl Lueger, Ring 12, Postfach 200, A-1014 Vienna, Austria.

FONTI E STUDI PER LA STORIA DI BOLOGNA E DELLE PROVINCE EMILIANE E ROMAGNOLE. see *ART*

945   IT   ISSN 0071-6901
FONTI SUI COMUNI RURALI TOSCANI. 1962. irreg., no. 9, 1984. price varies. (Deputazione di Storia Patria, Florence) Casa Editrice Leo S. Olschki, Casella Postale 66, 50100 Florence, Italy. Ed. Ernesto Sestan. circ. 1,000.

948.1   NO   ISSN 0071-7436
FORENINGEN TIL NORSKE FORTIDSMINNESMERKERS BEVARING. AARBOK. (Text in English and Norwegian) 1845. a. Kr.135. Foreningen til Norske Fortidsminnesmerkers Bevaring, Dronningensgt. 11, 0152 Oslo 1, Norway. adv. bk. rev.

943.6   AU
FORSCHUNGEN ZUR GESCHICHTE OBEROESTERREICHS. 1950. irreg. Oberoesterreichisches Landesarchiv, Anzengrubenstr. 19, A-4020 Linz, Austria. Eds. Alois Zauner, Georg Heilingsetzer. circ. 500. (back issues avail.) Indexed: M.L.A.

940   GE   ISSN 0071-7673
FORSCHUNGEN ZUR MITTELALTERLICHEN GESCHICHTE. 1956. irreg., vol.31, 1984. price varies. Hermann Boehlaus Nachfolger, Meyerstr. 50a, 5300 Weimar, Postfach 260, E. Germany (D.D.R.)

940 900   UK   ISSN 0261-586X
FORT; the international journal of military architecture and fortification. 1976. a. £10. University of Liverpool, School of Architecture, Fortress Study Group, School of Architecture, P.O. Box 147, Liverpool L69 3BX, England. Ed. Quentin Hughes. bk. rev. circ. 450. (also avail. in microfiche) Indexed: Br.Archaeol.Abstr. RILA.

940 956   UK
FOUNDATIONS OF MEDIEVAL HISTORY. 1979. irreg. price varies. Edward Arnold (Publishers) Ltd., 41 Bedford Square, London WC1B 3DQ, England. Ed. M.T. Clanchy.

940   UK
FOUNDATIONS OF MODERN HISTORY. 1966. irreg. price varies. Edward Arnold (Publishers) Ltd., 41 Bedford Square, London WC1B 3DQ, England.

948   DK   ISSN 0085-0845
FRA ALS OG SUNDEVED. 1928. a., lastest no.64, 1986. price varies. Historisk Samfund for Als og Sundeved, Soenderborg Slot, DK-6400 Soenderborg, Denmark. Ed. J. Slettebo. illus. circ. 1,500-2,000. Indexed: Numis.Lit.
Local

948   DK   ISSN 0107-2757
FRA BJERRINGBRO KOMMUNE. 1980. biennial. Kr.35. Bjerringbro Kommunes Lokalhistoriske Arkiv, EKSP. Bjerringbro Bibliotek, Realskolevej 12, 8850 Bjerringbro, Denmark. illus. circ. 350.

FRA BOV MUSEUM. see *MUSEUMS AND ART GALLERIES*

948   DK
FRA FREDERIKSBORG AMT. AARBOG. 1906. a. Kr.65. Frederiksborg Amts Historiske Samfund, Toftemosevej 23, 3100 Hornbaek, Denmark. Ed. Henning Ring. stat. illus. index. circ. 85.

948   DK
FRA HIMMERLAND OG KJAER HERRED. 1912. a. Historisk Samfund for Himmerland og Kjaer Herred, Danmarksgade 96, 9000 Alborg, Denmark.

948   DK
FRA HOLBACK AMT: HISTORISKE AARBOEGER. 1907. a. Kr.50($6) Historisk Samfund for Holbaek Amt, Museet for Holbaek og Omegn, Klosterstraede 14-16, 4300 Holbaek, Denmark. Ed. Else Asmussen. adv. bk. rev. charts. illus. circ. 500.
Local

948   DK
FRA KOEBENHAVNS AMT. irreg. Historisk Samfund for Koebenhavns Amt, 4000 Roskilde, Denmark. illus.
     Formerly (until 1925): Historisk Samfund for Koebenhavns Amt. Arbog.

948.9   DK   ISSN 0107-895X
FRA KVANGAARD TIL HUMLEKULE. 1971. a. membership. Havebrugshistorisk Selskab, Copenhagen, Denmark. illus.

948   DK   ISSN 0046-4864
FRA RIBE AMT. 1903. a. Kr.75. Historisk Samfund for Ribe Amt, DK-6700 Esbjerg, Denmark. Ed. Hans Joergen L. Larsen. bk. rev. index every 3 yrs. circ. 1,500.
Local

948   DK   ISSN 0085-0853
FRA VIBORG AMT. AARBOG. 1929. a. Kr.45. Historisk Samfund for Viborg Amt, Landsarkivet, 8800 Viborg, Denmark. Ed. Paul G. Oerberg. adv. bk. rev.
Local

940   FR   ISSN 0071-8440
FRANCE. COMITE DES TRAVAUX HISTORIQUES ET SCIENTIFIQUES. SECTION D'HISTOIRE MODERNE ET CONTEMPORAINE. ACTES DU CONGRES NATIONAL DES SOCIETES SAVANTES. 1951. a. price varies. Ministere de l'Education Nationale, Comite des Travaux Historiques et Scientifiques, 3-5 bd. Pasteur, 75015 Paris, France. cum.index: 1950-60. circ. 650.

944   FR   ISSN 0071-8459
FRANCE. COMITE DES TRAVAUX HISTORIQUES ET SCIENTIFIQUES. SECTION D'HISTOIRE MODERNE ET CONTEMPORAINE. BULLETIN. 1965. irreg. price varies. Ministere de l'Education National, Comite des Travaux Historiques et Scientifiques, 3-5 bd. Pasteur, 75015 Paris, France. Ed.Bd. cum.index: 1956-60. circ. 650. (back issues avail.)
     Formerly: France. Comite des Travaux Historiques et Scientifiques. Section d'Histoire Moderne et Contemporaine (Depuis 1610). Bulletin (ISSN 0399-9726)

944   FR
FRANCE. COMMISSION DEPARTEMENTALE D'HISTOIRE ET D'ARCHEOLOGIE. MEMOIRES. 1889. irreg., no.23, 1986. price varies. Commission Departementale d'Histoire et d'Archeologie, Archives Departementales, Prefecture, 62020 Arras Cedex, France.
     Formerly: France. Commission Departementale des Monuments Historiques du Pas-de-Calais. Memoires.
Local

940   FR
FRANCE-IBERIE RECHERCHE. THESES ET RECHERCHES. 1970. irreg. price varies. Universite de Toulouse II (le Mirail), Institut d'Etudes Hispaniques, Hispanoamericaines, 5 Allees Antonio Machado, 31058 Toulouse, France.
     Formerly: France-Iberie Recherche. These et Documents (ISSN 0082-5417)

940   GW
FRANKFURTER ALTHISTORISCHE STUDIEN.
1968. irreg. price varies. (Universitaet Frankfurt, Seminar fuer Alte Geschichte) Verlag Michael Lassleben, Lange Gasse 19, Postfach 20, 8411 Kallmuenz, W. Germany (B.R.D.) Eds. Jochen Bleicken, Helga Gesche.

940   GW   ISSN 0170-3226
FRANKFURTER HISTORISCHE ABHANDLUNGEN. (Text in English and German) irreg., vol.28, 1987. price varies. Franz Steiner Verlag Wiesbaden GmbH, Birkenwaldstr. 44, Postfach 347, D-7000 Stuttgart 1, W. Germany (B.R.D.) Ed.Bd.

940   GW   ISSN 0170-3293
FRANKFURTER HISTORISCHE VORTRAEGE. irreg., no. 10, 1985. price varies. (Frankfurter Kreis fuer Historische Forschungen) Franz Steiner Verlag Wiesbaden GmbH, Birkenwaldstr. 44, Postfach 347, D-7000 Stuttgart 1, W. Germany (B.R.D.) Ed.Bd.

943 200   GW
FRANKFURTER KIRCHLICHES JAHRBUCH. 1967. a. Evangelischer Gemeindeverband Frankfurt am Main, 6000 Frankfurt, W. Germany (B.R.D.) illus.

948   DK   ISSN 0108-8777
FREDERIKSBERG GENNEM TIDERNE. biennial. Kr.30. (Historisk-Topografisk Selskab for Frederiksberg) Bibliotekscentralen, Telegrafvej 5, DK-2750 Ballerup, Denmark.

948.9   DK   ISSN 0107-9476
FREDERIKSVAERKEGNENS MUSEUMSFORENING. AARSSKRIFT. 1983. a. Kr.100. Frederiksvaerkegnens Museumsforening, c/o Museumsgaarden, Jernbanegade 4, 3300 Frederiksvaerk, Denmark. Ed. Karen Follett. illus. circ. 700.
Formerly: Frederiksvaerkegnens Museumsforening. Aarbog.

942   UK
FREEMAN. 1908. a. membership. ‡ Guild of Freemen of the City of London, P.O. Box 153, 40a Ludgate Hill, London EC4M 7DE, England. Ed. Colin Dyer. adv. circ. 3,000. Indexed: P.A.I.S.

FREIE UNIVERSITAET BERLIN. OSTEUROPA-INSTITUT. BERICHTE. see HUMANITIES: COMPREHENSIVE WORKS

947   GW   ISSN 0067-5903
FREIE UNIVERSITAET BERLIN. OSTEUROPA-INSTITUT. HISTORISCHE VEROEFFENTLICHUNGEN; Forschungen zur Osteuropaeischen Geschichte. 1954. irreg., vol.39, 1986. price varies. Verlag Otto Harrassowitz, Taunusstr. 14, Postfach 2929, 6200 Wiesbaden 1, W. Germany (B.R.D.) Ed. H.T. Torke. Indexed: Hist.Abstr. Amer.Hist.& Life.

944   US
FRENCH COLONIAL HISTORICAL SOCIETY. PROCEEDINGS OF THE MEETING. (Text in English and French) 1976. irreg., 10th, 1985. University Press of America, 4720 Boston Way, Lanham, MD 20706. TEL 301-459-3366. Ed. James J. Cooke. circ. 300.

FRENCH XX BIBLIOGRAPHY. see PUBLISHING AND BOOK TRADE — Abstracting, Bibliographies, Statistics

940   GW
FRUEHMITTELALTERLICHE STUDIEN; Jahrbuch. 1967. a. price varies. (Universitaet Muenster, Institut fuer Fruehmittelalterforschung) Walter de Gruyter und Co., Genthiner Str. 13, 1000 Berlin 30, W. Germany (B.R.D.) (U.S. addr.: Walter de Gruyter, Inc., Saw Mill Rd., Hawthorne, N.Y. 10532) Ed. Karl Hauck. adv. bk. rev. Indexed: Br.Archaeol.Abstr. RILA.

943   GW   ISSN 0016-2612
FULDAER GESCHICHTSBLAETTER. 1902. a. DM.25. Fuldaer Geschichtsverein, Stadtschloss, 6400 Fulda, W. Germany (B.R.D.) Ed. Otto Berge. bk. rev. illus. tr.lit. index. circ. 1,000. (looseleaf format)
Local

948   DK   ISSN 0107-8399
FYENS STIFTSBOG. 1969. a. Kr.40. Fyens Stifts Landemode, Stiftsoevrighedens Kontor, Klaregade 17, 5000 Odense, Denmark. Ed. Poul Erik Andersen. illus. circ. 2,300.

948   DK   ISSN 0085-0918
FYNSKE AARBOEGER. 1939. a. Kr.60. Historisk Samfund for Fyns Stift, c/o H. H. Jacobsen, Ed., Hyrdinden 5, 5270 Odense N, Denmark. bk. rev.
Local

948 913   DK   ISSN 0427-7945
FYNSKE MINDER. 1951. a. Kr.50. Odense Bys Museer - City of Odense Museums, 5000 Odense, Denmark. Ed. Niels Oxenvad. cum.index: 1951-1976. circ. 1,000. Indexed: Br.Archaeol.Abstr.

G.W. LEIBNIZ: SAEMLICHE SCHRIFTEN UND BRIEFE. see PHILOSOPHY

948.9   DK   ISSN 0108-0032
GALTEN EGNSARKIV. ANNALES. 1982. a. Kr.55. Galten Egnsarkiv, Roeddikvej 18, 8464 Galten, Denmark. TEL 06-94 35 50. Ed. Ernst Johansen. adv. illus. circ. 650.

948   DK   ISSN 0108-3791
GAMLE LOEJT. 1978. a. Kr.70. Loejt Sogns Lokalhistoriske Forening, Stennevej 10, Stollig, 6200 Aabenraa, Denmark. illus.

948.1   NO
GAULDALSMINNE; arbok for bygdehistorie og folkeminne. 1926. irreg. Kr.30. Gauldal Historielag, c/o Jens Haukdal, 7450 Soknedal, Norway. Ed. Eirik Karstad. adv. bk. rev.

914.03 913   PO
GAYA. 1983. a. price varies. (Gabinete de Historia e Arqueologia) Camara Municipal de Vila Nova de Gala, Av. da Republica, 4400 Vila Nova Gala, Portugal. circ. 1,000.

943.8 913   PL   ISSN 0072-0410
GDANSKIE TOWARZYSTWO NAUKOWE. WYDZIAL 1. NAUK SPOLECZNYCH I HUMANISTYCZNYCH. KOMISJA ARCHEOLOGICZNA. PRACE. (Text in Polish; summaries in English and German) 1959. irreg., no. 9, 1983. price varies. (Gdanskie Towarzystwo Naukowe) Ossolineum, Publishing House of the Polish Academy of Sciences, Rynek 9, Wroclaw, Poland (Dist. by Ars Polona-Ruch, Krakowskie Przedmiescie 7, Warsaw, Poland) Ed.Bd. charts. illus. circ. 500.

943.8   PL   ISSN 0433-230X
GDANSKIE TOWARZYSTWO NAUKOWE. WYDZIAL 1. NAUK SPOLECZNYCH I HUMANISTYCZNYCH. SERIA MONOGRAFII. 1959. irreg., no.83, 1986. price varies. (Gdanskie Towarzystwo Naukowe) Ossolineum, Publishing House of the Polish Academy of Sciences, Rynek 9, Wroclaw, Poland (Dist. by: Ars Polona-Ruch, Krakowskie Przedmiescie 7, Warsaw, Poland) Ed.Bd. bibl. illus. circ. 1,500.

943.8   PL   ISSN 0072-0429
GDANSKIE TOWARZYSTWO NAUKOWE. WYDZIAL 1. NAUK SPOLECZNYCH I HUMANISTYCZNYCH. SERIA POPULARNONAUKOWA "POMORZE GDANSKIE". 1965. irreg., no.16, 1984. price varies. (Gdanskie Towarzystwo Naukowe) Ossolineum, Publishing House of the Polish Academy of Sciences, Rynek 9, Wroclaw, Poland (Dist. by Ars Polona-Ruch, Krakowskie Przedmiescie 7, Warsaw, Poland) Ed. Z. Ciesielski. circ. 740.

943.8   PL   ISSN 0072-0437
GDANSKIE TOWARZYSTWO NAUKOWE. WYDZIAL 1. NAUK SPOLECZNYCH I HUMANISTYCZNYCH. SERIA ZRODEL. irreg., no.11, 1984. (Gdanskie Towarzystwo Naukowe) Ossolineum, Publishing House of the Polish Academy of Sciences, Rynek 9, Wroclaw, Poland (Dist. by Ars Polona-Ruch, Krakowskie Przedmiescie 7, Warsaw, Poland) Ed. Z. Binerowski. circ. 600.

940   NE
GELDERSE HISTORISCHE REEKS. 1971. a. price varies. Walburg Pers, Zaadmarkt 84a-86, Box 222, 7200 AE Zutphen, Netherlands. TEL 05750-10522. (Co-sponsor: Stichting Gelderse Historische Reeks)

940   NE
GENOOTSCHAP AMSTELODAMUM. JAARBOEK. 1902. a. fl.35 includes the Jaarboek and six bi-m. issues. De Bussy, Eilerman Harms N. V., Warmoesstraat 151, Amsterdam, Netherlands. Ed. J.H.A. Ringeling. bibl. illus.

948   DK
GENTOFTE-BOGEN. 1924. a. Kr.70. Historisk Topografisk Selskab for Gentofte, Ahlmanns Alle 6, 2900 Hellerup, Denmark.
Formerly: Historisk-Topografisk Selskab for Gjentofte Kommune. Meddelelser.

943   GW
GERMANIA SLAVICA. 1980. irreg. Duncker & Humbolt, Dietrich-Schafer-Weg 9, Postfach 410329, 1000 Berlin 41, W. Germany (B.R.D.)

940   GE   ISSN 0075-2665
GESCHICHTE DER SOZIALISTISCHEN LAENDER EUROPAS. JAHRBUCH. 1969. a. price varies. (Akademie der Wissenschaften der DDR, Zentralinstitut fuer Geschichte) VEB Deutscher Verlag der Wissenschaften, Postfach 1216, 1080 Berlin, E. Germany (D.D.R.)
Formerly: Jahrbuch fuer Geschichte der USSR und der Volksdemokratischen Laender Europas.

943   GW   ISSN 0072-4203
GESCHICHTLICHE LANDESKUNDE. 1964. irreg., vol.29, 1986. price varies. (Universitaet Mainz, Institut fuer Geschichtliche Landeskunde) Franz Steiner Verlag Wiesbaden GmbH, Birkenwaldstr. 44, Postfach 347, D-7000 Stuttgart 1, W. Germany (B.R.D.) Ed. Alois Gerlich. (back issues avail.)

943 949   BE
GESCHICHTLICHES EUPEN. (Text in German) 1839. a. Eupener Geschichts-und Museumsverein, Obere Ibern 12, 4700 Eupen, Belgium.

943 398   GW   ISSN 0342-0965
GESCHICHTSBLAETTER FUER WALDECK. 1901. a. DM.20. Waldeckischer Geschichtsverein e.V. Arolsen, Am Sonderrein 14, 3590 Bad Wildungen, W. Germany (B.R.D.) Ed.Bd. bk. rev. cum.index. circ. 1,300.

940   BE   ISSN 0591-1133
GESCHIED- EN OUDHEIDKUNDIGE KRING VAN RONSE EN HET TENEMENT VAN INDE. ANNALEN/CERCLE HISTORIQUE ET ARCHEOLOGIQUE DE RENAUX ET DU TENEMENT D'INDE. ANNALES. (Editions in Flemish and French) 1948. a. 400 Fr. Geschied- en Oudheidkundige Kring van Ronse en Het Tenement van Inde, Cercle Historique and Archeologique de Renaix et du Tenement d'Inde, Glorieuxlaan 17, 9600 Ronse, Belgium. circ. 400.

940   BE   ISSN 0433-8456
GESCHIED- EN OUDHEIDKUNDIGE KRING VOOR LEUVEN EN OMGEVING. JAARBOEK. (Text in Flemish) 1961. a. Geschied- en Oudheidkundige Kring voor Leuven en Omgeving, Brusselsestr. 46, 3000 Louvain, Belgium. bk. rev.

943.6 284   AU
GESELLSCHAFT FUER DIE GESCHICHTE DES PROTESTANTISMUS IN OESTERREICH. JAHRBUCH. 1880. a. DM.30. Gesellschaft fuer die Geschichte des Protestantismus in Oesterreich, Severin-Schreiber-G. 3, A-1180 Vienna, Austria. Ed. Peter F. Barton. bk. rev. circ. 30. Indexed: Hist.Abstr. Amer.Hist.& Life.

943 284   GW   ISSN 0072-4238
GESELLSCHAFT FUER NIEDERSAECHSISCHE KIRCHENGESCHICHTE. JAHRBUCH. 1896. a. DM.15 to individuals; institutions DM.20. (Gesellschaft fuer Niedersaechsische Kirchengeschichte) Buchdruckerei Willi Rihn, 4733 Blomberg, W. Germany (B.R.D.) Ed. Hans-Walter Krumwiede. bk. rev. circ. 250.

943.6   AU
GESELLSCHAFT FUER SALZBURGER LANDESKUNDE. MITTEILUNGEN. 1861. a. Gesellschaft fuer Salzburger Landeskunde, Landesarchiv Michael-Pacher-Str. 40, 5020 Salzburg, Austria. Indexed: Hist.Abstr. Amer.Hist.& Life.

948.9   DK   ISSN 0109-6656
GILLELEJE MUSEUM. 1984. a. Kr.36. Gilleleje Museum, Rostgaardsvej 2, 3250 Gilleleje, Denmark. Ed. Soeren Frandsen. illus.

HISTORY — HISTORY OF EUROPE

945   IT   ISSN 0017-050X
GIORNALE STORICO DELLA LUNIGIANA E DEL TERRITORIO LUCENSE. 1950. a. L.20000. Istituto Internazionale di Studi Liguri, Via Romana 39, 18012 Bordighera, Italy. bk. rev. illus. cum.index every 5 yrs. circ. 1,000.
    Formerly (until 1960): Giornale Storico della Lunigiana.

949   YU
GLASNIK ARHIVA I DRUSTAVA ARHIVSKIH RADNIKA BOSNE I HERCEGOVINE. 1961. a. price varies. Drustvo Arhivskih Radnika Bosne i Hercegovine, Arhiv, Save Kovacevica 6, 71000 Sarajevo, Yugoslavia. Ed. Bozo Madzar. bk. rev. circ. 350. (also avail. in microfilm)

943   GW   ISSN 0436-1024
GODESBERGER HEIMATBLAETTER. 1963. a. DM.20. Verein fuer Heimatpflege und Heimatgeschichte, Bad Godesberg e.V., Eschenweg 2, 5300 Bonn 2, W. Germany (B.R.D.) Ed. Herbert Strack. bk. rev. circ. 1,400.

947   BU   ISSN 0204-4048
GODISHNIK NA MUZEITE OT SEVERNA BULGARIIA. 1975. irreg. Knigoizdatelstvo G. Bakalov, Blvd. Kristo Botev 3, Varna, Bulgaria (Subscr. to: Hemus Foreign Trade Co., 6 Ruski Blvd., 1000 Sofia, Bulgaria)

943   GW   ISSN 0072-4882
GOETTINGER JAHRBUCH. 1952. a. price varies. (Geschichtsverein fuer Goettingen und Umgebung) Reise Verlag, Hanssenstr. 24, Postfach 359, 3400 Goettingen, W. Germany (B.R.D.) Ed. W. Roehrbein.

940   UK
GOVERNANCE OF ENGLAND. 1984. irreg. price varies. Edward Arnold (Publishers) Ltd., 41 Bedford Sq., London WC1B 3DQ, England.

943.6   AU
GRAEZER BEITRAEGE; Zeitschrift fuer Klassische Altertumswissenschaft. (Text in English, French, German and Italian) 1973. a. S.890. (Universitaet Graz, Institut fuer Klassische Philologie) Verlag Ferdinand Berger und Soehne, Wiener Str. 21-23, A-3580 Horn, Austria.

940   FR   ISSN 0072-5404
GRANDES FIGURES DE LA CHARITE.* 1970. irreg. price varies. Editions S.O.S., 106 rue du Bac, 75007 Paris, France.

942   UK   ISSN 0072-5722
GREAT BRITAIN. CENTRAL OFFICE OF INFORMATION. OVERSEAS PUBLICATIONS DIVISION. REFERENCE PAMPHLETS SERIES. 1955. irreg. Central Office of Information, Overseas Publications Division, Hercules Rd., London SE1 7DU, England (Avail. from: Government Bookshop, 49 High Holborn, London WC1V 6HB or British Information Services, 845 Third Ave., New York, N.Y. 10022, U.S.A.)

GREAT BRITAIN. DEPARTMENT OF THE ENVIRONMENT. ARCHAEOLOGICAL REPORTS. see *ARCHAEOLOGY*

942 020   UK   ISSN 0072-6516
GREAT BRITAIN. KEEPER OF PUBLIC RECORDS. ANNUAL REPORT OF THE KEEPER OF PUBLIC RECORDS ON THE WORK OF THE PUBLIC RECORD OFFICE AND THE REPORT OF THE ADVISORY COUNCIL ON PUBLIC RECORDS. 1959. a. price varies. H.M.S.O., Box 569, London SE1 9NH, England. (reprint service avail. from UMI)

942 571   UK
GREAT BRITAIN. ROYAL COMMISSION ON ANCIENT AND HISTORICAL MONUMENTS IN WALES. INTERIM REPORT. 1909. irreg. price varies. H.M.S.O., Box 569, London SE1 9NH, England. (Co-sponsor: Royal Commission on Ancient and Historical Monuments in Wales)
    Formerly: Great Britain. Royal Commission on the Ancient and Historical Monuments and Constructions in Wales and Monmouthshire. Interim Report (ISSN 0072-7075)

942 571   UK
GREAT BRITAIN. ROYAL COMMISSION ON THE HISTORICAL MONUMENTS OF ENGLAND. INTERIM REPORT. 1910. irreg., 34th, 1977. price varies. Royal Commission on the Historical Monuments of England, Fortress House, 23 Savile Row, London W1X 1AB, England (Avail. from H.M.S.O., Publications Centre, 51 Nine Elms Lane, London SW8 5DR, England)
    Formerly: Great Britain. Royal Commission on the Ancient and Historical Monuments and Constructions of England. Interim Report (ISSN 0072-7067)

948   DK   ISSN 0107-8372
GRENAA OG NOERRE DJURS FOER OG NU. 1981. a. Kr.93.50. Postbox 156, 8500 Grenaa, Denmark. illus.
    Formed by the merger of: Grenaa og Omegn Foer og Nu & Noerre Djurs Egnsarkiv.

949.2   NE   ISSN 0169-2801
GRONIEK. 1967. irreg. fl.35. University of Groningen, Department of History, Grote Rozenstraat 38, 9712 Groningen TJ, Netherlands. Ed.Bd. adv. bk. rev. circ. 1,000.
    Formerly: Groniek. Onafhankelijk Gronings Historisch Studentenblad.

949.4   SZ   ISSN 0072-7725
GROSSE HEIMATBUECHER. (Text in English, French and German) 1965. irreg. 58 Fr. Paul Haupt AG, Falkenplatz 14, CH-3001 Berne, Switzerland.

944 914   FR   ISSN 0220-276X
GWECHALL. 1978. a. 50 F. (to non-members) Societe Finisterienne d'Histoire et d'Archeologie, 4 rue du Palais, Quimper, France. Ed. Claude Fagnen.

948   DK
HADERSLEV STIFTSBOG. 1946. a. (Haderslev Stiftsfond) J. D. Nielsens Forlag, 6100 Haderslev, Denmark.
    Formerly: Haderslav Stifts Arbog.

943   GE
HALLESCHE STUDIEN ZUR GESCHICHTE DER SOZIALDEMOKRATIE. 1978. irreg. Martin Luther Universitaet, Forschungsgruppe "Sozialdemokratie", August Bebel Str. 13, 401 Halle, E. Germany (D.D.R.) Ed. Johannes Glasneck. circ. 500.

948   FI
HAMEENLINNA-WANAJA. 1951. a. Hameenlinna Seura Wanaja Seura, Hainaronkatu 4, 13200 Hameenlinna 20, Finland. cum.index: 1951-70.
    Formerly: Hameenlinna.

948   FI
HAMEENMAA. 1928. irreg. (Hameen Heimoliitto) Karisto Oy, Paroistentie 2, 13600 Hameenlinna, Finland. Ed. Kanerva Unto. cum.index: 1928-59 in vol. 11, 1962. circ. 1,500.

HAMPSHIRE FIELD CLUB AND ARCHAEOLOGICAL SOCIETY PROCEEDINGS. see *ARCHAEOLOGY*

940   GW   ISSN 0073-0327
HANSISCHE GESCHICHTSBLAETTER. 1882. a. price varies. (Hansischer Geschichtsverein) Boehlau Verlag GmbH, Niehler Str. 272-274, 5000 Cologne 60, W. Germany (B.R.D.) Eds. Klaus Friedland, E. Irsigles. Indexed: Bibl.Cart.

948   DK   ISSN 0046-6840
HARDSYSSELS AARBOG. 1907; N.S. 1967. a. Kr.125 for non-members; members Kr.75. Historisk Samfund for Ringkoebing Amt, c/o Kr. Bjerregaard, Doesvej 69, 7500 Holstebro, Denmark. Ed. Knud Erik Nielsen. bk. rev. bibl. illus. index. cum.index: 1907-1966. circ. 2,000.
Local

940   US   ISSN 0073-0459
HARVARD ARMENIAN TEXTS AND STUDIES. 1965. irreg., no.7, 1984. price varies. Harvard University Press, 79 Garden St., Cambridge, MA 02138. TEL 617-495-2600. Ed. Avedis K. Sanjian.

HARVARD CELTIC COLLOQUIUM. PROCEEDINGS. see *LINGUISTICS*

947   US   ISSN 0073-0831
HARVARD UNIVERSITY. RUSSIAN RESEARCH CENTER. RUSSIAN RESEARCH CENTER STUDIES. (Text in English; one vol. in Russian) 1950. irreg., no.83, 1985. price varies. Harvard University Press, 79 Garden St., Cambridge, MA 02138. TEL 617-495-2600.

943   GW   ISSN 0073-0882
HARZ-ZEITSCHRIFT. 1868; N.S. 1948. a. DM.24. Harzverein fuer Geschichte und Altertumskunde, c/o Brannschweigisches Landesmuseum, Maenchstr. 1, 33 Braunschweig, W. Germany (B.R.D.) (Affiliate: Braunschweigisches Landesmuseum fuer Geschichte und Volkstum) Ed. Ralf Busch. bk. rev.

940   SZ   ISSN 0073-0955
HAUTES ETUDES MEDIEVALES ET MODERNES. 1964. irreg., no.56, 1986. price varies. (Ecole Pratique des Hautes Etudes, Centre de Recherches d'Histoire et de Philologie, FR) Librarie Droz, 11, rue Massot, 1211 Geneva 12, Switzerland. circ. 1,000.

940   BE
HEEMKRING OKEGEM. ANNALEN. (Text in Flemish) 1975. a. Heemkring Okegem, Hazelarr 23, 9471 Okegem, Belgium.

943   GW
HEIMAT AM INN. 1972. a. Rudolf Vierlinger, Ed. & Pub., Jakob-Weindler Str. 4, 8346 Simbach/Inn, W. Germany (B.R.D.) circ. 1,200.

943.6   AU
HEIMAT IM WEINLAND; Heimatkundliches Beiblatt zum Amtsblatt der Bezirkshauptmannschaft Mistelbach. 1950. irreg. Bezirkshauptmannschaft Mistelbach, Hauptplatz 4-5, 2130 Mistelbach, Austria. cum.index: 1960-69.
    Formerly: Heimatkundliches Beiblatt (ISSN 9086)

943 398   GW
HEIMATBRIEF DER STADT GERMERSHEIM. 1960. a. DM.7. Stadtverwaltung Germersheim, Stadthaus Kolpingplatz 3, 6728 Germersheim, W. Germany (B.R.D.) circ. 1,150.

947.5   GW   ISSN 0440-6230
HEIMATGRUSS. 1956. a. DM.6.30. Landsmannschaft der Deutschen aus Litauen, c/o Alfred Franzkeit, In den Wiesen 3, 2839 Wehrbleck, W. Germany (B.R.D.) Ed. Alfred Franzkeit. circ. 2,000.

943.6   AU
HEIMATKUNDE, KULTURPFLEGE, STADTGESCHICHTE; kulturbeilage zum Amtsblatt der Stadt Klosterneuburg. 1968. irreg. Arbeitskreis zur Foerderung der Heimatkunde in Klosterneuburg, Rathausplatz 1, 3400 Klosterneuberg, Austria.

943.6   AU
HEIMATKUNDLICHE NACHRICHTEN. 1970. irreg. free. Heimatmuseum Traiskirchen, Stadtgemeinde Traiskirchen, 2514 Traiskirchen, Austria. Ed. Franz Schlogl.

943   GW
HEIMATKUNDLICHES JAHRBUCH FUER DEN KREIS SEGEBERG. 1955. a. DM.19.80. (Heimatverein des Kreises Segeberg) Verlag C. H. Waeser, Hamburger Str. 26, 2360 Bad Segeberg, W. Germany (B.R.D.) bk. rev. bibl. illus. circ. 1,200.

943   GE   ISSN 0437-3014
HERBERGEN DER CHRISTENHEIT; Beitraege zur deutschen Kirchengeschichte. 1965. biennial. price varies. (Arbeitsgemeinschaft fuer Kirchengeschichte der Evangelischen Landeskirchen der DDR, Arbeitsgemeinschaft fuer das kirchliche Archiv- und Bibliothekswesen in der DDR) Evangelische Verlagsanstalt, Krautstr. 52, 1017 Berlin, E. Germany (D.D.R.) Ed. Karlheinz Blaschke. bk. rev. circ. 1,500.

943   GW
HERFORDER JAHRBUCH; BEITRAEGE ZUR GESCHICHTE DER STADT DES KREISES UND DES STIFTES HERFORD. 1960. a. DM.39.80. (Herforder Verein fuer Heimatkunde) Maximilian Verlag, Steintorwall 17, Postfach 2352, 4900 Herford, W. Germany (B.R.D.)
    Formerly: Herforder Jahrbuch; Beitraege zur Geschichte der Stadt und des Stiftes Herford (ISSN 0073-196X)

948.9　　　　　　DK　ISSN 0108-8017
HERNING-BOGEN. 1982. a. Kr.64.50. Historisk
Forening for Herning Kommune, Herning,
Denmark. adv. illus. circ. 500.

943　331.88　　　　　　GW
HESSISCHE BEITRAEGE ZUR GESCHICHTE
DER ARBEITERBEWEGUNG. irreg. price varies.
Historischer Verein fuer Hessen, Staatsarchiv,
Schloss, 6100 Darmstadt, W. Germany (B.R.D.)

943　　　　　　GW
HESSISCHE STAATSARCHIV DARMSTADT.
REPERTORIEN. 1971. irreg. price varies.
Historische Kommission fuer Hessen, Schloss, D-
6100 Darmstadt, W. Germany (B.R.D.) Ed.Bd.

943　　　　　　GW　ISSN 0073-2001
HESSISCHES JAHRBUCH FUER
LANDESGESCHICHTE. 1951. a. price varies.
Hessisches Landesamt fuer Geschichtliche
Landeskunde, Krummbogen 28c, 3550 Marburg, W.
Germany (B.R.D.) bk. rev. Indexed: Bibl.Cart.
Numis.Lit. RILA.

948　913　　　　　　DK　ISSN 0105-8118
HIKUIN. (Text in Danish, English, German and
Swedish) 1974. a. Kr.140. Forlaget Hikuin,
Moesgard, 8270 Hoejbjerg, Denmark. Ed. Jens
Vellev.

944　　　　　　FR
HISTOIRE ET THEORIE. irreg. price varies. Editions
Syros, 1 rue de Varenne, 75006 Paris, France.

HISTORIA ARCHAEOLOGICA. see
ARCHAEOLOGY

946　　　　　　SP
HISTORIA DE ESPANA EN EL MUNDO
MODERNO. ESTUDIOS. irreg., no. 2, 1981.
Consejo Superior de Investigaciones Cientificas,
Escuela de Historica, Madrid, Spain.

946　　　　　　SP
HISTORIA GRAFICA DE CATALUNYA DIA A
DIA. 1978. a. Edicions 62, S.A., Provenca 278,
Barcelona-8, Spain. Dir. Ramon Bastardes.

947.1　　　　　　FI　ISSN 0073-2540
HISTORIALLINEN ARKISTO. (Text in Finnish or
Swedish; summaries in English or German) 1866.
irreg., no.88, 1986. Fmk.80. Suomen Historiallinen
Seura - Finnish Historical Society, Vuorikatu 6 A 4,
00100 Helsinki 10, Finland. cum.index: nos. 1-50,
1886-1944. circ. 400. Indexed: Hist.Abstr.
Amer.Hist.& Life.

947.1　　　　　　FI　ISSN 0073-2559
HISTORIALLISIA TUTKIMUKSIA. (Text in Finnish
or Swedish; summaries in English or German)
1918/1920. irreg., no.136, 1986. Fmk.120. Suomen
Historiallinen Seura - Finnish Historical Society,
Vuorikatu 6 A 4, 00100 Helsinki 10, Finland. circ.
300.

940　　　　　　FI
HISTORIAN OPETTAJIEN VUOSIKIRJA. (Text in
Finnish and Swedish) 1953. irreg. Historian
Yhteiskuntaopin ja Taloustiedon Opettajat,
Mariankatu 28 B, 00170 Helsinki 17, Finland.
Former titles (until 1955): Historianopettajain
Liitto. Vuosikirja. Arsbok; (until 1958):
Historianopettajain Liiton Vuosikirja.

940　　　　　　US　ISSN 0883-3559
HISTORIANS OF EARLY MODERN EUROPE.
1966. a. $10. Sixteenth Century Journal Publishers,
Inc., Northeast Missouri State University, LB 115,
Kirksville, MO 63501. TEL 816-785-4665. (Co-
sponsors: Society for Reformation Research;
Sixteenth Century Studies Conference) Ed. R.V.
Schnucker. adv. circ. 1,800. (back issues avail.)
Incorporating: American Society for Reformation
Research. Newsletter.

942　　　　　　UK
HISTORIC HOUSES, CASTLES AND GARDENS
IN GREAT BRITAIN AND IRELAND. 1952. a.
£3.25. British Leisure Publications, Windsor Court,
East Grinstead House, East Grinstead, West Sussex
RH19 1XA, England. Ed. Sheila Alcock. adv. circ.
80,000.
Formerly: Historic Houses, Castles and Gardens
(ISSN 0073-2567)

942　　　　　　UK　ISSN 0140-332X
HISTORIC SOCIETY OF LANCASHIRE AND
CHESHIRE. TRANSACTIONS. 1848. a.
membership. ‡ Historic Society of Lancashire and
Cheshire, School of History, University of
Liverpool, Box 147, Liverpool L69 3BX, England
(Subscr. to: Hon. Sec. Miss J. E. Hollinshead,
Liverpool Institute of Higher Education, Stand Park
Rd., Liverpool L16 9JD, England). Eds. Dr. C.B.
Phillips, Mrs. J.I. Kermode. bk. rev. charts. illus.
index. cum.index. circ. 600. (also avail. in
microfiche) Indexed: Br.Hum.Ind.
Br.Archaeol.Abstr. Geo.Abstr.

943.7　　　　　　CS
HISTORICA. (Text in English, French, German and
Russian) 1959. irreg. exchange basis only. Academia
Nakladatelstvi C S A V, Vodickova 40, 112 29
Prague 1, Czechoslovakia (Subscr. to: Artia, Ve
Smeckach 30, 111 27 Prague 1, Czechoslovakia) bk.
rev. Indexed: Hist.Abstr. Arts & Hum.Cit.Ind.
Amer.Hist.& Life.

940　　　　　　UK
HISTORICAL RESEARCH. SPECIAL
SUPPLEMENT. 1936, no.3. irreg., no.12, 1982. free
with I.H.R. Bulletin. (University of London,
Institute of Historical Research) Basil Blackwell
Ltd., 108 Cowley Rd., Oxford OX4 1JF, England.
circ. 1,500.
Formerly: University of London. Institute of
Historical Research Bulletin. Special Supplement
(ISSN 0076-082X)

HISTORICAL SOCIETY OF THE CHURCH IN
WALES. JOURNAL. see RELIGIONS AND
THEOLOGY — Protestant

HISTORICAL SOCIETY OF THE PRESBYTERIAN
CHURCH OF WALES. JOURNAL. see
RELIGIONS AND THEOLOGY — Protestant

943　　　　　　UK　ISSN 0075-0743
HISTORICAL STUDIES. 1958. irreg. price varies.
Committee for Irish Historical Studies, Queen's
University, Belfast, N. Ireland. circ. 1,000
(controlled) Indexed: Br.Hum.Ind. Curr.Cont.
Arts & Hum.Cit.Ind. Aus.P.A.I.S.

943.6　　　　　　AU　ISSN 0440-9728
HISTORICHES JAHRBUCK DER STADT GRAZ.
1968. a. Stadtarchiv Graz, Magistrat der
Landeshaupstadt Graz, Hans Sachs Gasse 1, 8010
Graz, Austria.

943.7　　　　　　CS　ISSN 0323-0937
HISTORICKA DEMOGRAFIE. (Text in Czech,
Russian, Slovak; summaries in English, German)
1967. irreg. Ustav Ceskoslovenskych a Svetovych
Dejin CSAV, Vysehradska 49, 128 26 Prague 2,
Czechoslovakia. Ed. Lubomir Slezak. bk. rev. bibl.

943.7　　　　　　CS　ISSN 0323-0988
HISTORICKA GEOGRAFIE. (Text in Czech,
English, German, Russian) 1968. irreg. exchange
basis only. Ustav Ceskoslovenskych a Svetovych
Dejin CSAV, Vysehradska 49, 128 26 Prague 2,
Czechoslovakia. bk. rev. bibl.

943.7　　　　　　CS　ISSN 0440-9515
HISTORICKE STUDIE. (Text in Slovak; summaries
in German and Russian) irreg., vol. 22, 1977. fl.35
per no. (Slovenska Akademia Vied, Historicky
Ustav) Veda, Publishing House of the Slovak
Academy of Sciences, Klemensova 19, 814 30
Bratislava, Czechoslovakia (Distributor in Western
Countries: John Benjamins B.V., Amsteldijk 44,
Amsterdam (Z.), Netherlands) Ed. Vladimir Matula.
Indexed: Hist.Abstr. Amer.Hist.& Life.

949　　　　　　NE
HISTORISCH JAARBOEK VLAARDINGEN. 1977.
a. $17. (Historische Vereniging Vlaardingen)
Uitgeverij De Draak, Vlaardingen, Netherlands.
Ed.Bd. circ. 1,200.
Supersedes: Historische Vereniging Vlaardingen.
Tijdschrift.

943　　　　　　GW
HISTORISCHE STUDIEN. irreg., vol. 441, 1986.
price varies. Matthiessen Verlag GmbH,
Nordbahnhofstr. 2, 2250 Husum, W. Germany
(B.R.D.) Ed. Werner Poels.

943　　　　　　GW　ISSN 0073-2680
HISTORISCHER VEREIN DER PFALZ.
MITTEILUNGEN. 1870. a. price varies.
Historischer Verein der Pfalz, Gr. Pfaffengasse 7,
6720 Speyer, W. Germany (B.R.D.) Ed. L. Anton
Doll.

949.4　　　　　　SZ
HISTORISCHER VEREIN DES KANTONS BERN.
ARCHIV. 1848. a. price varies. Historischer Verein
des Kantons Bern, Stadt- und
Universitaetsbibliothek, Muenstergasse 61, CH-3000
Berne 7, Switzerland. charts. illus. cum.index:
vols.1-38; vols.39-55. circ. 1,750.

940　　　　　　SZ
HISTORISCHER VEREIN DES KANTONS ST.
GALLEN. NEUJAHRSBLATT. 1861. a. price
varies. ‡ Verlagsgemeinschaft St. Gallen in
Kommission, 9001 St. Gallen, Switzerland. Ed.Bd.
bibl. illus. circ. 300.
Local history

943　　　　　　GW　ISSN 0073-2699
HISTORISCHER VEREIN DILLINGEN AN DER
DONAU. JAHRBUCH. 1888. a. price varies.
Historischer Verein Dillingen an der Donau, Am
Hafenmarkt 11, PF 1210, 8880 Dillingen, W.
Germany (B.R.D) Ed. Rudolf Poppa. bk. rev. circ.
1,000.

943　914　　　　　　LH
HISTORISCHER VEREIN FUER DAS
FUERSTENTUM LIECHTENSTEIN.
JAHRBUCH. 1901. a. sfr.30. Historischer Verein
fuer das Fuerstentum Liechtenstein, Staedtle 43,
9490 Vaduz, Liechtenstein. cum.index: 1901-1950;
1950-1960. Indexed: Hist.Abstr. Amer.Hist.& Life.

943.6　　　　　　AU
HISTORISCHER VEREIN FUER STEIERMARK.
ZEITSCHRIFT. 1909. a. S.240. Historische Verein
fuer Steiermark, Hamerlinggasse 3, 8010 Graz,
Austria. Ed.Bd. bk. rev. circ. 1,400.

943.6　　　　　　AU　ISSN 0440-9736
HISTORISCHES JAHRBUCH DER STADT LINZ.
1935. a. S.330. Archiv der Stadt Linz, Neues
Rathaus, Hauptstr. 1-5, A-4041 Linz, Austria. Eds.
Fritz Mayrhofer, Willibald Katzinger. bk. rev.
cum.index. Indexed: Hist.Abstr. Amer.Hist.& Life.
Bibl.Cart.

948.9　　　　　　DK　ISSN 0109-2138
HISTORISK AARBOG FOR FELSTED SOGN.
1983. a. Kr.50. (Historisk Forening for Felsted
Skovboel) Peter Petersen, Eskedalvej 8, Ny
Skovboel, 6200 Abenraa, Denmark. Ed. Peter
Petersen. circ. 300.

948　　　　　　DK　ISSN 0107-783X
HISTORISK AARBOG FOR ROEDDING
KOMMUNE. 1981. a. Kr.50. Roedding Bibliotek,
Kongevej 6, 6630 Roedding, Denmark. Ed. Niels H.
Kragh Nielsen. illus. circ. 500.

948　　　　　　DK　ISSN 0107-721X
HISTORISK AARBOG FOR SKIVE OG OMEGN.
1909. a. Kr.44. Historisk Samfund for Skive og
Omegn, Lyngbakken 13, Thise, DK 7870 Roslev,
Denmark. Ed. Steen Sorensen. bk. rev. circ. 2,000.
Indexed: Hist.Abstr.
Local

948　　　　　　DK　ISSN 0108-4100
HISTORISK AARBOG FRA RANDERS AMT.
1907. a. Kr.85. Randers Amts Historiske Samfund,
Slynborggade 21, 8900 Randers, Denmark. Ed.Bd.
adv. illus. circ. 1,450. Indexed: Numis.Lit.

948　　　　　　DK
HISTORISK ARBOG FOR THY, MORS OG
VESTER HANHERRED. 1906. a. Historisk
Samfund for Thy, Mors og Vester Hanherred, 7700
Vestervig, Denmark.
Former titles: Historisk Arbog for Thy og Mors;
Which superseded: Historisk Arbog for Thisted
Amt.

948　　　　　　DK
HISTORISK ARBOG FRA ROSKILDE AMT. 1910.
a. Historisk Samfund for Roskilde Amt, Baldersvej
22, 4000 Roskilde, Denmark. cum.index: 1910-1968.

HISTORY — HISTORY OF EUROPE

948.9   DK   ISSN 0109-0674
HISTORISK ARKIV FOR BROERUP OG OMEGN. AARSSKRIFT. 1974. biennial. Kr.10. Historisk Arkiv for Broerup og Omegn, c/o Johs. Godsk Hansen, Soendergade 50, 6650 Broerup, Denmark. illus. circ. 250.

948   DK   ISSN 0108-6804
HISTORISK FORENING FOR VAERLOESE KOMMUNE. ARSSKRIFT. 1949. a. Kr.40. Historisk Forening for Vaerloese Kommune, Skovgards Alle 37, 3500 Vaerloese, Denmark. circ. 1,500.

948   DK
HISTORISK SAMFUND FOR ARHUS STIFT. ARBOGER. a. Kr.55. Historisk Samfund for Arhus Stift, 8000 Arhus, Denmark.

948   DK   ISSN 0107-6868
HISTORISK SAMFUND FOR PRAESTO AMT. AARBOG. 1912. a. Kr.75. Nils Hartmann, Gavnovej 155, 4700 Naestved, Denmark. Ed. Nils Hartmann. bk. rev. illus. circ. 1,500.

948   DK   ISSN 0109-9264
HISTORISK SAMFUND FOR SOENDERJYLLAND. SKRIFTER. 1985. a. Kr.110. Historisk Samfund for Soenderjylland, Haderslevvej 45, 6200 Aabenraa, Denmark.

948   DK
HISTORISK SAMFUND FOR SORO AMT. ARBOG. 1912. a. Kr.75. Historisk Samfund for Soro Amt, Kristinelundsvej 39, 4200 Slagelse, Denmark. Ed. Erling Petersen. bk. rev. cum.index: 1912-1978. circ. 800.

948   FI   ISSN 0356-1496
HISTORISKA SAMFUNDET I ABO. SKRIFTER UTGIVNA. (Text in Swedish) 1942. irreg. Historiska Samfundet i Abo, Abo Akademi, 20500 Abo, Finland. circ. 200.

940   DK
HISTORISKE MEDDELELSER OM KOEBENHAVN. 1907. a. Kr.90. Stadsarkiv, Raadhuset, DK-1599 Copenhagen V, Denmark. Ed. Helle Linde. bk. rev. bibl. illus. cum.index (every 4 yrs.) circ. 1,450. (back issues avail.) Indexed: Hist.Abstr. Amer.Hist.& Life.
Local

HISTORY OF UNIVERSITIES. see EDUCATION — Higher Education

940   PL   ISSN 0073-277X
HISTORYKA; STUDIA METODOLOGICZNE. (Text in Polish; summaries in English, and French) 1967. a. price varies. (Polska Akademia Nauk, Oddzial w Krakowie, Komisja Nauk Historycznych) Ossolineum, Publishing House of the Polish Academy of Sciences, Rynek 9, Wroclaw, Poland (Dist. by: Ars Polona-Ruch, Krakowskie Przedmiescie 7, Warsaw, Poland) Ed. Celina Bobinska. bk. rev. (reprint service avail.)

948.9   DK   ISSN 0900-2596
HOEJE-TASTRUP KOMMUNES. LOKALHISTORISKE ARKIV. AARSKRIFT. 1983. a. free. Hoeje-Taastrup Kommunes Lokalhistoriske Arkiv, Hoejgaardstoften 13, 2630 Taastrup, Denmark. illus.

943 323   US   ISSN 0738-0739
HOLOCAUST STUDIES ANNUAL. 1984. a. price varies. Penkevill Publishing Company, Box 212, Greenwood, FL 32443. TEL 904-569-2811. Eds. Sanford Pinsker, Jack Fischel. circ. 250.

948   DK   ISSN 0107-6752
HOLSTEBRO MUSEUM. AARSSKRIFT. 1969. a. Kr.75. Holstebro Museum, Museumsvej 3, 7500 Holstebro, Denmark. Ed. Torben Skov.

943.7   CS
HORNA NITRA. 1962. irreg. Vydavatel'stvo Osveta, Osloboditelov 21, 036 54 Martin, Czechoslovakia (Subscr. to: Slovart, Gottwaldovo Nam. 6, 805 32 Bratislava, Czechoslovakia)

942   UK   ISSN 0268-7836
HORNSEY HISTORICAL SOCIETY. BULLETIN. 1973. a. £1.95. Hornsey Historical Society, The Old Schoolhouse, 136 Tottenham Lane, London N8 7EL, England. adv. bk. rev. circ. 7,000.

942   UK
HORNSEY HISTORICAL SOCIETY. OCCASIONAL PAPERS. 1976; N.S. 1978. irreg., no.4, 1985. Hornsey Historical Society, The Old Schoolhouse, 136 Tottenham Lane, London N8 7EL, England.

940 398   BE
HOUTLAND. (Text in Flemish) 1959. a. 250 Fr. Heemkundige Kring Houtland, Markt 1, 8100 Torhout, Belgium.

948   DK
HUGIN. 1975. a. Lokalhistorisk Forening for Egebjerg Kommune, Stenstrup, Denmark.

940 929   UK   ISSN 0309-8346
HUGUENOT SOCIETY OF LONDON. PROCEEDINGS. 1885. a. £15($5) to non-members. Huguenot Society of London, c/o Barclay's Bank Ltd., 1 Pall Mall East, London SW1X 5AX, England. Ed. Irene Scouloudi. bk. rev. illus. cum.index.

900 929   UK   ISSN 0309-8354
HUGUENOT SOCIETY OF LONDON. QUARTO SERIES. 1885. irreg. (2-4/yr.) £15($15) to non-members. Huguenot Society of London, c/o Barclays Bank Ltd., 1 Pall Mall East, London SW1X 5AX, England. Ed. Irene Scouloudi.

940   US   ISSN 0742-115X
HUMANA CIVILITAS;* sources and studies relating to the Middle Ages and the Renaissance. 1976. irreg., latest no.8. price varies. (University of California, Los Angeles, Center for Medieval and Renaissance Studies) Undena Publications, 6355 Green Valley Circle, No.213, Culver City, CA 90230-7064. Ed.Bd. (back issues avail.)

943.7   CS
HUSITSKY TABOR. 1978. a. 30 Kcs. Muzeum Husitskeho Revolucniho Hnuti, 390 01 Tabor, Czechoslovakia (Subscr. to: Artia, Ve Smeckach 30, 111 27 Prague 1, Czechoslovakia) Ed. Milos Drda. bk. rev. circ. 70.

IBSEN AARBOKEN/IBSEN YEARBOOK. see LITERATURE

943 398   GW
IMMENSTAADER HEIMATBLAETTER. 1978. a. DM.12. Heimatverein Immenstaad, Frickenwaesele 18, 7997 Immenstaad, W. Germany (B.R.D.) illus. circ. 600. (back issues avail.)

946   SP
INSTITUCION PRINCIPE DE VIANA. COLECCION HISTORIA. no. 3, 1974. irreg. 350 ptas. Diputacion Foral de Navarra, Institucion Principe de Viana, Avda. Carlos III, 2, Pamplona, Spain.

943   FR   ISSN 0079-0001
INSTITUT D'ETUDES SLAVES, PARIS. COLLECTION HISTORIQUE. 1920. irreg., vol.32, 1986. price varies. Institut d'Etudes Slaves, 9 rue Michelet, 75006 Paris, France.

INSTITUT D'ETUDES SLAVES, PARIS. TRAVAUX. see LITERATURE

949   BE   ISSN 0073-8522
INSTITUT HISTORIQUE BELGE DE ROME. BIBLIOTHEQUE.* 1949. irreg. price varies. Institut Historique Belge de Rome, c/oArchives Generales du Royaume, 2-6 rue de Ruysbroeck, B-1000 Brussels, Belgium.

949   BE   ISSN 0073-8530
INSTITUT HISTORIQUE BELGE DE ROME. BULLETIN.* (Text in French or Italian) 1919. a. price varies. Institut Historique Belge de Rome, c/o Archives Generales du Royaume, 2-6 rue de Ruysbroeck, B-1000 Brussels, Belgium. circ. controlled. Indexed: Hist.Abstr. Amer.Hist.& Life. RILA.

949   BE   ISSN 0073-8557
INSTITUT JULES DESTREE. ETUDES ET DOCUMENTS. Alternate title: Institut Jules Destree. Collection: Etudes et Documents. irreg., no. 21. price varies. Institut Jules Destree, Rue du Chateau 3, 6100 Mont-sur-Marchienne Charleroi, Belgium.

945   GR   ISSN 0073-862X
INSTITUTE FOR BALKAN STUDIES. PUBLICATIONS/IDRYMA MELETON CHERSONESOU AIMOU. EKTHOSEIS. (Text in English, French, German and Greek) 1953. irreg., no.208, 1986. price varies. Institute for Balkan Studies, 45 Tsimiski St., 54110 Thessaloniki, Greece.

INSTITUTE OF EUROPEAN STUDIES. ANNALI I S E. see POLITICAL SCIENCE

946.73   SP   ISSN 0534-3364
INSTITUTO DE ESTUDIOS TARRACONENSES RAMON BERENGUER IV. PUBLICACION. 1952. irreg. Instituto de Estudios Tarraconenses Ramon Berenguer IV, Diputacion Provincial de Tarragona, Calle Santa Ana 8, Tarragona, Spain. bibl. illus.

946   SP
INSTITUTO PROVINCIAL DE INVESTIGACIONES Y ESTUDIOS TOLEDANOS. PUBLICACIONES. no. 4, 1976. irreg. Instituto Provincial de Investigaciones y Estudios Toledanos, Servicios Culturales, Diputacion Provincial de Toledo, Plaza de la Merced 4, Toledo, Spain.

INSTITUTUL DE ISTORIE SI ARHEOLOGIE "A.D. XENOPOL" - IASI. ANUARUL. see ARCHAEOLOGY

INSTITUTUL DE ISTORIE SI ARHEOLOGIE - CLUJ-NAPOCA. ANUARUL. see ARCHAEOLOGY

949.5   GR   ISSN 0571-5857
INTERNATIONAL ASSOCIATION FOR BYZANTINE STUDIES. BULLETIN D'INFORMATION ET DE COORDINATION. 1964. irreg. International Association for Byzantine Studies, c/o D. A. Zakythinos, Pres., Rue Sissini 31, Athens 612, Greece. Ed. Helene Ahrweiler. circ. 1,000.

949.5   GR   ISSN 0074-3542
INTERNATIONAL CONGRESS FOR BYZANTINE STUDIES. ACTS/CONGRES INTERNATIONAL DES ETUDES BYZANTINES. ACTES.* (Published in host country) irreg., 1971, 14th, Bucharest. International Association for Byzantine Studies, Rue Sissimi 31, Athens 612, Greece.

INTERNATIONAL DOCUMENTATION ON MACEDONIA. see POLITICAL SCIENCE — Civil Rights

940   CN
INTERUNIVERSITY CENTRE FOR EUROPEAN STUDIES. INTERNATIONAL COLLOQUIUM PROCEEDINGS. 1974. irreg. Can.$8.50. Interuniversity Centre for European Studies, Box 8892, Montreal, Que. H3C 3P3, Canada. TEL 514-282-6193.

940   CN
INTERUNIVERSITY CENTRE FOR EUROPEAN STUDIES. RESEARCH REPORT. 1980. irreg. Can.$2.50. Interuniversity Centre for European Studies, Box 8892, Montreal, Que. H3C 3P3, Canada. TEL 514-282-6193.

949.2   BE   ISSN 0075-0166
INVENTARIS VAN HET KUNSTPATRIMONIUM VAN OOST-VLAANDEREN. 1951. irreg., no. 17, 1982. price varies. Bestendige Deputatitie van Oost-Vlaanderen, Bisdomplein 3, 9000 Ghent, Belgium. index. circ. 1,250.

946   SP
INVESTIGACIONES HISTORICAS.* 1975. irreg. Universidad de Valladolid, Valladolid 8, Spain. circ. 500.
Formerly (until 1979): Cuadernas Simancas de Investigaciones Historicas. Monografias.

941 300   IE   ISSN 0332-4893
IRISH ECONOMIC AND SOCIAL HISTORY. 1974. a. $20. Economic and Social History Society of Ireland, History Department, University College, Galway, Ireland. Eds. T. Bartlett, S. Connolly. adv. bk. rev. abstr. bibl. stat. circ. 550. (back issues avail.) Indexed: Hist.Abstr. Amer.Hist.& Life.

941 IE ISSN 0332-3633
IRISH HISTORY WORKSHOP/SAOTHARLANN
STAIRE EIREANN. 1981. irreg. Irish History
Workshop Co-op, 127 Bothar na Tra, Baile Atha
Cliath, Dublin, Ireland. Ed.Bd. illus.

941 947 UK ISSN 0260-2067
IRISH SLAVONIC STUDIES. (Special issue (no.5,
1984): Irish-Russian Contacts) 1980. a. £5($8) Irish
Slavists' Association, Department of Slavonic
Studies, Queen's University, Belfast BT7 1NN, N.
Ireland. Ed. Neil Cornwell. adv. bk. rev. circ. 300.
Indexed: M.L.A.

948 914 IC
ISLENZKA FORNLEIFAFELAGS. ARBOK. (Text
in Icelandic; summaries in English) 1881. a.
National Museum of Iceland, Archeological Society
of Iceland, P.O.Box 1489, 121 Reykjavik, Iceland.
Ed. Inga Lara Baldvinsdoettir. circ. 750.

930 949.5 IT ISSN 0075-1502
ISTITUTO ELLENICO DI STUDI BIZANTINI E
POSTBIZANTINI, VENICE. BIBLIOTECA. 1962.
irreg., no.11, 1983. prices varies. Istituto Ellenico di
Studi Bizantini e Post-Bizantini, Castello 3412, 3412
Venezia, Italy. circ. 1,500.

945 001.3 300 IT ISSN 0080-391X
ISTITUTO GIAPPONESE DI CULTURA, ROME.
ANNUARIO. (Text in Italian) 1963. a. free.
(Kokusai Koryu Kikin) Istituto Giapponese di
Cultura in Roma, Via Antonio Gramsci 74, 00197
Roma, Italy. circ. 1,000. (back issues avail.)

949.5 IT ISSN 0075-1545
ISTITUTO SICILIANO DI STUDI BIZANTINI E
NEOELLENICI. QUADERNI. 1965. irreg., no. 12,
1984. price varies. Istituto Siciliano di Studi
Bizantini e Neoellenici, Via Noto, 34, 90141
Palermo, Italy.

949.5 880 IT ISSN 0075-1553
ISTITUTO SICILIANO DI STUDI BIZANTINI E
NEOELLENICI. TESTI E MONUMENTI. TESTI.
1954. irreg., no. 13, 1979. price varies. Istituto
Siciliano di Studi Bizantini e Neoellenici, Via Noto,
34, 90141 Palermo, Italy.

940 IT ISSN 0391-8211
ISTITUTO STORICO ARTISTICO ORVIETANO.
BOLLETTINO. 1945. a. L.10000 free to
institutions. Istituto Storico Artistico Orvietano,
Piazza Febei N.1, Orvieto 05018, Italy. Dir. Franco
Crisanti. adv. bk. rev. circ. controlled.

940 IT
ISTITUTO STORICO ITALO-GERMANICO IN
TRENTO. ANNALI/ITALIENISCH-
DEUTSCHEN HISTORISCHEN INSTITUTS.
JAHRBUCH. (Text in English, German, Italian;
summaries in Italian) 1975. a. L.60000. Istituto
Storico Italo-Germanico, Via S. Croce 77, 38100
Trento, Italy. circ. 1,000.

907 947 UR
ISTOCHNIKOVEDENIE OTECHESTVENNOI
ISTORII. 1973. irreg. price varies. (Akademiya
Nauk S.S.S.R., Institut Istorii S.S.S.R.) Izdatel'stvo
Nauka, Podsosenskii per., 21, Moscow K-62,
Russian S.F.S.R., U.S.S.R. (Subscr. to:
Mezhdunarodnaya Kniga, Moscow, G-200, Russian
S.F.S.R., U.S.S.R.) Ed. N.I. Pavlenko. bibl.

947 UR
ISTORIYA I ISTORIKI. a. price varies. Izdatel'stvo
Nauka, Podsosenskii Per., 21, Moscow K-62,
Russian S.F.S.R., U.S.S.R. (Subscr. to:
Mezhdunarodnaya Kniga, Moscow, G-200, Russian
S.F.S.R., U.S.S.R.) Ed. M.V. Nechkina. circ. 3,200.

ITALIAN GENEALOGIST. see GENEALOGY
AND HERALDRY

945 850 UK ISSN 0261-4340
ITALIANIST. (Text in English and Italian) 1981. a.
£5.50($12) Nova Graphics Ltd., 22-25 Bartholomew
Sq., London EC1, England (Subscr. to: Dept. of
Italian Studies, University of Reading, Whiteknights,
Reading, Berks. RG6 2AA, England) Eds. Z.G.
Baranski, B.K. Jones. bk. rev. (back issues avail.)
Indexed: M.L.A.

948 FI
ITAVIITTA. 1955. irreg. Fmk.20. Pitkapaasi-Seura,
Tammitie 18 A 8, 00330 Helsinki 33, Finland. Ed.
Hellin Erasaari. adv. cum.index: 1955-1972. circ.
500.

940 BU
IZSLEDOVANIIA PO BULGARSKA ISTORIIA.
1976. irreg. 5 lv. per issue. (Bulgarska Akademiia na
Naukite, Institut za Istoriia) Publishing House of the
Bulgarian Academy of Sciences, Acad. G. Boncev
St., Bldg. 6, 1113 Sofia, Bulgaria. circ. 2,000.

947 BU
IZSLEDOVANIYA ZA ISTORIIATA NA
BULGARSKIYA NAROD. 1970. irreg. (Bulgarska
Akademiya na Naukite) Publishing House of the
Bulgarian Academy of Sciences, Ul. Akad. G.
Bonchev, 1113 Sofia, Bulgaria (Subscr. to: Hemus
Foreign Trade Co., 6 Ruski Blvd., 1000 Sofia,
Bulgaria)

IZVESTIYA NA MUZEITE OT IUGOIZTOCHNA
BULGARIYA. see ARCHAEOLOGY

IZVESTIYA NA MUZEITE OT IUZHNA
BULGARIYA. see ARCHAEOLOGY

947 913 BU ISSN 0204-4013
IZVESTIYA NA MUZEITE V SEVEROZAPADNA
BULGARIYA. 1977. a. Hemus Foreign Trade Co.,
6 Ruski Blvd., 1000 Sofia, Bulgaria. bk. rev. illus.

948 NE
JAARBOEK ACHTERHOEK EN LIEMERS. 1980.
a. fl.25. Walburg Pers, Zaadmarkt 84-86, Box 222,
7200 AE Zutphen, Netherlands.

943 GW ISSN 0341-9177
JAHRBUCH DER HISTORISCHEN FORSCHUNG
IN DER BUNDESREPUBLIK DEUTSCHLAND.
1974. a. price varies. (Arbeitsgemeinschaft
Ausseruniversitaren Historischen
Forschungsrichtungen der Bundesrepublik) K.G.
Saur Verlag KG, Poessenbacherstr. 12B, Postfach
711009, 8000 Munich 71, W. Germany (B.R.D.)
(U.S. and Canadian subscr. to: K.G. Saur Inc., 175
Fifth Ave., N.Y., N.Y., 10010) Ed. Fritz Wagner.

943 GW ISSN 0075-2436
JAHRBUCH DES BALTISCHEN DEUTSCHTUMS.
1952. a. DM.18. Carl Schirren Gesellschaft, Am
Berge 35, 2120 Lueneburg, W. Germany (B.R.D.)
Eds. H. Kroeger, G.v. Mickwitz, D. Osteneck. adv.
bk. rev. circ. 1,000.

943 GW
JAHRBUCH DES SCHWALM-EDER-KREISES.
1975. a. DM.6. Kreisausschuss des Schwalm-Eder-
Kreises, Parkstr. 6, 3588 Homberg, W. Germany
(B.R.D.) adv. index. circ. 15,000.

943 GW ISSN 0448-150X
JAHRBUCH FUER DEN KREIS PINNEBERG.
1967. a. DM.22. (Heimatverband fuer den Kreis
Pinneberg) A. Beig Verlag, Damm 9-15, Postfach
1220, 2080 Pinneberg, W. Germany (B.R.D.) Ed.
Dr. Mannfred Peters. bk. rev. bibl. illus. circ. 1,300.

943 312 GW ISSN 0446-3943
JAHRBUCH FUER FRAENKISCHE
LANDESFORSCHUNG. (Text in English, French,
German; summaries in English) 1935. a. DM.50.
Universitaet Erlangen-Nuernberg, Zentralinstitut
fuer Fraenkische Landeskunde und Allgemeine
Regionalforschung, Kochstrasse 4, D-8520 Erlangen,
W. Germany (B.R.D.) Ed. Alfred Wendehorst. adv.
cum.index. circ. 700. Indexed: M.L.A.

940 GE ISSN 0448-1526
JAHRBUCH FUER GESCHICHTE. 1967. irreg.
Zentralinstitut fuer Geschichte, Akademie der
Wissenschaften der DDR, Clara Zetkin Str. 26,
Postfach 1216, 108 Berlin, E. Germany (D.D.R.)
cum.index: 1974. Indexed: Hist.Abstr. Amer.Hist.&
Life.

940 GE
JAHRBUCH FUER GESCHICHTE DES
FEUDALISMUS. 1977. a. M.48. (Akademie der
Wissenschaften der DDR, Zentralinstitut fuer
Geschichte) Akademie-Verlag, Leipziger Strasse 3-4,
1086 Berlin, E. Germany (D.D.R.)

940 GE ISSN 0085-2341
JAHRBUCH FUER REGIONALGESCHICHTE.
1965. irreg., vol.12, 1985. price varies. (Saechsische
Akademie der Wissenschaften, Leipzig, Historische
Kommission) Hermann Boehlaus Nachfolger,
Meyerstr. 50A, 53 Weimar, E. Germany (D.D.R.)
bk. rev.

943 GW ISSN 0075-2754
JAHRBUCH FUER SALESIANISCHE STUDIEN.
1963. a. price varies. (Arbeitsgemeinschaft fuer
Salesianische Studien) Franz-Sales-Verlag, Rosental
1, Abholfach, D-8078 Eichstaett/Bay., W. Germany
(B.R.D.) Ed. P. Anton Nobis. bk. rev.

940 GW ISSN 0170-2025
JAHRBUCH FUER WESTDEUTSCHE
LANDESGESCHICHTE. 1975. a. price varies.
Landesarchivverwaltung Rheinland-Pfalz,
Karmeliterstr. 1/3, 5400 Koblenz, W. Germany
(B.R.D.) Ed.Bd. Indexed: Bibl.Cart.

943.6 AU
JAHRBUCH FUER ZEITGESCHICHTE. 1978. a.
S.315. Geyer-Edition Wien-Salzburg, Seilergasse 3,
A-1010 Vienna, Austria.

943 GW
JAHRBUCH LANDKREIS KASSEL. 1973. a. DM.8.
Kreisausschuss des Landkreises Kassel, Humboldtstr.
24, 3500 Kassel, W. Germany (B.R.D.) Ed. Helmut
Burmeister. adv. bk. rev. circ. 7,000. (back issues
avail.)

940 GE
JAHRBUCH ZUR GESCHICHTE DRESDENS.
(Subseries of the Institute's Informationsdienst) a.
M.4. Institut und Museum fuer Geschichte der
Stadt Dresden, Ernst-Thaelmann-Str. 2, 801
Dresden A 1, E. Germany (D.D.R.) bk. rev. bibl.
illus.

940 GE ISSN 0075-2932
JAHRESSCHRIFT FUER MITTELDEUTSCHE
VORGESCHICHTE. 1964. a. price varies. VEB
Deutscher Verlag der Wissenschaften, Postfach
1216, 1080 Berlin, E. Germany (D.D.R.) Ed. H.
Behrens.

948 FI
JATULI. 1949. irreg. Kr.40. Kemin Kotiseutu- ja
Museoyhdistys, Kemin Museo, Meripuisto, Kemi,
Finland. Ed. Ossi Hedman. cum.index: 1949-75, in
vol.15.

943 GE ISSN 0138-3604
JENAER BEITRAEGE ZUR
PARTEIEGESCHICHTE; Mitteilungsblatt der
Forschungsgemeinschaft Geschichte der
Buergerlichen Parteien in Deutschland. 1957. irreg.
Historisches Institut der Friedrich -Schiller-
Universitaet Jena, Goetheallee 1, 69 Jena, E.
Germany (D.D.R.) Indexed: Hist.Abstr.
Amer.Hist.& Life.
Formerly: Arbeitsgemeinschaft der Sektion
Geschichte der Akademie der Wissenschaften
Geschichte der Buergerlichen Parteien in
Deutschland. Mitteilungsblatt.

940 913 BE
JESCHEIDENIS VAN WORTEL. (Text in Dutch)
1932. a. 600 Fr. Hoogstratens Oudheidkundige
Kring, Begynhof 1-2, 2320 Hoogstraten, Belgium.
bk. rev. circ. 500.
Formerly: Hok.

943.7 CS ISSN 0449-0436
JIZNI MORAVA. 1965. a. Teps Praha, Hybernska 10,
Prague 1, Czechoslovakia (Subscr. to: Artia, Ve
Smeckach 30, 111 27 Prague 1, Czechoslovakia) bk.
rev. bibl. cum.index: vols.1-10, 1975.

948 FI
JOUKO. 1910. irreg. Fmk.60. Pohjois-Pohjalainen
Osakunta, Toolonkatu 3A, 00100 Helsinki 10,
Finland.

947 UK ISSN 0075-4161
JOURNAL OF BYELORUSSIAN STUDIES. (Text in
English, Byelorussian and German) 1965. a.
£3.50($9) Anglo-Byelorussian Society, 39 Holden
Rd., London N12 8HS, England. Ed. Peter Mayo.
adv. bk. rev. cum.index: every 3 years (1977-80)
circ. 800. Indexed: M.L.A.

949.7 US ISSN 0075-4218
JOURNAL OF CROATIAN STUDIES; annual
review of the Croatian Academy of America. 1960.
a. $15. Croatian Academy of America, Inc., Box
1767 Grand Central Sta., New York, NY 10017.
Eds. Jerome Jareb, Karlo Mirth. bk. rev. circ. 1,000.
Indexed: Hist.Abstr. M.L.A. P.A.I.S. Amer.Hist.&
Life.

940 MM ISSN 0075-4285
JOURNAL OF MALTESE STUDIES. (Text in English, French and Italian) 1961. irreg. price varies. University of Malta, Department of Maltese, Msida, Malta. Ed. O. Friggieri. bk. rev. circ. 500.

947 YU ISSN 0449-3648
JUGOSLAVENSKA AKADEMIJA ZNANOSTI I UMJETNOSTI. HISTORIJSKI INSTITUT, DUBROVNIK. ANALI. (Text in Croatian; summaries in English, French or other languages) 1952. a. Jugoslavenska Akademija Znanosti i Umjetnosti, Historijski Institut, Dubrovnik., Yugoslavia. Ed.Bd. illus.

948 DK ISSN 0107-5446
JUL I FREDERIKSSUND. 1979. a. Kr.19. Thorsgaard, Tvaerstraede 5, 3600 Frederikssund, Denmark. adv. illus. circ. 6,000.

948 DK ISSN 0108-2965
JUL I LEJRE. 1981. a. Kr.10. Lejre-Posten, Munkedammen 5, 4320 Lejre, Denmark. illus.

948 913 DK ISSN 0107-2854
JYSK ARKAEOLOGISK SELSKABS. SKRIFTER/ JUTLAND ARCHAEOLOGICAL SOCIETY. PUBLICATIONS. 1951. a. Jysk Arkaeologisk Selskab - Jutland Archeological Society, 8270 Hoejbjerg, Denmark (Distr. By: Aarhus University Press, Aarhus University, DK-8000 Aarhus, Denmark) Ed. Poul Kjaerum. circ. 1,000.

949.7 200 YU ISSN 0453-0578
KACIC. (Text in Croatian; summaries in English, French, German, Italian) 1967. a. DM.30. Franjevacka Provincija Presvetoga Otkupitelja, Trg. G. Bulata 3, 5800 Split, Yugoslavia. adv. bk. rev. circ. 800. (also avail. in microform)

948 FI
KAIKUJA HAMEESTA. 1872. irreg. Hamalais-Osakunta, Kampinkatu 4-6 D, 00100 Helsinki 10, Finland.

948 FI
KARJALA. 1910. irreg. Karjalainen Osakunta, Liisankatu 17 B, 00170 Helsinki 17, Finland. circ. 1,000.

948 FI
KARLEBYNEJDEN. (Text in Swedish) 1970. irreg. Karlebynejdens Bygde- och Slaktforskare, SF-68410 Nedervetil, Finland. Ed. Jan-Erik Nygren. circ. 350.

943 GW
KARPATEN JAHRBUCH. 1950. a. DM.14. Arbeitsgemeinschaft der Karpatendeutschen, Schlosstrasse 92, 7000 Stuttgart 1, W. Germany (B.R.D.) Ed. Adalbert Wanhoff. adv. circ. 3,200.

948.9 DK ISSN 0280-8463
KATTEGAT-SKAGERRAK-PROJECTET. MEDDELELSER; regionens kulturudvikling under 1800-tallet. (Text in Danish, Norwegian and Swedish) 1982. irreg., no.11, 1986. free. Kattegat-Skagerrak-Projectet, c/o Fiskeri og Soefartsmuseet, 6700 Esbjerg, Denmark. Ed.Bd. circ. 600.

948 FI
KAUKOMIELI. 1876. irreg. Vilpurilainen Osakunto, Liisankatu 17 B, 00170 Helsinki 17, Finland.

948 FI
KELLON - HAUKIPUTAAN KOTISEUTUJULKAISU. 1961. irreg. Kellon-Haukiputaan Kotiseutuyhdistys, Oiva Kurkela, 90830 Haukipudas, Finland.

941 US ISSN 0192-1207
KELTICA; the Inter-Celtic journal. 1980. a. $5.95. Society of Inter-Celtic Arts and Culture, 96 Marguerite Ave., Waltham, MA 02154. TEL 617-899-2204. Ed. Kevin Dixon Gilligan. adv. bk. rev. circ. 2,500. (back issues avail.)

949 BE
KEN UW DORP EN UW FAMILIE: TIJDSCHRIFT VAN DE HEEMKUNDIGE KRING. (Text in Flemish) 1966. a. Heemkundige Kring, Kasteeldreef 17, Lede, Belgium.

948 FI ISSN 0355-1393
KESKI-SUOMI. (Text in Finnish; summaries in English) 1935. irreg., No.19, 1986. Fmk.35. Keski-Suomen Museo, Ruusupuisto, 40600 Jyvaskyla, Finland. Ed. Janne Vilkuna.

947 UR
KHABAROVSKII GOSUDARSTVENNYI PEDAGOGICHESKII INSTITUT. VOPROSY ISTORII DAL'NEGO VOSTOKA. 1972. irreg. Khabarovskii Gosudarstvennyi Pedagogicheskii Institut, Khabarovsk, Russian S.F.S.R., U.S.S.R.

943.7 CS
KMETIANUM. 1968. irreg. Osveta, Osloboditelov 21, 036 54 Martin, Czechoslovakia (Subscr. to: Slovart, Gottwaldovo Nam. 6, 805 32 Bratislava, Czechoslovakia)

KNIHOVNA. see *LIBRARY AND INFORMATION SCIENCES*

948 DK ISSN 0107-976X
KOEBENHAVNERLIV FOER OG NU. 1981. a. Kr.148. Herluf Stockholm, Kaerparken 6, 2800 Lyngby, Denmark. illus.

948 DK ISSN 0105-9254
KOEBSTADSMUSEET DEN GAMLE BY. 1928. a. Kr.150. 8000 Arhus, Denmark. Eds. Erik Kjersgaard, Henrik Nyrop-Christiensen. cum.index; 1927-72. circ. 4,500.

940 309 330 GW
KOELNER VORTRAEGE ZUR SOZIAL- UND WIRTSCHAFTSGESCHICHTE. 1969. irreg., no.37, 1983. price varies. Universitaet zu Koeln, Forschungsinstitut fuer Sozial- und Wirtschaftsgeschichte, Unter Sachsenhausen 10-26, 5000 Cologne 1, W. Germany (B.R.D.) Ed. Friedrich-Wilhelm Henning.

948 DK
KOLDING BOGEN. 1970. a. Kr.35. (Kolding Kommunes Udvalg for Kulturelle Anliggender) Konrad Joergensen A-S, 6000 Kolding, Denmark. Ed. Birgitte Dedenroth-Schou. cum.index: 1970-1976. circ. 1,500.

943.7 CS
KOMISE PRO DEJINY ZAVODU V C S S R. ZPRAVODAJ. 1962. irreg. Komise pro Dejiny Zavodu v C S S R, Ustredni Skola Revolucniho Odboroveho Hnuti Antonina, Francouzska 4, 120 00 Prague, Czechoslovakia. bk. rev. Formerly: Komise pro Dejiny Zavodu v C S S R Zpravy.

943 GW ISSN 0067-2831
KOMMISSION FUER GESCHICHTLICHE LANDESKUNDE IN BADEN-WUERTTEMBERG. VEROEFFENTLICHUNGEN. REIHE A. QUELLEN. 1958. irreg. price varies. Kommission fuer Geschichtliche Landeskunde in Baden-Wuerttemberg, Eugen-Str. 7, 7000 Stuttgart 1, W. Germany (B.R.D.) circ. 800.

943 GW ISSN 0521-9884
KOMMISSION FUER GESCHICHTLICHE LANDESKUNDE IN BADEN-WUERTTEMBERG. VEROEFFENTLICHUNGEN. REIHE B: FORSCHUNGEN. 1958. irreg. price varies. Kommission fuer Geschichtliche Landeskunde in Baden-Wuerttemberg, Eugen-Str. 7, 7000 Stuttgart 1, W. Germany (B.R.D.) circ. 800.

943.6 AU
KOMMISSION FUER NEUERE GESCHICHTE OESTERREICHS. VEROEFFENTLICHUNGEN. 1924. irreg., vol. 70, 1981. price varies. Hermann Boehlaus Nachf, c/o Dr. Karl Lueger, Ring 12, A-1010 Vienna, Austria. Ed. Erich Zoellner. circ. 700. (back issues avail.)

949 BE
KONINKLIJKE GESCHIED- EN OUDHEIDKUNDIGE KRING VAN KORTRIJK. HANDELINGEN/CERCLE ROYAL HISTORIQUE ET ARCHEOLOGIQUE DE COURTRAI. MEMOIRES. (Text in Flemish and French) 1903. a. Koninkijke Gescheid- en Oudheidkundige Kring van Kortrijke - Cercle Royal Historique et Archeologique de Courtrai, Aalbeeksesteenweg 84, 8500 Kortrijk, Belgium. bk. rev. illus. Indexed: Numis.Lit.

949 913 BE
KONINKLIJKE KRING VOOR OUDHEIDKUNDE LETTEREN EN KUNST VAN MECHELEN. HANDELINGEN. (Text in Flemish) 1889. a. Koninklijke Kring voor Oudheidkunde, Letteren en Kunst van Mechelen, Steenweg 1, 2800 Mechelen, Belgium. bibl.

943.6 AU ISSN 0023-4087
KORNEUBURGER KULTURNACHRICHTEN;* fuer die Bezirke Korneuburg und Stockerau. 1961. irreg. Manfred Kmoch, Parkring 45, Bisamberg, Austria. Ed. Dr. Rudolf Finz. bk. rev. abstr. index. (processed)
Local

948 FI
KOTISEUTUKUVAUKSIA LOUNAIS-HAEMEESTAE. 1925. irreg. Lounais-Haemeen kotiseutu-ja Museoyhdistys, Wahreninkatu, SF-30100 Forssa, Finland. cum.index 1925-64.

943.7 CS
KRAJSKE KULTURNI STREDISKO V HRADCI KRALOVE. KOMENTOVANA VYROCI. a. Krajske Kulturni Stredisko v Hradci Kralove, Hradci Kralove, Czechoslovakia.

943.7 CS
KRAJSKE MUZEUM V TEPLICICH. ZPRAVY A STUDIE. 1965. a. 15 Kcs. Krajske Muzeum v Teplicich, Zamecke Nam 14, 415 01 Teplice, Czechoslovakia (Subscr. to: Artia, Ve Smeckach 30, 111 27 Prague 1, Czechoslovakia) Formerly: Oblastni Vlastivedne Muzeum v Teplicich. Zpravy a Studie.

943.8 PL ISSN 0075-7020
KRAKOW DAWNIEJ I DZIS. 1952. irreg., vol. 20, 1978. price varies. Towarzystwo Milosnikow Historii i Zabytkow Krakowa, Ul. Sw. Jana 12, 31-018 Krakow, Poland (Dist. by Ars Polona-Ruch, Krakowskie Przedmiescie 7, Warsaw, Poland) Ed. Jan M. Malecki.

948 DK
KULTURMINDER. 1939; N.S. 1955, 1973. a. Selskabet for Dansk Kulturhistorie, Nationalmuseet, 1220 Copenhagen, Denmark.

943.7 CS
KULTURNO-POLITICKY A HISTORICKY KALENDAR MESTA BRATISLAVY. 1965. a. Archiv hl.mesta S.S.R. Bratislavy, Regionalna Kniznica, Primacialna Nam C.1, 886 23 Bratislava, Czechoslovakia.

948.5 SW ISSN 0083-6796
KUNGLIGA VITTERHETS- , HISTORIE- OCH ANTIKVITETS AKADEMIEN. AARSBOK. 1926. a. Kr.50. Kungliga Vitterhets-, Historie- och Antikvitets Akademien - Royal Academy of Letters, History and Antiquities, Villagatan 3, 114 32 Stockholm, Sweden (Dist. by: Almqvist & Wiksell International, P.O. Box 45150, S-104 30 Stockholm, Sweden) Indexed: Br.Archaeol.Abstr.

948.5 SW ISSN 0083-6761
KUNGLIGA VITTERHETS- , HISTORIE- OCH ANTIKVITETS AKADEMIEN. HANDLINGAR. ANTIKVARISKA SERIEN/ROYAL ACADEMY OF LETTERS, HISTORY AND ANTIQUITIES. PROCEEDINGS. ANTIQUARIAN SERIES. (Text in English, French, German and Swedish) 1954. irreg., no.37, 1986. price varies. Kungliga Vitterhets- , Historie- och Antikvitets Akademien, Villagatan 3, 114 32 Stockholm, Sweden (Dist. by: Almqvist & Wiksell International, P.O. Box 45150, S-104 30 Stockholm, Sweden)

940 SW ISSN 0083-6788
KUNGLIGA VITTERHETS- , HISTORIE- OCH ANTIKVITETS AKADEMIEN. HANDLINGAR. HISTORISKA SERIEN/ROYAL ACADEMY OF LETTERS, HISTORY AND ANTIQUITIES. PROCEEDINGS. HISTORICAL SERIES. (Text in German and Swedish; summaries in English and French) 1957. irreg., no. 21, 1979. price varies. Kungliga Vitterhets-, Historie- och Antikvitets Akademien, Villagatan 3, 114 32 Stockholm, Sweden (Dist. by: Almqvist & Wiksell International, P.O. Box 45150, S-104 30, Stockholm, Sweden) index.

HISTORY — HISTORY OF EUROPE

940   SW   ISSN 0083-6753
KUNGLIGA VITTERHETS- , HISTORIE- OCH ANTIKVITETS AKADEMIEN. HISTORISKT ARKIV. (Text in English, French, German or Swedish) 1954. irreg., no.18, 1986. price varies. Kungliga Vitterhets, Historie- och Antikvitets Akademien - Royal Academy of Letters, History and Antiquities, Villagatan 3, 114 32 Stockholm, Sweden (Dist. by: Almqvist & Wiksell International, P.O. Box 45150, S-104 30 Stockholm, Sweden) index.

948   FI   ISSN 0454-8086
KYTOESAVUT. 1945. irreg. Fmk.75. Etelae-Pohjanmaan Maakuntaliitto Ry, Vapaudentie 32 A 17, 60100 Seinajoki 10, Finland. Ed. Einar Ahlberg. adv.

941   UK
LANCASHIRE AND CHESHIRE ANTIQUARIAN SOCIETY. NEWSLETTER. 1977. irreg. membership. Lancashire and Cheshire Antiquarian Society, 59 Malmesbury Rd., Cheadle Hulme, Cheadle, Cheshire SK8 7QL, England. Ed. M. Garratt. bk. rev. circ. 300.

948.9 630   DK
LANDBOHISTORISK TIDSSKRIFT; bol og by. 1956; N.S. 1977. irreg. price varies. Landbohistorisk Selskab, H. C. Andersens Boulevard 38, DK-1553 Copenhagen K, Denmark. Eds. Erik Helmer Pedersen, Michael Hertz.
    Formerly: Bol og by (ISSN 0067-9550)

LANDESMUSEUM FUER VORGESCHICHTE, DRESDEN. VEROEFFENTLICHUNGEN. see *MUSEUMS AND ART GALLERIES*

LANDESMUSEUM FUER VORGESCHICHTE, HALLE. VEROEFFENTLICHUNGEN. see *MUSEUMS AND ART GALLERIES*

940 720   UK   ISSN 0143-3768
LANDSCAPE HISTORY. 1979. a. £9 to non-members. Society for Landscape Studies, c/o Department of Geography, University of Birmingham, P.O. Box 363, Birmingham B15 2TT, England. Ed. Dr. Della Hooke. adv. bk. rev. charts. illus. circ. 300. Indexed: Br.Archaeol.Abstr. Geo.Abstr.

943.6   AU
LANDESKUNDE VON NIEDEROESTERREICH. JAHRBUCH; neue Folge. 1865. irreg (Vol. 53, 1987) Verein fuer Landeskunde von Niederoesterreich, Herrengasse 11, 1014 Vienna, Austria.

948   NO
LANDSLAGET FOR LOKALHISTORIE. 1965. irreg. Norwegian University Press, Kolstadgt. 1, Postboks 2959, Toeyen, 0608 Oslo 6, Norway.
    Formerly: Landslaget for Bygde og Byhistorie. Skrifter (ISSN 0458-7073)

948.9   DK   ISSN 0109-0178
LANGAA; lokalhistorisk aarbog. 1972. a. Kr.25. Langaa Lokalhistoriske Forening, Bredgade 34, 8870 Langaa, Denmark. illus.

945   IT
LATIUM. a. L.25000 per no. Istituto di Storia e di Arte del Lazio Meridionale, Centro di Anagni, Via Umberto I, 29. Palazzo Longhi, I-03010 Fumone, Italy. Dir. Gioacchino Giammaria.

LEEDS MEDIEVAL STUDIES. see *LITERATURE*

LEICESTERSHIRE ARCHAEOLOGICAL AND HISTORICAL SOCIETY. TRANSACTIONS. see *ARCHAEOLOGY*

943   GE
LEIPZIG AUS VERGANGENHEIT UND GEGENWART; Beitraege zur Stadtgeschichte. 1963. irreg. Museum fuer Geschichte der Stadt Leipzig, Markt 1, 7010 Leipzig, E. Germany (D.D.R.)
    Former titles (until 1981): Geschichte der Stadt Leipzig. Jahrbuch; (1963-1974): Arbeitsberichte zur Geschichte der Stadt Leipzig.

LEO BAECK INSTITUTE. YEAR BOOK. see *RELIGIONS AND THEOLOGY — Judaic*

943.7 634.9   CS
LESNICKE DREVARSKE A POL'OVNICKE MUZEUM. 1961. irreg. Osveta, Osloboditelov 21, 036 54 Martin, Czechoslovakia (Subscr. to: Slovart, Gottwaldovo Nam. 6, 805 32 Bratislava, Czechoslovakia) illus. bibl. Indexed: Hist.Abstr.

943   GE   ISSN 0522-5078
LETOPIS. REIHE B. GESCHICHTE; Jahresschrift des Instituts fuer Sorbische Volksforschung. 1953. a. (Institut fuer Sorbische Volksforschung, Akademie der Wissenschaften der DDR.) Domowina Verlag, Tuchmacher-Str. 27, 86 Bautzen, E. Germany (D.D.R.) cum.index 1974.

943   GE   ISSN 0522-5086
LETOPIS. REIHE C. VOLKSKUNDE. 1958. a. (Institut fuer Sorbische Volksforschung, Wissenschaften der DDR.) Domowina Verlag, Tuchmacher-Str. 27, 86 Bautzen, E. Germany (D.D.R.)

947   UK   ISSN 0267-7105
LIBERTARIAN ALLIANCE. HISTORICAL NOTES. 1985. irreg. £5($10) Libertarian Alliance, 3 Langley Court, Covent Garden, London WC2E 9JY, England. Ed.Bd. adv. bk. rev. bibl. film rev. circ. 1,000. (back issues avail.)

947   US   ISSN 0091-4347
LIETUVIU TAUTOS PRAEITIS/LITHUANIAN HISTORICAL REVIEW. (Text in English, French, German and Lithuanian) 1959. a. price varies. Lithuanian Historical Society, Inc., 5620 S. Claremont Ave., Chicago, IL 60636. TEL 312-434-4545. Ed. John A.Rackauskas. bk. rev. circ. 1,000. Indexed: Hist.Abstr. Amer.Hist.& Life.

LINCOLNSHIRE HISTORY AND ARCHAEOLOGY. see *ARCHAEOLOGY*

949   NE
LINSCHOTEN-VEREENIGING. WERKEN. vol. 80, 1977. irreg. price varies. Walburg Pers, Zaadmarkt 84a-86, Box 222, 7200 AE Zutphen, Netherlands. (back issues avail.)

943.7   CS
LIPTOV. 1970. irreg. 32 Kcs. (Liptovske Muzeum v Ruzomberku) Vydavatel'stvo Osveta, Osloboditelov 21, 036 54 Martin, Czechoslovakia (Subscr. to: Slovart, Gottwaldovo Nam 6, 805 32 Bratislava, Czechoslovakia) Ed. Libusa Chrastekova. bk. rev.

943.7   CS
LITERARNI ARCHIV. 1966. a. Pamatnik Narodniho Pisemnictvi, Strahovske Nadv. 132, Prague 1, Czechoslovakia (Subscr. to: Artia, Ve Smeckach 30, 111 27 Prague 1, Czechoslovakia) bibl. illus. Indexed: Hist.Abstr. Amer.Hist.& Life.

943.7   CS   ISSN 0075-9988
LITOMERICKO; vlastivedny sbornik. 1964. a. 15 Kcs. Okresni Vlastivedne Muzeum, Mirove nam. 171, 412 01 Litomerice, Czechoslovakia. Ed. Eva Stibrova.

949.6   UR
LITUANISTIKA V S.S.S.R. ISTORIYA; nauchno-referativnyi sbornik. 1977. a. 1.70 Rub. per issue. Akademiya Nauk Litovskoi S.S.R., Nauchno-Informatsionnyi Tsentr, Michurino g-ve 1/46, Vilnius, Lithuanian S.S.R., U.S.S.R. Ed. A. Balsys. circ. 500.

940.53   IS
LO NISHKACH. a. Association of Greek Concentration Camp Survivors in Israel, 68 Levinsky St., Tel Aviv, Israel. Ed. Shmuel Refael.

948.9   DK   ISSN 0106-0430
LOEGUMKLOSTER-STUDIER. 1978. irreg. Kr.100. Historisk Forening for Loegumkloster Kommune, Museet Holmen Loegumkloster, DK-6240 Loegumkloster, Denmark.

948   DK   ISSN 0108-3244
LOKALHISTORIEN FOR TORSLUNDE ISHOEJ OG TRANEGILDE. vol.7, 1982. irreg. (2-3/yr.) Thorslunde Ishoej Lokalhistoriske Forening, Lille Bygade 6, 2635 Ishoej, Denmark. illus.
    Formerly: Thorslunde Ishoej Lokalhistoriske Forening (ISSN 0108-3805)

948.9   DK   ISSN 0109-6699
LOKALHISTORISK ARKIV, AALESTRUP. AARSSKRIFT. 1983. biennial. Kr.50. Lokalhistorisk Arkiv, Aalestrup, c/o Bogcentret, Jernbanegade 6, 9620 Aalestrup, Denmark. Eds. Jonna Bisgaard, Poul Gade. illus. circ. 600.

948.9   DK   ISSN 0900-3126
LOKALHISTORISK ARKIV FOR FREDERICIA OG OMEGN. AARSSKRIFT. 1984. a. free. Lokalhistorisk Arkiv for Fredericia og Omegn, Vendersgade 28, 7000 Fredericia, Denmark. illus.

948.9   DK   ISSN 0109-8551
LOKALHISTORISK ARKIV, ROEDBY. AARSSKRIFT. (Text in Danish) 1980. a. Kr.20. Lokalhistorisk Arkiv, Roedby, c/o Roedby Bibliotek, Kirkealle 11, 4970 Roedby, Denmark. Ed. Hans Ivar Bentsen.

948.9   DK   ISSN 0109-2162
LOKALHISTORISK ARKIV STUBBEKOEBING. AARSSKRIFT. 1983. a. Kr.20. Lokalhistorisk Arkiv Stubbekoebing, Stubbekoebing Bibliotek, Dosseringen 3, 4850 Stubbekoebing, Denmark. bk. rev. illus.

948.9   DK   ISSN 0109-2839
LOKALHISTORISK FORENING FOR HOERUP SOGN. AARSSKRIFT. 1983. a. Kr.25. Lokalhistorisk Forening for Hoerup Sogn, c/o Hans Thomsen Taekker, Nedergaden 18, Mjang, 6400 Soenderborg, Denmark. Ed. Jens Verner Nielsen. illus. circ. 500.

948   DK   ISSN 0106-9748
LOKALHISTORISK FORENING FOR SEJLFLOD KOMMUNE. Nr. 4, 1981. irreg. price varies. Lokalhistorisk Forening for Sejlflod Kommune, Sekretariat, Gl. Egensevej 31 A, Mou, 9280 Storvorde, Denmark. illus.

948   DK   ISSN 0109-4017
LOKALHISTORISK FORENING FOR SOENDERHALD KOMMUNE. AARSSKRIFT. 1977. a. Kr.30. Lokalhistorisk Forening for Soenderhald Kommune, c/o Helga Soerensen, Aarslev, 8900 Randers, Denmark. Ed.Bd.

948   DK   ISSN 0107-8798
LOLLAND-FALSTERS HISTORISKE SAMFUND. AARBOG. vol. 50, 1962. a. Kr.60 to non-members; members Kr. 35. Lolland-Falsters Historiske Samfund, Taagense Engvej 1, 4880 Nysted, Denmark, Denmark. Ed. Verner Hansen. adv. bk. rev. illus. circ. 1,260. Indexed: Chem.Abstr.

948   DK   ISSN 0542-6820
LOLLAND-FALSTERS STIFTSMUSEUMS AARSKRIFT. 1939. a. Kr.50. Lolland-Falsters Stiftsmuseum, Museumsgade 1, 4930 Maribo, Denmark. Ed. Else-Marie Boyhus. circ. 1,000.

942   UK   ISSN 0085-2848
LONDON RECORD SOCIETY. PUBLICATIONS. 1965. a. price varies. London Record Society, c/o Institute of Historical Research, Senate House, London WC1E 7HU, England. Ed. V. Harding. circ. 350. (back issues avail.)

948   FI
LOUNAIS-HAEMEEN KOTISEUTU JA MUSEOYHDISTYS. VUOSIKIRJA. 1924. a. Lounais-Haemeen Kotiseutu ja Museoyhdistys, Wahreninkatu, SF-30100 Forssa, Finland. cum.index: 1924-61 in vol.31; 1962-71 in vol.40; 1972-81 in vol.50; 1982-1986 in vol.55.

940   PO
LUGAR DA HISTORIA. no. 18, 1982. irreg. Edicoes 70, Avenida Duque de Avila, 69 r/c, 1000 Lisbon, Portugal.

940   PL   ISSN 0076-1516
LUSTRACJE DOBR KROLEWSKICH XVI-XVIII WIEKU. 1959. irreg. price varies. (Polska Akademia Nauk, Instytut Historii) Panstwowe Wydawnictwo Naukowe, Miodowa 10, 00-251 Warsaw, Poland (Dist. by: Ars Polona, Krakowskie Przedmiescie 7, 00-068 Warsaw, Poland) Ed. Leonid Zytkowicz.

948.9   DK   ISSN 0107-1238
LYBOEN. 1979. a. Kr.20. Lokalhistorisk Forening for Lyoe, Redaktionen, Nygade 6, 6760 Ribe, Denmark. illus.

HISTORY — HISTORY OF EUROPE

948   DK
LYNGBY-BOGEN. 1933. a. Kr.50. (Historisk-Topografisk Selskab for Lyngby-Taarbaek Kommune) Stadsbiblioteket i Lyngby, Lyngby Hovedgade 28, 2800 Lyngby, Denmark. Ed. Jeppe Toensberg. illus.

948   DK
M I V: MUSEERNE I VIBORG AMT. 1971. a. Viborg Stiftsmuseum, DK-8800 Viborg, Denmark (Subscr. to: Museumstjenesten, Sjorupvej, Lysgaard, DK-8800 Viborg, Denmark) Ed. Marianne Bro-Joergensen. illus. circ. 1,000.

943   GE
MAERKISCHEN MUSEUM. JAHRBUCH. 1975. a. Maerkisches Museum, Kultur Historisches Museum der Stadt Berlin, Am Koellinischen Park 5, 1020 Berlin, E. Germany (D.D.R.) illus.

943   HU   ISSN 0076-2407
MAGYAR KOZLONY; official gazette. irreg. $79. (Minisztertanacs) Lapkiado Vallalat, Lenin korut 9-11, 1073 Budapest, Hungary (Distr. by: Kultura, Box 149, 1389 Budapest, Hungary) Ed. Kiss Eleher.

MAGYARORSZAG MUEMLEKI TOPOGRAFIAJA. see *ART*

MAIHAUGEN. see *ARCHAEOLOGY*

943 709   GW   ISSN 0076-2725
MAINFRAENKISCHES JAHRBUCH FUER GESCHICHTE UND KUNST. 1949. a. DM.40. Freunde Mainfraenkischer Kunst und Geschichte, Karl-Straeub-Str. 9, 8700 Wuerzburg, W. Germany (B.R.D.) Ed. Dr. Ernst G. Krenig. bk. rev. circ. 900. Indexed: Numis.Lit. RILA.

MAINZER ZEITSCHRIFT; Mittelrheinisches Jahrbuch fuer Archaeologie, Geschichte und Kunst. see *ART*

949.5 398 913 400   GR   ISSN 0076-289X
MAKEDONIKA. (Text and summaries in English, French, German, Greek) 1940. a. Dr.900($16) Society for Macedonian Studies, Ethnikis Amymis 4, 546 21 Salonika, Greece. Indexed: Hist.Abstr. Amer.Hist.& Life.

940   UK
MALAGO. 1975. irreg. price varies. Malago Society, 10 Valley Rd., Bedminster Down, Bristol BS13 7JT, England. Ed. Miss B. Chappell. bk. rev. circ. 1,200.

942   UK   ISSN 0076-4264
MANX MUSEUM, DOUGLAS, ISLE OF MAN. JOURNAL. 1924. irreg. price varies. Manx Museum and National Trust, Douglas, Isle of Man, British Isles. TEL 0624-75522. Eds. S. Harrison, Ann M. Harrison. index. circ. 750. Indexed: Br.Hum.Ind. Br.Archaeol.Abstr. RILA.

948   DK   ISSN 0108-2868
MARIAGER AARBOG. 1982. a. (in 2 parts) Kr.50 for each part. Lokalhistorisk Forlag-Mariager, Vestparken 53, 9550 Mariager, Denmark. illus.

942   UK
MARITIME STORY OF SOUTHERN ENGLAND. 1982. irreg. £1.50. Heritage Publications, 6 Brook Court, Middlebridge St., Romsey, Hants. SO51 8HR, England. Ed. James Dunning.

948   DK   ISSN 0105-0826
MARK OG MONTRE; fra sydvestjyske museer. 1965. a. Kr.50. Kulturhistoriske Museer i Ribr Amt, Noerregade 25, DK-6700 Esbjerg, Denmark. Ed.Bd. illus.
Formerly: Fra Esbjerg Museums Virke.

944   US   ISSN 0076-4671
MARQUETTE SLAVIC STUDIES. 1955. irreg. price varies. (Marquette University, Slavic Institute) Marquette University Press, 1324 W. Wisconsin Ave., Milwaukee, WI 53233. TEL 414-224-1564.

940   AU
MATERIALIEN ZUR WIRTSCHAFTS- UND SOZIALGESCHICHTE. 1978. irreg. Verlag fuer Geschichte und Politik, Neulinggasse 26, A-1030 Vienna, Austria. Eds. Alfred Hoffmann, Herbert Matis, Micael Mitterauer.

940   PL   ISSN 0076-5236
MATERIALY ZACHODNIO-POMORSKIE. (Text in Polish; summaries in English, French and German) 1957. a. price varies. Muzeum Narodowe, Szczecin, Staromlynska 27, 70-561 Szczecin, Poland (Dist. by: Ars Polona- Ruch, Krakowskie Przedmiescie 7, Warsaw, Poland) Ed. Wladyslaw Filipowiak. bk. rev. circ. 700. Indexed: Numis.Lit.

942.5 410   IE
MEDIAEVAL AND MODERN BRETON SERIES. no. 3, 1975. irreg. £6. Dublin Institute for Advanced Studies, Dublin, Ireland.

948   DK   ISSN 0076-5864
MEDIAEVAL SCANDINAVIA; a journal devoted to the study of mediaeval civilization in Scandinavia and Iceland. (Text in English and German) 1968. a. price varies. Odense University Press, 36, Pjentedamsgade, DK-5000 Odense, Denmark. Ed. Hans Bekker-Nielsen. (back issues avail.) Indexed: M.L.A.

948   DK   ISSN 0106-102X
MEDIAEVAL SCANDINAVIA SUPPLEMENTS. (Text in English) 1980. irreg. price varies. Odense University Press, 36 Pjentedamsgade, DK-5000 Odense, Denmark. Ed. Hans Bekker-Nielsen.

MEDIAEVAL SOURCES IN TRANSLATION. see *LITERATURE*

940   CN   ISSN 0076-5872
MEDIAEVAL STUDIES. (Text in English; occasionally in French, German, Latin and other languages) 1939. a. $30. Pontifical Institute of Mediaeval Studies, 59 Queen's Park Crescent E., Toronto, Ont.M5S 2C4, Canada. TEL 416-926-7144. Ed. Virginia Brown. cum.index: vols.1-25; supplement index: vols. 26-30; 31-40. circ. 1,100. Indexed: Cath.Ind. Curr.Cont. M.L.A. Arts & Hum.Cit.Ind. Amer.Bibl.Slavic & E.Eur.Stud. M.L.A. Phil.Ind. RILA.

940   US   ISSN 0361-946X
MEDIAEVALIA. 1975. a. $25. State University of New York at Binghamton, Center for Medieval and Early Renaissance Studies, Binghamton, NY 13901. TEL 607-798-2730. Ed. Bernard S. Levy. circ. 400. (reprint service avail. from ISI) Indexed: Curr.Cont. M.L.A. RILA.

940   BE
MEDIAEVALIA LOVANIENSIA. SERIES I. (Text in Dutch, English, French and German) 1972. irreg., vol.14, 1986. price varies. (Katholieke Universiteit te Leuven, Instituut voor Middeleeuwse Studies) Leuven University Press, Krakenstraat 3, 3000 Louvain, Belgium.

940   US
MEDIEVAL ACADEMY BOOKS. 1928. irreg., no.94, 1985. Medieval Academy of America, 1430 Massachusetts Ave., Cambridge, MA 02138.
Formerly: Medieval Academy of America. Publications (ISSN 0076-583X)

940   CN
MEDIEVAL ACADEMY REPRINTS FOR TEACHING. 1978. irreg., no. 10, 1980. price varies. (Medieval Academy of America) University of Toronto Press, Front Campus, Toronto, Ont. M5S 1A6, Canada. TEL 613-667-7791.

MEDIEVAL ARCHAEOLOGY. see *ARCHAEOLOGY*

946   NE   ISSN 0076-6100
MEDIEVAL IBERIAN PENNINSULA. 1961. irreg., 1971, no. 4. price varies. E. J. Brill, P.O. Box 9000, 2300 PA Leiden, Netherlands.

940   US
MEDIEVALIA ET HUMANISTICA. 1981. a. price varies. (Modern Language Association) Rowman and Littlefield, 81 Adams Dr., Totowa, NJ 07512. TEL 201-256-8600. Ed. Paul Maurice Clogan. Indexed: M.L.A. RILA.

970   US   ISSN 0543-5056
MERCHANT EXPLORER. 1961. a. membership. James Ford Bell Library, 472 Wilson Library, University of Minnesota, Minneapolis, MN 55455. TEL 612-373-2403. Ed. John Parker. bk. rev. bibl. circ. 500.

940   US
MIDDLE AGES. 1897. irreg., latest 1986. University of Pennsylvania Press, Philadelphia, PA 19104. TEL 215-898-8452. Ed. Edward M. Peters.
Supersedes: Translations and Reprints from the Original Sources of European History (ISSN 0082-593X)

942   UK   ISSN 0047-729X
MIDLAND HISTORY. 1971. a. £8. University of Birmingham, School of History, Box 363, Birmingham B15 2TT, England. Ed. C. Dyer. adv. bk. rev. circ. 500. Indexed: Br.Hum.Ind. Hist.Abstr. Amer.Hist.& Life. Br.Archaeol.Abstr.

948.5 355   SW
MILITAERHISTORISK TIDSKRIFT. (Text in Swedish; summaries in English; sometimes French or German) 1963. a. Kr.20. Kungliga Militaerhoegskolan, Militaerhistoriska Avdelningen - Royal Armed Forces Staff College, Box 80 007, 104 50 Stockholm, Sweden. Eds.B. Hugemark, K.R. Boehme. circ. 2,000. Indexed: Hist.Abstr. Amer.Hist.& Life.
Formerly (until 1979): Aktuellt och Historiskt (ISSN 0065-5619)

943.7   CS
MINULOSTI A PRITOMNOSTI TURCA. 1970. irreg. Osveta, Osloboditelov 21, 036 54 Martin, Czechoslovakia (Subscr. to: Slovart, Gottwaldovo Nam. 6, 805 32 Bratislava, Czechoslovakia)

943.7   CS
MINULOSTI ROKYCANSKA. 1967. irreg. Zapadoceske Nakladatelstvi, Moskevska 36, 301 00 Pizen, Czechoslovakia (Subscr. to: Artia, Ve Smeckach 30, 111 27 Prague 1, Czechoslovakia) cum.index: vol.1-11 1967-1972.

943.7   CS
MINULOSTI ZAPADOCESKEHO KRAJE. 1962. irreg. Zapadoceske Nakladatelstvi, Moskevska 36, 301 00 Pizen, Czechoslovakia (Subscr. to: Artia, Ve Smeckach 30, 111 27 Prague 1, Czechoslovakia) bk. rev. bibl.

946   SP
MISCEL-LANIA DE TEXTOS MEDIEVALS. 1972. irreg. price varies. Institucion Mila y Fontanals, Departamento de Estudios Medievales, Egipciacas 15, 08001 Barcelona, Spain. adv. bk. rev. bibl. circ. 1,000.
Formerly: Miscelanea de Texos Medievales (ISSN 0213-2257)

949.5 809   GW   ISSN 0076-9347
MISCELLANEA BYZANTINA MONACENSIA. 1965. irreg., no. 23, 1978. price varies. Universitaet Muenchen, Institut fuer Byzantinistik und Neugriechische Philologie, Geschwister Scholl Platz 1, 8000 Munich 22, W. Germany (B.R.D.) Eds. Hans-Georg Beck, Armin Hohlweg. index.

MISHUA. see *ETHNIC INTERESTS*

943.6   AU
MISTELBACH IN VERGANGENHEIT UND GEGENWART; heimatkundliche Beilage zu den Mitteilungen der Stadtgemeinde. 1961. a. Stadtgemeinde Mistelbach, Hauptplatz 4-5, 2130 Mistelbach, Austria. circ. 4,500.

940   NE   ISSN 0076-9754
MITTELLATEINISCHE STUDIEN UND TEXTE. 1965. irreg., vol. 11, 1979. price varies. E. J. Brill, P.O. Box 9000, 2300 PA Leiden, Netherlands. Ed. K. Langosch.

948.5   DK   ISSN 0106-4479
MOELDRUP KOMMUNES LOKALHISTORISKE ARKIV. AARSSKRIFT. 1978. biennial. Kr.60. Lokalhistorisk Udvag-Moeldrup, Noerregade 15, 9632 Moeldrup, Denmark. TEL 06-691200. illus. circ. 600.

948.9   DK   ISSN 0106-1917
MOELPOSEN. 1978. a. Kr.20. Spoettrup Lokalhistoriske Arkiv, Ramsing, Denmark (Subscr. to: Spoettrup Bibliotek, Aalbaekvej 18, Lihme, 7861 Balling, Denmark) illus.

948   DK   ISSN 0900-8764
MOLSBIBLIOTEKETS LOKALHISTORISK ARKIV. a. Kr.35. Svinget 9, DK-8400 Ebeltoft, Denmark. Ed. Niels Berthelsen.

942 UK ISSN 0077-0299
MONARCHIST PRESS ASSOCIATION.
HISTORICAL SERIES. 1964. irreg. Monarchist
Press Association, 7 Sutherland Rd., West Ealing,
London, W13 0DX, England. circ. 3,000.

MONDES HISPANOPHONE ET LUSOPHONE. see *LITERATURE*

943.8 PL ISSN 0077-0523
MONOGRAFIE SLASKIE OSSOLINEUM. 1960.
irreg., vol.37, 1984. price varies. Ossolineum,
Publishing House of the Polish Academy of
Sciences, Rynek 9, 50-106 Wroclaw, Poland (Dist.
by: Ars Polona-Ruch, Krakowskie Przedmiescie 7,
Warsaw, Poland) Ed. Jan Gierowski.

MONOGRAFIE SLAWISTYCZNE. see *LITERATURE*

943.7 CS ISSN 0231-9136
MONOGRAPHIA HISTORICA BOHEMICA. 1985.
irreg. Ustav Ceskoslovenskych a Svetovych Dejin
CSAV, Vysehradska 49, 128 26 Prague 2,
Czechoslovakia. Ed. Josef Zemlicka.

943 GW ISSN 0026-9832
MONOGRAPHIEN ZUR GESCHICHTE DES
MITTELALTERS. 1970. irreg., vol.33, 1987. price
varies. Anton Hiersemann Verlag, Rosenbergstr.
113, Postfach 723, 7000 Stuttgart 1, W. Germany
(B.R.D.) Eds. Karl Bosl, Friedrich Prinz.

940 US
MONOGRAPHS ON EUROPE. 1980. irreg., no.4,
1981. Harvard University, Center for European
Studies, 5 Bryant St., Cambridge, MA 02138.

940 GW ISSN 0080-6951
MONUMENTA GERMANIAE HISTORICA.
SCHRIFTEN. 1938. irreg., vol.30, 1986. price
varies. Anton Hiersemann Verlag, Rosenbergstr.
113, Postfach 723, 7000 Stuttgart 1, W. Germany
(B.R.D.) circ. 1,200.

940 GW ISSN 0340-8035
MONUMENTA GERMANIAE HISTORICA.
STAATSSCHRIFTEN DES SPAETEREN
MITTELALTERS. (Text in German and Latin)
1941. irreg., vol. 3, part 3, 1984. price varies. Anton
Hiersemann Verlag, Rosenbergstr. 113, Postfach
723, 7000 Stuttgart 1, W. Germany (B.R.D.)

943 HU ISSN 0077-1430
MONUMENTA HISTORICA BUDAPESTINENSIA.
(Text in French, German and Hungarian) 1959.
irreg. price varies. (Magyar Tudomanyos Akademia)
Akademiai Kiado, Publishing House of the
Hungarian Academy of Sciences, Box 24, H-1363
Budapest, Hungary.

943.7 CS
MONUMENTORUM TUTELA. OCHRANA
PAMIATOK. (Text in Czech, English, French,
German and Russian) 1966. irreg. Vydavatel'stvo
Pallas, Sturova 1-b, 882 09 Bratislava,
Czechoslovakia (Subscr. to: Slovart, Gottwaldovo
Nam. 6, 805 32 Bratislava, Czechoslovakia) illus.

943.7 914 CS ISSN 0323-0570
MORAVSKE MUZEUM BRNO. CASOPIS. (Text in
Czech, German and Russian) 1901. a. Moravske
Muzeum, Nam. 25, Unora 6, 659 37 Brno,
Czechoslovakia (Subscr. to: Artia, Smeckach 30,
111 27 Prague 1, Czechoslovakia) bk. rev. Indexed:
Bull.Signal. Numis.Lit.
Formerly: Moravske Muzeum Zemskeho.
Casopis.

940 UK ISSN 0545-0373
MORGANNWG. 1957. a. £4. Glamorgan History
Society, c/o Dr. Matthew Griffiths, 24 Canon St.,
Barry, S. Glamorgan, Wales. Eds. B.L. James, J.R.
Alban. bk. rev. illus. circ. 500. Indexed:
Br.Archaeol.Abstr.

MUENCHENER BEITRAEGE ZUR
MEDIAEVISTIK UND RENAISSANCE-
FORSCHUNG. see *CLASSICAL STUDIES*

943 GW ISSN 0170-8929
MUENCHENER ZEITSCHRIFT FUER
BALKANKUNDE. 1978. a. DM.88. Dr. Rudolf
Trofenik Verlag, Elsabethstr. 18, 8000 Munich 40,
W. Germany (B.R.D.) Ed. Peter Bartl. bk. rev.

943.6 AU
MUSEALVEREIN WELS. JAHRBUCH. 1954. a.
S.200. Musealverein Wels, Wels, Austria. Ed. Kurt
Holter.

945 IT ISSN 0523-9478
MUSEO RISORGIMENTO. BOLLETINO. 1956. a.
Museum Risorgimento, Via dei Musei, 8, Bologna,
Italy. TEL 051-225583. bk. rev.

946.9 PO ISSN 0870-3876
MUSEU MUNICIPAL DO FUNCHAL. BOLETIM.
1945. a. exchange basis. (Camara Municipal do
Funchal) Museu Municipal do Funchal, Rua da
Mouraria, 31, 9000 Funchal, Madeira, Portugal.
Eds. Manuel Jose Biscoito, G.E. Maul. circ. 450.
Indexed: Biol.Abstr. Zoo.Rec.

943.8 PL ISSN 0077-2577
MUZEA WALKI. 1968. a. 50 Zl. Muzeum Historii
Polskiego Ruchu Rewolucyjnego, Plac
Dzierzynskiego 1, 00-139 Warsaw, Poland (Dist. by:
Ars Polona-Ruch, Krakowskie Przedmiescie 7,
Warsaw, Poland) Ed.Bd. bk. rev. circ. 800.

940.8 RM
MUZEUL DE ISTORIE AL REPUBLICII
SOCIALISTE ROMANIA. CERCETARI
ISTORICE. 1979. irreg. Muzeul de Istorie al
Republicii Socialiste Romania, Calea Victoriei 12,
Bucharest, Rumania. Ed.Bd.

943.8 PL ISSN 0068-4651
MUZEUM GORNOSLASKIE W BYTOMIU.
ROCZNIK. SERIA HISTORIA. 1963. irreg. price
varies. Muzeum Gornoslaskie, Pl. Thaelmanna 2,
41-902 Bytom, Poland (Dist. by Ars Polona-Ruch,
Krakowskie Przedmiescie 7, Warsaw, Poland)

949.8 RM
MUZEUM MILITAR CENTRAL ROMANIA.
STUDII SI MATERIALE DE MUZEOGRAFIE SI
ISTORIE MILITARA. a. Muzeum Militar Central
Romania, Str. Izvor nr.137, sector 6, 76111
Bucharest, Rumania.

943.7 CS
MUZEUM SLOVENSKEHO NARODNEHO
POVSTANIA. ZBORNIK. 1976. irreg. Osveta,
Oslobodietlov 21, 036 54 Martin, Czechoslovakia
(Subscr. to: Slovart, Gottwaldovo Nam. 6, 805 32
Bratislava, Czechoslovakia) bk. rev. bibl.
Formerly: Pamatnika - Muzeum Slovenskeho
Narodneho Povstania. Zbornik.

943.7 CS
MUZEUM UKRAJINSKEJ KULTURY VO
SVIDNIKU. VEDECKY ZBORNIK. (Text in
Slovak and Ukrainian) 1965. irreg. Slovenske
Pedagogicke Nakladatelstvo, Sasinkova 5, 891 12
Bratislava, Czechoslovakia (Subscr. to: Slovart,
Gottwaldovo Nam. 6, 805 32 Bratislava,
Czechoslovakia) bk. rev. bibl.

948 FI ISSN 0355-9106
NARINKKA. (Text in English, Finnish and Swedish)
1976. a. price varies. Helsingin Kaupunginmuseo -
Helsinki City Museum, Dagmarinkatu 6, 00100
Helsinki 10, Finland. Ed. Marja-Liisa Roenkkoe.

947 BU ISSN 0584-0007
NARODNA BIBLIOTEKA KIRIL I METODII.
IZVESTIYA. (Table of Contents in English and
Russian) 1953. irreg. price varies. Narodna
Biblioteka Kiril i Metodii, c/o Hemus Foreign Trade
Co., 6 Ruski Blvd., 1000 Sofia, Bulgaria. bk. rev.
bibl. charts. graphs. illus. Indexed: Hist.Abstr.
Amer.Hist.& Life.
Formerly (1959-1965): Izvestiya na Narodnata
Biblioteka Kiril i Metodii na Biblioeката na
Sofiiskiya Universitet Kliment Okhridski.

943 GW ISSN 0077-2887
NASSAUISCHE ANNALEN. 1827. a. DM.79.
Verein fuer Nassauische Altertumskunde und
Geschichtsforschung e.V., Mosbacher Str. 55, D-
6200 Wiesbaden, W. Germany (B.R.D.) Ed. Hans-
Joachim Haebel. adv. bk. rev. circ. 2,000.

948 DK
NATIONALMUSEETS ARBEJDSMARK. 1928. a.
Nationalmuseet, Frederiksholms Kanal 12, 1220
Copenhagen, Denmark. cum.index: 1928-1977.
Indexed: Art & Archaeol.Tech.Abstr.
Br.Archaeol.Abstr. Numis.Lit.
Formerly: Fra Nationalmuseets Arbejdsmark.

NATSIONALEN VOENNOISTORICHESKI
MUZEI, SOFIA. IZVESTIYA. see *MILITARY*

947 US
NAUKOVE TOVARYSTVO IMENI
SHEVCHENKA. BIBLIOTEKA
UKRAINOZNAVSTVA/LIBRARY OF
UKRAINIAN STUDIES. (Text in English and
Ukrainian) 1949. irreg. price varies. Shevchenko
Scientific Society, 63 Fourth Ave., New York, NY
10003.

949.2 914 NE
NEDERLANDS INSTITUUT TE ROME.
MEDEDELINGEN. (Text in Dutch and English)
1921. a. Staatsuitgeverij, Nederlands Instituut te
Rome, Chr. Plantijnstr. 1, 2500 The Hague,
Netherlands. cum.index: 1939-1959. Indexed: RILA.
Formerly: Nederlands Historisch Institutute
Rome. Mededelingen.

948 NE
NEDERLANDSE HISTORISCHE BRONNEN.
1979. irreg. price varies. (Nederlands Historisch
Genootschap) Uitgeverij S.M. Ontwikkeling, Box
33, 2300 AA Leiden, Netherlands.

949 NE
NETHERLANDS. RIJKSINSTITUUT VOOR
OORLOGSDOCUMENTATIE. PROGRESS
REPORT. 1953. irreg. free. Rijksinstituut voor
Oorlogsdocumentatie - Netherlands State Institute
for War Documentation, Herengracht 474, 1000 GT
Amsterdam, Netherlands. Ed. A. H. Paape. circ.
300.

943 GW
NEUES TRIERISCHES JAHRBUCH FUER
HEIMATPFLEGE UND HEIMATGESCHICHTE.
1961. a. DM.9.50. Verein Trierisch e.V.,
Loewenbrueckener Str. 23, 5500 Trier, W. Germany
(B.R.D.) Ed. Claus Zander.
Neues Trierisches Jahrbuch (ISSN 0077-7765)

943 GW ISSN 0077-7862
NEUSSER JAHRBUCH FUER KUNST,
KULTURGESCHICHTE UND HEIMATKUNDE.
1956. a. DM.10. Clemens-Sels-Museum, Im
Obertor, 4040 Neuss, W. Germany (B.R.D.) Ed.Bd.
circ. 2,000.

940 UK
NEW HISTORY OF ENGLAND. 1977. irreg. price
varies. Edward Arnold (Publishers) Ltd., 41 Bedford
Square, London WC1B 3DQ, England.

940 UK
NEW HISTORY OF SCOTLAND. 1981. irreg. price
varies. Edward Arnold (Publishers) Ltd., 41 Bedford
Square, London WC1B 3DQ, England.

940 GW
NIEDERSACHSISCHES JAHRBUCH. 1924. a.
DM.52.80. (Historische Kommission fuer
Niedersachsen und Bremen) Verlag August Lax,
Postfach 10 08 65, Kreuzstr. 21, 3200 Hildesheim,
W. Germany (B.R.D.)
Formerly: Niedersaechsisches Jahrbuch fuer
Landesgeschichte (ISSN 0078-0561)

948.8 US
NIEPODLEGLOSC; czasopismo poswiecone
najnowszym dziejom Polski. 1948. a. $12. J.
Pilsudski, 381 Park Ave. S., New York, NY 10016.
TEL 212-683-4342. Ed. Michal Budny. circ. 600.

948 DK ISSN 0106-6145
NOERRE-ALSLEV KOMMUNE.
LOKALHISTORISK ARKIV. AARSSKRIFT. 1979.
a. Kr.54.75. Noerre-Alslev Kommune,
Lokalhistorisk Arkiv, Eksp. Schleyer, Egelevgade
26, 4840 Noerre-Alslev, Denmark. illus.

NOMINA; a journal of name studies relating to Great
Britain and Ireland. see *LINGUISTICS*

940 NE
NOORDBRABANTS HISTORISCH JAARBOEK.
1984. a. fl.39.50. (Het Noordbrabants Genootschap)
Walburg Pers, Zaadmarkt 84a-86, Box 222, 7200
AE Zutphen, Netherlands. TEL 05750-10522.

HISTORY — HISTORY OF EUROPE

943 GW ISSN 0078-1037
NORDELBINGEN; Beitraege zur Kunst- und Kulturgeschichte. a. price varies. (Gesellschaft fuer Schleswig-Holsteinische Geschichte) Westholsteinische Verlagsanstalt Boyens und Co., Am Wulf-Isebrand-Platz, Postfach 1880, 2240 Heide, W. Germany (B.R.D.) Ed.Bd. Indexed: M.L.A. RILA.

943 GE ISSN 0138-2802
NORDEUROPA STUDIEN. 1966. a. DM.17.60. Sektion Nordeuropa Wissenschaften der Ernst-Moritz-Arndt Universitaet, Hans Fallada Str. 20, 22 Greifswald, E. Germany (D.D.R.) Indexed: Hist.Abstr. Amer.Hist.& Life.
Formerly: Nordeuropa. Jahrbuch fuer Nordische Studien.

949.2 GW ISSN 0078-1045
NORDFRIESISCHES JAHRBUCH. 1965. a. price varies. Nordfriisk Instituut, Osterstr. 63, 2257 Bredstedt, W. Germany (B.R.D.) Ed.Bd. bk. rev. circ. 950. Indexed: M.L.A.

948 DK
NORDSLESVIGSKE MUSEER. 1974. a. Kr.85. Museumsrad for Soenderjyllands Amt, Dalgade 7, 6100 Haderslev, Denmark.

942 UK ISSN 0078-1169
NORFOLK RECORD SOCIETY. PUBLICATIONS. 1931. a. membership. Norfolk Record Society, 425 Unthank Rd., Norwich NR4 7QB, England. Eds. A. Hassell Smith, R. Virgoe. circ. 300. Indexed: Br.Hum.Ind.

359 NO
NORSK SJOEFARTSMUSEUM. AARSBERETNING. (Text in Norwegian; summaries in English) 1965. a. Kr.140. Norsk Sjoefartsmuseum - Norwegian Maritime Museum, Bygdoeynesveien 37, 0286 Oslo 2, Norway. Ed. Baard Kollveit. adv. illus. cum.index. circ. 2,000.

948 NO ISSN 0549-6896
NORSK SKOGBRUKSMUSEUM. AARBOK. (Text in Norwegian; summaries in English) 1958. biennial, latest vol.11, 1986. Kr.120. Norsk skogbruksmuseum, Elverum, Norway. Ed. Tore Fossum. bk. rev. circ. 2,500.

913 UK ISSN 0078-1649
NORTH STAFFORDSHIRE JOURNAL OF FIELD STUDIES. irreg. £3.50($8) University of Keele, Keele, Staffordshire ST5 5BG, England. Ed. C.J. Hanison. Indexed: Br.Hum.Ind. Br.Archaeol.Abstr. Geo.Abstr. Numis.Lit.

914.2 UK ISSN 0140-9131
NORTHAMPTONSHIRE PAST AND PRESENT. 1948. a. membership. Northamptonshire Record Society, Delapre Abbey, Northampton, England. Ed.Bd. adv. bk. rev. illus. cum.index (every 5 or 6 years) circ. 3,000. Indexed: Br.Hum.Ind. Br.Archaeol.Abstr. RILA.
Local

942 UK ISSN 0078-172X
NORTHERN HISTORY; a review of the history of the North of England and the Borders. 1966. a. £8.50($26) University of Leeds, School of History, Leeds, LS2 9JT, England. Ed.Bd. G.C.F. Forster. bk. rev. circ. 800. Indexed: Br.Hum.Ind. Curr.Cont. Hist.Abstr. Arts & Hum.Cit.Ind. Br.Archaeol.Abstr.

941 UK ISSN 0306-5278
NORTHERN SCOTLAND. 1972. a. £6. University of Aberdeen, Centre for Scottish Studies, Old Aberdeen AB9 2UB, Scotland. Ed. D. Stevenson. bk. rev. circ. 400. Indexed: Br.Archaeol.Abstr.

NORTH WESTERN EUROPEAN LANGUAGE EVOLUTION. see LINGUISTICS

940 UK ISSN 0078-2122
NOTTINGHAM MEDIEVAL STUDIES. 1957. a. £4($7) University of Nottingham, German Department, Nottingham NG7 2RD, England. Ed. Antonia Gransden. bk. rev. circ. 500. Indexed: Br.Hum.Ind. M.L.A. Abstr.Engl.Stud. Br.Archaeol.Abstr.

943.7 CS ISSN 0546-8051
NOVE OBZORY. 1959. a. 38 Kcs. (Muzeum S R R v Presove) Vychodoslovenske Vydavatel'stvo v Kosiciach, Alejova 3, 040 01 Kosice 1, Czechoslovakia (Subscr. to: Slovart, Gottwaldovo Nam 6, 805 32 Bratislava, Czechoslovakia) Ed. I. Michnovic. bk. rev. circ. 800.

943 GW ISSN 0078-2653
NUERNBERGER FORSCHUNGEN. irreg. price varies. Verein fuer Geschichte der Stadt Nuernberg, Egidienplatz 23, 8500 Nuernberg 1, W. Germany (B.R.D.) Ed. Gerhard Hirschmann. circ. 850.

NUMISMATICKY SBORNIK. see NUMISMATICS

940 IT ISSN 0391-6049
NUOVO MEDIOEVO. 1976. irreg., no.26, 1986. price varies. Liguori Editore s.r.l., Via Mezzocannone 19, 80134 Naples, Italy. TEL 081/20 6077. Ed. Massimo Oldoni.

949 NE
O S G N WETENSCHAPPELIJKE PUBLIKATIE. 1967. irreg., no. 4, 1977. price varies. Organisatie van Studenten in de Geschiedenis van Nederland, Groningen, Netherlands. (Co-sponsor: Stichting Ter Bevordering van de Studie in de Geschiedenis van Nederland) adv.

943.6 913 AU
OBEROESTERREICHISCHER MUSEALVEREIN. JAHRBUCH. 1840. a. S.270. Oberoesterreichischer Musealverein, Gesellschaft fuer Landeskunde, Landstrasse 31, 4010 Linz, Austria. Eds. Dr. Heilingsetzer, Dr. Schwanzar. bk. rev. circ. 1,000. Indexed: Hist.Abstr. Amer.Hist.& Life. Br.Archaeol.Abstr. GeoRef.

943.6 AU ISSN 0572-192X
OBEROESTERREICHISCHES LANDESARCHIV. MITTEILUNGEN. 1950. a. Hermann Boehlaus Nachf., Schmalzhofgasse 4, Postfach 167, 1061 Vienna, Austria. bk. rev. illus. Indexed: Hist.Abstr. Amer.Hist.& Life.

943.7 320 CS
OBLASTNI MUZEUM V GOTTWALDOVE. ZPRAVY. 1956. a. Oblastni Muzeum Jihovychodni Moravy, Soudni 1, Gottwaldov, Czechoslovakia (Subscr. to: Artia, Ve Smeckach 30, 111 27 Prague 1, Czechoslovakia) Ed. Petr Starosta. bibl. circ. 600.
Formerly (1962-1966): Oblastni Muzeum Jihovychodni Moravy v Gottwaldove. Zpravy.

949.4 SZ
OBWALDNER GESCHICHTSBLAETTER. irreg. Historisch-Antiquarischer Verein Obwalden, CH-6060 Sarnen, Switzerland. illus.

942 UK ISSN 0078-303X
OCCASIONAL PAPERS IN ENGLISH LOCAL HISTORY. 1969. irreg., 4th series. price varies. ‡ Leicester University Press, Fielding Johnson Bldg., Univ. of Leicester, University Rd., Leicester, England. Eds. H. Fox, C. Phythian-Adams.

OCCASIONAL PAPERS IN GERMAN STUDIES. see LITERATURE

949.2 839.31 UK ISSN 0144-3070
OCCASIONAL PAPERS IN MODERN DUTCH STUDIES. 1980. irreg. Hull University Press, Hull HU6 7RX, England. Ed. P.K. King.

900 300 DK ISSN 0078-3307
ODENSE UNIVERSITY STUDIES IN HISTORY AND SOCIAL SCIENCES. (Text in Danish and English; summaries in English) 1970. irreg., no.100, 1986. price varies. Odense University Press, 36, Pjentedamsgade, DK-5000 Odense, Denmark. (back issues avail.)

947 PL ISSN 0029-8514
ODRODZENIE I REFORMACJA W POLSCE. (Summaries in English) 1956. a. price varies. (Polska Akademia Nauk, Instytut Historii) Ossolineum, Publishing House of the Polish Academy of Sciences, Rynek 9, Wroclaw, Poland (Dist. by: Ars Polona-Ruch, Krakowskie Przedmiescie 7, Warsaw, Poland) Ed. J. Tazbir.

943.6 AU
OESTERREICH ARCHIV. 1959. irreg. price varies. (Institut fuer Oesterreichkunde) Verlag fuer Geschichte und Politik, Neulinggasse 26, A-1030 Vienna, Austria. Ed. Erich Zoellner.

943.6 AU
OESTERREICHISCHE AKADEMIE DER WISSENSCHAFTEN. ARCHIV FUER OESTERREICHISCHE GESCHICHTE. 1848. irreg. price varies. (Oesterreichische Akademie der Wissenschaften, Historische Kommission) Verlag der Oesterreichischen Akademie der Wissenschaften, Ignaz Seipelplatz 2, A-1010 Vienna, Austria.

940 930 AU
OESTERREICHISCHE AKADEMIE DER WISSENSCHAFTEN. KOMMISSION FUER DIE TABULA IMPERII BYZANTINI. VEROEFFENTLICHUNGEN. (Subseries of: Oesterreichische Akademie der Wissenschaften. Philosophisch-Historische Klasse. Denkschriften) 1973. irreg. Verlag der Oesterreichischen Akademie der Wissenschaften, Ignaz Seipel-Platz 2, A-1010 Vienna, Austria. bibl. illus.

940 100 AU ISSN 0378-8652
OESTERREICHISCHE AKADEMIE DER WISSENSCHAFTEN. PHILOSOPHISCH-HISTORISCHE KLASSE. ANZEIGER. 1864. a. price varies. Verlag der Oesterreichischen Akademie der Wissenschaften, Dr. Ignaz Seipel-Platz 2, A-1010 Vienna, Austria. Indexed: Hist.Abstr. M.L.A. Amer.Hist.& Life.

OESTERREICHISCHE AKADEMIE DER WISSENSCHAFTEN. PHILOSOPHISCH-HISTORISCHE KLASSE. SITZUNGSBERICHTE. see PHILOSOPHY

940 AU ISSN 0065-5376
OESTERREICHISCHE AKADEMIE DER WISSENSCHAFTEN. PRAEHISTORISCHE KOMMISSION. MITTEILUNGEN. 1887. irreg. price varies. Verlag der Oesterreichischen Akademie der Wissenschaften, Dr. Ignaz Seipel-Platz 2, A-1010 Vienna, Austria.

949.5 AU ISSN 0378-8660
OESTERREICHISCHE BYZANTINISTIK. JAHRBUCH. (Text in English, French, German, ancient and modern Greek and Latin) 1951. a. price varies. (Oesterreichische Akademie der Wissenschaften, Kommission fuer Byzantinistik) Verlag der Oesterreichischen Akademie der Wissenschaften, Dr. Ignaz Seipel-Platz 2, A-1010 Vienna, Austria. Ed. Herbert Hunger. bk. rev. Indexed: M.L.A. RILA.
Formerly: Oesterreichische Byzantinische Gesellschaft Jahrbuch.

940 AU
OESTERREICHISCHES KULTURINSTITUT, ROM. ABTEILUNG FUER HISTORISCHE STUDIEN. PUBLIKATIONEN I. ABTEILUNG: ABHANDLUNGEN. (Text in English, French and German) 1954. irreg. price varies. Verlag der Oesterreichischen Akademie der Wissenschaften, Dr. Ignaz Seipel-Platz 2, A-1010 Vienna, Austria. Eds. Leo Santifaller, H. Schmidinger.

940
OESTERREICHISCHES KULTURINSTITUT, ROM. ABTEILUNG FUER HISTORISCHE STUDIEN. PUBLIKATIONEN II. ABTEILUNG: QUELLEN. 1968. irreg. price varies. Verlag der Oesterreichischen Akademie der Wissenschaften, Dr. Ignaz Seipel-Platz 2, A-1010 Vienna, Austria.

940 AU ISSN 0078-3439
OESTERREICHISCHES OST- UND SUEDOSTEUROPA INSTITUT. SCHRIFTENREIHE. 1967. irreg., vol.11, 1985. price varies. ‡ Verlag fuer Geschichte und Politik, Neulinggasse 26, A-1030 Vienna, Austria. Eds. R. G. Plaschka, K. Mack.

940 020 AU ISSN 0067-2297
OESTERREICHISCHES STAATSARCHIV. MITTEILUNGEN. (Supplements avail.) (Text in English, French, German and Italian) 1948. a. price varies. Verlag Ferdinand Berger und Soehne OHG, Wienerstr. 21-23, A-3580 Horn, Austria. Eds. Gerhard Rill, Christiane Thomas. bk. rev. bibl. illus. cum.index (every 25 years) circ. 500(controlled) Indexed: Hist.Abstr. Amer.Hist.& Life.

940 GW ISSN 0078-3714
OFFA-JAHRBUCH; VOR- UND FRUEHGESCHICHTE. a. Karl Wachholtz Verlag, Gaensemarkt 1, Postfach 255, 2350 Neumuenster, W. Germany (B.R.D.) circ. 500.

943.7 913 CS
OKRESNI ARCHIV OLOMOUC. VYROCNI
ZPRAVA. 1974. a. Okresni Archiv v Olomouci,
Krizkovskeho 2, Olomouc, Czechoslovakia (Subscr.
to: Artia, Ve Smeckach 30, 111 27 Prague 1,
Czechoslovakia)

943.7 912 CS
OKRESNI MUZEUM V BLANSKU. SBORNIK.
1969. a. Okresni Muzeum v Blansku, Blansko,
Czechoslovakia (Subscr. to: Artia, Ve Smeckach 30,
111 27 Prague 1, Czechoslovakia)
Formerly: Okresni Vlastivedneho Muzeum v
Blansku. Sbornik.

941 IE ISSN 0475-1388
OLD ATHLONE SOCIETY JOURNAL. 1969. irreg.,
(approx. biennial) £6 to non-members. ‡ Old
Athlone Society, c/o G. O'Brien, Ed., 52 Roslevin
Lawn, Athlone, Ireland. Ed. Gearoid O'Brien. adv.
charts. illus. circ. 750.

940 FR ISSN 0078-4591
OMBRES DE L'HISTOIRE.* 1969. irreg. price varies.
R. Laffont, 6 Place Saint-Sulpice, Paris 6e, France.

944 FR
OR DU RHINE.* 1977. irreg. Editions Copernic, 14
rue d'Armorique, 75015 Paris, France. Ed. Alain de
Benoist.

943.7 CS
OSTAVA. 1963. irreg. Nakladatelstvi Profil, Cihlarska
51, 701 00 Ostrava 1, Czechoslovakia (Subscr. to:
Artia, Ve Smeckach 30, 111 27 Prague 1,
Czechoslovakia) bk. rev. bibl.

943 GW ISSN 0078-6845
OSTBAIRISCHE GRENZMARKEN. 1957. a.
DM.25. Universitaet Passau, Institut fuer
Ostbairische Heimatforschung, Schusterg. 19/21,
Postfach 2540, D-8390 Passau, W. Germany
(B.R.D.) Ed. August Leidl. bk. rev. circ. 600.
Indexed: RILA.

948 FI ISSN 0473-8063
OSTERBOTTEN. (Text in Swedish) 1953. a. Svensk-
Osterbottniska Samfundet, Kyrkoesplanaden 19,
65100 Vasa 10, Finland.
Formerly (until 1964): Osterbottnisk Arsbok.

940 GW ISSN 0078-687X
OSTEUROPA INSTITUT, MUNICH.
VEROEFFENTLICHUNGEN. REIHE
GESCHICHTE. 1953. irreg., vol. 54, 1986. Verlag
Otto Harrassowitz, Taunusstr. 14, Postfach 2929,
6200 Wiesbaden 1, W. Germany (B.R.D.) Ed. G.
Stadtmueller. (back issues avail.)

910 AU ISSN 0078-6896
OSTPANORAMA. 1965. a. S.420. Gesellschaft fuer
Ost- und Suedostkunde, Bismarckstr. 5, A-4020
Linz, Austria. Ed. Ruediger Zellentin. adv. bk. rev.
circ. 5,000.

940 US
OXFORD HISTORICAL MONOGRAPHS. irreg.
price varies. Oxford University Press, 200 Madison
Ave., New York, NY 10016 TEL 212-679-7300.
(And Ely House, 37 Dover St., London W1X 4AH,
England) Ed.Bd.

949.7 890 UK
OXFORD SLAVONIC PAPERS. a. £22.50($45)
Oxford University Press, Walton St., Oxford OX2
6DP, England. Ed. G.C. Stone. (also avail. in
microform from UMI) Indexed: Br.Hum.Ind.
M.L.A.

941 UK
OXFORDSHIRE RECORD SOCIETY. 1919. irreg.
£8($15) Bodleian Library, Oxford OX1 3BG,
England. circ. 300.

OXONIENSIA. see *ARCHAEOLOGY*

940 282 GW ISSN 0340-7993
PAEPSTE UND PAPSTTUM. (Text in German and
English) 1971. irreg., vol.24, 1987. Anton
Hiersemann Verlag, Rosenbergstr. 113, Postfach
723, 7000 Stuttgart 1, W. Germany (B.R.D.) Ed. G.
Denzler.

948 FI
PAIMIO-SEURAN VUOSIKIRJA. 1956. irreg., latest
1985. Fmk.10. Paimio-Seuran, Paimio, Finland.

940 929 UK
PANORAMA. 1956. a. 40p.($2) Thurrock Local
History Society, Thurrock Museums Dept., Orsett
Rd., Grays, Essex RM17 5DX, England. Ed. Randal
Bingley. circ. 400. Indexed: Br.Archaeol.Abstr.
Local

940 CN ISSN 0228-8605
PAPERS IN MEDIAEVAL STUDIES. 1981. irreg.
price varies. Pontifical Institute of Mediaeval
Studies, 59 Queen's Park Crescent E., Toronto, Ont.
M5S 2C4, Canada. TEL 416-926-7144.

943 GW ISSN 0078-9410
PAPYROLOGICA COLONIENSIA. 1964. irreg.?
price varies. (Rheinisch-Westfaelische Akademie der
Wissenschaften) Westdeutscher Verlag GmbH,
P.O.B. 30 03 20, 5090 Leverkusen 3, W. Germany
(B.R.D.)

943.7 CS ISSN 0139-6595
PEDAGOGICKA FAKULTA V OSTRAVE.
SBORNIK PRACI. RADI C: DEJEPIS-ZEMEPIS.
(Text in Czech, English, French and German) 1966.
irreg. Statni Pedagogicke Nakladatelstvi, Ostrovni
30, 113 01 Prague 1, Czechoslovakia (Subscr. to:
Artia, Ve Smeckach 30, 111 27 Prague 1,
Czechoslovakia)

943.7 CS ISSN 0139-7346
PEDAGOGICKA FAKULTA V PLZNI. SBORNIK.
DEJEPIS. 1959. irreg. Statni Pedagogicke
Nakladatelstvi, Ostrovni 30, 113 01 Prague 1,
Czechoslovakia (Subscr. to: Artia, Ve Smeckach 30,
111 27 Prague 1, Czechoslovakia)
Formerly: Vyssi Pedagogicke Skoly v Plzni.
Sbornik: Pedagogickeho Institutu v Plzni. Sbornik.

948 FI
PEDERSORE. (Text in Swedish) 1909. a. Jakobstads
Tidning, Jakobsgatan 13, 68600 Jakobstad 60,
Finland. cum. index 1909-48.

942 UK
PEMBROKESHIRE HISTORICAL SOCIETY.
JOURNAL. 1985. a. £2. Pembrokeshire Historical
Society, The Castle, Haverfordwest, Dyfed SA61
2EF, Wales. Ed. C. Hughes. bk. rev. illus. circ. 300.
(back issues avail.)

940 410 IE ISSN 0332-1592
PERITIA. (Text in English, French and German)
1982. a. $30. Medieval Academy of Ireland, c/o
Department of Irish History, University College,
Cork, Ireland. TEL 353-21-276871. Ed. Donnchadh
O. Corrain. adv. bk. rev. circ. 600. (back issues
avail.) Indexed: M.L.A. Br.Archaeol.Abstr.

940 IT
PLUTEUS. a. L.30000. Edizioni dell' Orso, Via
Piacenza 66, 15100 Alessandria, Italy. Ed.
Alessandro Vitale-Brovarone. bk. rev. circ. 750.

940 327 US
POLITICS OF LIBERATION SERIES. 1985. irreg.
Holmes & Meier Publishers, Inc., 30 Irving Pl., New
York, NY 10003. TEL 212-254-4100. Eds. Geoffrey
Warner, David W. Ellwood.

940 PL ISSN 0079-3388
POLSKA AKADEMIA NAUK. ODDZIAL W
KRAKOWIE. KOMISJA NAUK
HISTORYCZNYCH. PRACE. (Text in Polish;
summaries in English, French or Russian) 1958.
irreg., no.46, 1985. price varies. Ossolineum,
Publishing House of the Polish Academy of
Sciences, Rynek 9, Wroclaw, Poland (Dist. by Ars
Polona-Ruch, Krakowskie Przedmiescie 7, Warsaw,
Poland)

947 PL ISSN 0137-5288
POLSKA KLASA ROBOTNICZA. STUDIA
HISTORYCZNE. irreg., vol.10, 1983. $10. (Polska
Akademia Nauk, Instytut Historii) Panstwowe
Wydawnictwo Naukowe, Miodowa 10, 00-251
Warsaw, Poland (Dist. by: Ars Polona, Krakowskie
Przedmiescie 7, 00-068 Warsaw, Poland) Ed. S.
Kalabinski. charts.

POLSKA 2000. see *SOCIOLOGY*

947 PL ISSN 0556-0691
POMORANIA ANTIQUA. irreg., vol. 12, 1986. price
varies. (Muzeum Archeologiczne, Gdansk)
Ossolineum, Publishing House of the Polish
Academy of Sciences, Rynek 9, Wroclaw, Poland
(Dist. by: Ars Polona-Ruch, Krakowskie
Przedmiescie 7, Warsaw, Poland) Ed. L. Luka.

947 BU
POMOSHTNI ISTORICHESKI DISTSIPLINI. irreg.
Hemus Foreign Trade Co., 6 Ruski Blvd., 1000
Sofia, Bulgaria.

940 CN ISSN 0082-5328
PONTIFICAL INSTITUTE OF MEDIAEVAL
STUDIES. STUDIES AND TEXTS. 1955. irreg.
price varies. Pontifical Institute of Mediaeval
Studies, 59 Queen's Park Crescent E., Toronto
Ontario M5S 2C4, Canada. TEL 416-926-7144.
circ. 500. Indexed: M.L.A.

947 BU ISSN 0554-7040
POREDITSA BALKANI. 1966. irreg. (Bulgarska
Akademiya na Naukite) Publishing House of the
Bulgarian Academy of Sciences, Ul. Akad. G.
Bonchev, Bldg. 6, 1113 Sofia, Bulgaria (Subscr. to:
Hemus Foreign Trade Co., 6 Ruski Blvd., 1000
Sofia, Bulgaria)

946.9 PO
PORTUGALIAE HISTORICA.* irreg. Universidade
de Lisboa, Instituto Historico Infante Dom
Henrique, Alameda da Universidade, 1699 Lisbon,
Portugal.

940 GW ISSN 0079-421X
PORTUGIESISCHE FORSCHUNGEN DER
GOERRESGESELLSCHAFT. REIHE 1:
AUFSAETZE ZUR PORTUGIESISCHEN
KULTURGESCHICHTE. 1960. irreg. price varies.
(Goerres-Gesellschaft) Aschendorffsche
Verlagsbuchhandlung, Soester Str. 13, 4400
Muenster, W. Germany (B.R.D.) Ed. Hans Flasche.
Indexed: M.L.A.

940 GW ISSN 0079-4228
PORTUGIESISCHE FORSCHUNGEN DER
GOERRESGESELLSCHAFT. REIHE 2:
MONOGRAPHIEN. 1961. irreg. price varies.
(Goerres-Gesellschaft) Aschendorffsche
Verlagsbuchhandlung, Soester Str. 13, 4400
Muenster, W. Germany (B.R.D.) Ed. Hans Flasche.

940 GW ISSN 0171-290X
PORTUGIESISCHE FORSCHUNGEN DER
GOERRESGESELLSCHAFT. REIHE 3: VIEIRA-
TEXTE UND VIEIRA-STUDIEN. 1972. irreg.
price varies. (Goerres-Gesellschaft) Aschendorffsche
Verlagsbuchhandlung, Soester Str. 13, 4400
Muenster, W. Germany (B.R.D.) Ed. Hans Flasche.

940 PL ISSN 0079-4465
POWSTANIE STYCZNIOWE. MATERIALY I
DOKUMENTY. irreg., vol.44, 1985. price varies.
(Polska Akademia Nauk) Ossolineum, Publishing
House of the Polish Academy of Sciences, Rynek 9,
50-106 Wroclaw, Poland (Dist. by: Ars Polona-
Ruch, Krakowskie Przedmiescie 7, Warsaw, Poland)

940 PL ISSN 0079-4651
POZNANSKIE TOWARZYSTWO PRZYJACIOL
NAUK. KOMISJA HISTORYCZNA. PRACE.
(Text in Polish; summaries in French, German)
vol.29, 1976. irreg., vol.37, 1983. price varies.
Panstwowe Wydawnictwo Naukowe, Miodowa 10,
00-251 Warsaw, Poland (Dist. by: Ars Polona,
Krakowskie Przedmiescie 7, 00-068 Warsaw,
Poland) Ed. W.R. Rzepka. bibl. charts. illus. circ.
750.

743.7 CS
PRACE Z DEJIN PRIRODNICH VED. (Text in
Czech, Slovak) 1969. irreg. avail. on exchange basis
only. Ustav Ceskoslovenskych a Svetovych Dejin
CSAV, Vysehradska 49, 128 26 Prague,
Czechoslovakia. Ed. Jan Janko. bk. rev. bibl.

943.7 913 CS
PRAZSKY SBORNIK HISTORICKY. 1962. a. price
varies. (Archiv Hlavniho Mesta Prahy)
Nakladatelstvi Panorama, Halkova 1, 120 72 Prague
2, Czechoslovakia (Subscr. to: Artia, Ve Smeckach
30, 111 27 Prague 1, Czechoslovakia) Ed. Frantisek
Holec. bk. rev. bibl. Indexed: Numis.Lit.

948 301.16 DK ISSN 0106-6579
PRESSENS ARBOG. (Text in Danish, Norwegian and
Swedish) 1963. a. (Dansk Pressehistorisk Selskab)
C. A. Reitzels Boghandel, Noerregade 20, 1165
Copenhagen, Denmark.

HISTORY — HISTORY OF EUROPE

943.64   LH   ISSN 0048-5306
PRINCIPALITY OF LIECHTENSTEIN - A DOCUMENTARY HANDBOOK. (Text in English, French and German) 1966. irreg. Press and Information Office, FL-9490 Vaduz, Principality of Liechtenstein. circ. 7,000.

937   IT   ISSN 0079-5682
PROBLEMI E RICERCHE DI STORIA ANTICA. 1951. irreg., no.7. price varies. Erma di "Bretschneider", Via Cassiodoro 19, 00193 Rome, Italy.

PROBLEMI SJEVERNOG JADRANA. see *ANTHROPOLOGY*

940   UK
PROJECT DEFNYDDIAU AC ADNODDAU Y SWYDDFA GYMREIG. 1982. irreg. price varies. (Welsh Joint Education Committee) University of Wales Press, 6 Gwennyth St., Cathays, Cardiff CF2 4YD, Wales. Ed. Carl J. Dodson.

940   GW
PROVINZIALINSTITUT FUER WESTFAELISCHE LANDES- UND VOLKSFORSCHUNG DES LANDSCHAFTSVERBANDES WESTFALEN-LIPPE. VEROEFFENTLICHUNGEN. 1937. irreg. price varies. Aschendorffsche Verlagsbuchhandlung, Soester Str. 13, 4400 Muenster, W. Germany (B.R.D.) Eds. Alfred Hartlieb von Wallthor, Karl-Heinz Kirchhoff.
    Formerly: Provinzialinstitut fuer Westfaelische Landes- und Volkforschung. Veroeffentlichungen (ISSN 0171-3736)

PRUMYSLOVE OBLASTI. see *BUSINESS AND ECONOMICS — Labor And Industrial Relations*

PUBBLICAZIONI DI VERIFICHE. see *PHILOSOPHY*

936 100   US   ISSN 0079-7677
PUBLICATIONS IN MEDIEVAL STUDIES. (Text in Latin) 1935? irreg., vol.22, no.1, 1984. price varies. ‡ (University of Notre Dame, Medieval Institute) University of Notre Dame Press, Notre Dame, IN 46556. TEL 219-239-6346.

930 930.1   IT
PUTEOLI; studi di storia antica. (Text in English, French, German and Italian) 1977. a. price varies. Azienda Autonoma di Cura, Soggiorno e Turismo, Via Campi Flegrei (S.S. Domiziana), 3, 80078 Pozzuoli (NA), Italy. Ed. Giuseppe Camodeca. bk. rev. circ. 1,000. (back issues avail.)

945   IT
QUADERNI DI CULTURA MATERIALE. 1977. irreg., vol. 3, 1981. Erma di Bretschneider, Via Cassiodoro 19, 00193 Rome, Italy. Ed. Andrea Carandini.

940   IT
QUADERNI DI STUDI STORICI TOSCANI. irreg., 3-4/yr. price varies. (Centro di Studi Storici Toscani) Libreria L. del Re, Via dei Pucci 45 R., Florence, Italy. Ed. M. Leopps Pegna. bibl. charts. illus. circ. 500.

945 300   IT   ISSN 0066-2283
QUADERNI INTERNAZIONALI DI STORIA ECONOMICA E SOCIALE/INTERNATIONAL JOURNAL OF ECONOMIC AND SOCIAL HISTORY/CAHIERS INTERNATIONAUX D'HISTOIRE ECONOMIQUE ET SOCIALE. (Text in English, French, German, Spanish and Italian) 1960. a. 80 Fr. Istituto Italiano per la Storia dei Movimenti Sociali e delle Structure Sociali, Via G. B. Ruoppolo 69, Naples, Italy (and Librairie Droz, rue Massot 11, Geneva, Switzerland) Ed. Domenico Demarco. adv. bk. rev. Indexed: Hist.Abstr. Amer.Hist.& Life.
    Formerly: Annali di Storia Economica e Sociale.

949.4   SZ   ISSN 0079-9076
QUELLEN UND FORSCHUNGEN ZUR BASLER GESCHICHTE. 1966. irreg., no. 12, 1983. price varies. (Staatsarchiv) Friedrich Reinhardt Verlag, Missionsstr. 36, 4012 Basel, Switzerland. Ed. Andreas Staehelin. circ. 500.

940   GW
QUELLEN UND STUDIEN ZU DEN FRIEDENSVERSUCHEN DES ERSTEN WELTKRIEGES. irreg., vol.5, 1984. price varies. Franz Steiner Verlag Wiesbaden GmbH, Birkenwaldstr. 44, Postfach 3479, D-7000 Stuttgart 1, W. Germany (B.R.D.) Ed. Wolfgang Steglich.
    Formerly: Quellen und Forschungen zur Geschichte des Ersten Weltkriees (ISSN 0722-8167)

940   GW   ISSN 0170-3595
QUELLEN UND STUDIEN ZUR GESCHICHTE DES OESTLICHEN EUROPA. irreg., vol.26, 1986. price varies. (Arbeitskreis der Osteuropahistoriker an den Hochschulen des Landes Nordrhein-Westfalen) Franz Steiner Verlag Wiesbaden GmbH, Birkenwaldstr. 44, Postfach 347, D-7000 Stuttgart 1, W. Germany (B.R.D.)

940   GE   ISSN 0079-9114
QUELLEN UND STUDIEN ZUR GESCHICHTE OSTEUROPAS. 1958. irreg., vol.27, 1984. price varies. Akademie-Verlag, Leipziger Str. 3-4, 1086 Berlin, E. Germany (D.D.R.) Eds. Eduard Winter, Heinz Lemke.

943   GW
RADIKALE HISTORIKER. 1978. irreg. J. Klein, Rektor-Ritter-Str. 1, 2000 Hamburg, W. Germany (B.R.D.)

942   UK   ISSN 0306-848X
RADNORSHIRE SOCIETY. TRANSACTIONS. 1931. a. £3 to individuals; institutions £4. Radnorshire Society, c/o Radnor College of Further Education, Llandrindod Wells, Radnorshire, England. Ed. R.W.D. Fenn. bk. rev. index: 1956-1980. circ. 500. (also avail. in microform from UMI; reprint service avail. from UMI) Indexed: Br.Hum.Ind. Br.Archaeol.Abstr.

948   DK   ISSN 0106-9616
RAETHINGE-POSTEN. 1978. a. membership. Ringe Museumsforening, Ringe Museum, 5750 Ringe, Denmark. (Co-sponsor: Ringe Lokalhistoriske Forening) illus.

940   FR
RECHERCHES SUR LA RENAISSANCE (PARIS) (Text in French) 1975. a. price varies. (Universite de Paris-Sorbonne, Institute de Recherches sur les Civilisations de l'Occident Moderne) Librarie Touzot, 38 rue Saint Sulpice, 75278 Paris Cedex 06, France.

943   GW
RECHTSRHEINISCHES KOELN; Jahrbuch fuer Geschichte und Landeskunde. 1975. a. price varies. Geschichts und Heimatverein Rechtsrheinisches, Friedrich-Ebert-Ufer 64-70, 5000 Cologne 90, W. Germany (B.R.D.) Eds. Gebhard Aders, Wilhelm Becker. adv. bk. rev. circ. 2,000.

942   UK   ISSN 0034-1738
RECORDS OF HUNTINGDONSHIRE. 1965. a. £50. Huntingdonshire Local History Society, 7 Post St., Godmanchester, Huntingdon, Cambs. PE18 8BA, England. Ed. J. Hadley. bk. rev. abstr. charts. illus. circ. 350. Indexed: Br.Archaeol.Abstr.

940   FR   ISSN 0080-1151
REPERTOIRE INTERNATIONAL DES MEDIEVISTES. 1965. irreg. 350 F.($28.80) Centre d'Etudes Superieures de Civilisation Medievale, Hotel Berthelot, 24, rue de la Chaine, 86000 Poitiers, France. adv. bk. rev. cum.index. in vol. published in 1971.

940   GW   ISSN 0724-9578
REPERTORIEN ZUR ERFORSCHUNG DER FREUHEN NEUZEIT. 1977. irreg., vol.10, 1987. price varies. Verlag Otto Harrassowitz, Taunusstr. 14, Postfach 2929, D-6200 Wiesbaden 1, W. Germany (B.R.D.) Ed. Bd.

REPERTORIUM VAN BOEKEN EN TIJDSCHRIFTARTIKELEN BETREFFENDE DE GESCHIEDENIS VAN NEDERLAND. see *HISTORY — Abstracting, Bibliographies, Statistics*

942   UK   ISSN 0261-5061
RETROSPECT (BURNLEY) 1980. a. 45p. Burnley and District Historical Society, c/o Central Library, Burnley, Lancs., England. Ed. Roger Frost. circ. 150.

940   SW   ISSN 0348-9078
REVISIONIST HISTORY. (Text in Arabic, English, French, German, Japanese, Polish, Russian and Spanish; summaries in English) 1980. irreg. Kr.150($20) Revisionist History, Marknadsvagen 289 2tr, S183 34 Taby, Sweden. Ed. Ditlieb Felderer. bk. rev. circ. 5,000. (back issues avail.)

944   FR   ISSN 0556-7335
REVUE ANNUELLE D'HISTOIRE DU QUATORZIEME ARRONDISSEMENT DE PARIS. 1955. a. 35 F. Societe Historique du Quatorzieme Arrondissement de Paris, 2 place Ferdinand Brunot, 75675 Paris Cedex 14, France. Ed. G. N. Perroy. adv. illus.

REVUE BELGE DE NUMISMATIQUE ET DE SIGILLOGRAPHIE. see *NUMISMATICS*

944   FR
REVUE DE LA SAINTONGE ET DE L'AUNIS. 1975. a. Societe d'Archeologie et d'Histoire de la Charente Maritime, Musee Archeologique, Esplanade A. Malraux, 17100 Saintes, France.

949.4   SZ
REVUE DU VIEUX GENEVE. 1921. a. 19 Fr. Promoedition SA, 2 Rue Bovy-Lysberg, Case Postale 418, 1211 Geneve 11, Switzerland. Ed. Bernard Lescaze. adv. bibl. charts. illus. circ. 3, 000.
    Formerly: Almanach du Vieux Geneve.

944   FR
REVUE HISTORIQUE DE BORDEAUX ET DU DEPARTEMENT DE LA GIRONDE. 1952, N.S. a. 150 F. Archives Municipales, 71 rue du Loup, 33000 Bordeaux, France. Ed. Jean Paul Avisseau. bk. rev. circ. 450. (back issues avail. (1908-1945))

REVUE HISTORIQUE ET ARCHEOLOGIQUE DU MAINE. see *ARCHAEOLOGY*

REVUE HISTORIQUE VAUDOISE. see *ARCHAEOLOGY*

943 398 572   GW   ISSN 0556-8218
RHEINISCH-WESTFAELISCHE ZEITSCHRIFT FUER VOLKSKUNDE. 1954. a. Volkskundliche Abteilung Institut fuer Geschichtliche Landeskunde der Rheinlande, Universitaet Bonn, Am Hofgarten 22, 5300 Bonn, W. Germany (B.R.D.) Ed.Bd. bk. rev.

943   GW   ISSN 0067-9976
RHEINISCHES LANDESMUSEUM IN BONN. BONNER JAHRBUECHER. 1846. irreg., vol. 180, 1980. price varies. Rheinland-Verlag, Kennedy-Ufer 2, 5000 Cologne 21, W. Germany (B.R.D.) (Dist. by: Rudolf Habelt Verlag, Am Buchenhang 1, 5300 Bonn 1, W. Germany (B.R.D.)) cum.index.

948   DK   ISSN 0108-0806
RIBE STIFTSBOG. 1970. a. Kr.35. Stiftsoevrigheds-og Bispekontoret, Korsbroedregade 7, 6760 Ribe, Denmark.
    Formerly: Ribe Stift.

945   IT
RICERCHE DI STORIA MODERNA. 1976. irreg. (Universita degli Studi di Pisa, Istituto di Storia Medioevale e Moderna) Pacini Editore, Via della Faggiola 17, Pisa, Italy.

949   NE
RIJKS GESCHIEDKUNDIGE PUBLICATIEN. GROTE SERIE. vol. 163, 1978. irreg. price varies. Uitgeverij S.M. Ontwikkeling, Box 566, 2501 CN The Hague, Netherlands.

949   NE
RIJKS GESCHIEDKUNDIGE PUBLICATIEN. KLEINE SERIE. vol. 44, 1976. irreg. price varies. Uitgeverij S.M. Ontwikkeling, Box 33, 2300 AA Leiden, Netherlands.

940   NE   ISSN 0066-1287
RIJKSINSTITUUT VOOR OORLOGSDOCUMENTATIE. DOCUMENTEN. 1967. irreg. Uitgeverij S.M. Ontwikkeling, Box 33, 2300 AA Leiden, Netherlands.

940   NE   ISSN 0066-1295
RIJKSINSTITUUT VOOR OORLOGSDOCUMENTATIE. MONOGRAFIEEN. irreg. price varies. Uitgeverij S.M. Onwickkeling, Box 33, 2300 AA Leiden, Netherlands.

RINASCIMENTO. see *HUMANITIES: COMPREHENSIVE WORKS*

948   DK
RINGKOEBING ARBOG. 1926. a. A. Rasmussens Bogtrykkeri, 6950 Ringkoebing, Denmark. Eds. S.A. Jacobsen, Helle Rasmussen.

940   956   IT
RIVISTA DI STUDI BIZANTINI E SLAVI. (Text in several languages) 1981. a. L.30000($30) (University of Bologna) Patron Editore, Via Badini 12, 40127 Bologna, Italy. bk. rev. bibl. charts. illus. circ. 4,000. (back issues avail.)

940   800   US   ISSN 0195-8453
ROCKY MOUNTAIN MEDIEVAL AND RENAISSANCE ASSOCIATION. JOURNAL. 1980. a. $10. Rocky Mountain Medieval and Renaissance Association, Northern Arizona University, Box 6032, Flagstaff, AZ 86011. TEL 602-523-9011. Ed. James B. Fitzmaurice. adv. bk. rev. illus. circ. 200. (also avail. in microform) Indexed: Hist.Abstr. M.L.A. Amer.Hist.& Life.

943.8   PL   ISSN 0080-3421
ROCZNIK BIALOSTOCKI. (Text in Polish; summaries in English and Russian) 1961. a. price varies. (Muzeum Okresgowe in Bialymstoku) Panstwowe Wydawnictwo Naukowe, Miodowa 10, 00-251 Warsaw, Poland (Dist. by: Ars Polona, Krakowskie Przedmiescie 7, 00-068 Warsaw, Poland) illus. Indexed: Numis.Lit.

940   PL   ISSN 0080-3456
ROCZNIK GDANSKI. (Text in Polish; summaries in English and Russian) 1927. a. price varies. (Gdanskie Towarzystwo Naukowe) Ossolineum, Publishing House of the Polish Academy of Sciences, Rynek 9, Wroclaw, Poland (Dist. by: Ars Polona-Ruch, Krakowskie Przedmiescie 7, Warsaw, Poland) Ed. Andrzej Bukowski. illus. circ. 750.

943.8   PL   ISSN 0080-3464
ROCZNIK GRUDZIADZKI.* 1960. a. price varies. Polskie Towarzystwo Historyczne, Oddzial w Grudziadzu, Murowa 29, Grudziadz, Poland (Dist. by Ars Polona-Ruch, Krakowskie Przedmiescie 7, Warsaw, Poland) Eds. Marian Biskup, Adam Wolnikowski.

943.8   PL   ISSN 0080-3480
ROCZNIK JELENIOGORSKI. 1963. a. price varies. (Towarzystwo Przyjaciol Ziemi Jeleniogorskiej) Ossolineum, Publishing House of the Polish Academy of Sciences, Rynek 9, 50-106 Wroclaw, Poland (Dist. by: Ars Polona-Ruch, Krakowskie Przedmiescie 7, Warsaw, Poland) Ed. Stanislaw Lejde. Indexed: Numis.Lit.

940   PL   ISSN 0137-3501
ROCZNIK KALISKI. 1968. a. price varies. (Polskie Towarzystwo Historyczne, Oddzial in Kalisz) Wydawnictwo Poznanskie, Ul. Newtona 8a/3, Poznan, Poland. (Co-sponsor: Muzeum Okregowe Ziemi Kaliskiej in Kalisz) Ed. Andrzej Nowak. bk. rev. illus. circ. 1,000.

940   PL   ISSN 0080-3499
ROCZNIK KRAKOWSKI. 1898. irreg., vol.50, 1980. price varies. (Towarzystwo Milosnikow Historii i Zabytkow Krakowa) Ossolineum, Publishing House of the Polish Academy of Sciences, Rynek 9, Wroclaw, Poland (Dist. by: Ars Polona-Ruch, Krakowskie Przedmiescie 7, Warsaw, Poland) Ed. J. M. Malecki. circ. 600. Indexed: Numis.Lit.

943.8   PL
ROCZNIK KULTURALNY ZIEMI GDANSKIEJ. 1965. irreg., 1973, vol. 6. 15 Zl. per volume. (Gdanskie Towarzystwo Przyjaciol Sztuki) Wydawnictwo Morskie, Szeroka 38-40, 80-835 Gdansk, Poland.
   Formerly: Gdanski Rocznik Kulturalny (ISSN 0435-1568)

943   PL   ISSN 0080-3502
ROCZNIK LODZKI. (Text in Polish; contents in English, Russian) 1958. a. price varies. Polskie Towarzystwo Historyczne, Oddzial w Lodzi) Panstwowe Wydawnictwo Naukowe, Miodowa 10, 00-251 Warsaw, Poland (Dist. by: Ars Polona, Krakowskie Przedmiescie 7, 00-068 Warsaw, Poland) Ed. B. Wachowska. bk. rev. charts. circ. 1, 230.

943.8   PL   ISSN 0080-3510
ROCZNIK LUBELSKI. (Text in Polish; summaries in French and Russian) 1959. a. price varies. (Polskie Towarzystwo Historyczne, Oddzial w Lublinie - Polish Historical Society) Wydawnictwo Lubelskie, Okopowa 7, Lublin, Poland (Dist. by Ars Polona-Ruch, Krakowskie Przedmiescie 7, Warsaw, Poland) Ed. Kazimierz Myslinski. circ. 500.

943.8   PL   ISSN 0080-3537
ROCZNIK OLSZTYNSKI. (Text in Polish; summaries in German and Russian) 1958. a. 400 Zl. Muzeum Warmii i Mazur, Ul. Zamkowa 2, 10-074 Olsztyn, Poland (Dist. by Ars Polona-Ruch, Krakowskie Przedmiescie 7, Warsaw, Poland) Ed. Jerzy Sikorski. bk. rev.

ROCZNIK SADECKI. see *FOLKLORE*

943.8   PL   ISSN 0080-3618
ROCZNIK WROCLAWSKI. 1957. a. (Towarzystwo Milosnikow Wroclawia) Ossolineum, Publishing House of the Polish Academy of Sciences, Rynek 9, 50-106 Wroclaw, Poland.

947   PL
ROCZNIK ZIEMI KLODZKIEJ. a. price varies. (Towarzystwo Milosnikow Ziemi Klodzkiej) Ossolineum, Publishing House of the Polish Academy of Sciences, Rynek 9, Wroclaw, Poland (Dist. by) Ars Polona-Ruch, Krakowskie Przedmiescie 7, Warsaw, Poland)

943.8   PL   ISSN 0080-3634
ROCZNIKI DZIEJOW SPOLECZNYCH I GOSPODARCZYCH/ANNALES D'HISTOIRE SOCIALE ET ECONOMIQUES. (Text in Polish; summaries in French) 1931. irreg., a. vol.44, 1983. price varies. (Poznanskie Towarzystwo Przyjaciol Nauk) Panstwowe Wydawnictwo Naukowe, Ul. Miodowa 10, 00-251 Warsaw, Poland (Dist. by: Ars Polona, Krakowskie Przedmiescie 7, 00-068 Warsaw, Poland) Ed. Wladyslaw Rusinski. bk. rev. bibl. charts. circ. 430.

900   069   GW   ISSN 0076-2741
ROEMISCH-GERMANISCHES ZENTRALMUSEUM, MAINZ. JAHRBUCH. 1954. a. DM.96. Dr. Rudolf Habelt GmbH, Am Buchenhang 1, 5300 Bonn 1, W. Germany (B.R.D.) bk. rev.

940   AU   ISSN 0080-3790
ROEMISCHE HISTORISCHE MITTEILUNGEN. 1958. a. price varies. (Oesterreichisches Kulturinstitut, Rome, IT) Verlag der Oesterreichischen Akademie der Wissenschaften, Dr. Ignaz Seipel-Platz 2, A-1010 Vienna, Austria. circ. 500.

945   NE
ROMA AETERNA. 1964. irreg. vol. 10, 1978. price varies. E. J. Brill, P.O. Box 9000, 2300 PA Leiden, Netherlands. Ed. Raoul Verdiere.

ROMANTIZM V RUSSKOI I SOVETSKOI LITERATURE. see *LITERATURE*

940   UK   ISSN 0306-1140
ROMFORD RECORD. no.4, 1971. a. 25p. Romford and District Historical Society, c/o Central Library, Romford, Essex, England. Ed. Brian D. Evans. charts. illus.

943   GW   ISSN 0722-7531
ROTTENBUERGER JAHRBUCH FUER KIRCHENGESCHICHTE. 1982. a. price varies. Jan Thorbecke Verlag GmbH & Co., Karlstr. 10, Postfach 546, D-7480 Sigmaringen, W. Germany (B.R.D.) bk. rev. (back issues avail.)

948.9   DK   ISSN 0106-5327
ROUGSOE LOKALHISTORISKE FORENING. AARSSKRIFT. 1979. a. membership. Rougsoe Lokalhistoriske Forening, Postbox 15, 8961 Allingaabro, Denmark. illus.

942   UK   ISSN 0080-4398
ROYAL HISTORICAL SOCIETY. GUIDES AND HANDBOOKS. (Supplementary Series) 1938; N.S. 1974. irreg. membership. Royal Historical Society, University College London, Gower St., London WC1E 6BT, England.

942   UK   ISSN 0080-4401
ROYAL HISTORICAL SOCIETY. TRANSACTIONS. FIFTH SERIES. 1872. a. membership. Royal Historical Society, University College London, Gower St., London WC1E 6BT, England. Indexed: Br.Hum.Ind. Br.Archaeol.Abstr. Geo.Abstr.

ROYAL IRISH ACADEMY. PROCEEDINGS. SECTION C: ARCHAEOLOGY, CELTIC STUDIES, HISTORY, LINGUISTICS AND LITERATURE. see *ARCHAEOLOGY*

RUHR-UNIVERSITAET. INSTITUT ZUR GESCHICHTE DER ARBEITERBEWEGUNG. MITTEILUNGSBLATT. see *LABOR UNIONS*

947   NE
RUMANIAN STUDIES; an international annual of the humanities and social sciences. 1970. irreg. price varies. E. J. Brill, P.O. Box 9000, 2300 PA Leiden, Netherlands. illus.

947   GW   ISSN 0721-9431
RUSSIA MEDIAEVALIS. (Text in English, German, Russian) 1973. irreg. price varies. Wilhelm Fink Verlag GmbH & Co KG, Ohmstr. 5, 8000 Munich 40, W. Germany (B.R.D.) Ed.Bd.

942   US   ISSN 0080-4886
RUSSIAN AND EAST EUROPEAN STUDIES. 1958. irreg. price varies. University of California Press, 2120 Berkeley Way, Berkeley, CA 94720. TEL 415-642-4247.

RUSSIAN ARCHIVAL SERIES. see *ETHNIC INTERESTS*

948   IC   ISSN 0558-1257
SAFN TIL SOEGU ISLANDS OG ISLENZKRA BOKMENTA. 1856. irreg. Kr.700. Islenzka Bokmenntafelag, Pingholtsstraeti 3, Reykjavik, Iceland. circ. 700.

SAGA OCH SED. see *FOLKLORE*

947   SZ   ISSN 0254-1521
SAMISDAT; Stimmen aus den "anderen Russland". 1972. irreg. price varies. Kuratorium Geistige Freiheit, Postfach 227, 3601 Thun, Switzerland. Ed. Udo Robe. circ. 2,000.
   Supersedes: Russischer Samisdat.

943.6   AU
SANCTA CRUX; Zeitschrift des Zisterzienserstiftes und der Philosophisch-Theologischen H ochschule. 1933. irreg. price varies. Stift Heiligenkreuz, 2532 Heiligenkreuz, Austria. Ed. P. Meinrad Tomann. bk. rev. circ. 1,000.

943.7   CS   ISSN 0577-3725
SBORNIK HISTORICKY. (Text in English, French, German and Russian) 1953. a. Academia Nakladatelstvi C S A V, Vodickova 40, 112 29 Prague 1, Czechoslovakia (Subscr. to: Artia, Ve Smeckach 30, 111 27 Prague 1, Czechoslovakia) Indexed: Hist.Abstr. CERDIC.

943.7   CS   ISSN 0231-6153
SBORNIK K DEJINAM 19 A 20 STOLETI. (Text in Czech) 1972. irreg. exchange basis only. Ustav Ceskoslovenskych a Svetovych Dejin CSAV, Vysehradska 49, 128 26 Prague 2, Czechoslovakia. Ed. Jurij Krizek.

943.7   CS   ISSN 0231-620X
SBORNIK K PROBLEMATICE DEJIN IMPERIALISMU. (Text in Czech, Russian and Slovak) 1972. irreg. exchange basis only. Ustav Ceskoslovenskych a Svetovych Dejin CSAV, Vysehradska 49, 128 26 Prague 2, Czechoslovakia. Ed. Karel Herman.

943.7   CS
SBORNIK PRACI HISTORICKYCH. (Text in Czech, German and Russian) 1954. irreg. Statni Pedagogicke Nakladatelstvi, Ostrovni 30, 113 01 Prague 1, Czechoslovakia (Subscr. to: Artia, Ve Smeckach 30, 111 27 Prague 1, Czechoslovakia) illus. Indexed: Hist.Abstr.
   Formerly (1954-1959): Olomouc. Vysoke Skoly Pedagogicke. Sbornik. Historie.

943.7   CS
SBORNIK PRACI VYCHODOCESKYCH ARCHIVU. 1970. irreg. Nakladatelstvi Kruh, Hradec Kralove, Czechoslovakia (Subscr. to: Artia, Ve Smeckach 30, 111 27 Prague 1, Czechoslovakia)

HISTORY — HISTORY OF EUROPE

943.7　　　　　CS
SBORNIK VLASTIVEDNYCH PRACI Z PODBLANNICKA. 1957. a. Statni Zemedelske Nakladatelstvi, Vaclavske Nam. 47, 113 78 Prague 1, Czechoslovakia (Subscr. to: Artia, Ve Smeckach 30, 111 27 Prague 1, Czechoslovakia) cum.index: vol.1-15, 1957-1974.

SCHATZKAMMER; der deutschen Sprache, Dichtung und Geschichte. see *HISTORY — History Of North And South America*

940　　　　　GW　　ISSN 0340-6490
SCHRIFTEN ZUR GEISTESGESCHICHTE DES OESTLICHEN EUROPA. 1967. irreg., vol. 16, 1983. price varies. Verlag Otto Harrassowitz, Taunusstr. 14, Postfach 2929, 6200 Wiesbaden 1, W. Germany (B.R.D.) Ed.Bd.

SCHRIFTEN ZUR PHILOSOPHIE UND IHRER GESCHICHTE. see *PHILOSOPHY*

940　320　322.4　　GW
SCHRIFTENREIHE DAS ANDERE DEUTSCHLAND. 1981. irreg. price varies. Donat & Temmen Verlag, Slevogtstr. 20, D-2800 Bremen, W. Germany (B.R.D.) Ed.Bd. circ. 2,000.

943　　　　　SZ　　ISSN 0080-7273
SCHWEIZERISCHE BEITRAEGE ZUR ALTERTUMSWISSENSCHAFT. (Text in French and German) 1942. irreg., no. 17, 1984. price varies. Friedrich Reinhardt Verlag, Missionsstr. 36, CH-4012 Basel, Switzerland (Dist. by: Albert J. Phiebig Books, Box 352, White Plains, NY 10602) Ed. Christoph Schaeublin. circ. 1,000.

930　　　　　SZ
SCHWEIZERISCHE GESELLSCHAFT FUER UR- UND FRUEHGESCHICHTE. JAHRBUCH. (Text in French, German and Italian) 1908. a. 90 Fr. ‡ Petersgraben 9-11, 4001 Basel, Switzerland. bk. rev. index. Indexed: Br.Archaeol.Abstr. Numis.Lit.

SCOTTISH LABOUR HISTORY SOCIETY. JOURNAL. see *BUSINESS AND ECONOMICS — Labor And Industrial Relations*

941　301　　　UK　　ISSN 0036-9411
SCOTTISH STUDIES. (Text in English; occasionally in Gaelic and Scots) 1957. a. £6($14) ‡ University of Edinburgh, School of Scottish Studies, 27 George Square, Edinburgh EH8 9LD, Scotland. Ed. Daphne J. Hamilton. bk. rev. illus. circ. 800. Indexed: Br.Hum.Ind. Curr.Cont. M.L.A. Arts & Hum.Cit.Ind. Br.Archaeol.Abstr. Ind.Bk.Rev.Hum.

941　　　　　CN
SCOTTISH TRADITION. 1968. a. Can.$15. Canadian Association for Scottish Studies, Department of History, University of Guelph, Guelph, Ont., Canada. TEL 519-824-4120. Eds. R.M. Sunter and Edward Cowan. bk. rev. circ. 250.
Incorporating: Colloquium on Scottish Studies. Proceedings (ISSN 0069-5823)

948　　　　　FI　　ISSN 0358-710X
SCRIPTA HISTORICA. (Text in English, Finnish, German and Swedish) 1967. irreg. Fmk.80. Oulun Historiaseura, PL 31, 90101 Oulu, Finland. TEL 981-220066. circ. 500.

944　840　　　UK　　ISSN 0265-1068
SEVENTEENTH CENTURY FRENCH STUDIES. 1979. a. £4. Society for Seventeenth Century French Studies, School of Modern Languages and European History, University of East Anglia, Norwich NR4 7TJ, England. Ed. C.N. Smith. bk. rev. circ. 300.
Formerly (until 1984): Society for Seventeenth Century French Studies. Newsletter (ISSN 0142-5080)

943.6　　　　　AU
SIMMERINGER MUSEUMSBLAETTER. 1977. irreg. Bezirksmuseum Simmering, Enkplatz 2, 1110 Vienna, Austria.

940　　　　　NE
SIR THOMAS BROWNE INSTITUUT. PUBLICATIONS. GENERAL SERIES AND SPECIAL SERIES. 1962. irreg. Leiden University Press, c/o E.J. Brill Publishers, Postbus 9000, 2300 PA Leiden, Netherlands.
Formerly: Sir Thomas Browne Instituut. Publications. General Series (ISSN 0080-9799)

940　　　　　NO　　ISSN 0080-9888
SJOEFARTSHISTORISK AARBOK/NORWEGIAN YEARBOOK OF MARITIME HISTORY. (Text in English and Norwegian; summaries in English) 1965. a. Kr.60. Bergens Sjoefartsmuseum - Bergen Maritime Museum, Box 2736, 5010 Bergen, Norway. Eds. Lauritz Pettersen, Atle Thowsen. adv. circ. 1,100. Indexed: Hist.Abstr. A.B.C.Pol.Sci.

948　　　　　DK　　ISSN 0108-397X
SKAEPPEN; aarsskrift for Herrested Sogn. 1982. a. Kr.20. Herrested Sogns Lokalhistoriske Arbejdsgruppe, c/o Poul Erik Steffansen, Odensevej 59, Herrested, 5853 Oerbaek, Denmark. illus. circ. 100.

948　　　　　DK　　ISSN 0108-0342
SKANDERBORG MUSEUM. AARSSKRIFT. no. 14, 1982. a. Kr.20. Skanderborg Museum, Adelgade 5, 8660 Skanderborg, Denmark. (Co-sponsor: Museumsforeningen for Skanderborg og Omegn.) Ed. Joergen Brinch. illus.
Formerly: Skvaet.

948　　　　　IC
SKIRNIR. 1827. a. Kr.900. Islenzka Bokmenntafelag Hid, Pingholtsstraeti 3, Reykjavik, Iceland. adv. bk. rev. cum.index. circ. 2,500. Indexed: M.L.A.
Formerly: Islenzk Sagnabloed.

948　　　　　DK　　ISSN 0106-2697
SKIVE-EGNENS JUL. 1978. a. Kr.35. Lokalhistorisk Forlag-Skiveegnen, Lyngbakken 13, Sdr. Thise, 7870 Roslev, Denmark. Ed. E. Steen Soerensen. adv. bk. rev. illus. circ. 3,000. Indexed: Hist.Abstr.
Formerly: Jul i Skive.

948　　　　　FI
SKOLHISTORISKT ARKIV; Uppsatser och Urkunder. (Text in Swedish) 1952. irreg. Ekenas Tryckeri Aktiebolags Foerlag, Stationsvagen 1, 10600 Eknas 60, Finland.

948　　　　　FI
SLAKT OCH HAVD (TERJARV) (Text in Swedish) 1961. irreg. Terjarv Hembygdsforening, Terjarv, Finland.

572　943.7　　CS　　ISSN 0081-0061
SLOVACI V ZAHRANICI. (Text in Slovak; summaries in English and Russian) 1971. a. price varies. Matica Slovenska, Mudronova 35, 036 52 Martin, Czechoslovakia. bk. rev.

947　　　　　CS　　ISSN 0081-007X
SLOVANSKE HISTORICKE STUDIE. (Text in Czech; summaries in English, French, German and Russian) 1955. irreg., vol.13, 1982. price varies. (Ceskoslovenska Akademie Ved) Academia, Publishing House of the Czechoslovak Academy of Sciences, Vodickova 40, 112 29 Prague 1, Czechoslovakia.

947　　　　　CS　　ISSN 0583-564X
SLOVANSKE STUDIE. vol. 17, 1976. irreg. fl.45. (Slovenska Akademia Vied, Udesk Sav) Veda, Publishing House of the Slovak Academy of Sciences, Klemensova 19, 814 30 Bratislava, Czechoslovakia (Distributor in Western countries: John Benjamins B.V., Amsteldijk 44, Amsterdam (Z.), Netherlands) Ed. J. Hroziencik.

SLOVENSKE BANSKE MUZEUM. ZBORNIK. see *MINES AND MINING INDUSTRY*

943.7　913　737　　CS
SLOVENSKE NARODNE MUZEUM. ZBORNIK. 1961. a. Osveta, Osloboditelov 21, 036 54 Martin, Czechoslovakia (Subscr. to: Slovart, Gottwaldovo Nam. 6, 805 32 Bratislava, Czechoslovakia) Indexed: Bull.Signal.
Formerly: Slovenske Narodne Muzeum. Historicky Sbornik.

943.7　　　　　CS　　ISSN 0139-5378
SLOVENSKE NARODNE MUZEUM. ZBORNIK ETNOGRAFIA. 1952. a. Osveta, Osloboditelov 21, 036 54 Martin, Czechoslovakia (Subscr. to: Slovart, Gottwaldovo Nam. 6, 805 32 Bratislava, Czechoslovakia) illus. cum.index: vol.1-8, 1952-67; vol.9-16, 1968-75.

945　　　　　IT　　ISSN 0081-0681
SOCIETA DI STUDI ROMAGNOLI. GUIDE. 1967. irreg., no.5, 1983. L.5000. c/o Biblioteca Malatestiana, 47023 Cesena, Italy. circ. controlled.

948　　　　　FI　　ISSN 0371-2885
SOCIETAS SCIENTIARUM FENNICA. AARSBOK VUOSIKIRJA. (Text in Finnish and Swedish) 1923. a. price varies. Finska Vetenskaps Societeten - Finnish Society of Sciences and Letters, Snellmaninkatu 9-11, 00170 Helsinki 17, Finland. Ed. Johan Chydenius. circ. 700. Indexed: Biol.Abstr. GeoRef.

SOCIETE ARCHEOLOGIQUE DE TOURAINE. MEMOIRES. see *ARCHAEOLOGY*

SOCIETE D'ARCHEOLOGIE, D'HISTOIRE ET DE FOLKLORE DE NIVELLES ET DU BRABANT WALLON. ANNALES. see *ARCHAEOLOGY*

944　　　　　FR
SOCIETE D'EMULATION DE MONTBELIARD. BULLETIN ET MEMOIRES. 1852. a. 120 F. Societe d'Emulation de Montbeliard, Musee Beurnier-Rossel, 8 place Saint-Martin, 25200 Montbeliard, France. Ed.Bd. circ. 700.
Formerly: Societe d'Emulation de Montbeliard. Memoires.
Local

944　　　　　FR　　ISSN 0081-0819
SOCIETE D'EMULATION HISTORIQUE ET LITTERAIRE D'ABBEVILLE. BULLETIN. 1888. a. 100 F.($10) Societe d'Emulation Historique et Litteraire d'Abbeville, Hotel de Ville, 80101 Abbeville, France. bk. rev. cum.index (at approx 4-5 yr. intervals) circ. 400.

944　　　　　FR　　ISSN 0081-0940
SOCIETE D'HISTOIRE DE FRANCE. ANNUAIRE. 1834. a. price varies. Editions Klincksieck, 11 rue de Lille, 75005 Paris, France. Ed. Michel Francois.

SOCIETE D'HISTOIRE ET D'ARCHEOLOGIE DE LA GOELE. BULLETIN D'INFORMATION. see *ARCHAEOLOGY*

944　　　　　FR
SOCIETE DES ANTIQUAIRES DE L'OUEST. MEMOIRES. 1834. irreg. price varies. Societe des Antiquaires de l'Ouest, Rue Paul Guillon, B.P. 179, 86004 Poitiers Cedex, France.
Local

944　　　　　FR
SOCIETE DES ANTIQUAIRES DE PICARDIE. MEMOIRES. 1838. irreg. price varies. Societe des Antiquaires de Picardie, Musee de Picardie, 48 rue de la Republique, 8000 Amiens, France. Indexed: Numis.Lit.

942　　　　　UI　　ISSN 0144-1973
SOCIETE GUERNESIAISE. REPORT AND TRANSACTIONS. (Text in English) 1882. a. membership. Societe Guernesiaise, Candie Gardens, St. Peter Port, Guernsey, Channel Islands. Ed. R Hocart. bk. rev. bibl. illus. index. circ. 1,200. Indexed: Br.Archaeol.Abstr.

944　　　　　FR
SOCIETE HISTORIQUE DE VILLIERS SUR MARNE ET DE LA BRIE FRANCAISE. REVUE.* 1968. a. 10 F. Centre Culturel du Belvedere, 94350 Villiers S/Marne, France.

949.2　　　　　NE　　ISSN 0085-6266
SOCIETE HISTORIQUE ET ARCHEOLOGIQUE DANS LE LIMBOURG. PUBLICATIONS. (Text in Dutch) 1864. a. fl.60. Limburgs Geschied- en Oudheidkundig Genootschap, Bogaardenstraat 43, Postbus 83, 6200 AB Maastricht, Netherlands. Ed.Bd. bk. rev. circ. 3,000.

944　　　　　FR
SOCIETE HISTORIQUE ET ARCHEOLOGIQUE DE PONTOISE, DU VAL D'OISE ET DU VEXIN. MEMOIRES. irreg. Societe Historique et Archeologique de Pontoise, du Val d'Oise et du Vexin, 43 rue de la Roche, Pontoise, France. illus.

944　　　　　FR
SOCIETE PHILOMATIQUE VOSGIENNE. BULLETIN. 1875. a. 150 F. Societe Philomatique Vosgienne, Bibliotheque Municipale, Rue St.-Charles, 88100 Saint-die, France. Ed. Albert Ronsin. adv. bk. rev. circ. 650.

HISTORY — HISTORY OF EUROPE

945 US ISSN 0081-1424
SOCIETY FOR ITALIAN HISTORICAL STUDIES. NEWSLETTER. 1963. a. free to members. ‡ Boston College, Society for Italian Historical Studies, Dept. of History, Chestnut Hill, MA 02167. TEL 617-969-0100. Ed. Alan Reinerman. circ. 350.

SOCIETY FOR LINCOLNSHIRE HISTORY AND ARCHAEOLOGY. ANNUAL REPORT AND STATEMENT OF ACCOUNTS. see *ARCHAEOLOGY*

947 407 US
SOCIETY FOR SLOVENE STUDIES. DOCUMENTATION SERIES. 1975. irreg. price varies. Society for Slovene Studies, 420 W. 118 St., New York, NY 10027. Ed. Rado L. Lencek. index. circ. 350.

942 UK ISSN 0265-1785
SOCIETY OF ANTIQUARIES OF NEWCASTLE UPON TYNE. MONOGRAPH SERIES. 1979. irreg. price varies. Society of Antiquaries of Newcastle Upon Tyne, The Black Gate, Newcastle upon Tyne, England. Ed. John Philipson. bk. rev.

942 913 UK ISSN 0263-3191
SOCIETY OF ANTIQUARIES OF SCOTLAND. MONOGRAPH SERIES. 1982. irreg. price varies. Society of Antiquaries of Scotland, Royal Museum of Scotland, Queen St., Edinburgh EH2 1JD, Scotland. Ed. Dr. Ian B.M. Ralston. Indexed: Br.Archaeol.Abstr.

942 UK ISSN 0081-1564
SOCIETY OF ANTIQUARIES OF SCOTLAND. PROCEEDINGS. 1851. a. £18 to non-members. Society of Antiquaries of Scotland, Royal Museum of Scotland, Queen Street, Edinburgh EH2 1JD, Scotland. Ed. Ian A.G. Shepherd. index. circ. 2,600. Indexed: Br.Archaeol.Abstr. Numis.Lit. RILA.

480 938 CY ISSN 0081-1580
SOCIETY OF CYPRIOT STUDIES. BULLETIN/ KYPRIAKAI SPOUDAI. (Text in Greek and other languages) 1937. a. $12 cyprus pounds 6. Society of Cypriot Studies, Box 1436, Nicosia, Cyprus. Ed. Theodore Papadopoullos. bk. rev. circ. 500. Indexed: Hist.Abstr. M.L.A. Amer.Hist.& Life.

948 DK ISSN 0085-6339
SOELLEROEDBOGEN. 1942. a. Kr.110. Historisk-Topografisk Selskab for Soelleroed Kommune, Byhistorisk Arkiv, Gl. Holtegaard, Attemosevej 170, 2840 Holte, Denmark. Ed. Niels Peter Stilling. circ. 1,600.

948 DK ISSN 0106-4452
SOENDERJYSKE ARBOEGER. 1889. a. Historisk Samfund for Soenderjylland, Haderslevvej 45, 6200 Abenra, Denmark. cum.index: 1889-1940.

948.5 SW ISSN 0349-0297
SOERMLANDSBYGDEN. 1932. a. Kr.60. Soedermanlands Hembygdsfoerbund, O. Kyrkogatan 48, S-611 33, Nykoeping, Sweden. Ed. R. Ryberg. adv. bk. rev. circ. 6,000.

940 GW
SOESTER BEITRAEGE. 1949. irreg. price varies. Verein fuer Geschichte und Heimatpflege Soest, Stadtarchiv, P.O. Box 525, Jakobistr. 13, D-4770 Soest, W. Germany (B.R.D.) bibl.

940 GW ISSN 0176-3946
SOESTER ZEITSCHRIFT. 1881. a. DM.20. Verein fuer Geschichte und Heimatpflege Soest, Stadtarchiv, P.O. Box 525, Jakobistr. 13, D-4770 Soest, W. Germany (B.R.D.) Indexed: Numis.Lit.

940 BU ISSN 0081-184X
SOFIISKI UNIVERSITET. FILOSOFSKI FAKULTET. GODISNIK/UNIVERSITE DE SOFIA. FACULTE DE PHILOSOPHIE. ANNUAIRE. (Summaries in various languages) vol. 67, 1973. price varies. Publishing House of the Bulgarian Academy of Sciences, Acad. G. Bonchev St., Bldg. 6, 1113 Sofia, Bulgaria. circ. 555.
Continues in part: Sofiiski Universitet. Filosofski-Istoriceski Fakultet. Godisnik.

948 355 FI ISSN 0357-816X
SOTAHISTORIALLINEN AIKAKAUSKIRJA. (Text in Finnish and Swedish, summaries in English) 1945. a. Fmk.50. Sotahistoriallinen Seura, Maurinkatu 1, 00170 Helsinki 17, Finland. Ed.Bd. circ. 1,000.

944 FR ISSN 0248-5516
SOURCES ET TRAVAUX D'HISTOIRE HAUT-PYRENEENNE. 1980. irreg. 70 Fr. Association Guillaume Mauran, Archives Departementales des Hautes-Pyrenees, Rue des Ursulines, 65000 Tarbes, France.

940 UK ISSN 0142-4688
SOUTHERN HISTORY. 1979. a. £12.50 to institutions; individuals £10. Southern History Society, c/o J.G. Rule, Ed., University of Southampton, Department of History, Southampton SO9 5NH, England. adv. bk. rev. circ. 450. (also avail. in microfiche) Indexed: Hist.Abstr. Br.Archaeol.Abstr.

940 100 NE
SOVIETICA. PUBLICATIONS AND MONOGRAPHS. 1959. irreg. price varies. (Universite de Fribourg, Institute of East-European Studies, SZ) D. Reidel Publishing Co., Box 17, 3300 AA Dordrecht, Netherlands (And 190 Old Derby St., Hingham, MA 02043) Ed.Bd.
Formed by the merger of: Sovietica. Publication (ISSN 0081-3206) & Sovietica. Monographs (ISSN 0081-3192)

946 GW ISSN 0342-1058
SPANISCHE FORSCHUNGEN DER GOERRESGESELLSCHAFT. REIHE 1: GESAMMELTE AUFSAETZE ZUR KULTURGESCHICHTE SPANIENS. 1928. irreg. price varies. (Goerres-Gesellschaft) Aschendorffsche Verlagsbuchhandlung, Soester Str. 13, 4400 Muenster, W. Germany (B.R.D.) Ed. Odilo Engels.

946 GW ISSN 0081-3494
SPANISCHE FORSCHUNGEN DER GOERRESGESELLSCHAFT. REIHE 2: MONOGRAPHIEN. 1931. irreg. price varies. (Goerres-Gesellschaft) Aschendorffsche Verlagsbuchhandlung, Soester Str. 13, 4400 Muenster, W. Germany (B.R.D.) Ed. Odilo Engels.

909.07 US
SPECULUM ANNIVERSARY MONOGRAPHS. 1977. irreg., no.11, 1985. price varies. Medieval Academy of America, 1430 Massachusetts Ave., Cambridge, MA 02138. TEL 617-491-1622.

940 296 IS
SPIEGEL LECTURES IN EUROPEAN JEWISH HISTORY. 1982. irreg. $5 per no. Tel Aviv University, School of Jewish Studies, Ramat-Aviv, Tel Aviv, Israel. Ed. Lloyd P. Gartner. circ. 1,500.

SRPSKI ETNOGRAFSKI ZBORNIK. NASELJA I POREKLO STANOVNISTVA. see *ANTHROPOLOGY*

SRPSKI ETNOGRAFSKI ZBORNIK. RASPRAVE I GRADJA. see *ANTHROPOLOGY*

SRPSKI ETNOGRAFSKI ZBORNIK. SRPSKE NARODNE UMOTVORINE. see *ANTHROPOLOGY*

SRPSKI ETNOGRAFSKI ZBORNIK. ZIVOT I OBICAJI NARODNI. see *ANTHROPOLOGY*

943.6 AU
STADTARCHIV KREMS. MITTEILUNGEN. 1961. irreg. price varies. Kulturamt der Stadt Krems, Koernermarkt 13, 3500 Krems an der Donau, Austria. Ed. Harry Kuehnel. bk. rev. circ. 400.

940 NE
HET STARING INSTITUUT. WERKEN. 1980. a. price varies. Walburg Pers, Zaadmarkt 84a-86, Box 222, 7200 AE Zutphen, Netherlands. TEL 05750-10522. (Co-sponsor: Het Staring Instituut)

949.5 CY
STASINOS. (Text in English and Greek) 1963. irreg. Syndesmos Hellenon Philologon Kyprou Stasinos, Stasinos, Pankyprion Oikonomikon Lykeion, Nicosia, Cyprus.

947 US
STATE UNIVERSITY OF NEW YORK. COLLEGE AT BUFFALO'S PROGRAM IN EAST EUROPEAN AND SLAVIC STUDIES. PUBLICATIONS. 1969. irreg. Hungarian Cultural Foundation, c/o J.M. Ertavy-Barath, Ed., Box 364, Stone Mountain, GA 30086.
Formerly: State University of New York, College at Buffalo. Program in Soviet and East Central European Studies. Publications (ISSN 0077-9385)

943.7 CS
STATNI ARCHIV V OPAVE. SBORNIK. 1969. irreg. Statni Archiv v Opava, Opava, Czechoslovakia (Subscr. to: Artia, Ve Smeckach 30, 111 27 Prague, Czechoslovakia) bk. rev. illus.

943.6 AU ISSN 0434-3883
STEIERMAERKISCHES LANDESARCHIV. MITTEILUNGEN. 1951. a. Steiermaerkisches Landesarchiv, Buergergasse 2-A, 8010 Graz, Austria. circ. 2,275. Indexed: Hist.Abstr. Amer.Hist.& Life.

943.6 AU ISSN 0490-9348
STEIRISCHER BURGENVEREIN. MITTEILUNGEN. 1951. a. Steirischer Burgenverein, Burgergasse 2A, 8010 Graz, Austria. bk. rev.

949.2 340 NE
STICHTING TOT UITGAVE DER BRONNEN VAN HET OUD-VADERLANDSCHE RECHT. 2 SERIES: WERKEN, AND VERSLAGEN EN MEDEDELINGEN. (Issued in two parts) 1885. irreg. fl.35. (Juridisch Instituut) Wlaburg Pers, Postbus 222, 7200 AE Zutphen, Netherlands. Ed. F.C.J. Ketelaar. circ. 500. Indexed: Hist.Abstr.
Formerly: Vereniging tot Uitgave der Bronnen van het oud Vaderlandsche Recht. Verslagen en Mededelingen.

940 NE
STICHTSE HISTORISCHE REEKS. 1975. a. price varies. Walburg Pers, Zaadmarkt 84a-86, Box 222, 7200 AE Zutphen, Netherlands. TEL 05750-10522. (Co-sponsor: Stichting Stichtse Historische Reeks)

060 GW ISSN 0342-0124
STIFTUNG PREUSSISCHE KULTURBESITZ. JAHRBUCH. 1962. a. price varies. Gebr. Mann Verlag, Lindenstr. 76, D-1000 Berlin 61, W. Germany (B.R.D.)

STILLE SCHAR. see *RELIGIONS AND THEOLOGY — Roman Catholic*

945 IT
STORIA E SOCIETA. 1976. irreg. (Istituto di Storia Contemporanea del Movimento Operaio e Contadino di Ferrera) Ricardo F. Levi Editore S.p.A., 1085-2 via Vaciglio, 41010 Modena, Italy.

945 IT
STORIA, LETTERATURA E ARTE NEL MEZZOGIORNO. irreg., no. 4, 1976. L.2000. Edizioni Dehoniane, Via Marechiaro 46, Naples, Italy. Ed. Fiorenzo F. Mastroianni.

945 IT
STORIADENTRO; rivista di studi su conegliano e il coneglianese. 1977. biennial. Comune, Piazza Beccaria-Biblioteca Civica, 31015 Conegliano, Italy. TEL 0438 35041.

940 IT
STUDI ETRUSCHI. 1927. a. price varies. Giorgio Bretschneider, Via Crescenzio 43, 00193 Rome, Italy. Eds. M. Pallottino, A. Neppi Modona.

945 IT ISSN 0081-6205
STUDI ROMAGNOLI. 1950. a. L.25000. Societa di Studi Romagnoli, c/o Biblioteca Malatestiana, 47023 Cesena, Italy. Indexed: Numis.Lit. RILA.

945 IT ISSN 0081-6213
STUDI ROMAGNOLI. ESTRATTI DI SEZIONE. 1951. irreg. price varies. Societa di Studi Romagnoli, c/o Biblioteca Malatestiana, 47023 Cesena, Italy.

945 IT ISSN 0081-6221
STUDI ROMAGNOLI. QUADERNI. 1962. irreg., no.13, 1984. price varies. Societa di Studi Romagnoli, c/o Biblioteca Malatestiana, 47023 Cesena, Italy.

945 IT ISSN 0081-6248
STUDI SECENTESCHI. 1960. a. price varies. Casa Editrice Leo S. Olschki, Casella Postale 66, 50100 Florence, Italy. Eds. Uberto Limentani, Martino Capucci. bk. rev. index. circ. 1,000. Indexed: M.L.A. RILA.

945 IT ISSN 0081-6264
STUDI VENEZIANI. 1959. a. price varies.
(Fondazione Giorgio Cini) Giardini Editori e
Stampatori, Via Santa Bibbiana 28, 56100 Pisa,
Italy. Ed. A. Pertusi. bk. rev. circ. 1,000. Indexed:
Numis.Lit.
 Continues: Societa e Dello Stato Veneziano.
Istituto di Storia. Bollettino.

947 BU
STUDIA BALCANICA. (Text in English, French,
German and Russian) irreg., no.3, 1970. price
varies. Publishing House of the Bulgarian Academy
of Sciences, Acad. G. Boncev St., Bldg. 6, 1113
Sofia, Bulgaria.

STUDIA CELTICA. see *LINGUISTICS*

STUDIA HIBERNICA. see *LITERATURE*

947.1 FI ISSN 0081-6493
STUDIA HISTORICA. (Text in English, French or
German) 1959. irreg., no.21, 1986. Fmk.80. Suomen
Historiallinen Seura - Finnish Historical Society,
Vuorikatu 6 A 4, 00100 Helsinki 10, Finland. circ.
350.

945 IT ISSN 0081-6507
STUDIA HISTORICA. 1964. irreg., no. 127, 1981.
price varies. Erma di "Bretschneider", Via
Cassiodoro, 19, 00193 Rome, Italy.

947.1 FI ISSN 0081-6523
STUDIA HISTORICA JYVASKYLAENSIA. (Text in
English, Finnish, French, German and Swedish;
summaries in English and German) 1962. irreg.
price varies. Jyvaskylan Yliopisto - University of
Jyvaskyla, Seminaarinkatu 15, 40100 Jyvaskyla 10,
Finland. Ed. Mauno Jokipii. circ. 450.

940 FI ISSN 0356-8199
STUDIA HISTORICA SEPTENTRIONALIA. (Text
in English) 1978. a. Fmk.90($14) Pohjois-Suomen
Historiallinen Yhdistys, Oulun Yliopisto, Historian
Laitos - Historical Association of Northern Finland,
Postilokero 191, 90101 Oulu, Finland. Ed. Kyoesti
Julku.

918 930 PL ISSN 0301-6420
STUDIA HISTORICA SLAVO-GERMANICA. (Text
in German and Polish; summaries in German) 1973.
irreg., vol. 5, 1976. price varies. Adam Mickiewicz
University Press, Marchlewskiego 128, 61-874
Poznan, Poland. Ed. Antoni Czubinski. bk. rev. bibl.

943.7 CS
STUDIA HISTORICA SLOVACA. (Text in English,
French, German and Russian) 1963. a. Veda
Vydavatel'stvo Slovenskej Akademie Vied,
Klemensova 19, 895 30 Bratislava, Czechoslovakia
(Subscr. to: Slovart, Gottwaldovo Nam. 6, 805 32
Bratislava, Czechoslovakia) bk. rev. Indexed:
Hist.Abstr.

940 SW ISSN 0081-6531
STUDIA HISTORICA UPSALIENSIA. (Subseries of
Acta Universitatis Upsala) (Text in French, English,
German, Norwegian, Swedish; summaries in
English, French and German) 1960. irreg., vol. 103,
1978. price varies. (Uppsala Universitet, Historiska
Institutionen) Almqvist & Wiksell International, Box
62, S-101 20 Stockholm, Sweden. Ed.Bd. index.

943.8 PL ISSN 0081-654X
STUDIA I MATERIALY DO DZIEJOW
WIELKOPOLSKI I POMORZA. 1955. irreg.,
vol.15, 1984. price varies. (Polskie Towarzystwo
Historyczne, Oddzial w Poznaniu) Panstwowe
Wydawnictwo Naukowe, Ul. Miodowa 10, 00-251
Warsaw, Poland (Dist. by: Ars Polona, Krakowskie
Przedmiescie 7, 00-068 Warsaw, Poland) Ed. Jerzy
Topolski. bk. rev. illus. circ. 300.

STUDIA I MATERIALY DO HISTORII
WOJSKOWOSCI. see *MILITARY*

STUDIA I MATERIALY Z DZIEJOW NAUKI
POLSKIEJ. SERIA A. HISTORIA NAUK
SPOLECZNYCH. see *SOCIAL SCIENCES:
COMPREHENSIVE WORKS*

914.38 PL ISSN 0081-6752
STUDIA NAD ZAGADNIENIAMI
GOSPODARCZYMI I SPOLECZNYMI ZIEM
ZACHODNICH. 1960. irreg. price varies. Instytut
Zachodni, Stary Rynek 78/79, 61-772 Poznan,
Poland (Dist. by Ars Polona-Ruch, Krakowskie
Przedmiescie 7, Warsaw, Poland)

949.7 US ISSN 0585-5543
STUDIA SLOVENICA. 1958. irreg., no. 15, 1983.
Studia Slovenica, Box 232, New York, NY 10032
TEL 212-927-4246. (And Box 4531, Washington,
DC 20017) Ed. John A. Arnez.

949.7 US ISSN 0081-6922
STUDIA SLOVENICA. SPECIAL SERIES. 1966.
irreg., no. 4, 1984. Studia Slovenica, P. O. Box 232,
New York, NY 10032 TEL 212-927-4246. (and P.
O. Box 4531, Washington, D. C. 20017) Ed. John
A. Arnez.

947 PL ISSN 0081-7082
STUDIA Z DZIEJOW ZSRR I EUROPY
SRODKOWEJ. (Text in Polish; summaries in
English and Russian) 1966. a. price varies. (Polska
Akademia Nauk, Instytut Historii) Ossolineum,
Publishing House of the Polish Academy of
Sciences, Rynek 9, Wroclaw, Poland (Dist. by: Ars
Polona-Ruch, Krakowskie Przedmiescie 7, Warsaw,
Poland) Ed. P. Lossowski. bk. rev. circ. 700.

943.8 PL ISSN 0081-7147
STUDIA ZRODLOZNAWCZE. (Text in Polish;
summaries in English, French, German, Polish,
Russian) 1957. irreg., vol.28, 1983. price varies.
(Polska Akademia Nauk, Instytut Historii)
Panstwowe Wydawnictwo Naukowe, Ul. Miodowa
10, 00-251 Warsaw, Poland (Dist. by: Ars Polona,
Krakowskie Przedmiescie, 00-068 Warsaw, Poland)
Ed. A. Gieysztor. bk. rev. illus. circ. 440. Indexed:
Numis.Lit.

943.7 CS
STUDIE O RUKOPISECH. (Text in Czech, German
and Latin) 1962. a. Ustredni Archiv C S A V,
Karlova 2, Prague 1, Czechoslovakia. bibl. Indexed:
CERDIC.

STUDIE Z DEJIN HORNICTVI. see *MINES AND
MINING INDUSTRY*

940 AU
STUDIEN UND QUELLEN ZUR
OESTERREICHISCHEN ZEITGESCHICHTE.
1978. irreg. (Wissenschaftliche Kommission zur
Erforschung der Geschichte der Republik
Oesterreich) Verlag fuer Geschichte und Politik,
Neulinggasse 26, A-1030 Vienna, Austria. Eds.
Rudolf Neck, Isabella Ackerl.

940 NE ISSN 0585-5837
STUDIEN UND TEXTE ZUR
GEISTESGESCHICHTE DES MITTELALTERS.
(Text in English and German) 1950. irreg., vol.16,
1984. price varies. E. J. Brill, P.O. Box 9000, 2300
PA Leiden, Netherlands.

940 GW ISSN 0081-7252
STUDIEN ZUR EUROPAEISCHEN GESCHICHTE.
1955. irreg. price varies. Colloquium Verlag, Unter
den Eichen 93, 1000 Berlin 45, W. Germany
(B.R.D.) circ. 1,000.

940 NE ISSN 0081-7317
STUDIEN ZUR GESCHICHTE OSTEUROPAS/
STUDIES IN EAST EUROPEAN HISTORY.
1954. irreg., vol. 22, 1981. price varies. E. J. Brill,
P.O. Box 9000, 2300 PA Leiden, Netherlands (Dist.
in U.S. by: Humanities Press, Inc., 171 First Ave.,
Atlantic Highlands, NJ 07716)

942 UK ISSN 0585-6515
STUDIES IN ANGLESEY HISTORY. 1966. irreg.
(approx. biennial) price varies. Anglesey Antiquarian
Society and Field Club, c/o Hon. Secretary, 1
Fronheulog, Tregarth, Bangor, Gwynedd, Wales. Ed.
Helen Ramage. bk. rev.

940 US
STUDIES IN BRITISH HISTORY. 1986. irreg., vol.5,
1987. $39.95 per no. Edwin Mellen Press, Box 450,
Lewiston, NY 14092.

940 GW ISSN 0081-7910
STUDIES IN EUROPEAN HISTORY. 1964. irreg.
price varies. Walter de Gruyter & Co., Mouton
Publishers, Postfach 110240, D-1000 Berlin 11, W.
Germany (B.R.D.) (U.S. addr: Mouton Publishers,
division of Walter de Gruyter, Inc., 200 Saw Mill
River Road, Hawthorne, NY 10532)

STUDIES IN GERMAN THOUGHT AND
HISTORY. see *ETHNIC INTERESTS*

940.1 US ISSN 0081-8224
STUDIES IN MEDIEVAL AND RENAISSANCE
HISTORY. (Text in English and French) 1963; N.S.
1978. a. $42.50. A M S Press, Inc., 56 E. 13th St.,
New York, NY 10003. TEL 212-777-4700. Eds.
J.A.S. Evans, R.W. Unger. index. (back issues avail.)

940 US ISSN 0098-275X
STUDIES IN MODERN EUROPEAN HISTORY
AND CULTURE. 1975. a. $9. Institute for the
Study of Nineteenth Century Europe, 188 Lawton
Rd., Riverside, IL 60546. bk. rev. circ. 500. (also
avail. in microform from UMI; reprint service avail.
from UMI) Indexed: Hist.Abstr.

940 UK
STUDIES IN RUSSIAN AND EAST EUROPEAN
HISTORY. irreg. price varies. (University of
London, School of Slavonic and East European
Studies) Macmillan Press Ltd., 4 Little Essex St.,
London WC2R 3LF, England.

940 UK ISSN 0141-030X
STUDIES IN WELSH HISTORY. 1977. irreg. price
varies. (Board of Celtic Studies) University of Wales
Press, 6 Gwennyth St., Cathays, Cardiff CF2 4YD,
Wales. Ed.Bd.

940.53 320 PL ISSN 0137-1126
STUDIES ON FASCISM AND HITLERITE
CRIMES. (Text in Polish; summaries in French,
German) 1974. a. 400 Zl. University of Wroclaw,
Faculty of Law, Ul. Uniwersytecka 22/26, 50-145
Wroclaw, Poland (Subscr. addr.: University of
Wroclaw, Ul. Kuznicza 35, Poland) (tabloid format)

STUDIES ON VOLTAIRE AND THE
EIGHTEENTH CENTURY. see *LITERATURE*

949 RM
STUDII SI ARTICOLE DE ISTORIE. irreg.
Societatea de Stiinte Istorice din Republica
Socialista Romania, Bd. Republicii Nr. 55,
Bucharest, Romania. illus.
 Formerly: Societatea de Stiinte Istorice si
Filologice Din R.P.R. Studii si Articole de Istorie.

940 RM
STUDII SI MATERIALE DE ISTORIE MEDIE.
(Text in Rumanian; summaries in English, French,
German, Russian) 1956. irreg., vol.9, 1978.
(Academia de Stiinte Sociale si Politice) Editura
Academiei Republicii Socialiste Rumania, Calea
Victoriei 125, 79717 Bucharest, Rumania (Subscr.
to: ARTEXIM, Export-Import Presa, Str. Piata
Scinteii nr.1, P.O. Box 33-16, 70055 Bucharest,
Rumania) adv. bk. rev. circ. 800. Indexed:
Numis.Lit.

940 RM
STUDII SI MATERIALE DE ISTORIE MODERNA.
(Text in Rumanian; summaries in French) 1970.
irreg., vol.7, 1983. (Academia de Stiinte Sociale si
Politice, Institutul de Istorie "N. Iorga") Editura
Academiei Republicii Socialiste Rumania, Calea
Victoriei 125, 79717 Bucharest, Rumania (Subscr.
to: ARTEXIM, Export-Import Presa, Str. Piata
Scinteii nr.1, P.O. Box 33-16, 70055 Bucharest,
Rumania) Eds. N. Adaniloaie, D. Berindei. adv. bk.
rev.

940 800 AT ISSN 0311-2233
STUDIUM. 1972. irreg. Aus.$3 for non-members.
Sydney Medieval and Renaissance Group, History
Department, University of Sydney, Sydney, NSW
2006, Australia. Eds. J.O. Ward, L.S. Davidson.
adv. bk. rev. circ. 200.

940 PL ISSN 0081-8941
STUDIUM NIEMCOZNAWCZE. (Text in Polish;
summaries in English or Russian) 1946. irreg., vol.
26, 1975. price varies. Instytut Zachodni, Stary
Rynek 78/79, 61-772 Poznan, Poland (Dist. by Ars
Polona-Ruch, Krakowskie Przedmiescie 7, Warsaw,
Poland) Ed. Maria Morkowska. circ. 1,750.

947 890 UK
STUDY GROUP ON EIGHTEENTH-CENTURY
RUSSIA. NEWSLETTER. 1973. a. £2.50($5) to
individuals; £5($10) to institutions. Study Group on
Eighteenth-Century Russia, c/o Prof. A.G. Cross,
Ed., Department of Slavonic Studies, University of
Cambridge, Sidgwick Ave., Cambridge CB3 9DA,
England. bk. rev. bibl. circ. 200.

HISTORY — HISTORY OF EUROPE

940   CN   ISSN 0316-0769
SUBSIDIA MEDIAEVALIA. 1972. irreg. price varies. Pontifical Institute of Mediaeval Studies, 59 Queen's Park Crescent E., Toronto, Ont. M5S 2C4, Canada. TEL 416-926-7144. circ. 600.

943.7   GW   ISSN 0081-9077
SUEDOST-FORSCHUNGEN; Internationale Zeitschrift fuer Geschichte, Kultur und Landeskunde Suedosteuropas. (Text in English, French and German) 1936. a. DM.95. Suedost-Institut, Guellstr. 7, 8000 Munich 2, W. Germany (B.R.D.) Ed. Mathias Bernath. bk. rev. Indexed: M.L.A. Numis.Lit.

940   GW
SUEDOSTDEUTSCHE HISTORISCHE KOMMISSION. BUCHREIHE. 1958. irreg. price varies. R. Oldenbourg Verlag GmbH, Rosenheimer Str. 145, 8000 Munich 80, W. Germany (B.R.D.) Ed. Adam Wandruszka.

940 398   GW   ISSN 0081-9085
SUEDOSTDEUTSCHES ARCHIV. 1958. a. DM.40. (Suedostdeutsche Historische Kommission) R. Oldenbourg Verlag GmbH, Rosenheimer Str. 145, 8000 Munich 80, W. Germany (B.R.D.) Ed. Adam Wandruszka, Felix v. Schroeder. Indexed: Numis.Lit.

943 800   GW   ISSN 0081-9093
SUEDOSTDEUTSCHES KULTURWERK, MUNICH. KLEINE SUEDOSTREIHE. 1957. irreg. price varies. Suedostdeutsches Kulturwerk, Guellstr. 7, 8000 Munich 2, W. Germany (B.R.D.)

943 831 700   GW   ISSN 0081-9107
SUEDOSTDEUTSCHES KULTURWERK, MUNICH. SCHRIFTENREIHEN. REIHE A. KULTUR UND DICHTUNG. 1953. irreg. price varies. Suedostdeutsches Kulturwerk, Guellstr. 7, 8000 Munich 2, W. Germany (B.R.D.)

943 830   GW   ISSN 0081-9115
SUEDOSTDEUTSCHES KULTURWERK, MUNICH. SCHRIFTENREIHEN. REIHE B. WISSENSCHAFTLICHE ARBEITEN. 1954. irreg. price varies. Suedostdeutsches Kulturwerk, Guellstr. 7, 8000 Munich 2, W. Germany (B.R.D.)

940 800   GW   ISSN 0081-9123
SUEDOSTDEUTSCHES KULTURWERK, MUNICH. SCHRIFTENREIHEN. REIHE C. ERINNERUNGEN UND QUELLEN. 1958. irreg. price varies. Suedostdeutsches Kulturwerk, Guellstr. 7, 8000 Munich 2, W. Germany (B.R.D.)

940   GW   ISSN 0081-914X
SUEDOSTEUROPA - JAHRBUCH. 1957. irreg., vol.16, 1986. price varies. Suedosteuropa-Gesellschaft e.V., Widenmayerstr. 49, 8000 Munich 22, W. Germany (B.R.D.) Indexed: RILA.

940   GW   ISSN 0081-9166
SUEDOSTEUROPA - STUDIEN. 1962. irreg.,no.37, 1984. price varies. Suedosteuropa-Gesellschaft e.V., Widenmayerstr. 49, 8000 Munich 22, W. Germany (B.R.D.)

940   GW
SUEDOSTEUROPAEISCHE ARBEITEN. no.13, 1937. irreg., vol.83, 1986. price varies. (Suedost-Institut) R. Oldenbourg Verlag GmbH, Rosenheimer Str. 145, 8000 Munich 80, W. Germany (B.R.D.) Ed. M. Bernath.

SUFFOLK INSTITUTE OF ARCHAEOLOGY AND HISTORY. PROCEEDINGS. see ARCHAEOLOGY

947.1   FI   ISSN 0081-9425
SUOMEN HISTORIAN LAEHTEITAE/SOURCE MATERIAL OF FINNISH HISTORY. (Text in Finnish or Swedish) 1936. irreg., no.9, 1985. price varies. Suomen Historiallinen Seura - Finnish Historical Society, Vuorikatu 6 A 4, 00100 Helsinki 10, Finland. circ. 342.

SVENSKA. RIKSARKIVET. MEDDELANDEN. see LIBRARY AND INFORMATION SCIENCES

948   FI
SVENSKA FOLKSKOLANS VAENNERS KALENDER. (Text in Swedish) 1886. a. Fmk.50. Svenska Folkskolans Vaenner, Annegatan 12, 00120 Helsinki 12, Finland. adv. circ. 12,000.

948.5   SW
SVENSKA HISTORISKA FOERENINGEN. SKRIFTER. irreg., no. 8, 1978. price varies. Almqvist & Wiksell International, Box 62, S-101 20 Stockholm, Sweden.

948.9   DK   ISSN 0900-2103
SYDTHY AARBOG. 1984. a. Kr.60. Egnshistorisk Forening for Sydthy, c/o Elly Mardahl, Burhoejgaardvej 2, Boddum, 7760 Hurup, Denmark.

943.8   UK   ISSN 0085-4956
TEKI HISTORYCZNE. (Text in Polish; summaries in English) 1947. a. Polish Historical Society in Great Britain, 20 Princes Gate, London SW7 1QA, England.

943   IS
TEL AVIV UNIVERSITY. INSTITUT FUER DEUTSCHE GESCHICHTE. JAHRBUCH. (Text in German; summaries in Hebrew) 1972. a. $17. Tel-Aviv University, Institute for German History, Ramat Aviv, Tel Aviv 69 978, Israel. Ed. Walter Grab. bk. rev. circ. 1,200. Indexed: Hist.Abstr.

948   FI
TELJAN TANHUVILTA. 1964. irreg. Kokemaki-Seura, Esko Pertola, 32800 Kokemaki, Finland.

946   SP
TEMAS DE HISTORIA Y POLITICA CONTEMPORANEAS. 1977. irreg. Ediciones Peninsula, Provenza 278, Barcelona 8, Spain.

940.5472   CS
TEREZINSKE LISTY. (Text in Czech; summaries in English, German and Russian) 1970. a. 10 Kcs. (Pamatnik Terezin) Severoceske Nakladatelstvi, P.O. Box 134, Velka hradebni 33, 400 11 Usti nad Labem, Czechoslovakia. Ed. Oldrich Skrbel. bk. rev. illus. circ. 1,000.

945   IT
TESTI MEDIEVALI DI INTERESSE DANTESCO. 1977. irreg., vol. 2, 1978. price varies. (Istituto Dantesco Europeo) Casa Editrice Leo S. Olschki, Casella Postale 66, 50100 Florence, Italy. Ed.Bd.

TEXTS AND STUDIES IN THE HISTORY OF MEDIAEVAL EDUCATION. see EDUCATION

948   DK   ISSN 0107-2676
THEMATA. 1980. irreg. free. Aarhus Universitet, Institut for Oldtids-og Middelalderforskning, Bygn. 323, 800 Aarhus C, Denmark. Ed. Soeren Soerensen. bk. rev. circ. 1,000.

944   US
THIRD REPUBLIC/TROISIEME REPUBLIQUE. (Text in English and French) 1976. irreg. $9. c/o William Logue, Ed., Northern Illinois University, Department of History, Dekalb, IL 60115. TEL 815-753-1000. Ed. William Logue. circ. 110. (microfiche; also avail. in microfiche) Indexed: Hist.Abstr.

940   NE
THORBECKE-COLLEGES. 1975. irreg., vol. 10, 1985. price varies. Leiden University Press, c/o E.J. Brill Publishers, Postbus 9000, 2300 PA Leiden, Netherlands.

THOROTON SOCIETY OF NOTTINGHAMSHIRE. TRANSACTIONS. see ARCHAEOLOGY

947   RM
TIBISCUS. SERIA ISTORIE. (Text in Rumanian: summaries in German) a. Muzeul Banatului, Piata Huniade Nr. 1, Timisoara, Rumania.

948   FI
TIEDE JA ASE. 1933. a. Fmk.55. Suomen Sotatieteellinen Seura ry, Sotatieteen Laitos, Box 223, 00171 Helsinki 17, Finland. circ. 1,250.

940.53 296   FI
TIKUFAT HASHOAH. 1979. irreg. Haifa University, Holocaust Research Center, Hacarmel, Haifa 31 999, Israel.

943.6   AU
TIROLER GESCHICHTSQUELLEN. 1976. irreg., 2-3/yr. price varies. Tiroler Landesarchiv, Herrengasse, A-6010 Innsbruck, Austria. Ed. Fridolin Doerrer.

943.6   AU
TIROLER HEIMAT; Jahrbuch fuer Geschichte und Volkskunde. 1920. a. Universitaetsverlag Wagner, Andreas-Hofer-Str. 13, Postfach 165, A-6020 Innsbruck, Austria. Eds. Josef Riedmann, Fridolin Dorrer. bk. rev. circ. 500.

943.6   AU
TIROLER LANDESARCHIV. VEROEFFENTLICHUNGEN. 1972. irreg. price varies. Tiroler Landesarchiv, Herrengasse 1, A-6010 Innsbruck, Austria. Ed. Fridolin Doerrer.

943.6   AU
TIROLER ORTSCHRONIKEN. 1973. irreg., 2-3/yr. price varies. Tiroler Landesarchiv, Herrengasse 1, A-6010 Innsbruck, Austria. Ed. Fridolin Doerrer.

948   FI
TORNIONLAAKSON VUOSIKIRJA. 1963. a. Tornionlaakson Kotiseututoimikunta, Vesaisenkatu 4 B, 95400 Tornio, Finland.

TORONTO MEDIAEVAL LATIN TEXTS. see LITERATURE

942 820   CN
TORONTO OLD ENGLISH SERIES. 1970. irreg. price varies. University of Toronto Press, Front Campus, Toronto, Ont. M5S 1A6, Canada TEL 613-667-7791. (U.S. address: 33 E. Tupper St., Buffalo, NY 14203) Ed. Roberta Frank.

948   FI
TOTTO. 1952. irreg. Kotiseutuyhdistys Rovaniemen Totto, Ylikyla, 96100 Rovaniemi 10, Finland. cum.index 1952-1968.

TOURING IN FROM SALISBURY. see TRAVEL AND TOURISM

940   PL   ISSN 0082-5506
TOWARZYSTWO NAUKOWE W TORUNIU. FONTES. (Text in Polish; summaries in English, German) 1897. irreg., vol.69, 1980. price varies. (Towarzystwo Naukowe w Toruniu) Panstwowe Wydawnictwo Naukowe, Miodowa 10, 00-251 Warsaw, Poland (Dist. by: Ars Polona, Krakowskie Przedmiescie 7, 00-068 Warsaw, Poland) Ed. Artur Hutnikiewicz.

940   US   ISSN 0362-1529
TRADITIO; studies in ancient and medieval history, thought, and religion. 1943. a. $34. Fordham University Press, University Box L, Bronx, NY 10458-5172. TEL 212-579-2319. circ. 1,000. (back issues avail.) Indexed: Curr.Cont. M.L.A. Arts & Hum.Cit.Ind. CERDIC. New Test.Abstr. Rel.Ind.One.

940 800 900   SZ   ISSN 0082-6081
TRAVAUX D'HUMANISME ET RENAISSANCE. irreg., no.215, 1986. price varies. Librarie Droz, 11, rue Massot, 1211 Geneva 12, Switzerland. circ. 1, 000.

948   FI   ISSN 0085-7440
TURUN HISTORIALLINEN ARKISTO. Variant title: Turun Historiallisen Yhdistyksen Julkaisuja. 1924. a. price varies. Turun Historiallinen Yhdistys, Turun Yliopisto, SF-20500 Turku 50, Finland. Ed. Eero Kuparinen. circ. 600. Indexed: Hist.Abstr.

948   FI
TURUN YLIOPPILAS. 1929. irreg. Turun Yliopiston Ylioppilaskunta, Rehtorinpellontie 4, 20500 Turku 50, Finland.

940   BE
TYPOLOGIE DES SOURCES DU MOYEN AGE OCCIDENTAL. 1972. irreg., 3-7/yr. (Institut d'Etudes Medievales U.C.L.) N.V. Brepols I.G.P., Rue Baron Francois du Four 8, B-2300 Turnhout, Belgium. Ed.Bd.

947   US
U C I S SERIES IN RUSSIAN & EAST EUROPEAN STUDIES. 1977. irreg. University of Pittsburgh Press, 127 N. Bellefield Ave., Ruskin Hall, Pittsburgh, PA 15260. TEL 412-624-4110.

943.7 373.246   CS
UCITELSKE VZDELANI. irreg. Ustav pro Ucitelske Vzdelani Univerista Karlova, Ovocny Trh. 5, 116 36 Prague 1, Czechoslovakia. charts. illus. Indexed: Hist.Abstr.

HISTORY — HISTORY OF EUROPE

940   UK   ISSN 0082-7371
ULSTER YEAR BOOK. a. price varies. H.M.S.O. (N. Ireland), 80 Chichester Street, Belfast BT1 4JY, Northern Ireland. (reprint service avail. from UMI)

943.91   GW   ISSN 0082-755X
UNGARN - JAHRBUCH; Zeitschrift fuer die Kunde Ungarns und Verwandte Gebiete. 1969. a. DM.80. (Ungarisches Institut) Verlag Dr. Rudolf Trofenik, Elisbethstr. 18, 8000 Munich 40, W. Germany (B.R.D.) Ed.Bd. bk. rev.

UNITARIAN HISTORICAL SOCIETY, LONDON. TRANSACTIONS. see *RELIGIONS AND THEOLOGY — Protestant*

940   US   ISSN 0083-0070
U.S. DEPARTMENT OF STATE. EUROPEAN AND BRITISH COMMONWEALTH SERIES. 1948. irreg. price varies. U.S. Department of State, Bureau of Public Affairs, 2201 C St. N.W., Washington, DC 20520 TEL 202-632-1394. (Orders to Supt. of Documents, Washington, DC 20402)

944   FR
UNIVERS DE LA FRANCE ET DES PAYS FRANCOPHONES. vol. 44, 1979. irreg. Editions Edouard Privat, 14 rue des Arts, 31000 Toulouse, France. Dir. Philippe Wolff.

946   SP
UNIVERSIDAD DE LA LAGUNA. COLECCION ESTUDIOS DE HISTORIA. no. 2, 1976. irreg. Universidad de la Laguna, Secretariado de Publicaciones, Laguna, Canary Islands, Spain.

946   SP   ISSN 0212-6559
UNIVERSIDAD DE MURCIA. ANALES DE HISTORIA CONTEMPORANEA. 1982. a. ($1100) Universidad de Murcia, Secretariado de Publicaciones e Intercambio Cientifico, Santo Cristo, 1, 30001 Murcia, Spain. TEL 968 24 92 00.

946 913   SP
UNIVERSIDAD DE MURCIA. ANALES DE PREHISTORIA Y ARQUEOLOGIA. 1985. a. ($1300) Universidad de Murcia, Secretariado de Publicaciones e Intercambio Cientifico, Santo Cristo, 1, 30001 Murcia, Spain. TEL 968 24 92 00.

946   SP   ISSN 0213-5477
UNIVERSIDAD DE MURCIA. CONTRASTES: REVISTA DE HISTORIA MODERNA. 1985. a. ($1100) Universidad de Murcia, Secretariado de Publicaciones e Intercambio Cientifico, Santo Cristo, 1, 30001 Murcia, Spain. TEL 968 24 92 00.

UNIVERSIDAD DE MURCIA. IMAFRONTE. DEPARTMENTO DE HISTORIA DEL ARTE. see *ART*

946   SP   ISSN 0210-4903
UNIVERSIDAD DE MURCIA. MISCELANEA MEDIEVAL MURICIANA. 1973. irreg., vol.13, 1986. ($1000) Universidad de Murcia, Secretariado de Publicaciones e Intercambio Cientifico, Santo Cristo, 1, 30001 Murcia, Spain. TEL 968 24 92 00.

940   SP
UNIVERSIDAD DE NAVARRA. DOCUMENTOS MEDIEVALES. 1965. irreg., no.2, 1965. price varies. (Departamento de Historia Medieval) Ediciones Universidad de Navarra, S.A., Apdo. 396, 31080 Pamplona, Spain.

940   SP
UNIVERSIDAD DE OVIEDO. CENTRO DE ESTUDIOS DEL SIGLO XVIII. BOLETIN. 1973. irreg. $5. Universidad de Oviedo, Centro de Estudios del Siglo XVIII, Calle San Francisco, Oviedo, Spain.

900   IT
UNIVERSITA DEGLI STUDI DI GENOVA. ISTITUTO DI MEDIEVISTICA. COLLANA STORICA DI FONTI E STUDI. (Text in Enlgish, French, German, Italian, Portuguese, Spanish) 1958. irreg. price varies. Universita degli Studi di Genova, Istituto di Medievistica, Via Lomellini 8, 16124 Genoa, Italy (Dist. by: Libreria Bozzi, via Cairoli 2, Genoa, Italy) Ed. Geo Pistarino. circ. 400.
Formerly: Universita degli Studi di Genova. Istituto di Paleografia e Storia Medievale. Collana Storica di Fonti e Studi (ISSN 0072-0860)

945   IT   ISSN 0078-771X
UNIVERSITA DEGLI STUDI DI PADOVA. CENTRO PER LA STORIA DELLA TRADIZIONE ARTISTOTELICA NEL VENETO. SAGGI E TESTI. 1961. irreg., no.20, 1983. price varies. Editrice Antenore, Via G. Rusca 15, 35100 Padua, Italy.

943.7   CS   ISSN 0556-1183
UNIVERSITA KARLOVA. PEDAGOGICKY FAKULTA. SBORNIK. HISTORIE. (Text in Czech, German and Russian) 1966. a. Universita Karlova, (Subscr. to: Artia, Ve Smeckach 30, 111 27 Prague 1, Czechoslovakia) Indexed: Hist.Abstr.

943.7   CS
UNIVERSITA PALACKEHO OLOMOUC. PEDAGOGICKA FAKULTA. SBORNIK PRACI. HISTORIE. 1971. irreg. Statni Pedagogicke Nakladatelstvi, Ostrovni 30, 113 01 Prague 1, Czechoslovakia (Subscr. to: Artia, Ve Smeckach 30, 111 27 Prague 1, Czechoslovakia)

UNIVERSITATEA BUCURESTI. ANALELE. FILOZOFIE. ISTORIE. DREPT. see *PHILOSOPHY*

940   FR   ISSN 0065-5007
UNIVERSITE D'AIX-MARSEILLE I. INSTITUT D'HISTOIRE DES PAYS D'OUTRE-MER. ETUDES ET DOCUMENTS. 1970. irreg. 25 F. Universite d'Aix-Marseille I, Institut d'Histoire des Pays d'Outre-Mer, 29 Avenue Robert Schuman, 13621 Aix- en- Provence, France. circ. 250. (also avail. in microform)

949.4   SZ
UNIVERSITE DE FRIBOURG. HISTORISCHE SCHRIFTEN. 1976. irreg. Editions Universitaires de Fribourg, 42 Bd. de Perolles, 1700 Fribourg, Switzerland.

940   SZ   ISSN 0072-0836
UNIVERSITE DE GENEVE. SECTION D'HISTOIRE. DOCUMENTS. 1966. irreg., no.14, 1985. price varies. Librarie Droz, 11, rue Massot, 1211 Geneva 12, Switzerland. circ. 1,600.

944   FR
UNIVERSITE DE NANTES. CENTRE DE RECHERCHES SUR L'HISTOIRE DU MONDE ATLANTIQUE. ENQUETES ET DOCUMENTS. 1971. a. price varies. Universite de Nantes, Centre de Recherches sur l'Histoire du Monde Atlantique, Chemin de la Sensive du Tertre, Boite Postal 1025, 44036 Nantes Cedex, Brittany, France. bk. rev. illus. stat.
Formerly: Universite de Nantes. Centre de Recherches sur l'Histoire de la France Atlantique. Enquetes et Documents (ISSN 0395-3203)

940   FR   ISSN 0079-256X
UNIVERSITE DE POITIERS. CENTRE D'ETUDES SUPERIEURES DE CIVILISATION MEDIEVALE. PUBLICATIONS. 1958. irreg. price varies. Universite de Poitiers, Centre d'Etudes Superieures de Civilisation Medievale, 24 rue de la Chaine, 86022 Poitiers, France.

949.3   BE
UNIVERSITE LIBRE DE BRUXELLES. GROUPE D'ETUDE DU DIX-HUITIEME SIECLE. ETUDES SUR LE DIX-HUITIEME SIECLE. 1974. a. (Groupe d'Etude de Dix-Huitieme Siecle) Editions de l'Universite de Bruxelles, Avenue P. Heger, 26-C.P. 163, B-1050 Brussels, Belgium.

940   BE
UNIVERSITE LIBRE DE BRUXELLES. INSTITUT POUR L'ETUDE DE LA RENAISSANCE ET DE L'HUMANISME. COLLOQUES. 1963. irreg., 5th, 1976. Editions de l'Universite de Bruxelles, Av. P. Heger 26, C.P. 163, B-1050 Brussels, Belgium.

UNIVERSITETS OLDSAKSAMLING. AARBOK. see *ARCHAEOLOGY*

940   UK   ISSN 0141-0008
UNIVERSITY OF NOTTINGHAM. DEPARTMENT OF ADULT EDUCATION. BULLETIN OF LOCAL HISTORY, EAST MIDLANDS REGION. 1966. a. price varies. University of Nottingham, Department of Adult Education, Publications Unit, Cherry Tree Buildings, University Park, Nottingham NG7 2RD, England. Eds. David Marcombe, Colin Griffin. adv. bk. rev. bibl. cum.index. circ. 300.

947   CN
UNIVERSITY OF OTTAWA. UKRAINIANS STUDIES/UNIVERSITE D'OTTAWA. ETUDES UKRAINIENNES. (Text in English, French and Ukrainian) 1977. irreg. University of Ottawa Press, 603 Cumberland, Ottawa, Ont. K1N 6N5, Canada. TEL 613-564-2270. Ed. Theofil Kus.

940 340   UK
UNIVERSITY OF WALES. BOARD OF CELTIC STUDIES. HISTORY AND LAW SERIES. 1929. irreg. University of Wales Press, 6 Gwennyth St., Cathays, Cardiff CF2 4YD, Wales. Ed. Glanmor Williams.

943 947   CS   ISSN 0231-7710
UNIVERZITA J. E. PURKYNE. FILOZOFICKA FAKULTA. SBORNIK PRACI. C: RADA HISTORICKA. irreg. (approx. a.) Univerzita J. E. Purkyne, Filozoficka Fakulta, A. Novaka 1, 602 00 Brno, Czechslovakia.

UNIVERZITA J. E. PURKYNE. FILOZOFICKA FAKULTA. SBORNIK PRACI. E: RADA ARCHEOLOGICKO-KLASICKA. see *ARCHAEOLOGY*

943.7   CS   ISSN 0139-5548
UNIVERZITA KOMENSKEHO TRNAVE. PEDAGOGICKE FAKULTA. ZBORNIK. SPOLOCENSKE VEDY. HISTORIA. 1968. irreg. Slovenske Pedagogicke Nakladatelstvo v Bratislave, Sasinkova 5, 891 12 Bratislava, Czechoslovakia (Subscr. to: Slovart, Gottwaldovo Nam. 6, 805 32 Bratislava, Czechoslovakia)
Formerly: Univerzita Komenskeho v Bratislave so Sidlom v Trnva. Pedagogicka Fakulta. Zbornik.

943.7   CS
UNIVERZITA PAVLA JOZEFA SAFARIKA. USTAV MARXIZMU-LENINIZMU. ZBORNIK PRAC UCITELOV. 1974. a. exchange basis only. Vychodoslovenske Vydavatel'stvo v Kosiciach, Alejova 3, 040 01 Kosice 1, Czechoslovakia.
Formerly: Marxizmus-Leninizmus. Zbornik Ustav Marxizmu-Leninizmu Univerzity P.J. Safarika.

943.8   PL   ISSN 0072-0461
UNIWERSYTET GDANSKI. WYDZIAL HUMANISTYCZNY. ZESZYTY NAUKOWE. HISTORIA. 1965. irreg. Uniwersytet Gdanski, Ul. Czerwonej Armii 110, 81-824 Sopot, Poland (Dist. by: Ars Polona-Ruch, Krakowskie Przedmiescie 7, Warsaw, Poland)

943.8   PL   ISSN 0083-4351
UNIWERSYTET JAGIELLONSKI. ZESZYTY NAUKOWE. PRACE HISTORYCZNE. (Text in English, French, German, Russian) 1955. irreg., no.643, 1984. price varies. Panstwowe Wydawnictwo Naukowe, Miodowa 10, 00-251 Warsaw, Poland (Dist. by: Ars Polona, Krakowskie Przedmiescie 7, 00-068 Warsaw, Poland) Ed. St. Cynarski. circ. 690.

948   SZ
UNSERE HEIMAT (WOHLEN) 1927. a. Historische Gesellschaft Freiamt, 5610 Wohlen, Switzerland.

900   US   ISSN 0042-0786
URAL-ALTAISCHE JAHRBUECHER/URAL-ALTAIC YEARBOOK. (Text in English, French, German and Russian) 1921. a. $52. Eurolingua, Box 101, Bloomington, IN 47402-0101. TEL 812-332-8918. Eds. Gyula Decsy, A.E.J. Bodrogligeti. adv. bk. rev. charts. index. illus. circ. 450. Indexed: M.L.A. Lang.& Lang.Behav.Abstr.
Formerly: Ungarische Jahrbuecher.

940 300   UK   ISSN 0306-0845
URBAN HISTORY YEARBOOK. 1974. a. price varies. Leicester University Press, Fielding Johnson Bldg., Univ. of Leicester, University Rd., Leicester, England. Ed. David Reeder. bk. rev. bibl. Indexed: Br.Tech.Ind. Br.Archaeol.Abstr. Geo.Abstr.

948.5   SW
VAESTERBOTTENS NORRA FORNMINNESFOERENING. SKELLEFTEA MUSEUM. MEDDELANDE. no. 37, 1975. irreg. Kr.18.50. Vaesterbottens Norra Fornminnesfoerening, Skelleftea Museum, Skelleftea, Sweden. Eds. Peter Gustafsson, Stig-Henrik Viklund. illus.

940   NO   ISSN 0800-0999
VALDRES HISTORIELAG. AARBOK. 1916. a. price varies. Valdres Historielag, Box 55-2901 Fagernes, Norway. Ed.Bd. bk. rev. bibl. illus. circ. 2,500.

948.9   DK   ISSN 0106-1283
VARNAES BIRK. 1976. a. Kr.50. Varnaes Birk Borgerforening, c/o Svend Agertoft, Vodagergaard, Noerskov 5, Varnaes, 6200 Abenraa, Denmark. illus. index.

948   FI
VARSINAIS SUOMEN MAAKUNTAKIRJA. 1928. irreg. Varsinais Suomen Maakuntaliitto, Puutarhakatu 8 B D, 20100 Turku 10, Finland.

949.7   YU   ISSN 0350-9494
VARSTVO SPOMENIKOV/MONUMENT CONSERVATION. 1948. a. 450 din. Zavod S R Slovenije za Varstvo Naravne i Kulturne Dediscine, Plecnikov Trg 2, P.O. Box 176, 61 001 Ljubljana, Yugoslavia. Ed. Iva Curk. cum.index: 1948-1975. circ. 850.

948   DK
VEJLE AMTS ARBOG. 1905. a. Kr.75. Vejle Amts Historiske Samfund, Vejle Kulturhistoriske Museum, Flegborg 18, 7100 Vejle, Denmark. Ed. K.E. Reddersen.

948   DK   ISSN 0085-7645
VENDSYSSEL AARBOG. 1915. a. Kr.40($5) ‡ (Historisk Samfund for Vendsyssel) Joergen Joergensen Ed. & Pub., Jensensvej 14, DK-9493 Saltum, Denmark. circ. 3,500.
Formerly: Vendsysselske Aarboeger.
Local

948.9   DK   ISSN 0108-867X
VENDSYSSEL HISTORISKE MUSEUM. 1982. a. Kr.10. Museumsgade 2, 9800 Hjoerring, Denmark. illus. circ. 1,000.

948   DK   ISSN 0105-2608
VENDSYSSEL NU OG DA. 1977. a. Kr.88. Vendsyssel Historiske Museum, Museumsgade 2, 9800 Hjoerring, Denmark. illus. circ. 2,000.

943   GW   ISSN 0083-5579
VEREIN FUER GESCHICHTE DER STADT NUERNBERG. MITTEILUNGEN. 1879. a. price varies. Verein fuer Geschichte der Stadt Nuernberg, Egidienplatz 23, 8500 Nuernberg 1, W. Germany (B.R.D.) Eds. G. Hirschmann, K. Ulshoefer. bk. rev. circ. 1,200.

943.6   AU
VEREIN FUER GESCHICHTE DER STADT WIEN. JAHRBUCH. 1939. a. price varies. Verein fuer Geschichte der Stadt Wien, Wiener Stadt- und Landesarchiv, Rathaus, A-1082 Vienna, Austria. Ed. Peter Csendes. adv. circ. 2,000. (back issues avail.) Indexed: Hist.Abstr. Amer.Hist.& Life.

943   GW   ISSN 0083-5587
VEREIN FUER HAMBURGISCHE GESCHICHTE. ZEITSCHRIFT. 1841. a. DM.30. Verein fuer Hamburgische Geschichte, ABC-Str. 19, 2000 Hamburg 36, W. Germany (B.R.D.) Ed. Hans-Dieter Lose. adv. bk. rev. cum.index. circ. 1,650.

943   GW   ISSN 0083-5609
VEREIN FUER LUEBECKISCHE GESCHICHTE UND ALTERTUMSKUNDE. ZEITSCHRIFT. 1920. a. DM.48. ‡ Max Schmidt-Roemhild Verlag, Mengstr. 16, 2400 Luebeck 1, W. Germany (B.R.D.) (Co-sponsor: Archiv de Hausestadt Lubeck) Ed. A. Grassmann. bk. rev.

949   SZ   ISSN 0083-5641
VEREINIGUNG PRO SIHLTAL. BLAETTER. 1951. a. 12 Fr. Vereinigung Pro Sihltal, Postfach 8039 Zurich Selnau, Switzerland. cum.index: 1951-1979.

347   GW   ISSN 0532-596X
VEROEFFENTLICHUNGEN DES OSTASIATISCHEN SEMINARS DER JOHANN-WOLFGANG-GOETHE-UNIVERSITAET, FRANKFURT. REIHE A. SUEDOSTASIENKUNDE. 1965. irreg. vol. 5, 1976. price varies. Verlag Otto Harrassowitz, Taunusstr. 14, Postfach 2929, 6200 Wiesbaden 1, W. Germany (B.R.D.) Eds. Otto Karow, Hans A. Dettmer.

943   GW
VEROEFFENTLICHUNGEN ZUR VERFASSUNGSGESCHICHTE VON BADEN-WUERTTEMBERG SEIT 1945. 1983. irreg. Kommission fuer geschichtliche Landeskunde in Baden-Wuerttemberg, Eugenstr. 7, 7000 Stuttgart 1, W. Germany (B.R.D.) circ. 1,000.

948.9   DK   ISSN 0108-6391
VESTFYNSK HJEMSTAVN. 1931. a. Kr.40. (Vestfyns Hjemstavnsforening) Vestfyns Hjemstavnsgaard, Klaregade 23, Gummerup, DK-5620 Glamsbjerg, Denmark. illus. circ. 1,000.

948   DK   ISSN 0107-8925
VIBORG STIFTS AARBOG. 1972. a. Viborg Stiftsoevrighed, Bispegaarden, 8800 Viborg, Denmark. Ed. Poul Nielsen. illus. circ. 3,200.

VIENNA CIRCLE COLLECTION. see BIOGRAPHY

948   UK   ISSN 0305-9219
VIKING SOCIETY FOR NORTHERN RESEARCH. SAGA BOOK. a. £10. Viking Society for Northern Research, c/o Dept. of Scandinavian Studies, University College, London WC1E 6BT, England. Indexed: Br.Archaeol.Abstr.

943.7   CS   ISSN 0139-9462
VLASTIVEDNY SBORNIK OKRESU NOVY JICIN. 1967. irreg. $2. Vlastivedny Ustav v Novem Jicine, Ul. 28, rijna 12, 741 11 Novy Jicin, Czechoslovakia. bk. rev. cum.index: vol.11-20, 1979.

VLASTIVEDNY ZBORNIK. see HUMANITIES: COMPREHENSIVE WORKS

943.7 913   CS
VLASTIVEDNY ZBORNIK POVAZIA. 1958. irreg. Osveta, Osloboditelov 21, 036 54 Martin, Czechoslovakia (Subscr. to: Slovart, Gottwaldovo Nam. 6, 805 32 Bratislava, Czechoslovakia) bibl. cum.index: vol.1-9, 1958-68.
Formerly: Vlastivedny Zbornik Zilinskeho Kraja.

943.6   AU
VORARLBERGER LANDESMUSEUMSVEREIN. JAHRBUCH. 1928. a. Vorarlberger Landesmuseumsverein, Kornmarkt, Bregenz, Austria. Eds. Paul Rachbauer, Christine Spiegel, Helmut Swozilek. bk. rev.

VRIJE FRIES. see LINGUISTICS

940 920   UR
VSPOMOGATEL'NYE ISTORICHESKIE DISTSIPLINY. 1968. a. Izdatel'stvo Nauka, Mendeleevskaya Liniya 1, Leningrad B-164, Russian S.F.S.R., U.S.S.R. Ed.V.A. Shishkin. circ. 2,000.

948.9   DK   ISSN 0108-691X
VULKANEN: REN L A V A. 1982. irreg., 2-3/yr. Kr.5 per no. Lokalhistoriske Arkiver i Vestsjaellands Amt, c/o Gitte Strange Joergensen, Malivej 12, 4200 Slagelse, Denmark. Ed. Inger Stig Hansen. circ. 250.

VYZKUMY V CECHACH. see ARCHAEOLOGY

940   UK
WAKEFIELD COURT ROLLS SERIES. 1976. a. £10. Yorkshire Archaeological Society, 23 Clarendon Rd., Leeds LS2 9NZ, England. Ed. Dr. M. Fraser. circ. 200.

940   UK   ISSN 0307-5281
WATFORD AND DISTRICT INDUSTRIAL HISTORY SOCIETY. JOURNAL. 1971. a. price varies. ‡ Watford and District Industrial History Society, c/o Mr. R.C. Kennell, 79 Abbots Rd., Abbots Langley, Herts. WD5 0BJ, England. Ed. D.G.N. English. charts. illus. circ. 100.
Formerly: Watford and District Industrial History Society Bulletin.
Local

943 330   GW   ISSN 0433-7603
WELTWIRTSCHAFT AM JAHRESWECHSEL. 1958. a. DM.4. (Bundesministerium fuer Wirtschaft) Bundesstelle fuer Aussenhandelsinformation, Blaubach 13, 5000 Cologne 1, W. Germany (B.R.D.)

949   NE
WERKGROEP ELITES. BULLETIN. 1978. a. free. Werkgroep Elites, Rijksuniversiteit Leiden, Doelensteeg 16, 2311 VL Leiden, Netherlands. circ. 250.

940 910   GE   ISSN 0138-3213
WERTE UNSERER HEIMAT; Ergebnisse der heimatkundlichen Bestandsaufnahme in der DDR. 1957. irreg., no.44, 1986. M.18. (Akademie der Wissenschaften der DDR, Geographisches Institut) Akademie-Verlag, Leipziger Str. 3-4, 1086 Berlin, E. Germany (D.D.R.)

942   UK   ISSN 0143-8158
WEST MIDLANDS ARCHIVES NEWSLETTER. 1979. irreg. free. Birmingham Public Libraries, Chamberlain Square, Birmingham, England. Eds. P. Basset, L.S. Latimer. bk. rev. illus. circ. 500.
Local

944   US   ISSN 0099-0329
WESTERN SOCIETY FOR FRENCH HISTORY. PROCEEDINGS OF THE ANNUAL MEETING. 1974. a. $25 to individuals; institutions $35. Western Society for French History, c/o William Roosen, Ed., History Dept., Box 6023, Northern Arizona University, Flagstaff, AZ 86011. TEL 913-864-3569. circ. 250. Indexed: Hist.Abstr. M.L.A. Amer.Hist. & Life. Key Title: Proceedings of the Annual Meeting of the Western Society for French History.

943   GW   ISSN 0083-9027
WESTFAELISCHE FORSCHUNGEN. a. price varies. (Provinzialinstitut fuer Westfaelische Landes- und Volksforschung) Aschendorffsche Verlagsbuchhandlung, Soester Str. 13, Postfach 1124, 4400 Muenster, W. Germany (B.R.D.) Ed. K. H. Kirchhoff. bk. rev. Indexed: Bibl.Cart.

943   GW   ISSN 0083-9043
WESTFAELISCHE ZEITSCHRIFT. 1948. irreg., vol.128, 1978. DM.42. (Verein fuer Geschichte und Altertumskunde Westfalens) Verlag Regensberg, Daimlerweg 58, Postfach 6748/6749, 4400 Muenster, W. Germany (B.R.D.) Eds. Klemens Honselmann, Alfred Hartlieb von Wallthor. circ. 3, 000. Indexed: Bibl.Cart.

WESTFALIA SACRA; Quellen und Forschungen zur Kirchengeschichte Westfalens. see RELIGIONS AND THEOLOGY

943   GW   ISSN 0511-8484
WESTPREUSSEN-JAHRBUCH. 1950. a. DM.22. (Landsmannschaft Westpreussen e.V.) Verlagsgesellschaft C. J. Fahle, Neubrueckenstr. 8-11, 4400 Muenster, W. Germany (B.R.D.) Eds. Herbert Lange, Hans-Juergen Schuch. bibl. illus. stat. circ. 2,000.

943   AU
WIENER BEITRAEGE ZUR GESCHICHTE DER NEUZEIT. 1974. a. price varies. Verlag fuer Geschichte und Politik, Neulinggasse 26, A-1030 Vienna, Austria. Ed.Bd.

WIENER RINGSTRASSE-BILD EINER EPOCHE; die Erweiterung der Inneren Stadt Wien unter Kaiser Franz Joseph. see ART

949.2   NE
WINKLER PRINS ENCYCLOPEDISCH JAARBOEK. 1976. a. fl.65. Uitgeversmaatschappij Elsevier, Amsteldijk 166, 1079 LH Amsterdam, Netherlands. Ed. J.N.M Brugge. illus. circ. 50,000.
Former titles (1972-1975): Het Jaar in Woord en Beeld; (1970-1972): Winkler Prins Jaarboek.

943 500   GW   ISSN 0178-6768
WISSENSCHAFTEN IN DER D.D.R. 1975. a. Institut fuer Gesellschaft und Wissenschaft, Aeussere Brucker Str. 33, Postfach 1409, 8520 Erlangen, W. Germany (B.R.D.)
Formerly: Wissenschaftsentwicklung und Wissenschaftspolitik in der DDR. Jahresbericht.

940 AU
WISSENSCHAFTLICHE KOMMISSION ZUR ERFORSCHUNG DER GESCHICHTE DER REPUBLIK OESTERREICH. VEROEFFENTLICHUNGEN. 1973. irreg. price varies. Verlag fuer Geschichte und Politik, Neulinggasse 26, A-1030 Vienna, Austria. Eds. R. Neck, Isabelle Ackerl.
Formerly: Wissenschaftliche Kommission des Theodor-Koerner-Stiftungsfonds und des Leopold-Kunschak-Preises zur Enforschung der Oesterreichischen Geschichte der Jahre 1918 bis 1938. Veroeffentlichungen.

940 GW ISSN 0724-956X
WOLFENBUETTLER ABHANDLUNGEN ZUR RENAISSANCEFORSCHUNG. 1981. irreg., vol.6, 1986. price varies. Verlag Otto Harrassowitz, Taunusstr. 14, Postfach 2929, D-6200 Wiesbaden 1, W. Germany (B.R.D.) Ed. August Buck.

940 GW ISSN 0724-472X
WOLFENBUETTLER ARBEITEN ZUR BAROCKFORSCHUNG. 1973. irreg., vol.16, 1987. price varies. Verlag Otto Harrassowitz, Taunusstr. 14, Postfach 2929, D-6200 Wiesbaden 1, W. Germany (B.R.D.) Ed. Martin Bircher.

940 GW ISSN 0724-9594
WOLFENBUETTLER FORSCHUNGEN. 1977. irreg., vol.38, 1987. Verlag Otto Harrassowitz, Taunusstr. 14, Postfach 2929, D-6200 Wiesbaden, W. Germany (B.R.D.) Ed.Bd.

940 US ISSN 0090-3868
WORLD TODAY SERIES: SOVIET UNION AND EASTERN EUROPE. 1970. a. $5.50. Stryker-Post Publications, 888 Seventeenth St., N.W., Washington, DC 20006. TEL 202-342-6055. Ed. M. Wesley Shoemaker.

940 US ISSN 0084-2338
WORLD TODAY SERIES: WESTERN EUROPE. a. $11. Stryker-Post Publications, 888 Seventeenth St., N.W., Washington, DC 20006. TEL 202-342-6055. Ed. Wayne C. Thompson.

943 GW ISSN 0084-2613
DER WORMSGAU; Wissenschaftliche Zeitschrift der Stadt Worms und des Altertumsvereins Worms. (Supplement avail.: Beiheft) 1926. a. DM.30. Stadtarchiv im Raschi-Haus, Hintere Judengasse 6, 6520 Worms, W. Germany (B.R.D.) Dir. Fritz Reuter. bk. rev.

943 GW ISSN 0084-3067
WUERTTEMBERGISCH FRANKEN. 1847. a. DM.40. Historischer Verein fuer Wuerttembergisch Franken, A. Rothmund, Muenzstr. 1, 7170 Schwaebisch Hall, W. Germany (B.R.D.) Ed. Gerhard Taddey. bk. rev.

943 GW
WUERZBURGER DIOEZESANGESCHICHTSBLAETTER. 1933. a. DM.20. Wuerzburger Dioezesangeschichtsverein, Domerschulstrasse, 8700 Wuerzburg 1, W. Germany (B.R.D.) bk. rev. charts. illus. circ. 800. (tabloid format) Indexed: CERDIC.

940 PL ISSN 0078-5393
WYZSZA SZKOLA PEDAGOGICZNA, OPOLE. ZESZYTY NAUKOWE. SERIA A. HISTORIA. (Text in Polish; summaries in English, German, Russian) 1960. irreg., vol. 20, 1982. price varies; available on exchange. Wyzsza Szkola Pedagogiczna, Opole, Oleska 48, 45-052 Opole, Poland (Dist. by: Ars Polona-Ruch, Krakowskie Przedmiescie 7, Warsaw, Poland)

945 IT
YEARBOOK OF ITALIAN STUDIES. 1971. irreg. price varies. (Italian Cultural Institute, CN) Casalini Libri, 50014 Fiesole, Italy. Eds. Antonio d'Andrea, Dante della Terza. circ. 1,500. Indexed: M.L.A.

YEARBOOK OF ROMANIAN STUDIES. see LITERATURE

942 UK ISSN 0084-4047
YEARBOOK OF THE COMMONWEALTH. 1969 under new title. a. H.M.S.O., Box 569, London SE1 9NH, England. (reprint service avail. from UMI)
Supersedes: Great Britain. Commonwealth Office. Yearbook.

940 UK
YORKSHIRE ARCHAEOLOGICAL SOCIETY RECORD SERIES. 1885. a. £12. Yorkshire Archaeological Society, Claremont, 23 Clarendon Rd., Leeds LS2 9NZ, England. Ed. R.B. Dobson. index. circ. 350.

943.7 CS
ZAPADNE SLOVENSKO. (Table of Contents in German and Russian) 1973. a. Obzor, Ceskoslovenskej Armady 29, 893 36 Bratislava, Czechoslovakia (Subscr. to: Slovart, Gottwaldovo Nam. 6, 805 32 Bratislava, Czechoslovakia)

949.7 YU ISSN 0084-5191
ZBORNIK ZA ISTORIJU, JEZIK I KNJIZEVNOST SRPSKOG NARODA. FONTES RERUM SLAVORUM MERIDIONALIUM. (Text in Serbo-Croatian; summaries in English, French, German or Russian) 1932. irreg. price varies. Srpska Akademija Nauka i Umetnosti, Knez Mihailova 35, 11001 Belgrade, Yugoslavia (Dist. by: Prosveta, Terazije 16, Belgrade, Yugoslavia) circ. 1,000.

949.7 YU ISSN 0084-5213
ZBORNIK ZA ISTORIJU, JEZIK I KNJIZEVNOST SRPSKOG NARODA. SPOMENICI NA TUDJIM JEZICIMA. 1904. irreg. price varies. Srpska Akademija Nauka i Umetnosti, Knez Mihailova 35, 11001 Belgrade, Yugoslavia (Dist. by: Prosveta, Terazije 16, Belgrade, Yugoslavia) circ. 1,000.

943 GW
ZEITSCHRIFT FUER DIE GESCHICHTE DES OBERRHEINS. 1850. a. DM.64. Kommission fuer Geschichtliche Landeskunde in Baden-Wuerttemberg, Eugen-Str. 7, 7000 Stuttgart 1, W. Germany (B.R.D.) bk. rev. circ. 800. Indexed: Numis.Lit.

943 GW ISSN 0514-8561
ZEITSCHRIFT FUER HOHENZOLLERISCHE GESCHICHTE. 1964. a. DM.30. Hohenzollerischer Geschichtsverein Sigmaringen, Karlstr. 3, D-7480 Sigmaringen, W. Germany (B.R.D.) Ed.Bd. bk. rev. bibl. illus. index. circ. 1,000. (back issues avail.)

946.3 AU ISSN 0049-8645
ZEITSCHRIFT FUER LATEINAMERIKA WIEN. (Summaries in Spanish) 1971. irreg. (approx. 2/yr.) S.180($10) Osterreichisches Lateinamerika Institut, Schmerlingplatz 8, A-1010 Vienna, Austria. Ed. Gerhard Drekonja. adv. bk. rev. circ. 500.

943 GW ISSN 0044-3786
ZEITSCHRIFT FUER WUERTTEMBERGISCHE LANDESGESCHICHTE. 1937. a. DM.64. Kommission fuer Geschichtliche Landeskunde in Baden-Wuerttemberg, Eugen-Str. 7, 7000 Stuttgart 1, W. Germany (B.R.D.) bk. rev. bibl. index. circ. 1, 300. Indexed: Bibl.Cart.

ZEMEDELSKE MUZEUM. VEDECKE PRACE/ MUSEUM OF AGRICULTURE. SCIENTIFIC WORKS. see AGRICULTURE

943 YU
ZENTAI FUZETEK. 1960. irreg. 25 din.($3) Udruzenje Prijatelja Muzeja i Arhiva "Dudas Gyula", 24400 Senta, Yugoslavia (Dist. by: Forum NIP, Vojvode Misica 1, 21000 Novi Sad, Yugoslavia) Ed. Janos Szloboda. circ. 650.
Local

943.8 913 PL ISSN 0514-3446
ZESZYTY GLIWICKIE. 1963. biennial. 100 Zl. Towarzystwo Przyjaciol Gliwic, Rynek 23, 44-100 Gliwice, Poland. Ed. Wlodzimierz Blaszczyk. circ. 1, 000. (back issues avail.)

943.8 PL ISSN 0084-5507
ZIEMIE ZACHODNIE. STUDIA I MATERIALY. (Text in Polish; summaries in English, Russian) 1957. irreg. price varies. Instytut Zachodni, Stary Rynek 78/79, 61-772 Poznan, Poland (Dist. by Ars Polona-Ruch, Krakowskie Przedmiescie 7, Warsaw, Poland) circ. 2,000.

943.8 PL ISSN 0084-568X
ZRODLA DO DZIEJOW BYDGOSZCZY. 1963. irreg. price varies. Bydgoskie Towarzystwo Naukowe, Jezuicka 4, Bydgoszcz, Poland (Dist. by Ars Polona-Ruch, Krakowskie Przedmiescie 7, Warsaw, Poland)

949.4 SZ ISSN 0084-5809
ZUR LAGE DER SCHWEIZ; beitraege zu einem Rueckblick. 1962. a. 10 Fr. Schweizerische Arbeitsgemeinschaft fuer Demokratie, Feldeggstrasse 65, 8034 Zurich, Switzerland. Ed.Bd.

940 NE
ZWISCHEN HAUSMANNSTURM UND WALBECKER WARTE. (Text in German) vol. 17, 1976. irreg. price varies. Europese Bibliotheek, Waalkade 34, Postbus 49, 5300 AA Zaltbommel, Netherlands. Ed. R. Schaper.

942 UK
1745 ASSOCIATION AND NATIONAL MILITARY HISTORY SOCIETY. QUARTERLY NOTES. 1967. irreg., 3-4/yr. £5. 1745 Association and National Military History Society, c/o Barbara Fairweather, Ed., Invercoe House, Glencoe, Argyll, Scotland (Subscr. to: Mrs Hart, 45 Ann St., Edinburgh, Scotland) bk. rev. circ. 325.

HISTORY — History Of North And South America

979.8 US
A P U PRESS ALASKANA BOOK SERIES. 1963. irreg., no.40, 1983. price varies. (Alaska Pacific University) Alaska Pacific University Press, Anchorage, AK 99508. TEL 907-564-8301. Ed. B. Harris. index. circ. 3,000. (also avail. in microform from UMI) Indexed: Hist.Abstr. Amer.Hist.& Life.
Former titles: A P U Press Alaskana Series & A M U Press Alaskana Series (Alaska Methodist University) (ISSN 0002-4554); Alaska Review.

ACADEMIA DE GEOGRAFIA E HISTORIA DE GUATEMALA. ANALES. see GEOGRAPHY

972.9 DR ISSN 0567-5871
ACADEMIA DOMINICANA DE LA HISTORIA. PUBLICACIONES. 1955. irreg., vol.57, 1980. price varies. (Academia Dominicana de la Historia) Editora Taller, Isabel la Catolica 309, Apdo. de Correos 2190, Z-1, Santo Domingo, Dominican Republic.

972 MX
ACADEMIA MEXICANA DE LA HISTORIA. MEMORIAS. vol. 30, 1978. irreg. Academia Mexicana de la Historia, Plaza de Carlos Pacheco 21, Mexico 1, D.F., Mexico. Ed. Edmundo O'Gorman.

987 AG ISSN 0539-242X
ACADEMIA NACIONAL DE LA HISTORIA. INVESTIGACIONES Y ENSAYOS. 1966. irreg, latest no.31. $6. Academia Nacional de la Historia, Balcarce 139, Buenos Aires, Argentina (Orders to: Libreria Platero S.R.L., Talcahuano 485, C.P. 1013 Bs. As., Argentina)

982 AG ISSN 0567-6029
ACADEMIA PROVINCIAL DE LA HISTORIA. BOLETIN.* 1971, no. 6. a. Academia Provincial de la Historia, Avda. Jose I de la Roza, San Juan, Argentina. Ed.Bd. bk. rev. bibl.

ACTA UNIVERSITATIS DE ATTILA JOZSEF NOMINATAE. ACTA HISTORICA. see HISTORY — History Of Europe

986 EC
ACTAS DEL CABILDO COLONIAL DE GUAYAQUIL. 1972. irreg. Archivo Historico del Guayas, Casilla 1333, Guayaquil, Ecuador.

974.7 028.5 US ISSN 0001-883X
ADVENTURES IN WESTERN NEW YORK HISTORY. 1960. irreg. $1.25 per no. Buffalo and Erie County Historical Society, 25 Nottingham Court, Buffalo, NY 14216. TEL 716-873-9644. bibl. illus.
Junior high school level

960 301.45 US
AFRICAN - AMERICAN HERITAGE SERIES. irreg., 1-2/yr. price varies. Alkebu-Lan Books, 209 W. 125th St., Room 218, New York, NY 10027. TEL 212-866-0641. circ. 1,500.

979.8　　　　　　　US　ISSN 0084-6139
ALASKA. STATE LIBRARY, JUNEAU.
HISTORICAL MONOGRAPHS. 1970. irreg.
Department of Education, Division of State
Libraries, Box G, Juneau, AK 99811. TEL 907-465-
2925. Ed. Phyllis DeMuth. circ. controlled. (tabloid
format)

918.5　　　　　　　PE
ALMANAQUE DEL PERU.* 1973. a. Selecciones
Tauro S.A., Jr. Huancavelica 421, Of. 402, Lima,
Peru. illus. stat.

980　　　　　　　UY
AMERICA MERIDIONAL. 1983. irreg. Sociedad
Regional de Ciencias Humanas, Manuel Errazquin
2351 (Punta Carretas), Montevideo, Uruguay. Ed.
Raul Federico Abadie-Aicardi.

910 917　　　　　US　ISSN 0065-8219
AMERICAN EXPLORATION AND TRAVEL.
1937. irreg. price varies. University of Oklahoma
Press, 1005 Asp Ave., Norman, OK 73019. TEL
405-325-5111. Indexed: M.L.A.

973　　　　　　　US
AMERICAN FOREIGN POLICY LIBRARY. irreg.
price varies. Harvard University Press, 79 Garden
St., Cambridge, MA 02138. TEL 617-495-2600.

AMERICAN INDIAN TREATIES PUBLICATIONS
SERIES. see LAW

970　　　　　　　US　ISSN 0065-8936
AMERICAN JEWISH COMMUNAL HISTORY.
1954. irreg., 1969, no. 5. price varies. American
Jewish Historical Society, 2 Thornton Rd.,
Waltham, MA 02154. TEL 617-891-8110. index.
circ. 1,000.

970　　　　　　　US　ISSN 0193-6859
AMERICAN POPULAR CULTURE. 1980. irreg.
price varies. Greenwood Press, 88 Post Rd. W., Box
5007, Westport, CT 06881. TEL 203-226-3571. Ed.
M. Thomas Inge.

973　　　　　　　US
AMERICAN PROBLEMS STUDIES. irreg. price
varies. Holt, Rinehart and Winston, Inc., 383
Madison Ave., New York, NY 10017. TEL 212-
688-9100.

973　　　　　　　II　ISSN 0066-0795
AMERICAN STUDIES RESEARCH CENTRE.
NEWSLETTER. (Text in English) 1964. irreg.
membership. American Studies Research Centre,
Osmania University Campus, Hyderabad 500007,
India. circ. 3,000.

910.2　　　　　　　US　ISSN 0066-0884
AMERICAN TRAIL SERIES. irreg. Arthur H. Clark
Co., Box 230, Glendale, CA 91209-0230.

970　　　　　　　US
ANNUAL EDITIONS: AMERICAN HISTORY.
1973. a., (in 2 vols.) Dushkin Publishing Group,
Inc., Sluice Dock, Guildford, CT 06437. TEL 203-
453-4351. Ed. Ian Nielsen.

917.3　　　　　　　US　ISSN 0090-4511
ANNUAL EDITIONS: READINGS IN AMERICAN
HISTORY. 1972/73. a. $9.50 per vol. (2 vols.)
Dushkin Publishing Group, Inc., Sluice Dock,
Guilford, CT 06437. TEL 203-453-4351. Ed. Ian
Nielsen. illus.
　　Formerly: Readings in American History.

973　　　　　　　US　ISSN 0066-4618
ANSON G. PHELPS LECTURESHIP ON EARLY
AMERICAN HISTORY. 1932. irreg., latest 1984.
price varies. New York University Press,
Washington Square, New York, NY 10003. TEL
212-598-2886.

979.4　　　　　　　US　ISSN 0044-8362
ANTEPASADOS. (Text in English and Spanish)
1970. a. $12.50 (includes noticias para los
Californianos) Los Californianos, Inc., Box 5155,
San Francisco, CA 94101. Ed. Rudecinda Lo
Buglio. bk. rev. illus. circ. 450. (processed; back
issues avail.)

970 918.5　　　　　PE　ISSN 0066-5223
ANUARIO GEOGRAFICO DEL PERU. 1962. a.
price varies. Sociedad Geografica de Lima, Jiron
Puno 456, Apdo. 1176, Lima, Peru.

982 020.6　　　　　AG　ISSN 0325-3899
ANUARIO INTERAMERICANO DE ARCHIVOS.
1974. a. $8. Centro Interamericano de Desarrollo de
Archivos, Avd. Hipolito Irigoye 174, 5000 Cordoba,
Argentina. Ed. Aurelio Tanodi. adv. bk. rev. bibl.
index. circ. 700,273. Indexed: Hist.Abstr.
Amer.Hist.& Life. Hisp.Amer.Per.Ind.
　　Formerly (until 1982): Boletin Interamericano de
Archivos.

977　　　　　　　US
ARCHAEOLOGICAL COMPLETION REPORT
SERIES. 1977. irreg. (approx. a.) price varies.
Mackinac Island State Park Commission, Box
30028, Lansing, MI 48909. TEL 906-847-3328. bibl.
illus. circ. 500.

986.6　　　　　　　EC
ARCHIVO HISTORICO DEL GUAYAS.
COLECCION MONOGRAFICA. 1972. irreg.
Archivo Historico del Guayas, Casilla 1333,
Guayaquil, Ecuador.

985 398　　　　　PE
ARCHIVOS DE HISTORIA ANDINA. irreg., no. 5,
1986. Centro de Estudios Rurales Andinos
"Bartolome de las Casas", Apdo. 477, Cusco, Peru.

ARGENTINA. DEPARTAMENTO DE ESTUDIOS
HISTORICOS NAVALES. SERIE E:
DOCUMENTOS. see MILITARY

355 982　　　　　AG　ISSN 0066-7293
ARGENTINA. SECRETARIA DE GUERRA.
DIRECCION DE ESTUDIOS HISTORICOS.
BOLETIN BIBLIOGRAFICO.* 1967. irreg. $350.
Secretaria de Guerra, Comando en Jefe del Ejercito,
Azopardo 250 Planta Baja, Buenos Aires, Argentina.

979.1　　　　　　　US
ARIZONA HISTORICAL SOCIETY. HISTORICAL
MONOGRAPHS. 1973. irreg., no.7, 1983. price
varies. Arizona Historical Society, 949 E. Second
St., Tucson, AZ 85719. TEL 602-628-5774.

970　　　　　　　US
ARIZONA HISTORICAL SOCIETY. MUSEUM
MONOGRAPH SERIES. 1964. irreg., no.7, 1976.
price varies. Arizona Historical Society, 949 East
Second St., Tucson, AZ 85719. TEL 602-628-5774.
Ed.Bd. bibl. charts. illus.

973.05　　　　　　US
ARKANSAS TECH UNIVERSITY. DEPARTMENT
OF HISTORY. OCCASIONAL PAPERS. 1970.
irreg., vol.6, 1984. $1. Arkansas Tech University,
Department of History, Russellville, AR 72801.
TEL 501-968-0389. Ed. B.B. McCool. bk. rev. circ.
100.

975.5　　　　　　　US　ISSN 0066-7684
ARLINGTON HISTORICAL MAGAZINE. 1957. a.
$8. Arlington Historical Society, Box 402,
Arlington, VA 22210. Ed. Phyllis W. Johnson.
index. cum.index: 1957 to present. circ. 600.
Indexed: Hist.Abstr. Amer.Hist.& Life. Geo.Abstr.
Va.Hist.Abstr.

ASIEN - AFRIKA - LATEINAMERIKA.
JAHRBUCH; Bilanz und Chronik. see
HISTORY — History Of Asia

BAJA CALIFORNIA TRAVELS SERIES. see
TRAVEL AND TOURISM

975　　　　　　　US
BALTIMORE/ANNAPOLIS (YEAR); a
comprehensive directory of the area's major
institutions and the people who run them. 1987. a.
$40. Columbia Books, Inc., 1350 New York Ave.,
N.W., Ste. 207, Washington, DC 20005. TEL 202-
737-3777. Ed. John Russell. index.

BAMPTON LECTURES IN AMERICA. see
RELIGIONS AND THEOLOGY

972.9　　　　　　　BB　ISSN 0005-5891
BARBADOS MUSEUM AND HISTORICAL
SOCIETY. JOURNAL. 1933. a. $10. Barbados
Museum and Historical Society, St. Ann's Garrison,
Barbados, W. Indies. Ed. P. F. Campbell. bk. rev.
circ. 500. Indexed: Hist.Abstr. Amer.Hist.& Life.

979.2　　　　　　　US
BEEHIVE HISTORY. 1975. a. $2.50. Utah State
Historical Society, 300 Rio Grande, Salt Lake City,
UT 84101. TEL 801-533-6024. Ed. Miriam B.
Murphy. circ. 3,300.

980　　　　　　　BM　ISSN 0409-2163
BERMUDA HISTORICAL SOCIETY.
OCCASIONAL PUBLICATIONS. irreg., 1972, no.
8. price varies. Bermuda Historical Society, Museum
Par La Ville, Hamilton, Bermuda. Ed.Bd.

986.6　　　　　　　EC
BIBLIOTECA AZUAYA. a. Consejo Provincial del
Azuay, Departamento de Cultura, Cuenca, Ecuador.

989.2 100　　　　　PY
BIBLIOTECA DE ESTUDIOS PARAGUAYOS.
1981. irreg., vol.18, 1987. price varies. Universidad
Catolica Nuestra Senora de la Asuncion, Centro de
Estudios Antropologicos, Casilla de Correo,
Asuncion, Paraguay. Ed. Adriano Irala-Burgos. adv.
circ. 1,000. (back issues avail.)

980　　　　　　　PN
BIBLIOTECA DE LA CULTURA PANAMENA.
irreg., no. 5, 1983. Universidad de Panama, Panama
City, Panama.

987　　　　　　　VE
BIBLIOTECA DE TEMAS Y AUTORES DE
ANZOATEGUI. no.4,1980. irreg. Ediciones de la
Presidencia de la Republica, Caracas, Venezuela.

972.9　　　　　　　GP
BIBLIOTHEQUE D'HISTOIRE ANTILLAISE. no. 3,
1978. irreg. Societe d'Histoire de la Guadeloupe,
Basse-Terre, Guadeloupe.

976　　　　　　　US
BIRMINGHAM HISTORICAL SOCIETY.
JOURNAL. 1960. a. $10. Birmingham Historical
Society, No. 1 Sloss Quarters, Birmingham, AL
35222-1243. TEL 203-251-1880. Eds. Marvin
Yeomans Whiting, Alicia McGivaren. circ. 2,400.

984　　　　　　　BO
BOLETIN DEL ARCHIVO DE LA PAZ. 1976. irreg.
free. Universidad Mayor de San Andres, Archivo de
la Paz, Casilla 6548, La Paz, Bolivia. circ. 300.

BOLSILIBROS. see LITERATURE

BORDER ISSUES AND PUBLIC POLICY.
RESEARCH PAPERS. see POLITICAL SCIENCE

BORDER PERSPECTIVES. RESEARCH PAPERS.
see POLITICAL SCIENCE

917.3　　　　　　　US　ISSN 0092-4571
BORDER STATES. 1973. a. $4. American Studies
Association, Kentucky-Tennessee Chapter, c/o
William Berge, Oral History Center, Easter
Kentucky University, Richmond, KY 40475. TEL
606-622-2446.

971　　　　　　　CN　ISSN 0068-0303
BOREAL INSTITUTE, EDMONTON.
OCCASIONAL PUBLICATIONS. 1964. irreg.
price varies. Boreal Institute for Northern Studies,
University of Alberta, Edmonton, Alberta T6G 2E9,
Canada. TEL 403-432-4999. Indexed: GeoRef.

971　　　　　　　CN　ISSN 0820-988X
BOREAL INSTITUTE FOR NORTHERN STUDIES.
REPORT OF ACTIVITIES. 1963/64. a. free.
Boreal Institute for Northern Studies, University of
Alberta, Edmonton, Alta. T6G 2E9, Canada.
Indexed: Biol.Abstr.
　　Former titles: Boreal Institute, Edmonton. Report
of Activities (ISSN 0316-7828); Boreal Institute,
Edmonton. Annual Report (ISSN 0068-0281)

974　　　　　　　US　ISSN 0190-3586
BOSTONIAN SOCIETY. PROCEEDINGS. 1881.
irreg., latest 1983. $9 per no. Bostonian Society, Old
State House, 206 Washington St., Boston, MA
02109. TEL 617-242-5614. circ. 1,500 (controlled)

970　　　　　　　CN　ISSN 0068-0524
BOUNDARY HISTORICAL SOCIETY. REPORT.
1958. irreg. Can.$3.50. Boundary Historical Society,
12 Street, S.E., Grand Forks, B.C., Canada. TEL
604-422-3737.

791.8　　　　　　　US
BRAND BOOK. 1972? biennial. $25. Westerners, San
Diego Corral, Box 7174, San Diego, CA 92107.

973　　　　　　　BL
BRAZIL. ARQUIVO NACIONAL. SERIE DE
PUBLICACOES. irreg. Arquivo Nacional, Praca da
Republica 26, Rio de Janeiro, R.J., Brazil. illus.

HISTORY — HISTORY OF NORTH AND SOUTH AMERICA

572 069   BL   ISSN 0101-0484
BRAZIL. MUSEU DO INDIO. BOLETIM. DOCUMENTACAO. 1976. irreg. Museu do Indio, Biblioteca Marechal Rondon, Rua das Palmeiras 55, Botafogo, CEP 22270 Rio de Janeiro, Brazil.

981   BL   ISSN 0100-7475
BRAZIL. MUSEU DO INDIO. BOLETIM. ETNO-HISTORIA. 1979. irreg. Museu do Indio, Biblioteca Marechal Rondon, Rua das Palmeiras 55, Botafogo, CEP 22270 Rio de Janeiro, Brazil.

971   CN   ISSN 0381-6206
BROME COUNTY HISTORICAL SOCIETY. PUBLICATION. 1937. irreg. Brome County Historical Society, Knowlton, Que., Canada. TEL 514-243-6782. illus. Key Title: Publication - Brome County Historical Society.

974   US
BROOKSIDE COLUMNS. irreg. Saratoga County Historical Society, Ballston Spa, NY 12020.

971   CN   ISSN 0084-8115
BRUCE COUNTY HISTORICAL SOCIETY. YEAR BOOK. 1967. a. Can.$8.00. Bruce County Historical Society, Box 1900, Port Elgin, Ont. N0H 2C0, Canada. Ed. Marion McGillivray. adv. illus. circ. 1,000.

982   AG   ISSN 0524-9864
BUENOS AIRES (PROVINCE). ARCHIVO HISTORICO. PUBLICACIONES. SEXTA SERIE. 1951. irreg. Ministerio de Educacion, Archivo Historico, La Plata, Argentina.

970   US   ISSN 0068-4287
BURT FRANKLIN AMERICAN CLASSICS IN HISTORY AND SOCIAL SCIENCES. 1966. irreg., 1973, no. 246. price varies. Lenox Hill Publishing and Distributing Corporation, 235 E. 44th St., New York, NY 10017. (back issues avail.)

987   VE   ISSN 0068-5259
CAIN.* 1969. a. Bs.3($0.70) Universidad del Zulia, Facultad de Humanidades y Educacion, Maracaibo, Venezuela.

980   UK   ISSN 0068-6689
CAMBRIDGE LATIN AMERICAN STUDIES. 1967. irreg., no.48, 1984. $49.50 for latest vol. Cambridge University Press, Edinburgh Bldg., Shaftesbury Rd., Cambridge CB2 2RU, England (and 32 E. 57th St., New York, NY 10022) Ed. Malcolm Deas.

971   CN   ISSN 0068-8193
CANADIAN ALMANAC AND DIRECTORY. 1847. a. Can.$84.95($60) Copp Clark Pitman Ltd., 495 Wellington St. W., Toronto, Ont. M5V 1E9, Canada (Dist. in the U.S. by: Gale Research Co., Book Tower, Detroit, MI 48226) Ed. Susan Bracken. index. circ. 8,000. (also avail. in microfiche from UMI)

971   CN   ISSN 0315-1433
CANADIAN ANNUAL REVIEW OF POLITICS AND PUBLIC AFFAIRS. 1961. a. price varies. University of Toronto Press, Front Campus, Toronto, Ont. M5S 1A6, Canada TEL 613-667-7791. (and 33 East Tupper St., Buffalo, N. Y. 14023) Ed. R. B. Byers. index.
    Formerly: Canadian Annual Review (ISSN 0068-8215)

971   CN   ISSN 0068-886X
CANADIAN HISTORICAL ASSOCIATION. HISTORICAL BOOKLETS. BROCHURES HISTORIQUES. (Text in English and French) 1953. irreg. Can.$1.50 per issue. ‡ Canadian Historical Association, 395 Wellington St., Ottawa, Ont. K1A 0N3, Canada. TEL 613-233-7885. Ed. T. Cook. circ. 4,000.

970 016   CN   ISSN 0068-9165
CANADIAN LOCAL HISTORIES TO 1950. A BIBLIOGRAPHY. HISTOIRES LOCALES ET REGIONALES CANADIENNES DES ORIGINES A 1950. 1967. irreg. price varies. (Centennial Commission) University of Toronto Press, Front Campus, Toronto, Ont. M5S 1A6, Canada TEL 613-667-7791. (and 33 East Tupper St., Buffalo, N. Y. 14203) Ed. W.F.E. Morley. (also avail. in microfiche)

971.006   CN   ISSN 0383-6894
CANADIAN ORAL HISTORY ASSOCIATION. JOURNAL. (Text in English and French) 1976. a. Can.$10 to individuals; Can.$20 to institutions. Canadian Oral History Association, Box 2064, Station "D", Ottawa, Ont. K1P 5W3, Canada. Ed. Richard Lochead. bk. rev. circ. 300. Indexed: Hist.Abstr. M.L.A.

970 630   CN
CANADIAN PAPERS IN RURAL HISTORY. 1978. biennial. $20. Langdale Press, RR1, Gananoque, Ont. K7G 2V3, Canada. Ed. Prof. D.H. Akenson. circ. 1,000. (back issues avail.) Indexed: Hist.Abstr. M.L.A. Amer.Hist.& Life. Geo.Abstr.

972.9   PR   ISSN 0069-0511
CARIBBEAN MONOGRAPH SERIES. 1964. irreg; no.15, 1980. price varies. Universidad de Puerto Rico, Institute of Caribbean Studies, Box BM, Rio Piedras, PR 00931. Ed. Sybil Farrell Lewis. adv. bk. rev. circ. 1,020.
    Incorporating: Universidad de Puerto Rico. Institute of Caribbean Studies. Special Studies (ISSN 0079-788X)

972.9 574   VI
CARIBBEAN RESEARCH INSTITUTE. REPORT. 1965. irreg., latest tenth anniv. issue, 1975. free. Caribbean Research Institute, University of the Virgin Islands, St. Thomas, VI 00801. Ed. Clara Wimbro Mitchell Lewis. circ. 750.
    Formerly: Caribbean Islands Research Institute. Annual Report (ISSN 0069-0503)

972.9   PR
CARRIBBEAN OCCASIONAL SERIES. irreg., latest no.4. Universidad de Puerto Rico, Institute of Caribbean Studies, Box BM, Rio Piedras, PR 00931.

972.91   CU
CENTRO DE ESTUDIOS MARTIANOS. ANUARIO. 1979. Centro de Estudios Martianos, Apdo. Postal 6640, Havana 6, Cuba. bk. rev. bibl. Supersedes (1969-1978, no.8): Anuario Martiano (ISSN 0066-524X)

989.5   VE   ISSN 0411-5023
CENTRO DE HISTORIA DEL TACHIRA. BOLETIN. 1943. irreg. exchange basis. Centro de Historia del Tachira, Av. 19 Abril 9-111, San Cristobal, Tachira, Tachira, Venezuela. Ed. Xuan Tomas Garcia-Tamayo. circ. 1,000.

977 770   US
CHAMPAIGN COUNTY HISTORICAL ARCHIVES HISTORICAL PUBLICATIONS SERIES. 1977. irreg., no.10, 1984. price varies. Champaign County Historical Archives, Urbana Free Library, 201 S. Race St., Urbana, IL 61801-3283. TEL 217-367-4025. Ed. Frederick A. Schlipf. (back issues avail.)
    Formerly: Historical Reprint Series.

971   CN   ISSN 0078-5091
CHAMPLAIN SOCIETY. ONTARIO SERIES. 1957. irreg. membership. University of Toronto Press, Front Campus, Toronto, Ont. M5S 1A6, Canada. TEL 613-667-7791.

971   CN   ISSN 0316-6724
CHARLOTTES. 1971. irreg. price varies. Queen Charlotte Islands Musuem Society, Second Beach Skidegate, Queen Charlotte, B.C. V0T 1S0, Canada. TEL 604-559-4643. Eds. T. & N. Gessler. circ. 2,500.

971   CN
CHATEAUGUAY VALLEY HISTORICAL SOCIETY ANNUAL JOURNAL/JOURNAL ANNUEL DE LA SOCIETE HISTORIQUE DE LA VALLEE DE LA CHATEAUGUAY. a. $6.50. Chateauguay Valley Historical Society, P.O. Box 61, Howick, Que. H0S 1G0, Canada. illus. circ. 1,000.

970   US   ISSN 0069-3278
CHICAGO HISTORY OF AMERICAN CIVILIZATION. 1956. irreg., latest 1982. price varies. University of Chicago Press, 5801 S. Ellis Ave., Chicago, IL 60637 TEL 312-962-7600. (Orders to: 11030 Langley Ave., Chicago IL 60628) Ed. Daniel J. Boorstin. adv. bk. rev. (reprint service avail. from UMI,ISI)

970.1   US   ISSN 0069-4304
CIVILIZATION OF THE AMERICAN INDIAN. 1932. irreg. price varies. University of Oklahoma Press, 1005 Asp Ave., Norman, OK 73019. TEL 405-325-5111.

917.97   US   ISSN 0090-449X
CLARK COUNTY HISTORY. 1960. a. $5. ‡ Fort Vancouver Historical Society, Box 1834, Vancouver, WA 98668. TEL 206-574-0358. bibl. circ. 1,000.

974   US
CLINTON HISTORICAL SOCIETY. NEWSLETTER. 1963. irreg. membership. Clinton Historical Society, Inc., Box 42, Clinton, NY 13323. Ed. Philip E. Munson. circ. 300.

981   BL
COLECAO DE ESTUDOS HISTORICOS. 1978. irreg. Fundacao Casa de Rui Barbosa, Rua Sao Clemente 134, Botafogo 22260, Rio de Janeiro, RJ, Brazil. Dir. Olavo Brasil de Lima Junior.

981   BL
COLECAO TEMAS BRASILEIROS. no. 13, 1972. irreg. Conquista, Av. 28 de Setembro 174, Rio de Janeiro GB, Brazil. Dir. Arthur C. Ferreira Reis. illus.

COLECCION ESTUDIOS LATINOAMERICANOS. see *LITERATURE*

987   VE   ISSN 0069-5084
COLECCION "FOROS Y SEMINARIOS." SERIE FOROS. 1965. irreg., 1968, no. 5. ‡ Universidad Central de Venezuela, Direccion de Cultura, Biblioteca Piso 10, Cuidad Universitaria, Caracas, Venezuela.

987   VE   ISSN 0069-5092
COLECCION "FOROS Y SEMINARIOS." SERIE SEMINARIOS. 1964. irreg., no. 2, 1966. Universidad Central de Venezuela, Direccion de Cultura, Biblioteca, Piso 10, Ciudad Universitaria, Caracas, Venezuela.

989.2   PY
COLECCION HISTORIA. 1982. irreg. El Lector, 25 de Mayo y Antequera, Asuncion, Paraguay.

974   US
COLONIAL SOCIETY OF MASSACHUSETTS. PUBLICATIONS. (Transactions and Collections) 1895. irreg., vol.63, 1985. $30. Colonial Society of Massachusetts, 87 Mount Vernon St., Boston, MA 02108. Ed. Frederick S. Allis, Jr. circ. 500.

COLONIAL WILLIAMSBURG ARCHAEOLOGICAL SERIES. see *ARCHAEOLOGY*

975   US
CONFEDERATE CALENDAR. 1975. a. $7.95. Confederate Calendar Works, Drawer 2084, Austin, TX 78768. Ed. Lawrence T. Jones. circ. 6,000.

970   US   ISSN 0069-9357
CONTEMPORARY AMERICAN HISTORY SERIES. 1969. irreg., 1977, no.10. Columbia University Press, 562 W. 113th St., New York, NY 10025. TEL 212-678-6777. Ed. William E. Leuchtenburg.

CONTRIBUTIONS IN AFRO-AMERICAN AND AFRICAN STUDIES. see *HISTORY — History Of Africa*

973   US   ISSN 0084-9219
CONTRIBUTIONS IN AMERICAN HISTORY. 1970. irreg. price varies. Greenwood Press, 88 Post Rd. W., Box 5007, Westport, CT 06881. TEL 203-226-3571. Ed. Jon L. Wakelyn.

973   US   ISSN 0084-9227
CONTRIBUTIONS IN AMERICAN STUDIES. 1969. irreg., latest no.76. price varies. Greenwood Press, 88 Post Rd. W., Box 5007, Westport, CT 06881. TEL 203-226-3571. Ed. Robert H. Walker.

970   US   ISSN 0163-3813
CONTRIBUTIONS IN COMPARATIVE COLONIAL STUDIES. 1979. irreg., latest no.15. price varies. Greenwood Press, 88 Post Rd. W., Box 5007, Westport, CT 06881. TEL 203-226-3571.

979.4   US   ISSN 0574-3680
COVERED WAGON. a. $2. Shasta Historical Society, Box 277, Redding, CA 96001. TEL 916-243-4995. illus.

HISTORY — HISTORY OF NORTH AND SOUTH AMERICA

978 US
COVERED WAGON WOMEN. 1982. irreg. $25. Arthur H. Clark Company, Box 230, Glendale, CA 91209. TEL 818-245-9119. Ed. Kenneth L. Holmes. circ. 1,500.

974 US
COW NECK PENINSULA HISTORICAL JOURNAL. 1965. a. membership. Cow Neck Peninsula Historical Society, 336 Port Washington Blvd., Port Washington, NY 11050. TEL 516-365-9074. Ed. Catherine E. Sandy. illus. cum.index 1965-1980. circ. 500.

983 CL ISSN 0716-1832
CUADERNOS DE HISTORIA. 1981. a. $10. Universidad de Chile, Facultad de Filosofia Humanidades Educacion, Departamento de Ciencias Historicas, Santiago, Chile. Ed. Rolando Mellafe. bk. rev. circ. 1,000.

971.4 CN ISSN 0825-2777
CULTURES DU CANADA FRANCAIS. 1970. a. Can.$7. University of Ottawa Press, 603 Cumberland, Ottawa, Ont. K1N 6N5, Canada. TEL 613-231-2270. Ed.Bd. bk. rev. bibl. illus. circ. 1, 200.
Formerly (until 1984): Centre de Recherche en Civilisation Canadienne-Francaise. Bulletin (ISSN 0045-608X)
French Canadian interests

980 US
DELLPLAIN LATIN AMERICAN STUDIES. irreg., no.15, 1984. Westview Press, 5500 Central Ave., Boulder, CO 80301. Ed. Krista Hayenga.

983 CL ISSN 0716-1484
DIMENSION HISTORICA DE CHILE. 1984. a. $7. Academia Superior de Ciencias Pedagogicas de Santiago, Departamento de Historia y Geografia, Av. Jose Pedro Alessandri 774, Santiago, Chile. Ed. Gonzalo Vial Correa. circ. 1,000.

918 US
DIRECTORY OF A S U LATIN AMERICANISTS. 1972/73. a. free. Arizona State University, Center for Latin American Studies, Tempe, AZ 85281. TEL 602-965-5127. Ed. J. R. Ladman.
Formerly: Directory of Latin Americanists (ISSN 0091-3235)

973 US ISSN 0070-5659
DIRECTORY OF HISTORICAL SOCIETIES AND AGENCIES IN THE UNITED STATES AND CANADA. triennial. $64.95. American Association for State and Local History, 172 2nd Ave., N., Ste. 102, Nashville, TN 37201. TEL 615-255-2971. adv.

970 980 AG ISSN 0325-9404
DOCUMENTOS DE GEOHISTORIA REGIONAL. 1980. irreg. Instituto de Investigaciones Geohistoricas, Consejo Nacional de Investigaciones Cientificas y Tecnicas, Av. Castelli 930, Casilla de Correo 438, 3500 Resistencia, Argentina.

970 JA ISSN 0420-0918
DOSHISHA AMERICAN STUDIES. (Text in English and Japanese; summaries in English) 1963. a. free. Doshisha University, Center for American Studies, Karasuma Imadega, Kamikyo-ku, Kyoto, Japan. bk. rev. index. circ. 700. Indexed: Jap.Per.Ind.

974 US
DUTCHESS COUNTY HISTORICAL SOCIETY. YEARBOOK. 1915. a. $15. Dutchess County Historical Society, Box 88, Poughkeepsie, NY 12602. Eds. John and Mary Lou Jeanneney. adv. bk. rev. bibl. charts. illus. index. cum.index: 1976-1980. circ. 650. (back issues avail.) Indexed: Amer.Hist & Life.

970 US ISSN 0070-8089
EAST CAROLINA UNIVERSITY PUBLICATIONS IN HISTORY. 1964. irreg., vol.6, 1985. $19.95 for cloth; paper $9.95. ‡ East Carolina University, Department of History, Greenville, NC 27834. TEL 919-757-6587. Ed. Fred D. Ragan. circ. 500.
Formerly: East Carolina College Publications in History.

970 US ISSN 0361-6193
EAST TENNESSEE HISTORICAL SOCIETY'S PUBLICATIONS. 1929. a. $12 with membership. East Tennessee Historical Society, Lawson McGhee Library, Knoxville, TN 37902. TEL 615-523-0781. Ed. Mark V. Wetherington. circ. 2,000. Indexed: Hist.Abstr. Amer.Hist.& Life.

970 US
ELLIS ISLAND SERIES: IMMIGRATION & THE PLURALIST SOCIETY. 1987. irreg. Holmes & Meier Publishers, Inc., I U B Bldg., 30 Irving Pl., New York, NY 10003. TEL 212-254-4100. Eds. Ira Glazier, Luigi de Rosa.

980 320 NQ
ENVIO. (Text in English, French, German and Spanish) 1982. m. $27 to individuals; institutions $50. Instituto Historico Centroamericano, Apdo. A-194, Managua, Nicaragua (Subscr. to: Central American Historical Institute, ICC, Georgetown University, Washington, DC 20057) circ. 4,000. (also avail. in microfilm) Indexed: HR Rep.

975.9 US
ESCRIBANO; St. Augustine Journal of History. 1959. a. $10 to institutions and libraries. ‡ St. Augustine Historical Society, 271 Charlotte St., St. Augustine, FL 32084. TEL 904-824-2872. Ed. Jacqueline K. Fretwell. illus. cum.index: 1959-1984. circ. 750. (back issues avail.) Indexed: Hist.Abstr. Amer.Hist.& Life.
Formerly: Escribano (ISSN 0014-0376)

ESSAYS FOR THE THIRD CENTURY. see *POLITICAL SCIENCE*

970.1 MX ISSN 0071-1667
ESTUDIOS DE CULTURA MAYA. (Text in English and Spanish) 1960. irreg. price varies. Universidad Nacional Autonoma de Mexico, Centro de Estudios Mayas, Torre de Humanidades II, Piso 11, Ciudad Universitaria, Mexico 04510, D.F., Mexico. bk. rev. circ. 1,500. Indexed: M.L.A. Hisp.Amer.Per.Ind.

972 MX
ESTUDIOS DE CULTURA NAHUATL. 1959. irreg., no.16, 1973. price varies. Universidad Nacional Autonoma de Mexico, Instituto de Investigaciones Historicas, Torre Humanidades, Ciudad Universitaria, 04510 Mexico, D.F., Mexico. Indexed: M.L.A.

972 MX ISSN 0014-147X
ESTUDIOS DE HISTORIA MODERNA Y CONTEMPORANEA DE MEXICO. 1965. irreg; vol. 9, 1983. price varies. Universidad Nacional Autonoma de Mexico, Instituto de Investigaciones Historicas, Delegacion Coyoacan, Ciudad Universitaria, 04510, Mexico, D.F., Mexico. Ed.Bd. bk. rev. bibl. illus. index. circ. 2,000. Indexed: Hist.abstr. Amer.Hist.& Life. Hisp.Amer.Per.Ind.

972 MX ISSN 0185-2523
ESTUDIOS DE HISTORIA NOVOHISPANA. 1947. irreg; no. 8, 1984. price varies. Universidad Nacional Autonoma de Mexico, Instituto de Investigaciones Historicas, Delegacion Coyoacan, Ciudad Universitaria, 04510 Mexico, D.F., Mexico. Indexed: Hist.Abstr. Amer.Hist.& Life.
Formerly: Universidad Nacional Autonoma de Mexico. Instituto de Investigaciones Historicas. Serie de Historia Novohispana (ISSN 0076-7379)

986.6 572 EC
ESTUDIOS ETNOHISTORICOS DEL ECUADOR. 1976. irreg. Casa de la Cultura Ecuatoriana, Nucleo de Guayas, Quito, Ecuador.

985 PE
ESTUDIOS HISTORICOS. (Text in Spanish) 1972. irreg, latest no.10. $12. (Instituto de Estudios Peruanos) I E P Ediciones, Horacio Urteaga 694 (Campe de Marte), Lima 11, Peru. (back issues avail.)

980 PL ISSN 0137-3080
ESTUDIOS LATINOAMERICANOS. (Text in Portuguese and Spanish) a., latest vol.10, 1985. price varies. (Polska Akademia Nauk, Instytut Historii) Ossolineum, Publishing House of the Polish Academy of Sciences, Rynek 9, Wroclaw, Poland (Dist. by: Ars Polona-Ruch, Krakowskie Przedmiescie 7, Warsaw, Poland) Ed Tadeusz Lepkowski. Indexed: Hisp.Amer.Per.Ind.

EXECUTIVE BIO-PICTORIAL DIRECTORY. see *POLITICAL SCIENCE*

980 US
FLORIDA INTERNATIONAL UNIVERSITY. LATIN AMERICAN AND CARIBBEAN CENTER. OCCASIONAL PAPERS SERIES. 1982. irreg. Florida International University, Latin American and Caribbean Center, Miami, FL 33199. TEL 305-554-2894. Eds. Mark B. Rosenberg, A. Douglas Kincaid.

982 AG ISSN 0325-8238
FOLIA HISTORICA DEL NORDESTE. 1974. irreg. $10. Universidad Nacional del Nordeste, Instituto de Historia, Casilla de Correo 438, 3500 Resistencia, Argentina. (Co-sponsor: Instituto de Investigaciones Geohistoricas) Ed.Bd. bk. rev. circ. 500.

978.9 US ISSN 0071-7754
FORT BURGWIN RESEARCH CENTER. PUBLICATIONS. 1961. irreg. price varies. Fort Burgwin Research Center, Inc., Southern Methodist University, Dallas, TX 75275. bk. rev. circ. 1,000. Indexed: GeoRef.

978 US
FORT POINT SALVO. 1967. a. plus q. supplement. $15. Fort Point and Army Museum Association, Box 29163, Presidio of San Francisco, CA 94129. TEL 415-921-8193. Ed. M.B. Halsey, Jr. charts, illus. circ. 900. (looseleaf format; back issues avail.) Indexed: Hist.Abstr. Amer.Hist.& Life.

970 GW
FREIE UNIVERSITAET BERLIN. JOHN F. KENNEDY-INSTITUT FUER NORDAMERIKA STUDIEN. MATERIALIEN. (Text in English and German) 1972. irreg., no. 2, 1973. price varies. Freie Universitaet Berlin, John F. Kennedy-Institut fuer Nordamerika-Studien, Lansstr. 7-9, 1000 Berlin 33, W. Germany (B.R.D.) bibl. circ. 400.

970 CN ISSN 0069-1771
FRENCH-CANADIAN CIVILIZATION RESEARCH CENTER. CAHIERS/CENTRE DE RECHERCHE EN CIVILISATION CANADIENNE-FRANCAISE. CAHIERS. 1968. irreg. price varies. University of Ottawa Press, 603 Cumberland, Ottawa, Ont. K1N 6N5, Canada. TEL 613-564-2270. Eds. J. Menard, J. Hare.
Formerly: Centre de Recherche en Litterature Canadienne-Francaise. Cahiers.

FRONTIER MILITARY SERIES. see *MILITARY*

985 PE
FUENTES E INVESTIGACIONES PARA LA HISTORIA DEL PERU. 1966. irreg., latest no.7. price varies. (Instituto de Estudios Peruanos) I E P Ediciones, Horacio Urteaga 694 (Campe de Marte), Lima 11, Peru. (back issues avail.)

970.1 MX ISSN 0071-9773
FUENTES INDIGENAS DE LA CULTURA NAHUATL. (Title varies: Fuentes Indigenas de la Cultura Nahuatl. Textos de los Informantes de Sahagun) 1958. irreg., no.7, 1969. price varies. Universidad Nacional Autonoma de Mexico, Instituto de Investigaciones Historicas, Villa Obregon, Ciudad Universitaria, Mexico 20, D.F., Mexico. Ed.Bd. circ. 3,000.
Translations from Classic Nahuatl language texts

981.6 BL
FUNDACAO CULTURAL DE CURITIBA. RELATORIO. 1974. irreg. Fundacao Cultural de Curitiba, Curitiba, Brazil. illus.

GERMAN-CANADIAN YEARBOOK/ DEUTSCHKANADISCHES JAHRBUCH. see *ETHNIC INTERESTS*

970.1 CN ISSN 0072-467X
GLENBOW-ALBERTA INSTITUTE. OCCASIONAL PAPER. 1966. irreg. Glenbow-Alberta Institute, 130-9th Ave. S.E., Calgary, Alta. T2G OP3, Canada. TEL 403-264-8300. illus.
Formerly: Glenbow Foundation. Occasional Paper (ISSN 0700-6365)

970.1 CN
GLENBOW MUSEUM. ARCHIVES SERIES. no.6, 1974. irreg. free. Glenbow-Alberta Institute, 130-9th Ave, S.E., Calgary, Alta. T2G OP3, Canada. TEL 403-264-8300. Ed. Anthony Rees. illus. circ. 500.
Formerly: Glenbow Foundation. Archives Series (ISSN 0436-0605)

HISTORY — HISTORY OF NORTH AND SOUTH AMERICA

971   CN   ISSN 0316-2702
GRAND MANAN HISTORIAN. 1934. a. Can.$3. ‡ Grand Manan Historical Society, c/o Secretary, Grand Manan, New Brunswick EOG IL0, Canada. Ed. L. Keith Ingersoll. circ. 300.

970   US   ISSN 0148-771X
GRASS ROOTS PERSPECTIVES ON AMERICAN HISTORY. 1978. irreg. price varies. Greenwood Press, 88 Post Rd. W., Box 5007, Westport, CT 06881. TEL 203-226-3571. Ed. David Thelen.

978 970.1   US   ISSN 0072-7342
GREAT WEST AND INDIAN SERIES. 1945. irreg. price varies. ‡ Westernlore Press, Box 35305, Tucson, AZ 85740. TEL 602-297-5491. Ed. Lynn R. Bailey.

975 929   US
GREENBRIER HISTORICAL SOCIETY. JOURNAL. 1963. a. $7 to non-members. Greenbrier Historical Society, North House, 100 Church St., Lewisburg, WV 24901. TEL 304-645-3503. circ. 550.

GUIDE TO DEPARTMENTS OF HISTORY (YEAR); colleges, universities, and research institutions in the United States and Canada. see EDUCATION — Guides To Schools And Colleges

946.9   PO
GUIMARAES. ARQUIVO MUNICIPAL "ALFREDO PIMENTA." BOLETIM DE TRABALHOS HISTORICOS; elementos para a historia Vimaranese. a. Arquivo Municipal "Alfredo Pimenta", Largo Conego Jose Maria Gomes, 4800 Guimaraes, Portugal. Dir. Manuel Alves de Oliveira.

973   US
GULF COAST CONFERENCE PROCEEDINGS. 1969. irreg. $15 for cloth; paper $10. (Gulf Coast History and Humanities Conference) University of West Florida, John C. Pace Library, Pensacola, FL 32514. TEL 904-474-2492. (back issues avail.)

972   US   ISSN 0072-9833
HANDBOOK OF LATIN AMERICAN STUDIES: A SELECTED AND ANNOTATED GUIDE TO RECENT PUBLICATIONS. 1935. a. beginning with no. 36, even numbered vols. cover humanities; odd numbered vols. cover social sciences. price varies. (U.S. Library of Congress, Hispanic Division) University of Texas Press, Box 7819, Austin, TX 78713. TEL 512-471-4278. Ed. Dolores Moyano Martin. bk. rev. circ. 1,500.

996.9   US   ISSN 0073-1145
HAWAII SERIES. 1968. irreg., no. 7, 1985. price varies. (University of Hawaii, Social Science Research Institute) University of Hawaii Press, 2840 Kolowalu St., Honolulu, HI 96822. TEL 808-948-8697. (reprint service avail. from UMI,ISI)

976   US
HEMPSTEAD COUNTY HISTORICAL SOCIETY. JOURNAL. 1977. irreg. Hempstead County Historical Society, Box 1257, Hope, AR 71801. TEL 202-785-2047.
    Formerly: Hempstead County Historical Society (Publication)

974   US
HERKIMER COUNTY HISTORICAL SOCIETY. 1976. a. Herkimer County Historical Society, 400 N. Main St., Herkimer, NY 13350. TEL 315-866-6413.

983   CL   ISSN 0073-2435
HISTORIA. 1961. a. $20. Pontificia Universidad Catolica de Chile, Instituto de Historia, Av. Diagonal Oriente 3300, Santiago, Chile. Ed.Bd. adv. bk. rev. circ. 1,000. Indexed: Hist.Abstr. Amer.Hist.& Life. Hisp.Amer.Per.Ind.

989.7   US
HISTORIA MILITAR DEL PARAGUAY. 1985. a. Academia de Historia Militar del Paraguay, Calle Paraguari No. 657, Asuncion, Paraguay.

980   CR
HISTORIA NATURAL DE COSTA RICA. (Text in English, French or Spanish) a. Museo Nacional de Costa Rica, Departamento de Historia Natural, Box 749, San Jose, Costa Rica.

985   PE   ISSN 0073-2486
HISTORIA Y CULTURA. (Text in Spanish) 1965. a. $10. Museo Nacional de Historia, Plaza Bolivar, Pueblo Libre, Apdo. 1992, Lima, Peru. Ed. Amalia Castelli. bk. rev. circ. 1,000. Indexed: Hist.Abstr. Amer.Hist.& Life. Hisp.Amer.Per.Ind.

974   US
HISTORIC BETHLEHEM. NEWSLETTER. no. 13, 1977. irreg. membership. Historic Bethlehem, Inc., 501 Main St., Bethlehem, PA 18018. TEL 215-691-5300. Ed. Nancy H. Horvath. illus. circ. 1,500.

970 980   US
HISTORIC DOCUMENTS. 1972. a. Congressional Quarterly Inc., 1414 22nd St. N.W., Washington, DC 20037. TEL 202-887-8500. bibl.

971   CN   ISSN 0709-5562
HISTORIC GUELPH; the royal city. 1977. a. Can.$5. Guelph Historical Society, P.O. Box 1502, Guelph, Ont. N1H 6N9, Canada. TEL 519-822-1709. Eds. Ruth and Eber Pollard. circ. 700. (back issues avail.)

977.5   US   ISSN 0361-574X
HISTORIC MADISON. JOURNAL. 1975. a. $3.50. Historic Madison, Inc., of Wisconsin, Box 4004, Madison, WI 53711. Ed. John Gruber. bk. rev. illus. circ. 500. Key Title: Journal of Historic Madison, Inc. of Wisconsin.

972   US
HISTORY OF THE AZTEC CLUB OF 1847; Mexican War Society. 1880. a. Aztec Club, c/o John C. Hunt, 5225 Westpath Way, Washington, DC 20816. circ. 125.

976   US
HISTORYGRAM. 1974. irreg. free. Metropolitan Historical Commission, Customs House, 701 Broadway, Nashville, TN 37203.

976   US
HUMPHREYS COUNTY HISTORICAL SOCIETY. PUBLICATION. 1978. irreg. c/o Mrs. John H. Whitfield, 105 1/2 Carroll Ave., Waverly, TN 37185.

980 860 460   CS
IBEROAMERICANA PRAGENSIA. 1966. irreg., (approx. every 18 mos.) price varies. Universita Karlova, Centro de Estudios Iberoamericanos, Nam. Krasnoarmejcu 2, 116 38 Prague 1, Czechoslovakia. Ed. Lubomir Vebr. circ. 700.

973   II   ISSN 0301-9101
IDEAS; Indian doctoral engagements in American studies. (Text in English) 1971. irreg. membership. American Studies Research Centre, Osmania University Campus, Hyderabad 500007, India. abstr. circ. 3,000.

ILLINOIS. STATE MUSEUM. SCIENTIFIC PAPERS SERIES. see SCIENCES: COMPREHENSIVE WORKS

917   US   ISSN 0360-0289
ILLINOIS. STATE MUSEUM. STORY OF ILLINOIS SERIES. 1943. irreg., no.14, 1982. Illinois State Museum, Springfield, IL 62706. TEL 217-782-7386.

IMAGO MUSICAE. see MUSIC

977.402   US
IMPRINTS ON THE SANDS OF MARQUETTE COUNTY. vol. 2, 1978. a. membership. Marquette County Historical Society, c/o Mrs. Grace R. Kerst, Rt. 1, Westfield, WI 53964. TEL 608-296-2480. Ed. Mary Lou Schmidt. circ. 250.
    Local

970 980   II
INDIAN ASSOCIATION OF AMERICAN STUDIES. PAPERS. 1973, no. 9. a. Indian Association of American Studies, c/o Dwijendra Tripathi, Indian Institute of Management, Vastrapur, Ahmedabad 380015, India. bibl.
    Formerly: Indian Congress of American History. Papers.

INDIANA; contributions to ethnology and linguistics, archaeology and physical anthropology of Indian America. see ANTHROPOLOGY

973   US   ISSN 0073-6880
INDIANA HISTORICAL COLLECTIONS. 1916. irreg. price varies. Indiana Historical Bureau, 408 State Library and Historical Bldg., 140 N. Senate Ave., Indianapolis, IN 46204. TEL 317-232-2537. bk. rev. index. circ. 600.

973   US   ISSN 0073-6902
INDIANA HISTORICAL SOCIETY. PUBLICATIONS. 1897. irreg., vol.27, no.1, 1984. $15. Indiana Historical Society, 315 W. Ohio St., Indianapolis, IN 46202. TEL 317-232-1882. circ. 5, 800.

977   US
INDIANA HISTORICAL SOCIETY NEWS. 1978. bi-m. $15. Indiana Historical Society, 315 W. Ohio St., Indianapolis, IN 46202. TEL 317-232-1882. Ed. J. Kent Calder.
    Supersedes (as of 1986): Indiana Historical Society Newsletter.

977   US
INDIANA HISTORY RESOURCE SERIES. 1980. irreg. price varies. Indiana Historical Bureau, 408 State Library and Historical Bldg., 140 N. Senate Ave., Indianapolis, IN 46204. TEL 317-232-2537. index. circ. 600.

980   PE
INEDITA. 1973. irreg. Universidad Nacional de San Agustin, Direccion Universitaria de Investigacion, Apdo. 23, Arequipa, Peru. Ed. Alejandro Malaga Medina.

980 972   FR
INSTITUT DES HAUTES ETUDES DE L'AMERIQUE LATINE. COLLECTION DES TRAVAUX ET MEMOIRES. 1957. a. price varies. Institut des Hautes Etudes de l'Amerique Latine, 28 rue Saint-Guillaume, 75007 Paris, France.
    Formerly: Institut des Hautes Etudes de l'Amerique Latine. Travaux et Memoires (ISSN 0073-8298)

INSTITUT FRANCAIS D'ETUDES ANDINES. TRAVAUX. see ANTHROPOLOGY

973 290   US   ISSN 0020-2843
INSTITUTE OF EARLY AMERICAN HISTORY AND CULTURE. NEWS LETTER. 1952. irreg. free to individual subscribers of William & Mary Quarterly. Institute of Early American History & Culture, Box 220, Williamsburg, VA 23187. TEL 804-253-5117. Ed. Michael McGiffert. circ. 3,800.

980   PE
INSTITUTO DE ESTUDIOS PERUANOS. HISTORIA ANDINA. 1973. irreg., latest no.12. price varies. I E P Ediciones, Horacio Urteaga 694 (Campo de Marte), Lima 11, Peru.

983 574   CL
INSTITUTO DE LA PATAGONIA. ANALES. SOCIAL SCIENCIES. (Text in Spanish; summaries in English) 1970. a. Esc.2000($10) Instituto de la Patagonia, Casilla de Correo 113-D, Punta Arenas, Magallanes, Chile. Ed. Mateo Martinic. adv. bk. rev. bibl. charts. illus. circ. 500. Indexed: Biol.Abstr. Chem.Abstr. Aqua.Sci.& Fish.Abstr.
    Supersedes in part (as of vol.15, 1984): Instituto de la Patagonia. Anales (ISSN 0085-1922)

980 300   US   ISSN 0074-0918
INTER-AMERICAN ECONOMIC AND SOCIAL COUNCIL. FINAL REPORT OF THE ANNUAL MEETING AT THE MINISTERIAL LEVEL. (Text in English, French, Portuguese and Spanish) 1962. a. $2. Organization of American States, Department of Publications, Washington, DC 20006. TEL 703-941-1617. circ. 2,000.

980   GW   ISSN 0075-2673
JAHRBUCH FUER GESCHICHTE VON STAAT, WIRTSCHAFT UND GESELLSCHAFT LATEINAMERIKAS. 1964. a. price varies. Boehlau Verlag GmbH, Niehler Str. 272-274, 5000 Cologne 60, W. Germany (B.R.D.) Ed. R. Konetzke. Indexed: Hist.Abstr. Amer.Hist.& Life. Hisp.Amer.Per.Ind.

989   JM
JAMAICAN HISTORICAL REVIEW. 1946. a. $10. Jamaican Historical Society, c/o Institute of Jamaica, 12-16 East St., Kingston, Jamaica. Ed. Carl Campbell. adv. bk. rev. illus. circ. 600.

HISTORY — HISTORY OF NORTH AND SOUTH AMERICA

973 US ISSN 0075-3599
JEFFERSON MEMORIAL LECTURE SERIES.
1962. irreg. price varies. University of California
Press, 2120 Berkeley Way, Berkeley, CA 94720.
TEL 415-642-4247.

980 US
JOHNS HOPKINS STUDIES IN ATLANTIC
HISTORY AND CULTURE. 1977. irreg. price
varies. Johns Hopkins University Press, 701 W. 40th
St., Ste. 275, Baltimore, MD 21211. TEL 301-338-
6900. Eds. Richard Price, Franklin W. Knight.
(reprint service avail. from UMI)

975 US ISSN 0094-8039
JOURNAL OF MUSCLE SHOALS HISTORY. 1973.
a. price varies. Tennessee Valley Historical Society,
Box 149, Sheffield, AL 35660. TEL 205-760-4307.
Ed. Kenneth R. Johnson. circ. 1,000. (back issues
avail.)

975 US ISSN 0739-1943
JOURNAL OF SOUTHWEST GEORGIA
HISTORY. 1983. a. membership. Thronateeska
Heritage Foundation, 100 Roosevelt Ave., Albany,
GA 31701. Ed. Lee W. Formwalt. adv. bk. rev. circ.
400. Indexed: Amer.Hist. & Life.

975 US ISSN 0276-7449
JOURNAL OF THE ALLEGHENIES. 1963. a.
membership. Council of the Alleghenies, Box 514,
Frostburg, MD 21532. Ed. Jeanne M. Cordts. bk.
rev. cum.index: 1963-1984. circ. 150. (back issues
avail.)

980 AG ISSN 0076-6380
JUNTA DE ESTUDIOS HISTORICOS DE
MENDOZA. REVISTA. 1934. biennial. price
varies. Junta de Estudios Historicos de Mendoza,
Calle Montevideo 544, 5500 Mendoza, Argentina.
Ed. Dr. Edmundo Correas. bk. rev. illus. circ. 1,300.

KENTUCKY. ADJUTANT-GENERAL'S OFFICE.
REPORT. see *MILITARY*

980 CN
L A R U WORKING PAPER. no. 28, Aug. 1980.
irreg., (3-4/yr.) Latin American Research Unit, Box
673, Adelaide St. P.O., Toronto, Ont. M5C 2J8,
Canada. Ed.Bd.

978 US
LAKE CHELAN HISTORY NOTES.* vol. 5, 1977.
irreg. Lake Chelan Historical Society, Box 1948,
Chelan, WA 98816. Ed. James E. Lindston.

980 US
LATIN AMERICAN HISTORICAL
DICTIONARIES SERIES. 1967. irreg., no.21,
1981. price varies. Scarecrow Press, Inc., 52 Liberty
St., Box 4167, Metuchen, NJ 08840. TEL 201-548-
8600. Ed. Lawrence Hallewell.

972 016 US
LATIN AMERICAN STUDIES WORKING
PAPERS. (Text in English and Spanish) 1972. irreg.
price varies. Indiana University, Center for Latin
American & Carribbean Studies, Lindley Hall 311,
Bloomington, IN 47405. (back issues avail.)

LATINOAMERICANA. see *BIBLIOGRAPHIES*

977 US
LEE COUNTY HISTORICAL SOCIETY.
HISTORICAL YEARBOOK. 1972? a. price varies.
Lee County Historical Society, Box 58, Dixon, IL
61021. Ed. Marion Snively. illus.

974.4 US ISSN 0024-8185
M.H.S. MISCELLANY. 1955. a. free. Massachusetts
Historical Society, 1154 Boylston St., Boston, MA
02215. TEL 617-536-1608. Ed. Conrad E. Wright.
circ. 1,500.

974 US
MADISON COUNTY HERITAGE. 1977. a.
membership. Madison County Historical Society,
435 Main St., Box 415, Oneida, NY 13421. TEL
315-363-4136. Ed.Bd. bk. rev. cum.index every 5
yrs. circ. 1,000.

975 US ISSN 0076-2342
MAGAZINE OF ALBEMARLE COUNTY
HISTORY. 1940. a. $15. ‡ Albemarle County
Historical Society, Publications Committee, 220
Court Sq., Charlottesville, VA 22901. TEL 804-296-
1492. Ed. Richard Lindenmann. bk. rev. cum.index:
vols. 1-20, 1940-1962. circ. 900. (back issues avail.)
Indexed: Hist.Abstr. Amer.Hist.& Life.

974.1 US ISSN 0076-2652
MAINE HERITAGE SERIES.* 1970. irreg. (Maine
State Museum) Bond Wheelwright Co., Box 1082,
Portland, ME 04104-1082.

974.1 US
MAINE HISTORICAL SOCIETY. RESEARCH
SERIES. 1977. irreg. price varies. Maine Historical
Society, 485 Congress St., Portland, ME 04101.
TEL 207-774-1822.

MALTESE DIRECTORY: CANADA, UNITED
STATES. see *ETHNIC INTERESTS*

980 UK
MANCHESTER LATIN AMERICAN STUDIES.
1981. irreg. price varies. Manchester University
Press, Oxford Rd., Manchester M13 9PL, England.
TEL 061-273-5539.

971 CN ISSN 0076-3896
MANITOBA RECORD SOCIETY.
PUBLICATIONS. (Text in English; occasionally
French) 1965. a. Can.$30. Manitoba Record
Society, Room 401, Fletcher Argue Bldg.,
University of Manitoba, Winnipeg, Man. R3T 2N2,
Canada. Ed. J.M. Bumsted. circ. 1,000.

970 US ISSN 0076-4981
MASSACHUSETTS HISTORICAL SOCIETY.
PROCEEDINGS. 1859. a. $20 paper; $25 cloth.
Massachusetts Historical Society, 1154 Boylston St.,
Boston, MA 02215. TEL 617-536-1608. Ed. Conrad
E. Wright. circ. 600. Indexed: Curr.Cont.
Hist.Abstr. Arts & Hum.Cit.Ind. Amer.Hist.& Life.
Abstr.Engl.Stud.

978 US
MEADE COUNTY HISTORIAN. 1974. a. Meade
County Historical Society, 200 E. Carthage, Meade,
KS 67864. TEL 316-873-2359. Ed. W.P. Bunyan.
circ. 1,500. (looseleaf format)

MEETING GROUND. see *ETHNIC INTERESTS*

972 DK
MELLEMAMERIKA NYT; avis. 1981. irreg. Kr.35
per no. El Salvadore Kampagnen, Noerrebrogade
32/4, 2200 Copenhagen N, Denmark. Ed. Stig
Nielsen. bk. rev. illus. circ. 3,000.
    Formerly: El Salvador Nyt (ISSN 0108-6510)

981 BL
MEMORIA E HISTORIA. irreg., no. 2, 1982. Livraria
Editora Ciencias Humanas, Rua 7 de Abril, 264
Subsolo B-Sala 5, Sao Paulo, Brazil.

977 020 US
MICHIGAN GAZETTE. 1967. a. free. University of
Michigan, Bentley Historical Library, 1150 Beal
Ave., Ann Arbor, MI 48109-2113. TEL 313-764-
3482. Ed. W.K. Wallace. circ. 800.

980 US ISSN 0076-8189
MICHIGAN STATE UNIVERSITY. LATIN
AMERICAN STUDIES CENTER.
MONOGRAPH SERIES. irreg. price varies. ‡
Michigan State University, Latin American Studies
Center, 103 International Center, East Lansing, MI
48824. TEL 517-355-1855. (reprint service avail.
from UMI)

980 US ISSN 0076-8200
MICHIGAN STATE UNIVERSITY. LATIN
AMERICAN STUDIES CENTER. RESEARCH
REPORTS. 1968. irreg. price varies. ‡ Michigan
State University, Latin American Studies Center,
103 International Center, East Lansing, MI 48824.
TEL 517-335-1855. (reprint service avail. from
UMI)

977 US
MIDDLETOWN HISTORICAL SOCIETY.
NEWSLETTER. no. 17, 1977. irreg. Middletown
Historical Society, 7426 Hubbard Ave., Middletown,
WI 53562.

MISSISQUOI HISTORICAL SOCIETY REPORTS.
see *GENEALOGY AND HERALDRY*

970 US ISSN 0076-9630
MISSOURI HANDBOOK SERIES. 1961. irreg., no.5,
1964. price varies. University of Missouri Press, 200
Lewis Hall, Columbia, MO 65211. TEL 314-882-
7641.

970 980 US
MONOGRAPHS IN INTERNATIONAL STUDIES:
LATIN AMERICA SERIES. 1977. irreg. price
varies. Ohio University, Center for International
Studies, Burson House, 56 E. Union St., Athens,
OH 45701 TEL 614-594-5511. (Orders to: Ohio
University Press, Scott Quad., Athens, OH 45701)
Ed. Thomas Walker. bibl. charts. illus. circ. 500.
(back issues avail.) Indexed: SSCI.
    Formerly: Papers in International Studies: Latin
American Series (ISSN 0149-4880)

MONUMENTA AMERICANA. see
ARCHAEOLOGY

980 860 UY ISSN 0077-2844
NARRATIVA LATINOAMERICANA.* irreg.
Editorial Arca, Colonia 1263, Montevideo, Uruguay.

974 US
NASSAU COUNTY HISTORICAL SOCIETY
JOURNAL. 1937. a. $5. Nassau County Historical
Society, Box 207, Garden City, NY 11530. Ed. Dr.
Myron H. Luke. circ. 600.

973 320 US ISSN 0077-7935
NEVADA STUDIES IN HISTORY AND
POLITICAL SCIENCE. 1960. irreg. price varies.
(University of Nevada, Departments of History and
Political Science) University of Nevada Press, Attn:
Katie Gude, Reno, NV 89557. TEL 702-784-6573.
Ed. Wilbur S. Shepperson. circ. 1,300.

974 US ISSN 0734-2802
NEW CANAAN HISTORICAL SOCIETY
ANNUAL. 1943. a. $3. New Canaan Historical
Society, 13 Oenoke Ridge, New Canaan, CT 06840.
TEL 203-966-1776. Ed. Elizabeth Marting. circ. 1,
000. (back issues avail.)

974 US
NEW HAVEN COLONY HISTORICAL SOCIETY.
JOURNAL. 1952. irreg. $6.65. New Haven Colony
Historical Society, 114 Whitney Ave., New Haven,
CT 06510. Ed. Lawrence Kenney. circ. 1,200.

976 US
NEW PERSPECTIVES ON THE SOUTH. 1979.
irreg., latest 1985. price varies. University Press of
Kentucky, Lexington, KY 40506-0024. TEL 606-
257-2951. Ed. Charles P. Roland. (reprint service
avail. from UMI)

970 980 US
NEW WORLD JOURNAL. 1975. a. $5.
(Netzahaulcoyotl Historical Society) Turtle Island
Foundation, 2845 Buena Vista Way, Berkeley, CA
94708. TEL 415-845-0984. Ed. Bob Callahan. bk.
rev. circ. 1,000.

NEW YORK (CITY). MUSEUM OF THE CITY OF
NEW YORK. ANNUAL REPORT. see
MUSEUMS AND ART GALLERIES

982 AG
NORTE. 1975 (third series) irreg. Consejo Provincial
de Difusion Cultural, Departamento de Literatura,
San Miguel de Tucuman, Argentina.

387.5 US ISSN 0198-7194
NORTH AMERICAN SOCIETY FOR OCEANIC
HISTORY. PROCEEDINGS. 1977. a. North
American Society for Oceanic History, c/o History
Department, U.S. Naval Academy, Annapolis, MD
21402. TEL 301-267-2248. bk. rev. circ. 200.

NORTH AMERICAN SOCIETY FOR SPORT
HISTORY. PROCEEDINGS. see *SPORTS AND
GAMES*

974 US
NORTH CASTLE HISTORY. 1974. a. $2.50 to non-
members. North Castle Historical Society, 440
Bedford Rd., Armonk, NY 10504. Ed. Norman
Stone. bibl. charts. illus. circ. 700. (back issues
avail.)

HISTORY — HISTORY OF NORTH AND SOUTH AMERICA

979 US ISSN 0272-1570
NORTHWEST DISCOVERY; the journal of northwest history and natural history. 1980. irreg., vol. 3, 1982. $15 for 4 nos. Northwest Press, 1439 E. Prospect St., Seattle, WA 98112. Ed. Harry M. Majors. Indexed: GeoRef.

973 US ISSN 0078-1789
NORTHWEST HISTORICAL SERIES. 1923. irreg. price varies. Arthur H. Clark Co., Box 230, Glendale, CA 91209-0230. index.

900 325 US ISSN 0078-1967
NORWEGIAN-AMERICAN HISTORICAL ASSOCIATION. NEWSLETTER. 1934. irreg. free. ‡ Norwegian-American Historical Association, St. Olaf College, Northfield, MN 55057. TEL 507-663-3221. Ed. Lloyd Hustvedt. circ. 1,300.

948 973 US ISSN 0085-4352
NORWEGIAN-AMERICAN HISTORICAL ASSOCIATION. TOPICAL STUDIES. 1971. irreg., vol.3, 1981. price varies. ‡ Norwegian-American Historical Association, St. Olaf College, Northfield, MN 55057. TEL 507-663-3221. Ed. Odd S. Lovoll. circ. 1,500. (reprint service avail. from UMI)

900 US ISSN 0078-1975
NORWEGIAN AMERICAN HISTORICAL ASSOCIATION. TRAVEL AND DESCRIPTION SERIES. 1926. irreg., vol.10, 1984. price varies. ‡ Norwegian-American Historical Association, St. Olaf College, Northfield, MN 55057. TEL 506-663-3221. Ed. Odd S. Lovoll. circ. 1,500. (reprint service avail. from UMI)

900 US ISSN 0078-1983
NORWEGIAN-AMERICAN STUDIES. 1926. irreg., vol.31, 1986. $15. ‡ Norwegian-American Historical Association, St. Olaf College, Northfield, MN 55057. TEL 507-663-3221. Ed. Odd S. Lovoll. circ. 1,500. (also avail. in microform from UMI; reprint service avail. from UMI) Indexed: M.L.A.
Formerly: Norwegian-American Studies and Records.

980 US ISSN 0078-6403
O A S. GENERAL SECRETARIAT. ANNUAL REPORT. 1960. a. $20. Organization of American States, General Secretariat, Department of Publications, 17th and Constitution Ave., N.W., Washington, DC 20006. TEL 703-941-1617.

974 US
OFFICE FOR METROPOLITAN HISTORY. RESEARCH AND REMARKS ON CURRENT TOPICS.* no. 11, 1977. irreg. Office for Metropolitan History, 255 W. 90th St., New York, NY 10024. TEL 212-799-0520.

978.9 US ISSN 0732-3093
OFFICIAL NEW MEXICO BLUE BOOK. 1882. biennial. free. ‡ Secretary of State, Executive Legislative Bldg., Santa Fe, NM 87503. TEL 505-827-3600. Ed. Edmundo Delgado. bibl. charts. illus. stat. circ. 3,000.
Former titles: New Mexico Blue Book (ISSN 0196-3929) & Historical Blue Book of New Mexico.

971 CN ISSN 0830-0739
OKANAGAN HISTORY; report of Okanagan historical society. 1926. a. Can.$10. Okanagan Historical Society, P.O. Box 313, Vernon, B.C. V1T 6M3, Canada. Ed. Jean Webber. circ. 2,000. (back issues avail.)
Formerly(until 1984): Okangan Historical Society. Report.

970 US
OLD GLORY; the story of our flag. 1972. a. $2. Snibbe Books, 1115 Ponce de Leon, Clearwater, FL 33516. Ed. M.R. Bennett. circ. 3,000,000.

974 US
OLD YORK ROAD HISTORICAL SOCIETY BULLETIN. 1936. a. membership; free to libraries. Old York Road Historical Society, c/o Jenkintown Library, York and Vista Rds., Jenkintown, PA 19046. TEL 215-884-0593. Ed. Suzanne M. Hilton. circ. 265.

971 CN
ONTARIO HISTORICAL STUDIES SERIES. 1977. irreg. (Ministry of Culture and Recreation) University of Toronto Press, Front Campus, Toronto, Ont. M5S 1A6, Canada TEL 613-667-7791. (U.S. address: 33 E. Tupper St., Buffalo, NY 14203) Ed.Bd.

980 016 US ISSN 0078-642X
ORGANIZATION OF AMERICAN STATES. OFFICIAL RECORDS. INDICE Y LISTA GENERAL. Spanish edition: Documentos Oficiales de la Organizacion de los Estados Americanos: Lista General Indice Analitico (ISSN 0078-6365) (Editions also in French and Portuguese) 1960. a. price varies. Organization of American States, General Secretariat, Department of Publications, 17th and Constitution Ave. N.W., Washington, DC 20006. TEL 703-941-1617. circ. 2,000.

980 341.8 US ISSN 0078-6438
ORGANIZATION OF AMERICAN STATES. PERMANENT COUNCIL. DECISIONS TAKEN AT MEETINGS (CUMULATED EDITION) (Text in English and Spanish) 1951. a. price varies. Organization of American States, Department of Publications, Washington, DC 20006. TEL 703-941-1617. circ. 1,000.

972 800 382 US ISSN 0190-2229
PACIFIC COAST COUNCIL ON LATIN AMERICAN STUDIES. PROCEEDINGS. (Text in English, Portuguese and Spanish) 1972. a. $12. San Diego State University Press, San Diego State University, San Diego, CA 92182. TEL 619-265-5200. Ed. Roger L. Cunniff. bk. rev. film rev. bibl. circ. 600(controlled) (back issues avail.)

979 US
PACIFIC ISLANDS MONGRAPH SERIES. 1983. irreg., no.3, 1986. (University of Hawaii, Center for Pacific and Asian Studies) University of Hawaii Press, 2840 Kolowalu St., Honolulu, HI 96822.

971 CN
PACIFIC MARITIME STUDIES SERIES. 1980. irreg. price varies. University of British Columbia Press, 303-6344 Memorial Rd., Vancouver, B.C. V6T 1W5, Canada. TEL 604-228-3259.

980 MX ISSN 0078-8813
PAN AMERICAN INSTITUTE OF GEOGRAPHY AND HISTORY. COMMISSION ON HISTORY. BIBLIOGRAFIAS. (Text in English, French, Portuguese or Spanish) 1953. irreg., vol.4, 1070. price varies. Instituto Panamericano de Geografia e Historia, Ex-Arzobispedo 29, Col. Observatorio, Deleg. Miguel Hidalgo, 11860 Mexico, D.F., Mexico.

980.2 MX ISSN 0078-883X
PAN AMERICAN INSTITUTE OF GEOGRAPHY AND HISTORY. COMMISSION ON HISTORY. HISTORIOGRAFIAS AMERICANAS. 1953. irreg., vol.5, 1979. Instituto Panamericano de Geografia e Historia, Ex-Arzobispedo 29, Col. Observatorio, Deleg. Miguel Hidalgo, 11860 Mexico, D.F., Mexico.

980 MX ISSN 0078-8848
PAN AMERICAN INSTITUTE OF GEOGRAPHY AND HISTORY. COMMISSION ON HISTORY. HISTORIADORES DE AMERICA. (Text in English, French, Portuguese or Spanish) 1949. irreg., vol.12, 1967. price varies. Instituto Panamericano de Geografia e Historia, Commission on History, Ex-Arzobispedo 29, Col. Observatorio, Deleg. Miguel Hidalgo, 11860 Mexico, D.F., Mexico.

980.2 MX ISSN 0078-8856
PAN AMERICAN INSTITUTE OF GEOGRAPHY AND HISTORY. COMMISSION ON HISTORY. MONUMENTOS HISTORICOS Y ARQUEOLOGICOS. 1950. irreg., vol.18, 1984. price varies. Instituto Panamericano de Geografia e Historia, Commission on History, Ex-Arzobispedo 29, Col. Observatorio, Deleg. Miguel Hidalgo, 11860 Mexico, D.F., Mexico.

976 US ISSN 0148-7795
PANHANDLE-PLAINS HISTORICAL REVIEW. 1928. a. $10. Panhandle-Plains Historical Society, Box 967 W.T. Station, Canyon, TX 79016. TEL 806-655-7191. Ed. Dianna Everett. index. circ. 1, 000. (back issues avail.)

PENNSYLVANIA. HISTORICAL AND MUSEUM COMMISSION. ANTHROPOLOGICAL SERIES. see *ANTHROPOLOGY*

970 UK ISSN 0266-1322
PERSPECTIVES IN AMERICAN HISTORY. 1984. a. $47 to individuals; institutions $42. (Charles Warren Center for Studies in American History, Harvard) Cambridge University Press, Edinburgh Bldg., Shaftesbury Rd., Cambridge CB2 2RU, England (And 32 E. 57th St., New York, NY 10022) Ed.Bd.

975 976 US ISSN 0275-584X
PERSPECTIVES ON THE AMERICAN SOUTH. 1981. irreg., latest vol.3, 1985. Gordon and Breach Science Publishers, 50 West 23rd St., New York, NY 10010. TEL 212-206-8900. Eds. J. Cobb, C. Wilson.

974 US
PETTAQUAMSCUTT REPORTER. vol.13, 1977. irreg. membership. Pettaquamscutt Historical Society, c/o William D. Metz, Box 59, Kingston, RI 02881. TEL 401-783-1328. Ed. Shirley Barrett. circ. 300.

917.4 US
PINERY. 1956; N.S. 1977. irreg. (3-4/yr.) membership. ‡ Portage County Historical Society, University of Wisconsin, Stevens Point, WI 54481. TEL 715-346-2586. Ed. William G. Paul. bk. rev. bibl. circ. 250.
Local

973 398 US
PIONEER AMERICA SOCIETY. TRANSACTIONS. 1977. a. $20. (Pioneer Society of America) University of Akron, Department of Geography, Akron, OH 44325 TEL 314-651-2354. (Subscr. to: c/o Keith Sculle, Illinois Historical Preservation Agency, Old State Capitol, Springfield, MO 62701) Ed. Russel Swenson. adv. bk. rev. abstr. illus. stat. index. (back issues avail.)

970 US
POPULAR CULTURE BIO-BIBLIOGRAPHIES. 1982. irreg. price varies. Greenwood Press, 88 Post Rd. W., Box 5007, Westport, CT 06881. TEL 203-226-3571. Ed. M. Thomas Inge.

917.8 US ISSN 0092-8313
PRAIRIE SCOUT. 1973. irreg., latest vol.5. $15. Westerners, Kansas Corral, Box 531, Abilene, KS 67410. Ed. Leo E. Oliva. illus. circ. 250.

390 973 UK ISSN 0361-2333
PROSPECTS; annual journal of American cultural studies. 1975. a. $37 to individuals; institutions $68. Cambridge University Press, The Edinburgh Bldg., Shaftesbury Rd., Cambridge CB2 2RU, England. Ed. Jack Salzman.

970 US
PUBLIC WORKS HISTORICAL SOCIETY NEWSLETTER. irreg., no.33, 1984. Public Works Historical Society, 1313 E. 60th St., Chicago, IL 60637. TEL 312-667-2200. Ed. Howard Rosen.

973 US ISSN 0085-5227
PUBLICATIONS IN THE AMERICAN WEST. 1969. irreg., latest issue, 1984. price varies. (American West Center) University of Utah Press, Salt Lake City, UT 84112. TEL 801-581-6771.

970 980 GW ISSN 0079-9157
QUELLENWERKE ZUR ALTEN GESCHICHTE AMERIKAS. irreg., vol.13, 1981. price varies. (Ibero-Amerikanisches Institut Preussischer Kulturbesitz Berlin) Gebr. Mann Verlag, Lindenstr. 76, Postfach 110303, 1000 Berlin 61, W. Germany (B.R.D.) Ed. Gerdt Kutscher.

980 EC
QUITUMBE. 1971. a., no.2, 1972. S/40($2) Pontificia Universidad Catolica del Ecuador, Departamento de Historia y Geografia, Avda. 12 de Octubre 1076 y Carrion, Apdo. 2184, Quito, Ecuador. adv. circ. 1, 000.

974 US
RADNOR HISTORICAL SOCIETY. BULLETIN. 1950. a. $3. Radnor Historical Society, 113 W. Beech Tree Lane, Wayne, PA 19087. TEL 215-688-2668. Eds. John Dale, Jean LaRouche. adv. circ. 300. (back issues avail.)

HISTORY — HISTORY OF NORTH AND SOUTH AMERICA

971　　　　　　CN　ISSN 0315-2804
RAINCOAST CHRONICLES. 1972. irreg. Can.$16. (Raincoast Historical Society) Harbour Publishing Co. Ltd., Box 219, Madeira Park, B.C. V0N 2H0, Canada. Ed. Howard White. bk. rev. illus. circ. 5,000.

974　　　　　　US
READINGS IN LONG ISLAND ARCHAEOLOGY AND ETHNOHISTORY. 1977. a. latest vol.7, 1986. price varies. (Suffolk County Archaeological Association) Ginn Press, 191 Spring St., Lexington, MA 02173 TEL 516-929-8725. (Subscr. to: Suffolk Co. Archaeological Assoc., Drawer AR, Stony Brook, NY 11790) Ed. Gaynell Stone. circ. 1,000. (back issues avail.)

981　　　　　　BL
RECIFE, BRAZIL. SECRETARIA DE EDUCACAO E CULTURA. ARQUIVOS. irreg. Secretaria de Educacao e Cultura, Recife, Pernambuco, Brazil.
Archives

971　　　　　　CN
RECOLLECTIONS OF THE PIONEERS OF BRITISH COLUMBIA. 1975. irreg. price varies. University of British Columbia Press, 303-6344 Memorial Rd., Vancouver, B.C. V6T 1W5, Canada. TEL 604-228-3259. Ed. Bd.
Formerly: British Columbia Historical Documents Series.

977 917　　　　US
REPORTS IN MACKINAC HISTORY AND ARCHAEOLOGY. 1972. irreg. (approx. a.) price varies. ‡ Mackinac Island State Park Commission, Box 30028, Lansing, MI 48909. TEL 906-847-3328. Ed. David A. Armour. bibl. illus.

980　　　　　　CL　ISSN 0080-2093
REVISTA CHILENA DE HISTORIA Y GEOGRAFIA. 1911. a. $15. Sociedad Chilena de Historia y Geografia, Casilla 1386, Santiago, Chile. bk. rev. cum.index. circ. 1,000. Indexed: Hisp.Amer.Per.Ind.

986.6　　　　　EC　ISSN 0556-5987
REVISTA DE HISTORIA DE LAS IDEAS. 1959. irreg. Instituto Panamericano de Geografia e Historia, Casa de la Cultura Ecuatoriana, Quito, Ecuador. Indexed: Hisp.Amer.Per.Ind.

982　　　　　　AG　ISSN 0556-5995
REVISTA DE HISTORIA DE ROSARIO. 1963. a. $5. Sociedad de Historia de Rosario, 1 de Mayo 1082, 2000 Rosario, Argentina. Ed. Wladimir C. Mikielievich. adv. bk. rev. circ. 1,100.

989　　　　　　UY
REVISTA HISTORICA. vol.67, 1973. a. Museo Historico Nacional, Casa Rivera, Rincon 437, Montevideo, Uruguay. Ed.Bd. Indexed: Hisp.Amer.Per.Ind.

REVISTA 13 GRAFICO. see *GENERAL INTEREST PERIODICALS — Guatemala*

970　　　　　　US　ISSN 0146-1869
RIO GRANDE HISTORY. 1973. irreg. $10. New Mexico State University Library, Rio Grande Historical Collections, Box 3475, Las Cruces, NM 88003. TEL 505-646-3839. Ed. Austin Hoover. bk. rev. illus. circ. 500. Indexed: Hist.Abstr. Amer.Hist. & Life.

RIPLEY P. BULLEN MONOGRAPHS IN ANTHROPOLOGY AND HISTORY. see *ARCHAEOLOGY*

975.5　　　　　US
ROANOKE VALLEY HISTORICAL SOCIETY JOURNAL. 1964. a. $4 to non-members; members $3. ‡ Roanoke Valley Historical Society, Box 1904, Roanoke, VA 24008. TEL 703-344-3418. Ed. George Kegley. illus. circ. 500 (approx.) (back issues avail.)
Formerly: Roanoke Historical Society. Journal (ISSN 0035-7359)

970　　　　　　US　ISSN 0080-3383
ROCKBRIDGE HISTORICAL SOCIETY, LEXINGTON, VIRGINIA. PROCEEDINGS. 1939. irreg., vol.9, 1982. $7.70. Rockbridge Historical Society, Box 514, Lexington, VA 24450. TEL 703-463-3281. Ed. Larry I. Bland. cum.index: vols. 1-6 in vol. 6. circ. 750.

980　　　　　　US　ISSN 0081-2951
S E C O L A S ANNALS. 1970. a. $12 to individuals; institutions $20. (Southeastern Council on Latin American Studies) Georgia Southern College, c/o T. Ray Shurbutt, Ed., Statesboro, GA 30460. TEL 912-681-5586. circ. 500. (also avail. in microfilm from UMI; back issues avail.) Indexed: Hist.Abstr. M.L.A. P.A.I.S. Amer.Hist.&Life.

970　　　　　　US
S M R C NEWSLETTER. 1967. irreg., vol.20, 1986. $10. ‡ Southwestern Mission Research Center, Inc., Arizona State Museum, University of Arizona, Tucson, AZ 85721. TEL 602-621-6278. Ed. Bernard Fontana. bk. rev. bibl. circ. 1,000.

979.2　　　　　US
SAGA OF THE SANPITCH. 1969. a. $2.50. ‡ Church of Jesus Christ of Latter-day Saints, Manti Region, Box 66, Sterling, UT 84665. TEL 801-835-2291. Ed. Pamela Jensen. circ. 2,000.

977.3　　　　　US　ISSN 0095-3911
ST. CLAIR COUNTY HISTORICAL SOCIETY. JOURNAL. a. $1.75. St. Clair County Historical Society, c/o Rose Mansfield, Ed., 20 Sherwood Forest, Belleville, IL 62223. TEL 618-234-0600. illus. (back issues avail.) Key Title: Journal of the St. Clair County Historical Society.

978　　　　　　US
SANTA ANA MOUNTAIN SERIES. 1977. irreg. price varies. California Classics, Box 291, Trabuco Canyon, CA 92678. Ed. Jim Sleeper. circ. 5,000.

981　　　　　　BL　ISSN 0034-9216
SAO PAULO (CITY) ARQUIVO MUNICIPAL. REVISTA. 1934-1984; resumed 1987 (no. 197) irreg. free. Arquivo Municipal, Divisao de Arquivo Historico, Rua da Consolacao 1024, Sao Paulo, Brazil. illus. circ. 1,000 (controlled)

SCANDINAVIAN HERITAGE. see *ETHNIC INTERESTS*

970 940 430 375.4　US　ISSN 0740-1965
SCHATZKAMMER; der deutschen Sprache, Dichtung und Geschichte. 1975. a. $7.50. University of South Dakota, c/o Werner Kitzler, Mg. Ed., Department of History, Vermillion, SD 57069. TEL 605-677-5011. Ed. Donald Pryce. adv. bk. rev. circ. 1,000. Indexed: Lang.& Lang.Behav.Abstr.
German-American history

SEMINAR ON THE ACQUISITION OF LATIN AMERICAN LIBRARY MATERIALS. PAPERS. see *LIBRARY AND INFORMATION SCIENCES*

981　　　　　　BL
SERIE CADERNOS DE HISTORIA.* no.2, 1977. irreg. Thesaurus Editora, SIG-Quadra 8-Lote 2356, 70610 Brasilia, Brazil. TEL X.

981 320　　　　BL
SERIE NOVAS PERSPECTIVAS. irreg., no.2, 1982. price varies. Editora Mercado Aberto, Rua Santos Dumont, 1186, C.P. 1432, 90000 Porto Alegre, RS, Brazil.

979.4　　　　　US　ISSN 0583-4449
SISKIYOU PIONEER AND YEARBOOK. 1946. a. $10 includes monthly newsletter, Nuggets. Siskiyou County Historical Society, 910 S. Main St., Yreka, CA 96097. adv. charts. illus. circ. 1,500.

971　　　　　　CN　ISSN 0085-6207
SOCIAL HISTORY OF CANADA. 1971. irreg. price varies. University of Toronto Press, Front Campus, Toronto, Ont. M5S 1A6, Canada TEL 613-667-7791. (and 33 East Tupper St., Buffalo, N.Y. 14203) Ed. Prof. H.V. Nelles.

SOCIEDAD GEOLOGICA DEL PERU. BOLETIN. see *EARTH SCIENCES — Geology*

985　　　　　　PE
SOCIEDAD PERUANA DE HISTORIA. SERIE: ACTOS ACADEMICOS. irreg. Universidad Nacional Mayor de San Marcos, Lima, Peru.

572 917 918　　SZ　ISSN 0582-1592
SOCIETE SUISSE DES AMERICANISTES. BULLETIN/SCHWEIZERISCHE AMERIKANISTEN-GESELLSCHAFT. BULLETIN. (Text in French and German) 1950; N.S. 1980. a. 25 Fr. Societe Suisse des Americanistes - Schweizerische Amerikanisten-Gesellschaft, 65-67, Boulevard Carl-Vogt, 1205 Geneva, Switzerland. Ed. Rene Fuerst. bibl. charts. illus. circ. 750.

SONS AND DAUGHTERS OF THE SODDIES. REPORTS; sod houses and dugouts in North America. see *GENEALOGY AND HERALDRY*

SOURCES OF MUSIC AND THEIR INTERPRETATION, DUKE STUDIES IN MUSIC. see *MUSIC*

980　　　　　　UK　ISSN 0268-0661
SOUTH AMERICA, CENTRAL AMERICA AND THE CARIBBEAN. 1985. biennial. $90. Europa Publications Ltd., 18 Bedford Sq., London WC1B 3JN, England. bibl. stat.

975　　　　　　US
SOUTH CAROLINA. DEPARTMENT OF ARCHIVES AND HISTORY. ANNUAL REPORT. 1906. a. free. Department of Archives and History, 1430 Senate St., Box 11669, Columbia, SC 29211. circ. 325.

975　　　　　　US　ISSN 0361-6207
SOUTH CAROLINA HISTORICAL ASSOCIATION. PROCEEDINGS. 1932. a. $10. South Carolina Historical Association, 171 University Pkwy., University of South Carolina at Aiken, Aiken, SC 29801. TEL 803-648-6851. Ed. Valdis O. Lumans. adv. index. circ. 300. (also avail. in microform from UMI; back issues avail.; reprint service avail. from UMI) Key Title: Proceedings of the South Carolina Historical Association.

977　　　　　　US
SOUTH DAKOTA HISTORICAL COLLECTIONS. 1902. irreg. price varies. South Dakota State Historical Society, 800 Governors Dr., Pierre, SD 57501. TEL 605-773-3458. Ed. Nancy Koupal. circ. 1,400. (reprint service avail. from UMI)
Former titles: South Dakota State Historical Society. Collections (ISSN 0081-2773); South Dakota. Department of History. Historical Collections; (until 1974): South Dakota. Department of History. Report and Historical Collections (ISSN 0092-198X)

977　　　　　　US
SOUTH WOOD COUNTY HISTORICAL CORPORATION. NEWSLETTER. 1962. irreg. free. South Wood County Historical Corporation, 540 Third St. So., Wisconsin Rapids, WI 54494. TEL 715-423-1580. Ed. J. Marshall Buehler. circ. 250.

973　　　　　　US　ISSN 0081-315X
SOUTHWESTERN STUDIES. MONOGRAPHS. 1963. irreg. (3-4/yr.) $12. (University of Texas at El Paso) Texas Western Press, University of Texas at El Paso, El Paso, TX 79968. TEL 915-747-5688. Ed. Dale L. Walker. bk. rev. circ. 1,500. (also avail. in microform from UMI) Indexed: SSCI.

SPECTRUM (ST. PAUL) see *POPULATION STUDIES*

971　　　　　　CN　ISSN 0081-4369
STANSTEAD COUNTY HISTORICAL SOCIETY. JOURNAL. 1965. biennial. Can.$10. Stanstead County Historical Society, Box 268, Stanstead, Que. J0B 3E0, Canada. TEL 819-876-5425. Ed. Ann Pelley. circ. 600.

972　　　　　　US
STATE UNIVERSITY OF NEW YORK AT ALBANY. INSTITUTE FOR MESOAMERICAN STUDIES. PUBLICATION. irreg., no.7, 1982. State University of New York at Albany, Institute for Mesoamerican Studies, Albany, NY 12222.

STORIES FROM THE HILLS. see *LITERATURE*

SURVEY OF PRESS FREEDOM IN LATIN AMERICA. see *JOURNALISM*

975.9　　　　　　US　　ISSN 0363-3705
TEQUESTA. 1941. a. $25 includes Update. ‡
Historical Association of Southern Florida, 101 W.
Flagler St., Miami, FL 33130. TEL 305-375-1492.
Ed.Bd. bk. rev. bibl. circ. 3,800.

985　　　　　　　PE
TESTIMONIOS (EN HISTORIETA) 1979. irreg. $40
includes subscr. to: Cuadernos de Estudio,
Cuadernos de Capacitation and Cuadernos
Populares. Comision Evangelica Latinoamericana de
Educacion Cristiana, Av. General Garzon 2267,
Lima 11, Peru.

976.4　　　　　　　US
TEXAS ALMANAC AND STATE INDUSTRIAL
GUIDE. Cover title: Texas Almanac. 1857. biennial.
$14.95 hardbound; paperbound $8.95. (Dallas
Morning News) A.H. Belo Corp., Communications
Center, Dallas, TX 75265. TEL 214-977-8393. Ed.
Mike Kingston. adv. charts. illus. stat. index. circ.
100,000. (also avail. in microform)

THESES IN LATIN AMERICAN STUDIES AT
BRITISH UNIVERSITIES IN PROGRESS OR
RECENTLY COMPLETED. see
BIBLIOGRAPHIES

975　　　　　　　US
THREE RIVERS CHRONICLE. 1981. irreg. Three
Rivers Historical Society, Box 723, Hemingway, SC
29554. Ed. Dr. Johnstone Parr.

970　　　　　　CN　　ISSN 0082-4283
THUNDER BAY HISTORICAL MUSEUM
SOCIETY. PAPERS AND RECORDS. 1908. irreg.
Can.$4. Thunder Bay Historical Museum Society,
219 S. May St., Thunder Bay, Ont. P7E 1B5,
Canada. TEL 807-623-0801. Ed. Roy H. Piovesana.
circ. 1,000.

971　　　　　　CN　　ISSN 0226-7209
TORONTO HISTORICAL BOARD. YEAR BOOK.
1975. a. Toronto Historical Board, General Office,
Stanley Barracks, Toronto, Ont. M6K 3C3, Canada.
TEL 416-595-1567. illus. circ. 600.

973　　　　　　　SP
TRABAJOS MONOGRAFICOS SOBRE LA
INDEPENDENCIA DE NORTEAMERICA.
1977. irreg. Ministerio de Asuntos Exteriores,
Direccion General de Relaciones Culturales,
Madrid, Spain.

980 910 551　　　　CL
TRAPANANDA. 1978. a. $5. Co-Austral y Chile
Futuro, Coyhaique, Chile. Ed. Antonio Horvath
Kiss. circ. 3,000.

981　　　　　　　BL
TUDO E HISTORIA. 1981. irreg., latest no.105.
Editora Brasiliense, S.A., 01223 R. General Jardim,
160, Sao Paulo, Brazil. Ed. Luiz Schwarcz. circ. 5,
000.

980　　　　　　　US
U C L A LATIN AMERICAN CENTER. SPECIAL
STUDIES SERIES. 1980. irreg. University of
California, Los Angeles, Latin American Center,
405 Hilgard Ave., Los Angeles, CA 90024. TEL
213-825-6634. Ed. Ludwig Lauerhass, Jr.

970 001.3 677
301.412　　　　　US　　ISSN 0277-0628
UNCOVERINGS; research papers. 1981. a. $12.
American Quilt Study Group, 105 Molino Ave.,
Mill Valley, CA 94941. TEL 415-388-1382. Ed.
Sally Garoutte. illus. index. circ. 750.

989.5　　　　　　UY
UNIVERSIDAD DE LA REPUBLICA. FACULTAD
DE HUMANIDADES Y CIENCIAS. REVISTA.
SERIE HISTORIA. irreg. exchange basis.
Universidad de la Republica, Facultad de
Humanidades y Ciencias, Seccion Revista, Tristan
Narvaja 1674, Montevideo, Uruguay. Dir. Beatriz
Martinez Osorio.
Supersedes in part: Universidad de la Republica.
Facultad de Humanidades y Ciencias. Revista.

970.1　　　　　　MX　　ISSN 0076-7166
UNIVERSIDAD NACIONAL AUTONOMA DE
MEXICO. CENTRO DE ESTUDIOS MAYAS.
CUADERNOS. 1969. irreg. price varies.
Universidad Nacional Autonoma de Mexico, Centro
de Estudios Mayas, Torre 12 de Humanidades, Piso
11, Ciudad Universitaria 04510, Mexico, D.F.,
Mexico (Subscr. to: Porto Alegre N. 260, Col. San
Andres Tetepilco, Mexico 09440 D.F.) Ed.
Mercedes de la Garza. bk. rev. circ. 2,000. Indexed:
M.L.A.

972　　　　　　MX　　ISSN 0076-7271
UNIVERSIDAD NACIONAL AUTONOMA DE
MEXICO. INSTITUTO DE INVESTIGACIONES
HISTORICAS. CUADERNOS SERIE
DOCUMENTAL. 1963. irreg., no.6, 1968. price
varies. Universidad Nacional Autonoma de Mexico,
Instituto de Investigaciones Historicas,
Departamento de Distribucion de Libros
Universitarias, Insurgentes sur 299, Mexico 11,
D.F., Mexico.

972　　　　　　MX　　ISSN 0076-7301
UNIVERSIDAD NACIONAL AUTONOMA DE
MEXICO. INSTITUTO DE INVESTIGACIONES
HISTORICAS. SERIE BIBLIOGRAFICA. 1948.
irreg., no.5, 1969. price varies. Universidad
Nacional Autonoma de Mexico, Instituto de
Investigaciones Historicas, Departamento de Distribucion de Libros
Universitarias, Insurgentes sur, 299, Mexico 11,
D.F., Mexico.

972　　　　　　MX　　ISSN 0076-731X
UNIVERSIDAD NACIONAL AUTONOMA DE
MEXICO. INSTITUTO DE INVESTIGACIONES
HISTORICAS. SERIE DOCUMENTAL. 1947.
irreg., no.11, 1974. price varies. Universidad
Nacional Autonoma de Mexico, Instituto de
Investigaciones Historicas, Departamento de
Distribucion de Libros Universitarias, Insurgentes
sur, 299, Mexico 11, D.F., Mexico.

972　　　　　　MX　　ISSN 0076-7328
UNIVERSIDAD NACIONAL AUTONOMA DE
MEXICO. INSTITUTO DE INVESTIGACIONES
HISTORICAS. SERIE DE CULTURAS
MESOAMERICANAS. 1967. irreg.; no. 2, 1968.
price varies. Universidad Nacional Autonoma de
Mexico, Instituto de Investigaciones Historicas,
Departamento de Distribucion de Libros
Universitarias, Insurgentes sur 299, Mexico 11,
D.F., Mexico.

972　　　　　　MX　　ISSN 0071-1675
UNIVERSIDAD NACIONAL AUTONOMA DE
MEXICO. INSTITUTO DE INVESTIGACIONES
HISTORICAS. SERIE DE CULTURA
NAHUATL. ESTUDIOS DE CULTURA
NAHUATL. 1959. irreg., vol.12, 1976. price varies.
Universidad Nacional Autonoma de Mexico,
Instituto de Investigaciones Historicas, Villa
Obregon, Ciudad Universitaria, Mexico 20, D.F.,
Mexico.

972　　　　　　MX　　ISSN 0076-7212
UNIVERSIDAD NACIONAL AUTONOMA DE
MEXICO. INSTITUTO DE INVESTIGACIONES
HISTORICAS. SERIE DE CULTURA
NAHUATL. FUENTES. 1958. irreg., no.7, 1969.
price varies. Universidad Nacional Autonoma de
Mexico, Instituto de Investigaciones Historicas,
Departamento de Distribucion de Libros
Universitarias, Insurgentes sur 299, Mexico 11,
D.F., Mexico.

972　　　　　　MX　　ISSN 0076-7344
UNIVERSIDAD NACIONAL AUTONOMA DE
MEXICO. INSTITUTO DE INVESTIGACIONES
HISTORICAS. SERIE DE CULTURA
NAHUATL. MONOGRAFIAS. 1959. irreg., no.19,
1975. price varies. Universidad Nacional Autonoma
de Mexico, Instituto de Investigaciones Historicas,
Departamento de Distribucion de Libros
Universitarias, Insurgentes sur 299, Mexico 11,
D.F., Mexico.

972　　　　　　MX　　ISSN 0076-7352
UNIVERSIDAD NACIONAL AUTONOMA DE
MEXICO. INSTITUTO DE INVESTIGACIONES
HISTORICAS. SERIE DE HISTORIA
GENERAL. 1949. irreg., no.8, 1972. Universidad
Nacional Autonoma de Mexico, Instituto de
Investigaciones Historicas, Departamento de
Distribucion de Libros Universitarias, Insurgentes
sur 299, Mexico 11, D.F., Mexico.

972　　　　　　MX　　ISSN 0076-7387
UNIVERSIDAD NACIONAL AUTONOMA DE
MEXICO. INSTITUTO DE INVESTIGACIONES
HISTORICAS. SERIE DE HISTORIADORES Y
CRONISTAS. 1967. irreg., no.6, 1977. price varies.
Universidad Nacional Autonoma de Mexico,
Instituto de Investigaciones Historicas,
Departamento de Distribucion de Libros
Universitarias, Insurgentes sur 299, Mexico 11,
D.F., Mexico.

985　　　　　　　PE
UNIVERSIDAD NACIONAL FEDERICO
VILLAREAL. DEPARTAMENTO DE CIENCIAS
HISTORICO SOCIALES. PUBLICACIONES.
1976. irreg. Universidad Nacional Federico Villareal,
Departamento de Ciencias Historico Sociales,
Colmena 412, Lima, Peru.

981　　　　　　　BL
UNIVERSIDADE DE SAO PAULO.
DEPARTAMENTO DE HISTORIA. BOLETIM.
1977; N.S. irreg., latest no.18. Universidade de Sao
Paulo, Departamento de Historia, Caixa Postal
8.105, Sao Paulo, Brazil. Dir. Myriam Ellis. bibl.

980.2　　　　　　BL　　ISSN 0080-6374
UNIVERSIDADE DE SAO PAULO. MUSEU
PAULISTA. ANAIS. (Text in Portuguese;
summaries in English) 1922. a. Universidade de Sao
Paulo, Museu Paulista, C. P. 42.503, 04263 Sao
Paulo, Brazil.

708　　　　　　　BL
UNIVERSIDADE DE SAO PAULO. MUSEU
PAULISTA. COLECAO. SERIE DE HISTORIA.
1963. irreg. Universidade de Sao Paulo, Museu
Paulista, C. P. 42503, Parque da Independencia,
04263 Sao Paulo, Brazil. Ed. Setembrino Petri.
Supersedes in part (since 1975): Museu Paulista.
Colecao (ISSN 0080-6382)

981　　　　　　　BL
UNIVERSIDADE FEDERAL DO RIO GRANDE
DO SUL. GABINETE DE PESQUISA DE
HISTORIA. BOLETIM. 1973. irreg. Universidade
Federal do Rio Grande do sul, Gabinete de Pesquisa
de Historia, 90000 Porto Alegre, Rio Grande do
Sul, Brazil.

UNIVERSITE CATHOLIQUE DE LOUVAIN.
CENTRE D'ETUDES POLITIQUES. WORKING
GROUP "AMERICAN FOREIGN POLICY."
CAHIER. see *POLITICAL SCIENCE —
International Relations*

UNIVERSITE DE BORDEAUX III. CENTRE DE
RECHERCHES SUR L'AMERIQUE
ANGLOPHONE. ANNALES. see *POLITICAL
SCIENCE*

971　　　　　　CN　　ISSN 0079-8347
UNIVERSITE LAVAL. CENTRE D'ETUDES
NORDIQUES. TRAVAUX ET DOCUMENTS.
(Text in English, Eskimo and French; summaries in
English and French) 1963. irreg., no.7, 1974. price
varies. Presses de l'Universite Laval, C.P. 2447
Quebec G1K 7R4, Canada. TEL 418-656-2590.

972　　　　　　　US
UNIVERSITY OF CALIFORNIA, LOS ANGELES.
CHICANO STUDIES RESEARCH CENTER.
MONOGRAPHS. 1970. irreg. price varies.
University of California, Los Angeles, Chicano
Studies Research Center, 405 Hilgard Ave., Los
Angeles, CA 90024. TEL 213-825-2363. (reprint
service avail. from UMI)
Formerly: University of California, Los Angeles.
Chicano Studies Center. Monographs (ISSN 0045-
3994)

980　　　　　　US　　ISSN 0075-8132
UNIVERSITY OF CALIFORNIA, LOS ANGELES.
LATIN AMERICAN CENTER. LATIN
AMERICAN STUDIES SERIES. 1965. irreg.,
no.59, 1984. price varies. University of California,
Los Angeles, Latin American Center, 405 Hilgard
Ave., Los Angeles, CA 90024. TEL 213-825-6634.
Ed. Johannes Wilbert.

980　　　　　　US　　ISSN 0068-6263
UNIVERSITY OF CALIFORNIA, LOS ANGELES.
LATIN AMERICAN CENTER. REFERENCE
SERIES. 1962. irreg., vol.10, 1983. price varies.
University of California, Los Angeles, Latin
American Center, 405 Hilgard Ave., Los Angeles,
CA 90024. TEL 213-825-6634. Ed. Ludwig
Lauerhass, Jr.

980   UK   ISSN 0076-0846
UNIVERSITY OF LONDON. INSTITUTE OF LATIN AMERICAN STUDIES. MONOGRAPHS. 1969. irreg., no.13, 1985. Athlone Press Ltd., 44 Bedford Row, London WC1R 4LY, England (Dist. in U.S. by: Athlone Press, Atlantic Highlands, NJ 07716)

980   UK   ISSN 0142-1875
UNIVERSITY OF LONDON. INSTITUTE OF LATIN AMERICAN STUDIES. OCCASIONAL PAPERS. irreg. (2-3/yr.) University of London, Institute of Latin American Studies, 31 Tavistock Sq., London WC1H 9HA, England.
Formerly: University of London. Institute of Latin American Studies. Working Papers.

UNIVERSITY OF MISSOURI MONOGRAPHS IN ANTHROPOLOGY. see *ANTHROPOLOGY*

980   US
UNIVERSITY OF WISCONSIN-MILWAUKEE. CENTER FOR LATIN AMERICA. BIBLIOGRAPHIC SERIES. 1970. irreg., no.3, 1977. price varies. ‡ University of Wisconsin-Milwaukee, Center for Latin America, Milwaukee, WI 53201. TEL 414-963-4401.
Former titles: University of Wisconsin-Milwaukee. Center for Latin America. Special Studies Series; University of Wisconsin, Milwaukee. Language and Area Center for Latin America. Special Studies Series (ISSN 0084-0858)

980   US
UNIVERSITY OF WISCONSIN-MILWAUKEE. CENTER FOR LATIN AMERICA. COMMUNITY RESOURCES SERIES. 1973. irreg., no. 4, 1981. $1. University of Wisconsin-Milwaukee, Center for Latin America, Milwaukee, WI 53201. TEL 414-963-4401. (back issues avail.)
Formerly: University of Wisconsin-Milwaukee. Center for Latin America. Special Papers Series (ISSN 0146-2598)

980   US
UNIVERSITY OF WISCONSIN-MILWAUKEE. CENTER FOR LATIN AMERICA. DISCUSSION PAPER SERIES. 1968. irreg., no.74, 1986. $1. ‡ University of Wisconsin-Milwaukee, Center for Latin America, Milwaukee, WI 53201. TEL 414-963-4401.
Former titles: University of Wisconsin, Milwaukee. Center for Latin America. Discussion Papers (ISSN 0146-258X) & University of Wisconsin, Milwaukee. Language and Area Center for Latin America. Discussion Papers (ISSN 0084-0831)

980   US   ISSN 0084-084X
UNIVERSITY OF WISCONSIN-MILWAUKEE. CENTER FOR LATIN AMERICA. ESSAY SERIES. 1968. irreg., no.8, 1980. price varies. University of Wisconsin-Milwaukee, Center for Latin America, Milwaukee, WI 53201. TEL 414-963-4401.

979   US   ISSN 0887-3771
UTAH CENTENNIAL SERIES. 1985. a. price varies. University of Utah Press, Salt Lake City, UT 84112. TEL 801-581-6771. Ed. Charles S. Peterson.

973   US   ISSN 0083-5781
VERMONT YEAR BOOK. 1818. a. $21. ‡ National Survey, Chester, VT 05143. TEL 802-875-2121. Ed. Cecil Waldo. adv. circ. 3,000.
Formerly: Walton's Register.

972.9   VI
VIRGIN ISLANDS (U.S.) DIVISION OF LIBRARIES, MUSEUMS AND ARCHAEOLOGICAL SERVICES. OCCASIONAL PAPER SERIES. 1977. irreg. $5 per no. Division of Libraries, Museums and Archaeological Services, Department of Conservation and Cultural Affairs, 23 Dronningens Gade, St. Thomas, VI 00802. circ. 500.
Formerly: Virgin Islands (U.S.) Bureau of Libraries, Museums and Archaeological Services. Occasional Paper Series.

975.5   US   ISSN 0083-6389
VIRGINIA HISTORICAL SOCIETY. DOCUMENTS. 1961. irreg., vol.16, 1984. price varies. University Press of Virginia, Box 3608, University Sta., Charlottesville, VA 22903. TEL 804-924-3468. circ. 1,500.

973   US   ISSN 0083-7121
WALTER LYNWOOD FLEMING LECTURES IN SOUTHERN HISTORY. 1937. irreg. price varies. Louisiana State University Press, University Station, Baton Rouge, LA 70803. TEL 504-388-3202.

975.3   US   ISSN 0083-7393
WASHINGTON (YEAR); a comprehensive directory of the Nation's Capital, its people and institutions. 1966. a. $40. Columbia Books, Inc., 1350 New York Ave., Ste. 207, Washington, DC 20005. TEL 202-737-3777. Ed. John Russell. index. (back issues avail.)
Formerly: Washington.

975.3   US
WASHINGTON INFORMATION DIRECTORY. 1976. a. Congressional Quarterly Inc., 1414 22nd St. N.W., DC 20037. TEL 202-887-8620.

971   CN   ISSN 0083-7733
WATERLOO HISTORICAL SOCIETY. REPORT. 1913. a. membership. Waterloo Historical Society, c/o Mrs. Robert Woolner, 49 Stirling Ave. N., Kitchener, Ont. N2H 3G4, Canada. Ed.Bd. circ. 600.

976   US   ISSN 0361-6215
WEST TENNESSEE HISTORICAL SOCIETY. PAPERS. 1947. a. $12. ‡ West Tennessee Historical Society Inc., Box 111046, Memphis, TN 38111-1046. TEL 901-458-4996. (Affiliate: Tennessee Historical Commission) Ed. Berkley Kalin. adv. bk. rev. bibl. illus. circ. 500.

976   US
WEST TEXAS HISTORICAL ASSOCIATION YEARBOOK. 1924. a. $10. Rupert Richardson Press, Box 152-Hardin-Simmons University, Abilene, TX 79698. TEL 915-677-7281. Eds. B.W. Aston, Ken Jacobs. bk. rev. circ. 350. (also avail. in microfilm; back issues avail.)

975.4   US   ISSN 0043-325X
WEST VIRGINIA HISTORY. 1939. a. $10. Department of Culture and History, Archives and History Division, Cultural Center, Charleston, WV 25305. TEL 304-348-0230. Ed. Fredrick H. Armstrong. bk. rev. bibl. illus. circ. 1,000. Indexed: Amer.Hist. & Life. Hist.Abstr.

978   US   ISSN 0083-887X
WESTERN FRONTIER LIBRARY. 1953. irreg. price varies. University of Oklahoma Press, 1005 Asp Ave., Norman, OK 73019. TEL 405-325-5111. Indexed: M.L.A.

973   US   ISSN 0083-8888
WESTERN FRONTIERSMEN SERIES. 1937. irreg. price varies. Arthur H. Clark Co., Box 230, Glendale, CA 91209-0230. index.

978   GW
WESTERN MAGAZIN; Zeitschrift fuer Western Historik. 1972. irreg. K.F. Bender Verlag, Bessunger Str. 47, 6100 Darmstadt, W. Germany (B.R.D.)

979   US   ISSN 0083-9019
WESTERNLORE GHOST TOWN SERIES. 1963. irreg. price varies. Westernlore Press, Box 35305, Tucson, AZ 85740. TEL 602-975-5491. Ed. Lynn R. Bailey.

976.7   US   ISSN 0043-4906
WHITE COUNTY HERITAGE. 1963. a. $6. White County Historical Society, Box 537, Searcy, AR 72143. Ed. Eloise Scott. circ. 60. (processed)

975.5   US   ISSN 0084-0297
WILLIAMSBURG IN AMERICA SERIES. 1950. irreg., vol.10, 1975. University Press of Virginia, Box 3608, University Station, Charlottesville, VA 22903. TEL 804-924-3468.

975   US   ISSN 0084-0300
WILLIAMSBURG RESEARCH STUDIES. 1965. irreg., unnumbered. price varies. ‡ Colonial Williamsburg Foundation, Williamsburg, VA 23187. TEL 804-229-1000. Ed. Cary Carson. index.

976   US
WILLIAMSON COUNTY HISTORICAL SOCIETY PUBLICATION. 1970. a. $8 membership. Williamson County Historical Society, Box 71, Franklin, TN 37064. Ed. Katharine Trickey. circ. 250.
Formerly: Williamson County Historical Society Newsletter.

971   US   ISSN 0883-8135
WORLD TODAY SERIES: CANADA. a. $5.50. Stryker-Post Publications, 888 Seventeenth St., N.W., Washington, DC 20006. TEL 202-342-6055. Ed. Wayne C. Thompson.

980   US   ISSN 0092-4148
WORLD TODAY SERIES: LATIN AMERICA. 1967. a. $5.50. Stryker-Post Publications, 888 Seventeenth St., N.W., Washington, DC 20006. TEL 202-342-6055. Ed. Pierre Etienne Dostert. circ. 15,000.

975.8 920   US   ISSN 0084-2621
WORMSLOE FOUNDATION. PUBLICATIONS. 1955. irreg., no.15, 1982. price varies. University of Georgia Press, Athens, GA 30602. TEL 404-542-2830. (reprint service avail. from UMI)

973   US   ISSN 0084-3393
YALE PUBLICATIONS IN AMERICAN STUDIES. 1957. irreg., no.20, 1970. price varies. Yale University Press, 92A Yale Sta., New Haven, CT 06520. TEL 203-432-0940.

978   US   ISSN 0084-3563
YALE WESTERN AMERICANA SERIES. 1962. irreg., no.33, 1982. price varies. Yale University Press, 92A Yale Sta., New Haven, CT 06520. TEL 203-432-0940.

971   CN   ISSN 0513-2711
YORK PIONEER. 1952. a. after 1985, previously s-a. $6 to non-members. York Pioneer and Historical Society, P.O. Box 481, Sta. "K", Toronto, Ont. M4P 2G9, Canada. TEL 416-481-8848. bk. rev. circ. 600. *Local*

HISTORY — History Of The Near East

956   LE
A J M E NEWS. 1974. irreg. (8-12/yr.) $12. Americans for Justice in the Middle East, P.O. Box 113-5581, Beirut, Lebanon. Ed. Marilyn Raschka. bk. rev. circ. 900. (processed) Indexed: HR Rep.
Supersedes (1961-1974): Middle East Newsletter.

956   NE   ISSN 0240-8910
ABSTRACTA IRANICA. (Supplement to: Studia Iranica) (Text in French) 1978. a. (Institut Francais de Recherche en Iran) E.J. Brill, P.O.B. 9000, 2300 PA Leiden, Netherlands.

956   NE
ACTA IRANICA. 1974. irreg., vol.25, 1986. price varies. E. J. Brill, P.O. Box 9000, 2300 PA Leiden, Netherlands.

930 913 722   US
AEGYPTOLOGISCHE FORSCHUNGEN. irreg. vol. 1-25, 1973. price varies. J. J. Augustin, Inc., Locust Valley, NY 11560. TEL 516-676-1510.

956   US   ISSN 0732-6505
AIDS AND RESEARCH TOOLS IN ANCIENT NEAR EASTERN STUDIES.* Short title: ARTANES. 1977. irreg., latest no.4. price varies. (International Institute of Mesopotamian Area Studies) Undena Publications, 6355 Green Valley Circle, No. 213, Culver City, CA 90230-7064. Ed. Giorgio Buccellati. bibl. charts. illus. circ. 500. (back issues avail.)

956   US
AIDS AND RESEARCH TOOLS IN MIDDLE EASTERN STUDIES.* Abbreviated title: A R T M E S. 1983. irreg. price varies. Undena Publications, 6355 Green Valley Circle, No. 213, Culver City, CA 90230-7064. charts. illus. index.

HISTORY — HISTORY OF THE NEAR EAST

950   US   ISSN 0066-0035
AMERICAN SCHOOLS OF ORIENTAL RESEARCH. ANNUAL. irreg., latest issue 1980/81. A S O R Publications Office, Box HM, Duke Sta., Durham, NC 27706. Eds. William G. Dever, Eric M. Meyers. (also avail. in microform from UMI)

956   US
ANCIENT NEAR EASTERN TEXTS AND STUDIES. 1986. irreg., vol.1. $39.95 per no. Edwin Mellen Press, Box 450, Lewiston, NY 14092.

956   SP   ISSN 0212-159X
ANDALUCIA ISLAMICA. TEXTOS Y ESTUDIOS. 1980. a. 2500 ptas. Universidad de Granada, Facultad de Filosofia y Letras, Departamento de Historia del Islam, Campus Universitario de Cartuja, Granada, Spain. Ed. J. Bosch-Vila. adv. bk. rev. circ. 1,000.

956   UK
ARABIA PAST & PRESENT SERIES. 1972. irreg. (approx. 2/yr.) price varies. Oleander Press, 17 Stansgate Ave., Cambridge CB2 2QZ, England (U.S. address: 210 Fifth Ave., New York, N.Y. 10010) Ed. Philip Ward. circ. 1,500.

953 320   UK   ISSN 0305-036X
ARABIAN STUDIES. 1974. a. price varies. (Cambridge University, Middle East Centre) Scorpion Publishing Ltd., Victoria House, Victoria Rd., Buckhurst Hill, Essex IG9 5ES, England. Eds. R.B. Serjeant and R.L. Bidwell. bk. rev. bibl. charts. circ. 1,000.

956   AU   ISSN 0066-6440
ARCHIV FUER ORIENTFORSCHUNG; Internationale Zeitschrift fuer die Wissenschaft vom Vorderen Orient. irreg., vol.29/30, 1984. Verlag Ferdinand Berger und Soehne OHG, Postfach 11, A-3580 Horn, A 3580 Horn, Austria.

956 297   GW   ISSN 0378-2808
ARCHIVUM OTTOMANICUM. (Text in English, French, German) 1969. a. DM.116 (approx.) Verlag Otto Harrassowitz, Tounusstr. 14, Postfach 2929, 6200 Wiesbaden, W. Germany (B.R.D.) Ed. Bd. bk. rev. circ. 350. (back issues avail.) Indexed: Hist.Abstr. Amer.Hist.& Life.

956   US   ISSN 0145-6334
ASSUR.* (Subseries of: Monographic Journals of the Near East) 1974. irreg., latest vol.3, no.3. $24. (International Institute of Mesopotamian Area Studies) Undena Publications, 6355 Green Valley Circle, No. 213, Culver City, CA 90230-7064. Ed. Dr. Claudio Saporetti. bibl. charts. illus. circ. 500. (back issues avail.) Indexed: M.L.A. Old Test.Abstr.

BEER-SHEVA. see *RELIGIONS AND THEOLOGY — Judaic*

950   GW   ISSN 0067-4931
BEIRUTER TEXTE UND STUDIEN. (Text in Arabic and German) 1964. irreg., vol.34, 1984. price varies. (Deutsche Morgenlaendische Gesellschaft Beirut, Orient-Institut, LE) Franz Steiner Verlag Wiesbaden GmbH, Birkenwaldstr. 44, Postfach 347, D-7000 Stuttgart 1, W. Germany (B.R.D.)

956   US   ISSN 0732-6440
BIBLIOTHECA MESOPOTAMICA.* 1975. irreg., latest no.16. price varies. (International Institute of Mesopotamian Area Studies) Undena Publications, 6355 Green Valley Circle, No. 213, Culver City, CA 90230-7064. Ed. Giorgio Buccellati. bibl. charts. illus. circ. 500. (back issues avail.)

956   II
BIHAR RESEARCH SOCIETY. JOURNAL.* (Text in English) vol.57, 1971. a. Rs.30. Bihar Research Society, Patna, India. Ed. S. Sohoni. bk. rev.

956   US   ISSN 0742-1141
BYZANTINA KAI METABYZANTINA.* 1978. irreg., latest no.3. price varies. Undena Publications, 6355 Green Valley Circle, No. 213, Culver City, CA 90230-7064. Ed. Speros Vyronis, Jr. (back issues avail.)

956.94 915   IS   ISSN 0334-4657
CATHEDRA. (Text in English) 1971. a. price varies. Yad Izhak Ben-Zvi Institute, Box 7660, Jerusalem 91076, Israel. Ed. Aharon Oppenheimer. bk. rev. circ. 2,000.
    Formerly: Jerusalem Cathedra (ISSN 0333-7618)

026 296   IS
CENTRAL ARCHIVES FOR THE HISTORY OF THE JEWISH PEOPLE NEWSLETTER/ ARKHIYON HA-MERKAZI LE-TOLDOT HA-AM HA-YEHUDI. YEDIOT. 1961. a. $5. Central Archives for the History of the Jewish People, Hebrew University Campus, Sprinzak Bldg., Box 1149, 91010 Jerusalem, Israel. Eds. Daniel J. Cohen, Aryeh Segall. illus. circ. 1,200.

CENTRE DE RECHERCHE D'HISTOIRE ET CIVILISATION DE BYZANCE. TRAVAUX ET MEMOIRES. see *HISTORY — History Of Europe*

956   US   ISSN 0742-2334
COMPUTER AIDED RESEARCH IN NEAR EASTERN STUDIES.* Short title: CARNES. (Subseries of: Cybernetica Mesopotamia) 1983. irreg. $24. (International Institute of Mesopotamian Area Studies) Undena Publications, 6355 Green Valley Circle, No. 213, Culver City, CA 90230-7064. Eds. G. Buccellati, O. Rouault.
    Formerly: Computer Aided Research in Ancient Near Eastern Studies.

956   SP
CUADERNOS DE HISTORIA DEL ISLAM. 1967. irreg. 2500 ptas. Universidad de Granada, Facultad de Filosofia y Letras, Departamento de Historia del Islam, Campus Universitario de Cartuja, Granada, Spain. Ed. J. Bosch-Vila. adv. bk. rev. index. circ. 1, 000. Indexed: Hist.Abstr. Amer.Hist.& Life.
    Formerly: Cuadernos de Historia del Islam. Serie Monografica Islamica Occidentalia (ISSN 0070-1696)

956   US   ISSN 0742-1427
DATA SETS: CUNEIFORM TEXTS;* electronic data processing of Mesopotamian materials, philological and artifactual. 1979. irreg., latest no.3. price varies. (International Institute of Mesopotamian Area Studies) Undena Publications, 6355 Green Valley Circle, No. 213, Culver City, CA 90230-7064. Ed. Jacques Maquet. (back issues avail.)
    Formerly: Data Sets: Cuneiform Sources.

956   GW   ISSN 0342-118X
DEUTSCHE ORIENT-GESELLSCHAFT. MITTEILUNGEN. (Text and summaries in English, French, German) 1898. a. membership. Deutsche Orient-Gesellschaft, Museum fuer Vor- und Fruehgeschichte, Schloss Charlottenburg, Langhansbau, 1000 Berlin 19, W. Germany (B.R.D.) Ed.Bd. circ. 800. (back issues avail.) Indexed: M.L.A.

956.94   IS   ISSN 0334-8903
DISPERSION Y UNIDAD. (Text in Spanish) 1978. a. IS.27($35) Semana Publishing Co., P.O. Box 2427, Jerusalem 91023, Israel. Ed. Julio Adin. bk. rev. circ. 2,000.

956   NE
DOCUMENTA ET MONUMENTA ORIENTIS ANTIQUI. 1947. irreg., vol.20, 1983. price varies. E. J. Brill, P.O. Box 9000, 2300 PA Leiden, Netherlands. illus.

932   NE
EGYPTOLOGISCHE UITGAVEN. 1982. irreg. price varies. Nederlands Instituut voor het Nabije Oosten - Netherlands Institute for the Near East, Witte Singel 24, Box 9515, 2300 RA Leiden, Netherlands. Ed.Bd.

FIHRIST; index to Arabic periodical literature. see *BIBLIOGRAPHIES*

FOUNDATIONS OF MEDIEVAL HISTORY. see *HISTORY — History Of Europe*

956   NE
GESCHICHTE DES ARABISCHEN SCHRIFTTUMS. 1967. irreg., vol.9, 1984. price varies. E.J. Brill, P.O. Box 9000, 2300 PA Leiden, Netherlands. Ed. Fuat Sezgin.

350   US   ISSN 0340-6369
GIORGIO LEVI DELLA VIDA CONFERENCES. REPORTS OF THE CONFERENCE.* 1970. biennial. $18.50. (University of California, Los Angeles, G. E. Von Grunebaum Center for Near Eastern Studies) Undena Publications, 6355 Green Valley Circle, No. 213, Culver City, CA 90230-7064. circ. 500. (back issues avail.)

956   US
GULF HANDBOOK; a guide to the eight Persian Gulf countries. 1977. irreg. $15.95. Garrett Park Press, Box 190F, Garrett Park, MD 20896. TEL 301-946-2553. Eds. Peter Kilner, Jonathan Wallace. illus.

932   GW
HABELTS DISSERTATIONSDRUCKE. REIHE AEGYPTOLOGIE. 1976. irreg., no.5, 1985. price varies. Dr. Rudolf Habelt GmbH, Am Buchenhang 1, 5300 Bonn 1, W. Germany (B.R.D.)

955   US
HARVARD IRANIAN SERIES. 1973. irreg., no.3, 1981. price varies. 79 Garden St., Cambridge, MA 02138. TEL 617-495-2600.

956   US   ISSN 0073-0580
HARVARD MIDDLE EASTERN STUDIES. 1958. irreg., latest vol.19, 1986. price varies. (Harvard University, Center for Middle Eastern Studies) Harvard University Press, 79 Garden St., Cambridge, MA 02138. TEL 617-495-2600.

930   US   ISSN 0073-0645
HARVARD SEMITIC SERIES. 1912. irreg., no.21, 1970. price varies. Scholars Press, 101 Salem St., Box 1608, GA 30031-1608.

950   SZ   ISSN 0073-0947
HAUTES ETUDES ISLAMIQUES ET ORIENTALES D'HISTOIRE COMPAREE. 1970. irreg, no.8, 1978. price varies. (Ecole Pratique des Hautes Etudes, Centre de Recherches d'Histoire et de Philologie, FR) Librarie Droz, 11 rue Massot, 1211 Geneva 12, Switzerland. Ed. Jean Aubin. circ. 1,000.

956 960   FR   ISSN 0073-2400
HISTOIRE ET CIVILISATION ARABE. 1969. irreg. price varies. Editions Cujas, 4,6,8 rue de la Maison-Blanche, 75013 Paris, France.

HOLY PLACES OF PALESTINE. see *RELIGIONS AND THEOLOGY*

956.94   LE
INSTITUTE FOR PALESTINE STUDIES. ARABS UNDER ISRAELI OCCUPATION SERIES. (Text in English and French) 1969. a. $7. Institute for Palestine Studies, Box 11-7164, Beirut, Lebanon (U.S. subscr. to: Georgetown Station, P.O.Box 25301, Washington, DC 20007)

956.94   LE
INSTITUTE FOR PALESTINE STUDIES. I.P.S. PAPERS SERIES. (Text in Arabic, English or French) 1979. irreg., no.23, 1984. $2. Institute for Palestine Studies, Box 11-7164, Beirut, Lebanon (U.S. subscr. to: Georgetown Station, P.O.Box 25301, Washington, DC 20007)

956.94   LE
INSTITUTE FOR PALESTINE STUDIES. ISRAELI KNESSET SERIES. (Text in Arabic) 1971. a. $30. Institute for Palestine Studies, Box 11-7164, Beirut, Lebanon (U.S. subscr. to: Georgetown Station, P.O.Box 25301, Washington, DC 20007)

956.94   LE
INSTITUTE FOR PALESTINE STUDIES. ZIONIST CONGRESS SERIES. (Text in Arabic) 1971. quadrennial. $20. Institute for Palestine Studies, Box 11-7164, Beirut, Lebanon (U.S. subscr. to: Georgetown Station, P.O.Box 25301, Washington, DC 20007)

INTERNATIONAL ASSOCIATION FOR BYZANTINE STUDIES. BULLETIN D'INFORMATION ET DE COORDINATION. see *HISTORY — History Of Europe*

INTERNATIONAL CONGRESS FOR BYZANTINE STUDIES. ACTS/CONGRES INTERNATIONAL DES ETUDES BYZANTINES. ACTES. see *HISTORY — History Of Europe*

INTERNATIONAL JOURNAL OF TURKISH STUDIES. see *GEOGRAPHY*

956   US   ISSN 0742-1133
INVITED LECTURES ON THE MIDDLE EAST AT THE UNIVERSITY OF TEXAS AT AUSTIN.* 1976. irreg., latest no.4. (University of Texas, Austin) Undena Publications, 6355 Green Valley Circle, No. 213, Culver City, CA 90230-7064. Ed. D. Schmandt-Bisserat. (back issues avail.)

HISTORY — HISTORY OF THE NEAR EAST

956 319   IR
IRAN YEARBOOK; a complete directory and encyclopedia of facts, data and statistics on Iran. a. Kayhan Group of Newspapers, Kayhan Research Associates, Ferdowsi Ave., Teheran, Iran.

ISLAMIC ART AND ARCHITECTURE. see *ART*

ISTITUTO ELLENICO DI STUDI BIZANTINI E POSTBIZANTINI, VENICE. BIBLIOTECA. see *HISTORY — History Of Europe*

JORDANIAN NATIONAL BIBLIOGRAPHY; annual register of book production in Jordan. see *BIBLIOGRAPHIES*

956.1   US
JOURNAL OF TURKISH STUDIES. 1977. a. Harvard University, Near Eastern Languages and Civilizations, 6 Divinity Ave., Cambridge, MA 02138. TEL 617-495-1000.

956.1   US
JOURNAL OF TURKISH STUDIES (DUXBURY)/ TURKLUK BILGISI ARASTIRMALARI. 1977. a. $100. Journal of Turkish Studies, 398 Summer St., Box 1447, Duxbury, MA 02332. Eds. Sinasi Tekin, Gonul A. Tekin. adv. bk. rev. circ. 53. (back issues avail.)

956 297   US   ISSN 0888-9007
JUSUR; the U C L A journal of Middle Eastern studies. 1985. a. $6 to individuals; students $4.50. University of California, Los Angeles, Von Grunebaum Center for Near Eastern Studies, 10286 Bunche Hall, Los Angeles, CA 90024. TEL 213-825-1181. Ed. William C. Young. bk. rev. film rev. circ. 200. (back issues avail.) Indexed: Amer.Hist.& Life. Hist.Abstr.

KATIB AL-FILASTINI. see *POLITICAL SCIENCE — International Relations*

KENTRON EPISTEMONIKON EREUNON. EPETERIS/CYPRUS RESEARCH CENTER. ANNUAL. see *LINGUISTICS*

943   GW   ISSN 0344-449X
MATERIALIA TURCICA. 1975. irreg. price varies. (Ruhr-Universitaet, Bochum, Sprachwissenschaftliches Institut, Lektorat fuer Tuerksprachen) Studienverlag Dr. N. Brockmeyer, Querenburger Hoehe 281, 4630 Bochum, W. Germany (B.R.D.) Ed. Hermann Vary. bk. rev.

956.94   IS
ME'ASEF; studies in the history and problems of the Israeli labor movement. a. Documentation and Research of Hashamer Hatzair, Givat Haviva 37 850, Israel. Ed. Haim Kahana.

956   SW   ISSN 0585-3214
MEDELHAVSMUSEET. BULLETIN. 1961. a. Medelhavsmuseet, Storgatan 41, 114 55 Stockholm, Sweden.

916   UK   ISSN 0076-8502
MIDDLE EAST AND NORTH AFRICA; survey and directory of lands of Middle East and North Africa. 1948. a. $135. Europa Publications Ltd., 18 Bedford Sq., London WC1B 3JN, England.

956   US   ISSN 0163-5476
MIDDLE EAST CONTEMPORARY SURVEY. 1976/77. a. $198. Westview Press, 5500 Central Ave., Boulder, CO 80301 TEL 212-254-4100. (U.K. address: Hillview House, 1 Halleswelle Parade, London NW1 ODL, England) Ed.Bd. bibl. index. circ. 2,000. (back issues avail.)

956   IS   ISSN 0076-8529
MIDDLE EAST RECORD. 1960. irreg., vol.5, 1977. (Tel-Aviv University, Shiloah Center for Middle Eastern and African Studies) Keter Publishing House Ltd., Box 7145, Jerusalem, Israel (U.S. Orders to: Keter Inc., 440 Park Ave. South, New York, NY 10016)

900   US   ISSN 0732-6491
MONOGRAPHS ON THE ANCIENT NEAR EAST.* 1974. irreg., latest vol. 2, no. 2. $24. (International Institute of Mesopotamian Area Studies) Undena Publications, 6355 Green Valley Circle, No. 213, Culver City, CA 90230-7064. Eds. Dr. Giorgio Buccellati, M. Kelly-Buccellati. bibl. charts. illus. circ. 500. (back issues avail.)

MUENCHENER ZEITSCHRIFT FUER BALKANKUNDE. see *HISTORY — History Of Europe*

956   GW
NEAR AND MIDDLE EAST MONOGRAPHS. 1973. irreg. price varies. Walter de Gruyter & Co., Mouton Publishers, Postfach 110240, D-1000 Berlin 11, W. Germany (B.R.D.) (U.S. addr.: Mouton Publishers, division of Walter de Gruyter, Inc., 200 Saw Mill River Road, Hawthorne, NY 10532)

NETHERLANDS INSTITUTE OF ARCHAEOLOGY AND ARABIC STUDIES IN CAIRO. PUBLICATIONS. see *ARCHAEOLOGY*

956   US   ISSN 0732-6475
OCCASIONAL PAPERS ON THE NEAR EAST.* (Sub-series of: Monographic Journals of the Near East) 1979. a. $24. (International Institute of Mesopotamian Area Studies) Undena Publications, 6355 Green Valley Circle, No. 213, Culver City, CA 90230-7064. Ed. Dr. Giorgio Buccellati. bibl. charts. illus. circ. 500. (back issues avail.) Indexed: Old Test.Abstr.

932   NE
ORIENTALIA MONSPELIENSIA. 1979. irreg. price varies. (Universite Paul Valery, Institut d'Egyptology, FR) E. J. Brill, P.O. Box 9000, 2300 PA Leiden, Netherlands.

935.63 319   QA
QATAR YEARBOOK. (Text in English) 1976. a. free. Ministry of Information, Box 1836, Doha, Qatar. circ. 10,000.

QUADERNI DE "LA TERRA SANTA". see *RELIGIONS AND THEOLOGY*

956   FR   ISSN 0766-5598
REVUE DES ETUDES BYZANTINES. (Text and summaries in English, French and German) 1943. a. 300 F. Association de l'Institut Francais d'Etudes Byzantines, 14 rue Seguier, 75006 Paris, France. adv. bk. rev. circ. 600. (back issues avail.)

RIVISTA DI STUDI BIZANTINI E SLAVI. see *HISTORY — History Of Europe*

956   TU   ISSN 0578-9761
SARKIYAT MECMUASI. 1956. irreg. TL.34. Istanbul University, Sarkiyat Enstitusu, Istanbul, Turkey. bk. rev. circ. 1,000.

956   GW   ISSN 0342-4839
SCHRIFTEN DES OESTERREICHISCHEN KULTURINSTITUTS KAIRO. ARCHAEOLOGISCH-HISTORISCHE ABTEILUNG. 1969. irreg., vol.3, 1982. price varies. Verlag Otto Harrassowitz, Taunusstr. 14, Postfach 29 29, 6200 Wiesbaden, W. Germany (B.R.D.)

956 913 572   CN
SCRIPTA MEDITERRANEA. (Text in English, French and German) 1980. a. Can.$18($18) to non-members. (Society for Mediterranean Studies) Benben Publications, 1483 Carmen Drive, Mississauga, Ont. M5S 1A1, Canada TEL 416-274-4380. (Subscr. to: Society for Mediterranean Studies, University of Toronto, New College, Box 308, Toronto, Ont. M5S 1A1 Canada.) Ed. Anthony Percival. bk. rev. bibl. circ. 250.

915.3   UK
SEMINAR FOR ARABIAN STUDIES. PROCEEDINGS. 1971. a. price varies. Seminar for Arabian Studies, 31-34 Gordon Square, London WC1H 0PY, England. circ. 200.

956 960   US
SHILOACH CENTER FOR MIDDLE EASTERN & AFRICAN STUDIES. MONOGRAPH SERIES. irreg., unnumbered, latest vol. 1973. Halsted Press (Subsidiary of: John Wiley & Sons, Inc.) 605 Third Ave., New York, NY 10016. TEL 212-850-6000.

956   NE   ISSN 0085-6193
SOCIAL, ECONOMIC AND POLITICAL STUDIES OF THE MIDDLE EAST. 1971. irreg., vol.40, 1986. price varies. E. J. Brill, P.O. Box 9000, 2300 PA Leiden, Netherlands (Dist. in U.S. by: Humanities Press, Inc., 171 First Ave., Atlantic Highlands, NJ 07716)

956   US   ISSN 0732-6424
SOURCES FROM THE ANCIENT NEAR EAST.* 1974. irreg. $24. (International Institute of Mesopotamian Area Studies) Undena Publications, 6355 Green Valley Circle, No. 213, Culver City, CA 90230-7064. Eds. G. Buccellati, M. Kelly-Buccellati. (back issues avail.) Indexed: Old Test.Abstr.

956   UK   ISSN 0266-6030
SOUTH ASIAN STUDIES. 1978. a. £10($25) to individuals; institutions £18($50) Society for South Asian Studies, c/o British Academy, 20-21 Cornwall Terrace, London NW1 4QP, England. Ed. B. Allchin. adv. bk. rev. circ. 300. Indexed: Geo.Abstr. Numis.Lit.
    Formerly (until 1985): Afghan Studies (ISSN 0265-4822)

STUDI CLASSICI E ORIENTALI. see *CLASSICAL STUDIES*

950 960   US
STUDIES IN MIDDLE EASTERN HISTORY. 1974. irreg., no.7, 1985. price varies. Bibliotheca Islamica, Inc., Box 14474, Univ. Station, Minneapolis, MN 55414.

956   US   ISSN 0742-1168
STUDIES IN NEAR EASTERN CULTURE AND SOCIETY.* 1977. irreg., latest no.5. price varies. (University of California, Los Angeles, G.E. von Grunebaum Center for Near Eastern Studies) Undena Publications, 6355 Green Valley Circle, No. 213, Culver City, CA 90230-7064. Ed.Bd. (back issues avail.)

956   SJ
SUDAN NOTES AND RECORDS. (Text in English) 1918. a. $16. Box 555, Khartoum, Sudan. Ed. Yusuf Fadl Hasan. adv. bk. rev. circ. 2,000. (back issues avail.) Indexed: Biol.Abstr. GeoRef.

956   US   ISSN 0732-6483
SYRO-MESOPOTAMIAN STUDIES.* (Subseries of: Monographic Journals of the Near East) 1974. a. $24. (International Institute of Mesopotamian Area Studies) Undena Publications, 6355 Green Valley Circle, No. 213, Culver City, CA 90230-7064. Ed. Dr. Giorgio Buccellati. bibl. charts illus. circ. 500. (back issues avail.) Indexed: Old Test.Abstr.

930   GW
TUEBINGER AEGYPTOLOGISCHE BEITRAEGE. 1973. irreg., no.2, 1976. price varies. Dr Rudolf Habelt GmbH, Am Buchenhang 1, 5300 Bonn 1, W. Germany (B.R.D.) Eds. Hellmut Brunner, Ingrid Gamer-Wallert.

956   TU   ISSN 0085-7432
TURKIYAT MECMUASI. 1925. irreg. price varies. Istanbul University, Institute of Turcology - Istanbul Universitesi, Turkiyat Enstitusu, Ayniyat, Istanbul, Turkey. Ed. M. Kaplan. circ. 1,000.

913.39   AG   ISSN 0325-1209
UNIVERSIDAD DE BUENOS AIRES. INSTITUTO DE HISTORIA ANTIGUA ORIENTAL. REVISTA. 1972. a. Universidad de Buenos Aires, Instituto de Historia Antigua Oriental, 25 de Mayo 217, Buenos Aires, Argentina. bk. rev. bibl. illus. circ. 800.

913   AG
UNIVERSIDAD DE BUENOS AIRES. INSTITUTO DE HISTORIA ANTIGUO ORIENTAL. COLECCION ESTUDIOS. irreg., no.8, 1978. Universidad de Buenos Aires, Instituto de Historia Antigua Oriental, 25 de Mayo 217, 3 Piso, Buenos Aires, Argentina.

955   IR
UNIVERSITY OF TEHERAN. FACULTY OF LETTERS AND HUMANITIES. BULLETIN OF IRANIAN STUDIES/DANESHGAH-E TEHRAN. DANESHKADE-YE ADABIYAT VA 'OLUM-E ENSANI. MAJALLE-YE IRANSHENASI. Short title: Bulletin of Iranian Studies. (Text in Persian) 1963. irreg. price varies. University of Teheran, Faculty of Letters and Humanities, Shahreza Ave., Teheran, Iran. Ed. Fereydun Badre'I.

930   GW
VETUS TESTAMENTUM COPTICE. 1973. irreg. price varies. Dr. Rudolf Habelt GmbH, Am Buchenhang 1, 5300 Bonn 1, W. Germany (B.R.D.)

VICINO ORIENTE. see *ORIENTAL STUDIES*

HOBBIES

956 IR
WISDOM OF PERSIA. 1971. irreg., no.38, 1986. McGill University, Teheran Branch, Institute of Islamic Studies, Box 13-145-133, Teheran, Iran. Ed. Mehdi Mohaghegh.

956 US ISSN 0084-3385
YALE NEAR EASTERN RESEARCHES. 1967. irreg., no.9, 1983. price varies. Yale University Press, 302 Temple St., New Haven, CT 06520. TEL 203-432-0940. Ed. William W. Hallo.

935 US
YALE ORIENTAL SERIES. BABYLONIAN TEXTS. 1915. irreg., vol.17, 1980. Yale University Press, 92A Yale Sta., New Haven, CT 06520. TEL 203-432-0940.

HOBBIES

see also Antiques; Needlework; Numismatics; Philately; Sports and Games

790.132 760 US ISSN 0275-1569
AMERICAN SOCIETY OF BOOKPLATE COLLECTORS AND DESIGNERS. YEAR BOOK. 1922. irreg. $27.50. American Society of Bookplate Collectors and Designers, 605 N. Stoneman Ave., No. F, Alhambra, CA 91801. TEL 213-283-1936. Ed. Audrey Spencer Arellanes. bk. rev. bibl. illus. cum.index: 1922-1950;1951-1972. circ. 200.

AMERICAN WINE SOCIETY. BULLETIN. see *BEVERAGES*

790.13 FR
ANNUAIRE INTERNATIONAL DES COLLECTIONNEURS. 1973. biennial. Editions Dany Thibaud, 52 rue Labrouste, 75015 Paris, France.

745.5 US
ART, CRAFTS & RELATED FIELDS. biennial. free. International Specialized Book Services, Inc., 3602 N.E. Hassalo St., Portland, OR 97213. TEL 800-547-7734. circ. 20,00.

B T H A BUYERS GUIDE. (British Toy & Hobby Manufacturers Association) see *GIFTWARE AND TOYS*

BETTER HOMES AND GARDENS CHRISTMAS IDEAS. see *HOME ECONOMICS*

745.5 US
BETTER HOMES AND GARDENS HOLIDAY CRAFTS. 1974. a. $2.50. Meredith Corporation, Special Interest Publications, 1716 Locust St., Des Moines, IA 50336. TEL 515-284-3000. adv.

BLACK & DECKER BUILD IT. see *HOME ECONOMICS*

623.4 US ISSN 0590-6776
CORD SPORTFACTS GUNS GUIDE. Short title: Guns Guide. a. $2.50. Cord Communications Corp., 130 W. 42nd St., New York, NY 10036. TEL 212-840-0660. illus. circ. 100,000.

790.13 791.43 US
DUCKBURG TIMES. 1977. irreg. $5. 400 Valleyview, Selah, WA 98942. TEL 509-697-4634. Eds. Dana Gabbard, Patricia Corbin. adv. bk. rev. circ. 1,000.

790.13 IT
FAR DA SE ALMANACCO. 1977. a. L.7000. Edizioni Fardase, Casella Postale 100, 15066 Gavi (Al.), Italy. Ed. Massimo Casolaro.

745.5 US
GOODFELLOW CATALOG OF WONDERFUL THINGS; a mail order treasury of America's finest crafts. (Each issue covers a specific product category) 1974. triennial. $14.95. ‡ Goodfellow Catalog Press, Box 4520, Berkeley, CA 94704. TEL 415-845-2062. Ed. Christopher Weills. adv. illus. circ. 100,000.

790.132 US
GUN TRADERS GUIDE. 1953. biennial. $13.95. Stoeger Publishing Co., 55 Ruta Ct., S. HackensacK, NJ 07405. TEL 201-440-2700.

790.2 746 US
HOBBY PUBLICATIONS ANNUAL TRADE DIRECTORY. a. $25. Hobby Publications, Inc., Box 420, Englishtown, NJ 07726. TEL 201-972-1022. Ed. Jack Harris. circ. 25,000.
Former titles: Craft and Needlework Age/World of Miniatures Annual Trade Directory & Craft, Model and Hobby Industry Annual Trade Directory & Annual Basic Hobby Industry Trade Directory (ISSN 0066-3778)

790.13 016 DK
HOBBYINDEKS FOR BOERNEBIBLIOTEKER. 1974. a. Kr.149.50. Bibliotekscentralen, Tempivej 7-11, DK-2750 Ballerup, Denmark.

795.4 UK
I P M CATALOGUE OF PICTURE POSTCARDS & YEAR BOOK. 1975. a. £5.95. I P M Publications, 2 Frederick Gardens, Brigton BN1 4TB, England. Ed. J.H.D. Smith. adv. index. circ. 4,000. (back issues avail.)

790.13 US
INTERNATIONAL DIRECTORY OF CONCHOLOGISTS. biennial. Shell Cabinet, Box 29, Falls Church, VA 22046. TEL 703-256-0707. Eds. Isabelle E. Welch, M. E. Young.

JOURNAL OF MAGIC HISTORY. see *THEATER*

790.13 US ISSN 0277-0725
KNIVES (YEAR) 1981. a. price varies. D B I Books, Inc., 4092 Commercial Ave., Northfolk, IL 60062. Ed. Ken Warner.

748.8 US
KOVELS' BOTTLE PRICE LIST. a. $10.95. Crown Publishers, Inc., One Park Ave., New York, NY 10016. TEL 212-532-9200. Eds. Ralph Kovel, Terry Kovel.
Formerly: Kovel's Complete Bottle Price List.

790 US
MINIATURES CATALOG; for hobbyists and collectors. 1978. a. $16.70. Boynton & Associates, Inc., Clifton House, Clifton, VA 22024. TEL 703-830-1000. Ed. Sybil Harp. adv. bk. rev. illus, tr. lit. circ. 30,000.

629.133 US
MODEL ROCKET NEWS MAGAZINE. 1961. irreg. (3-4/yr.) free to qualified personnel. ‡ Estes Industries, Penrose, CO 81240. TEL 303-372-6565. Eds. Robert Cannon, Mary Roberts. adv. charts. illus. tr.lit. circ. controlled. (looseleaf format)
Formerly: Model Rocket News.
Model rockets

790.132 US
NEWES. 1950. irreg. International Newspaper Collectors' Club, Box 5090, Phoenix, AZ 85010. TEL 602-273-7288. Ed. Charles J. Smith. adv. bk. rev. illus. circ. 150. (processed)

790.13 US
OFFICIAL OVERSTREET COMIC BOOK PRICE GUIDE. 1970. a. $11.95. Overstreet Publications, Inc., c/o Bob Overstreet, Ed., 780 Hunt Cliff Dr., N.W., Cleveland, TN 37311 TEL 615-472-4135. (Dist. by: House of Collectibles, 201 E. 50th St., New York, NY 10022) adv. illus. stat. tr.lit. circ. 65,000.
Formerly: Comic Book Price Guide (ISSN 0730-2916)

790.13 US
SCANDAL SHEET.* 1971. irreg. $2. Scandalous Bohemians of New Jersey, c/o Norman Nolan, 68 Crest Rd., Middletown, NJ 07748. Ed. Robert A.W. Lowndes. (back issues avail.)
Sherlockiana

659.1 FI ISSN 0037-4970
SIGNAL INTERNATIONAL; for penpals, collectors and traders. (Text in English) 1960. irreg. (2-3/yr.) $15. Moniposti, Box 150, SF-15111 Lahti, Finland. Ed. Raimo Kaarna. adv. bk. rev. illus. tr.lit. circ. 8,000.

355 US
SOLDIER SHOP ANNUAL. 1972. a. $10. ‡ Soldier Shop, Inc., 1222 Madison Ave., New York, NY 10128. Ed. Peter J. Blum. bk. rev. charts. illus. circ. 15,000.
Formerly: Soldier Shop Quarterly.

769.56 US ISSN 0276-7244
UNITED STATES POSTAL CARD CATALOG. quinquennial. United Postal Stationery Society, Cental Office, Box 48, Redlands, CA 92373.

790.13 NO
VI FORNYER OSS; magasinet for farve og miljoe. a. Farveraadet, Postboks 165, 1322 Hoevik, Norway. adv. circ. 40,000.

790.13 US
WHERE-TO-SELL-IT DIRECTORY. 1979. irreg. $3.95. Pilot Books, 103 Cooper St., Babylon, NY 11702. TEL 516-422-2225. Eds. Margaret A. Boyd, Sue Scott-Martin.

790.132 917 US
WHO'S WHO IN INDIAN RELICS. 1960. quadrennial. $25. Ben W. Thompson Publishing Co., 1757 W. Adams, St. Louis, MO 63122. TEL 314-822-2409. Ed. Ben W. Thompson. illus. circ. 3,000.

HOBBIES — Abstracting, Bibliographies, Statistics

790.13 DK ISSN 0105-8134
GOER DET SELV INDEKS. 1977. a. Kr.347.15. Bibliotekscentralen, Tempovej 7-11, DK-2750 Ballerup, Denmark.

016 US
NUMISMATIC BOOKS IN PRINT. 1975. a. $2. Sanford J. Durst Numismatic Publications, 29-28 41 Ave., Long Island City, NY 11101. TEL 718-706-0303. Ed. Sanford J. Durst. circ. 10,000.

HOME ECONOMICS

see also Interior Design and Decoration; Nutrition and Dietetics

AICHI KYOIKU DAIGAKU KENKYU HOKOKU. see *ART*

747 200 US ISSN 0405-6590
BETTER HOMES AND GARDENS CHRISTMAS IDEAS. 1952. a. $2.50 per no. Meredith Corporation, Special Interest Publications, 1716 Locust St., Des Moines, IA 50336. TEL 515-284-3000. adv.

640 635 US
BETTER HOMES AND GARDENS HOME PLAN IDEAS. 1978. a. $2.95 per no. Meredith Corporation, Locust at 17th, Des Moines, IA 50336. TEL 515-284-3000. adv.

640 790.13 US
BLACK & DECKER BUILD IT. 1984. a. Agua-Field Publications, Inc., 656 Shrewsbury Ave., Shrewsbury, NJ 07701. TEL 201-842-8300. adv. circ. 167,633.

CONSUMER-FARMER COOPERATOR. see *HOUSING AND URBAN PLANNING*

641 FR ISSN 0339-7963
CUISINE CHEZ SOL. 1975. irreg. 7 F. per no. Editions Beaulieu, 1 Place Alphonse Deville, 75006 Paris, France. Ed. Andre Guerber.

643 US
EDUCATORS GUIDE TO FREE HOME ECONOMICS MATERIALS. 1984. a. $20.50. Educators Progress Service, Inc., Randolph, WI 53956. TEL 414-326-3126. Ed. Patricia Suttles.

640 JA
FUKUI UNIVERSITY. FACULTY OF EDUCATION. MEMOIRS. SERIES 4: APPLIED SCIENCE AND HOME ECONOMICS. (Text in Japanese; summaries in English, Japanese) 1964. a. Fukui University, Faculty of Education, 9-1, 3-chome, Bunkyo, Fukui 910, Japan.

HANDBOOK OF FOOD PREPARATION. see *FOOD AND FOOD INDUSTRIES*

HOMOSEXUALITY 615

640 CN ISSN 0018-4004
HOME EC NEWS. (Supplement to: Alberta Teachers' Association. Journal of Home Economics Education) 1962. irreg. (2-3/yr.) Alberta Teachers' Association, Home Economics Council, 11010 142nd St., Edmonton, Alta. T5N 2R1, Canada. TEL 403-453-2411. Ed. Mary Davidson. bk. rev. charts. illus. circ. 621. (looseleaf format) Indexed: Can.Educ.Ind.

640 US ISSN 0073-3105
HOME ECONOMICS IN INSTITUTIONS GRANTING BACHELORS OR HIGHER DEGREES. 1965. biennial. $6. ‡ American Home Economics Association, 2010 Massachusetts Ave., N.W., Washington, DC 20036. TEL 202-862-8300. Ed. Laura Jane Harper.

640 UK
HOME ECONOMICS YEARBOOK. 1981. a. £6.95. Maypole Press Ltd., 18 High St., Maldon, Essex CM9 7PJ, England. Ed. James Robinson. adv. bk. rev. circ. 3,000.

HOME SEWING INDUSTRY RESOURCE DIRECTORY. see BUSINESS AND ECONOMICS — Trade And Industrial Directories

640 US
HOMEMAKER'S GUIDE. 1970. a. $2. Snibbe Books, 1115 Ponce de Leon, Clearwater, FL 33516. TEL 813-586-1779. Eds. John M. Benson Jr., Bern Fleming. circ. 700,000.
    Former titles: Homemaker's Handbook; Four Things Every Woman Should Know (ISSN 0073-3156); Homemaker's Guide.

HUMAN LIFE MATTERS. see POPULATION STUDIES

640 DK ISSN 0108-786X
HUSHOLDNINGSARBEJDET. 1975. a. free. Husmandsforeningernes Husholdningsudvalg, Vester Farimagsgade 6/3, 1606 Copenhagen K, Denmark. adv. illus. circ. 1,300.

640 FR ISSN 0074-3712
INTERNATIONAL CONGRESS OF HOME ECONOMICS. REPORT. (Text in English, French and German) quadrennial; 15th, 1984, Oslo. 40 F. International Federation for Home Economics, 5 av. de la Porte Brancion, 75015 Paris, France.

IOWA AGRICULTURE AND HOME ECONOMICS EXPERIMENT STATION. RESEARCH BULLETIN. see AGRICULTURE

KALNIRNAY. see ASTROLOGY

640 JA
KOBE WOMEN'S UNIVERSITY. FACULTY OF HOME ECONOMICS. BULLETIN. (Text in English and Japanese; summaries in English) 1967. a. members only. Kobe Women's University, Faculty of Home Economics, Aoyama, Suma-ku, Kobe-Shi, 654, Japan. Ed. Tokuya Harada. circ. 3, 000. (back issues avail.)

641.5 US ISSN 0094-0305
MCCALL'S COOKING SCHOOL. 1973. a. $2.50 per no. McCall Publishing Co., 230 Park Ave., New York, NY 10169. illus.

640 US
MCCALL'S HOLIDAY BAKE-IT BOOK. 1979. a. $1.75. McCall Publishing Co., 230 Park Ave., New York, NY 10017.

640 US
MCCALL'S TIME SAVING MEALS. 1981. a. McCall Publishing Co., 230 Park Ave, New York, NY 10017. Ed. Mary Eckley. circ. 300,000. (back issues avail.)

MAGAZIN POLOVNIKA. see SPORTS AND GAMES — Outdoor Life

MY BABY. see CHILDREN AND YOUTH — About

NATIONWIDE DIRECTORY OF GIFT, HOUSEWARES & HOME TEXTILE BUYERS. see GIFTWARE AND TOYS

640 US
NEW CONNECTIONS; your guide to living in Manhattan from New York Telephone. 1984. a. Reuben H. Donnelley (Subsidiary of: Dun & Bradstreet) 711 Third Ave., New York, NY 10017. TEL 212-972-7100. Ed. Georgia Orcutt. adv.

640 640.73 GW ISSN 0170-5768
SCHRIFTTUMS FUER DEN BEREICH HAUSHALT UND VERBAUCH. BIBLIOGRAPHIE. 1969. a. DM.10. Bundesforschungsanstalt fuer Ernaehrung, Garbenstr. 13, D-7000 Stuttgart 70, W. Germany (B.R.D.) Ed. Hans-Joachim Ulrich. bk. rev. circ. 500. (back issues avail.)

640 746 US ISSN 0080-9446
SHUTTLE CRAFT GUILD. MONOGRAPHS. 1960. irreg., latest no.37. price varies. H T H Publishers, Box 550, Coupeville, WA 98239. TEL 206-678-4447. Ed. Jim Anderst.

013 640 US ISSN 0082-4534
TITLES OF DISSERTATIONS AND THESES COMPLETED IN HOME ECONOMICS. (Formerly an annual compilation published in the Journal of Home Economics) 1962/63. a. $7.50. ‡ American Home Economics Association, 2010 Massachusetts Ave., N.W., Washington, DC 20036 TEL 202-862-8300. (Order from: University Microfilms Internatinal, Box 1764, Ann Arbor, MI 48106)

640 JA
TOKYO COLLEGE OF DOMESTIC SCIENCE. BULLETIN/TOKYO KASEI DAIGAKU KENKYU KIYO. (Text in English or Japanese) 1960. a. Tokyo College of Domestic Science - Tokyo Kasei Daigaku, 1-18-1 Kaga, Itabashi-ku, Tokyo 173, Japan. Indexed: Chem.Abstr. Psychol.Abstr.

640 US ISSN 0073-3113
U.S. DEPARTMENT OF AGRICULTURE. HOME ECONOMICS RESEARCH REPORT. 1957. irreg. U.S. Department of Agriculture, Washington, DC 20250. TEL 202-655-4000. Indexed: Nutr.Abstr.

641.5 IT
VIAGGI INTORNO ALLA TAVOLA. 1975. irreg. Edizioni Il Formichiere s.r.l., Via del Lauro 3, 20121 Milan, Italy.

640 AT
WEDDING GUIDE MAGAZINE. 1954. a. Aus.$3.25. Wescolour Press, 340 High St., East Fremantle, W.A. 6158, Australia. circ. 10,000.

641.8 US
WILTON YEARBOOK OF BAKING AND CAKE DECORATING. 1975. a. $3.99. Wilton Enterprises, 2240 W. 75th St., Woodridge, IL 60517. TEL 312-963-7100. Ed. Diane Pierson. adv. illus. circ. 1,000, 000.
    Former titles: Wilton Cake Decorating Yearbook & Celebrate; the Annual for Cake Decorators (ISSN 0361-0896)

WOODHEAT. see ENERGY

HOME ECONOMICS — Abstracting, Bibliographies, Statistics

301.5 645 CN ISSN 0318-5273
CANADA. STATISTICS CANADA. HOUSEHOLD FACILITIES AND EQUIPMENT/ L'EQUIPMENT MENAGER. (Catalogue 64-202) (Text in English and French) 1947. a. Can.$20($21) Statistics Canada, Communications Division, 3rd Floor, R.H. Coats Bldg., Ottawa, Ont. K1A 0T6, Canada TEL 613-993-7276. (Subscr. to: Publications Sales and Services, Ottawa, Ont. K1A 0T6, Canada) (also avail. in microform from MML)

640 314 HU ISSN 0439-9285
HUNGARY. KOZPONTI STATISZTIKAI HIVATAL. HAZTARTASSTATISZTIKA. a. 80 Ft. Statisztikai Kiado Vallalat, Kaszasdulo u. 2, Box 99, 1300 Budapest 3, Hungary (Subscr. to: Kultura, Box 149, H-1389 Budapest, Hungary)

310 640 JA
JAPAN. STATISTICS BUREAU. ANNUAL REPORT ON FAMILY INCOME AND EXPENDITURE SURVEY. a. 4.900 Yen. Statistics Bureau - Management and Coordination Agency, 19-1 Wakamatsu-cho, Shinjuku-ku, Tokyo 162, Japan (Subscr. to: Government Publications Service Centre, 1-2-1 Kasumigaseki, Chiyoda-ku, Tokyo 100, Japan)
    Formerly: Japan. Statistics Bureau. Annual Report on Family Income and Expenditures (ISSN 0075-3173)

640 MF
MAURITIUS. CENTRAL STATISTICAL OFFICE. HOUSEHOLD EXPENDITURE SURVEY. 1983. irreg. Rs.40 per no. Central Statistical Office, Rose Hill, Mauritius (Orders to: G.P.O., Elizabeth II, Port Louis, Mauritius)

310 640 PP
PAPUA NEW GUINEA. NATIONAL STATISTICAL OFFICE. HOUSEHOLD EXPENDITURE SURVEY. PRELIMINARY BULLETIN. (Text in English) 1975. irreg. National Statistical Office, P.O. Wards Strip, Papua New Guinea. Ed. J.J. Shadlow. charts. stat. circ. 385.

315 640 SI
SINGAPORE. DEPARTMENT OF STATISTICS. REPORT ON THE HOUSEHOLD EXPENDITURE SURVEY. 1972. quinquennial. S.$12. Department of Statistics, Maxwell Road PO Box 3010, Singapore 9050, Singapore, Singapore. charts. stat.

HOMOSEXUALITY

301.4157 301.412 US
BETTER HOMES & DYKES. irreg. $2 per no. Iowa City Lesbian Alliance, 130 N. Madison, Iowa City, IA 55240.

BIG APPLE DYKE NEWS. see WOMEN'S INTERESTS

CONDITIONS; a feminist magazine of writing by women, with an emphasis on writing by lesbians. see WOMEN'S INTERESTS

301 US
DIRECTORY OF HOMOSEXUAL ORGANIZATIONS AND PUBLICATIONS. a. $6. Homosexual Information Center, 6758 Hollywood Blvd., No. 208, Hollywood, CA 90028. TEL 213-464-8431. Ed. Ursula Enters Copely. (back issues avail.)

301.4157 301.412 US
DYKE DIANNIC WICCA SEPARATIST AMAZON MAGICK. irreg $3 per no. Box 486, Berkeley, CA 94701-0486. Ed. Amethyst/Artemis.

EARTH CIRCLES. see AGRICULTURE

301.4157 US ISSN 0046-3167
FAG RAG. 1970. a. $10. Fag Rag, Inc., Box 331, Kenmore Sta., Boston, MA 02215. TEL 617-661-7534. Ed.Bd. bk. rev. illus. circ. 5,000. (tabloid format; also avail. in microform from UMI; back issues avail.) Indexed: Abstr.Pop.Cult. Alt.Press Ind.

FEMALE IMPERSONATOR NEWS. see THEATER

GAIA'S GUIDE. see TRAVEL AND TOURISM

301.4157 157.734 AT ISSN 0705-5935
GAY COUNSELLING. 1980. a. Aus.$4($3) Gays Counselling Service of NSW, GPO Box 5074, Sydney 2001, Australia. Ed. Terry Goulden. bk. rev. circ. 350. (back issues avail.)

GAY INFORMATION; a journal of Gay studies. see POLITICAL SCIENCE — Civil Rights

380.1 301.4157 US ISSN 0363-826X
GAYELLOW PAGES; classified directory of gay U S A and Canada organizations and businesses. 1973. a. $10. Renaissance House, Box 292, Village Station, New York, NY 10014. Ed. Frances Green. adv. circ. 50,000.

616 HOMOSEXUALITY — ABSTRACTING, BIBLIOGRAPHIES, STATISTICS

323.4 301 US
HOMOSEXUAL INFORMATION CENTER. NEWSLETTER. irreg. free. Homosexual Information Center, 6758 Hollywood Blvd., No. 208, Hollywood, CA 90028. TEL 213-464-8431. bk. rev. (back issues avail.)

301.4157 301.412 US
IN THE LIFE. 1982. irreg. free to qualified personnel. West Coast Lesbian Collections, Box 23/53, Oakland, CA 94623. illus.

301.41 DK ISSN 0108-1888
KVINDER, KVINDER. 1972. a. Lesbisk Bevaegelse, Kvindehuset, Gothersgade 37, 1153 Copenhagen K, Denmark. illus.

301.4157 301.412 US
L A R C NEWSLETTER. 1980. irreg. $5. Radcliffe College, Lesbian Alumni, 70 W. 95 St., New York, NY 10025. Ed. Eleanor Batchelder. circ. 100.

301.4157 US
LESBIAN HERSTORY ARCHIVES NEWSLETTER. 1975. irreg. Lesbian Herstory Educational Foundation, Inc., c/o Deborah Edel, Box 1258, New York, NY 10116. TEL 212-874-7232. bibl. circ. 5,000. Indexed: Alt.Press Ind.

SAPPHIC TOUCH; a journal of lesbian erotica. see WOMEN'S INTERESTS

SPARTACUS INTERNATIONAL GAY GUIDE. see TRAVEL AND TOURISM

301.415 AT ISSN 0155-5936
SYDNEY GAY GUIDE. 1975. a. Gay Society of the University of NSW, Union Box 67, P.O. Box 1, Kensington, NSW 2033, Australia. circ. 5,000.

T V SWINGERS. see THEATER

307 US
WHOLE GAY CATALOG. 1983. a. $2. Lambda Rising, Inc., 1625 Connecticut Ave., N.W., Washington, DC 20009-1013. TEL 202-462-6969. Ed. Robert Dirmeyer. bk. rev. film rev. circ. 50,000.

HOMOSEXUALITY — Abstracting, Bibliographies, Statistics

301.415 US
GAY BIBLIOGRAPHY. 1971. irreg., every 3-4 yrs. $1.25. Box 2383, Philadelphia, PA 19103. TEL 215-471-3322. Ed. Barbara Gittings. circ. 30,000.

011 301 US
SELECTED BIBLIOGRAPHY OF HOMOSEXUALITY. biennial. $0.50. Homosexual Information Center, 6758 Hollywood Blvd., No. 208, Hollywood, CA 90028. TEL 213-464-8431. Ed. Leslie Colfax. (back issues avail.)

HORSES AND HORSEMANSHIP

see Sports and Games—Horses and Horsemanship

HOSPITALS

see also Medical Sciences; Nutrition and Dietetics

362.1 AT
A H A HEALTH SERVICES MONOGRAPHS. irreg. Aus.$1.15. Australian Hospital Association, 42 Thesiger Court, Deakin, A.C.T. 2600, Australia.

ALBERTA. HEALTH CARE INSURANCE PLAN. ANNUAL REPORT. see INSURANCE

658 610 CN ISSN 0227-7883
ALBERTA HOSPITALS AND MEDICAL CARE. ANNUAL REPORT. 1978. a. free. Alberta Hospitals and Medical Care, Communication Branch, 11010-101 St., Box 2222, Edmonton, Alta. T5J 2P4, Canada. TEL 403-427-1400. Ed.Bd. stat. circ. 1,000. (back issues avail.)

AMERICAN ANIMAL HOSPITAL ASSOCIATION. ANNUAL MEETING SCIENTIFIC PROCEEDINGS. see VETERINARY SCIENCE

362 US
AMERICAN COLLEGE OF HEALTHCARE EXECUTIVES. DIRECTORY. 1960. biennial. $60 to non-members. American College of Healthcare Executives, 840 N. Lake Shore Dr., Chicago, IL 60611. TEL 312-943-0544. Ed. Earl Tanis. circ. 4,000.
Formerly: American College of Hospital Administrators. Directory (ISSN 0065-7794)

362 US ISSN 0098-2377
AMERICAN GROUP PRACTICE ASSOCIATION DIRECTORY. 1952. a. $75. American Group Practice Association, 1422 Duke St., Alexandria, VA 22314. TEL 703-838-0033. adv. circ. 2,500.
Formerly: American Association of Medical Clinics. Directory (ISSN 0569-2679)

ANNUAIRE MEDICAL DE L'HOSPITALISATION FRANCAISE. see MEDICAL SCIENCES

362.15 610.736 US
ANNUAL REPORT OF ADVOCACY FOR NURSING HOME REFORM. 1977. a. $12. National Citizens Coalition for Nursing Home Reform, 1424 16th St., N.W., L-2, Washington, DC 20036. bk. rev. circ. 1,500. (back issues avail.)
Formerly (until 1986): Collation.

362.1 AT ISSN 0312-5599
AUSTRALIAN HOSPITALS AND HEALTH SERVICES YEARBOOK. 1975. a. Aus.$80 per no. (University of New South Wales, School of Health Administration) Peter Isaacson Publications, 45-50 Porter St., Prahran, Vic. 3181, Australia. Ed. Peter Finlayson. adv. circ. 2,500.
Formerly: Australian and New Zealand Hospitals and Health Services Yearbook (ISSN 0084-7208)

658 GW
BLAUE DATEI DER KRANKENHAUSLIEFERANTEN. 1979. a. DM.45. Verlag E.C. Baumann KG, E.C. Baumann Str. 5, 8650 Kulmbach, W. Germany (B.R.D.) Ed. Willibald Hock. adv. circ. 5,000.
Formerly: Blaue Datei der Krankenhauslieferanten mit Krankenhausverzeichnis.

658 BL
BRAZIL. COORDENACAO DE ASSISTENCIA MEDICA E HOSPITALAR. CADASTRO DE ESTABELECIMENTOS DE SAUDE. 1973. irreg. free. Ministerio da Saude, Secretaria Nacional de Acoes Basicas em Saude - Health Ministry, Brasilia, Brazil. stat. circ. 1,000.
Formerly: Brazil. Coordencacao de Assistencia Medica e Hospitalar. Cadastro Hospitalar Brasileiro.

362 326.16 UK ISSN 0068-208X
BRITISH HOSPITALS CONTRIBUTORY SCHEMES ASSOCIATION. DIRECTORY OF CONVALESCENT HOMES SERVING THE PROVINCES.* 1963. biennial. 25p. British Hospitals Contributory Schemes Association, 30 Lancaster Gate, London W2 4LT, England. Ed. A.A. Case.

362 368.4 UK ISSN 0068-2098
BRITISH HOSPITALS CONTRIBUTORY SCHEMES ASSOCIATION. DIRECTORY OF HOSPITALS CONTRIBUTORY SCHEME BENEFITS. 1954. biennial. £1. British Hospitals Contributory Schemes Association, 30 Lancaster Gate, London W2 3LT, England. Ed. A.A. Case. circ. 500.

362 UK ISSN 0068-2101
BRITISH HOSPITALS CONTRIBUTORY SCHEMES ASSOCIATION. REPORT.* 1949. a. 5p. British Hospitals Contributory Schemes Association, 30 Lancaster Gate, London W2 3LT, England. Ed. A.A. Case.

CALIFORNIA HEALTH FACILITIES COMMISSION. ANNUAL REPORT TO THE GOVERNOR AND LEGISLATURE OF THE STATE OF CALIFORNIA. see MEDICAL SCIENCES

362.1 US
CALIFORNIA STATE HEALTH PLAN. 1980. a. $25. Office of Statewide Health Planning Development, 1600 9th St., Rm. 440, Sacramento, CA 95814. TEL 916-322-7425. Ed. Larry Meeks. stat. circ. 5,000. Indexed: Ind.Med.
Former titles (until 1955): California State Plan for Hospital and Health Center Construction (ISSN 0098-9983); California State Plan for Hospitals and Related Health Facilities (ISSN 0526-9288); California State Plan for Hospitals (ISSN 0575-2221)

362 CN ISSN 0068-8932
CANADIAN HOSPITAL DIRECTORY/ ANNUAIRE DES HOPITAUX DU CANADA. (Text in English and French) 1953. a. Can.$65. ‡ Canadian Hospital Association, 17 York St., Ste. 100, Ottawa, Ont. K1N 9J6, Canada. TEL 613-238-8005. Ed. T. Radford. adv. circ. 5,000. (reprint service avail. from UMI)

658 371.42 AT
CAREERS IN HOSPITALS AND HEALTH SERVICES IN VICTORIA. 1969. biennial. Aus.$3.50. Health Department, Victoria, Mayfield Centre, 11-27 Mayfield Ave., Malvern, Vic. 3144, Australia. Ed. Leigh Brown. circ. 2,500.

362 200 US
CATHOLIC HEALTH ASSOCIATION OF THE UNITED STATES. GUIDEBOOK. a. Catholic Health Association of the United States, 4455 Woodson Rd., St. Louis, MO 63134. TEL 314-427-2500.
Formerly: Guidebook of Catholic Hospitals (ISSN 0090-2535)

658 US
CLARK'S DIRECTORY OF SOUTHERN HOSPITALS. 1934. a. $30. Billian Publishing Co., 2100 Powers Ferry Rd., Ste. 125, Atlanta, GA 30339. TEL 404-955-5656. adv. bk. rev. circ. 10, 654(controlled) Indexed: CINAHL.
Formerly: Southern Hospitals.

362 IT ISSN 0589-3267
CONGRESSO EUROPEO DI STORIA OSPITALIERA. ATTI.* 1960. irreg. Centro Italiano di Storia Ospitaliera, Reggio Emilia, Via Roma 31, Rome, Italy.

362.11 DK ISSN 0106-6706
D S I NOTAT. 1979. irreg. price varies. Dansk Sygehus Institut - Danish Hospital Institute, Copenhagen, Denmark. illus. circ. 1,000.

610 GW
DEUTSCHE KRANKENHAUSGESELLSCHAFT. JAHRESBERICHT. biennial. free. Deutsche Krankenhausgesellschaft, Tersteegenstr. 9, 4000 Duesseldorf 30, W. Germany (B.R.D.)

DIRECTORY OF ARCHITECTS FOR HEALTH FACILITIES. see ARCHITECTURE

658 371.42 AT ISSN 0157-2784
DIRECTORY OF INTERNSHIPS, RESIDENCIES AND REGISTRARSHIPS AVAILABLE IN VICTORIAN HOSPITALS. 1967. a. Aus.$6. Victorian Medical Postgraduate Foundation Inc., Trawalla 22 Lascelles Ave., Toorak, Vic. 3142, Australia. Ed. P.M. Jewell. circ. 900.

362.1 US ISSN 0095-5191
DIRECTORY OF INVESTOR-OWNED HOSPITALS, HOSPITAL MANAGEMENT COMPANIES AND HEALTH SYSTEMS. a. $40. F A H S Review, Inc., 1405 N. Pierce St., Ste. 308, Little Rock, AR 72207. TEL 501-661-9555. (reprint service avail. from UMI)
Formerly: Directory of Investor-Owned Hospitals and Hospital Management Companies.

658 US ISSN 0731-8510
DIRECTORY OF MULTIHOSPITAL SYSTEMS. 1980. a. $40. American Hospital Publishing, Inc., 211 E. Chicago Ave., Ste. 700, Chicago, IL 60611. TEL 312-951-1100. Ed. Dorothy Cobbs.

HOSPITALS

610   UK   ISSN 0260-8820
DIRECTORY OF PRIVATE HOSPITALS AND HEALTH SERVICES; a comprehensive guide to the independent health care sector in the U.K. vol.4, 1983. a. £25. Longman Group Ltd., Fourth Ave., Harlow, Essex CM19 5AA, England.

362   UK
ENGLAND AND WALES NATIONAL HEALTH SERVICE. HEALTH SERVICES COSTING RETURNS. 1976. a. £6. Department of Health and Social Security, Alexander Fleming House, Elephant and Castle, London SE1 6BY, England (Subscr. to: D H S S (Leaflets), P.O. Box 21, Stanmore, Middlesex HA7 1AY, England) (also avail. in microform) Indexed: Hosp.Abstr.
Former titles: Great Britain. National Health Service. Health Services Costing Returns; Great Britain National Health Service. Hospital Costing Returns (ISSN 0072-6966)

355.72 387.7   AT
FLYING DOCTOR YEARBOOK. 1976. a. (Royal Flying Doctor Service of Australia) Magazine Art Pty. Ltd., 35 Willis Street, Hampton, Victoria 3188, Australia. Ed. John Taylor. circ. 5,000.

362.11   DK   ISSN 0107-7627
FORBRUGET AF SOMATISKE SENGEPLADSER. 1982. a. Kr.25. Sundhedsstyrelsen, St. Kongensgade 1, 1264 Copenhagen K, Denmark (Orders to: Danske Boghendleres Kommissionsanstalt, Siljangade 6, 2300 Copenhagen S, Denmark) illus.

662.15 610   UK   ISSN 0262-1010
G P GUIDE TO EMERGENCY & MEDICAL SERVICES. 1981. a. £5. Asgard Publishing Co. Ltd., 4A The Square, Petersfield, Hants. GU32 3HJ, England. Ed. James Wroe. adv. circ. 26,000.

658 310   US   ISSN 0891-2173
GERIATRIC LENGTH OF STAY BY DIAGNOSIS AND OPERATION, UNITED STATES. 1964. a. price varies. Commission on Professional and Hospital Activities, 1968 Green Rd., Box 1809, Ann Arbor, MI 48106. TEL 800-521-6210. stat. (also avail. in microfiche; magnetic tape; back issues avail.)

362.11   UK
GREAT BRITAIN. DEPARTMENT OF HEALTH AND SOCIAL SECURITY. HEALTH BUILDING NOTES. 1961. irreg. price varies. H.M.S.O., P.O. Box 569, London SE1 9NH, England. (reprint service avail. from UMI)
Formerly: Great Britain. Department of Health and Social Security. Hospital Building Notes (ISSN 0072-601X)

362.11   UK   ISSN 0141-1403
GREAT BRITAIN. DEPARTMENT OF HEALTH AND SOCIAL SECURITY. HEALTH EQUIPMENT NOTES. 1975. irreg. price varies. H.M.S.O., Box 569, London SE1 9NH, England. (reprint service avail. from UMI)
Formerly: Great Britain. Department of Health and Social Security. Hospital Equipment Notes (ISSN 0072-6028)

362   UK
GREAT BRITAIN. DEPARTMENT OF HEALTH AND SOCIAL SECURITY. NOTES ON GOOD PRACTICES. 1975. irreg. price varies. H.M.S.O., Box 569, London SE1 9NH, England. abstr, charts, illus. stat. (looseleaf format; reprint service avail. from UMI) Indexed: Hosp.Abstr.
Former titles (until 1977): Abstracts of Efficiency Studies in the National Health Service; Abstracts of Efficiency Studies in the Hospital Service (ISSN 0001-3552)

362.1 614   UK
GREAT BRITAIN. DEPARTMENT OF HEALTH AND SOCIAL SECURITY. STATISTICAL AND RESEARCH REPORT SERIES. 1965. irreg. price varies. H.M.S.O., Box 569, London SE1 9NH, England. (reprint service avail. from UMI)
Formerly (until 1972): Great Britain. Department of Health and Social Security. Statistical Report Series (ISSN 0072-6125)

610   FR   ISSN 0072-8144
GUIDE MEDICAL ET HOSPITALIER; publics et prives de France. 1959. a. 530 F. Editions Boileau, 45 rue Saint Charles, 75015 Paris, France. adv. illus.

HANDBOOK ON HOSPITAL-ASSOCIATED INFECTIONS. see *BIOLOGY — Microbiology*

362   US
HAWAII. DEPARTMENT OF HEALTH. WAIMANO TRAINING SCHOOL AND HOSPITAL DIVISION (REPORT) 1962. a. free. Department of Health, Waimano Training School and Hospital Division, Box 3378, Honolulu, HI 96801. TEL 808-456-6223.
Former titles: Hawaii. Department of Health. Division of Mental Health. Children's Health Services; Hawaii, Department of Health Research and Planning Statistical Office. (Report on) Waimano Training School and Hospital (ISSN 0073-1056)

362 658.8   US
HAYES DIRECTORY OF MEDICAL SUPPLY HOUSES. 1935. a. $140. Edward N. Hayes, Ed. & Pub., 4229 Birch St., Newport Beach, CA 92660. TEL 714-756-9063.
Formerly: Hayes Directory of Physician and Hospital Supply Houses (ISSN 0073-1412)

362   US   ISSN 0889-0331
HEALTH AND HEALTH CARE IN NEW YORK CITY: LOCAL, STATE, AND NATIONAL PERSPECTIVES. a. $30. United Hospital Fund of New York, 55 Fifth Ave., New York, NY 10003. TEL 212-645-2500.

360   AT
HEALTH DEPARTMENT VICTORIA. ANNUAL REPORT. 1979. a. free. Health Department Victoria, 555 Collins St., Melbourne, Vic. 3000, Australia. Ed. Max Sims. circ. 1,700.
Former Titles: Health Commision of Victoria. Annual Report & Victoria. Hospitals and Charities Commision. Annual Report.

HEALTH DEVICES SOURCEBOOK. see *MEDICAL SCIENCES*

362   US   ISSN 0888-7039
HEALTH FACILITIES IN SOUTHERN NEW YORK: A GUIDE TO INPATIENT, OUTPATIENT, AND LONG-TERM CARE. a. $20. United Hospital Fund of New York, 55 Fifth Ave., New York, NY 10003. TEL 212-645-2500.

362.1   UK   ISSN 0140-5748
HEALTH SERVICE BUYERS GUIDE. 1966. a. £30. Sell's Publications Ltd., 55 High St., Epsom, Surrey KT19 8DW, England. adv. bk. rev. circ. 5,000.
Former titles: Sell's Health Service Buyers Guide (ISSN 0308-7107); Sell's Hospital and Surgical Supplies (ISSN 0073-3458)

HEALTH SYSTEMS MANAGEMENT. see *PUBLIC HEALTH AND SAFETY*

658   US
HEALTHCARE MARKETING ABSTRACTS. 1986. m. $68. C O R Research Inc., Box 6336, Torrance, CA 90504. TEL 213-833-3316. Ed. Dean H. Anderson. bk. rev.

900 610   GW
HISTORIA HOSPITALIUM. 1966. a. DM.45. Deutsche Gesellschaft fuer Krankenhausgeschichte, Schneebergweg, D-5100 Aachen, W. Germany (B.R.D.) Ed. Axel Hinrich Murken. bk. rev. circ. 600.

658   AT
HOSPITAL & HEALTH SERVICES YEARBOOK AUSTRALIA. 1975. a. Peter Isaacson Publications, 46 Porter St., Prahan, Vic. 3181, Australia. Ed. Peter Finlayson. adv. circ. 2,500.

362 610.73   SA   ISSN 0441-2613
HOSPITAL AND NURSING YEARBOOK OF SOUTHERN AFRICA. 1960. a. R.60 to individuals; hospitals R.25. Thomson Publications S.A. (Pty) Ltd., Thomson House, Cnr. Will Scarlet & Hendrik Verwoerd Dr., Randburg, P.O. Box 56182, Pinegowrie 2123, South Africa. Ed. Heinz Engelhardt. adv.

362.11   UK
HOSPITAL CONSULTANTS AND SPECIALISTS ASSOCIATION YEAR BOOK. 1982. a. free. Websters Publications Ltd., Onslow Hse., 60-66 Saffron Hill, London, EC1N 8AY, England. Ed. S.T. Chorkham. adv. circ. 6,000.

658   US
HOSPITAL CONTRACTS MANUAL. a. (plus s-a. supplements) $255. Aspen Publishers, Inc., 1600 Research Blvd., Rockville, MD 20850. TEL 301-251-5000.

658   BL
HOSPITAL-ESCOLA SAO CAMILO E SAO LUIS. BOLETIM. a. Hospital-Escola Sao Camilo e Sao Luis, Macapa, Brazil.

658   US   ISSN 0193-0486
HOSPITAL MANAGEMENT SYSTEMS SOCIETY. ANNUAL CONFERENCE PROCEEDINGS. 1976. a. price varies. American Hospital Association, 840 N. Lake Shore Dr., Chicago, IL 60611. TEL 312-280-6000. Ed. Richard P. Covert.

658   US
INSTITUTE OF INDUSTRIAL ENGINEERS. HEALTH SERVICES DIVISION. ANNUAL CONFERENCE PROCEEDINGS. 1975. a. price varies. American Hospital Association, 840 N. Lake Shore Dr., Chicago, IL 60611. TEL 312-280-6000. Ed. Richard P. Covert.
Formerly: American Institute of Industrial Engineers. Health Services Division. Annual Conference Proceedings (ISSN 0194-1135)

362   SZ   ISSN 0074-977X
INTERNATIONALER SPITALBEDARF. (Text in French, German) 1958. a. 20 Fr. Vogt-Schild AG, Dornacherstr. 39, 4501 Solothurn 1, Switzerland. Ed. Dr Eleonore Baumberger. adv. circ. 5,000.

ISRAEL. CENTRAL BUREAU OF STATISTICS. DIAGNOSTIC STATISTICS OF HOSPITALIZED PATIENTS. see *SOCIAL SERVICES AND WELFARE*

362   JA   ISSN 0408-0904
JAPANESE HOSPITAL DIRECTORY/BYOIN YORAN. (Text in Japanese) 1958/59-1964; resumed 1983. a. 13000 Yen. (Ministry of Health and Welfare - Koseisho Imukyoku Somuka) Igaku-Shoin Ltd., 24-3 5-chome Hongo, Bunkyo-ku, Tokyo 113-91, Japan.

658   GW
KRANKENHAUS KALENDER; Beschaffung-Organisation-Haustechnik-Medizin. 1980. a. DM.25. Ecomed Verlagsgesellschaft mbh, Justus-von-Liebig-Str. 1, 8910 Landsberg, W. Germany (B.R.D.) circ. 10,000.

362.11   DK   ISSN 0107-1165
LAEGESTILLINGER OG SENGEPLADSER PAA INSTITUTIONER. 1974. a. Kr.10. Sundhedstyrelsen, St. Kongensgade 1, 1264 Copenhagen K, Denmark.
Formerly: Normerede og Besatte Laegestillinger Samt Sengepladser paa Institutioner.

658 310   US   ISSN 0891-2114
LENGTH OF STAY BY DIAGNOSIS, CANADA. 1964. a. price varies. Commission on Professional and Hospital Activities, 1968 Green Rd., Box 1809, Ann Arbor, MI 48106. TEL 800-521-6210. stat. (also avail. in microfiche; magnetic tape; back issues avail.)

658 310   US   ISSN 0891-2149
LENGTH OF STAY BY DIAGNOSIS, UNITED STATES. 1964. a. price varies. Commission on Professional and Hospital Activities, 1968 Green Rd., Box 1809, Ann Arbor, MI 48106. TEL 800-521-6210. stat. (also avail. in microfiche; magnetic tape; back issues avail.)

658 310   US   ISSN 0891-2165
LENGTH OF STAY BY DIAGNOSIS, UNITED STATES, NORTH CENTRAL REGION. 1964. a. price varies. Commission on Professional and Hospital Activities, 1968 Green Rd., Box 1809, Ann Arbor, MI 48106. TEL 800-521-6210. stat. (also avail. in microfiche; magnetic tape; back issues avail.)

658 310   US   ISSN 0891-2122
LENGTH OF STAY BY DIAGNOSIS, UNITED STATES, NORTHEASTERN REGION. 1964. a. price varies. Commission on Professional and Hospital Activities, 1968 Green Rd., Box 1809, Ann Arbor, MI 48106. TEL 800-521-6210. stat. (also avail. in microfiche; magnetic tape; back issues avail.)

HOSPITALS — ABSTRACTING, BIBLIOGRAPHIES, STATISTICS

658 310   US   ISSN 0891-2130
LENGTH OF STAY BY DIAGNOSIS, UNITED STATES, SOUTHERN REGION. 1964. a. price varies. Commission on Professional and Hospital Activities, 1968 Green Rd., Box 1809, Ann Arbor, MI 48106. TEL 800-521-6210. stat. (also avail. in microfiche; magnetic tape; back issues avail.)

658 310   US   ISSN 0891-2157
LENGTH OF STAY BY DIAGNOSIS, UNITED STATES, WESTERN REGION. 1964. a. price varies. Commission on Professional and Hospital Activities, 1968 Green Rd., Box 1809, Ann Arbor, MI 48106. TEL 800-521-6210. stat. (also avail. in microfiche; magnetic tape; back issues avail.)

658 310   US   ISSN 0891-2181
LENGTH OF STAY BY OPERATION, CANADA. 1964. a. price varies. Commission on Professional and Hospital Activities, 1968 Green Rd., Box 1809, Ann Arbor, MI 48106. TEL 800-521-6210. stat. (also avail. in microfiche; magnetic tape; back issues avail.)

658 310   US   ISSN 0891-2203
LENGTH OF STAY BY OPERATION, UNITED STATES. 1964. a. price varies. Commission on Professional and Hospital Activities, 1968 Green Rd., Box 1089, Ann Arbor, MI 48106. TEL 800-521-6210. stat. (also avail. in microfiche; magnetic tape; back issues avail.)

658 310   US   ISSN 0891-222X
LENGTH OF STAY BY OPERATION, UNITED STATES, NORTH CENTRAL REGION. 1964. a. price varies. Commission on Professional and Hospital Activities, 1968 Green Rd., Box 1809, Ann Arbor, MI 48106. TEL 800-521-6210. stat. (also avail. in microfiche; magnetic tape; back issues avail.)

658 310   US   ISSN 0888-2673
LENGTH OF STAY BY OPERATION, UNITED STATES, NORTHEASTERN REGION. 1964. a. price varies. Commission on Professional and Hospital Activities, 1968 Green Rd., Box 1809, Ann Arbor, MI 48106. TEL 800-521-6210. stat. (also avail. in microfiche; magnetic tape; back issues avail.)

658 310   US   ISSN 0891-219X
LENGTH OF STAY BY OPERATION, UNITED STATES, SOUTHERN REGION. 1964. a. price varies. Commission on Professional and Hospital Activities, 1968 Green Rd., Box 1809, Ann Arbor, MI 48106. TEL 800-521-6210. stat. (also avail. in microfiche; magnetic tape; back issues avail.)

658 310   US   ISSN 0891-2211
LENGTH OF STAY BY OPERATION, UNITED STATES, WESTERN REGION. 1964. a. price varies. Commission on Professional and Hospital Activities, 1968 Green Rd., Box 1809, Ann Arbor, MI 48106. TEL 800-521-6210. stat. (also avail. in microfiche; magnetic tape; back issues avail.)

362.11   UK
LIST OF APPROVED HOSPITALS AND RECOGNISED HOUSE OFFICER POSTS. 1952. irreg. £10. General Medical Council, 44 Hallam St., London W1N 6AE, England.

658   GW   ISSN 0721-6076
MEDIZIN IN BERLIN (WEST); aktuelle Anschriften und Telefonnummern des Berliner Gesundheitswesens. 1936. a. DM.32.64. Verlag Joachim Kugler, Machnower Str. 7a, Postfach 37 03 45, 1000 Berlin 37, W. Germany (B.R.D.) Ed.Bd. adv. circ. 4,200.

658 371.42   AT   ISSN 0155-9567
NATIONAL DIRECTORY OF INTERNSHIPS, RESIDENCIES & REGISTRARSHIPS. 1978. a. Aus.$8. Victorian Medical Postgraduate Foundation Inc., Trawalla, 22 Lascelles Ave., Toorak, Vic. 3142, Australia. Ed. P.M. Jewell. circ. 500. (back issues avail.)

362.11   UK
NEW ST. GEORGE HOSPITAL GAZETTE. 1893. a. £1.05. St. George Hospital, Medical School, Cranmer Terrace, Tooting, London SW17 0RE, England. circ. 750.

658   US
NEW YORK (STATE). COMMISSION ON QUALITY OF CARE FOR THE MENTALLY DISABLED. ANNUAL REPORT. 1979. a. $3. Commission on Quality of Care for the Mentally Disabled, 99 Washington Ave., Albany, NY 12210. TEL 518-473-8683. Ed. Marcus A. Gigliotti. circ. 7, 500.

658   DK   ISSN 0109-9957
OPERATIONSMOENSTERET PAA DANSKE SYGEHUSE. 1982. a. Kr.40. Sundehdsstyrelsen, St. Kongensgade 1, 1264 Copenhagen K, Denmark (Subscr. to: Danske Boghendleres Kommisionsanstalt, Siljangade 6, 2300 Copenhagen S, Denmark)

362   SA   ISSN 0078-5547
ORANGE FREE STATE. DIRECTOR OF HOSPITAL SERVICES. REPORT/ORANGE FREE STATE. DIREKTEUR VAN HOSPITALDIENSTE. VERSLAG. 1965. a. R.9.50. ‡ Director of Hospital Services, Box 517, Bloemfontein 9300, South Africa. circ. controlled.

658 310   US   ISSN 0891-1223
PEDIATRIC LENGTH OF STAY BY DIAGNOSIS AND OPERATION, UNITED STATES. 1964. a. price varies. Commission on Professional and Hospital Activities, 1968 Green Rd., Box 1809, Ann Arbor, MI 48106. TEL 800-521-6210. stat. (also avail. in microfiche; magnetic tape; back issues avail.)

658   AT
PERMAIL HOSPITAL BOOK. 1965. biennial. Aus.$95. Permail Pty. Ltd., Box 56, Artarmon, NSW 2064, Australia.

658   DK   ISSN 0107-1173
PERSONALE- OG OEKONOMISTIK FOR SYGEHUSVAESENET. 1976. a. Kr.15. Sundhedsstyrelsen, St. Kongensgade 1, 1264 Copenhagen K, Denmark.
Formerly: Personale og Sengepladser ved de Sygedomsbehandlende Institutioner.

362   PR
PUERTO RICO. DIVISION OF HEALTH FACILITIES. PLAN FOR HOSPITAL AND MEDICAL FACILITES. (Text and summaries in English) 1949. a. Department of Health, Division of Health Facilites, Stop 19, Santurce, PR 00907. circ. 250. (processed)

362.11   CN
QUEEN ALEXANDRA HOSPITAL FOR CHILDREN. ANNUAL REPORT. 1927. a. Can.$5. Arbutus Society for Children, 2400 Arbutus Road, Victoria, B.C. V8N 1V7, Canada. TEL 604-477-1826. Ed. G.F. Fisher. circ. 700. (processed)
Formerly: Queen Alexandra Solarium for Crippled Children Annual Report (ISSN 0085-526X)

RHODE ISLAND. DEPARTMENT OF MENTAL HEALTH, RETARDATION AND HOSPITALS. MENTAL HEALTH, RETARDATION AND HOSPITALS. see PUBLIC HEALTH AND SAFETY

642.59 613.7   US   ISSN 0191-961X
RX HOME CARE BUYER'S GUIDE. 1983. a. $30. Brentwood Publishing Corp. (Subsidiary of: Simon & Schuster, unit of Gulf & Western, Inc.) 1640 5th St., Santa Monica, CA 90401 TEL 213-395-0234. (Subscr. to: Box 2178, Santa Monica, CA 90406-2178) Ed. Kris Kyes. adv. tr.lit. circ. 25,000. (back issues avail.)

610   UK   ISSN 0036-2840
SAINT GEORGE'S HOSPITAL GAZETTE. 1893. a. £1.05. St. George's Hospital Medical School, Cranmer Terrace, Tooting, London S.W. 17, England. Ed.Bd. adv. bk. rev. charts. illus. cum.index. circ. 1,000.

362.11   DK   ISSN 0107-8380
SYGDOMSMOENSTERET VED SOMATISKE SYGEHUSAFDELINGEN. 1979. triennial. Kr.40. Sundhedsstyrelsen, St. Kongensgade 1, 1264 Copenhagen K, Denmark (Orders to: Danske Boghendleres Kommissionsanstalt, Siljangade 6, 2300 Copenhagen S, Denmark)

362.11   DK   ISSN 0107-508X
SYGEHUSKLASSIFIKATION OG KOMMUNEKODER. 1974. a. Sundhedsstyrelsen, Store Kongensgade 1, 1264 Copenhagen K, Denmark.

362.11   DK   ISSN 0107-4954
SYGEHUSVAESENET. 1981. a. Sundhedsstyrelsen, St. Kongensgade 1, 1264 Copenhagen K, Denmark (Orders to: Indenrigsministeriet, 2 Sundhedskontor, Christiansborg Slotsplads 1, 1218 Copenhagen K, Denmark)

658 610   UK
TOO MUCH - UNIVERSITY COLLEGE HOSPITAL MAGAZINE. 1910. irreg. £1.50 for 4 nos. University College Hospital Medical School, University St., London W.C. 1, England. Eds. Susan Horsman, Robert F.K. Hughes. adv. bk. rev. play rev. circ. 1,000.
Formerly: University College Hospital Magazine (ISSN 0041-9273)

U.S. NATIONAL CENTER FOR HEALTH STATISTICS. VITAL AND HEALTH STATISTICS. SERIES 13. DATA ON HEALTH RESOURCES UTILIZATION. see PUBLIC HEALTH AND SAFETY

362   UN   ISSN 0510-8845
WORLD HEALTH ORGANIZATION. REGIONAL OFFICE FOR THE WESTERN PACIFIC. REPORT ON THE REGIONAL SEMINAR ON THE ROLE OF THE HOSPITAL IN THE PUBLIC HEALTH PROGRAMME. 1963. irreg. World Health Organization, Regional Office for the Western Pacific, Box 2932, Manila, Philippines.

HOSPITALS — Abstracting, Bibliographies, Statistics

362 016   US   ISSN 0194-4908
ABSTRACTS OF HEALTH CARE MANAGEMENT STUDIES. 1963/64. a. $65. (Foundation of the American College of Healthcare Executives) Health Administration Press, 1021 E. Huron St., Ann Arbor, MI 48104-9990 TEL 313-764-1380. (Subscr. to: Order Processing center, 1951 Cornell, Melrose Park, IL 60160) Ed. Gene Regenstreif. abstr. index. circ. 1,000. (also avail. in microfilm from UMI; reprint service avail. from UMI)
Formerly: Abstracts of Hospital Management Studies (ISSN 0001-3595)

362   US   ISSN 0094-8969
AMERICAN HOSPITAL ASSOCIATION. GUIDE TO THE HEALTH CARE FIELD. 1945. a. $88 to non-members; members $66. American Hospital Association, 840 N. Lake Shore Dr., Chicago, IL 60611. TEL 312-280-6000. Ed. Ellit H. Gage. adv. stat. tr. lit. circ. 30,000.

362.1   CN   ISSN 0225-5642
CANADA. STATISTICS CANADA. LIST OF CANADIAN HOSPITALS AND SPECIAL CARE FACILITIES/LISTE DES HOPITAUX CANADIENS ET DES ETABLISSEMENTS DE SOINS SPECIAUX. (Catalogue 83-201) (Text in English and French) 1942. a. Can.$35($36.50) Statistics Canada, Communications Division, 3rd Floor, R.H. Coats Bldg., Ottawa, Ont. K1A 0T6, Canada TEL 613-993-7276. (Subscr. to: Publications Sales and Services, Ottawa, Ont. K1A 0T6, Canada) (also avail. in microform from MML)
Formerly: Canada. Statistics Canada. Hospitals Section. List of Canadian Hospitals and Related Institutions and Facilities/Liste des Hopitaux Canadiens et des Etablissements et Installations Connexes (ISSN 0319-8014)

610   UK   ISSN 0267-1182
CHARTERED INSTITUTE OF PUBLIC FINANCE AND ACCOUNTANCY. NON-TEACHING HOSPITAL COSTS. STATISTICS. 1984. a. £8. Chartered Institute of Public Finance and Accountancy, 3 Robert St., London WC2N 6BH, England.

HOTELS AND RESTAURANTS

see also Nutrition and Dietetics; Travel and Tourism

610 UK ISSN 0267-1174
CHARTERED INSTITUTE OF PUBLIC FINANCE AND ACCOUNTANCY. TEACHING HOSPITAL STATISTICS. ACTUALS. 1984. a. £8. Chartered Institute of Public Finance and Accountancy, 3 Robert St., London WC2N 6BH, England. circ. 500.

658 CY
CYPRUS. MINISTRY OF HEALTH. DEPARTMENT OF MEDICAL & PUBLIC HEALTH SERVICES. ANNUAL REPORT. (Text in English) 1920. a. Ministry of Health, Department of Medical & Public Health Services, Nicosia, Cyprus. circ. 200.

613 016 NE ISSN 0300-5321
EXCERPTA MEDICA. SECTION 36: HEALTH ECONOMICS AND HOSPITAL MANAGEMENT. 1971. 10/yr. $210. Elsevier Science Publishers B.V., Box 211, 1000 AE Amsterdam, Netherlands. adv. bk. rev. abstr. charts. index; cum.index. Indexed: Excerp.Med.
●Also available online. Vendors: BRS, DIALOG.
Formerly: Excerpta Medica. Section 36: Health Economics.

362.2 US ISSN 0094-2294
FLORIDA. MENTAL HEALTH PROGRAM OFFICE. STATISTICAL REPORT OF HOSPITALS. (Former name of issuing body: Division of Mental Health) 1960. a. Department of Health and Rehabilitative Services, Alcohol, Drug Abuse and Mental Health Program Office, 1323 Winewood Blvd., Tallahassee, FL 32301. TEL 904-488-8304. circ. 50. Key Title: Statistical Report of Hospitals (Tallahassee)

362 NZ ISSN 0548-9938
HOSPITAL AND SELECTED MORBIDITY DATA. a. NZ.$16. National Health Statistics Centre, Private Bag 2, Upper Willis St., Wellington, New Zealand.

362 016 US ISSN 0018-5736
HOSPITAL LITERATURE INDEX. (Fourth quarterly is annual cum.) 1945. q. $168.75 to non-members; members $135. American Hospital Association, 840 N. Lake Shore Dr., Chicago, IL 60611. TEL 312-280-6263. Ed. Connie Poole. index. circ. 3,200. (also avail. in microform from UMI)
●Also available online. Vendors: DIMDI.
Formerly: Hospital Periodical Literature Index. *Hospital administration*

362 US
HOSPITAL STATISTICS (YEAR) 1946. a. $60.50 to non-members; members $49.50. American Hospital Association, 840 N. Lake Shore Dr., Chicago, IL 60611. TEL 312-280-6000. Ed. Elliot H. Gage. charts. stat. index. circ. 15,000. Key Title: Hospital Statistics.
Former titles: Hospital Statistics; Data from American Hospital Association Annual Survey (ISSN 0090-6662); Survey of Hospital Charges (ISSN 0360-9316)

KEY STATISTICAL INDICATORS FOR NATIONAL HEALTH SERVICE MANAGEMENT IN WALES. see *PUBLIC HEALTH AND SAFETY — Abstracting, Bibliographies, Statistics*

362 NZ ISSN 0110-1900
NEW ZEALAND. DEPARTMENT OF HEALTH. HOSPITAL MANAGEMENT DATA. 1926. a. price varies. National Health Statistics Centre, Private Bag 2, Upper Willis St., Wellington, New Zealand. circ. controlled.
Formerly: Hospital Statistics of New Zealand (ISSN 0073-3466)

362.11 DK ISSN 0109-3002
STATISTIK OM HJEMMESSYGEPLEJERKEVIRKSOMHEDEN. (Subseries: Primaer Sundhedstjenestatistik) 1980. a. Kr.30. Sundhedsstyrelsen, St. Kongensgade 1, 1264 Copenhagen K, Denmark (Subscr.to: Danske Boghendleres Kommissionsanstalt, Siljangade 6, 2300 Copenhagen S, Denmark)

362 UY ISSN 0041-8455
UNIVERSIDAD DE LA REPUBLICA. HOSPITAL DE CLINICAS. INFORME ESTATISTICO. 1962. a. $1. Hospital de Clinicas "Dr. Manuel Quintela", Universidad de la Republica, Avda. Italia S/N, Montevideo, Uruguay. Ed. Bd. circ. 400.

642.5 US
A LA CARTE; a menu guide to the restaurants of Western North Carolina. 1983. a. $3. Mountain Meadows Publications, 959 Merrimon Ave., Box 1513, Asheville, NC 28802. TEL 704-253-9299. Ed. Bobbi Cannon. adv. circ. 10,000.

647.94 IT
AGENDA/GUIDA DELL'OSPITALITA. a. L.18000. Publihotel International, Via Zanella 36, 20133 Milan, Italy. adv. circ. 12,000.

647 910 UK
AGENT'S HOTEL GAZETTEER: AMERICA. a. £22.50. C.H.G. Travel Publications, Waterside House, West Common, Gerrards Cross, Bucks, England.

647 UK
AGENT'S HOTEL GAZETTEER: CITIES OF EUROPE. a. £24. C.H.G. Travel Publications, Waterside House, West Common, Gerrards Cross, Bucks, England. illus.
Formerly: Agent's Hotel Gazetteer: Tourist Cities (ISSN 0308-9584)

647 910 UK
AGENT'S HOTEL GAZETTEER: RESORTS OF EUROPE. a. £25.50. C.H.G. Travel Publications, Waterside House, West Common, Gerrards Cross, Bucks, England. illus.
Formerly: Agent's Hotel Gazetteer: Resorts.

647.9 US
AMERICAN HOTEL AND MOTEL ASSOCIATION. BUYERS GUIDE FOR HOTELS & MOTELS. 1976. a. American Hotel and Motel Association, 888 Seventh Ave., New York, NY 10019. TEL 212-265-4506. adv. illus. circ. 14,000.
Supersedes: American Hotel and Motel Association. Product News. (ISSN 0032-9789)

ARABIAN HOTEL & TRAVEL GUIDE. see *TRAVEL AND TOURISM*

ATLANTIC CITY ACTION. see *BUSINESS AND ECONOMICS — Investments*

919.4 AT
AUSTRALIAN ACCOMMODATION GUIDE. 1963/64. a. $1 ea. Royal Automobile Association of South Australia Inc., 41 Hindmarsh Sqe., Adelaide, S.A. 5000, Australia. (Co-sponsor: Royal Automobile Club of Victoria) adv. circ. 120,000.
Formerly: Royal Automobile Association of South Australia. Accommodation Guide (ISSN 0085-5782)

BRITISH HOTEL INDUSTRY. see *BUSINESS AND ECONOMICS — Trade And Industrial Directories*

642.47 UK
BRITISH HOTELS, RESTAURANTS & CATERERS ASSOCIATION DIARY. a. Welbecson Ltd., Strawberry Street, Hull, Humberside, HU9 1EX, England.

647 916.8 SA
C V R HOTEL GUIDE TO SOUTHERN AFRICA. (Text in Afrikaans and English) 1966. a. R.16.50. Chris van Rensburg Publications (Pty) Ltd., Box 29159, Melville, 2109, South Africa.
Former Titles: C V R Travel and Hotel Guide to Southern Africa & Guide to Hotels in South Africa (ISSN 0533-5450)

647.9 US
CALIFORNIA LODGING INDUSTRY. 1983. a. $35. Laventhol & Horwath, 1845 Walnut St., Philadelphia, PA 19103. circ. 3,000.

647.9 US
CALIFORNIA RESTAURANT OPERATIONS. 1976. a. $35. Laventhol & Horwath, 1845 Walnut St., Philadelphia, PA 19103. charts. circ. 3,000.

658.91 CN
CANADIAN HOTEL & RESTAURANT. 1923. a. Can.$28. Maclean-Hunter Ltd., Business Publication Division, 777 Bay St., Toronto, ON M5W 1A7, Canada. TEL 416-596-5782. Ed. Andrew Douglas. adv. circ. 24,017.
Formerly: Canadian Hotel and Restaurant's Product Hot Lines/Produits Vedettes.

CANADIAN HOTEL, RESTAURANT, INSTITUTION & STORE EQUIPMENT DIRECTORY. see *BUSINESS AND ECONOMICS — Trade And Industrial Directories*

642.47 658.8 UK
CATERING (LONDON, 1984) 1984. irreg. £95($150) Jordan & Sons Ltd., Jordan House, 47 Brunswick Place, London N1 6EE, England.

642 UK
CHEWTON GLEN HOTEL MAGAZINE. 1985. a. Kingsclere Publications Ltd., Highfield House, 2 Highfield Ave., Newbury, Berks., England. Ed. Hilary Armfield. adv. circ. 15,000.

647.94 642.47 UK
CUMBRIA AND NORTH LANCASHIRE CATERING AND HOTEL YEAR BOOK. a. Border Press Agency Ltd., 12 Lonsdale St., Carlisle CA1 1DD, England.
Former titles: Lakeland and North Lancashire Catering and Hotel Year Book & Lakeland Hotel and Catering Year Book.

DIRECTORY OF CHAIN RESTAURANT OPERATORS. see *BUSINESS AND ECONOMICS — Trade And Industrial Directories*

642.5 US
DIRECTORY OF HIGH-VOLUME INDEPENDENT RESTAURANTS. 1987. a. $249. Chain Store Guide, 425 Park Ave., New York, NY 10022. TEL 212-371-9400.

647 US
DIRECTORY OF HOTEL AND MOTEL SYSTEMS. a. $24.50. American Hotel and Motel Association, 888 7th Ave., New York, NY 10019. TEL 212-265-4506.

647.94 KE
DIRECTORY OF HOTELS IN KENYA.* Cover title: Kenya Directory of Hotels. biennial. Kenya Marketing and Publications Co., Biashara St., Box 73400, Nairobi, Kenya.

647.954 914 UK
EGON RONAY'S GUIDE TO 500 GOOD RESTAURANTS IN MAJOR CITIES OF EUROPE. 1983. a. £7.95. Egon Ronay's Guides, Greencoat House, Francis St., London SW1 1DH, England (Dist. in U.S. & Canada by: St. Martin's Press, 175 Fifth Ave., New York, NY 10010) Ed. Egon Ronay. circ. 35,000.
Former titles: Egon Ronay's TWA Guide: 500 Good Restaurants in Major Cities, Europe and United States; Egon Ronay's TWA Guide to Good Restaurants in 35 European Business Cities.

647.954 UK
EGON RONAY'S GUINNESS PUB GUIDE TO FOOD AND ACCOMMODATION. 1980. a. £4.50($6.95) Egon Ronay's Guides, Greencoat House, Francis St., London SW1P 1DH, England (Dist. in U.S. & Canada by: St. Martin's Press, 175 Fifth Ave., New York, NY 10010)
Formerly: Egon Ronay's Bulmer Pub Guide to Food and Accommodation.

647.954 UK
EGON RONAY'S LUCAS GUIDE TO HOTELS, RESTAURANTS AND INNS IN GREAT BRITAIN AND IRELAND. 1957. a. £8.60($14.95) Egon Ronay's Guides, Greencoat House, Francis St., London SW1P 1DH, England (Dist. in U.S. & Canada by: St. Martin's Press, 175 Fifth Ave., New York, NY 10010) adv. circ. 100,000.
Former titles: Egon Ronay's Dunlop Guide to Hotels and Restaurants in the British Isles (ISSN 0070-9468); Egon Ronay's Guide to Hotels, Restaurants, Pubs and Inns.

HOTELS AND RESTAURANTS

647.9   UK   ISSN 0308-8464
FINANCIAL TIMES INTERNATIONAL YEAR BOOKS: WORLD HOTEL DIRECTORY. 1975/76. a. £30. Longman Group Ltd., Fourth Ave., Harlow, Essex CM19 5AA, England (Dist. in USA and Canada by: Longman Group USA Inc., 500 North Dearborn St, Chicago, IL 60610)

            US
FLORIDA LODGING INDUSTRY. 1979. a. $35. Laventhol & Horwath, 1845 Walnut St., Philadelphia, PA 19103. TEL 215-299-1600. charts. circ. 3,000.

GERMAN DEMOCRATIC REPUBLIC. CONSUMER CO-OPERATIVE SOCIETIES. MAGAZINE. see BUSINESS AND ECONOMICS — Cooperatives

647.95   UK   ISSN 0072-5005
GOOD FOOD GUIDE. 1951. a. £9.95. Consumers' Association, 14 Buckingham St., London W.C.2, England (Subscr. to: Castlemead, Gascoyne Way, Hertford SG13 7LZ, England) Ed. Drew Smith. circ. 60,000. (also avail. in microfiche)

647.95   UK
GOOD HOTEL GUIDE. a. £9.95. Consumers Association, 14 Buckingham St., London WC2N 6DS, England (Subscr. to: Castlemead, Gascoyne Way, Hertford, SG13 7LZ, England) Ed. Hilary Rubinstein. circ. 30,000.

642.57   910.09   SP
GOURMETOUR; gastronomy & travel guide. 1979. irreg. 1900 ptas.($18) Club G., S.A., Velayos, 4, Bajo, 28035 Madrid, Spain. Ed. Francisco Lopez Canis. adv. bk. rev. bibl. circ. 50,000. (back issues avail.)

647   US   ISSN 0093-4585
GUIDE TO THE RECOMMENDED COUNTRY INNS OF NEW ENGLAND. 1974. a. $9.95. Globe Pequot Press, P.O. Drawer Q, Chester, CT 06412. TEL 203-526-9571. Ed. Linda Kennedy. illus.

642.5   GW
GUT ESSEN/EATS & TREATS; hospitality in Frankfurt and Rhine Main Area. (Text in English, German) 1979. biennial. DM.5.80($2.75) Verlagscomptoir, Wasserhofstr. 44/46, 6000 Frankfurt M, W. Germany (B.R.D.) Ed. Manfred M. Gorselewski. adv. circ. 32,000. (back issues avail.)

919.4   AT   ISSN 0085-1485
HERALD MOTEL GUIDE. 1965. a. Aus.$1 ea. Herald Travel Bureau, Newspaper House, 247 Collins St., Melbourne, Vic. 3000, Australia. Ed. D.H. Day.

650   640   AT   ISSN 0156-3688
HOSPITALITY BUYERS GUIDE. a. Aus.$30. Peter Isaacson Publications, 45-50 Porter St., Prahran, Vic. 3181, Australia.
     Former titles: Hospitality Buyers Guide and Diary; Hospitality Yearbook (ISSN 0311-2969)

647.94   330   US
HOTEL & MOTEL MANAGEMENT SHOW DAILY. a. (in 3 edts.) free to convention attendees. Harcourt Brace Jovanovich, Inc., 7500 Old Oak Blvd., Cleveland, OH 44130 TEL 216-243-8100. (Subscr. addr.: 1 E. First St., Duluth, MN 55802) Ed. Michael DeLuca. circ. 6,500.

647.94   US   ISSN 0073-3490
HOTEL AND MOTEL RED BOOK. 1886. a. $59. (American Hotel and Motel Association) Pactel Publishing, P.O. Box 8124, Walnut Creek, CA 94704. TEL 415-932-6300. Ed. Valerie A. Dow. circ. 75,000.

919.4   AT   ISSN 0156-3661
HOTEL, MOTEL INDEX. Variant title: Travelweek Hotel, Motel Index. 1965. biennial. Aus.$50. Peter Isaacson Publications, 45-50 Porter St., Prahran, Vic. 3181, Australia.
     Former titles: Hotel, Motel and Travel Directory.

647.9   SA
HOTELIER & CATERER BUYER'S GUIDE. 1982. a. R.25. Ramsay, Son & Parker (Pty) Ltd., Box 180, Howard Place 7450, Cape Town, South Africa. TEL 021-531 391. Ed. Andrew Moth. circ. 1,500.
     Formerly: Hotelier and Caterer.

647.94   FR
HOTELS DE LA FRANCE. 1962. a. 161 F. Hotels de la France, 83 rue Amelot, 75011 Paris, France.
     Formerly: Hotels de la France et d'Outre-Mer (ISSN 0073-3539)

642.56   DK   ISSN 0107-8313
I BYEN'S SPISEGUIDE; politiken anmelder, gode spisteder. 1980. a. Kr.55. Politiken Plus, Vestergade 24/3, 1456 Copenhagen K, Denmark. illus.

INTERNATIONAL GUIDE. see TRAVEL AND TOURISM

647.94   FR   ISSN 0074-624X
INTERNATIONAL HOTEL GUIDE. 1948. a. 165 F. International Hotel Association, 80 rue de la Roquette, 75011 Paris, France. circ. 15,000.

647   JA   ISSN 0446-6217
JAPAN HOTEL GUIDE. (Text in English) irreg. Japan Tourist Association, 1 Marunouchi, Chuo-ku, Tokyo, Japan. illus.

647.954   UK
JUST A BITE; Egon Ronay's Lucas guide for gourmets on a family budget. 1979. a. £4.50($6.95) Egon Ronay's Guides, Greencoat House, Francis St., London SW1P 1DH, England (Dist. in U.S. & Canada by: St. Martin's Press, 175 Fifth Ave., New York, NY 10010)

642.56   UK
LAKESCENE - EATING OUT IN LAKELAND AND NORTH LANCASHIRE. 1975. a. £0.60. Border Press Agency Ltd., 12 Lonsdale St., Carlisle, Cumbria CA1 1DD, England. Ed. John Barker. adv.

647.94   910.09   388.411   GW   ISSN 0343-4192
LINKS UND RECHTS DER AUTOBAHN; der Reisefuehrer und Reiseatlas speziell fuer die Autobahn. 1961. a. DM.7.50. Verlag Holger Stuenings, Luisenstr. 100, 4150 Krefeld, W. Germany (B.R.D.) adv. charts. circ. 185,000. (back issues avail.)

642.5   CN
MANITOBA RESTAURANT & FOODSERVICES ROSTER. a. (Manitoba Restaurant & Foodservice Association) Naylor Communications Ltd., 124 W. 8th St., North Vancouver, B.C. V7M 3H2, Canada (Subscr. addr.: 100 Sutherland Ave., Winnipeg, Man. R2W 3C7, Canada) circ. 1,200.

MICHELIN RED GUIDE SERIES: GREATER LONDON. see TRAVEL AND TOURISM

647   US   ISSN 0095-0386
MORT'S GUIDE TO LOW-COST VACATIONS & LODGINGS ON COLLEGE CAMPUSES. 1974. irreg. $7. C M G Publications, Box 630, Princeton, NJ 08540. TEL 609-924-7503. illus.

647   US   ISSN 0099-0205
N A A WHERE TO STAY BOOK.* a. membership. National Automobile Association, 1730 Northeast Expwy. Acces Rd N.E., Atlanta, GA 30329. TEL 404-329-0123. illus.

647.94   US
NATIONAL DIRECTORY OF BUDGET MOTELS; a nation-wide guide to low-cost chain motel accommodations. 1975. a. $3.95. Pilot Books, 103 Cooper St., Babylon, NY 11702. TEL 516-422-2225. Ed. Raymond Carlson.

NIGERIA TOURIST GUIDE/GUIDE DU TOURISME NIGERIEN. see TRAVEL AND TOURISM

642.5   US
NORTH EAST FOOD SERVICE BU'YER'S GUIDE. 1982. a. $7.50. Trade Winds Publishing Co., Box 332, Braintree, MA 02184. TEL 617-848-5039. Ed. Dorothy Delano. adv. circ. 23,111.
     Formerly (until 1986): New England Food Service Buyer's Guide.

674.94   UK   ISSN 0307-062X
OFFICIAL GUIDE TO HOTELS & RESTAURANTS IN GREAT BRITAIN, IRELAND AND OVERSEAS. 1928. a. £4.95. British Hotels, Restaurants and Caterers Association, 40 Duke St., London W1M 6HR, England.
     Formerly: B H R C A Guide to Hotels and Restaurants (ISSN 0068-2128)

647.94   US
OFFICIAL HOTEL & RESORT GUIDE. 1963. a. in 18 geographical segments. $220. Murdoch Magazines (Secaucus), 500 Harmon Meadow Blvd., Secaucus, NJ 07904. TEL 212-503-5800. adv. circ. 21,000. (looseleaf format)

647.9   642.5   PK   ISSN 0250-4340
PAKISTAN HOTEL AND RESTAURANT GUIDE. (Text in English) 1980. a. Rs.35($4.50) Maulai Enterprise, J-6/2, al-Naseer, Sharifabad, Federal B Area, Blk. No. 1, Karachi 19, Pakistan. Ed. Syed Wali Ahmad Maulai. adv. stat. circ. 5,000.
     Incorporating (1973-1986): Pakistan Business and Shopping Guide.

647.9   PK   ISSN 0250-3654
PAKISTAN HOTEL GUIDE; (including business & shopping chapter) (Text in English) 1957. a. Rs.35($4.50) Maulai Enterprise, J-6/2 al-Naseer, Federal B Area, Block No. 1, Karachi 19, Pakistan. Ed. Syed Wali Ahmad Maulai. adv. charts. stat. circ. 5,000. (back issues avail.)

658.91   US
RESORTS & PARKS PURCHASING GUIDE. 1965. a. $8.95. Klevens Publications, Inc., 7600 Ave. V, Littlerock, CA 93543. TEL 805-944-4111. adv. tr.lit. circ. 16,874.
     Formerly: Resorts and R V Parks Purchasing Guide.

642.5   US
RESTAURANT INDUSTRY OPERATIONS REPORT. 1976. a. $38 to non members; members $19. (National Restaurant Association) Laventhol & Horwath, 1845 Walnut St., Philadelphia, PA 19103. TEL 215-299-1600. circ. 2,500.
     Former titles: Restaurant Operations Report for Tableservice Restaurants; (until 1978?): Tableservice Restaurant Operations Report; Restaurant Operations (ISSN 0190-9452)

ROUTIERS GUIDE TO FRANCE. see TRAVEL AND TOURISM

647   US   ISSN 0098-4507
SAV-ON-HOTELS (YEAR) Cover title: Sav-on-Hotels Across Europe. 1974. a. $4.95. Travel Tips, Box 11061, Oakland, CA 94611. Ed. Henry Seegall.

647.9   UK
SCOTTISH YOUTH HOSTELS ASSOCIATION HANDBOOK. 1980. a. £0.60. Scottish Youth Hostels Association, 7 Glebe Crescent, Stirling FK8 2JA, Scotland. adv. circ. 32,000.

SOPHISTICATED LEISURE TRAVEL DIRECTORY. see TRAVEL AND TOURISM

658.91   SA   ISSN 0489-8567
SOUTH AFRICAN LICENSEE'S GUARDIAN. 1964. a. R.28. Ramsay, Son & Parker (Pty) Ltd., Box 180, Howard Place 7450, Cape Town, South Africa. TEL 021-531 391. Ed. Andrew Moth. circ. 2,000.

647.9   US
TEXAS LODGING INDUSTRY. 1979. a. $35. Laventhol & Horwath, 1845 Walnut St., Philadelphia, PA 19103. TEL 215-299-1600. charts. circ. 3,000.

647   TU
TURKEY: HOTELS-CAMPING. (Text in English, French, German, Italian and Turkish) 1964. a. free. Ministry of Culture and Tourism - Turizm ve Tanitma Bakanligi, Gazi Mustafa Kemal Bulvari 33, Ankara, Turkey. adv. circ. 20,000.
     Formerly: Hotel Guide to Turkey.

647.9   US
U S ECONOMY LODGING INDUSTRY. 1981. a. $35. Laventhol & Horwath, 1845 Walnut St., Philadelphia, PA 19103. TEL 215-299-1600. charts. circ. 3,000.

658.91   US   ISSN 0361-2198
U S LODGING INDUSTRY; annual report on hotel and motor hotel operations. 1932. a. $50. Laventhol & Horwath, 1845 Walnut St., Philadelphia, PA 19103. TEL 215-299-1600. charts. circ. 20,000.
     Formerly: Lodging Industry.

642.56 CN ISSN 0706-5302
VANCOUVER GASTRONOMIC. 1977. a. $5 per no.
Apogee Enterprises Ltd, Box 48525, Sta. Bentall,
Vancouver, B.C. V7X 1A2, Canada. TEL 604-685-
7798. Ed. Elliot Cristall. adv. circ. 20,000.

647.94 UK ISSN 0083-6273
VILLA GUIDE. 1970. a. 25p. Villa Guide Ltd., 51
Brompton Road, London, SW3, England.
Formerly: Euro Property.

642.5 915 SI
WHERE TO EAT & ENTERTAIN - SINGAPORE.
1980. a. S.$5. Times Directories Private Ltd., 422
Thomson Rd., Singapore 1129, Singapore. circ. 12,
000.

642 UK
WHERE TO EAT IN AND AROUND GLASGOW.
1985. a. £1.50. Kingsclere Publications Ltd.,
Highfield House, 2 Highfield Ave., Newbury, Berks,
England. Ed. Michael Buckley. adv. circ. 10,000.

914.2 642.5 UK
WHERE TO EAT IN BERKSHIRE. 1980. a. £1.50.
Kingsclere Publications Ltd., Highfield House, 2
Highfield Ave., Newbury, Berkshire RG14 5DS,
England. Ed. Michael Buckley. adv. circ. 10,000.

647.95 914.2 UK
WHERE TO EAT IN BOURNEMOUTH, POOLE
AND DORSET. 1980. a. £1.50. Kingsclere
Publications Ltd., Highfield House, 2 Highfield
Ave., Newbury, Berkshire RG14 5DS, England. Ed.
Michael Buckley. adv. circ. 10,000.

914.2 642.5 UK
WHERE TO EAT IN BRISTOL, BATH & AVON.
1981. a. £1.50. Kingsclere Publications Ltd.,
Highfield House, 2 Highfield Ave., Newbury,
Berkshire RG14 5DS, England. Ed. Michael
Buckley. adv. circ. 10,000.

642 917.1 CN ISSN 0315-3088
WHERE TO EAT IN CANADA. 1971. a. $10.95.
Oberon Press, 401a Delta Ottawa, 350 Sparks St.,
Ottawa, Ont. K1R 7S8, Canada. TEL 613-238-2375.
Ed. Anne Hardy.

647.95 914.2 UK
WHERE TO EAT IN CARDIFF, SWANSEA &
SOUTH WALES. 1983. a. £1.50. Kingsclere
Publications Ltd., Highfield House, 2 Highfield
Ave., Newbury, Berkshire RG14 5DS, England. Ed.
Michael Buckley. adv. circ. 10,000.
Supersedes (from 1983): Where to Eat in Cardiff
and South Wales.

914.2 642.5 UK
WHERE TO EAT IN DEVON. 1981. a. £1.50.
Kingsclere Publications Ltd., Highfield House, 2
Highfield Ave., Newbury, Berkshire RG14 5DS,
England. Ed. Michael Buckley. adv. circ. 10,000.

647.95 914.2 UK
WHERE TO EAT IN EDINBURGH, FIFE AND
THE LOTHIANS. 1983. a. £1.50. Kingsclere
Publications Ltd., Highfield House, 2 Highfield
Ave., Newbury, Berkshire RG14 5DS, England. Ed.
Michael Buckley. circ. 10,000.
Formerly (until 1985): Where to Eat in
Edinburgh.

647.95 914.2 UK
WHERE TO EAT IN GLOUCESTERSHIRE AND
THE COTSWOLDS. 1985. a. £1.50. Kingsclere
Publications Ltd., Highfield House, 2 Highfield
Ave., Newbury, Berkshire RG14 5DS, England. Ed.
Michael Buckley. adv. circ. 10,000.

647.95 914.2 UK
WHERE TO EAT IN GREATER MANCHESTER.
1985. a. £1.50. Kingsclere Publications Ltd.,
Highfield House, 2 Highfield Ave., Newbury,
Berkshire RG14 5DS, England. Ed. Michael
Buckley. adv. circ. 10,000.

914.2 642.5 UK
WHERE TO EAT IN HAMPSHIRE AND THE
NEW FOREST. 1980. a. £1.50. Kingsclere
Publications Ltd., Highfield House, 2 Highfield
Ave., Newbury, Berkshire RG14 5DS, England. Ed.
Michael Buckley. adv. circ. 10,000.
Formerly: Where to Eat in Hampshire.

642 UK
WHERE TO EAT IN IRELAND. 1985. a. £1.50.
Kingsclere Publications Ltd., Highfield House, 2
Highfield Ave., Newbury, Berks, England. Ed.
Michael Buckley. adv. circ. 10,000.

647.95 914.2 UK
WHERE TO EAT IN KENT. 1985. a. £1.50.
Kingsclere Publications Ltd., Highfield House, 2
Highfield Ave., Newbury, Berkshire RG14 5DS,
England. Ed. Michael Buckley. adv. circ. 10,000.

914.2 642.5 UK
WHERE TO EAT IN OXFORD AND
OXFORDSHIRE. 1981. a. £1.50. Kingsclere
Publications Ltd., Highfield House, 2 Highfield
Ave., Newbury, Berkshire RG14 5DS, England. Ed.
Michael Buckley. adv. circ. 10,000.
Formerly: Where to Eat in Oxfordshire.

914.2 642.5 UK
WHERE TO EAT IN SOMERSET. 1980. a. £1.50.
Kingsclere Publications Ltd., Highfield House, 2
Highfield Ave., Newbury, Berkshire RG14 5DS,
England. Ed. Michael Buckley. adv. circ. 10,000.

914.2 642.5 UK
WHERE TO EAT IN SURREY. 1982. a. £1.50.
Kingsclere Publications Ltd., Highfield House, 2
Highfield Ave., Newbury, Berkshire RG14 5DS,
England. Ed. Michael Buckley. adv. circ. 10,000.

914.2 642.5 UK
WHERE TO EAT IN SUSSEX. 1982. a. £1.50.
Kingsclere Publications Ltd., Highfield House, 2
Highfield Ave., Newbury, Berkshire RG14 5DS,
England. Ed. Michael Buckley. adv. circ. 10,000.

914.2 642.5 UK
WHERE TO EAT IN THE CHANNEL ISLANDS.
1982. a. £1.50. Kingsclere Publications Ltd.,
Highfield House, 2 Highfield Ave., Newbury,
Berkshire RG14 5DS, England. Ed. Michael
Buckley. adv. circ. 10,000.

647.95 914.2 UK
WHERE TO EAT IN WILTSHIRE. 1979. a. £1.50.
Kingsclere Publications Ltd., Highfield House, 2
Highfield Ave., Newbury, Berkshire RG14 5DS,
England. Ed. Michael Buckley. adv. circ. 10,000.

WHERE TO STAY IN LONDON. see *TRAVEL
AND TOURISM*

338.4 US
WORLDWIDE HOTEL INDUSTRY; annual report
on international hotel operations. 1971. a. $65.
Horwath & Horwath International, 919 Third Ave.,
New York, NY 10022. TEL 212-980-3100. charts.
circ. 12,000.
Formerly: Worldwide Lodging Industry (ISSN
0361-218X)

647.94 CN
WRIGLEY'S HOTEL-MOTEL DIRECTORY. 1910.
a. Can.$8.50. Wrigley Directories Ltd., 7385
Laburnum St., Vancouver, B.C. V6P 5N2, Canada.
adv.

647 YU
YUGOSLAVIA; HOTEL AND TOURIST
DIRECTORY. Spine title: Hotelsko-Turisticki
Adresar. (Text in English, French, German,
Serbocroatian) irreg. Privredni Pregled, Marsala
Birjuzova 3, Belgrade, Yugoslavia. illus.

HOTELS AND RESTAURANTS —
Abstracting, Bibliographies, Statistics

647.94 IT
ATTREZZATURA ALBERGHIERA IN ITALIA. a.
L.5500. Istituto Centrale di Statistica, Via Cesare
Balbo 16, 00100 Rome, Italy.

647.95 US
BIBLIOGRAPHY OF HOTEL AND RESTAURANT
ADMINISTRATION. Variant title: Bibliography of
Hotel and Restaurant Administration and Related
Subjects. 1960. a. $20. Cornell University, School of
Hotel Administration, 327 Statler Hall, Ithaca, NY
14853. Ed. Margaret Oaksford. index. circ. 500.
(back issues avail.; reprint service avail. from UMI)

647 SI ISSN 0129-6760
SINGAPORE. DEPARTMENT OF STATISTICS.
REPORT ON THE CENSUS OF WHOLESALE,
RETAIL TRADES, RESTAURANTS & HOTELS.
biennial. S.$8.20. Department of Statistics, Maxwell
Road PO Box 3010, Singapore 9050, Republic of
Singapore.

HOUSING AND URBAN PLANNING

*see also Building and Construction; Real
Estate*

352.7 US
ALABAMA PLANNING RESOURCE CHECKLIST;
county/counties and substate planning and
development districts in Alabama. 1976. a. $25.
Development Office, c/o State Capitol,
Montgomery, AL 36130. TEL 205-284-8910. (Co-
sponsor: U.S. Department of Housing and Urban
Development) Ed. Mark Worsham. bibl. cum.index.
circ. 275. (back issues avail.)

711.4 US
ALASKA. STATE HOUSING AUTHORITY.
ANNUAL REPORT. a. free. State Housing Authority,
624 W. International Airport Rd., Anchorage, AK
99502-1307. TEL 907-562-2813.

352.7 DK ISSN 0107-1572
ALMENNYTTIGE BOLIGSELSKABERS
REGNSKABER. 1978. a. Kr.40. Boligministeriet -
Ministry of Housing, Departementets 4 Kontor,
Slotholmsgade 12, 1216 Copenhagen K, Denmark.
Formerly: Beretning om de Almennyttige
Boligselskabers Regnskaber.

352.7 301.15 949.5 GR
ANCIENT GREEK CITIES REPORT. 1971. irreg.,
no.24, 1978. price varies. Athens Center of Ekistics,
24, Strat. Syndesmou St., Box 3471, Athens 102 10,
Greece. Ed. P. Psomopoulos.

352.7 UK ISSN 0261-5932
ANGUS DISTRICT COUNCIL. HOUSING PLANS
AND PROGRAMMES. 1979. irreg., latest 1986/
87. £1.50. Angus District Council, Planning
Department, County Buildings, Forfar DD8 3LG,
Scotland. circ. 200.

352.7 360 FR
ANNUAIRE H L M. (Habitations a Loyer Modere)
Short title: Guide Annuaire des H.L.M. 1968. a. 365
F. to non-members; members 216 F. Union
Nationale des Federations d'Organismes
d'Habitations a Loyer Modere, Editions
Department, 14 rue Lord Byron, 75384 Paris Cedex
08, France. adv. index. circ. 5,600.

ANNUARIO EUROPEO DELL'AMBIENTE. see
ENVIRONMENTAL STUDIES

350.865 AG
ARGENTINA. CAJA FEDERAL DE AHORRO Y
PRESTAMO PARA LA VIVIENDA. MEMORIA
Y BALANCE. a. free. Caja Federal de Ahorro y
Prestamo para la Vivienda, Alsina 301 E.P., Buenos
Aires, Argentina. Dir. Salomon Herman. charts.
stat.

711 GR ISSN 0067-0073
ATHENS CENTER OF EKISTICS. RESEARCH
REPORT. 1967. irreg., latest no.13, 1973. price
varies. Athens Center of Ekistics, 24, Strat.
Syndesmou Street, Box 3471, Athens 102 10,
Greece. Ed. P. Psomopoulos. circ. 275.

711 AT ISSN 0067-1517
AUSTRALIA. NATIONAL CAPITAL
DEVELOPMENT COMMISSION. ANNUAL
REPORT. 1958. a. Aus.$2. National Capital
Development Commission, G.P.O. Box 373,
Canberra, A.C.T. 2601, Australia. circ. 2,500.

352.7 620 614.7 AT ISSN 0313-9948
AUSTRALIA. NATIONAL CAPITAL
DEVELOPMENT COMMISSION. TECHNICAL
PAPERS. 1974. irreg. Aus.$10 price varies.
National Capital Development Commission, G.P.O.
Box 373, Canberra, A.C.T. 2601, Australia.

HOUSING AND URBAN PLANNING

388.3 US
AUTOMATION IN HOUSING & MANUFACTURED HOME DEALER ANNUAL BUYERS' GUIDE. 1977. a. C M N Publications (Subsidiary of: C M N Associates) Box 120, 4371 Carpinteria Ave., Carpinteria, CA 93013. TEL 805-684-7659. adv. circ. 26,000. (reprint service avail. from UMI)
  Formerly: Automation in Housing/Systems Building News Annual Buyers' Guide.

352.7 BL
BANCO NACIONAL DA HABITACAO. RELATORIO DE ATIVIDADES. irreg. Banco Nacional da Habitacao, Secretaria de Divulgacao, Av. Republica do Chile 230, Rio de Janeiro, Brazil. charts. stat.

352.7 SZ
BERICHTE ZUR ORTS-, REGIONAL- UND LANDESPLANUNG. 1968. irreg. price varies. Eidgenoessische Technische Hochschule Zuerich, Institut fuer Orts-, Regional- und Landesplanung, Redaktion DISP - Swiss Federal Institute of Technology, Institute for Local, Regional and National Planning, 8093 Zurich, Switzerland.

352.7 IT
BIBLIOTECA MARSILIO: ARCHITETTURA E URBANISTICA. no.26, 1974. irreg. L.8300. Biblioteca Marsilio, Marsilio, Padua, Italy. bibl. charts. stat.

309.26 BL
BRAZIL. SUPERINTENDENCIA DO DESENVOLVIMENTO DO NORDESTE. SU D E N E PLANO DE ACAO. Cover title: S U D E N E Plano de Acao. irreg. Superintendencia do Desenvolvimento do Nordeste, Av. Prof. Moraes Rego, Cidade Universitaria, Recife-PE, Brazil. illus.
  Regional planning

352.7 CN ISSN 0225-509X
BRITISH COLUMBIA. HOUSING MANAGEMENT COMMISSION. ANNUAL REPORT. 1978. a. Housing Management Commission, Suite 1701, 4330 Kingsway, Burnaby, B.C. V5H 4G7, Canada. TEL 604-387-3502. illus. circ. 1,000.

352.7 CN ISSN 0702-6641
BRITISH COLUMBIA. MINISTRY OF MUNICIPAL AFFAIRS. MUNICIPAL STATISTICS, INCLUDING REGIONAL DISTRICTS. 1951. a. Ministry of Municipal Affairs, Victoria, B.C., Canada. TEL 604-387-5925. illus. circ. 2,000.

711.4 GW ISSN 0930-3839
BUNDESFORSCHUNGSANSTALT FUER LANDESKUNDE UND RAUMORDNUNG. SEMINARE - SYMPOSIEN - ARBEITSPAPIERE. 1981. irreg., vol.17, 1984. price varies. Am Michaelshof 8, Postfach 200130, D-5300 Bonn 2, W. Germany (B.R.D.)

352.7 BG
C U S BULLETIN. (Text in English) biennial. Centre for Urban Studies, c/o Dept. of Geography, University of Dacca, Ramna, Dacca 2, Bangladesh.

333.77 BE ISSN 0575-0970
CAHIERS DU SART TILMAN. 1963. irreg. 200 Fr. Universite de Liege, Batiment B 12, 4000 Sart-Tilman, Liege, Belgium.

711 720 UK
CAMBRIDGE URBAN AND ARCHITECTURAL STUDIES. 1972. irreg., no.8, 1984. $49.50 (cloth); $14.95 (paper) for latest vol. (Cambridge University, Cambridge School of Architecture) Cambridge University Press, Edinburgh Bldg., Shaftesbury Rd., Cambridge CB2 2RU, England. Eds. Leslie Martin, Lionel March.

352 CN ISSN 0226-0336
CANADA MORTGAGE AND HOUSING CORPORATION. ANNUAL REPORT. a. Canada Mortgage and Housing Corporation, Montreal Rd., Ottawa, Ont. K1A 0P7, Canada. TEL 613-748-2000.
  Formerly: Central Mortgage and Housing Corporation. Annual Report.

388.3 UK
CARAVAN INDUSTRY SUPPLIES & SERVICES DIRECTORY. 1980. a. £5.75. A.E. Morgan Publications Ltd., Stanley House, 9 West St., Epsom, Surrey, England. adv. circ. 2,500.

711 AT
CARLTON NEWSLETTER. 1967. irreg. Aus.$2. Carlton Association, Box 52, North Carlton, Vic. 3054, Australia. Ed. Richard Malone.

352.7 UK
CATHOLIC HOUSING AID SOCIETY. ANNUAL REPORT. 1956. a. free. Catholic Housing Aid Society, 189A Old Brompton Rd., London SW5 OAR, England. Ed. Robert Kahn. circ. 1,300.

352.7 US
CENTRAL MISSISSIPPI PLANNING AND DEVELOPMENT DISTRICT. ANNUAL REPORT. a. free. Central Mississippi Planning and Development District, 2675 River Ridge Rd., Box 4935, Jackson, MS 39216. TEL 601-981-1511. Ed. M.L. Smith. circ. 700.

312 301 352.7 CN ISSN 0316-4691
CENTRE FOR URBAN AND COMMUNITY STUDIES. BIBLIOGRAPHIC SERIES. 1969. irreg., approx. 2/yr. Centre for Urban and Community Studies, 455 Spadina Ave., University of Toronto, Toronto, Ont. M5S 2G8, Canada. TEL 416-978-7162. Indexed: Urb.Aff.Abstr.

312 301 352.7 CN ISSN 0319-4620
CENTRE FOR URBAN AND COMMUNITY STUDIES. MAJOR REPORT SERIES. 1974. irreg. (3-4/yr.) price varies. Centre for Urban and Community Studies, 455 Spadina Ave., University of Toronto, Toronto, Ont. M5S 2G8, Canada. Indexed: Urb.Aff.Abstr.

312 301 352.7 CN ISSN 0316-0068
CENTRE FOR URBAN AND COMMUNITY STUDIES. RESEARCH PAPERS. 1968. irreg. (5-10/yr.) price varies. Centre for Urban and Community Studies, 455 Spadina Ave., University of Toronto, Toronto, Ont. M5S 2G8, Canada.

338.4 FR
CHAMBRE DE COMMERCE ET D'INDUSTRIE DE PARIS. CONTRIBUTION DES EMPLOYEURS A L'EFFORT DE CONSTRUCTION. irreg. free. Chambre de Commerce et d'Industrie de Paris, 27 Av. de Driedland, 75008 Paris, France.

711.59 SP ISSN 0069-5068
COLECCION CIENCIA URBANISTICA. irreg. (Laboratorio de Urbanismo de la Escuela Tecnica Superior de Arquitectura de Barcelona) Editorial Gustavo Gili, S.A., Rosellon 87-89, Apdo. de Correos 35.149, Barcelona 29, Spain.

350.086 IT
COLLANA DI STUDI SU PROBLEMI URBANISTICI FIORENTINO. no.2, 1974. irreg. L.5500. Ufficio della Provincia, Florence, Italy. bibl. illus.

352.7 US
CONDOMINIUM DEVELOPMENT GUIDE. a. (to update base volume) $76 for base vol. plus supp. Warren, Gorham and Lamont, Inc., 210 South St., Boston, MA 02111. TEL 800-922-0066.

352.7 US
CONNECTICUT HOUSING MARKET. ANNUAL REPORT. 1980. a. Department of Housing, Planning Unit, 1179 Main St., Hartford, CT 06103. TEL 203-566-5264. Ed. Sandy Bergin. circ. 800.

CONSTRUCTION INDUSTRY EUROPE. see *BUILDING AND CONSTRUCTION*

352.7 US
CONSUMER-FARMER COOPERATOR. 1938. a. free. ‡ Consumer-Farmer Foundation, Inc., 101 E. 15th St., New York, NY 10003. TEL 312-673-5600. Ed. Harry DeRienzo. charts. illus. circ. 5,000.

352 BL
CONTRIBUICOES EM DESENVOLVIMENTO URBANO. irreg. Editora Campus Ltda. (Subsidiary of: Elsevier North-Holland Inc.) Rua Barao de Itapagipe 55, Rio Comprido, 20261 Rio de Janeiro RJ, Brazil.

352.7 US ISSN 0589-6355
COOPERATIVE HOUSING JOURNAL. resumed 1963. a. $35 (includes Cooperative Housing Bulletin) National Association of Housing Cooperatives, 2501 M St. N.W., Ste. 451, Washington, DC 20037. TEL 202-887-0706. Ed. Linda Baron. adv. bk. rev. circ. 1,500. (back issues avail.)

333.77 US
CORNELL UNIVERSITY. CITY AND REGIONAL PLANNING PUBLICATIONS. OCCASIONAL PAPERS. 1974. irreg., no.10, 1980. Cornell University, City and Regional Planning Publications, 106 W. Sibley Hall, Ithaca, NY 14853. (reprint service avail. from UMI)
  Formerly: Cornell University. Program in Urban and Regional Studies. Occasional Papers; Supersedes (as of 1976): Cornell University. Center for Urban Development Research. Occasional Papers.

352.7 333.77 US
CORNELL UNIVERSITY. CITY AND REGIONAL PLANNING PUBLICATIONS. RESEARCH REPORTS. 1955. irreg., latest 1981. Cornell University, City and Regional Planning Publications, 106 W. Sibley Hall, Ithaca, NY 14853. (reprint service avail. from UMI)
  Formerly: Cornell University. Program in Urban and Regional Studies. Research Reports; Supersedes (as of 1970): Cornell University. Center for Housing and Environmental Studies. Research Reports (ISSN 0070-0061)

333.77 PE
CUADERNOS PARA EL DEBATE REGIONAL. irreg., no.28, 1986. Centro de Estudios Rurales Andinos "Bartolome de las Casas", Apdo. 477, Cusco, Peru.

301.5 US
CURRENT CONSTRUCTION REPORTS: HOUSING UNITS AUTHORIZED BY BUILDING PERMITS; states and selected standard metropolitan statistical areas. (Series C-40) 1959. m. (plus a. issue) $49. U.S. Bureau of the Census, Customer Services, Washington, DC 20233 TEL 301-763-4100. (Subscr. to: Supt. of Documents, Washington, DC 20402) (also avail. in microfiche)
  Formerly: Current Construction Reports: Housing Units Authorized by Building Permits and Public Contracts (ISSN 0363-8790)

333.33 US ISSN 0363-8537
CURRENT CONSTRUCTION REPORTS: NEW ONE FAMILY HOMES SOLD AND FOR SALE. (Series C-25) 1963. m. (plus annual issue) $21. U.S. Bureau of the Census, Customer Services, Washington, DC 20233 TEL 301-763-4100. (Orders to: Supt. of Documents, Washington, DC 20402) (also avail. in microfiche)

301.5 US
CURRENT HOUSING REPORTS. (Published in several series, avail. separately) irreg. U.S. Bureau of the Census, Customer Services, Washington, DC 20233. TEL 301-763-4100.

333.33 US
CURRENT HOUSING REPORTS: AMERICAN HOUSING SURVEY: METROPOLITAN AREAS. (Series H-170; 6 titles in series) a. price varies. U.S. Bureau of the Census, Data User Services Division, Customer Services, Washington, DC 20233. TEL 301-763-4100. (also avail. in microfiche)
  Formerly: Current Housing Reports: Annual Housing Survey: Metropolitan Areas.

333.33 US
CURRENT HOUSING REPORTS: AMERICAN HOUSING SURVEY: UNITED STATES AND REGIONS. (Series H-150; 6 titles in series) biennial. price varies. U.S. Bureau of the Census, Data User Services Division, Customer Services, Washington, DC 20233. TEL 301-763-4100. (also avail. in microfiche)
  Formerly: Current Housing Reports: Annual Housing Survey: United States and Regions.

352 301.5 US ISSN 0498-8450
CURRENT HOUSING REPORTS: HOUSING CHARACTERISTICS. (Series H-121) irreg. U.S. Bureau of the Census, Data User Services Division, Customer Services, Washington, DC 20233 TEL 301-763-4100. (Subscriptions to: Supt. of Documents, Washington, DC 20402) (also avail. in microform)

HOUSING AND URBAN PLANNING

301.5 US ISSN 0498-8469
CURRENT HOUSING REPORTS: HOUSING VACANCIES. Quarterly reports are titled: Housing Vacancies. Annual reports are titled: Vacancy Rates and Characteristics of Housing in the United States. (Series H-111; 6 titles in series) q. and a. $13. U.S. Bureau of the Census, Data User Services Division, Customer Services, Washington, DC 20233 TEL 301-763-4100. (Subscr. to: Supt. of Documents, Washington, DC 20402) (also avail. in microfiche)

301.5 331.83 US ISSN 0363-8286
CURRENT HOUSING REPORTS: MARKET ABSORPTION OF APARTMENTS. (Series H-130) q. (and annual) $11. U.S. Bureau of the Census, Data User Services Division, Customer Services, Washington, DC 20233 TEL 301-763-4100. (Subscr. to: Supt. of Documents, Washington, DC 20402) (Issued jointly with: U.S. Department of Housing and Urban Development) (also avail. in microfiche)

352.7 US
D P E D NEWSLETTER. irreg. free. Department of Planning and Economic Development, Box 2359, Honolulu, HI 96804. TEL 808-548-4025.

DANMARKS TEKNISKE HOEJSKOLE. INSTITUTET FOR VEJE, TRAFIK OG BYPLAN. NOTAT/TECHNICAL UNIVERSITY OF DENMARK. INSTITUTE OF ROADS, TRANSPORT AND TOWN PLANNING. PAPER. see *TRANSPORTATION — Roads And Traffic*

333.77 DK ISSN 0108-6901
DENMARK. MILJOEMINISTERIET. MILJOEMINISTERENS REDEGOERELSE OM LANDSPLANLAEGNING. (Text in Danish) 1975. a. free. Miljoeministeriet, Plantstyrelsen - Danish national Agency for Physical Planning, Ministry of the environment, Holbergsgade 23, 1057 Copenhagen K, Denmark.
Formerly: Denmark. Miljoeministeriet. Redegoerelse fra Miljoeministeren om Landsplanlaegning.

352.7 DK ISSN 0105-9602
DENMARK. PLANSTYRELSEN. REGIONPLANORIENTERING. no.13, 1983. irreg. price varies. Planstyrelsen, Copenhagen, Denmark (Orders to: Danske Boghendleres Kommissionsanstalt, Siljangade 6, 2300 Copenhagen S, Denmark) illus.

712 711 NE
DEVELOPMENTS IN LANDSCAPE MANAGEMENT AND URBAN PLANNING. 1975. irreg., vol.6, 1984. price varies. Elsevier Science Publishers B.V., Box 211, 1000 AE Amsterdam, Netherlands.

301.5 AT
DIRECTORY: RESEARCH IN HOUSING - AUSTRALIA AND NEW ZEALAND. (Subseries of: Ian Buchan Fell Research Project on Housing. Report) irreg. Aus.$2. Ian Buchan Fell Research Project on Housing, Sydney, Australia.

DISCUSSIONS IN ENVIRONMENTAL HEALTH PLANNING. see *ENVIRONMENTAL STUDIES*

ENVIRONMENTAL DESIGN RESEARCH ASSOCIATION. ANNUAL CONFERENCE PROCEEDINGS. see *ARCHITECTURE*

FEDERAL FUNDING GUIDE. see *PUBLIC ADMINISTRATION — Municipal Government*

301.54 FR ISSN 0081-1262
FEDERATION NATIONALE DES SOCIETES D'ECONOMIE MIXTE DE CONSTRUCTION, D'AMENAGEMENT ET DE RENOVATION. ANNUAIRE. (Special number of Collectivites et Habitations) 1965. triennial. Federation Nationale des Societes d'Economie Mixte de Construction, d'Amenagement et de Renovation, 66 bd. Malesherbes, 75008 Paris, France. adv.

331.83 FJ
FIJI. HOUSING AUTHORITY. REPORT. (Subseries of: Fiji Parliament. Parliamentary Paper) 1959. a. $2. Housing Authority, Box 1263, Suva, Fiji. circ. 550.

309.2 US
FLORIDA. DIVISION OF STATE PLANNING. ANNUAL REPORT ON STATE AND REGIONAL PLANNING. 1973. a. free. Department of Administration, Division of State Planning, 660 Apalachee Pkwy., Tallahassee, FL 32301.

352.7 DK
FLYTNINGER. 1984. a. Kr.10. (Koebenhavns Statistike Kontor) Bibliotekscentralen, Telegrafvej 5, DK-2750 Ballerup, Denmark.

350 GW ISSN 0341-244X
FORSCHUNGEN ZUR RAUMENTWICKLUNG. 1975. irreg. vol.15, 1985. price varies. Bundesforschungsanstalt fuer Landeskunde und Raumordnung, Am Michaelshof 8, Postfach 200130, 5300 Bonn 2, W. Germany (B.R.D.)
Formerly (1953-1974): Institut fuer Raumordnung. Mitteilungen.

G A HOUSES. (Global Architecture) see *ARCHITECTURE*

GOLD BOOK OF MULTIHOUSING. see *BUILDING AND CONSTRUCTION*

711 352 UK ISSN 0072-6818
GREAT BRITAIN. DEPARTMENT OF THE ENVIRONMENT. STATISTICS FOR TOWN AND COUNTRY PLANNING. SERIES 1. (Joint publication with the Welsh Office) 1969. irreg. price varies. H.M.S.O., Box 569, London SE1 9NH, England.

711 352 UK ISSN 0072-6826
GREAT BRITAIN. DEPARTMENT OF THE ENVIRONMENT. STATISTICS FOR TOWN AND COUNTRY PLANNING. SERIES 2. (Joint publication with the Welsh Office) 1968. irreg. price varies. H.M.S.O., Box 569, London SE1 9NH, England.

301.54 FR
GUIDE DE L'HABITAT ET DE L'AMENAGEMENT RURAL. 1967. a. Federation Nationale de l'Habitat Rural et de l'Amenagement du Territoire Rural, 27 rue La Rochefoucauld, 75009 Paris, France.
Former titles: Guide de l'Habitat Rural; Annuaire des Organismes d'Habitat Rural (ISSN 0066-2917)

301.363 US
HARVARD STUDIES IN URBAN HISTORY. irreg., latest 1985. price varies. Harvard University Press, 79 Garden St., Cambridge, MA 02138. TEL 617-495-2600.

333.7 KE
HIGHLANDS FIELD STATION REPORT. 1978. irreg., latest no.2. University of Nairobi, Department of Urban and Regional Planning, Box 30197, Nairobi, Kenya.

301.54 UK ISSN 0073-3644
HOUSING AND PLANNING YEAR BOOK. 1900. a. 75p. National Housing and Town Planning Council, 14-18 Old St., London EC1V 9AB, England.

352.7 KE
HOUSING AND URBAN DEVELOPMENT DIGEST. 1985. irreg. free. Regional Housing and Urban Development Office for East and Southern Africa, P.O. Box 30261, Nairobi, Kenya. Ed. Fredrik Hansen. bk. rev. circ. 500.

352.7 SW
HOUSING AND URBAN PLANNING IN SWEDEN. ANNUAL REPORT/SVENSKA BOSTAEDER. AARSREDOVISNING. a. SB Svenska Bostaeder, Vaellingbyplan 2, Box 95, 16212 Vaellingby, Sweden. illus. stats.

352.7 332 KE
HOUSING FINANCE COMPANY OF KENYA. ANNUAL REPORT AND ACCOUNTS. 1970. a. Housing Finance Company of Kenya, Rehani House, Kenyatta Ave., Box 30088, Nairobi, Kenya. circ. 1,000.

352.7 UK ISSN 0264-5181
HOUSING YEAR BOOK. 1983. a. £26. Longman Group Ltd., Fourth Ave., Harlow, Essex CM19 5AA, England.

333.77 300 CN
HUMAN SETTLEMENT ISSUES. 1978. irreg. (University of British Columbia, Centre for Human Settlements) University of British Columbia Press, 303-6344 Memorial Rd., Vancouver, B.C. V6T 1W5, Canada. TEL 604-228-3259.

352.7 DK ISSN 0108-562X
HUMAN SETTLEMENTS SITUATION AND RELATED TRENDS AND POLICIES. 1982. quinquennial. Kr.30. Boligministeriet, Slotsholmsgade 12, 1216 Copenhagen K, Denmark (Orders to: Danske Boghendleres Kommissionsanstalt, Siljangade 6, 2300 Copenhagen S, Denmark) (Co-sponsor: Danish National Agency for Physical Planning)

352.7 US ISSN 0090-3248
ILLINOIS. HOUSING DEVELOPMENT AUTHORITY. ANNUAL REPORT. 1970. a. free. Housing Development Authority, 401 N. Michigan Ave., Chicago, IL 60611. TEL 312-836-5200. Ed. Don Rose. charts. illus. stat. circ. 5,000.

331.83 IO
INDONESIA. DIREKTORAT PERUMAHAN RAKJAT. LAPORAN KERDJA. 1970. a. free. Direktorat Perumahan Rakjat, Jalan Wijaya I/68, Kebayoran Baru, Jakarta, Indonesia. circ. controlled.

352.7 YU ISSN 0351-0174
INFORMATIVNI BILTEN URBANISTICNEGA INSTITUTA SR SLOVENIJE. SPOROCILA. (Text in Slovenian; index in English) 1977. irreg. (1-2/yr.) , latest no.10, 1983. Urbanisticni Institut SR Slovenije, Jamova 18, Box 3, 61111 Ljubljana, Yugoslavia. bk. rev. circ. 700.

INSTITUT ZA ARHITEKTURU I URBANIZAM SRBIJE. ZBORNIK RADOVA. see *ARCHITECTURE*

301.5 NE
INTERNATIONAL FEDERATION FOR HOUSING AND PLANNING. DIRECTORY. (Text in English, French or German) 1972. biennial. membership. ‡ International Federation for Housing and Planning. Wassenaarseweg 43, 2596 CG The Hague, Netherlands. circ. 1,500(controlled)
Former titles: International Federation for Housing and Planning. Yearbook; International Federation for Housing and Planning. List of Members.

333.77 US
INTERNATIONAL STUDIES IN PLANNING. 1978. irreg. Cornell University, City and Regional Planning Publications, 106 W. Sibley Hall, Ithaca, NY 14853. (Co-sponsor: Cornell University, Department of City and Regional Planning, Program on International Studies in Planning) (reprint service avail. from UMI)

711 JA ISSN 0074-8897
INTERNATIONAL SYMPOSIUM ON REGIONAL DEVELOPMENT. PAPERS AND PROCEEDINGS. (Text in English) 1967. irreg., 1974, 4th. 3700 Yen. Japan Center for Area Development Research - Nihon Chiiki Kaihatsu Senta, Iino Bldg., 2-1-1 Uchisaiwaicho, Chiyoda-ku, Tokyo 100, Japan. circ. 500.

333.77 UK
INTERNATIONAL YEARBOOK OF RURAL PLANNING. 1980. a. price varies. Geo Books, Regency House, 34 Duke St., Norwich NR3 3AP, England. Ed. A.W. Gilg. Indexed: Br.Archaeol.Abstr. Geo.Abstr. Rural Recreat.Tour.Abstr. World Agri.Econ. & Rural Sociol.Abstr.
Formerly: Countryside Planning Yearbook (ISSN 0143-8190)

301.54 IS ISSN 0075-109X
ISRAEL. CENTRAL BUREAU OF STATISTICS. SURVEY OF HOUSING CONDITIONS. (Subseries of its Special Series) (Text in English and Hebrew) 1963. irreg., latest issue, no.641, 1978. price varies. Central Bureau of Statistics, Box 13015, Jerusalem, Israel.

JERUSALEM URBAN STUDIES. see *SOCIOLOGY*

309.26 US ISSN 0075-3947
JOINT CENTER FOR URBAN STUDIES.
PUBLICATIONS. irreg., latest ed. 1973. Harvard University Press, 79 Garden St., Cambridge, MA 02138. TEL 617-495-2600. (Co-publisher: M I T Press)

352.7 US
JOURNAL OF URBAN AFFAIRS. 1976. irreg., no.3, 1977. $1.50 per no. Virginia Polytechnic Institute and State University, College of Architecture and Urban Studies, 201 Architecture Annex, Blacksburg, VA 24061.
 Formed by the 1982 merger of: Urban Affairs Papers & Urban Interest Journal.

624 US ISSN 0733-9488
JOURNAL OF URBAN PLANNING AND DEVELOPMENT. 1956. irreg. (2-3/yr.) $36 to non-members. American Society of Civil Engineers, 345 E. 47th St., New York, NY 10017. TEL 212-705-7275. circ. 3,900. (reprint service avail. from UMI) Indexed: A.S.& T.Ind. Curr.Cont. Eng.Ind. SSCI. Br.Rail.Bd. Fluidex. GeoRef. HRIS.
 Formerly (until 1982): American Society of Civil Engineers. Urban Planning and Development Division. Journal (ISSN 0569-8081)

352.7 JA
JUTAKU SANGYO HANDBOOK; statistical handbook for Japanese housing industry. (Text in Japanese) 1976. a. 3000 Yen. Jutaku Sangyo Johoh Services, 23 Mori Bldg., 1-23-7, Toranomon, Minato-ku, Tokyo 105, Japan. Ed. Tsuneshi Miwa. adv. (back issues avail)
 Formerly: Jutaku Sangyo Handobukku.

690 SW ISSN 0022-7293
K B S-RAPPORTER. 1961. irreg. (5-15/yr.) price varies. Byggnadsstyrelsen - National Board of Public Building, S-106 43 Stockholm, Sweden.

354.4 SW
K B S TEKNISKA FOERESKRIFTER/K B S TECHNICAL REGULATIONS; krav och raad/ requirements and recommendations. (In four parts) 1966. irreg. (4-5/yr.) price varies. Byggnadsstyrelsen - National Board of Public Building, S-106 43 Stockholm 27, Sweden.
 Supersedes as of 1979: K B S Anvisningar/K B S Directions (ISSN 0022-7285)

352.7 KE
KENYA. MINISTRY OF HOUSING. ANNUAL REPORT. 1967. a. Government Printing and Stationery Department, P.O. Box 30128, Nairobi, Kenya.
 Supersedes in part: Kenya. Ministry of Health and Housing. Annual Report (ISSN 0075-5877)

350.865 KE
KENYA. NATIONAL HOUSING CORPORATION. ANNUAL REPORT. a. EAs.4. National Housing Corporation, Box 30257, Nairobi, Kenya. charts. illus. stat.

352.7 DK ISSN 0573-9799
KOEBENHAVN BOLIGKOMMISSIONEN. AARSBERETNING. 1984. a. (Koebenhavn Boligkommissionen - Copenhagen's Housing Commission) Bibliotekscentralen, Telegrafvej 5, DK-2750 Ballerup, Denmark.

352.7 GW ISSN 0340-1170
KOMMUNALWISSENSCHAFTLICHE DISSERTATIONEN. 1970. a. DM.30. Deutsches Institut fuer Urbanistik, Strasse des 17. Juni 110, D-1000 Berlin 12, W. Germany (B.R.D.) circ. 500.

352.7 DK ISSN 0106-7362
KOMMUNEPLANORIENTERING. No. 4, 1981. irreg. Planstyrelsen, Copenhagen, Denmark. illus.

KUNST AM BAU. see ARCHITECTURE

350 US
LINCOLN INSTITUTE OF LAND POLICY. BASIC CONCEPT SERIES. 1978. irreg., latest no. 107. $6. Lincoln Institute of Land Policy, 26 Trowbridge St., Cambridge, MA 02138. TEL 617-661-3016. Ed. Sharon E. Shed. circ. 500.

352.7 UK ISSN 0261-0752
LINCOLNSHIRE, HOUSING. 1980. a. Lincolnshire County Council, County Planning Officer, County Offices, Newland, Lincoln LN1 1YL, England. illus. charts.

352.7 910.4 US ISSN 0278-9485
LIVABILITY DIGEST. 1981. irreg. $5 per no. Partners for Livable Places, 1429 21st St., N.W., Washington, DC 20036. TEL 202-887-5990. (back issues avail.)

352.7 UK ISSN 0260-3756
LOCAL AUTHORITY SPECIFIERS' REFERENCE BOOK AND BUYERS GUIDE. a. £20. (District Council Technical Association) Sterling Publications Ltd., 86-88 Edgware Rd., London W2, England.
 Formerly: Housing Managers Buyers Guide.

309.26 UK ISSN 0076-0633
LONDON PAPERS IN REGIONAL SCIENCE. 1969. a. price varies. Pion Ltd., 207 Brondesbury Park, London NW2 5JN, England (Dist. by: Methuen Inc., 29 W. 35th St., New York, NY 10001)

352 UK ISSN 0024-6158
LONDON SOCIETY. JOURNAL. 1913. a. £2. London Society, City University, Room G210, St. John St., London EC1V 0HB, England. Ed. S.J. Teague. bk. rev. illus. index. circ. 550. Indexed: Br.Hum.Ind.

331.83 MW ISSN 0581-0892
MALAWI HOUSING CORPORATION. ANNUAL REPORT AND ACCOUNTS. 1964. a. free. Malawi Housing Corporation, Box 414, Blantyre, Malawi.

MAN - ENVIRONMENT SYSTEMS. see ENVIRONMENTAL STUDIES

331.83 US ISSN 0076-499X
MASSACHUSETTS HOUSING FINANCE AGENCY. ANNUAL REPORT. 1969. a. free. Massachusetts Housing Finance Agency, 50 Milk St., Boston, MA 02109. TEL 617-451-3480. Ed. Martha Vaananen. circ. 18,000.

352.7 SP
MATERIALES DE LA CIUDAD. irreg. Editorial Gustavo Gili, S.A., Rosellon 87-89, Barcelona 15, Spain.

333 711 MF ISSN 0076-552X
MAURITIUS. MINISTRY OF HOUSING, LANDS AND TOWN AND COUNTRY PLANNING. ANNUAL REPORTS. a. price varies. Government Printing Office, Elizabeth II Ave., Port Louis, Mauritius.

352.7 MF
MAURITIUS HOUSING CORPORATION. REPORT AND ACCOUNTS. (Text in English) 1964. a. Mauritius Housing Corporation, Box 478, Port Louis, Mauritius. Ed.Bd. circ. 500.

350.086 US
MEMPHIS 2000 ANNUAL REPORT. 1982. irreg. free. Office of Planning and Development, 125 Mid American Mall N., Memphis, TN 38103. Ed. David Adams. circ. 500. (microfiche)

353.9 US
MICHIGAN STATE HOUSING DEVELOPMENT AUTHORITY. ANNUAL REPORT. 1970. a. State Housing Development Authority, Plaza One, Fourth Floor, 401 South Washington Square, Box 30044, Lansing, MI 48909. TEL 517-373-8370. Ed. Ann M. Harrison. illus. stat. circ. 7,500.

388.3 US ISSN 0026-7198
MOBILE LIVING. 1953. irreg. membership. National Association of Trailer Owners, Inc., 1323 Main St., Box 1418, Sarasota, FL 33578. TEL 813-953-2730. Ed. Frances Neel. adv. charts. illus. tr.lit. circ. 42,000.

352.7 BO
MONOGRAFIAS URBANAS. 1975. irreg., no.3, 1985. $12. Centro de Investigaciones Sociales, Casilla 6931 - C.C., La Paz, Bolivia.

309.2 NO ISSN 0085-4263
N I B R RAPPORT. (Text in Norwegian; summaries in English) 1965. irreg. price varies. Norsk Institutt for By- og Regionforskning - Norwegian Institute of Urban and Regional Research, Nycoveien 1, Box 15 Grefsen, Oslo 4, Norway.

352.7 UK
NATIONAL HOUSING AND TOWN PLANNING COUNCIL. CONFERENCE AND EXHIBITION GUIDE.* a. National Housing and Town Planning Council Inc., 14-18 Old St, London EC1V 9AB, England. circ. 1,200.

301.54 UK ISSN 0077-4707
NATIONAL HOUSING AND TOWN PLANNING COUNCIL. HANDBOOK AND YEAR BOOK. 1950. a. £0.75. National Housing and Town Planning Council, 14-18 Old St., London ECIV 9AB, England.

301.36 US
NATIONAL URBAN LEAGUE ANNUAL REPORT. a. $1. National Urban League, 500 E. 62nd St., New York, NY 10021. TEL 212-310-9000. illus.
 Formerly: National Urban League Progress Report (ISSN 0098-7735)

352 US ISSN 0028-5722
NEW JERSEY FEDERATION OF PLANNING OFFICIALS. FEDERATION PLANNING INFORMATION REPORTS. 1966. irreg., 4-5/yr. $85 (includes: Federation Planner) ‡ New Jersey Federation of Planning Officials, 66 Morris Ave., Springfield, NJ 07081-1409. Exec. Dir. James P. Grassi. circ. 1,000. (processed)

352.7 AT
NEW SOUTH WALES. DEPARTMENT OF HOUSING. ANNUAL REPORT. 1942. a. Department of Housing, G.P.O. Box 4121, Sydney, N.S.W. 2001, Australia. illus.
 Former titles: New South Wales. Housing Commission. Annual Report & New South Wales. Commonwealth Housing Commission. Annual Report.

350 US
NORTHEAST REGIONAL SCIENCE REVIEW. 1971. a. $8.50. Peace Society (International), School of Management, State University of New York at Binghamton, Binghamton, NY 13901. TEL 607-777-2475. Ed. Manas Chatterji. (back issues avail.)
 Formerly: Regional Science Review.

711 CK
NOTICIERO I.D.U.N. 1976. irreg. Instituto de Desarrollo Urbano, Division de Documentacion, Comunicacion y Archivo, Apartado Aereo 034176, Bogota, Colombia.

350.086 BL
NUCLEO DE ESTUDOS SOCIAIS PARA HABITACAO E URBANISMO. Variant title: N E U R B. irreg. Pontificia Universidade Catolica do Rio de Janeiro, Nucleo de Estudos Sociais para Habitacao e Urbanismo, Rua Marques de Sao Vicente 209, 20000 Rio de Janeiro, Brazil. Dir. Alexandre Luiz Mandina.

333.77 US
O D C PLANNING REPORTS. no.86, 1968. irreg. membership. Oahu Development Conference, 141 Merchant St., Honolulu, HI 96813. TEL 808-537-5721.

333.77 US
OAHU DEVELOPMENT CONFERENCE. ANNUAL REPORT. a. membership. Oahu Development Conference, 141 Merchant St., Honolulu, HI 96813. TEL 808-537-5271. illus.

309.26 301 AU
OESTERREICHISCHES INSTITUT FUER RAUMPLANUNG. OEIR-FORUM. 1957. irreg. price varies. Oesterreichisches Institut fuer Raumplanung, Franz Josefs Kai 27, A-1011 Vienna, Austria. Ed. Michael Sauberer.
 Formerly: Oesterreichisches Institut fuer Raumplanung. Veroeffentlichungen (ISSN 0078-3625)

711 AU ISSN 0078-3617
OESTERREICHISCHES INSTITUT FUER RAUMPLANUNG. TAETIGKEITSBERICHT. 1957. a. free. Oesterreichisches Institut fuer Raumplanung, Franz Josefs Kai 27, A-1011 Vienna, Austria. Ed. Michael Sauberer. circ. 1,300.

301.54 CN ISSN 0078-4885
ONTARIO. MINISTRY OF MUNICIPAL AFFAIRS AND HOUSING. ANNUAL REPORT. 1966. a. Can.$2 per no. Ministry of Municipal Affairs and Housing, 777 Bay St., 17th Fl., Toronto, Ont. M5G 2E5, Canada. TEL 416-585-7020. circ. 2,000.

352.7 DK ISSN 0108-4151
OVERSIGT OVER BY- OG REGIONFORSKNING. English edition: Urban and Regional Research in Denmark. (Editions in Danish and English) 1980. biennial. free. Statens Byggeforskningsinstitut, Planstyrelsen, Holbergsgade 23, 1057 Copenhagen K, Denmark. bk. rev. circ. 700.

352.7 336 US
OWNER OCCUPIED HOUSING STATISTICS FROM HOMESTEAD REBATE AND INCOME TAX DATA MATCH. 1978. a. free. Division of Taxation, Office of Tax Analysis, 50 Barrack St., Trenton, NJ 08646. TEL 609-292-7167. circ. 600.

350.86 PR ISSN 0048-4466
P L E R U S. (Planning-Economic, Regional, Urban, Social) (Text in English and Spanish) 1967. a. $5 (to individuals; $6 to institutions) Universidad de Puerto Rico, Escuela Graduada de Planificacion, Apartado B.E., Rio Piedras, PR 00931. Ed. Jose A. Vega. adv. bk. rev. circ. 1,000.

352.7 PN
PANAMA. MINISTERIO DE VIVIENDA. MEMORIA. a. Instituto de Vivienda y Urbanismo, Panama City, Panama. illus. stat.
Supersedes (since 1973): Instituto de Vivienda y Urbanismo. Memoria Presentada por el Director General.

301.54 SP ISSN 0067-4168
PATRONATO MUNICIPAL DE LA VIVIENDA DE BARCELONA. MEMORIA. 1947. a. free. Patronato Municipal de la Vivienda, Plaza F. de Lesseps, 12, Barcelona 6, Spain. Ed. Fernando Aramburo Campoy. bk. rev. index. circ. 1,500.

PLANNING AND ADMINISTRATION. see *PUBLIC ADMINISTRATION*

711.4 PL ISSN 0079-3493
POLSKA AKADEMIA NAUK. KOMITET PRZESTRZENNEGO ZAGOSPODAROWANIA KRAJU. BIULETYN. 1960. irreg. price varies. Panstwowe Wydawnictwo Naukowe, Ul. Miodowa 10, 00-251 Warsaw, Poland (Dist. by: Ars Polona, Krakowskie Przedmiescie 7, 00-068 Warsaw, Poland) Ed. A. Kuklinski. index. circ. 1,300.

711 PL ISSN 0079-3507
POLSKA AKADEMIA NAUK. KOMITET PRZESTRZENNEGO ZAGOSPODAROWANIA KRAJU. STUDIA. (Text in English, French, Polish or Russian: summaries in English and Russian) 1961. irreg., vol.83, 1984. price varies. Panstwowe Wydawnictwo Naukowe, Ul. Miodowa 10, 00-251 Warsaw, Poland (Dist. by: Ars Polona, Krakowskie Przedmiescie 7, 00-068 Warsaw, Poland) Ed. Michal Kaczorowski.

POLSKA AKADEMIA NAUK. ODDZIAL W KRAKOWIE. KOMISJA URBANISTYKI I ARCHITEKTURY. TEKA. see *ARCHITECTURE*

350.086 CL
PONTIFICIA UNIVERSIDAD CATOLICA DE CHILE. INSTITUTO DE ESTUDIOS URBANOS. DOCUMENTOS DE TRABAJO. 1969. irreg., no.251, 1984. price varies. Pontificia Universidad Catolica de Chile, Instituto de Estudios Urbanos, Los Navegantes 1919, Casilla 16002-Correo 9, Santiago, Chile.
Formerly: Universidad Catolica de Chile. Instituto de Planificacion del Desarrollo Urbano. Documentos de Trabajo.

350.086 US ISSN 0163-8602
PRESIDENT'S NATIONAL URBAN POLICY REPORT. 1978. biennial. U.S. Department of Housing and Urban Development, Washington, DC 20410. TEL 202-655-4000.

240 AU
PROBLEME GRENZNAHER RAEUME. 1973. irreg.? (Oesterreichische Gesellschaft und Raumplannung) Manz Verlag, Kohlmarkt 16, A-1014 Vienna 1, Austria. TEL (0222)631781. Ed. Franz Heigl.

711 309.62 US ISSN 0305-9006
PROGRESS IN PLANNING. 1973. 6/yr. (in 2 vols., 3 nos./vol.) $125 (annual bound volume $120) Pergamon Press, Inc., Journals Division, Maxwell House, Fairview Park, Elmsford, NY 10523 TEL 914-592-7700. (And Headington Hill Hall, Oxford OX3 0BW, England) Eds. D.R. Diamond, J.B. McLoughlin. (also avail. in microform from MIM, UMI) Indexed: SSCI. Geo.Abstr. HRIS. Sage Urb.Stud.Abstr.

350.086 PR
PUERTO RICO. DEPARTAMENTO DE LA VIVIENDA. SECRETARIA AUXILIAR DE PLANIFICATION Y PROGRAMACION. INFORME ANUAL. 1953. a. free. Department of Housing, Urban Renewal and Housing Corporation, San Juan, Puerto Rico. circ. 2,000.

352.7 333.33 US
RAND MCNALLY PLACES RATED ALMANAC. 1981. irreg. (approx. every 3 yrs.) $14.95 paper; hardbound $24.95. Rand McNally & Co., Box 7600, Chicago, IL 60680. TEL 312-673-9100.

352.7 US
RAND MCNALLY RETIREMENT PLACES RATED. 1983. irreg $9.95. Rand McNally & Co., Box 7600, Chicago, IL 60680. TEL 312-673-9100.
Formerly: Rand McNally Places Rated Retirement Guide.

352.7 614 SZ
RAUMPLANUNG UND UMWELTSCHUTZ IM KANTON ZURICH. (Text in German) 1964. irreg. 12 Fr. Amt fuer Raumplanung, Stampfenbach Str. 14, 8090 Zurich, Switzerland. (Co-sponsor: Amt fuer Regionalplanung) bibl. charts. illus. circ. 5,000.
Formerly (no. 1-7): Regionalplanung in Kanton Zurich.

309.26 FR
RECHERCHE URBAINE. 1973. irreg. price varies. Ecole des Hautes Etudes en Sciences Sociales, 131 bd. St. Michel, 75005 Paris, France.

352 US
REGIONAL PLAN NEWS. 1929. irreg., no.116, 1983. $7 per no. to non-members. Regional Plan Association, Inc., 1040 Ave. of the Americas, New York, NY 10018. TEL 212-398-1140. Ed. Wm. B. Shore. bk. rev. charts. illus. circ. 3,500. Indexed: P.A.I.S.
Former titles: R P A News; R P A Bulletin (ISSN 0483-7738); Regional Plan News (ISSN 0034-3374); Regional Plan Association. News Letter.

333.77 US
REGIONAL SCIENCE DISSERTATION AND MONOGRAPH SERIES. 1972. irreg., latest 1982. Cornell University, Program in Urban and Regional Studies, 209 W. Sibley Hall, Ithaca, NY 14853. (Co-sponsor: Cornell University Field of Regional Science) (reprint service avail. from UMI)

352 US ISSN 0034-3420
REGION'S AGENDA. 1970. irreg; vol.11, 1982. $3 per no. to non-members. Regional Plan Association, Inc., 1040 Ave. of the Americas, New York, NY 10018. TEL 212-398-1140.

352.7 JA
REPORT ON URBAN RESEARCH/TOSHI KENKYU HOKOKU. (Text in Japanese) 1969. irreg. free. Tokyo Metropolitan University - Tokyo-toritsu Daigaku, 1-1-1 Yakumo, Meguro-ku, Tokyo 152, Japan. illus.

RESEARCH IN URBAN ECONOMICS. see *PUBLIC ADMINISTRATION — Municipal Government*

350.865 VE
REVISTA INTERNACIONAL DE VIVIENDA RURAL/INTERNATIONAL RURAL HOUSING JOURNAL. (Text in English and Spanish) 1970. a. (with bi-m. supplements) $10. ‡ International Rural Housing Association, Apto. 16224, Caracas, Venezuela. Ed. Arturo R. Ortiz. adv. bk. rev. charts. illus. circ. 6,000.

354 AT
RURAL ADJUSTMENT AND FINANCE CORPORATION OF WESTERN AUSTRALIA. ANNUAL REPORT. 1971/72. a. free. Rural Adjustment and Finance Corporation of Western Australia, 16th Floor, St. Martins Tower, 44 St. George's Terrace, Perth, W.A. 6000, Australia. stat.
Former titles: Rural Adjustment of Western Australia. Annual Report & Rural Reconstruction Authority of Western Australia. Annual Report (ISSN 0310-4923)

338.7 CN
SASKATCHEWAN HOUSING CORPORATION. ANNUAL REPORT. 1973. a. free. Saskatchewan Housing Corporation, 900-2500 Victoria Ave., Regina, Sask. S4P 3V7, Canada. TEL 306-787-4177. Ed.Bd. illus. stat. circ. 2,000.

711.4 338.9 AU ISSN 0558-9746
SCHRIFTENREIHE FUER RAUMFORSCHUNG UND RAUMPLANUNG. 1957. irreg., vol.17, 1979. Amt der Kaerntner Landesregierung, Abteilung Landesplanung, A-9010 Klagenfurt, Austria. Ed. Oskar Glanzer. circ. 300.
Regional planning

352.7 SZ
SCHRIFTENREIHE ZUR ORTS-, REGIONAL- UND LANDESPLANUNG. 1969. irreg. price varies. Eidgenoessische Technische Hochschule Zuerich Institut fuer Orts- , Regional- und Landesplanung, Redaktion DISP - Swiss Federal Institute of Technology, Institute for Local, Regional and National Planning, 8093 Zurich, Switzerland.

352.7 BL
SERIE DEBATES URBANOS. irreg., no. 5, 1983. Zahar Editores S.A., Caixa Postal 207 (ZC-00), Rio de Janeiro, Brazil.

350.865 US
SHELBY COUNTY URBAN DEVELOPMENT REPORT. 1979. a. Memphis and Shelby County Office of Planning and Development, 125 Mid America Mall N., Memphis, TN 38103-2084. Ed. Louise Mercuro. circ. 500.
Supersedes: Urban Growth Indicators and Residential Activity Permit Report.

352.7 GW
SIN-STAEDTEBAUINSTITUT. INFORMATION. Short title: S I N Information. irreg. DM.10 per no. SIN-Staedtebauinstitut Forschungsgesellschaft mbH, Neutorgraben 1A, 8500 Nuernberg 111, W. Germany (B.R.D.) (looseleaf format)

352.7 GW
SIN-STAEDTEBAUINSTITUT. JAHRESBERICHTE. Short title: S I N Jahresberichte. a. free. SIN-Staedtebauinstitut Forschungsgesellschaft mbH, Neutorgraben 1A, 8500 Nuernberg 111, W. Germany (B.R.D.)

711 690 GW ISSN 0078-2807
SIN-STAEDTEBAUINSTITUT. SCHRIFTENREIHE. 1965. irreg. price varies. SIN-Staedtebauinstitut Forschungsgesellschaft mbH, Neutorgraben 1A, 8500 Nuernberg 111, W. Germany (B.R.D.) Ed. Gerhard G. Dittrich.

711 690 GW ISSN 0078-2815
SIN-STAEDTEBAUINSTITUT. STUDIENHEFTE. 1965. irreg. price varies. SIN-Staedtebauinstitut Forschungsgesellschaft mbH, Neutorgraben 1A, 8500 Nuernberg 111, W. Germany (B.R.D.) Ed. Gerhard G. Dittrich.

711 690 GW ISSN 0078-2823
SIN-STAEDTEBAUINSTITUT. WERKBERICHTE. 1968. irreg. price varies. SIN-Staedtebauinstitut Forschungsgesellschaft mbH, Neutorgraben 1A, 8500 Nuernberg 111, W. Germany (B.R.D.) Ed. Gerhard G. Dittrich.

350.086 SI
SINGAPORE. HOUSING AND DEVELOPMENT BOARD. ANNUAL REPORT. (Text in English) 1960. a. S.$20. Housing and Development Board, Ministry of National Development Building, Maxwell Road, Singapore 0106, Singapore. charts. illus. stat. circ. controlled. (back issues avail.)

352.7　　　　　　SI
SINGAPORE. MINISTRY OF NATIONAL DEVELOPMENT. ANNUAL REPORT. 1975. a. S.13. Ministry of National Development, National Development Bldg., Maxwell Rd., Singapore 0106, Singapore. circ. 1,500.

352.7　　　　　　AG
SOCIEDAD INTERAMERICANA DE PLANIFICACION. EDICIONES S I A P. 1974. irreg. (Sociedad Interamericana de Planificacion) Ediciones S.I.A.P., Chenaut 1968, 1426 Buenos Aires, Argentina (Distrib. by: Ediciones Nueva Vision, Viamonte 494, Buenos Aires, Argentina) Dir. Martha S. de Kaplan. circ. 3,000.

352　　　　　BE　ISSN 0067-5652
SOCIETE NATIONAL DU LOGEMENT. RAPPORT ANNUEL. Dutch edition: Nationale Maatschappij voor de Huisvesting. Jaarverslag (ISSN 0522-7739) (Text in Dutch and French) 1920 (French edt.); 1934 (Dutch edt.) a. free. Societe Nationale du Logement, Rue Breydel 12, 1040 Brussels, Belgium. circ. 3,000.

352.7　　　　　　US
SOUTH ATLANTIC URBAN STUDIES. 1977. a. $10 paperback; hardcover $14.95. College of Charleston, Urban Studies Center, Charleston, SC 29401. TEL 803-792-5737. Ed.Bd. bk. rev. circ. 500.

711　　　　　　US
SOUTHERN ILLINOIS UNIVERSITY, EDWARDSVILLE. REGIONAL RESEARCH AND DEVELOPMENT SERVICES. REPORT. 1969. irreg., no.10, 1979. Southern Illinois University, Edwardsville, Regional Research and Development Services, Box 32, Edwardsville, IL 62026-1001. TEL 618-692-3032. circ. 100.
Formerly (until 1985): Southern Illinois University, Edwardsville. Center For Urban and Environmental Research and Services. C U E R S Report. (ISSN 0073-4993)

352 711　　　　　　GW
DIE STADT. 1972. irreg. price varies. SIN-Staedtebauinstitut Forschungsgesellschaft mbH, Neutorgraben 1A, 8500 Nuernberg 111, W. Germany (B.R.D.) Ed. Gerhard G. Dittrich. adv.

352 333　　　　　　US
STATE OF FLORIDA LAND DEVELOPMENT GUIDE. a. free. Department of Administration, Division of State Planning, Bureau of Comprehensive Planning, 660 Apalachee Pkwy., Tallahassee, FL 32304. charts. illus.

STATISTISCHES JAHRBUCH DER STADT NUERNBERG. see *STATISTICS*

STUDIA I MATERIALY DO TEORII I HISTORII ARCHITEKTURY I URBANISTYKI. see *ARCHITECTURE*

352.7　　　　　　UK
STUDIES IN URBAN HISTORY. 1974. irreg. price varies. Edward Arnold (Publishers) Ltd., 41 Bedford Square, London WC1B 3DQ, England.

301.364　　　　US　ISSN 0081-8801
STUDIES OF URBAN SOCIETY. 1968. irreg., latest 1979. price varies. University of Chicago Press, 5801 S. Ellis Ave., Chicago, IL 60637. TEL 312-962-7700. Ed. David P. Street. (reprint service avail. from UMI,ISI)

SWEDEN. STATENS RAAD FOER BYGGNADSFORSKNING. DOCUMENT. see *BUILDING AND CONSTRUCTION*

SWEDEN. STATENS RAAD FOER BYGGNADSFORSKNING. RAPPORT. see *BUILDING AND CONSTRUCTION*

SWEDEN. STATENS RAAD FOER BYGGNADSFORSKNING. VERKSAMHETSPLAN. see *BUILDING AND CONSTRUCTION*

352.7　　　　　　UK
SYMPOSIUM ON URBAN RENEWAL. PAPERS. 1965. irreg. University of Salford, Department of Engineering, Salford, Lancs. M5 4WT, England.

350.865　　　　UK　ISSN 0261-197X
T P A S NOTES. 1980. irreg. price varies. Scottish Council of Social Service, Tenant Participation Advisory Service, 266 Clyde St., Glasgow G1 4JH, Scotland. Eds. Robina Goodlad, Roger Popplewell. circ. 1,000. (back issues avail.)

350.086　　　　　　TZ
TANZANIA. CAPITAL DEVELOPMENT AUTHORITY. REPORT AND ACCOUNTS. 1974. a. EAs.10. Capital Development Authority, Box 913, Dodoma, Tanzania. illus. circ. 110.

354　　　　　　TZ
TANZANIA. MINISTRY OF LANDS, HOUSING AND URBAN DEVELOPMENT. URBAN PLANNING DIVISION. ANNUAL REPORT. 1974. a. Ministry of Lands, Housing and Urban Development, Urban Planning Division, Box 20671, Dar es Salaam, Tanzania. Ed. I.J. Mitiro.

TECHNICAL UNIVERSITY OF DENMARK. INSTITUTE OF ROADS, TRANSPORT AND TOWN PLANNING. REPORT. see *TRANSPORTATION — Roads And Traffic*

711　　　　　HU　ISSN 0040-2680
TELEPULESTUDOMANYI KOZLEMENYEK. (Text in Hungarian; summaries in English, German & Russian) 1952. a. free. (Budapesti Muszaki Egyetem, Varosepitesi Tanszek) Muszaki Konyvkiado, Bajcsy-Zsilinszky Ut 22, 1051 Budapest, Hungary. (Co-sponsors: Magyar Urbanisztikai Tarsasag. Varosepitesi Tudomanyos es Tervezo Intezet) Ed. Dr. Kalman Farago. bk. rev. bibl. charts. illus. circ. 1,030.

309.2　　　　UK　ISSN 0308-082X
TOWN AND COUNTRY PLANNING ASSOCIATION. ANNUAL REPORT. 1899. a. £1.50($2.50) Town and Country Planning Association, 17 Carlton House Terrace, London SW1Y 5AS, England. Ed. David Boyle.

711　　　　　UK　ISSN 0078-2114
TOWN AND COUNTRY PLANNING SUMMER SCHOOL; REPORT OF PROCEEDINGS. 1936. a. Royal Town Planning Institute, 26 Portland Place, London W1N 4BE, England. Ed. Anthony Fyson. circ. 14,800.

TVAI; periodical for architecture, town planning, industrial design & the plastic arts. see *ARCHITECTURE*

352.7　　　　　　CN
U B C PLANNING PAPERS. 1981. irreg. University of British Columbia, School of Community and Regional Planning, Vancouver, B.C. V6T 1W5, Canada. TEL 604-228-3276. Ed. David Hulchanski. circ. 150.
Supersedes: University of British Columbia. School of Community and Regional Planning. Planning Papers; Formerly: University of British Columbia. School of Community and Regional Planning. Occasional Papers.

350.865　　　　US　ISSN 0565-2820
U.S. DEPARTMENT OF HOUSING AND URBAN DEVELOPMENT. ANNUAL REPORT. 1965. a. U.S. Department of Housing and Urban Development., Washington, DC 20410 TEL 202-655-4000. (Orders to: Supt.of Documents, Washington, DC 20402)

301.54　　　　US　ISSN 0091-4932
U.S. FEDERAL HOUSING ADMINISTRATION. F H A HOMES; data for states on characteristics of FHA operations under Section 203. 1956. irreg. U.S. Federal Housing Administration, 451 Seventh St., S.W., Washington, DC 20410. TEL 202-755-5995. stat. circ. 1,500. Key Title: F.H.A. Homes.

309 711.4　　　UK　ISSN 0067-8953
UNIVERSITY OF BIRMINGHAM. CENTRE FOR URBAN AND REGIONAL STUDIES. OCCASIONAL PAPERS. 1968; N.S. 1981. irreg., no.4, 1982. University of Birmingham, Centre for Urban and Regional Studies, J. G. Smith Bldg., Box 363, Birmingham B15 2TT, England.

309 711.4　　　UK　ISSN 0306-4034
UNIVERSITY OF BIRMINGHAM. CENTRE FOR URBAN AND REGIONAL STUDIES. RESEARCH MEMORANDUM. irreg., no.87, 1981. price varies. University of Birmingham, Centre for Urban and Regional Studies, J. G. Smith Bldg., Box 363, Birmingham B15 2TT, England. Indexed: Geo.Abstr.

309 711.4　　　UK　ISSN 0067-8961
UNIVERSITY OF BIRMINGHAM. CENTRE FOR URBAN AND REGIONAL STUDIES. URBAN AND REGIONAL STUDIES. 1971. irreg., no.11, 1984. George Allen & Unwin (Publishers) Ltd., 40 Museum St., London W.C. 1, England (U.S. addr.: Allen & Unwin Inc., 8 Winchester Place, Winchester, MA 01890) Indexed: Geo.Abstr.

309 711.4　　　　　UK
UNIVERSITY OF BIRMINGHAM. CENTRE FOR URBAN AND REGIONAL STUDIES. WORKING PAPER. irreg. price varies. University of Birmingham, Centre for Urban and Regional Studies, J. G. Smith Bldg., Box 363, Birmingham B15 2TT, England. Indexed: Rural Recreat.Tour.Abstr. World Agri.Econ. & Rural Sociol.Abstr.

352.7　　　　　　US
UNIVERSITY OF PENNSYLVANIA. DEPARTMENT OF CITY AND REGIONAL PLANNING. RESEARCH REPORTS SERIES. 1983. irreg., approx. 6/yr. price varies. University of Pennsylvania, Department of City and Regional Planning, Philadelphia, PA 19104. TEL 215-898-5731. Ed. Robert E. Coughlin. circ. 250.

350 711　　　　　　CN
UNIVERSITY OF TORONTO. DEPARTMENT OF GEOGRAPHY. PAPERS ON PLANNING & DESIGN. 1971. irreg., no.33, 1985. price varies. University of Toronto, Department of Geography, Toronto, Ont. M5S 1A1, Canada. Ed. J. Hitchcock.
Formerly: University of Toronto. Department of Urban & Regional Planning. Papers on Planning & Design.

UNIVERSITY OF WATERLOO. DEPARTMENT OF GEOLOGY. WORKING PAPERS SERIES. see *ENVIRONMENTAL STUDIES*

711.4 301.3　　　US　ISSN 0083-4688
URBAN AFFAIRS ANNUAL REVIEWS. 1967. biennial. $29.95 for hardcover; softcover $14.95. Sage Publications, Inc., 2111 W. Hillcrest Dr., Newbury Park, CA 91320 TEL 805-499-0721. (And Sage Publications, Ltd., 28 Banner St., London EC1Y 8QE, England) (back issues avail.)

711.4　　　　　　UK
URBAN AND REGIONAL PLANNING SERIES. 1970. irreg., vol.30, 1983. price varies. Pergamon Press Ltd., Headington Hill Hall, Oxford OX3 0BW, England (U.S. subscr. to: Maxwell House, Fairview Park, Elmsford, NY 10523)
Regional planning

338.7　　　　　　JM
URBAN DEVELOPMENT CORPORATION. ANNUAL REPORT. 1970. a. free. Urban Development Corporation, 12 Ocean Blvd., Kingston, Jamaica. illus. circ. 500.

307.76　　　　　　SA
URBAN FOUNDATION. ANNUAL REVIEW. (Text in Afrikaans and English) 1979/80. a. Urban Foundation, Box 1198, Johannesburg 2000, South Africa. circ. 6,000. (back issues avail.)
Formerly: Urban Foundation. Progress Report.

352.7 364　　　US　ISSN 0736-6272
URBAN INSIGHTS MONOGRAPH SERIES. 1979. irreg., 14th, 1985. price varies. Loyola University of Chicago, Center for Urban Policy, 820 N. Michigan Ave., Chicago, IL 60611. TEL 312-670-3112.

309.2　　　　　US　ISSN 0092-7481
URBAN INSTITUTE. ANNUAL REPORT. 1969/70. a. Urban Institute, 2100 M. Street, N. W., Washington, DC 20037. Ed. K. Storck. circ. 5,000. Indexed: Med.Care Rev. Key Title: Urban Institute Report.

309.5　　　　US　　ISSN 0741-8485
URBAN INSTITUTE. POLICY AND RESEARCH REPORT. 1971. irreg., latest vol.16, no.1, 1986. free. Urban Institute, 2100 M St. N.W., Washington, DC 20037. TEL 202-833-7200. Ed. K. Storck. bk. rev. charts. illus. circ. 8,500. (back issues avail.)
　　Formerly (until 1979): Search (Washington, D.C.) (ISSN 0048-9921)

711　　　　AT
URBAN ISSUES. 1970. irreg. Aus.$5 to libraries. Australian Institute of Urban Studies, Queensland Division, c/o Department of Geography, University of Queensland, St. Lucia, Qld. 4067, Australia (Subscr. address: Hon. Secretary, AIUS (Qld. Division), G.P.O. Box 1989, Brisbane, Qld. 4001, Australia) Ed. J. H. A. Dick. Indexed: Aus.P.A.I.S.

352.7　　　　AT
URBAN STUDIES YEARBOOK. a. Aus.$22.50. George Allen & Unwin, 8 Napier St., North Sydney, NSW 2060, Australia.

711　　　　AT　　ISSN 0310-5601
URBANOLOGY. 1971. irreg. University of New South Wales, School of Town Planning, P.O. Box 1, Kensington, NSW 2033, Australia. Ed. J.H. Shaw.

352.7　　　　SZ
VADEMECUM. 1970. irreg. 10 Fr. Eidgenoessische Technische Hochschule Zuerich, Institut fuer Orts-, Regional- und Landesplanung, Redaktion DISP - Swiss Federal Institute of Technology, Hoenggerberg HIL, CH-8093 Zurich, Switzerland.

352.7　　　　AT　　ISSN 0810-4972
VICTORIA. MINISTRY OF HOUSING. ANNUAL REPORT. 1938. a. free. Ministry of Housing, 250 Elizabeth St., Melbourne, Vic. 3000, Australia. illus. circ. 2,000.

630　　　　US
WORKING PAPERS IN PLANNING. 1979. irreg., no.43, 1980. $14. Cornell University, Program in Urban and Regional Studies, 209 W. Sibley Hall, Ithaca, NY 14853. (Co-sponsor: Cornell University Department of City and Regional Planning) (reprint service avail. from UMI)

309.26　301.364　　US　　ISSN 0084-3520
YALE STUDIES OF THE CITY. 1969. irreg. Yale University Press, 92A Yale Sta., New Haven, CT 06520. TEL 203-432-0940.

ZONING LAW ANTHOLOGY. see *LAW*

HOUSING AND URBAN PLANNING — Abstracting, Bibliographies, Statistics

352.7　600　016　　US　　ISSN 0163-1535
ABSTRACT NEWSLETTER: URBAN AND REGIONAL TECHNOLOGY AND DEVELOPMENT. w. $79. U.S. National Technical Information Service, 5285 Port Royal Rd., Springfield, VA 22161. TEL 703-487-4630. Ed. Linda J. LaGarde. index. (back issues avail.)
　　Former titles: Weekly Abstract Newsletter: Urban and Regional Technology and Development; Weekly Government Abstracts. Urban and Regional Technology and Development; Weekly Government Abstracts. Urban Technology (ISSN 0363-7417)

352.7　　　　AT　　ISSN 0155-9508
ANNUAL REVIEW OF THE RESIDENTIAL PROPERTY MARKET. 1978. a. Aus.$25($25) Real Estate Institute of Australia, Real Estate House, 16 Thesiger Court, Deakin, A.C.T. 2600, Australia. Ed. Ron Arnold. charts. stats. circ. 5,000. (back issues avail.)

352.7　016　　　　BL
BANCO NACIONAL DA HABITACAO. ASSESSORIA TECNICA DE DOCUMENTACAO. BOLETIM BIBLIOGRAFICO. 1976. irreg. Banco Nacional da Habitacao, Assessoria Tecnica de Documentacao, Biblioteca, Av. Chile 230, Rio de Janeiro, Brazil. bibl.
　　City planning

301.54　　　　CN　　ISSN 0068-8940
CANADIAN HOUSING STATISTICS. 1955. a. with monthly supplements. free. Canada Mortgage and Housing Corporation, Montreal Road, Ottawa, Ont. K1A OP7, Canada. TEL 613-748-2000.
　　Formerly: Housing in Canada.

352.7　　　　UK　　ISSN 0144-4514
CHARTERED INSTITUTE OF PUBLIC FINANCE AND ACCOUNTANCY. HOMELESSNESS STATISTICS. 1980. a. £10. Chartered Institute of Public Finance and Accountancy, 3 Robert St., London WC2N 6BH, England.

352.7　　　　UK　　ISSN 0307-0468
CHARTERED INSTITUTE OF PUBLIC FINANCE AND ACCOUNTANCY. HOUSING MAINTENANCE & MANAGEMENT. ACTUALS STATISTICS. 1967. a. £14. Chartered Institute of Public Finance and Accountancy, 3 Robert St., London WC2N 6BH, England. (back issues avail.)

352.7　　　　UK　　ISSN 0260-4078
CHARTERED INSTITUTE OF PUBLIC FINANCE AND ACCOUNTANCY. HOUSING REVENUE ACCOUNTS. ACTUALS STATISTICS. 1951. a. £14. Chartered Institute of Public Finance and Accountancy., 3 Robert St., London WC2N 6BH, England. (back issues avail.)
　　Formerly: Chartered Institute of Public Finance and Accountancy. Housing Part 2: Revenue Accounts. Actuals Statistics (ISSN 0307-1316)

352.7　　　　UK
CHARTERED INSTITUTE OF PUBLIC FINANCE AND ACCOUNTANCY. HOUSING REVENUE ACCOUNT ESTIMATE STATISTICS. 1975. a. £14. Chartered Institute of Public Finance and Accountancy, 3 Robert St., London WC2N 6BH, England. (back issues avail.)
　　Formerly: Chartered Institute of Public Finance and Accountancy. Housing Estimate Statistics (ISSN 0260-4086)

352.7　　　　UK　　ISSN 0260-406X
CHARTERED INSTITUTE OF PUBLIC FINANCE AND ACCOUNTANCY. HOUSING RENTS. STATISTICS. 1969. a. £14. Chartered Institute of Public Finance and Accountancy, 3 Robert St., London WC2N 6BH, England. (back issues avail.)
　　Formerly: Chartered Institute of Public Finance and Accountancy. Housing Part 1: Rents. Actuals Statistics (ISSN 0307-1308)

EKISTIC INDEX. see *SOCIOLOGY — Abstracting, Bibliographies, Statistics*

314　352.7　　FI　　ISSN 0355-2152
FINLAND. TILASTOKESKUS. ASUNTOTUOTANTO/FINLAND. STATISTIKCENTRALEN. BOSTADSPRODUKTIONEN/FINLAND. CENTRAL STATISTICAL OFFICE. CONSTRUCTION OF DWELLINGS. (Section XVIII D of Official Statistics of Finland) (Text in Finnish, Swedish and English) 1968. a. Fmk.35. Central Statistical Office, P.O. Box 504, SF-00101 Helsinki, Finland.

360　　　　FI　　ISSN 0430-5604
FINLAND. TILASTOKESKUS. TALONRAKENNUSTILASTO/FINLAND. STATISTIKCENTRALEN. HUSBYGGNADSSTATISTIK/FINLAND. CENTRAL STATISTICAL OFFICE. BUILDING CONSTRUCTION STATISTICS. (Section XVIII C of Official Statistics of Finland) (Text in Finnish, Swedish and English) 1961. a. Fmk.58. Tilastokeskus, Annankatu 44, SF-00100 Helsinki 10, Finland (Subscr. to: Government Printing Centre, Box 516, SF-00100 Helsinki 10, Finland)

352　016　　　　UK　　ISSN 0268-7925
GEOGRAPHICAL ABSTRACTS F (REGIONAL AND COMMUNITY PLANNING) 1972. 6/yr. £43.50. Geo Abstracts Ltd., Regency House, 34 Duke St., Norwich NR3 3AP, England. Ed. R. Land. index; cum.index: 1972-1976. circ. 1,100. (back issues avail.)
　　Formerly: Geo Abstracts F (Regional and Community Planning) (ISSN 0305-1943)

350　016　　US　　ISSN 0046-8908
INDEX TO CURRENT URBAN DOCUMENTS. 1972. q. (with a. cumulation) $250. Greenwood Press, 88 Post Rd. W., Box 5007, Westport, CT 06881. TEL 203-226-3511. Ed. Mary Kalb. index. (also avail. in microfiche)

352.7　310　　　　NR
NIGERIA. FEDERAL OFFICE OF STATISTICS. REPORT ON RURAL HOUSEHOLD SURVEY. a. £N2. Federal Office of Statistics, P.M.B. 12528, Lagos, Nigeria.

352.7　310　　　　NR
NIGERIA. FEDERAL OFFICE OF STATISTICS. REPORT ON URBAN HOUSEHOLD SURVEY. a. £N2. Federal Office of Statistics, P.M.B. 12528, Lagos, Nigeria.

350.865　312　　　　PH
PHILIPPINES. NATIONAL CENSUS AND STATISTICS OFFICE. LISTING OF CITIES, MUNICIPALITIES AND MUNICIPAL DISTRICTS BY PROVINCE. irreg. P.12($4) National Census and Statistics Office, Ramon Magsaysay Blvd., Box 779, Manila, Philippines.

352.7　016　　US　　ISSN 0090-5747
SAGE URBAN STUDIES ABSTRACTS. 1973. q. $60 to individuals; institutions $125. Sage Publications, Inc., 2111 W. Hillcrest Dr., Newbury Park, CA 91320. TEL 805-499-0721. Ed. Bd. adv. index. (back issues avail.)

352.7　　　　US
SAN DIEGO COUNTY. INFO BULLETIN. POPULATION & HOUSING ESTIMATES. 1965. a. $5. County Department of Planning and Land Use, 5201 Ruffin Road, San Diego, CA 92123. TEL 619-565-3025. Ed. Joey Perry. charts. stat. circ. controlled. (looseleaf format)
　　Former titles: San Diego County. Department of Planning and Land Use. County Data Base; San Diego County Planning Department. Planning Data.

352.7　316　　　　SA
SOUTH AFRICA. CENTRAL STATISTICAL SERVICE. CENSUS OF TOWNSHIP DEVELOPERS/SENSUS VAN DORPSONTWIKKELAARS. (Text in Afrikaans and English) biennial. Central Statistical Service, Private Bag X44, Pretoria, South Africa. stat.
　　Formerly: South Africa. Department of Statistics. Census of Township Developers.

301.54　　　　SA
SOUTH AFRICA. CENTRAL STATISTICAL SERVICE. STATISTICS OF HOUSES AND DOMESTIC SERVANTS AND OF FLATS. (Report No. 11-03) (Text in Afrikaans and English) a. Central Statistical Service, Private Bag X44, Pretoria 0001, South Africa (Orders to: Government Printer, Bosman St., Private Bag X85, Pretoria 0001, South Africa)
　　Formerly: South Africa. Department of Statistics. Statistics of Houses and Domestic Servants and of Flats.

301.54　　　　CE
SRI LANKA. CENSUS OF POPULATION AND HOUSING. (Text in English) every 10 yrs., last issue 1981. Rps.35. Department of Census and Statistics, P.O. Box 563, 6 Albert Crescent, Colombo 7, Sri Lanka. circ. 2,920.

352.7　310　　　　SW
SWEDEN. STATISTISKA CENTRALBYRAAN. ALLMAAN FASTIGHETSTAXERING. 1975. irreg. Statistiska Centralbyraan, Distribution, S-701 89 Oerebro, Sweden.

301.54　　　　US　　ISSN 0082-9366
U.S. BUREAU OF THE CENSUS. CENSUS OF HOUSING. (Issued in several series) 1940. decennial. price varies. U.S. Bureau of the Census, Customer Service, Washington, DC 20233 TEL 301-763-4100. (Orders to: Supt. of Documents, Washington, DC 20402)

352.7 310 US ISSN 0147-7870
U.S. DEPARTMENT OF HOUSING AND URBAN DEVELOPMENT. STATISTICAL YEARBOOK. a. $7.50. U.S. Department of Housing and Urban Development, Washington, DC 20410 TEL 202-655-4000. (Orders to: Supt. Doc., Washington, DC 20402) Key Title: Statistical Yearbook of the U.S. Department of Housing and Urban Development.
Formerly: H U D Statistical Yearbook (ISSN 0190-275X)

314 IT ISSN 0041-896X
UNIVERSITA DEGLI STUDI DI FIRENZE. ISTITUTO DI STATISTICA. DOCUMENTAZIONE; Ricerca sul problema delle abitazioni in Italia. (Summaries in English and French) 1965. irreg. price varies. Universita degli Studi di Firenze, Istituto di Statistica, Via Curtatone N.1, Florence, Italy. (Co-sponsor: Consiglio Nazionale delle Ricerche) Ed. Renzo Ricci. circ. 500. (processed)

HUMANITIES: COMPREHENSIVE WORKS

001.3 GW ISSN 0724-9624
DAS ABENDLAND; Forschungen zur Geschichte europaeischen Geisteslebens. Neue Folge. 1972. irreg., vol.16, 1986. price varies. Vittorio Klostermann, Frauenlobstr. 22, Postfach 900601, 6000 Frankfurt 90, W. Germany (B.R.D.) Eds. E. Heftrich.

001.3 BE
ACADEMIAE ANALECTA. MEDEDELINGEN VAN DE KONINKLIJKE ACADEMIE VOOR WETENSCHAPPEN, LETTEREN EN SCHONE KUNSTEN VAN BELGIE. SERIES 2. KLASSE DER LETTEREN. (Text in Dutch and English; summaries in English) 1938. irreg. price varies. Koninklijke Academie voor Wetenschappen, Letteren en Schone Kunsten van Belgie, 1 Hertogsstraat, B 1000 Brussels, Belgium (Subscr. to: Brepols Publishers, Baron Frans du Fourstraat, B-2300 Turnhout, Belgium) Ed. G. Verbeke. circ. 1,000. (back issues avail.)

001.3 500 BE
ACADEMIE ROYALE DES SCIENCES, DES LETTRES ET DES BEAUX-ARTS DE BELGIQUE. ANNUAIRE. 1835. a. 200 Fr. Academie Royale des Sciences, des Lettres et des Beaux-Arts de Belgique, Palais des Academies, 1 rue Ducale, 1000 Brussels, Belgium (Subscr. to: Office International des Periodiques, 114 Bd. Brand Whitlock, 1040 Brussels, Belgium)

001.3 BE
ACADEMIE ROYALE DES SCIENCES, DES LETTRES ET DES BEAUX-ARTS DE BELGIQUE. CLASSE DES LETTRES ET DES SCIENCE MORALES ET POLITIQUES. MEMOIRES. 1904. irreg. price varies. Academie Royale des Sciences, des Lettres et des Beaux-Arts de Belgique., Classe des Lettres et des Science Morales et Politiques, Palais des Academies, 1 rue Ducale, 1000 Brussels, Belgium (Subscr. to: Office International des Periodiques, 114 Bld. Brand Withloch, 1040 Brussels, Belgium) Ed.Bd. circ. 1, 000.

ACCADEMIA LIGURE DI SCIENZE E LETTERE. ATTI. see *SCIENCES: COMPREHENSIVE WORKS*

001.3 SW ISSN 0072-4823
ACTA REGIAE SOCIETATIS SCIENTIARUM ET LITTERARUM GOTHOBURGENSIS. HUMANIORA. (Contributions in various languages) 1967. irreg., no.24, 1986. price varies; also exchange basis. Kungliga Vetenskaps- och Vitterhets-Samhaellet i Goeteborg, c/o Goeteborgs Universitetsbibliotek, Box 5096, S-402 22 Goeteborg, Sweden (Dist. in U.S., Canada and Mexico by: Humanities Press, Inc., 171 First Ave., Atlantic Highlands, NJ 07716)
Supersedes in part: Goeteborgs Kungliga Vetenskaps- och Vitterhets- Samhaelle. Handlingar.

001.3 500 SW ISSN 0347-4925
ACTA REGIAE SOCIETATIS SCIENTIARUM ET LITTERARUM GOTHOBURGENSIS. INTERDISCIPLINARIA. 1977. irreg., no.2, 1979. price varies; also exchange basis. Kungliga Vetenskaps- och Vitterhets-Samhaellet i Goeteborg, c/o Goeteborgs Universitetsbibliotek, Box 5096, S-402 22 Goeteborg, Sweden (Dist. in U.S., Canada and Mexico by: Humanities Press, Inc., 171 First Ave., Atlantic Highlands, NJ 07716)

001.3 370 PL
ACTA UNIVERSITATIS LODZIENSIS: FOLIA SCIENTIARUM ARTIUM ET LIBRORUM POLITOLOGIA. (Text in Polish; summaries in various languages) irreg. Uniwersytet Lodzki, Drukarnia Wojskowa, Ul. Gdanska 130, Lodz, Poland (Dist. by: Ars Polona-Ruch, Krakowskie Przedmiescie 7, Warsaw, Poland)

001.3 SJ ISSN 0302-8844
ADDAB JOURNAL. (Text in English & French) 1972. a. (University of Khartoum, Faculty of Arts) Khartoum University Press, Box 321, Khartoum, Sudan. Ed. Ali Abdalla Abbas. bk. rev.

300 001.3 GW ISSN 0002-2977
AKADEMIE DER WISSENSCHAFTEN UND DER LITERATUR. GEISTES- UND SOZIALWISSENSCHAFTLICHE KLASSE. ABHANDLUNGEN. 1950. irreg. price varies. Franz Steiner Verlag Wiesbaden GmbH, Birkenwaldstr. 44, Postfach 347, D-7000 Stuttgart 1, W. Germany (B.R.D.) bibl. charts. illus. index.

AKADEMIE DER WISSENSCHAFTEN UND DER LITERATUR, MAINZ. JAHRBUCH. see *SCIENCES: COMPREHENSIVE WORKS*

001.3 370 VE
ALBARREGAS.* 1976. irreg. Universidad de los Andes, Facultad de Humanidades y Educacion, Via los Chorras de Milla, C.P. 5101, Merida, Venezuela (Orders to: Oficina Distribucion de Publicaciones, Av. Andres Bello-Via la Parroquia, Merida, Venezuela) Ed. Ramon Palomares. circ. 2,500.

001.3 378 GW ISSN 0342-6785
ALEXANDER VON HUMBOLDT FOUNDATION. ANNUAL REPORT. German edition: Alexander von Humboldt-Stiftung. Jahresbericht (ISSN 0172-3111) 1954. a. free. Alexander von Humboldt-Stiftung, Jean-Paul-Str. 12, D-5300 Bonn 2, W. Germany (B.R.D.) Ed. Heinrich Pfeiffer. index. cum.index: 1953-1983.

001.3 US ISSN 0065-6216
ALFRED P. SLOAN FOUNDATION. REPORT. a. free. Alfred P. Sloan Foundation, 630 Fifth Ave., New York, NY 10020. TEL 212-889-5666. circ. 3, 000. Indexed: Biol.Abstr.

001.3 061 US ISSN 0145-8493
AMERICAN ACADEMY AND INSTITUTE OF ARTS AND LETTERS. PROCEEDINGS. 1951. a. $15 to individuals; libraries $12. American Academy and Institute of Arts and Letters, 633 W. 155 St., New York, NY 10032. TEL 212-368-5900. circ. 600. (back issues avail.) Indexed: Curr.Cont.
Formerly: American Academy of Arts and Letters. Proceedings (ISSN 0065-6836)

ANALES DE LA UNIVERSIDAD HISPALENSE. SERIE: FILOSOFIA Y LETRAS. see *SCIENCES: COMPREHENSIVE WORKS*

060 US ISSN 0066-1694
ANDREW W. MELLON FOUNDATION. REPORT. (Supersedes Report of the Avalon Foundation and Report of the Old Dominion Foundation) 1969. a. free. Andrew W. Mellon Foundation, 140 E. 62nd St., New York, NY 10021. TEL 212-838-8400. circ. 3,000.
Supersedes: Avalon Foundation. Report & Old Dominion Foundation. Report.

942 UK ISSN 0263-6751
ANGLO-SAXON ENGLAND. 1972. a. $45 to individuals; $69 to institutions. Cambridge University Press, Edinburgh Bldg., Shaftesbury Rd., Cambridge CB2 2RU, England (And 32 E. 57th St., New York, NY 10022) Ed.Bd. adv. Indexed: M.L.A. Br.Archaeol.Abstr. RILA. Rel.Ind.Two.

001.3 FI ISSN 0355-113X
ANNALES ACADEMIAE SCIENTIARUM FENNICAE. DISSERTATIONES HUMANARUM LITTERARUM. (Text in English, French, German and Latin) 1973. irreg. Suomalainen Tiedeakatemia - Academia Scientiarum Fennicae, Snellmanikatu 9-11, 00170 Helsinki, Finland. Ed. Yrjo Blomstedt. circ. 500. (reprint service avail. from UMI) Indexed: M.L.A.

900 940 UK ISSN 0263-7383
ANNALES BENJAMIN CONSTANT. 1980. a. £20. Voltaire Foundation, Taylor Institution, St. Giles, Oxford OX1 3NA, England. Ed. Etienne Hofman. (back issues avail.)

ASLIB DIRECTORY OF INFORMATION SOURCES IN THE UNITED KINGDOM. VOLUME 2: SOCIAL SCIENCES, MEDICINE AND THE HUMANITIES. see *SOCIAL SCIENCES: COMPREHENSIVE WORKS*

020 US ISSN 0067-057X
AUGUSTANA LIBRARY PUBLICATIONS. Variant title: Augustana College Library Publications. 1898. irreg., latest no.35, 1981. price varies. Augustana College, Library, Rock Island, IL 61201. TEL 309-794-7266. Ed. John Caldwell. circ. 1,000.

001.3 AT ISSN 0067-1592
AUSTRALIAN ACADEMY OF THE HUMANITIES. PROCEEDINGS. 1970. triennial. price varies. Australian Academy of the Humanities, G.P.O. Box 93, Canberra, A.C.T. 2601, Australia. Ed. G.E.O. Schulz. circ. 1,000.

370 US ISSN 0073-6821
BALL STATE MONOGRAPHS. 1963. irreg., no.32, 1986. free. Ball State University, Faculty Publications Committee, Publications Office, Muncie, IN 47306. TEL 317-285-5946. Ed. Patricia Martin Gibby. circ. 900. (reprint service avail. from UMI) Indexed: Abstr.Engl.Stud.
Earlier issues under former name of organization: Indiana Ball State Teachers College.

BANCO DE LA REPUBLICA. BIBLIOTECA LUIS ANGEL ARANGO. BOLETIN CULTURAL Y BIBLIOGRAFICO. see *BIBLIOGRAPHIES*

900 GW ISSN 0005-710X
BAYERISCHE AKADEMIE DER WISSENSCHAFTEN. PHILOSOPHISCH-HISTORISCHE KLASSE. ABHANDLUNGEN. 1929. biennial. price varies. Bayerische Akademie der Wissenschaften, 8 Marstallplatz, 8000 Munich 22, W. Germany.

900 GW ISSN 0342-5991
BAYERISCHE AKADEMIE DER WISSENSCHAFTEN. PHILOSOPHISCH-HISTORISCHE KLASSE. SITZUNGSBERICHTE. irreg. (3-6/yr.) Bayerische Akademie der Wissenschaften, Marstallplatz 8, 8000 Munich 22, W. Germany(B.R.D.) Indexed: M.L.A.

001.3 GW
BIBLIOGRAPHIA HUMBOLDTIANA. 1977. a. free. Alexander von Humboldt-Stiftung, Jean-Paul-Str. 12, D-5300 Bonn 2, W. Germany (B.R.D.) Ed. Heinrich Pfeiffer. circ. 14,000.
Formerly: Humboldtiana (ISSN 0171-2063)

080 IT ISSN 0067-7434
BIBLIOTECA DI LABEO. 1964. irreg. price varies. Casa Editrice Dott. Eugenio Jovene, Via Mezzocannone, 109, Naples 80134, Italy. Ed.Bd. bk. rev.

080 PO ISSN 0067-7469
BIBLIOTECA DO EDUCADOR PROFISSIONAL. 1968. irreg., no.86, 1984. price varies. Livros Horizonte, Lda., Rua das Chagas, 17, Lisbon 2, Portugal. Ed. Rogenio Mendes de Moura.

001.3 SP
BIBLIOTECA N T; coleccion cultural de bolsillo. 1975. irreg., no.113, 1986. price varies. Ediciones Universidad de Navarra S.A., Apdo. 396, 31080 Pamplona, Spain.
Formerly: Temas N T.

001.3 CN
BIBLIOTHEQUE DES LETTRES QUEBECOISES. irreg. price varies. Presses de l'Universite de Montreal, C.P. 6128, Succ. A, Montreal, Que. H3C 3J7, Canada. TEL 514-343-6929.

BIDRAG TILL KAENNEDOM AV FINLANDS NATUR OCH FOLK. see *SOCIAL SCIENCES: COMPREHENSIVE WORKS*

001.3 407   CL
BIZANTION NEA HELLAS. 1970. a. Universidad de Chile, Centro de Estudios Bizantinos y Neohelenicos, Facultad de Filosofia, Humanidades y Educacion, Av. Larrain 9925, Casilla 10136, Santiago, Chile. Ed. Fotios Malleros. bk. rev. circ. 1,000. Indexed: M.L.A.

BOOK FORUM. see *PUBLISHING AND BOOK TRADE*

742   CN   ISSN 0068-029X
BOREAL INSTITUTE, EDMONTON. MISCELLANEOUS PUBLICATIONS. 1969. irreg. price varies. Boreal Institute for Northern Studies, University of Alberta, Edmonton, Alberta T6G 2E9, Canada. TEL 403-432-4999.

BULLETIN SCIENTIFIQUE. SECTION B: SCIENCES HUMANIES. see *HUMANITIES: COMPREHENSIVE WORKS — Abstracting, Bibliographies, Statistics*

981   BL
CADERNOS DE ESTUDOS BRASILEIROS. 1972. irreg. Cr.$3. Universidade Federal do Rio de Janeiro, Forum de Ciencia e Cultura., Av. Pasteur 250, Praia Vermelha, Rio de Janeiro, Brazil. illus. stat. circ. 5,000.

CAMBRIDGE COMMONWEALTH SERIES. see *HISTORY*

001.3   CN   ISSN 0225-6932
CANADIAN FEDERATION FOR THE HUMANITIES. ANNUAL REPORT. 1945. a. free. ‡ Canadian Federation for the Humanities, 151 Slater St., Ste. 407, Ottawa K1P 5H3, Canada. TEL 613-236-4686. circ. 1,500.
    Formerly: Humanities Research Council of Canada. Report (ISSN 0073-3946)

001.3   US   ISSN 0069-0635
CARNEGIE CORPORATION OF NEW YORK. ANNUAL REPORT. 1921. a. free. Carnegie Corporation of New York, 437 Madison Ave., New York, NY 10022. TEL 212-371-3200. Ed. Avery Russell. circ. 18,000.
    Formerly: Carnegie Corporation of New York. Reports of the Officers.

001.3   US   ISSN 0098-0900
CENTER FOR HERMENEUTICAL STUDIES IN HELLENISTIC AND MODERN CULTURE. PROTOCOL SERIES OF THE COLLOQUIES. 1970. irreg. (3-7/yr.) $6.75 per no. Center for Hermeneutical Studies, 2465 Le Conte Ave., Berkeley, CA 94709. TEL 415-642-6000. (Co-Sponsors: Graduate Theological Union; University of California, Berkeley) circ. 200. (back issues avail.) Indexed: New Test.Abstr.

001.3   FR   ISSN 0069-1976
CENTRE NATIONAL DE LA RECHERCHE SCIENTIFIQUE. COLLOQUES INTERNATIONAUX. SCIENCES HUMAINES. irreg. price varies. Editions du C N R S, 295 rue St. Jacques, 75005 Paris, France.

001.3   US
CHARLES ELIOT NORTON LECTURES. 1938/39. irreg. Harvard University Press, 79 Garden St., Cambridge, MA 02138. TEL 617-495-2600.

051   US   ISSN 0069-2786
CHARTER; Gonzaga University's journal of Liberal Arts. 1961. a. $0.50. ‡ Gonzaga University, Spokane, WA 99258. TEL 509-328-4220. circ. 500.

700   US   ISSN 0009-7349
CIRCULO; revista de cultura. (Text in English and Spanish) 1970. a. $8. Circulo de Cultura Panamericano, 16 Malvern Pl., Verona, NJ 07044. Ed. Elio Alba-Buffill. adv. bk. rev. abstr. bibl. cum.index. circ. 800. Indexed: M.L.A.

001.3   VE   ISSN 0069-5114
COLECCION "HUMANISM Y CIENCIA". (Some vols. issued in more than one part) irreg., no.12, 1977. Universidad Central de Venezuela, Direccion de Cultura, Biblioteca, Piso 10, Ciudad Universitaria, Caracas, Venezuela.

001.3   100   CN
COLLECTED WORKS OF ERASMUS. 1974. irreg. (approx. 2/yr.) price varies. University of Toronto Press, Toronto, Ont. M5S 1A6, Canada. TEL 613-667-7791.

001.3   FI   ISSN 0069-6587
COMMENTATIONES HUMANARUM LITTERARUM. (Text in English, German and Italian) 1923. irreg. price varies. Finnish Society of Sciences and Letters, Snellmansgatan 9-11, SF-00170 Helsinki 17, Finland. Ed. Henrik Zilliacus. circ. 1,000 (approx.) Indexed: Abstr.Engl.Stud. Bull.Signal. M.L.A. Lang.& Lang.Behav.Abstr.

001.3   PL   ISSN 0079-3167
CONFERENZE. (Text in Italian) irreg., vol.91, 1984. price varies. (Polska Akademia Nauk, Stacja Naukowa w Rzymie, IT) Ossolineum, Publishing House of the Polish Academy of Sciences, Rynek 9, 50-106 Wroclaw, Poland (Dist. by: Ars Polona-Ruch, Krakowskie Przedmiescie 7, Warsaw, Poland) Indexed: Math.R.

CONNECTICUT ACADEMY OF ARTS AND SCIENCES. MEMOIRS. see *SCIENCES: COMPREHENSIVE WORKS*

700 060 500   US   ISSN 0069-8989
CONNECTICUT ACADEMY OF ARTS AND SCIENCES. TRANSACTIONS. 1866. irreg., vol.46, 1985. price varies. Archon Books (Subsidiary of: Shoe String Press, Inc.) 925 Sherman Ave, Box 4327, Hamden, CT 06514. TEL 203-248-6307. Ed. Dorothea Rudnick. cum.index in vol.38, 1949. Indexed: Biol.Abstr. GeoRef.

001.3   IT
COSCIENZA DEL TEMPO. irreg. price varies. Edizioni Studium, Via Cassiodoro 14, 00193 Rome, Italy.

CRISI E LETTERATURA; periodico di lettere filosofia arti. see *LITERATURE*

001.3   MX
CRITERIO UNIVERSITARIO. irreg., no.8, 1978. Universidad Autonoma de Chiapas, 2a Poniente Sur 118, Tuxtla Gutierrez, Chiapas, Mexico.

800   IS   ISSN 0084-9456
CRITICISM AND INTERPRETATION; journal for literature, linguistics, history and aesthetics. (Text in Hebrew; summaries in English) 1970. irreg. Bar-Ilan University, Ramat-Gan, Israel. Ed. A. Shanan. Indexed: Ind.Heb.Per.

001.3   US
CROSS-REFERENCE. 1978. irreg. free. Tennessee Committee for the Humanities, Inc., Box 24767, Nashville, TN 37202.

001.3   PR
CRUZ ANSATA. 1978. a. $6. Universidad Central de Bayamon, Bayamon, PR 00619. Dir. Angel Sanz. circ. 3,000.

001.3   SP
CUADERNOS N T. 1975. irreg., no.9, 1980. price varies. Ediciones Universidad de Navarra, S.A., Apdo. 396, 31080 Pamplona, Spain.

001.3   IT   ISSN 0391-8505
CULTURA. 1974. irreg., no.31, 1985. price varies. Edizioni Studium, Via Cassiodoro 14, 00193 Rome, Italy.

CURRENT CONTENTS ADDRESS DIRECTORY-SOCIAL SCIENCES/ARTS & HUMANITIES. see *SOCIAL SCIENCES: COMPREHENSIVE WORKS*

001.3   UK   ISSN 0267-1972
CURRENT RESEARCH IN BRITAIN. HUMANITIES. 1986. a. £34. British Library, Document Supply Centre, Boston Spa, Wetherby, W. Yorkshire LS23 7BQ, England. Ed. A. Young.

001.3 300   US   ISSN 0590-417X
CURRENT RESEARCH IN BRITISH STUDIES BY AMERICAN AND CANADIAN SCHOLARS. 1953. irreg. price varies. (Conference on British Studies) Robin Higham, Ed.& Pub., Eisenhower Hall, Kansas State University, Manhattan, KS 66506-7189. TEL 913-532-6733. (Co-sponsor: the journals Military Affairs, Aerospace Historian) Ed. R. Kent Donovan. circ. 150.

001.3 100 350 352   US
DALLAS INSTITUTE OF HUMANITIES AND CULTURE. INSTITUTE NEWSLETTER. a. $5. Dallas Institute of Humanities and Culture, 2719 Routh St., Dallas, TX 75201. TEL 214-871-2440. Ed. Robert J. Sardello. circ. 10,000.

DISCRETIO. see *LITERARY AND POLITICAL REVIEWS*

940   FR   ISSN 0070-6760
DIX-HUITIEME SIECLE. 1969. a. 95 F. per no. (Societe Francaise d'Etude du Dix Huitieme Siecle) Editions Garnier Freres, 19 rue des Plantes, 75014-Paris, France. Ed. Roland Desne. adv. bk. rev. circ. 2,500. Indexed: M.L.A.

001.4   US   ISSN 0419-8050
DUKE ENDOWMENT. ANNUAL REPORT. 1963. a. free. ‡ Duke Endowment, 200 South Tryon St., Ste. 1100, Charlotte, NC 28202-3214. Ed. Elizabeth H. Locke. illus. circ. 7,500.

EAST AND MAGHREB. see *ETHNIC INTERESTS*

100   CN   ISSN 0071-1063
ERASMUS IN ENGLISH. 1970. irreg. (approx. a.) free. University of Toronto Press, Front Campus, Toronto, Ont. M5S 1A6, Canada. TEL 613-667-7791. Eds. R.M. Schoeffel, P. Tracy. bk. rev. circ. 3,300. Indexed: Hist.Abstr. M.L.A. Amer.Hist.& Life.

100   CN   ISSN 0318-3319
ERASMUS STUDIES. 1973. irreg. price varies. University of Toronto Press, Front Campus, Toronto, Ont. M5S 1A6, Canada TEL 613-667-7791. (U.S. address: 33 E. Tupper St., Buffalo, NY 14203)

001.3   UY   ISSN 0256-3061
ESTUDIOS DE CIENCIAS Y LETRAS. 1981. irreg., latest no.10. Universidad Catolica del Uruguay "Damaso Antonio Larranaga", Instituto de Filosofia, Ciencias y Letras, Avda. 8 de Octubre 2738, Montevideo, Uruguay. bk. rev. circ. 1,000.

001.3   BL
ESTUDOS UNIVERSITARIOS. 1970. irreg., latest 1973. (Faculdades Unidas Catolicas de Mato Grosso, Faculdade Dom Aquino de Filosofia, Ciencias e Letras) Edicoes F U C M T, Av. Mato Grosso 491, Caixa Postal 801, Campo Grande, Mato Grosso, Brazil. Dir. A. Maria da Gloria Sa Rosa. illus.

001.3 890   US   ISSN 0882-3030
FOLIO (BROCKPORT); essays on foreign languages and literature. (Text in English, French, and Spanish) 1970. irreg., no.16, 1984. $8. State University of New York, Department of Foreign Languages, Brockport, NY 14420. TEL 716-395-2269. Ed. Martha O'Nan. adv. bk. rev. circ. 500. (back issues avail.) Indexed: M.L.A.

FORD FOUNDATION ANNUAL REPORT. see *SOCIAL SCIENCES: COMPREHENSIVE WORKS*

940 335   GW   ISSN 0409-1477
FREIE UNIVERSITAET BERLIN. OSTEUROPA-INSTITUT. BERICHTE. 1952. irreg. price varies. Freie Universitaet Berlin, Osteuropa-Institut, Garystr. 55, 1000 Berlin 33 (Dahlem), W. Germany (B.R.D.) circ. 300.

001.3   SP
FUERA DE COLECCION. 1954. irreg., no.9, 1978. price varies. Ediciones Universidad de Navarra, S.A., Apdo. 396, 31080 Pamplona, Spain.

GEOGRAPHICAL SOCIETY OF CHINA. BULLETIN. see *GEOGRAPHY*

551   SW   ISSN 0436-113X
GOETEBORGS KUNGLIGA VETENSKAPS- OCH VITTERHETS-SAMHAELLE. AARSBOK. 1967. a. Kr.40 exchange basis. Kungliga Vetenskaps- och Vitterhets-Samhaellet i Goeteborg, Box 5096, S-402 22 Goeteborg, Sweden (Dist. in U.S., Canada, and Mexico by: Humanities Press, 171 First Ave., Atlantic Highlands, NJ 07716)
    Formerly: Goeteborgs Kungliga Vetenskaps- och Vitterhets-Samhaelle. Handlingar Bihang.

HUMANITIES: COMPREHENSIVE WORKS

001.3   JA   ISSN 0367-4061
GUNMA JOURNAL OF LIBERAL ARTS AND SCIENCES. 1967. a. exchange basis. Gunma University, Faculty of General Studies, Gunma University Library, 1375 Aramaki-cho, Maebashi, Gunma 371, Japan. Ed.Bd. circ. 640.

001.3   JA   ISSN 0386-4294
GUNMA UNIVERSITY. FACULTY OF EDUCATION. ANNUAL REPORT: CULTURAL SCIENCE SERIES. 1950. a. exchange basis. Gunma University, Faculty of Education, Gunma University Library, 4-2, Aramaki, Maebashi, Gunma, Japan. Indexed: M.L.A.

HEBREW ANNUAL REVIEW; a journal of biblical and Hebraic studies. see *LITERATURE*

HELLENIKA; Zeitschrift fuer deutsch-griechische kulturelle und wirtschaftliche Zusammenarbeit. see *LITERATURE*

001.3   FI   ISSN 0073-2702
HISTORISKA OCH LITTERATURHISTORISKA STUDIER. (Subseries of: Svenska Litteratursaellskapet i Finland. Skrifter) (Text in Swedish) 1925. a. Fmk.40. Svenska Litteratursaellskapet i Finland, Snellmansgatan 9-11, 00170 Helsinki 17, Finland. Ed. Torsten Steinby. Indexed: Hist.Abstr. M.L.A. Amer.Hist.& Life.

HITOTSUBASHI JOURNAL OF ARTS AND SCIENCES. see *SCIENCES: COMPREHENSIVE WORKS*

HUMAN SCIENCES RESEARCH COUNCIL. ANNUAL REPORT. see *SOCIAL SCIENCES: COMPREHENSIVE WORKS*

300 700 800   GT   ISSN 0018-7356
HUMANIDADES. vol.8, 1970. irreg. (2-3/yr.) Universidad de San Carlos de Guatemala, Ciudad Universitaria, Guatemala 12, Guatemala. Ed.Bd. bk. rev. bibl.

001.3   PO
HUMANIDADES. 1982. irreg. Universidade do Porto, Associacao de Estudantes da Faculdade de Letras, Porto, Portugal. circ. 1,000.

001.3   DK   ISSN 0107-9573
HUMANIST. 1982. irreg. (approx. 15/yr) free. Koebenhavns Universitet, Humanistisk Facultets Kontor - University of Copenhagen, Faculty of Humanities, Njalsgade 80, 2300 Copenhagen S, Denmark. Ed. Henrik Aegidius. bk. rev. illus. circ. 4,000.

001.3   UK
HUMANITIES IN REVIEW. 1982. irreg. price varies. (New York Institute for the Humanities) Cambridge University Press, Edinburgh Bldg., Shaftesbury Rd., Cambridge CB3 2RU, England (U.S. dist. addr.: 32 E. 57th St., New York, NY 10022) Ed.Bd.

I I A S OCCASIONAL PAPERS. (Indian Institute of Advanced Study) see *EDUCATION — Higher Education*

001.3 060   II   ISSN 0073-6465
INDIAN INSTITUTE OF ADVANCED STUDY. TRANSACTIONS AND MONOGRAPHS. 1965. irreg. price varies. Indian Institute of Advanced Study, Rashtrapati Nivas, Summer Hill, Simla 171005, India.

001.3   II
INDIAN INSTITUTE OF WORLD CULTURE. ANNUAL REPORT. no.18, 1977. a. Indian Institute of World Culture, 6 Shri B.P. Wadia Rd., P.O. Box 402, Basavangudi, Bangalore 560004, India.

054 001.3   FR   ISSN 0980-3637
INSTITUT D'ETUDES SLAVES INFORMATIONS. 1969. irreg. free to members and universities. Institut d'Etudes Slaves, 9 rue Michelet, 75006 Paris, France. bibl.
Formerly: I N E S Informations (ISSN 0339-4212)

INSTITUT DE FRANCE. ANNUAIRE. see *SCIENCES: COMPREHENSIVE WORKS*

054.1   SZ
INSTITUT NATIONAL GENEVOIS. ACTS. 1853. irreg. free. Institut National Genevois, 1, Promenade du Pin, Geneva, Switzerland.

001.3   CK
INSTITUTO CARO Y CUERVO. PUBLICACIONES. 1944. irreg., latest issue, no.70. 1985. price varies. Instituto Caro y Cuervo, Seccion de Publicaciones, Apdo. Aereo 51502, Botoga, Colombia. (back issues avail.)

001.3   SP   ISSN 0584-6374
INSTITUTO DE ESTUDIOS MADRILENOS. ANALES. 1966. irreg. price varies. (Consejo Superior de Investigaciones Cientificas, Instituto de Estudios Madrilenos) Espasa-Calpe, S.A., Carretera de Irun, Km. 12,200, Variente de Fuencarral, Apartado 547, Madrid 34, Spain. Indexed: Hist.Abstr. Amer.Hist.& Life.

001.3   UY
INSTITUTO DE FILOSOFIA, CIENCIAS Y LETRAS. CUADERNOS. no.6, 1980. irreg. Instituto de Filosofia, Ciencias y Letras, Av. 8 de Octubre 2738, Montevideo, Uruguay.

001.3   BL
INSTITUTO DO PATRIMONIO HISTORICO E ARTISTICO NACIONAL. PUBLICACOES. 1937. irreg. Instituto do Patrimonio Historico e Artistico Nacional, Palacio da Cultura, Rua da Imprensa 16, Rio de Janeiro, Brazil. Dir. Renato Soeiro. bibl. charts. illus.

001.3   PO
INSTITUTO NACIONAL DE INVESTIGACAO CIENTIFICA. TEXTOS HUMANISTICOS PORTUGUESES. irreg. Instituto Nacional de Investigacao Cientifica, Centro de Estudos Classicos, Coimbra, Portugal.

INTERNATIONAL CONFERENCE OF ORIENTALISTS IN JAPAN. TRANSACTIONS. see *HISTORY*

001.3 100   UN
INTERNATIONAL COUNCIL FOR PHILOSOPHY AND HUMANISTIC STUDIES. BULLETIN. (Editions in English and French) 1949. biennial. free. ‡ International Council for Philosophy and Humanistic Studies, c/o Maison de l'Unesco, 1 rue Miollis, 75732 Paris Cedex 15, France. circ. 3,200. (back issues avail.)
Formerly: International Council for Philosophy and Humanistic Studies. General Assembly. Compte Rendu (ISSN 0074-4298)

900   UK
INTERNATIONAL DIRECTORY OF EIGHTEENTH-CENTURY STUDIES/ REPERTOIRE INTERNATIONAL DES DIX-HUITIEMISTES. 1969. quadrennial. Voltaire Foundation, Taylor Institution, Oxford OX1 3NA, England. adv. circ. 5,000.

001.3   FR   ISSN 0074-6819
INTERNATIONAL LITERARY AND ARTISTIC ASSOCIATION. PROCEEDINGS AND REPORTS OF CONGRESS. (Text in English and French) irreg., 54th, 1972, Paris. International Literary and Artistic Association, c/o A. Francon, 55 rue des Mathurins, 75008 Paris, France.

001.3   UK   ISSN 0578-6967
IRAN. (Text in English, French, German) 1963. a. £20($40) British Institute of Persian Studies, 13 Cambrian Rd., Richmond, Surrey TW10 6JQ, England. Ed. Vesta Curtis. circ. 600. (back issues avail.)

ISTITUTO GIAPPONESE DI CULTURA, ROME. ANNUARIO. see *HISTORY — History Of Europe*

001.3 300   JA   ISSN 0385-4132
IWATE MEDICAL UNIVERSITY SCHOOL OF LIBERAL ARTS & SCIENCES. ANNUAL REPORT. (Text in English, German and Japanese) 1966. a. free. Iwate Ika Daigaku Kyoyobu, 16-1, 3-Chome, Honcho-Dori, Morioka-shi, Iwate-Ken, Japan. circ. 350. (back issues avail.)

001.3   GW
JAHRBUCH KREIS EUSKIRCHEN. 1951. a. DM.7. Kreis Euskirchen, Ed. & Pub., Julicher Ring 32, 5350 Euskirchen, W. Germany (B.R.D.) adv. circ. 7,000.

JAHRBUCH LANDKREIS KASSEL. see *HISTORY — History Of Europe*

001.3   JA
JAPAN FOUNDATION ANNUAL REPORT. (Text in English) a. free. Japan Foundation, Park Bldg., 3-6, Kioi-cho, Chiyoda-ku, Tokyo 102, Japan.

001.3   IS   ISSN 0333-9831
JERUSALEM INSTITUTE FOR ISRAEL STUDIES. DISCUSSION PAPERS. irreg. Jerusalem Institute for Israel Studies, 20A Radak St., Jerusalem 92 186, Israel. TEL 02-630175.

001.3 060   JA   ISSN 0084-5515
JIMBUN. (Text in English or French) 1957. a. Kyoto University, Research Institute for Humanistic Studies - Kyoto Daigaku Jimbun Kagaku Kenkyujo, 50 Kitashirakawa Oiwake-cho, Sakyo-ku, Kyoto 606, Japan. circ. controlled.

060   JA   ISSN 0521-7903
JOURNAL OF CULTURAL SCIENCES/BUNKA KAGAKU KIYO. (Text in Japanese) 1959. a. Chiba University, Faculty of Humanities and Social Sciences, 1-33 Yayoicho, Chiba 280, Japan.

700   UK   ISSN 0075-4390
JOURNAL OF THE WARBURG AND COURTAULD INSTITUTES. 1937. a. £30. Warburg Institute, University of London, Woburn Square, London, WC1H 0AB, England. Ed.Bd. index. cum.index: vols.1-37. circ. 1,300. Indexed: Curr.Cont. Arts & Hum.Cit.Ind. RILA.

001.3 300   CE
KALYANI; journal of humanities and social sciences of the University of Kelaniya. 1982. a. Rs.100($15) University of Kelaniya, c/o Librarian, Kelaniya, Sri Lanka. Eds. Prof. A. Liyanagamage, Prof. Y. Karunadasa, Prof. S. Bandaranayake. bk. rev. circ. 550.

089   JA
KANAGAWA UNIVERSITY. INSTITUTE OF HUMANITIES. BULLETIN. (Text in Japanese; summaries in English) 1965. a. Kanagawa University, Institute of Humanities, 3-chome Rokkaku-bashi, Kanagawa-ku, Yokahama, Japan.

001.3   II   ISSN 0075-515X
KARNATAK UNIVERSITY, DHARWAD, INDIA. JOURNAL. HUMANITIES. (Text mainly in English; occasionally in French, German and Sanskrit) 1957. a. Rs.8($4) Karnatak University, Director, Prasaranga, Dharwad 580003, Karnataka, India. Ed. C.G. Dubey. circ. 500.

001.3 080   US   ISSN 0075-5265
KATHERINE ASHER ENGEL LECTURES. 1958. irreg., latest 1983. price varies. Smith College Library, Office of Director of Technical Services, Northampton, MA 01063. TEL 413-584-2700. (reprint service avail. from UMI)

001.3   KE
KENYA NATIONAL ACADEMY FOR ADVANCEMENT OF ARTS AND SCIENCES. FOUNDATION LECTURES. 1965. irreg. no.6, 1974. Kenya National Academy for Advancement of Arts and Sciences, P.O. Box 47288, Nairobi, Kenya.
Formerly: East African Academy. Foundation Lectures.

001.3 060   KE
KENYA NATIONAL ACADEMY FOR ADVANCEMENT OF ARTS AND SCIENCES. PROCEEDINGS. 1964. a. EAs.70($9) Kenya National Academy for Advancement of Arts and Sciences, Box 47288, Nairobi, Kenya.
Formerly: East African Academy. Proceedings (ISSN 0070-7945)

KNOWLEDGE AND SOCIETY; studies in the sociology of culture past and present. see *SOCIOLOGY*

001.3 300   JA
KOBE UNIVERSITY OF MERCANTILE MARINE. REVIEW. PART 1. STUDIES IN HUMANITIES AND SOCIAL SCIENCE. (Text in Japanese; abstracts in English) 1952. a. Kobe University of Mercantile Marine, 5-1-1 Fukae-Minami-machi, Higashinada-ku, Kobe 658, Japan.

001.3   SZ   ISSN 0075-6520
KOELNER ROMANISTISCHE ARBEITEN. irreg., no.63, 1985. price varies. (Universitaet zu Koeln, Romanisches Seminar, GW) Librarie Droz, 11, rue Massot, 1211 Geneva 12, Switzerland. circ. 500.

HUMANITIES: COMPREHENSIVE WORKS

001.3 100   DK   ISSN 0106-0481
KONGELIGE DANSKE VIDENSKABERNES SELSKAB. HISTORISK-FILOSOFISKE MEDDELELSER. (Text in Danish and English, summaries in English) 1917. irreg., vol.52, no.3, 1985. price varies. Kongelige Danske Videnskabernes Selskab - Royal Danish Academy of Sciences and Letters, H.C. Andersens Blvd. 35, DK-1553 Copenhagen V, Denmark (Orders to: Munksgaard Export and Subscription Service, Noerre Soegade 35, DK-1370 Copenhagen K, Denmark) Ed. Erik Dal. bibl. circ. 800. (back issues avail) Indexed: M.L.A.

001.3   DK   ISSN 0023-3307
KONGELIGE DANSKE VIDENSKABERNES SELSKAB. HISTORISK-FILOSOFISKE SKRIFTER. (Text mainly in English) 1940. irreg., vol.11, 1985. price varies. Kongelige Danske Videnskabernes Selskab - Royal Danish Academy of Sciences and Letters, H.C. Andersens Blvd. 35, DK-1553 Copenhagen V, Denmark (Orders to: Munksgaard Export and Subscription Service, Noerre Soegade 35, DK-1370 Copenhagen K, Denmark) bibl. illus. index.

001.3   DK   ISSN 0368-7201
KONGELIGE DANSKE VIDENSKABERNES SELSKAB. OVERSIGT OVER SELSKABETS VIRKSOMHED. ANNUAL REPORT. (Text in Danish; summary in English) 1814. a. Kongelige Danske Videnskabernes Selskab - Royal Danish Academy of Sciences and Letters, H.C. Andersens Blvd. 35, DK-1553 Copenhagen V, Denmark (Orders to: Munksgaard Export and Subscription Service, Noerre Soegade 35, DK-1370 Copenhagen K, Denmark) illus. Indexed: Biol.Abstr. Chem.Abstr.

KONGELIGE NORSKE VIDENSKABERS SELSKAB. see *SCIENCES: COMPREHENSIVE WORKS*

KONGELIGE NORSKE VIDENSKABERS SELSKAB. SKRIFTER/ROYAL NORWEGIAN SOCIETY OF SCIENCES. PUBLICATIONS. see *SCIENCES: COMPREHENSIVE WORKS*

001.3   NE   ISSN 0065-5511
KONINKLIJKE NEDERLANDSE AKADEMIE VAN WETENSCHAPPEN. AFDELING LETTERKUNDE. VERHANDELINGEN. NIEUWE REEKS. (Text in Dutch, English, French and German) 1896. irreg., vol.129, 1985. price varies. ‡ Elsevier Science Publishers B.V., P.O. Box 211, 1000 AE Amsterdam, Netherlands. Ed. A.M. Verheggen. adv. bk. rev. circ. 1,000.

001.3   PL   ISSN 0075-7179
KSIAZKA W DAWNEJ KULTURZE POLSKIEJ. 1951. irreg., vol.12, 1984. price varies. (Polska Akademia Nauk, Instytut Badan Literackich) Ossolineum, Publishing House of the Polish Academy of Sciences, Rynek 9, 50-106 Wroclaw, Poland (Dist. by: Ars Polona-Ruch, Krakowskie Przedmiescie 7, Warsaw, Poland) Ed.Bd.

001.3   DK   ISSN 0107-3591
KULTUR OG SAMFUND; tekster. 1979. irreg. free. (Roskilde Universitetscenter, Institut VI) Academic Forlag, Postboks 260, 4000 Roskile, Denmark. Eds. Michel Olsen, Soeren Schou. illus. circ. 300.

001.3   JA   ISSN 0075-7381
KYOTO PREFECTURAL UNIVERSITY. SCIENTIFIC REPORTS: HUMANITIES/KYOTO-FURITSU DAIGAKU GAKUJUTSU HOKOKU JIMBUN. (Text in Japanese; summaries in English) 1952. irreg., no.28, 1976. exchange basis. Kyoto Prefectural University - Kyoto-furitsu Daigaku, Shimogamo Hangi-cho, Sakyo-ku, Kyoto 606, Japan. Ed. Z. Hayashino.

300   JA   ISSN 0453-0349
KYUSHU INSTITUTE OF TECHNOLOGY. BULLETIN: HUMANITIES, SOCIAL SCIENCES/KYUSHU KOGYO DAIGAKU KENKYU HOKOKU, JINBUN-SHAKAI-KAGAKU. (Text in Japanese, English or German) 1953. a. exchange basis. Kyushu Institute of Technology - Kyushu Kogyo Daigaku, 1-1 Sensui-cho, Tobata, Kitakyushu 804, Japan.

LATIN AMERICAN MONOGRAPH AND DOCUMENT SERIES. see *SOCIAL SCIENCES: COMPREHENSIVE WORKS*

001.3   PL   ISSN 0208-4996
LUBELSKIE TOWARZYSTWO NAUKOWE. WYDZIAL HUMANISTYCZNY. PRACE. MONOGRAFIE. irreg., no.6, 1967. (Lubelskie Towarzystwo Naukowe) Panstwowe Wydawnictwo Naukowe, Miodowa 10, 00-251 Warsaw, Poland (Dist. by: Ars Polona, Krakowskie Przedmiescie 7, 00-068 Warsaw, Poland) Ed. M. Wawrzyniak. bibl. circ. 470.

MAISON FRANCO-JAPONAISE. BULLETIN. see *ORIENTAL STUDIES*

MAKEDONSKA AKADEMIJA NA NAUKITE I UMETNOSTITE. LETOPIS. see *SCIENCES: COMPREHENSIVE WORKS*

001.3 700   GW
MASSSTAEBE. 1964. irreg. DM.21.50. Verlag der Massstaebe, Hafenstr. 6, Postfach 143, 2890 Nordenham, W. Germany (B.R.D.) Ed. Norbert Weiss. bk. rev. Indexed: Sociol.Abstr. RILM.

001.3   CK   ISSN 0120-1344
MEMORIAS MARTES DEL PARANINFO. 1980. irreg. exchange basis. Universidad de Antioquia, Extension Cultural, Medellin, Colombia.

001.3   GW
MINERVA; INTERNATIONALES VERZEICHNIS WISSENSCHAFTLICHER INSTITUTIONEN. 1891. irreg. price varies. Walter de Gruyter & Co., Mouton Pulishers, Genthiner Str. 13, 1000 Berlin 30, W. Germany (B.R.D.) adv.
Formerly: Minerva; Jahrbuch der Gelehrten Welt (ISSN 0076-8960)

001.3   UK
MODERN HUMANITIES RESEARCH ASSOCIATION. PUBLICATIONS. 1969. a. price varies. Modern Humanities Research Association, King's College, Strand, London WC2R 2LS, England.
Formerly: Modern Humanities Research Association. Monograph (ISSN 0076-9983)

060   VE
MONTALBAN. 1972. a. Bs.120($40) ‡ Universidad Catolica Andres Bello, Facultad de Letras, Departamento de Humanidades, Apdo. 29068, Caracas, Venezuela. Ed. Jose del Ray Fayardo. circ. 1,200. Indexed: Hist.Abstr. Amer.Hist.& Life. Hisp.Amer.Per.Ind. Lang.& Lang.Behav.Abstr.

001.3 300   BE
MUSEE ROYAL DE L'AFRIQUE CENTRALE. ANNALES. SERIE IN 8. SCIENCES HUMAINES/KONINKLIJK MUSEUM VOOR MIDDEN-AFRIKA. ANNALEN. REEKS IN 8. MENSELIJKE WETENSCHAPPEN. irreg., no.120, 1985. price varies. Musee Royal de l'Afrique Centrale, 13 Steenweg op Leuven, B-1980 Tervuren, Belgium. Indexed: Lang.& Lang.Behav.Abstr.

MUSICAL INTERPRETATION RESEARCH. see *MUSIC*

001.3   US   ISSN 0083-2111
NATIONAL ENDOWMENT FOR THE HUMANITIES. ANNUAL REPORT. 1966. a. U.S. National Endowment for the Humanities, 1100 Pennsylvania Ave., N.W., Washington, DC 20506. TEL 202-786-0435. circ. 3,000.

001.3   PY
NEMITY; revista bilingue de cultura. 1977. irreg. $12. Distribuidora Comuneros, Pte. Franco 480, Casella 930, Asuncion, Paraguay. Ed. Natalia K. de Canese. bk. rev.

491 940 300   NZ   ISSN 0028-8683
NEW ZEALAND SLAVONIC JOURNAL. (Text mainly in English; Cyrillic script occasionally) 1967. a. NZ.$12. Victoria University of Wellington, Department of Russian, Private Bag, Wellington, New Zealand. Ed. P.H. Waddington. bk. rev. play rev. circ. 175. (processed) Indexed: Hist.Abstr. M.L.A. Ind.N.Z.Per. Amer.Hist.& Life.

001.3   SW   ISSN 0078-0901
NOBEL SYMPOSIUM SERIES. (Publisher varies) 1966. irreg., no.54, 1982. price varies. Nobel Foundation, Nobel House, P.O. Box 5232, 102 45 Stockholm, Sweden. Indexed: Biol.Abstr. Chem.Abstr.

NORTHERN ILLINOIS UNIVERSITY. CENTER FOR SOUTHEAST ASIAN STUDIES. OCCASIONAL PAPERS SERIES. see *HISTORY — History Of Asia*

NORTHERN ILLINOIS UNIVERSITY. CENTER FOR SOUTHEAST ASIAN STUDIES. SPECIAL REPORT SERIES. see *HISTORY — History Of Asia*

001.3 800   US
NOTEBOOKS IN CULTURAL ANALYSIS. 1984. a. price varies. (New York University, Institute for Cultural Analysis) Duke University Press, 6697 College Sta., Durham, NC 27708. TEL 919-684-2173. Eds. Norman F. Cantor, Nathalia King.

930 800 001.3   MX
NOVA TELLUS. (Text in Greek, Latin, Spanish) 1983. a. Universidad Nacional Autonoma de Mexico, Direccion General de Publicaciones, Ciudad Universitaria, 04510 Mexico, D.F., Mexico. (back issues avail.)

001.3 100   IT
NUOVI ANNALI DELLA FACOLTA DI MAGISTERO DELL'UNIVERSITA DI MESSINA. (Text in Italian) 1983. a. L.102000($90) (Facolta di Magistero) Herder Editrice e Liberia, Piazza Montecitorio 117-120, 00186 Roma, Italy. Ed. Antonio Mazzarino.

001.3   IT   ISSN 0078-2769
NUOVI SAGGI. 1953. irreg., no.93, 1985. price varies. Edizioni dell' Ateneo S.p.A., P.O. Box 7216, 00100 Rome, Italy. circ. 2,000.

OESTERREICHISCHE AKADEMIE DER WISSENSCHAFTEN. ALMANACH. see *SCIENCES: COMPREHENSIVE WORKS*

083   AU
OESTERREICHISCHE AKADEMIE DER WISSENSCHAFTEN. IRANISCHE KOMMISSION. VEROEFFENTLICHUNGEN. (Subseries of: Oesterreichische Akademie der Wissenschaften. Philosophisch-Historische Klasse. Sitzungsberichte) 1973. irreg. Verlag der Oesterreichischen Akademie der Wissenschaften, Ignaz Seipelplatz 2, A-1010 Vienna, Austria.

100 001.3 830   GW   ISSN 0078-5539
OPUSCULA - AUS WISSENSCHAFT UND DICHTUNG. 1962. irreg. DM.7.80. Verlag Guenther Heske, Kloster, 7417 Pfullingen, W. Germany (B.R.D.)

054.1   FR   ISSN 0031-0387
PALLAS; revue interuniversitaire. 1952. a. 60 F. Universite de Toulouse II (le Mirail), Service des Publications, 56 rue du Taur, 31069 Toulouse Cedex, France. (Co-sponsors: Universite de Limoges; Universite de Montpellier; Universite de Pau; Universite de Perpignan) Ed. M.P. Duminil. illus.

001.3   SP
PARERGA. 1970. irreg., no.10, 1973. price varies. Ediciones Universidad de Navarra, S.A., Apdo. 396, 31080 Pamplona, Spain.

001.3   AT
PEASANTS IN HISTORY AND LITERATURE. 1981. a. Aus.$2.40. Australian Academy of the Humanities, GPO Box 93, Canberra, A.C.T. 2601, Australia.

001.3   PL   ISSN 0079-3531
POLSKA AKADEMIA NAUK. ODDZIAL W KRAKOWIE. ROCZNIK. 1959. a. price varies. Ossolineum, Publishing House of the Polish Academy of Sciences, Rynek 9, 50-106 Wroclaw, Poland (Dist. by: Ars Polona-Ruch, Krakowskie Przedmiescie 7, Warsaw, Poland)

POLSKIE TOWARZYSTWO NAUKOWE NA OBCZYZNIE. ROCZNIK. see *SCIENCES: COMPREHENSIVE WORKS*

001.3   SA   ISSN 0079-4333
POTCHEFSTROOM UNIVERSITY FOR CHRISTIAN HIGHER EDUCATION. WETENSKAPLIKE BYDRAES. REEKS A: GEESTESWETENSKAPPE. (Text in Afrikaans and English) 1971. irreg. free. Potchefstroom University for Christian Higher Education, Potchefstroom, South Africa. circ. 350.

HUMANITIES: COMPREHENSIVE WORKS

001.3   AT
PRESS, THE LAW AND BEYOND; a view from the press council. 1985. triennial. price varies. Australian Academy of the Humanities, G.P.O. Box 93, Canberra, A.C.T. 2601, Australia. Ed. G.E.O. Schultz. circ. 500.

001.3   701.18   US
PRINCETON ESSAYS ON THE ARTS. 1975. irreg. price varies. Princeton University Press, 3175 Princeton Pike, Lawrenceville, NJ 08648. TEL 609-452-4900. (reprint service avail. from UMI)

PROBLEMATA. see *PHILOSOPHY*

060   BG   ISSN 0483-9218
RAJSHAHI UNIVERSITY STUDIES.* vol.4, 1972. a. University of Rajshahi, c/o M. Rahman, Rajshahi, Bangladesh. Ed. A.F.S. Ahmed. adv.

001.3   UK   ISSN 0486-3720
RENAISSANCE AND MODERN STUDIES. 1957. a. £6. (University of Nottingham) Sisson & Parker, 25 Wheeler Gate, Nottingham NG1 2NF, England. (Co-sponsor: Renaissance & Modern Studies) Eds. R.A. Cardwell, M.C.E. Jones. adv. bibl. circ. 500. (also avail. in microform from UMI; reprint service avail. from UMI) Indexed: Br.Hum.Ind. M.L.A. Abstr.Engl.Stud.

REPERTOIRE INTERNATIONAL DES MEDIEVISTES. see *HISTORY — History Of Europe*

378.54   II
RESEARCH JOURNAL: HUMANITIES AND SOCIAL SCIENCES. (Text in English and Hindi) 1972. irreg. Rs.5. University of Indore, University House, Indore 452001, Madhya Pradesh, India. bibl. illus.

001.3   JA
REVIEW ON LIBERAL ARTS/KYOYO RONSHU. (Text in English or Japanese) 1975. irreg. Kokushikan University, Society of Liberal Arts - Kokushikan Daigaku Kyoyo Gakkai, 4-28-1 Setagaya, Setagaya-ku, Tokyo 154, Japan.

001.3   056.1   PR   ISSN 0378-7974
REVISTA DE ESTUDIOS HISPANICOS; estudios de lengua y litertura. (Text in English, French, Spanish) 1971. a. $3.50 to individuals; students $2; institutions $5. University of Puerto Rico, Seminario de Estudios Hispanicos "Federico de Onis", Rio Piedras, PR 00931 TEL 809-764-0000. (Subscr. to: Oficina de Publicaciones, Facultad de Humanidades, Universidad de Puerto Rico, Rio Piedras, PR 00931) Ed. Jose Luis Vega. adv. bk. rev. bibl. circ. 1,000. (also avail. in microform from UMI; reprint service avail. from UMI) Indexed: M.L.A.

001.3   VE
REVISTA NACIONAL DE CULTURA.* irreg., no.246, 1981. (Consejo Nacional de la Cultura) Venezuelan book Service, Apdo. Postal 47963, Caracas 1041-A, Venezuela. Ed. Francisco Perez Perdomo. adv. Indexed: Abstr.Engl.Stud. Hisp.Amer.Per.Ind.

001.3   FR
REVUE DE PAU ET DU BEARN. 1973. a. 70 F. Societe de Sciences, Lettres et Arts de Pau, 13 av. Trespoey, 64000 Pau, France. Ed.Bd. bibl. illus.

001.3   IT   ISSN 0080-3073
RINASCIMENTO. (Text in English, French, German and Italian) 1938. a. L.50000. Istituto Nazionale di Studi sul Rinascimento, Palazzo Strozzi, Piazza Strozzi, 50213 Florence, Italy. Ed. Eugenio Garin. circ. 800. Indexed: Arts & Hum.Cit.Ind. RILA.
   Formerly (until 1950): Rinascita.

001.3   PL
ROCZNIK DOLNOSLASKI. 1972. irreg. price varies. (Dolnoslaskie Towarzystwo Oswiatowe) Panstwowe Wydawnictwo Naukowe, Miodowa 10, 00-251 Warsaw, Poland. bk. rev. illus. circ. 1,800.

SAECULA SPIRITALIA. see *HISTORY*

060   II   ISSN 0080-5416
SAHITYA AKADEMI, NEW DELHI. REPORT. (Text in English) 1954/55. a. free. National Academy of Letters - Sahitya Akademi, Rabindra Bhavan, New Delhi 110001, India.

300   SZ   ISSN 0080-5807
SAMMLUNG DALP. 1946. irreg., vol.106, 1978. price varies. ‡ Francke Verlag, Postfach, CH-3000 Berne 26, Switzerland.

001.3   US   ISSN 0161-7729
SCHOLARS' FACSIMILES & REPRINTS. 1936. irreg., vol.420, 1986. price varies. Scholars' Facsimiles & Reprints, Inc., Box 344, Delmar, NY 12054. Ed. Norman Mangouni. (also avail. in microfiche; back issues avail.)

040   IS   ISSN 0080-8369
SCRIPTA HIEROSOLYMITANA. (Text in English) 1954. irreg. price varies. (Hebrew University of Jerusalem) Magnes Press, Jerusalem, Israel. Indexed: Biol.Abstr.

001.3   FR   ISSN 0085-6037
SEMITICA. 1948. a., vol.35, 1985. 180 F. (Universite de Paris III (Sorbonne-Nouvelle), Institut d'Etudes Semitiques) Adrien Maisonneuve, 11 rue St Sulpice, 75006 Paris, France. (Co-sponsor: Centre National de la Recherche Scientifique) Ed.Bd. Indexed: Old Test.Abstr.

001.3   500   II   ISSN 0080-9314
SHIVAJI UNIVERSITY, KOLHAPUR, INDIA. JOURNAL. HUMANITIES AND SCIENCES. (Text in English) 1968. a. (in 2 parts) Rs.10. Shivaji University, Registrar, Kolhapur, 416004 Maharashtra, India. Eds. V.B. Ghuge, A.T. Varute. bk. rev. circ. 377. Indexed: Biol.Abstr. Chem.Abstr.

001.3   YU   ISSN 0352-8650
SLAVONSKI POVIJESNI ZBORNIK. 1963. biennial. 2000 din. Centar za Povijest Slavonje i Baranje (C.P.S.B.), Starceviceva 8, 55000 Slavonski Brod, Yugoslavia. Ed. Mile Konjevic. circ. 500.
   Former titles: Centar za Drustvena Istrazivanja Slavonije i Baranje. Zbornik (ISSN 0352-1168); (until 1983): Historijski Institut Slavonije i Baranje. Zbornik.

001.3   YU
SLOVENSKO MORJE IN ZALEDJE. (Text in Slovene; summaries in English, Italian) 1977. biennial. Zalozba Lipa, Muzejski trg. 7, 66000 Koper, Yugoslavia. bk. rev. circ. 350.

001.3   BE   ISSN 0085-6169
SNOECK'S ALMANACH. 1782. a. 70 Fr. Snoeck-Ducaju en Zoon N.V., Begijnhoflaan 464, B-9000 Ghent, Belgium. Ed. Serge Snoeck. adv. circ. 100, 000.

001.3   BE   ISSN 0085-6177
SNOECK'S; LITERATUUR KUNST FILM TONEEL MODE REIZEN. 1923. a. 230 Fr. Snoeck-Ducaju en Zoon N.V., Begijnhoflaan 464, B-9000 Ghent, Belgium. Ed. Serge Snoeck. adv. bk. rev. circ. 126, 000.

001.3   CH
SOOCHOW JOURNAL OF HUMANITIES. 1976. a. $10 per no. Soochow University, Wai Shuang Shi, Shih Lin, Taipei, Taiwan, Republic of China.

001.3   IT   ISSN 0490-4788
SPOLETIUM; rivista di arte storia cultura. 1954. a. L.15000. Academia Spoletina, Palazzo Mauri, Via Brignone 14, 06049 Spoleto, Italy. circ. 1,500.

001.3   500   YU   ISSN 0081-4032
SRPSKA AKADEMIJA NAUKA I UMETNOSTI SPOMENICA. (Text in Serbo-Croatian; summaries in English, French, German or Russian) 1888. irreg. price varies. Srpska Akademija Nauka i Umetnosti, Knez Mihailova 35, 11001 Belgrade, Yugoslavia (Dist. by: Prosveta, Terazije 16, Belgrade, Yugoslavia) circ. 700.

301.2   UN   ISSN 0586-6898
STUDIES AND DOCUMENTS ON CULTURAL POLICIES. (Subseries of Unesco. Documents) irreg. Unesco, 7 Place de Fontenoy, 75700 Paris, France (Dist. in U.S. by: Bernan Associates-Unipub, 4611-F Assembly Dr., Lanham, MD 20706-4391)

001.3   900   US
STUDIES IN EIGHTEENTH CENTURY CULTURE; American Society for Eighteenth Century Studies. Proceedings of the Annual Meeting. (Vols.1-3 published by Case Western Reserve) irreg., vol.7, 1978. price varies. University of Wisconsin Press, 114 N. Murray St., Madison, WI 53715. TEL 608-262-4952. (reprint service avail. from UMI) Indexed: M.L.A.

001.3   500   300   SJ   ISSN 0453-8129
SUDAN RESEARCH INFORMATION BULLETIN. (Issued in two sections) 1965. irreg. University of Khartoum, Sudan Unit, Box 321, Khartoum, Sudan.

SURREALIST TRANSFORMACTION. see *ART*

060   US
SURVEY OF GRANT-MAKING FOUNDATIONS.* 3rd edt., 1977. a. $15.95. Public Service Materials Center, 5130 Macarthur Blvd.,N.W., Apt. 200, Washington, DC 20016-3316.

080   SA   ISSN 0082-1330
T.B. DAVIE MEMORIAL LECTURE. 1959. a. R.0.50. University of Cape Town, Private Bag, Rondebosch 7700, South Africa.

001.3   US   ISSN 0082-2779
TENNESSEE TECH JOURNAL. 1966. a. free. Tennessee Technological University, Box 5183, Cookeville, TN 38501. TEL 615-528-3368. Ed. Homer D. Kemp. abstr. circ. 1,300. (back issues avail.)

600   US   ISSN 0082-3198
TEXAS TECH UNIVERSITY. GRADUATE STUDIES. 1972. irreg. price varies. Texas Tech University Press, Box 4139, Lubbock, TX 79409. TEL 806-742-1593. Ed. Wendell W. Broom.

001.3   JA   ISSN 0285-3825
TOHOKU INSTITUTE OF TECHNOLOGY. MEMOIRS. SERIES 2: HUMANITIES AND SOCIAL SCIENCE. (Text in English or Japanese; summaries in English) 1981. a. Tohoku Institute of Technology, 35-1 Yagiyama-Kasumicho, Sedai 982, Japan. (back issues avail.)

040   JA   ISSN 0495-7601
TOKUSHIMA UNIVERSITY. JOURNAL OF GAKUGEI/TOKUSHIMA DAIGAKU GAKUGEI KIYO. (Text in Japanese; summaries in English) 1951. a. Tokushima University, Faculty of Education - Tokushima Daigaku Kyoiko Gakubu, Kyoiku-gakubu, Tokushima, Japan. circ. 450. Indexed: Biol.Abstr.
   Formerly: Journal of Cultural Sciences.

300   700   800   US   ISSN 0049-4127
TOPIC; a journal of the liberal arts. 1961. a. $1. Washington & Jefferson College, Washington, PA 15301. TEL 412-222-4400. circ. 1,000. Indexed: M.L.A. Amer.Bibl.Slavic & E.Eur.Stud. Abstr.Engl.Stud.

TRADITIO; studies in ancient and medieval history, thought, and religion. see *HISTORY — History Of Europe*

TURKIYAT MECMUASI. see *HISTORY — History Of The Near East*

001.3   FI   ISSN 0082-6987
TURUN YLIOPISTO. JULKAISUJA. SARJA B. HUMANIORA. (Latin title: Annales Universitatis Turkuensis) (Text in English, Finnish, French, German) 1923. irreg. price varies. Turun Yliopisto - University of Turku, SF-20500 Turku 50, Finland (Dist. by: Akateeminen Kirjakauppa, SF-00100 Helsinki10, Finland)

001.3   500   FI   ISSN 0082-6995
TURUN YLIOPISTO. JULKAISUJA. SARJA C. SCRIPTA LINGUA FENNICA EDITA. (Latin title: Annales Universitatis Turkuensis) (Text in Finnish; summaries in English, French, German) 1965. irreg. price varies. Turun Yliopisto, SF-20500 Turku 50, Finland (Dist. by: Akateeminen Kirjakauppa, SF-00100 Helsinki 10, Finland)

U P RESEARCH MONITOR. (University of the Philippines) see *SCIENCES: COMPREHENSIVE WORKS*

001.3   SW   ISSN 0345-0155
UMEAA STUDIES IN THE HUMANITIES. (Subseries of Acta Universitatis Umensis) 1975. irreg., no.8, 1975. Kr.37.25. Almqvist & Wiksell International, P.O. Box 45150, S-10430 Stockholm, Sweden. Ed. Per G. Raberg.

UNCOVERINGS; research papers. see *HISTORY — History Of North And South America*

060   BE   ISSN 0074-9346
UNION ACADEMIQUE INTERNATIONALE.
COMPTE RENDU DE LA SESSION
ANNUELLE DU COMITE. 1920. irreg., 57th,
1983. (International Union of Academies) Office
International de Librairie, 30 av. Marnix, B-1050
Brussels, Belgium.

001.3   CK
UNIVERSIDAD DE ANTIOQUIA.
DEPARTAMENTO DE HISTORIA.
COLECCION PAPELES DE TRABAJO. 1977.
irreg. Universidad de Antioquia, Departamento de
Historia, Medellin, Colombia.
   Formerly: Universidad de Antioquia.
Departamento de Humanidades. Coleccion Papeles
de Trabajo.

001.3   SP   ISSN 0072-5382
UNIVERSIDAD DE GRANADA. COLLECCION
MONOGRAFICA. 1970. irreg. price varies.
Universidad de Granada, Departamento de Historia
del Arte, Secretariado de Publicaciones, Granada,
Spain.

001.3   SP   ISSN 0463-9863
UNIVERSIDAD DE MURCIA. ANALES DE
LETRAS. 1930. irreg., vol.43, 1985. ($1000)
Universidad de Murcia, Secretariado de
Publicaciones e Intercambio Cientifico, Santo Cristo,
1, 30001 Murcia, Spain. TEL 968 24 92 00.
   Former titles (until 1980): Universidad de
Murcia. Filosofia y Letras; Until 1954: Universidad
de Murcia. Anales de Letras.

001.3   GT
UNIVERSIDAD DE SAN CARLOS ANUAL. 1945.
a. Universidad de San Carlos de Guatemala, Ciudad
Universitaria, Guatemala 12, Guatemala. Ed.Bd. bk.
rev. bibl.

001.3 080   AG   ISSN 0068-3485
UNIVERSIDAD DEL SALVADOR. ANALES. 1963.
a. $3. Universidad del Salvador, Alberti 158, Buenos
Aires, Argentina.

001.3   VE
UNIVERSIDAD DEL ZULIA. REVISTA. 1947; N.S.
1958. irreg. Universidad del Zulia, Direccion de
Cultura, Apartado 526, Maracaibo, Venezuela.
Indexed: Biol.Abstr.

001.3   CK   ISSN 0120-095X
UNIVERSIDAD INDUSTRIAL DE SANTANDER.
REVISTA - HUMANIDADES. (Text in Spanish;
summaries in English, French, German and Spanish)
1969. irreg. $2 per no. or exchange basis.
Universidad Industrial de Santander, Apdo. Aereo
678, Bucaramanga, Santander, Colombia. adv. bk.
rev. bibl. charts. illus. cum.index every 5 yrs.
   Supersedes in part: Universidad Industrial de
Santander. Revista.

UNIVERSIDAD INDUSTRIAL DE SANTANDER.
REVISTA - INVESTIGACIONES. see
ENGINEERING

001.3   MX
UNIVERSIDAD NACIONAL AUTONOMA DE
MEXICO. INSTITUTO DE INVESTIGACIONES
ESTETICAS. MONOGRAFIAS. SERIE MAYOR.
1977. irreg., latest issue 1977. price varies.
Universidad Nacional Autonoma de Mexico,
Instituto de Investigaciones Esteticas, Torre I de
Humanidades, Ciudad Universitaria, Mexico 20,
D.F., Mexico.

060   AG   ISSN 0564-4070
UNIVERSIDAD NACIONAL DE TUCUMAN.
FACULTAD DE FILOSOFIA Y LETRAS.
CUADERNOS DE HUMANITAS.* 1959. irreg.,
no.40, 1972. Universidad Nacional de Tucuman,
Facultad de Filosofia y Letras, Ayacucho 482, San
Miguel de Tucuman, Argentina. Ed. Bd. bibl.

001.3   VE   ISSN 0076-4345
UNIVERSIDAD NACIONAL DEL ZULIA.
FACULTAD DE HUMANIDADES Y
EDUCACION. CONFERENCIAS Y
COLOQUIOS.* irreg. Bs.7($1.60) Universidad del
Zulia, Facultad de Humanidades y Educacion,
Apartado 526, Maracaibo, Venezuela.

001.3   IT
UNIVERSITA DEGLI STUDI DI BARI. CENTRO
STUDI BIZANTINI. CORSI DI STUDI. 1976.
irreg., approx. every 3 yrs. price varies. L'erma di
Bretschneider, Via Cassiodoro 19, 00193 Rome,
Italy.

060   IT
UNIVERSITA DEGLI STUDI DI CAGLIARI.
FACOLTA DI LETTERE - FILOSOFIA.
ANNALI. 1976. irreg. L.10000. Universita degli
Studi di Cagliari, Facolta di Lettere-Filosofia,
Cagliari, Italy (Orders to: Libreria Cocco, Bargo
Carlo Felice 76, I-09100 Cagliari, Italy) abstr. illus.
circ. 425.
   Supersedes in part (1936-1975): Universita di
Cagliari. Facolta di Lettere - Filosofia e Magistero.
Annali.

060   IT
UNIVERSITA DEGLI STUDI DI CAGLIARI.
FACOLTA DI MAGISTERO. ANNALI. 1976.
irreg., no.2, 1977. Universita degli Studi di Cagliari,
Facolta di Magistero, 09100 Cagliari, Italy. abstr.
illus. circ. 425.
   Supersedes in part (1936-1975): Universita di
Cagliari. Facolta di Lettere-Filosofia e Magistero.
Annali.

001.3   IT
UNIVERSITA DI NAPOLI. FACOLTA DI
LETTERE E FILOSOFIA. ANNALI. 1950/51. a.
exchange basis only. Universita di Napoli, Facolta di
Lettere e Filosofia, Via Porta Di Massa 1, 80134
Napoli, Italy. Ed. Prof. Marcello Gigante. circ. 600.

085   RM
UNIVERSITATEA DIN CRAIOVA. ANALELE:
SERIA ISTORIE, GEOGRAFIE, FILOLOGIE.
(Text in Rumanian; summaries in French and/or
English, German, Italian, Russian) 1972. irreg. $10.
Universitatea din Craiova, Str. A.I. Cuza Nr. 13,
1100 Craiova, Rumania (Subscr. to: ILIXIM, Str. 13
Decembrie Nr. 3, P.O. Box 136-137, Bucharest,
Rumania) illus.

001.3   BE   ISSN 0076-1222
UNIVERSITE CATHOLIQUE DE LOUVAIN.
FACULTE DE PHILOSOPHIE ET LETTRES.
TRAVAUX. 1967. irreg. 1348 Louvain-la-Neuve,
Belgium. TEL tel: 32-10-434880. Ed. Tony
Hachens. circ. 2,000.

001.3   BE
UNIVERSITE DE LIEGE. FACULTE DE
PHILOSOPHIE ET LETTRES. PUBLICATIONS.
1897. irreg. Universite de Liege, Faculte de
Philosophie et Lettres, 7 Place du 20-Aout, Liege,
Belgium.

UNIVERSITE DE PARIS. FACULTE DES
LETTRES ET SCIENCES HUMAINES.
PUBLICATIONS. SERIE ACTA. see SCIENCES:
COMPREHENSIVE WORKS

001.3   FR   ISSN 0751-4239
UNIVERSITE DE PROVENCE. CENTRE D'AIX.
CAHIERS D'ETUDES GERMANIQUES. a.
Universite de Provence, Centre d'Aix, 29 Avenue
Robert Schuman, 13621 Aix-en-Provence, France.

001.3   FR   ISSN 0223-9469
UNIVERSITE DE SAINT ETIENNE. CENTRE
JEAN PALERNE. MEMOIRES. 1978. irreg. 80 F.
Universite de Saint Etienne, Centre Jean Palerne, 2
rue Trefilerie, 42100 Saint Etienne, France.

UNIVERSITE DE STRASBOURG II. INSTITUT DE
PHONETIQUE. TRAVAUX. see LINGUISTICS

001.3   BE
UNIVERSITE LIBRE DE BRUXELLES. FACULTE
DE PHILOSOPHIE ET LETTRES. TRAVAUX.
1930. irreg. Editions de l'Universite de Bruxelles,
Avenue P. Heger, 26-C.P. 163, B-1050 Brussels,
Belgium.

001.3   SA   ISSN 0070-7740
UNIVERSITY OF DURBAN-WESTVILLE.
JOURNAL/UNIVERSITEIT VAN DURBAN-
WESTVILLE. TYDSKRIF. (Text in English and
Afrikaans) 1965. a. exchange basis. University of
Durban-Westville, Private Bag X54001, Durban
4000, South Africa. Ed. G.A. Rauche. bk. rev. circ.
1,000. Indexed: Biol.Abstr. Ind.S.A.Per.

001.3   US   ISSN 0071-6189
UNIVERSITY OF FLORIDA MONOGRAPHS.
HUMANITIES. (Text in English, French and
Spanish) 1959. irreg., no.57, 1985. price varies.
University Presses of Florida, 15 N.W. 15 St.,
Gainesville, FL 32603. TEL 904-392-1351. Ed.
Raymond Gay-Crosier.

001.3   NR
UNIVERSITY OF IFE. FACULTY OF ARTS.
LECTURE SERIES. 1974. irreg. University of Ife,
Faculty of Arts, Ile-Ife, Nigeria.

001.3   US   ISSN 0085-2473
UNIVERSITY OF KANSAS HUMANISTIC
STUDIES. 1912. irreg. (approx. a.) price varies. ‡
University of Kansas, Lawrence, KS 66045. TEL
913-864-3347. Ed. David Bergeron.

001.3   NR   ISSN 0075-7675
UNIVERSITY OF LAGOS. HUMANITIES SERIES.
1971. irreg. price varies. (University of Lagos) Lagos
University Press, P.O. Box 132, Akoka, Yaba,
Lagos, Nigeria.

001.3   NR   ISSN 0075-7659
UNIVERSITY OF LAGOS. INAUGURAL
LECTURE SERIES. 1968. irreg. price varies.
(University of Lagos) Lagos University Press, P.O.
Box 132, Akoka, Yaba, Lagos, Nigeria.

001.3   US   ISSN 0076-9703
UNIVERSITY OF MISSOURI STUDIES. 1926.
irreg., no.69, 1980. price varies. University of
Missouri Press, 200 Lewis Hall, Columbia, MO
65211. TEL 314-882-2121. Indexed: Biol.Abstr.
Abstr.Engl.Stud.

001.3   US   ISSN 0077-6386
UNIVERSITY OF NEBRASKA STUDIES. NEW
SERIES. 1946. irreg., no.67, 1984. available on
exchange basis only. University of Nebraska-
Lincoln, Committee on Scholarly Publications,
Serials Department, Lincoln, NE 68588-0410. TEL
402-472-3874. Ed. Susan Rosowski. circ. 600. (also
avail. in microfilm) Indexed: M.L.A.

UNIVERSITY OF PITTSBURGH. CENTER FOR
INTERNATIONAL STUDIES. LATIN
AMERICAN REPRINT SERIES. see SOCIAL
SCIENCES: COMPREHENSIVE WORKS

060   SA
UNIVERSITY OF PORT ELIZABETH.
PUBLICATIONS. BIBLIOGRAPHIES. (Text in
Afrikaans and English) 1977. irreg., no.E 3, 1986.
University of Port Elizabeth, Library, Private Bag
X6058, Port Elizabeth 6000, South Africa. Ed.Bd.

001.3 060   SA   ISSN 0079-3957
UNIVERSITY OF PORT ELIZABETH.
PUBLICATIONS. GENERAL SERIES. (Text in
Afrikaans and English) 1965. irreg., latest no.A 16,
1984. price varies. University of Port Elizabeth,
Library, Private Bag X6058, Port Elizabeth 6000,
South Africa. Ed.Bd.

001.3   SA   ISSN 0085-5022
UNIVERSITY OF PORT ELIZABETH.
PUBLICATIONS. INAUGURAL AND
EMERITUS ADDRESSES. (Text in Afrikaans and
English) 1971. irreg., no. D14, 1986. price varies.
University of Port Elizabeth, Library, Private Bag
X6058, Port Elizabeth 6000, South Africa. Ed.Bd.

001.3 060   SA   ISSN 0079-3965
UNIVERSITY OF PORT ELIZABETH.
PUBLICATIONS. RESEARCH PAPERS. (Text in
Afrikaans and English) 1970. irreg., no.C 24, 1986.
price varies. University of Port Elizabeth, Library,
Private Bag X6058, Port Elizabeth 6000, South
Africa. Ed. Bd. circ. 500.

001.3 060   SA
UNIVERSITY OF PORT ELIZABETH.
PUBLICATIONS. SYMPOSIA, SEMINARS, AND
LECTURES. (Text in Afrikaans and English) 1969.
irreg., no.B 13,1986. price varies. University of Port
Elizabeth, Library, Private Bag X6058, Port
Elizabeth 6000, South Africa. Ed.Bd.
   Formerly: University of Port Elizabeth.
Publications. Symposia and Seminars (ISSN 0079-
3973)

001.3   PH   ISSN 0069-1321
UNIVERSITY OF SAN CARLOS. SERIES A: HUMANITIES. (Text in English) 1964. irreg., no.16, 1985. P.145($9.50) price varies. (University of San Carlos) San Carlos Publications, Cebu City 6401, Philippines (Dist. by: Cellar Book Shop, 18090 Wyoming, Detroit, MI 48221) Ed. Joseph Baumgartner. circ. 547.

UNIVERSITY OF SIND. RESEARCH JOURNAL. ARTS SERIES: HUMANITIES AND SOCIAL SCIENCES. see *ART*

UNIVERSITY OF WISCONSIN-MILWAUKEE. CENTER FOR LATIN AMERICA. BIBLIOGRAPHIC SERIES. see *HISTORY — History Of North And South America*

001.3   US
UNIVERSITY OF WYOMING AMERICAN STUDIES CONFERENCE. PROCEEDINGS. irreg., no.2, 1982. University of Wyoming, School of American Studies, Laramie, WY 82071. TEL 307-766-1121.

001.3   PL   ISSN 0208-4740
UNIWERSYTET GDANSKI. WYDZIAL HUMANISTYCZNY. ZESZYTY NAUKOWE. SLAWISTYKA. (Text in Polish; summaries in English and Russian) 1978. irreg. price varies. Uniwersytet Gdanski, Ul. Armii Czerwonej 110, 81-824 Sopot, Poland. Ed. Leszek Moszynski.

001.3   PL   ISSN 0076-034X
UNIWERSYTET LODZKI. PRACE. irreg. price varies. Uniwersytet Lodzki, Narutowicza 65, Lodz, Poland (Dist. by: Ars Polona-Ruch, Krakowskie Przedmiescie 7, Warsaw, Poland)

001.3   IT
VERIFICHE E PROPOSTE. 1975. irreg. Tringale Editore, Via Vecchia Ognina 90, 95129 Catania, Italy. Ed. Ermanno Scuderi.

943.7   CS
VLASTIVEDNY ZBORNIK. (Text in Slovak; summaries in German and Russian) 1973. irreg. 25.50. Matica Slovenska, Mudronova 35, 036 52 Martin, Czechoslovakia. illus.

700   UK
WARBURG INSTITUTE. OXFORD-WARBURG STUDIES. 1963. irreg. price varies. (Warburg Institute) Oxford University Press, Walton St., Oxford OX2 6DP, England. (Co-sponsor: Clarendon Press)

700   UK   ISSN 0083-7199
WARBURG INSTITUTE. STUDIES. 1939. irreg. price varies. Warburg Institute, University of London, Woburn Square, London WC1H 0AB, England.

700   UK   ISSN 0266-1772
WARBURG INSTITUTE. SURVEYS AND TEXTS. 1963. irreg. price varies. Warburg Institute, University of London, Woburn Square, London WC1H 0AB, England.
   Formerly: Warburg Institute. Surveys (ISSN 0083-7202)

060   US   ISSN 0083-9167
WHERE AMERICA'S LARGE FOUNDATIONS MAKE THEIR GRANTS;* who gets them and how much each receives. 1971/1972. irreg., latest 1983/84. $44.50. Public Service Materials Center, 5130 Macarthur Blvd., N.W., Apt. 200, Washington, DC 20016-3316. Ed. Joseph Dermer.

001.3   PL   ISSN 0084-3016
WROCLAWSKIE TOWARZYSTWO NAUKOWE. PRACE. SERIA A. HUMANISTYKA. (Text in English, French, German and Polish; summaries in English, French and German) 1947. irreg., no.236, 1986. price varies. Ossolineum, Publishing House of the Polish Academy of Sciences, Rynek 9, Wroclaw, Poland (Dist. by: Ars Polona-Ruch, Krakowskie Przedmiescie 7, Warsaw, Poland) Indexed: Math.R.

001.3   PL   ISSN 0078-544X
WYZSZA SZKOLA PEDAGOGICZNA, OPOLE. ZESZYTY NAUKOWE. SERIA B. STUDIA I MONOGRAFIE. (Text in Polish; summaries in English, German, Polish, Russian) 1956. irreg., no.92, 1983. price varies. Wyzsza Szkola Pedagogiczna, Opole, Oleska 48, Opole, Poland (Dist. by: Ars Polona-Ruch, Krakowskie Przedmiescie 7, Warsaw, Poland) bk. rev.

001.3   PH   ISSN 0084-3229
XAVIER UNIVERSITY. MUSEUM AND ARCHIVES PUBLICATIONS. 1970. irreg., no.18, latest issue. price varies. Xavier University, Cagayan de Oro 8401, Philippines. Ed. Francisco Demetrio y Radaza. (processed)

001.3   080   US   ISSN 0084-3318
YALE COLLEGE SERIES. 1964. irreg., no.14, 1976. price varies. Yale University Press, 92A Yale Station, New Haven, CT 06520. TEL 203-432-0940.

001.3   JA   ISSN 0085-834X
YAMAGATA UNIVERSITY. BULLETIN. (Bulletin issued in 6 parts) (Text in English, German, Japanese; summaries in English and German) 1950. a. Yamagata University, Main Library, 1-4-12 Koshirakawa-machi, Yamagata City, Japan. Indexed: Biol.Abstr. Sci.Abstr.

001.3   800   UK   ISSN 0306-2473
YEARBOOK OF ENGLISH STUDIES. 1971. a. $48. Modern Humanities Research Association, King's College, Strand, London WC2R 2CS, England. Ed. C.J. Rawson. bk. rev. bibl. Indexed: M.L.A. Abstr.Engl.Stud. Ind.Bk.Rev.Hum.

YEARBOOK ON HUMAN RIGHTS. see *POLITICAL SCIENCE — Civil Rights*

HUMANITIES: COMPREHENSIVE WORKS — Abstracting, Bibliographies, Statistics

016   810   US   ISSN 0361-0144
AMERICAN HUMANITIES INDEX. 1975. q. $165. Whitston Publishing Co. Inc., Box 958, Troy, NY 12181. TEL 518-283-4363. Ed. Jean Goode. bibl. cum.index. circ. 200. (back issues avail.)

001.3   016   SZ   ISSN 0067-7000
BIBLIOGRAPHIE INTERNATIONALE DE L'HUMANISME ET DE LA RENAISSANCE. 1965. a. price varies. (International Federation of Societies and Institutes for the Study of the Renaissance) Librarie Droz, 11, rue Massot, 1211 Geneva 12, Switzerland. circ. 1,200.

700   800   016   UK   ISSN 0007-0815
BRITISH HUMANITIES INDEX. 1915. 4/yr. (plus annual cumulation) £165($376) Library Association Publishing Ltd., 7 Ridgmount St., London WC1E 7AE, England. Ed. M. Duffus. (also avail. in microform from MIM)

001.3   YU   ISSN 0350-1604
BULLETIN SCIENTIFIQUE. SECTION B: SCIENCES HUMANIES. 1965. s-a. 1000 din.($50) Jugoslovenska Akademija Znanosti i Umjetnosti, Zrinski trg. 11, 41000 Zagreb, Yugoslavia. Ed. Milan Mogus. index. circ. 1,000. (back issues avail.)

001.3   016   US   ISSN 0069-2824
CHECKLISTS IN THE HUMANITIES AND EDUCATION. 1971. irreg. Trinity University Press, Trinity University, 715 Stadium Dr., San Antonio, TX 78284. TEL 512-736-7619. Ed. Harry B. Caldwell. index.

CLIO BIBLIOGRAPHY SERIES. see *HISTORY — Abstracting, Bibliographies, Statistics*

001.3   016   US   ISSN 0163-3155
CURRENT CONTENTS/ARTS & HUMANITIES. Short title: C C/A & H. (Includes Author Index and Address Directory, Current Book Contents, and Title Word Index) 1979. w. $283 domestic. Institute for Scientific Information, 3501 Market St., Philadelphia, PA 19104 TEL 215-386-0100. (And 132 High St., Uxbridge, Middlesex, UB8 1DP, England) (also avail. in magnetic tape) Indexed: SSCI.

300   016   US   ISSN 0419-4209
DISSERTATION ABSTRACTS INTERNATIONAL. SECTION A: HUMANITIES AND SOCIAL SCIENCES. 1938. m. $155. University Microfilms International, 300 N. Zeeb Rd., Ann Arbor, MI 48106. TEL 313-761-4700. abstr. index. circ. 2,000(combined) (also avail. in microfiche from UMI; reprint service avail. from UMI) Indexed: Biol.Abstr. Chem.Abstr. M.L.A. Psychol.Abstr. GeoRef. Geotech.Abstr. Music Ind. Popul.Ind. RAPRA. Rural Recreat.Tour.Abstr. World Agri.Econ.& Rural Sociol.Abstr.
   Formerly: Dissertation Abstracts.

001.3   US   ISSN 0095-5981
HUMANITIES INDEX; an author and subject index to periodicals in the fields of archaeology and classical studies, area studies, folklore, history, language and literature, literary and political criticism, performing arts, philosophy, religion and theology, and related subjects. 1974. q. (annual cumulations) service basis. ‡ H.W. Wilson Co., 950 University Ave., Bronx, NY 10452. TEL 212-588-8400. Ed. Elizabeth Pingree. (avail. on CD-ROM)
●Also available online. Vendors: Wilsonline.
   Supersedes in part: Social Sciences and Humanities Index (ISSN 0037-7899)

001.3   016   II
INDEX ASIA SERIES IN HUMANITIES. 1965. irreg. price varies. Centre for Asian Dokumentation, P.O. Box 7015, New Delhi 110002, India. Ed. S. Chaudhuri. bk. rev. index.
   Bibliographies and indexes

001.3   028   US   ISSN 0073-5892
INDEX TO BOOK REVIEWS IN THE HUMANITIES. 1960. a. $30. Phillip Thomson, Ed. & Pub., 836 Georgia St., Williamston, MI 48895. TEL 517-655-2930. circ. 1,050. (back issues avail.)

300   016   JA   ISSN 0021-5341
JAPANESE PERIODICALS INDEX. HUMANITIES AND SOCIAL SCIENCE SECTION/ZASSHI KIJI SAKUIN. JIMBUN SHAKAI-HEN. (Text in Japanese) 1948. q. 21200 Yen. National Diet Library - Kokuritsu Kokkai Toshokan, 1-10-1 Nagata-cho, Chiyoda-ku, Tokyo 100, Japan. index. circ. 1,200.

THESIS ABSTRACTS. see *AGRICULTURE — Abstracting, Bibliographies, Statistics*

HUMANITIES: COMPREHENSIVE WORKS — Computer Applications

200   001.6   BE
CENTRE; Bible data bank. (Text in English, French, German) 1981. biennial. 250 Fr. (Association Internationale "Bible et Informatique") N.V. Brepols I.G.P., Rue Baron du Four 8, B-2300 Turnhout, Belgium. Ed. R.F. Poswick. bibl. stat. circ. 1,200. (also avail. in magnetic tape)

301.16   001.53   US
COMMUNICATION THEORY IN THE CAUSE OF HUMANITY; notes on the application of theory to the strengthening of democratic institutions. 1970. irreg., approx. 2/yr. $6 for 4 nos. 2346 Lansford Ave., Box 5095, San Jose, CA 95150. Ed. Frederick B. Wood. circ. 150. (back issues avail.)
●Also available online.
   Former titles: Communication Theory in the Cause of Mankind & Communication Theory in the Cause of Man (ISSN 0162-8216)

COMPUTERS AND PEOPLE SERIES. see *COMPUTERS*

001.3   380.3   US
JOURNAL OF HUMAN COMMUNICATIONS RESEARCH; a forum for bio-medical communications research. (Text in English; summaries in German and Spanish) 1981. a. $3500. (Communications Research Labs) C R L Publishing Co., 223 W. 38th St., Box 62, New York, NY 10018. Ed. Gary A. Henderson. adv. bk. rev. abstr. bibl. charts. index. cum.index. (also avail. in microfiche)

HYDRAULIC ENGINEERING

see Engineering—Hydraulic Engineering

HYDROLOGY

see Earth Sciences—Hydrology

INDUSTRIAL HEALTH AND SAFETY

see also Business and Economics—Labor and Industrial Relations

614.7 US
AMERICAN CONFERENCE OF GOVERNMENTAL INDUSTRIAL HYGIENISTS. TRANSACTIONS OF THE ANNUAL MEETING. vol.39, 1976. a. $40. American Conference of Governmental Industrial Hygienists, Inc., 6500 Glenway Ave., Bldg. D-7, Cincinnati, OH 45211. TEL 513-661-7881. circ. 3,500. (back issues avail.)

613.62 US
AMERICAN INDUSTRIAL HYGIENE ASSOCIATION. CONFERENCE PROCEEDINGS. a. $3. American Industrial Hygiene Association, 475 Wolf Ledges Pkwy., Akron, OH 44311-1087. TEL 216-762-7294.

613 DK
ARBEJDSBETINGEDE LIDELSER. YEARBOOK. (Illness at Work) no.20, 1979. a. free. Arbejdstilsynets Ulykkesstatistik - Directorate of National Labor Inspection, Postboks 858, 2100 Copenhagen OE, Denmark. Eds. Ole Svane, Ole Brun. circ. 1,000.

614.8 NE
ARBO JAARBOEK. 1959. a. fl.77.50. Veiligheidsinstituut, Postbus 5665, 1007 AR Amsterdam, Netherlands. adv. circ. 5,000.
Formerly: Veiligheidsjaarboek (ISSN 0083-534X)

613.62 FR ISSN 0066-927X
ASSOCIATION FRANCAISE DES TECHNICIENS ET INGENIEURS DE SECURITE ET DES MEDECINS DU TRAVAIL. ANNUAIRE. 1965. a. 250 F. 118 rue de la Tombe Issoire, 75014 Paris, France. adv.

614.85 US ISSN 0090-7480
BEST'S SAFETY DIRECTORY; safety-industrial hygiene-security. 1946. a. $15. A.M. Best Co., Ambest Rd., Oldwick, NJ 08858. TEL 201-439-2200. Ed. Paul E. Wish. adv. circ. 19,500.

BRITISH COLUMBIA. MINISTRY OF LABOUR. NEGOTIATED WORKING CONDITIONS. see BUSINESS AND ECONOMICS — Labor And Industrial Relations

331 US
C C H/O S H A COMPLIANCE GUIDE. a. (plus m. reports) $255. Commerce Clearing House, Inc., 4025 W. Peterson Ave., Chicago, IL 60646. TEL 312-583-8500.

CALIFORNIA. DEPARTMENT OF INDUSTRIAL RELATIONS. ANNUAL REPORT. see BUSINESS AND ECONOMICS — Labor And Industrial Relations

613.62 US ISSN 0278-6265
CHEMICAL INDUSTRY INSTITUTE OF TOXICOLOGY SERIES. 1980. irreg., unnumbered, latest 1983. price varies. (Chemical Industry Institute of Toxicology) Hemisphere Publishing Corporation, 79 Madison Ave., New York, NY 10016. bibl. charts. illus. index. (back issues avail.) Indexed: Curr.Cont.

613.62 614.85 NE
CHEMIEKAARTEN. 1977. triennial. fl.160. Veiligheidsinstituut, Postbus 5665, 1007 AR Amsterdam, Netherlands. circ. 10,000.

614.85 CN
CORPUS OCCUPATIONAL HEALTH AND SAFETY MANAGEMENT HANDBOOK. 1985. every 18 months. Can.$157. Corpus Information Services, Division of Southam Communications Ltd., 1450 Don Mills Road, Don Mills, Ont. M3B 2X7, Canada. TEL 416-445-6641. Ed. Frances Makedessian. charts. graphs. illus. circ. 1,300.

331 313.62 US ISSN 0093-1535
EMPLOYMENT SAFETY AND HEALTH GUIDE. 3/yr. (plus w. reports) $505. Commerce Clearing House, Inc., 4025 W. Peterson Ave., Chicago, IL 60646. TEL 312-583-8500.

614.85 DK ISSN 0109-5129
FRAVAER VED ANMELDTE ARBEJDSULYKKER. 1981. quinquennial. free. (Direktoratet for Arbejdstilsynet) Bibliotekscentralen, Telegrafvej 5, DK-2750 Ballerup, Denmark.

613.62 669 EI
GENERAL COMMISSION ON SAFETY AND HEALTH IN THE IRON AND STEEL INDUSTRY. REPORT. (First edition in French only; later editions in Dutch, French, German and Italian) 1966. a. General Commission on Safety and Health in the Iron and Steel Industry, Rue de la Loi 200, 1040 Brussels, Belgium. circ. controlled.

613.62 UK
HANDBOOK OF INDUSTRIAL SAFETY AND HEALTH. 1980. irreg. Trade & Technical Press Ltd., Crown House, Morden, Surrey, SM4 5EW, England.

660 NE
HANDLING CHEMICALS SAFELY. 1980. a. fl.43.50. Veiligheidsinstituut - Safety Instituut, Postbus 5665, 1007 AR Amsterdam, Netherlands. patents. circ. 6,000.

614 UK ISSN 0267-2014
HEALTH AND SAFETY OFFICER'S HANDBOOK. 1983. a. £25. Millbank Publications, 25 Catherine St., London WC2B 5JW, England. TEL 01-379-3036. Ed. A.E. Waring. adv. charts. illus. circ. 4,000.

622 613.62 UK ISSN 0263-3094
HEALTH AND SAFETY: QUARRIES. 1979. a. £3.50. H.M.S.O., Box 569, London SE1 9NH, England.

614.82 FR
I N R S LETTRE D'INFORMATION SUR LA RECHERCHE. English Edition: Safety Research News (ISSN 0765-913X) 1982. irreg. free. Institut National de Recherche et de Securite pour la Prevention des Accidents du Travail et des Maladies Professionnelles, 30 rue Olivier Noyer, 75680 Paris Cedex 14, France. (Co-sponsors: International Social Security Association; International Section for Research on Prevention of Occupational Risks) Eds. M. Thanh & C. Skornik.

614.85 CN ISSN 0073-7305
INDUSTRIAL ACCIDENT PREVENTION ASSOCIATION. ANNUAL REPORT. 1918. a. Industrial Accident Prevention Association, 2 Bloor St. W., Toronto, Ont. M4W 3N8, Canada. TEL 416-965-8888. circ. 12,000.

614.84 UK
INDUSTRIAL FIRE PROTECTION & SECURITY HANDBOOK. 1976. irreg. £72. Trade & Technical Press Ltd., Crown House, Morden, Surrey, SM4 5EW, England.

613.62 US ISSN 0073-7488
INDUSTRIAL HEALTH FOUNDATION. CHEMICAL-TOXICOLOGICAL SERIES. BULLETIN. 1947. irreg., no.8, 1969. price varies. ‡ Industrial Health Foundation, Inc., 34 Penn Circle West, Pittsburgh, PA 15206. TEL 412-363-6600.
Formerly: Industrial Hygiene Foundation. Chemical-Toxicological Series. Bulletin (ISSN 0537-5215)

613.2 US ISSN 0073-7496
INDUSTRIAL HEALTH FOUNDATION. ENGINEERING SERIES. BULLETIN. 1936. irreg., no. 8, 1971. price varies. ‡ Industrial Health Foundation, Inc., 34 Penn Circle West, Pittsburgh, PA 15206. TEL 412-363-6600.

331.8 613.62 US ISSN 0073-750X
INDUSTRIAL HEALTH FOUNDATION. LEGAL SERIES BULLETIN. 1936. irreg., no. 9, 1972. price varies. ‡ Industrial Health Foundation, Inc., 34 Penn Circle West, Pittsburgh, PA 15206. TEL 412-363-6600.
Formerly: Industrial Hygiene Foundation of America. Legal Series Bulletin.

613.62 US ISSN 0073-7518
INDUSTRIAL HEALTH FOUNDATION. MEDICAL SERIES. BULLETIN. 1937. irreg., no.21, 1982. price varies. ‡ Industrial Health Foundation, Inc., 34 Penn Circle West, Pittsburgh, PA 15206. TEL 412-363-6600.

613.62 US
INDUSTRIAL HEALTH FOUNDATION. NURSING SERIES. BULLETINS. 1965. irreg., no.3, 1971. price varies. Industrial Health Foundation, Inc., 34 Penn Circle West, Pittsburgh, PA 15206. TEL 412-363-6600.
Formerly: Industrial Hygiene Foundation. Nursing Series. Bulletins (ISSN 0073-7526)

331 614 US
INDUSTRIAL HEALTH FOUNDATION. TECHNICAL BULLETIN. MANAGEMENT SERIES. 1971. irreg., no.2, 1978. price varies. Industrial Health Foundation, Inc., 34 Penn Circle West, Pittsburgh, PA 15206. TEL 412-363-6600. (back issues avail.)

INDUSTRIAL VENTILATION; A MANUAL OF RECOMMENDED PRACTICE. see HEATING, PLUMBING AND REFRIGERATION

331.8 614.8 UN ISSN 0579-8140
INTERNATIONAL DIRECTORY OF OCCUPATIONAL SAFETY AND HEALTH SERVICES AND INSTITUTIONS. (Subseries of the office's Occupational Safety and Health Series) a. International Labour Office, Publications Sales Service, CH-1211 Geneva 22, Switzerland (U.S. Distributor: I L O Branch Office, 1750 New York Ave. N.W., Washington, DC 20006)

613.62 331 US ISSN 0092-6299
IOWA. BUREAU OF LABOR. OCCUPATIONAL INJURIES AND ILLNESSES SURVEY. 1973. a. free. Bureau of Labor, Research and Statistics Division, 307 E. Seventh St., Des Moines, IA 50319. TEL 515-281-3606. stat. circ. 300. (processed)

614.85 JA
JAPAN INDUSTRIAL SAFETY AND HEALTH ASSOCIATION. RESEARCH AND SURVEY DIVISION. BAROMETER OF OCCUPATIONAL SAFETY. (Text in Japanese) a. Japan Industrial Safety and Health Association, Research and Survey Division, 5-35-1 Shiba Minato-ku, Tokyo 108, Japan.

613.62 JA
JAPAN INDUSTRIAL SAFETY AND HEALTH ASSOCIATION. RESEARCH AND SURVEY DIVISION. GUIDEBOOK ON OCCUPATIONAL HEALTH. (Text in Japanese) a. Japan Industrial Safety and Health Association, Research and Survey Division, 5-35-1 Shiba Minato-ku, Tokyo 108, Japan.

614.85 JA
JAPAN INDUSTRIAL SAFETY AND HEALTH ASSOCIATION. RESEARCH AND SURVEY DIVISION. YEARBOOK OF INDUSTRIAL SAFETY. (Text in Japanese) a. Japan Industrial Safety and Health Association, Research and Survey Division, 5-35-1 Shiba Minato-ku, Tokyo 108, Japan.

KOKUTETSU CHUO HOKEN KANRIJOHO; health control. see PUBLIC HEALTH AND SAFETY

610 613.62 SA ISSN 0026-4490
MINE MEDICAL OFFICERS' ASSOCIATION OF SOUTH AFRICA. PROCEEDINGS. (Text in English) 1921. irreg. (2-3/yr.). membership. Mine Medical Officers' Association of South Africa, P.O. Box 61809, Marshalltown, Johannesburg 2107, South Africa (And Chamber of Mines, Hollard St., Johannesburg, South Africa) Ed. Dr. J.P. Lowe. charts. illus. cum.index. circ. 200. Indexed: Excerp.Med. Ind.Med. Abstr.Hyg. Ind.S.A.Per. Trop.Dis.Bull.

MINES SAFETY AND HEALTH COMMISSION. REPORT/ORGANE PERMANENT POUR LA SECURITE DANS LES MINES DE HOUILLE. RAPPORT. see *MINES AND MINING INDUSTRY*

614.85 616.2   SA   ISSN 0374-9800
NATIONAL CENTRE FOR OCCUPATIONAL HEALTH. ANNUAL REPORT. (Text in Afrikaans and English) 1957. irreg. Department of Health and Welfare, National Centre for Occupational Health, Box 4788, Johannesburg 2000, South Africa. circ. 200.
Formerly: National Institute for Occupational Diseases. Annual Report.

614.85   AT   ISSN 0813-1694
NATIONAL SAFETY COUNCIL OF AUSTRALIA. ANNUAL REPORT. 1947. a. National Safety Council of Australia, 370 St. Kilda Rd., Melbourne, Vic. 3004, Australia.
Safety education

613.62 614.85   US
OCCUPATIONAL HEALTH & SAFETY PURCHASING SOURCEBOOK. a. Stevens Publishing Corp., 225 N. New Rd., Waco, TX 76710. TEL 817-776-9000. adv.

613.62   UK   ISSN 0141-7568
OCCUPATIONAL HYGIENE MONOGRAPHS. 1978. irreg. price varies. Science Reviews Ltd., 40 The Fairway, Northwood, Middx. HA6 3DY, England (Subscr. to: Northern Office, 28 High Ash Dr., Leeds LS17 8RA, England) Ed. Dr. Donald Hughes. circ. 5,000. (back issues avail.)

344   US   ISSN 0092-3435
OCCUPATIONAL SAFETY AND HEALTH DECISIONS. 1973. irreg. $29.50. Commerce Clearing House, Inc., 4025 W. Peterson Ave., Chicago, IL 60646. TEL 312-583-8500.

613.62   UN   ISSN 0078-3129
OCCUPATIONAL SAFETY AND HEALTH SERIES. (Editions in English, French and Spanish) 1963. irreg. price varies. International Labour Office, Publications Sales Service, CH-1211 Geneva 22, Switzerland (U.S. Distributor: I L O Branch Office, 1750 New York Ave. N.W., Washington, DC 20006)

613.62   UK
RECENT ADVANCES IN OCCUPATIONAL HEALTH. 1981. irreg. Churchill Livingstone Medical Journals, 1-3 Baxter's Place, Leith Walk, Edinburgh EH1 3AF, Scotland.

614.85   JA
RESEARCH INSTITUTE OF INDUSTRIAL SAFETY. ANNUAL REPORT. (Text in Japanese) 1968. a. free. Research Institute of Industrial Safety, 35-1, 5-Chome, Shiba, Minato-ku, Tokyo 108, Japan. circ. 2,000. (back issues avail.)

613.82 620   US
RESPIRATOR NEWS. 1983. irreg. $375 for 12 issues. Darrell Bevis Associates, Inc., 14640 Flint Lee Rd., Ste. D, Chantilly, VA 22021. TEL 703-378-0333. Ed. Darell A. Bevis. bk. rev. circ. 200.

613.62   UK   ISSN 0144-4301
S P A I D NEWS. 1980? irreg. £5. Society for the Prevention of Asbestosis and Industrial Diseases, 38 Drapers Rd., Enfield, Middx. EN2 8LU, England. Ed. Nancy Tait. circ. 2,000.

331.1   JA   ISSN 0081-928X
SUMITOMO BULLETIN OF INDUSTRIAL HEALTH/SUMITOMO SANGYO EISEI. (Text in Japanese; summaries in English) 1965. a. $15 approx. Institute of Industrial Health, Sumitomo Hospital, 5-2-2 Nakanoshima, Kita-ku, Osaka 530, Japan. Ed. Osamu Wadaka. bk. rev. (also avail. in microfiche) Indexed: Biol.Abstr. Chem.Abstr. Excerp.Med. Ind.Med. C.I.S. Abstr.

363.1   US   ISSN 0198-8360
U.S. NUCLEAR REGULATORY COMMISSION. OCCUPATIONAL RADIATION EXPOSURE, ANNUAL REPORT. 1970. a. U.S. Nuclear Regulatory Commission, Office of Nuclear Regulatory Research, 1717 H St. N.W., Washington, DC 20555. TEL 202-492-7000. circ. 1,000. Indexed: Geo.Abstr. Key Title: Occupational Radiation Exposure, Annual Report.
Formerly: U.S. Nuclear Regulatory Commission. Annual Occupational Radiation Exposure Report.

614.85   US
UNIVERSITY OF DELAWARE. DISASTER RESEARCH CENTER. MISCELLANEOUS REPORTS. no.32, 1982. irreg. University of Delaware, Disaster Research Center, Newark, DE 19716. TEL 302-451-6618.
Formerly: Ohio State University, Columbus. Disaster Research Center. Miscellaneous Reports.

WORKERS' COMPENSATION LAW REPORTER. see *INSURANCE*

614.8   SZ   ISSN 0084-165X
WORLD CONGRESS ON THE PREVENTION OF OCCUPATIONAL ACCIDENTS AND DISEASES. PROCEEDINGS. (Proceedings published by national organizing committee) 1955. triennial, 10th, 1983 Ottawa. International Social Security Association, P.O. Box 1, 1211 Geneva 22, Switzerland.

INDUSTRIAL HEALTH AND SAFETY — Abstracting, Bibliographies, Statistics

614.85   DK   ISSN 0106-9683
ARBEJDSULYKKER. AARSSTATISTIK. 1977. biennial. free. Arbejdstilsynet, Statistik Kontor, Postbox 858, 2100 Copenhagen OE, Denmark. Eds. Ole Brunn, Joergen Raffansoe. circ. 1,000.

AUSTRALIA. BUREAU OF STATISTICS. WESTERN AUSTRALIAN OFFICE. INDUSTRIAL ACCIDENTS. see *BUSINESS AND ECONOMICS — Abstracting, Bibliographies, Statistics*

614.8 016   GW
BERUF UND GESUNDHEIT/OCCUPATIONAL HEALTH. (Text in English and German) 1975. irreg. (3-4/yr.) Institut fuer Dokumentation und Information ueber Sozialmedizin und Oeffentliches Gesundheitswesen, Westerfeldstr. 35-37, Postfach 201012, 4800 Bielefeld 1, W. Germany (B.R.D.) Ed. H. Lange. bk. rev. circ. 600. Indexed: Ergon.Abstr.
Formerly (until 1985): Dokumentation Arbeitsmedizin/Documentation Occupational Health (ISSN 0340-3238)

614.8 016   UN   ISSN 0302-7651
C I S ABSTRACTS. French edition: Bulletin C I S (ISSN 0250-4235) (Editions in English, French, Italian, Russian, Serbocroatian, Spanish) 1974. 8/yr. $200. International Labour Office, International Occupational Safety and Health Information Centre - Centre International d'Informations de Securite et d'Hygiene du Travail, CH-1211 Geneva 22, Switzerland. Ed.Bd. adv. bk. rev. abstr. index. cum.index. circ. 20,000. (tabloid format) Indexed: Ergon.Abstr. Lab.Haz.Bull.
●Also available online. Vendors: European Space Agency.
Former English edition: Occupational Safety and Health Abstracts (ISSN 0029-7984); Former French edition: Bulletin Bibliographique de la Prevention (ISSN 0045-3498)

331.11   US   ISSN 0164-1530
CALIFORNIA WORK INJURIES AND ILLNESSES. 1945. a. free. Department of Industrial Relations, Division of Labor Statistics and Research, Box 603, San Francisco, CA 94101. TEL 415-557-1924.
Supersedes in part (as from 1975): California Work Injuries.

331.8 016 613   UN   ISSN 0074-2147
INTERNATIONAL CATALOGUE OF OCCUPATIONAL SAFETY AND HEALTH FILMS. (Subseries of Occupational Safety and Health Series) (Text in English, French and Spanish) 1969. irreg. International Labour Office, Publications Sales Service, CH-1211 Geneva 22, Switzerland (U.S. Distributor: I L O Branch Office, 1750 New York Ave. N.W., Washington, DC 20006)

331.11   US
OCCUPATIONAL DISEASE IN CALIFORNIA. (Formerly published by California Department of Health) 1979. a. free. Department of Industrial Relations, Division of Labor Statistics and Research, Box 603, San Francisco, CA 94101. TEL 415-557-2184.

610 613.62   UK
SELECTED ABSTRACTS ON OCCUPATIONAL DISEASES. 1982. q. £6.40. Department of Health and Social Security, Alexander Fleming House, Elephant and Castle, London SE1 6BY, England (Subscr. to: DHSS (Leaflets), P.O. Box 21, Stanmore, Middlesex HA7 1AY, England) Ed. C. Price.

INFORMATION SCIENCE AND INFORMATION THEORY

see *Computers — Information Science and Information Theory*

INORGANIC CHEMISTRY

see *Chemistry — Inorganic Chemistry*

INSTRUMENTS

see also *Jewelry, Clocks and Watches; Metrology and Standardization*

681.2   US   ISSN 0065-2814
ADVANCES IN INSTRUMENTATION. (Consists of: Instrument Society of America. International Conference Proceedings) a. price varies. Instrument Society of America, 67 Alexander Dr., Box 12277, Research Triangle Park, NC 27709. TEL 919-549-8411. (reprint service avail. from UMI, ISI and publisher) Indexed: Chem.Abstr. Excerp.Med.

BIOMEDICAL SCIENCES INSTRUMENTATION. see *MEDICAL SCIENCES*

BLUEGRASS DIRECTORY. see *MUSIC*

CLINICAL LABORATORY REFERENCE. see *MEDICAL SCIENCES — Experimental Medicine, Laboratory Technique*

CONFERENCE ON PRECISION ELECTROMAGNETIC MEASUREMENTS. DIGEST. see *ELECTRICITY AND ELECTRICAL ENGINEERING*

681.2 607   US   ISSN 0046-144X
EDUCATION NEWS FROM METROLOGIC. 1971. a. free. ‡ Metrologic Instruments Inc., 143 Harding Ave., Bellmawr, NJ 08030. TEL 609-933-0100. Ed. Herbert H. Gottlieb. adv. bk. rev. charts. illus. circ. 5,000.

681 617   US
ELECTROMEDICAL & ELECTROSURGICAL EQUIPMENT SPEC BOOK. 1985. a. Gordon Publications, Inc., Box 1952, Dover, NJ 07801. TEL 201-986-7492. Ed. Val DeGeiso. adv. circ. 13,500.

681   MX
GUIA DE LA INDUSTRIA: LABORATORIOS DE ESPECIALADES Y CONTROL. 1963. a. Mex.$2000($25) Editorial Cosmos, Espana No. 396, 09880 Mexico, D.F., Mexico. Dir. Cesar Macazaga Orodono. circ. 5,000.

681.2 542   US   ISSN 0533-5426
GUIDE TO SCIENTIFIC INSTRUMENTS. Variant title: Science Guide to Scientific Instruments. 1964. a. $4. American Association for the Advancement of Science, 1333 H St., N.W., Washington, DC 20005. TEL 202-326-6500. Ed. Riehard Sommer. adv. circ. 160,000. (also avail. in microfiche from BLH,UMI; microfiche from UMI; back issues avail.)

681 619   US   ISSN 0883-0762
HEALTH CARE INSTRUMENTATION. the information journal of current medical technology. 1985. irreg. $45 to individuals; institutions $70. Excerpta Medica, Inc., Box 3085, Princeton, NJ 08543-3085. TEL 609-896-3085. Ed. Michael Anbar. charts. illus. circ. 1,850. (back issues avail.)

681 US
HOME HEALTH CARE PRODUCTS DIRECTORY & RESOURCE GUIDE. 1981. a. $25. Miramar Publishing Co., 2048 Cotner Ave., Los Angeles, CA 90025. TEL 213-477-1033. Ed. A Segedy. adv. bk. rev. tr.lit. circ. 15,000. (reprint service avail.)

I & C S BUYERS' GUIDE. see *ENGINEERING*

681 US
I E C O N: INTERNATIONAL CONFERENCE ON INDUSTRIAL ELECTRONICS, CONTROL AND INSTRUMENTATION. PROCEEDINGS. Variant title: I E E E Industrial Electronics Society Conference. (Former name of issuing body: Industrial Electronics and Control Instrumentation Society) a. (I E E E, Industrial Electronics Society) Institute of Electrical and Electronics Engineers, Inc., 345 E. 47th St., New York, NY 10017. TEL 212-705-7900.
 Former titles (1982-1983): I E E E/I E C O N. Proceedings; Until 1981: I C E I Industrial and Control Applications of Microprocessors. Proceedings; Industrial Applications of Microprocessors.

681.2 US
I E E E INSTRUMENTATION AND MEASUREMENT TECHNOLOGY CONFERENCE. PROCEEDINGS. Short title: I M T C. 1984. a. price varies. (I E E E, Instrumentation and Measurement Society) Institute of Electrical and Electronics Engineers, Inc., 345 E. 47th St., New York, NY 10017 TEL 212-705-7900. (Subscr. to: 445 Hoes Lane, Piscataway, NJ 08854)

681 US ISSN 0272-8141
I S A DIRECTORY OF INSTRUMENTATION. (In 2 parts: International Volume & North American Volume) 1979. a. price varies. Instrument Society of America, 67 Alexander Dr., Box 27709, Research Triangle Park, NC 27709. TEL 919-549-8411. Ed. L.K. Ray. circ. 40,000.
 Incorporates: I S A Transducer Compendium.

681 660 US ISSN 0074-0551
INSTRUMENTATION IN THE CHEMICAL AND PETROLEUM INDUSTRIES. (Includes: International Instrument Society of America Chemical and Petroleum Instrumentation Syposium Proceedings) 1965. a. price varies. Instrument Society of America, 67 Alexander Dr., Box 12277, Research Triangle Park, NC 27709. TEL 919-549-8411. (reprint service avail. from UMI, ISI and publisher)

681 664 US ISSN 0095-0777
INSTRUMENTATION IN THE FOOD INDUSTRY. irreg., vol.3, 1980. price varies. Instrument Society of America, 67 Alexander Dr., Box 12277, Research Triangle Park, NC 27709. TEL 919-549-8411. (reprint service avail. from UMI,ISI and publisher)

681.7 US ISSN 0074-056X
INSTRUMENTATION IN THE POWER INDUSTRY. (Includes: International Instrument Society of America Power Symposium Proceedings) 1967. a. price varies. Instrument Society of America, 67 Alexander Dr., Box 12277, Research Triangle Park, NC 27709. TEL 919-549-8411. (reprint service avail. from UMI,ISI and publisher)

681.2 US ISSN 0738-3231
INSTRUMENTATION SYMPOSIUM FOR THE PROCESS INDUSTRIES. Variant title: Symposium on Instrumentation for the Process Industries. 35th, 1980. a. price varies. Instrument Society of America, 67 Alexander Dr., Box 12277, Research Triangle Park, NC 27709. TEL 919-549-8411. (reprint service avail. from UMI,ISI and publisher) Indexed: Chem.Abstr.

681 UK
INSTRUMENTS AND INSTRUMENTATION HANDBOOK. 1977. every 4 yrs. £45. Trade and Technical Press Ltd., Crown House, Morden, Surrey SM4 5EW, England.

681.2 540 UK
INTERNATIONAL GUIDE TO SCIENTIFIC INSTRUMENTS & CHEMICALS. 1976. a. $50. Labmate Ltd., 12 Alban Park, Hatfield Rd., St. Albans AL4 0JJ, England. Ed. M.H. Pattison. circ. 36,000. (back issues avail.)

338.4 UK ISSN 0141-8963
LABORATORY EQUIPMENT DIRECTORY. 1972. a. £24. Morgan-Grampian Book Publishing Co. Ltd., 30 Calderwood St., Woolwich, London SE18 6QH, England. Ed. Phil Brown. circ. 1,500.
 Formerly: Laboratory Equipment Directory and Buyers Guide.

621 US
M & C DATA ACQUISITION AND RECORDER HANDBOOK & BUYERS GUIDE. 1982. a. $15. Measurements and Data Corp., 2994 W. Liberty Ave., Pittsburgh, PA 15216. TEL 412-343-9666. Eds. Harish Saluja, Elisa Behnk. adv. circ. 10,000.
 Former titles: M & C Temperature Handbook and Buyers Guide; M & C Pressure and Force Handbook Buyers Guide.

681.2 918 US
SCIENTIFIC INSTRUMENTS: LATIN AMERICAN INDUSTRIAL REPORT. 1985. a. $235 per country report. Aurora International, Box 9099, Bridgeport, CT 06601-2099. TEL 203-368-0579. Ed. Andres C. Aquino.

681 UK
SIRA REVIEW ANNUAL BROCHURE. 1980. a. Sira Ltd., South Hill, Chislehurst, Kent BR7 5EH, England. circ. 3,000.
 Formerly: Sira Review.

681.2 US ISSN 0074-0527
STANDARDS AND PRACTICES FOR INSTRUMENTATION. INSTRUMENT SOCIETY OF AMERICA. 1963. triennially, 8th ed., 1986. price varies. Instrument Society of America, 67 Alexander Dr., Box 12277, Research Triangle Park, NC 27709. TEL 919-549-8411. Ed. L.M. Ferson. index. (reprint service avail. from UMI, ISI and publisher)

INSTRUMENTS — Abstracting, Bibliographies, Statistics

338.4 CN ISSN 0384-4242
CANADA. STATISTICS CANADA. SCIENTIFIC AND PROFESSIONAL EQUIPMENT INDUSTRIES/FABRICATION DE MATERIEL SCIENTIFIQUE ET PROFESSIONNEL. (Catalogue 47-206) (Text in English and French) 1960. a. Can.$20($21) Statistics Canada, Communications Division, 3rd Floor, R.H. Coats Bldg., Ottawa, Ont. K1A 0T6, Canada TEL 613-993-7276. (Subscr. to: Publications Sales and Services, Ottawa, Ont. K1A 0T6, Canada) (also avail. in microform from MML)

KEY ABSTRACTS - ELECTRONIC INSTRUMENTATION. see *METROLOGY AND STANDARDIZATION — Abstracting, Bibliographies, Statistics*

KEY ABSTRACTS - MEASUREMENTS IN PHYSICS. see *METROLOGY AND STANDARDIZATION — Abstracting, Bibliographies, Statistics*

INSURANCE

368 AT ISSN 0084-697X
A.I.J. MANUAL OF AUSTRALASIAN LIFE ASSURANCE. (Australasian Insurance Journal) 1930/31. a. $10. Bushell Publishing Co. Pty. Ltd., 1987 Pittwater Rd., Bayview, N.S.W. 2104, Australia.

A S A MONOGRAPH. (American Society of Appraisers) see *REAL ESTATE*

368.4 SZ ISSN 0379-7074
AFRICAN NEWS SHEET. French edition: Nouvelles Africaines de Securite Sociale. 1967. irreg. International Social Security Association, Box 1, 1211 Geneva 22, Switzerland (Dist. by: I S S A Regional Office for Africa, Boite Postale 10113, Lome, Togo)
 Formerly: African Social Security Series (ISSN 0065-4043)

368.012 US ISSN 0065-4272
AGENT'S AND BUYER'S GUIDE. 1948. a. $16.75. National Underwriter Co., 420 E. 4th St., Cincinnati, OH 45202. TEL 513-721-2140. adv.

368.382 354.7 CN
ALBERTA. HEALTH CARE INSURANCE PLAN. ANNUAL REPORT. 1970. a. Health Care Insurance Commission, 118th Ave. & Groat Rd., Edmonton, Alta. T5J 2M3, Canada. TEL 403-427-1400. Ed.Bd. illus.
 Formerly (until 1978): Alberta. Health Care Insurance Commission. Annual Report (ISSN 0383-3615)
 Health

ALBERTA HAIL AND CROP INSURANCE CORPORATION. ANNUAL REPORT. see *AGRICULTURE — Crop Production And Soil*

368 CN ISSN 0712-9343
ALBERTA INSURANCE DIRECTORY; insurance companies, agents and adjusters. 1982. a. Can.$20. Arbutus Publications Ltd., P.O. Box 35070, Sta. E., Vancouver, B.C. V6M 4G1, Canada. TEL 604-687-8003. Ed. W.D.S. Earle. adv. circ. 1,000.

368 333.33 CN ISSN 0229-7108
ALBERTA INSURANCE REPORT. 1976. irreg. Office of the Superintendent of Insurance and Real Estate, 10065 Jasper Ave., Edmonton, Alta. T5J 3B1, Canada. stat. circ. 700.
 Formerly (until 1984): Alberta. Office of the Superintendent of Insurance and Real Estate. Annual Report (ISSN 0705-596X)

368.4 NE ISSN 0401-331X
ALGEMEEN WERKLOOSHEIDSFONDS. JAARVERSLAG/ANNUAL REPORT. 1949. a. fl.50. Social Security Council, Postbus 100, 2700 AC Zoetermeer, Netherlands. circ. 1,000.

368 US
AMERICAN INSURANCE SERVICES GROUP. ENGINEERING AND SAFETY SERVICE. SPECIAL INTEREST BULLETIN. (Former name of issuing body: American Insurance Association) 1933. irreg. $15 per set. American Insurance Services Group, Inc., Engineering and Safety Service Information Center, 85 John St., New York, NY 10038. TEL 212-669-0478. circ. 16,000. (looseleaf format)

ANALYSIS OF WORKERS' COMPENSATION LAWS. see *SOCIAL SERVICES AND WELFARE*

ANKENAEVNET FOR ARBEJDSLOESHEDSFORSIKRINGEN. BERETNING. see *BUSINESS AND ECONOMICS — Labor And Industrial Relations*

368 FR
ANNUAIRE DES ASSURANCES ET L'ASSUREUR-CONSEIL. a. 2 rue de Chateaudun, 75009 Paris, France.

368 IT ISSN 0084-6635
ANNUARIO ITALIANO DELLE IMPRESE ASSICURATRICI. 1949. a. L.25000. Associazione Nazionale fra le Imprese Assicuratrici, Via della Frezza, 70, 00186 Rome, Italy. Ed. Fabrizio Moretti. circ. 5,000.

368 SP
ANUARIO ESPANOL DE SEGUROS. 1910. a. 5500 ptas.($60) Club del Ejecutivo de Seguros, Santa Engracia, 151, Madrid 3, Spain. circ. 7,500.

368 UK
ARABIAN INSURANCE GUIDE. a. $35. Beacon Publications PLC, York House, Newton Close, Park Farm, Wellingborough, Northamptonshire NN8 3UW, England.

368.4 NE
ARBEIDSONGESCHIKTHEIDSFONDS EN ALGEMEEN ARBEIDSONGESCHIKTHEIDSFONDS. JAARVERSLAG. 1977. a. fl.50. Social Security Council, Postbus 100, 2700 AC Zoetermeer, Netherlands. circ. 1,000.
 Former titles: Algemeen Arbeidsongeschiktheidsfonds. Jaarverslag; Arbeidsongeschiktheidsfonds. Jaarverslag.

INSURANCE

368.4 　　　　SW　ISSN 0562-861X
ARBETSSKADOR.* (Text in Swedish; summaries in English) 1979. a. Kr.110. National Central Bureau of Statistics, c/o Barbro Loogna, S-113 81 Stockholm, Sweden (And National Board of Occupational Safety and Health, S-115 81 Stockholm, Sweden)
　Supersedes (1955-1978): Sweden. Riksfoersaekringsverket. Yrkesskador.

368.1　　　　US　ISSN 0360-8921
ARGUS F C & S CHART. (Fire Casualty & Surety) a. $13.25. National Underwriter Co., Statistical Department, 420 E. 4th St., Cinncinnati, OH 45202. TEL 513-721-2140.
　Formerly: Argus Insurance Chart.

368.3　　　　US　ISSN 0066-9598
ASSOCIATION OF LIFE INSURANCE MEDICAL DIRECTORS OF AMERICA. TRANSACTIONS. 1889. a. $15. Association of Life Insurance Medical Directors of America, 140 Garden St., Hartford, CT 06115. Ed. Dr. Walter S. Clough. cum.index every 5 yrs. circ. 1,000(controlled) (also avail. in microform from UMI) Indexed: Ind.Med.

368.4　　　　AT
AUSTRALIA. DEPARTMENT OF SOCIAL SECURITY. ANNUAL REPORT OF THE DIRECTOR-GENERAL. 1972/73. a. price varies. Australian Government Publishing Service, Publishing Branch, G.P.O. Box 84, Canberra 2601, A.C.T., Australia. illus. stat.

328.94 368.9　　　　AT
AUSTRALIA. INSURANCE COMMISSIONER. ANNUAL REPORT. 1974. a. price varies. Australian Government Publishing Service, G.P.O. Box 84, Canberra, A.C.T. 2601, Australia. illus. stat.

AUSTRALIAN SUPERANNUATION AND EMPLOYEE BENEFITS GUIDE. see *SOCIAL SERVICES AND WELFARE*

368.4　　　　BE
BELGIUM. INSTITUT NATIONAL D'ASSURANCES SOCIALES POUR TRAVAILLEURS INDEPENDANTS. RAPPORT ANNUEL. Flemish edition: Belgium. Rijkinstituut voor de Sociale Verzekeringen der Zelfstandigen. Jaarverslag. 1970. a. free. Institut National d'Assurances Sociales pour Travailleurs Independants, Bibliotheque - Bureau 4-7 (Wat.), Place Jean Jacobs 6, 1000 Brussels, Belgium.

368　　　　BE
BELGIUM. INSTITUT NATIONAL D'ASSURANCES SOCIALES POUR TRAVAILLEURS INDEPENDANTS. STATISTIQUES DES BENEFICIAIRES DE PRESTATIONS DE RETRAITE ET DE SURVIE/ BELGIUM. RIJKINSTITUUT VOOR DE SOCIAL VERZEKERINGEN DER ZELFSTANDIGEN. STATISTIEK VAN DE PERSONEN DIE EEN RUST- EN OVERLEVINGSPRESTATIE GENIETEN. (Text in Flemish and French) 1970. a. free. Institut National d'Assurances Sociales pour Travailleurs Independants, Bibliotheque - Bureau 4-7 (Wat.), Place Jean Jacobs, 6, 1000 Brussels, Belgium. stat.

368.4　　　　BE
BELGIUM. INSTITUT NATIONAL D'ASSURANCES SOCIALES POUR TRAVAILLEURS INDEPENDANTS. STATISTIQUES DES PERSONNES ASSUJETTIES AU STATUT SOCIAL DES TRAVAILLEURS INDEPENDANTS/BELGIUM. RIJKSINSTITUUT VOOR DE SOCIALE VERZEKERINGEN DER ZELFSTANDIGEN. STATISTIEK VAN DE PERSONEN DIE ONDER DE TOEPASSING VALLEN VAN HET SOCIAAL STATUUT VAN DE ZELFSTANDIGEN. (Text in Flemish and French) 1970. a, latest 1983. free. Institut National d'Assurances Sociales pour Travailleurs Independants, Bibliotheque - Bureau 4-7 (Wat.), Place Jean Jacobs, 6, 1000 Brussels, Belgium.

368.4　　　　BE　ISSN 0067-558X
BELGIUM. MINISTERE DE LA PREVOYANCE SOCIALE. RAPPORT GENERAL SUR LA SECURITE SOCIALE/ALGEMEEN VERSLAG OVER DE SOCIALE ZEKERHEID. (Text in French or Flemish) 1962. a. 300 Fr. Ministere de la Prevoyance Sociale, Rue de la Vierge Noire 3 C, B-1000 Brussels, Belgium. Ed.Bd.

368　　　　US　ISSN 0094-9973
BEST'S AGENTS GUIDE TO LIFE INSURANCE COMPANIES. 1974. a. $40. A.M. Best Co., Oldwick, NJ 08858. TEL 201-439-2200. Ed. Robert J. King. stat.

368　　　　US
BEST'S DIRECTORY OF RECOMMENDED INSURANCE ADJUSTERS. 1930. a. $45. A.M. Best Co., Oldwick, NJ 08858. TEL 201-439-2200. Ed. E.C. Krisak.
　Former titles: Best's Directory of Recommended Independent Insurance Adjusters (ISSN 0271-0927); Best's Recommended Independent Insurance Adjusters (ISSN 0091-830X); Bests Recommended Insurance Adjusters.

368　　　　US　ISSN 0277-1551
BEST'S DIRECTORY OF RECOMMENDED INSURANCE ATTORNEYS. 1928. a. $50. A.M. Best Co., Oldwick, NJ 08858. TEL 201-439-2200. Ed. E.C. Krisak.
　Formerly: Best's Recommended Insurance Attorneys.

368　　　　US
BEST'S INSURANCE REPORT: LIFE-HEALTH. 1906. a. $220. A.M. Best Co., Oldwick, NJ 08858. TEL 201-439-2200. Ed. Robert J. King. stat.

368　　　　US　ISSN 0148-3218
BEST'S INSURANCE REPORT: PROPERTY-CASUALTY. 1900. a. $375. A.M. Best Co., Oldwick, NJ 08858. TEL 201-439-2200. Ed. Robert A. Bailey. stat.
　Formerly: Best's Insurance Report: Property-Liability.

BIBLIOGRAPHY OF APPRAISAL LITERATURE. see *REAL ESTATE — Abstracting, Bibliographies, Statistics*

368　　　　CN
BLUE CHART REPORT. 1984. a. Can.$10. Stone and Cox Limited, 323-366 Adelaide St. E., Toronto, Ont. M5A 3X9, Canada. TEL 416-864-0453. Ed. John D. Wyndham.

368　　　　BO
BOLIVIA. SUPERINTENDENCIA NACIONAL DE SEGUROS Y REASEGUROS. COLECCION ESTUDIOS. 1976. irreg. Superintendencia Nacional de Seguros y Reaseguras, La Paz, Bolivia.

368.4　　　　BL
BRAZIL. INSTITUTO NACIONAL DE PREVIDENCIA SOCIAL. BALANCO GERAL. a. Instituto Nacional de Assistencia Medica da Previdencia Social, Secretaria de Contabilidade e Autonomia, Rua Mexico 128, Caixa Postal 1290, Rio de Janeiro, Brazil. charts. stat.

368.4　　　　CN
BRITISH COLUMBIA. WORKERS' COMPENSATION BOARD. WORKERS' COMPENSATION REPORTER. 1973. irreg. Can.$35 per vol. Workers' Compensation Board, Community Relations Department, 6951 Westminster Highway, Richmond, B.C. V7C 1C6, Canada. TEL 604-273-2266. circ. 750.

368　　　　CN　ISSN 0068-1598
BRITISH COLUMBIA INSURANCE DIRECTORY. INSURANCE COMPANIES, AGENTS AND ADJUSTERS. 1964. a. Can.$23. Arbutus Publications Ltd., P.O. Box 35070, Sta. E, Vancouver, B.C. V6M 4G1, Canada. TEL 604-687-8003. Ed. W.D.S. Earle. adv. bk. rev. circ. 1,400.

368　　　　AG
BRUJULA. Variant title: Compania Argentina de Seguros. Memoria y Balance General. no.14, 1975. irreg. Compania Argentina de Seguros, San Martin 439, Buenos Aires, Argentina.

368　　　　US
BUYER STUDY; a market study of new insured and ordinary life insurance purchased. (In 2 edts., U.S. and Canada) a. $50. Life Insurance Marketing and Research Association (LIMRA), Box 208, Hartford, CT 06141. TEL 203-677-0033.

368　　　　US
C P C U PUBLIC AFFAIRS FORUM; a digest of current events about insurance & related issues. irreg. Society of Chartered Property & Casualty Underwriters, Kahler Hall, 720 Providence Rd. (CB No. 9), Malvern, PA 19355. TEL 215-251-2728. Ed. Margaret Kalalian.

368.4 355.115　　　　US
CAL-VET INSURANCE PLANS. ANNUAL REPORT. 1980. a. Department of Veterans Affairs, 1227 O St., Sacramento, CA 95814. TEL 916-322-1796.

368　　　　CN　ISSN 0380-1020
CANADA. DEPARTMENT OF INSURANCE. LIST OF SECURITIES. (Text in English and French) 1972. a. Can.$15.60. Department of Insurance, Ottawa, Ont., Canada. TEL 613-996-8587. circ. 1, 000.

332 368　　　　CN　ISSN 0068-7383
CANADA. DEPARTMENT OF INSURANCE. REPORT. CO-OPERATIVE CREDIT ASSOCIATIONS. 1956. a. price varies. Supply and Services Canada, Publishing Centre, Ottawa, Ont. K1A OS9, Canada. TEL 819-997-2560.

368　　　　CN　ISSN 0068-7405
CANADA. DEPARTMENT OF INSURANCE. REPORT OF THE SUPERINTENDENT OF INSURANCE. (Issued in 3 vols) a. price varies. Supply and Services Canada, Publishing Centre, Ottawa, Ont. K7A OS9, Canada. TEL 819-997-2560.

332　　　　CN　ISSN 0068-7413
CANADA. DEPARTMENT OF INSURANCE. REPORT. SMALL LOANS COMPANIES AND MONEY-LENDERS. a. price varies. Supply and Services Canada, Publishing Centre, Ottawa, Ont. K1A OS9, Canada. TEL 819-997-2560.

332.1 368　　　　CN　ISSN 0068-7391
CANADA. DEPARTMENT OF INSURANCE. REPORT. TRUST AND LOAN COMPANIES. a. price varies. Supply and Services Canada, Publishing Centre, Ottawa, Ont. K1A OS9, Canada. TEL 819-997-2560.

CANADIAN CASES ON THE LAW OF INSURANCE. see *LAW*

368　　　　CN　ISSN 0068-9025
CANADIAN INSURANCE. ANNUAL STATISTICAL ISSUE. 1905. a. Can.$16. Stone and Cox Ltd., 323-366 Adelaide St. E., Toronto, Ont. M5A 3X9, Canada. TEL 416-864-0453. Ed. M. Steeler. adv. circ. 11,338. (back issues avail.)

368　　　　CN　ISSN 0068-9157
CANADIAN LIFE AND HEALTH INSURANCE FACTS; an authoritative source of factual information about life and health insurance in Canada. (Editions in English and French) 1955. a. free. ‡ Canadian Life and Health Insurance Association Inc., Communications Department, 20 Queen St., W., Ste. 2500, Toronto, Ont. M5W 3S2, Canada. TEL 416-977-2221. Ed. Lydia M. Boyko. circ. 20,000. Indexed: CS Ind.
　Formed by 1985 merger of: Canadian Health Insurance Facts & Canadian Life Insurance Facts.

368.01　　　　US
CASUALTY ACTUARIAL SOCIETY. PROCEEDINGS.* vol.62, 1975. a. $30. Casualty Actuarial Society, 250 W. 34th St., One Penn Plaza, New York, NY 10119. TEL 212-560-1018. (also avail. in microform from UMI; reprint service avail. from UMI)

368.4　　　　CL
CHILE. SUPERINTENDENCIA DE SEGURIDAD SOCIAL. SEGURIDAD SOCIAL: ESTADISTICAS. 1969. irreg. exchange basis. Superintendenica de Seguridad Social, Santiago, Chile.
　Continues: Chile. Superintendencia de Seguridad Social. Boletin de Estadisticas de Seguridad.

368　　　　SA
COLIMPEX INSURANCE BROKERS EXECUPAD. (Text in Afrikaans and English) a. Colimpex Africa (Pty.) Ltd., Box 889, Wendywood 2144, South Africa. adv.

INSURANCE 639

368.01   US   ISSN 0069-5718
COLLEGE OF INSURANCE. GENERAL
BULLETIN. 1962/63. biennial. free. ‡ College of
Insurance, One Insurance Plaza, 101 Murray St.,
New York, NY 10007. TEL 212-962-4111. circ. 20,
000.

COLOMBIA. MINISTERIO DE TRABAJO Y
SEGURIDAD SOCIAL. MEMORIA. see
BUSINESS AND ECONOMICS — Labor And
Industrial Relations

COLOMBIA. SUPERINTENDENCIA BANCARIA.
SEGUROS Y CAPITALIZACION. see BUSINESS
AND ECONOMICS

CYPRUS. MINISTRY OF LABOUR AND SOCIAL
INSURANCE. ANNUAL REPORT. see
BUSINESS AND ECONOMICS — Labor And
Industrial Relations

368   DK   ISSN 0106-2735
DANSK FORSIKRINGS AARBOG. 1900. a. Kr.175.
Forlaget Forsikring, Amaliegade 10, DK-1256
Copenhagen K, Denmark. Ed. Erik Heimann Olsen.
circ. 1,500.

368.8   II   ISSN 0304-6966
DEPOSIT INSURANCE CORPORATION.
ANNUAL REPORT: DIRECTORS' REPORT,
BALANCE SHEET AND ACCOUNTS.* (Text in
English) a. Deposit Insurance & Credit Guarantee
Corp., New India Centre, 17 Cooperage Rd.,
Bombay 400039, India.

368   GW   ISSN 0070-4237
DIE DEUTSCHE LEBENSVERSICHERUNG.
JAHRBUCH. a. free. (Verband der
Lebensversicherungsunternehmen e.V.) Verlag
Versicherungswirtschaft e.V., Eduard-Pflueger-Str.
55, 5300 Bonn 1, W. Germany (B.R.D.) (Subscr. to:
Verlag Versicherungswirtschaft e.V., Klosestr. 20,
7500 Karlsruhe, W. Germany (B.R.D.)) Ed. Michael
Glueck. circ. 22,000. (back issues avail.)

368   US   ISSN 0070-5691
DIRECTORY OF INSURANCE COMPANIES
LICENSED IN NEW YORK STATE. a. $1 per no.
(single copies free to NY residents) Insurance
Department, Empire State Plaza, Agency Bldg. No.
1, Albany, NY 12257. circ. 5,000.

368   ES
EL SALVADOR. SUPERINTENDENCIA DE
BANCOS Y OTRAS INSTITUCIONES
FINANCIERAS. ESTADISTICAS: SEGUROS,
FINANZAS, BANCOS. Variant title: Estadisticas,
Seguros, Fianzas, Bancos. 1963. irreg., no.20, 1984.
free. Superintendencia de Bancos y Otras
Instituciones Financieras, Asesoria Actuarial y
Estadistica, Junta Monetaria, Edificio B C R, San
Salvador, El Salvador. charts. circ. 750.
    Formerly (until 1976, no.14): El Salvador.
Superintendencia de Bancos y Otras Instituciones
Financieras. Estadisticas: Seguros, Fianzas,
Capitalizacion (ISSN 0067-3234)

368   UK
EXECUTIVE PENSIONS. 1976. irreg. Financial
Times Business Information, 102 Clerkenwell Rd.,
London EC1M 5SA, England. circ. 4,500. (tabloid
format)

368.08   UK   ISSN 0071-3686
FACULTY OF ACTUARIES IN SCOTLAND.
TRANSACTIONS. 1901. irreg. (approx. 2/yr.)
£6.50 per issue. Faculty of Actuaries, 23 St. Andrew
Sq., Edinburgh EH2 1AQ, Scotland. Ed. D.
Morrice. bk. rev. index. circ. 1,100.

FEDERAL BENEFITS FOR VETERANS AND
DEPENDENTS, IS-1 FACT SHEET. see
MILITARY

368.8 332.2   US
FEDERAL HOME LOAN BANK SYSTEM. LIST
OF MEMBER INSTITUTIONS.* 1962. a. U.S.
Federal Home Loan Bank Board, Box 37248,
Washington, DC 20013. TEL 202-377-6000. Ed.
John Ghizzoni. circ. 500. Key Title: List of Member
Institutions - Federal Saving and Loan Insurance
Corporation.
    Formerly: Federal Savings and Loan Insurance
Corporation. List of Member Institutions (ISSN
0428-1365)

FEDERAL RESERVE BANK OF CLEVELAND.
WORKING PAPER. see BUSINESS AND
ECONOMICS — Banking And Finance

368.4   NE   ISSN 0071-4151
FEDERATIE VAN BEDRIJFSVERENIGINGEN.
JAARVERSLAG. 1930. a. free. Federatie van
Bedrijfsverenigingen, Postbus 8300, 1005 C A
Amsterdam, Netherlands. circ. 400.

368   UK   ISSN 0309-751X
FINANCIAL TIMES INTERNATIONAL YEAR
BOOKS: WORLD INSURANCE. a. £49. Longman
Group Ltd., Fourth Ave., Harlow, Essex CM19
5AA, England (Dist. in USA and Canada by:
Longman Group USA Inc., 500 North Dearborn St.,
Chicago, IL 60610)

368   CN
FINANCIAL TIMES OF CANADA. GUIDE TO R
R S PS. 1981. irreg. Financial Times of Canada, Ste.
500, 920 Yonge St., Toronto, Ont. M4W 3L5,
Canada. TEL 416-922-1133.

368.1   FI   ISSN 0355-5003
FINLAND KANSANELAKELAITOS.
TOIMINTAKERTOMUS. English edition: Finland.
Social Insurance Institution. Annual Report.
Swedish edition: Finland. Folkpensionsanstalten.
Beraettelse. 1938. a. Social Insurance Institution,
Information Division, P.O. Box 450, SF-00101
Helsinki 10, Finland. circ. 18,000.

568   DK   ISSN 0108-7304
FORSIKRINGSTILSYNET. BERETNING OM
TILSYNETS VIRKSOMHED. (Text in Danish,
English and French) 1981. a. Kr.100 for part 1-3.
Forsikringstilsynet, Hammerichsgade 14, 1611
Copenhagen V, Denmark (Orders to: Danske
Boghendleres Kommissionsanstalt, Siljangade 6,
2300 Copenhagen S, Denmark) circ. 1,500.
    Formerly: Forsikringsraadet. Beretning om
Raadets Virksomhed.

368   AG
GALICIA Y RIO DE LA PLATA. COMPANIA DE
SEGUROS. MEMORIA Y BALANCE
GENERAL. 1974. a. Compania de Seguros,
Rivadavia 717, Buenos Aires, Argentina. stat.

368   GW   ISSN 0302-5608
GERMANY (FEDERAL REPUBLIC, 1949-).
BUNDESAUFSICHTSAMT FUER DAS
VERSICHERUNGSWESEN.
GESCHAEFTSBERICHT. 1953. a. price varies.
Bundesaufsichtsamt fuer das Versicherungswesen,
Ludwigkirchplatz 3-4, Postfach 180, 1000 Berlin 15,
W. Germany (B.R.D.) bk. rev. stat. index. circ. 1,
400.

368.32 355.15   US
GOVERNMENT LIFE INSURANCE PROGRAMS
FOR VETERANS AND MEMBERS OF THE
SERVICES. ANNUAL REPORT. a. U.S. Veterans
Administration, Department of Veterans Benefits,
Washington, DC 20420.

368   UK   ISSN 0308-499X
GREAT BRITAIN. DEPARTMENT OF TRADE.
INSURANCE BUSINESS: ANNUAL REPORT. a.
H.M.S.O., P.O.Box 569, London SE1 9NH,
England. stat. (reprint service avail. from UMI)
    Continues: Great Britain. Board of Trade.
Insurance Business: Annual Report (ISSN 0072-
5684)

368.3   CN   ISSN 0317-2678
GUIDE DE REUSSITE DANS LA CARRIERE
D'ASSUREUR-VIE. English edition: Guide to a
Successful Life Insurance Career (ISSN 0381-6532)
(Text in French) 1971. a. Life Underwriters
Association of Canada - Association des Assureurs-
Vie du Canada, 41 Lesmill Rd., Don Mills, Ont.
M3B 2T3, Canada. TEL 416-444-5251.
    Formerly: Guide d'Une Carriere a Succes (ISSN
0317-2686)

368.32   CN   ISSN 0381-6532
GUIDE TO A SUCCESSFUL LIFE INSURANCE
CAREER. French edition: Guide de Reussite dans
la Carriere d'Assureur-Vie (ISSN 0317-2678) 1971.
a. Life Underwriters Association of Canada, 41
Lesmill Rd., Don Mills, Ont. M3B 2T3, Canada.
TEL 416-444-5251.

368   GY
GUYANA. NATIONAL INSURANCE BOARD.
ANNUAL REPORT. a. National Insurance Board,
Georgetown, Guyana.

368   US   ISSN 0073-1110
HAWAII. INSURANCE DIVISION. REPORT OF
THE INSURANCE COMMISSIONER OF
HAWAII. 1903. a. free. Department of Commerce
and Consumer Affairs, Insurance Division, Box
3614, Honolulu, HI 96811. TEL 808-548-5450. circ.
1,000.

368.3   US
HEALTH CARE VIEWPOINT. 1961. irreg. free.
Health Insurance Association of America, Public
Relations Div., 1850 K St., N.W., Washington, DC
20006. Ed. Dona DeSanctis. charts. circ. 2,500.
    Formerly: Health Insurance Viewpoints (ISSN
0017-9027)

368   US
HINE'S DIRECTORY OF INSURANCE
ADJUSTERS. 1936. a. $15. Hine's Legal Directory,
Inc., Box 71, Glen Ellyn, IL 60138. TEL 312-469-
3983. Ed. James R. Collins. circ. 8,000.

HINE'S INSURANCE COUNSEL. see LAW

368   GW   ISSN 0073-3350
HOPPENSTEDT VERSICHERUNGS-JAHRBUCH.
1957. a. DM.448. Verlag Hoppenstedt und Co.,
Havelstr. 9, Postfach 4006, 6100 Darmstadt, W.
Germany (B.R.D.) adv.

368   US
HUEBNER FOUNDATION MONOGRAPH. 1972.
irreg. price varies. University of Pennsylvania,
Wharton School, S.S. Huebner Foundation for
Insurance, 3641 Locust Walk-CE, Philadelphia, PA
19104 TEL 215-898-5644. (Dist. by: Richard D.
Irwin, Inc., Homewood, IL 60430) Ed. J. David
Cummins. circ. 1,000. Indexed: J.of Econ.Lit.

368   US
INDEX OF INSURANCE AND EMPLOYEE
BENEFITS PROCEEDINGS. 1982. a. $50. Badger
Infosearch, Box 11943, Milwaukee, WI 53211. TEL
414-964-2377. Ed. Darlene E. Waterstreet.
(looseleaf format; back issues avail.)

368   CK
INDUSTRIA ASEGURADORA COLOMBIANA.
ESTADISTICAS ANUALES. 1976. a. $15. Union
de Aseguradores Colombianos, Carrera 7a. No. 26-
20, Piso 11, Apdo. Aereo 5233, Bogota, Colombia.

368   UK   ISSN 0020-269X
INSTITUTE OF ACTUARIES STUDENTS'
SOCIETY. JOURNAL. 1916. a. price varies. Alden
Press Ltd., Osney Mead, Oxford OX2 OEF,
England. Eds. D.E. Purchase, P.J. Cooper. bk. rev.
charts. stat. index. cum.index. circ. 4,000.

368   UK   ISSN 0267-3673
INSTITUTE OF INSURANCE CONSULTANTS.
REFERENCE BOOK AND LIST OF MEMBERS
(YEAR) 1985. a. £19.95. Millbank Publications, 25
Catherine St., London WC2B 5JW, England. TEL
01-379-3036. Ed. K.J. Allen. adv. circ. 2,000.

368.4   HO   ISSN 0074-0233
INSTITUTO HONDURENO DE SEGURIDAD
SOCIAL. DEPARTAMENTO DE ESTADISTICA
Y PROCESAMIENTO DE DATOS. ANUARIO
ESTADISTICO. a. (with supplements) exchange.
Instituto Hondureno de Seguridad Social,
Departamento de Estadistica y Actuarial, Apartado
555, Tegucigalpa, D.C., Honduras.

368.4   CR
INSTITUTO NACIONAL DE SEGUROS
MEMORIA ANUAL. 1934. a. free. Instituto
Nacional de Seguros, Apdo. 10061, San Jose, Costa
Rica. charts. illus. stat. circ. 2,000.
    Former titles: Instituto Nacional de Seguros.
Memoria Anual I.N.S & Instituto Nacional de
Seguros. Informe Anual (ISSN 0074-0268)

368   US   ISSN 0074-0675
INSURANCE ALMANAC; WHO, WHAT, WHEN
AND WHERE IN INSURANCE. 1912. a. $75.
Underwriter Printing and Publishing Co., 50 E.
Palisade Ave., Englewood, NJ 07631. TEL 201-569-
8808. Ed. Donald E. Wolff. adv. circ. 10,000.

INSURANCE

368   PH
INSURANCE COMPANY PROFILE. 1982. a. price varies. Philippine Insurance Commission, Insurance Commission Bldg., 1071 United Nations Ave., P.O. Box 3589, Manila, Philippines. circ. 300.

368   UK   ISSN 0074-0691
INSURANCE DIRECTORY AND YEAR BOOK. 1841. a. £20. Buckley Press Ltd., The Butts, Half Acre, Brentford, Middlesex TW8 8BN, England. adv. charts.
    Formerly: Post Magazine Almanack. Insurance Directory.

368   NZ
INSURANCE DIRECTORY OF NEW ZEALAND. a. NZ.$8. Mercantile Gazette of New Zealand Ltd., P.O. Box 20-034, Christchurch 5, New Zealand. Ed. B.M. Stoop.

368   AT   ISSN 0811-0905
INSURANCE IN AUSTRALIA AND NEW ZEALAND. 1966. a. Aus.$45. Craftsman Publishing Pty. Ltd., 125 Highbury Rd., Burwood, Vic. 3000, Australia. Ed. David Anderson. adv. bk. rev. circ. 1,600.

368   US
INSURANCE LAW ANTHOLOGY. 1986. a. $99.95. International Library, 7315 Wisconsin Ave., Ste. 229E, Bethesda, MD 20814. Ed. Allison P. Zabriskie.

368   US   ISSN 0538-2629
INSURANCE MARKETPLACE; the agents and brokers guide to non-standard & specialty lines, aviation, marine & international insurance. 1962. a. free. Rough Notes Co., Inc., 1200 N. Meridian, Box 564, Indianapolis, IN 46206. TEL 317-634-1541. Ed. Wallace L. Clapp, Jr. circ. 110,000.

368   UK   ISSN 0950-3668
INSURANCE STATISTICS (1981-1985) 1952. a. free. Association of British Insurers, Aldermary House, Queen St., London EC4N 1TU, England. circ. 7,000.
    Supersedes: Insurance Facts and Figures & Life Insurance in the United Kingdom.

368   SZ   ISSN 0074-1264
INTERNATIONAL ACTUARIAL CONGRESS. TRANSACTIONS. (Published by host country) quadrennial, 22nd, 1984, Sydney. 280 Fr. (Association of Swiss Actuaries) Staempfli & Cie AG, Bern, c/o Prof. Heinz Schmid, Institut fuer math. Statistik, Sidlerstr. 5, CH-3012 Bern, Switzerland.

368   US
INTERNATIONAL CLAIM ASSOCIATION PROCEEDINGS. 1910. a. $7. International Claim Association, c/o Ernest Beane, Modern Woodmen of America, Mississippi River at 17th St., Rock Island, IL 61201 (Orders to: Professional Book Distributors, Inc., Box 16539, Columbus, OH 43216) Ed. Herbert A. Saari. circ. 3,000.

368.3 610   SZ   ISSN 0074-3747
INTERNATIONAL CONGRESS OF LIFE ASSURANCE MEDICINE. PROCEEDINGS. triennial, 15th, 1986, Tokyo. Permanent International Committee for the Study of Life Assurance Medicine, c/o Dr. E. Tanner, Secretary-General, Swiss Reinsurance Company, 60 Mythenquai, Box 172, 8022 Zurich, Switzerland.

368.4   SZ
INTERNATIONAL SOCIAL SECURITY ASSOCIATION. ETUDES ET RECHERCHES/ STUDIES AND RESEARCH. (Editions in English and French) 1970. irreg. (1-2/yr.) 25 Fr. per no. International Social Security Association, Box 1, CH-1211 Geneva 22, Switzerland.

368.4   SZ   ISSN 0251-1339
INTERNATIONAL SOCIAL SECURITY ASSOCIATION. REPORTS OF THE GENERAL ASSEMBLIES OF THE ISSA. triennial, 22nd, 1986, Montreal. price varies. International Social Security Association, Box 1, 1211 Geneva 22, Switzerland.
    Formerly: International Social Security Association. Technical Reports of Assemblies (ISSN 0074-8439)

368   IS   ISSN 0077-5037
ISRAELI LIFE TABLE. (Text in English) 1969. irreg. National Insurance Institute, Weizmann Ave., Jerusalem, Israel.

368   NE
JAARBOEK/VADEMECUM VOOR HET VERZEKERINGSWEZEN. (Issued in 2 Parts) vol.1975. a. fl.275.50. Drukkerij Korthuis, Marnixstraat 16, The Hague, Netherlands. adv.
    Formed by merger of: Vademecum voor Het Nederlandsche Verzekeringswezen; Jaarboek voor Het Assurantie- en Hypotheekwezen.

368   JM
JAMAICA. MINISTRY OF SOCIAL SECURITY. REPORT. irreg. free. Ministry of Social Security, 14 National Heroes Circle, Box 10, Kingston 5, Jamaica.
    Formerly: Jamaica. Ministry of Pensions and Social Security. Report; Incorporating: Jamaica. National Insurance Scheme. Annual Reports (ISSN 0077-5053)

368   CN   ISSN 0318-8116
L U A C MONITOR. French Edition (ISSN 0318-8213) (Editions in English and French) 1957. irreg. membership. ‡ Life Underwriters Association of Canada, 41 Lesmill Rd., Don Mills, Ont. M3B 2T3, Canada. TEL 416-444-5251. circ. 14,000 (English edt.); 4,400 (French edt.) (also avail. in microform from UMI) Indexed: LII.

368   CH
LIFE INSURANCE BUSINESS IN TAIWAN (YEAR) (Text in Chinese and English) 1972. a. free. Taipei Life Insurance Association, Suite 152, 5th Floor, Sung Chiang Rd., Taipei, Taiwan, Republic of China. Ed.Bd.
    Formerly: Annual Report of Life Insurance, Republic of China.

368.3   US   ISSN 0075-9406
LIFE INSURANCE FACT BOOK. 1946. biennial. single copy free; additional copies $1 ea. American Council of Life Insurance, 1850 K St., N.W., Washington, DC 20006-2284. TEL 202-862-4000. Ed. Suzanne K. Stemnock. circ. 110,000. (also avail. in microform from UMI) Indexed: LII.

368.3   US
LIFE INSURANCE MARKETING AND RESEARCH ASSOCIATION. PROCEEDINGS OF THE ANNUAL MEETING. 1946. a. $5. ‡ Life Insurance Marketing and Research Association (LIMRA), Box 208, Hartford, CT 06141. TEL 203-677-0033. Ed. M.B. Petersen. circ. 1,000.
    Formerly: Life Insurance Agency Management Association. Proceedings of the Annual Meeting (ISSN 0075-9392)

368   US
LIFE RATES & DATA. 1971. a. $17.85. National Underwriter Co., 420 E. Fourth St., Cincinnati, OH 45202. TEL 513-721-2140.

368   US
LONG ISLAND TELEPHONE TICKLER FOR INSURANCE MEN & WOMEN. a. $5. Underwriter Printing and Publishing Co., 50 E. Palisade Ave., Englewood, NJ 07631. TEL 201-569-8808. Ed. Donald E. Wolff. adv. circ. 17,000.

368   LU
LUXEMBOURG. INSPECTION GENERALE DE LA SECURITE SOCIALE. RAPPORT GENERAL SUR LA SECURITE SOCIALE AU GRAND-DUCHE DE LUXEMBOURG. 1974. a. 780 Fr. Inspection Generale de la Securite Sociale, Ministere de la Securite Sociale, Luxembourg, Luxembourg. circ. 700.

368   US
M D R T ANNUAL MEETING. PROCEEDINGS. 1927. a. $20. Million Dollar Round Table, 2340 River Rd., Des Plaines, IL 60018. TEL 312-477-4700. Ed. H. William Woulfe. circ. 20,000. (also avail. in microform from UMI; microfiche; audio cassette; video cassette) Indexed: LII.

368   MW   ISSN 0076-3349
MALAWI. REGISTRAR OF INSURANCE. REPORT. a., latest 1972. K.0.50. Government Printer, P.O. Box 37, Zomba, Malawi.

368   CN
MANITOBA. PENSION COMMISSION. UPDATE STUDY. 1975. a. Pension Commission, 1004-401 York Ave., Winnipeg, Man. R3C 0P8, Canada. TEL 204-945-2740. circ. 500.
    Formerly: Manitoba. Pension Commission. Annual Report (ISSN 0381-3215)

368 631   CN   ISSN 0542-5395
MANITOBA CROP INSURANCE CORPORATION. ANNUAL REPORT. 1962. a. free. Manitoba Crop Insurance Corporation, 25 Tupper St., N., Portage la Prairie, Man. R1N 3K1, Canada. charts. circ. 325.

368   MF
MAURITIUS. REGISTRAR OF INSURANCE. ANNUAL REPORT. 1972. a. Rs.20. Registrar of Insurance, Treasury Building, Port Louis, Mauritius (Orders to: Government Printing Office, Elizabeth II Ave., Port Louis, Mauritius) stat.

368.382   US
MEDICARE AND MEDICAID DATA BOOK. a. U.S. Health Care Financing Administration, Department of Health and Human Services, Baltimore, MD 21207. TEL 301-597-3000.
    Formerly: Data on the Medicaid Program: Eligibility/Service/Expenditures.

368   MX
MEXICO. COMISION NACIONAL BANCARIA Y DE SEGUROS. ANUARIO ESTADISTICO DE SEGUROS. 1945. a. free. Comision Nacional Bancaria y de Seguros, Codigo Postal 06080, Republica de el Salvador No. 47, 1 Mexico, D.F., Mexico. stat. index.

368   US
MISSOURI. DIVISION OF INSURANCE. ANNUAL REPORT AND STATISTICAL DATA. 1870. a. $5. Division of Insurance, Statistical Section, Box 690, Jefferson City, MO 65102. TEL 314-751-4126. Ed. Mary Perrey. circ. 1,800. (also avail. in microfiche)

368   TZ
NATIONAL INSURANCE CORPORATION OF TANZANIA. ANNUAL REPORT AND ACCOUNTS. (Text in English) a. National Insurance Corporation of Tanzania Ltd., Box 9264, Dar es Salaam, Tanzania.

368.01   IS   ISSN 0075-1324
NATIONAL INSURANCE INSTITUTE, JERUSALEM. FULL ACTUARIAL REPORT. (Text in English and Hebrew) triennial. price varies. National Insurance Institute, Jerusalem, Israel.

368   UK
NATIONAL UNION OF INSURANCE WORKERS. PRUDENTIAL SECTION. GAZETTE. irreg. National Union of Insurance Workers, Prudential Section, 91-93 Gray's Inn Rd., London WC1X 8TX, England.
    Continues: Prudential Staff Gazette.

368   NE   ISSN 0077-5975
NATIONALE-NEDERLANDEN. ANNUAL REPORT. (Text in Dutch and English) 1963. a. free. Nationale-Nederlanden N.V., Prinses Beatrixlaan 15, Box 90504, 2509 LM The Hague, Netherlands. TEL 70-417045. circ. 21,500.

368   NE
NEDERLANDSE SCHADEVERZEKERINGSMAATSCHAPPIJEN/ NETHERLANDS NON-LIFE INSURANCE COMPANIES. (Text in Dutch and English) 1967. irreg. fl.11.25. Centraal Bureau voor de Statistiek, Prinses Beatrixlaan 428, Voorburg, Netherlands (Orders to: Staatsuitgeverij, Christoffel Plantijnstraat, The Hague, Netherlands)

368.4 314   NE   ISSN 0168-4108
NETHERLANDS. CENTRAAL BUREAU VOOR DE STATISTIEK. DIAGNOSESTATISTIEK BEDRIJFSVERENIGINGEN (OMSLAGLEDEN). SOCIAL INSURANCE SICKNESS STATISTICS. (Text in Dutch and English) 1958. a. fl.15. Centraal Bureau voor de Statistiek, Prinses Beatrixlaan 428, Voorburg, Netherlands (Orders to: Staatsuitgeverij, Christoffel Plantijnstraat, The Hague, Netherlands)

INSURANCE 641

368.382   US
NEW GROUP HEALTH INSURANCE. 1961. biennial. free. Health Insurance Association of America, 1850 K St. N.W., Washington, DC 20006. TEL 202-862-4000. Ed. Suzanne K. Stemnock. circ. 6,000.

368   US
NEW YORK (STATE). INSURANCE DEPARTMENT. ANNUAL REPORT OF THE SUPERINTENDENT OF INSURANCE TO THE NEW YORK LEGISLATURE. a. free. Insurance Department, Empire State Plaza, Agency Bldg. No. 1, Albany, NY 12257. circ. 2,500.

368   US
NEW YORK (STATE). INSURANCE DEPARTMENT. FEES AND TAXES CHARGED INSURANCE COMPANIES UNDER THE LAWS OF NEW YORK TOGETHER WITH ABSTRACTS OF FEES, TAXES AND OTHER REQUIREMENTS OF OTHER STATES. 1906. a. $2.50. Insurance Department, Empire State Plaza, Agency Bldg. No. 1, Albany, NY 12257. circ. 2,000.

368   US   ISSN 0467-6769
NEW YORK (STATE). INSURANCE DEPARTMENT. LOSS AND EXPENSE RATIOS. 1951. a. $2.50. Insurance Department, Empire State Plaza, Agency Bldg. No. 1, Albany, NY 12257. circ. 3,000. (back issues avail.)

368.4   US
NEW YORK (STATE). WORKMEN'S COMPENSATION BOARD. SUMMARY OF ACTIVITIES. 1956. a. free. Worker's Compensation Board, 180 Livingston St., Brooklyn, NY 11201. TEL 718-488-4141. circ. 700.

368   US
NEW YORK TELEPHONE TICKLER FOR INSURANCE MEN AND WOMEN. a. $9. Underwriter Printing and Publishing Co., 50 E. Palisade Ave., Englewood, NJ 07631. TEL 201-569-8808. Ed. Donald E. Wolff. adv. circ. 27,500.
    Formerly: Telephone Tickler for Insurance Men and Women (ISSN 0082-2663)

368   US
NORTH JERSEY TELEPHONE TICKLER FOR INSURANCE MEN & WOMEN. a. $5. Underwriter Printing and Publishing Co., 50 E. Palisade Ave., Englewood, NJ 07631. TEL 201-569-8808. Ed. Donald E. Wolff. adv. circ. 17,000.

368   CN
ONTARIO INSURANCE DIRECTORY. a. Can.$22. Wadham Publications Ltd., 109 Vanderhoof Ave., Ste. 101, Toronto, Ont. M4G 2J2, Canada. TEL 416-425-9021. circ. 3,000.

368   PK   ISSN 0078-8236
PAKISTAN INSURANCE YEAR BOOK. (Text in English) a. Rs.3. Department of Insurance, Karachi, Pakistan (Order from: Manager of Publications, Government of Pakistan, 2nd Floor, Ahmad Chamber, Tariq Rd., P.E.C.H.S., Karachi 29, Pakistan)

368   US
PENSION FACTS. 1974. biennial. American Council of Life Insurance, Information Department, 1850 K St., N.W., Washington, DC 20006. circ. 35,000.

368   PH
PHILIPPINES. INSURANCE COMMISSION. ANNUAL REPORT. 1949. a. price varies. Insurance Commission, Insurance Commission Bldg., 1071 United Nations Ave., Box 3589, Manila, Philippines. circ. 1,000.

368   CN   ISSN 0227-437X
PROVINCIAL RESULTS IN CANADA OF GENERAL INSURANCE COMPANIES. (Text in English and French) 1935. a. Can.$50. Stone & Cox Ltd., 323-366 Adelaide St., Toronto, Ont. M5A 3X9, Canada. TEL 416-864-0453. Ed. John S. Wyndham. circ. 500.
    Formerly: Provincial Results in Canada of Fire & Casualty Companies.

368   CN   ISSN 0701-5666
QUEBEC (PROVINCE) REGIE DE L'ASSURANCE-DEPOTS DU QUEBEC. RAPPORT ANNUEL.* a. Editeur Officiel du Quebec, 1283 Bd. Charest Ouest, Quebec, P.Q. G1N 2C9, Canada. TEL 413-643-3895.

368.4   658.3   CN   ISSN 0712-8231
QUEBEC (PROVINCE). REGIE DES RENTES DU QUEBEC. STATISTICAL OUTLOOK. French edition: Quebec (Province). Regie des Rentes du Quebec. Perspectives Statistiques (ISSN 0712-8223) (Text in English and French) 1982. a. free. Regie des Rentes du Quebec, C.P. 5200, Quebec, P.Q. G1K 7S9, Canada. TEL 418-643-8309. circ. 2,500.

368   US
RALPH H. BLANCHARD MEMORIAL ENDOWMENT SERIES. 1977. irreg. $10 for vol.1. (University of Pennsylvania, Wharton School of Finance and Commerce. Pension Research Council) Richard D. Irwin, Inc., Homewood, IL 60430. TEL 312-785-6000.

368.3   CN   ISSN 0080-6544
SASKATCHEWAN. MEDICAL CARE INSURANCE COMMISSION. ANNUAL REPORT. 1962. a. free. Medical Care Insurance Commission, T.C. Douglas Bldg., 3475 Albert St., Regina, Sask. S4S 6X6, Canada. TEL 306-565-3475. circ. 2,500.

SASKATCHEWAN. PRESCRIPTION DRUG PLAN. ANNUAL REPORT. see *PHARMACY AND PHARMACOLOGY*

368   UY
SEGUROS. 1975. irreg. Banco de Seguros, Av. Libertador Brigadier General Juan A. Lavalleja No. 1465, Montevideo, Uruguay. illus.
    Formerly: Bancoseguros.

368   UK
SELF-EMPLOYED PENSIONS. 1975. irreg. Financial Times Business Information, 102 Clerkenwell Road, London EC1M 5SA, England. circ. 3,500. (tabloid format)
    Formerly: Handbook of Self-Employed Pensions.

SINGAPORE BANKING, FINANCE & INSURANCE. see *BUSINESS AND ECONOMICS — Banking And Finance*

368   SZ   ISSN 0379-704X
SOCIAL SECURITY DOCUMENTATION: AFRICAN SERIES. 1977. irreg. 15 Fr. per no. International Social Security Association, Box 1, CH-1211 Geneva 22, Switzerland.

368   SZ   ISSN 0250-4057
SOCIAL SECURITY DOCUMENTATION: ASIAN SERIES. 1979. irreg. 15 Fr. per no. International Social Security Association, Box 1, Ch-1211 Geneva 22, Switzerland.

368   SZ
SOCIAL SECURITY DOCUMENTATION: EUROPEAN SERIES. (Editions in English, French, German and Spanish) 1979. irreg. 20 Fr. per no. International Social Security Association, Box 1, CH-1211 Geneva 22, Switzerland.

368.4   US   ISSN 0081-0495
SOCIAL SECURITY HANDBOOK. 1944. a. $1.25. ‡ R & R Newkirk (Subsidiary of: Longman Financial Publishing Service) 500 N. Dearborn, Chicago, IL 60610-4901. Ed. John D. Wells.
    Social security

368   DK   ISSN 0107-5047
SOCIALE YDELSER, HVEM, HVAD, OG HVORNAAR; en Kort oversigt over Danmarks Sociale lovgivning med Regler og Ydelser. 1968. a. Kr.4. Forsikringsoplysningen, Amaliegade 10, 1256 Copenhagen K, Denmark. illus.

368   US   ISSN 0037-9794
SOCIETY OF ACTUARIES. TRANSACTIONS (GENERAL) 1949. a. $44. Society of Actuaries, 500 Park Blvd., Itasca, IL 60143. Ed. Douglas A. Eckley. bk. rev. abstr. bibl. charts. index. cum.index every 5 yrs. circ. 10,000. (also avail. in microform from UMI) Indexed: LII.

368   US
SOCIETY OF ACTUARIES. TRANSACTIONS: REPORTS OF MORTALITY AND MORBIDITY EXPERIENCE. 1951. a. $13.25 (foreign $19.80) Society of Actuaries, 500 Park Blvd., Itasca, IL 60143. TEL 312-773-3010. Ed. Douglas A. Eckley. charts. index. circ. 12,000.

368   US
SOCIETY OF ACTUARIES. YEARBOOK. 1950. a. $60 (foreign $90) Society of Actuaries, 500 Park Blvd., Itasca, IL 60143. TEL 312-773-3010. Ed. Linda M. Delgadillo. index. circ. 12,000.

368.38   US   ISSN 0073-148X
SOURCE BOOK OF HEALTH INSURANCE DATA. 1959. biennial. single copy free. Health Insurance Association of America, Public Relations Division, 1850 K St. N.W., Washington, DC 20006. index. circ. 45,000.

368.4   331.2   SA
SOUTH AFRICA. UNEMPLOYMENT INSURANCE FUND. REPORT/SOUTH AFRICA. WERKLOOSHEIDVERSEKERINGSFONDS. VERSLAG. (Text in Afrikaans and English) a. R.1. Unemployment Insurance Fund, Box 1851, Pretoria 0001, South Africa.

368   UK   ISSN 0038-8637
SPRINKLER BULLETIN. 1892. every 6-9 mos. contr.circ. Mather and Platt Ltd., Park Works, Manchester M10 6BA, England. Ed. M.L.A. Jones. charts. illus. stat. circ. 10,000.

368.4   US   ISSN 0099-2100
STATE HEALTH BENEFITS PROGRAM OF NEW JERSEY. ANNUAL REPORT. a. State Health Benefits Commission, 20 W. Front St., Trenton, NJ 08625. TEL 609-292-7060.

368   JA   ISSN 0910-5727
STATISTICS OF JAPANESE NON-LIFE INSURANCE BUSINESS. 1948. a. $26. Insurance Research Institute Ltd. - Hoken Kenkyujo Ltd., 17-3 Honmachi, 1-chome, Shibuya-ku, Tokyo, Japan. circ. 10,000.
    Formerly: Japanese Insurance Business Statistics: Non-Life; Supersedes in part: Insurance Life/Non-Life Annual Statistics (ISSN 0085-1930)

368   JA   ISSN 0910-5719
STATISTICS OF LIFE INSURANCE BUSINESS IN JAPAN. 1948. a. $26. Insurance Research Institute Ltd. - Hoken Kenkyujo Ltd., 17-3 Honmachi 1-chome, Shibuya-ku, Tokyo, Japan. circ. 10,000.
    Formerly: Japanese Insurance Business Statistics: Life; Which supersedes in part: Insurance Life/Non-Life Annual Statistics (ISSN 0085-1930)

368   CN
STONE AND COX GENERAL INSURANCE REGISTER. 1920. a. Can.$27. Stone and Cox Ltd., 323-366 Adelaide St. E., Toronto, Ont. M5A 3X9, Canada. TEL 416-864-0453. Ed. J.D. Wyndham. adv. circ. 2,500.
    Formerly: Stone and Cox General Insurance Year Book (ISSN 0081-5772)

368.3   CN   ISSN 0081-5780
STONE AND COX LIFE INSURANCE TABLES. (Text in English and French) 1912. a. Can.$20. Stone and Cox Ltd., 323-366 Adelaide St. E., Toronto, Ont. M5A 3X9, Canada. TEL 416-864-0453. Ed. J.D. Wyndham. adv. circ. 6,000.

368   PL   ISSN 0137-9704
STUDIA UBEZPIECZENIOWE. (Text in Polish; summaries in English, Russian) 1973. irreg., vol.7, 1984. price varies. (Polskie Towarzystwo Ekonomiczne, Oddzial w Poznaniu) Panstwowe Wydawnictwo Naukowe, Miodowa 10, 00-251 Warsaw, Poland. bibl. illus.

368   FI   ISSN 0356-7826
SUOMEN VAKUUTUSVUOSIKIRJA/FINNISH INSURANCE YEARBOOK. Swedish edition: Foersaekringsaarsbok foer Finland (ISSN 0356-7834) (Text in Finnish and Swedish with English glossary) 1912. a. Fmk.100. Suomen Vakuutusyhdistys - Finnish Insurance Society, Bulevardi 28, 00120 Helsinki 12, Finland. Ed. Goesta Wahlstroem. adv. stat. circ. 1,200 (Finnish edt.); 600 (Swedish edt.)

368.4   SW   ISSN 0082-0075
SWEDEN. RIKSFOERSAEKRINGSVERKET. ALLMAEN FOERSAEKRING. (Text in Swedish; summaries in English) 1963. a. Kr.110. Riksfoersaekringsverket - National Social Insurance Board, S-103 51 Vaellingby, Sweden (Orders to: Liber Foerlag, S-162 89 Vaellingby, Sweden) circ. 1,200.

INSURANCE — ABSTRACTING, BIBLIOGRAPHIES, STATISTICS

368 SW
SWEDEN. STATENS ARBETSGIVARVERK. FOERESKRIFTER OM STATLIG TJAENSTEPENSIONERING; F S P. 1970. a. Statens Arbetsgivarverk - National Swedish Agency for Government Employers, Box 2243, S-103 16 Stockholm, Sweden (Dist. by: Liber Foerlag, Fack, S-162 89 Vaellingby, Sweden)
    Former titles (until 1979): Sweden. Statens Avtalsverk. Foereskrifter om Statlight Tjaenstepensionering; F S P; Sweden. Statens Avtalsverk Foerfattningar om Statligt Tjaenstepensionering; F S P.

368 US
T A P REPORT. 1970. irreg. free. American Council of Life Insurance, Trend Analysis Program, 1850 K St., N.W., Washington, DC 20006. TEL 202-862-4000. bk. rev. circ. 7,000.

368 US
TAX FACTS 1; taxation on insurance. a. $9. National Underwriter Co., 420 E. 4 St., Cincinnati, OH 45202. TEL 513-721-2140. (also avail. in microform from UMI) Indexed: LII.
    Formerly: Tax Facts on Life Insurance (ISSN 0145-1847)

368.32 US ISSN 0739-4691
TEXAS BLUE BOOK OF LIFE INSURANCE STATISTICS. 1944. a. $22. Record Publishing Co. (Dallas), Box 225770, Dallas, TX 75265. TEL 214-630-0687. Ed. John H. Leslie. circ. 1,000.

368 AG
TUTORA. MEMORIA Y BALANCE GENERAL. no.13, 1975. a. Compania Sudamericana de Seguros, Rivadavia 717, Buenos Aires, Argentina.

368 CN ISSN 0576-4157
UNEMPLOYMENT INSURANCE CANADA. ANNUAL REPORT/ASSURANCE-CHOMAGE CANADA. RAPPORT ANNUEL. (Text in English and French) no.32, 1973. a. free. Unemployment Insurance Commission, c/o Public Relations, 222 Nepean, Ottawa K1A 0J5, Canada. charts. stat. circ. 10,000.

UNITED CHURCH OF CHRIST. PENSION BOARDS (ANNUAL REPORT) see *RELIGIONS AND THEOLOGY* — Other Denominations And Sects

U.S. DEPARTMENT OF LABOR. EMPLOYEE RETIREMENT INCOME SECURITY ACT. REPORT TO CONGRESS. see *BUSINESS AND ECONOMICS* — Labor And Industrial Relations

332.17 368.85 US ISSN 0083-0658
U.S. FEDERAL DEPOSIT INSURANCE CORPORATION. ANNUAL REPORT. 1934. a. U.S. Federal Deposit Insurance Corporation, 550 17th St., N.W., Washington, DC 20429. TEL 202-389-4221.

U.S. VETERANS ADMINISTRATION. ANNUAL REPORT. see *MILITARY*

368 SA ISSN 0259-0034
VITAE YEARBOOK. (Text in English) 1973. a. R.50. Vitae Insurance Publications (Pty.) Ltd., P.O. Box 39089, Bramley, 2018, South Africa. Ed. S.W. Bishop. adv. index. circ. 1,000.
    Formerly: Vitae S A Life Assurance Yearbook.

368 US
WHO WRITES WHAT IN LIFE AND HEALTH INSURANCE. a. $15.25. National Underwriter Co., 420 E. 4th St., Cincinnati, OH 45202. TEL 513-721-2140. adv.

WHO'S WHO IN INSURANCE. see *BIOGRAPHY*

WHO'S WHO IN INSURANCE. see *BIOGRAPHY*

368 US
WHO'S WHO IN RISK MANAGEMENT. 1971. a. $50. Underwriter Printing and Publishing Co., 50 E. Palisade Ave., Englewood, NJ 07631. TEL 201-569-8808. Ed. Donald E. Wolff. circ. 10,000.

368 US
WORKERS' COMPENSATION LAW REPORTER. a. (plus fortn. updates) $580. Commerce Clearing House, Inc., 4025 W. Peterson Ave., Chicago, IL 60646. TEL 312-583-8500. Ed. A.E. Schecter. (also avail. in looseleaf format)

368 ZA
ZAMBIA STATE INSURANCE CORPORATION. REPORT AND ACCOUNTS. 1971. a. Zambia State Insurance Corporation, Box 894, Lusaka, Zambia. circ. 3,000.

368 RH ISSN 0556-8692
ZIMBABWE. REGISTRAR OF INSURANCE. REPORT. (Text in English) 1974. a. Rhod.$1.50. Registrar of Insurance, Private Bag 7705, Causeway, Salisbury, Zimbabwe. stat. circ. 500.
    Formerly: Rhodesia. Central Statistical Office. Insurance Statistics.

INSURANCE — Abstracting, Bibliographies, Statistics

368 319 332 HO
BANCO CENTRAL DE HONDURAS. SECCION DE SEGUROS. BOLETIN DE ESTADISTICAS DE SEGUROS. 1974. irreg. (Banco Central de Honduras) Honduras. Superintendencia de Bancos, Seccion de Seguros, Tegucigalpa, Honduras.

314 368.4 BE
BELGIUM. INSTITUT NATIONAL D'ASSURANCES SOCIALES POUR TRAVAILLEURS INDEPENDANTS. STATISTIQUE DES ENFANTS BENEFICIAIRES D'ALLOCATIONS FAMILIALES/BELGIUM. RIJKSINSTITUUT VOOR DE SOCIALE VERZEKERINGEN DER ZELFSTANDIGEN. STATISTIEK VAN DE KINDEREN DIE RECHT GEVEN OP KINDERBIJSLAG. (Text in Dutch and French) 1970. a. Institut National d'Assurances Sociales pour Travailleurs Independants, 6 place Jean Jacobs, 1000 Brussels, Belgium.

368 CN ISSN 0701-5488
CANADA. STATISTICS CANADA. PENSION PLANS IN CANADA/REGIMES DE PENSIONS AU CANADA. (Catalogue 74-401) (Text in English and French) 1970. biennial. Can.$7.75($9.30) per issue. Statistics Canada, Communications Division, 3rd Floor, R.H. Coats Bldg., Ottawa, Ont. K1A 0T6, Canada TEL 613-993-7276. (Subscr. to: Publications Sales and Services, Ottawa, Ont. K1A 0T6, Canada) circ. 10,000. (also avail. in microform from MML)

368.4 314 FI ISSN 0071-5247
FINLAND. KANSANELAKELAITOS. TILASTOLLINEN VUOSIKIRJA/FINLAND. FOLKPENSIONSANSTALT. STATISTISK AARSBOK/FINLAND. SOCIAL INSURANCE INSTITUTION. STATISTICAL YEARBOOK. (Subseries of its Julkaisuja. Series T: 1) (Text in Finnish and Swedish; summaries in English) 1965. a. Fmk.45. Kansanelakelaitos - Social Insurance Institution of Finland, Estimating and Statistics Department, Nordenskioldinkatu 12, SF-00250 Helsinki 25, Finland. Ed. F. Gustafsson. charts. stat. circ. 4,000.

368.4 314 FR
FRANCE. CAISSE NATIONALE DE L'ASSURANCE MALADIE DES TRAVAILLEURS SALARIES. STATISTIQUES DE L'ANNEE. a. Caisse Nationale de l'Assurance Maladie des Travailleurs Salaries, 44-46 bd. de Grenelle, 75015 Paris, France. illus.

368 314 GW ISSN 0435-7442
GESAMTSTATISTIK DER KRAFTFAHRTVERSICHERUNG. 1958. a. free. Verband der Haftpflicht-, Unfall- und Kraftverkehrsversicherer e.V., Glockengiesserwall 1, 2000 Hamburg 1, W. Germany (B.R.D.) stat. circ. controlled.

368 314 AU
HANDBUCH DER OESTERREICHISCHEN SOZIALVERSICHERUNG. 1971. a. Hauptverband der Oesterreichischen Sozialversicherungstraeger, Kundmanng. 21, A-1037 Vienna, Austria.
    Formerly: Statistiches Handbuch der Oesterreichischen Sozialversicherung; Which superseded in part: Jahrbuch der Oesterreichischen Sozialversicherung.

368.01 US ISSN 0074-0713
INSURANCE FACTS. 1961. a. $12. Insurance Information Institute, 110 William St., New York, NY 10038. TEL 212-699-9200. Ed. Sean Mooney. circ. 25,000.
    Property-liability insurance and related fields

368 016 UK ISSN 0144-6304
INSURANCE INDEX. 1979. m. £39. Insurance Index Ltd., Bremar House, Sale Place, London W2 1PT, England.

368 016 US ISSN 0074-073X
INSURANCE PERIODICALS INDEX. 1964. a. $90. (Special Libraries Association, Insurance and Employee Benefits Division) N I L S Publishing Company, Box 2507, Chatsworth, CA 91311 TEL 818-998-8830. (Address of Association: 1700 19th St., N.W., Washington, DC 20009) Ed. Oriole Anderson. circ. 450. (back issues avail.)
    ●Also available online. Vendors: Mead Data Central.

368 319 FJ
INSURANCE STATISTICS OF FIJI. 1969. a. $2.50 free. Commissioner of Insurance, Government Printer, Box 98, Suva, Fiji. stat. circ. 200.

368 315 IS ISSN 0074-0705
ISRAEL. CENTRAL BUREAU OF STATISTICS. INSURANCE IN ISRAEL/ISKE HA-BITUAH BE-YISRAEL. (Subseries of the Bureau's Special Series) (Text in English, Hebrew) 1950/52. a. price varies. Central Bureau of Statistics, P.O. Box 13015, Jerusalem, Israel.

368 314 IT ISSN 0075-1790
ITALY. ISTITUTO CENTRALE DI STATISTICA. ANNUARIO STATISTICO DELL'ASSISTENZA E DELLA PREVIDENZA SOCIALE. a., 1979-82 in prep. L.12000. Istituto Centrale di Statistica, Via Cesare Balbo 16, 00100 Rome, Italy. circ. 1,200.

368.382 315 JA
JAPAN. MINISTRY OF HEALTH AND WELFARE. STATISTICS AND INFORMATION DEPARTMENT. REPORT ON SURVEY OF NATIONAL MEDICAL CARE INSURANCE SERVICES. a. 3.300 Yen. Ministry of Health and Welfare, Statistics and Information Department, 7-03 Ichigaya-Honmura cho, Shinjuku-ku, Tokyo 162, Japan (Order from: Health & Welfare Statistics Association, c/o Mezon Azabu, 5-13-14 Roppongi, Minato-ku, Tokyo, Japan)
    Health

310 IS
NATIONAL INSURANCE INSTITUTE, JERUSALEM. ANNUAL SURVEY. 1981. a. free. National Insurance Institute, 13 Sderot Weizman, Jerusalem, Israel.
    Formerly: National Insurance Institute, Jerusalem. Statistical Abstracts.

368 317 US
NEW YORK (STATE) INSURANCE DEPARTMENT. STATISTICAL TABLES FROM ANNUAL STATEMENTS. 1944. a. $6.50. Insurance Department, Empire State Plaza, Agency Bldg. No. 1, Albany, NY 12257. circ. 2,000. (back issues avail.)

368 319 NZ ISSN 0110-3474
NEW ZEALAND. DEPARTMENT OF STATISTICS. INSURANCE STATISTICS. a. NZ.$7.15. Department of Statistics, Private Bag, Wellington, New Zealand (Subscr. to: Government Printing Office, Publications, Private Bag, Wellington, New Zealand)

368 NZ ISSN 0111-0225
NEW ZEALAND. DEPARTMENT OF STATISTICS. NEW ZEALAND LIFE TABLES. quinquennial. NZ.$7.15. Department of Statistics, Private Bag, Wellington, New Zealand (Subscr. to: Government Printing Office, Publications, Private Bag, Wellington, New Zealand)
    Formerly: New Zealand. Department of Statistics. Life Annuity Tables.

368.4 319   PP
PAPUA NEW GUINEA. NATIONAL STATISTICAL OFFICE. WORKER'S COMPENSATION CLAIMS. (Text in English) 1966. a. free. National Statistical Office, P.O. Wards Strip, Papua New Guinea. Ed. J.J. Shadlow. circ. 367.
Former titles: Papua New Guinea. Bureau of Statistics. Industrial Accidents; Papua New Guinea. Bureau of Statistics. Workers' Compensation Statistics (ISSN 0078-9267)

368.4 317   CN
QUEBEC (PROVINCE) REGIE DE L'ASSURANCE-MALADIE. STATISTIQUES ANNUELLES. (Text in French) 1971. a. free. ‡ Regie de l'Assurance-Maladie, Case Postale 6600, Quebec, Que. G1K 7T3, Canada. TEL 418-643-3445. Ed.Bd. circ. 1,000.

368.382   DK   ISSN 0107-8437
SYGESIKRINGSSTATISTIK. 1981. a. free. Sygesikringens Forhandlingsudvalg, c/o Amtsraadsforeningen i Danmark, Landmaerket 10, 1119 Copenhagen K, Denmark. Ed. Frank I. Jensen. circ. 500.
Formerly: Statistik over Afregning af Ydelser indem for den Offentlige Sygesikring.

INTERIOR DESIGN AND DECORATION

see also Interior Design and Decoration—Furniture and House Furnishings

747   US
APPLIANCES: LATIN AMERICAN INDUSTRIAL REPORT. (Avail. for each of 22 Latin American countries) 1985. a. $435 per country report per industry covered. Aurora International, Box 9099, Bridgeport, CT 06601-2099. TEL 203-368-0579.

747   IT
BAGNOGUIDA. 1978. a. Faenza Editrice S.p.A, Via Pier de Crescenzi no.44, 48018 Faenza (RA), Italy. adv.

747 690   UK   ISSN 0260-9169
BARBOUR COMPENDIUM BUILDING PRODUCTS. 1977. a. £35. Barbour-Builder Ltd., New Lodge, Drift Rd., Windsor, Berks SL4 4RQ, England. Ed. Carol Barnes. adv. circ. 22,000.

747   US   ISSN 0277-836X
BETTER HOMES AND GARDENS WINDOW & WALL IDEAS. 1975. a. $2.50. Meredith Corporation, Special Interest Publications, 1716 Locust St., Des Moines, IA 50336. TEL 515-284-3000. illus.
Formerly: Window and Wall Decorating Ideas (ISSN 0363-5406)

747   UK   ISSN 0263-2047
BRITISH INSTITUTE OF INTERIOR DESIGN MEMBERS' REFERENCE BOOK. 1983. a. £20. Sterling Publications Ltd., 86-88 Edgware Road, London, W2 2YW, England. adv.

747   SP
COLOR Y DECORACION EN EL HOGAR. irreg. Editorial Gustavo Gili S.A., Rosellon 87-89, Barcelona 15, Spain.

747   UK
COMMERCIAL INTERIORS INTERNATIONAL. 1985. a. $29.95. Grosvenor Press International, West Garden Place, Kendal St., London W2 2AQ, England. Ed. Richard Parkes. circ. 30,000.

747   UK
CONTRACT INTERIOR'S CATALOGUE; 350 pages of manufacturers' contract furniture and furnishings. biennial. £12.50. Standard Catalogue Information Services Ltd., Medway Wharf Rd., Tonbridge, Kent TN9 1QR, England. circ. 3,750.
Former titles: I D Mini-File & Interior Design Catalogues.

747   DK   ISSN 0108-982X
DANISH CONTRACT; commercial furnishings and interior design. (Text in English, French and German) 1983. a. Kr.65. N O V A Kommunikation, Holte Midtpunkt 23/3, 2840 Holte, Denmark. Ed. Poul Jacobson. adv. illus. circ. 22,000.

747   GW
DECO; Magazin der Textilen Raumausstattung. 1979. a. DM.10. Peter Winkler Verlag, Maximiliansplatz 9, 8000 Munich 2, W. Germany (B.R.D.) circ. 40,000.

747   UK   ISSN 0070-3192
DECORATING CONTRACTOR ANNUAL DIRECTORY. 1903. a. £8.75. Ridgway Press, Sunrise House, 23 Midford Lane, Limpley Stoke, Bath BA3 6JR, England. Ed. Laurence Ridgeway. adv. bk. rev.

DESIGN DIRECTORY; a listing of firm and consultants in industrial, graphic, interior and environmental design. see *BUSINESS AND ECONOMICS — Trade And Industrial Directories*

DESIGN FROM SCANDINAVIA; a Scandinavian production in furniture, textiles, illumination, arts and crafts and industrial design. see *INTERIOR DESIGN AND DECORATION — Furniture And House Furnishings*

747   FI
DESIGN IN FINLAND. 1960. a. Fmk.45. Finnish Foreign Trade Association, Arkadiankatu 4-6B, 00100 Helsinki 10, Finland. illus. circ. 55,000.
Formerly: Designed in Finland (ISSN 0418-7717)

645 720   US
DESIGNERS WEST RESOURCE DIRECTORY. (Supplement to Designers West) 1973. a. $10 per no. Arts Alliance Corp., Box 48968, 8770 Beverly Blvd., Los Angeles, CA 90048. TEL 213-657-8231. Ed. Barbara L. Shepherd. adv. circ. 21,228.

DIRECTORY OF CONTRACT WALLCOVERINGS AND SPECIFICATIONS. see *BUSINESS AND ECONOMICS — Trade And Industrial Directories*

747   II   ISSN 0256-4025
DIRECTORY OF INTERIOR DESIGNERS. (Text in English) 1984. biennial. Rs.100. Architects Publishing Corp. of India, 51 Sujata, Ground Floor, Rani Sati Marg, Malad East, Bombay 400097, India. Ed. A.K. Gupta. adv. bk. rev. charts. illus. circ. 2,000.

747   US
FURNITURE: LATIN AMERICAN INDUSTRIAL REPORT. (Avail. for each of 22 Latin American countries) 1985. a. $435 per country report per industry covered. Aurora International, Box 9099, Bridgeport, CT 06601-2099. TEL 203-368-0579. Ed. Andres C. Aquino.

GABRIEL'S HOME IMPROVEMENT ANNUAL. see *BUILDING AND CONSTRUCTION*

GABRIEL'S KITCHENS AND BATHROOMS ANNUAL. see *BUILDING AND CONSTRUCTION*

INTERIOR DESIGN BUYERS GUIDE. see *BUSINESS AND ECONOMICS — Trade And Industrial Directories*

747   UK
INTERIOR DESIGNER'S HANDBOOK. 1981. a. £19.95. Grosvenor Press International, West Garden Place, Kendal St., London W2 2AQ, England. Ed. Richard Parkes. adv. circ. 10,000.

747   UK
THE INTERNATIONAL COLLECTION OF INTERIOR DESIGN. 1984. a. $29.95. Grosvenor Press International, West Garden Place, Kendal St., London W2 2AQ, England. Ed. Richard Parkes. adv. circ. 30,000.

745   US   ISSN 0534-9710
INTERNATIONAL DESIGN CONFERENCE IN ASPEN. REPORT.* 1951. a. International Design Conference, Box 664, Aspen, CO 81612.

747   IT
LIBRO DI CASA. 1935. a. $12. Editoriale Domus, Via Grandi 5/7, 20089 Rozzano (MI), Italy. adv.

745.05   US   ISSN 0272-4499
MCCALL'S COUNTRY DECORATING; do-it-yourself ideas. a. McCall Publishing Co., 230 Park Ave., New York, NY 10017.

747   UK
NATIONAL FEDERATION OF PAINTING AND DECORATING CONTRACTORS YEAR BOOK. 1982. a. Comprint Ltd., 177 Hagden Lane, Watford WD1 8LW, England. adv.

747   IT
OFFICE FURNITURE; rivista annual di arredamento per l'ufficio. 1981. a. $20. Alberto Greco Editore, Via G. Sidoli 20, 20129 Milan, Italy. Ed. Alessandro Ubertazzi. adv. circ. 21,500.
Formerly: Habitat Ufficio.

747.85   US   ISSN 0192-8732
STORES OF THE YEAR; a pictorial report on store interiors. biennial. Retail Reporting Bureau, 101 Fifth Ave., New York, NY 10003. TEL 212-255-9595. illus.

747   US
SWEET'S CONTRACT INTERIORS FILE. a. free to qualified personnel. Sweet's Catalog Files (Subsidiary of: McGraw-Hill Information Systems Co.) 1221 Ave. of the Americas, New York, NY 10020. TEL 212-512-4303. circ. 7,000.

TOY AND DECORATION FAIR DIRECTORY. see *GIFTWARE AND TOYS*

747 645   GE   ISSN 0138-2810
WOHNEN. 1978. a. M.4.70. Verlag Fuer die Frau, Friedrich-Ebert-Str. 76-78, 7010 Leipzig, E. Germany (D.D.R.)

747.05   US   ISSN 0361-638X
WOMAN'S DAY HOME DECORATING IDEAS. Short title: Home Decorating Ideas. a. $2.25. C B S Publications, Woman's Day, 1515 Broadway, New York, NY 10036. TEL 201-719-6816. Ed. Carolyn Gatto. adv. illus.

INTERIOR DESIGN AND DECORATION — Abstracting, Bibliographies, Statistics

338.4   US
CARPET AND RUG INDUSTRY REVIEW. a. $10. Carpet and Rug Institute, Box 2048, Dalton, GA 30720. TEL 404-278-3176.
Formerly: Carpet and Rug Institute. Review-State of the Industry (ISSN 0092-0495)

INTERIOR DESIGN AND DECORATION — Furniture And House Furnishings

684   FR
ANNUAIRE DE L'AMEUBLEMENT. 1908. a. 340 F. Editions Louis Johanet, 68 rue Boursault, 75017 Paris, France.
Former titles: Annuaire de l'Ameublement et des Industries s'y Rattachant (ISSN 0066-2615); Annuaire de l'Ameublement.

645 666   IT
ANNUARIO ARTICOLI CASALINGHI E ARTICOLI REGALO. (Editions in English, French and Italian) 1980. a. L.16000($30) Edispe s.n.c., Via Melchiorre Gioia 71, 20144 Milan, Italy. Ed. Vincenzo Vaccaro. adv. circ. 9,500.

AUSTRALIAN CONTRACT FURNISHING CYCLOPAEDIA. see *BUSINESS AND ECONOMICS — Trade And Industrial Directories*

645   AT
AUSTRALIAN CONTRACT YEARBOOK. 1972. a. Aus.$30. Furnishing Media Pty. Ltd., 162 Williams Rd., Prahran, Vic. 3181, Australia. Ed. Gunther Vance. adv. illus. patents. tr.lit. circ. 5,951.

381   AG
CAMARA DE COMERCIANTES EN ARTEFACTOS PARA EL HOGAR. REVISTA. irreg. Camara de Comerciantes en Artefactos para el Hogar, Bartolome Mitre 2162, Buenos Aires, Argentina. illus.

CANADIAN FURNITURE & FURNISHINGS
DIRECTORY. see *BUSINESS AND
ECONOMICS — Trade And Industrial Directories*

CONTRACT INTERIOR'S CATALOGUE; 350
pages of manufacturers' contract furniture and
furnishings. see *INTERIOR DESIGN AND
DECORATION*

747   DK   ISSN 0108-0695
DESIGN FROM SCANDINAVIA; a Scandinavian
production in furniture, textiles, illumination, arts
and crafts and industrial design. (Text in English,
French, German and Scandinavian languages) 1966.
a. Kr.120($17) World Pictures, Martinsvej 8, DK-
1926 Frederiksberg C, Denmark (U.S. subscr. to:
World Pictures, P.O. Box 305, Racine, WI 53401
U.S.A.) Ed. Kirsten Bjerregaard. illus. circ. 50,000.
Formerly: Design from Denmark.

645   US
DIRECTORY OF HOME FURNISHINGS
RETAILERS. 1987. a. $249. Chain Store Guide,
425 Park Ave., New York, NY 10022. TEL 212-
371-9400.

684.1   UK   ISSN 0070-6604
DIRECTORY TO THE FURNISHING TRADE;
cabinet maker directory. 1957. a. £60. Benn
Business Information Services Ltd., P.O. Box 20,
Sovereign Way, Tonbridge, Kent TN9 1RQ,
England. adv. index. circ. 3,515.

643.3   SW
ELECTROLUX. ANNUAL REPORT. (Text in
English) a. Electrolux, Lilla Essingen, S-10545
Stockholm, Sweden.
Appliances

GABRIEL'S HOME IMPROVEMENT ANNUAL.
see *BUILDING AND CONSTRUCTION*

GABRIEL'S KITCHENS AND BATHROOMS
ANNUAL. see *BUILDING AND
CONSTRUCTION*

GUIDE TO RESTORATION EXPERTS. see
BUILDING AND CONSTRUCTION

HOME CENTER OPERATORS & HARDWARE
CHAINS (YEAR) see *BUSINESS AND
ECONOMICS — Trade And Industrial Directories*

747   UK
HOME FURNISHINGS SURVEY. 1981. biennial.
£160. Euromonitor Publications Ltd., 87-88
Turnmill St., London EC1M 5QU, England.

677   US
LINENS, DOMESTICS & BATH PRODUCTS
ANNUAL DIRECTORY. 1927. a. $10. Columbia
Communications, Inc., 370 Lexington Ave., New
York, NY 10017. TEL 212-532-9290. adv. circ. 10,
011.

684   GW   ISSN 0077-0205
MOEBEL-INDUSTRIE UND IHRE HELFER. 1957.
a. DM.38. Industrieschau-Verlagsgesellschaft,
Berliner Allee 8, 6100 Darmstadt, W. Germany
(B.R.D.)

NATIONWIDE DIRECTORY OF GIFT,
HOUSEWARES & HOME TEXTILE BUYERS.
see *GIFTWARE AND TOYS*

684.1   DK   ISSN 0109-1573
NORMTAL. 1955. a. free to libraries.
Moebelfabrikanterforeningen, Center Boulevard 5,
DK-2300 Copenhagen S, Denmark. illus. circ. 500.

747.4   US
SPECIFIER'S GUIDE TO CONTRACT FLOOR
COVERINGS. 1977. a. $15. Hearst Business Media
Corporation, F C W Division, 919 Third Ave., New
York, NY 10022 (Subscr. to: Floor Covering
Weekly, 645 Stewart Ave., Garden City, NY
11530) Ed. Albert Wahnon.
Formerly: Handbook of Contract Floor Covering.

UNIVERSIDADE DE SAO PAULO. MUSEU
PAULISTA. COLECAO. SERIE DE
MOBILIARIO. see *MUSEUMS AND ART
GALLERIES*

WOMAN'S DAY HOME DECORATING IDEAS.
see *INTERIOR DESIGN AND DECORATION*

INTERNATIONAL COMMERCE

see *Business and Economics — International
Commerce*

INTERNATIONAL DEVELOPMENT AND ASSISTANCE

see *Business and Economics — International
Development and Assistance*

INTERNATIONAL EDUCATION PROGRAMS

see *Education — International Education
Programs*

INTERNATIONAL LAW

see *Law — International Law*

INTERNATIONAL RELATIONS

see *Political Science — International
Relations*

INVESTMENTS

see *Business and Economics — Investments*

ISLAM

see *Religions and Theology — Islamic*

JEWELRY, CLOCKS AND WATCHES

736   FR   ISSN 0066-3581
ANNUAIRE PARIS: BIJOUX. 1913. a. 62 rue
Beaubourg, 75003 Paris, France. Ed. J. Cangardel.

681.11   SP   ISSN 0066-510X
ANUARIO DE RELOJERIA Y ARTE EN METAL
PARA ESPANA E HISPANOAMERICA. 1959. a.
5000 ptas. Ediciones CEDEL, Calle Mallorca 257,
Barcelona 8, Spain.
Formerly: Anuario de la Relojeria en Espana.

739.27   BE
AURIFEX. (Subseries of: Universite Catholique de
Louvain. Institut Superieur d'Archeologie et Histoire
de l'Art. Publications; includes series and subseries
numbering) 1978. irreg., latest vol.5, 1983. price
varies. Universite Catholique de Louvain, Institut
Superieur d'Archeologie et d'Histoire de l'Art, 1
place Blaise Pascal, 1348 Louvain-La-Neuve,
Belgium. Ed. T. Hackens.

681.11   UK
BRITISH JEWELLER. BUYER'S GUIDE. biennial.
British Jewellery & Giftware Federation, 27
Frederick St., Birmingham B1 3HJ, England. circ. 6,
000.

739.27   658.7   UK
BRITISH JEWELLERS ASSOCIATION. BUYER'S
GUIDE. 1960. biennial. £8. British Jewellers
Association, 27 Frederick Street, Birmingham,
England. Ed. Shena Mason. adv. circ. 5,000.

CANADIAN JEWELLERY & GIFTWARE
DIRECTORY. see *BUSINESS AND
ECONOMICS — Trade And Industrial Directories*

681.1   GW   ISSN 0070-4040
DEUTSCHE GESELLSCHAFT FUER
CHRONOMETRIE. JAHRBUCH. 1950. a. DM.35.
Deutsche Gesellschaft fuer Chronometrie e.V.,
Christophstr. 5, Postfach 590, 7000 Stuttgart 1, W.
Germany (B.R.D.)

681.11   SZ
FEDERATION DE L'INDUSTRIE HORLOGERE
SUISSE. ANNUAL REPORT. (Text in French and
German) 1925. a. free. ‡ Federation de l'Industrie
Horlogere Suisse - Federation of the Swiss Watch
Manufacturers Industry, 6 rue d'Argent, 2501
Bienne, Switzerland (Dist. in the U.S. by:
Watchmakers of Switzerland Information Center,
Inc., 608 Fifth Ave., 8th Fl., NY 10020) circ. 3,300.
Formerly: Federation Horlogere Suisse. Annual
Report (ISSN 0071-4259)

736   553.8   II
GEM & JEWELLERY YEARBOOK. 1974. a.
Rs.100($32) Gem and Jewellery Information Centre
of India, A-95 Janta Colony, Jaipur 302004, India.
Eds. Vidya Vinod Kala and Alok Kala. adv. bk. rev.
charts. illus. stat. tr.lit. circ. 4,500.

739   681   GW
GOLDSCHMIEDE- UND UHRMACHER-
JAHRBUCH. 1903. a. DM.18.50. Ruehle-Diebener
Verlag GmbH und Co. KG, Wolfschlugener Str. 5a,
Postfach 700450, 7000 Stuttgart 70, W. Germany
(B.R.D.) adv. circ. 2,500.
Formerly: Diebeners Goldschmiede- und
Uhrmacher-Jahrbuch (ISSN 0070-4814)

681.11   SZ
GUIDE DES ACHETEURS: HORLOGERIE,
BIJOUTERIE ET BRANCHES ANNEXES/
BUYERS' GUIDE: WATCH INDUSTRY,
JEWELLERY AND ALLIED TRADES. (Text in
English, French, German and Spanish) 1930. a. $20.
Hugo Buchser S.A., Tour-de-l'Ile 4, 1211 Geneva
11, Switzerland. adv. circ. 4,000.
Continues: Guide des Acheteurs pour l'Horlogerie
et les Branches Annexes.

739.27   681.11   HK
HONG KONG JEWELLERY & WATCHES. (Text in
English) 1985. a. Hong Kong Trade Development
Council, Great Eagle Centre, 31st floor, 23 Harbour
Rd., Hong Kong, Hong Kong. Ed. Saul Lockhart.
circ. 12,500.

681.1   739.27   UK
JEWELLERS' REFERENCE BOOK. 1931. a. £15.
Whitehall Press Ltd., Earl House, Maidstone ME14
1PE, England. Ed. Ken Blakemore. adv.
Formerly: Watchmaker, Jeweller and Silversmith
Directory of Trade Names and Punch Marks (ISSN
0083-7628)

739.27   US
JEWELRY FASHION GUIDE. 1976. a. Gralla
Publications, 1515 Broadway, New York, NY
10036. TEL 212-869-1300. Ed. Gerry Gewirtz. adv.
illus. circ. 26,188 (controlled)

681.114   SZ   ISSN 0077-1309
MONTRE SUISSE. ANNUAIRE/WATCH REVIEW.
CURRICULUM. (Text in French and German)
1924. a. 18 Fr. Vogt-Schild AG, Dornacherstr. 39,
CH-4501 Solothurn 1, Switzerland. Ed. Marcel
Hammer.

646   US
NATIONAL JEWELER ANNUAL FASHION
GUIDE. 1976. a. Gralla Publications, 1515
Broadway, New York, NY 10036. TEL 212-869-
1300. adv. circ. 28,000.

736   FR   ISSN 0078-9496
PARIS - BIJOUX EXPORTATION. 9th edt., 1913. a.
free. 62 rue Beaubourg, 75003 Paris, France. Ed. M.
Cangardel. adv.

681.11   GW   ISSN 0082-7290
UHRMACHER - JAHRBUCH FUER HANDWERK
UND HANDEL. 1950. a. DM.5. Bielefelder
Verlagsanstalt KG, Niederwall 53, Postfach 1140,
4800 Bielefeld, W. Germany (B.R.D.) adv. circ. 4,
000.

JEWELRY, CLOCKS AND WATCHES — Abstracting, Bibliographies, Statistics

739.27   CN   ISSN 0828-9832
CANADA. STATISTICS CANADA. JEWELLERY AND PRECIOUS METAL INDUSTRIES/INDUSTRIES DE LA BIJOUTERIE ET DE L'ORFEVRERIE. (Catalogue 47-211) (Text in English and French) 1961. a. Can.$20($21) Statistics Canada, Communications Division, 3rd Floor, R.H. Coats Bldg., Ottawa, Ont. K1A 0T6, Canada TEL 613-993-7276. (Subscr. to: Publications Sales and Services, Ottawa, Ont. K1A 0T6, Canada)
   Former titles: Canada. Statistics Canada. Jewellery and Silverware Manufacturers; Canada. Statistics Canada. Jewellery and Silverware Industry (ISSN 0384-3378)

JOURNALISM

071   US
A P S DIRECTORY. 1972. biennial. $6. Alternative Press Syndicate, Box 1347, Ansonia Station, New York, NY 10023. Ed. RJ Smith. adv. bk. rev. circ. 5,000. (also avail. in microfilm from BLH)

070   US
A S N E 19. (Proceedings of the Society's annual convention) a. $25. American Society of Newspaper Editors, Box 17004, Washington, DC 20041. TEL 703-620-6087.
   Formerly: Problems of Journalism.

AARETS PRESSEFOTO. see PHOTOGRAPHY

070   GW   ISSN 0065-0323
ABHANDLUNGEN UND MATERIALEN ZUR PUBLIZISTIK. 1962. irregr. price varies. (Freie Universitaet Berlin, Institut fuer Publizistik) Colloquium Verlag, Unter den Eichen 93, 1000 Berlin 45, W. Germany (B.R.D.) Ed. Bernd Soesemann. circ. 1,000.

070   US
ACCREDITED JOURNALISM AND MASS COMMUNICATION EDUCATION. 1910. a. free. Accrediting Council on Education in Journalism and Mass Communications, University of Kansas, School of Journalism, Stauffer-Flint Hall, Lawrence, KS 66045. TEL 913-864-3973.
   Former titles: Accredited Journalism Education; Education for a Journalism Career; Accredited Programs in Journalism (ISSN 0079-6018)

070   US
AMERICAN NEWSPAPER MARKETS CIRCULATION. Cover title: Circulation. 1961. a. $60. American Newspaper Markets, Inc., Box 994, Malibu, CA 90265. TEL 213-456-1863. Ed. Peter S. Sinding. adv. circ. 7,750.

070   FR   ISSN 0066-2585
ANNUAIRE DE LA PRESSE ET DE LA PUBLICITE. 1879. a. 24 Place du General Catroux, 75017 Paris, France. adv.
   Before 1969: Annuaire de la Presse Francaise et Etrangere.

079   KO
ASIAN PRESS.* a. $3. Institute for Communication Research, Readership Research Center, Seoul National University, Dong Song-Dong, Seoul, S. Korea. illus.

ASSEMBLING ANNUAL. see PUBLISHING AND BOOK TRADE

ASSOCIATION DES JOURNALISTES AGRICOLES. ANNUAIRE. see AGRICULTURE

BEITRAEGE ZUR KOMMUNIKATIONSWISSENSCHAFT UND MEDIENFORSCHUNG. see COMMUNICATIONS

070   659.1   UK   ISSN 0269-8358
BENN'S MEDIA DIRECTORY. (In two volumes: vol.1 U.K. Media; vol.2 Overseas Press) 1846. a. £105 for both vols. Benn Business Information Services Ltd., P.O. Box 20, Sovereign Way, Tonbridge, Kent TN9 1RQ, England. adv. index. circ. 4,200.
   Former titles: Benn's Press Directory (ISSN 0141-1772); Newspaper Press Directory (ISSN 0078-043X)

081   US   ISSN 0195-895X
BEST NEWSPAPER WRITING; winners, The American Society of Newspaper Editors' competition. 1979. a. $7.95. Poynter Institute, 801 Third St. South, St. Petersburg, FL 33701. TEL 813-821-9494. Ed. Don Fry. circ. 5,000.

070   UK   ISSN 0007-0238
BRITISH AMATEUR JOURNALIST.* 1890. irreg. membership. ‡ British Amateur Press Association, 18 Hillview Rd., Minehead, Somerset TA24 8EG, England. bk. rev. circ. 200.

070   US
CALIFORNIA NEWSPAPER PUBLISHERS ASSOCIATION. DIRECTORY AND RATE BOOK. 1923. a. $30. California Newspaper Publishers Association, Inc., 1127 11th St., Ste. 1040, Sacramento, CA 95814. TEL 916-443-5991. Ed. Jackie Nava. adv. circ. 2,800.
   Formerly: California Newspaper Publishers' Association. Newspaper Directory; Which supersedes: California Newspaper Directory (ISSN 0068-5763)

CALIFORNIA STREET; San Francisco adventures and some that only began here. see LITERARY AND POLITICAL REVIEWS

070   FR
CEUX QUI FONT LA PRESSE. 1979. biennial. 490 F. Publications Professionnelles Francaises, 15 Square de Vergennes, 75015 Paris, France. (Affiliate: France Expansion)

070   IT
CHI E' CHI DEL GIORNALISMO DELL'AUTO. (Text in English, Italian) 1986. a. L.25000. Crisalide Editrice, Via Brusuglio 66, 20161 Milan, Italy. Ed. Bianca Carretto. circ. 15,000.

070   US
CHICAGO MEDIA DIRECTORY. a. free. Chicago Convention and Tourism Bureau, Inc., McCormick Place on the Lake, Chicago, IL 60616. TEL 312-255-5000. Ed. John Clegg. circ. 1,000.

070   BL
COLECAO JORNALISMO CATARINENSE. 1978. irreg. (Sindicato dos Jornalistas) Editora Lunardelli, Rua Victor Meirelles 28, 880000 Florianopolis SC, Brazil.

CONGRES INTERNATIONAL D'HISTOIRE DES SCIENCES. ACTES. see SCIENCES: COMPREHENSIVE WORKS

808.02   US   ISSN 0277-5956
CONNECTICUT NEWS HANDBOOK. 1977. a. $79.95. Connecticut Information Co., Box 2402, Short Beach, CT 06405. TEL 203-397-4511. Ed. Thomas C. Clarie. circ. 50.

070   II
COOPERATIVE PRESS IN SOUTH-EAST ASIA. 1965. irreg. Rs.7.50($1) International Co-Operative Alliance, Regional Office and Education Centre for South-East Asia, Box 3312, 43 Friends Colony, New Delhi 110014, India.

DANMARKS JOURNALISTHOEJSKOLES AARSKRIFT. see EDUCATION — Higher Education

DIRECTORY OF FLORIDA WRITERS. see ADVERTISING AND PUBLIC RELATIONS

073   GW   ISSN 0417-9994
DORTMUNDER BEITRAEGE ZUR ZEITUNGSFORSCHUNG. 1958. irreg., no.41, 1985. price varies. (Institut fuer Zeitsforschung der Stadt Dortmund Koysk) K.G. Saur Verlag KG, Poessenbacherstr. 12 B, Postfach 711009, 8000 Munich 71, W. Germany (B.R.D.) (U.S. and Canadian subscr. to: K.G. Saur Inc., 175 Fifth Ave., New York, N.Y. 10010) Ed. Kurt Koszyk. (reprint service avail. from UMI, ISI)

070   FR   ISSN 0070-8321
ECOLE FRANCAISE DES ATTACHES DE PRESSE. ASSOCIATION DES ANCIENS ELEVES. ANNUAIRE.* 2nd edt., 1962. a. price varies. Association des Anciens Eleves de l'Ecole Francaise des Attaches de Presse, 61 rue Pierre-Charron, 75008 Paris, France.

EDITOR & PUBLISHER INTERNATIONAL YEAR BOOK; encyclopedia of the newspaper industry. see COMMUNICATIONS

070   US
EIGHT BALL. 1947. m. (plus a. edition) membership. Greater Los Angeles Press Club, 600 N. Vermont Ave., Los Angeles, CA 90004. TEL 213-665-1141. Ed. Lucie Lowery. adv. bk. rev. circ. 2,500. (tabloid format)

070   FR   ISSN 0071-2299
EUROPA. REVUE DE PRESSE EUROPEENNE.* 1969. irreg. 0.50 f. each. Cercle Europe de la Faculte de Droit et des Sciences Economiques de Paris, 92 rue d'Assas, 75006 Paris, France.

070   DK   ISSN 0108-2027
FAGPRESSENOEGLEN. 1976. a. membership (Kr.40 to non-members) Dansk Fagpresse Service, Sommerstedgade 7, 1718 Copenhagen V, Denmark. illus.
   Formerly: Dansk Fagpresseforenings Medlemsliste.

070.5   FJ
FIJI. PRINTING DEPARTMENT REPORT. (Text in English) a. price varies. Government Printing Department, Box 98, Suva, Fiji.

070   FI   ISSN 0071-5301
FINLAND. POSTI-JA LENNATINLAITOS. ULKOMAISTEN SANOMALEHTIEN HINNASTO. UTLANDSK TIDNINGSTAXA. (Text in Finnish and Swedish) 1853. a. Fmk.7. Posti- ja Lennatinlaitos - General Direction of Posts and Telegraphs, Mannerheimintie 11, SF-00100 Helsinki 10, Finland. index.

070   US
FUTURE JOURNALISTS OF AMERICA. NEWSLETTER. 1958. irreg. membership. University of Oklahoma, School of Journalism and Mass Communication, Norman, OK 73019. TEL 405-325-2721. Ed. J.F. Paschal.

GADNEY'S GUIDE TO INTERNATIONAL CONTESTS, FESTIVALS & GRANTS IN FILM & VIDEO, PHOTOGRAPHY, TV-RADIO BROADCASTING, WRITING, POETRY, PLAYWRITING & JOURNALISM. see MOTION PICTURES

GENERAL DIRECTORY OF THE PRESS AND PERIODICALS IN JORDAN AND KUWAIT. see PUBLISHING AND BOOK TRADE

GENERAL DIRECTORY OF THE PRESS AND PERIODICALS IN SYRIA. see PUBLISHING AND BOOK TRADE

GUILD OF AGRICULTURAL JOURNALISTS YEAR BOOK. see AGRICULTURE

070   US   ISSN 0742-5538
HISTORICAL GUIDES TO THE WORLD'S PERIODICALS AND NEWSPAPERS. 1982. irreg. price varies. Greenwood Press, Box 5007, 88 Post Rd. West, Westport, CT 06881. TEL 203-226-3511.

070   US
HUDSON'S DIRECTORY. 1977. a. $60. Newsletter Clearinghouse (Rhinebeck), 44 W. Market St., Box 311, Rhinebeck, NY 12572. TEL 914-876-2081. Ed. Howard Penn Hudson. adv. circ. 1,035.
   Formerly: Newsletter Yearbook Directory.

070   US   ISSN 0441-389X
HUDSON'S WASHINGTON NEWS MEDIA CONTACTS DIRECTORY. 1968. a. $99. ‡ 44 W. Market St., Box 311, Rhinebeck, NY 12572. TEL 914-876-2081. Ed. Howard Penn Hudson. adv.

079   II
INDIAN & EASTERN NEWSPAPER SOCIETY PRESS HANDBOOK. Spine title: I.E.N.S. Press Handbook. (Text in English) irreg. Rs.25. Indian and Eastern Newspaper Society, I.E.N.S. Bldgs., Rafi Marg, New Delhi 110001, India.

070   US
INTER AMERICAN PRESS ASSOCIATION. MINUTES OF THE ANNUAL MEETING. a. $35. Inter American Press Association, 2911 N.W. 39th St., Miami, FL 33142. TEL 305-634-2465.

070.43   US
INVESTIGATIVE REPORTS. 1978. a. $3. Center for Investigative Reporting, 54 Mint St., 4th Fl., San Francisco, CA 94103. TEL 415-543-1200. Ed. Laura Lent. circ. 500.

070   US
JOURNAL OF PUBLIC COMMUNICATION AND MEMBERSHIP DIRECTORY. 1976. a. membership. National Association of Government Communicators, 80 S. Early St., Alexandria, VA 22304. TEL 703-823-4821. Ed. Robin PanLener. circ. 1,000.
    Formerly: Journal of Public Communication.

070 016   US   ISSN 0075-4412
JOURNALISM ABSTRACTS; M.A., M.S., and Ph.D. theses in journalism and mass communication. 1963. a. $10 to non-members; institutions $15. Association for Education in Journalism and Mass Communication, 1621 College St., University of South Carolina, Columbia, SC 29208-0251. TEL 803-777-2005. Ed. Frances Wilhoit. circ. 700. (also avail. in microform from UMI; reprint service avail. from UMI)

070 371.0025   US
JOURNALISM AND MASS COMMUNICATION DIRECTORY. 1983. a. $15. Association for Education in Journalism and Mass Communications, University of South Carolina, 1621 College St., Columbia, SC 29208-0251. TEL 803-777-2005. Ed. Lillian S. Coleman. adv. circ. 2,500. (also avail. in microform)
    Formerly: J D: Journalism Directory (ISSN 0735-3103)

070   US
JOURNALISM CAREER AND SCHOLARSHIP GUIDE; information on journalism career scholarships available for the study of journalism and directory of college journalism programs. 1962. a. single copies free. ‡ Dow Jones Newspaper Fund, Inc., Box 300, Princeton, NJ 08543-0300. TEL 609-452-2820. Ed. Janice M. Maressa. bibl. stat. index.
    Formerly: Journalism Scholarship Guide (ISSN 0449-3362)

JOURNALISM CAREER GUIDE FOR MINORITIES. see OCCUPATIONS AND CAREERS

070   IS   ISSN 0334-2948
JOURNALISM YEARBOOK. a. Association of Journalists, 4 Kaplan St., Tel Aviv, Israel. TEL 03-256141. Ed. Dov Atzman.

070   NE   ISSN 0022-555X
JOURNALIST. 1946. a. fl.126. Nederlandse Vereniging van Journalisten - Netherlands Association of Journalists, Johannes Vermeerstraat 55, Amsterdam, Netherlands. Ed. W. Verbei. adv. bk. rev. circ. 6,000. Indexed: Key to Econ.Sci.

073   GW
JOURNALISTEN - HANDBUCH. At head of title: Wer Schreibt und Spricht Worueber? irreg. DM.54. Verlag Chmielorz GmbH und Co, Wilhelmstr. 42, 6200 Wiesbaden, W. Germany.
    Formerly: Wer Schreibt Worueber? Journalisten-Handbuch.

070 301.16   GW   ISSN 0176-9707
JOURNALISTEN JAHRBUCH. 1983. a. DM.29.80. Verlag Oelschlaeger GmbH, Georgenstr. 112, D-8000 Munich 40, W. Germany (B.R.D.) Ed. Bernd-Juergen Martini. adv. circ. 3,000. (back issues avail.)

808.02 740   US
JUNIOR AUTHORS AND ILLUSTRATORS SERIES. 1951. irreg., 5th edt., 1983. price varies. H.W. Wilson Company, 950 University Ave., Bronx, NY 10452. Ed. Sally Holmes Holtze. index.
    Formerly: Book of Junior Authors and Illustrators.

070.48   US
KAPPA TAU ALPHA. NEWSLETTER. 1983. irreg. (3-4/yr.) membership. Kappa Tau Alpha, National Headquarters, 107 Sondra Ave., Columbia, MO 65202. TEL 314-443-3521. Ed. William H. Taft. circ. 1,700 (controlled)
    Alummni

073   GW
KOMMUNIKATION UND POLITIK. irreg., no.16, 1983. price varies. K.G. Saur Verlag KG, Poessenbacherstr. 12 B, Postfach 711009, 8000 Munich 71, W. Germany (B.R.D.) (U.S. and Canadian subscr. to: K.G. Saur Inc., 175 Fifth Ave., New York, N.Y. 10010) Ed.Bd. (reprint service avail. from UMI, ISI)

070.43   KO
KOREAN PRESS ANNUAL/HANGUK SINMUN PANGSONG YONGAM. (Text in Korean) 1976. a. 38,000 Won. Korean Press Institute, Korea Press Center Bldg., 12th floor, 1-31 Taepyung-ro, Chung-Ku, Seoul, Korea. Ed. Rho Chul-Yong. adv. circ. 1, 000.

LITERARY AGENTS OF NORTH AMERICA MARKETPLACE. see LITERATURE

MEDIA OWNERSHIP IN AUSTRALIA. see BUSINESS AND ECONOMICS — Trade And Industrial Directories

070   US
MEDIA PERSONNEL DIRECTORY. 1979. irreg. $80. Gale Research Company, Book Tower, Detroit, MI 48226. TEL 313-961-2242. Ed. Alan E. Abrams. Indexed: Child.Auth.& Illus.

070.172   US
N N A NATIONAL DIRECTORY OF WEEKLY NEWSPAPERS. 1921. a. $35. National Newspaper Association, 1627 K St., N.W., Ste. 400, Washington, DC 20006. TEL 202-466-7200. adv. charts. stat.

070   UK
N U J FREELANCE DIRECTORY. biennial. £2.50. National Union of Journalists, Acorn House, 314 Grays Inn Rd., London WC1X 8DP, England.

070   US   ISSN 0342-9148
NACHRICHTENTECHNIK. (Text in German) 1977. irreg., vol.10, 1983. price varies. Springer-Verlag, 175 Fifth Ave., New York, NY 10010 TEL 212-460-1500. (Also Berlin, Heidelberg, Tokyo and Vienna) Ed. H. Marko. (reprint service avail. from ISI)

070   US   ISSN 0147-538X
NEW YORK TIMES INDEX. 1913. s-m. (plus 3 quarterly & a. cumulations) $475. (New York Times Co.) University Microfilms International, 300 N. Zeeb Rd., Ann Arbor, MI 48106.
    ●Also available online.

NEWES. see HOBBIES

070.4   US   ISSN 0090-2209
NEWSPAPER GUILD. ANNUAL T.N.G. CONVENTION OFFICERS' REPORT. a. Newspaper Guild, AFL-CIO, CLC., 1125 15th St., N.W., Washington, DC 20005. TEL 202-296-2990. Key Title: Annual T N G Convention Officers' Report.

070.4   US
NEWSPAPER GUILD. PROCEEDINGS OF THE ANNUAL CONVENTION. 1940. a. Newspaper Guild, AFL-CIO, 1125 15th St. N.W., Washington, DC 20005. TEL 202-296-2990. (also avail. in microform from UMI; reprint service avail. from UMI)

070   UK
NEWSPAPER PUBLISHERS HANDBOOK. a. £9.95. Adprint, 69 Thorpe Rd., Norwich, Norfolk NR1 1TB, England. circ. 4,000.

070   US
NEWSPAPERS RECEIVED CURRENTLY. 1968. biennial. price varies. U.S. Library of Congress, Washington, DC 20540 TEL 202-287-6100. (Orders to: Supt. of Documents, Washington, DC 20402)
    Formerly: Newspapers Currently Received and Permanently Retained in the Library of Congress (ISSN 0083-1646)

O P M A OVERSEAS MEDIA GUIDE. (Overseas Press and Media Association) see ADVERTISING AND PUBLIC RELATIONS

070.4   US   ISSN 0195-6124
OUTDOOR WRITERS ASSOCIATION OF AMERICA. DIRECTORY. a. Outdoor Writers Association of America, Inc., 2017 Cato Ave., Ste. 101, State College, PA 16801. TEL 814-234-1011.
    Formerly: O W A A Outdoor Writers Directory.

070.1   CN
PERIODICAL WRITERS ASSOCIATION OF CANADA. DIRECTORY. 1982. a. Can.$15. Periodical Writers Association of Canada, 24 Ryerson Ave., Toronto, Ont. M5T 2P3, Canada. TEL 416-868-6913. circ. 2,000.

070.1   CN
PERIODICAL WRITERS ASSOCIATION OF CANADA. FEES SURVEY. 1979. a. Can.$10. Periodical Writers Association of Canada, 24 Ryerson Ave., Toronto, Ont. M5T 2P3, Canada. TEL 416-868-6913. circ. 1,000.

079   AT   ISSN 0079-5046
PRESS RADIO AND T.V. GUIDE. 1914. triennial. Aus.$49.50 per no. Neville Jefffress Advertising Agency, 7-13 Parraween St., Cremorne, N.S.W. 2900, Australia. Ed. N.V. Buchanan. adv. circ. 2, 500.
    Formerly: Press Directory of Australia and New Zealand.

PRESSEHANDBUCH (YEAR) see PUBLISHING AND BOOK TRADE

070 800   US
PROFESSIONAL FREELANCE WRITERS DIRECTORY. 1970. a. $7.50. National Writers Club, 1450 S. Havana, Ste. 620, Aurora, CO 80012. TEL 303-751-7844. Ed. James L. Young. circ. 1, 500. (processed; back issues avail.) Indexed: Text.Tech.Dig.
    Supersedes: National Writers Club. Bulletin for Professional Members (ISSN 0028-0429)

073   GW
PUBLIZISTIK-HISTORISCHE BEITRAEGE. irreg., no.5, 1982. price varies. K.G. Saur Verlag KG, Poessenbacherstr. 12 B, Postfach 711009, 8000 Munich 71, W. Germany (B.R.D.) (U.S. and Canadian subscr. to: K.G. Saur Inc., 175 Fifth Ave., New York, N.Y. 10010) Ed. Heinz-Dietrich Fischer. (reprint service avail. from UMI, ISI)

SOCIAL RESPONSIBILITY: BUSINESS, JOURNALISM, LAW, MEDICINE. see LAW

SPECTRUM; a guide to the independent press and informative organizations. see LIBRARY AND INFORMATION SCIENCES

073   GW   ISSN 0585-6175
STUDIEN ZUR PUBLIZISTIK. BREMER REIHE. 1958. irreg., vol.25, 1985. price varies. (Deutsche Presseforschung) K.G. Saur Verlag KG, Peossenbacherstr. 2, 8000 Munich 71, W. Germany (B.R.D.) (U.S. and Canadian subscr. to: K.G. Saur Inc., 175 Fifth Ave., New York, N.Y. 10010) Ed. Elger Bluehm. (reprint service avail. from UMI, ISI)

STUDIES IN MEDIA MANAGEMENT. see BUSINESS AND ECONOMICS — Management

070 327 980   US   ISSN 0743-4324
SURVEY OF PRESS FREEDOM IN LATIN AMERICA. 1983. a. $8.95. Council on Hemispheric Affairs, 1612 20th St., N.W., Washington, DC 20009. TEL 202-745-7000. (Co-Sponsor: Newspaper Guild) Ed.Bd. circ. 4,000.

070   US
SYNDICATED COLUMNISTS. 1975. biennial. $30 includes semi-annual revisions. Public Relations Publishing Co., 888 Seventh Ave., New York, NY 10106. TEL 212-535-8000. Ed. Richard Weiner. bibl. circ. 1,000.

TASCHENBUCH FUER AGRARJOURNALISTEN. see AGRICULTURE

070   SP
UNIVERSIDAD DE NAVARRA. FACULTAD DE CIENCIAS DE LA INFORMACION. COLECCION DE TRABAJO. 1964. irreg., no.49, 1986. price varies. Ediciones Universidad de Navarra, S.A., Apdo. 396, 31080 Pamplona, Spain.

070   SP   ISSN 0078-8783
UNIVERSIDAD DE NAVARRA. FACULTAD DE CIENCIAS DE LA INFORMACION. MANUALES: PERIODISMO. 1967. irreg., no.11, 1985. price varies. Ediciones Universidad de Navarra, S.A., Apdo. 396, 31080 Pamplona, Spain.

070   US   ISSN 0077-6378
UNIVERSITY OF NEBRASKA. SCHOOL OF JOURNALISM. DEPTH REPORT. 1961. a. free. University of Nebraska-Lincoln, School of Journalism, Lincoln, NE 68508. TEL 402-472-3047. Ed. Jack Botts. circ. 9,500.

070   CS   ISSN 0083-422X
UNIVERZITA KOMENSKEHO. FILOZOFICKA FAKULTA. ZBORNIK: ZURNALISTIKA. (Text in Slovak; summaries in German and Russian) 1968. irreg. exchange basis. (Univerzita Komenskeho, Filozoficka Fakulta) Slovenske Pedagogicke Nakladatelstvo, Sasinkova 5, 818 06 Bratislava, Czechoslovakia. Ed. Frano Ruttkay. circ. 674.

070   US   ISSN 0084-1323
WORKING PRESS OF THE NATION. (Issued in 5 vols.: Vol.1 The Newspaper Directory, Vol.2 The Magazine Directory, Vol.3 The Radio and Television Directory, Vol.4 The Feature Writers and Photographer Directory, Vol.5 Internal Publications Directory) 1949. a. $115 per vol., $250 per set. National Research Bureau, Inc., 310 S. Michigan Ave., Chicago, IL 52601. TEL 319-663-5580. Ed. Nancy Veatch.

070   GR
YEARBOOK OF GREEK PRESS. 1965. a. free. ‡ Secretariat General of Press and Information, Zalokosta 10, Athens, Greece. Ed.Bd. annual index. circ. 2,000. (tabloid format)

070   IS
ZSHURNALIST. (Text in Yiddish) 1974. irreg. World Federation of Jewish Journalists, Jerusalem, Israel. (Co-sponsor: World Zionist Organization. Information Department)

JOURNALISM — Abstracting, Bibliographies, Statistics

070.172   US   ISSN 0093-1179
ATLANTA CONSTITUTION: A GEORGIA INDEX. 1971. a. price varies. (Georgia State University, Library) University Microfilms International, 300 N. Zeeb Rd., Ann Arbor, MI 48106. TEL 313-761-4700. (back issues avail.)

070 016   CN   ISSN 0225-7459
CANADIAN NEWS INDEX. 1977. m. (with a. cumulation) Can.$850. Micromedia Ltd., 158 Pearl St., Toronto, Ont. M5H 1L3, Canada. TEL 416-593-5211. Ed. Virve Wiland. index. (also avail. in microfiche)
●Also available online. Vendors: CISTI, DIALOG, QL Systems Ltd.
    Formerly: Canadian Newspaper Index (ISSN 0384-983X)

011   DK   ISSN 0106-147X
DANSK ARTIKELINDEKS: AVISER OG TIDSSKRIFTER/DANISH INDEX OF ARTICLES: NEWSPAPERS AND PERIODICALS. 1940. m. (plus a. cum.) Kr.4366. Bibliotekscentralen, Tempovej 7-11, DK-2750 Ballerup, Denmark. bibl. index. circ. 300. (back issues avail.)
    Formed by the merger of: Avis-Kronik-Index (ISSN 0005-2280) & Dansk Tidsskrift Index.

070   DK   ISSN 0109-0968
DANSK FAGPRESSKATALOG. 1984. a. Kr.140. Dansk Fagpresse Service, Sommerstedgade 7, 1718 Copenhagen V, Denmark.

070   US   ISSN 0741-5281
INDEX TO THE BOSTON GLOBE. 1983. m. (plus a. cumulation) $495. University Microfilms International, 300 N. Zeeb Rd., Ann Arbor, MI 48106. TEL 313-761-4700. Ed. Jean Austin.

070 011   US   ISSN 0098-1184
INDEX TO THE CHRISTIAN SCIENCE MONITOR. 1945. m. (plus a. cumulation) $170. Bell & Howell Co., Newspaper Indexing Center, Microphoto Division, Old Mansfield Rd., Wooster, OH 44691. TEL 216-264-6666. Ed. Jean E. Austin. Indexed: Bus.Ind. Bk.Rev.Ind. Child.Bk.Rev.Ind. Tr.& Indus.Ind.
●Also available online.
    Formerly: Christian Science Monitor. Cumulated Index (ISSN 0578-0152)

070   US   ISSN 0195-6434
INDEX TO THE DENVER POST. 1979. m. (plus q. & a. cum.) $510. Bell & Howell Co., Newspaper Indexing Center, Microphoto Division, Old Mansfield Rd., Wooster, OH 44691. TEL 216-264-6666. Ed. Jean E. Austin.

070 011   US
INDEX TO THE DETROIT NEWS. 1976. m. (plus q. & a. cum.) $510. Bell & Howell Co., Newspaper Indexing Center, Microphoto Division, Old Mansfield Rd., Wooster, OH 44691. TEL 216-264-6666. Ed. Jean Austin. Key Title: Bell & Howell's Newspaper Index to the Detroit Area.
    Formerly: Detroit News. Newspaper Index (ISSN 0361-6983)

070 011   US
INDEX TO THE HOUSTON POST. 1976. m. (plus q. & a. cum.) $510. Bell & Howell Co., Newspaper Indexing Center, Microphoto Division, Old Mansfield Rd., Wooster, OH 44691. TEL 216-264-6666. Ed. Jean E. Austin.
    Formerly: Houston Post. Newspaper Index (ISSN 0363-7824)

070 011   US   ISSN 0195-6418
INDEX TO THE LOS ANGELES TIMES. 1972. m. (plus q. & a. cum.) $510. Bell & Howell Co., Newspaper Indexing Center, Microphoto Division, Old Mansfield Rd., Wooster, OH 44691. TEL 216-264-6666. Ed. Jean E. Austin. Indexed: Art & Archaeol.Tech.Abstr. Bus.Ind. Med.Care Rev.
●Also available online.
    Formerly: Los Angeles Times. Newspaper Index (ISSN 0098-1192)

011   US
INDEX TO THE NATIONAL OBSERVER. irreg. University Microfilms International, 300 N. Zeeb Rd., Ann Arbor, MI 48106. TEL 313-761-4700. (back issues avail.)

070 011   US   ISSN 0195-640X
INDEX TO THE NEW ORLEANS TIMES-PICAYUNE. 1972. m. (plus q. & a. cum.) $510. Bell & Howell Co., Newspaper Indexing Center, Microphoto Division, Old Mansfield Rd., Wooster, OH 44691. TEL 216-264-6666. Ed. Jean E. Austin.
    Formerly: New Orleans Times-Picayune. Newspaper Index (ISSN 0098-1206)

070   US   ISSN 0275-858X
INDEX TO THE ST. LOUIS POST-DISPATCH (WOOSTER) 1980. m. (plus a. cum.) $510. Bell & Howell Co., Newspaper Indexing Center, Microphoto Division, Old Mansfield Rd., Wooster, OH 44691. TEL 216-264-6666. Ed. Jean Austin.

011   US
INDEX TO THE ST. PAUL PIONEER PRESS AND DISPATCH. 1967. m. (plus a. cumulation) $150. St. Paul Public Library, 90 W. Fourth St., St. Paul, MN 55102. TEL 612-292-6206. Ed. Norman Lathrop. bk. rev. circ. 42. (looseleaf format; back issues avail.)
    Formerly: St. Paul Dispatch & Pioneer Press Newspaper Index (ISSN 0048-900X)

070 011   US   ISSN 0195-6396
INDEX TO THE SAN FRANCISCO CHRONICLE. 1976. m. (plus q. & a. cum.) $510. Bell & Howell Co., Newspaper Indexing Center, Microphoto Division, Old Mansfield Rd., Wooster, OH 44691. TEL 216-264-6666. Ed. Jean E. Austin.
    Formerly: San Francisco Chronicle. Newspaper Index (ISSN 0363-7816)

070   US   ISSN 0736-9999
INDEX TO USA TODAY. 1982. m. (plus a. cum.) $170. Bell & Howell Co., Newspaper Indexing Center, Microphoto Division, Old Mansfield Rd., Wooster, OH 44691. TEL 216-264-6666. Ed. Jean Austin.

070 016   US   ISSN 0742-3985
INTERNATIONAL PERIODICALS AND REFERENCE WORKS. 1974. irreg. free to libraries. Maxwell Scientific International (Subsidiary of: Pergamon Press, Inc.) Fairview Park, Elmsford, NY 10523. TEL 914-592-7700. Ed. Edward Gray. adv. bibl. circ. 15,000.
    Former titles: Guide to International Periodicals & Librarians' Guide to Back Issues of International Periodicals; Reference Guide and Comprehensive Catalog of International Serials (ISSN 0094-0151)

016   US
LATHROP REPORT ON NEWSPAPER INDEXES. 1979. irreg. $60. Norman Lathrop Enterprises, 2342 Star Dr., Box 198, Wooster, OH 44691. TEL 216-262-5587.

070   SA
PROMADATA; promotion, marketing & advertising data. (Text in English) 1948. a. R.57($67.72) incl. updating supplements. Clarion Communications Media (Pty.) Ltd., Business Press Division, Nedbank Centre, Hawthorne Rd., Box 375, Claremont 7735, South Africa. Ed. R. Brown. adv.
    Former titles: Advertising and Press Annual of Southern Africa; Advertising and Press Annual of Africa (ISSN 0065-3594)

070 016   GW   ISSN 0552-6981
PUBLIZISTIKWISSENSCHAFTLICHER REFERATEDIENST. Short title: P R D. 1966. a. price varies. (Freie Universitaet Berlin, Institut fuer Publizistik und Dokumentationswissenschaft) K.G. Saur Verlag KG, Poessenbacherstr. 12 B, Postfach 711009, 8000 Munich 71, W. Germany (B.R.D.) (U.S. and Canadian subscr. to: K.G. Saur Inc., 175 Fifth Ave., New York, N.Y. 10010) circ. 1,000. (Reprint service avail. from UMI, ISI)

070 011   US   ISSN 0041-1116
TRANSDEX INDEX. Variant title: Bell and Howell Transdex. 1974. m. (plus microform a. cum.) $645. Bell & Howell Co., Newspaper Indexing Center, Microphoto Division, Old Mansfield Rd., Wooster, OH 44691. TEL 216-264-6666. Ed. Jean Austin. Key Title: Transdex.

U S PROGRESSIVE PERIODICALS DIRECTORY. see *PUBLISHING AND BOOK TRADE — Abstracting, Bibliographies, Statistics*

JUDAISM

see *Religions and Theology—Judaic*

LABOR AND INDUSTRIAL RELATIONS

see *Business and Economics—Labor and Industrial Relations*

LABOR UNIONS

see also *Business and Economics—Labor and Industrial Relations*

331   AT
A C T U NATIONAL YOUTH BROCHURE. a. Australian Council of Trade Unions, 393-397 Swarston St., Melbourne, Vic. 3000, Australia.

331.8   US
A F L - C I O CONVENTION PROCEEDINGS. 1955. biennial. $15. A F L-C I O, 815 16th St., N.W., Washington, DC 20006. TEL 202-637-5041. index. circ. 5,000. (back issues avail.)

331.88 370   US
A F T ISSUES BULLETIN. irreg. American Federation of Teachers, 555 New Jersey Ave., N.W., Washington, DC 20001. TEL 202-879-4400. (reprint service avail. from UMI)

LABOR UNIONS

791 US
A G V A NEWSLETTER.* 1958. irreg. membership. American Guild of Variety Artists, 184 Fifth Ave., New York, NY 10010. TEL 212-675-1003. adv. bk. rev. illus. circ. 16,500.
Formerly: A G V A News (ISSN 0001-1371)

A T F ANNUAL REPORT. (Australian Teachers' Federation) see EDUCATION

331.88 BE ISSN 0065-4027
AFRICAN REGIONAL TRADE UNION CONFERENCE. REPORT.* 1957. irreg., 4th, 1964, Addis Ababa. (African Regional Organization of ICFTU) International Confederation of Free Trade Unions, 37-47, rue Montagne aux Herbes Potàgeres, Brussels 1, Belgium.

331.88 370 US
AMERICAN FEDERATION OF TEACHERS. CONVENTION PROCEEDINGS (ABRIDGED) a. price varies. American Federation of Teachers, 555 New Jersey Ave., N.W., Washington, DC 20001. TEL 202-879-4400. (reprint service avail. from UMI)

792.028 331.88 AG
ASOCIACION ARGENTINA DE ACTORES. MEMORIA Y BALANCE.* no.58, 1977. a. free. Asociacion Argentina de Actores, Alsina 1766, Buenos Aires, Argentina. circ. 3,000.

331 AT
AUSTRALIAN CONGRESS OF TRADE UNIONS. DECISIONS. biennial. Aus.$3. Australian Council of Trade Unions, 393-397 Swanston St., Melbourne, Vic. 3000, Australia.

331.8 AT ISSN 0314-2868
AUSTRALIAN COUNCIL OF TRADE UNIONS. BULLETIN. irreg. free to qualified personnel. Australian Council of Trade Unions, 393-397 Swanston St., Melbourne, Vic. 3000, Australia.

331.88 AT
AUSTRALIAN WORKERS' UNION. OFFICIAL REPORT OF THE ANNUAL CONVENTION. 1886. a. Aus.$5. Australian Workers' Union, Box a-252, Sydney S., N.S.W. 2000, Australia. Ed. F.V. Mitchell.

331.88 622 GW
BERGBAU-BERUFSGENOSSENSCHAFT. JAHRESBERICHT. 1887. a. free. Bergbau-Berufsgenossenschaft, Hunscheidtstr. 18, 4630 Bochum, W. Germany (B.R.D.) adv. bk. rev. stat. circ. 1,600. Indexed: GeoRef.
Formerly: Bergbau-Berufsgenossenschaft. Geschaeftsbericht (ISSN 0343-0510)

331.8 BB ISSN 0576-7547
CARIBBEAN CONGRESS OF LABOUR. REPORT. 1962. a. Caribbean Congress of Labour, Norman Centre, Rm.405, Broad St., Bridgetown, Barbados, W. Indies.

331.88 US ISSN 0069-1615
CENTRAL CONFERENCE OF TEAMSTERS. OFFICERS' REPORT. 1954. irreg., latest 1979. membership. Central Conference of Teamsters, 8550 W. Bryn Mawr Ave., Ste. 707, Chicago, IL 60631. TEL 312-693-6200. circ. 200,000.
Formerly: Central Conference of Teamsters. Chairman's Report.

331.88 SP
COLECCION PRIMERO DE MAYO. no.6, 1977. irreg. price varies. Editorial Laia S.A., Constitucion 18-20, Barcelona 14, Spain.

COLLECTIVE BARGAINING IN HIGHER EDUCATION AND THE PROFESSIONS. ANNUAL BIBLIOGRAPHY. see EDUCATION — Higher Education

301.16 331.88 BL
CONFEDERACAO NACIONAL DOS TRABALHADORES EM COMUNICACOES E PUBLICIDADE. RELATORIO ANUAL. 1967. a. free. Confederacao Nacional dos Trabalhadores Em Comunicacoes e Publicidade, Edificio Serra Dourada, Conj. 705, Brasilia, Brazil. Ed. Alceu Portocarrero. illus. circ. 1,500.
Trade unions telecommunication

DEMOKRATIE- UND ARBEITERGESCHICHTE. see HISTORY — History Of Europe

DEUTSCHES BANKEN-HANDBUCH (YEAR) see BUSINESS AND ECONOMICS — Banking And Finance

331.8 US ISSN 0419-2052
DIRECTORS GUILD OF AMERICA. DIRECTORY OF MEMBERS. 1967/68. a. $15. Directors Guild of America, 7950 Sunset Blvd., Hollywood, CA 90046. TEL 213-656-1220. adv. circ. 15,000.

DIRECTORY OF FACULTY CONTRACTS AND BARGAINING AGENTS IN INSTITUTIONS OF HIGHER EDUCATION. see EDUCATION — Higher Education

331.8 US
DIRECTORY OF LABOR UNIONS AND EMPLOYEE ORGANIZATIONS IN NEW YORK STATE. 1948. biennial. $10. Department of Labor, Division of Research and Statistics, One Main St., Brooklyn, NY 11201. Ed. Hilda Giberstone. circ. 5, 000.
Formerly: Directory of Labor Organizations in New York State.

331.88 CN ISSN 0075-7578
DIRECTORY OF LABOUR ORGANIZATIONS IN CANADA/REPERTOIRE DES ORGANISATIONS DE TRAVAILLEURS AU CANADA. (Text in English and French) 1911. a. Can.$6.50. Labour Canada, Ottawa, Ont. K1A 0J2, Canada TEL 613-997-2617. (Subscr. to: Canadian Government Publishing Centre, Supply and Services Canada, Ottawa, Ont. K1A 0S9, Canada) circ. 10, 500.

331.8 US
DIRECTORY OF MAINE LABOR ORGANIZATIONS. (Subseries of: Maine. Bureau of Labor Standards. B L S Bulletin) 1969. a. Department of Labor, State House Station 45, Augusta, ME 04333. TEL 207-289-4313. Ed. William A. Peabody. circ. 600.

331.8 US ISSN 0734-6786
DIRECTORY OF U.S. LABOR ORGANIZATIONS. 1982. biennial. $17.50. The Bureau of National Affairs, Inc., B N A Books, 1231 25th St., Washington, DC 20037. Ed. Courtney D. Gifford.

331.88 BL
FEDERACAO DOS TRABALHADORES NA AGRICULTURA DO ESTADO DO PARANA. RELATORIO. irreg. Federacao dos Trabalhadores na Agricultura do Estado do Parana, Curitiba, Brazil.

331.88 UK ISSN 0014-9411
FEDERATION NEWS. 1950. irreg. (3-4/yr.) free. General Federation of Trade Unions, Central House, Upper Woburn Pl., London W.C.1, England. bk. rev. charts. illus. stat. circ. 1,000.
Trade union

HESSISCHE BEITRAEGE ZUR GESCHICHTE DER ARBEITERBEWEGUNG. see HISTORY — History Of Europe

331.88 II ISSN 0073-2273
HIND MAZDOOR SABHA. REPORT OF THE ANNUAL CONVENTION. 1952. a. price varies. Hind Mazdoor Sabha, Nagindas Chambers, 167 P. d'Mello Rd., Bombay 400001, India.

331.88 EI ISSN 0073-7909
INFORMATION SERVICE OF THE EUROPEAN COMMUNITIES. TRADE UNION NEWS.* 1965. irreg. (approx. 4/yr.) limited distribution. Commission of the European Communities, Direction Generale de la Presse et Information, Rue de la Loi 200, B-1049 Brussels, Belgium.

331.88 BE ISSN 0074-2872
INTERNATIONAL CONFEDERATION OF FREE TRADE UNIONS. WORLD CONGRESS REPORTS. 1949. irreg., 13th, 1983, Oslo. $15. International Confederation of Free Trade Unions (I C F T U), 37-47 rue Montagne aux Herbes Potageres, 1000 Brussels, Belgium. Ed. John Vanderveken.

INTERNATIONAL FEDERATION OF PLANTATION, AGRICULTURAL AND ALLIED WORKERS. REPORT OF THE SECRETARIAT TO THE I F P A A W WORLD CONGRESS. see AGRICULTURE — Agricultural Economics

331.88 SZ ISSN 0074-6177
INTERNATIONAL GRAPHICAL FEDERATION. REPORT OF ACTIVITIES. (Text in English, French, German, Swedish) 1950. triennial. ‡ International Graphical Federation, Monbijoustrasse 73, CH-3007 Berne, Switzerland. Ed. Alfred Kaufmann. circ. 1,800.

INTERNATIONAL TRADE UNION CONFERENCE FOR ACTION AGAINST APARTHEID. RESOLUTION. see POLITICAL SCIENCE — Civil Rights

331.88 UK ISSN 0539-0915
INTERNATIONAL TRANSPORT WORKERS' FEDERATION REPORT ON ACTIVITIES. (Editions in English, French, German, Spanish and Swedish) 1897. irreg. ‡ International Transport Workers' Federation, 133-135 Great Suffolk St., London SE1 1PD, England. circ. 500 (approx.) (controlled)

331.88 664 SZ ISSN 0579-8299
INTERNATIONAL UNION OF FOOD AND ALLIED WORKERS' ASSOCIATIONS. MEETING OF THE EXECUTIVE COMMITTEE. I. DOCUMENTS OF THE SECRETARIAT. II. SUMMARY REPORT. a. 100 Fr. International Union of Food and Allied Workers' Associations - Union Internationale des Travailleurs de l'Alimentation et des Branches Connexes, Secretariat, Rampe du Pont-Rouge 8, CH-1213 Petit-Lancy/Geneva, Switzerland.

INTERNATIONAL YEARBOOK OF ORGANIZATIONAL DEMOCRACY. see POLITICAL SCIENCE

331.88 CS
KALENDAR ODBORARA. a. 8 Kcs. (Slovenska Odborova Rada) Praca, Publishing House of the Slovak Trade Unions Council, Obrancov mieru 19, 812 71 Bratislava, Czechoslovakia. TEL 33-58-37. Ed. Igor Mitterpach.

331.8 US
KENTUCKY. DEPARTMENT OF LABOR. DIRECTORY OF LABOR ORGANIZATIONS. a. Department of Labor, Division of Administrative Services, 127 South, Frankfort, KY 40601.

331 US ISSN 0023-6519
LABOR CHRONICLE. 1904. irreg. $2. ‡ New York City Central Labor Council, AFL-CIO, 386 Park Ave. S., New York, NY 10016. TEL 212-685-9552. Ed. Ted H. Jacobsen. adv. bk. rev. abstr. illus. (tabloid format)

331.8 IS ISSN 0023-6969
LABOUR IN ISRAEL. French edition: Israel au Travail (ISSN 0021-1966); German edition: Histadrut Nachrichten (ISSN 0333-7782); Spanish edition: Trabajo en Israel (ISSN 0041-0225) 1947. irreg. (3-4/yr.) free. Histadrut, 93 Arlosoroff St., Tel Aviv, Israel. illus. circ. 7,000(Eng. edt.); 3,500(Fr. edt.); 6,000(Sp. edt.); 5,000(Ger. edt.)

331.88 CN ISSN 0383-3437
LABOUR ORGANIZATIONS IN NOVA SCOTIA. 1970. a. free. Department of Labour, Economics and Research Division, P.O. Box 697, Halifax, Nova Scotia, Canada. TEL 902-424-4125. (processed)
Formerly: Directory of Labour Unions in Nova Scotia.

331.8 SW
LANDSORGANISATIONEN I SVERIGE. YTTRANDEN TILL OFFENTLIG MYNDIGHET. irreg. Landsorganisationen i Sverige, Barnhusgatan 18, 105 53 Stockholm, Sweden.

MAGYAR MUNKASMOZGALMI MUZEUM. EVKONYV. see POLITICAL SCIENCE

MEATWORKER. see FOOD AND FOOD INDUSTRIES

331.8 380.1 US
MEDICAL LABORATORY DIRECTORY (YEAR) irreg., latest 1987/88. $98. U S Directory Service, 655 N.W., 128th St., Box 68-1700, Miami, FL 33168. TEL 305-769-1700.

NATIONAL CENTER FOR THE STUDY OF COLLECTIVE BARGAINING IN HIGHER EDUCATION AND THE PROFESSIONS. ANNUAL CONFERENCE PROCEEDINGS. see *EDUCATION — Higher Education*

331.8   US   ISSN 0545-6061
NEW YORK CITY TRADE UNION HANDBOOK. 1950. irreg., latest edt. 1981. free. New York City Central Labor Council AFL-CIO, 386 Park Ave. S., New York, NY 10016.

331.88   NZ
NEW ZEALAND FEDERATION OF LABOUR. OFFICIAL TRADE UNION DIRECTORY. 1971. a. free. New Zealand Federation of Labour, Box 6161, Lukes Lane, Wellington, New Zealand. Ed.Bd. adv.

331.88   SW
NORDISKA SAMARBETSORGAN. 1975. irreg. Nordisk Raad, Tyrgatan 7, Boks 19506, S-104 32 Stockholm, Sweden.

331.8   FR
PAGES JURIDIQUES DE LA VIE OUVRIERE. a. Vie Ouvriere, 33 rue Bouret, 75940 Paris Cedex, France.

331.88   US   ISSN 0031-319X
PATTERN MAKERS' JOURNAL. 1890. a. Pattern Makers' League of North America, 501 15th St., No. 204, Moline, IL 61265-2180. Ed. Jack L. Gabelhausen, Sr. illus. circ. 10,500.
    Formerly: Pattern Makers & Allied Crafts Journal.

331.88   PE
PONTIFICIA UNIVERSIDAD CATOLICA. TALLER DE ESTUDIOS URBANO INDUSTRIALES. SERIE: ESTUDIOS SINDICALES. no.3, 1976. irreg. Pontificia Universidad Catolica, Taller de Estudios Urbanos Industriales, Fundo Pando s/n, Lima, Peru.

331.88   PR
PUERTO RICO. DEPARTMENT OF LABOR. DIRECTORIO DE ORGANIZACIONES DEL TRABAJO. 1965. a. free. Department of Labor, Bureau of Labor Statistics, 505 Munoz Rivera Ave., Hato Rey, PR 00918. Ed. Federico Irizarry. circ. 900. (also avail. in microform)

331.8   YU   ISSN 0033-7463
RAD. 1945. a. 320 din. Savez Sindikata Jugoslavije, Trg Marksa i Engelsa 5, 11000 Belgrade, Yugoslavia. Ed. Stanislav Marinkovic. Indexed: Math.R.

331.88   CS   ISSN 0557-1693
ROCENKA ODBORARA. a. 15 Kcs. (Slovenska Odborova Rada) Praca, Publishing House of the Slovak Trade Unions Council, Obrancov mieru 19, 812 71 Bratislava, Czechoslovakia. TEL 33-58-37. Ed. Igor Mitterpach.

943 331 327   GW   ISSN 0173-2471
RUHR-UNIVERSITAET. INSTITUT ZUR GESCHICHTE DER ARBEITERBEWEGUNG. MITTEILUNGSBLATT. a. Ruhr-Universitaet, Institut zur Erforschung der Europaeischen Arbeiterbewegung, Postfach 10 21 48, D-4630 Bochum 1, W. Germany (B.R.D.)

331.88   US
SERVICE EMPLOYEES INTERNATIONAL UNION. INTERNATIONAL CONVENTION. OFFICIAL PROCEEDINGS. 17th edt., 1980. quadrennial. Service Employees International Union, 1313 L St., N.W., Washington, DC 20005. TEL 202-898-3200.

STEUER-GEWERKSCHAFTS-HANDBUCH. see *BUSINESS AND ECONOMICS — Public Finance, Taxation*

331.88   SW
STUDIER I ARBETARROERELSENS HISTORIA. irreg. Saellskapet foer Studier i Arbetarroerelsens Historia, Box 16 393, Stockholm, Sweden.

331.8   SW   ISSN 0347-724X
SWEDEN. STATENS ARBETSGIVARVERK. FOERFATTNINGAR OM STATLIGT REGLERADE TJAENSTER: F S T. 1969. a. Statens Arbetsgivarverk - National Swedish Agency for Government Employers, Box 2243, S-103 16 Stockholm, Sweden (Dist. by: Allmaenna Forlaget, Fack, S-162 89 Vaellingby, Sweden)
    Formerly (until 1979): Sweden. Statens Avtalsverk. Foerfattningar om Statligt Reglerade Tjaenster: F S T.

SYNDICAT GENERAL DE LA CONSTRUCTION ELECTRIQUE. ANNUAIRE. see *ELECTRICITY AND ELECTRICAL ENGINEERING*

331.8   IS   ISSN 0002-4074
TA'AWUN; cooperation, economics and social welfare. (Text in Arabic) 1960. irreg. (2-3/yr.) Histadrut, Arab Workers' Department, Box 303, Tel Aviv, Israel. Ed. Mahmoied Youners.

331.8   US   ISSN 0738-7911
TALKIN' UNION. 1981. irreg. $7.50 to individuals; institutions $12. Box 5349, Takoma Park, MD 20912. TEL 301-587-0349. Ed. Saul Schniderman. circ. 500.

331.88   II   ISSN 0445-6289
TRADE UNIONS IN INDIA. (Text in English) biennial. Rs.34($12.24) Labour Bureau, Simla 171004, India (Order from: Controller of Publications, Government of India, Civil Lines, Delhi 110054, India)
    Supersedes: Review on the Working of the Trade Unions Act, 1926.

331.88   HU   ISSN 0084-1544
TRADE UNIONS INTERNATIONAL OF CHEMICAL, OIL AND ALLIED WORKERS. INTERNATIONAL TRADE CONFERENCE. DOCUMENTS. irreg., 7th, Tarnow, Poland. free. ‡ Trade Unions International of Chemical, Oil and Allied Workers, Benczur u. 45, Budapest 6, Hungary.

331.88   UK
TRADES UNION CONGRESS. REPORT. Cover title: T U C Report. 1868. a. £12. Trades Union Congress, Congress House, Great Russell St., London WC1B 3LS, England. Ed. B.P. Barber. circ. 3,000. (also avail. in microfilm)

331.8   AT
TRADES UNION DIRECTORY. 1970. a. Trades and Labor Council of Queensland, Room 1, Trades Hall, Edward Street, Brisbane, Qld. 4000, Australia.

331.8   UK   ISSN 0260-7891
UNION FACT SHEET. 1979. irreg. membership. General Federation of Trade Unions, Central House, Upper Woburn Place, London WC1, England.
    Trade union

331.8   SZ   ISSN 0503-2334
UNION MONDIALE DES ORGANISATIONS SYNDICALES SUR BASES ECONOMIQUE ET SOCIALE LIBERALES. CONFERENCES: RAPPORT. 1960. a., latest 29th, 1984, Bern. World Union of Liberal Trade Union Organisations, 41 Badenerstrasse, 8004 Zurich, Switzerland.

UNIVERZITA J. E. PURKYNE. FILOZOFICKA FAKULTA. SBORNIK PRACI. G: RADA SOCIALNEVEDNA. see *BUSINESS AND ECONOMICS — Economic Systems And Theories, Economic History*

WORLD FEDERATION OF TEACHERS' UNIONS. INFORMATION LETTER. see *EDUCATION*

LABOR UNIONS — Abstracting, Bibliographies, Statistics

FUNDHEFT FUER ARBEITS- UND SOZIALRECHT; systematischer Nachweis der deutschen Rechtsprechung, Zeitschriftenaufsaetze und selbstaendigen Schriften. see *LAW — Abstracting, Bibliographies, Statistics*

331.881 314   NE   ISSN 0168-4035
STATISTIEK DER VAKBEWEGING IN NEDERLAND/STATISTICS OF THE TRADE UNIONS IN THE NETHERLANDS. (Text in Dutch and English) 1946. a. fl.10. Centraal Bureau voor de Statistiek, Prinses Beatrixlaan 428, Voorburg, Netherlands (Orders to: Staatsuitgeverij, Christoffel Plantijnstraat, The Hague, Netherlands)
    Formerly: Omvang der Vakbeweging in Nederland (ISSN 0077-6904)

LABORATORY TECHNIQUE

see *Medical Sciences — Experimental Medicine, Laboratory Technique*

LAW

see also *Law — Computer Applications; Law — International Law; Criminology and Law Enforcement; Patents, Trademarks and Copyrights;*

also specific subjects

345.01   US
A A A ANNUAL REPORT. a. American Arbitration Association, 140 W. 51st St., New York, NY 10020.

A A L L PUBLICATIONS SERIES. (American Association of Law Libraries) see *LIBRARY AND INFORMATION SCIENCES*

346   US   ISSN 0361-3763
A B A LAWYERS' TITLE GUARANTY FUNDS NEWSLETTER. Variant title: Lawyers' Title Guaranty Funds. irreg. $1 per no. American Bar Association, Standing Committee on Lawyers' Title Guaranty Funds, 1155 East 60th St., Chicago, IL 60637. TEL 312-947-4000. circ. 5,000. Indexed: C.L.I. L.R.I.

340   US
A D L LAW REPORT. 1965. irreg. (1-2/yr.) Anti Defamation League of B'nai B'rith, 823 United Nations Plaza, New York, NY 10017. TEL 212-490-2525. Ed.Bd. circ. 5,000(controlled) (reprint service avail. from UMI)
    Formerly: Law (ISSN 0023-916X)

340   AT
A L R C REPORT SERIES. (Australia Law Reform Commission) 1975. irreg. price varies. Australian Government Publishing Service, G.P.O. Box 84, Canberra, A.C.T. 2601, Australia. Indexed: Aus.Leg.Mon.Dig.

A M S STUDIES IN CRIMINAL JUSTICE. see *CRIMINOLOGY AND LAW ENFORCEMENT*

340   US   ISSN 0161-1402
A S I L S INTERNATIONAL LAW JOURNAL. 1977. a. $9. Association of Student International Law Societies, Tillar House, 2223 Massachusetts Ave., N.W., Washington, DC 20008. Ed. Jonathan Clark Green. adv. bk. rev. circ. 500. Indexed: Leg.Per. C.L.I. L.R.I. Peace Res.Abstr.

340   GW   ISSN 0065-0307
ABHANDLUNGEN AUS DEM GESAMTEN BUERGERLICHEN RECHT, HANDELSRECHT UND WIRTSCHAFTSRECHT. 1954. irreg., no.57, 1984. price varies. Verlagsgesellschaft Recht und Wirtschaft mbH, Haeusserstr. 14, Postfach 105960, 6900 Heidelberg 1, W. Germany (B.R.D.) Eds. E. Steindorf, P. Ulmer.

340 388.324   US   ISSN 0571-6373
ABSTRACTS OF SUPREME COURT DECISIONS INTERPRETING THE INTERSTATE COMMERCE ACT. 1954. irreg. Association of Transportation Practitioners, 1211 Connecticut Ave., N.W., Ste. 510, Washington, DC 20036.

LAW

340 320 HU ISSN 0524-904X
ACTA FACULTATIS POLITICO-JURIDICAE UNIVERSITATIS SCIENTIARUM BUDAPESTIENSIS DE ROLANDO EOTVOS NOMINATAE. (Text in Hungarian; summaries in French, German and Russian) 1959. irreg. Eotvos Lorand Tudomanyegyetem, Allam- es Jogtudomanyi Kar, Egyetem ter 1-3, Budapest 5, Hungary. Indexed: Hist.Abstr. Amer.Hist.& Life.

340 SA ISSN 0065-1346
ACTA JURIDICA. 1947. a. R.54. Juta & Co. Ltd., Box 123, Wetton 7790, South Africa. Ed.Bd. circ. 500. Indexed: Leg.Per. Ind.S.A.Per.
    Formerly (until 1959): Butterworths South African Law Review.

340 320 HU ISSN 0563-0606
ACTA UNIVERSITATIS DE ATTILA JOZSEF NOMINATAE. ACTA IURIDICA ET POLITICA. (Text in English, French, German, Hungarian or Russian) 1955. a. exchange basis. Attila Jozsef University, c/o E. Szabo, Exchange Librarian, Dugonics ter 13, P.O.B. 393, Szeged H-6701, Hungary (Subscr. to: Kultura, Box 149, H-1389 Budapest, Hungary) Ed.Bd. circ. 500.

340 370 PL
ACTA UNIVERSITATIS LODZIENSIS: FOLIA IURIDICA. (Text in Polish; summaries in various languages) irreg. Uniwersytet Lodzki, Drukarnia Wojskowa, Ul. Gdanska 130, Lodz, Poland (Dist. by: Ars Polona-Ruch, Krakowskie Przedmiescie 7, Warsaw, Poland)

340 PL ISSN 0208-5283
ACTA UNIVERSITATIS NICOLAI COPERNICI. PRAWO. 1961. irreg. price varies. Uniwersytet Mikolaja Kopernika, Fosa Staromiejska 3, Torun, Poland (Dist. by: Osrodek Rozpowszechniania Wydawnictw Naukowych PAN, Palac Kultury i Nauki, 00-901 Warsaw, Poland)
    Formerly: Uniwersytet Mikolaja Kopernika, Torun. Nauki Humanistyczno-Spoleczne. Prawo (ISSN 0083-4513)

ADELPHIA LAW JOURNAL. see *CLUBS*

340 US
ADMINISTRATION OF JUSTICE MEMORANDA. 1975. irreg. price varies. University of North Carolina, Chapel Hill, Institute of Government, Knapp Bldg., 059-A, Chapel Hill, NC 27514. Ed. Robert L. Farb.

340 364 US
ADMINISTRATION OF JUVENILE JUSTICE IN CALIFORNIA. Department of Justice, Division of Law Enforcement, 4949 Broadway, Box 13427, Sacramento, CA 95813.

340 AT ISSN 0726-5816
ADMINISTRATIVE LAW DECISIONS. 1976. irreg, vol.8, 1986. Aus.$95. Butterworths Pty. Ltd., 271-273 Lane Cove Rd., North Ryde, N.S.W. 2113, Australia (Subscr. to: P.O. Box 345, North Ryde, N.S.W. 2113, Australia) Ed. D.C. Pearce.

340 CN
ADMINISTRATIVE LAW REPORTS. 1983. a $57.50. Carswell Legal Publications, 2330 Midland Ave., Agincourt, Ont. M1S 1P7, Canada. TEL 416-291-8421. (looseleaf format)

ADVANCES IN LAW AND CHILD DEVELOPMENT. see *CHILDREN AND YOUTH — About*

346.066 US
ADVERTISING LAW ANTHOLOGY. 1973. a. $59.95. Book Publishers, Inc., Wisconsin Ave., Ste. 229 E, Bethesda, MD 20814. Ed. Donald J. Hoyes. bibl.

340 US ISSN 0462-3134
ADVOCACY INSTITUTE. PROCEEDINGS. 23rd, 1972. a. price varies. Institute of Continuing Legal Education, 2010 Greene St., Ann Arbor, MI 48103. TEL 313-764-0533.

340 CN ISSN 0382-456X
ADVOCATE. 1964. irreg. University of Toronto, Faculty of Law, Toronto, Ont. M5S 1A1, Canada. TEL 416-978-3725.

342 AF
AFGHANISTAN. MINISTRY OF JUSTICE. OFFICIAL GAZETTE/RASMI JARIDAH. (Text in Persian) irreg. $15. Ministry of Justice, Darrul Aman, Kabul, Afghanistan.

340 GW ISSN 0722-2181
AFRIKANISCHES RECHT. JAHRBUCH. (Text in English, French and German; summaries in English and French) 1980. a. price varies. Juristischer Verlag GmbH, Postfach 102 640, 6900 Heidelberg, W. Germany (B.R.D.) Ed. C.F. Mueller. bk. rev.

340 BL
AJURIS. 1974. irreg. (Associacao dos Juizes do Rio Grande do Sul) Livraria Sulina, Av. Borges de Medeiros 1030-1036, Porto Alegre, Brazil.

340 CN
ALBERTA REPORTS. 1976. irreg. Can.$83 per vol. Maritime Law Book Ltd., Box 302, Fredericton, N.B. E3B 4Y9, Canada. TEL 506-454-9921. (back issues avail.)
    ●Also available online. Vendors: QL Systems Ltd.

347.9 CN
ALBERTA STATUTES AND RULES OF COURT - JUDICIALLY CONSIDERED; case annotations. 1980. a. Carswell Legal Publications (Western), 800 Rocky Mountain Plaza, 615 Macleod Trail, S.E., Calgary, Alb. T2G 4T8, Canada. TEL 403-233-9300. Ed. John Leeder.

340 BE
ALGEMENE PRACTISCHE RECHTVERZAMELING. Short title: A P R. 1972. irreg. price varies. E. Story-Scientia, Eekhout 2, B-9000 Ghent, Belgium.

340 UK ISSN 0265-766X
ALL ENGLAND LAW REPORTS. ANNUAL REVIEW. 1983. a. Butterworth & Co. (Publishers) Ltd., c/o John Lord, Promo. Mgr., 88 Kingsway, London WC2B 6AB, England.

AMERICAN AUTOMOBILE ASSOCIATION. DIGEST OF MOTOR LAWS. see *TRANSPORTATION — Automobiles*

340 US ISSN 0094-3584
AMERICAN BAR - THE CANADIAN BAR - THE INTERNATIONAL BAR. 1919. a. $180. Reginald Bishop Forster & Associates, Inc., 3280 Ramos Circle, Sacramento, CA 95827. Ed. Mindy Toomay. circ. 33,000.
    Formerly: American Bar Reference Handbook.

340 US
AMERICAN BENCH; judges of the nation. 1977. biennial. $170. Reginald Bishop Forster & Associates, Inc., 3287 Ramos Circle, Sacramento, CA 95827. TEL 916-362-3276. Ed.Bd.

340 970 US
AMERICAN INDIAN TREATIES PUBLICATIONS SERIES. 1975. irreg. University of California, Los Angeles, American Indian Studies Center, 3220 Campbell Hall, U.C.L.A., Los Angeles, CA 90024. TEL 213-825-4777. Ed. William Oandasan. (back issues avail.)

340 US ISSN 0065-8995
AMERICAN JOURNAL OF JURISPRUDENCE. 1956. a. $11. (University of Notre Dame, Law School) Western Publishing, 537 E. Ohio St., Indianapolis, IN 46204-2173. TEL 219-255-2938. Eds. Charles E. Rice, Robert E. Rodes. adv. bk. rev. circ. 1,000. (also avail. in microform from UMI, WSH; back issues avail.; reprint service avail. from UMI) Indexed: Cath.Ind. Leg.Per. A.B.C.Pol.Sci. C.L.I. L.R.I.
    Formerly: Natural Law Forum.

340 US ISSN 0732-1031
AMERICAN JUDICATURE SOCIETY. ANNUAL REPORT. 1917. a. free. American Judicature Society, 25 E. Washington, Ste. 1600, Chicago, IL 60602-1805. Ed. David Richert. circ. 50,000. (reprint service avail. from UMI,ISI)

340 US ISSN 0065-9045
AMERICAN LAW INSTITUTE. ANNUAL MEETING. PROCEEDINGS. 1923. a. $35. American Law Institute, 4025 Chestnut St., Philadelphia, PA 19104. TEL 215-243-1600. index from 1967. (also avail. in microfiche)

020 340 US
AMERICAN LIBRARY LAWS. irreg., 5th edt., 1984. $110 cloth bound. American Library Association, 50 E. Huron St., Chicago, IL 60611. TEL 312-944-6780. Ed. Alex Ladenson.

342 940 US ISSN 0740-0470
AMERICAN UNIVERSITY STUDIES. SERIES 10. POLITICAL SCIENCE. 1983. irreg. Peter Lang Publishing, Inc., 62 W. 45th St., New York, NY 10036. TEL 212-302-6740. Ed. Jay Wilson.

340 SP ISSN 0210-7686
ANALES DE LA UNIVERSIDAD HISPALENSE. SERIE: DERECHO. irreg, latest no.25. price varies. Universidad de Sevilla, San Fernando 4, Seville, Spain.

340 BL
ANALISE JURISPRUDENCIAL. 1976. irreg. (Instituto dos Advogados de Sao Paulo) Editora Resenha Tributaria, Rue Xavier de Toledo 210, Sao Paulo, Brazil.

ANALYSIS OF WORKERS' COMPENSATION LAWS. see *SOCIAL SERVICES AND WELFARE*

343 DK ISSN 0108-7169
ANKLAGEMYNDIGHEDENS AARSBERETNING. 1973. a. free. Rigsadvokaturen, Rigspolitchefen, Porthusgade 3, 1213 Copenhagen K, Denmark. circ. 3,000.

340 PL ISSN 0458-4317
ANNALES UNIVERSITATIS MARIAE CURIE-SKLODOWSKA. SECTIO G. IUS. (Text in English, French, German, Polish; summaries in French, German, Polish, Russian) 1954. a. price varies. Uniwersytet Marii Curie-Sklodowskiej, Plac Marii Curie-Sklodowskiej 5, 20-031 Lublin, Poland. Ed. W. Skrzydlo. circ. 500. Indexed: Hist.Abstr. Amer.Hist.& Life.

340 GW
ANNALES UNIVERSITATIS SARAVIENSIS. RECHTSWISSENSCHAFTLICHE ABTEILUNG. SCHRIFTENREIHE. 1963. irreg., vol.120, 1986. price varies. (Universitaet des Saarlandes, Rechtswissenschaftliche Fakultaet) Carl Heymanns Verlag KG, Luxemburgerstr. 449, 5000 Cologne 41, W. Germany (B.R.D.)

ANNALS OF AIR AND SPACE LAW/ANNALES DE DROIT AERIEN ET SPATIAL. see *AERONAUTICS AND SPACE FLIGHT*

340 FR ISSN 0066-2658
ANNUAIRE DE LEGISLATION FRANCAISE ET ETRANGERE. a. (Centre National de la Recherche Scientifique, Service de Recherches Juridiques Comparatives) Editions du C N R S, 295 rue St. Jacques, 75005 Paris, France.

ANNUAL ENERGY LITIGATION INSTITUTE. EFFECTIVE STRATEGIES AND TECHNIQUES. see *ENERGY*

ANNUAL INSTITUTE ON SECURITIES REGULATION. see *BUSINESS AND ECONOMICS — Banking And Finance*

ANNUAL REVIEW OF BANKING LAW. see *BUSINESS AND ECONOMICS — Banking And Finance*

340 CN
ANNUAL REVIEW OF CRIMINAL LAW (YEAR) 1982. a. price varies. Carsell Legal Publications, 2330 Midland Avenue, Agincourt, Ont. M1S 1P7, Canada.

340 UK ISSN 0066-4405
ANNUAL SURVEY OF AFRICAN LAW. 1970. a. price varies. Rex Collings Ltd., 6 Paddington St., London W.1., England. Eds. N.N. Rubin, E. Cotran. index.

340 US
ANNUAL SURVEY OF BANKRUPTCY LAW. 1979. a. $98.50. Callaghan and Company Inc., 3201 Old Glenview Rd., Wilmette, IL 60091. Ed. William L. Norton. index. (back issues avail.)

340 II ISSN 0570-2666
ANNUAL SURVEY OF INDIAN LAW. (Text in English) 1965. a. Rs.100. Indian Law Institute, Bhagwandas Rd., New Delhi 110001, India. bibl.

LAW

340 US ISSN 0570-2674
ANNUAL SURVEY OF MASSACHUSETTS LAW.
1954. a. $24.50. Boston College, School of Law, 885
Centre St., Newton Centre, MA 02159. TEL 617-
969-0100. Indexed: Leg.Per. C.L.I. L.R.I.

340.5 IT ISSN 0003-5149
ANNUARIO DI DIRITTO COMPARATO E DI
STUDI LEGISLATIVI. (Text in English, French
and Italian) 1927. a. L.16000. Istituto Italiano di
Studi Legislativi, Via Bertolini, 8, 00197 Rome,
Italy. Dir. Riccardo Monaco. index. circ. 500.

340 IT
ANNUARIO DI STATISTICHE GIUDIZIARIE -
TOMO 2. a. L.14000. Istituto Centrale di Statistica,
Via Cesare Balbo 16, 00100 Rome, Italy.

ANNUARIO EUROPEO DELL'AMBIENTE. see
ENVIRONMENTAL STUDIES

340 UK ISSN 0262-3234
ANTHONY AND BERRYMAN'S MAGISTRATES'
COURT GUIDE. a. Butterworth & Co. (Publishers)
Ltd., c/o John Lord, Promo. Mgr., 88 Kingsway,
London WC2B 6AB, England. Ed. A.P. Carr.

353.73 US ISSN 0162-7996
ANTITRUST. 1978. irreg. membership only. American
Bar Association, Antitrust Law Section, 750 N.
Lake Shore Drive, Chicago, IL 60611. TEL 312-
988-5555.

340 US ISSN 0738-5919
ANTITRUST LAW HANDBOOK. 1987. a. $58.50.
Clark Boardman Co., 435 Hudson St., New York,
NY 10014. TEL 212-929-7500.

340 UY
ANUARIO DE DERECHO CIVIL URUGUAYO.
1970. a. $40. Fundacion de Cultura Universitaria,
25 de Mayo, No. 568, Casilla de Correo No. 1155,
Montevideo, Uruguay.

340 SP
ANUARIO DE FILOSOFIA DEL DERECHO. 1953;
N.S. 1984. a. 3300 ptas. Instituto Nacional de
Estudios Juridicos, Seccion de Publicaciones, Duque
de Medinaceli St., No. 8, 28014 Madrid, Spain. Ed.
L. Legaz Lacambra.

340 301 SP ISSN 0210-1785
ANUARIO DE SOCIOLOGIA Y PSICOLOGIA
JURIDICAS. 1974. a. 1000 ptas. (Colegio de
Abogados de Barcelona) Instituto de Psicologia y
Sociologia Juridicas, Calle Mallorca 283, Barcelona,
Spain. bk. rev. bibl. index. circ. 1,000. Indexed:
Psychol.Abstr.

340 MX ISSN 0185-3295
ANUARIO JURIDICO. 1974. a. $30. Universidad
Nacional Autonoma de Mexico, Instituto de
Investigaciones Juridicas, Ciudad Universitaria,
Delegacion Coyoacan, 04510 Mexico, DF, Mexico.
Ed. Jose L. Soberanes. adv. bk. rev. abstr. bibl.
index.

340 CE
AQUINAS LAW JOURNAL.* (Text in English)
1972. irreg. Rs.15. Aquinas College of Higher
Studies, Colombo 8, Sri Lanka.

340 GW ISSN 0066-5703
ARBEITEN ZUR RECHTSVERGLEICHUNG. 1958.
irreg., vol.134, 1986. price varies. (Gesellschaft fuer
Rechtsvergleichung) Alfred Metzner Verlag,
Zeppelinallee 43, D-6000 Frankfurt/Main 97, W.
Germany (B.R.D.)

ARBEITSRECHT DER GEGENWART. see
*BUSINESS AND ECONOMICS — Labor And
Industrial Relations*

ARBEJDSRETLIGT TIDSSKRIFT; arbejdsrettens
domme, arbejdsretlige kendelser. see *BUSINESS
AND ECONOMICS — Labor And Industrial
Relations*

ARBITRATION & THE LAW. see *BUSINESS AND
ECONOMICS — Labor And Industrial Relations*

ARCHIV FUER RECHTS- UND
SOZIALPHILOSOPHIE. BEIHEFTE. see
PHILOSOPHY

340 FR ISSN 0066-6564
ARCHIVES DE PHILOSOPHIE DU DROIT. 1952.
a. Editions Sirey-Diffusion Dalloz, 11 rue Soufflot,
75240 Paris Cedex 05, France. Ed. Michel Villey.

340 PL ISSN 0066-6882
ARCHIVUM IURIDICUM CRACOVIENSE. (Text
in English, French and German) 1968. a. price
varies. (Polska Akademia Nauk, Oddzial w
Krakowie, Komisja Nauk Prawnych) Ossolineum,
Publishing House of the Polish Academy of
Sciences, Rynek 9, Wroclaw, Poland (Dist. by: Ars
Polona-Ruch, Krakowskie Przedmiescie 7, Warsaw,
Poland) Ed. Franciszek Studnicki. circ. 600.

348 US ISSN 0094-4246
ARIZONA LEGISLATIVE SERVICE. Cover title: A
R S Legislative Service. irreg. West Publishing Co.,
Box 3526, St. Paul, MN 55165. TEL 612-228-2500.

348 US
ARIZONA REPORTS. 1913. irreg. (Supreme Court)
West Publishing Co., Box 3526, St. Paul, MN
55165. TEL 612-228-2500.
Formerly: Report of Cases Argued and
Determined in the Supreme Court of the State of
Arizona.

340 NO ISSN 0004-2102
ARKIV FOR SJOERETT/SCANDINAVIAN
JOURNAL OF MARITIME LAW. (Text in
English and Scandinavian languages) 1951. irreg. (4-
5/vol.) price varies. (Norske Sjoeretts-Forening)
Universitetsforlaget, Kolstadgt. 1, Box 2959-Toeyen,
0608 Oslo 6, Norway (U.S. address: Publications
Expediting Inc., 200 Meacham Ave., Elmont, NY
11003) Ed. Thor Falkanger. adv. bk. rev. circ. 1,
500.

340 US
ASIAN LAW SERIES. 1969. irreg., no.7, 1980. price
varies. University of Washington Press, Seattle, WA
98105. TEL 206-543-4050.

340 UY ISSN 0376-5024
ASOCIACION DE ESCRIBANOS DEL
URUGUAY. REVISTA. 1904. irreg. price varies.
Asociacion de Escribanos del Uruguay, Av. 18 de
Julio 1730, Piso 11, Montevideo, Uruguay. Ed.
Gonzalo Sere Pineyrua. bk. rev. bibl. index. circ. 3,
900.

346 US ISSN 0066-9407
ASSOCIATION OF AMERICAN LAW SCHOOLS.
PROCEEDINGS. 1901. a. $10 per vol. Association
of American Law Schools, Ste. 370, 1 Dupont
Circle, N.W., Washington, DC 20036. TEL 202-
296-8851. Ed. Noel Augustyn. 50-yr.cum.index.
(processed; also avail. in microfiche)

340 CN
ATLANTIC PROVINCES REPORTERS. 1974. irreg.
Can.$67 per vol. Maritime Law Book Ltd., Box 302,
Fredericton, N.B. E3B 4Y9, Canada. TEL 506-454-
9921. (back issues avail.)

ATTORNEY'S DIRECTORY OF FORENSIC
PSYCHIATRISTS IN THE UNITED STATES
AND CANADA; a biographical professional and
reference directory of legal psychiatrists. see
MEDICAL SCIENCES — Forensic Sciences

346 NZ ISSN 0067-0510
AUCKLAND UNIVERSITY LAW REVIEW. 1967.
a. NZ.$7. Auckland University Law Students
Society, Inc., Private Bag, Auckland, New Zealand.
Eds. L.A. McGregor Godwin, H. Winkelmann. adv.
bk. rev. circ. 1,500. Indexed: Leg.Per. C.L.I. L.R.I.

338.7 340 GW ISSN 0067-0669
AUSLAENDISCHE AKTIENGESETZE. 1955. irreg.,
vol.18, 1983. price varies. (Gesellschaft fuer
Rechtsvergleichung) Alfred Metzner Verlag,
Zeppelinallee 43, D-6000 Frankfurt/Main 97, W.
Germany (B.R.D.)

328.94 328.9 AT
AUSTRALASIAN AND PACIFIC
PARLIAMENTARY SEMINAR. SUMMARY
REPORT OF PROCEEDINGS. 1972. biennial.
free. Australasian and Pacific Parliamentary
Association, Regional Secretariat, Canberra,
Australia. circ. 250.
Formerly (until 1980): Australia Parliamentary
Seminar. Summary Report of Proceedings.

AUSTRALIA. FISHING INDUSTRY RESEARCH
COMMITTEE. ANNUAL REPORT. see *FISH
AND FISHERIES*

340 AT ISSN 0312-6994
AUSTRALIA. LAW REFORM COMMISSION.
ANNUAL REPORT. 1975. a. price varies.
Australian Government Publishing Service, G.P.O.
Box 84, Canberra, A.C.T. 2601, Australia. (back
issues avail.) Indexed: Aus.Leg.Mon.Dig.

340 AT ISSN 0313-8445
AUSTRALIAN COMPANY LAW REPORTS;
reports of leading cases in company law in
Australia. 1977. biennial. Aus.$85($78) Butterworths
Pty. Ltd, 271-273 Lane Cove Rd., North Ryde,
N.S.W. 2113, Australia. Ed. W.E. Paterson. circ. 1,
608. (back issues avail.)

346 AT ISSN 0067-1843
AUSTRALIAN DIGEST; a digest of all the Australian
law reports. 1961. irreg., vol.42, 1986. Aus.$80. Law
Book Co. Ltd., 44-50 Waterloo Rd., North Ryde,
N.S.W. 2113, Australia. Ed. Kathy Fitzhenry.

347 AT
AUSTRALIAN FAMILY LAW CASES. 1976. a.
Aus.$69. C C H Australia Ltd., P.O. Box 230,
North Ryde, N.S.W. 2113, Australia. charts.

340 AT ISSN 0729-3356
AUSTRALIAN JOURNAL OF LAW AND
SOCIETY. 1982. a. Aus.$14. Macquarie University,
School of Law, Balaclava Rd., North Ryde, N.S.W.
2113, Australia. Ed. Brendan Edgeworth. circ. 500.
(back issues avail.)

345.01 AT
AUSTRALIAN LEGAL AID REVIEW
COMMITTEE. REPORT. 1974. a. Australian Legal
Aid Review Committee, 187 Macquarie St., Sydney,
N.S.W. 2000, Australia.

AUSTRALIAN LEGAL DIRECTORY. see
*BUSINESS AND ECONOMICS — Trade And
Industrial Directories*

AUSTRALIAN TAX CASES. see *BUSINESS AND
ECONOMICS — Public Finance, Taxation*

340 AU
AUSTRIA. OBERLANDESGERICHT WIEN IM
LEISTUNGSSTREITVERFAHREN ZWEITER
INSTANZ DER SOZIALVERSICHERUNG (SSV).
ENTSCHEIDUNGEN. 1961. a. price varies.
Manzsche Verlags- und Universitaetsbuchhandlung,
Kohlmarkt 16, A-1014 Vienna, Austria. circ. 2,000.

347 US ISSN 0099-1244
B A R - B R I BAR REVIEW. CIVIL PROCEDURE.
a. B A R-B R I Bar Review, 11801 W. Olympic
Blvd., Los Angeles, CA 90064. TEL 213-477-2542.
Key Title: Civil Procedure.

346 US
B A R - B R I BAR REVIEW. COMMUNITY
PROPERTY. a. B A R-B R I Bar Review, 11801
W. Olympic Blvd., Los Angeles, CA 90064. TEL
213-477-2542.

342.73 US ISSN 0098-7638
B A R - B R I BAR REVIEW. CONSTITUTIONAL
LAW. a. B A R-B R I Bar Review, 11801 W.
Olympic Blvd., Los Angeles, CA 90064. TEL 213-
477-2542. Key Title: Constitutional Law.

346.73 US ISSN 0098-762X
B A R - B R I BAR REVIEW. CONTRACTS. a. B A
R-B R I Bar Review, 11801 W. Olympic Blvd., Los
Angeles, CA 90064. TEL 213-477-2542. Key Title:
Contracts.

346 US ISSN 0099-1236
B A R - B R I BAR REVIEW. CORPORATIONS. a.
B A R-B R I Bar Review, 11801 W. Olympic Blvd.,
Los Angeles, CA 90064. TEL 213-477-2542. Key
Title: Corporations.

347.73 US
B A R - B R I BAR REVIEW. EVIDENCE. a. B A
R-B R I Bar Review, 11801 W. Olympic Blvd., Los
Angeles, CA 90064. TEL 213-477-2542.

652 LAW

174 US
B A R - B R I BAR REVIEW. PROFESSIONAL RESPONSIBILITY. a. B A R-B R I Bar Review, 11801 W. Olympic Blvd., Los Angeles, CA 90064. TEL 213-477-2542.
    Formerly: Bay Area Review Course. Legal Ethics (ISSN 0098-7980)

346.73 US
B A R - B R I BAR REVIEW. REAL PROPERTY. a. B A R-B R I Bar Review, 11801 W. Olympic Blvd., Los Angeles, CA 90064. TEL 213-477-2542.

347 US ISSN 0098-7999
B A R - B R I BAR REVIEW. REMEDIES. irreg. B A R-B R I Bar Review, 11801 W. Olympic Blvd., Los Angeles, CA 90064. TEL 213-477-2542. Key Title: Remedies.

346 US
B A R - B R I BAR REVIEW. WILLS. a. B A R-B R I Bar Review, 11801 W. Olympic Blvd., Los Angeles, CA 90064. TEL 213-477-2542.

B O C A BASIC NATIONAL BUILDING CODE. (Building Officials and Code Administrators International) see *BUILDING AND CONSTRUCTION*

B O C A BASIC-NATIONAL EXISTING STRUCTURES CODE. (Building Officials and Code Administrators International) see *BUILDING AND CONSTRUCTION*

B O C A BASIC-NATIONAL MECHANICAL CODE. (Building Officials and Code Administrators International) see *BUILDING AND CONSTRUCTION*

B O C A BASIC-NATIONAL PLUMBING CODE. (Building Officials and Code Administrators International) see *HEATING, PLUMBING AND REFRIGERATION*

342 BG
BANGLADESH JATIYA AINJIBI SAMITY SOUVENIR. Variant title: Bangladesh Jatiya Ainjibi Samity. Annual Law Journal. (Text in English or Bengali) 1977. a. Tk.25. Bangladesh Jatiya Ainjibi Samity - National Bar Associaton of Bangladesh, Dhanmandi R.A. 87, Road 7A, Dhaka, Bangladesh. Ed. Mr.Sobhan. adv. bk. rev. circ. 10,000.

BANK INCOME TAX RETURN MANUAL. see *BUSINESS AND ECONOMICS — Banking And Finance*

BANKING LAW ANTHOLOGY. see *BUSINESS AND ECONOMICS — Banking And Finance*

BANKING LAW JOURNAL DIGEST (SUPPLEMENT) see *BUSINESS AND ECONOMICS — Banking And Finance*

340 IS
BAR ILAN LAW STUDIES. (Text in Hebrew) a. $16. Bar Ilan University Press, Ramat Gat 52 100, Israel.

340.1 NR ISSN 0331-0086
BARRISTER. (Suspended 1968-70) 1967. irreg. 6 n. University of Nigeria, Law Student's Association, Nsukka, Nigeria. Ed. Emeka Ihene. adv. bk. rev. circ. 2,000. Indexed: Leg.Per.

340 SZ
BASLER STUDIEN ZUR RECHTSWISSENSCHAFT. 1932. irreg. price varies. Helbing und Lichtenhahn Verlag AG, Freie Strasse 82, CH-4051 Basel, Switzerland (Subscr. to: Sauerlaender AG, Postfach, CH-5001 Aarau, Switzerland)

BEITRAEGE ZUM RUNDFUNKRECHT. see *COMMUNICATIONS — Radio And Television*

340 AU
BEITRAEGE ZUM UNIVERSITAETSRECHT. 1982. irreg. price varies. Manzsche Verlags- und Universitaetsbuchhandlung, Kohlmarkt 16, A 1014 Vienna, Austria. Ed. Rudolf Strasser. circ. 1,500.

343.73 US ISSN 0270-5206
BENDER'S DICTIONARY OF 1040 DEDUCTIONS. 1980. a. Matthew Bender & Co., Inc., 235 E. 45 St., New York, NY 10017. TEL 212-661-5050. Ed. Kevin Egan.

BIBLIOTECA DE ESTUDIOS PARAGUAYOS. see *HISTORY — History Of North And South America*

340 SP
BOLETIN DE PEQUENA JURISPRUDENCIA. 1965. irreg. (approx. m.) free. Ilustre Colegio Provincial de Abogados de San Sebastian, Fuenterrabia A-2, Guipuzcoa, Spain. bibl. circ. 800.

340 CU
BOLETIN INFORMATIVO S A E. irreg. (Organo Arbitraje Estatal) Cientifico-Tecnico Organo de Arbitraje Estatal Nacional, Calle 5th No. 306, E/C y D, Vedado, Havana, Cuba.

BOSTON UNIVERSITY JOURNAL OF TAX LAW. see *BUSINESS AND ECONOMICS — Public Finance, Taxation*

BRAZIL. INSTITUTO DO ACUCAR E DO ALCOOL. CONSELHO DELIBERATIVO. COLETANEA DE RESOLUCOES (E) PRESIDENCIA. COLETANEA DE ATOS. see *AGRICULTURE — Crop Production And Soil*

340 BL
BRAZIL. SUPREMO TRIBUNAL FEDERAL. INDICES DE LEGISLACAO FEDERAL. (Subseries of: D.I.N.-Divulgacao) a. price varies. Supremo Tribunal Federal, Departamento de Imprensa Nacional, SIG -Quadra 6- Lote 800, CEP 70604 Brasilia-DF, Brazil.

340 BL
BRAZIL. SUPREMO TRIBUNAL FEDERAL. JURISCIVEL DO S.T.F. 1972. irreg. Cultural Distribuidora de Livros, Praca dos Tres Poderes, Brasilia, D.F., Brazil.

340 BL
BRAZIL. SUPREMO TRIBUNAL FEDERAL. RELATORIO DOS TRABALHOS REALIZADOS. 1916. a. Supremo Tribunal Federal, Departamento de Imprensa Nacional, SIG - Quadra 6- Lote 800, CEP 70604 Brasilia-DF, Brazil.

340 CN ISSN 0381-2510
BRITISH COLUMBIA. LAW REFORM COMMISSION. ANNUAL REPORT.* 1970. a. Law Reform Commission, Secretary to the Attorney General, Parliament Buildings, Victoria, BC V8V 1X4, Canada. TEL 604-660-2366. circ. 2,000.

340 CN
BRITISH COLUMBIA COURT FORMS. irreg. $495. Butterworth & Co. (Canada) Ltd., 2265 Midland Ave., Scarborough, Ont. M1P 4S1, Canada. TEL 416-292-1421. Eds. Beverly M. McLachlin, James P. Taylor. (looseleaf format)

340 CN
BRITISH COLUMBIA PRACTICE. a. $401.50. Butterworth & Co. (Canada) Ltd., 2265 Midland Avenue, Scarborough, Ont. M1P 4S1, Canada. TEL 416-292-1421. Eds. Beverly M. McLachlin, James P. Taylor. (looseleaf format)

348 US ISSN 0146-2989
BULLETIN OF MEDIEVAL CANON LAW. NEW SERIES. (Text in English, French, German, Italian, Latin and Spanish) 1971. a. $15. Institute of Medieval Canon Law, University of California, Berkeley, Boalt Hall, Berkeley, CA 94720. TEL 415-642-5094. Ed. Stephan Kuttner. bibl. circ. 500. Indexed: Canon Law Abstr. CERDIC.

340 BE
BULLETIN USUEL DES LOIS ET ARRETES. 1850. irreg. (10-25/m) 20.000 Fr. Etablissements Emile Bruylant, 67 rue de la Regence, 1000 Brussels, Belgium.

BUSINESS FRANCHISE GUIDE. see *BUSINESS AND ECONOMICS — Small Business*

346.066 CN ISSN 0703-5551
BUSINESS LAW REPORTS. 1977. a $59.25. Carswell Legal Publications, 2330 Midland Ave., Agincourt, Ont. M1S 1P7, Canada. TEL 416-291-8421. Ed. Robert L. Shirriff. (looseleaf format) Indexed: C.L.I. L.R.I.

340 381 UK
BUSINESS LAWS OF ARAB EMIRATES. a. (plus s-a. supplements) £280($448) Graham & Trotman Ltd., Sterling House, 66 Wilton Rd., London SW1V 1DE, England (Distr. in U.S. and Canada by: Trotman & Graham Inc., 13 Park Ave., Graithersburg, MD 20877) Ed. M.J. Hall.

340 381 UK
BUSINESS LAWS OF EGYPT. a. (plus q. supplements) £280($448) Graham & Trotman Ltd., Sterling House, 66 Wilton Rd., London SW1V 1DE, England (Distr. in U.S. and Canada by: Graham & Trotman Inc., 13 Park Ave., Gaithersburg, MD 20877) Ed. N.H. Karam.

340 381 UK
BUSINESS LAWS OF IRAQ. a. (plus q. supplements) £280($448) Graham & Trotman Ltd., Sterling House, 66 Wilton Rd., London SW1V 1DE, England (Distr. in U.S. and Canada by: Graham & Trotman Inc., 13 Park Ave., Gaithersburg, MD 20877) Ed. N.H. Karam.

340 381 UK
BUSINESS LAWS OF KUWAIT. a. (plus q. supplements) £280($448) Graham & Trotman Ltd., Sterling House, 66 Wilton Rd., London SW1V 1DE, England (Distr. in U.S. and Canada by: Graham & Trotman Inc., 13 Park Ave., Gaithersburg, MD 20877) Ed. N.H. Karam.

340 381 UK
BUSINESS LAWS OF OMAN. a. (plus q. supplements) £280($448) Graham & Trotman Ltd., Sterling House, 66 Wilton Rd., London SW1V 1DE, England (Distr. in U.S. and Canada by: Graham & Trotman Inc., 13 Park Ave., Gaithersburg, MD 208777) Ed. M.J. Hall.

340 381 UK
BUSINESS LAWS OF SAUDI ARABIA. a. (plus q. supplements) £280($448) Graham & Trotman Ltd., Sterling House, 66 Wilton Rd., London SW1V 1DE, England (Distr. in U.S. and Canada by: Graham & Trotman Inc., 13 Park Ave., Gaithersburg, MD 20877) Ed. N.H. Karam.

340 BL
CADERNO DE DIREITO ECONOMICO. 1983. biennial. Centro de Estudos de Extensao Universitaria, Av. Alfonso Bovero, 175, 01254 S. Paulo SP, Brazil. circ. 1,000.

340 BL
CADERNO DE PESQUISAS TRIBUTARIAS. 1976. a. Centro de Estudos de Extensao Universitaria, Av. Alfonso Bovero, 175, 01254 S. Paulo SP, Brazil.

CAISSES CENTRALES DE MUTUALITE SOCIALE AGRICOLE. STATISTIQUES. see *SOCIOLOGY*

347.9 US ISSN 0068-5488
CALIFORNIA. ADMINISTRATIVE OFFICE OF THE COURTS. ANNUAL REPORT. (Incorporates annual report of Judicial Council of California) 1962. a. free. Judicial Council of California, Administrative Office of the Courts, State Bldg. Rm. 3154, 350 McAllister St., San Francisco, CA 94102. Ed. Ralph J. Gampell. circ. 4,000.

340 US
CALIFORNIA. LAW REVISION COMMISSION. REPORTS, RECOMMENDATIONS AND STUDIES. 1955. irreg., vol.17, 1984. pamphlets free; bound vols. $12.85. Law Revision Commission, 4000 Middlefield Rd., Ste. D-2, Palo Alto, CA 94303-4739 (Bound vols. and priced pamphlets avail. from Department of General Services, Documents Section, Box 1015, North Highlands, CA 95660) index. circ. 1,500.
    Includes its Annual Reports, Recommendations and Studies issued as pamphlets; bound every 2 yrs.

350 US
CALIFORNIA. OFFICE OF ADMINISTRATIVE LAW. ANNIVERSARY REPORT. a. Office of Administrative Law, 1414 K St., Ste. 600, Sacramento, CA 95814. TEL 916-323-6225. Dir. Linda Stockdale Brewer.

CALIFORNIA. STATE BOARD OF COSMETOLOGY. RULES AND REGULATIONS. see *BEAUTY CULTURE*

LAW 653

340 US
CALIFORNIA AND NEVADA LEGAL SERVICES PROGRAMS DIRECTORY. 1974. a. $5.90. Western Center on Law and Poverty, Inc., 3535 W. Sixth St., Los Angeles, CA 90020-2898. TEL 213-487-7211. circ. 120. (back issues avail.)

340 352 US ISSN 0068-5879
CALIFORNIA COUNTY LAW LIBRARY BASIC LIST. 1961. irreg. free. State Library, Law Library, Box 942837, Sacramento, CA 94237-0001. TEL 916-324-4868. circ. 600.

340 US
CALIFORNIA NOTARY LAW PRIMER. a. $7.95. National Notary Association, 23012 Ventura Blvd., Box 4625, Woodland Hills, CA 91365. TEL 818-347-2035. (reprint service avail. from UMI)

340 UK ISSN 0084-8328
CAMBRIAN LAW REVIEW. 1970. a. £3. University College of Wales, Aberystwyth, Department of Law, Aberystwyth, Wales. Ed. J.E. Trice. adv. bk. rev. illus. circ. 700. (also avail. in microfilm from WSH) Indexed: Leg.Per. Abstr.Bk.Rev.Curr.Leg.Per. C.L.I. L.R.I.

410 UK
CAMBRIDGE STUDIES IN ENGLISH LEGAL HISTORY. irreg. price varies. Cambridge University Press, Edinburgh Bldg., Shaftesbury Rd., Cambridge CB2 2RU, England (And 32 E. 57th St., New York NY 10022) Ed. D.C. Yale.

340 341 UK ISSN 0068-6751
CAMBRIDGE STUDIES IN INTERNATIONAL AND COMPARATIVE LAW. 1967. irreg. price varies. Cambridge University Press, Edinburgh Bldg., Shaftesbury Rd., Cambridge CB2 2RU, England (and 32 E. 57 St., New York, NY 10022) Ed. R.Y. Jennings. index.

342 350 IT
CAMERA DEI DEPUTATI. BOLLETTINO DI INFORMAZIONI COSTITUZIONALI E PARLAMENTARI. 1981. biennial. L.30000. Camera dei Deputati, Palazzo Montecitorio, Rome, Italy. circ. 2,000. (back issues avail.)

340 IT
CAMERA DEI DEPUTATI. BOLLETTINO DI LEGISLAZIONE E DOCUMENTAZIONE REGIONALE. 1975. biennial. L.80000. Camera dei Deputati, Palazzo Montecitorio, Rome, Italy. circ. 4, 000. (back issues avail.)

340 US ISSN 0742-8987
CAMPBELL'S LIST; a directory of selected lawyers. 1879. a. (plus supp.) $10. Campbell's List, Inc., Campbell Bldg., 100 E. Ventris Ave., Maitland, FL 32751. TEL 305-644-8298. Ed. John A. Campbell, Jr. circ. 6,000.

340 CN
CANADA. LAW REFORM COMMISSION. ADMINISTRATIVE LAW SERIES. STUDY PAPERS. (Text in English and French) 1976. irreg. free. Law Reform Commission, 130 Albert St., Ottawa, Ont. K1A 0L6, Canada. TEL 613-996-7844. (back issues avail., reprint service avail. from MML)

340 CN ISSN 0382-1463
CANADA. LAW REFORM COMMISSION. ANNUAL REPORT. (Text in English and French) 1971. a., latest 1984-85. free. Law Reform Commission, 130 Albert St., 7th Floor, Ottawa, Ont. K1A 0L6, Canada. TEL 613-996-7844. (reprint service avail. from MML)

343 CN
CANADA. LAW REFORM COMMISSION. CRIMINAL LAW SERIES. STUDY PAPERS. (Text in English and French) irreg. free. Law Reform Commission, 130 Albert St., Ottawa, Ont. K1A 0L6, Canada. TEL 613-996-7844. (reprint service avail. from MML)

340 CN
CANADA. LAW REFORM COMMISSION. MODERNIZATION OF STATUTES. STUDY PAPERS. (Text in English and French) 1981. irreg. free. Law Reform Commission, 130 Albert St., Ottawa, Ont. K1A 0L6, Canada. TEL 613-996-7844. (reprint service avail. from MML)

340 CN
CANADA. LAW REFORM COMMISSION. PROTECTION OF LIFE SERIES. STUDY PAPERS. (Text in English and French) 1979. irreg. free. Law Reform Commission, 130 Albert St., Ottawa, Ont. K1A 0L6, Canada. TEL 613-996-7844. (back issues avail., reprint service avial. from MML)

340 CN
CANADA. LAW REFORM COMMISSION. REPORT TO PARLIAMENT. (Text in English and French) 1975. irreg. free. Law Reform Commission, 130 Albert St., Ottawa, Ont. K1A 0L6, Canada. TEL 613-996-7844. (back issues avail., reprint service avail. from MML)

340 CN
CANADA. LAW REFORM COMMISSION. WORKING PAPER. (Text in English and French) irreg. free. Law Reform Commission, 130 Albert St., Ottawa, Ont. K1A 0L6, Canada. TEL 613-996-7844. circ. 10,000(controlled) (back issues avail., reprint service avail. from MML)

CANADA. WOMEN'S BUREAU. WOMEN IN THE LABOUR FORCE. see BUSINESS AND ECONOMICS — Labor And Industrial Relations

346.71 CN ISSN 0317-6649
CANADA BUSINESS CORPORATIONS ACT WITH REGULATIONS. vol.5, 1983. irreg. Can.$7.75. C C H Canadian Ltd., 6 Garamond Ct., Don Mills, Ont. M3C 1Z5, Canada. TEL 416-441-2992. index.

340 CN
CANADA LEGAL DIRECTORY. 1911. a. Can.$55($55) Richard De Boo Publishers, 81 Curlew Dr., Don Mills, Ont. M3A 3P7, Canada. TEL 416-445-4940. Ed. Elizabeth F.V. Griffiths. circ. 3,000. (back issues avail.)

340 CN
CANADA PENSION PLAN AND OLD AGE SECURITY LEGISLATION. irreg., 6th edt., 1984. Can.$9.50. C C H Canadian Ltd., 6 Garamond St., Don Mills, Ont. M3C 1Z5, Canada. TEL 416-441-2992.

340 CN
CANADA STATUTE CITATOR. irreg. (4-5/yr.) Can.$102. Canada Law Book Inc., 240 Edward St., Aurora, Ont. L4G 3S9, Canada.

340 CN
CANADIAN BAR ASSOCIATION. ANNUAL REPORT OF PROCEEDINGS. a. Can.$30. Canadian Bar Foundation, Suite 1700, 130 Albert St., Ottawa, Ont. K1P 5G4, Canada. TEL 613-237-2925.

340 CN ISSN 0384-5753
CANADIAN BAR ASSOCIATION. BRITISH COLUMBIA BRANCH. PROGRAM REPORT.* 1971. irreg. Canadian Bar Association, British Columbia Branch, 130 Albert St., 1700, Ottawa, Ont. K1P 5G4, Canada.

340 658.3 CN
CANADIAN CASES ON EMPLOYMENT LAW REPORTS. 1983. a. (q. updates) $59.25. Carswell Legal Publications, 2330 Midland Ave., Agincourt, Ont. M1S 1P7, Canada. TEL 416-291-8421. Ed. David Harris.
Formerly: Employment Law Reports.

340 368 CN
CANADIAN CASES ON THE LAW OF INSURANCE. 1983. a. (q. updates) $56.25. Carswell Legal Publications, 2330 Midland Ave., Agincourt, Ont. M1S 1P7, Canada. TEL 416-291-8421. Eds. Marvin F. Baer, James A. Rendall.

340 CN ISSN 0701-1733
CANADIAN CASES ON THE LAW OF TORTS. 1976. a. (q. updates) $59.25. Carswell Legal Publications, 2330 Midland Ave., Agincourt, Ont. M1S 1P7, Canada. TEL 416-291-8421. Ed. John Irvine. Indexed: C.L.I. L.R.I.

340 CN ISSN 0704-0857
CANADIAN COMMUNITY LAW JOURNAL/ REVUE CANADIENNE DE DROIT COMMUNAUTAIRE. (Text in English and French) 1977. a. University of Windsor, Faculty of Law, Windsor, Ont. N9B 3P4, Canada. TEL 519-885-1211. Indexed: Abstr.Bk.Rev.Curr.Leg.Per. C.L.I. L.R.I.

340 614.7 CN
CANADIAN ENVIRONMENTAL LAW. a. $649. Butterworth & Co. (Canada) Ltd., 2265 Midland Avenue, Scarborough, Ont. M1P 4S1, Canada. TEL 416-292-1421. Eds. Robert T. Franson, Alastair R. Lucas. (looseleaf format)

340 301 CN ISSN 0829-3201
CANADIAN JOURNAL OF LAW AND SOCIETY. a. $18 to individuals; institutions $25. University of Calgary Press, 2500 University Dr., N.W., Calgary, Alta. T2N 1N4, Canada. TEL 403-220-7578.

340 CN ISSN 0084-8573
CANADIAN LAW LIST. a. Can.$72.00. ‡ Canada Law Book Inc., 240 Edward St., Aurora, Ont. L4G 3S9, Canada. TEL 416-773-6300. Ed. Mrs. P. Egan.

340 CN
CANADIAN UNEMPLOYMENT INSURANCE LEGISLATION. (Text in English or French) vol.8, 1984. irreg. Can.$9.95. C C H Canadian Ltd., 6 Garamond Court, Don Mills, Ontario M3C 1Z5, Canada. TEL 416-441-2992.

CAPITULO CRIMINOLOGICO. see CRIMINOLOGY AND LAW ENFORCEMENT

340 CN ISSN 0706-5388
CARSWELL'S PRACTICE CASES. 1976. a. (q. updates) $61.50. Carswell Legal Publications, 2330 Midland Ave., Agincourt, Ontario M1S 1P7, Canada. TEL 416-291-8421. Ed. Michael McGowan. (also avail. in looseleaf format) Indexed: C.L.I. L.R.I.

340 US
CASES AND MATERIALS ON CONSTITUTIONAL LAW. irreg. price varies. Foundation Press, Inc., 170 Old Country Rd., Mineola, NY 11501. TEL 516-248-5580.

340 US
CASES AND MATERIALS ON TRADE REGULATION. irreg. price varies. Foundation Press, Inc., 170 Old Country Rd., Mineola, NY 11501. TEL 516-248-5580.

CENTER FOR LAW AND EDUCATION. NEWSNOTES. see EDUCATION

CENTRO DE ESTUDIOS PUBLICOS. DOCUMENTO DE TRABAJO. see BUSINESS AND ECONOMICS — Economic Situation And Conditions

340 US
CHICANO LAW REVIEW. 1972. irreg. $10. (La Raza Law Students Association) University of California, Los Angeles, School of Law, Los Angeles, CA 90024. TEL 213-825-2894. Ed. Frances N. Araiza. adv. circ. 600. (back issues avail.) Indexed: Leg.Per. C.L.I. L.R.I.

CHRONICLE OF PARLIAMENTARY ELECTIONS AND DEVELOPMENTS. see POLITICAL SCIENCE

340 320 355 301 US
CIVILIAN CONGRESS; persons holding military office in Congress. 1964. biennial. $6. 2361 Mission St., Rm. 238, San Francisco, CA 94110-1868. TEL 415-695-1597. Ed. Jack Fitch. circ. 500. (looseleaf format; back issues avail.)

340 US ISSN 0276-752X
CLIENT COUNSELING UPDATE; developments in client counseling. 1980. irreg. $5. American Bar Association, Law Student Division, 750 N. Lake Shore Dr., Chicago, IL 60611. TEL 312-988-5621. Ed. Sherry L. Van Donk.

CODE OF MARYLAND REGULATIONS. see PUBLIC ADMINISTRATION

349 BE ISSN 0010-0188
CODES LARCIER. (Includes Mise a Jour) a. 19750 Fr. Maison Larcier Editeurs, Rue des Minimes 39, 1000 Brussels, Belgium. charts. index.

340 BL ISSN 0530-0657
COLECAO DE ESTUDOS JURIDICOS. 1956. irreg., latest 1982. Fundacao Casa de Rui Barbosa, Rua Sao Clemente 134, Botafogo 22260, Rio de Janeiro, RJ, Brazil. Dir. Olavo Brasil de Lima Junior.

340 SP ISSN 0069-5122
COLECCION JURIDICA. 1954. irreg., no.89, 1986. price varies. (Universidad de Navarra, Facultad de Derecho.) Ediciones Universidad de Navarra, S.A., Apdo. 396, 31080 Pamplona, Spain. index vols.1-6.

340 SP
COLECCION JURISPRUDENCIA Y TEXTOS LEGALES. 1973. irreg., no.6, 1984. price varies. (Universidad de Navarra, Facultad de Derecho) Ediciones Universidad de Navarra S.A., Apdo. 396, 31080 Pamplona, Spain.

342 VE
COLECCION TEXTOS LEGISLATIVOS. a. Editorial Juridica Venezolana, Apdo. 17598 Parque Central, Caracas, Venezuela.

340 CE ISSN 0069-5939
COLOMBO LAW REVIEW.* 1969. a. Rs.15($3) (Sri Lanka University Law Review Association) Hansa Publishers Ltd., Sri Lanka Law College, 244 Hulftsdorp St., Colombo 12, Sri Lanka. Ed. M. Sonnarajah.

COMMISSION ROYALE DES ANCIENNES LOIS ET ORDONNANCES DE BELGIQUE. BULLETIN/KONINKLIJKE COMMISSIE VOOR DE UITGAVE DER OUDE WETTEN EN VERORDENINGEN VAN BELGIE. HANDELINGEN. see HISTORY

346 AT ISSN 0069-7133
COMMONWEALTH LAW REPORTS. 1903. irreg. (approx. 10 issues per year) Aus.$97.50. Law Book Co. Ltd., 44-50 Waterloo Rd., North Ryde, N.S.W. 2112, Australia. index. cum.index: vols.1-127. Indexed: Leg.Per. Curr.Aus.N.Z.Leg.Lit.Ind. C.L.I.

347.01 UK ISSN 0307-6539
COMMONWEALTH MAGISTRATES' CONFERENCE. REPORT. 1972. irreg., 7th, 1985, Cyprus. £20. Commonwealth Magistrates' Association, 28 Fitzroy Square, London W1P 6DD, England. circ. 500.

340 US ISSN 0069-7893
COMPARATIVE JURIDICAL REVIEW. (Text in English and Spanish) 1964. a. free. (Rainforth Foundation) Pan American Institute of Comparative Law, 3001 Ponce de Leon Blvd., Coral Gables, FL 33134. TEL 305-446-7856. Ed. Mario Diaz Cruz. bk. rev. cum.index in vol.11, 1973. circ. 1,000. Indexed: C.L.I. L.R.I.

COMPENSATION OF ATTORNEYS (NON-LAW FIRMS) see BUSINESS AND ECONOMICS — Labor And Industrial Relations

340 US
COMPILATION OF STATE AND FEDERAL PRIVACY LAWS. 1975. irreg., latest issue 1984/85. $22. Privacy Journal, Box 15300, Washington, DC 20003. TEL 202-547-2865. Ed. Robert Ellis Smith. circ. 2,000.

349 PE ISSN 0573-4347
CONFERENCIA DE FACULTADES LATINOAMERICANAS DE DERECHO. (DOCUMENTOS OFICIALES)* 1959. a. Universidad Nacional, Apartado 524, Lima, Peru.

340 350 TT
CONGRESS OF MICRONESIA. SENATE. JOURNAL. (Text in English) irreg. Senate, Capitol Hill, Saipan 96950, Mariana Islands.

340 US
CONGRESSIONAL INDEX. 2 biennial vols. plus w. updates during session. $580. Commerce Clearing House, Inc., 4025 W. Peterson Ave., Chicago, IL 60646. TEL 312-583-8500.

353.9 US ISSN 0098-8138
CONNECTICUT. JUDICIAL DEPARTMENT. REPORT.* irreg. (approx. biennial) Judicial Department, 231 Capitol Ave., Hartford, CT 06106. TEL 203-566-5914. illus. Key Title: Report of the Judicial Department, State of Connecticut.

320 US
CONNECTICUT. LAW REVISION COMMISSION. ANNUAL REPORT. a. Law Revision Commission, Legislative Office Bldg., 18-20 Trinity St., Hartford, CT 06106. TEL 203-566-8254.

CONNECTICUT EDUCATION ASSOCIATION. LEGISLATIVE BULLETIN. see EDUCATION

342 US
CONSORTIUM FOR COMPARATIVE LEGISLATIVE STUDIES. PUBLICATIONS. 1975. irreg. price varies. Duke University Press, 6697 College Sta., Durham, NC 27708. TEL 919-684-2173.

340 690 CN
CONSTRUCTION LAW REPORTS. 1983. a. (q. updates) $60.00. Carswell Legal Publications, 2330 Midland Ave., Agincourt, Ont. M1S 1P7, Canada. TEL 416-291-8421. Ed. Harvey J. Kirsh. (also avail. in looseleaf format)

340 UK
CONSUMER CREDIT CONTROL. irreg. Longman Professional, 21-27 Lambs Conduit St., London WC1N 3NJ, England.

340 US ISSN 0147-1074
CONTRIBUTIONS IN LEGAL STUDIES. 1978. irreg., no.28, 1984. price varies. Greenwood Press, 88 Post Rd. W., Box 5007, Westport, CT 06881. TEL 203-226-3571. Ed. Paul L. Murphy.

340 SP ISSN 0589-8056
CORPUS HISPANORUM DE PACE. 1963. irreg. Consejo Superior de Investigaciones Cientificas, Instituto Francisco de Vitoria, Medinaceli 4, Madrid, Spain (Orders to: Consejo Superior de Investigaciones Cientificas. Distribution de Publicaciones, Viturbio 8, Madrid 6, Spain)

340 011 UK ISSN 0305-411X
COUNCIL OF LEGAL EDUCATION. CALENDAR. 1901/2. a. price varies. Council of Legal Education, 4, Gray's Inn Place, London WC1R 5DX, England. circ. 2,000.

340 UK ISSN 0269-3291
COUNTY COURT PRACTICE. a. Butterworth & Co. (Publishers) Ltd., 88 Kingsway, London WC2B 6AB, England. Ed. R.C.L. Gregory.

340 CN ISSN 0227-6178
COURT CASES OF INTEREST TO THE OMBUDSMAN INSTITUTION. a. $20. International Ombudsman Institute, Faculty of Law, University of Alberta, Edmonton, Alta. T6G 2H5, Canada. TEL 403-432-3196.

342 361 CN
CRIMINAL INJURIES COMPENSATION. (Text in English, French) 1980. irreg. Can.$25. Statistics Canada, Health Division, R.H. Coats Bldg., 18th floor, Ottawa K1A 0T6, Ont., Canada (Subscr. to: Publication Sales & Service, Statistics Canada, Ottawa K1A 0T6, Ont., Canada) circ. 1,300.
Formerly (until 1986): Criminal Injury Compensation.

340 AT ISSN 0705-7385
CRIMINAL LAW IN NEW SOUTH WALES. VOLUME 2: SUMMARY OFFENCES. 1978. irreg. Aus.$250. Law Book Company Limited, 44-50 Waterloo Rd., North Ryde, N.S.W. 2113, Australia. Eds. R. Watson, R. Bartley.

343 US ISSN 0145-7322
CRIMINAL LAW OUTLINE. 1966. a. $10. National Judicial College, Judicial College Bldg., University of Nevada, Reno, NV 89557. TEL 702-784-6747. Ed. William A. Grimes.

340 CN
CRIMINAL LAWYERS COMMONPLACE BOOK. a. $137.50. Butterworth & Co. (Canada) Ltd., 2265 Midland Avenue, Scarborough, Ont. M1P 4S1, Canada. TEL 416-292-1421. Ed. Paul Richard Meyers. (looseleaf format)

343 CN
CRIMINAL PROCEDURE; Canadian law and practice. a. $192.50. Butterworth & Co. (Canada) Ltd., 2265 Midland Ave., Scarborough, Ont. M1P 4S1, Canada. TEL 416-292-1421. Ed.Bd. (looseleaf format)

CRITICAL ISSUES. see ENVIRONMENTAL STUDIES

342 AG
CUADERNOS DE LOS INSTITUTOS. 1957. irreg. Universidad Nacional de Cordoba, Instituto de Derecho Constitucional, Calle Obispo Trejo y Sanabria 242, Cordoba, Argentina.

340 UK ISSN 0070-1998
CURRENT LEGAL PROBLEMS. 1948. a. £26. (University College, London) Sweet & Maxwell Stevens Journals, 11 New Fetter Lane, London, EC4, England (Dist. in U.S. & Canada by: Carswell Co Ltd., 233 Midland Ave., Agincourt, Ont., Canada) Eds. Lord Lloyd of Hampstead, Roger Rideout. Indexed: Leg.Per. C.L.I. L.R.I.

CURRENT MUNICIPAL PROBLEMS. see PUBLIC ADMINISTRATION — Municipal Government

D I N. CATALOG OF TECHNICAL RULES. (Deutsches Institut fuer Normung (DIN)) see TECHNOLOGY: COMPREHENSIVE WORKS

349 DK ISSN 0108-3627
D J OE F - HAANDBOGEN; opslagsbog for tillidsrepraesentanter i D J OE F. 1981. biennial. Kr.183. Danmarks Juris- og Oekonomforbund, Gothersgade 133, 1123 Copenhagen K, Denmark.

340 TZ ISSN 0418-3770
DAR ES SALAAM UNIVERSITY LAW JOURNAL. 1963. irreg. EAs.27. University of Dar es Salaam, Faculty of Law, Box 35034, Dar es Salaam, Tanzania. Ed. Ernest L. Kembela Mwipopo.
Formerly (until 1971): Denning Law Society. Journal.

348 US ISSN 0091-5564
DELAWARE REPORTER. (Vol. numbering adopted from that of the Atlantic Reporter) irreg. West Publishing Co., Box 3526, St. Paul, MN 55165. TEL 612-228-2500.
Supersedes: Delaware. Court of Chancery. Delaware Chancery Reports; Delaware. Courts. Delaware Reports.

340 II
DELHI LAW REVIEW. 1972. irreg. $2 per no. University of Delhi, Faculty of Law, Delhi 110007, India. adv. bk. rev. circ. 275.

DEMOCRATIC REPUBLIC OF THE SUDAN GAZETTE. LEGISLATIVE SUPPLEMENT. see PUBLIC ADMINISTRATION

DENMARK. LOVINFORMATION FRA MILJOESTYRELSEN. see ENVIRONMENTAL STUDIES

340 US
DEPAUL LAW REVIEW: ILLINOIS LAW ISSUE. 1952. a. $5. DePaul University, College of Law, 25 E. Jackson Blvd., Chicago, IL 60604. TEL 312-341-8554. Eds. C. Morris, Gatle Erjauac. adv. bk. rev. index. circ. 1,200. (also avail. in microfilm from WSH) Indexed: Leg.Per. C.L.I.
Formerly: Annual Survey of Illinois Law.

340 PE
DERECHO. 1944. a. $7.50. Pontificia Universidad Catolica del Peru, Facultad de Derecho, Apdo. 1761, Lima 100, Peru. Ed. Marcial Rubio Correo. adv. circ. 2,000.

340 GE ISSN 0138-1644
DEUTSCHE DEMOKRATISCHE REPUBLIK. GESETZBLATT; Gesetze und andere allgemeinverbindliche Rechtsvorschriften mit Ausnahme von voelkerrechtlichen Vertraegen. 1949. irreg. M.20. Staatsverlag der Deutschen Demokratischen Republik, Otto-Grotewohlstr. 17, DDR-1086 Berlin, E. Germany (D.D.R.) Ed.Bd.

340 BG
DHAKA LAW REPORTS: CIVIL DIGEST. (Text in English) 1949-1984; N.S. 1986. irreg. $35. Dacca Law Reports Office, Malibagh, Dacca, Bangladesh. Ed. Obaidul Hua.
Formerly: Up-to-Date Civil Reference.
Bangladesh legal system

LAW 655

347 US ISSN 0070-4857
DIGEST OF LEGAL ACTIVITIES OF
INTERNATIONAL ORGANIZATIONS AND
OTHER INSTITUTIONS. 1969. irreg. $100.
(Unidroit (International Institute for the Unification
of Private Law)) Oceana Publications, Inc., Dobbs
Ferry, NY 10522. Ed.Bd. (looseleaf format)

340 IS ISSN 0070-4903
DINE ISRAEL; an annual of Jewish Law: Past and
Present. (Absorbed Current Bibliography of Hebrew
Law with No. 8, 1969) (Text in English and
Hebrew) 1969. a. $14. Tel Aviv University, Faculty
of Law, Tel Aviv, Israel. Ed. Aaron Kirschenbaum.
bk. rev. circ. 500. Indexed: Ind.Heb.Per.

020 US
DIRECTORY OF LAW LIBRARIES. 1946. a. $5 to
members; $10 to non-members. American
Association of Law Libraries, 53 W. Jackson Blvd.,
Rm. 703, Chicago, IL 60604. TEL 312-939-4764.
Ed.Bd. circ. 3,600.

340 378 US ISSN 0070-573X
DIRECTORY OF LAW TEACHERS. 1922. a. $15. ‡
(Association of American Law Schools) West
Publishing Co., Box 3526, St. Paul, MN 55165 TEL
612-228-2500. (Order from: Association of
American Law Schools, One Dupont Circle, Ste.
370, Washington, DC 20036)

340 CN ISSN 0383-8358
DIRECTORY OF LAW TEACHERS/ANNUAIRE
DES PROFESSEURS DE DROIT. (Text in English
and French) 1972. a. Can.$13.50. Canadian
Association of Canadian Law Teachers, c/o
Canadian Bar Association, Suite 1700, 130 Albert
St., Ottawa, Ont. K1P 5G4, Canada. Ed. Louis
Perret. adv. circ. 500.

340 US
DIRECTORY OF LAWYER REFERRAL
SERVICES. 1976. a. $1.50. American Bar
Association, Standing Committee on Lawyer
Referral and Information Service, 750 N. Lake
Shore Dr., Chicago, IL 60611. TEL 312-988-5760.
Ed. C. Berg. circ. 1,000.

345.01 US ISSN 0276-5365
DIRECTORY OF LEGAL AID AND DEFENDER
OFFICES IN THE UNITED STATES. biennial.
National Legal Aid & Defender Association, 1625
K. St., N.W., 8th Fl., Washington, DC 20006. TEL
202-452-0620.
 Formerly: National Legal Aid and Defender
Association Directory.

340 US ISSN 0092-9174
DIRECTORY OF SAN FRANCISCO ATTORNEYS.
a. $35 to non-members; members $25. Bar
Association of San Francisco, 220 Bush St., San
Francisco, CA 94104. adv. circ. 6,600.

340 IT ISSN 0390-8542
DIRITTO E SOCIETA (NAPLES) (Numbers not
published consecutively) 1976. irreg., no.15, 1984.
price varies. Liguori Editore s.r.l., Via
Mezzocannone 19, 80134 Naples, Italy. TEL 081/
20 6077. Ed. Gustavo Minervini.

340 SP
DIVISION INTERDISCIPLINAR PARA LA
FAMILIA. 1982. irreg., no.4, 1986. price varies.
(Universidad de Navarra, Facultad de Derecho)
Ediciones Universidad de Navarra, S.A., Apdo. 396,
31080 Pamplona, Spain.

DIVORCE CHATS. see SOCIOLOGY

340 FR
DOCUMENTS D'ETUDES. (Includes 4 Series: Droit
Constitutionnel et Institutions Politiques; Droit
Administratif; Droit International Public; Libertes
Publiques) 1970. irreg. Documentation Francaise,
29-31 Quai Voltaire, 75340 Paris Cedex 07, France.
Ed. F. Gallouedec-Genuys. bibl. (also avail. in
microfiche)

340 US ISSN 0733-6098
EASTERN MINERAL LAW FOUNDATION.
ANNUAL INSTITUTE. PROCEEDINGS. 1980. a.
$99.50. Matthew Bender and Co., Inc., 235 E. 45th
St., New York, NY 10017. circ. 750. Indexed:
Leg.Per.

340 388.324 US ISSN 0271-437X
EASTERN TRANSPORTATION LAW SEMINAR
PAPERS AND PROCEEDINGS. 1971. a.
Association of Transportation Practitioners, 1211
Connecticut Ave., N.W., Ste. 310, Washington, DC
20036.
 Supersedes in part: Transportation Law Seminar.
Papers and Proceedings (ISSN 0164-1689)

EDUCATION LAW BULLETIN. see EDUCATION

340 AU ISSN 0531-674X
EHE- UND FAMILIENRECHTLICHE
ENTSCHEIDUNGEN. 1966. a. price varies.
Manzsche Verlags- und Universitaetsbuchhandlung,
Kohlmarkt 16, A-1014 Vienna, Austria. Eds.
Friedrich Hluze, Wolfgang Melber. circ. 2,500.

347.9 US
ELECTED AND APPOINTED BLACK JUDGES IN
THE UNITED STATES. biennial. $10. Joint Center
for Political Studies, 1301 Pennsylvania Ave., N.W.,
Washington, DC 20004.

342 US
ELECTION LAWS OF HAWAII HANDBOOK. a.
free. Office of the Lieutenant Governor, State
Capitol, Honolulu, HI 96813. TEL 808-548-2544.
 Formerly: Election Laws of Hawaii (ISSN 0091-
9101)

340 US
EMPLOYERS GUIDE TO LAW SCHOOLS.* a. $30.
National Association for Law Placement, 440 First
St., N.W., Ste. 302, Washington, DC 20001.
 Formerly: Employers Guide to A B A Approved
N A L P Member Law Schools (ISSN 0275-2832)

EMPLOYMENT SAFETY AND HEALTH GUIDE.
see INDUSTRIAL HEALTH AND SAFETY

340 SZ
ENGLISH LEGAL MANUSCRIPTS. 1975. irreg.
Inter-Documentation Company, Poststrasse 14, Zug,
Switzerland.

ENVIRONMENTAL STATUTES. see
ENVIRONMENTAL STUDIES

ERFDEEL VAN DE KLASSIEKE ROMEINSE
JURISTEN. see HISTORY

340 NR
ETHIOPE LAW SERIES. no.4, 1976. irreg. Ethiope
Publishing Corporation, 34 Murtala Mohammed St.,
P.M.B. 1192, Benin City, Nigeria. Ed. T.O. Elias.

340 BE
ETUDES DE LOGIQUE JURIDIQUE. irreg., latest
no.7. price varies. Etablissements Emile Bruylant, 67
rue de la Regence, 1000 Brussels, Belgium.

349 940 FR ISSN 0531-2671
EUROPEAN ASPECTS, LAW SERIES; a collection
of studies relating to European integration. 1962.
irreg. Council of Europe, Publications Section,
67000 Strasbourg, France (Dist. in U.S. by
Manhattan Publishing Co., P.O. Box 650, Croton-
on-Hudson, N.Y. 10520)

340 NE
EUROPEAN STUDIES IN LAW. 1977. irreg., vol.9,
1980. price varies. Elsevier Science Publishers B.V.,
Box 211, 1000 AE Amsterdam, Netherlands. Ed.
A.G. Chloros.

340 UK
EVERYMANS OWN LAWYER. 1856. triennial. £15.
Macmillan Press Ltd., 4 Little Essex St., London
WC2R 3LF, England.

348 CN ISSN 0380-2639
F M COMPILATION OF THE STATUTES OF
CANADA. (Text in English and French) 1972. a.
Municipal Forms Ltd., Farnham, Que. J2N 2R6,
Canada. TEL 514-293-5377. Ed. Pierrette Gregoire.
adv. bk. rev. (looseleaf format)

340 BE
FACULTE DE DROIT DE NAMUR. TRAVAUX.
no.12, 1975. irreg. price varies. (Societe d'Etudes
Morales, Sociales et Juridiques) Maison Ferdinand
Larcier S.A., Rue des Minimes 39, 1000 Brussels,
Belgium.

340 DK ISSN 0108-142X
FAEROESK LOVREGISTER. 1966. irreg. Kr.50.
Faeroernes Landsstyre, Rigsombudsmanden paa
Faeroerne, Torshavn, Denmark. circ. 450.

340 AT ISSN 0706-7666
FAMILY LAW REPORTS. 1976. m. Aus.$50.
Butterworths Pty.Ltd., PO Box 345, North Ryde,
N.S.W. 2113, Australia. circ. 800. (back issues
avail.)

342 AT ISSN 0085-0462
FEDERAL LAW REPORTS. 1956. irreg. Aus.$94.
Law Book Co. Ltd., 44-5- Waterloo Rd., North
Ryde, N.S.W. 2112, Australia. Indexed:
Curr.Aus.N.Z.Leg.Lit.Ind. C.L.I.

FEDERAL MARITIME COMMISSION SERVICE.
see TRANSPORTATION — Ships And Shipping

328.96 FJ
FIJI. OFFICE OF THE OMBUDSMAN. ANNUAL
REPORT OF THE OMBUDSMAN. (Text in
English) 1973. a. price varies. Office of the
Ombudsman, Suva, Fiji. circ. 200.

328 US ISSN 0090-1520
FLORIDA. LEGISLATURE. JOINT LEGISLATIVE
MANAGEMENT COMMITTEE. SUMMARY OF
GENERAL LEGISLATION. 1955. a. free. ‡
Legislature, Joint Legislative Management
Committee, 827, The Capitol, Tallahassee, FL
32304. TEL 904-488-2194. Ed. B. Gene Baker. circ.
500. (processed)

340 US
FLORIDA NOTARY LAW PRIMER. a. $7.95.
National Notary Association, 23012 Ventura Blvd.,
Box 4625, Woodland Hills, CA 91365. TEL 818-
347-2035. (reprint service avail. from UMI)

328.759 US ISSN 0093-4089
FLORIDA SENATE. 1965. biennial. free. Legislature,
Senate, Tallahassee, FL 32304. TEL 904-487-5270.
Ed. Joe Brown. illus. stat. circ. 75,000.

340 SW
FOERTECKNING OEVER ADVOKATER OCH
ADVOKATBYRAAER. a. Kr.30. ‡ Sveriges
Advokatsamfund - Swedish Bar Association, Box
27321, 102 54 Stockholm, Sweden.

FONTES RERUM AUSTRIACARUM. REIHE 3.
FONTES JURIS. see HISTORY — History Of
Europe

FOOD ADDITIVES - DESCRIPTIONS,
FUNCTIONS AND U.K. LEGISLATIONS. see
FOOD AND FOOD INDUSTRIES

FOOD LEGISLATION SURVEYS. see FOOD AND
FOOD INDUSTRIES

FOREIGN INVESTMENTS IN BRAZIL.
LEGISLATION. see BUSINESS AND
ECONOMICS — International Commerce

340 US ISSN 0192-3145
FORENSIC SERVICES DIRECTORY; national
register of experts, engineers, scientific advisors,
medical specialists, technical consultants and sources
of specialized knowledge. 1980. a. $79.50. National
Forensic Center, Box 3161, Princeton, NJ 08540.
TEL 609-883-0550. Ed. Betty S. Lipscher. adv.

340 US ISSN 0071-7657
FORSCHUNGEN AUS STAAT UND RECHT.
irreg., vol.66, 1983. price varies. Springer-Verlag,
175 Fifth Ave., New York, NY 10010 TEL 212-
460-1500. (Also Berlin, Heidelberg, Tokyo and
Vienna) (reprint service avail. from ISI)

340 AU
FORSCHUNGEN ZUR EUROPAEISCHEN UND
VERGLEICHENDEN RECHTSGESCHICHTE.
1977. irreg., vol.2, 1979. price varies. Hermann
Boehlaus Nachf., c/o Dr. Karl Lueger, Ring 12, A-
1010 Vienna, Austria. Ed. Berthold Sutter. circ. 600.
(back issues avail.)

340 SZ
FORSCHUNGEN ZUR RECHTSARCHAEOLOGIE
UND RECHTLICHEN VOLKSKUNDE. 1978.
irreg., vol.8, 1986. price varies. Schulthess
Polygraphischer Verlag AG, Zwingliplatz 2, 8022
Zurich, Switzerland. Ed. Louis Carlen.

LAW

FRANCE. DIRECTION GENERALE DES IMPOTS. PRECIS DE FISCALITE. see *BUSINESS AND ECONOMICS — Public Finance, Taxation*

FRANCE. I.F.RE.MER. CENTRE DE BREST. PUBLICATIONS. SERIE: RAPPORTS ECONOMIQUES ET JURIDIQUES. (Institut Francais de Recherche pour l'Exploitation de la Mer (IFREMER)) see *EARTH SCIENCES — Oceanography*

FRANCHISE LAW REVIEW. see *BUSINESS AND ECONOMICS*

340   614.7   US
FREEDOM OF INFORMATION FACT SHEETS. 1980. irreg. $2. Fund for Open Information and Accountability, 145 W. 4th St., New York, NY 10012. TEL 212-477-3188. Ed. Loretta Benjamin.

340   GW   ISSN 0343-835X
FREIE UNIVERSITAET BERLIN. OSTEUROPA-INSTITUT. RECHTSWISSENSCHAFTLICHE VEROEFFENTLICHUNGEN. 1974. irreg. price varies. Freie Universitaet Berlin, Osteuropa-Institut, Garystr. 55, 1000 Berlin 33 (Dahlem), W. Germany (B.R.D.) Eds. Klaus Westen, Herwig Roggemann. circ. 500.

340   GW   ISSN 0071-9919
FUNDHEFT FUER OEFFENTLICHES RECHT. 1948. a. price varies. C.H. Beck'sche Verlagsbuchhandlung, Wilhelmstr. 9, 8000 Munich 40, W. Germany (B.R.D.) Ed. Otto Stroessenreuther. circ. 3,000.

340   GW   ISSN 0071-9927
FUNDHEFT FUER ZIVILRECHT. 1948. a. price varies. C.H. Beck'sche Verlagsbuchhandlung, Wilhelmstr. 9, 8000 Munich 40, W. Germany (B.R.D.) Ed. Heinz Thomas. circ. 2,900.

344   US   ISSN 0362-5931
GEORGIA LEGISLATIVE REVIEW. 1974. irreg. Southern Center for Studies in Public Policy, Clark College, Atlanta, GA 30314. TEL 404-681-3080.

340   AU
GESAMTREGISTER MIT DEN RECHTSSAETZEN UND FUNDSTELLEN DER ENTSCHEIDUNGEN DER ZEITSCHRIFT FUER VERKEHRSRECHT. 1956. irreg. price varies. Manzsche Verlags- und Universitaetsbuchhandlung, Kohlmarkt 16, Postfach 163, A-1014 Vienna, Austria. circ. 2,400.

340   938   AU
GESELLSCHAFT FUER GRIECHISCHE UND HELLENISTISCHE RECHTSGESCHICHTE. AKTEN. irreg. Hermann Boehlaus Nachf., c/o Dr. Karl Lueger, Ring 12, A-1010 Vienna, Austria.

340   GW
GESETZ- UND VERORDNUNGSBLATT FUER BERLIN. 1945. irreg. (approx. 60/yr.) DM.232. Kulturbuch-Verlag GmbH, Passauer Strasse 4, D-1000 Berlin 30, W. Germany (B.R.D.) (back issues avail.)

349   GH   ISSN 0072-436X
GHANA LAW REPORTS. 1959. a. $79. Council for Law Reporting, Box M.165, Accra, Ghana. Ed. S.Y. Bimpong-Buta. adv. circ. 2,000.

340   US   ISSN 0193-8010
GILBERT LAW SUMMARIES. CRIMINAL PROCEDURE. 1968. irreg., 11th edt., 1983. $10.50. (Gilbert Law Summaries) H B J Legal & Professional Publication Inc., 14415 S. Main St., Gardena, CA 90248. TEL 213-321-3275. Ed. Marcus Whitebread.
  Formerly: Criminal Practices (ISSN 0193-922X)

343   IT
GIURISPRUDENZA ANNOTATA DI DIRITTO INDUSTRIALE. (Issued in pts.) 1972. a. price varies. Casa Editrice Dott. A. Giuffre, Via B. Arsizio 40, 20151 Milan, Italy.

340   IT
GIUSTIZIA CIVILE. REPERTORIO GENERALE ANNUALE. 1955. a. price varies. Casa Editrice Dott. A. Giuffre, Via B. Arsizio 40, 20151 Milan, Italy. Ed. Angelo Jannuzzi.

340   GW
GOETTINGER STUDIEN ZUR RECHTSGESCHICHTE. 1969. irreg. price varies. Muster-Schmidt-Verlag, Gruenbergerweg 6, Postfach 2741, 3400 Goettingen, W. Germany (B.R.D.) Ed. Dr. Kroeschell.

340   UK
GREAT BRITAIN. OFFICE OF FAIR TRADING. REPORT. 1975. a. H.M.S.O., P.O. Box 569, London SE1 9NH, England. (reprint service avail. from UMI)

349   UK   ISSN 0080-7915
GREAT BRITAIN. SCOTTISH LAW COMMISSION. ANNUAL REPORT. 1965/66. a. price varies. Scottish Law Commission, 140 Causewayside, Edinburgh EH9 1PR, Scotland (Subscr. avail. from: H.M.S.O., 13a Castle St., Edinburgh EH2 3AR, Scotland) circ. 1,000.

340   664   UK
GUIDE TO THE FOOD REGULATIONS IN THE U.K. 1984. a. £35 to members, non-members £105. British Food Manufacturing Industries Research Association, Randalls Rd., Leatherhead, Surrey, KT22 7RY, England.

344.73   US   ISSN 0196-7975
GUIDEBOOK TO FAIR EMPLOYMENT PRACTICES. (Supplement to: Labor Law Reports: Employment Practices.) a. $6. Commerce Clearing House, Inc., 4025 W. Peterson Ave., Chicago, IL 60646. TEL 312-583-8500.

GUIDEBOOK TO LABOR RELATIONS. see *BUSINESS AND ECONOMICS — Labor And Industrial Relations*

340   UK   ISSN 0308-4388
HALSBURY'S LAWS OF ENGLAND ANNUAL ABRIDGMENT. Short title: Laws of England Annual Abridgment. 1974. a. Butterworth & Co. (Publishers) Ltd., 88 Kingsway, London WC2B 6AB, England.

340   GW   ISSN 0072-9507
HAMBURGER ABHANDLUNGEN. 1950. irreg., no.65, 1983. price varies. (Universitaet Hamburg, Seminar fuer Oeffentliches Recht und Staatslehre) Gerold und Appel Verlagsgesellschaft, Neumann-Reichardt-Str. 29-33, 2000 Hamburg 70, W. Germany (B.R.D.) Eds. Rudolf Laun, Hans Peter Ipsen.

340   GW   ISSN 0341-3179
HAMBURGER JURISTISCHE STUDIEN. 1970. irreg., no.4, 1982. price varies. Verlag Helmut Buske, Schlueterstr. 14, 2000 Hamburg 13, W. Germany (B.R.D.).

340   341   GW   ISSN 0072-9574
HAMBURGER OEFFENTLICH-RECHTLICHE NEBENSTUNDEN. 1960. irreg., vol.31, 1979. price varies. (Universitaet Hamburg, Institut fuer Internationale Angelegenheiten) Nomos Verlagsgesellschaft mbH und Co. KG, Waldseestr. 3-5, Postfach 610, 7570 Baden Baden, W. Germany (B.R.D.) Ed. Herbert Krueger.

340   296   US   ISSN 0094-9701
HA-MESIVTA. (Text in Hebrew) 1940. a. $4. Yeshivath Torah Vodaath, Inc., 452 E. 9th St., Brooklyn, NY 11218. TEL 718-462-6087. Ed. Elie Goldberg. adv. circ. 1,000.

340   350   GW   ISSN 0438-5004
HANDAKTEN FUER DIE STANDESAMTLICHE ARBEIT. 1962. irreg. price varies. Verlag fuer Standesamtswesen GmbH und Co. KG, Hanauer Landstr. 197, 6000 Frankfurt 1, W. Germany (B.R.D.) Eds. August Simader, Berthold Gaaz.

340   DK   ISSN 0901-0602
HANDBOG I SOCIALLOVGIVNING; Social Legislation Handbook. a. Kr.183.30. Bibliotekscentralen, Telegrafvej 5, DK-2750 Ballerup, Denmark.

344.73   US   ISSN 0886-7402
HANDBOOK OF LIVING WILL LAWS. (Supplement avail.) 1975. a. $5. Society for the Right to Die, Inc., 250 W. 57 St., New York, NY 10107. TEL 212-246-6973. Ed. Peg Cameron. bibl. charts. circ. 6,000. (back issues avail.)
  Former titles: Society for the Right to Die. Handbook (ISSN 0198-8786); Legislative Manual (ISSN 0193-550X)

340   GW   ISSN 0073-0092
HANDBUCH DER JUSTIZ. 1953. biennial. DM.48. (Deutscher Richterbund) R. V. Decker's Verlag, G. Schenck GmbH, Im Weiher 10, 6900 Heidelberg, W. Germany (B.R.D.) Ed. R. Ziegler. adv. circ. 4,000.

HANDBUCH DES GRUNDSTUECKS- UND BAURECHTS. see *BUILDING AND CONSTRUCTION*

340   AU   ISSN 0567-1469
HANDELSRECHTLICHE ENTSCHEIDUNGEN. 1961. a. price varies. Manzsche Verlags- und Universitaetsbuchhandlung, Kohlmarkt 16, A-1014 Vienna, Austria. Ed. Gerhard Friedl. circ. 2,000.

340   AU
HANS KELSEN-INSTITUT. SCHRIFTENREIHE. 1974. irreg., vol.10, 1985. price varies. Manzsche Verlags- und Universitaetsbuchhandlung, Kohlmarkt 16, A-1014 Vienna, Austria.

349.73   US   ISSN 0270-1456
HARVARD WOMEN'S LAW JOURNAL. 1978. a. $7. Harvard University Law School, Women's Law Journal, Langdell Hall, Cambridge, MA 02138. TEL 617-495-3100. Ed. Ruth Borenstein. adv. bk. rev. circ. 1,200. (also avail. in microfilm from WSH; back issues avail.) Indexed: Leg.Per. P.A.I.S. Alt.Press Ind. Abstr.Bk.Rev.Curr.Leg.Per. C.L.I. HR Rep. L.R.I.
  ●Also available online. Vendors: WESTLAW.

347.9   US
HAWAII. COMMISSION ON JUDICIAL DISCIPLINE. ANNUAL REPORT. 1980. a. Commission on Judicial Discipline, Box 2560, Honolulu, HI 96804. Ed. Sandra L. Gorla. circ. 250.

HAWAII. STATE COMMISSION ON THE STATUS OF WOMEN. ANNUAL REPORT. see *WOMEN'S INTERESTS*

347.9   US
HAWAII. STATE JUDICIARY. ANNUAL REPORT. 1962. a. Judiciary Department, Box 2560, Honolulu, HI 96811. TEL 808-548-2458. Ed. Van Horne Diamond. illus. stat. circ. 4,500.
  Formerly: Hawaii. Judiciary Department. Annual Report.

340   UK
HAZELL'S GUIDE TO THE JUDICIARY & THE COURTS WITH THE HOLBORN LAW SOCIETY'S BAR LIST BY CHAMBERS. 1985. a. £15($25) Court & Judicial Publishing Co. Ltd., P.O. Box 39, Henley-on-Thames, Oxfordshire RG9 5UA, England. (Co-publisher: R. Hazell & Co.) Ed. C.G.A. Parker. adv. index.
  Formerly: Hazell's Guide to the Judiciary and the Courts with the Holborn Law Society's List of Barristers by Chambers (ISSN 0266-3597)

HEALTH LAW BULLETIN. see *PUBLIC HEALTH AND SAFETY*

340   AT
HEALTH SERVICES LAW VICTORIA. 1978. irreg. Mount Eagle Publications, P.O. Box 84, Heidelberg, Vic. 3084, Australia (Subscr. to: VHA, Miles St., Mulgrave, Victoria 3170, Australia)

347   IS   ISSN 0075-9740
HEBREW UNIVERSITY OF JERUSALEM. LIONEL COHEN LECTURES. (Text in English) 1953. irreg. price varies. Magnes Press, Hebrew University of Jerusalem, Jerusalem, Israel.

340   GW
HEIDELBERGER RECHTSVERGLEICHENDE UND WIRTSCHAFTSRECHLICHE STUDIEN. 1967. a. price varies. Carl Winter Universitaetsverlag, Lutherstr. 59, 6900 Heidelberg, W. Germany (B.R.D.)

340   GW   ISSN 0073-165X
HEIDELBERGER RECHTSWISSENSCHAFTLICHE ABHANDLUNGEN. NEUE FOLGE. 1957. irreg. price varies. (Universitaet Heidelberg, Juristische Fakultaet) Carl Winter Universitaetsverlag, Lutherstr. 59, 6900 Heidelberg, W. Germany (B.R.D.)

330 US
HERITAGE FOUNDATION. ISSUE BULLETINS. irreg., no.126, 1986. $2 per no. Heritage Foundation, 214 Massachusetts Ave., N.E., Washington, DC 20002. TEL 202-546-4400.

HIGHWAY CODE. see *TRANSPORTATION — Roads And Traffic*

340 US
HINE'S INSURANCE COUNSEL. 1908. a. $15. Hine's Legal Directory, Inc., Box 71, Glen Ellyn, IL 60138. TEL 312-469-3983. Ed. James R. Collins. adv. circ. 9,000.

320 340 JA ISSN 0073-2796
HITOTSUBASHI JOURNAL OF LAW AND POLITICS. 1960. a. Hitotsubashi University, Hitotsubashi Academy, 2-1 Naka, Kunitachi, Tokyo 186, Japan. Ed. T. Aruga. circ. 900. Indexed: P.A.I.S.

340 HU ISSN 0441-4411
HUNGARIAN LAW REVIEW. (Text in English) 1968. a. $9. Magyar Jogasz Szovetseg, Szemere u. 10, Budapest 5, Hungary (Subscr. to: Kultura, Box 149, H-1389 Budapest, Hungary) Ed. Dr. Gyorgy Antalffy. bibl.

340 NE
I C C A CONGRESS SERIES. 1983. a. price varies. Kluwer Law and Taxation Publishers, Box 23, 7400 GA Deventer, Netherlands (Orders to: Kluwer Academic Publishers Group, Distribution Center, Box 322, 3300 AH Dordrecht, Netherlands) Ed. Prof. P. Sanders.

347 US ISSN 0536-3713
ILLINOIS. ADMINISTRATIVE OFFICE OF ILLINOIS COURTS. ANNUAL REPORT TO THE SUPREME COURT OF ILLINOIS. 1959. a. Administrative Office of Illinois Courts, Supreme Court Bldg., Springfield, IL 62706. TEL 217-782-2000. stat. circ. 1,500. Key Title: Annual Report to the Supreme Court of Illinois.

340 US
ILLINOIS ATTORNEY GENERAL'S REPORT AND OPINIONS. 1874. a. Attorney General, 500 S. Second St., Springfield, IL 62706. TEL 217-782-1090. index. circ. 1,400. (also avail. in microfiche; back issues avail.)

340 US
ILLINOIS STATE BAR ASSOCIATION. LEGISLATIVE BULLETIN. irreg. during Assembly session. $20 to non-members; members $10. Illinois State Bar Association, Illinois Bar Center, Springfield, IL 62701. TEL 217-525-1760.

340 325.1 US ISSN 0149-9807
IMMIGRATION AND NATIONALITY LAW REVIEW. 1986. a. $65. Clark Boardman Company, Ltd., 435 Hudson St., New York, NY 10014. TEL 212-929-7500. Ed. Maurice A. Roberts.

IMMIGRATION LAW REPORTER. see *POPULATION STUDIES*

340 CE ISSN 0073-5728
INCORPORATED LAW SOCIETY OF SRI LANKA. ANNUAL REPORT.* 1960/61. a. Incorporated Law Society of Sri Lanka, 129/5 Hultsdorf St., Colombo 12, Sri Lanka.

340 CE ISSN 0073-5736
INCORPORATED LAW SOCIETY OF SRI LANKA. JOURNAL.* irreg. Incorporated Law Society of Sri Lanka, 129/5 Hultsdorf St., Colombo 12, Sri Lanka.

340 AU
INDEX DER RECHTSMITTELENTSCHEIDUNGEN UND DES SCHRIFTTUMS. 1947. a. price varies. Manzsche Verlags- und Universitaetsbuchhandlung, Kohlmarkt 16, Postfach 163, A-1014 Vienna, Austria. circ. 2,400.

347 AT ISSN 0312-4029
INDUSTRIAL ARBITRATION SERVICE. 1948. irreg. Aus.$82. Law Book Co. Ltd., 44-50 Waterloo Rd., North Ryde, N.S.W. 2112, Australia.

INDUSTRIAL HEALTH FOUNDATION. LEGAL SERIES BULLETIN. see *INDUSTRIAL HEALTH AND SAFETY*

346.066 UK
INDUSTRIAL PROPERTY LAW. ANNUAL. 1975. irreg. price varies. European Law Centre Ltd., 7 Swallow Place, Off Princes St., London W1R 8AB, England. Indexed: C.L.I. L.R.I.

340 GW
INDUSTRIEGESELLSCHAFT UND RECHT. 1974. irreg., vol.5, 1975. price varies. Gieseking-Verlag, Deckerstr. 2, Postfach 42, 4813 Bielefeld-Bethel, W. Germany (B.R.D.) Eds. Manfred Rehbinder, Bernd Rebe.

340 CU
INFORMACION JURIDICA. 1975. irreg. Fiscalia General de la Republica, San Rafael 3, Havana, Cuba. illus.

340 GW ISSN 0073-8492
INSTITUT FUER OSTRECHT. STUDIEN. 1958. irreg. price varies. Bundesanzeiger-Verlag, 5000 Cologne, W. Germany (B.R.D.) circ. 1,000.

INSTITUTE OF EUROPEAN STUDIES. ANNALI I S E. see *POLITICAL SCIENCE*

INSTITUTE OF PATENT ATTORNEYS OF AUSTRALIA. ANNUAL PROCEEDINGS. see *PATENTS, TRADEMARKS AND COPYRIGHTS*

340 SP
INSTITUTO DE ESTUDIOS TARRACONENSES RAMON BERENGUER IV. SECCION DE ESTUDIOS JURIDICOS. PUBLICACION. (Text in Catalan and/or Castilian) 1972. irreg. Instituto de Estudios Tarraconenses Ramon Berenguer IV, Calle Santa Ana 8, Tarragona, Spain.

340 VE
INSTITUTO DE FILOSOFIA DEL DERECHO. BOLETIN INFORMATIVO. 1973. biennial. free. (Universidad del Zulia, Faculdado de Derecho) Ediluz, Apdo. 526, Maracaibo 72687, Venezuela. circ. 1,000.

INSTITUTO INTERAMERICANO DEL NINO. JURIDICO SOCIAL. INFORMES TECNICOS. see *SOCIOLOGY*

INSTITUTO PERUANO DE DERECHO AGRARIO. CUADERNOS AGRARIOS. see *AGRICULTURE*

INSURANCE LAW ANTHOLOGY. see *INSURANCE*

340 US
INTER-AMERICAN BAR ASSOCIATION. CONFERENCE PROCEEDINGS. 1941. biennial. $6. Inter-American Bar Association, 1889 F. St., N.W., Ste. 450, Washington, DC 20016. TEL 202-789-2747.

340 BE ISSN 0074-1604
INTERNATIONAL ASSOCIATION OF DEMOCRATIC LAWYERS. CONGRESS REPORT. quadrennial, 12th, 1984, Athens. International Association of Democratic Lawyers, 263 av. Albert, 1180 Brussels, Belgium.

340 IS
INTERNATIONAL ASSOCIATION OF JEWISH LAWYERS AND JURISTS. BULLETIN. (Text in English) a. International Association of Jewish Lawyers and Jurists, 10 Daniel Frish St., Tel Aviv, Israel.

340 539 UN ISSN 0074-1868
INTERNATIONAL ATOMIC ENERGY AGENCY. LEGAL SERIES. (Text in English) 1959. irreg. price varies. International Atomic Energy Agency, Wagramer Str. 5, Box 100, A-1400 Vienna, Austria (Dist. in U.S. by: Bernan Associates-Unipub, 4611-F Assembly Dr., Lanham, MD 20706-4391)

340 IS
INTERNATIONAL CONGRESS OF COMPARTATIVE LAW. ISRAEL REPORTS. (Text in English) quadrennial. IS.45($30) P.O. Box 24100, Mt. Scopus, Jerusalem, Israel.

341.52 US
INTERNATIONAL INSTITUTE OF SPACE LAW. COLLOQUIUM. PROCEEDINGS. a., 28th, Stockholm, Sweden, 1985. $59.50. (American Institute of Aeronautics & Astronautics) American Institute of Aeronautics & Astronautics, Inc., 1633 Broadway, New York, NY 10019. TEL 212-581-4300.

347.9 NE
INTERNATIONAL LABOUR LAW REPORTS. 1978. a. price varies. Martinus Nijhoff Publishers, Postbus 163, 3300 AD Dordrecht, Netherlands. Ed.Bd.

INTERNATIONAL MARITIME LAW SEMINAR. PUBLICATION. see *LAW — International Law*

340 AU
INTERNATIONALE GESELLSCHAFT FUER URHEBERRECHT. SCHRIFTENREIHE. 1955. irreg., vol.61, 1984. price varies. (Internationale Gesellschaft fuer Urheberrecht e.V., GW - International Copyright Society) Manzsche Verlags- und Universitaetsbuchhandlung, Kohlmarkt 16, A-1014 Vienna, Austria.

347.9 IS ISSN 0075-1030
ISRAEL. CENTRAL BUREAU OF STATISTICS. JUDICIAL STATISTICS. (Subseries of its Special Series) (Text in English, Hebrew) 1951. irreg., latest issue, no.748, 1983. price varies. Central Bureau of Statistics, Box 13015, Jerusalem, Israel.

ISRAEL YEARBOOK ON HUMAN RIGHTS. see *POLITICAL SCIENCE — Civil Rights*

340 IT
ISTITUTO DI DIRITTO ROMANO. BOLLETTINO. (Text in various European Languages) 1888. a. price varies. Casa Editrice Dott. A. Giuffre, Via B. Arsizio 40, Milan 20151, Italy. Ed. Prof. Edoardo Volterra. adv. bk. rev. index. circ. 500.

340 IT ISSN 0075-1715
ITALY. ISTITUTO CENTRALE DI STATISTICA. ANNUARIO DI STATISTICHE GIUDIZIARIE-TOMO 1. 1962. a. L.8500. Istituto Centrale di Statistica, Via Cesare Balbo 16, 00100 Rome, Italy. circ. 1,050.

340 IT ISSN 0021-3241
IURA; rivista internazionale di diritto romano e antico. (Text in various languages) 1950. irreg. price varies. Casa Editrice Dott. Eugenio Jovene, 109 via Mezzocannone, Naples, Italy. Ed. Prof. Cesare Sanfilippo. bk. rev.

340 IT ISSN 0075-2037
IUS ROMANUM MEDII AEVI. (Text in English, French, German, Italian and Spanish) 1961. irreg. price varies. Casa Editrice Dott. A. Giuffre, Via B. Arsizio 40, 20151 Milan, Italy.

340 YU
IZVORI SRPSKOG PRAVA/SOURCES DE DROIT SERBE/SERBISCHE RECHTSQUELLEN. (Subseries of: Srpska Akademija Nauka i Umetnosti. Odeljenje Drustvenih Nauka. Posebna Izdanja) (Text in Serbian; summaries in English, French, German, Russian) 1967. irreg. Srpska Akademija Nauka i Umetnosti, Odeljenje Drustvenih Nauka, Knez Mihailova 35, 11001 Belgrade, Yugoslavia. illus.

340 GW ISSN 0075-2517
JAHRBUCH DES OEFFENTLICHEN RECHTS DER GEGENWART. N.S. 1951. a. price varies. Verlag J.C.B. Mohr (Paul Siebeck), Wilhelmstr. 18, Postfach 2040, 7400 Tuebingen, W. Germany (B.R.D.) Ed. Peter Haeberle. Indexed: CERDIC.

340 GW ISSN 0075-2746
JAHRBUCH FUER OSTRECHT. 1960. a. (2 pts.) DM.48. (Institut fuer Ostrecht, Munich) Bundesanzeiger-Verlag, 5000 Cologne, W. Germany (B.R.D.) Ed. Erhardt Gralla. circ. 750.

JAHRESFACHKATALOG RECHT-WIRTSCHAFT-STEUERN. see *BUSINESS AND ECONOMICS*

340 JM
JAMAICAN BAR ASSOCIATION. ANNUAL REPORT. a. Jamaican Bar Association, 11 Duke Street, Kingston, Jamaica.

JEWISH LAW ANNUAL. see *RELIGIONS AND THEOLOGY — Judaic*

LAW

340   NE
JEWISH LAW ANNUAL SUPPLEMENTS. 1980. irreg., vol.2, 1980. price varies. E.J. Brill, P.O. Box 9000, 2300 PA Leiden, Netherlands. Ed. B.S. Jackson.

340   US   ISSN 0270-854X
JOHN MARSHALL LAW REVIEW. 1967. a. $16. John Marshall Law School, 315 S. Plymouth Ct., Chicago, IL 60604. TEL 312-987-1415. adv. bk. rev. bibl. charts. illus. index. cum.index. circ. 2,500. (also avail. in microform from UMI; reprint service avail. from UMI) Indexed: Leg.Per. Crim.Just.Abstr. C.L.I. HRIS. L.R.I.
●Also available online. Vendors: WESTLAW.
Formerly (until 1979): John Marshall Journal of Practice and Procedure (ISSN 0021-7212)

JORNADAS NACIONALES DE DERECHO AERONAUTICO Y ESPACIAL. TRABAJOS. see *TRANSPORTATION — Air Transport*

347.9   JA   ISSN 0075-4188
JOURNAL OF CIVIL PROCEDURE/MINJI SOSHO ZASSHI. (Text in Japanese; summaries in English or German) 1954. a. 1500 Yen. (Japan Association of Civil Procedure - Minji Soshoho Gakkai) Horitsu Bunka Sha, 71 Kamigamo-Iwagz-Kakiuchi-Cho, Kita-ku, Kyoto, Japan. adv. bk. rev. circ. 1,500.

JOURNAL OF CRIME & JUSTICE. see *CRIMINOLOGY AND LAW ENFORCEMENT*

340   PL   ISSN 0075-4277
JOURNAL OF JURISTIC PAPYROLOGY. (Text in English, German, Italian and Russian) 1949. irreg., vol.19, 1983. price varies. (Uniwersytet Warszawski, Instytut Papirologii i Prawa Antycznego - Warsaw University, Institute of Papyrology and Ancient Laws) Panstwowe Wydawnictwo Naukowe, Ul. Miodowa 10, 00-251 Warsaw, Poland (Dist. by: Ars Polona, Krakowskie Przedmiescie 7, 00-068 Warsaw, Poland) Ed. H. Kupiszewski. bk. rev. circ. 510.

340   JA
JOURNAL OF LAW AND POLITICS/DAITO HOGAKU. (Text in Japanese) 1974. a. Daito Bunka University, Law Society - Daito Bunka Daigaku Hogakkai, 1-9-1 Takashimadaira, Itabashi-ku, Tokyo, Japan.

340   US   ISSN 0732-9113
JOURNAL OF LEGAL PLURALISM AND UNOFFICIAL LAW. 1969. a. $12.50 to individuals; institutions $26. (Foundation for the Journal of Legal Pluralism) Fred B. Rothman & Co., 10368 W. Centennial Rd., Littleton, CO 80127. TEL 303-979-5657. (Co-sponsor: University of California, Los Angeles, African Studies Center) Ed. John Griffiths. (back issues avail.) Indexed: Leg.Per. C.L.I. Curr.Cont.Africa. Foreign Leg.Per.
Formerly (1969-1981): African Law Studies (ISSN 0002-0060)

347.016   US
JOURNAL OF NOTARIAL ACTS AND RECORDKEEPING PRACTICES. 1974. a. $7.85. National Notary Association, 23012 Ventura Blvd., Box 4625, Woodland Hills, CA 91365. TEL 818-347-2035. Ed.Bd. (reprint service avail. from UMI)
Supersedes in part: Customs and Practices of Notaries Public and Digest of Notary Laws in the U.S.

340   US
JOURNAL OF THE LEGAL PROFESSION. 1976. a. $6. University of Alabama, School of Law, Box 1976, University, AL 35486. TEL 205-348-5930. Indexed: Leg.Per. Abstr.Bk.Rev.Curr.Leg.Per. C.L.I. L.R.I.

340 350   US
JUDICIAL STAFF DIRECTORY. 1986. a. $45. Congressional Staff Directory, Ltd., Box 62, Mount Vernon, VA 22121. TEL 703-765-3400. Eds. Charles B. Brownson, Anna L. Brownson.

340   MX
JURIDICA. (Published under a different title each year.) 1969. a. Mex.$300($12) Universidad Iberoamericana, Departamento de Derecho, Av. Cerro de las Torres 395, Campestre-Churubusco, Coyoacan, 04200 Mexico, D.F., Mexico.

348.46   SP
JURISPRUDENCIA ARAGONESA. 1972. a. Colegio de Abogados de Zaragoza., Zaragoza, Spain.

340   AG
JURISPRUDENCIA ARGENTINA. (In 5 vols. including an index) a. $100 per volume. Jurisprudencia Argentina S.A., Talcahuano 650, 1013 Buenos Aires, Argentina.
Formerly: Anuario de Jurisprudencia Argentina.

340   GW   ISSN 0449-4342
JURISTISCHE ABHANDLUNGEN. 1964. irreg., vol.19, 1984. price varies. Vittorio Klostermann, Frauenlobstr. 22, Postfach 900601, 6000 Frankfurt 90, W. Germany (B.R.D.)

340   US
JUSTICE IN AMERICA SERIES. 1969. irreg. $9.20 (6 vols.) (Law in American Society Foundation) Houghton Mifflin Co., One Beacon Street, Boston, MA 02107. TEL 617-725-5000. Ed. Robert H. Ratcliffe. bibl. illus.
Formerly: Justice in Urban America Series.

JUSTICE INSTITUTE OF BRITISH COLUMBIA. ANNUAL REPORT. see *EDUCATION — Higher Education*

KANAZAWA UNIVERSITY. FACULTY OF LAW AND LITERATURE. STUDIES AND ESSAYS. see *LITERATURE*

KANO STATE OF NIGERIA GAZETTE. see *PUBLIC ADMINISTRATION*

340   AU   ISSN 0259-0727
KANON. 1973. irreg., no.7, 1985. price varies. (Gesellschaft fuer das Recht der Ostkirchen) Verband der Wissenschaftlichen Gesellschaften Oesterreichs, Lindengasse 37, A-1070 Vienna, Austria. Indexed: CERDIC.

340   US
KANSAS JUSTICE INFORMATION SYSTEM. RESOURCE DIRECTORY (YEAR) a. Bureau of Investigation, Statistical Analysis Center, 1620 Tyler, Topeka, KS 66612. TEL 913-232-6000.

340   SJ
KHARTOUM LAW REVIEW. 1979. a. (University of Khartoum, Faculty of Law) Khartoum University Press, Box 321, Khartoum, Sudan.

KINDEX; an index to legal periodical literature concerning children. see *LAW — Abstracting, Bibliographies, Statistics*

340   AU   ISSN 0259-0735
KIRCHE UND RECHT. irreg., no.17, 1985. price varies. Verband der Wissenschaftliche Gesellschaften Oesterreichs, Lindengasse 37, A-1070 Vienna, Austria.

340 388.3   UK   ISSN 0308-8987
KITCHIN'S ROAD TRANSPORT LAW. 1959. biennial. Butterworth & Co. (Publishers) Ltd., 88 Kingsway, London WC2B 6AB, England. Ed. James Duckworth.

340   JA   ISSN 0075-6423
KOBE UNIVERSITY LAW REVIEW. INTERNATIONAL EDITION. (Text in English, French, German and other languages) 1961. a. avail. on exchange. Kobe University Law Review Association, Faculty of Law, Kobe University, Rokko, Kobe, Japan. Ed. Hiroshi Hanawa. circ. 460.

340   DK   ISSN 0108-9811
KOEBENHAVNS UNIVERSITET. RETSVIDENSKABELIGT INSTITUT B. STUDIER. 1983. irreg. free. Koebenhavns Universitet, Retsvidenskabeligt Institut B, Studiegaarden, Studiestraede 6, 1455 Copenhagen K, Denmark. Ed. Peter Blume. circ. 150.

340   PL   ISSN 0023-4478
KRAKOWSKIE STUDIA PRAWNICZE. (Text in Polish; summaries in English, French, German or Russian) 1968. a. price varies. (Polska Akademia Nauk, Oddzial w Krakowie, Komisja Nauk Prawnych) Ossolineum, Publishing House of the Polish Academy of Sciences, Rynek 9, Wroclaw, Poland (Dist. by: Ars Polona-Ruch, Krakowskie Przedmiescie 7, Warsaw, Poland) Ed. Joseph Filipek.

340   II
KURUKSHETRA LAW JOURNAL. (Text in English) 1971. a. Rs.7.50($2) Kurukshetra University, Faculty of Law, Kurukshetra 132118, Haryana, Punjab, India. Ed. S.C. Srivastava. bk. rev. circ. 700.

347   US
L C A QUARTERLY. 1981. irreg. $35. Lawyers for the Creative Arts, 623 S. Wabash, No. 300-N, Chicago, IL 60605. Ed. Tammi Franke. bk. rev. circ. 2,000.
Formerly: Lawyers for the Creative Arts. Bulletin.

LABOUR LAW CASES. see *BUSINESS AND ECONOMICS — Labor And Industrial Relations*

LABOUR LEGISLATION IN NOVA SCOTIA. see *BUSINESS AND ECONOMICS — Labor And Industrial Relations*

340   CN
LAND USE PLANNING; practice, procedure, policy. a. $165. Butterworth & Co. (Canada) Ltd., 2265 Midland Avenue, Scarborough, Ont. M1P 4S1, Canada. TEL 416-292-1421. Eds. Craig B. MacFarlane, Robert W. Macaulay. (looseleaf format)

LANSKY: BIBLIOTHEKSRECHTLICHE VORSCHRIFTEN. see *LIBRARY AND INFORMATION SCIENCES*

340   AU   ISSN 0259-0816
LAW & ANTHROPOLOGY; internationales Jahrbuch fuer Rechtsanthropologie. 1986. a. S.287. Verband der Wissenschaftliche Gesellschaften Oesterreichs, Lindengasse 37, A-1070 Vienna, Austria. (Co-sponsor: Klaus Renner Verlag)

340   US
LAW AND ETHICS SERIES. (Former name of issuing body: Academy for Contemporary Problems) 1977. irreg. Academy for State and Local Government, 444 N. Capitol St., N.W., Ste. 349, Washington, DC 20001. TEL 202-638-1445.

340   US   ISSN 0737-089X
LAW & INEQUALITY; a journal of theory and practice. 1983. irreg. (approx. 2-3/yr.) $10. University of Minnesota Law School, 229 19th Ave. S., Minneapolis, MN 55455. TEL 612-625-5807. Ed. Debra Shetka. bk. rev. circ. 5,500. (back issues avail.) Indexed: Leg.Per.

340   US
LAW AND LEGAL INFORMATION DIRECTORY. 1980. irreg., latest 4th edt., 1986. $280. Gale Research Company, Book Tower, Detroit, MI 48226. TEL 313-961-2242. Eds. Jacqueline Wasserman O'Brien, Steven Wasserman.

340 100   NE
LAW AND PHILOSOPHY LIBRARY. 1985. irreg., vol.2, 1985. price varies. D. Reidel Publishing Company, Box 17, 3300 AA Dordrecht, Netherlands. Eds. Michael Bayles, Alan Mabe.

340 320   KO
LAW AND POLITICAL REVIEW. (Text in Korean; table of contents in English) 1958. a. Ewha Women's University, College of Law and Political Science, 11-1 Dai-Hyun Dong, Seodaimoon Ku, Seoul, S. Korea. bibl.

340 300 616.8   US   ISSN 0098-5961
LAW AND PSYCHOLOGY REVIEW. 1975. a. $10. University of Alabama, School of Law, Box 1435, Tuscaloosa, AL 35487-1435. TEL 205-348-4527. adv. bk. rev. circ. 1,200. (also avail. in microfilm from WSH) Indexed: Leg.Per. Psychol.Abstr. Adol.Ment.Hlth.Abstr. C.L.I. Crim.Just.Abstr. L.R.I. Psycscan.

323.42   US
LAW & WOMEN SERIES. 1972. irreg. $2 per no. Today Publications & News Service, Inc., 621 National Press Bldg., Washington, DC 20045. TEL 202-638-0348. Ed. Myra E. Barrer.

340   HK
LAW ANNUAL REPORT OF CHINA. 1982. a. Kingsway International Publications Ltd., 20 Durham Rd, Kowloon Tong, Kowloon, Hong Kong. Ed. Fang Chun-ie.

340 016　　　　　US　ISSN 0075-8221
LAW BOOKS IN PRINT; books in English published throughout the world. (Supplemented 3 times a year by Law Books Published) 1957. irreg., revised every 3-5 years. $260. Glanville Publishers, Inc., 75 Main St., Dobbs Ferry, NY 10522. TEL 914-693-5956. Ed. Robert L. Buckwalter. index.

340.05　　　　　US
LAW FORUM. a. University of Baltimore, School of Law, 1420 N. Charles St., Baltimore, MD 21202. TEL 301-576-2303. (also avail. in microform from UMI; reprint service avail. from UMI)
　Former titles: Forum Law Journal (ISSN 0360-2044); Forum (Baltimore) (ISSN 0094-1948)

340　　　　　NR　ISSN 0458-8592
LAW IN SOCIETY. 1964. irreg. (1-2/yr.) Ahmadu Bello University, Law Society, Zaria, Nigeria.

340　　　　　US
LAW REPRINTS. 1984. irreg. price varies. Congressional Information Service, Inc., 4520 East-West Highway, Ste. 800, Bethesda, MD 20814-3389. TEL 301-564-1550.

340 332.6　　　　　US
LAW REPRINTS: SECURITIES REGULATION SERIES. 1976. irreg. $245. Congressional Information Service, Inc., 4520 East-West Hwy., Ste. 800, Bethesda, MD 20814. TEL 800-638-8380.
　Former titles: B N A's Law Reprints: Securities Regulation Series (ISSN 0275-696X); Law Reprints. Securities Regulation Series.

340 336　　　　　US
LAW REPRINTS: TAX LAW SERIES. 1968. irreg. $245. Congressional Information Service, Inc., 4520 East-West Hwy., Ste. 800, Bethesda, MD 20814. TEL 800-638-8380. index.
　Former titles: Law Reprints: Tax Regulation Series; B N A'S Law Reprints: Tax Regulation Series (ISSN 0275-6951); Law Reprints. Tax Series.

340　　　　　US
LAW, SOCIETY, AND POLICY. 1982. irreg. Plenum Publishing Corp., 233 Spring St., New York, NY 10013. Ed.Bd.

340　　　　　CN　ISSN 0316-5310
LAW SOCIETY OF UPPER CANADA. SPECIAL LECTURES. 1950. a. price varies. (Law Society of Upper Canada) Richard De Boo Publishers, 81 Curlew Drive, Don Mills, Ont. M3A 3P7, Canada. TEL 416-445-4940.

LAW, STATE AND SOCIETY. see SOCIOLOGY

340　　　　　KE
LAWS OF KENYA. SUPPLEMENT. (Text in English) 1963. irreg. Government Printing and Stationery Department, Box 30128, Nairobi, Kenya.

340　　　　　US
LAWYER STATISTICAL REPORT. irreg. price varies. American Bar Foundation, Publications Dept., 750 N. Lake Shore Dr., Chicago, IL 60611.
　Supersedes: Lawyers in the United States. Distribution and Income.

340　　　　　CN　ISSN 0317-8668
LAWYER'S PHONE BOOK (YEAR) a. $26.50. Canada Law Book Inc., 240 Edward St., Aurora, Ont. L3Y 1B4, Canada. TEL 416-773-6300. Ed. Patricia Egan. adv.

340　　　　　US
LAWYERS PROFESSIONAL LIABILITY UPDATE. 1981. a. $40. American Bar Association, Standing Committee on Lawyers Professional Liability, 750 N. Lake Shore Dr., Chicago, IL 60611. TEL 312-988-5755. Ed. Sheree L. Swetin. bk. rev. circ. 200.

340　　　　　US
LAWYERS REGISTER BY SPECIALTIES AND FIELDS OF LAW. 1978. a. $89.50. Lawyer's Register Publishing Co., 30700 Bainbridge Rd., Ste. H, Solon, OH 44139. TEL 216-248-0135. Ed. Margaret A. Schultz. circ. 4,000. (back issues avail.)

340　　　　　UK　ISSN 0142-7490
LAWYER'S REMEMBRANCER. a. Butterworth & Co. (Publishers) Ltd., 88 Kingsway, London WC2B 6AB, England. Ed. L.A. Whitbourn.

340　　　　　UK
LEASEHOLD LAW. irreg. Longman Professional, 21-27 Lambs Conduit St., London WC1N 3NJ, England.

340 900　　　　　AG
LECCIONES DE HISTORIA JURIDICA. irreg. (Universidad de Buenos Aires, Instituto de Historia del Derecho Ricardo Levene) Editorial Perrot, Azcuenaga 1846, Buenos Aires, Argentina.

342 341　　　　　AG
LECCIONES Y ENSAYOS. 1956. irreg. Universidad de Buenos Aires, Facultad de Derecho y Ciencias Sociales, Av. Figueroa Alcorta 2263, Buenos Aires, Argentina. illus.

345.01　　　　　CN　ISSN 0381-2049
LEGAL AID NEW BRUNSWICK ANNUAL REPORT/AIDE JURIDIQUE NOUVEAU BRUNSWICK RAPPORT ANNUEL. (Text in English and French) 1972. a. Barristers' Society of New Brunswick, P.O. Box 1063, Fredericton, New Brunswick E3B 5C2, Canada. TEL 506-455-6458. circ. 1,500.

340　　　　　US　ISSN 0075-8582
LEGAL ALMANAC SERIES. 1952. irreg. price varies. Oceana Publications Inc., Dobbs Ferry, NY 10522. TEL 914-693-1320. Ed. Irving J. Sloan.

340.023　　　　　US　ISSN 0272-1961
LEGAL ASSISTANTS UPDATE. 1980. a. $6. American Bar Association, Standing Committee on Legal Assistants, 750 North Shore Dr., Chicago, IL 60611. TEL 312-988-5555. Ed. Roger Larson. circ. 3,500. Indexed: Anbar.

340　　　　　US　ISSN 0270-3424
LEGAL CONNECTION: CORPORATIONS AND LAW FIRMS; a directory of publicly-held corporations and their law firms. 1979. a. Box 801, Menlo Park, CA 94025. Ed. S.P. Harris.

340 020　　　　　US　ISSN 0747-9298
LEGAL INFORMATION MANAGEMENT INDEX. 1984. bi-m. (plus a. cum.) $108. Legal Information Services, Box 67, Newton Highlands, MA 02161. TEL 617-443-4798. Ed. Elyse H. Fox.

340　　　　　CN　ISSN 0225-2287
LEGAL INFORMATION SERVICE REPORTS. 1979. irreg. price varies. University of Saskatchewan, Native Law Centre, Diefenbaker Centre, Saskatoon, Sask. S7N 0W0, Canada. TEL 306-966-6189. Ed. Zandra MacEachern. (back issues avail.)

340　　　　　US　ISSN 0275-4088
LEGAL LOOSELEAFS IN PRINT. 1981. a. $65. Infosources Publishing, 118 W. 79 St., New York, NY 10024. TEL 212-595-3161. Ed. Arlene L. Eis. adv. circ. 1,000.

340　　　　　US　ISSN 8755-416X
LEGAL NEWSLETTERS IN PRINT. 1985. a. $50. Infosources Publishing, 118 W. 79th St., New York, NY 10024. TEL 212-595-3161. Ed. Arlene L. Eis. adv. circ. 1,000.

LEGAL RESOURCES FOR THE MENTALLY DISABLED: A DIRECTORY OF LAWYERS AND OTHER SPECIALISTS. see MEDICAL SCIENCES — Psychiatry And Neurology

340　　　　　NE　ISSN 0458-9998
LEIDSE JURIDISCHE REEKS. 1954. irreg., vol.15, 1981. price varies. Leiden University Press, c/o E.J. Brill Publishers, Postbus 9000, 2300 PA Leiden, Netherlands.

340　　　　　LB
LIBERIA. MINISTRY OF JUSTICE. ANNUAL REPORT TO THE LEGISLATURE. 1973. a. Ministry of Justice, Monrovia, Liberia.

340　　　　　UK　ISSN 0267-7083
LIBERTARIAN ALLIANCE. LEGAL NOTES. 1985. irreg. £5($10) Libertarian Alliance, 3 Langley Court, Covent Garden, London WC2E 9JY, England. Ed.Bd. adv. bk. rev. bibl. film rev. circ. 1,000. (back issues avail.)

340 301　　　　　US　ISSN 0075-9120
LIBRARY OF LAW AND CONTEMPORARY PROBLEMS. 1961. irreg., no.19, 1974. price varies. (Duke University, School of Law) Oceana Publications Inc., Dobbs Ferry, NY 10522. TEL 914-693-1320.

340　　　　　US
LICENSING LAW AND BUSINESS INSTITUTE. SEMINAR. 1979. a. Boardman Educational Programs, 435 Hudson St., New York, NY 10014. TEL 212-929-7500.
　Formerly: Licensing Law and Business Institute. Annual (ISSN 0271-3489)

340 382 600　　　　　US　ISSN 0731-5783
LICENSING LAW HANDBOOK. 1979. a. $45. Clark-Boardman Company, Ltd., 435 Hudson St., New York, NY 10014. TEL 212-929-7500. index.

340　　　　　UR　ISSN 0202-2028
LITUANISTIKA V S.S.S.R. PRAVO; nauchno-referativnyi sbornik. (Text in Russian) 1978. a. 0.35 Rub. Akademiya Nauk Litovskoi S.S.R., Nauchno-Informatsionnyi Tsentr, Michurino g-ve 1/46, Vilnius, Lithuanian S.S.R., U.S.S.R. Ed. A. Balsys. circ. 250.

340　　　　　UK
LONGMAN PROFESSIONAL DIRECTORY OF LOCAL AUTHORITIES. a. £13.95. Longman Professional, 21-27 Lambs Conduit St., London WC1N 3NJ, England. Ed.Bd.

340　　　　　BL
M P. vol.8, 1979. a. Ministerio Publico, Curitaba, Parana, Brazil. Ed.Bd. bibl.

340　　　　　US
MAINE BAR DIRECTORY (YEAR) 1970. a. $21. Tower Publishing Co., 34 Diamond St., Box 7220, Portland, ME 04112. TEL 207-774-9813.

340　　　　　UG　ISSN 0075-4781
MAKERERE UNIVERSITY. FACULTY OF LAW. HANDBOOK. 1970/71. a. Makerere University, Faculty of Law, Box 17062, Kampala, Uganda.

347.9　　　　　MW　ISSN 0076-3160
MALAWI. MINISTRY OF JUSTICE. ANNUAL REPORT. a., latest 1969. K.0.50. Government Printer, P.O. Box 37, Zomba, Malawi.

340　　　　　MW
MALAWI. MINISTRY OF JUSTICE. LAWS AMENDMENTS. (Text in English) 1969. a. Government Printer, Box 37, Zomba, Malawi.

340　　　　　MW
MALAWI LAW REPORTS. a. Government Printer, Box 37, Zomba, Malawi. Ed. James B. Kalaile.
　Formerly (until 1973): African Law Reports: Malawi Series.

340　　　　　CN　ISSN 0380-0008
MANITOBA DECISIONS, CIVIL AND CRIMINAL CASES. 1975. a. (updated monthly) Can.$199.50. Western Legal Publications, 301-1 Alexander St., Vancouver, B.C. V6A 1B2, Canada. TEL 604-687-5671.

340　　　　　CN
MANITOBA REPORTS. irreg. Can.$84 per vol. Maritime Law Book Ltd., Box 302, Fredericton, N.B. E3B 4Y9, Canada. TEL 506-454-9921. (back issues avail.)
●Also available online. Vendors: QL Systems Ltd.

344　　　　　UK
MANUAL OF AIR FORCE LAW-AMENDMENTS. irreg. price varies. H.M.S.O., Box 569, London SE1 9NH, England. circ. 4,650.

344　　　　　UK
MANUAL OF MILITARY LAW - AMENDMENTS. irreg. price varies. H.M.S.O., Box 569, London SE1 9NH, England. circ. 13,000.

340　　　　　US
MARTINDALE - HUBBELL LAW DIRECTORY. (In 8 vols.) 1868. a. $160. ‡ Martindale-Hubbell, Inc., Box 1001, Summit, NJ 07901. TEL 201-464-6800.

LAW

340 CN ISSN 0527-7892
MARTIN'S ANNUAL CRIMINAL CODE. a. Can.$35. Canada Law Book Inc., 240 Edward St., Aurora, Ont. L4G 3S9, Canada. Ed. Edward L. Greenspan.

340 US
MARYLAND. GENERAL ASSEMBLY. SUBJECT INDEX TO BILLS INTRODUCED IN THE SESSION. 1976. a. $7.50. Department of Legislative Reference, 90 State Circle, Annapolis, MD 21401. TEL 301-841-3810.

340 US
MARYLAND. HOUSE OF DELEGATES. JOURNAL OF PROCEEDINGS. REGULAR SESSION. 1826. a. $75. Department of Legislative Reference, 90 State Circle, Annapolis, MD 21401. TEL 301-841-3810.

340 US
MARYLAND. SENATE. JOURNAL OF PROCEEDINGS. REGULAR SESSION. 1826. a. $75. Department of Legislative Reference, 90 State Circle, Annapolis, MD 21401. TEL 301-841-3810.

348.752 US ISSN 0093-0520
MARYLAND. STATE DEPARTMENT OF LEGISLATIVE REFERENCE. SYNOPSIS OF LAWS ENACTED BY THE STATE OF MARYLAND. 1916. a. $15. Department of Legislative Reference, 90 State Circle, Annapolis, MD 21401. TEL 301-841-3810. Key Title: Synopsis of Laws Enacted by the State of Maryland.

340 US ISSN 0542-836X
MARYLAND LAWYER'S MANUAL. 1968. a. $52.50 to non-members. ‡ Maryland State Bar Association, 520 W. Fayette St., Baltimore, MD 21201. TEL 301-685-7878. Ed. Brian W. Norris. adv. circ. 16,500.

340 MF
MAURITIUS. JUDICIAL DEPARTMENT. ANNUAL REPORT. (Text in English) a. Government Printing Office, Elizabeth II Ave., Port Louis, Mauritius.

340 GW
MAX-PLANCK-INSTITUT FUER AUSLAENDISCHES OEFFENTLICHES RECHT UND VOELKERRECHT. FONTES IURIS GENTIUM. (Deutsche Rechtssprechung Zum Voelkerrecht 1879-1980) 1931. irreg. price varies. Max-Planck-Institut fuer Auslaendisches Oeffentliches Recht und Voelkerrecht, Berliner Str. 48, 6900 Heidelberg, W. Germany (B.R.D.) Ed.Bd. adv. circ. 700.
Formerly: Max-Planck-Institut fuer Auslaendisches Oeffentliches Recht und Voelkerrecht. Fontes (ISSN 0076-5651)

340 GW ISSN 0579-2428
MAX-PLANCK-INSTITUTE FUER EUROPAISCHE RECHTSGESCHICHTE. VEROEFFENTLICHUNGEN. IUS COMMUNE. irreg., vol.13, 1985. price varies. Vittorio Klostermann, Frauenlobstr. 22, Postfach 900601, D-6000 Frankfurt 90, W. Germany (B.R.D.) Eds. Dieter Simon, Walter Wilhelm.

340 GW ISSN 0175-6532
MAX-PLANCK-INSTITUTE FUER EUROPAISCHE RECHTSGESCHICHTE. VEROEFFENTLICHUNGEN. JUSCOMMUNE. SONDERHEFTE. irreg., vol.26, 1986. price varies. Vittorio Klostermann, Frauenlobstr. 22, Postfach 900601, D-6000 Frankfurt 90, W. Germany (B.R.D.) Ed. H. Coing.

344.041 AT ISSN 0047-6587
MEDICO-LEGAL SOCIETY OF NEW SOUTH WALES. PROCEEDINGS. 1960/62. triennial. Aus.$30 per vol. Medico-Legal Society of New South Wales, Wardell Chambers, 39 Martin Place, Sydney, N.S.W. 2000, Australia. Ed. J.M. Bennett. circ. 1,000.

340 610 GW ISSN 0340-9511
MEDIZIN IM RECHT UND ETHIK. 1976. irreg., latest vol.15, 1985. price varies. Ferdinand Enke Verlag, Postfach 1304, D 7000 Stuttgart 1, W. Germany (B.R.D.) Eds. A. Eser, E. Seidler.

340 PP
MELANESIAN LAW JOURNAL. 1970. a. K.12. University of Papua New Guinea, Faculty of Law, Box 317, University P.O., Papua New Guinea (Overseas subscr. to: Methuen LBC Ltd., 301 Kent St., Sydney N.S.W., Australia) Ed. John Kaburise. bk. rev. circ. 1,000. Indexed: Leg.Per. C.L.I. L.R.I.

340 FR
MEMENTO PRATIQUE DES SOCIETES COMMERCIALES. a. 329 F. Editions Francis Lefebvre, 5 rue Jacques Bingen, 75017 Paris, France.

340 364 US ISSN 8756-0615
MICHIGAN YEARBOOK OF INTERNATIONAL LEGAL STUDIES. 1979. a. $40. University of Michigan Law School, Hutchins Hall, Ann Arbor, MI 48109. TEL 313-763-2050. bibl. index. Indexed: Leg.Per. L.R.I.

340 US
MIDWEST LAW REVIEW. 1981. a. $3. Midwest Business Law Association, School of Business, University of Kansas, Lawrence, KS 66045. TEL 913-864-3536. Ed. John W. Gergacz. bk. rev. circ. 250.

346 AU
MIETRECHTLICHE ENTSCHEIDUNGEN. Abbreviated title: MietSlg. 1951. irreg., vol.36, 1985. price varies. Manzsche Verlags- und Universitaetsbuchhandlung, Kohlmarkt 16, Postfach 163, A-1014 Vienna, Austria. Ed. Viktor Heller. (back issues avail.)

340 US ISSN 0026-5543
MINNESOTA LEGAL REGISTER: OPINIONS OF THE MINNESOTA ATTORNEY GENERAL. 1968. m. & a. $35 to residents for 2 yrs. (non-residents $37) Philip G. Bradley, Ed. & Pub., Box 3253, Minneapolis, MN 55403. TEL 612-332-0726. index. circ. 390. (looseleaf format)

349 US
MINNESOTA RULES. 1983. biennial. $125. Office of Revisor of Statutes, 700 State Office Bldg., St. Paul, MN 55155. TEL 612-296-2868. circ. 1,000.

349 US
MINNESOTA RULES. SUPPLEMENT. 1984. biennial (2/yr. in even-numbered years) $15. Office of Revisor of Statutes, 700 State Office Bldg., St. Paul, MN 55155. TEL 612-296-2868.

348 US ISSN 0191-1562
MINNESOTA STATUTES. 1941. biennial. $135. Office of Revisor of Statutes, 700 State Office Bldg., St. Paul, MN 55155. TEL 612-296-2868. circ. 3,500.

348 US ISSN 0094-1727
MINNESOTA STATUTES. SUPPLEMENT. 1973. biennial. $23. Office of Revisor of Statutes, 700 State Office Bldg., St. Paul, MN 55155. TEL 612-296-2868. circ. 2,800.

340 US
MINNESOTA TAX COURT DECISIONS. 1985. m. & a. $40. Philip G. Bradley, Ed. & Pub., Box 3253, Minneapolis, MN 55403. TEL 612-332-0726. index. circ. 140. (looseleaf format)

340 US
MISSOURI NOTARY LAW PRIMER. a. $7.95. National Notary Association, 23012 Ventura Blvd., Box 4625, Woodland Hills, CA 91365. TEL 818-347-2035. (reprint service avail. from UMI)

340 SP ISSN 0077-0442
MONOGRAFIAS DE FILOSOFIA JURIDICA Y SOCIAL/MONOGRAPHS OF SOCIAL AND LEGAL PHILOSOPHY.* 1967. a. 70 ptas.($1.) Universidad de Granada, Facultad de Derecho, Granada, Spain.

MONOGRAPHS ON INDUSTRIAL PROPERTY AND COPYRIGHT LAW. see *PATENTS, TRADEMARKS AND COPYRIGHTS*

340 SA
NATAL UNIVERSITY LAW AND SOCIETY REVIEW. 1972. a. $5. University of Natal, Howard College School of Law, King George V Ave., Durban, Natal 4001, South Africa. Ed. C. Patel. adv. bk. rev. circ. 700. (back issues avail.) Indexed: Foreign.Leg.Per. Ind.S.A.Per.
Formerly: Natal University Law Review.

340 US ISSN 0098-2857
NATIONAL BAR EXAMINATION DIGEST. 1975. a. $1. Harcourt Brace Jovanovich Legal and Professional Publications, Inc., 1909 K St. N.W., Washington, DC 20006. TEL 202-296-6882.

340 US
NATIONAL CENTER FOR STATE COURTS. PUBLICATIONS. irreg. National Center for State Courts, 300 Newport Ave., Williamsburg, VA 23187-8798. TEL 804-253-2000.

340 US
NATIONAL CONFERENCE OF COMMISSIONERS ON UNIFORM STATE LAWS. HANDBOOK AND PROCEEDINGS. 1892. a. price varies. (National Conference of Commissioners on Uniform State Laws) William S. Hein & Co., Inc., 1285 Main St., Buffalo, NY 14209. TEL 800-828-7571. Ed. Alicia J. Pond. circ. 800. Indexed: Leg.Per. C.L.I.

340 US
NATIONAL LAW JOURNAL INDEX. 1983. a. $55. New York Law Publishing Co., Marketing Dept., 111 Eighth Ave., New York, NY 10011. TEL 212-741-8300.

340 US
NATIONAL REFERRAL DIRECTORY. 1986. a. $15. National Lawyers Guild, 853 Broadway, Rm. 1705, New York, NY 10003. TEL 212-260-1360.

340 CN
NATIONAL REPORTER. (Text in English; occasionally in French) irreg. (6 vols. per year) Can.$79 per vol. Maritime Law Book Ltd., Box 302, Fredericton, N.B. E3B 4Y9, Canada. TEL 506-454-9921. Ed. Eric B. Appleby. (back issues avail.)
●Also available online. Vendors: QL Systems Ltd.

340 US
NATIONAL TRIAL AND DEPOSITION DIRECTORY. 1980. a. $35 to reporters. Richard Tackman, 421 W. Franklin, Box 1758, Boise, ID 83701. adv.

344 US
NAVAL LAW REVIEW. 1947. irreg. price varies. Naval Justice School, Naval Education and Training Center, Newport, RI 02840. bk. rev. illus. index. cum.index every 4 yrs. circ. 11,000. (also avail. in microform from UMI; reprint service avail. from UMI) Indexed: Leg.Per. P.A.I.S. C.L.I. Ind.U.S.Gov.Per. L.R.I. Mar.Aff.Bibl.
Formerly (until vol.33): J A G Journal (ISSN 0021-3519)
Martial law

343 US
NEBRASKA CRIMINAL JUSTICE PLAN. a. Nebraska Commission on Law Enforcement and Criminal Justice, 301 Centennial Mall South, Lincoln, NE 68509.

340 US
NEBRASKA TRANSCRIPT. irreg. free to qualified personnel. University of Nebraska-Lincoln, College of Law, Lincoln, NE 68583-0902. TEL 402-472-2161. Ed. Mark C. Quandahl. illus. circ. 4,500.

340 NP
NEPAL MISCELLANEOUS SERIES. (Text in English) 1964. irreg. Rs.900 per year. Regmi Research (Pvt.) Ltd., Lazimpat, Kathmandu, Nepal. Ed. Mahesh C. Regmi. (also avail. in microfilm from LCP)
Formerly: Nepal Law Translation Series (ISSN 0077-6572)

418.02 NP
NEPAL RECORDER. (Text in English) 1957. irreg. (2-3/mo.) Rs.900($50) Nepal Press Digest (Pvt) Ltd., Lazimpat, Kathmandu, Nepal. Ed. Mahesh C. Regmi. index. (also avail. in microfilm from LCP)
Formerly: Nepal Gazette Translation Service (ISSN 0028-2707)

340 MY
NERACA. (Text in English and Malaysian) 1973. a. University of Malaya, Law Society - Universiti Malaya, Persatuan Undang-Undang, Lembah Pantai, Kuala Lumpur 22-11, Malaysia. bk. rev.

LAW   661

347.9   NE
NETHERLANDS. CENTRAAL BUREAU VOOR DE STATISTIEK. CIVIL AND ADMINISTRATIVE JURISDICTION. BURGERLIJKE EN ADMINISTRATIEVE RECHTSPRAAK. (Text in Dutch and English) 1951. a. fl.12.45. Centraal Bureau voor de Statistiek, Prinses Beatrixlaan 428, Voorburg, Netherlands (Orders to: Staatsuitgeverij, Christoffel Plantijnstraat, The Hague, Netherlands)
Formerly: Netherlands. Centraal Bureau voor de Statistiek. Justitiele Statistiek. Judicial Statistics.

340   CN
NEW BRUNSWICK REPORTS. 1968. irreg. Can.$86 per vol. Maritime Law Book Ltd., Box 302, Fredericton, N.B. E3B 4Y9, Canada. TEL 506-454-9921. (back issues avail.)
●Also available online. Vendors: QL Systems Ltd.

NEW INITIATIVES IN ENERGY LEGISLATION; a state by state guide. see ENERGY

340   US
NEW JERSEY. ADMINISTRATIVE OFFICE OF THE COURTS. ANNUAL REPORT OF THE NEW JERSEY JUDICIARY. 1949. a. free. Administrative Office of the Courts, RJH Justice Complex CN-037, Trenton, NJ 08625. TEL 609-292-9580. illus. circ. 2,000.
Formerly: New Jersey. Administrative Office of the Courts. Annual Report of the Administrative Director of the Courts.

340   US
NEW JERSEY STATE BAR ADVOCATE. 1974. irreg. (approx. 10/yr.) membership. New Jersey State Bar Association, 172 W. State St., Trenton, NJ 08608. TEL 609-394-1101. Ed. Anne Rivera. circ. 15,000.

340.3   AT   ISSN 0085-400X
NEW SOUTH WALES. LAW REFORM COMMISSION. REPORT. 1966. irreg., no.15, 1972. price varies. Law Reform Commission, Goodsell Bldg., 8-12 Chifley Square, Sydney 2000, Australia.

340   AT
NEW SOUTH WALES BAR ASSOCIATION. ANNUAL REPORT. 1926. a. membership. (New South Wales Bar Association) Standard Publishing Co., Selborne Chambers, 174 Phillip St., Sydney, N.S.W. 2000, Australia. circ. 1,350.

340   AT   ISSN 0312-1674
NEW SOUTH WALES LAW REPORTS. 1971. irreg. (6-8/yr.) Aus.$61.50 per vol. (Council of Law Reporting for New South Wales) Law Book Co. Ltd., 44-50 Waterloo Rd., North Ryde, N.S.W. 2112, Australia. index.
Supersedes: New South Wales Weekly Notes (ISSN 0023-9232) & New South Wales State Reports (ISSN 0085-6703)

340   364   US
NEW YORK (CITY). DEPARTMENT OF JUVENILE JUSTICE. ANNUAL REPORT. a. Department of Juvenile Justice, 365 Broadway, New York, NY 10013-3991. TEL 212-925-7779. Ed.Bd.

340   US
NEW YORK (STATE) OPINIONS OF THE ATTORNEY GENERAL. 1890. a. $10. Department of Law, Office of the Attorney General, The Capitol, Albany, NY 12224. circ. 3,000.

340   US
NEW YORK STATE COMMITTEE ON OPEN GOVERNMENT. ANNUAL REPORT. 1978. a. New York State Committee on Open Government, Department of State, 162 Washington Ave., Albany, NY 12231. TEL 518-474-2518. cum.index. circ. 1,000. (back issues avail.)

NEW YORK UNIVERSITY. INSTITUTE ON FEDERAL TAXATION. CONFERENCE ON CHARITABLE FOUNDATIONS. see BUSINESS AND ECONOMICS — Public Finance, Taxation

340   NZ   ISSN 0112-4447
NEW ZEALAND. DEPARTMENT OF STATISTICS. JUSTICE STATISTICS: PART A. a. NZ.$12.10. Department of Statistics, Private Bag, Wellington, New Zealand (Subscr. to: Government Printing Office, Publications, Wellington, New Zealand)
Formerly: New Zealand. Department of Statistics. Justice Statistics (ISSN 0110-3482)

340   NZ   ISSN 0112-4501
NEW ZEALAND. DEPARTMENT OF STATISTICS. JUSTICE STATISTICS: PART B. 1983. a. NZ.$12.10. Department of Statistics, Private Bag, Wellington, New Zealand.

NEW ZEALAND INCOME TAX LEGISLATION. see BUSINESS AND ECONOMICS — Public Finance, Taxation

346   NZ   ISSN 0078-0081
NEW ZEALAND LAW REGISTER. 1950. a. NZ.$27. Sweet and Maxwell (N.Z.) Ltd., Private Bag, Auckland, New Zealand. circ. 3,500.

340   CN
NEWFOUNDLAND & PRINCE EDWARD ISLAND REPORTS. 1970. irreg. Can.$86 per vol. Maritime Law Book Ltd., Box 302, Fredericton, N.B. E3B 4Y9, Canada. TEL 506-454-9921. (back issues avail.)
●Also available online. Vendors: QL Systems Ltd.

347.7   NQ
NICARAGUA. CORTE SUPREMA DE JUSTICIA. BOLETIN JUDICIAL. irreg. Corte Suprema de Justicia, Managua, Nicaragua.

370.26   JA
NIHON KYOIKUHO GAKKAI NEMPO. Added title: Educational Law Review. 1972. a. 1000 Yen. (Nihon Kyoikuho Gakkai) Yuhikaku Publishing Co. Ltd., 2-17 Kanda Jimbocho, Chiyoda-ku, Tokyo 101, Japan. circ. 2,000.

340   CE
NITI VIMAMSA. (Text in Sinhalese) a. Rs.12. Sri Lanka Nitivedi Shishya Sanvidhanaya, Sevana, Seeduwa North, Sri Lanka.

340   SW   ISSN 0300-3094
NORDISK STATUTSAMLING. (Subseries of Nordisk Utredningsserie) (Text in Danish, Finnish, Icelandic, Norwegian, or Swedish) 1970. a. Nordiska Raadet, Box 19506, S-104 32 Stockholm, Sweden.

340   NO   ISSN 0085-4220
NORDISKE DOMME I SJOFARTSANLIGGENDER. 1900. irreg. Kr.80. Nordisk Skibsrederforening, Kristinelundvei 22, 0207 Oslo 2, Norway. adv. index. cum.index every 10 yrs. circ. 900. (tabloid format)

340   US
NORTH DAKOTA DIRECTORY OF LAWYERS AND JUDGES. a. $4. State Bar Board, State Capitol, Bismarck, ND 58505. TEL 701-224-2221.
Former titles: North Dakota Directory of Judges and Attorneys & Directory of North Dakota Lawyers.

347.016   US
NOTARY PUBLIC PRACTICES & GLOSSARY. 1978. biennial. $15.95. National Notary Association, 23012 Ventura Blvd., Box 4625, Woodland Hills, CA 91365. TEL 818-347-2035. Ed. Raymond C. Rothman. (reprint service avail. from UMI)
Supersedes in part: Customs and Practices of Notaries Public and Digest of Notary Laws in the U.S.

NOTICIAS DEL TRABAJO. see BUSINESS AND ECONOMICS — Labor And Industrial Relations

340   CN
NOVA SCOTIA BARRISTERS' SOCIETY. ANNUAL REPORT. a. Nova Scotia Barristers' Society, 1475 Hollis St., Halifax, N.S. B3J 3M4, Canada. TEL 902-422-1491.

340   CN   ISSN 0048-0983
NOVA SCOTIA REPORTS. 1970. irreg. (6 vols. per year) Can.$86 per vol. Maritime Law Book Ltd., Box 302, Fredericton, N.B. E3B 4Y9, Canada. TEL 902-667-3889. Ed.Bd. (back issues avail.)
●Also available online. Vendors: QL Systems Ltd.

NOW HIRING; government jobs for lawyers. see OCCUPATIONS AND CAREERS

340   SA
OBITER. (Text in Afrikaans and English) 1979. a. R.7.00. University of Port Elizabeth, Faculty of Law, Box 1600, Port Elizabeth 6000, South Africa. Ed. C. van Loggerenberg. adv. circ. 450. Indexed: Ind.S.A.Per.

950   340   US   ISSN 0730-0107
OCCASIONAL PAPERS/REPRINT SERIES IN CONTEMPORARY ASIAN STUDIES. 1977. bi-m. $15. University of Maryland, School of Law, 500 W. Baltimore St., Baltimore, MD 21201. TEL 301-528-7579. Ed. Hungdah Chiu. circ. 800.

OCEAN DUMPING CONTROL ACT ANNUAL REPORT. see ENVIRONMENTAL STUDIES

340   US   ISSN 0173-1718
OESTERREICHISCHE ZEITSCHRIFT FUER OEFFENTLICHES RECHT UND VOELKERRECHT. SUPPLEMENT. 1971. irreg., no.4, 1976. Springer-Verlag, 175 Fifth Ave., New York, NY 10010 TEL 212-460-1500. (also Berlin, Heidelberg, Vienna) (also avail. in microform from UMI; reprint service avail. from ISI)
Formerly: Oesterreichische Zeitschrift fuer Oeffentliches Recht. Supplement (ISSN 0078-3552)

345.01   US
OHIO LEGAL RIGHTS SERVICE. ANNUAL REPORT. 1976. a. $1. Ohio Legal Rights Service, Atlas Bldg., 8 E. Long St., Columbus, OH 43215. TEL 614-466-7264. Ed. David E. Merry. circ. 300.

340   US   ISSN 0078-4095
OHIO STATE UNIVERSITY. COLLEGE OF LAW. LAW FORUM SERIES. 1961. irreg., no.10, 1977. price varies. Ohio State University Press, 1050 Carmack Rd., Columbus, OH 43210. TEL 614-292-6930.

340   US   ISSN 0475-0926
OKLAHOMA. ATTORNEY GENERAL'S OFFICE. OPINIONS OF THE ATTORNEY GENERAL. 1968. a. price varies. Attorney General's Office, Rm. 112, State Capitol, Oklahoma City, OK 73105. TEL 405-521-3921. circ. 1,000. (back issues avail.)

340   CN   ISSN 0710-538X
OMBUDSMAN JOURNAL. a. $30. International Ombudsman Institute, Faculty of Law, University of Alberta, Edmonton, Alta. T6G 2H5, Canada. TEL 403-432-3196.

340   CN
ONTARIO ANNUAL PRACTICE. a. Can.$42. ‡ Canada Law Book Inc., 240 Edward St., Aurora, Ont. L4G 3S9, Canada. TEL 416-773-6300.
Formerly: Chitty's Ontario Annual Practice (ISSN 0084-8751)

340   CN
ONTARIO APPEAL CASES. 1984. irreg. Can.$59 per vol. Maritime Law Book Ltd., Box 302, Fredericton, N.B. E3B 4Y9, Canada. TEL 506-454-9921.
●Also available online. Vendors: QL Systems Ltd.

340   CN
ONTARIO DIGEST. a. $302.50. Butterworth & Co. (Canada) Ltd., 2265 Midland Avenue, Scarborough, Ont. M1P 4S1, Canada. TEL 416-292-1421. (looseleaf format)

340   CN
ONTARIO LABOUR RELATIONS BOARD LAW AND PRACTICE; citation up-dater. a. $44. Butterworth & Co. (Canada) Ltd., 2265 Midland Ave., Scarborough, Ont. M1P 4S1, Canada. TEL 416-292-1421. Ed. C. Michael Mitchell. (looseleaf format)

340   CN
ONTARIO SECURITIES LEGISLATION. irreg. 12th ed., 1983/84. Can.$12.50. C C H Canadian Ltd, 6 Garamond Court, Don Mills, Ontario M3C 1Z5, Canada. TEL 416-441-2992.

340   UK
ORGANISATION AND MANAGEMENT OF A SOLICITORS PRACTICE. irreg. Longman Professional, 21-27 Lambs Conduit St., London WC1N 3NJ, England. (looseleaf format)

LAW

340 NZ ISSN 0078-6918
OTAGO LAW REVIEW. 1965. a. NZ.$25. Otago Law Review Trust Board, c/o Faculty of Law, University of Otago, Dunedin, New Zealand (Dist. in U.S. by: Wm. M. Gaunt & Sons, Inc., Gaunt Bldg., 3011 Gulf Dr., Holmes Beach, FL 33510) Eds. P. Skegg, A. Beck. adv. bk. rev. circ. 1,200. Indexed: Leg.Per. C.L.I. L.R.I. Manage.Cont.

340 DK ISSN 0107-2412
OVERSAETTELSER AF DANSK LOVGIVNING MED ALFABETISK REGISTER. FORTEGNELSE/GUIDE TO TRANSLATION OF DANISH LEGISLATION WITH AN ALPHABETIC INDEX. (Text in Danish, English, French and German) 1981. irreg. Kr.50. Schultz Publishing House, Moentergade 21, 1116 Copenhagen K, Denmark. circ. 600.

340 CN ISSN 0475-1671
OYEZ. 1970. irreg. University of Windsor, Faculty of Law, Student Law Society, Windsor, Ont., Canada. TEL 519-253-4232. illus.

PAKISTAN. NATIONAL ASSEMBLY. DEBATES. OFFICIAL REPORT. see *PUBLIC ADMINISTRATION*

340 PK ISSN 0078-785X
PAKISTAN ANNUAL LAW DIGEST. (Text in English) 1947. a. Rps.600($5) P.L.D. Publishers, Nabha Rd., Lahore 1, Pakistan. (reprint service avail. from UMI)

340 CY
PALESTINE YEARBOOK OF INTERNATIONAL LAW. (Text in English) 1984. a. $25. Al-Shaybani Society of International Law Ltd., P.O. Box 4247, Nicosia, Cyprus. Ed. Anis F. Kassim. bk. rev. (back issues avail.)

340 IO
PANTA-RHEI. 1975. irreg. University of North Sumatra, Faculty of Law - Universitas Sumatera Utara, Fakultas Hukum, Jalan Universitas 4, Medan, Indonesia.

340 AT ISSN 0085-4689
PAPUA AND NEW GUINEA LAW REPORTS. 1963. irreg. Aus.$81. Law Book Co. Ltd., 44-50 Waterloo Rd., North Ryde, N.S.W. 2112, Australia.

346 AT
PAPUA NEW GUINEA COMPANIES LEGISLATION. 1980. irreg. Aus.$208. C C H Australia Ltd., P.O. Box 230, North Ryde, N.S.W. 2113, Australia. adv.

345 US ISSN 0196-6138
PARKER DIRECTORY OF CALIFORNIA ATTORNEYS. 1925. a. $20.94. Parker and Son Publications, Inc., Box 60001, Los Angeles, CA 90060. TEL 213-727-1088. Ed. Yvonne Anderson. adv. circ. 55,000.
Formerly: Parker Directory of Attorneys (ISSN 0079-0044)

346 UK ISSN 0079-0095
PARLIAMENT HOUSE BOOK. 1824. a. (regular updating) W. Green and Son Ltd., St. Giles St., Edinburgh EH1 1PU, Scotland. Ed. P. Nicholson. (looseleaf format)

340 UK ISSN 0269-3658
PATERSON'S LICENSING ACTS. a. Butterworth & Co. (Publishers) Ltd., 88 Kingsway, London WC2B 6AB, England. Ed. J.N. Martin.

340 AT ISSN 0728-3210
PAUL'S POLICE OFFENCES. (Text and summaries in English) 1982. irreg. price varies. Law Book Company Ltd., 44-50 Waterloo Road, North Ryde, N.S.W. 2113, Australia. Ed.Bd. circ. 574. (back issues avail.)

340 150 US
PERSPECTIVES IN LAW AND PSYCHOLOGY. 1977. irreg., vol.7, 1986. price varies. Plenum Publishing Corp., 233 Spring St., New York, NY 10013. TEL 212-620-8047. Ed. Bruce Dennis Sales. bibl.

PHARMACY AND LAW DIGEST. see *PHARMACY AND PHARMACOLOGY*

340 US
PHILADELPHIA BAR ASSOCIATION. LEGAL DIRECTORY. 1880. a. $15. (Philadelphia Bar Association) Packard Press, Inc., 10th & Spring Garden Sts., Philadelphia, PA 19123. TEL 215-236-2000. adv. circ. 27,500.

PHILIPPINES YEARBOOK OF THE FOOKIEN TIMES. see *BUSINESS AND ECONOMICS — Banking And Finance*

PLANO DA SAFRA ACUCAR E ALCOOL. see *AGRICULTURE — Crop Production And Soil*

340 PO
PORTUGAL. MINISTERIO DA JUSTICIA. BOLETIN. no.241, 1974. a. Esc.1500($80) Ministerio da Justicia, Gabinete de Gestao Financeira, Of. Subdirector-Geral, Praca do Comercio, 1194 Lisbon Codex, Portugal. bk. rev. bibl. circ. 5,500.

340 PL
PRACE POPULARNONAUKOWE. BIBLIOTECZKA PRAWNICZA. 1978. irreg. price varies. Towarzystwo Naukowe w Toruniu, Ul. Wysoka 16, 87-100 Torun, Poland (Dist. by: Ars-Polona Ruch, Krakowskie Przedmiescie 7, 00-068 Warsaw, Poland)
Supersedes in part: Prace Popularnonaukowe (ISSN 0079-4805)

340 UK
PRACTICAL CONVEYANCING PRECEDENTS. irreg. Longman Professional, 21-27 Lambs Conduit St., London WC1N 3NJ, England. (looseleaf format)

340 AT ISSN 0048-508X
PRACTICAL FORMS AND PRECEDENTS (NEW SOUTH WALES) 1957. irreg., vol.7, 1972. price varies. Law Book Co. Ltd., 44-50 Waterloo Rd., North Ryde, NSW 2113, Australia.

340 CS ISSN 0079-4929
PRAVNEHISTORICKE STUDIE. (Text in Czech; summaries in French, German, Russian) 1955. irreg., vol.25, 1983. price varies. (Ceskoslovenska Akademie Ved) Academia, Publishing House of the Czechoslovak Academy of Sciences, Vodickova 40, 112 29 Prague 1, Czechoslovakia. Indexed: CERDIC.

340 CS ISSN 0551-9039
PRAVNICKE STUDIE. (Text in Slovak; summaries in German and Russian; contents page in French, German, Russian and Slovak) 1953. a. fl.30 per no. (Slovenska Akademia Vied, Ustav Statu a Prava) Veda, Publishing House of the Slovak Academy of Sciences, Klemensova 19, 814 30 Bratislava, Czechoslovakia (Distributor in Western countries: John Benjamins B.V., Amsteldijk 44, Amsterdam (Z.), Netherlands) charts. stat. Indexed: Geo.Abstr.

340 PL
PRAWO. (Text in Polish; summaries in Russian and English or French) 1961. irreg. price varies. Adam Mickiewicz University Press, Marchlewskiego 128, 61-874 Poznan, Poland. Indexed: Canon Law Abstr.
Formerly: Uniwersytet im. Adama Mickiewicza w Poznaniu. Wydzial Prawa. Prace (ISSN 0083-4262)

340 YU
PREGLED SUDSKE PRAKSE. (Issued as Supplement to Nasa Zakonitost, by Ustavni Sud Hrvatske and Other Legislative Bodies) 1972. irreg. (Vrhovni Sud) Narodne Novine, Zagreb, Ratkajev Prolaz 4, Zagreb, Yugoslavia. (Co-sponsors: Croatia. Ustavni Sud; Visi Privredni Sud u Zagrebu) Ed. Ivan Salinovic.

340 US ISSN 0075-8264
PRELAW HANDBOOK. OFFICIAL LAW SCHOOL GUIDE. 1967. a. $14. ‡ Law School Admission Council, Law School Admission Services, Box 2000, Newtown, PA 18940. TEL 215-968-1001. Ed.Bd. circ. 140,000. (processed)
Formerly: Law Study and Practice in the United States: Pre-Law Handbook.

347 UK
PRIVATE LEGISLATION (SCOTLAND) PROCEDURE JOURNAL. irreg. price varies. H.M.S.O., Box 569, Cornwall House, London SE1 9NH, England. circ. 225.

343 PL ISSN 0208-6336
PROBLEMY PRAWA KARNEGO. (Text in Polish; summaries in German, Russian) 1975. irreg. price varies. Uniwersytet Slaski w Katowicach, Ul. Bankowa 14, 40-007 Katowice, Poland.

343.093 PL ISSN 0208-5518
PROBLEMY PRAWA PRZEWOZOWEGO. (Text in Polish; summaries in English, German, Russian) 1979. price varies. Uniwersytet Slaski w Katowicach, Ul. Bankowa 14, 40-007 Katowice, Poland. Indexed: Mar.Aff.Bibl.

340 622 PL ISSN 0208-5488
PROBLEMY PRAWNE GORNICTWA. (Text in Polish; summaries in German and Russian) 1977. irreg. price varies. Uniwersytet Slaski w Katowicach, Ul. Bankowa 14, 40-007 Katowice, Poland.

346.066 PL ISSN 0208-5496
PROBLEMY PRAWNE HANDLU ZAGRANICZNEGO. (Text in Polish; summaries in English and Russian) 1977. irreg. price varies. Uniwersytet Slaski w Katowicach, Ul. Bankowa 14, 40-007 Katowice, Poland.
Business law

340 IT
PROCESSO LEGISLATIVO NEL PARLAMENTO ITALIANO. no.3, 1974. irreg. (Universita degli Studi di Firenze, Facolta di Scienze Politiche) Casa Editrice Dott. A. Giuffre, Via B. Arsizio 40, 20151 Milan, Italy. Ed. Alberto Predieri.

349 LE ISSN 0032-9649
PROCHE-ORIENT ETUDES JURIDIQUES. (Text in Arabic, French) 1967. a. £L120. Universite Saint Joseph, Faculte de Droit et des Sciences Politiques, Rue Huvelin, Box 293, Beirut, Lebanon (Foreign subscr. address: Office du Livre, 14 bis rue Jean Ferrandi, 75006 Paris, France) Ed. I. Najjar.
Formerly: Etudes de Droit Libanais.

340 US
PUBLIC INTEREST CLEARINGHOUSE DIRECTORY; guide to 600 Bay Area public interest organizations. 1980. triennial, latest 1986/87. $15.98. Public Interest Clearinghouse, 200 McAllister St., San Francisco, CA 94102. circ. 1, 000.

340 US ISSN 0095-5086
PUBLIC UTILITIES LAW ANTHOLOGY. 1974. a. $99.95. International Library, 7315 Wisconsin Ave., Ste. 229 E, Bethesda, MD 20814. Ed. Donald J. Hoyes.

340 IT
QUADERNI CAMERTI DI STUDI ROMANISTICI. INDEX/INTERNATIONAL SURVEY OF ROMAN LAW. INDEX. (Vols. for 1970-72 issued by the Facolte Giuridica (under a variant name: Facolta di Giurisprudenza), Universita di Camerino) (Text in English, French, German, Italian, Spanish) 1970. a. L.90000. Edizioni Scientifiche Italiane S.p.A., Via Chiatamone 7, Naples, Italy. Ed. Luigi Labruna. adv. circ. 700.

340 900 IT
QUADERNI FIORENTINI PER LA STORIA DEL PENSIERO GIURIDICO MODERNO. (Text in English, French, German, Italian and Spanish) 1972. a. (University of Florence, Centro di Studi per la Storia del Pensiero Giuridico Moderno) Editore Giuffre, Via B. Arsizio 40, 20151 Milan, Italy.

354 CN
QUEBEC (PROVINCE) COMMISSION DES SERVICES JURIDIQUES. RAPPORT ANNUEL. 1973. a. Commission des Services Juridiques, C.P. 123, Succursale Desjardins, Montreal, Que. H5B 1B3, Canada. TEL 514-873-3562. Ed. Jacques Lemaitre-Auger. circ. 1,600.

QUEBEC CORPORATION AND INCOME TAX LEGISLATION. see *BUSINESS AND ECONOMICS — Public Finance, Taxation*

340 AU
RECHT-WIRTSCHAFT-AUSSENHANDEL SCHRIFTENREIHE. 1981. irreg. price varies. Manzsche Verlags-und Universitaetsbuchhandlung, Kohlmarkt 16, A 1014 Vienna, Austria. Eds. Helmut H. Haschek, Peter Doralt. circ. 1,500.

340 320   US   ISSN 0080-0163
RECHTS- UND STAATSWISSENSCHAFTEN.
1947. irreg., vol.24, 1975. price varies. Springer-
Verlag, 175 Fifth Ave., New York, NY 10010 TEL
212-460-1500. (Also Berlin, Heidelberg, Tokyo and
Vienna) (reprint service avail. from ISI)

340   NE
RECHTSHISTORISCHE STUDIES. 1976. irreg.,
vol.11, 1985. price varies. Leiden University Press,
c/o E.J. Brill Publishers, Postbus 9000, 2300 PA
Leiden, Netherlands.

340   GW   ISSN 0080-018X
RECHTSPFLEGE JAHRBUCH. 1954. a. Gieseking-
Verlag, Deckerstr. 2-10, Postfach 42, 4813 Bielefeld-
Bethel, W. Germany (B.R.D.)

RECHTSSTAAT IN DER BEWAEHRUNG. see
LAW — International Law

340   GW   ISSN 0034-1398
RECHTSTHEORIE; Zeitschrift fuer Logik,
Methodenlehre, Kybernetik und Soziologie des
Rechts. 1970. a. DM.144. Duncker und Humblot
GmbH, Dietrich-Schaefer-Weg 9, 1000 Berlin 41,
W. Germany (B.R.D.) Ed.Bd. adv. bk. rev. index.
Indexed: Phil.Ind.

340 320   AU
RECHTSWISSENSCHAFT UND SOZIALPOLITIK.
1966. irreg., vol.15, 1985. price varies. Manzsche
Verlags- und Universitaetsbuchhandlung, Kohlmarkt
16, A-1014 Vienna, Austria. Eds. H. Floretta, R.
Strasser.

370   BL
RECIFE, BRAZIL. SECRETARIA DE ASSUNTOS
JURIDICOS. REVISTA. irreg. Secretaria de
Assuntos Juridicos, Recife, Brazil. illus.

340   SP
RECOPILACION DE DOCTRINA LEGAL. a. price
varies. (Consejo de Estado) Spain. Boletin Oficial
del Estado, Trafalgar 29, 28010 Madrid, Spain.

342   BE
RECUEIL ANNUEL DE JURISPRUDENCE
BELGE. 1950. a. 14553 Fr. Maison Ferdinand
Larcier S.A., Rue des Minimes 39, 1000 Brussels,
Belgium.

346   UK
REFORM IN NORTHERN IRELAND. irreg.
(approx. 1/yr.) H.M.S.O. (N. Ireland), Chichester
House, Chichester St., Belfast BT1 4JY, N. Ireland.
(reprint service avail. from UMI)

343   SZ
REIHE STRAFRECHT. 1976. irreg. Verlag Ruegger,
Rechts- und Wirschaftsliteratur, Underdorf 65, CH-
7214 Grusch, Switzerland.

340   IT
REPERTORIO DEL FORO ITALIANO. 1876. a.
price varies. Zanichelli Editore, Via Irnerio 34,
Bologna 40126, Italy. abstr. bibl.

342   IT
REPERTORIO DELLE DECISIONI DELLA
CORTE COSTITUZIONALE. 1956. biennial. price
varies. Casa Editrice Dott. A. Giuffre, Via B.
Arsizio 40, 20151 Milan, Italy. Ed. Nicola Lipari.

347.9   IT
REPERTORIO DI GIURISPRUDENZA DEL
LAVORO. 1968. biennial. price varies. Casa
Editrice Dott. A. Giuffre, Via B. Arsizio 40, 20151
Milan, Italy. Eds. Mario Pacifico, Enrico Pacifico.

348   US   ISSN 0094-7148
REPORT OF CASES DETERMINED IN THE
SUPREME COURT AND COURT OF APPEALS
OF THE STATE OF NEW MEXICO. Spine title:
New Mexico Reports. 1968. irreg. (Supreme Court)
West Publishing Co., Box 3526, St. Paul, MN
55165. TEL 612-228-2500.

340   ISSN 8755-7509
REPORTER ON THE LEGAL PROFESSION. 1979.
a. $120. Legal-Medical Studies, Inc., 79 Joy St., Box
8219, Boston, MA 02114. TEL 617-742-7959. bk.
rev. abstr. bibl. index. (looseleaf format; back issues
avail.) Indexed: Leg.Per. C.L.I.

RESEARCH IN LAW AND ECONOMICS; a
research annual. see BUSINESS AND
ECONOMICS

340.1 301   US
RESEARCH IN LAW, DEVIANCE AND SOCIAL
CONTROL. 1978. a. $23.75 to individuals;
institutions $47.50. J A I Press Inc., Box 1678, 36
Sherwood Pl., Greenwich, CT 06836. TEL 203-661-
7602. Eds. Steven Spitzer, Andrew T. Scull.
Indexed: Leg.Per. C.L.I. L.R.I. Lang.&
Lang.Behav.Abstr.
 Formerly (until 1981): Research in Law and
Sociology (ISSN 0163-6588)

340   SA   ISSN 0486-5588
RESPONSA MERIDIANA;* an annual law review.
(Text in English and Afrikaans) 1964. a. $5.
(University of Cape Town, Student Law Society
Consulting) Butterworth Publishers Pty. Ltd., 152-
154 Gale St., P.O.B. 792, 4000 Durban, South
Africa. (Co-sponsor: University of Stellenbosch,
Student Law Society) Ed. I. Leeman. adv. bk. rev.
circ. 350. Indexed: Ind.S.A.Per.

340   US
RESTATEMENT IN THE COURTS. POCKET
PARTS. 1977. a. price varies. (American Law
Institute) American Law Institute Publishers, Box
64526, 50 West Kellogg Blvd., St. Paul, MN 55164-
0526. TEL 215-243-1650. Ed. Violet Meehan. circ.
2,400.
 Formerly (until 1976): Restatement in the Courts.
Supplements.

340   GH   ISSN 0034-6578
REVIEW OF GHANA LAW. 1969. a. $46.50.
Council for Law Reporting, Box M.165, Accra,
Ghana. Ed. S.Y. Bimpong-Buta. adv. bk. rev. index.
circ. 2,000. (also avail. in microform from UMI;
reprint service avail. from UMI)

340   AG   ISSN 0325-0601
REVISTA DE CIENCIAS JURIDICAS SOCIALES.
1922. irreg. exchange basis. Universidad Nacional
del Litoral, Facultad de Ciencias Juridicas y
Sociales, Candido Pujato 2751, 3000 Santa Fe,
Argentina. bk. rev. circ. 500.

340   AG
REVISTA DE DERECHO PUBLICO. 1950. irreg.
Universidad Nacional de Tucuman, Instituto de
Derecho Publico, Tucuman, Buenos Aires,
Argentina.

340   EC   ISSN 0484-6923
REVISTA DE DERECHO SOCIAL
ECUATORIANO. 1952-1956; resumed 1958. irreg.
Universidad Central del Ecuador, Box 2349, Quito,
Ecuador. Ed. H. Valencia.

340 630   VE
REVISTA DE DERECHO Y REFORMA
AGRARIA. 1969. a. $7. (Universidad de los Andes,
Instituto Iberoamericano de Derecho Agrario y
Reforma Agraria) Talleres Graficos, Merida,
Venezuela. bk. rev. bibl. circ. 1,200.

340   BL
REVISTA DE DIREITO DO TRABALHO
(PETROPOLIS)* 1973. irreg. Industrias Graficas
Centrograf Ltd, Rua Alencar Lima, 35- Grupo 903/
7, Petropolis, Brazil.

340   CL
REVISTA DE ESTUDIOS HISTORICO JURIDICO.
1976. a. $16. (Universidad Catolica de Valparaiso,
Escuela de Derecho) Ediciones Universitarias de
Valparaiso, Casilla 1415, Valparaiso, Chile. Ed.
Alejandro Guzman B. bk. rev. circ. 300.

340   AG
REVISTA DE HISTORIA DE DERECHO. 1973. a.
(Instituto de Investigaciones de Historia del
Derecho) Librart s.r.l., Departamento de
Publicaciones Cientificas Argentinas, Avda.
Corrientes 127, Casilla Correo Central 5047,
Buenos Aires, Argentina. Dir. Ricardo Zorraquin
Becu.

340   SP
REVISTA DE HISTORIA DEL DERECHO. a.
Universidad de Granada, Secretariado de
Publicaciones, Hospital Real, Granada, Spain. Ed.
Jose M. Perez Prendes.

340   AG   ISSN 0034-8481
REVISTA DE LEGISLACION ARGENTINA.
Variant title: Anuario de Legislacion Argentina. (In
2 volumes) 1966. a. $100 per volume.
Jurisprudencia Argentina S.A., Buenos Aires 1013,
Buenos Aires, Argentina. Ed.Bd. adv. charts. illus.
stat.

340   BL   ISSN 0034-9739
REVISTA JURIDICA. 1977. irreg., (1-3/yr.)
Cr.$30($7.) Av. Paris 72, ZC-24 Bonsucesso, 20000
Rio de Janeiro, Brazil. Eds. Angelito A. Aiquel,
Jamil A. Aiquel. illus. charts.

340   CN   ISSN 0556-7963
REVUE JURIDIQUE THEMIS. Running title:
Themis. (Text in English and French) 1953. a.
Can.$20. Editions Themis, C.P. 6201, Succursale A,
Montreal, Que. H3C 3T1, Canada. TEL 514-739-
9945. adv. bk. rev. bibl. index. circ. 1,700. (also
avail. in microfilm from WSH) Indexed: Leg.Per.
C.L.I. L.R.I. Mar.Aff.Bibl. Pt.de Rep.
 Supersedes: Revue Juridique Themis de
l'Universite de Montreal.

340   US
SAINT LOUIS UNIVERSITY PUBLIC LAW
REVIEW. 1981. a. $10 per 2 nos. Saint Louis
University School of Law, Thomas J. White Family
Center, 3700 Lindell Blvd., Saint Louis, MO 63108.
TEL 314-658-3067. Ed. Christopher Dysart. circ.
900. Indexed: Leg.Per. P.A.I.S. C.L.I. L.R.I.
 Formerly: Saint Louis University Public Law
Forum (ISSN 0738-5390)

340   AT   ISSN 0310-6861
ST. THOMAS MORE SOCIETY. JOURNAL. 1971.
irreg. St. Thomas More Society, Box 282 G.P.O.,
Sydney, N.S.W. 2001, Australia. Ed. John D. Traill.

340 320   GW   ISSN 0080-5823
SAMMLUNG GELTENDER
STAATSANGEHOERIGKEITSGESETZE. 1949.
irreg., vol.39, 1982. price varies. (Universitaet
Hamburg, Institut fuer Internationale
Angelegenheiten) Nomos Verlagsgesellschaft mbH
und Co. KG, Waldseestr. 3-5, Postfach 610, 7570
Baden Baden, W. Germany (B.R.D.)

340 664   GW   ISSN 0080-5831
SAMMLUNG LEBENSMITTELRECHTLICHER
ENTSCHEIDUNGEN. 1959. irreg., vol.16, 1986.
DM.500. Carl Heymanns Verlag KG,
Luxemburgerstr. 449, 5000 Cologne 41, W.
Germany (B.R.D.) Ed. K.H. Nuese.

340 341   AS
SAMOAN PACIFIC LAW JOURNAL. (Text in
English & Samoan) 1973. a. $7. American Samoa
Bar Association, Box 1509, Pago Pago 96799,
American Samoa. Ed.Bd. adv. bk. rev. illus. circ.
150. (back issues avail) Indexed: C.L.I. L.R.I.
 Formerly: American Samoa Bar Association.
Newsletter.

340   SZ
ST. GALLER STUDIEN ZUM WETTBEWERBS
UND IMMATERIALGUETERRECHT. 1971.
irreg. price varies. Verlag Ostschweiz, Oberer
Graben 8, Postfach 716, CH-9001 St. Gallen,
Switzerland. Ed. Mario M. Pedrazzini.

SAO PAULO, BRAZIL (STATE). SECRETARIA DA
EDUCACAO. ATIVIDADES DESENVOLVIDAS.
see EDUCATION

340   CN
SASKATCHEWAN REPORTS. 1979. irreg. Can.$84
per vol. Maritime Law Book Ltd., Box 302,
Fredericton, N.B. E3B 4Y9, Canada. TEL 506-454-
9921. (back issues avail.)
 ●Also available online. Vendors: QL Systems Ltd.

340   GE   ISSN 0084-5264
SAVIGNY-STIFTUNG FUER
RECHTSGESCHICHTE. ZEITSCHRIFT.
GERMANISTISCHE, ROMANISTISCHE UND
KANONISTISCHE ABTEILUNG. 1861. a. price
varies. ‡ Hermann Boehlaus Nachfolger, Meyerstr.
50A, 53 Weimar, E. Germany (D.D.R.) Ed.Bd. bk.
rev. Indexed: CERDIC.

340   SW   ISSN 0085-5944
SCANDINAVIAN STUDIES IN LAW. (Text in
English) 1957. a. Kr.120. (Stockholms Universitet)
Almqvist & Wiksell International, Box 62, S-101 20
Stockholm, Sweden.

LAW

SCHRIFTENREIHE FINANZWIRTSCHAFT UND FINANZRECHT. see *BUSINESS AND ECONOMICS — Banking And Finance*

SCHRIFTENREIHE FUER AGRARWIRTSCHAFT. see *AGRICULTURE*

340   AU
SCHRIFTENREIHE: GESELLSCHAFT UND BETRIEB. 1974. irreg., vol.4, 1980. price varies. (Institut fuer Partnerschaftliche Betriebsverfassung) Manzsche Verlags- und Universitaetsbuchhandlung, Kohlmarkt 16, A-1014 Vienna, Austria. circ. 1,800.

340   UK
SCOTS LAW TIMES CHRISTMAS CHARITY. SUPPLEMENT. a. W. Green & Son Ltd., 2-10 St. Giles St., Edinburgh EH1 1PU, Scotland.

340   UK   ISSN 0265-6159
SCOTTISH CURRENT LAW YEAR BOOK. 1948. a. £80. W. Green & Son Ltd., 2-10 St. Giles St., Edinburgh EH1 1PU, Scotland.

346   UK   ISSN 0080-8083
SCOTTISH LAW DIRECTORY. 1892. a. £21.50. William Hodge & Co. Ltd., 34/6 N. Frederick St., Glasgow G1 2BT, Scotland.

SECURITIES LAW REVIEW. see *BUSINESS AND ECONOMICS — Banking And Finance*

942   UK
SELDEN SOCIETY, LONDON. HANDBOOK: PUBLICATIONS, LIST OF MEMBERS AND RULES. 1952. every 4-5 years. £2 to non-members. Selden Society, Queen Mary College, Faculty of Laws, Mile End Rd., London E1 4NS, England.

942   UK
SELDEN SOCIETY, LONDON. LECTURES. 1953. every 2-3 years. price varies. Selden Society, Queen Mary College, Faculty of Laws, Mile End Rd., London E1 4NS, England.

942   UK
SELDEN SOCIETY, LONDON. MAIN (ANNUAL) SERIES. (Text in English, French, Latin; summaries in English) 1887. a. £5($40) to individuals; £6 ($50) to libraries. Selden Society, Queen Mary College, Faculty of Laws, Mile End Road, London E1 4NS, England. bibl. charts. illus. cum.index: vols. 1-79. circ. 1,600.

942   UK   ISSN 0582-4788
SELDEN SOCIETY, LONDON. SUPPLEMENTARY SERIES. 1965. irreg. price varies. Selden Society, Queen Mary College, Faculty of Laws, Mile End Rd., London E1 4NS, England.

SERIE LEGISLACION EDUCATIVA ARGENTINA. see *EDUCATION*

340   UK   ISSN 0037-282X
SESSION CASES; the official Law Reports of Scotland. 1904. irreg., (approx. 3-4/yr.) £35. (Scottish Council of Law Reporting) T. & T. Clark Ltd., 59 George St., Edinburgh EH2 2LQ, Scotland. Ed. J. R. Fiddes. index. cum.ind. circ. 1,000.

340   UK   ISSN 0264-312X
SHAW'S DIRECTORY OF COURTS IN THE UNITED KINGDOM. 1970. a. £9.50. Shaw & Sons Ltd., Shaway House, Bell Green Lane, London SE26 5AE, England. Ed. Gordon Morris. bk. rev. circ. 2,750.
Former titles (until 1983): Shaw's Directory of Courts in England and Wales (ISSN 0085-6061); Shaw's Directory of Magistrates' Courts and Crown Courts; Directory of Magistrates Courts.

345   US   ISSN 0080-9233
SHEPARD'S ACTS AND CASES BY POPULAR NAMES, FEDERAL AND STATE. 1968. irreg., latest edt. 1986, a. supplement. $200. Shepard's McGraw-Hill, Box 1235, Colorado Springs, CO 80901. TEL 303-475-7230.

343   US   ISSN 0363-0978
SHEPARD'S CRIMINAL JUSTICE CITATIONS. 1975. 3/yr. supplements to base vols. $70. Shepard's McGraw-Hill, Box 1235, Colorado Springs, CO 80901. TEL 303-475-7230.

340   US   ISSN 0730-7039
SHEPARD'S FEDERAL CIRCUIT TABLE. 1981. a. supplement. $34. Shepard's McGraw-Hill, Box 1235, Colorado Springs, CO 80901. TEL 303-475-7230.

340   US   ISSN 0582-9887
SHEPARD'S LAW REVIEW CITATIONS. 1968. irreg., latest edt. 1986; 3/yr. supplements to base vol. $186. Shepard's McGraw-Hill, Box 1235, Colorado Springs, CO 80901. TEL 303-475-7230.

340   US   ISSN 0582-9909
SHEPARD'S UNITED STATES ADMINISTRATIVE CITATIONS. 1967. irreg., latest edt. 1976; q. supplements to base vol. $138. Shepard's McGraw-Hill, Box 1235, Colorado Springs, CO 80901. TEL 303-475-7230.

348.7   US   ISSN 0162-0444
SIGNIFICANT DECISIONS OF THE SUPREME COURT. a. price varies. (American Enterprise Institute for Public Policy Research) Fred B. Rothman & Co., 10368 W. Centennial Rd., Littleton, CO 80127. TEL 303-979-5657.

349   SI   ISSN 0080-9705
SINGAPORE LAW REVIEW. (Text in English) 1969. a. $10. National University of Singapore Law Club, c/o Law Faculty, Kent Ridge Campus, Singapore 0511, Singapore. Eds. Ong Keng Sen, Sylvia Lim. adv. circ. 1,350.
Supersedes (1958-69): Me Judice.

SKATTEBVE; til studiebrug. see *BUSINESS AND ECONOMICS — Public Finance, Taxation*

170   US
SOCIAL RESPONSIBILITY: BUSINESS, JOURNALISM, LAW, MEDICINE. 1975. a. Washington and Lee University, Social Responsibility: Business, Journalism, Law, Medicine, Lexington, VA 24450. TEL 703-463-8786. Ed. Louis W. Hodges. circ. 8,000. (also avail. in microfilm from WSH) Indexed: Leg.Per. C.L.I. L.R.I.
Formerly: Social Responsibility: Journalism, Law, Medicine.

340   UK
SOCIAL WELFARE LAW. irreg. Longman Professional, 21-27 Lambs Conduit St., London WC1N 3NJ, England. (looseleaf format)

340   SP   ISSN 0213-0483
SOCIEDAD DE ESTUDIOS VASCOS. CUADERNOS DE SECCION. DERECHO. 1984. irreg. Eusko Ikaskuntza, S.A., Churruca, 7 - 2, 20004 Donostia, Spain.

SOCIEDADES POR ACOES. see *BUSINESS AND ECONOMICS*

340   IT   ISSN 0391-3260
SOCIETA E DIRITTO DI ROMA. 1975. irreg., no.4, 1979. price varies. Liguori Editore s.r.l., Via Mezzocannone 19, 80134 Naples, Italy. TEL 081/ 20 6077. Ed. Antonio Guarino.

340   FR   ISSN 0081-0843
SOCIETE DES AUTEURS, COMPOSITEURS, EDITEURS POUR LA GERANCE DES DROITS DE REPRODUCTION MECANIQUE. BULLETIN. (Title varies: A.C.E. Bulletin) irreg. price varies. Societe des Auteurs, Compositeurs, Editeurs pour la Gerance des Droits de Reproduction Mecanique, 62 rue Blanche, 75009 Paris, France.

SOCIETY OF MARITIME ARBITRATORS. AWARD SERVICE. see *TRANSPORTATION — Ships And Shipping*

340   BU   ISSN 0081-1866
SOFIISKI UNIVERSITET. JURIDIHESKI FAKULTET. GODISNIK. (Summaries in English, French, and German) irreg., vol.72, 1979. price varies. Publishing House of the Bulgarian Academy of Sciences, Acad. G. Bonchev St., Bldg. 6, 1113 Sofia, Bulgaria. Ed. G. Boychev. circ. 550.

340   UK
SOLICITORS' AND BARRISTERS' DIRECTORY AND DIARY. 1844. a. £33.80($75) Waterlow (Publishers) Ltd., Maxwell House, 74 Worship St., London EC2A 2EN, England. TEL 01 377 4602. adv. circ. 14,000.
Formerly: Solicitors' Diary and Directory.

340.3   SA
SOUTH AFRICA. LAW COMMISSION. JAARVERSLAG VAN DIE SUID-AFRIKAANSE REGSKOMMISSIE/ANNUAL REPORT OF THE SOUTH AFRICAN LAW COMMISSION. (Text in Afrikaans and English) 1974. a. Government Printer, Bosman St., Private Bag X85, Pretoria 0001, South Africa.

340   341   US   ISSN 0561-1784
SOUTHWESTERN LEGAL FOUNDATION. ANNUAL REPORT. 1955. a. free. Southwestern Legal Foundation, Box 830707, Richardson, TX 75083-0707. TEL 214-690-2377. Ed. Janice R. Moss. circ. 2,000. (back issues avail.)

340   AU
SOZIALVERSICHERUNGSRECHTLICHE ENTSCHEIDUNGEN. 1953. a. price varies. Manzsche Verlags- und Universitaetsbuchhandlung, Kohlmarkt 16, A-1014 Vienna, Austria. Eds. Albert Nowak, Hellmut Teschner. circ. 2,000.

340   SA   ISSN 0584-8652
SPECULUM JURIS. (Text in Afrikaans and English) a. R.5. (University of Fort Hare, Faculty of Law) Fort Hare University Press, Private Bag X1322, Alice, Republic of Ciskei, South Africa. Ed. J. Labuschagne. bibl. Indexed: Ind.S.A.Per.

340   GE   ISSN 0138-5208
STAATS- UND RECHTSTHEORETISCHE STUDIEN. 1976. irreg., vol.15, 1985. (Akademie der Wissenschaften der DDR) Akademie Verlag Berlin, Postfach 1233, Leipziger Str. 3-4, DDR-1086 Berlin, E. Germany (D.D.R.)

344.73   US   ISSN 0892-7138
STANFORD ENVIRONMENTAL LAW JOURNAL. 1978. a. $8. Stanford Environmental Law Society, Stanford Law School, Stanford, CA 94305. TEL 415-723-4421. circ. 2,000. Indexed: Leg.Per. C.L.I. L.R.I.
Formerly (until 1985): Stanford Environmental Law Annual (ISSN 0197-7873)

340.115   CS
STAT A PRAVO. 1956. irreg., vol.21, 1983. price varies. (Ceskoslovenska Akademie Ved, Ustav Statu a Prava) Academia, Publishing House of the Czechoslovak Academy of Sciences, Vodickova 40, 112 29 Prague 1, Czechoslovakia.

340   US   ISSN 0276-7651
STATE LAWS AND PUBLISHED ORDINANCES, FIREARMS. a. U.S. Department of the Treasury, Bureau of Alcohol, Tobacco and Firearms, 15th and Pennsylvania Ave. N.W., Washington, DC 20224. TEL 202-566-7777.
Formerly: Firearms, State Laws and Published Ordinances.

346   GW   ISSN 0170-6845
STEUER-TRAINING. a. DM.142.50. Verlag Dr. Peter Deubner GmbH, Fuerst-Puecklerstr. 30, Postfach 410268, 5000 Cologne, W. Germany (B.R.D.)

STICHTING TOT UITGAVE DER BRONNEN VAN HET OUD-VADERLANDSCHE RECHT. 2 SERIES: WERKEN, AND VERSLAGEN EN MEDEDELINGEN. see *HISTORY — History Of Europe*

340   UK   ISSN 0269-3682
STONE'S JUSTICES' MANUAL. a. Butterworth & Co. (Publishers) Ltd., 88 Kingsway, London WC2B 6AB, England. Eds. S.J. Richman, A.T. Draycott.

340   333.33   NE
STRUCTURING FOREIGN INVESTMENT IN U.S. REAL ESTATE. (Text in English) 1982. base volume plus a. updates. fl.225($95) Kluwer Law and Taxation Publishers, Box 23, 7400 GA Deventer, Netherlands (Orders to: Kluwer Academic Publishers Group, Distribution Center, Box 322, 3300 AH Dordrecht, Netherlands) Ed. W. Donald Knight.

340   US
STUDENT GUIDE TO GRADUATE LAW STUDY PROGRAMS. biennial. $19. Joint Committee on Law Study Programs, 154 Stuart St., Boston, MA 02116. TEL 617-451-0010. Eds. Ellen Wayne, Betsy McCombs.

340.07 US ISSN 0197-6656
STUDENT GUIDE TO SUMMER LAW STUDY PROGRAMS. 1980. a. $11. Joint Committee on Law Study Programs, 154 Stuart St., Boston, MA 02116. TEL 617-451-0010. Eds. Ellen Wayne, Betsy McCombs.
Formerly: Directory of Summer Law Programs.

STUDIA ET DOCUMENTA HISTORIAE ET IURIS. see HISTORY

340 PL ISSN 0081-6671
STUDIA IURIDICA. (Text in Polish; summaries in English, French and German) 1962. irreg. price varies. Towarzystwo Naukowe w Toruniu, Wysoka 16, 87-100 Torun, Poland (Dist. by: Ars Polona-Ruch, Krakowskie Przedmiescie 7, P.O. Box 1001 Warsaw, Poland) circ. 500.

340 HU ISSN 0324-5934
STUDIA IURIDICA AUCTORIATATE UNIVERSITATIS PECS PUBLICATA. (Text in Hungarian; summaries in English, French, German and Russian) 1958. irreg., no.87, 1977. exchange basis. Janus Pannonius Tudomanyegyetem, Allames Jogtudomanyi Karanak Tudomanyos Bizottsaga, 48-as ter 1, Pecs, Hungary. Ed. Antal Adam. circ. 400.

347 PL ISSN 0208-502X
STUDIA IURIDICA SILESIANA. (Text in German, Polish and Russian; summaries in French, German, Polish and Russian) 1976. irreg. price varies. Uniwersytet Slaski w Katowicach, Ul. Bankowa 14, 40-007 Katowice, Poland.

347.9 IT ISSN 0081-6698
STUDIA JURIDICA. 1964. irreg., no.83, 1979. price varies. Erma di "Bretschneider", Via Cassiodoro, 19, 00193 Rome, Italy.

340 RM ISSN 0578-5464
STUDIA UNIVERSITATIS "BABES-BOLYAI" IURISPRUDENTIA. (Text in Romanian; summaries in English, French and Russian) 1958. a. exchange basis. Universitatea "Babes-Bolyai", Biblioteca Centrala Universitara, Str. Clinicilor nr. 2, Cluj-Napoca, Rumania. bk. rev. cum.index: 1956-1963, 1964-1970.

900 340 330 AU
STUDIEN ZUR RECHTS-, WIRTSCHAFTS- UND KULTURGESCHICHTE. (Subseries of: Universitaet Innsbruck. Veroeffentlichungen) 1969. irreg., vol.10, 1974. price varies. (Universitaet Innsbruck) Oesterreichische Kommissionsbuchhandlung, Maximilianstr. 17, A-6020 Innsbruck, Austria. Ed. Nikolaus Grass.

STUDIES IN ABORIGINAL RIGHTS. see ETHNIC INTERESTS

340 US
STUDIES IN LEGAL HISTORY. 1973. irreg., latest 1983. price varies. (American Society for Legal History) University of North Carolina Press, Box 2288, Chapel Hill, NC 27514. TEL 919-966-3561. Ed. Stanley N. Katz.

340 US
STUDIES IN TRANSNATIONAL LEGAL POLICY. Variant title: American Society of International Law. Occasional Papers. irreg., latest no.20. price varies. American Society of International Law, 2223 Massachusetts Ave, N.W., Washington, DC 20008-2864. TEL 202-265-4313.

343 US ISSN 0362-2983
STUDY OF FEDERAL TAX LAW. INCOME TAX VOLUME: BUSINESS ENTERPRISES. 1975. irreg. $47. Commerce Clearing House, Inc., 4025 W. Peterson Ave., Chicago, IL 60646. TEL 312-583-8500.
Formerly: Study of Federal Tax Law. Income Tax Materials, Business Enterprises; Continues in part: Study of Federal Tax Law. Income Tax Volume.

343 US
STUDY OF FEDERAL TAX LAW. INCOME TAX VOLUME: INDIVIDUALS. 1976. irreg. $47. Commerce Clearing House, Inc., 4025 W. Peterson Ave., Chicago, IL 60646. TEL 312-583-8500.
Supersedes in part: Study of Federal Tax Law. Income Tax Volume (ISSN 0362-5230)

340 CN
SUBJECT MATTER INDEX TO PUBLIC AND PRIVATE STATUES OF NEW BRUNSWICK. 1971. a. Can.$87. Maritime Law Book Ltd., Box 302, Fredericton, N.B. E3B 4Y9, Canada. TEL 506-454-9921.

340 SJ ISSN 0585-8631
SUDAN LAW JOURNAL AND REPORTS. 1956. a. Judiciary, Khartoum, Sudan.

340 US ISSN 0736-9921
SUPREME COURT ECONOMIC REVIEW. 1983. a. $23.95. (Emory University, Law and Economics Center) Macmillan Publishing Company, 866 Third Ave., New York, NY 10022. Ed. Peter H. Aranson.

347 US ISSN 0362-5249
SUPREME COURT HISTORICAL SOCIETY. YEARBOOK.* 1976. a. $15 hardcover; softcover $10. Supreme Court Historical Society, 111 Second St., N.E., Washington, DC 20002. Ed. Dr. William Swindler. illus. circ. 2,850. Indexed: C.L.I. L.R.I. Key Title: Yearbook - Supreme Court Historical Society.

340 UK ISSN 0039-5978
SUPREME COURT PRACTICE. 1967. triennial. price varies. Sweet & Maxwell Stevens Journals, 11 New Fetter Lane, London E.C.4, England. Ed.Bd.
Formerly: Annual Practice.

345 347.9 US ISSN 0081-9557
SUPREME COURT REVIEW. 1960. a. University of Chicago Press, 5801 S. Ellis Ave., Chicago, IL 60637 TEL 312-962-7600. (Orders to: Box 37005, Chicago, IL 60637) Ed.Bd. (also avail. in microform from UMI; reprint service avail. from UMI,ISI) Indexed: Leg.Per. SSCI. ASCA. A.B.C.Pol.Sci. C.L.I. L.R.I.

SURVEY OF PHARMACY LAW. see PHARMACY AND PHARMACOLOGY

347 AT ISSN 0082-0512
SYDNEY LAW REVIEW. 1953. a. Aus.$12. University of Sydney, Faculty of Law, 173 Phillip St., Sydney, N.S.W. 2000, Australia (U.S. subscr. to: Wm. Gaunt & Sons, Inc., 3011 Gulf Drive, Holmes Beach, FL 33510) Ed.Bd. adv. bk. rev. index. circ. 1,250. (also avail. in microform from UMI; reprint service avail. from UMI) Indexed: Leg.Per. SSCI. Aus.Leg.Mon.Dig. Aus.P.A.I.S. C.C.L.P. C.L.I. L.R.I.

340 AT ISSN 0085-7106
TASMANIAN STATE REPORTS. 1905. a. Aus.$75. Law Book Co. Ltd., 44-50 Waterloo Rd., North Ryde, N.S.W. 2112, Australia.

TAX SHELTERED INVESTMENTS HANDBOOK. see BUSINESS AND ECONOMICS — Investments

TENDENCIAS ECONOMICAS: LEGISLACION ECONOMICAS ARGENTINA/BUSINESS TRENDS: ARGENTINE ECONOMIC LEGISLATION. see BUSINESS AND ECONOMICS

340 US
TEXAS NOTARY LAW PRIMER. a. $7.95. National Notary Association, 23012 Ventura Blvd., Box 4625, Woodland Hills, CA 91365. TEL 818-347-2035. (reprint service avail. from UMI)

340 FR
TEXTES D'INTERET GENERAL. irreg. Direction des Journaux Officiels, 26 rue Desaix, 75732 Paris Cedex 15, France.

346.73 US ISSN 0092-6175
TRANSPORTATION AND PRODUCTS LEGAL DIRECTORY.* 1973. a. Spangler, Jennings, Spangler & Dougherty, 8396 Mississippi St., Merrillville, IN 46410.

349.41 UK ISSN 0309-8990
TRENT LAW JOURNAL. 1977. a. £1.40. Trent Polytechnic, Department of Legal Studies, Burton St., Nottingham NG1 4BU, England. Ed. I.R. Storey. adv. bk. rev. circ. 400. Indexed: Leg.Per. C.L.I. L.R.I.

349 FR ISSN 0071-9129
TRIBUNAL DE COMMERCE, PARIS. ANNUAIRE.* 1969. a. price varies. Tribunal de Commerce de Paris, 1 Bld. du Palais, Paris, France.

340 CU
TRIBUNAL SUPREMO POPULAR. BOLETIN. a. Tribunal Supremo Popular, San Rafael No. 3, Habana 2, Havana, Cuba.

340 GW ISSN 0082-6731
TUEBINGER RECHTSWISSENSCHAFTLICHE ABHANDLUNGEN. 1961. irreg. price varies. (Universitaet Tuebingen, Rechts- und Wirtschaftswissenschaftliche Fakultaet) Verlag J.C.B. Mohr (Paul Siebeck), Wilhelmstr. 18, Postfach 2040, 7400 Tuebingen, W. Germany (B.R.D.)

340 BE
TWEETALIGE LOSBLADIGE WETBOEKEN. 1965. irreg. price varies. E. Story-Scientia, Eekhout 2, B-9000 Ghent, Belgium.

340 330 US ISSN 0082-7088
TWENTIETH CENTURY LEGAL PHILOSOPHY SERIES. irreg., no.8, 1970. Harvard University Press, 79 Garden St., Cambridge, MA 02138. TEL 617-495-2600.

340 341 MW
U M A STUDENTS LAW JOURNAL. 1978. a. k.4.00. University of Malawi, Students Law Society, Chancellor College, Box 280, Zomba, Malawi.

340 BB
U W I STUDENTS' LAW REVIEW. 1976. a. $5 bds. $4. University of the West Indies, Faculty of Law, Student's Law Review Committee, Cave Hill Campus, P.O. Box 64, Bridgetown, Barbados, W. Indies. Ed. Rudolph Muir. adv. bk. rev.

665.5 UK
UNITED KINGDOM OFFSHORE LEGISLATION GUIDE. 1980. a. £75. Benn Technical Books, Tolley House, 17 Scarbrook Rd., Croydon, Surrey CR0 1SQ, England. Ed. Harry Whitehead. circ. 400. (looseleaf format)

341.13 II ISSN 0503-4663
UNITED SCHOOLS INTERNATIONAL. DOCUMENTS OF THE BIENNIAL CONFERENCE.* irreg. United Schools International, Uso House, Arya Samaj Rd., New Delhi, India.

347 US ISSN 0097-7977
U.S. ADMINISTRATIVE OFFICE OF THE UNITED STATES COURTS. REPORT ON APPLICATIONS FOR ORDERS AUTHORIZING OR APPROVING THE INTERCEPTION OF WIRE OR ORAL COMMUNICATIONS. 1972. a. since 1977. U.S. Administrative Office of the United States Courts, U.S. Supreme Court Bldg., Washington, DC 20544. TEL 202-633-6247. Key Title: Report on Applications for Orders Authorizing or Approving the Interception of Wire or Oral Communications.

341.1 US ISSN 0082-8769
U.S. ARMS CONTROL AND DISARMAMENT AGENCY. ANNUAL REPORT TO CONGRESS. 1961. a. U.S. Arms Control and Disarmament Agency, Dept. of State Bldg., Washington, DC 20451 TEL 202-632-8715. (Also available from: Supt. of Documents, Washington DC 20402)

345 US ISSN 0082-9943
U.S. DEPARTMENT OF JUSTICE. ANNUAL REPORT OF THE ATTORNEY GENERAL OF THE UNITED STATES. 1870. a. price varies. U.S. Department of Justice., Office of Legal Policy, Constitution & 10th St., N.W., Washington, DC 20530 TEL 202-633-4601. (Orders to: Supt. of Documents, Washington, DC 20402)

U.S. DEPARTMENT OF JUSTICE. OFFICE OF LEGAL COUNSEL. OPINIONS. see POLITICAL SCIENCE

345 US ISSN 0082-9951
U.S. DEPARTMENT OF JUSTICE. OPINIONS OF ATTORNEY GENERAL. 1789. irreg. price varies. U.S. Department of Justice, Office of Legal Counsel, Constitution & 10th St., N.W., Washington, DC 20530 TEL 202-633-2041. (Orders to: Supt. of Documents, Washington, DC 20402) Ed. Margaret C. Love. cum.indexes issued separately. (also avail. in microfiche)

U.S. FEDERAL TRADE COMMISSION. COURT DECISIONS PERTAINING TO THE FEDERAL TRADE COMMISSION. see *BUSINESS AND ECONOMICS — Domestic Commerce*

U.S. FEDERAL TRADE COMMISSION. FEDERAL TRADE COMMISSION DECISIONS, FINDINGS, ORDERS AND STIPULATIONS. see *BUSINESS AND ECONOMICS — Domestic Commerce*

346   US   ISSN 0093-4631
U.S. FISH AND WILDLIFE SERVICE. SELECTED LIST OF FEDERAL LAWS AND TREATIES RELATING TO SPORT FISH AND WILDLIFE. irreg. $1.75. U.S. Fish & Wildlife Service, Washington, DC 20240 TEL 202-343-1100. (Orders to: Supt. of Documents, Washington, DC 20402) (looseleaf format) Key Title: Selected List of Federal Laws and Treaties Relating to Sport Fish and Wildlife.

340   US
U.S. LIBRARY OF CONGRESS. CONGRESSIONAL RESEARCH SERVICE. DIGEST OF PUBLIC GENERAL BILLS AND RESOLUTIONS. 1936. irreg. (per session of Congress) U.S. Library of Congress, Congressional Research Service, Washington, DC 20540 TEL 202-287-5000. (Subscr. to: Supt. of Documents, Washington, DC 20402) Ed. Terry G. Guertin. abstr. cum.index for session. circ. 5,000.
     Former titles: U.S. Library of Congress. Congressional Research Service. Digest of Public Bills and Resolutions (ISSN 0012-2785); U.S. Library of Congress. Legislative Reference Service. Digest of Public General Bills and Selected Resolutions (ISSN 0090-0125); U.S. Library of Congress. Legislative Reference Service. Digest of Public General Bills (ISSN 0090-0117)

345   US   ISSN 0083-3401
UNITED STATES STATUTES AT LARGE. 1873. a. U.S. Office of the Federal Register, National Archives and Records Administration, Washington, DC 20408 TEL 202-523-5240. (Orders to: Supt. of Documents, Washington, DC 20402) (also avail. in microform from UMI)
     Cumulation of daily slip law prints, annotated pamphlets of public laws enacted by congress

340   CL
UNIVERSIDAD CATOLICA DE VALPARAISO. REVISTA DE DERECHO. 1977. a. $10. (Universidad Catolica de Valparaiso, Escuela de Derecho) Ediciones Universitarias de Valparaiso, Casilla 1415, Valparaiso, Chile. Ed. Tito Solari P. circ. 300.

340   SP   ISSN 0075-773X
UNIVERSIDAD DE LA LAGUNA. FACULTAD DE DERECHO. ANALES. 1963. a. 150 ptas. Universidad de la Laguna, Secretariado de Publicaciones, Laguna, Canary Islands, Spain. Indexed: Hist.Abstr. Amer.Hist.& Life.

340   VE   ISSN 0076-6550
UNIVERSIDAD DE LOS ANDES. FACULTAD DE DERECHO. ANUARIO.* 1970. irreg. Universidad de Los Andes, Facultad de Derecho, Centro de Investigaciones Juridicas, Via los Chorras, C.P. 5101, Merida, Venezuela. Ed.Bd. bibl.
     Supersedes (1955-19??): Universidad de Los Andes. Facultad de Derecho. Revista.

340   SP   ISSN 0210-539X
UNIVERSIDAD DE MURCIA. ANALES DE DERECHO. 1977. a. ($1000) Universidad de Murcia, Secretariado de Publicaciones e Intercambio Cientifico, Santo Cristo, 1, 30001 Murcia, Spain. TEL 968 24 92 00.
     Supersedes (1954-1976): Universidad de Murcia. Anales. Derecho; (1930-1954): Universidad de Murcia. Anales: Anales de Derecho.

340   SP
UNIVERSIDAD DE MURCIA. DEPARTAMENTO DE DERECHO POLITICO. PUBLICACIONES. SERIE MONOGRAFIAS. 1977. irreg. Universidad de Murcia, Departamento de Derecho Politico, Murcia, Spain.

349   SP
UNIVERSIDAD DE NAVARRA. COLECCION MANUALES DE DERECHO. irreg., no.13, 1982. price varies. (Universidad de Navarra, Facultad de Derecho) Ediciones Universidad de Navarra, S.A., Apdo. 396, 31080 Pamplona, Spain.
     Formerly: Universidad de Navarra. Manuales: Derecho Notarial Espanol (ISSN 0078-8767)

340   PN
UNIVERSIDAD DE PANAMA. CENTRO DE INVESTIGACION JURIDICA. ANUARIO. a. price varies. Universidad de Panama, Centro de Investigacion Juridica, Estafeta Universitaria, Panama, Panama.

340   PN
UNIVERSIDAD DE PANAMA. CENTRO DE INVESTIGACION JURIDICA. JURISPRUDENCIA CONSTITUCIONAL. 1968. irreg. price varies. Universidad de Panama, Centro de Investigacion Juridica, Estafeta Universitaria, Panama, Panama. Ed. Aura G. de Villalaz.

340   PN
UNIVERSIDAD DE PANAMA. CENTRO DE INVESTIGACION JURIDICA. LEGISLACION PANAMENA. INDICES CRONOLOGICOS Y ANALITICO DE LEYES (O DECRETOS EJECUTIVOS) 1958. quinquennial. price varies. Universidad de Panama, Centro de Investigacion Juridica, Estafeta Universitaria, Panama, Panama. Dir. Aura G. de Villalaz.

340 327   PN
UNIVERSIDAD DE PANAMA. FACULTAD DE DERECHO Y CIENCIAS POLITICAS. CUADERNOS. 1960. irreg. Universidad de Panama, Facultad de Derecho y Ciencias Politicas, Oficina de Informacion y Publicaciones, Panama City, Panama.

340 658   SP   ISSN 0582-8929
UNIVERSIDAD DE SEVILLA. INSTITUTO GARCIA OVIEDO. PUBLICACIONES. irreg. price varies. Universidad de Sevilla, Instituto Garcia Oviedo, San Fernando 4, Seville, Spain.

340   VE
UNIVERSIDAD DEL ZULIA. FACULTAD DE DERECHO. REVISTA. (Not published 1976, 1977) 1961. irreg; no.49, 1977. Bs.15($3.50) Universidad del Zulia, Facultad de Derecho, Apdo. 526, Maracaibo, Venezuela. Dir. Alice Adrianza Alvarez. circ. 2,500. Indexed: P.A.I.S.

340   PO
UNIVERSIDADE DE LISBOA. FACULDADE DE DIREITO. REVISTA. 1944. a. Universidade de Lisboa, Faculdade de Direito, Lisbon, Portugal. bk. rev.

340   BL   ISSN 0080-6250
UNIVERSIDADE DE SAO PAULO. FACULDADE DE DIREITO. REVISTA. 1893. a. Cr.$2000. Universidade de Sao Paulo, Faculdade de Direito, Biblioteca Central, Largo de Sao Francisco, 95-1 Andar, 01005 Sao Paolo, Brazil. Ed. Antonio Augusto Machado de Campos. bk. rev. circ. 1,500.

340   BL   ISSN 0102-1397
UNIVERSIDADE FEDERAL DE UBERLANDIA. CURSO DE DIREITO. REVISTA. 1972. a. free. Universidade Federal de Uberlandia, Curso de Direito, Campus Umuarama-Bloco E, Sala 2E25, 38400 Uberlandia, MG, Brazil. Eds. Jacy de Assis, Dinah Fernandes de Carvalho. bibl. circ. 5,000.
     Formerly (until 1978): Universidade de Uberlandia. Faculdade de Direito. Revista.

340   RM   ISSN 0379-7872
UNIVERSITATEA "AL. I. CUZA" DIN IASI. ANALELE STIINTIFICE. SECTIUNEA 3D: STIINTE JURIDICE. (Text in Rumanian; summaries in foreign languages) 1955. a. 35 lei. Universitatea "Al. I. Cuza" din Iasi, Calea 23 August Nr. 11, Jassy, Rumania (Subscr. to: ILEXIM, Str. 13 Decembrie Nr. 3, P.O. Box 136-137, Bucharest, Rumania) Ed. I. Macovei. bk. rev. abstr. charts. illus. circ. 250.

UNIVERSITATEA BUCURESTI. ANALELE. FILOZOFIE. ISTORIE. DREPT. see *PHILOSOPHY*

340 300   FR
UNIVERSITE DE DROIT, ECONOMIE ET DE SCIENCES SOCIALES DE PARIS. TRAVAUX DU SEMINAIRE DE RECHERCHES SUR LES FAITS ELECTORAUX DE MONSIEUR LE PROFESSEUR ROBERT VILLERS. irreg. price varies. (Universite de Droit, Economie et de Sciences Sociales de Paris) Librarie Touzot, 38 rue Saint Sulpice, 75278 Paris Cedex 06, France.

340   CN   ISSN 0317-9656
UNIVERSITE DE SHERBROOKE. REVUE DE DROIT. (Text in English & French) 1970. a. Can.$18($19) Universite de Sherbrooke, Faculte de Droit, Sherbrooke, Que. J1K 2R1, Canada. TEL 819-821-7510. adv. bk. rev. circ. 1,500. (also avail. in microform from UMI) Indexed: Leg.Per. C.L.I. L.R.I.

340   FR
UNIVERSITE JEAN MOULIN. ANNALES. 1968. irreg. price varies. Editions Hermes, 31 Pasteur, 69007 Lyon, France. bk. rev. circ. 500.
     Former titles (until 1975): Universite de Lyon III. Faculte de Droit. Annales (ISSN 0336-1357); Universite de Lyon. Faculte de Droit et des Sciences Economiques. Annales (ISSN 0076-1664)

340   ZR
UNIVERSITE NATIONALE DU ZAIRE, KINSHASA. FACULTE DE DROIT. ANNALES. 1972. a. Universite Nationale du Zaire, Kinshasa, Faculte du Droit, B.P. 125, Kinshasa XI, Zaire.

346   US   ISSN 0537-9768
UNIVERSITY OF MIAMI, CORAL GABLES. LAW CENTER. ANNUAL INSTITUTE ON ESTATE PLANNING. 1967. a. $68.50. Matthew Bender & Co., Inc., 235 E. 45 St., New York, NY 10017. TEL 212-661-5050. Ed. Philip Heckerling. (back issues avail.)

346   CN   ISSN 0077-8141
UNIVERSITY OF NEW BRUNSWICK LAW JOURNAL. 1947. a. Can.$12. University of New Brunswick, Faculty of Law, Bag Service 44999, Fredericton, N.B. E3B 6C9, Canada TEL 506-453-4670. (Subscr. to: Carswell Co. Ltd., 2330 Midland Ave., Agincourt Ont., Canada) Ed. Howard A. Baker. adv. bk. rev. circ. 1,650. (also avail. in microform from UMI; microfilm from WSH; reprint service avail. from UMI) Indexed: Leg.Per. C.L.I. L.R.I.

UNIVERSITY OF OSAKA PREFECTURE. BULLETIN. SERIES D: SCIENCES OF ECONOMY, COMMERCE AND LAW. see *BUSINESS AND ECONOMICS*

340   AT   ISSN 0083-4041
UNIVERSITY OF QUEENSLAND LAW JOURNAL. 1948. a. Aus.$19($18) University of Queensland Press, P.O. Box 42, St. Lucia, Queensland 4067, Australia. Eds. R. O'Hair, D. Gifford. adv. bk. rev. circ. 750. (also avail. in microform from UMI) Indexed: Leg.Per. Aus.P.A.I.S. C.L.I. L.R.I.

340   AT   ISSN 0082-2108
UNIVERSITY OF TASMANIA LAW REVIEW. Title varies: Tasmanian University Law Review. 1958. a. Aus.$8. University of Tasmania Law Review, Box 252 C, Hobart, Tas. 7001, Australia. Ed. F.A. Bates. adv. bk. rev. index. circ. 450. (also avail. in microfilm from WSH) Indexed: Leg.Per. Aus. P.A.I.S. C.C.L.P. C.L.I. L.R.I.

UNIVERSITY OF WALES. BOARD OF CELTIC STUDIES. HISTORY AND LAW SERIES. see *HISTORY — History Of Europe*

340   US   ISSN 0083-4068
UNIVERSITY OF WEST LOS ANGELES LAW REVIEW. 1967. a. $5. University of West Los Angeles, Law Review, 12201 Washington Pl., Los Angeles, CA 90066. TEL 213-313-1011. adv. bk. rev. circ. 1,000. (also avail. in microfilm from WSH) Indexed: Leg.Per. C.L.I. L.R.I.

340   PL   ISSN 0208-4910
UNIWERSYTET GDANSKI. WYDZIAL PRAWA I ADMINISTRACJI. ZESZYTY NAUKOWE. PRAWO. (Text in Polish; summaries in English and Russian) 1972. a. price varies. Uniwersytet Gdanski, Ul. Czerwonej Armii 110, 81-824 Sopot, Poland. Ed. Marian Cieslak.

LAW 667

340 PL ISSN 0208-4929
UNIWERSYTET GDANSKI. WYDZIAL PRAWA I ADMINISTRACJI. ZESZYTY NAUKOWE. PRACE INSTYTUTU ADMINISTRACJI I ZARZADZANIA. (Text in Polish; summaries in English, Russian) 1976. irreg. price varies. Uniwersytet Gdanski, Ul. Armii Czerwonej 110, 81-824 Sopot, Poland (Dist. by: Ars Polona-Ruch, Krakowskie Przedmiescie 7, 00-680 Warsaw, Poland)

349 PL ISSN 0083-4394
UNIWERSYTET JAGIELLONSKI. ZESZYTY NAUKOWE. PRACE PRAWNICZE. (Text in Polish; summaries in English, Russian) 1955. irreg., no.110, 1984. price varies. Panstwowe Wydawnictwo Naukowe, Miodowa 10, 00-251 Warsaw, Poland (Dist. by: Ars Polona, Krakowskie Przedmiescie 7, 00-068 Warsaw, Poland) Ed. W. Litewski. circ. 500.

VEREENIGING TOT UITGAAF DER BRONNEN VAN HET OU-VADERLANDSCHE RECHT. WERKEN. see HISTORY

VERFASSUNG UND VERFASSUNGSWIRKLICHKEIT. see POLITICAL SCIENCE

340 AT
VICTORIAN BAR COUNCIL. ANNUAL REPORT. 1964. a. members only. Victorian Bar Council, Owen Dixon Chambers, 205 William St., Melbourne, Vic. 3000, Australia. Ed.Bd. circ. 1,200.

340 AT ISSN 0314-5204
VICTORIAN STATUTES CUMULATIVE SUPPLEMENT. 1962. a. Aus.$105. Law Book Company Limited, 44-50 Waterloo Rd., North Ryde, N.S.W. 2113, Australia.

340 331 AT
VICTORIAN WORKERS COMPENSATION PRACTICE GUIDE. 1980. irreg. Aus.$388. C C H Australia Ltd., P.O. Box 230, North Ryde, N.S.W. 2113, Australia.

342 US ISSN 0360-7453
VIOLATIONS OF HUMAN RIGHTS IN SOVIET OCCUPIED LITHUANIA; a report. 1971. a. $8. Lithuanian American Community of USA, Inc., 708 Custis Rd., Glenside, PA 19038. TEL 215-886-5849. Eds. Ginte Damusis, Casimir Pugevicius. circ. 4,000. (also avail. in microfiche) Indexed: HR Rep.

353.9 US
VIRGINIA. CRIMINAL JUSTICE SERVICES COMMISSION. ANNUAL REPORT. a. free. Criminal Justice Services Commission, 9 N. Twelfth St., Richmond, VA 23219. TEL 804-786-0000.
Former titles (1974-1976): Virginia. Criminal Justice Officers Training and Standards Commission. Biennial Report; (until 1974): Virginia. Law Enforcement Officers Training Standards Commission. Biennial Report (ISSN 0095-1846)

340 US
VIRGINIA LEGAL STUDIES. irreg. University Press of Virginia, Box 3608 University Sta., Charlottesville, VA 22903. TEL 804-924-3468.

347.9 CN ISSN 0509-5166
W.C.J. MEREDITH MEMORIAL LECTURES. 1961. a. (McGill University, Faculty of Law) Richard de Boo Publishers, 81 Curlew Dr., Don Mills, Ont. M3A 3P7, Canada. TEL 416-445-4940.
Formerly: Lectures Bar Extension.

347.9 US ISSN 0742-1095
WANT'S FEDERAL-STATE COURT DIRECTORY. 1984. a. $19.95. Want Publishing Company, 1511 K St., N.W., Washington, DC 20005. TEL 202-783-1887. Ed. Robert S. Want. circ. 5,000.

WASSERRECHT UND WASSERWIRTSCHAFT. see WATER RESOURCES

340 AT
WEST AUSTRALIAN REPORTS. 1960. biennial. Aus.$45. Law Book Co. Ltd., 44-50 Waterloo Rd., North Ryde, N.S.W. 2113, Australia.

350 AT
WESTERN AUSTRALIA. LAW REFORM COMMISSION. ANNUAL REPORT. 1973. a. free. Law Reform Commission, St. Martins' Tower, 16th Fl., 44 St. Georges Terrace, Perth, W.A. 6000, Australia. stat. circ. 300(AP)

340 AT ISSN 0085-8161
WESTERN AUSTRALIA LAW ALMANAC. 1913. a. Aus.$7.50. Crown Law Department, 109 St. George's Terrace, Perth, W.A. 6000, Australia. Ed. S.B.J. Currie. circ. 1,000.

346 AT ISSN 0083-8764
WESTERN AUSTRALIAN REPORTS. 1899. irreg., with annual cumulation. price on application. Butterworths Pty. Ltd., 271-273 Lane Cove Rd., North Ryde, N.S.W. 2113, Australia.

WESTERN TRANSPORTATION LAW SEMINAR. PAPERS AND PROCEEDINGS. see TRANSPORTATION

340 AT ISSN 0085-820X
WHITEACRE.* 1967. irreg. free. University of Sydney, Law Graduates Association, 173-175 Phillip St., Sydney, N.S.W. 2000, Australia.

340 US ISSN 0162-7880
WHO'S WHO IN AMERICAN LAW. 1977. irreg., 3rd edt., 1983. $165. Marquis Who's Who, Macmillan Directory Division, 3002 Glenview Rd., Wilmette, IL 60091. TEL 312-441-2387. Indexed: Child.Auth.& Illus.

WHO'S WHO IN CANADIAN LAW. see BIOGRAPHY

340 AU ISSN 0084-0025
WIENER RECHTSWISSENSCHAFTLICHE STUDIEN. 1964. irreg., no.19, 1985. price varies. (Universitaet Wien, Institut fuer Rechtsvergleichung) Manzsche Verlags- und Universitaetsbuchhandlung, Kohlmarkt 16, A-1014 Vienna, Austria. (Co-sponsor: Oesterreichische Gesellschaft fuer Rechtsvergleichung) Ed. Fritz Schwind.

340 CN
WILLISTON & POLLS COURT FORMS. irreg. Butterworth & Co. (Canada) Ltd., 2265 Midland Avenue, Scarborough, Ont. M1P 4S1, Canada. TEL 416-292-1421. Ed. R.J. Rolls. (looseleaf format)

347.91 CN ISSN 0710-0841
WINDSOR YEARBOOK OF ACCESS TO JUSTICE/RECUEIL ANNUEL DE WINDSOR D'ACCES A LA JUSTICE. (Text in English and French) 1981. a. Can.$25. University of Windsor, Faculty of Law, Windsor N9B 3P4, Canada. TEL 519-253-4232. Ed.Bd. Indexed: Curr.Cont. Leg.Per. PAIS. SSCI. C.L.I.

WIRTSCHAFTSWISSENSCHAFTLICHE UND WIRTSCHAFTSRECHTLICHE UNTERSUCHUNGEN. see BUSINESS AND ECONOMICS

340 US
WISCONSIN LEGISLATIVE COUNCIL RULES CLEARINGHOUSE. ANNUAL REPORT. 1980. a. Wisconsin Legislative Council, 147 North State Capitol, Madison, WI 53702. TEL 608-266-1304. Ed. Ronald Sklansky. (back issues avail.)

340 346.013 US
WISCONSIN WOMEN'S LAW JOURNAL. 1985. a. $8 to individuals; institutions $15. University of Wisconsin-Madison, Law School, 975 Bascom Mall, Madison, WI 53706. TEL 608-262-8294. bk. rev. circ. 500. (back issues avail.)

340 GW
WISSENSCHAFT UND GEGENWART. JURISTISCHE REIHE. 1970. irreg., no.6, 1973. price varies. Vittorio Klostermann, Frauenlobstr. 22, Postfach 900601, 6000 Frankfurt 90, W. Germany (B.R.D.)

301 340 GW ISSN 0084-0939
WISSENSCHAFTLICHE GESELLSCHAFT FUER PERSONENSTANDSWESEN UND VERWANDTE GEBIETE. SCHRIFTENREIHE. NEUE FOLGE. 1960. irreg., vol.24, 1984. price varies. Verlag fuer Standesamtswesen GmbH und Co. KG, Hanauer Landstr. 197, 6000 Frankfurt 1, W. Germany (B.R.D.) Ed.Bd.

346 GW ISSN 0721-6890
WISTRA. 1982. a. DM.198. Verlag Dr. Peter Deubner GmbH, Fuerst-Pueckleustr. 30, Postfach 410268, 5000 Cologne, W. Germany (B.R.D.)

347 US ISSN 0074-0837
WORK ACCOMPLISHED BY THE INTER-AMERICAN JURIDICAL COMMITTEE DURING ITS MEETING. Spanish edition: Trabajos Realizados por el Comite Juridico Interamericano Durante el Periodo Ordinario de Sesiones. (Editions in Spanish, English, French and Portuguese) a. price varies. Organization of American States, Department of Publications, Washington, DC 20006. TEL 703-789-3533. circ. 2,000.

355 GW ISSN 0084-3083
WUERZBURGER WEHRWISSENSCHAFTLICHE ABHANDLUNGEN. 1967. irreg., vol.5. 1975. price varies. (Universitaet Wuerzburg, Institut fuer Wehrrecht) Holzner-Verlag, Neubaustr. 22, Postfach 130, 8700 Wuerzburg 1, W. Germany (B.R.D.)

340 US ISSN 0513-1405
YALE LAW SCHOOL STUDIES. 1950. irreg. Yale University, School of Law, New Haven, CT 06520. TEL 203-436-2211. Indexed: Leg.Per. C.L.I.

340 510.78 UK ISSN 0269-3712
YEARBOOK OF LAW COMPUTERS AND TECHNOLOGY. 1984. a. Butterworth & Co. (Publishers) Ltd., c/o John Lord, Promo. Mgt., 88 Kingsway, London WC2B 6AB, England. Ed. Christopher Arnold. bk. rev.

340 US
YEARBOOK OF SCHOOL LAW. 1972. a. price varies. National Organization on Legal Problems of Education, 3601 S.W. 29th, Ste. 223, Topeka, KS 66614. TEL 913-273-3550. circ. 3,000. Indexed: Educ.Ind.

YEARBOOK ON SOCIALIST LEGAL SYSTEMS. see POLITICAL SCIENCE

342 II
YEARLY SUPREME COURT DIGEST. (Supplement to Shree Krishan Agarwal's "Twenty-One Years Supreme Court Digest, 1950-1970") (Text in English) 1966. a. Rs.45. Law Book Co., Sardar Patel Marg, Box 4, Allahabad 1, India. Ed. S.K. Agarwal. circ. 2,600.

340 PL ISSN 0208-5003
Z PROBLEMATYKI PRAWA PRACY I POLITYKI SOCJALNEJ. (Text in Polish; summaries in French and Russian) 1977. irreg. Uniwersytet Slaski w Katowicach, Ul. Bankowa 14, 40-007 Katowice, Poland.

328.675 ZR
ZAIRE. CONSEIL LEGISLATIF NATIONAL. COMPTE RENDU ANALYTIQUE. 1972. irreg. Conseil Legislatif National, Kinshasa, Zaire.
Continues: Zaire. Assemblee Nationale. Compte Rendu Analytique.

345.01 ZA
ZAMBIA. DEPARTMENT OF LEGAL AID. ANNUAL REPORT. (Text in English) a. Government Printer, Box 30136, Lusaka, Zambia.

340 ZA
ZAMBIA. HIGH COURT. LAW DIRECTORY AND LEGAL CALENDAR. (Text in English) a. Government Printer, Box 30136, Lusaka, Zambia.

340 ZA
ZAMBIA LAW JOURNAL. (Text in English) 1969. a. K.10($12) University of Zambia, School of Law, Box 32379, Lusaka, Zambia. Ed. S. Mumba. adv. bk. rev. bibl. circ. 300.

348 ZA
ZAMBIA LAW REPORTS. 1963. a. Z.$15. Council of Law Reporting, Box 50067, Lusaka, Zambia. Ed. Margaret S. Sekaggya. cum.index. circ. 500.

340 SZ ISSN 0254-945X
ZEITSCHRIFT FUER SCHWEIZERISCHES RECHT/REVUE DE DROIT SUISSE. (Text in German and French) 1860. irreg. (8-10/yr.) 118 Fr. Helbing und Lichtenhahn Verlag AG, Freie Strasse 82, CH-4051 Basel, Switzerland (Subscr. to: Sauerlaender AG, Postfach, CH-5001 Aarau, Switzerland) Ed.Bd. bk. rev. index. cum.index every 10 yrs.

668 LAW — ABSTRACTING, BIBLIOGRAPHIES, STATISTICS

340 RH
ZIMBABWE LAW REVIEW. 1985. a. Z.$40. University of Zimbabwe, Department of Law, Box MP 167, Harare, Zimbabwe. Ed. R.H.F. Austin. adv. bk. rev. circ. 600.

340 352.7 US ISSN 0193-757X
ZONING LAW ANTHOLOGY. 1978. a. $99.95. Book Publishers, Inc., 7315 Wisconsin Ave., Ste. 229, Bethesda, MD 20814. Ed.Donald J. Hoyes.

LAW — Abstracting, Bibliographies, Statistics

A B C POL SCI; a bibliography of contents: political science and government. see *POLITICAL SCIENCE* — *Abstracting, Bibliographies, Statistics*

ABSTRACTS OF BULGARIAN SCIENTIFIC LITERATURE. ECONOMICS AND LAW. see *BUSINESS AND ECONOMICS* — *Abstracting, Bibliographies, Statistics*

347.788 US ISSN 0094-7504
ANNUAL STATISTICAL REPORT OF THE COLORADO JUDICIARY. 1970. a. $6. Office of the Court Administrator, 2 E. 14th Ave., Denver, CO 80203. Ed.Bd. circ. 1,100.

340 AU
AUSTRIA. STATISTISCHES ZENTRALAMT. STATISTIK DER RECHTSPFLEGE. a. S.380. Oesterreichische Staatsdruckerei, Rennweg 120, 1037 Vienna, Austria.

340 BE
BELGIUM. INSTITUT NATIONAL DE STATISTIQUE. STATISTIQUES JUDICIAIRES. irreg. 290 Fr. Institut National de Statistique, 44 rue de Louvain, 1000 Brussels, Belgium. Indexed: P.A.I.S.For.Lang.Ind.

340 016 BL ISSN 0067-6616
BIBLIOGRAFIA BRASILEIRA DE DIREITO. (Formerly issued in Bibliografia Brasileira de Ciencias Sociais) 1967. irreg. Cr.$600($25) Instituto Brasileiro de Informacao em Ciencia e Tecnologia, SCRN 708/709 Bloco B Loja 18E 30, 70740 Brasilia DF, Brazil. bk. rev. circ. 300.

340 016 US ISSN 0360-2745
BIBLIOGRAPHIC GUIDE TO LAW. 1975. a. G.K. Hall & Co., 70 Lincoln St., Boston, MA 02111. TEL 617-423-3990.
Formerly: Law Book Guide (ISSN 0146-3861)

349 016 SZ
BIBLIOGRAPHIE DES SCHWEIZERISCHEN RECHTS. (Text in French, German, Italian) a. price varies. Helbing und Lichtenhahn Verlag AG, Freie Strasse 82, CH-4051 Basel, Switzerland (Subscr. to: Sauerlaender AG, Postfach, CH-5001 Aarau, Switzerland) Ed. Alfred Muller. bibl. index. cum.index every 5 yrs.

340 016 FR
BIBLIOGRAPHIE EN LANGUE FRANCAISE D'HISTOIRE DU DROIT DE 987 A 1914. vol.13, 1975. a. (since 1962) price varies. (Centre National de la Recherche Scientifique) Faculte de Droit de Saint-Maur, c/o Mme. Boulet-Sautel, Universite de Paris II (Universite de Droit d'Economie et des Sciences Social), 12 pl. du Pantheon, 75005 Paris, France. Ed.Bd.
Formerly: Bibliographie en la Langue Francaise d'Histoire du Droit de 987 a 1875 (ISSN 0067-6985)

340 320 US ISSN 0742-6909
BIBLIOGRAPHIES AND INDEXES IN LAW AND POLITICAL SCIENCE. 1984. irreg. price varies. Greenwood Press, 88 Post Rd. W., Box 5007, Westport, CT 06881. TEL 203-226-3571.

016 US ISSN 0067-7329
BIBLIOGRAPHY ON FOREIGN AND COMPARATIVE LAW: BOOKS AND ARTICLES IN ENGLISH. 1953. quinquennial with a. supplements. price varies. (Columbia University, Parker School of Foreign and Comparative Law) Oceana Publications, Inc., Dobbs Ferry, NY 10522. TEL 914-693-1320. Ed. Charles Szladits.

340 US ISSN 0882-7052
BIO-BIBLIOGRAPHIES IN LAW AND POLITICAL SCIENCE. 1985. irreg. price varies. Greenwood Press, Box 5007, 88 Post Rd. W., Westport, CT 06881. TEL 203-226-3571.

340 016 US ISSN 0000-0752
BOWKER'S LAW BOOKS AND SERIALS IN PRINT. (Issued in 3 vols.) 1982. a. with Updates 10/yr. $425. R.R. Bowker Company, Database Publishing Group, 245 W. 17th St., New York, NY 10011. TEL 800-521-8110.
Formerly: Law Information (ISSN 0000-0701)

340 IT
CAMERA DEI DEPUTATI. NOTIZIARIO DI STATISTICHE. 1972. biennial. L.20000. Camera dei Deputati, Palazzo Montecitorio, Rome, Italy. TEL 67179307. circ. 1,200. (back issues avail.)

016 340 AT ISSN 0310-5415
CURRENT AUSTRALIAN AND NEW ZEALAND LEGAL LITERATURE INDEX. 1974. q. Aus.$75. Law Book Co. Ltd., 44-50 Waterloo Rd., North Ryde, N.S.W. 2112, Australia. Ed. Gwenda Fischer. abstr. bibl.

340 US ISSN 0196-1780
CURRENT LAW INDEX. m. with 3 q. and 1 a. cumulations. Information Access Company, 11 Davis Dr., Belmont, CA 94002. TEL 800-227-8431. (Co-sponsor: American Association of Law Libraries)

340 016 US ISSN 0011-3859
CURRENT PUBLICATIONS IN LEGAL AND RELATED FIELDS. 1953. m. (except Jun., Jul. & Sep.) plus annual cumulation. $115. (American Association of Law Libraries) Fred B. Rothman & Co., 10368 W. Centennial Rd., Littleton, CO 80127. TEL 303-979-5657. index. circ. 500. (back issues avail.)

347.9 IT ISSN 0419-4632
DIZIONARIO BIBLIOGRAFICO DELLE RIVISTE GIURIDICHE ITALIANE. 1956. a. price varies. Casa Editrice Dott. A. Giuffre, Via B. Arsizio 40, 20151 Milan, Italy. Ed. Vincenzo Napoletano.

318 PN ISSN 0378-259X
ESTADISTICA PANAMENA. SITUACION POLITICA, ADMINISTRATIVA Y JUSTICIA. SECCION 631. JUSTICIA. 1967. a. Bl.0.75. Direccion de Estadistica y Censo, Contraloria General, Apartado 5213, Panama 5, Panama. circ. 900.

340 016 FR ISSN 0252-0648
EXCHANGE OF INFORMATION ON RESEARCH IN EUROPEAN LAW/ECHANGE D'INFORMATIONS SUR LES RECHERCHES EN DROIT EUROPEEN. (Text in English & French) 1971. a. $6. Council of Europe, Directorate of Legal Affairs - Conseil de l'Europe, Publications Section, 67006 Strasbourg, France (Dist. in U.S. by: Manhattan Publishing Co., 80 Brook St., Box 650, Croton, NY, 10520)

331 340 GW ISSN 0173-1688
FUNDHEFT FUER ARBEITS- UND SOZIALRECHT; systematischer Nachweis der deutschen Rechtsprechung, Zeitschriftenaufsaetze und selbstaendigen Schriften. 1945. a. $228. C.H. Beck'sche Verlagsbuchhandlung, Wilhelmstr. 9, 8000 Munich 40, W. Germany (B.R.D.) Ed. Wolfgang Blomeyer. circ. 1,500.
Formerly (until 1977): Fundheft fuer Arbeitsrecht (ISSN 0071-9900)

340 314 GW ISSN 0072-1859
GERMANY (FEDERAL REPUBLIC, 1949-). STATISTISCHES BUNDESAMT. FACHSERIE 10. RECHTSPFLEGE. (Consists of several subseries) 1959. a. price varies. W. Kohlhammer-Verlag GmbH, Abt. Veroeffentlichungen des Statistischen Bundesamtes, Philipp-Reis-Str. 3, Postfach 421120, 6500 Mainz 42, W. Germany (B.R.D.)

I C E L REFERENCES; to publications concerning legal, administrative and policy aspects of environmental conservation. (International Council on Environmental Law) see *ENVIRONMENTAL STUDIES* — *Abstracting, Bibliographies, Statistics*

340 016 CH
INDEX TO CHINESE LEGAL PERIODICALS. 1970. a. $18. Soochow University, Wai Shuang Hsi, Taipei, Taiwan, Republic of China.

340 016 US ISSN 0019-400X
INDEX TO FOREIGN LEGAL PERIODICALS. (Subject headings in English with translation into French, German and Spanish included in a. cumulation) 1960. q. (a. cumulations) $350. (University of California, Berkeley, School of Law Library) University of California Press, 2120 Berkeley Way, Berkeley, CA 94720 (Subscr. address: American Association of Law Libraries, 53 W. Jackson Blvd., Ste. 703, Chicago, IL 60604) Ed. T.H. Reynolds. circ. 780.

340 016 US ISSN 0019-4077
INDEX TO LEGAL PERIODICALS. 1908. m. (Oct.-Aug.) (q. and a. cumulations) $130. ‡ H.W. Wilson Co., 950 University Ave., Bronx, NY 10452. TEL 212-588-8400. Ed. Stephen Rosen. (avail. on CD-ROM) Indexed: C.L.I.
●Also available online. Vendors: Mead Data Central, Wilsonline.

340 016 US ISSN 0019-4093
INDEX TO PERIODICAL ARTICLES RELATED TO LAW; selected journals not included in the Index to Legal Periodicals. 1959. q. $35. Glanville Publishers, Inc., 75 Main St., Dobbs Ferry, NY 10522. TEL 914-693-5956. Eds. Roy M. Mersky, J. Myron Jacobstein. cum.index: 1959-1985. circ. 250.

340 010 SP
INSTITUTO INTERNACIONAL DE HISTORIA DEL DERECHO INDIANO. ACTAS Y ESTUDIOS. a. 1500 ptas. Instituto Nacional de Estudios Juridicos, Duque de Medinacelli St., No. 8, Madrid, Spain.
History

340 016 CN
INTERNATIONAL OMBUDSMAN INSTITUTE BIBLIOGRAPHY. a. (cum. vol. every 5 yrs.) $75. International Ombudsman Institute, Faculty of Law, University of Alberta, Edmonton, Alta. T6G 2H5, Canada. TEL 403-432-3196.
●Available only online.

340 IT ISSN 0392-7571
ISTITUTO PER LA DOCUMENTAZIONE GIURIDICA. BIBLIOGRAFIA. DIRITTO CIVILE. 1979. a. L.23000. Giuffre Editore, Via Busto Arsizio 40, 20151 Milan, Italy. Ed. Mario Ragona. circ. 400.

340 IT
ISTITUTO PER LA DOCUMENTAZIONE GIURIDICA. BIBLIOGRAFIA. DIRITTO INTERNAZIONALE; rassegna automatica di dottrina giuridica. a. Istituto per la Documentazione Giuridica, Via Panciatichi, 56/16, 50127 Florence, Italy (Subscr. to: Casa Editrice Giuffre, Via Statuto, 2, 20121 Milan, Italy) Ed.Bd.

340 362.7 US ISSN 0733-8937
KINDEX; an index to legal periodical literature concerning children. 1976. a. $25. National Center for Juvenile Justice, 701 Forbes Ave., Pittsburgh, PA 15219. TEL 412-227-6950. Ed. Cathy Gable. index. circ. 300. (back issues avail.)

340 016 US ISSN 0279-5787
LEGAL CONTENTS; semi-monthly compilation of tables of contents from more than 320 business magazines and journals. 1972. s-mw. $95. Find-S V P, 500 Fifth Ave., New York, NY 10110. TEL 212-354-2424. Ed. Karen O'Connor. adv. circ. 1,000. (also avail. in microform from UMI; reprint service avail. from UMI)
●Also available online. Vendors: DIALOG.
Former titles (until 1980): C C L P: Contents of Current Legal Periodicals (ISSN 0147-0493); Until 1976: Contents of Current Legal Periodicals (ISSN 0300-7391); Incorporating: Survey of Law Reviews (ISSN 0360-7372)

340 US
LEGAL RESOURCE INDEX. m. Information Access Company, 11 Davis Dr., Belmont, CA 94002. TEL 800-227-8431. (Co-sponsor: American Association of Law Libraries) (microfilm)
●Also available online. Vendors: BRS, DIALOG, Mead Data Central.

011 341   CN   ISSN 0226-8361
MARINE AFFAIRS BIBLIOGRAPHY; a
comprehensive index to marine law and policy
literature. (Text in French, German, Italian and
Spanish) 1980. q. Can.$95($95) Dalhousie Law
Library, Dalhousie University, Halifax, N.S. B3H
4H9, Canada. Eds. Christian L. Wiktor, Leslie A.
Foster. circ. 350.

347   US   ISSN 0098-7875
MICHIGAN. STATE COURT ADMINISTRATOR.
ANNUAL REPORT. (Supplement avail.) 1961. a.
State Court Administrative Office, Box 30048,
Lansing, MI 48909. TEL 517-373-0130. circ. 1,500.
Key Title: Judicial Statistics.

347   US
NORTH DAKOTA. JUDICIAL CONFERENCE.
ANNUAL REPORT. 1928. a. free. Judicial
Council, State Capitol, Bismarck, ND 58505. TEL
701-224-4216. Ed. William G. Bohn. stat. circ. 1,
000(controlled)
    Former titles: North Dakota. Judicial Council.
Annual Report & North Dakota. Judicial Council.
Statistical Compilation and Report (ISSN 0095-
6120)

340 016   US
PIMSLEUR'S CHECKLIST OF BASIC AMERICAN
LEGAL PUBLICATIONS. irreg. price varies.
(American Association of Law Libraries) Fred B.
Rothman & Co., 10368 W. Centennial Rd.,
Littleton, CO 80123. TEL 303-979-5657. Ed.
Marcia S. Zubrow. (looseleaf format)
    Formerly: Checklist of Basic American Legal
Publications.

016 340   SZ   ISSN 0250-5940
RECHTSBIBLIOGRAPHIE/BIBLIOGRAPHIE
JURIDIQUE/LAW BIBLIOGRAPHY. (In 2 vols.:
Vol.1 Switzerland; Vol.2 Austria, Liechtenstein)
1978. a. 33 Fr. per vol. Studio Verlag, CH-8023
Zurich, Switzerland. Ed. N. Mario Cerutti. bk. rev.
circ. 5,000. (also avail. in microfiche)

340 016   GE   ISSN 0081-3680
SPEZIALBIBLIOGRAPHIEN ZU FRAGEN DES
STAATES UND DES RECHTS. 1963. irreg. price
varies. Akademie fuer Staats- und
Rechtswissenschaft der DDR, Informationszentrum
Staat und Recht, August-Bebel-Str. 89, 1502
Potsdam-Babelsberg, E. Germany (D.D.R.)

340   SW   ISSN 0082-0318
SWEDEN. STATISTISKA CENTRALBYRAAN.
STATISTISKA MEDDELANDEN. SUBGROUP R
(JUDICIAL STATISTICS. LAW AND SOCIAL
WELFARE) (Text in Swedish; table heads and
summaries in English) 1963 N.S. irreg. Kr.320.
Statistiska Centralbyraan, Distribution, S-701 89
Oerebro, Sweden. circ. 1,400.

340   US
UNIVERSITY OF SOUTHERN CALIFORNIA.
LAW CENTER. BIBLIOGRAPHY SERIES. irreg.
University of Southern California, Law Center, Los
Angeles, CA 90089-0071. TEL 213-743-6366.

016 340   US   ISSN 0085-7092
UNIVERSITY OF TEXAS, AUSTIN. TARLTON
LAW LIBRARY. LEGAL BIBLIOGRAPHY
SERIES. 1970. irreg., no.29, 1985. price varies.
University of Texas at Austin, Tarlton Law Library,
727 E. 26 St., Austin, TX 78705-5799. TEL 512-
471-7726. bibl. (processed)

LAW — Computer Applications

340 026   FR
COUNCIL OF EUROPE. SYMPOSIUM ON
LEGAL PROCESSING. PROCEEDINGS. no.5,
1979. irreg. price varies. Council of Europe,
Publications Section, Strasbourg, France (Dist. in
U.S. by: Manhattan Publishing Co., 225 Lafayette
St., New York, NY 10012)

364 658.478   US
DIRECTORY OF CRIMINAL JUSTICE
INFORMATION SOURCES. 1972. biennial. U.S.
Department of Justice, National Institute of Justice,
National Criminal Justice Reference Service, Box
6000, Rockville, MD 20850. TEL 301-251-5500.
(also avail. in microfiche)
    Formerly: Directory of Automated Criminal
Justice Information Systems.

340 621.381 001.642   US
LAW OFFICE GUIDE IN COMPUTERS (YEAR)
DIRECTORY. 1984. a. $110. Rey R. Montez, Ed.
& Pub., 3315 Sacramento, Ste. 407, San Franscisco,
CA 94118. TEL 415-927-1747.

YEARBOOK OF LAW COMPUTERS AND
TECHNOLOGY. see LAW

LAW — International Law

341   US   ISSN 0272-5045
AMERICAN SOCIETY OF INTERNATIONAL
LAW. PROCEEDINGS OF THE ANNUAL
MEETING. 1907. a. $15. American Society of
International Law, 2223 Massachusetts Ave. N.W.,
Washington, DC 20008-2864. TEL 202-265-4313.
index. cum.index: 1907-1920, 1921-1940, 1941-
1960, 1961-1970, 1971-1980. (also avail. in
microform from UMI) Indexed: Hist.Abstr.
Leg.Per. Amer.Hist.& Life. C.L.I. L.R.I.
Mar.Aff.Bibl.
    Formerly (until 1974): American Society of
International Law. Proceedings (ISSN 0066-0647)

341 323.4   FR
ANNEE AFRICAINE. 1963. a. price varies. Editions
A. Pedone, 13 rue Soufflot, 75005 Paris, France.
Ed. A. Pedone.

341   FR   ISSN 0066-3085
ANNUAIRE FRANCAIS DE DROIT
INTERNATIONAL. 1955. a. price varies.
(Academie de Droit International de la Haye,
Groupe Francais des Anciens Auditeurs, NE)
Editions du C N R S, 295 rue St. Jacques, 75005
Paris, France.

341   SP
ANUARIO DE DERECHO INTERNACIONAL.
1975. a. 2500 ptas.($30) (Universidad de Navarra,
Departamento de Derecho Internacional) Ediciones
Universidad de Navarra, S.A., Apdo. 396, 31080
Pamplona, Spain. Dir. Jose Antonio Corriente
Cordoba. bk. rev.

ANUARIO DE HISTORIA DEL DERECHO
ESPANOL. see HISTORY — History Of Europe

341   EC   ISSN 0570-4251
ANUARIO ECUATORIANO DE DERECHO
INTERNACIONAL. 1964. a. $15. Universidad
Central del Ecuador, Instituto de Investigaciones
Internationales, Apdo. 9078, Quito, Ecuador. Ed.
Mario A. Gomez de la Torre. bk. rev. circ. 2,000.

341   US
ANUARIO INTERAMERICANO DE DERECHOS
HUMANOS/INTER-AMERICAN YEARBOOK
ON HUMAN RIGHTS. (Text in English and
Spanish) biennial. $15. (Inter-American Commission
on Human Rights) Organization of American States,
Department of Publications, Washington, DC
20006. TEL 202-789-3533.

341   NE   ISSN 0066-8923
ASSOCIATION OF ATTENDERS AND ALUMNI
OF THE HAGUE ACADEMY OF
INTERNATIONAL LAW. YEARBOOK. 1925. a.
price varies. (Association of Attenders and Alumni
of the Hague Academy of International Law)
Martinus Nijhoff Publishers, Postbus 163, 3300 AD
Dordrecht, Netherlands.

341.18   FR   ISSN 0519-3125
ATLANTIC MAIL.* irreg. Atlantic Treaty
Association, c/o Jean de Madre, 185 rue de la
Pompe, 75116 Paris, France.

ATMA JAYA RESEARCH CENTRE.
INTERNATIONAL CONTRACT LABOUR. see
BUSINESS AND ECONOMICS — Labor And
Industrial Relations

341   GW
AUGSBURGER SCHRIFTEN ZUM STAATS- UND
VOELKERRECHT. 1975. irreg. Verlag Peter Lang
GmbH, Hinter den Ulmen 19, D-6000 Frankfurt/
Main 50, W. Germany (B.R.D.) Ed. Dieter
Blumenwitz.

341.2   AT
AUSTRALIAN TREATY SERIES. irreg. price varies.
Australian Government Publishing Service, G.P.O.
Box 84, Canberra, A.C.T. 2601, Australia.
    Formerly: Australian Treaty List.

341   AT   ISSN 0084-7658
AUSTRALIAN YEARBOOK OF
INTERNATIONAL LAW. 1965. irreg. price on
application. Butterworths Pty. Ltd., 271-273 Lane
Cove Rd., North Ryde, N.S.W. 2113, Australia
(Dist. in U.S. by: Oceana Publications, Inc., Dobbs
Ferry, NY 10522) Indexed: Leg.Per. C.L.I. L.R.I.
Mar.Aff.Bibl.

BAILRIGG PAPERS ON INTERNATIONAL
SECURITY. see POLITICAL SCIENCE —
International Relations

341   US   ISSN 0172-4770
BEITRAEGE ZUM AUSLAENDISCHEN
OEFFENTLICHEN RECHT UND
VOELKERRECHT. (Text mainly in German)
vol.86, 1984. irreg., vol.91, 1986. price varies.
Springer-Verlag, 175 Fifth Ave., New York, NY
10010 TEL 212-460-1500. (Also Berlin, Heidelberg,
Tokyo and Vienna) (reprint service avail. from ISI)

341   US   ISSN 0068-2195
BRITISH INTERNATIONAL LAW CASES; a
collection of decisions of courts in the British Isles
on points of international law. 1964. irreg., no.9,
1973. price varies. (International Law Fund) Oceana
Publications Inc., Dobbs Ferry, NY 10522. TEL
914-693-1320. (Co-sponsor: British Institute of
Foreign and Comparative Law) Ed. C. Parry.

341.058   UK   ISSN 0068-2691
BRITISH YEAR BOOK OF INTERNATIONAL
LAW. 1920? a. £55($120) (Royal Institute of
International Affairs, UK) Oxford University Press,
Walton St., Oxford OX2 6DP, England (U.S.
address: 200 Madison Ave., New York, NY 10016)
Eds. D.W. Bowett, I. Brownlie. adv. bk. rev. index.
Indexed: Leg.Per. C.L.I. L.R.I.

341   BE
C E E INTERNATIONAL. DROIT ET AFFAIRES.
a. 10500 Fr. (Communaute Economique
Europeenne - European Communities)
Etablissements Emile Bruylant, 67 rue de la
Regence, 1000 Brussels, Belgium.

341.7   NE
CAHIERS DE DROIT FISCAL INTERNATIONAL.
1939. a. price varies. International Fiscal
Association, c/o General Secretariat, Box 1738,
Burg. Oudlaan 50, 3000 DR Rotterdam,
Netherlands (Subscr. addr.: Kluwer Publishers Law
and Taxation, Box 23 7400 GA Deventer,
Netherlands)

341 323.4   CN
CANADA. INFORMATION COMMISSIONER.
ANNUAL REPORT. (Text in English and French)
1983. a., latest 1984/85. free. Information
Commissioner, 112 Kent St., Ste. 1400, Ottawa, Ont
K1A 1H3, Canada. TEL 613-995-2410. stat. circ. 7,
000. (back issues avail)

CANADA. PRIVACY COMMISSIONER. ANNUAL
REPORT. see COMPUTERS — Computer Security

341   US   ISSN 0163-6391
CANADA-UNITED STATES LAW JOURNAL.
(Text in English and French) 1978. a. $6. Case
Western Reserve University, School of Law, 11075
East Blvd., Cleveland, OH 44106. TEL 216-368-
3291. adv. bk. rev. circ. 650. (also avail. in
microfilm from WSH) Indexed: Leg.Per. P.A.I.S.
Abstr.Bk.Rev.Curr.Leg.Per. C.L.I. Foreign Leg.Per.
L.R.I.

341   CN   ISSN 0069-0058
CANADIAN YEARBOOK OF INTERNATIONAL
LAW/ANNUAIRE CANADIEN DE DROIT
INTERNATIONAL. (Editions in English and
French) 1963. a. price varies. University of British
Columbia Press, 303-6344 Memorial Rd.,
Vancouver, B.C. V6T 1W5, Canada. TEL 604-228-
3259. Ed. C.B. Bourne. bk. rev. Indexed: Leg.Per.
Amer.Bibl.Slavic & E.Eur.Stud. Can.Ind. C.L.I.
Foreign Leg.Per. L.R.I. Mar.Aff.Bibl.

LAW — INTERNATIONAL LAW

341.11   BE   ISSN 0503-2407
COLLECTION OF DOCUMENTS FOR THE STUDY OF INTERNATIONAL NON-GOVERNMENTAL RELATIONS. Alternate title: Union of International Associations. Documents. (Text in English or French) 1956. irreg. Union of International Associations, c/o Robert Fenaux, Rue Washington 40, 1050 Brussels, Belgium.

COLLOQUIUM ON THE LAW OF OUTER SPACE. PROCEEDINGS. see *AERONAUTICS AND SPACE FLIGHT*

COMMISSION OF THE EUROPEAN COMMUNITIES. COLLECTION OF AGREEMENTS. see *BUSINESS AND ECONOMICS — International Commerce*

341.18   EI   ISSN 0590-6563
COMMISSION OF THE EUROPEAN COMMUNITIES. COMMUNITY LAW. (Editions also in Dutch, French, German, Italian) 1968. a. free. Commission of the European Communities, Service de Renseignement et de Diffusion des Documents, Rue de la Loi 200, 1049 Brussels, Belgium.
Extracts from its General Report on the Activities of the Communities

341.11   EI   ISSN 0591-1745
COMMISSION OF THE EUROPEAN COMMUNITIES. DIRECTORY. 1968. irreg. price varies. Office for Official Publications of the European Communities, P.O. Box 1003, L-2985 Luxembourg, Luxembourg (Dist. in the U.S. by: European Community Information Service, 2100 M St., N.W., Ste. 707, Washington, DC 20037)

341.18   FR   ISSN 0070-105X
COUNCIL OF EUROPE. EUROPEAN TREATY SERIES. (Text in English and French) 1949. irreg., no.124, 1986. $5. Council of Europe, Publications Section, Strasbourg, France (Dist. in U.S. by: Manhattan Publishing Co., 80 Brook St., Box 650, Croton-on-Hudson, NY 10520)

341.18   FR   ISSN 0252-0656
COUNCIL OF EUROPE. PARLIAMENTARY ASSEMBLY. DOCUMENTS; WORKING PAPERS/DOCUMENTS DE SEANCE. (Text in English and French) 1949. a. $24 per vol. Council of Europe, Parliamentary Assembly, Publications Section, F 67006 Strasbourg, France (Dist. in U.S. by Manhattan Publishing Co., Box 650, Croton-on-Hudson, NY 10520)
Continues (since vol.26, pt.3, 1974): Council of Europe. Consultative Assembly. Documents; Working Papers/Documents de Seance (ISSN 0070-1009)

341.8   FR   ISSN 0252-0664
COUNCIL OF EUROPE. PARLIAMENTARY ASSEMBLY. OFFICIAL REPORT OF DEBATES. (Text in English or French) 1949. a. (in 3 vols.) $24 per vol. Council of Europe, Parliamentary Assembly, Publications Section, F 67006 Strasbourg, France (Dist. in U.S. by: Manhattan Publishing Co., 80 Brook St., Box 650, Croton-on-Hudson, NY 10520)

341.18   FR   ISSN 0377-6093
COUNCIL OF EUROPE. PARLIAMENTARY ASSEMBLY. TEXTS ADOPTED BY THE ASSEMBLY/TEXTES ADOPTES PAR L'ASSEMBLEE. (Text in English and French) 1949. a. (in 3 vols.) $6.25 per vol. Council of Europe, Parliamentary Assembly, Publications Section, F 67006 Strasbourg, France (Dist. in U.S. by: Manhattan Publishing Co., 80 Brook St., Box 650, Croton-on-Hudson, NY 10520)
Continues (since 1974): Council of Europe. Consultative Assembly. Texts Adopted by the Assembly/Textes Adoptes Par l'Assemblee (ISSN 0070-1033)

341   EI
COURT OF JUSTICE OF THE EUROPEAN COMMUNITIES. REPORT OF CASES OF THE COURT. (Text in Dutch, English, French, German, Italian) 1954. a. Office for Official Publications of the European Communities, P.O. Box 1003, L-2985 Luxembourg, Luxembourg (Dist. in the U.S. by: European Community Information Service, 2100 M St., N.W., Ste. 707, Washington, DC 20037)
Court of Justice of the European Communities. Recueil de la Jurisprudence (ISSN 0070-1386)

341   UY
CUADERNOS DE DERECHO INTERNACIONAL PRIVADO. 1975. irreg. Fundacion de Cultura Universitaria, 25 de Mayo no. 568, Casilla de Correo No. 1155, Montevideo, Uruguay.

341.2   US   ISSN 0731-8189
CURRENT TREATY INDEX; a cumulative index to the United States slip treaties and agreements. 1982. a. $49.50. William S. Hein & Co., Inc., 1285 Main St., Buffalo, NY 14209 TEL 800-828-7571. Eds. Igor I. Kavass, Adolf Sprudzs. circ. 400.

341.18 330   EI   ISSN 0071-3015
DEBATES OF THE EUROPEAN PARLIAMENT. 1958. irreg. price varies. (European Parliament) Office for Official Publications of the European Communities, P.O. Box 1003, L-2985 Luxembourg, Luxembourg (Dist. in the U.S. by: European Community Information Service, 2100 M St., N.W., Ste. 707, Washington, DC 20037) (also avail. in microfiche)

341.57 382   US   ISSN 0419-1285
DIGEST OF COMMERCIAL LAWS OF THE WORLD. 1968. irreg. $850. (National Association of Credit Management) Oceana Publications, Inc., Dobbs Ferry, NY 10522. TEL 914-693-1320. Ed. Lester Nelson. bibl. (looseleaf format)

341   US   ISSN 0095-3369
DIGEST OF THE UNITED STATES PRACTICE IN INTERNATIONAL LAW. 1973. a. $11. U.S. Department of State, 2201 C St. N.W., Washington, DC 20250 TEL 202-634-3600. (Orders to: Supt. of Documents, Washington, DC 20402)

341.18   EI   ISSN 0250-5754
E P NEWS. (Editions in Danish, Dutch, French, German, Greek and Italian) 1967. irreg.; issued in relation to its sessions. free. European Parliament, Secretariat, Centre Europeen, Case Postale 1601, Luxembourg, Luxembourg. Ed. P. Davis. bk. rev. circ. 25,000.
Formerly (until 1979): European Parliament News (ISSN 0531-4321)

341.4   UA   ISSN 0080-259X
EGYPTIAN REVIEW OF INTERNATIONAL LAW/REVUE EGYPTIENNE DE DROIT INTERNATIONAL. (Text in Arabic, English, French) 1945. a. $30. Egyptian Society of International Law, 16 Ramses St., Cairo, Egypt (Dist. by Oceana Publications, Inc., Dobbs Ferry, NY 10522) Ed. Waheed Raafat. bk. rev. cum.index: 1945-49. Indexed: A.B.C.Pol.Sci. Mar.Aff.Bibl.

341.1   FR   ISSN 0589-9575
EUROPEAN CO-OPERATION. irreg. Council of Europe, Publications Section, 67000 Strasbourg, France (Dist. in U.S. by: Manhattan Publishing Co., Box 650, Croton-on-Hudson, NY 10520)

341.18   EI
EUROPEAN PARLIAMENT. WORKING DOCUMENTS. 1958. irreg. price varies. Office for Official Publications of the European Communities, P.O. Box 1003, L-2985 Luxembourg, Luxembourg (Dist. in the U.S. by: European Community Information Service, 2100 M St., N.W., Ste. 707, Washington, DC 20037) (also avail. in microfiche)
Formerly: European Parliament. Documents de Seance (ISSN 0071-3023)

341   US   ISSN 0426-7230
FONTES IURIS GENTIUM. SECTION 2. (Text in English, French and German) irreg. price varies. Springer-Verlag, 175 Fifth Ave., New York, NY 10010 TEL 212-460-1500. (Also Berlin, Heidelberg, Tokyo and Vienna) Eds. H. Mosler, R. Bernhardt. (reprint service avail. from ISI)
Supersedes in part: Fontes Iuris Gentium (ISSN 0428-903X)

341   FR   ISSN 0071-8971
FRANCE. MINISTERE DES AFFAIRES ETRANGERES. RECUEIL DES TRAITES ET ACCORDS DE LA FRANCE. 1961. a. price varies. Ministere des Affaires Etrangeres, 37, Quai d'Orsay, 75700 Paris, France.

341   GW
DAS GELTENDE SEEVOELKERRECHT IN EINZELDARSTELLUNGEN. 1970. irreg., vol.11, 1979. price varies. (Universitaet Hamburg, Institut fuer Internationale Angelegenheiten) Nomos Verlagsgesellschaft mbH und Co. KG, Walderstr. 3-5, Postfach 610, 7570 Baden-Baden, W. Germany (B.R.D.)
Formerly: Geltende Seekriegsrecht in Einzeldarstellungen (ISSN 0435-1924)

341   GW   ISSN 0344-3094
GERMAN YEARBOOK OF INTERNATIONAL LAW. 1948. a. price varies. (Universitaet Kiel, Institut fuer Internationales Recht) Duncker und Humblot GmbH, Dietrich-Schaefer-Weg 9, Postfach 410329, 1000 Berlin 41, W. Germany (B.R.D.) Indexed: Hist.Abstr. Amer.Hist.& Life.
Formerly: Jahrbuch fuer Internationales Recht (ISSN 0021-3993)

341   UN
GILBERTO AMADO MEMORIAL LECTURE. 1972. a. (United Nations International Law Commission) United Nations International Law Seminar, Secretary, Palais des Nations, CH-1211 Geneva 10, Switzerland. circ. 500.

341   NE   ISSN 0072-9272
HAGUE CONFERENCE ON PRIVATE INTERNATIONAL LAW. ACTES ET DOCUMENTS. (Text in English and French) 1893. quadrennial since 1951; latest 1985. price varies. Hague Conference on Private International Law, Permanent Bureau, Javastraat 2C, The Hague, Netherlands. circ. 1,000.

HAMBURGER OEFFENTLICH-RECHTLICHE NEBENSTUNDEN. see *LAW*

341   NE
I F A SEMINAR SERIES. 1976. a. price varies. International Fiscal Association, c/o General Secretariat, Box 1738, Burg. Oudlaan 50, 3000 DR Rotterdam, Netherlands (Subscr. address: Kluwer Publishers Law and Taxation, Box 23, 7400 GA Deventer, Netherlands)

341   SZ
INSTITUT FUER INTERNATIONALES RECHT UND INTERNATIONALE BEZIEHUNGEN. SCHRIFTENREIHE. (Text mainly in German; occasionally in English or French) 1939. irreg. price varies. Helbing und Lichtenhahn Verlag AG, Freie Strasse 82, CH-4051 Basel, Switzerland (Subscr. to: Sauerlaender AG, Postfach, CH-5001 Aarau, Switzerland)

INTERNATIONAL BOUNDARY STUDY. see *GEOGRAPHY*

INTERNATIONAL CENTRE FOR SETTLEMENT OF INVESTMENT DISPUTES. ANNUAL REPORT. see *BUSINESS AND ECONOMICS — Investments*

341   UN   ISSN 0074-445X
INTERNATIONAL COURT OF JUSTICE. YEARBOOK/ANNUAIRE. (Editions in English and French) 1946/47. a., latest vol.38, 1983/84. price varies. International Court of Justice, Peace Palace, 2517 KJ The Hague, Netherlands (Or United Nations Publications, New York, NY 10017; or Distribution and Sales Section, Palais des Nations, CH-12 Geneva, Switzerland) Ed.Bd. circ. 2,000.

341.7   NE
INTERNATIONAL FISCAL ASSOCIATION. YEARBOOK. a. membership. International Fiscal Association, c/o General Secretariat, P.O. Box 1738, Burg. Oudlaan 50, 3000 DR Rotterdam, Netherlands.

341   US
INTERNATIONAL LAW ASSOCIATION. AMERICAN BRANCH. PROCEEDINGS. biennial. $35. International Law Association, American Branch, c/o P. Nicholas Kourides, Chase Manhattan Bank, N.A., One Chase Manhattan Plaza, 29th Fl., New York, NY 10081. Ed. Theordore Giuttari. bibl. circ. 650.

341 UK ISSN 0074-6738
INTERNATIONAL LAW ASSOCIATION.
REPORTS OF CONFERENCES. (Text in English; some papers in French) 1875. biennial; 61st. 1984. Paris. price varies. International Law Association, 3 Paper Bldgs., The Temple, London EC4Y 7EU, England. cum.index: 1873-1972. circ. 4,000. Indexed: Leg.Per. C.L.I.
Formerly: Association Internationale du Droit Commercial. Et du Droit Affaires. Groupe Francais. Travaux (ISSN 0571-5873)

341 UN
INTERNATIONAL LAW COMMISSION YEARBOOK. (Issued in 2 vols.) (Text in English) 1949. a., latest 1984. price varies. United Nations Publications, Room DC2-853, New York, NY 10017 (Or Distribution and Sales Section, Palais des Nations, CH-1211 Geneva 10, Switzerland) (also avail. in microfiche)
Fomerly (until 1982): International Law Commission. Yearbook (ISSN 0082-8289)

341 CN
INTERNATIONAL MARITIME LAW SEMINAR. PUBLICATION. 1979. irreg., 3rd 1986. price varies. Continuing Legal Education Society of B.C., 200-1148 Hornby St., Vancouver, B.C. V6Z 2C3, Canada TEL 604-669-3544. (Subscr. addr.: Lloyd's of London, Sheepen Place, Colchester, Essex CO3 3LP, England) Ed. Karen M. Imeson. circ. 500. (looseleaf format; back issues avail.)

341 GW ISSN 0020-9503
INTERNATIONALES RECHT UND DIPLOMATIE. (Text mainly in German with quotations from other languages) 1956. irreg. DM.35($14) Verlag Wissenschaft und Politik Berend von Nottbeck, Salierring 14, 5000 Cologne 1, W. Germany (B.R.D) Ed. Boris Meissner. adv. bk. rev. index. cum.index. circ. 1,000. Indexed: Hist.Abstr. Amer.Hist.& Life.

341 IT
ISTITUTO DI STUDI E DOCUMENTAZIONI SULL'EST EUROPEO. SERIE GIURIDICA. 1969. irreg., latest issue no.6. price varies. Istituto di Studi e Documentazione sull'Est Europeo, Corso Italia 27, 34122 Trieste, Italy. circ. 700.

341 IT
ITALIAN YEARBOOK OF INTERNATIONAL LAW.* 1975. a. $25. Editoriale Scientifica (Naples), Via Chiatamone 606, 80121 Naples, Italy (Subscr. to: Oceana Publications, Inc., Dobbs Ferry, N.Y. 10522) Indexed: Mar.Aff.Bibl.

341 UK ISSN 0075-6040
KIME'S INTERNATIONAL LAW DIRECTORY. 1892. a. £21($30) Kime's International Law Directory, Ltd, 170 Sloane St., London SW1X 9QG, England. Ed. James M. Matthews. index.

341.57 380.5 FR
LAMY TRANSPORT. a. 1427 F.($206) Lamy S.A., 155 rue Legendre, 75850 Paris Cedex 17, France. Ed.Bd. bk. rev. tr.lit. index.

341 FR ISSN 0085-2686
LANGUE INTERNATIONALE. 1950. a. 20 F. ‡ Societe Idiste Francaise, c/o Georges Moureaux, Ed., 18 rue Emile Ecuyer, 01100 Oyonnax, France. bk. rev. (processed)

340 NE ISSN 0075-823X
LAW IN EASTERN EUROPE. (Text in English) 1958. irreg., no.30, 1985. price varies. (Rijksuniversiteit te Leiden, Documentation Office for East European Law) Martinus Nijhoff Publishers, Postbus 163, 3300 AD Dordrecht, Netherlands. Ed. F.J. Feldbrugge. index. circ. 900.

LAW REPRINTS: TRADE REGULATION SERIES. see BUSINESS AND ECONOMICS — International Commerce

LECCIONES Y ENSAYOS. see LAW

341 NE
LEGAL ASPECTS OF INTERNATIONAL ORGANIZATION. 1983. irreg. Kluwer Academic Publishers Group, Distribution Center, Box 322, 3300 AH Dordrecht, Netherlands.

341.44 US ISSN 0092-6426
LIMITS IN THE SEAS. (Subseries of International Boundary Study) irreg., no.101, 1984. free. ‡ U.S. Department of State, Office of the Geographer, c/o Bureau of Intelligence and Research, 2201 C St. N.W., Washington, DC 20520. TEL 202-632-2250.

341.2 MW ISSN 0076-3357
MALAWI TREATY SERIES. (Text in English) a, latest 1970/71. K.0.60. Government Printer, Box 37, Zomba, Malawi. Ed. James S. Friedlander. cum.index (1964-69)

341 610 US
MEDICOLEGAL LIBRARY. 1984. irreg., vol.6, 1985. price varies. Springer-Verlag, 175 Fifth Ave., New York, NY 10010 TEL 212-460-1500. (Also Berlin, Heidelberg, Tokyo, Vienna) (reprint service avail. from ISI)

341 UK
MELLAND SCHILL MONOGRAPHS IN INTERNATIONAL LAW. 1961; N.S. 1984. irreg. price varies. ‡ Manchester University Press, Oxford Rd., Manchester M13 9PL, England. Ed. G.M. White.
Formerly: Melland Schill Lectures on International Law (ISSN 0076-6313)

341 NE
NETHERLANDS YEARBOOK OF INTERNATIONAL LAW. (Text in English) 1970. a. 120. (T.M.C. Asser Institute) Martinus Nijhoff Publishers, Postbus 163, 3300 AD Dordrecht, Netherlands. Ed. Ko Swan Sik. bk. rev. bibl. circ. 750. Indexed: Foreign Leg.Per. Mar.Aff.Bibl.

OCEAN DUMPING CONTROL ACT ANNUAL REPORT. see ENVIRONMENTAL STUDIES

ORGANIZATION OF AMERICAN STATES. PERMANENT COUNCIL. DECISIONS TAKEN AT MEETINGS (CUMULATED EDITION) see HISTORY — History Of North And South America

341 PH
PHILIPPINE YEARBOOK OF INTERNATIONAL LAW. vol.3, 1974. a. P.18($7) Philippine Society of International Law, University of the Philippines, College of Law, Diliman, Quezon City, Philippines. Ed. Esteban B. Bautista. bibl. stat. Indexed: Leg.Per. C.L.I. Ind.Phil.Per. Mar.Aff.Bibl.

341 PL ISSN 0554-498X
POLISH YEARBOOK OF INTERNATIONAL LAW/ANNUAIRE POLONAIS DE DROIT INTERNATIONAL. (Text in English and French) 1966/67. a. price varies. (Polska Akademia Nauk, Instytut Nauk Prawnych) Ossolineum, Publishing House of the Polish Academy of Sciences, Rynek 9, Wroclaw, Poland (Dist. by: Ars Polona-Ruch, Krakowskie Przedmiescie 7, Warsaw, Poland) Ed. Janusz Symonides.

341 327 US ISSN 0079-5267
PRINCETON UNIVERSITY. CENTER OF INTERNATIONAL STUDIES POLICY MEMORANDUM. 1952. irreg., no.41, 1982. ‡ Princeton University, Center of International Studies, Princeton, NJ 08544. TEL 609-452-4851. (reprint service avail. from UMI)

PRINCETON UNIVERSITY. CENTER OF INTERNATIONAL STUDIES. RESEARCH MONOGRAPH SERIES. see POLITICAL SCIENCE — International Relations

PRIVATE INVESTORS ABROAD; problems and solutions in international business. see BUSINESS AND ECONOMICS — Investments

341 NE
PROBLEMS IN PRIVATE INTERNATIONAL LAW. 1977. irreg., vol.3, 1982. price varies. Elsevier Science Publishers B.V., Box 211, 1000 AE Amsterdam, Netherlands.

341 US
PROCEDURAL ASPECTS OF INTERNATIONAL LAW. irreg. price varies. University Press of Virginia, Box 3608 University Sta., Charlottesville, VA 22903. TEL 804-924-3468.

341 551.46 NE
PUBLICATIONS ON OCEAN DEVELOPMENT; a series of studies on the international, legal, institutional and policy aspects of the ocean development. (Text in English) 1976. irreg. price varies. Martinus Nijhoff Publishers, Postbus 163, 3300 AD Dordrecht, Netherlands. Ed. Shigeru Oda.
Formerly: Sijthoff Publications on Ocean Development.

340 341 GW
RECHTSSTAAT IN DER BEWAEHRUNG. 1975. irreg. price varies. C.F. Mueller Juristischer Verlag GmbH, Im Weiher 10, Postfach 102640, 6900 Heidelberg 1, W. Germany (B.R.D.)

SAMOAN PACIFIC LAW JOURNAL. see LAW

341 GW
SCHMERZENSGELD-BETRAEGE. biennial. DM.44. ADAC Verlag GmbH, Am Westpark 8, Postfach 70 01 86, 8000 Munich 70, W. Germany (B.R.D.)

341 SA ISSN 0379-8895
SOUTH AFRICAN YEARBOOK OF INTERNATIONAL LAW/SUID-AFRIKAANSE JAARBOEK VIR VOLKEREG. 1975. a. Z.$25. VerLoren van Themaat Centre for Public International Law, University of South Africa, Box 392, Pretoria 0001, South Africa. Ed. D.H. Van Wyk. bk. rev. Indexed: Ind.S.A.Per.

SOUTHWESTERN LEGAL FOUNDATION. ANNUAL REPORT. see LAW

341 US ISSN 0731-5082
STANFORD JOURNAL OF INTERNATIONAL LAW. 1966. a. $8. Stanford University, Stanford Law School, Stanford, CA 94305. TEL 415-497-2465. adv. bk. rev. circ. 500. Indexed: Leg.Per. P.A.I.S. SSCI. A.B.C.Pol.Sci. ASCA. Ind.Per.Art.Relat.Law. C.L.I. L.R.I. Mar.Aff.Bibl.
●Also available online. Vendors: WESTLAW.
Formerly: Stanford Journal of International Studies (ISSN 0081-4326)

341.7 NE
STUDIES IN TRANSNATIONAL ECONOMIC LAW. 1980. irreg., latest 1984. price varies. Kluwer Law and Taxation Publishers, Box 23, 7400 GA Deventer, Netherlands (Orders to: Kluwer Academic Publishers Group, Distribution Center, Box 322, 3300 AH Dordrecht, Netherlands) Ed. Norbert Horn. bibl.

TOLLEY'S TAXATION IN THE REPUBLIC OF IRELAND (YEAR) see BUSINESS AND ECONOMICS — Public Finance, Taxation

U M A STUDENTS LAW JOURNAL. (University of Malawi) see LAW

341 UN
U N I T A R CONFERENCE REPORTS. 1973. irreg. price varies. United Nations Institute for Training and Research, Publications Office, 801 United Nations Plaza, New York, NY 10017 (Order from: United Nations Publications Sales, DC 2 Room 874, New York, NY 10017; or Distribution and Sales Section, Palais des Nations, CH 1211 Geneva 10, Switzerland) bk. rev.

341.2 UN
UNITED NATIONS. MULTILATERAL TREATIES DEPOSITED WITH THE SECRETARY-GENERAL. (Text in English and French) 1967. irreg., latest 1985. $60. United Nations Publications, Room DC2-853, New York, NY 10017 (Or Distribution and Sales Section, Palais des Nations, CH-1211 Geneva 10, Switzerland) (also avail. in microfiche)
Formerly (until 1980): United Nations. Multilateral Treaties in Respect of Which the Secretary-General Performs Depository Functions (ISSN 0082-8319)

341.7 UN
UNITED NATIONS COMMISSION ON INTERNATIONAL TRADE LAW. REPORT ON THE WORK OF ITS SESSION. (Subseries of United Nations. General Assembly. Official Records. Supplement) 1968. a; latest issue vol.19, 1986. United Nations Commission on International Trade Law (UNCITRAL), Vienna International Centre, P.O. Box 500, A-1400 Vienna, Austria TEL 2631-4060. (Or Distribution and Sales Section, Palais des Nations, CH-1211 Geneva 10, Switzerland) Sec. Eric Bergsten.

672 LEATHER AND FUR INDUSTRIES

341 382   UN   ISSN 0251-4265
UNITED NATIONS COMMISSION ON
INTERNATIONAL TRADE LAW. YEARBOOK.
(Editions in English, French, Russian and Spanish)
irreg. (approx. a.), vol.14, 1983. price varies. United
Nations Commission on International Trade Law
(UNCITRAL), Vienna International Centre, P.O.
Box 500, A-1400 Vienna, Austria (Or Distribution
and Sales Section, Palais des Nations, CH-1211
Geneva 10, Switzerland) Sec. Eric Bergsten. bibl.

341   UN   ISSN 0082-8297
UNITED NATIONS JURIDICAL YEARBOOK.
(Text in English) 1962. a., latest 1981. $25. United
Nations Publications, Room DC2-853, New York,
NY 10017 (Or Distribution and Sales Section, CH-
1211 Geneva 10, Switzerland) (also avail. in
microfiche)

341   UN   ISSN 0082-8300
UNITED NATIONS LEGISLATIVE SERIES. 1951.
irreg., no.21, 1983. $35. United Nations
Publications, Room DC2-853, New York, NY
10017 (Or Distribution and Sales Section, CH-1211
Geneva 10, Switzerland) (also avail. in microfiche)

327 341.2   US   ISSN 0083-0186
U.S. DEPARTMENT OF STATE. TREATIES AND
OTHER INTERNATIONAL ACTS SERIES.
(Texts of individual treaties; collected and issued in
bound form as United States Treaties and Other
International Agreements, ISSN 0083-3487) 1946.
irreg., vol.32, pt.5, 1979/80. price varies. U.S.
Department of State, Office of the Legal Adviser,
2201 C. St.N.W., Washington, DC 20520 TEL 202-
647-1394. (Orders to Supt. of Documents,
Washington, DC 20402)

341.2   US   ISSN 0083-0194
U.S. DEPARTMENT OF STATE. TREATIES IN
FORCE. 1956. a. price varies. U.S. Department of
State, Office of the Legal Adviser, 2201 C St.N.W.,
Washington, DC 20520 TEL 202-647-1394. (Orders
to Supt. of Documents, Washington, DC 20402)

327 341.2   US   ISSN 0083-3487
UNITED STATES TREATIES AND OTHER
INTERNATIONAL AGREEMENTS. 1950. a.
price varies. U.S. Department of State, Office of the
Legal Adviser, 2201 C St. N.W., Washington, DC
20520 TEL 202-647-1394. (Orders to Supt. of
Documents, Washington, DC 20402)

341 327   GW   ISSN 0341-3241
UNIVERSITAET HAMBURG. INSTITUT FUER
INTERNATIONALE ANGELEGENHEITEN.
WERKHEFTE. 1965. irreg., vol.38, 1982. price
varies. Nomos Verlagsgesellschaft mbH und Co.
KG, Waldseestr. 3-5, Postfach 610, 7570 Baden
Baden, W. Germany (B.R.D.) (Co-sponsor:
Deutscher Verein fuer Internationales Seerecht)
    Formerly: Forschungstelle fuer Voelkerrecht und
Auslaendisches Oeffentliches Recht. Werkhefte
(ISSN 0072-9493)

WIENER RECHTSWISSENSCHAFTLICHE
    STUDIEN. see *LAW*

341   US   ISSN 0743-7951
WISCONSIN INTERNATIONAL LAW JOURNAL.
1983. a. $8. University of Wisconsin-Madison, Law
School, 975 Bascom Mall, Madison, WI 53706. TEL
608-262-2240. Ed. Teresa J. Welch. circ. 1,000.
(back issues avail.)

341.57   NE
YEARBOOK COMMERCIAL ARBITRATION.
(Text in English) 1976. a. price varies. Kluwer Law
and Taxation Publishers, Box 23, 7400 GA
Deventer, Netherlands (Orders to: Kluwer
Academic Publishers Group, Distribution Center,
Box 322, 3300 AH Dordrecht, Netherlands) Ed. P.
Sanders.

341   UK   ISSN 0266-7223
YEARBOOK OF EUROPEAN LAW. 1981. a.
£45($90) Oxford University Press, Walton St.,
Oxford OX2 6DP, England. Ed. F. Jacobs.

LEATHER AND FUR INDUSTRIES

see also *Clothing Trade; Shoes and Boots*

685   FR   ISSN 0066-2526
ANNUAIRE DE LA CHAUSSURE ET DES CUIRS.
1905. a. 325 F. Editions Louis Johanet, 68 rue
Boursault, 75017 Paris, France.

675.2   NE   ISSN 0067-4834
BEDRIJFSCHAP VOOR DE
LEDERWARENINDUSTRIE. JAARVERSLAG.
1957. a. fl.25. Bedrijfschap voor de
Lederwarenindustrie, Postbus 90154, 5000 LG
Tilburg, Netherlands. Ed. L. Ploeger. circ. 400.

636.088   US
BLUE BOOK OF FUR FARMING. 1943. a. $20.
Communications Marketing, Inc., 7535 Office Ridge
Circle, Eden Prairie, MN 55344. TEL 612-941-
5820. adv. circ. 2,100.

CANADIAN FOOTWEAR & LEATHER
    DIRECTORY. see *BUSINESS AND
    ECONOMICS — Trade And Industrial Directories*

685   GW   ISSN 0070-9530
EINKAUFSFUEHRER DURCH DIE PELZ- UND
LEDERMODE. 1968. a. DM.31. Otto Teubel
Verlag, Heinrich-Stamme-Str. 6, 3000 Hannover, W.
Germany (B.R.D.)

675   SA   ISSN 0085-2724
L I R I RESEARCH BULLETIN. 1942. irreg.
(approx. 20/yr.) price varies. Rhodes University,
Leather Industries Research Institute, Box 185,
Grahamstown 6140, South Africa. charts. illus.

675   SA
L I R I TECHNICAL BULLETIN. 1975. irreg.
(approx. 10/yr.) Rhodes University, Leather
Industries Research Institute, Box185, Grahamstown
6140, South Africa.

685 685.31   JA
LEATHER & FOOTWEARS/KAWA TO
HAKIMONO. (Text in Japanese) irreg. Tokyo-to
Sangyo Rodo Kaikan, 1-1-6 Hashiba, Taito-ku,
Tokyo, Japan. illus.

675.2   US   ISSN 0075-8345
LEATHER BUYERS GUIDE AND LEATHER
TRADE MARKS.* 1963. a. $6.50 (free with subscr.
to Leather and Shoes) Nickerson & Collins Co.,
Rumpf Publishing Division, 850 Busse Hwy., Park
Ridge, IL 60068-5980.

675.2   UK
LEATHER GUIDE. 1970. a. £55. Benn Business
Information Services Ltd., P.O. Box 20, Sovereign
Way, Tonbridge, Kent TN9 1RQ, England. adv.
index. circ. 1,500.
    Formerly: European Leather Guide (ISSN 0071-
2906)

685   US
LEATHER: LATIN AMERICAN INDUSTRIAL
REPORT. (Avail. for each of 22 Latin American
countries) 1985. a. $435 per country report per
industry covered. Aurora International, Box 9099,
Bridgeport, CT 06601-2099. TEL 203-368-0579. Ed.
Andres C. Aquino.

685 670   US
LEATHER MANUFACTURER'S DIRECTORY.
1986. a. $20. Shoe Trades Publishing Co., 65
Creighton St., Cambridge, MA 02140. TEL 617-
492-2387. adv. circ. 2,000. (back issues avail.)

685   II
LEXPORT. vol.11, 1974/75. a. Export Promotion
Council for Finished Leather & Leather
Manufacturers, 15-46 Civil Lines, Box 198, Kanpur
208001, India.

685 333.7   CN   ISSN 0705-4831
NOVA SCOTIA TRAPPERS NEWSLETTER. 1964.
a. free. Nova Scotia Lands and Forests, Box 68,
Truro, N.S. B2N 5B8, Canada. TEL 902-895-1519.
Ed. A.P. Duke. circ. 6,800.

338.7   II   ISSN 0302-4881
RAJASTHAN STATE TANNERIES LIMITED.
ANNUAL REPORT. (Text in English) 1973. a.
Rajasthan State Tanneries Limited, P-6 Tilak Marg,
C Scheme, Jaipur, India. Key Title: Annual Report -
Rajasthan State Tanneries Limited.

TRAVELWARE RESOURCES DIRECTORY. see
    *BUSINESS AND ECONOMICS — Trade And
    Industrial Directories*

675.3   UK
WINCKELMANN'S FUR DIRECTORIES. 1909. a.
£5. Winckelmann Publications Ltd., 4 Great St.,
Thomas Apostle, London EC4V 2BH, England.

LEATHER AND FUR INDUSTRIES — Abstracting, Bibliographies, Statistics

636.088   CN   ISSN 0318-7888
CANADA. STATISTICS CANADA. REPORT ON
FUR FARMS/RAPPORT SUR LES FERMES A
FOURRURE. (Catalog 23-208) (Text in English
and French) 1919. a. Can.$30($31) Statistics
Canada, Communications Division, 3rd Floor, R.H.
Coats Bldg., Ottawa, Ont. K1A 0T6, Canada TEL
613-993-7276. (Subscr. to: Publications Sales and
Services, Ottawa, Ont. K1A 0T6, Canada) (also
avail. in microform from MML)

675 016   II   ISSN 0011-3638
CURRENT LEATHER LITERATURE. (Text in
English) 1968. m. Rs.100($50) Central Leather
Research Institute, Adyar, Madras 600020, India.
TEL 412616. (Affiliate: Council of Scientific and
Industrial Research) Ed. R. Vengan. index. circ.
500.

LIBRARY AND INFORMATION SCIENCES

see also *Bibliographies*

021   AT   ISSN 0812-6267
A A C O B S ANNUAL REPORT. 1982. a.
Aus.$7.95. Australian Advisory Council on
Bibliographical Services, c/o National Library of
Australia, Canberra, A.C.T. 2600, Australia. circ.
500.
    Supersedes in part: Australian Advisory Council
on Bibliographical Services. Library Services for
Australia (ISSN 0310-8856)

020   US   ISSN 0065-7255
A A L L PUBLICATIONS SERIES. 1960. irreg.,
no.26, 1986. price varies. (American Association of
Law Libraries) Fred B. Rothman & Co., 10368 W.
Centennial Rd., Littleton, CO 80123. TEL 303-979-
5657. (back issues avail.)

020   UK   ISSN 0263-6832
A C O L A M NEWSLETTER. 1980. a. free.
Standing Conference of National and University
Libraries (SCONUL), Advisory Committee on Latin
American Materials, 102 Euston St., London NW1
2HA, England. Ed. A. Harvey Wood. circ. 100.
(back issues avail.)

020.622   US   ISSN 0084-6406
A L A HANDBOOK OF ORGANIZATION. a.
American Library Association, 50 E. Huron St.,
Chicago, IL 60611. TEL 312-944-6780.
    Formerly: A L A Handbook of Organization and
Membership Directory (ISSN 0273-4605)

020   US   ISSN 0065-907X
A L A STUDIES IN LIBRARIANSHIP. 1971. irreg.
price varies. American Library Association, 50 E.
Huron St., Chicago, IL 60611. TEL 312-944-6780.

020.6   US   ISSN 0364-1597
A L A YEARBOOK; a review of library events of
previous year. 1976. a. price varies. American
Library Association, 50 E. Huron St., Chicago, IL
60611. TEL 312-944-6780. illus. index.

020.6   US   ISSN 0361-5669
A R L ANNUAL SALARY SURVEY. 1968. a. $15.
Association of Research Libraries, 1527 New
Hampshire Ave., N.W., Washington, DC 20036.
TEL 202-232-2466. Ed. Gordon Fretwell. circ. 1,
000. (back issues avail.)

020   US
ABSTRACTS STRENGTHENING RESEARCH
LIBRARY RESOURCES PROGRAM. 1978. a.
free. U.S. Department of Education, Office of
Education, Research and Improvement, Washington,
DC 20208. Ed. Frank A. Stevens. circ. 1,000. (back
issues avail.)

LIBRARY AND INFORMATION SCIENCES

020   SW   ISSN 0065-1060
ACTA BIBLIOTHECAE REGIAE STOCKHOLMIENSIS. 1961. irreg. price varies. Kungliga Biblioteket, Box 5039, 102 41 Stockholm, Sweden.

020   SW   ISSN 0065-1079
ACTA BIBLIOTHECAE UNIVERSITATIS GOTHOBURGENSIS. 1941. irreg., no.23, 1984. price varies; also exchange basis. Goeteborgs Universitet, Universitetsbibliotek, Centralbiblioteket, Box 5096, S-402 22 Goeteborg, Sweden (Dist. in U.S., Canada and Mexico by: Humanities Press, Inc., 171 First Ave., Atlantic Highlands, NJ 07716)
    Formerly: Acta Bibliothecae Gothoburgensis.

010 020   HU   ISSN 0001-7175
ACTA UNIVERSITATIS SZEGEDIENSIS DE ATTILA JOZSEF NOMINATAE. ACTA BIBLIOTHECARIA. (Text in English, German or Hungarian; summaries in English, French, German or Russian) 1955. irreg. exchange basis. Attila Jozsef University, c/o E. Szabo, Exchange Librarian, Dugonics ter 13, P.O.B. 393, Szeged H-6701, Hungary (Subscr. to: Kultura, Box 149, H-1389 Budapest, Hungary) Ed. Bela Karacsonyi. charts. circ. 500.

027.7   ET
ADDIS ABABA UNIVERSITY. LIBRARY. ANNUAL REPORT. a. Addis Ababa University, Library, University College, Addis Ababa, Ethiopia.

020   US   ISSN 0065-2830
ADVANCES IN LIBRARIANSHIP. 1970. irreg., vol.14, 1986. Academic Press, Inc., Orlando, FL 32887. TEL 305-345-2000. Ed. Melvin J. Voigt.

025   US   ISSN 0732-0671
ADVANCES IN LIBRARY ADMINISTRATION AND ORGANIZATION. 1982. a. $23.75 to individuals; institutions $47.50. J A I Press Inc., Box 1678, 36 Sherwood Pl., Greenwich, CT 06836. TEL 203-661-7602. Ed.Bd.

AFRICANA JOURNAL; a bibliographic library journal and review annual. see *BIBLIOGRAPHIES*

027.4   US
ALABAMA. PUBLIC LIBRARY SERVICE. ANNUAL REPORT. 1956. a. free to Alabama libraries. Public Library Service, 6030 Monticello Dr., Montgomery, AL 36130. TEL 205-277-7330. circ. 1,200. (also avail. in microform from EDR)
    Supersedes: Alabama. Public Library Service. Basic State Plan and Annual Program (ISSN 0095-361X)

020   US
ALABAMA DEPARTMENT OF EDUCATION. LIBRARY MEDIA OUTPUT. vol.2, 1975. irreg. free. Department of Education, Montgomery, AL 36104. TEL 205-832-3316.

070   US
ALABAMA PRESS ASSOCIATION. RATE AND DATA GUIDE. (Cover title: Alabama Rate and Data) a. $15. Alabama Press Association, Box 1800, Tuscaloosa, AL 35403. TEL 205-345-5611. Ed. Mike Ryland. adv. circ. 1,500.
    Formerly: A P A Newspaper Directory (ISSN 0065-5643)

021   US
ALASKA LIBRARY. 1973. a. Alaska Library Association, c/o Rita Dursi, Treasurer, 1319 Chirikof Court, Anchorage, AK 99507. TEL 907-562-4161. circ. controlled.
    Formerly: Alaska Libraries and Library Personnel Directory.

027   CN   ISSN 0383-3712
ALBERTA. LEGISLATURE LIBRARY. ANNUAL REPORT. 1974. a. free. Legislature Library, 216 Legislature Bldg., Edmonton, Alta. T5K 2B6, Canada. TEL 403-422-5070. Ed. D.B. McDougall. circ. 250.

025   CN
ALBERTA LIBRARY BOARD. ANNUAL REPORT. 1979. a. free. Department of Culture, Library Services Branch, 16214-114 Ave., Edmonton, Alta. T5M 2Z5, Canada. TEL 403-427-2565. circ. 650.

AMERICAN INDIAN LIBRARIES NEWSLETTER. see *ETHNIC INTERESTS*

020   US
AMERICAN LIBRARY ASSOCIATION. ANNUAL CONFERENCE PROGRAM. a. American Library Association, Conference Arrangements Office, 50 E. Huron St., Chicago, IL 60611. TEL 312-944-6780. Ed. Mary Cilluffo. adv. circ. 11,000.

020   US   ISSN 0065-910X
AMERICAN LIBRARY DIRECTORY. 1908. a. $149.95. (Jaques Cattell Press) R. R. Bowker Company, Database Publishing Group, 245 W. 17th St., New York, NY 10011. TEL 800-521-8110.
● Also available online. Vendors: DIALOG.

AMERICAN LIBRARY LAWS. see *LAW*

026   US   ISSN 0065-938X
AMERICAN MERCHANT MARINE LIBRARY ASSOCIATION. REPORT. a. free. American Merchant Marine Library Association, One World Trade Center, Ste. 1365, New York, NY 10048. TEL 212-775-1038.

AMERICAN PETROLEUM INSTITUTE. CENTRAL ABSTRACTING AND INDEXING SERVICE. THESAURUS. see *PETROLEUM AND GAS*

029.7   US
AMERICAN SOCIETY FOR INFORMATION SCIENCE. HANDBOOK AND DIRECTORY. a. $50 to non-members. American Society for Information Science, 1424 16th St., N.W., Ste. 404, Washington, DC 20036. adv.
    Formerly: A S I S Handbook and Directory (ISSN 0066-0124)

020   CN   ISSN 0318-9937
AMERICAN SOCIETY FOR INFORMATION SCIENCE, WESTERN CANADA CHAPTER. ANNUAL MEETING PROCEEDINGS. 1969. a. price varies. American Society for Information Science, Western Canada Chapter, c/o G.A. Cooke, Ed., 8734 119th St., Edmonton, Alta. T6G 1W8, Canada. circ. 150. (back issues avail.)

025   US   ISSN 0066-0868
AMERICAN THEOLOGICAL LIBRARY ASSOCIATION. CONFERENCE. SUMMARY OF PROCEEDINGS. 1947. a. $20. American Theological Library Association, Office of the Executive Secretary, St. Meinrad School of Theology, Archabbey Library, St. Meinrad, IN 47577. TEL 812-357-6718. Ed. Betty O'Brien. 40 yr. cum. index 1986. circ. 700. (also avail. in microfilm) Indexed: Rel.Ind.One.

027.4   US
ANALYSES OF NEW JERSEY PUBLIC LIBRARY STATISTICS FOR (YEAR) 1981. a. free. State Library, 185 W. State St., Trenton, NJ 08625-0520. Ed. Oliver Gillock. circ. 600.

ANNOTATED BIBLIOGRAPHIES OF SERIALS: A SUBJECT APPROACH. see *BIBLIOGRAPHIES*

020   US
ANNUAL DIRECTORY OF OKLAHOMA LIBRARIES. 1984. a. Department of Libraries, 200 N.E. 18th St., Oklahoma City, OK 73105. TEL 405-521-2502.
    Supersedes in part: Oklahoma. Department of Libraries. Annual Report and Directory of Libraries in Oklahoma (ISSN 0066-4065)

027   US
ANNUAL REPORT OF OKLAHOMA LIBRARIES. 1955. a. free. ‡ Department of Libraries, 200 N.E. 18th St., Oklahoma City, OK 73105. TEL 405-521-2502. Ed. Beverly Jones.
    Supersedes in part (as of 1984): Oklahoma. Department of Libraries. Annual Report and Directory of Libraries in Oklahoma (ISSN 0066-4065)

001.5   NE   ISSN 0066-4200
ANNUAL REVIEW OF INFORMATION SCIENCE AND TECHNOLOGY. 1966. a. $52.50 to non-members; members $42. (American Society for Information Science, Information & Business Division (North-Holland) Elsevier Science Publishers B.V., P.O. Box 1991, 1000 BZ Amsterdam, The Netherlands. Ed. Martha E. Williams. bibl. index. cum.index: vols.1-10. (back issues avail.) Indexed: Biol.Abstr. Curr.Cont. SSCI. Sci.Abstr. Compumath.

ANUARIO INTERAMERICANO DE ARCHIVOS. see *HISTORY — History Of North And South America*

020   GW   ISSN 0518-2220
ARBEITSGEMEINSCHAFT DER PARLAMENTS- UND BEHOERDENBIBLIOTHEKEN. ARBEITSHEFTE. 1958. a. Arbeitsgemeinschaft der Parlaments- und Behoerdenbibliotheken, c/o Bibliothek des Deutschen Patentamtes, Zweibrueckenstr. 12, 8000 Munich 2, W. Germany (B.R.D.) circ. 600.

027.7   GW   ISSN 0177-8358
ARBEITSGEMEINSCHAFT KATHOLISCH-THEOLOGISCHER BIBLIOTHEKEN. MITTEILUNGSBLATT. 1952. a. DM.13. Arbeitsgemeinschaft Katholisch-Theologischer Bibliotheken (AKThB), Bibliothek des Priester Seminars, Jesuitenstr. 13, Postfach 1330, D-5500 Trier, W. Germany (B.R.D.) Ed. Franz Rudolf Reichert. bk. rev. cum.index. circ. 250.

025.17   UK   ISSN 0066-653X
ARCHIVES AND THE USER. 1970. irreg. price varies. British Records Association, c/o John Davies, Birmingham Central Library, Chamberlain Sq., Birmingham B3 3HQ, England. Ed. Alan Thacker.

ARCHIVES ET BIBLIOTHEQUES DE BELGIQUE/ ARCHIEF- EN BIBLIOTHEEKWEZEN IN BELGIE. see *HISTORY — History Of Europe*

029   PH
ARCHIVINIANA. (Text in English) 1968. a. National Archives, Bureau of Records Management, c/o National Library Building, Box 779, Manila, Philippines. Ed. Dr. Domingo Abella. circ. 500.

930.25   AG   ISSN 0325-2868
ARCHIVO GENERAL DE LA NACION. REVISTA. (Suspended during 1975) 1971. a. Archivo General de la Nacion, Leandro N. Alem 246, 1003 Buenos Aires, Argentina. Ed. Enrique M. Barba. bk. rev. bibl. circ. 1,000. Indexed: Hist.Abstr. *Archives*

020   GW   ISSN 0066-6793
ARCHIVUM. (Every 4 yrs. includes: International Congress of Archives. Proceedings) (Text in English, French, German, Spanish, Italian) 1951. a. price varies. (International Council on Archives, FR) K.G. Saur Verlag KG, Poessenbacherstr. 2, Postfach 711009, D-8000 Munich 71, W. Germany (B.R.D.) (U.S. and Canadian subscr. to: K.G. Saur Inc., 175 Fifth Ave., N.Y., N.Y., 10010) Ed. Michel Duchein. circ. 2,000. Indexed: Hist.Abstr. A.B.C.Pol.Sci. Amer.Hist.& Life.

020   SW   ISSN 0349-0505
ARKIV, SAMHAELLE OCH FORSKNING. 1953. a. Kr.60. Svenska Arkivsamfundet - Swedish Archival Association, Riksarkivet, Box 12541, S-10229 Stockholm, Sweden. Ed. Helmut Backhaus. bk. rev. circ. 500.
    Formerly: Svenska Arkivsamfundet Skrifter (ISSN 0562-7451)

020   UK
ASLIB ANNUAL REPORT. a. free. Aslib, Association for Information Management, Publications Department, Information House, 26-27 Boswell St., London WC1N 3JZ, England (Dist.in U.S. by Learned Information, 143 Old Marlton Pike, Medford, NJ 08055)
    Formerly: Work of Aslib: Annual Report (ISSN 0084-1285)

020   UK   ISSN 0066-8532
ASLIB OCCASIONAL PUBLICATIONS. 1968. irreg., no.29, 1984. Aslib, Association for Information Management, Publications Department, Information House, 26-27 Boswell St., London WC1N 3JZ (Dist.in U.S. by Learned Information, 143 Old Marlton Pike, Medford, NJ 08055)

020   CR   ISSN 0004-4784
ASOCIACION COSTARRICENSE DE BIBLIOTECARIOS. BOLETIN. 1955. irreg. free. Asociacion Costarricense de Bibliotecarios, Apdo. 3308, San Jose, Costa Rica. circ. 500. Indexed: Lib.Sci.Abstr.

LIBRARY AND INFORMATION SCIENCES

020.6 MX
ASOCIACION DE BIBLIOTECARIOS DE INSTITUCIONES DE ENSENANZA SUPERIOR E INVESTIGACION. ARCHIVOS.* 1976. irreg. Asociacion de Bibliotecarios de Instituciones de Ensenanza Superior e Investigaciones, Apartado Postal 20-671, Mexico 20, D.F., Mexico.

ASOCIACION INTERAMERICANA DE BIBLIOTECARIOS Y DOCUMENTALISTAS AGRICOLAS. BOLETIN ESPECIAL. see *AGRICULTURE*

020 VE ISSN 0066-8591
ASOCIACION VENEZOLANA DE ARCHIVEROS. COLECCION DOCTRINA.* 1970. irreg. Asociacion Venezolana de Archiveros, Archivo General de la Nacion, Santa Capilla a Carmelitas 15, Av. Urdaneta, Caracas 100, Venezuela.

020 FR ISSN 0066-8877
ASSOCIATION DE L'ECOLE NATIONALE SUPERIEURE DES BIBLIOTHECAIRES. ANNUAIRE. 1969. biennial. 100 F. Association de l'Ecole Nationale Superieure des Bibliothecaires, 17-21 Bd. du 11 Novembre, 69100 Villeurbanne, France. adv. circ. 1,200.

020.6 FR ISSN 0066-8931
ASSOCIATION DES BIBLIOTHECAIRES FRANCAIS. ANNUAIRE. 1906. triennial. 70 F. Editions Person, 34 rue de Penthievre, 75008 Paris, France. circ. 3,000.

020 US ISSN 0748-5786
ASSOCIATION FOR LIBRARY AND INFORMATION SCIENCE EDUCATION. DIRECTORY. (Special annual edition of Journal of Education for Library and Information Science) a. $10. Association for Library and Information Science Education, 471 Park Lane, State College, PA 16803. Ed. Janet Phillips. circ. 2,000. (also avail. in microfilm from UMI)
Formerly: Association of American Library Schools Directory.

029.7 378 GH
ASSOCIATION OF AFRICAN UNIVERSITIES. NEW ACQUISITIONS LIST. irreg. free. Association of African Universities, Box 5744, Accra, Ghana.

025 US
ASSOCIATION OF RESEARCH LIBRARIES. OFFICE OF MANAGEMENT STUDIES. OCCASIONAL PAPER. 1971. irreg., no.9, 1985. $15 per issue. Association of Research Libraries, Office of University Library Management Studies, 1527 New Hampshire Ave. N.W., Washington, DC 20036. TEL 202-232-8656. Ed. Maxine K. Sitts.
Formerly: Association of Research Libraries. University Library Management Studies Office. Occasional Paper (ISSN 0091-4479)

020 CN ISSN 0316-0955
ASSOCIATION POUR L'AVANCEMENT DES SCIENCES ET DES TECHNIQUES DE LA DOCUMENTATION. RAPPORT. 1945. a. Association pour l'Avancement des Sciences et des Techniques de la Documentation, 7243 Rue St. Denis, Montreal, Que. H2R 2E3, Canada. TEL 514-271-3349. circ. 1,200.
Formerly: Association Canadienne des Bibliothecaires de Langue Francaise. Rapport (ISSN 0066-8826)

020 IT ISSN 0519-2048
ASSOCIAZIONE ITALIANA BIBLIOTECHE. QUADERNI DEL BOLLETTINO D'INFORMAZIONI. (Supplement to: Associazione Italiana Biblioteche. Bollettino d'Informazioni) 1965. irreg., no.6, 1978. price varies. Associazione Italiana Biblioteche, Casella Postale 2461, 00100 Rome A-D, Italy. Ed. Diego Maltese. adv. bk. rev. circ. 1, 000. (back issues avail)

AUCHMUTY LIBRARY PUBLICATION. see *BIBLIOGRAPHIES*

027.8 DK ISSN 0107-9654
AUDIO-VISUELLE MATERIALER: SKOLEBIBLIOTEKET. 1976. biennial. Kr.110.90. Bibliotekscentralen, Tempovej 7-11, DK-2750 Ballerup, Denmark.

020 AT ISSN 0313-1971
AUSTRALIA. NATIONAL LIBRARY. ANNUAL REPORT. 1961. a. price varies. National Library of Australia, Sales and Subscriptions Section, Canberra, A.C.T. 2600, Australia.
Formerly: Australia. National Library. Annual Report of the Council (ISSN 0069-0082)

027 US ISSN 0067-3412
BANCROFTIANA. 1950. 3-4/yr. membership. Friends of the Bancroft Library, University of California, Berkeley, Bancroft Library, Berkeley, CA 94720. TEL 415-642-3781. Ed. James D. Hart. cum.index: 1950-1966. circ. 1,500.

020 GW ISSN 0342-0221
BAYERISCHE STAATSBIBLIOTHEK, MUNICH. JAHRESBERICHT. 1972. a. Bayerische Staatsbibliothek, Ludwigstr. 16, Postfach 34 0150, 8000 Munich 34, W. Germany (B.R.D.)

020 GW ISSN 0408-8107
BEITRAEGE ZUM BUCH- UND BIBLIOTHEKSWESEN. 1965. irreg., vol.23, 1987. price varies. Verlag Otto Harrassowitz, Taunusstr. 14, Postfach 2929, 6200 Wiesbaden 1, W. Germany (B.R.D.) Ed. Max Pauer.

BEITRAEGE ZUR INKUNABELKUNDE. DRITTE FOLGE. see *PUBLISHING AND BOOK TRADE*

027.7 US ISSN 0362-6881
BENTLEY HISTORICAL LIBRARY ANNUAL REPORT. 1935. a. free. University of Michigan, Bentley Historical Library, 1150 Beal Ave., Ann Arbor, MI 48109-2113. TEL 313-764-1817. Ed. William K. Wallach. circ. 500.

020 016 GE
BERGAKADEMIE FREIBERG. WISSENSCHAFTLICHES INFORMATIONSZENTRUM. VEROEFFENTLICHUNGEN. 1964. irreg., no.106, 1985. exchange. Bergakademie Freiberg, Wissenschaftliches Informationszentrum, Agricolastr. 10, 9200 Freiberg, E. Germany (D.D.R.) Ed. Dieter Schmidmaier. Indexed: LISA.

020 US ISSN 0067-6357
BETA PHI MU CHAPBOOK. 1953. irreg., no.10, 1974. price varies. Beta Phi Mu, International Honor Society, c/o University of Pittsburgh, School of Library and Information Science, Pittsburgh, PA 15260. Ed. Wayne A. Wiegand. Indexed: LISA. Lib.Lit.

011 VE ISSN 0006-1085
BIBLIOGRAFIA VENEZOLANA. (Text in Castellano) 1970. a. $20. Instituto Autonomo Biblioteca Nacional y de Servicios de Bibliotecas, Apdo. 6525, Caracas 1010A, Venezuela. bibl. circ. 1,500. (processed)
Formerly: Bibliografia Venezuela Anuario.

020 CS ISSN 0139-8539
BIBLIOGRAFIE CESKEHO KNIHOVNICTVI. BIBLIOGRAFIE A V T I. 1977. a. 32 Kcs. Statni Knihovna C S R, Klementinum 190, 110 01 Prague 1, Czechoslovakia (Subscr. address: Artia, Ve Smeckach 30, 111 27 Prague 1, Czechoslovakia) Ed. Miloslava Nepovimova.
Formerly: Bibliograficky Katalog C S S R. Ceske Knihy. Zvlastni Sesit. Bibliografie a V T I (ISSN 0323-1666)

BIBLIOGRAPHY OF EDUCATION THESES IN AUSTRALIA. see *EDUCATION — Abstracting, Bibliographies, Statistics*

021 SP ISSN 0006-1646
BIBLIOTECA DE MENENDEZ PELAYO. BOLETIN. 1919. a. 1500 ptas.($24) Sociedad "Menendez Pelayo", Santander, Spain. Ed. Manuel Revuelta Sanudo. bk. rev. index. cum.index: 1919-1960. circ. 600. Indexed: Hist.Abstr. M.L.A.

027.7 NQ
BIBLIOTECAS UNIVERSITARIAS. 1981. 1/yr. free to universities. Universidad Nacional Autonoma de Nicaragua, Biblioteca Central, Apartado 68, Leon CA, Nicaragua. Ed. Walterio Lopez Adaros.

020 MX
BIBLIOTECAS Y ARCHIVOS. a. $4. Escuela Nacional de Biblioteconomia y Archivonomia, Viaducto M. Aleman 155, Col. Alamos, Mexico 13, D.F., Mexico. Ed. Guillermo Oropeza Quiroz. bibl. charts. circ. 1,200. (back issues avail.) Indexed: Ref.Zh. I.R.E.B.I. Lib.Sci.Abstr.

020 PY
BIBLIOTECOLOGIA Y DOCUMENTACION PARAGUAYA. 1972. irreg. 1.50 g. per no. Asociacion de Bibliotecarios del Paraguay, Casilla de Correo 1505, Asuncion, Paraguay. circ. 200. (processed)

020 PL ISSN 0551-3790
BIBLIOTEKA KORNICKA. PAMIETNIK. (Text in Polish; summaries in English) 1929. irreg., vol.21, 1986. price varies. (Polska Akademia Nauk, Biblioteka Kornicka) Ossolineum, Publishing House of the Polish Academy of Sciences, Rynek 9, Wroclaw, Poland (Dist. by Ars Polona-Ruch, Krakowskie Przedmiescie 7, Warsaw, Poland) Ed. H. Chlopocka. circ. 700. (also avail. in microfilm)

020 PL ISSN 0083-7261
BIBLIOTEKA NARODOWA. ROCZNIK/ NATIONAL LIBRARY YEAR-BOOK. (List of contents in English, French, German, Russian; summaries in English) 1964. a. 300 Zl.($5.40) Biblioteka Narodowa, Ul. Hankiewicza 1, 00-973 Warsaw, Poland (Dist. by: Ars Polona-Ruch, Ul. Krakowskie Przedmiescie 7, 00-068 Warsaw, Poland) Ed. Stanislaw Czajka. bk. rev. circ. 657.

020 PL
BIBLIOTEKA SLASKA. KSIAZNICA SLASKA. 1956. irreg. free. Biblioteka Slaska, Ul. Francuska 12, 40-015 Katowice, Poland. bk. rev. bibl. cum. index (5 yrs.)
Formerly (until 1980): Biblioteka Slaska. Biuletyn Informacyjny.

020 YU ISSN 0006-1832
BIBLIOTEKARSTVO/LIBRARIANSHIP. (Text in Serbocroatian; summaries in English, German) 1956. a. 100 din.($6.25) Drustvo Bibliotekara Bosne i Hercegovine - Library Association of Bosnia and Hercegovina, Vojvode Stepe Obala 42, 71000 Sarajevo, Yugoslavia. Ed. Tatjana Prastalo. adv. bk. rev. circ. 750.

020 UR
BIBLIOTEKOVEDENIE, BIBLIOGRAFIYA I INFORMATIKA. 1974. irreg. 0.60 Rub. Moskovskii Gosudarstvennyi Institut Kul'tury, Moscow, Russian S.F.S.R., U.S.S.R.

020 016 BU ISSN 0324-1858
BIBLIOTEKOZNANIE, BIBLIOGRAFIIA, KNIGOZNANIE, NAUCHNA INFORMATSIIA. 1969. a. price varies. Narodna Biblioteka "Kiril i Metodii", 11, Tolbukhin Blvd., 1504 Sofia, Bulgaria. circ. 770.

027 DK ISSN 0084-957X
BIBLIOTEKSAARBOG. 1939. a. Kr.351($35) Danmarks Biblioteksforening - Danish Library Association, Trekronergade 15, DK-2500 Valby, Denmark. Ed. Hanne Wiberg. circ. 1,200.

020 DK ISSN 0109-923X
BIBLIOTEKSHISTORIE. a. Kr.141.20 free for members. (Dansk Bibliotekhistorisk Selskab) Bibliotekscentralen, Telegrafvej 5, DK-2750 Ballerup, Denmark.

027 DK
BIBLIOTEKSVEJVISER/GUIDE TO DANISH LIBRARIES. (Subtitles and index in English) 1970. a. Kr.270($26) Danmarks Biblioteksforening - Danish Library Association, Trekronergade 15, DK-2500 Valby, Denmark. Ed. Hanne Wiberg. circ. 2, 000.

070 GW ISSN 0340-8051
BIBLIOTHEK DES BUCHWESENS (B B) 1972. irreg., vol.10, 1987. price varies. Anton Hiersemann Verlag, Rosenbergstr. 113, Postfach 723, 7000 Stuttgart 1, W. Germany (B.R.D.) Ed. R.W. Fuchs.

020 GW ISSN 0067-8236
BIBLIOTHEK UND WISSENSCHAFT. (Text in English, French, German and Italian) 1964. a. DM.98 (approx.) Verlag Otto Harrassowitz, Taunusstr. 14, Postfach 2929, 6200 Wiesbaden 1, W. Germany (B.R.D.) Ed.Bd. adv. circ. 600. (back issues avail.)

LIBRARY AND INFORMATION SCIENCES

020 GW ISSN 0175-6796
BIBLIOTHEKEN DER BUNDESREPUBLIK DEUTSCHLAND. DATIERTE HANDSCHRIFTEN. 1984. irreg., vol.2, 1987. price varies. Anton Hiersemann Verlag, Rosenbergstr. 113, Postfach 723, 7000 Stuttgart 1, W. Germany (B.R.D.) Ed. J. Autenrieth.

020 GW
BIBLIOTHEKS TASCHENBUCH. a. DM.9.80. Bock & Herchen Verlag, Reichenberger Str. 11e, 5340 Bad Honnef, W. Germany (B.R.D.)

020 GW ISSN 0300-287X
BIBLIOTHEKSPRAXIS. irreg., vol.25, 1980. price varies. K.G. Saur Verlag KG, Poessenbacherstr. 2B, Postfach 711009, 8000 Munich 71, W. Germany (B.R.D.) (U.S. and Canadian subscr. to: K.G. Saur Inc., 175 Fifth Ave., New York, N.Y. 10010) Ed.Bd. (Reprint service avail. from UMI, ISI)

020 GW
BIBLIOTHEKSSTUDIEN. irreg., no.5, 1986. price varies. K.G. Saur Verlag KG, Poessenbacherstr. 2B, Postfach 711009, 8000 Munich 71, W. Germany (B.R.D.) (U.S. and Canadian subscr. to: K.G. Saur Inc., 175 Fifth Ave., New York, N.Y. 10010) Ed. Harro Heim. (Reprint service avail. from UMI, ISI)

020 BE ISSN 0770-4526
BIBLIOTHEQUE ROYALE ALBERT 1ER. RAPPORT ANNUEL. Dutch edition: Koninklijke Bibliotheek Albert I. Jaarverslag (ISSN 0770-447X) a. free to institutions. Bibliotheque Royale Albert 1er - Koninklijke Bibliotheek Albert I, 4 bd. de l'Empereur, 1000 Brussels, Belgium. stat.
Formerly: Bibliotheque Royale de Belgique. Rapport Annuel.

020 BE ISSN 0067-8538
BIJDRAGEN TOT DE BIBLIOTHEEKWETENSCHAP/ CONTRIBUTIONS TO LIBRARY SCIENCE. 1961. irreg. price varies. Rijksuniversiteit te Gent, Rozier 9, B-9000 Ghent, Belgium.

027.4 US
BINGHAMTON PUBLIC LIBRARY. ANNUAL REPORT. a. Binghamton Public Library, 78 Exchange St., Binghamton, NY 13901. TEL 607-723-6457.

029 UK ISSN 0520-2795
BLISS CLASSIFICATION BULLETIN. 1954. a. membership. Bliss Classification Association, c/o Library, Commonwealth Institute, Kensington High St., London W8 6NQ, England. Ed. T. Curwen. bk. rev. circ. 200.

020 GW ISSN 0068-0028
BONNER BEITRAEGE ZUR BIBLIOTHEKS- UND BUECHERKUNDE. 1954. irreg., vol.30, 1985. price varies. Bouvier Verlag Herbert Grundmann, Am Hof 32, Postfach 1268, 5300 Bonn 1, W. Germany (B.R.D.) Eds. Hartwig Lohse, Irmgard Ooms.

020 686 AT ISSN 0310-0391
BOOKMARK; diary and directory for readers and writers, libraries and librarians, publishers and booksellers. 1974. a. Aus.$21. Australian Library Promotion Council, State Library of Victoria, 328 Swanston St., Melbourne, Vic. 3000, Australia. Eds. J.S. Hamilton, M. Dugan. adv. bk. rev. circ. 1,650.

020 US ISSN 0006-7407
BOOKMARK (ALBANY); news about library services. 1949. irreg., approx. q. $4 or exchange. State Library, Albany, NY 12230. Ed. Joseph F. Shubert. bibl. circ. 5,000. (also avail. in microform from UMI; reprint service avail. from UMI) Indexed: Lib.Lit. P.A.I.S. LHTN.
Formerly: J P S Bookmark (ISSN 0275-8539)

021.7 US ISSN 0006-7393
BOOKMARK (CHAPEL HILL) 1944. irreg. membership. (Friends of the University of North Carolina Library) University of North Carolina, Academic Affairs Library, Wilson Library 024-A, Chapel Hill, NC 27514. TEL 919-962-1143. Ed. Charles B. McNamara. circ. 600.

027.7 US ISSN 0006-7458
BOOKS AND LIBRARIES AT THE UNIVERSITY OF KANSAS. 1952. irreg. free. University of Kansas Libraries, Lawrence, KS 66045. TEL 913-864-4334. Ed. James Helyar. bibl. illus. circ. controlled.

027.8 070.5 US ISSN 0068-0184
BOOKS FOR SECONDARY SCHOOL LIBRARIES. 1961. irreg., 6th edt., 1981. $34.95. (National Association of Independent Schools, Ad Hoc Library Committee) R.R. Bowker Company, 245 W. 17th St., New York, NY 10011. TEL 800-521-8110.
Formerly: Three Thousand Books for Secondary School Libraries.

028.5 US ISSN 0068-0192
BOOKS FOR THE TEEN AGE. 1929. a. $5. New York Public Library, Office of Young Adult Services, 455 Fifth Ave., New York, NY 10016. TEL 212-340-0907. Ed. Ruth Rausen. index. circ. 15,000.

020 US
BOOKS IN LIBRARY AND INFORMATION SCIENCE SERIES. 1972. irreg., vol.48, 1986. price varies. Marcel Dekker, Inc., 270 Madison Ave., New York, NY 10016. TEL 212-696-9000. Ed. A. Kent.

026 BS
BOTSWANA. NATIONAL ARCHIVES. REPORT ON THE NATIONAL ARCHIVES. 1975. a. free. National Archives, c/o T. Masisi Lekaukau, Director, Box 239, Gaborone, Botswana. circ. 200.

021 BS
BOTSWANA. NATIONAL LIBRARY SERVICE. REPORT. (Text in English) irreg. National Library Service, Private Bag 0036, Gaborone, Botswana. illus.

020 070.5 US ISSN 0068-0540
BOWKER ANNUAL; of library and book trade information. 1955. a. $89.95. R.R. Bowker Company, 245 W. 17th St., New York, NY 10011. TEL 800-521-8110. cum. index 1972-1976 in 1976 edt.

020 BL ISSN 0100-1922
BRAZIL. BIBLIOTECA NACIONAL. ANAIS. 1876. a. $10. Biblioteca Nacional, Av. Rio Branco 219, 20042 Rio de Janeiro, Brazil. circ. 1,000.

020 BL
BRAZIL. INSTITUTO NACIONAL DO LIVRO. RELATORIO DE ATIVIDADES. 1974. a. Instituto Nacional do Livro, Brasilia, D.F., Brazil.

020 UK
BRITISH LIBRARIANSHIP & INFORMATION WORK. (In two volumes) 1972. quinquiennial. £29.50 per vol. Library Association Publishing Ltd., 7 Ridgmount St., London WC1E 7AE, England. Ed. L.J. Taylor. index.
Former titles: British Librarianship & Information Science (ISSN 0071-5662) & Five Years Work in Librarianship.

027 UK ISSN 0305-7887
BRITISH LIBRARY. ANNUAL REPORT. 1974. a. £3.50. British Library, Board, 2 Sheraton St., London W1V 4BH, England. Indexed: Apic.Abstr.

020 UK ISSN 0262-0278
BRITISH LIBRARY. BIBLIOGRAPHIC SERVICES DIVISION. CATALOGUING PRACTICE NOTES FOR UKMARC RECORDS. 1981. irreg. British Library, Bibliographic Services, 2 Sheraton St., London W1V 4BH, England.

020 UK ISSN 0261-2178
BRITISH LIBRARY RESEARCH REVIEWS. 1981. irreg. price varies. British Library, Research and Development Department, 2 Sheraton St., London W1V 4BH, England (Distr. in U.S. and Canada by: Longwood Publishing Group Inc., 27 South Main St., Wolfeboro, New Hampshire 03894-2069)

BUSINESS INFORMATION SOURCEBOOK. see BUSINESS AND ECONOMICS

BUY BOOKS WHERE, SELL BOOKS WHERE; a directory of out of print book dealers and their author-subject specialties. see PUBLISHING AND BOOK TRADE

026 UK
C I C R I S DIRECTORY. 1968. irreg., 6th, 1986. £2. Cooperative Industrial and Commercial Reference and Information Service, Central Library, Cecil Rd., Enfield EN2 6TW, England. Ed. Peter E. Jones. circ. 200.
Formerly: C I C R I S Directory and Guide to Resources (ISSN 0069-9829)

020 CN
C L A DIRECTORY. 1950. irreg. price varies. Canadian Library Association, 200 Elgin Street, Ste.602, Ottawa, Ont K2P 1L5, Canada. TEL 613-232-9625.
Former titles: C L A Organization Handbook and Membership List (ISSN 0068-9130); Canadian Library Directory.

CALLISTO. see LIBRARY AND INFORMATION SCIENCES — Computer Applications

029 BL ISSN 0101-6903
CAMARA BRASILEIRA DO LIVRO. CENTRO DE CATALOGACO NA FONTE. OFICINA DE LIVROS: NOVIDADES CATALOGADAS NA FONTE. 1974. a. free. Camara Brasileira do Livro, Centro de Catalogacao na Fonte, Av. Ipiranga, 1267, 10 andar, Sao Paulo 01039, Brazil. Ed. Regina Carneiro. bk. rev. bibl. circ. 1,000.

020 UK
CAMBRIDGE UNIVERSITY LIBRARY LIBRARIANSHIP SERIES. irreg. £1 per no. Cambridge University Press, Edinburgh Bldg., Shaftesbury Rd., Cambridge CB2 2RY, England (And 32 E. 57th St., New York, NY 10022)

020 CN ISSN 0068-9092
CANADIAN LIBRARY ASSOCIATION. OCCASIONAL PAPERS. 1953. irreg. price varies. Canadian Library Association, 200 Elgin Street, Ste. 602, Ottawa, Ont. K2P 1L5, Canada. TEL 613-232-9625.

020 CN ISSN 0827-3715
CANADIAN LIBRARY YEARBOOK. a. Can.$55. Micromedia Ltd., 158 Pearl St., Toronto, Ont. M5H 1L3, Canada. Ed. Diane Gallagher.
Supersedes: Canadian Library Handbook (ISSN 0707-9680)

021.7 US ISSN 0008-6894
CARRELL. 1960. a. $5. (Friends of the University of Miami Library) University of Miami Library, Box 248214, Coral Gables, FL 33124. TEL 305-284-4585. Eds. Ronald P. Naylor, Laurence Donovan. bibl. illus. cum.index: vol.1-13, 1972. circ. 4,585. Indexed: M.L.A. Bibl.Engl.Lang.& Lit. Numis.Lit.

CASSETTE BOOKS. see BLIND

020 UK ISSN 0144-9931
CATALYST; information from the University of London Shared Automated Library Services. 1980; N.S. 1985. irreg. free. University of London, Library Resources Co-ordinating Committee, Senate House, Malet St., London WC1E 7HU, England. Ed. Paul McLaughlin. Indexed: LISA.

020 US
CENTER FOR RESEARCH LIBRARIES. HANDBOOK. irreg. $10 to non-members. Center for Research Libraries, 6050 S. Kenwood, Chicago, IL 60637. TEL 312-955-4545. index.

020 US ISSN 0193-7405
CENTRAL SERIALS RECORD. 1979. 2-3/yr. $25 per no. University of Washington Libraries, M171 Suzzallo Library, Seattle, WA 98195. TEL 206-543-1760.

020 MX
CENTRO DE BIBLIOTECOLOGIA, ARCHIVOLOGIA E INFORMACION. ANUARIO. 1961. a. Universidad Nacional Autonoma de Mexico, Centro de Bibliotecologia, Archivologia e Informacion, Villa Obregon, Ciudad Universitaria, Mexico 20, D.F., Mexico. Ed. Alicia Perales de Mercado. bk. rev. cum. index. circ. 1,000. (back issues avail)
Formerly: Anuario de Bibliotecologia, Archivologia e Informatica.

CERCLE BELGE DE LA LIBRAIRIE. ANNUAIRE. see PUBLISHING AND BOOK TRADE

020 CS
CESKOSLOVENSKA AKADEMIE VED. USTREDNI ARCHIV. ARCHIVNI ZPRAVY. 1970. 1-2/yr. free. ‡ Academia, Publishing House of the Czechoslovak Academy of Sciences, Vodickova 40, 112 29 Prague 1, Czechoslovakia. Ed. Jindrich Schwippel. bk. rev. bibl. circ. 500.

020 266 200   UK   ISSN 0309-4170
CHRISTIAN LIBRARIAN. 1976. a. £1.40. Librarians' Christian Fellowship, c/o Graham Hedges, Ed., 34 Thurlestone Ave., Seven Kings, Ilford, Essex IG3 9DU, England. adv. bk. rev. abstr. circ. 450. (back issues avail.) Indexed: Chr.Per.Ind.

020   US   ISSN 0009-885X
CLEVELAND PUBLIC LIBRARY STAFF ASSOCIATION. NEWS AND VIEWS. 1937. irreg. membership. Cleveland Public Library Staff Association, 325 Superior Ave., Cleveland, OH 44114. TEL 216-623-2800. bk. rev. circ. 350. (processed)

020   US
CODE NAME DIRECTORY. 1963. irreg. $50. Gale Research Company, Book Tower, Detroit, MI 48226. TEL 313-961-2242. Eds. Frederick G. Ruffner, Robert C. Thomas.

020   US   ISSN 0084-8905
COLORADO STATE UNIVERSITY LIBRARIES. PUBLICATION. 1966. irreg., no.22, 1979. free. ‡ Colorado State University, University Library, Fort Collins, CO 80523. TEL 303-491-5911. circ. 300.

COMPANY INFORMATION SOURCEBOOK. see *BUSINESS AND ECONOMICS*

347   SI
CONFERENCE OF SOUTHEAST ASIAN LIBRARIANS. PROCEEDINGS. 1970. irreg. price varies. Chopmen Publishers, Katong Shopping Centre, Mountbatten Road 05-28, Singapore 1543, Singapore.

020.6   SP
CONGRESO NACIONAL DE BIBLIOTECAS. PONENCIAS, COMUNICACIONES Y CRONICA. 1966. irreg., latest 1984. 1000 ptas. Asociacion Espanola de Archiveros, Bibliotecarios, Museologos y Documentalistas (A N A B A D), Paseo de Recoletos, 20, Madrid 1, Spain. bk. rev. (also avail. in microfilm)

025   US   ISSN 0069-9136
CONSERVATION OF LIBRARY MATERIALS. (Subseries of: American Library Association. Library Technology Program. L T P Publications) 1967. irreg. American Library Association, Library Technology Program, 50 E. Huron St., Chicago, IL 60611. TEL 312-944-6780.

029.7   US   ISSN 0084-9243
CONTRIBUTIONS IN LIBRARIANSHIP AND INFORMATION SCIENCE. 1972. irreg., no.43, 1983. price varies. Greenwood Press, 88 Post Rd. W., Box 5007, Westport, CT 06881. TEL 203-226-3571. Ed. Paul Wasserman.

025   US
COUNCIL ON LIBRARY RESOURCES ANNUAL REPORT. 1957. a. free. ‡ Council on Library Resources, Inc., 1785 Massachusetts Ave., N.W., Washington, DC 20036. circ. 4,600. (also avail. in microform from EDR) Indexed: ERIC.
Formerly: Council on Library Resources Report (ISSN 0070-1181)

025   US
CURRENT STUDIES IN LIBRARIANSHIP. 1977. a. $10. Texas Womens University, School of Library Science, c/o Bernie Schlessinger, Box 22905, Denton, TX 76204. Ed. Shelly Karp. circ. 600. Indexed: Lib.Lit.

029   GW   ISSN 0344-5372
D G D SCHRIFTENREIHE. irreg., latest 1985. price varies. (Deutsche Gesellschaft fuer Dokumentation e.V.) K.G. Saur Verlag KG, Poessenbacherstr. 12 B, Postfach 711009, 8000 Munich 71, W. Germany (B.R.D.) (U.S. and Canadian subscr. to: K.G. Saur Inc., 175 Fifth Ave., New York, N.Y. 10010) (Reprint service avail. from UMI, ISI)

020   US
D.H. HILL LIBRARY FOCUS. 1964. irreg. free. North Carolina State University, D.H. Hill Library, Box 7111, Raleigh, NC 27695-7111. TEL 919-737-2935. Ed. William C. Lowe. circ. 705. (processed)

020   CN   ISSN 0315-0054
DALHOUSIE UNIVERSITY. SCHOOL OF LIBRARY SERVICE. NEWSLETTER. 1971. a. $5. ‡ Dalhousie University, School of Library Service, Halifax, Nova Scotia B3H 4H8, Canada. TEL 902-424-3656. Ed. MAry Dykstra. circ. 800.

020   CN   ISSN 0701-8894
DALHOUSIE UNIVERSITY. SCHOOL OF LIBRARY SERVICE. Y-A HOTLINE. 1977. irreg. Can.$9.50 for 4 nos. Dalhousie University, School of Library Service, Halifax, N.S. B3H 4H8, Canada. TEL 902-424-3656. Ed. L.J. Amey. circ. 400.

020   DK   ISSN 0069-9861
DANMARKS BIBLIOTEKSSKOLE. SKRIFTER. 1965. a. price varies. Danmarks Biblioteksskole, 6 Birketinget, 2300 Copenhagen S, Denmark. bk. rev.

020   DK
DANMARKS BIBLIOTEKSSKOLE. STUDIER. 1974. irreg., 8-10/yr. price varies. Danmarks Biblioteksskole, 6 Birketinget, 2300 Copenhagen S, Denmark.

020   DK   ISSN 0900-4645
DANMARKS TEKNISKE BIBLIOTEK. KATALOG. a. (Tekniske Bibliotek) Bibliotekscentralen, Telegrafvej 5, DK-2750 Ballerup, Denmark.

027   DK   ISSN 0069-9896
DENMARK. KONGELIGE BIBLIOTEK. FUND OG FORSKNING. (Text in Danish; summaries in English) 1954. a. price varies. Kongelige Bibliotek, Christians Brygge 8, DK-1219 Copenhagen K, Denmark. cum.index: 1954-73.
Findings and research in the collections of the Royal Library

020   DK   ISSN 0107-8003
DENMARK BIBLIOTEKSTILSYNET. BERETNING. 1974. a. free. Bibliotekstilsynet, Nyhavn 31 E, 3, DK-1051 Copenhagen K, Denmark. circ. 2,500.

029 070.5   GE   ISSN 0323-374X
DEUTSCHES BUECHERVERZEICHNIS. 1911/14. irreg. VEB Bibliographisches Institut, Gerichtsweg 26, 7010 Leipzig, E. Germany (D.D.R.)

025.4   US   ISSN 0083-1573
DEWEY DECIMAL CLASSIFICATION ADDITIONS, NOTES AND DECISIONS. Cover title: D C & 1959. irreg., vol.4, no.5. ‡ U.S. Library of Congress, Decimal Classification Division, Washington, DC 20541 (Free to subscr. of LC Card Service, purchasers of 19th edition of Dewey Decimal Classification, and teachers of library science, upon request to: Forest Press, 85 Watervliet Ave., Albany, NY 12206) Ed. John P. Comaromi.

026   CK
DIRECTORIO COLOMBIANO DE UNIDADES DE INFORMACION. 1973. irreg. Fondo Colombiano de Investigaciones Cientificas y Proyectos Especiales, Apdo. Aereo 051580, Bogota, Colombia. adv. bk. rev. circ. 10,000. (also avail. in microform from NTI)

020   US   ISSN 0162-0290
DIRECTORY AND STATISTICS OF OREGON LIBRARIES. 1913. a. $20. State Library, Salem, OR 97310-0640. TEL 503-378-2112. circ. 800.
Formerly: Directory of Oregon Libraries.

DIRECTORY OF CANADIAN MAP COLLECTIONS. see *GEOGRAPHY*

023   US
DIRECTORY OF CHINESE AMERICAN LIBRARIANS. (Text in English and Chinese) 1977. irreg., latest edt., 1986. $6. Chinese Culture Service, Box 444, Oak Park, IL 60303. Ed. Tze-chung Li. circ. 500.

027   US   ISSN 0070-5276
DIRECTORY OF COLLEGE AND UNIVERSITY LIBRARIES IN NEW YORK STATE. 1965. irreg. free to libraries in New York State; on exchange basis with other libraries. State Library, Library Development, Albany, NY 12230. circ. 1,000.

020   US   ISSN 0094-8403
DIRECTORY OF COLORADO LIBRARIES. a. $10. State Library, 201 E. Colfax Ave., Denver, CO 80203. TEL 303-866-6745. Ed. Dan Petro.

DIRECTORY OF COMPUTERIZED DATA FILES. see *BIBLIOGRAPHIES*

027.4   US
DIRECTORY OF CONNECTICUT LIBRARIES AND MEDIA CENTERS INCLUDING BUYERS' GUIDE. a. $34.95. L D A Publishers, 42-36 209 St., Bayside, NY 11361. TEL 718-224-0486. adv.
Formerly: Directory of Connecticut Libraries and Media Centers and Buyers' Guide.

026 959   US   ISSN 0148-0065
DIRECTORY OF EAST ASIAN COLLECTIONS IN NORTH AMERICAN LIBRARIES. a. $5. Association for Asian Studies, Inc., Committee on East Asian Libraries, c/o Karl K. Lo, Chairperson, University of Washington, East Asia Library DO-27, Seattle, WA 98195. TEL 206-543-4490.

020   US   ISSN 0147-1678
DIRECTORY OF FEE-BASED INFORMATION SERVICES. 1978. a. $24.95. Burwell Enterprises, 5106 F.M. 1960 West Ste. 349, Houston, TX 77069. TEL 713-537-9051. Ed. Helen P. Burwell.

020   US   ISSN 0276-959X
DIRECTORY OF GOVERNMENT DOCUMENT COLLECTIONS AND LIBRARIANS. 1974. biennial. $37.50. Congressional Information Service, 4520 East-West Hwy., Bethesda, MD 20814.

020   US
DIRECTORY OF INSTITUTIONS OFFERING OR PLANNING PROGRAMS FOR THE TRAINING OF LIBRARY TECHNICAL MEDIA ASSISTANTS. 1968. triennial; latest, 1984. Council on Library-Media Technical Assistants, Cuyahoga Community College, 2900 Community College Ave., Cleveland, OH 44115. Ed. Myron Allman. stat. (also avail. in microfiche)
Former titles: Directory of Institutions Offering of Planning Programs for the Training of Library Technical Assistants; (until 1971): Council on Library Technology. Directory of Institutions in the United States and Canada Offering or Developing Courses in Library Technology.

DIRECTORY OF LAW LIBRARIES. see *LAW*

027   US
DIRECTORY OF LIBRARIES AND LIBRARY RESOURCES IN THE SOUTH CENTRAL RESEARCH LIBRARY COUNCIL REGION. 1969. a. $25. South Central Research Library Council, DeWitt Bldg., 215 N. Cayuga St., Ithaca, NY 14850. TEL 607-273-9106. Ed. Janet E. Steiner. circ. 700.
Formerly: South Central Research Library Council. Library Directory (ISSN 0081-2722)

021   CN   ISSN 0317-8536
DIRECTORY OF LIBRARIES IN MANITOBA. 1973. biennial. Public Library Services, 139 Hamelin St., Winnipeg, Man.R3T 4H4, Canada. TEL 204-945-6460.

778.1   US   ISSN 0160-6077
DIRECTORY OF LIBRARY REPROGRAPHIC SERVICES. 1959. biennial. $29.95. Meckler Publishing, 11 Ferry Lane West, Westport, CT 06880. TEL 203-226-6967. Ed. Joseph Z. Nitecki.

027   US
DIRECTORY OF LIBRARY SYSTEMS IN NEW YORK STATE. 1976. a. free to libraries in New York State; on exchange basis with other libraries. New York State Education Department, State Library, Library Development, Albany, NY 12230. circ. 1,250.
Formed by the merger of (1960-1975): Directory of New York State Public Library Systems (ISSN 0070-5950); (1967-1975): Directory of Reference and Research Library Resource Systems in New York State (ISSN 0070-6183)

020   US
DIRECTORY OF MASSACHUSETTES LIBRARIES AND MEDIA CENTERS INCLUDING BUYER'S GUIDE. 1985. a. $39.95. L D A Publishers, 42-36 209 St., Bayside, NY 11361. TEL 718-224-0485. Ed. Paul V. Ippolito.
Former titles: Directory of Massachusetts Libraries and Media Centers and Buyers' Guide; (until 1985): Directory of Massachusetts Libraries and Media Centers.

LIBRARY AND INFORMATION SCIENCES

027 US ISSN 0070-5810
DIRECTORY OF MEDICAL LIBRARIES IN NEW YORK STATE. 1967. irreg., 8th edt., 1985. free to libraries in New York State; on exchange basis with other libraries. State Library, Library Development, Albany, NY 12230. circ. 800.

027 US ISSN 0092-4067
DIRECTORY OF MISSOURI LIBRARIES; public, college, university & special libraries. 1965. a. free. State Library, Box 387, Jefferson City, MO 65102. TEL 314-751-3615. stat. circ. 750. (reprint service avail. from UMI)

020 025 US
DIRECTORY OF PERIODICALS ONLINE. VOL. 1: NEWS, LAW & BUSINESS; indexed, abstracted & full-text. (Updates avail.) a. Federal Document Retrieval, Inc., 514 C St. N.E., Washington, DC 20002. Ed. Catherine Chung.

DIRECTORY OF PLANS, EXECUTIVES, POLICIES FOR PCS, OFFICE AUTOMATION, DATACOM, ELECTRONIC MAIL. see *COMMUNICATIONS*

026 GH
DIRECTORY OF RESEARCH AND SPECIAL LIBRARIES IN GHANA. 1974. irreg. Council for Scientific and Industrial Research, Box M32, Accra, Ghana. Ed. L. Agyei-Gyane. circ. 500.
Formerly: Directory of Special Libraries in Ghana.

DIRECTORY OF RESEARCH INSTITUTES IN ISRAEL. see *SCIENCES: COMPREHENSIVE WORKS*

026 US
DIRECTORY OF SPECIAL LIBRARIES AND INFORMATION CENTERS. (In 3 vols.) 1963. biennial. vol.1, $335; vol.2, $275; vol.3, $285. Gale Research Company, Book Tower, Detroit, MI 48226. TEL 313-961-2242. Ed. Brigitte T. Darnay.
Formerly: Directory of Special Libraries and Information Centers in the U S and Canada (ISSN 0731-633X)

026 IO
DIRECTORY OF SPECIAL LIBRARIES AND INFORMATION SOURCES. (Text in Indonesian & English) 1961. irreg., latest issue 1985. $10 per no. Indonesian National Scientific Documentation Center - Pusat Dokumentasi Ilmiah Nasional, Jalan Jenderal Gatot Subroto, Box 3065/Jkt., Jakarta, Indonesia. Eds. Sudaisman Dwinarto, Setya Iswanti. circ. 1,000. (also avail. in microfiche)
Formerly: Directory of Special Libraries in Indonesia (ISSN 0376-8600)

026 IS
DIRECTORY OF SPECIAL LIBRARIES IN ISRAEL. (Text in English and Hebrew) 1961. irreg., 6th edt., 1985. $50. National Center of Scientific and Technological Information, Box 20125, Tel-Aviv, Israel. index.

020 CN
DIRECTORY OF SPECIAL LIBRARIES IN THE MONTREAL AREA/REPERTOIRE DES BIBLIOTHEQUES SPECIALISEES DE LA REGION DE MONTREAL. (Text in English and French) biennial. Can.$20. Special Libraries Association, Eastern Canada Chapter, Box 1538, Station B, Montreal, Que. H3B 3K3, Canada. circ. 350.
Formerly: Directory of Special Libraries in Montreal (ISSN 0070-6396)

025 US
DIRECTORY OF WESTCHESTER LIBRARIES AND MEDIA CENTERS INCLUDING BUYERS' GUIDE. a. $28.95. L D A Publishers, 42-36 209 St., Bayside, NY 11361. TEL 718-224-0485. adv.
Formerly: Directory of Westchester Libraries and Media Centers and Buyers' Guide.

020 US ISSN 0070-6663
DISCOURSE UNITS IN HUMAN COMMUNICATION FOR LIBRARIANS. 1969. irreg., no.27, 1983. price varies. University of Pittsburgh, Communications Media Research Center, c/o Patrick R. Penland, Graduate School of Library and Information Science, 135 No. Bellefield, Pittsburgh, PA 15260. TEL 412-624-4469. Ed. Patrick R. Penland. (back issues avail.) Indexed: Lib.Lit. ERIC.

020 AG ISSN 0070-6841
DOCUMENTACION BIBLIOTECOLOGICA. 1970. irreg; latest issue, 1974. $2. available on exchange. Universidad Nacional del Sur, Centro de Documentacion Bibliotecologica, Av. Alem 1253, Bahia Blanca, Argentina. Ed. Atilio Peralta. circ. 300.

020 UN
DOCUMENTATION, LIBRARIES AND ARCHIVES: STUDIES AND RESEARCH. (Editions in English, French and Spanish) 1972. irreg. price varies. Unesco Press, 7 Place de Fontenoy, F-75700 Paris, France (Dist. in U.S. by: Bernan Associates - Unipub, 10033-F King Highway, Lanham, MD 20706)
Formerly (1951-1971): Unesco Manuals for Libraries (ISSN 0082-7495)

DOKUMENTATION SPRACHWISSENSCHAFTLICHE FORSCHUNGSVORHABEN. see *LINGUISTICS*

027 IE ISSN 0332-0006
DUBLIN. NATIONAL LIBRARY OF IRELAND. COUNCIL OF TRUSTEES REPORT. 1901. a. price varies. Stationery Office, Bishop St., Dublin 8, Ireland (Avail. from: Government Publications Postal Sales Office, St. Martin's House, Waterloo Rd., Dublin 4, Ireland) illus. circ. 500.

027.7 US ISSN 0012-7108
DUKE UNIVERSITY LIBRARY NEWSLETTER. 1953. irreg. free. Duke University, Library, Perkins Library, Durham, NC 27706. TEL 919-684-2034.

027.4 SA
DURBAN MUNICIPAL LIBRARY. ANNUAL REPORT. (Text in English) 1854. a. free. Durban Municipal Library, Box 917, Durban 4000, South Africa. circ. 75.

020 UK
EALING MISCELLANY. 1973. irreg. £1 per no. Ealing College of Higher Education, St. Mary's Rd., Ealing W5 5RF, England. Ed. J.B. Tooley. circ. 200. Indexed: LISA.

020 US
EDUCATION AND TRAINING IN INDEXING AND ABSTRACTING. 1977. irreg. $12 to members; nonmembers $20. American Society of Indexers, 1700 18th St. N.W., Washington, DC 20009.

026 UK ISSN 0076-079X
EDUCATION LIBRARIES BULLETIN SUPPLEMENTS. 1958. irreg., no.23, 1985. price varies. University of London, Institute of Education Library, 11-13 Ridgmount St., London WC1E 7AH, England. Ed. Claire E. Drinkwater. adv. circ. 500. Indexed: Br.Educ.Ind. Lib.Sci.Abstr.

020 SZ ISSN 0514-0668
EIDGENOESSISCHE TECHNISCHE HOCHSCHULE ZUERICH. BIBLIOTHEK. SCHRIFTENREIHE. 1948. irreg. 20 Fr. per no. E T H - Bibliothek (Eidgenossische Technische Hochschule), CH-8092 Zurich, Switzerland. circ. 100.

027.8 372.21 US
ELEMENTARY SCHOOL LIBRARY COLLECTION. 1965. biennial. $79.95. Brodart Publishing Co., 500 Arch St., Williamsport, PA 17705. TEL 800-233-8467. Ed. Lois Winkel. bk. rev. bibl. circ. 10,000.

020 CK ISSN 0071-1314
ESCUELA INTERAMERICANA DE BIBLIOTECOLOGIA. ESTADISTICAS. a. free. Universidad de Antioquia, Apartado Aereo 1226, Medellin, Colombia.

020 GW ISSN 0723-4384
EUROPAEISCHE INTEGRATION - DOKUMENTATION; Informationen fuer Bibliothekare. 1982. a. free. Kommission der Europaeischen Gemeinschaft, Presse- und Informationsbuero, Zitelmannstr. 22, D-5300 Bonn 1, W. Germany (B.R.D.) circ. 1,500. (back issues avail.)

029 NE ISSN 0014-5424
EXTENSIONS AND CORRECTIONS TO THE U D C. (Text in English, French, German) 1950. a. price varies. International Federation for Documentation, Committee on Research on the Theoretical Basis of Information, P.O.Box 90402, 2509 LK The Hague, Netherlands. circ. 800.

029.7 NE ISSN 0379-3680
F I D DIRECTORY. 1958. biennial. fl.25. International Federation for Documentation, Committee on Research on the Theoretical Basis of Information, P.O.Box 90402, 2509 LK The Hague, Netherlands. circ. 1,000.
Formerly: F I D Yearbook (ISSN 0074-5839)

029 NE
F I D/R I MEETINGS REPORTS. 1970. irreg., no.2, 1974. varies. International Federation for Documentation, Committee on Research on the Theoretical Basis of Information, P.O. Box 90402, 2509 LK The Hague, Netherlands (And Vsesoyuznyi Institut Nauchno-Tekhnicheskoi Informatsii, Ul. Baltiiskaya 14, Moscow, U.S.S.R.)

029 NE ISSN 0203-6495
F I D/R I SERIES ON PROBLEMS OF INFORMATION SCIENCE. 1969. irreg., no.7, 1981. price varies. International Federation for Documentation, Committee on Research on the Theoretical Basis of Information, P.O. Box 90402, 2509 LK The Hague, Netherlands (And Vsesoyuznyi Institut Nauchno-Tekhnicheskoi Informatsii, Ul. Baltiiskaya 14, Moscow, U.S.S.R.) Ed. A.I. Mikhailov.
Formerly: F I D /R I Series of Collected Articles.

020 US ISSN 0882-908X
F L I C C NEWSLETTER. 1965. irreg., latest no.134, 1985. free. U.S. Library of Congress, Federal Library and Information Center Committee, Washington, DC 20540. TEL 202-287-6055. Ed. Christina Zirps. bk. rev. stat. circ. controlled. (processed)
Formerly: F L C Newsletter (ISSN 0014-5939)

070.5 GW ISSN 0071-3627
FACHLITERATUR ZUM BUCH- UND BIBLIOTHEKSWESEN/INTERNATIONAL BIBLIOGRAPHY OF THE BOOK TRADE AND LIBRARIANSHIP. 1961. irreg., latest 1981. price varies. K.G. Saur Verlag KG, Poessenbacherstr. 12 B, Postfach 711009, 8000 Munich 71, W. Germany (B.R.D.) (U.S. and Canadian subscr. to: K.G. Saur Inc., 175 Fifth Ave., New York, N.Y. 10010) Eds. Helga Lengenfelder, Gitta Hausen. adv. (Reprint service avail. from UMI, ISI)
Formerly: Literature About the Book and Librarianship.

026 686.2 UK ISSN 0141-3635
FACTOTUM. 1978, no.14,1982. irreg. (3-4/yr.) free. British Library, Humanities and Social Sciences, Great Russell St., London WC1B 3DG, England. Eds. A.D. Sterenberg, J.L. Wood. bibl. cum.index. circ. 2,000. (back issues avail.)

023 US ISSN 0273-1061
FEDERAL LIBRARIAN. 1972. irreg. American Library Association, Federal Librarians Round Table, 50 Huron St., Chicago, IL 60611. TEL 312-944-6780. Ed. Claire Tozier. circ. 500.
Supersedes (as of 1986): F L I R T Newsletter (ISSN 0090-9661)

020 US
FEDERAL LIBRARY RESOURCES; a user's guide to research collections. irreg. $37.50. Science Associates International, Inc., 1841 Broadway, New York, NY 10023.

028 PE ISSN 0015-0002
FENIX; revista. 1944. a. $4. Biblioteca Nacional, Apartado 2335, Lima, Peru. Ed. Lucila Valderrama. bk. rev. music rev. bibl. cum.index. circ. 1,000. Indexed: Hist.Abstr. Amer.Hist.& Life.

020 FJ
FIJI LIBRARY DIRECTORY. irreg., latest 1981. $2.50 per no. Fiji Library Association, Government Buildings, Box 2292, Suva, Fiji. circ. 55.

FINANCIAL ASSISTANCE FOR LIBRARY EDUCATION. see *EDUCATION — Higher Education*

026 820   US   ISSN 0428-8211
FOLGER SHAKESPEARE LIBRARY ANNUAL
REPORT. 1969, N.S. a. Folger Shakespeare Library,
201 E. Capitol St., S.E., Washington, DC 20003.
TEL 202-544-4600. stat. annual index. circ. 1,200.

027.4   DK   ISSN 0105-6077
FOLKEBIBLIOTEKSSTATISTIK, BUDGETTER,
VIRKSOMHED. 1977. a. Kr.129.40.
Bibliotekstilsynet - Directorate of Public Libraries,
Nyhavn 31 E,3, DK-1051 Copenhagen K, Denmark
(Subscr. to: Bibliotekscentralen, Tempovej 7-11,
DK-2750 Ballerup, Denmark) circ. 1,000.

020   US
FOUNDATIONS IN LIBRARY AND
INFORMATION SCIENCE; a series of
monographs, texts and treatises. 1980. irreg., vol.20,
1984. $23.75 47.50. J A I Press Inc., Box 1678, 36
Sherwood Pl., Greenwich, CT 06836. TEL 203-661-
7602. Ed. Robert D. Stueart.

020 070   UK
FRIENDS OF THE NATIONAL LIBRARIES.
ANNUAL REPORT. 1932. a. £7($15) to
individuals; institutions £10($25) Friends of the
National Libraries, c/o British Library, Great
Russell St., London WC1B 3DG, England. circ.
900.

020   PE   ISSN 0433-0730
GACETA BIBLIOTECARIA DEL PERU. 1963.
irreg. Instituto Nacional de Cultura, Biblioteca
Nacional, Oficina Nacional de Bibliotecas Publicas,
Apartado 2335, Lima, Peru. Ed. Carmen Checa de
Silva. illus. circ. 1,000.

020   GW   ISSN 0724-6358
GEMEINSAME KOERPERSCHAFTSDATEI. 1980.
a. Verlag Otto Harrassowitz, Taunusstr. 14, Postfach
2929, D-6200 Wiesbaden 1, W. Germany (B.R.D.)
Ed. Bd. (microfiche)

027.4   CN   ISSN 0380-8068
GEORGIAN BAY REGIONAL LIBRARY
SYSTEM. DIRECTORY-MEMBER LIBRARIES.
1968. irreg. Georgian Bay Regional Library System,
30 Morrow Rd., Barrie, Ont. L4N 3V8, Canada.
TEL 705-726-8251. circ. 100.

020   GH   ISSN 0016-9552
GHANA LIBRARY JOURNAL. 1963. irreg. Ghana
Library Association, Box 60, Legon, Ghana. Ed.
D.E.M. Oddoye. adv. bk. rev. abstr. charts. illus.
stat. index; cum.index. circ. 500. (also avail. in
microform) Indexed: Lib.Sci.Abstr.

020   SW   ISSN 0347-884X
GOETEBORGS UNIVERSITET.
UNIVERSITETSBIBLIOTEK.
AARSBERAETTELSE. 1907-27; N.S. 1930. a.
exchange basis. Goeteborgs Universitet,
Universitetsbibliotek, Centralbiblioteket, Box 5096,
S-402 22 Goeteborg, Sweden.

020   US
GOLDA MEIR LIBRARY NEWSLETTER. 1974.
irreg. free. ‡ University of Wisconsin-Milwaukee,
Golda Meir Library, 2311 E. Hartford Ave.,
Milwaukee, WI 53201. TEL 414-963-4785. Ed.
Jeane Knapp. circ. 4,000.
Formerly: U W M Library Newsletter.

002   US
GOVERNMENT DOCUMENTS AND
INFORMATION CONFERENCE.
PROCEEDINGS. irreg., no.3, 1982. Meckler
Publishing, 11 Ferry Lane West, Westport, CT
06880. Ed. Peter Hernon. bibl.
Formerly: Library Government Documents and
Information Conference. Proceedings.

026 950   II
GOVERNMENT ORIENTAL MANUSCRIPTS
LIBRARY. BULLETIN. (Text in English and
various Indic languages) 1948. a. Rs.14.
Government Oriental Manuscripts Library, Curator,
University Library Buildings, Chepauk, Madras
600005, India. Ed. R.N. Sampata. bk. rev.

GREAT BRITAIN. KEEPER OF PUBLIC
RECORDS. ANNUAL REPORT OF THE
KEEPER OF PUBLIC RECORDS ON THE
WORK OF THE PUBLIC RECORD OFFICE
AND THE REPORT OF THE ADVISORY
COUNCIL ON PUBLIC RECORDS. see
HISTORY — History Of Europe

025.17   UK   ISSN 0072-7016
GREAT BRITAIN. PUBLIC RECORD OFFICE.
HANDBOOKS. 1954. irreg. price varies. H.M.S.O.,
P.O. Box 569, London SE1 9NH, England. (reprint
service avail. from UMI)

020   US
GREAT PLAINS LIBRARIES. 1982. a. $5. (Emporia
State University, School of Library and Information
Management) Emporia State Press, 1200
Commercial St., Emporia, KS 66801. TEL 316-343-
1200. Ed. Robert Grover. illus. stat. circ. 500.
Supersedes: Library School Review (ISSN 0453-
2406)

GUIDE TO MICROFORMS IN PRINT. AUTHOR,
TITLE. see BIBLIOGRAPHIES

027.5   UN   ISSN 0072-8608
GUIDE TO NATIONAL BIBLIOGRAPHICAL
INFORMATION CENTRES. (Text in English and
French) 1962. irreg., 3rd edt., 1970. 23 F. Unesco,
7-9 Place de Fontenoy, 75700 Paris, France (Dist.
in U.S. by: Bernan Associates-Unipub, 4611-F
Assembly Dr., Lanham, MD 20706)

011   US
GUIDE TO REFERENCE BOOKS FOR SCHOOL
MEDIA CENTERS. irreg. no subscr. Libraries
Unlimited, Inc., Box 263, Littleton, CO 80160. TEL
303-770-1220. Ed. Christine Genrt Wynar.

020   US
H L A JOURNAL. 1944. a. $4 to non-members.
Hawaii Library Association, Box 4441, Honolulu,
HI 96813. charts. illus. circ. 600. (also avail. in
microfilm from UMI; reprint service avail. from
UMI) Indexed: LISA. Lib.Lit.
Formerly: Hawaii Library Association Journal
(ISSN 0017-8586)

HAIKU REVIEW. see LITERATURE — Poetry

HANDBOOK FOR LIBRARIES & OTHER
ORGANIZATIONAL USERS WHICH COPY
FROM SERIALS & SEPARATES; procedures for
using the programs of the Copyright Clearance
Center, Inc. see PUBLISHING AND BOOK
TRADE

029   GW   ISSN 0340-1332
HANDBUCH DER INTERNATIONALEN
DOKUMENTATION UND INFORMATION/
HANDBOOK OF INTERNATIONAL
DOCUMENTAION AND INFORMATION.
irreg., no.17, 1983. price varies. K.G. Saur Verlag
KG, Poessenbacherstr. 12 B, Postfach 711009, 8000
Munich 71, W. Germany (B.R.D.) (U.S. and
Canadian subscr. to: K.G. Saur Inc., 175 Fifth Ave.,
New York, N.Y. 10010) (Reprint service avail. from
UMI, ISI)
Formerly: Handbuch der Technischen
Dokumentation und Bibliographie.

020   GW   ISSN 0301-9225
HANDBUCH DER OEFFENTLICHEN
BIBLIOTHEKEN. 1952. biennial. DM.46.
Deutsches Bibliotheksinstitut, Bundesallee 185, 1000
Berlin 31, W. Germany (B.R.D.) stat. circ. 1,200.
(back issues avail.)

027   US   ISSN 0073-0564
HARVARD LIBRARIAN. 1957. 3-4/yr. free. ‡
Harvard University Library, Office of the Director,
Cambridge, MA 02138. TEL 617-495-3650. Ed.
Pamela J. Matz. circ. 3,000. (reprint service avail.
from UMI) Indexed: CALL.

510.78 410   US   ISSN 0073-0769
HARVARD UNIVERSITY. COMPUTATION
LABORATORY. MATHEMATICAL
LINGUISTICS AND AUTOMATIC
TRANSLATION; REPORT TO NATIONAL
SCIENCE FOUNDATION. 1959. irreg., no.27,
1970. free. Harvard University, Aiken Computation
Laboratory, Cambridge, MA 02138 (Orders to:
National Technical Information Service, Operations
Division, Springfield, VA 22151) Ed. Susumu Kuno.

020   US
HAWAII. DEPARTMENT OF EDUCATION.
OFFICE OF LIBRARY SERVICES. ANNUAL
REPORT. 1962/63. a. free. Research and
Evaluation Services, Office of Library Services,
Kekuanaoa Bldg., Rm. B-1, 465 S. King St.,
Honolulu, HI 96813. TEL 808-548-4775.

027   FI   ISSN 0355-1350
HELSINGIN YLIOPISTON KIRJASTON.
JULKAISUJA/HELSINGFORS UNIVERSITETS
BIBLIOTEKS SKRIFTER/HELSINKI
UNIVERSITY LIBRARY. PUBLICATIONS. 1918.
irreg., no.47, 1983. Helsingin Yliopiston, Kirjasto,
Box 312, 00171 Helsinki, Finland.

020   II   ISSN 0018-0521
HERALD OF LIBRARY SCIENCE. (Special
Numbers issued irregularly) 1962. q. Rs.150($48) P.
Kaula Endowment for Library and Information
Science, C-239 Indira Nagar, Lucknow 226016,
India. Ed. P.N. Kaula. adv. bk. rev. charts. illus.
index. (also avail. in microform from UMI; reprint
service avail. from UMI) Indexed: LISA. Lib.Lit.
Sci.Abstr. Indian Lib.Sci.Abstr.

020   JA   ISSN 0018-3431
HOKKAIDO LIBRARIANS STUDY CIRCLE.
BULLETIN/HOKKAIDO TOSHOKAN
KENKYUKAI. KAIHO. (Text in Japanese) 1954. a.
1000 Yen. Hokkaido Librarians Study Circle -
Hokkaido Toshokan Kenkyukai, c/o Sapporo Ika
Daigaku Fuzoku Toshokan, Nishi-17-chome,
Minami 1-jo, Sapporo, Japan. adv. circ. 300.

020   HK   ISSN 0073-3237
HONG KONG LIBRARY ASSOCIATION.
JOURNAL. (Text in English and Chinese) 1969. a.
price varies. Hong Kong Library Association, c/o
Univ. of Hong Kong Library, Pokfulum Rd., Hong
Kong, Hong Kong (Subscr. to: G.P.O. Box 10095,
Hong Kong) Ed. M. Quinn. adv. bk. rev. circ. 300.

020   GE   ISSN 0522-9898
HUMBOLDT-UNIVERSITAET ZU BERLIN.
UNIVERSITAETSBIBLIOTHEK.
SCHRIFTENREIHE. 1967. irreg., no.55, 1986.
price varies. Humboldt-Universitaet zu Berlin,
Universitaets-Bibliothek, Clara-Zetkin-Str. 27, PF
1236, 1086 Berlin, E. Germany (D.D.R.) Ed.
Waltraud Irmscher.

020   US   ISSN 0257-3229
I A S L CONFERENCE PROCEEDINGS. 1972. a.
price varies. International Association of School
Librarianship, c/o Secretariate, Box 1486,
Kalamazoo, MI 49005. TEL 616-343-5728. Ed. J.
Lowrie. circ. 250. (looseleaf format; back issues
avail.) Indexed: ERIC.

026   II   ISSN 0073-6279
I A S L I C SPECIAL PUBLICATION; working
papers of seminars and conferences. (Text in
English) 1960. a. price varies. Indian Association of
Special Libraries and Information Centres, P-291
C.I.T. Scheme No. 6M, Kankurgachi, Calcutta
700054, India.

026   II   ISSN 0073-6260
I A S L I C TECHNICAL PAMPHLETS. 1964. a.
price varies. Indian Association of Special Libraries
and Information Centres, P-291 C.I.T. Scheme No.
6M, Kankurgachi, Calcutta 700054, India.

020   SW
I A T U L QUARTERLY. 1963. irreg. Kr.80.
International Association of Technological
Universities Libraries, Chalmers University of
Technology, S-412 96 Gothenburg, Sweden. Ed.
Sinikka Koskiala. adv. bk. rev. bibl. illus. circ. 600.
Indexed: LISA. Lib.Lit. Sci.Abstr.
Inform.Sci.Abstr.
Former titles: I A T U L Proceedings (ISSN
0018-8476); I A T U L Newsletter.

020   SZ
I F I P INFORMATION BULLETIN. a. International
Federation for Information Processing, Secretariat, 3
rue du Marche, CH-1204 Geneva, Switzerland. bibl.

020   GW   ISSN 0074-5987
I F L A ANNUAL; proceedings of the General
Council Meetings. (Text in English) 1927. a.
DM.64. (International Federation of Library
Associations and Institutions) K.G. Saur Verlag KG,
Poessenbacherstr. 12 B, Postfach 711009, 8000
Munich 71, W. Germany (B.R.D.) (U.S. and
Canadian subscr. to: K.G. Saur, Inc., 175 Fifth
Ave., New York, N.Y. 10010) Ed.Bd. (Reprint
service avail. from UMI, ISI)

020   NE   ISSN 0074-6002
I F L A DIRECTORY. 1969. biennial. fl.50.
International Federation of Library Associations and
Institutions, Box 95312, 2509 C H The Hague,
Netherlands. Ed.Bd. circ. 2,000.

LIBRARY AND INFORMATION SCIENCES

025   GW
I F L A PUBLICATIONS. (Text in English and French) 1974. irreg. vol.36, 1987. (International Federation of Library Associations and Institutions) K.G. Saur Verlag KG, Poessenbacherstr. 2B, Postfach 711009, 8000 Munich 71, W. Germany (B.R.D.) (U.S. and Canadian subscr. to: K.G. Saur, 175 Fifth Ave., New York, N.Y. 10010) Eds. W.R. Koops, P. Havard-Williams. (Reprint service avail. from UMI,ISI)

020   DK
I N F A A RAPPORT. 1983. irreg. Kr.55. Aabenraa Proevecenter for Ny Informationsteknologi, c/o Det Soenderjydske Landsbibliotek, Haderslevvej 3, 6200 Aabenraa, Denmark. Ed. Ib Madsen.

539   UN
I N I S REFERENCE SERIES. 1969. irreg. price varies. International Atomic Energy Agency, Wagramer Str. 5, Box 100, A-1400 Vienna, Austria (Dist. in U.S. by: Bernan Associates-Unipub, 4611-F Assembly Dr., Lanham, MD 20706-4391) (some issues also avail. in microfiche)

I S B N REVIEW. (International Standard Book Number) see *PUBLISHING AND BOOK TRADE*

021.7   US   ISSN 0360-8409
ICARBS. 1973. irreg. $5. Friends of Morris Library, Southern Illinois University, Morris Library, Carbondale, IL 62901. TEL 618-453-2516. Eds. David V. Koch, Alan M. Cohn. adv. circ. 500. (back issues avail.) Indexed: M.L.A. Amer.Hum.Ind. Abstr.Engl.Stud.

027   IC
ICELAND. LANDSBOKASAFN ISLANDS. ARBOK. NYR FLOKKUR. N.S. 1976. a. Kr.300($8) Landsbokasafn Islands - National Library of Iceland, Safnahusinu, Hverfisgotu 15, 101 Reykjavik, Iceland. Ed. Finnbogi Gudmundsson.
Supersedes in part: Iceland. Landsbokasafn Islands. Arbok.

020   UN   ISSN 0073-6074
INDEX TRANSLATIONUM. (Text in English and French) 1950. a. price varies. Unesco, 7-9 Place de Fontenoy, 75700 Paris, France (Dist. in U.S. by: Bernan Associates-Unipub, 4611-F Assembly Dr., Lanham, MD 20706)

020   II   ISSN 0067-3439
INDIAN STATISTICAL INSTITUTE. DOCUMENTATION RESEARCH AND TRAINING CENTRE. D R T C ANNUAL SEMINAR. 1963. a. price varies. Indian Statistical Institute, Documentation Research and Training Centre, 8th Mile, Mysore Road, Bangalore 560 059, India. circ. 500. (also avail. in microfilm; microfiche) Indexed: LISA. Inform.Sci.Abstr.

020   II
INDIAN STATISTICAL INSTITUTE. DOCUMENTATION RESEARCH AND TRAINING CENTRE. D R T C REFRESHER SEMINAR. 1969. a. price varies. Indian Statistical Institute, Documentation Research and Training Centre, 8th Mile, Mysore Road, Bangalore 560 059, India. circ. 500. (also avail. in microform) Indexed: LISA. Inform.Sci.Abstr.

020   US   ISSN 0275-777X
INDIANA LIBRARIES. 1981. irreg. (2-4/yr.) $10. ‡ State Library, 140 N. Senate Ave., Indianapolis, IN 46204. TEL 317-636-6059. (Co-sponsor: Indiana Library Association/Indiana Library Trustee Association) Ed. Dan Callison. bibl. charts. illus. circ. 2,000. (also avail. in microform from UMI; back issues avail.) Indexed: Lib.Lit.
Supersedes (1906-1981): Library Occurrent (ISSN 0024-2454)

027.4   SA   ISSN 0256-4106
INFORMAT. irreg. Department of National Education, State Library, Norex Group Bldg., Edison St., Pretoria West, South Africa.

020   US
INFORMATION MANAGEMENT SOURCE BOOK. a. free to new members, $25 thereafter; non-members $40. Association for Information & Image Management, 1100 Wayne Ave., Siver Springs, MD 20910. TEL 301-587-8202. adv. circ. 8,000.

020   US
INFORMATION SCIENCES SERIES. 1963. irreg., latest 1981. price varies. John Wiley & Sons, Inc., 605 Third Ave., New York, NY 10016. TEL 212-850-6000. Eds. R.M. Hayes, J. Becker.
Formerly: Hayes & Becker Information Sciences Series.

020   GE
INFORMATIONSDIENST UEBERSETZUNGEN. irreg. Zentralinstitut fuer Information und Dokumentation, Koepenicker Str. 80/82, 1020 Berlin, E. Germany (D.D.R.) (microfiche)

INFOTERM SERIES. (International Information Centre for Terminology, Vienna) see *LINGUISTICS*

INSTITUT PROVINCIAL D'ETUDES ET RECHERCHES BIBLIOTHECONOMIQUES. MEMOIRES. see *BIBLIOGRAPHIES*

020   SI   ISSN 0073-9723
INSTITUTE OF SOUTHEAST ASIAN STUDIES. LIBRARY BULLETIN. (Text in English) 1971. irreg., no.16, 1985. price varies. Institute of Southeast Asian Studies, Heng Mui Keng Terrace, Pasir Panjang, Singapore 0511, Singapore. Indexed: Bibl.Asian Stud.

020   UK
INTERNATIONAL AFRICAN LIBRARY. 1986. irreg. price varies. (International African Institute) Manchester University Press, Oxford Rd., Manchester M13 9PL, England. TEL 061-273 5539. Eds. J.D.Y. Peel, D. Parkin.

026   US
INTERNATIONAL ASSOCIATION OF LAW LIBRARIES. DIRECTORY. 1977. irreg., latest edt. 1980. $15. International Association of Law Libraries, c/o Dr. Ivan Sipkov, U.S. Library of Congress, Law Library, Washington, DC 20540. adv. bk. rev. circ. 1,000. Indexed: Leg.Per. C.L.I.

INTERNATIONAL ASSOCIATION OF PERFORMING ARTS LIBRARIES AND MUSEUMS. CONGRESS PROCEEDINGS. see *ART*

020.6   UK
INTERNATIONAL ASSOCIATION OF SOUND ARCHIVES. DIRECTORY OF MEMBER ARCHIVES. 1982. irreg. £6.50. International Association of Sound Archives, Secretariat, Media Librarian, Open University Library, Walton Hall, Milton Keynes MK7 6AA, England. Ed. Grace Koch. circ. 700.

020   US
INTERNATIONAL BIBLIOGRAPHICAL AND LIBRARY SERIES. 1971. irreg., vol.3, 1973. Academic Press, Inc., Orlando, FL 32887. TEL 305-345-2000. Ed. G. Chandler.

020   US   ISSN 0364-3670
INTERNATIONAL CODEN DIRECTORY. every 5 yrs. (plus a. supplements) $750 for base vol.; $200 for each supplement. (American Chemical Society) Chemical Abstracts Service, 2540 Olentagy River Rd., Box 3012, Columbus, OH 43210. TEL 614-421-3600. (microfiche)

025.17   SP   ISSN 0255-3139
INTERNATIONAL COUNCIL ON ARCHIVES. COMMITTEE ON CONSERVATION AND RESTAURATION. COMMITTEE ON ARCHIVAL REPROGRAPHY (BULLETIN) (Text in English with summaries in English, French, Spanish, Italian and German) 1972. a. free. (Ministerio de Cultura, FR) Centro Nacional de Conservacion y Microfilmacion Documental y Bibliografica (C E C O M I), c/o Sra. Carmen Crespo Nogueira, Ed., Serrano 115, 28006 Madrid, Spain. illus. circ. 2,350.
Formerly: International Council on Archives. Microfilm Committee. Bulletin.

026   LO
INTERNATIONAL COUNCIL ON ARCHIVES. EAST AND CENTRAL AFRICA REGIONAL BRANCH. GENERAL CONFERENCE PROCEEDINGS. 1969. a. $15.50. International Council on Archives, Eastern and Southern Africa Regional Branch, c/o National University of Lesotho Library, P.O. Roma 180, Lesotho, Nairobi, Kenya. Ed. R.J. Kukubo.

025   US
INTERNATIONAL DIRECTORY OF NEWS LIBRARIES INCLUDING BUYER'S GUIDE (YEAR) 1985. a. $34.95. (Special Libraries Association, Newspaper Division) L D A Publishers, 42-36 209 St., Bayside, NY 11361. TEL 718-224-0485. adv.
Formerly: International Directory of News Libraries and Buyers' Guide (Year)

029   NE   ISSN 0378-7656
INTERNATIONAL FEDERATION FOR DOCUMENTATION. P-NOTES. 1931. irreg. (20-30/yr.) fl.40. International Federation for Documentation, Box 90402, 2509 LK The Hague, Netherlands.

029.7   NE   ISSN 0074-5812
INTERNATIONAL FEDERATION FOR DOCUMENTATION. PROCEEDINGS OF CONGRESS. 1895. irreg., latest issue 1984. price varies. International Federation for Documentation, Box 90402, 2509 LK The Hague, Netherlands.

020   GW   ISSN 0000-0221
INTERNATIONALES BIBLIOTHEKS-HANDBUCH/WORLD GUIDE TO LIBRARIES. (Text in English and German) 1966. irreg., 7th ed., 1985. price varies. K.G. Saur Verlag KG, Poessenbacherstr. 12 B, Postfach 711009, 8000 Munich 71, W. Germany (B.R.D.) (U.S. and Canadian subscr. to: K.G. Saur Inc., 175 Fifth Ave., New York, N.Y. 10010) Ed. Helga Lengenfelde. adv. (Reprint service avail. from UMI, ISI)

026 025   IE
IRISH ARCHIVES BULLETIN. (Text in English & Gaelic) 1971. a. £4.50. Irish Society for Archives, Dublin Diocesan Archives, Archbishop's House, Drum Condra, Dublin 9, Ireland. Ed. Ailsa C. Holland. bk. rev. circ. 200. (back issues avail.)

016   IT
ITALY. ISTITUTO DI STUDI SULLA RICERCA E DOCUMENTAZIONE SCIENTIFICA. NOTE DI BIBLIOGRAFIA E DOCUMENTAZIONE SCIENTIFICA. 1955. irreg., vol.47, 1985. price varies. Istituto di Studi sulla Ricerca e Documentazione Scientifica, Via Cesare do Lollis 12, 00185 Rome, Italy. Ed. Maria Pia Carosella. circ. 1,000. Indexed: Bull.Signal.
Former titles: Italy. Laboratorio di Studi sulla Ricerca e sulla Documentazione. Note di Bibliografia e Documentazione Scientifica; Italy. Consiglio Nazionale delle Ricerche. Nota di Bibliografia e di Documentazione Scientifica (ISSN 0085-2309)

020   SA   ISSN 0256-0070
JAGGER JOURNAL. 1980. a. R.5. University of Cape Town, Libraries, Rondebosch 7700, South Africa. Ed. B.H. Watts. Indexed: Ind.S.A.Per.

JAHRBUCH DER AUKTIONSPREISE FUER BUECHER, HANDSCHRIFTEN UND AUTOGRAPHEN; Ergebnisse der Auktionen in Deutschland, Holland, Oesterreich und der Schweiz. see *MUSEUMS AND ART GALLERIES*

020   GE   ISSN 0075-2215
JAHRBUCH DER BIBLIOTHEKEN, ARCHIVE UND INFORMATIONSTELLEN DER DEUTSCHEN DEMOKRATISCHEN REPUBLIK. Title varies: Jahrbuch der Bibliotheken, Informationsstellen und Archive der D D R. 1959. triennial. M.45. VEB Bibliographisches Institut, Gerichtsweg 26, 7010 Leipzig, E. Germany (D.D.R.) (Co-Sponsor: Bibliotheksverband der DDR) Eds. Heinz Gittig, Wolfgang Horscht. adv. bk. rev. circ. 3,500.

020   GW   ISSN 0075-2223
JAHRBUCH DER DEUTSCHEN BIBLIOTHEKEN. 1902. biennial, latest vol.52, 1987. DM.88.80 (approx.) (Verein Deutscher Bibliothekare) Verlag Otto Harrassowitz, Taunusstr. 14, Postfach 2929, 6200 Wiesbaden 1, W. Germany (B.R.D.) adv. circ. 2,400.

020.6   JM
JAMAICA LIBRARY ASSOCIATION. BULLETIN. 1950. a. Jamaica Library Association, P.O. Box 58, Kingston 5, Jamaica.
Formerly: Jamaica Library Association. Annual Bulletin (ISSN 0448-2174)

LIBRARY AND INFORMATION SCIENCES

027   JA   ISSN 0385-325X
JAPAN. NATIONAL DIET LIBRARY. ANNUAL REPORT/KOKURITSU KOKKAI TOSHOKAN NENPO. 1948. a. National Diet Library - Kokuritsu Kokkai Toshokan, 1-10-1 Nagata-cho, Chiyoda-ku, Tokyo 100, Japan. circ. 1,880.

027.4   SA
JOHANNESBURG PUBLIC LIBRARY. ANNUAL REPORT. (Text in English) 1891. a. free. Johannesburg Public Library, Market Square, Johannesburg 2001, South Africa. (back issues avail.)

017   AT   ISSN 0726-9587
JOINT SERIALS CATALOGUE OF WESTERN AUSTRALIAN ACADEMIC LIBRARIES. 1981. a. Aus.$63. Western Australian Institute of Technology. Library, Kent St., Bentley, W.A. 6102, Australia.
Formerly: University of Western Australia. Joint Serials Catalogue of Murdoch University.

050   US   ISSN 0362-4544
JOURNAL HOLDINGS IN THE WASHINGTON-BALTIMORE AREA. 1969. biennial. $160. Interlibrary Users Association, c/o Metropolitan Washington Library Council, 1875 Eye St. N.W., Ste. 200, Washington, DC 20006. TEL 202-223-6800. Ed. Mary Lynn Kingston. charts. circ. 160 (controlled) (processed)

029   UK   ISSN 0022-0418
JOURNAL OF DOCUMENTATION; devoted to the recording, organization and dissemination of specialized knowledge. 1945. q. £65 to non-members. Aslib, Association for Information Management, Publications Department, Information House, 26-27 Boswell St., London WC1N 3JZ, England (Dist. in U.S. by Learned Information, 143 Old Marlton, Pike, Medford, New Jersey 08055) Ed. R.T. Kimber. adv. bk. rev. abstr. bibl. index. circ. 3,500. Indexed: Biol.Abstr. Chem.Abstr. Curr.Cont. Excerp.Med. Lib.Lit. M.L.A. SSCI. Sci.Abstr. Sci.Cit.Ind. Abstr.Bull.Inst.Pap.Chem. Br.Ceram.Abstr. C.I.J.E. Compumath. Dairy Sci.Abstr. Fluidex. Ind.Sci.Rev. Ind.Vet. Key to Econ.Sci. Lang.& Lang.Behav.Abstr. Vet.Bull.

020   US
JUNIOR HIGH SCHOOL LIBRARY CATALOG. 4th edt., 1980. quinquennial, plus a. supplements. H. W. Wilson Co., 950 University Ave., Bronx, NY 10452. TEL 212-588-8400. Ed. Juliette Yaakov.

020   US
JUST B'TWX US: AN INTERLIBRARY LOAN INFORMATION BULLETIN. 1970. irreg., vol.5, no.3, 1981. $5 for 2 yrs. University of Colorado Libraries, Interlibrary Loan Service, Campus Box 184, Boulder, CO 80309. TEL 303-492-7477. Ed. Virginia Boucher. circ. 375. (processed)
Former titles: Just B'twx Us: An Interlibrary Loan Newsletter; Just B'twx Us: An Interlibrary Loan Service Newsletter (ISSN 0075-4587)

020   US   ISSN 0075-5311
KEEPSAKE. (Each issue has also a distinctive title) 1966. irreg., no.11, 1984. $7.50 per no. Library Associates, University of California, Davis, Davis, CA 95616. TEL 916-752-3222. circ. 1,200.

020   KE   ISSN 0075-5923
KENYA. NATIONAL LIBRARY SERVICE BOARD. ANNUAL AND AUDIT REPORT. 1967/68. a. available on exchange. National Library Services, P.O. Box 30573, Nairobi, Kenya.

020   KE
KENYA LIBRARY ASSOCIATION CHAIRMAN'S ANNUAL REPORT. a. Kenya Library Association, Box 46031, Nairobi, Kenya. Ed. Johnston L. Abukutsa.

020   CS
KNIHA. 1976. a. 25 Kcs. Matica Slovenska, Mudronova 35, 036 52 Martin, Czechoslovakia.
Formerly: Knizna Kultura.

020   943.7   CS   ISSN 0139-5335
KNIHOVNA. 1957. irreg. Statni Pedagogicke Nakladatelstvi, Ostrovni 30, 113 01 Prague 1, Czechoslovakia (Subscr. to: Artia, Ve Smeckach 30, 111 27 Prague, Czechoslovakia)

020   CS   ISSN 0075-6369
KNIZNICNY ZBORNIK/LIBRARY STUDIES. (Text in Slovak; summaries in German and Russian) 1957. irreg. price varies. Matica Slovenska, Mudronova 35, 036 52 Martin, Czechoslovakia. bk. rev.

020   GW   ISSN 0721-7587
KOELNER ARBEITEN ZUM BIBLIOTHEKS- UND DOKUMENTATIONSWESEN. 1981. irreg. price varies. (Fachhochschule fuer Bibliotheks und Dokumentationswesen in Koeln) Greven Verlag, Neue Weyerstr. 1-3, D-5000 Cologne 1, W. Germany (B.R.D.) circ. 700.
Continues: Bibliothekar-Lehrinstitut des Landes Nordrhein-Westfalen. Arbeiten aus dem B L I (ISSN 0069-5858) & Bibliothekar-Lehrinstitut des Landes Nordrhein-Westfalen. Bibliographische Hefte (ISSN 0069-5866)

020   DK   ISSN 0105-3167
KONGELIGE BIBLIOTEK. PUBLIKUMSORIENTERINGER. 1974. irreg., latest no.18 1985. Kongelige Bibliotek - Royal Library, Christians Brygge 8, DK-1219 Copenhagen k, Denmark.

020   HU   ISSN 0139-1305
KONYV ES KONYVTAR. (Text in Hungarian; summaries in English, French, German and Russian) 1958. irreg., vol.14, 1985. $8. Kossuth Lajos Tudomanyegyetem Konyvtara, Egyetem ter 1, 4010 Debrecen, Hungary. TEL 36-52-16-835. Ed. Olga Gomba. bk. rev. circ. 400.

020   398   US   ISSN 0736-4903
L C FOLK ARCHIVE FINDING AID. 1983. irreg. free. U.S. Library of Congress, Archive of Folk Culture, American Folklife Center, 10 First St., S.E., Washington, DC 20540. TEL 202-287-5510. Ed. Joseph C. Hickerson. circ. 1,000.

021   US   ISSN 0095-4721
L.S.C.A. ANNUAL PROGRAM, HAWAII STATE LIBRARY SYSTEM. (Library Services and Construction Act) a. free to libraries. Office of Library Services, Research Evaluation Services, 465 S. King St., Rm. B-1, Honolulu, HI 96813. TEL 808-548-5585. circ. 50.

023   NR   ISSN 0047-3901
LAGOS LIBRARIAN. 1966. irreg., latest vol.11, no.2, 1984. $20. ‡ Nigerian Library Association, Lagos Division, c/o University Library, University of Lagos, Yaba, Lagos, Nigeria. Ed. S.O. Olanlokun. adv. bk. rev. circ. 400.

020   340   GW   ISSN 0175-6524
LANSKY: BIBLIOTHEKSRECHTLICHE VORSCHRIFTEN. irreg., 4th, 1986. price varies. Vittorio Klostermann, Frauenlobstr. 22, Postfach 900601, D-6000 Frankfurt 90, W. Germany (B.R.D.)

020   US   ISSN 0170-8643
LECTURE NOTES IN CONTROL AND INFORMATION SCIENCES. 1978. irreg., vol.88, 1986. price varies. Springer-Verlag, 175 Fifth Ave., New York, NY 10010 TEL 212-460-1500. (Also Berlin, Heidelberg, Tokyo and Vienna) Eds. A.V. Balakrishnan, M. Thoma. (report service avail. from ISI)

LEGAL INFORMATION MANAGEMENT INDEX. see LAW

020   UK
LIBRARIAN'S HANDBOOK. irreg., vol.2, 1980. price varies. Library Association Publishing, 7 Ridgmount St., London WC1E 7AE, England. Ed. L.J. Taylor.

020   AT   ISSN 0728-7429
LIBRARIES AND RESOURCES CENTRES IN THE NORTHERN TERRITORY. LIST. 1980. a. Aus.$7.50 to non-members. Library Association of Australia, Northern Territory, G.P.O. Box 1837, Darwin NT S794, Australia. Eds. Julii Tyson and Frieda Evans. circ. 80. (back issues avail.)

020   UK
LIBRARIES IN THE UNITED KINGDOM & THE REPUBLIC OF IRELAND. a. price varies. Library Association Publishing Ltd., 7 Ridgmount St., London WC1E 7AE, England.

021   US   ISSN 0092-833X
LIBRARIES OF MAINE; DIRECTORY AND STATISTICS. 1966. a. free. ‡ State Library, Department of Educational and Cultural Services, State House Sta. 64, Augusta, ME 04333. TEL 207-289-5620. stat.

LIBRARIES YEARBOOK. see MUSEUMS AND ART GALLERIES

020   JA   ISSN 0373-4447
LIBRARY AND INFORMATION SCIENCE. (Text in English and Japanese) 1963. a. $17. Mita Society for Library and Information Science - Mita Toshokan Joho Gakkai, c/o Keio University, 2-15-45 Mita, Minato-ku, Tokyo 108, Japan. Ed. Yoshinari Tsuda. bk. rev. circ. 1,750. Indexed: Curr.Cont. Lib.Lit. SSCI. Lib.Sci.Abstr.

020.622   UK
LIBRARY ASSOCIATION. CONFERENCE. PROCEEDINGS, PAPERS AND SUMMARIES OF DISCUSSIONS. a. Library Association Publishing Ltd., 7 Ridgmount St., London WC1E 7AE, England.

026   UK
LIBRARY ASSOCIATION. INDUSTRIAL GROUP NEWSLETTER. irreg. membership. Library Association, Industrial Group, c/o Mrs. D. Palmer, Technical Librarian, Smith Kline & French Laboratories Ltd., Welwyn Garden City, Herts., England.

020.6   MM
LIBRARY ASSOCIATION (VALLETTA). GHAQDA BIBLIOTEKARJI/LIBRARY ASSOCIATION NEWSLETTER. (Text in English) 1969. irreg. membership. Library Association (Valletta), c/o John XXIII Library, 226 St. Paul Street, Valletta, Malta. Ed. Anthony F. Sapienza. bk. rev. circ. 150.
Formerly (until no. 30, 1978): Malta Library Association Newsletter.

020   UK   ISSN 0075-9066
LIBRARY ASSOCIATION. YEAR BOOK. 1892. a. price varies. Library Association Publishing Ltd., 7 Ridgmount St., London WC1E 7AE, England.

020   CN   ISSN 0075-904X
LIBRARY ASSOCIATION OF ALBERTA. OCCASIONAL PAPERS. 1969. irreg. Can.$10. Library Association of Alberta, 1122 Crescent Rd N.W., Calgary 41, Alberta, Canada. bk. rev. circ. 700.

020   AT   ISSN 0155-560X
LIBRARY ASSOCIATION OF AUSTRALIA. HANDBOOK. 1952. a. Aus.$18. Library Association of Australia, 376 Jones St., Ultimo, N.S.W. 2007, Australia. circ. 4,000.

020.6   BB
LIBRARY ASSOCIATION OF BARBADOS. BULLETIN. 1968. irreg., no.12, 1985. $5. Library Association of Barbados, P.O. Box 827E, Bridgetown, Barbados, W. Indies.

020   TR   ISSN 0521-9590
LIBRARY ASSOCIATION OF TRINIDAD AND TOBAGO. BULLETIN. 1964. a. T.T.$20. Library Association of Trinidad and Tobago, P.O. Box 1275, Port of Spain, Trinidad, W.I. Ed.Bd. adv. circ. 200.

020.6   UK
LIBRARY ASSOCIATION YEARBOOK. 1892. a. price varies. Library Association Publishing, 7 Ridgmount St., London WC1E 7AE, England.

029   US
LIBRARY BIBLIOGRAPHIES AND INDEXES. 1975. irreg. $80. Gale Research Company, Book Tower, Detroit, MI 48226. TEL 313-961-2242. Eds. Paul Wasserman, Esther Herman.

020   US   ISSN 0094-8829
LIBRARY DEVELOPMENT IN ALASKA: LONG RANGE PROGRAM. a. $5. Department of Education, Division of State Libraries, Box G, Juneau, AK 99811.

021　　　　　US　ISSN 0024-2330
LIBRARY KEYNOTES;* news and views of library activities in Maryland. 1964. irreg., 2-3/yr. free contr. circ. Department of Education, Library Development and Services Division, 200 W. Baltimore St., Baltimore, MD 21201. circ. 2,000. (processed)

020　　　　　II
LIBRARY LITERATURE IN INDIA SERIES. no.2, 1975. irreg. price varies. Library Literature House, Chandigarh, India. illus.

027.7　　　　　KE
LIBRARY MAGAZINE. Variant title: University of Nairobi Library Magazine. (Text in English) 1979. irreg., no.3, 1980. University of Nairobi, Library, Box 30197, Nairobi, Kenya.

027.7　　　　　US　ISSN 0024-2438
LIBRARY NOTES. 1936. irreg., no.50, 1982. membership. (Friends of Duke University Library) Duke University, Library, Durham, NC 27706. TEL 919-684-2034. bibl. circ. 1,500. (also avail. in microfilm) Indexed: Abstr.Engl.Stud.

020　　　　　US　ISSN 0162-6426
LIBRARY OF CONGRESS; a brief summary of major activities. 1976. a. free. U.S. Library of Congress, Washington, DC 20540. TEL 202-287-5000.

027　　　　　US　ISSN 0364-1236
LIBRARY RESOURCES FOR THE BLIND AND PHYSICALLY HANDICAPPED (LARGE PRINT EDITION) 1968. a. free. U.S. Library of Congress, National Library Service for the Blind and Physically Handicapped, 1291 Taylor St., N.W., Washington, DC 20542. TEL 202-287-5100. Indexed: ERIC.
Formerly: Directory of Library Resources for the Blind and Physically Handicapped (ISSN 0278-7857)

026　　　　　US
LIBRARY SERVICE TO THE PEOPLE OF NEW YORK STATE: A LONG RANGE PLAN. 1978. a. $1.50. New York State Library, State Education Department, Cultural Education Center, Albany, NY 12230 (Subscr. to: New York State Library Gift and Exchange Section, Albany, NY 12230) circ. 5,000.

020.6　　　　　JA
LIBRARY YEARBOOK/TOSHOKAN NENKAN. 1982. a. 12000 Yen. Japan Library Association - Nihon Toshokan Kyokai, 1-1-10 Taishido, Setagaya-ku, Tokyo 154, Japan.

020　　　　　US　ISSN 0273-0227
LINDA HALL LIBRARY. MISCELLANY. 1980. irreg. free. Linda Hall Library, 5109 Cherry St., Kansas City, MO 64110. TEL 816-363-4600. Ed. Paul A. Peterson. bk. rev. illus. circ. 3,000.

027　　　　　US　ISSN 0085-2759
LOUISIANA STATE UNIVERSITY. LIBRARY. LIBRARY LECTURES. 1965. irreg., no.6, 1979. free. Louisiana State University Library, Baton Rouge, LA 70803. TEL 504-388-2217. Ed. Caroline Wire. circ. controlled. (also avail. in microform from EDR) Indexed: LISA. Lib.Lit. Inform.Sci.Abstr.

027.4　　　　　ZA
LUSAKA CITY LIBRARY. ANNUAL REPORT. 1977. a. free. Lusaka City Library, Box 1304, Katondo Rd., Lusaka, Zambia. circ. 150. (processed)

MAGAZINES FOR LIBRARIES; for the general reader and school, junior college, university and public libraries. see *BIBLIOGRAPHIES*

026.025　　　　　US　ISSN 0091-0759
MAINE. STATE LIBRARY. SPECIAL SUBJECT RESOURCES IN MAINE. irreg., latest issue 1972. State Library, State House Sta. 64, Augusta, ME 04333. TEL 207-289-5600. Key Title: Special Subject Resources in Maine.

020　　　　　MY　ISSN 0126-7809
MAJALLAH PERPUSTAKAAN MALAYSIA. (Text in English and Malay) 1972. a. M.8. Persatuan Perpustakaan Malaysia, Box 2545, Kuala Lumpur, Malaysia. Ed. Lim Hucktee. adv. bk. rev. circ. 500. Indexed: LISA.

026　610　　　　　UG
MAKERERE UNIVERSITY. ALBERT COOK LIBRARY. LIBRARY BULLETIN AND ACCESSION LIST. irreg., no.2, 1977. free. Makerere University, Albert Cook Library, Makerere Medical School, Box 7072, Kampala, Uganda. Ed. Maria Gioretti musoke. circ. controlled. (processed/back issues avail.)

020　　　　　UG　ISSN 0075-4854
MAKERERE UNIVERSITY. LIBRARY. MAKERERE LIBRARY PUBLICATIONS. Short title: Makerere Library Publications. 1961. irreg. free. Makerere University, Library, Box 16002, Kampala, Uganda.

027.5689　　　　　MW
MALAWI. NATIONAL LIBRARY SERVICE BOARD. ANNUAL REPORT. 1969. a. free. National Library Service Board, Box 30314, Lilongwe 3, Malawi. circ. controlled.
Formerly: Malawi. National Library. Annual Report (ISSN 0581-0906)

020　　　　　UK　ISSN 0260-8502
MANCHESTER POLYTECHNIC. DEPARTMENT OF LIBRARY AND INFORMATION STUDIES. OCCASIONAL PAPERS. 1980. irreg. price varies. Manchester Polytechnic, Department of Library and Information Studies, All Saints, Manchester M15 6BH, England. Ed. A.E. Day. circ. 200.

021　　　　　CN　ISSN 0706-7798
MANITOBA. PUBLIC LIBRARY SERVICES. NEWSLETTER. 1978. irreg. Public Library Services, 139 Hamelin St., Winnipeg, Man. R3T 4H4, Canada. TEL 204-945-6460.

027.8　　　　　CN　ISSN 0315-9124
MANITOBA SCHOOL LIBRARY AUDIO VISUAL ASSOCIATION JOURNAL. 1968. 3-4/yr. $20 to members. ‡ Manitoba School Library Audio Visual Association, c/o Manitoba Teachers' Society, Winnipeg, Man. R3J 3H2, Canada. TEL 204-888-7961. bk. rev. illus. index. circ. 400. Indexed: Can.Ind.
Formerly: Manitoba Association of School Librarians Newsletter (ISSN 0025-2204)

021.7　　　　　US
MARGINAL NOTES; an interim newsletter. no.17, Nov.1977. irreg. $25. Friends of the Duke University Library, Durham, NC 27706. circ. 700.

MARIAN LIBRARY STUDIES. NEW SERIES. see *RELIGIONS AND THEOLOGY*

020　　　　　MF　ISSN 0076-5481
MAURITIUS. ARCHIVES DEPARTMENT. ANNUAL REPORT. (Includes yearly supplement Bibliography of Mauritius) (Text in English; bibliographical supplement in English and French) 1950 (covers 1949) a. Rs.15. Archives Department, Development Bank of Mauritius Complex, Coromandel, Beau-Bassin, Mauritius (Orders to: Government Printing Office, Elizabeth II Ave., Port Louis, Mauritius)

020　　　　　US　ISSN 0363-1257
METRO C A P CATALOG; a dictionary catalog of materials purchased through the Cooperative Acquisitions Program. 1976. irreg. price varies. New York Metropolitan Reference & Research Library Agency, 57 Willoughby St., Brooklyn, NY 11201. TEL 718-852-8700.

020　　　　　US
METRO HANDBOOK AND DIRECTORY OF MEMBERS (YEAR) 1980. a. $18.95 to members; non-members $23.95. ‡ (New York Metropolitan Reference & Research Library Agency) L D A Publishers, 42-36 209 St., Bayside, NY 11361. TEL 718-224-0485. circ. 1,030.
Former titles: METRO; New York Metropolitan Reference and Research Agency. Handbook and Directory of Members; New York Metropolitan Reference and Research Agency. Directory of Members (ISSN 0362-8744)

026　　　　　US　ISSN 0076-7018
METRO; NEW YORK METROPOLITAN REFERENCE AND RESEARCH LIBRARY AGENCY. METRO MISCELLANEOUS PUBLICATIONS SERIES. 1968. irreg., latest no.28. ‡ New York Metropolitan Reference & Research Library Agency, 57 Willoughby St., Brooklyn, NY 11201. TEL 718-852-8700.

025　　　　　CN　ISSN 0700-4532
METROPOLITAN TORONTO LIBRARY BOARD. ANNUAL REPORT. 1968. a. Metropolitan Toronto Library Board, Public Relations Office, 789 Yonge St., Toronto, Ont. M4W 2G8, Canada. TEL 416-824-5150. Ed. Margaret Chartrand. illus. circ. 3,000.

MICHIGAN GAZETTE. see *HISTORY — History Of North And South America*

021　　　　　US
MICHIGAN LIBRARY DIRECTORY. 1967. a. free. Library of Michigan, Box 30007, Lansing, MI 48909. TEL 517-373-1593. Ed. Donald C. Leaf. circ. 2,000.
Continues in part: Michigan Library Directory and Statistics (ISSN 0076-8081); Formerly: Michigan Library News.

778.1　　　　　US　ISSN 0362-0999
MICROFORM MARKET PLACE. Short title: M M P. 1974. biennial. $39.95. Meckler Publishing, 11 Ferry Lane West, Westport, CT 06880. TEL 203-226-6967. adv.

020　　　　　US
MICROGRAPHICS AND OPTICAL STORAGE EQUIPMENT REVIEW. 1976. a. $185 (institutional price varies) Meckler Publishing, 11 Ferry Lane West, Westport, CT 06880. TEL 203-226-6967. Ed. William Saffady. Indexed: Consum.Ind.
Formerly (until 1985): Micrographics Equipment Review (ISSN 0362-1006)

MODSZERTANI KIADVANYOK/METHODS OF INFORMATION AND DOCUMENTATION. see *TECHNOLOGY: COMPREHENSIVE WORKS*

021　　　　　US　ISSN 0094-873X
MONTANA LIBRARY DIRECTORY, WITH STATISTICS OF MONTANA PUBLIC LIBRARIES. a. State Library, 1515 E. 6th Ave., Helena, MT 59620. TEL 406-444-3115. stat.

020　060　　　　　AU　ISSN 0077-2208
MUSEION. 1957. irreg. price varies. (Oesterreichische Nationalbibliothek) Brueder Hollinek, Gallgasse 40A, A-1130 Vienna, Austria. (reprint service avail. from ISI)

026　　　　　US　ISSN 0094-5099
MUSIC LIBRARY ASSOCIATION. TECHNICAL REPORTS; information for music media specialists. 1973. irreg. price varies. Music Library Association, Box 487, Canton, MA 02021. Ed. Michael Fling. circ. 150. Indexed: RILM.

020　　　　　US　ISSN 0161-1704
MUSIC O C L C USERS GROUP. NEWSLETTER. 1977. irreg. $5 to individuals; institutions $10. Music O C L C Users Group, c/o Pamela K. Juengling, University of Massachusetts Music Library, Amherst, MA 01003. TEL 413-545-2870. Ed. Ann McCollough. circ. 500.

020　　　　　UN
N A T I S - NEWS. French edition: N A T I S-Nouvelles. Spanish edt.: N A T I S Noticias. (Newsletter containing information on the implementation in Unesco member states of national information systems) (Text in English, French, Spanish) 1975. irreg. free. Unesco, 7-9 Place de Fontenoy, 75700 Paris, France.

020　　　　　FI　ISSN 0358-7045
N O R D I N F O PUBLIKATION. 1981. irreg., no.9, 1985. price varies. Nordiska Samarbetsorganet for Vetenskaplig Information - Nordic Council for Scientific Information and Research Libraries, c/o Helsinki University of Technology Library, Otnaesvaegen 9, SF-02150 Esbo, Finland. circ. 2,500.

600　　　　　US
N T I S DIGEST. 1984. irreg. free. U.S. National Technical Information Service, 5285 Port Royal Rd., Springfield, VA 22161. TEL 703-487-4600.

020　　　　　YU　ISSN 0350-3569
NARODNA IN UNIVERZITETNA KNJIZNICA. ZBORNIK. (Text in Slovenian; summaries in French and German) 1974. irreg. Narodna in Univerzitetna Knjiznica, Turjaska 1, 61001 Ljubljana, Yugoslavia. TEL 061-332-853. illus.

LIBRARY AND INFORMATION SCIENCES

025.17   ZA   ISSN 0084-4942
NATIONAL ARCHIVES OF ZAMBIA. ANNUAL REPORT. 1964. a. National Archives, Box RW 50010, Ridgeway, Lusaka, Zambia.

020   NP
NATIONAL COUNCIL FOR SCIENCE & TECHNOLOGY. DIRECTORY; scientists and technologists of Nepal. (Text in English) 1977. a. $20. National Council for Science & Technology, Kirtipur, Kathmandu, Nepal. circ. 500.

026   US   ISSN 0884-9536
NATIONAL DIRECTORY OF BULLETIN BOARD SYSTEMS. 1985. m. $29.95. Meckler Publishing Corporation, 11 Ferry Lane West, Westport, CT 06880-5808. Ed. Nancy Melin.

020   RH
NATIONAL FREE LIBRARY OF ZIMBABWE. ANNUAL REPORT. 1961/62. a. free on exchange. ‡ National Free Library of Zimbabwe, P.O. Box 1773, Bulawayo, Zimbabwe. circ. 450.
   Former titles: National Free Library Service. Annual Report & National Free Library of Rhodesia. Annual Report (ISSN 0068-3612)

027.571   CN   ISSN 0078-7000
NATIONAL LIBRARY OF CANADA. ANNUAL REPORT. (Text in English and French) 1963. a. free. ‡ National Library of Canada, Public Relations Office, 395 Wellington St., Ottawa, Ont. K1A 0N4, Canada. TEL 613-995-7969. circ. 6,000.

020   US   ISSN 0093-0393
NATIONAL LIBRARY OF MEDICINE. PROGRAMS AND SERVICES. a. $10 for 1984 edt. ‡ U.S. National Library of Medicine, 8600 Rockville Pike, Bethesda, MD 20894 TEL 703-487-4650. (Orders to: NTIS, Springfield, VA 22161) (reprint service avail. from UMI)
   Formerly (until 1972): U.S. National Library of Medicine. Annual Report (ISSN 0083-2243)

021   US
NEBRASKA LIBRARY COMMISSION. LIBRARY DIRECTORY. biennial. Library Commission, 1420 P St, Lincoln, NE 68508. TEL 402-471-2045. Ed. John Kopischke. circ. 1,200.
   Former titles: Nebraska Library Commission. Biennial Report & Nebraska Library Commission. Annual Report (ISSN 0099-0299)

020   NE
NEDERLANDSE BIBLIOTHEEK- EN DOCUMENATIEGIDS;* adresboek van in Nederland gevestigde bibliotheken en documentatieinstellingen. biennial. (Nederlands Bibliotheek en Lektuur Centrum) Samsom Vakbladen, P.O.B. 93054, 2509 AB the Hague, Netherlands.
   Formerly: Venadam Bibliotheekgids.

027.4   NE   ISSN 0168-3462
NETHERLANDS. CENTRAAL BUREAU VOOR DE STATISTIEK. STATISTIEK VAN DE OPENBARE BIBLIOTHEKEN. a. fl.24. Centraal Bureau voor de Statistiek, Prinses Beatrixlaan 428, Voorburg, Netherlands (Orders to: Staatsuitgeverij, Christoffel Plantijnstraat, The Hague, Netherlands) stat.

020   GE   ISSN 0457-3897
NEUJAHRSGABE DER DEUTSCHEN BUECHEREI. 1956. a. Deutsche Buecherei, Deutscher Platz 1, 7010 Leipzig, E. Germany(D.D.R.)

020   US
NEVADA LIBRARY DIRECTORY AND STATISTICS. 1975. a. free. State Library, Capitol Complex, Carson City, NV 89710. TEL 702-885-5145.

025   US   ISSN 0147-1090
NEW DIRECTIONS IN LIBRARIANSHIP. 1978. irreg. price varies. Greenwood Press, 88 Post Rd. W., Box 5007, Westport, CT 06881. TEL 203-226-3571. Ed. Daniel Gore.

027   US   ISSN 0077-930X
NEW YORK. STATE LIBRARY, ALBANY. LIBRARY DEVELOPMENT. EXCERPTS FROM NEW YORK STATE EDUCATION LAW, RULES OF THE BOARD OF REGENTS, AND REGULATIONS OF THE COMMISSIONER OF EDUCATION PERTAINING TO PUBLIC AND FREE ASSOCIATION LIBRARIES, LIBRARY SYSTEMS, TRUSTEES AND LIBRARIANS. 1959. irreg. free to libraries in New York State; on exchange basis with other libraries. State Library, Library Development, Albany, NY 12234. circ. 1, 500.

027   US   ISSN 0077-9318
NEW YORK. STATE LIBRARY, ALBANY. LIBRARY DEVELOPMENT. INSTITUTION LIBRARIES STATISTICS. 1954. a. free to libraries in New York State; on exchange basis with other libraries. ‡ State Library, Library Development, Albany, NY 12230. circ. 1,000.

027   US   ISSN 0077-9326
NEW YORK. STATE LIBRARY, ALBANY. LIBRARY DEVELOPMENT. PUBLIC AND ASSOCIATION LIBRARIES STATISTICS. 1950. a. free to libraries in New York State; on exchange basis with other libraries. State Library, Library Development, Albany, NY 12230. circ. 1,250.

026   US   ISSN 0077-9490
NEW YORK UNIVERSITY. LIBRARIES. BULLETIN OF THE TAMIMENT LIBRARY. 1957. irreg., no.50, 1983. free. ‡ New York University, Tamiment Library, 70 Washington Sq. So., New York, NY 10012. TEL 212-598-3708. Ed. Dorothy Swanson. circ. 500. (also avail. in microfilm) Indexed: P.A.I.S.

025   GW   ISSN 0072-4866
NIEDERSAECHSISCHE STAATS- UND UNIVERSITAETSBIBLIOTHEK, GOETTINGEN. ARBEITEN. 1954. irreg., no.19, 1985. price varies. (Niedersaechsische Staats- und Universitaetsbibliothek) Vandenhoeck und Ruprecht, Theaterstr. 13, 3400 Goettingen, W. Germany (B.R.D.)

026   NO
NORSKE VITENSKAPELIGE OG FAGLIGE BIBLIOTEKER; en haandbok. (Text in Norwegian; contents and subject index in English) 1963. irreg., no.6, 1987. price varies. Riksbibliotektjenesten, Box 2439, Solli, 0202 Oslo 2, Norway TEL 02-43 08 80. (Dist. by: A/L Biblioteksentralen, Malerhaugveien 20, 0661 Oslo 6, Norway) Ed. Libena Vokac. bk. rev.

020   US   ISSN 0048-0789
NORTHERN LIBRARIES BULLETIN. 1972. irreg. (approx. 3/yr.) free. ‡ Department of Education, Division of State Libraries, Box G, Juneau, AK 99811. TEL 907-465-2910. Ed. Phyllis DeMuth. bk. rev. bibl. circ. 150.

020   NO   ISSN 0800-4153
NORWAY. RIKSBIBLIOTEKTJENESTEN. AARSMELDING. a. free. Riksbibliotektjenesten, Box 2439, Solli, 0202 Oslo 2, Norway.

020   NO   ISSN 0800-4129
NORWAY. RIKSBIBLIOTEKTJENESTEN. SKRIFTER/PAPERS. (Text in English and Norwegian; summaries in English) irreg., (1-3/yr.) free. Riksbibliotektjenesten, Box 2439, Solli, 0202 Oslo 2, Norway.

020.6   SW   ISSN 0349-3210
NYTT FRAAN D F I. (Text in Swedish) 1980. irreg., (3-4/yr.) free. Delegationen foer Vetenskaplig och Teknisk Informationsfoersoerjning - Delegation for Scientific and Technical Information, Box 43 033, 100 72 Stockholm, Sweden. Ed. Margareta Sundberg. circ. 2,000.

021.6   US   ISSN 0730-5125
O C L C ANNUAL REPORT. a. free. Online Computer Library Center, Inc., 6565 Frantz Rd., Dublin, OH 43017. TEL 614-764-6000.
   Formerly: Ohio College Library Center. Annual Report (ISSN 0090-8673)

025   US   ISSN 0278-7946
O M S ANNUAL REPORT. 1971. a. free. Association of Research Libraries, Office of Management Studies, 1527 New Hampshire Ave., N.W., Washington, DC 20036. TEL 202-232-8656. Ed. Maxine K. Sitts. circ. 500. Indexed: ERIC.

020   YU
OBVESTILA REPUBLISKE MATICNE SLUZBE. 1975. irreg. Narodna in Univerzitetna Knjiznica, Turjaska 1, 61001 Ljubljana, Yugoslavia. TEL 061-332-853.
   Formerly (until 1975): Obvestila Republiske Maticne Knjiznice (ISSN 0350-3577)

020   US   ISSN 0278-4882
OCCASIONAL PAPERS IN MIDDLE EASTERN LIBRARIANSHIP. 1981. irreg. $7. Middle East Librarians' Association, c/o Dona Straley, 1858 Neil Ave. Mall, Ohio State University, Columbus, OH 43210. TEL 614-292-3362. Ed. David H. Partington. circ. 175.

026 016   AU
OESTERREICHISCHES STAATSARCHIV. PUBLIKATIONEN; Inventare oesterreichischer staatlicher Archive. 1909. irreg., vol.36, 1984. price varies. Verlag Ferdinand Berger und Soehne OHG, Wiener Str. 21-23, A-3580 Horn, Austria.

027.4   US   ISSN 0748-2469
OFFICIAL DIRECTORY OF NEW JERSEY LIBRARIES MEDIA CENTERS INCLUDING BUYERS' GUIDE. a. $29.95. (New Jersey Library Association) L D A Publishers, 42-36 209 St., Bayside, NY 11361. TEL 718-224-0485. adv.
   Formerly: Official Directory of New Jersey Libraries and Media Centers.

027   US
OHIO. STATE LIBRARY. ANNUAL REPORT. 1972. a. free. State Library Board, 65 S. Front St., Columbus, OH 43266-0334. TEL 614-462-6875. Ed. Peggy Campbell. charts. illus. stat.
   Formerly: Ohio. State Library. State Library Review.

020   JA
OKINAWA LIBRARY ASSOCIATION. ANNALS/OKINAWA TOSHOKAN KYOKAI SHI. 1964. a. 500 Yen. Okinawa Library Association - Okinawa Toshokan Kyokai, c/o Okinawa Prefectural Library, 1-2-16 Yorimiya, Naha, Japan. adv. bk. rev. circ. 1, 000.

ONLINE BUSINESS SOURCEBOOK. see *BUSINESS AND ECONOMICS*

020   US   ISSN 0078-6381
ORGANIZATION OF AMERICAN STATES. DEPARTMENT OF CULTURAL AFFAIRS. MANUALES DEL BIBLIOTECARIO. 1961. irreg., latest no.9. $15. Organization of American States, Department of Publications, Washington, DC 20006. TEL 703-941-1617. circ. 2,000.

020   HU   ISSN 0524-8868
ORSZAGOS SZECHENYI KONYVTAR EVKONYVE. (Text in Hungarian; summaries in English, French, German, Russian) 1958. a. 130 Ft. Orszagos Szechenyi Konyvtar, Budavari Palota F, H-1827 Budapest 1, Hungary. Ed. Maria Nemeth. circ. 800.

020   US   ISSN 0146-2237
P L A REPORT. 1973. a. free. Post Library Association, Long Island Univ., C.W. Post Center, Greenvale, NY 11548. TEL 516-299-2303. Ed. Joan H. Huntoon. bk. rev. bibl. illus. circ. 2,000.

020   AT   ISSN 0814-771X
P L NEWS. (Public Library) 1982. irreg. free. Library Council of Victoria, 328 Swanson St., Melbourne, Vic. 3000, Australia. Ed. C. Ely. circ. 500. (back issues avail.)

020   US   ISSN 0079-0656
PENNSYLVANIA STATE UNIVERSITY. LIBRARIES. BIBLIOGRAPHICAL SERIES. 1969. irreg., latest no.10. price varies. ‡ Pennsylvania State University, University Libraries, University Park, PA 16802. TEL 814-865-0401. Ed. Charles H. Ness. circ. 500.

020   PE   ISSN 0031-6067
PERU. BIBLIOTECA NACIONAL. BOLETIN. 1943. a. $2.50. Biblioteca Nacional, Apdo. 2335, Lima, Peru. Ed. Lucila Valderrama. bk. rev. abstr. bibl. illus. circ. 1,000.

PHAEDRUS; international annual of children's literature research. see *LITERATURE*

LIBRARY AND INFORMATION SCIENCES

020   PH
PHILIPPINE LIBRARY ASSOCIATION.
BULLETIN. (Text in English) vol.8, 1973. a.
P.10($6) Philippine Library Association, c/o
National Library, T.M. Kalaw St., Manila,
Philippines. Ed. Conrado D. David. bk. rev. circ. 1,
000. (back issues avail.) Indexed: Ind.Phil.Per.

PHILIPPINES. GOVERNMENT PRINTING
OFFICE. ITEMIZATION OF PERSONAL
SERVICES AND ORGANIZATIONAL CHARTS.
see *PUBLIC ADMINISTRATION*

PIVOT. see *EDUCATION — Adult Education*

020   US
POINTS NORTHWEST. 1972. irreg., (4-6/yr.) $5 to
non-members. American Society for Information
Science, Pacific Northwest Chapter, Owen Science
& Engineering Library, Washington State University,
Pullman, WA 99164. adv. bk. rev. circ. 120.

026   060   PL   ISSN 0079-3140
POLSKA AKADEMIA NAUK. BIBLIOTEKA,
KRAKOW. ROCZNIK. (Text in Polish; summaries
in English and Russian) 1955. a. price varies.
Ossolineum, Publishing House of the Polish
Academy of Sciences, Rynek 9, 50-106 Wroclaw,
Poland (Dist. by: Ars Polona-Ruch, Krakowskie
Przedmiescie 7, Warsaw, Poland) Ed. Zbigniew
Jablonski. index.

020   UR
PROGNOZIROVANIE RAZVITIYA
BIBLIOTECHNOGO DELA V S.S.S.R. 1972.
irreg. 0.53 Rub. Moskovskaya Publichnaya
Biblioteka, Moscow, Russian S.F.S.R., U.S.S.R.

PROGRESS IN COMMUNICATION SCIENCES.
see *COMMUNICATIONS*

025   UK   ISSN 0263-9181
PUBLIC LIBRARY EXPENDITURE IN
SCOTLAND. 1982. a. £10. Scottish Library
Association, Motherwell Business Centre,
Coursington Rd., Motherwell 1ML 1PW, Scotland.

020   US   ISSN 0555-6031
PUBLIC LIBRARY REPORTER. Title varies; 1954-
58: P L D Reporter. 1954. irreg. price varies.
(Public Library Association) American Library
Association, 50 East Huron St., Chicago, IL 60611.
TEL 312-944-6780.

020   US
PUBLICATIONS IN THE INFORMATION
SCIENCES. (Each vol. has distinctive title) 1978.
irreg., latest 1981. price varies. Van Nostrand
Reinhold Company, 7625 Empire Dr., Florence, KY
41042. TEL 606-525-6600. Ed. R. G. Lerner. illus.
index.

PUBLISHERS' CATALOGS ANNUAL. see
BIBLIOGRAPHIES

020   CN   ISSN 0380-7150
Q L A BULLETIN/BULLETIN A B Q. (Text in
English and French) 3/yr. irreg. membership.
Quebec Library Association, Box 2216, Dorval,
Que. H9S 5J4, Canada. TEL 514-631-7616. Ed.
Gretchen Cheung. adv. bk. rev. circ. 225.

020   US   ISSN 0146-8677
QUEENS COLLEGE STUDIES IN
LIBRARIANSHIP. 1977. irreg. (approx. 1/yr.)
price varies. Queens College Press, c/o Dyanne
Maue, Kiely 1310, Flushing, NY 11367. TEL 718-
520-7599. Ed. Robert A. Colby. (back issues avail.)

027.7   CN
QUEEN'S UNIVERSITY AT KINGSTON.
ANNUAL REPORT ON THE LIBRARIES. a.
Queen's University, Kingston, Ont. K7L 3N6,
Canada. TEL 613-547-5511.

027   UR
RAIONNYE BIBLIOTEKI BELORUSSII; analiz
sostoyaniya raboty i metodicheskie rekomendatsii.
1957. a. free. Gosudarstvennaya Biblioteka
Belorusskoi S.S.R. im V.I. Lenina,
Krasnozmanennaya ul., 9, Minsk, Byelorussian
S.S.R., U.S.S.R. Ed. E.N. Tsygankov. circ. 370.
(also avail. in microfilm)

025   US   ISSN 0277-5948
RECOMMENDED REFERENCE BOOKS FOR
SMALL & MEDIUM-SIZED LIBRARIES AND
MEDIA CENTERS. 1981. a. $30.00. Libraries
Unlimited, Inc., Box 263, Littleton, CO 80160. TEL
303-770-1220. Ed. Bohdan S. Wynar. bk. rev.

029   US
REGISTER OF INDEXERS. 1974. a. $20. American
Society of Indexers, Inc., 1700 18th St., N.W.,
Washington, DC 20009. circ. 500.

029   370   SP
REPERTORIO DE SERVICIOS DE
DOCUMENTACION E INFORMACION
EDUCATIVA IBEROAMERICANOS. (Text in
Portuguese and Spanish) 1982. biennial. 1500
ptas.($11) Organizacion de Estados Iberoamericanos
(OEI), Ciudad Universitaria, 28040 Madrid, Spain.

020   US   ISSN 0733-1142
RESEARCH MATERIALS IN MICROFORM
AVAILABLE IN THE HARVARD UNIVERSITY
LIBRARY. 1981. irreg. Harvard University Library,
Cambridge, MA 02138.

020   SW   ISSN 0280-3046
RIKSARKIVETS RAPPORTER. 1981. irreg. price
varies. Riksarkivet, Box 12541, S-102 29 Stockholm,
Sweden.

027   US   ISSN 0080-3227
RIVER BEND LIBRARY SYSTEM. REPORT OF
THE DIRECTOR. 1966. a. free. ‡ River Bend
Library System, Box 125, Coal Valley, IL 61240.
TEL 309-799-3155. Ed. Robert W. McKay. (back
issues avail.) Indexed: Lib.Lit.

020   DK   ISSN 0105-564X
ROSKILDE UNIVERSITETSBIBLIOTEK.
SKRIFTSERIE. (Text in Danish) 1977. irreg., latest
no.11. free. Roskilde Universitetsbibliotek - Library
of Roskilde University, Postboks 258, DK-400
Roskilde, Denmark. circ. 500. (back issues avail)

620   025.33   US
S H E. (Subject Headings for Engineering) 1972.
irreg., latest 1983, plus supplements. $45.
Engineering Information, Inc., 345 E. 47th St., New
York, NY 10017. TEL 212-705-7600.

026   023   US
S L A TRIENNIAL SALARY SURVEY. 1964.
triennial. $25. Special Libraries Association, 1700
Eighteenth St., N.W., Washington, DC 20009. TEL
202-234-4700. (reprint service avail. from UMI)

010   NE   ISSN 0581-2674
SAFAHO-MONOGRAPHS. 1962. irreg. price varies.
(Safaho-Stiftung zur Foerderung Bibliographischer
Forschung) Erasmus Antiquariaat & Boekhandel,
Spui 2, Amsterdam, Netherlands. Ed. A. Horodisch.
circ. 500.
Formerly (1962-1969): Safaho-Monographien.

025   US
SCARECROW LIBRARY ADMINISTRATION
SERIES. irreg. Scarecrow Press, Inc., 52 Library St.,
Box 4167, Metuchen, NJ 08840.

027.8   CN   ISSN 0706-2915
SCHOOL LIBRARY NEWSLETTER. 1972. irreg.
free. Prince Edward Island Provincial Library,
Enman Cres., Box 7500, Charlottetown, P.E.I. C1A
8T8, Canada. TEL 902-892-3504. Eds. Bill Ledwell,
Sandra Taylor Richardson. bk. rev. circ. 200.
Formerly (until Apr. 1978): School Library
Association Newsletter (ISSN 0706-2907)

025.2   500   US   ISSN 0080-746X
SCIENCE AND TECHNOLOGY (PITTSBURGH); a
purchase guide for branch and public libraries. 1960.
a. $5. Carnegie Library of Pittsburgh, Science and
Technology Department, 4400 Forbes Ave.,
Pittsburgh, PA 15213. TEL 412-622-3141. circ. 500.
(also avail. in microform from EDR)
Continues: Basic Collection of Science and
Technology Books.
Annotated bibliography

020   FR
SCIENCES DE L'INFORMATION. LEXIQUE.
(Text in English) 1978. a. 265 F.($280) Centre
National de la Recherche Scientifique, Centre de
Documentation Scientifique et Technique, 26 rue
Boyer, 75971 Paris Cedex 20, France.

027   UK   ISSN 0080-8091
SCOTTISH LIBRARIES. 1966. quinquennial. Scottish
Library Association, Motherwell Business Centre,
Coursington Rd., Motherwell 1ML 1PW, Scotland.
adv. circ. 600.

021   UK
SCOTTISH LIBRARY AND INFORMATION
RESOURCES. 1984. irreg. £20. Scottish Library
Association, Motherwell Business Centre,
Coursington Rd., Motherwell ML1 1PW, Scotland.
Formerly: Library Resources in Scotland.

020   US
SEARCH INFORM. 1983. irreg., 3rd ed. 1986. $65.
Data Courier, 620 S. Fifth St., Louisville, KY
40202. TEL 800-626-2823. (looseleaf format)

027.4   MY
SELANGOR PUBLIC LIBRARY. ANNUAL
REPORT/PERBADANAN PERPUSTAKAAN
AWAM SELANGOR. LAPURAN TAHUNAN.
1972. a. Selangor Public Library, 21 Jalan Raja,
Kuala Lumpur 01-02, Malaysia. stat. circ. 500.

070   980   US   ISSN 0080-8857
SEMINAR ON THE ACQUISITION OF LATIN
AMERICAN LIBRARY MATERIALS.
MICROFILMING PROJECTS NEWSLETTER.
1964. a. $3. Seminar on the Acquisition of Latin
American Library Materials, Memorial Library,
University of Wisconsin-Madison, Madison, WI
53706. TEL 608-262-3240. Ed. Basil Malish.
cum.index (nos. 1-20) circ. 325. (processed)
Indexed: Lib.Lit.

025   US
SEMINAR ON THE ACQUISITION OF LATIN
AMERICAN LIBRARY MATERIALS. PAPERS.
1956. a. membership; price varies for individual nos.
‡ Seminar on the Acquisition of Latin American
Library Materials, SALALM Secretariat, Memorial
Library, University of Wisconsin-Madison, Madison,
WI 53706. TEL 608-262-3240. cum.index (nos. 1-
25) Indexed: Lib.Lit.
Former titles: Seminar on the Acquisition of
Latin American Library Materials. Final Report and
Working Papers (ISSN 0080-8849) & Seminar on
the Acquistion of Latin American Library Materials.
Working Papers.

026   SG   ISSN 0850-010X
SENEGAL. ARCHIVES DU SENEGAL. RAPPORT
ANNUEL. 1976. a. free. Archives du Senegal,
Immeuble Administratif, Av. Roume, Dakar,
Senegal. Ed. Saliou Mbaye. circ. 250.

020   US
SENIOR HIGH SCHOOL LIBRARY CATALOG.
quinquennial, with a. supplements. $70. ‡ H.W.
Wilson Co., 950 University Ave., Bronx, New York,
NY 10452. TEL 212-588-8400. Ed. Juliette Yaakov.
bk. rev.

SERIALS IN EDUCATION IN AUSTRALIAN
LIBRARIES: A UNION LIST. see
*EDUCATION — Abstracting, Bibliographies,
Statistics*

020   SL   ISSN 0583-2268
SIERRA LEONE. LIBRARY BOARD. REPORT.
1961. a. Library Board, Box 326, Freetown, Sierra
Leone. (back issues avail.)

020   SI   ISSN 0217-1546
SINGAPORE. NATIONAL LIBRARY. ANNUAL
REPORT. 1963. a. exchange basis. National
Library, Stamford Road, Singapore 0617, Singapore.
circ. 1,000.

027   SI   ISSN 0085-6118
SINGAPORE LIBRARIES. (Text mainly in English;
occasionally in Chinese, Malay and Tamil) 1971. a.
$15. Library Association of Singapore, c/o National
Library, Stamford Road, Singapore 0617, Singapore.
Ed. Poh Guan-Huat. adv. bk. rev. circ. 600.
Indexed: LISA. Lib.Lit.

020   SW   ISSN 0346-8488
SKRIFTER UTGIVNA AV SVENSKA
RIKSARKIVET. 1931. irreg. price varies.
Riksarkivet, Box 12541, S-102 29 Stockholm,
Sweden.

020 CN
SOCIETE DE DEVELOPPEMENT DU LIVRE ET DU PERIODIQUE. ANNUAIRE. 1965. a. free. Edi-Quebec Inc., 1151 Alexandre DeSeve, Montreal, Que. H2L 2T7, Canada. TEL 514-524-7528. circ. 4,000.
  Formerly: Conseil Superieur du Livre. Annuaire (ISSN 0084-9197)

SOFTWARE PUBLISHERS' CATALOGS ANNUAL. see COMPUTERS — Software

891.8 070.5 UK ISSN 0038-0903
SOLANUS; international journal for Russian & East European bibliographic, library & publishing studies. 1966; N.S. 1987. a. Standing Conference of National and University Libraries, c/o Dr. Gregory Walker, Ed., Slavonic Section, Bodleian Library, Oxford OX1 3BG, England. adv. bk. rev. circ. 100. (back issues avail.) Indexed: LISA.

020.6 US
SOLINET. ANNUAL REPORT. a. free. Southeastern Library Network, 400 Colony Square, 1201 Peachtree St., N.E., Atlanta, GA 30361. TEL 404-892-0943. charts. stat. circ. 1,500.
  Formerly: Southeastern Library Network. Annual Report (ISSN 0099-085X)

020 US ISSN 0038-1853
SOUNDINGS (SANTA BARBARA); collections of the University Library. 1969. a. $4 to non-members. ‡ University of California, Santa Barbara, University Library, Santa Barbara, CA 93106. TEL 805-961-3014. Ed. Donald E. Fitch. bibl. illus. circ. 850. Indexed: Hist.Abstr. M.L.A.

SOURCES FOR THE STUDY OF RELIGION IN MALAWI. see RELIGIONS AND THEOLOGY

027.568 SA
SOUTH AFRICA. STATE LIBRARY COUNCIL. REPORT/VERSLAG. (Text in English and Afrikaans) 1933. a. free. State Library, P.O. Box 397, Pretoria 0001, South Africa. illus.

025 AT ISSN 0081-2633
SOUTH AUSTRALIA. LIBRARIES BOARD. ANNUAL REPORT. 1884/5. a. free. Libraries Board of South Australia, Box 419 G.P.O., Adelaide 5001, Australia. Ed. Philip W. Pike. circ. 350.

027 US ISSN 0361-6479
SOUTH CAROLINA STATE LIBRARY. ANNUAL REPORT. 1943. a. free. State Library, 1500 Senate St., Box 11469, Columbia, SC 29211. TEL 803-734-8666. Ed. Betty E. Callaham. circ. 500(controlled) Indexed: ERIC.

020 950 UK ISSN 0308-4035
SOUTH EAST ASIA LIBRARY GROUP NEWSLETTER. 1968. irreg. (approx. 2/yr.) £5($11) for 4 nos. ‡ South East Asia Library Group, c/o Brynmor Jones Library, University of Hull, Hull HU6 7RX, England. Ed. M. Smyth. adv. bk. rev. bibl. circ. 200. Indexed: E.I.

020 CN ISSN 0707-6894
SOUTHEAST REGIONAL LIBRARY (SASK.) LIBRARY DIRECTORY. Variant title: Directory of Libraries in Southeast Saskatchewan. 1975. a. free contr. circ. Southeast Regional Library (Sask.), Box 550, Weyburn, Sask. S4H 2K7, Canada. TEL 306-842-3432. illus.

020 070 051 US ISSN 0883-282X
SPECTRUM; a guide to the independent press and informative organizations. 1973. irreg., 16th edt., 1986. $10 per no. Spectrum Publications, 762 Ave. N., S.E., Winter Haven, FL 33880. TEL 813-294-5555. Ed. Bayliss Corbett. circ. 500.
  Former titles: Censored (ISSN 0163-2280); Some Hard-to-Locate Sources of Information on Current Affairs.

020 US ISSN 0720-678X
SPRINGER SERIES IN INFORMATION SCIENCES. 1980. irreg., vol.15, 1986. Springer-Verlag, 175 Fifth Ave., New York, NY 10010 TEL 212-460-1500. (Also Berlin, Heidelberg, Tokyo and Vienna) Eds. K.S. Fu, T.S. Huang. (reprint service avail. from ISI) Indexed: Sci.Abstr.

026 GW ISSN 0340-0700
STAATSBIBLIOTHEK PREUSSISCHER KULTURBESITZ. AUSSTELLUNGSKATALOGE. 1970. irreg. price varies. Staatsbibliothek Preussischer Kulturbesitz, Potsdamer Str. 33, Postfach 1407, 1000 Berlin 30, W. Germany (B.R.D.) (Order from: Dr. Ludwig Reichert Verlag, Reisstr. 10,6200 Wiesbaden, W. Germany (B.R.D.))

026 GW ISSN 0340-2274
STAATSBIBLIOTHEK PREUSSISCHER KULTURBESITZ. JAHRESBERICHT. 1950. a. Staatsbibliothek Preussischer Kulturbesitz, Potsdamer Str. 33, Postfach 1407, 1000 Berlin 30, W. Germany (B.R.D.) stat. (back issues avail.)

020 US
STATE UNIVERSITY OF NEW YORK AT ALBANY. SCHOOL OF LIBRARY AND INFORMATION SCIENCE. BULLETIN. 1967/68. biennial. free. State University of New York at Albany, School of Library and Information Science, 135 Western Ave., Albany, NY 12222. TEL 518-455-6288. Ed. Richard S. Halsey. illus. circ. 3,000.

027 BU ISSN 0204-4684
STATISTICESKI DANNI ZA BIBLIOTEKITE V BULGARIA/STATISTICAL DATA ON LIBRARIES IN BULGARIA. 1966. a. price varies. Narodna Biblioteka "Kiril i Metodii", 11, Tolbukhin Blvd., 1504 Sofia, Bulgaria. Ed. H. Hadjihzistov. charts. stat. circ. 600. (processed)

027 US ISSN 0081-5152
STATISTICS OF INDIANA LIBRARIES. 1890. a. $2.50. ‡ State Library, 140 N. Senate Ave., Indianapolis, IN 46204. TEL 317-232-3697. circ. 300.

027.4 US ISSN 0731-8464
STATISTICS OF VIRGINIA PUBLIC LIBRARIES AND INSTITUTIONAL LIBRARIES. 1923. a. free. State Library, Library Development Branch, Richmond, VA 23219. TEL 804-786-1489. Ed. Christina J. Dunn. circ. 1,900.
  Formerly: Statistics of Virginia Public Libraries (ISSN 0095-3490)

020 070.5 PL ISSN 0137-3404
STUDIA O KSIAZCE. (Text in Polish; summaries in French and Russian) 1970. a. price varies. (Uniwersytet Wroclawski) Ossolineum, Publishing House of the Polish Academy of Sciences, Rynek 9, Wroclaw, Poland. Ed. Krzysztof Migon. bk. rev. bibl.

020 AU
STUDIEN ZUR BIBLIOTHEKSGESCHICHTE. 1973. irreg. price varies. Akademische Druck- und Verlagsanstalt, Neufeldweg 75, 8010 Graz, Austria.

020 US
STUDIES IN LIBRARY MANAGEMENT. 1972. irreg., vol.7, 1982. price varies. Archon Books (Subsidiary of: Shoe String Press, Inc.) 925 Sherman Ave., Box 4327, Hamden, CT 06514.

025 UK ISSN 0307-0808
STUDIES IN LIBRARY MANAGEMENT. 1972. irreg. price varies. Clive Bingley Ltd., 7 Ridgmount St., London WC1E 7AE, England. Ed. Anthony Vaughan. circ. 1,500. Indexed: LISA.

026 US
SUBJECT DIRECTORY OF SPECIAL LIBRARIES AND INFORMATION CENTERS. 1975. irreg. $650 for 5-vol. set; $150/vol. Gale Research Company, Book Tower, Detroit, MI 48226. TEL 313-961-2242. Ed. Brigitte T. Darnay.

020 SA
SUID-AFRIKAANSE ARGIEFBLAD/SOUTH AFRICAN ARCHIVES JOURNAL. (Text in Afrikaans and English) 1959. a. R.5. South African Society of Archivists, c/o Treasurer, Government Archives, Union Buildings, Private Bag X236, Pretoria 0001, South Africa. Eds. C. Kirkwood, K.L. de Vries. adv. bk. rev. bibl. circ. 300.

020 651 940 SW ISSN 0039-6893
SVENSKA. RIKSARKIVET. MEDDELANDEN. 1877. irreg. Kr.15. Riksarkivet - National Swedish Record Office, Box 12541, 102 29 Stockholm, Sweden.

SVENSKA BARNBOKSINSTITUTET. SKRIFTER/ SWEDISH INSTITUTE FOR CHILDREN'S BOOKS. STUDIES. see CHILDREN AND YOUTH — For

SWARBICA JOURNAL. see HISTORY — History Of Asia

020 US ISSN 0095-0874
SYMBOLS OF AMERICAN LIBRARIES. 1932. irreg. $13. U.S. Library of Congress, Catalog Management and Publication Division, Washington, DC 20540 TEL 202-287-6100. (Subscr. to: Cataloging Distribution Service, Washington, DC 20541) circ. 2,500.

020 CN ISSN 0380-2973
TALKING BOOKS IN THE PUBLIC LIBRARY SYSTEMS OF METROPOLITAN TORONTO. 1974. irreg. Can.$29.50. Metropolitan Toronto Library Board, 789 Yonge St., Toronto, Ont. M4W 2G8, Canada. TEL 416-824-5150. bibl.

020 TZ ISSN 0856-1621
TANZANIA LIBRARY SERVICE. OCCASIONAL PAPER. irreg. price varies. Library Services Board, Box 9283, Dar es Salaam, Tanzania.

027.4 US ISSN 0363-7158
TENNESSEE PUBLIC LIBRARY STATISTICS. 1965? a. free. State Library and Archives, Development and Extension Services Section, Office of Secretary of State, Nashville, TN 37219. TEL 615-741-2451. circ. 1,500.

027 US ISSN 0082-3120
TEXAS PUBLIC LIBRARY STATISTICS. 1965. a. free. ‡ State Library, Library Development Division, Box 12927, Austin, TX 78711. TEL 512-463-5465. Ed. Mitchell Gidseg. circ. 1,650.

026 US ISSN 0082-3163
TEXAS SPECIAL LIBRARIES DIRECTORY. 1969. biennial. free. State Library, Library Develpment Division, Texas Archives and Library Bldg., Box 12927, Capitol Sta., Austin, TX 78711. TEL 512-463-5465. (Co-sponsor: Special Library Association, Texas Chapter) Ed. Mitchell E. Gidseg. circ. 800.

THESAURUS OF E R I C DESCRIPTORS. (Educational Resources Information Center) see EDUCATION

027.4 US ISSN 0040-6252
THIS MONTH IN YOUR LIBRARY. 1955. irreg. (6-8/yr.) free. ‡ Dayton & Montgomery County Public Library, 215 E. Third St., Dayton, OH 45402. TEL 513-224-1651. Ed. Lisa Gooding-Jones. circ. 8,000. (processed)

020 II ISSN 0563-5489
TIMELESS FELLOWSHIP; annual journal of comparative librarianship. (Text in English) 1964. a. Rs.40($9) Karnatak University Library Association, Karnatak University, Dharwar 580003, Karnataka, India. Eds. K. S. Deshpande, M. R. Kumbhar. adv. bk. rev. circ. 500. Indexed: LISA.

020 UK
TOP 3,000 DIRECTORIES AND ANNUALS: A GUIDE TO THE MAJOR TITLES USED IN BRITISH LIBRARIES. 1980. a. £30. Alan Armstrong & Associates Ltd., 76 Park Rd., London NW1 5SH, England.
  Formerly: Top 2,000 Directories and Annuals: A Guide to the Major Titles Used in British Libraries (ISSN 0262-0219)

020 KO
TOSOGUIAN HAK. 1970. a. 400 Won($1) Korean Library Science Society, Yonsei University Library, Seoul 120, S. Korea.

029 HU ISSN 0373-5354
TUDOMANYOS TAJEKOZTATAS ELMELETE ES GYAKORLATA/THEORY AND PRACTICE OF SCIENTIFIC INFORMATION. (Text in Hungarian; summaries in English, German, Russian) 1966. irreg., no.21, 1976. price varies. Orszagos Muszaki Informacios Kozpont es Konyvtar (O.M.I.K.K.) - National Technical Information Centre and Library, Muzeum u. 17, Box 12, 1428 Budapest, Hungary.

020 060 FI ISSN 0082-7010
TURUN YLIOPISTO. KIRJASTO. JULKAISUJA. (Text in English, Finnish, French; summaries in English, French, German) 1948. irreg., no.12, 1983. price varies. Turun Yliopisto, Kirjasto - University of Turku, Kirjasto, SF-20500 Turku 50, Finland. circ. 300.

020 MX
U N A M DIRECTORIO DE BIBLIOTECAS. 1976. biennial. $8 (or exchange) Universidad Nacional Autonoma de Mexico, Direccion General de Bibliotecas, Ciudad Universitaria, Mexico 20, D.F., Mexico.

020 UN ISSN 0300-2519
U N I S I S T NEWSLETTER. (Unesco Programme of International Cooperation in Scientific and Technological Information) Russian edition (ISSN 0304-0070) (Editions in English, French, Russian and Spanish) 1973. 4-6/yr. (q. Russian edt.) free. ‡ Unesco, Division of Scientific and Technological Information and Documentation, 7-9 Place de Fontenoy, 75700 Paris, France. Indexed: Nutr.Abstr. Field Crop Abstr. Herb.Abstr.

355 US
U S M A LIBRARY BULLETIN. 1945. irreg., vol.18, 1981. controlled circ. ‡ U.S. Military Academy Library, West Point, NY 10996. TEL 914-938-4560. Ed. Egon A. Weiss. bibl. illus. circ. 750.

027 DK ISSN 0106-3014
U VEJVISER. 1979. a. Kr.45($5) Mellemfolkeligt Samvirke, Borgergade 14, DK-1300 Copenhagen K, Denmark. Ed. Helle Leth-Moeller. circ. 1,500.

027.4 UG
UGANDA. PUBLIC LIBRARIES BOARD. PROCEEDINGS. irreg. Public Libraries Board, Box 4262, Kampala, Uganda.

UMBRELLA (GLENDALE) see *ART*

020 025 US ISSN 0083-1565
U.S. LIBRARY OF CONGRESS. ANNUAL REPORT OF THE LIBRARIAN OF CONGRESS. 1866. a. price varies. U.S. Library of Congress, Washington, DC 20540 TEL 202-287-5000. (Free to libraries upon request to LC Central Services Division; foreign libraries apply to LC Exchange and Gift Division)

020 SP
UNIVERSIDAD DE BARCELONA. BIBLIOTECA. MEMORIA ANUAL. 1969/70. a. free. Universidad de Barcelona, Biblioteca, Gran via de les Corts Catalanes, 585, Barcelona-7, Spain. illus. circ. controlled.

020 AG ISSN 0068-3493
UNIVERSIDAD DE BUENOS AIRES. INSTITUTO BIBLIOTECOLOGICO. PUBLICACION. irreg., no.59, 1981. Universidad de Buenos Aires, Instituto Bibliotecologico, Casilla de Correo 901, 1000 Buenos Aires, Argentina. Ed. Hans Gravenhorst.

020 SP ISSN 0078-8740
UNIVERSIDAD DE NAVARRA. ESCUELA DE BIBLIOTECARIAS. COLECCION BIBLIOTECARIAS. 1969. irreg., no.4, 1977. price varies. Ediciones Universidad de Navarra, S.A., Apdo. 396, 31080 Pamplona, Spain.
Formerly: Universidad de Navarra. Escuela de Bibliotecarias. Manuales: Bibliotecarias.

020 MX
UNIVERSIDAD NACIONAL AUTONOMA DE MEXICO. INSTITUTO DE INVESTIGACIONES BIBLIOGRAFICA. INSTRUMENTA BIBLIOGRAPHICA; catalogo de seudonimos, anagramas, iniciales otros alias usados por escritores Mexicanos y extranjeros que han publicado en Mexico. 1973. irreg., latest 1985. $10. Universidad Nacional Autonoma de Mexico, Instituto de Investigaciones Bibliograficas, Ciudad Universitaria, Coyoacan, Mexico 04510, D.F., Mexico. (Co-sponsor: Biblioteca Nacional) Ed. Maria del Carmen Ruiz Castaneda. (back issues avail.)

020 PY
UNIVERSIDAD NACIONAL DE ASUNCION. ESCUELA DE BIBLIOTECOLOGIA. INFORMACIONES. 1972. biennial. $3. Universidad Nacional de Asuncion, Escuela de Bibliotecologia, Espana 1098, Casilla de Correo 1408, Asuncion, Paraguay. bk. rev. circ. 200.

020 010 AG ISSN 0076-6402
UNIVERSIDAD NACIONAL DE CUYO. BIBLIOTECA CENTRAL. CUADERNOS DE LA BIBLIOTECA. 1961. irreg., no.9, 1986. exchange basis. ‡ Universidad Nacional de Cuyo, Biblioteca Central, Centro Universitario-C.C. 420, Mendoza, Argentina.

020 PO
UNIVERSIDADE DE COIMBRA. ARQUIVO. BOLETIM. 1973. irreg. Universidade de Coimbra, Arquivo, Paco das Escolas, Coimbra, Portugal. Ed. Antonio de Oliveira.

020 GE ISSN 0438-4415
UNIVERSITAETS- UND LANDESBIBLIOTHEK SACHSEN-ANHALT. ARBEITEN. 1952. irreg., vol.30, 1985. price varies. Universitaets- und Landesbibliothek Sachsen-Anhalt, August-Bebel-Str. 13, 401 Halle (Saale) 1, E. Germany (D.D.R.)

027 GW ISSN 0072-4483
UNIVERSITAETSBIBLIOTHEK GIESSEN. BERICHTE UND ARBEITEN. 1962/63. irreg. price varies. Universitaetsbibliothek Giessen, Otto-Behaghel-Str. 8, 6300 Giessen, W. Germany (B.R.D.) Ed. B. Dugall. circ. 500.

020 SA ISSN 0379-7104
UNIVERSITEIT VAN PRETORIA. BIBLIOTEEKDIENS. VERSLAGREEKS. (Text in Afrikaans) 1979. irreg. price varies. University of Pretoria, Library Services, Pretoria 0002, South Africa. circ. 100.

027.7 NO
UNIVERSITETET I TRONDHEIM. BIBLIOTEKET. AVDELING B. RAPPORT. 1971. irreg. Universitetet i Trondheim, Biblioteket. Avdeling B, Trondheim, Norway. circ. 200. Indexed: LISA.

027 NR
UNIVERSITY OF BENIN. LIBRARY. ANNUAL REPORT. (Title varies slightly) 1970/71. a. University of Benin, Library, P.M.B. 1154, Eken Wan Rd., Benin City, Nigeria. stat.

027.7 SA ISSN 0576-6885
UNIVERSITY OF CAPE TOWN. LIBRARIES. STATISTICAL REPORT. a. free. University of Cape Town, Libraries, Rondebosch 7700, South Africa.

020 US ISSN 0069-3375
UNIVERSITY OF CHICAGO STUDIES IN LIBRARY SCIENCE. 1939. irreg., latest 1984. price varies. University of Chicago Press, 5801 S. Ellis Ave., Chicago, IL 60637. TEL 312-962-7700. Ed. Don R. Swanson. (back issues avail.; reprint service avail. from UMI,ISI)

020 GH
UNIVERSITY OF GHANA. DEPARTMENT OF LIBRARY AND ARCHIVAL STUDIES. OCCASIONAL PAPERS. irreg., no.15, 1976. University of Ghana, Department of Library and Archival Studies, Box 60, Legon, Ghana. circ. 200.

027 NR ISSN 0073-4322
UNIVERSITY OF IBADAN. LIBRARY. ANNUAL REPORT. 1948. a. free. University of Ibadan, Library, Ibadan, Nigeria. bk. rev. circ. 750.

025 US ISSN 0069-4789
UNIVERSITY OF ILLINOIS AT URBANA-CHAMPAIGN. CLINIC ON LIBRARY APPLICATIONS OF DATA PROCESSING. PROCEEDINGS. 1963. a. price varies. University of Illinois at Urbana-Champaign, Graduate School of Library and Information Science, 249 Armory Bldg., 505 E. Armory St., Champaign, IL 61820. TEL 217-333-1359. Ed. James Dowling. index. (back issues avail.)

020 US
UNIVERSITY OF ILLINOIS AT URBANA-CHAMPAIGN. GRADUATE SCHOOL OF LIBRARY AND INFORMATION SCIENCE. ALLERTON PARK INSTITUTE. PAPERS. 1954. a. price varies. University of Illinois at Urbana-Champaign, Graduate School of Library and Informaion Science, 249 Armory Bldg., 505 E. Armory St., Champaign, IL 61820. TEL 217-333-1359. Ed. James Dowling. index. (back issues avail.)
Formerly: University of Illinois at Urbana-Champaign. Graduate School of Library Science. Allerton Park Institute. Papers. (ISSN 0536-4604)

020 US
UNIVERSITY OF ILLINOIS AT URBANA-CHAMPAIGN. GRADUATE SCHOOL OF LIBRARY AND INFORMATION SCIENCE. DOWNS FUND PUBLICATIONS SERIES. 1972. irreg. price varies. University of Illinois at Urbana-Champaign, Graduate School of Library and Information Science, 249 Armory Bldg., 505 E. Armory St., Champaign, IL 61820. TEL 217-333-1266. Ed. Dederick Ward. Indexed: Lib.Lit. M.L.A.
Formerly: University of Illinois at Urbana-Champaign. Graduate School of Library Science. Downs Fund Publications Series.

020 US
UNIVERSITY OF ILLINOIS AT URBANA-CHAMPAIGN. GRADUATE SCHOOL OF LIBRARY AND INFORMATION SCIENCE. LIBRARY RESEARCH CENTER. ANNUAL REPORT. 1961/62. a. free. University of Illinois at Urbana-Champaign, Graduate School of Library and Information Science, 249 Armory Bldg., 505 E. Armory St., Champaign, IL 61820. TEL 217-333-4333.
Formerly: University of Illinois at Urbana-Champaign. Graduate School of Library Science. Library Research Center. Annual Report. (ISSN 0073-5361)

020 US
UNIVERSITY OF ILLINOIS AT URBANA-CHAMPAIGN. GRADUATE SCHOOL OF LIBRARY AND INFORMATION SCIENCE. MONOGRAPH SERIES. 1963. irreg. price varies. University of Illinois at Urbana-Champaign, Graduate School of Library and Information Science, 249 Armory Bdlg., 505 E. Armory St., Champaign, IL 61820. TEL 217-333-1359.
Formerly: University of Illinois at Urbana-Champaign. Graduate School of Library Science. Monograph Series. (ISSN 0073-5302)

020 US
UNIVERSITY OF ILLINOIS AT URBANA-CHAMPAIGN. GRADUATE SCHOOL OF LIBRARY AND INFORMATION SCIENCE. OCCASIONAL PAPERS. 1949. irreg., (5-6/yr.) $13. ‡ University of Illinois at Urbana-Champaign, Graduate School of Library and Information Science, 249 Armory Bldg., 505 E. Armory St., Champaign, IL 61820. TEL 217-333-3280. Ed. Donald Krummel. circ. 558. (back issues avail.) Indexed: Biol.Abstr.
Formerly: University of Illinois at Urbana-Champaign. Graduate School of Library Science. Occasional Papers.

020 US
UNIVERSITY OF IOWA. SCHOOL OF LIBRARY AND INFORMATION SCIENCE. NEWSLETTER. 1966. a. free. University of Iowa, School of Library and Information Science, Iowa City, IA 52242. TEL 319-353-3644. Ed. Ethel Bloesch. bibl. circ. 4,000.
Formerly: University of Iowa. School of Library Science. Newsletter (ISSN 0041-9648)

020 US ISSN 0075-5001
UNIVERSITY OF KANSAS LIBRARIES. LIBRARY SERIES. 1935. irreg. price varies. University of Kansas Libraries, Lawrence, KS 66045. TEL 913-864-4334. Ed. James Helyar.

020 US ISSN 0743-8915
UNIVERSITY OF KENTUCKY LIBRARIES. OCCASIONAL PAPERS. 1980. irreg., no.4, 1983. price varies. University of Kentucky Library, Margaret I. King Library, University of Kentucky, Lexington, KY 40506. Ed. Terry L. Birdwhistell. circ. 300.

027.7 SJ
UNIVERSITY OF KHARTOUM. LIBRARY BULLETIN. (Text in Arabic or English) 1977. a. University of Khartoum, Library, Box 321, Khartoum, Sudan.

020 NR ISSN 0075-7705
UNIVERSITY OF LAGOS. LIBRARY. ANNUAL REPORT. 1962/63. a. free. (University of Lagos, Library) Lagos University Press, P.O. Box 132, Akoka, Yaba, Lagos, Nigeria. Ed. E. B. Bankole. circ. 1,000.

UNIVERSITY OF LONDON. SCHOOL OF SLAVONIC AND EAST EUROPEAN STUDIES. LIBRARY. BIBLIOGRAPHICAL GUIDES. see *BIBLIOGRAPHIES*

LIBRARY AND INFORMATION SCIENCES

027   MW   ISSN 0085-3038
UNIVERSITY OF MALAWI LIBRARIES. REPORT TO THE SENATE ON THE UNIVERSITY LIBRARIES. 1965. a. free. University of Malawi Libraries, Central Library Services, Box 280, Zomba, Malawi. Ed. Steve S. Mwiyeriwa. circ. 200. (processed)

020   US   ISSN 0076-4833
UNIVERSITY OF MARYLAND. COLLEGE OF LIBRARY AND INFORMATION SERVICES. CONFERENCE PROCEEDINGS. 1968. irreg. price varies. University of Maryland, College of Library and Information Services, c/o Esther Herman, Director of Publications, College Park, MD 20742. TEL 301-454-2590. Indexed: Lib.Lit.

020   US   ISSN 0076-4841
UNIVERSITY OF MARYLAND. COLLEGE OF LIBRARY AND INFORMATION SERVICES. STUDENT CONTRIBUTION SERIES. 1967. irreg., no.10, 1977. price varies. University of Maryland, College of Library and Information Services, c/o Esther Herman, Director of Publications, College Park, MD 20742. TEL 301-454-2590. Indexed: Lib.Lit.

020   US
UNIVERSITY OF MISSOURI AT KANSAS CITY. FRIENDS OF THE LIBRARY. PUBLICATION SERIES. 1980. irreg. price varies. University of Missouri-Kansas City, Friends of the Library, Kansas City, MO 64110. TEL 816-276-1000.

027.7   US
UNIVERSITY OF MISSOURI, COLUMBIA. LIBRARY SERIES. 1908. irreg., no.29, 1985. exchange basis. University of Missouri-Columbia, Ellis Library, Columbia, MO 65201. TEL 314-882-4701. circ. 500.

020   AT   ISSN 0313-427X
UNIVERSITY OF NEW SOUTH WALES. LIBRARY. ANNUAL REPORT. 1978 (1975 report) a. free. University of New South Wales, Library, Box 1, Kensington, N.S.W. 2033, Australia. circ. 500.

020   AT
UNIVERSITY OF NEW SOUTH WALES. LIBRARY. STAFF PAPERS. 1966. irreg. University of New South Wales Library, P.O. Box 1, Kensington 2033 N.S.W., Australia. circ. 100.

020   US
UNIVERSITY OF RHODE ISLAND. LIBRARY. LIBRARY LETTER. 1967. a. free to qualified personnel. University of Rhode Island, Association of Friends of the Library, Kingston, RI 02881. Ed. Edna L. Steeves. bk. rev. circ. controlled.

027.7   US   ISSN 0041-9974
UNIVERSITY OF ROCHESTER LIBRARY BULLETIN. 1945. a. membership. University of Rochester, Rush Rhees Library, Rochester, NY 14627. TEL 716-275-3302. Ed. Catherine D. Hayes. illus. circ. 1,000. (back issues avail.) Indexed: Lib.Lit.

020 800   CN   ISSN 0380-9676
UNIVERSITY OF SASKATCHEWAN. LIBRARY. NOTABLE WORKS AND COLLECTIONS. 1975. a. free. University of Saskatchewan, Library, Saskatoon, Sask. S7N 0W0, Canada. TEL 306-966-5965. Ed. S.K. Lakhanpal. circ. 700. Indexed: M.L.A.

027   US   ISSN 0081-2706
UNIVERSITY OF SOUTH CAROLINA. LIBRARIES. REPORT OF THE DIRECTOR OF LIBRARIES. 1960. a. free. ‡ University of South Carolina Libraries, Director of Libraries, Columbia, SC 29208. TEL 803-777-4866. Ed. Kenneth Toombs. circ. 350(controlled)

025   UK   ISSN 0081-2935
UNIVERSITY OF SOUTHAMPTON. LIBRARY. AUTOMATION PROJECT REPORT. 1970. irreg. price varies. University of Southampton, Library, Highfield, Southampton, Hants S09 5NH, England. Ed. R.G. Woods. circ. 400. Indexed: LISA.

020   IR   ISSN 0497-1000
UNIVERSITY OF TEHERAN. CENTRAL LIBRARY. LIBRARY BULLETIN/ DANESHGAH-E TEHRAN. KETABKHANE-YE MARKAZI. NASHRIYE-YE KETABKHANEH. (Text in Persian) 1966. irreg. price varies. University of Teheran, Central Library, Shahreza Ave., Teheran, Iran. Ed. Iraj Afshar.

013   US   ISSN 0270-059X
UNIVERSITY OF TENNESSEE. LIBRARY LECTURES. 1952. triennial. $2 per copy. University of Tennessee, Publications Service Bureau, 293 Communications Building, Knoxville, TN 37996. TEL 615-974-0111. circ. 1,500. Key Title: Library Lectures (Knoxville)

020   US   ISSN 0362-854X
UNIVERSITY OF TEXAS AT AUSTIN. GENERAL LIBRARIES. NEWSLETTER. 1974. irreg. free. ‡ University of Texas at Austin, General Libraries, Austin, TX 78713-7330. TEL 512-471-3811. Ed. Mary Pound. bibl. circ. 450.

027.7   SA
UNIVERSITY OF THE WITWATERSRAND, JOHANNESBURG. LIBRARY. AFRICANA SERIES. 1987. irreg. University of Witwatersrand, Johannesburg, Library, Private Bag 31550, Braamfontein 2017, South Africa.

027   SA   ISSN 0075-3807
UNIVERSITY OF THE WITWATERSRAND, JOHANNESBURG. LIBRARY. ANNUAL REPORT OF THE UNIVERSITY LIBRARIAN. 1932. a. free. ‡ University of the Witwatersrand, Johannesburg, Library, Private Bag 31550, Braamfontein 2017, South Africa.

027.7   SA
UNIVERSITY OF THE WITWATERSRAND, JOHANNESBURG. LIBRARY. ARCHIVAL SERIES. irreg., no.13, 1985. University of the Witwatersrand, Johannesburg, Library, Private Bag 31550, Braamfontein 2017, South Africa.

027.7   SA
UNIVERSITY OF THE WITWATERSRAND, JOHANNESBURG. LIBRARY. OCCASIONAL PUBLICATIONS. 1976. irreg., no.12, 1986. University of the Witwatersrand, Johannesburg, Library, Private Bag 31550, Braamfontein 2017, South Africa.

020 900   UK
UNIVERSITY OF WARWICK LIBRARY. OCCASIONAL PUBLICATIONS. 1971. irreg. price varies. ‡ University of Warwick Library, Coventry, Warwickshire, CV4 7AL, England. Ed. P.E. Tucker. circ. controlled. (processed)

020   CN   ISSN 0076-0595
UNIVERSITY OF WESTERN ONTARIO. D.B. WELDON LIBRARY. LIBRARY BULLETIN. 1941. irreg., no.9, 1976. free. University of Western Ontario, D.B. Weldon Library, London, Ont., Canada. TEL 519-885-1211. Ed. Edward Phelps. circ. 500.

020.6   BB
UPDATE (BRIDGETOWN); occasional newsletter of the Library Association of Barbados. 1974. irreg., latest issue no.9, Sep. 1986. membership. Library Association of Barbados, Box 827E, Bridgetown, Barbados, W. Indies.
Formerly: Library Association of Barbados. Occasional Newsletter.

020   UY   ISSN 0544-9189
URUGUAY. BIBLIOTECA NACIONAL. REVISTA. 1966. irreg. (Donation or exchange requested) Biblioteca Nacional, Guayabo 1795, Casilla de Correo 452, Montevideo, Uruguay. Ed. Alvaro Miranda. adv. bk. rev. circ. 750. Indexed: Hisp.Amer.Per.Ind.

015   UK   ISSN 0065-0293
WALES. NATIONAL LIBRARY. HANDLIST ON MANUSCRIPTS IN THE NATIONAL LIBRARY OF WALES. (Supplement Series 2 of the National Library of Wales Journal) 1940. a. (occasionally irreg.) price varies. National Library of Wales, Aberystwyth, Dyfed SY23 3BU, Wales. index. circ. 550.

026 610   US
WASHINGTON UNIVERSITY. SCHOOL OF MEDICINE LIBRARY. LIBRARY NEWSLETTER; an occasional publication. 1961. irreg., approx. 4/yr. ‡ Washington University, School of Medicine Library, 4580 Scott Ave., St. Louis, MO 63110. TEL 314-362-7080. Ed Barbara Halbrook. bibl. charts. illus. stat. circ. 250. (processed)
Formerly: Washington University. School of Medicine Library. Library Notes (ISSN 0024-242X)

020   US
WEST VIRGINIA LIBRARY COMMISSION. NEWSLETTER. 1972. irreg. West Virginia Library Commission, Cultural Center, Charleston, WV 25305. TEL 304-348-2041. circ. 1,500.

020   US
WESTERN ASSOCIATION OF MAP LIBRARIES. OCCASIONAL PAPERS. 1973. irreg., no.10, 1986. price varies. Western Association of Map Libraries, c/o Stanley D. Stevens, Ed., University Library, University of California, Santa Cruz, CA 95064. TEL 408-429-2364. Indexed: Geo.Abstr. GeoRef.

027.7   AT
WESTERN AUSTRALIAN INSTITUTE OF TECHNOLOGY. LIBRARY. ANNUAL REPORT. 1976. a. free. Western Australian Institute of Technology. Library, Kent St., Bentley, W.A. 6102, Australia.

020   AT   ISSN 0810-5030
WESTERN AUSTRALIAN INSTITUTE OF TECHNOLOGY. LIBRARY. WESTERN LIBRARY STUDIES. 1983. irreg. Western Australian Institute of Technology. Library, Kent St., Bentley, W.A. 6102, Australia.

WHO KNOWS ABOUT INDUSTRIES AND MARKETS. see *BUSINESS AND ECONOMICS*

020 920   US
WHO'S WHO IN LIBRARY AND INFORMATION SERVICES. 1982. irreg. $150. American Library Association, 50 E. Huron St., Chicago, IL 60611. TEL 312-944-6780. Ed. Joel M. Lee.

026   US   ISSN 0278-842X
WHO'S WHO IN SPECIAL LIBRARIES. 1981. a. $25. Special Libraries Association, 1700 Eighteenth St., N.W., Washington, DC 20009. TEL 202-234-4700. Ed. Bill Johnson. circ. 12,000. (back issues avail.)

025.5   US   ISSN 0361-2848
WISCONSIN LIBRARY SERVICE RECORD. (Subseries of: Wisconsin. Department of Public Instruction. Bulletin) 1973. a. free. Department of Public Instruction, Division for Library Services, 125 S. Webster St., 3rd Fl., Box 7848, Madison, WI 53707. TEL 608-266-2205. (reprint service avail. from UMI)

027.7   SA
WITS JOURNAL OF LIBRARIANSHIP AND INFORMATION SCIENCE. 1982. a. R.10. University of the Witwatersrand, Johannesburg, Library, Private Bag 31550, Braamfontein 2017, South Africa. Ed. Reuben Musiker. Indexed: Ind.S.A.Per.

020   GW   ISSN 0300-2012
WOLFENBUETTLER BEITRAEGE. 1972. irreg., vol.6, 1983. price varies. (Herzog-August-Bibliothek, Wolfenbuettel) Vittorio Klostermann GmbH, Frauenlobstr. 22, D-6000 Frankfurt/Main 95, W. Germany (B.R.D.) Ed. Paul Raabe. cum.index. (back issues avail.)

025.3   US
WORK RELATED ABSTRACTS SUBJECT HEADING LIST. 1972. biennial. $15. Information Coordinators, Inc., 1435-37 Randolph St., Detroit, MI 48226. TEL 313-962-9720. circ. 500.
Formerly (until 1973): Employment Relations Abstracts: Subject Heading List (ISSN 0092-1432)

510.78   SZ   ISSN 0074-3127
WORLD CONGRESSES ON INFORMATION PROCESSING. PROCEEDINGS. 1959. triennial, 8th 1983, Paris. International Federation for Information Processing, Secretariat, 3 rue du Marche, CH-1204 Geneve, Switzerland.
Formerly: International Conference on Information Processing. Proceedings.

029 US
WORLD GUIDE TO ABBREVIATIONS OF
ORGANIZATIONS. 1974, 5th ed. irreg., 7th edt.,
1984. $115. Gale Research Company, Book Tower,
Detroit, MI 48226. TEL 313-961-2242. Ed. F.A.
Buttress.

026 PL ISSN 0137-5172
Z BADAN NAD POLSKIMI KSIEGOZBIORAMI
HISTORYCZNYMI. (Text in Polish) 1975. irreg.
121 Zl. per no. Uniwersytet Warszawski, Instytut
Bibliotekoznawstwa i Informacji Naukowej,
Krakowskie Przedmiescie 26/28, 00-325 Warsaw,
Poland. Ed. Barbara Bienkowska. index. circ. 500.

ZAMBIA. MINISTRY OF LEGAL AFFAIRS.
ANNUAL REPORT. see *BUSINESS AND
ECONOMICS*

020 GW ISSN 0514-6364
ZEITSCHRIFT FUER BIBLIOTHEKSWESEN UND
BIBLIOGRAPHIE. SONDERHEFTE. 1963. irreg.,
vol.43, 1986. price varies. Vittorio Klostermann,
Frauenlobstr. 22, Postfach 900601, D-6000
Frankfurt 90, W. Germany(B.R.D.)

020 070 UK
5001 HARD TO FIND PUBLISHERS. 1981. a.
£16.50. Alan Armstrong & Associates Ltd., 76 Park
Rd., London NW1 4SH, England.

LIBRARY AND INFORMATION SCIENCES — Abstracting, Bibliographies, Statistics

616.863 016 AT
A D F A AUDIO VISUAL CATALOGUE. 1980. a.
free. Alcohol and Drug Foundation, Australia,
G.P.O. Box 477, Canberra, ACT 2601, Australia.
circ. 300.
 Former titles: A F A D D Audio Visual
Catalogue & A F A D D Audio Visual Acquisitions
List.

027 US ISSN 0147-2135
A R L STATISTICS. 1964. a. $15. Association of
Research Libraries, 1527 New Hampshire Ave.,
N.W., Washington, DC 20036. TEL 202-232-2466.
Ed. Nicola Daval. circ. 1,400. (back issues avail.)
 Formerly: Academic Library Statistics (ISSN
0571-6519)

020 CN ISSN 0080-1569
ALBERTA RESEARCH COUNCIL. LIST OF
PUBLICATIONS. 1968. a. free. Alberta Research
Council, Publications Dept., P.O. Box 8330, Sta. F,
Edmonton, Alta. T6H 5X2, Canada. TEL 403-450-
5111.

016 US ISSN 0065-9959
AMERICAN REFERENCE BOOKS ANNUAL.
1970. a. $70.00. Libraries Unlimited, Inc., Box 263,
Littleton, CO 80160. TEL 303-770-1220. Ed.
Bohdan S. Wynar. cum.index every 5 yrs. Indexed:
Bk.Rev.Ind. Leg.Info.Manage.Ind.

020 011 PL ISSN 0509-6413
BIBLIOGRAFIA BIBLIOGRAFII I NAUKI O
KSIAZCE/BIBLIOGRAPHY OF
BIBLIOGRAPHIES AND LIBRARY SCIENCE.
(Appears in 2 parts: Part 1: Bibliografia Bibliografii
Polskich and Part 2: Polska Bibliografia
Bibliologiczna) 1947. a. 267 Zl. Biblioteka
Narodowa, Instytut Bibliograficzny, Ul. Hankiewicza
1, 00-973 Warsaw, Poland TEL 48-22-22-46-21.
(Dist. by: Ars Polona-Ruch, ul. Krakowskie
Przedmiescie 7, 00-068 Warsaw, Poland) index. circ.
750.

020 016 AG ISSN 0067-656X
BIBLIOGRAFIA BIBLIOTECOLOGICA
ARGENTINA. 1963. irreg. price varies.
(Universidad Nacional del Sur) Centro de
Documentacion e Informacion Educativa, Paraguay
1657-ler. piso, 1062-Capital Federal, Argentina. bk.
rev. author index in each issue. circ. 300.
Argentine bibliography on library science

029 015 PL ISSN 0239-4421
BIBLIOGRAFIA WYDAWNICTW CIAGLYCH/
BIBLIOGRAPHY OF POLISH SERIALS. 1958. a.
260 Zl. Biblioteka Narodowa, Instytut
Bibliograficzny, Ul. Hankiewicza 1, 00-973 Warsaw,
Poland TEL 48-22-22-46-21. (Dist. by: Ars Polona-
Ruch, ul. Krakowskie Przedmiescie 7, 00-068
Warsaw, Poland) Ed. Leokadia Dybowiczowa.
index. circ. 1,000.

020 US ISSN 0742-6879
BIBLIOGRAPHIES AND INDEXES IN LIBRARY
AND INFORMATION SCIENCE. irreg. price
varies. Greenwood Press, 88 Post Rd. W., Box
5007, Westport, CT 06881. TEL 203-226-3571.

020 011 US ISSN 0145-3084
BIBLIOGRAPHY NEWSLETTER. Abbreviated title:
BiN. 1973. irreg. (approx. 4/yr) $15. c/o Terry
Belanger, Ed., 21 Claremont Ave, New York, NY
10027. TEL 212-280-2292. Eds. Terry Belanger,
Daniel Traister. bk. rev. illus. index. circ. 800. (back
issues avail.)

020 PO ISSN 0253-343X
BOLETIM DE BIBLIOGRAFIA PORTUGUESA.
DOCUMENTOS NAO TEXTUAIS. 1981. a.
Biblioteca Nacional, Campo Grande 83, 1751
Lisbon Codex, Portugal. index. circ. 750.
 Supersedes in part (1935-1981): Boletim de
Bibliografia Portuguesa (ISSN 0006-5897)

020 PO ISSN 0253-3421
BOLETIM DE BIBLIOGRAFIA PORTUGUESA.
PUBLICACOES EM SERIE. 1981. a. Biblioteca
Nacional, Campo grande 83, 1751 Lisbon Codex,
Portugal. index. circ. 750.
 Supersedes in part (1935-1980): Boletim de
Bibliografia Portuguesa (ISSN 0006-5897)

027 CN
BRITISH COLUMBIA PUBLIC LIBRARIES,
STATISTICS. 1965. a. free. Library Services
Branch, Parliament Buildings, Victoria, B.C. V8V
1X4, Canada. stat. circ. 750.
 Formerly: British Columbia. Library Development
Commission. Public Libraries, Statistics (ISSN 0084-
8034)

020 UK
BRITISH LIBRARY. PRECIS VOCABULARY
FICHE. a. (or bi-m. cumulations) £35 (or £83 for
bi-m. cumulations) British Library, Bibliographic
Services, 2 Sheraton St., London W1V 4BH,
England. (microfiche)

020 UK
BRITISH LIBRARY. SUBJECT AUTHORITY
FICHE. a. (or bi-m. cumulations or four-monthly
cumulations) £135 (or £224 for four-monthly
cumulations; £394 for bi-m. cumulations) British
Library, Bibliographic Services, 2 Sheraton St.,
London W1V 4BH, England. (microfiche)

016.051 020 CN ISSN 0000-0345
CANADIAN SERIALS DIRECTORY/
REPERTOIRE DES PUBLICATIONS SERIEES
CANADIENNES. (Text in English and French)
irreg., latest issue 1977. University of Toronto Press,
Toronto, Ont., Canada. TEL 613-667-7791. bibl.

020 US ISSN 0084-6902
CENTER FOR CHINESE RESEARCH
MATERIALS. BIBLIOGRAPHICAL SERIES.
1968. irreg. price varies. Association of Research
Libraries, Center for Chinese Research Materials,
Box 3090, Oakton, VA 22124. TEL 703-281-7731.
Ed. Pingfeng Chi.

029 011 PL ISSN 0239-8931
CENTRALNY KATALOG ZAGRANICZNYCH
WYDAWNICTW CIAGLYCH W
BIBLIOTEKACH POLSKICH. ALFABETYCZNY
WYKAZ TYTULOW. (Supplement avail: Centralny
Katalog Zagranicznych Wydawnictw Ciaglych w
Bibliotekach Polskich. Nowe Tytuly w Roku) 1971/
1972. a. 810 Zl. Biblioteka Narodowa, Zaklad
Katalogow Centralnych, Ul. Aleje Niepodleglosci
213, 00-973 Warsaw, Poland TEL 48-22-25-96-99.
(Dist. by: Ars Polona-Ruch, ul. Krakowskie
Przedmiescie 7, 00-068 Warsaw, Polona) Ed. Joanna
Pasztaleniec-Jarzynska. index. circ. 450.
 Formerly (until 1982): Centralny Katalog
Biezacych Czasopism Zagranicznych w Bibliotakach
Polskich.

310 UK ISSN 0309-6629
CHARTERED INSTITUTE OF PUBLIC FINANCE
AND ACCOUNTANCY. PUBLIC LIBRARY
STATISTICS. ACTUALS. 1957/58. a. £14.
Chartered Institute of Public Finance and
Accountancy, 3 Robert St., London WC2N 6BH,
England. stat. (back issues avail.)

310 UK ISSN 0307-0522
CHARTERED INSTITUTE OF PUBLIC FINANCE
AND ACCOUNTANCY. PUBLIC LIBRARY
STATISTICS. ESTIMATES. 1974. a. £10.
Chartered Institute of Public Finance and
Accountancy, 3 Robert St., London WC2N 6BH,
England. (back issues avail.)

015 UK ISSN 0084-8085
CHECKLIST OF BRITISH OFFICIAL SERIAL
PUBLICATIONS. 1967. irreg. (approx. biennial)
£12. ‡ British Library, Humanities and Social
Sciences, Great Russell St., London WC1B 3DG,
England. Ed. Geoffrey Hamilton.

011 020 US
COLLEGE READING ASSOCIATION.
MONOGRAPHS. irreg. College Reading
Association, c/o Dr. Norman A. Stahl, Bus. Mgr.,
Box 872, University Plaza, Georgia State University,
Atlanta, GA 30303. TEL 404-658-3354. (reprint
service avail. from UMI)

CURRENT RESEARCH IN BRITAIN.
BIOLOGICAL SCIENCES. see *BIOLOGY —
Abstracting, Bibliographies, Statistics*

CURRENT RESEARCH IN BRITAIN. PHYSICAL
SCIENCES. see *SCIENCES: COMPREHENSIVE
WORKS — Abstracting, Bibliographies, Statistics*

CURRENT RESEARCH IN BRITAIN. SOCIAL
SCIENCES. see *SOCIAL SCIENCES:
COMPREHENSIVE WORKS — Abstracting,
Bibliographies, Statistics*

027.4 US
DIRECTORY OF LONG ISLAND LIBRARIES
AND MEDIA CENTERS INCLUDING BUYERS'
GUIDE. 1974. a. $29.95. L D A Publishers, 42-36
209 St., Bayside, NY 11361. TEL 718-224-0485.
Ed. Paul Ippolito. circ. 1,500.
 Formerly: Directory of Long Island Libraries and
Media Centers and Buyers' Guide.

010 020 UN
DOCUMENTATION, LIBRARIES AND
ARCHIVES: BIBLIOGRAPHIES AND
REFERENCE WORKS. 1972. irreg. price varies.
Unesco, Place de Fontenoy, F-75700 Paris, France
(Dist. in U.S. by: Bernan Associates-Unipub, 4611-F
Assembly Dr., Lanham, MD 20706)
 Formerly: Unesco Bibliographical Handbooks
(ISSN 0082-7460)

029 011 SA
GREY BIBLIOGRAPHIES. 1946. irreg., no.13, 1984.
price varies. South African Library, P.O. Box 496,
Cape Town 8000, South Africa. (reprint service
avail. from UMI)

011 AT ISSN 0156-6717
GUIDELINES; a subject guide for Australian libraries.
1969. 9/yr. (plus a. cumulation) Aus.$48.
Bibliographic Services, Box 2, Mount Waverley, Vic.
3149, Australia. Ed. Keith S. Darling. adv. circ. 1,
700. (also avail. in microfiche)

020 011 CR ISSN 0487-1596
I C A P LISTA DE NUEVAS ADQUISICIONES.
1958. irreg. Instituto Centroamericano de
Administracion Publica, Departamento de
Biblioteca, Apartado 10025, San Jose, Costa Rica.

020.6 DK ISSN 0109-5366
I F L A COMMUNICATIONS; bibliography of IFLA
conference papers. 1984. a. Kr.118,03.
Bibliotekscentralen, International Federation of
Library Associations and Institutions, Tempovej 7-
11, 2750 Ballerup, Denmark. Ed. Mona Madsen.
circ. 100.

029 KO
INDEX TO THE NATIONAL ASSEMBLY
RECORDS/KUK HOE HOE EU ROK SAEGIN.
(Text in Korean) 1963. irreg. free. National
Assembly, Library, Processing & Reference Bureau,
Yoido-Dong 1, Yoengdeungpo-gu, Seoul, S. Korea.
circ. 700.

020 II
INDIAN LIBRARY AND INFORMATION
SCIENCE INDEXES SERIES. irreg. Gina House
Publishers, 71 Sector 27-A, Chandigarh 160019,
India.

020 016 II ISSN 0019-5790
INDIAN LIBRARY SCIENCE ABSTRACTS. (Text
in English) 1967. q. Rs.25($5) Indian Association of
Special Libraries and Information Centres, P-291
C.I.T. Scheme No. 6M, Kankurgachi, Calcutta
700054, India. Ed.Bd.

029.7 651.8 016 US ISSN 0020-0239
INFORMATION SCIENCE ABSTRACTS. 1966. m.
$350 to non-members. (American Society for
Information Science) Plenum Press, Electronic
Publishing Division, 233 Spring St., New York, NY
10013. TEL 212-620-8468. (Co-sponsors: Special
Libraries Association; American Chemical Society,
Division of Chemical Information; American
Society of Indexers) Ed. Harry Allcock. adv. bk.
rev. index. circ. 1,000.
  ●Also available online. Vendors: DIALOG.
  Formerly: Documentation Abstracts.

020 US ISSN 0272-0310
INTERNATIONAL MICROGRAPHICS SOURCE
BOOK. 1972. biennial. $79.50. Microfilm
Publishing, Inc., Box 950, Larchmont, NY 10538-
0950. TEL 914-834-3044. Ed. Mitchell M. Badler.
adv. bk. rev. illus. stat. circ. 4,000.
  Former titles: International Microfilm Source
Book (ISSN 0362-4498); Microfilm Source Book
(ISSN 0090-2861)

020 016 IT ISSN 0075-0026
INVENTARI DEI MANOSCRITTI DELLE
BIBLIOTECHE D'ITALIA. 1890. irreg., vol.101,
1981. price varies. Casa Editrice Leo S. Olschki,
Casella Postale 66, 50100 Florence, Italy. Eds. A.
Sorbelli, L. Ferrari. cum.index in prep. circ. 1,000.

020 011 IC
ISLENSK BOKASKRA/ICELANDIC NATIONAL
BIBLIOGRAPHY. 1975. a. Kr.400($10)
Landsbokasafn Islands - National Library of Iceland,
Safnahusinu, Hverfisgotu 15, 101 Reykjavik,
Iceland.
  Supersedes in part: Iceland. Landsbokasafn
Islands. Arbok.

020 KE
KENYA NATIONAL BIBLIOGRAPHY. (Text in
English) 1980. a. EAs.95($15.50) Kenya National
Library Services, P.O. Box 30573, Nairobi, Kenya.
Ed. Francis W. Ochola. circ. 500. (back issues
avail.)

020 KE
KENYAN PERIODICALS DIRECTORY. (Text in
English) 1984. biennial. EAs.75($9.50) Kenya
National Library Services, National Reference and
Bibliographic Department, P.O. Box 30573, Nairobi,
Kenya. Ed. Francis W. Ochola.

029 011 UK ISSN 0143-9553
KEYWORD INDEX TO SERIAL TITLES. 1980. q.
£193. British Library, Document Supply Centre,
Publications Section, Boston Spa, Wetherby, West
Yorkshire LS23 7BQ, England. (microfiche)

020 US ISSN 0093-1888
LIBRARIANS' HANDBOOK. 1971. a. free to
qualified personnel. Ebsco Subscription Services,
Title Information Department, Box 1943,
Birmingham, AL 35201-1943. Ed. Sandra Gipson.
adv. circ. 25,000.

020 029.7 016 UK ISSN 0024-2179
LIBRARY & INFORMATION SCIENCE
ABSTRACTS. (Also avail. on CD-ROM) 1969. m.
(plus a. cum.) £157($357) Library Association
Publishing Ltd., 7 Ridgmount St., London WC1E
7AE, England. Ed. N. Moore. index. cum.index.
circ. 2,500. (also avail. in magnetic tape)
  ●Also available online. Vendors: DIALOG, Orbit
Information Technologies.
  Supersedes: Library Science Abstracts.

020 US ISSN 0085-2767
LIBRARY LIT. 1971. a. price varies. Scarecrow Press,
Inc., 52 Liberty St., Metuchen, NJ 08840. TEL 201-
548-8600. Ed. William A. Katz, Kathleen Weibel.
circ. 1,500.

020 029 016 US ISSN 0024-2373
LIBRARY LITERATURE; an index to library and
information science. 1921. bi-m. (a. cumulations)
service basis. ‡ H.W. Wilson Co., 950 University
Ave., Bronx, NY 10452. TEL 212-588-8400. Ed.
Cathy Rentschler. (avail. on CD-ROM)
  ●Also available online. Vendors: Wilsonline.

020 US
LIBRARY OF CONGRESS CLASSIFICATION
SCHEDULES: A CUMULATION OF
ADDITIONS AND CHANGES. 1971. irreg. price
varies. Gale Research Company, Book Tower,
Detroit, MI 48226. TEL 313-961-2242. Ed. Helen
Savage.

020 011 IE ISSN 0024-631X
LONG ROOM. 1970. a. £6. Trinity College, Friends
of the Library, College St., Dublin 2, Ireland. Ed.
W. E. Mackey. adv. bibl. illus. circ. 700. (back
issues avail.) Indexed: Br.Hum.Ind.

MAGYAR TUDOMANYOS AKADEMIA
KONVYTARANAK KIADVANYAI. see
SCIENCES: COMPREHENSIVE WORKS —
Abstracting, Bibliographies, Statistics

027.4 US ISSN 0164-0496
MISSOURI UNION LIST OF SERIAL
PUBLICATIONS. 1975. a. $50. St. Louis Public
Library, Board of Directors, 1301 Olive St., St.
Louis, MO 63103. Ed. Dorothy Knipmeyer. (avail.
only in microfiche)

MUSIC, BOOKS ON MUSIC AND SOUND
RECORDINGS. see MUSIC — Abstracting,
Bibliographies, Statistics

020 310 US
NEW JERSEY PUBLIC LIBRARY STATISTICS
FOR (YEAR) 1958. a. free. State Library, 185 W.
State St., Trenton, NJ 08625-0520. TEL 609-292-
8151. Ed. Oliver Gillock. circ. 600.
  Formerly: New Jersey Public Libraries. Statistics
(ISSN 0093-1098)

021 027.7 US
NORTH DAKOTA LIBRARY STATISTICS. a. free.
State Library, Capitol Grounds, Bismarck, ND
58505. TEL 701-224-2490.
  Formerly: North Dakota Academic Library
Statistics. (ISSN 0094-5455)

OHIO STATE UNIVERSITY. INSTITUTE OF
POLAR STUDIES. CONTRIBUTION SERIES. see
EARTH SCIENCES

808.81 US ISSN 0736-3966
POETRY INDEX ANNUAL. 1982. a. $54.99. Poetry
Index Press, Roth Publishing, Inc., Box 406, Great
Neck, NY 11022. TEL 516-466-3676. circ. 2,000.

020 AT ISSN 0156-4374
PUBLIC LIBRARIES OF VICTORIA. ANNUAL
STATISTICAL BULLETIN. 1969. a. Aus.$3.
Library Council of Victoria, Consultancy and Public
Libraries Services, 328 Swanston St., Melbourne,
Vic. 3000, Australia. circ. 500.

020 US
PUBLIC LIBRARY CATALOG. quinquennial, with a.
supplements. $140. ‡ H.W. Wilson Co., 950
University Ave., Bronx, NY 10452. TEL 212-588-
8400. Eds. Gary L. Bogove, John Greenfieldt. bk.
rev.
  Formerly: Standard Catalog for Public Libraries.

020 CN ISSN 0075-6113
QUEEN'S UNIVERSITY AT KINGSTON.
DOUGLAS LIBRARY. OCCASIONAL PAPERS.
1969. irreg. Can.$3. Queen's University, Douglas
Library, Kingston, Ont., Canada. TEL 613-547-
5511. circ. 300. (also avail. in microfilm)

026 US
S A L A L M BIBLIOGRAPHY AND REFERENCE
SERIES. (Text in English, French, Portuguese,
Spanish) 1969. irreg., approx. a. price varies.
Seminar on the Acquisition of Latin American
Library Materials, Memorial Library, University of
Wisconsin-Madison, Madison, WI 53706. TEL 608-
262-3240.
  Incorporating: Seminar on the Acquisition of
Latin American Library Materials. Report on
Bibliographic Activities; Formerly: S A L A L M
Bibliography Series.

SERIALS IN C L W LIBRARY. (College of
Librarianship Wales) see BIBLIOGRAPHIES

011 029 SL
SIERRA LEONE PUBLICATIONS. 1964. a. $6.
Library Board, Box 326, Freetown, Sierra Leone.
(back issues avail.)

020 US
STATISTICS OF SOUTHERN COLLEGE AND
UNIVERSITY LIBRARIES. 1929. a. free contr.
circ. Louisiana State University Library, Baton
Rouge, LA 70803. Ed. D.W. Schneider.

010 US ISSN 0081-7600
STUDIES IN BIBLIOGRAPHY. 1948. a. $25.
(Bibliographical Society of the University of
Virginia) University Press of Virginia, Box 3608
University Station, Charlottesville, VA 22903. TEL
804-924-3468. Eds. Fredson Bowers, L.A. Beaurline.
circ. 2,000. Indexed: M.L.A.

026 US ISSN 0000-0140
SUBJECT COLLECTIONS; a guide to special book
collections and subject emphasis in libraries. 1958.
irreg., 6th edt., 1985. $165. R.R. Bowker Company,
245 W. 17th St., New York, NY 10011. TEL 800-
521-8110. Ed. Lee Ash. subject index.

026 011 US
U.S. DEPARTMENT OF STATE. LIBRARY.
COMMERCIAL LIBRARY PROGRAM.
PUBLICATIONS LIST. 1978. irreg. U.S.
Department of State, 2201 C St., N.W.,
Washington, DC 20520 (Orders to: Supt. of
Documents, Washington, DC 20402)

020 016 US ISSN 0083-1603
U.S. LIBRARY OF CONGRESS. LIBRARY OF
CONGRESS PUBLICATIONS IN PRINT. 1935. a.
free. ‡ U.S. Library of Congress, Washington, DC
20540. TEL 202-287-5000. circ. 10,000.

020 UK ISSN 0268-3539
UNIVERSITY LIBRARY EXPENDITURE
STATISTICS. 1981. a. £12.50. Standing Conference
of National & University Libraries (SCONUL), 102
Euston St., London NW1 2HA, England. stat. circ.
250. (looseleaf format; back issues avail.)

020 070.5 011 US
UNIVERSITY MICROFILMS INTERNATIONAL
NEWSLETTER. 1978. irreg., vol.17, 1984. free.
University Microfilms International, 300 N. Zeeb
Rd., Ann Arbor, MI 48106. TEL 313-761-4700. Ed.
Stevens Rice. circ. 15,000. (back issues avail.)

LIBRARY AND INFORMATION SCIENCES — Computer Applications

015 029.7 BL ISSN 0067-6624
BIBLIOGRAFIA BRASILEIRA DE
DOCUMENTACAO. 1811; N.S. 1960. irreg.
Cr.$600($25) Instituto Brasileiro de Informacao em
Ciencia e Tecnologia, SCRN 708/709 Bloco B Loja
18E 30, 70740 Brasilia DF, Brazil. bk. rev. circ.
300.

020 025 UK
CALLISTO. 1984. irreg. £5. (Newcastle upon Tyne
Polytechnic, School of Librarianship) Newcastle
upon Tyne Polytechnic Products Ltd., Ellison Place,
Newcastle upon Tyne NE1 8ST, England. (Co-
sponsor: British Library Research and Development
Department) Eds. Joan M. Day, D. Alasdair Kemp.

025 US ISSN 0272-037X
D L A BULLETIN. 1981. irreg. University of
California, Division of Library Automation, 186
University Hall, Berkeley, CA 94720. TEL 415-642-
9485. Ed. Mary Engle. bk. rev. circ. 2,000.
  ●Also available online.

020 001.6 CN
DALHOUSIE UNIVERSITY. UNIVERSITY
LIBRARIES AND SCHOOL OF LIBRARY
SERVICE. OCCASIONAL PAPERS. irreg. price
varies. Dalhousie University, School of Library
Service, Halifax, N.S. B3H 4H8, Canada. TEL 902-
424-3656. Ed. Mary Dykstra.
  Formerly: Dalhousie University. School of
Library Service. Occasional Papers (ISSN 0318-
7403)

DIRECTORY OF PERIODICALS ONLINE. VOL. 1: NEWS, LAW & BUSINESS; indexed, abstracted & full-text. see *LIBRARY AND INFORMATION SCIENCES*

020 010   GW   ISSN 0074-5804
F.I.D./C.R. REPORT SERIES. 1964. irreg., no.20, 1982. price varies. International Federation for Documentation, Committee on Classification Research, Woogstr. 36a, D-6000 Frankfurt 50, West Germany (B.R.D.) Ed. Ingetraut Dahlberg. circ. 300.

INFORMATION PROCESSING ASSOCIATION OF ISRAEL. NATIONAL CONFERENCE ON DATA PROCESSING. PROCEEDINGS. see *COMPUTERS — Information Science And Information Theory*

MICRO SOFTWARE EVALUATIONS. see *COMPUTERS — Software*

025   US   ISSN 0743-0302
MICROCOMPUTERS FOR LIBRARIES; product review and procurement guide. 1984. irreg., base vol. plus q. updates. $115. James E. Rush Associates, Inc., 2223 Carriage Rd., Powell, OH 43065-9703. TEL 614-881-5949. Ed. James E. Rush. adv. bibl. circ. 400.

PLUS; Plus System newsletter. see *PUBLISHING AND BOOK TRADE — Computer Applications*

025   US   ISSN 0193-273X
S O L I N E W S. 1973. irreg. free. Southeastern Library Network, Inc., Plaza Level, 400 Colony Sq., 1201 Peachtree St., N.E., Atlanta, GA 30361. TEL 404-892-0943. Ed.Bd. circ. 1,500. (back issues avail.)

UNIVERSITY OF SOUTHAMPTON. LIBRARY. AUTOMATION PROJECT REPORT. see *LIBRARY AND INFORMATION SCIENCES*

025   US   ISSN 0884-593X
WIRED LIBRARIAN'S NEWSLETTER. 1983. irreg., approx. m. $15. Micro Libraries, No. 2C, Andover Dr., Athens, OH 45702. TEL 614-594-7757. Ed. Eric Anderson. bk. rev. software rev. circ. 800.

LINGUISTICS

see also Classical Studies; Oriental Studies

410   FI   ISSN 0356-8156
A FIN L A YEARBOOK; Yearbook. (Text in English) 1977. a. Fmk.40. Association Finlandaise de Linguistique Appliquee, Department of English, University of Jyvaeskylae, SF-40100 Jyvaeskylae, Finland. circ. 600.

410   DK   ISSN 0106-441X
A R K; sproginstitutternes arbejdspapirer. vol.9, 1981. irreg. Handelshoejskolen i Koebenhavn, Erhvervssproglige Fakultet, Fabrikvej 7, DK-2000 Copenhagen F, Denmark. Ed. Hans-Peder Kromann. circ. 200.

460   DK   ISSN 0107-6531
AARHUS UNIVERSITET. ROMANSK INSTITUT. SPANSK AFDELINGEN. INFORMATION. 1975. irreg., no.36, 1983. Kr.15 per no. Aarhus Universitet, Romansk Institut, 512 Spansk Agfdelingen, Willemoesgade 15, 8200 Aarhus N, Denmark. illus.

460   BO
ACADEMIA BOLIVIANA DE LA LENGUA. ANALES. 1985. a. Academia Boliviana de la Lengua, Casilla de Correos 4154, La Paz, Bolivia. Dir. Carlos Castanon Barrientos. bk. rev. circ. 400.

ACADEMIA DE CIENCIAS. ANUAL DE LITERATURA Y LINGUISTICA. see *LITERATURA*

400 060   HO   ISSN 0065-0471
ACADEMIA HONDURENA DE LA LENGUA. BOLETIN. 1957. a. $10. Academia Hondurena de la Lengua, Apdo. Postal 38, Tegucigalpa, Honduras. Ed. Jorge Fidel Duron. bk. rev. circ. 500. (back issues avail.)

ACADEMIA PAULISTA DE LETRAS. REVISTA. see *LITERATURA*

400 840   FR   ISSN 0065-0544
ACADEMIE DES INSCRIPTIONS ET BELLES-LETTRES. ETUDES ET COMMENTAIRES. 1946. irreg. price varies. Editions Klincksieck, 11 rue de Lille, 75007 Paris, France. (also avail. in microfiche)

840   BE   ISSN 0567-6584
ACADEMIE ROYALE DE LANGUE ET DE LITTERATURE FRANCAISES. ANNUAIRES. a. price changes. Academie Royale de Langue et de Litterature Francaises, Palais des Academies, 1 rue Ducale, Brussels, Belgium. Ed. Thomas Owen. bibl.

492.4   IS   ISSN 0065-0692
ACADEMY OF THE HEBREW LANGUAGE. SPECIALIZED DICTIONARIES. irreg. Academy of the Hebrew Language, Box 3449, 91034 Jerusalem, Israel.

492.4   IS
ACADEMY OF THE HEBREW LANGUAGE. TEXTS & STUDIES. irreg. Academy of the Hebrew Language, Box 3449, Jerusalem 91034, Israel.
Formerly: Academy of the Hebrew Language. Linguistic Studies (ISSN 0075-9643)

423.1   US   ISSN 0270-4404
ACRONYMS, INITIALISMS AND ABBREVIATIONS DICTIONARY; a guide to alphabetic designations, contractions, acronyms, initialisms, and similar condensed appellations. 11th edt., 1986. a. $180. Gale Research Company, Book Tower, Detroit, MI 48226. TEL 313-961-2242. Eds. Julie Towell, Helen Sheppard.
Formerly (until 1976): Acronyms and Initialisms Dictionary (ISSN 0065-0889)

410   SA   ISSN 0065-1141
ACTA CLASSICA. (Text mainly in English; occasionally in Afrikaans, French or German) 1958. a. R.20 per vol. Classical Association of South Africa, P.O. Box 392, Pretoria 0001, South Africa (And: Box 1675, Rotterdam, Netherlands; in the U.S. and Canada: Box 230, Accord, MA 02018) Ed. U.R.D. Vogel-Weidemann. bk. rev. circ. 500. Indexed: Ind.S.A.Per.

480 470   BE
ACTA COLLOQUII DIDACTICI CLASSICI; didactica classica gandensia. (Text in Dutch, English, French, German and Latin) 1963. a. 350 Fr. International Bureau for the Study of the Problems in the Teaching of Greek and Latin, Blandijnberg 2, B-9000 Ghent, Belgium. Eds. J. Veremans, F. Decreus.

430   SA
ACTA GERMANICA. (Text in English, French and German) 1966. a. R.43. (Suedafrikanischer Germanistenverband) Peter Lang Verlag, Rhodes University, Department of German, Grahamstown 6140, South Africa. Ed. Dieter Welz. bk. rev. circ. 400. (back issues avail.) Indexed: M.L.A.

410   DK   ISSN 0374-0463
ACTA LINGUISTICA HAFNIENSIA; international journal of general linguistics. (Text in English, French or German) 1939. irreg., latest vol.19, no.1-2, 1985. Kr.250. (Institute of Linguistics) C A Reitzel A-S, Noerregade 20, 1165 Copenhagen K, Denmark. Ed.Bd. bk. rev. bibl. circ. 90. (reprint service avail. from ISI) Indexed: Curr.Cont. M.L.A. Lang.& Lang.Behav.Abstr.
Formerly: Acta Linguistica (ISSN 0105-001X)

459   IT   ISSN 0065-1516
ACTA PHILOLOGICA. (Contributions in Italian, Rumanian, English, French, German and Spanish) 1958. irreg. price varies. Societa Accademica Romena, Foro Traiano 1a, 00187 Rome, Italy.

410   PL   ISSN 0065-1524
ACTA PHILOLOGICA. (Text in English, French, German and Polish) 1968. irreg., vol.12, 1983. price varies. (Uniwersytet Warszawski, Wydzial Neofilologii) Wydawnictwa Uniwersytetu Warszawskiego, Ul. Obozna 8, 00-927 Warsaw, Poland (Distr. by: CHZ ARS Polona, Krakowskie Przedmiescie 7, 00-068 Warsaw, Poland) Eds. J. Reychman, Witold Tyloch. circ. 500.

489   AU   ISSN 0065-1532
ACTA PHILOLOGICA AENIPONTANA. 1962. irreg., vol.4, 1979. price varies. (Gesellschaft fuer Klassische Philologie in Innsbruck) Universitaetsverlag Wagner, Andreas-Hofer-Str. 13, Postfach 165, A-6010 Innsbruck, Austria. Ed. Robert Muth. circ. 600.

439   DK   ISSN 0001-6691
ACTA PHILOLOGICA SCANDINAVICA; tidsskrift for nordisk sprogforskning. (Text in several languages; summaries in English) 1926 (suspended vol.33, 1982; will resume 1985) irreg. price varies. Sortedam Dossering 77, DK-2100 Copenhagen OE, Denmark. Ed. Joergen Larsen. bk. rev. bibl. illus. index. circ. 300. (reprint service avail. from ISI) Indexed: Curr.Cont. M.L.A.

ACTA REGIAE SOCIETATITIS HUMANIORUM LITTERATUM LUNDENSIS. see *ARCHAEOLOGY*

440 840   HU   ISSN 0567-8099
ACTA UNIVERSITATIS DE ATTILA JOZSEF NOMINATAE. ACTA ROMANICA. (Text in French and Italian) 1964; N.S. 1972. a. exchange basis. Attila Jozsef University, c/o E. Szabo, Exchange Librarian, Dugonics ter 13, P.O.B. 393, Szeged H-6701, Hungary (Subscr. to: Kultura, Box 149, H-1389 Budapest, Hungary) Ed. Miklos Palfy. circ. 300.

420 810 820   HU   ISSN 0230-2780
ACTA UNIVERSITATIS DE ATTILA JOZSEF NOMINATAE. PAPERS IN ENGLISH AND AMERICAN STUDIES. (Text in English) 1980. a. exchange basis. Attila Jozsef University, c/o E. Szabo, Exchange Librarian, Dugonics ter 13, P.O.B. 393, Szeged H-6701, Hungary (Subscr. to: Kultura, Box 149, H-1389 Budapest, Hungary) Ed. B. Rozsnyai. circ. 400. Indexed: M.L.A.

410 370   PL   ISSN 0208-6077
ACTA UNIVERSITATIS LODZIENSIS: FOLIA LINGUISTICA. (Text in Polish; summaries in various languages) irreg. Uniwersytet Lodzki, Drukarnia Wojskowa, Ul. Gdanska 130, Lodz, Poland (Dist. by: Ars Polona-Ruch, Krakowskie Przedmiescie 7, Warsaw, Poland)

400   PL   ISSN 0208-5259
ACTA UNIVERSITATIS NICOLAI COPERNICI. FILOLOGIA GERMANSKA. 1974. irreg. price varies. Uniwersytet Mikolaja Kopernika, Fosa Staromiejska 3, Torun, Poland (Dist. by: Osrodek Rozpowszechniania Wydawnictw Naukowych PAN, Palac Kultury i Nauki, 00-901 Warsaw, Poland)

491.85   PL   ISSN 0208-5321
ACTA UNIVERSITATIS NICOLAI COPERNICI. FILOLOGIA POLSKA. 1959. irreg. price varies. Uniwersytet Mikolaja Kopernika, Fosa Staromiejska 3, Torun, Poland (Dist. by: Osrodek Rozpowszechniania Wydawnictw Naukowych PAN, Palac Kultury i Nauki, 00-901 Warsaw, Poland)
Formerly: Uniwersytet Mikolaja Kopernika, Torun. Nauki Humanistyczno-Spoleczne. Filologia Polska (ISSN 0083-4483)

491.7 891.7   HU
ACTA UNIVERSITATIS SZEGEDIENSIS DE ATTILA JOZSEF NOMINATAE. DISSERTATIONES SLAVICAE. SECTIO LINGUISTICA. (Text in Russian) 1962. a. exchange basis. Attila Jozsef University, c/o E. Szabo, Exchange Librarian, Dugonics ter 13, P.O. Box 393, Szeged H-6701, Hungary (Subscr. to: Kultura, Box 149, H-1389 Budapest, Hungary) Ed. Imre H. Toth. circ. 400.
Supersedes in part: Acta Universitatis Szegediensis de Attila Jozsef Nominatae. Dissertationes Slavicae (ISSN 0586-3732)

494.511   HU   ISSN 0209-9543
ACTA UNIVERSITATIS SZEGEDIENSIS DE ATTILA JOZSEF NOMINATAE. SECTIO ETHNOGRAPHICA ET LINGUISTICA. (Its subseries: Neprajz es Nyelvtudomany. HU 0586-3716) (Summaries in English, French, German and Russian) 1957. a. exchange basis. Attila Jozsef University, c/o E. Szabo, Exchange Librarian, Dugonics ter 13, P.O.B. 393, Szeged H-6701, Hungary (Subscr. to: Kultura, Box 149, H-1389 Budapest, Hungary) Ed.Bd. bk. rev. circ. 500. Indexed: M.L.A.

491.7 891.7 HU
ACTA UNIVERSITATIS SZEGEDIENSIS DE ATTILA JOZSEF NOMINATAE. SECTIO HISTORIAE LITTERARUM. a. Attila Jozsef University, c/o E. Szabo, Exchange Librarian, Dugonics ter 13, P.O. Box 393, Szeged H-6701, Hungary. Ed. Katalin Szoke. circ. 400.
Supersedes in part (as of 1982): Acta Universitatis Szegediensis de Attila Jozsef Nominatae. Dissertations Slavicae (ISSN 0586-3732)

410 US
ADVANCES IN DISCOURSE PROCESSES. 1977. irreg., vol.21, 1986. price varies. Ablex Publishing Corp., 355 Chestnut St., Norwood, NJ 07648. TEL 201-767-8450. Ed. Roy O. Freedle. (reprint service avail. from ISI)

AFRO-ASIA. see *HISTORY*

492 US ISSN 0732-6416
AFROASIATIC DIALECTS.* 1977. irreg., latest no. 4. price varies. Undena Publications, 6355 Green Valley Circle, No. 213, Culver City, CA 90230-7064. Ed. Dr. Thomas Penchoen. bibl. charts. illus. circ. 500. (back issues avail.) Indexed: Lang.& Lang.Behav.Abstr.

492 US ISSN 0362-3637
AFROASIATIC LINGUISTICS.* (Subseries of: Monographic Journals of the Near East) 1974. irreg., vol.9, no.1, 1984. $24. Undena Publications, 6355 Green Valley Circle, No. 213, Culver City, CA 90230-7064. Eds. Robert Hetzron, Russel Schuh. bibl. charts. illus. circ. 500. (back issues avail.) Indexed: M.L.A. Old Test.Abstr. Curr.Cont.Africa. Lang.& Lang.Behav.Abstr.

400 900 GW ISSN 0065-5287
AKADEMIE DER WISSENSCHAFTEN, GOETTINGEN. NACHRICHTEN 1. PHILOLOGISCH-HISTORISCHE KLASSE. (Text in English, German, occasionally French) 1893. irreg. price varies. Vandenhoeck und Ruprecht, Theaterstr. 13, Postfach 37 53, 3400 Goettingen, W. Germany (B.R.D.) index. Indexed: Hist.Abstr. Amer.Hist.& Life.

AKADEMIJA NAUKA I UMJETNOSTI BOSNE I HERCEGOVINE. ODELJENJE ISTORIJSKO FILOLOSKIH NAUK. DJELA. see *HISTORY — History Of Europe*

491 UR
AKTUAL'NYE PROBLEMY LEKSIKOLOGII I SLOVOOBRAZOVANIYA. 1972. irreg. 0.70 Rub. Novosibirskii Gosudarstvennyi Universitet, Novosibirsk, 99 Akademgorodok, Russian S.F.S.R., U.S.S.R. bibl. illus.

410 572 US ISSN 0883-8526
ALASKA NATIVE LANGUAGE CENTER RESEARCH PAPERS. 1979. irreg., no.7, 1985. price varies. University of Alaska, Alaska Native Language Center, Box 111, Fairbanks, AK 99775-0120. TEL 907-474-7874. Ed. Michael Krauss. circ. 200. (back issues avail.)

400 800 BL ISSN 0002-5216
ALFA; revista de linguistica. (Text in Portuguese; summaries in English and Portuguese) 1962-1979; resumed 1980. a. $30 or exchange basis. Universidade Estadual Paulista, Av. Vicente Ferreira, 1278, Caixa Postal 603, 17.500 Marilia, SP, Brazil. Ed.Bd. bk. rev. bibl. index. circ. 1,000. Indexed: M.L.A. Sociol.Abstr. Lang.& Lang.Behav.Abstr.

ALGONQUIAN CONFERENCE PAPERS. see *ANTHROPOLOGY*

400 II
ALL-INDIA CONFERENCE OF LINGUISTS. PROCEEDINGS. (Text in English) 1970. a. price varies. Linguistic Society of India, c/o Deccan College Postgraduate and Research Institute, Poona 411006, India. Ed. R.V. Dhongde.

400 II
ALL-INDIA CONFERENCE OF LINGUISTS. SOUVENIR. 1970. irreg. $2. Linguistic Society of India, c/o Deccan College Postgraduate and Research Institute, Poona 411006, India. Ed. R.V. Dhongde. adv.

410 GE
ALTHOCHDEUTSCHES WOERTERBUCH. 1952. a. (Saechsische Akademie der Wissenschaften zu Leipzig) Akademie-Verlag Berlin, Leipzig 3-4, 1086 Berlin, E. Germany (D.D.R.) Ed. Rudolf Grasse.

400 US ISSN 0278-5943
AMERICAN CLASSICAL STUDIES. no.8, 1981. irreg. (American Philological Association) Scholars Press, 101 Salem St., Box 1608, Decatur, GA 30031-1608. Ed. Susan Treggiari.

427 US ISSN 0002-8207
AMERICAN DIALECT SOCIETY. PUBLICATIONS. Abbreviated title: P A D S. 1944. irreg. price varies. (American Dialect Society) University of Alabama Press, Box 2877, University, AL 35486. TEL 205-348-5180. circ. 800. Indexed: Lang.Behav.Abstr.

420 375.4 US ISSN 0734-7545
AMERICAN LANGUAGE JOURNAL; a journal for intensive English studies. 1982. a. $5.50. University of Arizona, Center for English as a Second Language, CESL 100, Tuscon, AZ 85721. TEL 602-621-1362. circ. 1,000. (also avail. in microform from UMI; back issues avail.) Indexed: Lang.& Lang.Behav.Abstr.

400 US ISSN 0044-779X
AMERICAN PHILOLOGICAL ASSOCIATION. DIRECTORY OF MEMBERS. 1970. irreg. (approx. biennial) price varies. (American Philological Association) Scholars Press, Box 1608, Decatur, GA 30031-1608. circ. 3,000.

480 478 US ISSN 0065-9703
AMERICAN PHILOLOGICAL ASSOCIATION. SPECIAL PUBLICATIONS. 1946. irreg. price varies. (American Philological Association) Scholars Press, Box 2268, Chico, CA 95927. TEL 916-891-4541.

406 US ISSN 0360-5949
AMERICAN PHILOLOGICAL ASSOCIATION. TRANSACTIONS. 1870. a. $40. (American Philological Association) Scholars Press, Box 1608, Decatur, GA 30031-1608. Ed. James E.G. Zetzel. cum.index 1869-1969. circ. 3,000. Indexed: Curr.Cont.
Formerly: American Philological Association. Transactions and Proceedings (ISSN 0065-9711)

430 374.4 833.91 US ISSN 0721-1392
AMERICAN UNIVERSITY STUDIES. SERIES 1. GERMANIC LANGUAGES AND LITERATURE. 1981. irreg. Peter Lang Publishing, Inc., 62 W. 45th St., New York, NY 10036. TEL 213-302-6740. Ed. Jay Wilson.

410 495.1 US
AMERICAN UNIVERSITY STUDIES. SERIES 6. FOREIGN LANGUAGE INSTRUCTION. 1983. irreg. Peter Lang Publishing, Inc., 62 W. 45th St., New York, NY 10036. TEL 212-302-6740. Ed. Jay Wilson.

891.733 US ISSN 0740-0497
AMERICAN UNIVERSITY STUDIES. SERIES 12. SLAVIC LANGUAGES AND LITERATURE. 1983. irreg. Peter Lang Publishing, Inc., 62 W. 45th St., New York, NY 10036. TEL 212-302-6740. Ed. Jay Wilson.

447 US ISSN 0740-4557
AMERICAN UNIVERSITY STUDIES. SERIES 13. LINGUISTICS. 1984. irreg. Peter Lang Publishing, Inc., 62 W. 45th St., New York, NY 10036. TEL 212-302-6740. Ed. Jay Wilson.

410 US ISSN 0304-0712
AMSTERDAM STUDIES IN THE THEORY AND HISTORY OF LINGUISTIC SCIENCE. SERIES 1: AMSTERDAM CLASSICS IN LINGUISTICS, 1800-1925. Short title: A C I L. (Text in English and German) 1974. irreg., vol.15, 1984. price varies. John Benjamins Publishing Co., One Buttonwood Sq., Philadelphia, PA 19130. TEL 215-564-6379. Ed. E.F.K. Koerner. Indexed: M.L.A.

410 150 US ISSN 0165-716X
AMSTERDAM STUDIES IN THE THEORY AND HISTORY OF LINGUISTIC SCIENCE. SERIES 2: CLASSICS IN PSYCHOLINGUISTICS. Short title: C I P L. (Text in English and German) 1978. irreg., vol.4, 1986. price varies. John Benjamins Publishing Co., One Buttonwood Sq., Philadelphia, PA 19130. TEL 215-564-6379. Ed. E.F.K. Koerner. Indexed: M.L.A.

410 US
AMSTERDAM STUDIES IN THE THEORY AND HISTORY OF LINGUISTIC SCIENCE. SERIES 3: STUDIES IN THE HISTORY OF THE LANGUAGE SCIENCES. Short title: S I H O L S. 1973. irreg., vol.39, 1986. price varies. John Benjamins Publishing Co., One Buttonwood Sq., Philadelphia, PA 19130. TEL 215-564-6379. Ed. E.F.K. Koerner. Indexed: M.L.A.
Formerly: Amsterdam Studies In the Theory and History of the Linguistic Science. Series 3: Studies In the History of Linguistics (ISSN 0304-0720)

410 US ISSN 0304-0763
AMSTERDAM STUDIES IN THE THEORY AND HISTORY OF LINGUISTIC SCIENCE. SERIES 4: CURRENT ISSUES IN LINGUISTIC THEORY. Short title: C I L T. (Text in English) 1975. irreg., vol.45, 1986. price varies. John Benjamins Publishing Co., One Buttonwood Sq, Philadelphia, PA 19130. TEL 215-564-6379. Ed. E.F.K. Koerner. Indexed: M.L.A.

AMSTERDAMER PUBLIKATIONEN ZUR SPRACHE UND LITERATUR. see *LITERATURE*

440 840 GW ISSN 0569-986X
ANALECTA ROMANICA. (Beihefte zu den Romanischen Forschungen) 1955. irreg., vol.51, 1986. price varies. Vittorio Klostermann, Frauenlobstr. 22, Postfach 900601, 6000 Frankfurt 90, W. Germany (B.R.D.) Ed. Wido Hempel.

420 DK ISSN 0105-9963
ANGLICA ET AMERICANA. no.14, 1981. irreg. price varies. Koebenhavns Universitet, Department of English, Njalsgade 84-96, 2300 Copenhagen S, Denmark (Dist. by: Atheneum Booksellers, 6 Norregade, DK-1165 Copenhagen K, Denmark) Ed.Bd. circ. 600.

430 792 UK
ANGLICA GERMANICA: SERIES 2. irreg. price varies. Cambridge University Press, Edinburgh Bldg., Shaftesbury Rd., Cambridge CB2 2RU, England (And: 32 E. 57th St., New York NY 10022) Ed.Bd.

ANGLO-AMERICAN FORUM. see *LITERATURE*

420 820 HU ISSN 0570-0973
ANGOL FILOLOGIAI TANULMANYOK/ HUNGARIAN STUDIES IN ENGLISH. (Text in English) 1967. irreg., vol.14, 1981. Kossuth Lajos Tudomanyegyetem, Angol Tanszek, Egyetem Ter 1, Debrecen 4010, Hungary. bibl. illus. Indexed: M.L.A.

ANNALES AEQUATORIA. see *ANTHROPOLOGY*

400 PL
ANNALES UNIVERSITATIS MARIAE CURIE-SKLODOWSKA. SECTIO FF. PHILOLOGIAE. (Text in English, French, German, Polish and Russian; summaries in English, French, Polish and Russian) 1983. a. price varies. Uniwersytet Marii Curie-Sklodowskiej, Plac Marii Curie-Sklodowskiej 5, 20-031 Lublin, Poland. Ed. Alina Aleksandrowicz. circ. 550.

470 FR ISSN 0066-2348
ANNEE EPIGRAPHIQUE; REVUE DES PUBLICATIONS EPIGRAPHIQUES RELATIVES A L'ANTIQUITE ROMAINE. 1962. a. 275 F. Presses Universitaires de France, 108 bd. Saint Germain, 75279 Paris Cedex 6, France (Service des Periodiques, 12 rue Jean Beauvais, 75005 Paris) (reprint service avail. from KTO) Indexed: Br.Archaeol.Abstr.

410 US ISSN 0271-9800
ANNUAL OF ARMENIAN LINGUISTICS. (Text in English, French, German, Italian) 1980. a. $17 to individuals; institutions $22, for 2 yrs. c/o John A.C. Greppin, Ed., Cleveland State University, Cleveland, OH 44115. adv. bk. rev. bibl. circ. 190. (back issues avail.) Indexed: M.L.A. Amer.Bibl.Slavic & E.Eur.Stud.

LINGUISTICS

410 950 US
ANNUAL OF URDU STUDIES. 1981. a. $12. 1130 E. 59th St., Chicago, IL 60637. TEL 312-962-7547. Ed. C.M. Naim. bk. rev. bibl. illus. circ. 100. (back issues avail.) Indexed: M.L.A.

407 UK
ANNUAL REVIEW OF APPLIED LINGUISTICS. 1981. a. $22 to individuals; institutions $37. Cambridge University Press, The Edinburgh Bldg., Shaftesbury Rd., Cambridge CB2 2RU. Ed. Robert B. Kaplan. bibl. charts. stat. Indexed: M.L.A.

ANTICHITA CLASSICA E CRISTIANA. see *HISTORY*

400 VE ISSN 0066-507X
ANUARIO DE FILOLOGIA.* 1962. a. Bs.10($2.25) Universidad del Zulia, Facultad de Humanidades y Educacion, Apdo. 526, Maracaibo, Venezuela. Indexed: M.L.A.

400 800 SP ISSN 0210-1343
ANUARIO DE FILOLOGIA. (Text in various European languages) 1975. a. 1200 ptas.($20) Universidad de Barcelona, Facultad de Filologia, 08007 Barcelona, Spain. Ed. Fernando Diaz Esteban. adv. bk. rev. cum.index. circ. 600. (back issues avail.) Indexed: Old Test.Abstr.
Formerly: Universidad de Barcelona. Facultad de Filologia. Anuario.

491.8 AU ISSN 0066-5282
ANZEIGER FUER SLAVISCHE PHILOLOGIE. 1966. irreg., vol.17, 1986. Akademische Druck- und Verlagsanstalt, Neufeldweg 75, 8010 Graz, Styria, Austria.

410 572 FR ISSN 0755-9291
APPLICATIONS ET TRANSFERTS. 1982. irreg. price varies. Societe d'Etudes Linguistiques et Anthropologiques de France (SELAF), 5 rue de Marseille, 75010 Paris, France.

410 US
APPLIED LANGUAGE STUDIES. 1981. irreg., latest vol.8, 1984. Academic Press Inc., Orlando, FL 32887. TEL 305-345-2000. Ed. D. Crystal.

410
APPLIED LINGUISTICS. ANNUAL REVIEW. a. $22 to individuals; institutions $37. Cambridge University Press, 32 E. 57th St., New York, NY 10022. Ed.Bd. adv. bk. rev.

410 GW ISSN 0066-5576
APPROACHES TO SEMIOTICS. 1969. irreg. price varies. (Walter de Gruyter und Co.) Walter de Gruyter & Co., Mouton Publishers, Postfach 110240, D-1000 Berlin 11, W. Germany (B.R.D.) (U.S. addr.: Mouton Publishers, division of Walter de Gruyter, Inc., 200 Saw Mill River Road, Hawthorne, NY 10532)

492.7 370 US ISSN 0889-8731
AL-ARABIYYA. (Text in Arabic and English) 1967. 1-2/yr. $15 to individuals; institutions $20; students $10. American Association of Teachers of Arabic, 256 Dieter Cunz Hall, 1841 Millikin Rd., Columbus, OH 43210. Ed. Frederic Cadora. adv. bk. rev. bibl. circ. 300. (back issues avail.) Indexed: M.L.A. Ind.Islam.
Formerly (until vol. 8): Al-Nashra (ISSN 0003-2387)

450 IT ISSN 0066-6696
ARCHIVIO LINGUISTICO VENETO. QUADERNI. 1962. irreg., no.5, 1969. price varies. (Fondazione Giorgio Cini) Casa Editrice Leo S. Olschki, Casella Postale 66, 50100 Florence, Italy. circ. 1,000.

410 709 880 IT
ARCHIVIO PER L'ALTO ADIGE; rivista di studi alpini. 1906. a. L.50000. Istituto di Studi per l'Alto Adige, Via Cesare Battisti 4, 50122 Florence, Italy. circ. 150. Indexed: M.L.A.

407 GW ISSN 0721-0442
ARCHIVUM CALDERONIANUM. (Text in Spanish) 1982. irreg., vol.3, 1985. price varies. Franz Steiner Verlag Wiesbaden GmbH, Birkenwaldstr. 44, Postfach 347, D-7000 Stuttgart 1, W. Germany (B.R.D.) Ed. Hans Flasche.

450 IT ISSN 0066-6815
ARCHIVUM ROMANICUM. BIBLIOTECA. SERIE 2: LINGUISTICA. (Text in French, German or Italian) 1921. irreg., no.40, 1984. price varies. Casa Editrice Leo S. Olschki, Casella Postale 66, 50100 Florence, Italy. circ. 1,500.

480 470 PL ISSN 0066-6866
ARCHIWUM FILOLOGICZNE. (Vols. are not issued in chronological order) (Text in French, German, Latin and Polish; summaries in French) 1958. irreg., vol.41, 1984. price varies. (Polska Akademia Nauk, Komitet Nauk o Kulturze Antycznej) Ossolineum, Publishing House of the Polish Academy of Sciences, Rynek 9, Wroclaw, Poland (Dist. by: Ars Polona-Ruch, Krakowskie Przedmiescie 7, Warsaw, Poland) Ed. J. Wolski. circ. 500-1,000.

491.85 891.85 PL ISSN 0208-7596
ARCHIWUM TLUMACZEN Z TEORII LITERATURY I METODOLOGII BADAN LITERACKICH. 1966. irreg. price varies. Katolicki Uniwersytet Lubelski, Katedra Teorii Literatury, Al. Raclawickie 14, 20-950 Lublin, Poland. Ed. Jozef Japola. index. circ. 225.

ARCTOS; ACTA PHILOLOGICA FENNICA. see *CLASSICAL STUDIES*

439 SW ISSN 0066-7668
ARKIV FOR NORDISK FILOLOGI/ARCHIVES FOR SCANDINAVIAN PHILOLOGY. (Text in Danish, English, French, German, Norwegian and Swedish) 1882. a. Kr.160. Student Litteratur AB, Box 141, S-221 00 Lund, Sweden. Ed. Bengt Pamp. bk. rev. circ. 470. Indexed: M.L.A.

ARNAMAGNAEAN INSTITUTE AND DICTIONARY. BULLETIN. see *LITERATURE*

408 UK ISSN 0587-3584
ART - LANGUAGE. irreg. £6. Art & Language Press, 13 Milverton Crescent, Leamington Spa, Warwickshire, England.

410 CK
ARTICULOS EN LINGUISTICA Y CAMPOS AFINES. 1974. irreg. $3.50 per no. Instituto Linguistico de Verano, Division Operative de Asuntos Indigenas, Apdo. Aereo 27744, Bogota, Colombia. Indexed: Social.Abstr.
South American Indian languages

410 FR ISSN 0224-2680
ASIE DU SUD-EST ET MONDE INSULINDIEN. 1976. irreg. price varies. Societe d'Etudes Linguistiques et Anthropologiques de France (SELAF), 5 rue de Marseille, 75010 Paris, France. Indexed: E.I.

400 CN ISSN 0066-9016
ASSOCIATION DES TRADUCTEURS ET INTERPRETES DE L'ONTARIO. REPERTOIRE/ ASSOCIATION OF TRANSLATORS AND INTERPRETERS OF ONTARIO. DIRECTORY. (Text in English, French) 1970. a. Can.$13. Association des Traducteurs et Interpretes de l'Ontario, 969 Bronson, Suite 212, Ottawa, Ont. K1S 4G8, Canada. TEL 613-233-6395. Ed.Bd. adv. circ. 2,500.

410 US ISSN 0066-9903
ASSYRIOLOGICAL STUDIES. 1931. irreg., vol.21, 1980. price varies. University of Chicago, Oriental Institute, 1155 E. 58th St., Chicago, IL 60637. TEL 312-962-9508.

410 CN ISSN 0820-8204
ATLANTIC PROVINCES LINGUISTIC ASSOCIATION. ANNUAL MEETING. PAPERS. (Text in English, French) 1977. a. Can.$15 includes Atlantic Provinces Linguistic Association. Journal. Atlantic Provinces Linguistic Association, Linguistics Department, Memorial University, St. John's, Nfld. A1B 3X9, Canada. TEL 709-737-8134. circ. 150.

410 CN ISSN 0706-6910
ATLANTIC PROVINCES LINGUISTIC ASSOCIATION JOURNAL. 1978. a. Can.$15. Atlantic Provinces Linguistic Association, c/o S. Clarke, Ed., Memorial University, Linguistics Department, St. John's, Nfld. A1B 3X9, Canada. TEL 709-737-8134. bk. rev. circ. 200. Indexed: Sociol.Abstr.

491.7 891.7 AT
AUSTRALIAN SLAVONIC AND EAST EUROPEAN STUDIES. (Text in English and Russian) 1967. a. Aus.$10. University of Melbourne, Department of Russian and Language Studies, Parkville, Victoria 3052, Australia. Eds. Paul Cubberley, Roland Sussex. adv. bk. rev. circ. 100. (also avail. in microfilm from UMI) Indexed: M.L.A.
Formerly: Melbourne Slavonic Studies (ISSN 0076-6267)

430 375.4 GW ISSN 0170-8007
BALKAN-ARCHIV NEUE FOLGE. 1976. irreg., no.11, 1986. price varies. Verlag Helmut Buske, Schlueterstr. 14, 2000 Hamburg 13, W. Germany (B.R.D.) Eds. Johannes Kramer, Wolfgang Dahmen.

430 GW ISSN 0720-0994
BALKAN-ARCHIV NEUE FOLGE BEIHEFT. 1981. irreg. price varies. Verlag Helmut Buske, Schlueterstr. 14, 2000 Hamburg 13, W. Germany (B.R.D.)

430 GE
BAUSTEINE ZUR SPRACHGESCHICHTE DES NEUHOCHDEUTSCHEN. 1970. irreg. price varies. (Akademie der Wissenschaften der DDR, Zentralinstitut fuer Sprachwissenschaft) Akademie-Verlag, Leipziger Strasse 3-4, 1086 Berlin, E. Germany (D.D.R.)
Formerly: Bausteine zur Geschichte des Neuhochdeutschen (ISSN 0067-463X)

430 375.4 GW ISSN 0721-4383
BAYREUTHER BEITRAEGE ZUR SPRACHWISSENSCHAFT. 1978. irreg., vol.6, 1986. price varies. Verlag Helmut Buske, Schlueterstr. 14, 2000 Hamburg 13, W. Germany (B.R.D.) Eds. Hans-Werner Eroms, Robert Hinderling.

410 GW ISSN 0721-8923
BAYREUTHER BEITRAEGE ZUR SPRACHWISSENSCHAFT. DIALEKTOLOGIE. 1980. irreg. price varies. Verlag Helmut Buske, Schlueterstr. 14, 2000 Hamburg 13, W. Germany (B.R.D.)

430 375.4 GW
BEITRAEGE ZUR DEUTSCHEN PHILOLOGIE. 1962. irreg. price varies. Wilhelm Schmitz Verlag, Kattenbachstr. 5, D-6300 Lahn-Wissmer, W. Germany (B.R.D.) (And: Postfach 111108, 6300 Giessen, W. Germany (B.R.D.)) Ed.Bd. circ. 100. Indexed: M.L.A.

430 GE ISSN 0232-2714
BEITRAEGE ZUR ERFORSCHUNG DER DEUTSCHEN SPRACHE. (Text and summaries in English, German) 1981. a. M.56. VEB Bibliographisches Institut, PSF 130, Gerichtsweg 26, 7010 Leipzig, E. Germany (D.D.R.) Ed. Wolfgang Fleischer.

480 GW
BEITRAEGE ZUR KLASSISCHEN PHILOLOGIE. 1960. irreg., no.173, 1985. price varies. Verlag Anton Hain GmbH, Adelheid Str. 2, Postfach 1220, 6240 Koenigstein, W. Germany (B.R.D.) Ed.Bd.

409 LU
BEITRAEGE ZUR LUXEMBURGISCHEN SPRACH- UND VOLKSKUNDE. (Text in French, German) 1925. irreg. price varies. Institut Grand-Ducal de Luxembourg, Section de Linguistique, de Folklore et de Toponymie, 5 rue Large, Luxembourg, Luxembourg. circ. 750. (back issues avail.)

410 GW ISSN 0178-1723
BEITRAEGE ZUR PHONETIK UND LINGUISTIK. (Text in German, English, French) 1972. irreg., no.54, 1986. price varies. Verlag Helmut Buske, Schlueterstr. 14, 2000 Hamburg 13, W. Germany (B.R.D.)
Formerly: Hamburger Phonetische Beitraege (ISSN 0341-3187)

BEITRAEGE ZUR ROMANISCHEN PHILOLOGIE DES MITTELALTERS. see *LITERATURE*

430 375.4 AU ISSN 0259-0662
BEITRAEGE ZUR SPRACHINSELFORSCHUNG. 1981. irreg., no.4, 1986. price varies. Verband der Wissenschaftlichen Gesellschaften Oesterreichs, Lindengasse 37, A-1070 Vienna, Austria. Ed. Maria Hornung.

LINGUISTICS

400   SP
BIBLIOTECA DE FILOLOGIA HISPANICA ONOMASTICA Y TOPONIMIA. 1975. irreg. Ediciones el Albir, Calle de los Angeles 8, Barcelona 1, Spain. circ. 500.

460   375.4   SP
BIBLIOTECA DE LINGUISTICA. irreg., no.5, 1983. Editorial Anagrama, S.A., Calle Pedro de la Creu, 58, 08034 Barcelona, Spain.

499.9   IT   ISSN 0067-7450
BIBLIOTECA DI STUDI ETRUSCHI. 1963. irreg., vol.13, 1980. price varies. (Istituto di Studi Etruschi, Florence) Casa Editrice Leo S. Olschki, Casella Postale 66, 50100 Florence, Italy. circ. 1,000.

410   SP
BIBLIOTECA FILOLOGICA. ENSAYOS. irreg. Editorial Bello, Barcas 5, Valencia, Spain.

410   SP
BIBLIOTECA FILOLOGICA. MANUALES. no.4, 1977. irreg. Editorial Bello, Barcas 5, Valencia, Spain.

BIBLIOTHECA AEGYPTIA; the philology and archaeology of ancient Egypt. see *ARCHAEOLOGY*

490   US   ISSN 0742-1117
BIBLIOTHECA AFROASIATICA.* 1982. irreg. price varies. Undena Publications, 6355 Green Valley Circle, No. 213, Culver City, CA 90230-7064. Ed.Bd. Indexed: M.L.A.

450   IT   ISSN 0067-7868
BIBLIOTHECA ATHENA. 1965. irreg., no.25, 1983. price varies. (Universita degli Studi di Roma, Scuola di Filologia Classica) Edizioni dell' Anteneo S.P.A., Box 7216, 00100 Rome, Italy. Ed. Scevola Mariotti. circ. 2,500.

430   324   SZ   ISSN 0067-7477
BIBLIOTHECA GERMANICA. HANDBUECHER, TEXTE UND MONOGRAPHIEN AUS DEM GEBIETE DER GERMANISCHEN PHILOLOGIE. 1951. irreg., vol.25, 1982. price varies. Francke Verlag, Postfach, CH-3000 Berne 26, Switzerland. Ed.Bd.

430   440   SZ   ISSN 0067-7515
BIBLIOTHECA ROMANICA. (Text in French, German or Italian) 1945. irreg., vol.13, 1977. price varies. Francke Verlag, Postfach, CH-3000 Berne 26, Switzerland. Ed. C. Th. Gossen.

800   GW   ISSN 0341-3217
BIBLIOTHECA RUSSICA. 1979. irreg., no.3, 1983. price varies. Verlag Helmut Buske, Schlueterstr. 14, 2000 Hamburg 13, W. Germany (B.R.D.) Ed. Irene Nowikowa.

491   943   FR   ISSN 0067-8325
BIBLIOTHEQUE D'ETUDES BALKANIQUES. 1925. irreg., vol.8, 1965. price varies. Institut d'Etudes Slaves, 9 rue Michelet, F 75006 Paris, France.

440   FR   ISSN 0067-8341
BIBLIOTHEQUE FRANCAISE ET ROMANE. SERIE A: MANUELS ET ETUDES LINGUISTIQUES. 1960. irreg. price varies. (Universite de Strasbourg II, Centre de Philologie et de Litteratures Romanes) Editions Klincksieck, 11 rue de Lille, 75007 Paris, France. Ed. Georges Straka.

800   479   FR   ISSN 0067-8384
BIBLIOTHEQUE FRANCAISE ET ROMANE. SERIE E: LANGUE ET LITTERATURE FRANCAISES AU CANADA. 1966. irreg., no.8, 1973. price varies. (Universite de Strasbourg II, Centre de Philologie et de Letteratures Romanes) Editions Klincksieck, 11 rue de Lille, 75005 Paris, France. Ed. Georges Straka.

491.8   PL   ISSN 0137-5431
BIULETYN SLAWISTYCZNY. vol.4, 1979. irreg., vol.7, 1983. (Polska Akademia Nauk, Instytut Slowianoznawstwa) Panstwowe Wydawnictwo Naukowe, Ul. Miodowa 10, 00-251 Warsaw, Poland (Dist. by: Ars Polona, Krakowskie Przedmiescie 7, 00-068 Warsaw, Poland) Ed. M. Basaj. circ. 320.

BIZANTION NEA HELLAS. see *HUMANITIES: COMPREHENSIVE WORKS*

BOARD OF CELTIC STUDIES. BULLETIN. see *LITERATURE*

400   CL   ISSN 0067-9674
BOLETIN DE FILOLOGIA. (Text in English, French, German, Spanish) 1934. a. $14. Universidad de Chile, Departamento de Linguistica, Facultad de Filosofia, Humanidades y Educacion, Casilla 10136, Correo Central, Santiago, Chile. Ed. Luis Prieto Vera. adv. bk. rev. cum.index. circ. 1,000. Indexed: Hist.Abstr. M.L.A. Amer.Hist.& Life.

410   IT
BOLLETTINO DELL'ATLANTE LINGUISTICO ITALIANO. 1976. a. L.10000. Bottega d'Erasmo s.a.s., Via Gaudenzio Ferrari 9, 10124 Turin, Italy. Ed.Bd. circ. 250. (back issues avail.) Indexed: M.L.A.

400   GW
BONNER ROMANISTISCHE ARBEITEN. 1977. irreg. Universitaet Bonn, Romanisches Seminar, Am Hof 1, D-5300 Bonn 1, W. Germany (B.R.D.) Ed.Bd. (back issues avail.) Indexed: M.L.A.

410   GE
BRANDENBURG-BERLINISCHES WOERTERBUCH. 1968. a. (Saechsische Akademie der Wissenschaften zu Leipzig) Akademie-Verlag Berlin, Leipziger Str. 3-4, 1086 Berlin, E. Germany (D.D.R.)

410   BL   ISSN 0101-0530
BRAZIL. MUSEU DO INDIO. BOLETIM. LINGUISTICA. 1980. irreg. Museu do Indio, Biblioteca Marechal Rondon, Rua das Palmeiras 55, Botafogo, CEP 22270 Rio de Janeiro, Brazil.

BRITISH COLUMBIA ENGLISH TEACHERS' ASSOCIATION. JOURNAL. see *EDUCATION — Teaching Methods And Curriculum*

491.81   BU   ISSN 0068-3787
BULGARSKA AKADEMIIA NA NAUKITE. INSTITUT ZA BULGARSKI EZIK. IZVESTIIA. (Summaries in various languages) vol.19, 1970. irreg. 4.68 lv. per no. Publishing House of the Bulgarian Academy of Sciences, Acad. G. Bonchev St., Bldg. 6, 1113 Sofia, Bulgaria (Dist. by: Hemus, 6, Rouski Blvd., 1000 Sofia, Bulgaria) circ. 577.

410   572   LU   ISSN 0068-4066
BULLETIN LINGUISTIQUE ET ETHNOLOGIQUE. (Text in French, German, Luxembourgeois) 1953. irreg. price varies. Institut Grand-Ducal de Luxembourg, Section de Linguistique, de Folklore et de Toponymie, 5 rue Large, Luxembourg, Luxembourg. circ. 500. (back issues avail.)

400   800   PL   ISSN 0068-4570
BYDGOSKIE TOWARZYSTWO NAUKOWE. WYDZIAL NAUK HUMANISTYCZNYCH. PRACE. SERIA B (JEZYK I LITERATURA) 1965. irreg. price varies. Bydgoskie Towarzystwo Naukowe, Jezuicka 4, Bydgoszcz, Poland (Dist. by: Ars Polona-Ruch, Krakowskie Przedmiescie 7, Warsaw, Poland)

410   800   UK   ISSN 0307-0131
BYZANTINE AND MODERN GREEK STUDIES. (Text in English; quotations in Greek) 1975. a. £12($30) to individuals; £18.50 ($44.25)to institutions. c/o Prof. Anthony Bryer, Centre for Byzantine Studies & Modern Greek, University of Birmingham, Box 363, Birmingham B15 2TT, England. Ed. J.F. Haldon. adv. circ. 300. Indexed: Curr.Cont. Hist.Abstr. M.L.A. Amer.Bibl.Slavic & E.Eur.Stud. Amer.Hist.& Life.

410   800   UK   ISSN 0261-314X
C E C T A L CONFERENCE PAPERS SERIES. 1981. irreg. price varies. Centre for English Cultural Tradition and Language, Division of Continuing Education, University of Sheffield, Sheffield S10 2TN, England. Ed. J.D.A. Widdowson.

410   US
C E T A BULLETIN. 1972. irreg. Chinese-English Translation Assistance Group, 3910 Knowles Ave., Box 400, Kensington, MD 20895. TEL 301-946-7006. Ed. J. Mathias. bk. rev. circ. 300. Indexed: CERDIC.

407   II
C I I L BILINGUAL HINDI SERIES. (Text in English) 1976. irreg. Central Institute of Indian Languages, Manasagangotri, Mysore 570006, India. bibl.

491   II
C I I L GRAMMAR SERIES. 1975. irreg., latest 1980. Rs.10. Central Institute of Indian Languages, Manasagangotri, Mysore 570006, India. bibl.
Study and teaching

491   II
C I I L OCCASIONAL MONOGRAPH SERIES. no.8, 1974. irreg., latest 1980. Central Institute of Indian Languages, Manasagangotri, Mysore 570006, India.

910   US
C U N Y FORUM; papers in linguistics. 1976. a. $5. City University of New York, Ph.D. Program in Linguistics, Graduate Center, 33 W. 42nd St., New York, NY 10036. TEL 212-790-4602. Ed. Robert M. Vago. circ. 125. Indexed: ERIC.

410   BL
CADERNOS DE ESTUDOS LINGUISTICOS/ CADERNOS DE ESTVDOS LINGVISTI. 1978. irreg. Cr.$500 exchange basis. Universidade Estadual de Campinas, Instituto de Estudos da Linguagem, Departamento de Linguistica, Caixa Postal 6045, 13100 Campinas SP, Brazil. Ed.Bd. bibl. charts.

CAHIERS D'ETUDES MONGOLES ET SIBERIENNES. see *ANTHROPOLOGY*

410   FR
CAHIERS DE LINGUISTIQUE HISPANIQUE MEDIEVALE. 1976. irreg., no.8, 1983. (Universite de Paris XIII) Editions Klincksieck, 11 rue de Lille, 75005 Paris, France.

400   FR   ISSN 0153-5048
CAHIERS DE PHILOLOGIE. (Includes supplements) 1976. irreg. (Universite de Lille III, Centre de Recherche Philologique) Presses Universitaires de Lille, Rue du Barreau, B.P. 199, 59654 Villeneuve d'Ascq Cedex, France. Dir. Jean Bollack.

400   CN   ISSN 0068-5070
CAHIERS DE PSYCHOMECANIQUE DE LANGAGE. irreg. price varies. (Universite Laval, Department de Linguistique) Presses de l'Universite Laval, C.P. 2447, Quebec, Que. G1K 7R4, Canada. TEL 418-656-2590.
Formerly: Cahiers de Linguistique Structurale.

418.02   CN
CAHIERS DE TRADUCTOLOGIE. 1979. irreg. University of Ottawa Press, 603 Cumberland, Ottawa, Ont. K1N 6N5. TEL 613-564-2270.

410   SZ   ISSN 0068-516X
CAHIERS FERDINAND DE SAUSSURE; review de linguistique general. 1941. irreg., no.39, 1985. price varies. (Cercle Ferdinand de Saussure) Librarie Droz, 11 rue Massot, 1211 Geneva 12, Switzerland. bk. rev. circ. 1,000. Indexed: M.L.A.

470   870   UK
CAMBRIDGE LATIN TEXTS. irreg. price varies. Cambridge University Press, Edinburgh Bldg., Shaftesbury Rd., Cambridge CB2 2RU, England (And: 32 E. 57th St., New York, NY 10022)

CAMBRIDGE PHILOLOGICAL SOCIETY. PRCCEEDINGS. see *CLASSICAL STUDIES*

CAMBRIDGE PHILOLOGICAL SOCIETY. PROCEEDINGS. SUPPLEMENT. see *CLASSICAL STUDIES*

400   UK   ISSN 0068-676X
CAMBRIDGE STUDIES IN LINGUISTICS. 1969. irreg., no.38, 1984. $59.50 cloth; 19.95 paper. Cambridge University Press, Edinburgh Bldg., Shaftesbury Rd., Cambridge CB2 2RU, England (And: 32 E. 57 St., New York, NY 10022) Ed.Bd. index. Indexed: M.L.A.

LINGUISTICS

410 UK ISSN 0263-0362
CARDIFF WORKING PAPERS IN WELSH
LINGUISTICS/PAPURAN GWAITH
IEITHYDDOL CYMRAEG CAERDYDD. (Text
in English; introduction in Welsh) 1981. a. National
Museum of Wales, Cathays Park, Cardiff CF1 3NP,
Wales. (Co-sponsors: University College Cardiff,
Welsh Language Research Unit; Welsh Folk
Museum) charts. illus.

407 DK
CEBAL. (Text and summaries in English, French,
German) 1970. biennial. Kr.69. Nyt Nordisk Forlag,
Arnold Busck A/S, Kobmagergade 49, 1150
Copenhagen K, Denmark. Ed. Jens Rasmussen. bk.
rev. circ. 800. (back issues avail.)

407 US
CENTRAL STATES CONFERENCE ON THE
TEACHING OF FOREIGN LANGUAGES.
EDUCATION SERIES. 1972. a. $10.95. (Central
States Conference on the Teaching of Foreign
Languages) National Textbook Co., 4255 W. Touhy
Ave., Lincolnwood, IL 60646. TEL 312-679-5500.
Ed. Maurice W. Conner.

410 ZR
CENTRE D'ETUDES ETHNOLOGIQUES.
PUBLICATIONS. SERIE 3: TRAVAUX
LINGUISTIQUES. 1972. irreg., no.11, 1984. C E E
B A Publications, B.P. 246, Bandundu, Zaire
(Foreign subscriptions to: Steyler-Presse-Vertrieb,
Box 2460, D-4054 Nettetal 2, W. Germany (B.R.D))
circ. 700.

410 FR
CENTRE INTERNATIONAL DE
DOCUMENTATION OCCITANE.
BIBLIOTHEQUE. CATALOGUE. (Text in French
and Occitan) 1976. irreg. Centre International de
Documentation Occitane, Bibliotheque, Boite
Postale 4202, 34325 Beziers Cedex, France.

CHIAKA CHRONIKA. see HISTORY — History Of
Europe

410 US ISSN 0577-7240
CHICAGO LINGUISTIC SOCIETY. PAPERS
FROM THE REGIONAL MEETINGS. 1965. a.
price varies. Chicago Linguistic Society, University
of Chicago, Classics 314A, 1050 E. 59th St.,
Chicago, IL 60637. Ed.Bd. circ. 1,500. (back issues
avail.) Indexed: Lang.& Lang.Behav.Abstr.
Former titles: Parasession: Non-Declarative
Sentences; Parasession: Interplay of Phonology,
Morphology & Syntax.

410 US ISSN 0163-2809
CHILDREN'S LANGUAGE. 1978. irreg., vol.5,
1986. Lawrence Erlbaum Associates, Inc., 365
Broadway, Box 237, Hillsdale, NJ 07642. TEL 201-
666-4110. Ed. Keith Nelson. (back issues avail.)

440 375.4 CN ISSN 0316-599X
CHUCHOTERIES. 1979. irreg. (included with subscr.
to Echange) Alberta Teachers' Association, Conseil
Francais, 11010 142nd St., Edmonton, Alta. T5N
2R1, Canada. Ed. Huguette Szucs. circ. 919.

450 IT ISSN 0069-4339
CIVILTA VENEZIANA. DIZIONARI DIALETTALI
E STUDI LINGUISTICI. 1960. irreg., no.5, 1976.
price varies. (Fondazione Giorgio Cini) Casa
Editrice Leo S. Olschki, Casella Postale 66, 50100
Florence, Italy. circ. 1,000.

400 BL ISSN 0587-6435
COLECAO DE ESTUDOS FILOLOGICOS. 1956.
irreg. Fundacao Casa de Rui Barbosa, Rua Sao
Clemente 134, Botafogo 22260, Rio de Janeiro, RJ,
Brazil. Dir. Olavo Brasil de Lima Junior.

460 375.4 MX
COLECCION LINGUISTICA INDIGENA. irreg.,
no.2, 1982. Universidad Nacional Autonoma de
Mexico, Instituto de Investigaciones Filologicas,
Ciudad Universitaria, Coyoacan 04510, Mexico,
D.F., Mexico.

410 FR ISSN 0220-746X
COLLECTION ORALITES-DOCUMENTS. 1978.
irreg. Societe d'Etudes Linguistiques et
Anthropologiques de France (SELAF), 5 rue de
Marseille, 75010 Paris, France.

460 US
COLLOQUIUM ON HISPANIC LINGUISTICS.
PROCEEDINGS. irreg., 2nd, 1976, Tampa.
(Linguistic Society of America) Georgetown
University Press, Washington, DC 20057. TEL 202-
625-3385.

400 JA ISSN 0069-598X
COLOQUIO DE ESTUDOS LUSO BRASILEIROS.
ANAIS. (Text in Portuguese) 1967. a. $15.
Associacao Japonesa de Estudos Luso-Brasileiros,
Brazilian Center, Sophia University, 7-1 Kioicho,
Chiyoda-Ku, Tokyo 102, Japan. Ed. Vendelino
Lorscheiter. bk. rev. bibl. index(1976) circ. 220.
(back issues avail.)

420 375.4 US
COLUMBIA UNIVERSITY. AMERICAN
LANGUAGE PROGRAM. BULLETIN; instruction
in English as a foreign language. 1953. biennial.
free. Columbia University, School of General
Studies, American Language Program, 505
Lewisohn Hall, New York, NY 10027. TEL 212-
280-3768. Ed. Louis Levi. circ. 6,000.

418 EI
COMMISSION OF THE EUROPEAN
COMMUNITIES. SPECIALIZED DEPARTMENT
TERMINOLOGY AND COMPUTER
APPLICATIONS. BULLETIN DE
TERMINOLOGIE ET DE TRADUCTION. (Text
in Danish, Dutch, English, French, German, Greek
and Italian) 1964. irreg. (3-4/yr.) fl.600($9)
Commission of the European Communities,
Terminologie et Applications Informatiques (TAI) -
Terminology and Computer Applications, Batiment
Jean Monnet A2/100, L-1615 Luxembourg-
Kirchberg, Luxembourg. Ed. J. Goetschal. bk. rev.
circ. 1,100.
Supersedes (1964-1984): Commission of the
European Communities. Terminology Bureau.
Terminology Bulletin/Bulletin de Terminologie.

COMMUNITY STUDIES SERIES. see SOCIAL
SCIENCES: COMPREHENSIVE WORKS

CONTRIBUTIONS TO THE SOCIOLOGY OF
LANGUAGE. see SOCIOLOGY

420 810 SZ ISSN 0069-9780
COOPER MONOGRAPHS ON ENGLISH AND
AMERICAN LANGUAGE AND LITERATURE.
(Text in English or German) 1956. irreg., vol.31,
1983. price varies. ‡ Francke Verlag, Postfach, CH-
3000 Berne 26, Switzerland. Ed. R. Stamm.
Indexed: M.L.A.

410 NE
CORNELL LINGUISTIC CONTRIBUTIONS. (Text
in English) 1977. irreg., vol.5, 1986. price varies.
(Cornell University, US) E. J. Brill, P.O. Box 9000,
2300 PA Leiden, Netherlands. Eds. Frans van
Coetsem, Linda R. Waugh.

420 810 820 US
COSTERUS; essays in English and American language
and literature. (Text in English) 1972. irreg. price
varies. Humanities Press, Inc., 171 First Ave.,
Atlantic Highlands, NJ 07716. TEL 201-872-1441.
Ed. James L.W. West, III. adv. bk. rev. illus. circ.
500. Indexed: M.L.A. Lang.& Lang.Behav.Abstr.

400 ISSN 0391-1535
CRONACHE ERCOLANESI. (Text in English,
French, German, Italian) 1971. a. L.18000. Gaetano
Macchiaroli Editore, Via Carducci 59, Naples
80121, Italy.
Study of papyri

410 MX
CUADERNOS DE LINGUISTICA. 1975. irreg. price
varies. Universidad Nacional Autonoma de Mexico,
Instituto de Investigaciones Filologicas, Centro de
Linguistica Hispanica, Torre de Humanidades II,
Ciudad Universitaria, Mexico 20, D.F., Mexico. Ed.
Juan M. Lope Blanch.

410 UY
CUADERNOS DE SEMIOTICA. 1978. irreg.
Editorial Anfora Solar, Garibaldi 2844, Montevideo,
Uruguay. Eds. Pilar Barreiro Muraccide, Luis
Ernesto Behares.

D S L PRAESENTATIONSHAEFTE. (Danske Sprog
og Litteraturselskab) see LITERATURE

840 440 GW
DACOROMANIA; Jahrbuch fuer oestliche Latinitaet.
1973. a. Karl Alber GmbH, Hermann-Herder-Str. 4,
7800 Freiburg, W. Germany (B.R.D.) Ed. Paul
Miron.

DANCE NOTATION BUREAU NEWSLETTER. see
DANCE

410 PE
DATOS ETNO-LINGUISTICOS. irreg., latest no.73,
1985. price varies. Instituto Linguistico de Verano,
Departamento de Estudios Etno-Linguisticos, Casilla
2492, Lima 100, Peru. (microfiche; back issues
avail.)

DECCAN COLLEGE. POSTGRADUATE &
RESEARCH INSTITUTE. BULLETIN. see
SOCIAL SCIENCES: COMPREHENSIVE
WORKS

407 US
DELAWARE SYMPOSIA ON LANGUAGE
STUDIES SERIES. 1985. irreg. price varies. Ablex
Publishing Corp., 355 Chestnut St., Norwood, NJ
07648. TEL 201-767-8450. Ed. Robert Di Pietro.
Formerly: Delaware Symposia Series.

491.7 GW ISSN 0070-3826
DESCRIPTION AND ANALYSIS OF
CONTEMPORARY STANDARD RUSSIAN.
irreg. price varies. Walter de Gruyter & Co.,
Mouton Publishers, Postfach 110240, D-1000 Berlin
11, W. Germany (B.R.D.) (U.S. addr.: Mouton
Publishers, division of Walter de Gruyter, Inc., 200
Saw Mill River Road, Hawthorne. NY 10532)

410.5 JA ISSN 0385-8960
DESCRIPTIVE AND APPLIED LINGUISTICS.
ANNUAL REPORTS. (Subseries of the
University's Publication 6-A) (Text in English)
1961. a. 1,500 Yen. International Christian
University, Division of Languages - Kokusai
Kirisutokyo Daigaku, 3-10-2 Osawa, Mitaka, Tokyo
181, Japan. Ed.Bd. bibl. circ. 500.
Continues: Summer Institute in Linguistics.
Studies in Descriptive and Applied Linguistics.

DEUTSCH-SLAWISCHE FORSCHUNGEN ZUR
NAMENKUNDE UND
SIEDLUNGSGESCHICHTE. see HISTORY —
History Of Europe

491 GW ISSN 0070-3923
DEUTSCHE AKADEMIE FUER SPRACHE UND
DICHTUNG. JAHRBUCH. 1953. a. DM.26. Verlag
Lambert Schneider, Hausackerweg 16, D-6900
Heidelberg, W. Germany (B.R.D.) Ed. Marieluise
Huebscher-Bitter. Indexed: M.L.A.

410 GW
DEUTSCHE DIALEKTGEOGRAPHIE. (Text in
English, German) 1908. irreg. price varies. N.G.
Elwert Verlag, Reitgasse 7/9, Postfach 1128, D-
3550 Marburg/Lahn, W. Germany (B.R.D.) Ed.
Reiner Hildebrandt. Indexed: M.L.A.

430 375.4 GW ISSN 0170-3153
DEUTSCHE SPRACHE IN EUROPA UND
UEBERSEE. irreg., vol.11, 1986. price varies.
(Institut fuer Deutsche Sprache, Mannheim) Franz
Steiner Verlag Wiesbaden GmbH, Birkenwaldstr. 44,
Postfach 347, D-7000 Stuttgart 1, W. Germany
(B.R.D.) Ed.Bd. Indexed: Lang.& Lang.Behav.Abstr.

447.9 BE
DIALECTES DE WALLONIE. Spine title: D W.
(Text in French) 1972. a. 450 Fr. Societe de Langue
et de Litterature Wallonnes, Place du Vingt-Aout 7,
B-4000 Liege, Belgium. Ed. Jean Lechanteur. bk.
rev. bibl. illus. circ. 600. Indexed: M.L.A.

460 NE
DIALOGOS HISPANICOS DE AMSTERDAM.
(Text in Spanish) 1980. a. price varies. Editions
Rodopi B.V., Keizersgracht 302-304, 1016 EX
Amsterdam, Netherlands. Ed.Bd. circ. 750. (back
issues avail.) Indexed: M.L.A.

440 375.4 FR ISSN 0226-6881
DIALOGUES ET CULTURES. 1970. a. 60 F. ‡
Federation Internationale des Professeurs de
Francais, c/o Sec. Gen., 1 av. Leon Journault,
92310 Sevres, France. Ed. Jean Pierre Beland. adv.
bk. rev. circ. 1,500.
Former titles: Dialogues & Federation
Internationale des Professeurs de Francais. Bulletin.
Study and teaching

LINGUISTICS

DICTIONARY OF CONTEMPORARY QUOTATIONS. see *LITERATURE*

DIMENSION: LANGUAGES; proceedings of the Southern Conference on Language Teaching. see *EDUCATION — Teaching Methods And Curriculum*

DIRECTORY OF PERIODICALS PUBLISHING ARTICLES ON ENGLISH AND AMERICAN LITERATURE AND LANGUAGE. see *LITERATURE*

410   US
DIRECTORY OF PROGRAMS IN LINGUISTICS; in the United States and Canada. 1962. triennial. $15. Linguistic Society of America, 1325 18th St., N.W., Ste. 211, Washington, DC 20036-6501. adv.
Former titles: Guide to Programs in Linguistics; University Resources in the United States and Canada for the Study of Linguistics; University Resources in the United States for Linguistics and the Teaching of English as a Foreign Language (ISSN 0511-3040)

428   UK   ISSN 0307-1006
DISCOURSE ANALYSIS MONOGRAPHS. 1976. irreg., latest no.13, July 1986. price varies. University of Birmingham, English Language Research, Birmingham B15 2TT, England. Ed.Bd. circ. 400. (also avail. in microfiche)

407   GW   ISSN 0343-3420
DOKUMENTATION NEUSPRACHLICHER UNTERRICHT. 1976. a. DM.22. Max Hueber Verlag GmbH & Co. KG, Max-Hueber-Str. 4, D-8045 Ismaning, W. Germany (B.R.D.) Ed.Bd.

410 378 020   GW   ISSN 0724-4320
DOKUMENTATION SPRACHWISSENSCHAFTLICHE FORSCHUNGSVORHABEN. 1981. biennial. DM.32. Institut fuer Deutsche Sprache, Friedrich-Karl-Strasse 12, 6800 Mannheim 1, W. Germany (B.R.D.) cum.index. (back issues avail.)

DOSHISHA LITERATURE; journal of English literature and philology. see *LITERATURE*

400 800   US
DUQUESNE STUDIES. LANGUAGE AND LITERATURE SERIES. 1960. irreg. price varies. Duquesne University Press, 600 Forbes Ave., Pittsburgh, PA 15282 TEL 412-434-6610. (Dist. by: Humanities Press, Inc., Atlantic Highlands, NJ 07716) Ed. Albert Labriola. Indexed: M.L.A.
Formerly (until vol.17): Duquesne Studies. Philological Series (ISSN 0070-7694)

410 890   TZ
E A C R O T A N A L INFORMATION. (Text in English and French) 1979. a. $3.50 per no. Eastern African Centre for Research on Oral Traditions and African National Languages, Box 600, Zanzibar, Tanzania. Ed. Didier Rapanoel. bk. rev. bibl. (back issues avail.)

410 890   TZ
E A C R O T A N A L STUDIES & DOCUMENTS. (Text in English; occasionally in French) 1980. a. $4. Eastern African Centre for Research on Oral Traditions and African National Languages, Box 600, Zanzibar, Tanzania. Ed. Didier Rapanoel. (back issues avail)

440 375.4   CN   ISSN 0831-5825
ECHANGE. 1970. irreg. (1-2/yr.) Can.$15. Alberta Teachers' Association, Conseil Francais, 11010 142nd St., Edmonton, Alta. T5N 2R1, Canada. Ed. Gerald Fallon. circ. 919.
Formerly (until 1985): Notre Langue et Notre Culture (ISSN 0380-5352)

EDITIONES ARNAMAGNAEANAE. SERIES A. see *LITERATURE*

EDITIONES ARNAMAGNAEANAE. SERIES B. see *LITERATURE*

410   US   ISSN 0163-3848
EDWARD SAPIR MONOGRAPH SERIES IN LANGUAGE, CULTURE, AND COGNITION. (Supplement to: Forum Linguisticum) 1977. irreg., approx. 2/yr. price varies. (Linguistic Association of Canada and the United States) Jupiter Press, Box 101, Lake Bluff, IL 60044. TEL 312-234-3997. Ed. Adam Makkai. circ. 1,000. (back issues avail.) Indexed: M.L.A.

491.62 891.62   IE   ISSN 0013-2608
EIGSE; a journal of Irish studies. 1939. a. (in one vol.) £10. National University of Ireland, 49 Merrion Square, Dublin 2, Ireland. Ed. Radraig Breatnack. bk. rev. circ. 400. Indexed: Curr.Cont. M.L.A. Arts & Hum.Cit.Ind.

493   GW   ISSN 0340-627X
ENCHORIA; Zeitschrift fuer Demotistik und Koptologie. (Text in English, French, German and Italian) 1971. a. DM.80 (approx.) Verlag Otto Harrassowitz, Taunusstr. 14, Postfach 2929, 6200 Wiesbaden 1, W. Germany (B.R.D.) Ed.Bd. bk. rev. circ. 400. (back issues avail.)

400   GW   ISSN 0071-0490
ENGLISH AND AMERICAN STUDIES IN GERMAN; summaries of theses and monographs. (Supplement to: Anglia - Zeitschrift fuer Englische Philologie) (Text in English) 1969. a. price varies. (German Congress of Scholars of English) Max Niemeyer Verlag, Pfrondorfer Str. 4, 7400 Tuebingen, W. Germany (B.R.D.) Ed. Horst Weinstock. (back issues avail.)

420 375.4   UK
ENGLISH LANGUAGE RESEARCH JOURNAL. 1980. a. price varies. University of Birmingham, English Language Research, P.O. Box 363, Birmingham B15 2TT, England. Ed. C.J. Kennedy.

410   UK   ISSN 0308-0129
ENGLISH PHILOLOGICAL STUDIES. irreg. price varies. (University of Birmingham) Heffers Printers Ltd., Kings Hedges Rd., Cambridge CB4 2PQ, England. Ed. Allan S.C. Ross. bibl.
Formerly: English and Germanic Studies.

420 422   UK   ISSN 0071-0636
ENGLISH PLACE-NAME SOCIETY. 1922. a. membership. ‡ English Place-Name Society, c/o Mrs. M.D. Pattison, School of English Studies, University of Nottingham, Nottingham NG7 2RD, England. Ed. Kenneth Cameron. index. circ. 740. Indexed: Br.Archaeol.Abstr. Geo.Abstr.

410   BL
ENSAIOS LINGUISTICOS. 1978. irreg. price varies. Summer Institute of Linguistics, Departamento de Estudos Tecnicos, SAI/NO Lote D, Bloco 3, 70770 Brasilia DF, Brazil.

EPIGRAPHIC SOCIETY. OCCASIONAL PUBLICATIONS. see *ARCHAEOLOGY*

410   NE   ISSN 0165-2524
ESPERANTO-DOKUMENTOJ. NOVA SERIO.
English edition: Esperanto Documents. New Series.
French edition: Documents sur l'Esperanto.
Nouvelle Serie (ISSN 0165-2621) (Text in Esperanto) 1976. irreg. fl.35 for 10 nos. Universala Esperanto-Asocio - Universal Esperanto Association, Nieuwe Binnenweg 176, 3015 BJ Rotterdam, Netherlands. circ. 550.

410   NE
ESSAIS DE DIALECTOLOGIE INTERLINGUALE. 1978. irreg. price varies. Van Gorcum, Box 43, 9400 AA Assen, Netherlands.

408   JA
ESSAYS IN FOREIGN LANGUAGES AND LITERATURES/GAIKOKUGO GAIKOKU BUNGAKU KENKYU. (Text in English, French, German, or Japanese) irreg. Hokkaido University, Faculty of Literature, Library, Kita-10, Nishi-7, Kita-ku, Sapporo 060, Japan. Indexed: M.L.A.

400   CL   ISSN 0071-1713
ESTUDIOS FILOLOGICOS. 1965. a. Esc.800($12) Universidad Austral de Chile, Facultad de Filosofia y Humanidades, Casilla 567, Valdivia, Chile. Dir. Guido Mutis. adv. bk. rev. circ. 700. Indexed: Hist.Abstr. M.L.A. Art & Hum.Cit.Ind. Amer.Hist.& Life.

ETUDES AEQUATORIA. see *ANTHROPOLOGY*

400   FR
ETUDES CELTIQUES. (Text in English and French) a. price varies. Editions du C N R S, 295 rue St. Jacques, 75005 Paris, France. Ed. Edward Bachellery. bk. rev. bibl. illus. cum.index. Indexed: M.L.A. Br.Archaeol.Abstr.

400   BE   ISSN 0071-1926
ETUDES DE PHILOLOGIE, D'ARCHEOLOGIE ET D'HISTOIRE ANCIENNE.* 1934. irreg. price varies. Institut Historique Belge de Rome, c/o Archives Generales de Royaume, 2-6 Rue de Ruysbroeck, B-1000 Brussels, Belgium. circ. controlled.

410 572   FR   ISSN 0757-7699
ETUDES ETHNO-LINGUISTIQUES MAGHREB-SAHARA. 1982. irreg. price varies. Societe d'Etudes Linguistiques et Anthropologiques de France (SELAF), 5 rue de Marseille, 75010 Paris, France.

ETUDES FINNO-OUGRIENNES. see *LITERATURE*

400   FR   ISSN 0071-2124
ETUDES LINGUISTIQUES. 1962. irreg. price varies. Editions Klincksieck, 11 rue de Lille, 75005 Paris, France. Indexed: M.L.A. Lang.& Lang.Behav.Abstr.

440 375.4   BE
ETUDES NERVALIENNES ET ROMANTIQUES. (Text in French) 1978. a. 350 Fr. Presses Universitaires de Namur, 8 Rempart de la Vierge, 5000 Namur, Belgium (Subscr. to: 8 Rempart de la Vierge, 5000 Namur, Belgium) Ed. Pierre Rummens. bk. rev. circ. 750. (back issues avail.)

410   SW
ETUDES ROMANES DE LUND. (Text in French) 1940. irreg., no.39, 1984. price varies. Liber Forlag, S-205 10, Malmo, Sweden. Ed. Alf Lombard.

410   IT
EUROASIATICA; journal of neohistorical linguistics. (Text in various European languages) 1970. irreg., vol.4, 1978. price varies. Giardini Editori e Stampatori, Via Santa Bibbiana 28, 56100 Pisa, Italy. Ed. Nullo Minissi.

410 572   FR   ISSN 0755-9313
EUROPE DE TRADITION ORALE. 1982. irreg. price varies. Societe d'Etudes Linguistiques et Anthropologiques de France (SELAF), 5 rue de Marseille, 75010 Paris, France. Ed. Fanny de Sivers. adv. bk. rev. circ. 250.

410   UK
EXPLORATIONS IN LANGUAGE STUDY. 1973. irreg. price varies. Edward Arnold (Publishers) Ltd., 41 Bedford Square, London WC1B 3DQ, England.

430 375.4   AU
FAUSTCHEN. 1973. irreg. Oesterreichische Hochschuelerschaft, S T R V Germanistik, Universitaetsstr. 7, A-1010 Vienna, Austria. Ed.Bd. bk. rev. bibl. circ. 1,000.
Formerly (until 1980): Beitraege zum Deutschstudium.

490   GW   ISSN 0341-311X
FENNO-UGRICA. 1973. irreg. price varies. Verlag Helmut Buske, Schlueterstr. 14, 2000 Hamburg 13, W. Germany (B.R.D.) Eds. Harald Haarmann, Janos Pusztay.

400   AG   ISSN 0071-495X
FILOLOGIA. 1949. a. exchange basis. Instituto de Filologia y Literaturas Hispanicas "Dr. Amado Alonso", 25 de Mayo 217, Buenos Aires 1002, Argentina (Subscr. to: Oficina de Venta de Publicaciones de la Facultad de Filosofia y Letras, Marcelo T. de Alvear 2230, C.P. 1122-Buenos Aires, Argentina) Ed. Ana Maria Barrenechea. adv. bk. rev. circ. 1,000. Indexed: Hist.Abstr. M.L.A. Amer.Hist.& Life.

420   PL   ISSN 0554-8144
FILOLOGIA ANGIELSKA. (Text in English, Polish; summaries in English) 1972. irreg. price varies. Adam Mickiewicz University Press, Marchlewskigo 128, 61-874 Poznan, Poland. Ed. Jacek Fisiak. bk. rev. circ. 1,250.
Formerly: Uniwersytet im. Adama Mickiewicza w Poznaniu. Wydzial Filologiczny. Seria Filologia Angielska.

491.9 891.9   PL
FILOLOGIA BALTYCKA/BALTIC PHILOLOGY. (Text in Baltic languages and Polish) 1977. irreg., no.3, 1978. price varies. Adam Mickiewicz University Press, Marchlewskiego, 61-874 Poznan, Poland.

LINGUISTICS

480 880   PL   ISSN 0554-8160
FILOLOGIA KLASYCZNA. (Text in Polish; summaries in various languages) 1966. irreg. price varies. Adam Mickiewicz University Press, Marchlewskiego 128, 61-874 Poznan, Poland.
     Formerly: Uniwersytet im. Adama Mickiewicza w Poznaniu. Wydzial Filologiczny. Seria Filologia Klasyczna.

400   CK   ISSN 0071-4976
FILOLOGOS COLOMBIANOS. 1954. irreg., no.9, 1979. price varies. Instituto Caro y Cuervo, Seccion de Publicaciones, Apdo. Aereo 51502, Bogota, Colombia.

491   YU   ISSN 0352-3055
FILOLOSKI FAKULTET. KATEDRA ZA ISTOCNOSLOVENSKI I ZAPADNOSLOVENSKI JAZICI I KNIZEUNOSTI. SLAVISTICKI STUDII. (Text in all Slavic languages; summaries in English) 1976. biennial. 100 din. Filoloski Fakultet, Katedra za Istocnoslovenski i Zapadnoslovenski Jazici i Knizeunosti, 91000 Skopje, Yugoslavia. Eds. Boris Markov, Milan Gjurchinov. circ. 300.

FINNISCH-UGRISCHE FORSCHUNGEN; Zeitschrift fuer Finnish-Ugrische Sprach und Volkskunde. see HISTORY — History Of Europe

410   US   ISSN 0160-9394
FOLIA SLAVICA. 1977. irreg., vol.7, 1984. $20 to individuals; institutions $30. Slavica Publishers, Inc., Box 14388, Columbus, OH 43214. TEL 614-268-4002. Ed. Charles E. Gribble. bk. rev. circ. 350. (back issues avail.) Indexed: M.L.A. Amer.Bibl.Slavic & E.Eur.Stud.

410   GW
FORUM LINGUISTICUM. (Text in English and German; summaries in English) 1974. irreg., no.19, 1977. price varies. Verlag Peter Lang GmbH, Hinter den Ulmen 19, D-6000 Frankfurt/Main 50, W. Germany (B.R.D.) Ed. Christoph Gutknecht. bk. rev. abstr. bibl. circ. 400 (controlled) (back issues avail.) Indexed: M.L.A.

410   GW   ISSN 0341-3144
FORUM PHONETICUM. 1973. irreg., no.37, 1986. price varies. Verlag Helmut Buske, Schlueterstr. 14, 2000 Hamburg 13, W. Germany (B.R.D.) Ed.Bd.

491.7   GW   ISSN 0473-5277
FRANKFURTER ABHANDLUNGEN ZUR SLAVISTIK. irreg., vol.24, 1977. price varies. Franz Steiner Verlag Wiesbaden GmbH, Birkenwaldstr. 44, Postfach 347, D-7000 Stuttgart 1, W. Germany (B.R.D.) Ed. Alfred Rammelmeyer.

FRANKFURTER BEITRAEGE ZUR GERMANISTIK. see LITERATURE

057 375   GW   ISSN 0170-1533
FREIE UNIVERSITAET BERLIN. OSTEUROPA-INSTITUT. BALKANOLOGISCHE VEROEFFENTLICHUNGEN. 1979. irreg., vol.11, 1986. price varies. (Freie Universitaet Berlin, Osteuropa-Institut) Verlag Otto Harrassowitz, Taunusstr. 14, Postfach 2929, 6200 Wiesbaden, W. Germany (B.R.D.) Ed. Norbert Reiter. circ. 500.

FREIE UNIVERSITAET BERLIN. OSTEUROPA-INSTITUT. SLAVISTISCHE VEROEFFENTLICHUNGEN. see LITERATURE

FU JEN STUDIES; literature & linguistics. see LITERATURE

410   DK   ISSN 0106-0872
G I P. (Germansk Institut Publikationer) no.28, 1981. irreg. free. Odense Universitet, Institut for Germansk Filologi, Campusvej 55, DK-5230 Odense M, Denmark. Eds. Uwe Helen Petersen, Thomas Jensen. circ. 200.

420 375.4   UK
GAELIC SOCIETY OF INVERNESS. TRANSACTIONS. (Text in English, Gaelic) 1872. biennial. Gaelic Society of Inverness, Granary, Ness-side, Dores Rd., Inverness, Scotland. circ. 500.

423.1   UK   ISSN 0072-0542
GEIRIADUR PRIFYSGOL CYMRU. (Text in English and Welsh) 1953. a. £2 per part. (Board of Celtic Studies) University of Wales Press, 6 Gwennyth St., Cathays, Cardiff CF2 4YD, Wales. Ed. G. A. Bevan. circ. 1,500.
     Dictionary of the Welsh language

412   US   ISSN 0072-0771
GENERAL SEMANTICS BULLETIN. 1950. a. $15. Institute of General Semantics, 163 Engle St., Englewood, NJ 07631. TEL 201-568-0551. Ed. Stuart Mayor. adv. bk. rev. cum.index: 1-37. circ. 600. (also avail. in microform from UMI; reprint service avail. from UMI) Indexed: Sociol.Abstr. Lang.& Lang.Behav.Abstr.
     For information and inter-communication among workers in the non-aristotelian discipline formulated by Alfred Korzybski

400   US   ISSN 0196-7207
GEORGETOWN UNIVERSITY ROUND TABLE ON LANGUAGES AND LINGUISTICS. 1951. a. price varies. (Georgetown University, School of Languages and Linguistics) Georgetown University Press, Washington, DC 20057. TEL 202-625-3385. circ. 2,000. Indexed: M.L.A. Lang.& Lang.Behav.Abstr.
     Former titles: Georgetown University. Institute of Languages and Linguistics. Report of the Annual Round Table Meeting on Linguistics and Language Studies (ISSN 0072-1212); Monograph Series on Languages and Linguistics (ISSN 0077-0612)

430 375.4   UK
GERMAN TEXTS. 1953. irreg. price varies. Manchester University Press, Oxford Rd., Manchester M13 9PL, England. TEL 061-273 5539.

430   GW   ISSN 0072-1492
GERMANISTISCHE LINGUISTIK. 1969/70. irreg., no. 5/6, 1979. price varies. (Forschunginstitut fuer Deutsche Sprache, Marburg) Georg Olms Verlag, Hagentorwall 7, 3200 Hildesheim, W. Germany (B.R.D.) (Dist. in U.S. by: Hy Cohen, Literary Agency Ltd., 111 West 57 St., New York, NY 10019) Ed.Bd. adv. bk. rev. index. circ. 1,000.

400   PL   ISSN 0072-4769
GLOTTODIDACTICA; AN INTERNATIONAL JOURNAL OF APPLIED LINGUISTICS. (Text in English, French, German, and Russian) 1966. irreg., vol.8, 1975. price varies. Adam Mickiewicz University Press, Marchlewskiego 128, 61-874 Poznan, Poland. Ed. Waldemar Pfeiffer. bk. rev. circ. 1,500. Indexed: M.L.A. Lang.& Lang.Behav.Abstr.

430 830   SW   ISSN 0072-4793
GOETEBORGER GERMANISTISCHE FORSCHUNGEN. (Subseries of Acta Universitatis Gothoburgensis) (Text in German) 1955. irreg., no.29, 1985. price varies; also exchange basis. Acta Universitatis Gothoburgensis, Box 5096, S-402 22 Goeteborg, Sweden (Dist. in U. S., Canada, and Mexico by: Humanities Press, Inc., 171 First Ave., Atlantic Highlands, NJ 07716) Ed. Sven-Gunnar Andersson.

430   GW
GOETHE-INSTITUT ZUR PFLEGE DER DEUTSCHEN SPRACHE IM AUSLAND UND ZUR FOERDERUNG DER INTERNATIONALEN KULTURELLEN ZUSAMMENARBEIT. JAHRBUCH. 1965. a. DM.11. Goethe-Institut zur Pflege der Deutschen Sprache im Ausland und zur Foederung der Internationalen Kulturellen Zusammenarbeit, Lenbachplatz 3, 8000 Munich 2, W. Germany (B.R.D.) Ed. Kajo Niggestich. circ. 4,000.
     Formerly: Goethe-Institut zur Pflege Deutscher Sprache und Kultur im Ausland. Jahrbuch (ISSN 0072-4858)

400 830   SW   ISSN 0072-503X
GOTHENBURG STUDIES IN ENGLISH. (Subseries of Acta Universitatis Gothoburgensis) 1952. irreg., no.61, 1986. price varies; also exchange basis. Acta Universitatis Gothoburgensis, Box 5096, S-402 22 Goeteborg, Sweden (Dist. in U. S., Canada, and Mexico by: Humanities Press, Inc., 171 First Ave., Atlantic Highlands, NJ 07716) Eds. Alvar Ellegaard, Erik Frykman. Indexed: M.L.A.

GRIECHISCHEN CHRISTLICHEN SCHRIFTSTELLER DER ERSTEN JAHRHUNDERTE. see RELIGIONS AND THEOLOGY

410   FR
GROUPE LINGUISTIQUE D'ETUDES CHAMITO-SEMITIQUES. COMPTES RENDUS. (Suspended publication 1940-1945) 1934. irreg. (Groupe Linguistique d'Etudes Chamito-Semitiques) Librarie Orientaliste Paul Geuthner, 12 rue Vavin, 75006 Paris, France.

430   GW
GRUNDLAGEN DER GERMANISTIK. irreg. Erich Schmidt Verlag GmbH, Viktoriastr. 44a, Postfach 7380 u. 7340, 4800 Bielefeld 1, W. Germany (B.R.D.) Eds. Hugo Moser, Hartmut Steinecke. (back issues avail.) Indexed: M.L.A.

420 375.4   US
GUIDE TO GRANTS AND FELLOWSHIPS IN LINGUISTICS. 1987. triennial. Linguistic Society of America, 1325 18th St., N.W., Ste. 211, Washington, DC 20036-6501. TEL 202-835-1714.

GUIDE TO PRIVATE ENGLISH LANGUAGE SCHOOLS IN THE U.K. FOR OVERSEAS STUDENTS. see EDUCATION — Guides To Schools And Colleges

GYPSY LORE SOCIETY. NORTH AMERICAN CHAPTER. PUBLICATIONS. see ANTHROPOLOGY

480   GW   ISSN 0072-9191
HABELTS DISSERTATIONSDRUCKE. REIHE KLASSISCHE PHILOLOGIE. 1953. irreg., no.38, 1986. price varies. Dr. Rudolf Habelt GmbH, Am Buchenhang 1, 5300 Bonn 1, W. Germany (B.R.D.) Eds. W. Schetter, W. Schmid.

491.7   GW   ISSN 0072-9515
HAMBURGER BEITRAEGE FUER RUSSISCHLEHRER. 1964. irreg., no.35, 1986. price varies. Verlag Hemlmut Buske, Schlueterstr. 14, 2000 Hamburg 13, W. Germany (B.R.D.) Ed. Irene Nowikowa.

430   GW   ISSN 0072-9582
HAMBURGER PHILOLOGISCHE STUDIEN. 1966. irreg., no.60, 1984. price varies. Verlag Helmut Buske, Schlueterstr. 14, 2000 Hamburg 13, W. Germany (B.R.D.) Indexed: M.L.A.

496   NR
HARSUNAN NIJERIYA. (Text in English and Hausa) 1971. a. $2. Ahmadu Bello University, Centre for the Study of Nigerian Languages, Private Bag 3011, Zaria, Nigeria. Ed. Roxana Ma Newman. circ. 500. (processed)

410 890 940   US
HARVARD CELTIC COLLOQUIUM. PROCEEDINGS. (Text in Breton, English, Irish and Welsh) 1981. a. $16. Harvard University, Department of Celtic Languages and Literature, Cambridge, MA 02138. Eds. Paul Jefferiss, William Mahon. circ. 250.

HARVARD ENGLISH STUDIES. see LITERATURE

492 220   US   ISSN 0073-0637
HARVARD SEMITIC MONOGRAPHS. 1968. irreg., no.6, 1973. price varies. Scholars Press, 101 Salem St., Box 1608, GA 30031-1608.

489   US   ISSN 0073-0688
HARVARD STUDIES IN CLASSICAL PHILOLOGY. 1890. a. latest vol.90, 1986. price varies. Harvard University Press, 79 Garden St., Cambridge, MA 02138. TEL 617-495-2600.

HARVARD-YENCHING INSTITUTE. MONOGRAPH SERIES. see HISTORY — History Of Asia

HAUTES ETUDES DU MONDE GRECO-ROMAIN. see CLASSICAL STUDIES

492.4   IS
HEBREW COMPUTATIONAL LINGUISTICS. (Text in English & Hebrew) 1969. 1-2/yr. $3.50. Bar Ilan University, Department of Hebrew and Semitic Languages, Ramat Gan, Israel. Ed. Ora Schwarzwald. bibl. circ. 400. Indexed: M.L.A. Lang.& Lang.Behav.Abstr.

480   GW   ISSN 0341-0064
HERMES-EINZELSCHRIFTEN. (Supplement to: Hermes) (Text in English and German) irreg., vol.52, 1987. price varies. Franz Steiner Verlag Wiesbaden GmbH, Birkenwaldstr. 44, Postfach 347, D-7000 Stuttgart 1, W. Germany (B.R.D.) Ed.Bd.

HERON; essays on language & literature. see LITERATURE

430 GW ISSN 0073-201X
HEUTIGES DEUTSCH. REIHE I: LINGUISTISCHE GRUNDLAGEN. 1971. irreg., vol.6, 1975. price varies. (Institut fuer Deutsche Sprache) Max Hueber Verlag, Max-Hueber-Str.4, 8045 Ismaning, W. Germany (B.R.D.) (Co-sponsor: Goethe-Institut, Munich) Ed.Bd.

400 410 US ISSN 0073-2710
HISTORY AND STRUCTURE OF LANGUAGES. 1967. irreg., no.4, 1978. price varies. University of Chicago Press, 5801 S. Ellis Ave., Chicago, IL 60637. TEL 312-962-7600. Ed. Eric P. Hamp. (reprint service avail. from UMI,ISI)

HUEBER HOCHSCHULREIHE. see *EDUCATION*

HUMAN COMMUNICATION AND ITS DISORDERS. see *EDUCATION — Special Education And Rehabilitation*

410 US
IDIOMS AND PHRASES INDEX. 1983. a. $220. Gale Research Company, Book Tower, Detroit, MI 48226. Ed. Laurence Urdang.

410 IT
INCONTRI LINGUISTICI. 1974. a. L.12000($14) (Universita degli Studi di Udine e Trieste) Giardini, Via di Santa Bibbiana 28, 56100 Pisa, Italy. Ed.Bd. adv. bk. rev. circ. 3,000. Indexed: M.L.A. Lang.& Lang.Behav.Abstr.

491 II ISSN 0073-6589
INDIAN LINGUISTICS MONOGRAPH SERIES. (Text in English) 1958. irreg. price varies. Linguistic Society of India, c/o Deccan College Postgraduate and Research Institute, Poona 411006, India. Ed. R.V. Dhongde.

400 US ISSN 0073-7097
INDIANA UNIVERSITY. RESEARCH INSTITUTE FOR INNER ASIAN STUDIES. URALIC AND ALTAIC SERIES. Short title: Uralic and Altaic Series. (Text in English unless reprints, or text editions preceeded by English introduction.) 1960. irreg., no.149, 1985. price varies. ‡ Indiana University, Research Institute for Inner Asian Studies, Goodbody Hall 344, Bloomington, IN 47405. TEL 812-335-1605. Ed. Denis Sinor. Indexed: M.L.A.

494 950 HU ISSN 0073-7194
INDICES VERBORUM LINGUAE MONGOLIAE MONUMENTIS TRADITORUM. (Text in Mongolian with transcriptions in Roman letters and introduction in French) 1970. irreg. price varies. (Magyar Tudomanyos Akademia) Akademiai Kiado, Publishing House of the Hungarian Academy of Sciences, Box 24, H-1363 Budapest, Hungary. Ed. L. Ligeti.

418 025 GW
INFOTERM SERIES. irreg., no.4, 1986. price varies. (International Information Centre for Terminology, Vienna, AU) K.G. Saur Verlag KG, Poessenbacherstr. 2B, Postfach 711009, 8000 Munich 71, W. Germany (B.R.D.) (U.S. and Canadian subscr. to: K.G. Saur, 175 Fifth Ave., New York, N.Y. 10010) (Reprint service avail. from UMI,ISI)

400 FR ISSN 0073-8018
INITIATION A LA LINGUISTIQUE. SERIE A. LECTURES. 1970. irreg. price varies. Editions Klincksieck, 11 rue de Lille, 75005 Paris, France. Eds. Pierre Guiraud, Alain Rey. Indexed: M.L.A.

400 FR ISSN 0073-8026
INITIATION A LA LINGUISTIQUE. SERIE B. PROBLEMES ET METHODES. 1970. irreg. price varies. Editions Klincksieck, 11 rue de Lille, 75005 Paris, France. Eds. Pierre Guiraud, Alain Rey.

410 FR ISSN 0154-0157
INSTITUT D'ETUDES SLAVES. LEXIQUES. 1978. irreg., vol.7, 1984. price varies. Institut d'Etudes Slaves, 9 rue Michelet, 75006 Paris, France.

491 FR ISSN 0078-9984
INSTITUT D'ETUDES SLAVES, PARIS. COLLECTION DE GRAMMAIRES. 1921. irreg., vol.7, 1980. price varies. Institut d'Etudes Slaves, 9 rue Michelet, 75006 Paris, France.

491 943 FR ISSN 0078-9992
INSTITUT D'ETUDES SLAVES, PARIS. COLLECTION DE MANUELS. 1923. irreg., vol.7, 1976. price varies. Institut d'Etudes Slaves, 9 rue Michelet, 75006 Paris, France.

375.4 FR ISSN 0300-2594
INSTITUT D'ETUDES SLAVES, PARIS. DOCUMENTS PEDAGOGIQUES. 1970. irreg., vol.28, 1986. price varies. Institut d'Etudes Slaves, 9 rue Michelet, 75006 Paris, France.

INSTITUT D'ETUDES SLAVES, PARIS. TRAVAUX. see *LITERATURE*

400 BE
INSTITUT DE LINGUISTIQUE DE LOUVAIN. BIBLIOTHEQUE DE LA C I L L. (Text in English, French, German and Italian) 1976. irreg., no.21, 1981. Editions Peeters s.p.r.l., Bondgenotenlaan, B-3000 Louvain, Belgium.

410 SW
INSTITUT DE LINGUISTIQUE DE LUND. TRAVAUX. (Text in English, French or German) 1959. irreg., no.19, 1983. price varies. Liber Forlag, S-205 10, Malmo, Sweden. Eds. Eva Gaarding, Bengt Sigurd.

410 CK
INSTITUTO CARO Y CUERVO. SEMINARIO ANDRES BELLO. CUADERNOS. 1978. irreg. Instituto Caro y Cuervo, Seccion de Publicaciones, Apdo. Aereo 51502, Bogota, Colombia.

INSTITUTO CARO Y CUERVO. SERIE MINOR. see *LITERATURE*

460 PE
INSTITUTO LINGUISTICO DE VERANO. DOCUMENTOS DE TRABAJO. 1973. irreg., no.20, 1981. price varies. Instituto Linguistico de Verano, Departamento de Estudios Etno-Linguisticos, Casilla 2492, Lima 100, Peru. Ed. Mary Ruth Wise. (also avail. in microfiche; back issues avail.)

407 CK
INSTITUTO LINGUISTICO DE VERANO. SERIE SINTACTICA. 1975. irreg. Instituto Linguistico de Verano, Division Operativa de Asuntos Indigenas, Apdo. Aereo 27744, Bogota, Colombia. circ. 300. (also avail. in microfiche)
South American Indian languages

460 375.4 PO
INSTITUTO NACIONAL DE INVESTIGACAO CIENTIFICA. TEXTOS DE LINGUISTICA. 1980. irreg., no.6, 1982. (Instituto Nacional de Investigacao Cientifica, Centro de Linguistica) Universidad de Lisboa, Centro de Linguistica, Av. 5 de Octubre, 85-5,6, 1000 Lisbon, Portugal. circ. 25, 000.

410 RM
INSTITUTUL PEDAGOGIC ORADEA. LUCRARI STIINTIFICE: SERIA LINGVISTICA. (Continues in part its Lucrari Stiintifice: Seria Filologie (1971-72), its Lucrari Stiintifice: Seria A and Seria B (1969-1970), and its Lucrari Stiintifice (1967-68).) (Text in Rumanian, occasionally in English or French; summaries in English, French, German or Rumanian) a. Institutul Pedagogic Oradea, Calea Armatei Rosii Nr. 5, Oradea, Rumania.

410 BE ISSN 0074-2791
INTERNATIONAL COMMITTEE FOR ONOMASTIC SCIENCES. CONGRESS PROCEEDINGS. (Proceedings published in host country) 1938. triennial, 13th, 1978, Krakow. price varies. International Centre of Onomastics, Blijde-Inkomststr. 21, 3000 Louvain, Belgium.

410 NE ISSN 0074-3755
INTERNATIONAL CONGRESS OF LINGUISTS. PROCEEDINGS. (Published in host country) 1928. quinquennial, 13th, 1982, Tokyo. price varies. Permanent International Committee of Linguists, c/o E. M. Uhlenbeck, Dr. Kuyperlaan 11, 2215 NE Voorhout, Netherlands. Eds. M. Borkent, M. Tanse. circ. 1,700.

400 US ISSN 0074-6797
INTERNATIONAL LINGUISTIC ASSOCIATION. MONOGRAPH. (Supplement to: Word) 1951. irreg. International Linguistic Association, c/o Fichtner, Department of Germanic Languages, City University of New York, Queens College, Flushing, NY 11367-0904.

400 US ISSN 0074-6800
INTERNATIONAL LINGUISTIC ASSOCIATION. SPECIAL PUBLICATIONS. 1964. irreg. International Linguistic Association, c/o Fichtner, Department of Germanic Languages, City University of New York, Queens College, Flushing, NY 11367-0904.

400 IT
ISTITUTO DI FILOLOGIA GRECA. BOLLETTINO. 1974. irreg. L.35000. Erma di Bretschneider, Via Cassiodoro 19, 00193 Rome, Italy. TEL 06 687 41 27. circ. 500.

ISTITUTO UNIVERSITARIO ORIENTALE. ANNALI; studi Nederlandesi, studi Nordici. see *ETHNIC INTERESTS*

457 IT ISSN 0085-2295
ITALIA DIALETTALE; rivista di Dialettologia Italiana. 1925. a. L.10000. (Universita degli Studi di Pisa, Istituto di Glottologia) Giardini Editori e Stampatori, Via S. Maria 36, Pisa, Italy. Ed. Tristano Bolelli. bk. rev. Indexed: M.L.A.

ITALIAN PRIVATE ENGLISH LANGUAGE SCHOOLS & ITALIAN LANGUAGE SCHOOLS FOR OVERSEAS & ITALY. see *EDUCATION — Guides To Schools And Colleges*

350 375.4 UK
ITALIAN TEXTS. 1963. irreg. price varies. Manchester University Press, Oxford Rd., Manchester M13 9PL, England. TEL 061-273 5539. Ed. Kathleen Speight.

ITALICA. see *EDUCATION*

430 375.4 GW ISSN 0083-5617
JAHRBUCH DES VEREINS FUER NIEDERDEUTSCHE SPRACHFORSCHUNG. (Text in English, German) 1875. a. DM.35. Karl Wachholtz Verlag, Postfach 2769, 2350 Neumunster, W. Germany (B.R.D.) Ed. Joachim Hartig. circ. 800. (back issues avail.)

JAHRBUCH DEUTSCH ALS FREMDSPRACHE. see *EDUCATION — Higher Education*

410 GW
JANUA LINGUARUM. SERIES ANASTATICA. irreg. price varies. Walter de Gruyter & Co., Mouton Publishers, Postfach 110240, D-1000 Berlin 11, W. Germany (B.R.D.) (U.S. addr.: Mouton Publishers, division of Walter de Gruyter, Inc., 200 Saw Mill River Road, Hawthorne, NY 10532) Indexed: M.L.A.

400 GW ISSN 0075-3092
JANUA LINGUARUM. SERIES CRITICA. 1971. irreg. price varies. Walter de Gruyter & Co., Mouton Publishers, Postfach 110240, D-1000 Berlin 11, W. Germany (B.R.D.) (U.S. addr.: Mouton Publishers, division of Walter de Gruyter, Inc., 200 Saw Mill River Road, Hawthorne, NY 10532) Indexed: M.L.A.

400 410 GW ISSN 0075-3106
JANUA LINGUARUM. SERIES DIDACTICA. 1973. irreg. price varies. Walter de Gruyter & Co., Mouton Publishers, Postfach 110240, D-1000 Berlin 11, W. Germany (B.R.D.) (U.S. addr.: Mouton Publishers, division of Walter de Gruyter, Inc., 200 Saw Mill River Road, Hawthorne, NY 10532) Indexed: M.L.A.

400 GW ISSN 0075-3114
JANUA LINGUARUM. SERIES MAJOR. 1959. irreg. price varies. Walter de Gruyter & Co., Mouton Publishers, Postfach 110240, D-1000 Berlin 11, W. Germany (B.R.D.) (U.S. addr.: Mouton Publishers, division of Walter de Gruyter, Inc., 200 Saw Mill River Road, Hawthorne, NY 10532) Indexed: M.L.A.

400 410 GW ISSN 0075-3122
JANUA LINGUARUM. SERIES MINOR. irreg.
price varies. Walter de Gruyter & Co., Mouton
Publishers, Postfach 110240, D-1000 Berlin 11, W.
Germany (B.R.D.) (U.S. addr.: Mouton Publishers,
division of Walter de Gruyter, Inc., 200 Saw Mill
River Road, Hawthorne, NY 10532) Indexed:
M.L.A.

410 GW ISSN 0075-3130
JANUA LINGUARUM. SERIES PRACTICA. 1963.
irreg. price varies. Walter de Gruyter & Co.,
Mouton Publishers, Postfach 110240, D-1000 Berlin
11, W. Germany (B.R.D.) (U.S. addr.: Mouton
Publishers, division of Walter de Gruyter, Inc., 200
Saw Mill River Road, Hawthorne, NY 10532)
Indexed: M.L.A.

JAPANESE STUDIES IN GERMAN LANGUAGE
AND LITERATURE/JAPANISCHE STUDIEN
ZUR DEUTSCHEN SPRACHE UND
LITERATUR. see *LITERATURE*

410 NE ISSN 0075-3491
JARLIBRO. (Text in Esperanto) 1908. a. fl.28($14)
Universala Esperanto Asocio, Nieuwe Binnenweg
176, 3015 BJ Rotterdam, Netherlands. adv. index.
circ. 7,000. (back issues avail.)

400 491.87 CS ISSN 0448-9241
JAZYKOVEDNE STUDIE. (Text in Slovak;
summaries in German and Russian) irreg., vol.13,
1976. fl.25 per no. (Slovenska Akademia Vied,
Jazykovedny Ustav L. Stura) Veda, Publishing
House of the Slovak Academy of Sciences,
Klemensova 19, 814 30 Bratislava, Czechoslovakia
(Distributor in Western countries: John Benjamins
B.V., Amsteldijk 44, Amsterdam (Z.), Netherlands)

410 296 800 IS ISSN 0333-8347
JEWISH LANGUAGE REVIEW. (Text mainly in
English, occasionally in French and Hebrew) 1981.
a. $18 to individuals; institutions $24. Association
for the Study of Jewish Languages, 1610 Eshkol
Tower, University of Haifa, Mount Carmel, Haifa
31 999, Israel. Eds. David L. Gold, Leonard Prager.
adv. bk. rev. bibl. (back issues avail) Indexed:
Bull.Signal. Curr.Cont. M.L.A. Sociol.Abstr. Arts
& Hum.Cit.Ind. Lang.& Lang.Behav.Abstr.

410 PL ISSN 0137-1444
JEZYKOZNAWSTWO STOSOWANE/APPLIED
LINGUISTICS. 1975. irreg. price varies. Adam
Mickiewica University Press, Marchlewskiego 128,
61-874 Poznan, Poland.

890 GW ISSN 0720-6666
JIDISCHE SCHTUDIES. 1981. irreg. price varies.
Verlag Helmut Buske, Schlueterstr. 14, 2000
Hamburg 13, W. Germany (B.R.D.) Ed. Walter
Roll.

JOURNAL OF HELLENIC STUDIES. see
CLASSICAL STUDIES

KATOLICKI UNIWERSYTET LUBELSKI
WYDZIAL HISTORYCZNO-FILOLOGICZNY.
ROZPRAWY. see *HISTORY*

KEILSCHRIFTTEXTE AUS BOGHAZKOI. see
ARCHAEOLOGY

400 956.4 CY ISSN 0071-0954
KENTRON EPISTEMONIKON EREUNON.
EPETERIS/CYPRUS RESEARCH CENTER.
ANNUAL. (Text in English, French, German and
Greek) 1967/1968. a. £C12. Ministry of Education,
Cyprus Research Centre, Box 1952, Nicosia,
Cyprus. Ed. Costas P. Kyrris. bk. rev. bibl. charts.
illus. circ. 500. (back issues avail.) Indexed: M.L.A.

491 UR
KHAR'KOVSKII GOSUDARSTVENNYI
UNIVERSITET. FILOLOGIYA. (Subseries of its:
Khar'kovski Gosudarstvennyi Universitet. Vestnik)
irreg. Khar'kovskii Gosudarstvennyi Universitet,
Kharkov, Ukrainian S.S.R., U.S.S.R.

496 TZ ISSN 0023-1886
KISWAHILI. (Text in English, Swahili) a. $10.
University of Dar es Salaam, Institute of Kiswahili
Research, Box 35110, Dar es Salaam, Tanzania.
Eds. M.M. Mulokozi & D.P.B. Massamba. Indexed:
M.L.A.

410 800 GW ISSN 0453-9842
KLAUS-GROTH-GESELLSCHAFT.
JAHRESGABEN. 1964. a. price varies.
Westholsteinische Verlagsanstalt Boyens und Co.,
Am Wulf-Isebrand-Platz, Postfach 1880, 2240
Heide, W. Germany (B.R.D.) Ed.Bd. illus. Indexed:
M.L.A.

410 510 DK ISSN 0106-8563
KOEBENHAVNS UNIVERSITET. INSTITUT FOR
ANVENDT OG MATEMATISK LINGVISTIK.
SKRIFTER. 1974. irreg. free. Koebenhavns
Universitet, Institut for Anvendt og Matematisk
Lingvistik, Njalsgade 96, Copenhagen S, Denmark.
Ed.Bd. circ. 300.

410 DK ISSN 0107-3265
KOEBENHAVNS UNIVERSITETS SLAVISKE
INSTITUT. RAPPORTER. 1984. a. Kr.45.75.
Bibliotekscentralen, Telegrafvej 5, DK-2750
Ballerup, Denmark.

400 NE ISSN 0083-3851
KONGRESA LIBRO. (Text in Esperanto) 1905. a.
fl.12($5) Universala Esperanto-Asocio, Nieuwe
Binnenweg 176, 3015 BJ Rotterdam, Netherlands.
adv. circ. 2,500.

410 800 BE ISSN 0770-7762
KONINKLIJKE ACADEMIE VOOR
NEDERLANDSE TAAL- EN LETTERKUNDE.
JAARBOEK. 1887. a. price varies. Koninklijke
Academie voor Nederlandse Taal- en Letterkunde,
Koningstraat 18, B-9000 Ghent, Belgium.

KOROSI CSOMA KISKONYVTAR. see
HISTORY — History Of Asia

410 890 YU ISSN 0454-4617
KOVCEZIC. (Text in Russian, Serbian) 1958. biennial.
400 din.($1.50) Narodni Vukov i Dositejev Muzej,
Trg. Republike 1A, Belgrade, Yugoslavia. Ed. J.
Jevtovic. circ. 500.

430 GW ISSN 0023-4567
KRATYLOS; kritisches Berichts- und Rezensionsorgan
fuer indogermanische und allgemeine
Sprachwissenschaft. (Text in English, French,
German and Italian) 1956. a. DM.56. Dr. Ludwig
Reichert Verlag, Tauernstr. 11, 6200 Wiesbaden, W.
Germany (B.R.D.) Ed. Ruediger Schmitt. adv. bk.
rev. circ. 700.

430 375.4 GW ISSN 0720-9983
KREOLISCHE BIBLIOTHEK. 1981. irreg., vol.7,
1985. price varies. Verlag Helmut Buske,
Schlueterstr. 14, 2000 Hamburg 13, W. Germany
(B.R.D.) Ed. Annegret Bollee.

400 SW ISSN 0083-6745
KUNGLIGA VITTERHETS-, HISTORIE- OCH
ANTIKVITETS AKADEMIEN. FILOLOGISKT
ARKIV. (Text in English, French, German, Spanish
or Swedish) 1955. irreg., no.34, 1985. price varies.
Kungliga Vitterhets-, Historie- och Antikvitets
Akademien - Royal Academy of Letters, History
and Antiquities, Villagatan 3, 114 32 Stockholm,
Sweden (Dist. by: Almqvist & Wiksell International,
P.O. Box 45150, S-104 30 Stockholm, Sweden)
index.

400 100 SW ISSN 0083-677X
KUNGLIGA VITTERHETS-, HISTORIE- OCH
ANTIKVITETS AKADEMIEN. HANDLINGAR.
FILOLOGISK-FILOSOFISKA SERIEN/ROYAL
ACADEMY OF LETTERS, HISTORY AND
ANTIQUITIES. PROCEEDINGS.
PHILOLOGICAL-PHILOSOPHICAL SERIES.
(Text in English, French, German and Swedish)
1954. irreg., no.20, 1983. price varies. Kungliga
Vitterhets-, Historie, och Antikvitets Akademien,
Villagatan 3, 114 32 Stockholm, Sweden (Dist. by:
Almqvist & Wiksell International, P.O. Box 45150,
S-1-4 30 Stockholm, Sweden) index.

410 GW ISSN 0721-4340
KUSCHITISCHE SPRACHSTUDIEN CUSHITIC
LANGUAGE STUDIES. 1982. irreg., vol.6, 1986.
price varies. Verlag Helmut Buske, Schlueterstr. 14,
2000 Hamburg 13, W. Germany (B.R.D.)

410 US ISSN 0195-377X
L A C U S FORUM. 1974. a. $12.95. (Linguistic
Association of Canada and the United States) L A
C U S, Box 7060044, Lake Bluff, IL 60044. TEL 803-
782-7667.

410 572 FR ISSN 0754-2445
LACITO DOCUMENTS AFRIQUE. 1978. irreg.
price varies. Societe d'Etudes Linguistiques et
Anthropologiques de France (SELAF), 5 rue de
Marseille, 75010 Paris, France.

410 572 FR ISSN 0751-4875
LACITO DOCUMENTS ASIE-AUSTRONESIE.
1977. irreg. price varies. Societe d'Etudes
Linguistiques et Anthropologiques de France
(SELAF), 5 rue de Marseille, 75010 Paris, France.

410 572 FR ISSN 0751-4883
LACITO DOCUMENTS EURASIE. 1978. irreg. price
varies. Societe d'Etudes Linguistiques et
Anthropologiques de France (SELAF), 5 rue de
Marseille, 75010 Paris, France.

410 UK
LAKELAND DIALECT. 1939. a. £2. Lakeland
Dialect Society, c/o James T. Relph, Holly Cottage,
Crosby Ravensworth, Penrith, Cumbria, CA10 3JP,
England. Ed. Ted Relph. bk. rev. circ. 600.
Formerly: Lakeland Dialect Society. Journal
(ISSN 0307-9341)

427 UK ISSN 0075-7799
LANCASHIRE DIALECT SOCIETY. JOURNAL.
1951. a. £1.50. ‡ Lancashire Dialect Society, c/o
Paul Salveson, 6 Alfred St., Farnworth, Bolton,
England. Ed. John Levitt. bk. rev. cum.index nos.1-
14 (1951-65): nos.15-35 (1966-86) circ. 300.

410 II ISSN 0253-9071
LANGUAGE FORUM. (Text in English) 1975. irreg.
(3-4/yr.) Rs.100($35) Bahri Publications Pvt. Ltd.,
57 Santnagar (East of Kailash), Box 7023, New
Delhi 110065, India (Distr. by: Biblia Impex Pvt.
Ltd., 2/18 Ansari Rd., New Delhi 110065, India)
Ed. Ujjal Singh Bahri. adv. bk. rev.

410 II ISSN 0254-0207
LANGUAGE FORUM MONOGRAPH SERIES.
1978. irreg. price varies. Bahri Publications Pvt.
Ltd., 57 Santnagar (East of Kailash), Box 7023,
New Delhi 110065, India. Ed. Ujjal Singh Bahri.

410 SZ ISSN 0085-2678
LANGUE ET CULTURES; etudes et documents.
(Text and summaries in French or English) 1971.
irreg. no.16, 1985. price varies. Librarie Droz, 11
rue Massot, 1211 Geneva 12, Switzerland. circ. 1,
000.

410 CM
LANGUES DU CAMEROUN. irreg., no.5, 1976. B.P.
5351, Douala, Cameroun.

410 301.2 FR ISSN 0240-2041
LANGUES ET CIVILISATIONS A TRADITION
ORALE. 1972. irreg. Societe d'Etudes Linguistiques
et Anthropologiques de France (SELAF), 5 rue de
Marseille, 75010 Paris, France.

410 572 FR ISSN 0755-9305
LANGUES ET CULTURES AFRICAINES. 1982.
irreg. price varies. Societe d'Etudes Linguistiques et
Anthropologiques de France (SELAF), 5 rue de
Marseille, 75010 Paris, France.

410 572 FR ISSN 0750-2036
LANGUES ET CULTURES DU PACIFIQUE. 1982.
irreg. price varies. Societe d'Etudes Linguistiques et
Anthropologiques de France (SELAF), 5 rue de
Marseille, 75010 Paris, France. adv. bk. rev. circ.
250.

LANGUES ET STYLES. see *LITERATURE*

410 UR
LATVIESU VALODAS KULTURAS JAUTAJUMI.
1965. a. Avots, 24, Padomju Blvd., 226047 Riga,
Latvian S.S.R., U.S.S.R. (Dist. by:
Mezhdunarodnaya Kniga, 32/34 Smolenskaya-
Sennaya, 121200 Moscow, Russian S.F.S.R.,
U.S.S.R.) Ed. L. Ceplitis. circ. 3,000.

420 UK ISSN 0075-8574
LEEDS TEXTS AND MONOGRAPHS. 1967. a.
price varies. University of Leeds, School of English,
Leeds LS2 9JT, England. Ed. P. Meredith. Indexed:
M.L.A.

479 879 NE ISSN 0075-8647
LEIDSE ROMANISTISCHE REEKS. (Text in French, Italian and Spanish) 1954. irreg., vol.22, 1975. price varies. Leiden University Press, c/o E.J. Brill Publishers, Postbus 9000, 2300 PA Leiden, Netherlands.

460 375.4 PE
LENGUA Y SOCIEDAD. (Text in Castellano) 1974. irreg., latest no.7. price varies. (Instituto de Estudios Peruanos) I E P Ediciones, Horacio Urteaga 694 (Campe de Marte), Lima 11, Peru. (back issues avail.)

410 CK ISSN 0120-3479
LENGUAJE. 1972. irreg. Col.$110($5) Universidad del Valle, Division de Humanidades, Departamento de Idiomas, Apdo. Aereo 25360, Cali, Colombia. Ed. Samuel Estrada. circ. 1,000. Indexed: M.L.A. Lang.& Lang.Behav.Abstr.

450 IT ISSN 0075-8825
LESSICO INTELLETTUALE EUROPEO. 1969. irreg., no.38, 1986. price varies. Edizioni dell' Ateneo S.p.A., P.O. Box 7216, 00100 Rome, Italy. circ. 1,500.

410 GW ISSN 0175-6206
LEXICOGRAPHICA; international annual for lexicography. (Text and summaries in English, French, German) 1985. a. DM.144. Max Niemeyer Verlag, Postfach 2140, D-7400 Tuebingen, W. Germany (B.R.D.) Ed. Antonin Kucera. (back issues avail.)

410 UR ISSN 0130-0172
LIETUVIU KALBOTYROS KLAUSIMAI/ PROBLEMS OF LITHUANIAN LINGUISTICS. (Text in Lithuanian or Russian; summaries in English, German, Lithuanian or Russian) 1957. a. price varies. (Akademiya Nauk Litovskoi S.S.R., Lietuviu Kalbos ir Literaturos Institutas - Institute of Lithuanian Language and Literature) Izdatel'stvo Mokslas, Zvaigzdziu 23, Vilnius 232050, Lithuanian S.S.R., U.S.S.R. Ed. S. Keinys. circ. 800. Indexed: M.L.A.

400 800 GW
LILI. BEIHEFTE. (Zeitschrift fuer Literaturwissenschaft und Linguistik) 1975. irreg., no.13, 1985. price varies. Vandenhoeck und Ruprecht, Theaterstr. 13, Postfach 37 53, 3400 Goettingen, W. Germany (B.R.D.) Indexed: Can.Rev.Comp.Lit.

400 800 BL ISSN 0047-4711
LINGUA E LITERATURA. (Text in various languages) 1972. a. Universidade de Sao Paulo, Faculdade de Filosofia, Letras e Ciencias Humanas, Ciudade Universitaria, C.P. 01000, Sao Paulo, Brazil. Eds. Aida Costa, Carlos Drumond, Paulo Vizioli. bk. rev. charts. illus. bibl. circ. 1,000. Indexed: Hisp.Amer.Per.Ind.

491.85 PL ISSN 0079-4740
LINGUA POSNANIENSIS. (Text in various languages) 1949. a. price varies. (Poznanskie Towarzystwo Przyjaciol Nauk) Panstwowe Wydawnictwo Naukowe, Ul.Miodowa 10, Warsaw, Poland (Dist. by: Ars Polona-Ruch, Krakowskie Przedmiescie 7, Warsaw, Poland) Ed. Jerzy Banczerowski. Indexed: M.L.A. Ind.Bk.Rev.Hum. Lang.& Lang.Behav.Abstr.

410 900 GW ISSN 0341-3225
LINGUARUM MINORUM DOCUMENTA HISTORIOGRAPHICA. 1977. irreg., no.5, 1983. price varies. Verlag Helmut Buske, Schlueterstr. 14, 2000 Hamburg 13, W. Germany (B.R.D.) Ed. H. Haarmann.

400 IT
LINGUE E ISCRIZIONI DELL'ITALIA ANTICA. 1977. irreg., no.5, 1985. Casa Editrice Leo S. Olschki, Viuzzo del Pozzetto, Casella Postale 66, 50100 Florence, Italy. Dir. Aldo Prosdocimi. circ. 1, 000.

410 IT ISSN 0391-3228
LE LINGUE E LE CIVILTA STRANIERE MODERNE. 1981. irreg., no.6, 1984. price varies. Liguori Editore s.r.l., Via Mezzocanone 19, 80134 Naples, Italy. TEL 081/20 6077. Ed. Elio Chinol.

410 800 US ISSN 0165-7712
LINGUISTIC & LITERARY STUDIES IN EASTERN EUROPE. Short title: L L S E E. 1979. irreg., vol.20, 1986. price varies. John Benjamins Publishing Co., One Buttonwood Sq, Philadelphia, PA 19130. TEL 215-564-6379. Ed.Bd. Indexed: M.L.A. Math.R.

400 NE
LINGUISTIC CALCULATION. (Text in English, French and German) 1961. a. Kr.75 price varies. D. Reidel Publishing Co., P.O. Box 17, 479-483 Voorstraat, 3300 AA Dordrecht, Netherlands (And: 190 Old Derby St., Hingham, MA 02043) Ed. Dr. Hans Karlgren. Indexed: M.L.A. SSCI.
  Former titles: S M I L Quarterly Journal of Linguistic Calculus; (until 1977): Statistical Methods in Linguistics (ISSN 0039-0437)

410 US ISSN 0075-9597
LINGUISTIC CIRCLE OF MANITOBA AND NORTH DAKOTA. PROCEEDINGS. 1959. irreg., (approx. a.) membership. ‡ University of North Dakota, Department of English, Grand Forks, ND 58202. (Co-sponsors: University of Winnipeg; University of Manitoba) Ed. Ben L. Collins. circ. 500.

410 US ISSN 0737-4720
LINGUISTIC NOTES FROM LA JOLLA. no.5, 1973. irreg. $8 per no. University of California, San Diego, Department of Linguistics, C-008, La Jolla, CA 92093. TEL 619-452-3600. Ed. Michael B. Smith. charts. circ. 75.

400 US ISSN 0075-9600
LINGUISTIC SOCIETY OF AMERICA. MEETING HANDBOOKS. 1965. a. price varies. Linguistic Society of America, 1325 18th St., N.W., Ste. 211, Washington, DC 20036-6501. adv. circ. 1,000.

491 II ISSN 0075-9627
LINGUISTIC SOCIETY OF INDIA. BULLETIN. (Supplement to Indian Linguistics) 1958. irreg., no.3, 1970. included with subscription to Indian Linguistics. Linguistic Society of India, c/o Deccan College Postgraduate and Research Institute, Poona 411006, India. Ed. R.V. Dhongde.

400 YU ISSN 0024-3922
LINGUISTICA. (Text in various languages) 1955. a. $8. Univerza Edvarda Kardelja v Ljubljani, Filozofska Fakulteta, Askerceva 12, 61000 Ljubljana, Yugoslavia. Ed. Mitja Skubic. circ. 600. Indexed: M.L.A. Lang.& Lang.Behav.Abstr.

410 PL ISSN 0208-4228
LINGUISTICA SILESIANA. (Text in English, French or Russian; summaries in Polish, Russian) 1975. irreg. price varies. Uniwersytet Slaski w Katowicach, Ul. Bankowa 14, 40-007 Katowice, Poland.

LINGUISTICS ABSTRACTS. see *LINGUISTICS — Abstracting, Bibliographies, Statistics*

410 US
LINGUISTICS OF THE TIBETO-BURMAN AREA. 1974. irreg. $5.50 per no. California State University, Fresno, Department of Linguistics, Fresno, CA 93740. Ed. Graham Thurgood. bk. rev. circ. 150. Indexed: M.L.A.

410 US ISSN 0166-0829
LINGUISTIK AKTUELL; Amsterdamer Arbeiten zur theoretischen und angewandten Linguistik. 1980. irreg., vol.4, 1986. price varies. John Benjamins Publishing Co., One Buttonwood Sq, Philadelphia, PA 19130. TEL 215-564-6379. Ed. Werner Abraham. Indexed: M.L.A.

410 375.4 MG
LINGUISTIQUE ET ENSEIGNEMENT. (Text in French or Malagasy) 1971. irreg. (approx. s-a) Universite de Madagascar, Institut de Linguistique Appliquee, B.P. 4099, Antananarivo, Malagasy Republic.

410 GW ISSN 0344-6727
LINGUISTISCHE ARBEITEN. 1973. irreg. price varies. Max Niemeyer Verlag, Postfach 2140, 74 Tuebingen, W. Germany (B.R.D.) Ed. Hans Altmann et al. (back issues avail.)

410 GW ISSN 0075-9686
LINGUISTISCHE REIHE. 1970. irreg., vol.22, 1975. price varies. Max Hueber Verlag, Max-Hueber-Str.4, 8045 Ismaning, W. Germany (B.R.D.) Eds. Klaus Baumgaertner, Hugo Steger.

410 440 US ISSN 0165-7569
LINGVISTICAE INVESTIGATIONES: SUPPLEMENTA; studies in French and general linguistics/etudes en linguistique francaise et generale. (Companion series to Lingvisticae Investigationes) 1979. irreg., vol.13, 1985. price varies. (Universite de Paris VIII (Paris-Vincennes), Departement de Linguistique, FR) John Benjamins Publishing Co., One Buttonwood Sq, Philadelphia, PA 19130. TEL 215-564-6379. (Co-sponsor: Laboratoire d'Automatique Documentaire et Linguistique (C.N.R.S.)) Ed.Bd. Indexed: M.L.A.

410 UR ISSN 0301-6900
LINGVISTICHESKIE ISSLEDOVANIYA. irreg. 0.96 Rub. Akademiya Nauk S.S.S.R., Institut Yazykoznaniya, Ul. Marksa i Engel'sa 1/14, Moscow, Russian S.F.S.R., U.S.S.R.

410 CS
LINGVISTICKE CITANKY/READINGS IN LINGUISTICS. 1970. irreg. 10 Kcs. Universita Karlova, Filosoficka Fakulta, Nam. Krasnoarmejcu 1, 116 38 Prague 1, Czechoslovakia. Ed. Bohumil Palek. circ. 500.

410 UR ISSN 0202-201X
LITUANISTIKA V S.S.S.R. YAZYKOZNANIE; nauchno-referativnyi sbornik. (Text in Russian) 1978. a. 0.40 Rub. Akademiya Nauk Litovskoi S.S.R., Nauchno-Informatsionnyi Tsentr, Michurino g-ve 1/46, Vilnius, Lithuanian S.S.R., U.S.S.R. Ed. B. Tolutiene. circ. 400.

400 PL ISSN 0076-0390
LODZKIE TOWARZYSTWO NAUKOWE. ROZPRAWY KOMISJI JEZYKOWEJ. 1954. irreg., vol.31, 1985. price varies. Ossolineum, Publishing House of the Polish Academy of Sciences, Rynek 9, 50-106 Wroclaw, Poland (Dist. by: Ars Polona-Ruch, Krakowskie Przedmiescie 7, 00-068 Warsaw, Poland) (Co-sponsor: Polska Akademia Nauk) Ed. Karol Dejna. circ. 500.

499.992 CN ISSN 0024-7367
LUMO; Kanada Esperanto-Revuo. (Text in Esperanto) 1957. a. Can.$3. Canadian Esperanto Association, Box 126, Sta. Beaubien, Montreal, Que. H2G 3C8, Canada. TEL 604-290-6010. Ed. Brian Kaneen. adv. bk. rev. illus. circ. 500.

420 SW ISSN 0076-1451
LUND STUDIES IN ENGLISH. 1933. irreg., no.73, 1985. price varies. Liber Forlag, S-205 10, Malmo, Sweden. Eds. Claes Schaar, Jan Svartvik. Indexed: M.L.A.

M L A INTERNATIONAL BIBLIOGRAPHY OF BOOKS AND ARTICLES ON THE MODERN LANGUAGES AND LITERATURES. (Modern Language Association of America) see *BIBLIOGRAPHIES*

407 AT ISSN 0310-9674
M.L.T.A. NEWS. 1973. irreg. Modern Language Teachers' Association of New South Wales, c/o School of Modern Languages, Macquarie University, North Ryde, NSW 2113, Australia. Ed. K.A.B. Strong. circ. 650(controlled)

440 370 AT ISSN 0815-7138
MACQUARIE UNIVERSITY FRENCH MONOGRAPHS. 1967-1972; N.S. 1973. irreg. Aus.$3 per no. ‡ Macquarie University, School of Modern Languages, North Ryde, N.S.W. 2113, Australia. Eds. Angus Martin & K.R. Dutton. circ. 250.
  Supersedes: Monographs for Teachers of French (ISSN 0047-7907)

410 HU ISSN 0541-9298
MAGYAR NYELVJARASOK. (Summaries in German and Russian) 1951. irreg., vol.25, 1983. Kossuth Lajos Tudomanyegyetem, Egyetem Ter 1, 4010 Debrecen, Hungary. bibl. Indexed: M.L.A.

400 GW ISSN 0542-1551
MAINZER ROMANISTISCHE ARBEITEN. (Text in English, French, and German) irreg.,vol.11, 1976. price varies. Franz Steiner Verlag Wiesbaden GmbH, Birkenwaldstr. 44, Postfach 347, D-7000 Stuttgart 1, W. Germany (B.R.D.) Eds. W.T. Elwert, H. Kroell.

MAINZER STUDIEN ZUR AMERIKANISTIK. see *LITERATURE*

400　　　　　GW　ISSN 0170-3560
MAINZER STUDIEN ZUR SPRACH- UND
VOLKSFORSCHUNG. irreg., vol.9, 1987. price
varies. (Universitaet Mainz, Institut fuer
Geschichtliche Landeskunde) Franz Steiner Verlag
Wiesbaden GmbH, Birkenwaldstr. 44, Postfach 347,
D-7000 Stuttgart 1, W. Germany (B.R.D.) Ed.Bd.

MAKEDONIKA. see *HISTORY — History Of Europe*

491.81　　　　　YU　ISSN 0025-1089
MAKEDONSKI JAZIK. (Text in Macedonian and
other languages) 1950. a. Institut za Makedonski
Jazik, Skopje - Institute of Macedonian Language,
P.O. Box 434, 91000 Skopje, Yugoslavia. (Co-
sponsor: Republicka Zaednica za Naucni Dejnosti)
Ed. Bozidar Vidoeski. bk. rev. circ. 2,000. Indexed:
M.L.A.

418.02　　　　　US　ISSN 0363-9037
MALEDICTA PRESS PUBLICATIONS. 1976. irreg.,
vol.5, 1979. price varies. Maledicta Press, 331 S.
Greenfield Ave., Waukesha, WI 53186. TEL 414-
542-5853. Ed. Reinhold Aman. circ. 4,000.

418.02　　　　　US　ISSN 0363-3659
MALEDICTA: THE INTERNATIONAL JOURNAL
OF VERBAL AGGRESSION. 1977. a. $19 to
individuals; institutions $25. (International
Maledicta Society) Maledicta Press, 331 S.
Greenfield Ave., Waukesha, WI 53186-6492. TEL
414-542-5853. Ed. Reinhold Aman. bk. rev. bibl.
index. cum. index: 1977-1986. circ. 4,000. (back
issues avail.) Indexed: M.L.A. Sociol.Abstr. Lang.&
Lang.Behav.Abstr.

MARI ANNALES DE RECHERCHES
INTERDISCIPLINAIRES. see *ARCHAEOLOGY*

410　　　　　AT
MATERIALS IN LANGUAGES OF INDONESIA.
1980. irreg. price varies. Australian National
University, Research School of Pacific Studies,
Department of Linguistics, G.P.O. Box 4, Canberra,
A.C.T. 2601, Australia. Ed. S.A. Wurm. cum.index:
1963-1981.

491.7　　　　　UR
MATERIALY I ISSLEDOVANIYA PO SIBIRSKOI
DIALEKTOLOGII. 1974. a. 1.10 Rub.
Krasnoyarskii Gosudarstvennyi Pedagogicheskii
Institut, Krasnoyarsk, Russian S.F.S.R., U.S.S.R. Ed.
N. Tsomakion. circ. 1,000.

410　　　　　FR
MATERIAUX POUR L'ETUDE DE L'ASIE
ORIENTALE MODERNE ET
CONTEMPORAINE. 1966. irreg., latest 1986.
price varies. Editions de l' Ecole des Hautes Etudes
en Sciences Sociales, 131 bd. Saint-Michel, 75005
Paris, France.

410　　　　　GE
MECKLENBURGISCHES WOERTERBUCH. 1955.
a. (Saechsische Akademie der Wissenschaften zu
Leipzig) Akademie-Verlag Berlin, Leipziger Str. 3-4,
1086 Berlin, E. Germany (D.D.R.)

MEDIAEVAL AND MODERN BRETON SERIES.
see *HISTORY — History Of Europe*

MICHIGAN SLAVIC MATERIALS. see
LITERATURE

470　　　　　GW　ISSN 0076-9762
MITTELLATEINISCHES JAHRBUCH. 1964. a.
Anton Hiersemann Verlag, Rosenbergstr. 113,
Postfach 723, 7000 Stuttgart 1, W. Germany
(B.R.D.) Eds. Karl Langosch, Fritz Wagner. circ.
600. Indexed: M.L.A.

410　　　　　US　ISSN 0736-5268
MODELS OF SCIENTIFIC THOUGHT; a series of
monographs and tracts. 1983. irreg. Harwood
Academic Publishers, Box 786, Cooper Sta., NY
10276.

420　375.4　　　　　JA
MODERN ENGLISH JOURNAL/EIGO KYOIKU
JAANARU. 1970. a. 900 Yen($6) Seido Language
Institute, 12-6 Funado-cho, Ashiya, Hyogo 659,
Japan. Ed. David Sell. adv. bk. rev. circ. 3,000. (also
avail. in microform from UMI) Indexed: Lang.&
Lang.Behav.Abstr.
English language study and teaching

410　　　　　HU　ISSN 0076-9967
MODERN FILOLOGIAI FUZETEK. 1966. irreg.,
vol.39, 1986. price varies. (Magyar Tudomanyos
Akademia) Akademiai Kiado, Publishing House of
the Hungarian Academy of Sciences, Box 24, H-
1363 Budapest, Hungary.

410　　　　　DK　ISSN 0107-2390
MODERSMAAL SELSKABET. AARBOG. 1980. a.
Kr.122. Modersmaal Selskabet, 3 Hammerichsvej,
DK-4760 Vordingborg, Denmark.

410　　　　　US　ISSN 0147-5207
MON-KHMER STUDIES. (Text in English, French
and German) 1972? a. $10 per vol. University of
Hawaii Press, 2840 Kolowalu St., Honolulu, HI
96822. TEL 808-948-8697. Ed. Stephen O'Harrow.
Indexed: M.L.A.

400　　　　　GW　ISSN 0077-1910
MUENCHENER STUDIEN ZUR
SPRACHWISSENSCHAFT. (Text in English,
French and German) 1954. irreg. (1-2/yr) price
varies. R. Kitzinger, Schellingstr. 25, 8000 Munich
40, W. Germany (B.R.D.) Eds. Bernhard Forssman,
Johanna Narten.

MUENCHNER GERMANISTISCHE BEITRAEGE.
see *LITERATURE*

410　　　　　TZ　ISSN 0856-0129
MULIKA. 1971. a. $5 per no. University of Dar es
Salaam, Institute of Kiswahili Research, Box 35110,
Dar es Salaam, Tanzania. Eds. E.D.Y. Mbogo & J.S.
Mdee.

400　　　　　NE
MUSEUM PHILOLOGUM LONDINIENSE. 1975.
irreg., no.2, 1977. price varies. Ed. J. C. Gieben,
Uithoorn, Netherlands. Ed. Giuseppe Giangrande.

100　　　　　SP
MYRTIA: REVISTA DE FILOLOGIA CLASICA.
1986. irreg. Universidad de Murcia, Secretariado de
Publicaciones e Intercambio Cientifico, Santo Cristo,
1, 30001 Murcia, Spain. TEL 968 24 92 00.

400　　　　　JA
NATIONAL LANGUAGE RESEARCH
INSTITUTE. ANNUAL REPORT/KOKURITSU
KOKUGO KENKYUSHO NENPO. 1951. a.
National Language Research Institute - Kokuritsu
Kokugo Kenkyusho, 3-9-14 Nisigaoka, Kita-ku,
Tokyo 115, Japan.

410　　　　　YU
NAUCNI SASTANAK SLAVISTA U VUKOVE
DANE. REFERATI I SAOPSTENJA. 1971. a.
Medjunarodni Slavisticki Centar SR Srbije,
Studetski trg 3/1, Belgrade, Yugoslvaia. illus.
Indexed: M.L.A.

400　　　　　HU　ISSN 0418-4580
NEMET FILOLOGIAI TANULMANYOK/
ARBEITEN ZUR DEUTSCHEN PHILOLOGIE.
(Text in German) 1965. irreg., vol.17, 1984.
Kossuth Lajos Tudomanyegyetem, Nemet Tanszek,
Egyetem Ter 1, 4010 Debrecen, Hungary. bibl.
Indexed: M.L.A.

440　　　　　CN　ISSN 0380-9366
NEOLOGIE EN MARCHE. SERIE A. LANGUE
GENERALE. 1973. irreg., no.8, 1978. Office de la
Langue Francaise, 700bd. Saint-Cyrille Est, 2e,
Quebec, P.Q. G1R 5A9, Canada. TEL 418-643-
6954. illus.

440　　　　　CN　ISSN 0701-7995
NEOLOGIE EN MARCHE. SERIE B. LANGUES
DE SPECIALITES. 1976. irreg., no.10, 1978.
Office de la Langue Francaise, 700 Bd. Saint-Cyrille
Est, 2e, Quebec, P.Q. G1R 5A9, Canada. TEL 418-
643-6954.

410　　　　　PL　ISSN 0208-5550
NEOPHILOLOGICA. (Text in West-European
languages; summaries in Polish and Russian) 1980.
irreg. Uniwersytet Slaski w Katowicach, Ul.
Bankowa 14, 40-007 Katowice, Poland.

410　　　　　NE
NETHERLANDS PHONETIC ARCHIVES. (Text in
English) irreg. Foris Publications, P.O. Box 509,
3300 AM Dordrecht, Netherlands. Ed. Marcel P.R.
van den Broecke.

490　350　　　　　GW　ISSN 0340-6385
NEUINDISCHE STUDIEN. 1970. irreg., vol.10,
1985. price varies. Verlag Otto Harrassowitz,
Taunusstr. 14, Postfach 2929, 6200 Wiesbaden 1,
W. Germany (B.R.D.) Ed.Bd.

NEUROLINGUISTICS; international series devoted
to speech physiology and speech pathology. see
*MEDICAL SCIENCES — Psychiatry And
Neurology*

423.1　　　　　US　ISSN 0148-866X
NEW ACRONYMS, INITIALISMS AND
ABBREVIATIONS. (Supplement to Acronyms,
Initialisms and Abbreviations Dictionary) a. $155.
Gale Research Company, Book Tower, Detroit, MI
48226. TEL 313-961-2242. Eds. Julie Towell, Helen
Sheppard.
  Formerly (until 1976): New Acronyms and
Initialisms (ISSN 0077-7986)

NEW CEYLON WRITING; creative and critical
writing of Sri Lanka. see *LITERATURE*

439　　　　　GW　ISSN 0078-0545
NIEDERDEUTSCHES WORT; Beitraege zur
niederdeutschen Philologie. 1960. irreg. price varies.
Aschendorffsche Verlagsbuchhandlung, Soester Str.
13, 4400 Muenster, W. Germany (B.R.D.) Ed. Jan
Goossens. Indexed: M.L.A.

420　940　　　　　UK　ISSN 0141-6340
NOMINA; a journal of name studies relating to Great
Britain and Ireland. 1977. a. £4. Council for Name
Studies in Great Britain and Ireland, c/o I.A.
Fraser, Esq., School of Scottish Studies, 27 George
Sq., Edinburgh EH8 9LD, Scotland (Subscr. addr.:
13 Church St., Chesterton, Cambridge CB4 1DT,
England) Ed.Bd. adv. bk. rev. bibl. circ. 200.
(looseleaf format; back issues avail.) Indexed:
M.L.A. Br.Archaeol.Abstr.

439　　　　　SW　ISSN 0078-1134
NORDISTICA GOTHOBURGENSIA. (Subseries of
Acta Universitatis Gothoburgensis) (Text in
Swedish; summaries in English and German) 1965.
irreg., no.12, 1980. price varies; also exchange basis.
Acta Universitatis Gothoburgensis, Box 5096, S-402
22 Goeteborg, Sweden (Dist. in U. S., Canada, and
Mexico by: Humanities Press, Inc., 171 First Ave.,
Atlantic Highlands, NJ 07716) Ed. Bo Ralph.

410　　　　　SW　ISSN 0346-6728
NORNA - RAPPORTER. (Text in English, German
and Swedish) 1973. irreg. price varies. Nordiska
Samarbetskommitten foer Namnforskning, Sankt
Johannesgatan 11, S-752 21 Uppsala, Sweden. bk.
rev. charts. circ. 500.

400　　　　　NE　ISSN 0078-1592
NORTH-HOLLAND LINGUISTIC SERIES. 1970.
irreg., vol.4, 1979. price varies. Elsevier Science
Publishers B.V., Box 211, 1000 AE Amsterdam,
Netherlands. Indexed: M.L.A.

NORTHEAST CONFERENCE ON THE
TEACHING OF FOREIGN LANGUAGES.
NORTHEAST CONFERENCE REPORTS. see
*EDUCATION — Teaching Methods And
Curriculum*

410　948　　　　　DK　ISSN 0900-8675
NORTH WESTERN EUROPEAN LANGUAGE
EVOLUTION. a. Kr.158.60. Odense University
Press, 36 Pjentedamsgade, DK-5000 Odense,
Denmark.

400　　　　　IT
NOVANTIQUA; biblioteca di filologia, curiosita e
dialettologia. 1977. irreg., no.13, 1984. price varies.
Societa Editrice Napoletana s.r.l., Corso Umberto I
34, Naples, Italy. Ed. Antonio Altamura.

410　　　　　DK
NYDANSKE STUDIER OG ALMEN
KOMMUNIKATIONSTEORI. 1971. irreg. price
varies. Akademisk Forlag, Store Kannikestraede 8,
P.O. Box 54, 1002 Copenhagen K, Denmark.

410　　　　　HU　ISSN 0078-2858
NYELVESZETI TANULMANYOK. 1951. irreg.,
vol.29, 1986. price varies. (Magyar Tudomanyos
Akademia) Akademiai Kiado, Publishing House of
the Hungarian Academy of Sciences, Box 24, H-
1363 Budapest, Hungary.

410   HU   ISSN 0078-2866
NYELVTUDOMANYI ERTEKEZESEK. 1953. irreg., vol.122, 1986. price varies. (Magyar Tudomanyos Akademia, Nyelvtudomanyi Intezet) Akademiai Kiado, Publishing House of the Hungarian Academy of Sciences, Box 24, H-1363 Budapest, Hungary.

410   SW   ISSN 0345-8768
NYSVENSKA STUDIER; tidsskrift foer Svensk stil och spraakforskning. 1921. a. Kr.60. (Institut for Nordiska Spraak) Lennart Elmevik, Ed. & Pub., Box 513, 75120 Uppsala, Sweden. circ. 600.

OCCASIONAL PAPERS IN GERMAN STUDIES. see LITERATURE

410   US
OCCASIONAL PAPERS IN LINGUISTICS. 1972. irreg., no.5, 1984. price varies. University of California, Los Angeles, Department of Linguistics, 405 Hilgard Ave., Los Angeles, CA 90024. TEL 213-825-0634.

410   UK   ISSN 0308-2075
OCCASIONAL PAPERS IN LINGUISTICS AND LANGUAGE LEARNING. 1976. irreg. price varies. University of Ulster, Linguistics Panel, Coleraine, N. Ireland. Ed. R. Thelwall. bibl. circ. 175. Indexed: M.L.A.

OCCASIONAL PAPERS IN SLAVIC LANGUAGES AND LITERATURE. see LITERATURE

410   US
OCCASIONAL PAPERS ON LINGUISTICS. 1978. irreg., latest, vol.13, 1986. varies. Southern Illinois University, Department of Linguistics, Carbondale, IL 62901. TEL 618-536-3385. Ed. James E. Redden. bibl. charts. illus. circ. 400.

499   US   ISSN 0078-3188
OCEANIC LINGUISTICS. SPECIAL PUBLICATIONS. 1966. irreg., no.21, 1986. price varies. (University of Hawaii, Social Science Research Institute) University of Hawaii Press, 2840 Kolowalu St., Honolulu, HI 96822. TEL 808-948-8697. Ed. George W. Grace. (reprint service avail. from UMI, ISI) Indexed: M.L.A.

410   DK   ISSN 0078-3277
ODENSE UNIVERSITY SLAVIC STUDIES. (Text in English and Russian) 1970. irreg., no.5, 1986. price varies. Odense University Press, 36, Pjentedamsgade, DK-5000 Odense, Denmark. (back issues avail.)

420   DK   ISSN 0078-3293
ODENSE UNIVERSITY STUDIES IN ENGLISH. (Text in English) 1969. irreg., no.9, 1985. price varies. Odense University Press, 36, Pjentedamsgade, DK-5000 Odense, Denmark. (back issues avail.) Indexed: M.L.A.

400   DK   ISSN 0078-3315
ODENSE UNIVERSITY STUDIES IN LINGUISTICS. 1968. irreg., no.5, 1986. price varies. Odense University Press, 36, Pjentedamsgade, DK-5000 Odense, Denmark. (back issues avail.)

439.5 839.5   DK   ISSN 0078-3331
ODENSE UNIVERSITY STUDIES IN SCANDINAVIAN LANGUAGES AND LITERATURES. (Text in Danish) 1968. irreg., no.14, 1986. price varies. Odense University Press, 36, Pjentedamsgade, DK-5000 Odense, Denmark. (back issues avail.)

410 401   AU
OESTERREICHISCHE AKADEMIE DER WISSENSCHAFTEN. KOMMISSION FUER LINGUISTIK UND KOMMUNIKATIONSFORSCHUNG. VEROEFFENTLICHUNGEN. (Subseries of: Oesterreichische Akademie der Wissenschaften. Philosophisch-Historische Klasse. Sitzungsberichte) 1973. irreg. Verlag der Oesterreichischen Akademie der Wissenschaften, Dr.-Ignaz-Seipel-Platz 2, A-1010 Vienna, Austria.

410   US
OHIO UNIVERSITY. WORKING PAPERS IN LINGUISTICS AND LANGUAGE TEACHING. 1974. irreg. $4 to individuals; institutions $6. Ohio University, Department of Linguistics, 103 Gordy, Athens, OH 45701. TEL 614-594-4892. Ed. Melanie L. Schneider. abstr. bibl. charts. illus. circ. 250.
Formerly: Working Papers in Applied Linguistics (ISSN 0163-0016)

400   US
OLOGIES AND ISMS; a thematic dictionary. 1979. irreg., latest 3rd edt., 1986. $92. Gale Research Company, Book Tower, Detroit, MI 48226. TEL 313-961-2242. Ed.Bd.

491.79   PL   ISSN 0078-4648
ONOMASTICA; pismo poswiecone nazewnictwu geograficznemu i osobowemu. (Summaries in French) 1955. a. price varies. (Polska Akademia Nauk, Komitet Jezykoznawstwa) Ossolineum, Publishing House of the Polish Academy of Sciences, Rynek 9, 50-106 Wroclaw, Poland (Dist. by: Ars Polona-Ruch, Krakowskie Przedmiescie 7, Warsaw, Poland) Ed. Kazimierz Rymut.

491.7 891.7   GW
OPERA SLAVICA. NEUE FOLGE. 1961. irreg., vol.6, 1985. price varies. Verlag otto Harrassowitz, Taunusstr. 14, Postfach 2929, 6200 Wiesbaden 1, W. Germany (B.R.D.) Ed. Reinhard Lauer.
Formerly (until 1981): Opera Slavica (ISSN 0085-4514)

439 800   DK   ISSN 0108-8025
ORD & SAG. 1981. a. free. Aarhus Universitet, Institut for Jysk Sprog- og Kulturforskning, Niels Juels Gade 84, 8200 Aarhus N., Denmark. Ed. Viggo Soerensen. illus. circ. 1,500.

410   IT
ORIENTAMENTI LINGUISTICI. 1977. irreg. price varies. (Universita degli Studi di Pisa, Istituto di Glottologia) Giardini Editori e Stampatori, Via Santa Bibbiana 28, 56100 Pisa, Italy. Ed. Tristano Bolelli.

418.02   SW   ISSN 0473-4351
ORTNAMNSSALLSKAPET I UPPSALA. AARSSKRIFT. (Text in English, German and Swedish; summaries in English) 1936. a. Kr.40($5) Ortnamnssallskapet i Uppsala - Place-Name Society of Uppsala, St. Johannesgatan 11, 752 21 Uppsala, Sweden. Ed. Karl I. Sandred. bk. rev. circ. 1,200. (back issues avail.)

OTTAWA HISPANICA. see LITERATURE

OXFORD GERMAN STUDIES. see LITERATURE

400   US   ISSN 0078-7469
PACIFIC COAST PHILOLOGY. (Text mainly in English; occasionally in French and German) 1966. a. $4. Philological Association of the Pacific Coast, c/o Louise Westling, Department of English, University of Oregon, Eugene, OR 97403. circ. 1,300.

499   AT   ISSN 0078-7531
PACIFIC LINGUISTICS. SERIES A: OCCASIONAL PAPERS. 1963. irreg. price varies. Australian National University, Research School of Pacific Studies, Dept. of Linguistics, Box 4, Canberra, A.C.T. 2601, Australia. Ed. S.A. Wurm. cum.index 1963-81 in Series D, no.40.

499   AT   ISSN 0078-754X
PACIFIC LINGUISTICS. SERIES B: MONOGRAPHS. 1963. irreg. price varies. Australian National University, Research School of Pacific Studies, Dept. of Linguistics, Box 4, Canberra, A.C.T. 2601, Australia. Ed. S.A. Wurm. cum.index 1963-1981 in Series D, no. 40.

499   AT   ISSN 0078-7558
PACIFIC LINGUISTICS. SERIES C: BOOKS. 1965. irreg. price varies. Australian National University, Research School of Pacific Studies, Dept. of Linguistics, Box 4, Canberra, A.C.T. 2601, Australia. Ed. S.A. Wurm. cum.index 1963-1981 in Series D, no. 40.

499   AT   ISSN 0078-7566
PACIFIC LINGUISTICS. SERIES D: SPECIAL PUBLICATIONS. 1964. irreg. price varies. Australian National University, Research School of Pacific Studies, Dept. of Linguistics, Box 4, Canberra, A.C.T. 2601, Australia. Ed. S.A. Wurm. cum.index 1963-81 in Series D, no. 40.

499   GE
PACO; bulteno de la Mondpaca Esperantista Movado, sekcio de GDR. (Text in Esperanto) 1966. a. Kulturbund der DDR, Esperanto-Verband, Charlottenstr. 60, 1080 Berlin, E. Germany (D.D.R.) (U.S. Subscr. to: J. M. Deer, 12946 N.E. Nancock, Portland, OR 97230) Ed. Detlev Blanke. bk. rev. illus.

491.8   PL   ISSN 0078-866X
PAMIETNIK SLOWIANSKI. 1950. a. $13.50. (Polska Akademia Nauk, Komitet Slowianoznawstwa) Ossolineum, Publishing House of the Polish Academy of Sciences, Rynek 9, 50-106 Wroclaw, Poland (Dist. by: Ars Polona-Ruch, Krakowskie Przedmiescie 7, Warsaw, Poland) Ed. Ludwik Bazylow.

400   IT
PAN; studi dell'Istituto di Filologia Latina. 1973. a. exchange basis. Universita degli Studi, Istituto di Filologia Latina, Viale delle Scienze, 90134 Palermo, Italy.

410   US
PAPERS AND REPORTS ON CHILD LANGUAGE DEVELOPMENT. 1970. irreg. $12. Stanford University, Department of Linguistics, Stanford, CA 94305 TEL 415-497-4284. (Available from: E R I C, National Institute of Education, U.S. Dept. of H.H.S., Washington DC 20208) Ed. E.V. Clark. circ. 200. Indexed: Lang.& Lang.Behav.Abstr.

410   PL   ISSN 0137-2459
PAPERS AND STUDIES IN CONTRASTIVE LINGUISTICS. (Text in English) 1973. irreg. price varies. Adam Mickiewicz University Press, Marchlewskiego 128, 61-874 Poznan, Poland. (Co-sponsor: Center for Applied Linguistics, Arlington, VA, USA) Ed. Jacek Fisiak. Indexed: M.L.A. Lang.& Lang.Behav.Abstr.

499   AT   ISSN 0078-9062
PAPERS IN AUSTRALIAN LINGUISTICS. (Subseries of Pacific Linguistics. Series A: Occasional Papers) 1967. irreg. price varies. Australian National University, Research School of Pacific Studies, Dept. of Linguistics, Box 4, Canberra, A.C.T. 2601, Australia. Ed. S.A. Wurm. cum.index 1963-1981 in Pacific Linguistics, Series D, no. 40. Indexed: M.L.A.

499   AT   ISSN 0078-9070
PAPERS IN BORNEO LINGUISTICS. (Subseries of Pacific Linguistics. Series A: Occasional Papers) 1969. irreg. price varies. Australian National University, Research School of Pacific Studies, Dept. of Linguustics, Box 4, Canberra, A.C.T. 2601, Australia. Ed. S.A. Wurm. cum.index 1963-1981 in Pacific Linguistics, Series D, no.40. Indexed: M.L.A.

410 375.4   JA
PAPERS IN JAPANESE LINGUISTICS.* (Text in English) 1972. a. $10. Kurosio Syuppan Co., Ltd., 3-24, Kanda Ogawa-Mati, Tiyoda-Ku, Tokyo 101, Japan. Ed. Masayoshi Shibatani. bk. rev. circ. 300.

499.5   AT   ISSN 0078-9127
PAPERS IN LINGUISTICS OF MELANESIA. (Subseries of Pacific Linguistics. Series A: Occasional Papers) 1968. irreg. price varies. Australian National University, Research School of Pacific Studies, Dept. of Linguistics, Box 4, Canberra, A.C.T. 2601, Australia. Ed. S.A. Wurm. cum.index 1963-81 in Pacific Linguistics, Series D, no.40. Indexed: M.L.A.

499   AT   ISSN 0078-9135
PAPERS IN NEW GUINEA LINGUISTICS. (Subseries of Pacific Linguistics. Series A: Occasional Papers) 1964. irreg. price varies. Australian National University, Research School of Pacific Studies, Dept. of Linguistics, Box 4, Canberra, A.C.T. 2601, Australia. Ed. S.A. Wurm. cum.index 1963-1981 in Pacific Linguistics, Series D, no.40. Indexed: M.L.A.

499　　　　　　AT　ISSN 0078-9143
PAPERS IN PHILIPPINE LINGUISTICS. (Subseries of Pacific Linguistics. Series A: Occasional Papers) 1966. irreg. price varies. Australian National University, Research School of Pacific Studies, Dept. of Linguistics, Box 4, Canberra, A.C.T. 2601, Australia. Ed. S.A. Wurm. cum.index 1963-1981 in Pacific Linguistics, Series D, no.40. Indexed: M.L.A.

410　　　　　　　　AT
PAPERS IN PIDGIN AND CREOLE LINGUISTICS. 1978. irreg. price varies. Australian National University, Research School of Pacific Studies, Department of Linguistics, G.P.O. Box 4, Canberra, A.C.T. 2601, Australia. Ed. S.A. Wurm. cum.index: 1963-1981.

410　　　　　　UK　ISSN 0263-5798
PAPERS IN SLAVONIC LINGUISTICS. 1982. irreg., latest vol.2, 1984. price varies. Aston Modern Languages Club, Aston University, Department of Modern Languages, Aston Triangle, Birmingham B4 7ET, England. Ed. F.K. Knowles. adv. bk. rev. circ. 100.

495　　　　　　AT　ISSN 0078-9178
PAPERS IN SOUTH EAST ASIAN LINGUISTICS. (Subseries of Pacific Linguistics. Series A: Occasional Papers) 1967. irreg. price varies. Australian National University, Research School of Pacific Studies, Dept. of Linguistics, Box 4, Canberra, A.C.T. 2601, Australia. Ed. S.A. Wurm. cum.index 1963-1981 in Pacific Linguistics, Series D, no.40. Indexed: M.L.A.

400　　　　　　GW　ISSN 0341-3195
PAPIERE ZUR TEXTLINGUISTIK/PAPERS IN TEXTLINGUISTICS. irreg., no.57, 1986. price varies. (Universitaet Bielefeld) Verlag Helmut Buske, Schlueterstr. 14, 2000 Hamburg 13, W. Germany (B.R.D.) Ed.Bd. Indexed: M.L.A.

491.86　　　　　　CS
PEDAGOGICKA FAKULTA V USTI NAD LABEM. SBORNIK: RADA BOHEMISTICKA. (Text in Czech; summaries in English, German, Russian) irreg. 16 Kcs. Statni Pedagogicke Nakladatelstvi, Ostrovni 30, 113 01 Prague 1, Czechoslovakia.

PERITIA. see *HISTORY — History Of Europe*

PHI THETA PAPERS. see *ORIENTAL STUDIES*

410　370　　　　PH　ISSN 0076-3780
PHILIPPINE NORMAL COLLEGE. LANGUAGE STUDY CENTER. OCCASIONAL PAPER. 1967. irreg., no.11, 1974. price varies. Philippine Normal College, Language Study Center, Manila 2801, Philippines. circ. 500. Indexed: Lang.& Lang.Behav.Abstr.

410　　　　　　GW　ISSN 0079-1598
PHILOLOGEN-JAHRBUCH. a. DM.20. Verlag Jahrbuch der Lehrer der Hoeheren Schulen, Richard Wagner Str. 1, 5000 Cologne 10, W. Germany (B.R.D.) Ed. K. Mueller.

439　　　　　　　　NE
PHILOLOGIA FRISICA. (Text in Dutch, English, French, Frisian and German) 1956. triennial. Fryske Akademy, Doelestrjitte 8, 8911 DX Ljouwert/Leeuwarden, Netherlands. TEL 058-131414.

401　　　　　　US　ISSN 0079-1628
PHILOLOGICAL MONOGRAPHS. 1931. irreg., no.31, 1973. (American Philological Association) Scholars Press, Box 1608, Decatur, GA 30031-1608. Ed. Susan Treggiari. circ. 1,000.

400　　　　　　UK　ISSN 0079-1636
PHILOLOGICAL SOCIETY TRANSACTIONS. 1842. a. £23.25($48.65) to individuals; institutions £34.75($72.50) Basil Blackwell Ltd., 108 Cowley Road, Oxford OX4 1JF, England. Ed. J.H.W. Penney. index.

410　　　　　　UK　ISSN 0265-8062
PHONOLOGY YEARBOOK. a. $30 to individuals; institutions $51. Cambridge University Press, Edinburgh Bldg., Shaftesbury Rd., Cambridge CB2 2RU, England. Eds. John Anderson, Colin Ewen.

450　055.1　　　DK　ISSN 0108-9935
PIRANESI; italienske Studier. 1983. a. Kr.75. Museum Tusculanums Forlag, Njalsgade 94, DK-2300 Copenhagen S, Denmark. illus.

420　375.4　　　　US
PITT SERIES IN ENGLISH AS A SECOND LANGUAGE. 1974. irreg. price varies. University of Pittsburgh Press, 127 North Bellefield Ave., Pittsburgh, PA 15260. TEL 412-624-4110. Eds. Lionel Mennsche, Christina Bratt Paulston.

410　　　　　　　　BE
PLURILINGUA. (Text in Dutch, English, French, German) 1983. irreg., latest 1986. 1,200 Fr. Research Centre on Multilingualism, Vrijheidslaan 17, Av. de la Liberte, 1080 Brussels, Belgium (Subscr. to: F. Dummler Verlag, Postfach 1480, D-5200 Bonn, West Germany (B.D.R.)) Ed. Peter Hans Nelde. circ. 500.

410　　　　　　DK　ISSN 0109-2820
POETICA ET ANALYTICA. 1984. irreg. Kr.75. Aarhus Universitet, Romansk Institut, Willemoesgade 15, 8200 Aarhus N, Denmark. Formerly: Matieres (ISSN 0107-4946)

407　　　　　　PL　ISSN 0208-8371
POLITECHNIKA WROCLAWSKA. STUDIUM PRAKTYCZNEJ NAUKI JEZYKOW OBCYCH. PRACE NAUKOWE. MONOGRAFIE. 1980. irreg., no.2, 1981. price varies. Politechnika Wroclawska, Wybrzeze Wyspianskiego 27, 50-370 Wroclaw, Poland (Distr. by: Ars Polona-Ruch, Krakowskie Przedmiescie 7, Warsaw, Poland) Ed. Jerzy Ciekot.

407　　　　　　PL　ISSN 0137-6349
POLITECHNIKA WROCLAWSKA. STUDIUM PRAKTYCZNEJ NAUKI JEZYKOW OBCYCH. PRACE NAUKOWE. STUDIA I MATERIALY. (Text in German, Polish, Russian; summaries in English) 1974. irreg., no.20, 1987. price varies. Politechnika Wroclawska, Wybrzeze Wyspianskiego 27, 50-370 Wroclaw, Poland (Dist. by: Ars Polona-Ruch, Krakowskie Przedmiescie 7, Warsaw, Poland) Ed. Jeny Ciekot. circ. 380.

490　　　　　　PL　ISSN 0137-9712
POLONICA. (Text in Polish; summaries in English) 1975. a. price varies. (Polska Akademia Nauk, Instytut Jezyka Polskiego) Ossolineum, Publishing House of the Polish Academy of Sciences, Rynek 9, 50-106 Wroclaw, Poland. Ed. S. Urbanczyk.

400　　　　　　PL　ISSN 0079-3272
POLSKA AKADEMIA NAUK. ODDZIAL W KRAKOWIE. KOMISJA FILOLOGII KLASYCZNEJ. PRACE. (Text in English, French, German, Latin and Polish; summaries in English and French) 1960. irreg., no.20, 1986. price varies. Ossolineum, Publishing House of the Polish Academy of Sciences, Rynek 9, Wroclaw, Poland (Dist. by: Ars Polona-Ruch, Krakowskie Przedmiescie 7, Warsaw, Poland)

400　　　　　　PL　ISSN 0079-3310
POLSKA AKADEMIA NAUK. ODDZIAL W KRAKOWIE. KOMISJA JEZYKOZNAWSTWA. PRACE. (Text in Polish, Latin and French) 1964. irreg., no.53, 1986. price varies. Ossolineum, Publishing House of the Polish Academy of Sciences, Rynek 9, 50-106 Wroclaw, Poland (Dist. by: Ars Polona-Ruch, Krakowskie Przedmiescie 7, Warsaw, Poland)

400　　　　　　PL　ISSN 0079-3329
POLSKA AKADEMIA NAUK. ODDZIAL W KRAKOWIE. KOMISJA JEZYKOZNAWSTWA. WYDAWNICTWA ZRODLOWE. (Text in Polish; summaries in English) irreg. price varies. Ossolineum, Publishing House of the Polish Academy of Sciences, Rynek 9, 50-106 Wroclaw, Poland (Dist. by: Ars Polona-Ruch, Krakowskie Przedmiescie 7, Warsaw, Poland) Indexed: M.L.A.

410　　　　　　PL　ISSN 0032-3802
POLSKIE TOWARZYSTWO JEZYKOZNAWCZE. BIULETYN. (Text in English, German and Polish) irreg., vol.40, 1986. price varies. Ossolineum, Publishing House of the Polish Academy of Sciences, Rynek 9, Wroclaw, Poland (Dist. by: Ars Polona-Ruch, Krakowskie Przedmiescie 7, Warsaw, Poland) Ed. K. Polanski.

410　　　　　　　　GE
POLYBIOS-LEXICON. (Text in Greek) 1968. irreg., latest 1975. (Akademie der Wissenschaften der DDR) Akademie-Verlag Berlin, Leipziger Str. 3-4, 1086 Berlin, E. Germany (D.D.R.)

410　　　　　　　　GE
POMORANISCHES WOERTERBUCH. (Text in German and Pomoran) 1958. irreg., latest 1983. (Akademie der Wissenschaften der DDR) Akademie-Verlag Berlin, Leipziger Str. 3-4, 1086 Berlin, E. Germany (D.D.R.)

059　　　　　　GW　ISSN 0554-7342
PORTA LINGUARUM ORIENTALIUM. 1965. irreg., vol.17, 1984. price varies. Verlag Otto Harrassowitz, Taunusstr. 14, Postfach 2929, 6200 Wiesbaden 1, W. Germany (B.R.D.) Ed.Bd.

410　　　　　　PL　ISSN 0079-4678
POZNANSKIE TOWARZYSTWO PRZYJACIOL NAUK. KOMISJA JEZYKOZNAWCZA. PRACE. (Text in English, German or Polish; summaries in English, French, German) 1962. irreg., vol.13, 1981. price varies. (Poznanskie Towarzystwo Przyjaciol Nauk) Panstwowe Wydawnictwo Naukowe, Ul.Miodowa 10, Warsaw, Poland (Dist by Ars Polona-Ruch, Krakowskie Przedmiescie 7, Warsaw, Poland) Ed. Jerzy Wislocki. Indexed: Lang. & Lang.Behav.Abstr.

400　　　　　　PL　ISSN 0079-3485
PRACE JEZYKOZNAWCZE. (Text in French and Polish) 1954. irreg., vol.110, 1986. price varies. (Polska Akademia Nauk, Komitet Jezykoznawstwa) Ossolineum, Publishing House of the Polish Academy of Sciences, Rynek 9, 50-106 Wroclaw, Poland (Dist. by: Ars Polona-Ruch, Krakowskie Przedmiescie 7, Warsaw, Poland)

491.8　　　　　　PL　ISSN 0079-4775
PRACE ONOMASTYCZNE. (Text in Polish; summaries in English, French and German) 1955. irreg., vol.30, 1984. price varies. (Polska Akademia Nauk, Komitet Jezykoznawstwa) Ossolineum, Publishing House of the Polish Academy of Sciences, Rynek 9, 50-106 Wroclaw, Poland (Dist. by: Ars Polona-Ruch, Krakowskie Przedmiescie 7, Warsaw, Poland)

410　100　　　　　　NE
PRAGMATICS AND DISCOURSE ANALYSIS. (Text and summaries in English) 1984. irreg. Foris Publications, Postbus 509, 3300 AM Dordrecht, Netherlands. Eds. Frans H. van Eemeren, Rob Grootendorst.

PRAKRIT TEXT SOCIETY. PUBLICATIONS. see *LITERATURE*

491.86　　　　　　CS　ISSN 0079-4902
PRAMENY CESKE A SLOVENSKE LINGVISTIKY. RADA CESKA. 1970. irreg. price varies. (Ceskoslovenska Akademie Ved) Academia, Publishing House of the Czechoslovak Academy of Sciences, Vodickova 40, 112 29 Prague 1, Czechoslovakia. Ed. Josef Vachek.

400　　　　　　　　UK
PRINCETON-CAMBRIDGE SERIES IN CHINESE LINGUISTICS. 1970. irreg., no.6, 1976. $69.50 for latest vol. (Princeton University, Chinese Linguistics Project) Cambridge University Press, Edinburgh Bldg., Shaftesbury Rd., Cambridge CB2 2RU, England (And: 32 E. 57 St., New York, N.Y. 10022)
Formerly: Princeton-Cambridge Studies in Chinese Linguistics (ISSN 0079-5178)

PROFESSION; selected articles from the Bulletins of the Association of Departments of English and the Association of Departments of Foreign Languages. see *LITERATURE*

490　956　　　　GW　ISSN 0079-7715
PUBLICATIONS IN NEAR AND MIDDLE EAST STUDIES. SERIES B. irreg. price varies. Columbia University, Department of Middle East Languages and Cultures, US) Walter de Gruyter & Co., Mouton Publishers, Postfach 110240, D-1000 Berlin 11, W. Gemany (B.R.D.) (U.S. addr.: Mouton Publishers, division of Walter de Gruyter, Inc., 200 Saw Mill River Road, Hawthorne, NY 10532) (Co-sponsor: Middle East Institute)

PUBLICATIONS OF THE NEW SOCIETY OF LETTERS AT LUND. see *ART*

PUBLICATIONS ROMANES ET FRANCAISES. see *LITERATURE*

LINGUISTICS

410 840 US ISSN 0165-8743
PURDUE UNIVERSITY MONOGRAPHS IN ROMANCE LANGUAGE. Short title: P U M R L. 1979. irreg., vol.23, 1986. price varies. John Benjamins Publishing Co., One Buttonwood Sq., Philadelphia, PA 19130. TEL 215-564-6379. Ed.Bd. Indexed: M.L.A.

410 800 IT ISSN 0033-4960
QUADERNI IBERO-AMERICANI; attualita culturale Penisola Iberica America-Latina. (Text in English, Italian, Portuguese and Spanish) 1946. irreg. L.30.000($30) c/o Giuliano Soria, Via Montebello 21, 10124 Turin, Italy. TEL 011 83 27 43. adv. bk. rev. cum.index. circ. 800. (back issues avail.)

410 IT
QUADERNI PATAVINI DI LINGUISTICA. (Text in English, French, German and Italian) 1979. a. L.15000($20) (Universita di Padova, Dipartimento di Linguistica) C.L.E.S.P., Via Seminario 12, 35122 Padua, Italy. circ. 100. (back issues avail.)
Formerly: Rivista di Grammatica Generative.

440 CN ISSN 0079-8770
QUEBEC (PROVINCE) OFFICE DE LA LANGUE FRANCAISE. CAHIERS. 1965. irreg., no.28, 1978. free. Office de la Langue Francaise, 700 Bd. Saint-Cyrille Est, 2e, Quebec, P.Q. G1R 5A9, Canada. TEL 418-643-6954. illus.

440 CN
QUEBEC (PROVINCE) OFFICE DE LA LANGUE FRANCAISE. RAPPORT D'ACTIVITES. a. Office de la Langue Francaise, 700 Bd. St. Cyrille Est., 2e, Quebec, P.Q. G1R 5A9, Canada. TEL 418-643-6954.

QUELLEN UND UNTERSUCHUNGEN ZUR LATEINISCHEN PHILOLOGIE DES MITTELALTERS. see *CLASSICAL STUDIES*

420 SI ISSN 0129-7716
R E L C ANNUAL REPORT. (Text in English) 1968/69. a. S.$11($9) Southeast Asian Ministers of Education Organization, Regional Language Centre, 30 Orange Grove Road, Singapore 1025, Singapore. charts. stat. circ. 400. (back issues avail.)

407 SI ISSN 0129-8844
R E L C OCCASIONAL PAPERS. irreg. S.7($6) Southeast Asian Ministers of Education Organization, Regional Language Centre, 30 Orange Grove Rd., Singapore 1025, Singapore. (back issues avail.)

407 SI
R E L C SEMINAR REPORT. 1970. a. S.$9($8) Southeast Asian Ministers of Education Organization, Regional Language Centre, 30 Orange Grove Rd., Singapore 1025, Singapore. (back issues avail.)

418 CL ISSN 0033-698X
R L A; revista de linguistica teorica y aplicada. (Text in Spanish; occasionally in English & French; abstracts in English) 1963. a. $6. Universidad de Concepcion, Facultad de Educacion, Humanidades y Artes, Casilla 2307, Concepcion, Chile. Ed. Max S. Echeverria. adv. bk. rev. charts. circ. 700. Indexed: Lang.& Lang.Behav.Abstr. Lang.Teach.& Ling.Abstr.

400 CN ISSN 0079-9335
R L S: REGIONAL LANGUAGE STUDIES, NEWFOUNDLAND. 1968. irreg. free. ‡ Memorial University of Newfoundland, Folklore and Language Archive, St. John's, Nfld. A1C 5S7, Canada. TEL 709-737-8000. Ed. William Kirwin. bk. rev. circ. 250. Indexed: M.L.A. Lang.& Lang.Behav.Abstr.

RAJASTHAN UNIVERSITY STUDIES IN ENGLISH. see *LITERATURE*

410 PR
READINGS IN SPANISH-ENGLISH CONTRASTIVE LINGUISTICS. (Text in English, Spanish) 1973. irreg. Inter American University Press, Call Box 5100, San German, PR 00753. Ed. Rose Nash. (reprint service avail. from UMI)

418.02 FR
RECHERCHES EN LINGUISTIQUE ETRANGERE. Variant title: Universite de Besancon. Annales Litteraires. 1973. irreg. (Universite de Besancon, Faculte des Lettres et Sciences Humaines) Societe d'Edition les Belles Lettres, 95 Bd. Raspail, Paris 75006, France.

RECHERCHES GERMANIQUES. see *LITERATURE*

410 FR
RECHERCHES LINQUISTIQUES. 1975. irreg. price varies. Universite de Metz, Centre d'Analyse Syntaxique, Metz, France (Subscr. to: Librairie Klincksieck, 11 rue de Lille, 75007 Paris, France)

REGENSBURGER BEITRAEGE ZUR DEUTSCHEN SPRACH- UND LITERATURWISSENSCHAFT. REIHE A: QUELLEN. see *LITERATURE*

REGENSBURGER BEITRAEGE ZUR DEUTSCHEN SPRACH- UND LITERATURWISSENSCAHFT. REIHE B: UNTERSUCHUNGEN. see *LITERATURE*

400 US ISSN 0270-4390
REVERSE ACRONYMS, INITIALISMS AND ABBREVIATIONS DICTIONARY. 1972. irreg., latest 11th edt., 1986. $205. Gale Research Company, Book Tower, Detroit, MI 48226. TEL 313-961-2242. Eds. Julie Towell, Helen Sheppard.
Formerly (until 1976): Reverse Acronyms and Initialisms Dictionary.

REVIEW (CHARLOTTESVILLE) see *LITERATURE*

410 869 BL
REVISTA BRASILEIRA DE LINGUA E LITERATURA. 1978. a. Sociedade Brasileira de Lingua e Literatura, Av. Epitacio Pessoa 2094/102, 22471 Rio de Janeiro, Brazil. Ed. Leodegario A. de Azevedo Filho. adv. bk. rev. circ. 3,000. Indexed: M.L.A.

REVISTA LETRAS. see *LITERATURE*

469 PO ISSN 0080-2433
REVISTA PORTUGUESA DE FILOLOGIA. 1978. a., (2 nos./vol.) 800 esc. Universidade de Coimbra, Instituto de Estudos Romanicos, Casa do Castelo, Rua da Sofia 47, Coimbra, Portugal. Ed. Manuel de Paiva Boleo. Indexed: M.L.A.

REVISTA SIGNOS DE VALPARAISO; estudios de lengua y literatura. see *LITERATURE*

REVUE DES ETUDES LATINES. see *CLASSICAL STUDIES*

450 IT ISSN 0080-293X
RICERCHE DI STORIA DELLA LINGUA LATINA. 1967. irreg., no.19, 1985. price varies. Edizioni dell' Ateneo S.p.A., Box 7216, 00100 Rome, Italy. Ed. Alfonso Traina. circ. 1,000.

410 800 IT ISSN 0391-4127
RICERCHE SLAVISTICHE. (Text in English, Italian, Russian; summaries in English) 1952. a. price varies. Licosa SpA, Via Lamarmora 45, 50121 Florence, Italy. Eds. Sante Graciotti, Lionello Costantini. circ. 1,000.

410 IT
RIVISTA DI GRAMMATICA GENERATIVA. (Text in English, French and Italian) L.15000($15) C.L.E.S.P., Via Seminario 12, 35122 Padua, Italy. (back issues avail.)

491.8 PL ISSN 0080-3588
ROCZNIK SLAWISTYCZNY. (Text in French, German and Polish) 1908. a. price varies. (Polska Akademia Nauk, Komitet Slowianoznawstwa) Ossolineum, Publishing House of the Polish Academy of Sciences, Rynek 9, 50-106 Wroclaw, Poland (Dist. by: Ars Polona-Ruch, Krakowskie Przedmiescie 7, Warsaw, Poland) Ed. F. Slawski. Indexed: M.L.A.

479.1 BE ISSN 0080-3855
ROMANICA GANDENSIA. 1953. irreg. price varies. ‡ Rijksuniversiteit te Gent, Section de Philologie Romane, Blandijnberg 2, B-9000 Gent, Belgium. Indexed: M.L.A.

430 830 SW ISSN 0080-3863
ROMANICA GOTHOBURGENSIA. (Subseries of Acta Universitatis Gothoburgensis) 1955. irreg., no.27, 1985. price varies; also exchange basis. Acta Universitatis Gothoburgensis, Box 5096, S-402 22 Goeteborg, Sweden (Dist. in U. S., Canada, and Mexico by: Humanities Press, Inc., 171 First Ave., Atlantic Highlands, NJ 07716) Ed. Gunnar von Proschwitz.

400 SZ ISSN 0080-3871
ROMANICA HELVETICA. (Text in German, French, or Italian) 1935. irreg., vol.97, 1984. price varies. (Collegium Romanicium Helvetiorum a Curatoribus Vocis Romanicae) Francke Verlag, Postfach, CH-3000 Berne 26, Switzerland.

410 IT ISSN 0391-1950
ROMANICA NEAPOLITANA. 1969. irreg., no.18, 1986. price varies. Liguori Editore s.r.l., Via Mezzocannone 19, 80134 Naples, Italy. TEL 081/20 6077. Eds. Francesco Bruni, Alberto Varvaro.

410 GW ISSN 0344-676X
ROMANISTISCHE ARBEITSHEFTE. 1973. irreg. price varies. Max Niemeyer Verlag, Postfach 2140, 7400 Tuebingen, W. Germany (B.R.D.) (back issues avail.)

400 GW
ROMANISTISCHE VERSUCHE UND VORARBEITEN. 1956. irreg. Universitaet Bonn, Romanisches Seminar, Am Hof 1, 5300 Bonn 1, W. Germany (B.R.D.) Indexed: M.L.A.

400 870 GW ISSN 0080-3898
ROMANISTISCHES JAHRBUCH. 1947. irreg., vol.35, 1985. price varies. (Universitaet Hamburg, Ibero-Amerikanisches Forschungsinstitut) Walter de Gruyter und Co., Genthiner Str. 13, 1000 Berlin 30, W. Germany (B.R.D.) (U.S. adress: Walter de Gruyter, Inc., 200 Saw Mill Rd., Hawthorne, N.Y. 10532) bk. rev. Indexed: M.L.A. Can.Rev.Comp.Lit.

410 DK ISSN 0106-0821
ROSKILDE UNIVERSITETSCENTER. LINGVISTGRUPPEN. ROLIG-PAPIR. 1974. irreg. free. Roskilde Universitetscenter, Lingvistgruppen, Postboks 260, 4000 Roskilde, Denmark. Eds. Karen Risager, Hartmut Haberland. circ. 350.

491.7 891.7 CS
ROSSICA OLOMUCENSIA. (Text in Czech or Russian; summaries in Russian) 1968. a. free. Univerzita Palackeho, Filozoficka Fakulta, Katedra Rusistiky, Krizkovskeho 10, 771 80 Olomouc, Czechoslovakia. Ed. Jaroslav Reska. circ. 350.

RUSSIAN POETICS IN TRANSLATION. see *LITERATURE*

400 US
S I L PUBLICATIONS IN LINGUISTICS. Abbreviated title: S I L P L Series. 1958. irreg. price varies. Summer Institute of Linguistics, Inc., Academic Publications, 7500 W. Camp Wisdom Rd., Dallas, TX 75236. TEL 214-298-3331. (Co-Sponsor: University of Texas at Arlington) Eds. Virgil Poulter, Desmond C. Derbyshire.
Formerly: S I L Publications on Linguistics and Related Fields (ISSN 0079-7669)

400 900 GE ISSN 0080-5297
SAECHSISCHE AKADEMIE DER WISSENSCHAFTEN, LEIPZIG. PHILOLOGISCH-HISTORISCHE KLASSE. ABHANDLUNGEN. 1896. irreg., vol.71, 1986. price varies. Akademie-Verlag, Leipziger Str. 3-4, 1086 Berlin, E. Germany (D.D.R.)

410 900 GE ISSN 0138-3957
SAECHSISCHE AKADEMIE DER WISSENSCHAFTEN, LEIPZIG. PHILOLOGISCH-HISTORISCHE KLASSE. SITZUNGSBERICHTE. vol.126, 1985. irreg. price varies. Akademie-Verlag, Leipziger Str. 3-4, 1086 Berlin, E. Germany (D.D.R.)

SAGA OCH SED. see *FOLKLORE*

410 GE ISSN 0138-550X
SAMMLUNG AKADEMIE-VERLAG: SPRACHE. 1968. irreg., vol.34, 1985. Akademie-Verlag Berlin, Leipziger Str. 3-4, 1086 Berliner, E. Germany (D.D.R.)

SAMMLUNG GROOS. see *EDUCATION — Higher Education*

430 375.4 GW
SAMMLUNG KURZER GRAMMATIKEN GERMANISCHER DIALEKTE. 1880. irreg. price varies. Max Niemeyer Verlag, Postfach 2140, 74 Tuebingen, W. Germany (B.R.D.) Ed. Hans Eggers. (back issues avail.)

410 FI
SANANJALKA. (Text in Finnish; abstracts in English or German) 1959. a. Suomen Kielen Seura - Finnish Language Society, Fennicum Henrikink 3, 20500 Turku 50, Finland. Ed. Osmo Ikola. adv. bk. rev. abstr. circ. 700. (back issues avail.)
Formerly: Suomen Kielen Seuran Vuosikirja (ISSN 0558-4639)

440 375.4 UR
SBORNIK STATEI PO FRANTSUZSKOI LINGVISTIKE I METODIKE PREPODAVANIYA INOSTRANNOGO YAZIKA V V U ZE. vol.3, 1971. irreg. 0.35 Rub. Moskovskii Gosudarstvennyi Pedagogicheskii Institut Inostrannykh Yazykov, Rostokinskii pr., 13, Moscow B-14, Russian S.F.S.R., U.S.S.R. bibl.
French language study and teaching

491.8 891.8 DK ISSN 0080-6765
SCANDO-SLAVICA. (Text in English, French, German, Italian or Russian) 1955. a. Kr.300. (Association of Scandinavian Slavicists and Baltologists) Munksgaard, 35 Noerre Soegade, DK-1370 Copenhogen K, Denmark. Ed. Gunnar Jacobsson. bk. rev. index. circ. 800. (reprint service avail. from ISI) Indexed: Curr.Cont. M.L.A.

491.8 891.8 DK
SCANDO-SLAVICA. SUPPLEMENTUM. irreg. price varies. (Association of Scandinavian Slavicists and Baltologists) Munksgaard, 35 Noerre Soegade, DK-1370 Copenhagen K, Denmark. (reprint service avail. from ISI)

SCHATZKAMMER; der deutschen Sprache, Dichtung und Geschichte. see *HISTORY — History Of North And South America*

410 GE ISSN 0558-9274
SCHRIFTEN ZUR PHONETIK, SPRACHWISSENSCHAFT UND KOMMUNIKATIONSFORSCHUNG. 1960. irreg., vol.7, 1987. Akademie-Verlag Berlin, Leipziger Str. 3-4, 1086 Berlin, E. Germany (D.D.R.)

400 800 SZ ISSN 0080-7214
SCHWEIZER ANGLISTISCHE ARBEITEN/SWISS STUDIES IN ENGLISH. (Text in German or English) 1935. irreg., no. 112, 1983. price varies. ‡ Francke Verlag, Postfach, CH-3000 Berne 26, Switzerland. Ed.Bd. Indexed: M.L.A.

410 800 SW ISSN 0582-3234
SCRIPTA ISLANDICA. (Text in English and Scandinavian languages) 1949. a. Kr.75. (Islaenska Saellskapet) Almqvist & Wiksell, Co-sponsor: Swedish Council for Research in the Humanities and Social Sciences, P.O. Box 45150, S-104 30 Stockholm, Sweden. index.

400 US ISSN 0277-0598
SELECTA (CORVALLIS) (Text in English, French, German, Italian and Spanish) 1950. a. $16. Pacific Northwest Council on Foreign Languages, c/o Franz Langhammer, Bus.Mgr., Department of Foreign Languages & Literatures, Portland State University, Portland, OR 97207. TEL 503-229-3522. Ed. Robert Aker. circ. 400. (also avail. in microfiche) Indexed: Amer.Bibl.Slavic & E.Eur.Stud. M.L.A.
Former titles: Pacific Northwest Council on Foreign Languages. Proceedings (ISSN 0363-8391) & Pacific Northwest Conference on Foreign Languages. Proceedings (ISSN 0078-7612) Pacific Northwest Conference of Foreign Language Teachers. Proceedings.

439 DK ISSN 0108-822X
SELSKAB FOR NORDISK FILOLOGI. AARSBERETNING. 1934. a. Kr.20. Selskab for Nordisk Filologi, Det Arnamagnaenske Institut, Njalsgde 76, 2300 Copenhagen S, Denmark. circ. 500.

499.992 DK ISSN 0108-3759
SEMAJNA BULTENO; europa semajna esperanto gazeto. (Text in Esperanto) 1976. irreg., (40-45/yr.) Kr.200. Esperanto Domo, Haslevangsvej 30, DK-8210 Aarhus V, Denmark. Ed. Eckhard Bick. adv. bk. rev. illus.
Formerly: Centra Bulteno (ISSN 0108-450X)

410 II
SEMINAR ON DRAVIDIAN LINGUISTICS. PROCEEDINGS. irreg., 5th, 1975. Annamalai University, Department of Linguistics, Annamalainagar P.O., Tamil Nadu, India. Eds. S. Agesthialingom, P.S. Subrahmanyam. bibl.

400 SP
SEMINARIO DE FILOLOGIA VASCA JULIO DE URQUIJO. ANUARIO. (Text in English, French, Spanish) a. 250 ptas. Seminario de Filologia Vasca Julio de Urquijo, Palacio de la Diputacion de Guipuzcoa, San Sebastian (Guipuzcoa), Spain.

492 892 SA ISSN 0256-6044
SEMITICS. (Subseries of University of South Africa. Miscellanea) (Text in English) 1970. irreg. price varies. University of South Africa, Box 392, Pretoria 0001, South Africa. Ed. H.J. Dreyer. bk. rev. circ. 600(controlled) Indexed: M.L.A. Old Test.Abstr.

460 572 914.6 398 MX
SERIE DE VOCABULARIOS Y DICCIONARIOS INDIGENAS "MARIANO SILVA Y ACEVES". 1959. irreg. price varies. Instituto Linguistico de Verano, Apdo. 22067, 14000 Mexico, D.F., Mexico (Subscr. to: Box 8987, C R B, Tucson, AZ 85738-0987) Eds. Doris Bartholmew, Louise Schoenhals. bibl. circ. 1,000. (also avail. in microform; back issues avail.)

410 PE
SERIE LINGUISTICA PERUANA. 1963. irreg., no.22, 1986. price varies. Instituto Linguistico de Verano, Departamento de Estudios Etno-Linguisticos, Casilla 2492, Lima 100, Peru. Ed. Mary Ruth Wise. (also avail. in microfiche; back issues avail.) Indexed: M.L.A.

410 DK ISSN 0106-1992
SERIE OM FREMMEDSPROG. no.20, 1981. irreg. Aalborg Universitetscenter, Institut for Sprog, Kommunikation og Kulturhistorie, Aalborg, Denmark.

410 058 DK ISSN 0105-7405
SERIE OM VIDENSKABSFORSKNING. no.15, 1981. irreg. Aalborg Universitetscenter, Institut for Sprog Kommunikation og Kulturhistorie, Aalborg, Denmark.

SERIES IN ENGLISH LANGUAGE AND LITERATURE. see *LITERATURE*

407 II
SERIES IN INDIAN LANGUAGES AND LINGUISTICS. 1972. irreg. price varies. Bahri Publications Pvt. Ltd., 57 Santnagar (East of Kailash), Box 7023, New Delhi 110065, India. Ed. Ujjal Shingh Bahri.

410 FR ISSN 0223-0100
SIGMA. 1976. a. 60 F. Centre d'Etudes Linguistiques d'Aix, Universite de Provence, 29, avenue Robert Schumann, 13100 Aix-en-Provence, France. Ed. Rene Rivara. adv. bk. rev. circ. 300.

869 FR
SILLAGES. (Text in French and Portuguese; summaries in English) 1972. a. 15 F.($4.50) Universite de Poitiers, Departement d'Etudes Portugaises et Bresiliennes, 95 Avenue du Recteur Pineau, 86022 Poitiers, France. Ed. R.A. Lawton. circ. 750.
Portuguese language study and teaching

490 PL ISSN 0081-0002
SLAVIA OCCIDENTALIS. (Text in Czech, Polish, Russian; summaries in French) 1922. irreg., vol.37, 1980. price varies. (Poznanskie Towarzystwo Przyjaciol Nauk) Panstwowe Wydawnictwo Naukowe, Ul. Miodowa 10, Warsaw, Poland (Dist. by: Ars Polona-Ruch, Krakowskie Przedmiescie 7, Warsaw, Poland) Ed. Wladyslaw Kuraszkiewicz. Indexed: Lang.& Lang.Behav.Abstr.

400 800 SW ISSN 0081-0010
SLAVICA GOTHOBURGENSIS. (Subseries of Acta Universitatis Gothoburgensis) 1958. irreg., no.7, 1980. price varies; also exchange basis. Acta Universitatis Gothoburgensis, Box 5096, S-402 22 Goeteborg, Sweden (Dist. in U.S., Canada, and Mexico by: Humanities Press, Inc., 171 First Ave., Atlantic Highlands, NJ 07716) Ed. Gunnar Jacobsson.

491.8 891.8 SW ISSN 0346-8712
SLAVICA LUNDENSIA. (Text in English, German, Slavic and Swedish; summaries in English and Russian) 1973. a. price varies. Lunds Universitet, Slaviska Institutionen, Finngatan 12, S-223 62 Lund, Sweden. Ed. Lubomir Durovic. circ. 400. (also avail. in microfilm from UMI; back issues avail.)

491 DK ISSN 0106-1313
SLAVICA OTHINIENSIA. (Text in English, German or Russian) 1978. a. free. Odense Universitet, Slaviske Institut, Odense, Denmark. Ed.Bd. bk. rev.

SLAVISTISCHE BEITRAEGE. see *LITERATURE*

491.8 GW ISSN 0583-5445
SLAVISTISCHE STUDIENBUECHER; neue Folge. 1984. irreg., vol.2, 1984. price varies. Verlag Otto Harrassowitz, Taunusstr. 14, Postfach 2929, D-6200 Wiesbaden 1, W. Germany (B.R.D.) Ed. Bd.

490 UR
SLAVYANSKAYA FILOLOGIYA. 1964. irreg. 0.72 Rub. Leningradskii Universitet, Universitetskaya nab. 7/9, Leningrad B-164, Russian S.F.S.R., U.S.S.R. bibl.

SLOVACI V ZAHRANICI. see *HISTORY — History Of Europe*

491.79 CN ISSN 0583-6263
SLOVO NA STOROZHI/WORD ON GUARD. 1964. a. Can.$6($6) Ukrainian Language Association, 911 Carling Ave., Ottawa, Ont., Canada. TEL 613-225-4447. Ed. J.B. Rudnyckyj. adv. bk. rev. circ. 500. (back issues avail.) Indexed: M.L.A.

SOCIEDAD DE ESTUDIOS VASCOS. CUADERNOS DE SECCION. HIZKUNTZA ETA LITERATURA. see *LITERATURE*

490 GW ISSN 0340-6423
SOCIETAS URALO-ALTAICA. VEROEFFENTLICHUNGEN. 1969. irreg., vol.21, 1986. price varies. Verlag Otto Harrassowitz, Taunusstr. 14, Postfach 2929, 6200 Wiesbaden 1, W. Germany (B.R.D.) Eds. A. V. Gabain, W. Veenker.

410 301.2 FR ISSN 0249-7069
SOCIETE D'ETUDES LINGUISTIQUES ET ANTHROPOLOGIQUES DE FRANCE. NUMEROS SPECIAUX. 1971. irreg. price varies. Societe d'Etudes Linguistiques et Anthropologiques de France (SELAF), 5 rue de Marseille, 75010 Paris, France.

410 FI
SOCIETE FINNO-OUGRIENNE. MEMOIRES; suomalais-ugrilaisen seuran toimituksia. (Text in English, Finnish, German) 1890. irreg. price varies. Suomalais-Ugrilainen Seura, Snellmaninkatu 9-11, 00170 Helsinki 17, Finland. Ed. Juha Janhunen. circ. 800. (back issues avail.)

400 FI
SOCIETE NEOPHILOLOGIQUE DE HELSINKI. MEMOIRES. (Text in English, French, German) 1893. irreg. price varies. Modern Language Society of Helsinki, Hallituskatu 11-13, 00100 Helsinki, Finland. Ed.Bd. cum.index. circ. 500. (back issues avail.)

SOCIETY FOR SLOVENE STUDIES. DOCUMENTATION SERIES. see *HISTORY — History Of Europe*

410 US
SOCIETY OF FEDERAL LINGUISTS. NEWSLETTER. 1946. irreg., approx. 9/yr. membership. Society of Federal Linguists, Inc., Box 7765, Washington, DC 20044. Ed. E.E. Larson. bk. rev. circ. 150 (controlled)

410 572 FR
SOCIOLINGUISTIQUE; systemes de langues et interactions sociales et culturelles. 1984. irreg. price varies. Societe d'Etudes Linguistiques et Anthropologiques de France (SELAF), 5 rue de Marseille, 75010 Paris, France. Ed. Jean Pierre Caprile. adv. bk. rev. circ. 500.

410 PL
SOCJOLINGWISTYKA. (Text in Polish; summaries in English, Russian) 1977. irreg. Uniwersytet Slaski w Katowicach, Ul. Bankowa 14, 40-007 Katowice, Poland.

410 BU
SOFIISKI UNIVERSITET. FAKULTET PO KLASICESKI I NOVI FILOLOGII. GODISNIK/ UNIVERSITE DE SOFIA. FACULTE DES LETTRES CLASSIQUES ET MODERNES. ANNUAIRE. (Text in various languages) irreg., vol.71, 1976. price varies. Publishing House of the Bulgarian Academy of Sciences, Acad. G. Bonchev St., Bldg. 6, 1113 Sofia, Bulgaria. bibl. circ. 550.
Formerly: Sofiiski Universitet. Fakultet po Zapadni Filologii. Godisnik (ISSN 0584-0252)

491 BU ISSN 0081-1831
SOFIISKI UNIVERSITET. FAKULTET PO SLAVIANSKA FILOLOGIIA. GODISHNIK. (Text in various languages) irreg., vol.63, 1970. price varies. Publishing House of the Bulgarian Academy of Sciences, Acad. G. Bonchev St., Bldg. 6, 1113 Sofia, Bulgaria. Ed. I. Duridanov. bibl. circ. 550.

410 CH
SOOCHOW JOURNAL OF FOREIGN LANGUAGES AND LITERATURES. (Text in Chinese, English, German, and Japanese) 1985. a. $12 per no. Soochow University, Wai Shuang Hsi, Shih Lin, Taipei, Taiwan, Republic of China.

SPANISH STUDIES; modern literature, history and politics. see *LITERATURE*

460 375.4 UK
SPANISH TEXTS. 1957. irreg. price varies. Manchester University Press, Oxford Rd., Manchester M13 9PL, England. TEL 061-273-5539. Ed. Herbert Ramsden.

491.7 890 GW ISSN 0170-1320
SPECIMINA PHILOLOGIAE SLAVICAE. (Text in English, German, Russian and other Slavic languages) 1972. irreg. price varies. Verlag Otto Sagner, Postfach 34 01 08, Hessstr. 39/41, D-8000 Munich 34, W. Germany (B.R.D.) Eds. Olexa Horbatsch, Gerd Freihof. circ. 100. (back issues avail.)

440 FR
SPICAE; cahiers de l'atelier Vincent de Beauvais. 1978. irreg. (Universite de Nancy II, Centre de Recherches et d'Applications Linguistiques) Editions du C N R S, 295 rue St. Jacques, 75005 Paris, France. (Co-sponsor: Institut de Recherche et d'Histoire des Textes) Eds. Helene Nais, Jean Schneider.

400 SZ ISSN 0081-3826
SPRACHE UND DICHTUNG. NEUE FOLGE. 1956. irreg., vol.36, 1985. price varies. Paul Haupt AG, Falkenplatz 14, 3001 Berne, Switzerland. Ed.Bd. Indexed: M.L.A.

430 GW ISSN 0170-5946
SPRACHE UND GESCHICHTE IN AFRIKA. Short title: S U G I A. (Text in English, French, German) 1979. irreg., approx. a. price varies. (Universitaet Bayreuth, Koeln, Institut fuer Afrikanistik) Verlag Helmut Buske, Schlueterstr. 14, 2000 Hamburg 13, W. Germany (B.R.D.)

400 943 GE ISSN 0138-5852
SPRACHE UND GESELLSCHAFT. 1974. irreg., vol.19, 1984. price varies. (Akademie der Wissenschaften der DDR, Zentralinstitut fuer Sprachwissenschaft) Akademie-Verlag, Leipziger Str. 3-4, 1086 Berlin, E. Germany (D.D.R.) adv.
Formerly: Akademie der Wissenschaften, Berlin. Zentralinstitut fuer Sprachwissenschaft. Schriften (ISSN 0065-5260)

410 US ISSN 0172-620X
SPRINGER SERIES IN LANGUAGE AND COMMUNICATION. 1978. irreg., vol.20, 1986. price varies. Springer-Verlag, 175 Fifth Ave., New York, NY 10010 TEL 212-460-1500. (Also Berlin, Heidelberg, Tokyo and Vienna) Ed. W.J.M. Levelt. (reprint service avail. from ISI)

410 DK
SPROGFORENINGENS ALMANAK. 1984. a. Kr.38. (Sprogforeningen) Dy-Po Bogforlag, Soenderborg, Denmark (Orders to: Boghendleres Kommissionsanstalt, Siljangade 6, 2300 Copenhagen S, Denmark)

400 891.1 II ISSN 0081-3915
SRI VENKATESWARA UNIVERSITY. DEPARTMENT OF SANSKRIT. SYMPOSIUM. (Text in Sanskrit and English) 1962. irreg., no.4, 1967. Rs.4. Sri Venkateswara University, Department of Sanskrit, Tirupati, Andhra Pradesh, India. Ed. E.R. Sreekrishna Sarma.

SRI VENKATESWARA UNIVERSITY. ORIENTAL JOURNAL. see *HISTORY — History Of Asia*

400 YU ISSN 0081-3958
SRPSKA AKADEMIJA NAUKA I UMETNOSTI. ODELJENJE JEZIKA I KNJIZEVNOSTI. GLAS. (Text in Serbo-Croatian; summaries in French, English, German or Russian) 1951, N.S. irreg. price varies. Srpska Akademija Nauka i Umetnosti, Knez Mihailova 35, 11001 Belgrade, Yugoslavia (Dist. by: Prosveta, Terazije 16, Belgrade, Yugoslavia) circ. 1,000. Indexed: Hist.Abstr. Amer.Hist.& Life.

SRPSKA AKADEMIJA NAUKA I UMETNOSTI. ODELJENJE JEZIKA I KNJIZEVNOSTI. POSEBNA IZDANJA. see *LITERATURE*

420 SW
STOCKHOLM STUDIES IN ENGLISH. (Subseries of Acta Universitatis Stockholmiensis) (Text in English) 1937. irreg., vol.49, 1978. price varies. (Stockholms Universitet) Almqvist & Wiksell International, Box 62, S-101 20 Stockholm, Sweden. Eds. Alarik Rynell, Lennart A. Bjork. (back issues avail.) Indexed: M.L.A.

410 800 UK ISSN 0261-099X
STRATHCLYDE MODERN LANGUAGE STUDIES. 1981. a. £2. University of Strathclyde, Department of Modern Languages, Livingstone Tower, Glasgow G1 1XH, Scotland. Eds. D. Johnston, G. Martin. cum.index. circ. 200. (back issues avail.)

410 IT ISSN 0391-1942
STRUMENTI LINGUISTICI. 1975. irreg., no.15, 1986. price varies. Liguori Editore s.r.l., Via Mezzocannone 19, 80134 Naples, Italy. TEL 081/20 6077. Ed. Gianfranco Folena.

491.9 891.9 IT ISSN 0081-6116
STUDI ALBANESI. STUDI E TESTI. 1967. irreg., no.6, 1986. price varies. (Universita degli Studi di Roma, Istituto Studi Albanesi) Casa Editrice Leo S. Olschki, Casella Postale 66, 50100 Florence, Italy. Ed. Ernesto Koliqi. circ. 1,000.

410 IT ISSN 0085-6827
STUDI E SAGGI LINGUISTICI; supplemento alla rivista l'Italia Dialettale. (Text in Italian; summaries in English) 1961. a. L.10000. (Universita degli Studi di Pisa, Istituto di Glottologia) Giardini Editori e Stampatori, Via Santa Bibbiana 28, Pisa, Italy. Ed. Tristano Bolelli. index. circ. 350. Indexed: M.L.A.

450 IT
STUDI LINGUISTICI SALENTINI.* 1965. Associazione Linguistica Salentina, Villa Sebaste, Via per Campi, 73051, Novoli (Lecce), Italy. illus.

400 PL ISSN 0081-6272
STUDIA ANGLICA POSNANIENSIA; international review of English Studies. (Text in English) 1969. irreg., vol.8, 1976. price varies. Adam Mickiewicz University Press, Marchlewskiego 128, 61-874 Poznan, Poland. Ed. Jacek Fisiak. adv. bk. rev. circ. 1,300. Indexed: M.L.A. Lang.& Lang.Behav.Abstr.

420 SW ISSN 0562-2719
STUDIA ANGLISTICA UPSALIENSES. (Subseries of Acta Universitatis Upsaliensis) 1963. irreg. price varies. Almqvist & Wiksell International, Box 62, S-101 20 Stockholm, Sweden. Eds. Johannes Soderlind, Olov Fryckstedt, Gunnar Sorelius. (back issues avail.) Indexed: Abstr.Engl.Stud.

491.6 UK ISSN 0081-6353
STUDIA CELTICA. (Text in English and Welsh; occasionally in French and German) 1966. biennial. £20 per double vol. (University of Wales, Board of Celtic Studies) University of Wales Press, 6 Gwennith St., Cathays, Cardiff CF2 4YD, Wales. Ed. J.E. Caerwyn Williams. adv. bk. rev. circ. 200. (reprint service avail. from UMI) Indexed: M.L.A. Br.Archaeol.Abstr.

STUDIA FENNICA; review of finnish linguistics and ethnology. see *ANTHROPOLOGY*

439 BE ISSN 0081-6442
STUDIA GERMANICA GANDENSIA. (Text in Dutch, English, German) 1959. a. 300 Fr. Rijksuniversiteit te Ghent, Faculteit der Letteren en Wijsbeegerte, Blandijnberg 2, B-9000 Ghent, Belgium. Ed. G.A.R. De Smet. index. circ. 150. Indexed: M.L.A.

430 GE ISSN 0081-6469
STUDIA GRAMMATICA. 1962. irreg., vol.24, 1985. price varies. (Akademie der Wissenschaften der DDR, Zentralinstitut fuer Sprachwissenschaft) Akademie-Verlag, Leipziger Str. 3-4, 1086 Berlin, E. Germany (D.D.R.) Indexed: M.L.A. Lang.& Lang.Behav.Abstr.

400 IT
STUDIA HISTORICA ET PHILOGIA: SECTIO ROMANICA. 1974. irreg. L.10000. Licosa S.p.A., Via Lamarmora 45, 50121 Florence, Italy. Ed. R. Picchio. circ. 2,000.

400 IT
STUDIA HISTORICA ET PHILOGICA: SECTIO SLAVICA. irreg. L.36000. Licosa S.p.A., Via Lamarmora 45, 50121 Florence, Italy.

400 IT
STUDIA HISTORICA ET PHILOGICA: SECTIO SLAVO-ROMANICA. irreg. L.60000. Licosa S.p.A., Via Lamarmora 45, 50121 Florence, Italy. Ed. Riccardo Picchio.

407 US
STUDIA LINGUISTICA ET PHILOLOGICA. 1975. irreg. $20 per vol. Anma Libri, Box 876, Saratoga, CA 95070. TEL 415-497-4186. Indexed: M.L.A.

410 SW ISSN 0081-6809
STUDIA PHILOLOGIAE SCANDINAVICAE UPSALIENSIA. (Subseries of Acta Universitatis Upsaliensis) 1961. irreg., vol.15, 1979. price varies; exchange avail. (Uppsala Universitet) Almqvist & Wiksell International, 26 Gamla Brogatan, S-101 20 Stockholm, Sweden. Ed.Bd.

400 FI ISSN 0585-5462
STUDIA PHILOLOGICA JYVASKYLAENSIA. (Text in English, Finnish, French, German and Swedish) 1966. irreg. price varies. Jyvaskylan Yliopisto - University of Jyvaskyla, Seminaarinkatu 15, 40100 Jyvaskyla 10, Finland. Ed. Raija Markkanen. circ. 450.

400 JA ISSN 0300-1067
STUDIA PHONOLOGICA/ONSEI KAGAKU KENKYU. (Text in English, German or Japanese) 1961. annual. Kyoto University, Institution for Phonetic Sciences - Kyoto Daigaku Onsei Kagaku Sogo Kenkyu Bukai, Nihonmatsucho, Yoshida, Sakyo-ku, Kyoto 606, Japan. Ed. Toshiyuki Sakai. illus. circ. 1,000. Indexed: Lang.& Lang.Behav.Abstr.

400 PL ISSN 0137-4370
STUDIA POLONISTYCZNE. (Text in Polish; summaries in English, French, German or Russian) 1973. irreg., vol.4, 1977. price varies. Adam Mickiewicz University Press, Marchlewskiego 128, 61-874 Poznan, Poland. Eds. Wladyslaw Kuraszkiewicz, Tadeusz Witczak. Indexed: Lang.& Lang.Behav.Abstr.

410 SW ISSN 0562-3022
STUDIA ROMANICA UPSALIENSIA. (Text in French, Italian and Spanish; summaries in English or French) 1961. irreg. (Uppsala University, Acta Universitatis Upsaliensis) Almqvist & Wiksell International, Box 256, 751 05 Uppsala, Sweden. Ed. Lennart Carlsson. circ. 600. (back issues avail.) Indexed: M.L.A.

410 PL ISSN 0137-6608
STUDIA SEMIOTYCZNE. a. price varies. (Polskie Towarzystwo Semiotyczne) Ossolineum, Publishing House of the Polish Academy of Sciences, Rynek 9, Wroclaw, Poland (Dist. by: Ars Polona-Ruch, Krakowskie Przedmiescie 7, Warsaw, Poland) Ed. Jerzy Pelc.

400 080 NE ISSN 0081-6957
STUDIA THEODISCA. (Summaries occasionally in English, French and German) 1965. irreg., no.13, 1974. price varies. Van Gorcum, Box 43, 9400 AA Assen, Netherlands.

400 RM ISSN 0039-3444
STUDIA UNIVERSITATIS "BABES-BOLYAI".
PHILOLOGIA. (Text in Romanian; summaries in English, French, German, Italian, Russian) 1956. a. exchange basis. Universitatea "Babes Bolyai", Biblioteca Centrala Universitara, Str. Clinicilor Nr. 2, Cluj-Napoca, Rumania. bk. rev. charts. illus. index.

410 AU ISSN 0259-0808
STUDIA URALICA. 1978. irreg., no.3, 1984. price varies. (Universitaet Wien, Institut fuer Finno-Ugristik) Verband der Wissenschaftlichen Gesellschaften Oesterreichs, Lindengasse 37, A-1070 Vienna, Austria.

494 SW ISSN 0081-7015
STUDIA URALICA ET ALTAICA UPSALIENSIA. (Subseries of Acta Universitatis Upsaliensis) (Text in English and Swedish) 1964. irreg., vol.11, 1976. price varies. (Uppsala Universitet) Almqvist & Wiksell International, Box 62, S-101 20 Stockholm, Sweden. Ed. Bo Wickman. bibl. charts.

491.8 PL ISSN 0081-7090
STUDIA Z FILOLOGII POLSKIEJ I SLOWIANSKIEJ. (Text in Polish; papers and summaries in Slavonic languages) 1955. irreg., vol.22, 1984. price varies. (Polska Akademia Nauk, Komitet Slowianoznawstwa) Panstwowe Wydawnictwo Naukowe, Miodowa 10, 00-251 Warsaw, Poland (Dist. by: Ars Polona, Krakowskie Przedmiescie 7, 00-068 Warsaw, Poland) Ed. J. Siatkowski. circ. 500.

490 GW ISSN 0585-5853
STUDIEN ZU DEN BOGAZKOEY-TEXTEN. 1965. irreg., vol.30, 1985. price varies. (Akademie der Wissenschaften und der Literatur, Kommission fuer den Alten Orient) Verlag Otto Harrassowitz, Taunusstr. 14, Postfach 2929, 6200 Wiesbaden, W. Germany (B.R.D.) Indexed: M.L.A.

430 GW
STUDIEN ZUM KLEINEN DEUTSCHEN SPRACHATLAS. 1982. irreg. Max Niemeyer Verlag, Pfrondorfer Str. 4, D-7400 Tuebingen, W. Germany (B.R.D.) Eds. Werner H. Veith, Wolfgang Putschke. circ. 500. (back issues avail.)

410 GW ISSN 0081-7244
STUDIEN ZUR ENGLISCHEN PHILOLOGIE, NEUE FOLGE. (Text in English or German) 1963. irreg., no.25, 1986. price varies. Max Niemeyer Verlag, Pfrondorfer Str. 4, 7400 Tuebingen, W. Germany (B.R.D.) Ed.Bd. (back issues avail.) Indexed: M.L.A.

STUDIEN ZUR INDOLOGIE UND IRANISTIK. see HISTORY — History Of Asia

400 SW
STUDIER I MODERN SPRAAKVETENSKAP/ STOCKHOLM STUDIES IN MODERN PHILOLOGY. (Text in English, French and German) 1898. triennial. (Humanistisk-Samhaellsvetenskapliga Forskning Raadet) Almqvist & Wiksell International, Box 45150, 104 30 Stockholm, Sweden. Ed.Bd.

430 375.4 GW ISSN 0171-6794
STUDIES IN DESCRIPTIVE LINGUISTICS. (Text in English; summaries in French, German) 1978. irreg. price varies. Julius Groos Verlag, Hertzstr. 6, Postfach 102423, D-6900 Heidelberg 1, W. Germany (B.R.D.) Ed. D. Nehls. circ. 1,000. (back issues avail.)

485 475 NE
STUDIES IN GREEK AND LATIN LINGUISTICS. 1980. irreg. price varies. Van Gorcum, Box 43, 9400 AA Assen, Netherlands.

411 II
STUDIES IN INDIAN EPIGRAPHY/BHARATIYA PURABHILEKHA PATRIKA. 1975. a. Epigraphical Society of India, University Buildings, Mysore 570005, India. Eds. Z.A. Desai, Ajay Mitra Shastri. illus.

410 II
STUDIES IN INDIAN PLACE NAMES/ BHARATIYA STHALANAMA PATRIKA. (Text in English) 1980. a. (Place Names Society of India) Geetha Book House, K.R. Circle, Mysore 570 001, India. Ed. Mandhav N. Katti.

400 US ISSN 0586-6928
STUDIES IN LANGUAGE AND LINGUISTICS. 1970. irreg. price varies. Texas Western Press, University of Texas at El Paso, El Paso, TX 79968. TEL 915-747-5688. Ed. Dale L. Walker.

410 800 US ISSN 0165-7763
STUDIES IN LANGUAGE COMPANION SERIES. Short title: S L C S. 1978. irreg., vol.14, 1986. price varies. John Benjamins Publishing Co., One Buttonwood Sq., Philadelphia, PA 19130. TEL 215-564-6379. Eds. John W.M. Verhaar, Werner Abraham. Indexed: M.L.A. Math.R.

410 370 UK ISSN 0144-3127
STUDIES IN LANGUAGE DISABILITY AND REMEDIATION. 1976. irreg. price varies. Edward Arnold (Publishers) Ltd., 41 Bedford Square, London WC1B 3DQ, England.

410 US
STUDIES IN LANGUAGE LEARNING; an interdisciplinary review of language acquistion, language pedagogy, stylistics, and language planning. 1975. irreg. (1-2/yr.) price varies. University of Illinois at Urbana-Champaign, Language Learning Laboratory, G70 Foreign Languages Bldg., 707 S. Mathews, Urbana, IL 61801. TEL 217-333-9776. Ed. Bd. bk. rev. circ. 300. (also avail. in microfiche) Indexed: Sociol.Abstr. ERIC.

STUDIES IN LINGUISTICS AND PHILOSOPHY. see PSYCHOLOGY

417 480 UK ISSN 0081-8275
STUDIES IN MYCENAEAN INSCRIPTIONS AND DIALECT. 1956. biennial. £5($7) British Association for Mycenaean Studies, Laundress Lane, Faculty Rooms, Cambridge CB2 1SD, England. Ed. John T. Killen. bk. rev. circ. 250.

410 NE
STUDIES IN NATURAL LANGUAGE AND LINGUISTIC THEORY. (Text in English) 1985. irreg. price varies. D. Reidel Publishing Company, P.O. Box 17, 3300 AA Dordrecht, Netherlands (And 190 Old Derbr St., Hingham, MA 02043) Eds. Frank Heny, Joan Maling.

410 890 II
STUDIES IN SEMIOTICS AND LITERATURE. 1979. irreg. price varies. Bahri Publications Pvt. Ltd., 57 Santnagar (East of Kailash), Box 7023, New Delhi 110065, India. Ed. Ujjal Singh Bahri.

492 NE ISSN 0081-8461
STUDIES IN SEMITIC LANGUAGES AND LINGUISTICS. 1967. irreg., vol.13, 1985. price varies. E. J. Brill, P.O. Box 9000, 2300 PA Leiden, Netherlands.

491 410 NE ISSN 0169-0124
STUDIES IN SLAVIC AND GENERAL LINGUISTICS. (Text in English, German, Polish or Russian) 1980. irreg. price varies. Editions Rodopi, Keizersgracht 302-304, 1016 EX Amsterdam, Netherlands. Ed.Bd. adv. circ. 500. Indexed: M.L.A.

491.7 UK ISSN 0081-8631
STUDIES IN THE MODERN RUSSIAN LANGUAGE. 1967. irreg., no.8, 1970. $64.50 for latest vol. Cambridge University Press, Edinburgh Bldg., Shaftesbury Rd., Cambridge CB2 2RU, England (and 32 E. 57 St., New York NY 10022) Ed. D. Ward.

410 150 NE
STUDIES IN THEORETICAL PSYCHOLINGUISTICS. 1983. irreg. price varies. D. Reidel Publishing Co., Box 17, 3300 AA Dordrecht, Netherlands. Eds. T. Roeper, K. Wexler.

SUGIA; Sprache und Geschichte in Afrika. see HISTORY — History Of Africa

418 US
SUMMER INSTITUTE OF LINGUISTICS. LANGUAGE DATA. AFRICAN SERIES. 1971. irreg., no.21, 1981. price varies. Summer Institute of Linguistics, Inc., Academic Publications, 7500 W. Camp Wisdom Rd., Dallas, TX 75236. TEL 214-298-3331. Ed. Pamela Bendor-Samuel. (also avail. in microfiche)

410 US
SUMMER INSTITUTE OF LINGUISTICS. LANGUAGE DATA. AMERINDIAN SERIES. 1973. irreg., no.7, 1979. price varies. Summer Institute of Linguistics, Inc., Academic Publications, 7500 W. Camp Wisdom Rd., Dallas, TX 75236. TEL 214-298-3331. Ed. Dr. Viola Waterhouse. bibl. charts. (also avail. in microfiche)

418 US
SUMMER INSTITUTE OF LINGUISTICS. LANGUAGE DATA. ASIA-PACIFIC SERIES. 1971. irreg., no.13, 1981. price varies. Summer Institute of Linguistics, Inc., Academic Publications, 7500 W. Camp Wisdom Rd., Dallas, TX 75236. TEL 214-298-3331. Eds. Phyllis Healey, David Thomas. (also avail. in microfiche)

498 BL
SUMMER INSTITUTE OF LINGUISTICS. SERIE LINGUISTICA. 1974. irreg. price varies. Summer Institute of Linguistics, Departamento de Estudos Tecnicos, SAI/NO Lote D, Bloco 3, 70770 Brasilia DF, Brazil. circ. 300.

410 US
SUMMER INSTITUTE OF LINGUISTICS. UNIVERSITY OF NORTH DAKOTA SESSION. WORK PAPERS. vol.21, 1977. a. price varies. Academic Publications (Dallas), 7500 W. Camp Wisdom Rd., Dallas, TX 75236 TEL 214-298-3331. (Subscr. address: c/o Dallas Center Bookstore, International Linguistics Center, 7500 West Camp Wisdom Rd., Dallas TX 75236) Ed. Desmond C. Derbyshire. (also avail. in microfiche)

410 572 FI ISSN 0355-0214
SUOMALAIS-UGRILAISEN SEURAN. AIKAKAUSKIRJA/SOCIETE FINNO-OUGRIENNE. JOURNAL. (Text in English, Finnish, French and Russian) 1886. a. Suomalais-Ugrilainen Seura, Snellmaninkatu 9-11, 00170 Helsinki 17, Finland. circ. 600.

SVENSKA LITTERATURSAELLSKAPET I FINLAND. SKRIFTER. see HISTORY

420 375.4 AT
SYDNEY STUDIES IN ENGLISH. (Text in English) 1975. a. $6.50. English Association, Sydney Branch, University of Sydney, Department of English, Sydney, N.S.W. 2006, Australia. Eds. G.A. Wilkes, A.P. Riemer. (back issues avail.)

410 US ISSN 0092-4563
SYNTAX AND SEMANTICS. 1972. irreg., vol.18, 1986. Academic Press, Inc., Orlando, FL 32887. TEL 305-345-2000. Ed. John Kimball. Indexed: M.L.A. ASCA.

410 FR ISSN 0066-9776
T.A. DOCUMENTS. (Traduction Automatique) 1966. irreg. price varies. Editions Klincksieck, 11 rue de Lille, 75005 Paris, France (Dist. by: University of Alabama Press, Drawer 2877, University, AL 35486)

400 820 US
T S E: TULANE STUDIES IN ENGLISH. 1949. a. $28. Tulane University, Department of English, New Orleans, LA 70118. TEL 504-865-5160. Ed. Huling E. Ussery. circ. 2,000. Indexed: Abstr.Engl.Stud. Curr.Cont. M.L.A. Arts & Hum.Cit.Ind.
Formerly: Tulane Studies in English (ISSN 0082-6758)

410 NZ ISSN 0494-8440
TE REO; journal of the Linguistic Society of New Zealand. (Text in English, French, Italian) 1958. a. NZ.$18 to individuals; institutions NZ$ 28. Linguistic Society of New Zealand, c/o University of Auckland, Private Bag, Auckland 1, New Zealand. Ed. J.C. Corne. adv. bk. rev. bibl. circ. 350. Indexed: Bull.Signal. M.L.A. E.I.

439.5 SW ISSN 0081-573X
TEKNISKA NOMENKLATURCENTRALEN PUBLIKATIONER. 1941. irreg., no.83, 1985. price varies. Tekniska Nomenklaturcentralen - Swedish Centre for Technical Terminology, Box 2303, S-103 17 Stockholm, Sweden (Dist. by: Svensk Byggtjaenst, AB, Box 7853,10399 Stockholm)

490 II
TELUGU AKADEMI LANGUAGE MONOGRAPH SERIES. 1974. irreg. Rs.16.25($8) Telugu Akademi, Hyderabad 500029, India.

LINGUISTICS

808.5 US ISSN 0363-8782
TEXAS SPEECH COMMUNICATION JOURNAL. 1976. a. $5. Texas Speech Communication Association, c/o Ann Harrell, Executive Secretary, Language Arts Department, McLennon Community College, Waco, TX 76708. adv. circ. 550.

TOHOKU GAKUIN UNIVERSITY REVIEW; essays and studies in English language and literature. see *LITERATURE*

410 JA ISSN 0389-3081
TOKAI UNIVERSITY. FOREIGN LANGUAGE CENTER. BULLETIN. (Text in Japanese; summaries in English) 1980. a., latest no.6, 1986. free. Tokai University, Foreign Language Center, 1117 Kitakaname, Hiratsuka-ku, Kanagawa-ken, Japan. circ. 700.

410 US
TRANSLATION SERVICES DIRECTORY. 1965. irreg., 6th, 1986. $30 to non-members; members $25. American Translators Association, 109 Croton Ave., Ossining, NY 10562 TEL 914-941-1500. (Distr. by: Learned Information, Inc., 143 Old Marlton Pike, Medford, NJ 08055)
Formerly: A T A Professional Services Directory (ISSN 0567-4263)

400 BE ISSN 0082-6049
TRAVAUX DE LINGUISTIQUE. (Text in French) 1969. irreg. price varies. ‡ Rijksuniversiteit te Gent, Dienst voor Franse Linguistiek - State University of Ghent, Department of French Linguistics, Blandijnberg 2, B-9000 Gent, Belgium. bk. rev. Indexed: Lang.& Lang.Behav.Abstr.

410 FR
TRAVAUX DE LINGUISTIQUE JAPONAISE. 1974. irreg. Universite de Paris VII, Groupe de Linguistique Japonaise, 2 Place Jussieu, 75005 Paris, France. Ed. Andre Wlodarczyk.
Formerly: Universite de Paris VII. Groupe de Linguistique Japonaise. Travaux (ISSN 0339-8811)

410 GW
TRENDS IN LINGUISTICS. 1976. irreg. price varies. Walter de Gruyter & Co., Mouton Publishers, Postfach 110240, D-1000 Berlin 11, W. Germany (B.R.D.) (U.S. addr.: Mouton Publishers, division of Walter de Gruyter, Inc., 200 Saw Mill River Road, Hawthorne, NY 10532) Ed. W. Winter.

410 GW
TUDUV-STUDIE. REIHE SPRACH- UND LITERATURWISSENSCHAFTEN. 1975. irreg. price varies. Tuduv Verlagsgesellschaft mbH, Gabelsbergerstr. 15, 8000 Munich 2, W. Germany (B.R.D.)

400 BE ISSN 0082-6847
TURCICA; REVUE D'ETUDES TURQUES. (Text in English, French and German) 1969. a. price varies. Editions Peeters s.p.r.l., Bondgenotenlaan 153, 2B-3000 Louvain, Belgium. Ed. I. Melikoff. bk. rev.

TURUN YLIOPISTO. KLASSILLISEN FILOLOGIAN LAITOS. OPERA EX INSTITUTO PHILOLOGIAE CLASSICAE UNIVERSITATIS TURKUENSIS EDITA. see *CLASSICAL STUDIES*

410 UY ISSN 0250-6548
UNIVERSIDAD DE LA REPUBLICA. FACULTAD DE HUMANIDADES Y CIENCIAS. REVISTA. SERIE LINGUISTICA. N.S. 1979. irreg. exchange basis. Universidad de la Republica, Facultad de Humanidades y Ciencias, Seccion Revista, Tristan Narvaja 1674, Montevideo, Uruguay. Dir. Beatriz Martinez Osorio.
Supersedes in part: Universidad de la Republica. Facultad de Humanidades y Ciencias. Revista.

410 860 SP ISSN 0210-4911
UNIVERSIDAD DE MURCIA. ESTUDIOS ROMANICOS. 1978. irreg., vol.3, 1986. $700. Universidad de Murcia, Secretariado de Publicaciones e Intercambio Cientifico, Santo Cristo 1, 30001 Murcia, Spain.

410 SP
UNIVERSIDAD DE NAVARRA. COLECCION I.L.C.E. 1976. irreg., no. 1, 1982. 490 ptas. (Instituto de Lengua y Cultura Espanola) Ediciones Universidad de Navarra, S.A., Apdo. 396, 31080 Pamplona, Spain.

UNIVERSIDAD NACIONAL AUTONOMA DE MEXICO. INSTITUTO DE INVESTIGACIONES FILOSOFICAS. CUADERNOS. see *PHILOSOPHY*

489 IT ISSN 0072-0852
UNIVERSITA DEGLI STUDI DI GENOVA. ISTITUTO DI FILOLOGIA CLASSICA E MEDIEVALE. PUBBLICAZIONI. 1952. irreg. price varies. Universita degli Studi di Genova, Istituto di Filologia Classica e Medievale, Genoa, Italy. Ed. Francesco Della Corte.

UNIVERSITA DEGLI STUDI DI MACERATA. FACOLTA DI LETTERE E FILOSOFIA. ANNALI. see *ARCHAEOLOGY*

491.7 891.7 CS
UNIVERSITA PALACKEHO. PEDAGOGICKA FAKULTA. SBORNIK PRACI: RUSKY JAZYK A LITERATURA. (Text in Czech or Russian, summaries in Czech, English, German, and Russian.) 1972. irreg. price varies. Statni Pedagogicke Nakladatelstvi, Ostrovni 30, 113 01 Prague 1, Czechoslovakia. Ed. Ljubov Ordeltova. bibl. circ. 300. Key Title: Rusky Jazyk a Literatura.

410 RM ISSN 0379-7880
UNIVERSITATEA "AL. I. CUZA" DIN IASI. ANALELE STIINTIFICE. SECTIUNEA 3E: LINGVISTICA. (Text in English, French, German, Rumanian, Russian, Spanish) 1955. a. 35 lei. Universitatea "Al. I. Cuza" din Iasi, Calea 23 August Nr.11, Jassy, Rumania (Subscr. to: ILEXIM, Str. 13 Decembrie Nr. 3, Box 136-137, Bucharest, Rumania) Ed. D. Irimia. bk. rev. abstr. charts. illus. circ. 300.

410 RM
UNIVERSITATEA BUCURESTI. ANALELE. FILOLOGIE. (Text in English, French, Italian, Rumanian; summaries in Russian) a. $10. Universitatea Bucuresti, Bd. Gh. Gheorghiu-Dej Nr. 64, Bucharest, Rumania.

400 RM ISSN 0082-4461
UNIVERSITATEA DIN TIMISOARA. ANALELE. STIINTE FILOLOGICE. 1962. a. $30. Universitatea din Timisoara, Faculty of Philology - University of Timisoara, Bd. Vasile Parvan nr.4, 1900 Timisoara, Romania (Subscr. to: ILEXIM, Calea Grivitei 64-66, Box 136-137, Bucharest, Romania) (Co-sponsor: Ministry of Education) Ed. Vasile Serban. bk. rev. circ. 250.

400 HU ISSN 0583-5356
UNIVERSITATIS DEBRECENIENSIS DE LUDOVICO KOSSUTH NOMINATAE. INSTITUTI PHILOLOGIAE SLAVICAE. ANNALES. SLAVICA. (Text in several languages) 1961. irreg., vol.20, 1983. $10. Kossuth Lajos Tudomanyegyetem, Szlav Filologiai Intezet, Egyetem Ter 1, 4010 Debrecen, Hungary. Eds. Endre Igloi, Ferenc Papp. adv. bk. rev. bibl. circ. 700.

410 BE ISSN 0577-1765
UNIVERSITE CATHOLIQUE DE LOUVAIN. CENTRE INTERNATIONAL DE DIALECTOLOGIE GENERALE. TRAVAUX. 1955. irreg. price varies. Universite Catholique de Louvain, Centre International de Dialectologie Generale, 3000 Louvain, Belgium.

400 BE ISSN 0076-1249
UNIVERSITE CATHOLIQUE DE LOUVAIN. INSTITUT DES LANGUES VIVANTES. CAHIERS. (Text in various languages) 1967. irreg., no.22, 1972. price varies. 1348 Louvain-la-Neuve, Belgium.

400 900 BE ISSN 0076-1311
UNIVERSITE CATHOLIQUE DE LOUVAIN. RECUEIL DE TRAVAUX D'HISTOIRE ET DE PHILOLOGIE. (Text in Dutch, English and French) 1904. irreg., 6th series, no.31, 1985. price varies. Editions Peeters s.p.r.l., Bondgenotenlaan 153, B-3000 Louvain, Belgium.

400 BE ISSN 0076-129X
UNIVERSITE CATHOLIQUE DE LOUVAIN. SECTION DE PHILOLOGIE GERMANIQUE. SERIE MICROFICHES.* 1970. irreg. Editions Nauwelaerts, 148 Mechelsestraat, 3000 Louvain, Belgium.

440 840 DK ISSN 0107-7392
UNIVERSITE D'ODENSE. ETUDES ROMANES. (Text in Danish, English and French) 1971. irreg., no.22, 1986. price varies. Odense University Press, 36, Pjentedamsgade, DK-5000 Odense, Denmark. (back issues avail.)

400 FR ISSN 0068-0273
UNIVERSITE DE BORDEAUX. COLLECTION SINOLOGIQUE. 1969. irreg. 27 F. Universite de Bordeaux III, Societe Bordelaise de Diffusion de Travaux des Lettres et Sciences Humaines, Domaine Universitaire, 33405 Talence, France.

414 FR
UNIVERSITE DE GRENOBLE III. INSTITUT DE PHONETIQUE. BULLETIN. 1972. a. 25 F. per issue. Universite de Grenoble III (Universite des Langues et Lettres), Institut de Phonetique, Domaine Universitaire de Saint-Martin-d'Heres, B. P. 25-X, 38040 Grenoble Cedex, France. Indexed: M.L.A.

410 FR
UNIVERSITE DE GRENOBLE III. INSTITUT DE PHONETIQUE. TRAVAUX: SERIE A: MANUALS. irreg. price varies. Universite de Grenoble III (Universite des Langues et Lettres), Institut de Phonetique, Domaine Universitaire de Saint-Martin-d'Heres, Boite Postale 25-X, 38040 Grenoble Cedex, France.
Formerly: Universite de Grenoble. Institut de Phonetique. Manuels. Serie A (ISSN 0085-1264)

410 FR ISSN 0085-1272
UNIVERSITE DE GRENOBLE III. INSTITUT DE PHONETIQUE. TRAVAUX. SERIE B: ETUDES LINGUISTIQUES. 1967. irreg. price varies. Universite de Grenoble III (Universite des Langues et Lettres), Institut de Phonetique, Domaine Universitaire de Saint-Martin-d'Heres, B.P. 25-X, 38040 Grenoble Cedex, France.

440 RE ISSN 0337-6176
UNIVERSITE DE LA REUNION. CAHIER. 1971. irreg., no.10, 1979. price varies. Universite de la Reunion, 24-26 av. de la Victoire, 97489 Saint-Denis, Reunion. bk. rev.
Formerly: Centre Universitaire de la Reunion. Cahier.

410 FR ISSN 0756-7138
UNIVERSITE DE LILLE III. LEXIQUE. 1982. a. (University of Lille III) Presses Universitaires de Lille, B.P. 199, 59654 Villeneuve d'Ascq cedex, France. Ed. Pierre Corbin.

410 ZR
UNIVERSITE DE LUBUMBASHI. CENTRE DE LINGUISTIQUE THEORIQUE ET APPLIQUEE AFRICANISTIQUE. irreg., no.14, 1985. Universite de Lubumbashi, Centre de Linguistique Theorique et Appliquee, B.P. 1607, Lubumbashi, Zaire.
Formerly: Universite Nationale du Zaire, Lubumbashi. Centre de Linguistique Theorique et Appliquee Africanistique.

410 ZR
UNIVERSITE DE LUBUMBASHI. CENTRE DE LINGUISTIQUE THEORIQUE ET APPLIQUEE. BULLETIN DE LIAISON, ENSEIGNMENT DES LANGUES. 1974. irreg., no.14. Universite de Lumbumbashi, Centre de Linguistique Theorique et Appliquee, B.P. 1607, Lubumbashi, Zaire.
Former titles: Universite National de Zaire, Lumbumbashi. Centre de Linguistique Theorique et Applique. Bulletin de Liaison, Enseignment des Langues; Universite Nationale du Zaire, Lubumbashi. Centre de Linguistique Theorique et Appliquee. Bulletin de Liaison.

410 ZR
UNIVERSITE DE LUBUMBASHI. CENTRE DE LINGUISTIQUE THEORIQUE ET APPLIQUEE. LINGUISTIQUE ET SCIENCES HUMAINES. BULLETIN D'INFORMATION. irreg., no.26, 1984. Universite de Lubumbashi, Centre de Linguistique Theorique et Appliquee, B.P. 1607, Lubumbashi, Zaire.
Former titles: Universite Nationale du Zaire, Lubumbashi. Centre de Linguistique Theorique et Appliquee. Linguistique et Sciences Humaines. Bulletin d'Information; Universite Nationale du Zaire, Lubumbashi. Centre de Linguistique Theorique et Appliquee. Bulletin d'Information.

UNIVERSITE DE NANCY II. CENTRE DE
RECHERCHES ET D'APPLICATIONS
PEDAGOGIQUES EN LANGUES. MELANGES.
see *EDUCATION — Teaching Methods And
Curriculum*

479   FR ISSN 0081-5918
UNIVERSITE DE STRASBOURG II. CENTRE DE
PHILOLOGIE ET LITTERATURES ROMANES.
ACTES ET COLLOQUES. 1963. irreg. price varies.
(Universite de Strasbourg II, Centre de Philologie et
de Litteratures Romanes) Editions Klincksieck, 11
rue de Lille, 75007 Paris, France.

400   FR ISSN 0081-5934
UNIVERSITE DE STRASBOURG II. INSTITUT DE
PHONETIQUE. TRAVAUX. 1970. a. free.
Universite de Strasbourg II, Institut de Phonetique,
22 rue Descartes, 67084 Strasbourg Cedex, France.
circ. 600.

UNIVERSITE DE TUNIS. ECOLE NORMALE
SUPERIEURE. SECTION A: LETTRES ET
SCIENCES HUMAINES. SERIE 1: LANGUE ET
LITTERATURE. see *LITERATURE*

UNIVERSITE SAINT-JOSEPH. FACULTE DES
LETTRES ET DES SCIENCES HUMAINES.
RECHERCHE. SERIE A: LANGUE ARABE ET
PENSEE ISLAMIQUE. see *RELIGIONS AND
THEOLOGY — Islamic*

410   NE
UNIVERSITEIT VAN AMSTERDAM. INSTITUUT
VOOR ALGEMENE TAALWETENSCHAP.
PUBLIKATIES. (Text in English and Dutch) 1971.
irreg., vol.51, 1986. price varies. Universiteit van
Amsterdam, Instituut voor Algemene
Taalwetenschap, Spuistraat 210, 1012 VT
Amsterdam, Netherlands. Eds. Hans den Besten,
Norval Smith. bk. rev. circ. 150.

491.8 375.4 891.8 NO
UNIVERSITETET I OSLO. SLAVISK-BALTISK
INSTITUTT. MEDDELELSER. (Text in
Norwegian, Russian and English) 1972. irreg. (3-5/
yr.) price varies. Universitetet i Oslo, Slavisk-Baltisk
Instiutt, Postboks 1028, Blindern, Oslo 3, Norway.
Ed.Bd. circ. 400.

400   US
UNIVERSITY OF CALIFORNIA, BERKELEY.
LANGUAGE BEHAVIOR RESEARCH
LABORATORY. WORKING PAPER SERIES.
1967. irreg., no.47, 1977. price varies. University of
California, Berkeley, Language-Behavior Research
Laboratory, Box 190, Arlington, VA 22210 TEL
703-841-1212. (Vols. 40-47 avail. from the
Laboratory, 2229 Piedmont Ave., Berkeley, CA
94720)

400   US ISSN 0068-6484
UNIVERSITY OF CALIFORNIA PUBLICATIONS
IN LINGUISTICS. 1945. irreg. price varies.
University of California Press, 2120 Berkeley Way,
Berkeley, CA 94720.

400   US ISSN 0068-6492
UNIVERSITY OF CALIFORNIA PUBLICATIONS
IN MODERN PHILOLOGY. 1909. irreg. price
varies. University of California Press, 2120 Berkeley
Way, Berkeley, CA 94720. TEL 415-642-4247.

810 410 SA
UNIVERSITY OF CAPE TOWN. STUDIES IN
ENGLISH. Variant title: U C T Studies in English.
1970. a. exchange basis. University of Cape Town,
Department of English, Rondebosch 7700, South
Africa. Ed.Bd. adv. bk. rev. circ. 450. Indexed:
M.L.A. Abstr.Engl.Stud.
 Formerly (until 1972): Studies in English.

410   DK ISSN 0589-6681
UNIVERSITY OF COPENHAGEN. INSTITUTE OF
PHONETICS. ANNUAL REPORT. 1967. a. free.
University of Copenhagen, Institute of Phonetics,
Njalsgade 96, DK-2300 Copenhagen, Denmark.
Joergen Rishel. circ. 350. (back issues avail.)
Indexed: M.L.A.

410   GH
UNIVERSITY OF GHANA. INSTITUTE OF
AFRICAN STUDIES. COLLECTED
LANGUAGE NOTES. no.13, 1972. irreg. price
varies. University of Ghana, Institute of African
Studies, Box 73, Legon, Ghana.

496   NR ISSN 0041-9613
UNIVERSITY OF IBADAN. DEPARTMENT OF
LINGUISTICS AND NIGERIAN LANGUAGES.
RESEARCH NOTES.* 1967. irreg. University of
Ibadan, Department of Linguistics and Nigerian
Languages, Ibadan, Nigeria.

494   II
UNIVERSITY OF KERALA. DEPARTMENT OF
TAMIL. RESEARCH PAPERS. (Text in English or
Tamil) 1970. a. University of Kerala, Department of
Tamil, Kariavattom, Trivandrum 685001, Kerala,
India.
 Continues (vol. 5, 1974): University of Kerala.
Department of Tamil. Journal.

490   II ISSN 0076-2237
UNIVERSITY OF MADRAS. KANNADA SERIES.*
irreg. University of Madras, Chepauk, Triplicane,
Madras 600005, Tamil Nadu, India.

490   II ISSN 0076-2245
UNIVERSITY OF MADRAS. MALAYALAM
SERIES.* irreg. University of Madras, Chepauk,
Triplicane, Madras 600005, Tamil Nadu, India.

490   II ISSN 0076-2261
UNIVERSITY OF MADRAS. SANSKRIT SERIES.*
irreg. University of Madras, Chepauk, Triplicane,
Madras 600005, Tamil Nadu, India.

490   II ISSN 0076-227X
UNIVERSITY OF MADRAS. TAMIL SERIES.*
irreg. University of Madras, Chepauk, Triplicane,
Madras 600005, Tamil Nadu, India.

490   II ISSN 0076-2288
UNIVERSITY OF MADRAS. TELUGU SERIES.*
irreg. University of Madras, Chepauk, Triplicane,
Madras 600005, Tamil Nadu, India.

490   II ISSN 0076-2296
UNIVERSITY OF MADRAS. URDU SERIES.* irreg.
University of Madras, Chepauk, Triplicane, Madras
600005, Tamil Nadu, India.

495.1   MY ISSN 0553-0644
UNIVERSITY OF MALAYA. CHINESE
LANGUAGE SOCIETY. JOURNAL/MAJALLAH
PANTAI/PAN T'AI HSUEH PAO.* (Text in
Chinese, English, and Malay) irreg. University of
Malaya, Chinese Language Society, Lembah Pantai,
Kuala Lumpur, 22-11, Malaysia. illus.

UNIVERSITY OF MANITOBA ANTHROPOLOGY
PAPERS. see *ANTHROPOLOGY*

410   US ISSN 0085-123X
UNIVERSITY OF NORTHERN COLORADO.
MUSEUM OF ANTHROPOLOGY.
OCCASIONAL PUBLICATIONS IN
ANTHROPOLOGY. LINGUISTICS SERIES.
1970. irreg. price varies. University of Northern
Colorado, Museum of Anthropology, Attn. George
E. Fay, Ed., Greeley, CO 80639. TEL 303-351-
1890. circ. 300. (processed)

491.1   II ISSN 0079-3809
UNIVERSITY OF POONA. CENTRE OF
ADVANCED STUDY IN SANSKRIT.
PUBLICATIONS. (Text in English and Sanskrit)
1965. irreg. price varies. University of Poona,
Centre of Advanced Study in Sanskrit,
Ganeshkhind, Poona 411007, India.

UNIVERSITY OF RAJASTHAN. STUDIES IN
SANSKRIT AND HINDI. see *LITERATURE*

410   SW
UNIVERSITY OF STOCKHOLM. INSTITUTE OF
LINGUISTICS. MONOGRAPHS. Abbbreviated
title: M I L U S. (Text in English) 1974. irreg.,
no.5, 1979. Kr.25. Stockholms Universitet, Institute
of Linguistics, Drottninggatan 116, Box 6801, S-106
91 Stockholm, Sweden. Eds. Benny Brodda, Bjoern
Lindblom.

479   CN ISSN 0082-5336
UNIVERSITY OF TORONTO ROMANCE SERIES.
(Text in English; occasionally in French) 1949.
irreg. price varies. (Department of Romance
Languages) University of Toronto Press, Front
Campus, Toronto, Ont. M5S 1A6, Canada TEL
613-667-7761. (And 33 East Tupper St., Buffalo,
N.Y. 14203) Indexed: M.L.A.

410 491.8 CS ISSN 0231-7567
UNIVERZITA J. E. PURKYNE. FILOZOFICKA
FAKULTA. SBORNIK PRACI. A: RADA
JAZYKOVEDNA. irreg., approx. a. Univerzita J. E.
Purkyne, Filozoficka Fakulta, A. Novaka 1, 602 00
Brno, Czechoslovakia.

420 430 CS ISSN 0231-5351
UNIVERZITA J. E. PURKYNE. FILOZOFICKA
FAKULTA. SBORNIK PRACI. K: RADA
GERMANISTICKO - ANGLISTICKA. irreg.,
approx. a. Univerzita J. E. Purkyne, Filozoficka
Fakulta, A. Novaka 1, 602 00 Brno,
Czechoslovakia.

440 809.02 CS ISSN 0231-7532
UNIVERZITA J. E. PURKYNE. FILOZOFICKA
FAKULTA. SBORNIK PRACI. L: RADA
ROMANISTICA. irreg., approx. a. Univerzita J. E.
Purkyne, Filozoficka Fakulta, A. Novaka 1, 602 00
Brno, Czechoslovakia.

410   CS ISSN 0083-4173
UNIVERZITA KOMENSKEHO. FILOZOFICKA
FAKULTA. ZBORNIK: PHILOLOGICA. (Text
and summaries in German, Slovak and several other
languages) 1949. a. exchange basis. ‡ (Univerzita
Komenskeho, Filozoficka Fakulta) Slovenske
Pedagogicke Nakladatelstvo, Sasinkova 5, 818 06
Bratislava, Czechoslovakia. Ed. Alexander Csanda.
illus. maps. circ. 649.

491.86 891.86 CS
UNIVERZITA PALACKEHO. PEDAGOGICKA
FAKULTA. SBORNIK PRACI: CESKY JAZYK A
LITERATURA. (Text in Czech; summaries and
contents page in Czech, German and Russian) irreg,
vol.2, 1973. 28 Kcs. Statni Pedagogicke
Nakladatelstvi, Ostrovni 30, 113 01 Prague 1,
Czechoslovakia. Eds. Eva Doupalova, Miloslav
Krbec. charts.

420 375.4 PL ISSN 0208-5240
UNIWERSYTET GDANSKI. WYDZIAL
HUMANISTYCZNY. ZESZYTY NAUKOWE.
FILOLOGIA ANGIELSKA. (Text in English)
1979. irreg. price varies. Uniwersytet Gdanski, Ul.
Armii Czerwonej 110, 81-824 Sopot, Poland (Dist.
by: Ars Polona-Ruch, Krakowskie Przedmiescie 7,
00-680 Warsaw, Poland)
 English language study and teaching

400   PL ISSN 0302-2315
UNIWERSYTET GDANSKI. WYDZIAL
HUMANISTYCZNY. ZESZYTY NAUKOWE.
FILOLOGIA POLSKA. PRACE
JEZYKOZNAWCZE. 1973. irreg. price varies.
Uniwersytet Gdanski, Ul. Armii Czerwonej 110, 81-
824 Sopot, Poland. Ed. Edward Breza.

491.7 375.4 PL ISSN 0208-4678
UNIWERSYTET GDANSKI. WYDZIAL
HUMANISTYCZNY. ZESZYTY NAUKOWE.
FILOLOGIA ROSYJSKA. (Text in Polish and
Russian) 1971. irreg. price varies. Uniwersytet
Gdanski, Ul. Armii Czerwonej 110, 81-824 Sopot,
Poland. Eds. Janina Domin, Janina Salajczyk.

410   PL ISSN 0138-063X
UNIWERSYTET GDANSKI. WYDZIAL
HUMANISTYCZNY. ZESZYTY NAUKOWE.
STUDIA SCANDINAVICA. (Text in Polish and
Scandinavian languages) 1978. irreg. price varies.
Uniwersytet Gdanski, Ul. Armii Czerwonej 110, 81-
824 Sopot, Poland. Ed. Zenon Ciesielski.

375   PL ISSN 0324-8895
UNIWERSYTET GDANSKI. WYDZIAL
HUMANYSTYCZNY. ZESZYTY NAUKOWE.
STUDIUM PRAKTYCZNEJ NAUKI JEZYKOW
OBCYCH. (Text in English, French, German,
Russian and Polish; summaries in German and
Russian) 1976. irreg. price varies. Uniwersytet
Gdanski, Ul. Armii Czerwonej 110, 81-824 Sopot,
Poland.
 Formerly: Uniwersytet Gdanski. Zeszyty
Naukowe Praktycznej Nauk i Jezykow Obcych.

410 PL ISSN 0083-4378
UNIWERSYTET JAGIELLONSKI. ZESZYTY
NAUKOWE. PRACE JEZYKOZNAWCZE. (Vol.
3- called also vol. 6- , continuing the volume
numbering of Seria Nauk Spolecznych, Filologia,
which it supersedes) (Text in Polish; summaries in
French) 1956. irreg., 1984. price varies. Panstwowe
Wydawnictwo Naukowe, Miodowa 10, 00-251
Warsaw, Poland (Dist. by: Ars Polona, Krakowskie
Przedmiescie 7, 00-068 Warsaw, Poland) Ed. A.
Heinz. circ. 550.

400 PL
UNIWERSYTET SLASKI W KATOWICACH.
PRACE HISTORYCZNOLITERACKIE. (Text in
English, French and Polish; summaries in English,
French, Polish and Russian) 1959. irreg. price
varies. Uniwersytet Slaski w Katowicach, Ul.
Bankowa 14, 40-007 Katowice, Poland.

491.47 PL ISSN 0208-5445
UNIWERSYTET SLASKI W KATOWICACH.
PRACE JEZYKOZNAWCZE. (Text in Polish and
Russian; summaries in English, Polish and Russian)
1969. irreg. price varies. Uniwersytet Slaski w
Katowicach, Ul. Bankowa 14, 40-007 Katowice,
Poland.

479 GW ISSN 0083-4580
UNTERSUCHUNGEN ZUR SPRACH- UND
LITERATURGESCHICHTE DER
ROMANISCHEN VOELKER. 1959. irreg., vol.10,
1980. price varies. (Akademie der Wissenschaften
und der Literatur, Mainz, Kommission fuer
Romanische Philologie) Franz Steiner Wiesbaden
GmbH, Birkenwaldstr. 44, Postfach 347, D-7000
Stuttgart 1, W. Germany (B.R.D.)

491.7 375.4 GW ISSN 0174-0652
URAL-ALTAISCHE JAHRBUECHER. NEUE
FOLGE. 1981. a. price varies. Verlag Otto
Harrassowitz, Taunusstr. 14, Postfach 2929, D-6200
Wiesbaden 1, W. Germany (B.R.D.) Ed.Bd. bk. rev.
circ. 400. Indexed: M.L.A.

460 375.4 SP
VERBA; anuario Galego de filoloxia. 1974. a. 2500
ptas.($18) Universidade de Santiago, Servicio de
Publicaciones e Intercambio Cientifico, Campus
Universitario, 15706 Santiago de Compostela, Spain.
TEL 81 593500. charts. index; cum.index. circ. 700.
(back issues avail.)

440 375.4 UK ISSN 0264-5564
VINAVER STUDIES IN FRENCH. 1984. irreg. price
varies. Francis Cairns (Publications), P.O. Box 147,
The University, Liverpool L69 3BX, England. Eds.
Jane H.M. Taylor, A.R.W. James.

491 954 II ISSN 0083-6621
VISHVESHVARANAND INDOLOGICAL SERIES.
(Text in English and Sanskrit) 1950. irreg., vol.73,
1982. price varies. Vishveshvaranand Vedic
Research Institute, Sadhu Ashram, Hoshiarpur
146021, Punjab, India. Ed. S. Bhaskaran Nair.

491.7 UR
VOPROSY RUSSKOGO YAZYKOZNANIYA. 1976.
irreg. 1.21 Rub. per issue. Moskovskii Universitet,
Leninskie Gory, Moscow V-234, Russian S.F.S.R.,
U.S.S.R. Ed. K. Gorshkova. circ. 4,760.

439 948 990 NE
VRIJE FRIES. (Text in Dutch and Frisian) 1955. a.
Fryske Akademy, Doelestrjitte 8, 8911 DX
Ljouwert/Leeuwarden, Netherlands. TEL 058-
131414. (Co-sponsor: Fries Genootschap)

410 NR ISSN 0331-0531
WEST AFRICAN JOURNAL OF MODERN
LANGUAGES/REVUE OUEST AFRICAINE
DES LANGUES VIVANTES. 1976. a. $20. West
African Modern Languages Association, c/o
University of Maiduguri, Department of Languages
and Linguistics, Borno State, Nigeria. Ed. C.M.B.
Brann. adv. bk. rev. circ. 1,000. Indexed: M.L.A.

420 820 AU ISSN 0083-9914
WIENER BEITRAEGE ZUR ENGLISCHEN
PHILOLOGIE. (Text in English, German) 1895.
irreg., vol.79, 1983. price varies. Wilhelm
Braumueller, Universitaets-Verlagsbuchhandlung
GmbH, Servitengasse 5, A-1092 Vienna, Austria.
Ed. Siegfried Korninger. index. circ. 600. Indexed:
M.L.A.

400 AU ISSN 0083-9922
WIENER BEITRAEGE ZUR
KULTURGESCHICHTE UND LINGUISTIK.
1930. irreg., vol.20, 1981. price varies. (Universitaet
Wien, Institut fuer Voelkerkunde) Verlag Ferdinand
Berger und Soehne OHG, Wienerstr. 21-23, A-3580
Horn, Austria.

400 800 AU ISSN 0084-0033
WIENER ROMANISTISCHE ARBEITEN. (Text in
French, German) 1962. a. price varies. Wilhelm
Braumueller, Universitaets-Verlagsbuchhandlung
GmbH, Servitengasse 5, A-1092 Vienna, Austria.
Ed. Wolfgang Pollack. index. circ. 600.

491.7 AU ISSN 0084-0041
WIENER SLAVISTISCHES JAHRBUCH/
VIENNESE SLAVONIC YEARBOOK. (Text in
English, French, German, Polish and Russian) 1950.
a. DM.100. (Universitaet Wien, Institut fuer
Slavische Philologie) Verlag der Oesterreichischen
Akademie der Wissenschaften, Dr. Ignaz Seipel-
Platz 2, A-1010 Vienna, Austria. Ed.Bd. adv. bk.
rev. bibl. illus. circ. 500. Indexed: M.L.A. Arts &
Hum.Cit.Ind. Can.Rev.Comp.Lit.

400 AU ISSN 0084-005X
WIENER STUDIEN. ZEITSCHRIFT FUER
KLASSISCHE PHILOLOGIE UND PATRISTIK.
(Text in Ancient Greek, English, German and
Latin) 1897. a. price varies. (Universitaet Wien,
Institut fuer Klassische Philologie) Verlag der
Oesterreichischen Akademie der Wissenschaften,
Dr. Ignaz Seipel-Platz 2, A-1010 Vienna, Austria.
Ed.Bd. adv. bk. rev. bibl. illus.

420 US
WORKING PAPERS IN LINGUISTICS. 1968. irreg.
(2-3/yr.) price varies. Ohio State University,
Department of Linguistics, 204 Dieter Cunz Hall,
1841 Millikin Rd., Columbus, OH 43210. TEL 614-
422-4052. circ. 400. (back issues avail.) Indexed:
M.L.A. Sociol.Abstr. ERIC.

407 US
WORLD HUMOR AND IRONY MEMBERSHIP
SERIAL YEARBOOK. Short title: W H I M S Y.
1983. a. $10. Arizona State University, English
Department, Tempe, AZ 85287. TEL 602-965-3168.
Ed. Don L.F. Nilsen. adv. bk. rev. circ. 1,000.
Indexed: Abstr.Engl.Stud. M.L.A. Bk.Rev.Ind.
Lang & Lang.Behav.Abstr.
Formerly: Western Humor and Irony
Membership Serial Yearbook (ISSN 0737-0342)

WRITING IN HOLLAND AND FLANDERS. see
LITERATURE

491.85 PL ISSN 0084-2990
WROCLAWSKIE TOWARZYSTWO NAUKOWE.
KOMISJA JEZYKOWA. ROZPRAWY. (Text in
English, German and Polish) 1957. irreg., vol.14,
1986. price varies. Ossolineum, Publishing House of
the Polish Academy of Sciences, Rynek 9, Wroclaw,
Poland (Dist. by Ars Polona-Ruch, Krakowskie
Przedmiescie 7, Warsaw, Poland)

400 870 880 GW
WUERZBURGER JAHRBUECHER FUER DIE
ALTERTUMSWISSENSCHAFT. 1975. a. DM.70.
F. Schoeningh Kommissionsverlag, Franziskaner
Platz 4, Postfach 129, D-8700 Wuerzburg, W.
Germany (B.R.D.) Ed. Joachim Latacz, Guenter
Neumann. circ. 600.

490 PL
WYZSZA SZKOLA PEDAGOGICZNA, KRAKOW.
PRACE JEZYKOZNAWCZE. 1970. a. 128.00
Zl. Wyzsza Szkola Pedagogiczna, Krakow,
Podchorazych 2, 30-084 Krakow, Poland. Ed.
Eugeniusz Pawlowski. illus.

400 800 PL ISSN 0324-9050
WYZSZA SZKOLA PEDAGOGICZNA, OPOLE.
ZESZYTY NAUKOWE. FILOLOGIA POLSKA.
irreg., vol.22, 1983. price varies; avail. on exchange.
Wyzsza Szkola Pedagogiczna, Opole, Oleska 48, 45-
052 Opole, Poland (Dist. by: Ars Polona-Ruch,
Krakowskie Przedmiescie 7, Warsaw, Poland)
Incorporates: Wyzsza Szkola Pedagogiczna,
Opole. Zeszyty Naukowe. Seria A. Historia
Literatury (ISSN 0078-5407)

WYZSZA SZKOLA PEDAGOGICZNA, OPOLE.
ZESZYTY NAUKOWE. SERIA A. FILOLOGIA
ROSYJSKA. see LITERATURE

410 PL ISSN 0078-5423
WYZSZA SZKOLA PEDAGOGICZNA, OPOLE.
ZESZYTY NAUKOWE. SERIA A.
JEZYKOZNAWSTWO. (Text in Polish) 1957.
irreg., no.8, 1982. avail. on exchange; price varies.
Wyzsza Szkola Pedagogiczna, Opole, Oleska 48,
Opole 45-052, Poland (Dist. by Ars Polona-Ruch,
Krakowskie Przedmiescie 7, Warsaw, Poland)

410 US ISSN 0731-0897
XIN TANG/NEW CHINA. 1982. a. $10 to
individuals; institutions $15. Institute for Advanced
Communication, Box 254, Swarthmore, PA 19081.
TEL 215-543-6286. Ed. Victor H. Mair. adv. bk.
rev. circ. 1,000. (back issues avail.)
Former titles: Xin Talng; (until 19784): Shin
Tarng.

400 US
YALE LANGUAGE SERIES. 1963. irreg., latest,
1983. Yale University Press, 92A Yale Sta., New
Haven, CT 06520. TEL 203-432-0940.
Formerly: Yale Linguistic Series (ISSN 0513-
4412)

410 296 800 IS
YIDDISH LITERARY AND LINGUISTIC
PERIODICALS AND MISCELLANIES; a
selective annotated bibliography. 1982. irreg.
Association for the Study of Jewish Languages,
1610 Eshkol Tower, University of Haifa, Mount
Carmel, Haifa 31 999, Israel (Subscr. to: Norwood
Editions, Box 38, Norwood, PA 19074, U.S.A.) Ed.
Leonard Prager.

492.49 US ISSN 0044-0442
YIDISHE SHPRAKH/YIDDISH LANGUAGE. (Text
in Yiddish) 1941. a. $5. Y I V O Institute for
Jewish Research, 1048 Fifth Ave., New York, NY
10028. TEL 212-535-6700. Ed. Mordkhe
Schaechter. bk. rev. circ. 1,000. (also avail. in
microform) Indexed: M.L.A.

410 UK ISSN 0513-2762
YORKSHIRE DIALECT SOCIETY. SUMMER
BULLETIN. 1953. a. £1. Yorkshire Dialect Society,
c/o S. Ellis, School of English, University of Leeds,
Leeds LS2 9JT, England. Ed. J. Danby. bk. rev.
circ. 750.

410 UK
YORKSHIRE DIALECT SOCIETY
TRANSACTIONS. 1897. a. £1. Yorkshire Dialect
Society, School of English, University of Leeds,
Leeds LS2 9JT, England. Ed. K.E. Smith. circ. 800.
(also avail. in microfiche)

410 YU
YUGOSLAV SERBO-CROATIAN-ENGLISH
CONTRASTIVE PROJECT. SERIES B: STUDIES.
(Text in English) 1969. irreg. 50 din. Institute of
Linguistics, Zagreb, Djure Salaja 3, 41000 Zagreb,
Yugoslavia. Ed. Rudolf Filipovic. circ. 500. Indexed:
Sociol.Abstr.

491.85 PL ISSN 0208-5011
Z TEORII I PRAKTYKI DYDAKTYCZNEJ
JEZYKA POLSKIEGO. (Text in Polish; summaries
in English and Russian) 1977. irreg. Uniwersytet
Slaski w Katowicach, Ul. Bankowa 14, 40-007
Katowice, Poland.

491 YU
ZBORNIK ZAGREBACKE SLAVISTICKE SKOLE.
1973. irreg. Medjunarodni Slavisticki Centar SR
Hrvatske, Djure Salaja 3, Zagreb, Yugoslavia. (Co-
sponsor: Sveucilista u Zagrebu, Filozofski Fakultet)
Eds. Franjo Grcevic and Mladen Kuzmanovic.

491.6 GW ISSN 0084-5302
ZEITSCHRIFT FUER CELTISCHE PHILOLOGIE.
(Text in English, French, German or Irish) 1904; no
issues published between 1944 and 1952. irreg.
DM.120. Max Niemeyer Verlag, Pfrondorfer Str. 4,
7400 Tuebingen, W. Germany (B.R.D.) (back issues
avail.) Indexed: M.L.A. Arts & Hum.Cit.Ind.

400 GW ISSN 0341-0838
ZEITSCHRIFT FUER DIALEKTOLOGIE UND
LINGUISTIK. BEIHEFTE. irreg., vol.53, 1986.
price varies. Franz Steiner Verlag Wiesbaden
GmbH, Birkenwaldstr. 44, Postfach 347, D-7000
Stuttgart 1, W. Germany (B.R.D.) Ed. Joachim
Goeschel.

440   GW   ISSN 0341-0811
ZEITSCHRIFT FUER FRANZOESISCHE
SPRACHE UND LITERATUR. BEIHEFTE.
NEUE FOLGE. irreg., vol.12, 1986. price varies.
Franz Steiner Verlag Wiesbaden GmbH,
Birkenwaldstr. 44, Postfach 347, D-7000 Stuttgart 1,
W. Germany (B.R.D.) Eds. H. Stimm, A. Noyer-
Weidner.

400 830   GW   ISSN 0084-5396
ZEITSCHRIFT FUER ROMANISCHE
PHILOLOGIE. BEIHEFTE. (Text in English,
French or German) 1906. irreg., no.211, 1986. Max
Niemeyer Verlag, Pfrondorfer Str. 4, 7400
Tuebingen, W. Germany (B.R.D.) Ed. Kurt
Baldinger. (back issues avail.)

460 375.4   GW
ZIELSPRACHE SPANISCH; Zeitschrift fuer den
Spanischunterricht in der Weiterbildung. 1974. irreg.
DM.16 per no. Max Hueber Verlag, Max-Hueber-
Str.4, 8045 Ismaning, W. Germany (B.R.D.) Ed.
Alberto Barrera-Vidal. circ. 1,200.

LINGUISTICS — Abstracting, Bibliographies, Statistics

016 410   US   ISSN 0165-7267
AMSTERDAM STUDIES IN THE THEORY AND
HISTORY OF LINGUISTIC SCIENCE. SERIES
5: LIBRARY AND INFORMATION SOURCES
IN LINGUISTICS. Short title: L I S L. (Text in
English) 1977. irreg., vol.17, 1985. price varies.
John Benjamins Publishing Co., One Buttonwood
Sq, Philadelphia, PA 19130. TEL 215-564-6379. Ed.
E.F.K. Koerner. Indexed: M.L.A.

BIBLIOGRAPHIE LINGUISTISCHER LITERATUR.
see LITERATURE — Abstracting, Bibliographies,
Statistics

400 016   FR   ISSN 0007-5590
BULLETIN SIGNALETIQUE. PART 524:
SCIENCES DU LANGAGE. 1947. q. 325 F.
Centre National de la Recherche Scientifique,
Centre de Documentation Sciences Humaines, 54
bd. Raspail, 75260 Paris Cedex, France. cum.index.
●Also available online. Vendors: European Space
Agency.

016 460   SP   ISSN 0590-1545
CUADERNOS BIBLIOGRAFICOS. no.33, 1976.
irreg. price varies. Consejo Superior de
Investigaciones Cientificas, Vitruvio 8, Apartado 14-
458, Madrid 6, Spain. bibl. illus. index.

440 840   UK
CURRENT RESEARCH IN FRENCH STUDIES AT
UNIVERSITIES AND POLYTECHNICS IN THE
UNITED KINGDOM. (Text in English and
French) 1969. biennial. £6($12) Society for French
Studies, c/o Dr. M.J. Tilby, Selwyn College,
Cambridge CB3 9DQ, England. index. circ. 400.
(back issues avail.)
  Formerly: Current Research in French Studies at
Universities and University Colleges in the United
Kingdom (ISSN 0263-4538)

400 016   US
DICTIONARIES, ENCYCLOPEDIAS, AND
OTHER WORD-RELATED BOOKS. irreg., latest
3rd edt., 1982. price varies. Gale Research
Company, Book Tower, Detroit, MI 48226. TEL
313-961-2242. Ed. Annie M. Brewer.

E I. (Excerpta Indonesica) see ANTHROPOLOGY —
Abstracting, Bibliographies, Statistics

440 016   CN   ISSN 0712-7561
ETUDES STRATEGIQUES ET MILITAIRES
(COLLECTION) 1981. a. Can.$10. Centre
Quebecois de Relations Interntionales, Faculte des
Sciences Sociales, Universite Laval, Quebec G1K
7P4, Canada. TEL 418-656-2462. Ed. Claude
Basset. circ. 500. Indexed: A.B.C.Pol.Sci.
  Formerly (until 1981): Communautes
Francophones: Bibliographie, Chroniques.

410   CK
INSTITUTO LINGUISTICO DE VERANO EN
COLOMBIA. BIBLIOGRAFIA. 1975. irreg. $2.
Instituto Linguistico de Verano en Colombia,
Technical Studies Department, Apdo. Aereo 27744,
Bogota, Colombia. circ. 1,000.

LANGUAGE TEACHING. see EDUCATION —
Abstracting, Bibliographies, Statistics

016 410   NE
LINGUISTIC BIBLIOGRAPHY. (Text in English and
French) 1949. a. fl.195 price varies. (International
Permanent Committee of Linguistics) Martinus
Nijhoff Publishers, Spuiboulevard 50, 3311 GR
Dordrecht, Netherlands (U.S. addr.: Kluwer
Academic Publishers Group, 190 Old Derby St.,
Hingham, MA 02043) Eds. H. Borkent, M. Janse.

410   UK   ISSN 0267-5498
LINGUISTICS ABSTRACTS. 1985. q. £25.90($45.50)
to individuals; institutions £47.50(82.50) Basil
Blackwell Ltd., 108 Cowley Rd., Oxford OX4 1JF,
England. Ed. David Crystal. adv. circ. 300. (also
avail. in microform)

400 016   US   ISSN 0888-8027
LINGUISTICS AND LANGUAGE BEHAVIOR
ABSTRACTS. Short title: L L B A. 1967. q. $150
($198 including annual index) Sociological
Abstracts, Inc., Box 22206, San Diego, CA 92122.
TEL 619-565-6603. adv. abstr. bibl. index.
cum.index. circ. 1,100. (back issues avail.)
●Also available online. Vendors: BRS, DIALOG.
  Formerly (until 1985): Language and Language
Behavior Abstracts (ISSN 0023-8295)

M L A DIRECTORY OF PERIODICALS; a guide to
journals and series in languages and literatures.
(Modern Language Association of America) see
LITERATURE — Abstracting, Bibliographies,
Statistics

479 016   GW   ISSN 0080-388X
ROMANISCHE BIBLIOGRAPHIE/
BIBLIOGRAPHIE ROMANE/ROMANCE
BIBLIOGRAPHY. (Supplement to: Zeitschrift fuer
Romanische Philologie) (Text in German, French
and English) 1965. a. price varies. Max Niemeyer
Verlag, Pfrondorfer Str. 4, 7400 Tuebingen, W.
Germany (B.R.D.) Ed. Gustav Ineichen. (back
issues avail.)

491.79   CN
RUDNYCKIANA. 1985. a. Can.$5. Ukrainian
Language Association, 911 Carling Ave., Ottawa,
Ont., Canada. Ed.Bd.

808.5 371.9   US   ISSN 0081-3656
SPEECH INDEX; an index to 259 collections of
orations and speeches for various occasions. 1935.
irreg., 1966, 4th edt., supp. 1982. price varies.
Scarecrow Press, Inc., 52 Liberty St., Box 4167,
Metuchen, NJ 08840. TEL 201-548-8600. Ed.
Charity Mitchell. circ. 3,000.

400 016   US
SUMMER INSTITUTE OF LINGUISTICS.
PUBLICATIONS CATALOG. 1968. biennial.
Summer Institute of Linguistics, Inc., Academic
Publications, 7500 W. Camp Wisdom Rd., Dallas,
TX 75236. TEL 214-298-3331. circ. 10,000.

YEAR'S WORK IN MODERN LANGUAGE
STUDIES. see LITERATURE — Abstracting,
Bibliographies, Statistics

LINGUISTICS — Computer Applications

410   UK
COMPENDIA; computer generated aids to literary
and linguistic research. 1968. irreg. price varies.
W.S. Maney & Son Ltd., Hudson Rd., Leeds LS9
7DL, England. Ed. R.A. Wisbey. stat. (back issues
avail.) Indexed: M.L.A.

410   FR   ISSN 0085-4786
DOCUMENTS DE LINGUISTIQUE
QUANTITATIVE. 1969. irreg. price varies.
(Association Jean-Favard pour le Developpement de
la Linguistique Quantitative) Editions Jean Favard,
37 rue du Four a Chaux, 91910 St. Sulpice de
Favieres, France. Ed. Daniel J. Herault. circ. 850.
Indexed: Bull.Signal.

410   US
I E E E COMPUTER SOCIETY WORKSHOP ON
VISUAL LANGUAGES. 1984. biennial. price
varies. (Institute of Electrical and Electronics
Engineers, Inc., Computer Society) I E E E
Computer Society Press, 1073 Massachusetts Ave.,
N.W., Washington, DC 20036-1903 TEL 202-371-
0101. (And 345 E. 47th St., New York, NY 10017-
2394)

410   GW
INTERNATIONAL CONFERENCE ON
COMPUTATIONAL LINGUISTICS.
PROCEEDINGS. irreg. (11th, 1986) Institut fuer
angewandte Kommunikations- und Sprachforschung
e.V., Poppelsdorfer Allee 47, D-5300 Bonn 1, W.
Germany (B.R.D.) (Co-sponsor: International
Committee on Computational Linguistics)

439   NE
RANDGEBIEDEN; een interdisciplinaire serie. vol.4,
1982. irreg. price varies. Dick Coutinho B.V.,
Badlaan 2, Muiderberg, Netherlands. bibl.

LITERARY AND POLITICAL REVIEWS

323.4   US
A IS A; writings on freedom and individualism. 1971.
irreg. $4 for 12 issues. Mega, 9730 Hyne Rd.,
Brighton, MI 48116. Ed. Dale Haviland. adv. bk.
rev. play rev. illus. circ. 500. (back issues avail.)
  Formerly: A Is A Newsletter (ISSN 0044-569X)

ABHANDLUNGEN ZUR KUNST-, MUSIK- UND
LITERATURWISSENSCHAFT. see ART

ACADEMIE ROYALE DE LANGUE ET DE
LITTERATURE FRANCAISES. ANNUAIRES.
see LINGUISTICS

808.8   US
THE ACTS THE SHELFLIFE. 1980. a. $5. c/o
Miekal And, 1341 Williamson Blvd., Madison, WI
53703. circ. 500.

056.1   VE
ACTUALIDADES. 1976. irreg. Bol.$10 per no.
Centro de Estudios Latinoamericanos "Romulo
Gallegos", Departamento de Documentacion e
Intercambio de Informacion, Apdo. Postal 75667,
Caracas 1062, Venezuela. bk. rev. Indexed: M.L.A.
Hisp.Amer.Per.ind.

052   UK
AGENT. a. Nominal Agency, 46 Denbigh St., London
SW1, England.

053   GW
DIE AKTION; Zeitschrift fuer Politik, Literatur,
Kunst. 1981. irreg. DM.48. Edition Nautilus Verlag
Lutz Schulenburg, Hassestr. 22, D-2050 Hamburg
80, W. Germany (B.R.D.) Ed. Lutz Schulenburg.
adv. bk. rev. film rev. circ. 3,000.

ALLMENDE; eine alemannische Zeitschrift. see
LITERATURE — Poetry

800   US
ALTERNATIVE PRESS ANNUAL. 1984. a. $34.95.
Temple University Press, Broad & Oxford Sts.,
Philadelphia, PA 19122. TEL 215-787-8787. Ed.
Patricia J. Case. bibl. illus. index. (back issues
avail.)

ANOTHER SEASON. see LITERATURE

700   PE   ISSN 0570-4006
ANUARIO CULTURAL DEL PERU. (Publication
suspended 1959-1977) 1954. a. Libreria-Editorial
Juan Mejia Baca, Azangaro 722, Lima, Peru. Ed.
Julio Vargas Prada.

800   US
APOCALYPSO. 1984. a. $3.50. Apocalypso Fourth
World Ltd., 673 9th Ave., New York, NY 10036.
TEL 212-247-8609. Ed. Oliver Trager. circ. 2,500.
(back issues avail.)

LITERARY AND POLITICAL REVIEWS

860 VE
ARAISA. 1975. irreg. Centro de Estudios Latinoamericanos "Romulo Gallegos", Departamento de Documentacion e Intercambio de Informacion, Apdo. Postal 75667, Caracas 1062, Venezuela. bk. rev. Indexed: Hisp.Amer.Per.Ind.

808.8 US ISSN 0883-9824
ARGONAUT. 1972. a. $8 for 3 nos. Argo Press, Box 4201, Austin, TX 78765-4201. TEL 512-451-6466. Ed. Michael E. Ambrose. adv. bk. rev. circ. 500.

053 GW ISSN 0722-964X
ARGUMENT-BEIHEFT. 1979. a. DM.14.60 to individuals; students DM.12.60. Argument-Verlag GmbH, Tegeler Str. 6, D-1000 Berlin 65, W. Germany (B.R.D.)

056.1 VE
ARTE Y VIDA; hacia un nuevo mundo. 1977. irreg. Arte y Vida Editorial, Apdo. 51494, Caracas, Zona 105, Venezuela.

AXE FACTORY REVIEW. see LITERATURE

820 UK
BACONIANA. 1885. a. £1. Francis Bacon Society Inc., Canonbury Tower, Islington, London N.1, England. Ed.Bd. bk. rev. bibl. index. circ. 200.

808.8 US
BARNWOOD.* 1980. irreg. (3-4/yr.) $2.50 for 4 nos. (Barnwood Press Cooperative, Inc.) Barnwood Press, c/o Tom Koontz, RR 2, Box 11C, Daleville, IN 47334-9602. bk. rev. circ. 500.

808.87 US
BAWL STREET JOURNAL; annual lampoon of the financial community. a. $3. Box 445, Wall St. Sta., New York, NY 10005.
Wit & humor

810 US ISSN 0005-920X
BERKSHIRE REVIEW. 1965. a. $2. Williams College, Box 633, Williamstown, MA 01267. TEL 413-597-3131. circ. 2,100. (also avail. in microform from UMI; reprint service avail. from UMI)

741.5 808.87 US ISSN 0091-2220
BEST EDITORIAL CARTOONS OF THE YEAR. 1973. a. $13.95 hardcover; $9.95 paperback. (Association of American Editorial Cartoonists) Pelican Publishing Co., 1101 Monroe St., Box 189, Gretna, LA 70053. TEL 504-368-1175. Ed. Charles Brooks. circ. 6,000.

808.8 US
BIG SCREAM. 1974. irreg., 2-3/yr. $8. Nada, 2782 Dixie, SW, Grandville, MI 49418. TEL 616-531-1442. Eds. David Cope, Susan Cope. circ. 100.

808.87 US
BIGGEST GREATEST CRACKED ANNUAL.* a. $1.50. Candar Publishing Corp., Major Magazines Division, 15/05 Jorden Ct., 102-B Uppr., Bayside, NY 11360-1148. circ. 425,000.
Wit and humor

808.8 US
BIKINI GIRL; a serial anthology of unconventional literature and graphics. 1976. a. $12. Vortex Publications, Box 371, Midwood Sta., Brooklyn, NY 11230-0371. Ed. Keith Rahmmings. adv. bk. rev. illus. circ. 1,500.
Formerly (until vol.2, no.2, 1981): Blank Tape.

808.8 US
BIRD EFFORT. 1975. a. $5 to individuals; institutions $6. Bird Effort Press, 25 Mudford Ave., Easthampton, NY 11937. Eds. Robert Long, Josh Dayton. adv. bk. rev. circ. 500. Indexed: Ind.Amer.Per.Verse.

051 US
BLACK BART. 1971. irreg., 1-3/yr. $10 institutions. Black Bart Brigade, Box 48, Canyon, CA 94516. Ed. Irv Thomas. bk. rev. circ. 500.
Former titles: Black Bart Brigade & Yin Times of Black Bart.

700 US ISSN 0364-3344
BOX 749; a magazine of the printable arts. 1972. a. $7 for 4 nos. Printable Arts Society, Inc., Box 749, Old Chelsea Station, New York, NY 10011. Ed. David Ferguson. bibl. illus. circ. 5,000. (also avail. in microform) Indexed: Access.

051 CN ISSN 0381-856X
CALEDONIAN. vol.8, 1978. irreg. free. College of New Caledonia, 3330 22nd Ave., Prince George, B.C. V2N 1P8, Canada. TEL 604-562-2131. Ed. Hans Allgaier. bk. rev. circ. 300. Indexed: Can.Ind.

808.8 070 US
CALIFORNIA STREET; San Francisco adventures and some that only began here. 1980. irreg., no.3, 1983. $9.95 per no. (Sons of Ojo Sarco) California Street Editions, 723 Dwight Way, Berkeley, CA 94710. TEL 415-549-2461. Ed. R.S. Loyce. circ. 2, 000. (back issues avail.)

CHARIOTEER; an annual review of modern Greek culture. see LITERATURE — Poetry

059 GR
CHRONICO. 1970. a. Dr.600($10) Athens Cultural Center "ORA", 7 Xenofondos St., Athens 118, Greece. Ed. A. Baharian. bk. rev. film rev. index. circ. 2,000.

800 SA
CLASSIC; magazine of creative writing and art. (Text in Afrikaans and English) 1982. biennial. R.1.50($3.00) (African Writers Association (AWA)) Skotaville Publishers, P.O. Box 32483, Braamfontein, Johannesburg 2017, South Africa. Ed. Jaki Seroke. film rev. illus. play rev. circ. 3,000. (back issues avail.) Indexed: Ind.S.A.Per.

056 BL
COLECAO ENCANTO RADICAL. Short title: Encanto Radical. no.33, 1983. irreg. Editora Brasiliense S.A., 01223-Rua General Jardim, 160, Sao Paulo, Brazil.

056 BL
COLECAO POLEMICAS DO NOSSO TIEMPO. no.5, 1983. irreg. Cortez Editora, Rua Bartira, 387, 05009 Sao Paulo, SP, Brazil.

056 BL
COLECAO PRIMEIROS PASSOS. no.98, 1983. irreg., latest no. 154. Editora Brasiliense S.A., 01223-Rua General Jardim, 160, Sao Paulo, Brazil.

COLECCAO N'GOLA. see HISTORY — History Of Africa

056.1 AG
COLECCION ENSAYOS. no.16, 1976. irreg. Editorial Plus Ultra, Viamonte 1755, 1055 Buenos Aires, Argentina.

056 MX
COLECCION LIBRO DE BOLSILLO. SERIE ENSAYO.* 1883. biennial. Editorial Katun, S.A., Republica de Colombia No. 7A, Col. Centro, Mexico 01, DF, Mexico.

840 CN
COLLECTION LIGNES QUEBECOISES. irreg. price varies. Presses de l'Universite de Montreal, C.P. 6128, Succ. A, Montreal, Que. H3C 3J7, Canada. TEL 514-343-6929.
Formerly: Collection Lignes Quebecoises. Textuelles.

808.8 US
COLONNADES. 1937. a. free. Box 5246, Elon College, NC 27244. Ed. Andrew J. Angyal. circ. 2, 500.

COLUMBIA REVIEW. see LITERATURE

808.8 334 335 910.09 GW
CONNEXIONS; address book of alternative projects. (World wide editions) 1981. irreg. DM.19.80($10) Mandala Verlag, Klingelbach, P.O. Box 60, 5429 Katzenelnbogen, W. Germany (B.R.D.) Ed. Peter H. Meyer. adv. bk. rev. index. circ. 10,000.

808.8 US
CONTEMPORARY ISSUES CRITICISM. 1982. irreg., latest vol.2, 1984. $90. Gale Research Company, Book Tower, Detroit, MI 48226. Ed. Dedria Bryfonski.

800 320 FR
CONTINENT. 1975. irreg. Editions Gallimard, 5 rue Sebastien-Bottin, 75007 Paris, France.
Literary and political review of translations from Russian

CUADERNOS DE CRITICA (MEXICO) see PHILOSOPHY

059 BD
CULTURE ET SOCIETE. (Text in French) 1978. a. $4. Ministere de la Jeunesse, des Sports et de la Culture, Centre de Civilisation Burundaise, B.P. 1095, Bujumbura, Burundi. Ed.Bd.

056.1 UY
DESTABANDA. 1977. irreg. Mario A. Aiello, Ed. & Pub., Gaboto 1918, Montevideo, Uruguay.

800 IT ISSN 0012-3668
DISCRETIO. 1962. irreg. Via F. M. Penna 20, 97018 Sicily, Italy. Ed. Dr. Giovanni Rossino. circ. 1,000. (tabloid format)
Translations from modern and classical languages

DOSTOEVSKY STUDIES. see LITERATURE

808.8 US
DUCK SOUP. 1978. a. free. 5001 N. MacArthur Blvd., Irving, TX 75062. TEL 214-659-5270. Ed. Nancy Jones. circ. 3,000.

056.9 BL
EDICOES CADERNOS CULTURAIS; uma revista de cultura do nordeste para o Brasil. irreg. Cr.$10 per no. (Universidade Federal de Pernambuco) Editora Universitaria, Recife, Brazil. illus.

811 US
EIGHTIES; a magazine of poetry and opinion. (Text in Danish, French, German and Swedish) 1958-19??; to resume in 1987. irreg. $10 for 4 nos. Eighties Press, 308 First St., Moose Lake, MN 55767 (Dist. by: Book People, 2940 Seventh St., Berkeley, CA 94710) Ed. Robert Bly. bk. rev. circ. 3,000. (also avail. in microfilm from UMI; back issues avail.; reprint service avail. from UMI)
Former titles: Seventies (ISSN 0037-5969); Sixties (ISSN 0583-4570)

800 US ISSN 0148-8627
ENSAYISTAS; Georgia series on Hispanic thought. (Text in English and Spanish) 1976. a. $5. University of Georgia, Latin American Studies Center, Athens, GA 30602. TEL 404-542-1075. Ed.Bd. bk. rev. bibl. circ. 200. (back issues avail.)

808.8 US
ESSENCE (WAYNE) 1963. a. free. William Paterson College, 300 Pomton Rd., Wayne, NJ 07570. TEL 201-595-2000. Ed. Richard Voza. adv. illus. circ. 1, 625.

052 CH
EVENSONGS/YEH KO. (Text in Chinese or English) irreg., no.25, 1981. (English Department Evening School) Tamkang University, 18 Lishui St., Taipei, Taiwan, Republic of China. Ed. Lin Wienhsiang. adv. bk. rev. illus. circ. 3,000.

808.87 US
EXTRA SPECIAL CRACKED.* a. $1.75 per no. Candar Publishing Corp., Major Magazines Division, 15/05 Jorden Ct., No. 102-B Upper, Bayside, NY 11360-1148. illus. circ. 400,000.
Wit and humor

053 GW
FABULA PRESS AWARD READER. 1983. a. $1. Fabula Press Agency, Bezgenrieter Str. 85, 7326 Heiningen, W. Germany (B.R.D.) Ed. Peter H. Feldmann. adv. illus. circ. 1,250. (back issues avail.)

808.8 052 UK
FANATIC; a paper of passion. 1977. irreg. price varies. Open Head Press, 2 Blenheim Cresc., London W11 1NN, England. (back issues avail.)

700 SP
FORMA ABIERTA; cuadernos de creacion e investigacion artistica. (Supplement of: Instituto de Estudios Alicantinos. Revista) 1974. irreg. Instituto de Estudios Alicantinos, Diputacion Provincial, Alicante, Spain. Ed. Juan Orts Serrano.

808.8 US
FROZEN WAFFLES. 1976. irreg. $4.50 per no. Frozen Waffles Press & Tapes, Recre-Acres, Lot 61, 4111 Vernal Pike, Bloomington, IN 47401. Eds. Bro Dimitrios, David Wade. circ. 300.

FURMAN STUDIES. see LITERATURE

GAY INFORMATION; a journal of Gay studies. see POLITICAL SCIENCE — Civil Rights

808.838　　　　　　AT　ISSN 0310-9968
GEGENSCHEIN. 1971. irreg., no.52, 1986. Aus.$1 for 2 nos.; US$1 for 2 nos. ‡ c/o Eric B. Lindsay, Ed., 6 Hillcrest Ave., Faulconbridge, N.S.W. 2776, Australia. bk. rev. circ. 245. (also avail. in microfiche)

658　808　　　　　US　ISSN 8756-2898
GELOSOPHIST. 1985. irreg. (3-6/yr.) $11. Lone Star Publications of Humor, Box 29000, Ste. 103, San Antonio, TX 78229. TEL 512-271-2632. Ed. Lauren I. Barnett. bk. rev. film rev. play rev. abstr. illus. stat. (looseleaf format; back issues avail.)

GESHER. see *RELIGIONS AND THEOLOGY — Judaic*

055.1　　　　　　IT　ISSN 0017-0526
GIOVANE CRITICA. no.19, 1968. irreg., (5-6/yr.) Via della Trinita dei Pellegrini 19, 00186 Rome, Italy. Ed. Giampiero Mughini. bk. rev. play rev.

808.8　　　　　　US　ISSN 0533-2869
GREYFRIAR/SIENA STUDIES IN LITERATURE. 1960. a. free. ‡ Siena College, Department of English, Loudonville, NY 12211. TEL 518-783-2300. Ed. Peter A. Fiore. bibl. circ. 750. Indexed: M.L.A. Abstr.Engl.Stud.

051　　　　　　　CN　ISSN 0017-453X
GRONK.* 1967. irreg. Can.$12 for 6 nos. Ganglia Press, c/o The Village Bookstore, 239 Queen St. W., Toronto, Ont. M5V 1Z4, Canada. Ed. B.P. Nichol. circ. 200.
  Formerly: Ganglia.

059　　　　　　　MG
HAITENY, HAISORATA, HAIRAHA. 1978. irreg. Academie Malgache, Section 1, B.P. 6217, Tsimbazaza, Antananarivo, Malagasy Republic. circ. 300.

808.8　　　　　　US　ISSN 0737-7169
HEMLOCKS AND BALSAMS. 1980. a. $3. Lees-McRae College, Box 128, Banner Elk, NC 28604. TEL 704-898-5241. Ed. Allen Speer. adv. bk. rev. circ. 500.

059　　　　　　　FR
HOR YEZH. (Text in Breton) 1954. irreg. 40 F. for 4 nos. c/o P. Denis, Le Ris, Ploare, 29100 Douarnenez, Brittany, France. Ed. Arzel Even. Indexed: M.L.A.

808.8　　　　　　US
HOT LOGARITHM. 1982. a. $5. 201 Maple Ave., Sea Cliff, NY 11579. Ed. Julius Vitali. adv. bk. rev. illus.

057　　　　　　　UR
IMPERIALISM: EVENTS, FACTS, DOCUMENTS. 1985. a. 0.65 Rub. Izdatel'stvo Muzyka, Ul. Neglinnaya 14, Moscow 103031, Russian S.F.S.R., U.S.S.R.

700　　　　　　　PO
INFORMACAO CULTURAL. 1976. irreg. Secretaria da Estado da Cultura, Av. da Republica 16, Lisboa 1, Portugal.

059　　　　　　　NE　ISSN 0167-3696
INS AND OUTS; a magazine of awareness. (Text in English) 1978. irreg. $30 for 6 issues. Ins & Outs Press, Box 3759, Amsterdam, Netherlands. Ed. Edward Woods. adv. bk. rev. circ. 2,500.

INVISIBLE CITY. see *LITERATURE — Poetry*

059.8　　　　　　GR　ISSN 0021-0404
IOS.* (Text in Greek; summaries in English) 1938. irreg. (3-12/yr.) Dr.150.($8.) C. Papagheorghiou, 209 Leoforos Alexandras, Athens, Greece. adv. illus. circ. 5,000.

051　960　　　　US　ISSN 0047-1607
ISSUE; a quarterly journal of opinion. 1972. irreg. membership. African Studies Association, U C L A, 255 Kinsey Hall, 405 Hilgard Ave., Los Angeles, CA 90024. TEL 213-206-8011. Ed. Donald Cosentino. adv. bibl. circ. 2,200. (also avail. in microfilm) Indexed: Hist.Abstr. Amer.Hist.& Life. HR Rep.

JOURNAL OF CROATIAN STUDIES; annual review of the Croatian Academy of America. see *HISTORY — History Of Europe*

700　　　　　　　TR
KAIRI. 1976. a. 22 Fitt St., Woodbrook, Port-of-Spain, Trinidad. Ed. Christopher Laird. bk. rev. bibl. illus.

051　　　　　　　YE
AL-KALIMA; majallat al-muthaqqafiyn al-yamaniyiyn. irreg. 2 rials. Box 1109, Sana'a, Yemen. Ed. Ibrahim al-Maqhafi. adv. bk. rev.

810　　　　　　　US　ISSN 0022-8990
KARAMU. 1967. a. $1.75. Karamu Association, English Department, Eastern Illinois University, Charleston, IL 61920. Ed.Bd. bk. rev. illus. cum.index. circ. 400. (processed)

808.87　　　　　　US
KING SIZED CRACKED.* a. $1.75. Candar Publishing Corp., Major Magazines Division, 15/05 Jorden St., No. 102-B Upper, Bayside, NY 11360-1148. circ. 500,000.
  Wit and humor

320　　　　　　　CN　ISSN 0316-3393
L A W G LETTER. 1973. irreg. Can.$35. Latin American Working Group, Box 2207, Sta. P, Toronto, Ont. M5S 2T2, Canada. TEL 416-533-4221. Ed.Bd. bk. rev. illus. circ. 1,200. Indexed: HR Rep.

052　　　　　　　UK　ISSN 0262-575X
L T P. 1982. a. £1.50. L T P Cambridge, New Hall, Cambridge, England. circ. 1,250. (back issues avail.)

808.8　　　　　　US
LAPIS. 1977. a. $4. Lapis Educational Association, Inc., c/o Karen Degenhart, Ed., 5757 S. University Ave., Apt. 20B, Chicago, IL 60637-1507. (Co-publisher: New Vision Publications) bk. rev. circ. 200. Indexed: M.L.A.

808.87　　　　　　US
LAUGH FACTORY.* 1981. m. $15. Fell Great Publishing Co., 1370 Windsor Rd., Teaneck, NJ 07666. TEL 201-833-1336. Eds. Vince Donato, Gary Poole.

700　　　　　　　US　ISSN 0160-1857
LEFT CURVE. 1974. irreg. $15 for 3 nos. to individuals; institutions $20. Box 472, Oakland, CA 94604. TEL 415-763-7193. Ed. Csaba Polony. adv. bk. rev. film rev. play rev. illus. circ. 1,000. (back issues avail.) Indexed: Alt.Press Ind.

051　　　　　　　FR
LIGNE CREATRICE. 1971. irreg., 14 nos. published through 1975. 20 F. per no. c/o J. Tarkieltaub, 69 rue d'Hauteville, Paris, France. Ed. Isidore Isou. bibl. illus.

800　　　　　　　US　ISSN 0147-2593
LION & THE UNICORN; a critical journal of children's literature. 1977. a. $14 to individuals; institutions $25. Johns Hopkins University Press, 701 W. 40 St., Ste. 275, Baltimore, MD 21211. TEL 301-338-6987. Eds. Geraldine DeLuca, Roni Natov. adv. bk. rev. bibl. circ. 750. (reprint service avail. from ISI) Indexed: Curr.Cont. M.L.A. Arts & Hum.Cit.Ind. Abstr.Engl.Stud.

053　　　　　　　GW
LITERARISCHER WEIHNACHTSKATALOG. 1877. a. DM.1.80. Koch, Neff & Oetinger & Co., Schockenriedstr. 37, 7000 Stuttgart 80, W. Germany (B.R.D.) adv. bk. rev. (back issues avail.)

808.57　　　　　　US
LONE STAR HUMOR. 1983. irreg. (4-6/yr.) $14.95. Lone Star Publications of Humor, Box 29000, Ste. 103, San Antonio, TX 78229. TEL 512-271-2632. Ed. Lauren I. Barnett. adv. bk. rev. film rev. play rev. charts. illus. tr.lit. circ. 1,000. (back issues avail.)
  Formerly: Lone Star (ISSN 0735-1623)
  Wit and humor

808.8　　　　　　US
LUCKY HEART BOOKS. 1939. irreg. price varies. Salt Lick Press, 1804 E. 38 1/2 St., Austin, TX 78722. Ed. James Haining.

808.8　　　　　　US
MENOMONIE REVIEW. 1982. a. $2. University of Wisconsin, Stout English Department, Menomonie, WI 54751. TEL 715-235-8040. Ed. William O'Neill. circ. 500.

052　791.43　　　AT　ISSN 0814-8805
METAPHYSICAL REVIEW. 1984. irreg., approx. 4/yr. Aus.$35($25) Bruce Gillespie, Ed. & Pub., 59 Keele St., Collingwood, Vic. 3066, Australia. adv. bk. rev. circ. 200. (back issues avail.)

MIDAMERICA (EAST LANSING) see *LITERATURE*

808.8　　　　　　CN
MITRE; students' literary magazine. (Text in English) 1893. a. Can.$2.50($2.50) Bishop's University, Student's Representative Council, Lennoxville, Que., Canada. TEL 819-569-9551. adv. bk. rev. illus. circ. controlled. (tabloid format)
  Former titles: New Mitre; Mitre.

800　　　　　　　US
NEIHARDT FOUNDATION NEWSLETTER. 1970. a. $5 membership. John G. Neihardt Foundation, Inc., Bancroft, NE 68004. TEL 402-648-3388. Eds. Carol Peterson, Rosalie Nebraska. bk. rev. circ. 350.

320.5　800　　　　CN　ISSN 0702-7532
NEW LITERATURE AND IDEOLOGY. French edition: Nouvelle Litterature et Ideologie (ISSN 0703-8011) 1969. irreg. Can.$6 for 4 nos. Canadian Cultural Workers Committee, Box 727, Adelaide Station, Toronto M5C 2J8 Ont., Canada (Subscr. to: National Publications Centre, Box 727, Adelaide Station, Toronto, Ont., Canada) bk. rev. circ. 5,000. Indexed: Abstr.Engl.Stud.
  Incorporating: Literature and Ideology (ISSN 0024-4740)

808.8　700　　　　CN
NEW TOY. 1977. irreg. Can.$5. Taralble Mistakes, 1812-415 Willowdale Ave., Willowdale, Ont. M2N 5B4, Canada. Ed. Taral Wayne. circ. 250.
  Former Titles: Hominids, Oh; March to the Beat of a Red Shift Drum.

NEW YORK UNIVERSITY. STUDIES IN NEAR EASTERN CIVILIZATION. see *SOCIOLOGY*

808.8　　　　　　GW　ISSN 0720-6542
NIESPULVER. 1967. irreg. DM.2.50. Satire-Verlag, P.O. Box 210 207, 3000 Hannover, W. Germany (B.R.D.) Ed. Hans Firzlaff. adv. bk. rev. illus. circ. 20,000.
  Former titles: Hannover Extra; Satire (Magazine); Steintor.

800　　　　　　　NR
NIGERIA. WORK IN PROGRESS. (Text in English) 1972. biennial. 2.50 n. Ahmadu Bello University, Department of English, Zaria, Nigeria. Ed.Bd. bk. rev.

NIGHTSUN. see *LITERATURE*

056.1　　　　　　AG　ISSN 0029-1242
NORDESTE. 1960. irreg. Universidad Nacional del Nordeste, Facultad de Humanidades, Av. Las Heras 727, Corrientes, Resistencia, Argentina. Ed.Bd. bk. rev. charts. illus. circ. 2,400.

058　　　　　　　DK　ISSN 0109-3967
NORDICA; tidsskrift for nordisk tekshistorie og aestetik. (Text in Danish, Norwegian and Swedish) 1984. a. Kr.100. (Odense Universitet, Nordisk Institut) Odense University Press, Pjentedamsgade 136, 5000 Odense, Denmark.

058　　　　　　　DK　ISSN 0105-5100
NORDISK KULTURELT SAMARBEJDE. (Text in Danish, Norwegian and Swedish) 1975. a. free. Nordisk Ministerraad, Store Strandstraede 18, 1255 Copenhagen K, Denmark.

052　　　　　　　UK　ISSN 0265-7295
NORTH WIND. 1982. a. George MacDonald Society, The Library, King's College, Strand, London WC2R 2LS, England. Ed. K. Triggs. adv. bk. rev. circ. 100.

NOTEBOOKS IN CULTURAL ANALYSIS. see *HUMANITIES: COMPREHENSIVE WORKS*

808.8　　　　　　US
NU YU. 1981. irreg. Data Day Communications, Box 251, Philadelphia, PA 19105.

700　　　　　　　US
OJITO. 1976. a. $6. New Mexico State University, Department of English, Box 3C, Las Cruces, NM 88003. TEL 505-646-3931. adv. circ. 1,000. (back issues avail.)

ORD & SAG. see *LINGUISTICS*

808 US
OTHER SCENES. Title varies: Yellow Journal Pocket Press. John Wilcock's Secret Diary. 1966. irreg. $10. Other Scenes, 421 W. 43rd St., New York, NY 10036. Ed. John Wilcock. bk. rev. circ. 1,500. (reprint service avail. from UMI)

051 US
OTTERBEIN MISCELLANY. (Text in English, French and German) 1965. a. $1. Otterbein College, Westerville, OH 43081. TEL 614-890-3000. Ed. Norman Chaney. bk. rev. circ. 200 (controlled)

808.8 US
PAPER NEWS. 1980. irreg. Vanity Press, 160 6th Ave., New York, NY 10013. TEL 212-925-3823. Ed. Tuli Kupferberg. circ. 500.

058 DK ISSN 0901-201X
PARA - NYT; kritisk forum for off-beat litteratur og pseudovidenskab. 1981. irreg. price varies. Wegner Forlag, Postbox 6, 9320 Hjallerup, Denmark. bk. rev. illus. circ. 300.
Formerly: Skeptika (ISSN 0107-2900)

051 US
PARAMETERS; an occasional newsletter of critical issues. irreg. Circle Forum, Box 176, Portland, OR 97207. Indexed: Air Un.Lib.Ind. Amer.Bibl.Slavic & E.Eur.Stud. PROMT.

810 US ISSN 0097-496X
PEMBROKE MAGAZINE. 1969. a. $3. (North Carolina Arts Council) Pembroke State University, Box 60, Pembroke, NC 28372. TEL 919-521-4214. Ed. Shelby Stephenson. adv. bk. rev. illus. cum.index: 1969-73. circ. 1,500. (also avail. in microfilm from UMI; reprint service avail. from UMI) Indexed: Amer.Hum.Ind. A.I.P.P.

057 UR
PERSONALITIES. EVENTS. TIMES; albums. 1982. a. 6 Rub. Izdatel'stvo Muzyka, Ul. Neglinnaya 14, Moscow 103031, Russian S.F.S.R., U.S.S.R.

053.1 GW ISSN 0031-6784
DIE PFORTE; Zeitschrift und Schriften fuer wertidealistische Philosophie und Kultur. 1947. a. DM.12. Dr. Kurt Port Verlag GmbH, Dulkweg 9, 7300 Esslingen, W. Germany (B.R.D.) bk. rev. index. circ. 3,000.

PIRANESI; italienske Studier. see *LINGUISTICS*

056.1 AG
PLUMA Y PINCEL; para la difusion del arte y la cultura latinoamericanos. 1976. irreg. Editorial Arte y Letras de America, Nicaragua 5925, Buenos Aires, Argentina. Ed. Romeo Medina.

800 808 US ISSN 0731-5236
POETICS JOURNAL. 1982. irreg. $15. 2639 Russell St., Berkeley, CA 94705. Eds. Lyn Hejinian, Barrett Watten. bk. rev. circ. 750.

058 DK ISSN 0108-9943
PRESSEBLOMSTER. 1982. a. Kr.25. Pirattrykkeriet, Strandvej 13, 5700 Svendborg, Denmark. Eds. Erik Mathiasen, Bendt Gammeltoft-Hansen. illus.

800 IT
PUBBLICO; rassegna annuale di fatti letterari. 1977. a. L.10000. Milano Libri Edizioni s.r.l., Via A. Rizzoli 2, 20137 Milan, Italy. Ed. Vittorio Spinazzola. circ. 4,500.

320 US
RAMPART INDIVIDUALIST; a journal of free market libertarian scholarship. 1981. biennial. $10 to non-members. Rampart Institute, Inc., Box 26044, Santa Ana, CA 92799. Ed. Lawrence Samuels.

808.8 US
RASPBERRY PRESS.* 1974. a. $2. Rte. 1, Box 81, Puposky, MN 56601. Ed. Susan Hauser. circ. 300.

808.8 US
RE: PRINT; an occasional magazine. irreg.? $0.75. Printable Arts Society Inc., Box 749, Old Chelsea Sta., New York, NY 10011. Ed. David Ferguson. circ. 5,000.

808.8 UK ISSN 0143-0122
REALITY STUDIOS. 1978. a. $6. Reality Studios, 85 Balfour St., London SE17, England (Subscr. to: Small Press Distribution Inc., 1814 San Pablo Ave., Berkeley, CA 94702) Ed. Ken Edwards. bk. rev. bibl. cum.index. circ. 400. (also avail. in microfiche)

957 CS
REVUE SVETOVEJ LITERATURY. irreg. (Slovak Literary Fund) Slovensky Spisovatel', Gajova 9, 801 00 Bratislava, Czechoslovakia.

808.8 US
ROAR; tapebook series. 1979. irreg. $10. Lionhead Publishing - Roar Recording, 2521 E. Stratford Court, Shorewood, WI 53211. TEL 414-332-7474. Ed. Martin J. Rosenblum. bk. rev. (also avail. in audio cassette)

ROMANTIST. see *LITERATURE*

056.1 PE
RUNA. irreg. S.150 per no. Instituto Nacional de Cultura, Azangaro 235, Lima, Peru. Eds. Maruja Barrig, Luis Freire. illus.

809 JA
SAITAMA UNIVERSITY. COLLEGE OF LIBERAL ARTS. JOURNAL. (Text in English) vol.26, 1978. irreg. free. Saitama University, College of Liberal Arts, 1255 Shimookubo, Urawa-shi 338, Japan. circ. 500.

810 US
SARAH LAWRENCE REVIEW. 1957. irreg. contr. free circ. Sarah Lawrence College, Bronxville, NY 10708. TEL 914-337-0700.
Former titles: Sarah Lawrence Literary Review; S.L. Literary Review (ISSN 0036-4746)

SERIE OM VIDENSKABSFORSKNING. see *LINGUISTICS*

051 US ISSN 0271-3012
SEVEN; an Anglo-American literary review. 1980. a. $11. (Marion E. Wade Collection at Wheaton College) Bookmakers Guild, Inc., 1430 Florida Ave., Ste. 202, Longmont, CO 80501. TEL 303-442-5774. Ed. Barbara Reynolds. adv. bk. rev. circ. 1,000.

808.87 CN ISSN 0824-7870
DER SHMAISER/SPANKER. 1984. irreg. Can.$1 per no. David Botwinik, Ed. & Pub., 5775 Wentworth, Cote St. Luc, Montreal, Que. H4W 2S3, Canada. TEL 514-488-4469. circ. 1,000.
Wit and humor

943.7 GW ISSN 0037-7058
SLOWAKEI/SLOVAKIA; kulturpolitische Revue. 1963. a. DM.6. Matus-Cernak-Institut, Kulturelles Zentrum der Slowaken in Deutschland, Postfach 100924, 5000 Cologne 1, W. Germany (B.R.D.) Ed. Alba Greiner. bk. rev. circ. 1,500.

SNOECK'S; LITERATUUR KUNST FILM TONEEL MODE REIZEN. see *HUMANITIES: COMPREHENSIVE WORKS*

054.1 FR
SOCIETE J.K. HUYSMANS. BULLETIN. 1928. irreg., approx. 2/yr. 60 F. membership only. ‡ Societe J.K. Huysmans, 22 rue Guynemer, 75006 Paris, France. adv. bk. rev. circ. 600(controlled)

296.67 IS ISSN 0082-4585
SOURCES OF CONTEMPORARY JEWISH THOUGHT/MEKEVOT. Title varies: To the Source/El Ha'ayin. (Text in English, French, Spanish, Hebrew) 1968. irreg., no.6, 1975. price varies. World Zionist Organization, Department for Torah Education and Culture in the Diaspora, Box 92, Jerusalem, Israel (Subscr. to: Jewish Agency, Publication Service, 515 Park Ave., New York, NY 10022) Ed.Bd.

052 700 UK ISSN 0584-8067
SPANNER (LONDON, 1974) 1974. irreg. £6 for 3 issues to individuals; institutions £9. 64 Lancerost Rd., London SW2 3DN, England. Ed. Allen Fisher. adv. bk. rev.

STONE LION REVIEW. see *HISTORY — History Of Asia*

808.8 US
STORM; a journal for free spirits. 1976. irreg. approx. 1-2/yr. $2 per no. Mackay Society, Box 131, Ansonia Sta., New York, NY 10023. TEL 212-595-1669. Ed.Bd. adv. bk. rev. circ. 300. (back issues avail.)

320 UK ISSN 0260-2563
STUDENT NATIONALIST; the paper for the independent-minded Scot. 1979? irreg. contributions. Federation of Student Nationalists, c/o Student Union, Aberdeen University, Upper Kirkgate, Aberdeen, Scotland. Ed. Eric Herring. illus. circ. 5, 000.
Formerly: Nor'-easter.

808.87 US ISSN 0163-4143
STUDIES IN CONTEMPORARY SATIRE. 1973. a. $3. Clarion University, English Department, Clarion, PA 16214. Ed. C. Darrel Sheraw. adv. bk. rev. circ. 350. (back issues avail.) Indexed: M.L.A. Amer.Bibl.Slavic & E.Eur.Stud. Abstr.Engl.Stud.

SUBTERRANEAN SOCIOLOGY NEWSLETTER. see *SOCIOLOGY*

800 US
SYMPOSIUM SERIES. 1974. irreg., vol.18, 1986. $39.95 per no. Edwin Mellen Press, Box 450, Lewiston, NY 14092.

051 US
U AND I. 1985. a. $5. United Illuminating, Inc., Box 93427, Los Angeles, CA 90093. Ed.Bd. circ. 5,000. (back issues avail.)

UGANDA JOURNAL. see *HISTORY — History Of Africa*

378.1 US ISSN 0041-9524
UNIVERSITY OF DAYTON REVIEW. 1964. irreg., approx. 3/yr. free on request. (University of Dayton) University of Dayton Press, 300 College Park Ave., Dayton, OH 45469. TEL 513-229-0123. Ed. Robert C. Conard. charts. illus. index. circ. 1, 000. Indexed: M.L.A. Amer.Hum.Ind. Amer.Bibl.Slavic & E.Eur.Stud. Abstr.Engl.Stud.

UNMUZZLED OX. see *LITERATURE — Poetry*

808.8 US
VANISHING CAB.* 1976. a. $3.50. c/o The Segue Foundation, 300 Bowery, New York, NY 10012. Ed. Jerry Estrin. circ. 500.

808.7 UK
VING. 1980. irreg. free. Outcrowd, 3 Pleasant Villas, 189 Kent St., Mereworth, Maidstone, Kent ME18 5QN, England. Ed. R. Earl. illus. circ. 100.

320 PO
VOZ DO OPERARIO. 1879. irreg. membership. Sociedad de Instrucao e Beneficiencia a Voz do Operario, R. da Voz do Operaro, 13, Lisbon-2, Portugal. Ed. A. Falcao. bk. rev. illus. circ. 5,000.

808.87 UK
WEEKEND BOOK OF JOKES. 1961. a. £0.60. Associated Newspapers Group Ltd., Carmelite House, London EC4Y 0JA, England.

808.8 US
WILD FENNEL. 1970. irreg. $1. 2510 48th St., Bellingham, WA 98226. Ed. Pauline Palmer. circ. 350.

808.81 US
YET ANOTHER SMALL MAGAZINE. 1982. a. $2. Andrew Mountain Press, Box 14353, Hartford, CT 06114. Ed. Candace C. Hall.

LITERARY AND POLITICAL REVIEWS — Abstracting, Bibliographies, Statistics

011 020 016 US ISSN 0002-662X
ALTERNATIVE PRESS INDEX; an index to alternative and radical publications. 1969. q. $25 to individuals; institutions $100. Alternative Press Center, Inc., Box 33109, Baltimore, MD 21218. TEL 301-243-2471. Ed.Bd. bk. rev. circ. 550. (back issues avail.)

FRENCH 17; an annual descriptive bibliography of French seventeenth century studies. see *HISTORY — Abstracting, Bibliographies, Statistics*

GUIDE TO ALTERNATIVE PERIODICALS. see *SOCIAL SCIENCES: COMPREHENSIVE WORKS — Abstracting, Bibliographies, Statistics*

808.8 016 CN
WINTERGREEN; a directory of progressive periodicals. 1979. a. Can.$5($6) Alternative Research, Box 1294, Kitchener, Ont. N2G 4G8, Canada. Ed.Bd. circ. 1,500.

LITERATURE

see also *Literature–Poetry; Adventure and Romance; Publishing and Book Trade*

800 US ISSN 0270-2983
A M S STUDIES IN MODERN LITERATURE. 1973. irreg., no.16, 1986. price varies. A M S Press, Inc., 56 E. 13th St., New York, NY 10003. TEL 212-777-4700. (back issues avail.)

800 US ISSN 0275-8407
A M S STUDIES IN MODERN SOCIETY. 1972. irreg., no.19, 1986. price varies. A M S Press, Inc., 56 E. 13th St., New York, NY 10003. TEL 212-777-4700. (back issues avail.)

800 US ISSN 0196-6561
A M S STUDIES IN THE EIGHTEENTH CENTURY. 1970. irreg., no.9, 1986. price varies. A M S Press, Inc., 56 E. 13th St., New York, NY 10003. TEL 212-777-4700. (back issues avail.) Indexed: M.L.A.

A M S STUDIES IN THE MIDDLE AGES. see *HISTORY*

800 US ISSN 0196-657X
A M S STUDIES IN THE NINETEENTH CENTURY. 1980. irreg., no.4, 1986. A M S Press, Inc., 56 E. 13th St., New York, NY 10003. TEL 212-777-4700. (back issues avail.)

800 792.02 US ISSN 0195-8011
A M S STUDIES IN THE RENAISSANCE. 1976. irreg., no.15, 1986. price varies. A M S Press, Inc., 56 E. 13th St., New York, NY 10003. TEL 212-777-4700. (back issues avail.)

809 US ISSN 0731-2342
A M S STUDIES IN THE SEVENTEENTH CENTURY. 1986. irreg. price varies. (Abrahams Magazine Service) A M S Press, Inc., 56 E. 13th St., New York, NY 10003. TEL 212-777-4700.

A P U PRESS ALASKANA BOOK SERIES. (Alaska Pacific University Press) see *HISTORY — History Of North And South America*

A S C A P BIOGRAPHICAL DICTIONARY. (American Society of Composers, Authors and Publishers) see *MUSIC*

820 UK
A S L S NEWSLETTER. 1974. irreg. membership. Association for Scottish Literary Studies, c/o Dr. David Robb, Ed., Dept. of English, University of Dundee, Dundee DD1 4HN, Scotland. circ. 750.

800 GW
AACHENER BEITRAEGE ZUR KOMPARATISTIK. 1977. irreg., no.6, 1981. price varies. Bouvier Verlag Herbert Grundmann, Am Hof 32, Postfach 1268, 5300 Bonn 1, W. Germany (B.R.D.) Ed. Hugo Dyserinck. Indexed: M.L.A.

810 US ISSN 0361-1663
ABRAXAS. 1968. irreg. $12. Abraxas Press, Inc., 2518 Gregory St., Madison, WI 53711. TEL 608-238-0175. Ed. Ingrid Swanberg. adv. bk. rev. cum.index: 1968-1982. circ. 500. (back issues avail.)

898 BL
ACADEMIA BRASILEIRA DE LITERATURA. REVISTA. 1985. irreg. exchange basis. Academia Brasileira de Literatura, Rua Marques de Abrantes, 127-Apt.904, CEP 22230 Flamengo, Rio de Janeiro, Brazil. Dir. Leodegario A. de Azevedo Filho.

869 BL ISSN 0065-0447
ACADEMIA CAMPINENSE DE LETRAS. PUBLICACOES. 1958. irreg., no.44, 1983. Cr.$10000 or exchange. Academia Campinense de Letras, Rua Marechal Deodoro, 525, 13100 Campinas SP, Brazil. Ed. Lycurgo de Castro Santos Filho. circ. 500(controlled)

800 US
ACADEMIA DE CIENCIAS. ANUAL DE LITERATURA Y LINGUISTICA. a. Academia de Ciencias, Instituto de Documentacion e Informacion Cientifico-Tecnica (I D I C T), Ave. Salvador Allende, No. 117, Havana, Cuba.

800 SP ISSN 0065-0455
ACADEMIA ESPANOLA, MADRID. ANEJOS DEL BOLETIN. 1959. irreg., latest no. 38. price varies. Real Academia Espanola, Calle de Felipe IV No. 4, Madrid 14, Spain.

860 US
ACADEMIA NORTEAMERICANA DE LA LENGUA ESPANOLA. BOLETIN. (Text in Spanish) 1976. irreg. $8 to individuals; institutions $12. Academia Norteamericana de la Lengua Espanola, Box 7, F.D.R. Post Office, New York, NY 10022 (Subscr. to: Odon Betanzos, 125 Queen St., Staten Island, NY 10314) Ed. Eugenio Chang-Rodriguez. bk. rev. illus. circ. 3,000. Indexed: M.L.A.

800 BL ISSN 0001-3846
ACADEMIA PAULISTA DE LETRAS. REVISTA. 1937. irreg. free. Academia Paulista de Letras, Largo do Arouche 312, Sao Paulo, Brazil. Ed. Leonardo Arroyo. bibl. circ. 1,500. Indexed: Hisp.Amer.Per.Ind.

860 BL
ACADEMIA PERNAMBUCANA DE LETRAS. REVISTA. 1901. irreg. Academia Pernambucana de Letras, Av. Rui Barbosa, 1596, Recife, Brazil. illus.

840 FR ISSN 0065-0587
ACADEMIE FRANCAISE. ANNUAIRE; documents et notices sur les membres de l'Academie. 1966. irreg. Academie Francaise, 23 Quai de Conti, Paris 6e, France.

890 IS ISSN 0568-7306
ACHSAV. a. P.O. Box 3421, Tel Aviv 63 415, Israel. TEL 03-245120.

860 CL ISSN 0716-0909
ACTA LITERARIA. 1975. a. $9. Universidad de Concepcion, Departamento de Espanol, Casilla 2307, Concepcion, Chile. Dir. Luis Munoz G. bk. rev. circ. 600. Indexed: M.L.A.

057 YU ISSN 0567-784X
ACTA NEOPHILOLOGICA. (Text in various languages) 1968. a. $6. Univerza Edvarda Kardelja V Ljubljani, Filozofska Fakulteta, Askerceva 12, 61000 Ljubljana, Yugoslavia. Ed. Janez Stanonik. bk. rev. bibl. circ. 400. Indexed: M.L.A.

894.511 HU ISSN 0586-3708
ACTA UNIVERSITATIS DE ATTILA JOZSEF NOMINATAE. ACTA HISTORIAE LITTERARUM HUNGARICARUM. (Text in Hungarian; summaries in English, French, German or Russian) 1961. a. exchange basis. Attila Jozsef University, c/o E. Szabo, Exchange Librarian, Dugonics ter 13, P.O.B. 393, Szeged H-6701, Hungary (Subscr. to: Kultura, Box 149, H-1389 Budapest, Hungary) Eds. Ferenc Grezsa, Balint Keseru. circ. 500. Indexed: M.L.A.

ACTA UNIVERSITATIS DE ATTILA JOZSEF NOMINATAE. ACTA ROMANICA. see *LINGUISTICS*

ACTA UNIVERSITATIS DE ATTILA JOZSEF NOMINATAE. PAPERS IN ENGLISH AND AMERICAN STUDIES. see *LINGUISTICS*

800 370 PL
ACTA UNIVERSITATIS LODZIENSIS: FOLIA LITTERARIA. (Text in Polish; summaries in various languages) irreg. Uniwersytet Lodzki, Drukarnia Wojskowa, Ul. Gdanska 130, Lodz, Poland (Dist. by: Ars Polona-Ruch, Krakowskie Przedmiescie 7, Warsaw, Poland)

ACTA UNIVERSITATIS SZEGEDIENSIS DE ATTILA JOZSEF NOMINATAE. DISSERTATIONES SLAVICAE. SECTIO LINGUISTICA. see *LINGUISTICS*

ACTA UNIVERSITATIS SZEGEDIENSIS DE ATTILA JOZSEF NOMINATAE. SECTIO HISTORIAE LITTERARUM. see *LINGUISTICS*

890 SW ISSN 0440-9078
ACTA UNIVERSITATIS UPSALIENSIS. HISTORIA LITTERARUM. (Text in English, French, German and Swedish; summaries in French, English and German) 1962. a. $20. (Uppsala University, Historia Litterarum) Almqvist & Wiksell International, Box 256, 75105 Uppsala, Sweden. circ. 800. Indexed: M.L.A.

830 SW
ACTA UNIVERSITATIS UPSALIENSIS. STUDIA GERMANISTISCA UPSALIENSIS. (Text in German) 1964. irreg., latest no.27 1983. Almqvist & Wiksell International, Gamla Brogatan 26, S-11120 Stockholm, Sweden. Ed. John Evert Haerd. Indexed: M.L.A.

800 US ISSN 0065-1877
ADAPTATIONS SERIES. 1970. irreg., no.5, 1980. price varies. Proscenium Press, Box 361, Newark, DE 19711. TEL 302-737-5803. Ed. Robert Hogan. (reprint service avail. from UMI)

800 700 US
ADVANCEMENT 2: LITERATURE, MEDIA ARTS, OPERA-MUSICAL THEATRE, VISUAL ARTS. a. National Endowment for the Arts, Public Information Office, Washington, DC 20506. TEL 202-682-5400.

808 US ISSN 8756-1271
ADVANCES IN WRITING RESEARCH. 1985. a. price varies. Ablex Publishing Corp., 355 Chestnut St., Norwood, NJ 07648. TEL 201-767-8450. Ed. Marcia Farr.

AGE OF JOHNSON. see *HISTORY*

800 700 770 US
AILERON; a literary journal. 1980. a. $6. Aileron Press, Box 891, Austin, TX 78767-0891. Ed. Michael Gilmore. circ. 400.

800 FR ISSN 0065-4787
AILLEURS ET DEMAIN; CLASSIQUES.* 1970. irreg. price varies. Editions R. Laffont, 6 Place Saint-Sulpice, Paris 6e, France.

889 GR
AIOLIKA GRAMMATA. 1971. irreg. $15. Hodos Nireos 41, Palaion Phaliron, Athens, Greece. circ. 2,000. Indexed: M.L.A.

800 GW ISSN 0002-2985
AKADEMIE DER WISSENSCHAFTEN UND DER LITERATUR, MAINZ. KLASSE DER LITERATUR. ABHANDLUNGEN. 1950. irreg. price varies. Franz Steiner Verlag Wiesbaden GmbH, Birkenwaldstr. 44, Postfach 347, D-7000 Stuttgart 1, W. Germany (B.R.D.) index.

800 IS ISSN 0334-4827
ALAI SIACH; literary conversation. irreg. Brit Takam, Rehov Dobnov 10, Tel Aviv 64 732, Israel. Ed. Yadidiya Yitzhaki.

800 US
ALCATRAZ. 1979. irreg., no.3, 1984. price varies. (A E Foundation) Alcatraz Editions, 354 Hoover Rd., Soquel, CA 95073. Eds. Stephen Kessler, Hollis de Lancey. bk. rev. circ. 1,000. (back issues avail.)

800 CN ISSN 0384-8523
ALCHEMIST. 1974. irreg. Can.$10. Box 123, Lasalle, Quebec H8R 3T7, Canada. Ed. Marco Fraticelli. illus. circ. 500.

801 701 FR ISSN 0249-3446
ALEA. 1981. a. Christian Bourgois Editeur, 8 rue Garanciere, 75006 Paris, France. Ed. J. Christophe Bally. illus. circ. 2,000. (back issues avail.)

800 CN ISSN 0065-616X
ALEXANDER LECTURES. 1929. irreg. price varies. University of Toronto Press, Front Campus, Toronto, Ont. M5S 1A6, Canada TEL 613-667-7791. (U.S. address: 33 E. Tupper St., Buffalo, NY 14203)

ALFA; revista de linguistica. see *LINGUISTICS*

ALIF; journal of comparative poetics. see *LITERATURE — Poetry*

800 US ISSN 0742-096X
ALLEGHENY REVIEW; a national journal of undergraduate literature. 1983. a. $3. Allegheny College, Box 32, Meadville, PA 16335 TEL 814-724-6553. Eds. Catherine M. Forbes, Amy L. MacZuzak. circ. 800. (back issues avail.)

ALMANAK FOR TEOLOGI OG LITTERATUR. see *RELIGIONS AND THEOLOGY*

800 700 CN
ALPHA. 1976. irreg. (2-4/yr.) Can.$3. (Acadia University Students Unions) Either Or Publications, Acadia University, Wolfville, N.S. B0P 1X0, Canada. TEL 902-542-2201. Ed. Penny L. Ellis. adv. bk. rev. film rev. play rev. illus. (back issues avail.)

830 GW ISSN 0065-6607
ALTDEUTSCHE TEXTBIBLIOTHEK. ERGAENZUNGSREIHE. 1963. irreg. price varies. Max Niemeyer Verlag, Pfrondorfer Str. 4, 7400 Tuebingen, W. Germany (B.R.D.) (back issues avail.) Indexed: M.L.A.

809 GW
ALTE ABENTEUERLICHE REISEBERICHTE. 1966. irreg. price varies. K. Thienemanns Verlag, Edition Erdmann, Blumenstr. 36, 7000 Stuttgart 1, W. Germany (B.R.D.) circ. 4,000.

820 821 UK ISSN 0266-8521
ALTRIVE CHAPBOOKS. 1984. a. £2. James Hogg Society, The Haldane Room, The Library, University of Stirling, Stirling FK9 4LA, Scotland. bk. rev. circ. 100. (back issues avail.)

AMACADMY. see *ART*

814.008 US ISSN 0065-9142
AMERICAN LITERARY SCHOLARSHIP. 1963. a. price varies. Duke University Press, 6697 College Sta., Durham, NC 27708. TEL 919-684-2173. Eds. J. Albert Robbins, Warren G. French. (reprint service avail. from ISI, UMI) Indexed: M.L.A.

AMERICAN PHILOLOGICAL ASSOCIATION. DIRECTORY OF MEMBERS. see *LINGUISTICS*

AMERICAN PHILOLOGICAL ASSOCIATION. SPECIAL PUBLICATIONS. see *LINGUISTICS*

AMERICAN SOCIETY FOR ARMENIAN STUDIES. JOURNAL. see *ETHNIC INTERESTS*

800 US ISSN 0740-9257
AMERICAN UNIVERSITY STUDIES. SERIES 2. ROMANCE LANGUAGES AND LITERATURE. 1982. irreg. Peter Lang Publishing, Inc., 62 W. 45th St., New York, NY 10036. TEL 212-302-6740. Ed. Jay Wilson.

808.1 US ISSN 0724-1445
AMERICAN UNIVERSITY STUDIES. SERIES 3. COMPARATIVE LITERATURE. 1982. irreg. Peter Lang Publishing, Inc., 62 W. 45th St., New York, NY 10036. TEL 212-302-7640. Ed. Jay Wilson.

800 US ISSN 0741-0700
AMERICAN UNIVERSITY STUDIES. SERIES 4. ENGLISH LANGUAGE AND LITERATURE. 1983. irreg. Peter Lang Publishing, Inc., 62 W. 45th St., New York, NY 10036. Ed. Jay Wilson.
Formerly: American University Studies. Series 5. Anglo-Saxon Language and Literature (ISSN 0724-1453)

800 US ISSN 0741-9309
AMERICAN UNIVERSITY STUDIES. SERIES 17. CLASSICAL LANGUAGE AND LITERATURE. 1986. irreg. Peter Lang Publishing, Inc., 62 W. 45th St., New York, NY 10036. TEL 213-302-6740. Ed. Jay Wilson.

823 US ISSN 0742-1923
AMERICAN UNIVERSITY STUDIES. SERIES 18. AFRICAN LITERATURE. 1984. irreg. Peter Lang Publishing, Inc., 62 W. 45th ST., New York, NY 10036. TEL 212-302-6740. Ed. Jay Wilson.

810.9 US
AMERICAN UNIVERSITY STUDIES. SERIES 19. GENERAL LITERATURE. 1984. irreg. Peter Lang Publishing, Inc., 62 W. 45th St., New York, NY 10036. TEL 212-302-6740. Ed. Jay Wilson.

800 920 FR ISSN 0293-0773
AMIS DE RAMUZ. BULLETIN. 1981. a. 65 Fr. Les Amis du Ramuz, Universite Francois Rabelais, 3 rue des Tanneurs, F-37000 Tours, France. Ed. J.L. Pierre. adv. bk. rev. circ. 250. (back issues avail)

800 940 NE ISSN 0304-6257
AMSTERDAMER BEITRAEGE ZUR NEUEREN GERMANISTIK. 1972. irreg. price varies. Editions Rodopi B.V., Keizersgracht 302-304, 1016 EX Amsterdam, Netherlands. Ed. Gerd Labroisse. circ. 600. Indexed: M.L.A.

830 NE ISSN 0169-0221
AMSTERDAMER PUBLIKATIONEN ZUR SPRACHE UND LITERATUR. 1972. irreg., approx. 20/yr. price varies. Editions Rodopi B.V., Keizersgracht 302-304, 1016 EX Amsterdam, Netherlands (Dist. in the U.S. by: Humanities Press, Inc., 171 First Ave., Atlantic Highlands, NJ 07718) Ed. Cola Minis. circ. 500. Indexed: M.L.A.
Germanic languages

808.8 US
ANAIS: AN INTERNATIONAL JOURNAL. 1983. a. $7. Anais Nin Foundation, 2335 Hidalgo Ave., Los Angeles, CA 90039. Ed. Gunther Stuhlmann. bk. rev. circ. 1,250. Indexed: Amer.Hum.Ind.

ANALECTA CARTUSIANA; review for Carthusian history and spirituality. see *RELIGIONS AND THEOLOGY*

ANALECTA ROMANICA. see *LINGUISTICS*

860 SP ISSN 0210-4547
ANALES DE LITERATURA HISPANOAMERICANA. 1972. a. 900 ptas.($14) Universidad Complutense de Madrid, Departamento de Literature Hispanoamericana, Facultad de Estomatologia, Ciudad Universitaria, 28040 Madrid, Spain. (Co-sponsor: Instituto de Cultura Hispanica) bk. rev. bibl.

860 US
ANALES GALDOSIANOS. (Text in Spanish and English) 1966. a. $6. International Association of Galdos Scholars, Cornell University, Dept. Romance Studies, Goldwin Smith Hill, Ithaca, NY 14853. Ed. John Kronik. bk. rev. circ. 375. Indexed: M.L.A.

800 IT
ANALYSIS: QUADERNI DI ANGLISTICA. (Text in English and Italian) 1983. a. L.16.000($13) Editrice Tecnico Scientifica, Piazza Torricelli 4, I-56100 Pisa, Italy. Ed. Anthony L. Johnson. circ. 500. (back issues avail.)

ANANDA ACHARYA UNIVERSAL SERIES. see *PHILOSOPHY*

809 IR ISSN 0517-8045
ANCIENT IRANIAN CULTURAL SOCIETY. PUBLICATION/ANJOMAN-E FARHANG-E IRAN-E BASTAN. NASHRIYEH. (Text in Farsi) 1962. irreg., latest vol.17, 1979. Rs.30 per no. Ancient Iranian Cultural Society, Nadri Ave., Kuche-Ye Shahrowkh, Box 14-1262, Teheran, Iran. Ed. Farhang Mehr. circ. 1,500.

800 DK ISSN 0084-6465
ANDERSENIANA. (Text in Danish; occasionally in English and German; summaries in Danish, English, French, German) 1933. a. Kr.50. Hans Christian Andersen Museum, Hans Jensensstraede 39-43, DK-5000 Odense C, Denmark. Ed. Niels Oxenvad. adv. bk. rev. abstr. bibl. illus. cum.index. circ. 1,000. Indexed: Bio.Ind.

840 FR ISSN 0180-9350
ANDRE GIDE; la revue des lettres modernes. 1970. a. price varies. Lettres Modernes, 73 rue du Cardinal Lemoine, 75005 Paris, France. Ed. Claude Martin. bk. rev. (back issues avail.)

820 IE
ANGELA THIRKELL SOCIETY. JOURNAL. 1981. a. £3. Angela Thirkell Society, c/o Mrs. V. Ramsden, 14 Stanhope Ave., Hosforth, Leeds LS1 5AR, England (Subscr. addr.: c/o G. Wright, Esq., Madely Cottage, Church Hill, Carshalton, Surrey, England) bk. rev. circ. 200. (back issues avail.)

700 800 US
ANGELTREAD. 1984. irreg. (3-4/yr.) $8. c/o Tina W. Phillips, Ed., 73 University Apts., Charleston, IL 61920-9714. TEL 512-965-4842.

820 DK ISSN 0066-1805
ANGLISTICA. 1953. irreg. price varies. Rosenkilde og Bagger Ltd., 3 Kron-Prinsens-Gade, P.O.B. 2184, DK-1017, Denmark. Ed. T.J.B. Spencer. circ. 900. Indexed: Curr.Cont. Arts & Hum.Cit.Ind.

809 GW
ANGLISTISCHE FORSCHUNGEN. 1901. irreg., vol.134, 1978. price varies. Carl Winter Universitaetsverlag, Lutherstr. 59, 6900 Heidelberg, W. Germany (B.R.D.) Indexed: M.L.A.

940 820 410 GW
ANGLO-AMERICAN FORUM. (Text in English and German; summaries in English) 1975. irreg. price varies. Verlag Peter Lang GmbH, Hinter den Ulmen 19, D-6000 Frankfurt/Main 50, W. Germany (B.R.D.) Ed. Christoph Gutknecht. bk. rev. abstr. bibl. circ. 400 (controlled) (back issues avail.) Indexed: M.L.A.

ANGOL FILOLOGIAI TANULMANYOK/ HUNGARIAN STUDIES IN ENGLISH. see *LINGUISTICS*

850 IT
ANNALI ALFIERIANI. irreg. Centro Nazionale di Studi Alfieriani, Via Gaudenzi Ferrari, 9, I-14100 Asti, Italy.

850 US ISSN 0741-7527
ANNALI D'ITALIANISTICA. 1983. a. $10 to individuals; students $8; institutions $16. (University of Notre Dame, Department of Modern and Classical Languages) Annali d'Italianistica, Inc., Notre Dame, IN 46556. Ed. Dino S. Cervigni. adv. bk. rev. circ. 500. Indexed: M.L.A.

843 FR ISSN 0084-6473
ANNEE BALZACIENNE. 1960. a. 85 F. (Groupe d'Etudes Balzaciennes) Editions Garnier Freres, 19, rue des Plantes, 75014 Paris, France. Indexed: M.L.A.

840 FR ISSN 0066-3387
ANNUAIRE NATIONAL DES LETTRES. 1948. biennial. Editions Dany Thibaud, 52 rue Labrouste, 75015 Paris, France.

900 800 UK ISSN 0066-3832
ANNUAL BULLETIN OF HISTORICAL LITERATURE. 1911. a. £10. Historical Association, 59a Kennington Park Rd., London SE11 4JH, England. Ed. M. Greengrass. index. (reprint service avail. from UMI) Indexed: Br.Archaeol.Abstr.

ANNUAL WORLD'S BEST S F. see *ADVENTURE AND ROMANCE*

879 US ISSN 0066-4456
ANNUALE MEDIAEVALE. 1960. a. $18.50 to individuals; institutions $28.50. Humanities Press, Inc., 171 First Ave., Atlantic Highlands, NJ 07716. TEL 201-872-1441. Ed. Frank Zbozny. adv. (back issues avail.) Indexed: Curr.Cont. M.L.A. Arts & Hum.Cit.Ind.

810 US
ANON NINE. irreg. Street Fiction Press, 130 Touro St., Box 625, Newport, RI 01840. TEL 401-847-1067.

800 US ISSN 0735-8202
ANOTHER SEASON. 1982. a. $6. Gothaholm House, 3980 Cty.Rd. No. 10 N., Watertown, MN 55388-9339. Ed. John M. Becknell. illus. circ. 500.

ANUARIO DE FILOLOGIA. see *LINGUISTICS*

860   MX   ISSN 0543-758X
ANUARIO DE LETRAS. 1961. a. Universidad
Nacional Autonoma de Mexico, Instituto de
Investigaciones Filologicas, Villa Obregon, Ciudad
Universitaria, Mexico 20, D.F., Mexico. Indexed:
Hist.Abstr. Amer.Hist.& Life. Hisp.Amer.Per.Ind.

860   CR   ISSN 0587-5196
ANUARIO DEL CUENTO COSTARRICENSE.
1967. a. $10. Editorial Costa Rica, Calles la y 3a,
Apdo 2014, San Jose, Costa Rica.

891.7   UR
APPARAT UPRAVLENIYA
SOTSIALISTICHESKOGO GOSUDARSTVA.
(Izdanie v dvukh chastyakh) 1976. irreg.
(Akademiya Nauk S.S.S.R., Institut Gosudarstva i
Prava) Izdatel'stvo Yuridicheskaya Literatura,
Moscow, Russian S.F.S.R., U.S.S.R. Ed.Bd.

840   IS
APPROCHES. (Text in French) 1984. a. Haifa
University, Faculty of Humanities, Hacarmel, Haifa
31 999, Israel.

860   UY   ISSN 0066-5606
AQUI. 1983. irreg. Editorial Arca, Zabala 1322, Apdo.
102, Montevideo, Uruguay.

AL-ARABIYYA. see *LINGUISTICS*

800   GW   ISSN 0173-2307
ARBEITEN UND TEXT ZUR SLAVISTIK. (Text
mainly in Russian) 1973. irreg. price varies. Verlag
Otto Sagner, Postfach 34 01 08, Hessstr. 39/41, D-
8000 Munich 34, W. Germany (B.R.D.) Ed.
Wolfgang Kassack. circ. 200. (back issues avail.)

890   IS
ARC. (Text in English) 1982. a. IS.6($4) Israel
Association of Writers in English, 4 Nathan St.,
Ramat Gan 52 435, Israel.

ARCHIVE FOR REFORMATION HISTORY.
LITERATURE REVIEW/ARCHIV FUER
REFORMATIONSGESCHICHTE.
LITERATURBERICHT. see *RELIGIONS AND
THEOLOGY*

840   FR   ISSN 0066-6556
ARCHIVES CLAUDELIENNES. (Subseries of:
Archives des Lettres Modernes) 1958. irreg. price
varies. Lettres Modernes, 73 rue du Cardinal-
Lemoine, 75005 Paris, France.

800   CN   ISSN 0066-6572
ARCHIVES DES LETTRES CANADIENNES. 1961.
irreg. price varies. (University of Ottawa, Centre de
Recherches de Litterature Canadienne-Francaise)
Editions Fides, 5710 Ave. Decelles, Montreal, Que.
H3S 2C5, Canada. TEL 514-735-6406. Indexed:
RADAR.

809   FR   ISSN 0003-9675
ARCHIVES DES LETTRES MODERNES; etudes de
critique et d'histoire litteraire. 1957. irreg. (6-10/yr.)
345 F. for 60 "cahiers". Lettres Modernes, 73 rue du
Cardinal Lemoine, 75005 Paris, France. Ed. Michel
J. Minard. Indexed: M.L.A.

860   CK   ISSN 0066-6734
ARCHIVO EPISTOLAR COLOMBIANO. 1965.
irreg., latest no.18, 1983. price varies. Instituto Caro
y Cuervo, Seccion de Publicaciones, Apdo. Aereo
51502, Bogota, Colombia.

809   IT   ISSN 0066-6807
ARCHIVUM ROMANICUM. BIBLIOTECA. SERIE
1: STORIA LETTERATURA-PALEOGRAFIA.
(Text in French, German, Italian) 1921. irreg.,
vol.199, 1986. price varies. Casa Editrice Leo S.
Olschki, Casella Postale 66, 50100 Florence, Italy.
circ. 1,000.

800   PL   ISSN 0066-6904
ARCHIWUM LITERACKIE. (Text in Polish) 1956.
irreg., vol.25, 1982. price varies. (Polska Akademia
Nauk, Instytut Badan Literackich) Ossolineum,
Publishing House of the Polish Academy of
Sciences, Rynek 9, Wroclaw, Poland (Dist. by Ars
Polona-Ruch, Krakowskie Przedmiescie 7, Warsaw,
Poland) circ. 1,500.

ARCHIWUM TLUMACZEN Z TEORII
LITERATURY I METODOLOGII BADAN
LITERACKICH. see *LINGUISTICS*

840   PO
ARIANE; revue d'etudes litteraires francaises. (Text in
French) 1982. a. 40 F. (L'institut de Culture
Francaise, Groupe Universitaire d'Etudes de
Litterature Francaise) Universidade de Lisboa,
Cidade Universitaria, 1699 Lisbon Codex, Portugal.
circ. 1,000.

820   PK   ISSN 0254-3028
ARIEL. (Text in English) 1972. a. Rs.25. University of
Sind, Department of English, Jamshoro, Sind,
Pakistan. Ed. K.M. Larik. bk. rev. circ. 500.
Indexed: Curr.Cont. Hum.Ind. Arts &
Hum.Cit.Ind.

800   US
ARIZONA STATE UNIVERSITY. CENTER FOR
ASIAN STUDIES. MONOGRAPH SERIES. 1967.
irreg., no.18, 1985. $8 per vol. Arizona State
University, Center for Asian Studies, Tempe, AZ
85287. TEL 602-965-7184. Dir. Sheldon Simon.
circ. 500.
   Formerly: Arizona State University. Center for
Asian Studies. Occasional Papers.

839 439   DK   ISSN 0107-1475
ARNAMAGNAEAN INSTITUTE AND
DICTIONARY. BULLETIN. 1964. biennial. free.
Arnamagnaean Institute and Arnamagnaean
Dictionary, Njalsgade 76, DK-2300 Copenhagen S,
Denmark.
   Formerly (until 1975): Arnamagnaean Institute.
Bulletin (ISSN 0066-7765)

808   US   ISSN 0277-7053
ART ON THE LINE. 1981. a. $8. Curbstone Press,
321 Jackson St., Willimantic, CT 06226. Ed. James
Scully. adv.

800   US   ISSN 0196-691X
ARTFUL DODGE. 1979. a. $10 to individuals;
institutions $16. Artful Dodge Publications, Box
1473, Bloomington, IN 47402. TEL 812-966-2096.
Ed. Daniel Bourne. adv. bk. rev. illus. circ. 750.
(back issues avail.)

840   FR   ISSN 0180-9385
ARTHUR RIMBAUD. 1972. a. Lettres Moderne, 73
rue du Cardinal Lemoine, 75005 Paris, France. Ed.
Louis Forrestier. bk. rev. (back issues avail.)

800   US
ARTHURIAN LITERATURE. 1981. a. 33.50.
Littlefield, Adams & Co., 81 Adams Dr., Totowa,
NJ 07512. Ed. Richard Barber.

808   US
ASSAYS. 1981. a. price varies. University of
Pittsburgh Press, 127 N. Bellefield Ave., Pittsburgh,
PA 15260. TEL 412-624-4110.

840   FR   ISSN 0066-8893
ASSOCIATION DES AMIS D'ALFRED DE
VIGNY. BULLETIN. 1968. a. membership.
Association des Amis d'Alfred de Vigny, 6 av.
Constant-Coquelin, 75007 Paris, France. Eds. Andre
Jarry, C. Lefranc. adv. bk. rev. circ. 500. (also avail.
in microfiche)

800   IT
ATALANTA. 1976. irreg., no.2, 1977. L.4900.
Giardini Editori e Stampatori, Via Santa Bibbiana
28, 56100 Pisa, Italy. Eds. S.G. Mancini, M.
Pagnini. Indexed: Biol.Abstr.

860   BL
ATRAVES. 1976. irreg. Livraria Duas Cidades, Rua
Bento Freitas 158, 01220 Sao Paulo SP, Brazil.
Ed.Bd. illus.

806   US
AUGUST DERLETH SOCIETY. NEWSLETTER.*
1977. irreg. $1. August Derleth Society, c/o
Richard H. Fawcett, Ed., 61 Teecomwas Dr.,
Uncasville, CT 06382. TEL 203-848-0636. Ed.
Richard H. Fawcett. adv. bk. rev. circ. 200.

830 709   GW   ISSN 0341-1230
AURORA; Jahrbuch der Eichendorff-Gesellschaft.
(Text in German; summaries in English and
German) 1953. a. price varies. Jan Thorbecke
Verlag, Postfach 546, D-7480 Sigmaringen, W.
Germany (B.R.D.) Ed.Bd. bk. rev. bibl. illus. index.
circ. 1,000. Indexed: M.L.A.

800   US
AURORA (RICHMOND) 1935. a. $1. Eastern
Kentucky University, Richmond, KY 40475. TEL
606-622-0111. circ. 400. (back issues avail.)

830 709   GW   ISSN 0171-6530
AURORA-BUCHREIHE. 1974. irreg. price varies. Jan
Thorbecke Verlag, Postfach 546, D-7480
Sigmaringen, W. Germany (B.R.D.) Ed.Bd. circ. 1,
000.

809 700   GW
AUSGABE; ein Literatur- und Kunstmagazin. 1976. a.
DM.20. Armin Hundertmark Ed. & Pub., Bruesseler
Str. 29, D-5000 Cologne 1, W. Germany (B.R.D.)
adv.

830   SZ
AUSTRALIAN AND NEW ZEALAND STUDIES
IN GERMAN LANGUAGE AND LITERATURE.
(Text in English and German) 1971. irreg. Verlag
Peter Lang AG, Jupiterstrasse 15, CH-3015 Bern,
Switzerland. Ed. G. Schulz. circ. 400. (back issues
avail.)

AUSTRALIAN SLAVONIC AND EAST
EUROPEAN STUDIES. see *LINGUISTICS*

808 920   US   ISSN 0145-1499
AUTHORS IN THE NEWS; compilation of news
stories and feature articles from American
newspapers and magazines, covering prominent
writers in all fields. 1975. irreg., vol.1, 1976. $72 per
vol. Gale Research Company, Book Tower, Detroit,
MI 48226. TEL 313-961-2242. Ed. Barbara
Nykoruk. Indexed: Child.Auth.& Illus.
   Formerly: Contemporary Authors News.

869   BL
AUTORES AFRICANOS. 1982. irreg. Editora Atica,
S.A., Rua Barao de Iguape, 110, Caixa Postal 8656,
Sao Paulo, Brazil.

840   FR   ISSN 0067-2610
AVANT-SIECLE. 1967. irreg., no.15, 1978. price
varies. Lettres Modernes, 73, Rue du Cardinal-
Lemoine, 75005 Paris, France. Ed. Louis Forestier.

800   UY   ISSN 0067-2637
AVES DEL ARCA.* irreg. Editorial Arca, Colonia
1263, Montevideo, Uruguay.

AWRAQ YADIDA. see *HISTORY — History Of
Europe*

808 700 778.534   US
AXE FACTORY REVIEW. 1985. a. $5. (Axe Factory
Center for the Arts) Axe Factory Publications, Box
11186, Philadelphia, PA 19136. TEL 215-331-7389.
Eds. Louis McKee, Joesph Farley. adv. bk. rev. circ.
600.

B L A C. (Black Literature and Arts Congress) see
ETHNIC INTERESTS

820   UK   ISSN 0306-8404
BANDERSNATCH. 1973. irreg. membership. Lewis
Carroll Society, 69 Ashby Rd., Woodville, Burton-
on-Trent, Staffs, England (Subscr. addr.: c/o Peter
Shaw, 47 Summerville Gardens, Cheam, Surrey,
England) Ed. Alfreda Blanchard. bk. rev. circ.
350(controlled)

896   SA   ISSN 0067-4044
BANTU TREASURY. 1935. irreg. price varies.
Witwatersrand University Press, Jan Smuts Ave.,
Johannesburg 2001, South Africa.

840 700   FR
BARBACANE; revue des pierres et des hommes.
vol.11, 1975. a. 40 F. Cercle Culturel et Artisanal
de Bonaguil, Chateau de Bonaguil, Saint Front sur
Lemance, 47500 Fumel, France. Ed. Max Pons. adv.
bk. rev. circ. 500.

371 028.5   AU   ISSN 0067-4206
DIE BARKE; Lehrer-Jahrbuch. 1956. a.
Oesterreichischer Buchklub der Jugend,
Mayerhofgasse 6, A-1040 Vienna, Austria. (Co-
sponsor: International Institute for Children's
Literature and Reading Research) Ed. Gertrud Pott.

LITERATURE

800 FR ISSN 0067-4222
BAROQUE; revue internationale. 1963. irreg., latest vol.12, 1985. 160 Fr. (Centre International de Synthese du Baroque) Editions Cocagne, 30 rue de la Banque, 82 000 Montauban, France. (back issues avail.) Indexed: M.L.A.
 Former titles (until 1966): Journees Internationales d'Etude du Baroque. Actes; 1963-1965: Journees Internationales d'Etudes du Baroque.

830 430 SZ ISSN 0067-4508
BASLER STUDIEN ZUR DEUTSCHEN SPRACHE UND LITERATUR. 1954. irreg., vol.59, 1983. price varies. Francke Verlag, Postfach, CH-3000 Berne 26, Switzerland. Ed.Bd.

891.7 CN ISSN 0005-6952
BAYAVAYA USKALOS; Byelorussian literary magazine. (Text in Byelorussian) 1950. a. Can.$3 or donation. Byelorussian Literary Association, 24 Tarlton Rd., Toronto, Ont. M5P 2M4, Canada. Ed. Siergey Khmara. bk. rev. illus. circ. 500.

800 IE
BEAU; an annual publication of and about literature. 1981. a. £1.50. Billy Mills, Ed. & Pub., 39 Synge Rd., Dublin 8, Ireland. circ. 1,000.

800 US
BEAU FLEUVE SERIES. 1970. irreg., no.9, 1976. $1. Intrepid Press, Box 110, Buffalo, NY 14215. Ed. Allen De Loach.

BEBOP DRAWING CLUB BOOK. see ART

891.4 II ISSN 0005-769X
BEDUIN. (Text in Bengali) 1966. a. Rs.12. Rani Suhasini Roy, Tamluk Raj House, Tamluk, Midnapore, West Bengal, India. Ed. Bhabanee Mukhopadhyay.

BEITRAEGE ZUR DEUTSCHEN PHILOLOGIE. see LINGUISTICS

809 GW ISSN 0170-3315
BEITRAEGE ZUR LITERATUR DES 15.-18. JAHRHUNDERTS. (Text in English and German) irreg., vol.6, 1974. price varies. Franz Steiner Verlag Wiesbaden GmbH, Birkenwaldstr. 44, Postfach 347, D-7000 Stuttgart 1, W. Germany (B.R.D.) Ed. Hans-Gert Roloff.

479 GW ISSN 0067-5202
BEITRAEGE ZUR ROMANISCHEN PHILOLOGIE DES MITTELALTERS. 1968. irreg. price varies. Wilhelm Fink Verlag, Ohmstr. 5, 8000 Munich 40, W. Germany (B.R.D.) Eds. Hans-Wilhelm Klein, Ernstpeter Ruhe. Indexed: Curr.Cont. M.L.A. Arts & Hum.Cit.Ind.

830 GW
BEITRAEGE ZUR SCHWABISCHEN LITERATUR- UND GEISTESGESCHICHTE UND MITTEILUNGEN DES JUSTINIUS KERNER- VEREINS UND FRAUENVEREINS. 1981. biennial. price varies. Justinus-Kerner-Verein, Steiermaerker Str. 132, 7000 Stuttgart 30, W. Germany (B.R.D.) Ed. Hartmut Froeschke.

800 CN ISSN 0067-5733
BENT. (Text in English) 1969. irreg., no.7, 1971. Can.$0.25. 1111 Bewdley Avenue, Victoria, B. C., Canada. Ed. Byrd Lukinuk. adv. circ. 300.

820 UK
BERNARD SHAW SERIES. 1976. a. £5. Bernard Shaw Centre, 125 Markyate Rd., Dagenham, Essex RM8 2LB, England. circ. 600.

820 UK
BERNARD SHAW SOCIETY JOURNAL. 1976. a. £5. Bernard Shaw Society, High Orchard, 124 Markyate Rd., Dagenham, Essex RM8 2LB, England. Ed. E. Ford. adv. bk. rev. abstr. bibl. charts. film rev. illus. stat. tr.lit. index. circ. 200. (also avail. in microform) Indexed: Abstr.Engl.Stud.

813.08 US ISSN 0067-6233
BEST AMERICAN SHORT STORIES. 1915. a. price varies. Houghton Mifflin Co., One Beacon St., Boston, MA 02107. TEL 617-725-5000.

813.01 CN ISSN 0703-9476
BEST CANADIAN STORIES. 1971. a. $23.95 (clothbound); $12.95(paperbacks) Oberon Press, 401a Delta Ottawa, 350 Sparks St., Ottawa, Ont. K1R 7S8, Canada. TEL 613-238-2375. Eds. David Helwig, Sandra Martin. adv. bk. rev. circ. 2,500.
 Continues: New Canadian Stories (ISSN 0316-7518)

BEST SCIENCE FICTION OF THE YEAR. see ADVENTURE AND ROMANCE

812.5 US ISSN 0067-6284
BEST SHORT PLAYS. 1969. a. $10.50. Chilton Book Co., Chilton Way, Radnor, PA 19089. Ed. Stanley Richards.

800 GW
BESTSELLER ALMANACH; die 3000 meistverkauften Buecher. 1986. a. DM.4.80. Dr. Lothar Rossipaul Verlagsgesellscaft mbH, Bavariaring 24, D-8000 Munich 2, W. Germany (B.R.D.) Ed. Rainer Rossipaul. circ. 80,000.

800 US
BETWEEN TWO RIVERS. 1980. irreg., no.2, 1981. price varies. From Here Press, Box 219, Fanwood, NJ 07023. Eds. William J. Higginson, Penny Harter. circ. 750. (back issues avail.)

810 US
BEYOND SCIENCE FICTION. 1971. a. $5. c/o Rey King, Ed., 414 S. 41st St., Richmond, CA 94804. TEL 415-658-0233. circ. 2,000.
 Formerly: Cosmic Circus.

BIBLIOGRAPHIEN ZUR DEUTSCHEN LITERATUR DES MITTELALTERS. see LITERATURE — Abstracting, Bibliographies, Statistics

BIBLIOGRAPHIES OF MODERN AUTHORS. see BIBLIOGRAPHIES

BIBLIOLOGIA. see PUBLISHING AND BOOK TRADE

860 CK
BIBLIOTECA COLOMBIANA. 1970. irreg., latest no.23, 1985. price varies. Instituto Caro y Cuervo, Seccion de Publicaciones, Apdo. Aereo 51502, Bogota, Colombia. (back issues avail.)

860 SP
BIBLIOTECA DE AUTORES ESPANOLES. PUBLICACION. irreg., no.5, 1983. Editorial Trieste, Villanueva, 14, Madrid 1, Spain.

BIBLIOTECA DE MENENDEZ PELAYO. BOLETIN. see LIBRARY AND INFORMATION SCIENCES

800 IT
BIBLIOTECA DI LETTERATURA E ARTE. 1975. irreg. price varies. Giardini Editori e Stampatori, Via Santa Bibbiana 28, 56100 Pisa, Italy.

860 SP
BIBLIOTECA ROMANICA HISPANICA. 1950. irreg. Editorial Gredos, Sanchez Pacheco 81, Madrid 2, Spain.
 Formerly: Biblioteca Romanica Hispanica. Estudios y Ensayos (ISSN 0519-7201)

891.85 PL ISSN 0519-8631
BIBLIOTEKA PISARZOW POLSKICH. SERIA A. 1953. irreg. price varies. (Polska Akademia Nauk, Instytut Badan Literackich) Ossolineum, Publishing House of the Polish Academy of Sciences, Rynek 9, Wroclaw, Poland (Dist. by Ars Polona-Ruch, Krakowskie Przedmiescie 7, Warsaw, Poland) Ed. Jerzy Woronczak. circ. 1,500.
 Formerly: Biblioteka Pisarzow Polskich (ISSN 0067-7736)

439 839 DK ISSN 0067-7841
BIBLIOTHECA ARNAMAGNAEANA; a jon helgason condita, auspiciis praesidii Arnamagnaeani. (Text in Danish, English, German, Icelandic, Norwegian, and Swedish) 1941. irreg. price varies. Arnamagnaean Insitute and Arnamagnaean Dictionary, Njalsgade 76, DK-2300 Copenhagen S, Denmark (Dist. by: C.A. Reitzels Boghandel A-S, Noerregade 20, DK-1165 Copenhagen K, Denmark) Indexed: M.L.A.

839.6 439 DK ISSN 0067-785X
BIBLIOTHECA ARNAMAGNAEANA. SUPPLEMENTUM. 1956. irreg. price varies. Arnamagnaean Insitute and Arnamagnaean Dictionary, Njalsgade 76, DK-2300 Copenhagen S, Denmark (Dist. by: C.A. Reitzels Boghandel A-S, Noerregade 20, DK-1165 Copenhagen K, Denmark)

BIBLIOTHECA RUSSICA. see LINGUISTICS

BIBLIOTHEQUE D'ETUDES BALKANIQUES. see LINGUISTICS

840 FR ISSN 0067-835X
BIBLIOTHEQUE FRANCAISE ET ROMANE. SERIE B: EDITIONS CRITIQUES DE TEXTES. 1962. irreg. price varies. (Universite de Strasbourg II, Centre de Philologie et de Litteratures Romanes) Editions Klincksieck, 11 rue de Lille, 75005 Paris, France. Ed. Georges Straka.

840 FR ISSN 0067-8368
BIBLIOTHEQUE FRANCAISE ET ROMANE. SERIE C: ETUDES LITTERAIRES. 1960. irreg. price varies. (Universite de Strasbourg II, Centre de Philologie et de Litteratures Romanes) Editions Klincksieck, 11 rue de Lille, 75005 Paris, France. Ed. Paul Vernois.

840 FR ISSN 0067-8376
BIBLIOTHEQUE FRANCAISE ET ROMANE. SERIE D: INITIATION, TEXTES ET DOCUMENTS. 1964. irreg. price varies. (Universite de Strasbourg II, Centre de Philologie et de Litteratures Romanes) Editions Klincksieck, 11 rue de Lille, 75005 Paris, France. Ed. Georges Straka.

BIBLIOTHEQUE FRANCAISE ET ROMANE. SERIE E: LANGUE ET LITTERATURE FRANCAISES AU CANADA. see LINGUISTICS

840 FR ISSN 0067-8422
BIBLIOTHEQUE INTROUVABLE. 1966. irreg. Lettres Modernes, 73 rue du Cardinal Lemoine, 75005 Paris, France.

800 PO
BIBLOS. 1925. a. price varies. Universidade de Coimbra, Faculdade de Letras, 3049 Coimbra Codex, Portugal. bk. rev. circ. 500.

810 US
BLACK JACK. 1973. a. $10. Seven Buffaloes Press, Box 249, Big Timber, MT 59011. Ed. Art Cuelho. circ. 750.

810 301.412 US ISSN 0045-222X
BLACK MARIA. 1971. a. $14 to individuals; institutions $16. Black Maria Collective, Inc., Box 25187, Chicago, IL 60625. Ed.Bd. adv. bk. rev. circ. 3,000.

830 SZ
BLAETTER DER RILKE-GESELLSCHAFT. (Text in English, French and German) 1972. a. DM.30. Rilke-Gesellschaft, c/o Ingrid Metzger-Buddenberg, Adlerstr. 31, CH-4052 Basel, Switzerland. Ed.Bd. adv. bk. rev. circ. 1,000. (back issues avail.)

808.8 810 US ISSN 0161-2506
BLOODROOT (GRAND FORKS) 1976. a. $9 for 3 issues. Bloodroot, Inc., Box 891, Grand Forks, ND 58201-0891. TEL 701-746-5858. Ed.Bd. circ. 800. (also avail. in microfilm; back issues avail.)

820 IT
BLUE GUITAR; rivista annuale di letteratura inglese e americana. (Text in English and Italian) 1975. a. $30. (Universita degli Studi di Messina, Facolta di Magistero) Herder Editrice e Libreria s.r.l., Piazza Montecitorio, 120, 00186 Rome, Italy. Ed. Angela Giannitrapani.

800 US
BLUE HORSE. 1966. irreg. Box 6061, Augusta, GA 30906. Ed.Bd. bk. rev. circ. 500.

810 US ISSN 0198-9901
BLUELINE. 1979. a. $5. Blueline Press, Blue Mountain Lake, NY 12812. TEL 518-352-7365. Ed. Alice Gilborn. bk. rev. illus. circ. 750. (back issues avail.) Indexed: Ind.Amer.Per.Verse.

800 491.66 940   UK   ISSN 0142-3363
BOARD OF CELTIC STUDIES. BULLETIN. (Text in English and Welsh) a. £8. (University of Wales, Board of Celtic Studies) University of Wales Press, 6 Gwennyth St., Cathays, Cardiff CF2 4YD, Wales. Ed.Bd. circ. 400. (also avail. in microform from UMI; reprint service avail. from UMI) Indexed: Curr.Cont. Hist.Abstr. M.L.A. Abstr.Engl.Stud. Amer.Hist.& Life. Art & Archaeol.Tech.Abstr. Arts & Hum.Cit.Ind. Br.Archaeol.Abstr. Geo.Abstr.

820   NE   ISSN 0169-6165
BOCHUMER ANGLISTISCHE STUDIEN/ BOCHUM STUDIES IN ENGLISH. 1975. irreg. price varies. B.R. Gruener B.V., Nieuwe Herengracht 31, 1011 RM Amsterdam, Netherlands. Ed. Ulrich Suerbaum. Indexed: M.L.A.

810   US   ISSN 0882-648X
BOGG; a journal of American and British writing. 1968. irreg. (2-3/yr.) $8 for 3 issues. Bogg Publications, 422 N. Cleveland St., Arlington, VA 22201 (U.K. subscr. to: 31, Belle Vue St., Filey, North Yorkshire YO14 9HU) Ed. John Elsberg. bk. rev. circ. 600. (back issues avail.) Indexed: Ind.Amer.Per.Verse.

800   DK   ISSN 0108-2019
BOGHVEDEGRYN. 1981. irreg. (3-4/yr.) Kr.12 per no. Amatoerforfatterforeningen Skriv Selv, c/o Kristen Oesterby, Laerkevaenget 2, 5471 Soendersoe, Denmark. illus.

800 080   UY   ISSN 0067-9909
BOLSILIBROS.* irreg. Editorial Arca, Colonia 1263, Montevideo, Uruguay.

830   GW   ISSN 0068-001X
BONNER ARBEITEN ZUR DEUTSCHEN LITERATUR. 1961. irreg., no.44, 1986. price varies. Bouvier Verlag Herbert Grundmann, Am Hof 32, Postfach 1268, 5300 Bonn 1, W. Germany (B.R.D.) Ed. Benno von Wiese. Indexed: M.L.A.

BOOK FORUM. see PUBLISHING AND BOOK TRADE

800   UK   ISSN 0260-0315
BOOKMARK. 1978. a. £5. English Department, Moray House, Holyrood Rd., College of Education, Edinburgh EH8 8AQ, Scotland. Ed. J. Aldridge. bk. rev. illus. circ. 400. Indexed: Child.Lit.Abstr.

BOOKS AND ARTICLES ON ORIENTAL SUBJECTS PUBLISHED IN JAPAN. see HISTORY — History Of Asia

810   US   ISSN 0147-0787
BOOKS AT BROWN. 1938. a. $10. Brown University Library, Friends of the Library, Box A, Providence, RI 02912 TEL 401-863-2146. circ. 400. Indexed: M.L.A.

BOOKS IN ARABIC. see BIBLIOGRAPHIES

BOOKS IN ARMENIAN. see BIBLIOGRAPHIES

BOOKS IN BENGALI. see BIBLIOGRAPHIES

BOOKS IN CHINESE. see BIBLIOGRAPHIES

BOOKS IN DANISH. see BIBLIOGRAPHIES

BOOKS IN DUTCH. see BIBLIOGRAPHIES

BOOKS IN FINNISH. see BIBLIOGRAPHIES

BOOKS IN HINDI. see BIBLIOGRAPHIES

BOOKS IN HUNGARIAN. see BIBLIOGRAPHIES

BOOKS IN SPANISH. see BIBLIOGRAPHIES

BOOKS IN URDU. see BIBLIOGRAPHIES

BORGO BIOVIEWS. see BIOGRAPHY

BORGO POLITICAL SCENARIOS. see POLITICAL SCIENCE

BORGO REFERENCE LIBRARY. see HISTORY

810   US   ISSN 0006-792X
BOSS. 1966. irreg., latest no.5, 1979, no.6 in prep. for 1987. $6 to individuals; institutions $9. Boss Books, Box 370, Madison Square Sta., New York, NY 10159. TEL 212-683-3274. Ed. Reginald Gay. illus. circ. 1,000.

810   US
BOTTOMFISH. 1976. a. $3.50. (De Anza College, Language Arts Department) Bottomfish Press, 21250 Stevens Creek Blvd., Cupertino, CA 95014. TEL 408-996-4545. Ed. Robert Brock. circ. 500.

800   FR
BOUTEILLE A LA MER. irreg. price varies. c/o Ed. Marc Beigbeder, 8 rue Theo-Renaudot, 75015 Paris, France.

BRADFORD CENTER OCCASIONAL PAPERS. see HISTORY

800   UK   ISSN 0261-0353
BRADFORD OCCASIONAL PAPERS; essays in language, literature and area studies. 1980. a. £75. University of Bradford, Modern Language Centre, West Yorks BD7 1DP, England. Ed.Bd. circ. 125.

800 700   US   ISSN 8756-8217
BREATHLESS MAGAZINE. 1985. a. $2.50. Breathless Magazine Inc., 910 Broad St., Endicott, NY 13760. TEL 607-785-7790. Ed. Ron Joseph, Jr. adv. bk. rev. circ. 500. (back issues avail.)

806   US   ISSN 0734-8665
BRECHT YEARBOOK. (Title varies for each volume) (Text and summaries in English, French and German) a. price varies. (International Brecht Society) Wayne State University Press, 5959 Woodward Ave., Detroit, MI 48202. TEL 313-577-4603. Ed.Bd. Indexed: M.L.A.

800   US   ISSN 0068-1334
BRITISH AUTHORS SERIES. 1967. irreg. price varies. Cambridge University Press, Edinburgh Bldg., Shaftesbury Rd., Cambridge CB2 2RU, England (and 32 E. 57 St., New York, NY 10022) Ed. Robin Mayhead. index.

850   UK   ISSN 0260-9215
BRITISH PIRANDELLO SOCIETY. YEARBOOK. 1981. a. £4. British Pirandello Society, c/o Jennifer Lorch, Ed., Department of Italian, University of Warwick, Coventry CV4 7AL, England. bk. rev. illus. circ. 300.

806   US
BRONTE NEWSLETTER. a. membership. Bronte Society, American Branch, 335 Grove St., Oradell, NJ 07649. Ed. Katherine M. Reise.

820   UK   ISSN 0309-7765
BRONTE SOCIETY TRANSACTIONS. 1895. a. $15. Bronte Society Inc., Bronte Parsonage, Haworth, Keighley, West Yorks BD22 8DR, England. Ed. Mark R.D. Seaward. adv. bk. rev. bibl. illus. cum.index. circ. 2,600. Indexed: Br.Hum.Ind. Abstr.Engl.Stud.

808   US
BROOKLYN REVIEW. 1984. a. City University of New York, Brooklyn College, Department of English, Brooklyn, NY 11210. Ed. Robert Thompson.
  Formerly (until 1983): Junction Magazine.

821.8   US   ISSN 0092-4725
BROWNING INSTITUTE STUDIES. 1973. a. $30 to non-members. Browning Institute, Inc., Box 2983, Grand Central Sta., New York, NY 10163. TEL 316-221-2779. Ed. Adrienne Munich. adv. bk. rev. illus. index. circ. 1,000. Indexed: Curr.Cont. M.L.A. Arts & Hum.Cit.Ind.

810   US
BROWNS MILLS REVIEW.* 1980. a. $4. David Vajda, Ed.& Pub., Box 908, Browns Mills, NJ 08015. (Back issues avail.)

846   FR   ISSN 0338-0548
BULLETIN D'INFORMATIONS PROUSTIENNES. 1975. a. 75 F. Presses de l'Ecole Normale Superieure, 45 rue d'Ulm, 75230 Paris Cedex 05, France. (Co-sponsors: Centre National de la Recherche Scientifique; Centre des Textes et Manuscrits Modernes) Ed. Bernard Brun. adv. bk. rev. circ. 500.

820   UK
BULWER LYTTON CIRCLE CHRONICLE. 1973. a. $15. (Bulwer Lytton Circle) High Orchard Press, High Orchard, 125 Markyate Rd., Dagenham, Essex RM8 2LB, England. Eds. Eric F.J. Ford, Howard Cooper-Brown. bk. rev. index. (also avail. in microform from UMI) Indexed: Abstr.Engl.Stud.

800   UK
BURNS CHRONICLE CLUB DIRECTORY. (Text in English and Scottish) 1892. a. £9.50 cloth bound; £6 paper bound. Burns Federation, Dick Institute, Elmbank Ave., Kilmarnock KAI 3BU, Scotland. Ed. James A. Mackay. adv. bk. rev. bibl. charts. illus. circ. 2,700.

813   US   ISSN 0007-6333
BURROUGHS BULLETIN.* 1947. irreg. membership. (Burroughs Bibliophiles) House of Greystoke, 2661 Geraldine Dr., Cincinnati, OH 45239-5521. Ed. Vernell W. Coriell. bk. rev. bibl. film rev. illus. circ. 2,800. (processed)
  Covers the works of Edgar Rice Burroughs

800   US   ISSN 0068-4325
BURT FRANKLIN ESSAYS IN LITERATURE AND CRITICISM. (Text in English and Romance languages) 1968. irreg., no.200, 1973. price varies. Lenox Hill Publishing and Distributing Corporation, 235 E. 44th St., New York, NY 10003. (back issues avail.)

BYDGOSKIE TOWARZYSTWO NAUKOWE. WYDZIAL NAUK HUMANISTYCZNYCH. PRACE. SERIA B (JEZYK I LITERATURA) see LINGUISTICS

809   US   ISSN 0196-8998
BYRON SOCIETY NEWSLETTER. 1973. biennial. membership. Byron Society, American Committee, 259 New Jersey Ave., Collingswood, NJ 08108. Dir. Marsha M. Manns. circ. 2,000.

BYZANTINE AND MODERN GREEK STUDIES. see LINGUISTICS

C E C T A L CONFERENCE PAPERS SERIES. (Centre for English Cultural Tradition and Language) see LINGUISTICS

895.1 792   US   ISSN 0193-7774
C H I N O P E R L PAPERS. (Text in Chinese and English) 1969. a. $10 to individuals; institutions $20. (Conference on Chinese Oral and Performing Literature) Cornell University, China-Japan Program, 140 Uris Hall, Ithaca, NY 14853. TEL 607-255-6222. Ed. Harold Shadick. bk. rev. bibl. circ. 200.
  Formerly: C H I N O P E R L News.

800   US   ISSN 0736-3982
C U N Y ENGLISH FORUM. 1985. a. $45. A M S Press, Inc., 56 E. 13th St., New York, NY 10003. TEL 212-777-4700. Eds. Saul N. Brody, Harold Schechter. circ. 500.

840   FR   ISSN 0575-0415
CAHIERS CHARLES DU BOS. 1955. a. Societe des Amis de Charles Du Bos, 76 bis rue des Saints-Peres, 75007 Paris, France. circ. 400. (back issues avail.)

840   FR   ISSN 0575-0466
CAHIERS D'ANALYSE TEXTUELLE. 1959. a. (Les Lettres Belges, BE) Societe d'Edition les Belles Lettres, 95 Bd. Raspail, 75007 Paris, France. Ed. Paul Delbouille. (back issues avail.) Indexed: M.L.A. Sociol.Abstr. Lang.& Lang.Behav.Abstr.

840   FR
CAHIERS DE JULES ROMAINS. 1976. a. price varies. (Societe des Amis de Jules Romains) Flammarion, 26 rue Racine, 75006 Paris, France.

840   SZ   ISSN 0007-9847
CAHIERS DE LA RENAISSANCE VAUDOISE. 1926. irreg. (2-4/yr.) price varies. 18 Petit-Chene, 1003 Lausanne, Switzerland. Ed. Olivier Delacretaz. illus. circ. 5,750.

800   FR   ISSN 0068-5089
CAHIERS DE SAINT-MICHEL DE CUXA. 1970. irreg. Association Culturelle de Cuxa, Centre Permanent de Recherches et d'Etudes Pre-Romanes et Romanes, Abbaye de Saint-Michel de Cuxa, Prades-Codalet, France (Subscr. address: c/o Andre Delteil, 4, rue Louis Esparre, 66000 Perpignan, France) bk. rev. Indexed: RILA.

840   FR   ISSN 0753-4590
CAHIERS HENRI BOSCO. 1973. a. 80 F. Amitie Henri Bosco, Les Oliviers III, 76 av. des Baumettes, 06000 Nice, France. Ed. Claude Girault. bk. rev. cum.index 1973-1977; 1978-1982. (back issues avail.)
    Formerly: Amitie Henri Bosco. Cahiers (ISSN 0399-1121)

800   FR   ISSN 0008-0365
CAHIERS NATURALISTES. 1955. a. 130 F.($18) (Societe Litteraire des Amis d'Emile Zola) Editions Grasset et Fasquelle, 61 rue Saints-Peres, 75006 Paris, France. Dir. Henri Mitterand. adv. bk. rev. bibl. charts. cum.index. circ. 1,000. Indexed: M.L.A.

840   FR
CAHIERS SAINT-EXUPERY. a. (Association des Amis d'Antoine de Saint-Exupery) Editions Gallimard, 5 rue Sebastien-Bottin, 75007 Paris, France. illus.

840   SZ
CAHIERS SUISSES ROMAIN ROLLAND. 1977. irreg. price varies. Editions de la Baconniere S.A., Box 185, 2017 Boudry, Switzerland. (reprint service avail. from UMI)

820   FR   ISSN 0575-2124
CALIBAN; etudes anglaises et nord-americaines. (Text in English or French; summaries in other languages) 1964. a. 51 F. Universite de Toulouse II (le Mirail), Service des Publications, 56 rue du Taur, 31069 Toulouse Cedex, France. Ed. M. Levy. Indexed: M.L.A. Abstr.Engl.Stud.

870 880   UK
CAMBRIDGE GREEK AND LATIN CLASSICS. irreg. price varies. Cambridge University Press, Edinburgh Bldg., Shaftesbury Rd., Cambridge CB2 2RU, England (And 32 E. 57th St., New York NY 10022) Eds. E.J. Kenney, P.E. Easterling.

CAMBRIDGE LATIN TEXTS. see *LINGUISTICS*

800   US
CAMELS COMING NEWSLETTER. 1972. a. $2. Box 703, San Francisco, CA 94101. Ed. Richard Morris. bk. rev. illus. circ. 600.

820   CN
CANADIAN SHORT STORY LIBRARY. 1972. irreg. University of Ottawa Press, 603 Cumberland, Ottawa, Ont. K1N 6N5, Canada. TEL 613-564-2270.

830.9   CN   ISSN 0317-7254
CARLETON GERMANIC PAPERS. 1973. a. Can.$3. Carleton University, Department of German, Ottawa K1S 5B6, Canada. TEL 613-564-2605. Ed.Bd. circ. 140. (back issues avail.) Indexed: Curr.Cont. M.L.A.

CARLYLE NEWSLETTER. see *BIOGRAPHY*

800 821   AT   ISSN 0815-452X
CARRIONFLOWER WRIT. 1985. irreg. Aus.$3. Nosukumo, G.P.O. Box 994-H, Melbourne, Vic. 3001, Australia. Ed. Javant Biarujia. circ. 500.

800   UK   ISSN 0069-0961
CASSAL BEQUEST LECTURES. (Text in French) 1961. irreg. price varies. University of London, Senate House, London WC1E 7HU, England.

810   US   ISSN 0145-8310
CATHARTIC. 1974. irreg., approx. 2/yr. $3.75. c/o Patrick M. Ellingham, Ed., Box 1391, Fort Lauderdale, FL 33302. TEL 305-474-7120. adv. bk. rev. index. circ. 200. (back issues avail.)

700 800   IT   ISSN 0008-8935
CENACOLO; arte e letteratura. 1949. a. Associazione Cenacolo, Via Madama Cristina 90, 10126 Turin, Italy. Ed. Dr. Giacomo Negri. adv. bk. rev. bibl. illus.

820   UK   ISSN 0069-164X
CENTRAL LITERARY MAGAZINE. 1873. a. 25p. 45 Sandhills Lane, Barnt Green, Nr. Birmingham, England. Ed. W.H.M. Sparks.

800   AE   ISSN 0069-1720
CENTRE CULTUREL FRANCAIS, ALGER. RENCONTRES CULTURELLES.* 1970. irreg. price varies. Centre Culturel Francais, 7 rue Medecin-Capitaine Kassani Issad, Algiers, Algeria.

800   US
CHANEY CHRONICAL. (Companion to: What's New About London, Jack) 1972. irreg. (1-2/yr.) $0.50 per no. London Northwest, 929 South Bay Rd., Olympia, WA 98506. Ed. David H. Schlottman. bk. rev. bibl. (processed)

800   FR   ISSN 0395-7845
CHANTS DES PEUPLES. no.2, 1974. irreg. Editions Caracteres, 7 rue de l'Arbalete, 75005 Paris, France. Dir. Bruno Durocher. illus.

820   US
CHAUCER LIBRARY. 1978. irreg., no.3, 1984. price varies. University of Georgia Press, Athens, GA 30602. TEL 404-542-2830.

810   US   ISSN 0009-2185
CHELSEA; a magazine for poetry, plays, stories and translations. 1958. a. $9.50. Chelsea Associates, Inc., Box 5880 Grand Central Sta., New York, NY 10163. Ed. Sonia Raiziss. cum.index. circ. 1,100. (also avail. in microform from UMI; back issues avail.; reprint service avail. from UMI, ISI) Indexed: Curr.Cont. Arts & Hum.Cit.Ind. Ind.Amer.Per.Verse.

891.4   II   ISSN 0009-3432
CHHANDITA. (Text in Bengali) 1965. irreg. (10-12/yr.) Rs.10. B-59 Rabindra Nagar, Calcutta 700018, India. Ed. Gourgopal Das. adv. bk. rev. circ. 2,500. (also avail. in microform)

800 770   US
CHICAGO RENAISSANCE. 1976. a. $5.95. (Chicago Renaissance Workshop) Natural Resources Unlimited, 3531 Roesner Dr., Markham, IL 60426. Ed. Joe H. Mitchell. bk. rev. circ. 3,000.

800   CN   ISSN 0315-467X
CHIEN D'OR/GOLDEN DOG. (Text in English and French) 1972. irreg. c/o Editor, English Department, Carleton University, Ottawa, Ont., Canada. TEL 613-231-3847. Ed. Michael Gnarowski. illus.
    Supersedes: Yes (ISSN 0044-0353)

028.5   US   ISSN 0092-8208
CHILDREN'S LITERATURE (NEW HAVEN) 1972. a. price varies. (Children's Literature Foundation) Yale University Press, 302 Temple St., 92A Yale Sta., New Haven, CT 06520. TEL 203-432-4969. Ed. Francelia Butler. bk. rev. illus. cum.index.: vols.1-5, 6-10. circ. 3,000. (reprint service avail.) Indexed: M.L.A. Child.Lit.Abstr.

891.43   II
CHILDREN'S LITERATURE SERIES. (Text in Hindi) 1951. irreg., vol.29, 1963. price varies. Vishveshvaranand Vedic Research Institute, P.O. Sadhu Ashram, Hoshiarpur 146021, Punjab, India.

810   US   ISSN 0009-4285
CHIMES. a. free. Saint Mary's College, Notre Dame, IN 46556. TEL 219-284-4000. illus. circ. 1,600.

820   HK   ISSN 0069-3642
CHIMES.* 1961. irreg. free. University of Hong Kong, English Society, Hong Kong, Hong Kong. Indexed: Ind.Chem.

808   US   ISSN 0277-7223
CHIRICU. (Text in English and Spanish) 1977. a. $4.50. Indiana University, Chicano Riqueno Studies, 849 Ballantine Hall, Bloomington, IN 47405. TEL 812-332-0211. Ed. Steve Dupouy. circ. 300. Indexed: M.L.A.

818   US   ISSN 0069-3928
CHRISTMAS: AN AMERICAN ANNUAL OF CHRISTMAS LITERATURE AND ART. 1931. a. $14.50 hardbound; $6.95 paper. Augsburg Publishing House, 426 S. Fifth St., Minneapolis, MN 55440. TEL 612-330-3300. Ed. Leonard Flachman. circ. 67,000.

870   IT   ISSN 0009-6687
CICERONIANA; rivista di studi Ciceroniani. 1959. irreg. L.20000. Centro di Studi Ciceroniani, Piazza dei Cavalieri di Malta 2, Rome, Italy. Dir. Scevola Mariotti.

890 701   II
CINMAY SMRTI PATHAGARA. (Text in Bengali) 1970. a. Rs.8. 26-8A Mahatma Gandhi Rd., Calcutta 9, India. adv.

700 100   FR   ISSN 0069-4177
CIRCE. 1969. irreg. 360 F. for 10 nos. Lettres Modernes, 73 rue du Cardinal Lemoine, 75005 Paris, France. Ed. Jean Burgos.

810   US
CITY LIGHTS ANTHOLOGY. irreg., latest no.4. City Lights Books, 261 Columbus Ave., San Francisco, CA 94133. TEL 415-362-8193.

800   US
CITY LIGHTS JOURNAL. 1963. irreg., latest no.4. City Lights Books, 261 Columbus Ave., San Francisco, CA 94133. TEL 415-362-8193. Ed. Lawrence Ferlinghetti.

860   CK   ISSN 0069-4444
CLASICOS COLOMBIANOS. 1954. irreg., no.8, 1980. price varies. Instituto Caro y Cuervo, Seccion de Publicaciones, Apdo. Aereo 51502, Bogota, Colombia.

CLASSIC; magazine of creative writing and art. see *LITERARY AND POLITICAL REVIEWS*

870 930   UK   ISSN 0069-4460
CLASSICAL ASSOCIATION. PROCEEDINGS. 1904. a. £3. Classical Association, Department of Classics, P.O. Box 78, University College, Department of Classics, Cardiff CF1 1XL, Wales. Ed. J. Percival. adv. circ. 4,000. (also avail. in microfilm)

850   IT
CLASSICI ITALIANI MINORI. irreg. Angelo Longo Editore, Via Paolo Costa 33, P.O. Box 431, 48100 Ravenna, Italy. Ed. Enzo Esposito.

820   US   ISSN 0069-4509
CLASSICS OF BRITISH HISTORICAL LITERATURE. 1970. irreg., no.14, 1984. price varies. University of Chicago Press, 5801 S. Ellis Ave., Chicago, IL 60637. TEL 312-962-7700. Ed. John L. Clive. (reprint service avail. from UMI,ISI)

CLIPPER STUDIES IN THE AMERICAN THEATER. see *THEATER*

800   NE
CODICES MANUSCRIPTI, BIBLIOTHECA UNIVERSITATIS LEIDENSIS. 1910. irreg., vol.21, 1983. price varies. Leiden University Press, E.J. Brill Publishers, P.O. Box 9000, 2300 PA Leiden, Netherlands.

800   US
COE REVIEW. 1972. a. $4. Student Senate of Coe College, 1220 First Ave., Cedar Rapids, IA 52402. TEL 319-399-8660. Eds. Pedro San Antonio, Lisa Spellman-Trimble. circ. 500.
    Formerly: Caravan.

810   US   ISSN 0084-8816
COLD-DRILL. 1970. a. $5. Boise State University, Department of English, 1910 University Drive, Boise, ID 83725. TEL 208-385-1999. Ed. Tom Trusky. charts. illus. circ. 500. (looseleaf format)

869   BL
COLECAO ESCRITORES BRASILEIROS; antologia e estudos. 1982. irreg. Editora Atica, S.A., Rua Barao de Iguape, 110, Caixa Postal 8656, Sao Paulo, Brazil.

869   BL
COLECAO TIRANDO DE LETRA. 1984. irreg. EMW Editores Ltda., Caixa Postal 2025, CEP 01051 Sao Paulo, SP, Brazil. Ed. Alberto Avillas. circ. 3,000.

869   PO
COLECCAO ENSAIO. no.3, 1981. irreg. Edicoes Ro, Rua da Tojeirinha, 10, 2735 Cacem, Portugal.

869   PO
COLECCAO LITERATURA. irreg., no.12, 1982. Instituto Nacional de Investigacao Cientifica, Lisbon, Portugal.

800   AG
COLECCION ESTUDIOS LATINOAMERICANOS. 1972. irreg. Fernando Garcia Cambeiro (Dist.), Cochabamba 244, 1150 Buenos Aires, Argentina. Ed. Graciela Maturo.

808 PY
COLECCION LITERATURA. irreg., no.3, 1983. El Lector, 25 de Mayo y Antequera, Asuncion, Paraguay.

COLECCION MIGUEL SALGUERO. see *ETHNIC INTERESTS*

860 NQ
COLECCION POPULAR DE LITERATURA NICARAGUENSE. DOCUMENTOS. 1982. irreg. Ministerio de Cultura, Apdo. 3514, Managua, Nicaragua. Ed. Ernesto Cardenal.

800 IT ISSN 0069-5165
COLLANA DI CULTURA. 1963. irreg., no.43, 1985. price varies. Edizioni dell' Ateneo S.p.A., Box 7216, 00100 Rome, Italy. circ. 1,000.

850 IT ISSN 0069-5203
COLLANA DI STUDI E SAGGI. 1959. irreg. price varies. Societa Accademica Romena, Foro Traiano 1a, 00187 Rome, Italy.

809 IT
COLLANA DI TESTI E DI CRITICA. 1964. irreg., no.29, 1987. price varies. Liguori Editore s.r.l., Via Mezzocannone 19, 80134 Naples, Italy. TEL 081/ 20 6077. Ed. Giorgio Petrocchi.

860 SP
COLLECCION POLIEDRO. irreg., no.10, 1981. Ediciones Rayuela, Claudio Coello, 19, Madrid-1, Spain.

800 FR
COLLECTION "CHANTS DES PEUPLES". vol.2, 1974. irreg. Editions Caracteres, 7 rue de l'Arbalete, 75005 Paris, France.

895 BE
COLLECTION VIETNAMIENNE. 1973. irreg., no.7, 1985. price varies. Librairie-Editions Thanh-Long, 34 rue Dekens, 1040 Brussels, Belgium.

COLLEGE OF DAIRYING. JOURNAL; CULTURAL AND SOCIAL SCIENCES/ RAKUNO GAKUEN DAIGAKU KIYO, JINBUN SHAKAIKAGAKU HEN. see *AGRICULTURE*

810 US ISSN 0161-486X
COLUMBIA: A MAGAZINE OF POETRY AND PROSE. 1977. irreg. (1-2/yr.) $5. Columbia University School of the Arts, Writing Division, 404 Dodge Hall, Columbia University, New York, NY 10027. TEL 212-280-4931. Eds. Betsy Lerner, Michael Kirkpatrick. adv. circ. 825.

800 378.1 US ISSN 0010-1982
COLUMBIA REVIEW. 1815. a. Columbia University, Columbia Review, 206 Ferris Booth Hall, New York, NY 10027. TEL 212-280-3611. Ed. Lisa Shea. circ. 500. (also avail. in microform from MIM) Indexed: C.L.I.

820 US ISSN 0069-6412
COMITATUS; A JOURNAL OF MEDIEVAL AND RENAISSANCE STUDIES.* 1970. a. $7.50 to individuals; institutions $12.50. (University of California, Los Angeles, Center for Medieval and Renaissance Studies) Undena Publications, 6355 Green Valley Circle, No. 213, Culver City, CA 90230-7064. Ed. Gary Remer. bk. rev. circ. 500. (back issues avail.) Indexed: Curr.Cont. M.L.A. Arts & Hum.Cit.Ind.

COMMENTATIONES BALTICAE. see *HISTORY — History Of Europe*

809 US ISSN 0275-2069
COMMUNICATION AND THE HUMAN CONDITION. vol.2, 1973. irreg. price varies. Gordon and Breach Science Publishers, 50 W. 23rd St., New York, NY 10010. TEL 212-206-8900. Ed. Lee Thayer.

800 US ISSN 0195-7678
COMPARATIST. 1977. a. $12. Southern Comparative Literature Association, c/o Mechthild Cranston, Ed., Department of Languages, Clemson University, Clemson, SC 29634-1515. TEL 803-656-5393. bk. rev. circ. 500. Indexed: M.L.A. Amer.Hum.Ind. Amer.Bibl.Slavic & E.Eur.Stud. Can.Rev.Comp.Lit.

809 UK ISSN 0144-7564
COMPARATIVE CRITICISM; a yearbook. 1979. a. $43 to individuals; institutions $65. (British Comparative Literature Association) Cambridge University Press, Edinburgh Bldg., Shaftesbury Rd., Cambridge CB2 2RU, England (And 32 E. 57th St., New York, NY 10022) Ed. Elinor Shaffer. Indexed: M.L.A.

CONDITIONS; a feminist magazine of writing by women, with an emphasis on writing by lesbians. see *WOMEN'S INTERESTS*

800 940 700 US
CONFERENCE ON EDITORIAL PROBLEMS: UNIVERSITY OF TORONTO. 1965. a. $29.50. (University of Toronto) A M S Press, Inc., 56 E. 13th St., New York, NY 10003. TEL 212-777-4700. Ed. A.F. Johnston. index. (back issues avail.)

800 BE ISSN 0010-5694
CONFINS.* 1962. irreg., (7-8/yr.) 100 Fr.($2) ‡ Institut Catholique des Hautes Etudes Commerciales, Union des Etudiants, 2 Bd. Brand Whitlock, 1040 Brussels, Belgium. Ed. Jacques van der Moot. adv. bk. rev. film rev. illus. circ. 500. (processed)

890 FR ISSN 0589-3496
CONNAISSANCE DE L'ORIENT. COLLECTION UNESCO D'OEUVRES REPRESENTATIVES. 1956. (Unesco, UN) Editions Gallimard, 5 rue Sebastien-Bottin, 75007 Paris, France.

800 US
CONNECTICUT WRITER. 1974. a. $5. Connecticut Writers League Inc., Box 10536, West Hartford, CT 06110. Ed. Betty Hoffman. circ. 500. (back issues avail.)
Formerly (until 1981): Harvest (ISSN 0362-7888)

CONTEMPORANEA; studi e testi. see *HISTORY*

800 US ISSN 0069-9381
CONTEMPORARY DRAMA SERIES. 1971. irreg., no.4, 1979. $2.95. Proscenium Press, Box 361, Newark, DE 19711. TEL 302-737-5803. Ed. Robert Hogan. (reprint service avail. from UMI)

809 US ISSN 0091-3421
CONTEMPORARY LITERARY CRITICISM SERIES; excerpts from criticism of the works of today's novelists, poets, playwrights, and other creative writers. 1973. irreg., vol.41, 1986. $90 per vol. Gale Research Company, Book Tower, Detroit, MI 48226. TEL 313-962-2242. Ed. Daniel G. Marowski. cum.index. Indexed: Child.Auth.& Illus. Perf.Arts Biog.Master Ind.

800 UK ISSN 0144-3399
CONTEXT (LEEDS) irreg. University of Leeds, School of English, Leeds LS2 9JT, England.
Formerly: University of Leeds English Society Paper (ISSN 0309-8907)

800 US
CONTINUUM. 1987. a. (University of Virginia, Center for Advanced Studies) A M S Press, Inc., 56 E. 13th St., New York, NY 10003. TEL 212-777-4700.

800 US
CONTRABAND (FALMOUTH)* 1971. irreg. $5 for 5 nos. ‡ Contraband Press, 54 Babidge Rd., Falmouth, ME 04105. Ed.Bd. bk. rev. illus. circ. 750. Indexed: ACCESS.

892.4 IS ISSN 0010-7948
CONTRAST. 1969. a. $1.50. Bar-Ilan University, English Department, Ramat Gan, Israel. Ed. Daniela Grunfeld. bk. rev. charts. illus.

CONTRIBUTIONS TO THE STUDY OF SCIENCE FICTION AND FANTASY. see *ADVENTURE AND ROMANCE*

808 US ISSN 0738-9345
CONTRIBUTIONS TO THE STUDY OF WORLD LITERATURE. 1983. irreg. price varies. Greenwood Press, 88 Post Rd. W., Box 5007, Westport, CT 06881. TEL 203-226-3571. Ed. Leif Sjoberg. index.

801 100 US ISSN 0270-6687
CORONA. 1980. a. $7 to individuals; institutions $8.50. Montana State University, Department of History and Philosophy, Bozeman, MT 59717. TEL 406-994-5200. Eds. Lynda and Michael Sexson. adv. bk. rev. illus. circ. 2,000. Indexed: M.L.A. Amer.Hum.Ind.

COSTERUS; essays in English and American language and literature. see *LINGUISTICS*

800 US
CRAWL OUT YOUR WINDOW. 1975. a. $5. Foundation for New Literature, 4641 Park Blvd., San Diego, CA 92116. Eds. Melvyn Freilicher, Eleanor Bluestein. circ. 600.

800 700 IT ISSN 0011-1406
CRISI E LETTERATURA; periodico di lettere filosofia arti. 1961. a. Gaetano Salveti, Ed. & Pub., Via Bu Meliana 12, 00195 Rome, Italy (Subscr. to: Lago d'Iseo No.21, 00050 Santa Severa, Rome, Italy) bk. rev. bibl. illus. circ. 3,000. (tabloid format)

840 US
CRITICAL BIBLIOGRAPHY OF FRENCH LITERATURE. 1951. irreg., vol.6, 1980. price varies. Syracuse University Press, 1600 Jamesville Ave., Syracuse, NY 13244. TEL 315-423-2596. Ed. Richard A. Brooks.

800 US ISSN 0070-153X
CRITICAL ESSAYS IN MODERN LITERATURE. 1957. irreg. price varies. University of Pittsburgh Press, 127 N. Bellefield Ave., Pittsburgh, PA 15260. TEL 412-624-4110.

800 UK
CRITICAL HERITAGE SERIES. irreg. price varies. Routledge & Kegan Paul PLC, 11 New Fetter Lane, London EC4P 4EE, England (U.S. address: 9 Park St., Boston, MA 02108)

899 900 100 AT
CRITICAL REVIEW. 1958. a. Aus.$7($6) Australian National University, Research School of Social Sciences, History of Ideas Unit, P.O. Box 4, Canberra, A.C.T. 2601, Australia. Ed. S.L. Goldberg. bk. rev. circ. 1,000. (back issues avail.) Indexed: Br.Hum.Ind. Hum.Ind. M.L.A. Abstr.Engl.Stud. Aus.P.A.I.S.
Former titles: Critical Review Melbourne (ISSN 0070-1548); Critical Review. Melbourne-Sydney.

CRITICISM AND INTERPRETATION; journal for literature, linguistics, history and aesthetics. see *HUMANITIES: COMPREHENSIVE WORKS*

809 US
CRITICISM MONOGRAPHS. irreg. Wayne State University Press, 5959 Woodward Ave., Detroit, MI 48202. TEL 313-577-4603. (back issues avail.)

800 FR ISSN 0070-1556
CRITIQUES DE NOTRE TEMPS ET... 1970. irreg. 18.50 F. Editions Garnier Freres, 19, rue des Plantes, 75014 Paris, France. circ. 10,000.

808 US ISSN 0748-0164
CROSS CURRENTS. a. $15. University of Michigan, Department of Slavic Languages and Literatures, MLB 3040, Ann Arbor, MI 48109. TEL 313-764-5355. Ed. Ladislav Matejka. Indexed: CERDIC.

800 700 US ISSN 0741-6210
CROTON REVIEW. 1978. a. $8 (for 3 nos.) Croton Council on the Arts, Inc., Box 277, Croton-on-Hudson, NY 10520. Ed. Ruth Lisa Schechter. circ. 2,000. (back issues avail.)

807 860 AG
CUADERNOS PARA EL ESTUDIO DE LA ESTETICA Y LA LITERATURA. no.8, 1974. irreg. Universidad Nacional del Nordeste, Instituto de Letras, Resistencia, Chaco, Argentina.

891.66 UK
CYFRES CLASURON YR ACADEMI. (Text in Welsh) 1980. irreg. price varies. (Welsh Academy) University of Wales Press, 6 Gwennyth St., Cathays, Cardiff CF2 4YD, Wales. Ed. P.J. Donovan.

CYPHER. see *ADVENTURE AND ROMANCE*

800 410   DK   ISSN 0105-208X
D S L PRAESENTATIONSHAEFTE. 1985. a. Kr.12.20. Danske Sprog og Litteraturselskab - Danish Society of Language and Literature, Frederiksholm Kanal 18A, 1220 Copenhagen K, Denmark.

DACOROMANIA; Jahrbuch fuer oestliche Latinitaet. see *LINGUISTICS*

800 700   US   ISSN 0084-9537
DADA/SURREALISM. 1970. a. $10 to individuals; institutions $12. ‡ (Association for the Study of Dada and Surrealism) University of Iowa, 425 EPB, Iowa City, IA 52242. bibl. illus. (back issues avail.) Indexed: Amer.Hum.Ind. RILA.

891.7   UR
DALYAGLYADY LITARATURNY ZBORNIK. 1975. irreg. Vydavetstva Mastatskaya Litabatura, Minsk, Byelorussian S.S.R., U.S.S.R. Ed.Bd.

810   US
DAMASCUS ROAD. 1959. irreg., (approx. a.), latest vol.10. $2.95 per no. c/o C.S. Hanna, 6271 Hill Dr., Wacosville, PA 18106. circ. 500. (also avail. in microform from UMI; reprint service avail. from UMI)

800   US
DAN RIVER ANTHOLOGY (YEAR) 1984. a. $9.95 paper; cloth $15.95. (Conservatory of American Letters) Dan River Press, Box 123, South Thomaston, ME 04858. TEL 207-354-6550. Ed. Richard S. Danbury III. circ. 500.

800   DK   ISSN 0416-6981
DANSK TEKNISK LITTERATURSELSKAB. SKRIFTSERIE. a. Kr.50. (Dansk Teknisk Litteraturselskab) Bibliotekscentralen, Telegrafvej 5, DK-2750 Ballerup, Denmark.

850   US   ISSN 0070-2862
DANTE STUDIES; with the Annual Report of the Dante Society. 1881/82. a. $15. State University of New York Press, State University Plaza, Albany, NY 12246. TEL 518-472-5025. Ed. Anthony L. Pellegrini. adv. circ. 350. (also avail. in microform from UMI; reprint service avail. from UMI) Indexed: M.L.A.
     Formerly (until 1980): Dante Society of America. Report with Accompanying Papers.

810   US
DARK WINDS; decadence fantasy magazine. 1982. a. $4. Gibbelin's Gazette Publications, 3217-G Whisper Ln., Winter Park, FL 32792-5369. Ed. Vernon Clark. adv. bk. rev. illus. circ. 500.

410   GW
DE PROPRIETATIBUS LITTERARUM. SERIES DIDACTICA. 1972. irreg. price varies. Walter de Gruyter & Co., Mouton Publishers, Postfach 110240, D-1000 Berlin 11, W. Germany (B.R.D.) (U.S. addr.: Mouton Publishers, division of Walter de Gruyter Inc., 200 Saw Mill River Road, Hawthorne, NY 10532)

800   GW   ISSN 0070-3060
DE PROPRIETATIBUS LITTERARUM. SERIES MAJOR. 1967. irreg. price varies. Walter de Gruyter & Co., Mouton Publishers, Postfach 110240, D-1000 Berlin 11, W. Germany (B.R.D.) (U.S. addr.: Mouton Publishers, division of Walter de Gruyter, Inc., 200 Saw Mill River Road, Hawthorne, NY 10532)

800   GW   ISSN 0070-3079
DE PROPRIETATIBUS LITTERARUM. SERIES MINOR. 1966. irreg. price varies. Walter de Gruyter & Co., Mouton Publishers, Postfach 110140, D-1000 Berlin 11, W. Germany (B.R.D.) (U.S. addr.: Mouton Publishers, division of Walter de Gruyter, Inc., 200 Saw Mill River Road, Hawthorn, NY 10532)

800   GW   ISSN 0070-3087
DE PROPRIETATIBUS LITTERARUM. SERIES PRACTICA. 1966. irreg. price varies. Walter de Gruyter & Co., Mouton Publishers, Postfach 110240, D-1000 Berlin 11, W. Germany (B.R.D.) (U.S. addr.: Mouton Publishers, division of Walter de Gruyter, Inc., 200 Saw Mill River Road, Hawthorne, NY 10532)

810 705   US   ISSN 0070-3141
DECEMBER; a magazine of the arts and opinion. 1958. irreg. $15 for 4 issues. December Press, 3093 Dato, Highland Park, IL 60035. TEL 312-432-6804. Ed. Curt Johnson. adv. bk. rev. film rev. illus. circ. 1,200. (also avail. in microform from UMI; reprint service avail. from UMI,KTO; back issues avail.)

890   US   ISSN 0148-561X
DEGRE SECOND: STUDIES IN FRENCH LITERATURE. 1976. a. $17. Virginia Polytechnic Institute and State University, Department of Foreign Languages, Blacksburg, VA 24061. TEL 703-961-5313. Ed. W. Pierre Jacoebee. adv. bk. rev. circ. 180. (back issues avail.) Indexed: M.L.A.
     Formerly: Degre Second: Studies in French Literature from the Renaissance to the Present.

DEINE STADT; Kunst, Kultur und Leben in Braunschweig. see *ART*

DEUTSCHE AKADEMIE FUER SPRACHE UND DICHTUNG. JAHRBUCH. see *LINGUISTICS*

830   GW
DEUTSCHE AKADEMIE FUER SPRACHE UND DICHTUNG. PREISSCHRIFTEN. 1964. irreg. price varies. Verlag Lambert Schneider, Hausackerweg 16, D-6900 Heidelberg, W. Germany (B.R.D.)

830   GW
DEUTSCHE AKADEMIE FUER SPRACHE UND DICHTUNG. SCHRIFTENREIHE. 1954. irreg., no.60, 1986. price varies. Verlag Lambert Schneider, Hausackerweg 16, D-6900 Heidelberg, W. Germany (B.R.D.)

800   GE   ISSN 0420-0152
DEUTSCHE BIBLIOTHEK. 1968. irreg., vol.12, 1985. (Akademie der Wissenschaften der DDR) Akademie-Verlag Berlin, Leipziger Str. 3-4, 1086 Berlin, E. Germany (D.D.R.)

830   GW   ISSN 0070-4318
DEUTSCHE SCHILLER-GESELLSCHAFT. JAHRBUCH. 1957. a. price varies. Alfred Kroener Verlag, Reinsburgstr. 56, 7000 Stuttgart 1, W. Germany (B.R.D.) Ed.Bd. circ. 3,000. Indexed: M.L.A.

820   GW   ISSN 0070-4326
DEUTSCHE SHAKESPEARE-GESELLSCHAFT WEST. JAHRBUCH. 1948. a. price varies (1978-79 double vol. DM. 74) Verlag Ferdinand Kamp GmbH & Co. KG, Postfach 10 13 09, D-4630 Bochum, W. Germany (B.R.D.) Ed. Werner Habicht. bk. rev. circ. 2,000. Indexed: M.L.A. Abstr.Engl.Stud. Ind.Bk.Rev.Hum.

430 830   GE   ISSN 0070-4334
DEUTSCHE TEXTE DES MITTELALTERS. vol.42, 1942. irreg., vol.73, 1985. price varies. Akademie-Verlag, Leipziger Str. 3-4, 108 Berlin, E. Germany (D.D.R.) Indexed: M.L.A.

DEVONSHIRE ASSOCIATION FOR THE ADVANCEMENT OF SCIENCE, LITERATURE AND ART. REPORT AND TRANSACTIONS. see *ART*

DIALOGOS HISPANICOS DE AMSTERDAM. see *LINGUISTICS*

808   US
DIANA'S ALMANAC. 1972. a. $4.50. Diana's Press, 23 N. Fair St., Warsick, RI 02888-1645. Ed. Tom Ahern. circ. 1,000.

820   US   ISSN 0084-9812
DICKENS STUDIES ANNUAL. 1970. a. $45. (City University of New York, Victorian Committee) A M S Press, Inc., 56 E. 13th St., New York, NY 10003. TEL 212-777-4700. Ed.Bd. circ. 600. (back issues avail.) Indexed: M.L.A. Amer.Hum.Ind.

400   ISSN 0360-215X
DICTIONARY OF CONTEMPORARY QUOTATIONS. 1976. triennial. $45. John Gordon Burke Publishers, Inc., Box 1492, Evanston, IL 60204-1492.
● Also available online.

DICTIONARY OF LITERARY BIOGRAPHY. see *BIOGRAPHY — Abstracting, Bibliographies, Statistics*

800 920   US
DICTIONARY OF LITERARY BIOGRAPHY YEARBOOK. 1981. a. $95. Gale Research Company, Book Tower, Detroit, MI 48226. TEL 313-961-2242.

800   US
DIMENSIONS (WATERBURY) 1969. a. free. Mattatuck Community College, Student Legislative Congress, 750 Chase Pkwy., Waterbury, CT 06708. TEL 203-575-0328. Ed. Gloria Pond. circ. 1,000.

050 810 820   US   ISSN 0070-6094
DIRECTORY OF PERIODICALS PUBLISHING ARTICLES ON ENGLISH AND AMERICAN LITERATURE AND LANGUAGE.* 1959. irreg., 4th edt. 1975. $10 $3.50 paper. Swallow Press, Inc., Box 2080, Chicago, IL 60690-2080. Eds. Donna Gerstenberger, George Hendrick.

DIVREI HA-AKADEMIA HA-LEUMIT HA-YISRAELIT LEMADAIM. see *HISTORY*

860   US
DOCUMENTACION CERVANTINA. 1978. irreg., no.5, 1985. price varies. Juan de la Cuesta, Pub., Hispanic Monographs, 270 Indian Rd., Newark, DE 19711. Ed. Thomas A. Lathrop. circ. 500. Indexed: M.L.A.

891.7   US
DOCUMENTARY STUDIES IN MODERN RUSSIAN POETRY. 1980. irreg., no.3, 1981. University of California Press, 2120 Berkeley Way, Berkeley, CA 94720. TEL 415-642-4247.

057.87 891.87   CS
DOMOVA POKLADNICA. a. 30 Kcs. Priroda, Krizkova 9, 815 34 Bratislava, Czechoslovakia.

820 420   JA   ISSN 0046-063X
DOSHISHA LITERATURE; journal of English literature and philology. (Text in English) 1887. biennial. 1000 Yen($7) per no. Doshisha University, English Literary Society, Karasuma Imadegawa, Kamikyo-ku, Kyoto 602, Japan. Ed. Isamu Saito. bk. rev. circ. 2,000. Indexed: Curr.Cont. Arts & Hum.Cit.Ind. Lang.& Lang.Behav.Abstr.
     Formerly: Doshisha Bungaku.

800   JA
DOSHISHA STUDIES IN FOREIGN LITERATURE.* (Text in English, French, German or Japanese) 1971. irreg. 1000 Yen. Doshisha University, Gaikoku Bungakukai, Karasuma Imadegawa, Kamikyo-ku, Kyoto 602, Japan.

891.7   US
DOSTOEVSKY STUDIES. (Text in English, French, German and Russian) 1980. a. $10. International Dostoevsky Society, c/o Martin P. Rice, University of Tennessee, Department of Germanic and Slavic Languages, Knoxville, TN 37996. TEL 615-974-3421. Ed. Rudolf Neuhaeuser. bk. rev. bibl. circ. 300. (back issues avail.) Indexed: M.L.A. Amer.Bibl.Slavic & E.Eur.Stud.
     Supersedes: International Dostoevsky Society Bulletin (ISSN 0047-0686)

378.1   UK   ISSN 0012-589X
DRAGON. (Editions in English and Welsh) 1966. a. 10p. University College of Wales, Students' Union, Aberystwyth, Cardiganshire, Wales. Eds. G.J. Hill, Huw Jones. adv. bk. rev. film rev. illus. record rev. circ. 1,000.

800   DK   ISSN 0900-7350
DRAMAPAEDAGOGIK I NORDISK PERSPEKTIV. a. Bibliotekscentralen, Telegrafvej 5, DK-2750 Ballerup, Denmark.

822   UK   ISSN 0070-7198
DRAMASCRIPTS SERIES. (Text in English or bilingual with English translations) 1965. irreg., no.4, 1970. price varies. Oleander Press, 17 Stansgate Ave., Cambridge CB2 2QZ, England (U.S. address: 210 Fifth Ave., New York, N.Y. 10010) Eds. Philip Ward, Wayne Schlepp.

810   US
DRUM (AMHERST); black literary experience. 1970. a. $3. 115 New Africa House, University of Massachusetts, Amherst, MA 01003. TEL 413-545-0111. bk. rev. play rev. illus. circ. 4,000. (back issues avail.)

DUQUESNE STUDIES. LANGUAGE AND LITERATURE SERIES. see *LINGUISTICS*

E A C R O T A N A L INFORMATION. (Eastern African Centre for Research on Oral Traditions and African National Languages) see *LINGUISTICS*

E A C R O T A N A L STUDIES & DOCUMENTS. (Eastern African Centre for Research on Oral Traditions and African National Languages) see *LINGUISTICS*

830   GW   ISSN 0073-2885
E.T.A. HOFFMANN-GESELLSCHAFT. MITTEILUNGEN. 1938. a. DM.30. E.T.A. Hoffmann-Gesellschaft, Wetzelstr. 79, 8600 Bamberg, W. Germany (B.R.D.) bk. rev. circ. 850.

ECOLE PRATIQUE DES HAUTES ETUDES. CENTRE DE RECHERCHES SUR LE PORTUGAL DE LA RENAISSANCE. SERIES TEXTES. see *HISTORY — History Of Europe*

840   SZ   ISSN 0070-8879
ECRITURE; l'annnee litteraire en suisse romande. 1964. a. 20 Fr. Editions Bertil Galland, 29 rue du Lac, CH-1800 Vevey, Switzerland. Ed. Bertil Galland. circ. 2,000.

398   PE
EDICIONES DEL PUEBLO. no.38, 1983. irreg. Universidad Nacional "Daniel Aleides Carron", Av. Guzman Blanco 465, Of.204, Lima, Peru.

839   439   DK   ISSN 0070-9069
EDITIONES ARNAMAGNAEANAE. SERIES A. (Text in Danish, English, Icelandic) 1958. irreg. price varies. Arnamagnaean Insitute and Arnamagnaean Dictionary, Njalsgade 76, DK-2300 Copenhagen S, Denmark (Dist. by: C.A. Reitzels Boghandel A-S, Noerregade 20, DK-1165 Copenhagen K, Denmark)

839   439   DK   ISSN 0070-9077
EDITIONES ARNAMAGNAEANAE. SERIES B. (Text in Danish, English, German, Icelandic) 1960. irreg. price varies. Arnamagnaean Insitute and Arnamagnaean Dictionary, Njalsgade 76, DK-2300 Copenhagen S, Denmark (Dist. by: C.A. Reitzels Boghandel A-S, Noerregade 20, DK-1165 Copenhagen K, Denmark)

839   DK   ISSN 0070-9085
EDITIONES ARNAMAGNAEANAE. SUPPLEMENTUM. 1963. irreg. Arnamagnaean Institute and Arnamagnaean Dictionary, Njalsgade 76, DK-2300 Copenhagen S, Denmark (Dist. by: C.A. Reitzels Boghandel A-S, Noerregade 20, DK-1165 Copenhagen K, Denmark)

800   US
EDITOR'S CHOICE; poetry, fiction and art. 1980. irreg., every 4-5 yrs. $10 paperback; hardcover $16. Spirit That Moves Us, Inc., Box 1585, Iowa City, IA 52244. TEL 319-338-7502. Eds. Morty Sklar, Mary Biggs. bibl. illus. circ. 4,200. Indexed: Amer.Hum.Ind. Ind.Amer.Per.Verse.

820   792   UK
EDWARDIAN STUDIES. 1976. a. £5($15) (Edwardian Studies Association) High Orchard Press, High Orchard, 125 Markyate Rd., Dagenham, Essex RM8 2LB, England. adv. bk. rev. index.
Literature and drama of the Edwardian era

810   UK
EIGHTEEN NINETIES SOCIETY. JOURNAL. 1963. a. membership. Eighteen Nineties Society, 17 Meton Hall Road, Wimbledon, London SW19 3PP, England. Ed. G. Krishnamurti. adv. bk. rev. circ. 750. (processed) Indexed: Abstr.Engl.Stud.
Formerly: Francis Thompson Society. Journal (ISSN 0532-5781)

800   US   ISSN 0161-0996
EIGHTEENTH CENTURY: A CURRENT BIBLIOGRAPHY. 1975. a. $67.50. A M S Press, Inc., 56 E. 13th St., New York, NY 10003. TEL 212-777-4700. Ed. Jim Springer Brock. bk. rev. index. circ. 600. (back issues avail.)

EIRENE; studia graeca et latina. see *CLASSICAL STUDIES*

808   CN
ELIXIR. a. Glendon College, Student Union, 2275 Bayview Ave., Toronto, Ont. M4N 3M6, Canada. TEL 416-487-6720. adv. circ. 2,000.

820   AU
ELIZABETHAN AND RENAISSANCE STUDIES. (Text in English) 1972. irreg., no.109, 1986. S.245. Universitaet Salzburg, Institut fuer Englische Sprache, Akademiestr. 24, A-5020 Salzburg, Austria. Ed. James Hogg. circ. 250. Indexed: M.L.A.

809.02   US   ISSN 0363-4841
ENCOMIA. 1975. a. $7.50. International Courtly Literature Society, c/o Sandra Ihle, Sec.-Treas, School of Business, University of Wisconsin, Madison, WI 53706. adv. bk. rev. illus. circ. 600. Indexed: M.L.A.

800   US   ISSN 0071-0164
ENCORE. 1948. a. $2. National Association of Dramatic and Speech Arts, Shaw University, Box 124, Raleigh, NC 27611. TEL 919-755-4878. Ed. H.B. Caple. adv. bk. rev. circ. 1,000. (also avail. in microform from UMI; reprint service avail. from UMI) Indexed: Mag.Ind. T.D.S.I.
Scholarly and creative writing about Black theatre and rhetoric

830   UK
ENGLISH GOETHE SOCIETY. PUBLICATIONS. 1886. N.S. 1972/73. a. £4($18) English Goethe Society, University College, Gower St., London W.C.1., England. Ed. Prof. F.M. Fowler. circ. 500.

814   US   ISSN 0071-0598
ENGLISH INSTITUTE. SELECTED ESSAYS. 1939. a. price varies. Johns Hopkins University Press, 701 W. 40th St., Ste. 275, Baltimore, MD 21211 TEL 301-338-6900. (Vols. before 1978 pub. by: Columbia University Press, 136 S. Broadway, Irvington-on-Hudson, NY 10533) (reprint service avail. from UMI)

809   US   ISSN 0013-8312
ENGLISH LITERARY RENAISSANCE SUPPLEMENTS. 1972. irreg., no.3, 1977. price varies; free with subscription to English Literary Renaissance. University of Massachusetts, Department of English, Amherst, MA 01002. TEL 413-545-0372. Ed. Arthur F. Kinney. circ. 1,000.
Formerly: English Literary Renaissance Monographs.

080   800   UK   ISSN 0071-061X
ENGLISH LITTLE MAGAZINES. 1967. irreg., no.16, 1971. price varies. Frank Cass & Co. Ltd., Gainsborough House, 11 Gainsborough Rd., London E11 1RS, England (Dist. in U.S. by: Biblio Distribution Center, 81 Adams Dr., Totowa, NJ 07512)

808   IT   ISSN 0425-0575
ENGLISH MISCELLANY; a symposium of history, literature and the arts. 1950. a. price varies. Edizioni di Storia e Letteratura, Via Lancellotti 18, 00186 Rome, Italy. Ed. Mario Praz. Indexed: M.L.A. Abstr.Engl.Stud.

ENNEMI. see *ART*

860   UY   ISSN 0071-0679
ENSAYO Y TESTIMONIO.* irreg. Editorial Arca, Colonia 1263, Montevideo, Uruguay.

800   DK   ISSN 0900-2731
ERHVERVS OG SAMFUNDSBESKRIVELSE. NOTER OG OPGAVER. 1985. a. Kr.44.65. Biblioekscentralen, Telegrafvej 5, DK-2750 Ballerup, Denmark.

800   IE
ERIU; journal devoted to Irish philology and literature. 1904. a. Royal Irish Academy, 19 Dawson St., Dublin 2, Ireland. Eds. Proinsias MacCana, E.G. Quin. Indexed: M.L.A.

808   US   ISSN 0887-5057
EROTIC FICTION QUARTERLY; a journal of erotic & other sexual fiction. 1985. irreg. $9.95 per no. E F Q Publications, Box 4958, San Francisco, CA 94101-4958. Ed. Richard Hiller. circ. 1,000.

860   100   CK   ISSN 0120-1263
ESCRITOS. 1974. irreg. $.50 per no. Universidad Pontificia Bolivariana, Escuela de Educacio y Humanidades, Biblioteca Central - Seccion Canje, Aptdo 1178, Medellin, Colombia. Ed. Carlos Enrique Londoro R. adv. bk. rev. bibl. circ. 1,000.

800   GW
ESOTERIK ALMANACH. 1986. a. DM.12.80. Dr. Lothar Rossipaul Verlagsgesellschaft GmbH, Bavariaring 24, D-8000 Munich 2, W. Germany (B.R.D.) Ed. Rainer Rossipaul. circ. 40,000.

824   US   ISSN 0071-1357
ESSAYS AND STUDIES. 1910. a. price varies. Humanities Press, Inc., 171 First Ave., Atlantic Highlands, NJ 07716. TEL 201-872-1441. Indexed: Br.Hum.Ind. M.L.A. Abstr.Engl.Stud.

808   US
ESSAYS BY DIVERS HANDS.* 1979. a. price varies. Boydell & Brewer, Box 2069, Wolfeboro, NH 03894-2069. Indexed: M.L.A. Abstr.Engl.Stud.

ESSAYS IN FOREIGN LANGUAGES AND LITERATURES/GAIKOKUGO GAIKOKU BUNGAKU KENKYU. see *LINGUISTICS*

800   US   ISSN 0738-0763
ESSAYS IN GRAHAM GREENE: AN ANNUAL REVIEW. 1987. a. $20. Penkevill Publishing Company, Box 212, Greenwood, FL 32443. TEL 904-569-2811. Ed. Peter Wolfe.

800   US   ISSN 0071-1470
ESSENTIAL ARTICLES. 1961. irreg., no.11, 1985. price varies. Shoe String Press Inc., 925 Sherman Ave., Hamden, CT 06514.
Anthologies of articles essential to the study of various periods and authors in the field of literature

860   MX   ISSN 0071-1691
ESTUDIOS DE LITERATURA. 1958. irreg., latest issue, 1976. price varies. ‡ Universidad Nacional Autonoma de Mexico, Instituto de Investigaciones Esteticas, Torre de Humanidades, Ciudad Universitaria, Mexico 20, D.F., Mexico.

860   SP   ISSN 0071-1705
ESTUDIOS DE LITERATURA CONTEMPORANEA. 1968. irreg. price varies, $3-$5. Real Academia Espanola de la Lengua, Universidad de Santiago de Compostela, Coruna, Spain. circ. 2,000.

800   BL
ESTUDOS BAIANOS. 1970. irreg. Cr.$290. Universidade Federal da Bahia, Centro Editorial e Didatico, Rua A. Viana s/n, Canela, Salvador, Bahia, Brazil. Ed.Bd. circ. 1,000.

830   BL
ESTUDOS GERMANICOS. 1980. a. $1. Universidade Federal de Minas Gerais, Departamento de Letras Germanicas, Campus Pampulha, Av. Antonio Carlos, 6627, 30000 Belo Horizonte, Minas Gerais, Brazil. Ed. Julio Yeha. bk. rev. circ. 1,000.

ESTUDOS ITALIANOS EM PORTUGAL. see *ART*

869   PO
ETC. no.4, 1981. irreg. Publicacoes Culturais Engrenagem, Lda., Rua da Emenda, 30, 1200 Lisbon, Portugal.

840   SZ   ISSN 0531-9455
ETUDES BAUDELAIRIENNES. 1970. irreg., no.12, 1987. price varies. Editions de la Baconniere S.A., Box 185, CH-2017 Boudry, Switzerland. Eds. Marc Eigeldinger, Claude Pichois.

400   900   SZ   ISSN 0071-1934
ETUDES DE PHILOLOGIE ET D'HISTOIRE. (Text in English or French) 1967. irreg., no.40, 1985. price varies. Librarie Droz, 11, rue Massot, 1211 Geneva 12, Switzerland.

800   FR   ISSN 0071-2051
ETUDES FINNO-OUGRIENNES. 1964. irreg. price varies. (Universite de Paris X (Paris-Nanterre), Centre d'Etudes Finno-Ougriennes) Editions Klincksieck, 11 rue de Lille, 75005 Paris, France. bk. rev.

840   SZ
ETUDES RABELAISIENNES. (Text in English, French, German, Italian, Spanish) 1956. irreg., latest vol.18, 1985. Librairie Droz S.A., 11 rue Massot, 1211 Geneva 12, Switzerland. circ. 800. Indexed: M.L.A.

830 398 GW ISSN 0531-2159
EULENSPIEGEL-JAHRBUCH. 1960. a. DM.36.
Verlag Peter Lang, Hinter den Ulmen 19, D-6000
Frankfurt 50, W. Germany (B.R.D.) (Subscr. to:
Dieter Scheller, Rathaus, D-3307 Schoeppenstedt,
W. Germany (B.R.D.)) Ed. Werner Wunderlich.
adv. bk. rev. circ. 600. (back issues avail.)

EVENTI E INTERVENTI. see *ART*

709 UK
EXETER'S STUDIES IN AMERICAN &
COMMONWEALTH ARTS. 1970. irreg. (1-2/yr.)
£1($3.50) University of Exeter, American Arts
Documentation Centre, Queens Building, Exeter EX
4QH, England. Ed. R. Maltby. circ. 2,000.
Formerly: American Arts Pamphlet Series.

810 US ISSN 0421-9090
EXILE; contemporary literature. 1953. biennial.
Denison University, Granville, OH 43023. TEL
614-587-0810. illus. Indexed: Curr.Cont. Arts &
Hum.Cit.Ind.

800 US ISSN 0195-3516
EXIT; a journal of the arts. 1976. irreg. $7 for 3
issues. Rochester Routes-Creative Arts Projects, 50
Inglewood Dr., Rochester, NY 14619. Eds. Frank
Judge, Gregory FitzGerald. adv. circ. 2,000.
Formerly: Entrance.

808 910.09 US
EXPLORATION; journal on the literature of
exploration and travel. 1972. a. $3. Illinois State
University, Department of English, Normal, IL
61761. Ed. Steven E. Kagle. bk. rev. circ. 250. (back
issues avail.) Indexed: Abstr.Engl.Stud.

EXPLORATIONS IN RENAISSANCE CULTURE.
see *HISTORY — History Of Europe*

820 AT ISSN 0085-039X
EXPRESSION. 1964. a. Aus.$2. University of
Wollongong, School of Education, Box 1144,
Wollongong, N.S.W. 2500, Australia. Ed. R.W.
Colvin. bk. rev. circ. 400.

830 AU
FACETTEN. 1970. a. S.110. (Kulturamt) Jugend und
Volk Verlagsgesellschaft, Anschuetzg. 1, A-1153
Vienna, Austria.

808 US ISSN 0271-7808
FANTASY VOICES. 1982. irreg., approx. a. $13.95
(hardcover); $5.95 (paperback) per no. Borgo Press,
Box 2845, San Bernardino, CA 92406. TEL 714-
884-5813.

808 US ISSN 0276-2072
FAT TUESDAY. (Each issue has distinctive title)
1981. a. $5. Fat Tuesday Publications, 419 N.
Larchmont Blvd., Ste. 104, Los Angeles, CA 90004.
Ed. F.M. Cotolo. adv. illus. circ. 200. (back issues
avail.)

800 301.412 FR
FEMMES EN LITTERATURE. 1976. irreg. price
varies. Librairie Klincksieck, 11 rue de Lille, 75005
Paris, France. Dir. Patrice Laurent.

800 US ISSN 0092-1912
FICTION INTERNATIONAL. 1973. a. $14 to
individuals; institutions $20. San Diego State
University Press, San Diego, CA 92182. adv. bk.
rev. illus. circ. 2,000. (also avail. in microform from
UMI; reprint service avail. from UMI) Indexed:
Amer.Hum.Ind. Bk.Rev.Ind. Abstr.Engl.Stud.

808 US ISSN 0275-2123
FICTION WRITER'S MARKET. a. $18.95. F & W
Publications, Inc., 9933 Alliance Rd., Cincinnati,
OH 45242. TEL 513-984-0717. Ed. Laurie Henry.
circ. 20,000.
Creative writing

800 US
FIFTH SUN. 1979. irreg. Quincunx Press, 1134-B
Chelsea Ave., Santa Monica, CA 90403. Ed. Max
Benavidez.

FILOLOGIA BALTYCKA/BALTIC PHILOLOGY.
see *LINGUISTICS*

810 US ISSN 0071-5654
FITZGERALD/HEMINGWAY ANNUAL. 1969. a.
$64. ‡ Gale Research Company, Book Tower,
Detroit, MI 48226. TEL 313-961-2242. Eds.
Matthew J. Bruccoli, Richard Layman.
Interviews, reminiscences and book reviews

809 US ISSN 0091-4924
FLANNERY O'CONNOR BULLETIN. 1972. a. $4.
Georgia College, Department of English and
Speech, Box 44, Milledgeville, GA 31061. TEL 912-
453-4581. Ed.Bd. adv. bk. rev. circ. 1,000. (also
avail. in microform from UMI; back issues avail.;
reprint service avail. from UMI) Indexed:
Amer.Hum.Ind. Abstr.Engl.Stud.

810 US ISSN 0147-1686
FLOATING ISLAND. 1976. irreg., no.3, 1980. price
varies. Floating Island Publications, Box 516, Point
Reyes Station, CA 94956. Ed. Michael Sykes. illus.
circ. 1,000.

806 US
FLORIDA STATE UNIVERSITY. ROBERT
MANNING STROZIER LIBRARY.
COLLECTION SERIES. irreg., no.3, 1982. Florida
State University, Robert Manning Strozier Library,
Tallahassee, FL 53761.

FLORILEGIUM; annual papers on classical antiquity
and the Middle Ages. see *CLASSICAL STUDIES*

997 JM
FOCUS. 1983. a. $11.20. Caribbean Authors
Publishing Co., Ltd., 20 A & B North St., Kingston,
Jamaica, W. Indies. Ed. Mervyn Morris. circ. 2,000.

800 US
FOCUSES. 1987. irreg. $10 to individuals; libraries
$14.95. Appalachian State University, Department
of English, Boone, NC 28608. TEL 704-262-3098.
Ed. William C. Wolff.

FOLGER SHAKESPEARE LIBRARY ANNUAL
REPORT. see *LIBRARY AND INFORMATION
SCIENCES*

FOLIO (BROCKPORT); essays on foreign languages
and literature. see *HUMANITIES:
COMPREHENSIVE WORKS*

800 808.81 BE
FONDATION MAURICE CAREME; etablissement
d'utilite publique. (Text in French; special issues in
English) 1978. a. free. Fondation Maurice Careme,
B.P. 7, Anderlecht 1, Belgium. (Co-sponsor: Les
Amis Maurice Careme) circ. 11,000.

809 IT ISSN 0390-2153
FORME DEL SIGNIFICATO. 1972. irreg., no.31,
1984. price varies. Liguori Editore s.r.l., Via
Mezzocannone 19, 80134 Naples, Italy. TEL 081/
20 6077. Ed.Bd.

830 NE ISSN 0168-9770
FORSCHUNGSBERICHTE ZUR D D R-
LITERATUR. 1980. irreg. price varies. Editions
Rodopi B.V., Keizersgracht 302-304, Amsterdam,
Netherlands. Ed. Gerd Labroisse.

800 GW ISSN 0071-7703
FORSCHUNGSPROBLEME DER
VERGLEICHENDEN
LITERATURGESCHICHTE. 1951. irreg., no.7,
1978. price varies. Max Niemeyer Verlag,
Pfrondorfer Str. 4, 7400 Tuebingen, W. Germany
(B.R.D.) (back issues avail.)

810 US ISSN 0362-0247
FOUR ZOAS; journal of poetry and letters. 1972.
irreg. $4 per no. Four Zoas Press, 30 Main St., Box
111, Ashuelot, NH 03441. adv. bk. rev. circ. 500.

830 430 GW ISSN 0071-9226
FRANKFURTER BEITRAEGE ZUR
GERMANISTIK. 1967. irreg., no.15, 1977. price
varies. Carl Winter Universitaetsverlag, Lutherstr.
59, 6900 Heidelberg, W. Germany (B.R.D.)
Indexed: M.L.A.

FRANKFURTER JUDAISTISCHE BEITRAEGE. see
ETHNIC INTERESTS

FRANZ DELITZSCH-VORLESUNGEN. NEUE
FOLGE. see *HISTORY*

491 891 GW ISSN 0067-592X
FREIE UNIVERSITAET BERLIN. OSTEUROPA-
INSTITUT. SLAVISTISCHE
VEROEFFENTLICHUNGEN. (Title varies:
Veroffentlichungen der Abteilung fuer Slavische
Sprachen und Literaturen) 1953. irreg., vol.61, 1986.
price varies. (Freie Universitaet Berlin, Osteuropa
Institut) Verlag Otto Harrassowitz, Taunusstr. 14,
Postfach 2929, 6200 Wiesbaden, W. Germany
(B.R.D.) Ed.Bd. circ. 500.

800 GW ISSN 0071-9463
FREIES DEUTSCHES HOCHSTIFT, FRANKFURT
AM MAIN. JAHRBUCH. (Text in English and
German) 1962. a. price varies. Max Niemeyer
Verlag, Pfrondorfer Str. 4, 7400 Tuebingen, W.
Germany (B.R.D.) Ed. Christoph Perels. circ. 1,500.
(back issues avail) Indexed: M.L.A.

800 410 CH
FU JEN STUDIES; literature & linguistics. (Text in
English) 1968. a. $3. Fu Jen University, College of
Foreign Languages & Literature, Taipei, Taiwan,
Republic of China. Ed. Peter Venne. circ. 300.
(back issues avail.) Indexed: M.L.A.

800 US ISSN 0190-4701
FURMAN STUDIES. 1912. a. free. Furman
University, Greenville, SC 29613. TEL 803-294-
2066. Ed. Gilbert Allen. circ. 500. Indexed: M.L.A.
Formerly: Furman University Bulletin. Furman
Studies Issue.

808 US
GARLAND ENGLISH TEXTS.* irreg., no.8, 1982.
Garland Publishing, Inc., 136 Madison Ave., New
York, NY 10016. TEL 212-686-7492. Ed. Jane
Lytton Gooch.

830 GW
GASOLIN 23. 1973. irreg., no.7, 1979. DM.6 per no.
Nova Press, Friedrichstr. 60, 6000 Frankfurt, W.
Germany (B.R.D.) Eds. J. Ploog, W. Hartmann.
adv. illus. circ. 2,000.

800 GW ISSN 0720-2520
GAUKE'S JAHRBUCH. 1980. a. DM.26. Gauke
GmbH Verlag, Bergstr. 26, 3510 Hann. Muenden 1,
W. Germany (B.R.D.) Eds. Christoph and Gabriele
Gauke.

800 821 UK ISSN 0308-7999
GAZELLE REVIEW OF LITERATURE ON THE
MIDDLE EAST. irreg. £3 per no. Ithaca Press, 13
Southwark St., London SE1 1RQ, England. Ed.
Roger Hardy. index.

800 GW ISSN 0072-0550
GEISTIGE BEGEGNUNG; Moderne Erzaehler der
Welt. 1962. irreg. DM.28. (Institut fuer
Auslandsbeziehungen, Stuttgart) K. Thienemanns
Verlag, Edition Erdmann, Blumenstr. 36, 7000
Stuttgart, W. Germany (B.R.D.) circ. 4,000.

800 GE
GEORG FORSTER: SAEMLICHE SCHRIFTEN,
TAGEBUECHER, BRIEFE. (Text in English and
German) 1958. irreg., vol.5, 1986. (Akademie der
Wissenschaften der DDR) Akademie-Verlag Berlin,
Leipziger Str. 3-4, 1086 Berlin, E. Germany
(D.D.R.)

800 UK
GEORGE ELIOT FELLOWSHIP REVIEW. 1970. a.
£3. George Eliot Fellowship, 71 Stepping Stones
Rd., Coventry CV5 8JT, W. Midlands, England.
Eds. Kathleen Adams, Graham Handley. bk. rev.
circ. 400. Indexed: M.L.A.

800 US ISSN 0884-8696
GEORGIA STATE LITERARY STUDIES. irreg.
price varies. A M S Press, 56 E. 13th St., New
York, NY 10003. TEL 212-777-4700. Ed. James D.
Wilson.

808 US
GLENS FALLS REVIEW. 1983. a. $4. Loft Press, 42
Sherman Ave., Glens Falls, NY 12801-2753. TEL
518-798-8110. Ed. Jean Rikhoff. circ. 1,000.

GOETEBORGER GERMANISTISCHE
FORSCHUNGEN. see *LINGUISTICS*

LITERATURE

830 GE ISSN 0323-4207
GOETHE-JAHRBUCH. 1880. a. M.35. (Goethe-Gesellschaft, Weimar) Hermann Boehlaus Nachfolger, Meyerstr. 50a, 53 Weimar, E. Germany (D.D.R.) Ed. Karl-Heinz Hahn. bk. rev. Indexed: Curr.Cont. M.L.A. Arts & Hum.Cit.Ind.
Formerly: Goethe-Gesellschaft. Jahrbuch (ISSN 0072-484X)

830 GW
GOETHE WOERTERBUCH. 1966. a. Verlag W. Kohlhammer, Postfach 400263, D-5000 Cologne 40, W. Germany (B.R.D.)

830 US ISSN 0734-3329
GOETHE YEARBOOK. 1982. a. $25. (Goethe Society of North America) Camden House, Inc., Box 2025, Columbia, SC 29202. TEL 803-788-8689. Ed. Thomas P. Saine. bk. rev. bibl. circ. 700. (back issues avail.) Indexed: M.L.A.

GOTHENBURG STUDIES IN ENGLISH. see *LINGUISTICS*

800 808.838 US
GOTHIC. 1979-1980; resumed 1983. a. $6. Gothic Press, Box 80051, Baton Rouge, LA 70898. TEL 504-766-2906. Ed. Gary William Crawford. bk. rev. bibl. circ. 300. (also avail. in microform from UMI; back issues avail.; reprint service avail. from UMI) Indexed: M.L.A.
Former titles: Gothic Chapbook Series (ISSN 0193-0184); Gothic.

809 US ISSN 0363-8057
GRADIVA; a journal of contemporary theory and practice. 1976. a. $8. c/o George Carpetto, Department of French and Italian, State University of New York at Stony Brook, Stony Brook, NY 11794. Ed. J.M. Heumann. adv. bk. rev. abstr. illus. circ. 300. Indexed: Curr.Cont. M.L.A. Arts & Hum.Cit.Ind.

860 UY ISSN 0072-5439
GRANDES TODOS.* irreg. Editorial Arca, Colonia 1263, Montevideo, Uruguay.

800 US ISSN 0092-5268
GRANTS AND AWARDS AVAILABLE TO AMERICAN WRITERS. 1969. biennial. $6 to individuals; institutions $9.50. P E N American Center, 568 Broadway, New York, NY 10012. TEL 212-334-1660. Ed. John Morrone. circ. 4,000.
Formerly: List of Grants and Awards Available to American Writers (ISSN 0075-983X)

800 US ISSN 0743-7471
GRAYWOLF ANNUAL. 1984. a. Graywolf Press, 370 Selby Ave., No. 203, St. Paul, MN 55102. TEL 612-222-8342. Ed. Scott Walker. (back issues avail.)

GREAT ISSUES OF THE DAY. see *POLITICAL SCIENCE*

GREEN FEATHER. see *ADVENTURE AND ROMANCE*

800 US ISSN 0160-6565
GUEST AUTHOR; a directory of speakers. 1978. biennial. $9.95. Hermes Press, 51 Lenox St., Brockton, MA 02401. Ed. Jane Manthorne, Rose Moorachian. circ. 2,000.

H S G'S AARBOG. (Hvad Skovsoeen /Gemte) see *ADVENTURE AND ROMANCE*

830 GW
HABELTS DISSERTATIONSDRUCKE. REIHE GERMANISTIK. 1973. irreg. price varies. Dr. Rudolf Habelt GmbH, Am Buchenhang 1, 5300 Bonn 1, W. Germany (B.R.D.)

HARVARD CELTIC COLLOQUIUM. PROCEEDINGS. see *LINGUISTICS*

800 420 US ISSN 0073-0513
HARVARD ENGLISH STUDIES. 1970. irreg., latest vol.14, 1986. Harvard University Press, 79 Garden St., Cambridge, MA 02138. TEL 617-495-2600. Indexed: M.L.A. Rel.Ind.Two.

800 US ISSN 0073-0696
HARVARD STUDIES IN COMPARATIVE LITERATURE. 1910. irreg., no.37, 1984. price varies. Harvard University Press, 79 Garden St., Cambridge, MA 02138. TEL 617-495-2600. Indexed: M.L.A.

800 US ISSN 0073-0718
HARVARD STUDIES IN ROMANCE LANGUAGES. irreg., no.40, 1985. price varies. Harvard University, Department of Romance Languages and Literature, c/o Raymond La Charite, Ed., Box 5108, Lexington, KY 40505. Indexed: M.L.A.

HARVARD-YENCHING INSTITUTE. MONOGRAPH SERIES. see *HISTORY — History Of Asia*

800 700 US
HARVESTER. 1972. a. Lincoln Land Community College, Humanities Division, Shephard Rd., Springfield, IL 62708. TEL 217-786-2200. Ed. Marcel E. Pacatte, Sr. circ. 2,000. (back issues avail.)

830 GW ISSN 0073-1560
HEBBEL-JAHRBUECHER. a. price varies. (Hebbel-Gesellschaft) Westholsteinische Verlagsanstalt Boyens und Co., Am Wulf-Isebrand-Platz, Postfach 1880, 2240 Heide, W. Germany (B.R.D.) Ed.Bd.

059.927 001.3 US
HEBREW ANNUAL REVIEW; a journal of biblical and Hebraic studies. 1977. a. $20. Ohio State University, Department of Judaic and Near Eastern Languages and Literatures, 1841 Millikin Road, Columbus, OH 43210 TEL 614-422-9255. (Orders to: Student Book Exchange, 1086 N. High St., Columbus, OH 43201) Ed. Reuben Ahroni. adv. circ. 750. Indexed: Lang.& Lang.Behav.Abstr. Rel.& Theol.Abstr. Rel.Ind.One.

830 920 GW ISSN 0073-1692
HEINE-JAHRBUCH. 1962. a. DM.25. (Heinrich-Heine-Institut, Duesseldorf) Hoffmann und Campe Verlag, Harvestehuder Weg 45, 2000 Hamburg 13, W. Germany (B.R.D.) Ed. Joseph A. Kruse. bk. rev. circ. 1,300. Indexed: M.L.A.

800 GE
HEINE SAEKULARAUSGABE: WERKE-BRIEFWECHSEL-LEBENSZEUGNISSE. (Text in French and German) 1970. irreg., vol.3, 1986. Akademie-Verlag Berlin, Leipziger Str. 3-4, 1086 Berlin, E. Germany (D.D.R.)

880 480 GW ISSN 0018-0084
HELLENIKA; Zeitschrift fuer deutsch-griechische kulturelle und wirtschaftliche Zusammenarbeit. 1964. a. DM.20. (Ausgaben Neugriechische Studien) Verlag Ferdinand Kamp, Am Dornbusch 28, 4630 Bochum, W. Germany (B.R.D.) Ed. Isidora Rosenthal-Kamarinea. adv. bk. rev. abstr. bibl. circ. 3,000. Indexed: M.L.A.

820 UK ISSN 0073-1927
HERBERT READ SERIES. 1961. irreg. 52p.($1.25) Oleander Press, 17 Stansgate Ave., Cambridge CB2 2QZ, England (U.S. address: 210 Fifth Ave., New York, NY 10010) Ed. Philip Ward.

830 GW
HERMAEA; germanistische Forschungen N.F. irreg. Max Niemeyer Verlag, Pfrondorferstr. 4, 7400 Tuebingen, W. Germany (B.R.D.) Eds. Hans Fromm, Hans-Joachim Maehl. (back issues avail.) Indexed: M.L.A.

809 400 JA ISSN 0387-9348
HERON; essays on language & literature. (Text in English and Japanese) 1966. a. Saitama University, 255 Simo-Okubo, Urawa-shi, Saitama-ken, Japan. Ed.Bd. circ. 200.

810 US
HILL AND HOLLER; southern Appalachian mountains. 1983. a. $12. Seven Buffaloes Press, Box 249, Big Timber, MT 59011. Ed. Art Cuelho. circ. 500.

890 II
HINDI KAHANI. (Text in Hindi) 1977. a. Rs.40($8) Granthayan, 398, Sarvoday Nagar, Sasni Gate, Aligarh 202001, India. Eds. Rakeshgupta, R.K. Chaturvedi. circ. 1,100. (back issues avail.)

100 800 SZ ISSN 0073-2397
HISTOIRE DES IDEES ET CRITIQUE LITTERAIRE. 1954. irreg., no.241, 1986. price varies. Librarie Droz, 11 rue Massot, 1211 Geneva 12, Switzerland. circ. 1,500.

808 FR
HOMMES ET LES LETTRES. irreg., vol.2, 1977. Editions l' Hermes, 31 rue Pasteur, 69007 Lyon, France. Ed. Jacques Goudet.

800 US
HOR-TASY. 1980. irreg., approx a. $2.95. Ansuda Publications, Box 158-B, Harris, IA 51345. Ed. Daniel R. Betz.

808 US
HOT CHOCOLATE FAIRY TALE SERIES. 1983. irreg. Coffee House Press, Box 10870, Minneapolis, MN 55440-3870. TEL 612-338-0126. Ed. Allan Kornblum. circ. 1,200.

800 UK ISSN 0305-926X
HOUSMAN SOCIETY JOURNAL. 1974. a. £3. Housman Society, c/o Ms. B.E. Barley, 70 New Rd., Bromsgrove, Worcs. B60 2LA, England. Ed. J. Pugh. adv. bk. rev. bibl. circ. 350. (back issues avail.) Indexed: M.L.A.

894.51 HU ISSN 0439-9080
HUNGARIAN P.E.N/P.E.N. HONGROIS. (Text in English and French) 1961. a. free. Hungarian P.E.N. Club, Vorosmarty ter 1, 1051 Budapest, Hungary. Ed. Istvan Bart. adv. bk. rev. bibl. circ. 1,000. Indexed: M.L.A.

809 US ISSN 0271-9061
I.O. EVANS STUDIES IN THE PHILOSOPHY & CRITICISM OF LITERATURE. 1982. irreg., approx. 4/yr. $15.95 (hardcover); $7.95 (paperback) per no. Borgo Press, Box 2845, San Bernardino, CA 92406. TEL 714-884-5813.

839.82 920 NO ISSN 0073-4365
IBSEN AARBOKEN/IBSEN YEARBOOK. (Text in English) 1951/52. irreg. price varies. Norwegian University Press, Kolstadgt. 1, Box 2959-Toeyen, 0608 Oslo 6, Norway (U.S. address: Publications Expediting Inc., 200 Meacham Ave., Elmont, NY 11003) Ed. Daniel Haakonsen. Indexed: M.L.A.

809 BE
ICON. CAHIER. (Text in Dutch, English and French) 1970. a. 200 Fr. Les Amis de Jean Ray, 4 rue Vautier, Brussels, Belgium (Subscr. to: Martinus Nijhoff, P.O. Box 269, 2501 AX the Hague, The Netherlands) Ed. Jozef Peeters. bk. rev. bibl. circ. 400.
Former titles: Icon-Werkgroep Jean Ray. Cahier; Cahier Jean Ray.

800 900 US ISSN 0160-5305
IDAHO (MOSCOW) 1977. a. $3 per no. University of Idaho, Department of English, Moscow, ID 83843. TEL 208-885-6559. Ed. Bd. adv. circ. 200. (also avail. in microfiche; back issues avail.)
Supersedes (as of vol.10, 1987): Snapdragon.

890 IS
IGRA. a. P.O. Box 7145, Jerusalem 91 071, Israel. TEL 02-521201.

ILOCOS REVIEW. see *HISTORY — History Of Australasia And Other Areas*

810 US ISSN 0748-1780
IMAGE MAGAZINE; a magazine of the arts. (Text in English, German, Spanish) 1972. irreg., approx. 3/yr. $6. Cornerstone Press, Box 28048, St. Louis, MO 63119. TEL 314-296-9662. Eds. Anthony J. Summers, James J. Finnegan. bk. rev. illus. circ. 750. (also avail. in microfiche)

INDAGINI E PROSPETTIVE. see *POLITICAL SCIENCE*

830 NE ISSN 0169-037X
INDICES ZUM ALTDEUTSCHEN SCHRIFTTUM. 1976. irreg. price varies. Editions Rodopi B.V., Keizersgracht 302-304, 1016 EX Amsterdam, Netherlands. Ed. R. Ralph Anderson. circ. 300.

INDUSTRIAL SABOTAGE. see *LITERATURE — Poetry*

800 US ISSN 0190-0234
INKLINGS.* 1979. irreg. $5. Mudborn Press, 703 W. Micheltorena St., Santa Barbara, CA 93101. Ed. Judyl Mudfoot. circ. 800. Indexed: Graph.Arts Lit.Abstr.

808.1   US   ISSN 0085-1884
INLET. 1972. a. free. Virginia Wesleyan College, Department of English, Norfolk, VA 23502. TEL 804-461-3232. Ed. Joseph Harkey. circ. 1,000.

800   AT   ISSN 0314-285X
INPRINT; the short story journal. 1977. triennial. Aus.$13.50($20) Australian Council Literature Board, P.O. Box 666, Broadway, NSW 2007, Australia. Ed. Bill Turner. adv. bk. rev. circ. 1,000. (back issues avail.)

800   GW   ISSN 0443-2460
INSEL-ALMANACH. 1905. a. price varies. Insel-Verlag, Lindenstr. 29, 6000 Frankfurt, W. Germany (B.R.D.) Ed. Elizabeth Borchers. bk. rev. circ. 5, 000.

891.7 947   FR   ISSN 0078-9976
INSTITUT D'ETUDES SLAVES, PARIS. BIBLIOTHEQUE RUSSE. (Text and summaries in French and Russian) 1912. irreg., vol.79,1987. price varies. Institut d'Etudes Slaves, 9 rue Michelet, 75006 Paris, France. Indexed: M.L.A.

891.8   FR   ISSN 0079-001X
INSTITUT D'ETUDES SLAVES, PARIS. TEXTES. 1926. irreg., vol.8, 1968. price varies. Institut d'Etudes Slaves, 9 rue Michelet, 75006 Paris, France.

891 943   FR   ISSN 0079-0028
INSTITUT D'ETUDES SLAVES, PARIS. TRAVAUX. 1923. irreg., vol.32, 1985. price varies. Institut d'Etudes Slaves, 9 rue Michelet, 75006 Paris, France.

800   FR   ISSN 0073-8212
INSTITUT DE RECHERCHE ET D'HISTOIRE DES TEXTES, PARIS. DOCUMENTS, ETUDES ET REPERTOIRES. 1958. irreg., vol.22, 1976. price varies. Institut de Recherche et d'Histoire des Textes, Paris, 15 Quai Anatole-France, 75700 Paris, France.

800   FR   ISSN 0073-8263
INSTITUT DES ETUDES OCCITANES. PUBLICATIONS. 1970. irreg. price varies. Presses Universitaires de France, 108 bd. Saint Germain, 75279 Paris Cedex 6, France (Service des Periodiques, 12 rue Jean de Beauvais, 75005 Paris) (reprint service avail. from KTO)

INSTITUT FRANCAIS D'INDOLOGIE. PUBLICATIONS. see HISTORY — History Of Asia

INSTITUT PROVINCIAL D'ETUDES ET RECHERCHES BIBLIOTHECONOMIQUES. MEMOIRES. see BIBLIOGRAPHIES

860   CK
INSTITUTO CARO Y CUERVO. SERIE GRANADA ENTREABIERTA. 1973. irreg., latest issue, no.39, 1985. price varies. Instituto Caro y Cuervo, Seccion de Publicaciones, Apdo. Aereo 51502, Bogota, Colombia.

860 400   CK   ISSN 0073-9928
INSTITUTO CARO Y CUERVO. SERIE MINOR. 1950. irreg., no.25, 1984. price varies. Instituto Caro y Cuervo, Seccion de Publicaciones, Apdo. Aereo 51502, Bogota, Colombia. (back issues avail.)

800   RM
INSTITUTUL PEDAGOGIC ORADEA. LUCRARI STIINTIFICE: SERIA LITERATURA. (Continues in part its Lucrari Stiintifice: Seria Filologie (1971-72), its Lucrari Stiintifice: Seria A and Seria B (1969-1970), and its Lucrari Stiintifice (1967-68).) (Text in Rumanian, occasionally in English or French; summaries in English, French, German or Rumanian) irreg. Institutul Pedagogic Oradea, Calea Armatei Rosii Nr. 5, Oradea, Rumania.

840 700   FR   ISSN 0074-1140
INTERFERENCES, ARTS, LETTRES. 1968. irreg. price varies. Lettres Modernes, 73 rue du Cardinal-Lemoine, 75005 Paris, France.

840   FR   ISSN 0571-5865
INTERNATIONAL ASSOCIATION OF FRENCH STUDIES. CAHIERS. 1951. a. 120 Fr. International Association of French Studies, 11 place Marcelin-Berthelot, 75005 Paris, France. Ed. Robert Garapon. circ. 300.

INTERNATIONAL AUTHORS AND WRITERS WHO'S WHO. see BIOGRAPHY

800   GW   ISSN 0074-2813
INTERNATIONAL COMPARATIVE LITERATURE ASSOCIATION. PROCEEDINGS OF THE CONGRESS. 1955. triennial, 1978, 7th Montreal, Canada. DM.213. (International Comparative Literature Association - Association Internationale de Litterature Comparee) Kunst und Wissen Erich Bieber OHG, Wilhelmstr. 4, Postfach 46, 7000 Stuttgart 1, W. Germany (B.R.D.) 1970, 6th, Bordeaux, France.
Proceedings published in host country

800 860   US   ISSN 0074-6495
INTERNATIONAL INSTITUTE OF IBERO-AMERICAN LITERATURE. CONGRESS PROCEEDINGS. MEMORIA. 1939. biennial, 19th, Pittsburgh, 1979. $30. International Institute of Ibero-American Literature - Institute Internacional de Literatura Iberoamericana, c/o Keith McDuffie, Sec-Treas., 1312 C.L., University of Pittsburgh, Pittsburgh, PA 15260. TEL 412-624-4141. Ed. Alfredo A. Roggiano. adv. bk. rev. circ. 2, 000. (also avail. in microform from UMI)
Proceedings published by sponsoring university

800   UK   ISSN 0074-722X
INTERNATIONAL P.E.N. CONGRESS. REPORT. irreg., 39th, 1974, Jerusalem. International P.E.N., 38 King St., London WC2E 8JT, England.

INTERNATIONAL WOMEN'S WRITING GUILD. SYMPOSIUM MONOGRAPH. see WOMEN'S INTERESTS

830   GW   ISSN 0340-4528
INTERNATIONALES ARCHIV FUER SOZIALGESCHICHTE DER DEUTSCHEN LITERATUR. (Text in English, French, German) 1976. a. DM.96. Max Niemeyer Verlag, Pfrondorfer Str. 4, Postfach 2140, 7400 Tuebingen, W. Germany (B.R.D.) Ed.Bd. adv. bk. rev. bibl. (back issues avail.) Indexed: Curr.Cont. M.L.A. Arts & Hum.Cit.Ind. Can.Rev.Comp.Lit.

809   US
INTERPLAY (MALIBU); proceedings of symposia in comparative literature and the arts. 1982. irreg., latest no.4. price varies. (University of Southern California, Center for the Humanities, Comparative Literature Program) Undena Publications, 6355 Green Valley Circle, No. 213, Culver City, CA 90230-7064. Eds. Moshe Lazar, Ron Gottesman. (back issues avail.) Indexed: Hist.Abstr. Amer.Hist.& Life. PROMT.

850   IT
INTERPRETE. (Text in English or Italian) irreg. Angelo Longo Editore, Via Paolo Costa 33, P.O. Box 431, 48100 Ravenna, Italy. Ed. Aldo Scaglione.

800   US   ISSN 0363-9991
INTERSTATE; a magazine of creative acts. 1974. irreg. $10 for 2 nos. Noumenon Foundation, Box 7068, Austin, TX 78712. Eds. Loris Essary, Mark Loeffler. bk. rev. circ. 500. Indexed: Abstr.Mil.Bibl.

800 900 100 700   IT
INTERVENTI CLASSENSI. irreg. Angelo Longo Editore, Via Paolo Costa 33, P.O. Box 431, 48100 Ravenna, Italy.

IO. see ANTHROPOLOGY

IRISH DRAMA SELECTIONS. see THEATER

800   UK   ISSN 0140-895X
IRISH LITERARY STUDIES. 1977. irreg. Colin Smythe, Ltd., Box 6, Gerrards Cross, Buckinghamshire SL9 8XA, England (Pub. in U.S. by: Barnes & Noble Books, Littlefield Adams, 81 Adams Drive, Totowa, NJ 07512) circ. 1,500.

800   US   ISSN 0075-0816
IRISH PLAY SERIES. 1968. irreg., no.18, 1981. price varies. Proscenium Press, Box 361, Newark, DE 19711. TEL 302-737-5803. Ed. Robert Hogan. (reprint service avail. from UMI)

IRISH SLAVONIC STUDIES. see HISTORY — History Of Europe

820   US
IRISH STUDIES SERIES. irreg. Syracuse University Press, 1600 Jamesville Ave., Syracuse, NY 13244. TEL 315-423-2596. Ed. Richard Fallis.

894   HU   ISSN 0075-0824
IRODALOM - SZOCIALIZMUS. (Text in Hungarian; occasional summaries in German or Russian) 1959. irreg. price varies. (Magyar Tudomanyos Akademia) Akademiai Kiado, Publishing House of the Hungarian Academy of Sciences, Box 24, H-1363 Budapest, Hungary.

800   HU   ISSN 0075-0832
IRODALOMELMELET KLASSZIKUSAI. 1963. irreg. price varies. (Magyar Tudomanyos Akademia) Akademiai Kiado, Publishing House of the Hungarian Academy of Sciences, Box 24, H-1363 Budapest, Hungary.

809   HU   ISSN 0075-0840
IRODALOMTORTENETI FUZETEK. 1950. irreg., vol.114, 1986. price varies. (Magyar Tudomanyos Akademia) Akademiai Kiado, Publishing House of the Hungarian Academy of Sciences, Box 24, H-1363 Budapest, Hungary. Indexed: M.L.A.

809   HU   ISSN 0075-0859
IRODALOMTORTENETI KONYVTAR. (Text in Hungarian; occasional summaries in French or German) 1957. irreg., vol.38, 1983. price varies. (Magyar Tudomanyos Akademia) Akademiai Kiado, Publishing House of the Hungarian Academy of Sciences, Box 24, H-1363 Budapest, Hungary.

800   US   ISSN 0161-4622
ITALIAN CULTURE. (Former name of issuing body: American Association of University Professors of Italian) (Text in English, French, Italian) 1978. a. $15 to individuals; institutions $20. (American Association for Italian Studies) Medieval & Renaissance Texts & Studies, c/o Mario A. Di Cesare, Ed., University Center at Binghamton, State University of New York, Binghamton, NY 13901. adv. bk. rev. bibl. illus. circ. 1,000. Indexed: M.L.A.

ITALIAN PRIVATE ENGLISH LANGUAGE SCHOOLS & ITALIAN LANGUAGE SCHOOLS FOR OVERSEAS & ITALY. see EDUCATION — Guides To Schools And Colleges

850   UK   ISSN 0075-1634
ITALIAN STUDIES. 1937. a. £9.50. Society for Italian Studies, c/o Dr. C.S. Cairns, Department of Romance Studies, University College of Wales, Aberystwyth, Dyfed, Wales. Ed. Prof. B. Moloney. adv. bk. rev. bibl. circ. 750. (back issues avail.) Indexed: Br.Hum.Ind. M.L.A. Ind.Bk.Rev.Hum.

ITALIANIST. see HISTORY — History Of Europe

800 300 500 375   JA   ISSN 0367-7370
IWATE UNIVERSITY. FACULTY OF EDUCATION. ANNUAL REPORT. 1950. a. Iwate University, Faculty of Education, Ueda, Morioka, Iwate 020, Japan. Ed. Y. Saito. index. circ. 450. (back issues avail.) Indexed: Biol.Abstr.

JACOBEAN DRAMA STUDIES. see THEATER

800   II   ISSN 0448-1143
JADAVPUR JOURNAL OF COMPARATIVE LITERATURE. (Text mainly in English, occasionally in Bengali; summaries in English) 1961. a. Rs.12.50($3) Jadavpur University, Department of Comparative Literature, Calcutta 32, India. Ed. Amiya Dev. index. cum.index: vols.1-10. circ. 500. Indexed: M.L.A. Abstr.Engl.Stud.

807   BG
JAHANGIRNAGAR UNIVERSITY. DEPARTMENT OF ENGLISH. BULLETIN. (Text in English) vol.2, 1978. Tk.5. Jahangirnagar University, Department of English, Savar, Dacca, Bangladesh.

811   US   ISSN 0362-8302
JAM TO-DAY. 1973. a. $4.50. 372 Dunstable Rd., Tyngsborod, MA 01879. Eds. Don D. Stanford, Judith A. Stanford. bk. rev. circ. 300. (back issues avail.)

895   JA
JAPANESE LITERATURE TODAY. (Text in English) 1959-1969; N.S. 1976. a. $10. Japan P.E.N. Club - Nihon P E N Kurabu, 265 Shuwa Residential Hotel, 9-1-7 Akasaka, Minato-ku, Tokyo, Japan. Ed. Fusao Ohkuto. bk. rev. Supersedes (March, 1976): Japan P.E.N. News (ISSN 0075-3300)
Includes list of translations into foreign languages

890 430   SZ   ISSN 0721-3719
JAPANESE STUDIES IN GERMAN LANGUAGE AND LITERATURE/JAPANISCHE STUDIEN ZUR DEUTSCHEN SPRACHE UND LITERATUR. (Text in English, German) 1971. irreg. Verlag Peter Lang AG, Jupiterstrasse 15, CH-3015 Bern, Switzerland. Ed. Peter Lang. circ. 400. Indexed: M.L.A.

830   GW   ISSN 0075-3580
JEAN-PAUL-GESELLSCHAFT. JAHRBUCH. 1966. a. DM.55. C.H. Beck'sche Verlagsbuchhandlung, Wilhelmstr. 9, 8000 Munich 40, W. Germany (B.R.D.) Ed. Kurt Woelfel. bk. rev. circ. 750. Indexed: M.L.A.

700   US   ISSN 0021-5880
JEOPARDY.* 1964. a. $2. Western Washington University, 516 High St, Bellingham, WA 98225. TEL 206-676-3000. Ed. Randy Jay Landon. bk. rev. illus. circ. 4,000. (back issues avail.) Indexed: A.I.P.P.

JEWISH LANGUAGE REVIEW. see LINGUISTICS

JIDISCHE SCHTUDIES. see LINGUISTICS

200   UK
JOHN CLARE SOCIETY JOURNAL. 1982. a. £2.50($5) to non-members. John Clare Society, c/o Mrs. Daphne Faux, Secy., 86 Glinton Rd., Helpston, Peterborough PE6 7DQ, England (Subscr. to: c/o Treasurer, 8 Priory Rd., Peterborough, PE3 6EB, England) Ed. Pauline Buttery. adv. bk. rev. circ. 500. (back issues avail.)

800 950   NE   ISSN 0085-2376
JOURNAL OF ARABIC LITERATURE. 1970. a. price varies. E.J. Brill, P.O. Box 9000, 2300 PA Leiden, Netherlands. Indexed: Curr.Cont. M.L.A. Arts & Hum.Cit.Ind. Ind.Bk.Rev.Hum. Rel.Ind.One.

800 792   UK   ISSN 0309-5207
JOURNAL OF BECKETT STUDIES. 1977. irreg. £13 for 2 issues. John Calder (Publishers) Ltd., 18 Brewer St., London W1R 4AS, England. Ed. Stanley Gontarski. adv. bk. rev. illus. (back issues avail.) Indexed: Curr.Cont. M.L.A. Arts & Hum.Cit.Ind. Ind.Bk.Rev.Hum.

800 100   CN   ISSN 0381-6524
JOURNAL OF OUR TIME. 1977. irreg. price varies. Traditional Studies Press, Box 984, Adelaide St. Post Office, Toronto, Ont. M5C 2K4, Canada. Ed. Jack Cain. bk. rev. circ. 1,000.

800   FR
JOURNAL OF THE SHORT STORY IN ENGLISH. (Text in English) 1983. a. 155 Fr. (Centre d'Etudes et de Recherches sur la Nouvelle en Langue Anglaise) Presses de l'Universite d'Angers, Bibliotheque Universitaire, 5 Blvd. Lavoisier, 49045 Angers, France (Subscr. to: 5 Blvd. Lavoisier, Belle-Beille, 49045 Angers, France)

JYVASKYLA STUDIES IN THE ARTS. see ART

809   II
KAKATIYA JOURNAL OF ENGLISH STUDIES. Other title: K J E S. (Text in English) 1976. a. Rs.15($2) Kakatiya University, Department of English, Vidyaranyapuri, Warangal 506009, India. Ed. Dr. S. Lanmana Murthy. circ. 250.

890 700   CE
KALAVA HA SAHITYAYA. (Text in Sinhalese) 1976. irreg. Rs.1. Nava Parapura, 26 Clifford Ave., Colombo 3, Sri Lanka.

800   FI   ISSN 0355-0311
KALEVALASEURAN VUOSIKIRJA. 1921. a. Fmk.98. (Finnish Literature Society) Suomalaisen Kirjallisuuden Seura, Hallituskatu 1, SF-00170 Helsinki, Finland. TEL 358-0-171229. cum. index 1921-70. circ. 2,000. Indexed: M.L.A.

813   US   ISSN 0022-7994
KALKI; studies in James Branch Cabell. 1965. irreg. $10 individuals; institutions $20. James Branch Cabell Society, HC 63 Box 79, E. Alstead, NH 03602-7705. (Affiliate: East Texas State University) Ed. Paul Spencer. bk. rev. bibl. illus. index. circ. 300. (back issues avail.; also avail. on microfilm from Johnson Reprint Corp.) Indexed: M.L.A. Amer.Hum.Ind.

808 301.2   MW
KALULU; bulletin of Malawian oral literature and cultural studies. 1976. irreg. $5. Chancellor College, Writer's Group, Box 280, Zomba, Malawi.

860   PE
KANAN; revista anual de cultura. 1978. a. Instituto Nacional de Cultura, Filial Ancash, Plaza de Armas s/n, Huaras, Peru. Dir. Francisco Gonzales. bk. rev.

800 340   JA   ISSN 0453-1981
KANAZAWA UNIVERSITY. FACULTY OF LAW AND LITERATURE. STUDIES AND ESSAYS. (Text in English and Japanese) 1953. a. Kanazawa University, Faculty of Law and Literature, 1-1 Marunouchi, Kanazawa 920, Japan. bibl.

833   GW
KARL-MAY-GESELLSCHAFT. JAHRBUCH. 1970. a. price varies. Hansa Verlag, Nordbahnhofstrasse 2, Postfach 1480, 2250 Husum, W. Germany (B.R.D.) Ed.Bd. Indexed: M.L.A.

800   US
KESTREL CHAPBOOK SERIES. 1982. irreg. $3 per no. Holmgangers Press, 95 Carson Ct., Shelter Cove, CA 95489. TEL 707-986-7700. Ed. Gary Elder. circ. 250. (back issues avail.)

KLAUS-GROTH-GESELLSCHAFT. JAHRESGABEN. see LINGUISTICS

830   GW   ISSN 0075-6318
KLEINE DEUTSCHE PROSADENKMAELER DES MITTELALTERS; Erst und Neuausgaben der Forschungstelle fuer deutsche prosa des Mittelalters. 1965. irreg. price varies. (Seminar fuer Deutsche Philologie) Wilhelm Fink Verlag, Ohmstr. 5, 8000 Munich 40, W. Germany (B.R.D.) Ed. Georg Steer.

800   GW
KLEIST-JAHRBUCH. 1980. a. price varies. Erich Schmidt Verlag GmbH, Zweigniederlassung Bielefeld, Viktoriastr. 44a, Postfach 7330 u. 7340, 4800 Bielefeld 1, W. Germany (B.R.D.) Ed. Hans Joachim Kreutzer. bk. rev. (back issues avail.)

KONINKLIJKE ACADEMIE VOOR NEDERLANDSE TAAL- EN LETTERKUNDE. JAARBOEK. see LINGUISTICS

400 800   BE   ISSN 0023-3404
KONINKLIJKE ACADEMIE VOOR NEDERLANDSE TAAL- EN LETTERKUNDE. VERSLAGEN EN MEDEDELINGEN. 1887; N.S. 1958. irreg. price varies. Koninklijke Academie voor Nederlandse Taal- en Letterkunde, Koningstraat 18, B-9000 Ghent, Belgium. bibl. illus. index. Indexed: Nutr.Abstr.

890   UR
KONTEKST. a. $3. (Akademiya Nauk S.S.S.R., Institut Mirovoi Literatury) Izdatel'stvo Nauka, Podsosenskii per., 21, Moscow K-62, Russian S.F.S.R., U.S.S.R. (Subscr. to: Mezhdunarodnaya Kniga, Moscow, G-200, Russian S.F.S.R., U.S.S.R.) Ed.Bd. circ. 7,700.

KOVCEZIC. see LINGUISTICS

KRATYLOS; kritisches Berichts- und Rezensionsorgan fuer indogermanische und allgemeine Sprachwissenschaft. see LINGUISTICS

808   JA   ISSN 0388-0532
KYOTO REVIEW. (Text in English) 1976. irreg. 500 Yen($2) Kyoto Seika College, 137 Iwakura Kino, Sakyo-ku, Kyoto 606, Japan. Eds. Rebecca Jennison, Katagiri Yuzuru. bk. rev. circ. 500.

810   JA   ISSN 0454-8132
KYUSHU AMERICAN LITERATURE. (Text in English) 1960. a. (Kyushu American Literature Society - Kyushu Amerika Bungaku-Kai) Kyushu University, College of General Education, 4-2-1 Ropponmatsu, Chuo-Ku, Fukuoka 810, Japan. adv. bk. rev. bibl. Indexed: Curr.Cont. M.L.A.

800   FR   ISSN 0335-9190
L.S.I. 1971. irreg. Jean Jachymiak, Pub., 6 Square de la Dordogne, 75017 Paris, France. adv. bk. rev. circ. 2,000.
   Formerly: Litterature. Science. Ideologie. (ISSN 0075-9996)

800   US   ISSN 0889-6410
LAKE STREET REVIEW. 1976. a. $2. Lake Street Review Press, Box 7188, Powderhorn Sta., Minneapolis, MN 55407. Ed. Kevin FitzPatrick. circ. 500. Indexed: A.I.P.P.

LAMAR LECTURE SERIES. see HISTORY

800 400   FR   ISSN 0457-1320
LANGUES ET STYLES. 1959. irreg., no.9, 1981. price varies. Lettres Modernes, 73 rue du Cardinal Lemoine, 75005 Paris, France.

800   CN   ISSN 0382-8824
LAOMEDON REVIEW. vol. 2, 1976. irreg. (1-2/yr.) Can.$5. c/o Erindale College, University of Toronto, Mississauga, Ont. L5L 1C6, Canada. TEL 416-978-2011. Ed. Linda J. Kuschnir. illus.

LEA. see BIBLIOGRAPHIES

810 820   US   ISSN 0075-8396
LEBARON RUSSELL BRIGGS PRIZE HONORS ESSAYS IN ENGLISH. 1965. irreg. Harvard University, Department of English, Cambridge, MA 02138 (Distr. by: Harvard University Press, 79 Garden St., Cambridge, MA 02138)

800 792 942   UK   ISSN 0140-8089
LEEDS MEDIEVAL STUDIES. 1975. irreg. price varies. University of Leeds, Centre for Medieval Studies, Leeds LS2 9JT, England. (back issues avail.)

900 800   UK   ISSN 0024-0281
LEEDS PHILOSOPHICAL AND LITERARY SOCIETY. PROCEEDINGS. LITERARY AND HISTORICAL SECTION. 1925. irreg. (3-4/yr.) price varies. Leeds Philosophical and Literary Society, Central Museum, Calverley St., Leeds 2, England. Ed. I.S. Moxon. charts. illus. index. circ. 650. Indexed: Br.Hum.Ind. Sci.Abstr.

820   UK   ISSN 0075-8566
LEEDS STUDIES IN ENGLISH. N.S. 1967. a. price varies. University of Leeds, School of English, Leeds LS2 9JT, England. Ed. Elizabeth Williams. Indexed: M.L.A. Br.Archaeol.Abstr.
   Supersedes: Leeds Studies in English and Kindred Languages.

830   NE   ISSN 0458-9971
LEIDSE GERMANISTISCHE EN ANGLISTISCHE REEKS. 1962. irreg., vol.21, 1983. price varies. Leiden University Press, c/o E.J. Brill Publishers, Postbus 9000, 2300 PA Leiden, Netherlands.

LEIDSE ROMANISTISCHE REEKS. see LINGUISTICS

892   IS
LEKET. (Text in Hebrew; English translation available) irreg. World Zionist Organization, Box 92, Jerusalem, Israel. Ed. David Hardan. illus.

830   GW   ISSN 0075-8833
LESSING YEARBOOK. (Text in English or German) 1969. a. DM.50. (Lessing Society) Edition Text und Kritik, Postfach 8005294, Leveling Str.69, 8000 Munich 80, W. Germany (B.R.D.) Ed. G. Hillen. bk. rev. Indexed: M.L.A.

850   IT   ISSN 0075-8892
LETTERE ITALIANE. BIBLIOTECA. 1961. irreg., vol.31, 1984. price varies. Casa Editrice Leo S. Olschki, Casella Postale 66, 50100 Florence, Italy. Eds. Vittore Branca, Giovanni Getto. circ. 1,000.

850   IT
LETTERE ITALIANE. SAGGI. 1959. irreg., no.34, 1985. price varies. Casa Editrice Leo S. Olschki, Casella Postale 66, 50100 Florence, Italy. circ. 1, 200.

850   IT
LETTURE CLASSENSI; studi danteschi. (Text in Italian) 1966. a. Angelo Longo Editore, Via Paolo Costa 33, P.O. Box 431, 48100 Ravenna, Italy. adv. cum. index.

800   US   ISSN 8755-2108
LIBRARY SCIENCE ANNUAL. 1985. a. $37.50. Libraries Unlimited, Inc., Box 263, Littleton, CO 80160. TEL 303-770-1220. Ed. Bohdan S. Wynar.

830					GW
LICHTWARK-STIFTUNG.
VEROEFFENTLICHUNG. irreg. price varies. Hans Christians Verlag, Kl. Theaterstr. 9, 2000 Hamburg 36, W. Germany (B.R.D.) bk. rev. bibl. circ. controlled.

800			US	ISSN 0743-913X
LIGHT YEAR; the annual of light verse & funny poems. 1983. a. $13.95. Bits Press, English Department, Case Western Reserve University, Cleveland, OH 44106. TEL 216-795-2810. Ed. Robert Wallace. circ. 3,600. (back issues avail.)

LILI. BEIHEFTE. (Zeitschrift fuer Literaturwissenschaft und Linguistik) see *LINGUISTICS*

LINGUA E LITERATURA. see *LINGUISTICS*

LINGUISTIC & LITERARY STUDIES IN EASTERN EUROPE. see *LINGUISTICS*

830					GW
LITERARISCHE HEFTE. vol.11, 1972. irreg. DM.8.50. Raith Verlag, Herzog Heinrich Str. 21, 8000 Munich 2, W. Germany (B.R.D.) Ed.Bd. bk. rev. illus. circ. 1,200.

830			GW	ISSN 0340-7888
LITERARISCHER VEREIN IN STUTTGART. BIBLIOTHEK. Abbreviated title: B L V S. 1842. irreg., vol.312, 1987. price varies. Anton Hiersemann Verlag, Rosenbergstr. 113, Postfach 723, 7000 Stuttgart 1, W. Germany (B.R.D.)

830			GE	ISSN 0323-3766
LITERARISCHES SONDERHEFT; der Zeitschrift Deutsch als Fremdsprache. Issued with: Deutsch als Fremdsprache (ISSN 0011-9741) 1971. a. M.7.50. (Karl-Marx-Universitaet Leipzig, Herder-Institut) V E B Verlag Enzyklopaedie, Gerichtsweg 26, DDR-7010 Leipzig, E. Germany (D.D.R.) (Orders to: Buchexport, Postfach 160, DDR-7010 Leipzig, E. Germany (D.D.R.)) Ed. Erhard Hexelschneider. bk. rev.

891.87 780
LITERARNO - MUZEJNY LETOPIS. (Text in Slovak; summaries in German and Russian) 1967. a. price varies. Matica Slovenska, Mudronova 35, 036 52 Martin, Czechoslovakia. bk. rev.
Continues: Letopis Pamatnika Slovenskej Literatury (ISSN 0075-8841)

891.87			CS	ISSN 0075-9872
LITERARNY ARCHIV. (Text in Slovak; summaries in German and Russian) 1964. irreg. (1-2/yr.) price varies. Matica Slovenska, Mudronova 35, 036 52 Martin, Czechoslovakia. bk. rev.

891.87			CS
LITERARRIA. irreg, vol.16, 1973. price varies. (Slovenska Akademia Vied, Literarnovedny Ustav) Veda, Publishing House of the Slovak Academy of Sciences, Klemensova 19, 814 30 Bratislava, Czechoslovakia (Subscr. to: Slovart, Gottwaldovo nam. 6, 817 64 Bratislava) Ed. Karol Rosenbaum.

806 070.5 070		US
LITERARY AGENTS OF NORTH AMERICA MARKETPLACE. 1983. a. $19.95. Research Associates International, Author Aid, 340 E. 52 St., New York, NY 10022. TEL 212-PL8-4213. Eds. Arthur Orrmont, Leonie Rosenstiel. adv.

820 810			US	ISSN 0075-9902
LITERARY MONOGRAPHS. 1967. irreg. ‡ University of Wisconsin Press, 114 N. Murray St., Madison, WI 53715. TEL 608-262-4952. (reprint service avail. from UMI)

801			US	ISSN 0160-8703
LITERARY ONOMASTICS STUDIES. 1974. a. $10. State University of New York, College at Brockport, Department of Foreign Languages and Literatures, Brockport, NY 14420. TEL 716-395-2211. (American Name Society) Ed. Grace Alvarez-Altman. circ. controlled. Indexed: M.L.A.

800 028			PK	ISSN 0075-9929
LITERARY PRIZES IN PAKISTAN. (Text in English) 1964. a. Rs.4.($1.) National Book Council of Pakistan, Theosophical Hall, M.A. Jinnah Rd., Karachi, Pakistan.
Formerly: Incentives for Better Books in Pakistan.

800			US	ISSN 0197-2146
LITERARY VOICES. 1980. irreg., approx. a. $13.95 (hardcover); $5.95 (paperback) per no. Borgo Press, Box 2845, San Bernardino, CA 92406. TEL 714-884-5813.

830					GW
LITERATUR. 1983. a. DM.9.50. Lamuv Verlag GmbH, Martinstr. 7, 5303 Bornheim 3, W. Germany (B.R.D.) Eds. Christoph Heubner, Alwin Meyer. circ. 12,000. (back issues avail.)

830					GW
LITERATUR UND GESCHICHTE. EINE SCHRIFTENREIHE. 1970. irreg. price varies. Lothar Stiehm Verlag, Hausackerweg 16, D-6900 Heidelberg, W. Germany (B.R.D.) Indexed: M.L.A.

800			GE	ISSN 0232-315X
LITERATUR UND GESELLSCHAFT. 1972. irreg., vol.89, 1986. (Akademie der Wissenschaften der DDR) Akademie-Verlag Berlin, Leipziger Str. 3-4, 1086 Berlin, E. Germany (D.D.R.)

800			GW	ISSN 0075-9937
LITERATUR UND WIRKLICHKEIT. 1967. irreg., vol.24. price varies. Bouvier Verlag Herbert Grundmann, Am Hof 32, Postfach 1268, 5300 Bonn 1, W. Germany (B.R.D.) Ed. Karl Otto Conrady.

891.7					UR
LITERATURA DREVNEI RUSI. 1975. irreg. 1 Rub. Moskovskii Gosudarstvennyi Pedagogicheskii Institut, Kafedra Russkoi Literatury, Moscow, Russian S.F.S.R., U.S.S.R. circ. 1,000.

891.7					UR
LITERATURA OB ARKHANGEL'SKOI OBLASTI. 1973. a. (Arkhangel'skaya Oblastnaya Biblioteka, Bibliograficheskii Otdel) Severo-Zapadnoe Knizhnoe Izdatel'stvo, Arkhangel'sk, Russian S.F.S.R., U.S.S.R.

869					BL
LITERATURA POPULAR EM VERSO. 1983. irreg. Fundacao Casa de Rui Barbosa, Rua Sao Clemente 134, Botoga 22260, Rio de Janeiro RJ, Brazil.

LITERATURE AND BELIEF. see *RELIGIONS AND THEOLOGY*

808 610			US	ISSN 0278-9671
LITERATURE & MEDICINE. 1982. a. $12.95 to individuals; institutions $25. (University of Texas Medical Branch at Galveston, Institute for the Medical Humanities) Johns Hopkins University Press, Journals Publishing Division, 701 W. 40th St., Ste. 275, Baltimore, MD 21211 TEL 301-338-6987. (Order from: Allen Press, Inc., 1041 New Hampshire St., Box 368, Lawrence, KS 66044) Ed. Anne Hudson Jones. adv. circ. 250. (back issues avail.) Indexed: Curr.Cont. M.L.A. Arts & Hum.Cit.Ind.

839					NE
LITERATURE AND SOCIETY IN THE SEVENTEENTH CENTURY. 1983. irreg. price varies. Dick Coutinho B.V., Badlaan 2, Muiderberg, Netherlands.

830			GW	ISSN 0075-997X
LITERATURWISSENSCHAFTLICHES JAHRBUCH. NEUE FOLGE. 1961. a. price varies. (Goerres-Gesellschaft) Duncker und Humblot GmbH, Dietrich-Schaefer-Weg 9, Postfach 410329, 1000 Berlin 41, W. Germany (B.R.D.) Ed.Bd. bk. rev. Indexed: M.L.A. Can.Rev.Comp.Lit.

800					NE
LITTERAE TEXTUALES; a series on manuscripts and their texts. 1972. irreg. price varies. E.J. Brill, P.O. Box 9000, 2300 PA Leiden, Netherlands. Ed.Bd.

800			PL	ISSN 0084-3008
LITTERARIA; teoria literatury-metodologia-kultura-humanistyka. 1969. irreg., vol.17, 1985. price varies. (Wroclawskie Towarzystwo Naukowe) Ossolineum, Publishing House of the Polish Academy of Sciences, Rynek 9, Wroclaw, Poland (Dist. by: Ars Polona-Ruch, Krakowskie Przedmiescie 7, Warsaw, Poland) (Co-sponsor: Polska Akademia Nauk) Ed. Jan Trzynadlowski. bk. rev. circ. 700. (also avail. in microfilm)

800			FR	ISSN 0069-5459
LITTERATURES ANCIENNES. 1970. irreg. price varies. Presses Universitaires de France, 108 bd. Saint Germain, 75279 Paris Cedex 6, France (Service des Periodiques, 12 rue Jean de Beauvais, 75005 Paris) (reprint service avail. from KTO)

810			US	ISSN 0033-6300
LITTLE MAGAZINE. (Includes Supplements) 1965. irreg., vol.15, 1986. $16 per. vol. Dragon Press, Box 78, Pleasantville, NY 10570. TEL 914-769-5545. Ed. David G. Hartwell. adv. bk. rev. circ. 1,100. (also avail. in microform from UMI; back issues avail.; reprint service avail. from UMI) Indexed: Amer.Hum.Ind.
Formerly: Quest.

810			US	ISSN 0024-5054
LITTLE REVIEW. 1969. irreg. $4. Little Review Press, Marshall University, Huntington, WV 25701. TEL 304-696-3170. Ed. John McKernan. bk. rev. circ. 1,000. (also avail. in microfilm from UMI) Indexed: Ind.Amer.Per.Verse.

890			UR	ISSN 0207-1274
LITUANISTIKA V S.S.S.R. LITERATUROVEDENIE; nauchno-referativnyi sbornik. (Text in Russian) 1978. a. 0.35 Rub. Akademiya Nauk Litovskoi S.S.R., Nauchno-Informatsionnyi Tsentr, Michurino g-ve 1/46, Vilnius, Lithuanian S.S.R., U.S.S.R. Ed. A. Balsys. circ. 350.

860			UK	ISSN 0261-1538
LIVERPOOL MONOGRAPHS IN HISPANIC STUDIES. 1982. irreg. (1-3/yr.) price varies. Francis Cairns (Publications), P.O. Box 147, The University, Liverpool L69 3BX, England. Ed. James Higgins. Indexed: M.L.A.

800			CN	ISSN 0076-0153
LIVRES ET AUTEURS QUEBECOIS. 1936. a. Can.$15. Presses de l'Universite Laval, C.P. 2447, Quebec, P.Q. G1K 7R4, Canada. TEL 418-656-2590. Ed. Paul-Andre Bourque. bk. rev. circ. 2,000. Indexed: M.L.A. Pt.de Rep.
Formerly: Livres et Auteurs Canadiens.

800			UK	ISSN 0076-0188
LLEN CYMRU. (Text in Welsh) 1950. irreg. £3.50 per double part. (Board of Celtic Studies) University of Wales Press, 6 Gwennyth St., Cathays, Cardiff CF2 4YD, Wales. Ed. A.O.H. Jarman. adv. bk. rev. circ. 250. (also avail. in microfilm from UMI; reprint service avail. from UMI) Indexed: M.L.A.

800			PL	ISSN 0076-0404
LODZKIE TOWARZYSTWO NAUKOWE. PRACE WYDZIALU JEZYKOZNAWSTWA, NAUKI O LITERATURZE I FILOZOFII. (Text in Polish; summaries in English, French and Russian) 1947. irreg., no.85, 1985. price varies. Ossolineum, Publishing House of the Polish Academy of Sciences, Rynek 9, 50-106 Wroclaw, Poland (Dist. by: Ars Polona-Ruch, Krakowskie Przedmiescie 7, 00-068 Warsaw, Poland) (Co-sponsor: Polska Akademia Nauk)

800					US
LOEB CLASSICAL LIBRARY. irreg., no.466, 1985. $13.50. Harvard University Press, 79 Garden St., Cambridge, MA 02138. TEL 617-495-2600.

830			UK	ISSN 0076-0811
LONDON GERMAN STUDIES. 1980. irreg. price varies. University of London, Institute of Germanic Studies, 29 Russell Square, London WC1B 5DP, England. circ. 500.

800			US	ISSN 0741-4242
LONG STORY. 1983. a. $4. 11 Kingston St., North Andover, MA 01845. TEL 617-686-7638. Ed. R.P. Burnham. circ. 400. (back issues avail.) Indexed: A.I.P.P.

800			US	ISSN 0076-1001
LOST PLAY SERIES. 1965. irreg., no.13, 1979. $1.75-$2.95. Proscenium Press, Box 361, Newark, DE 19711. TEL 302-737-5803. Ed. Robert Hogan. (reprint service avail. from UMI)

LUMO; Kanada Esperanto-Revuo. see *LINGUISTICS*

890			DK	ISSN 0109-906X
LYRIK & PROSA. 1984. a. Kr.25. c/o Anette Giertsen, Odensegade 10, 2100 Copenhagen OE, Denmark.

M L A INTERNATIONAL BIBLIOGRAPHY OF BOOKS AND ARTICLES ON THE MODERN LANGUAGES AND LITERATURES. (Modern Language Association of America) see *BIBLIOGRAPHIES*

808 US
M S S MAGAZINE. 1961. irreg. (2-3/yr.) $10 to individuals; instutations $15. State University of New York at Binghamton, Binghamton, NY 13901. Ed. L.M. Rosenberg. adv. bk. rev. illus. circ. 1,000. (back issues avail.)

800 US
M W A ANNUAL. 1961. a. membership. Mystery Writers of America, 150 5th Av., New York, NY 10011. adv. circ. 3,000.

800 028.5 IS ISSN 0334-2867
MAAGALAI KAREYA. (Text in Hebrew) 1977. irreg. Haifa University, Center for Children's Literature, Hacarmel, Haifa 31 999, Israel.

890 920 011 IS
MABUA/FOUNTAIN; religious creation in literature, society and thought. (Text and summaries in Hebrew) 1965. a. IS.2500($15) Association of Religious Writers, 58 King George St., 91073 Jerusalem, Israel. Ed. Ya'akov Edelstein. adv. bk. rev. circ. 2,000. (back issues avail.) Indexed: Ind.Heb.Per.

800 US
MCWINNERS MAGAZINE.* 1975. irreg. $12 to individuals; institutions $15. Alex N. Scandalios, Ed. & Pub., Box 8611, Santa Fe, CA 92067-8611. adv. bk. rev. circ. 30,000.
Former titles: Winners Magazine & Willmore City.

MAGAZIN POLOVNIKA. see *SPORTS AND GAMES — Outdoor Life*

100 700 US ISSN 0196-8432
MAGIC CHANGES; the annual for independent artists. 1979. a. $5. (Order of the Celestial Otter) Celestial Otter Press, c/o John Sennett, Ed., 2S424 Emerald Green Dr., No. F, Warrenville, IL 60555-9269. adv. bk. rev. circ. 500. (back issues avail.)

028.1 US ISSN 0163-3058
MAGILL'S LITERARY ANNUAL. a. $55. Salem Press, Box 1097, Englewood Cliffs, NJ 07632. TEL 201-871-3700. Ed. F.N. Magill. Indexed: Amer.Bibl.Slavic & E.Eur.Stud.
Formerly: Masterplots Annual.

800 900 US
MAGILL'S LITERARY ANNUAL: HISTORY AND BIOGRAPHY. a. $30. Salem Press, Box 1097, Englewood Cliffs, NJ 07632. TEL 201-871-3700. Ed. F.N. Magill.
Formerly: Magill's History Annual.

830 831 700 GW
MAGIRA. 1967. a. $3 per no. Erster Deutscher Fantasy Club eV, Postfach 1371, D-8390 Passau, W. Germany (B.R.D.) Ed. Hubert Strassl. adv. bk. rev. bibl. illus. circ. 1,500.

894.51 HU ISSN 0076-2385
MAGYAR IRODALOMTORTENETIRAS FORRASAI; fontes ad historiam litterariam Hungariae spectantes. 1960. irreg. price varies. (Magyar Tudomanyos Akademia) Akademiai Kiado, Publishing House of the Hungarian Academy of Sciences, Box 24, H-1363 Budapest, Hungary.

820 UK ISSN 0025-0848
MAINLY.* 1965. irreg. (2-4/yr.) 2s. 6d. per no.($.75) Carregraff, Graig Las, Talybont, Brecon, Wales. Eds. Lyndon Puw, Chrissie Smith. bk. rev. illus. circ. 1,000.

830 GW ISSN 0076-2784
MAINZER REIHE. 1960. irreg. Akademie der Wissenschaften und der Literatur, Mainz, Geschwister-Scholl-Str. 2, 6500 Mainz, W. Germany (B.R.D.) Indexed: Math.R.

810 418.02 GW ISSN 0170-9135
MAINZER STUDIEN ZUR AMERIKANISTIK. (Text in English, German) 1972. irreg. Peter Lang Verlag, Hinter den Ulmen 19, 6000 Frankfurt am Main, W. Germany (B.R.D.) Ed. Hans Galinsky. circ. 225. (back issues avail.)

800 UK
MAJOR EUROPEAN AUTHOR SERIES. irreg. price varies. Cambridge University Press, Edinburgh Bldg., Shaftesbury Rd., Cambridge CB2 2RU, England (And 32 E. 57th St., New York NY 10022)

810 US
MANASSAS REVIEW. 1977. irreg. Northern Virginia Community College, Manassas Campus, Manassas, VA 22110. TEL 703-368-0184. Ed. Patrick Bizzaro.

810 US ISSN 0025-3979
MARQUETTE JOURNAL. 1903. irreg. (4-6/yr.) $12.50. Marquette University, 1131 W. Wisconsin Ave., Milwaukee, WI 53233. TEL 414-224-7057. adv.

810 US
MASIFORM D. 1971. a. $10. Poison Pen Press, 627 East 8th St., Brooklyn, NY 11218. TEL 718-853-8121. Ed. Devra Michele Langsam. illus. circ. 1,000. (reprint service avail.)

820 UK ISSN 0025-4711
MASQUE. 1918. a. 30p. University of Strathclyde, Students' Association, 90 John St., Glasgow G1 1JH, Scotland. Ed. Graham Brown. adv. bk. rev. film rev. play rev. illus. circ. 2,500 (controlled)
Formerly: Mask.

800 US ISSN 0271-7794
MASTERS OF SCIENCE FICTION. 1982. irreg., approx. a. $13.95 (hardcover); $5.95 (paperback) per no. Borgo Press, Box 2845, San Bernardino, CA 92406. TEL 714-884-5813.

890 UR
MASTERSKAYA; uroki literaturnogo masterstva. 1975. irreg. 0.28 Rub. Izdatel'stvo Molodaya Gvardiya, Ul. Sushevskaya, 21, Moscow A-55, Russian S.F.S.R., U.S.S.R.

800 940 CN ISSN 0316-0874
MEDIAEVAL SOURCES IN TRANSLATION. 1949. irreg. price varies. Pontifical Institute of Mediaeval Studies, 59 Queen's Park Crescent E., Toronto, Ont. M5S 2C4, Canada. TEL 416-926-7144. circ. 1,000.

MEDIAEVALIA. see *HISTORY — History Of Europe*

MEDIEVAL ACADEMY BOOKS. see *HISTORY — History Of Europe*

MEDIEVAL ACADEMY REPRINTS FOR TEACHING. see *HISTORY — History Of Europe*

800 NE
MEDIEVAL AND RENAISSANCE AUTHORS. 1976. irreg., vol.7, 1986. price varies. E.J. Brill, P.O. Box 9000, 2300 PA Leiden, Netherlands. Eds. John Norton-Smith, Douglas Gray.

056.1 PE
MELIBEA. 1975. irreg. Casimiro Ulloa, 125, Lima, Peru. illus.

800 700 AT
MEUSE. 1977. biennial (plus special nos.) Aus.$15 to individuals; Aus.$18 to institutions. Meuse Press, Box 61, Wentworth Bldg., Sydney University, Sydney, N.S.W. 2006, Australia. Eds. Les Wicks, Bill Farrow. bk. rev. circ. 1,000. (back issues avail.)
Merged with: Rochford St Press.

801 US ISSN 0076-8103
MICHIGAN SLAVIC CONTRIBUTIONS. (Text in English, Russian and Slavic languages) 1968. irreg. price varies. University of Michigan, Department of Slavic Languages and Literatures, 3040 Modern Language Bldg., Ann Arbor, MI 48109. TEL 313-764-5355. Ed. Ladislaw Matejka. Indexed: M.L.A.

890 491.8 375.4 US ISSN 0543-9930
MICHIGAN SLAVIC MATERIALS. 1961. a. University of Michigan, Department of Slavic Languages and Literatures, 3040 Modern Language Bldg., Ann Arbor, MI 48109. TEL 313-764-5355. Ed. Ladislav Matejka.

891.7 US
MICHIGAN SLAVIC TRANSLATIONS. 1972. irreg., no.5, 1983. University of Michigan, Department of Slavic Languages and Literatures, 3040 Modern Language Bldg., Ann Arbor, MI 48104. TEL 313-764-5355. Ed. Ladislav Matejka.

890 US
MICHIGAN STUDIES IN THE HUMANITIES. 1980. irreg., no.4, 1981. University of Michigan, Department of Slavic Languages and Literatures, 3040 Modern Language Bldg., Ann Arbor, MI 48109. TEL 313-764-5355. Ed. Ladislav Matejka. Indexed: M.L.A.

810 US ISSN 0272-717X
MID-HUDSON LANGUAGE STUDIES. 1978. a. $6. Mid-Hudson Modern Language Association, c/o George J. Sommer, Ed., Marist College, Poughkeepsie, NY 12601. TEL 914-471-3240. circ. 600. Indexed: M.L.A.

800 US ISSN 0190-2911
MIDAMERICA (EAST LANSING) 1973. a. $7.50 per no. Society for the Study of Midwestern Literature, Ernst Bessey Hall, Michigan State University, East Lansing, MI 48824. TEL 517-355-1855. Ed. David D. Anderson. bk. rev. circ. 1,000. (back issues avail.) Indexed: Abstr.Engl.Stud. M.L.A.
Formerly: Midwestern Annual.

800 770 US ISSN 0886-7976
MIDLAND REVIEW. 1985. a. $6. Oklahoma State University, English Department, Morrill Hall, Stillwater, OK 74078. TEL 405-624-6138. Ed. Nuala Archer. adv. circ. 500.

810 US
MIDWESTERN MISCELLANY. irreg. membership. Society for the Study of Midwestern Literature, 240 Ernst Bessey Hall, Michigan State University, East Lansing, MI 48824. TEL 517-355-1855. Indexed: Mich.Mag.Ind.

800 IS
MIFGASH. 1984. a. Jewish-Arab Institute, Beit Berl, Doar Kfar Saba 44 905, Israel.

800 US ISSN 0163-2469
MILFORD SERIES; popular writers of today. 1976. irreg. (6-10/yr.) $13.95 (hardcover); $5.95 (paperback) per no. Borgo Press, Box 2845, San Bernardino, CA 92406. TEL 714-884-5813. Ed. R. Reginald. circ. 2,000.

821.4 US ISSN 0076-8820
MILTON STUDIES. 1969. a. price varies. University of Pittsburgh Press, 127 N. Bellefield Ave., Pittsburgh, PA 15260. TEL 412-624-4110. Ed. James Simmonds. Indexed: M.L.A. Abstr.Engl.Stud.

809 860 BL
MIMESIS. (Text in English, Portuguese, Spanish) 1975. irreg. Instituto de Biociencias, Letras e Ciencias Exatas de Sao Jose do Rio Preto, Faculdade de Filosofia, Ciencias e Letras, Rua Cristovao Colombo 2265, 15000 Sao Jose do Rio Preto, Sao Paulo, Brazil. illus.
Formerly: Etudos Anglo-Hispanico.

MISCELLANEA BYZANTINA MONACENSIA. see *HISTORY — History Of Europe*

810 US
MISSISSIPPI MUD. 1973. irreg. $15. 1336 S.E. Marion St., Portland, OR 97202. TEL 503-236-9962. Ed. Joel Weinstein. bk. rev. circ. 1,500. (reprint service avail. from UMI,ISI)

810 US ISSN 0076-9649
MISSOURI LITERARY FRONTIERS SERIES. 1968. irreg. price varies. University of Missouri Press, 200 Lewis Hall, Columbia, MO 65211. TEL 314-882-7641.

810.9 US ISSN 0270-9406
MODERN JEWISH STUDIES ANNUAL. a. Queens College Press, c/o Dyanne Maue, Kiely 1310, Flushing, NY 11367. TEL 718-520-7599.
Formerly: Conference on Modern Jewish Studies Annual (ISSN 0270-9392)

800 FR ISSN 0761-2397
MONDES HISPANOPHONE ET LUSOPHONE. 1965, no. 5. a. price varies. ‡ Universite de Rennes II (Universite de Haute Bretagne), 6 Avenue Gaston Berger, 35043 Rennes, France. Ed.Bd. adv. bk. rev. circ. 1,000.
Formerly: Universite de Haute Bretagne. Centre d'Etudes Hispaniques, Hispano-Americanes et Luso-Bresiliennes. Travaux (ISSN 0080-0929)

LITERATURE

810 US
MONMOUTH REVIEW. 1972. a. Monmouth College, College Center, West Long Branch, NJ 07664. adv. circ. 2,000.
Formerly: Monmouth Reviews: Journal of the Literary Arts (ISSN 0085-3534)

891.8 940 PL ISSN 0077-0531
MONOGRAFIE SLAWISTYCZNE. 1959. irreg., vol.53, 1986. price varies. (Polska Akademia Nauk, Komitet Slowianoznawstwa) Ossolineum, Publishing House of the Polish Academy of Sciences, Rynek 9, 50-106 Wroclaw, Poland (Dist. by: Ars Polona-Ruch, Krakowskie Przedmiescie 7, Warsaw, Poland)

810 US
MONTANA REVIEW. 1979. biennial. $9. (Owl Creek Foundation) Owl Creek Press, 1620 N. 45th St. Rm. 205, Seattle, WA 98103. TEL 206-633-5929. Ed. Rich Ives. adv. bk. rev. illus. circ. 500.

830 NE
MONUMENTA LITERARIA NEERLANDICA. 1979. irreg. price varies. Elsevier Science Publishers B.V., Box 211, 1000 AE Amsterdam, Netherlands.

800 US ISSN 0196-2604
MOODY STREET IRREGULARS; a Jack Kerouac newsletter. (Text in English and French) 1978. irreg. (3-4/yr.) $7 to individuals; institutions $9. Moody Street Irregulars, Inc., Box 157, Clarence Center, NY 14032. Ed. Joy Walsh. adv. bk. rev. film rev. play rev. bibl. charts. illus. stat. tr.lit. circ. 1,000. (back issues avail.) Indexed: M.L.A.

MOVEMENTS IN THE ARTS. see *ART*

430 830 GW ISSN 0077-1872
MUENCHNER GERMANISTISCHE BEITRAEGE. 1968. irreg. price varies. Wilhelm Fink Verlag, Ohmstr. 5, 8000 Munich 40, W. Germany (B.R.D.) Ed.Bd.

830 GW ISSN 0077-1996
MUENSTERSCHE BEITRAEGE ZUR DEUTSCHEN LITERATURWISSENSCHAFT. 1966. irreg. price varies. Aschendorffsche Verlagsbuchhandlung, Soester Str. 13, 4400 Muenster, W. Germany (B.R.D.) Ed. Wolfdietrich Rasch.

892 US
MUNDUS ARABICUS. 1981. a. $30. Dar Mahjar Inc., Box 56, Cambridge, MA 02238. Ed.Bd. circ. 350. Indexed: Ind.Islam.

810 GW
MUNICH ROUND UP. vol.10, 1975. irreg. (3-4/yr.) $5.30. Waldemar Kumming, Ed. & Pub., Herzogspitalstr. 5, 8000 Munich 2, W. Germany (B.R.D.) (U.S. subscr. to: Andrew Porter, Box 4175, New York, NY 10017) bk. rev. circ. 300.

800 NR ISSN 0331-3468
MUSE; journal of creative and critical writing from Nsukka. 1963. a. £N2 per no. University of Nigeria, Department of English, Nsukka, Nigeria. Ed. Onyedika L. Okwuonu. adv. bk. rev. circ. 1,500.

809 IT
MUSEUM CRITICUM. vol.10, 1975. irreg., vol.12, 1977. price varies. Giardini Editori e Stampatori, Via Santa Bibbiana 28, 56100 Pisa, Italy. Ed. Benedetto Marzullo.

890 069.9 PL ISSN 0324-8925
MUZEUM LITERATURY IM. ADAMA MICKIEWICZA. BLOK-NOTES. 1959. irreg. 300 Zl. Muzeum Literatury im. Adama Mickiewicza, Rynek Starego Miasta 20, 00-272 Warsaw, Poland. Ed. Malgorzata Kucza-Kuczynska. circ. 600. (back issues avail.)

MYSTERY & DETECTION ANNUAL. see *ADVENTURE AND ROMANCE*

800 US
MYTHIC CIRCLE. 1981. q. $9. Mythopoeic Society, Box 6707, Altadena, CA 91001-6707. Eds. Lunn Maudlin, Christine Lowentrout. circ. 100.
Formerly (until Jul. 1987): Mythellany.

800 890 DK ISSN 0107-8232
NAAR LAMPEN TAENDES. FORTAELLINGER. a. Bibliotekscentralen, Telegrafsvej 5, DK-2750 Ballerup, Denmark.

860 UY ISSN 0077-2801
NARRADORES DE ARCA.* irreg. Editorial Arca, Colonia 1263, Montevideo, Uruguay.

NARRATIVA LATINOAMERICANA. see *HISTORY — History Of North And South America*

810 US ISSN 0077-2879
NASSAU REVIEW. 1964. a. free. Nassau Community College, SUNY, Department of English, Office of Community Relations, Garden City, NY 11530. TEL 516-222-7187. Ed. Paul A. Doyle. circ. 1,200. Indexed: M.L.A. Abstr.Engl.Stud.

810 US ISSN 0073-1382
NATHANIEL HAWTHORNE JOURNAL. 1971. a. $64. Gale Research Company, Book Tower, Detroit, MI 48226. TEL 313-961-2242. Ed. C.E. Frazer Clark, Jr. Indexed: M.L.A.

NATIONAL FOUNDATION FOR ADVANCEMENT IN THE ARTS. ANNUAL REPORT. see *ART*

890 US
NAUKOVE TOVARYSTVO IMENI SHEVCHENKA. UKRAINSK'VA LITERARURNA BIBLIOTEKA/UKRAINIAN LITERARY LIBRARY. (Text in Ukrainian; summaries in English) 1881. irreg. price varies. Shevchenko Scientific Society, 63 Fourth Ave., New York, NY 10003.

890 CN ISSN 0077-6300
NEAR AND MIDDLE EAST SERIES. 1949. irreg. price varies. University of Toronto Press, Front Campus, Toronto, Ont. M5S 1A6, Canada TEL 613-667-7791. (And 33 Tupper St., Buffalo, NY 14203)

810 US ISSN 0162-3818
NEBULA WINNERS. 1965. a. price varies. Arbor House Publishing Co., 235 E. 45th St., New York, NY 10017. TEL 212-599-3131. Ed. Marta Randall.
Formerly: Nebula Award Stories (ISSN 0077-6408)

NEMET FILOLOGIAI TANULMANYOK/ARBEITEN ZUR DEUTSCHEN PHILOLOGIE. see *LINGUISTICS*

830 GW ISSN 0077-7668
NEUDRUCKE DEUTSCHER LITERATURWERKE. 1961, N.S. irreg. price varies. Max Niemeyer Verlag, Pfrondorfer Str. 4, 7400 Tuebingen, W. Germany (B.R.D.) (back issues avail.) Indexed: M.L.A.
Continues: Neudrucke Deutscher Literaturwerke des XVI und XVII Jahrhunderts & Neudrucke Deutscher Literaturwerke des XVIII und XIX Jahrhunderts.

830 GW ISSN 0077-7676
NEUDRUCKE DEUTSCHER LITERATURWERKE. SONDERREIHE. 1964. irreg. price varies. Max Niemeyer Verlag, Pfrondorfer Str. 4, 7400 Tuebingen, W. Germany (B.R.D.) (back issues avail.)

NEW CANADIAN FANDOM. see *ADVENTURE AND ROMANCE*

800 410 AT
NEW CEYLON WRITING; creative and critical writing of Sri Lanka. 1970. irreg. Aus.$10. (Macquarie University, School of English & Linguistics) Yasmine Gooneratne, Ed. & Pub., North Ryde, N.S.W. 2113, Australia. adv. bk. rev. play rev. abstr. bibl. circ. 250.

800 700 UK
NEW DEPARTURES; international review of literature & the lively arts. 1959. a. $7.50. c/o Michael Horovitz, Ed., Mullions, Piedmont, Bisley, Stroud, Glos. GL6 7BU, England. adv. bk. rev. circ. 10,000.

800 792 US ISSN 0731-4523
NEW PLAYS U S A. 1982. biennial. $11.95 cloth; paperback $22.50. Theatre Communications Group, 355 Lexington Ave., New York, NY 10017. TEL 212-697-5230. Ed. James Leverett. circ. 3,500. (back issues avail.)

808 US
NEW RAIN. (Text in English, French and Spanish) 1981. a. $4.25. Blind Beggar Press, Box 437, Williamsbridge Station, Bronx, NY 10467. Eds. Gary Johnston, C.D. Grant. illus. circ. 1,000. (back issues avail.)

820 UK ISSN 0028-6540
NEW RAMBLER.* 1941. a. $4. Johnson Society of London, Round Chimey, Playden, Rye, E. Sussex TN31 7UR, England. Ed. James H. Leicester. adv. bk. rev. illus. play rev. circ. 300. (back issues avail.) Indexed: Abstr.Engl.Stud.

800 770 US
NEW VIRGINIA REVIEW. 1978. biennial. $20. New Virginia Review, Inc., Box 29791, Richmond, VA 23229. TEL 804-740-7506. Ed. Virginia Dabney. circ. 1,500.

810 US
NEW VOICES.* 1972. a. $3. Box 308, Clintondale, NY 12515. circ. 500.

NEW WORLD JOURNAL. see *HISTORY — History Of North And South America*

810 375 US ISSN 0548-9040
NEW YORK STATE ENGLISH COUNCIL. MONOGRAPH SERIES. 1950. biennial. price varies. New York State English Council (Liverpool), c/o John Andola, Box 2397, Liverpool, NY 13089. Ed. Charles Chew. adv. bk. rev. bibl. circ. 3,000. (also avail. in microform from EDR) Indexed: Sociol.Abstr. ERIC.

809 808.8 US ISSN 0077-9504
NEW YORK UNIVERSITY STUDIES IN COMPARATIVE LITERATURE. 1967. irreg., latest 1980. New York University Press, Washington Square, New York, NY 10003.

800 100 US ISSN 0278-6079
NIGHTSUN. 1981. a. $6. (Frostburg State College, Department of Philosophy) Adler Publishing Co., 2156 Carter Rd., Fairport, NY 14450. TEL 716-337-5804. Ed. Jorn K. Bramann. adv. bk. rev. circ. 1,500. (back issues avail.)

800 US
NINETEENTH-CENTURY LITERATURE (ANN ARBOR) irreg., vol.2, 1986. U M I Research Press, 300 N. Zeeb Rd., Ann Arbor, MI 48106. Ed. Juliet McMaster.

NORDISTICA GOTHOBURGENSIA. see *LINGUISTICS*

839.82 NO ISSN 0078-1266
NORSK LITTERAER AARBOK. (Text mainly in Norwegian; partly Danish and Swedish) 1966. a. Kr.168. Norske Samlaget, Trondheimsvn. 15, Oslo 5, Norway. Eds. Leif Maehle, Geir Mork. circ. 1, 500. Indexed: M.L.A.

840 US
NORTH CAROLINA STUDIES IN THE ROMANCE LANGUAGES AND LITERATURES. (Text in English, French, Italian, Latin, Spanish) 1940. irreg., no.222, 1984. price varies. University of North Carolina at Chapel Hill, Department of Romance Languages, Dey Hall 014A, Chapel Hill, NC 27514. TEL 919-962-1069. Indexed: M.L.A.
Formerly: Studies in the Romance Languages and Literatures (ISSN 0081-8666)

800 US
NORTHEAST JOURNAL. 1978. a. $5. Northeast Journal, Box 217, Kingston, RI 02881. TEL 401-461-6250. Eds. Tina Letcher, Indu Suryanarayan. bk. rev. circ. 500.

810 US
NORTHEAST/JUNIPER BOOKS. 1962. irreg. (6-7/yr.) $30 to individuals; institutions $35. Juniper Press, 1310 Shorewood Dr., La Crosse, WI 54601. Ed. John Judson. bk. rev. cum.index every 5 yrs. circ. 400. (formats include books and booklets) Indexed: Ind.Little Mag. A.I.P.P.

NORTHERN LIGHTS STUDIES IN CREATIVITY. see *ART*

800 US ISSN 0190-3012
NORTHERN NEW ENGLAND REVIEW. 1973. a. $3.50. Franklin Pierce College, Box 825, Rindge, NH 03461. TEL 603-899-5111. Ed. Michael Terault. adv. bk. rev. circ. 1,000. (back issues avail.) Indexed: M.L.A. A.I.P.P.

800 550 UK ISSN 0308-4809
NORTHUMBRIANA; true Northumberland's own magazine. (Text in English and Northumbrian) 1975. irreg., (approx. 3/yr.) 65p. Morpeth Northumbrian Gathering Committee, Westgate House, Dogger Bank, Morpeth, Northumberland NE61 1RF, England. Ed. Roland Bibby. adv. bk. rev. circ. 825.

840 920 FR ISSN 0078-2165
NOUVELLE BIBLIOTHEQUE NERVALIENNE. (Consists of two subdivisions: Textes and Etudes et Documents; subdivisions are numbered consecutively within the main series) 1959. irreg. Lettres Modernes, 73 rue du Cardinal Lemoine, 75005 Paris, France.

NOVA TELLUS. see *HUMANITIES: COMPREHENSIVE WORKS*

808 333.7 US
NOW AND THEN. 1984. triennial. $7.50. East Tennessee State University, Center for Appalachian Studies and Services, Box 19180-A, Johnson City, TN 37614-0002. TEL 615-929-5348. Ed. Pat Arnow. bk. rev. circ. 880.
Former Titles: Second Growth & Appalachian Nature and Culture.

850 IT ISSN 0391-8548
NUOVA UNIVERSALE STUDIUM. 1974. irreg., no.46, 1985. price varies. Edizioni Studium, Via Cassiodoro 14, 00193 Rome, Italy.

808 US
NYCTALOPS. 1970. irreg. $5. ‡ Silver Scarab Press, 502 Elm S.E., Albuquerque, NM 87102. TEL 505-242-8047. Ed. Harry O. Morris, Jr. bk. rev. illus. circ. 1,000.

891.7 UR
O LITERATURE DLYA DETEI. vol.20, 1976. irreg. 0.36 Rub. per no. Izdatel'stvo Detskaya Literatura, Nab. Kutuzova 6, 192187 Leningrad, Russian S.F.S.R., U.S.S.R. circ. 10,000.

891.85 PL ISSN 0078-2963
OBRAZ LITERATURY POLSKIEJ. 1965. irreg. price varies. (Polska Akademia Nauk, Instytut Badan Literackich) Ossolineum, Publishing House of the Polish Academy of Sciences, Rynek 9, 50-106 Wroclaw, Poland.

800 917.306 US
O'CASEY ANNUAL. 1982. a. $30. Humanities Press, Inc., 171 First Ave., Atlantic Highlands, NJ 07716. TEL 201-872-1441. Ed. Robert Lowery.

430 400 940 UK ISSN 0307-7497
OCCASIONAL PAPERS IN GERMAN STUDIES. (Text in English with German quotations) 1972. irreg. 75p. per no. University of Warwick, Department of German Studies, Coventry CV4 4AL, England. (Co-sponsor: Volkswagen Foundation) Ed. Tony Phelan. circ. 200.

OCCASIONAL PAPERS IN MODERN DUTCH STUDIES. see *HISTORY — History Of Europe*

800 UK ISSN 0078-3099
OCCASIONAL PAPERS IN MODERN LANGUAGES. (Text in all modern languages except English) 1966. irreg. individually priced. Hull University Press, Hull HU6 7RX, England. Ed. B. Moloney. Indexed: M.L.A.

807 407 US
OCCASIONAL PAPERS IN SLAVIC LANGUAGES AND LITERATURE. 1982. a. University of Washington, Department of Slavic Languages and Literature, DR-30, Seattle, WA 98195.

809 DK ISSN 0106-2212
ODENSE UNIVERSITET. LABORATORIUM FOR FOLKESPROGLIG MIDDELALDERLITTERATUR. MINDRE SKRIFTER. 1977. irreg. price varies. Odense Universitet, Laboratorium for Folkesproglig Middelalderlitteratur, Odense, Denmark. circ. 100.

800 DK ISSN 0078-3323
ODENSE UNIVERSITY STUDIES IN LITERATURE. (Text in Danish; summaries in English) 1969. irreg., no.19, 1985. price varies. Odense University Press, 36, Pjentedamsgade, DK-5000 Odense, Denmark. (back issues avail.)

ODENSE UNIVERSITY STUDIES IN SCANDINAVIAN LANGUAGES AND LITERATURES. see *LINGUISTICS*

838 AU
OESTERREICHISCHE AKADEMIE DER WISSENSCHAFTEN. KOMMISSION FUER LITERATURWISSENSCHAFT. VEROEFFENTLICHUNGEN. (Subseries of: Oesterreichische Akademie der Wissenschaften. Philosophisch-Historische Klasse. Sitzungsberichte) 1973. irreg. Verlag der Oesterreichischen Akademie der Wissenschaften, Dr. Ignaz Seipel Platz, A-1010 Vienna, Austria.

810 US
OFF MAIN STREET. 1986. a. $3.50. Ferris State College, Languages and Literature Department, Big Rapids, MI 49307. TEL 616-796-8762. Eds. David Vinopal, John Caserta.

052 GH ISSN 0048-1629
OKYEAME; Ghana's literary magazine. 1961. irreg. price varies. University of Ghana, Institute of African Studies, Box 73, Legon, Ghana. circ. 1,000.

810 US
OLD RED KIMONO. 1972. a. $2. Floyd Junior College, Humanities Division, Box 1864, Rome, GA 30163. TEL 404-295-6312. Eds. Jo Anne Starnes, Jon Hershey. index. circ. 1,000. (processed)

OPERA SLAVICA. NEUE FOLGE. see *LINGUISTICS*

ORBIT (NEW YORK); a science fiction anthology. see *ADVENTURE AND ROMANCE*

ORDEN POUR LE MERITE FUER WISSENSCHAFTEN UND KUENSTE. REDEN UND GEDENKWORTE. see *HISTORY*

800 UK
ORDINARY LIVES. 1976. irreg. £6.95. Dennis Dobson Books Ltd., 80 Kensington Church St., London W8 4BZ, England.

460 860 CN
OTTAWA HISPANICA. 1979. a. Can.$6. University of Ottawa, Department of Modern Languages, Ottawa, Ont. K1N 6N5, Canada. TEL 613-231-3311. Ed. Rodolfo A. Borello. adv. circ. 400. Indexed: M.L.A.

800 US ISSN 0739-4969
OUTERBRIDGE. 1975. a. $4. City University of New York, College of Staten Island, Department of English, 715 Ocean Terrace, Staten Island, NY 10301. TEL 718-390-7654. Ed. Charlotte Alexander. bk. rev. cum.index: vols.8-9, 1981-1982. circ. 500. (back issues avail.) Indexed: Ind.Amer.Per.Verse.

820 US
OXFORD ENGLISH MONOGRAPHS. irreg. price varies. Oxford University Press, 200 Madison Ave., New York, NY 10016 TEL 212-679-7300. (And Ely House, 37 Dover St., London W1x 4AH, England) Ed.Bd. Indexed: M.L.A.

830 410 UK ISSN 0078-7191
OXFORD GERMAN STUDIES. (Text and summaries in English and German) 1966. a. $15. (Fiedler Foundation) Willem A. Meeuws, Pub., 11 Broad St., Oxford OX1 3AR, England. Eds. P.F. Ganz, T.J. Reed. adv. bk. rev. circ. 500. (back issues avail.) Indexed: Curr.Cont. M.L.A.

800 US
OXFORD MODERN LANGUAGE AND LITERATURE MONOGRAPHS. irreg. price varies. Oxford University Press, 200 Madison Ave., New York, NY 10016 TEL 212-679-7300. (And Ely House, 37 Dover St., London W1X 4AH, England) Ed.Bd. Indexed: M.L.A.

OXFORD SLAVONIC PAPERS. see *HISTORY — History Of Europe*

OXFORD THEATRE TEXTS. see *THEATER*

810 US
OYEZ REVIEW. 1966. a. $3.50. Roosevelt University, 430 S. Michigan Ave., Chicago, IL 60605. TEL 312-341-2017. Ed. Constance Kwain. adv. illus. circ. 750. (back issues avail.)

OZIANA. see *CLUBS*

P S; tidsskrift for spontan satire, fjollet filosofi, funny fiction and lojerlig ligegyldighed. see *PHILOSOPHY*

PACIFIC COAST COUNCIL ON LATIN AMERICAN STUDIES. PROCEEDINGS. see *HISTORY — History Of North And South America*

860 972 US ISSN 0277-1535
LA PALABRA. 1979. a. $20. La Palabra, 1616 E. Westchester Dr., Tempe, AZ 85283. Ed. Justo S. Alarcon. Indexed: M.L.A.

810 US ISSN 0031-059X
PAN AMERICAN REVIEW.* (Text mainly in English, occasionally in Spanish) 1970. irreg. $6. Wade Press, Box 3427, Edinburg, TX 78540-3427. Ed. Seth Wade.

PAN-EROTIC REVIEW. see *ART*

810 US ISSN 0738-8705
PANHANDLER. 1976. a. $4. University of West Florida, English Department, Pensacola, FL 32514. TEL 904-474-2923. Ed. Michael Yots. adv. bk. rev. circ. 900.

800 808.81 CS
PANORAMA OF CZECH LITERATURE. German edition: Panorama der Tschechischen Literatur. Spanish edition: Panorama de la Literatura Checa. French edition: Panorama de la litterature Tcheque. Russian edition: Panorama Cheshskoi Literatury. (Editions in French, German, Russian and Spanish) 1980. irreg. (1-2/yr.) free. (Union of Czech Writers) Panorama, Halkova Ulice 1, 120 72 Prague 2, Czechoslovakia. (Co-sponsors: Czech Literary Fund, DILIA Theatrical and Literary Agency) Ed. Ivo Kral. circ. 5,000.

808 US ISSN 0736-9123
PAPERS IN COMPARATIVE STUDIES. 1981. a. $6. Ohio State University, Center for Comparative Studies in the Humanities, 306 Dulles Hall, 230 W. 17th Ave., Columbus, OH 43210. TEL 614-486-0003. Eds. Richard Bjornson, Marilyn R. Waldman. circ. 200. (back issues avail.)

807 US
PAPERS OF ROBERT MORRIS, 1781-1784. 1973. irreg. price varies. University of Pittsburgh Press, 127 North Bellefield Ave., Pittsburgh, PA 15260. TEL 412-624-4110. Eds. John Catanzariti.

800 NE
PAPYROLOGICA LUGDUNO-BATAVA. 1941. irreg., vol.24, 1983. price varies. E.J. Brill, P.O. Box 9000, 2300 PA Leiden, Netherlands. Ed.Bd.

800 FR ISSN 0078-9429
PARALOGUE. 1965. irreg. Lettres Modernes, 73 rue de Cardinal Lemoine, 75005 Paris, France.

800 AT ISSN 0313-6221
PARERGON. 1968. a. Aus.$25. Australian and New Zealand Association for Medieval and Renaissance Studies, Sydney University, Department of Modern Greek, Sydney, N.S.W. 2006, Australia. Ed. E.M. Jeffreys. bk. rev. circ. 350. Indexed: Curr.Cont. M.L.A. Arts & Hum.Cit.Ind. Aus.P.A.I.S.

808 US
PELLENNORATH. 1980. irreg., no. 5, 1982. $4 for five issues. Pandemonium Press, 1273 Crest Dr., Encinitas, CA 92024. Ed. R.C. Walker. (back issues avail.)

800 UK
PEOPLE LIKE THAT. 1970. irreg. Central London Adult Education Institute, 6 Bolt Court, Fleet St., London E.C.4, England. Ed. Bernard Miller. illus.

800 US ISSN 0098-7301
PERSPECTIVES ON CONTEMPORARY LITERATURE. 1975. a. $7.50. (University of Louisville, Conference on Twentieth Century Literature) University Press of Kentucky, Lexington, KY 40506-0024. TEL 606-257-2951. Ed. David Hershberg. adv. circ. 200. Indexed: M.L.A.

LITERATURE

809   US
PERSUASIONS. (Text in English) 1979. a. membership. Jane Austen Society of North America, Box 252, Wayne, PA 19087 TEL 215-687-4714. (Subscr. address: 221 Nevin St., Lancaster, PA 17603) Ed. Joan Austen-Leigh. circ. 2,000. (back issues avail.)

800   US
PERSUASIONS, OCCASIONAL PAPERS. 1984. irreg. price varies. Jane Austen Society of North America, Box 252, Wayne, PA 19087 TEL 215-687-4714. (Subscr. to: 221 Nevin St., Lancaster, PA 17603) illus.

800   HU   ISSN 0524-8906
PETOFI IRODALMI MUZEUM EVKONYVE/ YEARBOOK OF THE LITERARY MUSEUM. 1958. biennual. Muzsak, Kartacs u. 24/26, 1139 Budapest 13, Hungary. Ed. Ferenc Botka.

020 800   US   ISSN 0098-3365
PHAEDRUS; international annual of children's literature research. 1973. a. $20 to individuals; institutions $31. Phaedrus, Inc., Fairleigh Dickinson University, Madison, NJ 07940. Ed. James Fraser. adv. bk. rev. circ. 925. Indexed: Abstr.Engl.Stud. Lib.Lit. M.L.A. Amer.Hum.Ind. Amer.Bibl.Slavic & E.Eur.Stud. Child.Lit.Abstr.

PHI THETA PAPERS. see ORIENTAL STUDIES

800   GW
PHILOGISCHE STUDIEN UND QUELLEN. 1960. irreg. Erich Schmidt Verlag GmbH, Genthiner Str. 30 G, 1000 Berlin 30, W. Germany (B.R.D.) (Subscr. addr.: Zweigniederlassung Bielefeld Viktoriastr. 44a, 4800 Bielefeld 1, W. Germany (B.R.D.)) Ed.Bd.

810   US
PHILOMEL; a University of Pennsylvania magazine of commentary and literature. 1964. a. $4. Philomathean Society, University of Pennsylvania, Philadelphia, PA 19104. TEL 215-898-8907. Ed. Elizabeth E. Crane. adv. bk. rev. illus. circ. 2,000. Formerly: Era (ISSN 0013-9920)

800   NE
PHILOSOPHIA PATRUM; interpretations of patristic texts. 1971. irreg., vol. 8, 1986. price varies. E.J. Brill, P.O. Box 9000, 2300 PA Leiden, Netherlands. Eds. J.H. Waszink, J.C.M. van Winden.

800   CN   ISSN 0079-1784
PHOENIX. SUPPLEMENTARY VOLUMES. 1952. irreg. price varies. University of Toronto Press, Front Campus, Toronto, Ont. M5S 1A6, Canada TEL 613-667-7791. (And 33 East Tupper St., Buffalo, N.Y. 14203) Ed.Bd.

800   US   ISSN 0735-0317
PHOTRON. 1971. irreg., no.17, 1982. $1 per no. Allan Beatty Ed. & Pub., Box 1906, Ames, IA 50010. adv. bk. rev. film rev. play rev. circ. 500. (back issues avail.)

800   US   ISSN 0362-5214
PIG IRON. 1975. a. $10. Pig Iron Press, Box 237, Youngstown, OH 44501. TEL 216-783-1269. Eds. Jim Villani, Rose Sayre. bibl. illus. circ. 700. (also avail. in microfilm from GLB) Indexed: Ind.Amer.Per.Verse.

800   US   ISSN 0192-8716
PIKESTAFF FORUM. 1978. irreg. $10 for 6 nos. Pikestaff Publications, Inc., Box 127, Normal, IL 61761. TEL 309-452-4831. Eds. Robert D. Sutherland, James R. Scrimgeour. bk. rev. index. circ. 1,000. (tabloid format; back issues avail.) Indexed: Ind.Amer.Per.Verse.

891.85   PL   ISSN 0079-211X
PISARZE SLASCY 19 I 20 WIEKU.* 1965. irreg. price varies. Slaski Instytut Naukowy, Francuska 12, Katowice, Poland (Dist. by Ars Polona-Ruch, Krakowskie Przedmiescie 7, Warsaw, Poland)

808   US
PITT LATIN AMERICAN SERIES. 1965. irreg. price varies. University of Pittsburgh Press, 127 N. Bellefield Ave., Pittsburgh, PA 15260. TEL 412-624-4110. Ed. Cole Blasier.

806   AT   ISSN 0311-0753
PLAIN TURKEY. 1973. irreg. Mt. Isa Writers Workshop, 97 Trainor St., Mt. Isa, Qld. 4825, Australia. Ed. R. Algie.

PLAYS & PLAYWRIGHTS. see THEATER

800   IT
PLEIADI. irreg. Angelo Longo Editore, Via Paolo Costa 33, P.O. Box 431, 48100 Ravenna, Italy. Ed. Franco Mollia.

POE MESSENGER. see LITERATURE — Poetry

POESIE UND WISSENSCHAFT. SAMMLUNG. see LITERATURE — Poetry

POETES ET PROSATEURS DU PORTUGAL. see LITERATURE — Poetry

POETI E PROSATORI TEDESCHI. see LITERATURE — Poetry

POETIC DRAMA AND POETIC THEORY. see LITERATURE — Poetry

POETICS JOURNAL. see LITERARY AND POLITICAL REVIEWS

809   PL   ISSN 0554-579X
POLSKA AKADEMIA NAUK. ODDZIAL W KRAKOWIE. KOMISJA HISTORYCZNOLITERACKA. PRACE. (Text in English, French and Polish) 1961. irreg., no.44, 1984. price varies. Ossolineum, Publishing House of the Polish Academy of Sciences, Rynek 9, Wroclaw, Poland (Dist. by: Ars Polona-Ruch, Krakowskie Przedmiescie 7, Warsaw, Poland)

POLSKA AKADEMIA NAUK. ODDZIAL W KRAKOWIE. KOMISJA HISTORYCZNOLITERACKA. ROCZNIK. see HISTORY

891.8   PL   ISSN 0079-3434
POLSKA AKADEMIA NAUK. ODDZIAL W KRAKOWIE. KOMISJA SLOWIANOZNAWSTWA. PRACE. (Text in Polish; summaries in English and Russian) 1962. irreg., no.44, 1985. price varies. Ossolineum, Publishing House of the Polish Academy of Sciences, Rynek 9, 50-106 Wroclaw, Poland (Dist. by: Ars Polona-Ruch, Krakowskie Przedmiescie 7, Warsaw, Poland)

PONTINE DOSSIER. see ADVENTURE AND ROMANCE

839   NE
POPULAIRE LITERATUUR; een reeks teksten uit de late Middeleeuwen. 1979. irreg. price varies. Dick Coutinho B.V., Badlaan 2, Muiderberg, Netherlands.

839   NE
POPULAR ESSAYS FROM THE LATE REPUBLIC. 1983. irreg. price varies. Dick Coutinho B.V., Badlaan 2, Muiderberg, Netherlands.

800 850   IT
PORTICO. (In two parts: Letteratura Italiana; Letteratura Straniera) irreg. Angelo Longo Editore, Via Paolo Costa 33, P.O. Box 431, 48100 Ravenna, Italy. Ed. Antonio Piromalli.

POSTCARD ART/POSTCARD FICTION. see ART

808.838   CN   ISSN 0226-0840
POTTERSFIELD PORTFOLIO; fiction, plays, essays and poetry from Atlantic Canada. 1979. a. Can.$12 for 3 yrs. Crazy Quilt Press, 19 Oakhill Drive, Hallifax, Nova Scotia B3M 2V3, Canada. adv. bk. rev. circ. 3,000. Indexed: Amer.Hum.Ind.

820   FR   ISSN 0240-8864
POUVOIR DANS LA LITTERATURE ET LA PENSEE ANGLAISES. (Text in French) irreg., no.2, 1981. price varies. (Universite de Provence-Aix, Centre Aixois de Recherches Anglaises) Librarie Touzot, 38 rue Saint Sulpice, 75278 Paris Cedex 06, France.

891.85   PL   ISSN 0079-4791
PRACE POLONISTYCZNE. 1951. a. price varies. (Lodzkie Towarzystwo Naukowe) Ossolineum, Publishing House of the Polish Academy of Sciences, Rynek 9, 50-106 Wroclaw, Poland (Dist. by: Ars Polona-Ruch, Krakowskie Przedmiescie 7, 00-068 Warsaw, Poland) (Co-sponsor: Polska Akademia Nauk) Ed. Z. Skwarczynski. bk. rev. circ. 800. (also avail. in microfilm)

800   II
PRAKALPANA SAHITYA/PRAKALPANA LITERATURE. 1977. a. Rps.5. c/o Vattacharja Chandan, P-40 Nandana Park, Calcutta, India. circ. 1,000.

491 891   II
PRAKRIT TEXT SOCIETY. PUBLICATIONS. irreg. price varies. Prakrit Text Society, c/o Lalbhai Dalpatbhai Institute of Indology, Near Gujarat University, P.O. Navarangpura, Ahmedabao 380009, India.

891   UR
PRIAMUR'E MOE; literaturno-khudozhestvennyi sbornik. irreg. 1.05 Rub. Khabarovskoe Knizhnoe Izdatel'stvo, Ul. Lenina, 181, Blagoveshchensk, Russian S.F.S.R., U.S.S.R. illus.

PRIMAVERA (CHICAGO) see WOMEN'S INTERESTS

800   UK   ISSN 0269-2619
PRINCESS GRACE IRISH LIBRARY. 1986. irreg. price varies. Colin Smythe Ltd., P.O. Box 6, Gerrards Cross, Buckinghamshire SL9 8XA, England (Distr. in U.S. by: Barnes & Noble Books, Littlefield Adams, 81 Adams Dr., Totowa, NJ 07512) circ. 1,500.

800   UK   ISSN 0950-5121
PRINCESS GRACE IRISH LIBRARY LECTURES. 1986. irreg. £3.50 per issue. Colin Smythe Ltd., P.O. Box 6, Gerrards Cross, Buckinghamshire SL9 8XA, England. circ. 750.

800   US   ISSN 0079-5186
PRINCETON ESSAYS IN LITERATURE. 1964. irreg. price varies. Princeton University Press, 3175 Princeton Pike, Lawrenceville, NJ 08648. TEL 609-896-2111. (reprint service avail. from UMI)

813.5   US   ISSN 0079-5453
PRIZE STORIES; THE O. HENRY AWARDS. 1919. a. Doubleday & Company, Inc., 245 Park Ave., New York, NY 10017. TEL 212-984-7561. Ed. William Abrahams. circ. 20,000.

820   II
PROBITAS; devoted to literature and culture. (Text in English) Rs.3($2) per no. Aruna Printing Works, Berhampur 760002, India.

800   US
PROFESSION; selected articles from the Bulletins of the Association of Departments of English and the Association of Departments of Foreign Languages. 1977. a. $4. Modern Language Association of America, 10 Astor Pl., New York, NY 10003. TEL 212-614-6314. Eds. Richard I. Brod, Phyllis P. Franklin. circ. 28,000. (back issues avail.; reprint service avail. from UMI)

800   US
PUB. 1979. biennial. $5 for 3 issues. Ansuda Publications, Box 158-B, Harris, IA 51345. Ed. Daniel Betz. adv. circ. 350.

840 440   SZ   ISSN 0079-7812
PUBLICATIONS ROMANES ET FRANCAISES. no.9, 1933. irreg, no.172, 1986. price varies. Librarie Droz, 11, rue Massot, 1211 Geneva 12, Switzerland. circ. 1,000. Indexed: M.L.A.

PURDUE UNIVERSITY MONOGRAPHS IN ROMANCE LANGUAGE. see LINGUISTICS

810   US   ISSN 0149-7863
PUSHCART PRIZE: BEST OF THE SMALL PRESSES. 1976. a. $26. Pushcart Press, Box 380, Wainscott, NY 11975. Ed. Bill Henderson. circ. 10,000. (back issues avail.)

QUADERNI IBERO-AMERICANI; attualita culturale Penisola Iberica America-Latina. see LINGUISTICS

830 920   GW   ISSN 0075-2371
RAABE- GESELLSCHAFT. JAHRBUCH. 1960. a. DM.20. Waisenhaus Buchdruckerei und Verlag, Waisenhausdamm 13, 3300 Braunschweig, W. Germany (B.R.D.) bk. rev.

800 US ISSN 0731-4817
RACKHAM JOURNAL OF THE ARTS AND HUMANITIES. (Text in English, French, German) 1970. a. $3. University of Michigan, Romance Languages and Literatures, 4024 Modern Language Bldg., Ann Arbor, MI 48109. TEL 313-764-2537. Ed. Darcy Engholm. adv. circ. 500. Indexed: M.L.A. Amer.Hum.Ind. Abstr.Engl.Stud.
    Formerly: Rackham Literary Studies (ISSN 0360-7887)

820 420 II ISSN 0448-1690
RAJASTHAN UNIVERSITY STUDIES IN ENGLISH. (Text in English) 1963. a. $2. University of Rajasthan, Department of English, Gandhi Nagar, Jaipur 302004, India. bk. rev. Indexed: M.L.A.

800 US
RAMBUNCTIOUS REVIEW. 1984. a. Rambunctious Press, Inc., 1221 W. Pratt Blvd., Chicago, IL 60626. TEL 312-338-2439. Ed.Bd. circ. 500. (back issues avail.)

800 UR
RASSKAZ. a. Izdatel'stvo Sovremennik, Yartsevskaya 4, Moscow 121351, Russian S.F.S.R., U.S.S.R.

890 PK
RAVI. (Issued in 3 parts) (Text in English, Panjabi or Urdu) 1906. a. price varies. Government College, Lahore, Pakistan.

800 GW ISSN 0723-0338
REAL. (Text in English) 1982. a. price varies. Walter de Gruyter & Co., Genthiner Str. 13, D-1000 Berlin 30, W. Germany (B.R.D.) Ed.Bd. adv. bibl. circ. 800. (back issues avail.)

500 700 800 SP ISSN 0034-060X
REAL ACADEMIA DE CORDOBA DE CIENCIAS, BELLAS LETRAS Y NOBLES ARTES. BOLETIN. 1922. a. 200 ptas. Real Academia de Cordoba de Ciencias, Bellas Letras y Nobles Artes, Ambrosia de Morales 9, Cordoba, Spain. bk. rev. abstr. charts. illus. index. circ. 500. Indexed: Hist.Abstr. Amer.Hist.& Life.

REAL LIFE MAGAZINE. see *ART*

REALITY STUDIOS. see *LITERARY AND POLITICAL REVIEWS*

820 CN
REAPPRAISALS; Canadian writers. 1974. irreg. University of Ottawa Press, 603 Cumberland, Ottawa, Ont. K1N 6N5, Canada. TEL 613-564-2270. Ed. Lorraine McMullen.

830 430 FR ISSN 0399-1989
RECHERCHES GERMANIQUES. (Text in French and German) 1971. a. price varies. Universite de Strasbourg II, 22 rue Descartes, 67084 Strasbourg, France. Ed. G.L. Fink. bibl. circ. 1,200. (back issues avail.) Indexed: M.L.A.

800 US ISSN 0300-6425
RECOVERING LITERATURE; a journal of contextualist criticism. 1972. irreg. (1-3/yr.) $6. Box 805, Alpine, CA 92001. Ed. Gerald J. Butler. adv. bk. rev. circ. 250. (back issues avail.) Indexed: Abstr.Engl.Stud.

800 US
RECREATION: CURRENT SELECTED RESEARCH. 1987. a. A M S Press, Inc., 56 E. 13th St., New York, NY 10003. TEL 212-777-7400. Eds. James H. Humphrey, Fred Humphrey.

810 US
RED WEATHER; poems, translations, essays, reviews. irreg., approx. 4/yr. $2.50 per no. c/o Bruce Taylor, 1133 Barron St., Eau Claire, WI 54703. bk. rev. circ. 400.

811 US ISSN 0484-2650
REFLECTION (SPOKANE); Gonzaga's literary magazine. 1960. a. free. Gonzaga University, Spokane, WA 99258. TEL 509-328-4220. circ. 600.

830 430 375.4 GW
REGENSBURGER BEITRAEGE ZUR DEUTSCHEN SPRACH- UND LITERATURWISSENSCHAFT. REIHE A: QUELLEN. irreg. Verlag Peter Lang GmbH, Hinter den Ulmen 19, 6000 Frankfurt a.M. 50, W. Germany (B.R.D.) Ed. Bernhard Gajek.

830 430 GW
REGENSBURGER BEITRAEGE ZUR DEUTSCHEN SPRACH- UND LITERATURWISSENSCAHFT. REIHE B: UNTERSUCHUNGEN. irreg. Verlag Peter Lang GmbH, Hinter den Ulmen 29, 6000 Frankfurt a.M. 50, W. Germany (B.R.D.) Ed. Bernhard Gajek.

DER REGGEBOGE. see *ETHNIC INTERESTS*

894 HU ISSN 0080-0570
REGI MAGYAR PROZAI EMLEKEK. (Text in Hungarian; occasional summaries in German) 1968. irreg. price varies. (Magyar Tudomanyos Akademia) Akademiai Kiado, Publishing House of the Hungarian Academy of Sciences, Box 24, H-1363 Budapest, Hungary.

RENAISSANCE DRAMA. see *THEATER*

800 US
RENAISSANCE PAPERS. 1955. a. $14. Southeastern Renaissance Conference, 402 Allen Bldg., Duke University, Durham, NC 27706. TEL 919-684-2741. Eds. Dale B.J. Randall, Joseph A. Porter. circ. 400.

830 GW
REPERTORIA HEIDELBERGENSIA. 1976. irreg. price varies. Verlag Lambert Schneider, Hausackerweg 16, D-6900 Heidelberg, W. Germany (B.R.D.)

807 UK
REVELS PLAYS COMPANION LIBRARY, REVELS PLAYS. 1959. irreg. price varies. Manchester University Press, Oxford Rd., Manchester M13 9PL, England. TEL 061-273 5539. Ed.Bd.

809 420 375.4 US ISSN 0190-3233
REVIEW (CHARLOTTESVILLE) 1979. a. $24. (Virginia Polytechnic Institute and State University) University Press of Virginia, Box 3608 University Sta., Charlottesville, VA 22903. TEL 804-924-3468. Eds. James O. Hoge, James L.W. West III. circ. 1, 500.

800 US ISSN 0034-6640
REVIEW OF NATIONAL LITERATURES. 1970. a. membership (includes C N L/Quarterly World Report) (Council on National Literatures) Griffon House Publications, Box 81, Whitestone, NY 11357. TEL 718-767-8380. Ed. Anne Paolucci. adv. bk. rev. abstr. bibl. circ. 1,200. (back issues avail.) Indexed: Curr.Cont. M.L.A. Arts & Hum.Cit.Ind. Abstr.Engl.Stud.

REVISTA BRASILEIRA DE LINGUA E LITERATURA. see *LINGUISTICS*

869 BL ISSN 0101-3505
REVISTA DE LETRAS. (Text in Portuguese; summaries in English and Portuguese) 1959-1977; resumed 1980. a. $30 or exchange. Universidade Estadual Paulista, Av. Vicente Ferreira 1278, Caixa Posta 603, 17.500 Marilia SP, Brazil. bk. rev. bibl. circ. 1,000. Indexed: M.L.A. Sociol.Abstr. Hisp.Amer.Per.Ind. Lang.& Lang.Behav.Abstr.

869 BL ISSN 0100-0888
REVISTA LETRAS. 1953. a. exchange only. Universidade Federal do Parana, Setor de Ciencias Humanas, Letras e Artes, Curitiba, Parana, Brazil. Ed. Oswaldo Portella. bk. rev. circ. 800. Indexed: M.L.A.

850 IT ISSN 0080-2441
REVISTA SCRIITORILOR ROMANI. (Text in Rumanian) 1962. a. price varies. Societa Accademica Romena, Foro Traiano 1a, 00187 Rome, Italy.

400 800 CL ISSN 0035-0451
REVISTA SIGNOS DE VALPARAISO; estudios de lengua y literatura. Variant title: Revista Signos. (Text in Spanish; summaries in English, French and Spanish) 1967. a. $8. (Universidad Catolica de Valparaiso, Instituto de Literatura y Ciencias del Languaje) Ediciones Universitarias de Valparaiso, Casilla 1415, Valparaiso, Chile. Ed. Eduardo Godoy. bk. rev. bibl. circ. 300. Indexed: M.L.A.

809 FR ISSN 0035-2136
REVUE DES LETTRES MODERNES; histoire des idees et des litteratures. 1954. irreg. (5-8/yr.) 800 F. for 50 nos. Lettres Modernes, 73 rue du Cardinal Lemoine, 75005 Paris, France. Ed. M.J. Minard. bk. rev. bibl. Indexed: M.L.A.

840 FR ISSN 0425-4791
REVUE DES LETTRES MODERNES. ETUDES BERNANOSIENNES. 1960. a. price varies. Lettres Modernes, 73 rue du Cardinal Lemoine, 75005 Paris, France. Ed. Michel Esteve. bk. rev. (back issues avail.)

RICERCHE SLAVISTICHE. see *LINGUISTICS*

820 821 UK ISSN 0261-3042
RIVERSIDE INTERVIEWS. 1980. irreg. Binnacle Press, 106 Ladbroke Grove, London W11 1PY, England. Ed. Gavin Selerie. bibl. illus. circ. 600. (back issues avail.)

820 UK ISSN 0307-8957
ROBERT BURNS CHRONICLE. 1892. a. £9.50 cloth bound; £6 paper bound. Burns Federation, Dick Institute, Elmbank Avenue, Kilmarnock KAI 3BU, Scotland. Ed. James A. Mackay. adv. bk. rev. bibl. illus. cum.index. circ. 3,000.

ROCKY MOUNTAIN MEDIEVAL AND RENAISSANCE ASSOCIATION. JOURNAL. see *HISTORY — History Of Europe*

813 US ISSN 0145-5753
ROHMER REVIEW. 1968. irreg. $1.50 per no. ‡ 4 Forest Ave., Salem, MA 01970. TEL 617-744-0885. Ed. Robert E. Briney. bk. rev. illus. circ. 400. Indexed: Abstr.Pop.Cult.

800 GW ISSN 0557-2614
ROMANFUEHRER; der Inhalt der Romane und Novellen der Weltliteratur. 1952. irreg., vol.18, 1987. DM.120 per vol. Anton Hiersemann Verlag, Rosenbergstr. 113, Postfach 723, 7000 Stuttgart 1, W. Germany (B.R.D.)

ROMANICA GOTHOBURGENSIA. see *LINGUISTICS*

ROMANICA HELVETICA. see *LINGUISTICS*

890 920 DK ISSN 0106-8253
ROMANSERIER OG SELVBIOGRAFISKE SERIER. a. Kr.59.80. Bibliotekscentralen, Tempovej 7-11, DK-2750 Ballerup, Denmark.

820 AU
ROMANTIC REASSESSMENT. 1972. irreg., no.110, 1986. S.245. Universitaet Salzburg, Institut fuer Englische Sprache, Akademiestr. 24, A-5020 Salzburg, Austria. Ed. James Hogg. circ. 300. Indexed: M.L.A.

800 700 011 US ISSN 0161-682X
ROMANTIST. 1977. a. $10. F. Marion Crawford Memorial Society, Saracinesca House, 3610 Meadowbrook Ave., Nashville, TN 37205. TEL 615-292-9695. Ed.Bd. adv. bk. rev. abstr. circ. 300(controlled) (back issues avail.) Indexed: M.L.A.

800 UR
ROMANTIZM V RUSSKOI I SOVETSKOI LITERATURE. 1973. irreg. 68 Rub. Kazanskii Universitet, Ul. Lenina, 4/5, Kazan, Russian S.F.S.R., U.S.S.R.

ROSSICA OLOMUCENSIA. see *LINGUISTICS*

ROYAL IRISH ACADEMY. PROCEEDINGS. SECTION C: ARCHAEOLOGY, CELTIC STUDIES, HISTORY, LINGUISTICS AND LITERATURE. see *ARCHAEOLOGY*

820 UK
ROYAL SHAKESPEARE COMPANY. PUBLICATION. 1978. a. £3.75. R S C Publications, Barbican Theatre, London EC2Y 8BQ, England. Ed. Simon Trussler.

820 UK
ROYAL SOCIETY OF LITERATURE. ESSAYS BY DIVERS HANDS. 1825. biennial. Royal Society of Literature, 1 Hyde Park Gardens, London W2, England.

891.72 US ISSN 0048-881X
RUSSIAN LITERATURE TRIQUARTERLY. 1971. a. $70. Ardis Publishers, 2901 Heatherway, Ann Arbor, MI 48104. TEL 313-971-2367. Ed.Bd. adv. bk. rev. abstr. bibl. charts. illus. circ. 300. (back issues avail.) Indexed: Curr.Cont. M.L.A. Arts & Hum.Cit.Ind. Amer.Bibl.Slavic & E.Eur.Stud. Can.Rev.Comp.Lit.

891.7 491.7 700 UK
RUSSIAN POETICS IN TRANSLATION. 1973. irreg. price varies. (University of Essex, Department of Literature) R P T Publications, Old School House, Somerton, Oxford OX5 4NE, England. bibl. circ. 800. Indexed: M.L.A.

800 PL ISSN 0208-5038
RUSYCYSTYCZNE STUDIA LITERATUROZNAWCZE. (Text in Polish and Russian; summaries in Polish, English and Russian) 1977. irreg. price varies. Uniwersytet Slaski w Katowicach, Ul. Bankowa 14, 40-007 Katowice, Poland.

800 US
S C L A NEWSLETTER. 1975. a. $5. Southern Comparative Literature Association, c/o Eva Mills, Ed., Winthrop College, Department of English, Rock Hill, SC 29733. bibl. circ. 2,000.

800 US ISSN 0737-5506
SALTHOUSE.* 1975. irreg., nos.14-17, 1986. $6 for 4 issues. Salthouse Press, c/o Dept. of Engineering, 800 W. Main, Univ. of Wisconsin, Whitewater, WI 53190-1790. Ed. DeWitt Clinton. adv. bk. rev. circ. 450. (back issues avail.)

801 II
SAMBALPUR UNIVERSITY. POST-GRADUATE DEPARTMENT OF ORIYA. JOURNAL. (Text in Oriya) no.2, 1976. a. Sambalpur University, Post Graduate Department of Oriya, Jotibihara, Sambalpur, India.

800 US
SANDS; a literary magazine. 1979. a. $7. c/o Susan Charles Baugh, Ed., Box 638, Addison, TX 75001. TEL 214-931-1528. bk. rev. circ. 500.
Formerly: Sand.

SAPPHIC TOUCH; a journal of lesbian erotica. see *WOMEN'S INTERESTS*

890 II ISSN 0303-3074
SARVOTKRUSHTA MARATHI KATHA. (Text in Marathi) vol.9, 1974. a. Rs.16($2) c/o Mrs. Chhaya Kolarkar, Ed., 43/348 Sant Tukaram Nagar, Pimpri, Poona 411018, India. circ. 1,500. (back issues avail.)

890 II ISSN 0581-8532
SATAPITAKA. INDO-ASIAN LITERATURES. 1957. irreg. price varies. (International Academy of Indian Culture) Impex India, 2/18 Ansari Rd., New Delhi 110002, India. Ed. Lokesh Chandra. circ. 100.

SAVACOU; a journal of the Caribbean artists movement. see *ART*

SCANDO-SLAVICA. see *LINGUISTICS*

SCANDO-SLAVICA. SUPPLEMENTUM. see *LINGUISTICS*

830 GW
SCHLESWIG-HOLSTEINISCHER HEIMATKALENDER. 1938. irreg. DM.6.90. (Schleswig-Holsteinischer Heimatbund) Heinrich Moeller Soehne GmbH, Bahnhofstr. 12-16, 2370 Rendsburg, W. Germany (B.R.D.) illus.

809 GW ISSN 0430-5809
SCHRIFTEN AUS DEM FINNLAND-INSTITUT KOELN. 1961. irreg., no.15, 1987. price varies. Verlag Helmut Buske, Schlueterstr. 14, 2000 Hamburg 13, W. Germany (B.R.D.) Ed. Fritz Keese.

SCHRIFTEN ZUR JUGENDLEKTUERE. see *CHILDREN AND YOUTH — For*

800 FR
SCIENCE-FICTION ET FANTASTIQUE. (YEAR)* 1976. a. 75 F.($10) per issue. Editions Temps Futurs, 5 rue Cochin, 75005 Paris, France. Ed. Daniel Riche. adv. bibl. film rev. circ. 8,000.

808 US ISSN 0164-1093
SCIENCE FICTION VOICES. 1979. irreg., approx. a. $13.95 (hardcover); $5.95 (paperback) per no. Borgo Press, Box 2845, San Bernardino, CA 92406. TEL 714-884-5813.

SCRIPTA ISLANDICA. see *LINGUISTICS*

860 DR
SCRIPTURA. irreg. Universidad Autonoma de Santo Domingo, Depto. de Letras, Apdo. 1355, Santo Domingo, Dominican Republic. Indexed: New Test.Abstr. Rel.Ind.One.

810 811 US ISSN 0095-1730
SEEMS. 1971. irreg. $12. c/o Karl Elder, Ed., Lakeland College, Box 359, Sheboygan, WI 53081. TEL 414-565-3871. bk. rev. circ. 250. Indexed: Access.

895 MY
SEJAHTERA. (Text in English or Malay) a. Islamic Students' Union of the University of Malaya - Persatuan Mahasiswa Islam Universiti Malaya, Kuala Lumpur, Malaysia.

860 CR
SERIE ESTUDIOS LITERARIOS. 1975. irreg. free (not for international distribution) Ministerio de Cultura, Juventud y Deportes, Dept. de Publicaciones, Apdo. 10227, San Jose, Costa Rica.

800 410 II ISSN 0254-0193
SERIES IN ENGLISH LANGUAGE AND LITERATURE. (Text in English) 1978. irreg. price varies. Bahri Publications Pvt. Ltd., 57 Santnagar (East of Kailash), Box 7023, New Delhi 110065, India. Ed. Ujjal Singh Bahri.

SERIES IN SIKH HISTORY AND CULTURE. see *HISTORY — History Of Asia*

820 SA
SESAME. (Text in English) 1982. irreg. (2-3/yr.) R.10. Renoster Books, 1A Fifth Street, Victoria 2192, South Africa. Ed. L. Abrahams. adv. bk. rev. circ. 400. Indexed: Ind.S.A.Per.

SEVENTEENTH CENTURY FRENCH STUDIES. see *HISTORY — History Of Europe*

SEZ; a multi-racial journal of poetry & people's culture. see *ETHNIC INTERESTS*

807 UK
SHAKESPEARE IN PERFORMANCE. 1984. irreg. price varies. Manchester University Press, Oxford Rd., Manchester M13 9PL, England. TEL 061-273-5539. Eds. J.R. Mulryne, J. Bulman.

800 GE ISSN 0080-9128
SHAKESPEARE - JAHRBUCH. 1864. a., vol.121, 1985. M.35. (Deutsche Shakespeare Gesellschaft) Hermann Boehlaus Nachfolger, Meyerstr. 50a, 53 Weimar, E. Germany (D.D.R.) Eds. A. Schloesser, A.G. Kuckhoff. bk. rev. Indexed: M.L.A.

820 JA ISSN 0582-9402
SHAKESPEARE STUDIES. (Text in English) 1962. a. 5000 Yen($5) Shakespeare Society of Japan, 601 Kenkyusha Bldg. 9, 2-chome Kanda-Surugadai, Chiyoda-ku, Tokyo 101, Japan. Ed. Jiro Ozu. circ. 700. Indexed: Hum.Ind. M.L.A.

809 US ISSN 0582-9399
SHAKESPEARE STUDIES; an annual gathering of research, criticism & review. 1965. a. $25. Burt Franklin & Co., Inc., 235 E. 44 St., New York, NY 10017. TEL 212-687-5250. Indexed: M.L.A. Ind.Bk.Rev.Hum.

822 UK ISSN 0080-9152
SHAKESPEARE SURVEY. 1948. a. $39.50. Cambridge University Press, Edinburgh Bldg., Shaftesbury Rd., Cambridge CB2 2RU, England (and 32 E. 57 St., New York NY 10022) Ed. Stanley Wells. index. cum.index: vols. 1-10, 11-10, 21-30. Indexed: Curr.Cont. Hum.Ind. M.L.A. Arts & Hum.Cit.Ind. Abstr.Engl.Stud.

800 US
SHAKESPEARE WORLDWIDE. 1974. a. $45. A M S Press, Inc., 56 E. 13th St., New York, NY 10003. TEL 212-777-4700. (back issues avail.)
Formerly: Shakespeare Translation.

807 US
SHAKESPEAREAN CRITICISM. 1984. irreg., latest vol.4, 1986. $85. Gale Research Company, Book Tower, Detroit, MI 48226. Ed. Mark Scott. abstr. bibl. illus.

810 US
SHANKPAINTER. 1970. a. free. Fine Arts Work Center in Provincetown, Inc., Box 565, 24 Pearl St., Provincetown, MA 02657. TEL 617-487-9960. circ. 700.

820 UK ISSN 0037-3346
SHAVIAN. 1946. a. $15. (Bernard Shaw Society) High Orchard Press, High Orchard 125 Markyate Rd., Dagenham, Essex RM8 2LB, England. Ed. Eric F.J. Ford. adv. bk. rev. cum.index: vol.1, 1953-1959; vol.2, 1960-1963. circ. 500-600. (also avail. in microform from UMI; reprint service avail. from UMI) Indexed: Abstr.Engl.Stud. M.L.A.

820 US ISSN 0741-5842
SHAW ANNUAL. Variant title: Shaw: the annual of Bernard Shaw Studies. 1951. a. $22.50. Pennsylvania State University Press, 215 Wagner Bldg., University Park, PA 16802. TEL 814-865-1327. Ed. Dr. Stanley Weintraub. bk. rev. bibl. illus. index. cum.index: 1950-1975. circ. 600. (also avail. in microform from MIM,UMI; reprint service avail. from UMI) Indexed: Curr.Cont. M.L.A. Amer.Hum.Ind. Abstr.Engl.Stud. Ind.Bk.Rev.Hum.
Formerly: Shaw Review (ISSN 0037-3354)

822 UK
SHAW SOCIETY OF LONDON. JOURNAL. a. £5. Shaw Society of London, 125 Markyate Road, Dagenham, Essex, RM8 2LB, England. Ed. E. Ford. circ. 600.

SHILOACH CENTER FOR MIDDLE EASTERN & AFRICAN STUDIES. MONOGRAPH SERIES. see *HISTORY — History Of The Near East*

800 US ISSN 0080-9403
SHORT PLAY SERIES. 1966. irreg., no.8, 1982. price varies. Proscenium Press, Box 361, Newark, DE 19711. TEL 302-737-5803. Ed. Robert Hogan. (reprint service avail. from UMI)

840 FR
SIECLE ECLATE: DADA, SURREALISME ET LES AVANT-GARDES. (Subseries of: Revue des Lettres Modernes) 1974. irreg. price varies. Lettres Modernes, 73 rue du Cardinal Lemoine, 75005 Paris, France. circ. 2,500.

SILLAGES. see *LINGUISTICS*

SLAVICA LUNDENSIA. see *LINGUISTICS*

891 GW ISSN 0081-0029
SLAVISTIC PRINTING AND REPRINTINGS. irreg. price varies. Walter de Gruyter & Co., Mouton Publishers, Postfach 110240, D-1000 Berlin 11, W. Germany (B.R.D.) (U.S. addr.: Mouton Publishers, divison of Walter de Gruyter, Inc., 200 Saw Mill River Road, Hawthorne, NY 10532) Indexed: M.L.A.

830 430 GW ISSN 0583-5429
SLAVISTISCHE BEITRAEGE. (Text in English and German) 1960. irreg. price varies. Verlag Otto Sagner, P.O. Box 34 01 08, Hessstr. 39/41, D-8000 Munich 34, W. Germany (B.R.D.) Ed.Bd. circ. 300. (back issues avail.)

806 AG
SOCIEDAD ARGENTINA DE ESCRITORES. BOLETIN. 1975. Sociedad Argentina de Escritores, Uruguay 1371, Buenos Aires 1016, Argentina. Ed. Horacio Esteban Ratti.

800 PR
SOCIEDAD DE AUTORES PUERTORRIQUENOS. ANALES. 1981. a. Sociedad de Autores Puertorriquenos, San Juan, Puerto Rico.

800 410 SP ISSN 0212-3223
SOCIEDAD DE ESTUDIOS VASCOS. CUADERNOS DE SECCION. HIZKUNTZA ETA LITERATURA. 1982. irreg. (Sociedad de Estudios Vascos) Eusko Ikaskuntza, S.A., Churruca, 7 - 2, 20004 Donostia, Spain.

840 FR ISSN 0081-0754
SOCIETE CHATEAUBRIAND. BULLETIN. NOUVELLE SERIES. 1930; N.S. 1957. a. 170 F. Societe Chateaubriand, Secretariat General, 122 bd. de Courcelles, 75017 Paris, France (Subscr. to: Librairie Nizet, 3 bis Place de la Sorbonne, 75005 Paris, France) Ed.Bd. bk. rev. circ. 500.

800 FR ISSN 0583-8452
SOCIETE DES AMIS DE MARCEL PROUST ET DES AMIS DE COMBRAY. BULLETIN. 1950. a. 130 F.($20) Societe des Amis de Marcel Proust, BP 25 Illiers Combray 28120, France. Eds. Henry Bonnet, Elyanne Dezon-Jones. bk. rev. circ. 1,000. (back issues avail) Indexed: M.L.A.

SOCIETE DES SCIENCES ET DES LETTRES DE LODZ. BULLETIN. see *SCIENCES: COMPREHENSIVE WORKS*

800 700 FR
SOCIETE DES SCIENCES, LETTRES ET ARTS DE BAYONNE. BULLETIN. a. Societe des Sciences, Lettres et Arts de Bayonne, Musee Basque, 1 rue Marengo, 64100 Bayonne, France. (back issue avail.)

820 FR
SOCIETE FRANCAISE SHAKESPEARE. ACTES DU CONGRES. (Text in French) 1981. a. price varies. (Societe Francaise Shakespeare) Librarie Touzot, 38 rue Saint Sulpice, 75278 Paris Cedex 06, France.

800 SW
SOCIETE ROYALE DE LETTRES DE LUND. BULLETIN/KUNGLIGA HUMANISTISKA VETENSKAPSSAMFUNDET I LUND. ARSBERATTELSE. (Text in French) a. Almqvist & Wiksell International, Box 1034, S-171 21 Solna, Sweden.

800 FR ISSN 0221-7945
SOCIETE THEOPHILE GAUTIER. BULLETIN. 1977. a. 110 Fr. Universite Paul Valery, BP 5043, 34032 Montpelier, France. Ed. Claudine Lacoste.

800 700 100 UK
SOCIETY FOR RENAISSANCE STUDIES. OCCASIONAL PAPERS. 1973. irreg. price varies. Society for Renaissance Studies, Department of History of Art, Westfield College (University of London), Kidderpore Ave., London NW3 7ST, England. Ed. Peter Denley. circ. 500.

810 US
SOME FRIENDS. 1972. irreg., approx. 1/yr. $1.50. c/o Terry J. Cooper, Ed., Box 6395, Tyler, TX 76701. TEL 214-597-1258. circ. 500.

SOOCHOW JOURNAL OF FOREIGN LANGUAGES AND LITERATURES. see *LINGUISTICS*

SOUNDINGS (SANTA BARBARA); collections of the University Library. see *LIBRARY AND INFORMATION SCIENCES*

806 US
SOUTH ATLANTIC MODERN LANGUAGE ASSOCIATION AWARDS. 1977. a. price varies. University of Georgia Press, Athens, GA 30602. TEL 404-542-2830.

800 US
SOUTHEASTERN WRITING CENTER ASSOCIATION. SELECTED PAPERS. 1986. $8 to individuals; libraries $14.95. Appalachian State University, Department of English, Boone, NC 28608. TEL 704-262-3098. Ed. William C. Wolff.

891.7 UR
SOVETSKAYA LITERATURA, TRADITSII I NOVATORSTVO. 1976. irreg. 0.68 Rub. per issue. Leningradskii Universitet, Universitetskaya Nab. 7/9, Leningrad B-164, Russian S.F.S.R., U.S.S.R. Ed. L. Gladkovskaya. circ. 6,550.

891 FR ISSN 0303-111X
SOVETSKIE LJUDI SEGODNJA/VIE QUOTIDIENNE EN U.R.S.S. PRISE SUR LE VIF. (In two series Textes Litteraires and Dossiers) (Text in Russian; notes and comments in French or Russian) 1969. irreg. price varies. Institut d'Etudes Slaves, 9 rue Michelet, 75006 Paris, France.

860 460 UK
SPANISH STUDIES; modern literature, history and politics. 1979. a. £8.50 for 4 years. c/o Mrs. Olga Kenyon, Ed., 29 Woodsyre, Sydenham hill, London SE26 6SS, England. adv. bk. rev. play rev. circ. 300. (back issues avail.)

SPECIMINA PHILOLOGIAE SLAVICAE. see *LINGUISTICS*

SPECULUM ANNIVERSARY MONOGRAPHS. see *HISTORY — History Of Europe*

800 IT
SPECULUM ARTIUM. (Text in English, French and Italian) irreg. Angelo Longo Editore, Via Paolo Costa 33, P.O. Box 431, 48100 Ravenna, Italy. Ed. Aldo Scaglione. Indexed: M.L.A.

830 GW
SPEKTRUM DES GEISTES; Literaturkalender. 1951. a. DM.19.80. Husum Druck- und Verlagsgesellschaft, Nordbahnhofstr. 2, 2250 Husum, W. Germany (B.R.D.) Ed. Ehrhardt Heinold. circ. 10,000.

821.3 US ISSN 0195-9468
SPENSER STUDIES; a Renaissance poetry annual. 1980. a. $45. A M S Press, Inc., 56 E. 13 St., New York, NY 10003. TEL 212-777-4700. Eds. Patrick Cullen, Thomas P. Roche, Jr. circ. 600. (back issues avail.) Indexed: M.L.A.

SPIRAL. see *WOMEN'S INTERESTS*

800 CN ISSN 0383-283X
SQUATCHBERRY JOURNAL. 1975. a. Can.$5($8) Box 205, Geraldton, Ont. P0T 1M0, Canada. Ed. Edgar Lavoie. bk. rev. circ. 1,250.

891.92 491.92 YU ISSN 0081-3990
SRPSKA AKADEMIJA NAUKA I UMETNOSTI. ODELJENJE JEZIKA I KNJIZEVNOSTI. POSEBNA IZDANJA. (Text in Serbo-Croatian; summaries in English, French, German or Russian) 1950. irreg. price varies. Srpska Akademija Nauka i Umetnosti, Knez Mihailova 35, 11001 Belgrade, Yugoslavia (Dist. by: Prosveta, Terazije 16, Belgrade, Yugoslavia) circ. 1,000.

800 700 SA ISSN 0258-7211
STAFFRIDER MAGAZINE. (Text in English) 1978. irreg. R.2($4) Ravan Press Pty. Ltd., P.O. Box 31134, Braamfontein 2007, South Africa. Ed. Chris Van Wyk. adv. bk. rev. circ. 5,000.

840 850 US
STANFORD FRENCH & ITALIAN STUDIES. 1975. irreg., approx. 4 vols./yr. $25 per vol. (Stanford University, Department of French and Italian) Anma Libri, Box 876, Saratoga, CA 95071. TEL 415-851-3375. Ed. Alphonse Juilland. Indexed: M.L.A.

810 US ISSN 0272-7730
STARMONT READER'S GUIDES. irreg., latest no. 43. Borgo Press, Box 2845, San Bernardino, CA 92406. TEL 714-884-5813.

800 US ISSN 0738-0127
STARMONT REFERENCE GUIDES. irreg., latest no. 7. Borgo Press, Box 2845, San Bernardino, CA 92406. TEL 714-884-5813.

809 US ISSN 0737-1306
STARMONT STUDIES IN LITERARY CRITICISM. irreg., latest no. 21. Borgo Press, Box 2845, San Bernardino, CA 92406.

810 US ISSN 0085-6746
STEINBECK MONOGRAPH SERIES. 1971. irreg., no.12, 1986. price varies. Steinbeck Research Institute, Steinbeck Society, English Dept., Ball State University, Muncie, IN 47306. TEL 317-289-1241. Ed. Tetsumaro Hayashi. adv. bk. rev. circ. 600. (also avail. in microfilm from UMI; reprint service avail. from UMI) Indexed: Curr.Cont. M.L.A. Arts & Hum.Cit.Ind. Abstr.Engl.Stud.

809 SW ISSN 0491-0869
STOCKHOLM STUDIES IN HISTORY OF LITERATURE. (Subseries of Acta Universitatis Stockholmiensis) (Text in English and Spanish) 1956. irreg., latest no.21. price varies. (Stockholms Universitet) Almqvist & Wiksell International, Box 62, S-101 20 Stockholm, Sweden. Eds. O. Lindberger, I. Jonsson. (back issues avail.)

890 SW
STOCKHOLM STUDIES IN RUSSIAN LITERATURE. (Subseries of Acta Universitatis Stockholmiensis) (Text in Russian; summaries in English; latest no.9. price varies. (Stockholms Universitet) Almqvist & Wiksell International, Box 62, S-101 20 Stockholm, Sweden. Ed. Nils Ake Nilsson. Indexed: M.L.A.

STONY THURSDAY BOOK. see *LITERATURE — Poetry*

820 US ISSN 0081-5861
STORIES FROM THE HILLS. 1970. a. $4. Morris Harvey College Publications, Charleston, WV 25304. TEL 304-346-9471. Ed. William Plumley. circ. 2,000.

818.005 CN
STORY SO FAR. 1971. irreg. price varies. Coach House Press, 401(Rear) Huron St., Toronto, Ont. M5S 2G5, Canada. TEL 416-979-2217.

891.86 CS ISSN 0081-5896
STRAHOVSKA KNIHOVNA. (Text in Czech; summaries in French and German) 1966. a. price varies. Pamatnik Narodniho Pisemnictvi, Strahovske nadv. 132, Prague 1, Czechoslovakia. Ed. Pravoslav Kneidl.

STRATFORD-UPON-AVON STUDIES. see *THEATER*

STRATHCLYDE MODERN LANGUAGE STUDIES. see *LINGUISTICS*

810 US ISSN 0190-1737
STREET MAGAZINE. 1975. irreg. $10 for 4 issues. Street Press, Box 555, Port Jefferson, NY 11777. Ed. Bd. bk. rev. circ. 750. (back issues avail.)

STRINDBERGIANA. see *THEATER*

STUDI ALBANESI. STUDI E TESTI. see *LINGUISTICS*

810 IT ISSN 0085-6819
STUDI AMERICANI. (Text and summaries in English and Italian) 1955. a. price varies. Edizioni di Storia e Letteratura, Via Lancellotti 18, Rome 00186, Italy. Ed. Agostino Lombardo. Indexed: M.L.A.

840 IT ISSN 0585-4768
STUDI DI LETTERATURA FRANCESE. (Text in language of authors) 1967. a. price varies. (Universita degli Studi di Milano, Istituto di Letterature Straniere) Casa Editrice Leo S. Olschki, Casella Postale 66, 50100 Florence, Italy. Ed. Bd. circ. 1,000. Indexed: M.L.A.

809 IT
STUDI E TESTI DELL'ANTICHITA. 1975. irreg., no.18, 1984. price varies. Societa Editrice Napoletana s.r.l., Corso Umberto I 34, 80138 Naples, Italy. Ed. Fabio Cupaiuolo.

809 850 IT
STUDI E TESTI DI LETTERATURA ITALIANA. 1974. irreg., no.21, 1984. price varies. Societa Editrice Napoletana s.r.l., Corso Umberto I 34, 80138 Naples, Italy.

800 IT ISSN 0585-492X
STUDI ISPANICI. 1962. a. L.5000. Giardini Editori e Stampatori, Via Santa Bibbiana 28, 56100 Pisa, Italy. Ed.Bd. Indexed: M.L.A.

850 IT ISSN 0081-6256
STUDI TASSIANI. 1951. a. L.35000. Centro di Studi Tassiani, Piazza Vecchia 15, 24100 Bergamo, Italy. cum.index: vols.1-10; 11-20.

800 900 100 IT ISSN 0039-3088
STUDI URBINATI. SERIE B: LETTERATURA, STORIA, FILOSOFIA. N.S. 1950. a. L.15.000. (Universita degli Studi di Urbino, Facolta di Giurisprudenza) Edizioni Quattroventi, Via Saffi, 2, 61029 Urbino, Italy (Subscr. to: Edizioni Quattroventi, Casella Postale 156, 61029 Urbino, Italy) Ed. Carlo Bo. bk. rev. charts. illus. index. Indexed: Curr.Cont. Arts & Hum.Cit.Ind. Formerly: Studi Urbinati. Serie B: Letteratura.

STUDIA DELITZSCHIANA. NEUE FOLGE. see *HISTORY*

830 PL ISSN 0137-2467
STUDIA GERMANICA POSNANIENSIA. (Text in German) 1971. irreg., no.6, 1977. price varies. Adam Mickiewicz University Press, Marchlewskiego 128, 61-874 Poznan, Poland. Ed. Stefan H. Kaszynski. bk. rev. bibl. Indexed: Lang.& Lang.Behav.Abstr.

891 941.5   IE   ISSN 0081-6477
STUDIA HIBERNICA. 1961. a. £3. ‡ St. Patrick's
College, Editorial Committee, Dublin 9, Ireland. Ed.
D.F. Cregan. bk. rev. circ. 1,000. Indexed: M.L.A.
Br.Archaeol.Abstr.

800   HU   ISSN 0562-2867
STUDIA LITTERARIA. (Text in French and
Hungarian) 1963. irreg., vol.22, 1984. Kossuth Lajos
Tudomanyegyetem, Magyar Irodalomtorteneti
Intezet, Egyetem Ter 1, 4010 Debrecen, Hungary.
bibl. Indexed: M.L.A.

801 830   HU   ISSN 0209-9403
STUDIA POETICA. (Text in English, German) 1980.
irreg. exchange basis. Attila Jozsef University, c/o
E. Szabo, Exchange Librarian, Dugonics ter 13,
P.O.B. 393, Szeged H-6701, Hungary (Subscr. to:
Kultura, Box 149, H-1389 Budapest, Hungary) Eds.
Arpad Bernath, Karoly Csuri. circ. 500. Indexed:
Aqua.Sci.& Fish.Abstr. Entomol.Abstr.
Microbiol.Abstr.

809   PL   ISSN 0137-4389
STUDIA POLONO-SLAVICA ORIENTALIA.
ACTA LITTERARIA. a. price varies. (Polska
Akademia Nauk, Instytut Slowianoznawstwa,
Pracownia Literatur Wschodnioslowianskich)
Ossolineum, Publishing House of the Polish
Academy of Sciences, Rynek 9, Wroclaw, Poland
(Dist. by: Ars Polona-Ruch, Krakowskie
Przedmiescie 7, Warsaw, Poland) Ed. Bazyli
Bialokozowicz.

800   PL   ISSN 0081-6884
STUDIA ROSSICA POSNANIENSIA. (Text in
Polish and Russian; summaries in English and
Russian) 1970. irreg., vol. 7, 1976. price varies.
Adam Mickiewicz University Press, Marchlewskiego
128, 61-874 Poznan, Poland. Eds. Zbigniew
Baranski, Leszek Ossowski. bk. rev. circ. 700.
Indexed: Lang.& Lang.Behav.Abstr.

800   PL   ISSN 0081-6949
STUDIA STAROPOLSKIE. 1953. irreg., vol.52, 1984.
price varies. (Polska Akademia Nauk, Instytut
Badan Literackich) Ossolineum, Publishing House of
the Polish Academy of Sciences, Rynek 9, Wroclaw,
Poland (Dist. by: Ars Polona-Ruch, Krakowskie
Przedmiescie 7, Warsaw, Poland)

800   PL   ISSN 0081-7112
STUDIA Z OKRESU OSWIECENIA. (Text in Polish;
summaries in English and French) 1964. irreg.,
vol.20, 1986. price varies. (Polska Akademia Nauk,
Instytut Badan Literackich) Ossolineum, Publishing
House of the Polish Academy of Sciences, Rynek 9,
Wroclaw, Poland (Dist. by: Ars Polona-Ruch,
Krakowskie Przedmiescie 7, Warsaw, Poland)
Ed.Bd. bibl. circ. 500-1,500.

830   GW   ISSN 0081-7236
STUDIEN ZUR DEUTSCHEN LITERATUR. 1966.
irreg., no.90, 1986. price varies. Max Niemeyer
Verlag, Pfrondorfer Str. 4, 7400 Tuebingen, W.
Germany (B.R.D.) Ed.Bd. (back issues avail.)
Indexed: M.L.A.

830   GW   ISSN 0340-594X
STUDIEN ZUR GERMANISTIK, ANGLISTIK
UND KOMPARATISTIK. 1970. irreg., vol.116,
1985. price varies. Bouvier Verlag Herbert
Grundmann, Am Hof 32, Postfach 1268, 5300 Bonn
1, W. Germany (B.R.D.) Eds. A. Arnold, A. Hass.
Indexed: M.L.A.

800   GW   ISSN 0340-9023
STUDIEN ZUR LITERATUR DER MODERNE.
1976. irreg., vol.13, 1985. price varies. Bouvier
Verlag Herbert Grundmann, Am Hof 32, Postfach
1268, 5300 Bonn 1, W. Germany (B.R.D.) Ed.
Helmut Koopmann.

860 301   GW   ISSN 0340-5990
STUDIEN ZUR LITERATUR- UND
SOZIALGESCHICHTE SPANIENS UND
LATEINAMERIKAS. 1975. irreg., no. 7, 1984.
price varies. Bouvier Verlag Herbert Grundmann,
Am Hof 32, Postfach 1268, 5300 Bonn 1, W.
Germany(B.R.D.) Ed. Martin Franzbach.

STUDIEN ZUR PHILOSOPHIE UND LITERATUR
DES NEUNZEHNTEN JAHRHUNDERTS. see
PHILOSOPHY

807 296   US
STUDIES IN AMERICAN JEWISH LITERATURE.
1975; N.S. 1981. a. $12.95 to individuals;
institutions $25. Kent State University Press, Attn:
John Hubbell, Kent, OH 44242. TEL 216-672-7913.
Ed. Daniel Walden. adv. circ. 350. Indexed: M.L.A.
Amer.Bibl.Slavic & E.Eur.Stud. Abstr.Engl.Stud.
Jewish interests

808 910.03   US   ISSN 0738-0755
STUDIES IN BLACK AMERICAN LITERATURE.
1984. a. price varies. Penkevill Publishing Company,
Box 212, Greenwood, FL 32443. Eds. Joe
Weixlmann, Houston A. Baker, Jr. adv. circ. 500.

809   JA
STUDIES IN BRITISH & AMERICAN
LITERATURE/EI-BEIBUNGAKU. (Text in
English or Japanese) a. Komazawa University, 1-23-
1 Komazawa, Setagaya-ku, Tokyo 154, Japan.
Formerly: Gaikoku Bungaku Kenkyu.

820   US   ISSN 0095-4489
STUDIES IN BROWNING AND HIS CIRCLE; a
journal of criticism, history and bibliography. 1968.
a. $15. Baylor University, Armstrong Browning
Library, Waco, TX 76706. TEL 817-755-3566. bk.
rev. cum.index. circ. 600-700. Indexed:
Abstr.Engl.Stud. Curr.Cont. M.L.A.
Amer.Hum.Ind. Arts & Hum.Cit.Ind.
Ind.Bk.Rev.Hum.
Formerly: Browning Newsletter (ISSN 0007-
2532)

STUDIES IN CLASSICAL LITERATURE. see
CLASSICAL STUDIES

809   US   ISSN 0081-7775
STUDIES IN COMPARATIVE LITERATURE
(CHAPEL HILL) (Text in English, French,
German, Italian, Latin, and Spanish) 1950. irreg.,
no.61, 1978. price varies. ‡ University of North
Carolina Press, Box 2288, Chapel Hill, NC 27514.
TEL 919-966-3561. (reprint service avail. from
UMI)

820   UK
STUDIES IN ENGLISH LITERATURE. 1961. irreg.
price varies. Edward Arnold (Publishers) Ltd., 41
Bedford Square, London WC1B 3DQ, England.
Indexed: Abstr.Engl.Stud. LCR.

840   GW   ISSN 0081-7937
STUDIES IN FRENCH LITERATURE. 1964. irreg.
price varies. Walter de Gruyter & Co., Mouton
Publishers, Postfach 110240, D-1000 Berlin 11, W.
Germany (B.R.D.) (U.S. addr.: Mouton Publishers,
division of Walter de Gruyter, Inc., 200 Saw Mill
River Road, Hawthorne, NY 10532)

840   UK
STUDIES IN FRENCH LITERATURE. 1960. irreg.
price varies. Edward Arnold (Publishers) Ltd., 41
Bedford Sq., London WC1B 3DQ, England.

800   GW   ISSN 0081-7945
STUDIES IN GENERAL AND COMPARATIVE
LITERATURE. 1965. irreg. price varies. Walter de
Gruyter & Co., Mouton Publishers, Postfach
110240, D-1000 Berlin 11, W. Germany (B.R.D.)
(U.S. addr.: Mouton Publishers, division of Walter
de Gruyter, Inc., 300 Saw Mill River Road,
Hawthorne, NY 10532)

830   GW   ISSN 0081-797X
STUDIES IN GERMAN LITERATURE. 1964. irreg.
price varies. Walter de Gruyter & Co., Mouton
Publishers, Postfach 110240, D-1000 Berlin 11, W.
Germany (B.R.D.) (U.S. addr.: Mouton Publishers,
division of Walter de Gruyter, Inc., 200 Saw Mill
River Road, Hawthorne, NY 10532) Indexed:
M.L.A.

850   GW   ISSN 0081-8119
STUDIES IN ITALIAN LITERATURE. 1966. irreg.
price varies. Walter de Gruyter & Co., Mouton
Publishers, Postfach 110240, D-1000 Berlin 11, W.
Germany (B.R.D.) (U.S. addr.: Mouton Publishers,
division of Walter de Gruyter, Inc., 200 Saw Mill
River Road, Hawthorne, NY 10532)

STUDIES IN LANGUAGE COMPANION SERIES.
see *LINGUISTICS*

800   US
STUDIES IN LITERATURE AND CRITICISM.
irreg. price varies. Burt Franklin & Co., Inc., 235
East 44th St., New York, NY 10017. TEL 212-687-
5250.

STUDIES IN MEDIEVAL CULTURE. see
HISTORY

890   US
STUDIES IN MIDDLE EASTERN LITERATURES.
1972. irreg., no.11, 1984. price varies. Bibliotheca
Islamica, Inc., Box 14474, Univer. Station,
Minneapolis, MN 55414.

890   US
STUDIES IN MODERN HEBREW LITERATURE.
irreg. price varies. Cornell University Press, 124
Roberts Place, Ithaca, NY 14850. TEL 607-257-
7000.

800   US
STUDIES IN MODERN LITERATURE. irreg.,
vol.57, 1986. U M I Research Press, 300 N. Zeeb
Rd., Ann Arbor, MI 48106. Ed. A. Walton Litz.

479   US
STUDIES IN ROMANCE LANGUAGES &
LITERATURES. 1970. irreg., latest 1986. price
varies. University Press of Kentucky, Lexington, KY
40506-0024. TEL 606-257-2951. Ed. John E. Keller.
(reprint service avail. from UMI) Indexed: M.L.A.
Formerly: Studies in Romance Languages (ISSN
0085-6894)

STUDIES IN SEMIOTICS AND LITERATURE. see
LINGUISTICS

899   NE   ISSN 0169-0175
STUDIES IN SLAVIC LITERATURE AND
POETICS. Short title: S S P. 1981. irreg. price
varies. (Slavisch Instituut) Editions Rodopi B.V.,
Keizersgracht 302-304, 1016 EX Amsterdam,
Netherlands. Ed.Bd. Indexed: M.L.A.

800   US
STUDIES IN SPECULATIVE FICTION. irreg.,
vol.12, 1985. U M I Research Press, 300 N. Zeeb
Rd., Ann Arbor, MI 48106. Ed. Robert Scholes.

807   US   ISSN 0190-2407
STUDIES IN THE AGE OF CHAUCER. 1979. a.
$30. University of Tennessee, Department of
English, New Chaucer Society, Knoxville, TN
37916. Ed. Thomas J. Heffernan. bibl. index. circ.
700. (back issues avail.)

800   ISSN 0149-015X
STUDIES IN THE AMERICAN RENAISSANCE.
1978. a. $35. (University of South Carolina)
University Press of Virginia, Box 3608,
Charlottesville, VA 22903. TEL 617-423-3990. Ed.
Joel Myerson. bk. rev. bibl. illus. circ. 1,000.
Indexed: Hist.Abstr. M.L.A. Amer.Hist. & Life.
Amer.Hum.Ind. Rel.Ind.One.

830   US   ISSN 0081-8593
STUDIES IN THE GERMANIC LANGUAGES
AND LITERATURES. 1949. irreg., no.98, 1982.
price varies. University of North Carolina Press,
Box 2288, Chapel Hill, NC 27514. TEL 919-966-
3561. (reprint service avail. from UMI)

840 940   UK   ISSN 0435-2866
STUDIES ON VOLTAIRE AND THE
EIGHTEENTH CENTURY. (Text in English and
French) 1955. irreg., (approx. 12/yr.) price varies.
Voltaire Foundation, Taylor Institution, St. Giles,
Oxford OX1 3NA, England. Ed. Prof. H.T. Mason.
cum.index: 1955-64, 1965-70. (also avail. in
microfiche; back issues avail.) Indexed: M.L.A.

STUDY GROUP ON EIGHTEENTH-CENTURY
RUSSIA. NEWSLETTER. see *HISTORY —
History Of Europe*

800   GW
STUTTGARTER ARBEITEN ZUR GERMANISTIK.
(Text and summaries in English, German) 1975.
irreg. price varies. Verlag Hans-Dieter Heinz-
Akademischer Verlag Stuttgart, Steiermaerkerstrasse
132, 7000 Stuttgart 30, W. Germany (B.R.D.)
Ed.Bd. circ. 400. (back issues avail.) Indexed:
M.L.A.

869   BL
STYLOS. 1980. irreg., no. 43, 1981. Universidade Estadual Paulista Julio de Mesquita Filho, Instituto de Biociencias, Letras e Ciencias Exatas, Rua Cristovao Colombo 2265-J. Nazareth, 15100 Campus de Sao Jose do Rio Preto SP, Brazil.

840   HU   ISSN 0418-4572
SUDIA ROMANICA UNIVERSITATIS DEBRECENIENSIS DE LUDOVICO KOSSUTH NOMINATAE. SERIES LITTERARIA. (Text in French) 1962. irreg., vol.9, 1982. Kossuth Lajos Tudomanyegyetem, Roman Nyelvek es Irodalmak Tanszek, Egyetem Ter 1, 4010 Debrecen, Hungary. bibl.

SUEDOSTDEUTSCHES KULTURWERK, MUNICH. KLEINE SUEDOSTREIHE. see HISTORY — History Of Europe

SUEDOSTDEUTSCHES KULTURWERK, MUNICH. SCHRIFTENREIHEN. REIHE A. KULTUR UND DICHTUNG. see HISTORY — History Of Europe

SUEDOSTDEUTSCHES KULTURWERK, MUNICH. SCHRIFTENREIHEN. REIHE C. ERINNERUNGEN UND QUELLEN. see HISTORY — History Of Europe

SUN DANCE REPRINTS. see HISTORY

SURREALIST TRANSFORMACTION. see ART

806   SW
SVERIGES FOERFATTARFOERBUND. MEDLEMSFOERTECKNING. a. Sveriges Foerfattarfoerbund, Box 5087, 102 42 Stockholm, Sweden.

808   US   ISSN 0277-447X
SWIFT KICK. 1982. irreg., latest no.4, 1984. $10 for 4 nos. to individuals; institutions $20. 1711 Amherst St., Buffalo, NY 14214. Ed. Robin Kay Willoughby. circ. 100.

850   RM
SYNTHESIS; Bulletin du Comite National Roumain de Litterature Comparee. (Text in English, French, German, Italian, Spanish) 1972. a. 25 lei($42) Editura Academiei Republicii Socialiste Rumania, Calea Victoriri 125, 79717 Bucharest, Rumania (Subscr. to: ROMPRESFILATELIA, Calea Grivitei 64-66, P.O. Box 12-201, 78104 Bucharest, Rumania) Ed. Zoe Dumitrescu Busulenga. bk. rev.

800   II
TAGORE INTERNATIONAL. (Text in English) 1985. a. Rs.5($2) Tagore Research Institute, c/o Ms. Pronoti Mukerji, Rabindra Charcha Bhavan, Kalighat Park, Calcutta 700 026, India. Ed. Somendra Nath Bose. bk. rev. circ. 500.

860   CL
TALLER DE LETRAS. (Some vols. accompanied by supplements) 1971. a. Universidad Catolica de Chile, Instituto de Letras, Av. Bernardo O'Higgins 340, Casilla 114-D, Santiago, Chile. Ed. Cedomil Goic. bk. rev. bibl. illus. index. circ. 1,000.

808   US
TARASQUE. 1983. irreg. 302 Alamosa N.W., Albuquerque, NM 87107.

860   SP
TEMAS Y FORMAS DE LA LITERATURA. irreg., no. 2, 1982. Edi-6, S.A., Madrid, Spain.

800 100   FR
TEMPS DE LA REFLEXION. 1980. a. 91 F. Editions Gallimard, 15, rue Sebatien-Bottin, Paris(7e), France. Ed. J.B. Pontalis.

800   US   ISSN 0497-2384
TENNESSEE STUDIES IN LITERATURE. 1956. a. price varies. (University of Tennessee, Department of English) University of Tennessee Press, Knoxville, TN 37996-0325. TEL 615-974-3321. Eds. Allison R. Ensor, Thomas J. A. Heffernan. bk. rev. bibl. cum.index. circ. 1,000. (also avail. in microform from UMI; back issues avail.; reprint service avail. from UMI) Indexed: M.L.A. Amer.Hum.Ind.

820   UK   ISSN 0082-2841
TENNYSON RESEARCH BULLETIN. 1967. a. membership. Tennyson Society, Tennyson Research Centre, Central Library, Free School Lane, Lincoln, England. Ed.Bd. bk. rev. index. cum.index every 5 years. circ. 500. Indexed: M.L.A.

820   UK   ISSN 0082-285X
TENNYSON SOCIETY, LINCOLN, ENGLAND. MONOGRAPHS. 1969. irreg., no.10, 1985. membership. Tennyson Society, Tennyson Research Centre, Central Library, Free School Lane, Lincoln, England. Ed.Bd. circ. 500.

820   UK   ISSN 0307-3572
TENNYSON SOCIETY, LINCOLN, ENGLAND. OCCASIONAL PAPERS. 1974. irreg., no.6, 1984. membership. Tennyson Society, Tennyson Research Centre, Central Library, Free School Lane, Lincoln, England.

820   UK   ISSN 0082-2868
TENNYSON SOCIETY, LINCOLN, ENGLAND. REPORT. 1961. a. free. Tennyson Society, Tennyson Research Centre, Central Library, Free School Lane, Lincoln, England. circ. 500.

144   IT
TESTI E STUDI UMANISTICI. irreg. Angelo Longo Editore, Via Paolo Costa 33, P.O. Box 431, 48100 Ravenna, Italy.

808.8   US   ISSN 0084-9103
TEXAS TECH UNIVERSITY. INTERDEPARTMENTAL COMMITTEE ON COMPARATIVE LITERATURE. PROCEEDINGS OF THE COMPARATIVE LITERATURE SYMPOSIUM. 1968. a. price varies. Texas Tech University Press, Box 4139, Lubbock, TX 79409. TEL 806-742-1593. Ed. Wendell M. Aycock. illus. circ. 500. Indexed: Abstr.Engl.Stud. M.L.A.

800   US   ISSN 0736-3974
TEXT (NEW YORK) 1984. a. $45. (Society for Textual Scholarship) A M S Press, Inc., 56 E. 13th St., New York, NY 10003. TEL 212-777-4700. Eds. D.C. Greetham, W. Speed Hill. circ. 600. (back issues avail.)

800   GW
TEXT UND KONTEXT; Romanische Literaturen und allgemeine Literaturwissenschaft. irreg., vol.4, 1986. price varies. Franz Steiner Verlag Wiesbaden GmbH, Birkenwaldstr. 44, Postfach 347, 7000 Stuttgart 1, W. Germany (B.R.D.) Ed. Klaus W. Hempfer.

800 320   GE   ISSN 0081-3257
TEXTAUSGABEN ZUR FRUEHEN SOZIALISTISCHEN LITERATUR IN DEUTSCHLAND. 1963. irreg., vol. 23, 1982. price varies. (Akademie der Wissenschaften der DDR, Zentralinstitut fuer Literaturgeschichte) Akademie-Verlag, Leipziger Str. 3-4, 1086 Berlin, E. Germany (D.D.R.) Ed. Ursula Muenchow.

800   GW
TEXTE DES SPAETEN MITTELALTERS UND DER FRUEHEN NEURZEIT. 1956. irreg. Erich Schmidt Verlag GmbH, Genthiner Str. 30 G, 1000 Berlin 30, W. Germany (B.R.D.) (Subscr. addr.: Zweigniederlassung Bielefeld Viktoriastr. 44a, 4800 Bielefeld 1, W. Germany (B.R.D.)) Eds. Karl Stackmann, Stanley N. Werbow.

840   SZ
TEXTES LITTERAIRES FRANCAIS. 1895. irreg., no. 340, 1986. price varies. Librairie Droz, 11 rue Massot, 1211 Geneva 12, Switzerland.

800   NE
TEXTUS MINORES. 1948. irreg., vol.55, 1984. price varies. E.J. Brill, P.O. Box 9000, 2300 PA Leiden, Netherlands. Ed.Bd.

830 920   GW   ISSN 0082-3880
THEODOR-STORM-GESELLSCHAFT. SCHRIFTEN. 1952. a. price varies. Westholsteinische Verlagsanstalt Boyens und Co., Am Wulf-Isebrand-Platz, Postfach 1880, 2240 Heide, W. Germany (B.R.D.) Eds. Karl E. Laage, Friedrich Heitmann.

806   US
THOMAS HARDY ANNUAL. 1982. a. price varies. Humanities Press, Inc., Atlantic Highlands, NJ 07716. TEL 201-872-1441. Ed. Norman Page. bibl. Indexed: M.L.A.

820   UI   ISSN 0082-416X
THOMAS HARDY YEAR BOOK. 1970. a. 1p. Toucan Press, Saravia, Rue des Monts, Delancey Park, St. Sampson, Guernsey, Channel Islands. Eds. J. Stevens Cox, G. Stevens Cox. adv. bk. rev. circ. 2,000-3,000. Indexed: Br.Hum.Ind. M.L.A.

800   SZ   ISSN 0082-4186
THOMAS MANN GESELLSCHAFT. BLAETTER. 1958. a. price varies. Thomas Mann Gesellschaft, Raemistrasse 5, 8001 Zurich, Switzerland. bk. rev. circ. 1,000.

820   UK   ISSN 0040-6562
THRESHOLD. 1957. irreg., no. 31, 1980. price varies. Lyric Players Theatre, 55 Ridgeway St., Belfast 9, N. Ireland. Ed. John Boyd. bk. rev. circ. 1,000.

810   US   ISSN 0277-7800
THRESHOLD OF FANTASY; fantastic literature. 1982. a. $13. Fandom Unlimited Enterprises, Box 70868, Sunnyvale, CA 94086. TEL 415-960-1151. Ed. Randall D. Larson. adv. bk. rev. illus. circ. 1, 000. (back issues avail.)

820 810 410   JA   ISSN 0385-406X
TOHOKU GAKUIN UNIVERSITY REVIEW; essays and studies in English language and literature. (Text in English and Japanese) 1958. a. 2000 Yen($12) Literary, Economic and Juristic Association, Tohoku Gakuin University, 3-1 Tsuchitoi 1-Chome, Sendai 980, Japan. Ed. Yukio Igarashi. bk. rev. circ. 2,000. Indexed: MLA.

940   CN   ISSN 0082-5050
TORONTO MEDIAEVAL LATIN TEXTS. 1972. irreg. $4.75. ‡ Pontifical Institute of Mediaeval Studies, 59 Queen's Park Crescent. E., Toronto, Ont. M5S 2C4, Canada. TEL 416-926-7144. Ed.Bd.

TORONTO OLD ENGLISH SERIES. see HISTORY — History Of Europe

891.85   PL   ISSN 0067-7787
TOWARZYSTWO LITERACKIE IM. A. MICKIEWICZA. BIBLIOTEKA. 1960. irreg., vol.17, 1984. price varies. Ossolineum, Publishing House of the Polish Academy of Sciences, Rynek 9, 50-106 Wroclaw, Poland.

830   GE
TRAJEKT. 1970. a. free. VEB Hinstorff Verlag, Lagerstr. 7, DDR-2500 Rostock, E. Germany (D.D.R.) bk. rev. illus.

800   US
TRANSIENT. 1973. irreg., no. 6, 1977. $5. ‡ Transient Press, Box 4662, Albuquerque, NM 87106. TEL 505-242-6600. Ed. Ken Saville. circ. 250.
Formerly: Is.

TRAZA Y BAZA; cuadernos hispanos de simbologia, arte y literatura. see ART

800 700   UK
TRIVIUM. 1966. a. £5. Saint David's University College, Lampeter, Dyfed SA48 7ED, Wales. Ed. C.C. Eldridge. bk. rev. circ. 300. Indexed: M.L.A. Arts & Hum.Cit.Ind. Abstr.Engl.Stud.

420.5 809   JA   ISSN 0496-3547
TSUDA REVIEW. (Text in English) 1956. a. exchange basis. Tsuda College - Tsuda Daigaku, 2-1-1 Tsuda-machi, Kodaira City, Tokyo 187, Japan. circ. 1,000. Indexed: Abstr.Engl.Stud.

809   US
TWENTIETH-CENTURY LITERARY CRITICISM; excerpts from criticism of the works of novelists, poets, playwrights, and other creative writers of the era 1900-1960. 1978. irreg., latest vol.22, 1986. $90 per vol. Gale Research Company, Book Tower, Detroit, MI 48226. TEL 313-961-2242. Ed. Dennis Poupard. bibl. index. (back issues avail.) Indexed: Child.Auth.& Illus.

810   US
TYPEWRITER. 1971. irreg. (1-2/yr.) $2 per no. Bird in the Bush, Box 409, Iowa City, IA 52240. Eds. R. Caldwell, Claire Maric. circ. 200.

LITERATURE

810.8 CN ISSN 0226-3440
U.C. REVIEW. Variant title: University College Literary Review. a. University of Toronto, University College, Toronto, Ont. M5S 1A1, Canada. TEL 613-978-2011. illus.

808.81 808.81 US ISSN 0739-1609
U S 1 WORKSHEETS. 1973. irreg. (2-3/yr.) $5 for 6 nos. U S 1 Poets' Cooperative, 21 Lake Dr., Roosevelt, NJ 08555. circ. 500. (tabloid format; back issues avail.) Indexed: Ind.Amer.Per.Verse.

895 UN ISSN 0566-6201
UNESCO ASIAN FICTION SERIES. irreg. price varies. Unesco, 7 Place de Fontenoy, F-75700 Paris, France (Dist. in U.S. by: Bernan Associates-Unipub, 4611-F Assembly Dr., Lanham, MD 20706-4391)

890 SW
UNGA DIKTARA. a. Bokfoerlaget Inferi, Box 167, 821 01 Bollnaes 1, Sweden.

860 UY ISSN 0250-6556
UNIVERSIDAD DE LA REPUBLICA. FACULTAD DE HUMANIDADES Y CIENCIAS. REVISTA. SERIE LETRAS. N.S. 1979. irreg. exchange basis. Universidad de la Republica, Facultad de Humanidades y Ciencias, Seccion Revista, Tristan Narvaja 1674, Montevideo, Uruguay. Dir. Beatriz Martinez Osorio.
Supersedes in part: Universidad de la Republica. Facultad de Humanidades y Ciencias. Revista.

860 VE
UNIVERSIDAD DE LOS ANDES. ESCUELA DE LETRAS. ANUARIO.* 1975. a. exchange basis. Universidad de los Andes, Escuela de Letras, Via los Chorras de Milla, C.P. 5101, Merida, Venezuela. Ed.Bd.

UNIVERSIDAD DE MURCIA. ESTUDIOS ROMANICOS. see *LINGUISTICS*

860 SP
UNIVERSIDAD DE NAVARRA. DEPARTAMENTO DE LITERATURA ESPANOLA. COLECCION PUBLICACIONES. 1974. irreg., no.9, 1986. price varies. Ediciones Universidad de Navarra S.A., Apdo. 396, 31080 Pamplona, Spain.

860 UY ISSN 0077-1252
UNIVERSIDAD DE URUGUAY. DEPARTAMENTO DE LITERATURA IBEROAMERICANA PUBLICACIONES.* irreg. Universidad de Uruguay, Departamento de Literatura Iberoamericana, Montevideo, Uruguay.

869 BL ISSN 0079-9327
UNIVERSIDADE FEDERAL DE MINAS GERAIS. CORPO DISCENTE. REVISTA LITERARIA. Cover title: R L; Revista Literaria. 1966. a. free. Universidade Federal de Minas Gerais, Servico de Relacoes Universitarias, Rua Carangola 288, Caixa Postal 1621, 30000 Belo Horizonte, Minas Gerais, Brazil. Ed. Bd. bk. rev. illus. circ. 2,000.

UNIVERSITA DEGLI STUDI DI PADOVA. FACOLTA DI LETTERE E FILOSOFIA. OPUSCOLI ACCADEMICI. see *ART*

UNIVERSITA DEGLI STUDI DI PADOVA. FACOLTA DI LETTERE E FILOSOFIA. PUBBLICAZIONI. see *ART*

850 100 IT
UNIVERSITA DEGLI STUDI DI SIENA. FACOLTA DI LETTERE E FILOSOFIA. ANNALI. 1980. a. price varies. (Universita degli Studi di Siena, Facolta di Lettere e Filosofia) Casa Editrice Leo S. Olschki, Viuzzo del Pozzetto (Viale Europa), 50126 Florence, Italy.

491 CS
UNIVERSITA PALACKEHO. FILOSOFICKA FAKULTA. SLAVICA. (Subseries of its Philologica) (Text in Czech; summaries in French or German) 1971. irreg. 8.50 Kcs. Statni Pedagogicke Nakladatelstvi, Ostrovni 30, 113 01 Prague 1, Czechoslovakia. bibl. illus.
Continues: Series Slavica.

UNIVERSITA PALACKEHO. PEDAGOGICKA FAKULTA. SBORNIK PRACI: RUSKY JAZYK A LITERATURA. see *LINGUISTICS*

850 RM ISSN 0379-7899
UNIVERSITATEA "AL. I. CUZA" DIN IASI. ANALELE STIINTIFICE. SECTIUNEA 3F. : LITERATURA. (Text in English, French, German, Rumanian, Russian) 1955. a. 35 lei. Universitatea "Al. I. Cuza" din Iasi, Calea 23 August Nr. 11, Jassy, Rumania (Subscr. to: ILEXIM, Str. 13 Decembrie Nr. 3, P.O. Box 136-137, Bucharest, Rumania) Ed. C. Ciopraga. bk. rev. abstr. charts. illus. circ. 300.

880 FR ISSN 0065-4981
UNIVERSITE D'AIX-MARSEILLE I. CENTRE D'ETUDES ET DE RECHERCHES HELLENIQUES. PUBLICATIONS. 1958. irreg. Universite d'Aix-Marseille I (Universite de Provence), Centre d'Etudes et de Recherches Helleniques, Service des Publications, 13621 Aix en Provence, France.

UNIVERSITE D'ODENSE. ETUDES ROMANES. see *LINGUISTICS*

001.3 FR
UNIVERSITE DE DAKAR. FACULTE DES LETTRES ET SCIENCES HUMAINES. ANNALES. 1971? a. Presses Universitaires de France, 108 bd. Saint Germain, 75279 Paris Cedex 6, France (Service des Periodiques, 12 rue Jean de Beauvais, 75005 Paris) Ed. Jacques Gengoux. bibl. charts. illus. (reprint service avail. from KTO)

840 FR ISSN 0181-561X
UNIVERSITE DE HAUTE BRETAGNE. CENTRE D'ETUDES IRLANDAISES. CAHIER. 1976. a. 60 F. (Universite de Haute Bretagne, Centre d'Etudes Irlandaises) Presses Universitaires de Rennes II, 6 av. Gaston Berger, 35043 Rennes, France. Ed. Jean Noel. bk. rev. circ. 500.
Formerly: Universite de Haute Bretagne. Centre d'Etudes Anglo-Irlandaises. Cahier.

800 700 SZ ISSN 0041-915X
UNIVERSITE DE LAUSANNE. FACULTE DES LETTRES. PUBLICATIONS. 1930. irreg., no.26, 1983. price varies. Librarie Droz, 11 rue Massot, 1211 Geneva 12, Switzerland.

800 SZ ISSN 0077-7633
UNIVERSITE DE NEUCHATEL. FACULTE DES LETTRES. RECUEIL DE TRAVAUX. 1905. irreg., no.37, 1984. price varies. Librarie Droz, 11 rue Massot, 1211 Geneva 12, Switzerland. circ. 500-1, 000.

UNIVERSITE DE STRASBOURG II. CENTRE DE PHILOLOGIE ET LITTERATURES ROMANES. ACTES ET COLLOQUES. see *LINGUISTICS*

UNIVERSITE DE STRASBOURG II. INSTITUT DE PHONETIQUE. TRAVAUX. see *LINGUISTICS*

890 410 TI
UNIVERSITE DE TUNIS. ECOLE NORMALE SUPERIEURE. SECTION A: LETTRES ET SCIENCES HUMAINES. SERIE 1: LANGUE ET LITTERATURE. 1977. irreg. Universite de Tunis, Ecole Normale Superieure, Tunis, Tunisia.

UNIVERSITETET I OSLO. SLAVISK-BALTISK INSTITUTT. MEDDELELSER. see *LINGUISTICS*

UNIVERSITY OF CAPE TOWN. STUDIES IN ENGLISH. see *LINGUISTICS*

830 UK ISSN 0144-9850
UNIVERSITY OF LONDON. INSTITUTE OF GERMANIC STUDIES. BITHELL MEMORIAL LECTURES. 1975. a. £1.50. University of London, Institute of Germanic Studies, 29 Russell Square, London WC1B 5DP, England. Ed.Bd. circ. 1,000.

830 UK ISSN 0266-7932
UNIVERSITY OF LONDON. INSTITUTE OF GERMANIC STUDIES. BITHELL SERIES OF DISSERTATIONS. 1979. irreg. University of London, Institute of Germanic Studies, 29 Russell Square, London WC1B 5DP, England. Ed.Bd. circ. 500.

830 UK ISSN 0076-0803
UNIVERSITY OF LONDON. INSTITUTE OF GERMANIC STUDIES. LIBRARY PUBLICATIONS. 1961. irreg. price varies. ‡ University of London, Institute of Germanic Studies, 29 Russell Sq., London WC1B 5DP, England. circ. 500.

820 US ISSN 0081-7880
UNIVERSITY OF MISSISSIPPI STUDIES IN ENGLISH. 1960. a. $15. University of Mississippi, Department of English, University, Lafayette Co., MS 38677. TEL 601-232-7439. Ed. Benjamin F. Fisher IV. adv. bk. rev. circ. 450. Indexed: M.L.A. Abstr.Engl.Stud.
Formerly: University of Mississippi. Studies in English. New Series.

491.1 891.1 II ISSN 0448-1712
UNIVERSITY OF RAJASTHAN. STUDIES IN SANSKRIT AND HINDI. 1965. irreg. University of Rajasthan, Departments of Sanskrit and Hindi, Gandhi Nagar, Jaipur 302004, India.

UNIVERSITY OF SASKATCHEWAN. LIBRARY. NOTABLE WORKS AND COLLECTIONS. see *LIBRARY AND INFORMATION SCIENCES*

UNIVERSITY OF TORONTO ROMANCE SERIES. see *LINGUISTICS*

820 US
UNIVERSITY OF TULSA. MONOGRAPH SERIES. 1966. irreg., nos. 20 & 21, 1985. price varies. University of Tulsa, 600 S. College Ave., Tulsa, OK 74104. Ed. Thomas F. Staley. circ. 300. (also avail. in microfilm from UMI; back issues avail.) Indexed: M.L.A.
Formerly: University of Tulsa. Department of English. Monograph Series (ISSN 0082-6812)

809 491.8 CS ISSN 0231-7818
UNIVERZITA J. E. PURKYNE. FILOZOFICKA FAKULTA. SBORNIK PRACI. D: RADA LITERARNEVDNA. irreg., approx. a. Univerzita J. E. Purkyne, Filozoficka Fakulta, A. Novaka 1, 602 00 Brno, Czechoslovakia.

UNIVERZITA J. E. PURKYNE. FILOZOFICKA FAKULTA. SBORNIK PRACI. K: RADA GERMANISTICKO - ANGLISTICKA. see *LINGUISTICS*

UNIVERZITA J. E. PURKYNE. FILOZOFICKA FAKULTA. SBORNIK PRACI. L: RADA ROMANISTICA. see *LINGUISTICS*

UNIVERZITA KOMENSKEHO. FILOZOFICKA FAKULTA. ZBORNIK: PHILOLOGICA. see *LINGUISTICS*

UNIVERZITA PALACKEHO. PEDAGOGICKA FAKULTA. SBORNIK PRACI: CESKY JAZYK A LITERATURA. see *LINGUISTICS*

891.85 943 PL ISSN 0072-0488
UNIWERSYTET GDANSKI. WYDZIAL HUMANISTYCZNY. ZESZYTY NAUKOWE. PRACE HISTORYCZNO-LITERACKIE. 1965. irreg. Uniwersytet Gdanski, Ul. Czerwonej Armii 110, 81-824 Sopot, Poland (Dist. by: Ars Polona-Ruch, Krakowskie Przedmiescie 7, Warsaw, Poland)

891.85 PL ISSN 0083-436X
UNIWERSYTET JAGIELLONSKI. ZESZYTY NAUKOWE. PRACE HISTORYCZNOLITERACKIE. (Vol. 3- called also vol. 5-, continuing the volume numbering of Seria Nauk Spolecznych. Filologia, which it supersedes) (Text in Polish, rarely in English, French or Russian; summaries in English, French, German, Russian) 1955. irreg., 1984. price varies. Panstwowe Wydawnictwo Naukowe, Miodowa 10, 00-251 Warsaw, Poland (Dist. by: Ars Polona, Krakowskie Przedmiescie 7, 00-068 Warsaw, Poland) Ed. St. Jaworski. circ. 600.

811 US ISSN 0049-559X
UNSPEAKABLE VISIONS OF THE INDIVIDUAL. 1971. irreg. Tuvoti, Box 439, California, PA 15419. TEL 412-938-8956. Eds. Arthur W. Knight, Kit Knight. adv. bk. rev. illus. circ. 2,000.

830 GW ISSN 0083-4564
UNTERSUCHUNGEN ZUR DEUTSCHEN LITERATURGESCHICHTE. 1962. irreg., no.39, 1986. price varies. Max Niemeyer Verlag, Pfrondorferstr. 4, 7400 Tuebingen, W. Germany (B.R.D.) (back issues avail.) Indexed: M.L.A.

810 US
URTHONA. a. free. Boston University, 236 Bay State Rd., Boston, MA 02215. TEL 617-353-2000. illus.

840　　　　FR　ISSN 0760-5641
VALENCIENNES. 1976. a. 100 F. Presses Universitaires de Valenciennes, Le Mont Houy, 59326 Valenciennes Cedex, France. Ed. J.P. Giusto. adv. circ. 500. (back issues avail.)
　　Formerly (until 1981): Cahiers de l'U E R Froissart.

800　　　　US
VALLEY GRAPEVINE. 1978. a. $10. Seven Buffaloes Press, Box 249, Big Timber, MT 59011. Ed. Art Cuelho. circ. 750.

860　　　　AG
VENGA QUE LE CUENTO; publicacion periodica aleatoria de narradores argentinos. no. 1974. irreg. Prudan 1330, Buenos Aires, Argentina. adv. illus.

800　　　　GW　ISSN 0170-3633
VERSCHOLLENE UND VERGESSENE. irreg. price varies. (Akademie der Wissenschaften und der Literatur, Mainz, Klasse der Literatur) Franz Steiner Verlag Wiesbaden GmbH, Birkenwaldstr. 44, Postfach 347, D-7000 Stuttgart 1, W. Germany (B.R.D.) Ed. Bernd Goldmann.

800　　　　NE
VERZAMELING VAN MIDDELNEDERLANDSE BIJBELTEKSTEN. Added title page title: Corpus Sacrae Scripturae Neerlandicae Medii Aevii. 1970. irreg. E.J. Brill, P.O. Box 9000, 2300 PA Leiden, Netherlands.

890　　　　UR
VETER STRANSTVII. vol.11, 1976. irreg. 0.80 Rub. per no. Izdatel'stvo Fizkul'tura i Sport, Kalyaevskaya Ul., 27, Moscow K-6, Russian S.F.S.R., U.S.S.R. Ed.Bd. illus. circ. 100,000.

820.9　　　CN　ISSN 0703-5500
VICTORIAN STUDIES ASSOCIATION OF WESTERN CANADA. NEWSLETTER. 1972. biennial. Can.$15 membership to individuals; institutions Can.$10. Victorian Studies Association of Western Canada, c/o Prof. Isobel M. Findlay, Ed., English Department, University of Saskatchewan, Saskatoon, Sask. S7N 0W0, Canada TEL 306-966-5499. (Subsc. address: c/o Prof. Ian Dyck, Department of History, St. Thomas More College, University of Saskatchewan, Saskatoon, Sask. S7N 0W0) Ed. Isobel W. Findlay. adv. bk. rev. circ. 200. Indexed: Abstr.Engl.Stud.

839　　　　UK　ISSN 0083-6257
VIKING SOCIETY FOR NORTHERN RESEARCH. TEXT SERIES. 1953. a. Viking Society for Northern Research, University College, Gower St., London WC1E 6BT, England.

VINAVER STUDIES IN FRENCH. see LINGUISTICS

VOICES FROM WITHIN. see CRIMINOLOGY AND LAW ENFORCEMENT

800　　　　AT
VOID MAGAZINE. 1975. a. Aus.$12. Cory and Collins, Box 66, St. Kilda, Vic. 3182, Australia. Ed. Paul Collins. circ. 1,000.

891.7　　　UR
VOLOGODSKAYA BIBLIOTEKA IM. BABUSHKINA. LITERATURA O VOLOGOSKOI OBLASTI. 1976. a. Vologodskaya Oblastnaya Biblioteka, Spravochno-Bibliograficheskii Otdel, Zhdanova, i, 160000, Vologda, Russian S.F.S.R., U.S.S.R.

830　　　　NE
VOORZETTEN. 1985. irreg. price varies. (Nederlandse Taalunie) Stichting Bibliographia Neerlandica, P.O. Box 90407, 2509 LK The Hague, Netherlands. TEL (070)14 02 85. Ed. Oscar de Wandel.

820　　　　UK
WAKE NEWSLITTER MONOGRAPHS. 1962. irreg. £3($5) per issue. Awake Newsletter Press, c/o University of Essex, Department of Literature, Wivenhoe Park, Colchester, Essex CO4 3SQ, England. Ed. Clive Hart. bk. rev. circ. 900.

809　　　　US　ISSN 0083-7210
WARD - PHILLIPS LECTURES IN ENGLISH LANGUAGE AND LITERATURE. 1967. irreg., no. 10, 1979. price varies. ‡ (University of Notre Dame, Department of English) University of Notre Dame Press, Notre Dame, IN 46556. TEL 219-239-6346. Indexed: Cath.Ind.

810　　　　US　ISSN 0278-4947
WHAT'S COOKING IN CONGRESS? 1979. biennial. $7.95. (Harian Creative Associates) Harian Creative Press-Books, 47 Hyde Blvd., Ballston Spa, NY 12020. TEL 518-885-7397. Eds. Harry Barba, Marian Barba. circ. 5,000.
　　Former titles: Harian Creative Press; Harian Press (ISSN 0017-7776)

800　　　　US
WHAT'S NEW ABOUT LONDON, JACK? (Companion to Chaney Chronical) 1971. irreg. $5 for 10 nos. London Northwest, 929 South Bay Rd., Olympia, WA 98506. Ed. David H. Schlottman. adv. bk. rev. bibl. film rev. play rev. circ. 70. (processed)

808　　　　US
WHICH WAY.* irreg., no. 4, 1982. c/o Don Byrd, 51 Marlboro Rd., Delmar, NY 12054-2924. Eds. Jed Rasula, Don Byrd.

WHISPERS. see ADVENTURE AND ROMANCE

800　　　　GE
WIELANDS BRIEFWECHSEL. 1963. irreg., vol.5, 1983. (Akademie der Wissenschaften der DDR) Akademie-Verlag Berlin, Leipziger Str. 3-4, 1086 Berlin, E. Germany (D.D.R.)

830　　　　AU　ISSN 0083-9906
WIENER ARBEITEN ZUR DEUTSCHEN LITERATUR. 1970. a. price varies. Wilhelm Braumueller, Universitaets-Verlagsbuchhandlung GmbH, Servitengasse 5, A-1092 Vienna, Austria. Eds. Wendelin Schmidt-Dengler, Werner Welzig. index. circ. 1,000. Indexed: M.L.A.

WIENER BEITRAEGE ZUR ENGLISCHEN PHILOLOGIE. see LINGUISTICS

830 831　　AU　ISSN 0250-443X
WIENER-GOETHE-VEREIN. JAHRBUCH. 1878. a. S.150. Wiener-Goethe-Verein, Stallburggasse 2, A-1010 Vienna, Austria. Ed. Herbert Zeman. adv. bk. rev. circ. 550.

WIENER ROMANISTISCHE ARBEITEN. see LINGUISTICS

807 700　　US
WINTERFARE. a. Arts and Business Council, Inc., 130 E. 40 St., New York, NY 10016. TEL 212-683-5555.

808.83　　　UK　ISSN 0084-0394
WINTER'S TALES; an anthology of long short stories. 1955. a. £4.95($9.95) Macmillan Journals Ltd. (Subsidiary of: Macmillan Publishers Ltd.) 4 Little Essex St., London W.C.2, England. Ed. A.D. Maclean. circ. 4,000.

810 370　　US
WISCONSIN COUNCIL OF TEACHERS OF ENGLISH. SERVICE BULLETIN SERIES. no.24, 1979. irreg. price varies. Wisconsin Council of Teachers of English, c/o Nicholas J. Karolides, Ed., University of Wisconsin-River Falls, River Falls, WI 54022. TEL 715-425-3284. adv. bk. rev. circ. 600. (back issues avail.)

800 700　　US
WITTENBERG REVIEW OF LITERATURE AND ART. 1977. a. Wittenberg University, Box 1, Recitation Hall, Springfield, OH 45501. TEL 513-327-6231. Eds. Marty Lammon, Jill Gassaway. illus. circ. 900.

WOLFENBUETTELER STUDIEN ZUR AUFKLAERUNG. SCHRIFTENREIHE. see HISTORY

WOMEN & LITERATURE; a journal of women writers and the literary treatment of women. see WOMEN'S INTERESTS

WOOLNER INDOLOGICAL SERIES. see PHILOSOPHY

WORLD HUMOR AND IRONY MEMBERSHIP SERIAL YEARBOOK. see LINGUISTICS

800　　　　CN　ISSN 0316-3768
WRIT. 1970. a. Can.$12($12) for 2 nos. c/o Innis College, University of Toronto, 2 Sussex Ave., Toronto, Ont. M5S 1J5, Canada. TEL 416-978-4871. Ed. Roger Greenwald. index. circ. 700. (back issues avail.)

808　　　　UK　ISSN 0260-2776
WRITER (PENZANCE) 1963. a. £9. United Writers Publications Ltd., Ailsa, Castle Gate, Penzance TR20 8BG, Cornwall, England. Ed. Sydney Sheppard. adv. bk. rev. illus. mkt. tr.lit. circ. 4,000.
　　Incorporating: Writer's Review (ISSN 0043-9568)

808　　　　UK
WRITERS' AND POETS' YEARBOOK. a. United Writers Publications Ltd., Ailsa, Castle Gate, Penzance, Cornwall, England.

810　　　　US　ISSN 0960-2992
WRITERS FORUM. 1974. a. $8.95. University of Colorado at Colorado Springs, Colorado Springs, CO 80907. TEL 303-599-4023. Ed. Alex Blackburn. adv. circ. 1,000. (also avail. in microfiche; back issues avail.)

WRITERS INK. see PUBLISHING AND BOOK TRADE

800　　　　UK　ISSN 0141-5050
WRITERS OF WALES. 1970. irreg. price varies. (Welsh Arts Council) University of Wales Press, 6 Gwennyth St., Cathays, Cardiff CF2 4YD, Wales. Eds. Meic Stephens, R. Brinley Jones.

828　　　　II
WRITERS WORKSHOP LITERARY READER. (Text in English) 1972. irreg. Rs.60 hardback; Rs. 15 flexiback. Writers Workshop, 162-92 Lake Gardens, Calcutta 700045, India. Ed. P. Lal. circ. 1, 000.

810　　　　US　ISSN 0084-2745
WRITING (SAN FRANCISCO) 1964. irreg., no.43, 1983. price varies. Four Seasons Foundation, Box 31190, San Francisco, CA 94131 (Dist. by: Subco, Box 10233, Eugene, OR 97440) Ed. Donald Allen. circ. 3,000. (also avail. in microfiche from BLH)

890 418.02 407　　NE
WRITING IN HOLLAND AND FLANDERS. (Text in English) 1956. irreg. free. Foundation for the Promotion of the Translation of Dutch Literary Works, Singel 450, 1017 AV Amsterdam, Netherlands. Ed.Bd. bk. rev. bibl. illus. circ. 3,500.
　　Formerly: Literary Holland.

808　　　　US
WRITING RESEARCH. 1984. irreg. price varies. Ablex Publishing Corp., 355 Chestnut St., Norwood, NJ 07648. TEL 201-767-8450. Ed. Marcia Farr.

800　　　　GW　ISSN 0341-2172
WUPPERTALER SCHRIFTENREIHE LITERATUR. 1976. irreg., vol.22, 1982. price varies. Bouvier Verlag Herbert Grundmann, Am Hof 32, Postfach 1268, 5300 Bonn 1, W. Germany (B.R.D.) (Subscr. to: VVA Guetersloh, Postfach 7777, D-4830 Guetersloh 1, W. Germany) Ed.Bd.
　　Formerly: Gesamthochschule Wuppertalerschriftenreihe Literaturwissenschaft.

WYZSZA SZKOLA PEDAGOGICZNA, OPOLE. ZESZYTY NAUKOWE. FILOLOGIA POLSKA. see LINGUISTICS

890　　　　PL　ISSN 0474-2974
WYZSZA SZKOLA PEDAGOGICZNA, OPOLE. ZESZYTY NAUKOWE. SERIA A. FILOLOGIA ROSYJSKA. (Text in Polish and Russian; summaries in Russian) 1962. irreg., vol.23, 1983. price varies; avail. on exchange basis. Wyzsza Szkola Pedagogiczna, Opole, Oleska 48, 45-052 Opole, Poland (Dist. by: Ars Polona-Ruch, Krakowskie Przedmiescie 7, Warsaw, Poland)

800　　　　US
XTRAS. 1975. irreg., no.11, 1985. price varies. From Here Press, Box 219, Fanwood, NJ 07023. Eds. William J. Higginson, Penny Harter. circ. 750. (back issues avail.)

LITERATURE — ABSTRACTING, BIBLIOGRAPHIES, STATISTICS

820   CN   ISSN 0704-5697
Y E R MONOGRAPH SERIES. (Yeats Elliot Review) 1978. irreg. Can.$8. University of Victoria, Department of English, Victoria, B.C., Canada. TEL 604-721-7211. Indexed: M.L.A.

830   US   ISSN 0084-3334
YALE GERMANIC STUDIES. 1964. irreg., no.6, 1976. price varies. Yale University Press, 92A Yale Sta., New Haven, CT 06520. TEL 203-432-0940. Indexed: M.L.A.

879.9   US   ISSN 0084-3423
YALE ROMANIC STUDIES. SECOND SERIES. 1951. irreg., no.26, 1976. price varies. Yale University Press, 92A Yale Sta., New Haven, CT 06520. TEL 203-432-0940.

891.8   US   ISSN 0084-3431
YALE RUSSIAN AND EAST EUROPEAN STUDIES. 1966. irreg., no.14, 1978. Yale University Press, 92A Yale Sta., New Haven, CT 06520 TEL 203-432-0940. (Dist. by: Slavica Publishers, Inc., Box 14388, Columbus, OH 43214) Eds. Alexander M. Schenker, Edward Stankiewicz.

820 810   US   ISSN 0084-3482
YALE STUDIES IN ENGLISH. 1898. irreg., no.190, 1981. price varies. Yale University Press, 92A Yale Sta., New Haven, CT 06520. TEL 203-432-0940. Indexed: M.L.A.

800   US   ISSN 0084-3695
YEARBOOK OF COMPARATIVE AND GENERAL LITERATURE. (Issued 1952-60 as subseries of University of North Carolina, Studies in Comparative Literature) 1952. a. $10 per vol. Indiana University, Comparative Literature Program, Ballantine Hall 402, Bloomington, IN 47405 TEL 812-335-2140. (Vols.1-11, 1952-62; Available from Scribner Distribution Center, Inc., 12 Vreeland Ave., Totowa, NJ 07512) Ed. Claus Cluver. bk. rev. circ. 1,375. (also avail. in microform from UMI; reprint service avail. from UMI) Indexed: M.L.A. Amer.Hum.Ind. Amer.Bibl.Slavic & E.Eur.Stud. Abstr.Engl.Stud. Can.Rev.Comp.Lit. Ind.Bk.Rev.Hum. LCR.

809.915   US   ISSN 0084-3709
YEARBOOK OF COMPARATIVE CRITICISM. 1968. irreg., vol. 10, 1982. $22.50. Pennsylvania State University Press, 215 Wagner Bldg., University Park, PA 16802. TEL 814-865-1327. Ed. Joseph Strelka. (reprint service avail. from UMI) Indexed: M.L.A. Can.Rev.Comp.Lit.

YEARBOOK OF ENGLISH STUDIES. see
HUMANITIES: COMPREHENSIVE WORKS

800   US
YEARBOOK OF GERMAN-AMERICAN STUDIES. (Text and summaries in English and German) 1969. a. membership. Society for German-American Studies, c/o C. Richard Beam, Treasurer, 406 Spring Dr., Millersville, PA 17551. Eds. Helmut Huelsbergen, William Keel. adv. bk. rev. bibl. circ. 300. Indexed: M.L.A.
Supersedes (after vol.15): Journal of German-American Studies; Formerly (until vol. 11, 1976): German-American Studies (ISSN 0046-5836)

840 947   US   ISSN 0149-7219
YEARBOOK OF ROMANIAN STUDIES. 1976. a. $5. Romanian Studies Association of America, c/o Paul G. Teodorescu, Ed., 7 John Circle, No. 4, Salinas, CA 93905. adv. bk. rev. circ. 250. Indexed: M.L.A. Amer.Bibl.Slavic & E.Eur.Stud.

820.6   US   ISSN 0084-4144
YEAR'S WORK IN ENGLISH STUDIES. 1919. a. price varies. Humanities Press, Inc., 171 First Ave., Atlantic Highlands, NJ 07716. TEL 201-872-1441. bk. rev. index. Indexed: Br.Hum.Ind. Hum.Ind. M.L.A.

809   US
YEATS; an annual of critical and textual studies. 1983. a. Cornell University Press, Yeats: An Annual of Critical and Textual Studies, 124 Roberts Pl., Ithaca, NY 14850. Ed. Richard J. Finneran.

YEATS ELIOT REVIEW. see *LITERATURE — Poetry*

296 830   IS   ISSN 0334-9594
YERUSHOLAIMER ALMANAKH. (Text in Yiddish) 1973. a. $15. Yidishe Shrayber Grupe in Yerusholaim - Yiddish Writers Group in Jerusalem, Shederot Eshkol 12/6, Jerusalem, Israel. Ed. Yoysef Kerler. bk. rev. illus. circ. 700. Indexed: M.L.A.

YIDDISH LITERARY AND LINGUISTIC PERIODICALS AND MISCELLANIES; a selective annotated bibliography. see *LINGUISTICS*

891.85   PL   ISSN 0084-4411
Z DZIEJOW FORM ARTYSTYCZNYCH W LITERATURZE POLSKIEJ. (Text in Polish) 1963. irreg., vol.68, 1985. price varies. (Polska Akademia Nauk, Instytut Badan Literackich) Ossolineum, Publishing House of the Polish Academy of Sciences, Rynek 9, 50-106 Wroclaw, Poland (Dist. by: Ars Polona-Ruch, Krakowskie Przedmiescie 7, Warsaw, Poland)

891.82   YU   ISSN 0084-5183
ZBORNIK ISTORIJE KNJIZEVNOSTI/RECUEIL DES TRAVAUX DE L'HISTOIRE DE LA LITTERATURE. (Text in Serbo-Croatian; summaries in English, French, German or Russian) 1960. irreg. price varies. Srpska Akademija Nauka i Umetnosti, Odeljenje Jezika i Knjizevnosti, Knez Mihailova 35, 11001 Belgrade, Yugoslavia (Dist. by: Prosveta, Terazije 16, Belgrade, Yugoslavia) circ. 1, 000. Indexed: M.L.A.

891.82   YU   ISSN 0084-5205
ZBORNIK ZA ISTORIJU, JEZIK I KNJIZEVNOST SRPSKOG NARODA. SPOMENICI NA SRPSKOM JEZIKU. (Text in Serbo-Croatian; summaries in English, French, German or Russian) 1902. irreg. price varies. Srpska Akademija Nauka i Umetnosti, Knez Mihailova 35, 11001 Belgrade, Yugoslavia (Dist. by Prosveta, Terazije 16, Belgrade, Yugoslavia) circ. 1,000.

ZEITSCHRIFT FUER CELTISCHE PHILOLOGIE. see *LINGUISTICS*

ZEITSCHRIFT FUER ROMANISCHE PHILOLOGIE. BEIHEFTE. see *LINGUISTICS*

ZENTRALINSTITUTS FUER ALTE GESCHICHTE UND ARCHAEOLOGIE. VEROEFFENTLICHEN. see *HISTORY*

808   SZ
2 PLUS 2; collection of international writing. 1983. a. $15.95. Mylabris Press, Case Postale 35, 1000 Lausanne 25, Switzerland. Ed. James Gill. circ. 3, 500. (back issues avail.)

810 301.412   US   ISSN 0094-3320
13TH MOON; a feminist literary magazine. 1973. irreg. $13 per 2 vols. to individuals; institutions $26. 13th Moon, Inc., Box 309, Cathedral Sta., New York, NY 10025. Ed. Marilyn Hacker. adv. bk. rev. illus. circ. 3,000. Indexed: M L A. A.I.P.P. Abstr.Pop.Cult. Amer.Hum.Ind. Ind.Amer.Per.Verse.

808   US
23 CLUB SERIES. 1971. irreg. Intrepid Press, Box 110, Buffalo, NY 14215. Ed. Allen DeLoach. circ. 1,000.

LITERATURE — Abstracting, Bibliographies, Statistics

820 016   AT   ISSN 0084-7216
A.A.T.E. GUIDE TO ENGLISH BOOKS. 1970. a. Aus.$3 (or Aus.$12 for combined subscription with English in Australia) Australian Association for the Teaching of English, Box 203, Norwood, S.A. 5067, Australia. Ed. B. Devlin. adv. bk. rev. index. circ. 5, 000.

AMERICAN HUMANITIES INDEX. see
HUMANITIES: COMPREHENSIVE WORKS — Abstracting, Bibliographies, Statistics

001   US
AMERICAN POETRY INDEX. 1983. a. $46. Poetry Index Press, Roth Publishing, Inc., Box 406, Great Neck, NY 11022. TEL 516-466-3676.

016 820   US
ANNOTATED SECONDARY BIBLIOGRAPHY SERIES ON ENGLISH LITERATURE IN TRANSITION, 1880-1920. irreg. price varies. Northern Illinois University Press, Dekalb, IL 60115. TEL 815-753-1826.

420 016   UK   ISSN 0066-3786
ANNUAL BIBLIOGRAPHY OF ENGLISH LANGUAGE AND LITERATURE. 1920. a. $104.50. Modern Humanities Research Association, Kings College, London WC2R 2LS, England (Vols. 1-39 avail. from: Wm. Dawson & Sons Ltd., Cannon House, Folkstone, Kent, England) Eds. E. Erskine, M.J. De Marr.

016 820   UK   ISSN 0307-9864
ANNUAL BIBLIOGRAPHY OF SCOTTISH LITERATURE. 1969. a. $9. Library Association, Scottish Group, Edinburgh University Library, Edinburgh EH8 9LJ, Scotland. Eds. J. Kidd, R.H. Carnie. adv. bk. rev. circ. 400. Indexed: LISA. Abstr.Engl.Stud.

800 016   CN   ISSN 0227-1400
ANNUAL BIBLIOGRAPHY OF VICTORIAN STUDIES. 1977. a. LITIR Database, c/o Department of English, University of Alberta, Edmonton, Alta. T6G 2E5, Canada. TEL 403-432-3258. Ed. Brahma Chaudhuri. cum.index every 5 years.

811   US   ISSN 0882-195X
ANNUAL INDEX TO POETRY IN PERIODICALS. 1985. a. $39.99. Poetry Index Press, Roth Publishing, Inc., Box 406, Great Neck, NY 11022. TEL 516-466-3676. (back issues avail.)

800   FR
ARGUS DU LIVRE DE COLLECTION ET DE L'AUTOGRAPHE. (Text in English and French) 1981. a. 800 F. Promodis, 18 rue Dauphine, 75006 Paris, France. Ed. Jean-Pierre Vivet.
Formerly: Argus du Livre Ancien et Moderne (ISSN 0242-5823)

860 016   SP
BIBLIOGRAFIA DE LA LITERATURA HISPANICA. 1960. irreg. (Consejo Superior de Investigaciones Cientificas) Libreria Cientifica Medinaceli, Vitrubio 16, Madrid 6, Spain. Ed. Jose Simon Diaz.

809 016   IT
BIBLIOGRAFIA E STORIA DELLA CRITICA. irreg. Angelo Longo Editore, Via Paolo Costa 33, P.O. Box 431, 48100 Ravenna, Italy. Ed. Enzo Esposito.

016 830   GW   ISSN 0341-9363
BIBLIOGRAPHIE DER DEUTSCHEN SPRACH- UND LITERATURWISSENSCHAFT. 1957. a. DM.190 (approx.) Vittorio Klostermann, Frauenlobstr. 22, Postfach 900601, 6000 Frankfurt 90, W. Germany (B.R.D.) Ed. Bernhard Kossmann. circ. 2,000.
Formerly: Bibliographie der Deutschen Literaturwissenschaft.

800   SZ
BIBLIOGRAPHIE DER DEUTSCHSPRACHIGEN SCHWEIZERLITERATUR. (Text in French and German) 1976. a. 25 Fr. Bibliotheque National Suisse, Hallwylstr. 15, 3003 Berne, Switzerland. Ed. Gaby Rauch. bk. rev. circ. 75.

016 840   GW   ISSN 0523-2465
BIBLIOGRAPHIE DER FRANZOESISCHEN LITERATURWISSENSCHAFT. 1960. a. DM.250 (approx.) Vittorio Klostermann, Frauenlobstr. 22, 6000 Frankfurt 90, W. Germany (B.R.D.) Ed. Otto Klapp. circ. 1,500.

830 430 016   GW   ISSN 0172-3960
BIBLIOGRAPHIE LINGUISTISCHER LITERATUR. a. DM.434 (approx.) Vittorio Klostermann, Frauenlobstr. 22, Postfach 900601, D-6000 Frankfurt 90, W. Germany(B.R.D.)
Formerly (1976-1978): Bibliographie Unselbstaendiger Literatur-Linguistik.

830   GW   ISSN 0523-2767
BIBLIOGRAPHIEN ZUR DEUTSCHEN LITERATUR DES MITTELALTERS. 1966. irreg., latest vol.8, 1981. price varies. Erich Schmidt Verlag GmbH, Viktoriastr. 44a, 4800 Bielefeld 1, Berlin, W. Germany (B.R.D.) Eds. Ulrich Pretzel, Wolfgang Bachofer. (back issues avail.) Indexed: M.L.A.

840 GW ISSN 0171-0125
BIBLIOGRAPHIEN ZUR ROMANISTIK. (Text in French) 1981. irreg. price varies. Edition Gemini, Nonnenwerthstr. 66, D-5000 Koeln 41, West Germany (B.R.D.) Ed. Gernot U. Gabel. circ. 200. (back issues avail.)

810 US ISSN 0742-6860
BIBLIOGRAPHIES AND INDEXES IN AMERICAN LITERATURE. 1984. irreg. price varies. Greenwood Press, 88 Post Rd. W., Box 5007, Westport, CT 06881. TEL 203-226-3571.

808 US ISSN 0742-6801
BIBLIOGRAPHIES AND INDEXES IN WORLD LITERATURE. 1984. irreg. price varies. Greenwood Press, 88 Post Rd. W., Box 5007, Westport, CT 06881. TEL 203-226-3571.

800 016 DK ISSN 0067-8473
BIDRAG TIL H. C. ANDERSENS BIBLIOGRAFI. 1966. irreg., vol.10, 1979. price varies. Kongelige Bibliotek, Christians Brygge 8, DK-1219 Copenhagen K, Denmark.

810 US ISSN 0742-695X
BIO-BIBLIOGRAPHIES IN AMERICAN LITERATURE. 1984. irreg. price varies. Greenwood Press, 88 Post Rd. W., Box 5007, Westport, CT 06881. TEL 203-226-3571.

016 US ISSN 0524-0581
BOOK REVIEW INDEX: ANNUAL CLOTHBOUND CUMULATIONS. 1965. a. $160 per vol. Gale Research Company, Book Tower, Detroit, MI 48226. TEL 313-961-2242. Ed. Barbara Beach. (back issues avail.)

016 028.1 GW ISSN 0068-3396
EIN BUECHERTAGEBUCH; Buchbesprechungen aus der Frankfurter Allgemeinen Zeitung. 1967. a. DM.18. Frankfurter Allgemeine Zeitung, Postfach 100808, Hellerhofstr. 2-4, 6000 Frankfurt am Main 1, W. Germany (B.R.D.) bk. rev. circ. 15,000.

016 880 US ISSN 0528-2594
CATALOGUS TRANSLATIONEM ET COMMENTATORIUM; Medieval and Renaissance Latin translations. 1960. irreg., latest issue, vol.6. price varies. Catholic University of America Press, 620 Michigan Ave., N.E., Washington, DC 20064. TEL 202-635-5052. (reprint service avail. from UMI)

800 FR
CENTRO CULTURAL PORTUGUES. ARQUIVOS. 1969. a. 300 F. Centro Cultural Portugues, Fundacao Calouste Gulbencian, 51 Ave d'Iena, 75016 Paris, France (Subscr.to: Jean Touzot/Editeur Libraire, 38 rue de Saint-Sulpice, 75006 Paris, France) Ed. Jose Augusto Franca. bk. rev. circ. 1, 000.

CHILDREN'S AUTHORS AND ILLUSTRATORS; an index to biographical dictionaries. see BIOGRAPHY — Abstracting, Bibliographies, Statistics

028.5 370 US ISSN 0069-3480
CHILDREN'S BOOKS IN PRINT. 1962. a. $79.95. R.R. Bowker Company, Database Publishing Group, 245 W. 17th St., New York, NY 10011. TEL 800-521-8110.
●Also available online.
Formerly: Children's Books for Schools and Libraries.

CURRENT RESEARCH IN FRENCH STUDIES AT UNIVERSITIES AND POLYTECHNICS IN THE UNITED KINGDOM. see LINGUISTICS — Abstracting, Bibliographies, Statistics

015 DK ISSN 0070-2714
DANIA POLYGLOTTA; literature on Denmark in languages other than Danish and books of Danish interest published abroad. 1947; N.S. 1969. a. price varies. Kongelige Bibliotek, Danish Department, Christians Brygge 8, 1219 Copenhagen K, Denmark (Avail. on exchange from: I.D.E., Danmarks Institut for International Udveksling, Amaliegade 38, DK-1256 Copenhagen K, Denmark) Eds. Sven C. Jacobsen, Jan William Rasmussen.

DOCUMENTATIEBLAD: THE ABSTRACTS JOURNAL OF THE AFRICAN STUDIES CENTRE LEIDEN. see HISTORY — Abstracting, Bibliographies, Statistics

E I. (Excerpta Indonesica) see ANTHROPOLOGY — Abstracting, Bibliographies, Statistics

800 011 US ISSN 0160-4880
FICTION CATALOG. quinquennial w. annual supplements. $70. ‡ H. W. Wilson Co., 950 University Ave., Bronx, NY 10452. TEL 212-588-8400. Ed. Juliette Yaakov.

800 ISSN 0271-6607
FRENCH LITERATURE SERIES. 1974. a. $11. University of South Carolina, Department of Foreign Languages, Columbia, SC 29208. TEL 803-777-4881. Ed. A. Maynor Hardee. bibl. circ. 300. (back issues avail.) Indexed: M.L.A.

016 US ISSN 0090-9130
INDEX OF AMERICAN PERIODICAL VERSE. 1971. a. Scarecrow Press, Inc., 52 Liberty St., Box 4167, Metuchen, NJ 08840. TEL 201-548-8600. Ed. S.W. Zulauf. circ. 3,000.

800 016 UK
INDEX OF ENGLISH LITERARY MANUSCRIPTS. 1980. irreg. price varies. Mansell Publishing Ltd., 6 All Saints St., London N1 9RL, England (Dist. in U.S. by: H.W. Wilson Co., 950 University Ave., Bronx, NY 10452)

820 398 CN ISSN 0074-1388
INTERNATIONAL ARTHURIAN SOCIETY. BIBLIOGRAPHICAL BULLETIN/SOCIETE INTERNATIONALE ARTHURIENNE. BULLETIN BIBLIOGRAPHIQUE. (Text in English and French) 1949. a. $18 to non-members; members $15. International Arthurian Society, c/o Hans R. Runte, Sec.-Treas., Dalhousie University, Department of French, Halifax, Nova Scotia B3H 3J5, Canada. TEL 902-424-2430. Ed. Douglas Kelly. bk. rev. bibl. circ. 1,000. (back issues avail.) Indexed: MLA.
Supersedes: International Arthurian Society. Report on Congress (ISSN 0074-1396)

KOVCEZIC. see LINGUISTICS

890 NE
LITERAIRE TIJDSCHRIFTEN IN NEDERLAND; bibliografische beschrijvingen, analytische inhoudsopgaven en indices. 1975. irreg., latest no. 6, 1986. price varies. De Graaf Publishers, Postbus 6, 2420 AA Nieuwkoop, Netherlands.

809 011 US
LITERARY CRITICISM REGISTER; a monthly listing of studies in English and American literature. 1983. m. $34 to individuals; institutions $59. Literary Criticism Register, Drawer CC, DeLand, FL 32721. TEL 904-736-6029. Ed. Sims D. Kline. adv. cum.index. circ. 1,000.
Formerly: L C R (ISSN 0733-2165)

890 DK ISSN 0108-7215
LITTERATUR PAA INDVANDRERSPROG I DANSKE FOLKEBIBLIOTEKER. 1983. a. Kr.560. Bibliotekscentralen, Tempovej 7-11, 2750 Ballerup, Denmark.

890 DK ISSN 0108-9633
LITTERATUR PAA INDVANDRERSPROG I DANSKE FOLKEBIBLIOTEKER. SERBOKROATISK. 1983. a. Kr.262.30. Bibliotekscentralen, Telegrafvej 5, 2750 Ballerup, Denmark.

890 DK ISSN 0108-9641
LITTERATUR PAA INDVANDRERSPROG I DANSKE FOLKEBIBLIOTEKER. TYRKISK. 1983. a. Kr.585.20. Bibliotekscentralen, Tempovej 7-11, 2750 Ballerup, Denmark.

890 DK ISSN 0108-965X
LITTERATUR PAA INDVANDRERSPROG I DANSKE FOLKEBIBLIOTEKER. URDU. 1983. a. Kr.470.40. Bibliotekscentralen, Tempovej 7-11, 2750 Ballerup, Denmark.

800 400 016 US ISSN 0197-0380
M L A DIRECTORY OF PERIODICALS; a guide to journals and series in languages and literatures. 1979. biennial. $100. Modern Language Association of America, 10 Astor Pl., New York, NY 10011. TEL 212-614-6314. Ed. Eileen M. Mackesy.

808 US
PITTSBURGH SERIES IN BIBLIOGRAPHY. 1972. a. price varies. University of Pittsburgh Press, 127 North Bellefield Ave., Pittsburgh, PA 15260. TEL 412-624-4110. Ed. Matthew J. Bruccoli.

800 016 US ISSN 0554-3037
PLAY INDEX. quinquennial. $40. H. W. Wilson Co., 950 University Ave., Bronx, NY 10452. TEL 212-588-8400. Ed. Juliette Yaakov.

PLAYWRIGHTS UNION OF CANADA CATALOGUE OF CANADIAN PLAYS. see THEATER — Abstracting, Bibliographies, Statistics

891.85 016 PL ISSN 0079-3590
POLSKA BIBLIOGRAFIA LITERACKA. 1944. irreg. price varies. (Polska Akademia Nauk, Instytut Badan Literackich) Panstwowe Wydawnictwo Naukowe, Ul. Miodowa 10, 00-251 Warsaw, Poland (Dist. by: Ars Polona, Krakowskie Przedmiescie 7, 00-068 Warsaw, Poland) Ed. J. Czachowska. circ. 700.

890 SW ISSN 0348-6133
SAMLAREN; tidskrift for Svensk litteraturvetenskaplig forskning. (Text and summaries in English, German and Swedish) 1880. a. Kr.80. Humanistisk Samhallsvetenskapligt Centrum, Box 513, 75120 Uppsala, Sweden. Ed. Ulf Wittrock. circ. 1,000. (back issues avail.)

800 016 US ISSN 0360-9774
SHORT STORY INDEX; an index to stories in collections and periodicals. 1900. a. plus 5 yr. cumulation. $44. H. W. Wilson Co., 950 University Ave., Bronx, NY 10452. TEL 212-588-8400. Ed. Juliette Yaakov.

808 US ISSN 0742-8936
SOUTH DAKOTA AUTHORS' CATALOG. 1981. biennial. $5. South Dakota State Poetry Society, Box 326, Harrisburg, SD 57032. TEL 605-361-6942. Ed. Janet Leih. adv. bk. rev. circ. 200.

800 DK ISSN 0106-6641
UDENLANDSK LITTERATUR I DANSKE FOLKEBIBLIOTEKER. SKOENLITTERATUR. 1972. a. Kr.7737.50. Bibliotekscentralen, Tempovej 7-11, DK-2750 Ballerup, Denmark.

016 800 AT ISSN 0158-3921
VICTORIAN FICTION RESEARCH GUIDES. 1979. irreg. (3-4/yr.) Aus.$16($20) University of Queensland, Department of English, St. Lucia, Qld. 4067, Australia. Ed. P.D. Edwards. circ. 300. (back issues avail.) Indexed: M.L.A.

405 UK ISSN 0084-4152
YEAR'S WORK IN MODERN LANGUAGE STUDIES. 1929-30. a. $108. Modern Humanities Research Association, King's College, London WC2, England (Vols.1-29 avail. from: Wm. Dawson & Sons Ltd., Cannon House, Folkstone, Kent, England) Ed. G. Price. index. circ. 850. Indexed: Br.Hum.Ind. M.L.A.
Critical bibliography of language and literature (modern and Medieval) for all European languages except English

LITERATURE — Poetry

808.81 US
A M S ARS POETICA. 1983. irreg., no.3, 1986. price varies. A M S Press, Inc., 56 E. 13th St., New York, NY 10003. TEL 212-777-4700. (back issues avail.)
Formerly: A M S Studies in Ars Poetica (ISSN 0734-7618)

810 US
ACADEMY OF AMERICAN POETS. LAMONT POETRY SELECTION AND WALT WHITMAN SELECTION. 1954. a. $35. Academy of American Poets, 177 E. 87th St., New York, NY 10128.
Formerly: Academy of American Poets. Lamont Poetry Selections (ISSN 0515-2003)

861 MX ISSN 0185-3082
ACTA POETICA. 1979. a. price varies. Universidad Nacional Autonoma de Mexico, Instituto de Investigaciones Filologicas, Ciudad Universitaria, C.P. 04510, Mexico 21 D.F., Mexico.

LITERATURE — POETRY

861 SP
AKAL BOLSILLO. irreg., no. 63, 1983. Paseo de Sta. Maria de la Cabeza 132, Madrid 26, Spain. Ed. Ramon Akal Gonzalez.

ALCHEMIST. see LITERATURE

821 UK ISSN 0140-5136
ALEMBIC. 1973. a. $20 for 4 nos. Flat 2, 129 West End Lane, London N.W.6, England. Ed. Robert Hampson. adv. bk. rev. bibl. circ. 200. (back issues avail.)

808.81 UA
ALIF; journal of comparative poetics. (Text in Arabic and English) 1981. a. £E2($5) American University in Cario, Department of English and Comparative Literature, P.O. Box 2511, Cairo, Egypt. circ. 500. (back issues avail.)

831 053 GW ISSN 0720-3098
ALLMENDE; eine alemannische Zeitschrift. 1981. irreg. DM.16. Elster Verlag, Engelstr. 6, D-7580 Buehl/Moos, W. Germany (B.R.D.) Ed.Bd. adv. index. circ. 3,000. (back issues avail.)

811 US ISSN 0162-8208
ALTADENA REVIEW. 1978. irreg. $5 for 2 issues. Altadena Review, Inc., Box 212, Altadena, CA 91001. Ed. Robin Shectman. bk. rev. circ. 300. (back issues avail.) Indexed: A.I.P.P.

ALTRIVE CHAPBOOKS. see LITERATURE

811 US
AMERICAN POETRY ANTHOLOGY. 1981. irreg. (3-4/yr.) $35. American Poetry Association, Box 8403, Santa Cruz, CA 95061-8403. Ed. John Frost. circ. 10,000.

AMERICAN POETRY INDEX. see LITERATURE — Abstracting, Bibliographies, Statistics

811 US
AMERICAN POETRY SERIES. 1973. irreg., vol.32, 1985. price varies. Ecco Press Ltd., 18 W. 30 St., New York, NY 10001. TEL 212-685-8240.

808.81 US
ANDROGYNE; a rebus of poetry, fiction & graphic art. 1971. a. $2.50. Androgyne Books, 930 Shields St., San Francisco, CA 94132. Ed. Ken Weichel. adv. bk. rev. circ. 500. (back issues avail.)

800 US
ANGELSTONE. 1978. a. $5. Angelstone Press, 316 Woodland Dr., Birmingham, AL 35209. Ed.Bd. circ. 300.

811 US ISSN 0196-2221
ANTHOLOGY OF MAGAZINE VERSE AND YEARBOOK OF AMERICAN POETRY. 1980. a. $35. Monitor Book Co., Inc., 9441 Wilshire Blvd., Box 3668, Beverly Hills, CA 90212. TEL 213-271-5558. Ed. Alan F. Pater. Indexed: Child.Auth.& Illus.
Formerly: Anthology of Magazine Verse (ISSN 0270-3904)

861 AG
ANTOLOGIA POETICA DEL PARTIDO DE ESTEBAN ECHEVERRIA. 1979. a. Arg.$10000. (Asociacion de Artes y Letras de Esteban Echeverria) Ediciones Agon, Charcas 3918, 1425 Buenos Aires, Argentina. Dir. Maria E. Dubecq.

861 CK
AQUARIMANTIMA. 1973. irreg. Apdo. Aereo 3845, Medellin, Colombia.

861 AG
AQUARIO; revista internacional de poesia. 1977. irreg. $2.50. Paraguay 647, Buenos Aires, Argentina. Eds. Sergio Chaves, Sigfrido Radaelli.

ARC. see LITERATURE

808.81 US
ARCHIVE FOR NEW POETRY NEWSLETTER. 1978. irreg. price varies. (Archive for New Poetry) University of California, San Diego, Central University Library, La Jolla, CA 92903. TEL 619-452-3837. Ed. Michael Davidson.

808.1 FR ISSN 0066-734X
ARGUS DE LA POESIE FRANCAISE.* 1971. irreg. 30 F. Association Poesie Vivante France, B.P.8, 01210 Ferney-Voltaire, France.

ARSENAL; surrealist subversion. see ART

811 US
AVALON DISPATCH. irreg. (3-4/yr.) membership. (Avalon Poets) Vernon Payne, Ed. & Pub., 212 W. First St., San Angelo, TX 76901. circ. 500.

811 US ISSN 0067-5695
BELOIT POETRY JOURNAL. CHAPBOOK. 1951. irreg., approx. biennial, no.18, 1985. $2.50 included in subscr. to Beloit Poetry Journal. Beloit Poetry Journal, Box 154, RFD 2, Ellsworth, ME 04605. TEL 207-667-5598. Ed. Marion K. Stocking. circ. 1,100. Indexed: Amer.Hum.Ind. Ind.Amer.Per.Verse.

861 BL
BIBLIOTECA ALFA-OMEGA DE POESIA BRASILEIRA: SERIE 1. 1983. irreg. Editora Alfa-Omega, Rua Lisbon, 500, 05413 Sao Paulo, Brazil.

BIRTHSTONE. see ART

301 323 US ISSN 0084-7909
BLACK POSITION. 1971. irreg. no.3 & 4, 1974. $3. Broadside Press, Box 04257, Northwestern Station, Detroit, MI 38204-0257. Ed. Gwendolyn Brooks. circ. 2,000. Indexed: Ind.Per.Blacks.

811 US
BLACK RIVER REVIEW. a. $3. 855 Mildred, Lorain, OH 44052. TEL 216-244-9654. Eds. Jack Smith, Kaye Collier.

273 US
BLACKBERRY. (Chapbook series) 1974. irreg. (approx. 20/yr.) $2.50 per no. Blackberry Books, Chimney Farm, Nobleboro, ME 04555. Ed. Gary Lawless. bk. rev. circ. 650.

800 US
BLUE BUILDINGS. 1979. irreg. (1-2/yr.) $2. 1215 25th St., Apt. F, Des Moines, IA 50311-3005 (Or Department of English, Drake University, Des Moines, IA 50311) Ed.Bd. circ. 300.

811 US
BLUE PIG.* 1968. irreg. $5. 23 Cedar St., Northampton, MA 01060. circ. 250.

BOSS. see LITERATURE

808.81 US ISSN 0275-6080
BRAVO; the poet's magazine. 1980. a. $3.50. Bravo Editions, c/o John Edwin Cowen, Ltd, 1081 Trafalgar St., Teaneck, NJ 07666. TEL 201-836-5922. Ed. Jose Garcia Villa. circ. 1,000. (back issues avail.)

821 CN ISSN 0382-5272
BRITISH COLUMBIA MONTHLY. 1972. irreg. (6-10/yr.) Can.$20 to individuals; institutions Can.$35. B.C. Monthly Press, Box 48884, Vancouver, B.C. V7X 1A8, Canada. Ed. Gerry Gilbert. adv. bk. rev. index. circ. 350.

890 AT ISSN 0310-2467
BRONZE SWAGMAN BOOK OF BUSH VERSE. 1973. a. Aus.$6.50. Winton Tourist Promotion Association, Box 44, Winton, Qld. 4735, Australia. Ed.Bd. circ. 1,500.

821 UK ISSN 0301-7257
BYRON JOURNAL. 1973. a. £3. Byron Society Journal Ltd., 6 Gertrude St., London SW10 0JN, England. Ed.Bd. adv. bk. rev. circ. 2,000. (back issues avail.) Indexed: Curr.Cont. M.L.A. Arts & Hum.Cit.Ind.

811 US
CAFETERIA. 1971. irreg. $3. Cafeteria Press, 1724 Woodland Ave., Modesto, CA 95351. TEL 209-523-8916. Eds. Gordon Preston, Rick Robbins. bk. rev. circ. 300.

841 BE
CAHIERS NIVELLOIS. 1978. irreg. 250 Fr. Association Culturelle et Dialectale de la Region Nivelloise, Allee des Couterelles 4, 1400 Nivelles, Belgium.

841 FR
CAHIERS SAINT-JOHN PERSE. 1978. a. (Fondation St.-John Perse) Editions Gallimard, 5 rue Sebastien-Bottin, 75007 Paris, France. Ed. Jean-Louis Lalanne. circ. 1,200. (back issues avail.)

841 FR
CAHIERS TRISTAN L'HERMIT. 1979. a. price varies. Rougerie Editeur, Mortemart, 87330 Mezieres-sur-Issoire, France. Ed. M. Carriat. Indexed: Can.Rev.Vomp.Lit.

821 UK
CANDELABRUM. 1970. a. £1.50($4) Red Candle Press, 9 Milner Rd., Wisbech PE13 2LR, England. Eds. Basil Wincote, M.L. McCarthy. bk. rev. cum.index. circ. 1,000. (back issues avail.)

CARRIONFLOWER WRIT. see LITERATURE

811 US ISSN 0883-9174
CELEBRATION. 1975. irreg. $5 for 4 nos. Prospect Press, 2707 Lawina Rd., Baltimore, MD 21216. Ed. William J. Sullivan. circ. 300.

811 US
CENTERING. 1973. irreg. price varies. Years Press, ATL EBH, Michigan State University, East Lansing, MI 48824. TEL 517-332-5983. Ed. F. Richard Thomas. circ. 300.

808.81 IS
CHADARIM; magazine for poetry. 1981. a. $7.50. Gordon Gallery, Rehov Ben Yehuda 95, Tel Aviv 63 401, Israel. Ed. Helit Yeshurun. circ. 1,500.

808 US ISSN 0577-5574
CHARIOTEER; an annual review of modern Greek culture. (Text in English & Greek) 1960. a. $15. Pella Publishing, 337 W. 36th St., New York, NY 10018. Ed. Carmen Capri-Karka. adv. bk. rev. illus. circ. 1,000. (back issues avail.) Indexed: Amer.Bibl.Slavic & E.Eur.Stud.

CHILDHOOD IN POETRY. see CHILDREN AND YOUTH — Abstracting, Bibliographies, Statistics

811 760 US
CHOICE (BINGHAMTON); a magazine of poetry and graphics. 1961. a. $5. State University of New York at Binghamton, Box Z, Binghamton, NY 13901. TEL 607-798-2000. Eds. Milton Kessler, John Logan. circ. 1,000.

811 US
CIRCLE; a periodical of reversible poetry. 1975. biennial. $2 per no. ‡ Circle Forum, Box 176, Portland, OR 97207. Ed. J.M. Gates. bk. rev. circ. controlled. Indexed: CERDIC.

811 US
CIRCLETS; an occasional newsletter of reversible poetry. no. 4,1977. irreg. Circle Forum, Box 176, Portland, OR 97207.

861 US
CIRCULO POETICO; cuadernos de poesia. (Text in English, Spanish) 1970. a. $8. Circulo de Cultura Panamericano, 650 West Park Dr., Apt. 101, Miami, FL 33172. Ed. Ana H. Raggi. illus. circ. 800.

841 FR
CLIVAGES. 1974. irreg., no.8, 1986. Editions Clivages, 46 rue de l'Universite, Paris 75007, France. Ed. Jean P. Leger. adv. illus.

861 PO
COLECCAO FORMA. irreg., no. 16, 1983. Editorial Presenca, Lda., Rua Augusto Gil, 35-A, 1000 Lisbon, Portugal.

869 PO
COLECCAO: POESIA (LISBON) 1982. irreg. Edicoes CASO, R. Cons. A. Pedroso, 59-2 E, Lisbon, Portugal.

869 PO
COLECCAO POESIA (PORTO) no.3, 1982. irreg. Edicoes Afrontamento, Rua Costa Cabral, 859, 4200 Porto, Portugal.

861 SP
COLECCION "BAHIA". irreg., no.10, 1979. Ediciones Bahia, Fray Bartolome Bloque 1, Algeciras, Spain. Ed. Manual Fernandez Mota. circ. 700.

LITERATURE — POETRY

861   SP
COLECCION PENTESILEA. 1978. irreg. Ediciones Caballo Griego para la Poesia, Bolonia 3, Madrid 28, Spain. Ed. Maya Smerdou Altolaguirre.

861   AG
COLECCION POESIA DEL NUEVO TIEMPO. no. 3, 1976. irreg. Ediciones Tres Tiempos, Av. Belgrano 225, Buenos Aires, Argentina. Ed. Sigfrido Radaelli. illus.

861   MX
COLECCION SIGNO Y SOCIEDAD. irreg., no. 4, 1980. Universidad Autonoma de Puebla, 4 Sur 104, Puebla, Mexico.

851   IT
COLLANA DI POESIA. 1974; N.S. 1977. irreg., no.26, 1981. price varies. Societa Editrice Napoletana s.r.l., Corso Umberto I 34, 80138 Naples, Italy. Ed. Domenico Rea.

861   US   ISSN 0277-6782
COLLECCION VORTEX. irreg., no. 2, 1981. $2.50. c/o Julian Bacque, 3600 S.W. 9th Terrace, Apt. 2-B, Miami, FL 33135. circ. 425.

811   US   ISSN 0010-5201
CONCERNING POETRY. 1968. a. $8. Western Washington University, Department of English, Bellingham, WA 98225. TEL 206-676-3226. Ed. Ellwood Johnson. adv. bk. rev. circ. 370. (also avail. in microform from UMI; reprint service avail. from UMI, ISI) Indexed: Curr.Cont. M.L.A. A.I.P.P. Arts & Hum.Cit.Ind. Abstr.Engl.Stud. Ind.Bk.Rev.Hum. LCR.

CONFINS. see *LITERATURE*

808.81 792   US   ISSN 0277-7770
CONNECTICUT POETRY REVIEW. 1981. a. $3.50. Box 3783, New Haven, CT 06525. Eds. J. Claire White, James Wm. Chichetto. bk. rev. circ. 450. (back issues avail.)

811   US
CONNECTIONS. 1971. a. $3.50. Connections Magazine, Bell Hollow Rd., Putnam Valley, NY 10579. TEL 914-526-3420. Ed. Toni Ortner-Zimmerman. bk. rev. circ. 600.

808.81   US   ISSN 0162-7201
CONTEMPORARY QUARTERLY.* 1976. irreg., no. 10, 1980. $10 to individuals, institutions $20. L-A House, 1 W. California Blvd., Ste. 224, Pasadena, CA 91105. Ed. John Engle. adv. bk. rev. circ. 1,000. (back issues avail.)

CONTRAST. see *LITERATURE*

CRISI E LETTERATURA; periodico di lettere filosofia arti. see *LITERATURE*

821   UK
CYFRES BARDDONIAETH PWYLLGOR CYFIEITHIADAU YR ACADEMI. (Text in Welsh) 1980. irreg. price varies. (Welsh Academy) University of Wales Press, 6 Gwennyth St., Cathays, Cardiff CF2 4YD, Wales.

839   DK   ISSN 0107-4431
DANSK DIGTREGISTER. 1981. a. Kr.1237.70. Bibliotekscentralen, Tempovej 7-11, DK-2750 Ballerup, Denmark.
Formerly: Dansk Digtkatalog.

811   US   ISSN 0275-3073
DAY TONIGHT/NIGHT TODAY. 1981. irreg., no.30, 1985. $26. S.R. Jade, Ed. & Pub., Box 353, Hull, MA 02045. circ. 1,000.

841   FR   ISSN 0011-7889
DELIRANTE;* revue de poesie. (Text in French; occasionally in other languages) 1967. irreg. (2-4/yr.) 40 F. 54 rue de Seine, 75006 Paris, France.

DEUTSCHE BIBLIOTHEK. see *LITERATURE*

DICHTER UND ZEICHNER. see *ART*

808.81   II
DIPAVALI. (Text in Marathi) vol. 33, 1977. a. Rs.7. Ravindra Kesava Kothavale, 316 Prasad Chambers, Bombay 400004, India. Ed. Ashok Kothavale. adv. circ. 10,000.

811   US   ISSN 0734-0605
DIRECTORY OF AMERICAN POETS AND FICTION WRITERS. 1973. irreg., latest, 1985/1986. $14.95. ‡ Poets & Writers, Inc., 201 W. 54 St., New York, NY 10019. TEL 212-757-1766. (reprint service avail. from UMI) Indexed: Child.Auth.& Illus.
Formed by the merger of: Directory of American Poets & Directory of American Fiction Writers.

808.81   US
DIRECTORY OF LITERARY MAGAZINES. 1981. a. $5.95. Coordinating Council of Literary Magazines, 666 Broadway, New York, NY 10012. TEL 212-614-6551. index. circ. 3,000.

808.81 070.5   US
DIRECTORY OF POETRY PUBLISHERS. a. $9. Dustbooks, Box 100, Paradise, CA 95969.

808.81   US
DOCUMENTS FOR NEW POETRY. 1978. irreg. $3.75 per no. University of California, San Diego, Archive for New Poetry, Mandeville Department of Special Collections, University Library, La Jolla, CA 92093. TEL 619-452-2230.

861   UK   ISSN 0260-2113
ECUATORIAL; poetry. (Text in English, Portuguese and Spanish) 1978. irreg. King's College, Department of Spanish, c/o Dr. William Rowe, Strand, London WC2R, England.

EIGHTIES; a magazine of poetry and opinion. see *LITERARY AND POLITICAL REVIEWS*

890   II
EK BACHARER SRESTHA KABITA. (Text in Bengali) 1973. a. Rs.4($1) c/o Mrs. Bhaswati Sinha, 36 Ballygunge Place, Calcutta 19, India. Eds. M. Manindra Gupta, Ranjit Sinha. adv. illus. stat. circ. 1,000.

811   US   ISSN 0271-5023
EN PASSANT/POETRY. 1975. irreg. $6. (En Passant Literary Association) En Passant Press, 4612 Sylvanus Dr., Wilmington, DE 19803. Ed. James A. Costello. bk. rev. illus. circ. 500. Indexed: Ind.Amer.Per.Verse.
Formerly: En Passant Poetry Quarterly (ISSN 0363-3780)

ENGLISH GOETHE SOCIETY. PUBLICATIONS. see *LITERATURE*

ETUDES BAUDELAIRIENNES. see *LITERATURE*

811   US   ISSN 0014-4770
EXPERIMENT; a magazine of new poetry. 1944. irreg. $4.20. Experiment Press, 6565 N.E. Windermere Rd., Seattle, WA 98105. Ed. Carol Ely Harper. adv. bk. rev. illus. index. circ. 400.

811   US
FLORIDA STATE POETRY SOCIETY. SELECTED POEMS. 1966. a. membership. Florida State Poetry Society, Inc., 1110 No. Venetian Dr., Miami Beach, FL 33139. Ed. Frances Clark Handler. circ. 17,500.

FONDATION MAURICE CAREME; etablissement d'utilite publique. see *LITERATURE*

821   UK   ISSN 0015-7740
FORMAT. 1966. irreg. £0.50. ‡ Stilt Press, c/o Alan & Joan Tucker, The Bookshop, Stroud, Gloucestershire, England. Ed. Alan Tucker. circ. 150 (controlled) (processed)

FRAENKISCHER HAUSKALENDER UND CARITASKALENDER. see *BIOGRAPHY*

821   UK   ISSN 0306-1256
GALLERY. 1975. a. £2.50. Gallery Publications, c/o Valerie Sinason, Ed., 3 Honeybourne Rd., London NW6 1HH, England. adv. bk. rev. illus. circ. 1,000.

808.81   US
GALLERY WORKS. 1973. every 18 mos. $4 per no. Poet's Commune Publications, 25 Carlin St., Norwalk, CT 06851. Ed.Bd. circ. 500. (back issues avail.)

GAZELLE REVIEW OF LITERATURE ON THE MIDDLE EAST. see *LITERATURE*

821   UK
GENERA. 1971. irreg. £12 for 4 nos. c/o Colin Simms, Ed., Low Woodhead North, Bellingham, Northumberland NE48 2UX, England. illus. circ. 1, 000. (back issues avail.)
Formerly: North York Poetry.

821   AT   ISSN 0310-639X
GENTLE FOLK AND OTHER CREATURES. 1972. irreg. c/o Jamie Griffen, Union Building, Australian National University, P.O. Box 4, Canberra City, A.C.T. 2601, Australia.

GEORG FORSTER: SAEMLICHE SCHRIFTEN, TAGEBUECHER, BRIEFE. see *LITERATURE*

811   US   ISSN 0016-9633
GHOST DANCE; the international quarterly of experimental poetry. 1968. irreg. (1-2/yr.) $3. Ghost Dance Press, Dept. of American Thought and Language (EBH), Michigan State University, E. Lansing, MI 48823. Ed. Hugh B. Fox. circ. 300. (also avail. in microfilm from UMI; reprint service avail. from UMI)

811   US
GREENFIELD REVIEW CHAPBOOK. 1971. irreg., latest no. 47. price varies. Greenfield Review Press, R.D. 1, Box 80, Greenfield Center, NY 12833.

821   UK   ISSN 0261-5576
GREGORY AWARDS; poems. 1980. a. £4.50. Secker & Warburg, 54 Poland St., London W1V 3DF, England.

811   US
GRIST.* 1975. irreg. $50 per no. Grist Press, University of Rhode Island, Kingston, RI 02881. Ed.Bd. illus. circ. 1,000. (tabloid format)

821   UK
GUILDHALL POETS. a. £0.35. 19 Rugwood Rd., Flackwell Heath, High Wycombe HP10 9HA, England.

808.81 070.5 020   US
HAIKU REVIEW. 1980. biennial. $5. High-Coo Press, Route 1, Battle Ground, IN 47920. TEL 217-567-2596. Eds. Randy Brooks, Shirley Brooks. bk. rev. bibl. circ. 500. Indexed: M.L.A.

811   US   ISSN 0046-6832
HAPPINESS HOLDING TANK. 1970. irreg. $4. Stone Press, 9727 Reedway SE, Portland, OR 97266-3738. Ed. Albert Drake. bk. rev. illus. circ. 300. (processed; back issues avail.) Indexed: Bk.Rev.Ind.

808.81   US   ISSN 0887-5170
HAYDEN'S FERRY REVIEW. 1986. a. $4. Arizona State University, Student Publications, Tempe, AZ 85287. TEL 602-965-7572. circ. 2,000. (back issues avail.)

HEINE SAEKULARAUSGABE: WERKE-BRIEFWECHSEL-LEBENSZEUGNISSE. see *LITERATURE*

861   AG
HOJAS DE POESIA. irreg. $2.50. Aquario, Paraguay 647, Buenos Aires, Argentina. Ed. Sergio Chaves, Sigfrido Radaelli. (poster format)

800   US   ISSN 0278-4173
HOT WATER REVIEW. 1976. a. latest no.3, 1983. $6. Hot Water Review, Inc., 436 Ft. Washington Ave., No. 3E, New York, NY 10033. Eds. Peter Bushyeager, Richard Oosterom. adv. circ. 1,000.

811   PE   ISSN 0300-4031
IN TERRIS; revista de poesia. 1967. irreg. Livio Gomez Flores, Ed. & Pub., Francisco Cornejo 847, Tacna, Peru. adv. bk. rev. illus. circ. 1,000. (also avail. in microform; back issues avail.)

821   CN
INDUSTRIAL SABOTAGE. 1979. irreg. price varies. Curvd H & Z, 729A Queen Street E., Toronto, Ont. M4M 1H1, Canada. TEL 416-463-5867. circ. 150. (back issues avail.)

811   US
INKY TRAILS. 1967. irreg., (2-3/yr.) $17.50. Inky Trails Publications, Box 345, Middleton, ID 83644. Ed. Pearl Kirk. adv. bk. rev. bibl. circ. 150. (processed)

810.8　　　　　　　US　ISSN 0094-2715
INSCAPE (PASADENA) vol. 33, 1977. a. $1.
Pasadena City College, 1570 E. Colorado Blvd.,
Pasadena, CA 91106. TEL 818-578-7123. illus.
Continues (since vol. 30): Pipes of Pan.

861　　　　　　　　　US
INTERNATIONAL POETRY. (Text in English,
French, German, Italian, Portuguese and Spanish)
1973. a. $15. c/o Teresinka Pereira, Ed.,
Department of Spanish and Portuguese, University
of Colorado, Box 278, Boulder, CO 80301. TEL
303-492-7308. bk. rev. circ. 500.
Formerly: Poema Convidado.

051　　　　　　ISSN 0147-4936
INVISIBLE CITY. 1971. irreg. (approx. 1/yr.) $3
individuals; libraries $5. Red Hill Press, Box 2853,
San Francisco, CA 94126. Eds. John McBride, Paul
Vangelisti. bk. rev. circ. 3,000. (tabloid format; also
avail. in microform) Indexed: Access.
Formerly: Red Hill Press (ISSN 0034-2009)

830　　　　　　　　　GW
JAHRBUCH DEUTSCHER DICHTUNG. 1975. a.
Kurt Ruediger, Ed. & Pub., Friedenstr. 16, 7500
Karlsruhe, W. Germany (B.R.D.)

808.81　　　　　　　II
JAMINRAITU. (Text in Telugu) a. Zamin Ryot Press,
170 Thipparajuvari St, Nellore 524001, India.

JEOPARDY. see *LITERATURE*

890　　　　　KE　ISSN 0449-0738
JOHARI ZA KISWAHILI. (Text in Swahili) 1960.
irreg, vol. 13, 1975. Kenya Literature Bureau, Box
30022, Nairobi, Kenya.

JOHN CLARE SOCIETY JOURNAL. see
LITERATURE

808.81　　　　　CN　ISSN 0705-1328
JOURNAL OF CANADIAN POETRY. (Text in
English, French) 1978. a. Can.$12.50. Borealis Press
Limited, 9 Ashburn Dr., Nepean, Ont. K2E 6N4,
Canada. Ed. David Staines. adv. bk. rev. circ. 300.
(back issues avail.) Indexed: CMI.

811　　　　　　US　ISSN 0363-4205
JOURNAL OF NEW JERSEY POETS. 1976. a. $3
for 2 nos. Fairleigh Dickinson University, Florham-
Madison Campus, Creative Writing Program, 285
Madison Ave., Madison, NJ 07940. TEL 201-377-
4700. Ed.Bd. bk. rev. circ. 400. Indexed:
Ind.Amer.Per.Verse.

811　　　　　　　　　US
JUNCTION. 1973. a. $1.50. City University of New
York, Brooklyn College, Graduate Student
Association, La Guardia Hall, Room 237C,
Brooklyn, NY 11210. TEL 718-780-5485. Ed.
Marshall Scott Grossman. bk. rev. bibl. circ. 600.

811　700　　　　　　US
KALDRON. 1976. irreg. (1-2/yr.) $5 price varies. Box
7036, Halcyon, CA 93420-7036. Ed. Karl Kempton.
bk. rev.

821　　　　　　US　ISSN 0453-4387
KEATS-SHELLEY JOURNAL; Keats, Shelley, Byron,
Hunt, and their circles. 1952. a. $12.50 to
individuals; institutions $18. Keats-Shelley
Association of America, Inc., New York Public
Library, 5th Ave. at 42nd St.-Rm. 319, New York,
NY 10018. Ed. Stuart Curran. bk. rev. bibl. circ. 1,
000. (also avail. in microfilm) Indexed: Curr.Cont.
Hum.Ind. M.L.A. Arts & Hum.Cit.Ind.
Abstr.Engl.Stud. Ind.Bk.Rev.Hum. RILA.

LAKE STREET REVIEW. see *LITERATURE*

811　　　　　　　　　II
LAVA. 1975. irreg. Rs.24($10) for 12 issues. Lava
Publications, 26/53 W.E.A., New Delhi 110005,
India. Ed. G. P. Vimal. bk. rev.

861　　　　　　　　　NQ
LETRAS DE NICARAGUA. irreg., no. 3, 1982.
Editorial Nueva Nicaragua, Paseo Salvador Allende,
Km. 3 1/2 Carretera Sur, Apdo. Postal RP-073,
Managua, Nicaragua.

811　　　　　　US　ISSN 0743-2909
LIMBERLOST REVIEW. 1976. irreg. (1-2/yr.) $9.95.
Box 1563, Boise, ID 83701-1563. Ed. Richard
Ardinger. circ. 500.

LITERATUR UND GESELLSCHAFT. see
LITERATURE

800　　　　　DK　ISSN 0107-0916
LITTERATURTOLKNINGER. 1980. a. Kr.622.95.
Bibliotekscentralen, Tempovej 7-11, 2750 Ballerup,
Denmark.

821　　　　　　　　　UK
LITTLE WORD MACHINE. 1971. irreg. $8 for 4
nos. L.W.M. Publications, 5 Beech Terrace,
Undercliffe, Bradford, West Yorkshire BD3 OPY,
England. Ed. Nick Toczek. adv. bk. rev. circ. 1,000.

808.81　　　　　　　US
LOCKERT LIBRARY OF POETRY IN
TRANSLATION. 1967. a. price varies. Princeton
University Press, 3175 Princeton Pike,
Lawrenceville, NJ 08648. TEL 609-896-1344.
(reprint service avail. from UMI)

811　　　　　　　　　US
LONGHOUSE. 1973. a. $10. Green River R.F.D.,
Brattleboro, VT 05301. Ed. Bob Arnold. bk. rev.
circ. 200.

811　　　　　　　　　US
LOOK QUICK. 1975. irreg., approx. 2/yr. $7.50.
Quick Books, Box 222, Pueblo, CO 81002. Eds. Joel
Scherzer, Robbie Rubinstein. bk. rev. circ. 200. (also
avail. in microfilm; back issues avail.)

811　　　　　　US　ISSN 0076-1699
LYRICAL IOWA; poetry by Iowa authors. 1946. a.
$6. Iowa Poetry Association, c/o Virginia Blanck
Moore, Ed., 1724 E. 22nd St., Des Moines, IA
50317. circ. 750.

MABUA/FOUNTAIN; religious creation in literature,
society and thought. see *LITERATURE*

811　　　　　　US　ISSN 0047-5432
MADRONA;* a quarterly of poetry. 1971. irreg. $2.
Gemini Foundation, c/o Charles Webb, 3232
Palmer Dr., Los Angeles, CA 90065-4925. TEL
213-380-6762. Eds. Charles Webb, Jeff Powers. bk.
rev. circ. 500 (controlled) (also avail. in microform
from UMI)

MAGIRA. see *LITERATURE*

840　　　　　SZ　ISSN 0076-3748
LA MANDRAGORE QUI CHANTE. 1961. irreg.,
latest vol. 39. price varies. Editions de la Baconniere
S. A., Box 185, 2017 Boudry, Switzerland. Ed.
Marc Eigeldinger. (reprint service avail. from UMI)

808.81　　　　　US　ISSN 0275-6889
MANHATTAN REVIEW. 1980. a. $8 to individuals;
institutions $12. Manhattan Review Press, c/o
Philip Fried, 304 Third Ave., Suite 4A, New York,
NY 10010. Ed. Philip Fried. adv. circ. 500. (back
issues avail.) Indexed: Ind.Amer.Per.Verse.

ME. see *ART*

808.21　　　　　　　US
ME TOO.* 1974. a. $1.50. Me Too, Inc., 112 W. 34th
St., New York, NY 10001. TEL 212-594-9224.

811　　　　　　US　ISSN 0194-1313
MICKLE STREET REVIEW. 1979. a. $5. Walt
Whitman Association, 328 Mickle St., Camden, NJ
08103. TEL 609-541-8280. Ed. Geoffrey M. Sill.
adv. bk. rev. circ. 500.

821　　　　　　US　ISSN 0540-0961
MILTON SOCIETY OF AMERICA.
PROCEEDINGS. 1953. a. $3. Milton Society of
America, c/o Albert C. Labriola, Ed., Department
of English, Duquesne University, Pittsburgh, PA
15282. TEL 412-434-6420. circ. 450.

808.81　　　　　CN　ISSN 0228-7404
MOOSEHEAD REVIEW. 1978. a. Can.$5.50.
Moosehead Press, Box 169, Ayer's Cliff, Que. JOB
1C0, Canada. Ed. Robert Allen. bk. rev. circ. 350.

811　　　　　　　　　US
MOVING FINGER. vol. 4, 1974. biennial. $0.50.
Indiana State University, Evansville, 8600
University Blvd., Evansville, IN 47712. TEL 812-
464-4600. Eds. Chuck Connor, Debbie Miller. illus.

081　　　　　　　　　US
MR. COGITO. 1973. irreg. $4.50 for three nos. Mr.
Cogito Press, U.C. Box 627, Pacific University,
Forest Grove, OR 97116. TEL 503-357-6151. Eds.
Robert A. Davies, John M. Gogol. circ. 500.

821　　　　　　　　　IE
NEPTUNE'S KINGDOM; poetry review. (Text in
English) 1972. irreg. 10p.($1) per issue. c/o Martin
Gleeson, Ed., 5 Victoria Terrace, Kilkee, Co. Clare,
Ireland. bk. rev. illus. circ. 500.

808.81　　　　　　　US
NEW AMERICAN WRITING. 1971. a. $5 per no.
Oink! Press, Inc., 1446 W. Jarvis, Chicago, IL
60626. Eds. Maxine Chernoff, Paul Hoover. adv. bk.
rev. circ. 600.
Supersedes: Oink! (ISSN 0883-8518)

NEW LITERATURE AND IDEOLOGY. see
LITERARY AND POLITICAL REVIEWS

808　　　　　　　　　US
NEW VOICES (METHUEN) 1979. a. $4. 24
Edgeworth Terrace, Methuen, MA 01844. TEL 617-
685-3087. Ed. Lorraine Moreau-Laverriere. circ.
300. (back issues avail.)

821　　　　　　　　　AT
NIMROD'S QUARRY. 1965. irreg. Aus.$6 per no.
Nimrod Publications, University of Newcastle,
Dept. of English, Newcastle, N.S.W. 2308,
Australia. Ed. Norman Talbot. bk. rev. circ. 1,750.
Formerly (until 1981): Hunter Valley Poets.

820　　　　　　UK　ISSN 0078-1738
NORTHERN HOUSE PAMPHLET POETS. 1964.
irreg. price varies. Northern House, 19 Haldane
Terrace, Newcastle-upon-Tyne NE2 3AN, England.
Ed.Bd. adv. bk. rev. circ. 1,000. (back issues avail.)

871　　　　　　　　　SP
NUEVA POETICA ANDALUZA. 1981. irreg.
Editorial Cajal, Juez 3, 1, Almeria, Spain.

821　　　　　　　　　NR
OMABE; poetry from Nsukka. (Text in English) 1972.
irreg., (approx. 3/yr.) £N3($4.50) University of
Nigeria, Department of English, Nsukka, Nigeria.
Ed. Ossie Onuora Enekwe. illus. circ. 1,000. (back
issues avail.)
Formerly: Omaba.

821　　　　　　UK　ISSN 0030-459X
ORE. 1954. irreg., 1-2/yr. £3. c/o Ed. Eric Ratcliffe, 7
the Towers, Stevenage, Herts., SG1 1HE, England
(Subscr. addr.: Owles Warehouse, 4 Trinity St.,
Bungay, Suffolk, England) Ed. E. Ratcliffe. bk. rev.
circ. 6,000.

811　　　　　　US　ISSN 0030-7629
OX HEAD. 1966. irreg. $10 for 10 issues. Ox Head
Press, 414 N. Sixth St., Marshall, MN 56258. TEL
507-532-6459. Ed. Don Olsen. circ. 200-500.

P S; tidsskrift for spontan satire, fjollet filosofi, funny
fiction and lojerlig ligegyldighed. see *PHILOSOPHY*

808.81　　　　　US　ISSN 0092-5535
PANJANDRUM POETRY JOURNAL. 1972. 3/yr.
$14. Panjandrum Press, Inc., 11321 Iowa Ave., Ste.
1, Los Angeles, CA 90025. TEL 213-477-8771. Ed.
Dennis Koran. circ. 1,250.

PANORAMA OF CZECH LITERATURE. see
LITERATURE

410 811　　　　　　　US
PAPER AIR. 1976. irreg. $12 for 3 nos. to individuals;
institutions $24. Singing Horse Press, Box 40034,
Philadelphia, PA 19106. TEL 215-844-7429. Ed. Gil
Ott. adv. bk. rev. bibl. illus. circ. 800. (back issues
avail.)

811　　　　　　US　ISSN 0277-1098
PLAY THE RED. Sysyphus Press, 192 Spring St.,
New York, NY 10012.

811　　　　　　US　ISSN 0079-2438
POCKET POETS SERIES. 1955. irreg., no. 43, 1987.
price varies. City Lights Books, 261 Columbus Ave.,
San Francisco, CA 94133. TEL 415-362-8193.

809 US ISSN 0276-3737
POE MESSENGER. 1969. a. $3. Poe Foundation, Inc., 1914-16 E. Main St., Richmond, VA 23223. Ed. Agnes Bondurant Marcuson. bk. rev. play rev. illus. circ. 550. (back issues avail.) Indexed: Amer.Hum.Ind.

861 UY ISSN 0079-2462
POESIA.* irreg. Editorial Arca, Colonia 1263, Montevideo, Uruguay.

861 PN
POESIA PANAMENA ACTUAL. 1979. a. price varies. (Direccion Nacional de Extension Cultural, Departamento de Letras) Editorial Mariano Arosemena (INAC), Apdo. 662, Panama 1, Panama. TEL 22-7908 or 22-7953.

830 GW
POESIE UND WISSENSCHAFT. SAMMLUNG. 1967. irreg. price varies. Lothar Stiehm Verlag, Hausackerweg 16, D-6900 Heidelberg, W. Germany (B.R.D.) Indexed: M.L.A.

811 US
POET; peu a peu. 1973. a. $11.50. Fine Arts Society, 2314 W. Sixth St., Mishawaka, IN 46544. Ed. Doris Nemeth. adv. illus. circ. 1,000 (controlled) (reprint service avail. from UMI)

811 US ISSN 0032-1958
POET AND CRITIC. 1965. a. $17 for 3 nos. Iowa State University, Department of English, 203 Ross Hall, Ames, IA 50010. TEL 515-294-2180. Ed. Micheal Martone. adv. bk. rev. illus. circ. 350. (also avail. in microform from UMI; reprint service avail. from UMI) Indexed: Curr.Cont. A.I.P.P. Arts & Hum.Cit.Ind. Abstr.Engl.Stud. Ind.Amer.Per.Verse.

861 PY
POETAS.* 1977. irreg. (Paraguay PEN Centre) Fondo Editor Paraguayo, San Rafael 658, Asuncion, Paraguay.

811 FR ISSN 0079-2470
POETES ET PROSATEURS DU PORTUGAL. 1970. irreg. price varies. (Fundacao Calouste Gulbenkian, PO) Presses Universitaires de France, 108 bd. Saint Germain, 75279 Paris Cedex 6, France (Service des Periodiques, 12 rue Jean de Beauvais, 75005 Paris) (reprint service avail. from KTO)

811 US
POETESSA; the new woman's poetry journal. 1984. irreg. $30. Poetessa Press, Box 420, East Rockaway, NY 11518. Ed. Yvette E. Schneider. adv. bk. rev. circ. 700. (back issues avail.)

830 IT ISSN 0079-2500
POETI E PROSATORI TEDESCHI. 1962. irreg., no.7, 1982. price varies. Edizioni dell' Ateneo S.p.A., Box 7216, 00100 Rome, Italy. Ed. Paolo Chiarini. circ. 1,000.

820 AU
POETIC DRAMA AND POETIC THEORY. (Text in English) 1972. irreg., no. 78, 1986. S.245. Universitaet Salzburg, Institut fuer Englische Sprache, Akademiestr. 24, A-5020 Salzburg, Austria. Ed. James Hogg. circ. 200.

821 UK ISSN 0032-2083
POETRY MARKET. 1965. irreg. 25p. per mo. Aubrey Bush Publications, 17 Balmoral Rd., Forest Rd., Nottingham NG1 4HX, England. Ed. Aubrey Bush. adv. bk. rev. mkt. play rev.

821 UK
POETRY SUPPLEMENT. a. £3.95. Poetry Book Society Ltd., 21 Earls Court Sq., London SW5 9DE, England.

811 US ISSN 0883-5470
POET'S MARKET; where and how to publish your poetry. 1986. a. $16.95. Writer's Digest Books, 9933 Alliance Rd., Cincinnati, OH 45242. TEL 513-984-0717. Ed. Judson Jerome. index.

811 US
POETS NOW. 1982. irreg., approx. 6/yr. $13.50. Scarecrow Press, Inc., Box 4167, Metuchen, NJ 08840. TEL 201-548-8600. Ed. Robert Peters.

821 UK
POET'S YEARBOOK.* 1975. a. £2.45. Poet's Yearbook Ltd., 35 Rowston St., Cleethorpes DN35 8QR, England. Ed. S.T. Gardiner.

811 PL ISSN 0079-2527
POETYKA. ZARYS ENCYKLOPEDYCZNY. 1956. irreg., latest 1984. price varies. (Polska Akademia Nauk, Instytut Badan Literackich) Ossolineum, Publishing House of the Polish Academy of Sciences, Rynek 9, 50-106 Wroclaw, Poland (Dist. by: Ars Polona-Ruch, Krakowskie Przedmiescie 7, Warsaw, Poland) Eds. Maria Renata Mayenowa , Lucylla Pszczolowska.

899 UR
POEZIYA (MOSCOW) vol.20, 1977. irreg. 0.99 Rub. per issue. Izdatel'stvo Molodaya Gvardiya, Ul.Sushchevskaya, 21, 103030 Moscow, Russian S.F.S.R., U.S.S.R. Ed. N. Starshinov. illus. circ. 65,000.

811 US
PORTLAND REVIEW OF THE ARTS. 1980. a. $3. University of Southern Maine, 96 Falmouth St., Portland, ME 04103. TEL 207-780-4186. Ed. Barbara W. Cariddi. circ. 400.

POTTERSFIELD PORTFOLIO; fiction, plays, essays and poetry from Atlantic Canada. see LITERATURE

808.81 US ISSN 0196-822X
PRACTICES OF THE WIND; a magazine/anthology of poetry. 1980. irreg. $4 per no. Box 214, Kalamazoo, MI 49005. Eds. Nicolaus Waskowsky, David M. Marovich. circ. 500.

811 861 US ISSN 0747-9697
PRICKLY PEAR TUCSON. 1983. a. $7.50. 2833 E. Kaibab Vista, Tucson, AZ 85713. Eds. Burgess Needle, Michael Rattee. circ. 100.

811 US
PRIMARY WRITING. 1985. irreg. (1-3/yr.) $3 per no. c/o Phyllis Rosenzweig, 1545 18th St., N.W., No. 116, Washington, DC 20036. TEL 202-232-2472.

811 US
PRINCETON SERIES OF CONTEMPORARY POETS. 1975. a. price varies. Princeton University Press, 3175 Princeton Pike, Lawrenceville, NJ 08648. TEL 609-896-1344. (reprint service avail. from UMI)

821 UK
PROEM PAMPHLETS. 1976. irreg. price varies. Proem Pamphlets, Festival Office, Ilkley, West Yorkshire LS29 8DG, England. Ed. Michael Dawson. circ. 875.

861 SP
PROVINCIA; coleccion de poesia. no. 20, 1974. irreg. 1500 ptas.($20) (for 6 nos.) Institucion "Fray Bernardino de Sahagun", Edificio Fierro, Puerta de la Reina, 1, Leon, Spain. circ. 1,000.

861 AG
PROVINCIA. 1967. irreg, no.121, 1985. $2. Rafael M. Altamirano, Ed. & Pub., Calle Libertad, Casa 16 B, Barrio los Olivos 5870, Villa Dolores, Argentina. bk. rev.

811 US
PTOLEMY.* 1979. a. $2. David Vajda, Ed. & Pub., Box 908, Browns Mills, NJ 08015. circ. 250.

851 IT ISSN 0391-3104
QUADERNI DEL VITTORIALE. 1977. irreg. L.15000($24) Fondazione del Vittoriale, Corso Portanuova 34, Milan, Italy. Ed. Giuseppe Longo. illus. tr.lit. circ. 5,000. Indexed: M.L.A.

808 IT ISSN 0079-8274
QUADERNI DI POESIA NEOGRECA. 1967. irreg., no. 5, 1980. price varies. Istituto Siciliano di Studi Bizantini e Neoellenici, Via Noto, 34, 90141 Palermo, Italy.

800 US
QUARTERLY REVIEW OF LITERATURE POETRY SERIES. Variant title: Q R L Poetry Series. 1943. a. $15 paperback (2vols.); $20 hardback (1vol.) 26 Haslet Ave., Princeton NJ 08540. TEL 609-452-4703. Eds. Theodore & Renee Weiss. adv. circ. 4,000. (back issues avail.) Indexed: Curr.Cont. R.G. Ind.Little Mag. Arts & Hum.Cit.Ind. A.I.P.P.
Former titles: Quarterly Review of Literature Contemporary Poetry Series & Quarterly Review of Literature (ISSN 0033-5819)

808.81 US
QUERCUS. a. $15 includes Poet News. Sacramento Poetry Center, no. 8, 2791 24 St., Sacramento, CA 95818. TEL 916-739-1885. Ed. Susan Kelly-DeWitt. circ. 400.

811 US ISSN 0148-0162
RACCOON. 1977. irreg. (approx. 4/yr.) $12.50. Ion Books, Inc., 3387 Poplar, Ste. 205, Memphis, TN 38111. TEL 901-323-8858. Ed. David Spicer. bk. rev. index. circ. 500. (back issues avail.) Indexed: Amer.Hum.Ind.

811 US ISSN 0147-0396
REBIS CHAPBOOK SERIES. 1977. irreg., unnumbered. Allegany Mountain Press, 111 N. 10th St., Olean, NY 14760. Ed. H. Ruggieri. circ. 300.

811 US ISSN 0742-454X
RED FOX REVIEW AT MOHEGAN COMMUNITY COLLEGE. 1974. a. $6 for 2 yrs. Mohegan Fine Arts Committee, c/o James Coleman, Ed., Mohegan Community College, Norwich, CT 06360. TEL 203-886-1913. bk. rev. illus. circ. 1,250.
Formerly: Red Fox Review.

RIVERSIDE INTERVIEWS. see LITERATURE

811 US
RIVERWIND. 1977. $5. (Hocking Technical College) Riverwind Press, General Studies, Hocking Technical College, Nelsonville, OH 45764. TEL 614-753-3591. Ed.Bd. bk. rev. circ. 1,000.

811 US
ROAD/HOUSE. 1975. irreg. (5-6/yr.) $1.50. Todd Moore, Ed. & Pub., 900 W. 9th St., Belvidere, IL 61008. TEL 815-544-9581. bk. rev. circ. 100. (back issues avail.)

808.1 US
ROBERSON POETRY ANNUAL. a. Bellevue Press, 60 Schubert St., Binghamton, NY 13905.

811 US ISSN 0300-7936
ROBINSON JEFFERS NEWSLETTER. 1962. irreg. $4. Occidental College Library, c/o Ed. Tyrus G. Harmsen, 1600 Campus Rd., Los Angeles, CA 90041. TEL 213-259-2510. Ed. Dr. Robert Brophy. bk. rev. abstr. circ. 200. (processed) Indexed: M.L.A. Abstr.Engl.Stud. LCR.

821 UK ISSN 0144-7262
ROCK DRILL. 1980. irreg. £1.20($4.80) Supranormal Cassettes, 15 Oakapple Rd., Southwick, Sussex BN4 4YL, England. Eds. Robert Sheppard, Penelope Bailey. adv. bk. rev. circ. 200. (back issues avail.)

811 305.4 US
ROOM; a woman's literary journal. 1975. a. $3.50. Box 40610, San Francisco, CA 94110. Eds. Gail Newman, Kathy Barr. bk. rev. circ. 750. (back issues avail.)

821 UK
ROUTLEDGE HISTORY OF ENGLISH POETRY. 1977. irreg. price varies. Routledge and Kegan Paul PLC, 11 New Fetter Lane, London EC4P 4EE, England (U.S. orders to: 9 Park St., Boston, MA 02108) Ed. R. A. Foakes.

811 US
SAILING THE ROAD CLEAR. 1973. irreg. $5 (for 3 issues) c/o Jane Creighton, Box 238, Old Mystic, CT 06372. circ. 400.

811 US ISSN 0036-360X
SALT LICK. 1969. irreg. $10. Salt Lick Press, 1804 E. 38 1/2 St., Austin, TX 78722. TEL 512-480-9372. Ed. James Haining. bk. rev. illus. circ. 1,500. (processed; also avail. in microform from UMI; reprint service avail. from UMI)

SANDS; a literary magazine. see LITERATURE

808.1 CN ISSN 0080-6560
SASKATCHEWAN POETRY BOOK. 1936. biennial. Can.$3.92. Saskatchewan Poetry Society, 3104 College Avenue, Regina, Saskatchewan S4T 1V7, Canada. Ed.Bd. circ. 600. (back issues avail.)

SEEMS. see LITERATURE

841 FR
SENTIERS POESIE. no.2, 1973. irreg. 34 F. Editions Subervie, 21, rue de l'Embergue, F-12 Rodez, France.

LITERATURE — POETRY

811 US
SEVEN. 1958. irreg., latest vol.2, no.3, 1982. $7.50 for 4 nos. 3630 N.W. 22, Oklahoma City, OK 73107-2893. TEL 405-949-0675. Ed. James Neill Northe. circ. 1,000.

808.81 US ISSN 0037-329X
SHANTIH; new international writings. 1971. irreg. $8 for 4 issues. Box 125, Bay Ridge Station, Brooklyn, NY 11220. Eds. Irving Gottesman, John Friedman. adv. bk. rev. illus. circ. 1,000.

700 US
SO AND SO MAGAZINE.* 1973. a. $15. So and So Press, 1003 Kieth Ave., Berkeley, CA 94708. Ed. John Marron. bk. rev. circ. 500. (back issues avail.) Formerly: Bad Breath.

841 FR ISSN 0081-0908
SOCIETE DES POETES FRANCAIS. ANNUAIRE. 1902. a. Societe des Poetes Francais, Hotel de Massa, 38 rue du Faubourg Saint-Jacques, 75014 Paris, France.

821 UK ISSN 0260-4531
SPINDRIFT. 1977. irreg. £0.65. Scarborough Poetry Workshop, c/o Ms. D. Whalley, 14 Littledale, Pickering, North Yorkshire, England. Ed. Peggy Loosemore Jones. circ. 300.

SPIRAL. see WOMEN'S INTERESTS

SPIRIT WINGS. see RELIGIONS AND THEOLOGY

811 US
SPRING RAIN. 1971. irreg. (2-4/yr.) $4. Spring Rain Press, Box 15319, Seattle, WA 98115. Ed. Karen Gates. circ. 500.

831 GW ISSN 0720-0218
STADTANSICHTEN; Jahrbuch fuer Literatur und kulturelles Leben in Berlin (West) 1980. irreg. DM.12. Edition Neue Wege, Kaiserdamm 27, PB 191603, D-1000 Berlin (West) 19, W. Germany (B.R.D.) Ed. Peter Gerlinghoff. adv. bk. rev. circ. 2,000.

821 UK
STARDANCE.* 1972. a. 10p. c/o Marek Urbanowicz, Ed., 49 Sheen Park, Richmond, Surrey, England.

821 UK ISSN 0039-1212
STEREO HEADPHONES; an occasional magazine of the new experimental poetries. (Text in English, French, German and Italian) 1969. irreg. (2-3/yr.) £4($7.50) per no. Church Steps, Kersey, Near Ipswich, Suffolk, England (Also avail. from: Nicholas Zurbrugg, Ed., School of Humanities, Griffith University, Nathan, Brisbane, Qld. 4111, Australia) adv. bk. rev. bibl. illus. circ. 1,000. (tabloid format; also avail. in cards)

851 IT ISSN 0393-9480
STEVE; rivista di poesia. 1981. a. L.15000($20) Laboratorio di Poesia di Modena, Via Fosse 14, 41100 Modena, Italy. circ. 500.

891 UR
STIKHI. (Subseries of: Repertuar Khudozhestvennoi Samodeyatel'nosti. Seriya-Repertuarnye Sborniki) 1967. irreg. Izdatel'stvo Iskusstvo, Tsvetnoi bul'var, 25, Moscow K-51, Russian S.F.S.R., U.S.S.R.

811 US
STONE. 1967. irreg. $3.50. Stone Press, 1112-B Ocean St., Santa Cruz, CA 95060. Ed. Rich Jorgensen. circ. 500.

821 820 IE
STONY THURSDAY BOOK. (Text in English and Gaelic) 1975. irreg., no. 8, 1982/83. £2($4.50) John Liddy, Ed. & Pub., 128 Sycamore Ave., Rath Bhan, Limerick, Ireland. bk. rev. play rev. bibl. illus. circ. 1,000. (back issues avail.)

808.81 HU ISSN 0586-3783
SZEP VERSEK. 1964. a. ‡ Magveto Kiado, Vorosmarty ter 1, Budapest V, Hungary. Ed. Miklos Jovanovics.

808 418 US
TERRA POETICA; a multilingual magazine of poetry. 1979. irreg. $5. State University of New York at Buffalo, Department of Modern Languages, 910 Clemens Hall, Buffalo, NY 14260. TEL 716-636-2191. Ed. Jorge Guitar. circ. 500. (back issues avail.)

808.81 100 US
THOUGHTS FOR ALL SEASONS; the magazine of epigrams. 1976. irreg., vol.2, 1984. $5. Valley Press, 15 Second Street, Geneseo, NY 14454. TEL 716-243-2127. Ed. Michel P. Richard. adv. circ. 1,000. (back issues avail.)

821 US
THROUGH CASA GUIDI WINDOWS; the bulletin of the Browning Institute. 1975. irreg. Browning Institute Inc., Box 2983, Grand Central Sta., New York, NY 10163. Ed.Bd. adv. bibl.

U.C. REVIEW. see LITERATURE

U S 1 WORKSHEETS. see LITERATURE

811 HU ISSN 0082-7312
UJ MAGYAR NEPKOLTESI GYUJTEMENY. 1955. irreg. price varies. (Magyar Tudomanyos Akademia) Akademiai Kiado, Publishing House of the Hungarian Academy of Sciences, P.O. Box 24, H-1363 Budapest, Hungary.

943.1 US
UNICORN GERMAN SERIES. (Text in English and German) 1968. irreg. $5 paper; $15 cloth. Unicorn Press, Inc., Box 3307, Greensboro, NC 27402. Ed. Teo Savory. adv. bk. rev. circ. 2,000. (back issues avail.)

861 CK ISSN 0120-0992
UNIVERSIDAD DE LOS ANDES. CUADERNOS DE FILOSOFIA Y LETRAS. 1973. irreg. Universidad de los Andes, Facultad de Humanidades y Ciencias Sociales, Comite de Publicaciones, Bogota, Colombia. bibl. circ. 1,000. Formerly: Universidad de los Andes. Cuadernos de Letras.

811 US ISSN 0049-5557
UNMUZZLED OX. 1971. irreg. $20 to non-members; members $6. (Cultural Council Foundation, Ltd.) Unmuzzled Ox Foundation, Ltd., 105 Hudson St., New York, NY 10013. (Co-sponsor: Sotto Baroque Opera Company, Inc.) Ed. Michael Andre. adv. bk. rev. bibl. illus. circ. 20,000. Indexed: Ind.Amer.Per.Verse. Amer.Hum.Ind.

890 BG
UTSABA. (Text in Bengali) a. Tk.5. Syed Zafar Ali, 113 Jagannath Saha Rd., Dacca 1, Bangladesh.

811 US
VAGABOND CHAPBOOK.* vol. 6, 1976. irreg. $1 per no. Vagabond Press, Box 395, Ellensburg, WA 98926-0395.

861 SP
VERDE YERBA;* antologia Hispanoamericana de poesia. no.10, 1972. irreg. Carabela, General Sanjuro 53, Dpto. 50, Barcelona 12, Spain.

821 UK
VERMOUTH. irreg. £0.50. Ver Poets, 61 & 63 Chiswell Green Lane, St. Albans, Herts, AL2 3AG, England. Eds. May Badman, Jeff Cloves.

821 UK
VISION ON. a. £0.50. Ver Poets, 61 & 63 Chiswell Green Lane, St. Albans, Herts AL2 3AG, England. Ed. May Badman.

821 IS ISSN 0333-676X
VOICES - ISRAEL; magazine of English poetry in Israel. (Text in English) 1972. a. price varies. Voices Group of Israeli Poets in English, c/o R. Rose, Ed., 38 Nehemia St., Nave Sha'anan, Haifa 32 295, Israel. adv. circ. 500. (also avail. in microfiche)

890 US ISSN 0888-5257
VSTRECHI; almanac. (Text in Russian) 1977. a. $7. Encounters, 7738 Woodbine Ave., Philadelphia, PA 19151. Ed. Valentina Sinkevich. bk. rev. circ. 550. Formerly: Perekrestki (ISSN 0160-5534)
Cyrillic alphabet

811 US ISSN 0148-7132
WALLACE STEVENS JOURNAL. 1977. biennial. $15 to individuals; institutions $20. Wallace Stevens Society, Inc., c/o Clarkson University, Potsdam, NY 13676. TEL 315-268-3987. Ed. John N. Serio. adv. bk. rev. bibl. circ. 600. Indexed: Curr.Cont. M.L.A. Arts & Hum.Cit.Ind. Abstr.Engl.Stud.

811 US
WASHOUT REVIEW. 1975. irreg. $6. Washout Publishing Co., Box 9252, Schenectady, NY 12309. Eds. Ellen Biss, Kathryn Poppino. illus. circ. 500. (back issues avail.)

811 US
WEST HILLS REVIEW. 1979. a. $6.00. Walt Whitman Birthplace Association, 246 Old Walt Whitman Rd., Huntington Station, Long Island, NY 11746. TEL 516-427-5240. Ed.Bd. circ. 800.

811 US ISSN 0511-8832
WHITTIER NEWSLETTER. 1966. a. free. Whittier Clubs of Haverhill and Amesbury, c/o Howard W. Curtis, Ed., Haverhill Public Library, Haverhill, MA 01830. bk. rev. bibl. circ. 600. (looseleaf format; back issues avail)

800 US ISSN 0882-066X
WIDENER REVIEW; poetry, fiction, reviews. 1984. a. $3. Widener University, Humanities Division, Chester, PA 19013. TEL 215-499-4266. Ed. Michael Clark. bk. rev. circ. 250. (back issues avail.)

WIELANDS BRIEFWECHSEL. see LITERATURE

WIENER-GOETHE-VEREIN. JAHRBUCH. see LITERATURE

811 US ISSN 0043-5716
WINDLESS ORCHARD; a quarterly magazine of photography and contemporary poetry. 1970. irreg., no.47, 1986. $7 for 4 nos. Robert Novak, Ed. & Pub., c/o English Dept., Indiana University, Fort Wayne, IN 46805. TEL 219-482-5441. bk. rev. illus. circ. 300. (also avail. in microfilm from UMI; reprint service avail. from UMI) Indexed: Ind.Amer.Per.Verse.

811 US ISSN 0195-6183
WOMAN POET. 1980. a. $16.95 hardcover; paperback $11. Women-in-Literature, Inc., Box 60550, Reno, NV 89506. TEL 702-972-1671. Ed. Elaine Dallman. bk. rev. circ. 3,000. (back issues avail.)

811 305.4 US
WOMEN - POEMS. 1971. irreg. $1.50 per no. Women-Poems Press, 23 Meriam St., Lexington, MA 02173. Eds. Celia Gilbert, Pat Rabby. circ. 2,000.

811 US
WOMEN TALKING, WOMEN LISTENING. 1975. a. $3. Women Talking, Women Listening Press, Box 2414, Dublin, CA 94566. Ed. Sharon Lee. circ. 1,200.

811 US ISSN 0043-8154
WORLD. 1966. a. $10. Poetry Project, St. Marks Church In-The-Bowery, 10th St & Second Ave., New York, NY 10003. TEL 212-674-0910. Ed. Steve Levine. circ. 1,000. (processed) Indexed: Abstr.Mil.Bibl.

WRITERS' AND POETS' YEARBOOK. see LITERATURE

811 US ISSN 0146-0463
XANADU; a literary journal. 1975. a. $5. Long Island Poetry Collective, Inc., Box 773, Huntington, NY 11743. Ed.Bd. circ. 600. (back issues avail.)

811 US ISSN 0084-3458
YALE SERIES OF YOUNGER POETS. 1919. a. price varies. Yale University Press, 92A Yale Sta., New Haven, CT 06520. TEL 203-432-0940. Ed. James Merrill.

811 US
YEARBOOK OF WORKS RE APPALACHIA. 1969. a. $4. Morris Harvey College Publications, Charleston, WV 25304. TEL 304-346-9471. Ed. William Plumley. circ. 5,000. (tabloid format; also avail. in record)

820 CN ISSN 0704-5700
YEATS ELIOT REVIEW. 1974. a. Can.$12 for 2 years to institutions. c/o Shyamal Bagchee, Ed., Department of English, University of Victoria, Victoria, B.C. V8W 2Y2, Canada. TEL 604-721-7211. bk. rev. bibl. Indexed: Curr.Cont. M.L.A. Amer.Hum.Ind. Arts & Hum.Cit.Ind. Abstr.Engl.Stud. Ind.Bk.Rev.Hum.
Incorporating: T.S. Eliot Review (ISSN 0318-6342); T. S. Eliot Newsletter (ISSN 0315-1174)

YET ANOTHER SMALL MAGAZINE. see *LITERARY AND POLITICAL REVIEWS*

821   AT
YOUR FRIENDLY FASCIST. 1970. irreg. Aus.$2 per no. Pig's Arse Press, Box 297, Summer Hill, N.S.W. 2130, Australia. Eds. Rae Desmond Jones, John Edwards. circ. 300.

821   UK   ISSN 0260-7654
ZIP; poetry magazine. 1980. irreg. $4. Iris Services Co-operative, 1A Oldham St., Hyde, Cheshire SK14 1LJ, England. Ed. Sandy Gort. adv. illus. circ. 1,000. Indexed: Graph.Arts Lit.Abstr.

LUMBER AND WOOD

see Forests and Forestry—Lumber and Wood

MACHINERY

see also Agriculture—Agricultural Equipment

621.9   IT   ISSN 0393-0483
A M U. (Annuario Italiano Macchine Utensili e Complementari) 1966. a. L.80000. Tecniche Nuove s.r.l., Via Moscova 46/9a, 20121 Milan, Italy. circ. 7,000.

A T M DIRECTORY. (Automated Teller Machines) see *BUSINESS AND ECONOMICS — Banking And Finance*

621.9   FR
ANNUAIRE DE LA MECANIQUE. (Special edition in English, French, German and Spanish) a. 460 F. (Federation des Industries Mecaniques et Transformatrices des Metaux) Union Francaise d'Annuaires Professionnels, 13 av. Vladimir Komarov, B.P. 36, 78192 Trappes Cedex, France.

621.9   FR
ANNUAIRE NATIONAL DES MATIERES PREMIERES DE RECUPERATION ET DU MATERIEL D'OCCASION. 1953. a. 60 F. S E P Edition, 194-196 rue Marcadet, 75018 Paris, France. adv.

ANNUAIRE REPERTOIRE DE LA MOTOCULTURE DE PLAISANCE JARDINAGE. see *GARDENING AND HORTICULTURE*

621.9   FR
ANNUAIRE TECHNIQUE DE LA SOUS-TRAITANCE MECANIQUE. biennial. 200 F. (Federation des Industries Mecaniques et Transformatrices des Metaux) Union Francaise d'Annuaires Professionnels, 13 av. Vladimir Komarov, B.P. 36, 78192 Trappes Cedex, France.

ASSOCIATED EQUIPMENT DISTRIBUTORS. RENTAL RATES COMPILATION; nationally averaged rental rates for construction equipment including complete model specifications. see *BUILDING AND CONSTRUCTION*

621.9   FR
CATALOGUE DES CONSTRUCTEURS FRANCAIS D'EQUIPEMENTS POUR LES INDUSTRIES ALIMENTAIRES. irreg., latest 1981. 375 F. Societe d'Edition et de Promotion Agro-Alimentaires, Industrielles et Commerciales, B.P. 551, 42 rue du Louvre, 75027 Paris Cedex 01, France.

621.8   US
CENTRIFUGAL PUMP SPEC BOOK. 1981. a. Gordon Publications Inc., Box 1952, Dover, N.J. 07801, Randolph, NJ 07869. TEL 201-361-9060. adv.

CHINA, REPUBLIC. MACHINERY AND ELECTRICAL APPARATUS INDUSTRY YEARBOOK/CHUNG-HUA MIN KUO CHI CHI YU TIEN KUNG CHI TSAI NIEN CHIEN. see *ELECTRICITY AND ELECTRICAL ENGINEERING*

621.9   US
DESIGN NEWS ELECTRICAL/ELECTRONIC DIRECTORY. 1970. a. $15. Cahners Publishing Co., Inc., Manufacturing Group, Division of Reed Publishing USA, 275 Washington St., Newton, MA 02158 TEL 617-964-3030. (Subscr. to: 44 Cook St., Denver, CO 80206) Ed. Steven Kern. circ. controlled.
    Formerly: Design News Electrical/Electronic Reference Edition.

621.9   US
DESIGN NEWS FASTENING DIRECTORY. 1970. a. $15. Cahners Publishing Co., Inc., Manufacturing Group, Division of Reed Publishing USA, 275 Washington St., Newton, MA 02158 TEL 617-964-3030. (Subscr. to: 44 Cook St., Denver, CO 80206) Ed. Steven Kern. circ. controlled.
    Former titles: Design News Fastening Reference Edition; Design News. Fastening (ISSN 0190-2296); Design News Fastening Directory (ISSN 0190-2288)

621.9   US
DESIGN NEWS FLUID POWER DIRECTORY. 1970. a. $15. Cahners Publishing Co., Inc., Manufacturing Group, Division of Reed Publishing USA, 275 Washington St., Newton, MA 02158 TEL 617-964-3030. (Subscr. to: 44 Cook St., Denver, CO 80206) Ed. Steven Kern. circ. controlled.
    Former titles: Design News Fluid Power Reference Edition; Design News. Fluid Power (ISSN 0164-2871); Design News Annual. Fluid Power Edition.

621.9   US
DESIGN NEWS MATERIALS DIRECTORY. 1970. a. $15. Cahners Publishing Co., Inc., Manufacturing Group, Division of Reed Publishing USA, 275 Washington St., Newton, MA 02158 TEL 617-964-3030. (Subscr. to: 44 Cook St., Denver, CO 80206) Ed. Steven Kern. circ. controlled.
    Former titles: Design News Materials Reference Edition; Design News. Materials (ISSN 0164-2839); Design News Annual. Materials Edition.

621.9   US
DESIGN NEWS POWER TRANSMISSION DIRECTORY. 1970. a. $15. Cahners Publishing Co., Inc., Manufacturing Group, Division of Reed Publishing USA, 275 Washington St., Newton, MA 02158 TEL 617-964-3030. (Subscr. to: 44 Cook St., Denver, CO 80206) Ed. Steven Kern. circ. controlled.
    Formerly: Design News Power Transmission Reference Edition.

338.4 621.9   US   ISSN 0070-8550
ECONOMIC HANDBOOK OF THE MACHINE TOOL INDUSTRY. 1967. a. $35. National Machine Tool Builders' Association, 7901 Westpark Dr., McLean, VA 22102. TEL 703-893-2900. circ. 2,000.

621.9   MX
EQUIPO; materiales y servicio. 1962. a. Mex.$2000($25) Litoimpresores, S.A., Espana 396, 09880 Mexico, D.F., Mexico. Ed. Cesar Macazaga. adv.

FACULTAD NACIONAL DE AGRONOMIA MEDELLIN. see *AGRICULTURE*

621.9   SZ
FOERDERMITTELKATALOG; Foerdern-Lagern-Verteilen. 1969. a. 21 Fr. Verlag Binkert AG, CH-4335 Laufenburg, Switzerland. Ed. Silvan Binkert. adv. circ. 4,000.

FOOD MANUFACTURE INGREDIENT AND MACHINERY SURVEY. see *FOOD AND FOOD INDUSTRIES*

621.9   MX
GUIA DE LA INDUSTRIA: EQUIPO Y MATERIALES. 1968. a. Mex.$25. Editorial Cosmos, Espana No. 396, 09880 Mexico D.F., Mexico. Ed. Catalina Ramirez de Arellano. circ. 5,000.

621.9   GW
GUSS PRODUKTE. a. Verlag Hoppenstedt & Co., Havelstr. 9, P.O. Box 4006, D-6100 Darmstadt, W. Germany (B.R.D.)

621.9   US
INDUSTRIAL MACHINERY: LATIN AMERICAN INDUSTRIAL REPORT. (Avail. for each of 22 Latin American countries) 1985. a. $435 per country report per industry covered. Aurora International, Box 9099, Bridgeport, CT 06601-2099. TEL 203-368-0579.

621.9   US
INSIDE F M S; the comprehensive buying reference for factory automation. 1986. a. $50. Grant Publications, 155 E. 23rd St., New York, NY 10010. TEL 212-505-2600. Ed. Michael Ryan. adv. circ. 12,000.

INSTYTUT OBROBKI SKRAWANIEM. ZESZYTY NAUKOWE. see *ENGINEERING — Engineering Mechanics And Materials*

621.9   UK   ISSN 0074-6835
INTERNATIONAL MACHINE TOOL DESIGN AND RESEARCH CONFERENCE. PROCEEDINGS. 1960. a., 17th, 1977. £36.10. (University of Birmingham, Department of Mechanical Engineering) Macmillan Press Ltd., 4 Little Essex St., London WC2R 3LF, England. Ed. Prof. S.A. Tobias. circ. 550.

INTERNATIONAL TEXTILE MACHINERY. see *TEXTILE INDUSTRIES AND FABRICS*

INTERNATIONAL TRENDS IN MANUFACTURING TECHNOLOGY. see *TECHNOLOGY: COMPREHENSIVE WORKS*

JAPAN SOCIETY OF LUBRICATION ENGINEERS. JOURNAL. INTERNATIONAL EDITION. see *ENGINEERING*

621.9 918   US
LATIN AMERICAN METAL MECHANIC & ELECTRONIC INDUSTRY DIRECTORY. a. $150 per m. Aurora International, Box 9099, Bridgeport, CT 06601-2099. TEL 203-368-0579. Ed. Andres C. Aquino. adv.

621.9   UK   ISSN 0305-3121
MACHINERY BUYERS' GUIDE. 1926. a. £18. Findlay Publications Ltd., Franks Hall, Franks Lane, Horton Kirby, Kent DA4 9LL, England. Ed. F.A.J. Browne. adv. circ. 8,000.
    Formerly: Machinery's Annual Buyer's Guide (ISSN 0076-2040)

621   US
MACHINERY: LATIN AMERICAN INDUSTRIAL REPORT. 1985. a. $235 per country report. Aurora International, Box 9099, Bridgeport, CT 06601-2099. TEL 203-368-0579. Ed. Andres C. Aquino.

621.86   US
MATERIAL HANDLING ENGINEERING HANDBOOK AND DIRECTORY. biennial. $25. Penton Publishing, 1100 Superior Ave., Cleveland, OH 44114. TEL 216-696-7000. Ed. Bernie Knill. circ. 113,000. (reprint service avail. from UMI)

MINING AND ALLIED MACHINERY CORPORATION. ANNUAL REPORT. see *MINES AND MINING INDUSTRY*

621.75   US   ISSN 0026-8003
MODERN MACHINE SHOP. (Chinese edition avail.) 1928. a. $12 (free to qualified personnel) ‡ Gardner Publications, Inc., 6600 Clough Pike, Cincinnati, OH 45244. TEL 513-231-8020. Ed. Ken M. Gettelman. adv. charts. illus. tr.lit. circ. 106,000. (also avail. in microform from UMI; reprint service avail. from UMI) Indexed: Chem.Abstr. Met.Abstr. Sci.Abstr. Bus.Ind. ISMEC. Ind.Sci.Rev. Tr.& Indus.Ind. World Alum.Abstr.

338.45 621.9   US
MODERN MACHINE SHOP N C/C I M GUIDEBOOK. 1970. a. $10. Gardner Publications Inc., 6600 Clough Pike, Cincinnati, OH 45244. TEL 513-231-8020. Ed. Ken M. Gettelman. adv. circ. 66,000. (also avail. in microform from UMI; reprint service avail. from UMI)
    Formerly: Modern Machine Shop N C Guidebook and Directory (ISSN 0076-9991)

746 MACHINERY — ABSTRACTING, BIBLIOGRAPHIES, STATISTICS

621.9 US
NATIONAL TOOLING AND MACHINING
ASSOCIATION. BUYERS GUIDE. 1968. a. $90.
National Tooling and Machining Association, 9300
Livingston Rd., Ft. Washington, MD 20744. TEL
301-248-6200. Ed. Mark Jeschke. adv. circ. 25,000.
Formerly: National Tool, Die and Precision
Machining Association. Buyers Guide.

621.9 US ISSN 0028-9159
NEWS FROM THE GUTTER. 1961. irreg. (2-4/yr.)
free. Power Curbers Inc., Box 1639, Salisbury, NC
28144. TEL 704-636-5871. Ed. Richard Messinger.
charts. illus. stat. circ. 17,500.

NORTH CAROLINA METALWORKING
DIRECTORY. see BUSINESS AND
ECONOMICS — Trade And Industrial Directories

621.9 PL ISSN 0324-9646
POLITECHNIKA WROCLAWSKA. INSTYTUT
KONSTRUKCJI I EKSPLOATACJI MASZYN.
PRACE NAUKOWE. KONFERENCJE. 1973.
irreg., no.12, 1986. price varies. Politechnika
Wroclawska, Wybrzeze Wyspianskiego 27, 50-370
Wroclaw, Poland (Dist. by: Ars Polona-Ruch,
Krakowskie Przedmiescie 7, Warsaw, Poland) Ed.
Jerzy Ciekot. illus.

620 PL ISSN 0324-962X
POLITECHNIKA WROCLAWSKA. INSTYTUT
KONSTRUKCJI I EKSPLOATACJI MASZYN.
PRACE NAUKOWE. MONOGRAFIE. (Text in
Polish; summaries in English and Russian) 1969.
irreg., no.11, 1985. price varies. Politechnika
Wroclawska, Wybrzeze Wyspianskiego 27, 50-370
Wroclaw, Poland (Dist. by: Ars Polona-Ruch,
Krakowskie Przedmiescie 7, Warsaw, Poland) Ed.
Jerzy Ciekot.

620 PL ISSN 0324-9638
POLITECHNIKA WROCLAWSKA. INSTYTUT
KONSTRUKCJI I EKSPLOATACJI MASZYN.
PRACE NAUKOWE. STUDIA I MATERIALY.
(Text in Polish: summaries in English and Russian)
1970. irreg., no.23, 1984. price varies. Politechnika
Wroclawska, Wybrzeze Wyspianskiego 27, 50-370
Wroclaw, Poland (Dist. by: Ars Polona-Ruch,
Krakowskie Przedmiescie 7, Warsaw, Poland) Ed.
Jerzy Ciekot.

621.9 PL ISSN 0239-3182
POLITECHNIKA WROCLAWSKA. INSTYTUT
KONSTRUKCJI I EKSPLOATACJI MASZYN.
PRACE NAUKOWE. WSPOLPRACA. (Text in
Polish; summaries in English, Russian) 1979. irreg.,
no.3, 1985. price varies. Politechnika Wroclawska,
Wybrzeze Wyspianskiego 27, 50-370 Wroclaw,
Poland (Dist. by: Ars Polona-Ruch, Krakowskie
Przedmiescie 7, Warsaw, Poland) Ed. Jerzy Ciekot.

621.9 UR ISSN 0372-6053
POLITEKHNICHNYI INSTYTUT KIEV. VESTNIK.
SERIYA MASHINOSTROENIYA. (Text in
Russian; summaries in English) irreg. 1.21 Rub.
Politekhnichnyi Instytut, Brest-Litovskii pr., 39,
Kiev, Ukrainian S.S.R., U.S.S.R. illus.

621.9 669 DK ISSN 0106-0104
PRODUKTIONS NYTS
LEVERANDOERREGISTER. 1963. a. Thomson
Communications (Scandinavia) A-S, Struenseegade
7-9, DK-2200 Copenhagen N, Denmark. adv. circ.
13,168.

621.8 621 HU ISSN 0133-297X
PUBLICATIONS OF THE TECHNICAL
UNIVERSITY FOR HEAVY INDUSTRY. SERIES
C, MACHINERY. (Text in English, German,
Russian) irreg., vol.37, no.1/2, 1982. Nehezipari
Muszaki Egyetem, Miskolc, Hungary. Ed.Bd. bibl.
index. circ. 400.
Formerly: Publications of the Technical
University for Heavy Industry. Series C, Mechanical
Engineering.

621.9 669 US ISSN 0074-4557
S D C E INTERNATIONAL DIE CASTING
CONGRESS. TRANSACTIONS. 1960. biennial.
$65 to members; non-members $80. Society of Die
Casting Engineers, Inc., 2000 N. Fifth Ave., River
Grove, IL 60171. TEL 312-452-0700. cum.index:
1960-1983. circ. 500. (also avail. in microfilm from
UMI; reprint service avail. from UMI)
Formerly: National Die Casting Congress.
Transactions.

621.9 SA
SOUTH AFRICAN MECHANICS HANDBOOK.
(Text in Afrikaans and English) a. R.1.25. Union
Trades Directories (Pty) Ltd., 22-24 North Block,
Mutual Sq., Davenport Rd., Box 687, Durban 4000,
South Africa. adv.

621.9 UK ISSN 0263-5038
SPON'S PLANT AND EQUIPMENT PRICE
GUIDE. 1982. a. £85($190) E. & F.N. Spon Ltd.,
11 New Fetter Lane, London EC4P 4EE, England.
Formerly: Spon's Plant and Equipment Guide.

621.46 US ISSN 0092-1661
SYMPOSIUM ON INCREMENTAL MOTION
CONTROL SYSTEMS AND DEVICES.
PROCEEDINGS. 1972. a. $55. Incremental Motion
Control Systems Society, Box 2772, Station A,
Champaign, IL 61820. TEL 217-356-1523. Ed. B.C.
Kuo. illus. circ. 500. Indexed: Comput.Cont. Key
Title: Proceedings. Annual Symposium. Incremental
Motion Control Systems and Devices.

621.9 US
TURBOMACHINERY SYMPOSIUM.
PROCEEDINGS. 1972. a. $55. Texas A & M
University, Department of Mechanical Engineering,
Turbomachinery Laboratories, College Station, TX
77843. TEL 409-845-8943. Ed. Jean C. Bailey. circ.
1,500.

621.9 669 US
U S S R REPORT: MACHINE TOOLS AND
METAL-WORKING EQUIPMENT. irreg., approx.
10/yr. $5 per no. U.S. Joint Publications Research
Service, 1000 N. Glebe Rd., Arlington, VA 22201
TEL 703-487-4630. (Orders to: NTIS, Springfield,
VA 22161)

621.9 US ISSN 0085-6916
UNIVERSITAET STUTTGART. INSTITUT FUER
STEUERUNGSTECHNIK DER
WERKZEUGMASCHINEN UND
FERTIGUNGSEINRICHTUNGEN. I S W
BERICHTE. 1972. irreg., vol.45, 1982. price varies.
(GW) Springer-Verlag, 175 Fifth Ave., New York,
NY 10010 TEL 212-460-1500. (Also Berlin,
Heidelberg, Tokyo and Vienna) (reprint service
avail. from ISI)

621.9 DK
VEJVISER FOR MASKININDUSTRIEN. a. St.
Kongensgade 78, 1264 Copenhagen K, Denmark.
Ed. G.F. Kentorp. adv. circ. 3,500.

VEREIN DEUTSCHER INGENIEURE.
INFORMATIONSDIENST.
INSTANDHALTUNG. see ENGINEERING —
Abstracting, Bibliographies, Statistics

MACHINERY — Abstracting, Bibliographies, Statistics

620 621 016 PL ISSN 0032-3713
POLSKA BIBLIOGRAFIA ANALITYCZNA
MECHANIKI/POLISH SCIENTIFIC
ABSTRACTS ON MECHANICS. (Contents page
and captions in English) 1953. q. (Polska Akademia
Nauk, Instytut Podstawowych Problemow Techniki)
Panstwowe Wydawnictwo Naukowe, Miodowa 10,
00-251 Warsaw, Poland (Dist. by: Ars Polona,
Krakowskie Przedmiescie 7, 00-068 Warsaw,
Poland) Ed. M. Sokolowski. bk. rev. abstr. circ. 350.
Indexed: Appl.Mech.Rev. Math.R.

621.6 016 UK ISSN 0302-2870
PUMPS AND OTHER FLUIDS MACHINERY
ABSTRACTS. 1971. bi-m. £99($163) B H R A
Fluid Engineering, Cranfield, Bedford MK43 0AJ,
England (Dist. in U.S. by: Learned Information Inc.,
143 Old Marlton Pike, Medford, NJ 08055) bk. rev.
abstr. index. cum.index.
●Also available online. Vendors: European Space
Agency.

385.1 016 UR ISSN 0034-2556
REFERATIVNYI ZHURNAL. PROMYSHLENNYI
TRANSPORT. 1963. 12/yr. 60 Rub. (63.80 Rub.
including index) Vsesoyuznyi Institut Nauchno-
Tekhnicheskoi Informatsii (VINITI), Baltiiskaya ul.,
14, Moscow A-219, Russian S.F.S.R., U.S.S.R
(Subscr. to: Mezhdunarodnaya Kniga, Dimitrova ul.
39, 113095 Moscow, Russian S.F.S.R., U.S.S.R.)

621 016 UR ISSN 0034-2599
REFERATIVNYI ZHURNAL. TEKHNOLOGIYA
MASHINOSTROENIYA. 1956. m. 213.40 Rub.
(224.40 Rub. including index) Vsesoyuznyi Institut
Nauchno-Tekhnicheskoi Informatsii (VINITI),
Baltiiskaya ul., 14, Moscow A-219, Russian
S.F.S.R., U.S.S.R (Subscr. to: Mezhdunarodnaya
Kniga, Dimitrova ul. 39, 113095 Moscow, Russian
S.F.S.R., U.S.S.R.)

MACROECONOMICS

see Business and
Economics — Macroeconomics

MANAGEMENT

see Business and Economics — Management

MARKETING AND PURCHASING

see Business and Economics — Marketing
and Purchasing

MATHEMATICS

510 DK ISSN 0105-8533
AARHUS UNIVERSITET. MATEMATISK
INSTITUT. DATALOGISK AFDELING. DAIMI
FN. 1973. irreg. price varies. Aarhus Universitet,
Matematisk Institut, Datalogisk Afdeling, Ny
Munkegade, 8000 Aarhus C, Denmark.

510 DK ISSN 0106-9969
AARHUS UNIVERSITET. MATEMATISK
INSTITUT. DATALOGISK AFDELING. DAIMI
IR. 1973. irreg. price varies. Aarhus Universitet,
Matematisk Institut, Datalogisk Afdeling, Bygn.
540, Ny Munkegade, 8000 Aarhus C, Denmark.

510 DK ISSN 0105-8525
AARHUS UNIVERSITET. MATEMATISK
INSTITUT. DATALOGISK AFDELING. DAIMI
MD. 1973. irreg. price varies. Aarhus Universitet,
Matematisk Institut, Datalogisk Afdeling, Ny
Munkegade, 8000 Aarhus C, Denmark.

510 DK ISSN 0105-8517
AARHUS UNIVERSITET. MATEMATISK
INSTITUT. DATALOGISK AFDELING. DAIMI
PB. 1972. irreg. price varies. Aarhus Universitet,
Matematisk Institut, Datalogisk Afdeling, Ny
Munkegade, 8000 Aarhus C, Denmark.

510 DK ISSN 0106-8997
AARHUS UNIVERSITET. MATEMATISK
INSTITUT. ELEMENTAERAFDELING. 1957.
irreg. price varies. Aarhus Universitet, Matematisk
Institut, Aarhus, Denmark. illus.

510 DK ISSN 0065-017X
AARHUS UNIVERSITET. MATEMATISK
INSTITUT. LECTURE NOTES SERIES. 1963.
irreg., no.56, 1986. price varies. Aarhus Universitet,
Matematisk Institut, Ny Munkegade, 8000 Aarhus
C, Denmark.

510 DK
AARHUS UNIVERSITET. MATEMATISK
INSTITUT. MEMOIRS. 1974. irreg. Aarhus
Universitet, Matematisk Institut, Ny Munkegade,
8000 Aarhus C, Denmark.

510 DK ISSN 0065-0188
AARHUS UNIVERSITET. MATEMATISK
INSTITUT. VARIOUS PUBLICATIONS SERIES.
1962. irreg., no.36, 1985. price varies. Aarhus
Universitet, Matematisk Institut, Ny Munkegade,
8000 Aarhus C, Denmark.

MATHEMATICS

510   NR   ISSN 0001-3099
ABACUS. 1960. a. NC.5 per no. Mathematical Association of Nigeria, c/o Department of Education, University of Nigeria, Nsukka, Nigeria. Ed. R.O. Ohuche. bk. rev.

510 500 520   YU
ACADEMIE SERBE DES SCIENCES ET DES ARTS. CLASSE DES SCIENCES MATHEMATIQUES ET NATURELLES. BULLETIN. SCIENCES MATHEMATIQUES. (Text in English, French, Russian) 1952. a. price varies. Srpska Akademija Nauka i Umetnosti - Serbian Academy of Sciences and Arts, Knez Mihailova 35, 11001 Belgrade, Yugoslavia (Dist. by: Prosveta, Terazije 16, Belgrade, Yugoslavia) circ. 500. Indexed: Chem.Abstr. Math.R.
     Supersedes in part: Academie Serbe des Sciences et des Arts. Classe des Sciences Mathematiques et Naturelles. Bulletin. Nouvelle Serie (ISSN 0001-4184)

ACCADEMIA DELLE SCIENZE DI TORINO. MEMORIE. PART 1. CLASSE DI SCIENZE FISICHE, MATEMATICHE E NATURALI. see *SCIENCES: COMPREHENSIVE WORKS*

510 500 600   FI   ISSN 0001-5105
ACTA ACADEMIAE ABOENSIS, SERIES B: MATHEMATICA ET PHYSICA. (Text in English, German and Swedish) 1922. irreg., vol.45, 1985. price varies. Aabo Akademi, Domkyrkotorget 3, 20500 Aabo, Finland. charts. index. Indexed: Biol.Abstr. Math.R. Abstr.Bull.Inst.Pap.Chem.

510   PL   ISSN 0065-1036
ACTA ARITHMETICA. (Text in English, French, German, Italian and Russian) 1935. irreg., vol.44, 1984. $60 per vol. (Polska Akademia Nauk, Instytut Matematyczny) Panstwowe Wydawnictwo Naukowe, Ul. Miodowa 10, 00-251 Warsaw, Poland (Dist. by: Ars Polona, Krakowskie Przedmiescie 7, 00-068 Warsaw, Poland) Ed. A. Schinzel. bibl. charts. Indexed: Math.R. ASCA. Compumath. GeoRef.

510 370   PL   ISSN 0208-6204
ACTA UNIVERSITATIS LODZIENSIS: FOLIA MATHEMATICA. (Text in Polish; summaries in various languages) irreg. Uniwersytet Lodzki, Drukarnia Wojskowa, Ul. Gdanska 130, Lodz, Poland (Dist. by: Ars Polona-Ruch, Krakowskie Przedmiescie 7, Warsaw, Poland)

510   HU   ISSN 0001-6969
ACTA UNIVERSITATIS SZEGEDIENSIS DE ATTILA JOZSEF NOMINATAE. ACTA SCIENTIARUM MATHEMATICARUM. (Text in English, French, German, Italian and Russian) 1922. a. exchange basis. Attila Jozsef University, c/o E. Szabo, Exchange Librarian, Dugonics ter 13, P.O.B. 393, Szeged H-6701, Hungary (Subscr. to: Kultura, Box 149, H-1389 Budapest, Hungary) Ed. Laszlo Leindler. adv. bk. rev. index. circ. 1,000. Indexed: Curr.Cont. Math.R. Ref.Zh. Compumath.

510   US
ADVANCES IN PROBABILITY AND RELATED TOPICS. 1971. irreg., vol.7, 1984. price varies. Marcel Dekker, Inc., 270 Madison Ave., New York, NY 10016. TEL 212-696-9000. Eds. Peter Ney, Sidney Port. Indexed: Math.R.
     Formerly: Advances in Probability (ISSN 0065-3217)

510   PL   ISSN 0860-2727
AKADEMIA GORNICZO-HUTNICZA IM. STANISLAWA STASZICA. ZESZYTY NAUKOWE. OPUSCULA MATHEMATICA. (Text in English; summaries in Polish and Russian) 1985. irreg., no.3, 1987. price varies. (Akademia Gorniczo-Hutnicza im. Stanislawa Staszica) Wydawnictwo A G H, Manifestu Lipcowego 16, 31-109 Krakow, Poland (Dist. by: Ars Polona, Krakowskie Przedmiescie 7, 00-068 Warsaw, Poland) Ed. Z. Kleczek. illus. circ. 300.

510   PL   ISSN 0137-169X
AKADEMIA ROLNICZA, POZNAN. ROCZNIKI. ALGORYTMY BIOMETRYCZNE I STATYSTYCZNE. (Text in Polish; summaries in English, Russian) 1972. irreg. price varies. Akademia Rolnicza, Poznan, Ul. Wojska Polskiego 28, 60-637 Poznan, Poland. Indexed: Bibl.Agri.

510 530   GW   ISSN 0065-5295
AKADEMIE DER WISSENSCHAFTEN, GOETTINGEN. NACHRICHTEN 2. MATHEMATISCH-PHYSIKALISCHE KLASSE. (Text in English, German; occasionally in French) 1893. irreg. price varies. Vandenhoeck und Ruprecht, Theaterstr. 13, Postfach 37 53, 3400 Goettingen, W. Germany (B.R.D.) index. Indexed: Math.R. GeoRef.

510 530   GW
AKADEMIE DER WISSENSCHAFTEN IN GOETTINGEN. ABHANDLUNGEN. MATHEMATISCH-PHYSIKALISCHE KLASSE. DRITTE FOLGE. 1937. irreg. Vandenhoeck & Ruprecht, Robert-Bosch-Breite 6, Postfach 3753, D-3400 Goettingen, W. Germany (B.R.D.) Ed.Bd.

510   GW
AKADEMIE DER WISSENSCHAFTEN IN GOETTINGEN. ABHANDLUNGEN. MATHEMATISCH-PHYSIKALISCHE KLASSE. DRITTE SONDERHEFTE. 1951. irreg. Vandenhoeck & Ruprecht, Robert-Bosch-Breite 6, Postfach 3753, D-3753 Goettingen, W. Germany (B.R.D.) Ed.Bd.

510   CN   ISSN 0711-2521
ALBERTA TEACHERS' ASSOCIATION. MATH MONOGRAPH. 1973. a. price varies. Alberta Teachers' Association, Mathematics Council, Barnett House, 11010 142nd St., Edmonton. Alta T5N 2R1, Canada. TEL 403-453-2411. Ed. Thomas Schroeder. circ. 630.
     Formerly: Alberta Teachers' Association. Mathematics Monograph (ISSN 0317-8579); Supersedes: Mathematics Annual (ISSN 0085-3178)

510   YU
ALGEBRAIC CONFERENCE. PROCEEDINGS. 1980. irreg. $25. Institut za Matematiku, Prirodno-Matematicki Fakultet, Ul. Dr. Ilije Duricica 4, 21000 Novi Sad, Yugoslavia (Subscr. to: "FORUM", Izvozno Odelenje, ul. Vojvode Misica 1, 21000 Novi Sad, Yugoslavia)

510   US
ALGORITHMS AND COMBINATORICS. 1986. irreg. price varies. Springer-Verlag, 175 Fifth Ave., New York, NY 10160 TEL 212-460-1500. (Also Berlin, Heidelberg, Tokyo, Vienna) (reprint service avail. from ISI)

510   US   ISSN 0065-9258
AMERICAN MATHEMATICAL SOCIETY. COLLOQUIUM PUBLICATIONS. 1905. irreg., no.40, 1983. price varies. American Mathematical Society, Box 6248, Providence, RI 02940. TEL 401-272-9500. index in each vol. Indexed: Math.R. Zent.Math.

510   US   ISSN 0065-9290
AMERICAN MATHEMATICAL SOCIETY. TRANSLATIONS. SERIES 2. (Supersedes Series 1) 1955. irreg. price varies. American Mathematical Society, P.O. Box 6248, Providence, RI 02940. TEL 401-272-9500. Ed. Ben Silver. cum.index: 1966-1973.

510   FI   ISSN 0066-1953
ANNALES ACADEMIAE SCIENTIARUM FENNICAE. SERIES A, I: MATHEMATICA. (Text in English, French, German) 1941. a. $60. Suomalainen Tiedeakatemia - Academia Scientiarum Fennica, Snellmanink. 9-11, 00170 Helsinki, Finland. Ed. Olli Lehto. index, cum.index: 1941-1967 in vol. 400; 1967-1975 in vol. 600. circ. 725. (also avail. in microform; back issues avail.; reprint service avail. from UMI) Indexed: Bull.Signal. Math.R. Ref.Zh. Sci.Abstr. Sci.Cit.Ind. Compumath. Phys.Abstr. Zent.Math.

510   FI   ISSN 0355-0087
ANNALES ACADEMIAE SCIENTIARUM FENNICAE. SERIES A, I: MATHEMATICA DISSERTATIONES. (Text in English, French and German) 1975. irreg. price varies. Suomalainen Tiedeakatemia - Academia Scientiarum Fennica, Snellmanink 9-11, 00170 Helsinki, Finland. Ed. Olli Lehto. circ. 725. (also avail. in microform; back issues avail.; reprint service avail. from UMI) Indexed: Bull.Signal. Math.R. Ref.Zh. Sci.Cit.Ind. Phys.Abstr. Zent.Math.

510   PL   ISSN 0066-2216
ANNALES POLONICI MATHEMATICI. (Text in various languages) 1954. irreg., vol.44, 1984. $45 per vol. (Polska Akademia Nauk, Instytut Matematyczny) Panstwowe Wydawnictwo Naukowe, Ul. Miodowa 10, 00-251 Warsaw, Poland (Dist. by: Ars Polona, Krakowskie Przedmiescie 7, 00-068 Warsaw, Poland) Eds. Jozef Siciak, St. Lojasiewicz. bibl. Indexed: Math.R.

510   PL
ANNALES SOCIETATIS MATHEMATICAE POLONAE. SERIA 3: MATEMATYKA STOSOWANA. 1973. irreg. (3-4/yr.) 24 Zl. Polskie Towarzystwo Matematyczne, Ul. Sniadeckich 8, 00-950 Warsaw, Poland. Ed. Robert Bartoszynski. circ. 1,300. Indexed: Math.R.
     Formerly: Polskie Towarzystwo Matematyczne. Roczniki. Seria 3: Matematyka Stosowana.

510   PL   ISSN 0365-1029
ANNALES UNIVERSITATIS MARIAE CURIE-SKLODOWSKA. SECTIO A. MATHEMATICA. (Text in English, French, German, Polish) 1946. a. price varies. Uniwersytet Marii Curie-Sklodowskiej, Plac Marii Curie-Sklodowskiej 5, 20-031 Lublin, Poland. Eds. J. Krzyz, A. Bielecki. circ. 650. Indexed: Math.R.

510   IT   ISSN 0003-4622
ANNALI DI MATEMATICA; pura ed applicata. (Text in English, French, German and Italian) 1850. irreg., approx. 3-4/yr. Nicola Zanichelli Editore, Via Irnerio 34, Bologna 40126, Italy. bibl. charts. circ. 700. Indexed: Math.R.

510   US
ANNALS OF MATHEMATICS STUDIES. irreg., no.109, 1985. price varies. Princeton University Press, 3175 Princeton Pike, Lawrenceville, NJ 08648. TEL 609-896-2111. (reprint service avail. from UMI) Indexed: Math.R. Compumath.

510   US   ISSN 0172-4568
APPLICATIONS OF MATHEMATICS. 1975. irreg., vol.20, 1986. price varies. Springer-Verlag, 175 Fifth Ave., New York, NY 10010 TEL 212-460-1500. (Also Berlin, Heidelberg, Tokyo and Vienna) Eds. A.V. Balakrishnan, W. Hildenbrand. (reprint service avail. from ISI) Indexed: Math.R.

510   US   ISSN 0066-5452
APPLIED MATHEMATICAL SCIENCES. (Text in English) 1972. irreg., vol.62, 1986. price varies. Springer-Verlag, 175 Fifth Ave., New York, NY 10010 TEL 212-460-2500. (Also Berlin, Heidelberg, Tokyo and Vienna) (reprint service avail. from ISI) Indexed: Math.R.

510 531   US   ISSN 0066-5479
APPLIED MATHEMATICS AND MECHANICS; an international series of monographs. vol.2, 1957. irreg., vol.17, 1986. price varies. Academic Press Inc., Orlando, FL 32887. TEL 305-345-2000. Eds. F.N. Frenkiel, G. Temple. Indexed: Appl.Mech.Rev. Math.R. Sci.Abstr.

510   CN   ISSN 0700-9224
APPLIED MATHEMATICS NOTES/NOTES DE MATHEMATIQUES APPLIQUEES. (Text in English and French) vol.3, 1977. irreg. Can.$10. Canadian Mathematical Society - Societe Mathematique du Canada, 577 King Edward, Ottawa, Ont. K1N 6N5, Canada. Indexed: Math.R.
     Formerly: University of British Columbia. Department of Mathematics. Applied Mathematics Notes/Notes de Mathematiques Appliquees.

510   UR
ASIMPTOTICHESKIE METODY V TEORII SISTEM. 1971. irreg. 1 Rub. Irkutskii Gosudarstvennyi Universitet im. A.A. Zhdanova, Ul. Karla Marksa, 1, Irkutsk, Russian S.F.S.R., U.S.S.R. Ed. A.N. Panchenkov. circ. 600.

BALSKRISHNAN - NEUSTADT SERIES. see *TECHNOLOGY: COMPREHENSIVE WORKS*

BAYERISCHE AKADEMIE DER WISSENSCHAFTEN. MATHEMATISCH-NATURWISSENSCHAFTLICHE KLASSE. SITZUNGBERICHTE. see *SCIENCES: COMPREHENSIVE WORKS*

MATHEMATICS

510   GE   ISSN 0138-4821
BEITRAEGE ZUR ALGEBRA UND GEOMETRIE. 1971. irreg. M.25. VEB Deutscher Verlag der Wissenschaften, Postfach 1216, 1080 Berlin, E. Germany (D.D.R.) Ed.Bd. Indexed: Math.R.

510   US
BERKELEY SYMPOSIA ON MATHEMATICAL STATISTICS AND PROBABILITY. irreg., 6th, 1972. price varies. University of California Press, 2120 Berkeley Way, Berkeley, CA 94720. TEL 415-642-4247. Indexed: Biol.Abstr.

510   PL   ISSN 0519-8356
BIBLIOTEKA MATEMATYCZNA. 1953. irreg., vol.40, 1980. Panstwowe Wydawnictwo Naukowe, Miodowa 10, 00-251 00-251 Warsaw, Poland (Dist. by: Ars Polona, Krakowskie Przedmiescie 7, 00-068 Warsaw, Poland) bibl. Indexed: Math.R.

BIOMATHEMATICS. see *BIOLOGY*

510   BL
BOLETIM DE ANALISE E LOGICA MATEMATICA. 1969. irreg. Universidade Federal Fluminense, Instituto de Matematica, Niteroi, Brazil.

519.5   JA   ISSN 0286-522X
BULLETIN OF INFORMATICS AND CYBERNETICS. (Text in English) vol.4, 1950. a. 4000 Yen. Research Association of Statistical Sciences - Tokei Kagaku Kenkyukai, c/o Kyushu University 33, 10-1, Hakozaki 6-Chome, Higashi-Ku, Fukuoka, 812 Japan. Ed. T. Kitagawa. bibl. charts. circ. 600. Indexed: Math.R. Sci.Abstr. JCT. Zent.Math.
    Formerly (until vol.19, 1981): Bulletin of Mathematical Statistics (ISSN 0007-4993)

510   NE
C W I TRACTS. (Text in English) 1963. irreg. Stichting Mathematisch Centrum, Box 4079, 1009 AB Amsterdam, Netherlands. circ. 300.
    Formerly (until 1984): Mathematical Centre Tracts.

CAMBRIDGE MONOGRAPHS ON MATHEMATICAL PHYSICS. see *PHYSICS*

CAMBRIDGE MONOGRAPHS ON MECHANICS AND APPLIED MATHEMATICS. see *PHYSICS — Mechanics*

510   530.15   UK
CAMBRIDGE TRACTS IN MATHEMATICS. 1905. irreg., no.85, 1985. $32.50 for latest vol. Cambridge University Press, Edinburgh Bldg., Shaftesbury Rd., Cambridge CB2 2RU, England (and 32 E. 57 St., New York, NY 10022) Ed.Bd. Indexed: Math.R.
    Formerly: Cambridge Tracts in Mathematics and Mathematical Physics (ISSN 0068-6824)

510   CN
CANADIAN MATHEMATICAL SOCIETY. NOTES, NEWS AND COMMENTS. (Text in English and French) 1969. irreg. (8-9/yr.) Can.$10. Canadian Mathematical Society - Societe Mathematique du Canada, 577 King Edward, Ottawa, Ont. K1N 6N5, Canada. TEL adv. circ. 1,100.
    Formerly: Canadian Mathematical Congress. Notes, News and Comments (ISSN 0045-5164)

510   AT
CANBERRA MATHEMATICAL ASSOCIATION. NEWSLETTER. 1963. irreg. Aus.$0.75. Canberra Mathematical Association, Institute of Advanced Studies, Australian National University, Box 4, Canberra City, A.C.T. 2601, Australia. Ed. E. Lee. bk. rev. circ. 200.

510   CN   ISSN 0069-0600
CARLETON MATHEMATICAL SERIES. (Text in English and French) 1971. irreg. price varies. Carleton University, Department of Mathematics and Statistics, Ottawa, Ont. K1S 5B6, Canada. Ed. B.C. Mortimer. Indexed: Math.R.

510   CN   ISSN 0827-3669
CARLETON-OTTAWA MATHEMATICAL LECTURE NOTE SERIES. 1972. irreg. price varies. Carleton University, Department of Mathematics and Statistics, Ottawa, Ont. K1S 5B6, Canada. TEL 613-564-5500. Ed. B.C. Mortimer. Indexed: Math.R.
    Formerly (until 1985): Carleton Lecture Note Series.

510   SZ
CENTRE DE RECHERCHES EN MATHEMATIQUES PURES. PUBLICATIONS. SERIE 1. COURTES PUBLICATIONS. 1958. a. 24 Fr. Centre de Recherches en Mathematiques Pures, P.R. Gare 2, 2002 Neuchatel, Switzerland. Ed. S. Piccard. cum.index. Indexed: Math.R.
    Continues: Universite de Neuchatel. Seminaire de Geometrie. Publications. Serie 1. Courtes Publications (ISSN 0077-7641)

510   SZ
CENTRE DE RECHERCHES EN MATHEMATIQUES PURES. PUBLICATIONS. SERIE 2. MONOGRAPHIES. 1966. irreg. price varies. Centre de Recherches en Mathematiques Pures, P.R. Gare 2, 2002 Neuchatel, Switzerland. Ed. S. Piccard. Indexed: Math.R.
    Continues: Universite de Neuchatel. Seminaire de Geometrie. Publications. Serie 2. Monographies (ISSN 0077-765X)

510   SZ
CENTRE DE RECHERCHES EN MATHEMATIQUES PURES. PUBLICATIONS. SERIE 3. OEUVRES. irreg. Centre de Recherches en Mathematiques Pures, P.R. Gares 2, 2002 Neuchatel, Switzerland. Indexed: Math.R.

510   SZ
CENTRE DE RECHERCHES EN MATHEMATIQUES PURES. PUBLICATIONS. SERIE 4. CONFERENCES COMMUNICATIONS. a. 41.50 Fr. Centre de Recherches en Mathematiques Pures, P.R. Gares 2, 2002 Neuchatel, Switzerland. Indexed: Math.R.

CHANTIERS DE PEDAGOGIE MATHEMATIQUE. see *EDUCATION — Teaching Methods And Curriculum*

510   US   ISSN 0069-3286
CHICAGO LECTURES IN MATHEMATICS. 1964. irreg., latest 1984. price varies. University of Chicago Press, 5801 S. Ellis Ave., Chicago, IL 60637. TEL 312-962-7600. Ed. Irving Kaplansky. (reprint service avail. from UMI,ISI) Indexed: Math.R.

510   FR
COLLECTION FORMATION DES ENSEIGNANTS ET FORMATION CONTINUE. 1973. irreg. Editions Hermann, 293 rue Lecourbe, 75015 Paris, France. illus.
    Formerly: Collection Formation des Enseignants.

510   PL   ISSN 0010-1354
COLLOQUIUM MATHEMATICUM. (Text in various languages) 1947. irreg., vol.49, 1984. $45 per vol. (Polska Akademia Nauk, Instytut Matematyczny) Panstwowe Wydawnictwo Naukowe, Ul. Miodowa 10, 00-251 Warsaw, Poland (Dist. by: Ars Polona, Krakowskie Przedmiescie 7, 00-068 Warsaw, Poland) Ed. St. Hartman. bibl. circ. 900. Indexed: Math.R. GeoRef.

COMMENTATIONES PHYSICO-MATHEMATICAE. see *PHYSICS*

CONFERENCE ON PROBABILITY AND STATISTICS IN ATMOSPHERIC SCIENCES. PREPRINTS. see *METEOROLOGY*

510   CN   ISSN 0384-9864
CONGRESSUS NUMERANTIUM; a conference journal on numerical themes. 1970. irreg., approx. 3/yr. price varies. Utilitas Mathematica Publishing Inc., Box 7, University Centre, University of Manitoba, Winnipeg, Man. R3T 2N2, Canada. TEL 204-474-9423. Ed. Ralph G. Stanton. circ. 300. Indexed: Math.R. Zent.Math.
    Incorporating (until 1971): Manitoba Conference on Numerical Mathematics and Computing. Proceedings; (since 1970): Southeastern Conference on Combinatorics, Graph Theory and Computing Proceedings.

510   US   ISSN 0271-4132
CONTEMPORARY MATHEMATICS. 1980. irreg., latest, vol.59, 1986. American Mathematical Society, Box 6248, Providence, RI 02940. TEL 401-272-9500. Indexed: Math.R.

510   US   ISSN 0732-4405
CURRENT TOPICS IN CHINESE SCIENCE. SECTION C: MATHEMATICS. 1982. a., latest vol.3, 1985. Gordon & Breach Science Publishers, 50 W. 23rd St., New York, NY 10010. TEL 212-206-8900.

510   DK   ISSN 0106-6366
D C A M M REPORT. 1970. irreg. free. Danmarks Tekniske Hoejskole, Danish Center for Applied Mathematics and Mechanics, Department of Solid Mechanics, Technical University of Denmark, Lyngby, Denmark. circ. 500.

510   DK   ISSN 0106-9306
DANMARKS TEKNISKE HOEJSKOLE. MATEMATISK INSTITUT. MAT - P R. no. 2, 1984. irreg. Danmarks Tekniske Hoejskole, Matematisk Institut, 2800 Lyngby, Denmark. Ed. V. Lundsgaard Hansen. circ. 100.

DEVELOPMENTS IN GEOMATHEMATICS. see *EARTH SCIENCES — Geophysics*

510   HU   ISSN 0070-671X
DISQUISITIONES MATHEMATICAE HUNGARICAE. (Text in English, French, German or Hungarian) 1970. irreg., vol.13, 1984. price varies. (Magyar Tudomanyos Akademia) Akademiai Kiado, Publishing House of the Hungarian Academy of Sciences, P.O. Box 24, H-1363 Budapest, Hungary.

510   PL   ISSN 0012-3862
DISSERTATIONES MATHEMATICAE/ROZPRAWY MATEMATYCZNE. (Text in English, French, Polish, German and Russian; summaries in English and Russian) 1952. irreg., vol.232, 1984. price varies. (Polska Akademia Nauk, Instytut Matematyczny) Panstwowe Wydawnictwo Naukowe, Ul. Miodowa 10, 00-251 Warsaw, Poland (Dist. by: Ars Polona, Krakowskie Przedmiescie 7, 00-068 Warsaw, Poland) Ed. B. Bojavski. bibl. Indexed: Math.R.

DIVREI HA-AKADEMIA HA-LEUMIT HA-YISRAELIT LEMADAIM-HA-HATIVA LE-MADAEI HA-TEVA. see *PHYSICS*

510   UK   ISSN 0260-4884
DOZENAL JOURNAL. 1959. irreg. £5. Dozenal Society of Great Britain, Millside, Mill Rd., Denmead, Hampshire PO7 6PA, England. Ed. Donald Hammond. bk. rev. index. circ. 200. (tabloid format)
    Former titles (until winter 1980): Dozenal Review (ISSN 0309-8648); Until 1977: Duodecimal Review.

510   US   ISSN 0071-1136
ERGEBNISSE DER MATHEMATIK UND IHRER GRENZGEBIETE. NEUE FOLGE. (Text in German or English; occasionally French or Italian) 1955; 3rd series 1984. irreg., vol.13, 1987. price varies. Springer-Verlag, 175 Fifth Ave., New York, NY 10010 TEL 212-460-1500. (Also Berlin, Heidelberg, Tokyo and Vienna) Ed. P.Z. Hilton. circ. 2,000. (reprint service avail. from ISI) Indexed: Math.R.

510   530.15   UK   ISSN 0071-2248
EUREKA: THE ARCHIMEDEAN'S JOURNAL. 1939. a. £1. Cambridge University, Mathematical Society, Archimedeans, c/o Arts School, Bene't St., Cambridge CB2 3PY, England. Ed. E. Welbourne. adv. bk. rev. circ. 800. Indexed: Met.Abstr.

510   PL   ISSN 0044-4413
FASCICULI MATHEMATICI. (Text and summaries in English, French and Russian) irreg. price varies. Politechnika Poznanska, Pl. Curie Sklodowskiej 5, Poznan, Poland. illus. circ. 180. Indexed: Math.R. Ref.Zh.
    Formerly: Politechnika Poznanska. Zeszyty Naukowe. Matematyka (ISSN 0079-452X)

510   CS
FORMATOR SYMPOSIUM ON MATHEMATICAL METHODS FOR THE ANALYSIS OF LARGE-SCALE SYSTEMS. (Text in English) irreg., 4th 1983, Prague. $53.70 per no. (Ceskoslovenska Akademie Ved, Matematicky Ustav) Academia, Publishing House of the Czechoslovak Academy of Sciences, Vodickova 40, 112 29 Prague 1, Czechoslovakia.

510 FR
FRANCE. MINISTERE DE LA RECHERCHE ET DE L'INDUSTRIE. REPERTOIRE NATIONAL DES LABORATOIRES; LA RECHERCHE UNIVERSITAIRE; SCIENCES EXACTES ET NATURELLES. TOME 4: MATHEMATIQUES, SCIENCES DE L'ESPACE ET DE LA TERRE. 1966. irreg. price varies. (Centre National de la Recherche Scientifique) Documentation Francaise, 29-31 Quai Voltaire, 75007 Paris, France.
   Formerly: France. Delegation Generale a la Recherche Scientifique et Technique. Repertoire National des Laboratoires; la Recherche Universitaire; Sciences Exactes et Naturelles. Tome 4: Mathematiques, Sciences de l'Espace et de la terre (ISSN 0071-8564)

510 PL ISSN 0208-6573
FUNCTIONES ET APPROXIMATIO COMMENTARII MATHEMATICI. (Text in English) 1974. irreg., vol.14, 1984. price varies. Uniwersytet im. Adama Mickiewicza w Poznaniu, Instytut Matematyki, Matejki 48/49, 60-769 Poznan, Poland TEL 699 221. (Dist. by: Adam Mickiewicz University Press, Marchlewskiego 128, 61-874 Poznan, Poland) Eds. J. Musielak and A. Alexiewicz. circ. 600. Indexed: Math.R.

510 PL ISSN 0016-2736
FUNDAMENTA MATHEMATICAE. (Text in various languages) 1920. irreg., vol.123, 1984. $45 per vol. (Polska Akademia Nauk, Instytut Matematyczny) Panstwowe Wydawnictwo Naukowe, Miodowa 10, 00-251 Warsaw, Poland (Dist. by: Ars Polona, Krakowskie Przedmiescie 7, 00-068 Warsaw, Poland) Ed. R. Engellcing. Indexed: Math.R. Compumath.

510 500 PL ISSN 0072-0445
GDANSKIE TOWARZYSTWO NAUKOWE. WYDZIAL 3. NAUK MATEMATYCZNO-PRZYRODNICZYCH. ROZPRAWY. (Text in Polish; summaries in English and Russian) 1964. irreg. price varies. Ossolineum, Publishing House of the Polish Academy of Sciences, Rynek 9, 50-106 Wroclaw, Poland (Dist. by: Ars Polona-Ruch, Krakowskie Przedmiescie 7, Warsaw, Poland) Ed. Ryszard Piekos.

510 US ISSN 0072-5285
GRADUATE TEXTS IN MATHEMATICS. (Text in English) 1971. irreg., vol.111, 1986. price varies. Springer-Verlag, 175 Fifth Ave., New York, NY 10010 TEL 212-460-1500. (Also Berlin, Heidelberg, Tokyo and Vienna) Ed.Bd. (reprint service avail. from ISI) Indexed: Math.R.

510 GR ISSN 0072-7466
GREEK MATHEMATICAL SOCIETY. BULLETIN/ HELLENIKE MATHEMATIKE HETAIREIA. DELTION. (Text in English, French, German, Greek, and Italian) 1960. a. $20. Greek Mathematical Society, 34, E. Venizelou St., Athens 143, Greece. Ed.Bd. circ. 1,000.

510 US
GRUNDLEHREN DER MATHEMATISCHEN WISSENSCHAFTEN. (Text in English, occasionally in French and German) 1957. irreg., vol.286, 1987. price varies. Springer-Verlag, 175 Fifth Ave., New York, NY 10010 TEL 212-460-1500. (Also Berlin, Heidelberg, Tokyo and Vienna) (reprint service avail. from ISI) Indexed: Math.R.
   Formerly: Grundlehren der Mathematischen Wissenschaften in Einzeldarstellungen (ISSN 0072-7830)

510 II ISSN 0073-2281
HINDU ASTRONOMICAL AND MATHEMATICAL TEXT SERIES. (Text in English and Sanskrit; summaries in English) 1957. irreg. price varies. University of Lucknow, Department of Mathematics and Astronomy, Lucknow, Uttar Pradesh, India. Ed. R. P. Agarwala. Indexed: Math.R.

510 GE ISSN 0073-2842
HOCHSCHULBUECHER FUER MATHEMATIK. 1955. irreg. price varies. VEB Deutscher Verlag der Wissenschaften, Postfach 1216, 1080 Berlin, E. Germany (D.D.R.) Eds. H. Grell, R. Maruhn, W. Rinow. Indexed: Math.R.

I B M RESEARCH SYMPOSIA SERIES. see
PHYSICS

510 US
I M A VOLUMES IN MATHEMATICS AND ITS APPLICATIONS. 1986. irreg. price varies. Springer-Verlag, 175 Fifth Ave., New York, NY 10160 TEL 212-460-1500. (Also Berlin, Heidelberg, Tokyo, Vienna) (reprint service avail. from ISI)

510 US
I M S LECTURE NOTES. MONOGRAPH SERIES. 1981. irreg. Institute of Mathematical Statistics, 3401 Investment Blvd., Ste. 7, Hayward, CA 94545. TEL 415-783-8141. Ed. Shanti S. Gupta.

510 JA
IBARAKI UNIVERSITY. FACULTY OF SCIENCE. BULLETIN. SERIES A: MATHEMATICS. (Text in English; summaries in Japanese) 1968. a. exchange basis only. Ibaraki University, Department of Mathematics, 2-1-11 Bunkyo, Mito 310, Japan. circ. 250. Indexed: Math.R.

510 II ISSN 0019-5839
INDIAN MATHEMATICAL SOCIETY. JOURNAL. (Text in English) 1909; N.S. 1934. a. $50. Indian Mathematical Society, Meerut University, Department of Mathematics, Meerut 250 005, India. Ed. I.B.S. Passi. bk. rev. bibl. pat. tr.lit. index. circ. 1,200. Indexed: Math.R.

510 II
INDIAN NATIONAL SCIENCE ACADEMY. MATHEMATICAL TABLES. 1956. irreg. Rs.15($5) Indian National Science Academy, Bahadur Shah Zafar Marg, New Delhi 110002, India. Eds. M. S. Cheema and H. Gupta.
   Continues: National Institute of Sciences of India. Mathematical Tables (ISSN 0466-3276)

510 FR
INSTITUT HENRI POINCARE. GROUPE D'ETUDE D'ANALYSE ULTRAMETRIQUE. EXPOSES. 1974. a. 60 Fr. Institut Henri Poincare, Secretariat Mathematique, 11 rue Pierre et Marie Curie, F-75231 Paris Cedex 05, France (Subscr. address: Offilib, 48 rue Gay Lussac, F-75240 Paris Cedex 05, France) Ed. Paul Belgodere. circ. 200. (back issues avail) Indexed: Math.R. Ref.Zh. Zent.Math.

510 UK
INSTITUTE OF MATHEMATICS AND ITS APPLICATIONS. PROCEEDINGS. irreg. price varies. Institute of Mathematics and its Applications, Maitland House, Warrior Sq., Southend-on-Sea, Essex SS1 2JY, England.

510 AG ISSN 0326-0690
INSTITUTO DE MATEMATICA BEPPO LEVI. CUADERNOS. 1971. irreg. exchange basis. Universidad Nacional de Rosario, Avenida Pellegrini 250, 2000 Rosario, Argentina. Ed.Bd. circ. 500. Indexed: Appl.Mech.Rev. Math.R. Zent.Math.

510 DK ISSN 0107-5233
INSTITUTTET FOR MATEMATISK STATISTIK OG OPERATIONSANALYSE. WORKING PAPER. irreg. Instituttet for Matematisk Statistik og Operationsanalyse, Lyngby, Denmark. illus.

510 RM
INSTITUTUL PEDAGOGIC ORADEA. LUCRARI STIINTIFICE: SERIA MATEMATICA. (Continues in part its Lucrari Stiintfice: Seria Matematica, Fizica, Chimie (1971-72), its Lucrari Stiintifice: Seria A and Seria B (1969-1970), and its Lucrari Stiintifice (1967-68).) (Text in Rumanian, occasionally in English or French; summaries in English, French, German, Rumanian) 1967. a. Institutul Pedagogic Oradea, Calea Armatei Rosii Nr. 5, Oradea, Romania.

515 US
INTERNATIONAL CONFERENCE ON COMPUTING FIXED POINTS WITH APPLICATIONS. PROCEEDINGS. 1977. irreg., 1st, 1974, Clemson University (pub. 1977) Department of the Navy, Office of Naval Research, Arlington, VA 22217. TEL 202-545-6700. (Co-sponsor: U.S. Army Research Office)

510 530 II ISSN 0074-705X
INTERNATIONAL MONOGRAPHS ON ADVANCED MATHEMATICS AND PHYSICS. (Text in English) 1961. irreg. Hindustan Publishing Corp., 6-U.B. Jawahar Nagar, Delhi 110007, India.

510 UK
INTERNATIONAL SERIES IN NONLINEAR MATHEMATICS; theory, methods and applications. 1980. irreg., vol.4, 1981. Pergamon Press, Ltd., Headington Hill Hall, Oxford OX3 0BW, England (U.S. subscr. to: Maxwell House, Fairview Park, Elmsford, NY 10523) Eds. V. Lakshmikantham, C.P. Tsokos.

510 UK ISSN 0539-0125
INTERNATIONAL SERIES IN PURE AND APPLIED MATHEMATICS. 1957. irreg., vol.108, 1980. price varies. Pergamon Press, Ltd., Headington Hill Hall, Oxford OX3 0BW, England (U.S. subscr. to: Maxwell House, Fairview Park, Elmsford, NY 10523) Indexed: Math.R.
   Formerly: International Series of Monographs in Pure and Applied Mathematics.

IOWA STATE UNIVERSITY. STATISTICAL LABORATORY. ANNUAL REPORT. see
MATHEMATICS — Abstracting, Bibliographies, Statistics

ISSLEDOVANIA PO TEORII ALGORIFMOV I MATEMATICHESKOI LOGIKE. see
PHILOSOPHY

510 UR
ISTORIKO-MATEMATICHESKIE ISSLEDOVANIYA. vol.22, 1977. irreg. price varies. (Akademiya Nauk S.S.S.R., Institut Istorii Estestvoznaniya i Tekhniki) Izdatel'stvo Nauka, Podsosenskii per., 21, Moscow K-62, Russian S.F.S.R., U.S.S.R. (Subscr. to: Mezhdunarodnaya Kniga, Moscow, G-200, Russian S.F.S.R., U.S.S.R.) Ed. A.P. Yushkevich. abstr. bibl. illus. circ. 1,500. Indexed: Math.R.

510 UR ISSN 0202-7445
ITOGI NAUKI I TEKHNIKI: ALGEBRA - TOPOLOGIYA - GEOMETRIYA. irreg., latest vol.25, 1987. 8 Rub. Vsesoyuznyi Institut Nauchno-Tekhnicheskoi Informatsii (VINITI), Baltiiskaya ul. 14, Moscow A-219, Russian S.F.S.R., U.S.S.R. (Subscr. to: Mezhdunarodnaya Kniga, Dimitrova ul. 39, 113095 Moscow, Russian S.F.S.R., U.S.S.R.)

510 UR ISSN 0202-7453
ITOGI NAUKI I TEKHNIKI: MATEMATICHESKII ANALIZ. irreg., latest vol.25, 1987. price varies. Vsesoyuznyi Institut Nauchno-Tekhnicheskoi Informatsii (VINITI), Baltiiskaya ul. 14, Moscow A-219, Russian S.F.S.R., U.S.S.R. (Subscr. to: Mezhdunarodnaya Kniga, Dimitrova ul. 39, 113095 Moscow, Russian S.F.S.R., U.S.S.R.)

516 UR ISSN 0202-7461
ITOGI NAUKI I TEKHNIKI: PROBLEMY GEOMETRII. irreg., latest vol.19, 1987. price varies. Vsesoyuznyi Institut Nauchno-Tekhnicheskoi Informatsii (VINITI), Baltiiskaya ul. 14, Moscow A-219, Russian S.F.S.R., U.S.S.R. (Subscr. to: Mezhdunarodnaya Kniga, Dimitrova 39, 113095 Moscow, Russian S.F.S.R., U.S.S.R.)

510 001.53 UR ISSN 0202-7488
ITOGI NAUKI I TEKHNIKI: TEORIYA VEROYATNOSTEJ - MATEMATICHESKAYA STATISTIKA-TEORETICHESKAYA KIBERNETIKA. irreg., vol.25, 1987. price varies. Vsesoyuznyi Institut Nauchno-Tekhnicheskoi Informatsii (VINITI), Baltiiskaya ul. 14, Moscow A-219, Russian S.F.S.R., U.S.S.R. (Subscr. to: Mezhdunarodnaya Kniga, Dimitrova ul. 39, 113095 Moscow, Russian S.F.S.R., U.S.S.R.)

510 GW ISSN 0172-8512
JAHRBUCH UEBERBLICKE MATHEMATIK. 1975. a. price varies. Bibliographisches Institut, Dudenstr. 6, Postfach 311, 6800 Mannheim 1, W. Germany (B.R.D.) Ed.Bd.

510 JA ISSN 0075-4293
JOURNAL OF MATHEMATICS. (Text in English) 1967. a. exchange basis. Tokushima University, Faculty of Education - Tokushima Daigaku Kyoiku Gakubu, Kyoiku-gakubu, Tokushima, Japan. Indexed: Math.R.

510 FI ISSN 0075-4641
JYVASKYLAN YLIOPISTO. MATEMATIIKAN LAITOS. REPORT. 1967. irreg. exchange basis only. ‡ University of Jyvaskyla, Department of Mathematics - Jyvaskylan Yliopisto, Seminaarinkatu 15, SF-40100 Jyvaskyla 10, Finland. Ed. Olli Martio. Indexed: Math.R. Zent.Math.

MATHEMATICS

510 UR
KHAR'KOVSKII GOSUDARSTVENNYI UNIVERSITET. MATEMATIKA I MEKHANIKA. (Subseries of: Khar'kovskii Universitet. Vestnik) vol.41, 1976. irreg. 0.56 Rub. per issue. Izdatel'stvo Vysshaya Shkola-Khar'kov, Khar'kovskoe Otdelenie, Universitetskaya 16, 310003 Kharkov, Ukrainian S.S.R., U.S.S.R. Ed. I. Tarapov. circ. 1,000.

KOEBENHAVNS UNIVERSITET. INSTITUT FOR ANVENDT OG MATEMATISK LINGVISTIK. SKRIFTER. see *LINGUISTICS*

510 530 DK ISSN 0023-3323
KONGELIGE DANSKE VIDENSKABERNES SELSKAB. MATEMATISK-FYSISKE MEDDELELSER. (Text in English, French and German) 1919. irreg., vol.41, 1985. price varies. Kongelige Danske Videnskabernes Selskab - Royal Danish Academy of Sciences and Letters, H.C. Andersens 35, DK-1553 Copenhagen V, Denmark (Orders to: Munksgaard Export and Subscription Service, Noerre Soegade 35, DK-1370 Copenhagen K, Denmark) bibl. charts. illus. index. Indexed: Chem.Abstr. Math.R. Met.Abstr. Sci.Abstr.

510 UR
KRAEVYE ZADACHI DLYA DIFFERENTSIAL'NYKH URAVNENII. 1971. irreg. 1.10 Rub. Akademiya Nauk Uzbekskoi S.S.R., Institut Matematiki im. V.I. Romanovskogo, Astronomicheskii tup., 11, Tashkent, Uzbek S.S.R., U.S.S.R.

510 KU
KUWAIT UNIVERSITY. CONFERENCE ON ALGEBRA AND GEOMETRY. PROCEEDINGS. (Text in English) 1982. irreg. Kuwait University, Department of Mathematics, Kuwait. (Kuwait Foundation for the Advancement of Sciences) Ed.Bd. charts.

510 500 JA ISSN 0454-8221
KYUSHU INSTITUTE OF TECHNOLOGY. BULLETIN: MATHEMATICS, NATURAL SCIENCE/KYUSHU KOGYO DAIGAKU KENKYU HOKOKU, SHIZENKAGAKU. (Text in European languages) 1955. a. exchange basis. Kyushu Institute of Technology - Kyushu Kogyo Daigaku, Tobata, Kitakyushu 804, Japan. Indexed: Math.R. Sci.Abstr.

510 574 US ISSN 0341-633X
LECTURE NOTES IN BIOMATHEMATICS. 1974. irreg., vol.69, 1986. price varies. Springer-Verlag, 175 Fifth Ave., New York, NY 10010 TEL 212-460-1500. (Also Berlin, Heidelberg, Tokyo and Vienna) Ed. S. Levin. (reprint service avail. from ISI) Indexed: Biol.Abstr. Chem.Abstr.

510 330 US ISSN 0075-8442
LECTURE NOTES IN ECONOMICS AND MATHEMATICAL SYSTEMS; operations research, computer science, social science. 1968. irreg., vol.283, 1986. price varies. Springer-Verlag, 175 Fifth Ave., New York, NY 10010 TEL 212-460-1500. (Also Berlin, Heidelberg, Tokyo and Vienna) Eds. M. Beckmann, W. Krelle. cum.index nos. 1-170. (reprint service avail. from ISI) Indexed: SSCI. Sci.Abstr.
  Former titles (until 1971): Lecture Notes in Operations Research and Mathematical Systems; Which supersedes (1967-1969): Lecture Notes in Operations Research and Mathematical Economics; Lecture Notes in Operations Research and Mathematical Systems.

510 US ISSN 0075-8434
LECTURE NOTES IN MATHEMATICS. (Text in English; occasionally in German and French) 1964. irreg., vol.1221, 1986. price varies. Springer-Verlag, 175 Fifth Ave., New York, NY 10010 TEL 212-460-1500. (Also Berlin, Heidelberg, Tokyo and Vienna) Eds. A. Dold, B. Eckmann. (reprint service avail. from ISI) Indexed: Math.R. Compumath.

510 US ISSN 0075-8469
LECTURE NOTES IN PURE AND APPLIED MATHEMATICS. 1971. irreg., vol.105, 1986. price varies. Marcel Dekker, Inc., 270 Madison Ave., New York, NY 10016. TEL 212-696-9000. Ed.Bd.

510 US ISSN 0075-8485
LECTURES IN APPLIED MATHEMATICS. 1957. irreg., vol.24, 1986. price varies. American Mathematical Society, Box 6248, Providence, RI 02940. TEL 401-272-9500. Indexed: Biol.Abstr. Math.R. Zent.Math.

510 570 US ISSN 0075-8523
LECTURES ON MATHEMATICS IN THE LIFE SCIENCES. 1968. irreg., vol.18, 1986. price varies. American Mathematical Society, Box 6248, Providence, RI 02940. TEL 401-272-9500. Indexed: Biol.Abstr. Chem.Abstr. Math.R. Zent.Math.

510 370 GW
LEHRBUECHER UND MONOGRAPHIEN ZUR DIDAKTIK DER MATHEMATIK. 1985. irreg. price varies. Bibliographisches Institut, Dudenstr. 6, Box 311, D-6800 Mannheim 1, W. Germany (B.R.D.) Eds. N. Knoche, H. Scheid.

510 US ISSN 0278-5307
LIBERTAS MATHEMATICA. (Text in English, French, Rumanian) 1981. a. $20 to individuals; institutions $40. (American Romanian Academy of Arts and Sciences) A R A Publication, Department of French and Italian, University of California, Sproul Hall, Davis, CA 95616. TEL 916-752-6442. Ed. Constantin Corduneanu. bibl. illus. stat. circ. 250. (back issues avail.)

510 500 PL ISSN 0076-0412
LODZKIE TOWARZYSTWO NAUKOWE. WYDZIAL III. NAUK MATEMATYCZNO-PRZYRODNICZYCH. PRACE. (Text in Polish; summaries in English or French) 1947. irreg., 1973. price varies. Panstwowe Wydawnictwo Naukowe, Ul. Miodowa 10, 00-251 Warsaw, Poland (Dist. by: Ars Polona, Krakowskie Przedmiescie 7, 00-068 Warsaw, Poland) Indexed: Biol.Abstr.

510 UK ISSN 0076-0552
LONDON MATHEMATICAL SOCIETY. LECTURE NOTE SERIES. 1971. irreg., no.101, 1985. $19.95 for latest vol. Cambridge University Press, Edinburgh Bldg., Shaftesbury Rd., Cambridge CB2 2RU, England (and 32 E. 57 St., New York NY 10022) Ed. I.M. James. index. Indexed: Math.R.

510 US
LONDON MATHEMATICAL SOCIETY. MONOGRAPHS. NEW SERIES. 1986. irreg.? Academic Press Inc., Orlando, FL 32887. TEL 305-345-2000. Eds. P.M. Cain, D.A. Edwards. Indexed: Math.R.
  Supersedes (1970-1985): L M S Monographs (ISSN 0076-0560)

MATCH; informal communications in mathematical chemistry. see *CHEMISTRY*

510 530 UR
MATEMATICHESKAYA FIZIKA I FUNKTSIONAL'NYI ANALIZ. (Text in Russian; summaries in English) irreg. 1 Rub. Akademiya Nauk Ukrainskoi S.S.R., Fiziko-Tekhnicheskii Institut Nizkikh Temperatur, Pr. Lenina 47, Kharkov, Ukrainian S.S.R., U.S.S.R.

510 PL
MATEMATYKA. 1963. irreg. price varies. Adam Mickiewicz University Press, Marchlewskiego 128, 61-874 Poznan, Poland. Ed. Julian Musielak.
  Formerly: Uniwersytet im. Adama Mickiewicza w Poznaniu. Wydzial Matematyki, Fizyki i Chemii. Prace. Seria Matematyka (ISSN 0551-6625)

510 AG ISSN 0025-553X
MATHEMATICAE NOTAE. (Text in English, French, German, Italian and Spanish) 1941. a. exchange basis. ‡ (Instituto de Matematica Beppo Levi) Universidad Nacional de Rosario, Avenida Pellegrini 250, 2000 Rosario, Argentina. Ed.Bd. bk. rev. circ. 500. Indexed: Appl.Mech.Rev. Math.R. Zent.Math.

510 NZ ISSN 0581-1155
MATHEMATICAL CHRONICLE. 1969. irreg., vol.13, 1984. NZ.$8($10) to individuals, $10 to institutions. University of Auckland, Department of Mathematics & Statistics, Mathematical Chronicle Committee, Private Bag, Auckland, New Zealand. Ed. D.J. Smith. bk. rev. bibl. charts. cum.index vols: 1-10. circ. 300. Indexed: Math.R.

510 CN ISSN 0076-5333
MATHEMATICAL EXPOSITIONS. 1946. irreg. price varies. University of Toronto Press, Front Campus, Toronto, Ont. M5S 1A6, Canada TEL 613-667-7791. (and 33 East Tupper St., Buffalo, N. Y. 14203)

510 US
MATHEMATICAL NOTES (PRINCETON) 1966. a. price varies. Princeton University Press, Princeton, NJ 08540. TEL 609-896-2111. (Co-publisher: University of Tokyo Press) (reprint service avail. from UMI) Indexed: Math.R. Compumath.

519 530.15 NE
MATHEMATICAL PHYSICS AND APPLIED MATHEMATICS. 1976. irreg. price varies. D. Reidel Publishing Co., Box 17, 3300 AA Dordrecht, Netherlands (And 190 Old Derby St., Hingham, MA 02043) Eds. M. Flato, R. Raczka. Indexed: Math.R.

510 US
MATHEMATICAL SCIENCES RESEARCH INSTITUTE PUBLICATIONS. 1984. irreg., vol.6, 1986. price varies. Springer-Verlag, 175 Fifth Ave., New York, NY 10010 TEL 212-460-1500. (Also Berlin, Heidelberg, Tokyo, Vienna) (reprint service avail. from ISI)

510 JA ISSN 0549-4540
MATHEMATICAL SOCIETY OF JAPAN. PUBLICATIONS. (Text in English and European languages) 1955. irreg. Mathematical Society of Japan - Nihon Sugakkai, 25-9-203, Hongo 4-chome, Bunkyo-ku, Tokyo 113, Japan, Japan.

510 US
MATHEMATICAL SURVEYS & MONOGRAPHS. 1950. irreg., no.23, 1986. price varies. American Mathematical Society, Box 6248, Providence, RI 02940. TEL 401-272-9500. Indexed: Math.R. Zent.Math.
  Formerly: Mathematical Surveys (ISSN 0076-5376)

MATHEMATICAL SYSTEMS IN ECONOMICS. see *BUSINESS AND ECONOMICS — Economic Systems And Theories, Economic History*

510 US ISSN 0543-0941
MATHEMATICS AND ITS APPLICATIONS. 1971. a., vol.15, 1983. price varies. Gordon and Breach Science Publishers, 50 West 23rd St., New York, NY 10010. TEL 212-206-8900. Ed. Jacob T. Schwartz, Maurice Levy. Indexed: Math.R.
  Formerly: Notes on Mathematics and Its Applications.

510 NE
MATHEMATICS AND ITS APPLICATIONS. 1977. irreg. D. Reidel Publishing Co., Box 17, 3300 AA Dordrecht, Netherlands (And 190 Old Derby St., Hingham, MA 02043) Ed. M. Hazewinkel. Indexed: Math.R.

510 NE
MATHEMATICS AND ITS APPLICATIONS: EAST EUROPEAN SERIES. 1982. irreg. price varies. D. Reidel Publishing Co., Box 17, 3300 AA Dordrecht, Netherlands (And 190 Old Derby St., Hingham, MA 02043) Ed. M. Hazewinkel. Indexed: Math.R.

510 NE
MATHEMATICS AND ITS APPLICATIONS: JAPANESE SERIES. 1983. irreg. price varies. D. Reidel Publishing Co., Box 17, 3300 AA Dordrecht, Netherlands (And 190 Old Derby St., Hingham, MA 02043) Ed. M. Hazewinkel.

510 NE
MATHEMATICS AND ITS APPLICATIONS: SOVIET SERIES. 1984. irreg. price varies. D. Reidel Publishing Co., Box 17, 3300 AA Dordrecht, Netherlands (And 190 Old Derby St., Hingham, MA 02043) Ed. M. Hazewinkel. Indexed: Math.R.

MATHEMATICS EDUCATION LIBRARY. see *EDUCATION*

510 620 US ISSN 0076-5392
MATHEMATICS IN SCIENCE AND ENGINEERING; series of monographs and textbooks. 1961. irreg., vol.180, 1986. Academic Press Inc., Orlando, FL 32887. TEL 305-345-2000. Ed. Richard E. Bellman. Indexed: Math.R.

510   GE   ISSN 0543-100X
MATHEMATIK FUER NATURWISSENSCHAFT
UND TECHNIK. 1957. irreg. price varies. VEB
Deutscher Verlag der Wissenschaften, Postfach
1216, 1080 Berlin, E. Germany (D.D.R.) Eds. H.
Heinrich, H. Schubert.

510   GE   ISSN 0233-1063
MATHEMATIK UND IHRE ANWENDUNGEN IN
PHYSIK UND TECHNIK. (Text in English,
German) 1927. a. Akademische Verlagsgesellschaft
Geest & Portig K.-G., Sternwartenstrasse 8, 7010
Leipzig, E. Germany (D.D.R.) Ed.Bd.

510 531   GE   ISSN 0138-3019
MATHEMATISCHE FORSCHUNG.
SCHRIFTENREIHE. 1972. irreg. price varies.
(Akademie der Wissenschaften der DDR, Institut
fuer Mathematik) Akademie-Verlag, Leipziger Str.
3-4, 1086 Berlin, E. Germany (D.D.R.) Ed.Bd.
Indexed: Math.R.
    Formerly: Zentralinstitut fuer Mathematik und
Mechanik. Schriftenreihe.

510   GE   ISSN 0076-5430
MATHEMATISCHE LEHRBUECHER UND
MONOGRAPHIEN. ABTEILUNG 2:
MATHEMATISCHE MONOGRAPHIEN. 1952.
irreg., vol.61, 1983. price varies. (Akademie der
Wissenschaften der DDR, Institut fuer Mathematik)
Akademie-Verlag, Leipziger Str. 3-4, 1086 Berlin, E.
Germany (D.D.R.)

510   GE   ISSN 0543-1042
MATHEMATISCHE MONOGRAPHIEN. 1958.
irreg. price varies. VEB Deutscher Verlag der
Wissenschaften, Postfach 1216, 1080 Berlin, E.
Germany (D.D.R.) Eds. W. Groebner, H. Reichardt.

510   GE   ISSN 0076-5449
MATHEMATISCHE SCHUELERBUECHEREI.
1956. irreg. price varies. VEB Deutscher Verlag der
Wissenschaften, Postfach 1216, 1080 Berlin, E.
Germany (D.D.R.) Indexed: Math.R.

510 530   GW
METHODEN UND VERFAHREN DER
MATHEMATHISCHEN PHYSIK. 1969. irreg.,
vol.16, 1976. price varies. (Bibliographisches
Institut) Verlag Peter Lang GmbH, Hinter den
Ulmen 19, D-6000 Frankfurt/Main 50, W. Germany
(B.R.D.) Eds. Bruno Brosowski, Erich Martensen.

510   NE
METHODS IN GEOMATHEMATICS. (Text in
English) 1976. irreg., vol.2, 1976. Elsevier Science
Publishers B.V., Box 211, 1000 AE Amsterdam,
Netherlands. Ed. R.A. Reyment. charts.

MOBIUS. see EDUCATION — Teaching Methods
And Curriculum

510   BL
MONOGRAFIAS DE MATEMATICA. 1969. irreg.
price varies. Instituto de Matematica Pura e
Aplicada, Edificio Leio Gama, Estrada Dona
Castorina, 110 Jardim Botanico, 22460 Rio de
Janeiro, Brazil. Ed. Cesar Camacho. circ. 600.
Indexed: Math.R.

510   PL   ISSN 0077-0507
MONOGRAFIE MATEMATYCZNE. (Text in
English, French, German and Polish) 1932. irreg.,
vol.61, 1982. price varies. (Polska Akademia Nauk,
Instytut Matematyczny) Panstwowe Wydawnictwo
Naukowe, Miodowa 10, 00-251 Warsaw, Poland
(Dist. by: Ars Polona, Krakowskie Przedmiescie 7,
00-068 Warsaw, Poland) Indexed: Math.R.

510   RM
MONOGRAFII MATEMATICE. 1973. irreg. 30 lei.
Universitatea din Timisoara, Facultatea de Stiinte
ale Naturii, Bd. Vasile Pirvan Nr. 4, Timisoara,
Rumania. Ed. Dumitru Gaspar. circ. 150. Indexed:
Math.R.

510   US
MONOGRAPHS, ADVANCED TEXTS AND
SURVEYS IN PURE AND APPLIED
MATHEMATICS.* no.2, 1976. irreg, no.21, 1984.
Pitman Publishing Inc., c/o Longman Inc., 95
Church St., White Plains, NY 10601-1505. Ed.Bd.
    Formerly (until vol.25, 1986): Monographs and
Studies in Mathematics.

510   US
MONOGRAPHS ON NUMERICAL ANALYSIS.
irreg. price varies. Oxford University Press, 200
Madison Ave., New York, NY 10016 TEL 212-679-
7300. (And Ely House, 37 Dover St., London W1X
4AH, England) Ed. J. Walsh. Indexed: Math.R.

510.8   US   ISSN 0077-1554
MOSCOW MATHEMATICAL SOCIETY.
TRANSACTIONS. English edition of: Moskovskoe
Matematicheskoe Obshchestvo. Trudy. 1978.
Missing freq. noted 6.19.87--source not traceable.
$159 to non-members; institutional members $127.
American Mathematical Society, Box 6248,
Providence, RI 02940. TEL 401-272-9500. (Co-
sponsor: London Mathematical Society) Ed. Ben
Silver. circ. 500. Indexed: Math.R.

510   UR
MOSKOVSKOE MATEMATICHESKOE
OBSHCHESTVO. TRUDY. vol.34, 1977. irreg.
2.90 Rub. per no. Moskovskii Universitet,
Moskovskoe Matematicheskoe Obshchestvo,
Universitetskii Prospekt, 13, Moscow V-234,
Russian S.F.S.R., U.S.S.R. Ed. O. Oleinik. bibl.
illus. circ. 1,270. Indexed: Math.R.
Int.Aerosp.Abstr.

510 500   NE
N A T O ADVANCED SCIENCE INSTITUTE
SERIES. C: MATHEMATICAL AND PHYSICAL
SCIENCES. (Text in English) irreg. price varies.
(North Atlantic Treaty Organization, Scientific
Affairs Division, BE) D. Reidel Publishing Co.,
P.O. Box 17, 3300 AA Dordrecht, Netherlands
(And 190 Old Derby St., Hingham, MA 02043)
Indexed: GeoRef. Phys.Ber.

510 370   US
NATIONAL COUNCIL OF TEACHERS OF
MATHEMATICS. PROFESSIONAL
REFERENCE SERIES. 1980. irreg. National
Council of Teachers of Mathematics, 1906
Association Dr., Reston, VA 22091. TEL 703-620-
9840. (reprint service avail. from UMI)

510 370   US   ISSN 0077-4103
NATIONAL COUNCIL OF TEACHERS OF
MATHEMATICS. YEARBOOK. 1926. a. $14.50.
National Council of Teachers of Mathematics, 1906
Association Dr., Reston, VA 22091. TEL 703-620-
9840. circ. controlled. (also avail. in microform from
UMI; reprint service avail. from UMI) Indexed:
Educ.Ind.

510   UN   ISSN 0077-8893
NEW TRENDS IN MATHEMATICS TEACHING.
(Editions in English, French and Spanish) 1966.
irreg., latest 1979. $9.25. Unesco, 7-9 Place de
Fontenoy, 75700 Paris, France (Dist. in U.S. by:
Bernan Associates-Unipub, 4611-F Assembly Dr.,
Lanham, MD 20706-4391)

511   JA   ISSN 0369-576X
NIIGATA UNIVERSITY. FACULTY OF SCIENCE.
SCIENCE REPORTS. SERIES A:
MATHEMATICS. (Text in European languages)
1964. a. exchange basis. Niigata University, Faculty
of Science - Niigata Daigaku Rigakubu, 8050
Igarashi Nino-cho, Niigata-shi 950-21, Japan.
Indexed: Math.R.

510   NE
NORTH-HOLLAND MATHEMATICAL LIBRARY.
1971. irreg., vol.33, 1985. price varies. Elsevier
Science Publishers B.V., Box 211, 1000 AE
Amsterdam, Netherlands.

510   NE
NORTH-HOLLAND MATHEMATICS STUDIES.
1970. irreg., vol.117, 1985. price varies. Elsevier
Science Publishers B.V., Box 211, 1000 AE
Amsterdam, Netherlands.

620 510   NE   ISSN 0066-5460
NORTH-HOLLAND SERIES IN APPLIED
MATHEMATICS AND MECHANICS. 1967.
irreg., vol.29, 1985. price varies. Elsevier Science
Publishers B.V., Box 211, 1000 AE Amsterdam,
Netherlands. Ed.Bd. Indexed: Math.R.

510   AG   ISSN 0078-2009
NOTAS DE ALGEBRA Y ANALISIS. (Text in
English, French and Spanish) 1966. irreg., no.13,
1985. price varies. ‡ Universidad Nacional del Sur,
Instituto de Matematica, Av. Alem 1253, 8000
Bahia Blanca, Argentina. circ. 1,000. Indexed:
Math.R. Zent.Math.

510   AG   ISSN 0078-2017
NOTAS DE LOGICA MATEMATICA. (Text in
English, French, Portuguese, Spanish) 1963. irreg.,
no.33, 1974. price varies. ‡ Universidad Nacional
del Sur, Instituto de Matematica, Avda. Alem 1253,
8000 Bahia Blanca, Argentina. bibl. circ. 1,000.
Indexed: Math.R. Zent.Math.

510   AG   ISSN 0326-1336
NOTAS DE MATEMATICA DISCRETA. 1982.
irreg. Universidad Nacional del Sur, Instituto de
Matematica, Avda. Alem 1253, 8000 Bahia Blanca,
Argentina. charts. illus. Indexed: Math.R.

510   BL   ISSN 0085-5413
NOTAS E COMUNICACOES DE MATEMATICA.
(Text in English, French, Portuguese, Spanish) 1965.
irreg., latest no.130. price varies. Universidade
Federal de Pernambuco, Departamento de
Matematica, Edf. dos Institutos Basicos, 50.000
Recife, PE, Brazil. Ed. Jorge Hounie. circ. 125.

510   CL
NOTAS MATEMATICAS. English edition:
Mathematical Notes. 1972. a. free. Universidad
Catolica de Chile, Instituto de Matematicas, Casilla
114-D, Santiago, Chile (Subscr. to: Instituto de
Matematica, Vicuna Mackenna 4860, Santiago,
Chile) Ed. Alvaro Cofre. circ. 200.

510   AT
NOTES ON PURE MATHEMATICS. 1974. irreg.
price varies. Australian National University,
Department of Mathematics, IAS, G.P.O Box 4,
Canberra, 2601, Australia. Ed. M.F. Newman. circ.
200.

500 510   US   ISSN 0379-0207
OESTERREICHISCHE AKADEMIE DER
WISSENSCHAFTEN, VIENNA.
MATHEMATISCH-
NATURWISSENSCHAFTLICHE KLASSE.
DENKSCHRIFTEN. (Text in German) irreg. S.1,
020($67) (AU) Springer-Verlag, 175 Fifth Ave.,
New York, NY 10010 TEL 212-460-1500. (Also
Berlin, Heidelberg, Tokyo and Vienna) (reprint
service avail. from ISI) Indexed: Biol.Abstr.
Math.R.
    Formerly: Oesterreichische Akademie der
Wissenschaften, Vienna. Mathematisch-
Naturwissenschaftliche Klasse. Anzeiger (ISSN
0065-535X)

519   UR
OPTIMIZATSIYA. irreg. (5-6/yr.) 1 Rub. Akademiya
Nauk S.S.S.R., Sibirskoe Otdelenie, Institut
Matematiki, Novosibirsk, Akademgorodok, Russian
S.F.S.R., U.S.S.R. Ed. L.V. Vantorovich. Indexed:
Math.R.

510   US   ISSN 0078-6330
ORGANIZATION OF AMERICAN STATES.
DEPARTMENT OF SCIENTIFIC AFFAIRS.
SERIE DE MATEMATICA: MONOGRAFIAS.
no.2, 1965. irreg., no.22, 1979. $3.50 per no.
Organization of American States, Department of
Publications, Washington, DC 20006. TEL 703-941-
1617.

510   US
OXFORD MATHEMATICAL MONOGRAPHS.
irreg. price varies. Oxford University Press, 200
Madison Ave., New York, NY 10016 TEL 212-679-
7300. (And Ely House, 37 Dover St., London W1X
4AH, England) Indexed: Math.R.

510 530   CS
PEDAGOGICKA FAKULTA V OSTRAVE.
MATEMATIKA, FYZIKA. (Subseries of its
Sbornik Praci: Rada A) (Text in Czech; summaries
in English, German, Russian) 1971. irreg. Statni
Pedagogicke Nakladatelstvi, Ostrovni 30, 113 01
Prague 1, Czechoslovakia. illus.
    Supersedes in part : Prirodni Vedy a Matematika.

510   US   ISSN 0172-6641
PERSPECTIVES IN MATHEMATICAL LOGIC.
1975. irreg., latest 1986. Springer-Verlag, 175 Fifth
Ave., New York, NY 10010. TEL 212-460-1500.
(reprint service avail. from ISI) Indexed: Math.R.

510   US   ISSN 0031-8019
PHILOSOPHIA MATHEMATICA. (Text in English,
French and German) 1964-1981 (vol.18); N.S. 1986.
irreg. $12 per yr. Old Dominion University, c/o J.
Fang, Ed., Old Dominion University, Norfolk, VA
23508. TEL 804-440-4738. adv. bk. rev. circ. 600.
Indexed: Phil.Ind. Math.R. Zent.Math.

510   PL   ISSN 0137-6934
POLISH ACADEMY OF SCIENCES. MATHEMATICAL INSTITUTE. BANACH CENTER PUBLICATIONS. (Text in various languages) 1976. irreg., vol.12, 1984. price varies. (Polish Academy of Sciences. Institute of Mathematics) Panstwowe Wydawnictwo Naukowe, Miodowa 10, 00-251 Warsaw, Poland (Dist. by: Ars Polona, Krakowskie Przedmiescie 7, 00-068 Warsaw, Poland) Ed. Czeslaw Olech.

510   PL
POLITECHNIKA GDANSKA. INSTYTUT MATEMATYKI. RAPORT. 1982. a. price varies. Politechnika Gdanska, Ul. Majakowskiego 11/12, 80-592 Gdansk 6, Poland.

510   PL   ISSN 0072-0372
POLITECHNIKA GDANSKA. ZESZYTY NAUKOWE. MATEMATYKA. (Text in Polish; summaries in Russian and one West-European language) 1963. irreg. price varies. Politechnika Gdanska, Majakowskiego 11/12, 81-952 Gdansk 6, Poland (Dist. by: Osrodek Rozpowszechniania Wydawnictw Naukowych Pan, Palac Kultury i Nauki, 00-901 Warsaw, Poland)

510   PL   ISSN 0137-2572
POLITECHNIKA LODZKA. ZESZYTY NAUKOWE. MATEMATYKA. (Text in various languages; summaries in Polish and Russian) 1972. irreg. price varies. Politechnika Lodzka, Ul. Zwirki 36, 90-924 Lodz, Poland (Dist. by: Ars Polona-Ruch, Krakowskie Przedmiescie 7, Warsaw, Poland) Ed. Janusz Matkowski. circ. 283. Indexed: Math.R. Math. R.

510   PL   ISSN 0239-488X
POLITECHNIKA POZNANSKA. ZESZYTY NAUKOWE. GEOMETRIA. (Text in English, French) irreg. price varies. Politechnika Poznanska, Pl. Curie-Sklodowskiej 5, Poznan, Poland. Ed. Eugeniusz Korczak.
   Formerly: Politechnika Poznanska. Zeszyty Naukowe. Geometria Wykreslna.

510 530   PL   ISSN 0072-470X
POLITECHNIKA SLASKA. ZESZYTY NAUKOWE. MATEMATYKA-FIZYKA. (Text in Polish; summaries in English and Russian) 1961. irreg. price varies. Politechnika Slaska, W. Pstrowskiego 7, 44-100 Gliwice, Poland (Dist. by: Ars Polona, Krakowskie Przedmiescie 7, 00-068 Warsaw, Poland) Ed. Boguslaw Nosowicz. circ. 315. Indexed: Chem.Abstr. Math.R.

510   PL   ISSN 0137-6268
POLITECHNIKA WROCLAWSKA. INSTYTUT MATEMATYKI. PRACE NAUKOWE. KONFERENCJE. 1977. irreg., no.2 1986. price varies. Politechnika Wroclawska, Wybrzez Wyspianskiego 27, 50-370 Wroclaw, Poland. Ed. Jerzy Ciekot.

510   PL   ISSN 0324-9603
POLITECHNIKA WROCLAWSKA. INSTYTUT MATEMATYKI. PRACE NAUKOWE. MONOGRAFIE. (Text in Polish; summaries in English and Russian) 1974. irreg., no.4, 1977. price varies. Politechnika Wroclawska, Wybrzeze Wyspianskiego 27, 50-370 Wroclaw, Poland (Dist. by: Ars Polona-Ruch, Krakowskie Przedmiescie 7, Warsaw, Poland) Ed. Marian Kloza. circ. 475. Indexed: Math.R.

510 530   PL   ISSN 0324-9611
POLITECHNIKA WROCLAWSKA. INSTYTUT MATEMATYKI. PRACE NAUKOWE. STUDIA I MATERIALY. (Former Name of Institute: Instytut Matematyki i Fizyki Teoretycznej) (Text in Polish; summaries in English and Russian) 1970. irreg., no.15, 1980. price varies. Politechnika Wroclawska, Wybrzeze Wyspianskiego 27, 50-370 Wroclaw, Poland (Dist. by: Ars Polona-Ruch, Krakowskie Przedmiescie 7, Warsaw, Poland) Ed. Marian Kloza. Indexed: Math.R.

510   PL   ISSN 0079-3698
POLSKIE TOWARZYSTWO MATEMATYCZNE. ROCZNIKI. SERIA II. WIADOMOSCI MATEMATYCZNE. 1955. irreg. (3-4 yr.) 35 Zl.($3.50) per volume. Polskie Towarzystwo Matematyczne, Ul. Sniadeckich 8, 00-950 Warsaw, Poland (Dist. by: Ars Polona-Ruch, Krakowskie Przedmiescie 7, Warsaw, Poland) Ed. Zbigniew Semadeni. bk. rev. bibl. index. circ. 2,750.

510   PL   ISSN 0373-8299
POLSKIE TOWARZYSTWO MATEMATYCZNE. ROCZNIKI. SERIA 1: COMMENTATIONES MATHEMATICAE. PRACE MATEMATYCZNE. (Text in English, French, German, Polish or Russian; summaries in English, French or Russian) 1955. irreg., vol.24, 1984. Panstwowe Wydawnictwo Naukowe, Ul. Miodowa 10, 00-251 Warsaw, Poland (Dist. by: Ars Polona, Krakowskie Przedmiescie 7, 00-068 Warsaw, Poland) Ed. Wladyslaw Orlicz. bibl. index. Indexed: Math.R.

POZNANSKIE TOWARZYSTWO PRZYJACIOL NAUK. KOMISJA MATEMATYCZNO-PRZYRODNICZA. PRACE. see *PHYSICS*

510   US   ISSN 0079-5194
PRINCETON MATHEMATICAL SERIES. 1946. irreg., no.34, 1981. price varies. Princeton University Press, 3175 Princeton Pike, Lawrenceville, NJ 08648 TEL 709-452-4900. (and University of Tokyo Press, Tokyo, Japan) (back issues avail.; reprint service avail. from UMI)

PRINCETON STUDIES IN MATHEMATICAL ECONOMICS. see *BUSINESS AND ECONOMICS*

519   US   ISSN 0079-5607
PROBABILITY AND MATHEMATICAL STATISTICS; a series of monographs and textbooks. 1967. irreg., no.53, 1986. Academic Press Inc., Orlando, FL 32887. TEL 305-345-2000. Eds. Z. W. Birnbaum, E. Lukacs. Indexed: Math.R.

510   US
PROBABILITY: PURE AND APPLIED. 1984. irreg. price varies. Marcel Dekker, Inc., 270 Madison Ave., New York, NY 10016. TEL 212-696-9000. Ed. Marcel Neuts.

510   US
PROBLEM BOOKS IN MATHEMATICS. 1981. irreg., latest 1986. Springer-Verlag, 175 Fifth Ave., New York, NY 10010 TEL 212-460-1500. (And Berlin, Heidelberg, Tokyo and Vienna) Ed. P. Halmos.

510   UR
PROBLEMY ISTORII MATEMATIKI I MEKHANIKI. 1972. irreg. 1 Rub. Moskovskii Universitet, Leninskie Gory, Moscow V-234, Russian S.F.S.R., U.S.S.R. illus.

510   US   ISSN 0079-8169
PURE AND APPLIED MATHEMATICS; a series of monographs and textbooks. 1949. irreg., vol.122, 1986. $59. Academic Press Inc., Orlando, FL 32887. TEL 305-345-2000. Eds. Paul A. Smith, Samuel Eilenberg. Indexed: Math.R.

510   US
PURE AND APPLIED MATHEMATICS: A WILEY INTERSCIENCE SERIES OF TEXTS, MONOGRAPHS AND TRACTS. 1948. irreg., latest 1986. price varies. John Wiley & Sons, Inc., 605 Third Ave., New York, NY 10016. TEL 212-850-6000. Ed. L. Bers. Indexed: Math.R.
   Formed by the merger of: Interscience Tracts in Pure and Applied Mathematics (ISSN 0074-994X) & Pure and Applied Mathematics; a Series of Texts and Monographs (ISSN 0079-8185)

510   US   ISSN 0079-8177
PURE AND APPLIED MATHEMATICS SERIES. 1970. irreg., vol.105, 1986. price varies. Marcel Dekker, Inc., 270 Madison Ave., New York, NY 10016. TEL 212-696-9000. Ed. S. Kobayashi.

510   IT   ISSN 0391-3236
QUADERNI DI ANALISI MATEMATICA. 1977. irreg., no.2, 1978. price varies. Liguori Editore s.r.l., Via Mezzocannone 19, 80134 Naples, Italy. TEL 081/20 6077. Eds. Federico Cafiero, Antonio Zitarosa.

510   CN   ISSN 0079-8797
QUEEN'S PAPERS IN PURE AND APPLIED MATHEMATICS. (Text in English and French) 1966. irreg. price varies. ‡ Queen's University, Department of Mathematics and Statistics, Kingston, Ont. K7L 3N6, Canada. TEL 613-545-2390. Ed. Grace Orzech. Indexed: Math.R.
   Formerly: Queen's University at Kingston. Department of Mathematics. Research Report.

510   II   ISSN 0079-9602
RANCHI UNIVERSITY MATHEMATICAL JOURNAL. (Text in English) 1970. a. Rs.40($10) Ranchi University, Department of Mathematics, Ranchi 1, Bihar, India. Ed. R.C. Choudhary. circ. 150. Indexed: Math.R.

REPORTS ON MATHEMATICAL LOGIC. see *PHILOSOPHY*

510   US
RESEARCH NOTES IN MATHEMATICS.* 1975. irreg., no.109, 1984. Pitman Publishing, Inc., c/o Longman Inc., 95 Church St., White Plains, NY 10601-1505. Indexed: Math.R.

510   BL   ISSN 0102-0811
REVISTA DE MATEMATICA E ESTATISTICA. (Abstracts in English and Portuguese) 1983. a. $30 or exchange basis. Universidade Estadual Paulista, Av. Vicente Ferreira 1278, Caixa Posta 603, 17.500 Marilia SP, Brazil. bibl. charts.

510   UK   ISSN 0080-4614
ROYAL SOCIETY OF LONDON. PHILOSOPHICAL TRANSACTIONS. SERIES A. MATHEMATICAL AND PHYSICAL SCIENCES. 1665. irreg. £87 per vol. Royal Society of London, 6 Carlton House Terrace, London S.W.1, England. (reprint service avail. from ISI) Indexed: Appl.Mech.Rev. Biol.Abstr. Chem.Abstr. Eng.Ind. Math.R. Met.Abstr. Nutr.Abstr. Sci.Abstr. Br.Geol.Lit. Br.Archaeol.Abstr. Fluidex. Geo.Abstr. GeoRef. Mass Spectr.Bull. Petrol.Abstr. Soils & Fert.

500 510   UK   ISSN 0080-4630
ROYAL SOCIETY OF LONDON. PROCEEDINGS. SERIES A. MATHEMATICAL AND PHYSICAL SCIENCES. 1832. irreg. £42 per vol. Royal Society of London, 6 Carlton Terrace, London S.W.1, England. (reprint service avail. from ISI) Indexed: Chem.Abstr. Curr.Cont. Eng.Ind. Excerp.Med. Math.R. Met.Abstr. Sci.Abstr. Br.Archaeol.Abstr. Fluidex. GeoRef. Mass Spectr.Bull. Petrol.Abstr.

510   US   ISSN 0080-5084
S I A M - A M S PROCEEDINGS. 1969. irreg., vol.14, 1984. price varies. (Society for Industrial and Applied Mathematics) American Mathematical Society, P.O. Box 6248, Providence, RI 02940. TEL 401-272-9500. index in each vol. Indexed: Math.R. Zent.Math.
   Formerly: American Mathematical Society. Proceedings of Symposia in Applied Mathematics.

SAECHSISCHE AKADEMIE DER WISSENSCHAFTEN, LEIPZIG. MATHEMATISCH-NATURWISSENSCHAFTLICHE KLASSE. ABHANDLUNGEN. see *SCIENCES: COMPREHENSIVE WORKS*

SAECHSISCHE AKADEMIE DER WISSENSCHAFTEN, LEIPZIG. MATHEMATISCH-NATURWISSENSCHAFTLICHE KLASSE. SITZUNGSBERICHTE. see *SCIENCES: COMPREHENSIVE WORKS*

SAGA UNIVERSITY. FACULTY OF SCIENCE AND ENGINEERING. REPORTS. see *ENGINEERING*

510 530 540   JA
SAITAMA UNIVERSITY. SCIENCE REPORTS. SERIES A: MATHEMATICS. (Text in English) 1952. a. exchange basis. Saitama University, 255 Shimookubo, Urawa-shi 338, Japan. Indexed: Math.R. Sci.Abstr.
   Formerly: Saitama University. Science Reports. Series A: Mathematics, Physics and Chemistry (ISSN 0558-2431)

519.5   US   ISSN 0094-8837
SELECTED TABLES IN MATHEMATICAL STATISTICS. 1970. irreg., vol.10, 1986. American Mathematical Society, Box 6248, Providence, RI 02940. TEL 401-272-9500.

510 519   US   ISSN 0065-9274
SELECTED TRANSLATIONS IN MATHEMATICAL STATISTICS AND PROBABILITY. 1961. irreg., vol.16, 1985. price varies. (Institute of Mathematical Statistics) American Mathematical Society, P.O. Box 6248, Providence, RI 02940. TEL 401-272-9500. Ed. Ben Silver. cum.index 1966-1973.

510 RM
SEMINAR ARGHIRIADE. (Text in English, French, Rumanian, Russian) 1974. irreg. 20 lei. Universitatea din Timisoara, Facultatea de Stiinte ale Naturii, Bd. Vasile Pirvan Nr. 4, Timisoara, Rumania. Ed. Achim Dragomir. circ. 250. Indexed: Math.R. Zentr.Fur Math.

510 530 IT ISSN 0391-3252
SERIE DI MATEMATICA E FISICA. 1974. irreg., no.8, 1986. price varies. Liguori Editore s.r.l., Via Mezzocannone 19, 80134 Naples, Italy. TEL 081/20 6077. Ed. G. Vidossich.

510 530 IT
SERIE DI MATEMATICA E FISICA. PROBLEMI RISOLTI. 1978. irreg., no.6, 1982. price varies. Liguori Editore s.r.l., Via Mezzocannone 19, 80134 Naples, Italy. TEL 081/20 6077. Ed. Livio C. Piccinini.

SHINSHU UNIVERSITY. FACULTY OF TEXTILE SCIENCE AND TECHNOLOGY. JOURNAL. SERIES F: PHYSICS AND MATHEMATICS. see *PHYSICS*

510 BL ISSN 0102-3292
SOCIEDADE PARANAENSE DE MATEMATICA. MONOGRAFIAS. 1984. irreg. Sociedade Paranense de Matematica, Caixa Postal 1261, 80001 Curitiba, Parana, Brazil. Ed. C. Pereira da Silva. bibl. Indexed: Math.R. Zent.Math.

510 BU ISSN 0081-1858
SOFIISKI UNIVERSITET. FAKULTET PO MATEMATIKA I MEKHANIKA. GODISHNIK/UNIVERSITE DE SOFIA. FACULTE DES MATHEMATIQUES ET DE MECANIQUE. ANNUAIRE. (Text in Bulgarian and English) irreg. vol.67, 1972/73. price varies. Publishing House of the Bulgarian Academy of Sciences, Acad. G. Boncev St., Bldg. 6, 1113 Sofia, Bulgaria. Ed. M. Pecheva. circ. 550. Indexed: Chem.Abstr. Math.R.

510 500 CH
SOOCHOW JOURNAL OF MATHEMATICS. 1975. a. $15 per no. Soochow University, Wai Shuang Hsi, Shih Lin, Taipei, Taiwan, Republic of China. Indexed: Math.R.
 Former titles: Soochow Journal of Mathematical and Natural Sciences; Until 1978: Soochow Journal of Mathematics.

510 US ISSN 0172-6315
SOURCES IN THE HISTORY OF MATHEMATICS AND PHYSICAL SCIENCES. 1976. irreg., vol.8, 1985. price varies. Springer-Verlag, 175 Fifth Ave., New York, NY 10010 TEL 212-460-1500. (Also Berlin, Heidelberg, Tokyo, Vienna) (reprint service avail. from ISI)

SOVIET SCIENTIFIC REVIEWS. SECTION C: MATHEMATICAL PHYSICS REVIEWS. see *PHYSICS*

510 US
SPRINGER SERIES IN COMPUTATIONAL MATHEMATICS. 1983. irreg., vol.8, 1986. price varies. Springer-Verlag, 175 Fifth Ave., New York, NY 10010 TEL 212-460-1500. (Also Berlin, Heidelberg, Tokyo, Vienna) (reprint service avail. from ISI)

510 US
SPRINGER SERIES IN SOVIET MATHEMATICS. 1983. irreg., latest 1986. Springer-Verlag, 175 Fifth Ave., New York, NY 10010 TEL 212-460-1500. (Also Berlin, Heidelberg, Tokyo, Vienna) (reprint service avail. from ISI)

510 530 GE ISSN 0081-4113
STAATLICHE MATHEMATISCH-PHYSIKALISCHE SALONS, DRESDEN. VEROEFFENTLICHUNGEN. 1960. irreg. price varies. VEB Deutscher Verlag der Wissenschaften, Postfach 1216, 1080 Berlin, E. Germany (D.D.R.) Ed. H. Groetzsch.

510 CN ISSN 0085-6800
STUDENT MATHEMATICS. 1970. a. Can.$0.20. ‡ c/o S.K. Harburn, Ed., Faculty of Education, Rm. 373, University of Toronto, 371 Bloor St. West, Toronto M5S 2R7, Canada. TEL 416-978-2011. bk. rev. circ. 3,000.

510 PL ISSN 0039-3223
STUDIA MATHEMATICA. (Text in various languages) 1929. irreg., no.79, 1984. $45 per vol. (Polska Akademia Nauk, Instytut Matematyczny) Panstwowe Wydawnictwo Naukowe, Ul. Miodowa 10, 00-251 Warsaw, Poland (Dist. by: Ars Polona, Krakowskie Przedmiescie 7, 00-068 Warsaw, Poland) Ed. W. Orlicz. bibl. index. circ. 1,100. Indexed: Math.R. ASCA. Compumath.

510 RM
STUDIA UNIVERSITATIS "BABES-BOLYAI". MATHEMATICA. (Text in Rumanian; summaries in English, French, German, Russian) 1958. a. exchange basis. Universitatea "Babes-Bolyai", Biblioteca Centrala Universitara, Str. Clinicilor Nr. 2, Cluj-Napoca, Rumania. charts. illus. Indexed: Math.R.
 Formerly: Studia Universitatis "Babes-Bolyai". Series Mathematica-Physica (ISSN 0039-3436)

510 378 GW
STUDIENFUEHRER MATHEMATIK. 1973. a. free. Technical University Berlin, Department of Mathematics, Strasse des 17.Juni 135, 1000 Berlin 12, W. Germany (B.R.D.) illus. circ. 400.

511 NE ISSN 0049-237X
STUDIES IN LOGIC AND THE FOUNDATIONS OF MATHEMATICS. 1954. irreg., vol.117, 1985. price varies. Elsevier Science Publishers B.V., Box 211, 1000 AE Amsterdam, Netherlands. Ed.Bd.

510 US ISSN 0081-8208
STUDIES IN MATHEMATICS (WASHINGTON) Variant title: M A A Studies in Mathematics. 1962. irreg., no.25, 1985. Mathematical Association of America, 1529 Eighteenth St., N.W., Washington, DC 20036. TEL 202-687-5200. Ed. C.W. Curtis. (reprint service avail. from UMI)

510 NE
STUDIES IN MATHEMATICS AND ITS APPLICATIONS. 1975. irreg., vol.15, 1983. price varies. Elsevier Science Publishers B.V., Box 211, Amsterdam, Netherlands (Dist. in the U.S. and Canada by: Elsevier North-Holland, Inc., New York, 52 Vanderbilt Ave., New York, NY 10017) Ed.Bd. bibl. Indexed: Math.R.

509 US ISSN 0172-570X
STUDIES IN THE HISTORY OF MATHEMATICS AND PHYSICAL SCIENCES. 1975. irreg., vol.11, 1985. price varies. Springer Verlag, 175 Fifth Ave., New York, NY 10010 TEL 212-460-1500. (Also Berlin, Heidelberg, Tokyo and Vienna) Eds. M.J. Klein, G.J. Toomer. (reprint service avail. from ISI) Indexed: Biol.Abstr. Math.R.

510 US
SURVEYS & REFERENCE WORKS IN MATHEMATICS.* 1979. irreg., no.9, 1983. Pitman Publishing Inc., c/o Longman Inc., 95 Church St., White Plains, NY 10601-1505. Indexed: Math.R.

510 US ISSN 0082-0725
SYMPOSIA MATHEMATICA. (Contributions in English, French, German and Italian) 1969. irreg., vol.27, 1986. (Istituto Nazionale di Alta Matematica Francesco Severi) Academic Press Inc., Orlando, FL 32887. TEL 305-345-2000. Indexed: Math.R. Zent.Math.

510 530 II ISSN 0082-075X
SYMPOSIA ON THEORETICAL PHYSICS AND MATHEMATICS. Represents: Institute of Mathematical Sciences, Madras, India. Proceedigs of Symposia and Summer Schools. (Title of Summer School Proceedings varies, Vols.1 and 2: Matscience Summer School. Proceedings) (Text in English) 1963. irreg., vol. 10, 1970. $20. Institute of Mathematical Sciences, Adyar, Madras 20, India.

510 US
TATA INSTITUTE LECTURES ON MATHEMATICS. 1979. irreg. price varies. (Tata Institute of Fundamental Research, II) Springer-Verlag, 175 Fifth Ave., New York, NY 10010 TEL 212-460-1500. (Also Berlin, Heidelberg, Tokyo and Vienna) Eds. K.G. Ramanathan, B.V. Sreekantan. (reprint service avail. from ISI) Indexed: Math.R.
 Formerly: Tata Institute Lecture Notes; Which supersedes: Tata Institute of Fundamental Research. Lectures on Mathematics and Physic. Physics (ISSN 0496-9472) & Tata Institute of Fundamental Research. Lectures on Mathematics and Physics. Mathematics (ISSN 0406-6987)

510 US
TATA INSTITUTE STUDIES IN MATHEMATICS. 1978? irreg. price varies. (Tata Institute of Fundamental Research, II) Springer-Verlag, 175 Fifth Ave., New York, NY 10010 TEL 212-460-1500. (Also Berlin, Heidelberg, Tokyo and Vienna) Ed. K.G. Ramanathan. (reprint service avail. from ISI)

510 UR ISSN 0082-2191
TBILISSKII UNIVERSITET. INSTITUT PRIKLADNOI MATEMATIKI. SEMINAR. ANNOTATSII DOKLADOV. (Text in Russian; summaries in English and Georgian) 1969. irreg., no.4, 1971. price varies. Tbilisskii Universitet, Chavchavadze Ave., Tbilisi, Georgian S.S.R., U.S.S.R. Eds. T. Gegelia, L. Magnaradze. circ. 400.

510 NE
TECHNISCHE HOGESCHOOL EINDHOVEN. ONDERAFDELING DER WISKUNDE EN INFORMATICA. E U T REPORTS - W S K. 1968. irreg. Technische Hogeschool Eindhoven, Onderafdeling der Wiskunden Informatica - Eindhoven University of Technology. Department of Mathematics and Computing Science, Box 513, 5600 MB Eindhoven, Netherlands. circ. 100. Indexed: Math.R. Ref.Zh. Zent.Math.
 Former titles: Technische Hogeschool Eindhoven. Onderafdeling der Wiskunde. E U T Reports - W S K; Technische Hogeschool Eindhoven. Onderafdeling der Wiskunde. T H Report W S K.

510 530 DK ISSN 0106-6242
TEKSTER FRA I M F U F A. no.50, 1982. irreg. Roskilde Universitetscenter, Institut for Studiet af Matematik og Fysik Samt Deres Funktioner i Undervisning Forskning og Anvendelse, Postbus 260, 4000 Roskilde, Denmark. illus.

510 UR
TEORIYA FUNKTSII, FUNKTSIONAL'NYI ANALIZ I IKH PRILOZHENIYA. vol.27, 1977. irreg. 0.60 Rub. per issue. (Khar'kovskii Gosudarstvennyi Universitet) Izdatel'stvo Vysshaya Shkola, Khar'kovskoe Otdelenie, Ul. Universitetskaya 16, 310003 Kharkov, Ukrainian S.S.R., U.S.S.R. Ed. I. Ostrovskii. abstr. charts. circ. 1,000. Indexed: Math.R.

510 UR
TEORIYA FUNKTSII KOMPLEKSNOGO PEREMENNOGO I KRAEVYE ZADACHI. 1972. irreg. 0.80 Rub. Chuvashskii Gosudarstvennyi Universitet, Moskovskii prospekt, 15, Cheboksary, Chuvach Autonomous S.S.R., U.S.S.R.

510 UR ISSN 0321-3900
TEORIYA SLUCHAINYKH PROTSESSOV; respublikanskii mezhvedomstvennyi sbornik nauchnykh trudov. 1973. a. 1.38 Rub. (Akademiya Nauk Ukrainskoi S.S.R., Institut Prikladnoi Matematiki i Mekhaniki) Izdatel'stvo Naukova Dumka, c/o Yu.A. Khramov, Dir, Ul. Repina, 3, Kiev 252 601, Ukrainian S.S.R., U.S.S.R. (Subscr. to: Mezhdunarodnaya Kniga, Moscow, G-200, Russian S.F.S.R., U.S.S.R.) Ed. Yu.N. Linkov. circ. 1,400.

TEXTS AND MONOGRAPHS IN ECONOMICS AND MATHEMATICAL SYSTEMS. see *BUSINESS AND ECONOMICS — Economic Systems And Theories, Economic History*

510 620 US
TRANSLATION SERIES IN MATHEMATICS AND ENGINEERING. 1984. irreg. Springer-Verlag, 175 Fifth Ave., New York, NY 10010 TEL 212-460-1500. (Also Berlin, Heidelberg, Tokyo, Vienna) (reprint service avail. from ISI)

510 US ISSN 0065-9282
TRANSLATIONS OF MATHEMATICAL MONOGRAPHS. (Chiefly from Russian sources) 1962. irreg., vol.66, 1986. price varies. American Mathematical Society, Box 6248, Providence, RI 02940. TEL 401-272-9500. Ed. Ben Silver. circ. 400. Indexed: Math.R.

510 FR
TRAVAUX EN COURS. 1983. irreg. Editions Hermann, 293 rue Lecourbe, 75015 Paris, France.

MATHEMATICS

510   US   ISSN 0172-6056
UNDERGRADUATE TEXTS IN MATHEMATICS. 1974. irreg., latest 1986. Springer-Verlag, 175 Fifth Ave., New York, NY 10010 TEL 212-460-1500. (Also Berlin, Heidelberg, Tokyo and Vienna) (reprint service avail. from ISI)

510   US   ISSN 0083-1786
U.S. NATIONAL BUREAU OF STANDARDS. APPLIED MATHEMATICS SERIES. 1948. irreg. price varies. U.S. National Bureau of Standards, Gaithersburg, DC 20234 TEL 301-975-3058. (Orders to: Supt. of Documents, Washington, DC 20402)

510   UY
UNIVERSIDAD DE LA REPUBLICA. FACULTAD DE HUMANIDADES Y CIENCIAS. REVISTA. SERIE CIENCIAS EXACTAS. 1980. irreg. exchange basis. Universidad de la Republica, Facultad de Humanidades y Ciencias, Seccion Revista, Tristan Narvaja 1674, Montevideo, Uruguay. Dir. Beatriz Martinez Osorio.
     Supersedes in part: Universidad de la Republica. Facultad de Humanidades y Ciencias. Revista.

510   MX   ISSN 0076-7441
UNIVERSIDAD NACIONAL AUTONOMA DE MEXICO. INSTITUTO DE MATEMATICAS. ANALES. 1961. a. $15 per no. Universidad Nacional Autonoma de Mexico, Instituto de Matematicas, Area de la Investigacion Cientifica, Circuito Exterior, Ciudad Universitaria, Mexico 04510, DF, Mexico. bk. rev. cum.index: vols.1-25, 1961-1985. circ. 550. Indexed: Math.R.

510   MX
UNIVERSIDAD NACIONAL AUTONOMA DE MEXICO. INSTITUTO DE MATEMATICAS. MONOGRAFIAS. 1975. irreg., no.18, 1986. $15. Universidad Nacional Autonoma de Mexico, Instituto de Matematicas, Area de la Investigacion Cientifica, Circuito Exterior, Ciudad Universitaria, Mexico 04510, DF, Mexico. Indexed: Math.R.

510   BL
UNIVERSIDADE FEDERAL DO RIO DE JANEIRO. INSTITUTO DE MATEMATICA. ESTUDOS E COMUNICACOES. (Text in English, French, Portuguese, Spanish; summaries in English) 1983. irreg., no.26, 1986. $3 to institutions; free to individuals. Universidade Federal do Rio de Janeiro, Instituto de Matematica, C.P. 68530, 21944 Rio de Janeiro, RJ, Brazil. circ. (controlled)

510   BL
UNIVERSIDADE FEDERAL DO RIO DE JANEIRO. INSTITUTO DE MATEMATICA. TEXTOS DE METODOS MATEMATICOS. (Text in language of author) 1972. irreg., no.20, 1985. $4 institutions; free to individuals. Universidade Federal do Rio de Janeiro, Instituto de Matematica, C.P. 68.530, 21944 Rio de Janeiro, RJ, Brazil.
     Formerly: Universidade Federal do Rio de Janeiro. Instituto de Matematica. Notas de Matematica Fisica.

510   IT   ISSN 0035-6298
UNIVERSITA DEGLI STUDI DI PARMA. RIVISTA DI MATEMATICA. (Text in English, French, German, Italian and Spanish) 1950. a. L.90000($60) Universita degli Studi di Parma, Dipartimento di Matematica, Via Universita 12, 43100 Parma, Italy. Dir. Bianca Manfredi. bk. rev. bibl. charts. index. circ. 500. Indexed: Appl.Mech.Rev. Math.R.

510   GW
UNIVERSITAET GIESSEN. MATHEMATISCHES INSTITUT. VORLESUNGEN. (Text in English and German) 1974. irreg. price varies. Universitaet Giessen, Mathematisches Institut, Arndt Str. 2, 6300 Giessen, W. Germany (B.R.D.) Ed. F. Timmesfeld.

510   GW   ISSN 0025-5858
UNIVERSITAET HAMBURG. MATHEMATISCHES SEMINAR. ABHANDLUNGEN. 1922. a. price varies. Vandenhoeck und Ruprecht, Theaterstr. 13, Postfach 37 53, 3400 Goettingen, W. Germany (B.R.D.) Eds. K. Legrady, O. Riemenschneider. adv. tr.lit. circ. 410. Indexed: Math.R. Compumath.

510   AU
UNIVERSITAET INNSBRUCK. MATHEMATISCHE STUDIEN. (Subseries of: Universitaet Innsbruck. Veroefentlichungen) 1974. irreg. price varies. Oesterreichische Kommissionsbuchhandlung, Maximilian Str. 17, A-6020 Innsbruck, Austria. Ed. Roman Liedl.

510   530   570   RM
UNIVERSITATEA DIN BRASOV. BULETINUL. SERIA C. STIINTE ALE NATURRI SI PEDAGOGIE. (Text in Rumanian; summaries in English, French and German) vol.14, 1972. a. price varies. Universitatea din Brasov, Bd. Gh. Gheorghiu-Dej Nr. 29, Brasov, Rumania. bibl. illus. Indexed: Chem.Abstr. Math.R.

510   530   RM
UNIVERSITATEA DIN CRAIOVA. ANALE. SERIA: MATEMATICA, FIZICA-CHIMIE. (Text in English, French and German) a. Universitatea din Craiova, Str. A.I. Cuza Nr. 13, Craiova, Rumania. Indexed: Math.R.

514   516   RM
UNIVERSITATEA DIN TIMISOARA. FACULTATEA DE STIINTE ALE NATURII. LUCRARILE SEMINARULUI DE GEOMETRIE SI TOPOLOGIE. (Text in English, French, German and Rumanian) 1972. irreg. 20 lei. Universitatea din Timisoara, Facultatea de Stiinte ale Naturii, Bd. Vasile Pirvan Nr.4, Timisoara, Rumania. Ed. Dan I. Papuc. circ. 250.

510   RM
UNIVERSITATEA DIN TIMISOARA. FACULTATEA DE STIINTE ALE NATURII. SEMINARUL DE TEORIA PROBABILITATILOR SI APLICATII. (Text in English, French, German, Rumanian) 1973. irreg. 20 lei. Universitatea din Timisoara, Facultatea de Stiinte ale Naturii, Bd. Vasile Pirvan Nr.4, Timisoara, Rumania. Ed. Gh. Constantin. circ. 250.
     Formerly (until 1980, no.51): Universitatea din Timisoara. Facultatea de Stiinte ale Naturii. Seminarul de Teoria Functiilor si Matematici Aplicate. A: Spatii Metrice Probabiliste.

510   RM
UNIVERSITATEA DIN TIMISOARA. FACULTATEA DE STIINTE ALE NATURII. SEMINARUL DE TEORIA STRUCTURILOR. (Text in English, French, German, and Rumanian) 1971. irreg. 20 lei. Universitatea din Timisoara, Facultatea de Stiinte ale Naturii, Bd. Vasile Pirvan Nr. 4, Timisoara, Rumania. Ed. Constantin Popa. circ. 250.

510   RM
UNIVERSITATEA DIN TIMISOARA. SECTIA MATEMATICA INFORMATICA. SEMINARUL DE INFORMATICA SI ANALIZA NUMERICA. (Text in English, French, German, Rumanian) 1975. irreg. 20 lei. Universitatea din Timisoara, Sectia Matematica Informatica, Bd. Vasile Pirvan Nr.4, Timisoara, Rumania. Ed. S. Maruster. circ. 250.
     Formerly (until 1981): Universitatea din Timisoara. Facultatea de Stiinte ale Naturii. Seminarul de Teoria Functiilor si Matematici Aplicate. B: Analiza Numerica.

510   BE
UNIVERSITE CATHOLIQUE DE LOUVAIN. INSTITUT DE MATHEMATIQUE. RAPPORT DE MATHEMATIQUE. (Text and summaries in French and English) 1978. irreg. free. Cabay Libraire-Conseil S.A., Agora 11, 1348 Louvain-la-Neuve, Belgium. Ed.Bd. bibl. charts.
     Formerly: Universite Catholique de Louvain. Institut de Mathematique Pure et Appliquee. Rapport.

510   FR   ISSN 0069-472X
UNIVERSITE DE CLERMONT-FERRAND 2. ANNALES SCIENTIFIQUES. SERIE MATHEMATIQUE. 1962. irreg. price varies. Universite de Clermont-Ferrand II, Unite d'Enseignement et de Recherche de Sciences Exactes et Naturelles, B.P. 45, 63170 Aubiere, France. circ. 250. (back issues avail.)

UNIVERSITE DE MADAGASCAR. ETABLISSEMENT D'ENSEIGNEMENT SUPERIEUR DES SCIENCES. ANNALES: SERIE SCIENCES DE LA NATURE ET MATHEMATIQUES. see *SCIENCES: COMPREHENSIVE WORKS*

510   FR   ISSN 0373-0956
UNIVERSITE SCIENTIFIQUE ET MEDICALE DE GRENOBLE. INSTITUT FOURIER. ANNALES. (Text and summaries in English and French) 1949. a. 840 F. Association des annales de l'Institut Fourier, Universite Scientifique , Technologique et Medicale de Grenoble, B.P. 74, 38402 Saint-Martin d'Heres, France. Ed.Bd. adv. circ. 1,300. Indexed: Math.R. Zent.Math.

510   NE
UNIVERSITEIT VAN AMSTERDAM. MATHEMATISCH INSTITUUT. REPORT. (Text in English, French or German) 1970. irreg. exchange basis. ‡ Universiteit van Amsterdam, Mathematisch Instituut, Roetersstraat 15, 1018 WB Amsterdam, Netherlands. Ed. P. van Emde Boas. circ. 250.

510   530   US   ISSN 0172-5939
UNIVERSITEXTS. 1973. irreg., latest 1986. Springer-Verlag, 175 Fifth Ave., New York, NY 10010. TEL 212-460-1500. (reprint service avail. from ISI)

510   US
UNIVERSITY OF ARKANSAS. LECTURE NOTES IN THE MATHEMATICAL SCIENCES. irreg., vol.6, 1983. John Wiley & Sons, Inc., 605 Third Ave., New York, NY 10158. bibl. index. Indexed: Math.R.

510   NZ   ISSN 0110-4152
UNIVERSITY OF AUCKLAND. DEPARTMENT OF MATHEMATICS. REPORT SERIES. 1971. irreg., no.208, 1984. free to individuals or on exchange. University of Auckland, Department of Mathematics & Statistics, Private Bag, Auckland, New Zealand. circ. 175.

510   NO   ISSN 0084-778X
UNIVERSITY OF BERGEN. DEPARTMENT OF APPLIED MATHEMATICS. REPORT. (Text in English) 1964. irreg. exchange basis. Universitetet i Bergen, Department of Applied Mathematics, Allegt. 53-55, 5014 Bergen-U, Norway. circ. 100. (processed)

510   CN
UNIVERSITY OF CALGARY. DEPARTMENT OF MATHEMATICS AND STATISTICS. RESEARCH PAPERS. 1966. irreg. University of Calgary, Department of Mathematics and Statistics, Calgary, Alta, Canada. TEL 403-284-7578. Ed. Dr. K. Varadarajan.
     Formerly: University of Calgary. Department of Mathematics and Computing Science. Research Papers (ISSN 0575-206X)

510   PK
UNIVERSITY OF THE PUNJAB. DEPARTMENT OF MATHEMATICS. JOURNAL OF MATHEMATICS. (Text in English) no.6, 1973. a. $10. University of the Punjab, Department of Mathematics, New Campus, Lahore, Pakistan. circ. 500. Indexed: Math.R.

510   PL   ISSN 0072-0402
UNIWERSYTET GDANSKI. WYDZIAL MATEMATYKI, FIZYKI, CHEMII. ZESZYTY NAUKOWE. MATEMATYKA. (Text in Polish; summaries in English) 1972. irreg. price varies. Uniwersytet Gdanski, Ul. Czerwonej Armii 110, 81-824 Sopot, Poland. illus.

510   PL
UNIWERSYTET JAGIELLONSKI. ZESZYTY NAUKOWE. ACTA MATEMATICA. (Text in Polish; summaries in French, English, Russian) no.5, 1959. irreg. price varies. Panstwowe Wydawnictwo Naukowe, Miodowa 10, 00-251 Warsaw, Poland (Dist. by: Ars Polona, Krakowskie Przedmiescie 7, 00-068 Warsaw, Poland) Indexed: Math.R.
     Formerly (until 1984): Uniwersytet Jagiellonski. Zeszyty Naukowe. Prace Matematyczne (ISSN 0083-4386); Which supersedes in part: Seria Nauk Matematyczno-Przyrodniczych. Matematyka, Fizyka, Chimia.

510   PL
UNIWERSYTET SLASKI W KATOWICACH. ANNALES MATHEMATICAE SILESIANAE. (Text in English; summaries in Polish, Russian) 1969. irreg. price varies. Uniwersytet Slaski w Katowicach, Ul. Bankowa 14, 40-007 Katowice, Poland.
     Formerly: Uniwersytet Slaski w Katowicach. Prace Matematyczne (ISSN 0208-5410)

510   CN   ISSN 0382-0718
VECTOR. 1968. irreg. Can.$30 to non-members. (B.C. Association of Mathematics Teachers) B.C. Teachers' Federation, 2235 Burrard St., Vancouver, B.C. V6J 3H9, Canada. TEL 604-731-8121. illus. circ. 650. Indexed: Can.Educ.Ind.
  Formerly: British Columbia Association of Mathematics Teachers. Newsletter (ISSN 0382-0726)

530 510   GE   ISSN 0084-098X
WISSENSCHAFTLICHE TASCHENBUECHER. REIHE MATHEMATIK, PHYSIK. 1965. irreg. price varies. Akademie-Verlag, Leipziger Str. 3-4, 1086 Berlin, E. Germany (D.D.R.) Indexed: Biol.Abstr. Math.R.

510   CN   ISSN 0315-1700
WORLD DIRECTORY OF HISTORIANS OF MATHEMATICS. 1972. irreg., latest 1978. Can.$7 per vol. (Commission on History of Mathematics) University of Toronto Press, 21 King's College Circle, Toronto, Ont. M5S 1A1, Canada. TEL 613-978-2011. Ed. C.J. Scriba. circ. 1,000.

510   US   ISSN 0512-2740
WORLD DIRECTORY OF MATHEMATICIANS. 1958. quadrennial, 8th edt., 1986. (International Mathematical Union) American Mathematical Society, Box 6248, Providence, RI 02940. TEL 401-272-9500. Ed. G.D. Mostow. circ. 2,000.

510   PL   ISSN 0078-5431
WYZSZA SZKOLA PEDAGOGICZNA, OPOLE. ZESZYTY NAUKOWE. SERIA A. MATEMATYKA. (Text in Polish; summaries in English) 1961. irreg., vol.22, 1981. available on exchange. Wyzsza Szkola Pedagogiczna, Opole, Oleska 48, 45-052 Opole, Poland (Dist. by: Ars Polona-Ruch, Krakowskie Przedmiescie 7, Warsaw, Poland) Indexed: Math.R.

MATHEMATICS — Abstracting, Bibliographies, Statistics

500 016   BU   ISSN 0204-9449
ABSTRACTS OF BULGARIAN SCIENTIFIC LITERATURE. MATHEMATICAL AND PHYSICAL SCIENCES. (Editions in English and Russian) 1963. q. 3.44 lv.($2.) Bulgarska Akademiia na Naukite, Centur za Nauchna Informaciia, 7 Noemvri St., 1, 1040 Sofia, Bulgaria (Dist. by: RP, Klokotnica St., no.2A, 1202 Sofia, Bulgaria) Ed.Bd. abstr. index. circ. 800. Indexed: Chem.Abstr.
  Formerly: Abstracts of Bulgarian Scientific Literature. Mathematics, Physics, Astronomy, Geophysics, Geodesy (ISSN 0001-351X)

510   BL   ISSN 0067-6667
BIBLIOGRAFIA BRASILEIRA DE MATEMATICA. 1961. irreg. Cr.$600($25) Instituto Brasileiro de Informacao em Ciencia e Tecnologia, SCRN 708/709 Bloco B Loja 18E 30, 70740 Brasilia DF, Brazil. bk. rev. circ. 300.
  Supersedes in part: Bibliografia Brasileira de Matematica e Fisica.

510 523.013 530   HK
CHINA SCIENCE & TECHNOLOGY ABSTRACTS. SERIES 1: MATHEMATICS, ASTRONOMY, PHYSICS. 1980. bi-m. $36. International Information Service Ltd., Room 103, Wing on Plaza, Tsimshatsui East, Kowloon, Hong Kong, Hong Kong. Ed. C.N. Shum. circ. 2,000. (back issues avail.)

510 001.6   US   ISSN 0730-6199
COMPUMATH CITATION INDEX. Short title: C M C I. (Includes: Source Index, Research Front Speciality Index, Citation Index, Permuterm Subject Index, and Corporate Index) 3/yr. $925. Institute for Scientific Information, 3501 Market St., Philadelphia, PA 19104 TEL 215-386-0100. (And 132 High St., Uxbridge, Middx. UB8 1DP, England) cum.index: 1976-80. (also avail. in magnetic tape)
● Also available online. Vendors: BRS.

510 310   US   ISSN 0097-4455
CONFERENCE BOARD OF THE MATHEMATICAL SCIENCES. REGIONAL CONFERENCE SERIES IN APPLIED MATHEMATICS. 1971. irreg., no.58, 1983. Society for Industrial and Applied Mathematics, Conference Board of the Mathetical Sciences, Attn: C. Tanzer, 1405 Architects Bldg., 117 S. 17th St., Philadelphia, PA 19103. TEL 215-564-2929. Indexed: Appl.Mech.Rev.

510 016   US   ISSN 0361-4794
CURRENT MATHEMATICAL PUBLICATIONS. 1969. 17/yr. $233 to individual member; institutional member $186; reviewer $93. American Mathematical Society, Box 6248, Providence, RI 02940. TEL 401-272-9500. abstr. circ. 1,300. Indexed: Math.R.
● Also available online. Vendors: BRS, DIALOG, European Space Agency.
  Formed by the 1975 merger of: American Mathematical Society. New Publications (ISSN 0002-9912) & Contents of Contemporary Mathematical Journals (ISSN 0010-759X)

510 016   US   ISSN 0019-3917
INDEX OF MATHEMATICAL PAPERS. Variant title: Mathematical Reviews Annual Index. (Special issue of Mathematical Reviews) 1971. a. price varies. American Mathematical Society, Box 6248, Providence, RI 02940. TEL 401-272-9500. circ. 3,500.

510   US
IOWA STATE UNIVERSITY. STATISTICAL LABORATORY. ANNUAL REPORT. 1945. a. free. Iowa State University of Science and Technology, Statistical Laboratory, 102 Snedecor Hall, Ames, IA 50011. TEL 515-294-3440. Ed. Jauvanta M. Walker. bk. rev. abstr. bibl. illus. circ. 1,950. (back issues avail.) Indexed: Biol.Abstr.

512 016   UR
KOL'TSA; bibliografiya. irreg. 0.45 Rub. single issue. Akademiya Nauk S.S.S.R., Sibirskoe Otdelenie, Institut Matematiki, Novosibirsk, Akademgorodok, Russian S.F.S.R., U.S.S.R.

510 016   US   ISSN 0025-5629
MATHEMATICAL REVIEWS; a reviewing journal covering the world literature of mathematical research. (Text in English, French, German and Italian) 1940. m. $2950 to non-members; individual members $354; institutional members $2360; reviewer $236. American Mathematical Society, Box 6248, Providence, RI 02940. TEL 401-272-9500. Ed. R. Bartle. bk. rev. index. circ. 1,750. (also avail. in microfiche from AMS) Indexed: Appl.Mech.Rev. Math.R.
● Also available online. Vendors: BRS, DIALOG, European Space Agency.

510 016   UR   ISSN 0034-2467
REFERATIVNYI ZHURNAL. MATEMATIKA. 1953. m. 217.60 Rub. (285.60 Rub. including index) Vsesoyuznyi Institut Nauchno-Tekhnicheskoi Informatsii (VINITI), Baltiiskaya ul., 14, Moscow A-219, Russian S.F.S.R., U.S.S.R. (Subscr. to: Mezhdunarodnaya Kniga, Dimitrova ul. 39, 113095 Moscow, Russian S.F.S.R., U.S.S.R.) Ed. R.V. Gamkrelidze. circ. 2,296.

530 510   US
U S S R REPORT: PHYSICS AND MATHEMATICS. irreg., approx. 10/yr. $5 per no. U.S. Joint Publications Research Service, 1000 N. Glebe Rd., Arlington, VA 22201 TEL 703-487-4630. (Orders to: NTIS, Springfield, VA 22161)
  Formerly: U S S R and Eastern Europe Scientific Abstracts: Physics and Mathematics; Which was formed by the merger of: U S S R Scientific Abstracts: Physics and Mathematics; East European Scientific Abstracts: Physics and Mathematics.

510 310   BL
UNIVERSIDADE FEDERAL DO RIO DE JANEIRO. INSTITUTO DE MATEMATICA. MEMORIAS DE MATEMATICA. (Text in English, French, Portuguese, Spanish; summaries in English) 1971. irreg., no.146, 1985. $3 to institutions; free to individuals. Universidade Federal do Rio de Janeiro, Instituto de Matematica, C.P. 68.530, 21944 Rio de Janeiro, RJ, Brazil. Ed.Bd. circ. controlled.

510 016   US   ISSN 0044-4235
ZENTRALBLATT FUER MATHEMATIK UND IHRE GRENZGEBIETE/MATHEMATICS ABSTRACTS. (Text in English, French, German) 1931. 26/yr. $2968. (Deutsche Akademie der Wissenschaften zu Berlin, GW) Springer-Verlag, 175 Fifth Ave., New York, NY 10010 TEL 212-460-1500. (Also Berlin, Heidelberg, Tokyo and Vienna) (Co-sponsor: Heidelberger Akademie der Wissenschaften) Ed.Bd. cum.index: vols.1-25; 26-41; 60-61; 77-100; 221-249; 251-299; 301-349; 351-399. (also avail. in microform from UMI; reprint serivce avail. from ISI) Indexed: Appl.Mech.Rev. Math.R.
● Also available online. Vendors: STN International.

MATHEMATICS — Computer Applications

ACTA POLYTECHNICA SCANDINAVICA. MATHEMATICS AND COMPUTER SCIENCE SERIES. see COMPUTERS

COMPUTER SCIENCE AND APPLIED MATHEMATICS. see COMPUTERS

COMPUTERS AND MATH SERIES. see EDUCATION — Computer Applications

550 001.6   UR   ISSN 0301-6897
MATEMATICHESKIE PROBLEMY GEOFIZIKI. 1969. irreg. 1.41 Rub. Akademiya Nauk S.S.S.R., Vychislitel'nyi Tsentr, Ul. Vavilova, 40, Moscow V-333, Russian S.F.S.R., U.S.S.R. illus.

510   US   ISSN 0888-3262
PERSONAL COMPUTING SERIES. 1984. irreg. Computer Science Press, Inc., 1803 Research Blvd., Ste. 500, Rockville, MD 20850. TEL 301-251-9050. Ed. Arthur D. Friedman. (back issues avail.)

PRINCIPLES OF COMPUTER SCIENCE SERIES. see ENGINEERING — Computer Applications

MECHANICAL ENGINEERING

see Engineering — Mechanical Engineering

MECHANICS

see Physics — Mechanics

MEDICAL SCIENCES

see also Medical Sciences—Allergology and Immunology; Medical Sciences—Anaesthesiology; Medical Sciences—Cancer; Medical Sciences—Cardiovascular Diseases; Medical Sciences—Chiropractics, Homeopathy, Osteopathy; Medical Sciences—Communicable Diseases; Medical Sciences—Computer Applications; Medical Sciences—Dentistry; Medical Sciences—Dermatology and Venereology; Medical Sciences—Endocrinology; Medical Sciences—Experimental Medicine, Laboratory Technique; Medical Sciences—Forensic Sciences; Medical Sciences—Gastroenterology; Medical Sciences—Hematology; Medical Sciences—Nurses and Nursing; Medical Sciences—Obstetrics and Gynecology; Medical Sciences—Ophthalmology and Optometry; Medical Sciences—Orthopedics and Traumatology; Medical Sciences—Pediatrics; Medical Sciences—Psychiatry and Neurology; Medical Sciences—Radiology and Nuclear Medicine; Medical Sciences—Respiratory Diseases; Medical Sciences—Rheumatology; Medical Sciences—Sports Medicine; Medical Sciences—Surgery; Medical Sciences—Urology and Nephrology; Drug Abuse and Alcoholism; Gerontology and Geriatrics; Hospitals; Industrial Health and Safety; Nutrition and Dietetics; Pharmacy and Pharmacology; Physical Fitness and Hygiene; Public Health and Safety

A A M C CURRICULUM DIRECTORY. (Association of American Medical Colleges) see EDUCATION — Teaching Methods And Curriculum

A A M C DIRECTORY OF AMERICAN MEDICAL EDUCATION. (Association of American Medical Colleges) see EDUCATION — School Organization And Administration

610   US   ISSN 0884-1543
A B M S COMPENDIUM OF CERTIFIED MEDICAL SPECIALISTS. 1986. biennial. $200. American Board of Medical Specialties, One American Plaza, Ste. 805, Evanston, IL 60201. TEL 312-491-9091. Ed. Donald G. Langsley, M.D.

610   US
A B M S DIRECTORY OF CERTIFIED EMERGENCY PHYSICIANS. 1983. biennial. $24.95. American Board of Medical Specialties, One American Plaza, Ste. 805, Evanston, IL 60201. TEL 312-491-9091. Ed. Donald G. Langsley, M.D.

610   US   ISSN 0884-643X
A B M S DIRECTORY OF CERTIFIED FAMILY PRACTITIONERS. 1985. biennial. $49.95 hardcover; $39.95 softcover. American Board of Medical Specialties, One American Plaza, Ste. 805, Evanston, IL 60201. TEL 312-491-9091. Ed. Donald G. Langsley, M.D.

610   US   ISSN 0884-6448
A B M S DIRECTORY OF CERTIFIED INTERNISTS. 1985. biennial. $59.95 hardcover; $49.95 softcover. American Board of Medical Specialties, One American Plaza, Ste. 805, Evanston, IL 60201. TEL 312-491-9091. Ed. Donald G. Langsley, M.D.

610   US
A B M S DIRECTORY OF CERTIFIED PREVENTIVE MEDICINE PHYSICIANS. 1985. biennial. $24.95 softcover. American Board of Medical Specialties, One American Plaza, Ste. 805, Evanston, IL 60201. TEL 312-491-9091. Ed. Donald G. Langsley, M.D.

610 617   US   ISSN 0884-1462
A B M S DIRECTORY OF CERTIFIED THORACIC SURGEONS. 1983. biennial. $24.95. American Board of Medical Specialties, One American Plaza, Ste. 805, Evanston, IL 60201. TEL 312-491-9091. Ed. Donald G. Langsley, M.D.

610   US   ISSN 0748-5557
A M A DIRECTORY OF OFFICIALS AND STAFF. 1960. a. American Medical Association, 535 N. Dearborn St., Chicago, IL 60610. TEL 312-645-5000. circ. controlled. (reprint service avail. from UMI)
Formerly: American Medical Association. Directory of Officials and Staff (ISSN 0569-6534)

610   DK   ISSN 0109-9973
AARHUS UNIVERSITET. SOCIALMEDICINSK INSTITUT. RAPPORT. 1984. irreg. free. Aarhus Universitet, Socialmedicinsk Institut, Vesterbro Torv 1-3/6, 8000 Aarhus C, Denmark.

616.98   UK   ISSN 0260-5511
ABSTRACTS ON HYGIENE AND COMMUNICABLE DISEASES. 1926. m. $192. Bureau of Hygiene and Tropical Diseases, Keppel St., London WC1E 7HT, England. Ed. D.W. FitzSimons. adv. bk. rev. abstr. index. circ. 1,650. (also avail. in microform from UMI) Indexed: Biol.Abstr. Nutr.Abstr. C.I.S. Abstr. Ergon.Abstr. Ind.Vet. Rev.Appl.Entomol. Rev.Plant Path. Vet.Bull. World Text.Abstr.
Former titles: Abstracts on Hygiene (ISSN 0001-3692); Bulletin of Hygiene.

610   CL
ACADEMIA CHILENA DE MEDICINA. BOLETIN ANUAL. 1967. a. $25. Academia Chilena de Medicina, Clasificador 1349, Santiago 1, Chile. Eds. Dr. Amador Neghme, Dr. Alberto Donoso. index. circ. 1,000. (back issues avail.) Indexed: Ind.Med.
Formerly: Academia de Medicina. Boletin.

610   PL   ISSN 0303-4135
ACADEMIAE MEDICAE GEDANENSIS. ANNALES. (Text in English, Polish; summaries in English, Russian) 1971. a. 300 Zl.($14.50) Academia Medyczna w Gdansku, Ul. Marii Sklodowskiej-Curie 3a, 80-210 Gdansk, Poland. Ed. Stefan Raszeja. index. circ. 500. (back issues avail.) Indexed: Biol.Abstr.

610   IT   ISSN 0390-7783
ACCADEMIA DELLE SCIENZE DI SIENA DETTA DE FISIOCRITICI. ATTI. 1760; currently series 14. a. L.15000. Accademia delle Scienze di Siena Detta de Fisiocritici, Piazza S. Agostino 4, 53100 Siena, Italy. Indexed: Biol.Abstr.
Formerly: Accademia dei Fisiocritici, Siena. Sezione Medico-Fisica (ISSN 0065-0722)

610   IT   ISSN 0001-4427
ACCADEMIA MEDICA LOMBARDA. ATTI. (Issued in 4 vols.) a. L.12000. Accademia Medica Lombarda, Ospedale Policlinico "Paciglione Beretta Est", Via Festa del Perdona 37, 20122 Milan, Italy. bibl. illus. index. cum.index. circ. 1,200. Indexed: Biol.Abstr. Chem.Abstr. Excerp.Med. Ind.Med.

610   IT
ACCADEMIA MEDICA PISTOIESE "FILIPPO PACINI". BOLLETINO. 1928. a. L.5000($20) Accademia Medica Pistoiese "Filippo Pacini", Via della Rosa, Pistoia, Italy. Ed. Collatino Cantieri. adv.

615 610   FR
ACCESSOIREX. (Medical accessories available in pharmacies) 1971. a.(with 11 supplements) 363 F. Societe d'Editions Medico-Pharmaceutiques, 26 rue le Brun, 75013 Paris, France. circ. 10,000 (controlled) (looseleaf format; also avail. in microfiche)

610   CS
ACTA FACULTATIS MEDICAE UNIVERSITATIS BRUNENSIS. (Text and summaries in Czech, English, Russian) 1958. irreg. price varies. J.E. Purkyne University, Faculty of Medicine, Komenskeho nam.2, 66243 Brno, Czechoslovakia. Ed. M. Dokladal. circ. 700. Indexed: Biol.Abstr.

574   GE   ISSN 0065-1281
ACTA HISTOCHEMICA; Zeitschrift fuer histologische Topochemie. (Text in English, French, German; summaries in English) 1954. irreg.(4-6/yr.) M.120 per vol. VEB Gustav Fischer Verlag, Villengang 2, Postfach 176, 6900 Jena, E. Germany (D.D.R.) Ed.Bd. bk. rev. bibl. charts. illus. index. (reprint service avail. from ISI) Indexed: Biol.Abstr. Chem.Abstr. Curr.Cont. Excerp.Med. Ind.Med. Nutr.Abstr. Sci.Cit.Ind. ASCA. Dairy Sci.Abstr. Dent.Ind. Helmintol.Abstr. Ind.Sci.Rev. Ind.Vet. Vet.Bull.

ACTA HISTORICA LEOPOLDINA. see SCIENCES: COMPREHENSIVE WORKS

610   IT   ISSN 0065-1389
ACTA MEDICAE HISTORIAE PATAVINA. (Text in Italian or language of contributor; summaries in English, French, German and Italian) 1955. a. L.17000($8.) Universita degli Studi di Padova, Istituto di Storia della Medicina, Via Fallopia 50, 35100 Padua, Italy. Ed. Loris Premuda. index in vol.10. circ. 250.
History

ACTA PATHOLOGICA, MICROBIOLOGICA ET IMMUNOLOGICA SCANDINAVICA. SECTION A: PATHOLOGY. SUPPLEMENTUM. see BIOLOGY

636.089 610   AT   ISSN 0065-1907
ADELAIDE. INSTITUTE OF MEDICAL AND VETERINARY SCIENCE. ANNUAL REPORT OF THE COUNCIL. 1937/38. a. free. Institute of Medical and Veterinary Science, Frome Rd, Adelaide, S.A., Australia. Ed. Dr. R. G. Edwards. circ. 1,000.

ADVANCES IN BIOLOGICAL AND MEDICAL PHYSICS. see BIOLOGY — Biophysics

612.015 574.192   US   ISSN 0065-2571
ADVANCES IN ENZYME REGULATION. 1963. a. $170. Pergamon Press, Inc., Journals Division, Maxwell House, Fairview Park, Elmsford, NY 10523. TEL 914-592-7700. Ed. George Weber. adv. (also avail. in microform from MIM,UMI) Indexed: Biol.Abstr. Chem.Abstr. Ind.Med. Sci.Cit.Ind. Ind.Sci.Rev.

ADVANCES IN EXPERIMENTAL MEDICINE AND BIOLOGY. see BIOLOGY

610   US   ISSN 0197-8322
ADVANCES IN INFLAMMATION RESEARCH. 1979. irreg. price varies. Raven Press, 1185 Ave. of the Americas, New York, NY 10036. TEL 212-575-0335. Ed. Gerald Weissmann. Indexed: Biol.Abstr. Chem.Abstr. Curr.Cont.

616.026   US   ISSN 0065-2822
ADVANCES IN INTERNAL MEDICINE. 1954. a. $55. Year Book Medical Publishers, Inc., 35 E. Wacker Dr., Chicago, IL 60601. TEL 312-726-9733. Ed. G.H. Stollerman. (also avail. in microfilm from UMI; reprint service avail. from UMI) Indexed: Biol.Abstr. Chem.Abstr. Ind.Med. Sci.Cit.Ind. Dent.Ind. Ind.Sci.Rev.

ADVANCES IN MEDICAL SOCIAL SCIENCE: HEALTH AND ILLNESS AS VIEWED BY ANTHROPOLOGY, GEOGRAPHY, HISTORY, PSYCHOLOGY AND SOCIOLOGY. see SOCIAL SCIENCES: COMPREHENSIVE WORKS

612   US
ADVANCES IN PARENTERAL SCIENCES. 1985. irreg., vol. 3, 1986. price varies. Marcel Dekker, Inc., 270 Madison Ave., New York, NY 10016. TEL 212-696-9000. Ed. Joseph R. Robinson.

ADVANCES IN POLYAMINE RESEARCH. see BIOLOGY — Biological Chemistry

610   US   ISSN 0195-878X
ADVANCES IN SHOCK RESEARCH. 1979. a. price varies. Alan R. Liss, Inc., 41 E. 11th St., New York, NY 10003. TEL 212-475-7700. Indexed: Chem.Abstr. Ind.Med.

616.98 574   US
AEROSPACE MEDICINE & BIOLOGY (NASA) (National Aeronautics and Space Administration) irreg., approx. 12/yr. $8 per no. U.S. National Technical Information Service, 5285 Port Royal Road, Springfield, VA 22161. TEL 703-487-4600. (Compiled by: U.S. Library of Congress & American Institute of Aeronautics and Astronautics) index.
Formerly: Aerospace References in Medicine and Biology.

610   PL   ISSN 0067-6489
AKADEMIA MEDYCZNA IM. J.
MARCHLEWSKIEGO W BIALYMSTOKU.
ROCZNIKI/ANNALES ACADEMIAE
MEDICAE BIALOSTOCENSIS. (Text in Polish;
summaries in English, Polish, Russian) 1955. irreg.
free. Panstwowy Zaklad Wydawnictw Lekarskich,
Ul. Dluga 38/40, Warsaw, Poland (Subscr. to:
Redakcja Rocznikow A M B, ul. Mickiewicza 2,
Bialystok 12-230, Poland) circ. 800. (back issues
avail.) Indexed: Ind.Med.

610   PL   ISSN 0084-277X
AKADEMIA MEDYCZNA WE WROCLAWIU.
PRACE NAUKOWE. 1967. irreg., vol.15, 1981.
price varies. Akademia Medyczna we Wroclawiu,
Ul. Pasteura 1, 50-367 Wroclaw, Poland (Dist. by:
Ars Polona, Krakowskie Przedmiescie 7, 00-068
Warsaw, Poland) Ed. S. Iwankiewicz.

610   JA   ISSN 0002-368X
AKITA JOURNAL OF RURAL MEDICINE/
AKITA-KEN NOSON IGAKKAI ZASSHI. 1954.
irreg. 1000 Yen($3.) Akita Association of Rural
Medicine - Akita-ken Noson Igakkai, c/o Akita-ken
Kosei Nogyo Kyodo Kumiai Rengokai, 3 Omachi,
Akita-shi 010, Japan. Ed. Masakazu Tatsumi, M. D.
adv. abstr. charts. illus. stat. cum.index.

ALBERTA HOSPITALS AND MEDICAL CARE.
ANNUAL REPORT. see HOSPITALS

612 574   DK   ISSN 0065-6186
ALFRED BENZON SYMPOSIUM.
PROCEEDINGS. 1969. irreg. price varies.
Munksgaard, 35 Noerre Soegade, DK-1370
Copenhagen K, Denmark (Dist. in U.S. by:
Academic Press Inc., 171 First Ave., Atlantic
Highlands, NJ 07716) (reprint service avail. from
ISI) Indexed: Biol.Abstr. Chem.Abstr.

ALLIANCE (CHARLESTON) see COLLEGE AND
ALUMNI

610 574   US   ISSN 0589-1019
ALLIANCE FOR ENGINEERING IN MEDICINE
AND BIOLOGY. PROCEEDINGS OF THE
ANNUAL CONFERENCE. vol. 1, covering 12th
conference, 1959. a. $35 to non-members; members
$28. Alliance for Engineering in Medicine &
Biology, Attn: Patricia I. Horner, 1101 Connecticut
Ave., N.W., Ste. 700, Washington, DC 20036. TEL
202-857-1199. circ. 1,500. Indexed: Chem.Abstr.
Eng.Ind.

ALLIED HEALTH EDUCATION DIRECTORY. see
EDUCATION — Guides To Schools And Colleges

388.3 610   US   ISSN 0401-6351
AMERICAN ASSOCIATION FOR AUTOMOTIVE
MEDICINE. PROCEEDINGS. 1959. a. $40.
American Association for Automotive Medicine,
2350 E. Devon Ave., Ste. 205, Des Plaines, IL
60018. TEL 312-390-8927.

616.07 574.2 589.9 US ISSN 0065-7298
AMERICAN ASSOCIATION OF PATHOLOGISTS
AND BACTERIOLOGISTS. SYMPOSIUM.
MONOGRAPHS. Williams & Wilkins, 428 E.
Preston St., Baltimore, MD 21202. TEL 301-528-
4000. Ed. Nathan Kaufman.

610   US   ISSN 0272-9741
AMERICAN BOARD OF MEDICAL
SPECIALTIES. ANNUAL REPORT &
REFERENCE HANDBOOK. 1970. a. free.
American Board of Medical Specialties, One
American Plaza, Suite 805, Evanston, IL 60201.
TEL 312-491-9091. Ed. Donald G. Langsley, M.D.
circ. 6,000.
   Formerly: American Board of Medical
Specialties. Annual Report (ISSN 0146-5872)

616.98   US   ISSN 0065-7778
AMERICAN CLINICAL AND
CLIMATOLOGICAL ASSOCIATION.
TRANSACTIONS. 1881. a. $20. American Clinical
and Climatological Association, c/o James C. Allen,
M.D., Sec.-Treas., Medical University of South
Carolina, Rm. 803CSB, 171 Ashley Ave.,
Charleston, SC 29425. TEL 803-792-2914. Ed. Dr.
Theodore J. Abernethy. circ. 500. Indexed:
Biol.Abstr. Excerp.Med. Ind.Med.

610 534   US
AMERICAN INSTITUTE OF ULTRASOUND IN
MEDICINE. ANNUAL SCIENTIFIC
CONFERENCE. PROCEEDINGS. a. membership.
American Institute of Ultrasound in Medicine, Attn.
Michael Meinerz, Executive Office, 4405 East-West
Hwy., Ste. 504, Bethesda, MD 20814. TEL 301-
656-6117. adv. bk. rev. circ. 8,000.
   Formerly: American Institute of Ultrasound in
Medicine. Annual Scientific Conference. Program
(ISSN 0065-8871)

610   US
AMERICAN MEDICAL ASSOCIATION.
COUNCIL ON ETHICAL AND JUDICIAL
AFFAIRS. CURRENT OPINIONS. 1981. irreg.
$9.50. American Medical Association, Council on
Ethical and Judicial Affairs, 535 N. Dearborn St.,
Chicago, IL 60610. TEL 312-645-6000. Ed. Mary
M. Devlin. circ. 10,000.
   Formerly: American Medical Association.
Judicial Council. Current Opinions.

610   US
AMERICAN MEDICAL DIRECTORY. 1906. irreg.,
30th ed., 1986. $400 for 4 vols. American Medical
Association, 535 N. Dearborn St, Chicago, IL
60610. TEL 312-645-5000.
   Former titles: American Medical Directory of
Physicians; American Medical Directory (ISSN
0065-9339)

610   NE   ISSN 0066-1368
ANALECTA BOERHAAVIANA. 1959. irreg., no.8,
1979. price varies. E.J. Brill, P.O. Box 9000, 2300
PA Leiden, Netherlands. Ed. G.A. Lindeboom.

610   SP   ISSN 0586-9919
ANALES DE LA UNIVERSIDAD HISPALENSE.
SERIE: MEDICINAS. irreg. price varies.
Universidad de Sevilla, San Fernando 4, Seville,
Spain. charts. illus.

574.4 611   GE   ISSN 0066-1562
ANATOMISCHE GESELLSCHAFT.
VERHANDLUNGEN. (Supplement to:
Anatomischer Anzeiger) 1887. a. price varies. VEB
Gustav Fischer Verlag, Villengang 2, Postfach 176,
6900 Jena, E. Germany (D.D.R.) (reprint service
avail. from ISI) Indexed: Biol.Abstr. Chem.Abstr.
Excerp.Med. Ind.Med.
   Anatomy

574.4 611   GE   ISSN 0003-2786
ANATOMISCHER ANZEIGER; Zentralblatt fuer die
gesamte wissenschaftliche Anatomie. (Text in
English, French and German; summaries in English)
1886. irreg.(10-15/yr.) M.150 per vol. VEB Gustav
Fischer Verlag, Villengang 2, Postfach 176, 6900
Jena, E. Germany (D.D.R.) Ed. G.-H. Schumacher.
bk. rev. bibl. charts. illus. tr.lit. index per vol.
cum.index: vols.1-100. (reprint service avail. from
ISI) Indexed: Biol.Abstr. Chem.Abstr. Curr.Cont.
Excerp.Med. Ind.Med. Sci.Cit.Ind. Dairy
Sci.Abstr. Dent.Ind. Ind.Sci.Rev. Ind.Vet.
Vet.Bull.
   Anatomy

ANIMALS FOR RESEARCH - A DIRECTORY OF
SOURCES. see BIOLOGY — Zoology

610   PL   ISSN 0066-1945
ANNALES ACADEMIAE MEDICAE
STETINENSIS/ROCZNIKI POMORSKIEJ
AKADEMII MEDYCZNEJ W SZCZECINIE.
(Supplements available.) 1951. a. price varies.
(Pomorska Akademia Medyczna w Szczecinie)
Panstwowy Zaklad Wydawnictw Lekarskich, Ul.
Dluga 38-40, Warsaw 1, Poland (Subscr. to: Ars
Polona, Krakowskie Przedmiescie 7, 00-068
Warsaw, Poland) Indexed: Ind.Med. Dent.Ind.

610   FI   ISSN 0066-1996
ANNALES ACADEMIAE SCIENTIARUM
FENNICAE. SERIES A, V: MEDICA. (Text in
English, French, German) 1945. irreg. price varies.
Suomalainen Tiedeakatemia - Academia Scientiarum
Fennica, Snellmanink. 9-11, 00170 Helsinki,
Finland. Ed. Matti Bergstrom. circ. 400. (also avail.
in microform; back issues avail.; reprint service
avail. from UMI) Indexed: Biol.Abstr. Bull.Signal.
Chem.Abstr. Excerp.Med. Ind.Med. Ref.Zh.

610   PL   ISSN 0066-2240
ANNALES UNIVERSITATIS MARIAE CURIE-
SKLODOWSKA. SECTIO D. MEDICINA. (Text
in English or Polish; summaries and table of
contents in English and Russian) 1946. a. price
varies. Uniwersytet Marii Curie-Sklodowskiej, Plac
Marii Curie-Sklodowskiej 5, 20-031 Lublin, Poland.
Ed. Stanislaw Bryc. circ. 600. Indexed: Biol.Abstr.
Chem.Abstr. Excerp.Med. Ind.Med. Field Crop
Abstr. Herb.Abstr. Ind.Vet. Rev.Appl.Entomol.
Vet.Bull.

ANNALS OF CLINICAL RESEARCH.
SUPPLEMENTUM. see MEDICAL
SCIENCES — Experimental Medicine, Laboratory
Technique

610   FR   ISSN 0066-3298
ANNUAIRE MEDICAL DE L'HOSPITALISATION
FRANCAISE. (Includes supplement: Vademecum)
1949. a. 400 Fr. Edi-Publi-France, 8 rue Blanche,
75009 Paris, France. adv.

610   FR
ANNUAIRE MEDICAL DU DR. PORCHERON ET
PROF. G. BELTRAMI. 1912. a. 120 F. SO-GE-
CO-PRO S.A.R.L, 20-26 rue Caisserie, 13235
Marseille Cedex 1, France. adv.

610   FR   ISSN 0337-5935
ANNUAIRE NATIONAL DES MASSEURS
KINESITHERAPEUTES. vol. 2, 1975. a.
Federation Francaise des Masseurs-
Kinesitherapeutes Reeducateurs., 9 rue des Petits-
Hotels, 75010 Paris, France.
   Continues: Annuaire National M.K.D.E. France
(ISSN 0337-5927)

ANNUAL BOOK OF A S T M STANDARDS.
VOLUME 13.01. MEDICAL DEVICES. see
ENGINEERING — Engineering Mechanics And
Materials

ANNUAL EDITIONS: READINGS IN HUMAN
DEVELOPMENT. see BIOLOGY — Physiology

610   US
ANNUAL REVIEW OF MEDICINE: SELECTED
TOPICS IN THE CLINICAL SCIENCES. 1950. a.
$31. Annual Reviews Inc., 4139 El Camino Way,
Palo Alto, CA 94306. TEL 415-493-4400. Ed.
William P. Creger. bibl. index. cum.index. (back
issues avail.; reprint service avail. from ISI) Indexed:
Biol.Abstr. Chem.Abstr. Curr.Cont. Ind.Med.
Nutr.Abstr. Psychol.Abstr. Sci.Cit.Ind. Dent.Ind.
Helminthol.Abstr. Ind.Sci.Rev. Ind.Vet. M.M.R.I.
Vet.Bull.
   Formerly: Annual Review of Medicine (ISSN
0066-4219)

610   IT
ANNUARIO SANITARIO ITALIANO/ITALIAN
SANITARY DIRECTORY. 1955. a. £85000. Guida
Monaci S.p.A., Via Crispi 10, 00187 Rome, Italy.
adv. circ. 85,000.
   Formerly: Guida Monaci. Annuario Sanitario.

610   IT
ANTHOLOGIA MEDICA SANTORIANA. a. price
varies. Giardini Editori e Stampatori, Via Santa
Bibbiana 28, 56100 Pisa, Italy. Ed. Marcello Comel.

610   CL
ANUARIO ENFERMEDADES DE
NOTIFICACION OBLIGATORIA. 1947. a. $5.
Ministerio de Salud, Departamento de Control y
Evaluacion, Santiago, Chile.

610   UK   ISSN 0268-4861
ARAB MEDICARE; a guide to medical equipment
suppliers. 1986. a. $50. International Trade Press
Ltd., Queensway House, 2 Queensway, Redhill,
Surrey RH1 1QS, England. Ed. G.N. Napier. adv.

610 574   GW   ISSN 0066-5665
ARBEITEN AUS DEM PAUL-EHRLICH-
INSTITUT, DEM GEORG-SPEYER-HAUS UND
DEM FERDINAND-BLUM-INSTITUT. a. price
varies. Gustav Fischer Verlag, Wollgrasweg 49,
Postfach 720143, 7000 Stuttgart 70, W. Germany
(B.R.D.) Indexed: Excerp.Med. Ind.Med.

ARCHIVES D'ANATOMIE, D'HISTOLOGIE ET
D'EMBRYOLOGIE; normales et experimentales.
see BIOLOGY

MEDICAL SCIENCES

616.98   IT   ISSN 0003-9934
ARCHIVES OF MEDICAL HYDROLOGY. (Text in English, French, German, Italian) 1928. irreg. (3-4/yr.) $5. International Society of Medical Hydrology and Climatology, Via Rovereto 11, 00198 Rome, Italy. bibl. circ. 550. Indexed: Chem.Abstr.
Climatological medicine

616.07   IT   ISSN 0004-0061
ARCHIVIO DE VECCHI; per l'anatomia patologica e la medicina clinica. 1938. irreg. L.80000. Editrice Il Sedicesimo, Via Mannelli 29R, 50132 Florence, Italy. TEL 055/2476781. Ed. Prof. Antonio Costa. bibl. charts. illus. index. circ. 1,000. Indexed: Biol.Abstr. Chem.Abstr. Ind.Med.
Pathology

ARKANSAS. DIVISION OF REHABILITATION SERVICES. ANNUAL REPORT. see *SOCIAL SERVICES AND WELFARE*

616.07   PO   ISSN 0066-7854
ARQUIVOS DE PATOLOGIA GERAL E ANATOMIA PATOLOGICA. (Text in Portuguese; summaries in English and French) 1913. a. available on exchange. Universidade de Coimbra, Instituto de Anatomia Patologica, Faculdade de Medicina, 3049 Coimbra Codex, Portugal. Ed. Renato Trincao. circ. 400. Indexed: Biol.Abstr. Excerp.Med.
Pathology

610 572   SP   ISSN 0210-4466
ASCLEPIO; archivo Iberoamericano de historia de la medicina. 1949. a. 2000 ptas. Consejo Superior de Investigaciones Cientificas C.S.I.C), Instituto Arnau de Vilanova, Vitnuvio, 8. Apdo. 14.458, 28046 Madrid, Spain. Ed. Pedro Lain Entralgo. bk. rev. bibl. cum.index: 1949-1973.
History

ASLIB DIRECTORY OF INFORMATION SOURCES IN THE UNITED KINGDOM. VOLUME 2: SOCIAL SCIENCES, MEDICINE AND THE HUMANITIES. see *SOCIAL SCIENCES: COMPREHENSIVE WORKS*

610   BL
ASOCIACAO MEDICA BRASILEIRA. BOLETIM. 1962. irreg. Asociacao Medica Brasileira, Sao Carlos Pinhal 324, Sao Paulo, SP, Brazil. Ed. Pedro Kassab. adv. circ. 45,000.

610.7   MX   ISSN 0004-4857
ASOCIACION MEXICANA DE FACULTADES Y ESCUELAS DE MEDICINA. BOLETIN. 1962. irreg. free. Asociacion Mexicana de Facultades y Escuelas de Medicina, Queretaro No. 147, Oficinas 501 y 502, Apdo. Postal 12927, 06760 Mexico, D.F., Mexico. Ed. Dr. Manuel Loria-Mendez. bibl. charts. illus. index. circ. 750.
Study and teaching

610   IS   ISSN 0334-3871
ASSIA. (Text in English and Hebrew) 1970. irreg. $25 for 4 nos. (Shaare Zedek Medical Center, Falk Schlesinger Institute for Medical Halachic Research) Falk Schlesinger Institute for Medical-Halachic Research, Box 293, Jerusalem 91002, Israel. Ed. Rabbi Mordechai Halperin. adv. bk. rev. abstr. circ. 850. Indexed: Ind.Heb.Per.

610   US   ISSN 0066-9458
ASSOCIATION OF AMERICAN PHYSICIANS. TRANSACTIONS. 1886. a. $37 domestic; $21 foreign. William J. Dornan, Inc., Willows Ave., Collingdale, PA 19023. TEL 215-583-5741. Ed. Dr. K. Frank Austin. Indexed: Chem.Abstr. Excerp.Med. Ind.Med.

ASSOCIATION OF LIFE INSURANCE MEDICAL DIRECTORS OF AMERICA. TRANSACTIONS. see *INSURANCE*

610   IT   ISSN 0365-5377
ATENEO PARMENSE. COLLANA DI MONOGRAFIE. irreg. Ateneo Parmense, Via Gramsci 14, 43100 Parma, Italy. Ed. P. Bobbio. charts.

610 309   IO
ATMA JAYA RESEARCH CENTRE. SOCIO-MEDICAL RESEARCH REPORT/PUSAT PENELITIAN ATMA JAYA. PENELITIAN TENTANG KEBUTUHAN KESEHATAN MASYARAKAT DAN SISTEM PELEYANAN KESEHATAN DI KECAMATAN PENJARINGAN. 1978. irreg. Atma Jaya Research Centre - Pusat Penelitian Atma Jaya, Jalan Jenderal Sudirman 49a, Box 2639, Jakarta 10001, Indonesia.

610 028.5   AT
AUSTRALIAN ASSOCIATION FOR ADOLESCENT HEALTH. NEWSLETTER. 1978. irreg. Aus.$25. (Australian Association for Adolescent Health) Canberra College of Advanced Education, P.O. Box 1, Belconnen, A.C.T. 2616, Australia. Ed. Murray Williams. circ. 200. (back issues avail.)

610   DK   ISSN 0108-4739
AUTORISEREDE LAEGER, TANDLAEGER, DYRLAEGER I DANMARK; fortegnelse. 1982. biennial. Kr.80. Sundhedsstyrelsen, St. Kongensgade 1, 1264 Copenhagen K, Denmark (Orders to: Statens Informationtjeneste, Siljangade 6, 2300 Copenhagen S, Denmark) (Co-sponsor: Direktoratet for Statens Indkoeb)
Formerly: Fortegnelse over Autoriserede Laeger, Tandlaeger, Dyrlaeger i Danmark.

AVIATION MEDICAL EDUCATION SERIES. see *AERONAUTICS AND SPACE FLIGHT*

610   IT
AVVENIRE MEDICO. a. price varies. Giardini Editori e Stampatori, Via Santa Bibbiana 28, 56100 Pisa, Italy.

614.88   UK
BAILLIERE'S HANDBOOK OF FIRST AID. 1958. irreg. Bailliere Tindall, 1 Vincent Sq., London SW1P 2PN, England.

BASHAVIL HAREFUAH. see *RELIGIONS AND THEOLOGY — Judaic*

610 574   SZ   ISSN 0067-4524
BASLER VEROEFFENTLICHUNGEN ZUR GESCHICHTE DER MEDIZIN UND DER BIOLOGIE. 1953. irreg., no.35, 1985. price varies. Schwabe und Co. AG, Steinentorstr. 13, 4010 Basel, Switzerland. Eds. Heinrich Buess, Ulrich Troehler. index.

610   US   ISSN 0067-4672
BAYER-SYMPOSIEN. (Text in English) 1969. irreg., vol.9, 1986. price varies. (Bayer AG, GW) Springer-Verlag, 175 Fifth Avenue, New York, NY 10010 TEL 212-460-1500. (Also Berlin, Heidelberg, Tokyo and Vienna) (reprint service avail. from ISI) Indexed: Biol.Abstr.

610   SZ   ISSN 0378-8679
BEITRAEGE ZU INFUSIONSTHERAPIE UND KLIN. ERNAEHRUNG. 1978. a. price varies. S. Karger AG, P.O. Box, CH-4009 Basel, Switzerland. Ed.Bd. (back issues avail.) Indexed: Biol.Abstr. Chem.Abstr. Curr.Cont. Ind.Med.

616.02   SZ   ISSN 0254-8275
BEITRAEGE ZUR INTENSIV- UND NOTFALLMEDIZIN. (Text in German) 1983. irreg. price varies. S. Karger AG, P.O. Box, CH-4009 Basel, Switzerland. Ed. G. Kalff.

BEITRAEGE ZUR PSYCHOLOGIE UND SOZIOLOGIE DES KRANKEN MENSCHEN. see *PSYCHOLOGY*

BENCHMARK PAPERS IN HUMAN PHYSIOLOGY. see *BIOLOGY — Physiology*

BERICHTE NATURWISSENSCHAFTLICH-MEDIZINISCHEN VEREINS IN INNSBRUCK. see *BIOLOGY*

611 574.4   SZ   ISSN 0067-7833
BIBLIOTHECA ANATOMICA. (Text in English, French and German) 1961. irreg. (approx. a.) price varies. S. Karger AG, Allschwilerstrasse 10, P.O. Box, CH-4009 Basel, Switzerland. Ed. W. Lierse. (reprint service avail. from ISI, back issues avail.) Indexed: Biol.Abstr. Chem.Abstr. Curr.Cont. Ind.Med.
Incorporating: European Conference on Microcirculation. Proceedings.
Anatomy

BIOCHEMISTRY OF DISEASE. see *BIOLOGY — Biological Chemistry*

610.28 614   US
BIOMEDICAL ENGINEERING AND HEALTH SYSTEMS: A WILEY-INTERSCIENCE SERIES. (Issues not published consecutively) 1968. irreg., unnumbered, latest 1983. price varies. John Wiley & Sons, Inc., 605 Third Ave., New York, NY 10016. TEL 212-850-6000. Ed. John H. Milsum. Indexed: Math.R.
Formerly: Biomedical Engineering Series of Monographs (ISSN 0067-8848)

610.28   US   ISSN 0067-8856
BIOMEDICAL SCIENCES INSTRUMENTATION. 1963. a. since 1974. price varies. Instrument Society of America, 67 Alexander Dr., Box 12277, Research Triangle Park, NC 27709. TEL 919-549-8411. (also avail. in microform from UMI; reprint service avail. from UMI, ISI and publisher) Indexed: Appl.Mech.Rev. Biol.Abstr. Chem.Abstr. Eng.Ind. Excerp.Med. Ind.Med. Dent.Ind.
Medical instrumentation

BIOTECHNOLOGY AND GENETIC ENGINEERING REVIEWS. see *BIOLOGY*

616.043   US
BIRTH DEFECTS INSTITUTE. SYMPOSIA. 1971. a., vol.15, 1986. $33. Academic Press, Inc., Orlando, FL 32887. TEL 305-345-2000. Ed. Ernest B. Hook.
Congenital defects

616.043   US   ISSN 0547-6844
BIRTH DEFECTS ORIGINAL ARTICLE SERIES. (Former name of issuing body: National Foundation, March of Dimes) irreg., vol.22, no.5, 1983. price varies. (March of Dimes Birth Defects Foundation) Alan R. Liss, Inc., 41 E. 11th St., New York, NY 10003. TEL 212-475-7700. Indexed: Biol.Abstr. Chem.Abstr. Curr.cont. Excerp.Med. Ind.Med. Dent.Ind.
Congenital defects.

610   UK   ISSN 0045-2084
BLACK BAG. 1898. irreg. £10. Galenicals Society, Bristol University Medical School, Dolphin House, Bristol Royal Infirmary, Bristol 2, England. Ed. Paul T. Johns. adv. bk. rev. film rev. illus. circ. 1,000 (controlled)

610   UK
BLACK'S MEDICAL DICTIONARY. 1906. irreg., (every 2-3 yrs.) A & C Black (Publishers) Ltd., 35 Bedford Row, London WC1R 4JH, England. Ed. Dr. C.W.H. Havard.

610   CU
BOLETIN DE MEDICIANA TRADICIONAL GRUPO "JUAN TOMAS ROIG". a. Academia de Ciencias, Instituto de Documentacion e Informacion Cientifico-Tecnica (I D I C T), Capitolio Nacional, Prado y San Jose, La Habana 2, Havana, Cuba.

610   CN
BRITISH COLUMBIA. MEDICAL SERVICES PLAN. PRACTITIONERS' NEWSLETTER. 1977. irreg. free. Medical Services Plan, Box 1600, Victoria, B.C. V8V 2X9, Canada. TEL 604-669-4211. Ed. Dr. Bolton.
Formerly: British Columbia. Medical Services Plan. Physician's Newsletter (ISSN 0707-0462)

BUNDESARBEITSGEMEINSCHAFT HILFE FUER BEHINDERTE. JAHRESPIEGEL. see *EDUCATION — Special Education And Rehabilitation*

614.88 384.5   IT
C.I.R.M. 1935. a. free. Centro Internazionale Radio-Medico, Via Architettura 41, 00144 Rome, Italy.

610   US   ISSN 0276-8283
C P T. (Physicians' Current Procedural Terminology) 1966. irreg., 4th ed., 1987. $30. American Medical Association, 535 N. Dearborn St., Chicago, IL 60610. TEL 312-645-5000. (also avail. in microfiche; reprint service avail. from UMI)
Formerly (1st & 2nd edts.): Current Procedural Terminology (ISSN 0065-9312)

CALENDAR OF CONGRESSES OF MEDICAL SCIENCES. see *MEETINGS AND CONGRESSES*

MEDICAL SCIENCES 759

610 658 US
CALIFORNIA HEALTH FACILITIES
COMMISSION. ANNUAL REPORT TO THE
GOVERNOR AND LEGISLATURE OF THE
STATE OF CALIFORNIA. 1973. a. free. Health
Facilities Commission, Public Liaison Offic, 717 K
St., Sacramento, CA 95814. TEL 916-322-2810. Ed.
Sandra Salazar. circ. 1,750.

610 CN ISSN 0381-2561
CANADA HEALTH MANPOWER INVENTORY.
(Text in English and French) 1969. a. free.
Department of National Health and Welfare, Health
Information Division, Brooke Claxton Bldg.,
Ottawa, Ont. K1A 0K9, Canada. TEL 613-957-
1372. stat. circ. 1,200.

610.28 CN
CANADIAN CLINICAL ENGINEERING
CONFERENCE. PROCEEDINGS. irreg., 3rd,
1981, Saskatoon. Can.$15. Canadian Medical and
Biological Engineering Society, Rm. 164, Bldg. M-
50, National Research Council, Ottawa, Ont. K1A
0R8, Canada.

610.28 CN
CANADIAN MEDICAL AND BIOLOGICAL
ENGINEERING CONFERENCE. DIGEST OF
PAPERS. biennial, 9th, 1982, Fredericton. Can.$20.
Canadian Medical and Biological Engineering
Society, Rm. 164, Bldg. M-50, National Research
Council, Ottawa, Ont. K1A 0R8, Canada. TEL 613-
993-1686.

610 CN ISSN 0068-9203
CANADIAN MEDICAL DIRECTORY. 1955. a.
Can.$84.95. Southam Communications Ltd., 1450
Don Mills Rd., Don Mills, Ont. M3B 2X7, Canada.
TEL 416-445-6641.

610 CN ISSN 0068-9580
CANADIAN REHABILITATION COUNCIL FOR
THE DISABLED. ANNUAL REPORT. 1963. a.
free. Canadian Rehabilitation Council for the
Disabled, Suite 2110, One Yonge St., Toronto, Ont.
M5E 1E5, Canada. TEL 416-862-0340. Ed. Heather
Ney. circ. 2,000.

362.1 CN ISSN 0828-5748
CATHOLIC HEALTH ASSOCIATION OF
CANADA. DIRECTORY. Short title: C H A C
Directory. (Text in English and French) 1968.
biennial. Can.$17 to non-members. Catholic Health
Association of Canada, 1247 Kilborn Ave., Ottawa,
Ont. K1H 6K7, Canada. TEL 613-238-8471. Ed.
Freda Fraser. circ. 975.
 Formerly: Catholic Hospital Association of
Canada. Directory (ISSN 0380-8475)

616 JA ISSN 0078-6632
CENTER FOR ADULT DISEASES, OSAKA.
ANNUAL REPORT. (Text in English) 1961. a.
free. Center for Adult Diseases, Osaka, 1-3-3
Nakamichi, Higashinari-ku, Osaka 537, Japan. Ed.
Nobuyuki Senda, M.D. Indexed: Biol.Abstr.
Excerp.Med.

610 TU
CERRAHPASA MEDICAL REVIEW. (Supplements:
Cerrahpasa Medical Faculty. Journal) 1982. a.
TL.220($2) free to medical libraries. University of
Istanbul, Cerrahpasa Medical Faculty, Dergi Kurulu,
Cerrahpasa Tip Fakultesi, Aksaray, Istanbul, Turkey.
Ed. Altan Onat. bibl. charts. illus.

610 GE
CHARITE ANNALEN. NEUE FOLGE. 1981. a.
Akademie-Verlag Berlin, Leipziger Str. 3-4, 1086
Berlin, E. Germany (D.D.R.) Ed. Jurgen Grosser.

CHICAGO HISTORY OF SCIENCE AND
MEDICINE. see HISTORY

610 US ISSN 0069-3685
CHINA MEDICAL BOARD OF NEW YORK.
ANNUAL REPORT. 1951. a. membership. China
Medical Board of New York, 622 Third Ave., New
York, NY 10017. TEL 212-682-8000. circ. 300.

CHINESE JOURNAL OF PHYSIOLOGY. see
BIOLOGY — Physiology

610 US ISSN 0084-8786
CIBA COLLECTION OF MEDICAL
ILLUSTRATIONS. 1953. irreg., vol.7, 1979. price
varies. Ciba Giegy Corporation, Medical Education
Division, 14 Henderson Dr., W. Caldwell, NJ
07006. TEL 201-575-6510. illus. (avail. on slides)
Indexed: Biol.Abstr.

610 SP ISSN 0212-6052
CIENCIA MEDICA; para la practica diaria. irreg.
Alpe Editores, S.A., Arzobispo Morcillo, 24, 28029
Madrid, Spain. TEL 733 88 11/92.

CLINICAL AND BIOCHEMICAL ANALYSIS. see
BIOLOGY — Biological Chemistry

610 US ISSN 0730-0077
CLINICAL AND EXPERIMENTAL
HYPERTENSION. PART A: THEORY AND
PRACTICE. 1978. 12/yr. $555 ($635 Parts A & B
combined) Marcel Dekker Journals, 270 Madison
Ave., New York, NY 10016 TEL 212-696-9000.
(Prepaid subscr. to: Box 11305, Church St. Sta.,
New York, NY 10249) Ed. I.H. Slater. adv. bk. rev.
index. (also avail. in microform from RPI; back
issues avail.) Indexed: Chem.Abstr. Curr.Cont.
Excerp.Med. Ind.Med. Sci.Cit.Ind. Biol.Dig.
Biotech.Abstr. Dent.Ind. Ind.Sci.Rev.
 Supersedes in part: Clinical and Experimental
Hypertension (ISSN 0148-3927)

610 US ISSN 0191-7870
CLINICAL BIOMECHANICS. 1971. irreg. Clinical
Biomechanics Corp., Box 35185, Los Angeles, CA
90035.

610.28 US
CLINICAL ENGINEERING SERIES. 1972. irreg.,
vol.5, 1981. Academic Press, Inc., Orlando, FL
32887. TEL 305-345-2000. Ed. Cesar A. Caceres.
Biomedical engineering

610 616.9 US
CLINICAL TOPICS IN INFECTIOUS DISEASE.
1986. irreg. price varies. Springer-Verlag, 175 Fifth
Ave., New York, NY 10160 TEL 212-460-1500.
(Also Berlin, Heidelberg, Tokyo, Vienna) (reprint
service avail. from ISI)

610 GW
CLIO; eine periodische Zeitschrift zur Selbsthilfe.
1976. irreg. DM.20($10) for 4 nos. Feministisches
Frauen Gesundheitszentrum e.V., Bambergerstr. 51,
1000 Berlin 30, W. Germany (B.R.D.) adv. bk. rev.
illus. circ. 5,000. (back issues avail.) Indexed:
Abstr.Engl.Stud.

610 SP
COLECCION CIENCIAS MEDICAS DE
BOLSILLO. 1977. irreg., no.17, 1984. price varies.
(Universidad de Navarra, Facultad de Medicina)
Ediciones Universidad de Navarra, S.A., Apdo. 396,
31080 Pamplona, Spain.

610 SP
COLECCION LIBROS DE MEDICINA. 1974. irreg.,
no.21, 1986. price varies. (Universidad de Navarra,
Facultad de Medicina) Ediciones Universidad de
Navarra, S.A., Apdo. 396, 31080 Pamplona, Spain.
 Formerly: Coleccion Medicina.

610 SA
COLIMPEX MEDICAL EXECUPAD. (Text in
Afrikaans and English) a. free to qualified
personnel. Colimpex Africa (Pty) Ltd., Box 889,
Wendywood 2144, South Africa. adv.

610 CN
COLLEGE OF PHYSICIANS AND SURGEONS
OF BRITISH COLUMBIA. ANNUAL REPORT.
a. membership. College of Physicians and Surgeons
of British Columbia, 1807 W. 10th Ave., Vancouver,
B.C. V6J 2A9, Canada. TEL 604-736-5551.

610 CN ISSN 0069-5726
COLLEGE OF PHYSICIANS AND SURGEONS
OF BRITISH COLUMBIA. MEDICAL
DIRECTORY. a. Can.$28. College of Physicians
and Surgeons of British Columbia, 1807 W. 10th
Ave., Vancouver, B.C. V6J 2A9, Canada. TEL 604-
736-5551.

CONCEPTS IN TOXICOLOGY. see PHARMACY
AND PHARMACOLOGY

615.8 FR ISSN 0071-2817
CONFEDERATION EUROPEENNE POUR LA
THERAPIE PHYSIQUE. CONGRESS REPORTS.
irreg., 14th, 1971, Strasbourg. European
Confederation for Physical Therapy, 11 rue des
Petits - Hotels, 75010 Paris, France.
Physiotherapy

610.28 US
CONFERENCE ON ENGINEERING IN
MEDICINE AND BIOLOGY. RECORD. a.
Alliance for Engineering in Medicine and Biology,
1101 Connecticut Ave., N.W., Ste. 700,
Washington, DC 20036. TEL 202-857-1199.
 Formerly: Engineering in Medicine and Biology
Conference. Record (ISSN 0071-0334)
Biomedical engineering

610 MQ ISSN 0414-4406
CONGRESS INTERNATIONAL MEDICAL DE
PAYS DE LANGUE FRANCAISE DE
L'HEMISPHERE AMERICAIN. RAPPORTS ET
COMMUNICATIONS. 1951. biennial. price varies.
Societe Medicale des Antilles et Guyane Francaises,
Section Martiniquaise, 35 rue Victor Severe, Fort de
France, Martinique. circ. 1,000.

610 US ISSN 0147-1058
CONTRIBUTIONS IN MEDICAL HISTORY. 1978.
irreg. price varies. Greenwood Press, 88 Post Rd.
W., Box 5007, Westport, CT 06881. TEL 203-226-
3571. Ed. John Burnham.

612 SZ ISSN 0301-4193
CONTRIBUTIONS TO HUMAN DEVELOPMENT.
(Text in English) 1962. irreg.(approx. 1/yr.) price
varies. S. Karger AG, Allschwilerstrasse 10, CH-
4009 Basel, Switzerland. Ed. J.A. Meacham. (reprint
service avail. from ISI) Indexed: Biol.Abstr.
Chem.Abstr. Curr.Cont. Psychol.Abstr. Ind.Med.
 Formerly: Bibliotheca Vita Humana.

610 SZ ISSN 0250-3220
CONTRIBUTIONS TO ONCOLOGY/BEITRAEGE
ZUR ONKOLOGIE. (Text in English and German)
1979. irreg.(approx. 3/yr.) price varies. S. Karger
AG, P.O. Box, CH-1004 Basel, Switzerland. Ed.Bd.
index. Indexed: Biol.Abstr. Chem.Abstr.
Curr.Cont.

CONTRIBUTIONS TO SENSORY PHYSIOLOGY.
see BIOLOGY — Physiology

610 CN ISSN 0315-226X
CORPORATION PROFESSIONNELLE DES
MEDECINS DU QUEBEC. ANNUAIRE
MEDICAL. a. Can.$35. Corporation Professionnelle
des Medecins du Quebec, 1440 Ouest rue St.
Catherine, Suite 914, Montreal, Que. H3G 1S5,
Canada. TEL 514-878-4441.

610 CN ISSN 0315-2979
CORPORATION PROFESSIONNELLE DES
MEDECINS DU QUEBEC. BULLETIN. 1961.
irreg.(4-6/yr.) free. Corporation Professionnelle des
Medecins du Quebec, 1440 Ouest rue St. Catherine,
Suite 914, Montreal, Que H3G 1S5, Canada. TEL
514-878-4441. Indexed: Pt.de Rep.
 Formerly: College des Medecins et Chirurgiens
de la Province de Quebec. Bulletin (ISSN 0069-
5599)

610 GE ISSN 0070-0347
CORPUS MEDICORUM GRAECORUM. 1958.
irreg., vol.26, 1985. price varies. (Akademie der
Wissenschaften der DDR) Akademie-Verlag,
Leipziger Str. 3-4, 1086 Berlin, E. Germany
(D.D.R.) (Co-sponsors: Koenigliche Daenische
Akademie; Saechsische Akademie der
Wissenschaften, Leipzig)
History

610 668.5 US
COSMETIC SCIENCE AND TECHNOLOGY
SERIES. 1984. irreg., vol.4, 1985. price varies.
Marcel Dekker, Inc., 270 Madison Ave., New York,
NY 10016. TEL 212-696-9000. Ed. Eric Jungerman.

610.6 US ISSN 0196-2434
COST AND PRODUCTION SURVEY REPORT.
1970. a. $126.75. Medical Group Management
Association, 1355 S. Colorado Blvd., Ste. 900,
Denver, CO 80222. Ed.Bd. charts. stat. circ. 6,500.
(back issues avail.)

616.865　　　　　US　　ISSN 0361-1612
COUNCIL FOR TOBACCO RESEARCH--U.S.A.
REPORT. a. Council for Tobacco Research--U.S.A.
Inc., 900 Third Ave., New York, NY 10022. TEL
212-421-8885. abstr. Key Title: Report of the
Council for Tobacco Research-U.S.A., Inc.

610 500　　　　　SP　　ISSN 0011-2577
CUADERNOS VALENCIANOS DE HISTORIA DE
LA MEDICINA Y DE LA CIENCIA. (Text in
Spanish and classical languages) 1962. irreg., 2-3
nos. per yr. price varies. Universidad de Valencia,
Catedra Historia de la Medicina de Valencia, Avda.
Blasco Ibanez 17, Valencia 10, Spain. Ed.Bd. charts.
illus. circ. 500. (reprint service avail.)
　　History

616.97　　　　　US
CUMITECHS. (Cumulative Techniques and
Procedures in Clinical Microbiology) 1974. irreg.
(2-3/yr.) $7 per no. American Society for
Microbiology, 1913 I St. N.W., Washington, DC
20006. TEL 202-833-9680. Ed. Steven Specter.

610　　　　　US　　ISSN 0070-2005
CURRENT MEDICAL INFORMATION AND
TERMINOLOGY. Short title: C M I T. 1963.
irreg., 5th ed., 1981. $22. American Medical
Association, 535 N. Dearborn St., Chicago, IL
60610. TEL 312-645-5000. index. (also avail. in
microfiche; reprint service avail. from UMI)
　　Formerly: Current Medical Terminology.

610 615　　　　　UK　　ISSN 0300-7995
CURRENT MEDICAL RESEARCH AND
OPINION. 1972. irreg. $60. Clayton-Wray
Publications Ltd., 1A High St., Alton, Hants GU34
1BA, England. Ed. N.B. Clayton. index. circ. 6,000.
(also avail. in microform from UMI; reprint service
avail. from UMI; back issues avail.) Indexed:
Chem.Abstr. Curr.Cont. Excerp.Med. Ind.Med.
Nutr.Abstr. Sci.Cit.Ind. Abstr.Hyg. Biotech.Abstr.
Helminthol.Abstr. Ind.Sci.Rev. Rev.Plant Path.
Trop.Dis.Bull.

CURRENT PROBLEMS IN CLINICAL
BIOCHEMISTRY. see *BIOLOGY — Biological
Chemistry*

616.07 574.2　　　　　US　　ISSN 0090-8584
CURRENT TOPICS IN COMPARATIVE
PATHOBIOLOGY. 1971. irreg., vol.2, 1973.
Academic Press, Inc., Orlando, FL 32887. TEL
305-345-2000. Ed. Thomas C. Cheng. Indexed:
Biol.Abstr.
　　Pathology

610　　　　　UK　　ISSN 0260-1664
CURRENT TOPICS IN INFECTION. 1980. irreg.
price varies. Edward Arnold (Publishers) Ltd., 41
Bedford Square, London WC1B 3DQ, England. Ed.
I. Phillips.

616.07 574.2　　　　　US　　ISSN 0070-2188
CURRENT TOPICS IN PATHOLOGY. irreg., vol.75,
1986. price varies. Springer-Verlag, 175 Fifth Ave.,
New York, NY 10010 TEL 212-460-1500. (Also
Berlin, Heidelberg, Tokyo and Vienna) (reprint
service avail. from ISI) Indexed: Biol.Abstr.
Chem.Abstr. Ind.Med. Ind.Vet. Vet.Bull.
　　Formerly: Ergebnisse der Allgemeinen Pathologie
und Pathologischen Anatomie.

610　　　　　DK　　ISSN 0901-4500
CYSTISK FIBROSE. 1980. irreg. (4-6/yr.) free.
Landsforeningen til Bekaempelse af Cystisk Fibrose,
Hyrdebakken 246, 8800 Viborg, Denmark. adv.
illus.
　　Formerly: Hej (ISSN 0108-5409)

610　　　　　DK　　ISSN 0011-6092
DANISH MEDICAL BULLETIN. (Summaries in
Interlingua) 1954. irreg. (6-8/yr.) Kr.250 (free to
medical institutions on request) Almindelige Danske
Laegeforening - Danish Medical Association,
Trondhjemsgade 9, DK-2100 Copenhagen, Denmark
(Subscr. to: Laegeforeningens Forlag, Esplanaden 8
A, DK-1263 Copenhagen K, Denmark) Eds. John
Christiansen, Erik Juhl. adv. charts. illus. circ. 5,
300. (also avail. in microform from UMI; reprint
service avail. from UMI) Indexed: Biol.Abstr.
Chem.Abstr. Curr.Cont. Excerp.Med. Ind.Med.
Nutr.Abstr. Sci.Cit.Ind. Abstr.Hyg. Dairy
Sci.Abstr. Ind.Sci.Rev. Risk Abstr. Rehabil.Lit.
Trop.Dis.Bull.

610　　　　　DK　　ISSN 0084-9588
DANSK MEDICINHISTORISK AARBOG/
YEARBOOK OF DANISH MEDICAL HISTORY.
(Text in Danish; summaries in English) 1972. a.
Kr.100. Medical History Societies in Denmark,
Bredgade 62, DK-1260 Copenhagen, Denmark. Ed.
Anna-Elisabeth Brade. adv. circ. 1,500.
　　History

610　　　　　HU　　ISSN 0133-9060
DEBRECENI ORVOSTUDOMANYI EGYETEM
EVKONYVE. 1966. a. free; exchange basis. ‡
Debreceni Orvostudomanyi Egyetem, Nagyerdei
korut 98, 4012 Debrecen, Hungary. Ed. Alajos
Bolodar. abstr. bibl. stat. index. circ. 650.

610　　　　　DK　　ISSN 0108-9781
DENMARK. SUNDHEDSSTYRELSEN.
KURSUSOVERSIGT; specialistnaevnets udvalg for
den teoretiske videreuddanelse. 1983. a. Kr.45.
Sundhedsstyrelsen, St. Kongensgade 1, 1264
Copenhagen K, Denmark (Orders to: Danske
Boghandlers Kommissionsanstalt, Siljongade 6,
2300 Copenhagen S, Denmark)

616.02　　　　　US　　ISSN 0070-4067
DEUTSCHE GESELLSCHAFT FUER INNERE
MEDIZIN. VERHANDLUNGEN. 44th congress,
1932. irreg., 90th congress, 1984. price varies.
Springer-Verlag, 175 Fifth Ave., New York, NY
10010 TEL 212-460-1500. (Also Berlin, Heidelberg,
Tokyo and Vienna) Ed. B. Schlegel. (reprint service
avail. from ISI) Indexed: Biol.Abstr.

616.07 574.2　　　　　GW　　ISSN 0070-4113
DEUTSCHE GESELLSCHAFT FUER
PATHOLOGIE. VERHANDLUNGEN. a. price
varies. Gustav Fischer Verlag, Wollgrasweg 49,
Postfach 720143, 7000 Stuttgart 70, W. Germany
(B.R.D.) Indexed: Biol.Abstr. Chem.Abstr.
Ind.Med.
　　Pathology

DIARIO DE CONGRESOS MEDICOS. see
MEETINGS AND CONGRESSES

610　　　　　MY
DIRECTORY OF INFORMATION ON MEDICAL
PRACTITIONERS IN MALAYSIA. Cover title:
Directory of Medical Practitioners Malaysia.
(Supplement avail.) (Text in English) 1969. triennial,
latest 1978. Malaysian Medical Association, MMA
House, (1st Floor), 124 Jalan Pahang, 53000 Kuala
Lumpur, Malaysia. Eds. Dr. Lim Say Wan, Dr.
Yeoh Poh Hong. circ. 3,500(controlled) (back issues
avail.)

610 378.0025　　　　　US
DIRECTORY OF MEDICAL SCHOOLS
WORLDWIDE (YEAR) irreg., latest 1987/88.
$29.95. U S Directory Service, 655 N.W., 128th St.,
Box 68-1700, Miami, FL 33168. TEL 305-769-1700.

610　　　　　US　　ISSN 0070-5829
DIRECTORY OF MEDICAL SPECIALISTS. 1940.
biennial. $265 for 2-vol. set. Marquis Who's Who,
Macmillan Directory Division, 3002 Glenview Rd.,
Wilmette, IL 60091. TEL 312-441-2387.

616.07 574.2　　　　　US　　ISSN 0070-6086
DIRECTORY OF PATHOLOGY TRAINING
PROGRAMS. 1968. a. $400. ‡ Intersociety
Committee on Pathology Information, 4733
Bethesda Ave., Ste. 735, Bethesda, MD 20814. TEL
301-656-2944. Ed. Eileen Lavine. circ. 2,500.

DIRECTORY OF PRIVATE HOSPITALS AND
HEALTH SERVICES; a comprehensive guide to
the independent health care sector in the U.K. see
HOSPITALS

DIRECTORY OF RESIDENCY TRAINING
ACCREDITED BY THE ACCREDITATION
COUNCIL FOR GRADUATE MEDICAL
EDUCATION. see *EDUCATION — Higher
Education*

610　　　　　IS
DOCTOR'S MANUAL. 1969. a. $120. P.O. Box
8206, Ramat Gan 52 180, Israel. Ed. Ze'ev
Stavinsky.

610　　　　　GW
DOCUMENTA HOMOEOPATHICA. 1977. a.
DM.78. Karl F. Haug Verlag GmbH, Fritz-Frey-Str.
21, Postfach 10 28 40, 6900 Heidelberg 1, W.
Germany (B.R.D.) Ed. Dr. Mathias Dorcsi.

610　　　　　US
DOLAND'S MEDICAL DIRECTORY. NEW YORK
METROPOLITAN AREA EDITION. 1987. a. $45.
Packard Press, Inc., 10th & Spring Garden Sts.,
Philadelphia, PA 19123. TEL 215-236-2000. adv.
circ. 5,000.

610　　　　　JA　　ISSN 0288-1829
DONAN IGAKUKAI. 1948. a. Hakodate-shi Medical
Association, 33-19, Motomachi, Hakodate-shi,
Japan. Ed.Bd. circ. 850.

610　　　　　US
DORLAND'S MEDICAL DIRECTORY.
DELAWARE VALLEY EDITION. 1952. a. $45.
Packard Press, Inc., 10th & Spring Garden Sts.,
Philadelphia, PA 19123. TEL 215-236-2000. adv.
circ. 6,500.
　　Formerly: Dorland's Medical Directory.
Philadelphia Metropolitan Area.

610　　　　　US
DORLAND'S MEDICAL DIRECTORY. WESTERN
PHILADELPHIA TRI-STATE AREA EDITION.
1985. a. $40. Packard Press, Inc., 10th & Spring
Garden Sts., Philadelphia, PA 19123. TEL 215-236-
2000. adv. circ. 2,700.

610　　　　　SP　　ISSN 0211-9536
DYNAMIS. 1981. a. 1.500 ptas.($18) Universidad de
Granada, Departamento de Historia de la Medicina,
Facultad de Medicina, 18012 Granada, Spain.
Ed.Bd. bk. rev. circ. 150. Indexed: Bull.Signal.
Hist.Abstr. Bibl Hist.Med. Bull.Signal.
Amer.Hist.& Life. ISIS. Ind.Med.Esp.

610　　　　　UK
EARLY DIAGNOSIS PAPERS.* 1967. irreg. price
varies. Office of Health Economics, 12 Whitehall,
London SW1, England. Ed. J.C. McKenzie. charts.

352.3　　　　　US　　ISSN 0145-2037
EDUCATIONAL COMMISSION FOR FOREIGN
MEDICAL GRADUATES. ANNUAL REPORT.
1958. a. free. Educational Commission for Foreign
Medical Graduates, 3624 Market St., Philadelphia,
PA 19104. TEL 215-386-5900. Ed.Bd. circ. 5,000.
　　Formerly: Educational Council for Foreign
Medical Graduates. Annual Report (ISSN 0422-
6690)

610　　　　　US　　ISSN 0070-959X
ELDRIDGE REEVES JOHNSON FOUNDATION
FOR MEDICAL PHYSICS. COLLOQUIUM.
PROCEEDINGS.* 1963. irreg., 1969, 5th (pub.
1971) $13.50, vol. 1; $14.50, vol. 2. University of
Pennsylvania, Eldridge Reeves Johnson Foundation
for Medical Physics, Philadelphia, PA 19104.

610　　　　　UK
ELECTRO MEDICAL TRADE ASSOCIATION.
PRODUCTS DIRECTORY. (Text in English;
summaries in French, German and Spanish) 1965.
irreg. free to qualified personnel. ‡ Electro Medical
Trade Association Ltd., Leicester House, 8 Leicester
St., London WC2H 7BN, England. Ed. J.W.
Christopher. circ. 500 (approx.)

ENTWICKLUNGSLAENDER-STUDIEN;
Verzeichnis entwicklungslaenderbezogener
Forschungsarbeiten. see *BUSINESS AND
ECONOMICS — International Development And
Assistance*

614.49　　　　　EC
EPIDEMIOLOGIA CIENTIFICA: TEORIA Y
PRACTICA. 1979. irreg. $6. Centro de Estudios y
Asesoria en Salud, Roca No. 549-Dpto. 602, Quito,
Ecuador. circ. 1,000.

EPIDEMIOLOGIC REVIEWS. see *PUBLIC
HEALTH AND SAFETY*

616.026　　　　　US　　ISSN 0071-111X
ERGEBNISSE DER INNEREN MEDIZIN UND
KINDERHEILKUNDE. NEW SERIES/
ADVANCES IN INTERNAL MEDICINE AND
PEDIATRICS. (Text in German; occasionally in
English) 1949. irreg., vol.54, 1985. price varies.
Springer-Verlag, 175 Fifth Ave., New York, NY
10010 TEL 212-460-1500. (Also Berlin, Heidelberg,
Tokyo and Vienna) (reprint service avail. from ISI)
Indexed: Ind.Med.
　　Internal medicine

MEDICAL SCIENCES

611 US
ESO MONOGRAPHS. 1986. irreg. price varies. Springer-Verlag, 175 Fifth Ave., New York, NY 10160 TEL 212-460-1500. (Also Berlin, Heidelberg, Tokyo, Vienna) (reprint service avail. from ISI)

EXPERIMENTAL BIOLOGY AND MEDICINE. see BIOLOGY

610 SP ISSN 0210-8852
F A C: REVISTA PRACTICA DE MEDICINA. 1969. irreg.(4-5/yr.) free to qualified personnel. Laboratorio Alonga, S.A., Avda. Aragon, 18, 28027 Madrid, Spain. Ed. Francisco Llagostera Campillo. adv. bk. rev. circ. 30,000.
Formerly: F A C: Revista Practica del Estudiante de Medicina.

610 US
FEDERATION EXCHANGE. a. Federation of State Medical Boards, 2630 W. Freeway, Ste. 138, Fort Worth, TX 76102-7199 (Subscr. to: F S M B National Office, 3624 Market St., Philadelphia, PA 19104)

611 US
FIDIA RESEARCH SERIES. 1986. irreg. price varies. Springer-Verlag, 175 Fifth Ave., New York, NY 10160. TEL 212-460-1500. (reprint service avail. from ISI)

610 FI ISSN 0355-4813
FINLAND. KANSANELAKELAITOS. JULKAISUJA. SARJA AL. (Text in English and Finnish; summaries in English) 1975. irreg., no. AL28, 1986. Kansanelakelaitos - Social Insurance Institution of Finland, Research Institute for Social Security, P.O. Box 78, SF-00381 Helsinki 38, Finland.

616.39 FI ISSN 0355-4856
FINLAND. KANSANELAKELAITOS. JULKAISUJA. SARJA EL. (Text in English and Finnish; summaries in English) 1973. irreg., no. EL33, 1986. Kansanelakelaitos - Social Insurance Institution of Finland, Research Institute for Social Security, P.O. Box 78, SF-00381 Helsinki 38, Finland.

616.39 FI ISSN 0355-483X
FINLAND. KANSANELAKELAITOS. JULKAISUJA. SARJA ML. (Text in Finnish; summaries in English) 1973. irreg., ML58, 1986. Kansanelakelaitos - Social Insurance Institution of Finland, Research Institute for Social Security, P.O. Box 78, SF-00381 Helsinki 38, Finland.

610 617.6 FI
FINLAND. LAAKINTOHALLITUS. LAAKARIT, HAMMASLAAKARIT/LAKARE, TANDLAEKARE. (Text in Finnish and Swedish) 1976. a. Fmk.58. Valtion Painatuskeskus, Annankatu 44, 00100 Helsinki 10, Finland.
Formerly: Finland. Laakintohallitus. Laakarit, Hammaslaakarit, Sairaalat (ISSN 0430-5299)

FINLAND. TILASTOKESKUS. KUOLEMANSYYT/ FINLAND. STATISTIKCENTRALEN. DOEDSORSAKER/FINLAND. CENTRAL STATISTICAL OFFICE. CAUSES OF DEATH IN FINLAND. see BUSINESS AND ECONOMICS — Abstracting, Bibliographies, Statistics

610 YU ISSN 0350-0233
FOLIA ANATOMICA IUGOSLAVICA. (Supplement accompanies each vol.) (Text in Serbo-Croatian; summaries in English) 1972. a. $10. Anatomski Institut, Mose Pijade 6, 71000 Sarajevo, Yugoslavia. Ed. Mirko Cus. bk. rev. circ. 600. Indexed: Excerp.Med.

FORSKNING I GROENLAND-TUSAAT. see EARTH SCIENCES

610 FR ISSN 0763-7098
FRANCE. INSTITUT NATIONAL DE LA SANTE ET DE LA RECHERCHE MEDICALE. COLLOQUES. 1971. irreg. price varies. Institut National de la Sante et de la Recherche Medicale, 101 rue de Tolbiac, 75654 Paris Cedex 13, France.

G P GUIDE TO EMERGENCY & MEDICAL SERVICES. see HOSPITALS

610 US
GAP CONFERENCE REPORTS.* 1975. a. Cystic Fibrosis Foundation, 6931 Arlington Rd., No. 200, Bethesda, MD 20814-5205. (back issues avail.)

610 NE
GENEESKUNDIG ADRESBOEK. Cover title: Geneeskundig Adresboek voor Nederland. a. Nijgh Periodieken B.V., Postbus 122, 3100 AC Schiedam, Netherlands.
Supersedes in part: Geneeskundig Jaarboekje.

610 NE
GENEESKUNDIG JAARBOEK MEDICIJNEN. a. Nijgh Periodieken B.V., Postbus 122, 3100 AC Schiedam, Netherlands.
Supersedes in part: Geneeskundig Jaarboekje.

610 UK ISSN 0072-0763
GENERAL MEDICAL COUNCIL. MEDICAL REGISTER. 1859. a. £57. General Medical Council, 44 Hallam Street, London W1N 6AE, England.

610.6 UK
GENERAL MEDICAL COUNCIL. MINUTES. 1858. a. £25. General Medical Council, 44 Hallam St., London W1N 6AE, England.

GEOGRAPHIA MEDICA; international journal on geography of health/journal international de la geographie de la sante. see GEOGRAPHY

GREAT BRITAIN. GENERAL REGISTER OFFICE. STUDIES ON MEDICAL AND POPULATION SUBJECTS. see POPULATION STUDIES

610 UK ISSN 0141-2256
GREAT BRITAIN. MEDICAL RESEARCH COUNCIL. ANNUAL REPORT. a. price varies. Medical Research Council, 20 Park Crescent, London W1N 4AL, England.
Formerly (until 1965): Great Britain. Medical Research Council. Report (ISSN 0072-6567)

610 UK ISSN 0309-0132
GREAT BRITAIN. MEDICAL RESEARCH COUNCIL. HANDBOOK. a. price varies. Medical Research Council, 20 Park Crescent, London W1N 4AL, England.

GUIDE MEDICAL ET HOSPITALIER; publics et prives de France. see HOSPITALS

610 FR ISSN 0072-8209
GUIDE ROSENWALD: ANNUAIRE MEDICAL ET PHARMACEUTIQUE. 1887. a. 17 rue Tronchet, 75008 Paris, France.

610 US ISSN 0085-1353
GUIDE TO BIOMEDICAL STANDARDS. 1971. a. $15. ‡ Quest Publishing Co., 1351 Titan Way, Brea, CA 92621. TEL 714-738-6400. Ed. Allan F. Pacela.

610 IS ISSN 0072-923X
HADASSAH MEDICAL ORGANIZATION. REPORT. (Text in English) irreg., latest issue, 1972/73. Hadassah Medical Organization, Jerusalem, Israel. Eds. Hadassah Gillon, Philip Gillon. adv.

610 NE ISSN 0167-5567
HANDBOOK OF INFLAMMATION. irreg. Elsevier-North Holland Biomedical Press, Box 211, 1000 AE Amsterdam, Netherlands. Ed.Bd.

616.02 US ISSN 0072-9841
HANDBOOK OF MEDICAL TREATMENT.* 1949. biennial. $7.50. Jones Medical Publications, 355 Los Cerros Dr., Greenbrae, CA 94904. Ed. Milton J. Chatton.

610 615.9 US
HANDBOOK OF NATURAL TOXINS. 1983. irreg., vol.2 ,1984. Marcel Dekker, Inc., 270 Madison Ave., New York, NY 10016. TEL 212-696-9000.

612 US ISSN 0072-9906
HANDBOOK OF SENSORY PHYSIOLOGY. 1971. irreg., vol.7, part 6C. price varies. Springer-Verlag, 175 Fifth Ave., New York, NY 10010 TEL 212-460-1500. (Also Berlin, Heidelberg, Tokyo, Vienna) (reprint service avail. from ISI)

610 US
HANDBOOK OF THE SPINAL CORD. 1983. irreg., vol. 4, 1986. Marcel Dekker, Inc., 270 Madison Ave., New York, NY 10016. TEL 212-696-9000.

610 US ISSN 0073-0874
HARVEY LECTURES. 1953. irreg., series 79, 1985. $65. Academic Press, Inc., Orlando, FL 32887. TEL 305-345-2000. cum.index: series 1-50 in series 50 (1956) Indexed: Biol.Abstr. Chem.Abstr. Ind.Med. Sci.Cit.Ind. Ind.Sci.Rev.

HEALTH & MEDICAL HORIZONS. see PHYSICAL FITNESS AND HYGIENE

HEALTH CONSEQUENCES OF SMOKING. see DRUG ABUSE AND ALCOHOLISM

681 US ISSN 0278-3452
HEALTH DEVICES SOURCEBOOK. 1979. a. $140. (Emergency Care Research Institute) E C R I, 5200 Butler Pike, Plymouth Meeting, PA 19462. Ed. Robert Mosenkis.

610 US
HEALTH INDUSTRY BUYERS GUIDE. 1940. a. $45. J. B. Lippincott Co., E. Washington Sq., Philadelphia, PA 19105. TEL 215-238-4200. Ed. Laurie N. Cassak. adv. circ. 4,000.
Formerly: Surgical Trade Buyers Guide (ISSN 0081-9654)

HEALTH LAW BULLETIN. see PUBLIC HEALTH AND SAFETY

610 614 US ISSN 0440-5609
HEALTH ORGANIZATIONS OF THE U.S., CANADA AND THE WORLD; a directory of voluntary associations, professional societies and other groups concerned with health and related fields. 1961. irreg., 5th edt., 1981. $90. Gale Research Company, Book Tower, Detroit, MI 48226. TEL 313-961-2242. Eds. Paul Wasserman, Marek Kaszubski.

610 CN
HEALTH SCIENCES INFORMATION IN CANADA: ASSOCIATIONS/INFORMATION EN SCIENCES DE LA SANTE AU CANADA: ASSOCIATIONS. triennial. Can.$18. National Research Council Canada - Conseil National de Recherches du Canada, Ottawa, Ont. K1A 0S2, Canada. TEL 613-993-3736.

610 CN
HEALTH SCIENCES INFORMATION IN CANADA: LIBRARIES/INFORMATION EN SCIENCES DE LA SANTE AU CANADA: BIBLIOTHEQUES. triennial. Can.$20. National Research Council Canada - Conseil National de Recherches du Canada, Ottawa, Ont. K1A 0S2, Canada. TEL 613-993-3736.

610 US
HEALTHCARE TECHNOLOGY TRANSFER AND PRODUCT OPPORTUNITIES. Short title: H T T P O. a. $775. Biomedical Business International, 17722 Irvine Blvd., Tustin, CA 92680. TEL 714-838-8350.

610 616.1 JA ISSN 0910-0377
HIROSAKI DAIGAKU IGAKUBU EISEIGAKU KYOSHITSU GYOSEKISHU. (Text in Japanese; summaries in English) 1954. irreg. Hirosaki University, School of Medicine, 5, Zaifu-cho, Hirosaki-shi 036, Japan. Ed. Naosuke Sasaki. circ. 90.

HISTORIA HOSPITALIUM. see HOSPITALS

610 HK
HONG KONG MEDICAL ASSOCIATION. JOURNAL. (Text in English) 1948. q. $20 for non-members; free to members. Hong Kong Medical Association, Duke of Windsor Building, 15 Hennessy Road, 5th Floor, Hong Kong, Hong Kong. Ed. Dr. E.K. Yeoh. adv. circ. 4,000. (back issues avail.) Indexed: Excerp.Med.
Formerly(until 1985): Hong Kong Medical Association. Bulletin.

610 618.92 CN ISSN 0082-5034
HOSPITAL FOR SICK CHILDREN, TORONTO. RESEARCH INSTITUTE. ANNUAL REPORT. (Text in English) 1969. a. Hospital for Sick Children, 555 University Ave., Toronto, Ont. M5G 1X8, Canada. TEL 416-597-1500. Ed. Dr. A. Rothstein. circ. 500.

MEDICAL SCIENCES

610 612　　　　　　AT　ISSN 0314-6162
HOWARD FLOREY INSTITUTE OF
EXPERIMENTAL PHYSIOLOGY & MEDICINE.
ANNUAL REPORT AND NOTICE OF
MEETING. 1974. a. Howard Florey Institute of
Experimental Physiology & Medicine, Parkville,
Vic., Australia. illus. circ. 3,000.

613.7　　　　　　　　US
I C H P E R CONGRESS PROCEEDINGS. 1958.
biennial. price varies. International Council on
Health, Physical Education and Recreation, 1900
Association Dr., Reston, VA 22091. TEL 202-476-
3400. Indexed: Sportsearch.
　　Formerly: I C H P E R Congress Reports (ISSN
0074-4417)
　　Physical fitness

615.8　　　　　　　　II
INDIAN ASSOCIATION OF
PHYSIOTHERAPISTS. JOURNAL. 1965. a.
membership. Indian Association of Physiotherapists,
c/o Mrs. S. M. Sanghavi, 3rd Fl., 35 Chowpaty Sea
Face, Bombay 400007, India. adv. bk. rev. circ. 500.
　　Physiotherapy

610　　　　　　　II　ISSN 0367-9012
INDIAN JOURNAL OF MEDICAL RESEARCH.
SUPPLEMENT. (Text in English) 1922. irreg.
Rs.200($70) includes subscription to journal. Indian
Council of Medical Research, Box 4508, Ansari
Nagar, New Delhi 110029, India. Ed. Dr. G.V.
Satyavati. bk. rev. bibl. charts. circ. 1,000. Indexed:
Biol.Abstr. Chem.Abstr. Curr.Cont. Ind.Med.
Nutr.Abstr. Sci.Cit.Ind. Trop.Dis.Bull.

INDUSTRIAL HEALTH FOUNDATION.
MEDICAL SERIES. BULLETIN. see
INDUSTRIAL HEALTH AND SAFETY

INSTITUT FUER DEN WISSENSCHAFTLICHEN
FILM. PUBLIKATIONEN ZU
WISSENSCHAFTLICHEN FILMEN. SEKTION
MEDIZIN. see *MOTION PICTURES*

610　　　　　　　　CX
INSTITUT PASTEUR DE BANGUI. RAPPORT
BISANNUEL. 1961. biennial. $15. Institut Pasteur
de Bangui, B.P. 923, Bangui, Central African
Republic. adv. circ. 200. Indexed: Biol.Abstr.
　　Formerly (until 1984): Institut Pasteur de Bangui.
Rapport Annuel.

610　　　　　　US　ISSN 0073-8638
INSTITUTE FOR CLINICAL SCIENCE.
PROFICIENCY TEST SERVICE. REPORT.*
1949. a. (compilation of monthly reports) $150
(incl. also monthly samples) American Society of
Clinical Pathologists, 2100 W. Harrison St.,
Chicago, IL 60612. TEL 312-738-1336. Ed. F.W.
Sunderman. circ. 1,000.

610　　　　　　　　BL
INSTITUTO BUTANTAN. COLETANEA DE
TRABALHOS. 1901-1925; resumed 1950. irreg.
Instituto Butantan, Caixa Postal 65, Sao Paulo,
Brazil. circ. 800.

610　　　　　　NG　ISSN 0534-4735
INTER-AFRICAN CONFERENCE ON MEDICAL
CO-OPERATION. MEETING.* irreg.; 1955 3rd.
(Commission for Technical Co-Operation in Africa
South of the Sahara) Maison de l'Afrique, B.P. 878,
Niamey, Niger.

610　　　　　　　　SP
INTERCON. Spanish translation of: Vademecum.
1967. a. 2500 ptas. Editores Medicos, S.A., Primario
de la Castellana, 53, 28046 Madrid, Spain. TEL 442
88 56. circ. 40,000.

611 574.4　　　　UR　ISSN 0074-1353
INTERNATIONAL ANATOMICAL CONGRESS.
PROCEEDINGS. (Text in English, French and
German) 1905. quinquennial, 1970, 9th, Leningrad.
International Anatomical Congress, c/o Prof. Dr.
Shdanow, Karl Marx Prospekt 18, Moscow K-9,
Russian S.F.S.R., U.S.S.R.

610　　　　　　FR　ISSN 0074-1760
INTERNATIONAL ASSOCIATION OF
THALASSOTHERAPY. CONGRESS REPORTS.
(Proceedings published by organizing committee)
1954. triennial; 1975, 16th, Opatija, Yugoslavia.
International Association of Thalasso-Therapy, c/o
Professeur D. Leroy, 6, rue Lafayette, 35000
Rennes, France.
　　Marine medicine

610　　　　　　FR　ISSN 0074-3704
INTERNATIONAL CONGRESS OF HISTORY OF
MEDICINE. PROCEEDINGS. (Proceedings
Published in Host Country) 1920. biennial, 30th,
Dusseldorf, 1986. International Society for the
History of Medicine, 22 rue Francois Villenuve,
34000 Montpellier, France.
　　History

INTERNATIONAL CONGRESS OF LIFE
ASSURANCE MEDICINE. PROCEEDINGS. see
INSURANCE

615.8　　　　　　AT　ISSN 0074-3828
INTERNATIONAL CONGRESS OF
OCCUPATIONAL THERAPY. PROCEEDINGS.
1974. irreg., 7th, 1978, Jerusalem. World Federation
of Occupational Therapists, 20 Syree Court,
Marmion, W.A. 6020, Australia (Publisher of
proceedings varies) circ. 1,500.
　　Physiotherapy

619　　　　　　　　NO
INTERNATIONAL COUNCIL FOR
LABORATORY ANIMAL SCIENCE.
PROCEEDINGS OF THE SYMPOSIUM. 1958.
triennial, 7th, 1979, Utrecht. price varies (DM .85
for 6th) International Council for Laboratory
Animal Science, c/o Dr. Stian Erichsen, Sec.-Gen.,
National Institute of Public Health, Postuttak, Oslo
1, Norway. (also avail. in microfiche from NTI)
Indexed: Anim.Breed.Abstr.
　　Formerly: International Committee on Laboratory
Animals. Proceedings of Symposium (ISSN 0074-
2805)
　　Laboratory animals

610　　　　　　AU　ISSN 0074-6037
INTERNATIONAL FEDERATION OF MEDICAL
STUDENTS' ASSOCIATIONS. MINUTES AND
REPORTS OF THE GENERAL ASSEMBLY.
1951. a. free. International Federation of Medical
Students' Associations, Liechtensteinstr. 13, A-1090
Vienna, Austria. Ed. Fritz Mahrer. circ. 150.

INTERNATIONAL MEDICAL WHO'S WHO. see
BIOGRAPHY

610　　　　　　　　NE
INTERNATIONAL ORGANIZATION FOR
COOPERATION IN HEALTH CARE.
GENERAL ASSEMBLY. REPORT. 1979. a. free.
Medicus Mundi Internationalis, P.O. Box 1547,
6501 BM Nijmegen, Netherlands.
　　Supersedes: International Organization for
Medical Cooperation. General Assembly. Report
(ISSN 0579-3912)

362　　　　　　US　ISSN 0020-8477
INTERNATIONAL REHABILITATION REVIEW.
1949. triennial; latest 1985. $30. Rehabilitation
International, 25 E. 21st St., 4th Fl., New York, NY
10010. TEL 212-420-1500. Ed. Barbara Duncan.
adv. bk. rev. illus. circ. 20,000. (TA) Indexed:
Excerp.Med. CINAHL. Except.Child.Educ.Abstr.
Rehabil.Lit.

616.07　　　　　US　ISSN 0074-7718
INTERNATIONAL REVIEW OF EXPERIMENTAL
PATHOLOGY. 1962. irreg., vol.29, 1986.
Academic Press, Inc., Orlando, FL 32887. TEL
305-345-2000. Eds. G.W. Richter, M.A. Epstein.
index. Indexed: Biol.Abstr. Chem.Abstr.
Excerp.Med. Ind.Med. Sci.Cit.Ind. Abstr.Hyg.
Ind.Sci.Rev. Ind.Vet. Vet.Bull. Trop.Dis.Bull.

616　　　　　　SZ　ISSN 0074-8544
INTERNATIONAL SOCIETY OF INTERNAL
MEDICINE. CONGRESS PROCEEDINGS. 1950.
biennial, 1974, 12th, Tel Aviv. International Society
of Internal Medicine, c/o Dr. Rolf A. Streuli,
Regionalspital, 4900 Langenthal, Switzerland
(Proceedings of 12th and 13th Congress published
by: S. Karger AG, Arnold-Boecklin-Str. 25, 4011
Basel, Switzerland)

INTERNATIONAL UNION OF SCHOOL AND
UNIVERSITY HEALTH AND MEDICINE.
CONGRESS REPORTS. see *EDUCATION*

615.8　　　　　　IS　ISSN 0021-2199
ISRAEL JOURNAL OF PHYSIOTHERAPY. (Text
in English and Hebrew) irreg. (3-4/yr.) membership.
National Union of Physiotherapy in Israel, 93
Arlozorov St., Tel-Aviv, Israel. Ed.Bd. charts. illus.
　　Physiotherapy

JACKSON LABORATORY SCIENTIFIC REPORT.
see *BIOLOGY — Genetics*

610 574　　　　　　　　JA
JAPANESE COLLAGEN CLUB. PROCEEDINGS
OF THE ANNUAL MEETING. (Text in Japanese;
summaries in English) 1959. a. 2.000 Yen($10)
Japanese Collagen Club., c/o Tokyo Medical and
Dental University, Department of Tissue
Physiology, Kandasurugadai 2-3-10, Chiyoda-ku,
Tokyo 101, Japan. Ed. Yutaka Nagai. adv. circ. 300.
(back issues avail.)

610　　　　　　　　JA
JAPANESE MEDICAL RESEARCHERS
DIRECTORY. (Text in English and Japanese)
1960. a. 33000 Yen($157.14) (Office of Rural
Development) Igaku-Shoin Ltd., 5-24-3 Hongo,
Bunkyo-ku, Tokyo 113-91, Japan. Ed. Hiromasa
Kita. circ. 1,500. Indexed: Biol.Abstr.

JOURNAL OF CYTOLOGY AND GENETICS. see
BIOLOGY — Genetics

610　　　　　　JA　ISSN 0075-4579
JUNTENDO UNIVERSITY, TOKYO. MEDICAL
ULTRASONICS RESEARCH CENTER.
ANNUAL REPORT.* (Text in English) a.
Juntendo University, School of Medicine, Medical
Ultrasonics Research Center, 2-1-2 Hongo, Bunkyo-
ku, Tokyo 113, Japan.

610　　　　　　VE　ISSN 0075-5222
KASMERA. 1962. irreg., vol.4, 1983. exchange basis.
Universidad del Zulia, Departamento de
Microbiologia, Parasitologia y Medicina Tropical,
Facultad de Medicina, Maracaibo Apdo. Postal 526,
Codigo Postal 4011, Venezuela. Ed. Dr. Ricardo
Soto Urribarri. bibl. charts. illus. stat. circ. 1,000.
(also avail. in microform) Indexed: Biol.Abstr.
Abstr.Hyg. Trop.Dis.Bull.

170 610　　　　　　　US
KENNEDY INSTITUTE OF BIOETHICS. SCOPE
NOTE. 1982. irreg., no.7, 1986. $3 per no. Kennedy
Institute of Bioethics, National Reference Center for
Bioethics Literature, Georgetown University,
Washington, DC 20057. TEL 212-625-4117.

610　　　　　　　　KE
KENYA. MINISTRY OF HEALTH. ANNUAL
REPORT. a. Ministry of Health, P.O. Box 52,
Homa Bay, Kenya.

610　　　　　　KE　ISSN 1010-576X
KENYA MEDICAL RESEARCH INSTITUTE.
PROCEEDINGS OF THE ANNUAL MEDICAL
RESEARCH CONFERENCES. (Text and
summaries in English) 1980. a. EAs.200. Kenya
Medical Research Institute (KEMRI), P.O. Box
54840, Nairobi, Kenya. circ. 1,000. (back issues
avail.)

610　　　　　　　　JA
KETSUEKI JIGYO NO GENKYO. 1865. a. free.
Niigata kaen Niigatashi, Sinkocho 4-1, Niigata-shi,
Japan.

610　　　　　　JA　ISSN 0075-6431
KOBE UNIVERSITY. MEDICAL JOURNAL/KOBE
DAIGAKU IGAKUBU KIYO. (Continues: Kobe
Ika Daigaku. Kiyo) (Table of contents and abstracts
in English) 1949. a. free. (Kobe University Medical
Society - Kobe Daigaku Igakkai) Kobe University,
School of Medicine, 5-1 Kusunoki-cho 7 chome,
Chuo-Ku, Kobe 650, Japan. Ed. Kazushi Hirohata.
Indexed: Biol.Abstr. Ind.Med.

610　　　　　　DK　ISSN 0105-4139
KOEBENHAVNS UNIVERSITET. INSTITUT FOR
SOCIAL MEDICIN. PUBLIKATION. no.13, 1981.
irreg. Foreningen af Danske Laegestuderendes
Forlag, Copenhagen, Denmark. illus. circ. 500.

KOKUTETSU CHUO HOKEN KANRIJOHO; health
control. see *PUBLIC HEALTH AND SAFETY*

610　　　　　　HU　ISSN 0075-6792
KORANYI SANDOR TARSASAG.
TUDOMANYOS ULESEK. 1961. irreg. price
varies. Akademiai Kiado, Publishing House of the
Hungarian Academy of Sciences, P.O. Box 24, H-
1363 Budapest, Hungary.

MEDICAL SCIENCES

610   JA   ISSN 0075-7217
KUMAMOTO UNIVERSITY. INSTITUTE OF CONSTITUTIONAL MEDICINE. BULLETIN. SUPPLEMENT. (Text in English or European languages; summaries in English) 1951. a. available on exchange. Kumamoto University, Institute of Constitutional Medicine - Kumamoto Daigaku Taishitsu Igaku Kenkyusho, 4-24-1 Kuhonzi, Kumamoto 862, Japan.

610   DK
LAEGEFORENINGENS VEJVISER. 1976. irreg. (Almindelige Danske Laegeforening) Laegeforeningens Forlag, Esplanaden 8A, DK-1263 Copenhagen K, Denmark.
  Formerly: Almindelige Danske Laegeforening (ISSN 0105-1830)

610   DK
LAEGEN. a. Forlaget John Vaboe A-S, Svanemoellevej 34, 2100 Copenhagen OE, Denmark. adv. circ. 5,200.

610   US   ISSN 0172-7788
LECTURE NOTES IN MEDICAL INFORMATICS. 1978. irreg., vol.29, 1986. Springer-Verlag, 175 Fifth Ave., New York, NY 10010 TEL 212-460-1500. (Also Berlin, Heidelberg, Tokyo and Vienna) Eds. D.A.B. Lindberg, P.L. Reichertz. (reprint service avail. from ISI)

610   CS   ISSN 0075-8736
LEKARSKE PRACE. (Articles mainly in Slovak, some in English, German or Russian; summaries in one or two of the other languages) 1961. irreg., approx. s-a; vol. 10, no. 2, 1973. (Slovenska Akademia Vied) Veda, Publishing House of the Slovak Academy of Sciences, Klemensova 19, 814 30 Bratislava, Czechoslovakia (Subscr. to: Slovart, Gottwaldovo nam. 6, 817 64 Bratislava) Indexed: Biol.Abstr. Ind.Med.

610   AU
LIEFERKATALOG FUER KRANKENHAUS, ARZT, APOTHEKE UND LABOR; Lieferfirmen- und Bezugsquellennachweis. 1974. a. S.120. Verlag Dieter Goschl, Andergasse 10, A-1170 Vienna, Austria. adv. circ. 13,500.

LITERATURE & MEDICINE. see *LITERATURE*

610   PL   ISSN 0076-0420
LODZKIE TOWARZYSTWO NAUKOWE. WYDZIAL IV. NAUK LEKARSKICH. PRACE. (Text in Polish; summaries in French and Russian) 1951. irreg., 1967. price varies. Panstwowe Wydawnictwo Naukowe, Ul. Miodowa 10, 00-251 Warsaw, Poland (Dist. by: Ars Polona, Krakowskie Przedmiescie 7, 00-068 Warsaw, Poland)

610   SA
M I M S MEDICAL MEMORY AIDS. 1981. biennial. M I M S (Pty) Ltd., Box 2059, Pretoria 0001, Transvaal, South Africa. Ed. R. van Rooyen. adv. circ. 3,000.

610   CN   ISSN 0024-905X
MCGILL MEDICAL JOURNAL. 1931. irreg.(2-3/yr.) Can.$5 for 4 nos. McGill Medical Undergraduate Society, McIntyre Medical Sciences Bldg., 3655 Drummond St., Montreal, Que. H3G 1Y6, Canada. TEL 514-392-4311. Ed. D.K. Fast. adv. bk. rev. abstr. bibl. illus. index. circ. 5,000. Indexed: Chem.Abstr. Excerp.Med. Ind.Med.

610   GW   ISSN 0720-597X
MADE IN EUROPE - MEDICAL EQUIPMENT AND SUPPLY GUIDE. (Text in English) 1981. a. $25. Made in Europe Marketing Organisation GmbH & Co., Unterlindau 21-29, 6000 Frankfurt/ Main, W. Germany (B.R.D.) Ed. H.E. Reisner. adv. index. circ. 20,200. (back issues avail.)

610   UG   ISSN 0025-1119
MAKERERE MEDICAL JOURNAL. 1957. a. $5.75. Makerere University Medical Students' Association, Box 7072, Kampala, Uganda. adv. bk. rev. charts. illus. circ. 1,000. Indexed: Biol.Abstr. Chem.Abstr. Trop.Dis.Bull.

MAKERERE UNIVERSITY. ALBERT COOK LIBRARY. LIBRARY BULLETIN AND ACCESSION LIST. see *LIBRARY AND INFORMATION SCIENCES*

616.07   MY
MALAYSIAN JOURNAL OF PATHOLOGY. a. M.$10. Malaysian Society of Pathologists, Department of Pathology, Kuala Lumpur, Malaysia. Ed. K. Prathap. Indexed: Ind.Med.

616.07   US   ISSN 0732-9539
MASSON MONOGRAPHS IN DIAGNOSTIC CYTOPATHOLOGY.* 1979. irreg., vol. 4, 1983. price varies. Masson Publishing U.S.A. Inc., 133 E. 58th St., New York, NY 10016. TEL 212-838-8510. Ed. Dr. William W. Johnson.
  Pathology

610   US
MAUDSLEY MONOGRAPHS. irreg. price varies. Oxford University Press, 200 Madison Ave, New York, NY 10016 TEL 212-679-7300. (And Ely House, 37 Dover St., London W1X 4AH, England) Ed. Bd.

610   AU   ISSN 0253-7419
MEDEQUIP. 1982. irreg.(7-10/yr.) S.3.50. Brueder Hollinek, Gallgasse 40 A, A-1130 Vienna, Austria. Ed.Bd. adv. circ. 7,000.

MEDICAID RECIPIENT CHARACTERISTICS AND UNITS OF SELECTED MEDICAL SERVICES. see *SOCIAL SERVICES AND WELFARE*

MEDICAL AND HEALTHCARE MARKETPLACE GUIDE. see *BUSINESS AND ECONOMICS — Trade And Industrial Directories*

610   UK   ISSN 0076-5899
MEDICAL ANNUAL; A year book of treatment and practitioners' index. 1883. a. £19.50. John Wright, Techno House, Redcliffe Way, Bristol BS1 6NX, England. Ed. D.J. Pereira Gray. adv. index. circ. 3,000.

610   IR
MEDICAL COUNCIL OF IRAN. PUBLICATION/ NEZAM PEZESHKI-YE IRAN. NASHRIYEH. (Text in Persian) 1970. irreg. free to physicians. Medical Council of Iran, 40 Shirin Ave., Hafez Ave., P.O.B. 3474, Teheran, Iran. Ed. Mohammad Ali Hafizi.

610   UK   ISSN 0305-3342
MEDICAL DIRECTORY; an alphabetical listing of medical practitioners registered in Britain. a. £62. Longman Group Ltd., Fourth Ave., Harlow, Essex CM19 5AA, England.

610   US
MEDICAL DIRECTORY OF NEW YORK STATE. biennial. $70. Medical Society of the State of New York, 420 Lakeville Rd., Lake Success, NY 11042.

615.845   US
MEDICAL ELECTRONICS AND EQUIPMENT NEWS BUYERS' GUIDE. 1966. irreg., latest 1976. $5. Reilly Publishing Co., 532 Busse Highway, Park Ridge, IL 60068. TEL 312-696-3034. adv. charts. circ. controlled.
  Formerly: Medical Electronics and Equipment News Dictionary and Buyers' Guide.
  Medical electronics

610   US
MEDICAL GROUP MANAGEMENT ASSOCIATION. DIRECTORY. 1961. a. $95 to members; non-members $156. ‡ Medical Group Management Association, 1355 S. Colorado Blvd., Denver, CO 80222. TEL 303-753-1111. Ed. Dennis Barnhardt. circ. 6,311.
  Formerly: Medical Group Management Association. International Directory (ISSN 0094-9604)

610   530   US   ISSN 0076-5953
MEDICAL PHYSICS SERIES. 1969. irreg., vol.8, 1985. price varies. Academic Press Inc., Orlando, FL 32887. TEL 305-345-2000. Ed. P.N.T. Wells.

610   380.1   JA
MEDICAL PRODUCT OF JAPAN; directory of medical equipment. (Text in English) no. 7, 1983. biennial. 6000 Yen($67) Genyosha Publications, Inc, 3-18-2 Shibuya, Shibuya-ku, Tokyo 150, Japan. adv. circ. 6,500.

610   381   US
MEDICAL PRODUCTS MARKETERS DIRECTORY. 1981. a. $85. Fisher-Stevens Publications Division, 100 Campus Rd., Towowa, NJ 07512. TEL 201-890-1122. Ed. Marianne McCabe. circ. 2,310.

610   UK   ISSN 0076-5961
MEDICAL PROTECTION SOCIETY. ANNUAL REPORT. 1892. a. membership. ‡ Medical Protection Society Ltd., 50 Hallam Street, London W1N 6DE, England. Ed. Dr. R.N. Palmer. adv. circ. 105,000.

610   KE   ISSN 0076-5988
MEDICAL RESEARCH CENTRE, NAIROBI. ANNUAL REPORT. 1966. a. free. ‡ Medical Research Centre, Nairobi, Box 20752, Nairobi, Kenya. (Affiliate: Koninklijk Instituut voor de Tropen, Netherlands) Indexed: Biol.Abstr.

610   UK
MEDICAL RESEARCH CENTRES; a world directory of organizations and programmes. irreg., 6th edt. 1983. £185. ‡ Longman Group Ltd., Fourth Ave., Harlow, Essex CM19 5AA, England (Dist. in U.S. and Canada by: Gale Research Co. Ltd., Book Tower, Detroit, MI 48226)
  Formerly: Medical Research Index (ISSN 0076-6003)

610   GH
MEDICAL RESEARCH CENTRES IN GHANA: CURRENT RESEARCH PROJECTS. 1973. irreg. free. Council for Scientific and Industrial Research, Box M32, Accra, Ghana. Ed. D.K. Opare-Sem. (back issues avail.)

610   CN
MEDICAL RESEARCH COUNCIL OF CANADA. GRANTS AND AWARDS GUIDE/GUIDE DE SUBVENTIONS ET BOURSES. (Text and summaries in English and French) a. Medical Research Council, Ottawa K1A 0W9, Canada. TEL 613-954-1806. charts. circ. 7,400.

610.6   CN
MEDICAL RESEARCH COUNCIL OF CANADA. REFERENCE LIST OF HEALTH SCIENCE RESEARCH IN CANADA. (Text in English and French) 1968. a. free. Medical Research Council of Canada, Ottawa, Ont. K1A 0W9, Canada. TEL 613-954-1806. circ. 1,000.

610   CN
MEDICAL RESEARCH COUNCIL OF CANADA. REPORT OF THE PRESIDENT. (Text in English & French) 1960. a. free. Medical Research Council, Ottawa, Ont. K1A 0W9, Canada. TEL 613-954-1806. charts. illus. stat. index. circ. 2,300(controlled)

616.98   US
MEDICAL RESEARCH IN THE V.A. 1957. a. $0.40. U.S. Veterans Administration, Medical Research Service, 810 Vermont Ave., N.W., Washington, DC 20420 TEL 202-745-8000. (Orders to Supt. of Documents, U.S. Government Printing Office, Washington, DC 20402) Ed. Russell D. Bowman.
  Formerly: Highlights of V A Medical Research (ISSN 0073-2141)
  Military

MEDICAL SCHOOL ADMISSION REQUIREMENTS, UNITED STATES AND CANADA. see *EDUCATION — Higher Education*

610   UK   ISSN 0076-6011
MEDICAL SOCIETY OF LONDON. TRANSACTIONS. 1773. a. £10. Medical Society of London, 11 Chandos Street, Cavendish Square, London, W1N OEB, England. Ed. R.P. Rosswick. circ. 550. Indexed: Excerp.Med. Ind.Med.

610   US   ISSN 0565-811X
MEDICAL SUBJECT HEADINGS. (Issued as Pt. 2 of the January Index Medicus) 1960. a. $29. U.S. National Library of Medicine, 8600 Rockville Pike, Bethesda, MD 20894 TEL 202-783-3238. (Orders to: Supt. of Documents, Washington, DC 20402) circ. 8,000.

610.28   UK
MEDICAL TECHNOLOGIST DIARY & CLASSIFIED BUYER'S GUIDE. a. £6. A. E. Morgan Publications Ltd., Stanley House, 9 West St., Epsom, Surrey, England.

MEDICAL SCIENCES

610 US
MEDICINE (NEW YORK) a. John Wiley & Sons, Inc., 605 Third Ave., New York, NY 10016. TEL 212-850-6000.

610 DK ISSN 0461-6308
MEDICINSK AARBOG. 1957. a. price varies. Munksgaard, Noerre Soegade 35, 1370 Copenhagen K, Denmark. illus.

MEDICOLEGAL LIBRARY. see *LAW — International Law*

MEDIZIN IM RECHT UND ETHIK. see *LAW*

610 GE ISSN 0070-721X
MEDIZINISCHE AKADEMIE "CARL GUSTAV CARUS" DRESDEN. SCHRIFTEN. 1959. irreg., vol.20, 1984. price varies. Medizinische Akademie "Carl Gustav Carus", Zentralbibliothek, Fiedlerstr. 27, 8019 Dresden, E. Germany (D.D.R.) circ. 500.

610 US ISSN 0342-4103
MEDIZINISCHE INFORMATIK UND STATISTIK. (Text in German) 1976. irreg., vol.51, 1984. price varies. Springer-Verlag, 175 Fifth Ave., New York, NY 10010 TEL 212-460-1500. (Also Berlin, Heidelberg, Tokyo and Vienna) Ed.Bd. (reprint service avail. from ISI)

610 US ISSN 0076-6151
MEDIZINISCHE LAENDERKUNDE. GEOMEDICAL MONOGRAPH SERIES. Short title: Geomedical Monograph Series. (Text in German) 1967. irreg., no.6, 1980. Springer-Verlag, 175 Fifth Ave., New York, NY 10010 TEL 212-460-1500. (also Berlin, Heidelberg, Vienna) (reprint service avail. from ISI)

MEMBRANE TRANSPORT PROCESSES. see *BIOLOGY — Biophysics*

610 US ISSN 0076-6526
MERCK MANUAL: A HANDBOOK OF DIAGNOSIS AND THERAPY. 1899. irreg., 14th edt., 1982. $19.75. Merck and Co., Inc., Box 2000, Rahway, NJ 07065. TEL 201-574-4003. Ed. Dr. Robert Berkow.

616.07 SZ ISSN 0076-681X
METHODS AND ACHIEVEMENTS IN EXPERIMENTAL PATHOLOGY. (Text in English) 1965. irreg.(approx. 1/yr.) price varies. S. Karger AG, Allschwilerstrasse 10, P.O. Box, CH-4009 Basel, Switzerland. Ed. G. Jasmin. (reprint service avail. from ISI) Indexed: Biol.Abstr. Chem.Abstr. Ind.Med. Curr.Cont.
Pathology

MICROBIOS LETTERS; a prestige international biomedical journal for the rapid publication of biomedical communications. see *BIOLOGY — Cytology And Histology*

410 GE
MIKROBIELLE UMWELT UND ANTIMIKROBIELLE MASSNAHMEN; Schriftenreihe fuer Theorie und Praxis in Medizin, Pharmazie und Wirtschaft. 1977. irreg., vol.10, 1987. price varies. Johann Ambrosius Barth Verlag, Salomonstr. 186, DDR-7010 Leipzig, E. Germany (D.D.R.) (Orders to: Buchexport, Leninstr. 16, DDR-7010 Leipzig, E. Germany (D.D.R.)) Ed.Bd.

378 US ISSN 0085-3488
MINORITY STUDENT OPPORTUNITIES IN UNITED STATES MEDICAL SCHOOLS. 1970. biennial. $7.50. Association of American Medical Colleges, One Dupont Circle, N.W., Washington, DC 20036. TEL 202-828-0400.

MISSISSIPPI ACADEMY OF SCIENCE. JOURNAL. see *BIOLOGY*

610 US
MODERN TECHNICS IN SURGERY. SECTION OF THE EAR. 1981. irreg. price varies. Futura Publishing Company, 295 Main St., Box 330, Mount Kisco, NY 10549. TEL 914-666-7528. illus.

610 574.87 SZ ISSN 0077-0809
MONOGRAPHS IN CLINICAL CYTOLOGY. (Text in English) 1965. irreg. (approx. 1/yr.) price varies. S. Karger AG, Allschwilerstrasse 10, P.O. Box, CH-4009 Basel, Switzerland. Ed. G.L. Wied. Indexed: Biol.Abstr. Chem.Abstr. Curr.Cont. Ind.Med.
Embryology

610 JA ISSN 0469-4759
NAGOYA UNIVERSITY. RESEARCH INSTITUTE OF ENVIRONMENTAL MEDICINE. ANNUAL REPORT/NAGOYA DAIGAKU KANKYO IGAKU KENKYUSHO NENPO. (Text in English) 1951. a. exchange basis. Nagoya University, Research Institute of Environmental Medicine - Nagoya Daigaku Kankyo Igaku Kenkyusho, Furo-cho, Chikusa-ku, Nagoya 464, Japan. Ed. Nobuo Matsui. circ. 400. Indexed: Biol.Abstr. Chem.Abstr. Excerp.Med.
Formerly: Environmental Medicine (ISSN 0287-0517)

610 AT ISSN 0811-6199
NATIONAL HEALTH AND MEDICAL COUNCIL. MEDICAL RESEARCH. 1968. a. free. (National Health and Medical Council, Department of Health) Australian Government Publishing Service, P.O. Box 100, Woden, ACT 2606, Australia. Ed. A. Charlton. circ. 1,000. (back issues avail.)

616.1 AT
NATIONAL HEART NEWS. 1981. irreg. free. National Heart Foundation of Australia, National Office, P.O. Box 2, Woden, A.C.T. 2606, Australia. Ed. Linda Norton. bk. rev. circ. 20,000.

610 UK ISSN 0141-2116
NATIONAL INSTITUTE FOR MEDICAL RESEARCH. REPORT. 1973. a. free. Medical Research Council, Mill Hill, London NW7 1AA, England. circ. 500. Indexed: Biol.Abstr.
Formerly: National Institute for Medical Research. Scientific Report (ISSN 0307-076X)

NATIONAL INSTITUTE OF POLAR RESEARCH. MEMOIRS. SERIES E: BIOLOGY AND MEDICAL SCIENCE. see *BIOLOGY*

610 US ISSN 0149-9939
NATIONAL LIBRARY OF MEDICINE. AUDIOVISUALS CATALOG. 1978. q. with annual cumulation. $26 for quarterly; price of annual cumulation varies. U.S. National Library of Medicine, 8600 Rockville Pike, Bethesda, MD 20894 TEL 202-783-3238. (Orders to: Supt. of Documents, Washington, D.C. 20402)

610 617.6 US ISSN 0027-9676
NATIONAL MEDICAL AND DENTAL ASSOCIATION. BULLETIN. (Text mainly in English; occasionally in Polish) 1926. a. $12. (National Medical and Dental Association of America) Polstar Publishing Corp., c/o Raymond S. Dziejma, Ed., 72-41 Grand Ave., Maspeth, NY 11378. TEL 718-478-3333. adv. illus. circ. 3,000.

NATIONAL REHABILITATION CENTER FOR THE DISABLED. RESEARCH BULLETIN. see *BLIND*

NATIONAL RESEARCH COUNCIL, CANADA. DIVISION OF ELECTRICAL ENGINEERING. BULLETIN/CONSEIL NATIONAL DE RECHERCHES DU CANADA. DIVISION DE GENIE ELECTRIQUE. BULLETIN. see *ENGINEERING*

610 US ISSN 0276-2293
NATIONAL REYE'S SYNDROME FOUNDATION. 1980. a. $5. National Reye's Syndrome Foundation, 426 N. Lewis, Box 829, Bryan, OH 43506. TEL 419-636-2679. Ed. Dennis J. Pollack. charts. circ. 5,000. (back issues avail.)

610 CH ISSN 0028-0275
NATIONAL TAIWAN UNIVERSITY. COLLEGE OF MEDICINE. MEMOIRS. vol.16, 1971. a. National Taiwan University, College of Medicine, No. 1, Jen Ai Rd., 1st Section, Taipei, Taiwan, Republic of China. Ed.Bd. bibl. charts. illus. stat. circ. 1,500. Indexed: Biol.Abstr. Abstr.Hyg. Trop.Dis.Bull.

NAUKOVE TOVARYSTVO IMENI SHEVCHENKA. PROCEEDINGS OF THE SECTION OF CHEMISTRY, BIOLOGY AND MEDICINE. see *CHEMISTRY*

610 GW ISSN 0300-8371
NEUE MUENCHNER BEITRAEGE ZUR GESCHICHTE DER MEDIZIN UND NATURWISSENSCHAFTEN. MEDIZINHISTORISCHE SERIE. 1970. irreg., vol. 8, 1978. price varies. (Werner Fritsch Verlag) Theodor Ackermann, Ludwigstr. 7, 8000 Munich 22, W. Germany (B.R.D.) Eds. Heinz Goerke, Joern Wolf. index. Indexed: Ind.Med.
History

616 US
NEW HORIZONS IN THERAPEUTICS. 1984. irreg. price varies. Plenum Publishing Corp., 233 Spring St., New York, NY 10013. TEL 212-620-8047. Eds. George Poste, Stanley T. Crooke.

610.6 US
NEW YORK ACADEMY OF MEDICINE. ANNUAL REPORT. a. New York Academy of Medicine, 2 E. 103 St., New York, NY 10029. TEL 212-876-8200.

610 CN ISSN 0078-0316
NEWFOUNDLAND MEDICAL DIRECTORY. 1961. a. free. Newfoundland Medical Board, Registrar, 47 Queen's Rd., St. John's, Nfld., A1C 2A7, Canada. TEL 709-726-8546. circ. 700.

610 NR ISSN 0078-0782
NIGERIAN MEDICAL DIRECTORY. 1967. a. £N10. African Literary and Scientific Publications Ltd., 9 Kodesho St., Ikeja, Lagos, Nigeria. Ed. V.O. Awosika. adv. bk. rev. circ. 3,000.

610 SW ISSN 0078-1061
NORDISK MEDICINHISTORISK AARSBOK. (Text in Swedish; summaries in English) 1953. a. Kr.70. Medicinhistoriska Museet - Museum of Medical History, Aasoegatan 146, 116 32 Stockholm, Sweden. Ed. Wolfram Kock. adv. circ. 1,000. Indexed: Hist.Abstr. Amer.Hist.& Life.
Formerly: Medicinhistorisk Aarsbok.
History

610.6 US ISSN 0361-5537
NORTH CAROLINA MEDICAL SOCIETY. TRANSACTIONS. a. North Carolina Medical Society, 222 N. Person St., Raleigh, NC 27611. TEL 919-833-3836. Key Title: Transactions - North Carolina Medical Society.
Formerly: Medical Society of the State of North Carolina. Transactions.

610 US
NUCLEUS SCIENCE JOURNAL. 1957. a. $10. Queens College, Kissena & Melbourne Ave., Flushing, NY 11367. TEL 718-520-7000. Ed. Kenneth M Simckes. adv. bk. rev. bibl. charts. illus. stat. index. circ. 7,000. (back issues avail.)

610 574 JA ISSN 0469-2071
NUKADA INSTITUTE FOR MEDICAL AND BIOLOGICAL RESEARCH. REPORTS. (Text in English) irreg. exchange basis. Nukada Institute for Medical and Biological Research - Nukada Igaku Seibutsugaku Kenkyusho, 5-18 Inage-cho, Chiba-shi 280, Japan.

610 US
OAK RIDGE ASSOCIATED UNIVERSITIES. MEDICAL AND HEALTH SCIENCES DIVISION. RESEARCH REPORT. 1951. a. free. ‡ Oak Ridge Associated Universities, Inc., Office of Information Services, Box 117, Oak Ridge, TN 37831-0117. TEL 615-576-3000. Ed. William W. Burr. circ. 3,000.
Formerly: Oak Ridge Associated Universities. Medical Division. Research Report (ISSN 0078-2890)

610 575 US
OXFORD MONOGRAPHS ON MEDICAL GENETICS. irreg. price varies. Oxford University Press, 200 Madison Ave., New York, NY 10016 TEL 212-679-7300. (And Ely House, 37 Dover St., London W1X 4AH, England) Ed. Bd.

610 US
PAIN SERIES. 1968. irreg. price varies. F. A. Davis Co., 1915 Arch St., Philadelphia, PA 19103. TEL 800-523-4049. Ed. Rene Cailliet.

610   PR   ISSN 0078-8864
PAN AMERICAN MEDICAL WOMEN'S ALLIANCE. NEWSLETTER. (Text and summaries in English and Spanish) 1956. irreg. price varies. Pan American Medical Women's Alliance, c/o Dr. Rosa E. Fiol, Editor, Buzon No. 16, Carr. 859, Carolina, PR 00630.

610   PP   ISSN 0256-2901
PAPUA NEW GUINEA INSTITUTE OF MEDICAL RESEARCH. MONOGRAPH SERIES. 1970. irreg. price varies. Papua New Guinea Institute of Medical Research, P.O. Box 60, Goroka, Papua New Guinea. Ed. Dr. M.P. Alpers. bibl. charts. illus. circ. 1,000.

616.07 574.2   US
PATHOBIOLOGY ANNUAL. 1972. a. price varies. Raven Press, 1185 Ave. of the Americas, New York, NY 10036. TEL 212-575-0335. Ed. Harry L. Ioachim. bibl. charts. illus. circ. 4,000. Indexed: Biol.Abstr. Chem.Abstr. Excerp.Med. Ind.Med.
Pathology

616.07   GW   ISSN 0344-0338
PATHOLOGY, RESEARCH AND PRACTICE. (Text in English) 1886. irreg., 6 nos. per vol. DM.648. (European Society of Pathology) Gustav Fischer Verlag, Wollgrasweg 49, Postfach 720143, 7000 Stuttgart 70, W. Germany (B.R.D.) Ed. Dr. E. Grundmann. adv. bk. rev. charts. illus. index. circ. 750. Indexed: Biol.Abstr. Chem.Abstr. Curr.Cont. Ind.Med. Nutr.Abstr. Dent.Ind. Helminthol.Abstr. Ind.Vet. Vet.Bull.
Former titles: Pathology and Practice; Beitraege zur Pathologie (ISSN 0005-8165)
Pathology

PERSPECTIVES IN PEDIATRIC PATHOLOGY. see *MEDICAL SCIENCES — Pediatrics*

610 615   UK   ISSN 0142-1581
PHARMACEUTICAL MEDICINE. 1979. irreg., latest vol.2, 1980. £5. Cambridge Medical Publications Ltd., 3 Liverpool Gardens, Worthing, West Sussex BN11 1TF, England.

PHARMAKOTHERAPIE. see *PHARMACY AND PHARMACOLOGY*

610   UK   ISSN 0308-051X
PHARMATHERAPEUTICA. (Text and summaries in various languages) 1976. irreg. $60. Clayton-Wray Publications Ltd., 1A High St., Alton, Hants. GU34 1BA, England. Ed. Nigel Clayton. circ. 5,500. Indexed: Biol.Abstr. Chem.Abstr. Curr.Cont. Excerp.Med. Ind.Med. Nutr.Abstr. Abstr.Hyg. Biotech.Abstr. Dent.Ind. Helminthol.Abstr.

PHILOSOPHY AND MEDICINE. see *PHILOSOPHY*

610   US
PHYSICIAN ASSISTANT PROGRAMS, A NATIONAL DIRECTORY. 1975. biennial. $10. Association of Physician Assistant Programs, 1117 N. 19th St., Ste. 300, Arlington, VA 22209. TEL 703-525-4200. Ed. Nancy Tilson. circ. 10,000.
Former titles: National Health Practitioner Program Profile (ISSN 0277-3376); National New Health Practitioner Program Profile (ISSN 0145-3793)

610   US   ISSN 0731-0315
PHYSICIAN CHARACTERISTICS & DISTRIBUTION IN THE U S. 1943. a. $42. American Medical Association, 535 N. Dearborn St., Chicago, IL 60610. TEL 312-645-5000. Ed. G.A. Roback. (reprint service avail. from UMI)
Former titles: Physician Characteristics and Distribution & Physician Distribution and Medical Licensure in the U S (ISSN 0364-6610); Distribution of Physicians in the U S (ISSN 0146-4558); Distribution of Physicians, Hospital, Hospital Beds in the U S (ISSN 0419-4357)

610   US   ISSN 0093-4461
PHYSICIANS' DESK REFERENCE. 1947. a. $32.95. ‡ Medical Economics Co., 680 Kinderkamack Rd., Oradell, NJ 07649. TEL 201-262-3030. circ. 464,000 (controlled)
Formerly: Physicians' Desk Reference to Pharmaceutical Specialties and Biologicals (ISSN 0093-447X)

610   US
PHYSICIANS' DESK REFERENCE FOR NONPRESCRIPTION DRUGS. 1980. a. $19.95. Medical Economics Co., 680 Kinderkamack Rd., Oradell, NJ 07649. TEL 201-262-3030. circ. 300,000 (controlled)

610   UK   ISSN 0260-2946
PHYSIOLOGICAL PRINCIPLES IN MEDICINE. 1981. irreg. price varies. Edward Arnold (Publishers) Ltd., 41 Bedford Square, London WC1B 3DQ, England.

615.8   UK
PHYSIOTHERAPY RESEARCH NEWSLETTER. a. £1. Physiotherapy Research, King's College London, Strand, London WC2R 2LS, England. TEL 01-834-9268. Ed. Sue Carter.

362   US
POLLING. 1974. irreg? free. ‡ United Cerebral Palsy of New York City, Inc., 122 E. 23rd St., New York, NY 10010. TEL 212-677-7400. (Co-sponsor: Epilepsy Foundation of America) Ed. Daniel A. Poling, II. adv. bk. rev. illus. circ. 10,000.
Rehabilitation

610   PL   ISSN 0079-3558
POLSKA AKADEMIA NAUK. WYDZIAL NAUK MEDYCZNYCH. ROZPRAWY.* (Text in Polish; summaries in English and Russian) 1956. irreg. price varies. Politechnika Warszawska, Plac Jednosci Robotniczie, 00-661 Warsaw, Poland (Dist. by: Ars Polona-Ruch, Krakowskie Przedmiescie 7, 00-068 Warsaw, Poland) Ed. Witold Orlowski.

616.07   UK
PROBLEMS IN PATHOLOGY. irreg. price varies. W. B. Saunders Co. Ltd., 1 St. Anne's Rd., Eastbourne, East Sussex BN21 3UN, England. Ed. J.L. Bennington.

610   US   ISSN 0361-7742
PROGRESS IN CLINICAL AND BIOLOGICAL RESEARCH. 1975. irreg., vol.217, 1986. price varies. Alan R. Liss Inc., 41 E. 11th St., New York, NY 10003. TEL 212-475-7700. (reprint service avail. from ISI) Indexed: Biol.Abstr. Chem.Abstr. Excerp.Med. Ind.Med. Dent.Ind.

616.075   US   ISSN 0079-6174
PROGRESS IN CLINICAL PATHOLOGY. 1967. irreg., vol.9, 1984. Grune and Stratton, Inc. (Subsidiary of: Harcourt Brace Jovanovich, Inc.) Orlando, FL 32887 TEL 305-345-4200. (Dist. by: Academic Press, Inc., 1250 Sixth Ave., San Diego, CA 92101) Ed. Mario Stefanini, M.D. Indexed: Biol.Abstr. Chem.Abstr. Ind.Med.
Pathology

610   SZ   ISSN 0254-623X
PROGRESS IN CRITICAL CARE MEDICINE. (Text in English) 1984. irreg. price varies. S. Karger AG, Alschwilerstr. 10, P.O. Box, CH-4009 Basel, Switzerland. Ed. W.H. Massion. (reprint sevice avail.; back issues avail.) Indexed: Biol.Abstr. Chem.Abstr. Curr.Cont. Ind.Med.

612   US   ISSN 0721-9156
PROGRESS IN SENSORY PHYSIOLOGY. 1981. irreg., vol.7, 1986. Springer-Verlag, 175 Fifth Ave., New York, NY 10010 TEL 212-460-1500. (Also Berlin, Heidelberg, Tokyo and Vienna) (reprint service avail. from ISI)
Physiology

PROTEIN ABNORMALITIES. see *BIOLOGY*

610 614   UN   ISSN 0300-4880
PUBLIC HEALTH IN EUROPE. French edition (ISSN 0250-8419); Russian edition (ISSN 0250-8672) (Editions in English, French and Russian) 1972. irreg. World Health Organization, Regional Office for Europe, Scherfigsvej 8, 2100 Copenhagen OE, Denmark. Indexed: Curr.Cont. Abstr.Hyg. ERIC. Trop.Dis.Bull.

610   CN   ISSN 0079-8789
QUEEN'S MEDICAL REVIEW. 1951. a. Queen's University, Aesculapian Society, Kingston, Ontario, Canada. TEL 613-547-5511. Ed. R.B. Egerdie. adv. circ. 1,000.

MEDICAL SCIENCES   765

610   FR
REANIMATION ET MEDECINE D'URGENCE. 1968. a. (Societe de Reanimation de Langue Francaise) Expansion Scientifique Francaise, 15 rue St. Benoit, 75278 Paris Cedex 06, France. circ. 4,000.

613   US
RECENT ADVANCES IN OBESITY RESEARCH. 1977. irreg. price varies. Technomic Publishing Co., Inc., 851 New Holland Ave., Box 3535, Lancaster, PA 17604. TEL 717-291-5609. Eds. Dr. Alan N. Howard, Dr. George A. Bray. illus. Indexed: Chem.Abstr.

610   SA
REGISTER OF MEDICAL PRACTITIONERS, INTERNS AND DENTISTS FOR THE REPUBLIC OF SOUTH AFRICA. (Text and summaries in Afrikaans and English) a. with m. supplements. R.25 (plus R.5 for m. supplements) South African Medical & Dental Council, P.O. Box 205, Pretoria 0001, South Africa.

362   JA   ISSN 0036-0538
REHABILITATION/RYOIKU. (Text in Japanese) 1951. a. $12. Japanese Society for Disabled Children - Nihon Shitai Fujiyuji Kyokai, 3-13-15 Higashi Ikebukuro, Toshima-ku, Tokyo 170, Japan. Ed.Bd. circ. 2,000.
Rehabilitation

REHABILITATION DER ENTWICKLUNGSGEHEMMTEN. see *EDUCATION — Special Education And Rehabilitation*

362   US   ISSN 0172-6412
REHABILITATION UND PRAEVENTION. 1977. irreg., vol.18, 1986. price varies. Springer-Verlag, 175 Fifth Ave., New York, NY 10010 TEL 212-460-1500. (Also Berlin, Heidelberg, Tokyo and Vienna) (reprint service avail. from ISI)
Rehabilitation

REICHORUI KENKYUJO NENPO/KYOTO UNIVERSITY. PRIMATE RESEARCH INSTITUTE. ANNUAL REPORT. see *ANTHROPOLOGY*

610   NE
REPERTORIUM. 1967. a. fl.75.50. Association of the Dutch Pharmaceutical Industry "Nefarma" - Dutch Association of Pharmaceutical Industries, Postbus 9193, 3506 GD Utrecht, Netherlands. Ed.Bd. adv. abstr. cum.index. circ. 30,000.
Former titles: Repertorium Farmaceutische Specialites Periodiek Overzicht voor Artsen; Repertorium Verpakte Geneesmiddelen Periodiek Overzicht voor Artsen (ISSN 0034-463X)

614.5   US   ISSN 0197-7423
REPORT OF THE PATIENT REGISTRY.* a. Cystic Fibrosis Foundation, 6931 Arlington Rd., No. 200, Bethesda, MD 20814-5205.
Formerly: Report on Survival Studies of Patients With Cystic Fibrosis (ISSN 0161-472X)

RESEARCH AND CLINICAL CENTER FOR CHILD DEVELOPMENT. ANNUAL REPORT. see *CHILDREN AND YOUTH — About*

610   UK   ISSN 0143-3083
RESEARCH AND CLINICAL FORUMS. 1979. irreg. M C S Consultants, Chapel Place, Tunbridge Wells, Kent TN1 1BP, England. Indexed: Chem.Abstr.

614.8   US   ISSN 0275-4959
RESEARCH IN THE SOCIOLOGY OF HEALTH CARE; a research annual. 1980. a. $24.75 to individuals; institutions $49.50. J A I Press Inc., 36 Sherwood Place, Box 1678, Greenwich, CT 06830. TEL 203-661-7602. Ed. Julius A. Roth. Indexed: Lang.& Lang.Behav.Abstr.

610   TH   ISSN 0557-7330
RESEARCH INTO DISEASE.* 1967. irreg. South East Asia Treaty Organization, Sri Ayudhaya Road, P.O. Box 517, Bangkok, Thailand.

610   BE   ISSN 0773-7777
RESEAU AUTOMATIQUE BELGE DE LA POLLUTION ATMOSPHERIQUE. (Text in Dutch and French) 1978. a. $7. Instituut voor Hygiene en Epidemiologie (IHE), Juliette Wytsmanstraat 14, 1050 Brussels, Belgium. circ. 250.

MEDICAL SCIENCES

610   BL   ISSN 0101-322X
REVISTA DE CIENCIAS BIOMEDICAS. (Text in Portuguese; summaries in English and Portguese) 1980. a. $30 or exchange basis. Universidade Estadual Paulista, Av. Vicente Ferreira 1278, Caixa Postal 630, 17.500 Marilia SP, Brazil. bibl. charts. illus. stat. Indexed: Biol.Abstr. Bull.Signal. Chem.Abstr. Excerp.Med.

610   UK   ISSN 0266-0512
RISK IN SOCIETY. 1984. irreg. £25($30) John Libbey & Co. Ltd., 80/84 Bondway, London SW8 1SF, England. Ed. A.J. Jouhar.

610   IT
RIVISTA DI STORIA DELLE SCIENZE MEDICHE E NATURALI. BIBLIOTECA. 1947. irreg., no.24, 1986. price varies. Casa Editrice Leo S. Olschki, Casella Postale 66, 50100 Florence, Italy.
History

610 613   US   ISSN 0091-3472
ROBERT WOOD JOHNSON FOUNDATION. ANNUAL REPORT. 1971. a. free. Box 2316, Princeton, NJ 08540. TEL 609-452-8701. illus. circ. 20,000. Indexed: Med.Care Rev. Key Title: Annual Report - Robert Wood Johnson Foundation.

610   US
ROCKEFELLER UNIVERSITY, NEW YORK. SCIENTIFIC AND EDUCATIONAL PROGRAMS. 1979. biennial. free. Rockefeller University Press, 1230 York Ave., New York, NY 10021. TEL 212-570-8568. circ. 9,000. (reprint service avail. from ISI, UMI)
Supersedes (1955-1979): Rockefeller University, New York. Annual Report (ISSN 0080-3405)

610.69   CN   ISSN 0707-3542
ROLLCALL. 1974. irreg. Can.$5. University of British Columbia, Division of Health Services Research and Development, Vancouver, B.C. V6T 1W5, Canada. TEL 604-228-2211. illus.

610   UK
ROYAL COLLEGE OF GENERAL PRACTITIONERS. OCCASIONAL PAPERS. 1976. irreg. price varies. Royal College of General Practitioners, Alford House, 9 Marlborough Rd., Exeter EX2 4TJ, England. Ed. D.J. Pereira Gray. adv. bk. rev. circ. 1,500. Indexed: Excerp.Med. Ind.Med.

616.07 574.2   AT
ROYAL COLLEGE OF PATHOLOGISTS OF AUSTRALASIA. BROADSHEETS. 1967. irreg. Aus.$5 membership. Royal College of Pathologists of Australasia, 207 Albion St., Surry Hills, N.S.W. 2010, Australia. Ed. F.H. Smith. circ. 1,200.
Formerly: Royal College of Pathologists of Australia. Broadsheets.

610   UK
ROYAL COLLEGE OF PHYSICIANS OF EDINBURGH. DIRECTORY. 1910. irreg. Royal College of Physicians of Edinburgh, 9 Queen Street, Edinburgh EH2 1JQ, Scotland. circ. controlled.
Formerly: Royal College of Physicians of Edinburgh. Yearbook and Calendar.

610   UK   ISSN 0144-8676
ROYAL SOCIETY OF MEDICINE. ANNUAL REPORT OF THE COUNCIL. (Previously issued in the Society's Calendar) 1959/60. a. free. Royal Society of Medicine, 1 Wimpole St., London W1M 8AE, England. circ. 17,500. (reprint service avail. from UMI, ISI)

610   US   ISSN 0142-2367
ROYAL SOCIETY OF MEDICINE. INTERNATIONAL CONGRESS AND SYMPOSIUM SERIES. 1978. irreg., vol.60, 1983. Grune & Stratton, Inc. (Subsidiary of: Harcourt Brace Jovanovich, Publishers) Orlando, FL 32887. TEL 305-345-4200.

610   UK   ISSN 0268-3091
ROYAL SOCIETY OF MEDICINE. ROUND TABLE SERIES. 1980. irreg. Royal Society of Medicine, 1 Wimpole St., London W1M 8AE, England.
Formerly: Royal Society of Medicine. Forum Series (ISSN 0144-5618)

610   US   ISSN 0080-4797
RUDOLF VIRCHOW MEDICAL SOCIETY IN THE CITY OF NEW YORK. PROCEEDINGS. 1942. irreg., no.27, 1972. price varies. Rudolf Virchow Medical Society, 310 E. 14th St., New York, NY 10003. Indexed: Biol.Abstr. Excerp.Med. Ind.Med.

SAINT GEORGE'S HOSPITAL GAZETTE. see *HOSPITALS*

SCANDINAVIAN JOURNAL OF CLINICAL AND LABORATORY INVESTIGATION. SUPPLEMENT. see *MEDICAL SCIENCES — Experimental Medicine, Laboratory Technique*

616.98   GW   ISSN 0080-679X
SCHIFFAHRTMEDIZINISCHES INSTITUT DER MARINE, KIEL. VEROEFFENTLICHUNGEN. 1969. irreg. free. Schiffahrtmedizinisches Institut der Marine, Kopperpahler Allee 120, 2300 Kiel-Kronshagen, W. Germany (B.R.D.) Ed. K. Seemann. adv. circ. 2,000.
Military

610   DK   ISSN 0109-260X
SCHULTZ MEDICINALBIBLIOTEK. PUBLIKATION. a. Kr.25. Bibliotekscentralen, Telegrafvej 5, DK-2750 Ballerup, Denmark.

610   SZ
SCHWEIZERISCHE MEDIZINISCHE WOCHENSCHRIFT (SUPPLEMENTUM) (Text in French, German; summaries in English) 1975. irreg. price varies. Schwabe und Co. AG, Steinentorstr. 13, CH-4010 Basel, Switzerland. adv. circ. 4,000. (back issues avail.) Indexed: Ind.Med.

610   SZ   ISSN 0251-1762
SCHWEIZERISCHER MEDIZINALKALENDER. (Text in German) 1878. a. 47.50 Fr. Schwabe und Co. AG, Steinentorstr. 13, CH-4010 Basel, Switzerland. Ed. M. Soliva. adv. index. circ. 10,000.

610   SZ   ISSN 0080-7400
SCHWEIZERISCHES MEDIZINISCHES JAHRBUCH. (Text in French and German) 1968. a. 101 Fr. ‡ (Schweizerische Aerzteorganisation - Federation of Swiss Physicians) Schwabe und Co. AG, Steinentorstr. 13, CH-4010 Basel, Switzerland. adv. index. circ. 5,000.

SCIENCE, MEDICINE AND TECHNOLOGY IN EAST ASIA. see *SCIENCES: COMPREHENSIVE WORKS*

610   US
SCRIPPS CLINIC AND RESEARCH FOUNDATION. RESEARCH INSTITUTE. SCIENTIFIC REPORT. 1974/75. a. free to qualified personnel. Scripps Clinic and Research Foundation, Research Institute, 10666 N. Torrey Pines Rd., La Jolla, CA 92037. TEL 619-455-9100. Ed. Phyllis Minick. circ. 3,000(controlled)
Formerly (until 1976/77): Scripps Clinic and Research Foundation. Scientific Report (ISSN 0361-3054)

610   GW
SEIBT MEDIZINISCHE TECHNIK. (Text in English, French, German, Spanish) a. DM.84. Seibt Verlag, Pilgersheimer Str., D-8000 Munich 90, W. Germany (B.R.D.)

610 615   KO
SEOUL NATIONAL UNIVERSITY. FACULTY PAPERS.* (Text in English; summaries in Korean) 1972. a. Seoul National University, Research Committee, Seoul, S. Korea. Ed. Byong Seol Seo.

610   US
SERONO CLINICAL COLLOQUIA ON REPRODUCTION SERIES. 1980. irreg., vol.3, 1983. Grune & Stratton, Inc. (Subsidiary of: Harcourt Brace Jovanovich, Publishers) Orlando, FL 32887. TEL 305-345-4200.

610   US
SERONO FOUNDATION SYMPOSIA. 1973. irreg., vol.51, 1983. Academic Press Inc., Orlando, FL 32887. TEL 305-345-2000. Indexed: Chem.Abstr.

SHONI NO HOKEN/HEALTH FOR CHILDREN. see *CHILDREN AND YOUTH — About*

SOCIAL RESPONSIBILITY: BUSINESS, JOURNALISM, LAW, MEDICINE. see *LAW*

610   SP   ISSN 0213-3601
SOCIEDAD DE ESTUDIOS VASCOS. CUADERNOS DE SECCION. MEDICINA. 1984. irreg. (Sociedad de Estudios Vascos) Eusko Ikaskuntza, S.A., Churruca, 7-2, 20004 Donostia, Spain.

610   SP   ISSN 0583-7480
SOCIEDAD ESPANOLA DE HISTORIA DE LA MEDICINA. BOLETIN.* vol.14, 1974. a. Sociedad Espanola de Historia de la Medicina, Duque de Medinaceli 4, Madrid-14, Spain. bibl.
History

610   LU   ISSN 0037-9247
SOCIETE DES SCIENCES MEDICALES DU GRAND-DUCHE DE LUXEMBOURG. BULLETIN. (Text in English, French and German) 1863. irreg., (approx. 2-3/yr.) free to institutions. (Societe des Sciences Medicales, Institut Grand-Ducal) Imprimerie Saint Paul, Centre Hospitalier de Luxembourg, 4 rue Barble, Luxembourg, Luxembourg. Ed. Dr. M. Dicato. adv. bk. rev. bibl. charts. illus. circ. 850. Indexed: Biol.Abstr. Chem.Abstr. Excerp.Med. Ind.Med. Dent.Ind.

SOUTH AFRICAN INSTITUTE FOR MEDICAL RESEARCH. PUBLICATION. see *BIOLOGY*

616.21 371   SA
SOUTH AFRICAN JOURNAL OF COMMUNICATION DISORDERS/SUID-AFRIKAANSE TYDSKRIF VIR KOMMUNIKASIEAFWYKINGS. (Text mainly in English) 1948. a. R.7.50. South African Speech & Hearing Association - Suid-Afrikaanse Vereniging vir Spraak- en Gehoorheelkunde, Box 31782, Braamfontein 2017, South Africa. Ed. M.L. Aron. adv. bk. rev. circ. 1,000. Indexed: Biol.Abstr. Ind.Med. DSH Abstr. Ind.S.A.Per.
Former titles: South African Speech and Hearing Association. Journal (ISSN 0081-2471); South African Logopedic Society. Journal.

610 360   SA
SOUTH AFRICAN MEDICAL AND DENTAL COUNCIL. REGISTER OF SUPPLEMENTARY HEALTH SERVICES PROFESSIONS. a. (with m. supplements. R.15 (plus R.3 for supplements) South African Medical and Dental Council, Box 205, Pretoria 0001, South Africa.

610   SA   ISSN 0081-248X
SOUTH AFRICAN MEDICAL RESEARCH COUNCIL. ANNUAL REPORT/SUID-AFRIKAANSE MEDIESE NAVORSINGSRAAD. JAARVERSLAG. (Text in Afrikaans and English) 1969/70. a. free. South African Medical Research Council, P.O. Box 70, Tygerberg 7505, South Africa. Ed. Grace Townshend. circ. 1,000.

SOUTH AFRICAN SOCIETY OF PATHOLOGISTS. CONGRESS BROCHURE. see *MEETINGS AND CONGRESSES*

SOUTHEAST ASIAN REGIONAL SEMINAR ON TROPICAL MEDICINE & PUBLIC HEALTH. PROCEEDINGS. see *PUBLIC HEALTH AND SAFETY*

613   SZ   ISSN 0076-6186
SOZIALMEDIZINISCHE UND PAEDAGOGISCHE JUGENDKUNDE. (Text in German) 1965. irreg. (approx. 1/yr.) price varies. S. Karger AG, Allschwilerstrasse 10, P.O. Box, CH-4009 Basel, Switzerland. Ed. G. Ritzel. (reprint service avail. from ISI) Indexed: Biol.Abstr. Chem.Abstr. Curr.Cont. Ind.Med.
Formerly: Medizinische und Paedagogische Jugendkunde.

616.85   US   ISSN 0193-3434
SPEECH AND LANGUAGE: ADVANCES IN BASIC RESEARCH AND PRACTICE. 1979. a., vol.11, 1984. Academic Press, Inc., Orlando, FL 32887. TEL 305-345-2000.

616.07   US   ISSN 0081-3699
SPEZIELLE PATHOLOGISCHE ANATOMIE. 1966. irreg., vol.18, 1984. price varies. Springer-Verlag, 175 Fifth Ave., New York, NY 10010 TEL 212-460-1500. (Also Berlin, Heidelberg, Tokyo and Vienna) (reprint service avail. from ISI)
Pathology

MEDICAL SCIENCES 767

610 YU ISSN 0081-3966
SRPSKA AKADEMIJA NAUKA I UMETNOSTI. ODELJENJE MEDICINSKIH NAUKA. GLAS. (Text in Serbo-Croatian; summaries in English, French, German or Russian) 1949, N.S. irreg. price varies. Srpska Akademija Nauka i Umetnosti, Knez Mihailova 35, 11001 Belgrade, Yugoslavia (Dist. by: Prosveta, Terazije 16, Belgrade, Yugoslavia) circ. 1,000. Indexed: Ind.Med. Excerp.Med.

610 YU ISSN 0081-4016
SRPSKA AKADEMIJA NAUKA I UMETNOSTI. ODELJENJE MEDICINSKIH NAUKA. POSEBNA IZDANJA. (Text in Serbo-Croatian; summaries in English, French, German or Russian) 1950. irreg. price varies. Srpska Akademija Nauka i Umetnosti, Knez Mihailova 35, 11001 Belgrade, Yugoslavia (Dist. by: Prosveta, Terazije 16, Belgrade, Yugoslavia) circ. 1,000. Indexed: Chem.Abstr. Excerp.Med. Ind.Med.

STUDIA I MATERIALY Z DZIEJOW NAUKI POLSKIEJ. SERIA B. HISTORIA NAUK BIOLOGICZNYCH I MEDYCZNYCH. see *BIOLOGY*

610 GW ISSN 0081-7333
STUDIEN ZUR MEDIZINGESCHICHTE DES NEUNZEHNTEN JAHRUNDERTS. 1963. irreg., vol.9, 1979. Vandenhoeck und Ruprecht, Theaterstr. 13, Postfach 37 53, 3400 Goettingen, W. Germany (B.R.D.)
History

610 614 UK ISSN 0473-8837
STUDIES ON CURRENT HEALTH PROBLEMS.* 1962. irreg. price varies. (Association of the British Pharmaceutical Industry) Office of Health Economics, 12 Whitehall, London SW1, England. Ed.Bd. charts.

610 JA ISSN 0019-1612
STUDIES ON HISTORY OF MEDICINE/ IGAKUSHI KENKYU. (Text in Japanese) 1961. a. 1500 Yen($10.) (Collegium Ad Studium Historiae Medicae - Igakushi Kenkyukai) Osaka University Medical School, Department of Hygiene, 4-3 Nakanoshima, Kita-ku, Osaka 530, Japan. Ed. Hiroshi Maruyama. adv. bk. rev. abstr. bibl. illus. cum.index: 1961-1968. circ. 700. Indexed: Curr.Cont.
History

610 500 GW ISSN 0341-0773
SUDHOFFS ARCHIV. BEIHEFTE. irreg., vol.27, 1987. price varies. Franz Steiner Verlag Wiesbaden GmbH, Birkenwaldstr. 44, Postfach 347, D-7000 Stuttgart 1, W. Germany (B.R.D.) Ed.Bd. Indexed: Ind.Med. GeoRef.

610 SW ISSN 0346-6000
SWEDEN. SOCIALSTYRELSEN. FOERFATTNINGSSAMLING: MEDICAL. irreg. (approx. 40/yr.) Kr.125. Socialstyrelsen - National Board of Health and Welfare, 106 30 Stockholm, Sweden. index. circ. 8,000. (looseleaf format)
Supersedes in part (1883-1976): Sweden. Medicinalvaesendet. Foerfattningssamling (ISSN 0346-5837)

610 SW ISSN 0345-0171
SWEDEN. SOCIALSTYRELSEN. LEGITIMERADE LAEKARE/AUTHORIZED PHYSICIANS. irreg. Kr.80. (National Board of Health and Welfare) Allmaenna Foerlaget, Box 5227, 102 45 Stockholm, Sweden. index. circ. 10,000.

610 PL ISSN 0082-125X
SZCZECINSKIE TOWARZYSTWO NAUKOWE. WYDZIAL NAUK LEKARSKICH. PRACE. (Text in Polish; summaries in English, Polish and Russian) 1959. irreg. price varies. Panstwowy Zaklad Wydawnictw Lekarskich, Dluga 38/40, Warsaw, Poland (Dist. by: Ars Polona-Ruch, Krakowskie Przedmiescie 7, 00-068 Warsaw, Poland)

610 II ISSN 0970-1257
TIBETAN MEDICINE. 1980. irreg. $3 per no. Library of Tibetan Works and Archives, Dharamsala 176215, India. (back issues avail.)

610.28 JA ISSN 0082-4739
TOKYO MEDICAL AND DENTAL UNIVERSITY. INSTITUTE FOR MEDICAL AND DENTAL ENGINEERING. REPORTS/IYO KIZAI KENKYUSHO HOKOKU. (Table of contents and summaries in English) 1967. a. free. Tokyo Medical and Dental University, Institute for Medical and Dental Engineering - Tokyo Ika Shika Daigaku Iyo Kizai Kenkyusho, 2-3-10 Surugadai, Kanda, Chiyoda-ku, Tokyo, Japan. Ed. Tatsuo Togawa. Indexed: Dent.Ind.

610 JA ISSN 0082-4771
TOKYO METROPOLITAN RESEARCH LABORATORY OF PUBLIC HEALTH, ANNUAL REPORT/TOKYO-TORITSU EISEI KENKYUSHO KENKYU NENPO. (Text in Japanese; summaries occasionally in English) 1949-50. a. exchange basis. Tokyo Metropolitan Research Laboratory of Public Health - Tokyo-toritsu Eisei Kenkyusho, 3-24-1 Hyakunin-cho, Shinjuk-ku, Tokyo 160, Japan. Indexed: Dairy Sci.Abstr. Food Sci.& Tech.Abstr.

TOO MUCH - UNIVERSITY COLLEGE HOSPITAL MAGAZINE. see *HOSPITALS*

610 US
TREATMENT IN CLINICAL MEDICINE. 1984. irreg., latest 1986. Springer-Verlag, 175 Fifth Ave., New York, NY 10010 TEL 212-460-1500. (Also Berlin, Heidelberg, Tokyo, Vienna) (reprint service avail. from ISI)

616.988 UK ISSN 0041-3240
TROPICAL DISEASES BULLETIN. 1912. m. $146. Bureau of Hygiene and Tropical Diseases, Keppel St., London WC1E 7HT, England. Ed. C.A. Brown. adv. bk. rev. abstr. index. circ. 1,500. Indexed: Biol.Abstr. Ind.Med. Nutr.Abstr. Helminthol.Abstr. Ind.Vet. Rev.Appl.Entomol. Rev.Plant Path. Vet.Bull.
Tropical medicine

610 FI ISSN 0355-9483
TURUN YLIOPISTO. JULKAISUJA. SARJA D. MEDICA-ODONTOLOGICA. (Latin title: Annales Universitatis Turkuensis) (Text in English) 1972. irreg. price varies. Turun Yliopisto - University of Turku, SF-20500 Turku 50, Finland (Dist. by: Akateeminen Kirjakauppa, SF-00100 Helsinki 10, Finland) Indexed: Chem.Abstr.

610 US ISSN 0082-7134
U C L A FORUM IN MEDICAL SCIENCES. 1962. irreg., vol.27, 1986. (University of California, Los Angeles) Academic Press, Inc., Orlando, FL 32887. TEL 305-345-2000. Indexed: Biol.Abstr. Chem.Abstr. Ind.Med.

610.25 US ISSN 0091-8393
U S MEDICAL DIRECTORY. 1969. irreg., latest 1986/87. $125. U S Directory Service (Miami), 665 N.W. 128th St., Box 68-1700, Miami, FL 33168. TEL 305-769-1700. Ed. Stanley Alperin.

610 150 301.1 US
U S S R REPORT: LIFE SCIENCES, BIOMEDICAL AND BEHAVIORAL SCIENCES. 1973. irreg. (approx. 20/yr.) $5 5. U.S. Joint Publications Research Service, 1000 N. Glebe Rd., Arlington, VA 22201 TEL 703-487-4630. (Orders to: NTIS, Springfield, VA 22161)
Former titles: U S S R Report: Biomedical and Behavioral Sciences; U S S R and Eastern Europe Scientific Abstracts: Biomedical and Behavioral Sciences; U S S R and Eastern Europe Scientific Abstracts: Biomedical Sciences.

574 616.9 US
U S S R REPORT: SPACE BIOLOGY AND AEROSPACE MEDICINE. English translation of: Kosmicheskaya Biologiya i Aviakosmicheskaya Meditsina. irreg.(approx. 6/yr.) $5 per no. U.S. Joint Publications Research Service, 1000 N. Glebe Rd., Arlington, VA 22201 TEL 703-487-4630. (Orders to NTIS, Springfield, VA 22161)
Former titles: Space Biology and Aerospace Medicine; Space Biology and Medicine.
Translations of reports on Soviet technology in aerospace medicine

616.98 US
U.S. AIR FORCE. SCHOOL OF AEROSPACE MEDICINE. STANDARD TECHNICAL REPORT SERIES. 1958. irreg. U.S. Air Force, School of Aerospace Medicine, Aeromedical Library (USAFSAM/TSKD), Brooks Air Force Base, TX 78235-5301. TEL 512-536-3322. (also avail. in microfiche) Indexed: Excerp.Med. Ind.Med.
Incorporates (as of Oct., 1984): Aeromedical Reviews (ISSN 0065-3683)
Military

616.98 US ISSN 0083-355X
U.S. VETERANS ADMINISTRATION. MEDICAL RESEARCH PROGRAM. 1957. a. $0.40. U.S. Veterans Administration, Medical Research Service, 810 Vermont Ave., N.W., Washington, DC 20240 TEL 202-745-8000. (Orders to: Supt. of Documents, U.S. Government Printing Office, Washington, DC 20402) Ed. Russell D. Bowman.
Military

610 SP ISSN 0210-5527
UNIVERSIDAD DE OVIEDO. FACULTAD DE MEDICINA. ARCHIVOS. 1976. a. Universidad de Oviedo, Facultad de Medicina, Oviedo, Spain (Subscr. to: Servicio de Publicaciones, Un. de Oviedo, Calle Jesus Arias de Velasco s/n, 33005 Oviedo, Spain) Ed. Bernardo Marin Fernandez. abstr. illus. circ. 500.

610 VE ISSN 0542-6375
UNIVERSIDAD DEL ZULIA. FACULTAD DE MEDICINA. REVISTA. (Text in Spanish; summaries in English) 1968. irreg. Bs.32($9.50) (or exchange) Universidad del Zulia, Facultad de Medicina, Apartado 526, Maracaibo, Venezuela. Ed. G. Olivares. bibl. charts. illus. index. circ. 1,000. Indexed: Abstr.Hyg. Biol.Abstr. Excerp.Med. Trop.Dis.Bull.

UNIVERSIDAD INDUSTRIAL DE SANTANDER. REVISTA - INVESTIGACIONES. see *ENGINEERING*

610 CK ISSN 0120-0909
UNIVERSIDAD INDUSTRIAL DE SANTANDER. REVISTA - MEDICINA. (Text in Spanish; summaries in English, French, German and Spanish) 1969. irreg. $2 per no. or exchange basis. Universidad Industrial de Santander, Adpo. Aereo 678, Bucaramanga, Santander, Colombia. adv. bk. rev. bibl. charts. illus. cum.index every 5 yrs.

610 BL ISSN 0301-7729
UNIVERSIDADE FEDERAL DE MINAS GERAIS. FACULDADE DE MEDICINA. ANAIS. (Summaries in English and Portuguese) 1943? s-a. Universidade Federal de Minas Gerais, Faculdade de Medicina, Biblioteca "J. Baeta Vianna", Av. Alfredo Balena, 190-C.P. 340, 30.000 Belo Horizonte, Minas Gerais, Brazil. Ed.Bd. bibl. illus. stat. Indexed: Biol.Abstr.

610 BL ISSN 0085-042X
UNIVERSIDADE FEDERAL DO RIO GRANDE DO SUL. FACULDADE DE MEDICINA. ANAIS. (Text in Portuguese; summaries in English) 1938. irreg. free. ‡ Universidade Federal do Rio Grande do Sul, Faculdade de Medicina, Rua Sarmento Leite s/n, 90000 Porto Alegre, R.S, Brazil. Ed. Dr. Alaor Teixeira. circ. 1,000(approx.) Indexed: Biol.Abstr.

610 AU ISSN 0579-7772
UNIVERSITAET INNSBRUCK. MEDIZINISCHE FAKULTAET. ARBEITEN. 1970. irreg. price varies. Oesterreichische Kommissionsbuchhandlung, Maximilianstrasse 17, A-6020 Innsbruck, Austria. Ed. Hans Schroecksnadel.

UNIVERSITY OF CALIFORNIA. LAWRENCE BERKELEY LABORATORY. BIOLOGY AND MEDICINE DIVISION. ANNUAL REPORT. see *BIOLOGY — Biological Chemistry*

610 LB
UNIVERSITY OF LIBERIA. A.M. DOGLIOTTI COLLEGE OF MEDICINE. ANNUAL REPORT OF THE DEAN. a. University of Liberia, A.M. Dogliotti College of Medicine, Monrovia, Liberia.

610 010.7   UK   ISSN 0076-0854
UNIVERSITY OF LONDON. ROYAL
POSTGRADUATE MEDICAL SCHOOL.
REPORT. 1936. a. free. ‡ University of London,
Royal Postgraduate Medical School, Hammersmith
Hospital, Du Cane Rd., London W12 0HS,
England. circ. 500.

610   US
UPDATE IN INTENSIVE CARE AND
EMERGENCY MEDICINE. 1986. irreg. price
varies. Springer-Verlag, 175 Fifth Ave., New York,
NY 10160 TEL 212-460-1500. (Also Berlin,
Heidelberg, Tokyo, Vienna) (reprint service avail.
from ISI)

610   UK
UPDATE POSTGRADUATE CENTRE SERIES.
1970. irreg. Update-Siebert Publications Ltd., Friary
Court, 13-21 High St., Guildford GU1 3DX,
England. Ed. Caley Montgomery. adv. circ. 11,500.
(back issues avail.)

610   GW   ISSN 0340-241X
VEROEFFENTLICHUNGEN AUS DER
PATHOLOGIE. irreg. price varies. Gustav Fischer
Verlag, Wollgrasweg 49, Postfach 720143, 7000
Stuttgart 70, W. Germany (B.R.D.) Indexed:
Ind.Med. Dent.Ind.

610   US
VITAL SIGNS (FRESNO) 1949. a. $12. Fresno
Madera Medical Society, 3425 N. First St., Fresno,
CA 93726. TEL 209-224-4224. Ed.Bd. adv. illus.
circ. 1,100.
  Formerly: Fresno County Medical Society.
Bulletin (ISSN 0016-1160)
  Organization news

VITAMINS AND HORMONES: ADVANCES IN
RESEARCH AND APPLICATIONS. see
PHARMACY AND PHARMACOLOGY

610   UN   ISSN 0512-3054
W H O TECHNICAL REPORT SERIES. (Editions in
Arabic, Chinese, English, French, Russian and
Spanish) 1950. irreg., no.738, 1986. $45. World
Health Organization - Organisation Mondiale de la
Sante, Distribution and Sales, 20 Avenue Appia,
CH-1211 Geneva 27, Switzerland. TEL 91-21-11.
circ. 15,000 (combined) Indexed: Biol.Abstr.
Excerp.Med. I.P.A. Ind.Med. Nutr.Abstr.
Abstr.Hyg. Dent.Ind. Med.Care Rev. Rural
Recreat.Tour.Abstr. Trop.Dis.Bull. World
Agri.Econ.& Rural Sociol.Abstr.

WASHINGTON UNIVERSITY. SCHOOL OF
MEDICINE LIBRARY. LIBRARY
NEWSLETTER; an occasional publication. see
LIBRARY AND INFORMATION SCIENCES

615.89   UK   ISSN 0143-7984
WELLCOME UNIT FOR THE HISTORY OF
MEDICINE. RESEARCH PUBLICATIONS. 1979.
irreg., latest issue 7. price varies. Wellcome Unit for
the History of Medicine, University of Oxford, 45-
47 Banbury Rd., Oxford OX2 6PE, England. bibl.
circ. 200. (back issues avail.)

610   US   ISSN 0271-9347
WISTAR SYMPOSIUM SERIES. 1980. irreg., vol.3,
1985. price varies. (Wistar Institute of Anatomy and
Biology) Alan R. Liss, Inc., 41 E. 11th St., New
York, NY 10003. Indexed: Chem.Abstr.

610   US
WOMEN IN CONTEXT. 1978. irreg. price varies.
Plenum Publishing Corp., 233 Spring St., New
York, NY 10013. TEL 212-620-8047. Ed.Bd.
  Formerly: Women in Context: Development and
Stresses.

WORLD BIOLICENSING REPORT. see *BIOLOGY*

610   US   ISSN 0734-3299
YEAR BOOK OF CRITICAL CARE MEDICINE.
1983. a. $44.95. Year Book Medical Publishers, Inc.,
35 E. Wacker Dr., Chicago, IL 60601. TEL 312-
726-9733. Ed.Bd. illus.

610   US   ISSN 0147-1996
YEAR BOOK OF FAMILY PRACTICE. 1977. a.
$42.95. Year Book Medical Publishers, Inc., 35 E.
Wacker Dr., Chicago, IL 60601. TEL 312-726-9733.
Ed. Robert E. Rakel, M.D. illus.

610   US   ISSN 0084-3873
YEAR BOOK OF MEDICINE. 1933. a. $44.95. Year
Book Medical Publishers, Inc., 35 E. Wacker Dr.,
Chicago, IL 60601. TEL 312-726-9733. Ed. David
E. Rogers, M.D.

616.07   US   ISSN 0084-3946
YEAR BOOK OF PATHOLOGY AND CLINICAL
PATHOLOGY. 1940. a. $44.95. Year Book
Medical Publishers, Inc., 35 E. Wacker Dr.,
Chicago, IL 60601. TEL 312-726-9733. Ed. K.M.
Brinkhous, M.D. illus.
  Pathology

610 371   US
YEAR BOOK OF REHABILITATION. a. $39.95.
Year Book Medical Publishers, Inc., 35 E. Wacker
Dr., Chicago, IL 60601. TEL 312-726-9746. illus.

650 616.1   US
YEAR BOOK OF VASCULAR SURGERY. a.
$39.95. Year Book Medical Publishers, Inc., 35 E.
Wacker Dr., Chicago, IL 60601. TEL 312-726-9733.

615.8   GE   ISSN 0003-9357
ZEITSCHRIFT FUER PHYSIOTHERAPIE.
(Summaries in English, German and Russian) 1949.
irreg.(approx. 6/yr.) M.84. (Gesellschaft fuer
Physiotherapie der DDR) VEB Georg Thieme,
Hainstr. 17/19, Postfach 946, 7010 Leipzig, E.
Germany (D.D.R.) Eds. Prof. H. Jordan , Dr. J.C.
Cordes. adv. bk. rev. abstr. charts. illus. circ. 1,
100. Indexed: Biol.Abstr. Chem.Abstr. Ind.Med.
  Formerly: Archiv fuer Physikalische Therapie,
Balneologie und Klimatologie.
  Physiotherapy

616.07 574.2   GE   ISSN 0044-4030
ZENTRALBLATT FUER ALLGEMEINE
PATHOLOGIE UND PATHOLOGISCHE
ANATOMIE/GENERAL PATHOLOGY,
PATHOLOGICAL ANATOMY. (Text in English
and German) 1890. irreg.(6-12/yr.) M.150 per vol.
(Gesellschaft fuer Pathologie der DDR) VEB
Gustav Fischer Verlag, Villengang 2, Postfache 176,
6900 Jena, E. Germany (D.D.R.) (Co-sponsor:
Gesellschaft fuer Neuropathologie der DDR) Ed.Bd.
bk. rev. abstr. bibl. charts. illus. index. (reprint
service avail. from ISI) Indexed: Biol.Abstr.
Chem.Abstr. Excerp.Med. Ind.Med. Dent.Ind.
Ind.Vet. Vet.Bull.
  Pathology

ZENTRALINSTITUT FUER
VERSUCHSTIERZUCHT. JAHRESBERICHT. see
BIOLOGY

MEDICAL SCIENCES — Abstracting, Bibliographies, Statistics

610 016   BU   ISSN 0001-3536
ABSTRACTS OF BULGARIAN SCIENTIFIC
MEDICAL LITERATURE. (Editions in English
and Russian) vol.9, 1970. q. 11.28 lv.($16.92)
Tsentur za Nauchno-Meditsinska Informatsiia, 8, Ul.
Bialo More, Sofia 27, Bulgaria. Ed. I. Nikolov.
abstr. index. circ. 540 (English edt.) Indexed:
Chem.Abstr.

ABSTRACTS ON HYGIENE AND
COMMUNICABLE DISEASES. see *MEDICAL SCIENCES*

616.4   DK   ISSN 0300-9750
ACTA ENDOCRINOLOGICA CONGRESS.
ADVANCE ABSTRACTS. 1971. irreg. price varies;
free to subscribers to Acta Endocrinologica.
Periodica, Skolegade 12, DK-2500 Valby
Copenhagen, Denmark. Indexed: Biol.Abstr.
Curr.Cont. Ind.Med. Nutr.Abstr.

619   US
ANIMAL RESOURCES; a research resources
directory. 1978. biennial. free. U. S. National
Institutes of Health, Division of Research
Resources, Bldg. 31, Rm. 5B-10, 9000 Rockville
Pike, Bethesda, MD 20205. TEL 301-496-5545.
circ. 9,000.

610 013   PL   ISSN 0066-1937
ANNALES ACADEMIAE MEDICAE
CRACOVIENSIS. INDEX DISSERTATIONUM
EDITARUM. (Text in English, Polish and Russian)
1955. a. price varies. Akademia Medyczna, Krakow,
Botaniczna 3, Krakow, Poland (Dist. by Ars Polona-
Ruch, Krakowskie Przedmiescie 7, Warsaw, Poland)
Ed. Dr. Mieczyslaw Goldsztajn. circ. 1,000.

610 016   CS
ANNUAL OF CZECHOSLOVAK MEDICAL
LITERATURE. (Text in English) 1956. a. free.
Ustav Vedeckych Lekarskych Informaci, Sokolska
31, 121 32 Prague 2, Czechoslovakia. index. circ.
400. (microfiche)

617.6   US   ISSN 0084-6554
ANNUAL REPORT ON DENTAL AUXILIARY
EDUCATION. 1967. a. American Dental
Association, Division of Educational Measurements,
211 E. Chicago Ave., Chicago, IL 60611. TEL 312-
440-2500. Ed. David R. DeMarais. (also avail. in
microform from UMI)

617.6   US   ISSN 0065-8030
ANNUAL REPORT ON DENTAL EDUCATION.
1967. a. American Dental Association, Division of
Educational Measurements, 211 E. Chicago Ave.,
Chicago, IL 60611. TEL 312-440-2500. Ed. David
R. DeMarais. (also avail. in microform from UMI)
  Formerly: Dental Students' Register (ISSN 0065-
8049)

616.8   DK   ISSN 0107-4156
BEFOLKNINGENS FORBRUG AF
PSYKIATRISKE SENGEPLADSER. (Subseries of:
Sygehusstatistik) 1976. triennial. Sundhedsstyrelsen,
St. Kongensgade 1, 1264 Copenhagen K, Denmark.

610 016   BL   ISSN 0067-6675
BIBLIOGRAFIA BRASILEIRA DE MEDICINA.
1937. irreg. Cr.$600($25) Instituto Brasileiro de
Informacao em Ciencia e Tecnologia, SCRN 708/
709 Bloco B Loja 18E 30, 70740 Brasilia DF,
Brazil. bk. rev. circ. 300.
  Formerly (until 1958): Indice-Catalogo Medico
Brasileiro.

617.643   BL   ISSN 0100-6266
BIBLIOGRAFIA BRASILEIRA DE
ODONTOLOGIA. (Text in Portuguese;
introduction and information in English) 1966/67.
biennial. $6 individuals; free to institutions.
Universidade de Sao Paulo, Faculdade de
Odontologia, Seccao de Documentacao
Odontologica, Caixa Postal 8216, 01000 Sao Paulo,
Brazil. circ. 700.

610 016   YU   ISSN 0067-6799
BIBLIOGRAFIJA MEDICINSKE PERIODIKE
JUGOSLAVIJE/INDEX MEDICUS
IUGOSLAVICUS. (Text in Serbo-Croatian;
summaries in English, French, German and Russian)
1966. a. 150 din.($10) Opca Bolnica "Dr. Josip
Kajfes", Miskine 64, Zagreb, Yugoslavia.

BIBLIOGRAPHIES IN THE HISTORY OF
PSYCHOLOGY AND PSYCHIATRY. see
PSYCHOLOGY — Abstracting, Bibliographies, Statistics

610 016   US   ISSN 0363-0161
BIBLIOGRAPHY OF BIOETHICS. 1975. a. price
varies. Kennedy Institute of Ethics, National
Reference Center for Bioethics Literature,
Georgetown University, Washington, DC 20057.
Eds. LeRoy Walters, Tamar Joy Kahn. circ. 1,500.
Indexed: CERDIC.
  ●Also available online. Vendors: National Library of
Medicine.

616.8 016   UK   ISSN 0067-7183
BIBLIOGRAPHY OF DEVELOPMENTAL
MEDICINE AND CHILD NEUROLOGY.
BOOKS AND ARTICLES RECEIVED.
(Supplement to: Developmental Medicine and Child
Neurology ISSN 0012-1622) 1963. a. price varies.
Mac Keith Press, 5A Netherhall Gardens, London
NW3 5RN, England (Dist. in U.S. by: J.B.
Lippincott Co., E. Washington Square, Philadelphia,
PA 19105) Ed. Dr. M.C.O. Bax. circ. 5,200.
(reprint service avail. from UMI) Indexed:
Nutr.Abstr.

MEDICAL SCIENCES — ABSTRACTING, BIBLIOGRAPHIES, STATISTICS

617   US   ISSN 0067-7264
BIBLIOGRAPHY OF SURGERY OF THE HAND. 1967. a. $15. American Society for Surgery of the Hand, c/o Gail M. Gorman, Suite 65, 3025 S. Parker Rd., Aurora, CO 80014. TEL 303-755-4588. Ed. Dr. John P. Adams. circ. 800. (back issues avail.) Indexed: Ind.Med.

610 016   US   ISSN 0067-7280
BIBLIOGRAPHY OF THE HISTORY OF MEDICINE. 1965. a., quinquennial cumulation. price varies. U. S. National Library of Medicine, 8600 Rockville Pike, Bethesda, MD 20894 TEL 202-783-3238. (Orders to: Supt. of Documents, Washington, DC 20402)
History

614 617   CN   ISSN 0317-3720
CANADA. STATISTICS CANADA. SURGICAL PROCEDURES AND TREATMENTS/ INTERVENTIONS CHIRURGICALES ET TRAITEMENTS; a report on the surgical operations and non-surgical procedures performed on in-patients in Canadian hospitals/un rapport sur les interventions chirurgicales et les actes non chirurgicaux, effectues sur les malades hospitalises dans les hopitaux Canadiens. (Catalog 82-208) (Text in English and French) 1969. a. Can.$35($36.50) Statistics Canada, Communications Division, 3rd Floor, R.H. Coats Bldg., Ottawa, Ont. K1A 0T6, Canada TEL 613-993-7276. (Subscr. to: Publications Sales and Services, Ottawa, Ont. K1A 0T6, Canada) (also avail. in microform from MML)

016 610   CN   ISSN 0707-7629
CANADIAN LOCATIONS OF JOURNALS INDEXED FOR MEDICINE/DEPOTS CANADIENS DES REVUES INDEXEES POUR MEDECINE. 1970. a. Can.$37. (National Research Council of Canada) C.I.S.T.I. Publications, Ottawa, Ont. K1A 0S2, Canada. TEL 613-993-3736. circ. 300.
Formerly: Canadian Locations of Journals Indexed in Index Medicus (ISSN 0316-3938)

312.3   NZ
CANCER DATA: NEW REGISTRATIONS AND DEATHS. a. NZ.$22. National Health Statistics Centre, Private Bag 2, Upper Willis St., Wellington, New Zealand. stat. circ. controlled.
Formerly: Cancer Data: Deaths and Cases Reported (ISSN 0548-9415)

CANDLELIGHTERS CHILDHOOD CANCER FOUNDATION/ANNOTATED BIBLIOGRAPHY AND RESOURCE GUIDE. see *BIBLIOGRAPHIES*

616.994 016   US   ISSN 0008-6258
CARCINOGENESIS ABSTRACTS. 1962. m. $70. U.S. National Cancer Institute, Division of Cancer Cause and Prevention, National Institutes of Health, Bethesda, MD 20205 TEL 301-496-4000. (Orders to: Franklin Institute Press, Box 2266, Philadelphia, PA 19103) circ. 3,900.

618   US   ISSN 0190-4981
COMBINED CUMULATIVE INDEX TO PEDIATRICS.* 1979. triennial. $24.50. Numarc Book Corporation, 50 Alcona Ave., Buffalo, NY 14226. TEL 716-834-1390. Ed. Arnold C. Westphal. circ. 2,000. (back issues avail.)

610 016   US   ISSN 0090-1377
CUMULATED ABRIDGED INDEX MEDICUS. a. $43. U. S. National Library of Medicine, 8600 Rockville Pike, Bethesda, MD 20894 TEL 202-783-3238. (Orders to: Supt. of Documents, Washington, DC 20402) circ. 1,500.

610 016   US   ISSN 0090-1423
CUMULATED INDEX MEDICUS. a. $204. U. S. National Library of Medicine, 8600 Rockville Pike, Bethesda, MD 20894 TEL 202-783-3238. (Orders to: Supt. of Documents, Washington, DC 20402) circ. 5,000. (also avail. in microfilm from UMI; reprint service avail. from UMI)
Supersedes: Quarterly Cumulated Index Medicus.

610.73 016   US   ISSN 0146-5554
CUMULATIVE INDEX TO NURSING & ALLIED HEALTH LITERATURE (C I N A H L) 1961. bi-m. and a. $168 includes 5 bi-m. issues. (C I N A H L, Corp.) Glendale Adventist Medical Center, Box 871, Glendale, CA 91209. TEL 818-577-7233. Ed. Delauna Lockwood. adv. cum.index: 1956 to date. circ. 5,300. (also avail. in microform from UMI; reprint service avail. from UMI)
●Also available online. Vendors: BRS, BRS/ Saunders Colleague, Data-Star, DIALOG.
Incorporating: Nursing and Allied Health Index (ISSN 0744-8732); Which was formerly (1956-1976) : Nursing Literature Index; until 1977: Cumulative Index to Nursing Literature (ISSN 0011-3018); Incorporating: C I N A H L'S List of Subject Headings; Which was formerly (until 1977): Cumulative Index to Nursing Literature, Nursing Subject Headings (ISSN 0070-1793)

610 016   US
CURRENT CONTENTS/CLINICAL MEDICINE. Short title: C C/C M. (Includes Author Index and Address Directory, Current Book Contents and Title Word Index) 1973. w. $283 domestic. Institute for Scientific Information, 3501 Market St., Philadelphia, PA 19104 TEL 215-386-0100. (And 132 High St., Uxbridge, Middlesex, UB8 1DP, England) (also avail. in magnetic tape) Indexed: Sci.Cit.Inc. Compumath. Curr.Lit.Fam.Plan. Ind.Sci.Rev.
●Also available online. Vendors: BRS.
Formerly: Current Contents/Clinical Pratice (ISSN 0091-1704)

610 016   UK   ISSN 0011-3999
CURRENT WORK IN THE HISTORY OF MEDICINE; an international bibliography. 1954. q. £13 to individuals; institutions £20. (Wellcome Institute for the History of Medicine) Professional & Scientific Publications, Tavistock House East, Tavistock Square, London WC1H 9JR, England (U.S. distr. addr.: Box 560B, Kennebunkport, ME 04046) bibl. circ. 750.
History of medicine

618.92 016   US   ISSN 0070-2455
CYSTIC FIBROSIS CLUB ABSTRACTS.* no.3, 1962. a. free. Cystic Fibrosis Foundation, 6931 Arlington Rd., No. 200, Bethesda, MD 20814-5205. Ed. Anne Topham. circ. 2,000. Indexed: Excerp.Med.

617.6 016   US   ISSN 0011-8486
DENTAL ABSTRACTS. 1956. m. $24. American Dental Association, 211 E. Chicago Ave., Chicago, IL 60611. TEL 312-440-2500. Ed. Ellen Wade Beals. adv. bk. rev. abstr. charts. illus. stat. index. circ. 8,000. (also avail. in microform from UMI; reprint service avail. from UMI) Indexed: Biol.Abstr. Ind.Dent.Lit.

617.6   US
DENTAL STATISTICS HANDBOOK. irreg. (every 1-2 yrs.) $7.95. American Dental Association, Bureau of Economic Research and Statistics, 211 E. Chicago Ave., Chicago, IL 60611. TEL 312-440-2500.

616.8 016   US   ISSN 0012-2769
DIGEST OF NEUROLOGY & PSYCHIATRY. 1932. 10/yr. free to physicians and medical libraries. Institute of Living, 400 Washington St., Hartford, CT 06106. TEL 203-241-6824. Ed. Dr. William L. Webb, Jr. bk. rev. abstr. index. circ. 6,000. (also avail. in microfilm from UMI; reprint service avail. from UMI) Indexed: Rehabil.Lit.

616.4   US   ISSN 0749-8020
ENDOCRINOLOGY ABSTRACTS. m. $375. Cambridge Scientific Abstracts, 5161 River Rd., Bethesda, MD 20816. TEL 301-951-1400.

574.92 016   NE   ISSN 0014-4053
EXCERPTA MEDICA. SECTION 1: ANATOMY, ANTHROPOLOGY, EMBRYOLOGY & HISTOLOGY. 1947. 10/yr. fl.570. Elsevier Science Publishers B.V., Box 211, 1000 AE Amsterdam, Netherlands. adv. bk. rev. abstr. index; cum.index. Indexed: Chem.Abstr. Excerp.Med. Lab.Haz.Bull.
●Also available online. Vendors: BRS, DIALOG.

612 016   NE   ISSN 0014-4061
EXCERPTA MEDICA. SECTION 2: PHYSIOLOGY. 1948. 30/yr. $450. Elsevier Science Publishers B.V., Box 211, 1000 AE Amsterdam, Netherlands. adv. bk. rev. abstr. charts. index; cum.index. Indexed: Chem.Abstr. Excerp.Med.
●Also available online. Vendors: BRS, DIALOG.

616.4 016   NE   ISSN 0014-407X
EXCERPTA MEDICA. SECTION 3: ENDOCRINOLOGY. 1947. 20/yr. $306. Elsevier Science Publishers B.V., Box 211, 1000 AE Amsterdam, Netherlands. adv. bk. rev. abstr. charts. index. cum.index. Indexed: Chem.Abstr. Excerp.Med.
●Also available online. Vendors: BRS, DIALOG.

576 016   NE
EXCERPTA MEDICA. SECTION 4: MICROBIOLOGY: BACTERIOLOGY, MYCOLOGY AND PARASITOLOGY. 1948. 30/yr. $306. Elsevier Science Publishers B.V., Box 211, 1000 AE Amsterdam, Netherlands. Ed.Bd. adv. bk. rev. abstr. index. cum.index. Indexed: Chem.Abstr. Excerp.Med.
●Also available online. Vendors: BRS, DIALOG.
Formerly: Excerpta Medica. Section 4: Microbiology-Bacteriology, Virology, Mycology and Parasitology (ISSN 0014-4088)

616.07 016 574.2   NE   ISSN 0014-4096
EXCERPTA MEDICA. SECTION 5: GENERAL PATHOLOGY AND PATHOLOGICAL ANATOMY. 1948. 20/yr. fl.960. Elsevier Science Publishers B.V., Box 211, 1000 AE Amsterdam, Netherlands. adv. bk. rev. abstr. index; cum.index. Indexed: Chem.Abstr. Excerp.Med.
●Also available online. Vendors: BRS, DIALOG.

616.026 016   NE   ISSN 0014-410X
EXCERPTA MEDICA. SECTION 6: INTERNAL MEDICINE. 1947. 30/yr. fl.1110. Elsevier Science Publishers B.V., Box 211, 1000 AE Amsterdam, Netherlands. Ed.Bd. adv. bk. rev. abstr. index. cum.index. Indexed: Chem.Abstr. Excerp.Med.
●Also available online. Vendors: BRS, DIALOG.

618.92 016   NE
EXCERPTA MEDICA. SECTION 7: PEDIATRICS AND PEDIATRIC SURGERY. 1947. 20/yr. fl.960. Elsevier Science Publishers B.V., Box 211, 1000 AE Amsterdam, Netherlands. adv. bk. rev. abstr. cum.index. Indexed: Excerp.Med.
●Also available online. Vendors: BRS, DIALOG.
Formerly: Excerpta Medica. Section 7: Pediatrics (ISSN 0014-4118)

616.8 016   NE   ISSN 0014-4126
EXCERPTA MEDICA. SECTION 8: NEUROLOGY AND NEUROSURGERY. 1948. 32/yr. fl.1540. Elsevier Science Publishers B.V., Box 211, 1000 AE Amsterdam, Netherlands. Ed.Bd. adv. bk. rev. abstr. index; cum.index. Indexed: Excerp.Med.
●Also available online. Vendors: BRS, DIALOG.

617 016   NE   ISSN 0014-4134
EXCERPTA MEDICA. SECTION 9: SURGERY. 1947. 20/yr. fl.960. Elsevier Science Publishers B.V., Box 211, 1000 AE Amsterdam, Netherlands. Ed.Bd. adv. bk. rev. abstr. index. cum.index. Indexed: Chem.Abstr. Excerp.Med.
●Also available online. Vendors: BRS, DIALOG.

618 016   NE   ISSN 0014-4142
EXCERPTA MEDICA. SECTION 10: OBSTETRICS AND GYNECOLOGY. 1948. 20/yr. fl.960. Elsevier Science Publishers B.V., Box 211, 1000 AE Amsterdam, Netherlands. Ed.Bd. adv. bk. rev. abstr. index. cum.index. Indexed: Chem.Abstr. Excerp.Med.
●Also available online. Vendors: BRS, DIALOG.

616.21 016   NE   ISSN 0014-4150
EXCERPTA MEDICA. SECTION 11: OTORHINOLARYNGOLOGY. 1948. 10/yr. fl.655. Elsevier Science Publishers B.V., Box 211, 1000 AE Amsterdam, Netherlands. adv. bk. rev. abstr. index. cum.index. Indexed: Chem.Abstr. Excerp.Med.
●Also available online. Vendors: BRS, DIALOG.

MEDICAL SCIENCES — ABSTRACTING, BIBLIOGRAPHIES, STATISTICS

617.7 016   NE   ISSN 0014-4169
EXCERPTA MEDICA. SECTION 12: OPHTHALMOLOGY. 1947. 10/yr. fl.570. Elsevier Science Publishers B.V., Box 211, 1000 AE Amsterdam, Netherlands. adv. bk. rev. abstr. index. cum.index. Indexed: Chem.Abstr. Excerp.Med.
●Also available online. Vendors: BRS, DIALOG.

616.5 016   NE   ISSN 0014-4177
EXCERPTA MEDICA. SECTION 13: DERMATOLOGY AND VENEREOLOGY. 1947. 10/yr. fl.570. Elsevier Science Publishers B.V., Box 211, 1000 AE Amsterdam, Netherlands. adv. bk. rev. abstr. index. cum.index. Indexed: Chem.Abstr.
●Also available online. Vendors: BRS, DIALOG.

615.842 016   NE   ISSN 0014-4185
EXCERPTA MEDICA. SECTION 14: RADIOLOGY. 1947. 20/yr. fl.960. Elsevier Science Publishers B.V., Box 211, 1000 AE Amsterdam, Netherlands. adv. bk. rev. abstr. index. cum.index. Indexed: Chem.Abstr. Excerp.Med.
●Also available online. Vendors: BRS, DIALOG.

616.2 016   NE   ISSN 0014-4193
EXCERPTA MEDICA. SECTION 15: CHEST DISEASES, THORACIC SURGERY AND TUBERCULOSIS. 1948. 20/yr. $294. Elsevier Science Publishers B.V., Box 211, 1000 AE Amsterdam, Netherlands. adv. bk. rev. abstr. index. cum.index. Indexed: Chem.Abstr. Excerp.Med.
●Also available online. Vendors: BRS, DIALOG.

616.994 016   NE   ISSN 0014-4207
EXCERPTA MEDICA. SECTION 16: CANCER. 1953. 32/yr. $1540. Elsevier Science Publishers B.V., Box 211, 1000 AE Amsterdam, Netherlands. adv. bk. rev. abstr. index. cum.index. Indexed: Chem.Abstr. Excerp.Med.
●Also available online. Vendors: BRS, DIALOG.

EXCERPTA MEDICA. SECTION 17: PUBLIC HEALTH, SOCIAL MEDICINE & HYGIENE. see *PUBLIC HEALTH AND SAFETY — Abstracting, Bibliographies, Statistics*

612 016   NE   ISSN 0014-4231
EXCERPTA MEDICA. SECTION 19: REHABILITATION AND PHYSICAL MEDICINE. 1958. 10/yr. fl.545. Elsevier Science Publishers B.V., Box 211, 1000 AE Amsterdam, Netherlands. adv. bk. rev. abstr. index. cum.index. Indexed: Excerp.Med.
●Also available online. Vendors: BRS, DIALOG.

EXCERPTA MEDICA. SECTION 20: GERONTOLOGY AND GERIATRICS. see *GERONTOLOGY AND GERIATRICS — Abstracting, Bibliographies, Statistics*

615.842 016   NE   ISSN 0014-4274
EXCERPTA MEDICA. SECTION 23: NUCLEAR MEDICINE. 1964. 20/yr. fl.960. Elsevier Science Publishers B.V., Box 211, 1000 AE Amsterdam, Netherlands. adv. bk. rev. abstr. index. cum.index. Indexed: Chem.Abstr. Excerp.Med.
●Also available online. Vendors: BRS, DIALOG.

617.96 016   NE   ISSN 0014-4282
EXCERPTA MEDICA. SECTION 24: ANESTHESIOLOGY. 1966. 10/yr. fl.545. Elsevier Science Publishers B.V., Box 211, 1000 AE Amsterdam, Netherlands. adv. bk. rev. abstr. index. cum.index. Indexed: Excerp.Med.
●Also available online. Vendors: BRS, DIALOG.

616.15 016   NE   ISSN 0014-4290
EXCERPTA MEDICA. SECTION 25: HEMATOLOGY. 1967. 20/yr. $312. Elsevier Science Publishers B.V., Box 211, 1000 AE Amsterdam, Netherlands. Ed.Bd. adv. bk. rev. abstr. index. cum.index. Indexed: Excerp.Med.
●Also available online. Vendors: BRS, DIALOG.

615.37 016   NE   ISSN 0014-4304
EXCERPTA MEDICA. SECTION 26: IMMUNOLOGY, SEROLOGY AND TRANSPLANTATION. 1967. 30/yr. $418. Elsevier Science Publishers B.V., Box 211, 1000 AE Amsterdam, Netherlands. adv. bk. rev. abstr. index. cum.index. Indexed: Excerp.Med.
●Also available online. Vendors: BRS, DIALOG.

610.28 016   NE   ISSN 0014-4312
EXCERPTA MEDICA. SECTION 27: BIOPHYSICS, BIO-ENGINEERING AND MEDICAL INSTRUMENTATION. 1967. 10/yr. $102. Elsevier Science Publishers B.V., Box 211, 1000 AE Amsterdam, Netherlands. adv. bk. rev. abstr. index. cum.index. Indexed: Excerp.Med.
●Also available online. Vendors: BRS, DIALOG.
Biomedical engineering

616.6 016   NE   ISSN 0014-4320
EXCERPTA MEDICA. SECTION 28: UROLOGY AND NEPHROLOGY. 1967. 20/yr. $294. Elsevier Science Publishers B.V., Box 211, 1000 AE Amsterdam, Netherlands. Ed.Bd. adv. bk. rev. abstr. index. cum.index. Indexed: Excerp.Med.
●Also available online. Vendors: BRS, DIALOG.

574.192 016   NE   ISSN 0300-5372
EXCERPTA MEDICA. SECTION 29: CLINICAL BIOCHEMISTRY. 1948. 40/yr. $508. Elsevier Science Publishers B.V., Box 211, 1000 AE Amsterdam, Netherlands. adv. bk. rev. abstr. charts. index. cum.index. Indexed: Chem.Abstr. Excerp.Med.
●Also available online. Vendors: BRS, DIALOG.
Formerly: Excerpta Medica. Section 29: Biochemistry (ISSN 0014-4339)

616.742 016   NE   ISSN 0014-4355
EXCERPTA MEDICA. SECTION 31: ARTHRITIS AND RHEUMATISM. 1965. 10/yr. $172. Elsevier Science Publishers B.V., Box 211, 1000 AE Amsterdam, Netherlands. adv. bk. rev. abstr. index. cum.index. Indexed: Excerp.Med.
●Also available online. Vendors: BRS, DIALOG.

616.89 016   NE   ISSN 0014-4363
EXCERPTA MEDICA. SECTION 32: PSYCHIATRY. 1948. 20/yr. $312. Elsevier Science Publishers B.V., Box 211, 1000 AE Amsterdam, Netherlands. adv. bk. rev. abstr. index. cum.index. Indexed: Excerp.Med.
●Also available online. Vendors: BRS, DIALOG.

617.3 016   NE   ISSN 0014-4371
EXCERPTA MEDICA. SECTION 33: ORTHOPEDIC SURGERY. 1956. 10/yr. $102. Elsevier Science Publishers B.V., Box 211, 1000 AE Amsterdam, Netherlands. adv. bk. rev. abstr. index. cum.index. Indexed: Excerp.Med.
●Also available online. Vendors: BRS, DIALOG.

617.95 016   NE   ISSN 0014-438X
EXCERPTA MEDICA. SECTION 34: PLASTIC SURGERY. 1970. 10/yr. $102. Elsevier Science Publishers B.V., Box 211, 1000 AE Amsterdam, Netherlands. adv. bk. rev. abstr. index. cum.index. Indexed: Excerp.Med.
●Also available online. Vendors: BRS, DIALOG.

613.62 016   NE   ISSN 0014-4398
EXCERPTA MEDICA. SECTION 35: OCCUPATIONAL HEALTH AND INDUSTRIAL MEDICINE. 1971. 10/yr. $151. Elsevier Science Publishers B.V., Box 211, 1000 AE Amsterdam, Netherlands. adv. bk. rev. abstr. index. cum.index. Indexed: Excerp.Med. Ergon.Abstr.
●Also available online. Vendors: BRS, DIALOG.

EXCERPTA MEDICA. SECTION 36: HEALTH ECONOMICS AND HOSPITAL MANAGEMENT. see *HOSPITALS — Abstracting, Bibliographies, Statistics*

610 016   NE   ISSN 0001-8848
EXCERPTA MEDICA. SECTION 38: ADVERSE REACTIONS TITLES. 1966. 12/yr. Elsevier Science Publishers B.V., Box 211, 1000 AE Amsterdam, Netherlands. adv. bk. rev. index. cum.index. Indexed: Excerp.Med.
●Also available online. Vendors: BRS, DIALOG.

EXCERPTA MEDICA. SECTION 46: ENVIRONMENTAL HEALTH AND POLLUTION CONTROL. see *ENVIRONMENTAL STUDIES — Abstracting, Bibliographies, Statistics*

616.92 016 576.64   NE   ISSN 0304-4084
EXCERPTA MEDICA. SECTION 47: VIROLOGY. 1971. 10/yr. $102. Elsevier Science Publishers B.V., Box 211, 1000 AE Amsterdam, Netherlands. adv. bk. rev. Indexed: Excerp.Med.
●Also available online. Vendors: BRS, DIALOG.

616.3 016   NE   ISSN 0031-3580
EXCERPTA MEDICA. SECTION 48: GASTROENTEROLOGY. 1971. 20/yr. $294. Elsevier Science Publishers B.V., Box 211, 1000 AE Amsterdam, Netherlands. adv. bk. rev. abstr. index; cum.index. Indexed: Excerp.Med.
●Also available online. Vendors: BRS, DIALOG.

340.6 016   NE   ISSN 0031-0743
EXCERPTA MEDICA. SECTION 49: FORENSIC SCIENCE. 1975. 10/yr. $102. Elsevier Science Publishers B.V., Box 211, 1000 AE Amsterdam, Netherlands. adv. bk. rev. Indexed: Excerp.Med.
●Also available online. Vendors: BRS, DIALOG.

616.853 016   NE   ISSN 0303-8459
EXCERPTA MEDICA. SECTION 50: EPILEPSY. 1971. 12/yr. $132. Elsevier Science Publishers B.V., Box 211, 1000 AE Amsterdam, Netherlands. adv. bk. rev. abstr. index; cum.index. Indexed: Excerp.Med.
●Also available online. Vendors: BRS, DIALOG.
Epilepsy

016 616.998   NE   ISSN 0165-2222
EXCERPTA MEDICA. SECTION 51: LEPROSY AND RELATED SUBJECTS. 1979. m. $65. (Netherlands Leprosy Relief Association) Elsevier Science Publishers B.V., Box 211, 1000 AE Amsterdam, Netherlands. Indexed: Excerp.Med.
●Also available online. Vendors: BRS, DIALOG.

610 016   AT   ISSN 0227-2393
F A M L I. (Family Medicine Literature Index) 1980. a. Can.$48. World Organisation of National Colleges, Academies and Academic Associations of General Practitioners-Family Physicians, CN , 70 Jolimont St., 4th Fl., Jolimont, Vic. 3002, Australia (Subscr. to: College of Family Physicians of Canada, 4000 Leslie St., Willowdale, Ont. M2K 2R9, Canada) Ed. Lynn Dunikowski. cum.index. circ. 400. (back issues avail.)

614.84   UK   ISSN 0260-3098
FIRE STATISTICS UNITED KINGDOM. 1946. a. price varies. Home Office, 50 Queen Anne's Gate, London SW1H 9AT, England. circ. 900.
Former titles (until 1977): United Kingdom Fire Statistics; United Kingdom Fire and Loss Statistics (ISSN 0082-7959)

619   US
GENERAL CLINICAL RESEARCH CENTERS; a research resources directory. 1978. biennial. free. U.S. National Institutes of Health, Division of Research Resources, Bldg. 31, Rm. 5B-10, 9000 Rockville Pike, Bethesda, MD 20205. TEL 301-496-4000. circ. 9,000.

616.863 310   UK
GREAT BRITAIN. HOME OFFICE. STATISTICS OF THE MISUSE OF DRUGS IN THE UNITED KINGDOM, SUPPLEMENTARY TABLES. 1978. a. Home Office, 50 Queen Anne's Gate, London SW1H 9AT, England.

610   US   ISSN 0163-0458
HEALTH DEVICES ALERTS; a summary of reported problems, hazards, recalls, and updates. 1976. w. $235 (free to members) (Emergency Care Research Institute) E C R I, 5200 Butler Pike, Plymouth Meeting, PA 19462. TEL 215-825-6000. abstr. (back issues avail.)

610 310 574   GW   ISSN 0303-4577
I M B I S; Information fuer medizinisch-biologische Statistik und deren Grenzgebiete. 1973. irreg. free. Universitaet Marburg, Institut fuer Medizinisch-biologische Statistik, Ernst-Giller-str. 20, 3550 Marburg 1, W. Germany (B.R.D.) Ed. Dr. Peter Ihm. adv. circ. 300.

615.37 016   US   ISSN 0307-112X
IMMUNOLOGY ABSTRACTS. 1976. m. $532. Cambridge Scientific Abstracts, 5161 River Rd., Bethesda, MD 20816. TEL 301-951-1400. Ed. Pam Clare. adv. (also avail. in magnetic tape) Indexed: Cal.Tiss.Abstr. Chemorec.Abstr. Oncol.Abstr.
●Also available online. Vendors: DIALOG.

610 016   US   ISSN 0019-3879
INDEX MEDICUS. (Medical Subject Headings (MeSH) is published as Part 2 of the January Index Medicus) 1960. m. $163. U.S. National Library of Medicine, 8600 Rockville Pike, Bethesda, MD 20894 TEL 202-783-3238. (Orders to: Supt. of Documents, Washington, DC 20402) circ. 6,000. (also avail. in microform from MIM,UMI) Indexed: JAMA. Popul.Ind.
●Also available online. Vendors: DIALOG.

INDEX MEDICUS LATINOAMERICANO. see *ABSTRACTING AND INDEXING SERVICES*

617.6 016   US   ISSN 0019-3992
INDEX TO DENTAL LITERATURE; an alphabetical author and subject index to dental literature. q. (annual cumulation) $125 (including bound vol.) American Dental Association, Bureau of Library Services, 211 E. Chicago Ave., Chicago, IL 60611. TEL 312-440-2500. index. circ. 1,100. (also avail. in microform from UMI; reprint service avail. from UMI)
●Also available online. Vendors: DIALOG.

610 016   II   ISSN 0019-4042
INDEX TO INDIAN MEDICAL PERIODICALS. (Text in English) 1959. q. price varies per vol. Controller of Publications, Civil Lines, Delhi 110054, India. Ed. D.B. Bisht. bk. rev. quarterly index. circ. 250.

610 016   SP   ISSN 0019-7068
INDICE MEDICO ESPANOL. 1965. q. 3,000 ptas. (Centro de Documentation e Informatica Biomedica) Universidad de Valencia, Facultad de Medicina, Avda. Blasco Ibanez - 17, 46010 Valencia, Spain. Dir. Maria-Luz Terrada Ferrandis. circ. 5,000. (reprint service avail.) Indexed: Nutr.Abstr.

011 610   GW   ISSN 0340-8094
INDICES NATURWISSENSCHAFTLICH-MEDIZINISCHER PERIODICA BIS 1850. 1971. irreg., vol.4, 1987. price varies. Anton Hiersemann Verlag, Rosenbergstr. 113, Postfach 723, 7000 Stuttgart 1, W. Germany (B.R.D.) Ed. Armin Geus.

340.6 016   US   ISSN 0098-2393
INTERNATIONAL BIBLIOGRAPHY OF THE FORENSIC SCIENCES. 1975. a. $20. International Reference Organization in Forensic Medicine and Sciences, c/o Wm. G. Eckert, M.D., Box 8282, Wichita, KS 67208. TEL 316-268-5000.

617.11 016   US   ISSN 0090-0575
INTERNATIONAL BIBLIOGRAPHY ON BURNS. 1969. a. $20 includes annual supplement. National Institute for Burn Medicine, 909 E. Ann St., Ann Arbor, MI 48104. TEL 313-769-9000. Ed. Irving Feller, M.D. circ. 1,000.

610.73 016   US
INTERNATIONAL NURSING INDEX INCLUDING NURSING CITATION INDEX. 1966. q. $250. (American Nurses' Association) American Journal of Nursing Co., 555 W. 57th St., New York, NY 10019. TEL 212-582-8820. Ed. Frederick W. Pattison. index. circ. 1,917. (also avail. in microform from UMI; reprint service avail. from UMI) Indexed: JAMA.
●Also available online. Vendors: BRS, DIALOG.
Formerly: International Nursing Index (ISSN 0020-8124)
Covers over 240 international nursing journals

610 315   JA
JAPAN. MINISTRY OF HEALTH AND WELFARE. STATISTICS AND INFORMATION DEPARTMENT. STATISTICS ON ACTIVITIES OF HEALTH CENTERS. a. 2.000 Yen. Ministry of Health and Welfare, Statistics and Information Department, 7-3 Ichigaya-Honmura cho, Shinjuku-ku, Tokyo 162, Japan (Order from: Health & Welfare Statistics Association, c/o Mezon Azabu, 5-13-14 Roppongi, Minato-ku, Tokyo, Japan)

616.9 315   JA
JAPAN. MINISTRY OF HEALTH AND WELFARE. STATISTICS AND INFORMATION DEPARTMENT. STATISTICAL REPORT ON COMMUNICABLE DISEASES. a. 1.700 Yen. Ministry of Health and Welfare, Statistics and Information Department, 42 Ichigaya-Honmura cho, Shinjuku-ku, Tokyo 162, Japan (Order from: Health & Welfare Statistics Association, c/o Mezon Azabu, 5-13-14 Roppongi, Minato-ku, Tokyo, Japan)
Supersedes in part: Japan. Ministry of Health and Welfare. Statistics and Information Department. Statistical Report on Communicable Diseases and Food Poisonings.

616.9 315   JA
JAPAN. MINISTRY OF HEALTH AND WELFARE. STATISTICS AND INFORMATION DEPARTMENT. STATISTICAL REPORT ON FOOD POISONINGS. a. 1.200 Yen. Ministry of Health and Welfare, Statistics and Information Department, 7-3 Ichigaya-Honmura Cho, Shinjuku-ku, Tokyo 162, Japan (Subscr. to: Health and Welfare Statistics Association, c/o Mezon Azabu, 5-13-14 Roppongi, Minato-ku, Tokyo, Japan)
Supersedes in part: Japan. Ministry of Health and Welfare. Statistics and Information Department. Statistical Report on Communicable Diseases and Food Poisonings.

610   KE
KENYA MEDICAL ABSTRACTS. 1980. irreg. University of Nairobi, Medical Library, Box 30588, Nairobi, Kenya. Ed. R. Kiathe. circ. 150.

610 016   IS
KOROTH; a bulletin devoted to the history of medicine and science. (Text in English and Hebrew) 1952. a. $17. Israel Institute of the History of Medicine, Box 432, Jerusalem, Israel. Ed. Joshua O. Leibowitz, Samuel S. Kottek. bk. rev. circ. 250.
Formerly: Jerusalem Historical Medical Publications (ISSN 0449-4881)
History

610 016   SW   ISSN 0075-9813
LIST BIO-MED; BIOMEDICAL SERIALS IN SCANDINAVIAN LIBRARIES. (Text in English) 1965. irreg. Kr.125. Karolinska Institutets Bibliotek och Informationscentral, Box 60201, S-104 01 Stockholm, Sweden. circ. 600.

011 610   PR
LIST OF CURRENT SERIAL PUBLICATIONS BEING RECEIVED AT THE UNIVERSITY OF PUERTO RICO MEDICAL SCIENCES CAMPUS LIBRARY. a. free. Universidad de Puerto Rico, Medical Sciences Campus Library, G.P.O. Box 5067, San Juan, PR 00936. (processed)

610   US   ISSN 0093-3821
LIST OF JOURNALS INDEXED IN INDEX MEDICUS. 1960. a. $10. U.S. National Library of Medicine, 8600 Rockville Pike, Bethesda, MD 20894 TEL 202-783-3238. (Orders to: Supt. of Documents, Washington, DC 20402) circ. 3,500.

610 015   US
LIST OF SERIALS INDEXED FOR ONLINE USERS. 1980. a. $12 for 1986 edt. U.S. National Library of Medicine, 8600 Rockville Pike, Bethesda, MD 20894 TEL 202-487-4650. (Orders to: NTIS, Springfield, VA 22161)
Formerly: List of Serials and Monographs Indexed for Online Users (ISSN 0196-755X)

610 016   US   ISSN 0000-085X
MEDICAL AND HEALTH CARE BOOKS AND SERIALS IN PRINT; an index to literature in health sciences. 1972. a. $129.95. R.R. Bowker Company, Database Publishing Group, 245 W. 17th St., New York, NY 10011. TEL 800-521-8110.
●Also available online. Vendors: BRS, DIALOG.
Former titles: Medical Books and Serials in Print (ISSN 0000-0574); Medical Books in Print (ISSN 0076-5929)

MEDICAL CARE REVIEW. see *PUBLIC HEALTH AND SAFETY — Abstracting, Bibliographies, Statistics*

618   DK   ISSN 0107-7597
MEDICINSK FOEDSELSSTATISTIK. 1973. biennial. Kr.25. Sundhedsstyrelsen, St. Kongensgade, 1264 Copenhagen K, Denmark (Orders to: Statens Informationtjeneste, Bredgade 20, 1260 Copenhagen K, Denmark)

610   US   ISSN 0097-9732
MEDOC: INDEX TO U S GOVERNMENT PUBLICATIONS IN THE MEDICAL AND HEALTH SCIENCES. 1975. q. $68. Spencer S. Eccles Health Sciences Library, University of Utah, Bldg. 89, Salt Lake City, UT 84112. TEL 801-581-5268. Ed. Michael Thelin. bk. rev. circ. 400.

616.8   NZ   ISSN 0548-992X
MENTAL HEALTH DATA. a. price varies. National Health Statistics Centre, Private Bag 2, Upper Willis St., Wellington, New Zealand. circ. controlled.

616.89   UK   ISSN 0260-5252
MENTAL HEALTH STATISTICS FOR WALES. 1981. a. £3. Welsh Office, Economic and Statistical Services Division, New Crown Bldg., Cathays Park, Cardiff CF1 3NQ, Wales. Ed. E. Swires-Hennessy. stat. circ. 500.

619   US
MINORITY BIOMEDICAL RESEARCH SUPPORT PROGRAM; a research resources directory. 1977. biennial. free. U.S. National Institutes of Health, Division of Research Resources, Bldg. 31, Rm. 5B-10, 9000 Rockville Pike, Bethesda, MD 20205. TEL 301-496-5545. circ. 9,000.
Formerly: Minority Biomedical Support Program.

610 016   US   ISSN 0027-9641
NATIONAL LIBRARY OF MEDICINE. CURRENT CATALOG. 1966. q. with annual cumulation. $26 for q.; price of annual cumulation varies. U.S. National Library of Medicine, 8600 Rockville Pike, Bethesda, MD 20894 TEL 202-783-3238. (Orders to: Supt. of Documents, Washington, DC 20402) Indexed: Popul.Ind.
Incorporating (1965-1980): Notes for Medical Catalogers (ISSN 0078-2025)

016 610   US   ISSN 0083-2251
NATIONAL LIBRARY OF MEDICINE. LITERATURE SEARCH SERIES. 1966. irreg. free. ‡ U.S. National Library of Medicine, Reference Section, 8600 Rockville Pike, Bethesda, MD 20894. TEL 301-496-6095. circ. 1,000.

616.8 011   US   ISSN 0141-7711
NEUROSCIENCES ABSTRACTS. 1983. m. $415. Cambridge Scientific Abstracts, 5161 River Rd., Bethesda, MD 20816. Ed. M. Brazier.
●Also available online. Vendors: DIALOG.

618.92 319.4   NZ   ISSN 0111-8617
NEW ZEALAND. NATIONAL HEALTH STATISTICS CENTRE. FETAL AND INFANT DEATHS. 1964. a. price varies. National Health Statistics Centre, Private Bag 2, Upper Willis St., Wellington, New Zealand. circ. controlled circ.

617.6   US
NORTHWESTERN UNIVERSITY. DENTAL SCHOOL LIBRARY. CURRENT SUBSCRIPTIONS LIST. 1970. a. free. Northwestern University, Dental School Library, 311 East Chicago Ave., Chicago, IL 60611. TEL 312-649-8331. bibl. circ. 350. (processed)

610   NO   ISSN 0800-403X
NORWAY. STATISTISK SENTRALBYRAA. HELSEPERSONELLSTATISTIKK. (Subseries of Norges Offisielle Statistikk) 1979. biennial. Statistisk Sentralbyraa, Box 8131-Dep., 0033 Oslo 1, Norway. circ. 2,000.
Supersedes: Norway. Statistisk Sentralbyraa. Legestatistikk (ISSN 0377-8886)

016 610.73   US   ISSN 0195-3354
NURSING ABSTRACTS. 1979. bi-m. $295. Nursing Abstracts Co. Inc., Box 295, Forest Hills, NY 11375. Ed. D. Dolgins. abstr. index. (back issues avail.)

616.4   US
ONCOLOGY ABSTRACTS. 1986. m. $475. Cambridge Scientific Abstracts, 5161 River Rd., Bethesda, MD 20816. TEL 301-951-1400. index. Indexed: Cal.Tiss.Abstr. Chemorec.Abstr. Oncol.Abstr.

616.4 016　　　FR
P A S C A L EXPLORE. PART 64:
ENDOCRINOLOGIE HUMAINE ET
EXPERIMENTALE. ENDOCRINOPATHIES.
1985. 10/yr. 1080 F. Centre National de la
Recherche Scientifique, Centre de Documentation
Scientifique et Technique, Service des
Abonnements, 26 rue Boyer, 75971 Paris Cedex 20,
France.
　　Supersedes in part: Bulletin Signaletique. Part
361: Reproduction. Gynecologie. Obstetrique.
Embryologie. Endocrinologie (ISSN 0245-9884)

150　616.89 016　　　FR
P A S C A L EXPLORE. PART 65:
PSYCHOLOGIE. PSYCHOPATHOLOGIE.
PSYCHIATRIE. 1985. 10/yr. 1170 F. Centre
National de la Recherche Scientifique, Centre de
Documentation Scientifique et Technique, Service
des Abonnements, 26 rue Boyer, 75971 Paris 20,
France. abstr. index. cum.index. (also avail. in
microform from MIM)
　　Supersedes (1961-1984): Bulletin Signaletique.
Part 390: Psychologie. Psychopathologie. Psychiatrie
(ISSN 0007-5531)

617.7 016　　　FR
P A S C A L EXPLORE. PART 71:
OPHTALMOLOGIE. 1985. 10/yr. 710 F. Centre
National de la Recherche Scientifique, Centre de
Documentation Scientifique et Technique, Service
des Abonnements, 26 rue Boyer, 75971 Paris Cedex
20, France. abstr. index. cum.index.
　　Supersedes (1972-1984): Bulletin Signaletique.
Part 346: Ophtalmologie (ISSN 0301-3324); Which
supersedes in part: Bulletin Signaletique. Part 350.
Pathologie Generale et Experimentale.

616.21 016　　　FR
P A S C A L EXPLORE. PART 72:
OTORHINOLARYNGOLOGIE.
STOMATOLOGIE. PATHOLOGIE
CERVICOFACIALE. 1984. 10/yr. 725 F. Centre
National de la Recherche Scientifique, Centre de
Documentation Scientifique et Technique, 26 rue
Boyer, 75971 Paris 20, France. abstr. bibl. index.
cum.index.
　　Supersedes (1972-1984): Bulletin Signaletique.
Part 347: Oto-Rhino-Laryngologie, Stomatologie,
Pathologie Cervicofaciale (ISSN 0301-3375); Which
supersedes in part: Bulletin Signaletique. Part 350.
Pathologie Generale et Experimentale.

616.5 016　　　FR
P A S C A L EXPLORE. PART 73:
DERMATOLOGIE. MALADIES
SEXUELLEMENT TRANSMISSIBLES. 1985. 10/
yr. 740 F. Centre National de la Recherche
Scientifique, Centre de Documentation Scientifique
et Technique, Service des Abonnements, 26 rue
Boyer, 75971 Paris 20, France. abstr. index.
cum.index.
　　Supersedes (1972-1984): Bulletin Signaletique.
Part 348: Dermatologie - Venerologie (ISSN 0301-
3383); Which supersedes in part: Bulletin
Signaletique. Part 350. Pathologie Generale et
Experimentale.

616.2 016　　　FR
P A S C A L EXPLORE. PART 74:
PNEUMOLOGIE. 1985. 10/yr. 720 F. Centre
National de la Recherche Scientifique, Centre de
Documentation Scientifique et Technique, Service
des Abonnements, 26 rue Boyer, 75971 Paris 20,
France. abstr. index. cum.index. (also avail. in
microform from MIM)
　　Supersedes in part (1973-1984): Bulletin
Signaletique. Part 362: Maladies de l'Appareil
Respiratoire du Coeur et des Vaisseaux. Chirurgie
Thoracique et Vasculaire (ISSN 0301-3391); Which
supersedes in part: Bulletin Signaletique. Part 350:
Pathologie Generale et Experimentale.

616.2 016　　　FR
P A S C A L EXPLORE. PART 75: CARDIOLOGIE
ET APPAREIL CIRCULATOIRE. 1985. 10/yr.
1065 F. Centre National de la Recherche
Scientifique, Centre de Documentation Scientifique
et Technique, Service des Abonnements, 26 rue
Boyer, 75971 Paris Cedex 20, France.
　　Supersedes in part: Bulletin Signaletique. Part
352: Maladies de l'Appareil Respiratoire, du Coeur
et des Vaisseaux. Chirurgie Thoracique et
Vasculaire.

616.3 617 016　　　FR
P A S C A L EXPLORE. PART 76:
GASTROENTEROLOGIE, FOIE, PANCREAS,
ABDOMEN. 1985. 10/yr. 1110 F. Centre National
de la Recherche Scientifique, Centre de
Documentation Scientifique et Technique, Service
des Abonnements, 26 rue Boyer, 75971 Paris 20,
France. abstr. index. cum.index. (also avail. in
microform from MIM)
　　Supersedes (1973-1984): Bulletin Signaletique.
Part 354: Maladies de l'Appareil Digestif. Chirurgie
Abdominale (ISSN 0301-3405); Which supersedes
in part: Bulletin Signaletique. Part 350. Pathologie
Generale et Experimentale.

616.6 016 617　　　FR
P A S C A L EXPLORE. PART 77:
NEPHROLOGIE. VOIES URINAIRES. 1985. 10/
yr. 725 F. Centre National de la Recherche
Scientifique, Centre de Documentation Scientifique
et Technique, Service des Abonnements, 26 rue
Boyer, 75971 Paris 20, France. abstr. index;
cum.index. (also avail. in microform from MIM)
　　Supersedes (1973-1984): Bulletin Signaletique.
Part 355: Maladies des Reins et des Voies Urinaires.
Chirurgie (ISSN 0301-3413); Which was formerly:
Bulletin Signaletique. Part 355: Maladies des Reins
et des Voies Urinaires - Chirurgie de l'Appareil
Urinaire; Supersedes in part: Bulletin Signaletique.
Part 350. Pathologie Generale et Experimentale.

616.8 016　　　FR
P A S C A L EXPLORE. PART 78: NEUROLOGIE.
1985. 10/yr. 1220 F. Centre National de la
Recherche Scientifique, Centre de Documentation
Scientifique et Technique, Service des
Abonnements, 26 rue Boyer, 75971 Paris 20,
France. abstr. index. cum.index. (also avail. in
microform from MIM)
　　Supersedes (1973-1984): Bulletin Signaletique.
Part 356: Maladies du Systeme Nerveux
Myopathies-Neurochirurgie (ISSN 0301-3421);
Which supersedes in part: Bulletin Signaletique. Part
350. Pathologie Generale et Experimentale.

617.3 016　　　FR
P A S C A L EXPLORE. PART 79: PATHOLOGIE
ET PHYSIOLOGIE OSTEOARTICULAIRES.
1985. 10/yr. 760 F. Centre National de la
Recherche Scientifique, Centre de Documentation
Scientifique et Technique, Service des
Abonnements, 26 rue Boyer, 75971 Paris 20,
France. abstr. index. cum.index. (also avail. in
microform from MIM)
　　Supersedes (1973-1984): Bulletin Signaletique.
Part 357: Maladies des Os et des Articulations.
Chirurgie Orthopedique. Traumatologie (ISSN 0301-
343X); Which supersedes in part: Bulletin
Signaletique. Part 350. Pathologie Generale et
Experimentale.

616.15 016　　　FR
P A S C A L EXPLORE. PART 80:
HEMATOLOGIE. 1985. 10/yr. 830 F. Centre
National de la Recherche Scientifique, Centre de
Documentation Scientifique et Technique, Service
des Abonnements, 26 rue Boyer, 75971 Paris 20,
France. (also avail. in microform from MIM)
　　Supersedes (1973-1984): Bulletin Signaletique.
Part 359: Maladies du Sang (ISSN 0301-3448);
Which supersedes in part: Bulletin Signaletique. Part
350. Pathologie Generale et Experimentale.

616.462 016　　　FR
P A S C A L EXPLORE. PART 81: MALADIES
METABOLIQUES. 1985. 10/yr. 650 F. Centre
National de la Recherche Scientifique, Centre de
Documentation Scientifique et Technique, Service
des Abonnements, 26 rue Boyer, 75971 Paris 20,
France. Ed. E. Bernheim. abstr. index. cum.index.
(also avail. in microform from MIM) Indexed:
Nutr.Abstr.
　　Supersedes (1972-1984): Bulletin Signaletique.
Part 362: Diabete. Maladies Metaboliques;
Formerly: Bulletin Signaletique. 362: Diabete.
Obesite. Maladies. (ISSN 0007-5507) Indexed:
Diabetes

616.4 016　　　FR
P A S C A L EXPLORE. PART 82:
GYNECOLOGIE. OBSTETRIQUE.
ANDROLOGIE. 1985. 10/yr. 860 F. Centre
National de la Recherche Scientifique, Centre de
Documentation Scientifique et Technique, Service
des Abonnements, 26 rue Boyer, 75971 Paris Cedex
20, France.
　　Supersedes in part: Bulletin Signaletique. Part
361: Reproduction. Gynecologie. Obstetrique.
Embryologie. Endocrinologie (ISSN 0245-9884)

617.96 016　　　FR
P A S C A L EXPLORE. PART 83: ANESTHESIE
ET REANIMATION. 1985. 10/yr. 745 F. Centre
National de la Recherche Scientifique, Centre de
Documentation Scientifique et Technique, Service
des Abonnements, 26 rue Boyer, 75971 Paris 20,
France. abstr. index. cum.index. (also avail. in
microform from MIM)
　　Supersedes (1972-1984): Bulletin Signaletique.
Part 349: Anesthesie. Reanimation (ISSN 0301-
133X); Bulletin Signaletique. Part 350. Pathologie
Generale et Experimentale (ISSN 0007-5469)

610 016 574　　　FR
P A S C A L EXPLORE. PART 84: GENIE
BIOMEDICAL. INFORMATIQUE
BIOMEDICALE. 1985. 10/yr. 540 F. Centre
National de la Recherche Scientifique, Centre de
Documentation Scientifique et Technique, Service
des Abonnements, 26 rue Boyer, 75971 Paris 20,
France. abstr. index. cum.index. (also avail. in
microform from MIM)
　　Supersedes (1972-1984): Bulletin Signaletique.
Part 310: Genie Biomedical. Informatique
Biomedicale. Physique Biomedicale (ISSN 0398-
9941)

616.4 016　　　FR
P A S C A L FOLIO. PART 54: REPRODUCTION
DES VERTEBRES. EMBRYOLOGIE DES
VERTEBRES ET DES INVERTEBRES. 1985. 10/
yr. 595 F. Centre National de la Recherche
Scientifique, Centre de Documentation Scientifique
et Technique, Service des Abonnements, 26 rue
Boyer, 75971 Paris 20, France. (also avail. in
microform from MIM)
　　Supersedes in part (1961-1984): Bulletin
Signaletique. Part 361: Reproduction. Gynecologie.
Obstetrique. Embryologie. Endocrinologie (ISSN
0245-9884); Which was formerly: Bulletin
Signaletique. Part 361: Reproduction. Embryologie.
Endocrinologie (ISSN 0180-9989); Bulletin
Signaletique. Part 361. Endocrinologie et
Reproduction (ISSN 0007-5493)

610　574　　　FR
P A S C A L THEMA. PART 215:
BIOTECHNOLOGIES (EDITION FRANCAISE)
1985. 10/yr. 1115 F. Centre National de la
Recherche Scientifique, Centre de Documentation
Scientifique et Technique, Service des
Abonnements, 26 rue Boyer, 75971 Paris 20,
France. Ed.Bd. abstr. index. cum.index. (also avail.
in microform)
　　Supersedes (1982-1984): Bulletin Signaletique.
Part 215: Biotechnologies (French Edition) (ISSN
0245-954X)

610　574　　　FR
P A S C A L THEMA. PART 216:
BIOTECHNOLOGY (ENGLISH EDITION)*
(Text in English) 1985. 10/yr. 2000 F. Centre
National de la Recherche Scientifique, Centre de
Documentation Scientifique et Technique, Service
des Abonnements, 26 rue Boyer, 75971 Paris 20,
France. Ed.Bd. abstr. index. cum.index.
　　Supersedes (1982-1984): Bulletin Signaletique.
Part 215: Biotechnology (English Edition) (ISSN
0245-9868)

610 616.07　　　FR
P A S C A L THEMA. PART 235: MEDECINE
TROPICALE. 1985. 10/yr. 745 F. Centre National
de la Recherche Scientifique, Centre de
Documentation Scientifique et Technique, Service
des Abonnements, 26 rue Boyer, 75971 Paris 20,
France. Ed.Bd. abstr. index. cum.index.
　　Supersedes (1982-1984): Bulletin Signaletique.
Part 233: Medicine Tropicale (ISSN 0245-9558)

MEDICAL SCIENCES — ALLERGOLOGY AND IMMUNOLOGY

616.994 016   **FR**
PASCAL THEMA. PART 251:
CANCEROLOGIE (CANCERNET) 1985. 10/yr.
1050 F. Centre National de la Recherche
Scientifique, Centre de Documentation Scientifique
et Technique, Service des Abonnements, 26 rue
Boyer, 75971 Paris 20, France. (Co-sponsor: Institut
Gustave Roussy (Villejuif)) (also avail. in microform
from MIM)
     Supersedes (1968-1984): Bulletin Signaletique.
Part 351: Revue Bibliographique Cancer (ISSN
0007-5477)

POLICE SCIENCE ABSTRACTS. see
*CRIMINOLOGY AND LAW
ENFORCEMENT — Abstracting, Bibliographies,
Statistics*

619 016   **US**   **ISSN 0743-4456**
PROSTAGLANDINS BIBLIOGRAPHY. 1966. a.
price varies. College of Physicians of Philadelphia
(Subsidiary of: Medical Documentation Service) 19
S. 22nd St., Philadelphia, PA 19103. TEL 215-563-
1238. (Affiliate: Upjohn Company) Eds. June
Fulton, Pauline Sattler. circ. 550.

616.97 016   **UR**   **ISSN 0202-9154**
REFERATIVNYI ZHURNAL. IMMUNOLOGIYA -
ALLERGOLOGIYA. 1978. m. 66 Rub. 75 Rub.
with index. Vsesoyuznyi Institut Nauchno-
Tekhnicheskoi Informatsii (VINITI), Baltiiskaya ul.
14, Moscow A-219, Russian S.F.S.R., U.S.S.R.
(Subscr. to: Mezhdunarodnaya Kniga, Dimitrova ul.
39, 113095 Moscow, Russian S.F.S.R., U.S.S.R.)

610 016   **UR**   **ISSN 0034-2475**
REFERATIVNYI ZHURNAL. MEDITSINSKAYA
GEOGRAFIYA. m. 26.40 Rub. 30 Rub. including
index. Vsesoyuznyi Institut Nauchno-Tekhnicheskoi
Informatsii (VINITI), Baltiiskaya ul., 14, Moscow
A-219, Russian S.F.S.R., U.S.S.R (Subscr. to:
Mezhdunarodnaya Kniga, Dimitrova ul. 39, 113095
Moscow, Russian S.F.S.R., U.S.S.R.)

616.992 016   **UR**   **ISSN 0202-9197**
REFERATIVNYI ZHURNAL. ONKOLOGIYA.
1961. m. 160 Rub. (200 Rub. including index)
Vsesoyuznyi Institut Nauchno-Tekhnicheskoi
Informatsii (VINITI), Baltiiskaya ul., 14, Moscow
A-219, Russian S.F.S.R., U.S.S.R. (Subscr. to:
Mezhdunarodnaya Kniga, Dimitrova ul. 39, 113095
Moscow, Russian S.F.S.R., U.S.S.R.)

574.19 016   **UR**   **ISSN 0131-355X**
REFERATIVNYI ZHURNAL. RADIATSIONNAYA
BIOLOGIYA. 1973. m. 56 Rub. 60 Rub. including
index. Vsesoyuznyi Institut Nauchno-Tekhnicheskoi
Informatsii (VINITI), Baltiiskaya ul., 14, Moscow
A-219, Russian S.F.S.R., U.S.S.R. (Subscr. to:
Mezhdunarodnaya Kniga, Dimitrova ul. 39, 113095
Moscow, Russian S.F.S.R., U.S.S.R.) Indexed:
Chem.Abstr.

SELECTED ABSTRACTS ON OCCUPATIONAL
DISEASES. see *INDUSTRIAL HEALTH AND
SAFETY — Abstracting, Bibliographies, Statistics*

610   **US**
SELECTED PERIODICALS FOR THE MEDICAL
LIBRARY. 1967. a. free to qualified personnel.
Ebsco Industries, Inc., Box 1943, Birmingham, AL
35201-1943. Ed. Erdeal Moore. adv. tr.lit. circ. 18,
000.

616.95 011   **US**   **ISSN 0195-7708**
SEXUALLY TRANSMITTED DISEASES.
ABSTRACTS & BIBLIOGRAPHY. no.2, 1978. a?
U.S. Centers for Disease Control, 1600 Clifton Rd.,
N.E., Atlanta, GA 30333. Indexed: Trop.Dis.Bull.
     Formerly: Current Literature on Venereal Disease
(ISSN 0001-3544)

610.73   **DK**   **ISSN 0108-9714**
STATISTIK OM SUNDHEDSPLEJERSKERNES
VIRKSOMHED. (Subseries of: Primaer
Sundhedstjenestestatistik) 1983. a. Kr.30.
Sundhedsstyrelsen, St. Kongensgade 1, 1264
Copenhagen K, Denmark. illus.

TROPICAL DISEASES BULLETIN. see *MEDICAL
SCIENCES*

619   **US**   **ISSN 0278-5374**
U.S. NATIONAL INSTITUTES OF HEALTH.
DIVISION OF RESEARCH RESOURCES.
PROGRAM HIGHLIGHTS. 1980. a. free. U.S.
National Institutes of Health, Division of Research
Resources, Bldg. 31, Rm. 5B-10, 9000 Rockville
Pike, Bethesda, MD 20892. TEL 301-496-5545.
circ. 11,000.

616.92 016 576.64   **US**   **ISSN 0042-6830**
VIROLOGY ABSTRACTS. 1967. m. $463.
Cambridge Scientific Abstracts, 5161 River Rd.,
Bethesda, MD 20816. TEL 301-951-1400. Ed. B.
Engel. adv. (also avail. in magnetic tape) Indexed:
Cal.Tiss.Abstr. Chemorec.Abstr. Oncol.Abstr.
●Also available online. Vendors: DIALOG.
Virology

MEDICAL SCIENCES — Allergology And Immunology

616.97   **US**   **ISSN 0883-2994**
A B M S DIRECTORY OF CERTIFIED
ALLERGY-IMMUNOLOGY PHYSICIANS. 1985.
biennial. $29.95 hardcover; $24.95 softcover.
American Board of Medical Specialties, One
American Plaza, Ste. 805, Evanston, IL 60201. TEL
312-491-9091. Ed. Donald G. Langsley, M.D.

576 615.37   **DK**   **ISSN 0108-0210**
ACTA PATHOLOGICA, MICROBIOLOGICA ET
IMMUNOLOGICA SCANDINAVICA. SECTION
C: IMMUNOLOGY. SUPPLEMENTUM. irreg.
free to subscribers. Munksgaard, 35 Noerre Soegade,
DK-1370 Copenhagen K, Denmark. (reprint service
avail. from ISI) Indexed: Biol.Abstr. Chem.Abstr.
Ind.Med.
     Formerly: Acta Pathologica et Microbiologica
Scandinavica. Section C: Immunology.
Supplementum.

616.97   **US**   **ISSN 0065-2776**
ADVANCES IN IMMUNOLOGY. 1961. irreg.,
vol.39, 1986. Academic Press, Inc., Orlando, FL
32887. TEL 305-345-2000. Eds. Talia Ferrs, W.H.
Humphrey. index. Indexed: Biol.Abstr.
Chem.Abstr. Ind.Med. Nutr.Abstr. Sci.Cit.Ind.
Anim.Breed.Abstr. Abstr.Hyg. Dairy Sci.Abstr.
Helminthol.Abstr. Ind.Sci.Rev. Ind.Vet. Vet.Bull.
Trop.Dis.Bull.

616.97   **SZ**   **ISSN 0065-6372**
ALLERGOLOGICUM; TRANSACTIONS OF THE
COLLEGIUM INTERNATIONALE. (Text in
English) 1955. a. Collegium Internationale
Allergologicum, c/o P. Dukor, Ciba-Geigy Ltd.,
CH-4002 Basel, Switzerland.

616.97   **FI**
ALLERGY. SUPPLEMENTUM. (Text in English)
1950. irreg. Nordic Congress in Allergology,
University of Turku, SF-20500 Turku, Finland. adv.
(reprint service avail. from ISI) Indexed: Biol.Abstr.
Curr.Cont.
     Formerly: Acta Allergologica. Supplementum
(ISSN 0065-096X)

616.97   **US**
AMERICAN ACADEMY OF ALLERGY. POLLEN
AND MOLD COMMITTEE. STATISTICAL
REPORT. 1973. a. free. Ross Laboratories, 625
Cleveland Ave., Columbus, OH 43216. TEL 614-
227-3333. Ed. Bill Rohn. circ. 100. Indexed:
Biol.Abstr. Nutr.abstr.

616.97   **US**   **ISSN 0732-0582**
ANNUAL REVIEW OF IMMUNOLOGY. 1983. a.
$31. Annual Reviews, Inc., 4139 El Camino Way,
Palo Alto, CA 94306. TEL 415-493-4400. Ed.
William E. Paul. bibl. index. cum.index. (also avail.
in microform from UMI) Indexed: Biol.Abstr.
Chem.Abstr. Sci.Cit.Ind. Abstr.Hyg. Ind.Sci.Rev.

616.97 616.2   **JA**   **ISSN 0287-0185**
ARERUGIA. 1968. irreg. free. Japan Allergy
Foundation, 6-8 Minamidai, Sagamihara, Kanagawa
Prefecture, Japan. Ed. Prof. A. Kumagai. circ. 4,500.

615.37   **SZ**   **ISSN 0301-3782**
BASEL INSTITUTE FOR IMMUNOLOGY.
ANNUAL REPORT. (Text in English) 1972. a. free
to libraries and immunologists. Basel Institute for
Immunology, Grenzacherstrasse 487, CH-4058
Basel, Switzerland. Ed. C.M. Steinberg. circ. 3,500.
Indexed: Biol.Abstr.

616.97   **US**   **ISSN 0278-9566**
BI-ANNUAL REVIEW OF ALLERGY. 1973.
biennial. $48. Elsevier Science Publishing Co., Inc.
(New York), 52 Vanderbilt Ave., New York, NY
10017-3808. TEL 212-916-1150. Ed. Claude Frazie,
M.D. charts. illus.
     Formerly: Annual Review of Allergy (ISSN 0090-
1083)

615.37   **CN**   **ISSN 0068-9653**
CANADIAN SOCIETY FOR IMMUNOLOGY.
BULLETIN. 1967. a. membership. ‡ Canadian
Society for Immunology, c/o Department des
Sciences Biologiques, University of Quebec at
Montreal, C.P. 8888, suc. A, Montreal, PQ H3C
3P8, Canada. TEL 514-282-3345. Ed. Dr. M.
Fournier. adv. bk. rev. circ. 500. (also avail. in
microform from UMI; reprint service avail. from
UMI)

615.37 574   **US**
CLINICAL IMMUNOBIOLOGY. 1972. irreg., vol.4,
1980. Academic Press, Inc., Orlando, FL 32887.
TEL 305-345-2000. Ed. F.H. Bach.

616.97 574.2   **US**   **ISSN 0093-4054**
CONTEMPORARY TOPICS IN
IMMUNOBIOLOGY. 1972. irreg. price varies.
Plenum Publishing Corp., 233 Spring St., New
York, NY 10013. TEL 212-620-8047. illus. Indexed:
Biol.Abstr. Ind.Med. Sci.Cit.Ind. ASCA.
Int.Sci.Rev.

615.37   **US**   **ISSN 0090-8800**
CONTEMPORARY TOPICS IN MOLECULAR
IMMUNOLOGY. 1972. irreg. price varies. Plenum
Publishing Corp., 233 Spring St., New York, NY
10013. TEL 212-620-8047. Eds. F.P. Inman, Ralph
A. Reisfeld. Indexed: Biol.Abstr. Ind.Med.
Sci.Cit.Ind. Ind.Sci.Rev.

615.37 576   **SZ**   **ISSN 0301-3081**
CONTRIBUTIONS TO MICROBIOLOGY AND
IMMUNOLOGY. (Text in English) 1973. irreg.
(approx. 1/yr.) price varies. S. Karger AG,
Allschwilerstrasse 10, P.O. Box, CH-4009 Basel,
Switzerland. Eds. J.M. Cruse, R.E. Lewis Jr.
(reprint service avail. from ISI) Indexed: Biol.Abstr.
Chem.Abstr. Curr.Cont. Ind.Med. Ind.Vet.
Vet.Bull.
     Supersedes: Bibliotheca Microbiologia (ISSN
0067-8058)

574   **UK**
CURRENT TOPICS IN IMMUNOLOGY. 1975.
irreg. price varies. Edward Arnold (Publishers) Ltd.,
41 Bedford Sq., London WC1B 3DQ, England.

616.97   **NE**   **ISSN 0531-2612**
EUROPEAN ACADEMY OF ALLERGY.
PROCEEDINGS.* (Text in English, French and
German) 1960. a. European Academy of Allergy,
Pieterskerhot 38, Leyden, Netherlands.
Allergies

HOKKAIDO UNIVERSITY. INSTITUTE OF
IMMUNOLOGICAL SCIENCE. BULLETIN. see
MEDICAL SCIENCES — Respiratory Diseases

616.97   **SZ**   **ISSN 0074-4220**
INTERNATIONAL CONVOCATION ON
IMMUNOLOGY. PAPERS. 1968. irreg. price
varies. (Center for Immunology) S. Karger AG,
Allschwilerstrasse 10, P.O. Box, CH-4009 Basel,
Switzerland. (reprint service avail. from ISI)

616.97   **SZ**   **ISSN 0077-0760**
MONOGRAPHS IN ALLERGY. (Text in English)
1966. irreg., approx. 1/yr. price varies. S. Karger
AG, Allschwilerstrasse 10, P.O. Box, CH-4009
Basel, Switzerland. Ed.Bd. (reprint service avail.
from ISI) Indexed: Biol.Abstr. Chem.Abstr.
Curr.Cont. Ind.Med. Dent.Ind. Ind.Sci.Rev.

615.37   **US**
PERSPECTIVES IN IMMUNOLOGY; a series of
publications based on symposia. 1969. irreg., no.10,
1981. Academic Press, Inc., Orlando, FL 32887.
TEL 305-345-2000.

616.97   **SZ**   **ISSN 0079-6034**
PROGRESS IN ALLERGY. (Text in English) 1939.
irreg., approx. 1/yr. price varies. S. Karger AG,
Allschwilerstrasse 10, P.O. Box, CH-4009 Basel,
Switzerland. Ed.Bd. (back issues avail.) Indexed:
Biol.Abstr. Chem.Abstr. Curr.Cont. Excerp.Med.
Ind.Med.

MEDICAL SCIENCES — ANAESTHESIOLOGY

616.97 SZ ISSN 0250-8087
PSEUDO-ALLERGIC REACTIONS; involvement of drugs and chemicals. (Text in English) 1980. irreg. price varies. S. Karger AG, P.O. Box, CH-4009 Basel, Switzerland. Eds. P. Kallos, H.D. Schlumberger, G.B. West. (reprint service avail. from ISI)

616.97 SZ ISSN 0253-4843
SURVEY OF DRUG RESEARCH IN IMMUNOLOGIC DISEASE. (Text in English) 1983. biennial. 490 Fr.($293.50) S. Karger AG, Allschwilerstr. 10, CH-4009 Basel, Switzerland. Ed. V. St.Georgiev.

616.96 US
VACCINES (YEAR) a. Cold Spring Harbor Laboratory, Box 100JN, Cold Spring Harbor, New York, NY 11724. TEL 516-367-8423.

615.37 GW ISSN 0171-2985
ZEITSCHRIFT FUER IMMUNITAETSFORSCHUNG. IMMUNOBIOLOGY. (Text and summaries in English) 1909. irreg., (5 nos./vol.) DM.284 per vol. Gustav Fischer Verlag, Wollgrasweg 49, Postfach 720143, 7000 Stuttgart 70, W. Germany (B.R.D.) Ed. D. Gemsa. circ. 900. Indexed: Biol.Abstr. Chem.Abstr. Excerp.Med. Ind.Med.
Former titles: Zeitschrift fuer Immunitaetsforschung - Immunologie; Zeitschrift fuer Immunitaetsforschung, Experimentelle und Klinische Immunologie (ISSN 0300-872X)

MEDICAL SCIENCES — Anaesthesiology

617.96 US ISSN 0883-122X
A B M S DIRECTORY OF CERTIFIED ANESTHESIOLOGISTS. 1985. biennial. $34.95 hardcover; $29.95 softcover. American Board of Medical Specialties, One American Plaza, Ste. 805, Evanston, IL 60201. TEL 312-491-9091. Ed. Donald G. Langsley, M.D.

617.96 US ISSN 0363-471X
A S A REFRESHER COURSES IN ANESTHESIOLOGY. 1973. a. $15. (American Society of Anesthesiologists) J.B. Lippincott Co., E. Washington Square, Philadelphia, PA 19105. TEL 215-238-4200. Ed. Paul G. Barash, M.D. (also avail. in microform from UMI)

617.96 DK ISSN 0515-2720
ACTA ANAESTHESIOLOGICA SCANDINAVICA. SUPPLEMENTUM. irreg. free to subscribers. Munksgaard, 35 Noerre Soegade, DK-1370 Copenhagen K, Denmark. Indexed: Biol.Abstr. Chem.Abstr. Curr.Cont. Ind.Med.

617.96 US ISSN 0737-6146
ADVANCES IN ANESTHESIA. 1983. a. $55. Year Book Medical Publishers, Inc., 35 E. Wacker Dr., Chicago, IL 60601. TEL 312-726-9733. Ed. Robert K. Stoelting, M.D.

617.96 JO ISSN 0259-1162
ANAESTHESIA ESSAYS AND RESEARCHES. (Text in Arabic and English) 1985. a. $18. (Pan-Arabic Scientific Committee) Jordan House for Publication, Box 1121, Amman, Jordan. Ed. Dr. M. Takrouri. adv. bk. rev. circ. 3,000.

617.96 US ISSN 0171-1814
ANAESTHESIOLOGIE UND INTENSIVMEDIZIN/ANAESTHESIOLOGY AND INTENSIVE CARE MEDICINE. (Contributions in English, French and German) 1963. irreg., vol.185, 1987. price varies. Springer-Verlag, 175 Fifth Ave., New York, NY 10010 TEL 212-460-1500. (Also Berlin, Heidelberg, Tokyo, Vienna) (reprint service avail. from ISI)
Formerly: Anaesthesiology and Resuscitation (ISSN 0066-1341)

617.96 UK ISSN 0144-8684
CURRENT TOPICS IN ANAESTHESIA. 1979. irreg. price varies. Edward Arnold (Publishers) Ltd., 41 Bedford Square, London WC1B 3DQ, England.

617.96 SP ISSN 0071-2671
EUROPEAN CONGRESS OF ANAESTHESIOLOGY. PROCEEDINGS. (Proceedings published in host countries) 1962. quadrennial, 4th, Madrid, 1974. (World Federation of Societies of Anaesthesiologists) European Congress of Anaesthesiology, Inquire: Professor Arias, Arapiles 16, Madrid, Spain.

617.96 US ISSN 0099-1546
PROGRESS IN ANESTHESIOLOGY. 1975. irreg. Raven Press, 1185 Ave. of the Americas, New York, NY 10036. TEL 212-575-0335. Indexed: Biol.Abstr. Chem.Abstr.

617 UK
ROYAL COLLEGE OF SURGEONS OF ENGLAND. FACULTY OF ANAESTHETISTS. DEAN'S NEWSLETTER. 1965. a. membership. ‡ Royal College of Surgeons of England, Faculty of Anaesthetists, 35-43 Lincoln's Inn Fields, London WC2A 3PN, England. circ. 6,000(controlled)
Formerly: Royal College of Surgeons of England. Faculty of Anaesthetists. Newsletter.

617.96 US ISSN 0084-3652
YEAR BOOK OF ANESTHESIA. 1961. a. $44.95. Year Book Medical Publishers, Inc., 35 E. Wacker Dr., Chicago, IL 60601. TEL 312-726-9733. Ed. R.D. Miller, M.D. illus.

MEDICAL SCIENCES — Cancer

ACTA MANILANA. see CHEMISTRY — Organic Chemistry

616.994 US ISSN 0065-230X
ADVANCES IN CANCER RESEARCH. 1953. irreg., vol.47, 1986. Academic Press, Inc., Orlando, FL 32887. TEL 305-345-2000. Eds. George Klein, Sidney Weinhouse. Indexed: Biol.Abstr. Chem.Abstr. Ind.Med. Sci.Cit.Ind. Biotech.Abstr. Dent.Ind. Ind.Sci.Rev. Ind.Vet. Vet.Bull.

616.99 US
ADVANCES IN IMMUNITY AND CANCER THERAPY. 1985. irreg., vol.2, 1986. Springer-Verlag, 175 Fifth Ave., New York, NY 10010 TEL 212-460-1500. (Also Berlin, Heidelberg, Tokyo, Vienna) (reprint service avail. from ISI)

616.99 JA ISSN 0374-5295
AICHI CANCER CENTER RESEARCH INSTITUTE. ANNUAL REPORT. (Text in English) 1968. biennial. free. Aichi Cancer Center Research Institute, Tashirocho, Chikusa-ku, Nagoya, 464, Japan. Ed. Taijo Takahashi. circ. 800.

616.99 SW ISSN 0348-8799
ANNUAL REPORT ON RESULTS OF TREATMENT IN GYNECOLOGICAL CANCER. 1937. triennial, Vol.19, 1985. $20. International Federation of Gynecology and Obstetrics, Cancer Committee, Radiumhemmet, S-104 01 Stockholm, Sweden. Ed. Dr. Pettersson. adv. charts. circ. 2,000. Indexed: Excerp.Med.
Formerly (1937-1979): Annual Report on the Results of Treatment in Carcinoma of the Uterus, Vagina, and Ovary.

616.9 SP
ASOCIACION ESPANOLA CONTRA EL CANCER. MEMORIA TECNICO-ADMINISTRATIVA. 1958. a. free. Asociacion Espanola Contra el Cancer, Amador de los Rios 5, Madrid 4, Spain. charts. stat.
Formerly: Asociacion Espanola Contra el Cancer. Memoria de la Assemblea General (ISSN 0066-8540)

616.99 IS
BAMAH; journal for heaith professionals in the field of cancer. irreg. free. Israel Cancer Association, Rehov Hachashonaim 91, Tel Aviv, Israel. TEL 03-250361. Ed. Miri Ziv.

616.99 US
BRISTOL-MEYERS CANCER SYMPOSIA. PROCEEDINGS. 1979. irreg., vol.7, 1985. Academic Press, Inc., Orlando, FL 32887. TEL 305-345-2000. Eds. Stanley T. Cook, Maxwell Gordon. Indexed: Chem.Abstr.

616.992 CN
BRITISH COLUMBIA CANCER RESEARCH CENTRE. ANNUAL REPORT. 1950. a. free. British Columbia Cancer Research Centre, 601 W. 10th Ave., Vancouver, B.C. V5Z 1L3, Canada. TEL 604-877-6010. Ed. Maureen Molaro. circ. 6,000.
Formerly: British Columbia. Cancer Foundation. Annual Report (ISSN 0068-1423)

616.99 616.15 US ISSN 0737-9587
C R C CRITICAL REVIEWS IN ONCOLOGY-HEMATOLOGY. 1983. irreg. $104. C R C Press, Inc., 2000 Corporate Blvd., N.W., Boca Raton, FL 33431. Ed. Stephen Davis, M.D. Indexed: ASCA. Ind.Sci.Rev.

616.994 UK ISSN 0305-7232
CANCER BIOCHEMISTRY - BIOPHYSICS. 1975. 8/yr. (in 2 vols., 4 nos./vol.) $450 academic $276. Gordon and Breach Science Publishers, Ltd., P.O. Box 197., London WC2E 9PX, England. Ed. Harry Darrow Brown. adv. (also avail. in microform from MIM) Indexed: Biol.Abstr. Chem.Abstr. Curr.Cont. Excerp.Med. Ind.Med. Sci.Cit.Ind. Biotech.Abstr. Dairy Sci.Abstr. Helminthol.Abstr. Ind.Sci.Rev.

616.99 US ISSN 0198-6473
CANCER BIOLOGY REVIEWS. 1980. irreg., vol.3, 1982. Marcel Dekker, Inc., 270 Madison Ave., New York, NY 10016. TEL 212-696-9000. Indexed: Chem.Abstr.

616.99 GW ISSN 0342-8893
CANCER CAMPAIGN. 1978. irreg. price varies. Gustav Fischer Verlag, Wollgrasweg 49, Postfach 720143, 7000 Stuttgart 70, W. Germany (B.R.D.)

616.994 US ISSN 0361-090X
CANCER DETECTION AND PREVENTION. 1976. m. $390. Alan R. Liss, Inc., 41 E. 11th St., New York, NY 10003. TEL 212-475-7700. Ed. Herbert E. Nieburgs. (also avail. in microfilm; reprint service avail. from ISI) Indexed: Biol.Abstr. Chem.Abstr. Curr.Cont. Excerp.Med. Ind.Med. Abstr.Hyg. Dent.Ind. Trop.Dis.Bull.

616.994 US ISSN 0069-0147
CANCER FACTS AND FIGURES. 1951. a. free. ‡ American Cancer Society Inc., 4 W. 35th St., New York, NY 10001. TEL 212-736-3030. Ed. Gigi Marion. circ. 400,000.

616.9 CN ISSN 0315-9884
CANCER IN ONTARIO. 1946. a. free. Ontario Cancer Treatment and Research Foundation, 7 Overlea Blvd., Toronto, Ont. M4H 1A8, Canada. TEL 416-423-4240. Ed. J.O. Godden. circ. 17,000.
Formerly: Ontario Cancer Treatment and Research Foundation. Annual Report (ISSN 0078-4699)

616.9 PR
CANCER IN PUERTO RICO. (Text in English and Spanish) 1950. a. free. (Department of Health, Cancer Control Program, NCI-BIO Branch) Cancer Registry of Puerto Rico, Department of Health, Call Box 70184, San Juan, PR 00936 TEL 809-764-7453. Ed. Dr. Isidro Martinez. circ. 1,000. Indexed: Excerp.Med.

616.9 SW ISSN 0069-0155
CANCER INCIDENCE IN SWEDEN. 1960. a. Kr.29. (Swedish Cancer Registry) Allmaenna Foerlaget, Box 5227, 102 45 Stockholm, Sweden. circ. 2,000.

616.994 JA
CANCER INSTITUTE SCIENTIFIC REPORT. 1976. a. free. Japanese Foundation for Cancer Research, Cancer Institute, 1-37-1 Kami-Ikebukuro, Toshima-ku, Tokyo 170, Japan. Ed. Dr. Tadashi Utakoji. circ. 1,500.

616.994 US ISSN 0099-2372
CANCER NEWS JOURNAL. 1964. irreg. $20 membership. International Association of Cancer Victors and Friends, 7740 W. Manchester Ave., No. 110, Playa del Rey, CA 90293. TEL 213-822-5032. Ed. Ann Cinquina. adv. bk. rev. film rev. illus. stat. circ. 5,000.

616.994 UK ISSN 0365-9623
CANCER RESEARCH CAMPAIGN. ANNUAL REPORT. 1924. a. free to medical & scientific institutions. Cancer Research Campaign, 2 Carlton House Terrace, London SW1Y 5AR, England. circ. controlled.

MEDICAL SCIENCES — CANCER

616.9 US ISSN 0069-0171
CANCER SEMINAR PROCEEDINGS. 1950-1974; N.S. 1975. irreg. $10. University of South Florida, College of Medicine, Tampa, FL 33620. TEL 813-974-2196. Ed. J.A. del Regato, M.D.

616 US ISSN 0147-4006
CARCINOGENESIS; a comprehensive survey. 1976. irreg., vol.5, 1979. price varies. Raven Press, 1185 Ave. of the Americas, New York, NY 10036. TEL 212-575-0335. Indexed: Biol.Abstr. Chem.Abstr. Ind.Med. Sci.Cit.Ind. Dairy Sci.Abstr. Dent.Ind. Risk Abstr. Rev.Plant Path.

CURRENT HEMATOLOGY AND ONCOLOGY. see MEDICAL SCIENCES — Hematology

616.99 US
CURRENT TREATMENT OF CANCER. 1986. irreg. price varies. Springer-Verlag, 175 Fifth Ave., New York, NY 10160 TEL 212-460-1500. (Also Berlin, Heidelberg, Tokyo, Vienna) (reprint service avail. from ISI)

362.1 US ISSN 0095-6775
DAMON RUNYON-WALTER WINCHELL CANCER FUND. ANNUAL REPORT.* 1973. a. free. Damon Runyon Walter Winchell Cancer Fund, 131 E. 36th St., New York, NY 10016-3404. circ. 1,000. Key Title: Annual Report - Damon Runyon-Walter Winchell Cancer Fund.
Continues: Damon Runyon Memorial Fund for Cancer Research. Report.

616.9 GW ISSN 0070-4229
DEUTSCHES KREBSFORSCHUNGSZENTRUM. VEROEFFENTLICHUNGEN. 1965. a. Deutsches Krebsforschungszentrum, Institut fuer Epidemiologie und Biometrie, Im Neuenheimer Feld 280, D-6900 Heidelberg 1, W. Germany (B.R.D.) circ. 1,000.

619.99 NE
DEVELOPMENTS IN ONCOLOGY. 1980. irreg. (5-6 vols. yr.) price varies. Martinus Nijhoff Publishers, Box 163, 3300 AD Dordrecht, Netherlands. circ. 2,000. Indexed: Chem.Abstr.

616.99 FR
DIRECTORY OF ON-GOING RESEARCH IN CANCER EPIDEMIOLOGY. (Text in English) 1976. a. £18($20) International Agency for Research on Cancer, 150 cours Albert-Thomas, 69372 Lyon Cedex 08, France (Subscr. to: Oxford University Press, Walton St., Oxford OX2 6DP, England) Eds. C.S. Muir, G. Wagner. circ. 2,300.

616.99 310 GR ISSN 0302-9697
ETESIA STATISTIKE. EREVNA TOU KARKINOU/ANNUAL STATISTICAL SURVEY OF CANCER. 1967/69. biennial. Dr.100. (National Statistical Service of Greece) 14-16 Lycourgou St., GR 101 66 Athens, Greece. circ. 1,000.

616 US
EUROPEAN ORGANIZATION FOR RESEARCH ON TREATMENT OF CANCER. MONOGRAPH SERIES. 1975. irreg., vol.5, 1978. price varies. Raven Press, 1185 Ave. of the Americas, New York, NY 10036. TEL 212-575-0335. Ed. M.J. Staquet. Indexed: Biol.Abstr. Curr.Cont.

616.99 GE ISSN 0323-5084
FORTSCHRITTE DER ONKOLOGIE. (Text in English and German) 1975. irreg., vol.13, 1986. (Akademie der Wissenschaften der DDR) Akademie-Verlag Berlin, Leipziger Str. 3-4, 1086 Berlin, E. Germany (D.D.R.)

FRONTIERS OF RADIATION THERAPY AND ONCOLOGY. see MEDICAL SCIENCES — Radiology And Nuclear Medicine

616.994 FR ISSN 0072-7806
GROUPEMENT DES ENTREPRISES FRANCAISES DANS LA LUTTE CONTRE LE CANCER. BULLETIN NATIONAL DE LIAISON.* (Title varies) irreg., no.4, 1970. price varies. Federation Nationale des Groupements des Entreprises Francaises dans la Lutte Contre le Cancer, 4 rue Auber, Paris 8e, France.

616.994 UN ISSN 0250-9555
I A R C MONOGRAPHS ON THE EVALUATION OF THE CARCINOGENIC RISK OF CHEMICALS TO HUMANS. (Text in English) 1972. irreg. price varies. International Agency for Research on Cancer - Centre International de Recherche sur le Cancer, 150 cours Albert-Thomas, 69372 Lyon Cedex 08, France (U.S. subscr. addr.: World Health Organization, Box 5284, Church Street Station, New York, NY 10246) Indexed: Biol.Abstr. Curr.Cont. Ind.Med. Abstr.Hyg. Anal.Abstr. Food Sci.& Tech.Abstr. Trop.Dis.Bull.
Formerly: I A R C Monographs on the Evaluation of Carcinogenic Risk of Chemicals to Man.

616.994 UN ISSN 0300-5038
I A R C SCIENTIFIC PUBLICATIONS. 1971. irreg. price varies. International Agency for Research on Cancer - Centre International de Recherche sur le Cancer, 150 cours Albert-Thomas, 69372 Lyon Cedex 08, France (U.S. subscr. to: Oxford University Press, 200 Madison Ave., New York, N.Y. 10016, U.S.A.) Ed. E. Heseltine. Indexed: Biol.Abstr. Chem.Abstr. Curr.Cont. Excerp.Med. Ind.Med. Abstr.Hyg. Anal.Abstr. Dent.Ind. Food Sci.& Tech.Abstr. Trop.Dis.Bull.
Formerly: International Agency for Research on Cancer. I A R C Technical Publications.

616.99 573.21 US
I.C.R. SCIENTIFIC REPORT. 1948. a. free. Fox Chase Cancer Center, 7701 Burholme Ave., Philadelphia, PA 19111. Ed. Elizabeth Patterson. circ. 7,500.

616.994 UK
IMPERIAL CANCER RESEARCH FUND. SCIENTIFIC REPORT. 1973. a. private circulation to qualified personnel. Imperial Cancer Research Fund, Lincoln's Inn Fields, London WC2A 3PX, England. Ed. Angela H. Aldam. circ. 1,200.

616.9 YU ISSN 0079-9580
INCIDENCA RAKA V SLOVENIJI/CANCER INCIDENCE IN SLOVENIA. (Text in English and Slovenian) 1957. a. free. Onkoloski Institut, Zaloska C,2, 61005 Ljubljana, Yugoslavia. Ed. Vera Pompe Kirn. index. circ. 800.
Formerly: Rak v Sloveniji. Tabele.

616.99 SZ
INTERNATIONAL CATALOGUE OF FILMS, FILMSTRIPS AND SLIDES ON PUBLIC EDUCATION ABOUT CANCER. Variant title: International Catalogue of Films for Public Education About Cancer. (Subseries of U I C C Technical Report Series) (Text in English; summaries in English, French and Spanish) 1977. irreg. price varies. International Union Against Cancer, 3 rue de Conseil-General, 1205 Geneva, Switzerland. circ. 1,000.

616.99 SZ
INTERNATIONAL DIRECTORY OF SPECIALIZED CANCER RESEARCH AND TREATMENT ESTABLISHMENTS. (Subseries of U I C C Technical Report Series) 1976. every 4 years. 200 Fr. International Union Against Cancer, 3 rue de Conseil-General, 1205 Geneva, Switzerland.

610 SZ ISSN 0074-9192
INTERNATIONAL UNION AGAINST CANCER. MANUAL/UNION INTERNATIONALE CONTRE LE CANCER. MANUEL. (Text in English and French) 1963. irreg., latest 1983. free. ‡ International Union Against Cancer, 3 rue de Conseil-General, 1205 Geneva, Switzerland.

616.99 UR ISSN 0202-7127
ITOGI NAUKI I TEKHNIKI: ONKOLOGIYA. irreg., latest vol.16, 1987. price varies. Vsesoyuznyi Institut Nauchno-Tekhnicheskoi Informatsii (VINITI), Baltiiskaya ul. 14, Moscow A-219, Russian S.F.S.R., U.S.S.R. (Subscr. to: Mezhdunarodnaya Kniga, Dimitrova ul. 39, 113095 Moscow, Russian S.F.S.R., U.S.S.R.)

616.9 JA ISSN 0075-3327
JAPAN SOCIETY FOR CANCER THERAPY. PROCEEDINGS OF THE CONGRESS. (Text in English) 1963. a. 5000 Yen. Japan Society for Cancer Therapy - Nihon Gan Chiryo Gakkai, Kyoto University Medical School, Second Surgical Division, Shogoin Kawara-cho, Sakyo-ku, Kyoto 606, Japan.

616.994 JA ISSN 0022-2119
JOURNAL OF KARYOPATHOLOGY/ SAIBOKAKU BYORIGAKU ZASSHI; tumor and tumor virus. (Text in Japanese; summaries in English) 1953. irreg. $2. Okayama University, School of Medicine, Department of Pathology - Okayama Daigaku Igakubu Byorigaku Kyoshitsu, 2-5-1 Shikata-cho, Okayama 700, Japan. Ed. Y. Hamazaki. adv. (reprint service avail. from ISI) Indexed: Biol.Abstr. Ind.Med.

KAZAKHSKII NAUCHNO-ISSLEDOVATEL'SKII INSTITUT ONKOLOGII I RADIOLOGII. TRUDY. see MEDICAL SCIENCES — Radiology And Nuclear Medicine

616.99 US ISSN 0160-2454
M.D. ANDERSON CLINICAL CONFERENCES ON CANCER. 1978. a. (University of Texas System Cancer Center) Raven Press, 1185 Ave. of the Americas, New York, NY 10036. TEL 212-575-0335. (Co-sponsor: M.D. Anderson Hospital and Tumor Institute)

616.9 US ISSN 0066-1627
M.D. ANDERSON HOSPITAL AND TUMOR INSTITUTE. GENERAL REPORT. 1965. biennial. free. University of Texas, M.D. Anderson Hospital and Tumor Institute, Texas Medical Center, Houston, TX 77030. TEL 713-792-2121. circ. 5,000.

616.9 US ISSN 0066-1635
M.D. ANDERSON HOSPITAL AND TUMOR INSTITUTE. RESEARCH REPORT. 1955. a. free. University of Texas System Cancer Center, M.D. Anderson Hospital and Tumor Institute, Texas Medical Center, Houston, TX 77030. TEL 713-792-2121. circ. 4,000.

616.99 US
M.D. ANDERSON SYMPOSIA IN FUNDAMENTAL CANCER RESEARCH. 1978. a. (University of Texas System Cancer Center) Raven Press, 1185 Ave. of Americas, New York, NY 10036. TEL 212-575-0335. (Co-sponsor: M.D. Anderson Hospital and Tumor Insitute)

616.99 UK ISSN 0144-8692
MANAGEMENT OF MALIGNANT DISEASE SERIES. 1978. irreg. price varies. Edward Arnold (Publishers) Ltd., 41 Bedford Square, London WC1B 3DQ, England. Ed. M.J. Peckham.

616.9 CN ISSN 0076-3802
MANITOBA CANCER TREATMENT AND RESEARCH FOUNDATION. REPORT. 1957/58. a. free. Manitoba Cancer Treatment and Research Foundation, 100 Olivia St., Winnipeg, Man. R3E 0V9, Canada. TEL 204-787-1297. Ed. J. Singer. circ. 2,500.

616.99 US ISSN 0270-7950
N C I FACT BOOK; national cancer program. a. U.S. National Cancer Institute, Bethesda, MD 20205. TEL 301-496-4000.
Formerly: National Cancer Institute Fact Book.

616.994 US
N C I MONOGRAPHS. 1959. irreg., latest no.67, 1985. price varies. U.S. National Cancer Institute, Department of Health and Human Services, 9030 Old Georgetown Rd., Bethesda, MD 20892 TEL 301-496-8810. (Orders to: Supt. of Documents, Washington, DC 20402) Ed. Dr. Peter Greenwald. circ. 3,000. (microfiche; back issues avail.) Indexed: Biol.Abstr. Ind.Med.
Formerly: U.S. National Cancer Institute. Monograph (ISSN 0083-1921)

616.9 JA
NATIONAL CANCER CENTER. ANNUAL REPORT/KOKURITSU GAN SENTA NENPO. 1967. a. National Cancer Center - Kokuritsu Gan Senta, 5-1-1 Tsukiji, Chuo-ku, Tokyo 104, Japan.

616.9 JA ISSN 0077-3662
NATIONAL CANCER CENTER. COLLECTED PAPERS/KOKURITSU GAN SENTA, TOKYO. COLLECTED PAPERS. (Text in English) 1966. a. free to medical libraries and researchers. National Cancer Center - Kokuritsu Gan Senta, 5-1-1 Tsukiji, Chuo-ku, Tokyo 104, Japan. author index. circ. 225.

616.99 US ISSN 0195-8690
NATIONAL CANCER INSTITUTE. ANNUAL REPORT. a. U.S. National Cancer Institute, Bethesda, MD 20205. TEL 301-496-4000.

616.9 CN ISSN 0077-3689
NATIONAL CANCER INSTITUTE OF CANADA. ANNUAL REPORT. 1947. a. free. National Cancer Institute of Canada, 77 Bloor St. W., Suite 1702, Toronto, Ont. M5S 3A1, Canada. TEL 416-961-7223. Ed. Mrs. A. Vogel. circ. 800.

616 JA
OSAKA UNIVERSITY. INSTITUTE FOR CANCER RESEARCH. ANNUAL REPORT. (Text in English) irreg. exchange basis. Osaka University, Institute for Cancer Research - Osaka Daigaku Igakubu Fuzoku Gankenku Shisetsu, 3-12 Dojimahama-dori, Fukushima-ku, Osaka-shi 553, Japan.

616.994 IT ISSN 0069-8520
PERUGIA QUADRENNIAL INTERNATIONAL CONFERENCES ON CANCER. PROCEEDINGS. 1957. quadrennial. price varies. Universita degli Studi di Perugia, Division of Cancer Research, P.O. Box 327, 06100 Perugia, Monteluce, Italy. Ed. Lucio Severi. index.

616 US ISSN 0145-3726
PROGRESS IN CANCER RESEARCH AND THERAPY. 1976. irreg., vol.11, 1979. price varies. Raven Press, 1185 Ave. of the Americas, New York, NY 10036. TEL 212-575-0335. Indexed: Biol.Abstr. Chem.Abstr. Nutr.Abstr. Dairy Sci.Abstr. Hort.Abstr.

616.994 US ISSN 0079-6166
PROGRESS IN CLINICAL CANCER. 1965. irreg. price varies. Grune and Stratton, Inc. (Subsidiary of: Harcourt Brace Jovanovich, Inc.) Orlando, IL 32887 TEL 305-345-4200. (Dist. by: Academic Press Inc., 1250 Sixth Ave., San Diego, CA 92101) Ed. Dr. Irving M. Ariel. Indexed: Ind.Med.

616.994 SZ ISSN 0079-6263
PROGRESS IN EXPERIMENTAL TUMOR RESEARCH. (Text in English) 1960. irreg. (approx. 1/yr.) price varies. S. Karger AG, Allschwilerstrasse 10, CH-4009 Basel, Switzerland. Ed. F. Homburger. (reprint service avail. from ISI, back issues avail.) Indexed: Biol.Abstr. Chem.Abstr. Curr.Cont. Ind.Med.

616.994 US ISSN 0080-0015
RECENT RESULTS IN CANCER RESEARCH/FORTSCHRITTE DER KREBSFORSCHUNG. (Text in English; occasionally in French or German) 1965. irreg., vol.104, 1987. price varies. Springer-Verlag, 175 Fifth Ave., New York, NY 10010. TEL 212-460-1500. Ed. P. Rentchnick. (reprint service avail. from ISI) Indexed: Biol.Abstr. Chem.Abstr. Excerp.Med. Ind.Med. Dent.Ind.

616.99 BU
SCRIPTA SCIENTIFICA MEDICA. (Text in English; summaries in Russian) 1962. a. 10 lv. Izdatelstvo Meditsina i Fizkultura, Pl. Slaveikov 11, Sofia, Bulgaria (Subscr. to: Higher Institute of Medicine, 55 Marin Drinov St., Varna 9002, Bulgaria) Ed. Prof. Vanko Vankov. (back issues avail.) Indexed: Biol.Abstr. Ref.Zh. Abstr.Bulg.Sci.Med.Lit. Abstr.Hyg. Trop.Dis.Bull.

616.9 US ISSN 0081-0045
SLOAN-KETTERING INSTITUTE FOR CANCER RESEARCH. PROGRESS REPORT.* 1949. a. free. Sloan-Kettering Institute for Cancer Research, 410 E. 68 St., New York, NY 10021. TEL 212-794-7081.
Continues: Memorial Sloan-Kettering Cancer Center. New York. Report.

616.994 US ISSN 0082-0733
SYMPOSIA ON FUNDAMENTAL CANCER RESEARCH. PAPERS. no.2, 1947. a. price varies. American Association for Cancer Research, Inc., 428 E. Preston St., Baltimore, MD 21202. TEL 301-528-4000. Eds. R.W. Cumley, J. McCay.

616.9 SZ ISSN 0074-9222
U I C C TECHNICAL REPORT SERIES. 1968. irreg., latest vol.79. price varies. ‡ International Union Against Cancer, 3 rue de Conseil-General, 1205 Geneva, Switzerland. Indexed: Biol.Abstr. Excerp.Med.

616.99 US ISSN 0272-2836
U.S. NATIONAL TOXICOLOGY PROGRAM. ANNUAL REPORT ON CARCINOGENS. 1980. a. U.S. Public Health Service, 5600 Fishers Lane, Rockville, MD 20852. TEL 301-444-6656.

616.994 US ISSN 0084-3679
YEAR BOOK OF CANCER. 1957. a. $44.95. Year Book Medical Publishers, Inc., 35 E. Wacker Dr., Chicago, IL 60601. TEL 312-726-9733. Ed. Robert C. Hickey, M.D. illus.

MEDICAL SCIENCES — Cardiovascular Diseases

616.1 SZ ISSN 0065-2326
ADVANCES IN CARDIOLOGY. (Text in English) 1956. irreg., approx. 2/yr. price varies. S. Karger AG, Allschwilerstrasse 10, P.O. Box, CH-4009 Basel, Switzerland. Ed. J. Kellermann. (reprint service avail. from ISI) Indexed: Biol.Abstr. Chem.Abstr. Curr.Cont. Excerp.Med. Ind.Med. CINAHL.

616.1 SZ ISSN 0378-6900
ADVANCES IN CARDIOVASCULAR PHYSICS. (Text in English) a. price varies. S. Karger AG, Allschwilerstrasse 10, P.O. Box, CH-4009 Basel, Switzerland. Ed. D.N. Ghista. charts. (reprint service avail. from ISI) Indexed: Biol.Abstr. Chem.Abstr. Curr.Cont. Ind.Med.

612 591 SZ ISSN 0065-2938
ADVANCES IN MICROCIRCULATION. (Text in English) 1968. irreg., approx. 1/yr. price varies. S. Karger AG, Allschwilerstrasse 10, P.O. Box, CH-4009 Basel, Switzerland. Eds. B.M. Altura, E. Davis. (back issues avail.; reprint service avail. from ISI) Indexed: Biol.Abstr. Chem.Abstr. Curr.Cont. Ind.Med. Sci.Cit.Ind. Ind.Sci.Rev.

616.1 US
AMERICAN COLLEGE OF CARDIOLOGY. SYMPOSIA.* 1973. irreg. price varies. American College of Cardiology, 9111 Old Georgetown Rd., Bethesda, MD 20814.

616.6 US ISSN 0065-8499
AMERICAN HEART ASSOCIATION. MONOGRAPHS. 1960. irreg., no.44, 1974. price varies. American Heart Association, Inc., 7320 Greenville Ave., Dallas, TX 75231. TEL 214-706-1310. (reprint service avail. from UMI) Indexed: Biol.Abstr. Ind.Med.

616.1 IO ISSN 0587-5471
ASIAN PACIFIC CONGRESS OF CARDIOLOGY. SYMPOSIA.* irreg. Asian-Pacific Society of Cardiology, c/o Cardiac Centre, Jalan Diponegoro 69, Jakarta, Indonesia (Symposia from 4th Congress, 1968, pub. by Academic Press, US) Indexed: Biol.Abstr.
Cardiology

616.1 US
ATHEROSCLEROSIS. 1977. irreg., vol.6, 1983. Springer-Verlag, 175 Fifth Ave., New York, NY 10010 TEL 212-460-1500. (Also Berlin, Heidelberg, Tokyo and Vienna) (reprint service avail. from ISI) Indexed: Excerp.Med. Ind.Med. Nutr.Abstr. Sci.Cit.Ind. Biotech.Abstr. Risk Abstr. Vet.Bull.

616.136 US ISSN 0362-1650
ATHEROSCLEROSIS REVIEWS. 1975. irreg., vol.6, 1979. price varies. Raven Press, 1185 Ave. of the Americas, New York, NY 10036. TEL 212-575-0335. Eds. Antonio Gotto, Jr., Rodolfo Paoletti. Indexed: Biol.Abstr. Chem.Abstr. Curr.Cont. Sci.Cit.Ind. Ind.Sci.Rev.
Atherosclerosis

616.1 SZ ISSN 0067-7906
BIBLIOTHECA CARDIOLOGICA. (Text in English) 1939. irreg. price varies. S. Karger AG, Allschwilerstrasse 10, P.O. Box, CH-4009 Basel, Switzerland. Ed. J.J. Kellermann. (reprint service avail. from ISI) Indexed: Biol.Abstr. Chem.Abstr. Curr.Cont. Ind.Med.
Cardiology

616.1 CN ISSN 0068-8851
CANADIAN HEART FOUNDATION. ANNUAL REPORT. (Text in English and French) 1956. a. free. Canadian Heart Foundation, Suite 1200, One Nicholas St., Ottawa, Ont. K1N 7B7, Canada. TEL 613-237-4361. Ed. E. MacDonald. circ. 5,000.

616.1 US ISSN 0163-1675
CARDIOLOGY UPDATE; reviews for physicians. 1979. a. Elsevier Science Publishing Co., Inc. (New York), 52 Vanderbilt Ave., New York, NY 10017. TEL 212-370-5520. Ed. E. Rapaport.

616.1 US ISSN 0271-4779
CARDIOVASCULAR REVIEW. a. Williams & Wilkins, 428 E. Preston St., Baltimore, MD 21202. TEL 301-528-4000.

617.41 US ISSN 0069-0406
CARDIOVASCULAR SURGERY. (Subseries of: American Heart Association Monographs) 1962. a. price varies. American Heart Association, Inc., Council on Cardiovascular Surgery, 7320 Greenville Ave., Dallas, TX 75231. TEL 214-706-1310. Ed. Donald B. Doty, M.D. adv. circ. 23,000. Indexed: Ind.Med.

616.1 US
CLINICAL CARDIOLOGY MONOGRAPHS. 1972. irreg., latest 1978. price varies. Grune and Stratton, Inc. (Subsidiary of: Harcourt Brace Jovanovich, Inc.) Orlando, FL 32887 TEL 305-345-4200. (Dist. by: Academic Press Inc., 1250 Sixth Ave., San Diego, CA 92101) Eds. Drs. J. Willis Hurst, Dean T. Mason.
Formerly (vol.1): Cardiovascular Diseases; Current Status and Advances.

616.2 US ISSN 0069-5319
COLLECTED WORKS ON CARDIO-PULMONARY DISEASE. 1959. irreg.; latest issue, vol. 21, 1977. free. Heineman Medical Research Center, Box 4457, Charlotte, NC 28204. TEL 704-374-0505. Indexed: Biol.Abstr. Ind.Med.

616.1 US ISSN 0163-9501
CURRENT CARDIOLOGY. 1979. a. $30. Year Book Medical Publishers, Inc., 35 E. Wacker Dr., Chicago, IL 60601.

616.12 US
CURRENT PROBLEMS IN PULMONOLOGY. 1979. a. $69.95. Year Book Medical Publishers, Inc., 35 E. Wacker Dr., Chicago, IL 60601. Ed.Bd. illus.

616.1 UK
CURRENT TOPICS IN CARDIOVASCULAR MEDICINE. 1987. irreg. price varies. Edward Arnold (Publishers) Ltd., 41 Bedford Sq., London WC1B 3DQ, England.

616.1 NE ISSN 0421-7527
EUROPEAN CONGRESS OF CARDIOLOGY. ABSTRACTS OF PAPERS. (Text in English, French and German) 1952. quadrennial, 1980, 8th, Paris. European Society of Cardiology, c/o Prof. Paul G. Hugenholtz, Sec., P.O. Box 23410, 3001 KK Rotterdam, Netherlands.
Cardiology

616.1 NE ISSN 0423-7242
EUROPEAN CONGRESS OF CARDIOLOGY. (PROCEEDINGS) 1952. quadrennial, 1980, 8th, Paris. European Society of Cardiology, c/o Prof. Paul G. Hugenholtz, Sec., P.O. Box 23410, 3001 KK Rotterdam, Netherlands.
Cardiology

HIROSAKI DAIGAKU IGAKUBU EISEIGAKU KYOSHITSU GYOSEKISHU. see *MEDICAL SCIENCES*

616.1 DK ISSN 0105-9785
HJERTEFORENINGEN. 1978. a. free. Hjerteforeningen, Hauser Plads 10, 1127 Copenhagen K, Denmark. illus.

616.1 DK ISSN 0108-8904
HJERTENYT; orientering om sundhed og praeventiv medicin. 1982. irreg. free. Hjerteforeningen, Hauser Plads 10, 1127 Copenhagen K, Denmark.

616.12 US ISSN 0173-0282
INTERNATIONAL BOEHRINGER MANNHEIM SYMPOSIA. 1976. irreg., latest 1983. Springer-Verlag, 175 Fifth Ave., New York, NY 10010. TEL 212-460-1500. (reprint service avail. from ISI)

616.13 IT ISSN 0074-347X
INTERNATIONAL CONGRESS OF ANGIOLOGY. PROCEEDINGS. 1952. irreg., 1976, 10th, Tokyo. International Union of Angiology, c/o Marcello Tesi, Via Bonifacio Lupi 11, 20129 Florence, Italy.
Proceedings published in host country

INTERNATIONAL SOCIETY OF BLOOD TRANSFUSION. PROCEEDINGS OF THE CONGRESS. see MEDICAL SCIENCES — Hematology

616.1 US ISSN 0074-8765
INTERNATIONAL SYMPOSIUM ON ATHEROSCLEROSIS. PROCEEDINGS. 1966. irreg., 2nd, 1962, Chicago. Springer-Verlag, 175 Fifth Ave., New York, NY 10010. TEL 212-460-1500.

INTERNATIONAL SYMPOSIUM ON SURGICAL HEART DISEASE. PROCEEDINGS. see MEDICAL SCIENCES — Surgery

616.1 JA
JAPANESE CIRCULATION JOURNAL SUPPLEMENT. (Text in Japanese) irreg. (2-3/yr.) Japanese Circulation Society - Nihon Junkanki Gakkai, Kinki Invention Center, 14 Yoshida Kawaharacho, Sakyoku 606, Japan. Ed. Shoji Hayase.

616.1 SZ ISSN 0077-099X
MONOGRAPHS ON ATHEROSCLEROSIS. (Text in English) 1969. irreg., approx. 1/yr. price varies. S. Karger AG, Allschwilerstrasse 10, P.O. Box, CH-4009 Basel, Switzerland. Eds. D. Kritchevsky, O.J. Pollak. (reprint service avail. from ISI) Indexed: Biol.Abstr. Chem.Abstr. Curr.Cont. Ind.Med.
Atherosclerosis

616.1 SZ ISSN 0302-2293
MONOGRAPHS ON STANDARDIZATION OF CARDIOANGIOLOGICAL METHODS. Variant title: Standardization of Cardioangiological Methods. 1972. irreg. (International Committee for the Standardization of Angiological Methods) Verlag Hans Huber, Laenggassstr. 76 und Marktgasse 9, CH-3000 Berne 9, Switzerland. (Co-sponsor: Council on Clinical Science of the International Society of Cardiology)

616.1 AT ISSN 0077-4685
NATIONAL HEART FOUNDATION OF AUSTRALIA. RESEARCH-IN-PROGRESS. 1962. a. free. National Heart Foundation of Australia, Box 2, Woden, A.C.T. 2605, Australia. Ed. Robert Hodge. circ. 2,000.

NATIONAL HEART NEWS. see MEDICAL SCIENCES

616.1 AT ISSN 0550-0990
NOTES ON CARDIOVASCULAR DISEASES. (Supplement to: A M A Victoria Branch News) 1964. irreg. free to qualified personnel. Australian Medical Association, Victoria Branch, 293 Royal Parade, Parkville, Vic. 3052, Australia. (Co-sponsor: National Heart Foundation (Victoria)) Ed.Bd. circ. 20,000.

616.1 US ISSN 0361-0527
PERSPECTIVES IN CARDIOVASCULAR RESEARCH. 1976. irreg., vol.4, 1979. Raven Press, 1185 Ave. of the Americas, New York, NY 10036. TEL 212-575-0335. Ed. Arnold M. Katz. Indexed: Chem.Abstr.

PERSPECTIVES IN NEPHROLOGY AND HYPERTENSION. see MEDICAL SCIENCES — Urology And Nephrology

616.1 US
PRINCETON RESEARCH CONFERENCES ON CEREBROVASCULAR DISEASES. 1976. irreg., vol.11, 1979. price varies. Raven Press, 1185 Ave. of the Americas, New York, NY 10036. TEL 212-575-0335. index. Indexed: Chem.Abstr. Key Title: Cerebrovascular Diseases.
Former titles: Princeton Conference on Cerebrovascular Diseases (ISSN 0146-6917); Until 1976: Cerebral Vascular Diseases. Conference (ISSN 0069-2255)

616.1 SZ ISSN 0254-5195
PROGRESS IN APPLIED MICROCIRCULATION/ MIKROZIRKULATION IN FORSCHUNG UND KLINIK. 1983. irreg., 1-2/yr. price varies. S. Karger AG, Allschwilerstr. 10, CH-4009 Basel, Switzerland. Eds. K. Messmer, F. Hammersen. Indexed: Chem.Abstr.

616.1 US ISSN 0097-109X
PROGRESS IN CARDIOLOGY; a series. 1972. a. price varies. Lea & Febiger, 600 S. Washington Sq., Philadelphia, PA 19106. TEL 800-433-3850. Eds. Paul N. Yu, John F. Goodwin. illus. Indexed: Biol.Abstr.
Cardiology

618 US ISSN 0361-0233
PROGRESS IN CHEMICAL FIBRINOLYSIS AND THROMBOLYSIS. 1975. irreg., vol.3, 1979. price varies. Raven Press, 1185 Avenue of the Americas, New York, NY 10036. TEL 212-575-0335. Indexed: Biol.Abstr.
Formerly: International Conference on Synthetic Fibrinolytic--Thrombolytic Agents. Proceedings.

616.1 US
PROGRESS IN CORONARY SINUS INTERVENTIONS. 1986. irreg. price varies. Springer-Verlag, 175 Fifth Ave., New York, NY 10160 TEL 212-460-1500. (Distr. in Germany by: Dr. Dietrich /Steinkopff Verlag, Darmstadt, West Germany (B.R.D.)) (reprint service avail. from ISI)

616.15 US
PROGRESS IN HEMOSTASIS AND THROMBOSIS. 1972. irreg., vol.7, 1985. price varies. Grune and Stratton, Inc. (Subsidiary of: Harcourt Brace Jovanovich, Inc.) Orlando, FL 32887 TEL 305-345-4200. (Dist. by: Academic Press Inc., 1250 Sixth Ave., San Diego, CA 92101) Ed. Theodore H. Spaet, M.D. Indexed: Biol.Abstr. Chem.Abstr. Ind.Med.
Formerly: Progress in Hemostasis.

SCRIPTA SCIENTIFICA MEDICA. see MEDICAL SCIENCES — Cancer

362.1 US ISSN 0161-1917
U.S. NATIONAL HEART, LUNG, AND BLOOD ADVISORY COUNCIL. REPORT. (Subseries of: N I H Publication) 1973. a. U.S. National Heart, Lung, and Blood Advisory Council, 9000 Rockville Pike, Bethesda, MD 20205. TEL 301-496-7548. circ. 5,000.
Continues: U.S. National Heart and Lung Advisory Council. Annual Report (ISSN 0095-0262)

616.1005 US ISSN 0145-4145
YEAR BOOK OF CARDIOLOGY. 1968. a. $42.95. Year Book Medical Publishers, Inc., 35 E. Wacker Dr., Chicago, IL 60601. TEL 312-726-9733. Ed. W. Proctor Harvey, M.D. illus.
Former titles: Yearbook of Cardiovascular Medicine (ISSN 0360-6031) & Yearbook of Cardiovascular Medicine and Surgery (ISSN 0084-3687); Supersedes in part title issued 1962-67 as: Yearbook of Cardiovascular and Renal Disease.

YEAR BOOK OF VASCULAR SURGERY. see MEDICAL SCIENCES

MEDICAL SCIENCES — Chiropractics, Homeopathy, Osteopathy

615.53 US ISSN 0883-2986
A B M S DIRECTORY OF CERTIFIED PHYSICAL MEDICINE & REHABILITATION PHYSICIANS. 1985. biennial. $24.95 softcover. American Board of Medical Specialties, One American Plaza, Ste. 805, Evanston, IL 60201. TEL 312-491-9091. Ed. Donald G. Langsley, M.D.

615.533 US
A O A YEARBOOK AND DIRECTORY OF OSTEOPATHIC PHYSICIANS. 1908. a. $35. American Osteopathic Association, 212 E. Ohio St., Chicago, IL 60611. TEL 312-280-5800. Ed. George W. Northup, D.O. adv. stat. index. circ. 19,300.
Formerly: Yearbook and Directory of Osteopathic Physicians (ISSN 0084-358X)

615.533 US ISSN 0732-703X
AMERICAN ACADEMY OF OSTEOPATHY YEARBOOK. Variant title: Yearbook of Selected Osteopathic Papers. 1943. a. $15. American Academy of Osteopathy, Box 750, 12 W. Locust St., Newark, OH 43055. TEL 614-349-8701. illus. cum.index 1972, 1977. circ. 1,100 (controlled)
Osteopathy

ANNUAIRE NATIONAL DES MASSEURS KINESITHERAPEUTES. see MEDICAL SCIENCES

615.53 920 900 US ISSN 0736-4377
CHIROPRACTIC HISTORY. 1981. a. $24. Association for the History of Chiropractic, 4920 Frankford Ave., Baltimore, MD 21206. TEL 301-488-6604. Dir. William S. Rehm. circ. 500. (back issues avail.)

MEDICAL SCIENCES — Communicable Diseases

ADVANCES IN VIRUS RESEARCH. see BIOLOGY — Microbiology

CLINICAL TOPICS IN INFECTIOUS DISEASE. see MEDICAL SCIENCES

616.9 US ISSN 0195-3842
CURRENT CLINICAL TOPICS IN INFECTIOUS DISEASES. 1980. a. $45. McGraw-Hill Book Co., 1221 Ave. of the Americas, New York, NY 10020. TEL 212-512-2000. Eds. Jack Remington, M.D., Morton Swartz, M.D. illus.

616.9 TZ
EAST AFRICAN INSTITUTE OF MALARIA AND VECTORBORNE DISEASES. ANNUAL REPORT. (Text in English) a. East African Institute of Malaria and Vectorborne Diseases, Box 4, Amani, Tanzania. Indexed: Biol.Abstr. Rev.Appl.Entomol.

016.6 US ISSN 0197-8160
HUMAN GENETICS, INFORMATIONAL AND EDUCATIONAL MATERIALS. SUPPLEMENT. 1980. a. U.S. Public Health Service, 5600 Fishers Lane, Rockville, MD 20852. TEL 301-444-6656.

616.01 576.64 AE ISSN 0020-2460
INSTITUT PASTEUR D'ALGERIE. ARCHIVES. (Text in English and French) 1921. a. 30 din.($6.) (Institut Pasteur d'Algerie) Societe Nationale d'Edition et de Diffusion, Rue Docteur Laveran, Algiers, Algeria. bibl. charts. illus. stat. index. circ. 1,000. (also avail. in microfilm) Indexed: Biol.Abstr. Excerp.Med. Ind.Med. Helminthol.Abstr. Ind.Vet. Rev.Appl.Entomol. Vet.Bull. Trop.Dis.Bull.
Virology

616.01 576 GR ISSN 0004-6620
INSTITUT PASTEUR HELLENIQUE. ARCHIVES. (Text in French; summaries in English and Greek) 1923. a. free. ‡ Institut Pasteur Hellenique, 127 Ave. de la Reine Sophie, Athens 618, Greece. Dir. Charles Serie. adv. circ. 1,500. Indexed: Biol.Abstr. Abstr.Hyg. Bull.Inst.Pasteur. Ind.Vet. Vet.Bull. Trop.Dis.Bull.

INSTITUTO DE HIGIENE E MEDICINA TROPICAL. ANAIS. see PUBLIC HEALTH AND SAFETY

616.96 PL ISSN 0074-3356
INTERNATIONAL COMMISSION ON TRICHINELLOSIS. PROCEEDINGS. (Published as a No. of "Wiadomosci Parazytologiczne") 1962. irreg. 90 Zl. Polskie Towarzystwo Parazytologiczne, Norwida 29, 50-375 Wroclaw, Poland. Ed. Z. Zara. bk. rev. circ. 800.
Parasitology

616.9 GR ISSN 0074-4212
INTERNATIONAL CONGRESSES ON TROPICAL MEDICINE AND MALARIA. (PROCEEDINGS) (Proceedings issued at discretion of host country; none issued for 8th, Teheran.) 1948. quinquennial. 9th Athens. International Congresses on Tropical Medicine and Malaria, c/o Prof. J. Papa Vassilious, University of Athens, Athens, Greece. circ. 1,500.
Tropical medicine

616.988 US ISSN 0074-7777
INTERNATIONAL REVIEW OF TROPICAL MEDICINE. 1961. irreg., 1971, vol. 4. Academic Press, Inc., Orlando, FL 32887. TEL 305-345-2000. Ed. David R. Lincicome. index. Indexed: Biol.Abstr.
Tropical medicine

616.01 576.64 US ISSN 0076-6933
METHODS IN VIROLOGY. 1967. irreg., vol.8, 1984. price varies. Academic Press, Inc, Orlando, FL 32887. TEL 305-345-2000. Eds. Karl Maramorosch, Hilary Koprowski. Indexed: Biol.Abstr.

MEDICAL SCIENCES — COMPUTER APPLICATIONS

616.96   AG   ISSN 0524-952X
MUSEO ARGENTINO DE CIENCIAS
NATURALES "BERNARDINO RIVADAVIA."
INSTITUTO NACIONAL DE INVESTIGACION
DE LAS CIENCIAS NATURALES. REVISTA.
PARASITOLOGIA. 1968. irreg., latest vol.2, no.5,
1980. Museo Argentino de Ciencias Naturales
"Bernardino Rivadavia", Instituto Nacional de
Investigacion de las Ciencias Naturales, Avda.
Angel Gallardo 470, Casilla de Correo 220-Sucursal
5, Buenos Aires, Argentina.

614   616.998   JA   ISSN 0454-2029
NATIONAL INSTITUTE FOR LEPROSY
RESEARCH. ANNUAL REPORT/KOKURITSU
TAMA KENKYUSHO NENPO. (Text in Japanese)
1955. a. National Institute for Leprosy Research -
Kokuritsu Tama Kenkyusho, 4-1455 Aoba-cho,
Higashimurayama, Tokyo 189, Japan.
Leprosy

610   576.64   SZ   ISSN 0079-645X
PROGRESS IN MEDICAL VIROLOGY. (Text in
English) 1958. irreg., approx. 1/yr. price varies. S.
Karger AG, Allschwilerstrasse 10, P.O. Box, CH-
4009 Basel, Switzerland. Ed. J.L. Melnick. (reprint
service avail. from ISI) Indexed: Biol.Abstr.
Chem.Abstr. Curr.Cont. Ind.Med. Abstr.Hyg.
Dent.Ind. Ind.Vet. Vet.Bull.

616.9   614   UK   ISSN 0142-3517
PUBLIC HEALTH LABORATORY SERVICE
BOARD. ANNUAL REPORT. 1975. a. free. Public
Health Laboratory Service Board, 61 Colindale
Ave., London NW9 5DF, England. Ed. B. Guthrie.
circ. 1,500. (also avail. in microform; MI)
    Formerly: Public Health Laboratory Service
Board. Year Book (ISSN 0306-1531)

616.2   US   ISSN 0272-7900
PULMONARY DISEASE REVIEWS. 1980. irreg.,
vol.4, 1984. $69. John Wiley & Sons, Inc., 605
Third Ave., New York, NY 10016. TEL 212-850-
6000.

616.9   UK   ISSN 0144-1078
RECENT ADVANCES IN INFECTION. 1979. irreg.
Churchill Livingstone Medical Journals, Robert
Stevenson House, 1-3 Baxter's Place, Leith Walk,
Edinburgh EH3 3AF, Scotland.

616.988   BL   ISSN 0034-7256
REVISTA BRASILEIRA DE MALARIOLOGIA E
DOENCAS TROPICAIS. (Text in Portuguese;
summaries in English and Portuguese) 1949. a. free
to medical organizations. ‡ Ministerio da Saude,
Esplanada dos Ministerios Bloco G, 7 Andar, 70058
Brasilia DF, Brazil. Ed. Marcos A. Soares Porto. bk.
rev. abstr. charts. illus. stat. index. cum.index.
circ. 2,000. Indexed: Biol.Abstr. Chem.Abstr.
Ind.Med. Abstr.Hyg. Helminthol.Abstr.
Rev.Appl.Entomol. Trop.Dis.Bull.
Tropical medicine

616.988   UK   ISSN 0080-4711
ROYAL SOCIETY OF TROPICAL MEDICINE
AND HYGIENE, LONDON. YEARBOOK. 1908.
a. £15. Royal Society of Tropical Medicine and
Hygiene, Manson House, 26 Portland Place,
London, W1N 4EY, England. Ed. R.J. Baker. adv.
bk. rev. circ. 3,500. Indexed: Curr.Cont.
Tropical medicine

610   US   ISSN 0171-2160
TOPICS IN INFECTIOUS DISEASES. 1975. irreg.,
vol.3, 1978. price varies. Springer Verlag, 175 Fifth
Ave., New York, NY 10010 TEL 212-460-1500.
(And Berlin, Heidelberg, Tokyo and Vienna)
(reprint service avail. from ISI) Indexed:
Chem.Abstr.

616.9   SZ
TROPICAL DISEASES RESEARCH SERIES. 1979.
irreg., no.5, 1984. price varies. (Special Programme
for Research and Training in Tropical Diseases, UN)
Schwabe und Co. AG, Steinentorstr. 13, 4010
Basel, Switzerland. (Co-sponsors of program: United
Nations Development Programme; World Bank;
World Health Organization)

616.9   TH
TROPMED SEMINARS ON TROPICAL
MEDICINE. PROCEEDINGS. (Text in English)
irreg., no.29, 1986. $10. Southeast Asian Ministers
of Education Organisation, Regional Tropical
Medicine & Public Health Project, 420/6 Rajvithi
Road, Bangkok 10400, Thailand. circ. 500.
    Former titles: Tropmed Seminars on Parasitology
and Tropical Medicine. Proceedings & Southeast
Asian Seminar on Parasitology and Tropical
Medicine. Proceedings (ISSN 0085-6517)

610   US
U.S. ARMY MEDICAL RESEARCH INSTITUTE
OF INFECTIOUS DISEASES. ANNUAL
PROGRESS REPORT. 1968. a. free. U.S. Army
Medical Research Institute of Infectious Diseases,
Fort Detrick, Frederick, MD 21701 TEL 301-663-
8000. (Orders to: NTIS, Springfield, VA 22151) Ed.
K. Kenyon. Key Title: Annual Progress Report -
U.S. Army Medical Research Institute of Infectious
Diseases.
Military

616.9   US
U.S. CENTERS FOR DISEASE CONTROL.
DIPHTHERIA SURVEILLANCE REPORT. 1962.
irreg. U.S. Centers for Disease Control, Dept. of
Health and Human Services, 1600 Clifton Rd., NE,
Atlanta, GA 30333. TEL 404-329-3311. charts.
stat. (looseleaf format)

616.998   US
U.S. CENTERS FOR DISEASE CONTROL.
LEPROSY SURVEILLANCE REPORT. 1970.
irreg., no.2, 1972. U.S. Centers for Disease Control,
Dept. of Health and Human Services, 1600 Clifton
Rd., N.E., Atlanta, GA 30333. TEL 404-329-3311.
charts. stat.
Leprosy

616.9   US
U.S. CENTERS FOR DISEASE CONTROL.
LISTERIOSIS SURVEILLANCE REPORT. irreg.
U.S. Centers for Disease Control, Dept. of Health
and Human Services, 1600 Clifton Rd., N.E.,
Atlanta, GA 30333. TEL 404-329-3311. charts.
stat.

616.9   US   ISSN 0501-8390
U.S. CENTERS FOR DISEASE CONTROL.
MALARIA SURVEILLANCE REPORT. 1955. a.
free. U.S. Centers for Disease Control, Dept. of
Health and Human Services, 1600 Clifton Rd.,
N.E., Atlanta, GA 30333. TEL 404-329-3311. Ed.
Dr. Myron G. Schultz. circ. 2,000.

VIROLOGY MONOGRAPHS/VIRUSFORSCHUNG
IN EINZELDARSTELLUNGEN. see
BIOLOGY — Microbiology

610   KO
YONSEI REPORTS ON TROPICAL MEDICINE.
(Text in English) 1970. a. avail. on exchange.
Yonsei University, College of Medicine, Box 8044,
Seoul, S. Korea. Ed. Chin-Thack Soh. adv. abstr.
bibl. charts. stat. (tabloid format) Indexed:
Biol.Abstr. Excerp.Med.

616.96   574.524   GW   ISSN 0174-3031
ZENTRALBLATT FUER BAKTERIOLOGIE,
PARASITENKUNDE,
INFEKTIONSKRANKHEITEN UND HYGIENE.
SERIES A; MEDIZINISCHE MIKROBIOLOGIE
UND PARASITOLOGIE. irreg., 4 nos. per vol.
DM.284 per vol. Gustav Fischer Verlag,
Wollgrasweg 49, 7000 Stuttgart 70, W. Germany
(B.R.D.) Ed. G. Henneberg. circ. 1,100. Indexed:
Biol.Abstr. Chem.Abstr. Ind.Med. Dent.Ind.
Helminthol.Abstr. Rev.Appl.Entomol.
Parasitology

MEDICAL SCIENCES — Computer Applications

ADVANCES IN BIOMEDICAL COMPUTING
SERIES. see *ENGINEERING — Computer
Applications*

621.3   616   US   ISSN 0276-6574
COMPUTERS IN CARDIOLOGY. 1974. a. price
varies. (Institute of Electrical and Electronics
Engineers, Inc.) I E E E Computer Society Press,
1730 Massachusetts Ave., N.W., Washington, DC
20036-1903 (And 345 E. 47th St., New York, NY
10017) (Co-sponsors: U.S. National Institutes of
Health; European Society of Cardiology) Indexed:
Sci.Abstr.

610   615   US
COMPUTERTALK PHARMACY SYSTEMS
BUYERS GUIDE. 1982. a. $25. ComputerTalk
Associates, Inc., 1750 Walton Rd., Blue Bell, PA
19422. TEL 215-825-7686. Ed. Neil R. Bauman.
adv. circ. 50,000.
    Formerly: ComputerTalk Directory of Pharmacy
Systems (ISSN 0736-3877)

610   001.6   US
FRONTIERS OF ENGINEERING AND
COMPUTING IN HEALTH CARE. Represents: I
E E E Engineering in Medicine and Biology
Society. Annual Conference. Proceedings. 1983. a.
price varies. (I E E E, Engineering in Medicine and
Biology Society) Institute of Electrical and
Electronics Engineers, Inc., 345 E. 47th St., New
York, NY 10017 TEL 212-705-7900. (Subscr.
address: 445 Hoes Lane, Piscataway, NJ 08854)
    Formed by the merger of (1981-1982): I E E E
Frontiers of Computers in Medicine; (1979-1982): I
E E E Frontiers of Engineering in Health Care.

001.6   610   US   ISSN 0195-4210
SYMPOSIUM ON COMPUTER APPLICATIONS
IN MEDICAL CARE. PROCEEDINGS. 1977. a.
(Institute of Electrical and Electronics Engineers,
Inc.) I E E E Computer Society Press, 1730
Massachusetts Ave., N.W., Washington, DC 20036-
1903 TEL 202-371-0101. (And 345 E. 47th St.,
New York, NY 10017)

360   US
U.S. NATIONAL CENTER FOR HEALTH
STATISTICS. CATALOG OF PUBLIC USE
DATA TAPES. a. U.S. National Center for Health
Statistics, Scientific and Technical Information
Branch, 3700 East-West Highway, Hyattsville, MD
20782. TEL 301-436-8500.
    Formerly: U.S. National Center for Health
Statistics. Standardized Micro-Data Tape
Transcripts.

MEDICAL SCIENCES — Dentistry

617.6   CN   ISSN 0383-6355
A.D.A. NEWS INFORMATION. 1967. irreg.
membership. Alberta Dental Association, Suite 101,
8230 105 St., Edmonton, Alta., Canada. Ed. D.L.
Thompson. adv. circ. 1,375.

617.6   US   ISSN 0277-3619
A S D A HANDBOOK. a. $2 to members; $4 non-
members. American Student Dental Association,
211 E. Chicago Ave., Chicago, IL 60611. TEL 312-
440-2795. adv. circ. 23,000.

617.6   US   ISSN 0065-079X
ACCEPTED DENTAL THERAPEUTICS. 1934.
biennial. $16.50 to non-members; members $15.
American Dental Association, 211 E. Chicago Ave.,
Chicago, IL 60611. TEL 312-440-2500. Ed. Dr.
Edgar Mitchell. index.
    Formerly: Accepted Dental Remedies.

617.6   US   ISSN 0091-729X
ADMISSION REQUIREMENTS OF U S AND
CANADIAN DENTAL SCHOOLS. 1963. a.
$13.50. American Association of Dental Schools,
1625 Massachusetts Ave, N.W., Washington, DC
20036. TEL 202-667-9433. circ. 3,000. (reprint
service avail. from UMI)
    Formerly: Admission Requirements of American
Dental Schools (ISSN 0065-1990)

617.6   US   ISSN 0065-3020
ADVANCES IN ORAL BIOLOGY. 1964. irreg., vol.
4, 1970. Academic Press, Inc., Orlando, FL 32887.
TEL 305-345-2000. Ed. Peter H. Staple. index.
Indexed: Biol.Abstr.

MEDICAL SCIENCES — DENTISTRY

617.6   US
AMERICAN DENTAL ASSOCIATION. TRANSACTION SERIES: ANNUAL REPORTS AND RESOLUTIONS, SUPPLEMENTS ONE AND TWO, TRANSACTIONS. a. price varies. American Dental Association, 211 E. Chicago Ave., Chicago, IL 60611. TEL 312-440-2500.
    Formerly: American Dental Association. Annual Reports and Resolutions (ISSN 0090-3329)

617.6   US   ISSN 0065-8073
AMERICAN DENTAL DIRECTORY. 1947. a. $60. American Dental Association, 211 E. Chicago Ave., Chicago, IL 60611. TEL 312-440-2500.

617.6   FR   ISSN 0066-2712
ANNUAIRE DENTAIRE. 1936/37. a. 400 F.($65) Editions de Chabassol, 30 rue de Gramont, 75002 Paris, France. Ed. B. Laloup. adv. circ. 6,500.

618   US
ANNUAL REPORT ON ADVANCED DENTAL EDUCATION. 1972. a. free. American Dental Association, 211 E. Chicago Ave., Chicago, IL 60611. TEL 312-440-2500. Ed. David R. DeMarais. (also avail. in microform from UMI)

617.6   US   ISSN 0005-7258
BAYLOR DENTAL JOURNAL. 1951. a. free to qualified personnel. Baylor College of Dentistry, Alumni and Public Information Office, 3302 Gaston Ave., Dallas, TX 75246. TEL 214-828-8204. Ed. Dr. William Binnie. adv. abstr. illus. circ. 5,000(controlled) Indexed: Dent.Ind.

617.6   DK   ISSN 0108-6618
BOERNETANDPLEJEN I DANMARK. (Subseries: Primaer Sundhedstjenestestatistik) 1983. irreg. Kr.25. Sundhedsstyrelsen, St. Kongensgade 1, 1264 Copenhagen K, Denmark (Subscr.to: Danske Boghandleres Kommissionsanstalt, Siljangade 6, 2300 Copenhagen S, Denmark)

617.6   AG   ISSN 0069-9799
COOPERADOR DENTAL.* 1933. irreg. membership. Cooperativa Dental Argentina, M.T. de Alvear 2167, Buenos Aires, Argentina. Eds. H. B. Ferreri, Horacio Martinez. adv. bk. rev. circ. 6,000.

D M D. see *COLLEGE AND ALUMNI*

617.6   CN
DALHOUSIE DENTAL JOURNAL. 1961. a. free. Dalhousie Dental Students Society, Dalhousie University, Halifax, N.S. B3H 4H8, Canada. TEL 902-424-2211. Ed. Heather Carr-Kinnear. adv. circ. 1,000. (back issues avail.)

617.6   US
DENTAL ADMISSION TESTING PROGRAM. 1951. a. free. American Dental Association, Division of Educational Measurements, 211 E. Chicago Ave., Chicago, IL 60611. TEL 312-440-2500. Ed. David R. DeMarais. circ. 110,000.

617.6   UK   ISSN 0266-6073
DENTAL ANNUAL. 1985. a. £18.50. John Wright, Techno House, Redcliffe Way, Bristol BS1 6NX, England. index. circ. 2,000.

617.6   CN   ISSN 0070-3656
DENTAL GUIDE. 1965. a. Can.$20. Southam Communications Ltd., 1450 Don Mills Rd., Don Mills, Ont., Canada. TEL 416-445-6641. adv. circ. 13,663.

DENTAL LABORATORY REVIEW BUYER'S GUIDE. see *MEDICAL SCIENCES — Experimental Medicine, Laboratory Technique*

617.6   IE   ISSN 0084-9723
DENTAL REGISTER OF IRELAND. 1929. a. £1. Dental Board, 57 Merrion Sq., Dublin 2, Ireland. circ. 1,500.

617.6   UK
DENTAL TECHNICIAN YEARBOOK & DIRECTORY. 1979. a. £5.75. A.E. Morgan Publications Ltd., Stanley House, 9 West St., Epsom, Surrey KT18 7RL, England. Ed. D. Ritchie. adv.

617.6   JA   ISSN 0070-3737
DENTISTRY IN JAPAN. (Text in English) 1968. a. ‡ (Japanese Association for Dental Science - Nihon Shika Igakkai) Japan Dental Association, 3-16 Hayabusa-cho, Chiyoda-ku, Tokyo 102, Japan. Ed. Dr. S. Kikuchi. circ. 1,300 (controlled)

617.6   US
DENTIST'S DESK REFERENCE; materials, instruments & equipment. 1962. biennial. $17.55 to non-members; members $15.95. American Dental Association, 211 E. Chicago Ave., Chicago, IL 60611. TEL 312-440-2500. Ed. J. W. Stanford. bibl. charts. illus. circ. 10,000.
    Formerly: Guide to Dental Materials and Devices (ISSN 0093-9706)

617.6   GW
DEUTSCHER ZAHNAERZTEKALENDER. 1941. a. DM.48. Carl Hanser Verlag, Kolbergerstr. 22, Postfach 860420, 8000 Munich 80, W. Germany (B.R.D.) TEL 0049/89/926940. Ed. Dr. Werner Ketterl. adv. circ. 7,200.

DIRECTORY OF DENTAL EDUCATORS. see *EDUCATION — Higher Education*

617.6   US
DISTRIBUTION OF DENTISTS IN THE U S. triennial. free. American Dental Association, Bureau of Economic Research and Statistics, 211 E. Chicago Ave., Chicago, IL 60611. TEL 312-440-2500.

617.6   US   ISSN 0517-1024
FACTS ABOUT STATES FOR THE DENTIST SEEKING A LOCATION. 1953. irreg. (every 2-3 yrs.) American Dental Association, Bureau of Economic Research and Statistics, 211 E. Chicago Ave., Chicago, IL 60611. TEL 312-440-2500.

FINLAND. LAAKINTOHALLITUS. LAAKARIT, HAMMASLAAKARIT/LAKARE, TANDLAEKARE. see *MEDICAL SCIENCES*

614
FLUORIDATION CENSUS. 1954. irreg. U.S. Centers for Disease Control, Bureau of State Services, Dental Disease Prevention Activity, 1600 Clifton Rd., N.E., Atlanta, GA 30333. TEL 404-329-3311.

617.643   SZ   ISSN 0301-536X
FRONTIERS OF ORAL PHYSIOLOGY. (Text in English) 1974. irreg. (approx. 1/yr.) price varies. S. Karger AG, Allschwilerstrasse 10, P.O. Box, CH-4009 Basel, Switzerland. Ed. D.B. Ferguson. (reprint service avail. from ISI) Indexed: Biol.Abstr. Chem.Abstr. Ind.Med.

617.6   UK   ISSN 0072-0674
GENERAL DENTAL COUNCIL. DENTISTS REGISTER. 1878. a. £18.50. General Dental Council, 37 Wimpole St., London W1M 8DQ, England.

617.6   UK   ISSN 0072-0682
GENERAL DENTAL COUNCIL. MINUTES OF THE PROCEEDINGS. 1956. a. £10. General Dental Council, 37 Wimpole St., London W1M 8DQ, England.

617.6   US   ISSN 0073-1021
HAWAII DENTAL ASSOCIATION. TRANSACTIONS. a. Hawaii Dental Association, 1000 Bishop St., Suite 805, Honolulu, HI 96813. TEL 808-536-2135.

617.3   US   ISSN 0073-1404
HAYES DIRECTORY OF DENTAL SUPPLY HOUSES. 1935. a. $60. Edward N. Hayes, Ed. & Pub., 4229 Birch St., Newport Beach, CA 92660. TEL 714-756-9063.

617.6   JA   ISSN 0073-2915
HOKKAIDO DENTAL ASSOCIATION. JOURNAL/HOKKAIDO SHIKA ISHIKAISHI, DOSHIKAI TSUSHIN. (Text in Japanese) 1948. a. Hokkaido Dental Association - Hokkaido Shika Ishikai, 7-2 Odori Nishi, Chuo-ku, Sapporo 060, Japan.

INDICE DE LA LITERATURA DENTAL PERIODICA EN CASTELLANO. see *BIBLIOGRAPHIES*

617.6   DK   ISSN 0107-8097
INFODONT. 1980. irreg. (6-8/yr.) membership. Odontologisk Forening, Aarhus Tandlaegehoejskole, Vennelyst Boulevard, 8000 Aarhus C, Denmark.
    Formed by the merger of: Info & Odont (ISSN 0105-189X)

617.6   US   ISSN 0534-669X
INTERNATIONAL ASSOCIATION FOR DENTAL RESEARCH. ABSTRACTS OF THE GENERAL MEETING. 1919. a. $20. International Association for Dental Research, 1111 14 St., N.W., Ste. 1000, Washington, DC 20005. (Co-sponsor: American Association for Dental Research) Ed. Colin Dawes. adv. circ. 6,500. (also avail. in microform from UMI) Indexed: Dent.Abstr.

617.6   UK
INTERNATIONAL COLLEGE OF DENTISTS. EUROPEAN SECTION. NEWSLETTER. 1956. a. membership. International College of Dentists, European Section, 2 Haigh Lawn, St. Margaret's Rd., Altrincham, Cheshire WA14 2AP, England. Ed. Dr. H.D. Norton. circ. 500.

617.6   US   ISSN 0074-3216
INTERNATIONAL CONFERENCE ON ORAL BIOLOGY. PROCEEDINGS. (Special issue of Journal of Dental Research) triennial. American Association for Dental Research, 1111 14th St., N.W., Ste. 1000, Washington, DC 20005. TEL 202-898-1050. Ed. Colin Dawes. circ. 7,000. (reprint service avail. from UMI) Indexed: Dent.Abstr. Oral Res.Abstr.

617.6   JM
JAMAICA DENTAL ASSOCIATION. NEWSLETTER. irreg. Jamaica Dental Association, P.O. Box 19, Kingston 5, Jamaica.

617.632   DK   ISSN 0075-4331
JOURNAL OF PERIODONTAL RESEARCH. SUPPLEMENTUM. (Text in English) 1966. irreg. free to subscribers. Munksgaard, 35 Noerre Soegade, DK-1370 Copenhagen K, Denmark. Ed. Roy C. Page. adv. (reprint service avail. from ISI) Indexed: Biol.Abstr. Chem.Abstr. Ind.Med. Nutr.Abstr.

617.6   JA   ISSN 0385-1443
KANAGAWA DENTAL COLLEGE. BULLETIN. (Text in English) 1975. irreg. free. Kanagawa Dental College Society, 82, Inaoka-Cho, Yokosuka, Kanagawa-Ken, Japan. Ed. Taro Hisada. circ. 1,000.

617.6   CN   ISSN 0024-9025
MCGILL DENTAL REVIEW. 1934. irreg. McGill University, Dental Students' Society, Montreal, Quebec, Canada. TEL 514-392-4311. illus. Indexed: Dent.Ind.

MATSUMOTO DENTAL COLLEGE RESEARCH BULLETIN. see *BIOLOGY*

618   US
MEHARRY MEDICAL COLLEGE. SCHOOL OF DENTISTRY. PROCEEDINGS OF AN ORAL RESEARCH SEMINAR. 1973. biennial. free. Meharry Medical College, School of Dentistry, 1005 18th Ave. N., Nashville, TN 37208. TEL 615-327-6207. Ed. Theodore E. Bolden. (back issues avail)

617.6   CE
MIRROR AND PROBE.* (Text in English; summaries in Sinhala and Tamil) 1963. a. Dental Students' Association, University of Sri Lanka, University Park, Peradeniya, Sri Lanka. adv. charts. illus. stat. circ. controlled.

617.6   SZ   ISSN 0077-0892
MONOGRAPHS IN ORAL SCIENCE. (Text in English) 1972. irreg. (approx. 1/yr.) price varies. S. Karger AG, Allschwilerstrasse 10, P.O. Box, CH-4009 Basel, Switzerland. Ed. H.M. Myers. (reprint service avail. from ISI) Indexed: Biol.Abstr. Chem.Abstr. Curr.Cont. Ind.Med.

NATIONAL MEDICAL AND DENTAL ASSOCIATION. BULLETIN. see *MEDICAL SCIENCES*

617.6   JA   ISSN 0549-5245
NIPPON DENTAL UNIVERSITY. ANNUAL PUBLICATIONS. (Text in English) 1964. a. exchange basis. Nipon Dental University, 1-9-20 Fujimi, Chiyoda-ku, Tokyo 102, Japan. Ed. Osami Morita. circ. 2,000.
    Formerly: Society of Nippon Dental College. Annual Publications.

MEDICAL SCIENCES — DERMATOLOGY AND VENEREOLOGY

617.6   CN
NOVA SCOTIA DENTIST. irreg. membership. Nova Scotia Dental Association, 5991 Spring Garden Road, Suite 604, Halifax, N.S. B3H 1Y6, Canada. TEL 902-454-5449. Ed. D.V. Pamenter. circ. 500.
Formerly (until 1985): Nova Scotia Dental Association. Newsletter.

617.6   DK   ISSN 0105-0141
ODONTOLOGI. (Text in Danish, Norwegian and Swedish) 1976. irreg. price varies. Munksgaard, Noerre Soegade 35, DK-1370 Copenhagen K, Denmark. illus.

617.6   FI   ISSN 0078-3358
ODONTOLOGISKA SAMFUNDET I FINLAND. AARSBOK. 1946. a. Fmk.50. Odontologiska Samfundets i Finland, Bergmansg. 11 D 11, SF-00140 Helsinki 14, Finland. adv. bk. rev. circ. 500. Indexed: Biol.Abstr.

617.6   FR   ISSN 0078-6608
ORTHODONTIE FRANCAISE. (1921-1962 called also Comptes Rendus du Congres Annuel) 1921. a. 400 F. Julien Prelat, 17, rue du Petit-Pont, 75005 Paris, France. Indexed: Ind.Med.

617.6   AT   ISSN 0079-5631
PROBE. 1949. a. Aus.$5. University of Adelaide (AUDSS), Dental Students Society, School of Dentistry, Adelaide, Australia. Eds. S.R. Moore, H. Raets. adv. bk. rev. circ. 500.

617.6   UK
ROLLS OF ANCILLARY DENTAL WORKERS. a. £7.50. General Dental Council, 37 Wimpole St., London W1M 8DQq, England.

617.6   AT   ISSN 0158-1570
ROYAL AUSTRALASIAN COLLEGE OF DENTAL SURGEONS. ANNALS. 1967. irreg., vol.9, 1987. price varies. Royal Australasian College of Dental Surgeons, 64 Castlereagh St., Sydney, N.S.W. 2000, Australia. Ed. Dr. Robert Harris. circ. 1,000.
Former titles: Royal Australian College of Dental Surgeons. Annals (ISSN 0312-7923); Australian College of Dental Surgeons. Annals. (ISSN 0004-8895)

617.6   FR   ISSN 0081-1203
SOCIETE ODONTO-STOMATOLOGIQUE DU NORD-EST. REVUE ANNUELLE.* Called also: Revue Odonto-Stomatologique du Nord-Est. 1969. a. Societe Odonto-Stomatologique du Nord-Est, 9 rue Saint-Nicolas, 54000 Nancy, France.

617.6   FI   ISSN 0355-4651
SUOMEN HAMMASLAAKARISEURA. TOIMITUKSIA. SUPPLEMENTA/FINNISH DENTAL SOCIETY. PROCEEDINGS. SUPPLEMENT. (Text in English; summaries in Finnish) 1966. irreg., latest vol.81, 1985. Fmk.70($15) Finnish Dental Society - Suomen Hammaslaakariseura, Akavatalo, Rautatielaisenkatu 6, SF-00520 Helsinki 52, Finland. circ. 200. Indexed: Chem.Abstr.

617.6   US
SURVEY OF DENTAL PRACTICE. irreg., every 2-3/yrs. free. American Dental Association, Bureau of Economic Research and Statistics, 211 E. Chicago Ave., Chicago, IL 60611. TEL 312-440-2500.

617.6   DK
TANDLAEGEN. a. Forlaget John Vaboe A-S, Svanemoellevej 34, 2100 Copenhagen OE, Denmark. adv. circ. 4,500.

617.6   US
THIRTIETH DISTRICT DENTAL SOCIETY, FRESNO, CALIFORNIA. BULLETIN.* 1953. irreg. ‡ Fresno-Madera Dental Society, 4747 N. First St., No. 123, Fresno, CA 93726-0517. Ed. Dennis Shamlian. adv. circ. 600.
Former titles: Thirteenth District Dental Society. Bulletin; Fifth District Dental Society. Bulletin (ISSN 0071-9544)

TOKYO MEDICAL AND DENTAL UNIVERSITY. INSTITUTE FOR MEDICAL AND DENTAL ENGINEERING. REPORTS/IYO KIZAI KENKYUSHO HOKOKU. see *MEDICAL SCIENCES*

617.6   UY   ISSN 0083-4785
UNIVERSIDAD DE LA REPUBLICA. FACULTAD DE ODONTOLOGIA. ANALES. (Supplements accompany some numbers) 1955. irreg. exchange basis. Universidad de la Republica, Facultad de Odontologia, Gral. las Heras 1925, Montevideo, Uruguay. Indexed: Biol.Abstr. Dent.Ind.

617.6   BL
UNIVERSIDADE FEDERAL DE PERNAMBUCO. FACULDADE DE ODONTOLOGIA. ANAIS. (Text in Portuguese; summaries in English) 1960. a. Universidade Federal de Pernambuco, Faculdade de Odontologia, Recife, Pernambuco, Brazil.
Continues (with vol. 5): Universidade do Recife. Faculdade de Odontologia. Anais.

617.6   SW   ISSN 0076-3438
UNIVERSITY OF LUND. SCHOOL OF DENTISTRY. FACULTY OF ODONTOLOGY. ANNUAL PUBLICATIONS. Cover title: University of Lund. Faculty of Odontology. Annual Publications. (Text in English) 1958. a. free. University of Lund, Faculty of Odontology, School of Dentistry, 214 21 Malmoe, Sweden. Ed. Bengt Moeller. bk. rev. circ. 750.

617.6   US   ISSN 0076-843X
UNIVERSITY OF MICHIGAN. SCHOOL OF DENTISTRY. ALUMNI BULLETIN. 1937. a. University of Michigan, School of Dentistry, Ann Arbor, MI 48104. TEL 313-764-1817. Charles C. Kelsey. circ. 6,000. Indexed: Dent.Ind.

617.6   CN   ISSN 0042-0255
UNIVERSITY OF TORONTO UNDERGRADUATE DENTAL JOURNAL. 1964. a. $4 for 2 yrs. University of Toronto, Front Campus, Toronto, Ont. M5S 1A6, Canada. TEL 416-596-2552. Ed.Bd. adv. bk. rev. abstr. charts. illus.

617.6   US   ISSN 0083-7431
WASHINGTON STATE DENTAL JOURNAL. 1934. a. $10. Washington State Dental Association, Box 9824, Seattle, WA 98109. TEL 206-448-1914. adv. circ. 3,150. Indexed: Dent.Ind.

617.6058   US   ISSN 0084-3717
YEAR BOOK OF DENTISTRY. 1936. a. $45.95. Year Book Medical Publishers, Inc., 35 E. Wacker Dr., Chicago, IL 60601. TEL 312-726-9733. Ed. D. Walter Cohen. illus.

MEDICAL SCIENCES — Dermatology And Venereology

616.5   US   ISSN 0884-1489
A B M S DIRECTORY OF CERTIFIED DERMATOLOGISTS. 1984. biennial. $34.95 hardcover; $29.95 softcover. American Board of Medical Specialties, One American Plaza, Ste. 805, Evanston, IL 60201. TEL 312-491-9091. Ed. Donald G. Langsley, M.D.

616.5   US
ADVANCES IN DERMATOLOGY. 1985? a. $39.95. Year Book Medical Publishers, Inc., 35 E. Wacker Dr., Chicago, IL 60601. TEL 312-726-9746. illus.

616.5   UK   ISSN 0366-077X
BRITISH JOURNAL OF DERMATOLOGY. SUPPLEMENT. 1969. irreg. free. (British Association of Dermatologists) Blackwell Scientific Publications Ltd., Osney Mead, Oxford OX2 0EL, England. Ed. R.M. Mackie. adv. circ. 3,800. (also avail. in microfiche) Indexed: Biol.Abstr. Chem.Abstr. Curr.Cont. Excerp.Med. I.P.A. Ind.Med. Nutr.Abstr. Sci.Cit.Ind. ASCA. Helminthol.Abstr. Rev.Plant Path.

616.5   SZ   ISSN 0070-2064
CURRENT PROBLEMS IN DERMATOLOGY. (Text in English) 1959. irreg., approx. 1/yr. price varies. S. Karger AG, Allschwilerstrasse 10, P.O. Box, CH-4009 Basel, Switzerland. Ed. H. Honigsmann. (reprint service avail. from ISI) Indexed: Biol.Abstr. Chem.Abstr. Curr.Cont. Ind.Med. Dent.Ind.

616.5   US
DERMATOLOGY SERIES. 1982. irreg., vol.7, 1986. price varies. Marcel Dekker, Inc., 270 Madison Ave., New York, NY 10016. TEL 212-696-9000. Eds. Charles D. Calnan, Howard I. Mailbach.

616.5   US   ISSN 0163-1691
DERMATOLOGY UPDATE; reviews for physicians. 1979. a. Elsevier Science Publishing Co., Inc. (New York), 52 Vanderbilt Ave., New York, NY 10017. TEL 212-916-1150. Ed. S. Moschella.

616.5   616.95   US   ISSN 0071-7932
FORTSCHRITTE DER PRAKTISCHEN DERMATOLOGIE UND VENEROLOGIE. 1952. irreg., vol. 10, 1984. price varies. Springer-Verlag, 175 Fifth Ave., New York, NY 10010 TEL 212-460-1500. (Also Berlin, Heidelberg, Tokyo and Vienna) (reprint service avail. from ISI)

616.5   SZ
MODELS IN DERMATOLOGY. (Text in English) 1985. a. price varies. S. Karger AG, P.O. Box, CH-4009 Basel, Switzerland. Eds. H.I. Maibach, N.J. Lowe. Indexed: Biol.Abstr. Curr.Cont. Ind.Med.

PARAPHARMEX. see *PHARMACY AND PHARMACOLOGY*

616.951   CN
SEXUALLY TRANSMITTED DISEASE IN CANADA (YEAR) (Text in English, French) a. free. Health and Welfare Canada, Laboratory Centre for Disease Control, Rm. 145-B, Tunney's Pasture, Ottawa, Ont. K1A 0L2, Canada. TEL 613-957-1785. charts. stat. circ. 150. (back issues avail.)

616   312.39   CN
VENEREAL DISEASES IN CANADA. French edition: Maladies Veneriennes au Canada (ISSN 0319-0390) 1972. a. free. Department of National Health and Welfare, Brooke Claxton Bldg., Ottawa, Ont. K1A OK9, Canada. TEL 613-996-4650. illus.
Formerly: Canada. Epidemiology Division. Venereal Disease in Canada (ISSN 0319-0382)

616.505   US   ISSN 0093-3619
YEAR BOOK OF DERMATOLOGY. 1933. a. $45.95. Year Book Medical Publishers, Inc., 35 E. Wacker Dr., Chicago, IL 60601. TEL 312-726-9733. Ed. Arthur Sober, M.D. illus. Indexed: Biol.Abstr.
Formerly: Yearbook of Dermatology and Syphilology (ISSN 0093-3627)

MEDICAL SCIENCES — Endocrinology

616.4   DK
ACTA ENDOCRINOLOGICA. SUPPLEMENTUM. 1949. irreg. Periodica, Skolegade 12, DK-2500 Valby Copenhagen, Denmark. abstr. illus. Indexed: Biol.Abstr. Chem.Abstr. Excerp.Med. Ind.Med. Nutr.Abstr. Dairy Sci.Abstr.

ACTA ENDOCRINOLOGICA CONGRESS. ADVANCE ABSTRACTS. see *MEDICAL SCIENCES — Abstracting, Bibliographies, Statistics*

616.4   AG   ISSN 0065-1192
ACTA ENDOCRINOLOGICA PANAMERICANA.* irreg. Panamerican Federation of Endocrine Societies, c/o Dr. Noe Altschuler, 25 de Mayo no. 648, Vicente Lopez, Buenos Aires, Argentina.

616.4   618
ADVANCES IN HUMAN FERTILITY & REPRODUCTIVE ENDOCRINOLOGY. 1982. a. Raven Press, 1185 Ave. of the Americas, New York, NY 10036. TEL 212-575-0335. Ed. Daniel R. Mishell, Jr.

616.4   US   ISSN 0065-2903
ADVANCES IN METABOLIC DISORDERS. 1964. irreg., vol.10, 1983. $65. Academic Press, Inc., Orlando, FL 32887. TEL 305-345-2000. Indexed: Biol.Abstr.
Formerly: Advances in Metabolic Disorders. Supplements (ISSN 0587-4394)

616.4   US   ISSN 0361-5952
ADVANCES IN PROSTAGLANDIN AND THROMBOXANE RESEARCH. 1976. irreg., vol. 6, 1980. price varies. Raven Press, 1185 Ave. of the Americas, New York, NY 10036. TEL 212-575-0335. Eds. Bengt Samuelsson, Rodolfo Paoletti. Indexed: Biol.Abstr. Chem.Abstr. Curr.Cont. Ind.Med. Sci.Cit.Ind. Ind.Sci.Rev.

MEDICAL SCIENCES — EXPERIMENTAL MEDICINE, LABORATORY TECHNIQUE

616.4 US
BASIC & CLINICAL ENDOCRINOLOGY. 1981. irreg., vol.8, 1986. Marcel Dekker, Inc., 270 Madison Ave., New York, NY 10016. TEL 212-696-9000. Indexed: Chem.Abstr.

616.4 US ISSN 0160-242X
COMPREHENSIVE ENDOCRINOLOGY. 1978. irreg. Raven Press, 1185 Ave. of the Americas, New York, NY 10036. TEL 212-575-0335. Ed. Luciano Martini.

616.4 SZ ISSN 0255-7983
CONCEPTS IN IMMUNOPATHOLOGY. 1985. irreg. price varies. S. Karger AG, Allschwilerstr. 10, P.O. Box, CH-4009 Basel, Switzerland. Eds. J.M. Cruse, R.E. Lewis Jr.

616.4 US ISSN 0091-7397
CURRENT TOPICS IN EXPERIMENTAL ENDOCRINOLOGY. 1972. irreg., vol.5, 1983. Academic Press, Inc., Orlando, FL 32887. TEL 305-345-2000. Eds. L. Martini, V.H.T. James. Indexed: Biol.Abstr. Excerp.Med. Ind.Med.

CURRENT TOPICS IN NEUROENDOCRINOLOGY. see *MEDICAL SCIENCES — Psychiatry And Neurology*

616.4 NE
DEVELOPMENTS IN ENDOCRINOLOGY. 1977. irreg., vol.16, 1985. price varies. Elsevier Science Publishers B.V., Box 211, 1000 AE Amsterdam, Netherlands. Indexed: Chem.Abstr.

616.4 NE
DIABETES ANNUAL. a. Elsevier Science Publishers B.V., P.O. Box 1126, 1000 BC Amsterdam, Netherlands (Distr. in U.S. and Canada by: Elsevier Science Publishing Co. Inc., 52 Vanderbilt Ave., New York, NY 10017) Eds. K.G.M.M. Alberti, L.P. Krall.

616.4 UA ISSN 0070-9506
EGYPTIAN SOCIETY OF ENDOCRINOLOGY AND METABOLISM. JOURNAL.* (Publication suspended 1968-71) (Text in English) 1955. irreg. Egyptian Society of Endocrinology and Metabolism, 42 Sharia Kasr el-Aini, Cairo, Egypt.

616.4 AT ISSN 0312-4738
ENDOCRINE SOCIETY OF AUSTRALIA. PROCEEDINGS. 1958. a. Aus.$5. Endocrine Society of Australia, c/o Endocrine Unit, Royal Adelaide Hospital, Adelaide, S.A. 5000, Australia. Ed. P.E. Harding. adv. circ. 650. Indexed: Biol.Abstr. Excerp.Med.

616.4 SZ ISSN 0251-5342
FRONTIERS IN DIABETES. (Text in English) a. price varies. S. Karger AG, P.O. Box, CH-4009 Basel, Switzerland. Ed. F. Belfiore. (reprint service avail. from ISI) Indexed: Biol.Abstr.

616.4 616.8 US ISSN 0532-7466
FRONTIERS IN NEUROENDOCRINOLOGY. irreg., vol.5, 1978. price varies. Raven Press, 1185 Ave. of the Americas, New York, NY 10036. TEL 212-575-0335. Eds. L. Martini, William F. Ganong. Indexed: Biol.Abstr. Chem.Abstr. Curr.Cont. Sci.Cit.Ind. Ind.Sci.Rev.

616.4 SZ ISSN 0301-3073
FRONTIERS OF HORMONE RESEARCH. (Text in English) 1972. irreg. (approx. 1/yr.) price varies. S. Karger AG, Allschwilerstrasse 10, P.O. Box, CH-4009 Basel, Switzerland. Ed. T.H.B. van Wimersma Greidanus. (reprint service avail. from ISI) Indexed: Biol.Abstr. Chem.Abstr. Curr.Cont. Ind.Med. Sci.Cit.Ind. Ind.Sci.Rev.
Formerly: Monographs in Hormone Research (ISSN 0077-0868)

616.4 JA ISSN 0533-6724
GUMMA SYMPOSIA ON ENDOCRINOLOGY. (Text in English) 1964. a. $50. Center for Academic Publications, 4-16 Yayoi 2-chome, Bunkyo-ku, Tokyo 113, Japan. (Co Sponsor: V N U Science Press, Europalaan 93, 3526 KP Utrecht, the Netherlands) Ed.Bd. circ. 900. Indexed: Biol.Abstr.

616.4 IS
JOURNAL OF PEDIATRIC ENDOCRINOLOGY. 1985. a. $100. Freund Publishing House, Box 35010, 61 Nachmani St., Tel Aviv, Israel. Ed. Dan Herness.

616.4 FR ISSN 0075-4439
JOURNEES ANNUELLES DE DIABETOLOGIE DE L'HOTEL DIEU. 1961. a. price varies. (Hotel-Dieu, Clinique Medico-Sociale du Diabete et des Maladies Metaboliques) Flammarion Medecine Sciences, 4 rue Casimir Delavigne, 75006 Paris, France (U.S. subscr. address: S.F.P.A., c/o M. Benech, 14 E. 60 St., New York, NY 10022) Ed. Rathery, M.D. Indexed: Biol.Abstr. Chem.Abstr. Ind.Med. Dent.Ind.

616.4 US ISSN 0077-1015
MONOGRAPHS ON ENDOCRINOLOGY. 1967. irreg., vol.28, 1985. price varies. Springer-Verlag, 175 Fifth Ave., New York, NY 10010 TEL 212-460-1500. (Also Berlin, Heidelberg, Tokyo and Vienna) (reprint service avail. from ISI) Indexed: Biol.Abstr. Chem.Abstr. Ind.Med.

616.4 SZ ISSN 0304-4254
PEDIATRIC AND ADOLESCENT ENDOCRINOLOGY. (Text in English) 1976. irreg. (approx. 2/yr.) price varies. S. Karger AG, Allschwilerstrasse 10, P.O. Box, CH-4009 Basel, Switzerland. Ed. Z. Laron. (reprint service avail. from ISI) Indexed: Biol.Abstr. Chem.Abstr.

616.4 574.192 US ISSN 0079-9963
RECENT PROGRESS IN HORMONE RESEARCH. PROCEEDINGS OF THE LAURENTIAN HORMONE CONFERENCE. 1947. irreg., vol.42, 1986. $75. Academic Press, Inc, Orlando, FL 32887. TEL 305-345-2000. Ed. Gregory Pincus. index; cum.index: subject vols. 1-10 (1947-1954) in vol. 11 (1955) Indexed: Biol.Abstr. Chem.Abstr. Excerp.Med. Ind.Med. Nutr.Abstr. Anim.Breed.Abstr. Dairy Sci.Abstr. Ind.Vet. Vet.Bull.

616.4 591 UK ISSN 0081-136X
SOCIETY FOR ENDOCRINOLOGY (GREAT BRITAIN) MEMOIRS. 1959. irreg., no.20, 1973. $42.50 for latest vol. Cambridge University Press, Edinburgh Bldg., Shaftesbury Rd., Cambridge CB2 2RU, England (and 32 E. 57 St., New York NY 10022) Indexed: Biol.Abstr.

616.4058 US ISSN 0084-3741
YEAR BOOK OF ENDOCRINOLOGY. 1950. a. $45.95. ‡ Year Book Medical Publishers, Inc., 35 E. Wacker Dr., Chicago, IL 60601. TEL 312-726-9733. Eds. T.B. Schwartz, M.D., Will G. Ryan, M.D. Indexed: Anim.Breed.Abstr.

MEDICAL SCIENCES — Experimental Medicine, Laboratory Technique

A I CH E EQUIPMENT TESTING PROCEDURES. (American Institute of Chemical Engineers) see *ENGINEERING — Chemical Engineering*

ANIMAL RESOURCES; a research resources directory. see *MEDICAL SCIENCES — Abstracting, Bibliographies, Statistics*

ANLEITUNG FUER DIE CHEMISCHE LABORATORIUMSPRAXIS/CHEMICAL LABORATORY PRACTICE. see *CHEMISTRY*

616 FI ISSN 0066-2291
ANNALS OF CLINICAL RESEARCH. SUPPLEMENTUM. (Text in English) 1969. irreg. Fmk.100($60) free with subscription. Finnish Medical Society Duodecim, Kalevankatu 11 A, SF-00100 Helsinki, Finland. Ed. J. Huttunen. adv. index. (also avail. in microform from UMI) Indexed: Biol.Abstr. Curr.Cont. Ind.Med.
Incorporating since 1969: Annales Paediatriae Fenniae. Supplementum & Annales Medicinae Internae.

616 FR
ANNUAIRE DES LABORATOIRES D'ANALYSES DE BIOLOGIE MEDICALE DE FRANCE. a. Labo-France, 7 rue Godot de Mauroy, 75009 Paris, France. adv.
Formerly: Annuaire des Laboratoires d'Analyses de France.

ARCHIVOS DE BIOLOGIA Y MEDICINA EXPERIMENTALES. see *BIOLOGY*

ARQUIVOS DE CIRURGIA CLINICA E EXPERIMENTAL. see *MEDICAL SCIENCES — Surgery*

616 UR
BIOLOGIYA LABORATORNYKH ZHIVOTNYKH. irreg. 2 Rub. Akademiya Meditsinskikh Nauk S.S.S.R., Nauchno-Issledovatel'skaya Laboratoriya Eksperimental'no-Biologicheskikh Modelei, Moskovskaya Oblast', G. Khimki, Pos. Svetlye Gory, Russian S.F.S.R., U.S.S.R. bibl.
Laboratory animals

616 US
BIOPSY INTERPRETATION SERIES. irreg. price varies. Raven Press, 1185 Ave. of the Americas, New York, NY 10036. TEL 212-575-0335. Ed. Steven G. Silverberg. Indexed: Curr.Cont.

CANADIAN CLINICAL ENGINEERING CONFERENCE. PROCEEDINGS. see *MEDICAL SCIENCES*

CANADIAN MEDICAL AND BIOLOGICAL ENGINEERING CONFERENCE. DIGEST OF PAPERS. see *MEDICAL SCIENCES*

542 681.2 US ISSN 0093-8076
CLINICAL LABORATORY REFERENCE. Abbreviated title: C L R. 1974. a. $19. (Medical Laboratory Observer) Medical Economics Co., Inc., 680 Kinderkamack Rd., Oradell, NJ 07649. TEL 201-262-3030. Ed. Robert J. Fitzgibbon. adv. circ. 55,000(controlled)

DECHEMA MONOGRAPHIEN. see *CHEMISTRY — Analytical Chemistry*

618 US
DENTAL LABORATORY REVIEW BUYER'S GUIDE. 1975. a. $6. Dental Survey Publications (Subsidiary of: Harcourt Brace Jovanovich, Inc.) 7500 Old Oak Blvd., Cleveland, OH 44130 TEL 216-243-8100. adv. circ. 17,264.
Formerly: Dental Laboratory Buyer's Guide.

619 PO
FOLIA ANATOMICA UNIVERSITATIS CONIMBRICENSIS. (Text in English, French and Portuguese) 1926. a. free (exchange basis) Imprensa de Coimbra, Ltd., Largo de S. Salvador, Coimbra, Portugal. Ed. A. Simoes de Carvalho. bibl. illus. index. Indexed: Biol.Abstr.

GENERAL CLINICAL RESEARCH CENTERS; a research resources directory. see *MEDICAL SCIENCES — Abstracting, Bibliographies, Statistics*

616 US
GUIDE FOR THE CARE AND USE OF LABORATORY ANIMALS. 1963. irreg. $2.50 (single copy free) U.S. National Institutes of Health, Division of Research Resources, Bethesda, MD 20205 TEL 301-496-5545. (Orders to: Supt. of Documents, Washington, DC 20402)
Formerly until 1972: Guide for Laboratory Animal Facilities and Care (ISSN 0072-8098)
Laboratory animals

HEALTH CARE INSTRUMENTATION; the information journal of current medical technology. see *INSTRUMENTS*

HUMAN GENE MAPPING. see *BIOLOGY — Genetics*

616 UK
INSTITUTE OF MEDICAL LABORATORY SCIENCES. LONDON, ANNUAL REPORT. 1943. a. free. ‡ Institute of Medical Laboratory Sciences, 12 Queen Anne St., London W1M 0AU, England. circ. 17,000.
Formerly: Institute of Medical Laboratory Technology. London. Annual Report (ISSN 0073-9448)

INTERNATIONAL COUNCIL FOR LABORATORY ANIMAL SCIENCE. PROCEEDINGS OF THE SYMPOSIUM. see *MEDICAL SCIENCES*

619 NO
INTERNATIONAL WORKSHOP ON NUDE MICE. PROCEEDINGS. 1974. irreg., no. 2, 1977. International Council for Laboratory Animal Science, c/o Dr. S. Erichsen, Secretary-General, National Institute of Public Health, Posttutak, Oslo 1, Norway (Publisher varies; 2nd avail. from: University of Tokyo Press, 7-3-1 Hongo, Bunkyo-ku, Tokyo 113, Japan) Indexed: Chem.Abstr.
Laboratory animals

MEDICAL SCIENCES — FORENSIC SCIENCES

619   IS
ISRAEL INSTITUTE OF ANIMAL SCIENCE. SCIENTIFIC ACTIVITIES. triennial. $5. Agricultural Research Foundation, Volcani Centre, P.O. Box 6, Bet-Dagan, Israel. Indexed: Biol.Abstr.

542   MX
LABORATORIOS DE ESPECIALIDADES Y CONTROL. 1963. a. Mex.$2000($25) Litoimpresores, S.A., Espana 396, 09880 Mexico, D.F., Mexico. Ed. Cesar Macazaga. adv.

606   US   ISSN 0160-8584
LABORATORY AND RESEARCH METHODS IN BIOLOGY AND MEDICINE. 1978. irreg., vol.8, 1983. price varies. Alan R. Liss, Inc., 41 E. 11th St., New York, NY 10003. TEL 212-475-7700. Indexed: Biol.Abstr. Chem.Abstr. Curr.Cont. Ind.Med.
●Also available online.

616   UK   ISSN 0458-5933
LABORATORY ANIMAL HANDBOOKS. 1968. irreg. price varies. (Laboratory Animal Science Association) Laboratory Animals Ltd., 1 Thrifts Mead, Theydon Bois, Essex CM16 7NF, England. circ. 750-1,500. Indexed: Biol.Abstr. Excerp.Med.

619   UK
LABORATORY ANIMALS. BUYERS GUIDE. 1977/78. a. Laboratory Animals Ltd., 1 Thrifts Mead, Theydon Bois, Essex CM16 7NF, England.

542   UK   ISSN 0308-8367
LABORATORY EQUIPMENT INDEX. 1976. a. Technical Indexes Ltd., Willoughby Rd., Bracknell, Berks. RG12 4DW, England. Ed. P. Hughes. adv. circ. 1,305.

MADE IN EUROPE - MEDICAL EQUIPMENT AND SUPPLY GUIDE. see *MEDICAL SCIENCES*

MINORITY BIOMEDICAL RESEARCH SUPPORT PROGRAM; a research resources directory. see *MEDICAL SCIENCES — Abstracting, Bibliographies, Statistics*

619
MONOGRAPHS ON PATHOLOGY OF LABORATORY ANIMALS. 1983. irreg., latest 1986. (International Life Sciences Institute) Springer-Verlag, 175 Fifth Ave., New York, NY 10010 (Also Berlin, Heidelberg, Tokyo and Vienna) Ed. T.C. Jones.

619   NE
NEDERLANDSE VERENIGING VOOR KLINISCHE CHEMIE. ALMANAK. a. membership. Speciaal Uitgeverij van Verenigings-Almanakken, Elandweide 52, 3437 CS Nieuwegein, Netherlands. adv. circ. 650.

619   US   ISSN 0309-1848
RAT NEWS LETTER. 1977. irreg. £10($20) for 5 nos. University of Pittsburgh School of Medicine, Department of Pathology, Pittsburgh, PA 15261. Ed. Dr. D.V. Cramer. bk. rev. circ. 300(controlled) Indexed: Biol.Abstr. Excerp.Med. Anim.Breed.Abstr. Ind.Vet. Vet.Bull.

RAVEN PRESS SERIES IN EXPERIMENTAL PHYSIOLOGY. see *BIOLOGY — Physiology*

619   DK   ISSN 0105-9173
REGISTER OVER AUTORISEREDE LABORATORIER/REGISTER OF AUTORIZED LABORATORIES. 1978. a. free. Teknologistyrelsen - Danish National Agency of Technology, Tagensvej 135, 2200 Copenhagen N, Denmark. illus. circ. 3, 000.
Formerly: Autorisationsregister.

616   UK   ISSN 0085-591X
SCANDINAVIAN JOURNAL OF CLINICAL AND LABORATORY INVESTIGATION. SUPPLEMENT. (Text in English) 1951. irreg. (Scandinavian Society for Clinical Chemistry and Clinical Physiology) Blackwell Scientific Publications Ltd., Osney Mead, Oxford OX2 0EL, England. Ed. O. Stokke. adv. circ. 1,600. (back issues avail.; reprint service avail. from ISI) Indexed: Biol.Abstr. Chem.Abstr. Curr.Cont. Ind.Med. Nutr.Abstr.

SCHWEIZERISCHE GESELLSCHAFT FUER KLINISCHE CHEMIE. BULLETIN. see *BIOLOGY — Biological Chemistry*

574   UK   ISSN 0080-8210
SCOTTISH SOCIETY FOR PREVENTION OF VIVISECTION. ANNUAL PICTORIAL REVIEW. 1912. a. free. ‡ Scottish Society for Prevention of Vivisection, 10 Queensferry St., Edinburgh EH2 4PG, Scotland. Ed. Clive Hollands. bk. rev. circ. 10, 000.

SCRIPTA SCIENTIFICA MEDICA. see *MEDICAL SCIENCES — Cancer*

TECHNIQUES OF CHEMISTRY. see *CHEMISTRY*

619   UK
TECHNIQUES OF MEASUREMENT IN MEDICINE SERIES. 1978. irreg., no.7, 1982. $52.50 (cloth); $22.95 (paper) for latest vol. Cambridge University Press, Edinburgh Bldg., Shaftesbury Rd., Cambridge CB2 2RU, England (And 32 E. 57th St., New York, NY 10022) Indexed: Biol.Abstr.

ULTRASTRUCTURAL PATHOLOGY PUBLICATION. see *BIOLOGY — Cytology And Histology*

U.S. NATIONAL INSTITUTES OF HEALTH. DIVISION OF RESEARCH RESOURCES. PROGRAM HIGHLIGHTS. see *MEDICAL SCIENCES — Abstracting, Bibliographies, Statistics*

610 591   GW   ISSN 0300-1016
VERSUCHSTIERKUNDE. (Text in English, German) 1972. irreg. price varies. Verlag Paul Parey (Berlin), Lindenstr. 44-47, 1000 Berlin 61, W. Germany (B.R.D.) Eds. M. Merkenschlager, K. Gaertner. bibl. illus. index. (back issues avail.)

619   GE   ISSN 0044-3697
ZEITSCHRIFT FUER VERSUCHSTIERKUNDE/ JOURNAL OF EXPERIMENTAL ANIMAL SCIENCE. (Text and summaries in English and German) 1961. irreg. (6-12/yr.) M.120 per vol. VEB Gustav Fischer Verlag, Villengang 2, Postfach 176, 6900 Jena, E. Germany (D.D.R.) Ed.Bd. bk. rev. abstr. bibl. charts. illus. index. (reprint service avail. from ISI) Indexed: Biol.Abstr. Chem.Abstr. Curr.Cont. Excerp.Med. Ind.Med. Nutr.Abstr. Anim.Breed.Abstr. Biotech.Abstr. Dairy Sci.Abstr. Dent.Ind. Helminthol.Abstr. Ind.Vet. Vet.Bull.
Laboratory animals

MEDICAL SCIENCES — Forensic Sciences

614.19   US   ISSN 0883-1203
A B M S DIRECTORY OF CERTIFIED PATHOLOGISTS. 1985. biennial. $39.95 hardcover; $29.95 softcover. American Board of Medical Specialties, One American Plaza, Ste. 805, Evanston, IL 60201. TEL 312-491-9091. Ed. Donald G. Langsley, M.D.

ALCOHOL, DRUGS AND DRIVING: ABSTRACTS AND REVIEWS. see *DRUG ABUSE AND ALCOHOLISM*

614.19   GW   ISSN 0570-5886
ARBEITSMETHODEN DER MEDIZINISCHEN UND NATURWISSENSCHAFTLICHEN KRIMINALISTIK. 1962. irreg., vol. 15,1977. price varies. Max Schmidt-Roemhild Verlag, Mengstr. 16, 2400 Luebeck 1, W. Germany (B.R.D.)

616.8 340   US   ISSN 0278-0879
ATTORNEY'S DIRECTORY OF FORENSIC PSYCHIATRISTS IN THE UNITED STATES AND CANADA; a biographical professional and reference directory of legal psychiatrists. 1983. biennial. $20. (American College of Forensic Psychiatry) Edward Miller, Ed.& Pub., 26701 Quail Creek, No. 295, Laguna Hills, CA 92656. TEL 714-831-0236. circ. 1,000. (back issues avail.)

340.6   AU   ISSN 0067-5016
BEITRAEGE ZUR GERICHTLICHEN MEDIZIN. 1911. a., vol.69, 1986. S.2500. Franz Deuticke, Helferstorfer Strasse 4, A-1010 Vienna, Austria. Ed. Werner Boltz. cum.index (vols. 1-20 in vol. 20; vols. 21-30 in vol. 31) circ. 250. (back issues avail.) Indexed: Chem.Abstr. Ind.Med. Ind.Med. Dent.Ind.

CRIMINALIST'S SOURCE BOOK. see *CRIMINOLOGY AND LAW ENFORCEMENT — Abstracting, Bibliographies, Statistics*

614.19
FORENSIC SCIENCE PROGRESS. 1986. irreg. price varies. Springer-Verlag, 175 Fifth Ave., New York, NY 10160 TEL 212-460-1550. (Also Berlin, Heidelberg, Tokyo, Vienna) (reprint service avail. form ISI)

340.6 610   FR   ISSN 0075-9473
INSTITUT DE MEDECINE LEGALE ET DE MEDECINE SOCIALE. ARCHIVES. 1935. irreg; latest 1966. Institut de Medecine Legale et de Medecine Sociale, Place Theo Varlet, 59000 Lille, France.

340.6   IT   ISSN 0074-1248
INTERNATIONAL ACADEMY OF LEGAL MEDICINE AND OF SOCIAL MEDICINE. (CONGRESS REPORTS)* triennial, 1973, 9th, Rome. International Academy of Legal Medicine and Social Medicine, c/o Prof. Ferdinando Antoniotti, Viale Regina, Elena 336, 00161 Rome, Italy.

340.6   US   ISSN 0197-9981
LEGAL MEDICINE. 1969. a. price varies. W. B. Saunders Co., W. Washington Sq., Philadelphia, PA 19105. TEL 203-838-4400. Ed. Cyril H. Wecht. Indexed: Excerp.Med. Ind.Med. C.L.I. L.R.I.
Formerly: Legal Medicine Annual (ISSN 0075-8590)

340.6   CE
MEDICO-LEGAL SOCIETY OF SRI LANKA. PROCEEDINGS. irreg. Medico-Legal Society of Sri Lanka, 111 Francis Rd., Colombo 10, Sri Lanka.

614.19   JA   ISSN 0289-0755
RESEARCH AND PRACTICE IN FORENSIC MEDICINE. (Text in Japanese; summaries in English) 1954. a. 3.500 Yen. Tohoku University, School of Medicine, Department of Forensic Science, Sendai, Japan. Ed. Kaoru Sagisaka. circ. 1, 000. (back issues avail.)

MEDICAL SCIENCES — Gastroenterology

617   US   ISSN 0884-1470
A B M S DIRECTORY OF CERTIFIED COLON & RECTAL SURGEONS. 1985. biennial. $34.95. American Board of Medical Specialties, One American Plaza, Ste. 805, Evanston, IL 60201. TEL 312-491-9091. Ed. Donald G. Langsley, M.D.

617.5   US   ISSN 0065-7204
AMERICAN ASSOCIATION OF GENITO-URINARY SURGEONS. TRANSACTIONS. a. American Association of Genito-Urinary Surgeons, 22 W. Greene St., Baltimore, MD 21201. (also avail. in microform from UMI) Indexed: Ind.Med.

616.3   US   ISSN 0198-8085
CURRENT GASTROENTEROLOGY. 1980. a. $65. Year Book Medical Publishers, Inc., 35 E. Wacker Dr., Chicago, IL 60601. illus.

616.3   SZ
FRONTIERS OF GASTROINTESTINAL RESEARCH. (Text in English) 1960. irreg. (approx. 1/yr.) price varies. S. Karger AG, Allschwilerstrasse 10, P.O. Box, CH-4009 Basel, Switzerland. Ed. P. Rozen. (reprint service avail. from ISI) Indexed: Biol.Abstr. Chem.Abstr. Curr.Cont. Ind.Med.
Formerly: Bibliotheca Gastroenterologica (ISSN 0302-0665)

616.3   US
GASTROENTEROLOGY ANNUAL. 1983. a. $69. Elsevier Science Publishing Co., Inc. (New York), 52 Vanderbilt Ave., New York, NY 10017. TEL 212-916-1150. Ed. F. Kern, Jr. illus.

616.3
GASTROENTEROLOGY SERIES. irreg., vol.2, 1986. Marcel Dekker, Inc., 270 Madison Ave., New York, NY 10016. TEL 212-696-9000.

MEDICAL SCIENCES — NURSES AND NURSING

616.3 II
INDIAN SOCIETY OF GASTROENTEROLOGY. PROCEEDINGS OF THE ANNUAL CONFERENCE. 1962. a. $20. Indian Society of Gastroenterology, c/o Dr. Rakesh K. Tandon, All-India Institute of Medical Science, Ansari Nagar, New Delhi 110 029, India. adv. circ. 500. Indexed: Excerp.Med. Ind.Med.

617 US ISSN 0196-1918
MODERN TECHNICS IN SURGERY. ABDOMINAL SURGERY. 1980. irreg. (approx. a.) price varies. Futura Publishing Company, Inc., 295 Main St., Box 330, Mount Kisco, NY 10549. TEL 914-666-7528. Ed. Dr. Seymour I. Schwartz. index.

616.362 US ISSN 0079-6409
PROGRESS IN LIVER DISEASES. 1961. irreg., vol.8, 1986. price varies. Grune & Stratton, Inc., (Subsidiary of: Harcourt Brace Jovanovich, Inc.) Orlando, FL 32887 TEL 305-345-4200. (Dist. by: Academic Press Inc., 1250 Sixth Ave., San Diego, CA 92101) Eds. Hans Popper, M.D., Fenton Schaffner, M.D. index. Indexed: Biol.Abstr. Chem.Abstr. Ind.Med. ASCA.

616.3 NO ISSN 0085-5928
SCANDINAVIAN JOURNAL OF GASTROENTEROLOGY. SUPPLEMENT. (Text in English) 1968. irreg. $267 for Journal and its Supplements. Norwegian University Press, Kolstadgt. 1, Box 2959-Toeyen, 0608 Oslo 6, Norway (U.S. address: Publications Expediting Inc., 200 Meacham Ave., Elmont, NY 11003) Ed. E. Gjone. circ. 1,700. (also avail. in microform from UMI; back issues avail.) Indexed: Biol.Abstr. Chem.Abstr. Excerp.Med. Ind.Med. Nutr.Abstr. Dent.Ind.

616.3 US
TOPICS IN GASTROENTEROLOGY. 1979. irreg. price varies. Plenum Publishing Corp., 233 Spring St., New York, NY 10013. Ed. Howard M. Spiro. Indexed: Biol.Abstr.

616.3 US
YEAR BOOK OF DIGESTIVE DISEASES. a. $42.95. Year Book Medical Publishers, Inc., 35 E. Wacker Dr., Chicago, IL 60601. TEL 312-726-9746. illus.

MEDICAL SCIENCES — Hematology

616.15 YU ISSN 0523-6150
BILTEN ZA HEMATOLOGIJU I TRANSFUZIJU. 1973. a. 200 din. Zavod za Transfuziju Krvi, Belgrade, Svetosavska 39, Belgrade, Yugoslavia. (Co-sponsor: Udruzenje Hematologa i Transfuziologa Jugoslavije) Ed. Budimir Dinic. adv. circ. 500. Indexed: Ind.Med.

C R C CRITICAL REVIEWS IN ONCOLOGY-HEMATOLOGY. (C R C Press, Inc) see *MEDICAL SCIENCES — Cancer*

616.15 CN
CANADIAN RED CROSS BLOOD TRANSFUSION SERVICE. ANNUAL REPORT. (Text in English and French) 1946. a. free. Canadian Red Cross Society, National Headquarters, 95 Wellesley St. E., Toronto, Ont. M4Y 1H6, Canada. TEL 416-923-6692. circ. 6,000.

616.15 011 PH
CONGRESSI C C S S. BOLLETTINO; Comitato per la Collaborazione tra Societa Medico-Scientifiche. (Text in English and Italian) 1978. a. free. Centro Trasfusionale Ospedale Maggiore Policlinico di Milano, Via Francesco Sforza 35, 20122 Milan, Italy. adv. circ. 8,000.

616.15 US ISSN 0197-3649
CONTEMPORARY HEMATOLOGY/ONCOLOGY. 1977. biennial. Plenum Publishing Corp., 233 Spring St., New York, NY 10013. TEL 212-620-8047. Ed.Bd. Indexed: Biol.Abstr.
Formerly: Year in Hematology (ISSN 0160-7014)

616.15 616.99 US
CURRENT HEMATOLOGY AND ONCOLOGY. 1982? a. $65. Year Book Medical Publishers, Inc., 35 E. Wacker Dr., Chicago, IL 60601. TEL 312-726-9746. illus.

616.1 SZ
CURRENT STUDIES IN HEMATOLOGY AND BLOOD TRANSFUSION. (Text in English) 1955. irreg. (approx. 1/yr.) price varies. (European Society of Hematology) S. Karger AG, Allschwilerstrasse 10, P.O. Box, CH-4009 Basel, Switzerland. Ed. A. Haessig. (reprint service avail. from ISI) Indexed: Biol.Abstr. Chem.Abstr. Curr.Cont. Excerp.Med. Ind.Med.
Formerly: Bibliotheca Heamatologica.

616.15 US ISSN 0440-0607
HAEMATOLOGIE UND BLUTTRANSFUSION. (Supplement to Blut) (Text in English or German) 1962. irreg., vol. 28, 1982. price varies. Springer-Verlag, 175 Fifth Ave., New York, NY 10010 TEL 212-460-1500. (Also Berlin, Heidelberg, Tokyo and Vienna) Eds. W. Stich, G. Ruhenstroth-Bauer. (also avail. in microform from UMI; reprint service avail. from ISI) Indexed: Chem.Abstr.

616.15 US
HEMATOLOGY SERIES. irreg., vol.5, 1985. Marcel Dekker, Inc., 270 Madison Ave., New York, NY 10016. TEL 212-696-9000. Ed. Kenneth M. Brinkhous.

616.15 GW
INTERNATIONAL COMMITTEE FOR STANDARDIZATION IN HEMATOLOGY. SYMPOSIA. irreg., 13th, 1972. price varies. Institut fuer Standardisierung und Dokumentation im Med Laboratorium, Hugstetter Str. 55, D-7800 Freiburg im Breisgau, W. Germany (B.R.D.)

612.1 AG ISSN 0074-3682
INTERNATIONAL CONGRESS OF HEMATOLOGY. PROCEEDINGS. 1958. biennial, 21st Sydney, Australia. International Society of Hematology, c/o Dr. Miguel Pavlovsky, Sec.-Gen, Junin 1284, 1113 Buenos Aires, Argentina. circ. 2, 000.
Proceedings published in host country

616.5 612.1 FR ISSN 0074-8528
INTERNATIONAL SOCIETY OF BLOOD TRANSFUSION. PROCEEDINGS OF THE CONGRESS. biennial. International Society of Blood Transfusion - Societe Internationale de Transfusion Sanguine, c/o Secretariat, 6 rue Alexandre Cabanel, 75739 Paris Cedex 15, France. Indexed: Biol.Abstr.
Blood transfusion

616.1508 US ISSN 0079-6301
PROGRESS IN HEMATOLOGY. 1956. irreg., vol.13, 1984. price varies. Grune and Stratton, Inc. (Subsidiary of: Harcourt Brace Jovanovich, Inc.) Orlando, FL 43887 TEL 305-345-4200. (Dist. by: Academic Press Inc., 1250 Sixth Ave., San Diego, CA 92101) Ed. Elmer B. Brown, M.D. Indexed: Biol.Abstr. Chem.Abstr. Ind.Med. Trop.Dis.Bull.

616.15 DK ISSN 0080-6722
SCANDINAVIAN JOURNAL OF HAEMATOLOGY. SUPPLEMENTUM. (Text in English) 1964. irreg. free to subscribers of Journal. Munksgaard, 35 Noerre Soegade, Dk-1370 Copenhagen K, Denmark. Ed. Inge Olsson. adv. (reprint service avail. from ISI) Indexed: Biol.Abstr. Chem.Abstr. Curr.Cont. Ind.Med. Nutr.Abstr.

616.15 US
YEAR BOOK OF HEMATOLOGY. a. $39.95. Year Book Medical Publishers, Inc., 35 E. Wacker Dr., Chicago, IL 60601. TEL 312-726-9746. illus.

MEDICAL SCIENCES — Nurses And Nursing

see also Gerontology and Geriatrics; Hospitals

610.73 CK ISSN 0044-930X
A N E C. 1966. irreg. $7. Asociacion Nacional de Enfermeras de Colombia, Apdo. Aereo No. 059871, Bogota, D.E., Colombia. Ed.Bd. adv. bk. rev. illus. circ. 1,500,811. Indexed: Int.Nurs.Ind.
Formerly: Asociacion Nacional de Enfermeras de Colombia. A N E C. Revista.

610.73 US ISSN 0739-6686
ANNUAL REVIEW OF NURSING RESEARCH. 1984. a. price varies. Springer Publishing Company, 536 Broadway, New York, NY 10012. TEL 212-431-4370. Ed.Bd. circ. 1,212. Indexed: Int.Nurs.Ind.

610.73 VE ISSN 0066-8613
ASOCIACION VENEZOLANA DE ENFERMERAS PROFESIONALES. BOLETIN.* irreg. Asociacion Venezolana de Enfermeras Profesionales, Edificio Sur, 4 Piso, Oficina 412, el Silencio, Caracas, Venezuela.

610.73 378 US
ASSOCIATE DEGREE EDUCATION FOR NURSING. 1972. a. $4.95. National League for Nursing, 10 Columbus Circle, New York, NY 10019. TEL 212-582-1022.
Formerly: National League for Nursing. Associate Degree Education for Nursing (ISSN 0077-5118)

610.73 378 US ISSN 0069-5602
BACCALAUREATE EDUCATION IN NURSING: KEY TO A PROFESSIONAL CAREER IN NURSING. 1964. a. $4.95. National League for Nursing, 10 Columbus Circle, New York, NY 10019. TEL 212-582-1022.

610.73 UK
BAILLIERE'S NURSES' DICTIONARY. 1912. irreg. Bailliere Tindall, 1 Vincent Sq., London SW1P 2PN, England.

610.73 UK
BAILLIERE'S POCKET BOOK OF WARD INFORMATION. 1933. irreg. Bailliere Tindall, 1 Vincent Sq., London SW1P 2PN, England.

610.73 BB ISSN 0572-6042
BARBADOS NURSING JOURNAL. a. membership. Barbados Registered Nurses Association, Gibson House, Spry Street, Bridgetown, Barbados, W. Indies.

610.73 CN ISSN 0319-4787
CANADIAN NURSES ASSOCIATION. ENTRANCE REQUIREMENTS FOR DIPLOMA SCHOOLS OF NURSING AND SCHOOLS OF PRACTICAL NURSING. (Text in English and French) a. Can.$1. Canadian Nurses Association - Association des Infirmieres et Infirmiers du Canada, 50 the Driveway, Ottawa, Ont. K2P 1E2, Canada. TEL 613-237-2133.

610.73 CN ISSN 0229-7345
CANADIAN NURSES ASSOCIATION. NURSING PROGRAMS AND ENTRANCE REQUIREMENTS AT CANADIAN UNIVERSITIES. a. Can.$3. Canadian Nurses Association - Association des Infirmieres et Infirmiers du Canada, 50 the Driveway, Ottawa, Ont. K2P 1E2, Canada. TEL 613-237-2133.

610.73 SP
COLECCION LIBROS DE ENFERMERIA. 1975. irreg., no.10, 1979. price varies. (Universidad de Navarra, Escuela de Enfermeras) Ediciones Universidad de Navarra, S.A., Apdo. 396, 31080 Pamplona, Spain.

610.73 SA
COLIMPEX PAEDIATRIC EXECUPED. (Text in Afrikaans and English) a. free to nurses at clinics. Colimpex Africa (Pty) Ltd., 300 Bree St., Box 5838, Johannesburg 2000, South Africa. adv.

610.73 US
CONTEMPORARY NURSING SERIES. irreg., latest 1980. price varies. (American Nurses Association) American Journal of Nursing Co., 555 W. 57th St., New York, NY 10019. TEL 212-852-8820. (reprint service avail. from UMI)

610.73 CN ISSN 0226-5419
DIRECTORY OF LONG-TERM CARE CENTRES IN CANADA/REPERTOIRE DES CENTRES DE SOINS DE LONGUE DUREE AU CANADA. (Text in English and French) 1980. a. Can.$65. Canadian Hospital Association, 17 York St., Suite 100, Ottawa, Ont. K1N 9J6, Canada. TEL 613-238-8005. Ed. T. Radford. circ. 2,000.

610.73 US
DIRECTORY OF NURSES WITH DOCTORAL DEGREES. irreg. varies. American Nurses' Association, 2420 Pershing Rd., Kansas City, MO 64108. TEL 816-474-5720. (reprint service avail from UMI)

MEDICAL SCIENCES — OBSTETRICS AND GYNECOLOGY

610.73 378 US ISSN 0070-9166
EDUCATION FOR NURSING: THE DIPLOMA WAY. 1966. a. $4.95. National League for Nursing, 10 Columbus Circle, New York, NY 10019. TEL 212-582-1022.

610.73 US ISSN 0172-5238
FACHSCHWESTER - FACHPFLEGER. 1975. irreg.; latest, 1978. price varies. Springer-Verlag, 175 Fifth Ave., New York, NY 10010 TEL 212-460-1500. (Also Berlin, Heidelberg, Tokyo and Vienna) (reprint service avail. from ISI)

610.73 UK
HANDBOOK OF COMMUNITY NURSING. 1980. a. £5. Asgard Publishing Co. Ltd., 4A The Square, Petersfield, Hants. GU32 3HJ, England. Ed. James Wroe. adv. circ. 12,000.

610.73 AU ISSN 0073-0181
HANDBUCH FUER DIE SANITAETSBERUFE OESTERREICH. 1950. a. S.475. Verlag Dieter Goeschl, Andergaase 10, A-1170 Vienna, Austria. Ed. Walter Urbarz. adv. index. circ. 6,300.

HOME CARE SERVICES IN NEW YORK STATE. see *SOCIAL SERVICES AND WELFARE*

HOSPITAL AND NURSING YEARBOOK OF SOUTHERN AFRICA. see *HOSPITALS*

INDUSTRIAL HEALTH FOUNDATION. NURSING SERIES. BULLETINS. see *INDUSTRIAL HEALTH AND SAFETY*

610.73 CK
INVESTIGACION Y EDUCACION EN ENFERMERIA. 1983. a. Col.800($5) Universidad de Antioquia, Facultad de Enfermeria, Apdo. Aereo 1226, Medellin, Colombia. Ed. Consuelo Castrillon. bk. rev. circ. 1,000.

610.7 US ISSN 0075-0387
IOWA NURSES' ASSOCIATION. BULLETIN. vol.11, 1957. a. $5. Iowa Nurses' Association, 215 Shops Bldg., Des Moines, IA 50309. TEL 515-282-9169. Ed. Kay Myers. adv. circ. 2,000. Indexed: Int.Nurs.Ind. CINAHL.
Continues: Iowa State Nurses' Association. Bulletin.

610.73 371.42 JA ISSN 0911-0844
JAPANESE NURSING ASSOCIATION RESEARCH REPORT. (Text in Japanese; summaries in English) 1975. irreg. 1.000 Yen. Japanese Nursing Association, 8-2, 7-Chome, Minamiaoyama, Sibuya-Ku, Tokyo 150, Japan. circ. 1,200.

610.73 UK
LONDON HOSPITAL LEAGUE OF NURSES REVIEW. 1921. a. membership. London Hospital League of Nurses, London Hospital, Whitechapel, London E1 1BB, England. Ed. M.J. Deadman. adv. circ. 2,400(controlled)

610.73 US
LOUISIANA. STATE BOARD OF NURSING. REPORT (CALENDAR YEAR) 1973. a. $15. State Board of Nursing, 907 PereMarquette Bldg., New Orleans, LA 70112. TEL 504-568-5464. Ed. Marjorie M. Luc. circ. 100.
Formerly (until 1976): Louisiana. State Board of Nurse Examiners. Report (ISSN 0095-5884)

610.73 US
M L N NEW DIRECTIONS. 1975. irreg., (2-3/yr.) $3. Minnesota League for Nursing, 2353 N. Rice St., No. 220, St. Paul, MN 55113. Eds. Jan & Doug Hart. adv. circ. 700. Indexed: Ind.Nurs.Ind.
Formerly: M L N Bulletin - Newsletter; Supersedes (1953-1975): M L N Bulletin (ISSN 0047-7508)

610.73 378 US
MASTER'S EDUCATION: ROUTE TO OPPORTUNITIES IN CONTEMPORARY NURSING. 1966. a. $4.95. National League for Nursing, 10 Columbus Circle, New York, NY 10019. TEL 212-582-1022.
Formerly: Masters Education; Route to Opportunities in Modern Nursing (ISSN 0076-5104)

610.73 US
N L N NURSING DATA REVIEW. a. $24.95. National League for Nursing, 10 Columbus Circle, New York, NY 10019. TEL 212-582-1022.
Former titles: N L N Nursing Data Book; Until 1980: N L N Nursing Data Book: Statistical Information on Nursing Education and Newly Licensed Nurses; Some Statistics on Baccalaureate and Higher Degree Programs in Nursing (ISSN 0081-203X)

610.73 792 UK
NATIONAL ASSOCIATION OF THEATRE NURSES. ANNUAL CONGRESS HANDBOOK. 1965. a. Newton Mann Ltd., Sherwood House, Matlock, Derbyshire DE4 3LY, England. Ed. I.D. Curry.

610.73 US
NEW YORK L P N AND TECHNICIAN.* vol.34, 1973. irreg. membership (non-members $3) Licensed Practical Nurses and Technicians of New York, Inc., 233 W. 49th St., New York, NY 10019. TEL 212-247-7270. adv. charts. illus. circ. 4,500.
Formerly: New York L P N (ISSN 0028-730X)

610.73 NZ ISSN 0110-0890
NEW ZEALAND NURSING FORUM. 1973. irreg. NZ.$20. Nurses Society of New Zealand., P.O. Box 3195, Auckland 1, New Zealand. Ed. David Wills. adv. bk. rev. abstr. bibl. charts. illus. stat. circ. 10,000. Indexed: Int.Nurs.Ind. C.I.N.L.

610.73 US ISSN 0192-2394
NURSING (YEAR) CAREER DIRECTORY. 1979. a. free. Springhouse Corporation, 1111 Bethlehem Pike, Springhouse, PA 19477. TEL 215-646-8700. adv. charts. illus. tr.lit. index. circ. 100, 000(controlled)

610.73 US ISSN 0273-320X
NURSING (YEAR) DRUG HANDBOOK. a. Springhouse Book Company, 1111 Bethlehem Pike, Springhouse, PA 19477. TEL 215-646-8700. Ed. Helen Klusek Hamilton.

610.73 US
NURSING (YEAR) /NURSEPAC: STUDENTS. 1980. a. Springhouse Corporation, 1111 Bethlehem Pike, Springhouse, PA 19477. TEL 215-646-8700. circ. 40,000.

610.73 CE
NURSING JOURNAL. a. Sri Lanka Nurses Association, Post Basic School of Nursing, Regent St., Colombo 10, Sri Lanka. Indexed: CINAHL.

610.73 US
NURSING OPPORTUNITIES. 1970. a. $4.95. (R N Magazine) Medical Economics Company, Inc., 680 Kinderkamack Rd., Oradell, NJ 07649. TEL 201-262-3030. Ed. James A. Reynolds. adv. bk. rev. circ. 125,000.

610.73 US
NURSINGWORLD JOURNAL NURSING JOB GUIDE. 1979. a. $24. Prime National Publishing Corp., 470 Boston Post Rd., Weston, MA 02193. TEL 617-899-2702. Ed. Eileen F. DeVito. adv. charts. illus. stat. circ. 10,000. (back issues avail.)
Former titles: Nursingworld Journal Annual Hospital Directory; Nursing Job News: Annual Hospital Directory; Nursing Job News: Nursing Job Guide to Over 7000 Hospitals (ISSN 0162-9069)

610.7 AU
OESTERREICHISCHER KRANKENPFLEGERVERBAND. FORTBILDUNGSPROGRAMM. 1969. a. free. Oesterreichischer Krankenpflegeverband, Mollgasse 3a, A-1180 Vienna, Austria. Ed. Marianne Kriegl. circ. 6,500.

610.73 US
PRACTICAL NURSING CAREER. 1968. a. $3.95. National League for Nursing, 10 Columbus Circle, New York, NY 10019. TEL 212-582-1022.

610.73 JA ISSN 0385-1982
SHINSHU UNIVERSITY. SCHOOL OF ALLIED MEDICAL SCIENCES. TREATISES AND STUDIES. (Text in Japanese; summaries in English) 1975. a. free. Shinshu Daigaku Iryo-gijutsu Tanki Daigakubu, 3-1-1, Asahi, Matsumoto-shi 390, Japan. circ. 300. (back issues avail.)

610.73 US ISSN 0081-4423
STATE-APPROVED SCHOOLS OF NURSING - L.P.N./L.V.N. 1958. a. $15.95. National League for Nursing, 10 Columbus Circle, New York, NY 10019. TEL 212-582-1022.
Formerly (1959-1966): State-Approved Schools of Practical and Vocational Nursing (ISSN 0095-6570)

610.73 US ISSN 0081-4431
STATE-APPROVED SCHOOLS OF NURSING - R.N. a. $15.95. National League for Nursing, 10 Columbus Circle, New York, NY 10019. TEL 212-582-1022.

610.73 US
STUDIES IN NURSING MANAGEMENT. 1982. irreg., no.11, 1983. U M I Research Press, 300 N. Zeeb Rd., Ann Arbor, MI 48106. Eds. Philip A. Kalisch, Beatrice J. Kalisch.

610.73 UK ISSN 0302-1440
STUDY OF NURSING CARE: RESEARCH PROJECT SERIES. 1973. irreg. price varies. Royal College of Nursing, 20 Cavendish Square, London W1M 0AB, England. bibl.

WERKSTATTSCHRIFTEN ZUR SOZIALPSYCHIATRIE. see *PSYCHOLOGY*

610.73 UK
WESTMINSTER HOSPITAL NURSES' LEAGUE. PUBLICATION. a. membership. Westminster Hospital Nurses' League, Queen Mary Nurses' Home, Page St., Westminster, London SW1, England.

MEDICAL SCIENCES — Obstetrics And Gynecology

618 US ISSN 0884-1535
A B M S DIRECTORY OF CERTIFIED OBSTETRICIANS & GYNECOLOGISTS. 1985. biennial. $49.95 hardcover; $39.95 softcover. American Board of Medical Specialties, One American Plaza, Ste. 805, Evanston, IL 60201. TEL 312-491-9091. Ed. Donald G. Langsley, M.D.

ADVANCES IN HUMAN FERTILITY & REPRODUCTIVE ENDOCRINOLOGY. see *MEDICAL SCIENCES — Endocrinology*

AMERICAN ASSOCIATION OF GENITO-URINARY SURGEONS. TRANSACTIONS. see *MEDICAL SCIENCES — Gastroenterology*

618.1 618.2 US ISSN 0065-728X
AMERICAN ASSOCIATION OF OBSTETRICIANS AND GYNECOLOGISTS. TRANSACTIONS.* 1888. a. American Association of Obstetricians and Gynecologists, c/o Richard F. Mattingly, M.D., Medical College of Wisconsin, 8700 W. Wisconsin Ave., Milwaukee, WI 53226. circ. 250.

618.1 618.2 US
AMERICAN GYNECOLOGICAL AND OBSTETRICAL SOCIETY. TRANSACTIONS OF THE A G O S. 1878. a. $56. C. V. Mosby Co., 11830 Westline Industrial Dr., St. Louis, MO 63146. TEL 314-872-8370. circ. 200.
Formerly: American Gynecological Society. Transactions of the A G S (ISSN 0065-8480)

618 SP ISSN 0210-7171
AVANCES EN OBSTETRICIA Y GINECOLOGIA. 1975. irreg., approx. biennial. 4950 ptas. Salvat Editores, S.A., Mallorca 45, 08029 Barcelona, Spain. TEL 201-09-11. Ed. J. Gonzalez-Merlo. charts. illus. circ. 2,000. Indexed: Curr.Cont.

618.2 AG
B.I.M. BOLETIN DEL INSTITUTO DE MATERNIDAD "ALBERTO PERALTA RAMOS". (Text and summaries in Spanish; occasionally in English) 1941. irreg. Instituto de Maternidad "Alberto Peralata Ramos", Asociacion Medica, Buenos Aires, Argentina.

618.2 UK
BAILLIERE'S MIDWIVES' DICTIONARY. 1951. irreg. Bailliere Tindall, 1 Vincent Sq., London SW1P 2PN, England.

618.1　　　　　GW　ISSN 0068-337X
BUECHEREI DES FRAUENARZTES. (Beginning 1972, supplements Zeitschrift fuer Geburtshilfe und Perinatologie) 1956. irreg., vol.24, 1987. price varies. Ferdinand Enke Verlag, Postfach 1304, 7000 Stuttgart 1, W. Germany (B.R.D.) Eds. G. Martius, M. Schmidt-Gollwitzer. Indexed: Chem.Abstr.

618　　　　　US
CHILDBIRTH (YEAR) 1984. s-a. Cahners Publishing Co., Inc., American Baby Group, Division of Reed Publishing USA, 249 W. 17th St., New York, NY 10011. TEL 212-645-0067. Ed. Marsha Rehns. adv. circ. 1,300,000.

618　　　　　US
CLINICAL MONOGRAPHS IN OBSTETRICS AND GYNECOLOGY. 1975. irreg., no.3, 1981. John Wiley & Sons, Inc., 605 Third Ave., New York, NY 10016. TEL 212-850-6000. Ed. E.J. Quilligan, M.D.

618　　　　　US
CLINICAL PERSPECTIVES IN OBSTETRICS AND GYNECOLOGY. 1983. irreg., latest 1986. Springer-Verlag, 175 Fifth Ave., New York, NY 10010 TEL 212-460-1500. (Also Berlin, Heidelberg, Tokyo and Vienna)

618.1　618.2　SZ　ISSN 0304-4246
CONTRIBUTIONS TO GYNECOLOGY AND OBSTETRICS. (Text in English) 1950. irreg. (approx. 1/yr.) price varies. S. Karger AG, Allschwilerstrasse 10, P.O. Box, CH-4009 Basel, Switzerland. Ed. P.J. Keller. (reprint service avail. from ISI; back issues avail.) Indexed: Biol.Abstr. Chem.Abstr. Curr.Cont. Excerp.Med. Ind.Med.
　Formerly: Advances in Obstetrics and Gynaecology (ISSN 0065-2997)

FIRST YEAR OF LIFE; a guide to your baby's growth and development month by month. see *CHILDREN AND YOUTH — About*

HAROLD C. MACK SYMPOSIUM. PROCEEDINGS. see *BIOLOGY — Physiology*

MONTHLY EXTRACT. see *WOMEN'S INTERESTS*

NETWORK (RESEARCH TRIANGLE PARK) see *BIRTH CONTROL*

618.1　618.2　US　ISSN 0078-7442
PACIFIC COAST OBSTETRICAL AND GYNECOLOGICAL SOCIETY. TRANSACTIONS. 1944/46, vol. 14. a. (Pacific Coast Obstetrical and Gynecological Society) C. V. Mosby Co., 11830 Westline Industrial Dr., St. Louis, MO 63146. TEL 314-872-8370. Indexed: Ind.Med.
　Continues: Pacific Coast Society of Obstetrics and Gynecology. Transactions.

618　　　　　US
PERINATOLOGY/NEONATOLOGY BUYER'S GUIDE. 1984. a. $45. Brentwood Publishing Corp. (Subsidiary of: Simon & Schuster, unit of Gulf & Western, Inc.) 1649 5th St., Santa Monica, CA 90401. TEL 213-395-0234. Ed. Martin H. Waldman. adv. tr.lit. circ. 18,500.

618　380.1　US　ISSN 0147-7927
PERINATOLOGY-NEONATOLOGY BUYERS GUIDE. a. $45. Brentwood Publishing Corp. (Subsidiary of: Simon & Schuster, unit of Gulf & Western, Inc.) 1640 5th St., Santa Monica, CA 90401 TEL 213-395-0234. (Subscr. to: Box 2178, Santa Monica, CA 90406-2178) Ed. Kris Kyes. adv. charts. tr.lit. circ. 18,000. (back issuea avail.)

618　　　　　UK　ISSN 0261-0140
PROGRESS IN OBSTETRICS AND GYNAECOLOGY. 1981. a. £14. Churchill Livingstone Medical Journals, 1-3 Baxter's Place, Leith Walk, Edinburgh EH3 3AF, Scotland. illus.

618.3　　　　　US　ISSN 0362-5699
REVIEWS IN PERINATAL MEDICINE. 1976. a. price varies. Raven Press, 1185 Ave. of the Americas, New York, NY 10036. TEL 212-575-0335. Eds. Emile M. Scarpelli, Ermelando V. Cosmi. Indexed: Biol.Abstr.

618　　　　　US
TROPHOBLAST RESEARCH. 1984. irreg. price varies. Plenum Publishing Corp., 233 Spring St., New York, NY 10013. TEL 212-620-8047. Eds. Richard K. Miller, Henry A. Thiede.

618.1　　　　　SA
UNIVERSITY OF CAPE TOWN. DEPARTMENT OF OBSTETRICS AND GYNAECOLOGY. ANNUAL REPORT. (Text in English) 1952. a. free. University of Cape Town, Department of Obstetrics and Gynaecology, Medical School, Anzio Road, Observatory, Cape Town 7925, South Africa. (Co-sponsor: Cape Provincial Administration) Ed. Herman A. van Coeverden de Groot. circ. 250.
　Formerly: University of Cape Town. Department of Gynaecology. Annual Report (ISSN 0069-0228)

618.1　618.2　US　ISSN 0084-3911
YEAR BOOK OF OBSTETRICS AND GYNECOLOGY. 1933. a. $42.95. ‡ Year Book Medical Publishers, Inc., 35 E. Wacker Dr., Chicago, IL 60601. TEL 312-726-9733. Eds. R.M. Pitkin, M.D., Frank J. Zlatnik, M.D. illus.

MEDICAL SCIENCES — Ophthalmology And Optometry

617.7　　　　　US　ISSN 8756-9175
A B M S DIRECTORY OF CERTIFIED OPHTHALMOLOGISTS. 1983. biennial. $34.95 hardcover; $29.95 softcover. American Board of Medical Specialties, One American Plaza, Ste. 805, Evanston, IL 60201. TEL 312-491-9091. Ed. Donald G. Langsley, M.D.

617.7　　　　　NE　ISSN 0065-115X
ACTA CONCILIUM OPHTHALMOLOGICUM. (Text in English, French, German and Spanish) quadrennial, 1974, 22nd, Paris. (International Federation of Ophthalmological Societies) Kugler Publications, P.O. Box 516, 1180 AM Amsterdam, Netherlands. TEL 020-278070. circ. 8, 500(controlled) (reprint service avail. from ISI) Indexed: Curr.Cont. Excerp.Med.
　Represents: International Congress of Ophthalmology.

617.7　　　　　DK　ISSN 0065-1451
ACTA OPHTHALMOLOGICA. SUPPLEMENTUM. (Text in English) 1923. irreg. free to subscribers. Scriptor Publisher ApS, Gasvaerksvej 15, 1656 Copenhagen K, Denmark. adv. Indexed: Biol.Abstr. Curr.Cont. Ind.Med. Dent.Ind.

617.7　　　　　US　ISSN 0276-3508
ADVANCES IN OPHTHALMIC PLASTIC & RECONSTRUCTIVE SURGERY. 1982. a. $70. Pergamon Press, Inc., Journals Division, Maxwell House, Fairview Park, Elmsford, NY 10523 TEL 914-592-7700. (And Headington Hill Hall, Oxford OX3 0BW, England) Ed. Dr. Stephen Bosniak. (also avail. in microfilm; microfiche) Indexed: Curr.Cont.

617　　　　　II
ALL INDIA OPHTHALMOLOGICAL SOCIETY. PROCEEDINGS.* (Text in English) a. All India Ophthalmological Society, 111/112 Summerville, Bhulabhai De Sai Rd., Bombay 400 026, India.

617.7　　　　　US　ISSN 0065-9533
AMERICAN OPHTHALMOLOGICAL SOCIETY. TRANSACTIONS. 1864. a. $50 per vol. American Ophthalmological Society, c/o Thomas P. Kearns, M.D., Sec.-Treas., 200 First St., S.W., Rochester, MN 55901. Ed. Dr. Robert Welch. index. circ. 700. (back issues avail.) Indexed: Biol.Abstr. Excerp.Med. Ind.Med. Dent.Ind.

617.7　　　　　US　ISSN 0065-955X
AMERICAN ORTHOPTIC JOURNAL. 1950. a. $25. (American Association of Certified Othoptists) University of Wisconsin Press, 114 N. Murray St., Madison, WI 53715. TEL 608-262-4952. Ed. Dr. Thomas France. adv. cum.index: 1950-1960, 1971-1980. circ. 993. (also avail. in microform from UMI; back issues avail.; reprint service avail. from UMI) Indexed: Biol.Abstr.

617.7　　　　　FR　ISSN 0301-4495
ANNEE THERAPEUTIQUE ET CLINIQUE EN OPHTALMOLOGIE. 1950. a. 280 F. Fueri-Lamy, 21 rue Paradis, 13001 Marseille, France. adv. Indexed: Ind.Med.
　Formerly: Annee Therapeutique en Ophtalmologie (ISSN 0066-2402)

617.3　　　　　US　ISSN 0067-9283
BLUE BOOK OF OPTOMETRISTS. 1912. a. Professional Press Books, Inc., Book Division, 7 E. 12th St., New York, NY 10003. TEL 212-741-6640. index.

617.7　　　　　UK　ISSN 0068-2314
BRITISH ORTHOPTIC JOURNAL. 1939. a. $15. British Orthoptic Society, Tavistock House North, Tavistock Sq., London WC1H 9HX, England. Ed. A. Horwood. adv. bk. rev. cum.index every 5 yrs. circ. 1,800. Indexed: Biol.Abstr. Excerp.Med.

617.7　　　　　GW　ISSN 0068-3361
BUECHEREI DES AUGENARZTES. 1938. irreg., no.110, 1987. price varies. Ferdinand Enke Verlag, Postfach 1304, 7000 Stuttgart 1, W. Germany (B.R.D.) Ed.Bd. Indexed: Ind.Med.

617.7　　　　　US
CELL AND DEVELOPMENTAL BIOLOGY OF THE EYE. 1984. irreg., latest 1986. Springer-Verlag, 175 Fifth Ave., New York, NY 10010 TEL 212-460-1500. (Also Berlin, Heidelberg, Tokyo and Vienna) Eds. J.B. Sheffield, S.R. Hilfer.

617.752　　　　　GW　ISSN 0724-6226
CONTACTOLOGIA-BUCHEREI. (Supplement to: Contactologia) 1983. irreg. price varies. Ferdinand Enke Verlag, Postfach 1304, D 7000 Stuttgart 1, W. Germany (B.R.D.) Eds. W. Ehrich, R. Heitz.

617.7　　　　　US　ISSN 0190-2970
CURRENT TOPICS IN EYE RESEARCH. 1979. irreg., vol.4, 1984. Academic Press, Inc., Orlando, FL 32887. TEL 305-345-2000. illus. Indexed: Ind.Med.

618　　　　　DK
DANISH OPHTHALMOLOGICAL SOCIETY. TRANSACTIONS. Issued with: Acta Ophthalmologica (ISSN 0001-639X) (Text in English) a. (Danish Ophthalmological Society) Scriptor Publisher ApS, Gasvaerksvej 15, DK-1656 Copenhagen K, Denmark.

617.7　　　　　SZ　ISSN 0250-3751
DEVELOPMENTS IN OPHTHALMOLOGY. (Text in English and German) 1980. irreg. (approx. 2/yr.) price varies. S. Karger AG, Allschwilerstrasse 10, P.O. Box, CH-4009 Basel, Switzerland. Ed. W. Straub. (reprint service avail. from ISI, back issues avail.) Indexed: Biol.Abstr. Chem.Abstr. Curr.Cont. Ind.Med.
　Formed by the merger of: Advances in Ophthalmology (ISSN 0065-3004) & Bibliotheca Ophthalmologica (ISSN 0067-8090) & Modern Problems in Ophthalmology (ISSN 0077-0078)

617.7　　　　　NE
DOCUMENTA OPHTHALMOLOGICA PROCEEDINGS SERIES. (Text in English) 1973. irreg., vol. 33, 1982. price varies. Martinus Nijhoff-Dr. W. Junk Publishers, Box 163, 3300-AD Dordrecht, Netherlands (U.S. address: Kluwer Academic Publishers, Philip Dive 101, Assinippi Park, Norwell, MA 02061) Ed. H. E. Henkes. Indexed: Biol.Abstr. Nutr.Abstr. Psychol.Abstr.

617.7　　　　　NE　ISSN 0301-326X
EUROPEAN OPHTHALMOLOGICAL SOCIETY. CONGRESS ACTA. (Text in English, French and German) 1960. quinquennial, 6th, 1980, Brighton. 180 Fr.($76) (Royal Society of Medicine, London, UK) European Ophthalmological Society, c/o Harold E. Henkes, Eye Clinic, Schiedamse Vest 180, 3001 Rotterdam, Netherlands. (Co-sponsors: Academic Press, Grune and Stratton) Ed. P.D. Trevor-Roper. circ. 1,500.

617.7　　　　　II　ISSN 0255-4062
EYE CARE. (Text in English) 1979. a. Rs.200($20) (Chandulal Eye Centre) Dr. Narendra Kumar Ed. & Pub., P.O. Box 2812, New Delhi 110 060, India. adv. bk. rev. circ. 1,200.

617.7　　　　　　US　ISSN 0072-8977
GUILD OF PRESCRIPTION OPTICIANS OF
AMERICA. REFERENCE LIST. 1954. irreg.,
approx. biennial. $60. Guild of Prescription
Opticians of America, Box 10110, 10341
Democracy Ln., Fairfax, VA 22030-2505. (Affiliate:
Opticians Association of America) Ed. T.M. Schott.
circ. 15,000.

617.762　　　　　　NE　ISSN 0074-3844
INTERNATIONAL CONGRESS OF
ORTHOPTISTS. TRANSACTIONS.* 1967. irreg.,
1971, 2nd, Amsterdam. International Orthoptic
Association, Henriette Bosmansstraat 50,
Amsterdam (Zuid), Netherlands.

617.7　　　　　　UK
INTERNATIONAL OPTICAL YEAR BOOK. 1903.
a. £23. Business Press International Ltd., Quadrant
House, the Quadrant, Sutton, Surrey SM2 5AS,
England. Ed. Philip Mullins.

JAHRBUCH FUER BLINDENFREUNDE. see
BLIND

617.7　　　　　　FR　ISSN 0240-7914
JOURNAL FRANCAIS D'ORTHOPTIQUE. 1969. a.
100 Fr. Association Francaise des Orthoptistes, Les
Roussieres, 01390 St. Andre de Corcy, France. Ed.
A.P. Ravault. circ. 2,000.

617.7　　　　　　NE
MONOGRAPHS IN OPHTHALMOLOGY. (Text in
English) 1981. irreg. price varies. Martinus Nijhoff-
Dr. W. Junk Publishers, Box 163, 3300 AD
Dordrecht, Netherlands (U.S. address: Kluwer
Academic Publishers, 101 Philip Drive, Assinippi
Park, Norwell, MA 02061.) Indexed: Biol.Abstr.

617.7　　　　　　US　ISSN 0077-8605
NEW ORLEANS ACADEMY OF
OPHTHALMOLOGY. TRANSACTIONS. a. price
varies. C. V. Mosby Co., 11830 Westline Industrial
Dr., St. Louis, MO 63146. TEL 314-872-8370.
Ed.Bd. Indexed: Ind.Med.　Dent.Ind.

617.7　　　　　　US
OCULAR THERAPEUTICS AND
PHARMACOLOGY. 4th edt., 1973. irreg., 7th edt.,
1985. $47. C. V. Mosby Co., 11830 Westline
Industrial Dr., St. Louis, MO 63146. TEL 314-872-
8370. Ed. Philip P. Ellis.
　Formerly: Handbook of Ocular Therapeutics and
Pharmacology (ISSN 0072-985X)

617.7　　　　　　UA　ISSN 0078-5342
OPHTHALMOLOGICAL SOCIETY OF EGYPT.
BULLETIN. (Text in Arabic, English and French)
1902. a. $10. Ophthalmological Society of Egypt,
Dar el Hekma, 42 Kasr el-Aini St., Cairo, Egypt.
Indexed: Excerp.Med.　Ind.Med.　Ophthal.Lit.

617.7　　　　　　US　ISSN 0278-4327
PROGRESS IN RETINAL RESEARCH. 1982. a.
$80. Pergamon Press, Inc., Journals Division,
Maxwell House, Fairview Park, Elmsford, NY
10523 TEL 914-592-7700. (And Headington Hill
Hall, Oxford OX3 0BW, England) Eds. Neville
Osborne, G.J. Chader. (also avail. in microfilm/
microfiche) Indexed: Chem.Abstr.

617.7　　　　　　US　ISSN 0146-4582
RED BOOK OF OPHTHALMOLOGY. a.
Professional Press Books, Inc., 7 E. 12th St., New
York, NY 10003. TEL 212-741-6640. adv.
　Formerly: Red Book of Eye, Ear, Nose and
Throat Specialists.

617.7　　　　　　FR　ISSN 0081-1270
SOCIETE D'OPHTALMOLOGIE DE FRANCE.
BULLETIN. 1949. irreg. 290 F.($59) Publicite
Stephane Batard, 21 Rue Saint-Fiacre, Paris 2e,
France. Indexed: Biol.Abstr.　Chem.Abstr.
Ind.Med.

617.7　　　　　　US　ISSN 0082-1195
SYSTEM OF OPHTHALMOLOGY. 1958. irreg.
price varies. C.V. Mosby, 11830 Westline Industrial
Dr., St. Louis, MO 63146. TEL 314-872-8370.

617.705　　　　　　US　ISSN 0084-392X
YEAR BOOK OF OPHTHALMOLOGY. 1901. a.
$44.95. ‡ Year Book Medical Publishers, Inc., 35 E.
Wacker Dr., Chicago, IL 60601. TEL 312-726-9733.
Ed. J.T. Ernest, M.D.

617.7　　　　　　US
YEAR BOOK OF OPTHAMOLOGY. a. $44.95. Year
Book Medical Publishers, Inc., 35 E. Wacker Dr.,
Chicago, IL 60601. TEL 312-726-9746. illus.

MEDICAL SCIENCES — Orthopedics And Traumatology

617.3　　　　　　US　ISSN 0883-1211
A B M S DIRECTORY OF CERTIFIED
ORTHOPAEDIC SURGEONS. 1985. biennial.
$34.95 hardcover; $29.95 softcover. American
Board of Medical Specialties, One American Plaza,
Ste. 805, Evanston, IL 60201. TEL 312-491-9091.
Ed. Donald G. Langsley, M.D.

617.3　　　　　　DK　ISSN 0300-8827
ACTA ORTHOPAEDICA SCANDINAVICA.
SUPPLEMENTUM. irreg. free to subscribers.
(Scandinavian Orthopaedic Association)
Munksgaard, Noerre Soegade 35, DK-1370
Copenhagen K, Denmark. (reprint service avail.
from ISI) Indexed: Biol.Abstr.　Curr.Cont.
Ind.Med.

617.1　　　　　　US
ADVANCES IN TRAUMA. 1986. a. $49.95. Year
Book Medical Publishers, Inc., 35 E. Wacker Dr.,
Chicago, IL 60601. TEL 312-726-9746. illus.

617　　　　　　SZ
AKTUELLE PROBLEME IN CHIRURGIE UND
ORTHOPADIE. 1966. irreg. price varies. Verlag
Hans Huber, Laenggassstr. 76, CH-3000 Berne 9,
Switzerland (Subscr. to: Hans Huber Publ. Inc., 14
Bruce Park Av., Toronto, Ont. M4P 253, Canada)
Indexed: Ind.Med.
　Formerly: Aktuelle Probleme in der Chirurgie
(ISSN 0065-5589)

617.3　　　　　　US　ISSN 0065-6895
AMERICAN ACADEMY OF ORTHOPAEDIC
SURGEONS. COMMITTEE ON
INSTRUCTIONAL COURSES.
INSTRUCTIONAL COURSE LECTURES. 1944.
irreg., vol.35, 1986. (American Academy of
Orthopaedic Surgeons) C. V. Mosby Co., 11830
Westline Industrial Dr., St. Louis, MO 63146. TEL
314-872-8370. (reprint service avail. from UMI)
　*From 1961 to the present, lectures published
monthly in Journal of Bone and Joint Surgery*

617.3　　　　　　US　ISSN 0516-8856
AMERICAN ACADEMY OF ORTHOPAEDIC
SURGEONS. DIRECTORY. 1933. a. membership
only. American Academy of Orthopaedic Surgeons,
222 S. Prospect St., Park Ridge, IL 60068. TEL
312-823-7186. Ed. Pamela Winkler. circ. 12,000.

AMERICAN COLLEGE OF FOOT SPECIALISTS.
ANNUAL YEARBOOK. see *MEDICAL
SCIENCES — Surgery*

AMERICAN PODIATRIC MEDICAL
ASSOCIATION. DESK REFERENCE AND
DIRECTORY; with constitution, by-laws and code
of ethics. see *MEDICAL SCIENCES — Surgery*

617.3　　　　　　GW　ISSN 0068-3388
BUECHEREI DES ORTHOPAEDEN. 1969. irreg.,
no.50, 1987. price varies. Ferdinand Enke Verlag,
Postfach 1304, 7000 Stuttgart 1, W. Germany
(B.R.D.) Eds. P. Otte, K.-F. Schlegel.

610　　　　　　US　ISSN 0085-1469
HEFTE ZUR UNFALLHEILKUNDE. irreg., no.167,
1984. price varies. Springer Verlag, 175 Fifth Ave.,
New York, NY 10010 TEL 212-460-1500. (Also
Berlin, Heidelberg, Tokyo and Vienna) (also avail.
in microform from UMI; reprint service avail. from
ISI) Indexed: Biol.Abstr.　Excerp.Med.　Ind.Med.

617.58　　　　　　US　ISSN 0095-7216
HIP; proceedings of the Open Scientific Meeting of
the Hip Society. 1973. a. $62. (Hip Society) C. V.
Mosby Co., 11830 Westline Industrial Dr., St.
Louis, MO 63146. TEL 314-872-8370. illus. (back
issues avail.) Indexed: Ind.Med.

MEDICINE AND SPORT SCIENCE. see
MEDICAL SCIENCES — Sports Medicine

617.1　　　　　　US
NEUROORTHOPAEDIE. (Represents material
presented at annual Erlangen Workshops) 1983.
irreg. Springer-Verlag, 175 Fifth Ave., New York,
NY 10010.

NEUROTRAUMATOLOGY. see *MEDICAL
SCIENCES — Psychiatry And Neurology*

RECONSTRUCTION SURGERY AND
TRAUMATOLOGY. see *MEDICAL
SCIENCES — Surgery*

617.3　　　　　　FR　ISSN 0081-1033
SOCIETE FRANCAISE DE CHIRURGIE
ORTHOPEDIQUE ET TRAUMATOLOGIQUE.
CONFERENCES D'ENSEIGNEMENT. 1967.
irreg., latest 1973. price varies. Expansion
Scientifique, 15 rue Saint-Benoit, 75278 Paris Cedex
06, France. Ed. J. Duparc.

617.1　　　　　　FR　ISSN 0397-3999
TECHNIQUES ORTHOPEDIQUES. 1976. irreg.,
latest 1981. 800 F.($100) Expansion Scientifique
Francaise, 15 rue Saint Benoit, 75278 Paris Cedex
06, France. Eds. J. Casaing, L. Descamps.

617　　　　　　GW　ISSN 0510-5315
DIE WIRBELSAEULE IN FORSCHUNG UND
PRAXIS. 1956. irreg., latest vol.105, 1985. price
varies. Hippokrates Verlag GmbH, Ruedigerstr. 14,
Postfach 593, D-7000 Stuttgart 1, W.
Germany(B.R.D.) Ed. Klaus Peter Schulitz.
Indexed: Biol.Abstr.

617　　　　　　US　ISSN 0271-7964
YEAR BOOK OF EMERGENCY MEDICINE. 1981.
a. $44.95. Year Book Medical Publishers, Inc., 35 E.
Wacker Dr., Chicago, IL 60601. TEL 312-726-9733.
Ed. D.K. Wagner, M.D.

617.305　　　　　　US　ISSN 0276-1092
YEAR BOOK OF ORTHOPEDICS. 1940. a. $44.95.
‡ Year Book Medical Publishers, Inc., 35 E. Wacker
Dr., Chicago, IL 60601. TEL 312-726-9733. Ed.
Mark B. Coventry, M.D. illus.
　Former titles: Year Book of Orthopedics,
Traumatic and Plastic Surgery; Year Book of
Orthopedics and Traumatic Surgery (ISSN 0084-
3938)

617.3　　　　　　US
YEAR BOOK OF PODIATRIC MEDICINE AND
SURGERY. a. $39.95. Year Book Medical
Publishers, Inc., 35 E. Wacker Dr., Chicago, IL
60601. TEL 312-726-9746. illus.

MEDICAL SCIENCES — Otorhinolaryngology

616.21　　　　　　US　ISSN 0883-3001
A B M S DIRECTORY OF CERTIFIED
OTOLARYNGOLOGISTS. 1985. biennial. $39.95
hardcover; $29.50 softcover. American Board of
Medical Specialties, One American Plaza, Ste. 805,
Evanston, IL 60201. TEL 312-491-9091. Ed.
Donald G. Langsley, M.D.

371.9　617.8　612.85　　US　ISSN 0569-8553
A S H A REPORTS. 1972. irreg., no.16, 1986.
American Speech-Language-Hearing Association,
10801 Rockville Pike, Rockville, MD 20852. TEL
301-897-5700. Ed. Arnold Small. Indexed:
Biol.Abstr.　Educ.Ind.　Psychol.Abstr.

616.21　　　　　　DK　ISSN 0365-5237
ACTA OTO-LARYNGOLOGICA. SUPPLEMENT.
a. Kr.142. (Scandinavian Oto-Laryngological
Society) Biblioteksscentralen, Telegrafvej 5, DK-2750
Ballerup, Denmark.

616.21　　　　　　BE　ISSN 0001-6497
ACTA OTO-RHINO-LARYNGOLOGICA
BELGICA. vol.21,1967. irreg., approx. 6/yr. 3700
Fr. (Association des Societes Scientifiques
Medicales Belges) Publications Acta Medica
Belgica, Hotel des Societes Scientifiques, 43 rue des
Champs-Elysees, B-1050 Brussels, Belgium. Ed. Dr.
P. Hennebert. Indexed: Biol.Abstr.　Chem.Abstr.
Excerp.Med.　Ind.Med.　Dent.Ind.　Lang.&
Lang.Behav.Abstr.

617.89 SZ ISSN 0254-8747
ADVANCES IN AUDIOLOGY. (Text in English)
1983. irreg. price varies. S. Karger AG, P.O. Box,
CH-4009 Basel, Switzerland. Ed. M. Hoke.

616.21 SZ ISSN 0065-3071
ADVANCES IN OTO-RHINO-LARYNGOLOGY.
(Text in English) 1953. irreg. price varies. S. Karger
AG, Allschwilerstrasse 10, P.O. Box, CH-4009
Basel, Switzerland. Ed. C.R. Pfaltz. (reprint service
avail. from ISI) Indexed: Biol.Abstr. Chem.Abstr.
Curr.Cont. Ind.Med. Dent.Ind.

616.21 US ISSN 0065-7603
AMERICAN BRONCHO-ESOPHAGOLOGICAL
ASSOCIATION. TRANSACTIONS. 1921. a. $35.
American Broncho-Esophagological Association, c/o
Dr. Gerald B. Healy, Ed., 300 Longwood Ave.,
Boston, MA 02115.

616.21 US ISSN 0065-9037
AMERICAN LARYNGOLOGICAL,
RHINOLOGICAL AND OTOLOGICAL
SOCIETY. TRANSACTIONS. 1896. a. $25.
(American Laryngological Rhinological and
Otological Society) Laryngoscope Co., 9216 Clayton
Road, Ste. 18, St. Louis, MO 63124. TEL 314-997-
5070. Ed. Malcolm Stroud, M.D. adv. bk. rev. circ.
500. (also avail. in microform from UMI)

617.8 US
AMERICAN OTOLOGICAL SOCIETY.
TRANSACTIONS. 1868. a. price varies. (American
Otological Society) Annals Publishing Co., 4507
Laclede Ave., St. Louis, MO 63108. Ed. Jack D.
Clemis. circ. 500.

616.855 612.85 US
AMERICAN SPEECH - LANGUAGE - HEARING
ASSOCIATION. DIRECTORY. biennial. price
varies. American Speech-Language-Hearing
Association, 10801 Rockville Pike, Rockville, MD
20852. TEL 301-897-5700.
 Formerly: A S H A Directory (American Speech
and Hearing Association) (ISSN 0569-8561)

616.2 IT ISSN 0066-9865
ASSOCIAZIONE ITALIANA
LARINGECTOMIZZATI. ATTI (DEL)
CONVEGNO NAZIONALE. 1957. a. Associazione
Italiana Laringectomizzati, Piazza Bertarelli, 4,
Milan, Italy.

617.89 US ISSN 0197-3657
HOUSE EAR INSTITUTE. PROGRESS REPORT.
1973. a. House Ear Institute, 256 S. Lake St., Los
Angeles, CA 90057. TEL 213-483-4431.
 Formerly: Los Angeles Foundation of Otology.
Progress Report.

617.89 UK ISSN 0262-6853
I A P A BULLETIN. 1981. irreg. International
Association of Physicians in Audiology, c/o D.
Stephens, 309 Grays Inn Rd., London WC1 8DA,
England. charts. illus.
 Audiology

616.21 AT ISSN 0030-6614
OTO-LARYNGOLOGICAL SOCIETY OF
AUSTRALIA. JOURNAL. 1962. a. Aus.$30. ‡
Oto-Laryngological Society of Australia, 33-35
Atchison St., St. Leonards, N.S.W. 2065, Australia.
Ed. Dr. Rory Willis. adv. bk. rev. circ. 1,000. (also
avail. in microform from UMI; reprint service avail.
from UMI) Indexed: DSH Abstr. Excerp.Med.

SOUTH AFRICAN JOURNAL OF
COMMUNICATION DISORDERS/SUID-
AFRIKAANSE TYDSKRIF VIR
KOMMUNIKASIEAFWYKINGS. see MEDICAL
SCIENCES

616.21 US
SYMPOSIUM ON CARE OF THE
PROFESSIONAL VOICE. TRANSCRIPTS.
(Published in 2 parts) 1978. a., 13th symposium,
1984. $35. Voice Foundation, 157 E. 61 St., New
York, NY 10021. TEL 212-688-1897. Ed. Van
Lawrence. charts. illus. (back issues avail.)

616.21 US
YEAR BOOK OF OTOLARYNGOLOGY. 1900. a.
$44.95. Year Book Medical Publishers, Inc., 35 E.
Wacker Dr., Chicago, IL 60601. TEL 312-726-9733.
Eds. M.M. Paparella, M.D., B.J. Bailey, M.D. illus.
 Formerly (1958-1975): Year Book of the Ear,
Nose and Throat (ISSN 0084-4055); Supersedes in
part: Yearbook of the Eye, Ear, Nose and Throat.

MEDICAL SCIENCES — Pediatrics

618.92 US ISSN 0884-1497
A B M S DIRECTORY OF CERTIFIED
PEDIATRICIANS. 1984. biennial. $49.95
hardcover; $39.95 softcover. American Board of
Medical Specialties, One American Plaza, Ste. 805,
Evanston, IL 60201. TEL 312-491-9091. Ed.
Donald G. Langsley, M.D.

ADVANCES IN CHILD DEVELOPMENT AND
BEHAVIOR. see PSYCHOLOGY

618.92 US
ADVANCES IN DEVELOPMENTAL AND
BEHAVIORAL PEDIATRICS: a research annual.
1980. a. $23.75 to individuals; institutions $47.50. J
A I Press Inc., Box 1678, 36 Sherwood Pl.,
Greenwich, CT 06836. TEL 203-661-7602. Eds.
Mark Wolraich, Donald K. Routh. Indexed:
Psychol.Abstr.
 Formerly: Advances in Behavioral Pediatrics
(ISSN 0198-7089)

618.92 US ISSN 0732-9598
ADVANCES IN INFANCY RESEARCH. 1981. a.
$29.50 to individuals; institutions $45. Ablex
Publishing Corp., 355 Chestnut St., Norwood, NJ
07648. TEL 201-767-8450. Eds. Lewis P. Lipsitt,
Carolyn Rovee-Collier. (reprint service avail. from
ISI) Indexed: Psychol.Abstr.

618.92 UK
ADVANCES IN INTERNATIONAL MATERNAL
AND CHILD HEALTH. 1981. a. £22($45) Oxford
University Press, Walton St., Oxford OX2 6DP,
England. Ed. E.F.P. Jelliffe.

618.92 US ISSN 0065-3101
ADVANCES IN PEDIATRICS. 1942. a. $49.95. Year
Book Medical Publishers, Inc., 35 E. Wacker Dr.,
Chicago, IL 60601. TEL 312-726-9733. Ed. L.A.
Barness, M.D. illus. (also avail. in microform from
UMI; reprint service avail. from UMI) Indexed:
Ind.Med. CINAHL. Dent.Ind.

618.92 US ISSN 0065-6909
AMERICAN ACADEMY OF PEDIATRICS.
COMMITTEE ON INFECTIOUS DISEASES.
REPORT. 1938. irreg., 1982, 19th edt. $20.
American Academy of Pediatrics, 141 Northwest
Point Rd., Box 927, Elk Grove Village, IL 60007.
TEL 312-228-5005.

618.92 FR ISSN 0066-3514
ANNUAIRE NATIONAL DES SPECIALISTES
QUALIFIES EXCLUSIFS EN PEDIATRIE. 1962.
a. 50 F. (Revue de Pediatrie) Societe Internationale
d'Edition Medicale, 62 rue Ivan Tourgueniev, 78380
Bougival, France. Ed. Jeanine Guillin. adv.

616.8 367 GW ISSN 0067-5105
BEITRAEGE ZUR KINDERPSYCHOTHERAPIE.
1965. irreg., no.30, 1985. price varies. Ernst
Reinhardt, GmbH und Co., Verlag, Kemnatenstr.
46, 8000 Munich 19, W. Germany (B.R.D.) Ed.
Gerd Biermann. index.

618.92 PL
BIBLIOTEKA PEDIATRY. 1974. irreg. Panstwowy
Zaklad Wydawnictw Lekarskich, Ul. Dluga 38-40,
Warsaw, Poland. Ed. Krystyna Bozkowa.

618.92 UK
BREAST FEEDING. 1983. a. $2 free in U.K. B.
Edsall & Co. Ltd., 124 Belgrave Rd., London,
SW1V 2BL, England. Ed. Patricia Scowen. adv.
circ. 650,000.

618.92 GW ISSN 0373-3165
BUECHEREI DES PAEDIATERS. 1972. irreg.,
no.90, 1986. price varies. Ferdinand Enke Verlag,
Postfach 1304, 7000 Stuttgart 1, W. Germany
(B.R.D.) Ed.Bd. Indexed: Nutr.Abstr.
 Continues: Archiv fuer Kinderheilkunde. Beihefte
(ISSN 0066-6378)

618.92 155.4 616.89 US ISSN 0193-7421
CHILD BEHAVIOR AND DEVELOPMENT. 1975.
irreg. S P Medical & Scientific Books (Subsidiary of:
Spectrum Publications, Inc.) 175-20 Wexford
Terrace, Jamaica, NY 11432. TEL 718-658-0888.

612 UK ISSN 0069-4835
CLINICS IN DEVELOPMENTAL MEDICINE.
1959. irreg., (approx. 4/yr., latest no.95, 1985)
£35($60) Mac Keith Press, 5A Netherhall Gardens,
London NW3 5RN, England (Dist. in U.S. by: J.B.
Lippincott Company, E. Washington Square,
Philadelphia, PA 19105)

COMBINED CUMULATIVE INDEX TO
PEDIATRICS. see MEDICAL SCIENCES —
Abstracting, Bibliographies, Statistics

618.92 US
COMPREHENSIVE MANUALS IN PEDIATRICS.
1982. irreg., latest 1984. Springer-Verlag, 175 Fifth
Ave., New York, NY 10010 TEL 212-460-1500.
(Also Berlin, Heidelberg, Tokyo and Vienna) Eds.
M. Katz, E.R. Stiehm.

CONCEPTS IN PEDIATRIC NEUROSURGERY.
see MEDICAL SCIENCES — Psychiatry And
Neurology

618.92 US ISSN 0172-1232
CURRENT DIAGNOSTIC PEDIATRICS. 1977.
irreg., vol.3, 1980. price varies. Springer-Verlag, 175
Fifth Ave., New York, NY 10010 TEL 212-460-
1500. (Also Berlin, Heidelberg, Tokyo and Vienna)
Ed. A. Chrispin. (reprint service avail. from ISI)

618.92 DK ISSN 0105-9289
DANSK PAEDIATRISK SELSKAB. AARBOG.*
1977. a. Dansk Paediatrisk Selskab, c/o Dr.
Flemming Haft Hansen, Abrinken 155, DK-2830
Virum, Denmark. adv. circ. 400.

DEVELOPMENTAL & BEHAVIORAL
PEDIATRICS: SELECTED TOPICS. see
PSYCHOLOGY

EPIDEMIOLOGIA CIENTIFICA: TEORIA Y
PRACTICA. see MEDICAL SCIENCES

ERGEBNISSE DER INNEREN MEDIZIN UND
KINDERHEILKUNDE. NEW SERIES/
ADVANCES IN INTERNAL MEDICINE AND
PEDIATRICS. see MEDICAL SCIENCES

HAWAII. FAMILY HEALTH SERVICES
DIVISION. CRIPPLED CHILDREN SERVICES
BRANCH. REPORT. see SOCIAL SERVICES
AND WELFARE

618.92 SZ ISSN 0073-1811
HELVETICA PAEDIATRICA ACTA.
SUPPLEMENTUM. (Text in French and German;
summaries in English, German and Italian) 1945.
irreg. price varies. (Swiss Society of Paediatrics)
Schwabe und Co. AG, Steinentorstr. 13, 4010 Basel,
Switzerland. Indexed: Ind.Med. Nutr.Abstr.

HOSPITAL FOR SICK CHILDREN, TORONTO.
RESEARCH INSTITUTE. ANNUAL REPORT.
see MEDICAL SCIENCES

618.92 AU ISSN 0074-7300
INTERNATIONAL PEDIATRIC ASSOCIATION.
PROCEEDINGS OF CONGRESS.* triennial,
1971, 13th, Vienna. Wiener Medizinische
Akademie, 9 Alserstr. 4, Vienna, Austria.

JOURNAL OF PEDIATRIC ENDIOCRINOLOGY.
see MEDICAL SCIENCES — Endocrinology

618.92 FR ISSN 0075-4471
JOURNEES PARISIENNES DE PEDIATRIE. 1966.
a. price varies. (Hopital des Enfants Malades,
Centre d'Etudes sur les Maladies du Metabolisme
chez l'Enfant) Flammarion Medecine-Sciences, 4
rue Casimir Delavigne, 75006 Paris, France (U.S.
subscr. address: S.F.P.A., c/o M. Benech, 14 E.
60th St., New York, NY 10022) Ed. P. Royer.

618.92 US ISSN 0362-3173
LACTATION REVIEW. 1976. irreg. $25 to
individuals; institutions $35. Human Lactation
Center Ltd., 666 Sturges Hwy., Westport, CT
06880. Ed. Dana Raphael. adv. bk. rev. film rev.
abstr. circ. 3,500. (back issues avail.)

618.92 SZ ISSN 0077-0086
MODERN PROBLEMS IN PAEDIATRICS. (Text in
English) 1954. irreg. (approx. 1/yr.) price varies. S.
Karger AG, Allschwilerstrasse 10, P.O. Box, CH-
4009 Basel, Switzerland. Ed.Bd. (reprint service
avail. from ISI) Indexed: Biol.Abstr. Chem.Abstr.
Curr.Cont. Ind.Med.

618.92 SZ ISSN 0077-0914
MONOGRAPHS IN PAEDIATRICS. (Text in English) 1971. irreg. (approx. 1/yr.) price varies. S. Karger AG, Allschwilerstrasse 10, P.O. Box, CH-4009 Basel, Switzerland. Ed.Bd. (reprint service avail. from ISI) Indexed: Biol.Abstr. Chem.Abstr. Curr.Cont. Ind.Med.
Supersedes (1924-1970): Bibliotheca Paediatrica.

618.92 US
MONOGRAPHS ON INFANCY. 1981. irreg. price varies. Ablex Publishing Corp., 355 Chestnut St., Norwood, NJ 07648. TEL 201-767-8450. Ed. Lewis P. Lipsitt. Indexed: Psychol.Abstr.

618.92 US ISSN 0300-9556
PAEDIATRIE UND PAEDOLOGIE. SUPPLEMENT. 1972. irreg., vol.6, 1980. price varies. Springer-Verlag, 175 Fifth Ave., New York, NY 10010 TEL 212-460-1500. (Also Berlin, Heidelberg, Vienna) (reprint service avail. from ISI) Indexed: Ind.Med.

618.92 US
PAEDIATRIE: WEITER- UND FORTBILDUNG. (Text in German) 1980. irreg., vol.3, 1982. Springer-Verlag, 175 Fifth Ave., New York, NY 10010 TEL 212-460-1500. (Also Berlin, Heidelberg, Tokyo and Vienna) Ed. H. Ewerbeck. (reprint service avail. from ISI)

618.92 SZ ISSN 0078-7795
PAEDIATRISCHE FORTBILDUNGSKURSE FUER DIE PRAXIS. (Text in German) 1961. irreg. (approx. 2/yr.) price varies. S. Karger AG, Allschwilerstrasse 10, P.O. Box, CH-4009 Basel, Switzerland. Ed. E. Rossi. (reprint service avail. from ISI; back issues avail.) Indexed: Biol.Abstr. Chem.Abstr. Curr.Cont. Ind.Med.

610 SZ
PERSPECTIVES IN PEDIATRIC PATHOLOGY. (Text in English) 1973. irreg. S. Karger AG, Allschwilerstrasse 10, P.O. Box, CH-4009 Basel, Switzerland. Eds. H.S. Rosenberg, J. Bernstein.

618.92 PL ISSN 0079-4279
POSTEPY PEDIATRII. (Text in Polish; summaries in English, Polish, and Russian) 1955. a. Panstwowy Zaklad Wydawnictw Lekarskich, Dluga 38-40, Warsaw, Poland. Ed. Jana Raszka, M.D.

618.92 US
PRE-PARENT ADVISER. a. free contr. circ. (Johnson & Johnson) Whittle Communications, L.P., 50 Market St., Knoxville, TN 37902. TEL 615-595-5761. circ. 1,000,000.

618.92 617 US
PRINCIPLES OF PEDIATRIC NEUROSURGERY. 1986. irreg. price varies. Springer-Verlag, 175 Fifth Ave., New York, NY 10160 TEL 212-460-1500. (Also Berlin, Heidelberg, Tokyo, Vienna) (reprint service avail. from ISI)

618.92 SZ ISSN 0079-6646
PROGRESS IN PEDIATRIC RADIOLOGY. (Text in English) 1967. irreg. (approx. 1/yr.) price varies. S. Karger AG, Allschwilerstrasse 10, P.O. Box, CH-4009 Basel, Switzerland. Ed. H.J. Kaufmann. (reprint service avail. from ISI) Indexed: Biol.Abstr. Chem.Abstr. Curr.Cont. Ind.Med.

618.92 136.7 FR ISSN 0079-726X
PSYCHIATRIE DE L'ENFANT. 1958. a. (in 2 issues) 291 F. Presses Universitaires de France, 108 bd. Saint Germain, 75229 Paris Cedex 6, France. Ed.Bd. cum.index. (reprint service avail. from KTO) Indexed: Excerp.Med. Ind.Med. Psychol.Abstr. SSCI.

618.92 CK ISSN 0120-6311
REVISTA INTERNACIONAL DE PEDIATRIA. 1984. irreg. (4-6/yr.) (Miami Children's Hospital) Ediciones Lerner Ltda., Calle 8A No.68A-41, Bogota, Colombia. circ. 35,000.
Formerly (until Dec. 1984): Miami Children's Hospital Journal.

618.92 US
SALUD MATERNOINFANTIL Y ATENCION EN LAS AMERICAS. (Text in Spanish) irreg., no.461, 1984. Organizacion Mundial de la Salude, 525 23 St., N.W., Washington DC 20037.

THEIR WORLD. see CHILDREN AND YOUTH — About

THEORY AND RESEARCH IN BEHAVIORAL PEDIATRICS. see PSYCHOLOGY

618.92 US ISSN 0084-3954
YEAR BOOK OF PEDIATRICS. 1933. a. $42.95. Year Book Medical Publishers, Inc., 35 E. Wacker Dr., Chicago, IL 60601. TEL 312-726-9733. Eds. Frank A. Oski, M.D., James A. Stockman, III, M.D.

YOUR FIRST BABY. see CHILDREN AND YOUTH — About

MEDICAL SCIENCES — Psychiatry And Neurology

616.8 617 US ISSN 0882-2832
A B M S DIRECTORY OF CERTIFIED NEUROLOGICAL SURGEONS. 1983. biennial. $29.95 hardcover; $24.95 softcover. American Board of Medical Specialties, One American Plaza, Ste. 805, Evanston, IL 60201. TEL 312-491-9091. Ed. Donald G. Langsley, M.D.

616.8 US ISSN 0884-1500
A B M S DIRECTORY OF CERTIFIED NEUROLOGISTS. 1985. biennial. $34.95 hardcover; $29.95 softcover. American Board of Medical Specialties, One American Plaza, Ste. 805, Evanston, IL 60201. TEL 312-491-9091. Ed. Donald G. Langsley, M.D.

616.89 US ISSN 0884-1519
A B M S DIRECTORY OF CERTIFIED PSYCHIATRISTS. 1985. biennial. $49.95 hardcover; $39.95 softcover. American Board of Medical Specialties, One American Plaza, Ste. 805, Evanston, IL 60201. TEL 312-491-9091. Ed. Donald G. Langsley, M.D.

362.2 US ISSN 0001-1436
A H R C CHRONICLE. 1949. irreg. (3-4/yr.) membership. Association for the Help of Retarded Children, New York City Chapter, 200 Park Ave. S., New York, NY 10003. TEL 212-254-8203. Eds. John Wykert, Belle Press. adv. bk. rev. illus. circ. 10,000.
Mental retardation

616.8 US ISSN 0001-6268
ACTA NEUROCHIRURGICA. SUPPLEMENTA. 1950. irreg., vol.34, 1984. price varies. Springer-Verlag, 175 Fifth Ave., New York, NY 10010 TEL 212-460-1500. (Also Berlin, Heidelberg, Tokyo and Vienna) Ed. F. Loew. (also avail. in microform from UMI; reprint service avail. from ISI) Indexed: Biol.Abstr. Ind.Med.
Formerly: Acta Neurochirurgica. Supplement (ISSN 0065-1419)

616.8 DK ISSN 0065-1427
ACTA NEUROLOGICA SCANDINAVICA. SUPPLEMENTUM. (Text in English) 1932. irreg. free to subscribers. Munksgaard, 35 Noerre Soegade, DK-1370 Copenhagen, Denmark. Ed. Dr. H. Pakkenberg. adv. (reprint service avail. from ISI) Indexed: Chem.Abstr. Biol.Abstr. Curr.Cont. Ind.Med.

616.8 US ISSN 0065-1435
ACTA NEUROPATHOLOGICA. SUPPLEMENT. 1962. irreg., no.9, 1983. price varies. Springer-Verlag, 175 Fifth Ave., New York, NY 10010 TEL 212-460-1500. (Also Berlin, Heidelberg, Tokyo and Vienna) (also avail. in microform from UMI; reprint service avail. from ISI) Indexed: Biol.Abstr. Chem.Abstr. Ind.Med.

616.8 DK ISSN 0065-1591
ACTA PSYCHIATRICA SCANDINAVICA. SUPPLEMENTUM. (Text in English) 1932. irreg. free to subscribers of Acta Psychiatrica Scandinavica. Munksgaard, 35 Noerre Soegade, DK-1370 Copenhagen K, Denmark. Ed. Jan-Otto Ottosson. adv. (reprint service avail. from ISI) Indexed: Biol.Abstr. Chem.Abstr. Curr.Cont. Ind.Med.

616.8 US ISSN 0065-2008
ADOLESCENT PSYCHIATRY; development and clinical studies. Represents: American Society for Adolescent Psychiatry. Annals. 1971. a. $37.50. (American Society for Adolescent Psychiatry) University of Chicago Press, 5801 S. Ellis Ave., Chicago, IL 60637 TEL 312-962-7600. (Orders to: Box 37005, Chicago, IL 60637) Ed. Sherman C. Feinstein. (reprint service avail. from UMI,ISI) Indexed: Biol.Abstr. Psychol.Abstr. SSCI. ASCA. CINAHL.

616.8 US ISSN 0095-4829
ADVANCES AND TECHNICAL STANDARDS IN NEUROSURGERY. 1974. irreg., no.13, 1986. price varies. Springer-Verlag, 175 Fifth Ave., New York, NY 10010 TEL 212-460-1500. (Also Berlin, Heidelberg, Tokyo and Vienna) Ed.Bd. (reprint service avail. from ISI)

ADVANCES IN BIOCHEMICAL PSYCHOPHARMACOLOGY. see PHARMACY AND PHARMACOLOGY

616.8 SZ ISSN 0378-7354
ADVANCES IN BIOLOGICAL PSYCHIATRY. 1978. irreg. (approx. 2/yr.) price varies. S. Karger AG, Allschwilerstrasse 10, P.O. Box, CH-4009 Basel, Switzerland. Eds. H.M. van Praag, J. Mendlewicz. (reprint service avail. from ISI) Indexed: Biol.Abstr. Chem.Abstr. Curr.Cont. Psychol.Abstr.

ADVANCES IN FORENSIC PSYCHOLOGY AND PSYCHIATRY. see PSYCHOLOGY

ADVANCES IN HUMAN PSYCHOPHARMACOLOGY; a research annual. see PHARMACY AND PHARMACOLOGY

ADVANCES IN NEUROCHEMISTRY. see BIOLOGY — Biological Chemistry

ADVANCES IN NEUROGERONTOLOGY. see GERONTOLOGY AND GERIATRICS

616.8 US ISSN 0091-3952
ADVANCES IN NEUROLOGY. 1973. irreg., vol.27, 1979. price varies. Raven Press, 1185 Ave. of the Americas, New York, NY 10036. TEL 212-575-0335. Indexed: Biol.Abstr. Chem.Abstr. Curr.Cont. Ind.Med. Dent.Ind.

616.8 US ISSN 0302-2366
ADVANCES IN NEUROSURGERY. 1973. irreg., vol.14, 1986. price varies. Springer-Verlag, 175 Fifth Ave., New York, NY 10010 TEL 212-460-1500. (And Berlin, Heidelberg, Tokyo and Vienna) (reprint service avail. from ISI) Indexed: Biol.Abstr. Chem.Abstr.

616.8 US ISSN 0146-0722
ADVANCES IN PAIN RESEARCH AND THERAPY. 1976. irreg., vol.3, 1979. price varies. Raven Press, 1185 Ave. of the Americas, New York, NY 10036. TEL 212-575-0335. Ed. John J. Bonica. index. Indexed: Biol.Abstr. Chem.Abstr. Curr.Cont. Sci.Cit.Ind. Ind.Sci.Rev.

ADVANCES IN PERSONALITY ASSESSMENT. see PSYCHOLOGY

616.8 SZ ISSN 0065-3268
ADVANCES IN PSYCHOSOMATIC MEDICINE. (Text in English) 1960. irreg. (approx. 1/yr.) price varies. S. Karger AG, Allschwilerstrasse 10, P.O. Box, CH-4009 Basel, Switzerland. Ed. T.N. Wise. (reprint service avail. from ISI, back issues avail.) Indexed: Biol.Abstr. Chem.Abstr. Curr.Cont. Ind.Med. SSCI.

616.8 SZ ISSN 0065-3381
ADVANCES IN STEREOENCEPHALOTOMY. (Text in English) irreg. (approx. 1/yr.) price varies. S. Karger AG, Allschwilerstrasse 10, P.O. Box, CH-4009 Basel, Switzerland. Ed. L.P. Gildenberg. (reprint service avail. from ISI) Indexed: Biol.Abstr. Chem.Abstr. Curr.Cont. Ind.Med.

616.8 SZ ISSN 0065-5600
AKTUELLE PROBLEME IN DER PSYCHIATRIE, NEUROLOGIE, NEUROCHIRURGIE. 1968. irreg. price varies. Verlag Hans Huber, Laenggassstr. 76, CH-3000 Berne 9, Switzerland (Subscr. to: Hans Huber Publ. Inc., 14 Bruce Park Ave., Toronto, Ont. M4P 2S3, Canada) Ed.Bd.

MEDICAL SCIENCES — PSYCHIATRY AND NEUROLOGY

616.8 US ISSN 0002-7995
AMERICAN COLLEGE OF
NEUROPSYCHIATRISTS. BULLETIN.* vol.26,
1973. irreg. (2-3/yr.) membership. (American
College of Neuropsychiatrists) 405 Grand Ave.,
Dayton, OH 45405. TEL 513-222-4213. Ed. Sydney
Mark Kanev, D.O. illus.

616.89 US
AMERICAN ORTHOPSYCHIATRIC
ASSOCIATION. PAPERS PRESENTED AT THE
ANNUAL CONVENTION. a. price varies. Wayne
State University Press, 5959 Woodward Ave.,
Detroit, MI 48202. TEL 313-577-4603.

616.89 US ISSN 0090-1881
AMERICAN PSYCHIATRIC ASSOCIATION.
SCIENTIFIC PROCEEDINGS IN SUMMARY
FORM. a. $15. American Psychiatric Association,
1400 K St. N.W., Washington, DC 20005. TEL
202-682-6000.

616.89 US
AMERICAN PSYCHIATRIC ASSOCIATION.
TASK FORCE REPORTS. 1970. irreg., no.21,
1982. price varies. American Psychiatric
Association, 1400 K St. N.W., Washington, DC
20005. TEL 202-682-6268.

616.89 US ISSN 0091-7389
AMERICAN PSYCHOPATHOLOGICAL
ASSOCIATION. PROCEEDINGS OF THE
ANNUAL MEETING. 1945. a. price varies.
Guilford Publications, Inc., 200 Park Ave. S., New
York, NY 10003. TEL 212-674-1900. (reprint
service avail. from UMI)

616.8 US ISSN 0066-0132
AMERICAN SOCIETY FOR NEUROCHEMISTRY.
TRANSACTIONS. 1970. a. $10. (American Society
for Neurochemistry) Medical College of Virginia, c/
o Marion E. Smith, Sec., Department of Neurology
127A, V. A. Medical Center, Palo Alto, CA 94304.
adv. circ. 1,500.

618.928 US ISSN 0066-4030
ANNUAL PROGRESS IN CHILD PSYCHIATRY
AND CHILD DEVELOPMENT. 1968. a. price
varies. Brunner-Mazel, Inc., 19 Union Sq. W., New
York, NY 10003. TEL 212-924-3344. Eds. S.
Chess, A. Thomas. bk. rev. (reprint service avail.
from UMI) Indexed: Biol.Abstr. Psychol.Abstr.

616.8 US ISSN 0147-006X
ANNUAL REVIEW OF NEUROSCIENCE. 1977. a.
$31. Annual Reviews Inc., 4139 El Camino Way,
Palo Alto, CA 94306. TEL 415-493-4400. Ed. W.
Maxwell Cowan. bibl. index. cum.index. (back issues
avail.; reprint service avail. from ISI) Indexed:
Biol.Abstr. Chem.Abstr. Curr.Cont. Ind.Med.
Psychol.Abstr. Sci.Cit.Ind.

616.8 GW ISSN 0172-7311
ARBEITSGEMEINSCHAFT FUER KLINISCHE
NEPHROLOGIE. MITTEILUNGEN. a. DM.32.
(Arbeitsgemeinschaft fuer Klinische Nephrologie
e.V.) Vandenhoeck & Ruprecht, Postfach 3753,
Theaterstr. 13, D-3400 Goettingen, W. Germany
(B.R.D.) Ed. E. Quellhorst.

610 US ISSN 0091-7443
ASSOCIATION FOR RESEARCH IN NERVOUS
AND MENTAL DISEASE. RESEARCH
PUBLICATIONS. a. price varies. Raven Press,
1185 Ave. of the Americas, New York, NY 10036.
TEL 212-575-0335. Indexed: Biol.Abstr.
Chem.Abstr. Curr.Cont. Ind.Med. Dent.Ind.

ATTORNEY'S DIRECTORY OF FORENSIC
PSYCHIATRISTS IN THE UNITED STATES
AND CANADA; a biographical professional and
reference directory of legal psychiatrists. see
MEDICAL SCIENCES — Forensic Sciences

616.8 DK ISSN 0108-7819
BERETNING FOR PSYKIATRISKE
INSTITUTIONER I DANMARK. (Text in English
and Danish) 1979. irreg. Kr.25. Sundhedsstyrelsen,
St. Kongensgade 1, 1264 Copenhagen K, Denmark
(Orders to: Statens Informationtjeneste, Bredgade
20, 1260 Copenhagen K, Denmark)

616.8 SZ ISSN 0067-8147
BIBLIOTHECA PSYCHIATRICA. (Text in English
and German) 1917. irreg. (approx. 1/yr.) price
varies. S. Karger AG, Allschwilerstrasse 10, P.O.
Box, CH-4009 Basel, Switzerland. Eds. P. Berner, E.
Gabriel. (reprint service avail. from ISI, back issues
avail.) Indexed: Biol.Abstr. Chem.Abstr.
Curr.Cont. Ind.Med. SSCI.

BIOFEEDBACK SOCIETY OF AMERICA.
PROCEEDINGS OF THE ANNUAL MEETING.
see PSYCHOLOGY

616.8 UK ISSN 0260-0137
BUTTERWORTHS INTERNATIONAL MEDICAL
REVIEWS: NEUROLOGY. 1981. a. price varies.
Butterworth & Co. (Publishers) Ltd., Borough
Green, Sevenoaks, Kent TN15 8PH, England.
Indexed: Biol.Abstr.

616.8 157.61 AT
C C H R NEWSLETTER. 1972. irreg., latest Nov.
1985. Aus.$12($15) Citizens Committee on Human
Rights, 24 Waymouth St., Adelaide, S.A. 5000,
Australia. Ed. Colin Harris. circ. 350. (back issues
avail.)

616.858 UK
CARE MAGAZINE. 1973. a. £3. Care for Mentally
Handicapped People, c/o T.S. Doggett, 9a Weir
Rd., Kibworth, Leics. LE8 0LQ, England. Ed. A.H.
Franklin. circ. 4,000. Indexed: HR Rep.

616.858 UK
CARE NEWS. 1973. a. £3. Care for Mentally
Handicapped People, c/o T.S. Doggett, 9a Weir
Rd., Kibworth, Leics. LE8 0LQ, England. Ed. A.H.
Franklin. circ. 4,000.

616.8 US
CEREBRAL FUNCTION SYMPOSIUM.
PROCEEDINGS.* 1970. irreg., 2nd, 1972. price
varies. Charles C. Thomas, Publisher, 2600 S. First
St., Springfield, IL 62717. TEL 217-789-8980.

CHILD BEHAVIOR AND DEVELOPMENT. see
MEDICAL SCIENCES — Pediatrics

616.8 CN ISSN 0069-441X
CLARKE INSTITUTE OF PSYCHIATRY.
MONOGRAPH SERIES. 1967. irreg. price varies.
University of Toronto Press, Front Campus,
Toronto, Ont. M5S 1A6, Canada. TEL 613-667-
7791. Indexed: Biol.Abstr.

616.8 IT
CLINICA NEUROPSICHIATRICA. (Text in Italian;
summaries in English, French, German, Italian)
1965. irreg. Ospedale Neuropsichiatrico, Teramo,
Italy.

616.8 AT ISSN 0158-1597
CLINICAL AND EXPERIMENTAL NEUROLOGY.
1963. a. (Australian Association of Neurologists)
Williams & Wilkins Associates, 43 Herbert St.,
Artarmon, N.S.W. 2064, Australia. Eds. J.H. Tyrer,
M.J. Eadie. circ. 300. (also avail. in microfilm from
UMI) Indexed: Chem.Abstr. Excerp.Med.
Ind.Med.
Formerly: Australian Association of Neurologists
Proceedings (ISSN 0084-7224)

616.8 US
CLINICAL INFANT REPORTS. MONOGRAPH.
irreg., no.4 in prep. price varies. (National Center
for Clinical Infant Programs) International
Universities Press, Inc., 59 Boston Post Rd., Box
1524, Madison, CT 06443-1524. TEL 203-245-
4000. Indexed: Psychol.Abstr.

617.48 US ISSN 0069-4827
CLINICAL NEUROSURGERY; PROCEEDINGS.
1953. a. price varies. (Congress of Neurological
Surgeons) Williams & Wilkins, 428 E. Preston St.,
Baltimore, MD 21202. TEL 301-528-4000. Indexed:
Ind.Med.

CLINICS IN DEVELOPMENTAL MEDICINE. see
MEDICAL SCIENCES — Pediatrics

616.8 SZ ISSN 0251-2068
CONCEPTS IN PEDIATRIC NEUROSURGERY.
(Text in English) 1981. a. price varies. S. Karger
AG, P.O. Box, CH-4009 Basel, Switzerland.
Indexed: Biol.Abstr.

616.8 US ISSN 0069-9446
CONTEMPORARY NEUROLOGY SERIES. 1966.
irreg., vol.28, 1987. price varies. F.A. Davis Co.,
1915 Arch St., Philadelphia, PA 19103. TEL 800-
523-4049. Ed. Fred Plum, M.D. Indexed:
Chem.Abstr. Ind.Med.

CONTRIBUICOES EM PSICOLOGIA,
PSIQUIATRIA E PSICANALISE. see
PSYCHOLOGY

616.8 US ISSN 0161-780X
CURRENT NEUROLOGY. 1978. a. $60. Year Book
Medical Publishers, Inc., 35 E. Wacker Dr.,
Chicago, IL 60601. Ed. Stanley H. Appel, M.D.
illus. Indexed: Chem.Abstr.

616.4 US
CURRENT TOPICS IN
NEUROENDOCRINOLOGY. 1982. irreg., vol.7,
1986. Springer-Verlag, 175 Fifth Ave., New York,
NY 10010 TEL 212-460-1500. (Also Berlin,
Heidelberg, Tokyo and Vienna) Indexed:
Chem.Abstr.

616.8 NE ISSN 0166-5960
DEVELOPMENTS IN NEUROLOGY. 1978. irreg.,
vol.7, 1983. Elsevier Science Publishers B.V., Box
211, 1000 AE Amsterdam, Netherlands. illus.
Indexed: Chem.Abstr.

616.8 NE
DEVELOPMENTS IN NEUROSCIENCE. 1977.
irreg., vol.18, 1984. price varies. Elsevier Science
Publishers B.V., P.O. Box 211, 1000 AE
Amsterdam, Netherlands. Indexed: Chem.Abstr.
Sci.Cit.Ind. Ind.Sci.Rev.

616.8 NE ISSN 0166-2481
DEVELOPMENTS IN PSYCHIATRY. 1979. irreg.,
vol.6, 1983. Elsevier Science Publishers B.V., Box
211, 1000 AE Amsterdam, Netherlands. illus.
Indexed: Chem.Abstr.

DIRECTORY OF BEHAVIORAL GRADUATE
STUDY. see EDUCATION — Guides To Schools
And Colleges

616.8 US ISSN 0734-9890
EMOTIONS AND BEHAVIOR. MONOGRAPH.
irreg., no.7, in prep. price varies. (Chicago Institute
for Psychoanalysis) International Universities Press,
Inc., 59 Boston Post Rd., Box 1524, Madison, CT
06443-1524. TEL 203-245-4000. Ed. George H.
Pollock. Indexed: Psychol.Abstr.

ENCOUNTERER. see PSYCHOLOGY

616.8 US
EXPERIMENTAL AND CLINICAL PSYCHIATRY.
1979. irreg., vol.4, 1981. price varies. Marcel
Dekker, Inc., 270 Madison Ave., New York, NY
10016. Ed. Van Praag. Indexed: Psychol.Abstr.

616.8 US ISSN 0172-9039
EXPERIMENTAL BRAIN RESEARCH.
SUPPLEMENTA. 1976. irreg., vol.15, 1986.
Springer-Verlag, 175 Fifth Ave., New York, NY
10010. TEL 212-460-1500. (reprint service avail.
from ISI) Indexed: Chem.Abstr. Ind.Sci.Rev.

616.8 GW ISSN 0071-8025
FORUM DER PSYCHIATRIE. 1961; N.S. 1977.
irreg., vol.26, 1987. price varies. Ferdinand Enke
Verlag, Postfach 1304, 7000 Stuttgart 1, W.
Germany (B.R.D.) Ed.Bd.

616.8 US
FUNCTIONAL NEUROSCIENCE. 1977. irreg.,
vol.3, 1984. $70. Lawrence Erlbaum Associates,
Inc., 365 Broadway, Hillsdale, NJ 07642. TEL 201-
666-4110. Ed. T. Harmony. (back issues avail.)
Indexed: Curr.Cont. Psychol.Abstr.

616.8 US
GENERATIONS. irreg. National Ataxia Foundation,
600 Twelve Oaks Center, 15500 Wayzata Blvd.,
Wayzata, MN 55391. TEL 612-473-7666.

155 US
GENESIS OF BEHAVIOR. 1978. irreg. price varies.
Plenum Publishing Corp., 233 Spring St., New
York, NY 10013. TEL 212-620-8047. Eds. Michael
Lewis, Leonard A. Rosenblum.

616.89　　　　　　　　US
GROUP FOR THE ADVANCEMENT OF PSYCHIATRY. PUBLICATION. 1947. irreg., approx. 10 in 3 yrs. price varies. (Group for the Advancement of Psychiatry) Brunner-Mazel, Inc., 19 Union Sq. W., New York, NY 10003. TEL 212-924-3344. Dir. Alex Sareyan. cum.index. Indexed: Ind.Med.　Psychol.Abstr.

Supersedes (after 1977, vol.9): Group for the Advancement of Psychiatry. Report (ISSN 0072-775X) & Group for the Advancement of Psychiatry. Symposium.

616.89　　　　　GW　ISSN 0017-4947
GRUPPENPSYCHOTHERAPIE UND GRUPPENDYNAMIK. (Summaries in English and German) 1968. irreg. (4 nos. per vol.) DM.82. Vandenhoeck und Ruprecht, Theaterstr 13., Postfach 37 53, 3400 Goettingen, W. Germany (B.R.D.) Ed. Dr. Annelise Heigl-Evers. circ. 1,050. Indexed: Curr.Cont.　Excerp.Med.　SSCI.

616.8　　　　　US　ISSN 0271-521X
I B R O NEUROSCIENCE CALENDAR. 1980. a. $6 available only with a subscription to Neuroscience. (International Brain Research Organization) Pergamon Press, Inc., Journals Division, Maxwell House, Fairview Park, Elmsford, NY 10523 TEL 914-592-7700. (And Headington Hill Hall, Oxford OX3 0BW, England) Ed. David Smith. (also avail. in microform from MIM,UMI)

616.8　　　　　AU　ISSN 0539-0230
I E S A INFORMATION. (Editions in English) 1967. irreg. (3-4/yr.) membership. International Society for Electrosleep and Electroanaesthesia, Chirurgische Universitaetsklinik, A-8036 Graz, Austria. Ed.Bd. adv. bk. rev. abstr. bibl. charts. illus. circ. 300. (processed)

616.891　　　　　US
I U P STRESS AND HEALTH SERIES. irreg. price varies. International Universities Press, Inc., 59 Boston Post Rd., Box 1524, Madison, CT 06443-1524. TEL 203-245-4000. Ed. Leo Goldberger.

616.8　618.928　　US　ISSN 0074-963X
INTERNATIONAL ASSOCIATION FOR CHILD PSYCHIATRY AND ALLIED PROFESSIONS. YEARBOOK. Added title: Child in His Family. 1970. irreg., vol.7, 1982. price varies. John Wiley & Sons, Inc., 605 Third Ave., New York, NY 10016. TEL 212-850-6000. Eds. E. James Anthony, Cyrille Koupernik.

Formerly: International Yearbook for Child Psychiatry and Allied Disciplines.

616.89　　　　　IE　ISSN 0085-2007
INTERNATIONAL ASSOCIATION FOR SCIENTIFIC STUDY OF MENTAL DEFICIENCY. PROCEEDINGS OF INTERNATIONAL CONGRESS. 1967. triennial, 8th, 1988, Dublin. £40. International Association for Scientific Study of Mental Deficiency, c/o Dr. Michael Mulcahy, Stewards Hospital, Palmerstown, Ireland. Ed. J. Berg. circ. 4,000.

616.855　　　　SZ　ISSN 0074-1655
INTERNATIONAL ASSOCIATION OF LOGOPEDICS AND PHONIATRICS. REPORTS OF CONGRESS. 1947. triennial, 19th, 1980, Washington. 130.20 Fr.($74.20) International Association of Logopedics and Phoniatrics, c/o Dr. A. Muller,Gen.Sec., Av. de la Gare 6, CH-1003 Lausanne, Switzerland. adv. bk. rev.

610　　　　　US　ISSN 0361-0462
INTERNATIONAL BRAIN RESEARCH ORGANIZATION MONOGRAPH SERIES. 1975. irreg., vol.6, 1979. price varies. Raven Press, 1185 Ave. of the Americas, New York, NY 10036. TEL 212-575-0335. Ed. M.A.B. Brazier. Indexed: Biol.Abstr.　Chem.Abstr.　Curr.Cont.　Sci.Cit.Ind.

616.8　　　　　SZ
INTERNATIONAL COLLEGE OF PSYCHOSOMATIC MEDICINE. PROCEEDINGS OF THE CONGRESS. (Text in English) irreg. price varies. S. Karger AG, Allschwilerstrasse 10, P.O. Box, CH-4009 Basel, Switzerland. (reprint service avail. from ISI)

616.8　　　　　SZ　ISSN 0074-5847
INTERNATIONAL FEDERATION FOR MEDICAL PSYCHOTHERAPY. CONGRESS REPORTS. 1972. triennial, 8th, 1970, Milan: 10th, 1976, Paris. International Federation for Medical Psychotherapy, 11-bis rue Caroline, CH-1000 Lausanne, Switzerland (Order 8th report from: S. Karger AG, Arnold-Boecklin-Str. 25, CH-4011 Basel, Switzerland) Ed. Peter Sifueos.

INTERNATIONAL LEAGUE OF SOCIETIES FOR PERSONS WITH MENTAL HANDICAP. WORLD CONGRESS PROCEEDINGS. see *PSYCHOLOGY*

616.8　　　　　US
INTERNATIONAL PSYCHO-ANALYTICAL ASSOCIATION. MONOGRAPH. irreg., no.2, 1984. price varies. (International Psychoanalytical Association) International Universities Press, Inc., 59 Boston Post Rd., Box 1524, Madison, CT 06443-1524. TEL 212-684-7900. Indexed: Biol.Abstr.

616.8　　　　　US　ISSN 0074-7742
INTERNATIONAL REVIEW OF NEUROBIOLOGY. 1959. irreg., vol.27, 1985. Academic Press, Inc., Orlando, FL 32887. TEL 305-345-2000. Eds. Carl C. Pfeiffer, John R. Smythies. index. Indexed: Biol.Abstr.　Chem.Abstr.　Excerp.Med.　Ind.Med.　Sci.Cit.Ind.　Dent.Ind.　Ind.Sci.Rev.

157　616.858　　US　ISSN 0074-7750
INTERNATIONAL REVIEW OF RESEARCH IN MENTAL RETARDATION. 1966. irreg., vol.13, 1985. price varies. Academic Press, Inc., Orlando, FL 32887. TEL 305-345-2000. Ed. Norman R. Ellis. Indexed: SSCI.

JAMES ARTHUR LECTURE ON THE EVOLUTION OF THE HUMAN BRAIN. see *BIOLOGY — Genetics*

616.8　　　　　JA
JAPANESE NEUROCHEMICAL SOCIETY. BULLETIN/SHINKEI KAGAKU. (Text in Japanese) 1962. a. price varies. Japanese Neurochemical Society, c/o Dept. of Physiology, Keio University School of Medicine, Shinanomachi, Shinjuku-ku, Tokyo 160, Japan. Ed. Prof. Yasuzo Tsukada. adv. bk. rev. bibl. circ. 1,500. (processed) Indexed: Biol.Abstr.　Chem.Abstr.

Formerly: Nerve Chemistry (ISSN 0037-3796)

616.8　　　　　US　ISSN 0303-6995
JOURNAL OF NEURAL TRANSMISSION. SUPPLEMENT. no.11, 1974. irreg., no.19, 1983. Springer-Verlag, 175 Fifth Ave., New York, NY 10010 TEL 212-460-1500. (Also Berlin, Heidelberg, Tokyo and Vienna) (also avail. in microform from UMI; reprint service avail. from ISI) Indexed: Chem.Abstr.　Ind.Med.

Formerly: Journal of Neuro-Visceral Relations. Supplement (ISSN 0075-4323); Continues: Acta Neurovegetativa. Supplement.

616.8　　　　　JA　ISSN 0288-9617
KANAGAWA-KEN SEISHIN IGAKKAISHI/KANAGAWA ASSOCIATION OF PSYCHIATRY. JOURNAL. (Text in Japanese) 1959. a. 2,000 Yen. Kanagawa Association of Psychiatry, c/o Yokohama Shiritsu Seishingaku, 3-46, Urafune-Cho, Minami-Ku, Yokojama-Shi 232, Japan. Ed. Susumu Yokai. adv. circ. 600. (back issues avail.)

616.8　　　　　US　ISSN 0075-7608
LAFAYETTE CLINIC HANDBOOKS IN PSYCHIATRY. 1967. irreg. price varies. Wayne State University Press, 5959 Woodward Ave., Detroit, MI 48202. TEL 313-577-4603.

616.8　　　　　US　ISSN 0075-7616
LAFAYETTE CLINIC MONOGRAPHS IN PSYCHIATRY. 1965. irreg. price varies. Wayne State University Press, 5959 Woodward Ave., Detroit, MI 48202. TEL 313-577-4603.

616.89　340　　　US
LEGAL RESOURCES FOR THE MENTALLY DISABLED: A DIRECTORY OF LAWYERS AND OTHER SPECIALISTS. 1982. a. American Bar Association, 1800 M St., N.W., Washington, DC 20036. Ed. John Parry.

Formerly: Mental and Developmental Disabilities Directory of Legal Advocates.

616.8　　　　　US
MAKER. 1967. irreg. (3-4/yr.) free. Huntington's Disease Society of America, 140 W. 22nd St., 6th Fl., New York, NY 10011. TEL 212-242-1968. Ed. Gary Wallach. circ. 8,000. (processed)

Formerly: Committee to Combat Huntingtons Disease Newsletter.

618.9　　　　　US　ISSN 0091-6315
MENTAL RETARDATION AND DEVELOPMENTAL DISABILITIES. 1970. a. Plenum Publishing Corp., 233 Spring St., New York, NY 10013. TEL 212-620-8047. Ed. J. Wortis. Indexed: Biol.Abstr.　SSCI.　Adol.Ment.Hlth.Abstr.　Except.Child.Educ.Abstr.　Rehabil.Lit.

Continues: Mental Retardation.

616.8　　　　　SZ　ISSN 0077-0094
MODERN PROBLEMS OF PHARMACOPSYCHIATRY. (Text in English) 1968. irreg. (approx. 1/yr.) price varies. S. Karger AG, Allschwilerstr. 10, P.O. Box, CH-4009 Basel, Switzerland. Ed.Bd. (reprint service avail. from ISI) Indexed: Biol.Abstr.　Chem.Abstr.　Curr.Cont.　Ind.Med.　Psychol.Abstr.

MODERN TECHNICS IN SURGERY. NEUROSURGERY. see *MEDICAL SCIENCES — Surgery*

616.894　　　　　US　ISSN 0077-0620
MONOGRAPH SERIES ON SCHIZOPHRENIA. 1950. irreg., no.8, 1969. price varies. International Universities Press, Inc., 59 Boston Post Rd., Box 1524, Madison, CT 06443-1524. TEL 203-245-4000.

616.8　　　　　US　ISSN 0077-0671
MONOGRAPHIEN AUS DEM GESAMTGEBIETE DER PSYCHIATRIE - PSYCHIATRY SERIES. (Text in English and German) 1970. irreg., vol.42, 1986. price varies. Springer-Verlag, 175 Fifth Ave., New York, NY 10010 TEL 212-460-1500. (Also Berlin, Heidelberg, Tokyo and Vienna) (reprint service avail. from ISI) Indexed: Ind.Med.　Psychol.Abstr.

Supersedes in part: Monographien aus dem Gesamtgebiete der Neurologie und Psychiatrie.

616.8　　　　　SZ　ISSN 0300-5186
MONOGRAPHS IN NEURAL SCIENCES. (Text in English) 1972. irreg. (approx. 1/yr.) price varies. S. Karger AG, Allschwilerstr. 10, P.O. Box, CH-4009 Basel, Switzerland. Ed. M.M. Cohen. (reprint service avail. from ISI) Indexed: Biol.Abstr.　Chem.Abstr.　Curr.Cont.　Ind.Med.

Formerly: Monographs in Basic Neurology.

616　301　　　US　ISSN 0547-7115
NATIONAL GUILD OF CATHOLIC PSYCHIATRISTS. BULLETIN. (Not published in 1986) 1948. a. $12. National Guild of Catholic Psychiatrists, c/o Anne Polcino, M.D., 120 Hill St., Whitinsville, MA 01588. TEL 617-651-3893. Ed. Anna Polcino, M.D. bk. rev. circ. 300. (back issues avail.) Indexed: Cath.Ind.

612.78　　　　　NE　ISSN 0301-6412
NEUROLINGUISTICS; international series devoted to speech physiology and speech pathology. 1973. irreg. price varies. Swets Publishing Service (Subsidiary of: Swets en Zeitlinger B.V.) Heereweg 347, 2161 CA Lisse, Netherlands (Dist. in the U.S. and Canada by: Hogrefe International, Inc., 525 Eglinton Ave. East, Toronto, Ont. M4P 1N5, Canada) Eds. Yvan Lebrun, Richard Hoops. Indexed: Biol.Abstr.　Lang.& Lang.Behav.Abstr.

616.8　　　　　US
NEUROLOGY AND NEUROBIOLOGY. 1982. irreg., vol.21, 1986. price varies. Alan R. Liss, Inc., 41 E. 11th St., New York, NY 10003. TEL 212-475-7700. Indexed: Biol.Abstr.　Chem.Abstr.

NEUROORTHOPAEDIE. see *MEDICAL SCIENCES — Orthopedics And Traumatology*

616.8　　　　　US　ISSN 0077-7846
NEUROSCIENCES RESEARCH. 1968. irreg., vol.5, 1973. Academic Press Inc., Orlando, FL 32887. TEL 305-345-2000. Eds. S. Ehrenpreis, O. Solnitsky.

615.9　　　　　US　ISSN 0160-2748
NEUROTOXICOLOGY. 1977. irreg. Raven Press, 1185 Ave. of the Americas, New York, NY 10036. TEL 212-575-0335. Indexed: Chem.Abstr.　Curr.Cont.　Excerp.Med.　Dent.Ind.　Ind.Sci.Rev.

616.8 617.7   JA   ISSN 0389-5610
NEUROTRAUMATOLOGY. (Text in Japanese; summaries in English) 1978. a. 5000 Yen. Japanese Society of Neurotraumatology, Tokyo Jikei University School of Medicine, Department of Neurosurgery, 3-25-8, Nishi-Shimbashi, Minatoku, Tokyo 105, Japan. circ. 1,000. (back issues avail.)

NEW YORK (STATE). COMMISSION ON QUALITY OF CARE FOR THE MENTALLY DISABLED. ANNUAL REPORT. see *HOSPITALS*

610   AT
NOTES ON NEUROLOGY. (Supplement to: A M A Victoria Branch News) irreg. free. Australian Medical Association, Victoria Branch, 293 Royal Parade, Parkville, Vic. 3052, Australia. (Co-sponsor: Australian Brain Foundation) Ed. Dr. Robert Helme.

616.89 150   DK   ISSN 0105-0621
ODENSE UNIVERSITY STUDIES IN PSYCHIATRY AND MEDICAL PSYCHOLOGY. (Text in Danish and English) 1973. irreg., no.3, 1986. price varies. Odense University Press, 36, Pjentedamsgade, DK-5000 Odense, Denmark. (back issues avail.) Indexed: Excerp.Med.

616.835   IT   ISSN 0030-5618
ORIZZONTI APERTI; la voce dei poliomielitici. vol.4, 1970. irreg. (3-5/yr.) free. Associazione Nazionale Invalidi Esiti Poliomielite, Via Coltelli 7/D, 40124 Bologna, Italy. Ed. Gianni Selleri. circ. 16,000.
   Poliomyelitis

616.8   US
OXFORD NEUROLOGICAL MONOGRAPHS. irreg. price varies. Oxford University Press, 200 Madison Ave., New York, NY 10016 TEL 212-679-7300. (And Ely House, 37 Dover St., London W1X 4AH, England) Ed. W. Ritchie Russell.

616.8   SZ   ISSN 0255-3910
PAIN AND HEADACHE. (Text in English) 1967. irreg. (approx. 1/yr.) price varies. S. Karger AG, Allschwilerstrasse 10, P.O. Box, CH-4009 Basel, Switzerland. Ed. P.L. Gildenberg. (reprint service avail. from ISI) Indexed: Biol.Abstr. Chem.Abstr. Curr.Cont. Ind.Med.
   Formerly: Research and Clinical Studies in Headache (ISSN 0080-1453)
   Migraine

PRAXIS DER KINDERPSYCHOLOGIE UND KINDERPSYCHIATRIE. BEIHEFTE. see *PSYCHOLOGY*

616.8 612   SZ   ISSN 0378-4045
PROGRESS IN CLINICAL NEUROPHYSIOLOGY. (Text in English) 1977. irreg. price varies. S. Karger AG, Allschwilerstrasse 10, P.O. Box, CH-4009 Basel, Switzerland. Ed. J.E. Desmedt. (back issues avail.) Indexed: Biol.Abstr. Chem.Abstr. Curr.Cont. Ind.Med.

617.48   SZ   ISSN 0079-6492
PROGRESS IN NEUROLOGICAL SURGERY. (Text in English) 1966. irreg. (approx. 1/yr.) price varies. S. Karger AG, Allschwilerstrasse 10, P.O. Box, CH-4009 Basel, Switzerland. Ed. A.M. Landolt. (reprint service avail. from ISI) Indexed: Biol.Abstr. Chem.Abstr. Curr.Cont. Ind.Med.

616.8   US
PROGRESS IN NEUROPATHOLOGY. 1971. irreg., vol.4, 1979. price varies. Raven Press, 1185 Ave. of the Americas, New York, NY 10036. TEL 212-575-0335. Ed. H.M. Zimmerman, M.D. Indexed: Biol.Abstr.

616.8   FI   ISSN 0079-7227
PSYCHIATRIA FENNICA. (Text mainly in English) 1970. a. Fmk.125. Psychiatria Fennica, Arkadiankatu 35 B 37, 00100 Helsinki 10, Finland. adv. bk. rev. circ. 1,500. Indexed: Biol.Abstr. Excerp.Med. Psychol.Abstr. CINAHL.

616.8   FI   ISSN 0355-7707
PSYCHIATRIA FENNICA. MONOGRAFIASARJA/PSYCHIATRIA FENNICA. MONOGRAPHS. (Text in English and Finnish) 1970. irreg., no.11, 1984. Fmk.60. Psychiatria Fennica, Arkadiankatu 35 B 37, 00100 Helsinki 10, Finland. circ. 900. Indexed: Excerp.Med. Psychol.Abstr.

616.8   FI
PSYCHIATRIA FENNICA. REPORTS. (Text mainly in English and Finnish) 1970. irreg., no.65, 1985. Fmk.60. ‡ (Foundation for Psychiatric Research in Finland) Psychiatria Fennica, Arkadiankatu 35 B 37, 00100 Helsinki 10, Finland. Ed. K.A. Achte. circ. 150-300. Indexed: Excerp.Med. Psychol.Abstr.
   Former Titles: Psychiatria Fennica. Julkaisusarja (ISSN 0355-7693); Helsingin Yliopisto Keskussairaala. Psykiatrian Klinikka. Julkaisusarja (ISSN 0073-1730)

616.89   US   ISSN 0163-1721
PSYCHIATRIC MEDICINE UPDATE; Massachusetts General Hospital reviews for physicians. a. $75. Elsevier Science Publishing Co., Inc. (New York), 52 Vanderbilt Ave., New York, NY 10017. TEL 212-916-1050. Ed. T.C. Manschreck.

616.8   SZ
RECENT ACHIEVMENTS IN RESTORATIVE NEUROLOGY. (Text in English) 1985. irreg. price varies. S. Krager AG, Allschwilerstrasse 10, P.O. Box, CH-4009 Basel, Switzerland. Ed. M.R. Dimitrijevic. Indexed: Biol.Abstr. Curr.Cont. Ind.Med.

616.853   UK
RECENT ADVANCES IN EPILEPSY. 1983. irreg. price varies. Churchill Livingstone Journals, 1-3 Baxter's Place, Leith Walk, Edinburgh EH1 3AF, Scotland. Eds. Timothy A. Pedley, Brian S. Meldrum.

RESEARCH METHODS IN NEUROCHEMISTRY. see *BIOLOGY — Biological Chemistry*

616.8   US   ISSN 0095-7550
REVIEWS OF NEUROSCIENCE. 1974. irreg., vol.4, 1979. price varies. Raven Press, 1185 Avenue of the Americas, New York, NY 10036. TEL 212-575-0335.

616.8   BL   ISSN 0101-1693
SAO PAULO. COORDENADORIA DE SAUDE MENTAL. ARQUIVOS. (Supplement issue.) (Text in Portuguese; summaries in English) 1924. a. free. Hospital de Juqueri, Biblioteca, CEP 07780 Franco de Rocha, Brazil. Ed.Bd. bk. rev. circ. 1,000.

616.8   US   ISSN 0080-715X
SCHRIFTENREIHE NEUROLOGIE/NEUROLOGY SERIES. (Partly supersedes: Monographien aus dem Gesamtgebiete der Neurologie und Psychiatrie) (Text in German; occasionally in English) 1959. irreg., vol.26, 1984. price varies. Springer-Verlag, 175 Fifth Ave., New York, NY 10010 TEL 212-460-1500. (Also Berlin, Heidelberg, Tokyo and Vienna) (reprint service avail. from ISI) Indexed: Biol.Abstr. Ind.Med.

616.8   JA   ISSN 0080-8547
SEISHIN-IGAKU INSTITUTE OF PSYCHIATRY, TOKYO. BULLETIN/SEISHIN IGAKU KENKYUSHO, TOKYO. GYOSEKI SHU. (Text in Japanese; table of contents and summaries in English) 1954. a. free to qualified personnel. Seishin Igaku Institute of Psychiatry - Seishin Igaku Kenkyusho, 4-11-11 Komone, Itabashi-ku, Tokyo 173, Japan. Indexed: Biol.Abstr. Excerp.Med.

SEMINARS IN NEUROLOGICAL SURGERY. see *MEDICAL SCIENCES — Surgery*

616.8   US   ISSN 0093-0407
SLEEP RESEARCH. 1972. a. $85. Brain Information Service-Brain Research Institute, University of California, Los Angeles, Center for the Health Sciences, Los Angeles, CA 90024. Ed.Bd. bk. rev. bibl. circ. 2,000. (back issues avail.)

STUDIES IN NEUROSCIENCE. see *MEDICAL SCIENCES — Surgery*

616.8   US   ISSN 0172-5742
STUDIES OF BRAIN FUNCTION. 1977. irreg., vol.13, 1986. price varies. Springer-Verlag, 175 Fifth Ave., New York, NY 10010 TEL 212-460-1500. (Also Berlin, Heidelberg, Tokyo and Vienna) Ed.Bd. (reprint service avail. from ISI) Indexed: Biol.Abstr.

616.8   US   ISSN 0093-3317
STUDIES ON THE DEVELOPMENT OF BEHAVIOR AND THE NERVOUS SYSTEM. 1973. irreg. vol.4, 1978. Academic Press, Inc., Orlando, FL 32887. TEL 305-345-2000. Ed. Gilbert Gottlieb.

616.8   JA
TOKYO METROPOLITAN INSTITUTE OF NEUROSCIENCES. ANNUAL REPORT/TOKYO-TO SHINKEI KAGAKU SOGO KENKYUJO NEMPO. (Text in Japanese) 1972. a. Tokyo Metropolitan Institute of Neurosciences, 2-6 Musashidai, Fuchu-shi, Tokyo 183, Japan.

618.9   US
UNION OF EUROPEAN PEDOPSYCHIATRISTS. PROCEEDINGS.* (Text in English, French or German) irreg., 4th, Stockholm, 1971. $39.50. Halsted Press, 605 Third Ave., New York, NY 10016. Ed. Arna-Lisa Annell. bibl.

616.82   US
U.S. CENTER FOR DISEASE CONTROL. NEUROTROPIC VIRAL DISEASES SURVEILLANCE: ASEPTIC MENINGITIS. a. free. U.S. Center for Disease Control, 1600 Clifton Rd., Atlanta, GA 30333. TEL 404-329-3311.

616.832   US
U.S. CENTER FOR DISEASE CONTROL. NEUROTROPIC VIRAL DISEASES SURVEILLANCE: ENCEPHALITIS. a. free. U.S. Center for Disease Control, 1600 Clifton Rd., Atlanta, GA 30333. TEL 404-329-3311.

616.8   US
U.S. CENTER FOR DISEASE CONTROL. NEUROTROPIC VIRAL DISEASES SURVEILLANCE: ENTEROVIRUS. a. U.S. Center for Disease Control, 1600 Clifton Rd, Atlanta, GA 30333. TEL 404-329-3311.

616.835   US
U.S. CENTER FOR DISEASE CONTROL. NEUROTROPIC VIRAL DISEASES SURVEILLANCE: POLIOMYELITIS. a. free. U.S. Center for Disease Control, 1600 Clifton Rd., Atlanta, GA 30333. TEL 404-329-3311.

616.8   CN   ISSN 0083-5196
VANCOUVER NEUROLOGICAL CENTRE. ANNUAL REPORTS. a. free. Vancouver Neurological Centre, 1195 W. 8th Ave., Vancouver, B.C. V6H 1C5, Canada. TEL 604-734-2221.

WERKSTATTSCHRIFTEN ZUR SOZIALPSYCHIATRIE. see *PSYCHOLOGY*

616.89   AU   ISSN 0084-1609
WORLD CONGRESS OF PSYCHIATRY. PROCEEDINGS. 1950. irreg., 5th, 1971, Mexico. $100. World Psychiatric Association, c/o Prof. P. Berner, Psychiatrische Universitaetsklinik, Lazarettg. 14, A-1097 Vienna, Austria (Proceedings of 5th, 1971 avail. from: Excerpta Medica, Box 211, Amsterdam, Netherlands) Ed.Bd.

616.8 617   US
YEAR BOOK OF NEUROLOGY & NEUROSURGERY. 1902. a. $44.95. Year Book Medical Publishers, Inc., 35 E. Wacker Dr., Chicago, IL 60601. TEL 312-726-9733. Ed. Russell DeJong, M.D.
   Supersedes in part: Year Book of Neurology, Psychiatry and Neurosurgery.

616.89   US   ISSN 0084-3970
YEAR BOOK OF PSYCHIATRY AND APPLIED MENTAL HEALTH. 1970. a. $42.95. Year Book Medical Publishers, Inc., 35 E. Wacker Dr., Chicago, IL 60601. TEL 312-726-9733. Ed. Daniel Freedman, M.D.
   Supersedes in part: Yearbook of Neurology, Psychiatry and Neurosurgery.

150 616.89   GW   ISSN 0085-8412
ZEITSCHRIFT FUER PSYCHOSOMATISCHE MEDIZIN UND PSYCHOANALYSE. BEIHEFTE. 1970. irreg., no.11, 1983. price varies. Vandenhoeck und Ruprecht, Theaterstr. 13, 3400 Goettingen, W. Germany (B.R.D.) Indexed: Psychol.Abstr. SSCI.

MEDICAL SCIENCES — Radiology And Nuclear Medicine

615.842 US ISSN 0884-1454
A B M S DIRECTORY OF CERTIFIED NUCLEAR MEDICINE SPECIALISTS. 1984. biennial. $24.95 softcover. American Board of Medical Specialties, One American Plaza, Ste. 805, Evanston, IL 60201. TEL 312-491-9091. Ed. Donald G. Langsley, M.D.

615.842 US ISSN 0883-1238
A B M S DIRECTORY OF CERTIFIED RADIOLOGISTS. 1985. biennial. $49.95 hardcover; $39.95 softcover. American Board of Medical Specialties, One American Plaza, Ste. 805, Evanston, IL 60201. TEL 312-491-9091. Ed. Donald G. Langsley, M.D.

ADVANCES IN X-RAY ANALYSIS. see *TECHNOLOGY: COMPREHENSIVE WORKS*

615.842 UN
ANIMAL PRODUCTION AND HEALTH NEWSLETTER. (Text in English) 1976. irreg. free. International Atomic Energy Agency, Wagramer Str. 5, Box 100, A-1400 Vienna, Austria. (Co-sponsor: Food and Agriculture Organization) circ. 230. Indexed: Nutr.Abstr.

615.842 363.179 IT
ANNALI DI RADIOPROTEZIONE. (Summaries in English and Italian) 1979. a. $5 to non-members. Associazione Italiana di Protezione Contro le Radiozioni (AIRP), 21020 Ispra, Italy. circ. 600. (back issues avail.)

615.842 US
APPLIED RADIOLOGY BUYER'S GUIDE. 1984. a. $45 per no. Brentwood Publishing Corp. (Subsidiary of: Simon & Schuster, unit of Gulf & Western, Inc.) 1640 5the St., Santa Monica, CA 90401. TEL 213-395-0234. Ed. Martin H. Waldman. adv. tr.lit. circ. 23,500.

615.842 617 US
ARTHROLOGY. irreg. Springer-Verlag, 175 Fifth Ave., New York, NY 10010. TEL 212-460-1500. Ed. H.G. Jacobson.

615.842 US ISSN 0172-4843
COMPREHENSIVE MANUALS IN RADIOLOGY. 1978. irreg., latest 1980. price varies. Springer-Verlag, 175 Fifth Ave., New York, NY 10010 TEL 212-460-1500. (Also Berlin, Heidelberg, Tokyo, Vienna) (reprint service avail. from ISI)

615.8 US ISSN 0161-7818
CURRENT RADIOLOGY. 1978. a. $55. Year Book Medical Publishers, Inc., 35 E. Wacker Dr., Chicago, IL 60601. illus.

615.842 US
DIAGNOSTIC RADIOLOGY SERIES. 1983. irreg. price varies. Marcel Dekker, Inc., 270 Madison Ave., New York, NY 10017. TEL 212-696-9000. Indexed: Biol.Abstr.

615.842 US
FRONTIERS IN EUROPEAN RADIOLOGY. 1982. irreg., vol.4, 1984. Springer-Verlag, 175 Fifth Ave., New York, NY 10010 TEL 212-460-1500. (Also Berlin, Heidelberg, Tokyo, Vienna) (reprint service avail. from ISI)

615 616.9 SZ ISSN 0071-9676
FRONTIERS OF RADIATION THERAPY AND ONCOLOGY. (Text in English) 1967. irreg. (approx. 1/yr.) price varies. S. Karger AG, Allschwilerstrasse 10, P.O. Box, CH-4009 Basel, Switzerland. Ed. J.M. Vaeth. (reprint service avail. from ISI) Indexed: Biol.Abstr. Chem.Abstr. Curr.Cont. Ind.Med. Dent.Ind.

612.014 JA ISSN 0073-232X
HIROSHIMA UNIVERSITY. RESEARCH INSTITUTE FOR NUCLEAR MEDICINE AND BIOLOGY. PROCEEDINGS/HIROSHIMA DAIGAKU GENBAKU HOSHANO IGAKU KENKYUSHO NENPO. (Text in English and Japanese) 1960. a. Hiroshima University, Research Institute for Nuclear Medicine and Biology - Hiroshima Daigaku Genbaku Hoshano Kenkyusho, Kasumi, Hiroshima 734, Japan. Ed.Bd. circ. 450 (controlled)

615.842 UN
INFORMATION CIRCULAR ON RADIATION TECHNIQUES AND THEIR APPLICATIONS TO INSECT PESTS. (Text in English) 1963. irreg. free. International Atomic Energy Agency, Wagramer Strasse 5, Box 100, A-1400 Vienna, Austria. (Co-sponsor: Food and Agriculture Organization) circ. 600. Indexed: Rev.Appl.Entomol.

574.191 PL ISSN 0074-0640
INSTYTUT BADAN JADROWYCH. ZAKLAD RADIOBIOLOGII I OCHRONY ZDROWIA. PRACE DOSWIADCZAINE. (Text in English, French, German or Polish; summaries in English) 1960. irreg., vol.4, 1973. free. (Institute of Nuclear Research) Osrodek Informacji o Energii Jadrowej, Palac Kultury i Nauki, Warsaw, Poland. Ed. Maria Kopec. author index.

616.8 UK ISSN 0074-2759
INTERNATIONAL COMMISSION ON RADIOLOGICAL PROTECTION. REPORT. 1960. irreg., vol.36, 1983. price varies. Pergamon Press, Ltd., Headington Hill Hall, Oxford OX3 0BW, England (U.S. subscr. to: Maxwell House, Fairview Park, Elmsford, NY 10523)

615.84 612.014 SZ ISSN 0074-3933
INTERNATIONAL CONGRESS OF RADIOLOGY. (REPORTS) irreg., 13th, 1973, Madrid; 14th, 1977, Rio de Janeiro. International Society of Radiology, c/o Prof. Dr. W.A. Fuchs, University Hospital, Department of Diagnostic Radiology, Inselspital, CH-3010 Berne, Switzerland. Ed. Gomez Lopez Bonmati. circ. 10,000. Indexed: Excerp.Med.

615.842 UA ISSN 0021-1907
ISOTOPE AND RADIATION RESEARCH. (Text in English; summaries in Arabic) 1968. a. $5. Middle Eastern Regional Radioisotope Centre for the Arab Countries, Sh. Malaeb el Gamaa, Dokki 11321, Cairo, Egypt. Eds. M. Mokhtar & S. Hashish. adv. bk. rev. Indexed: Chem.Abstr. Excerp.Med. Soils & Fert.

615.8 UR ISSN 0075-529X
KAZAKHSKII NAUCHNO-ISSLEDOVATEL'SKII INSTITUT ONKOLOGII I RADIOLOGII. TRUDY. (Text in Russian; summaries in English) 1965. a. price varies. Kazakhskii Nauchno-Issledovatel'skii Institut Onkologii i Radiologii, Alma-Ata, Kazakh S.S.R., U.S.S.R. (Co-sponsor: Ministerstvo Zdravokhraneniya Kazakhskoi S.S.R.) Eds. O.K. Kabiev, S.B. Balmukhanov. circ. 400. Indexed: Biol.Abstr.

615.842 SZ
LITHIUM THERAPY MONOGRAPHS. 1987. irreg. price varies. S. Karger AG, Allschwilerstrasse 10, P.O. Box, CH-4009 Basel, Switzerland. Ed. F.N. Johnson.

615.842 US
MEDICAL RADIOLOGY. 1985. irreg., latest 1985. Springer-Verlag, 175 Fifth Ave., New York, NY 10010 TEL 212-460-1500. (Also Berlin, Heidelberg, Tokyo, Vienna) (reprint service avail. from ISI)

615.842 US
N C R P STATEMENTS. 1954. irreg. free. National Council on Radiation Protection and Measurements, 7910 Woodmont Ave., Ste. 1016, Bethesda, MD 20814. TEL 301-657-2652. Ed. W. Roger Ney.

574.191 UK ISSN 0550-8398
NON-IONIZING RADIATION; r.f., microwaves, infra-red, lasers. 1969. irreg. £14.50($39) Kendervic Ltd., 3 Erpingham Rd., London SW15 1BE, England. bk. rev. abstr. charts. illus. index. Indexed: Biol.Abstr.

615.842 US ISSN 0272-0108
NUCLEAR MEDICINE ANNUAL. a. Raven Press, 1185 Ave. of the Americas, New York, NY 10036. TEL 212-575-0335. Eds. Leonard M. Freeman, Heidi S. Weissman. Indexed: Biol.Abstr. Chem.Abstr.

NUCLEUS. see *PHYSICS — Nuclear Energy*

615.842 SZ ISSN 0079-6573
PROGRESS IN NUCLEAR MEDICINE. (Text in English) 1972. irreg. (approx. 1/yr.) price varies. S. Karger AG, Allschwilerstrasse 10, P.O. Box, CH-4009 Basel, Switzerland. Eds. A. Donath, A.N. Serafini. (reprint service avail. from ISI) Indexed: Biol.Abstr. Chem.Abstr. Ind.Med.

PROGRESS IN PEDIATRIC RADIOLOGY. see *MEDICAL SCIENCES — Pediatrics*

615 UN
RADIATION DOSIMETRY DATA; CATALOGUE. 1964. irreg. free. International Atomic Energy Agency, Wagramer Str. 5, Box 100, A-1400 Vienna, Austria. circ. 3,000.
Formerly (until 1969): International Atomic Energy Agency. Radiation Data for Medical Use; Catalogue (ISSN 0538-4850)

615.842 US
RADIOLOGISCHE KLINIK. 1983. irreg. Springer-Verlag, 175 Fifth Ave., New York, NY 10010. TEL 212-460-1500.

615.842 US
RADIOLOGY OF IATROGENIC DISORDERS. 1981. irreg., latest 1986. price varies. Springer-Verlag, 175 Fifth Ave., New York, NY 10010 TEL 212-460-1500. (Also Berlin, Heidelberg, Tokyo, Vienna) (reprint service avail. from ISI)

615.842 US
RADIOLOGY TODAY. 1981. irreg., vol.3, 1985. Springer-Verlag, 175 Fifth Ave., New York, NY 10010 TEL 212-460-1500. (Also Berlin, Heidelberg, Tokyo and Vienna) (reprint service avail. from ISI)

616.9 US ISSN 0163-6170
RECENT ADVANCES IN NUCLEAR MEDICINE. 1965. irreg., vol.6, 1983. price varies. Grune & Stratton Inc., (Subsidiary of: Harcourt Brace Jovanovich, Inc.) Orlando, FL 32887 TEL 305-345-4200. (Dist. by: Academic Press, Inc.) Eds. John H. Lawrence, M.D., Thomas Budinger, M.D.
Former titles: Progress in Nuclear Medicine (ISSN 0079-6581); Progress in Atomic Medicine (ISSN 0085-5189)

615.842 UK ISSN 0143-6961
RECENT ADVANCES IN RADIOLOGY AND MEDICAL IMAGING. 1979. irreg. Churchill Livingstone Medical Journals, 23 Ravelston Terr., Edinburgh EH4 3TL, Scotland.

615.8 SZ
S I N MEDICAL NEWSLETTER. (Text in English) 1978. a. Schweizerisches Institut fuer Nuklearforschung, CH-5234 Villigen, Switzerland.

615.842 UK ISSN 0260-4043
ULTRASOUND PATENTS & PAPERS. 1980. irreg. Scientific and Medical Information Services, Kingsbourne House, 229 High Holborn, London WC1V 7DA, England. illus.

618 574 UR
VOPROSY RADIOBIOLOGII I BIOLOGICHESKOGO DEISTVIYA TSITOSTATICHESKIKH PREPARATOV. 1969. irreg. (Tomskii Meditsinskii Institut, Tsentral'naya Nauchno-Issledovatel'skaya Laboratoriya) Izdatel'svo Tomskii Universitet, Prospekt Lenina, 36, Tomsk-10, Russian S.F.S.R., U.S.S.R. bibl. illus.

615.84 US ISSN 0098-1672
YEAR BOOK OF DIAGNOSTIC RADIOLOGY. 1932. a. $44.95. ‡ Year Book Medical Publishers, Inc., 35 E. Wacker Dr., Chicago, IL 60601. TEL 312-726-9733. Ed. David G. Bragg, M.D.
Formerly (until 1975): Year Book of Radiology (ISSN 0084-3989)

615.8 US ISSN 0084-3903
YEAR BOOK OF NUCLEAR MEDICINE. 1966. a. $44.95. ‡ Year Book Medical Publishers, Inc., 35 E. Wacker Dr., Chicago, IL 60601. TEL 312-726-9733. Ed. P. Hoffer, M.D. illus.

MEDICAL SCIENCES — Respiratory Diseases

ARERUGIA. see *MEDICAL SCIENCES — Allergology And Immunology*

616.2 PE ISSN 0069-2166
CENTRO DE SALUD "MAX ARIAS SCHREIBER", LIMA. CONGRESO NACIONAL DE TUBERCULOSIS Y ENFERMEDADES RESPIRATORIAS.* irreg., 1970, 9th. Dispensario Antituberculoso "Max Arias Schreiber", Raymondi 2da Cuadra (La Victoria), Lima, Peru.

MEDICAL SCIENCES — SURGERY 793

616.2   US   ISSN 0196-2418
CYSTIC FIBROSIS G A P CONFERENCE
REPORTS.* 1969. a. Cystic Fibrosis Foundation
(Rockville), 6931 Arlington Rd., No. 200, Bethesda,
MD 20814-5205. bibl. charts. illus. stat. circ. 2,
800.

616.2   DK   ISSN 0106-4347
EUROPEAN JOURNAL OF RESPIRATORY
DISEASES. SUPPLEMENTUM. (Text in English)
1920. irreg. free to subscribers. Munksgaard, 35
Noerre Soegade, DK-1370 Copenhagen K,
Denmark. Ed. E. Berglund. adv. (reprint service
avail. from ISI) Indexed: Biol.Abstr. Curr.Cont.
Ind.Med. Ind.Sci.Rev.
  Formerly (until 1980): Scandinavian Journal of
Respiratory Diseases. Supplementum (ISSN 0080-
6730)

616.2   JA
HOKKAIDO UNIVERSITY. INSTITUTE OF
IMMUNOLOGICAL SCIENCE. BULLETIN.
(Text in Japanese; summaries in English and
Japanese) 1953. a. exchange basis. Hokkaido
University, Institute of Immunological Science,
North 15, West 7, Sapporo 060, Japan. Ed. Ken-Ichi
Yamamoto. circ. 300. Indexed: Biol.Abstr.
  Until 1975: Kekkaku No Kenkyu. (ISSN 0075-
5354)

616.2   JA   ISSN 0075-3165
JAPAN ANTI-TUBERCULOSIS ASSOCIATION.
REPORTS ON MEDICAL RESEARCH
PROBLEMS/KEKKAKU YOBOKAI KENKYU
GYOSEKI. (Text in English) 1951. a. exchange
basis. Japan Anti-Tuberculosis Association -
Kekkaku Yobokai, 1-3-12 Misaki-cho, Chiyoda-ku,
Tokyo 101, Japan. Ed. Tadao Shimao, M.D. circ.
800. Indexed: Biol.Abstr.

616.2   US
LUNG BIOLOGY IN HEALTH AND DISEASE.
1976. irreg., vol.30, 1985. price varies. Marcel
Dekker, Inc., 270 Madison Ave., New York, NY
10016. TEL 212-696-9000. Indexed: Biol.Abstr.
Chem.Abstr.

NATIONAL CENTRE FOR OCCUPATIONAL
HEALTH. ANNUAL REPORT. see INDUSTRIAL
HEALTH AND SAFETY

616.2   SZ   ISSN 0079-6751
PROGRESS IN RESPIRATION RESEARCH. (Text
in English) 1963. irreg. (approx. 1/yr.) price varies.
S. Karger AG, Allschwilerstrasse 10, P.O. Box, CH-
4009 Basel, Switzerland. Ed. H. Herzog. (reprint
service avail. from ISI) Indexed: Biol.Abstr.
Chem.Abstr. Curr.Cont. Ind.Med.

RESPIRATOR NEWS. see INDUSTRIAL HEALTH
AND SAFETY

616.246   KE
RESPIRATORY DISEASES RESEARCH CENTRE.
ANNUAL REPORT. (Text in English) 1974. a.
free. Kenya Medical Research Institute, Kenya
Tuberculosis & Respiratory Diseases Research
Centre, Box 47855, Nairobi, Kenya. circ. 200. (back
issues avail.) Indexed: Biol.Abstr.
  Former Titles: Kenya Tuberculosis and
Respiratory Diseases Research Center. Annual
Report; Kenya Tuberculosis Investigation Centre.
Annual Report; Supersedes in part: East African
Tuberculosis Investigation Centre. Annual Report.

616.2   US
RESPIRATORY MANAGEMENT BUYER'S
GUIDE. a. $45. Brentwood Publishing Corp.
(Subsidiary of: Simon & Schuster, unit of Gulf &
Western, Inc.) 1640 5th St., Santa Monica, CA
90401. TEL 213-395-0234. Ed. Martin H.
Waldman. adv. circ. 19,800.
  Formerly: Respiratory Therapy Buyer's Guide.

616.2   SA   ISSN 0081-2501
S A N T A ANNUAL REPORT/S A N T A
JAARLIKSE VERSLAG. (Text in Afrikaans and
English) 1949. a. free. South African National
Tuberculosis Association, 621 Leisk House, 195
Bree St., Johannesburg 2001, South Africa. Ed.
Heather Basson. circ. 2,000.

616.2   FI   ISSN 0355-5011
TUBERCULOSIS AND RESPIRATORY DISEASES
YEARBOOK/TUBERKULOOSI JA
KEUHKOSAIRAUDET VUOSIKIRJA/
TUBERKULOS OCH LUNGSJUKDOMAR
AARSBOK. (Text in Finnish, English, or Swedish)
1972. irreg.(1 vol/yr; 2-3 nos./vol.) free. Suomen
Tuberkuloosin Vastustamisyhdistys - Finnish Anti-
Tuberculosis Association (Foereningen foer
Tuberkulosens Bekaempande i Finland),
Kalevankatu 9, 00100 Helsinki 10, Finland. Ed.Bd.
circ. 2,000.

616.246 614   US   ISSN 0149-2616
U.S. CENTER FOR DISEASE CONTROL.
TUBERCULOSIS IN THE UNITED STATES.
1974. a. free. U.S. Center for Disease Control,
Tuberculosis Control Division, 1600 Clifton Rd.
N.E., Atlanta, GA 30333. TEL 404-329-2501.
charts. illus. stat. circ. 7,000.
  Formed by the merger of: U.S. Center for
Disease Control. Reported Tuberculosis Data; U.S.
Center for Disease Control. Tuberculosis Program
Reports.

616.246 614   US
U.S. CENTER FOR DISEASE CONTROL.
TUBERCULOSIS STATISTICS: STATES AND
CITIES. a. U.S. Center for Disease Control,
Tuberculosis Control Division, 1600 Clifton Rd.,
N.E., Atlanta, GA 30333. TEL 404-329-2501. circ.
7,000.
  Formerly: U.S. Center for Disease Control.
Tuberculosis: States and Cities.

U.S. NATIONAL HEART, LUNG, AND BLOOD
ADVISORY COUNCIL. REPORT. see MEDICAL
SCIENCES — Cardiovascular Diseases

616.995   AG
UNIVERSIDAD DE BUENOS AIRES. CATEDRA
DE PATOLOGIA Y CLINICA DE LA
TUBERCULOSIS. ANALES. vol.29, 1970. irreg.
Universidad de Buenos Aires, Catedra de Patologia
y Clinica de la Tuberculosis, Avda. Velez Sarsfield
405, Buenos Aires, Argentina. Indexed: Biol.Abstr.

616.2   US
YEAR BOOK OF PULMONARY DISEASE. 1986.
a. $39.95. Year Book Medical Publishers, Inc., 35 E.
Wacker Dr., Chicago, IL 60601. TEL 312-726-9746.
illus.

616.2   ZA   ISSN 0084-5000
ZAMBIA. PNEUMOCONIOSIS MEDICAL AND
RESEARCH BUREAU AND
PNEUMOCONIOSIS COMPENSATION
BOARD. ANNUAL REPORTS. 1964. a. 25 n.
Government Printer, P.O. Box 136, Lusaka, Zambia.

MEDICAL SCIENCES — Rheumatology

616.742   FR   ISSN 0065-1818
ACTUALITE RHUMATOLOGIQUE PRESENTEE
AU PRATICIEN; cahier annuel d'informations et
de renseignements. a. price varies. Expansion
Scientifique, 15 rue Saint Benoit, 75278 Paris Cedex
06, France.

616.742   US
AMERICAN RHEUMATISM ASSOCIATION.
DIRECTORY. a. price varies. American
Rheumatism Association, 17 Executive Park Dr.,
N.E., Ste. 480, Atlanta, GA 30329. TEL 404-633-
3777.

616.7   US   ISSN 0191-2836
ARTHRITIS FOUNDATION ANNUAL REPORT.
1948. a. Arthritis Foundation, 1314 Spring St.,
N.W., Atlanta, GA 30309. TEL 404-872-7100.

616.742   GE   ISSN 0067-5199
BEITRAEGE ZUR RHEUMATOLOGIE. 1958. irreg.
price varies. VEB Verlag Volk und Gesundheit,
Neue Gruenstr. 18, 1020 Berlin, E. Germany
(D.D.R.) Ed. Kurt Seidel. (reprint service avail.
from ISI) Indexed: Biol.Abstr. Excerp.Med.
Ind.Med.

616.7   SW
BERTINE KOPERBERG CONFERENCE
(PROCEEDINGS) (Supplement to: Scandinavian
Journal of Rheumatology) 2nd, 1978. irreg. $28.50.
Almqvist & Wiksell International, Box 62, S-101 20
Stockholm, Sweden. Ed. T.W. Feltkamp. illus.

616.742   SZ   ISSN 0071-7851
FORTBILDUNGSKURSE FUER
RHEUMATOLOGIE. (Text in German) 1971.
irreg. (approx. 1/yr.) price varies. S. Karger AG,
Allschwilerstrasse 10, P.O. Box, CH-4009 Basel,
Switzerland. Ed.Bd. (reprint service avail. from ISI)
Indexed: Biol.Abstr. Chem.Abstr. Curr.Cont.
Ind.Med.

616.742   UK
MATHILDA AND TERENCE KENNEDY
INSTITUTE OF RHEUMATOLOGY. ANNUAL
REPORT. 1967. a. free. Mathilda and Terence
Kennedy Institute of Rheumatology, 6 Bute
Gardens, Hammersmith, London W6 7DW,
England. circ. 2,000(controlled)

616.742   IT   ISSN 0048-7449
REUMATISMO. (Supplements accompany some vols.)
1949. irreg. L.12000. (Societa Italiana per lo Studio
del Reumatismo e per la Lotta Contro le Malattie
Reumatiche) Longanesi & C., Sezione Redi, Via
Borghetto 5, 20122 Milan, Italy. Ed. Elisa Cirla.
adv. bk. rev. illus. Indexed: Biol.Abstr. Chem.Abstr.
Ind.Med.

616.742   SZ   ISSN 0080-2727
RHEUMATOLOGY. (Text in English) 1966. irreg.
(approx. 1/yr.) price varies. S. Karger AG,
Allschwilerstrasse 10, P.O. Box, CH-4009 Basel,
Switzerland. Ed. M. Schattenkirchner. (reprint
service avail. from ISI) Indexed: Biol.Abstr.
Chem.Abstr. Curr.Cont. Ind.Med.

616.7   US   ISSN 0190-5422
U.S. NATIONAL ARTHRITIS ADVISORY BOARD.
ANNUAL REPORT.* a. U.S. National Arthritis
Advisory Board, National Institute of Arthritis,
Diabetes and Digestive Diseases, Federal Bldg., Rm.
620, Bethesda, MD 20205. Key Title: Annual
Report - National Arthritis Advisory Board.

MEDICAL SCIENCES — Sports Medicine

ANNUAIRE NATIONAL DES MASSEURS
KINESITHERAPEUTES. see MEDICAL
SCIENCES

613.7   US   ISSN 0091-6331
EXERCISE AND SPORT SCIENCES REVIEWS.
1973. a. $27.50. (American College of Sports
Medicine) Macmillan Publishing Co., Medical-
Nursing Department, 866 Third Ave., New York,
NY 10022. Ed. Kent B. Randolf. charts. illus. circ.
1,000. (back issues avail.) Indexed: Biol.Abstr.
Ind.Med. Ind.Med. Sportsearch.

617.102   SZ   ISSN 0254-5020
MEDICINE AND SPORT SCIENCE. (Text in
English) 1966. irreg. (approx. 1/yr.) price varies. S.
Karger AG, Allschwilerstrasse 10, P.O. Box, CH-
4009 Basel, Switzerland. Eds. M. Hebbelinck, R.J.
Shephard. (reprint service avail. from ISI; back
issues avail.) Indexed: Biol.Abstr. Chem.Abstr.
Chem.Abstr. Curr.Cont. Ind.Med.
  Formerly: Medicine and Sport (ISSN 0076-6070)

PSYCHOLOGY AND SOCIOLOGY OF SPORT;
current selected research. see PSYCHOLOGY

617.102   GE   ISSN 0075-8655
SPORTMEDIZINISCHE SCHRIFTENREIHE. 1967.
irreg., vol.24, 1985. price varies. (Deutsche
Hochschule fuer Koerperkultur Leipzig) Johann
Ambrosius Barth Verlag, Salomonstr. 18b, DDR-
7010 Leipzig, E. Germany (D.D.R.) (Orders to:
Buchexport, Leninstr. 16, DDR-7010 Leipzig, E.
Germany (D.D.R.)) Ed.Bd. (back issues avail.)

617.1   US   ISSN 0162-0908
YEAR BOOK OF SPORTS MEDICINE. 1979. a.
$42.95. Year Book Medical Publishers, Inc., 35 E.
Wacker Dr., Chicago, IL 60601. TEL 312-726-9733.
Ed. L.J. Krakauer, M.D. illus.

MEDICAL SCIENCES — Surgery

A B M S DIRECTORY OF CERTIFIED
NEUROLOGICAL SURGEONS. (American Board
of Medical Specialties) see MEDICAL
SCIENCES — Psychiatry And Neurology

MEDICAL SCIENCES — SURGERY

617 US ISSN 0749-839X
A B M S DIRECTORY OF CERTIFIED PLASTIC SURGEONS. 1983. biennial. $44.95 hardcover; $34.95 softcover. American Board of Medical Specialties, One American Plaza, Ste. 805, Evanston, IL 60201. TEL 312-491-9091. Ed. Donald G. Langsley, M.D.

617 US ISSN 0884-1527
A B M S DIRECTORY OF CERTIFIED SURGEONS. 1985. biennial. $44.95 hardcover; $34.95 softcover. American Board of Medical Specialties, One American Plaza, Ste. 805, Evanston, IL 60201. TEL 312-491-9091. Ed. Donald G. Langsley, M.D.

A B M S DIRECTORY OF CERTIFIED THORACIC SURGEONS. (American Board of Medical Specialties) see MEDICAL SCIENCES

617 US ISSN 0081-9646
ACKERMAN'S SURGICAL PATHOLOGY. 6th edt., 1968. irreg., 6th edt., 1981. $170. C.V. Mosby Co., 11830 Westline Industrial Dr., St. Louis, MO 63146. TEL 314-872-8370. Ed. Juan Rosai. (reprint service avail. from UMI)

ACTA NEUROCHIRURGICA. SUPPLEMENTA. see MEDICAL SCIENCES — Psychiatry And Neurology

ADVANCES AND TECHNICAL STANDARDS IN NEUROSURGERY. see MEDICAL SCIENCES — Psychiatry And Neurology

ADVANCES IN NEUROSURGERY. see MEDICAL SCIENCES — Psychiatry And Neurology

617.95 US
ADVANCES IN PLASTIC AND RECONSTRUCTIVE SURGERY. 1984. a. $59.95. Year Book Medical Publishers, Inc., 35 E. Wacker Dr., Chicago, IL 60601. TEL 312-726-9746. Eds. Mutaz B. Hatal, William D. Morain. illus.

617.082 US ISSN 0065-3411
ADVANCES IN SURGERY. 1966. a. $47.95. Year Book Medical Publishers, Inc., 35 E. Wacker Dr., Chicago, IL 60601. TEL 312-726-9733. Ed. John Mannick, M.D. illus. (also avail. in microfilm from UMI; reprint service avail. from UMI) Indexed: Ind.Med.

617.585 US
AMERICAN COLLEGE OF FOOT SPECIALISTS. ANNUAL YEARBOOK. 1958. a. American College of Foot Specialists, 1801 Vauxhall Rd., Box 54, Union, NJ 02083. circ. 2,000.
Formerly (until 1980): American Association of Foot Specialists. Program Journal (ISSN 0065-7190)

617.585 US
AMERICAN PODIATRIC MEDICAL ASSOCIATION. DESK REFERENCE AND DIRECTORY; with constitution, by-laws and code of ethics. 1948. a. American Podiatric Medical Association, 20 Chevy Chase Circle, N.W., Washington, DC 20015. TEL 202-537-4900. circ. controlled.
Formerly: American Podiatry Association. Desk Reference and Directory (ISSN 0065-9770)

617 US
AMERICAN SOCIETY OF PLASTIC AND RECONSTRUCTIVE SURGEONS. SYMPOSIA. vol.5, 1973. irreg., vol.24, 1984. C.V. Mosby Co., 11830 Westline Industrial Dr., St. Louis, MO 63146. TEL 314-872-8370.

617 US ISSN 0066-0833
AMERICAN SURGICAL ASSOCIATION. TRANSACTIONS. 1882. a. $25. J.B. Lippincott Co., E. Washington Sq., Philadelphia, PA 19105.

617 AG ISSN 0066-1465
ANALES DE CIRUGIA. 1935. irreg. Calle Paraguay 40, Rosario, Prov. de Santa Fe, Argentina. Indexed: Biol.Abstr. Excerp.Med.

617 IT ISSN 0066-670X
ARCHIVIO PUTTI DI CHIRURGIA DEGLI ORGANI DI MOVIMENTO. (Text in Italian; summaries in English and Italian) 1951. a. L.35000($45) Aulo Gaggi Editore, Via Andrea Costa 131/5, 40134 Bologna, Italy. Ed. O. Scaglietti. bk. rev. circ. 1,500. Indexed: Excerp.Med. Ind.Med. Dent.Ind.

617 BL ISSN 0066-7846
ARQUIVOS DE CIRURGIA CLINICA E EXPERIMENTAL.* (Supplements accompany some issues) (Some summaries in English) 1937. irreg. $35. Universidade de Sao Paulo, Hospital das Clinicas, Caixa Postal 8091, Sao Paulo, Brazil. Ed. Ruy G. Bevilacqua. index. cum.index. circ. 10,000. Indexed: Biol.Abstr.

ARTHROLOGY. see MEDICAL SCIENCES — Radiology And Nuclear Medicine

617 370 ZA
ASSOCIATION OF SURGEONS OF EAST AFRICA. PROCEEDINGS. (Text and summaries in English) 1978. a. 15 n.($20) Association of Surgeons of East Africa, Box 320159, Woodlands, Lusaka, Zambia. Ed. John E. Jellis. adv. bk. rev. cum.index. circ. 800. (back issues avail.)

CARDIOVASCULAR SURGERY. see MEDICAL SCIENCES — Cardiovascular Diseases

CLINICAL NEUROSURGERY; PROCEEDINGS. see MEDICAL SCIENCES — Psychiatry And Neurology

617 US ISSN 0172-4827
COMPREHENSIVE MANUALS OF SURGICAL SPECIALITIES. 1975. irreg., latest 1986. Springer-Verlag, 175 Fifth Ave., New York, NY 10010 TEL 212-460-1500. (Also Berlin, Heidelberg, Tokyo and Vienna) Ed. R.H. Egdahl. (reprint service avail. from ISI)

617 US ISSN 0070-2196
CURRENT TOPICS IN SURGICAL RESEARCH. 1969. irreg., vol.3, 1971. Academic Press, Inc., Orlando, FL 32887. TEL 305-345-2000. Eds. G.D. Zuidema, D.B. Skinner.

ELECTROMEDICAL & ELECTROSURGICAL EQUIPMENT SPEC BOOK. see INSTRUMENTS

617 US ISSN 0071-8041
FORUM ON FUNDAMENTAL SURGICAL PROBLEMS. Variant title: Surgical Forum. 1950. a. $14. American College of Surgeons, 55 E. Erie St., Chicago, IL 60611. TEL 312-664-4050. Ed. Marjorie Pannell. circ. 4,000. (also avail. in microform from UMI; reprint service avail. from UMI) Indexed: Biol.Abstr. Curr.Cont. Excerp.Med. ASCA.

617.4 UK
INTERNATIONAL SYMPOSIUM ON SURGICAL HEART DISEASE. PROCEEDINGS.* irreg., 2nd, Auckland, N.Z, 1972. $28. Churchill Livingstone, 23 Ravelston Terr., Edinburgh EH4 3TL, Scotland (And Williams and Wilkins Co., 428 E. Preston St., Baltimore, MD 21202) Ed.Bd. bibl. illus.

617 US ISSN 0075-3815
JOHN ALEXANDER MONOGRAPH SERIES ON VARIOUS PHASES OF THORACIC SURGERY.* irreg. price varies. Charles C. Thomas, Publisher, 2600 S. First St., Springfield, IL 62717. TEL 217-789-8980. Indexed: Biol.Abstr.

607 IT
JOURNAL OF CARDIOVASCULAR SURGERY. CONGRESS PROCEEDINGS. irreg. price varies. (International Cardiovascular Society) Edizioni Minerva Medica, Corso Bramante 83-85, 10126 Turin, Italy.

616 US
MODERN NEUROSURGERY. (Consists of selected papers from the Congress of the World Federation of Neurosurgical Societies) 1982. quadrennial. Springer-Verlag, 175 Fifth Ave., New York, NY 10010 TEL 212-460-1500. (And Berlin, Heidelberg) Ed. M. Brock.

617.54 US ISSN 0163-7029
MODERN TECHNICS IN SURGERY. CARDIAC/THORACIC SURGERY. 1979. irreg. (approx. a.) price varies. Futura Publishing Company, Inc., 295 Main St., Box 330, Mount Kisco, NY 10549. TEL 914-666-7528. Ed. Dr. Lawrence H. Cohn. index.

617 US ISSN 0271-8219
MODERN TECHNICS IN SURGERY. HEAD AND NECK SURGERY. 1981. irreg. (approx. a.) price varies. Futura Publishing Company, Inc., 295 Main St., Box 330, Mount Kisco, NY 10549. TEL 914-666-7528. Ed. Dr. Moses Nussbaum. index.

617 US ISSN 0163-7037
MODERN TECHNICS IN SURGERY. NEUROSURGERY. 1979. irreg. (approx. a.) price varies. Futura Publishing Company, Inc., 295 Main St., Box 330, Mount Kisco, NY 10549. TEL 914-666-7528. Ed. Dr. Joseph Ransohoff. index.

617.95 US ISSN 0276-9387
MODERN TECHNICS IN SURGERY. PLASTIC SURGERY. 1981. irreg. (approx a.) price varies. Futura Publishing Company, Inc., 295 Main St., Box 330, Mount Kisco, NY 10549. TEL 914-666-7528. Eds. Drs. Sidney Kahn, Bernard E. Simon.

617 US ISSN 0193-8568
MODERN TECHNICS IN SURGERY. UROLOGIC SURGERY. 1980. irreg. (approx. a.) price varies. Futura Publishing Company, Inc., 295 Main St., Box 330, Mount Kisco, NY 10549. TEL 914-666-7528. Ed. Dr. Richard M. Ehrlich.

617.96 GW ISSN 0079-4899
PRAKTISCHE CHIRURGIE. 1936. irreg., no.97, 1984. price varies. Ferdinand Enke Verlag, Postfach 1304, 7000 Stuttgart 1, W. Germany (B.R.D.) Eds. K. Kremer, A. Encke.
Continues: Vortraege aus der Praktischen Chirurgie (ISSN 0083-6931)

616 US
PRAXIS DER CHIRURGIE. 1982. irreg. price varies. Springer-Verlag, 175 Fifth Ave., New York, NY 10010 TEL 212-460-1500. (Also Berlin, Heidelberg, Tokyo and Vienna)

PRINCIPLES OF PEDIATRIC NEUROSURGERY. see MEDICAL SCIENCES — Pediatrics

PROGRESS IN NEUROLOGICAL SURGERY. see MEDICAL SCIENCES — Psychiatry And Neurology

617 SZ ISSN 0079-6824
PROGRESS IN SURGERY. (Text in English) 1961. irreg. (approx. 1/yr.) price varies. S. Karger AG, Allschwilerstrasse 10, P.O. Box, CH-4009 Basel, Switzerland. Ed. E.H. Farthmann. (reprint service avail. from ISI) Indexed: Biol.Abstr. Chem.Abstr. Curr.Cont. Ind.Med.

617.95 SZ ISSN 0080-0260
RECONSTRUCTION SURGERY AND TRAUMATOLOGY. (Text in English) 1953. irreg. (approx. 1/yr.) price varies. S. Karger AG, Allschwilerstrasse 10, P.O. Box, CH-4009 Basel, Switzerland. Ed. H. Eberle. (reprint service avail. from ISI) Indexed: Biol.Abstr. Chem.Abstr. Curr.Cont. Ind.Med.

610 UK
ROYAL COLLEGE OF SURGEONS OF ENGLAND. HANDBOOK. quinquennial. Royal College of Surgeons of England, Lincoln's Inn Fields, London WC2A 3PN, England.

616 US ISSN 0160-2489
SEMINARS IN NEUROLOGICAL SURGERY. 1978. irreg., no.5, 1979. Raven Press, 1185 Ave. of the Americas, New York, NY 10036. TEL 212-575-0335. Indexed: Excerp.Med. ASCA.

617 US
SOUTHERN SURGICAL ASSOCIATION. TRANSACTIONS. a. $30. J.B. Lippincott Co., E. Washington Sq., Philadelphia, PA 19105.

616.8 UK
STUDIES IN NEUROSCIENCE. 1985. irreg. price varies. Manchester University Press, Oxford Rd., Manchester M13 9PL, England. TEL 061-273-5539. Ed. W. Winlow.

616 US ISSN 0081-9638
SURGERY ANNUAL. 1969. a. price varies. Appleton & Lange, 25 Van Zant St., E. Norwalk, CT 06855. TEL 203-838-4400. Ed. Dr. Lloyd Nyhos. Indexed: Biol.Abstr. Excerp.Med. Ind.Med. Dent.Ind.

617 US ISSN 0074-3984
TRANSPLANTATION TODAY. Represents: International Congress of the Transplantation Society. Proceedings. 1967. biennial, vol.8, 1985. Grune and Stratton, Inc. (Subsidiary of: Harcourt Brace Jovanovich, Inc.) Orlando, FL 32887 TEL 305-345-4200. (Dist. by: Academic Press, Inc.) Ed.Bd.

YEAR BOOK OF NEUROLOGY &
NEUROSURGERY. see *MEDICAL
SCIENCES — Psychiatry And Neurology*

617.95   US   ISSN 0084-3962
YEAR BOOK OF PLASTIC AND
RECONSTRUCTIVE SURGERY. 1970. a. $46.95.
Year Book Medical Publishers, Inc., 35 E. Wacker
Dr., Chicago, IL 60601. TEL 312-726-9733. Ed.
F.J. McCoy, M.D. illus.

YEAR BOOK OF PODIATRIC MEDICINE AND
SURGERY. see *MEDICAL SCIENCES —
Orthopedics And Traumatology*

617.005   US   ISSN 0090-3671
YEAR BOOK OF SURGERY. 1971. a. $44.95. ‡
Year Book Medical Publishers, Inc., 35 East Wacker
Drive, Chicago, IL 60601. TEL 312-726-9733. Ed.
S.I. Schwartz, M.D. illus.
    Formerly: Year Book of General Surgery.

MEDICAL SCIENCES — Urology And Nephrology

616.6   US   ISSN 0742-0374
A B M S DIRECTORY OF CERTIFIED
UROLOGISTS. 1983. biennial. $39.95 hardcover;
$29.95 softcover. American Board of Medical
Specialties, One American Plaza, Ste. 805,
Evanston, IL 60201. TEL 312-491-9091. Ed.
Donald G. Langsley, M.D.

616.6   FR   ISSN 0073-3326
ACTUALITES NEPHROLOGIQUES. 1960. a. price
varies. (Hopital Necker, Clinique Nephrologique)
Flammarion Medecine Sciences, 4 rue Casimir
Delavigne, 75006 Paris, France (U.S. subscr.
address: S.F.P.A., c/o Mr. Benech, 14 E. 60th St.,
New York, NY 10022) Ed. J.P. Grunfeld.
cum.index: 1960-69. Indexed: Chem.Abstr.
Excerp.Med.

616.6   US
ADVANCES IN NEPHROLOGY. 1971. a. $65. Year
Book Medical Publishers, Inc., 35 E. Wacker Dr.,
Chicago, IL 60601. TEL 312-726-9733. Ed. Dr.
Jean-Pierre Grunfeld. (also avail. in microfilm from
UMI; reprint service avail. from UMI) Indexed:
Biol.Abstr. Chem.Abstr. Ind.Med.
    Formerly: Advances in Nephrology from the
Necker Hospital (ISSN 0084-5957)

616.602   SZ   ISSN 0250-3212
BEITRAEGE ZUR UROLOGIE. (Text in German)
1979. irreg. S. Karger AG, Allschwilerstrasse 10,
P.O. Box, CH-4009 Basel, Switzerland. Eds. H.
Melchior. charts. illus. (back issues avail.) Indexed:
Biol.Abstr. Curr.Cont.

616.1   US
CLINICAL PRACTICE IN UROLOGY. 1982. irreg.,
latest 1986. Springer-Verlag, 175 Fifth Ave., New
York, NY 10010 TEL 212-460-1500. (And Berlin,
Heidelberg, Tokyo and Vienna) Ed. G.D. Chisholm.

616.6   US
CONTEMPORARY NEPHROLOGY. 1981. biennial.
price varies. Plenum Publishing Corp., 233 Spring
St., New York, NY 10013. TEL 212-620-8047. Eds.
Saulo Klahr, Shaul G. Massry.

610   US   ISSN 0148-4265
CURRENT NEPHROLOGY. 1977. a. $65. Year
Book Medical Publishers, Inc., 35 E. Wacker Dr.,
Chicago, IL 60601. Ed. Harvey C. Gonick, M.D.
illus. circ. 1,300. Indexed: Biol.Abstr. Chem.Abstr.

616.6   US
DEUTSCHE GESELLSCHAFT FUER UROLOGIE.
VERHANDLUNGEN. 19th Session, 1962. irreg.,
35th session, 1984. price varies. Springer-Verlag,
175 Fifth Ave., New York, NY 10010 TEL 212-
460-1500. (Also Berlin, Heidelberg, Tokyo and
Vienna) (reprint service avail. from ISI)
    Formerly: Deutsche Gesellschaft fuer Urologie.
Verhandlungsbericht (ISSN 0070-413X)

616.6   SW
EUROPEAN COLLOQUIUM ON RENAL
PHYSIOLOGY (PROCEEDINGS) (Supplement to:
Uppsala Journal of Medical Sciences) 3rd, 1979.
irreg. $23.80. Almqvist & Wiksell International, Box
62, S-101 20 Stockholm, Sweden. Ed. Hans R.
Ulfendahl.

616.6   GW   ISSN 0071-7975
FORTSCHRITTE DER UROLOGIE UND
NEPHROLOGIE. (Text in English and German)
1970. irreg., vol.25, 1986. price varies. Dr. Dietrich
Steinkopff Verlag, Saalburstr. 12, Postfach 11 14 42,
6100 Darmstadt 11, W. Germany (B.R.D.) Eds. A.
Gasser, W. Vahlensieck. index. circ. 2,000. Indexed:
Chem.Abstr.

616.6   GR   ISSN 0074-3771
INTERNATIONAL CONGRESS OF
NEPHROLOGY. ABSTRACTS OF REPORTS
AND COMMUNICATIONS.* 1960. irreg., 4th,
1969, Stockholm. International Society of
Nephrology, c/o Prof. Papadimitriou, Hopital Sainte
Sophia, Thessalolinki, Greece. Indexed: Chem.Abstr.

616.65   DK   ISSN 0106-1607
INTERNATIONAL JOURNAL OF ANDROLOGY.
SUPPLEMENT. 1978. irreg. price varies. Scriptor
Publisher ApS, Gasvaerksvej 15, DK-1656
Copenhagen V, Denmark. illus. Indexed: Biol.Abstr.
Chem.Abstr.

616.6   FR   ISSN 0074-8579
INTERNATIONAL SOCIETY OF UROLOGY.
REPORTS OF CONGRESS. (Reports published in
host country) irreg., 17th, 1975, Madrid.
International Society of Urology, c/o Prof. Rene
Kuess, 63 Ave. Niel, 75017 Paris, France.

616.6   US
KIDNEY DISEASES. 1979. irreg., vol.7, 1986. price
varies. Marcel Dekker, Inc., 270 Madison Ave.,
New York, NY 10016. TEL 212-696-9000. Indexed:
Chem.Abstr.

616.6   US
KIDNEY INTERNATIONAL. SUPPLEMENT. 1974.
irreg., vol.14, 1983. price varies (free to subscribers
of Kidney International) Springer-Verlag, 175 Fifth
Ave., New York, NY 10010 TEL 212-460-1500.
(Also Berlin, Heidelberg, Vienna) (reprint service
avail. from ISI) Indexed: Biol.Abstr. Chem.Abstr.
Ind.Med. Nutr.Abstr.

MODERN TECHNICS IN SURGERY. UROLOGIC
SURGERY. see *MEDICAL SCIENCES — Surgery*

616.6   US   ISSN 0077-5096
NATIONAL KIDNEY FOUNDATION. ANNUAL
REPORT. 1957/58. a. free. National Kidney
Foundation, 2 Park Ave., New York, NY 10016.
TEL 212-889-2210.

616.6   US   ISSN 0194-0090
NEPHROLOGY REVIEWS. 1980. a. $35. John Wiley
& Sons, Inc., 605 Third Ave., New York, NY
10158. TEL 212-850-6000.

616.6 616.132   US   ISSN 0092-2900
PERSPECTIVES IN NEPHROLOGY AND
HYPERTENSION. 1973. irreg., unnumbered, latest
1981. price varies. John Wiley & Sons, Inc., 605
Third Ave., New York, NY 10016. TEL 212-850-
6000. Ed. E.L. Becker. Indexed: Biol.Abstr.
Ind.Med.

616.6   FR   ISSN 0083-4769
URO-NEPHRO; ANNUAIRE DE L'UROLOGIE ET
DE LA NEPHROLOGIE.* 1969. irreg. price
varies. Laboratoires Winthrop, 92-98 Bld. Victor-
Hugo, Clichy, France.

616.6   US   ISSN 0084-4071
YEAR BOOK OF UROLOGY. 1933. a. $44.95. Year
Book Medical Publishers, Inc., 35 E. Wacker Dr.,
Chicago, IL 60601. TEL 312-726-9733. Eds. Jay Y.
Gillenwater, M.D., Stuart S. Howards, M.D. illus.

MEETINGS AND CONGRESSES

578 011   US   ISSN 0569-2628
A A F M PROCEEDINGS OF ANNUAL
MEETING. 1952. a. $15. American Association of
Feed Microscopists, 1118 Apple Dr.,
Mechanicsburg, PA 17055. TEL 717-766-6030. Ed.
Janet Windsor. circ. 200.

A U M A KALENDER AUSLAND. see *BUSINESS
AND ECONOMICS — Marketing And Purchasing*

A U M A KALENDER REGIONAL. see *BUSINESS
AND ECONOMICS — Marketing And Purchasing*

A U M A ZAHLENSPIEGEL REGIONAL. see
*BUSINESS AND ECONOMICS — Marketing
And Purchasing*

AMERICAN LIBRARY ASSOCIATION. ANNUAL
CONFERENCE PROGRAM. see *LIBRARY AND
INFORMATION SCIENCES*

011   BE
ANNUAL INTERNATIONAL CONGRESS
CALENDAR. (Text in English) 1961. a. 900 Fr.
Union of International Associations, c/o Robert
Fenaux, Rue Washington 40, 1050 Brussels,
Belgium. Ed. G. de Coninck. adv. index. cum.index.

011   US
B O M A INTERNATIONAL CONVENTION
DIRECTORY. 1907. a. Building Owners and
Managers Association International, 1250 Eye St.,
N.W., Ste. 200, Washington, DC 20005. TEL 202-
289-7000. Ed. Charles T. Glazer. adv. circ. 1,000.

610 011   SZ   ISSN 0301-2891
CALENDAR OF CONGRESSES OF MEDICAL
SCIENCES. (Text in English and French) 1949. a.
10 Fr.($5.50) Council for International
Organizations of Medical Sciences - Conseil des
Organisations Internationales des Sciences
Medicales, c/o World Health Organization, 20 Ave.
Appia, CH-1211 Geneva 27, Switzerland. Ed. Dr.
Zbigniew Bankowski. adv. circ. 2,000.
    Formed by the merger of, and assuming the
numbering of the former: Calendar of International
Congresses of Medical Sciences (ISSN 0589-915X)
& Calendar of Regional Congresses of Medical
Sciences (ISSN 0574-248X)

011 338   CN   ISSN 0068-8967
CANADIAN INDUSTRY SHOWS AND
EXHIBITIONS. 1964. a. (plus 3 updates) Can.$39.
Maclean-Hunter Ltd., Business Publication Division,
Maclean-Hunter Bldg., 777 Bay St., Toronto, Ont.
M5W 1A7, Canada. TEL 416-596-5891. Ed. Irvine
Brace.

011   UK   ISSN 0260-2431
THE CONFERENCE BLUE BOOK; your guaranteed
guide to conference venues in the British Isles.
1978. a. £20. Spectrum Communications Ltd.,
Spectrum House, 191 The Vale, London W3 7Q3,
England. Ed. Sally Greenhill. adv. illus. charts. circ.
8,000.

011   UK   ISSN 0260-2199
THE CONFERENCE GREEN BOOK; guide to
conference venues in the British Isles offering
sports, leisure, and "special interest" facilities. 1980.
a. £15. Spectrum Communications Ltd., Spectrum
House, 191 The Vale, London W3 7Q3, England.
Ed. Sally Greenhill. adv. charts. illus. circ. 9,000.

CONFERENCE PAPERS ANNUAL INDEX. see
ABSTRACTING AND INDEXING SERVICES

011   UK
CONFERENCES & EXHIBITIONS
INTERNATIONAL WORLDWIDE
CONVENTION CENTRES YEARBOOK. 1986. a.
$25. International Trade Publications Ltd.,
Queensway House, 2 Queensway, Redhill, Surrey
RH1 1QS, England.

011 910.2   UK   ISSN 0260-776X
CONFERENCES MEETINGS & EXHIBITIONS
WELCOME. 1979. a. free to qualified personnel.
Lewis Productions Ltd., 31 Castle St., Kingston
upon Thames, Surrey KT1 1ST, England. Ed.
Rosemary Bray. adv. circ. 30,000.

711   UK
CONGRESS IN PARK AND RECREATION
ADMINISTRATION. PROGRAMME. triennial.,
1983, Barcelona. International Federation of Park
and Recreation Administration, c/o J.S. Thornton,
Sec. Gen., The Grotto, Lower Basildon, Reading,
Berks. RG8 9NE, England.
    Formerly: World Congress in Public Park
Administration. Programme (ISSN 0510-8233)

060   BE   ISSN 0573-5661
CONGRESS OF INTERNATIONAL CONGRESS
ORGANIZERS AND TECHNICIANS.
PROCEEDING. (Subseries of International
Congress Sciences Series) irreg., 6th, 1977, Kyoto.
600 Fr. Union of International Associations, Rue
Washington 40, 1050 Brussels, Belgium.

CONGRESSI C C S S. BOLLETTINO; Comitato per la Collaborazione tra Societa Medico-Scientifiche. see *MEDICAL SCIENCES — Hematology*

011   CN   ISSN 0226-8922
CONVENTIONS & MEETINGS-CANADA. 1971. a. Can.$25. Effective Communications Ltd., 72 Wellington St. West, Ste. 207, Markham, Ont. L3P 1A8, Canada. TEL 416-471-1550. adv. circ. 10, 688(controlled) (back issues avail.)

COUNCIL OF LEGAL EDUCATION. CALENDAR. see *LAW*

610   011   SP   ISSN 0210-5578
DIARIO DE CONGRESOS MEDICOS. irreg. Ediciones Doyma S.A., Travesera de Gracia 17-21, Barcelona 21, Spain. adv. circ. 10,000.

011   US   ISSN 0417-5751
DIRECTORY OF CONVENTIONS. 1952. a. plus mid-year supplement. $80. Successful Meetings, Directory Department, 633 Third Ave., New York, NY 10017. TEL 212-986-4800. Ed. Toula de Prince. circ. 3,000.

DOMOVA POKLADNICA. see *LITERATURE*

011   EI
EUROPEAN PARLIAMENT. COMMITTEE REPORT. 1967. irreg. Office for Official Publications of the European Communities, Centre Europeen, Batiment Jean Monnet, 2920 Luxembourg, Luxembourg (Dist. in the U.S. by: European Community Information Service, 2100 M St., NW, Suite 707, Washington, DC 20037) Ed.Bd. charts.
European Parliament. Selected Documents.

FRANCE. INSTITUT NATIONAL DE LA SANTE ET DE LA RECHERCHE MEDICALE. COLLOQUES. see *MEDICAL SCIENCES*

GEOGRAPHICAL SOCIETY OF CHINA. BULLETIN. see *GEOGRAPHY*

011   AG   ISSN 0301-7567
GUIA DE REUNIONES CIENTIFICAS Y TECNICAS EN LA ARGENTINA. 1959. a. free. (Secretaria de Estado de Ciencia y Tecnologia, Ministerio de Cultura y Educacion) Fundacion para la Educacion la Ciencia y la Cultura, Moreno 431 (Guia de Reuniones) 1091, Buenos Aires, Argentina. adv. circ. 4,000.

011   BE   ISSN 0538-6772
INTERNATIONAL CONGRESS SCIENCE SERIES. 1961. irreg. price varies. Union of International Associations, Rue Washington 40, 1050 Brussels, Belgium.

011   PH   ISSN 0074-588X
INTERNATIONAL FEDERATION OF ASIAN AND WESTERN PACIFIC CONTRACTORS' ASSOCIATIONS. PROCEEDINGS OF THE ANNUAL CONVENTION. (Proceedings published by organizing committee) irreg. International Federation of Asian and Western Pacific Contractors Associations, Padilla Building, 3rd Fl., Ortigas Commercial Center, Emerald Ave., Pasig, Metro Manila, Philippines.

INTERNATIONAL SOCIETY OF CITRICULTURE. PROCEEDINGS. see *AGRICULTURE*

KALENDAR ODBORARA. see *LABOR UNIONS*

057.87   CS
KULTURNOPOLITICKY KALENDAR. a. 30 Kcs. Obzor, Ceskoslovenskej Armady 35, 815 85 Bratislava, Czechoslovakia. illus.

011   GW   ISSN 0175-3053
MEDIZINISCHE KONGRESSE; National - International. 1957. a. DM.14($6) Werbeagentur Frankfurt am Main R. Haack & Co. GmbH, W E F R A Haus, D-6078 Zeppelinheim, W. Germany (B.R.D.) circ. 40,000. (back issues avail.)

011   UK
SCOTLAND: CONFERENCES, MEETINGS, SEMINARS. irreg. free. Scottish Tourist Board, 23 Ravelston Terrace, Edinburgh EH4 3EU, Scotland.

011   616.07   SA
SOUTH AFRICAN SOCIETY OF PATHOLOGISTS. CONGRESS BROCHURE. (Text in Afrikaans and English) a. South Africa Society of Pathologists, Beatrix St., Pretoria, South Africa. adv.

658.8   US
SUCCESSFUL MEETINGS FACILITIES DIRECTORY. (Special issue of: Successful Meetings Magazine) a. $35. Bill Communications, Inc., 633 Third Ave, New York, NY 10017. TEL 212-986-4800.
Formerly: International Convention Facilities Directory.

TRADESHOW & EXHIBIT MANAGER BUYERS GUIDE. see *BUSINESS AND ECONOMICS — Trade And Industrial Directories*

669   011   UK
WORLD CALENDAR OF FORTHCOMING MEETINGS: METALLURGY AND MATERIALS SCIENCE. 1965. q. £50($80) Institute of Metals, Materials Information, 1 Carlton House Terrace, London SW1Y 5DB, England. Ed. L. Biggs.
Formerly: World Calendar of Forthcoming Meetings: Metallurgical and Related Fields (ISSN 0043-8294)

MEETINGS AND CONGRESSES —
Abstracting, Bibliographies, Statistics

020   015   UK
BRITISH LIBRARY. DOCUMENT SUPPLY CENTRE. INDEX OF CONFERENCE PROCEEDINGS RECEIVED. 1964. m. (annual, 5 year, 10 year, 18 year cumulations) £62. British Library, Document Supply Centre, Boston Spa, Wetherby, West Yorkshire LS23 7BQ, England. circ. 800. (back issues avail.) Indexed: Dairy Sci.Abstr. Rev.Appl.Entomol. Rev.Plant Path.
●Also available online.
Formerly: British Library. Lending Division. Index of Conference Proceedings Recieved (ISSN 0305-5183)

METALLURGY

see also Metallurgy — Welding

A I M M SYMPOSIA SERIES. (Australasian Institute of Mining and Metallurgy) see *MINES AND MINING INDUSTRY*

669   US
A I S E YEARBOOK. 1907. a. $50 to non-members; members $37. Association of Iron and Steel Engineers, Ste. 2350, Three Gateway Center, Pittsburgh, PA 15222. TEL 412-281-6323. Ed. Charles J. Labee. index. circ. 600.
Formerly: Association of Iron and Steel Engineers. A I S E Proceedings.

ACTA POLYTECHNICA SCANDINAVICA. CHEMICAL TECHNOLOGY AND METALLURGY. see *CHEMISTRY*

ADVANCES IN X-RAY ANALYSIS. see *TECHNOLOGY: COMPREHENSIVE WORKS*

669   FR   ISSN 0065-4256
AGENDA DE LA QUINCAILLERIE; fers et metaux. 1956. a. free to members of the Syndicat Confederation. Regie Publicite Industrielle, 36 rue du Fer-a-Moulin, 75005 Paris, France.

671   PL   ISSN 0075-7004
AKADEMIA GORNICZO-HUTNICZA IM. STANISLAWA STASZICA. ZESZYTY NAUKOWE. HUTNICTWO. (Text in Polish; summaries in English and Russian) 1959. irreg. price varies. Akademia Gorniczo-Hutnicza im. Stanislawa Staszica, Al. Mickiewicza 30, 30-059 Krakow, Poland (Dist. by: Ars Polona, Krakowskie Przedmiescie 7, 00-068 Warsaw, Poland) Ed. Michal Odlanicki-Poczobutt. Indexed: Geo.Abstr.

669   PL   ISSN 0137-6535
AKADEMIA GORNICZO-HUTNICZA IM. STANISLAWA STASZICA. ZESZYTY NUKOWE. METALURGIA I ODLEWNICTWO. (Text in English or Polish; summaries in English, Polish, Russian) 1954. irreg., no.106, 1986. price varies. (Akademia Gorniczo-Hutnicza im. Stanislaw Staszica) Wydawnictwo A G H, Manifestu Lipcowego 16, 31-109 Krakow, Poland (Dist. by: Ars Polona, Krakowskie Przedmiescie 7, 00-068 Warsaw, Poland) Ed. Z. Kleczek. illus. circ. 300.

669   UR
AKADEMIYA NAUK KAZAKHSKOI S.S.R. INSTITUT METALLURGII I OBOGASHCHENIYA. TRUDY. vol.52, 1977. irreg. 1.80 Rub. per no. Izdatel'stvo Nauka, Kazakhskoe Otdelenie, Ul. Shevchenko 28, 480021 Alma-Ata, Kazakh S.S.R., U.S.S.R. Ed. A. Kunaev. abstr. bibl. illus. circ. 1,000. Indexed: Chem.Abstr.

669.722   AT   ISSN 0084-6279
ALUMINIUM DEVELOPMENT COUNCIL OF AUSTRALIA. TECHNICAL PAPERS. 1967. irreg. Aluminium Development Council of Australia, 99 Elizabeth St., Sydney, N.S.W. 2000, Australia.

669   UK
ALUMINIUM INDUSTRY IN THE SOVIET UNION. irreg., latest 1982. £70($168) Metal Bulletin PLC, Park House, Park Terrace, Worcester Park, Surrey KT4 7HY, England (Dist. in U.S. by: Metal Bulletin Inc., 220 Fifth Ave., New York, NY 10001)

669.722   GW
ALUMINIUM INTERN: ALUMINIUM UND AUTOMOBIL. irreg. (approx. 4/yr.) (Aluminium-Zentrale e.V.) Aluminium-Verlag GmbH, Koenigsallee 30, Postfach 1207, 4000 Duesseldorf 1, W. Germany(B.R.D.) Indexed: Int.Packag.Abstr.

673   US   ISSN 0065-6658
ALUMINUM STANDARDS AND DATA. 1968. biennial. $12. Aluminum Association, Inc., 818 Connecticut Ave., N.W., Washington, DC 20006. TEL 202-862-5156. circ. 40,000.

673   US
ALUMINUM STANDARDS AND DATA-METRIC. biennial. $4. Aluminum Association, Inc., 818 Connecticut Ave., N.W., Washington, DC 20006. TEL 202-862-5156. circ. 40,000.

673   338.4   US   ISSN 0065-6666
ALUMINUM STATISTICAL REVIEW. (Title varies: Aluminum Industry Annual Statistical Review) 1962. a. $25. Aluminum Association, Inc., 818 Connecticut Ave., N.W., Washington, DC 20006. TEL 202-862-5156. circ. 15,000.

669.028   671.2   US   ISSN 0065-8375
AMERICAN FOUNDRYMEN'S SOCIETY. TRANSACTIONS. 1896. a. $100 to non-members. American Foundrymen's Society, Inc., Golf & Wolf Rds., Des Plaines, IL 60016. TEL 312-824-0181. cum.index: 10 years. (also avail. in microform from UMI; reprint service avail. from UMI) Indexed: Chem.Abstr.

ANNUAL BOOK OF A S T M STANDARDS. VOLUME 01.01. STEEL-PIPING, TUBING, FITTINGS. (American Society for Testing and Materials) see *ENGINEERING — Engineering Mechanics And Materials*

ANNUAL BOOK OF A S T M STANDARDS. VOLUME 01.02. FERROUS CASTINGS, FERRO ALLOYS; SHIPBUILDING. see *ENGINEERING — Engineering Mechanics And Materials*

ANNUAL BOOK OF A S T M STANDARDS. VOLUME 01.03. STEEL PLATE, SHEET, STRIP WIRE. see *ENGINEERING — Engineering Mechanics And Materials*

ANNUAL BOOK OF A S T M STANDARDS. VOLUME 01.04. STEEL-STRUCTURAL, REINFORCING, PRESSURE VESSEL; RAILWAY. see *ENGINEERING — Engineering Mechanics And Materials*

ANNUAL BOOK OF A S T M STANDARDS. VOLUME 01.05. STEEL-BARS, BEARINGS, FORGINGS, CHAIN, SPRINGS. see *ENGINEERING — Engineering Mechanics And Materials*

METALLURGY

ANNUAL BOOK OF A S T M STANDARDS. VOLUME 01.06. COATED STEEL PRODUCTS. see *ENGINEERING — Engineering Mechanics And Materials*

ANNUAL BOOK OF A S T M STANDARDS. VOLUME 02.01. COPPER AND COPPER ALLOYS. see *ENGINEERING — Engineering Mechanics And Materials*

ANNUAL BOOK OF A S T M STANDARDS. VOLUME 02.02. DIE-CAST METALS; ALUMINUM AND MAGNESIUM ALLOYS. see *ENGINEERING — Engineering Mechanics And Materials*

ANNUAL BOOK OF A S T M STANDARDS. VOLUME 02.04. NONFERROUS METALS-NICKEL, LEAD, TIN ALLOYS, PRECIOUS, PRIMARY, REACTIVE METALS. see *ENGINEERING — Engineering Mechanics And Materials*

ANNUAL BOOK OF A S T M STANDARDS. VOLUME 02.05. METALLIC AND INORGANIC COATINGS; METAL POWDERS, SINTERED P/M STRUCTURAL PARTS. see *ENGINEERING — Engineering Mechanics And Materials*

ANNUAL BOOK OF A S T M STANDARDS. VOLUME 03.01. METALS-MECHANICAL TESTING; ELEVATED AND LOW-TEMPERATURE TESTS METALLOGRAPHY. see *ENGINEERING — Engineering Mechanics And Materials*

ANNUAL BOOK OF A S T M STANDARDS. VOLUME 03.02. WEAR AND EROSION; METAL CORROSION. see *ENGINEERING — Engineering Mechanics And Materials*

ANNUAL BOOK OF A S T M STANDARDS. VOLUME 03.03. NONDESTRUCTIVE TESTS. see *ENGINEERING — Engineering Mechanics And Materials*

ANNUAL BOOK OF A S T M STANDARDS. VOLUME 03.05. CHEMICAL ANALYSIS OF METALS; METAL BEARING ORES. see *ENGINEERING — Engineering Mechanics And Materials*

669 CL
AREA METALURGIA. Short title: Metalurgia. (Text in Spanish; summaries in English) 1971. irreg. $5. Universidad de Santiago de Chile, Direccion de Investigaciones Cientificas y Tecnologicas, Avda. Ecuador 3469, Santiago, Chile. illus. circ. 1,000. Indexed: Chem.Abstr.

671.2 FR
ASSOCIATION TECHNIQUE DE FONDERIE. ANNUAIRE; ingenieurs et techniciens. 1911. biennial. Agence de Diffusion et de Publicite, 24 Place du General Catroux, 75017 Paris, France. adv.

669 AT
AUSTRALASIAN INSTITUTE OF METALS. PROCEEDINGS OF THE ANNUAL CONFERENCE. 1947. a. price varies. Australian Institute of Metals, 191 Royal Parade, Parkville, Vic. 3052, Australia. bibl. charts. illus. circ. 300. (also avail. in microfiche) Indexed: Met.Abstr.
Formerly: Australian Institute of Metals. Proceedings of the Annual Conference.

669 II
BANARAS METALLURGIST. (Text in English and Hindi) 1968. a. free. Banaras Hindu University, Institute of Technology, Department of Metallurgical Engineering, Varanasi 221005 U.P., Uttar Pradesh, India. adv. bk. rev. circ. 500. Indexed: Met.Abstr.

669 UK
BRITISH INDEPENDENT STEEL COMPANIES AND THEIR PRODUCTS. 1969. irreg. free. British Independent Steel Producers Association (B.I.S.P.A.), c/o B.D. Orchard, 5 Cromwell Rd., London SW7 2HX, England. Ed. B.D. Orchard. circ. 5,000.

669 UK ISSN 0068-2586
BRITISH STEEL CORPORATION. ANNUAL REPORT AND ACCOUNTS. a. £1. British Steel Corp., 9 Albert Embankment, London SE1 7SN, England. illus.

C.I.M. DIRECTORY. (Canadian Institute of Mining and Metallurgy) see *MINES AND MINING INDUSTRY*

669.1 MX
CAMARA NACIONAL DE LA INDUSTRIA DEL HIERRO Y DEL ACERO. INFORME DEL PRESIDENTE. a. $5. Camara Nacional de la Industria del Hierro y del Acero, Amores 338, Apdo. Postal 12783, Mexico 12, D.F., Mexico.

CANADA. STATISTICS CANADA. COMMUNICATIONS AND ENERGY WIRE AND CABLE INDUSTRY/INDUSTRIE DES FILS ET CABLES ELECTRIQUES ET DE COMMUNICATIONS. see *ELECTRICITY AND ELECTRICAL ENGINEERING*

669 CN ISSN 0384-4935
CANADA. STATISTICS CANADA. SMELTING AND REFINING/FONTE ET AFFINAGE. (Catalogue 41-214) (Text in English and French) 1927. a. Can.$20($21) Statistics Canada, Communications Division, 3rd Floor, R.H. Coats Bldg., Ottawa, Ont. K1A 0T6, Canada TEL 613-993-7276. (Subscr. to: Publications Sales and Services, Ottawa, Ont. K1A 0T6, Canada) (also avail. in microform from MML)

669.1 FR
CHAMBRE SYNDICALE DE LA SIDERUGIE FRANCAISE. BULLETIN STATISTIQUE. SERIE BLEUE. COMMERCE EXTERIEUR. a. 260 F. Societe d'Editions de la Siderurgie, 5 bis, rue de Madrid, 75379 Paris Cedex 08, France.

669.1 FR ISSN 0755-2025
CHAMBRE SYNDICALE DE LA SIDERUGIE FRANCAISE. BULLETIN STATISTIQUE. SERIE ROUGE. PRODUCTION. a. Societe d'Editions de la Siderurgie, 5 bis, rue de Madrid, 75379 Paris Cedex 08, France.

COKE OVEN MANAGERS' ASSOCIATION. YEAR BOOK. see *MINES AND MINING INDUSTRY*

669 FR ISSN 0069-5807
COLLOQUE DE METALLURGIE. a. Presses Universitaires de France, 108 bd. Saint Germain, 75279 Paris Cedex 6, France (Subscr. to: 12 rue Jean de Beauvais, 75005 Paris) (reprint service avail. from KTO) Indexed: Chem.Abstr.

669 CL ISSN 0589-2813
CONGRESO LATINAMERICANO DE SIDERURGIA. MEMORIA TECNICA.* 1961. irreg. Instituto Latinoamericano del Fierro y el Acero, Secretaria General, Moneda 1140, Casilla Postal 13810, Santiago, Chile. Indexed: Chem.Abstr.

620.112 US
CORROSION MONOGRAPH SERIES. 1966. irreg., unnumbered, latest 1986. price varies. John Wiley & Sons, Inc., 605 Third Ave., New York, NY 10016. TEL 212-850-6000. Ed. R.T. Foley.

CURRENT BIBLIOGRAPHIES ON SCIENCE AND TECHNOLOGY: METALLURGY, NATURAL RESOURCES & ENERGY. see *METALLURGY — Abstracting, Bibliographies, Statistics*

669 943.7 CS
Z DEJIN HUTNICTVI. (Text in Czech; summaries in English and German) 1972. irreg. exchange basis. Narodni Technicke Muzeum, Kostelni 42, 170 78 Prague 7, Czechoslovakia. illus. bibl.

669 US ISSN 0070-5039
DIRECTORY IRON AND STEEL PLANTS. 1917. a. $35. Association of Iron and Steel Engineers, Ste. 2350, Three Gateway Center, Pittsburgh, PA 15222. TEL 412-281-6323. Ed. Dorothy Sukits. adv. circ. 5,000.

DIRECTORY OF STEEL FOUNDRIES IN THE UNITED STATES, CANADA AND MEXICO. see *BUSINESS AND ECONOMICS — Trade And Industrial Directories*

669 380 US ISSN 0278-8799
DUN'S INDUSTRIAL GUIDE/METALWORKING DIRECTORY. 1961. a. $610. Dun's Marketing Services (Subsidiary of: Dun & Bradstreet, Inc.) 49 Old Bloomfield Rd., Mtn. Lakes, NJ 07046. TEL 201-299-8016. (also avail. in magnetic tape)
Formerly: Dun and Bradstreet Metalworking Directory (ISSN 0070-7597)

669.6 UK
E E C - TIN IN TINPLATE. 1981. irreg. £15. International Tin Council, 1 Oxendon St., London SW1Y 4EQ, England.

669 US
E/M J INTERNATIONAL DIRECTORY OF MINING. 1968. a. $70. McGraw-Hill Publications Co., 1221 Ave. of the Americas, New York, NY 10020. Ed. George F. Nielson.
Formerly: E/M J International Directory of Mining and Mineral Processing Operations.

ELEKTRYFIKACJA I MECHANIZACJA GORNICTWA I HUTNICTWA/ELECTRIFICATION AND MECHANIZATION IN MINING AND METALLURGY. see *MINES AND MINING INDUSTRY*

669 UK ISSN 0261-426X
EUROPEAN AND NORTH AMERICAN SCRAP DIRECTORY. 1976. irreg., latest 1981. £35($84) Metal Bulletin Books Ltd., Park House, Park Terrace, Worcester Park, Surrey KT4 7HY, England (Dist. in U.S. by: Metal Bulletin Inc., 220 Fifth Ave., New York, NY 10001) Ed. John Bailey.
Formerly: European Scrap Directory (ISSN 0308-7786)

671 UK ISSN 0014-5785
F E & Z N. (Editions in English, French, German, Italian and Spanish) 1960. irreg. free. Zinc Development Association, 34 Berkeley Square, W1X 6AJ, London, England. Ed. A.J. Wall. charts. illus. circ. 30,000.

671.2 BE
FEDERATION DES ENTREPRISES DE L'INDUSTRIE DES FABRICATIONS METALLIQUES, MECANIQUES, ELECTRIQUES ET DE LA TRANSFORMATION DES MATIERES PLASTIQUES. CENTRE DE RECHERCHES SCIENTIFIQUES ET TECHNIQUES. SECTION: FONDERIE (FD). RESEARCH REPORTS. 1965. irreg. Federation des Entreprises de l'Industrie des Fabrications Metalliques, Mecaniques, Electriques et de la Transformation des Matieres Plastiques, 21 rue des Drapiers, 1050 Brussels, Belgium.

669.6 FR ISSN 0085-0519
FER-BLANC EN FRANCE ET DANS LE MONDE. 1956. a. free. Chambre Syndicale des Producteurs de Fer-Blanc et de Fer-Noir, 5 rue Paul Cezanne, 75008 Paris, France. charts. stat. circ. 800.
Tin

669 UK ISSN 0266-3198
FERRO ALLOY DIRECTORY. 1984. irreg. £27.50($66) Metal Bulletin Books Ltd., Park House, Park Terrace, Worcester Park, Surrey KT4 7HY, England (Dist. in U.S. by: Metal Bulletin Inc., 220 Fifth Ave., New York, NY 10001) Ed. Danielle Donougher. adv.

671 UK ISSN 0071-5182
FINISHING HANDBOOK AND DIRECTORY. 1950. a. free to subscribers of monthly Product Finishing. Sawell Publications Ltd., 127, Stanstead Road, London SE23 1JE, England. Ed. R.S. Capp. adv. circ. 4,192.

669 PL ISSN 0208-578X
FIZYKA I CHEMIA METALI. (Text and summaries in English, Polish, Russian) 1976. irreg. price varies. Uniwersytet Slaski w Katowicach, Ul. Bankowa 14, 40-007 Katowice, Poland.

699 US
FOUNDRY DATABOOK & CATALOG FILE. 1970/71. a. $10. Penton Publishing, 1100 Superior Ave., Cleveland, OH 44114. TEL 216-696-7000. adv. circ. 24,000. (reprint service avail. from UMI)
Formerly: Foundry Catalog File (ISSN 0533-005X)

METALLURGY

669   UK   ISSN 0071-8130
FOUNDRY DIRECTORY AND REGISTER OF FORGES. 1959. biennial, latest edt. 1985. £27.50($66) Metal Bulletin Books Ltd., Park House, 3 Park Terr., Worcester Park, Surrey KT4 7HY, England (Dist. in U.S. by: Metal Bulletin Inc., 220 Fifth Ave., New York, NY 10001)

671.2   UK   ISSN 0306-4212
FOUNDRY YEARBOOK. 1972. a. £32. Fuel and Metallurgical Journals Ltd., Queensway House, 2 Queensway, Redhill, Surrey RH1 1QS, England. Ed. R. Sansom. adv. charts. tr.lit. circ. 3,000.
Founding

669   GE
FREIBERGER FORSCHUNGSHEFTE. MONTANWISSENSCHAFTEN: REIHE B. METALLURGIE UND WERSTOFFTECHNIK. 1951. irreg. price varies. (Bergakademie Freiberg) VEB Deutscher Verlag fuer Grundstoffindustrie, Karl-Heine-Str. 27, DDR-7031 Leipzig, E. Germany (D.D.R.) Indexed: Met.Abstr. World Alum.Abstr.
Formerly: Freiberger Forschungshefte. Montanwissenschaften: Reihe B. Metallurgie (ISSN 0071-9420)

GENERAL COMMISSION ON SAFETY AND HEALTH IN THE IRON AND STEEL INDUSTRY. REPORT. see *INDUSTRIAL HEALTH AND SAFETY*

GEOLOGICAL, MINING AND METALLURGICAL SOCIETY OF INDIA. BULLETIN. see *EARTH SCIENCES — Geology*

669   GW   ISSN 0340-8175
GIESSEREI-KALENDER. 1954. a. (Verein Deutscher Giessereifachleute) Giesserei-Verlag GmbH, Sohnstr. 65, 4000 Duesseldorf 1, W. Germany (B.R.D.)

620.112   UK   ISSN 0143-6082
GUIDES TO PRACTICE IN CORROSION CONTROL. 1978. irreg. Department of Industry, 1 Victoria St., London S.W.1., England.

669 540   US
I L Z R O ANNUAL REVIEW. 1963. a. free. International Lead Zinc Research Organization, Inc., 292 Madison Ave., New York, NY 10017. TEL 212-532-2373. Ed. A.L. Ponikvar. bibl. charts. illus. pat. stat. circ. 1,500.
Former titles: I L Z R O Annual Research Review.

669 540   US   ISSN 0146-7980
I L Z R O LEAD RESEARCH DIGEST. (Editions in French and Japanese) 1963. irreg., latest no.40, 1984. free. International Lead Zinc Research Organization, Inc., 292 Madison Ave., New York, NY 10017. TEL 212-532-2373. Ed. A.L. Ponikvar. bibl. charts. illus. pat. stat. circ. 3,500. Indexed: Met.Abstr.

669 540   US
I L Z R O ZINC/CADIUM RESEARCH DIGEST. (Editions in French and Japanese) 1963. a. free. International Lead Zinc Research Organization, Inc., 292 Madison Ave., New York, NY 10017. TEL 212-532-2373. Ed. A.L. Ponikvar. bibl. charts. illus. pat. stat. circ. 4,500. Indexed: Met.Abstr.
Formerly: I L Z R O Zinc Research Digest (ISSN 0146-7999)

669   II
INDIAN INSTITUTE OF METALS. PROCEEDINGS. irreg. Indian Institute of Metals, 2 Sambhunath Pandit St., Calcutta 700020, India. Indexed: Chem.Abstr.

669.1   MX
INDUSTRIA SIDERURGICA EN MEXICO. 1981. a. price varies. Instituto Nacional de Estadistica, Geografia e Informatica, Secretaria de Programacion y Presupuesto, Patriotismo 711 Torre "A" P.H., Col. San Juan Mixcoac, Deleg. Benito Juarez, 03910 Mexico, D.F., Mexico TEL 598-99-05. (Subscr. to: Rio Rhin No. 56, Col. Cuauhtemoc, 06500 Mexico, D.F., Mexico)

669   SW   ISSN 0015-7953
INSTITUTET FOER METALLFORSKNING. FORSKNINGSVERKSAMHETEN. 1952. a. free. Institutet foer Metallforskning - Swedish Institute for Metals Research, Drottning Kristinas Vaeg 48, S-114 28 Stockholm, Sweden. Ed. Rune Lagneborg. bibl.illus. circ. 2,400.

669   US   ISSN 0361-3070
INSTRUMENTATION IN THE MINING AND METALLURGY INDUSTRIES. 1975. irreg. price varies. Instrument Society of America, 67 Alexander Dr., Box 12277, Research Triangle Park, NC 27709. TEL 919-549-8411. (reprint service avail. from UMI, ISI and publisher) Indexed: Chem.Abstr.
Formerly: I S A Mining and Metallurgy Instrumentation Symposium. Proceedings.

669.4   UK   ISSN 0074-316X
INTERNATIONAL CONFERENCE ON LEAD. PROCEEDINGS. 1962. triennial, 7th, 1980, Madrid; 8th, 1983, Hague. Lead Development Association, 34 Berkeley Sq., London W1X 6AJ, England. Ed. A.T. Hughes. circ. 1,000.

620.112   GW   ISSN 0074-4123
INTERNATIONAL CONGRESS ON METALLIC CORROSION. (PROCEEDINGS) 1961. triennial (10th, 1987) DM.250. (International Corrosion Council) National Research Council Canada, Publication Sales and Ditribution, Ottawa, Ontario K1A 0R6, Canada.

669 692.1   US   ISSN 0074-6118
INTERNATIONAL FOUNDRY CONGRESS. PAPERS AND COMMUNICATIONS.* (Papers published in host countries) a., 39th, 1972, Philadelphia. Inquire: American Foundrymen's Society, Golf & Wolf Roads, Des Plaines, IL 60016. Indexed: Chem.Abstr.

338.2 672   BE   ISSN 0074-6630
INTERNATIONAL IRON AND STEEL INSTITUTE. REPORT OF CONFERENCE PROCEEDINGS. 1967. a., latest 18th, 1984 Chicago. 1000 Fr. ‡ International Iron and Steel Institute, 12-14 av. Hamoir, B-1080 Brussels, Belgium.

671.3   SZ   ISSN 0074-6983
INTERNATIONAL METALWORKERS' CONGRESS. REPORTS. quadrenial, 26th, 1985, Tokyo, Japan. $10. International Metalworkers' Federation, 54 bis, Rte. des Acacias, 1227 Geneva, Switzerland.

671.37   US   ISSN 0074-7513
INTERNATIONAL POWDER METALLURGY CONFERENCE. PROCEEDINGS-MODERN DEVELOPMENTS IN POWDER METALLURGY. 1960. triennial since 1973; 5th, Chicago. price varies. Metal Powder Industries Federation, 105 College Road East, Princeton, NJ 08540. TEL 609-452-7700. circ. 1,000. (reprint service avail. from UMI)

669.6   UK
INTERNATIONAL TIN RESEARCH INSTITUTE. ANNUAL REPORT. 1938. a. free. International Tin Research Institute, Kingston Lane, Uxbridge, Middlesex UB8 3PJ, England TEL (0895) 72406. (Subscr. to: Tin Research Institute, Inc., 1353 Perry St., Columbus, Ohio 43201) Ed. C.J. Evans. circ. 5, 000. Indexed: Met.Abstr. World Alum.Abstr.
Formerly: International Tin Research Council. Annual Report (ISSN 0074-9125)

669   UK   ISSN 0140-8402
IRON & MANGANESE ORES SURVEY. 1978. irreg. £15($36) Metal Bulletin PLC, Park House, 3 Park Terrace, Worcester Park, Surrey, England (Dist. in U.S. by: Metal Bulletin Inc., 220 Fifth Ave., New York, NY 10001)

669   UK
IRON & STEEL INDUSTRY IN CHINA; prospects and perspectives. 1981. irreg. £70($168) Metal Bulletin PLC, Park House, 3 Park Terrace, Worcester Park, Surrey KT4 7HY, England (Dist. in U.S. by: Metal Bulletin Inc., 220 Fifth Ave., New York, NY 10001)

669.1   UK   ISSN 0075-0875
IRON AND STEEL WORKS OF THE WORLD. 1952. irreg., 8th edt., 1983. £60($144) Metal Bulletin Books Ltd., Park House, 3 Park Terr., Worcester Park, Surrey KT4 7HY, England (Dist. in U.S. by: Metal Bulletin Inc., 220 5th Ave., New York, NY 10001) Ed.Bd. adv.

669.1   UK   ISSN 0950-2548
IRON ORE DATABOOK. 1986. irreg. £40($96) Metal Bulletin Books Ltd., Park House, 3 Park Terrace, Worcester Park, Surrey KT4 7HY, England (Distr. in U.S. by: Metal Bulletin Inc., 220 Fifth Ave., New York, NY 10001) Ed. Henry Cooke.

669.142   BG
ISPAT. (Text in Bengali or English) 1973. a. free. Chittagong Steel Mills Ltd., Box 429, Chittagong, Bangladesh. Ed.Bd. adv. circ. 2,500.

620.112   UR   ISSN 0202-7976
ITOGI NAUKI I TEKHNIKI: KORROZIYA I ZASHCHITA OT KORROZII. irreg., latest vol.13, 1987. price varies. Vsesoyuznyi Institut Nauchno-Tekhnicheskoi Informatsii (VINITI), Ul. Baltiiskaya 14, Moscow A-219, Russian S.F.S.R., U.S.S.R. (Subscr. to: Mezhdunarodnaya Kniga, Dimitrova ul. 39, 113095 Moscow, Russian S.F.S.R., U.S.S.R.) Indexed: Chem.Abstr.

669   UR   ISSN 0202-7739
ITOGI NAUKI I TEKHNIKI: METALLOVEDENIE I TERMICHESKAYA OBRABOTKA. irreg., latest vol.21, 1987. price varies. Vsesoyuznyi Institut Nauchno-Tekhnicheskoi Informatsii (VINITI), Ul. Baltiiskaya 14, Moscow A-219, Russian S.F.S.R., U.S.S.R. (Subscr. to: Mezhdunarodnaya Kniga, Dimitrova ul. 39, 113095 Moscow, Russian S.F.S.R., U.S.S.R.) Indexed: Chem.Abstr.

669   UR   ISSN 0202-7755
ITOGI NAUKI I TEKHNIKI: METALLURGICHESKAYA TEPLOTEKHNIKA; oborudovanie, izmerenie, kontrol' i avtomatizatsiyu v metallurgicheskom proizvodstve. irreg., latest vol.7, 1986. price varies. Vsesoyuznyi Institut Nauchno-Tekhnicheskoi Informatsii (VINITI), Ul. Baltiiskaya 14, Moscow A-219, Russian S.F.S.R., U.S.S.R. (Subscr. to: Mezhdunarodnaya Kniga, Dimitrova ul. 39, 113095 Moscow, Russian S.F.S.R., U.S.S.R.) Indexed: Chem.Abstr.

669   UR   ISSN 0202-7747
ITOGI NAUKI I TEKHNIKI: METALLURGIYA TSVETNYKH METALLOV. irreg., latest vol.17, 1987. price varies. Vsesoyuznyi Institut Nauchno-Tekhnicheskoi Informatsii (VINITI), Ul. Baltiiskaya 14, Moscow A-219, Russian S.F.S.R., U.S.S.R. (Subscr. to: Mezhdunarodnaya Kniga, Dimitrova ul. 39, 113095 Moscow, Russian S.F.S.R., U.S.S.R.) Indexed: Chem.Abstr.

669   GW   ISSN 0075-2819
JAHRBUCH OBERFLAECHENTECHNIK (YEAR) a. DM.90. Metall-Verlag GmbH, Hubertusallee 18, 1000 Berlin 33, W. Germany (B.R.D.) Ed.Bd. adv. circ. 4,200. Indexed: Chem.Abstr.

672   GW   ISSN 0724-8482
JAHRBUCH STAHL. 1951. a. DM.28. (Verein Deutscher Eisenhuettenleute) Verlag Stahleisen mbH, Sohnstr. 65, Postfach 8229, 4000 Duesseldorf 1, W. Germany (B.R.D.)
Former titles: Stahleisen Kalender (ISSN 0081-4180); Taschenbuch fuer die Stahlindustrie.

669   JA
JAPAN STEEL WORKS TECHNICAL NEWS. (Text in European languages) 1961. irreg. exchange basis. Japan Steel Works, Ltd. - Nihon Seikosho, 1-12 Yuraku-cho, Chiyoda-ku, Tokyo 100, Japan.

669.6   UK
JAPAN - TIN IN TINPLATE. 1984. irreg. £15. International Tin Council, 1 Oxendon St., London SW1Y 4EQ, England.

669.2   JA   ISSN 0075-3475
JAPAN'S IRON AND STEEL INDUSTRY. (Text in English) 1951. a. $19. Kawata Publicity Inc. - Kawata Paburishiti K. K., Central Box 1157, Tokyo 100-91, Japan. Ed Sukeyuki Kawata. adv. circ. 7, 500.

669   GW
KORROSIONSVERHALTEN VON ZINK. irreg., vol.4, 1977. DM.8.50. (Zinkberatung e.V.) Metall-Verlag GmbH, Hubertusallee 18, 1000 Berlin 33, W. Germany (B.R.D.)

669   UR   ISSN 0302-9069
LITEINOE PROIZVODSTVO, METALLOVEDENIE I OBRABOTKA METALLOV DAVLENIEM. irreg. 0.47 Rub. (Krasnoyarskii Institut Tsvetnykh Metallov) Krasnoyarskoe Knizhnoe Izdatel'stvo, Prospekt Mira, 89, Krasnoyarsk, Russian S.F.S.R., U.S.S.R. illus. Indexed: Chem.Abstr.

M.T.I.A. ANNUAL REPORT. (Metal Trades Industry Association of Australia) see *BUSINESS AND ECONOMICS — Labor And Industrial Relations*

METALLURGY 799

671 382 AT
M T I A N E G'S EXPORT NOTE PAD. 1969. irreg. Aus.$1. Metal Trades Industry Association National Export Group, National Office, 51 Walker St., North Sydney, NSW 2060, Australia. Ed. S.K. Myatt. adv. circ. 800.
Formerly: Australian Metal Trades Export Group's Export Note Pad.

338.4 US ISSN 0095-7976
MATERIALS PERFORMANCE BUYER'S GUIDE; the corrosion control products/services purchasing directory. 1940? a. $15. National Association of Corrosion Engineers, Box 218340, Houston, TX 77218. TEL 713-492-0535. adv. circ. 16,500.

669 US
MATERIALS RESEARCH AND ENGINEERING/ REINE UND ANGEWANDTE METALLKUNDE. 1980. irreg., latest 1986. price varies. Springer-Verlag, 175 Fifth Ave, New York, NY 10010 TEL 212-460-1500. (Also Berlin, Heidelberg, Tokyo and Vienna) Ed. B. Ilschner. (reprint service avail. from ISI)
Supersedes (1948-1976): Reine und Angewandte Metallkunde in Einzeldarstellungen (ISSN 0080-0791)

669 338.2 UK ISSN 0269-1698
METAL BULLETIN PRICES & DATA BOOK. 1968. a. £20($48) Metal Bulletin Books Ltd., Park House, 3 Park Terr., Worcester Park, Surrey, England (Dist. in U.S. by: Metal Bulletin Inc., 220 Fifth Ave., New York, NY 10001) Ed. R. Packard. adv. (back issues avail.)
Formerly (until 1986): Metal Bulletin Handbook (ISSN 0262-6454); Supersedes: Quin's Metal Handbook.

METAL-CENTER NEWS' METAL DISTRIBUTION. see BUSINESS AND ECONOMICS — Trade And Industrial Directories

381 US ISSN 0098-2210
METAL DISTRIBUTION. 1975. a. $10. (Metal Center News) Fairchild Publications, Inc., 7 E. 12th St., New York, NY 10003. TEL 212-741-4000. Ed. Joseph C. Marino. adv. illus. circ. 13,000.

669 US
METAL FINISHING GUIDEBOOK & DIRECTORY. 1932. a. $5.95. Metals and Plastics Publications, Inc., One University Plaza, Hackensack, NJ 07601. TEL 201-487-3700. Ed. Michael Murphy. adv. circ. 15,000.

METAL MARKETING CORPORATION OF ZAMBIA. ANNUAL REPORT. see BUSINESS AND ECONOMICS — Marketing And Purchasing

669 671 US ISSN 0076-6658
METAL STATISTICS. 1904. a. $65. Fairchild Publications, Inc., Metal Statistics (Subsidiary of: Capital Cities Media, Inc.) 7 East 12th St., New York, NY 10003. TEL 212-741-4140. adv. circ. 13,000.

669 UK ISSN 0143-7607
METAL TRADERS OF THE WORLD. 1980. irreg., 3rd edt., 1986. £45($108) Metal Bulletin Books Ltd., Park House, 3 Park Terrace, Worcester Park, Surrey KT4 7HY, England (Dist. in U.S. by: Metal Bulletin Inc., 220 Fifth Ave., New York, NY 10001) Ed. David Gilbertson. adv.

669 GW ISSN 0369-2345
METALLGESELLSCHAFT AKTIENGESELLSCHAFT. REVIEW OF THE ACTIVITIES. (Text in English and German) 1929; N.S. 1959. a. Metallgesellschaft AG, Volkswirtschaftliche Abteilung, Reuterweg 14, 6000 Frankfurt 1, W. Germany (B.R.D.) Eds. Hans Schreiber, Sylvia Noske. bibl. charts. illus. circ. 7,000. Indexed: Chem.Abstr. Eng.Ind. Met.Abstr.

669 II ISSN 0369-061X
METALLURGICAL ENGINEER. (Text in English) 1969. a. free or on exchange basis. (Metallurgical Engineering Association) Indian Institute of Technology, Bombay, Powai, Bombay, India. Ed. P. Ramakrishnan. adv. Indexed: Chem.Abstr. Eng.Ind. Met.Abstr. World Alum.Abstr.

669 UK ISSN 0308-7794
METALLURGICAL PLANTMAKERS OF THE WORLD. 1973. irreg., latest edt. 1981. £33($79) Metal Bulletin Books Ltd., Park House, Park Terr., Worcester Park, Surrey KT4 7HY, England (Dist. in U.S. by: Metal Bulletin Inc., 220 Fifth Ave., New York, NY 10001) Ed. R. Serjeantson. adv.

669 671.52 FR
METALLURGIE. LEXIQUE. (Text in English, French and German) 1978. a. 400 F.($420) Centre National de la Recherche Scientifique, Centre de Documentation Scientifique et Technique, 26 rue Boyer, 75971 Paris Cedex 20, France.

669 UK
METALLURGY AND MATERIAL SCIENCE. 1981. irreg. price varies. Edward Arnold (Publishers) Ltd., 41 Bedford Square, London WC1B 3DQ, England.

669 US ISSN 0094-5447
METALLURGY - MATERIALS EDUCATION YEARBOOK. (American Society for Metals) a. $20. A S M International, Materials Information, Metals Park, OH 44073. TEL 216-338-5151.

669 US
METALMECHANICS: LATIN AMERICAN INDUSTRIAL REPORT. (Avail. for each of 22 Latin American countries) 1985. a. $435 per country report per industry covered. Aurora International, Box 9099, Bridgeport, CT 06601-2099. TEL 203-368-0579. Ed. Andres C. Aquino.

METALURGIA. see ANTHROPOLOGY

669 AG
METALURGICA MODERNA. biennial. Sociedad Argentina de Metales, Santa Fe 1145, Buenos Aires, Argentina.

669 UK ISSN 0140-8399
MINOR METALS SURVEY. 1978. irreg., latest edt. 1981. £15($36) Metal Bulletin PLC, Park House, 3 Park Terrace, Worcester Park, Surrey, England (Dist. in U.S. by: Metal Bulletin Inc., 220 Fifth Ave., New York, NY 10001) adv. Indexed: GeoRef.

620.112 US
MOLY CORROSION INHIBITORS. 1981. a. Amax Specialty Chemicals, Box 1568, Ann Arbor, MI 48105. TEL 313-761-2300.

669 US ISSN 0730-9163
MOLYSULFIDE NEWSLETTER. 1956. irreg. free. Amax Specialty Chemical, Techical Information Department, 1600 Huron Parkway, Ann Arbor, MI 48105. TEL 313-761-2300. Ed. Kurt Miska. bk. rev. circ. 10,000.

672 UR
MOSKOVSKII INSTITUT STALI I SPLAVOV. NAUCHNYE TRUDY. 1972. irreg. 0.85 Rub. Izdatel'stvo Metallurgiya, 2-i Obydenskii Per., 14, Moscow G-34, Russian S.F.S.R., U.S.S.R. illus. Indexed: Chem.Abstr.

669 658.5 US ISSN 0077-3379
N A M F MANAGEMENT MANUAL.* 1960. irreg. $100 to non-members; members $25. National Association of Metal Finishers, 111 E. Wacker Dr., Chicago, IL 60601. TEL 312-644-6610. Ed. J.D. Carey. index.

NCHANGA CONSOLIDATED COPPER MINES LTD. ANNUAL REPORT AND ACCOUNTS. see MINES AND MINING INDUSTRY

671.37 US
NEW PERSPECTIVES IN POWDER METALLURGY. 1966. irreg., vol.7, 1980. price varies. Metal Powder Industries Federation, 105 College Road East, Princeton, NJ 08540. TEL 609-452-7700. circ. 1,000.
Formerly: Perspectives in Powder Metallurgy (ISSN 0079-1032)

669.1 JA
NIPPON STEEL REPORT. a. Nippon Steel Corporation, 2-6-3 Otemachi, Chiyoda-ku, Tokyo 100, Japan (U.S. address: 345 Park Ave., 41st Floor, New York, NY 10154)

669 US ISSN 0360-9553
NON-FERROUS METAL DATA. 1920. a. $120. American Bureau of Metal Statistics Inc., Box 1405, Plaza Sta., 400 Plaza Dr., Secaucus, NJ 07094-1405. TEL 201-863-6900. Ed. William J. Lambert. cum.index. circ. 3,000.
Formerly (until 1974): American Bureau of Metal Statistics. Year Book (ISSN 0065-7611)

673 UK ISSN 0078-0987
NON-FERROUS METAL WORKS OF THE WORLD. 1967. irreg., latest edt. 1985. £60($144) Metal Bulletin Books Ltd., Park House, Park Terr., Worcester Park, Surrey KT4 7HY, England (Dist. in U.S. by: Metal Bulletin Inc., 220 Fifth Ave., New York, NY 10001) Ed. R. Serjeantson. adv.

NORTH CAROLINA METALWORKING DIRECTORY. see BUSINESS AND ECONOMICS — Trade And Industrial Directories

669 UR
NOVYE ISSLEDOVANIYA V KHIMII, METALLURGII I OBOGASHCHENII. (Subseries of: Gornyi Institut, Leningrad. Nauchnye Trudy) irreg. 0.75 Rub. Leningradskii Gornyi Institut, Leningrad, Russian S.F.S.R., U.S.S.R. illus.

671 UR
OCHISTKA VODNOGO I VOZDUSHNOGO BASSEINOV NA PREDPRIYATIYAKH CHERNOI METALLURGII. irreg. 1.12 Rub.($18.60) Izdatel'stvo Metallurgiya, 2-i Obydenskii Per., 14, Moscow G-34, Russian S.F.S.R., U.S.S.R. (Co-sponsor: Ministerstvo Chernoi Metallurgii) illus. Indexed: Chem.Abstr.

669 GW ISSN 0078-3420
OERLIKON SCHWEISSMITTEILUNGEN. 1955. irreg. free. Oerlikon Elektrodenfabrik Eisenberg GmbH, 6719 Eisenberg/Pfalz, W. Germany (B.R.D.) (Co-sponsor: Schweissindustrie Oerlikon Buehrle AG, Zurich) Ed. K. Weigel. circ. 5,000. Indexed: Chem.Abstr. BMT.

338.47 672 FR ISSN 0474-5973
ORGANIZATION FOR ECONOMIC COOPERATION AND DEVELOPMENT. SPECIAL COMMITTEE FOR IRON AND STEEL. IRON AND STEEL INDUSTRY. 1953/54. irreg. $10. Organization for Economic Cooperation and Development, 2 rue Andre Pascal, 75016 Paris, France (U.S. orders to: O.E.C.D. Publications and Information Center. 1750 Pennsylvania Ave., N.W., Washington, D. C. 20006) (also avail. in microfiche)

669 US
ORGANOMETALLIC SYNTHESES. 1965. irreg., vol.2, 1982. Academic Press, Inc., Orlando, FL 32887. TEL 305-345-2000. Eds. John J. Eisch, R. Bruce King.

669 PL ISSN 0372-9699
POLITECHNIKA CZESTOCHOWSKA. ZESZYTY NAUKOWE. NAUKI TECHNICZNE. HUTNICTWO. (Text in Polish; summaries in English and Russian) 1969. irreg. Politechnika Czestochowska, Ul. Deglera 31, 42-200 Czestochowa, Poland (Dist. by: Ars Polona-Ruch, Krakowskie Przedmiescie 7, Warsaw, Poland) Ed. Stefan Szymura. Indexed: Chem.Abstr. Met.Abstr.

669 PL ISSN 0324-802X
POLITECHNIKA SLASKA. ZESZYTY NAUKOWE. HUTNICTWO. (Text in Polish; summaries in English and Russian) 1971. irreg. price varies. Politechnika Slaska, W. Pstrowskiego 7, 44-100 Gliwice, Poland (Dist. by: Ars Polona, Krakowskie Przedmiescie 7, 00-068 Warsaw, Poland) Ed. Izabella Hyla. circ. 200. Indexed: Chem.Abstr. Met.Abstr.

669 PL ISSN 0079-3345
POLSKA AKADEMIA NAUK. ODDZIAL W KRAKOWIE. KOMISJA METALURGICZNO-ODLEWNICZA. PRACE: METALURGIA. (Text in English and Polish; summaries in English and Russian) 1965. irreg., no.34, 1986. price varies. Ossolineum, Publishing House of the Polish Academy of Sciences, Rynek 9, Wroclaw, Poland (Dist. by: Ars Polona-Ruch, Krakowskie Przedmiescie 7, Warsaw, Poland) Ed. Czeslaw Podrzucki. circ. 500. Indexed: Chem.Abstr. Eng.Ind.
Formerly: Polska Akademia Nauk. Komisja Metalurgiiodlewnia. Metalurgia.

669 UR ISSN 0136-3557
POLUTEHNILINE INSTITUUT TALLINN.
SVOISTVA I TEKHNOLOGIYA
IZGOTOVLENIYA IZNOSOSTOIKIKH
MATERIALOV. (Subseries of its Toimetised) (Text in Russian; summaries in English or German) irreg. price varies. Polutehniline Instituut Tallinn, Ehitajate tee 5, Tallinn, Estonian S.S.R., U.S.S.R.

669 US ISSN 0149-3922
POWDER METALLURGY IN DEFENSE TECHNOLOGY. irreg. Metal Powder Industries Federation, 105 College Rd. East, Princeton, NJ 08540. TEL 609-452-7700.

669 NE
PROCESS METALLURGY. 1978. irreg., vol.3, 1984. price varies. Elsevier Science Publishers B.V., Box 211, 1000 AE Amsterdam, Netherlands. Eds. G.M. Ritcey, A.W. Ashbrook.

PRODUKTIONS NYTS LEVERANDOERREGISTER. see MACHINERY

671 US ISSN 0079-6719
PROGRESS IN POWDER METALLURGY; P-M Technical Conference proceedings. 1947. a. Metal Powder Industries Federation, 105 College Road East, Princeton, NJ 08540. TEL 609-452-7700. Indexed: Chem.Abstr.

669 HU ISSN 0324-4679
PUBLICATIONS OF THE TECHNICAL UNIVERSITY FOR HEAVY INDUSTRY. SERIES B, METALLURGY. (Text in English, German, Russian) irreg., vol.35, no.1-4, 1982. Nehezipari Muszaki Egyetem, Miskolc, Hungary. Ed.Bd. bibl. index. circ. 400. Indexed: Met.Abstr.

669 IT ISSN 0080-1216
REPERTORIO DELLE INDUSTRIE SIDERURGICHE ITALIANE. 1949. quinquennial. L.32000. Associazione Industrie Siderurgiche Italiane, Piazza Velasca 8, 20122 Milan, Italy. adv. circ. 1,000.

669 DK ISSN 0108-8599
RISOE INTERNATIONAL SYMPOSIUM ON METALLURGY AND MATERIALS SCIENCE. PROCEEDINGS. 1980. a. Kr.400. Risoe National Laboratory, P.O. Box 49, DK-4000 Roskilde, Denmark.

671 669 UK ISSN 0080-505X
RYLAND'S DIRECTORY. a. £38. Fuel and Metallurgical Journals Ltd., Queensway House, 2 Queensway, Redhill, Surrey RH1 1QS, England (Distr. by: Guardian Communications Ltd., Albany House, Hurst St., Birmingham B5 4BD, England) adv.

669 SZ
S M U V ZEITUNG. vol.72, 1973. irreg. 35 Fr. Schweizerischer Metall- und Uhrenarbeitnehmer-Verband - Federation Suisse des Travailleurs de la Metallurgie et de l'Horlogerie, Postfach 272, CH-3000 Bern 15, Switzerland. Ed.Bd. adv. bk. rev. charts. illus. (newspaper)

620.1 DK ISSN 0581-9431
SCANDINAVIAN CORROSION CONGRESS. PROCEEDINGS. (Text in English) 1954. irreg., no.10, 1986 (approx. triennial) $20. Korrosionscentralen, ATV, Park Alle 345, DK-2600 Glostrup, Denmark.

669 UK ISSN 0305-7798
SHEET METAL INDUSTRIES YEAR BOOK. a. £32. Fuel and Metallurgical Journals Ltd., Queensways House, 2 Queensway, Redhill, Surrey RH1 1QS, England. Ed. R. Sansom. adv. bibl. index.

669.142 BL
SIDERURGIA BRASILEIRA S.A. RELATORIO DE DIRETORIA. 1973. a. free. Siderurgia Brasileira S.A., Setor de Autarquias sul, Quadra 2, Bloco E, 70070 Brasilia, Brazil. illus. circ. 5,000.

669.23 336 US ISSN 0066-4332
SILVER MARKET. 1916. a. free. ‡ Handy and Harman, 850 Third Ave., New York, NY 10022. TEL 212-752-3400. Ed. Stephen Mudd. circ. 10, 000.

669 US
SOURCE JOURNALS IN METALS AND MATERIALS. 1981. biennial. $47.50. (Materials Information) A S M International, Metals Park, OH 44073. TEL 216-338-5151. Ed. W.A. Weida.
Formerly: Source Journals in Metallurgy.

669 US
SOURCES. 1962. a. $35. American Metal Stamping Association, 27027 Chardon Rd., Richmond Heights, OH 44143. adv. circ. 14,500.
Former titles: Sources for Stamping; (until 1979): Metal Stamping Buyer's Guide.

669 622 SA
SOUTH AFRICAN INSTITUTE OF MINING AND METALLURGY. MONOGRAPH SERIES. 1978. irreg. price varies. South African Institute of Mining and Metallurgy, Box 61019, Marshallton 2107, South Africa. Indexed: GeoRef.

669 UK
STAINLESS STEEL: AN INTERNATIONAL SURVEY AND DIRECTORY. 1957. irreg., latest edt. 1985. £27.75($66.60) Metal Bulletin PLC, Park House, Park Terrace, Worcester Park, Surrey KT4 7HY, England (Dist. in U.S. by: Metal Bulletin Inc., 220 Fifth Ave., New York, NY 10001) Eds. Milton Nurse, Debbie Hargreaves. adv.
Formerly: Stainless Steel: An International Directory (ISSN 0143-5442)

669.142 UK
STAINLESS STEEL DIRECTORY. 1975. biennial. £10.50. Modern Metals Publications Ltd., 14 Knoll Rd., Dorking, Surrey RH4 3EW, England. Ed. K.T. Rowland. adv. circ. 700.
Formerly: Directory of the Stainless Steel Industry.

669 AT ISSN 0085-6657
STANDARDS FOR AUSTRALIAN ALUMINIUM MILL PRODUCTS. (Metric Edition) irreg. Aus.$1. Aluminium Development Council of Australia, 99 Elizabeth St., Sydney, N.S.W. 2000, Australia.

669 US
STEEL AND AMERICA; an annual report. 1982. a. American Iron and Steel Institute, 1000 16th St. N.W., Washington, DC 20036. charts. illus. stat.

669.1 UN
STEEL MARKET. 1953. a. $16.50. (Economic Commission for Europe (ECE)) United Nations Publications, Room DC2-0853, New York, NY 10017 (Or Distribution and Sales Section, Palais des Nations, 1211 Geneva 10, Switzerland)

669 UK ISSN 0308-8006
STEEL TRADERS OF THE WORLD. 1976. irreg., latest edt. 1986. £45($108) Metal Bulletin Books Ltd., Park House, 3 Park Terrace, Worcester Park, Surrey KT4 7HY, England (Dist. in U.S. by: Metal Bulletin Inc., 220 Fifth Ave., New York, NY 10001) Ed. John Bailey. adv.

STEELMAKING CONFERENCE: PROCEEDINGS. see MINES AND MINING INDUSTRY

669.1 SW
SWEDISH STEEL MANUAL. (Text and summaries in English) 1962. irreg. Jernkontoret - Swedish Ironmasters' Association, Box 1721, S-111 87 Stockholm, Sweden. Ed. Hans von Delwig.

669 GW ISSN 0082-1772
TASCHENBUCH DER GIESSEREI-PRAXIS. 1952. a. DM.42. Fachverlag Schiele und Schoen GmbH, Markgrafenstr. 11, 1000 Berlin 61, W. Germany (B.R.D.) Ed. E. Brunhuber. adv. circ. 5,000.

669 GW ISSN 0494-9390
TECHNISCHE MITTEILUNGEN KRUPP. (Published in two parts) (Editions in English and German) 1986. irreg. (2-4/yr.) free. Friedrich Krupp GmbH, Postfach 10 22 52, 4300 Essen 1, W. Germany (B.R.D.) charts. illus. index. circ. 4,000. Indexed: Chem.Abstr. Eng.Ind. Met.Abstr. World Alum.Abstr.
Supersedes (1920-1986?): Technische Mitteilungen Krupp. Forschungsberichte; Technische Mitteilungen Krupp. Werksberichte.

669.6 UK
TIN PRODUCTION AND INVESTMENT. 1979. irreg. £40. International Tin Council, 1 Oxendon St., London SW1Y 4EQ, England.

669 UK ISSN 0264-8199
TRADING IN METALS. 1983. irreg. £25($60) Metal Bulletin Books Ltd., Park House, 3 Park Terrace, Worcester Park, Surrey KT4 7HY, England (Distr. in U.S. by: Metal Bulletin Inc., 220 Fifth Ave., New York, NY 10001) Eds. Trevor Tarrin, Peter Robbins.

TRANSACTIONS OF THE MONUMENTAL BRASS SOCIETY. see ARCHAEOLOGY

U S S R REPORT: MACHINE TOOLS AND METAL-WORKING EQUIPMENT. see MACHINERY

669.6 UK
UNITED KINGDOM - TIN IN TINPLATE. 1981. irreg. £10. International Tin Council, 1 Oxendon St., London SW1Y 4EQ, England.

669.6 UK
UNITED STATES OF AMERICA - TIN IN TINPLATE. 1983. irreg. £15. International Tin Council, 1 Oxendon St., London SW1Y 4EQ, England.

UNIVERSIDAD AUTONOMA DE SAN LUIS POTOSI. INSTITUTO DE GEOLOGIA Y METALURGIA. FOLLETO TECNICO. see EARTH SCIENCES — Geology

669 AT ISSN 0085-4018
UNIVERSITY OF NEW SOUTH WALES. METALLURGICAL SOCIETY. METALLURGICAL REVIEW. 1956/57. a. free. ‡ University of New South Wales, Metallurgical Society, Box 1, Kensington, N.S.W. 2033, Australia. Ed. B.J. Gale. adv. circ. 1,500. Indexed: Aus.P.A.I.S.

669 CS ISSN 0042-3726
VYSOKA SKOLA BANSKA. SBORNIK VEDECKYCH PRACI: RADA HUTNICKA/ INSTITUTE OF MINING AND METALLURGY. TRANSACTIONS: METALLURGICAL SERIES. (Text in Czech; summaries in English, German, Russian) 1955. irreg. (2-8/yr.) 25 Kcs.($1) per issue. Statni Pedagogicke Nakladatelstvi, Ostrovni 30, 113 01 Prague 1, Czechoslovakia. bk. rev. abstr. bibl. charts. illus. stat. index. Indexed: Met.Abstr. Fuel & Energy Abstr. Geo.Abstr. World Alum.Abstr.

671.2 JA ISSN 0511-1927
WASEDA UNIVERSITY. CASTING RESEARCH LABORATORY. REPORT. (Text in English) 1950. a. exchange basis. Waseda University, Casting Research Laboratory - Waseda Daigaku Imono Kenkyushitsu, 1-500 Totsuka-cho, Shinjuku-ku, Tokyo 160, Japan. Indexed: Chem.Abstr. Met.Abstr.

671.8 UK ISSN 0084-0424
WIRE INDUSTRY YEARBOOK; international buyers guide. (Text in English, French, German, Italian and Spanish) 1951. a. £24.50. Magnum Publications Ltd., 110-112 Station Rd. E., Oxted, Surrey RH8 0QA, England. Ed. P.A. Clayton. adv. circ. 5,702.

WIRE TECHNOLOGY BUYER'S GUIDE. see BUSINESS AND ECONOMICS — Trade And Industrial Directories

669 658.8 UK ISSN 0144-5960
WOLFF'S GUIDE TO THE LONDON METAL EXCHANGE. 1976. irreg., latest 1987. Metal Bulletin PLC, Park House, Park Terrace, Worcester Park, Surrey KT4 7HY, England. (Co-publisher: Rudolf Wolff and Co. Ltd.)

669 UK
WORLD ALUMINIUM SURVEY. 1954. irreg., latest edt. 1981. £20($48) Metal Bulletin PLC, Park House, Park Terrace, Worcester Park, Surrey KT4 7HY, England (Dist. in U.S. by: Metal Bulletin Inc., 220 Fifth Ave., New York, NY 10001) Ed. Norman Connell. adv.

WORLD CALENDAR OF FORTHCOMING MEETINGS: METALLURGY AND MATERIALS SCIENCE. see MEETINGS AND CONGRESSES

669.6 UK
WORLD CONFERENCE ON TIN. PROCEEDINGS. irreg., 4th, 1974 Kuala Lumpur. £36. International Tin Council, Haymarket House, 1 Oxendon St., London SW1Y 4EQ, England.

669 UK ISSN 0950-2262
WORLD COPPER DATABOOK. 1986. irreg.
£60($144) Metal Bulletin Books Ltd., Park House, 3
Park Terrace, Worcester Park, Surrey KT4 7HY,
England (Distr. in U.S. by: Metal Bulletin Inc., 220
Fifth Ave., New York, NY 10001) Ed. Dick
Sarjeantson.

669 UK
WORLD METAL STATISTICS. YEARBOOK. 1984.
a. $100. World Bureau of Metal Statistics, 41
Doughty St., London WC1N 2LF, England.

669 UK ISSN 0263-9661
WORLD PRECIOUS METALS SURVEY. 1982.
irreg. £15($36) Metal Bulletin PLC, Park House,
Park Terrace, Worcester Park, Surrey KT4 7HY,
England (Dist. in U.S. by: Metal Bulletin Inc., 220
Fifth Ave., New York, NY 10001) Ed. Norman
Connell. adv.

669.6 UK
WORLD - TIN IN TINPLATE. 1986. irreg. £25.
International Tin Council, 1 Oxendon St., London
SW1Y 4EQ, England.

669 UK
WORLD TIN MINING OPERATIONS,
EXPLORATION AND DEVELOPMENTS. a.
£20. International Tin Council, 1 Oxendon St.,
London SW1Y 4EQ, England.

669.142 UK
WORLD TRADE - STAINLESS, HIGH SPEED &
OTHER ALLOY STEEL. 1979. q.(quantities);
a.(values) £125. U.K. Iron and Steel Statistics
Bureau, NLA Tower, 12 Addiscombe Rd., Croydon
CR9 3JH, England.

669 UK
WORLD TRADE - STEEL. 1970. q.(quantities);
a.(values) £125. U.K. Iron and Steel Statistics
Bureau, NLA Tower, 12 Addiscombe Rd., Croydon
CR9 3JH, England.

663 UR ISSN 0130-1519
ZASHCHITNYE POKRYTIYA NA METALLAKH;
respublikanskii mezhvedomstvennyi sbornik
nauchnykh trudov. (Text in Russian) 1967. a.
(Akademii Nauk Ukrainskoi S.S.R., Institut
Problem Materialovedeniya) Izdatel'stvo Naukova
Dumka, c/o Yu.A. Khramov, Dir, Ul. Repina, 3,
Kiev 252 601, Ukrainian S.S.R., U.S.S.R. (Subscr.
to: Mezhdunarodnaya Kniga, Moscow, G-200,
Russian S.F.S.R., U.S.S.R.) Ed. J.M. Fedorchenko.
Indexed: Chem.Abstr.

METALLURGY — Abstracting, Bibliographies, Statistics

669 016 US ISSN 0001-2556
A S M BIBLIOGRAPHY SERIES. (American Society
for Metals) 1967. a. (109 topics avail.). $65 per
topic to non-members; members $55. A M S
International, Materials Information, Metals Park,
OH 44073. TEL 216-338-5151.

669 016 US ISSN 0094-8233
ALLOYS INDEX. (Auxiliary publication to Metals
Abstracts and Metals Abstracts Index) 1974. m.
$240. A M S International, Materials Information,
Metals Park, OH 44073. TEL 216-338-5151. (Co-
sponsor: Institute of Metals, London) Ed. H.D.
Chafe.
●Also available online. Vendors: CEDOCAR,
CISTI, DIALOG, European Space Agency, Orbit
Information Technologies.

669.142 310 UN
ANNUAL BULLETIN OF STEEL STATISTICS
FOR EUROPE. (Text in English, French and
Russian) 1974. a., latest vol.12, 1984. price varies.
Economic Commission for Europe (ECE), Palais
des Nations, 1211 Geneva 10, Switzerland (Or
United Nations Publications, Rm. DC2-853, New
York, NY 10017) Indexed: PROMT.

669 016 UK ISSN 0268-3393
B C I R A ABSTRACTS OF INTERNATIONAL
LITERATURE ON METAL CASTINGS
PRODUCTION. 1969. bi-m. £54. British Cast Iron
Research Association (BCIRA), Alvechurch,
Birmingham B48 7QB, England. Ed. D.M. Gore.
bk. rev. abstr. index. circ. 250.
Former titles: B C I R A Abstracts of
International Foundry Literature (ISSN 0141-2930);
(until 1978): B C I R A Abstracts of Foundry
Literature (ISSN 0005-2868)

669 UK
CADSCAN. 1977. q. £50. Cadmium Association, 34
Berkeley Sq., London W1X 6AJ, England. Ed. M.J.
Conway. adv. bk. rev. index. circ. 400. (back issues
avail.) Indexed: Br.Ceram.Abstr.
●Also available online. Vendors: Pergamon Infoline.
Formerly (until Oct. 1986): Cadmium Abstracts
(ISSN 0309-1139)

CANADA. STATISTICS CANADA.
COMMUNICATIONS AND ENERGY WIRE
AND CABLE INDUSTRY/INDUSTRIE DES
FILS ET CABLES ELECTRIQUES ET DE
COMMUNICATIONS. see ELECTRICITY AND
ELECTRICAL ENGINEERING

338.4 CN ISSN 0828-9921
CANADA. STATISTICS CANADA.
ORNAMENTAL AND ARCHITECTURAL
METAL PRODUCTS INDUSTRY/INDUSTRIE
DES PRODUITS METALLIQUES
D'ORNEMENT ET D'ARCHITECTURE.
(Catalogue 41-221) (Text in English and French)
1960. a. Can.$20($21) Statistics Canada,
Communications Division, 3rd Floor, R.H. Coats
Bldg., Ottawa, Ont. K1A 0T6, Canada TEL 613-
993-7276. (Subscr. to: Publications Sales and
Services, Ottawa, Ont. K1A 0T6, Canada) (also
avail. in microform from MML)
Formerly: Canada. Statistics Canada. Ornamental
and Architectural Metal Industry/Industrie des
Produits Metalliques d'Architecture et d'Ornement
(ISSN 0527-5997)

671.84 CN ISSN 0828-9913
CANADA. STATISTICS CANADA. WIRE AND
WIRE PRODUCTS INDUSTRIES/INDUSTRIES
DU FIL METALLIQUE ET DE SES PRODUITS.
(Catalogue 41-216) (Text in English and French)
1927. a. Can.$20($21) Statistics Canada,
Communications Division, 3rd Floor, R.H. Coats
Bldg., Ottawa, Ont. K1A 0T6, Canada TEL 613-
993-7276. (Subscr. to: Publications Sales and
Services, Ottawa, Ont. K1A 0T6, Canada)
Formerly: Canada. Statistics Canada. Wire and
Wire Products Manufacturers (ISSN 0576-0062)

620.112 016 US ISSN 0010-9339
CORROSION ABSTRACTS; abstracts of the world's
literature on corrosion and corrosion mitigation.
1962. bi-m. $200 individuals; libraries $250.
National Association of Corrosion Engineers, Box
218340, Houston, TX 77218. TEL 713-492-0535.
Ed. R.I. Lindberg. abstr. index. circ. 650. Indexed:
Art & Archaeol.Tech.Abstr.

620.112 016 UK ISSN 0010-9347
CORROSION CONTROL ABSTRACTS. English
translation of: Referativnyi Zhurnal. Korroziya i
Zashchita ot Korrozii. 1966. m. £670. Scientific
Information Consultants Ltd., 661 Finchley Rd.,
London NW2 2HN, England. Ed. Eugene Gros.
abstr.

016 621.9 669 KO
CURRENT BIBLIOGRAPHIES ON SCIENCE AND
TECHNOLOGY: MECHANICAL
ENGINEERING & CONSTRUCTION
ENGINEERING. 1962. m. $92. Korea Institute for
Economics and Technology, P.O.B. 250, Seoul, S.
Korea. circ. 300. (reprint service avail. from UMI)
Formerly: Current Index to Journals in Science
and Technology: Mechanical, Metallurgical, Natural
Resources and Construction Engineering;
Supersedes in part: Current Bibliography on Science
and Technology.

011 669 KO
CURRENT BIBLIOGRAPHIES ON SCIENCE AND
TECHNOLOGY: METALLURGY, NATURAL
RESOURCES & ENERGY. m. $92. Institute for
Economics and Technology, P.O. Box 205, Seoul,
South Korea. circ. 300.

EURO ABSTRACTS SECTION II. COAL AND
STEEL. see MINES AND MINING
INDUSTRY — Abstracting, Bibliographies,
Statistics

I M M ABSTRACTS; a survey of world literature on
the economic geology and mining of all minerals
(except coal), mineral processing and non-ferrous
extraction metallurgy. (Institution of Mining and
Metallurgy) see MINES AND MINING
INDUSTRY — Abstracting, Bibliographies,
Statistics

669.3 UK ISSN 0309-2216
INTERNATIONAL COPPER INFORMATION
BULLETIN; recent reports, publications and
abstracts on copper, its alloys and compounds. 1976.
q. £15. Copper Development Association, Orchard
House, Mutton Lane, Potters Bar, Herts. EN6 3AP,
England. Ed. G. Greetham. adv. bk. rev. circ. 7,000.
Indexed: Met.Abstr.
Supersedes: Copper Abstracts (ISSN 0010-8596);
Incorporates: Kupfer-Mitteilungen (ISSN 0023-
5628); Cuivre, Laitons, Alliages-Bibliographie;
Rame-Schede Bibliographiche; Cobre-Resumes
Bibliograficos.

310 671 UK
INTERNATIONAL STEEL STATISTICS -
COMPLETE SERIES. 1970. a. £500. U.K. Iron &
Steel Statistics Bureau, NLA Tower, 12 Addiscombe
Rd., Croydon CR9 3JH, England.

310 671 UK
INTERNATIONAL STEEL STATISTICS -
SUMMARY TABLES. 1970. a. £75. U.K. Iron &
Steel Statistics Bureau, NLA Tower, 12 Addiscombe
Rd., Croydon CR9 3JH, England.

669.1 338.4 UK ISSN 0075-0867
IRON AND STEEL. ANNUAL STATISTICS FOR
THE UNITED KINGDOM. 1918. a. £40. U.K.
Iron and Steel Statistics Bureau, NLA Tower, 12
Addiscombe Rd., Croydon CR9 3JH, England.

669 016 UK ISSN 0950-1584
LEADSCAN; a review of recent technical literature
on the uses of lead and its products. 1958. 4/yr.
£50($70) (Zinc-Lead Library and Abstracts Service)
Lead Development Association, 34 Berkeley Square,
London W1X 6AJ, England. Ed. M.J. Conway. bk.
rev. abstr. index. circ. 1,300. (also avail. in
microform from UMI) Indexed: Br.Ceram.Abstr.
Lead Abstr. World Surf.Coat.
●Also available online. Vendors: Pergamon Infoline.
Formerly: Lead Abstracts (ISSN 0023-9569)

669 JA ISSN 0451-6001
LIGHT METAL STATISTICS IN JAPAN/
KEIKINZOKU KOGYO TOKEI NENPO. (Text
mainly in Japanese) irreg. 1000 Yen. Japan Light
Metal Association - Keikinzoku Kyokai, c/o
Nihonbashi Asahi Seimeikan, 2-1-3 Nihonbashi,
Chuo-ku, Tokyo 102, Japan. stat.

669 UK
MATERIALS BUSINESS ABSTRACTS. 1985. m.
Institute of Metals, 1 Carlton House Terrace,
London SW1Y 5DB, England.

310 669 GW ISSN 0170-9933
METAL STATISTICS (YEARS) (Text in English,
German) 1889. a. DM.80($45) Metallgesellschaft
AG, Volkswirtschaftliche Abteilung, Reuterweg 14,
6000 Frankfurt/Main, W. Germany (B.R.D.) Ed.
Willy Bauer.

880 016 US ISSN 0026-0924
METALS ABSTRACTS. (American Society for
Metals) 1968. m. $1180. A S M International,
Materials Information, Metals Park, OH 44073.
TEL 216-338-5151. circ. 1,500. Indexed:
Br.Ceram.Abstr.
●Also available online. Vendors: CEDOCAR,
CISTI, DIALOG, European Space Agency, INKA,
Orbit Information Technologies.
Formed by the merger of: Review of Metal
Literature & Metallurgical Abstracts.

669 016 US ISSN 0026-0932
METALS ABSTRACTS INDEX. (American Society
for Metals) 1968. m. $500. A S M International,
Materials Information, Metals Park, OH 44073.
TEL 216-338-5151. cum.index. circ. 1,100.

669.23 016   US   ISSN 0095-9286
NEW SILVER TECHNOLOGY; silver summaries
from the current world literature. 1974. q. $45.
Silver Institute, Ste. 101, 1026 16th St., Washington,
DC 20036. TEL 202-331-1485. Ed. John H. Lutley.
cum.index 1974-1980. circ. 450. (back issues avail.)

669 016   FR
P A S C A L THEMA. PART 240: METAUX.
METALLURGIE. 1985. 10/yr. 1285 F. Centre
National de la Recherche Scientifique, Centre de
Documentation Scientifique et Technique, Service
des Abonnements, 26 rue Boyer, 75971 Paris 20,
France. abstr. index; cum.index. (also avail. in
microform from MIM) Indexed: World Alum.Abstr.
    Supersedes (1969-1984): Bulletin Signaletique.
Part 740: Metaux. Metallurgie (ISSN 0007-5655)

671.52 016   FR
P A S C A L THEMA. PART 245: SOUDAGE,
BRASAGE ET TECHNIQUES CONNEXES.
1985. 10/yr. 450 F. Centre National de la
Recherche Scientifique, Centre de Documentation
Scientifique et Technique, Service des
Abonnements, 26 rue Boyer, 75971 Paris 20,
France. abstr. index; cum.index. (also avail. in
microform from MIM)
    Supersedes (1972-1984): Bulletin Signaletique.
Part 745: Soudage, Brasage et Techniques Connexes
(ISSN 0301-3480)

671.52 016   GW   ISSN 0340-4749
REFERATE ORGAN: SCHWEISSEN UND
VERWANDTE VERFAHREN/BULLETIN OF
ABSTRACTS: WELDING AND ALLIED
PROCESSES. 1956. bi-m. DM.240. Bundesanstalt
fuer Materialpruefung, Unter den Eichen 87, 1000
Berlin 45, W. Germany (B.R.D.) (Co-sponsor:
Deutscher Verband fuer Schweisstechnik (DVS)) bk.
rev. abstr. charts. illus. cumulative author and
keyword index. circ. 1,500.
    Formerly: Selective Abstracting Service: Welding
and Allied Processes (ISSN 0037-1432)

620.1 016   UR   ISSN 0131-3533
REFERATIVNYI ZHURNAL. KORROZIYA I
ZASHCHITA OT KORROZII. 1968. m. 79.20 Rub.
Vsesoyuznyi Institut Nauchno-Tekhnicheskoi
Informatsii (VINITI), Baltiiskaya ul., 14, Moscow
A-219, Russian S.F.S.R., U.S.S.R. (Subscr. to:
Mezhdunarodnaya Kniga, Dimitrova ul. 39, 113095
Moscow, Russian S.F.S.R., U.S.S.R.) Indexed:
Chem.Abstr. Met.Abstr. World Alum.Abstr.

669 016   UR   ISSN 0034-2491
REFERATIVNYI ZHURNAL. METALLURGIYA.
1961. m. 244.20 Rub. 305 Rub. including index)
Vsesoyuznyi Institut Nauchno-Tekhnicheskoi
Informatsii (VINITI), Baltiiskaya ul., 14, Moscow
A-219, Russian S.F.S.R., U.S.S.R. (Subscr. to:
Mezhdunarodnaya Kniga, Dimitrova ul. 39, 113095
Moscow, Russian S.F.S.R., U.S.S.R.) abstr. bibl.
pat. circ. 1,649. Indexed: Chem.Abstr. Met.Abstr.
World Alum.Abstr.

671.52 316   UR   ISSN 0131-3525
REFERATIVNYI ZHURNAL. SVARKA. 1965. m.
72.60 Rub. Vsesoyuznyi Institut Nauchno-
Tekhnicheskoi Informatsii (VINITI), Baltiiskaya ul.,
14, Moscow A-219, Russian S.F.S.R., U.S.S.R
(Subscr. to: Mezhdunarodnaya Kniga, Dimitrova ul.
39, 113095 Moscow, Russian S.F.S.R., U.S.S.R.)

SOURCE JOURNALS IN METALS AND
MATERIALS. see *METALLURGY*

314 669   EI
STATISTICAL OFFICE OF THE EUROPEAN
COMMUNITIES. IRON AND STEEL.
YEARBOOK. (Text in Dutch, English, French and
Italian) 1977. a. 1,000 Fr.($21) Statistical Office of
the European Communities, B.P. 1903, L-2920
Luxembourg, Luxembourg. Ed.Bd.

338.4 669 310   EI   ISSN 0081-4954
STATISTICAL OFFICE OF THE EUROPEAN
COMMUNITIES. SIDERURGIE ANNUAIRE.
(Text in Dutch, French, German, Italian) 1964. a.
Rue Alcide de Gasperi, B.P. 1907, Luxembourg,
Luxembourg (Dist. in the U.S. by: European
Community Information Service, 2100 M St., NW,
Suite 707, Washington, DC 20037)

669.1 310   II   ISSN 0081-511X
STATISTICS FOR IRON AND STEEL INDUSTRY
IN INDIA. (Text in English) 1964. a. price varies.
Steel Authority of India Ltd., Ispat Bhavan, Lodi
Rd., New Delhi 110003, India. Eds. J. Prasad, M.
Usman. index.

669.142 310   UN   ISSN 0081-5195
STATISTICS OF WORLD TRADE IN STEEL. 1961.
a., latest 1984. price varies. Economic Commission
for Europe (ECE), Palais des Nations, 1211
Geneva, Switzerland (Or United Nations
Publications, Rm. DC2-853, New York, NY 10017)
(also avail. in microfiche)

310   UN
STATISTICS ON WORLD TRADE IN
ENGINEERING PRODUCTS. BULLETIN. (Text
in English, French and Russian; tables in English)
1963. a., latest 1983. price varies. Economic
Commission for Europe (ECE), Palais des Nations,
1211 Geneva 10, Switzerland (Or United Nations
Publications, Rm. DC2-853, New York, NY 10017)

669 310   GW   ISSN 0081-5365
STATISTISCHES JAHRBUCH DER EISEN- UND
STAHLINDUSTRIE. 1929. a. DM.49.
(Wirtschaftsvereinigung Eisen- und Stahlindustrie)
Verlag Stahleisen mbH, Sohnstr. 65, Postfach 8229,
4000 Duesseldorf 1, W. Germany (B.R.D.)

669 016   UK   ISSN 0950-5199
SURFACE TREATMENT TECHNOLOGY
ABSTRACTS. 1959. bi-m. £180($350) Finishing
Publications Ltd., 28 High St., Teddington,
Middlesex, England. Ed. R. Pinner. adv. bk. rev.
abstr. pat. index. circ. 1,000. Indexed: Art &
Archaeol.Tech.Abstr.
    Formerly: Metal Finishing Abstracts (ISSN 0026-
0584)

669 310   UK
TIN STATISTICS. 1973. a. £20. International Tin
Council, Haymarket House, 1 Oxendon St., London
SW1Y 4EQ, England.
    Supersedes in part: International Tin Council.
Statistical Yearbook (ISSN 0074-9117);
International Tin Council. Statistical Supplement.
Tin, Tinplate Canning (ISSN 0074-9109)

669   US   ISSN 0278-4238
TRANSLATIONS INDEX. (American Society for
Metals) 1977. q. $110. A S M International,
Materials Information, Metals Park, OH 44073.
    Formerly: A S M Translations Index (ISSN 0263-
2659)

U S S R REPORT: MATERIALS SCIENCE AND
METALLURGY. see *ENGINEERING —
Abstracting, Bibliographies, Statistics*

669.722 016   US   ISSN 0002-6697
WORLD ALUMINUM ABSTRACTS; a monthly
review of the world's technical literature on
aluminum. (Text in English) 1968. m. $240 to
individuals; libraries $150. Aluminum Association,
Inc., 818 Connecticut Ave., N.W., Washington, DC
20006. TEL 202-862-5156. (Co-sponsors: European
Aluminum Association; Japan Light Metal
Association; Aluminum Development Council)
abstr. index. circ. 1,100. (magnetic tape; also avail.
in microfiche from CIS) Indexed: Chem.Abstr.
●Also available online. Vendors: DIALOG,
European Space Agency.

669   UK
WORLD BUREAU OF METAL STATISTICS.
ANNUAL REPORT. a. World Bureau of Metal
Statistics, 41 Doughty St., London WC1N 2LF,
England.

WORLD METAL STATISTICS. YEARBOOK. see
METALLURGY

669.142   UK   ISSN 0141-0806
WORLD STAINLESS STEEL STATISTICS. 1972. a.
£150($360) World Bureau of Metal Statistics, 41
Doughty St., London WC1N 2LF, England (Subscr.
to: Metal Bulletin PLC, Park House, Park Terrace,
Worcester Park, Surrey KT4 7HY, England) Ed.
J.L.T. Davies.

669.142   UK   ISSN 0266-7347
WORLD WROUGHT COPPER STATISTICS. 1985.
a. £150($360) World Bureau of Metal Statistics, 41
Doughty St., London WC1N 2LF, England. Ed.
J.L.T. Davies.

669.5 016   UK   ISSN 0950-1592
ZINCSCAN; a review of recent technical literature on
the uses of zinc and its products. 1943. q. £50. Zinc
Development Association, 34 Berkeley Square,
London W1X 6AJ, England. Ed. M.J. Conway. adv.
bk. rev. abstr. index. circ. 1,000. Indexed:
Chem.Abstr. Br.Ceram.Abstr.
●Also available online. Vendors: Pergamon Infoline.
    Formerly: Zinc Abstracts (ISSN 0044-4731)

METALLURGY — Welding

671.52   US
AMERICAN WELDING SOCIETY ANNUAL
MEETING. ABSTRACTS OF PAPERS. a.
American Welding Society, Box 351040, Miami, FL
33135.

671.52   US
INTERNATIONAL THERMAL SPRAYING
CONFERENCE. PREPRINT OF PAPERS. irreg.
9th, 1980. $25. American Welding Society, Box
351040, Miami, FL 33135. TEL 305-443-9353.

671.52   UR   ISSN 0202-778X
ITOGI NAUKI I TEKHNIKI: SVARKA. irreg., latest
vol.18, 1987. price varies. Vsesoyuznyi Institut
Nauchno-Tekhnicheskoi Informatsii (VINITI), Ul.
Baltiiskaya 14, Moscow A-219, Russian S.F.S.R.,
U.S.S.R. (Subscr. to: Mezhdunarodnaya Kniga,
Dimitrova ul. 39, 113095 Moscow, Russian S.F.S.R.,
U.S.S.R.) Indexed: Chem.Abstr.

METALLURGIE. LEXIQUE. see *METALLURGY*

SHEET METAL INDUSTRIES YEAR BOOK. see
METALLURGY

671.5   US   ISSN 0278-7067
WELDING AND FABRICATING DATA BOOK.
1958. biennial. $27. Penton Publishing, 1100
Superior Ave., Cleveland, OH 44114. TEL 216-696-
7000. Ed. Rosalie Brosilow. adv. charts. illus. circ.
24,000. (reprint service avail. from UMI)
    Formerly: Welding Data Book (ISSN 0511-4365)

671.52   US
WELDING RESEARCH COUNCIL YEARBOOK.
1936. a. $1000 membership. Welding Research
Council, United Engineering Center, 345 E. 47th
St., New York, NY 10017. TEL 212-705-7956. circ.
700.

METEOROLOGY

ACTA GEOGRAPHICA DEDRECINA. see
GEOGRAPHY

551.6   HU   ISSN 0563-0614
ACTA UNIVERSITATIS DE ATTILA JOZSEF
NOMINATAE. ACTA CLIMATOLOGICA. (Text
in English) 1959. biennial. exchange basis. Attila
Jozsef University, c/o E. Szabo, Exchange
Librarian, Dugonics ter 13, P.O.B. 393, Szeged H-
6701, Hungary (Subscr. to: Kultura, P.O. Box 149,
H-1389 Budapest, Hungary) Ed. Laszlo Jakucs.
charts. illus. circ. 400.

551.5   SG   ISSN 0065-4248
AGENCE POUR LA SECURITE DE LA
NAVIGATION AERIENNE EN AFRIQUE ET A
MADAGASCAR. DIRECTION DE
L'EXPLOITATION METEOROLOGIQUE.
PUBLICATIONS. SERIE 1. 1966. irreg. price
varies. Agence pour la Securite de la Navigation
Aerienne en Afrique et a Madagascar, Direction de
l'Exploitation Meteorologique, B.P. 3144, Dakar,
Senegal.

551.5   SG   ISSN 0084-6015
AGENCE POUR LA SECURITE DE LA
NAVIGATION AERIENNE EN AFRIQUE ET A
MADAGASCAR. DIRECTION DE
L'EXPLOITATION METEOROLOGIQUE.
PUBLICATIONS. SERIE 2. 1965. irreg. price
varies. Agence pour la Securite de la Navigation
Aerienne en Afrique et a Madagascar, Direction de
l'Exploitation Meteorologique, B.P. 3144, Dakar,
Senegal.

551.5 ES ISSN 0084-6236
ALMANAQUE SALVADORENO. 1945. a. $.60. Ministerio de Agricultura y Ganaderia, Centro de Recursos Naturales, Servicio de Meteorologia e Hidrologia, 39 Av. Norte No. 214, San Salvador, El Salvador. adv. charts,illus,stat. circ. 2,000.

551.5 US ISSN 0065-9401
AMERICAN METEOROLOGICAL SOCIETY. METEOROLOGICAL MONOGRAPHS. 1947. irreg., vol.19, 1986. price varies. American Meteorological Society, 45 Beacon St., Boston, MA 02108. TEL 617-227-2425. Ed. John Dutton. Indexed: Biol.Abstr. Chem.Abstr. Sci.Abstr. Meteor.& Geoastrophys.Abstr.

551.5 GW ISSN 0072-4122
ANNALEN DER METEOROLOGIE. NEUE FOLGE. 1948; 1963 N.S. irreg., no.23, 1986. Deutscher Wetterdienst, Frankfurter Str. 135, Postfach 10 04 65, 6050 Offenbach (Main) 1, W. Germany (B.R.D.)

551.6 BD
ANNUAIRE PLUVIOMETRIQUE. a. Ministere des Transports et de l'Aeronautique, Centre National d'Hydrometeorologie, B.P. 331, Bujumbura, Burundi.

551.5 PK
ANNUAL GEOMAGNETIC BULLETIN OF PAKISTAN. vol.9-10, 1963/64. a. Meteorological Department, Headquarters Office, 34-J Block No. 6, P.E.C.H.S., Karachi 29, Pakistan.

551.5 PO ISSN 0870-2950
ANUARIO CLIMATOLOGICO. (Since 1977 issued in 3 parts: A: Continente(0870-6360); B: Acores (0870-6379); C: Madeira (0870-6387)) 1947. a. Esc.600 (or Part A, Esc. 500; Part B, Esc. 250; Part C, Esc. 250) Instituto Nacional do Meteorologia e Geofisica, Rua C do Aeroporto, 1700 Lisbon, Portugal. stat.

551.6 FR ISSN 0242-4002
ASSOCIATION NATIONALE D'ETUDE ET DE LUTTE CONTRE LES FLEAUX ATMOSPHERIQUES. RAPPORT DE CAMPAGNE. 1951. a. free. Association Nationale de Lutte Contre les Fleaux Atmospheriques, 52 rue Alfred-Dumeril, 31400 Toulouse, France. bk. rev. illus. circ. 200. Indexed: Meteor.& Geoastrophys. Abstr.
Formerly: Association Nationale de Lutte Contre les Fleaux Atmospheriques. Rapport de Campagne (ISSN 0373-7349) Continues the Rapport sur la Campagne issued by the association under its earlier name: Association d' Etudes des Moyens de Lutte Contre les Fleaux Atmospheriques.

551.5 UR ISSN 0135-1419
ATMOSFEROS FIZIKA/ATMOSPHERIC PHYSICS. (Text in Russian; summaries in English and Lithuanian) 1975. a. price varies. (Akademiya Nauk Litovskoi S.S.R., Institute of Physics) Izdatel'stvo Mokslas, Zvaigzdziu 23, Vilnius 232050, Lithuanian S.S.R., U.S.S.R. Ed. B. Styra. circ. 1,000.

551.5 AT ISSN 0067-1312
AUSTRALIA. BUREAU OF METEOROLOGY. BULLETIN. 1908. irreg., no.51, 1984. price varies. Australian Government Publishing Service, G.P.O. Box 84, Canberra, A.C.T., Australia. Indexed: Meteor.& Geoastrophys.Abstr.

551.5 AT ISSN 0067-1320
AUSTRALIA. BUREAU OF METEOROLOGY. METEOROLOGICAL STUDY. 1954. irreg., no.34, 1984. available on exchange. Australian Government Publishing Service, G.P.O. Box 84, Canberra, A.C.T., Australia. Indexed: Meteor.& Geoastrophys.Abstr.

551.5 551 AU ISSN 0067-2351
AUSTRIA. ZENTRALANSTALT FUER METEOROLOGIE UND GEODYNAMIK. JAHRBUCH. 1864. irreg. price varies. Zentralanstalt fuer Meteorologie und Geodynamik, Hohe Warte 38, A-1190 Vienna, Austria. circ. 500. Indexed: GeoRef.

551.5271 BE ISSN 0524-7780
BELGIUM. INSTITUT ROYAL METEOROLOGIQUE. ANNUAIRE: RAYONNEMENT SOLAIRE/JAARBOEK: ZONNESTRALING. irreg., latest 1982. 500 Fr. Institut Royal Meteorologique, 3 av. Circulaire, 1180 Brussels, Belgium. circ. 182.

551.5 551 BE ISSN 0020-255X
BELGIUM. INSTITUT ROYAL METEOROLOGIQUE. PUBLICATIONS. (Text in Dutch, English and French) 1952. irreg. (15-20/yr.) Institut Royal Meteorologique, 3 av. Circulaire, 1180 Brussels, Belgium. circ. 290.

551.5 PL ISSN 0239-6270
BIBLIOGRAFIA METEOROLOGII/ BIBLIOGRAPHY OF METEOROLOGY. (Text in English, French, German, Polish and Russian) 1963. irreg. $180. Instytut Meteorologii i Gospodarki Wodnej - Institute of Meteorology and Water Management, 61 Podlesna St., 01-673 Warsaw, Poland. circ. 500.

551.5 NE ISSN 0067-8902
BIOMETEOROLOGY; PROCEEDINGS. Represents: International Biometeorological Congress. Proceedings. triennial, 10th, 1984, Tokyo, Japan. fl.160. (International Society of Biometeorology) Swets Publishing Service (Subsidiary of: Swets en Zeitlinger B.V.) Heereweg 347, 2161 CA Lisse, Netherlands (Dist. in the U.S. and Canada by: Swets North America, Inc., Box 517 Berwyn, PA 19312) Indexed: Biol.Abstr. Chem.Abstr.

551.5 PL
BIULETYN METEOROLOGICZNY. (Subseries of its: Acta Universitatis Wratislaviensis) 1971. irreg. price varies. Wydawnictwa Uniwersytetu Wroclawskiego, Ul. Kuznicza 34, 50-138 Wroclaw, Poland.

551.5 BL ISSN 0067-9585
BOLETIM CLIMATOLOGICO. 1960. irreg., no.5, 1984. price varies; avail. on exchange. Universidade de Sao Paulo, Instituto Oceanografico, Cidade Universitaria, Butanta, 05508 Sao Paulo, SP, Brazil. circ. 100.

551.5 GW ISSN 0006-7156
BONNER METEOROLOGISCHE ABHANDLUNGEN. (Text in English and German) 1962. irreg. price varies. (Universitaet Bonn, Meteorologisches Institut) Ferd. Duemmlers Verlag, Postfach 1480-Kaiserstr. 31-37, D-5300 Bonn 1, W. Germany (B.R.D.) Ed. Michael Hantel. abstr. charts. illus. Indexed: Meteor.& Geoastrophys.Abstr. Geo.Abstr.

551.5 SP
CALENDARIO METEOROLOGICO. 1943. a. 400 ptas. Instituto Nacional de Meteorologia, Ministerio de Transportes, Turismo y Comunicaciones, Ciudad Universitaria, Apartado 285, Madrid, Spain.
Formerly: Calendario Meteoro-Fenologico.

551.5 CM
CAMEROUN. SERVICE D'HYDROMETEOROLOGIE. PLUVIOMETRIE MENSUELLE ET ANNUELLE. a. $17.75. Service d'Hydrometeorologie, Yaounde, Cameroon. charts. stat.

551.6 CN ISSN 0068-7715
CANADA. ATMOSPHERIC ENVIRONMENT SERVICE. CLIMATOLOGICAL STUDIES. 1965. irreg. price varies. Atmospheric Environment Service, 4905 Dufferin St., Downsview, Ont. M3H 5T4, Canada TEL 416-667-4882. (Subscr. to: Supply & Services Canada, Publishing Centre, Hull, Que. K1A 0S9, Canada)

551.5 CN ISSN 0068-7782
CANADA. ATMOSPHERIC ENVIRONMENT SERVICE. METEOROLOGICAL TRANSLATIONS. 1959. irreg., no.33, 1980. Can.$1.50. Atmospheric Environment Service, 4905 Dufferin St., Downsview, Ont M3H 5T4, Canada TEL 416-667-4882. (Subscr. to: Supply & Services Canada, Publishing Centre, Hull, Que. K1A 0S9, Canada) circ. 500.

551.538 CN ISSN 0068-7790
CANADA. ATMOSPHERIC ENVIRONMENT SERVICE. SNOW COVER DATA/DONNEES D'ENNEIGEMENT. (Text in English and French) 1954/55. a. free. Atmospheric Environment Service, 4905 Dufferin St, Downsview, Ont. M3H 5T4 Canada, Canada TEL 416-667-4882. (Subscr. to: Supply & Services Canada, Publishing Centre, Hull, Que. K1A 0S9, Canada) Ed. B.J. Yorke. circ. 800.

551.5 CN ISSN 0068-7804
CANADA. ATMOSPHERIC ENVIRONMENT SERVICE. TECHNICAL MEMORANDA. (Text in English; summaries in English and French) 1954. irreg., TEC 882, 1985. Can.$5. Atmospheric Environment Service, 4905 Dufferin St., Downsview, Ont., M3H 5T4, Canada. TEL 416-667-4882.

551.5 CN
CANADIAN METEOROLOGICAL AND OCEANOGRAPHIC SOCIETY. ANNUAL CONGRESS. 1967. a. $12. Canadian Meteorological and Oceanographic Society, 805-151 Slater St., Ottawa, Ont. K1P 5H3, Canada. Ed. E. Truhlar. adv. circ. 1,000. Indexed: Meteor.& Geoastrophys.Abstr.
Formerly: Canadian Meteorological Society. Annual Congress (ISSN 0068-9254)

551.5 CN ISSN 0068-9246
CANADIAN METEOROLOGICAL MEMOIRS. 1935. irreg., no.31, 1977. Can.$5. Atmospheric Environment Service, 4905 Dufferin St., Downsview, Ont., M3H 5T4, Canada. TEL 416-667-4882.

551.5 CN
CANADIAN METEOROLOGICAL RESEARCH REPORTS. (Text in English; summaries in English and French) 1968. irreg. Can.$5 per no. Atmospheric Environment Service, 4905 Dufferin St., Downsview, Ont. M3H 5T4, Canada. TEL 416-667-4882.

551.5 IO ISSN 0009-8957
CLIMATOLOGICAL DATA FOR JAKARTA OBSERVATORY. (Text in English) 1956. a. exchange basis. Meteorological and Geophysical Institute - Badan Meteorologi dan Geofisika, Jalan Arief Rakhman Hakim 3, Jakarta, Indonesia.

551.5 US ISSN 0067-0340
COLORADO STATE UNIVERSITY. ATMOSPHERIC SCIENCE PAPER. 1959. irreg. available on exchange. ‡ Colorado State University, Atmospheric Science Department, College of Engineering, Fort Collins, CO 80523. TEL 303-491-8360. Ed. T.B. McKee. (also avail. in microfiche) Indexed: Meteor.& Geoastrophys.Abstr.
Supersedes: Atmospheric Science Technical Paper & Atmospheric Science Research Report.

551.51 AT ISSN 0159-0219
COMMONWEALTH SCIENTIFIC AND INDUSTRIAL RESEARCH ORGANIZATION. DIVISION OF ATMOSPHERIC RESEARCH. RESEARCH REPORT. biennial. Aus.$3 per no. C.S.I.R.O., Division of Atmospheric Research, 314 Albert St., East Melbourne, Vic. 3002, Australia. illus.
Formerly: Commonwealth Scientific and Industrial Research Organization. Division of Atmospheric Physics. Annual Report (ISSN 0310-1908)

551.51 AT
COMMONWEALTH SCIENTIFIC AND INDUSTRIAL RESEARCH ORGANIZATION. DIVISION OF ATMOSPHERIC RESEARCH. TECHNICAL PAPER. 1983. irreg. (approx. 1-3/yr.) price varies. C.S.I.R.O., Division of Atmospheric Research, 314 Albert Street, East Melbourne, Vic. 3002, Australia. circ. 750. Indexed: Biol.Abstr.
Formerly: Commonwealth Scientific and Industrial Research Organization. Division of Atmospheric Physics. Technical Paper.

551.5 US
CONFERENCE ON AGRICULTURE & FOREST METEOROLOGY. PUBLICATION. 1978. irreg., 17th, 1985. $30. American Meteorological Society, 45 Beacon St., Boston, MA 02108. TEL 617-227-2425.

551.5 US
CONFERENCE ON ATMOSPHERIC ENVIRONMENT OF AEROSPACE SYSTEMS AND APPLIED METEOROLOGY. PREPRINTS. 9th, 1968. irreg., latest 1983. $20. ‡ American Meteorological Society, 45 Beacon St., Boston, MA 02108. TEL 617-227-2425. adv. Indexed: Meteor.& Geoastrophys.Abstr.
Former titles: Conference on Aerospace and Aeronautical Meteorology. Preprints; National Conference on Aerospace Meteorology. Proceedings (ISSN 0077-3913)

METEOROLOGY

551.5   US
CONFERENCE ON COASTAL METEOROLOGY. (PREPRINTS) irreg., 3rd, 1984. $20. American Meteorological Society, 45 Beacon St., Boston, MA 02108. TEL 617-227-2425.

551.5   US
CONFERENCE ON HYDROMETEOROLOGY. PREPRINT. 2nd, 1977. irreg., 6th, 1985. $30. American Meteorological Society, 45 Beacon St., Boston, MA 02108. TEL 617-227-2425. Indexed: GeoRef. Meteor.& Geoastrophys.Abstr.

551.5   US
CONFERENCE ON MOUNTAIN METEOROLOGY (PUBLICATION) 1981. irreg., 3rd, 1984. $20. American Meteorological Society, 45 Beacon St., Boston, MA 02108. TEL 617-227-2425.

551.5   US
CONFERENCE ON NUMERICAL WEATHER PREDICTION. (PUBLICATION) 3rd, 1977. irreg., 7th, 1985. $30. American Meteorological Society, 45 Beacon St., Boston, MA 02108. TEL 617-227-2425.

551.68   US
CONFERENCE ON PLANNED AND INADVERTENT WEATHER MODIFICATION. PREPRINTS. (In 1981 and 1984 issued as Extended Abstracts) 1968. irreg., 9th, 1984. $20. ‡ American Meteorological Society, 45 Beacon St., Boston, MA 02108. TEL 617-227-2425. adv. Indexed: Meteor.& Geoastrophys.Abstr.
    Former titles: Conference on Weather Modification. Preprints; National Conference on Weather Modification. Preprints (ISSN 0077-3956); National Conference on Weather Modification. Proceedings.

551.5   519.5   US
CONFERENCE ON PROBABILITY AND STATISTICS IN ATMOSPHERIC SCIENCES. PREPRINTS. 1968. irreg., 9th, 1985. $30. ‡ American Meteorological Society, 45 Beacon St., Boston, MA 02108. TEL 617-227-2425. adv. Indexed: Meteor.& Geoastrophys.Abstr.
    Formerly: Statistical Meteorological Conference. Proceedings.

551.635   US   ISSN 0069-8636
CONFERENCE ON RADAR METEOROLOGY. PREPRINTS. 1951. biennial. $32. ‡ American Meteorological Society, 45 Beacon St., Boston, MA 02108. TEL 617-227-2425. adv. Indexed: Meteor.& Geoastrophys.Abstr.

551.55   US   ISSN 0069-8679
CONFERENCE ON SEVERE LOCAL STORMS. PREPRINTS. 7th, 1971. irreg., 14th, 1985. $30. ‡ American Meteorological Society, 45 Beacon St., Boston, MA 02108. TEL 617-227-2425. adv. Indexed: Meteor.& Geoastrophys.Abstr.

551.63   US
CONFERENCE ON WEATHER FORECASTING AND ANALYSIS. (PUBLICATION) 6th, 1976. irreg., 10th, 1984. $30. American Meteorological Society, 45 Beacon St., Boston, MA 02108. TEL 617-227-2425.
    Former titles: Conference on Weather Forecasting and Analysis and Aviation Meteorology. Preprints; Conference on Weather Forecasting and Analysis. Preprints.

551.5   370   US
CURRICULA IN THE ATMOSPHERIC, OCEANIC AND RELATED SCIENCES. Variant title: Curricula in the Atmospheric Sciences. biennial. $12. American Meteorological Society, 45 Beacon St., Boston, MA 02108. TEL 617-227-2425.
    Formerly: Curricula in the Atmospheric and Oceanographic Sciences.

551.6   CY   ISSN 0379-0916
CYPRUS. METEOROLOGICAL SERVICE. SUMMARY OF THE WEATHER IN CYPRUS. (Text in English) 1971. a. Meteorological Service, Nicosia, Cyprus. circ. 120.

551.5   IO   ISSN 0303-1969
DATA-DATA IKLIM DI INDONESIA. (Text in English and Indonesian) 1971. a. Meteorological and Geophysical Institute - Badan Meteorologi dan Geofisika, Jalan Arif Rachman Hakim 3, Jakarta, Indonesia.

551.5   GW   ISSN 0072-4130
DEUTSCHER WETTERDIENST. BERICHTE. 1953. irreg., no.173, 1987. price varies. Deutscher Wetterdienst, Frankfurter Str. 135, Postfach 10 04 65, 6050 Offenbach (Main) 1, W. Germany (B.R.D.)

551.5   GW   ISSN 0072-1603
DEUTSCHER WETTERDIENST. SEEWETTERAMT. EINZELVEROEFFENTLICHUNGEN. 1953. irreg., no.113, 1985. price varies. Deutscher Wetterdienst, Seewetteramt, Bernhard Nocht-Str. 76, Postfach 180, 2000 Hamburg 4, W. Germany (B.R.D.) bk. rev. circ. 250.

551.5   NE
DEVELOPMENTS IN ATMOSPHERIC SCIENCE. 1974. irreg., vol.16, 1984. price varies. Elsevier Science Publishers B.V., Box 211, 1000 AE Amsterdam, Netherlands.

551.5   EC
ECUADOR. INSTITUTO NACIONAL DE METEOROLOGIA E HIDROLOGIA. ANUARIO METEOROLOGICO. 1959. a. available on exchange. Instituto Nacional de Meteorologia e Hidrologia, Daniel Hidalgo 132 y 10 de Agosto, Quito, Ecuador. index.
    Supersedes: Ecuador. Servicio Nacional de Meteorologia e Hidrologia. Anuario Meteorologico (ISSN 0070-8941)

551.5   UA
EGYPT. METEOROLOGICAL AUTHORITY. ANNUAL METEOROLOGICAL REPORT. a. $1.50. Meteorological Authority, Kubri-el-Qubbeh, Cairo, Egypt.

551.5   318   PN
ESTADISTICA PANAMENA. SITUACION FISICA. SECCION 121. METEOROLOGIA. 1952/57. a. Bl.0.75. Direccion de Estadistica y Censo, Contraloria General, Apartado 5213, Panama 5, Panama. circ. 800.
    Formerly: Estadistica Panamena. Situacion Fisica. Seccion 121-Clima. Meteorologia (ISSN 0378-6757)

551.5   FI   ISSN 0071-5190
FINNISH METEOROLOGICAL INSTITUTE. CONTRIBUTIONS. (Text in English) 1925. irreg., no.87, 1984. price varies. ‡ Ilmatieteen Laitos - Finnish Meteorological Institute, Box 503, SF-00101 Helsinki, Finland.

550   UR
FIZIKA AERODISPERSNYKH SISTEM. (Text in Russian; summaries in English) 1969. irreg. Izdatel'stvo Kievskii Universitet, Bul'var Tarasa Shevchenko, 14, Kiev, Ukrainian S.S.R., U.S.S.R. (Subscr. to: Mezhdunarodnaya Kniga, Moscow, G-200, Russian S.F.S.R., U.S.S.R.) illus. Indexed: Chem.Abstr.

550   UR
FIZIKA NIZHNEI ATMOSFERY. (Subseries of: Institut Eksperimental'noi Meteorologii. Trudy) 1972. irreg. (Institut Eksperimental'noi Meteorologii) Gidrometeoizdat, Vasil'evskii Ostrov, 3, Leningrad V-53, Russian S.F.S.R., U.S.S.R. illus.

551.5   AT
FLINDERS INSTITUTE FOR ATMOSPHERIC AND MARINE SCIENCES. COMPUTING REPORTS. 1972. irreg., no.11, 1978. Flinders Institute for Atmospheric and Marine Sciences, Bedford Park, S.A. 5042, Australia. Ed. Peter Schwerdtfeger. circ. 150.

551.5   AT
FLINDERS INSTITUTE FOR ATMOSPHERIC AND MARINE SCIENCES. RESEARCH REPORTS. 1972. irreg., no.33, 1980. Flinders Institute for Atmospheric and Marine Sciences, Bedford Park, S.A. 5042, Australia. Ed. Peter Schwerdtfeger. circ. 200.

551.5   AT
FLINDERS INSTITUTE FOR ATMOSPHERIC AND MARINE SCIENCES. TECHNICAL REPORTS. 1973. irreg., no.4, 1980. Aus.$20. Flinders Institute for Atmospheric and Marine Sciences, Bedford Park, S.A. 5042, Australia. Ed. Peter Schwerdtfeger. circ. 150.

551.5   GE   ISSN 0138-5658
GERMANY (DEMOCRATIC REPUBLIC, 1949-). METEOROLOGISCHER DIENST. ABHANDLUNGEN. 1964. irreg., no.135, 1986. price varies. Akademie-Verlag, Leipziger Strasse 3-4, 1086 Berlin, E. Germany (D.D.R.)

551.5   GH
GHANA. METEOROLOGICAL DEPARTMENT. CLIMATOLOGICAL NOTES. irreg., latest no.5. price varies. Meteorological Department, Box 87, Legon, Accra, Ghana.

551.5   GH
GHANA. METEOROLOGICAL DEPARTMENT. PROFESSIONAL NOTES. irreg., latest no.23. price varies. Meteorological Department, Box 87, Legon, Accra, Ghana.

551.5   GH
GHANA. METEOROLOGICAL DEPARTMENT. SUN AND MOON TABLES FOR GHANA. Short title: Sun and Moon Tables for Ghana. 1954. a. NC.1. Meteorological Department, Box 87, Legon, Accra, Ghana.

551.5   UK   ISSN 0072-6605
GREAT BRITAIN. METEOROLOGICAL OFFICE. ANNUAL REPORT. a. price varies. H.M.S.O., Box 569, London SE1 9NH, England. (reprint service avail. from UMI)

551.5   UK   ISSN 0072-6621
GREAT BRITAIN. METEOROLOGICAL OFFICE. SCIENTIFIC PAPER. 1960. irreg. price varies. H.M.S.O., Box 569, London SE1 9NH, England. (reprint service avail. from UMI)

551.6   GY
GUYANA. HYDROMETEOROLOGICAL SERVICE. ANNUAL CLIMATOLOGICAL DATA SUMMARY. (Subseries of: Guyana. Hydrometeorological Service) 1973. a. Hydrometeorological Service, Georgetown, Guyana. Ed. S. Raghunandan. illus. circ. 200.

551.5   IS
HEBREW UNIVERSITY OF JERUSALEM. DEPARTMENT OF ATMOSPHERIC SCIENCES. LIST OF CONTRIBUTIONS. 1970. a. Hebrew University of Jerusalem, Department of Atmospheric Sciences, Terra Santa College Building, Jerusalem, Israel.

551.5   HK
HONG KONG. ROYAL OBSERVATORY. OCCASIONAL PAPER. 1950. irreg. Royal Observatory, Nathan Rd., Kowloon, Hong Kong, Hong Kong.

551.5   HK
HONG KONG. ROYAL OBSERVATORY. TECHNICAL NOTE. 1949. irreg. Royal Observatory, Nathan Rd., Kowloon, Hong Kong, Hong Kong.
    Formerly: Hong Kong. Royal Observatory. Climatological Note.

551.5   BU   ISSN 0018-1331
HYDROLOGY AND METEOROLOGY/ HIDROLOGIJA I METEOROLOGIJA. (Summaries in various languages) 1964. irreg. price varies. Publishing House of the Bulgarian Academy of Sciences, Acad. G. Bonchev St., Bldg. 6, 1113 Sofia, Bulgaria (Dist. by: Hemus, 6, Rouski Blvd., 1000 Sofia, Bulgaria) Ed. I. Marinov. circ. 500.
    Formerly: Bulgarska Akademiia na Naukite. Institut po Khidrologiia i Meteorologiia. Izvestiia (ISSN 0068-3876)

551.5   CS
HYDROMETEOROLOGICKY USTAV. VYROCNI ZPRAVA. a. price varies. Statni Nakladatelstvi Technicke Literatury, Spalena 51, 113 02 Prague 1, Czechoslovakia.

551.57   CS
HYDROMETEOROLOGICKY USTAV, BRATISLAVA. ZBORNIK PRAC. (Text in Russian; summaries in Czech or Slovak, and in German) 1972. irreg., approx. biennial. 30 Kcs. Slovenske Pedagogicke Nakladatelstvo, Sasinkova 5, 815 60 Bratislava, Czechoslovakia. illus.

551.5 US
I A M P NEWS BULLETIN. irreg. International
Association of Meteorology and Atmospheric
Physics, c/o Stanley Ruttenberg, Sec.-Gen.,
University Corporation for Atmospheric Research,
Box 3000, Boulder, CO 80307. TEL 303-497-1658.

551.5 JA
IJO TENKO HOKOKU. 1974. irreg. 2100 Yen. Japan
Meteorological Agency, Ote-Machi, Hiyoda-ku,
Tokyo 100, Japan.

551.5 II
INDIA. METEOROLOGICAL DEPARTMENT.
MEMOIRS. (Text in English) irreg. price varies.
Meteorological Department, Lodi Rd., New Delhi
110003, India (Order from: Controller of
Publications, Government of India, Civil Lines,
Delhi 110054, India)

551.5 II ISSN 0250-6017
INDIAN INSTITUTE OF TROPICAL
METEOROLOGY. ANNUAL REPORT. 1971/72.
a. contr.circ. Indian Institute of Tropical
Meteorology, Ramdurg House, University Rd.,
Poona 411005, India. circ. controlled.

551.5 II ISSN 0252-1075
INDIAN INSTITUTE OF TROPICAL
METEOROLOGY. CONTRIBUTIONS. 1980.
irreg. Indian Institute of Tropical Meteorology,
Ramdurg House, University Rd., Poona 411005,
India. circ. controlled.
 Supersedes (1971-1980): Indian Institute of
Tropical Meteorology. Research Report (ISSN
0250-6009)

551.5 UR
INSTITUT EKSPERIMENTAL'NOI
METEOROLOGII. TRUDY. vol.16, 1977. irreg.
price varies. Gidrometeoizdat, Moskovskoe
Otdelenie, Ul. Buzheninovskaya, 42-1, Moscow
107061, Russian S.F.S.R., U.S.S.R. abstr. circ. 400.
Indexed: Chem.Abstr.

551.5 AO
INSTITUTO DE INVESTIGACAO AGRONOMICA
DE ANGOLA. DIVISAO DE METEOROLOGIA
AGRICOLA. ANUARIO. 1972. a. free. Instituto de
Investigacao Agronomica de Angola, C.P. 406,
Nova Lisboa, Angola. Indexed: Trop.Abstr.

551.5 US ISSN 0074-1663
INTERNATIONAL ASSOCIATION OF
METEOROLOGY AND ATMOSPHERIC
PHYSICS. REPORT OF PROCEEDINGS OF
GENERAL ASSEMBLY. 1924. every 3-4 yrs.;
18th, 1979, Canberra. free. International Association
of Meteorology and Atmospheric Physics, c/o
Stanley Ruttenberg, Sec.-Gen., University
Corporation for Atmospheric Research, Box 3000,
Boulder, CO 80307. TEL 303-497-8998. circ.
controlled.

INTERNATIONAL CONFERENCE ON
ATMOSPHERIC ELECTRICITY.
PUBLICATION. see PHYSICS — Heat

551.576 CN ISSN 0074-3011
INTERNATIONAL CONFERENCE ON CLOUD
PHYSICS. PROCEEDINGS. (Proceedings
published in host countries) 1968. irreg., 8th, 1982,
Aubiere, France. Can.$20. (International
Association of Meteorology and Atmospheric
Physics) International Commission on Cloud
Physics, c/o Prof. R. List, University of Toronto,
Toronto, Ont. M5S 1A6, Canada. adv. circ. 1,500.

551.5 SW ISSN 0349-0068
INTERNATIONAL METEOROLOGICAL
INSTITUTE IN STOCKHOLM. ANNUAL
REPORT. (Report year ends June 30) 1973. a. free.
International Meteorological Institute in Stockholm,
Arrhenius Laboratory, S-106 91 Stockholm, Sweden.
Ed. Marianne Skaarman. circ. 600.

551.5 333.91 IS
ISRAEL. METEOROLOGICAL SERVICE.
RAINFALL SEASON. (Text in English and
Hebrew) a. Meteorological Service, P.O. Box 25,
Beit Dagan 50 200, Israel. TEL 03-625231.

551.5 IS ISSN 0075-126X
ISRAEL. METEOROLOGICAL SERVICE. SERIES
B: OBSERVATIONAL DATA. ANNUAL
RAINFALL SUMMARY. (Text in Hebrew,
summaries in English and Hebrew) 1947/48. a.
Meteorological Service, Box 25, Bet Dagan, Israel.

551.5 IS ISSN 0075-1286
ISRAEL. METEOROLOGICAL SERVICE. SERIES
B: OBSERVATIONAL DATA. ANNUAL
WEATHER REPORT. (Text in Hebrew, and
summaries in English and Hebrew) 1948. a.
Meteorological Service, Box 25, Bet Dagan, Israel.

551.5 IS
ISRAEL. METEOROLOGICAL SOCIETY.
METEOROLOGIA BE-ISRAEL. (Text in Hebrew)
1963. irreg. $5. Meteorological Society, Box 25,
Bet-Dagan, Israel. Ed.Bd. bk. rev. charts. illus. circ.
300. (processed) Indexed: Meteor. &
Geoastrophys.Abstr.
 Formerly: Israel. Meteorologia Be-Israel. (ISSN
0026-1122)

551.51 IT ISSN 0075-191X
ISTITUTO DI FISICA DELL'ATMOSFERA,
ROME. CONTRIBUTI SCIENTIFICI:
PUBBLICAZIONI DI FISICA
DELL'ATMOSFERA E DI METTEOROLOGIA.
(Contributions in English, German and Italian)
1964. irreg. Istituto di Fisica dell'Atmosfera,
Piazzale Luigi Sturzo 31, 00144 Rome, Italy.
Indexed: Meteor.& Geoastrophys.Abstr.

551.51 IT ISSN 0075-1928
ISTITUTO DI FISICA DELL'ATMOSFERA,
ROME. PUBBLICAZIONI DIDATTICHE. 1962.
irreg. $10. Istituto di Fisica dell'Atmosfera, Piazzale
Luigi Sturzo 31, 00144 Rome, Italy. Indexed:
Meteor.& Geoastrophys.Abstr.

551.51 IT ISSN 0075-1936
ISTITUTO DI FISICA DELL'ATMOSFERA,
ROME. PUBBLICAZIONI SCIENTIFICHE.
(Contributions in English and Italian) 1962. irreg.
Istituto di Fisica dell'Atmosfera, Piazzale Luigi
Sturzo 31, 00144 Rome, Italy. Indexed: Meteor.&
Geoastrophys.Abstr.

551.51 IT ISSN 0075-1944
ISTITUTO DI FISICA DELL'ATMOSFERA,
ROME. PUBBLICAZIONI VARIE. (Contributions
in English and Italian) 1962. irreg. Istituto di Fisica
dell'Atmosfera, Piazzale Luigi Sturzo 31, 00144
Rome, Italy. Indexed: Meteor.& Geoastrophys.Abstr.

551.51 IT ISSN 0075-1952
ISTITUTO DI FISICA DELL'ATMOSFERA,
ROME. RAPPORTI INTERNI PROVVISORI
ADIFFUSIONE LIMITATA. (Contribution in
English and Italian) 1966. irreg. Istituto di Fisica
dell'Atmosfera, Piazzale Luigi Sturzo 31, 00144
Rome, Italy. Indexed: Meteor.& Geoastrophys.Abstr.

551.51 IT ISSN 0075-1960
ISTITUTO DI FISICA DELL'ATMOSFERA,
ROME. RAPPORTI SCIENTIFICI. (Contributions
in English and Italian) 1962. irreg. Istituto di Fisica
dell'Atmosfera, Piazzale Luigi Sturzo 31, 00144
Rome, Italy. Indexed: Meteor.& Geoastrophys.Abstr.

551.51 IT ISSN 0075-1979
ISTITUTO DI FISICA DELL'ATMOSFERA,
ROME. RAPPORTI TECNICI. (Contributions in
English, French and Italian) 1961. irreg. Istituto di
Fisica dell'Atmosfera, Piazzale Luigi Sturzo 31,
00144 Rome, Italy. Indexed: Meteor.&
Geoastrophys.Abstr.

551.4 IT ISSN 0082-6448
ISTITUTO SPERIMENTALE TALASSOGRAFICO,
TRIESTE. ANNUARIO. 1954. a. L.2000. Istituto
Sperimentale Talassografico, c/o Consiglio
Nazionale delle Ricerche, Servizio Pubblicazioni,
Piazzale Aldo Moro 7, I-00100 Rome, Italy.

551.65 IT ISSN 0075-1731
ITALY. ISTITUTO CENTRALE DI STATISTICA.
ANNUARIO DI STATISTICHE
METEOROLOGICHE. a. L.7000. Istituto Centrale
di Statistica, Via Cesare Balbo 16, 00100 Rome,
Italy. circ. 1,200.

551.5 GW ISSN 0433-8251
JAHRESBERICHT DES DEUTSCHEN
WETTERDIENSTES. 1953. a. DM.33. Bibliothek
des Deutschen Wetterdienstes, Frankfurter Str. 135,
6050 Offenbach (Main), W. Germany (B.R.D.) circ.
800.

551.65 JA ISSN 0448-3758
JAPAN. METEOROLOGICAL AGENCY.
ANNUAL REPORT/KISHO-CHO NENPO
ZENKOKU KISHOHYO. (Issued in two parts)
1886. a. $12. Japan Weather Association, c/o Japan
Meteorological Agency, 1-3-4 Otemachi, Chiyoda-
ku, Tokyo 100, Japan.

551.5 630 JA
JAPAN METEOROLOGICAL AGENCY.
AGRICULTURAL METEOROLOGY. ANNUAL
REPORT. (Text in Japanese) 1940. a. membership.
Japan Meteorological Agency, Ote-Machi, Chiyoda-
Ku, Tokyo, Japan. circ. 400.

551.5 US
JOINT CONFERENCE ON APPLICATIONS OF
AIR POLLUTION METEOROLOGY
(PUBLICATION) 1977. irreg., 4th, 1984. $30.
American Meteorological Society, 45 Beacon St.,
Boston, MA 02108. TEL 617-227-2425.

551.5 US
JOINT CONFERENCE ON FIRE AND FOREST
METEOROLOGY. (PUBLICATION) 5th, 1978.
irreg., 7th, 1983. $20. American Meteorological
Society, 45 Beacon St., Boston, MA 02108. TEL
617-227-2425.

551.63 US ISSN 0739-1781
JOURNAL OF WEATHER MODIFICATION. 1969.
a. $35. Weather Modification Association, Box
8116, Fresno, CA 93727. TEL 209-291-8466. Ed.
Thomas J. Henderson. adv. cum.index: 1969-1985.
circ. 500. (back issues avail.)

551.5 JA
KANSOKUJO KISHO NENPO. 1966. a. 2100 Yen.
Japan Meteorological Agency, Ote-Machi, Chiyoda-
ku, Tokyo 100, Japan. circ. 400.

551.656 KE
KENYA METEOROLOGICAL DEPARTMENT.
ANNUAL REPORT. 1929. a. Meteorological
Department, P.O. Box 30259, Dagoretti Corner,
Ngong Rd., Nairobi, Kenya. circ. 1,200.
 Supersedes in part: East African Community.
East African Meteorological Department. Annual
Report.

551.5 JA
KISHO-CHO KANSOKU GIJUTSU SHIRYO. 1956.
irreg. 1100 Yen. Japan Meteorological Agency, Ote-
Machi, Chihyoda-ku, Tokyo 100, Japan. circ. 400.

551.5 UR
KLIMAT I GIDROGRAFIYA ZABAIKAL'YA.
1972. irreg. 0.40 Rub. Geograficheskoe Obshchestvo
S.S.S.R., Zabaikal'skii Filial, Chita, Russian S.F.S.R.,
U.S.S.R. illus.

KOBE KAIYO KISHODAI IHO/KOBE MARINE
OBSERVATORY. BULLETIN. see EARTH
SCIENCES — Oceanography

551.5 KO
KOREA (REPUBLIC). CENTRAL
METEOROLOGICAL OFFICE. ANNUAL
REPORT. a. 1000 Won($2) Central Meteorological
Office, Seoul, S. Korea.

551.5 FI ISSN 0303-2485
KUUKAUSIKATSAUS SUOMEN ILMASTOON/
MAANADSOEVERSIKT OEVER FINLANDS
KLIMAT. (Text and summaries in Finnish and
Swedish) 1907. irreg. Fmk.55. Ilmatieteen Laitos -
Finnish Meteorological Institute, Box 503, SF-00101
Helsinki, Finland. (back issues avail.)

551.6 CN ISSN 0076-1931
MCGILL UNIVERSITY, MONTREAL.
DEPARTMENT OF GEOGRAPHY.
CLIMATOLOGICAL RESEARCH SERIES. 1966.
irreg. price varies. McGill University, Department
of Geography, 805 Sherbrooke St. W., Montreal,
Que. H3A 2R6, Canada. TEL 514-392-5700. Eds.
T. Moore, J. Lewis.

551.5 MW
MALAWI. METEOROLOGICAL DEPARTMENT.
TOTALS OF MONTHLY AND ANNUAL
RAINFALL. (Text and summaries in English) 1969.
a. K.1. Meteorological Department, Box 2, Chileka,
Malawi. stat.
 Formerly: Malawi. Meteorological Services. Totals
of Monthly and Annual Rainfall.

METEOROLOGY

551.5   MY
MALAYSIA. METEOROLOGICAL SERVICE. ANNUAL SUMMARY OF METEOROLOGICAL OBSERVATIONS. (Text and summaries in English) 1930. a. M.30. ‡ Malaysian Meteorological Service - Perkhidmatan Kajicuaca Malaysia, Jalan Sultan, Petaling Jaya, Selangor, Malaysia. circ. 210.
  Former titles: Malaysia. Meteorological Service. Summary of Observations for Malaysia (ISSN 0126-8864); Malaysia. Meterological Service. Summary of Observations for Malaya, Sabah and Sarawak.

551.5   PL   ISSN 0239-6262
MATERIALY BADAWCZE. SERIA: METEOROLOGIA/RESEARCH PAPERS SERIES: METEOROLOGY. (Text in Polish; summaries in English and Russian) 1974. irreg. $33. Instytut Meteorologii i Gospodarki Wodnej - Institute of Meteorology and Water Management, 61 Podlesna St., 01-673 Warsaw, Poland. circ. 350.

551.5   MF   ISSN 0076-5511
MAURITIUS. METEOROLOGICAL SERVICES. REPORT. a., latest issue 1973-74. price varies. Government Printing Office, Elizabeth II Ave., Port Louis, Mauritius.

551.5   FI   ISSN 0076-6747
METEOROLOGICAL YEARBOOK OF FINLAND. PART 1: CLIMATOLOGICAL DATA. (Text in English and Finnish) 1981. a. price varies. ‡ Ilmatieteen Laitos - Finnish Meteorological Institute, Box 503, SF-00101 Helsinki, Finland.

551.5   FI   ISSN 0076-6755
METEOROLOGICAL YEARBOOK OF FINLAND. PART 2: PRECIPITATION AND SNOW COVER DATA. (Text in English and Finnish) 1960. a. price varies. ‡ Ilmatieteen Laitos - Finnish Meteorological Institute, Box 503, SF-00101 Helsinki, Finland.

551.5   FI   ISSN 0780-7295
METEOROLOGICAL YEARBOOK OF FINLAND. PART 3. STATISTICS OF RADIOSONDE OBSERVATIONS 1961-1980. (Text in English and Finnish) 1984. irreg. price varies. Finnish Meteorological Institute, Box 503, SF-00101, Helsinki, Finland.

551.5   FI   ISSN 0076-6763
METEOROLOGICAL YEARBOOK OF FINLAND. PART 4: MEASUREMENTS OF RADIATION AND BRIGHT SUNSHINE. (Text in English and Finnish) 1966. a. price varies. ‡ Ilmatieteen Laitos - Finnish Meteorological Institute, Box 503, SF-00101 Helsinki, Finland.

551.5   GE   ISSN 0138-1105
METEOROLOGISCHEN DIENSTES DER D D R. VEROEFFENTLICHUNGEN. (Text in German; summaries in English, German and Russian) 1949. irreg., vol.26, 1985. (Meteorologischen Dienst der DDR) Akademie-Verlag Berlin, Leipziger Str. 3-4, 1086 Berlin, E. Germany (D.D.R.)

551.65   DK   ISSN 0106-6463
METEOROLOGISK AARBOG/METEOROLOGICAL YEARBOOK. (Text in Danish and English) 1873. a. Dansk Meteorologiske Institiut, Copenhagen, Denmark.

551.65   US
MINNESOTA WEATHER GUIDE CALENDAR. Short title: Weatherguide. 1975. a. $9.65. Freshwater Foundation, Box 90, Navarre, MN 55392. TEL 612-471-8407. Eds. Bruce Watson, Jim Gilbert. circ. 25,000.
  Former titles: Weather Guide Calendar (ISSN 0270-9031); Weather Guide Calendar Almanac (until 1977); Minnesota and Environs Weather Almanac (ISSN 0095-7348)

551.51   JA   ISSN 0077-264X
NAGOYA UNIVERSITY. RESEARCH INSTITUTE OF ATMOSPHERICS. PROCEEDINGS/NAGOYA DAIGAKU KUDEN KENKYUSHO HOKOKU. (Text in English) 1953. a. Nagoya University, Research Institute of Atmospherics - Nagoya Daigaku Kuden Kenkyusho, 3-13 Honohara, Toyokawa 442, Aichi-ken, Japan. Indexed: Int.Aerosp.Abstr.

551.65   JA   ISSN 0386-5525
NATIONAL INSTITUTE OF POLAR RESEARCH. MEMOIRS. SERIES B: METEOROLOGY. (Text and abstracts in English) 1969. irreg., no.2, 1974. exchange basis. National Institute of Polar Research - Kokuritsu Kyokuchi Kenkyujo, 9-10, Kaga 1-chome, Itabashi-ku, Tokyo 173, Japan. Ed. Tatsuro Matsuda. circ. 1,000. Indexed: Curr.Antarc.Lit.
  Supersedes: Japanese Antarctic Research Expedition, 1956-1962. Scientific Reports. Series B: Meteorology (ISSN 0075-336X)

551.5   II
NATIONAL REPORT FOR INDIA: METEOROLOGY AND ATMOSPHERIC ANALYSIS. (Text in English) quadrennial. Meteorological Department, Lodi Road, New Delhi 110003, India.

551.5   II
NATIONAL REPORT FOR INDIA: SEISMOLOGY AND PHYSICS OF THE EARTH'S INTERIOR. (Text in English) quadrennial. Meteorological Department, Lodi Rd., New Delhi 110003, India.
  Continues: India (Republic). Meteorological Department Report on Seismology (ISSN 0536-9029)

551.5   CU
NOTICIERO AGROPECUARIO. SUPLEMENTO AGROMETEOROLOGICO. irreg. Ministerio de la Agricultura, 11 No. 1057, Vedado, Havana, Cuba.

OHIO STATE UNIVERSITY. INSTITUTE OF POLAR STUDIES. MISCELLANEOUS SERIES. see *EARTH SCIENCES*

OHIO STATE UNIVERSITY. INSTITUTE OF POLAR STUDIES. REPORT SERIES. see *EARTH SCIENCES*

551.5   PL
OPADY ATMOSFERYCZNE/PRECIPITATION. (Text in Polish; table and chart titles in English and Russian) 1945. a. $240. Instytut Meteorologii i Gospodarki Wodnej - Institute of Meteorology and Water Management, Podlesna 61, 01-673 Warsaw, Poland (Dist. by: Ars Polona-Ruch, Krakowskie Przedmiescie 7, 00-068 Warsaw, Poland) charts. illus. circ. 400.

551.5   US
OXFORD MONOGRAPHS ON METEOROLOGY AND PHYSICAL OCEANOGRAPHY. irreg. price varies. Oxford University Press, 200 Madison Ave., New York, NY 10016 TEL 212-679-7300. (And Ely House, 37 Dover St., London W1X 4AH, England) Ed. P.A. Sheppard.
  Formerly: Oxford Monographs on Meterology.

551.5   CN   ISSN 0030-7777
OZONE DATA FOR THE WORLD/DONNEES MONDIALES SUR L'OZONE. (Text in English and French) 1960. bi-m. (plus supplements and annual cumulative catalog) Can.$1. Atmospheric Environment Service, 4905 Dufferin St., Downsview, Ont. M3H 5T4, Canada. TEL 416-667-4882. circ. 500. (back issues avail.)

551.5   PH
PHILIPPINE AGRICULTURAL METEOROLOGY BULLETIN. 1970. irreg. 42p.($3) Philippine Atmospheric, Geophysical and Astronomical Services Administration, Agricultural Meteorology Division, 424 Quezon Ave., Quezon City, Philippines. Ed.Bd. charts. stat. circ. 130.

PROBLEMY FIZIKI ATMOSFERY. see *PHYSICS*

610 551.5   NE
PROGRESS IN BIOMETEOROLOGY. (Text in English) 1972. irreg. price varies. Swets Publishing Service (Subsidiary of: Swets en Zeitlinger B.V.) Heereweg 347, 2161 CA Lisse, Netherlands (Dist. in the U.S. and Canada by: Swets North America, Inc. Box 517, Berwyn, PA 19312) circ. 600. Indexed: Biol.Abstr. Chem.Abstr.

551.5   PL
PROMIENIOWANIE SLONECZNE/SOLAR RADIATION. (Text in Polish; table titles in English and Russian) 1961. a. $300. Instytut Meteorologii i Gospodarki Wodnej - Institute of Meteorology and Water Management, Podlesna 61, 01-673 Warsaw, Poland (Dist. by: Ars Polona-Ruch, Krakowskie Przedmiescie 7, 00-068 Warsaw, Poland) charts. circ. 200.

551.6   US
PUBLICATIONS IN CLIMATOLOGY. 1948. a. vol. of 3 or 4 nos. price varies. (Laboratory of Climatology, Centerton, N.J.) C.W. Thornthwaite Associates, Rt. 1, Centerton, Elmer, NJ 08318. TEL 609-358-2350. Ed. John R. Mather. circ. 500. Indexed: GeoRef.

551.527   NO
RADIATION OBSERVATIONS IN BERGEN; radiation yearbook. 1965. a. free. Universitetet i Bergen - University of Bergen, Geophysical Institute, Bergen, Norway. Ed. A. Skartveit. circ. 300.

551.5   MH   ISSN 0460-3060
RESULTADOS DAS OBSERVACOES METEOROLOGICAS DE MACAU. (Text in English and Portuguese; summaries in Portuguese) 1952. m. (plus annual) free. Servicos Meteorologicos e Geofisicos de Macau, Caixa Postal 93, Macao. Ed.Bd. charts. stat. circ. 120.

551.5 551   BE   ISSN 0072-4440
RIJKSUNIVERSITEIT TE GENT. STERRENKUNDIG OBSERVATORIUM. MEDEDELINGEN: METEOROLOGIE EN GEOFYSICA. (Text and summaries in Dutch, English or French) 1961. irreg. free. Rijksuniversiteit te Gent, Sterrenkundig Observatorium, Krijgslaan 281, 9000 Ghent, Belgium.

551.5   PL   ISSN 0080-3448
ROCZNIK ELEKTRYCZNOSCI ATMOSFERYCZNEJ I METEOROLOGII. (Subseries of Prace Obserwatorium Geofizycznego Im. St. Kalinowskiego w Swidrze) (Text in French and Polish; summaries in French) 1961. irreg., 1974. price varies. (Polska Akademia Nauk, Instytut Geofizyki) Panstwowe Wydawnictwo Naukowe, Miodowa 10, 00-251 Warsaw, Poland (Dist. by: Ars Polona, Krakowskie Przedmiescie 7, 00-068 Warsaw, Poland) Ed. Roman Teisseyre.

551.656   MG
SAISON CYCLONIQUE A MADAGASCAR. (Text in French) 1973/74. a. Service de la Meteorologie Nationale, B.P. 1254, Antananarivo, Malagasy Republic.

551.6   CN
SASKATCHEWAN RESEARCH COUNCIL. CLIMATOLOGICAL REFERENCE STATION. ANNUAL SUMMARY. 1975. a. Can.$5. Saskatchewan Research Council., Environment Division, 15 Innovation Blvd., Saskatoon, Sask. S7N 2X8, Canada. TEL 306-933-8179. Ed. Elaine Wheaton. circ. 350.
  Former titles: Saskatoon S.R.C. Climatological Reference Station. Annual Summary; Saskatchewan Research Council. Physics Division. Annual Climatic Summary (ISSN 0706-9391)

551.5   SZ   ISSN 0080-7338
SCHWEIZERISCHE METEOROLOGISCHE ANSTALT. ANNALEN. 1864. a. 70 Fr. Schweizerische Meteorologische Anstalt - Swiss Meteorological Institute, Kraehbuehlstrasse 58, CH-8044 Zurich, Switzerland. index.

551.5   SZ
SCHWEIZERISCHE METEOROLOGISCHE ANSTALT. VEROEFFENTLICHUNGEN. (Text in French, German or Italian; summaries in English, French, German or Italian) 1962. irreg., no.45, 1984. price varies. Schweizerische Meteorologische Anstalt - Swiss Meteorological Institute, Kraehbuehlstr. 58, CH-8044 Zurich, Switzerland. Indexed: Field Crop Abstr. Geo.Abstr. Herb.Abstr.
  Formerly: Schweizerische Meterologische Zentralanstalt. Veroeffentlichungen (ISSN 0080-7346)

551.6   SA   ISSN 0379-6736
SOUTH AFRICA. WEATHER BUREAU. TECHNICAL PAPER/TEGNIESE VERHANDELINGE. 1974. irreg., no.14, 1983. Weather Bureau, Department of Environment Affairs, Private Bag X97, Pretoria 0001, South Africa.

551.5   SA   ISSN 0081-2331
SOUTH AFRICA. WEATHER BUREAU. W.B. SERIES. 1971. irreg., no.39, 1979. Weather Bureau, Department of Environment Affairs, Private Bag X97, Pretoria 0001, South Africa. circ. 1,500.

METEOROLOGY   807

551.5   US
SYMPOSIUM ON METEOROLOGICAL OBSERVATIONS AND INSTRUMENTATION. PREPRINTS. irreg., 5th, 1983. $20. American Meteorological Society, 45 Beacon St., Boston, MA 02108. TEL 617-227-2425.

551.5   US
SYMPOSIUM ON TURBULENCE AND DIFFUSION. PREPRINTS. (In 1981 and 1983 also called Extended Abstracts) irreg., 9th, 1985. $30. American Meteorological Society, 45 Beacon St., Boston, MA 02108. TEL 617-227-2425.
Former titles (until 1983): Symposium on Turbulence, Diffusion and Air Pollution. Preprints & Symposium on Atmospheric Turbulence, Diffusion and Air Quality. Preprints.

551.5 620   JA
SYMPOSIUM ON WIND EFFECTS ON STRUCTURES IN JAPAN. PROCEEDINGS. (Text in Japanese; summaries in English) 1970. biennial. price varies. Science Council of Japan, Meteorological Society of Japan, c/o Japan Meteorological Agency, 1-7, Ote-machi, Chiyoda-ku, Tokyo 100, Japan.
Formerly: National Symposium on Wind Engineering. Proceedings.

551.5   JA
TAIFU KEIROZU. 1940. a. 2100 Yen. Japan Meteorological Agency, Ote-Machi, Chiyoda-Ku, Tokyo 100, Japan. circ. 500.

551.5   US
TECHNICAL CONFERENCE ON HURRICANES AND TROPICAL METEOROLOGY (PUBLICATION) 11th, 1977. irreg., 16th, 1985. $20. American Meteorological Society, 45 Beacon St., Boston, MA 02108. TEL 617-227-2425.

551.5   TG
TOGO. DIRECTION DE LA METEOROLOGIE NATIONALE. RESUME ANNUEL DU TEMPS. a. Direction de la Meteorologie Nationale, B.P. 1505, Lome, Togo.

TOPICS IN ATMOSPHERIC AND OCEANOGRAPHIC SCIENCES. see *EARTH SCIENCES — Oceanography*

551.6   US
U.S. NATIONAL OCEANIC AND ATMOSPHERIC ADMINISTRATION. ANNUAL CLIMATE DIAGNOSTIC WORKSHOP. PROCEEDINGS. 1976. a. U.S. National Oceanic and Atmospheric Administration, 6010 Executive Blvd., Rockville, MD 20852 TEL 301-655-4000. (Orders to: N T I S, U.S. Dept. of Commerce, Sills Bldg., 5285 Port Royal Rd., Springfield, VA 22161)

551.552   US   ISSN 0092-2056
U.S. NATIONAL OCEANIC AND ATMOSPHERIC ADMINISTRATION. INTERDEPARTMENTAL COMMITTEE FOR METEOROLOGICAL SERVICES AND SUPPORTING RESEARCH. NATIONAL HURRICANE OPERATIONS PLAN. (Formerly issued by: Office of Federal Coordinator for Meteorological Services and Supporting Research) 1962. irreg. U.S. National Oceanic and Atmospheric Administration, Interdepartmental Committee for Meteorological Services and Supporting Research, Rockville, MD 20852. TEL 301-655-4000. illus. circ. 1,000. Key Title: National Hurricane Operations Plan.

UNIVERSITAET ZU KOELN. INSTITUT FUER GEOPHYSIK UND METEOROLOGIE. MITTEILUNGEN. see *EARTH SCIENCES — Geophysics*

UNIVERSITY OF ALASKA. GEOPHYSICAL INSTITUTE. REPORT SERIES. see *EARTH SCIENCES — Geophysics*

551.6   UK
UNIVERSITY OF EAST ANGLIA. CLIMATIC RESEARCH UNIT. RESEARCH PUBLICATION. 1973. irreg. price varies. University of East Anglia, Climatic Research Unit, School of Environmental Sciences, Norwich NR4 7TJ, England. Indexed: Geo.Abstr.

551.5271   US   ISSN 0193-9629
UNIVERSITY OF WISCONSIN, MADISON. ENGINEERING EXPERIMENT STATION. ANNUAL REPORT. a. free. University of Wisconsin-Madison, Engineering Experiment Station, Informational Resources Office, 1500 Johnson Dr., Madison, WI 53706. TEL 605-263-1610. Ed. Ann Bitter. charts. illus. Key Title: Annual Report - Engineering Experiment Station (Madison)

VIND - NYT. see *TRANSPORTATION — Ships And Shipping*

551.65   JA
WAKAYAMA PREFECTURE. ANNUAL REPORT OF METEOROLOGY/WAKAYAMA-KEN KISHO NENPO. (Text in Japanese) a. Wakayama Local Meteorological Observatory - Wakayama Chiho Kishodai, 4 Onoshiba-cho, Wakayama 640, Japan. charts.stat.

551.6   US   ISSN 0731-5627
WEATHER ALMANAC. 1974. irreg., 5th edt., 1986. $110. Gale Research Company, Book Tower, Detroit, MI 48226. TEL 313-961-2242. Eds. James A. Ruffner, Frank E. Bair.

551.5   UN   ISSN 0084-1927
WORLD METEOROLOGICAL CONGRESS. ABRIDGED REPORT WITH RESOLUTIONS. (Text in English, French, Russian, Spanish) 1952. quadrennial. price varies. World Meteorological Organization, 41 Av. Giuseppe Motta, CH-1211 Geneva 20, Switzerland (Dist. in U.S. by: American Meteorological Society, 45 Beacon St., Boston, MA 02108)

551.5   UN   ISSN 0084-1935
WORLD METEOROLOGICAL CONGRESS. PROCEEDINGS. (Text in English and French) 1952. quadrennial. World Meteorological Organization, 41 Av. Giuseppe Motta, CH-1211 Geneva 20, Switzerland (Dist. in U.S. by: American Meteorological Society, 45 Beacon St., Boston, MA 02108)

551.5   UN   ISSN 0084-1994
WORLD METEOROLOGICAL ORGANIZATION. ANNUAL REPORTS. 1953. a. price varies. World Meteorological Organization, 41 Av. Giuseppe Motta, CH-1211 Geneva 20, Switzerland (Dist. in U.S. by: American Meteorological Society, 45 Beacon St., Boston, MA 02108)

551.5   UN
WORLD METEOROLOGICAL ORGANIZATION. BASIC DOCUMENTS. irreg. World Meteorological Organization, 41 Av. Giuseppe Motta, CH-1211 Geneva 20, Switzerland (Dist. in U.S. by: American Meteorological Society, 45 Beacon St., Boston, MA 02108)
Former titles: World Meteorological Organization. Basic Documents and Official Reports; World Meteorological Organization. Basic Documents, Records and Reports (ISSN 0084-1943)

551.5   UN
WORLD METEOROLOGICAL ORGANIZATION. EXECUTIVE COUNCIL SESSION. ABRIDGED FINAL REPORTS WITH RESOLUTIONS. a. price varies. World Meteorological Organization, 41 Av. Giuseppe Motta, CH-1211 Geneva 20, Switzerland (Dist. in U.S. by: American Meteorological Society, 45 Beacon St., Boston, MA 02108)
Former titles: World Meteorological Organization. Executive Committee Reports. Abridged Final Reports with Resolutions; World Meteorological Organization. Executive Committee Sessions: Abridged Reports with Resolutions (ISSN 0084-196X)

551.5   UN
WORLD METEOROLOGICAL ORGANIZATION. REPORTS OF SESSIONS OF REGIONAL ASSOCIATIONS. irreg. price varies. World Meteorological Organization, 41 Av. Giuseppe Motta, CH-1211 Geneva 20, Switzerland (Dist. in U.S. by: American Meteorological Society, 45 Beacon St., Boston, MA 02108)
Formerly: World Meteorological Association. Regional Associations. Abridged Final Reports (ISSN 0084-1900)

551.5   UN
WORLD METEOROLOGICAL ORGANIZATION. REPORTS OF SESSIONS OF TECHNICAL COMMISSIONS. irreg. price varies. World Meteorological Organization, 41 Av. Giuseppe Motta, CH-1211 Geneva 20, Switzerland (Dist. in U.S. by: American Meteorological Society, 45 Beacon St., Boston, MA 02108)
Formerly: World Meteorological Association. Technical Commissions Abridged Final Reports (ISSN 0084-1919)

WORLD METEOROLOGICAL ORGANIZATION. SPECIAL ENVIRONMENTAL REPORTS. see *ENVIRONMENTAL STUDIES*

551.5   UN   ISSN 0084-201X
WORLD METEOROLOGICAL ORGANIZATION. TECHNICAL NOTES. 1954. irreg. price varies. World Meteorological Organization, 41 Av. Giuseppe Motta, CH-1211 Geneva 20, Switzerland (Dist. in U.S. by: American Meteorological Society, 45 Beacon St., Boston, MA 02108) Indexed: Biol.Abstr. GeoRef. Rural Recreat.Tour.Abstr. World Agri.Econ.& Rural Sociol.Abstr.

551.632   UN
WORLD METEOROLOGICAL ORGANIZATION. WEATHER REPORTING. VOLUME A: OBSERVING STATIONS. (Catalogue W M O No. 9) base vol. plus s-a updates. 134 Fr. for updates; 145 Fr. for basic volume. World Meteorological Organization, 41 Av. Giuseppe Motta, CH-1211 Geneva 20, Switzerland (Dist. in U.S. by: American Meteorological Society, 45 Beacon St., Boston, MA 02108) (looseleaf format)

551.632   UN
WORLD METEOROLOGICAL ORGANIZATION. WEATHER REPORTING. VOLUME B: DATA PROCESSING. (Catalogue W M O No.9) 1974. base vol. (plus irreg. updates) 30 Fr. for updates; basic volume 78 Fr. World Meteorological Organization, 41 Av. Giuseppe Motta, CH-1211 Geneva 20, Switzerland (Dist. in U.S. by: American Meteorological Society, 45 Beacon St., Boston, MA 02108) (looseleaf format)

551.632   UN
WORLD METEOROLOGICAL ORGANIZATION. WEATHER REPORTING. VOLUME C: TRANSMISSIONS. (Catalogue W M O No. 9) bi-m. (supplement to base vol.) 132 Fr. for supplement; fr.152 for basic volume. World Meteorological Organization, 41 Av. Giuseppe Motta, CH-1211 Geneva 20, Switzerland (Dist. in U.S. by: American Meteorological Society, 45 Beacon St., Boston, MA 02108) (looseleaf format)

551.632   UN
WORLD METEOROLOGICAL ORGANIZATION. WEATHER REPORTING. VOLUME D: INFORMATION FOR SHIPPING. (Catalogue W M O No.9) bi-m. (supplements to base vol.) 96 Fr. for supplement; fr. 183 for basic volume. World Meteorological Organization., 41 Av. Giuseppe Motta, CH-1211 Geneva 20, Switzerland (Dist. in U.S. by: American Meteorological Society, 45 Beacon St., Boston, MA 02108) (looseleaf format)

551.63   UN   ISSN 0084-2451
WORLD WEATHER WATCH PLANNING REPORTS. 1966. irreg. price varies. World Meteorological Organization, 41 Av. Giuseppe Motta, CH-1211 Geneva 20, Switzerland (Dist. in U.S. by: American Meteorological Society, 45 Beacon St., Boston, MA 02108)

551.5   ZA   ISSN 0302-5047
ZAMBIA. METEOROLOGICAL DEPARTMENT. TOTALS OF MONTHLY AND ANNUAL RAINFALL; for selected stations in Zambia. (Former name of issuing body: Department of Meteorology) K.1. Meteorological Department, Box 30200, Lusaka, Zambia (Orders to: Government Printer, Box 30136, Lusaka, Zambia)

551.5   RH   ISSN 0085-5693
ZIMBABWE. DEPARTMENT OF METEOROLOGICAL SERVICES. RAINFALL REPORT. a. ‡ Department of Meteorological Services, Box BE 150, Belvedere, Harare, Zimbabwe.

METEOROLOGY — ABSTRACTING, BIBLIOGRAPHIES, STATISTICS

551.5   RH   ISSN 0085-5707
ZIMBABWE. DEPARTMENT OF METEOROLOGICAL SERVICES. REPORT OF THE DIRECTOR. a. ‡ Department of Meteorological Services, Box BE 150, Belvedere, Harare, Zimbabwe. circ. 80. (back issues avail.)

METEOROLOGY — Abstracting, Bibliographies, Statistics

551.5   PL   ISSN 0239-958X
BIBLIOGRAFIA AGROMETEOROLOGII/ BIBLIOGRAPHY OF AGROMETEOROLOGY. (Text in English, Polish, Russian) 1958. a. $9. Instytut Meteorologii i Gospodarki Wodnej - Institute of Meteorology and Water Management, Ul. Podlesna 61, 01-673 Warsaw, Poland. circ. 120.
Formerly: Bibliografia z Zakresu Meteorologii Rolniczej i Lesnej.

551.5   US
CONFERENCE ON ATMOSPHERIC RADIATION. ABSTRACTS. 1972. irreg., 5th, 1983. $20. American Meteorological Society, 45 Beacon St., Boston, MA 02108. TEL 617-227-2425.

551.5 016   GW   ISSN 0072-4149
DEUTSCHER WETTERDIENST. BIBLIOGRAPHIEN. 1955. irreg., no.41, 1985. price varies. Deutscher Wetterdienst, Frankfurter Str. 135, Postfach 10 04 65, 6050 Offenbach (Main) 1, W. Germany (B.R.D.)

551.5 016   IT   ISSN 0075-1901
ISTITUTO DI FISICA DELL'ATMOSFERA, ROME. BIBLIOGRAFIA GENERALE. (Text in Italian; occasional English or French editions available) 1963. irreg. Istituto di Fisica dell'Atmosfera, Piazzale Luigi Sturzo 31, 00144 Rome, Italy. Indexed: Meteor.& Geoastrophys.Abstr.

551.5 523.01 016   US   ISSN 0026-1130
METEOROLOGICAL AND GEOASTROPHYSICAL ABSTRACTS. 1950. m. $450. American Meteorological Society, 45 Beacon St., Boston, MA 02108. TEL 617-227-2425. Ed. Malcolm Rigby. bk. rev. abstr. index. circ. 600. Indexed: Chem.Abstr. Sci.Abstr.
●Also available online. Vendors: DIALOG.

551.5 011   FR
P A S C A L EXPLORE. PART 49: METEOROLOGIE. 1985. 10/yr. 500 F. Centre National de la Recherche Scientifique, Centre de Documentation Scientifique et Technique, Service des Abonnements, 26 rue Boyer, 75971 Paris 20, France.
Supersedes in part: Bulletin Signaletique. Part 120: Astronomie - Physique Spatiale - Geophysique (ISSN 0240-849X)

METROLOGY AND STANDARDIZATION

389 658.5   US   ISSN 0360-6929
AMERICAN SOCIETY FOR QUALITY CONTROL. ANNUAL TECHNICAL CONFERENCE TRANSACTIONS. 1950? a. American Society for Quality Control, 310 W. Wisconsin Ave., Milwaukee, WI 53203. index by category, author and title. circ. 4,500. (also avail. in microfiche from UMI) Indexed: Eng.Ind.
Formerly: American Society for Quality Control. Transactions of Annual Technical Conferences (ISSN 0066-0159)

389   AU
AUSTRIA. BUNDESAMT FUER EICH- UND VERMESSUNGSWESEN. AMTSBLATT FUER DAS EICHWESEN. 1952. 8/yr. S.370. Kommissionsverlag der Oesterreichischen Staatsdruckerei, Rennweg 12a, A-1037 Vienna, Austria. index. circ. 500.

389   UK
B S I CATALOGUE. a. £26.75 to non-members. British Standards Institution, Linford Wood, Milton Keynes MK14 6LE, England. circ. 34,000.
Formerly: British Standards Year Book (ISSN 0068-2578)

389.6   CN
CANADIAN STANDARDS ASSOCIATION. ANNUAL REPORT. (Editions in English and French) 1919. a. free. ‡ Canadian Standards Association, Public Affairs, 178 Rexdale Blvd., Toronto (Rexdale), Ontario M9W 1R3, Canada. TEL 416-747-4129. Ed.Bd. circ. 10,000.

389.6   CN
CANADIAN STANDARDS ASSOCIATION. CATALOGUE. 1930. a. free. ‡ Canadian Standards Association, Standards Sales, 178 Rexdale Blvd., Toronto (Rexdale), Ont., M9W 1R3, Canada. TEL 416-747-4044. Ed.Bd. circ. 40,000.
Supersedes: Canadian Standards Association. Standards Catalogue & Canadian Standards Association. List of Publications.

389   FR
CATALOGUE AFNOR (NORMES FRANCAISES) vol.32, 1976. a. 185 F. Association Francaise de Normalisation, Tour Europe - Cedex, 92080 Paris la Defense, France. Ed. G. de Balathier. adv. circ. 15,000.
Formerly: Catalogue des Normes Francaises.

389.6   FR
COMITE CONSULTATIF POUR LA MASSE ET LES GRANDEURS APPARENTEES. 1981. irreg. 66 Fr. Bureau International des Poids et Mesures, Pavillon de Breteuil, 92310 Sevres, France. circ. 500.

621.3   FR
COMITE INTERNATIONAL DES POIDS ET MESURES. COMITE CONSULTATIF D'ELECTRICITE. (RAPPORT ET ANNEXES) (Travaux of sessions 1-8 (1928-57) issued in Proces-Verbaux du Comite International des Poids et Mesures) 1961, 9th. irreg., 16th session, 1983. 120 Fr. Bureau International des Poids et Mesures, Pavillon de Breteuil, 92310 Sevres, France.

535   FR   ISSN 0588-621X
COMITE INTERNATIONAL DES POIDS ET MESURES. COMITE CONSULTATIF DE PHOTOMETRIE ET RADIOMETRIE.(RAPPORT ET ANNEXES) (Sessions 1-4, 1937-1957 issued in Proces-Verbaux du Comite International des Poids et Mesures) irreg., 10th session, 1982. 97 Fr. Bureau International des Poids et Mesures, Pavillon de Breteuil, 92310 Sevres, France. charts. illus.

536.5   FR
COMITE INTERNATIONAL DES POIDS ET MESURES. COMITE CONSULTATIF DE THERMOMETRIE. RAPPORTS ET ANNEXES. (Sessions 1-5 (1939-1958) issued in Proces-Verbaux du Comite International des Poids et Mesures)) (Editions in English and French) 1950. biennial, 15th session, 1984. 121 Fr. Bureau International des Poids et Mesures, Pavillon de Breteuil, 92310 Sevres, France. bibl. charts. stat.

389   FR
COMITE INTERNATIONAL DES POIDS ET MESURES. COMITE CONSULTATIF DES UNITES (RAPPORT ET ANNEXES) (Editions in English and French) 1967. irreg., 9th session, 1984. 31 Fr. Bureau International des Poids et Mesures, Pavillon de Breteuil, 92310 Sevres, France.

389   FR   ISSN 0588-6228
COMITE INTERNATIONAL DES POIDS ET MESURES. COMITE CONSULTATIF POUR LA DEFINITION DE LA SECONDE. (RAPPORT ET ANNEXES) (First session issued in Proces-Verbaux du Comite International des Poids et Mesures) 1957. irreg., 10th session, 1985. 82 Fr. Bureau International des Poids et Mesures, Pavillon de Breteuil, 92310 Sevres, France.

389   FR   ISSN 0588-6236
COMITE INTERNATIONAL DES POIDS ET MESURES. COMITE CONSULTATIF POUR LA DEFINITION DU METRE (RAPPORT ET ANNEXES) (Sessions 1-2 (1953-1957) Issued in Proces-Verbaux du Comite International des Poids et Mesures) (Editions in English and French) 3rd, 1962. irreg., 7th session, 1982. 72 Fr. Bureau International des Poids et Mesures, Pavillon de Breteuil, 92310 Sevres, France.

389   FR
COMITE INTERNATIONAL DES POIDS ET MESURES. COMITE CONSULTATIF POUR LES ETALONS DES MESURE DES RAYONNEMENTS IONISANTS (RAPPORT ET ANNEXES) (First session issued in Proces-Verbaux du Comite International des Poids et Mesures) (Editions in English and French) 1959. irreg., 10th session, 1983. 30 Fr. Bureau International des Poids et Mesures, Pavillon de Breteuil, 92310 Sevres, France.
Formerly: Comite International des Poids et Mesures. Comite Consultatif pour les Etalons des Mesure des Radiations Ionisantes(Rapport et Annexes) (ISSN 0588-6244)

389   FR
COMITE INTERNATIONAL DES POIDS ET MESURES. PROCES-VERBAUX DES SEANCES. 1875. a., 74st session, 1985. 143 Fr. Bureau International des Poids et Mesures - International Bureau of Weights and Measures, Pavillon de Breteuil, 92310 Sevres, France. charts. illus. stat. index. circ. 650.

389   FR
COMITE INTERNATIONAL DES POIDS ET MESURES. SYSTEME INTERNATIONAL D'UNITES. 1970. irreg., 5th ed., 1985. 60 Fr. Bureau International des Poids et Mesures, Pavillon de Breteuil, F-92310 Sevres, France.

389.6   AT
COMMONWEALTH SCIENTIFIC AND INDUSTRIAL RESEARCH ORGANIZATION. DIVISION OF APPLIED PHYSICS. BIENNIAL REPORT. 1977. biennial. Aus.$5. C.S.I.R.O., Division of Applied Physics, Box 218, Lindfield, N.S.W. 2070, Australia. Ed. Paul L. Hewitt. circ. 2,000. Indexed: Biol.Abstr.
Former titles: Commonwealth Scientific and Industrial Research Organization. National Measurement Laboratory. Biennial Report; Commonwealth Scientific and Industrial Research Organization. National Standards Laboratory. Biennial Report; C.S.I.R.O. Division of Physics & Applied Physics. Annual Reports.

389.6   FR
CONFERENCE GENERALE DES POIDS ET MESURES. COMPTES RENDUS DES SEANCES. 1889. irreg., 17th, 1983. 86 Fr. Bureau International des Poids et Mesures, 92310 Sevres, France.

389.6   MX
CONGRESO MEXICANO DE CONTROL DE CALIDAD. ANNUAL PROCEEDINGS. (In 2 vols.) 1973. a. $30. Instituto Mexicano de Control de Calidad, Thiers 251-Col. Anzures, 11590 Mexico, D.F., Mexico. Ed. Patricia Gonzalez Prado. adv. bk. rev. circ. 3,000.

621.38   US   ISSN 0900-5579
D A N T E C INFORMATION. (Summaries in English, French and German) 1965. a. free. D A N T E C Electronics, 6 Pearl Court, Allendale, NJ 07401. TEL 201-825-3339. Ed. E. Bornhoeft. circ. 21,000. Indexed: Met.Abstr. Sci.Abstr. BMT. Fluidex. Int.Aerosp.Abstr. World Alum.Abstr.
Former titles: D I S A Information. Measurement and Analysis (ISSN 0070-6639); D I S A Information. Electronic Measurement of Mechanic Events.

389.1   GW   ISSN 0722-7337
D I N - HANDBOOK. 1982. irreg. price varies. (Deutsches Institut fuer Normung e.V. (D I N)) Beuth Verlag GmbH, Burggrafenstrasse 6, 1000 Berlin 30, W. Germany (B.R.D.) (Subscr. to: International Publisher Service, Hingham, MA 02043)

350.821   GW
D I N - KATALOG FUER TECHNISCHE REGELN. (Text in English and German) 1982. a. DM.198. Deutsches Institut fuer Normung e.V., Burggrafenstr. 4-10, 1000 Berlin 30, W. Germany (B.R.D.)
Formerly: Katalog fuer Technische Regeln (ISSN 0722-9313)

389.1   GW   ISSN 0342-801X
D I N - TASCHENBUECHER. 1963. irreg. price varies. (Deutsches Institut fuer Normung e.V. (D I N)) Beuth Verlag GmbH, Burggrafenstr. 6, 1000 Berlin 30, W. Germany (B.R.D.) (Order from: IPS International Service, Hingam, MA 02043 U.S.A.) circ. 2,000.

350.821   DK
DENMARK. DANTEST-NYT. AARSBERETNING. 1977. a. 20. Dantest-National Institute for Testing and Verification, Amager Blvd. 115, 2300 Copenhagen S, Denmark.
    Formerly (until 1979): Denmark. Justervaesenet. Aarsberetning.

389   US   ISSN 0070-6558
DIRECTORY OF UNITED STATES STANDARDIZATION ACTIVITIES. (Subseries of its Special Publication Series) irreg. U.S. National Bureau of Standards, Gaithersburg, MD 20899 TEL 301-975-3058. (Orders to: Supt. of Documents, Washington, DC 20402)

389   EI
E U R O N O R M. (Editions in Dutch, French, German and Italian) irreg. price varies. Office for Official Publications of the European Communities, P.O. Box 1003, L-2985 Luxemburg, Luxembourg (Avail. also from: Association Francaise de Normalisation, Paris La-Defense; Institut Belge de Normalisation, Brussels; Beuth-Vertries, Berlin; Ente Nazionale Italiano di Unificazione, Milan; and Nederlands Normalistie-Institut, The Hague)

389.1   GW   ISSN 0174-3805
ENGLISH TRANSLATIONS OF GERMAN STANDARDS. CATALOGUE. 1978. irreg. DM.36($16) per no. (Deutsches Institut fuer Normung e.V.) Beuth Verlag GmbH, Postfach 1145, 1000 Berlin 30, W. Germany (B.R.D.) circ. 10,000.
    Formerly: English Translations of German Standards (ISSN 0071-0660)

620   SZ   ISSN 0071-2981
EUROPEAN ORGANIZATION FOR QUALITY CONTROL. CONFERENCE PROCEEDINGS. 1970. a., 29th, 1985, Estoril, Portugal. European Organization for Quality Control, Box 2613, CH-3001 Berne, Switzerland.

389.152   UK   ISSN 0072-6869
GREAT BRITAIN. DEPARTMENT OF THE ENVIRONMENT. METRICATION IN THE CONSTRUCTION INDUSTRY. irreg., no.3, 1971. H.M.S.O., Box 569, London SE1 9NH, England.

389.6   US
HANDBOOK FOR METRIC USAGE. 1977. irreg. $6. American Home Economics Association, 2010 Massachusetts Ave. N.W., Washington, DC 20036. TEL 202-862-8300.

I E E E INSTRUMENTATION AND MEASUREMENT TECHNOLOGY CONFERENCE. PROCEEDINGS. see INSTRUMENTS

389.6   IR
I S I R I YEARBOOK. (Text in English) 1975. a. free. Institute of Standards and Industrial Research of Iran, Box 15875-4618, Teheran, Iran. Ed. F. Hazegh. circ. 1,000.

389.6   SZ   ISSN 0303-3309
I S O CATALOGUE. (Text in English and French) a. International Organization for Standardization, 1 rue de Varembe, 1211 Geneva 20, Switzerland (Dist. in U.S. by: American National Standards Institute, 1430 Broadway, New York, NY 10018)

389   SZ
I S O INTERNATIONAL STANDARDS. (Body of existing I S O Recommendations and I S O International Standards called I S O Standards) 1954. irreg. price varies. International Organization for Standardization, 1 rue de Varembe, 1211 Geneva 20, Switzerland (Dist. in the U.S. by: American National Standards Institute, 1430 Broadway, New York, NY 10018) Indexed: HRIS.

389   SZ   ISSN 0536-2067
I S O MEMENTO. (Text in English and French) a. International Organization for Standardization, 1 rue de Varembe, 1211 Geneva 20, Switzerland (Dist. in the U.S. by: American National Standards Institute, 1430 Broadway, New York, NY 10018)

389.6   US
IDENTIFIED SOURCES OF SUPPLY. 1960. a. $145. National Standards Association, Inc., 5161 River Rd., Bethesda, MD 20816. TEL 301-951-1389. Ed. K. Stover. (also avail. in microfiche)
    Formerly: Source (Washington)

389   US
INDEX AND DIRECTORY OF U.S. INDUSTRY STANDARDS. 1983. a. $195. Information Handling Services, 15 Inverness Way. E., Box 1154, Englewood, CO 80150 (Subscr. to: Global Engineering, 2625 Hickory St., Box 2504, Santa Ana, CA 92707) Ed. Liz Maynard Prigge. circ. 400. (tabloid format)

389.6   MW
MALAWI. MALAWI BUREAU OF STANDARDS. ANNUAL REPORT AND STATEMENT OF ACCOUNTS. (Text in English) a. Malawi Bureau of Standards, Box 946, Blantyre, Malawi.

MARINE STANDARDIZATION IN JAPAN. see TRANSPORTATION — Ships And Shipping

350.821   MF
MAURITIUS STANDARDS BUREAU. ANNUAL REPORT. (Text in English) a., latest 1978. Government Printing Office, Elizabeth II Ave., Port Louis, Mauritius.

389.6   CN   ISSN 0383-9184
METRIC FACT SHEETS. 1973. irreg. $5 (subscription includes Metric Message) Canadian Metric Association, Box 35, Fonthill, Ont. L0S 1E0, Canada.

389.1   US   ISSN 0077-3964
NATIONAL CONFERENCE ON WEIGHTS AND MEASURES. REPORT. 1905. a. approx. $6. U.S. National Bureau of Standards, Office of Weights and Measures, Gaithersburg, MD 20899. TEL 301-975-3058. cum.index: 1905-60.

POLITEKNIKA WROCLAWSKA. INSTYTUT METROLOGII ELEKTRYCZNEJ. PRACE NAUKOWE. KONFERENCJE. see ELECTRICITY AND ELECTRICAL ENGINEERING

POLITEKNIKA WROCLAWSKA. INSTYTUT METROLOGII ELEKTRYCZNEJ. PRACE NAUKOWE. MONOGRAFIE. see ELECTRICITY AND ELECTRICAL ENGINEERING

POLITEKNIKA WROCLAWSKA. INSTYTUT METROLOGII ELEKTRYCZNEJ. PRACE NAUKOWE. STUDIA I MATERIALY. see ELECTRICITY AND ELECTRICAL ENGINEERING

389   690   FR   ISSN 0335-3559
REPERTOIRE DE MATERIAUX ET ELEMENTS CONTROLES DU BATIMENT. 1965. a. 25 F. Association Francaise de Normalisation, Tour Europe - Cedex 7, 92080 Paris la Defense, France. adv. bibl. index. circ. 7,500.

389   SA   ISSN 0259-3602
S A B S CATALOGUE. Afrikaans Edition: S A B S Katalogus (ISSN 0259-3610) (Editions in Afrikaans or English) 1963. a. price varies. South African Bureau of Standards, Language Services, Private Bag X191, Pretoria 0001, South Africa. Ed. J.C. de Beer. circ. 2,000.
    Formerly: S A B S Yearbook (ISSN 0081-2137)

389.6   620   FI
S F S CATALOGUE; catalogue of Finnish national standards. (Text and summaries in English and Finnish) 1924. a. Fmk.60 (supplements 8/yr. Fmk. 15) Suomen Standardisoimisliitto - Finnish Standards Association, Box 205, Bulevardi 5 A 7, SF-00121 Helsinki, Finland. TEL 358-0-645 601. circ. 2,000.

389.6   CS
SEZNAM PLATNYCH CESKOSLOVENSKYCH STATNICH A OBOROVYCH NOREM. 1953. a. 98 Kcs. Urad pro Normalizaci a Mereni, Vaclavske nam. 19, 113 47 Prague 1, Czechoslovakia. circ. 25,000.

620   US
STANDARD SPECIFICATIONS FOR TRANSPORTATION MATERIALS AND METHODS OF SAMPLING AND TESTING. a. $50. American Association of State Highway and Transportation Officials, 444 N. Capital St., N.W., Suite 225, Washington, DC 20001. TEL 202-624-5800.

STANDARDS FOR AUSTRALIAN ALUMINIUM MILL PRODUCTS. see METALLURGY

620.1   TZ   ISSN 0856-0374
TANZANIA. BUREAU OF STANDARDS. DIRECTOR'S ANNUAL REPORT. 1976/77. a. Bureau of Standards, Box 9524, Dar es Salaam, Tanzania. Ed. N.N. Maingu. circ. controlled.

389   US
U.S. NATIONAL BUREAU OF STANDARDS. ANNUAL REPORT. 1902. a. price varies. U.S. National Bureau of Standards, Gaithersburg, MD 20899 TEL 301-975-3058. (Orders to: Supt. Doc., Washington, DC 20402)
    Formerly: Technical Highlights of the National Bureau of Standards (ISSN 0083-1905)

389   US
U.S. NATIONAL BUREAU OF STANDARDS. FEDERAL INFORMATION PROCESSING STANDARDS. irreg. price varies. U.S. National Bureau of Standards, Gaithersburg, MD 20899 TEL 301-975-3058. (Orders to: NTIS, Springfield, VA 22161)

389   US
U.S. NATIONAL BUREAU OF STANDARDS. MONOGRAPHS. irreg. price varies. U.S. National Bureau of Standards, Gaithersburg, MD 20899 TEL 301-975-3058. (Orders to: Supt. of Documents, Washington, DC 20402) Indexed: GeoRef.

389   US   ISSN 0083-1840
U.S. NATIONAL BUREAU OF STANDARDS. NATIONAL STANDARD REFERENCE DATA SERIES. irreg. price varies. U.S. National Bureau of Standards, Gaithersburg, MD 20899 TEL 301-975-3058. (Orders to: Supt. of Documents, Washington, DC 20402)

389.608   621.3   US
U.S. NATIONAL BUREAU OF STANDARDS. SEMICONDUCTOR MEASUREMENT TECHNOLOGY. irreg. U.S. National Bureau of Standards, Gaithersburg, MD 20899. TEL 301-975-3058. illus.
    Former titles: U.S. National Bureau of Standards. Semiconductor Measurement Technology. Quarterly Report (ISSN 0145-4676); Continues: U.S. National Bureau of Standards. Methods of Measurement for Semiconductor Materials, Process Control, and Devices; Quarterly Report (ISSN 0090-8541)

389   US   ISSN 0083-1913
U.S. NATIONAL BUREAU OF STANDARDS. TECHNICAL NOTES. 1959. irreg. price varies. U.S. National Bureau of Standards, Gaithersburg, MD 20899 TEL 301-975-3058. (Orders to: Supt. of Documents, Washington, DC 20402) Indexed: Chem.Abstr.

389   US
U.S. NATIONAL BUREAU OF STANDARDS. VOLUNTARY PRODUCT STANDARDS. irreg. U.S. National Bureau of Standards, Gaithersburg, MD 20899 TEL 301-975-3058. (Orders to: Supt. of Documents, Washington, DC 20402)
    Former titles: U.S. National Bureau of Standards. Commercial Standards (ISSN 0083-1808) & U.S. National Bureau of Standards. Product Standards (ISSN 0083-1859)

METROLOGY AND STANDARDIZATION — Abstracting, Bibliographies, Statistics

389.6   389.6   016   UK   ISSN 0950-480X
KEY ABSTRACTS - ELECTRONIC INSTRUMENTATION. 1976. m. $110 to non-members. INSPEC, I.E.E., Station House, Nightingale Rd., Hitchin, Herts SG5 1RJ, England (U.S. address: 445 Hoes Lane, Piscataway, NJ 08854) index. Indexed: Agri.Eng.Abstr.
Formerly (until 1987): Key Abstracts - Electrical Measurements and Instrumentation (ISSN 0307-7977)

621.3   389.6   016   UK   ISSN 0950-4818
KEY ABSTRACTS - MEASUREMENTS IN PHYSICS. 1976. m. $110 to non-members. INSPEC, I.E.E., Station House, Nightingale Rd., Hitchin, Herts SG5 1RJ, England (U.S. address: 445 Hoes Lane, Piscataway, NJ 08854) index. Indexed: Excerp.Med. Agri.Eng.Abstr.
Formerly (until 1987): Key Abstracts - Physical Measurements and Instrumentation (ISSN 0307-7969)

389.6   FR
P A S C A L EXPLORE. PART 32: METROLOGIE ET APPAREILLAGE EN PHYSIQUE ET PHYSICOCHIMIE. 1985. 10/yr. 580 F. Centre National de la Recherche Scientifique, Centre de Documentation Scientifique et Technique, Service des Abonnements, 26 rue Boyer, 75971 Paris 20, France.
Supersedes in part: Bulletin Signaletique. Part 130: Physique Mathematique, Optique, Acoustique, Mechanique, Chaleur (ISSN 0397-7757)

389   016   UR   ISSN 0034-2505
REFERATIVNYI ZHURNAL. METROLOGIYA I IZMERITEL'NAYA TEKHNIKA. 1963. m. 116 Rub. (123 Rub. including index) Vsesoyuznyi Institut Nauchno-Tekhnicheskoi Informatsii (VINITI), Baltiiskaya ul., 14, Moscow A-219, Russian S.F.S.R., U.S.S.R (Subscr. to: Mezhdunarodnaya Kniga, Dimitrova ul. 39, 113095 Moscow, Russian S.F.S.R., U.S.S.R.) Indexed: Chem.Abstr.

MICROBIOLOGY
see Biology—Microbiology

MICROCOMPUTERS
see Computers—Microcomputers

MICROSCOPY
see Biology—Microscopy

MILITARY
see also Civil Defense

355   658   US
A L A WORLDWIDE DIRECTORY AND FACT BOOK. 1982. a. $50. American Logistics Association, 1133 15th St., N.W., Suite 600, Washington, DC 20005. Ed. Paul Pierpoint. adv.

A M S STUDIES IN THE EMBLEM. (Abrahams Magazine Service) see GENEALOGY AND HERALDRY

355.31   FR
AGENDA DES ARMEES. 1977. a. Editions Charles Lavauzelle, Le Prouet, B.P. 8, 87350 Panazol, France.

358.4   UK
AIR FORCE LIST.* a. price varies. H.M.S.O., P.O. Box 276, London SW8 5DT, England. circ. 3,400.

358.4   SZ
AIR FORCES OF THE WORLD. a. 750 Fr.($375) per edition. Interavia S.A., 86 Av. Louis Casai, Case Postale 162, CH-1216 Cointrin-Geneva, Switzerland.

355   SZ
AIRCRAFT ARMAMENT. a. 900 Fr.($450) Interavia S.A., 86 Av. Louis Casai, Case Postale 162, CH-1216 Cointrin-Geneva, Switzerland.

359   US   ISSN 0736-3559
ALMANAC OF SEAPOWER. a. Navy League of the United States, 2300 Wilson Blvd., Arlington, VA 22201. TEL 703-528-1775. Ed. Vincent C. Thomas, Jr.

359   AG   ISSN 0066-703X
ARGENTINA. DEPARTAMENTO DE ESTUDIOS HISTORICOS NAVALES. SERIE A: CULTURA NAUTICA. 1961. irreg. Departamento de Estudios Historicos Navales, Instituto de Publicaciones Navales, Av. Cordoba 547, Buenos Aires, Argentina.

359   AG   ISSN 0066-7048
ARGENTINA. DEPARTAMENTO DE ESTUDIOS HISTORICOS NAVALES. SERIE B: HISTORIA NAVAL ARGENTINA. 1960. irreg., no.18, 1975. price varies. Departamento de Estudios Historicos Navales, Instituto de Publicaciones Navales, Av. Cordoba 547, Buenos Aires, Argentina.

359   920   AG   ISSN 0066-7056
ARGENTINA. DEPARTAMENTO DE ESTUDIOS HISTORICOS NAVALES. SERIE C: BIOGRAFIAS NAVALES ARGENTINAS. irreg. Departamento de Estudios Historicos Navales, Instituto de Publicaciones Navales, Av. Cordoba 547, Buenos Aires, Argentina.

359   980   AG
ARGENTINA. DEPARTAMENTO DE ESTUDIOS HISTORICOS NAVALES. SERIE E: DOCUMENTOS. 1977. irreg. Departamento de Estudios Historicos Navales, Instituto de Publicaciones Navales, Av. Cordoba 547, Buenos Aires, Argentina.

ARGENTINA. SECRETARIA DE GUERRA. DIRECCION DE ESTUDIOS HISTORICOS. BOLETIN BIBLIOGRAFICO. see HISTORY — History Of North And South America

355   949.2   NE
ARMAMENTARIA. 1965. irreg. fl.2500. Nederlands Leger- en Wapenmuseum Generaal Hoefer, Korte Geer 1, 2611 CA Delft, Netherlands.

355.31   UK
ARMY LIST. a. price varies. H.M.S.O., Box 569, London SE1 9NH, England.

355   069   UK
ARMY MUSEUM. 1981. a. £3.50. National Army Museum, Royal Hospital Rd., London SW3 4HT, England. Eds. E. Talbot Rice, A. Guy. circ. 1,450. (back issues avail.)

355   II   ISSN 0004-3826
ARTILLERY JOURNAL. 1948. a. Artillery Association, School of Artillery, Deolali, India. adv. bk. rev. circ. 5,000.

335   AT
AUSTRALIAN DEFENCE EQUIPMENT CATALOGUE. 1974. biennial. Aus.$45. (Department of Defence Support) Peter Isaacson Publications, 45-50 Porter St., Prahran, Vic. 3181, Australia. adv. illus.

355   CU
AVANTE. a. Ministerio de las Fuerzas Armadas Revolucionarias, Ave. del Puerto esq. a, Obrapia, Habana Vieja, Havana, Cuba.

355   GW
BERNARD UND GRAEFE AKTUELL.* 1967. irreg., no.18, 1976. price varies. (Arbeitskreis fuer Wehrforschung) Bernard und Graefe Verlag, Karl-Mand-Str. 2, Postfach 2060, 5400 Koblenz, W. Germany (B.R.D.)
Incorporating: Wehrwissenschaftliche Berichte (ISSN 0083-7822); Wehrforschung Aktuell; Beitraege zur Wehrforschung.

355   UK
BIBLIOTHECA HISTORICO MILITARIS. (Text in German) 1976. irreg. £3.50. Carl Slienger, Box 4ST, London W1P 1AA, England.
History

355   949.2   NE   ISSN 0523-5774
BIJDRAGE TOT DE GESCHIEDENIS VAN HET ZEEWEZEN. 1967. irreg. price varies. Afdeling Maritieme Historie van de Marinestaf, Jan van Nassaustraat 112, 2596 BW The Hague, Netherlands.
Formerly: Bureau Maritieme Historie van de Marinestaf. Mededelingenblad.

355   UK
BRITAIN'S DEFENCE SERVICE INDUSTRY. 1985. irreg. £95($150) Jordan & Sons Ltd., Jordan House, 47 Brunswick Place, London N1 6EE, England.

CAL-VET INSURANCE PLANS. ANNUAL REPORT. see INSURANCE

354   CN   ISSN 0383-4638
CANADA. DEPARTMENT OF NATIONAL DEFENCE. DEFENCE (YEAR) a. free. National Defence Headquarters, 101 Colonel By Drive, Ottawa, Ont. K1A 0K2, Canada. TEL 613-996-2353. illus.

355   CN
CANADA. DEPARTMENT OF NATIONAL DEFENCE. DIRECTORATE OF HISTORY. MONOGRAPH SERIES. 1976. irreg. price varies. Department of National Defence, Ottawa, Ont. K1A 0K2, Canada TEL 613-992-4582. (Avail. from: Canadian Government Publishing Centre, Supply and Services Canada, Ottawa, Ont. K1A 0S9, Canada)
Supersedes (as from 1983): Canada. Department of National Defence. Directorate of History. Occasional Paper.

355   CN   ISSN 0316-1919
CANADA. NATIONAL MUSEUM OF MAN. MERCURY SERIES. CANADIAN WAR MUSEUM. PAPERS/CANADA. MUSEE NATIONAL DE L'HOMME. COLLECTION MERCURE. MUSEE CANADIEN DE LA GUERRE. DOSSIERS. (Text in English or French) 1972. irreg., no.9, 1978. free. (National Museum of Man) National Museums of Canada, Ottawa, Ontario K1A 0M8, Canada. TEL 613-992-3497.

331.1   355.115   CN   ISSN 0382-1587
CANADA. PENSION REVIEW BOARD. REPORTS/RECUEIL DES ARRETS DU CONSEIL DE REVISION DES PENSIONS. 1972. irreg. ,latest 1986. free. Department of Veterans Affairs, Ottawa, Ont. K1A 0P4, Canada. TEL 613-992-7472. Ed. P.M. Giesler. index. circ. 1,000.

358   CN   ISSN 0068-8843
CANADIAN GUNNER. 1965. a. Can.$15. (Royal Regiment of Canadian Artillery) Leech Printing Ltd., Brandon, Man., Canada. TEL 204-728-3037. (back issues avail.)

355   II   ISSN 0069-2654
CHANAKYA DEFENCE ANNUAL. (Text in English) 1969. a. $10. ‡ Chanakya Publishing House, 3 Thornhill Rd., Allahabad 1, India. Ed. Ravi Kaul. adv. bk. rev. circ. 5,200. (back issues avail.)

CHINA REPORT: POLITICAL, SOCIOLOGICAL, AND MILITARY AFFAIRS. see POLITICAL SCIENCE

CIVIL WAR COLLECTORS' DEALER DIRECTORY. see ANTIQUES

CIVILIAN CONGRESS; persons holding military office in Congress. see LAW

359　US　ISSN 0364-3263
COMBAT FLEETS OF THE WORLD. 1897. biennial. (U.S. Naval Institute) Naval Institute Press, Annapolis, MD 21402. TEL 301-268-6110. Ed. Jean Labayle Couhat.

355　387　SZ
COMMERCIAL AIR TRANSPORT INDUSTRY. a. 900 Fr.($450) Interavia S.A., 86 Av. Louis Casai, Case Postale 162, CH-1216 Cointrin-Geneva, Switzerland.
Former titles: World Commercial Aircraft; World Helicopter Systems; Military Avionic Equipment.

CONFEDERATE CALENDAR. see *HISTORY — History Of North And South America*

909　US　ISSN 0883-6884
CONTRIBUTIONS IN MILITARY STUDIES. 1969. irreg. price varies. Greenwood Press, 88 Post Rd. W., Box 5007, Westport, CT 06881. TEL 203-226-3571. Eds. Thomas E. Griess, Jay Luvass.
Formerly: Contributions in Military History (ISSN 0084-9251)

CURRENT AIRCRAFT PRICES. see *AERONAUTICS AND SPACE FLIGHT*

DEFENSE ELECTRONICS. MARKETING DIRECTORY AND BUYERS GUIDE. see *ELECTRICITY AND ELECTRICAL ENGINEERING*

355　327　US
DEFENSE FOREIGN AFFAIRS HANDBOOK; political, economic & defense data on every country in the world. 1976. a. $185. Perth Corporation, 1777 T St N.W., Washington, DC 20009. TEL 202-223-4934. Ed. Michael Dunn. adv. circ. 2,500. (back issues avail.)

355　US　ISSN 0099-166X
DEFENSE REFERENCE. 1974. irreg. price varies. Government Business World Wide Reports, Box 5997, Washington, DC 20016. TEL 202-966-6379. Ed. J.H. Wagner. charts. stat.

355　GW　ISSN 0417-3635
DEUTSCHES SOLDATENJAHRBUCH. 1953. a. DM.59. Schild-Verlag GmbH, Federseestr. 1, 8000 Munich 60, W. Germany (B.R.D.) Ed. Helmut Damerau. adv. bk. rev. bibl. charts. illus. stat. circ. 7,000(controlled)

355.115　US
DIRECTORY OF VETERANS ORGANIZATIONS. 1984. a. U.S. Veterans Administration, Office of the Administrator, 810 Vermont Ave., N.W., Rm. 1018, Washington, DC 20420.

327.174　UN
DISARMAMENT; a periodic review by the United Nations. (Text in English, French and Spanish) 1978. irreg., 2-3/yr., latest vol.10, no.1. $6 per issue. United Nations Publications, Sales Section, Room DC2-853, New York, NY 10017. bibl. charts.
Indexed: P.A.I.S. Amer.Bibl.Slavic & E.Eur.Stud.

355　SZ
ELECTRONIC WARFARE. a. 1500 Fr.($750) Interavia S.A., 86 Ave. Louis Casai, Case Postale 162, CH-1216 Cointrin/Geneva, Switzerland.
Indexed: PROMT.

355.11　368.4　US
FEDERAL BENEFITS FOR VETERANS AND DEPENDENTS, IS-1 FACT SHEET. 1961. a. $2.25. U.S. Veterans Administration, 810 Vermont Ave., N.W., Washington, DC 20420 (Orders to: Supt. of Documents, Washington, DC 20402)
Formerly: U.S. Veterans Administration. V A Fact Sheets (ISSN 0083-3576)

FORT POINT SALVO. see *HISTORY — History Of North And South America*

355　973　US　ISSN 0071-9641
FRONTIER MILITARY SERIES. 1951. irreg. price varies. Arthur H. Clark Co., Box 230, Glendale, CA 91209-0230. index.

DAS GELTENDE SEEVOELKERRECHT IN EINZELDARSTELLUNGEN. see *LAW — International Law*

GLADIUS; etudes sur les armes anciennes, l'armement, l'art militaire et la vie culturelle en Orient et Occident. see *ANTIQUES*

GOVERNMENT LIFE INSURANCE PROGRAMS FOR VETERANS AND MEMBERS OF THE SERVICES. ANNUAL REPORT. see *INSURANCE*

GUIDE TO GOVERNMENT-LOAN FILMS. see *MOTION PICTURES*

335　US
HANDBOOK OF SERVICE MEMBERS' AND VETERANS' BENEFITS. 1956. irreg. $2.05. R & R Newkirk (Subsidiary of: Longman Financial Publishing Service) 500 N. Dearborn, Chicago, IL 60610-4901.
Formerly: Handbook of Servicemen's and Veterans' Benefits (ISSN 0072-9914)

355　GW
HANDBUCH ZUR DEUTSCHEN MILITAERGESCHICHTE.* 1964. irreg., vol.6, 1970. price varies. (Militaergeschichtliches Forschungsamt) Bernard und Graefe Verlag, Karl-Mund-Str. 2, Postfach 2060, 5400 Koblenz, W. Germany (B.R.D.)

355　US　ISSN 0073-0394
HARMON MEMORIAL LECTURES IN MILITARY HISTORY. 1959. a. free. United States Air Force Academy, Dept. of History, Colorado Springs, CO 80840. TEL 303-472-3230. circ. 1,000.

355　GW
HEERE INTERNATIONAL. 1981. irreg. DM.49.80. Verlag E.S. Mittler und Sohn GmbH, Postfach 371, 4900 Herford, W. Germany (B.R.D.) Ed.Bd. adv. abstr. charts. illus. stat. circ. 3,000.

HISTORIA MILITAR DEL PARAGUAY. see *HISTORY — History Of North And South America*

355　UK　ISSN 0305-0440
HISTORICAL BREECHLOADING SMALLARMS ASSOCIATION. JOURNAL. 1973. a. £4. Historical Breechloading Smallarms Association, c/o Imperial War Museum, Lambeth Road, London SE1 6HZ, England. Ed. J.B. Bell. bk. rev. bibl. charts. illus. circ. 2,000.
History

355　US　ISSN 0073-8670
INSTITUTE FOR DEFENSE ANALYSES. STUDIES. irreg. Institute for Defense Analyses, 1801 N. Beauregard St., Alexandria, VA 22311 (Avail. from: National Technical Information Service, Springfield, VA 22151)

INTERNATIONAL ASSOCIATION OF MUSEUMS OF ARMS AND MILITARY HISTORY. CONGRESS REPORTS. see *MUSEUMS AND ART GALLERIES*

355　US　ISSN 0145-2584
INTERNATIONAL COUNTERMEASURES HANDBOOK. 1975. a. $50. E W Communications, Inc., 1170 E. Meadow Dr., Palo Alto, CA 94303. TEL 415-494-2800. Ed. Richard V. Hartman. adv. bibl. charts. illus. stat. (back issues avail.)

355　SZ　ISSN 0256-7822
INTERNATIONAL DEFENSE DIRECTORY. (Text and summaries in English) a. 595 Fr.($325) Interavia S.A., Ave. Louis-Casai 86, CH-1216 Cointrin-Geneva, Switzerland. Ed. Colin Howard. adv.

359　IT　ISSN 0075-1588
ISTITUTO UNIVERSITARIO NAVALE, NAPLES. ANNALI. (Text in Italian; summaries in English) 1920. a. Istituto Universitario Navale, Via Acton 38, Naples 80100, Italy. Indexed: Int.Aerosp.Abstr.

358　623　GW　ISSN 0075-2428
JAHRBUCH DER WEHRTECHNIK. 1966. a. DM.32. Bernard & Graefe Verlag, Karl-Mand-Strasse 2, 5400 Koblenz, W. Germany (B.R.D.) Ed. Wolfgang Flume. adv. circ. 5,000.

355　UK
JANE'S ARMOUR AND ARTILLERY. 1979. a. £57($125) Jane's Publishing Co., 238 City Rd., London E.C.1, England (Subscr.to: Jane's Publishing Inc., 20 park Plaza, Boston, MA 02116) Ed. Christopher F. Foss. adv. index.

359　UK　ISSN 0075-3025
JANE'S FIGHTING SHIPS. 1897. a. £57.50($125) Jane's Publishing Co., 238 City Rd., London E.C.1, England (Subscr.to: Jane's Publishing Inc., 20 Park Plaza, Boston, MA 02116) Ed. Capt. John E. Moore. adv. inex.
Navy

355　UK　ISSN 0306-3410
JANE'S INFANTRY WEAPONS. 1975. a. £57.50($125) Jane's Publishing Co., 238 City Rd., London E.C.1, England (Subscr.to: Jane's Publishing Inc., 20 Park Plaza, Boston, MA 02116) Ed. Ian V. Hogg. adv. index.

355　UK　ISSN 0144-0004
JANE'S MILITARY COMMUNICATIONS. 1979. a. £59($125) Jane's Publishing Co., 238 City Rd., London E.C.1, England (Subscr.to: Jane's Publishing Inc., 20 Park Plaza, Boston, MA 02116) Ed. R.J. Raggett. adv. index.

355　UK
JANE'S MILITARY REVIEW. 1981. a. £16.95($14.95) Jane's Publishing Co. Ltd., 238 City Rd., London EC1V 2PU, England (Subscr. to: 20 Park Pl., Boston, MA 02116) Ed. Ian V. Hogg. charts. illus. stat.

355　UK
JANE'S MILITARY VEHICLES AND GROUND SUPPORT EQUIPMENT. 1978. a. £57.50($125) Jane's Publishing Co., 238 City Rd., London E.C.1., England (Subscr.to: Jane's Publishing Inc., 20 Park Plaza, Boston, MA 02116) Eds. Christopher F. Foss and Terry Gander. index.
Formerly: Jane's Combat Support Equipment.

355　UK　ISSN 0075-3068
JANE'S WEAPON SYSTEMS. 1969. a. £62($125) Jane's Publishing Co., 238 City Rd., London E.C.1, England (Subscr.to: Jane's Publishing Inc., 20 Park Plaza, Boston, MA 02116) Ed. Ronald T. Pretty. adv. index.

970.04　US
KENTUCKY. ADJUTANT-GENERAL'S OFFICE. REPORT. a. Adjutant-General's Office, Frankfort, KY 40601. TEL 502-564-8558.

KOEHLERS FLOTTENKALENDER. JAHRBUCH FUER SCHIFFAHRT UND HAEFEN. see *TRANSPORTATION — Ships And Shipping*

354　LB
LIBERIA. MINISTRY OF NATIONAL DEFENSE. ANNUAL REPORT. a. Ministry of National Defense, Monrovia, Liberia.

MANUAL OF AIR FORCE LAW-AMENDMENTS. see *LAW*

MANUAL OF MILITARY LAW - AMENDMENTS. see *LAW*

MEDDELANDE ARMEMUSEUM. YEARBOOK. see *MUSEUMS AND ART GALLERIES*

355　AT　ISSN 0157-4159
MELBOURNE PAPERS ON AUSTRALIAN DEFENCE. 1979. irreg. price varies. Australian Defence Association, Box 329, Nth Melbourne, Vic. 3051, Australia.

355　IS
MIDDLE EAST MILITARY BALANCE. (Text in English) a. Tel Aviv University, Jaffe Center for Stategic Studies, Ramat Aviv, Tel Aviv 69 978, Israel.

MILITAERHISTORISK TIDSKRIFT. see *HISTORY — History Of Europe*

355　NO　ISSN 0026-3842
MILITAERPSYKOLOGISKE MEDDELELSER. 1955. irreg. free. ‡ Forsvarets Psykologitjeneste, Oslo Mil, Oslo 1, Norway.

358.4　629.13　UK
MILITARY AIRCRAFT MARKINGS. 1980. a. Ian Allan Ltd., Coombelands House, Addlestone, Weybridge, Surrey KT15 1HU, England. Ed. Peter R. March. circ. 15,000.

MILITARY

355   UK   ISSN 0459-7222
MILITARY BALANCE. 1959. a. £13.50($21)
International Institute for Strategic Studies, 23
Tavistock St, London WC2E 7NQ, England (U.S.
dist: Marketing International, Inc., 1120
Connecticut Ave., N.W., Ste. 940, Washington, DC
20036) charts. stat. circ. 19,500.

355.27   SZ
MILITARY COMMUNICATIONS. a. 1500 Fr.($750)
Interavia S.A., 86 Av. Louis Casai, Case Postale
162, CH-1216 Cointrin/Geneva, Switzerland.

MILITARY DEALERS AND COLLECTORS
DIRECTORY. see *ANTIQUES*

355   UK
MILITARY INTELLIGENCE CRITICAL
ATTRIBUTES. 1981. irreg. $385. Aviation Studies
International, Sussex House, Parkside, Wimbledon,
London SW19 5NB, England.

355   621.3   UK
MILITARY MICROWAVES (YEAR).
PROCEEDINGS OF CONFERENCE. 1978.
biennial. price varies. Microwave Exhibitions &
Publishers Ltd., 90 Calverley Rd., Tunbridge Wells,
Kent TN1 2UN, England. circ. 1,500. (back issues
avail.)

355   US   ISSN 0275-5823
MILITARY OPERATIONS RESEARCH. 1981.
irreg., latest vol.2, 1982. Gordon and Breach
Science Publishers, 50 West 23rd St., New York,
NY 10010. TEL 212-206-8900. Ed. Stephen W.
Leibholz.

355   II   ISSN 0076-8782
MILITARY YEAR BOOK. (Text in English) 1965. a.
Rs.135. Guide Publications, 60-20 Prabhat Rd., New
Delhi 110005, India TEL 572-5793. (Dist. in U.S
by: International Publications Service, 114 E. 32 St.,
New York, N.Y 10016) Ed. S.P. Baranwal. adv.
circ. 5,800.

355   FR
NATION ARMEE.* irreg., vol.2, 1977. Editions
Copernic, 14 rue d'Armorique, 75015 Paris, France.
Dir. Philippe Conrad.

355   US   ISSN 0363-8618
NATIONAL GUARD ALMANAC. 1975. a. $4.25.
Federal and Military Personnel Publications
(Subsidiary of: Uniformed Services Almanac, Inc.)
Box 76, Washington, DC 20044 TEL 703-532-1631.
(Subscr. to:, Dept. G) Ed. Lt. Col. Sol Gordon,
USAF-Ret.
    Formerly: Uniformed Services Almanac. National
Guard Edition (ISSN 0363-8588)

355   US
NATIONAL STRATEGY INFORMATION
CENTER. AGENDA PAPERS. 1969. irreg. (2-3/
yr.) price varies. National Strategy Information
Center, 150 E. 58th St., New York, NY 10155.
TEL 212-838-2912. Ed. William Bodie. bibl. stat.
circ. 7,500.
    Formerly: National Strategy Information Center.
Strategy Papers.

355   947   BU   ISSN 0324-0835
NATSIONALEN VOENNOISTORICHESKI
MUZEI, SOFIA. IZVESTIYA. 1973. a. Durzhavno
Voenno Izdatelstvo, c/o Hemus Foreign Trade Co.,
6 Ruski Blvd., 1000 Sofia, Bulgaria. illus.

NAVAL LAW REVIEW. see *LAW*

355   UK
NAVY LIST OF RETIRED OFFICERS. a. price
varies. H.M.S.O., Box 569, Cornwall House,
London SE1 9HN, England.

353.9   US   ISSN 0094-7326
NEW MEXICO. VETERANS' SERVICE
COMMISSION. REPORT. a. Veterans' Service
Commission, Villagra Bldg., 408 Galisteo St., Box
2324, Santa Fe, NM 87503. TEL 505-827-6300.
charts. stat. circ. 100. Key Title: Report of the New
Mexico Veteran's Service Commission.

355.45   US
NEW YORK (STATE). ASSEMBLY. STANDING
COMMITTEE ON VETERANS' AFFAIRS.
ANNUAL REPORT. a. State Assembly, Room 524,
State Capitol, Albany, NY 12248. TEL 518-455-
4178.

355   NZ
NEW ZEALAND. MINISTRY OF DEFENCE.
REVIEW OF DEFENCE POLICY. 1957. irreg.
price varies. Ministry of Defence, Wellington, New
Zealand.

POLITICS OF LIBERATION SERIES. see
HISTORY — History Of Europe

355.1   UK
QUEEN'S REGULATIONS FOR THE ARMY
AMENDMENTS. irreg. price varies. H.M.S.O., Box
569, Cornwall House, London SE1 9NH, England.

358.4   343.01   UK
QUEEN'S REGULATIONS FOR THE R.A.F.
AMENDMENTS. irreg. price varies. H.M.S.O., Box
569, Cornwall House, London SE1 9NH, England.

355.3   US   ISSN 0363-860X
RESERVE FORCES ALMANAC. 1975. a. $4.25.
Federal and Military Personnel Publications
(Subsidiary of: Uniformed Services Alamanc, Inc.)
Box 76, Washington, DC 20044 TEL 703-532-1631.
(Subscr. to: Department R.) Ed. Lt. Col. Sol
Gordon, USAF-Ret.
    Formerly: Uniformed Services Almanac. Special
Reserve Forces Edition (ISSN 0360-554X)

355   US   ISSN 0149-7197
RETIRED MILITARY ALMANAC. 1978. a. $4.25.
Federal and Military Personnel Publications
(Subsidiary of: Uniformed Services Almanac, Inc.)
Box 76, Washington, DC 20044 TEL 703-532-1631.
(Subscr. to:, Dept M) Ed. Lt. Col. Sol Gordon,
USAF-Retired.

355   NE   ISSN 0254-8186
REVUE INTERNATIONALE D'HISTOIRE
MILITAIRE. (Text in English, French, German,
Italian, Russian and Spanish) 1939. irreg. 15 per no.
Commission Internationale d'Histoire Militaire, c/o
Secretary-General Dr. C.M. Schulten,
Frederikkazerne, Gebouw 103, P.O. Box 90701,
2509 LS The Hague, Netherlands. circ. 1,500.

358.4   UK   ISSN 0035-8606
ROYAL AIR FORCE COLLEGE JOURNAL. 1920.
a. £1($5) Royal Air Force College, Cranwell,
Sleaford, Lincs, England. Ed. Sgr. Ldr. Parker. adv.
bk. rev. circ. 1,800.

358.4   UK
ROYAL AIR FORCE EDUCATION BULLETIN.
1964. a. free. Royal Air Force School of Education
& Training Support, Educational and Training
Technology Development Unit, RAF Newton,
Nottingham NG13 8HL, England. (Co-sponsor:
Ministry of Defence) Ed. V. Hartley. circ. 1,500.
(back issues avail.) Indexed: Res.High.Educ.Abstr.

358.4   UK
ROYAL AIR FORCE YEARBOOK. 1975. a. £1.20.
Royal Air Force Benevolent Fund, De Worde
House, 283 Lonsdale Rd., London SW13 9QW,
England. Ed. William Green. adv. circ. 136,469.

358.4   629.1   AT
ROYAL AUSTRALIAN AIR FORCE ACADEMY
JOURNAL. a. free to qualified personnel. Magazine
Art Pty. Ltd., 35 Willis St., Hampton, Vic. 3188,
Australia. Ed. B. Williams. adv. illus. circ. 5,500.

355   UK
ROYAL BRITISH LEGION ANNUAL REPORT
AND ACCOUNTS. 1921. a. free. Royal British
Legion, National Executive Council, 48 Pall Mall,
London SW1Y 5JY, England. circ. 8,000.

355   UK
ROYAL WELSH FUSILIERS. JOURNAL. a.
Combined Service Publications Ltd., Box 4,
Farnborough, Hants. GU14 7LR, England.

355   US   ISSN 0080-5335
SAGAMORE ARMY MATERIALS RESEARCH
CONFERENCE. PROCEEDINGS. 1954-197?;
resumed 19?? a. price varies. Plenum Publishing
Corp., 233 Spring St., New York, NY 10013. TEL
212-620-8047. Indexed: Chem.Abstr.

359   US   ISSN 0080-9292
SHIPS AND AIRCRAFT OF THE UNITED
STATES FLEET. 1939. irreg., 13th edt., 1984.
$29.95. (U.S. Naval Institute) Naval Institute Press,
Annapolis, MD 21402. TEL 301-268-6110. Ed.
Norman Polmar. index.

SOLDIER SHOP ANNUAL. see *HOBBIES*

SOTAHISTORIALLINEN AIKAKAUSKIRJA. see
HISTORY — History Of Europe

355.03   SA
SOUTH AFRICA. DEPARTMENT OF DEFENSE.
WHITE PAPER ON DEFENSE AND
ARMAMENT PRODUCTION. (Text in: Afrikaans
and English) irreg. Department of Defense, Cape
Town, South Africa.

355   310   US
SOVIET ARMED FORCES REVIEW ANNUAL.
Abbreviated title: S A F R A. 1977. a. price varies.
Academic International Press, Box 1111, Gulf
Breeze, FL 32561. Ed. David R. Jones. bibl. charts.
illus. stat. (back issues avail.) Indexed:
Amer.Bibl.Slavic & E.Eur.Stud.

355   069   PL   ISSN 0137-5733
STUDIA DO DZIEJOW DAWNEGO UZBROJENIA
I UBIORU WOJSKOWEGO. (Text in Polish;
summaries in English) 1963. irreg., latest no.8, 1982.
400 Zl. National Museum in Crakow, Ul. Manifestu
Lipcowego 12, 30-109 Cracow, Poland. (Co-sponsor:
Association of Old Arms and Uniforms Amateurs)
Ed. Katarzyna Onderka. circ. 1,000. (also avail. in
microfilm)

355   943.8   PL   ISSN 0562-2786
STUDIA I MATERIALY DO HISTORII
WOJSKOWOSCI. vol.27, 1984. irreg., vol.28, 1985.
price varies. (Polska Akademia Nauk, Komitet Nauk
Historycznych) Ossolineum, Publishing House of
the Polish Academy of Sciences, Rynek 9, Wroclaw,
Poland (Dist by: Ars Polona-Ruch, Krakowskie
Przedmiescie 7, Warsaw, Poland) Ed. Benon
Miskiewicz.

355   320   US
STUDIES IN DEFENSE POLICY. 1971. irreg.,
no.33, 1984. price varies. Brookings Institution,
1775 Massachusetts Ave. N.W., Washington, DC
20036. TEL 202-797-6258.

355   NE
STUDIES IN U.S. NATIONAL SECURITY. 1977.
irreg. (U.S. Army War College, Strategic Studies
Institute, US) Martinus Nijhoff Publishers, Box
566, 2501 CN The Hague, Netherlands. Ed. James
A. Kuhlman.

355   FI   ISSN 0039-5633
SUOMI MERELLA. (Text in Finnish) 1934. biennial.
Fmk.25. Meriupseeriyhdistys, Varnank 41, 20310
Turku 31, Finland. Ed. V. Auvinen. adv. bk. rev.
abstr. illus. circ. 800.

355.155   UK   ISSN 0491-6204
SURMACH. (Text in Ukrainian) 1955. a. £1.50($2.30)
Association of Ukranian Former Combatants in
Great Britain, 49 Linden Gardens, London W2
4HG, England. Ed. S.M. Fostun. adv. bk. rev. circ.
1,000.

TEMPORARY MILITARY LODGING AROUND
THE WORLD. see *TRAVEL AND TOURISM*

355   FR   ISSN 0036-2794
TRIOMPHE SAINT-CYR; plaquette annuelle des
promotions de l'Ecole Special Militaire de St. Cyr et
de l'Ecole Militaire Interarmes. 1949. a. 43 F. Ecole
Speciale Militaire de Saint-Cyr, 56210 Coetquidan,
France. (Co-sponsor: Ecole Militaire Interarmes)
adv. circ. 1,000.
    Formerly: Triomphe.

U S M A LIBRARY BULLETIN. (U.S. Military
Academy Library) see *LIBRARY AND
INFORMATION SCIENCES*

355.1   US
U S S R REPORT: MILITARY AFFAIRS. irreg.
(approx. 70/yr.) $5 per no. U.S. Joint Publications
Research Service, 1000 N. Glebe Rd., Arlington,
VA 22201 TEL 703-487-4630. (Orders to: NTIS,
Springfield, VA 22161)
    Formerly: Translations on U S S R Military
Affairs.

355   US   ISSN 0503-1982
UNIFORMED SERVICES ALMANAC. 1959. a.
$4.25. Federal and Military Personnel Publications
(Subsidiary of: Uniformed Services Almanac, Inc.)
Box 76, Washington, DC 20044. TEL 703-532-
1631. Eds. Lee E. Sharff, Lt. Col. Sol Gordon,
USAF-Ret.

355 539.7 320　　　UN
UNITED NATIONS DISARMAMENT
YEARBOOK. irreg., latest vol.10, 1985. $25.
United Nations Publications, Room DC2-853, New
York, NY 10017 (Or Distribution and Sales Section,
Palais des Nations, CH-1211 Geneva 10,
Switzerland) (also avail. in microfiche)
　　Former titles: United Nations. Disarmament
Commission. Yearbook; United Nations.
Disarmament Commission. Official Records (ISSN
0082-8076)

355 539.7 320　　　UN
UNITED NATIONS ECONOMIC AND SOCIAL
COUNCIL. DISARMAMENT STUDY SERIES.
1981. irreg., latest no.16. price varies. United
Nations Publications, Room DC2-0853, New York,
NY 10017 (Or Distribution and Sales Section,
Palais des Nations, 1211 Geneva 10, Switzerland)

358 600　　　US
U.S. AIR FORCE GEOPHYSICS LABORATORY. A
F G L (SERIES) 1960? irreg. no subscriptions. U.S.
Air Force Geophysics Laboratory, Hanscom Air
Force Base, Bedford, MA 01730 TEL 617-861-
4441. (Order from: National Technical Information
Service, Springfield, VA 22151) (also avail. in
microform) Indexed: Geo.Abstr. GeoRef.
　　Supersedes: U.S. Air Force Cambridge Research
Laboratories. A F C R L (Series) (ISSN 0082-870X)

356.1　　　US
U.S. ARMY INFANTRY SCHOOL. HISTORY;
ANNUAL SUPPLEMENT. a. free to qualified
military agencies. U.S. Army Infantry School, Attn:
ATSH-SE, Fort Benning, GA 31905-5452. Key
Title: History. Annual Supplement.
　　Formerly: U.S. Army Infantry Center. History;
Annual Supplement (ISSN 0091-2271)

355　　　US　ISSN 0082-9862
U.S. DEPARTMENT OF DEFENSE. DEFENSE
PROGRAM AND DEFENSE BUDGET. (Also
called: Defense Budget and Defense Program) a.
U.S. Department of Defense., The Pentagon,
Washington, DC 20301 TEL 202-545-6700. (Orders
to: Supt. of Documents, Washington, DC 20402)
Indexed: DM & T.

355.6　　　US　ISSN 0098-3888
U.S. DEPARTMENT OF DEFENSE. REPORT OF
SECRETARY OF DEFENSE TO THE
CONGRESS. a. $4.00. U.S. Department of Defense,
The Pentagon, Washington, DC 20301 TEL 202-
545-6700. (Orders to: Supt. of Documents,
Washington, DC 20402) Key Title: Report of
Secretary of Defense to the Congress.

333.9　　　US　ISSN 0361-2651
U.S. DEPARTMENT OF THE ARMY. PROJECTS
RECOMMENDED FOR DEAUTHORIZATION,
ANNUAL REPORT. 1975. a. U.S. Department of
the Army, Corps of Engineers, Washington, DC
20310 TEL 202-545-6700. (Orders to: National
Technical Information Service, 5285 Port Royal
Rd., Springfield, VA 22151) Ed. Velma L. Payton.
circ. 500. Key Title: Projects Recommended for
Deauthorization, Annual Report.

359　　　US　ISSN 0077-6238
U.S. NAVAL INSTITUTE. NAVAL REVIEW; annual
review of world seapower. (May issue of U.S. Naval
Institute, Proceedings) 1962. a. $8 paperback;
hardbound $16. U.S. Naval Institute, Annapolis,
MD 21402. Ed. Paul Stillwell. adv. circ. 90,000.

359.07　　　US　ISSN 0500-1951
U.S. OFFICE OF NAVAL RESEARCH. ANNUAL
TASK SUMMARY: CONTRACT RESEARCH
PROGRAM. a. U.S. Office of Naval Research,
Arlington, VA 22217. TEL 202-545-6200. Key
Title: Annual Task Summary, Contract Research
Program.

355.11 368.4　　　US　ISSN 0083-3533
U.S. VETERANS ADMINISTRATION. ANNUAL
REPORT. 1931. a. free. U.S. Veterans
Administration, 810 Vermont Ave., N.W. (722 B),
Washington, DC 20420. TEL 202-389-2525.

355　　　DK　ISSN 0109-1239
VAABENKAPLOEB OG VAABENKONTROL.
1983. a. Kr.90. (Stockholm International Peace
Research Institute) Mellemfolkeligt Samvirke,
Borgergade 14, 1300 Copenhagen K, Denmark.
illus.

355　　　FR
VIVAT HUSSAR. 1966. a. 180 F. Association des
Amis du Musee International des Hussards, Jardin
Massey, 65000 Tarbes, France. Ed. Bd. adv. bk. rev.
bibl. illus. circ. 1,500.

355　　　YU　ISSN 0067-5660
VOJNI MUZEJ, BELGRADE. VESNIK/MILITARY
MUSEUM, BELGRADE. BULLETIN. (Text in
Serbocroatian; summaries in French and English)
1954. irreg. $0.60 per copy. Vojni Muzej,
Kalemegdan 66, 11000 Belgrade, Yugoslavia. Ed.
Voja Subotic. bk. rev. circ. 2,000.

350　　　GW
WEISSBUCH ZUR SICHERHEIT DER
BUNDESREPUBLIK DEUTSCHLAND UND
ZUR LAGE DER BUNDESWEHR. 1970. irreg.
$10. Bundesministerium der Verteidigung, Postfach
1328, D-5300 Bonn, W. Germany (B.R.D.) circ.
250,000.

355　　　GW　ISSN 0083-9078
WEYERS FLOTTENTASCHENBUCH/WARSHIPS
OF THE WORLD. 1900. a. DM.98. Bernard und
Graefe Verlag, Karl-Mand-Str. 2, D-5400 Koblenz,
W. Germany (B.R.D.)
　　Former titles: Taschenbuch der Kriegsflotten;
Taschenbuch der Deutschen Kriegsflotten.

355.115　　　US　ISSN 0083-9108
WHAT EVERY VETERAN SHOULD KNOW. 1937.
a. (with m. supplements) $6 (with supplements $22)
Veterans Information Service, Box 111, East
Moline, IL 61244. Ed. Patrick L. Murphy. index.

355　　　US
WORLD MILITARY EXPENDITURES AND
ARMS TRANSFERS. a. U.S. Arms Control and
Disarmament Agency, Dept. of State Bldg.,
Washington, DC 20451 TEL 202-632-8715. (Also
avail. from: Supt. of Documents, Washington, DC
20402)
　　Formerly: World Military Expenditures (ISSN
0363-7204); Which supersedes: World Military
Expenditures and Related Data (ISSN 0082-8793)

WORLDWIDE REPORT: ARMS CONTROL. see
POLITICAL SCIENCE — International Relations

355 539.7　　　US
WORLDWIDE REPORT: NUCLEAR
DEVELOPMENT AND PROLIFERATION. irreg.
(approx. 30/yr.) $5 per no. U.S. Joint Publications
Research Service, 1000 N. Glebe Rd., Arlington,
VA 22201 TEL 703-487-4630. (Orders to: NTIS,
Springfield, VA 22161)

WUERZBURGER WEHRWISSENSCHAFTLICHE
ABHANDLUNGEN. see LAW

MILITARY — Abstracting, Bibliographies, Statistics

355 016　　　AG
ABSTRACTS OF MILITARY BIBLIOGRAPHY.
(Text in English) 1967. q. $70. Ruben A. Ramirez
Mitchell, Ed. & Pub., Maipu 262, 1084 Buenos
Aires, Argentina. adv. bk. rev. abstr. tr.mks. index;
cum.index. circ. 2,000.
　　Former titles: Resumenes Analiticos Sobre
Defensa y Seguridad Nacional/Abstracts of Military
Bibliography (ISSN 0034-5873) & Resumenes
Analiticos de Bibliografia Militar.

355 011　　　US
AEROSPACE DEFENSE MARKETS AND
TECHNOLOGY. 1983. m. $850. Predicasts, Inc.,
200 University Circle Research Center, 11001
Cedar Ave., Cleveland, OH 44106. TEL 216-795-
3000. q. and a. cum.indexes. Indexed:
Abstr.Mil.Bibl.
　●Also available online. Vendors: DIALOG.
　　Formerly: Defense Markets and Technology.

355 016　　　US　ISSN 0002-2586
AIR UNIVERSITY LIBRARY INDEX TO
MILITARY PERIODICALS. 1949. q., cumulated
annually. free to libraries. U.S. Air Force, Air
University Library, Maxwell Air Force Base, AL
36112-5564. TEL 205-293-2504. Ed. A. Sue
Goodman. bk. rev. index; cum.index. circ. 1,575.

359 090　　　AG　ISSN 0066-7080
ARGENTINA. DEPARTAMENTO DE ESTUDIOS
HISTORICOS NAVALES. SERIE J: LIBROS Y
IMPRESOS RAROS. 1962. irreg., no.2, 1970.
Departamento de Estudios Historicos Navales,
Instituto de Publicaciones Navales, Av. Cordoba
547, Buenos Aires, Argentina.

359　　　AG　ISSN 0066-7331
ARGENTINA. SERVICIO DE INTELIGENCIA
NAVAL. BIBLIOTECAS DE LA ARMADA.
BOLETIN BIBLIOGRAFICO. 1943. a. Servicio de
Inteligencia Naval, Bibliotecas de la Armada,
Edificio Libertad, Comodoro Py y Corbeta Uruguay,
Buenos Aires, Argentina. Ed. Juan A. Manon.

011 355　　　II
UNIVERSAL MILITARY ABSTRACTS. (Text in
English) 1986. bi-m. $50. 10 A, Astley Hall,
Dehradun 248 001, India. Ed. S.K. Arora. adv. bk.
rev. abstr. charts illus. index.

VIRGINIA MILITARY INSTITUTE, LEXINGTON.
PUBLICATIONS, THESES, AND
DISSERTATIONS OF THE STAFF AND
FACULTY. see EDUCATION — Abstracting,
Bibliographies, Statistics

355.115 310　　　US
WISCONSIN. DEPARTMENT OF VETERANS
AFFAIRS. BIENNIAL REPORT. 1977. biennial.
free. Department of Veterans Affairs, 77 N.
Dickinson St., Box 7843, Madison, WI 53707. TEL
608-266-1311. Ed. Clifford C. Borden Jr. circ. 700.

MINES AND MINING INDUSTRY

see also Metallurgy

622 669　　　AT
A I M M SYMPOSIA SERIES. 1972. irreg. no.47,
1986. price varies. Australasian Institute of Mining
and Metallurgy, Clunies Ross House, 191 Royal
Parade, Parkville, Vic. 3052, Australia. Indexed:
Chem.Abstr. GeoRef.

622　　　US
A M A PRODUCT DIRECTORY. biennial. American
Monument Association, 6902 N. High St.,
Worthington, OH 43085. TEL 614-885-2713. Ed.
Pennie Sabel.
　　Former titles: American Monument Association.
Retailer's Guide & Granite and Marble Directory
(ISSN 0731-4094)

A M D E L BULLETIN. (Australia Mineral
Development Laboratories) see EARTH
SCIENCES — Geology

622 665.5　　　AT　ISSN 0157-2083
A M P L A YEARBOOK. 1977. a. Aus.$85.
Australian Mining and Petroleum Law Association
Ltd., 160 Queen St., 8th Fl., Melbourne, Vic. 3000,
Australia. Ed. Alfreda Stressac. circ. 600. (back
issues avail.) Indexed: C.L.I. L.R.I.
　　Formerly (until 1983): Australian Mining and
Petroleum Law Journal.

549 665.5　　　HU　ISSN 0365-8066
ACTA UNIVERSITATIS DE ATTILA JOZSEF
NOMINATAE. ACTA MINERALOGICA -
PETROGRAPHICA. (Text in English) 1943. a.
exchange basis. Attila Jozsef University, c/o E.
Szabo, Exchange Librarian, Dugonics ter 13, P.O.B.
393, Szeged H-6701, Hungary (Subscr. to: Kultura,
Box 149, H-1389 Budapest, Hungary) Ed. Gyula
Grasselly. bk. rev. charts. illus. circ. 600. Indexed:
Met.Abstr.

622　　　CM　ISSN 0575-7258
ACTIVITES MINERES AU CAMEROUN. 1962. a.,
latest 1975. Direction des Mines et de la Geologie,
Ministere des Mines et de l'Energie, Yaounde,
Cameroon.

MINES AND MINING INDUSTRY

622 PL ISSN 0372-9400
AKADEMIA GORNICZO-HUTNICZA IM. STANISLAWA STASZICA. INSTYTUT GORNICTWA PODZIEMNEGO. PRACE. (Subseries of Zeszyty Naukowe. Gornictwo) (Summaries in English and Russian) 1971. irreg. price varies. Akademia Gorniczo-Hutnicza im. Stanislawa Staszica, Al. Mickiewicza 30, 30-059 Krakow, Poland (Dist. by: Ars Polona, Krakowskie Przedmiescie 7, 00-068 Warsaw, Poland) illus.

622 PL ISSN 0452-6457
AKADEMIA GORNICZO-HUTNICZA IM. STANISLAWA STASZICA. ZESZYTY NAUKOWE. GEODEZJA. (Text in Polish; summaries in English and Russian) 1956. irreg., no.91, 1987. price varies. (Akademia Gorniczo-Hutnicza im. Stanislawa Staszica) Wydawnictwo A G H, Manifestu Lipcowego 17, 31-109 Krakow, Poland (Dist. by: Ars Polona, Krakowskie Przedmiescie 7, 00-068 Warsaw, Poland) Ed. Z. Kleczek. illus. circ. 300.

622 PL
AKADEMIA GORNICZO-HUTNICZA IM. STANISLAWA STASZICA. ZESZYTY NAUKOWE. GORNICTWO. (Text in English and Polish; summaries in English and Russian) 1954. irreg., no. 130, 1987. price varies. (Akademia Gorniczo-Hutnicza im. Stanislawa Staszica) Wydawnictwo A G H, Manifestu Lipcowego 16, 31-109 Krakow, Poland (Dist. by: Ars Polona, Krakowskie Przedmiescie 7, 00-068 Warsaw, Poland) Ed. Z. Kleczek. illus. circ. 300. Indexed: Chem.Abstr.

333.7 338.2 CN ISSN 0380-4321
ALBERTA COAL INDUSTRY, ANNUAL STATISTICS. 1973. a. Can.$15. Energy Resources Conservation Board, 640 5th Ave. S.W., Calgary, Alta. T2P 3G4, Alta, Canada. TEL 403-297-8311. illus. stat.
Formerly: Cumulative Annual Statistics, Alberta Coal Industry.

338.4 GW
ALUMINUM SMELTERS; Europe, Japan, USA. (Edts. in English, French and German) 1965. a. free. Organisation of European Aluminium Smelters, Graf-Adolf-Str. 18, 4000 Duesseldorf, W. Germany (B.R.D.) Ed. Guenter Kirchner. circ. 4,000.
Formerly: Organisation of European Aluminum Smelters. Economic Situation of the Aluminum Smelters in Europe (ISSN 0474-4829)

ANGOLA. DIRECCAO PROVINCIAL DOS SERVICOS DE GEOLOGIA E MINAS. BOLETIM. see EARTH SCIENCES — Geology

622 BE ISSN 0003-4290
ANNALES DES MINES DE BELGIQUE/ ANNALEN DER MIJNEN VAN BELGIE. (Text in Dutch and French; summaries in Dutch, English, French and German) 1896. a. 4000 Fr. Institut National des Industries Extractives - Nationaal Instituut voor de Extractiebedrijven, 200 rue du Chera, 4000 Liege, Belgium. adv. bk. rev. abstr. charts. illus. circ. 900. Indexed: Chem.Abstr. Eng.Ind. Excerp.Med. Art & Archaeol.Tech.Abstr. C.I.S. Abstr. Fuel & Energy Abstr. GeoRef.

622 FR
ANNUAIRE DE L'ADMINISTRATION DES MINES. (Compiled from information contained in Les Annales des Mines) 1852. a. 117 Fr.($13.50) Annales des Mines, 120 rue du Cherche-Midi, 75006 Paris, France (Orders to: G.E.D.I.M; 19, rue du Grand-Moulin, 42 Saint-Etienne Cedex, France) Ed. Michel Matheu. adv. circ. 1,500. (back issues avail.)
Formerly: Annuaire de l'Administration et du Corps des Mines (ISSN 0071-822X)

ANNUAL BOOK OF A S T M STANDARDS. VOLUME 05.05. GASEOUS FUELS; COAL AND COKE. see ENGINEERING — Engineering Mechanics And Materials

622 UN ISSN 0066-3808
ANNUAL BULLETIN OF COAL STATISTICS FOR EUROPE. (Text in English, French and Russian) 1966. a., latest vol.19, 1984. price varies. Economic Commission for Europe (ECE), Distribution and Sales Section, Palais des Nations, 1211 Geneva 10, Switzerland (Or United Nations Publications, Rm. DC2-853, New York, NY 10017)

338.7 II
ANNUAL REPORT OF THE WORKING AND AFFAIRS OF MYSORE MINERALS LIMITED. (Text in English) a. Mysore Minerals Ltd., Bangalore, Karnataka, India.

622 558 CL ISSN 0066-5096
ANUARIO DE LA MINERIA DE CHILE. 1961. a. $8 (or exchange basis) Servicio Nacional de Geologia y Mineria, Casilla 10465, Santiago, Chile. Ed. Juan Williams. circ. 700.

338.2 BL
ANUARIO MINERAL BRASILEIRO. 1972. a. Cr.$140. Departamento Nacional da Producao Mineral, Setor Autarquia Norte, Quadra 1 Bloco B, 70000 Brasilia D.F., Brazil. illus. stat.

549 US ISSN 0066-5487
APPLIED MINERALOGY. TECHNISCHE MINEROLOGIE. 1971. irreg., vol.12, 1981. price varies. Springer-Verlag, 175 Fifth Ave., New York, NY 10010 TEL 212-460-1500. (Also Berlin, Heidelberg, Tokyo and Vienna) (reprint service avail. from ISI) Indexed: GeoRef.

ARGENTINA. SERVICIO NACIONAL MINERO GEOLOGICO. ANALES. see EARTH SCIENCES — Geology

ARGENTINA. SERVICIO NACIONAL MINERO GEOLOGICO. BOLETIN. see EARTH SCIENCES — Geology

553 AG ISSN 0066-7161
ARGENTINA. SERVICIO NACIONAL MINERO GEOLOGICO. ESTADISTICA MINERA. 1909. irreg. price varies. Servicio Nacional Minero Geologico, Bibliotheca, Av. Santa Fe 1548, Buenos Aires, Argentina.
Formerly: Argentine Republic. Direccion Nacional de Geologia y Mineria. Estadistica Minera.

ASBESTOS PRODUCER/PRODUCTEUR D'AMIANTE. see BUILDING AND CONSTRUCTION

622 550 AT
AUSTRALIA. BUREAU OF MINERAL RESOURCES. GEOLOGY AND GEOPHYSICS. RESOURCE REPORT. 1987. irreg. price varies. Bureau of Mineral Resources, Geology and Geophysics, G.P.O. Box 378, Canberra, A.C.T. 2601, Australia.

338.2 AT ISSN 0311-8975
AUSTRALIA. BUREAU OF STATISTICS. MINERAL PRODUCTION, AUSTRALIA. 1971. a. free. Australian Bureau of Statistics, P.O. Box 10, Belconnen, A.C.T. 2616, Australia. circ. 2,000.

338.2 AT ISSN 0067-1762
AUSTRALIAN COAL INDUSTRY RESEARCH LABORATORIES. ANNUAL REPORT. 1966. a. free. Australian Coal Industry Research Laboratories Ltd., Box 83, Northryde, N.S.W. 2113, Australia. Ed. A. Robertson. Indexed: Chem.Abstr.

622 AT ISSN 0084-7488
AUSTRALIAN MINERAL INDUSTRY. ANNUAL REVIEW. 1948. a. price varies. Bureau of Mineral Resources, Geology and Geophysics, Box 378, Canberra, A.C.T. 2601, Australia. Indexed: GeoRef.
Formerly: Australia Mineral Industry Review (ISSN 0067-1509)

622 AT
AUSTRALIAN MINING INDUSTRY COUNCIL. DIRECTORY. 1983. biennial. free. Australian Mining Industry Council, Box 363, Dickson, A.C.T. 2602, Australia.

622 AT ISSN 0314-7762
AUSTRALIAN MINING YEAR BOOK. a. Aus.$65. Thomson Publications (Australia) Pty. Ltd., 47 Chippen St., Chippendale, N.S.W. 2008, Australia. Ed. Peter Barrett. circ. 2,000. (also avail. in microfiche)

622 CS
BANICKE LISTY/FOLIA MONTANA. (Text in Slovak; summaries in English, French and Russian) 1974. irreg. 9 Kcs. (Slovenska Akademia Vied, Banicky Ustav Sav) Veda, Publishing House of the Slovak Academy of Sciences, Klemensova 19, 814 30 Bratislava, Czechoslovakia (Subscr. to: Slovart, Gottwaldovo nam. 6, 817 64 Bratislava) illus.

BANYASZATI SZAKIRODALMI TAJEKOZTATO/ MINING ABSTRACTS. see MINES AND MINING INDUSTRY — Abstracting, Bibliographies, Statistics

622 BE
BELGIUM. ADMINISTRATION DES MINES. STATISTIQUES: HOUILLE, COKES, AGGLOMERES METALLURGIE, CARRIERES/ STATISTIEKEN: STEENKOLEN, COKES, AGGLOMERATEN, METAALNIJVERHEID, GROEVEN. 1954. irreg. Administration des Mines, 30 rue de Mot, 1040 Brussels, Belgium. illus. circ. 250.
Formerly: Belgium. Administration des Mines. Service: Statistiques. Siderurgie, Houille, Agglomeres, Cokes (ISSN 0525-4752)

BERGBAU-BERUFSGENOSSENSCHAFT. JAHRESBERICHT. see LABOR UNIONS

622 PH
BIBLIOGRAPHY ON PHILIPPINE GEOLOGY, MINING AND MINERAL RESOURCES. (Text in English) 1971. a. P.20($3) Bureau of Mines and Geo-Sciences, Sciences Mineral Economics and Information Division, Pedro Gill St., Ermita Metro Manila, Philippines. circ. 100. (back issues avail.)
Formerly: Philippine Geology, Mining and Mineral Resources.

622 AT
BLACK COAL IN AUSTRALIA. 1977. a. Aus.$12. Australia and New South Wales Joint Coal Board, Sydney, N.S.W., Australia. illus.

622 BO ISSN 0067-9852
BOLIVIA. SERVICIO GEOLOGICO. SERIE MINERALOGICA. CONTRIBUCIONE. 1968. irreg. Servicio Geologico, Casilla 2729, La Paz, Bolivia.

662 UR
BOR'BA S GAZOM V UGOL'NYKH SHAKHTAKH. irreg. 0.61 Rub. (Nauchno-Issledovatelskii Institut po Bezopasnosti Rabot v Gornoi Promyshlennosti, Makeevka) Izdatel'stvo Nedra, Tret'yakovskii proezd, 1, Moscow K-12, Russian S.F.S.R., U.S.S.R. illus.

622 BL
BRAZIL. DEPARTAMENTO NACIONAL DA PRODUCAO MINERAL. AVULSO. 1974. irreg. free. Departamento Nacional da Producao Mineral, Setor Autarcuia Norte, Quadra 1, Bloco B, Brasilia, D.F., Brazil.

622 BL
BRAZIL. DEPARTAMENTO NACIONAL DA PRODUCAO MINERAL. BOLETIM. 1973. irreg. price varies. Departamento Nacional da Producao Mineral, Setor Autarcuia Norte, Quadra 1, Bloco B, Brasilia, D.F., Brazil. (back issues avail.)

622 BL
BRAZIL. DEPARTAMENTO NACIONAL DA PRODUCAO MINERAL. PROGRAMACAO. a. free. Departmento Nacional da Producao Mineral, Setor Autarcuia Norte, Quadra 1, Bloco B, Brasilia, D.F., Brazil. circ. 150 (controlled)

622 665.5 CN ISSN 0365-9356
BRITISH COLUMBIA. MINISTRY OF ENERGY, MINES AND PETROLEUM RESOURCES. ANNUAL REPORT. a. free. Ministry of Energy, Mines and Petroleum Resources, Publications Distribution Section, 552 Michigan St., Victoira, B.C. V8V 1X4, Canada. TEL 604-387-5178.

622.33 333.7 CN ISSN 0707-3739
BRITISH COLUMBIA. MINISTRY OF THE ENVIRONMENT. NORTHEAST COAL STUDY PRELIMINARY ENVIRONMENTAL REPORT. 1977. a. Ministry of the Environment, Resource Analysis Branch, Parliament Bldgs., Victoria, B.C. V8V 1X5, Canada. TEL 604-387-5162. illus. Key Title: Northeast Coal Study. Preliminary Environmental Report.

622 CN ISSN 0705-5196
C A N M E T REPORT. 1974. irreg. price varies. Canada Centre for Mineral and Energy Technology 555 Booth St., Ottawa, Ont. K1A 0G1, Canada. Ed M. Close. circ. 1,000. Indexed: Chem.Abstr. Energy Ind. GeoRef.
Incorporating (as of 1977): C A N M E T Review.

MINES AND MINING INDUSTRY

622 669 CN ISSN 0068-9009
C.I.M. DIRECTORY. 1967. a. Can.$75. Canadian Institute of Mining and Metallurgy, 400-1130 Sherbrooke West, Montreal, Que. H3A 2M8, Canada. TEL 514-842-3461. Ed. Pierre Michaud. adv. circ. 12,750.

622 330 CN ISSN 0228-1821
C R S PERSPECTIVES. 1978. irreg. free. Centre for Resource Studies, Queen's University, Kingston, Ont. K7L 3N6, Canada. TEL 613-547-5957. Ed. David Yudelman. bk. rev. circ. 4,500.

CALIFORNIA. DIVISION OF MINES AND GEOLOGY. BULLETIN. see *EARTH SCIENCES* — *Geology*

CALIFORNIA. DIVISION OF MINES AND GEOLOGY. SPECIAL PUBLICATION. see *EARTH SCIENCES* — *Geology*

CALIFORNIA. DIVISION OF MINES AND GEOLOGY. SPECIAL REPORT. see *EARTH SCIENCES* — *Geology*

338.2 CN
CANADA. INDIAN AND NORTHERN AFFAIRS CANADA. MINES AND MINERAL ACTIVITIES (YEAR) 1972. a. free. Indian and Northern Affairs Canada, 355 River Road, Ottawa, Ont. K1A 0E4, Canada. TEL 613-997-0380.
Formerly: Canada. Northern Natural Resources and Environment Branch. Mining Section. North of 60: Mines and Mineral Activities; Supersedes: Canada. Department of Indian Affairs and Northern Development. Mines and Minerals, Activities (ISSN 0590-580X)

622 CN
CANADA. MINERAL POLICY SECTOR. MINERAL BULLETINS. 1953. irreg. price varies. Department of Energy, Mines and Resources, Mineral Policy Sector, Ottawa, Ont. K1A 0E4, Canada TEL 613-997-2560. (Orders to: Supply and Services Canada, Publishing Centre, Hull, Que. K1A OS5, Canada)
Former titles: Canada. Mineral Policy Sector. Mineral Information Bulletin; Canada. Mineral Development Sector. Mineral Information Bulletin; Canada. Mineral Resources Branch. Mineral Information Bulletin. (ISSN 0068-7812)

622 CN ISSN 0068-9270
CANADIAN MINERALS YEARBOOK/ ANNUAIRE DES MINERAUX DU CANADA. 1962. a. price varies. Department of Energy, Mines and Resources, Mineral Policy Sector, Publication Distribution Office, Ottawa, Ontario K1A OE4, Canada TEL 613-997-2560. (Orders to: Supply and Services Canada, Publishing Centre, Hull, Que. K1A OS5, Canada)

622 CN ISSN 0068-9289
CANADIAN MINES HANDBOOK. 1931. a. Can.$26 (paper); Can.$29 (hardcover) Northern Miner Press Ltd., 7 Labatt Ave., Toronto, Ont. M5A 3P2, Canada. TEL 416-368-3481. Ed. C.D. Gardiner. circ. 15,000.

338.2 622 CN ISSN 0068-9297
CANADIAN MINES REGISTER OF DORMANT AND DEFUNCT COMPANIES. 1960. irreg. Can.$35 including supplements. Northern Miner Press Ltd., 7 Labatt Ave., Toronto, Ont. M5A 3P2, Canada. TEL 416-368-3481. Ed. A. Worobec.

338.2 622 CN ISSN 0068-9300
CANADIAN MINES REGISTER OF DORMANT AND DEFUNCT COMPANIES. SUPPLEMENT. 1966. irreg., 3rd, 1976. Can.$15. Northern Miner Press Ltd., 7 Labatt Ave., Toronto, Ont. M5A 3P2, Canada. TEL 416-368-3481. Ed. A. Worobec.

622 CN ISSN 0315-9140
CANADIAN MINING JOURNAL'S REFERENCE MANUAL & BUYERS' GUIDE. 1891. a. Can.$22($32) Southam Communications Limited, 1450 Don Mills Road, Don Mills, Ontario M3B 2X7. TEL 416-445-6641. Ed. Richard Fish. adv. circ. 2,970.
Formerly: Canadian Mining Manual (ISSN 0068-9319)

622 665.5 CN ISSN 0710-622X
CANADIAN OIL & GAS HANDBOOK. a. Can.$26 (paper); Can.$29 (hardcover) Northern Miner Press Ltd., 7 Labatt Ave., Toronto, Ont. M5A 3P2, Canada. TEL 416-368-3481. Ed. G.D. Gardiner. Indexed: CS Ind.

622 CK
CARTA METALURGICA. 1958. a. free. Fedemetal, Calle 35 N. 4-81, Bogota, Colombia. Ed. Amparo Segura. adv. bk. rev. circ. 3,000.
Formerly: Metal.

622 II
CENTRAL MINE PLANNING & DESIGN INSTITUTE. MANUALS. (Text in English) 1976. irreg. free. Central Mine Planning & Design Institute Ltd. (Subsidiary of: Coal India Limited) Publications Wing, Gondwana Place, Kanke Rd., Ranchi 834008, Bihar, India.

622 II
CENTRAL MINING RESEARCH STATION, DHANBAD. ANNUAL REPORT. 1961. a. price varies. Central Mining Research Station, Barwa Rd., Dhanbad 826001, Bihar, India. (Affiliate: Council of Scientific and Industrial Research) Ed. V.S. Narayana. circ. 1,000.
Formerly: Central Mining Research Station, Dhanbad. Progress Research (ISSN 0070-4628)

622 CN
CENTRE FOR RESOURCE STUDIES. ANNUAL REPORT. a. Centre for Resource Studies, Queen's University, Kingston, Ont. K7L 3N6, Canada.

622 CN
CENTRE FOR RESOURCE STUDIES. PROCEEDINGS. 1978. irreg. price varies. Centre for Resource Studies, Queen's University, Kingston, Ont. K7L 3N6, Canada. TEL 613-547-5957. Ed. Margot Wojciechowski.

622 CN
CENTRE FOR RESOURCE STUDIES. TECHNICAL PAPERS. 1981. irreg. price varies. Centre for Resource Studies, Queen's University, Kingston, Ont. K7L 3N6, Canada. TEL 613-547-5957.

622 CN ISSN 0226-7616
CENTRE FOR RESOURCES STUDIES. WORKING PAPERS. no.3, 1977. irreg. price varies. Centre for Resource Studies, Queen's University, Kingston, Ont. K7L 3N6, Canada. TEL 613-547-5957.

338.2 CM ISSN 0069-2530
CHAMBRE DE COMMERCE, D'INDUSTRIE ET DES MINES DU CAMEROUN. RAPPORT ANNUEL. a. EAs.1000. Chambre de Commerce, d'Industrie et des Mines du Cameroun, B.P. 4011, Douala, Cameroon. circ. 350.

CHAMBRE SYNDICALE DE LA SIDERUGIE FRANCAISE. BULLETIN STATISTIQUE. SERIE BLEUE. COMMERCE EXTERIEUR. see *METALLURGY*

CHAMBRE SYNDICALE DE LA SIDERUGIE FRANCAISE. BULLETIN STATISTIQUE. SERIE ROUGE. PRODUCTION. see *METALLURGY*

338 FR ISSN 0069-259X
CHAMBRE SYNDICALE DES MINES DE FER DE FRANCE. RAPPORT D'ACTIVITE. a. Chambre Syndicale des Mines de Fer de France, 15 bis rue de Marignan, 75008 Paris, France. charts. stat.

622.33 FR ISSN 0009-1685
CHARBONNAGES DE FRANCE. PUBLICATIONS TECHNIQUES. (In two sections: Documents Techniques and Notes Techniques) (Text in French; summaries in English, German and Russian) 1965. irreg.; approx 4-5/yr. 615 F. Unite des Services Techniques des Charbonnages de France, 2 rue de Metz, 57802 Freyming Merlebach, France. Ed.Bd. bibl. charts. illus.
Coal

622 HK ISSN 0258-3062
CHINA COAL INDUSTRY YEARBOOK. (Text in English) 1982. a. HK.$250($45) Economic Information & Agency, 342 Hennessy Rd., 10th Fl., Hong Kong, Hong Kong. (back issues avail.)

622.33 CH
CHINA, REPUBLIC. MINING RESEARCH AND SERVICE ORGANISATION. M R S O SPECIAL REPORT. 1977. irreg. Mining Research and Service Organization, Industrial Technology Research Institute, Taipei, Taiwan, Republic of China.

553.61 US ISSN 0069-4592
CLAY RESOURCES BULLETIN. 1967. irreg., no.3, 1972. $3. Geological Survey, Box G, University Station, Baton Rouge, LA 70893. TEL 504-342-6754.

622.33 UK ISSN 0309-4979
COAL ABSTRACTS. 1977. m. £100. I.E.A. Coal Research, 14/15 Lower Grosvenor Place, London SW1W 0EX, England. index. circ. 1,200. (also avail. in microfiche)
●Also available online. Vendors: BELINDIS, CISTI, INKA.

622 US ISSN 0145-417X
COAL DATA. a. $75 to individuals; non-profit institutions $50. National Coal Association, Coal Bldg., 1130 17 St. N.W., Washington, DC 20036. TEL 202-463-2631. Indexed: GeoRef.
Formerly: Bituminous Coal Data (ISSN 0067-897X)

338.2 622 US
COAL FACTS. 1948. a. $10. National Coal Association, 1130 17th St. N.W., Washington, DC 20036. TEL 202-463-2625. Ed. Thomas B. Johnson. index.
Formerly (until 1972): Bituminous Coal Facts (ISSN 0067-8988)

622.33 US
COAL PRODUCTION (YEAR) Variant title: Annual Coal Production Report. 1976. a. $6. U.S. Energy Information Administration, National Energy Information Center, EI-22, Forrestal Bldg., 1000 Independence Ave., S.W., Washington, DC 20585. TEL 202-252-8800.
Formerly: Coal Production Annual; Incorporating (as of 1983): Coal-Pennsylvania Anthracite.

622 UK
COAL RESEARCH PROJECTS. 1981. a. £45. I.E.A. Coal Research, 14/15 Lower Grosvenor Place, London SW1, England. circ. 1,200. (also avail. in microfiche)
Formerly: Coal Research Projects. Coal Research Database.

553 US ISSN 0069-4916
COAL TRAFFIC ANNUAL. a. $75 to individuals; non-profit organizations $50. National Coal Association, Coal Bldg., 1130 17 St., N.W., Washington, DC 20036. TEL 202-463-2631. Ed. Bonnie L. King.

553 UK ISSN 0069-4991
COKE OVEN MANAGERS' ASSOCIATION. YEAR BOOK. 1917. a. £17. Waveney House, Adwick Road, Mexborough, Yorks S64 0BS, England. Ed. F.H. Metcalf. adv. circ. 750. Indexed: Br.Ceram.Abstr.

622 SA
COLIMPEX MINING EXECUPAD. (Text in Afrikaans and English) a. free to qualified personnel. Colimpex Africa (Pty.) Ltd., Box 889, Wendywood 2144, South Africa. adv.

622 550 560 US ISSN 0069-6056
COLORADO SCHOOL OF MINES. PROFESSIONAL CONTRIBUTIONS. 1965. irreg., no.11, 1983. $25. (Colorado School of Mines) Colorado School of Mines Press, Golden, CO 80401. TEL 303-273-3607. bibl. charts. illus. cum.index: 1953-1973. circ. 1,000. (reprint service avail. from UMI) Indexed: Chem.Abstr. GeoRef.

338.9 EI ISSN 0069-6757
COMMISSION OF THE EUROPEAN COMMUNITIES. INVESTMENTS IN THE COMMUNITY COAL MINING AND IRON AND STEEL INDUSTRIES. REPORT ON THE SURVEY. (Editions also in Dutch, French, German, and Italian) 1956. a. price varies. Office for Official Publications of the European Communities, P.O. Box 1003, L-2985 Luxembourg, Luxembourg (Dist. in U.S. by: European Community Information Service, 2100 M St., N.W., 707, Washington, DC 20037)

MINES AND MINING INDUSTRY

549   AT   ISSN 0728-7615
COMMONWEALTH SCIENTIFIC AND INDUSTRIAL RESEARCH ORGANIZATION. DIVISION OF FOSSIL FUELS. REPORT OF RESEARCH. 1982. biennial. C.S.I.R.O., Division of Fossil Fuels, Box 136, North Ryde, N.S.W. 2113, Australia. circ. 750.

622.33   AT   ISSN 0726-6510
COMMONWEALTH SCIENTIFIC AND INDUSTRIAL RESEARCH ORGANIZATION. DIVISION OF GEOMECHANICS. GEOMECHANICS OF COAL MINING REPORT. 1978. irreg. Aus.$5 per no. C.S.I.R.O., Division of Geomechanics, Box 54, Mt. Waverley, Vic. 3149, Australia.
Coal

624.176   AT   ISSN 0069-7249
COMMONWEALTH SCIENTIFIC AND INDUSTRIAL RESEARCH ORGANIZATION. DIVISION OF GEOMECHANICS. TECHNICAL REPORT. 1963. irreg. Aus.$5 per no. C.S.I.R.O., Division of Geomechanics, Box 54, Mt. Waverley 3149, Victoria, Australia. Indexed: Biol.Abstr.
Formerly: Commonwealth Scientific and Industrial Research Organization. Division of Soil Mechanics. Technical Report.

549   AT   ISSN 0729-056X
COMMONWEALTH SCIENTIFIC AND INDUSTRIAL RESEARCH ORGANIZATION. INSTITUTE OF ENERGY AND EARTH RESOURCES. ANNUAL REPORT. 1980. a. free. C.S.I.R.O., Institute of Energy and Earth Resources, Box 225, Dickson, A.C.T. 2602, Australia. Ed. J. North. circ. 2,000(controlled)
Supersedes: Commonwealth Scientific and Industrial Research Organization. Institute of Earth Resources. Annual Report. (ISSN 0158-7412)

549   AT
COMMONWEALTH SCIENTIFIC AND INDUSTRIAL RESEARCH ORGANIZATION. INSTITUTE OF ENERGY AND EARTH RESOURCES. DIVISION OF MINERAL PHYSICS & MINERALOGY. BIENNIAL REPORT. 1981. biennial. free. Division of Mineral Physics & Mineralogy, Box 136, North Ryde, N.S.W. 2113, Australia. circ. controlled.
Formerly: Commonwealth Scientific and Industrial Research Organization of Energy and Earth Resources. Division of Mineral Physics. Biennial Report (ISSN 0725-0142)

549   AT   ISSN 0726-1780
COMMONWEALTH SCIENTIFIC AND INDUSTRIAL RESEARCH ORGANIZATION. INSTITUTE OF ENERGY AND EARTH RESOURCES. INVESTIGATION REPORT. 1954. irreg. free. ‡ C.S.I.R.O., Institute of Energy and Earth Resources, Box 136, North Ryde. N.S.W.2113, Australia. Ed. J. Thomson. circ. 825(controlled) Indexed: Chem.Abstr.
Former titles: Commonwealth Scientific and Industrial Research Organization. Institute of Earth Resources. Investigation Report. (ISSN 0156-9953); Commonwealth Scientific and Industrial Research Organization. Minerals Research Laboratories. Investigation Report (ISSN 0084-8999); Commonwealth Scientific and Industrial Research Organization. Division of Coal Research. Investigation Report.

549   AT   ISSN 0726-1772
COMMONWEALTH SCIENTIFIC AND INDUSTRIAL RESEARCH ORGANIZATION. INSTITUTE OF ENERGY AND EARTH RESOURCES. TECHNICAL COMMUNICATION. 1953. irreg., (approx. 2/yr.) free. ‡ C.S.I.R.O., Institute of Energy and Earth Resources, Box 136, North Ryde, N.S.W. 2113, Australia. Ed. J. Thomson. circ. controlled. Indexed: Chem.Abstr.
Former titles: Commonwealth Scientific and Industrial Research Organization. Institute of Earth Resources. Technical Communication. (ISSN 0156-9945); Commonwealth Scientific and Industrial Research Organization. Minerals Research Laboratories. Technical Communication; Commonwealth Scientific and Industrial Research Organization. Division of Mineral Chemistry. Technical Communication.

CONSTRUCTION EQUIPMENT BUYERS GUIDE. see *BUILDING AND CONSTRUCTION*

622   CY
CYPRUS. MINES SERVICE. ANNUAL REPORT. 1921. a. free. Ministry of Commerce and Industry, Mines Department, Government Printing Office, Nicosia, Cyprus. Ed. G.C. Kronides. circ. 500.
Formerly: Cyprus. Mines Department. Annual Report of the Senior Mines Officer for the Year.

E/M J INTERNATIONAL DIRECTORY OF MINING. see *METALLURGY*

E N I ANNUAL REPORT. (Ente Nazionale Idrocarburi) see *ENERGY*

622 671   PL   ISSN 0070-9964
ELEKTRYFIKACJA I MECHANIZACJA GORNICTWA I HUTNICTWA/ ELECTRIFICATION AND MECHANIZATION IN MINING AND METALLURGY. (Subseries of: Akademia Gorniczo-Hutnicza im. Stanislawa Staszica. Zeszyty Naukowe) (Text and summaries in English) 1954. irreg. Akademia Gorniczo-Hutnicza im. Stanislawa Staszica, Al. Mickiewicza 30, 30-059 Krakow, Poland (Dist. by: Ars Polona, Krakowskie Przedmiescie 7, 00-068 Warsaw, Poland)

622.33   IT
ENERGIA ED IDROCARBURI/ENERGY AND HYDROCARBONS. (Text in English and Italian) irreg. Ente Nazionale Idrocarburi, Rome, Italy. charts.
Formerly: Energia ed Idrocarburi. Sommario Statistico.

622 338   SP   ISSN 0071-156X
ESTADISTICAS MINERA Y METALURGICA DE ESPANA.* a. 500 ptas. (Direccion General de Minas y Combustibles) Ministerio de Industria, Paseo de la Castellana 160, Madrid 16, Spain.

EXPLORATION IN BRITISH COLUMBIA. see *EARTH SCIENCES — Geology*

622   DK   ISSN 0107-3117
FAELLESRAADET VEDROERENDE MINERALISKE RAASTOFFER I GROENLAND. BERETNING. Eskimo edition: Kalatdlitnunane Augtitagssanik Atortugssiagssiat Pivdlugit. Faellesraadet Naluaerut. 1980. a. free. Faellesraadet Vedroerende Mineraliske Raastoffer i Groenland, c/o Raastofforvaltningen for Groenland, Hausergade 3, 1128 Copenhagen K, Denmark.

549   FJ   ISSN 0252-2462
FIJI. MINERAL RESOURCES DEPARTMENT. ANNUAL REPORT. (Text in English) 1953. a. price varies. Mineral Resources Department, P.M. Bag, Suva, Fiji. Ed. Peter Rodda.
Former titles: Fiji. Mineral Resources Division. Annual Report; (Until 1978): Fiji. Department of Lands, & Mineral Resources. Annual Report (ISSN 0252-2470); (Until 1972): Fiji. Geological Survey. Annual Report (ISSN 0252-2489)

549   FJ
FIJI. MINERAL RESOURCES DEPARTMENT. ECONOMIC INVESTIGATION. (Text in English) 1972. irreg. price varies. Mineral Resources Department, P.M. Bag, Suva, Fiji. Ed. Peter Rodda. circ. 300. Indexed: GeoRef.
Formerly: Fiji. Mineral Resources Division. Economic Investigation (ISSN 0379-296X); Supersedes (1962-1972): Fiji. Geological Survey. Economic Investigation (ISSN 0428-3279)

338.2 665.5   CN   ISSN 0227-1656
FINANCIAL POST SURVEY OF MINES AND ENERGY RESOURCES. 1980. a. Can.$59.95. Maclean Hunter Ltd., Financial Post Division, Maclean Hunter Bldg., 777 Bay St., Toronto, Ont. M5W 1A7, Canada. TEL 416-596-5585. Ed. John Byrne. adv. circ. 11,000.
Formed by the merger of: Financial Post Survey of Mines (ISSN 0071-5085); Financial Post Survey of Energy Resources (ISSN 0705-7091)
Investment and financial information on publicly owned mining and resource companies in Canada

622   UK   ISSN 0141-3244
FINANCIAL TIMES INTERNATIONAL YEAR BOOKS: MINING. 1887. a. £52. Longman Group Ltd., Fourth Ave., Harlow, Essex CM19 5AA, England (Distr. in U.S. and Canada by: Longman Group USA Inc., 500 North Dearborn St., Chicago, IL 60610)
Formerly: Mining Year Book.

FRANCE. BUREAU DE RECHERCHES GEOLOGIQUES ET MINIERES. MANUELS ET METHODES. see *EARTH SCIENCES — Geology*

FRANCE. BUREAU DE RECHERCHES GEOLOGIQUES ET MINIERES. MEMOIRES. see *EARTH SCIENCES — Geology*

FUNDACION BARILOCHE. INSTITUTO DE ECONOMIA DE LA ENERGIA. PUBLICACIONES. see *ENERGY*

338.7   ZR
GECAMINES ANNUAL REPORT/GECAMINES RAPPORT ANNUEL. (Editions in English and French) a. Generale des Carrieres et des Mines, Division des Relations Publiques, B.P. 8714, Kinshasa, Zaire. charts. stat.

622   ZR
GENERALE DES CARRIERES ET DES MINES. MONOGRAPHIE. irreg. (approx. 4/yr.) Generale des Carrieres et des Mines, Division des Relations Publiques, B.P. 450, Lubumbashi, Zaire.
Formerly: Generale des Carrieres et Mines du Zaire. Monographie.

GEOLOGICAL, MINING AND METALLURGICAL SOCIETY OF INDIA. BULLETIN. see *EARTH SCIENCES — Geology*

GEOLOGISCHES JAHRBUCH. REIHE D: MINERALOGIE. PETROGRAPHIE, GEOCHEMIE, LAGERSTAETTENKUNDE. see *EARTH SCIENCES — Geology*

622   US
GEORGIA. GEOLOGIC SURVEY. CIRCULAR 3. THE MINERAL INDUSTRY OF GEORGIA. 1977. irreg. free. Department of Natural Resources, Georgia Geologic Survey, 19 Martin Luther King Jr. Dr., S.W., Rm. 400, Atlanta, GA 30334. TEL 404-656-3214.

338.2   US
GEORGIA. GEOLOGICAL SURVEY. CIRCULAR 2. MINING DIRECTORY OF GEORGIA. irreg., 18th ed., 1981. free. ‡ Department of Natural Resources, Georgia Geologic Survey, 19 Martin Luther King Jr. Dr., S.W., Rm. 400, Atlanta, GA 30334. TEL 404-656-3214. Ed. E. Morrow.

338.2   US   ISSN 0433-5473
GEORGIA. GEOLOGICAL SURVEY. INFORMATION CIRCULAR. 1933. irreg. price varies. ‡ Department of Natural Resources, Georgia Geologic Survey, 19 Martin Luther King Jr. Dr., S.W., Rm. 400, Atlanta, GA 30334. TEL 404-656-3214. Ed. E. Morrow.

GREAT BRITAIN. BRITISH GEOLOGICAL SURVEY. MINERAL ASSESSMENT REPORT. see *EARTH SCIENCES — Geology*

GREAT BRITAIN. BRITISH GEOLOGICAL SURVEY. OVERSEAS GEOLOGY AND MINERAL RESOURCES. see *EARTH SCIENCES — Geology*

622.33   UK
GREAT BRITAIN. HEALTH AND SAFETY EXECUTIVE. HEALTH AND SAFETY: COAL MINES. a. H.M.S.O., Box 569, London SE1 9NH, England.

622   UK
GREAT BRITAIN. HEALTH AND SAFETY EXECUTIVE. HEALTH AND SAFETY: MINES. a. H.M.S.O., Box 569, London SE1 9NH, England.

622   UK
GREAT BRITAIN. HEALTH AND SAFETY EXECUTIVE. HEALTH AND SAFETY: QUARRIES. a. H.M.S.O., Box 569, London SE1 9NH, England.

338.2   BL
GUIA ECONOMICO E INDUSTRIAL DO ESTADO DE MINAS GERAIS. a. free. Federacao das Industrias do Estado de Minas Gerais, Av. Carandai 1115, 30000 Belo Horizonte, Brazil. Ed. Paulo A.S. Passos. adv. charts. stat.
Supersedes (since 1979): Anuario Industrial de Minas Gerais (ISSN 0066-5231)

MINES AND MINING INDUSTRY

553   UK   ISSN 0072-8713
GUIDE TO THE COALFIELDS. 1948. a. £28.50.
Fuel and Metallurgical Journals Ltd., Queensway House, 2 Queensway, Redhill, Surrey RH1 1QS, England. Ed. Glenda Kusay. adv.

HEALTH AND SAFETY: QUARRIES. see *INDUSTRIAL HEALTH AND SAFETY*

HIROSHIMA UNIVERSITY. JOURNAL OF SCIENCE. SERIES C. GEOLOGY AND MINERALOGY. see *EARTH SCIENCES — Geology*

622 557   US   ISSN 0734-3825
IDAHO. GEOLOGICAL SURVEY. BULLETIN. 1920. irreg., no.26, 1982. price varies. Idaho Geological Survey, Moscow, ID 83843. TEL 208-885-7991.
   Formerly (until 1984): Idaho. Bureau of Mines and Geology. Bulletin (ISSN 0073-442X)

622 517   US
IDAHO. GEOLOGICAL SURVEY. INFORMATION CIRCULAR. 1957. irreg., no.40, 1986. price varies. Idaho Geological Survey, Moscow, ID 83843. TEL 208-885-7991.
   Formerly (until 1984): Idaho. Bureau of Mines and Geology. Information Circular (ISSN 0073-4446)

338.2 553   US   ISSN 0094-9442
ILLINOIS MINERALS NOTES. 1954. irreg., no.94, 1986. $1.25 per no. ‡ State Geological Survey, Natural Resources Bldg., 615 E. Peabody Dr., Champaign, IL 61820. TEL 217-344-1481. abstr. bibl. charts. illus. stat. Indexed: Geo.Abstr. GeoRef.
   Formed by the merger of: Illinois. State Geological Survey. Industrial Mineral Notes (ISSN 0073-4853) & Illinois. State Geological Survey. Mineral Economic Briefs (ISSN 0073-5116)

622   US
ILLINOIS MINING INSTITUTE. PROCEEDINGS. 1892. a. $12 (free to members, mining schools and technical libraries) Illinois Mining Institute, 200 Natural Resources Building, Champaign, IL 61820. TEL 217-333-5115. Ed. H.H. Damberger. adv. circ. 1,400.

622   II   ISSN 0445-7897
INDIAN MINERALS YEAR BOOK. (Text in English) a. $63. Indian Bureau of Mines, New Secretariat Bldg., Nagpur 440001, India (Order from: Controller of Publications, Civil Lines, Delhi 110054, India)

622.07   II   ISSN 0304-1158
INDIAN SCHOOL OF MINES. ANNUAL REPORT. (Text in English) a. Indian School of Mines, Dhanbad 826004, Bihar, India. illus. Key Title: Annual Report - Indian School of Mines.

338.2 660   UK   ISSN 0269-1701
INDUSTRIAL MINERALS DIRECTORY - WORLD GUIDE TO PRODUCERS AND PROCESSORS. 1977. irreg., latest 3rd ed., 1986. £60($144) Metal Bulletin Books Ltd., Park House, 3 Park Terrace, Worcester Park, Surrey KT4 7HY, England (Dist. in U.S. by: Metal Bulletin Inc., 220 Fifth Ave., New York, NY 10001) Ed. Gerry Clarke. adv.
   Formerly: Industrial Minerals Directory (ISSN 0141-5263)

622   BE
INSTITUT NATIONAL DES INDUSTRIES EXTRACTIVES. RAPPORT ANNUEL. Dutch edition: Nationaal Instituut voor de Extractiebedrijven. Jaarbericht. (Editions in French and Dutch) 1968. a. free. Institut National des Industries Extractives, 200 rue du Chera, 4000 Liege, Belgium. circ. 3,200 (both edts.) (back issues avail.)

622 382   US
INTERNATIONAL COAL. a. $150 to individuals; institutions $95. National Coal Association, Coal Bldg., 1130 17th St. N.W., Washington, DC 20036. TEL 202-463-2631.
   Formerly: World Coal Trade (ISSN 0084-148X)

549   GW   ISSN 0074-7017
INTERNATIONAL MINERALOGICAL ASSOCIATION. PROCEEDINGS OF MEETINGS. (Proceedings usually published in host country) 1959. biennial. price varies. International Mineralogical Association, c/o Prof. Dr. S. Hafner, Fachbereich Geowissenschaften der Universitaet, Lahnberge, D-3550 Marburg, W. Germany (B.R.D.) Indexed: Mineral.Abstr.

622   IR   ISSN 0075-0514
IRANIAN MINERAL STATISTICS.* (Text in English and Persian) 1962. a. free. Ministry of Finance and Economic Affairs, Bureau of Statistics, Tehran, Iran.

ITOGI NAUKI I TEKHNIKI: GEOKHIMIYA - MINERALOGIYA - PETROGRAFIYA. see *EARTH SCIENCES — Geology*

549   UR   ISSN 0202-7437
ITOGI NAUKI I TEKHNIKI: OBOGASHCHENIE POLEZNYKH ISKOPAEMYKH. irreg., latest vol.21, 1987. price varies. Vsesoyuznyi Institut Nauchno-Tekhnicheskoi Informatsii (VINITI), Baltiiskaya ul. 14, Moscow A-219, Russian S.F.S.R., U.S.S.R. (Subscr. to: Mezhdunarodnaya Kniga, Dimitrova ul. 39, 113095 Moscow, Russian S.F.S.R., U.S.S.R.)

622   UR   ISSN 0202-7410
ITOGI NAUKI I TEKHNIKI: RAZRABOTKA MESTOROZHDENII TVERDYKH POLEZNYKH ISKOPAEMYKH. irreg., latest vol.37, 1987. price varies. Vsesoyuznyi Institut Nauchno-Tekhnicheskoi Informatsii (VINITI), Baltiiskaya ul. 14, Moscow A-219, Russian S.F.S.R., U.S.S.R. (Subscr. to: Mezhdunarodnaya Kniga, Dimitrova ul. 39, 113095 Moscow, Russian S.F.S.R., U.S.S.R.)

622   UR   ISSN 0202-7380
ITOGI NAUKI I TEKHNIKI: RUDNYE MESTOROZHDENIYA. irreg., latest vol.17, 1987. price varies. Vsesoyuznyi Institut Nauchno-Tekhnicheskoi Informatsii (VINITI), Baltiiskaya ul. 14, Moscow A-219, Russian S.F.S.R., U.S.S.R. (Subscr. to: Mezhdunarodnaya Kniga, Dimitrova ul. 39, 113095 Moscow, Russian S.F.S.R., U.S.S.R.)

556 338.2   IV
IVORY COAST. DIRECTION DES MINES ET DE LA GEOLOGIE. RAPPORT PROVISOIRE SUR LES ACTIVITIES DU SECTEUR.* irreg. Direction des Mines et de la Geologie, c/o Ministry of Mining, BP V50, Abidjan, Ivory Coast. Indexed: GeoRef.

622   GW
JAHRBUCH FUER BERGBAU, ENERGIE, MINERALOEL UND CHEMIE. 1893. a. DM.88. Verlag Glueckauf GmbH, Franz-Fischer-Weg 61, Postfach 103945, 4300 Essen 1, W. Germany (B.R.D.) adv. Indexed: GeoRef.
   Formerly: Jahrbuch des Deutschen Bergbaus.

338.7   II   ISSN 0304-7164
JAMMU & KASHMIR MINERALS LIMITED. ANNUAL REPORT. (Text in English) a. Jammu & Kashmir Minerals Limited, Srinagar, India. Key Title: Annual Report - Jammu & Kashmir Minerals Limited.

622   AT   ISSN 0075-3777
JOBSON'S MINING YEAR BOOK. 1957. a. Aus.$140. Dun & Bradstret (Australia) Pty. Ltd., 24 Albert Rd., Melbourne, Vic. 3205, Australia. Ed. David M. Newbold. adv. circ. 6,000.

KEMISK ANALYSE AF MINERALER OG BJERGARTER. see *CHEMISTRY*

KEYSTONE COAL INDUSTRY MANUAL. see *BUSINESS AND ECONOMICS — Trade And Industrial Directories*

KONINKLIJK NEDERLANDS GEOLOGISCH MIJNBOUWKUNDIG GENOOTSCHAP. VERHANDELINGEN. see *EARTH SCIENCES — Geology*

LANDESMUSEUM JOANNEUM. ABTEILUNG FUER GEOLOGIE, PALAEONTOLOGIE UND BERGBAU. MITTEILUNGEN. see *PALEONTOLOGY*

622   AU   ISSN 0259-0751
LEOBENER GRUENE HEFTE. NEUE FOLGE. irreg., no.5, 1984. price varies. (Montanhistorischer Verein fuer Oesterreich) Verband der Wissenschtlichen Gesellschaften Oesterreichs, Lindengasse 37, A-1070 Vienna, Austria.

LIBERIA. MINISTRY OF LANDS, MINES AND ENERGY. ANNUAL REPORT. see *ENGINEERING — Civil Engineering*

MANITOBA. ENERGY AND MINES. ANNUAL REPORT SERIES. see *ENERGY*

MANITOBA ENERGY AND MINES. GEOLOGICAL REPORT. see *EARTH SCIENCES — Geology*

622   FR
MEMENTO DES MINES ET CARRIERES. 1958. a. 320 F. Regie Publicite Industrielle, 36 rue du Fer a Moulin, 75005 Paris, France. bk. rev.

MEMOIRES POUR SERVIR A L'EXPLICATION DES CARTES GEOLOGIQUES ET MINIERES DE LA BELGIQUE. see *EARTH SCIENCES — Geology*

622   US
METAL MINING: LATIN AMERICAN INDUSTRIAL REPORT. (Avail. for each of 20 Latin American countries) 1985. a. $235 per country report. Aurora International, Box 9099, Bridgeport, CT 06601-2099. TEL 203-368-0579. Ed. Andres C. Aquino.

622   MX
MEXICO. DIRECCION GENERAL DE ESTADISTICA. ESTADISTICA MINEROMETALURGICA: PRODUCCION Y EXPORTACION. irreg. latest 1972. free. Direccion General de Estadistica, Secretaria de Programacion y Presupuesto, Balderas 71, Agencia de Correos 245, Mexico 1, D. F., Mexico. stat. circ. controlled.

622   AT   ISSN 0085-3453
MINE AND QUARRY MECHANISATION. 1960. a. Aus.$27. Magazine Associates Pty. Ltd., Box 5, Hamilton, N.S.W. 2303, Australia. Ed. Max Fiddler. adv. circ. 1,500. (back issues avail.)

549   AT
MINERAL FACTS. 1979. a. Australian Mining Industry Council, Box 363, Dickson, A.C.T. 2602, Australia.

549   AT
MINERALOGICAL SOCIETY OF NEW SOUTH WALES. JOURNAL. 1979. a. Aus.$3. Mineralogical Society of New South Wales, Box R35, Royal Exchange, Sydney, N.S.W., Australia. Ed. Richard Depledge. Indexed: GeoRef.

622   AT
MINERALS AND MINERAL DEVELOPMENT. 1974. a. free. State Printing Division, Department of Services, 22 Station St., Wembley, W.A. 6014, Australia.

MINERALS AND ROCKS; monograph series of theoretical and experimental studies. see *EARTH SCIENCES — Geology*

549   AT
MINERALS INDUSTRY SURVEY. 1978. a. Australian Mining Industry Council, Box 363, Dickson, A.C.T. 2602, Australia.

622 918   US
MINERALS: LATIN AMERICAN INDUSTRY REPORT. 1985. a. $235 per country report. Aurora International, Box 9099, Bridgeport, CT 06601-2099. TEL 203-368-0579. Ed. Andres C. Aquino.

622   MX
LA MINERIA EN MEXICO. 1981. biennial. Mex.$1000($4.92) Instituto Nacional de Estadistica Geografia e Informatica, Secretaria de Programacion y Presupuesto, Patriotismo No. 711, 1 piso, Col. San Juan Mixcoac, C.P. 03700 Mexico, D.F., Mexico.

MINES AND MINING INDUSTRY

622   UK
MINES & MINING EQUIPMENT AND SERVICE COMPANIES WORLDWIDE (YEAR) 1982. a. £48.50. E. & F.N. Spon Ltd., 11 New Fetter Ln., London EC4P 4EE, England.
    Formerly: Mines and Mining Equipment Companies Worldwide (ISSN 0262-7965)

622   US   ISSN 0096-4859
MINES DIRECTORY. 1910. a. $10. Colorado School of Mines Alumni Association, Inc., Chauvenet Hall, 14th and Illinois St., Golden, CO 80401. TEL 303-273-3293. Ed. Patricia C. Petty. adv. circ. 5,200.

622   US
MINES IN WEST VIRGINIA. 1964. irreg. $4 per issue. Geological and Economic Survey, Box 879, Morgantown, WV 26507-0879. TEL 304-594-2331.

622   613.62   EI   ISSN 0588-702X
MINES SAFETY AND HEALTH COMMISSION. REPORT/ORGANE PERMANENT POUR LA SECURITE DANS LES MINES DE HOUILLE. RAPPORT. 1967. a. free. Commission of the European Communities, 200 rue de la Loi, 1049 Brussels, Belgium.
    Issued 1959-1966 as: European Coal and Steel Community. Organe Permanent pour la Securite dans les Mines de Houille. Rapport (ISSN 0531-2922)

338.7   II
MINING AND ALLIED MACHINERY CORPORATION. ANNUAL REPORT. (Text in English) a. Mining and Allied Machinery Corporation, Durgapur, India. illus.

622   AT
MINING & CONSTRUCTION METHODS AND EQUIPMENT. 1973. irreg. Finecraft Publishing Co., Box 260, Neutral Bay Junction, N.S.W. 2089, Australia. Ed. Fiona Stewart.

622   UK   ISSN 0076-8995
MINING ANNUAL REVIEW. 1935. a. £30($45) Mining Journal Ltd., 60 Worship St., London EC2A 2HD, England. Ed. Michael West. adv. circ. 11,000. (also avail. in microfilm; reprint service avail. from UMI) Indexed: Br.Geol.Lit. GeoRef. Ref.Zh.

622   UK   ISSN 0307-9066
MINING DEPARTMENT MAGAZINE. 1948. a. £10. University of Nottingham, Mining Engineering Department, Nottingham NG7 2RD, England. Ed. D.J. Hodges. adv. circ. 5,000.

622   CN   ISSN 0316-2281
MINING IN CANADA - FACTS & FIGURES. French edition: Mines au Canada - Faits et Chiffres (ISSN 0316-2311) (Editions in English and French) 1964. a. free. Mining Association of Canada, 350 Sparks St., No.809, Ottawa, Ont. K1R 7S8, Canada. charts. stat. circ. 24,000. (back issues avail.) Indexed: CS Ind.

622   RH
MINING IN ZIMBABWE. 1950. a. $15. Thomson Publications Zimbabwe, Box 1683, Harare, Zimbabwe. Ed. T. Grundy. adv. circ. controlled.
    Formerly: Mining in Rhodesia (ISSN 0076-8987)

622   II
MINING INDUSTRY & TRADE ANNUAL. (Text in English) 1962. a. $15. Praveen Corp, Sayajiganj, Baroda 390005, India. Ed. C.M. Pandit.
    Formerly: Mining Industry and Trade Journal (ISSN 0026-5217)

622   US
MINING INDUSTRY OF IDAHO. ANNUAL REPORT. 1899. a. Department of Labor and Industrial Services, Mine Safety Bureau, 317 Main St., Rm. 4000, Statehouse, Boise, ID 83720. TEL 208-334-2320. stat. index. circ. controlled. (processed)

622   US
MINING INDUSTRY TECHNICAL CONFERENCE. CONFERENCE RECORD. 1979. biennial. price varies. (I E E E, Industry Applications Society) Institute of Electrical and Electronics Engineers, Inc., 345 E. 47th St., New York, NY 10017 TEL 212-705-7900. (Subscr to: 445 Hoes Lane, Piscataway, NJ 08865)

622   CN   ISSN 0317-9508
MINING - WHAT MINING MEANS TO CANADA. French edition: Mines - Pilier de l'Economie Canadienne (ISSN 0317-9524) 1964. biennial. free. Mining Association of Canada, 350 Sparks St., No.809, Ottawa, Ont. K1R 7S8, Canada. TEL 416-363-8019. circ. 100,000.

549   US   ISSN 0272-8583
MINNESOTA INDUSTRIAL MINERALS DIRECTORY. 1980. a. $7. University of Minnesota, Mineral Resources Research Center, 56 East River Rd., Minneapolis, MN 55455. TEL 612-625-3344. Ed. Rodney J. Lipp. circ. 400.

622.33   SA
MINTEK. SPECIAL PUBLICATIONS. irreg. Council for Mineral Technology (Mintek), Private Bag X3015, Randburg 2125, South Africa.
    Formerly: Council for Mineral Technology (MINTEK). Special Publication.

622.33   SA
MINTEK REPORTS. 1966. irreg. free. Council for Mineral Technology (Mintek), Private Bag X3015, Randburg 2125, South Africa. bibl. illus. Indexed: Chem.Abstr. Met.Abstr. Mineral.Abstr. Nucl.Sci.Abstr.
    Former Titles: M I N T E K Reports; N I M Reports.

MISSOURI DIRECTORY OF MANUFACTURING AND MINING. see *BUSINESS AND ECONOMICS — Trade And Industrial Directories*

MONTANA. BUREAU OF MINES AND GEOLOGY. BULLETIN. see *EARTH SCIENCES — Geology*

622   US   ISSN 0077-1104
MONTANA. BUREAU OF MINES AND GEOLOGY. DIRECTORY OF MINING ENTERPRISES. (Subseries of Bulletins) a. Bureau of Mines and Geology, Montana College of Mineral Science and Technology, Butte, MT 59701. TEL 406-496-4180.

MONTANA. BUREAU OF MINES AND GEOLOGY. MEMOIR. see *EARTH SCIENCES — Geology*

MONTANA. BUREAU OF MINES AND GEOLOGY. SPECIAL PUBLICATIONS. see *EARTH SCIENCES — Geology*

553   UK   ISSN 0077-3786
NATIONAL COAL BOARD. REPORT AND ACCOUNTS. a. H.M.S.O., Box 569, London SE1 9NH, England. (reprint service avail. from UMI)

622   669.3   ZA
NCHANGA CONSOLIDATED COPPER MINES LTD. ANNUAL REPORT AND ACCOUNTS. (Text in English) a. Nchanga Consolidated Copper Mines Ltd., Box 30048, Lusaka, Zambia.

NEVADA. BUREAU OF MINES AND GEOLOGY. BULLETIN. see *EARTH SCIENCES — Geology*

NEVADA. BUREAU OF MINES AND GEOLOGY. REPORT. see *EARTH SCIENCES — Geology*

622   CN
NEW BRUNSWICK. BEACH RESOURCES - EASTERN NEW BRUNSWICK. irreg. price varies. Department of Natural Resources, Mines Division, Fredericton, N.B. E3B 5H1, Canada. TEL 506-453-2260.

622   CN   ISSN 0077-8109
NEW BRUNSWICK. MINERAL RESOURCES BRANCH. REPORT OF INVESTIGATIONS. 1966. irreg. price varies. Department of Natural Resources, Geology Division, Fredericton, N.B. E3B 5H1, Canada. TEL 506-453-2260. Indexed: Chem.Abstr. GeoRef.

622   CN
NEW BRUNSWICK. WETLANDS - PEATLANDS RESOURCES. irreg. price varies. Department of Natural Resources, Mines Division, Fredericton, N.B. E3B 5H1, Canada. TEL 506-453-2260.

622   NL
NEW CALEDONIA. SERVICE DES MINES ET DE L'ENERGY. RAPPORT ANNUEL. 1915. a. 110 F. Service des Mines et de l'Energie, Noumea, New Caledonia. illus. circ. 250.

622   US
NEW MEXICO. BUREAU OF MINES AND MINERAL RESOURCES. BULLETIN. 1915. irreg., no.108, 1981. price varies. Bureau of Mines and Mineral Resources, Socorro, NM 87801. TEL 505-835-5410. Indexed: GeoRef.

622   US
NEW MEXICO. BUREAU OF MINES AND MINERAL RESOURCES. CIRCULAR. 1930. irreg., no.188, 1982. price varies. Bureau of Mines and Mineral Resources, Socorro, NM 87801. TEL 505-835-5410. Indexed: GeoRef.

622   US   ISSN 0548-5975
NEW MEXICO. BUREAU OF MINES AND MINERAL RESOURCES. MEMOIR. 1956. irreg., no.41, 1982. price varies. Bureau of Mines and Mineral Resources, Socorro, NM 87801. Indexed: GeoRef.

622   US   ISSN 0098-7077
NEW MEXICO. BUREAU OF MINES AND MINERAL RESOURCES. PROGRESS REPORT. 1972. irreg., no.10, 1978. price varies. Bureau of Mines and Mineral Resources, Socorro, NM 87801. Indexed: GeoRef. Key Title: Progress Report - New Mexico Bureau of Mines & Mineral Resources.

NEW MEXICO MANUFACTURING DIRECTORY (YEAR) see *BUSINESS AND ECONOMICS — Trade And Industrial Directories*

622   AT   ISSN 0727-9256
NEW SOUTH WALES. DEPARTMENT OF MINERAL RESOURCES. ANNUAL REPORT. 1875. a. price varies. Department of Mineral Resources, G.P.O. Box 5288, Sydney, N.S.W. 2001, Australia. index. circ. 500. Indexed: GeoRef.
    Former titles: New South Wales. Department of Mines. Annual Report (ISSN 0077-8664) & New South Wales. Department of Mineral Resources and Development. Annual Report.

NEW SOUTH WALES. GEOLOGICAL SURVEY. MINE DATA SHEETS AND METALLOGENIC STUDY. see *EARTH SCIENCES — Geology*

622   559   AT   ISSN 0077-8729
NEW SOUTH WALES. GEOLOGICAL SURVEY. MINERAL INDUSTRY SERIES. no.3, 1967. irreg., no.44, 1979. price varies. Department of Mineral Resources, Box 5288, Sydney, N.S.W. 2001, Australia. Ed. H. Basden. circ. 400. Indexed: GeoRef.

622   559   AT   ISSN 0077-8737
NEW SOUTH WALES. GEOLOGICAL SURVEY. MINERAL RESOURCES SERIES. Variant title: Geological Survey of N.S.W. Mineral Resources. 1898. irreg., no.45, 1983. price varies. Department of Mineral Resources, G.P.O. Box 5288, Sydney, N.S.W. 2001, Australia. Ed. H. Basden. index. circ. 400. Indexed: GeoRef.

338.2   NZ
NEW ZEALAND. MINISTRY OF ENERGY. REPORT. 1978. a. price varies. Ministry of Energy, Private Bag, Wellington, New Zealand. circ. 1,000.
    Incorporating: New Zealand. Ministry of Energy. Mines Division. Annual Report.

622   CN   ISSN 0078-0340
NEWFOUNDLAND. MINERAL DEVELOPMENT DIVISION. INFORMATION. 1934. irreg. price varies. Department of Mines and Energy, Mineral Development, 95 Bonaventure Ave., St. Johns, Newfoundland, Canada. TEL 709-576-3154.

622   CN   ISSN 0078-0359
NEWFOUNDLAND. MINERAL DEVELOPMENT DIVISION. INFORMATION CIRCULAR. 1934. irreg., no.15, 1974. price varies. Mineral Development Division, P.O. Box 4750, 95 Bonaventure Ave., St. John's, Newfoundland, Canada. TEL 709-576-3159.

622   CN   ISSN 0078-0367
NEWFOUNDLAND. MINES BRANCH. ANNUAL REPORT SERIES. 1953. a. price varies. Department of Mines and Energy, Mineral Development Division, 95 Bonaventure Ave., St. Johns, Newfoundland, Canada. TEL 709-576-3159. circ. 200.

622 550 NR
NIGERIAN MINING AND GEOSCIENCES
SOCIETY. JOURNAL. 1964. a. $20. Nigerian
Mining and Geosciences Society, c/o Department of
Geology, University of Nigeria, Nsukka, Nigeria.
Ed. A.C. Onyeagocha. adv. bk. rev. abstr. charts.
illus. stat. index. circ. 750. Indexed: Chem.Abstr.
GeoRef.
Formerly: Nigerian Mining, Geological and
Metallurgical Society. Journal.

NIIGATA UNIVERSITY. FACULTY OF SCIENCE.
SCIENCE REPORTS. SERIES E: GEOLOGY
AND MINERALOGY. see EARTH
SCIENCES — Geology

553 US
NORTH CAROLINA. GEOLOGICAL SURVEY
SECTION. BULLETIN. 1893. irreg., no.87, 1982.
price varies. Department of Natural Resources and
Community Development, Geological Survey
Section, Box 27687, Raleigh, NC 27611. TEL 919-
733-2423. Indexed: GeoRef.
Formerly: North Carolina. Division of Mineral
Resources. Bulletin.

553 US
NORTH CAROLINA. GEOLOGICAL SURVEY
SECTION. ECONOMIC PAPER. no.3, 1900.
irreg., no.68, 1970. Department of Natural
Resources and Community Development,
Geological Survey Section, Box 27687, Raleigh, NC
27611. TEL 919-733-2423. Indexed: GeoRef.
Formerly: North Carolina. Division of Mineral
Resources. Economic Paper.

553 US
NORTH CAROLINA. GEOLOGICAL SURVEY
SECTION. INFORMATION CIRCULAR. 1940.
irreg., no.25, 1982. price varies. Department of
Natural Resources and Community Development,
Geological Survey Section, Box 27687, Raleigh, NC
27611. TEL 919-733-2423. Indexed: GeoRef.
Formerly: North Carolina. Division of Mineral
Resources. Information Circular.

553 US
NORTH CAROLINA. GEOLOGICAL SURVEY
SECTION. SPECIAL PUBLICATION. 1965. irreg.,
no.8, 1983. price varies. ‡ Department of Natural
Resources and Community Development,
Geological Survey Section, Box 27687, Raleigh, NC
27611. TEL 919-733-2423. Indexed: GeoRef.
Formerly: North Carolina. Division of Mineral
Resources. Special Publication (ISSN 0078-1398)

622 665 US ISSN 0271-0315
OIL SHALE SYMPOSIUM PROCEEDINGS. 1964.
a. $25. (Colorado School of Mines) Colorado School
of Mines Press, Golden, CO 80401. TEL 303-273-
3607. (reprint service avail. from UMI) Indexed:
Chem.Abstr. GeoRef.

622 CN ISSN 0708-2061
ONTARIO. GEOLOGICAL SURVEY.
AGGREGATE RESOURCES INVENTORY
PAPER. 1979. irreg. Can.$2 per issue. Geological
Survey, 77 Grenville St., Rm. 719, Toronto, Ont.
M7A 1W4, Canada TEL 416-965-6511. (Subscr. to:
Ministry of Natural Resources, Public Service
Centre, Rm. 1640, Whitney Block, Queens Park,
Toronto, Ont. M7A 1W3, Canada)

622 551 CN
ONTARIO. GEOLOGICAL SURVEY. ANNUAL
REPORT OF THE REGIONAL AND RESIDENT
GEOLOGISTS. (Sub-Series of: Geological
Survey. Miscellaneous Paper (ISSN 0704-2752))
1967. a. Can.$2. Geological Survey, 77 Greenville
St., Rm. 719, Toronto, Ont. M7A 1W4, Canada
TEL 416-965-6511. (Subscr. to: Ministry of Natural
Resources, Public Service Centre, Room 1640,
Whitney Block, Queen's Park, Toronto, Ont. M7A
1W3 Canada) Ed. C.R. Kustra. circ. 1,500. (also
avail. in microfiche; back issues avail.)

622 CN ISSN 0826-791X
ONTARIO. GEOLOGICAL SURVEY.
EXPLORATION TECHNOLOGY
DEVELOPMENT FUND GRANTS. (Subseries of:
Ontario. Geological Survey. Miscellaneous Paper
(ISSN 0704-2752)) 1983. a. Can.$2. Geological
Survey, 77 Grenville St., Rm. 719, Toronto, Ont.
M7A 1W4, Canada (Subscr. to: Ontario Ministry of
Natural Resources, Public Service Centre, 99
Wellesley St. W., Toronto, Ont. M7A 1W3,
Canada)

622 557 CN
ONTARIO. GEOLOGICAL SURVEY.
GEOLOGICAL REPORT. 1960. irreg. (approx. 3-
10/yr.) price varies. Geological Survey, 77 Grenville
St., Rm. 719, Toronto, Ont. M7A 1W4, Canada
TEL 416-965-2000. (Subscr. to: Ministry of Natural
Resources, Public Service Centre, Room 1640,
Whitney Block, Queen's Park, Toronto, Ont. M7A
1W3 Canada) Indexed: Chem.Abstr. GeoRef.
Former titles: Ontario. Geological Survey. Report
(ISSN 0704-2582); Ontario. Division of Mines.
Geological Reports; Incorporating: Ontario. Division
of Mines. Geochemical Reports.

622 CN ISSN 0225-5316
ONTARIO. GEOLOGICAL SURVEY.
GEOSCIENCE RESEARCH GRANT
PROGRAM. SUMMARY OF RESEARCH.
(Supplement to: Ontario. Geological Survey. Annual
Report of the Regional and Resident Geologists)
1979. a. Can.$2. Geological Survey, 77 Grenville
St., Rm. 719, Toronto, Ont. M7A 1W4, Canada
TEL 416-965-2000. (Subscr. to: Ministry of Natural
Resources, Public Service Centre, Room 1640,
Whitney Block, Queen's Park, Toronto, Ont. M7A
1W3 Canada) Ed. V.G. Milne. (also avail. in
microfiche)

ONTARIO. GEOLOGICAL SURVEY. GUIDE
BOOKS. see EARTH SCIENCES — Geology

549 CN ISSN 0706-4551
ONTARIO. GEOLOGICAL SURVEY. MINERAL
DEPOSITS CIRCULAR. 1950. irreg. (1-2/yr.) price
varies. Geological Survey, 77 Grenville St., Rm.
719, Toronto, Ont., Canada TEL 416-965-2000.
(Subscr. to: Ministry of Natural Resources, Public
Service Centre, Room 1640, Whitney Block,
Queen's Park, Toronto, Ont. M7A 1W3, Canada)
Indexed: GeoRef.
Formerly: Ontario. Division of Mines. Mineral
Resource Circulars.

622 CN ISSN 0704-2752
ONTARIO. GEOLOGICAL SURVEY.
MISCELLANEOUS PAPER. 1960. irreg. (approx.
3-4/yr.) price varies. Geological Survey, 77
Grenville St., Rm. 719, Toronto, Ont., Canada TEL
416-965-2000. (Subscr. to: Ministry of Natural
Resources, Public Service Centre, Room 1640,
Whitney Block, Queen's Park, Toronto, Ont.
M7A1W3, Canada) Indexed: GeoRef.
Formerly: Ontario. Division of Mines.
Miscellaneous Papers.

622 CN ISSN 0709-4671
ONTARIO. GEOLOGICAL SURVEY. NORTHERN
ONTARIO ENGINEERING GEOLOGY
TERRAIN STUDY. irreg. Can.$2 per issue.
Geological Survey, 77 Grenville St., Rm. 719,
Toronto, Ont. M7A 1W4, Canada TEL 416-965-
2000. (Subscr. to: Ministry of Natural Resources,
Public Service Centre, Rm. 1640, Whitney Block,
Queens Park, Toronto, Ont. M7A 1W3, Canada)

622 CN ISSN 0704-2590
ONTARIO. GEOLOGICAL SURVEY. STUDY.
irreg. price varies. Geological Survey, 77 Grenville
St., Rm. 719, Toronto, Ont. M7A 1W4, Canada
TEL 416-965-2000. (Subscr. to: Ministry of Natural
Resources, Public Service Centre, Room 1640,
Whitney Block, Queens Park, Toronto, Ont.
M7A1W3 Canada) Indexed: Chem.Abstr. GeoRef.

622 CN ISSN 0829-8203
ONTARIO. GEOLOGICAL SURVEY. SUMMARY
OF FIELD WORK. (Sub-series of: Ontario.
Geological Survey. Miscellaneous Paper (ISSN
0704-2752)) 1968. a. Can.$2. Geological Survey, 77
Grenville St., Rm. 719, Toronto, Ont. M7A 1W4,
Canada (Subscr. to: Ministry of Natural Resources,
Public Service Centre, Rm. 1640, Whitney Block,
Queens Park, Toronto, Ont. M7A 1W3, Canada)

622 CN
ONTARIO. GEOLOGICAL SURVEY.
SUPPLEMENT. (Sub-series of: Ontario. Geological
Survey. Miscellaneous Paper (ISSN 0704-2752))
1978. a. price varies. Geological Survey, 77
Grenville St., Rm. 719, Toronto, Ont. M7A 1W4,
Canada (Subscr. to: Ministry of Natural Resources,
Public Service Centre, Rm. 1640, Whitney Block,
Queens Park, Toronto, Ont. M7A 1W3, Canada)

OREGON. STATE DEPARTMENT OF GEOLOGY
AND MINERAL INDUSTRIES. BULLETIN. see
EARTH SCIENCES — Geology

338.2 US
PENNSYLVANIA. DEPARTMENT OF
ENVIRONMENTAL RESOURCES. ANNUAL
REPORT ON MINING ACTIVITIES. 1870. a.
price varies. Department of Environmental
Resources, Bureau of Deep Mine Safety, Harrisburg,
PA 17120 TEL 717-783-7515. (Orders to:
Pennsylvania State Bookstore, Box 1365 Harrisburg,
PA 17125) Ed. Patsie Nichols. stat. circ. 1,000.
Former titles: Pennsylvania. Office of Mines and
Land Protection. Annual Report; (until 1973):
Pennsylvania. Anthracite, Bituminous Coal and Oil
and Gas Divisions. Annual Report.

622 PH ISSN 0085-4875
PHILIPPINE MINING AND ENGINEERING
JOURNAL. MINING ANNUAL AND
DIRECTORY. Included as July issue of Phillipine
Mining and Engineering Journal. 1971. a. P.3($15)
Business Masters International, 55 U.E. Tech.
Avenue, University Hills, Subdivision Malabon,
Rizal, Philippines. Ed. Luciano B. Quitlong. adv.
circ. 10,000.

622 333.7 PH
PHILIPPINES. BUREAU OF MINES. ANNUAL
REPORT. 1973. a. $3. Bureau of Mines and Geo-
Sciences, Manila, Philippines. Ed. Rolando V.
Quano. adv. circ. 1,000.

622 US
PIT & QUARRY HANDBOOK AND BUYERS
GUIDE;* equipment and technical reference manual
for nonmetallic industry. 1907. a. $80. Harcourt
Brace Jovanovich, Inc., 7500 Old Oak Blvd.,
Cleveland, OH 44130. TEL 312-726-7151. Ed. B.C.
Herod. adv. index. circ. 8,700.
Formerly: Pit and Quarry Handbook and
Purchasing Guide (ISSN 0079-2128)

622 PL ISSN 0372-9508
POLITECHNIKA SLASKA. ZESZYTY NAUKOWE.
GORNICTWO. (Text in Polish; summaries in
English and Russian) 1959. irreg. price varies.
Politechnika Slaska, W. Pstrowskiego 7, 44-100
Gliwice, Poland (Dist. by: Ars Polona, Krakowskie
Przedmiescie 7, 00-068 Warsaw, Poland) Ed.
Miroslaw Chudek. circ. 260. Indexed: Chem.Abstr.

622 PL ISSN 0324-9670
POLITECHNIKA WROCLAWSKA. INSTYTUT
GORNICTWA. PRACE NAUKOWE.
KONFERENCJE. (Text in Polish; summaries in
English and Russian) 1971. irreg., no.9, 1985. price
varies. Politechnika Wroclawska, Wybrzeze
Wyspianskiego 27, 50-370 Wroclaw, Poland (Dist
by: Ars Polona-Ruch, Krakowskie, Przedmiescie 7,
Warsaw, Poland) Ed. Jerzy Ciekot.

622 PL ISSN 0324-9689
POLITECHNIKA WROCLAWSKA. INSTYTUT
GORNICTWA. PRACE NAUKOWE.
MONOGRAFIE. (Text in Polish; summaries in
English and Russian) 1973. irreg., no.22, 1986. price
varies. Politechnika Wroclawska, Wybrzeze
Wyspianskiego 27, 50-370 Wroclaw, Poland (Dist.
by: Ars Polona-Ruch, Krakowskie Przediescie 7,
Warsaw, Poland) Ed. Jerzy Ciekot. illus.

622 PL ISSN 0370-0798
POLITECHNIKA WROCLAWSKA. INSTYTUT
GORNICTWA. PRACE NAUKOWE. STUDIA I
MATERIALY. (Text in Polish; summaries in
English and Russian) 1970. irreg., no.17, 1986. price
varies. Politechnika Wroclawska, Wybrzeze
Wyspianskiego 27, 50-370 Wroclaw, Poland (Dist.
by: Ars Polona-Ruch, Krakowskie Przedmiescie 7,
Warsaw, Poland) Ed. Jery Ciekot.

622 PL ISSN 0079-3280
POLSKA AKADEMIA NAUK. ODDZIAL W
KRAKOWIE. KOMISJA GORNICZO-
GEODEZYJNA. PRACE: GORNICTWO. (Text in
Polish; summaries in English and Russian) 1965.
irreg., no.24, 1986. price varies. Ossolineum,
Publishing House of the Polish Academy of
Sciences, Rynek 9, Wroclaw, Poland (Dist. by: Ars
Polona-Ruch, Krakowskie Przedmiescie 7, Warsaw,
Poland) Ed. Zbigniew Strzelecki.

PORTUGAL. SERVICOS GEOLOGICOS.
COMUNICACOES. see EARTH SCIENCES —
Geology

PROBLEMY PRAWNE GORNICTWA. see LAW

PRODUCCION Y EXPORTACIONES CHILENAS DE COBRE. see *BUSINESS AND ECONOMICS — Production Of Goods And Services*

622 HU ISSN 0324-4628
PUBLICATIONS OF THE TECHNICAL UNIVERSITY FOR HEAVY INDUSTRY. SERIES A, MINING. (Text in English, German and Russian) irreg., vol.37, no.1, 1982. Nehezipari Muszaki Egyetem, Miskolc, Hungary. Ed.Bd. bibl. index. circ. 450.

622 JA
REPORT OF OVERSEAS MINING INVESTIGATION: INDIA, PAKISTAN, BANGLADESH/KAIGAI KOGYO JIJO CHOSA HOKOKUSHO: INDO, PAKISUTAN, BANGURADISSHU. (Text in Japanese) irreg. Metal Mining Agency, Data Center - Kinzoku Kogyo Jigyodan. Shiryo Senta, 6-3 Shiba Nishikubo Saguragawa-cho, Shiba, Minato-ku, Tokyo 105, Japan. charts. illus.

622 JA
REPORT OF OVERSEAS MINING INVESTIGATION: MADAGASCAR, SWAZILAND/KAIGAI KOGYO JIJO CHOSA HOKOKUSHO: MADAGASUKARU, SUWAJIRANDO. (Text in Japanese) irreg. Metal Mining Agency, Data Center - Kinzoku Kogy Jigyodan. Shiryo Senta, 6-3 Shiba Nishikubo Saguragawa-cho, Shiba, Minato-ku, Tokyo 105, Japan. charts. illus.

338.2 US
REPORT ON OHIO MINERAL INDUSTRIES; with directories of reporting coal and industrial mineral operations. 1872. a. $4. ‡ Department of Natural Resources, Division of Geological Survey, Fountain Sq., Bldg. B, Columbus, OH 43224. TEL 614-265-6605. Ed. Sherry Weisgarber. index. circ. 1,600.
Former titles: Ohio. Division of Mines. Report (ISSN 0078-401X); Ohio. Division of Mines. Annual Report with Coal and Industrial Mineral Directories of Reporting Firms.

RESERVES OF COAL, PROVINCE OF ALBERTA. see *ENERGY*

338.2 TZ ISSN 0082-1659
REVIEW OF THE MINERAL INDUSTRY IN TANZANIA. Title varies: Tanzania. Mines Division. Review of the Mineral Industry. (Former name of issuing body: Mineral Resources Division) 1965. a. free. Ministry of Water, Energy and Minerals, Mines Division, Box 903, Dodoma, Tanzania. Ed. Anthony Muze. circ. 400.

622 SP ISSN 0210-8356
REVISTA DE MINAS. 1979. a. 2500 ptas. Universidad de Oviedo, Escuela Tecnica Superior de Ingenieros de Minas, Oviedo, Spain (Subscr. to: Servicio de Publicaciones, Un. de Oviedo, Calle J. Arias de Velasco s/n, 33005 Oviedo, Spain) Ed. Jose Martinez Alvarez. bk. rev. illus. circ. 500.

622 US ISSN 0080-3375
ROCK MECHANICS/FELSMECHANIK/ MECHANIQUE DES ROCHES. SUPPLEMENT. 1970. irreg., no.12, 1982. Springer-Verlag, 175 Fifth Ave., New York, NY 10010 TEL 212-460-1500. (Also Berlin, Heidelberg, Tokyo and Vienna) (also avail. in microform from UMI; reprint service avail. from ISI) Indexed: Geo.Abstr. GeoRef. Geotech.Abstr.
Continues: Felsmechanik und Ingenieurgeologie. Rock Mechanics and Engineering Geology. Supplement.

622 UK ISSN 0080-4495
ROYAL SCHOOL OF MINES, LONDON. JOURNAL. 1951. a. £1. Royal School of Mines Association, Prince Consort Road, London SW7 2BP, England. Ed. A.J. Carr. adv. bk. rev. circ. 1, 600.

622.33 CN
SASKATCHEWAN ENERGY & MINES. ANNUAL REPORT. 1954. a. Saskatchewan Energy & Mines, 1914 Hamilton St., Regina, Sask. S4P 4V4, Canada. TEL 306-787-2528. charts. illus.
Former titles: Saskatchewan Mineral Resources. Annual Report; Saskatchewan. Department of Mineral Resources. Annual Report (ISSN 0581-8109)

338.2 665.5 CN
SASKATCHEWAN ENERGY AND MINES. MINERAL STATISTICS YEARBOOK. 1964. a. Can.$30. ‡ Saskatchewan Energy and Mines, Marketing and Publications Office, 1914 Hamilton St., Regina, Sask. S4P 4V4, Canada. TEL 306-787-2528.
Former titles: Saskatchewan Mineral Resources. Mineral Statistical Yearbook; Saskatchewan. Department of Mineral Resources. Statistical Yearbook (ISSN 0707-2570)

622 943.7 CS
SLOVENSKE BANSKE MUZEUM. ZBORNIK. 1967. irreg. Osveta, Osloboditelov 21, 036 54 Martin, Czechoslovakia (Subscr. to: Slovart, Gottwaldovo Nam. 6, 805 32 Bratislava, Czechoslovakia)

338.2 FR ISSN 0081-0797
SOCIETE DE L'INDUSTRIE MINERALE. ANNUAIRE. 1855. a. 198 F. Societe de l'Industrie Minerale, 19 rue du Grand Moulin, 42029 St.-Etienne Cedex, France. adv. index.

338.7 IV ISSN 0250-3697
SOCIETE POUR LE DEVELOPPEMENT MINIER DE LA COTE D'IVOIRE. RAPPORT ANNUEL. 1962. a. free. Societe pour le Developpement Minier de la Cote d'Ivoire, B.P. 2816, Abidjan, Ivory Coast. illus. Indexed: GeoRef.

622 551 SA
SOUTH AFRICA. DEPARTMENT OF MINERAL AND ENERGY AFFAIRS. ANNUAL REPORT. (Text in Afrikaans and English) N.S. 1947. a. price varies. Department of Mineral and Energy Affairs, Private Bag X59, Pretoria 0001, South Africa (Orders to: Government Printer, Bosman St., Private Bag X85, Pretoria 0001, South Africa) circ. 1,000. Indexed: GeoRef.
Formerly: South Africa. Department of Mines. Annual Report; Includes: South Africa. Geological Survey. Report of the Chief Director of the Geological Survey.

SOUTH AFRICAN INSTITUTE OF MINING AND METALLURGY. MONOGRAPH SERIES. see *METALLURGY*

622 620 SA ISSN 0081-2498
SOUTH AFRICAN MINING AND ENGINEERING YEARBOOK. Variant title: S.A. Mining and Engineering Yearbook. 1915. a. R.100. Thomson Publications S.A. (Pty.) Ltd., Box 56182, Pinegowrie 2123, South Africa. Ed. Hendrick Vorster. adv.

SOUTH AUSTRALIA. DEPARTMENT OF MINES AND ENERGY. SPECIAL PUBLICATIONS. see *EARTH SCIENCES*

622 UK
SOUTHERN AFRICAN METALS & MINERALS CONFERENCE. PROCEEDINGS. 1981. irreg. £35. Metal Bulletin PLC, Park House, 3 Park Terrace, Worcester Park, Surrey KT4 7HY, England. Ed. Trevor Tarring.

622 SP
SPAIN. INSTITUTO GEOLOGICO Y MINERO. COLLECCION MEMORIAS.* 1854. irreg. 300 ptas. Instituto Geologico y Minero, Rios Rosas 23, Madrid 3, Spain. Indexed: GeoRef.

622 DK ISSN 0107-430X
SPECIFICATIONS OF MINERAL CONCESSIONS AND LICENSES IN GREENLAND. 1981. biennial. free. Ministeriet for Groenland, Mineral Resources Administration, Hausergade 3, 1128 Copenhagen K, Denmark.
Formerly: Specifications of Mineral Licenses and Concessions in Greenland.

338.2 MY ISSN 0302-6620
STATES OF MALAYA CHAMBER OF MINES. COUNCIL REPORT. (Text in English) a. States of Malaya Chamber of Mines, Ming Bldg., 6th Fl., Jalan Bukit Nanas, P.O. Box 12560, Kuala Lumpur, Malaysia.

338.2 MY
STATES OF MALAYA CHAMBER OF MINES. YEARBOOK. 1966. a. M.$10. States of Malaya Chamber of Mines, Ming Bldg., 6th Fl., Jalan Bukit Nanas, P.O. Box 12560, Kuala Lumpur, Malaysia. stat.

338.2 CN
STATISTICAL REVIEW OF COAL IN CANADA. 1971. a. Department of Energy, Mines and Resources, Energy Sector, 580 Booth St., Ottawa, Ontario, Canada. TEL 613-996-9533. stat.
Formerly: Coal in Canada, Supply and Demand (ISSN 0700-284X)

622 665.5 US
STEAM-ELECTRIC PLANT FACTORS (1978) a. $125 to individuals; non-profit organizations $100. National Coal Association, Coal Bldg., 1130 17 St., N.W., Washington, DC 20036. TEL 202-463-2631.
Former titles: Steam Electric Fuels (ISSN 0090-3884); Steam-Electric Plant Factors (ISSN 0081-5411)

669 622 665.5 US
STEELMAKING CONFERENCE: PROCEEDINGS. 1928. a., latest 69th. $25 to non-members; members $10.50. American Institute of Mining, Metallurgical and Petroleum Engineers, Inc., Iron and Steel Society, Steelmaking Division, 410 Commonwealth Dr., Warrendale, PA 15086. TEL 212-705-7695. Ed. Lawrence G. Kuhn. Indexed: Chem.Abstr.
Former titles: Steelmaking Proceedings & American Institute of Mining, Metallurgical and Petroleum Engineers. National Open Hearth and Basic Oxygen Steel Division. Proceedings of the Conference.

622 943.7 CS
STUDIE Z DEJIN HORNICTVI. (Text in Czech; summaries in German) 1971. irreg. exchange basis. Narodni Technicke Muzeum, Kostelni 42, Prague 7, Czechoslovakia. bibl. illus.

622 US ISSN 0085-7068
SYMPOSIUM ON COAL MINE DRAINAGE RESEARCH. PAPERS. 1965. a. or biennial. $10. ‡ (Coal Industry Advisory Committee to the Ohio River Valley Water Sanitation Commission) Bituminous Coal Research, Inc., 350 Hochberg Rd., Monroeville, PA 15146 TEL 412-327-1600. (Or National Coal Association, 1130 17th St. N.W., Washington, DC 20036) Indexed: GeoRef.

622 US
SYMPOSIUM ON SURFACE MINING AND RECLAMATION. 1973. a., latest 1977. $10. (National Coal Association) Bituminous Coal Research, Inc., 350 Hochberg Rd., Monroeville, PA 15146. TEL 412-327-1600.

622.33 551.4 US ISSN 0735-0686
SYMPOSIUM ON SURFACE MINING, HYDROLOGY, SEDIMENTOLOGY AND RECLAMATION. PROCEEDINGS. 1979. a. $45. (University of Kentucky, Office of Engineering Continuing Education) O E S Publications, 226 Anderson Hall, University of Kentucky, Lexington, KY 40506-0046. TEL 606-257-3343. Eds. R. William DeVore, Donald H. Graves. circ. 750.

622 US ISSN 0586-3031
U S SYMPOSIUM ON ROCK MECHANICS. PROCEEDINGS. 1977. irreg., 18th, 1977. $35. (Colorado School of Mines) Colorado School of Mines, Golden, CO 80401. TEL 303-273-3000. Eds. Tun-Den Wang, George B. Clark. (reprint service avail. from UMI)

338.2 UK ISSN 0308-5090
UNITED KINGDOM MINERAL STATISTICS. 1974. a. price varies. British Geological Survey, Keyworth, Nottingham NG12 5GG, England (Avail. from H.M.S.O., c/o Liaison Officer, Nine Elms, London SW8 5DR, England) stat.

550 UN ISSN 0082-8114
UNITED NATIONS. ECONOMIC AND SOCIAL COMMISSION FOR ASIA AND THE PACIFIC. MINERAL RESOURCES DEVELOPMENT SERIES. 1952. irreg., latest no.51, 1984. price varies. United Nations Economic and Social Commission for Asia and the Pacific, United Nations Bldg., Rajamnern Ave., Bangkok 2, Thailand (Dist. by: United Nations Publications, Room DC2-0853, New York, NY 10017; or Distribution and Sales Section, Palais des Nations, CH-1211 Geneva 10, Switzerland) (back issues avail.)

622   US   ISSN 0082-9129
U.S. BUREAU OF MINES. BULLETIN. 1910. irreg. price varies. U.S. Bureau of Mines, Dept. of the Interior, 4900 La Salle Rd., Avondale, MD 20782. TEL 301-436-8538. (also avail. in microfiche from NTI) Indexed: Petrol.Abstr.

622   US
U.S. BUREAU OF MINES. INFORMATION CIRCULAR. 1925. irreg. price varies. U.S. Bureau of Mines, Department of the Interior, 4900 La Salle Rd., Avondale, MD 20782. TEL 301-436-8538. (also avail. in microfiche from NTI) Indexed: Chem.Abstr. Pollut.Abstr. GeoRef. Petrol.Abstr.

622   US   ISSN 0160-5151
U.S. BUREAU OF MINES. MINERAL COMMODITY SUMMARIES. 1957. a. free. ‡ U.S. Bureau of Mines, Dept. of the Interior, 4900 La Salle Rd, Avondale, MD 20782. TEL 301-436-8538. Ed. Albert E. Schreck. circ. 5,000.
Formerly: U.S. Bureau of Mines. Commodity Data Summaries (ISSN 0082-9137)

549   US   ISSN 0076-8952
U.S. BUREAU OF MINES. MINERALS YEARBOOK. 1932. a. U.S. Bureau of Mines, Dept. of the Interior, 4900 La Salle Rd., Avondale, MD 20782 TEL 301-436-8538. (Orders to: Supt. Doc., Washington, DC 20402)

622   US
U.S. BUREAU OF MINES. REPORT OF INVESTIGATIONS. 1919. irreg. free. U.S. Bureau of Mines, Department of the Interior, 4900 La Salle Rd., Avondale, MD 20782. TEL 301-436-8538. (also avail. in microfiche from NTI) Indexed: Chem.Abstr. GeoRef. Petrol.Abstr. Soils & Fert.

622   338.2   US   ISSN 0082-9382
U.S. BUREAU OF THE CENSUS. CENSUS OF MINERAL INDUSTRIES. (Issued in subject, geographic areas and industry series) 1840. quinquennial. price varies. U.S. Bureau of the Census, Customer Service, Washington, DC 20233 TEL 301-763-4100. (Orders to: Supt. Doc., Washington, DC 20402)

622.8   US   ISSN 0097-9376
U.S. MINING ENFORCEMENT AND SAFETY ADMINISTRATION. INFORMATIONAL REPORT. irreg. U.S. Department of Labor, Mine Safety and Health Administration, 4015 Wilson Blvd., Arlington, VA 22203. Key Title: Informational Report- United States Department of the Interior, Mining Enforcement and Safety Administration.

622   CK   ISSN 0120-2561
UNIVERSIDAD NACIONAL DE COLOMBIA. FACULTAD NACIONAL DE MINAS. ANALES. 1911. irreg., no.60, 1985. price varies. Universidad Nacional de Colombia, Facultad Nacional de Minas, Apdo. Aereo 1027, Medellin, Colombia. Ed.Bd. circ. 1,000.

549   IT
UNIVERSITA DEGLI STUDI DI FERRARA. ISTITUTO DI MINERALOGIA. ANNALI. NUOVA SERIE. SEZIONE 17: SCIENZE MINERALOGICHE E PETROGRAFICHE. (Text in Italian; summaries in English, French and Italian) vol.1, no.7, 1973. irreg. Universita degli Studi di Ferrara, Istituto di Mineralogia, Ferrara, Italy. bibl. charts.

UNIVERSITE DE CLERMONT-FERRAND II. ANNALES SCIENTIFIQUES. SERIE GEOLOGIE ET MINERALOGIE. see *EARTH SCIENCES — Geology*

338.2   622   US   ISSN 0065-5961
UNIVERSITY OF ALASKA. MINERAL INDUSTRY RESEARCH LABORATORY. REPORT. 1964. irreg., no.65, 1985. price varies. University of Alaska, Mineral Industry Research Laboratory, Box 95303, Fairbanks, AK 99701. TEL 907-474-7135. Ed. Ernest N. Wolff. Indexed: GeoRef.

UNIVERSITY OF TEXAS, AUSTIN. BUREAU OF ECONOMIC GEOLOGY. MINERAL RESOURCE CIRCULARS. see *EARTH SCIENCES — Geology*

UTAH GEOLOGICAL AND MINERAL SURVEY. BULLETIN. see *EARTH SCIENCES — Geology*

UTAH GEOLOGICAL AND MINERAL SURVEY. SPECIAL STUDIES. see *EARTH SCIENCES — Geology*

622   665   VE
VENEZUELA. MINISTERIO DE ENERGIA Y MINAS. MEMORIA Y CUENTA. 1952. a. free. Ministerio de Energia y Minas, Torre Norte, Centro Simon Bolivar, Caracas, Venezuela. charts. stat. Indexed: GeoRef.
Formerly: Venezuela. Ministerio de Minas e Hidrocarburos. Memoria y Cuenta (ISSN 0083-5374)

553   622   US
VIRGINIA. DIVISION OF MINERAL RESOURCES. REPORTS. 1959. irreg. price varies. Department of Conservation and Economic Development, Division of Mineral Resources, Box 3667, Charlottesville, VA 22903. TEL 804-293-5121. Indexed: GeoRef.
Former titles: Virginia. Division of Mineral Resources. Publications; Virginia. Division of Mineral Resources. Bulletin; Virginia. Division of Mineral Resources. Information Circular (ISSN 0083-632X); Virginia. Division of Mineral Resources. Resources Report (ISSN 0083-6338); Virginia. Division of Mineral Resources. Report of Investigations (ISSN 0083-6346)

VIRGINIA INDUSTRIAL DIRECTORY. see *BUSINESS AND ECONOMICS — Trade And Industrial Directories*

WASHINGTON (STATE). DIVISION OF GEOLOGY AND EARTH RESOURCES. BULLETIN. see *EARTH SCIENCES — Geology*

557.97   US   ISSN 0147-1783
WASHINGTON (STATE). DIVISION OF GEOLOGY AND EARTH RESOURCES. INFORMATION CIRCULAR. 1939. irreg., no.79, 1985. price varies. Department of Natural Resources, Division of Geology and Earth Resources, Olympia, WA 98504. TEL 206-459-6372. Key Title: Information Circular - State of Washington, Department of Natural Resources, Division of Geology and Earth Resources.

338.2   US
WEST VIRGINIA. DEPARTMENT OF ENERGY. ANNUAL REPORT AND DIRECTORY. 1883. a. $10. Department of Energy, 1615 Washington St. E., Charleston, WV 25311. TEL 304-348-3500. circ. 2,500.
Formed by the merger of: West Virginia. Department of Mines. Annual Report & West Virginia. Department of Mines. Directory of Mines (ISSN 0083-8462)

622   US
WEST VIRGINIA. MINERAL INDUSTRY STATUS. a. free. Geological and Economic Survey, Box 879, Morgantown, WV 26507-0879. Ed. Fred Schroyer. circ. 500.

622   US   ISSN 0083-842X
WEST VIRGINIA COAL MINING INSTITUTE. PROCEEDINGS. 1919. irreg. $7.50. West Virginia Coal Mining Institute, 213 White Hall, Morgantown, WV 26506. Ed. Jay Hilary Kelley.

622   US
WEST VIRGINIA MINERAL PRODUCERS AND PROCESSORS DIRECTORY. 1971. a. $7.50 per no. Geological and Economic Survey, Box 879, Morgantown, WV 26507-0879.
Formerly: West Virginia Mineral Producers Directory.

622   AT
WHAT MINING MEANS TO AUSTRALIANS. 1978. biennial. free. Australian Mining Industry Council, Box 363, Dickson, A.C.T. 2602, Australia.

338.2   UK   ISSN 0260-3403
WORLD COPPER SURVEY. 1974. irreg., latest 1980. £18($43.20) Metal Bulletin PLC, Park House, Park Terrace, Worcester Park, Surrey KT4 7HY, England (Dist. in U.S. by: Metal Bulletin Inc., 220 Fifth Ave., New York, NY 10001) adv. illus.
Formerly: Copper Survey.

622   PL
WORLD MINING CONGRESS. REPORT. (Published in Host Country) (Text mainly in English) 1958. triennial since 1976; latest 12th, 1984, New Delhi. ‡ World Mining Congress, International Organizing Committee, c/o Ing. M. Najberg, Secretary-General, Al. Ujazdowskie 1-3, 00-583 Warsaw, Poland (Order 10th Report from: MTA, Ankara, Turkey) circ. 2,250.
Formerly: International Organizing Committee of World Mining Congresses. Report (ISSN 0074-2775)

338.2   ZA   ISSN 0076-9010
ZAMBIA MINING YEARBOOK. 1955. a. free. Copper Industry Service Bureau, Kitwe, Zambia (Dist. by American Metal Climax, Inc., 1270 Ave. of the Americas, New York, N.Y. 10026) circ. 500.
Formerly: Copperbelt of Zambia Mining Industry Year Book.

ZIMBABWE. MINISTRY OF LANDS AND NATURAL RESOURCES. REPORT OF THE SECRETARY FOR LANDS AND NATURAL RESOURCES. see *CONSERVATION*

MINES AND MINING INDUSTRY — Abstracting, Bibliographies, Statistics

338.2   NZ   ISSN 0112-2584
ANNUAL RETURNS OF PRODUCTION FROM QUARRIES AND MINERAL PRODUCTION STATISTICS. 1972. a. NZ.$1.50. Ministry of Energy, Mines Division, Private Bag, Wellington, New Zealand. Ed. P.G. Turner. circ. 200.
Former titles: New Zealand Mineral Production Statistics & New Zealand. Ministry of Energy. Mines Division. Annual Returns of Production from Quarries and Mineral Production Statistics; New Zealand. Mines Department. Annual Returns of Production from Quarries and Mineral Production Statistics.

622   AT   ISSN 0314-1888
AUSTRALIA. AUSTRALIAN BUREAU OF STATISTICS. TASMANIAN OFFICE. MINING TASMANIA. a. Australian Bureau of Statistics, Tasmanian Office, Box 66A, Hobart, Tasmania 7001, Australia.

622   319.4   AT
AUSTRALIA. BUREAU OF STATISTICS. MINERAL EXPLORATION, AUSTRALIA. 1974. a. free. Australian Bureau of Statistics, Box 10, Belconnen, A.C.T. 2616, Australia. circ. 1,500.

622   016   HU   ISSN 0231-0651
BANYASZATI SZAKIRODALMI TAJEKOZTATO/ MINING ABSTRACTS. 1949. m. (Text in Hungarian) Orszagos Muszaki Informacios Kozpont es Konyvtar (O.M.I.K.K.) - National Technical Information Centre and Library, Muzeum u. 17, Box 12, 1428 Budapest, Hungary (Subscr. to: Kultura, Box 149, H-1389 Budapest, Hungary) Ed. E. Vajda. abstr. index. circ. 260.
Supersedes (as of 1982): Muszaki Lapszemle. Banyaszat/Technical Abstracts. Mining (ISSN 0027-495X)

549   CN   ISSN 0380-7797
CANADA. STATISTICS CANADA. CANADA'S MINERAL PRODUCTION: PRELIMINARY ESTIMATE/PRODUCTION MINERALE DU CANADA, CALCUL PRELIMINAIRE. (Catalogue 26-202) (Text in English and French) 1927. a. Can.$20($21) Statistics Canada, Communications Division, 3rd Floor, R.H. Coats Bldg., Ottawa, Ont. K1A 0T6, Canada TEL 613-993-7276. (Subscr. to: Publications Sales and Services, Ottawa. Ont. K1A 0T6, Canada) (also avail. in microform from MML)

622.33   CN   ISSN 0705-436X
CANADA. STATISTICS CANADA. COAL MINES/ MINES DE CHARBON. (Catalogue 26-206) (Text in English and French) 1917. a. Can.$20($21) Statistics Canada, Communications Division, 3rd Floor, R.H. Coats Bldg., Ottawa, Ont. K1A 0T6, Canada TEL 613-993-7276. (Subscr. to: Publications Sales and Services, Ottawa, Ont. K1A 0T6, Canada) (also avail. in microform from MML)

MINICOMPUTERS

338.2   CN   ISSN 0575-8645
CANADA. STATISTICS CANADA. GENERAL REVIEW OF THE MINERAL INDUSTRIES/ REVUE GENERALE SUR LES INDUSTRIES MINERALES; mines, quarries and oil wells/mines, carrieres et puits de petrole. (Catalogue 26-201) (Text in English and French) 1949. a. Can.$20($21) Statistics Canada, Communications Division, 3rd Floor, R.H. Coats Bldg., Ottawa, Ont. K1A 0T6, Canada TEL 613-993-7276. (Subscr. to: Publications Sales and Services, Ottawa, Ont. K1A 0T6, Canada) (also avail. in microform from MML)

COAL ABSTRACTS. see *MINES AND MINING INDUSTRY*

016 622   UR
EKONOMIKA UGOL'NOI PROMYSHLENNOSTI. irreg. 0.76 Rub. Ministerstvo Ugol'noi Promyshlennosti, Moscow, Russian S.F.S.R., U.S.S.R. bibl.

622   EI   ISSN 0378-3472
EURO ABSTRACTS SECTION II. COAL AND STEEL. (Text in English) vol.4, 1978. m. price varies. (European Coal and Steel Community) Office for Official Publications of the European Communities, P.O. Box 1003, L-2985 Luxembourg, Luxembourg (Dist. in U.S. by European Community Information Service, 2100 M St., N.W., suite 707, Washington, D.C. 20037) Eds. H.-L. Scherff, B. Jay. abstr. bibl. patents. index. Indexed: Br.Ceram.Abstr.

338.2   GR   ISSN 0072-7415
GREECE. NATIONAL STATISTICAL SERVICE. ANNUAL STATISTICAL SURVEY OF MINES, QUARRIES AND SALTERNS. (Text in English and Greek) a., latest 1982. $2.50. National Statistical Service, Publications and Information Division, 14-16 Lycourgou St., 10166 Athens, Greece.

622   VE
HIERRO; y otros datos estadisticos. 1965. a. free. Ministerio de Energia y Minas, Oficina de Economia Minera, Piso 24, Torre Norte, Centro Simon Bolivar, Caracas, Venezuela.
    Formerly: Venezuela. Ministerio de Minas e Hidrocarburos. Oficina de Economia Minera. Hierro y Otros Datos Estadisticos (ISSN 0083-5382)

553 622 669 016   UK   ISSN 0019-0020
I M M ABSTRACTS; a survey of world literature on the economic geology and mining of all minerals (except coal), mineral processing and non-ferrous extraction metallurgy. 1950. bi-m. £75($150) to non-members. Institution of Mining and Metallurgy, 44 Portland Place, London W1N 4BR, England. Ed. M. McGarr. abstr. circ. 1,000. (reprint service avail. from OMP) Indexed: Fluidex.
    ●Also available online.

622   FR
INTERGOVERNMENTAL COUNCIL OF COPPER EXPORTING COUNTRIES. STATISTICAL BULLETIN. (Text in English) a. Intergovernmental Council of Copper Exporting Countries, 39 rue de la Bienfaisance, 75008 Paris, France.

622 016   US   ISSN 0148-9062
INTERNATIONAL JOURNAL OF ROCK MECHANICS AND MINING SCIENCES & GEOMECHANICS ABSTRACTS. 1964. bi-m. $455. Pergamon Press, Inc., Journals Division, Maxwell House, Fairview Park, Elmsford, NY 10523 TEL 914-592-7700. (and Headington Hill Hall, Oxford OX3 0BW, England) Ed. J.A. Hudson. adv. bk. rev. abstr. charts. illus. index. circ. 1,400. (also avail. in microform from MIM,UMI; reprint service avail. from UMI) Indexed: Appl.Mech.Rev. Curr.Cont. Eng.Ind. Excerp.Med. Sci.Abstr. Sci.Cit.Ind. C.I.S. Abstr. Fuel & Energy Abstr. Geo.Abstr. Geotech.Abstr. HRIS. Ind.Sci.Rev. Petrol.Abstr.
    ●Also available online. Vendors: Pergamon Infoline.
    Formerly: International Journal of Rock Mechanics and Mining Sciences (ISSN 0020-7624); Incorporating: Rock Mechanics Abstracts (ISSN 0035-7456)

338.2 315   KO   ISSN 0075-6849
KOREA (REPUBLIC). NATIONAL BUREAU OF STATISTICS. REPORT ON MINING AND MANUFACTURING SURVEY/ KWANGGONGUP TONGGYE ZO SA BOGO SEO. (Text in Korean and English) 1963. a. 20,010 Won. National Bureau of Statistics, Economic Planning Board, Gyeongun-Dong, Jongro-Gu, Seoul, S. Korea. Ed. Myong Hyun Sohn. circ. 1,000.

622 310   MY   ISSN 0126-818X
MALAYSIA. DEPARTMENT OF MINES. STATISTICS RELATING TO THE MINING INDUSTRY OF MALAYSIA. (Text in English and Malay) 1951. a. M.$6. Department of Mines, Survey Building, 6th Floor, Gurney Road, Kuala Lumpur, Malaysia.

338.2 016   FR
P A S C A L FOLIO. PART 41: GISEMENTS METALLIQUES ET NON-METALLIQUES. ECONOMIE MINIERE. 1985. 10/yr. 935 F. (Bureau de Recherches Geologiques et Minieres) Centre National de la Recherche Scientifique, Centre de Documentation Scientifique et Technique, Service des Abonnements, 26 rue Boyer, 75971 Paris 20, France.
    Supersedes (1972-1984): Bulletin Signaletique: Bibliographie des Sciences de la Terre. Section 221. Gisements Metalliques et Non Metalliques. Economie Miniere; Formerly: Bulletin Signaletique: Bibliographie des Sciences de la Terre. Section 221. Gisements Metalliques et Non Metalliques (ISSN 0304-1301); Supersedes: Bulletin Signaletique: Bibliographie des Sciences de la Terre. Section 221. Cahier B. Gitologie, Economie Miniere (ISSN 0300-9270)

553.21 016   IE   ISSN 0031-367X
PEAT ABSTRACTS. 1951. q. exchange basis only. ‡ Bord na Mona - Irish Peat Development Authority, Research & Development, Droichead Nua, Co. Kildare, Ireland. Ed. John Cooke. bk. rev. circ. controlled. (processed) Indexed: Hort.Abstr.

314 622   PL   ISSN 0079-2675
POLAND. GLOWNY URZAD STATYSTYCZNY. ROCZNIK STATYSTYCZNY GORNICTWA. YEARBOOK OF MINING STATISTICS. (Issued in its Seria Roczniki Branzowe. Branch Yearbooks) irreg., latest 1970. Glowny Urzad Statystyczny, Al. Niepodleglosci 208, 00-925 Warsaw, Poland.

622 016   UR   ISSN 0034-2386
REFERATIVNYI ZHURNAL. GORNOE DELO. 1964. m. 160 Rub. (187 Rub. including index) Vsesoyuznyi Institut Nauchno-Tekhnicheskoi Informatsii (VINITI), Baltiiskaya ul., 14, Moscow A-219, Russian S.F.S.R., U.S.S.R (Subscr. to: Mezhdunarodnaya Kniga, Dimitrova ul. 39, 113095 Moscow, Russian S.F.S.R., U.S.S.R.)

622 338.2   SA
SOUTH AFRICA. CENTRAL STATISTICAL SERVICE. MINING: FINANCIAL STATISTICS. (Report No. 16-01) a. R.2.50. Central Statistical Service, Private Bag X44, Pretoria 0001, South Africa (Orders to: Government Printer, Bosman St., Private Bag X85, Pretoria 0001, South Africa)
    Formerly: South Africa. Department of Statistics. Mining: Financial Statistics.

312 622   GW
STATISTISCHE MITTEILUNGEN DER BERGBEHOERDEN DER BUNDESREPUBLIK. a. DM.39.50. Ed. Piepersche Buchdruckerei und Verlagsanstalt, Osteroeder Str. 3, Postfach 10, 3392 Claustahl-Zellerfeld, W. Germany (B.R.D.) stat. (tabloid format)

VENEZUELA. MINISTERIO DE ENERGIA Y MINAS. APENDICE ESTADISTICO. see *ENERGY — Abstracting, Bibliographies, Statistics*

VENEZUELA. MINISTERO DE ENERGIA Y MINAS. MEMORIA. see *ENERGY — Abstracting, Bibliographies, Statistics*

338.2 310   UK
WORLD MINERAL STATISTICS; world production, exports and imports. 1977. a. price varies. British Geological Survey, Keyworth, Nottingham NG12 5GG, England (Avail. from H.M.S.O., c/o Liaison Officer, Nine ELms, London SW8 5DR, England) circ. 1,000.
    Supersedes: Institute of Geological Sciences, London. Statistical Summary of the Mineral Industry (ISSN 0073-9367)

MINICOMPUTERS

see *Computers — Minicomputers*

MOTION PICTURES

790   RM
ALMANAHUL CINEMA. a. 15 lei. Piata Scinteii Nr. 1, Bucharest, Rumania. illus.

778.534   SZ
AMATEURFILM JOURNAL. a. Alma-Verlag, Postfach 1020, 8953 Dietikon, Switzerland. Ed. Albert Haeusermann.
    Formerly: Super-8 Journal.

791.43   US
AMERICAN FILM AND VIDEO FESTIVAL GUIDE. 1959. a. $12. Educational Film Library Association, Inc., 45 John St., New York, NY 10038. TEL 212-227-5599. adv. index. cum.index: 1959-1963. circ. 7,000.
    Former titles: American Film Festival Guide & Festival Film Guide (ISSN 0071-4658)

791.4   US
AMERICAN FILM & VIDEO REVIEW. 1962. a. free. (American Educational Film and Video Center) Eastern College, St. Davids, PA 19087. Ed. John A. Baird, Jr. circ. 30,000.
    Formerly: American Film Review (ISSN 0065-8308)

778.5   FR
ANNEE DU CINEMA. 1977. a. price varies. Editions Calmann-Levy, 3 rue Auber, 75009 Paris, France. illus.

ANNUAIRE BIOGRAPHIQUE DU CINEMA ET DE LA TELEVISION EN FRANCE ET EN BELGIQUE. see *COMMUNICATIONS — Radio And Television*

791.43   FR
ANNUAIRE DU CINEMA ET TELEVISION-VIDEO. 1948. a. 651.50 F.($82) Editions Bellefaye, 1 av. de l'Abbe Roussel, 75016 Paris, France. adv.
    Formerly: Annuaire du Cinema et Television (ISSN 0066-2968)

791.4   RM
ANUL CINEMATOGRAFIC. 1966. a. free. Arhiva Nationala de Filme, Bd. Gh. Gheorghiu-Dej Nr. 65, Bucharest C.P. 1-126, Rumania. Ed. Georgeta Davidescu.

791   IT
ATTUALITA CINEMATOGRAFICHE. 1964. a. price varies. (Chiesa Parrocchiale Santa Maria della Scala in San Fedele) Edizioni Letture, Piazza San Fedele 4, 20121 Milan, Italy. circ. 1,500.

791.43   AT   ISSN 0045-0448
AUSTRALIAN FILMS; a catalogue of scientific, educational and cultural films. 1959. a. National Film & Sound Archive, McCoy Circuit, Acton, A.C.T. 2601, Australia. circ. 800.

AXE FACTORY REVIEW. see *LITERATURE*

384.1 791.4   US   ISSN 0098-5481
BACKSTAGE T V FILM/TAPE & SYNDICATION DIRECTORY. 1965. a. $25. Backstage Publications, Inc., 330 W. 42th St., New York, NY 10036. TEL 212-947-0020. Ed. Allen Zwerdling. adv. bk. rev. circ. 30,000.

BOERNEFILMKATALOGET. see *CHILDREN AND YOUTH — For*

791.43   UK   ISSN 0068-2004
BRITISH FILM FUND AGENCY. ANNUAL REPORT. 1958. a. price varies. H.M.S.O., P.O. Box 569, London SE1 9NH, England.

BUSINESS EDUCATION FILMS CATALOG. see *BUSINESS AND ECONOMICS*

778 UK ISSN 0068-4449
BUSINESS MONITOR: MISCELLANEOUS
SERIES. M2 CINEMAS. a. price varies.
Department of Industry, 29 Great Peter St., London
SW1P 3LW, England (Avail. from H.M.S.O., c/o
Liaison Officer, Atlantic House, Holborn Viaduct,
London EC1P 1BN, England) Indexed: BMT.
Int.Packag.Abstr. Rehabil.Lit. Paper & Bd.Abstr.

791 FR ISSN 0526-6513
C.I.C.A.E. BULLETIN D'INFORMATION.
(Confederation Internationale des Cinemas d'Art et
d'Essai) 1965. irreg. $20. International Art Cinemas
Confederation, c/o Jean Lescure, 22 rue d'Artois,
75008 Paris, France. Ed. Jean Lescure. circ. 1,000.

791.4 US ISSN 0007-9219
C T V D: CINEMA - TV - DIGEST; a quarterly
review of the serious, foreign-language cinema-TV-
press. 1961/62. irreg. $3 for 4 nos. Hampton Books,
Route 1, Box 202, Newberry, SC 29108. TEL 803-
276-6870. Ed. Ben Hamilton. adv. bk. rev. film rev.
illus. circ. 550. (back issues avail.)

790.2 US ISSN 0363-745X
C U DIRECTORY. 1953. a. $15 per no. Chicago
Unlimited, Inc., 619 N. Wabash, 2nd Fl., Chicago,
IL 60611-2713. adv. illus. circ. 7,000.

CANADA COUNCIL ANNUAL REPORT AND
SUPPLEMENT/RAPPORT ANNUEL DU
CONSEIL DES ARTS DU CANADA ET SON
SUPPLEMENT. see ART

791.43 CN ISSN 0705-548X
CANADIAN FILM SERIES. 1976. irreg., no.6, 1981.
price varies. Canadian Film Institute, 150 Rideau
St., Ottawa, Ont. K1N 5X6, Canada. TEL 613-232-
6727.

791.43 371.912 US
CATALOG OF CAPTIONED FILMS FOR THE
DEAF.* a. Associations for Education of the Deaf,
Special Materials Project, 7009 Varnum St.,
Landover, MD 20784-2109.

791.43 PL
CATALOGUE OF POLISH FEATURE FILMS.
(Text in English, French and German) a. Film
Polski, Ul. Mazowiecta 6-8, 00-048 Warsaw, Poland.
Formerly (until 1969): Polish Film Production.

791.43 780 US
CELEBRITY DIRECTORY; how to reach movie, tv
stars and other celebrities. 1984. a. $5.95. Scion
Information Services, Box 8013, Ann Arbor, MI
48107. TEL 313-761-4842. circ. 3,000.

CELEBRITY SERVICE INTERNATIONAL
CONTACT BOOK; trade directory/entertainment
industry. see THEATER

CENTRE INTERNATIONAL DE LIAISON DES
ECOLES DE CINEMA ET DE TELEVISION.
BULLETIN D'INFORMATIONS. see
COMMUNICATIONS — Radio And Television

791.43 UY ISSN 0069-4118
CINE CLUB DEL URUGUAY. CUADERNOS.*
1962. irreg. (approx. 1/yr.) Cine Club del Uruguay,
Rincon 567, Montevideo, Uruguay.

778.5 US ISSN 0277-5891
CINEFAN. 1974. biennial. $3.50. Fandom Unlimited
Enterprises, Box 70868, Sunnyvale, CA 94086. TEL
415-960-1151. Ed. Randall D. Larson. adv. bk. rev.
illus. film rev. circ. 1,000.

791.43 384.55 792 SP ISSN 0069-4134
CINEGUIA; annuario espanol del espectaculo y
audiovisuales. 1960. a. 3500 ptas. Jose Luis Barbero,
Ed. & Pub., Antonio Acuna, 13, 28009 Madrid,
Spain. adv. circ. 3,000.

778.5 SZ
CINEMA; unabhaengig schweizerische Filmzeitschrift/
revue cinematographique independent suisse. 1951.
a. 18 Fr. Arbeitsgemeinschaft Cinema, Postfach
5252, CH-8022 Zurich, Switzerland. adv. bk. rev.
illus. circ. 2,600. Indexed: Film Lit.Ind.

791.43 792 UK
CINEMA AND SOCIETY. irreg. price varies.
Routledge & Kegan Paul PLC, 11 New Fetter Lane,
London EC4P 4EE, England (U.S. address: 9 Park
St., Boston, MA 02108)

791.43 IT ISSN 0009-7152
CINEMA E SOCIETA. 1966. irreg. L.3000 per no.
Giorgio Trentin, Ed. & Pub., Via Porta Maggioreo,
81, 00185 Rome, Italy. bk. rev. film rev. illus. circ.
2,500. (tabloid format)

791.43 FR ISSN 0292-7292
CINEMA FRANCAIS PRODUCTION. 1977. a.
Unifrance Film International, 114, av. des Champs-
Elysees, 75008 Paris, France.

791.43 AT ISSN 0158-698X
CINEMA PAPERS YEARBOOK. 1980. a.
Aus.$19.95. MTV Publishing Ltd., 644 Victoria St.,
North Melbourne, Vic. 3051, Australia. Eds. Peter
Beilby, Ross Lansell.
  Formerly (until 1985): Australian Motion Picture
Yearbook.

791.43 UK
CINEMA PREVIEW. 1920. a. £0.25. Cinema Press
Ltd., 93-95 Wardour St., London W1, England.

778.5 US ISSN 0198-1064
CINEMACABRE; an appreciation of the fantastic.
1979. irreg. $8 for 3 nos. George Stover, Ed. &
Pub., Box 10005, Baltimore, MD 21204. TEL 301-
828-0286. adv. bk. rev. film rev. illus. circ. 3,000.
Indexed: Film Lit.Ind. Media Rev.Dig.
  Supersedes: Black Oracle (ISSN 0045-2246)

791.43 US ISSN 0886-6570
CINEMATOGRAPH. 1985. a. $7.50 for individuals;
institutions $13. Foundation of Art in Cinema, 480
Potrero, San Francisco, CA 94110. TEL 415-558-
8129. Ed. Scott Stark. adv. circ. 1,000. (also avail.
in microform from UMI)

778.534 US ISSN 0886-6570
CINEMATOGRAPH; a journal of film and media art.
1985. a. $13. San Francisco Cinematheque, 480
Potrero Ave., San Francisco, NY 94110. Ed.Bd.

778.5 US ISSN 0162-0126
CINEMONKEY;* a serious film journal. 1976. irreg.
$7. Cinemonkey Inc,,, 1435 N.E. Lemoine, Portland,
OR 97213. TEL 503-248-0849. Ed. Douglas Holm.
adv. bk. rev. film rev.
  Formerly: Scintilation (ISSN 0147-5789)

778 BL
COLECAO CINEMA. vol. 14, 1982. irreg. Editora
Paz e Terra, Rua Sao Jose 90, Centro, Rio de
Janeiro, RJ, Brazil.

778.5 FR
COLLECTION CA-CINEMA.* irreg; no. 8, 1978.
Editions Albatros, 21 rue Cassette, 75006 Paris,
France. Eds. Francois Barat, Joel Farges.

778.5 US
COUNCIL ON INTERNATIONAL
NONTHEATRICAL EVENTS. YEARBOOK;
Golden Eagle film awards. 1962. a. $7.50. Council
on International Nontheatrical Events, Inc., 1201
Sixteenth Street, N.W., Washington, DC 20036.
TEL 202-785-1136. film rev. illus. stat. circ. 1,200.

778.534 SP
CUADERNOS DE SESSION. CINEMATOGRAFIA.
1986. irreg. (Sociedad de Estudios Vascos) Eusko
Ikaskuntza, S.A., Churruca, 7 - 2, 20004 Donostia,
Spain. TEL 425111.

291.43 US ISSN 0748-8580
CURRENT RESEARCH IN FILM. 1984. a. price
varies. Ablex Publishing Corp., 355 Chestnut St.,
Norwood, NJ 07648. TEL 201-767-8450. Ed. Bruce
A. Austin.

791.43 GE
D D R FILM INFORMATION.* (Text in English,
French and German) 1974. irreg. D E E A Studio
for Shortfilms, Milastr. 2, 1058 Berlin, E. Germany
(D.D.R.)

778.5 DK ISSN 0418-3304
DANISH FILMS. (Text in English) a. Danske
Filminstitut, Store Soendervoldstraede, DK-1419
Copenhagen, Denmark. illus.

778.5 DK ISSN 0109-4076
DENMARK. STATENS FILMCENTRAL.
INFORMATION OG BERETNING. 1983. irreg.
free. Statens Filmcentral, Vestergade 27, 1456
Copenhagen K, Denmark. illus.
  Formerly: Statens Filmcentral.

791.43 DK
DENMARK. STATENS FILMCENTRAL. S F C
CATALOGUE. 1950. biennial (w. supplements)
free. Statens Filmcentral - Danish Government Film
Office, 27 Vestergade, 1456 Copenhagen K,
Denmark. Eds. Axel Jepsen, Tue Steen Mueller.
circ. 25,000.
  Formerly: Denmark. Statens Filmcentral. S F C
Film (ISSN 0070-3621)

778.5 DK ISSN 0105-5526
DENMARK. STATENS FILMCENTRAL. S F C,
16MM FILM. vol.84, 1983. biennial. free. Statens
Filmcentral, Vestergade 27, 1456 Copenhagen K,
Denmark.
  Formerly: Denmark. Statens Filmcentral. Katalog
over 16mm Film.

778.5 DK ISSN 0105-5070
DENMARK. STATENS FILMCENTRAL.
STATISTIK OVER UDLEJNING AF 16MM
FILM I FINANSAARET. 1976. a. Statens
Filmcentral, Vestergade 27, 1456 Copenhagen K,
Denmark.

778.5 UK
DISNEY MAGAZINE ANNUAL. a. £2.75. World
International Publishing Ltd., Box 111, Gt. Ducie
St., Manchester, M60 3 BL, England. Ed. Mae
Broadley. adv.

DRAGON. see LITERATURE

DUCKBURG TIMES. see HOBBIES

778.5 NE
DUTCH FILM. (Text in English) irreg. Ministerie van
Welzijn Volksgezondheid en Cultuur,
Steenvoordelaan 370, Rijswijk (Z.H.), Netherlands.
Ed. Pieter van Lierop. illus.

791.43 FR ISSN 0014-1992
ETUDES CINEMATOGRAPHIQUES. 1960. irreg.
150 F. for 10 nos. Lettres Modernes, 73 rue du
Cardinal-Lemoine, 75005 Paris, France. Ed. Michel
Esteve. bibl. illus. Indexed: Curr.Cont. Arts &
Hum.Cit.Ind.

778.53 US
FIELD OF VISION. 1976. a. $12. Island Cinema
Resources, 135 St. Paul's Ave., Staten Island, NY
10301. TEL 718-727-5593. Ed. Robert A. Haller.
adv. bk. rev. circ. 600. (back issues avail.)

791.43 US
FILAMENT. 1981. a. free. Wright State University,
Department of Theatre Arts, Dayton, OH 45435.
Ed. Glenn Lalich. circ. 1,500. (back issues avail.)
Indexed: Film Lit.Ind.

778.534 DK ISSN 0109-2774
FILM AARBOGEN. 1983. a. Kr.36.50.
Bibliotekscentralen, Telegrafvej 5, 2750 Ballerup,
Denmark.

791.43 US
FILM AND VIDEO MAKERS DIRECTORY. 1973.
a. $10 (Includes subscription to Film and Video
Makers Travel Sheet) Carnegie Institute, Museum
of Art, Section of Film and Video, 4400 Forbes
Ave., Pittsburgh, PA 15213. TEL 412-622-3212. Ed.
Matthew Yokobosky. circ. 2,000.

572 700 028.5 370 AT
FILM AUSTRALIA CATALOGUE. 1970. biennial.
Film Australia, Eton Rd., Lindfield, NSW 2070,
Australia. Ed. Max Keogh. (back issues avail.)

791 UK ISSN 0305-1706
FILM DOPE. 1972. irreg. (approx. 3/yr.) £3.70($9)
for 4 nos. 43 Willifield Way, London N.W. 11,
England. Eds. David Badder, Bob Baker. adv. bk.
rev. circ. 1,000. (back issues avail.) Indexed: Film
Lit.Ind.

791.43 GW ISSN 0071-4879
FILM-ECHO FILMWOCHE. VERLEIH-KATALOG.
1949. a. DM.63. Axtmann-Verlag, Wilhelmstr. 42,
6200 Wiesbaden 1, W. Germany (B.R.D.) Ed. Horst
Axtmann. adv. bk. rev. circ. 2,500.

778.5 CN ISSN 0704-9536
FILM EDMONTON. 1977. irreg. Can.$0.50 per no.
Edmonton Film Society, 501, 10015-119 St.,
Edmonton, Alta. T5K 1Y7, Canada.

MOTION PICTURES

778.5 780 US
FILM MUSIC BUYER'S GUIDE. 1977. a. $9.95. R T S, Box 1829, Dept. BW, Novato, CA 94948.

791.43
FILM READER. 1975. a. $8.50 to individuals; libraries $10. Swift Hall, Rm. 212, Northwestern University, Evanston, IL 60201. Ed. Annie May. adv. circ. 1,000. Indexed: Curr.Cont. Arts & Hum.Cit.Ind. Film Lit.Ind. Media Rev.Dig.

791.43 UK ISSN 0071-4917
FILM REVIEW. 1970. a. £10.95. W.H. Allen & Co. Ltd., 44 Hill St., London W1X 8LB, England. Ed. F. Maurice Speed. bk. rev.

778 US ISSN 0737-9080
FILM REVIEW ANNUAL. 1981. a. $75. Jerome S. Ozer, Publisher, 340 Tenafly Rd., Englewood, NJ 07631. TEL 201-567-7040. Ed. Jerome S. Ozer. index. circ. 800. (back issues avail.)

791.43 GW ISSN 0173-4970
FILM UND FERNSEHEN IN FORSCHUNG UND LEHRE. 1978. a. DM.15. Stiftung Deutsche Kinemathek, Pommernallee 1, 1000 Berlin 19, W. Germany (B.R.D.) (Co-sposor: Arbeitsstelle Filmgeschichte der Hochschule fuer Bildene Kuenste) index. circ. 1,000.

791.43 SW ISSN 0071-4925
FILMARSBOKEN/SWEDISH FILM ANNUAL. 1967/68. a. $10. (Swedish Film Institute) Proprius Forlag AB, Box 10251, S-100 55 Stockholm, Sweden. Ed. Bertil Wredlund. adv. circ. 1,500.

016 DK ISSN 0107-0940
FILMATISEREDE BOEGER. 1974. a. Kr.92.21. Bibliotekscentralen, Tempovej 7-11, DK-2750 Ballerup, Denmark.

FILMS ON VIDEO. see *COMMUNICATIONS — Radio And Television*

778.5 DK ISSN 0107-1033
FILMSAESONEN: DANSK FILMFORTEGNELSE. 1980. a. Kr.122.95. (Danske Filmmuseum) Bibliotekcentralen, Tempovej 7-11, DK-2750 Ballerup, Denmark. Ed. Per Calum. illus. circ. 1, 200.

791.43 GW ISSN 0071-4941
FILMSTATISTISCHES TASCHENBUCH. 1957. a. DM.20. Spitzenorganisation der Filmwirtschaft e.V., Langenbeckstr. 9, 6200 Wiesbaden, W. Germany (B.R.D.) Ed. Johannes Klingsporn. circ. 700.

778.5 DK
FILMVIDENSKABELIGT ARBOG. 1973. a. price varies. Koebenhavns Universitet, Filmvidenskabeligt Institut, Frue Plads, DK-1168 Copenhagen K, Denmark (Subscr. to: C. A. Reitzel Booksellers, 20 Noerregade, DK-1165 Copenhagen K, Denmark) illus. circ. 500.
Supersedes in part (as of 1978): Koebenhavns Universitet. Institut for Filmvidenskab. Skrifter.

778.5 DK ISSN 0900-6664
FORENINGEN AF FILMLAERERE I GYMNASIET. MEDDELELSER. 1978. irreg. (3-4/yr.) membership. Foreningen af Filmlaerere i Gymnasiet, c/o Karsten Koch, Ny Carlsbergvej 23, 1760 Copenhagen V, Denmark. illus.

778.5 AG
FOTO CINE GUIA. a. $2.50. Editorial Fotografia Universal, Muniz 1327/49, Buenos Aires, Argentina.

778.5 770 384.5
GADNEY'S GUIDE TO INTERNATIONAL CONTESTS, FESTIVALS & GRANTS IN FILM & VIDEO, PHOTOGRAPHY, TV-RADIO BROADCASTING, WRITING, POETRY, PLAYWRITING & JOURNALISM. 1979. biennial. $15.95. Festival Publications, Box 10180, Glendale, CA 91209. TEL 818-887-0034. Ed. Alan Gadney. adv. circ. 15,000.
Formerly: Gadney's Guide to 1800 International Contests, Festivals and Grants in Film and Video, Photography, TV-Radio Broadcasting, Writing, Poetry, Playwriting and Journalism.

778 UK ISSN 0072-5773
GREAT BRITAIN. CINEMATOGRAPH FILMS COUNCIL. ANNUAL REPORT. a. H.M.S.O., Box 569, London SE1 9NH, England. (reprint service avail. from UMI)

778 UK ISSN 0072-6958
GREAT BRITAIN. NATIONAL FILM FINANCE CORPORATION. ANNUAL REPORT. a. H.M.S.O., Box 569, London SE1 9NH, England. (reprint service avail. from UMI)

791.43 US ISSN 0072-8284
GUIDE TO COLLEGE COURSES IN FILM AND TELEVISION. 1969. irreg., latest 1980; 1986 in prep. price varies. American Film Institute, Box 27999, 2021 N. Western Ave., Los Angeles, CA 90027. TEL 213-856-7600. Ed. Peter Bukalski.

791 355 US
GUIDE TO GOVERNMENT-LOAN FILMS. irreg., latest 1975. $9.95. Serina Press, 70 Kennedy St., Alexandria, VA 22305. TEL 703-548-4080.
Formerly: Guide to Military-Loan Films (ISSN 0072-8586)

700 US ISSN 0278-419X
HOLLYWOOD REPORTER STUDIO BLU-BOOK DIRECTORY. 1978. a. $35. H. R. Industries, Inc., 6715 Sunset Blvd., Hollywood, CA 90028. Ed. Brenda Marshall. bk. rev. circ. 3,000.

015 II ISSN 0377-7359
INDIAN FILMS. (Text in English) 1972. a. Rs.40. Motion Picture Enterprises, Alaka Talkies, Poona 411030, India. Ed. B.V. Dharap. adv. illus. index. circ. 1,200.

791 II
INDIAN MOTION PICTURE ALMANAC. (Text in English) a. Rs.40. Shot Publications, 3-B Madan St., Calcutta 700013, India. illus.
Incorporating: Bengal Motion Picture Diary and General Information.

778.5 BL
INFORMACOES SOBRE A INDUSTRIA CINEMATOGRAFICA BRASILEIRA. ANUARIO. 1980. a. Empresa Brasileira de Filmes, Directoria Tecnica e de Operacoes nao Comerciais, R. Mayrink Veieta 28, 20090 Rio de Janeiro RJ, Brazil. circ. 3,000.

574 610 GW ISSN 0073-8417
INSTITUT FUER DEN WISSENSCHAFTLICHEN FILM. PUBLIKATIONEN ZU WISSENSCHAFTLICHEN FILMEN. SEKTION BIOLOGIE. (Text and summaries in English, French or German) 1963. irreg., series 16, 1983. Institut fuer den Wissenschaftlichen Film, Nonnenstieg 72, 3400 Goettingen, W. Germany (B.R.D.) Ed. H.K. Galle.

791.43 GW ISSN 0341-5910
INSTITUT FUER DEN WISSENSCHAFTLICHEN FILM. PUBLIKATIONEN ZU WISSENSCHAFTLICHEN FILMEN. SEKTION ETHNOLOGIE. (Text and summaries in English, French and German) 1963. irreg., series 13, 1983. Institut fuer den Wissenschaftlichen Film, Nonnenstieg 72, 3400 Goettingen, W. Germany (B.R.D.) Ed. H.K. Galle.
Formerly: Institut fuer den Wissenschaftlichen Film. Publikationen zu Wissenschaftlichen Filmen. Sektion Voelkerkunde.

791.43 900 GW ISSN 0341-5937
INSTITUT FUER DEN WISSENSCHAFTLICHEN FILM. PUBLIKATIONEN ZU WISSENSCHAFTLICHEN FILMEN. SEKTION GESCHICHTE, PUBLIZISTIK. (Text in German; summaries in English, French and German) 1963. irreg., series 6, 1983. Institut fuer den Wissenschaftlichen Film, Nonnenstieg 72, 34 Goettingen, W. Germany (B.R.D.) Ed. H.K. Galle.
Formerly: Publikationen zu Wissenschaftlichen Filmen. Sektion Geschichte, Paedagogik (ISSN 0073-8441)

610 791.43 GW ISSN 0341-5929
INSTITUT FUER DEN WISSENSCHAFTLICHEN FILM. PUBLIKATIONEN ZU WISSENSCHAFTLICHEN FILMEN. SEKTION MEDIZIN. (Text in English, French and German; summaries in English, French and German) 1970. irreg., series 6, 1983. Institut fuer den Wissenschaftlichen Film, Nonnenstieg 72, 3400 Goettingen, W. Germany (B.R.D.) Ed. H.K. Galle.

500 791.43 GW ISSN 0073-8433
INSTITUT FUER DEN WISSENSCHAFTLICHEN FILM. PUBLIKATIONEN ZU WISSENSCHAFTLICHEN FILMEN. SEKTION TECHNISCHE WISSENSCHAFTEN, NATURWISSENSCHAFTEN. (Text and summaries in English, French or German) 1963. irreg., series 8, 1983. Institut fuer den Wissenschaftlichen Film, Nonnenstieg 72, 3400 Goettingen, W. Germany (B.R.D.) Ed. H.K. Galle.

791 RM ISSN 0538-4281
INTERNATIONAL ANIMATED FILM ASSOCIATION. BULLETIN. 1967, no. 15. irreg. International Animated Film Association - Association Internationale du Film d'Animation, c/o Marin Paraianu, 45 Strada Olteni, Bucuresti 4, Rumania.

791 US ISSN 0074-462X
INTERNATIONAL DIRECTORY OF 16MM FILM COLLECTORS. 1971. irreg. (approx. biennial) $15. (16mm Filmland) Evan H. Foreman, Ed. & Pub., P.O. Drawer F, Mobile, AL 36601. TEL 205-432-8406. circ. 1,000. (tabloid format)

791.43 UK ISSN 0074-6053
INTERNATIONAL FILM GUIDE. 1964. a. $14.95. Tantivy Press, 136-148 Tooley St., London SE1 2TT, England (Dist. in U.S. by: New York Zoetrope Inc., 838 Broadway, New York, NY 10003) Ed. Peter Cowie. adv. bk. rev.

791.43 US ISSN 0074-7084
INTERNATIONAL MOTION PICTURE ALMANAC; reference tool of the film industry. 1929. a. $55. Quigley Publishing Co., 159 W. 53 St., New York, NY 10019. TEL 212-247-3100. Ed. Richard Gertner. adv. Indexed: Child.Auth.& Illus. Perf.Arts Biog.Master Ind.

791 IS
ISRAEL FILM CENTRE. INFORMATION BULLETIN. (Text in English) 1969. a. free. Israel Film Centre, Box 299, Jerusalem, Israel. TEL 210 297.

778.5 IS
ISRAEL FILM INDUSTRY DIRECTORY. (Text in English) 1976. irreg. Israel Film Centre, Box 299, Jerusalem, Israel. TEL 210 297. adv.
Formerly: Filmmakers and Film Production Services of Israel.

770 GW ISSN 0075-2509
JAHRBUCH DES KAMERAMANNS. 1959. a. DM.25. D D K-Verlag Ingeborg Weber, Rotbuchenstr. 21, 8000 Munich 90, W. Germany (B.R.D.) adv.

778.5 US ISSN 0146-5546
JUMP CUT; a review of contemporary media. 1974. irreg. (1-2/yr.) $10. Jump Cut Associates, Box 865, Berkeley, CA 94701. TEL 415-658-4482. Ed.Bd. adv. bk. rev. film rev. illus. circ. 6,000. (tabloid format; also avail. in microform from UMI; back issues avail.; reprint service avail. from UMI) Indexed: Sociol.Abstr. Alt.Press Ind. Film Lit.Ind. Int.Ind.Film Per. Media Rev.Dig.

791.43 UK
KEMPS INTERNATIONAL FILM AND TELEVISION YEAR BOOK. 1956. a. $55. Kemps Group (Printers & Publishers) Ltd., 1-5 Bath St., London EC1V 9QA, England (Dist. by: R.R. Bowker Company, 205 E. 42nd St., New York, NY 10017) adv.
Formerly: Kemps Film and Television Year Book (International) (ISSN 0075-5427)

791.43 YU
KINEMATOGRAFIJA U SRBIJI - UPOREDO SFRJ. (Subseries of: Biblioteka Dokumentacije) 1969. a. 120 din.($15) Institut za Film, Belgrade, Cika Ljubina 15, Belgrade, Yugoslavia. Ed. M. Ilic. stat. circ. 1,000.
Formerly: Kinematografija u Srbiji (ISSN 0350-2651)

778.5 KO
KOREA FILM CATALOG. a. International Cultural Society of Korea, C.P.O. Box 2147, Seoul, S. Korea. illus.

778 US
MAGILL'S CINEMA ANNUAL. a. $35. Salem Press, Box 1097, Englewood Cliffs, NJ 07632. TEL 201-871-3700. Ed. F.N. Magill. film rev.

791   US
MALCOLM HULKE STUDIES IN CINEMA &
TELEVISION. irreg., latest no. 1. Borgo Press, Box
2845, San Bernardino, CA 92406. TEL 714-884-
5813.

METAPHYSICAL REVIEW. see *LITERARY AND
POLITICAL REVIEWS*

791   JA   ISSN 0085-3577
MOVIE/T V MARKETING GLOBAL MOTION
PICTURE YEAR BOOK. (Text in English) 1955. a.
$45. Movie TV Marketing, Box 30, Central Post
Office, Tokyo 100-91, Japan. Ed. William J. Ireton.
adv. circ. 100,000. (also avail. in microform from
UMI)

791.43   US   ISSN 0362-3688
NEW YORK TIMES FILM REVIEWS. 1913.
biennial. Times Books (Subsidiary of: Random
House, Inc.) 201 E. 50th St., New York, NY
10022-7703. TEL 212-751-2600. illus.

384.8   CN
OFFICE DES COMMUNICATIONS SOCIALES,
MONTREAL. SELECTION DE FILMS EN 16
MM. 1966. irreg. Can.$15. ‡ Office des
Communications Sociales, 4005 rue de Bellechasse,
Montreal, Que. H1X 1J6, Canada. TEL 514-729-
6391. circ. 1,500.
    Formerly: Office des Communications Sociales,
Montreal. Selection de Films pour Cine Clubs.
(ISSN 0078-3730)

791.43   US
ON LOCATION DIRECTORY; the national film &
videotape production directory. 1977. a. $75. On
Location Publishing, P.O. Box 2810, Hollywood,
CA 90028. Ed. Steven Bernard.
    Formerly: On Location: Film and Videotape
Production Directory.

791.43   100   US
PERSISTENCE OF VISION. 1984. a. $13.50 to
individuals; institutions $15. City University of New
York, Film Faculty, c/o Tony Pipolo, Ed., 53-24
63rd St., Maspeth, NY 11378. TEL 718-779-3936.
adv. (back issues avail.) Indexed: M.L.A.

791.43   US   ISSN 0031-8833
PHOTON. 1963. irreg. $4. Mark Frank, Ed. & Pub.,
801 Ave. C, Brooklyn, NY 11218. adv. bk. rev. film
rev. illus. circ. 40,000. (back issues avail.)

791.43   FR   ISSN 0079-2535
POINTS. FILMS. 1971. irreg. price varies. Editions du
Seuil, 27 rue Jacob, 75261 Paris Cedex 06, Paris 6e,
France.

778.5   US   ISSN 0732-6653
PRODUCER'S MASTERGUIDE; the international
production manual for motion pictures, television,
commercials, cable and videotape industries in the
United States, Canada, the United Kingdom,
Ireland, Bermuda and the Caribbean Islands. 1979.
a. $85. New York Production Manual, Inc., 611
Broadway, Ste. 807, New York, NY 10012-2608.
TEL 212-777-4002. Ed. Shmuel Bension. adv.
charts. stat. circ. 20,000.
    Formerly (until 1982): New York Production
Manual (ISSN 0163-1276)

778.5   US
PYRAMID FILM AND VIDEO CATALOG. 1960.
biennial. free. Pyramid Film & Video, Box 1048,
Santa Monica, CA 90406-1048. TEL 213-828-7577.
Ed. Jean Phillips. film rev. circ. 60,000.

778.5   DK   ISSN 0109-0631
R F MEDLEMSBLAD. 1980. a. Romansk Filmklub,
Roarsvej 18/3 tv, 2000 Copenhagen F, Denmark.
    Formerly: Romansk Filmklub. Medlemsblad
(ISSN 0106-214X)

791   CN   ISSN 0085-543X
RECUEIL DES FILMS. 1955. a. Can.$12. ‡ Office
des Communications Sociales, 4005 rue de
Bellechasse, Montreal, Que. H1X 1J6, Canada. TEL
514-729-6391. adv. film rev. circ. 1,500.

778.5   DK
SAERRAKKE. 1978. irreg. (approx 1/yr.) Kr.18.50.
Koebenhavns Universitet, Filmvidenskabeligt
Institut, Frue Plads, DK-1168 Copenhagen K,
Denmark (Subscr. to: C.A. Reitzel Booksellers, 20
Noerregade, DK-1165 Copenhagen K, Denmark)
    Supersedes in part (as of 1978): Koebenhavns
Universitet. Institut for Filmvidenskab Skrifter.

791   UK
SCREEN INTERNATIONAL FILM AND T.V.
YEARBOOK. 1945. a. $50. King Publications Ltd.,
Kingsween House, 6/7 Great Chapel St., Soho,
London W1, England. Ed. Peter Noble. adv. illus.
circ. 6,000.
    Former titles: International Film and T.V.
Yearbook; British Film and T.V. Yearbook (ISSN
0068-1997)

791.43   US   ISSN 0080-8288
SCREEN WORLD. 1949. a. $19.95. Crown
Publishers, Inc., One Park Ave., New York, NY
10016. TEL 212-532-9200. Ed. John Willis.

778.5   DK   ISSN 0106-2484
SEKVENS; filmvidenskabelig aarbog. 1978. a.
Kr.85.40. University of Copenhagen, Institut of
Political Studies, Rosenborggade 15, DK-1130
Copenhagen K, Denmark. circ. 200.
    Supersedes in part: Koebenhavns Universitet.
Institut for Filmvidenskab. Skrifter.

791.43   GW   ISSN 0071-4933
SPIELFILMLISTE. 1958. a. DM.7. Institut Jugend,
Film, Fernsehen, Waltherstr. 23, 8000 Munich 2, W.
Germany (B.R.D.) Ed. Hans Strobel. adv. circ. 5,
000.
    Formerly: Filmliste.

778.5   AT
SPROCKET. 1966. irreg. membership. International
Film Theatre, Box 90, Subiaco, W.A. 6008,
Australia. circ. 300.

778.5   CE
SRI LANKA FILM ANNUAL. (Text in Sinhalese)
no. 28, 1975. a. Rs.6.95. National Catholic Film
Office, St. Phillip Neri's Church, Katukurunda,
Kalutara, Sri Lanka. film rev.

STAGECAST-IRISH STAGE AND SCREEN
DIRECTORY. see *THEATER*

STELLE FILANTI. see *BIOGRAPHY*

778.5   NE
STICHTING FILM EN WETENSCHAP.
CATALOGUE 16MM FILMS AND VIDEO
PROGRAMMES. 1978. irreg. Stichting Film en
Wetenschap, Box 9550, 3506 GN Utrecht,
Netherlands.
    Formerly: Stichting Film en Wetenschap.
Catalogue 16mm Films.

778   US
STUDIES IN CINEMA. irreg., vol.38, 1985. U M I
Research Press, 300 N. Zeeb Rd., Ann Arbor, MI
48106. Ed. Diane Kirkpatrick.

STUDII SI CERCETARI DE ISTORIA ARTEI.
SERIA TEATRU-MUZICA-CINEMATOGRAFIE.
see *THEATER*

778.534   780 792   RM
STUDII SI CERCETARI DE ISTORIA ARTEI.
SERIA TEATRU, MUZICA,
CINEMATOGRAFIE/STUDIES AND
RESEARCH IN ART HISTORY. SERIES:
THEATRE, MUSIC, CINEMATOGRAPHY. a.
$45. (Academy of Social and Political Sciences of
the S.R.R.) Editura Academiei Republicii Socialiste
Rumania, Calea Victoriei nr.125, sectorul 1, R-
79717 Bucharest, Rumania.

791.43   AT
SYDNEY FILM FESTIVAL PROGRAMME. 1954.
a. Aus.$5($15) Sydney Film Festival, P.O. Box 25,
Glebe, N.S.W. 2037, Australia. Ed. Rod Webb. adv.
film rev. circ. 4,000. (back issues avail.)

778.5   CN
TELEFILM CANADA ANNUAL REPORT. 1968. a.
free. Canadian Film Development Corporation,
Telefilm Canada, 600 de la Gauchetiere Street
West, 25th Floor, Montreal, Que. H3B 4L2,
Canada. TEL 514-283-6363. circ. 3,000.
    Formerly: C F D C Annual Report (ISSN 0382-
2273)

TELEVISION NETWORK MOVIES. see
COMMUNICATIONS — Radio And Television

792.43   US
VARIETY INTERNATIONAL MOTION PICTURE
MARKETPLACE.* a. Garland Publishing, Inc., 136
Madison Ave., New York, NY 10036. TEL 212-
686-7492. Ed. Mike Kaplan.

791.43   US   ISSN 0149-1830
VELVET LIGHT TRAP; review of cinema. 1971. a.
$12 to individuals; institutions $24; other rates avail.
Madcinema, Ltd., Box 9240, Madison, WI 53715.
Ed. Matthew Bernstein. adv. bk. rev. illus. circ. 3,
500. (also avail. in microform from UMI; reprint
service avail. from UMI) Indexed: Film Lit.Ind.
Int.Ind.Film Per.

778.5   AT   ISSN 0810-4476
VICTORIA. STATE FILM CENTRE. NEW FILMS
AND VIDEOTAPES. 1954. irreg. price varies.
State Film Centre of Victoria, 1 Macarthur St., East
Melbourne, Vic. 3002, Australia. Ed.Bd. circ. 2,000.
(also avail. in microfiche)
    Formerly: Victoria. State Film Centre. New
Films.

VIDEO REGISTER. see *BUSINESS AND
ECONOMICS — Trade And Industrial Directories*

778.534   US   ISSN 0277-3317
VIDEO SOURCE BOOK. 1979. a. $135. National
Video Clearinghouse, Inc., 100 Lafayette Dr.,
Syosset, NY 11791 (Libraries Order from: Gale
Research Co., Book Tower, Detroit, MI 48226) Ed.
Liz Doris. adv. index. circ. 5,000. (back issues
avail.)

778.5   FR
VIVRE LE CINEMA. 1977. irreg. Editions Jacques
Glenat, 6 rue Lieutenant Chanaron, 38000
Grenoble, France. Ed. Gilbert Hus.

WHO'S WHO IN CANADIAN FILM AND
TELEVISION. see *BIOGRAPHY*

WHO'S WHO ON THE SCREEN. see *BIOGRAPHY*

778.5   NE
3 D FILM GIDS; catalogus korte films (16mm) irreg.
Verenigde Filmdiensten, Postbus 515, Hilversum,
Netherlands. illus.

MOTION PICTURES — Abstracting, Bibliographies, Statistics

BOERNEBIBLIOTEKSKATALOG. DIAS, FILM,
VIDEO. see *CHILDREN AND YOUTH —
Abstracting, Bibliographies, Statistics*

778.5   DK   ISSN 0106-7990
BOERNEFILMKATALOGET. SUPPLEMENT.
1980. a. Kr.135.25. (Danske Filminstitut)
Bibliotekscentralen, Tempovej 7-11, 2750 Ballerup,
Denmark. illus.

791   016   UK   ISSN 0007-1552
BRITISH NATIONAL FILM CATALOGUE. 1963.
q. £44. British Film Institute, 127 Charing Cross
Rd., London WC2H 0EA, England. Ed. Maureen
Brown. bibl. index. circ. 1,000.

791.43   FR
C N C STATISTIQUES. a. Centre National de la
Cinematographie, 12 rue Lubeck, 75784 Paris
Cedex 16, France.

791.43   CN   ISSN 0380-6294
CANADA. STATISTICS CANADA. MOTION
PICTURE THEATRES AND FILM
DISTRIBUTORS/CINEMAS ET
DISTRIBUTEURS DE FILMS. (Catalogue 63-207)
(Text in English and French) 1930. a. Can.$20($21)
Statistics Canada, Communications Division, 3rd
Floor, R.H. Coats Bldg., Ottawa, Ont. K1A 0T6,
Canada TEL 613-993-7276. (Subscr. to: Publications
Sales and Services, Ottawa, Ont. K1A 0T6, Canada)
(also avail. in microform from MML)

EDUCATIONAL FILM AND VIDEO (YEAR); a
rental catalog. see *EDUCATION — Abstracting,
Bibliographies, Statistics*

791.4   US
EDUCATIONAL FILM/VIDEO LOCATOR. 2nd
edt., 1980. irreg. 3rd edt., 1986. $150. (Consortium
of University Film Centers) R.R. Bowker Company,
Database Publishing Group, 245 W. 17th St., New
York, NY 10011. TEL 800-521-8110.
    Formerly (until 3rd edt.): Educational Film
Locator (ISSN 0000-0590)

791.43 016   US   ISSN 0093-6758
FILM LITERATURE INDEX. 1973. q. $250 with bound cumulation. Filmdex Part II Inc., Film and Television Documentation Center, State University of New York, Albany, 1400 Washington Ave., Albany, NY 12222 TEL 518-442-5745. (Or 16 Bacon Lane, Albany, NY 12211) Eds. Vincent J. Aceto, Fred Silva. bk. rev. bibl.

FILM UND FERNSEHEN IN FORSCHUNG UND LEHRE. see *MOTION PICTURES*

778.5   DK   ISSN 0106-8180
FILMREGISTRET. 1962. a. Kr.688.50. Bibliotekscentralen, Tempovej 7-11, DK-2750 Ballerup, Denmark.

FILMS: THE VISUALIZATION OF ANTHROPOLOGY. see *ANTHROPOLOGY — Abstracting, Bibliographies, Statistics*

011   US
FLORIDA STATE UNIVERSITY. INSTRUCTIONAL SUPPORT CENTER. FILM AND VIDEO. 1954. biennial. free. Florida State University, Instructional Support Center, Tallahassee, FL 32306-1019. TEL 904-644-2820. Ed. Valarie Howington. circ. 5,000.
   Former titles: Florida State University. Instructional Support Center. Film; Florida State University. Media Services. Motion Pictures; Florida State University. Educational Media Center. Educational Motion Pictures (ISSN 0430-7313)

791   US   ISSN 0072-8462
GUIDE TO GOVERNMENT-LOAN FILMS VOLUME 1: THE CIVILIAN AGENCIES. 1969. irreg., 6th edt., 1980. $9.95. Serina Press, 70 Kennedy St., Alexandria, VA 22305. TEL 703-548-4080. Ed. Daniel Sprecher.

016.791 791.43   UK   ISSN 0000-0388
INTERNATIONAL INDEX TO FILM PERIODICALS. 1972. a. £37.50. International Federation of Film Archives (F.I.A.F.), 90-94 Shaftesbury Ave., London W1V 7DH, England (Distr. in U.S. by: St. James Press, 425 North Michigan Ave., Chicago 60611) Ed. Michael Moulds. (also avail. in microfiche)

778.5 016   US   ISSN 0363-7778
MEDIA REVIEW DIGEST; the only complete guide to reviews of non-book media. 1970. a. with one supplement. $198. Pierian Press, Box 1808, Ann Arbor, MI 48106. TEL 313-434-5530. Ed. Leslie Orlin. cum.index.
   Formerly: Multi Media Reviews Index (ISSN 0091-5858)
   Films, film strips, records, tapes, slides, transparencies, overlays, games, kits

778.5   MX
MEXICO. CENTRO DE INFORMACION TECNICA Y DOCUMENTACION. INDICE DE PELICULAS. a. (Centro de Informacion Tecnica y Documentacion) Mexico. Servicio Nacional de Adiestramiento Rapido de la Mano de Obra en la Industria, Calzada Atzcapotzalco-la Villa 209, Mexico 16, D.F., Mexico.

338 016   US
N I C E M INDEX TO PRODUCERS AND DISTRIBUTORS. 1971. a. $50. (National Information Center for Educational Media) Access Innovations, Inc, Box 40130, Albuquerque, NM 87196. TEL 505-265-3591.

791.4 016   DK   ISSN 0107-0894
NYE BOEGER OM FILM/TV/NEW BOOKS ON FILM/TV. (Text in Danish and English) 1967. a. Kr.223.50. Bibliotekscentralen, Tempovej 7-11, 2750 Ballerup, Denmark. Ed. Karen Jones. circ. 1,000.
   Formerly: Nye Boeger om Film (ISSN 0048-1238)

PERFORMING ARTS BIOGRAPHY MASTER INDEX. see *THEATER — Abstracting, Bibliographies, Statistics*

PSYCHOLOGICAL CINEMA REGISTER; films and video in the behavioral sciences. see *PSYCHOLOGY — Abstracting, Bibliographies, Statistics*

REFERATIVNYI ZHURNAL. FOTOKINOTEKHNIKA. see *PHOTOGRAPHY — Abstracting, Bibliographies, Statistics*

016 791.4   CN   ISSN 0315-7326
SIXTEEN MM FILMS AVAILABLE IN THE PUBLIC LIBRARIES OF METROPOLITAN TORONTO. 1969. irreg. Can.$31.00. Metropolitan Toronto Library Board, 789 Yonge St., Toronto, Ontario M4W 2G8, Canada.

016 371.42   DK   ISSN 0900-3479
UDDANNELSE OG ERHVERV KATALOG. 1967. a. free. Raadet for Uddannelses og Erhvervsvejledning, Aebeloegade 7, 2100 Copenhagen OE, Denmark. Ed. Bodit Sneslev. circ. 8,000.

MUNICIPAL GOVERNMENT

see *Public Administration — Municipal Government*

MUSEUMS AND ART GALLERIES

069.9   US
AFRICAN AMERICAN MUSEUMS ASSOCIATION. ANNUAL MEETING REPORT. a. African American Museums Association, 1318 Vermont Ave., N.W., Washington, DC 20005.

069 500   JA
AKIYOSHI-DAI MUSEUM OF NATURAL HISTORY. BULLETIN. (Text in English or Japanese; summaries in English) 1961. irreg., 1969, no. 6. Akiyoshi-dai Museum of Natural History, Akiyoshi-dai, Akiyoshi-cho Miya-gun, Yamaguchi 754-05, Japan. Ed. M. Ota.
   Formerly: Akiyoshi-dai Science Museum. Bulletin (ISSN 0065-5554)

069   HU   ISSN 0324-542X
ALBA REGIA. (Text in English, French, German) 1960. a. DM.70 (or exchange) Istvan Kiraly Muzeum, P.O. Box 12, Szekesfehervar 1, Hungary. bk. rev.

707.4   US
ALLIED ARTISTS OF AMERICA. ANNUAL EXHIBITION (BULLETIN) 1914. a. Allied Artists of America, 15 Gramercy Park South, New York, NY 10003. Ed.Bd. circ. 3,000.

708.1   US   ISSN 0065-6410
ALLIED ARTISTS OF AMERICA. EXHIBITION CATALOG. 1914. a. $3. Allied Artists of America, 15 Gramercy Park South, New York, NY 10003. adv. circ. 1,600.

945   IT   ISSN 0569-1346
ALTAMURA. a. L.5000 membership. Museo Civico, Biblioteca, Palazzo degli Studi, Altamura, Italy. Ed. Celio Sabini. bibl. illus.

069 500   US
AMERICAN MUSEUM OF NATURAL HISTORY. ANNUAL REPORT. 1870. a. American Museum of Natural History, 79th St. and Central Park W., New York, NY 10024. TEL 212-873-4225. Ed. Ann Breen Metcalfe. bibl. charts. illus. circ. 5,000.

AMERICAN MUSEUM OF NATURAL HISTORY. BULLETIN. see *SCIENCES: COMPREHENSIVE WORKS*

069.5   GR
ANNALES MUSEI GOULANDRIS; contributiones ad historiam naturalem graeciae et regionis mediterraneae. (Text in English, German, French and Latin; summaries in English and Greek) 1973. a. $15. Goulandris Natural History Museum, 13, Levidou Str., Kifissia, Greece. Ed. W.T. Stearn. circ. 1,000. Indexed: GeoRef.

069   GE   ISSN 0402-7817
ARBEITS UND FORSCHUNGSBERICHTE ZUR SAECHSISCHEN BODENDENKMALPFLEGE. 1953. a. price varies. (Landesmuseum fuer Vorgeschichte Dresden) VER Deutscher Verlag der Wissenschaften, Postfach 1216, 1080 Berlin, E. Germany (D.D.R.) Ed. Heinz-Joachim Vogt. Indexed: Br.Archaeol.Abstr.

ARCHIVES ET BIBLIOTHEQUES DE BELGIQUE/ ARCHIEF- EN BIBLIOTHEEKWEZEN IN BELGIE. see *HISTORY — History Of Europe*

ARMY MUSEUM. see *MILITARY*

700   HU   ISSN 0133-6673
ARS DECORATIVA; annuaire du Musee des Arts Decoratifs et du Musee d'Art d'Extreme Orient Ferenc Hopp. (Text in English, French and German) 1973. a. exchange basis. Iparmuveszeti Muzeum, Ulloi ut 33, 1091 Budapest 9, Hungary. Ed. Imre Jakabffy.
   Supersedes: Iparmuveszeti Muzeum. Evkonyv.

708   AT   ISSN 0066-7935
ART BULLETIN OF VICTORIA. (Supersedes its Annual Bulletin, 1959-1966) 1967/68. a. price varies. National Gallery of Victoria, Victoria Arts Centre, 180 St. Kilda Rd., Melbourne, Vic. 3004, Australia. Ed. Sonia Dean. circ. 2,500. Indexed: Artbibl. Aus.P.A.I.S. RILA.

708   CN   ISSN 0082-5018
ART GALLERY OF ONTARIO. ANNUAL REPORT. 1966/67. a. Art Gallery of Ontario, 317 Dundas St. W., Toronto, Ont. M5T 1G4, Canada. TEL 416-977-0414. circ. 2,500.

ART NEWS DIRECTORY OF CORPORATE ART COLLECTIONS. see *ART*

ARTISTS IN CANADA: UNION LIST OF ARTISTS FILES/ARTISTES DU CANADA. LISTE COLLECTIVE DES DOSSIERS D'ARTISTES. see *ART*

591 594   NZ   ISSN 0067-0456
AUCKLAND INSTITUTE AND MUSEUM. BULLETIN. 1941. irreg., no.14, 1984. price varies. Auckland Institute and Museum, Private Bag, Auckland 1, New Zealand. Ed. K. Wise. (back issues avail.) Indexed: Biol.Abstr. GeoRef.

069.7   NZ   ISSN 0067-0464
AUCKLAND INSTITUTE AND MUSEUM. RECORDS. 1930. a. price varies. Auckland Institute and Museum, Private Bag, Auckland 1, New Zealand. Ed. K. Wise. index. circ. 300. (back issues avail.) Indexed: Biol.Abstr. Ind.N.Z.Per. GeoRef.

708   SZ   ISSN 0067-0618
AUS DEM SCHWEIZERISCHEN LANDESMUSEUM. 1953. irreg., no. 41, 1978. price varies. Paul Haupt AG, Falkenplatz 14, CH-3001 Berne, Switzerland.

069.7   AT   ISSN 0812-7387
AUSTRALIAN MUSEUM, SYDNEY. SUPPLEMENTS. 1983. irreg. price varies. Australian Museum, 6-8 College St., Sydney, N.S.W., Australia. Ed. J.K. Lowry.
   Formerly: Australian Museum Memoirs.

AWARDS IN THE VISUAL ARTS. see *ART*

708.1   US   ISSN 0045-3242
B.A.C.A. CALENDAR OF CULTURAL EVENTS. 1971. a. $10. Brooklyn Arts and Culture Association, Inc.- Brooklyn Arts Council, 200 Eastern Parkway, Brooklyn, NY 11238. TEL 718-783-4469. Ed. Charles Reichenthal. circ. 15,000.

069   DK   ISSN 0109-8489
BANGSBOMUSEET. AARBOG. 1984. a. Kr.30. Bangsbomuseet, Frederikshavn, Denmark. Ed. Hans Munk Pedersen. circ. 1,000.

069   GE   ISSN 0138-4279
BEITRAEGE ZUR UR- UND FRUEHGESCHICHTE DER BEZIRKE ROSTOCK, SCHWERIN UND NEUBRANDENBURG. 1967. irreg. price varies. (Museum fuer Ur- und Fruehgeschichte Schwerin) VEB Deutscher Verlag der Wissenschaften, Postfach 1216, 1080 Berlin, E. Germany (D.D.R.) Ed. Horst Keiling.

BIBLIOTHEQUES ET MUSEES. see *HISTORY — History Of Europe*

BILDUNG IM GESCHICHTSMUSEUM. see *HISTORY — History Of Europe*

069　　　　　　　GE　ISSN 0067-9461
BODENDENKMALPFLEGE IN MECKLENBURG. 1964. a. price varies. (Museum fuer Ur- und Fruehgeschichte, Schwerin) VEB Deutscher Verlag der Wissenschaften, Postfach 1216, 1080 Berlin, E. Germany (D.D.R.) Ed. E. Schuldt. Indexed: Br.Archaeol.Abstr.

069　　　　　　　US　ISSN 0084-7992
BOWDOIN COLLEGE. MUSEUM OF ART. OCCASIONAL PAPERS. 1972. irreg., no.2, 1975. price varies. Bowdoin College, Museum of Art, Brunswick, ME 04011. TEL 207-725-3275. Indexed: RILA.
Formerly: Walker Art Museum. Bulletin.

BRAZIL. MUSEU DO INDIO. BOLETIM. DOCUMENTACAO. see HISTORY — History Of North And South America

708　　　　BX　ISSN 0084-8131
BRUNEI MUSEUM. SPECIAL PUBLICATION/ MUZIUM BRUNEI. PENERBITAN KHAS. (Text in English and Malay) 1972. irreg., latest no. 10. price varies. Brunei Museum, Kota Batu, Bandar Seri Begawan, Brunei. Ed. P.M. Dato Shariffiddin. circ. 1,000.

708　　　　BX　ISSN 0068-2918
BRUNEI MUSEUM JOURNAL. (Text in English) 1969. a. B.$10. Brunei Museum, Kota Batu, Brunei. Ed. P.M. Dato Shariffiddin. illus. circ. 3,000. Indexed: E.I.

063　　　　　　　BE
CAHIERS DE MARIEMONT. 1970. a. 200 Fr. Musee Royal de Mariemont, Ministere de la Communaute Francaise, Service de Documentation, B-6510 Morlanwelz-Mariemont, Belgium. Ed. Guy Donnay. circ. 1,000.

708 069　　　CN　ISSN 0711-2866
CANADA. NATIONAL MUSEUMS OF CANADA. ANNUAL BULLETIN/CANADA. MUSEES NATIONAUX DU CANADA. BULLETIN ANNUEL. (Text in English and French) 1979. a. Can.$10. National Museums of Canada, Ottawa, Ont. K1A 0M8, Canada TEL 613-990-1969. (Order from: National Gallery of Canada, Ottawa, Ont. K1P 5P8, Canada) Eds. Jean-Rene Ostiguy, Myron Laskin. illus. circ. 5,000. Indexed: RILA.
Formed by the merger of: National Gallery of Canada. Annual Review (ISSN 0078-6977) & National Gallery of Canada. Bulletin (ISSN 0027-9323)

069　　　　　　　UK
CARMARTHEN MUSEUM. PUBLICATION. 1975. irreg. £0.50. Carmarthen Museum, Abergwili, Carmarthen, Wales. Ed. C.J. Delaney. illus.

069　　　　　　　US
CARNEGIE INSTITUTE. ANNUAL REPORT. 1898. a. Carnegie Institute, 4400 Forbes Ave., Pittsburgh, PA 15213. TEL 412-622-3131. Ed. Patricia H. Snyder. circ. 2,100.

069.9　　　　　US
CARNEGIE INTERNATIONAL. a. Carnegie Institute, Museum of Art, 4400 Forbes Ave., Pittsburgh, PA 15213.

069　　　　　　　DK
CARTHA. 1982. a. Kr.50. Kerteminde Museum, Strandgade, 5300 Kerteminde, Denmark. Ed. Erland Porsmose. illus.
Formerly: Kerteminde Museum. Aarsskrift (ISSN 0109-047X)

708　　　　US　ISSN 0069-4061
CINCINNATI ART MUSEUM. BULLETIN. (Most issues are Annual Reports.) 1930; N.S. 1950. a. $5 per no. Cincinnati Art Museum, Publications Department, Eden Park, Cincinnati, OH 45202. TEL 513-721-5204. Dir. Millard F. Rogers, Jr. circ. 6,400. (also avail. in microform from UMI; reprint service avail. from UMI) Indexed: Art Ind. RILA.

708　　　　IT　ISSN 0070-0479
CORPUS VASORUM ANTIQUORUM. ITALIA. 1927. irreg. price varies. Erma di "Bretschneider", Via Cassiodoro 19, 00193 Rome, Italy. Ed. E. Mangani.

069　　　　　　　RM
CRESTEREA PATRIMONIULUI MUZEAL. 1978. irreg. Muzeul de Istorie al Republicii Socialiste Romania, Calea Victoriei 12, Bucharest, Rumania. Ed.Bd. bk. rev. illus.

069　　　　SW　ISSN 0070-2528
DAEDALUS. (Text in Swedish; occasional paper in English) 1931. a. Kr.150. Sveriges Tekniska Museum - National Museum of Science and Technology, S-115 27 Stockholm, Sweden. Ed. Jan-Erik Pettersson. adv. cum.index. circ. 5,000. Indexed: Curr.Cont. M.L.A. P.A.I.S. SSCI. Arts & Hum.Cit.Ind. Amer.Bibl.Slavic & E.Eur.Stud. Educ.Admin.Abstr. G.Soc.Sci.& Rel.Per.Lit. High.Educ.Curr.Aware.Bull. Mag.Ind.

708.1　　　　　US
DALLAS MUSEUM OF ART. ANNUAL REPORT. 1953. a. $50 includes Quarterly Bulletin and Calendar. Dallas Museum of Art, 1717 N. Harwood, Dallas, TX 75201. TEL 214-922-0220. Ed. Robert Rozelle. circ. 20,000.

708　　　　　　　US
DAYTON ART INSTITUTE. ANNUAL REPORT AND BULLETIN. 1931. a. $2.50. Dayton Art Institute, Box 941, Dayton, OH 45401. TEL 513-223-5277. Ed. Eileen Evans Carr. circ. 3,000.
Formerly (until 1984): Dayton Art Institute. Annual Report (ISSN 0070-3028)

DEINE STADT; Kunst, Kultur und Leben in Braunschweig. see ART

069　　　　DK　ISSN 0084-9308
DENMARK. NATIONALMUSEET. ARBEJDSMARKT. 1928. a. Nationalmuseet, Oplysningsafdelingen, Ny Vestergade 10, 1471 Copenhagen K, Denmark.

708.8　　　　　DK
DENMARK. NATIONALMUSEET. WORKING PAPERS. irreg. Nationalmuseet, Oplysningsafdelingen, Ny Vestergade 10, 1471 Copenhagen K, Denmark.

509　　　　GW　ISSN 0012-1339
DEUTSCHES MUSEUM. ABHANDLUNGEN UND BERICHTE. 1929. irreg. membership. R. Oldenbourg Verlag GmbH, Rosenheimer Str. 145, 8000 Munich 80, W. Germany (B.R.D.) bibl. charts. illus. circ. 7,000. Indexed: Chem.Abstr. History

707.4　　　　UK　ISSN 0267-9698
DIRECTORY OF MUSEUMS & LIVING DISPLAYS. quinquennial. Macmillan Press Ltd., 4 Little Essex St., London WC2R 3LF, England.

069 708.1　　CN　ISSN 0714-7023
DIRECTORY OF MUSEUMS, ART GALLERIES AND ARCHIVES OF BRITISH COLUMBIA. a. British Columbia Museums Association, 514 Government St., Victoria, B.C. V8V 4X4, Canada. TEL 604-387-3315. Ed. Richard A. Duckles.

069　　　　DK　ISSN 0108-3643
F R A M. (Fra Ringkoebing Amts Museer) 1982. a. Kr.68. Museumsraadet i Ringkoebing Amt, Holstebro Museum, Museumsvej 3, 7500 Holstebro, Denmark. Ed. Esben Graugaard. illus. circ. 3,000.

948　　　　DK　ISSN 0107-4849
FRA BORNHOLMS MUSEUM. 1980. a. Kr.40. Bornholms Museum, Sct. Mortensgade 29, 3700 Roenne, Denmark. Ed. Anne Vibeke Knudsen. illus.
Formerly: Nyt fra Bornholms Museum.

708.8 948.9　DK　ISSN 0106-8229
FRA BOV MUSEUM. vol. 2, 1979. a. Kr.35. Historisk Forening for Visherred, Bov Museum, Padborg, Denmark (Subscr. to: Th. Laursen, Oesterloekke 13, Bov, 6330 Padborg, Denmark)
Formerly: Fra Bov Sogns Museum.

069　　　　DK　ISSN 0105-9858
FREDERIKSBORGMUSEET. AARSSKRIFT. 1985. a. Kr.125. (Frederiksborgmuseet) Bibliotekscentralen, Telegrafvej 5, DK-2750 Ballerup, Denmark.

069　　　　IT　ISSN 0072-0070
GABINETTO DISEGNI E STAMPE DEGLI UFFIZI. CATALOGHI. 1951. irreg., no.64, 1985. price varies. Casa Editrice Leo S. Olschki, Casella Postale 66, 50100 Florence, Italy. circ. 2,000.

708　　　　GW　ISSN 0072-0089
GALERIE NIERENDORF, BERLIN. KUNSTBLAETTER. 1963. irreg., no.48, 1985. price varies. ‡ Galerie Nierendorf, Hardenbergstr. 19, 1000 Berlin 12, W. Germany (B.R.D.) Ed. Florian Karsch. circ. 2,000.

708　　　　　　　AU
GALERIE SANCT LUCAS. GEMAELDE ALTER MEISTER. 1930. a. S.350. Galerie Sanct Lucas, Josefsplatz 5, Palais Pallavicini, A-1010 Vienna, Austria. illus.

708.5　　　　　IT
GALLERIA DEL CAVALLINO. MOSTRE. 1956. a. $10 per no. Edizioni del Cavallino, San Marco 1725, 30124 Venice, Italy. Ed. Paolo Cardazzo. illus. circ. 3,000.

069　　　　YU　ISSN 0350-2929
GORISKI LETNIK. 1974. a. 400 din. Goriski Muzej, Grad Kromberk, 65000 Nova Gorica, Yugoslavia. Indexed: Hist.Abstr. Amer.Hist.& Life.

760　　　　UR　ISSN 0077-1562
GOSUDARSTVENNYI MUZEI IZOBRAZITEL'NYKH ISKUSSTV IM. PUSHKINA. SOOBSHCHENIYA. (Text in Russian; summaries in French) 1960. irreg. Gosudarstvennyi Muzei Izobrazitel'nykh Iskusstv im. Pushkina, Volkhonka 12, 121019 Moscow, Russian S.F.S.R., U.S.S.R.

708　　　　　　　UK
GREAT BRITAIN. VICTORIA AND ALBERT MUSEUM. ILLUSTRATED BOOKS. 1951. irreg. price varies. Victoria and Albert Museum, South Kensington, London S.W.7, England (Avail. from: Trefoil /V & A Book Services, 13 St. John's Hill, London SW11, England)
Formerly: Great Britain. Victoria and Albert Museum. Illustrated Booklets (ISSN 0083-5900)

708　　　　UK　ISSN 0083-5919
GREAT BRITAIN. VICTORIA AND ALBERT MUSEUM. MONOGRAPHS. irreg. price varies. Victoria and Albert Museum, South Kensington, London S.W. 7, England.

069　　　　UK　ISSN 0260-5570
HANDBOOKS IN MARITIME ARCHAEOLOGY. irreg. price varies. National Maritime Museum, Romney Rd., Greenwich SE10 9NF, England (U.S. subscr. to: Mystic Seaport Museum Stores, Mystic, CT 06355)

016.9173　　US　ISSN 0093-1047
HARRIS AUCTION GALLERIES. COLLECTORS' AUCTION. 1962. irreg. (8-10/yr.) $25. Harris Auction Galleries, Inc., 873-875 N. Howard St., Baltimore, MD 21201. TEL 301-728-7040. Eds. Barr Harris, Christopher Bready. circ. 1,000. Key Title: Collectors' Auction (Baltimore)

069　　　　DK　ISSN 0108-0393
HELSINGOER KOMMUNES MUSEER. AARBOG. 1981. a. Kr.85. Helsingoer Bymuseum, Hestemoellestraede 1, 3000 Helsingoer, Denmark. illus.
Formerly: Helsingoer Bymuseum. Aarbog.

069　　　　DK　ISSN 0106-5440
HELSINGOER SOM FOTOGRAFEN SAA DET. 1980. a. Kr.25. Helsingoer Bymuseum, Karmeliterhuset, Hestomoellestraede, 3000 Helsingoer, Denmark. illus.

069　　　　　　　US
IDAHO MUSEUM OF NATURAL HISTORY. SPECIAL PUBLICATION. no. 7, 1980. irreg. price varies. Idaho Museum of Natural History, Idaho State University, Box 8096, Pocatello, ID 83209-0009. Ed. Barry L. Keller.

069.095　　　II　ISSN 0019-5987
INDIAN MUSEUM BULLETIN. (Text in English) 1966. a. Rs.30($10) Indian Museum, Calcutta, 27 Jawaharlal Nehru Rd., Calcutta 700016, India. TEL 29-9902. Ed. Dr. R.C. Sharma. bk. rev. charts, illus. index. cum.index: 1966-1969. circ. 500. Indexed: Numis.Lit.

069.5　　　　　US
INDIANA UNIVERSITY ART MUSEUM BULLETIN. irreg. Indiana University Art Museum, Bloomington, IN 47405. TEL 812-335-5445. Ed. Linda Baden.

MUSEUMS AND ART GALLERIES

355 GW ISSN 0074-168X
INTERNATIONAL ASSOCIATION OF MUSEUMS OF ARMS AND MILITARY HISTORY. CONGRESS REPORTS. 1957. triennial., 1969, 5th, Rome, Naples, Brescia. membership. International Association of Museums of Arms and Military History, c/o Ernst Aichner, Bayerisches Armeemuseum, D-8070 Ingolstadt, Neues Schloss, Paradeplatz 4, W. Germany (B.R.D.) circ. controlled.
1981, 9th, Washington

INVENTAIRE GENERAL DES MONUMENTS ET DES RICHESSES ARTISTIQUES DE LA FRANCE. see *ARCHITECTURE*

069 IS ISSN 0333-7499
ISRAEL MUSEUM JOURNAL. (Text in English) 1965. a. $5. Israel Museum, Jerusalem, Israel. Ed.Bd. adv. charts. illus. circ. 3,000. Indexed: RILA.
Formerly: Israel Museum News (ISSN 0021-227X)

708.1 069.7 US ISSN 0021-356X
J. B. SPEED ART MUSEUM BULLETIN. 1940. irreg. (2-3/yr.) $4.50. ‡ J.B. Speed Art Museum, 2035 S. Third St., Box 8345, Louisville, KY 40208. TEL 502-636-2893. Ed. Addison Page. illus. circ. 2, 500. Indexed: RILA.

655.5 GW
JAHRBUCH DER AUKTIONSPREISE FUER BUECHER, HANDSCHRIFTEN UND AUTOGRAPHEN; Ergebnisse der Auktionen in Deutschland, Holland, Oesterreich und der Schweiz. 1950. a. DM.298. Dr. Ernst Hauswedell und Co. Verlag, Rosenberg Str. 113, D-7000 Stuttgart 1, W. Germany (B.R.D.) Ed. Ernst Hauswedell. adv. circ. 1,300. (back issues avail.)
Formerly: Jahrbuch der Auktionspreise (ISSN 0075-2193)

069 708 GW ISSN 0075-2207
JAHRBUCH DER BERLINER MUSEEN. 1959. a. price varies. (Staatliche Museen Preussischer Kulturbesitz Berlin) Gebr. Mann Verlag, Lindenstr. 76, Postfach 110303, 1000 Berlin 61, W. Germany (B.R.D.) Indexed: Curr.Cont. Arts & Hum.Cit.Ind. RILA.

069.7 700 GW ISSN 0344-712X
JAHRBUCH DER WERBUNG. 1964. a. DM.128. ECON Verlag GmbH, Kaiserwerter Strasse 282, Postfach 30 03 21, D-4000 Duesseldorf, W. Germany (B.R.D.) Eds. J.Jurgen Jeske, Eckhard Neumann, Wolfgang Sprang. adv. bk. rev. circ. 4, 000.
Formerly (until 1975): Werbung in Deutschland (ISSN 0083-8012)

069 UK ISSN 0260-9126
JOURNAL OF EDUCATION IN MUSEUMS. 1980. a. membership. Group for Education in Museums, c/o P. Dival, Kent County Museums Service, West Malling Air Station, West Malling, Kent ME19 6Q, England. illus.

069 II
JOURNAL OF INDIAN MUSEUMS.* (Text in English) a. Museums Association of India, c/o National Museum of Natural History, F I C C I, Museum Building, Barakhamba Road, New Delhi 110002, India. Indexed: Art & Archaeol.Tech.Abstr.

KAERNTNER MUSEUMSSCHRIFTEN. see *ART*

069 KE
KENYA MUSEUM SOCIETY. CHAIRMAN'S REPORT. (Text in English) a. Kenya Museum Society, c/o Kenya National Museums, Box 40658, Nairobi, Kenya. Ed. D. Chryssee.

708 GW ISSN 0075-6326
KLEINE MUSEUMSHEFTE. 1967. irreg. price varies. Rheinland-Verlag, Kennedy-Ufer 2, 5000 Cologne 21, W. Germany (B.R.D.) (Distr. by: Rudolf Habelt Verlag, Am Buchenhang 1, 5300 Bonn, W. Germany (B.R.D.))

069 DK ISSN 0107-931X
KOEGE MUSEUM. 1976. irreg. Kr.60. Koege Museum, Noerregade 4, 4600 Koege, Denmark.
Formerly: Koege Museum. Aarbog.

LAEGAEST: ARKEOLOGI I NORDLESVIG. see *ARCHAEOLOGY*

708 940 GE ISSN 0070-7201
LANDESMUSEUM FUER VORGESCHICHTE, DRESDEN. VEROEFFENTLICHUNGEN. 1952. irreg., vol.17, 1985. price varies. VEB Deutscher Verlag der Wissenschaften, Postfach 1216, 1080 Berlin, E. Germany (D.D.R.) Ed. Werner Coblenz.

708 940 GE ISSN 0072-940X
LANDESMUSEUM FUER VORGESCHICHTE, HALLE. VEROEFFENTLICHUNGEN. 1964. irreg. price varies. (Landesmuseum fuer Vorgeschichte, Halle) VEB Deutscher Verlag der Wissenschaften, Postfach 1216, 1080 Berlin, E. Germany (D.D.R.) Ed. H. Behrens.

708 069 UK
LIBRARIES YEARBOOK. 1897. biennial. £30($65) ‡ James Clarke & Co. Ltd., 7 All Saints Passage, Cambridge CB2 3LS, England. Ed. Adrian Brink. adv. index. circ. 3,500.
Formerly: Libraries, Museums and Art Galleries Year Book (ISSN 0075-899X)

LOCUS (NEW YORK) see *ART*

069 II
MAHARAJA SAWAI MAN SINGH II MEMORIAL SERIES. 1971. irreg., no. 3, 1978. Rs.40. Maharaja Sawai Man Singh II Museum, City Palace, Jaipur 302002, India. Ed. Gopal Narayan Bahura. circ. 1, 100.

069 II
MANIPUR STATE MUSEUM. BULLETIN. (Text in English) 1972. a. Rs.3. Manipur State Museum, Publications Sub-Committee, Imphal 759001, Manipur, India.

069 CN
MANITOBA MUSEUM OF MAN AND NATURE. ANNUAL REPORT. 1966. a. membership. Manitoba Museum of Man and Nature, 190 Rupert Ave., Winnipeg, Man. R3B ON2, Canada. TEL 204-956-2830. circ. 3,000.
Formerly (until 1984): Manitoba Museum of Man and Nature. Biennial Report (ISSN 0076-3888)

069 387 UK ISSN 0307-8590
MARITIME MONOGRAPHS AND REPORTS. 1970. irreg. price varies. National Maritime Museum, Romney Rd., Greenwich SE10 9NF, England (U.S. subscr. to: Mystic Seaport Museum Stores, Mystic, CT 06355) bibl. illus.

708.3 GW ISSN 0172-2115
MATERIALEN ZUR KUNST DES NEUNZEHNTEN JAHRHUNDERTS. 1971. irreg. price varies. Prestel-Verlag, Mandlstr. 26, 8000 Munich 40, W. Germany (B.R.D.)

MAURITIANA (ALTENBURG) see *SCIENCES: COMPREHENSIVE WORKS*

069 355 SW
MEDDELANDE ARMEMUSEUM. YEARBOOK. 1938. a. Kr.50. Armemuseum - Royal Army Museum, P.O.B. 14095, S-104 41 Stockholm, Sweden (Dist. by Liber Foerlag, Fack, S-162 89 Vaellingby, Sweden) Ed. Jan Von Konow. circ. 2, 000.
Formerly (until 1976): Foereningen Armemusei Vaenner. Meddelande: Kungliga Armemuseum (ISSN 0349-1048)

708 US ISSN 0077-8958
METROPOLITAN MUSEUM JOURNAL. 1968. a. $50. Metropolitan Museum of Art, Fifth Ave. and 82nd St., New York, NY 10028 (Orders to: Univeristy of Chicago Press, Box 37005, Chicago, IL 60637) Ed. M.E.D. Laing. illus. (back issues avail.) Indexed: Curr.Cont. Arts & Hum.Cit.Ind. RILA.

069 977.4 US ISSN 0076-8235
MICHIGAN STATE UNIVERSITY. MUSEUM PUBLICATIONS. CULTURAL SERIES. 1961. irreg., 1967, vol.1, no.3. price varies. ‡ Michigan State University, Museum, East Lansing, MI 48824 TEL 517-355-2370. (And Exchange Dept., MSU Library, East Lansing, MI 48824) index at end of each completed vol. circ. 1,850.

960 FR
MUSEE DE L'HOMME, PARIS. CATALOGUES. SERIE C: AFRIQUE NOIRE. (Supplement to: Objets et Mondes) 1970. irreg., no. 2, 1976. price varies. Museum Nationale d'Histoire Naturelle, Musee de l'Homme, Palais de Chaillot, Place du Trocadero, 75116 Paris, France.

900 FR
MUSEE DE L'HOMME, PARIS. CATALOGUES. SERIE H: AMERIQUE. (Supplement to: Objets et Mondes) 1963. irreg., no. 3, 1966. price varies. Museum Nationale d'Histoire Naturelle, Musee de l'Homme, Palais de Chaillot, Place du Trocadero, 75116 Paris, France.

950 FR
MUSEE DE L'HOMME, PARIS. CATALOGUES. SERIE K: ASIE. (Supplement to: Objets et Mondes) 1969. irreg., no. 2, 1972. price varies. Museum Nationale d'Histoire Naturelle, Musee de l'Homme, Palais de Chaillot, Place du Trocadero, 75116 Paris, France.

708 BE ISSN 0027-3856
MUSEES ROYAUX DES BEAUX-ARTS DE BELGIQUE. BULLETIN/KONINKLIJKE MUSEA VOOR SCHONE KUNSTEN VAN BELGIE. BULLETIN. (Text in Dutch, English, French, German, Italian and Spanish; summaries in Dutch and French) 1952. a. 600 Fr. Musees Royaux des Beaux-Arts de Belgique - Koninklijke Musea voor Schone Kunsten van Belgie, Museumstr. 9, 1000 Brussels, Belgium. Ed. Andre A. Moerman. illus. index. circ. 600. Indexed: Art Ind. RILA.

069 DK ISSN 0108-917X
MUSEET FOR HOLBAEK OG OMEGN. AARSBERETNING. 1921. a. Kr.6. Museumsforeningen for Holbaek og Omegn, Klosterstraede 14-16, 4300 Holbaek, Denmark. Ed. J.L. Oestergaard Christensen. illus. circ. 1,800.
Formerly: Museet for Holbaek og Omegn.

913 IT ISSN 0391-9293
MUSEO ARCHEOLOGICO DI TARQUINIA. MATERIALI. 1980. irreg. Giorgio Bretschneider, Via Crescenzio 43, I-00193 Rome, Italy. (back issues avail.)

708.5 IT
MUSEO BODONIANO. BOLLETTINO. 1972. irreg. L.60000 per no. Museo Bodoniano, Biblioteca Palatina, Palazzo della Pilotta, 43100 Parma, Italy. bk. rev. circ. 8,000. (also avail. in microfilm)

069 VE
MUSEO BOGGIO. CUADERNOS DE ARTE.* no. 3, 1976. irreg. Museo Emilio Boggio, Esquina las Monjas, Caracas 101, Venezuela. Ed. Peran Erminy. illus.

301.2 DR
MUSEO DEL HOMBRE DOMINICANO. SERIE CATALOGOS Y MEMORIAS. 1976. irreg., no. 13, 1982. Museo del Hombre Dominicano, Calle Pedro Henriquez Urena, Plaza de la Cultura, Santo Domingo, Dominican Republic. illus.

301.2 DR
MUSEO DEL HOMBRE DOMINICANO. SERIE MESA REDONDA. 1978. irreg. price varies. Museo del Hombre Dominicano, Calle Pedro Henriquez Urena, Plaza de la Cultura, Santo Domingo, Dominican Republic. illus.

708 IT
MUSEO DELLA CIVILTA ROMANA. STUDI E MATERIALI. 1938. irreg., no.11, 1984. price varies. Erma di "Bretschneider", Via Cassiodoro, 19, 00193 Rome, Italy.
Formerly: Museo dell'Impero Romano. Studi e Materiali (ISSN 0080-3936)

069 PE
MUSEO NACIONAL. REVISTA. 1932. a. $20. (Museo Nacional de la Cultura Peruana) Industrial Grafica S.A., Apdo.3048, Lima 100, Peru. Ed. Rosalia Avalos de Matos. circ. 1,000. Indexed: Hisp.Amer.Per.Ind.
Formerly: Museo Nacional de la Cultural Peruana. Revista.

MUSEO NACIONAL DE HISTORIA NATURAL. ANALES. see *SCIENCES: COMPREHENSIVE WORKS*

500.907　　　　　　　　CL　ISSN 0716-0224
MUSEO NACIONAL DE HISTORIA NATURAL.
PUBLICACION OCASIONAL. 1963. irreg., no.42,
1985. Museo Nacional de Historia Natural, Casilla
787, Santiago, Chile. Ed. Daniel Frassinetti Cabeza.

709.5　　　　　　　　　　　IT
MUSEO NAZIONALE D'ARTE ORIENTALE.
SCHEDE. no. 6, 1974. irreg. Museo Nazionale
d'Arte Orientale, Via Merulana 248, Rome 00185,
Italy. bibl.

069　　　　　　　　　　　IT
MUSEO NAZIONALE DI CASTEL SAN
ANGELO. QUADERNI. 1976. a. (Associazione
Amici di Castel San Angelo) De Luca Editore, Via
S. Anna 11, 00186 Rome, Italy. illus.

708.9　　　　　　　　　　　AG
MUSEO Y MONUMENTO NACIONAL "JUSTO
JOSE DE URQUIZA". SERIE 3. no. 14, 1981.
Museo y Monumento Nacional Justo Jose de
Urquiza, Palacio San Jose, Entre Rios, Argentina.

069　　　　　　　　　　　IT
MUSEOLOGIA. 1972. a. L.15000. Universita
Internazionale dell'Arte, Centro di Studi per la
Museologia, Via Incontri, 3, 50139 Florence, Italy.
(Co-sponsor: Societa di Museologia) Ed. Carlo L.
Ragghianti. adv. bk. rev.

069　　　　　　　　　　　US
MUSEOLOGY. 1975. irreg., no.7, 1986. price varies.
(Texas Tech University, Museum Science Program)
Texas Tech University Press, Box 4139, Lubbock,
TX 79409.

708　　　　　　　　BL　ISSN 0080-3111
MUSEU NACIONAL, RIO DE JANEIRO.
ARQUIVOS. (Text in Portuguese; summaries in
English) 1876. irreg., latest issue 1975. exchange
only. Museu Nacional, Quinta da Boa Vista, 20940
Rio de Janeiro, RJ, Brazil. charts. bibl. illus.
Indexed: Biol.Abstr. Rev.Appl.Entomol.

708　　　　　　　　NE　ISSN 0077-2275
MUSEUM BOYMANS-VAN BEUNINGEN.
AGENDA - DIARY. (Text in Dutch and English)
1949. a. fl.15. Museum Boymans-van Beuningen,
Mathenesserlaan 18-20, P.O. Box 2277, 3000 CG
Rotterdam, Netherlands. circ. 30,000.

MUSEUM FUER UR- UND FRUEHGESCHICHTE
DER BEZIRKE POTSDAM, FRANKFURT/
ODER UND COTTBUS.
VEROEFFENTLICHUNGEN. see HISTORY

069 398　　　　　　　GE　ISSN 0075-8663
MUSEUM FUER VOELKERKUNDE, LEIPZIG.
JAHRBUCH. irreg., vol.36, 1985. price varies.
Akademie-Verlag, Leipziger Str. 3-4, 1086 Berlin, E.
Germany (D.D.R.)

708 390　　　　　　　GE　ISSN 0075-8671
MUSEUM FUER VOELKERKUNDE, LEIPZIG.
VEROEFFENTLICHUNGEN. irreg., vol. 34, 1983.
price varies. Akademie-Verlag, Leipziger Str. 3-4,
1086 Berlin, E. Germany (D.D.R.)

500.907　　　　　　　　　FR
MUSEUM NATIONAL D'HISTOIRE
NATURELLE, PARIS. LABORATOIRE
D'ETHNOBOTANIQUE. PUBLICATIONS
DIVERSES. 1933. irreg. Museum National
d'Histoire Naturelle, Laboratoire d'Ethnobotanique,
57 rue Cuvier, 75005 Paris, France.

708　　　　　　　　SW　ISSN 0081-5691
MUSEUM OF FAR EASTERN ANTIQUITIES.
BULLETIN. 1929. a. price varies. Oestasiatiska
Museet - Museum of Far Eastern Antiquities,
Skeppsholmen, Box 16381, 103 27 Stockholm,
Sweden. Ed. Jan Wirgin. circ. 600. (back issues
avail.) Indexed: M.L.A.

069　　　　　　　　　　　AT
MUSEUM OF VICTORIA. MEMOIRS. 1906. a. plus
special issues. Aus.$20. Museum of Victoria
Council, 285-321 Russell St., Melbourne, Vic. 3000,
Australia. Ed. D. Stone. circ. 1,500. Indexed:
Geo.Abstr. Bull.Signal. Zoo.Rec. GeoRef.
 Formerly: National Museum of Victoria. Memoirs
(ISSN 0083-5986)

069　　　　　　　　AT　ISSN 0814-1819
MUSEUM OF VICTORIA. OCCASIONAL
PAPERS. 1984. irreg. Museum of Victoria Council,
285-321 Russel St., Melbourne, Vic. 3000, Australia.
Eds. Robert Edwards, Gary C.B. Poore.

069 700　　　　　　　US　ISSN 0740-0403
MUSEUM YEAR. a. $5. Museum of Fine Arts, 465
Huntington Ave., Boston, MA 02115. TEL 617-
267-9300. circ. 27,000.
 Formerly: Boston Museum of Fine Arts. Museum
Year. Annual Report.

708 059　　　　　　　UK　ISSN 0141-6723
MUSEUMS AND GALLERIES IN GREAT
BRITAIN AND IRELAND. 1955. a. £2.75. British
Leisure Publications, Windsor Court, East Grinstead
House, East Grinstead, West Sussex RH19 1XA,
England. adv. circ. 20,000.
 Formerly: Museums and Galleries (ISSN 0077-
2267)

708　　　　　　　　UN　ISSN 0077-233X
MUSEUMS AND MONUMENTS SERIES. (English,
French and Spanish editions) 1952. irreg., vol.19,
1984. price varies. Unesco, 7-9 Place de Fontenoy,
75700 Paris, France (Dist. in U.S. by: Bernan
Associates-Unipub, 4611-F Assembly Dr., Lanham,
MD 20706-4391) Indexed: GeoRef.

069　　　　　　　　UK　ISSN 0306-5332
MUSEUMS ASSOCIATION INFORMATION
SHEETS. 1970. irreg. Museums Association, 34
Bloomsbury Way, London WC1A 2SF, England.
Ed. Steve Caplin.

069　　　　　　　　AT　ISSN 0812-7883
MUSEUMS AUSTRALIA. 1983. a. Aus.$4. Museums
Association of Australia Inc, 304-328 Swanston St,
Melbourne, Vic 3000, Australia. Ed. Hayden J.
Downing. adv. circ. 1,300. (back issues avail.)

708　　　　　　　　PK　ISSN 0077-2348
MUSEUMS JOURNAL OF PAKISTAN. (Text in
English) a. Museums Association of Pakistan,
Victoria Memorial Hall, Peshawar, Pakistan.

069　　　　　　　　　　　II
MUSEUMS NEWSLETTER.* irreg. Museums
Association of India, c/o National Museum of
Natural History, F I C C I, Museum Building,
Barakhamba Road, New Delhi 110002, India.

069 708　　　　　　　　　GW
MUSEUMS OF THE WORLD/MUSEEN DER
WELT. (Text in English) 1973. irreg., 3rd edt.,
1981. price varies. K.G. Saur Verlag KG,
Poessenbacherstr. 12 B, Postfach 711009, 8000
Munich 71, W. Germany (B.R.D.) (U.S. and
Canadian subscr. to: K.G. Saur Inc., 175 Fifth Ave.,
New York, N.Y. 10010) adv. (reprint service avail.
from UMI, ISI)

069　　　　　　　　UK　ISSN 0307-7675
MUSEUMS YEARBOOK. (Including a Directory of
Museums and Art Galleries of the British Isles)
1956. a. £22 to non-members. Museums
Association, 34 Bloomsbury Way, London WC1A
2SF, England. Ed. Steve Caplin. circ. 1,800.
 Formerly: Museums Calendar (ISSN 0580-2652)

069　　　　　　　　DK　ISSN 0109-5854
MUSEUMSFORENINGEN FOR LAESOE.
LITTERATURE. 1983. a. Kr.20. Laesoe Museum,
Museumsforeningen for Laesoe, Oesterby Skole,
9960 Oesterby Havn, Denmark. Ed. Michael Teisen.
circ. 500.

MUZEJSKI VJESNIK/MUSEUM NEWS
MAGAZINE. see ARCHAEOLOGY

708　　　　　　　　　　　RM
MUZEUL NATIONAL. (Text in Rumanian;
summaries in English, French) 1974. a. Muzeul de
Istorie al Republicii Socialiste Romania, Calea
Victoriei Nr.12, Bucharest, Rumania. Ed.Bd. bk. rev.
illus. Indexed: Numis.Lit.

069　　　　　　　　　　　RM
MUZEUL SI EDUCATIA SOCIALISTA. 1977. irreg.
Muzeul de Istorie al Republicii Socialiste Romania,
Calea Victoriei 12, Bucharest, Rumania. Ed.Bd.

MUZEUM LITERATURY IM. ADAMA
MICKIEWICZA. BLOK-NOTES. see
LITERATURE

069　　　　　　　　PL　ISSN 0509-6936
MUZEUM NARODOWE W WARSZAWIE.
ROCZNIK/MUSEE NATIONAL DE VARSOVIE.
ANNUAIRE. (Text in French, Polish; summaries in
French, Russian) 1938. a. Muzeum Narodowe w
Warszawie, Al. Jerozolimskie 3, Warsaw, Poland.
Ed.Bd. circ. 575. (back issues avail.)

600 069　　　　　　　　　CS
NARODNI TECHNICKE MUZEUM.
CATALOGUES OF COLLECTIONS. (Text in
English) 1956. irreg. exchange basis. Narodni
Technicke Muzeum, Kostelni 42, 170 78 Prague 7,
Czechoslovakia.

NATIONAL GALLERY, LONDON. TECHNICAL
BULLETIN. see ART

354.689　　　　　　　　　RH
NATIONAL GALLERY OF ZIMBABWE.
ANNUAL REPORT AND BALANCE SHEET
AND INCOME AND EXPENDITURE
ACCOUNT. 1953. a. free. National Gallery of
Zimbabwe, Box 8155, Causeway, Harare, Zimbabwe.
illus. circ. 400.
 Former titles: National Gallery of Zimbabwe-
Rhodesia. Annual Report and Balance Sheet and
Income and Expenditure Account; National Gallery
of Rhodesia. Annual Report and Balance Sheet and
Income and Expenditure Account.

069 387　　　　　　　UK　ISSN 0141-1268
NATIONAL MARITIME MUSEUM.
OCCASIONAL LECTURES SERIES. 1978. irreg.
price varies. National Maritime Museum, Romney
Rd., Greenwich SE10 9NF, England. illus. Indexed:
Br.Archaeol.Abstr.

069　　　　　　　　　　　JA
NATIONAL MUSEUM OF MODERN ART.
ANNUAL REPORT. (Text in English and
Japanese) 1957. a. National Museum of Modern
Art, Tokyo, 3 Kitanomaru Koen, Chiyoda- ku,
Tokyo 102, Japan. Ed. Shigeo Chiba. circ. 1,000.

069　　　　　　　　NZ　ISSN 0110-9464
NATIONAL MUSEUM OF NEW ZEALAND.
BULLETIN. (Text and summaries in English) 1905.
irreg. National Museum of New Zealand, Buckle
Street, Wellington, New Zealand. Ed. P.J.
Brownsey. Indexed: Biol.Abstr.

069　　　　　　　　NZ　ISSN 0110-1447
NATIONAL MUSEUM OF NEW ZEALAND.
MISCELLENAEOUS SERIES. (Text in English)
1976. irreg. National Museum of New Zealand,
Buckle Street, Wellington, New Zealand. Ed. P.J.
Brownsey.

069　　　　　　　　NZ　ISSN 0110-943X
NATIONAL MUSEUM OF NEW ZEALAND
RECORDS. 1975. irreg. price varies. National
Museum of New Zealand, Board of Trustees, Buckle
Street, Wellington, New Zealand. Ed. P.J.
Brownsey. bk. rev. bibl. charts. illus. circ. 350.
Indexed: Biol.Abstr.
 Supersedes: Dominion Museum Records;
Dominion Museum Records in Ethnology.

708　　　　　　　　TZ　ISSN 0082-1675
NATIONAL MUSEUM OF TANZANIA. ANNUAL
REPORT. 1966. a. National Museum of Tanzania,
Box 511, Dar es Salaam, Tanzania. circ. 1,100.

708　　　　　　　　PH　ISSN 0076-3756
NATIONAL MUSEUM OF THE PHILIPPINES.
ANNUAL REPORT. (Text in English) 1966/67. a.
free. National Museum of the Philippines, Rizal
Park, Manila, Philippines. Ed. Rosario B. Tantoco.
circ. controlled. (processed)

069　　　　　　　　　　　UK
NATIONAL MUSEUM OF WALES. ANNUAL
REPORT. (Text in English, Welsh) 1907. a. 25p.
plus postage. National Museum of Wales, Cathays
Park, Cardiff CF1 3NP, Wales. Ed. D.A. Bassett.
circ. 1,000.

708　　　　　　　　US　ISSN 0077-7919
NEVADA. STATE MUSEUM, CARSON CITY.
OCCASIONAL PAPERS. 1968. irreg., no.4, 1980.
price varies. Nevada State Museum, Department of
Anthropology, Capitol Complex, Carson City, NV
89701. circ. 1,000.

MUSEUMS AND ART GALLERIES

708 US ISSN 0077-7927
NEVADA. STATE MUSEUM, CARSON CITY. POPULAR SERIES. 1965. irreg., no.20, 1987. price varies. Nevada State Museum, Department of Anthropology, Capitol Complex, Carson City, NV 89701. TEL 702-855-4217. Ed.Bd. circ. 1,000.

069 US
NEW YORK (CITY). MUSEUM OF THE CITY OF NEW YORK. ANNUAL REPORT. 1923. a. free. ‡ Museum of the City of New York, Fifth Ave. and 103 St., NY 10029. TEL 212-534-1672. Ed. Joseph P. Wells. charts. illus. circ. 5,000.
  Supersedes (1970?-1982): New York (City). Museum of the City of New York. Bulletin.

708 SZ ISSN 0067-4311
OEFFENTLICHE KUNSTSAMMLUNG. JAHRESBERICHT. 1904. irreg., latest 1977. price varies. ‡ Oeffentliche Kunstsammlung, Kunstmuseum Basel, St. Albangraben 16, CH-4010 Basel, Switzerland. Ed. Paul H. Boerlin.

708.1 AU ISSN 0029-909X
OESTERREICHISCHE GALERIE. MITTEILUNGEN. 1957. a. S.90. Oesterreichische Galerie, Postfach 12, A-1037 Vienna, Austria. Ed.Bd. illus. circ. 1,000. (tabloid format)

069 US ISSN 0090-6700
OFFICIAL MUSEUM DIRECTORY. 1961. a. $103 to non-members; members $76; institutions $89. (American Association of Museums) National Register Publishing Co. Inc., 3004 Glenview Rd., Wilmette, IL 60091. TEL 312-256-6067. Ed. Robert Weicherding. adv. abstr. circ. 4,000.

708 NE
ORANJE-NASSAU MUSEUM. JAARBOEK. a. fl.29.50. (Vereniging "Oranje-Nassau Museum") Walburg Pers, Zaadmarkt 84a-86, Box 222, 7200 AE Zutphen, Netherlands. TEL 05750-10522.

069 JA ISSN 0389-8105
OSAKA MUSEUM OF NATURAL HISTORY. ANNUAL REPORT. (Text in Japanese) 1964. biennial. Osaka Museum of Natural History, Nagai Park, Higashisumiyoshi-ku, Osaka 546, Japan. Ed. Fusato Ogawa. circ. 1,200.

069.097 US ISSN 0031-0158
EL PALACIO. 1913. triennial. $12. Museum of New Mexico, Box 2087-B, Santa Fe, NM 87504. TEL 505-827-6794. Ed. Sarah Nestor. bk. rev. bibl. charts. illus. index. circ. 3,000. Indexed: M.L.A.

069 500 US ISSN 0079-0354
PEARCE-SELLARDS SERIES. 1963. irreg., no.39, 1983. Texas Memorial Museum, University of Texas at Austin, 2400 Trinity, Austin, TX 78705. TEL 512-471-1604. Ed. Georg Zappler. (reprint service avail. from UMI) Indexed: Biol.Abstr.

069 US ISSN 0730-5435
PERCEPTIONS (INDIANAPOLIS); a scholarly publication of the Indianapolis Museum of Art. 1981. a. Indianapolis Museum of Art, 1200 W. 38th St., Indianapolis, IN 46208. TEL 317-923-1331. Ed. Robert A. Yassin. illus. circ. 1,500. Indexed: RILA.

708.1 US ISSN 0031-7160
PHAROS. 1963. a. membership. Museum of Fine Arts, St. Petersburg, 255 Beach Drive N., St. Petersburg, FL 33701. TEL 813-896-2667. Ed. Diane Lesko. illus. circ. 3,300. Indexed: RILA.

069.5 US ISSN 8755-2035
PORTICUS. 1978. a. $2.25. University of Rochester, Memorial Art Gallery, 490 University Ave., Rochester, NY 14607. Ed. Susan Dodge Peters. circ. 1,500. (back issues avail.) Indexed: Art Ind. RILA.

069 708 AT
QUEEN VICTORIA MUSEUM AND ART GALLERY. ANNUAL REPORT. 1902. a. free. Queen Victoria Museum and Art Gallery, c/o Kay Dimmack, Wellington St., Launceston, Tas. 7250, Australia. Ed. C.B. Tassell. circ. 500.

069 708 500 AT ISSN 0085-5278
QUEEN VICTORIA MUSEUM AND ART GALLERY. LAUNCESTON, TASMANIA. RECORDS. 1942. irreg., no.89, 1985. price varies. Queen Victoria Museum and Art Gallery, c/o Kaye Dimmack, Wellington Street, Launceston, Tasmania 7250, Australia. Ed. C.B. Tassell. circ. 500. Indexed: Biol.Abstr. GeoRef.

069.7 AT ISSN 0079-8835
QUEENSLAND MUSEUM, BRISBANE. MEMOIRS. 1912. a. price varies. ‡ Queensland Museum, Gregory Terrace, Fortitude Valley, Brisbane 4006, Australia. Eds. R.E. Molnar, P. Davie. circ. 650. Indexed: Biol.Abstr. Aus.Sci.Ind. Zoo.Rec. GeoRef. Rev.Appl.Entomol.

069 708 US
R C H A TECHNICAL INFORMATION SHEET. 1971. irreg. $12.50 to individuals; institutions $20 (includes: R C H A Newsletter) Regional Council of Historical Agencies, 1509 Park St., Syracuse, NY 13208. TEL 315-475-1525. Ed. Jackie Day. bibl. (tabloid format; back issues avail.)

708 CN ISSN 0035-7154
R.L.C.'S MUSEUM GAZETTE. 1966. irreg. Richard L. Coulton, Ed. & Pub., Bentley, Alberta T0C 0J0, Canada. adv. bk. rev. abstr. charts. tr.lit. cum.index. circ. 400. (processed)

069.5 US
REDDING MUSEUM. OCCASIONAL PAPERS. 1980. irreg. $10. Redding Museum and Art Center, Box 427, Redding, CA 96099. TEL 916-243-4994. Eds. James Dotta, Margaret Kardell. circ. 1,000.

069 AG
REVISTA DEL MUSEO AMERICANISTA. 1969. a. Museo Americanista de Antropologia, Historia, Numismatica y Ciencias Naturales, Manuel Castro 254, Lomas de Zamora, Buenos Aires, Argentina.

069 DK ISSN 0107-928X
ROMU. 1980. a. Kr.60. Roskilde Museum, Sct. Olsgade 17, 4000 Roskilde, Denmark. Eds. Flemming Rasmussen and Frank Birkebaek. illus. circ. 1,000.

069 NE
ROTTERDAM. DIENST GEMEENTELIJKE MUSEA. JAARVERSLAG. 1975. a. Dienst Gemeentelijke Musea, Clandstraat 7, P.O. Box 23053, 3001 KB Rotterdam, Netherlands. circ. 1,000.

708 CN ISSN 0082-5115
ROYAL ONTARIO MUSEUM. ANNUAL REPORT. 1949/50. a. free. Royal Ontario Museum, Publication Services, 100 Queen's Park, Toronto, Ont. M5S 2C6, Canada. TEL 416-586-5581.

069 II ISSN 0304-8152
SALAR JUNG MUSEUM. ANNUAL REPORT. (Text in English or Hindi) a. Salar Jung Museum, Hyderabad 500002, Andhra Pradesh, India.

500.907 US
SANTA BARBARA MUSEUM OF NATURAL HISTORY. OCCASIONAL PAPERS. 1932. irreg., no.11, 1981. price varies. Santa Barbara Museum of Natural History, 2559 Puesta del Sol Road, Santa Barbara, CA 93105. TEL 805-682-4711.

069 US
SCHOHARIE MUSEUM OF THE IROQUOIS INDIAN. MUSEUM NOTES. 1981. irreg., vol.6, 1986. $12. Schoharie Museum of the Iroquois Indian, Box 158, North Main St., Schoharie, NY 12157. TEL 518-295-8553. Ed. John P. Ferguson. circ. 500.

SEFUNIM. see ARCHAEOLOGY

069 BP
SOLOMON ISLANDS MUSEUM ASSOCIATION. JOURNAL. 1975. a. (Solomon Islands Museum Association) Solomon Islands Government Printing, Box 313, Honiara, British Solomon Islands.

574 500.907 US
SONORENSIS. ANNUAL REPORT. 1957. a. membership. ‡ Arizona-Sonora Desert Museum, Inc., 2021 N. Kinney Rd., Tucson, AZ 85743. TEL 602-833-1380.
  Formerly: Arizona-Sonora Desert Museum. Annual Report.

069 US ISSN 0073-4985
SOUTHERN ILLINOIS UNIVERSITY. UNIVERSITY MUSEUM STUDIES. 1968. irreg., no. 11, 1977. price varies. ‡ Southern Illinois University, Carbondale, University Museum, Carbondale, IL 62901. TEL 618-453-5388.

SPORVEJSMUSEET SKJOLDENAESHOLM. AARSBERETNING. see TRANSPORTATION — Railroads

709 GW ISSN 0075-5133
STAATLICHE KUNSTHALLE KARLSRUHE. BILDHEFTE. 1958. irreg. price varies. Staatliche Kunsthalle Karlsruhe, Hans-Thoma-Str. 2, 7500 Karlsruhe, W. Germany (B.R.D.)

709 GW ISSN 0075-5141
STAATLICHE KUNSTHALLE KARLSRUHE. GRAPHIK-SCHRIFTENREIHE. 1933. irreg. price varies. Staatliche Kunsthalle Karlsruhe, Hans Thoma-Str. 2, 7500 Karlsruhe, W. Germany (B.R.D.)

709 GW ISSN 0067-284X
STAATLICHE KUNSTSAMMLUNGEN IN BADEN-WUERTTEMBERG. JAHRBUCH. 1964. a. DM.60. Deutscher Kunstverlag GmbH, Vohburger Str. 1, 8000 Munich 21, W. Germany (B.R.D.) circ. 600. Indexed: RILA.

STAATLICHE MUSEEN ZU BERLIN. JAHRBUCH. FORSCHUNGEN UND BERICHTE. see ART

708 301.2 GE ISSN 0070-7295
STAATLICHES MUSEUM FUER VOELKERKUNDE DRESDEN. ABHANDLUNGEN UND BERICHTE. 1881. irreg., vol.42, 1986. price varies. Akademie-Verlag, Leipziger Str. 3-4, 1086 Berlin, E. Germany (D.D.R.) bk. rev.
  Supersedes (from vol. 21, 1962): Staatliches Museum fuer Voelkerkunde und Tierkunde. Abhandlungen und Berichte.

069 GW ISSN 0078-2777
STADTBIBLIOTHEK NUERNBERG. AUSSTELLUNGSKATALOG. 1955. irreg., vol. 95, 1984. Stadtbibliothek, Egidienplatz 23, 8500 Nuernberg 2, W. Germany (B.R.D.)

069.5 US
STANFORD ART BOOKS. 1964. irreg. (approx. a) price varies. Stanford University, Stanford Museum, Art Department, Stanford, CA 94305. TEL 415-723-4177.

708 US ISSN 0085-6665
STANFORD MUSEUM. 1971. biennial. $5. Stanford University, Stanford Museum, Art Department, Stanford, CA 94305. TEL 415-723-4177. Eds. Betsy G. Fryberger, Carol M. Osborne. circ. 3,000. Indexed: RILA.

069 NO ISSN 0333-0656
STAVANGER MUSEUM. AARBOK. (Summaries in English) 1890. a. Kr.100. Stavanger Museum, 4000 Stavanger, Norway. Indexed: Br.Archaeol.Abstr.

069 NO ISSN 0333-0664
STAVANGER MUSEUM. SKRIFTER. (Text in Norwegian; summaries in English) 1920. irreg., vol.11, 1985. Stavanger Museum, 4000 Stavanger, Norway. illus.

069 HU ISSN 0133-3046
STUDIA COMITATENSIA. (Text in Hungarian; summaries in English, German, and Russian) 1972. a. exchange basis. Pest Megyei Muzeumok Igazgatosaga, Studia Comitatensia - Direction of Pest County Museums, Fo ter 6, H-2000 Szentendre, Hungary. Ed. Nandor Ikvai. illus.

STUDIA DO DZIEJOW DAWNEGO UZBROJENIA I UBIORU WOJSKOWEGO. see MILITARY

069 II ISSN 0081-8259
STUDIES IN MUSEOLOGY. (Text in English) 1965. a. Rs.10($2.) Maharaja Sayajirao University of Baroda, Department of Museology, Sayaji Park, Baroda 390002, Gujarat, India. Ed. V. H. Bedekar. bk. rev. circ. 400.

STUDII SI CERCETARI DE ISTORIA ARTEI. SERIA ARTA PLASTICA. see ART

708 069 SW
SWEDEN. NATIONALMUSEI SKRIFTSERIE. 1954. irreg., no. 18, 1979. price varies. Nationalmusei - National Museum, Box 16176, 103 24 Stockholm, Sweden. Ed. Per Bjurstroem. adv. circ. 2,500.
  Formerly (until 1984): Sweden. Nationalmuseum. Skriftserie (ISSN 0081-5683)

708.9 MG
TALOHA. (Text in French and Malagasy) 1965. irreg., latest no.10, 1987. FMG.3600. Universite de Madagascar, Musee d'Art et d'Archeologie, B.P. 564 Isoraka, Antananarivo, Malagasy Republic.

060 US ISSN 0082-3074
TEXAS MEMORIAL MUSEUM. BULLETIN. 1960. irreg., no.32, 1984. price varies. Texas Memorial Museum, University of Texas at Austin, 2400 Trinity, Austin, TX 78705. TEL 512-471-1604. Ed. Georg Zappler. (reprint service avail. from UMI) Indexed: Biol.Abstr. GeoRef.

069 500 US ISSN 0082-3082
TEXAS MEMORIAL MUSEUM. MISCELLANEOUS PAPERS. 1968. irreg., no. 6, 1981. price varies. Texas Memorial Museum, University of Texas at Austin, 2400 Trinity, Austin, TX 78705. TEL 512-471-1604. Ed. Georg Zappler. (reprint service avail. from UMI) Indexed: Biol.Abstr. GeoRef.
Reprint series

060 US
TEXAS MEMORIAL MUSEUM. MUSEUM NOTES. 1938. irreg., no. 12, 1974. price varies. Texas Memorial Museum, University of Texas at Austin, 2400 Trinity, Austin, TX 78705. TEL 512-471-1604. Ed. Georg Zappler. (reprint service avail. from UMI)

069 US ISSN 0149-175X
TEXAS TECH UNIVERSITY. MUSEUM. OCCASIONAL PAPERS. 1971. irreg. (approx. 10/yr), no.107,1986. $19. Texas Tech University Press, University Library, Lubbock, TX 79409. TEL 806-742-1569. Indexed: Biol.Abstr. GeoRef.

069 500 US ISSN 0149-1768
TEXAS TECH UNIVERSITY. MUSEUM. SPECIAL PUBLICATIONS. 1972. irreg., no.25, 1986. price varies. (Texas Tech University) Texas Tech University Press, Box 4240, Lubbock, TX 79409. TEL 806-742-1569. circ. 1,200. (back issues avail.) Indexed: Biol.Abstr.

709 DK ISSN 0085-7262
THORVALDSENS MUSEUM. MEDDELELSER. (Text in Danish; summaries in English, French, German) 1917. irreg., latest 1982. price varies. Thorvaldsens Museum, Porthusgade 2, 1213 Copenhagen K, Denmark. illus. index. circ. 1,200.

069 SZ
THURGAUISCHE MUSEUM. MITTEILUNGEN. 1946. irreg., latest 1974. 3 Fr. Thurgauische Museumsgesellschaft, CH-8500 Frauenfeld, Switzerland. Ed. H. Guhl-Widmer.

069 AU
TIROLER LANDESMUSEUM FERDINANDEUM, INNSBRUCK. VEROEFFENTLICHUNGEN. 1825. a. S.300. Tiroler Landesmuseum Ferdinandeum, Museumstr. 15, A-6010 Innsbruck, Austria. Ed. Dr. Josef Ladurner. circ. 400.

069 SA ISSN 0496-1102
TRANSVAAL MUSEUM. BULLETIN. 1955. irreg., no.21, 1985. price varies. Transvaal Museum, Box 413, Pretoria, Transvaal, South Africa. Indexed: Biol.Abstr. Art & Archaeol.Tech.Abstr.

069 SA ISSN 0255-0172
TRANSVAAL MUSEUM. MONOGRAPHS. 1983. irreg., no.5, 1986. Transvaal Museum, Box 413, Pretoria, South Africa. Ed. D. Dippenaar.

069.9 BL
UNIVERSIDADE DE SAO PAULO. MUSEU PAULISTA. COLECAO. SERIE DE MOBILIARIO. irreg. Universidade de Sao Paulo, Museu Paulista, Caixa Posta 42503, Parque da Independencia, 04263 Sao Paulo, Brazil. Ed. Setembrino Petri.
Supersedes in part (since 1975): Museu Paulista. Colecao (ISSN 0080-6382)

069 US ISSN 0093-7436
UNIVERSITY OF ALASKA MUSEUM. ANNUAL REPORT. a. University of Alaska Museum, 907 Yukon Dr., Fairbanks, AK 99775-1200. TEL 907-474-7505. circ. controlled.

708 US ISSN 0270-1642
UNIVERSITY OF MICHIGAN. MUSEUMS OF ART AND ARCHAEOLOGY. BULLETIN. 1978. a. $5. University of Michigan Museum of Art, Alumni Memorial Hall, 525 S. State St., Ann Arbor, MI 48109. TEL 313-764-0395. (Co-sponsors: Kelsey Museum of Archaeology, Department of the History of Art) Eds. Marvin Eisenberg, Lauren Arnold. circ. 500. Indexed: RILA.
Supersedes (N.S. 1965-1977): University of Michigan. Museum of Art. Bulletin (ISSN 0076-8391)

708 US ISSN 0077-8583
UNIVERSITY OF NEW MEXICO ART MUSEUM. BULLETIN. 1965/66. a. $5. University of New Mexico, Art Museum, College of Fine Arts, Albuquerque, NM 87131. TEL 505-277-4001. Ed. Susan Corbin. circ. 1,000. Indexed: RILA.

708 CN ISSN 0083-5161
VANCOUVER ART GALLERY. ANNUAL REPORT. 1932. a. free. Vancouver Art Gallery, 750 Hornby St., Vancouver, B. C. V6Z 2H7, Canada. TEL 604-682-5621. circ. 9,000.

069 SW ISSN 0083-5536
VARBERGS MUSEUM. AARSBOK. 1950. a. Kr.35. Hallands Laensmuseer, 432 00 Varberg, Sweden. Ed. Bengt-Arne Person. adv. bk. rev.

954.9 069 BG
VARENDRA RESEARCH MUSEUM. JOURNAL. (Text in English) 1972. a. Tk.15($3) Varendra Research Museum, University of Rajshahi, Rajshahi, Bangladesh.

069.5 US
VISTAS. 1979. irreg. price varies. V.O.L.N. Press, Box 93, Merion Station, Montgomery County, PA 19066. Ed. Violette de Mazia. circ. 2,000.

600 NO ISSN 0048-2277
VOLUND. Represents: Norsk Teknisk Museum. Yearbook. (Text in Norwegian; summaries in English) 1953. a. Kr.60. ‡ Norsk Teknisk Museum - Norwegian Museum of Science and Industry, Kjelsaasveien 141, 0491 Oslo 4, Norway. TEL 02-22-52-50. Ed. Torleif Lindtveit. adv. bk. rev. illus. circ. 2,500.

090 CS
VYROCNE SPRAVY O CINNOSTI SLOVENSKYCH MUZEI A GALERTI. 1966. a. free. Ustredna Sprava Muzei a Galerii, Lodna 2, 815 77 Bratislava, Czechoslovakia. Ed.Bd.
Former titles: Ustredna Sprava Muzei a Galerii. Vyrocne Spravy o Cinnosti Slovenskych Muzei; Slovenske Narodne Muzeum. Muzeologicky Kabinet. Vyrocne Spravy o Cinnosti Slovenskych Muzei.

069 708 AT ISSN 0312-3162
WESTERN AUSTRALIAN MUSEUM. RECORDS. 1974. irreg. Aus.$7.50. Western Australian Museum, Francis St., Perth, WA 6000. Ed.Bd. circ. 150. Indexed: Biol.Abstr. Aus.Sci.Ind.
Formerly: Western Australia. Public Library, Museum and Art Gallery. Record.

069 AT ISSN 0313-122X
WESTERN AUSTRALIAN MUSEUM. RECORDS. SUPPLEMENT. 1975. irreg. Aus.$7.50. Western Australian Museum, Francis St., Perth, W.A. 6000, Australia. Indexed: Biol.Abstr. Aus.Sci.Ind.

069 AT
WESTERN AUSTRALIAN MUSEUM, PERTH. ANNUAL REPORT. a. Western Australian Museum, Perth, W.A., Australia. Indexed: GeoRef.
Formerly: Western Australia Museum, Perth. Report of the Museum Board (ISSN 0083-8721)

069 US
WHITNEY MUSEUM OF AMERICAN ART. BULLETIN. 1978. a. membership. Whitney Museum of American Art, 945 Madison Ave., New York, NY 10021. TEL 212-570-3657. Ed. Sheila Schwartz. circ. 5,000. (back issues avail.)

708 US ISSN 0511-8824
WHITNEY REVIEW. 1960/61. a. $2. Whitney Museum of American Art, 945 Madison Ave. at 75 St., New York, NY 10021. TEL 212-570-3600.

WHO'S WHO IN AMERICAN ART. see
BIOGRAPHY

069 US
WILLIAM HAMMOND MATHERS MUSEUM. OCCASIONAL PAPERS AND MONOGRAPHS. 1974. irreg. Indiana University, William Hammond Mathers Museum, 601 E. Eighth St., Bloomington, IN 47405. TEL 812-335-7224.
Formerly: Indiana University Museum. Occasional Papers and Monographs.

708.1 US ISSN 0193-9564
WORCESTER ART MUSEUM. JOURNAL. 1979. a. $6. Worcester Art Museum, 55 Salisbury St., Worcester, MA 01609-3196. Ed. Anne P. Gibson. illus. circ. 3,000. Indexed: RILA.
Supersedes (1935-1979): Worcester Art Museum Bulletin; Which was formerly titled: Worcester Art Museum. News Bulletin and Calendar (ISSN 0043-7891)

708 US ISSN 0084-3539
YALE UNIVERSITY ART GALLERY. BULLETIN. 1926. irreg. (2-3/yr.) $3.50 per no. Yale University Art Gallery, 2006 Yale Sta., New Haven, CT 06520. TEL 203-432-0602. Ed. Caroline Rollins. circ. 2,100. (also avail. in microform from UMI; reprint service avail. from UMI) Indexed: Artbibl. RILA. Key Title: Bulletin - Yale University Art Gallery.
Formerly: Yale Art Gallery Bulletin (ISSN 0360-3180)

069 708 IS ISSN 0334-1798
YISRAEL-AM VE'ERETZ. 1984. a. Haaretz Museum, P.O. Box 17068, Ramat Aviv, Tel Aviv, Israel. TEL 03-415244.

708 ZA ISSN 0084-4977
ZAMBIA. NATIONAL MUSEUMS BOARD. REPORT. a. K.1.00. National Museums Board, Livingstone Museum, Box 498, Livingstone, Zambia.

069 ZA
ZAMBIA MUSEUMS JOURNAL. 1970. irreg. K.8. National Museums Board, Livingstone Museum, Box 60498, Livingstone, Zambia. Eds. N. Mataa, M. Mukela. circ. 500.

MUSEUMS AND ART GALLERIES — Abstracting, Bibliographies, Statistics

060 US
CATALOG OF MUSEUM PUBLICATIONS AND MEDIA; a directory and index of publications and audiovisuals available from U.S. and Canadian institutions. 1972. irreg., latest edt. 1980. $265. Gale Research Company, Book Tower, Detroit, MI 48226. TEL 313-961-2242. Eds. Paul Wasserman, Esther Herman. index.
Former titles: Museum Catalog of Publications and Media; Museum Media.

069.5 011 II
CONCISE DESCRIPTIVE CATALOGUE OF ARABIC MANUSCRIPTS IN THE SALAR JUNG MUSEUM AND LIBRARY. (Text in English) 1957. irreg., vol. 4, 1981. price varies. Salar Jung Museum, Hyderabad 500002, Andhra Pradesh, India.
Formerly: Catalogue of Arabic Manuscripts in Salar Jung Museum.

069.5 011 II
CONCISE DESCRIPTIVE CATALOGUE OF THE PERSIAN MANUSCRIPTS IN THE SALAR JUNG MUSEUM AND LIBRARY. (Text in English) 1965. irreg., vol.8, 1983. price varies. Salar Jung Museum, Hyderabad 500002, Andhra Pradesh, India. illus.
Formerly: Catalogue of Persian Manuscripts in Salar Jung Museum.

069.5 011 II
CONCISE DESCRIPTIVE CATALOGUE OF THE URDU MANUSCRIPTS IN THE SALAR JUNG MUSEUM AND LIBRARY. (Text in Urdu) 1957 irreg. Rs.3($1.50) Salar Jung Museum, Hyderabad 500002, Andhra Pradesh, India. illus.
Formerly: Catalogue of Urdu Manuscripts in Salar Jung Museum.

778.5   US
FILM PROGRAMMER'S GUIDE TO 16MM RENTALS. 1972. irreg., 3rd edt., 1980. Foundation for Open Company, Reel Research, Box 6037, Albany, CA 94706. TEL 415-549-0923. Ed. Kathleen Weaver. adv. bibl. circ. 5,000.

708 010   AU
OESTERREICHISCHES MUSEUM FUER VOLKSKUNDE. KATALOGE. 1946. irreg. price varies. Verlag Ferdinand Berger und Soehne OHG, Wiener Str. 21-23, A-3580 Horn, Austria.

069 016   CS
SELECTED BIBLIOGRAPHY OF MUSEOLOGICAL LITERATURE. (Text in English) 1970. a. exchange basis. Ustredna Sprava Muzei a Galerii, Lodna 2, 815 77 Bratislava, Czechoslovakia. Eds. Milan Rybecky, Viera Schnappova. index.
Formerly: Bibliographical Selection of Museological Literature (ISSN 0067-6861)

016   CS
VYBEROVA BIBLIOGRAFIA MUZEOLOGICKEJ LITERATURY. 1962. a. exchange basis. Ustredna Sprava Muzei a Galerii, Lodna 2, 815 77 Bratislava, Czechoslovakia. Eds. Milan Rybecky, Viera Schnappova.

MUSIC

see also Dance; Sound Recording and Reproduction

780.42   CN   ISSN 0704-6138
A C M E NEWSLETTER. 1976. irreg. free. Academy of Country Music Entertainment, 9312 150 Ave., Edmonton, Alta. T5E 2N8, Canada. illus.

780   US
A I M S BULLETIN. 1969. biennial. $10. American Institute of Musical Studies, 2701 Fondren Dr., Dallas, TX 75206. TEL 214-691-6451. Ed. George Tepping. illus. circ. 10,000.

780 800 070.5 920   US
A S C A P BIOGRAPHICAL DICTIONARY.* irreg., 4th edt. 1980. $41.95. American Society of Composers, Authors and Publishers, 1 Lincoln Plaza, New York, NY 10023. Indexed: Child.Auth.& Illus. Perf.Arts Biog.Master Ind.

780   US
A S U C JOURNAL OF MUSIC SCORES. Variant title: Journal of Music Scores. 1973. irreg. (2-3/yr.) price varies. (American Society of University Composers) European American Music Corporation, Box 850, Valley Forge, PA 19482-0650. TEL 215-648-0506. Ed. Bruce Taub. circ. 175. Indexed: Music Ind.

ABHANDLUNGEN ZUR KUNST-, MUSIK- UND LITERATURWISSENSCHAFT. see *ART*

780   IT
ACCADEMIA DEI CONCORDI ROVIGO. COLLANA DI MUSICHE. no.12, 1977. irreg. price varies. Giardini Editori e Stampatori, Via Santa Bibbiana 28, 56100 Pisa, Italy.

786.5   GW   ISSN 0567-7874
ACTA ORGANOLOGICA. 1967. a. (Gesellschaft der Orgelfreunde e.V.) Verlag Merseburger Berlin GmbH, Motz Str. 13, 3500 Kassel, W. Germany (B.R.D.) illus. Indexed: RILM.

780   GW   ISSN 0001-6942
ACTA SAGITTARIANA. (Text in English, French and German) 1963. a. membership. Internationale Heinrich Schuetz-Gesellschaft e.V., Heinrich-Schuetz-Allee 35, 3500 Kassel-Wilhelmshoehe, W. Germany (B.R.D.) Ed. Sieglinde Froehlich-Spillner. adv. bk. rev. illus. circ. 1,500. Indexed: Music Ind.

780   US
AESTHETICS IN MUSIC SERIES. 1983. irreg., no.4, 1986. Pendragon Press, R.R. 1, Box 159, Stuyvesant, NY 12173-9720.

780   SA   ISSN 0065-4019
AFRICAN MUSIC. (Text in English and French) 1954. irreg. (approx. a.) R.10($15) International Library of African Music, Institute of Social and Economic Research, Rhodes University, Grahamstown 6140, South Africa. Ed. Andrew Tracey. adv. bk. rev. cum.index with each vol. (covers 4 nos.) circ. 500. (back issues avail.) Indexed: Curr.Cont. RILM. Curr.Cont.Africa. Ind.S.A.Per. Music Ind.
Supersedes (1948-1953): African Music Society. Newsletter.

781.7   KE
AFRICAN MUSICOLOGY. 1983. a. $5. (University of Nairobi, Institute of African Studies) Eleza Services Ltd., P.O. Box 14925, Nairobi, Kenya. Eds. A. Darkwa, W.A. Omondi. Indexed: M.L.A.

780   US
AFRO-AMERICAN MUSIC OPPORTUNITIES ASSOCIATION. RESOURCE PAPERS. irreg. price varies. Afro-American Music Opportunities Association, 2909 Wayzata Blvd., Minneapolis, MN 55440. TEL 612-377-3730.

780   PL
AKADEMIA MUZYCZNA. PRACE SPECJALNE. 1984. irreg. exchange basis. Akademia Muzyczna, Ul. 27 Stycznia 33, 40-025 Katowice, Poland (Distr. by: Ars Polona Ruch, Krakowskiw Przedmiescie 7, 00-068 Warsaw, Poland)
Formerly: Panstwowa Wyzsza Szkola Muzyczna.

780   PL
AKADEMIA MUZYCZNA. SKRYPTY. 1984. irreg. exchange basis. Akademia Muzyczna, Ul. 27 Stycznia 33, 40-025 Katowice, Poland (Distr. by: Ars Polona Ruch, Krakowskie Przemiescie 7, 00-068 Warsaw, Poland)
Formerly: Panstwowa Wyzsza Szkola Muzyczna.

780   PL
AKADEMIA MUZYCZNA. SPRAWOZDANIA. a. exchange basis. Akademia Muzyczna, Ul. 27 Stycznia 33, 40-025 Katowice, Poland (Dist. by: Ars Polona-Ruch, Krakowskie Przedmiescie 7, 00-068 Warsaw, Poland) Ed. B. Lankowska-Guzy.
Formerly: Panstwowa Wyzsza Szkola Muzyczna. Sprawozdania.

780   PL
AKADEMIA MUZYCZNA. WYDAWNICTWA OKOLICZNOSCIOWE. irreg. exchange basis. Akademia Muzyczna, Ul. 27 Stycznia 33, 40-025 Katowice, Poland (Dist. by: Ars Polona Ruch, Krakowskie Przedmiescie 7, 00-068 Warsaw, Poland)
Formerly: Panstwowa Wyzsza Szkola Myzyczna. Wydawnictwa Okolicznosciowe.

780   UR
AKADEMIYA NAUK AZERBAIDZHANSKOI S.S.R. MUZEI ISTORII. TRUDY. (Text in Azerbaijani and Russian) vol.9, 1973. irreg. 1.50 Rub. per no. Izdatel'stvo Elm, Ul. Narimanova, 31, Baku 370073, Azerbaijan S.S.R., U.S.S.R. Ed. P. Azizbekova. illus. circ. 500.

780   UR
ALBUM OF CONCERT PIECES. irreg. 1.40 Rub. Izdatel'stvo Muzyka, Ul. Neglinnaya 14, Moscow 103031, Russian S.F.S.R., U.S.S.R.

783 282   GW
ALLGEMEINER CAECILIEN-VERBAND. SCHRIFTENREIHE. irreg. latest no.15. price varies. Allgemeiner Caecilien-Verband, Andreasstr. 9, D-8400 Regensburg, W. Germany (B.R.D.)

780   US   ISSN 0065-6704
AMATEUR CHAMBER MUSIC PLAYERS. DIRECTORY. (Overseas Directory or North American Directory published in alternate years) 1948. a. contribution. Amateur Chamber Music Players, Inc., 545 Eighth Ave., New York, NY 10018. TEL 212-244-2778. Ed. Susan McIntosh Lloyd. circ. 4,500.

780   CN
AMATEUR MUSICIAN/MUSICIEN AMATEUR. irreg., 3-4/yr. $25 to individuals; students $13. Canadian Amateur Musicians (CAMMAC), P.O. Box 353, Westmount, PQ H3Z 2T5, Canada. TEL 514-932-8755. Ed. Claire Heistek. adv. circ. 2,000.

789.5   US   ISSN 0093-1330
AMERICAN BELL ASSOCIATION. DIRECTORY. a. (some vols. accompanied by supplemental directory) $12 to members. American Bell Association, Route 1, Box 286, Natrona Heights, PA 15065. TEL 412-295-9623. Key Title: Directory - American Bell Association.

780   US   ISSN 0065-8316
AMERICAN FOLK MUSIC OCCASIONAL. 1970. irreg. $2.95. Music Sales Corp., 24 E. 22nd St., New York, NY 10010. Eds. Chris Strachwitz, Pete Welding.

780   GW   ISSN 0065-8855
AMERICAN INSTITUTE OF MUSICOLOGY. MISCELLANEA. 1951. irreg. (American Institute of Musicology, US) Haenssler-Verlag, Postfach 1220, Bismarckstrasse 4, 7303 Nauhausen-Stuttgart, W. Germany (B.R.D.) Ed. Armen Carapetyan.

781.9   US   ISSN 0362-3300
AMERICAN MUSICAL INSTRUMENT SOCIETY. JOURNAL. 1975. a. membership. American Musical Instrument Society, c/o Shrine to Music Museum, 414 E. Clark St., Vermillion, SD 57069. Ed. Martha Maas. adv. bk. rev. bibl. charts. illus. circ. 1,000. Indexed: Curr.Cont. Arts & Hum.Cit.Ind. Music Ind. RILM. Key Title: Journal of the American Musical Instrument Society.

780   US
AMERICAN MUSICOLOGICAL SOCIETY. STUDIES AND DOCUMENTS. 1948. irreg., no.6, 1972. price varies. 201 S. 34th St., Philadelphia, PA 19104-6316. TEL 215-898-8698.

780   GW   ISSN 0569-9827
ANALECTA MUSICOLOGIA. (Vol. 1-11 Published by Boehlau-Verlag) 1963. irreg., vol.24, 1986. price varies. (Deutsches Historisches Institut in Rom, Musikgeschichtliche Abteilung, IT) Laaber-Verlag, Regensburger Str. 19, 8411 Laaber, W. Germany (B.R.D.) illus.

780   SZ
ANNALES PADEREWSKI. 1979. irreg., approx. 1/yr. 10 Fr. Societe Paderewski a Morges, Hotel de Ville, CH-1110 Morges, Switzerland. Ed. Maurice Giordani. bk. rev. circ. 1,000.

780   UK
ANNUAL CHART SUMMARIES. 1983. a. $4. Chart Watch, 17 Springfield, Ilminster, Somerset, England (Subscr. addr.: 191 Perne Rd., Cambridge CB1 3NT, England) circ. 70.

786   US
ANNUAL ORGAN HANDBOOK; regional survey of historical pipe organs. 1956. a. $22 (includes subscr. to: Tracker) Organ Historical Society, Inc., Box 26811, Richmond, VA 23261. TEL 804-353-9226. Ed. Alan Laufman. adv. illus. circ. 2,000.
Supersedes: Organ Historical Society. National Convention (Proceedings)

785.4   US   ISSN 0731-0641
ANNUAL REVIEW OF JAZZ STUDIES. 1982. a. $19.95. (Institute of Jazz Studies) Transaction Periodicals Consortium, Rutgers University, New Brunswick, NJ 08903. TEL 201-932-2280. Ed.Bd. adv. bk. rev. bibl. discographies. circ. 1,000. (also avail. in microform from MIM,UMI; reprint service avail. from UMI) Indexed: Curr.Cont. Hist.Abstr. Amer.Hist.& Life. Music Ind. RILM.
Supersedes (1973-vol.6, 1981): Journal of Jazz Studies; Incorporating: Studies in Jazz Discography (ISSN 0093-3686)

780   SP
ANNUARIO MUSICAL. a. 90 ptas. Consejo Superior de Investigaciones Cientificas, Instituto Espanol de Musicologia, 15 Barcelona 1, Spain. Indexed: Music Ind.

780   IT
ANNUARIO MUSICALE ITALIANO. 1981. biennial. L.60000. Comitato Nazionale Italiano Musica, Via Vittoria Colonna 18, 00193 Rome, Italy. Ed. Marcello Ruggieri. adv. circ. 6,000.

780.42   GW   ISSN 0344-2667
ANSCHLAEGE. 1978. irreg. price varies. Archiv fuer Populaere Musik GmbH, Ostertorsteinweg 3, D-2800 Bremen 1, W. Germany (B.R.D.) Ed. Klaus Kuhnke. adv. bk. rev. bibl. illus.

780 GW ISSN 0570-6769
ARCHIV FUER MUSIKWISSENSCHAFT.
BEIHEFTE. (Text in English and German) irreg.,
vol.26, 1987. price varies. Franz Steiner Verlag
Wiesbaden GmbH, Birkenwaldstr. 44, Postfach 347,
D-7000 Stuttgart 1, W. Germany (B.R.D.)

780.903 IT
ARCHIVUM MUSICUM; collana di testi rari. 1978.
irreg. price varies. Studio per Edizioni Scelte,
Lungarno Guicciadini 9, 50125 Florence, Italy.
Ed.Bd.

780 SA ISSN 0379-6485
ARS NOVA. (Text in Afrikaans and English) 1969. a.
R.3.25. University of South Africa, Department of
Musicology, Box 392, Pretoria, South Africa. Ed. F.
van der Merwe. adv. bk. rev. circ. 450. (back issues
avail.)

780 YU ISSN 0587-5455
ARTI MUSICES/MUSICOLOGICAL YEARBOOK.
(Text in Croatian; summaries in English) 1969. a.
80 din.($7) Muzicka Akademija u Zagrebu,
Muzikoloski Zavod - Zagreb Academy of Music,
Institute of Musicology, Gunduliceva 6, 41000
Zagreb, Yugoslavia. Ed.Bd. adv. bk. rev. bibl. illus.
Indexed: Music Ind. RILM.

780 US ISSN 0081-1319
ASIAN MUSIC PUBLICATIONS. SERIES A:
BIBLIOGRAPHIC AND RESEARCH AIDS.
1970. irreg., latest 1974. (Society for Asian Music)
Asian Music Publications, c/o Theodore Front
Musical Literature, Inc., 16122 Cohasset St., Van
Nuys, CA 91406. TEL 818-994-1902. Ed. Fredric
Lieberman. circ. 400. (back issues avail.) Indexed:
RILM.
Formerly: Society for Asian Music. Publication
Series. Series A: Bibliographic and Research Aids.

780 US ISSN 0081-1327
ASIAN MUSIC PUBLICATIONS. SERIES B.
TRANSLATIONS. irreg. (Society for Asian Music)
Asian Music Publications, c/o Theodore Front
Musical Literature, Inc., 16122 Cohasset St., Van
Nuys, CA 91406. TEL 818-994-1902. Ed. Fredric
Lieberman. Indexed: RILM.
Formerly: Society for Asian Music. Publication
Series. Series B: Translations.

780 US ISSN 0081-1335
ASIAN MUSIC PUBLICATIONS. SERIES C:
REPRINTS. irreg. (Society for Asian Music) Asian
Music Publications, c/o Theodore Front Musical
Literature, Inc., 16122 Cohasset St., Van Nuys, CA
91406. TEL 818-994-1902. Ed. Fredric Lieberman.
Indexed: RILM.
Formerly: Society for Asian Music. Publication
Series. Series C: Reprints.

780 US ISSN 0081-1343
ASIAN MUSIC PUBLICATIONS. SERIES D:
MONOGRAPHS. 1969. irreg., latest 1977. (Society
for Asian Music) Asian Music Publications, c/o
Theodore Front Musical Literature, Inc., 16122
Cohasset St., Van Nuys, CA 91406. TEL 818-994-
1902. Ed. Fredric Lieberman. circ. 400 (approx.)
Indexed: RILM.
Formerly: Society for Asian Music. Publications
Series. Series D: Monographs.

781.7 AT
AUSTRALASIAN COUNTRY MUSIC ANNUAL.
Variant title: Who's Who. 1973. a. Aus.$2. B.A.L.
Marketing, Box 497, Tamworth, N.S.W. 2340,
Australia. Ed. K. Knapp. adv. bk. rev. circ. 20,000.
Former titles: Passport; Australian Country Music
Annual.
Country

780 AT ISSN 0311-2764
AUSTRALIAN COMPOSER. 1972. irreg. free to
members. Fellowship of Australian Composers, P.O.
Box 522, Strathfield, NSW 2135, Australia. bk. rev.
circ. 250.
Formerly: Fellowship of Australian Composers.
Newsletter.

781.7 AT ISSN 0726-4941
AUSTRALIAN FOLK DIRECTORY. biennial.
Australian Folk Trust, P.O. Box 265, Paddington
4064, Australia.

780 AT ISSN 0706-6678
AUSTRALIAN MUSIC DIRECTORY. 1981. a.
Aus.$14.95. Australian Music Directory Pty Ltd.,
644 Victoria St., North Melbourne, Vic. 3051,
Australia. circ. 20,000.

780 US
B A MAGAZINE. vol.6, 1977. irreg. Brooklyn
Academy of Music, 30 Lafayette Ave., Brooklyn,
NY 11217. TEL 718-636-4100. illus.

780 US ISSN 0084-8018
B B C MUSIC GUIDES. (British Broadcasting Corp.
Music Guide) 1969. irreg., latest 1983. price varies.
University of Washington Press, Seattle, WA 98105.
TEL 206-543-4050.

780 GE ISSN 0084-7682
BACH-JAHRBUCH. 1904. a. price varies.
(International Union of the New Bach Society)
Evangelische Verlagsanstalt GmbH, Krautstr. 52,
1017 Berlin, E. Germany (D.D.R.) Eds. H.-J.
Schulze, C. Wolff. bk. rev. bibl. charts. illus. circ.
4,700. Indexed: RILM.

785 US ISSN 0084-7704
BAND MUSIC GUIDE. 1959. irreg. $22.
Instrumentalist Co., 200 Northfield Rd., Northfield,
IL 60093. TEL 312-446-5000.

780 GW ISSN 0522-5949
BEETHOVEN-JAHRBUCH. 1954. biennial. price
varies. Verein Beethoven-Haus Bonn, Postfach 2463,
5300 Bonn 1, W. Germany (B.R.D.) bibl. circ. 1,
000. Indexed: RILM.

780 AU ISSN 0067-5067
BEITRAEGE ZUR HARMONIKALEN
GRUNDLAGENFORSCHUNG. 1968. irreg.,
no.11, 1980. price varies. Musikverlag Elisabeth
Lafite, Hegelgasse 13/22, A-1010 Vienna, Austria.

780 AU
BEITRAEGE ZUR JAZZFORSCHUNG/STUDIES
IN JAZZ RESEARCH. (Text in German) 1969.
irreg., vol.8, 1986. price varies. (International
Society for Jazz Research) Akademische Druck-
und Verlagsanstalt, Neufeldweg 75, 8010 Graz,
Styria, Austria. Eds. Alfons M. Dauer, Franz
Kerschbaumer. (back issues avail.) Indexed: RILM.

780 PL
BIBLIOTEKA CHOPINOWSKA. 1959. irreg. price
varies. Polskie Wydawnictwo Muzyczne, Al.
Krasinskiego 11a, 31-111 Krakow, Poland (Distr.
by: Ars Polona, Krakowskie Przedmiescie 7, 00-068
Warsaw, Poland) Ed. Mieczyslaw Tomaszewski.

780 PL ISSN 0208-9963
BIBLIOTEKA RES FACTA. 1970. irreg. price varies.
Polskie Wydawnictwo Muzyczne, Al. Krasinskiego
11a, 31-111 Krakow, Poland (Distributed by: Ars
Polona-Ruch, Krakowskie, Przedmiescie 7, 00-068
Warsaw, Poland) Ed. Michal Bristiger. Indexed:
RILM.

780 PL ISSN 0067-7779
BIBLIOTEKA SLUCHACZA KONCERTOWEGO.
SERIA WPROWADZAJACA. 1954. irreg. price
varies. Polskie Wydawnictwo Muzyczne, Al.
Krasinskiego 11a, 31-111 Krakow, Poland (Dist. by
Ars Polona-Ruch, Krakowskie Przedmiescie 7, 00-
068 Warsaw, Poland)

780 US ISSN 0067-8600
BILLBOARD'S INTERNATIONAL BUYER'S
GUIDE OF THE MUSIC-RECORD-TAPE
INDUSTRY. 1958. a. $60. Billboard Directories,
1515 Broadway, New York, NY 10036 TEL 212-
764-7300. (And 9000 Sunset Blvd., Los Angeles,
CA 90069) (also avail. in microfilm from KTO)
Formerly (until 1960): Billboard. International
Buyer's Guide of the Music-Record Industry.

792 US
BILLBOARD'S YEAR-END ISSUE TALENT IN
ACTION. 1970. a. $9. Billboard Directories, 1515
Broadway, New York, NY 10036 TEL 212-764-
7300. (And 9000 Sunset Blvd., Los Angeles, CA
90069) circ. 45,000. (also avail. in microfilm from
KTO)
Former titles: Billboard's Year-End Awards/
Talent in Action & Billboard's Talent in Action.

780 681 US
BLUEGRASS DIRECTORY. 1981. biennial. $5.50. B
D Products, Box 412, Murphys, CA 95247. TEL
209-728-3379. Ed. Betty Deakins. adv. circ. 1,000.
(back issues avail.)

781.57 US
BLUES RESEARCH. 1959. irreg., no.17, 1975. $1 per
no. Record Research, 65 Grand Ave., Brooklyn, NY
11205. TEL 718-857-7003. Eds. Anthony Rotante,
Paul Sheatsley. charts. illus.

786 US
BOSTON ORGAN CLUB NEWSLETTER.* 1965.
irreg. $5. Organ Historical Society, Boston Organ
Club, Box 863, Claremont, NH 03743. Ed. E.A.
Boadway. adv. bk. rev. circ. 300.

780 920 GW
BRAHMS STUDIEN. 1976. a. membership. J.
Brahms-Gesellschaft, Internationale Vereinigung
e.V., Trostbruecke 4, D-2000 Hamburg 11, W.
Germany (B.R.D.) adv. bk. rev. illus. circ. 500.
Formerly: Brahms-Gesellschaft Hamburg.
Jahresgabe.

780 US
BRASS PLAYERS' GUIDE. 1975. a. $2. Robert King
Music Sales, Inc., 112A Main St., North Easton,
MA 02356. Ed. Nancy King. circ. 15,000.

780 US ISSN 0363-454X
BRASS RESEARCH SERIES. irreg. Brass Press, 136
Eighth Ave., N., Nashville, TN 37203. TEL 615-
254-8969. Ed. Stephen L. Glover.

BRAVURA STUDIES IN MUSIC. see *MUSIC —
Abstracting, Bibliographies, Statistics*

781.97 016 UK ISSN 0068-1407
BRITISH CATALOGUE OF MUSIC. 1957. a., with 2
interim issues. £40. British Library, Bibliographic
Services, 2 Sheraton St., London W1V 4BH,
England. bibl. index. circ. 600.

780.7 CN ISSN 0007-0564
BRITISH COLUMBIA MUSIC EDUCATOR. vol.13,
1970. irreg. Can.$32 to non-members. (B.C. Music
Educators' Association) B.C. Teachers' Federation,
2235 Burrard St., Vancouver, B.C. V6J 3H9,
Canada. TEL 604-731-8121. adv. bk. rev. illus. stat.
circ. 875. (processed) Indexed: Can.Educ.Ind.
Study and teaching

780 UK ISSN 0309-8044
BRITISH FEDERATION OF MUSIC FESTIVALS.
YEARBOOK.* 1974. a. £1.50. British Federation of
Music Festivals, 198 Park Lane, Macclesfield,
Cheshire SK11 6UD, England. circ. 2,500.

780.7 UK ISSN 0266-2329
BRITISH MUSIC EDUCATION YEARBOOK. 1984.
a. £8.95. Rhinegold Publishing Ltd., 239/241
Shaftesbury Ave., London WC2H 8EH, England.
Eds. Marianne Barton, Jacqueline Fowler.

780 UK ISSN 0306-5928
BRITISH MUSIC YEARBOOK. 1972. a. £9.95.
Rhinegold Publishing Ltd., 239/241 Swaftesbury
Ave., London WC2H 8EH, England. Ed. Marianne
Barton. adv. stat. index. Indexed: RILA.
Formerly: Music Yearbook.

780 NE
BRUSSELS MUSEUM OF MUSICAL
INSTRUMENTS. BULLETIN. vol.5, 1975. irreg.
price varies. (BE) Uitgeverij Frits Knuf B.V., Box
720, 4116 ZJ Buren, Netherlands. Indexed: Music
Ind. RILM.

780 US
BULLETIN OF RESEARCH IN MUSIC
EDUCATION. Cover title: P M E A. Bulletin of
Research. 1969. a. $5. Pennsylvania Music
Educators Association, Inc., c/o Keith Thompson,
265 Chambers Bldg., School of Music, Pennsylvania
State University, University Park, PA 19382. Ed.
Keith Thompson. circ. 4,000. Indexed: Music
Artic.Guide.

780 792.6 US
BUYERS GUIDE: FOOTNOTES. 1974. a. $2.
Stagestep, Box 328, Philadelphia, PA 19105. Ed.
Randy Swartz. adv. bk. rev. tr.lit. circ. 300,000.
(back issues avail.)

780   CN
C B C CLASSICAL RECORD REFERENCE BOOK. (Text in English and French) 1980. a. Canadian Broadcasting Corporation, 7925 Cote St. Luc Rd., Montreal, Que. H4W 1R5, Canada. TEL 514-285-3211.

780   AU   ISSN 0574-9468
C.I.A. REVUE.* 1953. irreg. Confederation Internationale des Accordeonistes, c/o Walter Mauer, Sec. Gen., Rasumovskygasse 32, Postbox 323, Vienna, Austria.

780   CN   ISSN 0820-7356
C L E M. (Text in English) 1981. a. Can.$12($12) Contact List of Electronic Music, P.O. Box 86010, North Vancouver, B.C. V7L 4J5, Canada. TEL 604-985-5996. Ed. Alex Douglas. bk. rev. circ. 2,000.

789.99   US
C M E ANNUAL REPORT. 1972. a. free. Center for Music Experiment, Q-037, University of California, San Diego, La Jolla, CA 92093. TEL 619-534-4383. Ed. John D. Lauer. circ. 500. (back issues avail.)

780.92   FR
CAHIERS DEBUSSY. 1974. irreg. 120 F. Centre de Documentation Claude Debussy, Jardin des Arts, 3 rue Henry IV, Saint Germain-en-Laye, France. Ed. Francois Lesure. adv. illus. Indexed: RILM.

CANADA'S ATLANTIC FOLKLORE AND FOLKLIFE SERIES. see FOLKLORE

781.6   CN   ISSN 0008-3259
CANADIAN COMPOSER/COMPOSITEUR CANADIEN. (Text and title in English and French) 1965. irreg., (approx. 10/yr.) $5. (Composers Authors & Publishers Association of Canada) Creative Arts Co., 1240 Bay, Suite 303, Toronto, Ont. M5R 2A7, Canada. Ed. Richard Flohil. bk. rev. illus. rec. rev. circ. 12,000. (also avail. in microform from MIM,UMI) Indexed: CMI. Can.Ind. Music Ind. Mag.Ind. Pt.de Rep. RILM.

780   CN
CANADIAN COMPOSERS SERIES. 1975. irreg. price varies. University of Toronto Press, Front Campus, Toronto, Ont. M5S 1A6, Canada. TEL 613-667-7791.

780   CN   ISSN 0068-8746
CANADIAN FOLK MUSIC JOURNAL. (Text in English and French) 1973. a. Can.$15 to individuals; Can.$20 to institutions (subscribers receive both Journal and Bulletin) Canadian Folk Music Society, P.O. Box 4232, Sta. C, Calgary, Alta. T2T 5N1, Canada. Ed. Edith Fowke. bk. rev. circ. 900. Indexed: M.L.A. Music Ind.

CANADIAN MUSIC DIRECTORY. see BUSINESS AND ECONOMICS — Trade And Industrial Directories

780   CN   ISSN 0710-0353
CANADIAN UNIVERSITY MUSIC REVIEW/ REVUE DE MUSIQUE DES UNIVERSITES CANADIENNES. (Text in English and French) 1971. N.S 1980. a. Can.$15. ‡ Canadian University Music Society - Societe de Musique des Universites Canadiennes, c/o Bruce Penny Cook, Dept. of Music, Queen's University, Kingston, Ont. K7L 3N6, Canada. TEL 613-547-5783. bk. rev. circ. 350. (also avail. in microfilm from UMI; back issues avail.; reprint service avail. from UMI) Indexed: Music Ind. RILM.
    Formerly: Canadian Association of University Schools of Music. Journal. (ISSN 0315-3541)

781.7 398   UK
CANU GWERIN/FOLK SONG. 1909. a. membership. Welsh Folk-Song Society, c/o Mrs. B. L. Roberts, Hafan, Cricieth, Gwynedd, Wales. Ed. D. Roy Saer. bk. rev. circ. 250. (back issues avail.)
    Formerly (until 1978): Welsh Folk-Song Society. Journal.
    Folk

780   AT
CATALOGUE OF AUSTRALIAN BRASS AND CONCERT BAND MUSIC. 1985. irreg. Aus.$20. Australian Music Centre Ltd., Box 49, Broadway, Sydney, N.S.W. 2007, Australia.

780   AT
CATALOGUE OF AUSTRALIAN CHORAL MUSIC. 1985. irreg. Aus.$12. Australian Music Centre Ltd., Box 49, Broadway, Sydney, N.S.W. 2007, Australia.

781.7   UK
CATALOGUE OF CONTEMPORARY WELSH MUSIC. irreg., latest vol.7, no.7. £1 per no. Guild for the Promotion of Welsh Music, 94 Walter Rd., Swansea SA1 5QA, Wales. Ed. Robert Smith.

780   GW   ISSN 0069-116X
CATALOGUS MUSICUS. 1963. irreg., no.7, 1975. price varies. (International Association of Music Libraries) Baerenreiter Verlag, Heinrich-Schuetz-Allee 31-37, 3500 Kassel-Wilhelmshoehe, W. Germany (B.R.D.) (Co-sponsor: International Musicological Society) Ed.Bd.

CELEBRITY DIRECTORY; how to reach movie, tv stars and other celebrities. see MOTION PICTURES

CENTRE CULTUREL FRANCAIS DE YAOUNDE. PROGRAMME SAISON. see ART

781.7   IE   ISSN 0009-0174
CEOL; a journal of Irish music. 1963. irreg. $5. Breandan Breathnach, Ed. & Pub., 47 Frascati Park, Blackrock, Dublin, Ireland. adv. bk. rev. record rev. illus. cum.index. circ. 1,000. (also avail. in microfilm) Indexed: M.L.A. Music Ind. RILM.
    Folk music

380.1   IT
CHI E DOVE. (Special issue of Musica e Dischi) 1971. a. L.15000. Musica e Dischi, Via De Amicis 47, 20123 Milan, Italy. Ed. Mario de Luigi.

780   IT   ISSN 0069-3391
CHIGIANA; rassegna annuale di studi musicologia. 1964. a. price varies. Accademia Musicale Chigiana, Siena, Via di Citta 89, 53100 Siena, Italy (Dist. by: Casa Editrice Leo S. /Olschki, Casella Postale 66, 50100 Florence, Italy) Ed. Guido Burchi. bk. rev. circ. 500. Indexed: RILM.
    Formerly: Accademia Musicale Chigiana. Quaderni (ISSN 0065-0714)

780.01   HK
CHINESE UNIVERSITY OF HONG KONG. CHUNG CHI COLLEGE. MUSIC DEPARTMENT. HOLDINGS OF THE CHINESE MUSIC ARCHIVES. (Text in English and Chinese) 1974. a. Chinese University of Hong Kong, Chung Chi College, Music Department, Shatin N.T., Hong Kong, Hong Kong. illus.

780   UR
CHOIR DIRECTOR'S LIBRARY. 1966. a. 0.70 Rub. Izdatel'stvo Muzyka, Ul. Neglinnaya 14, Moscow 103031, Russian S.F.S.R., U.S.S.R.

780   US   ISSN 0069-3758
CHORD AND DISCORD. 1933. irreg. (every 3-4 yrs.) free. Bruckner Society of America Inc., Box 2570, Iowa City, IA 52244. circ. 750.

784   GW   ISSN 0009-5036
DER CHORDIRIGENT; Nachrichtenblatt fuer Chorleiter. 1951. irreg. free. B. Schott's Soehne, Weihergarten 1-9, Postfach 3640, 6500 Mainz 1, W. Germany (B.R.D.) Ed. Hilger Schallehn. circ. 20,000.

780.7   SP
CICLO VIDA Y OBRA. no.6, 1983. Asociacion de Compositores Sinfonicos Espanoles, Teatro Real, Calle Carlos III, Madrid, Spain.

780   UK
CITY OF BIRMINGHAM SYMPHONY ORCHESTRA. ANNUAL PROSPECTUS. a. free. City of Birmingham Symphony Orchestra, Paradise Place, Birmingham B3 3RP, England. circ. 200,000.

780   UK
CITY OF BIRMINGHAM SYMPHONY ORCHESTRA. PROM PROSPECTUS. a. free. City of Birmingham Symphony Orchestra, Paradise Place, Birmingham B3 3RP, England. circ. 60,000.

780 700   SP
COLECCION ETHOS-ARTE. no.4, 1981. irreg. Universidad de Oviedo, Departamento de Arte-Musicologia, Servicio de Publicaciones, Oviedo, Spain.

780.9   IT   ISSN 0069-5270
COLLECTANEA HISTORIAE MUSICAE. 1953. irreg., vol.4, 1966. price varies. Casa Editrice Leo S. Olschki, Casella Postale 66, 50100 Florence, Italy. circ. 500.

780   FR
COLLECTION PSYCHOLOGIE ET PEDAGOGIE DE LA MUSIQUE. 1978. irreg. Editions Scientifiques et Psychologiques, 6 bis, rue A. Chenier, 92130 Issy-les-Moulineaux, France.

780   US   ISSN 0069-5696
COLLEGE MUSIC SYMPOSIUM. 1961. a. $16. College Music Society, 1444 Fifteenth St., Boulder, CO 80302. TEL 303-449-1611. adv. cum.index in vol. 12. circ. 6,500. Indexed: Curr.Cont. Arts & Hum.Cit.Ind. Music Ind. RILM.

780   US   ISSN 0147-0108
COLLEGIUM MUSICUM: YALE UNIVERSITY. 1955. irreg. $25. (Yale University, Department of Music) A-R Editions, Inc., 315 W. Gorham St., Madison, WI 53703. TEL 608-251-2114. Eds. Leon Plantinga, Jane Stevens. circ. 800. (back issues avail.) Indexed: Music Ind. RILM.

780   US
COMMUNIQUE (NASHVILLE) 1980. a. International Rock and Roll Music Association, Inc., Box 50111, Nashville, TN 37205. TEL 615-287-9072. Ed. Roy G. Biv. adv. bk. rev. circ. 2,000.

780 927   US   ISSN 0069-8016
COMPOSERS OF THE AMERICAS/ COMPOSITORES DE AMERICA. 1955. a. $7. Organization of American States, Department of Publications, Washington, DC 20006. TEL 703-941-1617. circ. 2,000.

780   UK
COMPOSERS OF WALES SERIES. 1978. irreg. price varies. (Welsh Arts Council) University of Wales Press, 6 Gwennyth St., Cathays, Cardiff CF2 4YD, Wales. Ed. Roy Bohana.

780   GW
CONCENTUS MUSICUS. 1973. irreg., vol.7, 1985. price varies. (Deutsches Historisches Institut in Rom, Musikgeschichtliche Abteilung, IT) Laaber-Verlag, Regensburger Str. 19, 8411 Laarber, W. Germany (B.R.D.) illus.

780   UK
CONSORT. 1929. a. (plus s-a bulletin) £9. Dolmetsch Foundation, c/o Mrs. P. Dutton, Sec., Derwen, Star Hill, Churt, Surrey GU10 2HS, England. Ed. Gwilym Beechey. adv. bk. rev. charts. illus. cum.index: 1929-1972. circ. 900. (also avail. in microfilm; reprint service avail. from UMI) Indexed: Br.Hum.Ind. Music Ind. RILM.

CONTACTS & FACILITIES; in the entertainment industry. see THEATER

780   US   ISSN 0190-4922
CONTRIBUTIONS TO MUSIC EDUCATION. 1972. a. $5. Ohio Music Education Association, c/o Duane Sample, Ed., Dana School of Music, Youngstown State University, Youngstown, OH 44555. TEL 216-742-1835. circ. 500. Indexed: Music Ind.

780   US   ISSN 0193-9041
CONTRIBUTIONS TO THE STUDY OF MUSIC AND DANCE. 1981. irreg., no.4, 1984. price varies. Greenwood Press, 88 Post Rd. W., Box 5007, Westport, CT 06881. TEL 203-226-3571.

780   GW   ISSN 0070-0363
CORPUS MENSURABILIS MUSICAE. 1948. irreg. (American Institute of Musicology, US) Haenssler-Verlag, Postfach 1220, Bismarckstrasse 4, 7303 Neuhausen-Stuttgart, W. Germany (B.R.D.) Ed. Frank D'Accone.
    Medieval and Renaissance

780   GW
CORPUS OF EARLY KEYBOARD MUSIC; transcription of all known sources of keyboard music of the 14th and 15th centuries. 1963. irreg. price varies. (American Institute of Musicology) Haenssler-Verlag, Postfach 1220, Bismarckstr. 4, 7303 Neuhausen-Stuttgart, West Germany. Ed. John Caldwell.

780 GW ISSN 0070-0460
CORPUS SCRIPTORUM DE MUSICA. (Text mainly in Latin) 1950. irreg. (American Institute of Musicology, US) Haenssler-Verlag, Postfach 1220, Bismarckstrasse 4, 7303 Neuhausen-Stuttgart, W. Germany (B.R.D.) Ed. Gilbert Reaney.

COUNTRY DANCE AND SONG. see *DANCE*

780 US ISSN 0273-1428
COUNTRY MUSIC SOURCEBOOK. Variant title: Billboard's Country Music Sourcebook. a. $27. Billboard Directories, 1515 Broadway, New York, NY 10026. adv. circ. 47,000. (also avail. in microfilm from KTO)

781.7 US ISSN 0277-1292
COUNTRY SONG ROUNDUP YEARBOOK. Running title: C S R Yearbook. a. Charlton Publications, Charlton Bldg., Derby, CT 06418. TEL 203-735-3381.

CURRENT ISSUES IN MUSIC EDUCATION. see *EDUCATION — Teaching Methods And Curriculum*

782.1 US ISSN 0731-8529
DALLAS OPERA MAGAZINE. 1977. a. $8. Dallas Opera, Majestic Theatre, Ste. 400, 1925 S. Elm, Dallas, TX 75201. TEL 214-747-8600. Ed. Roger G. Pines. adv. circ. 55,000.
Formerly: Dallas Civic Opera Magazine (ISSN 0277-0113)

780 DK ISSN 0105-8045
DANSK MUSIKFORTEGNELSE/DANISH NATIONAL BIBLIOGRAPHY: MUSIC. 1933. a. Kr.96.43. (Kongelige Bibliotek, Musikafdeling) Biblioteksentralen, Tempovej 7-11, DK-2750 Ballerup, Denmark. Ed. Susanne Sugar.

DEINE STADT; Kunst, Kultur und Leben in Braunschweig. see *ART*

780 US
DETROIT MONOGRAPHS IN MUSICOLOGY. 1971. irreg. price varies. Information Coordinators, Inc., 1435-37 Randolph St., Detroit, MI 48226. TEL 313-962-9720.

780 GW ISSN 0417-2051
DEUTSCHE GESELLSCHAFT FUER MUSIK DES ORIENTS. MITTEILUNGEN. (Text in English and German) 1962. irreg. DM.28. (Deutsche Gesellschaft fuer Musik des Orients) Verlag der Musikalienhandlung Karl Dieter Wagner, Rothenbaumchaussee 1, 2000 Hamburg 13, W. Germany (B.R.D.) illus. (back issues avail.)

780 GW
DEUTSCHES MOZARTFEST. a. DM.40 membership. Deutschen Mozart-Gesellschaft e.V., Karlstrasse 6, Augsburg, W. Germany (B.R.D.) Indexed: Music Ind.

780 GW
DEUTSCHES MUSIKLEBEN (YEAR) Enlish edition: Music in Germany. (Text in German) 1954. a. free. Inter Nations e.V., Kennedyallee 91-103, D-5300 Bonn 2, W. Germany (B.R.D.) Ed. Marianne Goebel. circ. 8,500.

780 AT ISSN 0815-5232
DIRECTORY OF AUSTRALIAN COMPOSERS. 1985. irreg. Aus.$4. Australian Music Centre Ltd., Box 49, Broadway, Sydney, N.S.W. 2007, Australia.

780 AT ISSN 0157-6402
DIRECTORY OF AUSTRALIAN MUSIC ORGANISATIONS. 1980. irreg. Aus.$12.50. Australian Music Centre Ltd., Box 49, Broadway, Sydney, N.S.W. 2007, Australia. Ed. Bill Flemming.

785 UK
DIRECTORY OF BRITISH BRASS BANDS.* irreg. £1. British Federation of Brass Bands, 28 Marigold St., Rochdale, Lancs., England.

785 CN ISSN 0705-6249
DIRECTORY OF CANADIAN ORCHESTRAS AND YOUTH ORCHESTRAS/ANNUAIRE CANADIEN DES ORCHESTRES ET ORCHESTRES. DES JEUNES. (Text in English and French) 1976. a. Can.$8. Association of Canadian Orchestras, 56 The Esplanade, Suite 311, Toronto, Ont. M5E 1A7, Canada. TEL 416-366-8834. (Co-sponsor: Ontario Federation of Symphony Orchestras)

780 US ISSN 0098-664X
DIRECTORY OF MUSIC FACULTIES IN COLLEGES & UNIVERSITIES U S AND CANADA. 1967. biennial. $35. ‡ College Music Society, Inc., 1444 Fifteenth St., Boulder, CO 80302. TEL 303-449-1611. Ed. Robby D. Gunstream. circ. 4,000. Indexed: Music Ind. RILM.
Continues: Directory of Music Faculties in American Colleges and Universities (ISSN 0419-3040)

780.42 UK
DISCO 80 ANNUAL. 1979. £1.95. Brown Watson Ltd., 44 Hill St., London, W1X 84B, England.

780.1 US ISSN 0095-8115
DISCOGRAPHY SERIES. 1969. irreg., no.20, 1987. price varies. J.F. Weber, Ed. & Pub., 194 Roosevelt Dr., Utica, NY 13502. bibl. circ. 300.

781.57 US
DISC'RIBE; a journal of discographical information. 1980. irreg. (approx. a) $5 for 4 issues. Wildmusic Company, Box 2138, Ann Arbor, MI 48106. Ed. David Wild. adv. circ. 200.

780 NE
DIVITIAE MUSICAE ARTIS. SERIES A. vol.3, 1975. irreg. price varies. Uitgeverij Frits Knuf B.V., Box 720, 4116 ZJ Buren, Netherlands.

780 BE
DOCUMENTA MUSICAE NOVAE; critical edition of contemporary music sources. (Text in Dutch, English and French) 1968. irreg. $12. Rijksuniversiteit te Gent, Seminarie voor Musicologie, Muinkkaai, 51, B-9000 Ghent, Belgium. Ed. Herman Sabbe. circ. 200. Indexed: RILM.

780 621.389 US
DOWN HOME MUSIC NEWSLETTER. 1978. irreg. (every 5-6 wks.) $3. Down Home Music Inc., 10341 San Pablo Ave., El Cerrito, CA 94530. TEL 415-525-1494. Ed. Franklyn Scott. bk. rev. rec. rev. circ. 9,000.

DRAGON. see *LITERATURE*

785.0671 CS
DYCHOVA HUDBA. irreg., vol.17, 1976. 8 Kcs. per no. Opus, Bratislava, Czechoslovakia.

787 US
EARLY CELLO SERIES. FACSIMILE REPRINT EDITION. 1982. irreg. (approx. 20 vols./yr.) $215 with supplements. Grancino International Ltd., 1109 Del Corto, Fullerton, CA 92633.

787 US ISSN 0884-1055
EARLY CELLO SERIES. MODERN EDITION. 1982. irreg. (approx. 20 vols./yr) $145 ; with supplement $250. Grancino International Ltd., 1109 Del Corto, Fullerton, CA 92633. Ed. Nona Pyron. circ. 500. (also avail. in microfiche)

780 UK ISSN 0261-1279
EARLY MUSIC HISTORY; studies in medieval and early modern music. 1982. a. $32.50 to individuals; institutions $60. Cambridge University Press, Edinburgh Bldg., Shaftesbury Rd., Cambridge CB2 2RU, England (And 32 E. 57th St., New York, NY 10022) Ed. Iain Fenlon. bk. rev.

780 US ISSN 0363-4558
EDWARD H. TARR SERIES. irreg. Brass Press, 136 Eighth Ave., N., Nashville, TN 37203. TEL 615-254-8969.

780.42 UK
ELVIS SPECIAL. 1983. a. £2.75. World International Publishing Ltd., Gt. Ducie St., Manchester, M60 3BL, England. Ed. Mae Broadley.

ENJOYING THE ARTS. see *DANCE*

780 US
ERNEST BLOCH SOCIETY. BULLETIN. 1967. a. $3.50. Ernest Bloch Society, c/o Susan Bloch, Ed., 448 Riverside Dr., New York, NY 10027. bk. rev. circ. 2,000.
Former titles: Ernest Bloch Society. Newsletter; (until 1983): Ernest Bloch Society. Bulletin (ISSN 0071-1195)

ESSAYS ON ASIAN THEATER, MUSIC AND DANCE. see *THEATER*

780 US
ESSAYS ON MODERN MUSIC. 1984. a. $5. League of Composers, International Society for Contemporary Music, Boston Section, Inc., c/o Division of Fine Arts, Northeastern University, 102 The Fenway, Boston, MA 02115. Ed. Martin Brody. circ. 1,000.

780 US ISSN 0364-9210
ETHNODISC JOURNAL OF RECORDED SOUND. 1972. irreg. $50 for 5 vols., cassette edt.; $140 for 5 vols., open reel edt. Pachart Publishing House, 1130 San Lucas Cir., Tucson, AZ 85733 TEL 602-297-4797. (Subscr. to: Box 35549, Tucson, AZ 85740) Ed. Dr. Joseph M. Pacholczyk. charts. illus. (magazine plus cassettes or open reel tape)
Formerly: Ethnodisc Recordings.

783 FR ISSN 0071-2086
ETUDES GREGORIENNES; revue de musicologie religieuse. (Text in English, French and Italian) 1954. irreg, latest vol.20, 1981. price varies. ‡ Editions Abbaye Saint-Pierre de Solesmes, 72300 Sable sur Sarthe, France. Dir. D. Jean Claire. bk. rev. circ. 500. Indexed: RILM.

780 GE ISSN 0073-0025
EUROPAEISCHE VOLKSMUSIKINSTRUMENTE. HANDBUCH. 1967. irreg. price varies. VEB Deutscher Verlag fuer Musik, Karlstr. 10, 701 Leipzig, E. Germany (D.D.R.) Eds. Ernst Emsheimer, Erich Stockmann.

EXETER'S STUDIES IN AMERICAN & COMMONWEALTH ARTS. see *LITERATURE*

FACE TO FACE WITH TALENT. see *COMMUNICATIONS — Radio And Television*

FACILITIES DIRECTORY/REPERTOIRE DES SALLES DE SPECTACLE. see *DANCE*

781.57 DK ISSN 0105-5933
FAJABEFA NYT. 1980. irreg. (2-3/yr.) free. Danske Jazzcenter, Borupvej 66, 4683 Roennede, Denmark.

780 UK
FANFARE. 1968. a. £1.60($5) Royal Military School of Music, Kneller Hall, Twickenham, Middx. TW2 7DU, England. Ed. John Pope. adv. bk. rev. circ. 5, 100.

780.1 US
FESTSCHRIFT SERIES. 1977. irreg., vol.5, 1985. Pendragon Press, Rt. 1, Box 159, Stuyvesant, NY 12173-9720. TEL 518-828-3008. (back issues avail.) Indexed: RILM.

FILM MUSIC BUYER'S GUIDE. see *MOTION PICTURES*

FLORIDA FOLKLIFE RESOURCE DIRECTORY. see *ART*

781.7 793.31 UK ISSN 0531-9684
FOLK MUSIC JOURNAL. 1965. a. English Folk Dance and Song Society, Cecil Sharp House, 2 Regents Park Rd., London NW1 7AY, England. Ed. Ian Russell. adv. bk. rev. cum.index. circ. 9,000. (also avail. in microform from UMI; reprint service avail. from UMI) Indexed: Br.Hum.Ind. Curr.Cont. M.L.A. Arts & Hum.Cit.Ind. Music Ind.
Supersedes: English Folk Dance and Song Society. Journal.

781.7 DK ISSN 0107-7074
FOLKEMUSIKHUSRINGEN. 1980. irreg. membership. Bent Doessing, Doellevangen 14, 2730 Herlev, Denmark.

781.7 US
FOLKLORICA PUBLICATIONS IN FOLKSONG AND BALLADRY. irreg., no.3, 1981. Folklorica Press, Inc., 301 E. 47 St., New York, NY 10017. Ed. Kenneth S. Goldstein.

780.01 AU
FORSCHUNGEN ZUR AELTEREN MUSIKGESCHICHTE. 1976. irreg., no.5, 1984. price varies. (Universitaet Wien, Musikwissenschaftliches Institut) W. Braumueller, Servitengasse 5, A-1092 Vienna, Austria. Ed. Walter Pass. circ. 500.

780.01 UK ISSN 0072-0127
GALPIN SOCIETY JOURNAL; for the Study of
Musical Instruments. 1948. a. £10 to non-members.
Galpin Society, c/o Miss Pauline Holden, 38
Eastfield Road, Western Park, Leicester LE3 6FE,
England. Ed. Maurice Byrne. adv. bk. rev. index.
circ. 1,600. (also avail. in microfilm from UMI;
reprint service avail. from UMI) Indexed:
Br.Hum.Ind. Curr.Cont. Arts & Hum.Cit.Ind.
Music Ind. RILM.

780 GW
GITARRE; Pressedienst der gitarristischen
Gesellschaft in Bayern. irreg. DM.12. Zupfmusik,
Breslauer Ring 9B, D-6382 Friedrichsdorf 4, W.
Germany (B.R.D.) Indexed: Music Ind.

782.1 UK ISSN 0434-1066
GLYNDEBOURNE FESTIVAL PROGRAMME
BOOK. 1952. a. £5. ‡ (Glyndebourne Festival
Opera) Glyndebourne Productions Ltd.,
Glyndebourne, Lewes, Sussex BN8 5UU, England.
Ed. Brian Dickie. adv. circ. 30,000.

783 NE
GOSPEL INFORMATIE-HANDBOEK. 1975. a. $10.
Continental Sound, Postbus 80165, 3009 GB
Rotterdam, Netherlands. Ed. Leen la Riviere. adv.
bk. rev. circ. 1,500.

783.7 US
GOSPEL MUSIC OFFICAL DIRECTORY. 1971. a.
$5. Gospel Music Association, Inc., Box 23201,
Nashville, TN 37202. TEL 615-255-1907. Ed.
Donald W. Butler. adv. illus. circ. 15,000.
Former titles: Complete Guide to Gospel Music;
Gospel Music (ISSN 0197-2715); Gospel Music
Association. Annual Directory; Gospel Music
Association. Annual Directory and Yearbook (ISSN
0362-7330); Gospel Music Directory and Yearbook.

781.7 US ISSN 0272-0264
GREENWOOD ENCYCLOPEDIA OF BLACK
MUSIC. 1981. irreg. price varies. Greenwood Press,
Box 5007, 88 Post Rd. West, Westport, CT 06881.
TEL 203-226-3571.

GUIDE TO A P R S MEMBER STUDIOS.
(Association of Professional Recording Studios) see
SOUND RECORDING AND REPRODUCTION

789.5 US ISSN 0827-5955
GUILD OF CARILLONNEURS IN NORTH
AMERICA. BULLETIN. 1969. a. $1. Guild of
Carillonneurs in North America, University of
California, Music Dept., Riverside, CA 92521. TEL
213-377-0741. Ed. Margo Halsted. circ. 525.
Former titles (until 1986): Carillon News (ISSN
0730-5001); Randschriften; a Newsletter for the
Guild of Carilloneurs (ISSN 0085-5383)

780.6 UK
HALLE YEAR BOOK. 1858. a. £2. Halle Concerts
Society, 30 Cross St., Manchester M2 7BA,
England. Ed. Clive F. Smart. adv. circ. 6,500.
Formerly: Halle Prospectus.

780 GW
HAMBURGER JAHRBUCH FUER
MUSIKWISSENSCHAFT. 1974. a. DM.82. Verlag
der Musikalienhandlung Karl Dieter Wagner,
Rothenbaumchaussee 1, 2000 Hamburg 13, W.
Germany (B.R.D.) Indexed: RILM.

780 US ISSN 0073-0629
HARVARD PUBLICATIONS IN MUSIC. 1967.
irreg., no.15, 1985. price varies. Harvard University
Press, 79 Garden St., Cambridge, MA 02138. TEL
617-495-2600.

780 920 GW ISSN 0440-5323
HAYDN-STUDIEN. (Text in English and German)
1965. irreg. (1-2/yr.) price varies. (Joseph Haydn-
Institut e.V.) G. Henle Verlag, Forstenrieder Allee
122, Postfach 710466, 8000 Munich 71, W.
Germany (B.R.D.) Ed. Georg Feder. adv. bk. rev.
illus. index. circ. 750. Indexed: Curr.Cont. Arts &
Hum.Cit.Ind. RILM.

780 DK ISSN 0441-5833
HI FI AARBOGEN. 1973. a. Kr.99.50. Forlaget
Audio A-S, St. Kongensgade 72, DK-1264
Copenhagen K, Denmark. Ed.Bd. adv. illus. tr.lit.
circ. 16,000. (back issues avail.)

780.904 GW
HINDEMITH-JAHRBUCH/ANNALES
HINDEMITH. 1971. a. DM.22.40 (single copy,
DM. 28) (Paul-Hindemith-Institut) B. Schott's
Soehne, Weihergarten 5, Postfach 3640, 6500 Mainz
1, W. Germany (B.R.D.) Ed. Dieter Rexroth. bk.
rev. circ. 1,200. Indexed: RILM.

HISPANIC AMERICAN ARTS; all you want or must
know, about everything, in all the fields of Hispanic
American arts. see ART

780 IT ISSN 0073-2516
HISTORIAE MUSICAE CULTORES BIBLIOTECA.
1952. irreg., vol.42, 1985. price varies. Casa Editrice
Leo S. Olschki, Casella Postale 66, 50100 Florence,
Italy. circ. 1,000.

780 US
HISTORICAL HARPSICHORD SERIES. 1984.
irreg., vol.2, 1985. Pendragon Press, R.R. 1, Box
159, Stuyvesant, NY 12173-9720.

780 CS
HUDOBNY ARCHIV. (Text in Slovak; summaries
also in German and Russian) 1974. irreg. price
varies. Matica Slovenska, Mudronova 35, 036 52
Martin, Czechoslovakia.

780 975 US
IMAGO MUSICAE. 1984. a. price varies. Duke
University Press, 6697 College Sta., Durham, NC
27708. TEL 919-684-2173. (Co-publisher:
Barenreiter-Verlag Basel) Ed. Tilman Seebass. (back
issues avail.)

780 US ISSN 0360-4365
IN THEORY ONLY. 1975. irreg. $12 to individuals;
institutions $15. Michigan Music Theory Society, c/o
School of Music, University of Michigan, Ann
Arbor, MI 48109. TEL 313-764-0583. Ed. William
E. Lake. bk. rev. bibl. charts. illus. index. circ.
425. (also avail. in microform from UMI; reprint
service avail. from UMI) Indexed: RILM. Music
Ind. Music Artic.Guide. RILM.

780 UK
INCORPORATED SOCIETY OF MUSICIANS
YEARBOOK. 1898. a. £8. Incorporated Society of
Musicians, 10 Stratford Place, London W1N 9AE,
England. circ. 7,500.
Formerly: Incorporated Society of Musicians
Handbook.

690 UK ISSN 0073-5744
INCORPORATED SOCIETY OF ORGAN
BUILDERS. JOURNAL. 1949. irreg. £2.50. ‡
Incorporated Society of Organ Builders, Petersfield,
Hants GU32 3AT, England. Ed. C.J. Gordon Wells.

780 II ISSN 0019-5995
INDIAN MUSIC JOURNAL; devoted to general
reader and student. (Text in English, Tamil, and
Sanskrit; summaries in English) 1964. a. Rs.15($9)
Tyaga Bharati Music Education Mission, Melkote-
571 431, India. Ed. Sri Rama Bharati. adv. bk. rev.
charts. illus. circ. 1,300.

INDIAN RECORDS. see SOUND RECORDING
AND REPRODUCTION

780 US
INDIANA DIRECTORY OF MUSIC TEACHERS.
1941. a. $12 (educators $9) ‡ Indiana University,
School of Music, Music Education Department,
Bloomington, IN 47405. TEL 812-335-2051. Ed.
Shirley W. Brown. index. circ. 220.

780 AU
INNSBRUCKER BEITRAEGE ZUR
MUSIKWISSENSCHAFT. 1977. irreg. price varies.
Musikverlag Helbling, Kaplanstr. 9, Postfach 416,
6021 Innsbruck/Neu Rum, Austria. Ed. Walter
Salmen. charts. illus. index.

780 IT ISSN 0073-8611
INSTITUTA ET MONUMENTA. SERIES 1:
MONUMENTA. 1954. irreg. price varies.
(Universita degli Studi di Pavia, Scuola di
Paleografia e Filologia Musicale) Fondazione
"Claudio Monteverdi", Corso Garibaldi 178, 26100
Cremona, Italy.

780 IT ISSN 0392-629X
INSTITUTA ET MONUMENTA. SERIES 2.
INSTITUTA. 1969. irreg., vol.8, 1979. price varies.
(Universita degli Studi di Pavia, Scuola di
Paleografia e Filologia Musicale) Fondazione
"Claudio Monteverdi", Corso Garibaldi 178, 26100
Cremona, Italy. circ. 500(controlled)

781.5 US
INSTITUTE FOR STUDIES IN AMERICAN
MUSIC. MONOGRAPHS. 1973. irreg., no.22,
1985. price varies. Institute for Studies in American
Music, City University of New York, Brooklyn
College, Conservatory of Music, Brooklyn, NY
11210. TEL 718-780-5655. Ed. H. Wiley Hitchcock.

781.7 398 VE
INSTITUTO INTERAMERICANO DE
ETNOMUSICOLOGIA Y FOLKLORE.
REVISTA. Short title: Revista I N I D E F. 1975.
irreg. $4. Instituto Interamericano de
Etnomusicologia y Folklore, Apdo. 81015, Caracas,
Venezuela. bk. rev. illus.

780 US
INTERNATIONAL ALBAN BERG SOCIETY
NEWSLETTER. 1968. a. $15. International Alban
Berg Society, Ph.D. Program in Music, City
University of New York, 33 W. 42 St., New York,
NY 10036. TEL 212-790-4554. Ed. Joan Smith.
circ. 300. (back issue avail.) Indexed: RILM.

780 IT
INTERNATIONAL CONGRESS OF VERDI
STUDIES. PROCEEDINGS. (Text in English,
German, French, Italian, Spanish) irreg. L.20000.
Istituto di Studi Verdiani, Strada della Repubblica
56, 43100 Parma, Italy.

781.7 SW
INTERNATIONAL FOLK MUSIC COUNCIL.
INTERNATIONALE ARBEITSTAGUNG DER
STUDY GROUP ON FOLK MUSICAL
INSTRUMENTS. (Supplement to: Musikhistoriska
Museets Skrifter) 6th, 1977. irreg. $57. Almqvist &
Wiksell International, Box 62, S-101 20 Stockholm,
Sweden. Ed. Erich Stockmann. illus.

780 UK
INTERNATIONAL MUSIC AND OPERA GUIDE.
a. $12.95. Tantivy Press, 136-148 Tooley St.,
London SE1 2TT, England (Dist. in U.S. by: New
York Zoetrope Inc., 838 Broadway, New York, NY
10003) Ed. Catriona Hall.
Formerly: International Music Guide.

780 US
INTERNATIONAL MUSICOLOGICAL SOCIETY
AND THE AMERICAN MUSICOLOGICAL
SOCIETY. REPORT. (Text in English, French,
German) irreg., Twelfth Congress Berkeley, 1977.
$55. International Musicological Society and the
American Musicological Society, 201 South 34th
St., Philadelphia, PA 19104. TEL 215-898-8698.
Eds. Daniel Heartz, Bonnie Wade.

780 US ISSN 0363-5708
INTERNATIONAL TROMBONE ASSOCIATION
SERIES. irreg. Brass Press, 136 Eighth Ave., N.,
Nashville, TN 37203. TEL 615-254-8969. Ed.
Stephen L. Glover.

787 US
INTERNATIONAL VIOLIN AND GUITAR
MAKERS ASSOCIATION. JOURNAL.* 1958-
1978; temporarily suspended; resumed 1980. a. $6. ‡
International Violin and Guitar Makers Association,
c/o Reid, Box 2392, Los Nietos, CA 90610-2392.
adv. bk. rev. illus. tr.lit. circ. 1,000.
String

780 UK ISSN 0307-2894
INTERNATIONAL WHO'S WHO IN MUSIC AND
MUSICIANS' DIRECTORY. 1935. triennial. price
varies. Melrose Press Ltd., 3 Regal Lane, Soham,
Ely, Cambridgeshire CB7 5BA, England (Dist. in
U.S. by: Gale Research Co., Detroit, MI 48226)
Indexed: Child.Auth.& Illus. Perf.Arts Biog.Master
Ind.
Formerly: Who's Who in Music and Musicians'
International Directory (ISSN 0083-9647)

780.01 US ISSN 0276-3052
INTERVAL; exploring the sonic spectrum. 1978.
irreg., vol.3, 1981. $12. Interval Foundation Press,
Box 8027, San Diego, CA 92102. TEL 619-239-
1713. Ed. Jonathan Glasier. adv. bk. rev. illus. circ.
400. Indexed: Music Ind.

780 IE
IRISH FOLK MUSIC STUDIES. 1972. irreg. £1. Folk Music Society of Ireland, c/o Hugh Shields, Ed., 3 Sydenham Road, Dundrum, Dublin 14, Ireland. Ed. Hugh Shields. adv. bk. rev. bibl. circ. 1,000. Indexed: RILM.

ISLENSK HLJODRITASKRA. see *BIBLIOGRAPHIES*

781.7 IS ISSN 0334-2026
ISRAEL STUDIES IN MUSICOLOGY. 1978. irreg. $15. Tel Aviv University, c/o Dept. of Musicology, Ramat Aviv, Israel. Ed. Shai Burstyn. bk. rev. circ. 1,000. Indexed: RILM.

JAHRBUCH FUER LITURGIK UND HYMNOLOGIE. see *RELIGIONS AND THEOLOGY*

780 398 GW ISSN 0075-2703
JAHRBUCH FUER MUSIKALISCHE VOLKS- UND VOELKERKUNDE. 1968. irreg. price varies. (Freie Universitaet Berlin, Vergleichende Musikwissenschaft) Breitkopf und Haertel, Walkmuehlstr. 52, Postfach 1707, 6200 Wiesbaden, W. Germany (B.R.D.) Ed. Josef Kuckertz. Indexed: RILM.

782 GW ISSN 0724-8156
JAHRBUCH FUER OPERNFORSCHUNG. (Text in English, French, and German) 1985. a. 44 Fr. Verlag Peter Lang, Hinter den Ulmen 19, 6000 Frankfurt, W. Germany (B.R.D.)
Opera

784.4 398 GW ISSN 0075-2789
JAHRBUCH FUER VOLKSLIEDFORSCHUNG. 1928. a. price varies. (Deutsches Volksliedarchiv) Erich Schmidt Verlag GmbH (Bielefeld), Viktoriastr. 44A, Postfach 7330, 4800 Bielefeld 1, W. Germany (B.R.D.) Ed. Rolf Wilhelm Brednich. adv. bk. rev. index. Indexed: Curr.Cont. M.L.A.

780 GW
JAHRBUCH PETERS. 1980. a. Verlag C. F. Peters, Kennedyallee 101, Postfach 700906, 6 Frankfurt 70, W. Germany (B.R.D.) (Distr. by: C. F. Peters Corp., 373 Park Ave. S., New York, NY 10016) Ed. Eberhard Klemm. Indexed: RILM.
Supersedes (1973-1977): Deutsches Jahrbuch der Musikwissenschaft (ISSN 0070-4504)

780 JA ISSN 0075-3459
JAPANESE PHONOGRAPH RECORDS OF FOLK SONGS, CLASSICAL AND POPULAR MUSIC. (Text in Japanese) a. Japan Phonograph Record Association, 8-9 Tsukiji, Chuo-ku, Tokyo, Japan.

781.57 DK ISSN 0900-064X
JAZZ FESTIVALS AND RELATED MAJOR JAZZ EVENTS. DIRECTORY. biennial. Kr.50. (Danish Jazz Center) Bibliotekscentralen, Telegrafvej 5, DK-2750 Ballerup, Denmark.

780 AU ISSN 0075-3572
JAZZFORSCHUNG/JAZZ RESEARCH. (Text and summaries in English and German) 1969. a. price varies; free to members. (International Society for Jazz Research) Akademische Druck- und Verlagsanstalt, A-8010 Graz, Neufeldweg 75, Austria. (Co-Sponsors: Hochschule fuer Musik und Institut fuer Jazz Darstellende Kunst) Indexed: Music Ind. RILM.

781.57 US
JAZZMEN'S REFERENCE BOOK; Jazz World Direct. 1973. a. $95 to non-members. Jazz World Society, Box 777, Times Square Sta., New York, NY 10108-0777. Ed. Jan Byrczek. adv. circ. 8,000.

781.57 US
JAZZOLOGIST. 1963. irreg. (4-6/yr.) $8. New Orleans Jazz Club of California, Box 1225, Kerrville, TX 78029. TEL 512-896-2285. Ed. Mort Enob. adv. bk. rev. rec. rev. bibl. circ. 5,000.

780 GW ISSN 0446-9577
JOSEPH HAAS GESELLSCHAFT. MITTEILUNGSBLATT. 1950. a. membership. Joseph Haas Gesellschaft e.V., Veroneserstr. 4, 8000 Munich 90, W. Germany (B.R.D.) Ed. Siegfried Bissinger. bk. rev. bibl. cum.index. circ. 300.

783.02 US ISSN 0197-0100
JOURNAL OF JEWISH MUSIC AND LITURGY. (Text in English and Hebrew) 1976. a. $6. Cantorial Council of America, c/o Yeshiva University, 500 W. 185th St., New York, NY 10033. TEL 212-960-5353. Ed. Macy Nulman. circ. 300.

780 US ISSN 0364-2216
JOURNAL OF THE GRADUATE MUSIC STUDENTS AT THE OHIO STATE UNIVERSITY. 1969. irreg., no.6, 1977. Ohio State University, School of Music, 1899 N. College Rd., Columbus, OH 43210. TEL 614-422-6571.

780 UR
KAZANSKII GOSUDARSTVENNYI PEDAGOGICHESKII INSTITUT. VOPROSY ISTORII, TEORII MUZYKI I MUZYKAL'NOGO VOSPITANIYA. SBORNIK. 1970. biennial. price varies. Kazanskii Gosudarstvennyi Pedagogicheskii Institut, Ul. Mezjlauk, 1, 420021 Kazan, Russian S.F.S.R., U.S.S.R. circ. 600.

780 UK
KEMPS INTERNATIONAL MUSIC AND RECORDING INDUSTRY YEARBOOK. 1965. a. $30. Kemps Group (Printers & Publishers) Ltd., 1-5 Bath St., London EC1V 9QA, England (Dist. by: R.R. Bowker Company, 205 E. 42nd St., New York, NY 10017) adv.
Former titles: Kemps International Music and Recording Yearbook & Kemps Music and Record Industry Year Book International (ISSN 0305-7100) ; Kemps Music and Record Industry Year Book (ISSN 0075-5451)

780 KE
KENYA CONSERVATOIRE OF MUSIC. NEWSLETTER. (Text in English) 1945. irreg. free to members. Kenya Conservatoire of Music, Box 41343, Nairobi, Kenya. Ed. Philip Mundey. circ. 400.

780 NE
KEY NOTES; musical life in the Netherlands. (Text in English) 1975. a. fl.15 (free abroad to individuals) Donemus Amsterdam, Paulus Potterstraat 14, 1071 CZ Amsterdam, Netherlands. Ed.Bd. illus. circ. 8,000. Indexed: RILM.
Formerly: Sonorum Speculum (ISSN 0038-1438)

780 NE
KIJKBOEKJES. (Text in Dutch and English) 1976. irreg., no.5, 1977. price varies. (Gemeentemuseum) Uitgeverij Frits Knuf B.V., Box 720, 4116 ZJ Buren, Netherlands. illus.

780 GW ISSN 0075-6199
KIRCHENMUSIKALISCHES JAHRBUCH. 1876. a. price varies. Allgemeiner Caecilien-Verband, Andreasstr. 9, D-8400 Regensburg, W. Germany (B.R.D.) Ed. Prof. Guenther Massenkeil. bk. rev. Indexed: Music Ind. RILM.

780 NE ISSN 0030-3836
KLANK EN WEERKLANK. 1970. irreg. (8-9/yr.) fl.25. Stichting Vrienden van het Brabants Orkest - Foundation Friends of the Brabant Orchestra, Postbox 442, 5201 AK s-Hertogenbosch, Netherlands. Ed.Bd. adv. bk. rev. illus. circ. 4,500.
Supersedes: Opmaat.

783 SZ ISSN 0023-2068
KLEINE CHORZEITUNG; Mitteilungsblatt fuer die katholischen Kirchenchoere. (Supplement to: Katholische Kirchenmusik) 1950. irreg. (2-3/yr.) 0.50 Fr. per no. Paulus-Verlag GmbH, Murbacherstr. 29, 6003 Lucerne, Switzerland.
Formerly: Kirchensaenger.

780 GW
KOELNER BEITRAEGE ZUR MUSIKFORSCHUNG. irreg., vol.150, 1986. price varies. Gustav Bosse Verlag, Von-der-Tann-Str. 38, Postfach 417, 8400 Regensburg 1, W. Germany (B.R.D.) Ed. Michael Trapp.

780.7 GW ISSN 0172-9624
KONGRESSBERICHT BUNDESSCHULMUSIKWOCHE; Medieninvasion - die kulturpolitische Verantwortung der Musikerziehung. 1972. biennial. price varies. Musikverlag B. Schott's Soehne, Weihergarten 5, D-6500 Mainz, W. Germany (B.R.D.) Ed. Karl Heinrich Ehrenforth. circ. 800. (back issues avail.)

780 GW
KONZERT ALMANACH; Termine, Programme, Sitzplaene und Preise klassischer Konzerte i.d. BRD. 1981. a. F.Ch. Heel Verlag, Koenigswinterer Strasse 528-536, 5300 Bonn 3 (Oberkassel), W. Germany (B.R.D.) adv. circ. 6,000.

780 JA
KUNITACHI COLLEGE OF MUSIC. MEMOIRS/ KUNITACHI ONGAKU DAIGAKU KENKYU KIYO. (Text in Japanese) 1966. a. 2500 Yen. Kunitachi College of Music - Kunitachi Ongaku Daigaku, 5-5-1 Kashiwa-cho, Tachikawa-shi, Tokyo 190, Japan. Ed.Bd. illus. circ. 800.

781.7 US
LATVJU MUZIKA. (Text in Latvian) 1968. a. $17. Latvian Choir Association in the United States, Inc., 4538 W. 156th St., Cleveland, OH 44135 (Subscr. to: 3322 St. Antoine Ave., Kalamazoo, MI 49007) Ed. Roberts Zuika. bk. rev. (back issues avail.)

781.57 DK ISSN 0109-1212
LISTE OVER RYTMISKE SPILLESTEDER I DANMARK. 1982. a. Kr.50. Danske Jazzcenter, Borupvej 66, 4683 Roennede, Denmark. Eds. Arnvid Meyer, Birgit Kabelmann. circ. 2,500.
Formerly: Liste over Danske Jazzklubber og Huse m.V.
Jazz

786 AU
LISZT INFORMATION-COMMUNICATION; Mitteilungsblatt. 1972. a. S.15. Prugg-Verlag Eisenstaedter Graphische GmbH, Joseph Haydngasse 10, A-7000 Eisenstadt, Austria. Ed. Emmerich Karl Horvath. bibl. illus. circ. 1,250. (looseleaf format; back issues avail.)

780 UK ISSN 0141-0792
LISZT SOCIETY. JOURNAL. 1976. a. membership. Liszt Society Ltd., 78 Wimbledon Park Side, London SW19 5LH, England. Ed. Adrian Williams. bk. rev. bibl. circ. 300.
Formerly: Liszt Society, London. Newsletter (ISSN 0459-5084)

LITERARNO - MUZEJNY LETOPIS. see *LITERATURE*

780 DK
LITTLE RICHARD NEWS. 1986. irreg. (approx. 4-5/yr.) Kr.100. Mjoelner Edition, Oregaardrvaengevej 15, DK-4720 Praestoe, Denmark. Ed. John Garadkin. adv. bk. rev. circ. 500.

780 RM
LUCRARI DE MUZICOLOGIE. (Text in Rumanian; summaries in English, or French, or German) 1965. a. price varies. Conservatorul de Muzica "George Dima", Str. 23 August Nr. 25, 3400 Cluj-Napoca, Rumania. Ed. Dan Voiculescu. circ. 300. Indexed: RILM.

780 UK ISSN 0460-007X
LUTE SOCIETY JOURNAL. 1959. a. £3($8) Lute Society, 71 Priory Rd., Kew Gardens, Richmond, Surrey TW9 3DH, England. Ed. Ian Harwood. (back issues avail.) Indexed: RILM.

780 US ISSN 0076-1524
LUTE SOCIETY OF AMERICA. JOURNAL. 1968. a. membership. Lute Society of America, c/o Beedle Hinely, Box 1328, Lexington, VA 24450. TEL 703-463-5812. Ed. James Meadors. adv. bk. rev. index. circ. 600. Indexed: RILM.

780 PL
MALA BIBLIOTEKA OPEROWA. 1955. irreg. price varies. Polskie Wydawnictwo Muzyczne, Al. Krasinskiego 11a, 31-111 Krakow, Poland (Distr. by: Ars Polona, Krakowskie Przedmiescie 7, 00-068 Warsaw, Poland) Ed. Mieczyslaw Tomaszewski.

MASQUE. see *LITERATURE*

784.3 787.61 CS
MELODIE PRE VAS. irreg, vol.7, 1974. 7 Kcs. per no. Opus, Bratislava, Czechoslovakia.

780 CS ISSN 0544-4136
MISCELLANEA MUSICOLOGICA. (Text in Czech; summaries in German) 1956. irreg. (approx. a.) 24.50 Kcs. Universita Karlova, Filosoficka Fakulta, Katedra Dejin Hudby, Divadla a Filmu, Nam. Krasnoarmejcu 1, 116 38 Prague 1, Czechoslovakia. Ed. Jiri V. Cerny. illus. circ. 700. Indexed: RILM. CERDIC.

MUSIC

780   US   ISSN 0085-350X
MISSOURI JOURNAL OF RESEARCH IN MUSIC EDUCATION. 1962. a. $2. ‡ Missouri Music Educators Association, c/o Jack Stephenson, Ed., Conservatory of Music, University of Missouri-Kansas City, 4420 Warwick Blvd., Kansas City, MO 64111. TEL 816-363-4300. circ. 800. Indexed: Music Ind.

781.57   IT
MODERN JAZZ. (Text in English) irreg. Ruggero Stiassi, Ed. & Pub., Via Putti 3, Bologna, Italy. adv. rec. rev. (processed)

780.01   US
MONOGRAPHS IN MUSICOLOGY SERIES. 1983. irreg., vol.4, 1986. Pendragon Press, Rt. 1, Box 159, Stuyvesant, NY 12173-9720. TEL 518-828-3008.

780   US   ISSN 0077-1503
MONUMENTS OF RENAISSANCE MUSIC. 1964. irreg., vol.7, 1983. price varies. University of Chicago Press, 5801 S. Ellis Ave., Chicago, IL 60637. TEL 312-962-7700. Ed. Edward E. Lowinsky. (reprint service avail. from UMI,ISI)

780   UR
MONUMENTS OF RUSSIAN MUSIC. 1972. irreg. Izdatel'stvo Muzyka, Ul. Neglinnaya 14, Moscow 103031, Russian S.F.S.R., U.S.S.R.

MOVEMENTS IN THE ARTS. see *ART*

780   GW   ISSN 0077-1805
MOZART - JAHRBUCH. (Text in English, French and German) 1950. a. price varies. (Internationale Stiftung Mozarteum, AU) Baerenreiter-Verlag, Heinrich-Schuetz-Allee 29-37, 3500 Kassel-Wilhelmshoehe, W. Germany (B.R.D.) Ed.Bd. adv. index. circ. 1,000. Indexed: RILM.

780   US
MUGWUMPS' INSTRUMENT HERALD. CATALOG REPRINT SERIES. 1972. irreg. Mugwumps' Instrument, 12704 Barbara Rd., Silver Spring, MD 20906.

780   II
MUSIC ACADEMY. CONFERENCE SOUVENIR. (Text in English, Sanskrit or Tamil) 1940. a. Music Academy, 306 T.T.K. Rd., Royapettah, Madras 600014, India.

780   II
MUSIC ACADEMY. JOURNAL. (Text in English, Sanskrit, Tamil) 1929. a. Rs.15($3) Music Academy, Royapettah, 306 T.T.K. Rd., Madras 600014, India.

780   UK   ISSN 0085-3607
MUSIC AND LIFE. 1950. irreg. (3-4/yr.) £1.20. Music Group of the Communist Party, c/o George Burn, Ed., 17 Huntingdon Rd., London N.2, England. circ. 300. (processed)

780   UR
MUSIC AND MUSICIANS IN THE REMINISCENCES OF CONTEMPORARIES. 1985. irreg. 0.80 Rub. Izdatel'stvo Muzyka, Ul. Neglinnaya 14, Moscow 103031, Russian S.F.S.R., U.S.S.R.

780   IE
MUSIC ASSOCIATION OF IRELAND. ANNUAL REPORT. 1975. a. Music Association of Ireland, 23 Upper Mount St., Dublin 2, Ireland. stat.

780   CN   ISSN 0820-0416
MUSIC DIRECTORY CANADA. 1982. a. Can.$20.95. Norris-Whitney Communications, Inc., 832 Mount Pleasant Rd., Toronto, Ont. M4P 2L3, Canada. TEL 416-485-1049. Ed. Ted Burley. circ. 10,000.

785   US
MUSIC EDUCATORS NATIONAL CONFERENCE. SELECTIVE MUSIC LISTS: INSTRUMENTAL SOLOS AND ENSEMBLES. 1972. irreg., latest edt. 1979. $5 members; non-members $6.25. ‡ Music Educators National Conference, 1902 Association Dr., Reston, VA 22091. TEL 703-860-4000.

788   US   ISSN 0077-2402
MUSIC EDUCATORS NATIONAL CONFERENCE. SELECTIVE MUSIC LISTS: VOCAL SOLOS AND ENSEMBLES. 1968. irreg., latest 1974. $4.50 to members; non-members $5.75. ‡ Music Educators National Conference, 1902 Association Dr., Reston, VA 22091. TEL 703-860-4000.

780.1   US
MUSIC FORUM. 1967. irreg., vol.4, 1977. price varies. Columbia University Press, 562 W. 113th St., New York, NY 10025. TEL 212-678-6777. Ed. Felix Salzer. illus. Indexed: Music Ind. RILM.

780   US
MUSIC IN AMERICAN LIFE. irreg. University of Illinois Press, 54 E. Gregory Dr., Champaign, IL 61820. TEL 217-333-0950. (reprint service avail. from UMI)

780   IS
MUSIC IN TIME. a. $5.95. Jerusalem Rubin Academy of Music and Dance, 7 Peretz Smolenskin St., Jerusalem, Israel. Ed. Tzvi Avni.

MUSIC LIBRARY ASSOCIATION. TECHNICAL REPORTS; information for music media specialists. see *LIBRARY AND INFORMATION SCIENCES*

780.1   US
MUSIC LOCATOR. 1976. biennial. $89.95. Resource Publications, Inc., 160 E. Virginia St., San Jose, CA 95112. TEL 408-286-8505. circ. 750.

789.91   UK
MUSIC MASTER CATALOGUE. 1974. a. (with m. supplements) £119.50. John Humphries (Publishing) Ltd., Music House, 2 De Cham Ave., Hastings, Sussex TN37 6H , England. TEL (0424) 715181/424376. adv. circ. 3,000.
Formerly: Music Master (ISSN 0308-9347); Incorporating: Singles Master & Record Prices.

789.91   UK
MUSIC MASTER LABELS LIST. 1980. a. £14.95. John Humphries (Publishing) Ltd., Music House, 1 De Cham Ave., Hastings, Sussex TN37 6HE, England. TEL (0424) 715181/424376. circ. 4,000.

789.91   UK
MUSIC MASTER YEARBOOK. 1981. a. £14.95. John Humphries (Publishing) Ltd., Music House, 1 De Cham Ave., Hastings, Sussex TN37 6HE, England. circ. 4,000.

MUSIC O C L C USERS GROUP. NEWSLETTER. see *LIBRARY AND INFORMATION SCIENCES*

781.7   UR
MUSIC OF THE PEOPLES OF THE U.S.S.R; collection of essays. a. 1.70 Rub. Izdatel'stvo Muzyka, Ul. Neglinnaya 14, Moscow 103031, Russian S.F.S.R., U.S.S.R.

780   JA
MUSIC RESEARCH/ONGAKU KENKYU. a. 1500 Yen. Osaka College of Music - Osaka Ongaku Daigaku, 1-1-8 Shonai-saiwaicho, Toyonaka, Osaka, Japan. Ed. Nobuo Nishioka. adv. illus. circ. 1,000.
Former titles: Music Cultures; (1976-1978): Date of Music in Western Japan; (1972-1975): Date of Music in Kansai District.

780   US   ISSN 0195-6167
MUSIC THEORY SPECTRUM. 1979. a. $20. Society for Music Theory, School of Music, Indiana University, Bloomington, IN 47405. TEL 812-335-7346. Ed. John Clough. adv. bk. rev. circ. 1,000. Indexed: Music Ind. RILM.

780   US   ISSN 0734-7367
MUSIC THERAPY. 1981. a. $16.25. (American Association for Music Therapy) Association Management Corp., 66 Morris Ave., Springfield, NJ 07081. TEL 201-379-1100. Ed. Karen Goodman. bk. rev. circ. 1,000. Indexed: Psychol.Abstr.

780 310   US
MUSIC U S A. 1957? a. $15. American Music Conference, 303 E. Wacker Dr.. Ste. 1214, Chicago, IL 60601. TEL 312-856-8888. Ed. Paul B.E. Jorneberg.

780   UK
MUSIC WEEK DIRECTORY. 1976. a. $14. Spotlight Publications Ltd., Greater London House, Hampstead Rd., London NW1 7QZ, England.
Former titles: Music and Video Week Directory (ISSN 0264-3383) & Music and Video Week Yearbook; Music Week Industry Year Book.

780   UK   ISSN 0077-2453
MUSIC WORLD YEAR BOOK. 1981. a. £1.25. (Music Trade Association) Turret-Wheatland Ltd., 12 Greycaine Rd., Watford, Herts. WD2 4JP, England. Ed. Peter Pulham. circ. 3,000.

780 950   US   ISSN 0140-6078
MUSICA ASIATICA. 1978. irreg. (approx. a.), latest vol.3, 1981. price varies. Oxford University Press, 200 Madison Ave., New York, NY 10016 TEL 212-679-7300. (And Ely House, 37 Dover St., London W1X 4AH, England) Ed. Laurence Picken. illus. Indexed: RILM.

780   UK   ISSN 0580-2954
MUSICA BRITANNICA; a national collection of music. 1951. irreg. price varies. (Musica Britannica Trust) Stainer and Bell Ltd., 82 High Rd., P.O. Box 110, London N2 9PW, England. Ed. Michael Tilmouth. circ. 1,100.

780.9   GW   ISSN 0077-2461
MUSICA DISCIPLINA; yearbook of the history of music, Medieval and Renaissance. (Text in English; occasionally in French and German) 1946. a. (American Institute of Musicology, US) Haenssler-Verlag, Postfach 1220, Bismarckstrasse 4, 7303 Neuhausen-Stuttgart, W. Germany (B.R.D.) Ed. Armen Carapetyan. Indexed: Curr.Cont. Arts & Hum.Cit.Ind. Music Ind. RILM.

780 700 792   IT
MUSICA, IMMAGINE, TEATRO. irreg. Angelo Longo Editore, Via Paolo Costa 33, P.O. Box 431, 48100 Ravenna, Italy.

781.7   US
MUSICA JUDAICA. (Text in English and Hebrew) 1976. a. $20. American Society for Jewish Music, 155 Fifth Ave., New York, NY 10010. TEL 212-533-2601. Ed. Israel J. Katz. adv. bk. rev. circ. 1, 500. Indexed: Ind.Jew.Per. Music Ind. RILM.

780   PL   ISSN 0077-247X
MUSICA MEDII AEVI. (Text in Polish; summaries in English) 1965. irreg. price varies. (Polska Akademia Nauk, Instytut Sztuki) Polskie Wydawnictwo Muzyczne, Al. Krasinskiego 11a, 31-111 Krakow, Poland (Dist. by: Ars Polona-Ruch, Krakowskie Przedmiescie 7, 00-068 Warsaw, Poland) Ed. Jerzy Morawski. Indexed: RILM.

783   GW   ISSN 0027-4569
MUSICAE SACRAE MINISTERIUM. 1964. irreg. $10 to non-members. Consociatio Internationalis Musicae Sacrae, c/o Robert A. Skeris, Ed., D-5471 Maria Laach, Haus der Kirchenmusik, W. Germany (B.R.D.) Ed. Rudolf Pohl. bk. rev. abstr. index. circ. 5,000. Indexed: RILM.
Sacred music

790   US
MUSICAL AMERICA INTERNATIONAL DIRECTORY OF THE PERFORMING ARTS. 1968/69. a. $55. A B C Leisure Magazines Inc., 825 Seventh Ave., New York, NY 10019. TEL 212-265-8360. Ed. Shirley Fleming. adv. circ. 9,000.
Formerly: Musical America Annual Directory Issue (ISSN 0580-308X)

780   DK   ISSN 0027-4585
MUSICAL DENMARK. 1952. a. Kr.20. Danske Selskab - Danish Cultural Institute, 2 Kultorvet, 1175 Copenhagen K, Denmark. bibl. illus. circ. 3, 000. (back issues avail.) Indexed: Music Ind.

781.7   KE
MUSICAL INSTRUMENTS OF EAST AFRICA. 1975. irreg. EAs.0.80. Nelson Africa Ltd., Box 73146, Nairobi, Kenya.

780 001.3   SW   ISSN 0349-988X
MUSICAL INTERPRETATION RESEARCH. Short title: M I R. 1982. irreg. price varies. Mirage, Stjarnvagen 9, S-352 41 Vaxjo, Sweden. Ed. Nils-Goran Sundin. bk. rev. (back issues avail.)

780.7   301.412   US   ISSN 0737-0032
MUSICAL WOMAN. 1983. irreg. price varies.
Greenwood Press, 88 Post Rd. W., Box 5007,
Westport, CT 06881. TEL 203-226-3571.

780.01   IT
MUSICHE RINASCIMENTALI SICILIANE. no.7,
1978. irreg., no.15, 1985. price varies. Casa Editrice
Leo S. Olschki, Casella Postale 66, 50100 Florence,
Italy. circ. 1,000.

780   US
MUSICK OF THE FIFES & DRUMS SERIES. 1976.
irreg. price varies. Colonial Williamsburg
Foundation, Box C, Williamsburg, VA 23187. TEL
804-229-1000. Ed. John C. Moon.

780.1   781.7   SP
MUSICOLOGIA ESPANOLA. 1975. irreg. Ministerio
de Educacion y Ciencia, Comisaria Nacional de la
Musica, Madrid 3, Spain.

780   HU   ISSN 0077-2488
MUSICOLOGICA HUNGARICA. (Text in German)
1967. irreg., vol.7, 1980. price varies. (Magyar
Tudomanyos Akademia) Akademiai Kiado,
Publishing House of the Hungarian Academy of
Sciences, P.O. Box 24, H-1363 Budapest, Hungary.

780.01   BE
MUSICOLOGICA NEOLOVANIENSIA STUDIA.
1980. irreg., latest no.5, 1986. price varies.
Universite Catholique de Louvain, Institut Superieur
d'Archeologie et d'Histoire de l'Art, 1 place Blaise
Pascal, 1348 Louvain-la-Neuve, Belgium.

780   CS   ISSN 0581-0558
MUSICOLOGICA SLOVACA. 1969. irreg. price
varies. (Slovenska Akademia Vied, Umenovedny
Ustav) Veda, Publishing House of the Slovak
Academy of Sciences, Klemensova 19, 814 30
Bratislava, Czechoslovakia (Subscr. to: Slovart,
Gottwaldovo nam. 6, 817 64 Bratislava) Indexed:
Music Ind. RILM.

780   GW   ISSN 0077-2496
MUSICOLOGICAL STUDIES AND DOCUMENTS.
(Text in English; occasionally in French) 1948.
irreg. (American Institute of Musicology, US)
Haenssler-Verlag, Postfach 1220, Bismarckstrasse 4,
7303 Neuhausen-Stuttgart, W. Germany (B.R.D.)
Ed. Armen Carapetyan.

780   AT   ISSN 0077-250X
MUSICOLOGY AUSTRALIA. 1965. a. Aus.$20.
Musicological Society of Australia, Union Box 67,
University of New South Wales, Box 1, Kensington,
N.S.W. 2033, Australia. Ed.Bd. bk. rev. circ. 350.
Indexed: Aus.P.A.I.S. Music Ind. RILM.

780   GW   ISSN 0930-8954
MUSIK - ALMANACH; Musikleben in der
Bundesrepublik Deutschland. biennial.
(Bundesministers der Innern) Gustav Bosse Verlag
GmbH & Co. KG, Postfach 417, D-8400
Regensburg 1, W. Germany (B.R.D.) (Co-sponsor:
Deutschen Stiftung Musikleben) Ed. Margot
Wallscheid.

780   GW
MUSIK AUS DER STEIERMARK. 1959. irreg. (4-6/
yr.) price varies. (Institut fuer Musikethnologie)
Fritz Schulz Verlag GmbH, Am Maerzengraben 6,
D-7800 Freiburg-Tiengen, W. Germany (B.R.D.)
Ed. Wolfgang Suppan. circ. 200.

780   SW   ISSN 0077-2518
MUSIK I SVERIGE. (Text in English and Swedish)
1969. irreg. price varies. Svenskt Musikhistoriskt
Arkiv, Box 16326, S-103 26 Stockholm, Sweden.
TEL 46-08 11 93 13. (Co-sponsor: Svenska
Samfundet foer Musikforskning) Indexed: RILM.

780   301   AU   ISSN 0259-076X
MUSIK UND GESELLSCHAFT. 1967. irreg., no.19,
1985. price varies. Verband der Wissenschaftlichen
Gesellschaft Oesterreichs, Lindengasse 37, A-1070
Vienna, Austria.

780   GW   ISSN 0077-2526
MUSIKALISCHE DENKMAELER. 1955. irreg.
Akademie der Wissenschaften und der Literatur,
Mainz, Geschwister-Scholl-Str. 2, 6500 Mainz, W.
Germany (B.R.D.)

780   DK   ISSN 0108-0040
MUSIKBRANCHENS AARBOG. 1982. a. Kr.29.75.
Danplay, Krohsgade 1, 2100 Copenhagen OE,
Denmark. Ed. Uffe Egekvist. adv. bk. rev. illus. circ.
7,000.

780   DK   ISSN 0109-2618
MUSIKHISTORISK MUSEUM OG CARL
CLAUDIUS SAMLING. MEDDELELSER. 1982.
biennial. Kr.30. Musikhistorisk Museum, Aabenraa
30, 1124 Copenhagen K, Denmark. Ed. Mette
Mueller. adv. illus.

780   SW
MUSIKMUSEETS SKRIFTER. 1964. irreg., no.12,
1986. price varies. Statens Musiksamlingar,
Musikmuseet, Box 16326, S-10326 Stockholm,
Sweden. circ. 1,000. Indexed: RILM.
Formerly: Musikhistoriska Museet. Skrifter (ISSN
0081-5675)

780   GW
MUSIKPAEDAGOGISCHE BIBLIOTHEK. 1962.
irreg., vol.32, 1985. DM.19.80. (Heinrichshofen
Buecher) Florian Noetzel Verlag, Heinrichshofen
Buecher, Valoisstrasse 11, 2940 Wilhelmshaven, W.
Germany (B.R.D.) (Dist. in U.S. by C.F. Peters
Corp., 373 Park Ave. S., New York, N.Y. 10016)
Ed. Walter Kolneder.

780   DK   ISSN 0107-654X
MUSIKPLADER OG -BAAND. KLASSISK MUSIK.
1980. a. Kr.867.85. Bibliotekscentralen, Tempovej 7-
11, DK-2750 Ballerup, Denmark.
Supersedes in part: Musikplader og -baand.

780   DK   ISSN 0107-8690
MUSIKPLADER OG -BAAND. RYTMISK MUSIK.
1980. a. Kr.1649.00. Bibliotekscentralen, Tempovej
7-11, DK-2750 Ballerup, Denmark.
Supersedes in part: Musikplader og -baand.

780   GW   ISSN 0177-350X
MUSIKPSYCHOLOGIE. 1984. DM.28. (Deutsche
Gesellschaft fuer Musikpsychologie) Florian Noetzel
Verlag, Heinrichshofen Buecher, Postfach 580, D-
2940 Wilhelmshaven, W. Germany (B.R.D.) Ed.Bd.
circ. 1,000. (back issues avail.)

780   YU   ISSN 0580-373X
MUZIKOLOSKI ZBORNIK/MUSICOLOGICAL
ANNUAL. (Text in various languages; summaries in
English and Slovene) 1965. a. price varies. Univerza
Edvarda Kardelja v Ljubljani, Oddelek za
Muzikologijo, Filozofska Fakulteta, Askerceva 12,
61000 Ljubljana, Yugoslavia. Ed. Andrej Rijavec.
illus. index. circ. 500. Indexed: RILM.

780   398   UR
MUZYKAL'NAYA FOL'KLORISTIKA. (Text in
Russian; summaries in English and German) 1973.
irreg. 2 Rub. (Soyuz Kompozitorov Rossiiskoi
S.F.S.R., Fol'klornaya Komissiya) Izdatel'stvo
Sovetskii Kompozitor, 14-12, Sadovaya-
Triumfalnaya St., 103006, Moscow, Russian
S.F.S.R., U.S.S.R. illus. Indexed: M.L.A.

371   780   UR   ISSN 0302-847X
MUZYKAL'NOE VOSPITANIE V SHKOLE. irreg.
0.57 Rub. Izdatel'stvo Muzyka, Neglinnaya ul., 14,
Moscow K-45, Russian S.F.S.R., U.S.S.R.

780   AT   ISSN 0811-7497
N M A. (New Music Articles) 1982. irreg. (1-2/yr.)
Aus.$25. N.M.A. Publications, 48 Greville St.,
Prahran, Victoria 3181, Australia (Subscr. addr.:
P.O. Box 185, Brunswick, Victoria 3056, Australia)
Eds. Rainer Linz, Richard Vella. adv. circ. 1,000.
(back issues avail.)

780   US   ISSN 0547-4175
NATIONAL ASSOCIATION OF SCHOOLS OF
MUSIC. DIRECTORY. 1950. a. $8. National
Association of Schools of Music, 11250 Roger
Bacon Dr., No. 5, Reston, VA 22090. TEL 703-
437-0700.

780   US   ISSN 0164-2847
NATIONAL ASSOCIATION OF SCHOOLS OF
MUSIC. HANDBOOK. 1930. biennial. $8. National
Association of Schools of Music, 11250 Roger
Bacon Dr., No. 5, Reston, VA 22090. TEL 703-
437-0700. circ. 2,200.

780.7   US   ISSN 0077-3409
NATIONAL ASSOCIATION OF SCHOOLS OF
MUSIC. PROCEEDINGS OF THE ANNUAL
MEETING. 1934. a. $9. National Association of
Schools of Music, 11250 Roger Bacon Dr., Reston,
VA 22090. TEL 703-437-0700. Indexed: Music Ind.

786   US
NATIONAL CONFERENCE ON PIANO
PEDAGOGY. PROCEEDINGS. 1980. biennial.
National Conference on Piano Pedagogy, 51 White
Pine Ln., Princeton, NJ 08540. TEL 201-924-3969.
Ed. Dr. Baker. circ. 1,000.

786.3   US   ISSN 0077-4642
NATIONAL GUILD OF PIANO TEACHERS.
GUILD SYLLABUS. 1943. a. $0.75. National
Guild of Piano Teachers, Box 1807, Austin, TX
78767. TEL 512-478-5775. Ed. Walter Merchant.
circ. 14,000.

782   US   ISSN 0085-381X
NATIONAL OPERA ASSOCIATION.
MEMBERSHIP DIRECTORY. 1955. a. $4.
National Opera Association, Inc., c/o Mary Elaine
Wallace, Route 2, Box 93, Commerce, TX 75428.
TEL 214-886-3830. circ. 850.

780   GW   ISSN 0077-7714
NEUE MUSIKGESCHICHTLICHE
FORSCHUNGEN. 1968. irreg. price varies. ‡
Breitkopf und Haertel, Walkmuehlstr. 52, Postfach
1707, 6200 Wiesbaden, W. Germany (B.R.D.) Ed.
Lothar Hoffman-Erbrecht.

781.7   UK
NEW CITY SONGSTER. 1968. a. £1($3) per no. 35
Stanley Ave., Beckenham, Kent BR3 2PU, England.
Eds. Ewan MacColl, Peggy Seeger. adv. illus. index.
circ. 4,000.

780.7   US   ISSN 0028-5315
NEW HAMPSHIRE QUARTER NOTES. vol.20,
1977. a. $10. New Hampshire Music Educators
Association, 14 Hill St., Dover, NH 03820. Ed. Nan
Arnstein. adv. bk. rev. circ. 750(controlled)

780.7   US
NEW OXFORD HISTORY OF MUSIC. irreg. price
varies. Oxford University Press, 200 Madison Ave.,
New York, NY 10016 TEL 212-679-7300. (And
Ely House, 37 Dover St., London W1X 4AH,
England) Ed.Bd.

780   US   ISSN 0085-4042
NEW YORK PRO MUSICA INSTRUMENTAL
SERIES.* 1967. irreg., no.6, 1970. $3.50. ‡
Associated Music Publishers, Inc., 24 E. 22nd St.,
New York, NY 10010-6110.

780   UK   ISSN 0261-5096
NORTHUMBRIAN PIPERS' SOCIETY
MAGAZINE. 1980. biennial. £0.50. Northumbrian
Pipers' Society, c/o R. Butler, Ed., 22 Newlyn
Drive, Parkside Dale, Cramlington, Northumberland
NE23 9RN, England. bk. rev. circ. 500.

780   NO   ISSN 0801-1087
NORWEGIAN MUSIC INFORMATION CENTER.
BULLETIN. a. free. Norwegian Music Information
Centre, Toftesgt. 69, N-0552 Oslo 5, Norway. TEL
02-37-09-09. Ed. Lisbeth Risnes.

780   PL
OBRZEDY I ZWYCZAJE LUDOWE. 1985. irreg.
price varies. Polskie Wydawnictwo Muzyczne, Al.
Krasinskiego 11, 31-111 Krakow, Poland (Dist. by:
Ars Polona, Krakowskie Przedmiescie 7, 00 068
Warsaw, Poland) Ed. Alexandra Bogucka.

780   AU   ISSN 0023-3048
OESTERREICHISCHE AKADEMIE DER
WISSENSCHAFTEN. KOMMISSION FUER
MUSIKFORSCHUNG. MITTEILUNGEN.
(Supplements) 1956. irreg. price varies. Verlag der
Oesterreichischen Akademie der Wissenschaften,
Dr. Ignaz Seipelplatz 2, A-1010 Vienna, Austria.

780   GW   ISSN 0078-3471
OESTERREICHISCHE GESELLSCHAFT FUER
MUSIK. BEITRAEGE. 1967. irreg. price varies.
(AU) Baerenreiter Verlag, Heinrich-Schuetz-Allee
31-37, 3500 Kassel-Wilhelmshoehe, W. Germany
(B.R.D.) Eds. R. Klein, K. Roschitz. Indexed:
RILM.

780 920	AU	ISSN 0078-3501
OESTERREICHISCHE KOMPONISTEN DES 20. JAHRHUNDERTS. 1964. irreg. price varies. Musikverlag Elisabeth Lafite, Hegelgasse 13/22, A-1010 Vienna, Austria (and Oesterreichischer Bundesverlag, Schwarzenbergstr. 5, 1015 Vienna 1, Austria)

784	AU	ISSN 0473-8624
OESTERREICHISCHES VOLKSLIEDWERK. JAHRBUCH. 1952. a. S.150. Oesterreichischer Bundesverlag, Schwarzenbergstr. 5, A-1010 Vienna, Austria. Ed. Gerlinde Haid. bk. rev. index. circ. 600. Indexed: RILM.
Supersedes: Volkslied, Volkstanz, Volksmusik.

786.6	US	ISSN 0048-1513
OFFICIAL ORGAN BLUE BOOK;* international used organ valuation guide. 1967. a. $30. ‡ c/o Zeb Billings, Sight & Sound International, Inc., 3200 S. 166th St., Box 27, New Berlin, WI 53151. Ed. Walter Kappelmann. illus. stat. index. cum.index. circ. 2,500.

780.1	UK	ISSN 0048-1653
OLD TIME MUSIC. 1971. irreg. (2-3/yr.) £6($12) c/o Tony Russell, Ed., 22 Upper Tollington Park, London N4 3EL, England. adv. bk. rev. record rev. bibl. illus. circ. 1,200. Indexed: Abstr.Pop.Cult. M.L.A. Pop.Mus.Per.Ind. Music Ind.
Country

780.7	CN	ISSN 0700-5318
OPUS. 1964. irreg. free. University of Western Ontario, Faculty of Music, London, Ont. N6A 3K7, Canada. TEL 519-885-1211. Ed. John James Nelder. illus. circ. 300.

780.01	IS	ISSN 0303-3937
ORBIS MUSICAE; Assaph studies in the arts. (Text in English, French, German) 1971. biennial. $12. Tel-Aviv University, Department of Musicology, Ramat-Aviv, Tel-Aviv, Israel. Ed.Bd. bk. rev. circ. 500. (back issues avail.) Indexed: Music Ind.

780	GW
ORGAN BUILDING PERIODICAL/ZEITSCHRIFT FUER ORGELBAU; I S O Information. (Text in English and German) 1969. irreg. DM.45 for 3 issues. (International Society of Organbuilders - Internationale Orgelbauer-Vereinigung) Orgelbau-Fachverlag, Postfach 226, 7128 Lauffen, W. Germany (B.R.D.) Ed. Richard Rensch. adv. bk. rev. circ. 2,200. Indexed: Music Ind.
Formerly: I S O Information (ISSN 0579-5613)

780	NE	ISSN 0078-6098
ORGAN YEARBOOK; a journal for the players and historians of keyboard instruments. (Text in English, French and German) 1970. a. fl.45. Uitgeverij Frits Knuf B. V., Box 720, 4116 ZJ Buren, Netherlands. Ed. Peter Williams. adv. bk. rev. circ. 3,000. (back issues avail.) Indexed: Music Ind. RILM.

786	UK
ORGANISTS' BENEVOLENT LEAGUE INC. ANNUAL REPORT. 1909. a. free. Organists' Benevolent League, c/o R.C. Lyne, Ed., 10 Stratford Place, London W1N 9AE, England. circ. 2,500.

700	US
OXFORD MONOGRAPHS ON MUSIC. irreg. price varies. Oxford University Press, 200 Madison Ave., New York, NY 10016 TEL 212-679-7300. (And Ely House, 37 Dover St., London W1X 4AH, England)

780	US	ISSN 0078-7264
OXFORD STUDIES OF COMPOSERS. irreg., no.19, 1982. price varies. Oxford University Press, 200 Madison Ave., New York, NY 10016 TEL 212-679-7300. (and Ely House, 37 Dover St., London W1X 4AH, England) Ed. Colin Mason.

780	PL	ISSN 0137-3935
PAGINE/PAGINE. ARGOMENTI MUSICALI POLACCO-ITALIANI; Polsko-wloskie materialy muzyczne. (Text in Italian and Polish; summaries in Italian) 1972. a. price varies. (Polish Music Council, Warsaw) Polskie Wydawnictwo Muzyczne, Al. Krasinskiego 11a, 31-111 Krakow, Poland (Distributed by: Ars Polona-Ruch, Krakowskie Przedmiescie 7, 00-068 Warsaw, Poland) Ed. Michal Bristiger. bk. rev. index. Indexed: RILM.

789.9	US	ISSN 0360-2109
PAUL'S RECORD MAGAZINE. 1975. irreg., nos.17/18, 1978. $2 per no. Paul E. Bezanker, Ed. & Pub., Box 2343, Enfield, CT 06082. adv. bk. rev. rec.rev. illus. stat. index. cum.index. circ. 1,500. Indexed: Pop.Mus.Per.Ind.

780	UK	ISSN 0309-0019
PERFORMING RIGHT NEWS. 1976. irreg. membership. Performing Right Society Ltd., c/o Lesley Bray, 29-33 Berners St., London W1P 4AA, England. circ. 20,000. Indexed: Mus.Ind.
Replaces: Performing Right (ISSN 0031-5257)

780	UK	ISSN 0309-0884
PERFORMING RIGHT YEAR BOOK. a. membership. Performing Right Society Ltd., c/o Lesley Bray, 29-33 Berners St., London W1P 4AA, England.

780	US	ISSN 0191-1554
PERFORMING WOMAN; a national directory of professional women musicians. 1978. a. $5. J.D. Dinneen, Ed. & Pub., 26910 Grand View Ave., Hayward, CA 94542. circ. 4,000.

780	US
PERGOLESI STUDIES/STUDI PERGOLESIANI. 1986. irreg. Pendragon Press, R.R. 1, Box 159, Stuyvesant, NY 12173-9720.

786	GW	ISSN 0173-8607
PIANO-JAHRBUCH; das deutschsprachige Klavierperiodikum. 1977. irreg. DM.38.40($14) Piano-Verlag Recklinghausen, Koernerplatz 8, D-4350 Recklinghausen, W. Germany (B.R.D.) Ed. Rainer M. Klaas. adv. bk. rev. bibl. illus. index. circ. 1,300. (back issues avail.)

780	UK	ISSN 0143-4918
PLAINSONG & MEDIAEVAL MUSIC SOCIETY. JOURNAL. 1978. a. £5($12) Plainsong & Mediaeval Music Society, 72 Brewery Rd., London N7 9NE, England. Ed. David Hiley. adv. bk. rev. circ. 400.

781.57	BE
POINT DU JAZZ. (Text in French) 1969. a. 500 Fr. for 3 nos. ‡ Sweet and Hot, c/o Jacques Denis, 36 rue Inchebroux, B-5890 Chaumont-Gistoux, Belgium (Subscr. to: Lucien Ravet, Rue de la Commune 66, B-1030 Brussels, Belgium) Ed. Jacques Tricot. adv. bk. rev. illus. circ. 1,000. Indexed: Music Ind.

781.7	US	ISSN 0741-9945
POLISH MUSIC HISTORY SERIES. 1982. irreg. price varies. Friends of Polish Music, University of Southern California, School of Music, Los Angeles, CA 90089-0851. TEL 213-887-1906. Ed. Wanda Wilk. circ. 1,000.

780	PL
POLSKA AKADEMIA NAUK. INSTYTUT SZTUKI. SERIES A: WORKS BY POLISH COMPOSERS. (Text mainly in Latin; occasionally in Polish and other languages) 1966. irreg. price varies. Polskie Wydawnictwo Muzyczne, Al. Krasinskiego 11a, 31-111 Krakow, Poland (Dist. by: Ars Polona, Krakowskie Przedmiescie 7, 00-068 Warsaw, Poland) Ed. Zygmunt M. Szweykowski.
Supersedes in part: Monumenta Musicae in Polonia (ISSN 0077-1465)

780	PL
POLSKA AKADEMIA NAUK. INSTYTUT SZTUKI. SERIES B: FONTES ARTIS MUSICAE. 1964. irreg. Polskie Wydawnictwo Muzyczne, Al. Krasinskiego 11a, 31-111 Krakow, Poland. Ed. Jozef M. Chominski.
Supersedes in part: Monumenta Musicae in Polonia (ISSN 0077-1465)

780	PL
POLSKA AKADEMIA NAUK. INSTYTUT SZTUKI. SERIES C: TRACTATUS DE MUSICA. 1984. irreg. Polskie Wydawnictwo Muzyczne, Al. Krasinskiego 11a, 31-111 Krakow, Poland. Ed. Henryk Kowalewicz.
Supersedes in part: Monumenta Musicae in Polonia (ISSN 0077-1465)

780	PL
POLSKA AKADEMIA NAUK. INSTYTUT SZTUKI. SERIES D: BIBLIOTHECA ANTIQUA. 1975. irreg. Polskie Wydawnictwo Muzyczne, Al. Krasinskiego 11a, 31-111 Krakow, Poland. Ed. Jerzy Morawski.
Supersedes in part: Monumenta Musicae in Polonia (ISSN 0077-1465)

780	PL	ISSN 0079-3612
POLSKA PIESN I MUZYKA LUDOWA. ZRODLA I MATERIALY. 1974. irreg. price varies. (Polska Akademia Nauk, Instytut Sztuki) Polskie Wydawnictwo Muzyczne, Al. Krasinskiego 11a, 31-111 Krakow, Poland (Dist. by Ars Polona-Ruch, Krakowskie Przedmiescie 7, 00-068 Warsaw, Poland)

780	PL
PRACE ARCHIVUM SLASKIEJ KULTURY MUZYCZNEJ. 1973. irreg., no.8, 1980. exchange basis. Akademia Muzyczna, Biblioteka Glowna, Ul. 27 Stycznia 33, 40-025 Katowice, Poland (Dist. by: Ars Polona-Ruch, Krakowskie Przedmiescie 7, 00-68 Warsaw, Poland)

780	US	ISSN 0079-5259
PRINCETON STUDIES IN MUSIC. 1964. irreg., no.7, 1980. price varies. Princeton University Press, 3175 Princeton Pike, Lawrenceville, NJ 08648. TEL 609-896-1344. (reprint service avail. from UMI)

780	UK
PROFESSIONAL REGISTER OF ARTISTS. 1976. a. Incorporated Society of Musicians, 10 Stratford Place, London W1N 9AE, England. circ. 4,000.

780	UK
PROFESSIONAL REGISTER OF PRIVATE TEACHERS OF MUSIC. 1978. a. Incorporated Society of Musicians, 10 Stratford Place, London W1N 9AE, England. circ. 6,000.

780	US
PURCHASER'S GUIDE TO THE MUSIC INDUSTRIES. 1897. a. free with subscription to Music Trades. Music Trades Corporation, c/o Paul A. Majeski, Box 432, 80 West St., Englewood, NJ 07631. TEL 201-871-1965. Ed. Brian T. Majeski. adv. circ. 8,000. (reprint service avail. from UMI)

780	IT
QUADERNI PUCCINIANI. a. Istituto di Studi Pucciniani, Lucca, Italy.

780	GW	ISSN 0079-905X
QUELLENKATALOGE ZUR MUSIKGESCHICHTE. 1966. irreg., vol.19, 1981. Florian Noetzel Verlag, Heinrichshofen Buecher, Valoisstrasse 11, 2940 Wilhelmshaven, W. Germany (B.R.D.) (Dist. in U.S. by C. F. Peters Corp., 373 Park Ave. S., New York, N.Y. 10016) Ed. Richard Schaal.

780	FR	ISSN 0080-0139
RECHERCHES SUR LA MUSIQUE FRANCAISE CLASSIQUE. 1960. a. price varies. Editions A. et J. Picard, 82, rue Bonaparte, 75006 Paris, France. Indexed: RILM.

780	US	ISSN 8755-6154
RECORD COLLECTOR'S MONTHLY. 1982. irreg. (4-5/yr.) 10 Record Collector's Monthly, Inc., Box 75, Mendham, NJ 07945. TEL 201-543-9520. Ed. Don Mennie. adv. bk. rev. rec.rev. circ. 5,000. (tabloid format; back issues avail.)

780	GW
REGER-STUDIEN. 1978. irreg. price varies. (Max-Reger-Institut, Bonn) Breitkopf und Haertel, Walkmuehlstr. 52, Postfach 1707, 6200 Wiesbaden, W. Germany (B.R.D.) Eds. Guenter Massenkeil, Susanne Popp.

780	CN	ISSN 0714-4369
REGGAE. (Text in English) 1982. irreg. (1-2/yr.) Can.$3.00 per no. Live Good Today, 10 Walmer Rd., No. 1501, Toronto, Ontario M5R 2W4, Canada. TEL 416-924-8519. Ed. Beth Lesser. adv. circ. 5,000. (back issues avail.)
Formerly: Reggae Quarterly.

780 HU ISSN 0080-0562
REGI MAGYAR DALLAMOK TARA/CORPUS
MUSICAE POPULARIS HUNGARICAE. (Text in
Hungarian; occasional summaries in German) 1958.
irreg. price varies. (Magyar Tudomanyos Akademia,
Nepzenekutato Csoport) Akademiai Kiado,
Publishing House of the Hungarian Academy of
Sciences, P.O. Box 24, H-1363 Budapest, Hungary.

780 GW
RENAISSANCE MANUSCRIPT STUDIES. 1973.
irreg., latest vol.1. (American Institute of
Musicology, US) Haenssler-Verlag, Postfach 1220,
Bismarckstrasse 4, 7303 Neuhausen-Stuttgart, W.
Germany (B.R.D.) Ed. Charles Hamm.

780 PL ISSN 0486-4689
RES FACTA; teksty o muzyce wspolczesnej. 1967.
irreg. price varies. Polskie Wydawnictwo Muzyczne,
Al. Krasinskiego 11a, 31-111 Krakow, Poland (Dist.
by: Ars Polona-Ruch, Krakowskie Przedmiescie 7,
00-068 Warsaw, Poland) Ed. Michal Bristiger.
Indexed: RILM.

780.01 US
RESEARCH SYMPOSIUM ON THE
PSYCHOLOGY AND ACOUSTICS OF MUSIC.
PROCEEDINGS. 1977. a. price varies. University
of Kansas, A M E M T Department, 311 Bailey
Hall, Lawrence, KS 66045-2344. TEL 913-864-
4784. Ed. George L. Duerksen. circ. 300.

780 UK ISSN 0080-1828
RESOURCES OF MUSIC. 1969. irreg., no.24, 1982.
$18.95 (cloth); $9.95 (paper) for latest vol.
Cambridge University Press, Edinburgh Bldg.,
Shaftesbury Rd., Cambridge CB2 2RU, England
(and 32 E. 57 St., New York NY 10022) Ed. John
Paynter.

780 BL
REVISTA BRASILEIRA DE MUSICA. irreg.
Universidade Federal de Rio de Janeiro, Escola de
Musica, Rua de Passeio, 98-200021 Rio de Janeiro,
Brazil. Indexed: Music Ind.

780.01 BE
REVUE BELGE DE MUSICOLOGIE/BELGISCH
TIJDSCHRIFT VOOR MUZIEKWETENSCHAP.
(Text in Dutch, English, French, and German)
1945. a. 700 Fr.($14) Societe Belge de Musicologie,
30 rue de la Regence, 1000 Brussels, Belgium. Eds.
H. Vanhulst, R. Wangermee. adv. bk. rev. illus. circ.
600. Indexed: Music Ind. RILM.

REVUE DES ARCHEOLOGUES ET HISTORIENS
D'ART DE LOUVAIN. see ART

780.01 IT
RIVISTA ITALIANA DI MUSICOLOGIA.
QUADERNI. 1966. irreg., no.9, 1984. price varies.
Casa Editrice Leo S. Olschki, Casella Postale 66,
50100 Florence, Italy.

ROAR; tapebook series. see LITERARY AND
POLITICAL REVIEWS

780.42 US ISSN 0275-9187
ROCK YEARBOOK. 1980. a. Grove Press, Inc., 196
W. Houston St., New York, NY 10014. TEL 212-
242-4900. Eds. Michael Gross, Maxim Jakubowski.
illus.

780 UK ISSN 0080-4320
ROYAL COLLEGE OF ORGANISTS. YEAR
BOOK. 1864/65. a. £2.35. ‡ Royal College of
Organists, Kensington Gore, London SW7 2QS,
England. adv. circ. 4,000.

780 IE
ROYAL IRISH ACADEMY OF MUSIC.
PROSPECTUS. 1973. a. 50p. ‡ Royal Irish
Academy of Music, 36/38 Westland Row, Dublin,
2, Ireland. circ. 1,000.

780 UK ISSN 0080-4460
ROYAL MUSICAL ASSOCIATION. R.M.A.
RESEARCH CHRONICLE. 1961. a. £10.50 to
non-members. Royal Musical Association, c/o
Rosemary Dooley, Secy., 5 Church St., Harston,
Cambridge CB2 5NP, England. Ed. John Milsom.
circ. 600. Indexed: Br.Hum.Ind. RILM. Music Ind.

780 PL
ROZPRAWY I SZKICE FILOZOFICZNO-
ESTETYCZNE O MUZYCE. 1972. irreg. price
varies. Polskie Wydawnictwo Muzyczne, Al.
Krasinskiego 11a, 31-111 Krakow, Poland (Dist. by:
Ars Polona, Krakowskie Przedmiescie 7, 00 068
Warsaw, Poland)

780 UR
RUSSIAN CLASSICAL MUSICAL CRITICS. a. 2.50
Rub. Izdatel'stvo Muzyka, Ul. Neglinnaya 14,
Moscow 103031, Russian S.F.S.R., U.S.S.R.

781.7 US
RUSSIAN MUSIC STUDIES. irreg., vol.12, 1984. U
M I Research Press, 300 N. Zeeb Rd., Ann Arbor,
MI 48106. Ed. Malcolm H. Brown.

780 GW ISSN 0080-519X
SAARBRUECKER STUDIEN ZUR
MUSIKWISSENSCHAFT. 1966. irreg. price varies.
(Universitaet des Saarlandes,
Musikwissenschaftliches Institut) Baerenreiter
Verlag, Heinrich-Schuetz-Allee 31-37, 3500 Kassel-
Wilhelmshoehe, W. Germany (B.R.D.) Ed. Walter
Wiora.

SADLER'S WELLS THEATRE PROGRAMME. see
THEATER

784 GW
SAENGER-TASCHENKALENDER. 1955. a. price
varies. (Deutscher Saengerbund e.V.) Verlag
Deutsche Saengerzeitung GmbH, Luepertzender Str.
157-163, Postfach 304, 4050 Moenchengladbach 1,
West Germany (B.R.D.) adv. circ. 12,000.

780 DK ISSN 0109-8438
SAMFUNDET TIL UDGIVELSE AF DANSK
MUSIK. BULLETIN. 1981. irreg. free. Samfundet
til Udgivelse af Dansk Musik - Society for
Publication of Danish Music, Valkendorfsgade 3,
1151 Copenhagen K, Denmark. Ed. Steen Pade.

780 GW ISSN 0085-588X
SAMMLUNG MUSIKWISSENSCHAFTLICHER
ABHANDLUNGEN/COLLECTION D'ETUDES
MUSICOLOGIQUES. (Text in English, French,
and German) 1932. irreg., no.75, 1987. price varies.
Verlag Valentin Koerner, H.-Sielcken-Str. 36,
Postfach 304, D-7570 Baden Baden 1, W. Germany
(B.R.D.)

780 CN
SASKATCHEWAN MUSIC FESTIVAL
ASSOCIATION OFFICIAL SYLLABUS. 1909. a.
Saskatchewan Music Festival Association, 210-3806
Albert St., Regina, S4S 3R2, Canada. Ed. Doris
Covey Lazecki. adv. circ. 2,500.

791 GW
SCHOTT AKTUELL. (Text in German) 1961. irreg.
free. B. Schott's Soehne, Weihergarten 1-9, Postfach
3640, 6500 Mainz 1, W. Germany (B.R.D.) Ed.Bd.
circ. 2,800. (tabloid format)
  Formerly: Schott-Kurier (ISSN 0036-6919)

780 GW
SCHUETZ-JAHRBUCH. 1980. a. membership.
(Internationale Heinrich Schuetz-Gesellschaft e.V.)
Baerenreiter Verlag, Heinrich-Schuetz-Allee 31-37,
3500 Kassel-Wilhelmshoehe, W. Germany (B.R.D.)
Indexed: Music Ind. RILM.
  Supersedes (1966-197?): Sagittarius (ISSN 0080-
5408)

780 SZ
SCHWEIZER BEITRAGE ZUR
MUSIKWISSENSCHAFT. (Text in German;
summaries vary) 1972. irreg. price varies. P. Haupt,
Falkenplatz 14, CH-3001 Berne, Switzerland. Ed.
Ernst Lichtenhahn.

780 SZ ISSN 0080-7354
SCHWEIZERISCHE MUSIKFORSCHENDE
GESELLSCHAFT. PUBLIKATIONEN. SERIE 2.
1952. irreg., no.33, 1983. price varies. Paul Haupt
AG, Falkenplatz 14, CH-3001 Berne, Switzerland.

781.7 UK
SCOTTISH FOLK DIRECTORY. 1973. a. £1.25. ‡
c/o Sheila Douglas, Ed., 12 Mansfield Rd., Perth,
Scotland. adv. bk. rev. circ. 650.

781.7 US ISSN 0361-6622
SELECTED REPORTS IN ETHNOMUSICOLOGY.
1966. a. price varies. (Council on Ethnomusicology)
University of California, Los Angeles, Department
of Music, Los Angeles, CA 90024. TEL 213-825-
5947. Ed. Roger Wright. illus. circ. 800. Indexed:
M.L.A. Music In: RILM.

780.01 IT
SEMINARIO DI STUDI E RICERCHE SUL
LINGUAGGIO MUSICALE. ATTI. 1971. a.
Istituto Musicale F. Canneti, Villa Cordellina-
Lombardi, Montecchio Maggiore, Vincenza, Italy.
illus.

SEVENTEENTH CENTURY FRENCH STUDIES.
see HISTORY — History Of Europe

783 US
SHALSHELET: THE CHAIN. vol.11, 1976. irreg.
membership. Hebrew Union College-Jewish Institute
of Religion, School of Sacred Music Cantorial
Alumni Association, One W. 4th St., New York,
NY 10012. TEL 212-674-5300. Ed. B. Ostfeld
Horowitz. circ. 200.

780 790 UK
SHOWCALL. 1973. a. £5.50 for 2 parts. Carson and
Comerford Ltd., Stage House, 47 Bermondsley St.,
London SE1 3XT, England. adv. illus. index.

780 DK ISSN 0108-4402
SKOLEMUSIKHAANDBOGEN. 1982. a. Kr.45.
Folkeskolens Musiklaererforening, Gudenaavej 162,
7400 Herning, Denmark.

SLOVENSKA NARODNA BIBLIOGRAFIA SERIA
H: HUDOBNINY. see MUSIC — Abstracting,
Bibliographies, Statistics

784.7691 786.97 CS
SLOVENSKE LUDOVE PIESNE PRE
AKORDEON. irreg., vol.3, 1974. 8 Kcs. per no.
Opus, Bratislava, Czechoslovakia.

780 SP ISSN 0213-0815
SOCIEDAD DE ESTUDIOS VASCOS.
CUADERNOS DE SECCION. MUSICA. 1983.
irreg. (Sociedad de Estudios Vascos) Eusko
Ikaskuntza, S.A., Churruca, 7 - 2, 20004 Donostia,
Spain.

780.65 US ISSN 0161-5971
SONGWRITER'S MARKET. 1979. a. $15.95. F & W
Publications, Inc., 9933 Alliance Rd., Cincinnati,
OH 45242. TEL 513-984-0717. Ed. Julie Whaley.
(reprint service avail. from UMI)

780 975
SOURCES OF MUSIC AND THEIR
INTERPRETATION, DUKE STUDIES IN
MUSIC. 1987. irreg. price varies. Duke University
Press, 6697 College Station, Durham, NC 27708.
TEL 919-684-2173. Ed. Peter Williams.

780 SP
SPAIN. DIRECCION GENERAL DE BELLAS
ARTES. SEMANA DE MUSICA EN LA
NAVIDAD. irreg. Direccion General de Bellas
Artes, Murcia, Spain. illus.

780 PL
SPOTKANIA. 1984. irreg. price varies. Polskie
Wydawnictwo Muzyczne, Al. Krasinskiego 11, 31-
111 Krakow, Poland (Dist. by: Ars Polona,
Krakowskie Przedmiescie 7, 00 068 Warsaw,
Poland)

780 YU ISSN 0490-6659
SRPSKA AKADEMIJA NAUKA I UMETNOSTI.
ODELJENJE LIKOVNE I MUZICKE
UMETNOSTI. MUZICKA IZDANJA. 1953. irreg.
avail. on exchange. Srpska Akademija Nauka i
Umetnosti, Odeljenje Likovne i Muzicke Umetnosti,
Knez Mihailova 35, 11001 Belgrade, Yugoslavia
(Dist. by: Prosveta export import Terazije 16, 11001
Belgrade) circ. 300.

SRPSKA AKADEMIJA NAUKA I UMETNOSTI.
ODELJENJE LIKOVNE I MUZICKE
UMETNOSTI. POSEBNA IZDANJA. see ART

780 UR
STUDENT CHOIR DIRECTOR'S LIBRARY. 1951.
a. 0.70 Rub. Izdatel'stvo Muzyka, Ul. Neglinnaya
14, Moscow 103031, Russian S.F.S.R., U.S.S.R.

MUSIC

780   IT
STUDI DI MUSICA VENETA. 1968. irreg., no.8, 1984. price varies. (Fondazione Giorgio Cini) Casa Editrice Leo S. Olschki, Casella Postale 66, 50100 Florence, Italy.

782.1   IT
STUDI VERDIANI. (Text in English, German and Italian) 1982. a. L.20000. Istituto di Studi Verdiani, Strada della Repubblica 56, 43100 Parma, Italy (U.S. subscr. to: Broude Brothers Ltd., 141 White Oaks Road, Williamstown, MA 01267)
Opera

780   PL
STUDIA I MATERIALY DO DZIEJOW MUZYKI POLSKIEJ. 1955. irreg. price varies. Polskie Wydawnictwo Muzyczne, Al. Krasinskiego 11a, 31-111 Krakow, Poland (Distr. by: Ars Polona, Krakowskie Przedmiescie 7, 00 068 Warsaw, Poland)
Formerly: Muzyka Polska w Dokumentacjach i Interpretacjach.

780.01   NO   ISSN 0332-5024
STUDIA MUSICOLOGICA NORVEGICA. (Text in English and Norwegian) 1968. a. Norwegian University Press, Kolstadgt. 1, Box 2959-Toeyen, 00-068 Oslo 6, Norway (U.S. address: Publications Expediting Inc., 200 Meacham Ave., Elmont, NY 11003) Ed. Ove Kr. Sundberg. Indexed: Music Ind. RILM.

780   SW   ISSN 0081-6744
STUDIA MUSICOLOGICA UPSALIENSIA. NOVA SERIES. (1952-58, vols. 1-8; 1965 designated as Nova Series and issued in Acta Universitatis Upsaliensis) irreg., vol. 6, 1979. price varies. (Uppsala Universitet) Almqvist and Wiksell International, Box 62, S-101 20 Stockholm, Sweden. Ed. Ingmar Bengtsson.

780   GW   ISSN 0081-7341
STUDIEN ZUR MUSIKGESCHICHTE DES NEUNZEHNTEN JAHRHUNDERTS. irreg. price varies. Baerenreiter Verlag, Heinrich-Schuetz-Allee 29-37, 3500 Kassel-Wilhelmshoehe, W. Germany (B.R.D.)

780.01   US
STUDIES IN BRITISH MUSICOLOGY. irreg., vol.7, 1982. U M I Research Press, 300 N. Zeeb Rd., Ann Arbor, MI 48106. Ed. Nigel Fortune. index.

780   AT   ISSN 0081-8267
STUDIES IN MUSIC. 1967. a. Aus.$12. University of Western Australia, Department of Music, Nedlands, 6009 W.A., Australia. Ed.Bd. circ. 950. Indexed: RILM. Aus.P.A.I.S. Music Ind.

780   CN   ISSN 0703-3052
STUDIES IN MUSIC. 1976. a. University of Western Ontario, Department of Music History, London, Ontario, Canada. Ed. Richard Semmens. circ. 300. Indexed: Music Ind.

780.01   US
STUDIES IN MUSICOLOGY. irreg., vol.92. 1985. U M I Research Press, 300 N. Zeeb Rd., Ann Arbor, MI 48106. Ed. George J. Buelow.

780 900   US
STUDIES IN THE HISTORY AND INTERPRETATION OF MUSIC. 1980. irreg., vol.2. $39.95 per no. Edwin Mellen Press, Box 450, Lewiston, NY 14092.

STUDII SI CERCETARI DE ISTORIA ARTEI. SERIA TEATRU-MUZICA-CINEMATOGRAFIE. see *THEATER*

STUDII SI CERCETARI DE ISTORIA ARTEI. SERIA TEATRU, MUZICA, CINEMATOGRAFIE/STUDIES AND RESEARCH IN ART HISTORY. SERIES: THEATRE, MUSIC, CINEMATOGRAPHY. see *MOTION PICTURES*

780 016   SW   ISSN 0586-0709
SVENSKT MUSIKHISTORISKT ARKIV. BULLETIN. (Text in Swedish; glossary in English) 1966. irreg. (approx. 1/yr.) free. Svenskt Musikhistoriskt Arkiv, Box 16326, S-103 26 Stockholm, Sweden. circ. 300. Indexed: RILM.

780   US   ISSN 0275-9381
SYMPHONY GOLD BOOK. a. $20. American Symphony Orchestra League, 633 E St., N.W., Washington, DC 20004. Ed. Karen Kittilstad. circ. 600.

780   PL   ISSN 0239-9148
SZKICE O KULTURZE MUZYCZNEJ XIX WIEKU. STUDIA I MATERIALY. (Text in Polish; summaries in English) irreg., vol.4, 1981. price varies. (Polska Akademia Nauk, Instytut Sztuki) Panstwowe Wydawnictwo Naukowe, Miodowa 10, 00-251 Warsaw, Poland (Dist. by: Ars Polona, Krakowskie Przedmiescie 7, 00-068 Warsaw, Poland) Ed. Z. Chechlinska. charts. illus.

780   US
T.U.B.A. SERIES. 1975. irreg. price varies. (Tubists Universal Brotherhood Association) Brass Press, 136 Eighth Ave., N., Nashville, TN 37203. TEL 615-254-8969. Ed. Stephen L. Glover.

780   II
TAMIL ICAIC CANKAM MATURAI. ANTU VILA MALAR. (Text in Tamil) 1978. a. Rs.7.50. Tamil Icaic Cankam Maturai, Tamil Isai Sangam Madurai, 7 Vallabai Rd, Madurai 600002, India.

780   GW   ISSN 0344-1407
TASCHENBUCH FUER LITURGIE KIRCHENMUSIK UND MUSIKERZIEHUNG. 1958 (did not appear in 1978; resumed with 1979 volume) a. DM.19.80. Verlag Friedrich Pustet, Gutenbergstr. 8, 8400 Regensburg 1, W. Germany (B.R.D.) Ed. Franz Johann Loeffler. adv. bk. rev. circ. 2,500.
Former titles: Taschenbuch fuer Liturgie und Kirchenmusik (ISSN 0082-187X); Taschenbuch fuer den Kirchenmusiker.

780   GW   ISSN 0082-1969
TASCHENBUECHER ZUR MUSIKWISSENSCHAFT. 1969. irreg., vol.104, 1986. DM.16.80. Florian Noetzel Verlag, Heinrichshofen Buecher, Valoisstrasse 11, 2940 Wilhelmshaven, W. Germany (B.R.D.) (Dist. in U.S. by: C. F. Peters Corp., 373 Park Ave. S., New York, N.Y. 10016) Ed. Richard Schaal.

780   US
THEMATIC CATALOGUE SERIES. (Text in English, French and German) 1972. irreg., vol.13, 1986. Pendragon Press, Rt. 1, Box 159, Stuyvesant, NY 12173-9720. TEL 518-828-3008.

780.42   UK
TOP OF THE POPS ANNUAL. a. £2.50. World International Publishing Ltd., P.O. Box 111, Gt. Ducie St., Manchester M6D 3BL, England. Ed. M. Broadley. adv.

780.904   US
TOP TENS AND TRIVIA OF ROCK AND ROLL AND RHYTHM AND BLUES. ANNUAL SUPPLEMENT. 1974. a. $6. Blueberry Hill Publishing Co., Box 24170, St. Louis, MO 63130. TEL 314-727-0880. Ed. Joe Edwards.

780   UK
TUTOR & TEXTBOOK - ELEMENTARY PIPING & DRUMMING. 1963. £2.50. ‡ Royal Scottish Pipe Band Association, 45, Washington Street, Glasgow, G3 8AZ, Scotland. adv.

780.904   DK   ISSN 0107-6116
TWIST; rockskrift. 1980. irreg. Kr.9.50 per no. Regensburggade 19/1, 8000 Aarhus C, Denmark. illus.

780.01   UY
UNIVERSIDAD DE LA REPUBLICA. FACULTAD DE HUMANIDADES Y CIENCIAS. REVISTA. SERIE MUSICOLOGIA. irreg. exchange basis. Universidad de la Republica, Facultad de Humanidades y Ciencias, Seccion Revista, Tristan Narvaja 1674, Montevideo, Uruguay. Dir. Beatriz Martinez Osorio.
Supersedes in part: Universidad de la Republica. Facultad de Humanidades y Ciencias. Revista.

UNIVERSIDAD NACIONAL DE COLOMBIA. CENTRO DE ESTUDIOS FOLKLORICOS. MONOGRAFIAS. see *FOLKLORE*

784.4   UK
UNIVERSITY FOLK. no.2, Jan. 1972. irreg. (1-2/yr.) membership. ‡ Manchester University Folk Song Society, University Union, Oxford Road, Manchester M13 9PR, England. circ. 500. (processed)

780   AT
UNIVERSITY OF WESTERN AUSTRALIA. DEPARTMENT OF MUSIC. MUSIC MONOGRAPH. no.2, 1975. irreg. $12.50 per no. University of Western Australia, Department of Music, Nedlands, W. A. 6009, Australia. Ed. David Tunley.

780.42   CS   ISSN 0231-522X
UNIVERZITA J. E. PURKYNE. FILOZOFICKA FAKULTA. SBORNIK PRACI. H: RADA HUDEBNEVEDNA. irreg. (approx. a) (Univerzita J. E. Purkyne, Filozoficka Fakulta) A. Novaka 1, 602 00 Brno, Czechoslovakia.

UNIVERZITA KOMENSKEHO. FILOZOFICKA FAKULTA. ZBORNIK: MUSAICA. see *ART*

780   UR
V MIRE MUZYKI; Kalendar' a. 1.07 Rub. Izdatel'stvo Sovetskii Kompozitor, 14-12, Sadovaya Triumfalnaya St., 103006 Moscow, Russian S.F.S.R., U.S.S.R. illus.

780   IT   ISSN 0042-3734
VERDI. (Text in English, German and Italian) 1960. irreg. L.20000 per no. Istituto di Studi Verdiani, Strada della Repubblica 56, 43100 Parma, Italy (U.S. subscr. to: Broude Brothers Ltd., 141 White Oaks Road, Williamstown, MA 01267) illus. index. cum.index every 3 nos. Indexed: RILM.

780   US
VERDI NEWSLETTER. (Text in English and Italian) 1976. a. $15. (American Institute for Verdi Studies) New York University, Department of Music, 24 Waverly Pl., New York, NY 10003. TEL 212-598-3431. Eds. Martin Chusid, Andrew Porter. adv. bk. rev. bibl. charts. illus. circ. 500. (back issues avail.) Indexed: RILM.

780.9   NE   ISSN 0042-3874
VERENIGING VOOR NEDERLANDSE MUZIEKGESCHIEDENIS. TIJDSCHRIFT. (Text in Dutch, English; summaries in English) 1882. a. fl.88($32) ‡ Vereniging voor Nederlandse Muziekgeschiedenis, P.O. Box 825, 2160 SZ Lisse, Netherlands. Ed. Willem Elders. bk. rev. cum. index: vols. 1-30. circ. 800. (also avail. in microfiche; back issues avail.) Indexed: Arts & Hum.Cit.Ind. Curr.Cont. RILM. Music Ind.

780   GW   ISSN 0543-1735
VEROEFFENTLICHUNGEN DES MAX-REGER-INSTITUTES. 1966. irreg. price varies. (Max-Reger-Institut) Ferd. Duemmlers Verlag, Kaiserstr. 32, D-5300, Bonn 1, W. Germany (B.R.D.)

780   GW
VEROEFFENTLICHUNGEN ZUR MUSIKFORSCHUNG. 1973. irreg., vol.7, 1986. price varies. Florian Noetzel Verlag, Heinrichshofen Buecher, Valoisstrasse 11, 2940 Wilhelmshaven, W. Germany (B.R.D.) (Dist. in U.S. by C.F. Peters Corp., 373 Park Ave. S., New York, NY 10016) Ed. Richard Schaal.

780   FR   ISSN 0083-6109
VIE MUSICALE EN FRANCE SOUS LES ROIS BOURBONS. SERIE 1: ETUDES. (Text in English and French: summaries in French) 1954. irreg. price varies. Editions A. et J. Picard, 82 rue Bonaparte, 75006 Paris, France. Ed. Norbert Dufourcq.

780   FR   ISSN 0083-6117
VIE MUSICALE EN FRANCE SOUS LES ROIS BOURBONS. SERIE 2: RECHERCHES SUR LA MUSIQUE CLASSIQUE FRANCAISE. (Text in English and French; summaries in French) 1960. a. price varies. Editions A. et J. Picard, 82 rue Bonaparte, 75006 Paris, France. Ed. Nobert Dufourcq.

780　　　　　　　US
VIERUNDZWANZIGSTELJAHRSSCHRIFT DER INTERNATIONALEN MAULTROMMELVIRTUO GENOSSENSCHAFT. (Text in English, French, German, Italian) 1982. irreg. (approx. 1/yr) $12 for 2 nos. V I M, 930 Talwrn Ct., Iowa City, IA 52240. Ed. Frederick Crane. adv. rec.rev. circ. 75. (back issues avail.) Indexed: RILM.
Jew's harp

780　　　　　　US　　ISSN 0507-0252
VIOLA DA GAMBA SOCIETY OF AMERICA. JOURNAL. 1964. a. $15. Viola da Gamba Society of America, Inc., c/o John A. Whisler, 1823 Valley Rd., No. D, Champaign, IL 61820-7141 (Subscr. to: 1536 Third St., Apt. 6, Charleston, IL 61920) Ed. Efrim Fruchtman. adv. bk. rev. bibl. illus. circ. 700. (back issues avail.) Indexed: Music Ind. RILM.

784　　　　　　　UR
VOPROSY UCHEBNO-VOSPITATEL'NOI RABOTY V SAMODEYATEL'NYKH KOLLEKTIVAKH. (Subseries of the Institute's Trudy) 1972. irreg. 0.33 Rub. (Nauchno-Issledovatel'skii Institut Kul'tury, Otdel Narodnogo Tvorchestva) Izdatel'stvo Sovetskaya Rossiya, Proezd Sapunova 13/15, Moscow K-12, Russian S.F.S.R., U.S.S.R.

790.2　　　　　US　　ISSN 0092-4113
W.P.A.S. MUSELETTER. 1970. irreg. membership. Washington Performing Arts Society, 1029 Vermont Ave., N.W., Ste. 1100, Washington, DC 20005. TEL 202-393-3600. Ed. Sharon Berg. circ. 6,500.

WHO'S WHO AMONG MUSIC STUDENTS IN AMERICAN HIGH SCHOOLS; a biographical dictionary of outstanding music students in American high schools. see *BIOGRAPHY*

WHO'S WHO IN AMERICAN MUSIC. see *BIOGRAPHY*

780　　　　　　AU　　ISSN 0084-0017
WIENER MUSIKHOCHSCHULE. PUBLIKATIONEN. 1967. irreg., no.7, 1978. price varies. Musikverlag Elisabeth Lafite, Hegelgasse 13/22, A-1010 Vienna, Austria.

780　　　　　　US　　ISSN 0740-1558
YEARBOOK FOR TRADITIONAL MUSIC. (Text in English, French, German) 1949. a. membership. International Council for Traditional Music, c/o Department of Music, Columbia University, New York, NY 10027. TEL 212-678-0332. Ed. Dieter Christensen. bk. rev. rec.rev. circ. 1,000. Indexed: M.L.A. Music Ind. RILM.
　Former titles (until 1980): International Folk Music Council. Yearbook; International Folk Music Council Journal (ISSN 0074-6096)

780　　　　　　　JA
YOUNG AUDIO NOW. (Text in Japanese) 1974. a. 680 price varies. Gakken Co. Ltd., 40-5, 4-chome, Kamiikedai, Ohta-ku, Tokyo 145, Japan. Ed. Akira Ohuchi.

780　　　　　　IS　　ISSN 0084-439X
YUVAL. (Text in English, French and Hebrew; summaries in English and Hebrew) 1968. irreg. price varies. (Jewish Music Research Centre) Magnes Press, The Hebrew University, Jerusalem, Israel. Ed. Israel Adler. Indexed: Ind.Heb.Per. RILM.

780　　　　　　PL　　ISSN 0084-442X
Z DZIEJOW MUZYKI POLSKIEJ. 1960. irreg. Bydgoskie Towarzystwo Naukowe, Jezuicka 4, Bydgoszcz, Poland (Dist. by Ars Polona-Ruch, Krakowskie Przedmiescie 7, Warsaw, Poland)

780　　　　　　GE　　ISSN 0232-9387
ZEITGENOESSISCHES MUSIKSCHAFFEN IN DER DEUTSCHEN DEMOKRATISCHEN REPUBLIK. URAUFFUEHRUNGEN. (Text in German) 1976. a. Saechsische Landesbibliothek, Mariaenalle 12, 8060 Dresden, E. Germany (D.D.R.) Ed. Ludwig Mueller.
　Formerly: Sozialistisches Musikschaffen der Deutschen Demokratischen Republik.

780　　　　　　PL　　ISSN 0084-571X
ZRODLA DO HISTORII MUZYKI POLSKIEJ. 1960. irreg. price varies. Polskie Wydawnictwo Muzyczne, Al. Krasinskiego 11a, 31-111 Krakow, Poland (Distr. by: Ars Polona-Ruch, Krakowskie Przedmiescie 7, 00-068 Warsaw, Poland)

780　　　　　　　PL
ZRODLA PAMIETNIKARSKO-LITERACKIE DO DZIEJOW MUZYKI POLSKIEJ. 1957. irreg. price varies. Polskie Wydawnictwo Muzyczne, Al. Krasinskiego 11a, 31-111 Krakow, Poland (Dist. by: Ars Polona, Krakowskie Przedmiescie 7, 00 068 Warsaw, Poland)

MUSIC — Abstracting, Bibliographies, Statistics

016　780　　　　　NE　　ISSN 0084-7844
BIBLIOGRAPHIA MUSICOLOGICA; a bibliography of musical literature. (Text in various languages) 1970. a. fl.225($100) Joachimsthal Publishers, Box 2238, 3500 GE Utrecht, Netherlands. Ed. A.M. Joachimsthal. (back issues avail.)

016.78　　　　　　US　　ISSN 0360-2753
BIBLIOGRAPHIC GUIDE TO MUSIC. (Text in English and French) a. price varies. G. K. Hall and Co., 70 Lincoln St., Boston, MA 02111. TEL 617-423-3990.
　Formerly: Music Book Guide (ISSN 0360-1943)

780　　　　　　GE　　ISSN 0232-7678
BIBLIOGRAPHIE MUSIK. (Text in German) 1975. a. Saechsische Landesbibliothek, Marienalle 12, 8060 Dresden, E. Germany (D.D.R.) Ed. Cornelia v. Ardenne.

780　016　　　　　US
BIBLIOGRAPHIES IN AMERICAN MUSIC. 1974. irreg. price varies. (College Music Society) Information Coordinators, Inc., 1435-37 Randolph St., Detroit, MI 48226. TEL 313-962-9720. Ed. Bunker J. Clark.

780　　　　　　US　　ISSN 0742-6968
BIO-BIBLIOGRAPHIES IN MUSIC. 1985. irreg. price varies. Greenwood Press, 88 Post Rd. W., Box 5007, Westport, CT 06881. TEL 203-226-3571.

016　　　　　　　DK　　ISSN 0106-729X
BOERNEBIBLIOTEKSKATALOG. GRAMMOFONPLADER KASSETTEBAND. 1979. a. (plus supplements) Kr.619.65. Bibliotekscentralen, Tempovej 7-11, DK-2750 Ballerup, Denmark.
　Formerly: Boerneplader Boernekassetter.

780　　　　　　　UK
BRAVURA STUDIES IN MUSIC. 1979. a. Bravura Publications, 2 Tudor Close, Grayshott, Hindhead, Surrey GU26 6HP, England. Ed. Alan Poulton. bibl. circ. 250. (back issues avail.)

015　789.91　　　BU　　ISSN 0323-9365
BULGARSKI GRAMOFONNI PLOCHI. 1979. a. price varies. Narodna Biblioteka Kiril i Metodii, 11, Tolbukhin Blvd., Sofia, Bulgaria. Ed. K. Zotova. bibl. circ. 360.

784　　　　　　DK　　ISSN 0108-2272
DANSK SANGINDEKS; register til sange for boern og voksne. 1982. a. Kr.631.65. Bibliotekscentralen, Telegrafvej 5, DK-2750 Ballerup, Denmark.

780　016　　　　　US　　ISSN 0070-3885
DETROIT STUDIES IN MUSIC BIBLIOGRAPHY. 1961. irreg., no.40, 1979. price varies. Information Coordinators, Inc., 1435-37 Randolph St., Detroit, MI 48226. TEL 313-962-9720.

780　016　　　　　GE　　ISSN 0075-2959
JAHRESVERZEICHNIS DER MUSIKALIEN UND MUSIKSCHRIFTEN; Veroeffentlichungen der DDR. der BRD und Westberlins sowie deutschsprachige Werke anderer Laender. (In 2 Vols: Teil 1 Alphabetischer Teil; Teil 2 Systematischer Teil und Registerteil) a. M.128 for both vols. VEB Friedrich Hofmeister Musikverlag, Karlstr. 10, 7010 Leipzig, E. Germany (D.D.R.)
　Formerly: Jahresverzeichnis der Musikalien und Musikschriften.

780　016　　　　　　JA
JAPAN FEDERATION OF COMPOSERS. CATALOGUE OF PUBLICATIONS. (Text in Japanese & English) 1970. a. free. Japan Federation of Composers, Shinanomachi Bldg., 602 33-Shinanomachi, Shinjuku-ku, Tokyo 160, Japan. Ed.Bd. circ. 1,000.

780　016　　　　　GW　　ISSN 0344-5399
JAZZ INDEX; bibliography of jazz literature in periodicals and collections. (Text in English) 1977. a. DM.48($24) to individuals; DM. 96($48) to libraries. Norbert Ruecker, Ed. & Pub., Postfach 14, D-6384 Schmitten 1, W. Germany (B.R.D.) Eds. Norbert Ruecker, Christa Reggentin-Scheidt. circ. 300. (back issues avail.)

780　371.3　016　　CN
KODALY INSTITUTE OF CANADA. MONOGRAPH; a selected bibliography of the Kodaly concept of music education. vol.2, 1979. irreg. Can.$8.50. Avondale Press, Box 451, Willowdale, Ont. M2N 5T1, Canada. Ed.Bd.

MEDIA REVIEW DIGEST; the only complete guide to reviews of non-book media. see *MOTION PICTURES — Abstracting, Bibliographies, Statistics*

MUSIC & MUSICIANS: BRAILLE SCORES CATALOG - CHORAL (LARGE PRINT EDITION) see *BLIND — Abstracting, Bibliographies, Statistics*

MUSIC & MUSICIANS: BRAILLE SCORES CATALOG - INSTRUMENTAL. see *BLIND — Abstracting, Bibliographies, Statistics*

MUSIC & MUSICIANS: BRAILLE SCORES CATALOG - ORGAN (LARGE PRINT EDITION) see *BLIND — Abstracting, Bibliographies, Statistics*

MUSIC & MUSICIANS: BRAILLE SCORES CATALOG - PIANO (LARGE PRINT EDITION) see *BLIND — Abstracting, Bibliographies, Statistics*

MUSIC & MUSICIANS: BRAILLE SCORES CATALOG - VOCAL (LARGE PRINT EDITION) see *BLIND — Abstracting, Bibliographies, Statistics*

MUSIC & MUSICIANS: INSTRUCTIONAL CASSETTE RECORDINGS CATALOG (LARGE PRINT EDITION) see *BLIND — Abstracting, Bibliographies, Statistics*

MUSIC & MUSICIANS: INSTRUCTIONAL DISC RECORDINGS CATALOG (LARGE PRINT EDITION) see *BLIND — Abstracting, Bibliographies, Statistics*

MUSIC & MUSICIANS: LARGE-PRINT SCORES AND BOOKS CATALOG (LARGE PRINT EDITION) see *BLIND — Abstracting, Bibliographies, Statistics*

780　016　　　　　US　　ISSN 0027-4240
MUSIC ARTICLE GUIDE. 1965/66. q. $35. Information Services, Inc., Box 27066, Philadelphia, PA 19118. Ed. Morris Henken. (also avail. in microfilm from UMI)

780　011　　　　　US　　ISSN 0092-2838
MUSIC, BOOKS ON MUSIC AND SOUND RECORDINGS. (Text in various languages) 1953. a. $105. U.S. Library of Congress, Catalog Management and Publication Division, Washington, DC 20540 TEL 202-287-6100. (Subscriptions to: Cataloging Distribution Service, Library of Congress, Washington, DC 20541)
　Formerly: U.S. Library of Congress Catalog - Music and Phonorecords (ISSN 0041-7793)

780　　　　　　US　　ISSN 0192-4729
MUSIC-IN-PRINT ANNUAL SUPPLEMENT. 1979. a. $90. Musicdata, Inc., Box 48010, Philadelphia, PA 19144-8010. TEL 215-842-0555. Ed.Bd. adv. circ. 700.

780　　　　　　US　　ISSN 0146-7883
MUSIC-IN-PRINT SERIES. 1974. irreg., vol.6, 1980. price varies. Musicdata, Inc., Box 48010, Philadelphia, PA 19144-8010. TEL 215-842-0555. Ed.Bd. adv. bibl. circ. 2,000.

780　016　　　　　US　　ISSN 0027-4348
MUSIC INDEX; a subject-author guide to over 300 current international periodicals. (Entries are in language of country of origin) 1949. m. $890 (including annual cumulation) Information Coordinators, Inc., 1435 Randolph St., Detroit, MI 48226. TEL 313-962-9720. Ed. Nadia Stratelak. bk. rev. bibl. index. circ. 500.

780 029.5   US   ISSN 0094-6478
MUSIC LIBRARY ASSOCIATION. INDEX AND
BIBLIOGRAPHY SERIES. 1964. irreg. price varies.
Music Library Association, Box 487, Canton, MA
02021. circ. 250.
Formerly: Music Library Association. Index
Series (ISSN 0077-2445)
*Analytical indexes to various serial publications
of music and bibliographies of musical material*

780   US   ISSN 0736-7740
MUSIC REFERENCE COLLECTION. 1983. irreg.
Greenwood Press, Box 5007, 88 Post Rd., Westport,
CT 06881.

780 016   DK   ISSN 0085-3623
MUSIKALIER I DANSKE BIBLIOTEKER/MUSIC
IN DANISH LIBRARIES; accessionskatalog/union
catalogue. (Text in Danish and English) 1970. a.
price varies. Bibliotekscentralen, Tempovej 7-11,
DK-2750 Ballerup, Denmark. (also avail. in
microfiche)

780 016   JA
ONGAKU BUNKEN YOSHI MOKUROKU. (Text in
Japanese, English, French, German) 1973. a. 1.500
Yen. R I L M National Committee of Japan,
Musashino Music College, 1-13 Hazawa, Nerima-
Ku, Tokyo 176, Japan. (Affiliate: International
Repertory of Music Literature) adv. bk. rev. circ. 1,
000.
Formerly: Nihon Ongaku Bunken Yoshi
Mokuroku.

780 016   US   ISSN 0033-6955
R I L M ABSTRACTS OF MUSIC LITERATURE.
1967. q. $36 to individuals; institutions $120.
(International Association of Music Libraries)
International Repertory of Music Literature, 33 W.
42 St., New York, NY 10036 TEL 212-790-4214.
(European subscr. to: Baerenreiter Verlag, Heinrich-
Schuetz Allen 31-37, D-3500 Kassel, W. Germany
(B.R.D.)) (Co-sponsor: International Musicological
Society) Ed. Barry S. Brook. bk. rev. abstr. index.
cum.index. circ. 1,500(controlled)
•Also available online. Vendors: DIALOG.

780 016   US   ISSN 0582-1487
SCHWANN ARTIST CATALOG. triennial. $6.95. A
B C Schwann Publications, Inc., 535 Boylston St.,
Boston, MA 02116. TEL 617-437-1350. Ed. Donna
Hieken. circ. 50,000.

780   CS
SLOVENSKA NARODNA BIBLIOGRAFIA SERIA
H: HUDOBNINY. (Text in Czech, Slovak;
summaries in English, French, German, Slovak)
1981. a. Matica Slovenska, Mudronova 35, 036 52
Martin, Czechoslovakia (Subscr. addr.: Ustredna
Expedicia a Dovoz Tlace; Gottwaldovo nam. 6, 813
81 Bratislava, Czechoslovakia) Ed. Anna
Foldvariova. (back issues avail.)

780 016   US
U C L A MUSIC LIBRARY BIBLIOGRAPHY
SERIES. 1977. irreg., no.5, 1986. free. University of
California, Los Angeles, Music Library, Schoenberg
Hall, Los Angeles, CA 90024. TEL 213-825-4881.
Ed. Stephen M. Fry. circ. 300. (back issues avail.)

MUSIC — Computer Applications

see also Computers—Computer Music

SYMPOSIUM ON SMALL COMPUTERS IN THE
ARTS. PROCEEDINGS. see *ART — Computer
Applications*

NEEDLEWORK

793   US
GRANNY SQUARE & CRAFT IDEAS. At head of
title: Woman's Day Super Special. 1973. a. $2.25. C
B S Publications, Woman's Day, 1515 Broadway,
New York, NY 10036. TEL 201-719-6812. Ed.
Marion Lyons. adv. bk. rev. charts. illus. tr.lit.
(back issues avail.)
Formerly: Woman's Day Granny Squares.

HOBBY PUBLICATIONS ANNUAL TRADE
DIRECTORY. see *HOBBIES*

362.5   US   ISSN 0360-1102
NEEDLEWORK GUILD OF AMERICA. ANNUAL
REPORT.* a. Needlework Guild of America, 1007
B Street Rd., Southampton, PA 18966-4230. illus.

746   US   ISSN 0740-4093
QUILT DIGEST. 1983. a. price varies. Quilt Digest
Press, 955 Fourteenth St., San Francisco, CA
94114. Ed. Michael M. Kile.

SHUTTLE CRAFT GUILD. MONOGRAPHS. see
HOME ECONOMICS

746   US
WOMAN'S DAY SWEATERS & CRAFTS. a. $2.28.
C B S Publications, Woman's Day, 1515 Broadway,
New York, NY 10036. TEL 201-719-6814. Ed.
Ellene Saunders. adv.
Formerly: Woman's Day Needlework Ideas.

746.4   US
101 SWEATER & CRAFT IDEAS. At head of title:
Woman's Day Special. 1981. a. C B S Publications,
Woman's Day, 1515 Broadway, New York, NY
10036. TEL 203-719-6812. Ed. Ellene Saunders. adv.
bk. rev. charts. illus. tr.lit. circ. 763,000. (back
issues avail.)
Former titles: 101 Needlework and Sweater Ideas
& Woman's Day 101 Sweaters You Can Knit and
Crochet.

NUCLEAR ENERGY

see *Physics—Nuclear Energy*

NUMISMATICS

737   US   ISSN 0569-6720
AMERICAN NUMISMATIC SOCIETY. ANNUAL
REPORT. a. free. American Numismatic Society,
Broadway at 155th St., New York, NY 10032. TEL
212-234-3130. illus. (reprint service avail. from
UMI)

737.4   US
ANCIENT COINS IN NORTH AMERICAN
COLLECTIONS. 1969. irreg. price varies.
American Numismatic Society, Broadway at 155th
St., New York, NY 10032. TEL 212-234-3130.
(reprint service avail. from UMI)
Formerly: Greek Coins in North American
Collections (ISSN 0072-744X)

737 954   II
ANDHRA PRADESH, INDIA. DEPARTMENT OF
ARCHAEOLOGY AND MUSEUMS. MUSEUM
SERIES. (Text in English) 1961. irreg., no.18, 1975-
76. price varies. Department of Archaeology and
Museums, Hyderabad 500001, Andhra Pradesh,
India (Or: Publications Bureau, Directorate of
Government Printing, Chanchalguda, Hyderabad,
Andhra Pradesh, India)
Former titles: Andhra Pradesh, India. Department
of Archaeology and Museums. Museum Objects and
Numismatics Series; Andhra Pradesh, India.
Department of Archaeology. Museum Series (ISSN
0066-166X)

737   AT   ISSN 0004-9875
AUSTRALIAN NUMISMATIC JOURNAL; devoted
to the study of coins, tokens, paper money and
medals, particularly the issues of Australia. 1949. a.,
no.34, 1984. membership. South Australian
Numismatic Society, Box 80 G.P.O., Adelaide,
South Australia, Australia. Ed. D.J. Rampling. bk.
rev. index. cum.index. circ. 200. Indexed:
Numis.Lit.

737   UK
BRITISH NUMISMATIC JOURNAL. (Includes the
Society's Annual Proceedings) 1905. a. £12($25)
membership. British Numismatic Society, c/o W.
Slayter, Hon. Sec., 63 West Way, Edgeware, Middx.
HA8 9LA, England. Eds. M. Delme-Radcliffe, N.J.
Mayhew. adv. bk. rev. bibl. charts. illus. index;
cum.index every 10 vols. circ. 650. Indexed:
Br.Hum.Ind.   Br.Archaeol.Abstr.   Numis.Lit.

737   CN   ISSN 0045-5202
CANADIAN NUMISMATIC RESEARCH
SOCIETY. TRANSACTIONS. (Text mainly in
English, occasionally in French) 1965. a. available
on exchange. Canadian Numismatic Research
Society, P.O. Box 1263, Guelph, Ont. N1H 6N6,
Canada. Ed. R. W. Irwin. bk. rev. circ. 50. Indexed:
Numis.Lit.

737   BE   ISSN 0069-2247
CERCLE D'ETUDES NUMISMATIQUES.
TRAVAUX. 1964. irreg. price varies. Cercle
d'Etudes Numismatiques, 4 Boulevard de
l'Empereur, B-1000 Brussels, Belgium.

737   UK   ISSN 0140-1149
COIN HOARDS. irreg. membership. Royal
Numismatic Society, British Museum, London
WC1B 3DG, England (Distr. by: Spink & Son Ltd.,
5-7 King St., St. James, London SW1, England) Ed.
M.J. Price. Indexed: Br.Archaeol.Abstr.

737.4   US   ISSN 0361-0845
COIN WORLD ALMANAC. 1976. irreg. $14.95.
Amos Press Inc., Box 150, Sidney, OH 45367. TEL
513-498-0800. illus.

737.4   UK   ISSN 0307-6571
COIN YEARBOOK. 1968. a. £10.70. Numismatic
Publishing Co., Sovereign House, Brentwood, Essex
CM14 4SE, England. illus. circ. 20,000.

737.4   UK   ISSN 0069-4983
COINS MARKET VALUES. a. £2.95. Link House
Magazines Ltd., Link House, Dingwall Ave,
Croydon, CR9 2TA, England. Ed. Richard West.
Indexed: Numis.Lit.
Formerly: Coins Annual.

737   CS
FOLIA NUMISMATICA. (Text in Czech; summaries
in English, French, German, Russian) 1986. a. 20
Kcs. Moravske Muzeum, Numismaticke Oddeleni,
Nam. 25, Unora 6, 65937 Brno, Czechoslovakia.
illus. index. circ. 700.

737.4   US   ISSN 0072-8829
GUIDEBOOK OF UNITED STATES COINS. 1946.
a. $6.95. Western Publishing Co., Inc., 1220 Mound
Ave., Racine, WI 53404. TEL 414-633-2431. Ed.
R.S. Yeoman. illus. index.

737   GW   ISSN 0072-9523
HAMBURGER BEITRAEGE ZUR NUMISMATIK.
1947. a. price varies. Hamburger Museumsverein,
Holstenwall 24, 2000 Hamburg 36, W. Germany
(B.R.D.) Eds. Walter Haevernick, Gert Hatz. bk.
rev. circ. 200. Indexed: Numis.Lit.

737.4   US   ISSN 0072-9949
HANDBOOK OF UNITED STATES COINS. 1941.
a. $3.95. Western Publishing Co., Inc., 1220 Mound
Ave., Racine, WI 53404. TEL 414-633-2431. Ed.
R.S. Yeoman. illus. index.

737   SZ   ISSN 0073-0963
HAUTES ETUDES NUMISMATIQUES. 1966. irreg.,
no.2, 1978. (Ecole Pratique des Hautes Etudes,
Centre de Recherches d'Histoire et de Philologie,
FR) Librarie Droz, 11, rue Massot, 1211 Geneva
12, Switzerland. circ. 1,000.

737   IT   ISSN 0578-9923
ISTITUTO ITALIANO DI NUMISMATICA.
ANNALI. 1954. a. Istituto Italiano di Numismatica,
Palazzo Barberini, Via Quattro Fontane 13, Rome
00195, Italy. (back issues avail.)

737.4   NE
JAARBOEK VOOR MUNT EN PENNINGKUNDE.
(Text in Dutch, occasionally in English, French,
German; summaries in English) 1914. a. price
varies. Koninklijk Nederlands Genootschap voor
Munt- en Penningkunde - Royal Dutch Society of
Numismatics, c/o The Netherlands Bank, Postbus
98, 1000 AB Amsterdam, Netherlands. Ed.Bd.
cum.index. circ. 500.

737   GW   ISSN 0075-2711
JAHRBUCH FUER NUMISMATIK UND
GELDGESCHICHTE. (Text mainly in German;
occasionally in English and French) 1949. a. price
varies. (Bayerische Numismatische Gesellschaft)
Verlag Michael Lassleben, Lange Gasse 19, Postfach
20, 8411 Kallmuenz, W. Germany (B.R.D.) Ed. J.
Kellner. Indexed: Br.Archaeol.Abstr. Numis.Lit.

LANDESMUSEUM FUER KAERNTEN. BUCHREIHE. see *ART*

737 900   AU   ISSN 0255-2809
LITTERAE NUMISMATICAE VINDOBONENSES. 1979. irreg. price varies. Verlag der Oesterreichischen Akademie der Wissenschaften, Dr. Ignaz-Seipel-Platz 2, A-1010 Vienna, Austria. circ. 250.

737   IQ   ISSN 0002-4058
AL-MASKUKAT. 1969. a. ID.5000($12) State Antiquities Organization, Jamal Abdul Nasr St., Baghdad, Iraq.

737   IT   ISSN 0392-5439
MEDAGLIA. (Text in Italian; summaries in English, French, German) 1971. a. L.35000. Stabilimento Stefano Johnson S.p.A., Piazza S. Angelo 1, 20121 Milan, Italy. TEL 6554812. bk. rev. bibl. illus. cum.index. (back issues avail.)

737   CS   ISSN 0077-152X
MORAVSKE NUMISMATICKE ZPRAVY. (Text in Czech; summaries in English, French, German) 1956/57. irreg., latest no.16, 1985. price varies. Moravske Muzeum, Numismaticke Oddeleni, Nam.25, Unora 6, 65937 Brno, Czechoslovakia. circ. 1,000. Indexed: Numis.Lit.

737.4   US   ISSN 0145-1413
MUSEUM NOTES (NEW YORK) a. membership. American Numismatic Society, Broadway at 155th St., New York, NY 10032. TEL 212-345-3130. (reprint service avail. from UMI)

737.4   PL   ISSN 0208-5062
MUZEUM ARCHEOLOGICZNE I ETNOGRAFICZNE, LODZ. PRACE I MATERIALY. SERIA NUMIZMATYCZNA I KONSERWATORSKA. (Text in Polish; summaries in English) 1981. a. price varies. Panstwowe Wydawnictwo Naukowe, Ul. Miodowa 10, 00-251 Warsaw, Poland (Dist. by: Ars Polona, Krakowskie Przedmiescie 7, 00-068 Warsaw, Poland) Ed. A. Mikolajczyk. circ. 600.

737   GR
NOMISMATIKA CHRONICA. (Summaries in English) 1972. irreg. $6. Hellenic Numismatic Society, Box 736, Athens, Greece. circ. 1,000. Indexed: Numis.Lit.

NORDISK JULEMAERKE KATALOG; Nordic Christmas seal catalogue. see *PHILATELY*

737   NO   ISSN 0078-107X
NORDISK NUMISMATISK AARSSKRIFT/ SCANDINAVIAN NUMISMATIC JOURNAL. (Text in English and Scandinavian languages; summaries in English) 1936. biennial. price varies. (Kungliga Vitterhets-, Historie- och Antikvitets Akademien, SW - Royal Academy of Letters, History and Antiquities) Norwegian University Press, Kolstadgt. 1, Box 2959-Toeyen, 0608 Oslo 6, Norway (U.S. address: Publications Expediting Inc., 200 Meacham Ave., Elmont, NY 11003) (Co-sponsor: Nordisk Numismatisk Union) Ed. Kolbjorn Skaare. cum.index: 1936-1970 in vol. 1971. Indexed: Numis.Lit.

737 900   UK   ISSN 0078-2696
NUMISMATIC CHRONICLE AND JOURNAL. 1839. a. membership. Royal Numismatic Society, British Museum, London, WC1B 3DG, England (Distr. by: Spink & Son Ltd., 5-7 King St., St. James, London SW1, England) Ed. Dr. K. Rutter. adv. bk. rev. circ. 1,400. Indexed: Br.Hum.Ind.

737   US   ISSN 0029-6031
NUMISMATIC LITERATURE. 1947. s-a. $8. American Numismatic Society, Broadway at 155th St., New York, NY 10032. TEL 212-234-3130. adv. abstr. bibl. index. (reprint service avail. from UMI) Indexed: Amer.Bibl.Slavic & E.Eur.Stud. Br.Archaeol.Abstr. Numis.Lit.

737   US   ISSN 0078-2718
NUMISMATIC NOTES AND MONOGRAPHS. 1920. irreg., no.162, 1983. price varies. American Numismatic Society, Broadway at 155th St., New York, NY 10032. TEL 212-234-3130. (reprint service avail. from UMI) Indexed: Numis.Lit.

737   US   ISSN 0517-404X
NUMISMATIC STUDIES. irreg. price varies. American Numismatic Society, Broadway at 155th St., New York, NY 10032. TEL 212-234-3130. (reprint service avail. from UMI) Indexed: Numis.Lit.

737   SZ
NUMISMATICA E ANTICHITA CLASSICHE. (Text in English, French, German, Italian) 1972. a. Secretariat, Casalla Postale 3157, 6901 Lugano CH, Switzerland.

737   BE
NUMISMATICA LOVANIENSIA. (Subseries of: Universite Catholique de Louvain. Institut Superieur d'Archeologie et d'Histoire de l'Art. Publications; includes series and subseries numbering) 1977. irreg., latest no.6, 1983. price varies. Universite Catholique de Louvain, Institut Superieur d'Archeologie et d'Histoire de l'Art, College Erasme, 1 place Blaise Pascal, 1348 Louvain-la-Neuve, Belgium. Ed. T. Hackens.

737   CS   ISSN 0078-2726
NUMISMATICA MORAVICA. (Text in Czech; summaries also in English, French, German, Russian) 1965. irreg., latest no.6, 1985. price varies. Moravske Muzeum, Numismaticke Oddeleni, Nam.25, Unora 6, 65937 Brno, Czechoslovakia. illus. index. circ. 1,200. Indexed: Numis.Lit.

737.4 943.7   CS   ISSN 0546-9414
NUMISMATICKY SBORNIK. (Text mainly in Czech and Slovak; occasionaly in German and other languages) 1953. biennial. Academia, Publishing House of the Czechoslovak Academy of Sciences, Vodickova 40, 112 29 Prague 1, Czechoslovakia (Subscr. to: Artia, Ve Smeckach 30, 111 27 Prague 1, Czechoslovakia) Ed. Jiri Sejbal. illus. circ. 1,000. Indexed: Numis.Lit.

737   SW   ISSN 0078-2734
NUMISMATISKA MEDDELANDEN/ NUMISMATIC COMMUNICATIONS. (Text in Swedish; summaries in English, French and occasionally German) 1874. irreg. price varies. Svenska Numismatiska Foereningen, Oestermalmsgatan 81, 114 50 Stockholm, Sweden. Ed.Bd. index. circ. 1,000. Indexed: Numis.Lit.

737   AU
OESTERREICHISCHE AKADEMIE DER WISSENSCHAFTEN. NUMISMATISCHE KOMMISSION. VEROEFFENTLICHUNGEN. (Subseries of: Oesterreichische Akademie der Wissenschaften. Philosophisch-Historische Klasse. Denkschriften) 1973. irreg. Verlag der Oesterreichischen Akademie der Wissenschaften, Dr. Ignaz-Seipel Platz 2, A-1010 Vienna, Austria. illus.

737   BE
REVUE BELGE DE NUMISMATIQUE ET DE SIGILLOGRAPHIE. 1842. a. 1800 Fr. Societe Royale de Numismatique de Belgique, 28a Av. Leopold, 1330 Rixensart, Belgium. Ed.Bd. adv. bk. rev. cum.index: nos. 1-110. circ. 500. Indexed: Numis.Lit.

737   FR   ISSN 0484-8942
REVUE NUMISMATIQUE. 1836. a. 310 F. (Societe Francaise de Numismatique) Societe d'Edition les Belles Lettres, 95 Boulevard Raspail, 75006 Paris, France. bk. rev. Indexed: Numis.Lit.

737   SZ   ISSN 0035-4163
REVUE SUISSE DE NUMISMATIQUE/ SCHWEIZERISCHE NUMISMATISCHE RUNDSCHAU. (Text in English, French and German) 1890. a. 50 Fr. Societe Suisse de Numismatique - Schweizerische Numismatische Gesellschaft, c/o Colin Martin, Petit-Chene 18, 1002 Lausanne, Switzerland. adv. illus. circ. 1,000. Indexed: Numis.Lit.

737   UK   ISSN 0080-4487
ROYAL NUMISMATIC SOCIETY. SPECIAL PUBLICATIONS. irreg. Royal Numismatic Society, British Museum, London WC1B 3DG, England.

737.4   UK
SEABY'S STANDARD CATALOGUE OF BRITISH COINS. 1978. a. £9.95. B.A. Seaby Ltd., 8 Cavendish Sq., London W1M 0AJ, England. illus.

737.4   DK   ISSN 0586-4496
SIEG'S MOENTKATALOG. DANMARK, DANSK VESTINDIEN, FAEROERNE, GROENLAND, ISLAND. (Text in Danish; summaries in English) 1968. a. Kr.45. Frovin Sieg, Skals, Denmark (Subscr. to: Danske Boghandleres Kommissionsanstalt, Siljangade 6, 2300 Copenhagen S, Denmark) illus.

737   CS   ISSN 0081-0088
SLOVENSKA NUMIZMATIKA. (Text in Slovak; summaries in German) 1970. approx. biennial. 35 Kcs. (Slovenska Akademia Vied) Veda, Publishing House of the Slovak Academy of Sciences, Klemensova 19, 814 30 Bratislava, Czechoslovakia (Subscr. to: Slovart, Gottwaldovo nam. 6, 817 64 Bratislava) Ed. Josef Hlinka. Indexed: Numis.Lit.

SLOVENSKE NARODNE MUZEUM. ZBORNIK. see *HISTORY — History Of Europe*

737   CS   ISSN 0081-6779
STUDIA NUMISMATICA ET MEDAILISTICA. (Text in Czech; summaries in English, French, German and Russian) 1970. irreg., no.6, 1985. price varies. Moravske Muzeum, Numismaticke Oddeleni, Nam.25, Unora 6, 65937 Brno, Czechoslovakia. illus. index. circ. 1,200.

737   RM   ISSN 0081-8887
STUDII SI CERCETARI DE NUMISMATICA. 1957. irreg., vol.8, 1984. (Academia Republicii Socialiste Romania) Editura Academiei Republicii Socialiste Rumania, Calea Victoriei 125, 79717 Bucharest, Rumania (Subscr. to: ARTEXIM, Export-Import Presa, Str. Piata Scinteii nr.1, P.O. Box 33-16, 70055 Bucharest, Rumania) Indexed: Numis.Lit.

737   US   ISSN 0271-3993
SYLLOGE NUMMORUM GRAECORUM. Short title: S N G A N S. 1972. irreg., vol.6, 1981. price varies. American Numismatic Society, Broadway at 155th St., New York, NY 10032. TEL 212-234-3130. (reprint service avail. from UMI)

SYLLOGE NUMMORUM GRAECORUM DEUTSCHLAND. STAATLICHE MUENZSAMMLUNG MUENCHEN. see *ARCHAEOLOGY*

TRIERER ZEITSCHRIFT FUER GESCHICHTE UND KUNST DES TRIERER LANDES UND SEINER NACHBARGEBIETE. see *ARCHAEOLOGY*

069.9 737   BL
UNIVERSIDADE DE SAO PAULO. MUSEU PAULISTA. COLECAO. SERIE DE NUMISMATICA. 1975. irreg. Universidade de Sao Paulo, Museu Paulista, Caixa Postal 42503, Parque da Independencia, 04263 Sao Paulo SP, Brazil. Ed. Antonio Rocha Penteado.
 Supersedes in part (since 1975): Museu Paulista. Colecao (ISSN 0080-6382)

NURSES AND NURSING

see Medical Sciences—Nurses and Nursing

NUTRITION AND DIETETICS

613.2   US   ISSN 0149-9483
ADVANCES IN NUTRITIONAL RESEARCH. 1977. a. Plenum Publishing Corp., 233 Spring St., New York, NY 10013. TEL 212-741-6680. Ed. Harold H. Draper. Indexed: Chem.Abstr. Ind.Med. Sci.Cit.Ind. Ind.Sci.Rev.

AGRICULTURA, LA PESCA Y LA ALIMENTACION ESPANOLAS. see *AGRICULTURE*

NUTRITION AND DIETETICS

613.2   US   ISSN 0199-9885
ANNUAL REVIEW OF NUTRITION. 1981. a. $31. Annual Reviews, Inc., 4139 El Camino Way, Palo Alto, CA 94306. TEL 415-493-4400. Ed. Robert E. Olson. bibl. index. cum.index. (also avail. in microform from UMI; back issues avail.) Indexed: Biol.Abstr. Chem.Abstr. Ind.Med. Sci.Cit.Ind. Abstr.Hyg. Dent.Ind. Ind.Sci.Rev.

641   US
BASIC AND CLINICAL NUTRITION. 1980. irreg., vol.3, 1981. price varies. Marcel Dekker, Inc., 270 Madison Ave., New York, NY 10016. TEL 212-696-9000. Indexed: Biol.Abstr. Chem.Abstr.

641.1   SZ   ISSN 0067-8198
BIBLIOTHECA NUTRITIO ET DIETA. (Text in English, French and German) 1960. irreg. (approx. 1/yr.) price varies. S. Karger AG, Allschwilerstrasse 10, P.O. Box, CH-4009 Basel, Switzerland. Ed. J.C. Somogyi. (reprint service avail. from ISI, back issues avail.) Indexed: Biol.Abstr. Chem.Abstr. Curr.Cont. Ind.Med. Nutr.Abstr. Dairy Sci.Abstr. Food Sci.& Tech.Abstr.

613.2   UK
BRITISH NUTRITION FOUNDATION BRIEFING PAPERS. 1980. irreg. £1. British Nutrition Foundation, 15 Belgrave Square, London SW1X 8PS, England.

613.2   UK
BRITISH NUTRITION FOUNDATION MONOGRAPH. 1980. irreg. British Nutrition Foundation, 15 Belgrave Sq., London SW1X 8PS, England. Indexed: Nutr.Abstr.
Formerly: British Nutrition Foundation Newsletter.

613.2   UK
BRITISH NUTRITION FOUNDATION TASK FORCE REPORTS. 1983. irreg. British Nutrition Foundation, 15 Belgrave Sq., London SW1X 8PS, England.

COMMENTS FROM C A S T. (Council for Agricultural Sciences and Technology) see *AGRICULTURE*

641.1   US   ISSN 0090-0443
CURRENT CONCEPTS IN NUTRITION. 1972. irreg., vol.16, 1987. price varies. John Wiley & Sons, Inc., 605 Third Ave., New York, NY 10016. TEL 212-850-6000. Ed. M. Winick. Indexed: Biol.Abstr. Chem.Abstr. Ind.Med.

616.39   US   ISSN 0191-2453
CURRENT TOPICS IN NUTRITION AND DISEASE. 1977. irreg. price varies. Alan R. Liss, Inc., 41 E. 11th St., New York, NY 10003. TEL 212-475-7700. bibl. illus. index. Indexed: Biol.Abstr. Chem.Abstr.

613.2   FR
ECOLE NATIONALE SUPERIEURE DE BIOLOGIE APPLIQUEE A LA NUTRITION ET A L'ALIMENTATION. CAHIERS. Cover title: E N S B A N A Cahiers. 1976. a. 200 F. ‡ Ecole Nationale Superieure de Biologie Appliquee a la Nutrition et a l'Alimentation (ENSBANA), 11 rue Lavoisier, 75384 Paris cedex 08, France. Ed. Denise Simatos. adv. bk. rev. bibl. charts. illus. circ. 3,000. Indexed: Bull.Signal. Chem.Abstr.
Former titles: Amis de l'E.N.S.B.A.N.A; Amis de l'I.B.A.N.A. (Publication) (ISSN 0003-1801)

EXERCISE PHYSIOLOGY; current selected research. see *PHYSICAL FITNESS AND HYGIENE*

613.2   UN
F A O FOOD AND NUTRITION SERIES. (Text in English, French and Spanish) irreg., no.21, 1981. price varies. Food and Agriculture Organization of the United Nations, Distribution and Sales Section, Via delle Terme di Caracalla, 00100 Rome, Italy (Dist. in U.S. by: Bernan Associates-Unipub, 4611-F Assembly Drive, Lanham, MD 20706-4391) Indexed: Nutr.Abstr. Ind.Med.
Formerly: F A O Nutritional Study (ISSN 0071-7088)

FINLAND. KANSANELAKELAITOS. JULKAISUJA. SARJA EL. see *MEDICAL SCIENCES*

FINLAND. KANSANELAKELAITOS. JULKAISUJA. SARJA ML. see *MEDICAL SCIENCES*

641.1 664   US   ISSN 0730-9198
I F T BASIC SYMPOSIUM SERIES. 1978. a. $59. (Institute of Food Technologists) A V I Publishing Company, 250 Post Road East, Box 831, Westport, CT 06881.

616.39   US
I L S I HUMAN NUTRITION REVIEWS. 1986. irreg. price varies. Springer-Verlag, 175 Fifth Ave., New York, NY 10160 TEL 212-460-1500. (Also Berlin, Heidelberg, Tokyo, Vienna) (reprint service avail. from ISI)

641   UN   ISSN 0533-4179
INSTITUTO DE NUTRICION DE CENTRO AMERICA Y PANAMA. INFORME ANUAL. (Editions in English and Spanish) 1950. a. exchange basis. Institute of Nutrition of Central America and Panama (INCAP) - Instituto de Nutricion de Centro America y Panama, Carretera Roosevelt, Apdo. Postal 1188, Guatemala City, Guatemala. Ed. Grace H. de Munoz. circ. 550. Indexed: Biol.Abstr. Nutr.Abstr.

INSTITUTO DE TECNOLOGIA DE ALIMENTOS. COLETANEA. see *FOOD AND FOOD INDUSTRIES*

641   BL   ISSN 0074-0144
INSTITUTO DE TECNOLOGIA DE ALIMENTOS. INSTRUCOES PRATICAS. 1968. irreg., no.21, 1985. $5 per no. ‡ Instituto de Tecnologia de Alimentos, C.P. 139, Campinas, S.P., Brazil.

641   BL   ISSN 0074-0152
INSTITUTO DE TECNOLOGIA DE ALIMENTOS. INSTRUCOES TECNICAS. 1968. irreg. $6 per no. ‡ Instituto de Tecnologia de Alimentos, C.P. 139, Campinas, S.P., Brazil.

612   NG   ISSN 0534-4700
INTER-AFRICAN CONFERENCE ON FOOD AND NUTRITION. PROGRAMA E INFORMACOES.* (Text in English, French and Portuguese) irreg. (Commission for Technical Co-Operation in Africa South of the Sahara) Maison de l'Afrique, B.P. 878, Niamey, Niger.

641   NG   ISSN 0538-2785
INTER-AFRICAN CONFERENCE ON FOOD AND NUTRITION. REPORT.* 1949. irreg. (Commission for Technical Co-Operation in Africa, South of the Sahara) Maison de l'Afrique, B.P. 878, Niamey, Niger.

919.204   UK
INTERNATIONAL VEGETARIAN HANDBOOK. 1956. biennial. £3.95. Vegetarian Society, c/o Publications Mgr., Parkdale, Dunham Rd., Altrincham, Cheshire WA14 4QG, England. adv. circ. 35,000.
Former titles: Vegetarian Health Food Handbook; Vegetarian Handbook (ISSN 0083-5315); Food Reformers' Yearbook.

641.1   II   ISSN 0377-3744
NATIONAL INSTITUTE OF NUTRITION. ANNUAL REPORT. (Text in English) 1946. a. free. National Institute of Nutrition, Indian Council of Medical Research, Jamai-Osmania, Hyderabad 500 007, India. circ. 1,400.
Continues: Nutrition Research Laboratories. Annual Report.

574.13   JA
NATIONAL INSTITUTE OF NUTRITION. ANNUAL REPORT/KOKURITSU EIYO KENKYUSHO HOKOKU. (Text in Japanese) 1949. a. exchange basis. National Institute of Nutrition - Kosei-sho Kokuritsu Eiyo Kenkyusho, 1 Toyama-cho, Shinjuku-ku, Tokyo 162, Japan. Indexed: Biol.Abstr.

613.2 616.39   SZ
NESTLE FOUNDATION. ANNUAL REPORT. 1969. a. free. Nestle Foundation, 4 Place de la Gare, 1003 Lausanne, Switzerland. Ed. B. Schuerch. circ. 1,000.

641.1   US
NEW YORK STATE. ASSEMBLY SUBCOMMITTEE ON FOOD, FARM AND NUTRITION POLICY. REPORT.* a. Subcommittee on Food, Farm and Nutrition Policy, Empire State Plaza, 13th Fl., A-4, Albany, NY 12248-0001.

641.1   US   ISSN 0362-0069
NEW YORK'S FOOD AND LIFE SCIENCES BULLETIN. 1971. irreg. (New York State College of Agriculture and Life Sciences) Cornell University, New York's Food and Life Sciences Bulletin, 292 Roberts Hall, Ithaca, NY 14853. TEL 607-255-5420. charts. illus. stat. circ. 1,500. (back issues avail.) Indexed: Biol.Abstr. Nutr.Abstr. Field Crop Abstr. Geo.Abstr. Herb.Abstr. Hort.Abstr. Plant Breed.Abstr. Rural Recreat.Tour.Abstr. World Agri.Econ.& Rural Sociol.Abstr.

641.1   NO
NORWAY. FISKERIDIREKTORATET. SKRIFTER. SERIE ERNAERING. (Text in English) 1976. irreg. price varies. Fiskeridirektoratet - Directorate of Fisheries, Box 185, 5001 Bergen, Norway. Ed. Georg Lambertsen. Indexed: Biol.Abstr. Chem.Abstr. Nutr.Abstr.& Rev.

613.2   CN   ISSN 0078-236X
NOVA SCOTIA. DEPARTMENT OF PUBLIC HEALTH. NUTRITION DIVISION. ANNUAL REPORT. a. free to qualified personnel. Department of Public Health, Halifax, N.S., Canada. TEL 902-424-4034. Ed. Jessie Rae.

618   US
NUTRITION AND THE BRAIN. 1975. irreg., vol.5, 1979. price varies. Raven Press, 1185 Ave. of the Americas, New York, NY 10036. TEL 212-575-0335. Eds. Richard J. and Judith J. Wurtman. Indexed: Biol.Abstr. Curr.Cont. Sci.Cit.Ind.

613.2   US   ISSN 0160-2470
NUTRITION IN HEALTH AND DISEASE. 1978. irreg., vol.2, 1980. Raven Press, 1185 Ave. of the Americas, New York, NY 10036. TEL 212-575-0335. Indexed: Biol.Abstr.

613.2 612.3   AT   ISSN 0314-1004
NUTRITION SOCIETY OF AUSTRALIA. PROCEEDINGS. 1976. a. Aus.$10. Nutrition Society of Australia, c/o C S I R O, Private Bag, PO, Wembley, S.A. 6014, Australia. Ed. A.J. Sinclair. index. circ. 1,000. (back issues avail.) Indexed: Biol.Abstr. Chem.Abstr. Curr.Cont.

641.4 630   II
NUTRITION SOCIETY OF INDIA. PROCEEDINGS. 1967. a. Rs.20($10) Nutrition Society of India, c/o National Institute of Nutrition, PO-Jamai Osmania, Hyderabad 500007, India. Ed.Bd. circ. 1,500. (back issues avail.)

641   US
OSPREY'S SEAFOOD NEWSLETTER. 1985. irreg. free. Osprey Books, Box 965, Huntington, NY 11743. TEL 516-549-0143. Ed. Peter Zees. circ. 30, 000.

641.1   PH
PHILIPPINES. FOOD AND NUTRITION RESEARCH INSTITUTE. ANNUAL REPORT. 1950. a. free. Food and Nutrition Research Institute, 727 Pedro Gil St., Box 774, Ermita, Manila, Philippines. Ed. Rodolfo F. Florentino. circ. controlled.
Formerly: Philippines. Food and Nutrition Center. Annual Report (ISSN 0071-7142)

664   MX
SECTOR ALIMENTARIO EN MEXICO (YEAR) 1981. irreg. price varies. Instituto Nacional de Estadistica, Geografia e Informatica, Secretaria de Programacion y Presupuesto, Patriotismo 711 Torre "A" P.H., Col. San Juan Mixcoac, Deleg. Benito Juarez, 03910 Mexico, D.F., Mexico TEL 598-99-05. (Subscr. to: Rio Rhin No. 56, Col. Cuauhtemoc, 06500 Mexico, D.F., Mexico)

641   SW   ISSN 0082-0415
SWEDISH NUTRITION FOUNDATION. SYMPOSIA. (Text in English) 1962. a. price varies. Almqvist & Wiksell International, Box 62, S-101 20 Stockholm, Sweden. Ed. Gunnar Blix. Indexed: Biol.Abstr.

664 BL
UNIVERSIDADE ESTADUAL DE CAMPINAS.
FACULDADE DE TECNOLOGIA DE
ALIMENTOS. INFORMATIVO ANUAL. (Text
in English or Portuguese) a. Universidade Estadual
de Campinas, Faculdade de Tecnologia de
Alimentos, Ciudade Universitaria, Barao Geraldo,
Caixa Postal 1170, Campinas, Sao Paulo, Brazil.
Formerly: Universidade Estadual de Campinas.
Faculdade de Engenharia de Alimentos e
Enpenhoria Agricola. Informativo Annual.

613.2 SW ISSN 0346-7341
VAAR FOEDA. SUPPLEMENT. (Text in Swedish;
summaries in English) 1973. irreg., (3-5/yr.) Kr.30
per issue. Statens Livsmedelswerk - National Food
Administration, Box 622, S-751 26 Uppsala,
Sweden. Ed. Leif Chrona. bk. rev. circ. 2,500.

VEGETARIAN ASTROLOGER. see *ASTROLOGY*

613.26 DK ISSN 0109-8861
VEGETARISK TIDSSKRIFT. irreg. (1-2/yr.) vol.77,
1983. Kr.30. Dansk Vegetar-og Raakostforening, Ny
Vestergaardsvej 6, 3500 Vaerloese, Denmark. illus.
Formerly: V F (ISSN 0109-8845)
Vegetarianism

WARSAW AGRICULTURAL UNIVERSITY. S G G
W-A R. ANNALS. FOOD TECHNOLOGY AND
NUTRITION. see *FOOD AND FOOD
INDUSTRIES*

613.2 US
WESTERN HEMISPHERE NUTRITION
CONGRESS. PROCEEDINGS. 1965. triennial.
$80. American Medical Association, Food &
Nutrition Program, 535 N. Dearborn St., Chicago,
IL 60610. TEL 312-751-6000. (Co-sponsors:
American Institute of Nutrition; Canadian Society
for Nutritional Sciences; Sociedad Latinoamericano
de Nutricion) Eds. P.L. White, N. Selvey. circ. 1,
200.

613.2 US
WOMAN'S DAY 101 WAYS TO LOSE WEIGHT
AND STAY HEALTHY. 1973. a. C B S
Publications, Woman's Day, 1515 Broadway, New
York, NY 10036. TEL 201-719-6814. Eds. Gale
Steves, Andrea Levine. adv. illus.

641.1 SZ ISSN 0084-2230
WORLD REVIEW OF NUTRITION AND
DIETETICS. (Text in English) 1964. irreg. (approx.
2/yr.) price varies. S. Karger AG, Allschwilerstrasse
10, P.O. Box, CH-4009 Basel, Switzerland. Ed.
G.H. Bourne. (reprint service avail. from ISI)
Indexed: Biol.Abstr. Chem.Abstr. Curr.Cont.
Ind.Med. Nutr.Abstr. Abstr.Hyg. Dairy Sci.Abstr.
Dent.Ind. Trop.Dis.Bull.

ZAMBIA. NATIONAL FOOD AND NUTRITION
COMMISSION. ANNUAL REPORT. see *FOOD
AND FOOD INDUSTRIES*

NUTRITION AND DIETETICS —
Abstracting, Bibliographies, Statistics

ABSTRACTS FROM CURRENT SCIENTIFIC AND
TECHNICAL LITERATURE. see *FOOD AND
FOOD INDUSTRIES — Abstracting,
Bibliographies, Statistics*

612.3 016 UK
C.A.B. INTERNATIONAL BUREAU OF
NUTRITION. ANNOTATED BIBLIOGRAPHIES.
(Former name of issuing body: Commonwealth
Agricultural Bureaux) no.2, 1967. irreg. price varies.
C.A.B. International, Bureau of Nutrition, Farnham
House, Farnham Royal, Slough SL2 3BN, England.
bk. rev. Indexed: Nutr.Abstr.& Rev.
•Also available online. Vendors: BRS, CISTI,
DIMDI, DIALOG, European Space Agency.
Formerly: Commonwealth Bureau of Nutrition.
Annotated Bibliographies (ISSN 0069-6935)

613.2 US ISSN 0883-1963
CONSUMER HEALTH AND NUTRITION INDEX.
1985. q. $79.50. Oryx Press, 2214 N. Central at
Encanto, Phoenix, AZ 85004-1483. TEL 602-254-
6156. Ed. Barbara D. Bernoff. bibl. (back issues
avail.)

641 016 UK ISSN 0309-1295
NUTRITION ABSTRACTS AND REVIEWS.
SERIES A: HUMAN AND EXPERIMENTAL.
Incorporating separate section: Reviews in Clinical
Nutrition. 1977. m. £250($440) to non-members.
C.A.B. International, Farnham House, Farnham
Royal, Slough SL2 3BN, England (U.S. subscr. to:
C.A.B. International, North American Office, 845
N. Park Ave., Tucson, AR 85719) Ed.Bd. adv. bk.
rev. index. cum.index: vols.1-10 (in 2 vols.) circ. 1,
750. (also avail. in microfiche; back issues avail.)
Indexed: Biol.Abstr. Chem.Abstr. Ind.Med.
Abstr.Hyg. Anim.Breed.Abstr. Dairy Sci.Abstr.
Forest.Abstr. JAMA. Trop.Dis.Bull.
•Also available online. Vendors: BRS, CISTI,
DIMDI, DIALOG, European Space Agency.
Supersedes in part: Nutrition Abstracts and
Reviews (ISSN 0029-6619)

613 016 US ISSN 0149-6743
NUTRITION PLANNING; an international journal of
abstracts about food and nutrition policy, planning
and programs. 1978. a. $75. Oelgeschlager, Gunn &
Hain, Inc., 131 Clarendon St., Boston, MA 02116
TEL 617-437-9620. (Or: 1130 Hill St., Ann Arbor,
MI 48104) (Co-sponsor: Tufts University, School of
Nutrition) Ed. Ellen Kramer. adv. bk. rev. charts.
stat. index. circ. 1,600. (back issues avail.) Indexed:
Nutr.Abstr.

OBSTETRICS AND GYNECOLOGY

see *Medical Sciences — Obstetrics and
Gynecology*

OCCUPATIONS AND CAREERS

see also *Business and Economics — Labor
and Industrial Relations*

371.42 387.7 US
AIRLINE GUIDE TO FLIGHT ATTENDANT
CAREER. 1968. a. $8.95. International Publishing
Co. of America, 665 La Villa Dr., Miami Springs,
FL 33166. TEL 305-887-1701. Ed. Alexander C.
Morton. circ. 25,000.
Former titles: Airline Guide to Stewardess &
Stewards Career (ISSN 0065-4914) & Annual Guide
to Stewardess Career.

371.42 AT
AUSTRALIAN SCHOOL LEAVERS YEARBOOK.
1967. a. Aus.$5.95. Hobson's Press Australia Pty
Ltd., 491 Kent St., Sydney, NSW 2000, Australia.
Eds. S. Seymour, L. Roberts. adv. circ. 30,000.
Fomerly (until 1981): Opportunities for School
Leavers in Australia.

BUSINESS RESOURCES TOURISM/
HOSPITALITY/RECREATION. see
EDUCATION — Higher Education

331.7 US
C P C ANNUAL. (In 3 vols.) 1957. a. $25. College
Placement Council, Inc., 62 Highland Ave.,
Bethlehem, PA 18017. TEL 215-868-1421. Ed. Joan
M. Bowser. adv. illus. circ. 1,000,000.
Formerly: College Placement Annual (ISSN
0069-5734)

371.42 US ISSN 8755-8378
C P C NATIONAL DIRECTORY; who's who in
career planning, placement, and recruitment. 1985.
a. $30 to non-members; members $20. College
Placement Council, Inc., 62 Highland Ave.,
Bethlehem, PA 18017. TEL 215-868-1421. Ed.
Marian R. Szakacs. circ. 4,000.

371.42 US
CALIFORNIA PERSONNEL & GUIDANCE
ASSOCIATION. MONOGRAPHS. 1960. irreg.,
no.11, 1977. price varies. California Personnel &
Guidance Association, 654 E. Commonwealth Ave.,
Fullerton, CA 92631. TEL 714-871-6460.

371.42 US ISSN 0740-7289
CAREER GUIDE: DUN'S EMPLOYMENT
OPPORTUNITIES DIRECTORY. a. $315. Dun's
Marketing Services (Subsidiary of: Dun & Bradstreet
International) 49 Old Bloomfield Rd., Mtn. Lakes,
NJ 07046.
Formerly: Dun's Employment Opportunities
Directory.

371.42 SA
CAREERING. 1978. a. free. University of Cape
Town, Careers Office, Private Bag, Rondebosch
7700, South Africa. Ed. Mervyn Wetmore. adv. circ.
5,000.

371.42 AT
CAREERS. 1955. a. free. Careers Publishing Pty Ltd.,
8 Elliott St., Ascot Vale, Vic. 3032, Australia.

371.42 UK
CAREERS ENCYCLOPEDIA. 1952. biennial.
£17.95. Cassell Ltd., 1 St. Anne's Rd., Eastbourne,
E. Sussex BN21 3UN, England. Ed. Audrey Segal.
adv.

371.42 CN ISSN 0318-6229
CAREERS FOR GRADUATES/CARRIERES POUR
DIPLOMES. (Text in English and French) 1973. a.
free to Canadian University graduates; others Can.
$2. Development Publications Ltd., Box 84, Sta. A,
Willowdale, Ont. M2N 5S7, Canada. TEL 416-636-
2230.

371.42 AT
CAREERS GUIDE. 1956. a. David Boyce Publishing
and Associates, 44 Regent St., Redfern, N.S.W.
2016, Australia.

371.42 US ISSN 0069-0449
CAREERS IN DEPTH; Exploring Careers. 1960.
irreg. $8.97. Rosen Publishing Group, Inc., 29 E. 21
St., New York, NY 10010. TEL 212-777-3017. Ed.
Ruth C. Rosen.

CAREERS IN HOSPITALS AND HEALTH
SERVICES IN VICTORIA. see *HOSPITALS*

371.42 II
CAREERS INFORMATION SERIES. irreg. price
varies. Ministry of Works and Housing, Department
of Publications, Civil Lines, Delhi 110054, India.
(Co-sponsor: Central Institute for Research and
Training in Employment Service)

371.42 331.1 US ISSN 0276-0355
CHRONICLE CAREER INDEX. a. $15.68.
Chronicle Guidance Publications, Inc., Box 1190,
Moravia, NY 13118. TEL 315-497-0330.
Former titles: Chronicle Career Index Annual
(ISSN 0190-4663) & Career Index (ISSN 0576-
7296)

371.42 US
COLLEGE PLANNING/SEARCH BOOK. 1975. a.
$6. American College Testing Program, 2201 N.
Dodge, Box 168, Iowa City, IA 52243. TEL 319-
337-1429.

331.1 330 US
CONSULTING RATES AND BUSINESS
PRACTICES. ANNUAL SURVEY. 1979. biennial.
$9.95. Professional and Technical Consultants
Association, 1330 S. Bascom Ave., San Jose, CA
95158. Eds. Gary Cunningham, John Stormes. circ.
2,000.

371.42 UK
D O G CAREER GUIDES SERIES. 1974. a. £2.25.
V N U Business Publications Ltd., 53-55 Frith St.,
London W1A 2HG, England. Ed. Iris Rosier. circ.
12,000.

920 CK
DIRECTORIO NACIONAL DE PROFESIONALES.
irreg. E C O C Ltda., Calle 17 no. 5-43, Apdo.
Aereo 30969, Bogota, Colombia. illus.

DIRECTORY OF COURSES/TOURISM/
HOSPITALITY/RECREATION. see
EDUCATION — Higher Education

DIRECTORY OF INTERNSHIPS, RESIDENCIES
AND REGISTRARSHIPS AVAILABLE IN
VICTORIAN HOSPITALS. see *HOSPITALS*

OCCUPATIONS AND CAREERS

DIRECTORY OF MODEL-TALENT AGENCIES AND SCHOOLS USA AND INTERNATIONAL. see *EDUCATION — Guides To Schools And Colleges*

371.42   UK   ISSN 0070-6019
DIRECTORY OF OPPORTUNITIES FOR GRADUATES. 1957. a. £12.50. V N U Business Publications BV, 53-55 Frith St., London W1A 2HG, England. Ed. Iris Rosier.

331.1   UK   ISSN 0070-6051
DIRECTORY OF OVERSEAS SUMMER JOBS. 1969. a. $8.95. Vacation-Work, 9 Park End St., Oxford, England (Dist. in U.S. by: Writer's Digest Books, 9933 Alliance Rd., Cincinnati, OH 45242) Ed. David Woodworth.

DIRECTORY OF PUBLIC VOCATIONAL TECHNICAL SCHOOLS AND INSTITUTES. see *EDUCATION — Guides To Schools And Colleges*

DIRECTORY OF SPECIAL OPPORTUNITIES FOR WOMEN. see *WOMEN'S INTERESTS*

DIRECTORY OF SPECIAL PROGRAMS FOR MINORITY GROUP MEMBERS; CAREER INFORMATION SERVICES, EMPLOYMENT SKILLS, BANKS, FINANCIAL AID SOURCES. see *EDUCATION — Guides To Schools And Colleges*

371.42   UK   ISSN 0308-7123
DIRECTORY OF SUMMER JOBS ABROAD. 1970. a. £4.95. Vacation-Work, 9 Park End St., Oxford OX1 1HJ, England. Ed. David Woodworth.

371.4   UK   ISSN 0143-3490
DIRECTORY OF SUMMER JOBS IN BRITAIN. 1970. a. $8.95. Vacation-Work, 9 Park End St., Oxford, England (Dist. in U.S. by: Writer's Digest Books, 9933 Alliance Rd., Cincinnati, OH 45242) Ed.Susan Griffith.

371.4   600   UK   ISSN 0309-5290
DIRECTORY OF TECHNICAL AND FURTHER EDUCATION. 1956. biennial. £35. Longman Group Ltd., Fourth Ave., Harlow, Essex CM19 5AA, England. index.
Former titles: Yearbook of Technical and Further Education; Yearbook of Technical Education and Training for Industry (ISSN 0084-4020)

658   UK
DOG VOLUME 3. ADMINISTRATION, MANAGEMENT, MARKETING AND SALES. 1980. a. £2.50. New Opportunity Press, Yeoman House, 76 St. James's Lane, London N10 3RD, England. Ed. A. Sich. charts.
Former titles (until 1984): Graduate Careers in Sales and Marketing for Graduates and Postgraduates (ISSN 0260-0706); Graduate Careers in Sales and Marketing.

EDUCATION & CAREERS IN SOUTH AFRICA. see *EDUCATION*

EMERGING PATTERNS OF WORK AND COMMUNICATIONS IN AN INFORMATION AGE. see *COMMUNICATIONS*

371.42   370.196   FR
EMPLOIS D'ETE EN FRANCE. (Text in French) 1974. a. £4.95. Vacation Work, 4 rue d'Alesia, 75014 Paris, Franced. Ed. Francois Armen.

331.7   CN   ISSN 0381-3711
EMPLOYERS OF NEW COMMUNITY COLLEGE GRADUATES: DIRECTORY. (Text in English and French) 1971. a. Can.$5. Department of Manpower and Immigration, Economic Analysis and Forecasts Branch, Ottawa, Ont. K1A 0J9, Canada. TEL 613-996-8211. illus.

331.7   370.7   CN   ISSN 0381-372X
EMPLOYERS OF NEW UNIVERSITY GRADUATES: DIRECTORY. French edition: Annuaire des Employeurs des Nouveaux Diplomes de College. (Text in English and French) 1971. a. Can.$5. Department of Manpower and Immigration, Economic Analysis and Forecasts Branch, Ottawa, Ont. K1A 0J9, Canada. TEL 613-996-8211. illus.
Formerly: Directory of Employers Offering Employment to New University Graduates (ISSN 0381-3738)

FREELANCERS OF NORTH AMERICA. see *PUBLISHING AND BOOK TRADE*

371.42   AT
GRADUATE OUTLOOK. 1977. a. Hobsons Press Australia Pty Ltd., 491 Kent St., Sydney, N.S.W. 2000, Australia. Ed. Gwen Seligman. adv. circ. 36,000.

371.42   IS
HADASSAH VOCATIONAL GUIDANCE INSTITUTE. ANNUAL REPORT FOR THE YEAR. (Editions in English & Hebrew) 1948. a. free. ‡ Hadassah Vocational Guidance Institute, P.O. Box 1406, Jerusalem, Israel. (Co-sponsor: Hadassah Women Zionist Organization of America) Ed. Y. Garty. circ. 1,200 (both edts.)
Formerly: Hadassah Vocational Guidance Institute. Report (ISSN 0072-9248)

331   US   ISSN 0085-1728
ILLINOIS LABOR HISTORY SOCIETY REPORTER. 1970. irreg. (approx. 3/yr.) $5. ‡ Illinois Labor History Society, 28 E. Jackson Blvd., Chicago, IL 60604. TEL 312-663-4107. Ed. Leslie F. Orear. bk. rev. circ. 500.
Labor force studies

INTERNATIONAL ASSOCIATION FOR EDUCATIONAL AND VOCATIONAL INFORMATION. STUDIES AND REPORTS. see *EDUCATION*

658.3   US   ISSN 0272-5460
INTERNSHIPS; 35,000 on-the-job training opportunities for all types of careers. 1981. a. $18.95. F & W Publications, Inc., 9933 Alliance Rd., Cincinnati, OH 45242. TEL 513-984-0717. Ed. Katherine Jobst.

JAPANESE NURSING ASSOCIATION RESEARCH REPORT. see *MEDICAL SCIENCES — Nurses And Nursing*

371.42   US   ISSN 0278-5706
JOB CATALOG; where to find that creative job in Washington DC and Baltimore. 1979. a. $9.50. Mail Order USA, Box 19083, Washington, DC 20036. Ed. Dorothy O'Callaghan. circ. 5,000.

331.1   US
JOB MARKET. 1987. a. American Vocational Association, 1410 King St., Alexandria, VA 22314. TEL 703-683-3111. Ed. William Hornung. circ. 1,000.

371.42   UK
JOBS IN THE 'GAP' YEAR. 1969. biennial, 8th edt., 1986. Independent Schools Careers Organisation, 12a-18a Princess Way, Camberley, Surrey GU15 3SP, England. Ed. Joan Hills. circ. 4,000.
Formerly: Temporary Occupations and Employment (ISSN 0264-7761)

371   US
JOURNALISM CAREER GUIDE FOR MINORITIES. 1985. a. Dow Jones Newspaper Funds, Inc., Box 300, Princeton, NJ 08542. TEL 609-452-2820.

371.42   UK   ISSN 0066-3972
N U T GUIDE TO CAREERS WORK. 1957. a. £1.50. (National Union of Teachers) Teacher Publishing Co. Ltd., Derbyshire House, Lower Street, Kettering, Northants, NN16 8BB, England. Ed. Stuart Skyte. adv. circ. 15,000.
Formerly: Annual Guide to Careers for Young People.

NATIONAL DIRECTORY OF EDUCATIONAL PROGRAMS IN GERONTOLOGY. see *GERONTOLOGY AND GERIATRICS*

NATIONAL DIRECTORY OF INTERNSHIPS, RESIDENCIES & REGISTRARSHIPS. see *HOSPITALS*

NATIONAL EMPLOYMENT LISTING SERVICE FOR THE CRIMINAL JUSTICE SYSTEM. POLICE EMPLOYMENT GUIDE. see *CRIMINOLOGY AND LAW ENFORCEMENT*

NATIONAL EMPLOYMENT LISTING SERVICE FOR THE CRIMINAL JUSTICE SYSTEM. SPECIAL EDITION: EDUCATION OPPORTUNITIES. see *CRIMINOLOGY AND LAW ENFORCEMENT*

331.1   378   US
NORTHWESTERN ENDICOTT REPORT; salary schedules and employment trends on the employment of college and university graduates in business and industry. 1946. a. $15. Northwestern University, Placement Center, Evanston, IL 60201. TEL 312-491-3707. Ed. Victor R. Lindquist. circ. 38,000. Indexed: PROMT.
Formerly: Endicott Report.

371.4   340   US
NOW HIRING; government jobs for lawyers. 1952. a. $14.95 to non-members; members $9.95. ‡ American Bar Association, Law Student Division, 750 N. Lake Shore Dr., Chicago, IL 60611. TEL 312-988-5000.
Former titles: Washington Want Ads & Federal Government Legal Career Opportunities (ISSN 0065-7476)

OCCUPATIONAL PROGRAMS IN CALIFORNIA PUBLIC COMMUNITY COLLEGES. see *EDUCATION — Guides To Schools And Colleges*

331.1   US
OFFICIAL GUIDE TO AIRLINE CAREERS. 1977. a. $8.95. International Publishing Co. of America, 665 La Villa Dr., Miami Springs, FL 33166. TEL 305-887-1701. Ed. Alex Morton. adv. circ. 20,000.

331.1   AT
ON STARTING WORK. irreg. Monash University, Careers and Appointments Services, Wellington Road, Clayton, Vic. 3168, Australia. Ed. Lionel Parrot.

371.42   UK
OPPORTUNITIES FOR GEOLOGISTS AND GEOPHYSICISTS. 1978. biennial. £1.50. Institution of Geologists, Burlington House, Piccadilly, London W1V 9HG, England. Ed. Peter Caswell. circ. 2,000.
Formerly (until 1985): Careers for Geologists.

371.42   SA
OPPORTUNITIES FOR GRADUATES IN SOUTHERN AFRICA. (Text in English) 1964. a. R.5. Bee Books, P.O. Box 47433, Parklands, Johannesburg 2121, South Africa. Ed. Grahan Hulley. adv. index. cum.index. circ. 15,000.

371.42   SA
OPPORTUNITIES FOR MATRICULANTS & SCHOOL LEAVERS IN SOUTHERN AFRICA. (Text in Afrikaans and English) 1964. a. R.5. Bee Books, P.O. Box 47433, Parklands, Johannesburg 2121, South Africa. Ed. Graham Hulley. adv. index. cum.index. circ. 55,000.

331.1   620   US
OPPORTUNITIES IN SCIENCE AND ENGINEERING. (Former name of issuing body: Scientific Manpower Commission) 1982. irreg. $15. Commission on Professionals in Science & Technology, 1500 Massachusetts Ave., N.W., Ste. 831, Washington, DC 20005. TEL 202-223-6995. Ed. Betty M. Vetter. charts.

371.42   UK
OXBRIDGE CAREERS HANDBOOK. 1979. a. £1.95. Oxford University Students Union, New Barnet House, Little Clarendon St., Oxford OX1 2HU, England. Ed. Danny Gittings. adv. circ. 15,000.

331   UN
P R E A L C NEWSLETTER. (Test and summaries in English and Spanish) 1985. irreg. (approx. 3/yr.) free. International Labor Office, Programa Regional del Empleo para America Latina y el Caribe, Casilla 618, Santiago, Chile. circ. 1,300. (looseleaf format)

331.1   US   ISSN 0749-5021
PETERSON'S GUIDE TO BUSINESS AND MANAGEMENT JOBS (YEAR) 1984. a. $14.95. Petersons's Guides, 166 Bunn Dr., Box 2123, NJ 08543-2123. TEL 609-924-5338. Ed. Christopher Billy. adv. tr.lit. circ. 17,000. (also avail. in microform)

371.42   US
PETERSON'S SUMMER OPPORTUNITIES FOR KIDS AND TEENAGERS. 1983. a. $12.95. Peterson's Guides, Box 2123, Princeton, NJ 08543-2123. TEL 609-924-5338. Ed. Christopher Billy.
Formerly: Peterson's Annual Guides: Summer Opportunities for Kids and Teenagers (ISSN 0739-9006)

371.42   US   ISSN 0190-1796
PROFESSIONAL WOMEN AND MINORITIES; a
manpower data resource service. (Former name of
issuing body: Scientific Manpower Commission)
1975. a. $75. Commission on Professionals in
Science & Technology, 1500 Massachusetts Ave.,
N.W., Ste. 813, Washington, DC 20005. TEL 202-
223-6995. Eds. B. Vetter, E. Babco. bibl. charts.
index. circ. 1,000. (reprint service avail. from UMI)

331.1   AT
REASONS FOR CHOOSING. irreg. Monash
University, Careers and Appointments Services,
Wellington Road, Clayton, Vic. 3168, Australia. Ed.
Lionel Parrot.

371.42   US
RECRUITING(YEAR) a. College Placement Council,
Inc., 62 Highland Ave., Bethlehem, PA 18017. TEL
215-868-1421.

331.1   US   ISSN 0146-5015
SALARIES OF SCIENTISTS, ENGINEERS AND
TECHNICIANS; a summary of salary surveys.
1965. biennial. $35. Commission on Professionals in
Science & Technology, 1500 Massachusetts Avenue,
N.W., Ste. 831, Washington, DC 20005. TEL 202-
223-6995. Ed. Eleanor L. Babco. charts. illus. stat.
circ. 1,000. (reprint service avail. from UMI)

331.1   US
SCIENCE, ENGINEERING, AND HUMANITIES
DOCTORATES IN THE UNITED STATES:
PROFILE. 1973. biennial. free. (National Science
Foundation) National Academy Press, 2101
Constitution Ave., Washington, DC 20418. TEL
202-334-2000. Ed. Betty D. Maxfield. charts. stat.
tr.lit. circ. 3,000. Indexed: ERIC.
  Formerly (until 1977): Doctoral Scientists and
Engineers in the United States. Profile (ISSN 0095-
0750)

331.1   US   ISSN 0081-9352
SUMMER EMPLOYMENT DIRECTORY OF THE
UNITED STATES. 1952. a. $9.95. F & W
Publications, Inc., 9933 Alliance Rd., Cincinnati,
OH 45242. TEL 513-984-0717. Ed. Pat Beusterien.
adv. bk. rev. circ. 25,000.
  Names and addresses of employers and summer
and part-time jobs available to students and teachers

331.1   US
SUMMER JOBS FOR (YEAR); Opportunities in the
Federal Government. a. U.S. Civil Service
Commission, U.S. Office of Personal Management,
1900 E. St., N.W., Washington, DC 20415.

TEACHER SUPPLY/DEMAND. see
EDUCATION — School Organization And
Administration

331.71   FR   ISSN 0082-2442
TECHNIQUES ARTISANALES MODERNES. 1970.
irreg. price varies. Editions C. Massin et Cie, 2 rue
de l'Echelle, 75001 Paris, France.

331.1   US
TECHNOLOGICAL MARKETPLACE: SUPPLY
AND DEMAND FOR SCIENTISTS AND
ENGINEERS. 1977. irreg. $25. Commission on
Professionals in Science & Technology, 1500
Massachusetts Ave., N.W., Ste. 831, Washington,
DC 20005. TEL 202-223-6995. Ed. Betty M.
Vetter. charts.
  Formerly: Supply and Demand for Scientists and
Engineers (ISSN 0732-2631)

TRAINING RESOURCES TOURISM/
HOSPITALITY/RECREATION. see
EDUCATION — Higher Education

371.42   NN
VANUATU. NATIONAL PLANNING AND
STATISTICS OFFICE. MANPOWER AND
EMPLOYMENT SURVEY. FINAL RESULTS/
ENQUETE SUR L'EMPLOI ET LA MAIN
D'OEUVRE. DEFINITIFS. (Text in English &
French) 1973 edt., 1978. irreg. free. Informations
Department, Statistics Division, NP 50, Port-Vila,
Vanuatu. stat. circ. 500.
  Formerly (until 1984): Vanuatu. Bureau of
Statistics. Manpower and Employment Survey. Final
Results/Enquete sur l'Emploi et la Main d'Oeuvre.
Definitifs.

331.1   US
WASHINGTON. EMPLOYMENT SECURITY
DEPARTMENT. ANNUAL DEMOGRAPHIC
INFORMATION. 1976. a. free. Employment
Security Department, LEMA Mailstop KG-11,
Olympia, WA 98504-5311. TEL 206-438-4800. Ed.
Jack Schillinger. circ. 400.

WORKING HOLIDAYS (YEAR) see CHILDREN
AND YOUTH — For

375   SW   ISSN 0513-6261
YRKE OCH FRAMTID. 1972. biennial. Kr.85.
(Arbetsmarknadsstyrelsen) Allmaenna Foerlaget,
Box 5227, 102 45 Stockholm, Sweden. illus.

354.689   ZA   ISSN 0514-5457
ZAMBIA. EDUCATIONAL AND
OCCUPATIONAL ASSESSMENT SERVICE.
ANNUAL REPORT. a. 20 n. Government Printer,
P.O. Box 2186, Lusaka, Zambia. stat.

OCCUPATIONS AND CAREERS —
Abstracting, Bibliographies, Statistics

371.42 016   UY   ISSN 0069-1046
CATALOGO DE PUBLICACIONES
LATINOAMERICANAS SOBRE FORMACION
PROFESIONAL. 1964. a. price varies. Centro
Interamericano de Investigacion y Documentacion
Sobre Formacion Profesional, Avda. Uruguay 1238,
Casilla de Correo 1761, Montevideo, Uruguay (Dist.
in U.S. by International Labour Office, Washington
Branch Office, 666 11th St., N.W., Washington,
D.C. 20001) Indexed: CIRF Abstr.

371.42   US   ISSN 0161-0562
CURRENT CAREER AND OCCUPATIONAL
LITERATURE. 1973. biennial. $30. H.W. Wilson
Co., 950 University Ave., Bronx, NY 10452. TEL
212-588-8400. Ed. Leonard H. Goodman.

331.1 315   JA
JAPAN. MINISTRY OF HEALTH AND
WELFARE. STATISTICS AND INFORMATION
DEPARTMENT. REPORT ON
OCCUPATIONAL STATISTICS ON VITAL
EVENTS. quinquennial. 5000 Yen. Ministry of
Health and Welfare, Statistics and Information
Department, 7-3 Ichigaya-Honmura cho, Shinjuku-
ku, Tokyo 162, Japan (Order from: Health &
Welfare Statistics Association, c/o Mezon Azabu, 5-
13-14 Roppongi, Minato-ku, Tokyo, Japan)

NETHERLANDS. CENTRAAL BUREAU VOOR
DE STATISTIEK. STATISTIEK VAN DE
VOORLICHTING BIJ SCHOLEN EN
BEROEPSKEUZE. STATISTICS OF
VOCATIONAL GUIDANCE. see
EDUCATION — Abstracting, Bibliographies,
Statistics

NETHERLANDS. CENTRAAL BUREAU VOOR
DE STATISTIEK. STATISTIEK VAN HET
BEROEPSONDERWIJS: TECHNISCH EN
NAUTISCH ONDERWIJS. STATISTICS ON
VOCATIONAL TRAINING. see
EDUCATION — Abstracting, Bibliographies,
Statistics

NETHERLANDS. CENTRAAL BUREAU VOOR
DE STATISTIEK. STATISTIEK VAN HET
HOGER BEROEPSONDERWIJS: AGRARISCH
ONDERWIJS. see EDUCATION — Abstracting,
Bibliographies, Statistics

371.42 317   US
U.S. BUREAU OF LABOR STATISTICS.
OCCUPATIONAL OUTLOOK HANDBOOK.
1946. biennial. price varies. U.S. Bureau of Labor
Statistics, 441 G. St., N.W., Washington, DC 20212
TEL 202-655-4000. (Orders to: Supt. of Documents,
Washington, DC 20402)

OCEANOGRAPHY

see Earth Sciences — Oceanography

OFFICE EQUIPMENT AND SERVICES

see Business and Economics — Office
Equipment and Services

OPHTHALMOLOGY AND OPTOMETRY

see Medical Sciences — Ophthalmology and
Optometry

OPTICS

see Physics — Optics

ORGANIC CHEMISTRY

see Chemistry — Organic Chemistry

ORIENTAL RELIGIONS

see Religions and Theology — Oriental

ORIENTAL STUDIES

see also History — History of Asia;
Linguistics

956   GW   ISSN 0173-1904
ABHANDLUNGEN DES DEUTSCHEN
PALAESTINAVEREINS. 1969. irreg., vol.7, 1985.
price varies. Verlag Otto Harrassowitz, Taunusstr.
14, Postfach 2929, 6200 Wiesbaden 1, W. Germany
(B.R.D.) Ed. Arnulf Kuschke.

950   GW   ISSN 0567-4980
ABHANDLUNGEN FUER DIE KUNDE DES
MORGENLANDES. (Text in English, French, and
German) irreg., vol.48, no.1, 1986. price varies.
(Deutsche Morgenlaendische Gesellschaft) Franz
Steiner Verlag Wiesbaden GmbH, Birkenwaldstr. 44,
Postfach 347, D-7000 Stuttgart 1, W. Germany
(B.R.D.) Ed. Ewald Wagner.

950   NE   ISSN 0065-0382
ABR-NAHRAIN. 1959/60. a. price varies. (University
of Melbourne, Department of Middle Eastern
Studies, AT) E.J. Brill, P.O. Box 9000, 2300 PA
Leiden, Netherlands.

950   NE   ISSN 0065-0390
ABR-NAHRAIN. SUPPLEMENTS. 1964. irreg. price
varies. (University of Melbourne, Department of
Middle Eastern Studies, AT) E.J. Brill, P.O. Box
9000, 2300 PA Leiden, Netherlands. Indexed:
M.L.A.

950   DK   ISSN 0001-6438
ACTA ORIENTALIA. (Text in English, French or
German) a. Kr.362. Munksgaard, 35 Noerre
Soegade, DK-1370 Copenhagen K, Denmark. Ed.
Soeren Egerod. bk. rev. circ. 500. (reprint service
avail. from ISI) Indexed: Curr.Cont. M.L.A.

950   GW   ISSN 0720-9061
AEGYPTEN UND ALTES TESTAMENT. 1979.
irreg., vol.11, 1987. price varies. Verlag Otto
Harrassowitz, Taunusstr. 14, Postfach 2929, D-6200
Wiesbaden 1, W. Germany (B.R.D.) Ed. Manfred
Goerg.

ORIENTAL STUDIES

956   GW ISSN 0568-0476
AEGYPTOLOGISCHE ABHANDLUNGEN. 1960. irreg., vol.44, 1986. price varies. Verlag Otto Harrassowitz, Taunusstr. 14, Postfach 2929, 6200 Wiesbaden 1, W. Germany (B.R.D.) Ed. Wolfgang Helck.

950   GW ISSN 0170-3196
AETHIOPISTISCHE FORSCHUNGEN. (Text in English and German) irreg., vol.25, 1987. price varies. Franz Steiner Verlag Wiesbaden GmbH, Birkenwaldstr. 44, Postfach 347, D-7000 Stuttgart 1, W. Germany (B.R.D.) Ed. E. Hammerschmidt.

AFRO-ASIA. see *HISTORY*

950   GW ISSN 0568-4447
AKADEMIE DER WISSENSCHAFTEN UND DER LITERATUR, MAINZ. ORIENTALISCHE KOMMISSION. VEROEFFENTLICHUNGEN. (Text in French and German) irreg., vol.38, 1985. price varies. Franz Steiner Verlag Wiesbaden GmbH, Birkenwaldstr. 44, Postfach 347, D-7000 Stuttgart 1, W. Germany (B.R.D.)

950   LE ISSN 0002-3973
AL-ABHATH. (Text in Arabic and English) 1948. a. $18. American University of Beirut, Box 1786, Beirut, Lebanon. Ed. R. Baalbaki. bk. rev. bibl. circ. 1,000. Indexed: Hist.Abstr. Numis.Lit.

954   II
ALL-INDIA ORIENTAL CONFERENCE. SUMMARIES OF PAPERS. (Text in English, Hindi or Sanskrit) irreg., 27th 1974. Kurukshetra University, Kurukshettra, India. Ed. Gopikamohan Bhattacharya.

950   NE ISSN 0065-6593
ALTBABYLONISCHE BRIEFE IM UMSCHRIFT UND UEBERSETZUNG. 1964. irreg., vol.11, 1986. price varies. E.J. Brill, P.O. Box 9000, 2300 PA Leiden, Netherlands.

950   US ISSN 0065-9541
AMERICAN ORIENTAL SERIES. 1925. irreg. price varies. American Oriental Society, 329 Sterling Memorial Library, Box 1603A, Yale Sta., New Haven, CT 06520 (Subscr. to: Eisenbrauns, Box 275, Winona Lake, IN 46590) bk. rev.

950   VC
ANALECTA ORIENTALIA. 1931. irreg., no.54, 1979. price varies. (Pontificio Istituto Biblico) Biblical Institute Press, Piazza della Pilotta 35, 00187 Rome, Italy.

950   US
ANCIENT NEAR EASTERN SOCIETY. JOURNAL. Short title: J A N E S. 1968. a. $15. Ancient Near Eastern Society, Jewish Theological Seminary, 122nd & Broadway, New York, NY 10027. TEL 212-678-8827. Eds. Edward L. Greenstein, David Marcus. adv. illus. circ. 400. (also avail. in microfilm; back issues avail.) Indexed: Old Test.Abstr. Rel.Ind.One. Rel.& Theol.Abstr.
Formerly: Columbia University. Ancient Near Eastern Society. Journal (ISSN 0010-2016)

956 297   UA ISSN 0570-1716
ANNALES ISLAMOLOGIQUES. (Text in Arabic, English and French) 1954. a. £E25($35) Institut Francais d'Archeologie Orientale du Caire, 37 Sharia Sheikh Aly Youssef, Mounira, Cairo, Egypt. circ. 800. (back issues avail.)

068.549 954   BG
ANNUAL GENERAL MEETING OF THE ASIATIC SOCIETY OF BANGLADESH; REPORT OF THE GENERAL SECRETARY. (Text in English) a. Asiatic Society of Bangladesh, Dacca Museum Bldgs., Ramna, Dacca 2, Bangladesh.

ANNUAL OF URDU STUDIES. see *LINGUISTICS*

956   GW ISSN 0724-8822
ARCHIVUM EURASIAE MEDII AEVI. (Text in English, French) 1975. a. Verlag Otto Harrassowitz, Taunusstr. 14, Postfach 2929, 6200 Wiesbaden, W. Germany (B.R.D.) Ed.Bd. bk. rev. Indexed: Numis.Lit.

950 709   US ISSN 0571-1371
ARS ORIENTALIS; the arts of Islam and the East. 1954. a. $25. Department of History of Art, Tappan Hall, University of Michigan, Ann Arbor, MI 48109. TEL 313-763-5840. Eds. Richard Edwards, Terry Allen. bk. rev. circ. 1,000.
Supersedes: Ars Islamica.

950   IT
ARTE ORIENTALE IN ITALIA. (Subseries of: Rome (City). Museo Nazionale d'Arte Orientale. Pubblicazione) 1971. irreg. price varies. Museo Nazionale d'Arte Orientale, Via Merulana 248, Rome 00185, Italy. Ed. Giovanni Poncini. illus. circ. 1,000.

ARTIBUS ASIAE SUPPLEMENTA. see *ART*

ARTS ASIATIQUES. see *ART*

950 960 490 890   CS ISSN 0571-2742
ASIAN AND AFRICAN STUDIES. (Text in English) 1965. a. price varies. (Slovenska Akademia Vied, Kabinet Orientalistiky) Veda, Publishing House of the Slovak Academy of Sciences, Klemensova 19, 814 30 Bratislava, Czechoslovakia (Dist. in Western countries by: Curzon Press Ltd., 42 Gray's Inn Rd., London WC1, England) Ed. I. Dolezal. bk. rev. index. Indexed: Curr.Cont.Africa. E.I.

950   UN
ASIAN CULTURAL CENTRE FOR UNESCO. ORGANIZATION AND ACTIVITIES. (Text in English) a. Asian Cultural Centre for Unesco, 6 Fukuro-machi, Shinjuku-ku, Tokyo 162, Japan. illus.

ASIAN CULTURAL STUDIES. see *HISTORY — History Of Asia*

950   PH ISSN 0004-4679
ASIAN STUDIES. 1963. a. $8.50. University of the Philippines, Asian Center, Diliman, Quezon City 3004, Philippines. charts. illus. stat. circ. 500. Indexed: M.L.A. E.I.

950   AT ISSN 0156-0182
ASIAN STUDIES ASSOCIATION OF AUSTRALIA. CONFERENCE PAPERS. 1978. biennial. price varies. (Asian Studies Association of Australia) University of New South Wales Library, P.O. Box 1, Kensington, N.S.W. 2033, Australia. Ed. Peter Dobrovits. (microfiche)

ASIAN STUDIES MONOGRAPHS SERIES. see *HISTORY — History Of Asia*

ASIAN STUDIES SERIES. see *HISTORY — History Of Asia*

950   II ISSN 0004-4709
ASIATIC SOCIETY, BOMBAY. JOURNAL. N.S. 1925. a. price varies. Asiatic Society, Bombay, Town Hall, Bombay 1, India (Subscr. to: Arthur Probsthain, 41 Great Russell St., London, W.C. 1, England) Ed.Bd. bk. rev. illus. circ. 1,000. Indexed: Hist.Abstr. Amer.Hist.& Life.

950   II ISSN 0571-3161
ASIATIC SOCIETY, CALCUTTA. JOURNAL. (Text in English) vol.18, 1976. a. $9. Asiatic Society, Calcutta, 1 Park St., Calcutta 16, India. bk. rev. bibl. charts. illus. (also avail. in microfilm from UMI; reprint service avail. from UMI) Indexed: Numis.Lit.

950   II
ASIATIC SOCIETY, CALCUTTA. MONOGRAPH SERIES. irreg. $10 per vol. Asiatic Society, Calcutta, 1 Park St., Calcutta 16, India.

950   II
ASIATIC SOCIETY, CALCUTTA. SEMINAR SERIES. irreg. Asiatic Society, Calcutta, 1 Park St., Calcutta 16, India.

956   GW ISSN 0571-320X
ASIATISCHE FORSCHUNGEN. 1959. irreg., vol.98, 1986. price varies. Verlag Otto Harrassowitz, Taunusstr. 14, Postfach 2929, D-6200 Wiesbaden 1, W. Germany (B.R.D.) Ed. Walther Heissig.

950   SP ISSN 0571-3692
ASOCIACION ESPANOLA DE ORIENTALISTAS. BOLETIN. (Text in European languages) 1965. a. 600 ptas.($14) (Asociacion Espanola de Orientalistas) F. Valderrama, Ed. & Pub., Universidad Autonoma, Edificio Rectorado, 28049 Madrid, Spain. bk. rev. charts. illus. circ. 500. (back issues avail.) Indexed: Hist.Abstr. Amer.Hist.& Life.

950 490   AU ISSN 0259-0654
BEIHEFTE ZUR WIENER ZEITSCHRIFT FUER DIE KUNDE DES MORGENLANDES. irreg., no.13, 1985. price varies. Verband der Wissenschaftlichen Gesellschaften Oesterreichs, Lindengasse 37, A-1070 Vienna, Austria. Eds. Arne A. Ambros, Anton C. Schaendlinger.

952   AU ISSN 0522-6759
BEITRAEGE ZUR JAPANOLOGIE. (Text in English and German, summaries in English and Japanese) 1955. irreg., vol.23, 1987. price varies. Universitaet Wien, Institut fuer Japanologie, Universitaetsstr. 7/4, A-1010 Vienna, Austria. Eds. Alexander Slawik, Sepp Linhart. bk. rev. circ. 300.

950   GE ISSN 0138-4228
BERLINER TURFANTEXTE. (Text in English and German) 1971. irreg., vol.15, 1985. (Akademie der Wissenschaften der DDR) Akademie-Verlag Berlin, Leipziger Str. 3-4, 1086 Berlin, E. Germany (D.D.R.)

954   II
BHANDARKAR ORIENTAL RESEARCH INSTITUTE. ANNALS. (Text in English) 1919. a. Rps.80. Bhandarkar Oriental Research Institute, Deccan Gymkhana, Pune 411 004, India. Eds. R.N. Dandekar, G.B. Palsule. bk. rev. circ. 1,250. Indexed: M.L.A.

BIBLICA ET ORIENTALIA. see *RELIGIONS AND THEOLOGY — Roman Catholic*

BIBLIOTECA DEGLI STUDI CLASSICI E ORIENTALI. see *CLASSICAL STUDIES*

BIBLIOTHECA ISLAMICA. see *RELIGIONS AND THEOLOGY — Islamic*

950 490   HU ISSN 0067-8104
BIBLIOTHECA ORIENTALIS HUNGARICA. (Text in English, French and German) 1955. irreg., vol.29, 1984. price varies. (Magyar Tudomanyos Akademia) Akademiai Kiado, Publishing House of the Hungarian Academy of Sciences, P.O. Box 24, H-1363 Budapest, Hungary. Indexed: Old Test.Abstr. New Test.Abstr.

954   II ISSN 0001-902X
BRAHMAVIDYA. Variant title: Adyar Library Bulletin. (Text in English and Sanskrit; occasionally French and German) 1937. a. Rs.50($10) Adyar Library and Research Centre, Theosophical Society, Adyar, Madras 600 020, India. Ed.Bd. adv. bk. rev. cum.index: vols.1-46. circ. 300. (back issues avail.) Indexed: M.L.A.

BULLETIN CRITIQUE DES ANNALES ISLAMOLOGIQUES. see *RELIGIONS AND THEOLOGY — Islamic*

951   US ISSN 0049-254X
BULLETIN OF SUNG AND YUAN STUDIES. (Text in Chinese and English) 1970. a. $8 to individuals; institutions $15. c/o John W. Chaffee, Ed., Department of History, State University of New York, Binghamton, Binghamton, NY 13901. bk. rev. bibl. illus. circ. 300.
Formerly (until vol.14, 1978): Sung Studies Newsletter.

950   GW ISSN 0177-1647
BULLETIN OF THE MIDDLE EASTERN CULTURE. 1984. irreg., vol.2,1987. price varies. Verlag Otto Harrassowitz, Taunusstr. 14, Postfach 2929, D-6200 Wiesbaden, W. Germany (B.R.D.) Eds. H.I.H. Prince, Takahito Mikasa.

950   LE
C E M A M REPORTS. 1974. a. price varies. (Universite Saint-Joseph, Center for the Study of the Modern Arab World) Dar el-Mashreq S.A.R.L., 2 rue Huvelin, Box 946, Beirut, Lebanon (Subscr. to: Librairie Orientale, Box 946, Beirut, Lebanon)

950 DK ISSN 0109-4203
C I N A - NYTT. (Text in Danish, English, Norwegian and Swedish) 1983. irreg. free. (Centralinstitut foer Nordisk Asienforskning) Scandinavian Institute of Asian Studies, Kejsergade 2, 1155 Copenhagen K, Denmark. (looseleaf format)
Formerly: Asien-Studier i Skandinavien (ISSN 0105-7340)

950 II
CHAUKHAMBHA ORIENTAL RESEARCH STUDIES. 1976. irreg., latest no.34, 1985. price varies. Chaukhambha Orientalia, Gokul Bhawan, K 37/109 Gopal Mandir Lane, Varanasi 221001, India.

CHINESE SCIENCE. see *SCIENCES: COMPREHENSIVE WORKS*

951 HK
CHINESE UNIVERSITY OF HONG KONG. INSTITUTE OF CHINESE STUDIES. JOURNAL. 1968. a. HK.$50($8.70) Chinese University of Hong Kong, Institute of Chinese Studies, Shatin, New Territories, Hong Kong, Hong Kong. Ed.Bd. adv. bk. rev. bibl. charts. illus. circ. 500. Indexed: Hist.Abstr. Amer.Hist.& Life.

CHRISTIAN INSTITUTE FOR ETHNIC STUDIES IN ASIA. BULLETIN. see *RELIGIONS AND THEOLOGY*

950 GW ISSN 0340-6393
CODICES ARABICI ANTIQUI. 1972. irreg., vol.4, 1986. price varies. Verlag Otto Harrassowitz, Taunusstr. 14, Postfach 2929, 6200 Wiesbaden, W. Germany (B.R.D.) Ed. R.G. Khoury.

950 AG
COLECCION ORIENTE-OCCIDENTE. 1976. irreg. price varies. Universidad del Salvador, Instituto Latinoamericano de Investigaciones Comparadas Oriente-Occidente, Collao 966, 1022 Buenos Aires, Argentina. Eds. F. Garcia Bazan, P. Matin. circ. 2, 000.

954 UK ISSN 0141-0156
COLLECTED PAPERS ON SOUTH ASIA. 1978. irreg. price varies. (University of London, School of Oriental and African Studies) Curzon Press, 42 Gray's Inn Rd., London W.C. 1., England.

951 FR
COLLEGE DE FRANCE. INSTITUT DES HAUTES ETUDES CHINOISES. MEMOIRS. 1975. irreg. Presses Universitaires de France, 108 bd. Saint Germain, 75279 Paris Cedex 6, France (Service des Periodiques, 12 rue Jean de Beauvais, 75005 Paris) illus. (reprint service avail. from KTO)

950 US
COLUMBIA UNIVERSITY. EAST ASIAN INSTITUTE. STUDIES. 1962. irreg., latest 1980. price varies. Columbia University Press, 562 W. 113th St., New York, NY 10025. TEL 212-678-6777.

950 US ISSN 8756-5293
CORNELL EAST ASIA PAPERS. 1973. irreg., no. 43, 1986. price varies. Cornell University, China-Japan Program, 140 Uris Hall, Ithaca, NY 14853. TEL 607-255-6222. Ed. Robert J. Smith. circ. 2,000.

959 US
CORNELL UNIVERSITY. MODERN INDONESIA PROJECT. INTERIM REPORTS. 1956. irreg., vol.63, 1984. price varies. Cornell University, Modern Indonesia Project, Southeast Asia Program, Ithaca, NY 14850. TEL 607-255-4359. Ed. Audrey Kahin.

959 011 US ISSN 0589-7300
CORNELL UNIVERSITY. MODERN INDONESIA PROJECT PUBLICATIONS. MONOGRAPHS, TRANSLATIONS, BIBLIOGRAPHIES. 1958. irreg., no.66, 1986. price varies. Cornell University, Cornell Modern Indonesia Project, Ithaca, NY 14850.
Formerly: Cornell University. Modern Indonesia Project. Monographs.

950 GW ISSN 0341-0803
DEUTSCHE MORGENLAENDISCHE GESELLSCHAFT. ZEITSCHRIFT. SUPPLEMENTA. irreg., vol.6, 1985. price varies. Franz Steiner Verlag Wiesbaden GmbH, Birkenwaldstr. 44, Postfach 347, D-7000 Stuttgart 1, W. Germany (B.R.D.)

954 II
DHANIRAM BHALLA GRANTHAMALA. (Text in Hindi and Sanskrit) irreg., vol.19, 1972. price varies. Vishveshvaranand Vedic Research Institute, P.O. Sadhu Ashram, Hoshiarpur 146021, Punjab, India. Ed. Vishva Bandhu.

950 895 495 CS
DISSERTATIONES ORIENTALES. (Text in Chinese and English) vol.35, 1975. irreg. price varies. (Ceskoslovenska Akademie Ved, Orientalni Ustav) Academia, Publishing House of the Czechoslovak Academy of Sciences, Vodickova 40, 112 29 Prague 1, Czechoslovakia. Ed. Jaroslav Cesar.

950 FR
DOCUMENTS D'HISTOIRE MAGHREBINE. irreg. Librairie Orientaliste Paul Geuthner, 12 rue Vavin, 75006 Paris, France. Ed. Ch. de la Veronne.

950 JA ISSN 0012-8414
EAST ASIAN CULTURAL STUDIES. (Text in English) 1962. a. price varies. Centre for East Asian Cultural Studies, Toyo Bunko (Oriental Library), 2-28-21 Honkomagome, Bunkyo-ku, Tokyo 113, Japan. Ed. Masao Mori. circ. 1,000.

950 US
EAST ASIAN HISTORICAL MONOGRAPHS. irreg. Oxford University Press, 200 Madison Ave., New York, NY 10016 TEL 212-679-7300. (And: Ely House, 37 Dover St., London W1X 4AH, England) Ed. Wang Gungiou.

950 FR
ECOLE FRANCAISE D'EXTREME-ORIENT. BULLETIN. 1901. irreg., vol.74, 1985. 640 Fr. Librairie Adrien Maisonneuve, 11 rue St. Sulpice, 75006 Paris, France. Indexed: Hist.Abstr. Amer.Hist.& Life. E.I.

959 BE ISSN 0531-1926
ETUDES ORIENTALES. 1963. irreg., no.11, 1983. price varies. Librairie-Editions Thanh-Long, 34 rue Dekens, 1040 Brussels, Belgium. (back issues avail.)

ETUDES PRELIMINAIRES AUX RELIGIONS ORIENTALES DANS L'EMPIRE ROMAIN. see *RELIGIONS AND THEOLOGY*

950 AT ISSN 0085-0586
FLINDERS ASIAN STUDIES LECTURE. 1970. a. Aus.$3. ‡ Flinders University of South Australia, School of Social Sciences, Director of Asian Studies, Bedford Park, S. A. 5042, Australia. Ed. L. Brennan.

950 AT
FLINDERS ASIAN STUDIES MONOGRAPH. 1981. irreg. price varies. Flinders University of South Australia, School of Social Sciences, Director of Asian Studies, Bedford Park, S.A. 5042, Australia.

950 PL ISSN 0015-5675
FOLIA ORIENTALIA. (Text in English, French and German) 1959. a. price varies. (Polska Akademia Nauk, Oddzial w Krakowie, Komisja Orientalistyczna) Ossolineum, Publishing House of the Polish Academy of Sciences, Rynek 9, Wroclaw, Poland. Ed. J. Lewicki. bk. rev. abstr. bibl. circ. 590. Indexed: M.L.A. Numis.Lit.

950 GW ISSN 0170-3307
FREIBURGER ALTORIENTALISCHE STUDIEN. irreg., vol.12, 1985. price varies. Franz Steiner Verlag Wiesbaden GmbH, Birkenwaldstr. 44, Postfach 347, D-7000 Stuttgart, W. Germany (B.R.D.) Ed. Burkhart Kienast.

956 GW ISSN 0340-6261
FREIBURGER BEITRAEGE ZUR INDOLOGIE. 1968. irreg., vol.17, 1985. price varies. Verlag Otto Harrassowitz, Taunusstr. 14, Postfach 2929, 6200 Wiesbaden, W. Germany (B.R.D.) Ed. Ulrich Schneider.

950 GW ISSN 0724-4703
FREIBURGER FERNOESTLICHE FORCHUNGEN. 1983. irreg. price varies. Verlag Otto Harrassowitz, Taunusstr. 14, Postfach 2929, D-6200 Wiesbaden 1, W. Germany (B.R.D.) Ed. Peter Greiner.

956 297 GW ISSN 0170-3285
FREIBURGER ISLAMSTUDIEN. irreg., vol.11, 1987. price varies. Franz Steiner Verlag Wiesbaden GmbH, Birkenwaldstr. 44, Postfach 347, D-7000 Stuttgart 1, W. Germany (B.R.D.) Ed. Hans Robert Roemer.

FU JEN STUDIES; literature & linguistics. see *LITERATURE*

890 297 YU ISSN 0350-1418
GAZI HUSREVBEGOVA BIBLIOTEKA. ANALI. (Text in Serbocroatian; summaries in English) 1972. a. Gazi Husrevbegova Biblioteka, Obala Pariske Komune 4, 71000 Sarajevo, Yugoslavia. (Co-sponsor: Starjesinstvo Islamske Zajednice) Ed. Abdurahman Hukic. circ. 1,500. Indexed: Hist.Abstr. Amer.Hist.& Life.

950 GW ISSN 0170-3455
GLASENAPP-STIFTUNG. irreg., vol.30, 1987. price varies. (Glasenapp-Stiftung) Franz Steiner Verlag Wiesbaden GmbH, Birkenwaldstr. 44, Postfach 347, D-7000 Wiesbaden 1, W. Germany (B.R.D.)

956 297 NE
GOEJE-STICHTING. UITGAVEN. 1956. irreg., vol.25, 1983. price varies. E. J. Brill, P.O. Box 9000, 2300 PA Leiden, Netherlands.

935 950 GW ISSN 0340-6326
GOETTINGER ORIENTFORSCHUNGEN. REIHE I: SYRIACA. irreg., vol.30, 1987. price varies. Verlag Otto Harrassowitz, Taunusstr. 14, Postfach 2929, 6200 Wiesbaden 1, W. Germany (B.R.D.)

950 GW ISSN 0173-2358
GOETTINGER ORIENTFORSCHUNGEN. REIHE II: STUDIEN ZUR SPAETANTIKEN UND FRUEHCHRISTLICHEN KUNST. 1980. irreg., vol.8, 1986. price varies. Verlag Otto Harrassowitz, Taunusstr. 14, Postfach 2929, D-6200 Wiesbaden 1, W. Germany (B.R.D.)

932 GW ISSN 0340-6342
GOETTINGER ORIENTFORSCHUNGEN. REIHE IV: AEGYPTEN. 1973. irreg., vol.17, 1986. price varies. Verlag Otto Harrassowitz, Taunusstr. 14, Postfach 2929, 6200 Wiesbaden 1, W. Germany (B.R.D.)

GOVERNMENT ORIENTAL MANUSCRIPTS LIBRARY. BULLETIN. see *LIBRARY AND INFORMATION SCIENCES*

410 SZ ISSN 0073-0971
HAUTES ETUDES ORIENTALES. 1968. irreg., no.22, 1986. (Ecole Pratique des Hautes Etudes, Centre de Recherches d'Histoire et de Philologie, FR) Librarie Droz, 11, rue Massot, 1211 Geneva 12, Switzerland. circ. 1,000.

950 GE ISSN 0232-3001
HILPRECHT: SAMMLUNG. 1961. irreg., vol.3, 1976. (Friedrich-Schiller-Universitaet, Prof. Hilprecht Sammlung Vorderasiatischer Aelterumer) Akademie-Verlag Berlin, Leipziger Str. 3-4, 1086 Berlin, E. Germany (D.D.R.) Eds. Rudolf Heyer, Friedmar Kuhnert.

INDICES VERBORUM LINGUAE MONGOLIAE MONUMENTIS TRADITORUM. see *LINGUISTICS*

954 FR
INDOLOGICA TAURINENSIA. (Text in various languages) 1973. a. L.25000. International Association of Sanscrit Studies, 22 av. du President Wilson, 75116 Paris, France (Dist. by: Herder Editrice e Libreria S.R.L., Piazza Montecitorio 120, 00186 Rome, Italy) Ed. Oscar Botto. (back issues avail.)

956 GW ISSN 0073-8387
INSTITUT FUER ASIENKUNDE. SCHRIFTEN. (Text in German; summaries in English) 1957. irreg., no.47, 1986. price varies. Verlag Otto Harrassowitz, Taunusstr. 14, Postfach 2929, 6200 Wiesbaden 1, W. Germany(B.R.D.)

950 371.0025 HK
INTERNATIONAL DIRECTORY OF CENTERS FOR ASIAN STUDIES. 1975. biennial. $30. Asian Research Service, G.P.O. Box 2232, Hong Kong, Hong Kong. Ed. Nelson Leung. circ. 1,000.

ORIENTAL STUDIES

IRANICA ANTIQUA; dealing with archaeology, history, religion, art and literature of ancient Persia. see *ARCHAEOLOGY*

IRAQ. see *ARCHAEOLOGY*

956   MY
ISLAMIYAT. (Text in English and Malay) 1977. a. National University of Malaysia - Universiti Kebangsaan Malaysia, Box 1124, Jalan Pantai Baru, Kuala Lumpur 22-12, Malaysia.

492   IS   ISSN 0334-4401
ISRAEL ORIENTAL STUDIES. (Text in English, French, German) 1971. a. $40. Tel-Aviv University, Faculty of Humanities, Department of Arabic Studies, P.O.B. 39040, Tel-Aviv 69 978, Israel (U.S. dist.: Transaction, Inc., Rutgers-The State University, New Brunswick, NJ 08903) Ed. Gideon Goldenberg. circ. 1,000.

ISTANBULER MITTEILUNGEN. see *ARCHAEOLOGY*

950   IT
ISTITUTO UNIVERSITARIO ORIENTALE. ANNALI. a. L.80000. (Istituto Universitario Orientale) Edizioni dell'Ateneo spa, Casella Postale 7216, 00100 Rome, Italy.

ISTITUTO UNIVERSITARIO ORIENTALE DI NAPOLI. SEMINARIO DI STUDI DEL MONDO CLASSICO. ANNALI. SEZIONE LINGUISTICA. see *CLASSICAL STUDIES*

JOURNAL OF ARABIC LITERATURE. see *LITERATURE*

950   US   ISSN 0162-6795
JOURNAL OF ASIAN CULTURE. 1977. a. $7. University of California, Los Angeles, Department of East Asian Languages and Cultures, Graduate Students in Asian Studies, 222 Royce Hall, Los Angeles, CA 90024. TEL 213-825-4321. adv. bk. rev. charts. illus. circ. 500. Indexed: Hist.Abstr. Amer.Hist.& Life.

JOURNAL OF CHINESE RELIGIONS. see *RELIGIONS AND THEOLOGY — Oriental*

950   II   ISSN 0022-3301
JOURNAL OF ORIENTAL RESEARCH. (Text in English and Sanskrit) 1927. irreg. $3. Kuppuswami Sastri Research Institute, 84 Royapettah High Rd., Madras 600004, India. Ed. S.S. Janaki. bk. rev. illus. index. circ. 400.

950   GW   ISSN 0720-6615
JOURNAL OF THE NEPAL RESEARCH CENTRE. (Text in English) 1977. a. DM.48. Franz Steiner Verlag Wiesbaden GmbH, Birkenwaldstr. 44, Postfach 347, D-7000 Stuttgart 1, W. Germany (B.R.D.) Ed. Albrecht Wezler.

KEILSCHRIFTTEXTE AUS BOGHAZKOI. see *ARCHAEOLOGY*

950   HU   ISSN 0133-6193
KELETI TANULMANYOK/ORIENTAL STUDIES. (Text in English, French, German, Hungarian, Russian and languages of the East) 1976. irreg. exchange basis. Magyar Tudomanyos Akademia Konyvtara, Akademia u.2, P.O. Box 7, 1361 Budapest 5, Hungary. Ed. Eva Apor. circ. 800.

956   GW   ISSN 0343-1088
KLEINE AEGYPTISCHE TEXTE. 1969. irreg., vol.9, 1986. price varies. Verlag Otto Harrassowitz, Taunusstr. 14, Postfach 2929, 6200 Wiesbaden 1, W. Germany (B.R.D.) Ed. Wolfgang Helck.

950   GW
KOELNER SARASVATI SERIE. irreg., vol.7, 1985. price varies. Franz Steiner Verlag Wiesbaden GmbH, Birkenwaldstr. 44, Postfach 347, D-7000 Stuttgart 1, W. Germany (B.R.D.) Ed. Klaus Ludwig Janert.

KUNST DES ORIENTS/ART OF THE ORIENT. see *ART*

950   895   II
LALBHAI DALPATBHAI INSTITUTE OF INDOLOGY. PUBLICATIONS. (Text in various languages) irreg. price varies. Lalbhai Dalpatbhai Institute of Indology, Near Gujarat University, P.O. Navarangpura, Ahmedabad 380009, India.

954   UK   ISSN 0142-601X
LONDON STUDIES ON SOUTH ASIA. 1980. irreg. price varies. (University of London, School of Oriental and African Studies) Curzon Press, 42 Gray's Inn Rd., London W.C.1., England. bibl. index.

M E E D PRACTICAL GUIDE. OMAN. (Middle East Economic Digest Ltd.) see *TRAVEL AND TOURISM*

M E E D PRACTICAL GUIDE. SAUDI ARABIA. see *TRAVEL AND TOURISM*

M E E D PRACTICAL GUIDE. U A E. (United Arab Emirates) see *TRAVEL AND TOURISM*

954   II
MADHYA PRADESH ITIHASA PARISHAD. JOURNAL. (Text in English or Hindi) 1959. irreg. (approx. a.) Rs.20. Madhya Pradesh Itihasa Parishad, 34/14, South T. T. Nagar, Bhopal 462003, India. Ed. S.D. Guru. bk. rev. circ. 500. (also avail. in microfilm)
History, art, archaeology, and civilization of Madhya Pradesh

952   001.3   300   FR   ISSN 0495-7725
MAISON FRANCO-JAPONAISE. BULLETIN. (Text in French; summaries in English and French) 1927; N.S. 1951. irreg. (approx. every 2-3 yrs.) price varies. (Maison Franco-Japonaise, JA) Presses Universitaires de France, 3, 2-chome, Kanda Surugadai, Chiyoda-ku, Tokyo 101, Japan (Subscr. to: Librairie-Editions Peeters, Bondgenotenlaan 153, 3000 Leuven, Belgium) Ed.Bd. bibl. circ. 7,000. (reprint service avail. from KTO) Indexed: MLA.

950   IT
MATERIALI PER IL VOCABOLARIO NEOSUMERICO. COLLANA. 1974. a. (Unione Accademica Nazionale) Multigrafica Editrice, Viale Quattro Venti 52/A, 00152 Rome, Italy. (back issues avail.)

950   327   GW
MATERIALIEN ZUM INTERNATIONALEN KULTURAUSTAUSCH/STUDIES IN INTERNATIONAL CULTURAL RELATIONS. 1972. irreg. Institut fuer Auslandsbeziehungen, Charlottenplatz 17, 7000 Stuttgart 1, W. Germany (B.R.D.) (back issues avail.)

956   950   GW   ISSN 0543-1719
MAX FREIHERR VON OPPENHEIM-STIFTUNG. SCHRIFTEN. 1955. irreg., vol.10, 1978. price varies. Verlag Otto Harrassowitz, Taunusstr. 14, Postfach 2929, 6200 Wiesbaden 1, W. Germany (B.R.D.)

950   GW   ISSN 0724-7567
MEDITERANEAN LANGUAGE REVIEW. (Text in English, French, German, and Italian) 1983. irreg., vol.2, 1986. Verlag Otto Harrassowitz, Taunusstr. 14, Postfach 2929, D-6200 Wiesbaden 1, W. Germany (B.R.D) Eds. A. Borg, P. Wexler.

950   GW   ISSN 0179-1621
MEDITERRANEAN LANGUAGE AND CULTURE MONOGRAPH SERIES. 1985. irreg., vol.2, 1986. price varies. Verlag Otto Harrassowitz, Taunusstr. 14, Postfach 2929, D-6200 Wiesbaden 1, W. Germany (B.R.D.) Ed.Bd.

950   GE   ISSN 0138-3663
MEROITICA. (Text in English, French, German) 1973. irreg., vol.8, 1985. (Humboldt-Universitaet zu Berlin, Bereich Aegyptologie und Sudan Archaeologie) Akademie-Verlag Berlin, Leipziger Str. 3-4, 1086 Berlin, E. Germany (D.D.R.)

MODERN EAST ASIAN STUDIES. see *HISTORY — History Of Asia*

MODERN MIDDLE EAST SERIES. see *HISTORY — History Of Asia*

950   US
MONGOLIAN STUDIES. 1974. a. $20. Mongolia Society, Inc., 321-322 Goodbody Hall, Indiana University, IN 47405. TEL 812-335-4078. Ed. John R. Krveger. adv. bk. rev. abstr. bibl. charts. stat. circ. 400. Indexed: Hist.Abstr. M.L.A. Amer.Bibl.Slavic & E.Eur.Stud. Amer.Hist.& Life.
Supersedes: Mongolian Society Bulletin (ISSN 0026-9654)

954   GW   ISSN 0170-8864
MONOGRAPHIEN ZUR INDISCHEN ARCHAEOLOGIE, KUNST UND PHILOLOGIE. irreg., vol.6, 1987. price varies. (Stiftung Ernst Waldschmidt) Franz Steiner Verlag Wiesbaden GmbH, Birkenwaldstr. 44, Postfach 347, D-7000 Stuttgart 1, W. Germany (B.R.D.) Ed. Herbert Haertel.

MONUMENTA GRAECA ET ROMANA. see *ART*

894.2   HU   ISSN 0230-8452
MONUMENTA LINGUAE MONGOLICAE COLLECTA. (Text in Mongolian with transcriptions in Roman letters and introduction in French) 1971. irreg. price varies. (Magyar Tudomanyos Akademia) Akademiai Kiado, Publishing House of the Hungarian Academy of Sciences, P.O. Box 24, H-1363 Budapest, Hungary. Ed. L. Ligeti.
Supersedes: Mongol Nyelvemlektar (ISSN 0540-6471)

950   SZ   ISSN 0077-149X
MONUMENTA SERICA; journal of oriental studies. (Text in English, French, German) 1934. irreg., vol.35, 1981-83. 115 Fr. Editions Saint-Paul, Perolles 42, CH-1700 Fribourg, Switzerland. Ed. Wilhelm Muller. bk. rev. circ. 500. (also avail. in microfilm) Indexed: Hist.Abstr. Amer.Hist.& Life.

956   GW   ISSN 0077-1880
MUENCHENER INDOLOGISCHE STUDIEN. 1955. irreg., vol.6, 1969. price varies. Verlag Otto Harrassowitz, Taunusstr. 14, Postfach 2929, 6200 Wiesbaden, W. Germany (B.R.D.) Ed. H. Hoffmann.

950   GW   ISSN 0170-3668
MUENCHENER OSTASIATISCHE STUDIEN. (Text in English and German) irreg., vol.43, 1986. price varies. Franz Steiner Verlag Wiesbaden GmbH, Birkenwaldstr. 44, Postfach 347, D-7000 Stuttgart 1, W. Germany (B.R.D.) Ed.Bd.

950   GW   ISSN 0170-3676
MUENCHENER OSTASIATISCHE STUDIEN. SONDERREIHE. (Text in English and German) irreg., vol.3, 1978. price varies. Franz Steiner Verlag Wiesbaden GmbH, Birkenwaldstr. 44, Postfach 347, D-7000 Stuttgart 1, W. Germany (B.R.D.) Ed.Bd.

MUSEO NAZIONALE D'ARTE ORIENTALE. SCHEDE. see *MUSEUMS AND ART GALLERIES*

950   BE
MUSEON; revue d'etudes orientales. (Text in English and French) 1881. a. 2000 Fr. Editions Peeters s.p.r.l., Bondgenotenlaan 153, B-3000 Louvain, Belgium. Indexed: New Test.Abstr. Numis.LIt.

MUSEUM OF FAR EASTERN ANTIQUITIES. BULLETIN. see *MUSEUMS AND ART GALLERIES*

MUSICA ASIATICA. see *MUSIC*

954   II   ISSN 0580-4396
MYSORE ORIENTALIST. (Text in English or Sanskrit) 1967. a. $5. Oriental Research Institute, University of Mysore, Mysore 5, Karnataka, India. Ed. H.P. Malledevaru. bk. rev. circ. 300.
Indological studies

NANZAN INSTITUTE FOR RELIGION AND CULTURE. BULLETIN. see *RELIGIONS AND THEOLOGY*

951   NP
NEPAL - ANTIQUARY. BIBLIOGRAPHICAL SERIES. 1976. irreg. Rs.250($30) Office of Nepal-Antiquary, 20/401 Naxal, Kathmandu, Nepal.

ORBIS MUSICAE; Assaph studies in the arts. see *MUSIC*

950   NE   ISSN 0078-6527
ORIENS. (Text in English, French, German) 1948. irreg., vol.28, 1981. price varies. (Internationale Gesellschaft fuer Orientforschung) E.J. Brill, P.O. Box 9000, 2300 PA Leiden, Netherlands. Ed. R. Sellheim. bk. rev. cum.index: vols.1-10.

950   AT   ISSN 0030-5340
ORIENTAL SOCIETY OF AUSTRALIA. JOURNAL. 1961. a. Aus.$10. Oriental Society of Australia, University of Sydney, Department of Oriental Studies, Sydney N.S.W. 2006, Australia. Ed. A.D. Stefanowska. adv. bk. rev. charts. circ. 500. Indexed: Aus.P.A.I.S. E.I.

950   297   JA
ORIENTAL STUDIES/TOHO GAKUHO. (Text in Japanese; table of contents in English) 1931. a. Kyoto University, Research Institute for Humanistic Studies - Kyoto Daigaku Jimbun Kagata Kenkyusyo, 50 Kitashurakawa, Ogura-machi, Sagyo-ku, Kyoto, Japan. illus.

950   200   VC
ORIENTALIA CHRISTIANA ANALECTA. 1923. irreg. price varies. Pontificio Istituto Orientale, Piazza S. Maria Maggiore 7, 00185 Rome, Italy. Ed. John F. Long. circ. 1,000.
     Continues (since 1935): Orientalia Christiana.

950   SW   ISSN 0078-656X
ORIENTALIA GOTHOBURGENSIA. (Subseries of: Acta Universitatis Gothoburgensis) 1969. irreg., no.9, 1986. price varies; also exchange basis. Acta Universitatis Gothoburgensis, Box 5096, S-402 22 Goeteborg, Sweden (Dist. in U.S., Canada and Mexico by: Humanities Press, Inc., 171 First Ave., Atlantic Highlands, NJ 07716) Ed. Fathi Talmoudi.

950   BE   ISSN 0085-4522
ORIENTALIA LOVANIENSIA PERIODICA. (Text in English, French, German; summaries in English) 1970. a. 1600 Fr. Katholieke Universiteit te Leuven, Departement Orientalistiek, Blijde Inkomststraat 21, B-3000 Louvain, Belgium. Ed. G. Pollet. bk. rev. abstr. charts. illus. cum.index. circ. 500. Indexed: M.L.A. Old Test.Abstr. Numis.Lit.

950   NE
ORIENTALIA RHENO-TRAIECTINA. 1949. irreg., vol.29, 1986. price varies. E.J. Brill, P.O. Box 9000, 2300 PA Leiden, Netherlands. Eds. J. Gonda, H.W. Obbink.

950   SW   ISSN 0078-6578
ORIENTALIA SUECANA. 1952. a. Kr.75($15) (Uppsala Universitet) Almqvist & Wiksell International, Box 62, S-101 20 Stockholm, Sweden. Ed. Frithiof Rundgren. circ. 600. Indexed: M.L.A. Numis.Lit.

950   GE   ISSN 0232-3257
PAPYRI AUS DEN STAATLICHEN MUSEEN ZU BERLIN. 1978. irreg., latest 1981. (Staatliche Museen zu Berlin) Akademie-Verlag Berlin, Leipziger Str. 3-4, 1086 Berlin, E. Germany (D.D.R.)

894   494   947.87   US   ISSN 0031-5508
PERMANENT INTERNATIONAL ALTAISTIC CONFERENCE (PIAC). NEWSLETTER. 1966. irreg., (2-3/yr.) free. Indiana University, Permanent International Altaistic Conference, Goodbody Hall 101, Bloomington, IN 47405. TEL 812-335-0959. Ed. Prof. Denis Sinor. adv. bibl. circ. 750. (processed)
     Organization news

950   490   890   US
PHI THETA PAPERS. (Text in English; occasionally in Chinese, Japanese) 1950. a. $7 to individuals; institutions $10. (Oriental Languages Student Association) University of California, Berkeley, Department of Oriental Languages, Durant Hall, Berkeley, CA 94720. Ed. G. Wiersma. circ. 150. (back issues avail.)

950   PL   ISSN 0079-3426
POLSKA AKADEMIA NAUK. ODDZIAL W KRAKOWIE. KOMISJA ORIENTALISTYCZNA. PRACE. (Text in English, French, German, Polish) 1962. irreg., no.18, 1985. price varies. Ossolineum, Publishing House of the Polish Academy of Sciences, Rynek 9, 50-106 Wroclaw, Poland (Dist. by: Ars Polona-Ruch, Krakowskie Przedmiescie 7, Warsaw, Poland) circ. 700.

PORTA LINGUARUM ORIENTALIUM. see *LINGUISTICS*

950   PL   ISSN 0079-4783
PRACE ORIENTALISTYCZNE. (Text and summaries in English, French, German, Polish, and Russian) 1954. irreg., vol.28, 1984. price varies. (Polska Akademia Nauk, Komitet Nauk Orientalistycznych) Panstwowe Wydawnictwo Naukowe, Ul. Miodowa 10, 00-251 Warsaw, Poland (Dist. by: Ars Polona, Krakowskie Przedmiescie 7, 00-068 Warsaw, Poland) circ. 1,200.

954   II
PUNJAB UNIVERSITY INDOLOGICAL SERIES. no.24, 1979. irreg. price varies. Vishveshvaranand Vedic Research Institute, P.O. Sadhu Ashram, Hoshiarpur 146021, Punjab, India. Ed. S. Bhaskaran Nair.

RECORDS OF CIVILIZATION. SOURCES AND STUDIES. see *HISTORY*

932   950   GW   ISSN 0340-8450
RECORDS OF THE ANCIENT NEAR EAST. (Text in English) 1972. irreg., vol.2, 1976. price varies. Verlag Otto Harrassowitz, Taunusstr. 14, Postfach 2929, 6200 Wiesbaden 1, W. Germany (B.R.D.)

950   PL   ISSN 0080-3545
ROCZNIK ORIENTALISTYCZNY. (Text in English, French, German or Russian and Polish) 1914. irreg., vol.42, 1982. price varies. (Polska Akademia Nauk, Komitet Nauk Orientalistycznych) Panstwowe Wydawnictwo Naukowe, Ul. Miodowa 10, 00-251 Warsaw, Poland (Dist. by: Ars Polona, Krakowskie Przedmiescie 7, 00-068 Warsaw, Poland) Ed. E. Tryjarski. circ. 470. Indexed: M.L.A.

950   HK   ISSN 0085-5774
ROYAL ASIATIC SOCIETY. HONG KONG BRANCH. JOURNAL. 1961. a. HK.$50. Royal Asiatic Society, Hong Kong Branch, Box 13864, Hong Kong, Hong Kong. Ed. David Faure. bk. rev. cum.index: vols. 1-10, 1961-1970. circ. 700. Indexed: Hist.Abstr. Amer.Hist.& Life.

960   DK   ISSN 0106-3871
SCANDINAVIAN INSTITUTE OF ASIAN STUDIES. ANNUAL NEWSLETTER. 1968. a. free. Scandinavian Institute of Asian Studies - Centralinstitut for Nordisk Asienforskning, 2 Kejsergade, DK-1155 Copenhagen K, Denmark. bk. rev. circ. 3,000.

930   950   UK   ISSN 0069-1712
SCANDINAVIAN INSTITUTE OF ASIAN STUDIES. MONOGRAPH SERIES. (Text in English) 1969. irreg., no.46, 1981. price varies. (Scandinavian Institute of Asian Studies, DK) Curzon Press, 42 Gray's Inn Rd., London W.C.1, England. circ. 1,100.

958   UK   ISSN 0266-206X
SCANDINAVIAN INSTITUTE OF ASIAN STUDIES. OCCASIONAL PAPERS. 1987. irreg. (Scandinavian Institute of Asian Studies, DK) Curzon Press Ltd., 42 Gray's Inn Rd., London WC1, England.

SCHRIFTEN ZUR GESCHICHTE UND KULTUR DES ALTEN ORIENTS. see *HISTORY — History Of Asia*

SCRIPTA MEDITERRANEA. see *HISTORY — History Of The Near East*

950   296   NE
SEMITIC STUDY SERIES. (Text in English) 1902; N.S. 1952. irreg., vol.5, 1981. E.J. Brill, P.O. Box 9000, 2300 PA Leiden, Netherlands.
     Jewish interests

952   UK   ISSN 0260-6674
SHEFFIELD STUDIES IN JAPANESE; scientific and technical Japanese. (Text in English; summaries in Japanese) 1979. irreg. University of Sheffield, Sheffield Centre of Japanese Studies, Sheffield S10 2TN, England. illus.

951   GW   ISSN 0170-3706
SINOLOGICA COLONIENSIS; Ostasiatische Beitraege der Universitaet zu Koeln. irreg., vol.13, 1985. price varies. (Universitaet zu Koeln) Franz Steiner Verlag Wiesbaden GmbH, Birkenwaldstr. 44, Postfach 347, D-7000 Stuttgart 1, W. Germany (B.R.D.) Ed. Martin Gimm.

950   GW   ISSN 0170-7787
SOUTH ASIAN DIGEST OF REGIONAL WRITING. (Text in English) irreg., vol.11, 1986. price varies. (Universitaet Heidelberg, Suedasien Institut) Franz Steiner Verlag Wiesbaden GmbH, Birkenwaldstr. 44, Postfach 347, D-7000 Stuttgart 1, W. Germany (B.R.D.) Ed. Guenther D. Sontheimer.

954   GW   ISSN 0584-3170
SOUTH ASIAN STUDIES. (Text in English) irreg., vol.16, 1986. price varies. (Universitaet Heidelberg, Suedasien Institut, New Delhi, II) Franz Steiner Verlag Wiesbaden GmbH, Birkenwaldstr. 44, Postfach 347, D-7000 Stuttgart 1, W. Germany (B.R.D.)

SOUTH EAST ASIA LIBRARY GROUP NEWSLETTER. see *LIBRARY AND INFORMATION SCIENCES*

959   US
SOUTHEAST ASIA PAPERS. (Text in English) 1973. irreg., (1-2/yr.) price varies. University of Hawaii, Southeast Asian Studies Program, Honolulu, HI 96822. TEL 808-948-8324. Ed. Walter F. Vella. bibl. circ. 150. Indexed: HR Rep.
     Formerly: Southeast Asian Studies Working Paper Series.

959   US
SOUTHEAST ASIA PROGRAM SERIES; monographs, translations, bibliographies. 1986. irreg. price varies. Cornell University, Southeast Asia Program, 120 Uris Hall, Ithaca, NY 14853-7601.

955   NE
STUDIA IRANICA. (Includes supplement: Abstract Iranica) (Text in English or French) 1972. a. price varies. E.J. Brill, P.O. Box 9000, 2300 PA Leiden, Netherlands. bibl. illus. stat. Indexed: M.L.A.

950   FI   ISSN 0039-3282
STUDIA ORIENTALIA. (Text in English, French and German) 1925. irreg. price varies. Finnish Oriental Society, c/o University of Helsinki, Department of Asian and African Studies, SF-00100 Helsinki, Finland. Ed. Tapani Harviainen. bk. rev. charts. illus. cum.index. circ. 700.

950   VC
STUDIA POHL. (Text in language of author) 1967. irreg. price varies. (Pontificio Istituto Biblico) Biblical Institute Press, Piazza della Pilotta 35, 00187 Rome, Italy.

950   VC
STUDIA POHL: SERIES MAIOR. 1969. irreg. price varies. (Pontificio Istituto Biblico) Biblical Institute Press, Piazza della Pilotta 35, 00187 Rome, Italy. charts. illus.

950   GW   ISSN 0171-9378
STUDIEN ZU NICHTEUROPAEISCHEN RECHTSTHEORIEN. 1979. irreg., vol. 2, 1986. price varies. Franz Steiner Verlag Wiesbaden GmbH, Birkenwaldstr. 44, Postfach 347, D-7000 Stuttgart 1, W. Germany (B.R.D.) Eds. Theodor Vieweg, Reinhard May.

STUDIEN ZUR OSTASIATISCHEN SCHRIFTKUNST. see *ART*

954   UK   ISSN 0142-6028
STUDIES ON ASIAN TOPICS. 1980. irreg. price varies. (Scandinavian Institute of Asian Studies, DK) Curzon Press, 42 Gray's Inn Rd., London WC1, England.

950   US
STUDIES ON EAST ASIA. (Text in English or Oriental languages) 1971. irreg., vol.17, 1984. price varies per no. ‡ Western Washington University, Center for East Asian Studies, Bellingham, WA 98225. TEL 206-676-3041. Ed. Henry G. Schwarz.
     Formerly (until vol.13): Western Washington State College. Program in East Asian Studies. Occasional Papers.

959   US
STUDIES ON SOUTHEAST ASIA. 1985. irreg. price varies. Cornell University, Southeast Asia Program, 120 Uris Hall, Ithaca, NY 14853-7601.

951 CH
SUI YUAN WEN HSIEN. (Text in Chinese) 1977. a. free. Association of Fellow Provincials of Sui Yuan - Sui Yuan Wen Hsien Sheh, 101 4th St., Chung Yang Hsin Ts'un, Hsin Tien, Taipei 231, Taiwan, Republic of China. Ed. Chi-Yuan Lee. circ. 1,500. (back issues avail.)

950 US
T'ANG STUDIES. 1982. a. $15. T'ang Studies Society, c/o Paul W. Kroll, Ed., University of Colorado, Department of Oriental Languages, Box 279, Boulder, CO 80309. circ. 250.

950 US ISSN 0735-1364
TIBET SOCIETY. JOURNAL. (Text in English, French, German and Tibetan) 1981. s-a. membership. Tibet Society, Inc., Indiana University, Goodbody Hall 157, Bloomington, IN 47405. TEL 812-335-2428. Ed. Christopher I. Beckwith. bk. rev. circ. 450. (back issues avail.)

950 GW ISSN 0344-5542
TUNGUSICA. 1978. irreg., vol.3, 1985. price varies. Verlag Otto Harrassowitz, Taunusstr. 14, Postfach 2929, D-6200 Wiesbaden 1, W. Germany (B.R.D.) Ed. Michael Weiers.

950 GW ISSN 0177-4743
TURCOLOGICA. 1984. irreg. price varies. Verlag Otto Harrassowitz, Taunusstr. 14, Postfach 2929, D-6200 Wiesbaden 1, W. Germany (B.R.D.) Ed. Lars Johnson.

950 AU
TURKOLOGISCHER ANZIEGER/TURKOLOGY ANNUAL. (Text in English, French and German) 1975. a. S.400($27) Orientalisches Institut, Universitaet Wien, 1010 Vienna, Austria. (Co-sponsor: Unesco) Eds. Georges Hanzai and Andreas Tietze. circ. 400. (back issues avail.)

950 BL
UNIVERSIDADE DE SAO PAULO. FACULDADE DE FILOSOFIA, LETRAS E CIENCIAS HUMANAS. DEPARTAMENTO DE LINGUISTICA E LINGUAS ORIENTAIS. BOLETIM. no.8, 1977 (N.S.) irreg. exchange requested. Universidade de Sao Paulo, Faculdade de Filosofia, Letras e Ciencias Humanas, Departamento de Linguistica e Linguas Orientais, Caixa Postal 8.105, 0.1000 Sao Paulo, Brazil.

950 GW ISSN 0340-6652
UNIVERSITAET FRANKFURT AM MAIN. OSTASIATISCHEN SEMINARS. VEROEFFENTLICHUNGE. 1970. irreg., vol.8, 1979. price varies. Verlag Otto Harrassowitz, Taunusstr. 14, Postfach 2929, D-6200 Wiesbaden 1, W. Germany (B.R.D.) Eds. Otto Karow, Hans A. Dettmer.

950 GW ISSN 0179-6755
UNIVERSITAET GOETTINGEN. VEROEFFENTLICHUNGEN DES SEMINARS FUER INDOLOGIE. irreg., vol.7, 1987. Franz Steiner Verlag Wiesbaden GmbH, Birkenwaldstr. 44, Postfach 347, 7000 Stuttgart 1, W. Germany (B.R.D.) Ed. Heinz Bechert.

UNIVERSITAETSBIBLIOTHEK GIESSEN. KURZBERICHTE AUS DEN PAPYRUS-SAMMLUNGEN. see HISTORY

UNIVERSITE CATHOLIQUE DE LOUVAIN. INSTITUT ORIENTALISTE. PUBLICATIONS. see HISTORY — History Of Asia

950 BE
UNIVERSITE LIBRE DE BRUXELLES. INSTITUT DE PHILOLOGIE ET D'HISTOIRE ORIENTALES ET SLAVES. ANNUAIRE. 1957? irreg. Editions de l'Universite de Bruxelles, Avenue P. Heger, 26-C.P. 163, B-1050 Brussels, Belgium. Indexed: M.L.A.

955 200 LE
UNIVERSITE SAINT-JOSEPH. FACULTE DES LETTRES ET DES SCIENCES HUMAINES. RECHERCHE. SERIE B: ORIENT CHRETIEN. (Previously published by its Institut des Lettres Orientales in 4 series) 1956; NS. 1971. irreg. price varies. Dar el-Mashreq S.A.R.L., 2 rue Huvelin, Box 946, Beirut, Lebanon (Subscr. to: Librairie Orientale, Box 946, Beirut, Lebanon)

950 HK ISSN 0378-2689
UNIVERSITY OF HONG KONG. CENTRE OF ASIAN STUDIES. OCCASIONAL PAPERS AND MONOGRAPHS. (Text in English or Chinese; summaries in English) 1970. irreg., nos. 59-61, 1984-85. price varies. University of Hong Kong, Centre of Asian Studies, Pokfulam Road, Hong Kong, Hong Kong. Ed. Edward K.Y. Chen. (processed)

951 UK ISSN 0085-2856
UNIVERSITY OF LONDON. SCHOOL OF ORIENTAL AND AFRICAN STUDIES. CONTEMPORARY CHINA INSTITUTE. PUBLICATIONS. 1970. irreg. price varies. Cambridge University Press, Edinburgh Bldg., Shaftesbury Rd., Cambridge CB2 2RU, England (And 32 E. 57th St., New York NY 10022) Ed.Bd.

915.4 II
UNIVERSITY OF RAJASTHAN. SOUTH ASIAN STUDIES CENTRE. ANNUAL REPORT. (Text in English) 1966. irreg., latest issue 1973. University of Rajasthan, South Asian Studies Centre, Gandhi Nagar, Jaipur 302004, India.

UNIVERZITA KOMENSKEHO. FILOZOFICKA FAKULTA. ZBORNIK: GRAECOLATINA ET ORIENTALIA. see CLASSICAL STUDIES

VARENDRA RESEARCH MUSEUM. JOURNAL. see MUSEUMS AND ART GALLERIES

950 GW ISSN 0506-7936
VERZEICHNIS DER ORIENTALISCHEN HANDSCHRIFTEN IN DEUTSCHLAND. Short title: V O H D. (Text in English and German) irreg., vol. 33,1987. price varies. (Deutsche Morgenlaendische Gesellschaft) Franz Steiner Verlag Wiesbaden GmbH, Birkenwaldstr. 44, Postfach 347, D-7000 Stuttgart 1, W. Germany (B.R.D.) Ed. Dieter George.

950 GW ISSN 0506-7944
VERZEICHNIS DER ORIENTALISCHEN HANDSCHRIFTEN IN DEUTSCHLAND. SUPPLEMENTBAENDE. Short title: V O H D Supplementbaende. (Text in English and German) irreg., vol.27, 1987. price varies. (Deutsche Morgenlaendische Gesellschaft) Franz Steiner Verlag Wiesbaden GmbH, Birkenwaldstr. 44, Postfach 347, D-7000 Stuttgart 1, W. Germany (B.R.D.) Ed. Dieter George.

950 956 IT
VICINO ORIENTE. 1978. a. $35. (Universita di Roma "La Sapienza") Herder Editrice e Libreria s.r.l., Piazza Montecitorio 120, 00186 Rome, Italy. Ed. Mario Liverani.

954 II
VISHVA VICHARAMALA. (Text in Hindi and Sanskrit) irreg. price varies. Vishveshvaranand Vedic Research Institute, P.O. Sadhu Ashram, Hoshiarpur 146021, Punjab, India. Ed. S. Bhaskaran Nair.

954 II
VISHVESHVARANAND VEDIC RESEARCH INSTITUTE. RESEARCH AND GENERAL PUBLICATIONS. (Text in English, Hindi, and Sanskrit) 1921. irreg. price varies. Vishveshvaranand Vedic Research Institute, P.O. Sadhu Ashram, Hoshiarpur 146021, Punjab, India.

VOORAZIATISCH-EGYPTISCH GENOOTSCHAP "EX ORIENTE LUX". JAARBERICHT; annuaire de la Societe Orientale Neerlandaise "Ex Oriente Lux". see HISTORY — History Of Asia

VOORAZIATISCH-EGYPTISCH GENOOTSCHAP "EX ORIENTE LUX". MEDEDELINGEN EN VERHANDELINGEN. see HISTORY — History Of Asia

950 GE ISSN 0138-4449
VORDERASIATISCHE SCHRIFTDENKMALER DER STAATLICHEN MUSSEN ZU BERLIN. 1971. irreg. (Vol.7, 1985) (Vorderasiatisches Museum DDR) Akademie-Verlag Berlin, Leipziger Str. 3-4, 1086 Berlin, E. Germany (D.D.R.)

956 AU ISSN 0084-0076
WIENER ZEITSCHRIFT FUER DIE KUNDE DES MORGENLANDES. (Text in English, French, German and Italian) 1887. a. price varies. Universitaet Wien, Institut fuer Orientalistik, Universitaets Str. 7/V, A-1010 Vienna, Austria. Eds. Arne A. Ambros, Anton C. Schaendlinger. adv. bk. rev. circ. 400. Indexed: M.L.A.

WISCONSIN CHINA SERIES. see HISTORY — History Of Asia

ORIENTAL STUDIES — Abstracting, Bibliographies, Statistics

TURKOLOGISCHER ANZIEGER/TURKOLOGY ANNUAL. see ORIENTAL STUDIES

950 016 HK ISSN 0441-1900
UNIVERSITY OF HONG KONG. CENTRE OF ASIAN STUDIES. BIBLIOGRAPHIES AND RESEARCH GUIDES. (Text in English and Chinese; summaries in English) 1970. irreg., no.23, 1984. price varies. ‡ University of Hong Kong, Centre of Asian Studies, Pokfulam Road, Hong Kong, Hong Kong. Ed. Edward K.Y. Chen. (processed)

ORNITHOLOGY

see Biology—Ornithology

ORTHOPEDICS AND TRAUMATOLOGY

see Medical Sciences—Orthopedics and Traumatology

OTORHINOLARYNGOLOGY

see Medical Sciences—Otorhinolaryngology

OUTDOOR LIFE

see Sports and Games—Outdoor Life

PACKAGING

ANNUAL BOOK OF A S T M STANDARDS. VOLUME 15.09. PAPER; PACKAGING; FLEXIBLE BARRIER MATERIALS; BUSINESS COPY PRODUCTS. see ENGINEERING — Engineering Mechanics And Materials

658.788 FR
B I C-CODE. (Bureau International des Containers-Code) (Text in English and French) 1972. a. 80 Fr. per no. Bureau International des Containers - International Container Bureau, 38 Cours Albert 1er, 75008 Paris, France. charts.

621 US ISSN 0360-8689
BEST IN PACKAGING. (Subseries of: Print Casebooks) 1975. a. $19.50. R C Publications, Inc., 104 Fifth Ave., 9th Fl., New York, NY 10011 TEL 301-229-9040. (Subscr. to: 6400 Goldsboro Rd., Bethesda, MD 20817) illus.

658.7884 US
CAN MANUFACTURERS INSTITUTE. ANNUAL CANS SHIPMENT REPORT. 1972. a. $75. Can Manufacturers Institute, 1625 Massachusetts Ave., N.W., Washington, DC 20036. TEL 202-232-4677. circ. 500.
Formerly: Can Manufacturers Institute. Annual Metal Cans Shipment Report (ISSN 0068-7014)

670 MX
ENVASE Y EMBALAJE. 1975. a. Mex.$2000($25) Litoimpresores, S.A., Espana 396, 09880 Mexico, D.F., Mexico. Ed. Cesar Macazaga. adv.

EXPORT GRAFICAS U S A; with an international buyer's guide and directory. see PRINTING

658.7884 663.19 US
GLASS PACKAGING INSTITUTE. ANNUAL REPORT. 1957. a. free. Glass Packaging Institute, 1133 20th St., N.W., Ste. 321, Washington, DC 20036-3408. circ. 24,000. Indexed: Br.Ceram.Abstr.
Formerly: Glass Containers (ISSN 0072-4637)

676.2 US
INTERNATIONAL CONTAINER DIRECTORY. a. $40. Harcourt Brace Jovanovich, Inc., 7500 Old Oak Blvd., Cleveland, OH 44130 TEL 216-243-8100. (Subscr. address: 1 E. First St., Duluth, MN 55802) Ed. Nancy Page. adv. circ. 1,540.

ISRAEL INSTITUTE OF PACKAGING. PACKAGING DIRECTORY. see BUSINESS AND ECONOMICS — Trade And Industrial Directories

658.788 JM
JAMAICAN PACKAGING DIRECTORY. 1982. quinquennial. Jam.$100($20) Bureau of Standards, Packaging Centre, 6 Winchester Rd., Kingston 10, Jamaica, W.I. Ed. Y. Allen. adv. circ. 1,500. (back issues avail.)

700 FR
J'EMBALLE.* 1965. a. 160.80 F. Societe des Editions de l' Imprimerie Nouvelle, 53 guai Seine 19e, Paris, France. adv. bk. rev. tr.lit. circ. 6,000. (tabloid format)
Formerly: Graphiq'emballage.

676 DK
LEVERANDOERHAANDBOGEN (SKOVLUNDE); emballage og pakkemaskiner. 1979. biennial. free. Emballage & Transportinstituttet, Meterbuen 15, 2740 Skovlunde, Denmark. Ed. Erik Munksoe. circ. 10,000.
Formerly: Emballageinstituttets Leverandoerhaandbog (ISSN 0107-3737)

MATERIAL HANDLING ENGINEERING HANDBOOK AND DIRECTORY. see MACHINERY

658.7884 UK ISSN 0078-768X
PACKAGING DIRECTORY. 1946. a. £22.50. Wheatland Journals Ltd., Penn House, Penn Place, Rickmansworth, Herts WD3 1SN, England. Ed. A.J. LaRoche.

658.7884 US
PACKAGING ENCYCLOPEDIA. 1929. a. $30 (included in subscr. to Packaging Magazine) Cahners Publishing Co., Inc., Foodservice and Packaging Group, Division of Reed Publishing USA, 1350 E. Touhy Ave, Des Plaines, IL 60018 TEL 617-232-5470. (Subscr. to: 44 Cook St., Denver, CO 80206) index. circ. 83,000.
Former titles: Packaging Reference Issue and (Year) Encyclopedia; (until 1986): Packaging Encyclopedia and Yearbook; (until 1985): Packaging Encyclopedia; Modern Packaging Encyclopedia (ISSN 0077-0035)

658.7884 US ISSN 0078-7698
PACKAGING MACHINERY MANUFACTURERS INSTITUTE. OFFICIAL PACKAGING MACHINERY DIRECTORY. Cover title: Packaging Machinery Directory. 1954. biennial. $3. Packaging Machinery Manufacturers Institute, 1343 L St., N.W., Washington, DC 20005. TEL 202-347-3838. Ed. Claude S. Breeden, Jr. index. circ. 50,000.

658.788 US
PACKAGING MARKETPLACE; the practical guide to packaging sources. 1978. irreg. $120. Gale Research Company, Book Tower, Detroit, MI 48226. TEL 313-961-2142. Ed. Joseph F. Hanlon.

658.788 UK
PACKAGING REVIEW DIRECTORY. a. £25. Benn Publications Ltd., Sovereign Way, Tonbridge, Kent TN9 1RW, England. Ed. Pauline Covell.

658.7 II
PACKAGING UPDATE. (Text in English) 1975. m. Rs.35. Indian Institute of Packaging, E-2 Marol Industrial Estate, MIDC, Andheri East, Bombay 400093, India. abstr.

PNEUMATIC PACKAGING. see ENGINEERING — Mechanical Engineering

PRODUCE MARKETING ALMANAC. see FOOD AND FOOD INDUSTRIES

664.09 US
PURE-PAK NEWS. 1940? irreg. (approx. 3/yr.) Ex-cell-o Corp., Packaging Systems Division, 850 Ladd Rd., Box 700, Walled Lake, MI 48088. TEL 313-624-7800. Ed. Keith M. Langham. circ. 12,000.
Formerly: Packaging Systems News.

670 SZ
SCHWEIZER VERPACKUNGSKATALOG. (Text in French and German) 1947. a. 23 Fr. Verlag Binkert AG, CH-4335 Lauferburg, Switzerland. Ed. Silvan Binkert. adv. circ. 4,100.

670 FR
TECH-EMBAL; annuaire des fournisseurs de l'emballage. 1966. a. 250 F. Editions Technorama, 31 Place Saint Ferdinand, 75017 Paris, France. Ed. R. Baschet. circ. 2,000.

676.3 US
TECHNICAL ASSOCIATION OF THE PULP AND PAPER INDUSTRY. CORRUGATED CONTAINERS CONFERENCE. PROCEEDINGS. (1981 held jointly with Testing Conference Proceedings) a. $64.95 to non-members; members $43.52. Technical Association of the Pulp and Paper Industry, Inc., Technology Park/Atlanta, Box 105113, Atlanta, GA 30348. TEL 404-446-1400.

PACKAGING — Abstracting, Bibliographies, Statistics

658.788 016 US ISSN 0091-0120
CURRENT PACKAGING ABSTRACTS. 1969. s-m. $120. Rutgers University, Ira S. Gotscho Packaging Information Center, Box 909, Piscataway, NJ 08854. TEL 201-932-3044. Ed. John C. Adams. circ. 250. (looseleaf format; back issues avail.)
Formerly: Packaging Bulletin (ISSN 0030-9095)

658.788 016 UK ISSN 0260-7409
INTERNATIONAL PACKAGING ABSTRACTS. 1944. m. $475 to non-members. Pergamon Press, Inc., Journals Division, Maxwell House, Fairview Park, Elmsford, NY 10523 TEL 914-592-7700. (And Headington Hill Hall,Oxford OX3 0BW, England) Ed. Marie Rushton. adv. bk. rev. abstr. index. circ. 900. (also avail. in microform from UMI; reprint service avail. from UMI) Indexed: Abstr.Bull.Inst.Pap.Chem. Curr.Pack.Abstr. World Text.Abstr.
●Also available online. Vendors: Orbit Information Technologies, Pergamon Infoline.
Formerly: Packaging Abstracts (ISSN 0030-9087)

658.788 011 UK ISSN 0722-3218
PACKAGING SCIENCE AND TECHNOLOGY ABSTRACTS/REFERATEDIENST VERPACKUNG. (Text in English and German) 1982. 6/yr. DM.420. International Food Information Service (IFIS), Lane End House, Shinfield, Reading RG2 9BB, England. index.

PAINTS AND PROTECTIVE COATINGS

ADVANCES IN ORGANIC COATINGS SCIENCE AND TECHNOLOGY. see CHEMISTRY — Organic Chemistry

ANNUAL BOOK OF A S T M STANDARDS. VOLUME 06.01. PAINT - TESTS FOR FORMULATED PRODUCTS AND APPLIED COATINGS. see ENGINEERING — Engineering Mechanics And Materials

ANNUAL BOOK OF A S T M STANDARDS. VOLUME 06.02. PAINT - PIGMENTS, RESINS AND POLYMERS. see ENGINEERING — Engineering Mechanics And Materials

ANNUAL BOOK OF A S T M STANDARDS. VOLUME 06.03. PAINT - FATTY OILS AND ACIDS, SOLVENTS, MISCELLANEOUS; AROMATIC HYDROCARBONS. see ENGINEERING — Engineering Mechanics And Materials

698 UK
BRITISH DECORATORS ASSOCIATION. MEMBERS REFERENCE HANDBOOK. 1932. a. British Decorators Association, 6 Haywra Street, Harrogate, North Yorkshire, HG1 5BL, England. Ed. Kenneth A.C. Blease. adv. abstr. charts. circ. 3, 500.

667.6 FR ISSN 0396-1214
CATALOGUE NATIONAL DU TRAITEMENT DES SURFACES DE L'ANTICORROSION ET DES TRAITEMENTS THERMIQUES. 1963. a. 63 F. Editions du Cartel, 51 rue Vivienne, 75002 Paris, France. Ed. A.L. Savu. adv. circ. 10,000.

338.4 UK
CHATFIELD'S EUROPEAN DIRECTORY OF PAINTS AND ALLIED PRODUCTS/ ANNUAIRE CHATFIELD EUROPEAN DE PEINTURES ET PRODUITS ASSIMILES/ CHATFIELDS EUROPAEISCHES ADRESSBUCH FUER ANSTRICHMITTEL-UND VERWANDTE PRODUKTE. Short title: European Directory of Paints and Allied Products. (Text in English, French, or German) 1973. irreg. price varies. Chatfield Applied Research Laboratories Ltd., 13 Stafford Rd., Croydon, Surrey CR0 4NG, England. Eds. C.J. Chatfield, H.W. Chatfield. adv. circ. 1,000.

667.6 667.7 FR ISSN 0071-416X
FEDERATION D'ASSOCIATIONS DE TECHNICIENS DES INDUSTRIES DES PEINTURES, VERNIS, EMAUX ET ENCRES D'IMPRIMERIE DE L'EUROPE CONTINENTALE. ANNUAIRE OFFICIEL. OFFICIAL YEARBOOK. AMTLICHES JAHRBUCH. (Text in English, French, German) 1955. biennial. Federation d'Associations de Techniciens des Industries des Peintures, Vernis, Emaux et Encres d'Imprimerie de l'Europe Continentale., Maison de la Chimie, 28 rue Saint Dominique, 75007 Paris, France. adv. circ. 3,000.

667.6 US
FEDERATION OF SOCIETIES FOR COATINGS TECHNOLOGY. YEARBOOK AND ANNUAL MEMBERSHIP DIRECTORY. 1928. a. $20. Federation of Societies for Coatings Technology, 1315 S. Walnut St., Ste. 830, Philadelphia, PA 19107. Ed. Rosemary Falvey. adv. circ. 7,000.
Formerly: Federation of Societies for Paint Technology. Yearbook (ISSN 0071-4437)

698 UK
FINISHING DIARY. 1950. a. $21. Wheatland Journals Ltd., Penn House, Penn Place, Rickmansworth, Herts WD3 1SN, England. Ed. David Pescod. adv. circ. 2,000.
Former titles: International Finishing Industries Manual (ISSN 0073-747X); Industrial Finishing Year Book.

667.6 FR ISSN 0071-9048
FRANCE-PEINTURE. 1953. biennial. 135 F. Creations, Editions et Productions Publicitaires, 1 Place d'Estienne d'Orves, 75009 Paris, France. Ed. Georges Prieux. adv. circ. 9,100.
Directory of painting, varnishes and annexed industries

667.6 US
INDUSTRIAL FINISHING BUYER'S GUIDE. 1984. a. Hitchcock Publishing Co. (Subsidiary of: American Broadcasting Companies, Inc.) Hitchcock Building, Wheaton, IL 60188. TEL 312-665-1000. adv. circ. 36,000.

PAINT RED BOOK; directory of the paint and coatings industry. see BUSINESS AND ECONOMICS — Trade And Industrial Directories

698 US
PAINTING AND DECORATING CRAFTSMAN MANUAL AND TEXTBOOK. irreg., 5th edt., 1975. $9.75. Painting and Decorating Contractors of America, 7223 Lee Highway, Falls Church, VA 22046. TEL 703-534-1201. charts. illus.

667.6 UK ISSN 0078-7817
POLYMERS PAINT AND COLOUR YEAR BOOK. 1961. a. £30.50. Fuel and Metallurgical Journals Ltd., Queensway House, 2 Queensway, Redhill, Surrey RH1 1QS, England. Ed. R. Read. adv.
Formerly: Paint, Oil Colour Year Book.

698 US ISSN 0478-4251
PRODUCTS FINISHING DIRECTORY. a. $10. Gardner Publications, Inc., 6600 Clough Pike, Cincinnati, OH 45202. TEL 513-231-8020. Ed. Gerard H. Poll, Jr. adv. circ. 30,000.

698 FR
QUI FABRIQUE ET FOURNIT QUOI. 1973. a. 120 F. Editions Ampere, 46 rue Ampere, 75017 Paris, France.

382 II ISSN 0304-8179
SHELLAC EXPORT PROMOTION COUNCIL. ANNUAL REPORT. (Text in English) a. Shellac Export Promotion Council, 14/1-B Ezra St., Calcutta 1, India. stat.

667.6 DK ISSN 0085-6126
SKANDINAVISK TIDSKRIFT FOR FAERG OCH LACK. AARSBOK.* (Text in Scandinavian languages; summaries in English) a. free to members. (Federation of Scandinavian Paint and Varnish Technicians) Dansk Bladforlag ApS, Hellerupvej 78, 2900 Hellerup, Denmark.

698 US
STEEL STRUCTURES PAINTING BULLETIN. 1955. biennial. free. Steel Structures Painting Council, 4400 Fifth Ave., Pittsburgh, PA 15213. TEL 412-578-3405. Ed. Bernard R. Appleman. circ. 30,000.

PAINTS AND PROTECTIVE COATINGS — Abstracting, Bibliographies, Statistics

REFERATIVNYI ZHURNAL. KORROZIYA I ZASHCHITA OT KORROZII. see METALLURGY — Abstracting, Bibliographies, Statistics

667.6 016 UK ISSN 0043-9088
WORLD SURFACE COATING ABSTRACTS. 1928. m. £295($590) (Paint Research Association) Pergamon Press Ltd., Headington Hill Hall, Oxford OX3 0BW, England. Ed. N. Morgan. (also avail. in magnetic tape) Indexed: Curr.Cont. Abstr.Bull.Inst.Pap.Chem. Anal.Abstr. BMT. Int.Packag.Abstr.
●Also available online. Vendors: Orbit Information Technologies, Pergamon Infoline.

PALEONTOLOGY

ACTA PALAEOBOTANICA. see BIOLOGY — Botany

AMERICAN ASSOCIATION OF STRATIGRAPHIC PALYNOLOGISTS. CONTRIBUTIONS SERIES. see EARTH SCIENCES — Geology

560 US ISSN 0192-737X
AMERICAN ASSOCIATION OF STRATIGRAPHIC PALYNOLOGISTS FOUNDATION. FIELD TRIP GUIDE. 1971. a. American Association of Stratigraphic Palynologists Foundation, c/o Robert T. Clarke, Mobil R & D Corp.-D R L, Box 819047, Dallas, TX 75381.

560 572 GW ISSN 0066-4723
ANTHROPOS; studie z oboru anthropologie, paleoethnologie, paleontologie a kvarterni geologie. (Text in Czech and German) 1959 (N.S.) irreg. price varies. (Moravske Museum, Brno, CS) Dr. Rudolf Habelt GmbH, Am Buchenhang 1, 5300 Bonn 1, W. Germany (B.R.D.) Indexed: CERDIC. Curr.Cont.Africa. E.I. Rel.Ind.One.

ARGENTINA. MUSEO PROVINCIAL DE CIENCIAS NATURALES. COMUNICACIONES. NUEVA SERIE. see BIOLOGY

560 AT ISSN 0810-8889
ASSOCIATION OF AUSTRALASIAN PALAEONTOLOGISTS. MEMOIRS. 1983. irreg. price varies. Geological Society of Australia, Association of Australasian Palaeontologists, 10 Martin Place, Sydney, N.S.W. 2000, Australia. Ed. P.A. Jell. (back issues avail.)

560 551 GW ISSN 0077-2070
BAYERISCHE STAATSSAMMLUNG FUER PALAEONTOLOGIE UND HISTORISCHE GEOLOGIE. MITTEILUNGEN. (Text and summaries in English and German) 1961. a. price varies. Bayerische Staatssammlung fuer Palaeontologie und Historische Geologie, Richard-Wagner-Strasse 10, 8000 Munich 2, W. Germany (B.R.D.) Ed. Dietrich Herm. Indexed: Biol.Abstr.

560 AU
BEITRAEGE ZUR PALAEONTOLOGIE VON OESTERREICH. (Text and summaries in English, German) 1976. a. price on request. Kommissionsverlag, Universitaetsstr. 7/II, A-1010 Vienna, Austria. Ed.Bd. (back issues avail.) Indexed: Biol.Abstr.

566 US ISSN 0272-8869
BIBLIOGRAPHY OF FOSSIL VERTEBRATES. 1940. a. $135. Society of Vertebrate Paleontology, c/o Natural History Museum of Los Angeles County, 900 Exposition Blvd., Los Angeles, CA 90007. TEL 213-747-6598. (back issues avail.) Indexed: GeoRef.

BUDOWA GEOLOGICZNA POLSKI. see EARTH SCIENCES — Geology

BULLETIN SCIENTIFIQUE DE BOURGOGNE. see SCIENCES: COMPREHENSIVE WORKS

560 FR ISSN 0068-5054
CAHIERS DE MICROPALEONTOLOGIE. 1965. irreg. (Ecole pratique des hautes etudes, Laboratoire de micropaleontologie) Editions du C N R S, 295 rue St. Jacques, 75005 Paris, France. Indexed: Br.Geol.Lit. Geo.Abstr. GeoRef.

CARNEGIE MUSEUM OF NATURAL HISTORY. ANNALS OF (THE) CARNEGIE MUSEUM. see SCIENCES: COMPREHENSIVE WORKS

CARNEGIE MUSEUM OF NATURAL HISTORY. BULLETIN. see SCIENCES: COMPREHENSIVE WORKS

COLORADO SCHOOL OF MINES. PROFESSIONAL CONTRIBUTIONS. see MINES AND MINING INDUSTRY

CONTRIBUTIONS IN BIOLOGY AND GEOLOGY. see EARTH SCIENCES — Geology

CURRENT RESEARCH IN THE PLEISTOCENE. see ARCHAEOLOGY

563 US ISSN 0070-2242
CUSHMAN FOUNDATION FOR FORAMINIFERAL RESEARCH. SPECIAL PUBLICATION. 1952. irreg. price varies. Cushman Foundation for Foraminiferal Research, Inc., E501 U.S. National Museum, Washington, DC 20560. Ed. Steven J. Culver. circ. 600. Indexed: Biol.Abstr. GeoRef.

CYPRIS; international ostracoda newsletter. see BIOLOGY — Zoology

560 560.17 NE
DEVELOPMENTS IN PALAEONTOLOGY AND STRATIGRAPHY. irreg., vol.7, 1984. Elsevier Science Publishers B.V., Box 211, 1000 AE Amsterdam, Netherlands.

DISTRICT MEMOIR. see EARTH SCIENCES — Geology

DORTMUNDER BEITRAEGE ZUR LANDESKUNDE. see BIOLOGY

EHIME UNIVERSITY. MEMOIRS. SERIE: NATURAL SCIENCE. see EARTH SCIENCES — Geology

560 GW ISSN 0424-7116
EISZEITALTER UND GEGENWART. 1951. a. E. Schweizerbart'sche Verlagsbuchhandlung, Johannesstr. 3a, 7000 Stuttgart 1, W. Germany (B.R.D) Ed. H.D. Lang. Indexed: Geo.Abstr.

F A C E N A. (Facultad de Ciencias Exactas y Naturales y Agrimensura) see BIOGRAPHY

560 PL ISSN 0015-573X
FOLIA QUATERNARIA. (Text in English and German) 1960. irreg., no.56, 1985. price varies. (Polska Akademia Nauk, Oddzial w Krakowie) Ossolineum, Publishing House of the Polish Academy of Sciences, Rynek 9, Wroclaw, Poland. Ed. Kazimierz Kowalski. Indexed: Biol.Abstr. Geo.Abstr. GeoRef.

560 NO
FOSSILS AND STRATA; a monograph series in palaeontology and stratigraphy. (Text in English) 1972. irreg. price varies. Norwegian University Press, Kolstadgt. 1, Box 2959-Toeyen, 0608 Oslo 6, Norway (U.S. address: Box 258, Irvington-on-Hudson, NY 10533) Ed. Stefan Bengtson. Indexed: Biol.Abstr. Br.Geol.Lit.

FREIBERGER FORSCHUNGSHEFTE. MONTANWISSENSCHAFTEN: REIHE C. GEOWISSENSCHAFTEN. see EARTH SCIENCES

GEOLOGICA ET PALAEONTOLOGICA. see EARTH SCIENCES — Geology

GEOLOGISCHE ABHANDLUNGEN HESSEN. see EARTH SCIENCES — Geology

GEOLOGISCHE BUNDESANSTALT, VIENNA. JAHRBUCH. see EARTH SCIENCES — Geology

GEOLOGISCHES JAHRBUCH. REIHE A: ALLGEMEINE UND REGIONALE GEOLOGIE B.R. DEUTSCHLAND UND NACHBARGEBIETE, TEKTONIK, STRATIGRAPHIE, PALAEONTOLOGIE. see EARTH SCIENCES — Geology

GEOLOGISCHES JAHRBUCH HESSEN. see EARTH SCIENCES — Geology

GESELLSCHAFT DER GEOLOGIE- UND BERGBAUSTUDENTEN. MITTEILUNGEN. see EARTH SCIENCES — Geology

INSTYTUT GEOLOGICZNY. PRACE. see EARTH SCIENCES — Geology

KYUSHU UNIVERSITY. DEPARTMENT OF GEOLOGY. SCIENCE REPORTS/KYUSHU DAIGAKU RIGAKUBU KENKYU HOKOKU CHISHITSUGAKU. see EARTH SCIENCES — Geology

560 622 551 AU
LANDESMUSEUM JOANNEUM. ABTEILUNG FUER GEOLOGIE, PALAEONTOLOGIE UND BERGBAU. MITTEILUNGEN. 1937. irreg. (approx. 1/yr.) price varies. Landesmuseum Joanneum, Abteilung fuer Geologie, Palaeontologie und Bergbau, Raubergasse 10, A-8010 Graz, Austria. illus.
Formerly (until 1972): Joanneum. Museum fuer Bergbau, Geologie und Technik. Mitteilungen.

LET ME TELL YOU ABOUT - DINOSAURS. see CHILDREN AND YOUTH — For

560.172 US ISSN 0076-1389
LOWER PALEOZIC ROCKS OF THE NEW WORLD. 1971. irreg., vol.4, 1985. $150. John Wiley & Sons, Inc., 650 Third Ave., New York, NY 10016. TEL 212-850-6000. Ed. C.H. Holland.

MAN & ENVIRONMENT. see ANTHROPOLOGY

560 US
MICHIGAN STATE UNIVERSITY. MUSEUM PUBLICATIONS. PALEONTOLOGICAL SERIES. 1972. irreg. price varies. ‡ Michigan State University Museum, East Lansing, MI 48824. TEL 517-335-2370. Ed.Bd. bibl. charts. illus. circ. 1,500.

563 US ISSN 0160-2071
MICROPALEONTOLOGY SPECIAL PUBLICATIONS. 1976. irreg., no.4, 1980. Micropaleontology Press, c/o American Museum of Natural History, Central Park W. at 79th St., New York, NY 10024. TEL 212-873-1300. Ed. John A. Van Couvering. (reprint service avail. from UMI) Indexed: GeoRef.

560 IS
MITEKUFAT HAEVEN; journal of the Israel prehistoric society. (Text in English and Hebrew) 1985. a. IS.12($12) Israel Prehistoric Society, P.O. Box 1502, Jerusalem 91 004, Israel.

560 NE ISSN 0168-6151
MODERN QUATERNARY RESEARCH IN SOUTHEAST ASIA. 1975. a. $18.50. A.A. Balkema, Box 1675, 3000 BR Rotterdam, Netherlands (And Box 230, Accord, MA 02018) Eds. G.-J. Bartstra, W.A. Casparie. Indexed: GeoRef.

MONOGRAPHS IN GEOLOGY AND PALEONTOLOGY. see *EARTH SCIENCES — Geology*

560 US ISSN 0736-3907
MOSASAUR. 1983. irreg. $6 to individuals; institutions $12. Delaware Valley Paleontological Society, c/o William B. Gallagher, Ed., Dept. of Geology, D-4, University of Pennsylvania, 240 S. 33rd St., Philadelphia, PA 19104. circ. 500.

560 AG ISSN 0524-9511
MUSEO ARGENTINO DE CIENCIAS NATURALES "BERNARDINO RIVADAVIA." INSTITUTO NACIONAL DE INVESTIGACION DE LAS CIENCIAS NATURALES. REVISTA. PALEONTOLOGIA. 1964. irreg., vol.3, no.2, 1981. Museo Argentino de Ciencias Naturales "Bernardino Rivadavia, Instituto Nacional de Investigacion de las Ciencias Naturales, Avda. Angel Gallardo 470, Casilla de Correo 220-Sucursal 5, Buenos Aires, Argentina. Indexed: GeoRef.

560 UY
MUSEO NACIONAL DE HISTORIA NATURAL. COMMUNICACIONES PALEONTOLOGICAS. (Summaries in English, Spanish) 1970. irreg. exchange basis. Museo Nacional de Historia Natural, Casilla de Correos 399, Montevideo, Uruguay.

NATIONAL MUSEUM. MEMOIRS. see *ARCHAEOLOGY*

NATURAL HISTORY CONTRIBUTIONS. see *BIOLOGY*

NATURHISTORISCHES MUSEUM BASEL. VEROEFFENTLICHUNGEN. see *ANTHROPOLOGY*

NATUURHISTORISCH GENOOTSCHAP IN LIMBURG. PUBLICATIES. see *BIOLOGY*

NEUES JAHRBUCH FUER GEOLOGIE UND PALAEONTOLOGIE. ABHANDLUNGEN. see *EARTH SCIENCES — Geology*

560 AT
NEW SOUTH WALES. GEOLOGICAL SURVEY. MEMOIRS: PALEONTOLOGY. 1888. irreg., no.19, 1982. price varies. Department of Mineral Resources, Box 5288, Sydney, N.S.W. 2001, Australia. Ed. H. Basden. circ. 400. Indexed: GeoRef.
Formerly: New South Wales. Department of Mines. Memoirs: Paleontology (ISSN 0077-8699)

560 NZ ISSN 0078-8589
NEW ZEALAND GEOLOGICAL SURVEY. PALEONTOLOGICAL BULLETIN. Short title: Paleontological Bulletins. 1913. irreg., no.52, 1984. price varies. Department of Scientific and Industrial Research, Science Information Publishing Centre, Box 9741, Wellington, New Zealand. Ed. I. Mackenzie. circ. 800. (back issues avail.) Indexed: Biol.Abstr. Geo.Abstr. GeoRef. Petrol.Abstr.

560 AT ISSN 0159-818X
NOMEN NUDUM. a. Geological Society of Australia, Association of Australasian Palaeontologists, Challis House, Martin Place, Sydney 2000, Australia. Ed. G.C. Young.

OESTERREICHISCHE GEOLOGISCHE GESELLSCHAFT. MITTEILUNGEN. see *EARTH SCIENCES — Geology*

560 PK ISSN 0078-8155
PAKISTAN. GEOLOGICAL SURVEY. MEMOIRS; PALEONTOLOGIA PAKISTANICA. (Text in English) 1956. irreg. price varies. ‡ Geological Survey of Pakistan, c/o Chief Librarian, Box 15, Quetta, Pakistan. circ. 1,500. Indexed: GeoRef.

560 GW ISSN 0085-4611
PALAEONTOGRAPHICA. SUPPLEMENTBAENDE. irreg., vol.8, pt.2B, 1980. price varies. E. Schweizerbart'sche Verlagsbuchhandlung, Johannesstr. 3A, 7000 Stuttgart 1, W. Germany (B.R.D.) Indexed: GeoRef.

560 US ISSN 0078-8546
PALAEONTOGRAPHICA AMERICANA. 1916. irreg., no.54, 1984. price varies. Paleontological Research Institution, 1259 Trumansburg Road, Ithaca, NY 14850. TEL 607-273-6623. Ed. Dr. Peter R. Hoover. bibl. charts. illus. stat. circ. 250. (back issues avail.) Indexed: Biol.Abstr. GeoRef.

PALAEONTOGRAPHICAL SOCIETY. MONOGRAPHS (LONDON) see *EARTH SCIENCES — Geology*

560 SA ISSN 0078-8554
PALAEONTOLOGIA AFRICANA. 1953. irreg. price varies. University of the Witwatersrand, Johannesburg, Bernard Price Institute for Palaeontological Research, Wits 2050, South Africa. Ed. M.A. Raath. bk. rev. circ. 600. Indexed: Biol.Abstr. Bull.Signal. Geo.Abstr. GeoRef. Ind.S.A.Per.

560 PL ISSN 0078-8562
PALAEONTOLOGIA POLONICA. (Text in English or French; summaries in Polish) 1929. irreg., no.46, 1984. price varies. (Polska Akademia Nauk, Zaklad Paleobiologii) Panstwowe Wydawnictwo Naukowe, Miodowa 10, 00-251 Warsaw, Poland (Dist. by: Ars Polona, Krakowskie Przedmiescie 7, 00-068 Warsaw, Poland) Ed. Zofia Kielan-Jaworowska. charts. illus. circ. 560. Indexed: Biol.Abstr. GeoRef.

PALEO DATA BANKS; for the improvement of communication in palynology, paleobotany, and related sciences. see *BIOLOGY — Botany*

560 551 US ISSN 0031-0298
PALEOBIOS. 1967. irreg. $3. University of California, Berkeley, Museum of Paleontology, Berkeley, CA 94720. TEL 415-642-1827. Eds. Jennifer A. Hogler, Laurie J. Bryant. bibl. charts. illus. circ. 800. (back issues avail.) Indexed: Biol.Abstr. GeoRef.

560 NE ISSN 0168-6208
PALEOECOLOGY OF AFRICA. 1965. a. fl.85($27.50) per no. A.A. Balkema, Box 1675, 3000 BR Rotterdam, Netherlands (And Box 230, Accord, MA 02018) Eds. A. Coetzee, E.M. van Zinderen Bakker. Indexed: GeoRef.
Former titles: Paleoecology of Africa and the Surrounding Islands; Palaeoecology of Africa and the Surrounding Islands and Antarctica (ISSN 0078-8538)

560 US ISSN 0078-8597
PALEONTOLOGICAL SOCIETY. MEMOIR. 1968. irreg. $8 per no. Paleontological Society (Chicago), Department of Geological Sciences, University of Chicago, 5734 S. Ellis Ave., Chicago, IL 60637. TEL 312-753-1234. Ed. Kenneth Caster. circ. 3,200. Indexed: Biol.Abstr. GeoRef.

560 BU
PALEONTOLOGIIA, STRATIGRAFIIA I LITOLOGIIA. (Text in various languages; summaries in Bulgarian, English, French, German) 1975. irreg. price varies. (Bulgarska Akademiia na Naukite, Geologicheski Institut) Publishing House of the Bulgarian Academy of Sciences, Acad. G. Bonchev St., Bldg. 6, 1113 Sofia, Bulgaria. Ed. C. Spasov. illus. circ. 470. Indexed: Biol.Abstr. GeoRef.
Supersedes in part: Bulgarska Akademiia na Naukite. Geologicheski Institut. Izvestiia.

PALYNOLOGY. see *EARTH SCIENCES — Geology*

PRIRODNJACKI MUZEJ U BEOGRADU. GLASNIK. SERIJA A: MINEROLOGIJA, GEOLOGIJA, PALEONTOLOGIJA. see *EARTH SCIENCES — Geology*

QUARTAERPALAEONTOLOGIE. see *EARTH SCIENCES*

560 UK ISSN 0266-4755
REPORT ON BRITISH PALAEOBOTANY & PALYNOLOGY. 1976. biennial. £1($5) University of London, Royal Holloway and Bedford New College, Botany Department, Huntersdale, Callow Hill, Virginia Water, Surrey GU25 4LN, England. Ed.Bd. bibl. circ. 125. Indexed: Biol.Abstr.

560 CS ISSN 0036-5297
SBORNIK GEOLOGICKYCH VED: PALEONTOLOGIE/JOURNAL OF GEOLOGICAL SCIENCES: PALEONTOLOGY. (Text in English, French or German; summaries also in Russian) 1949. irreg. Ustredni Ustav Geologicky, Malostranske nam. 19, 118 21 Prague 1, Czechoslovakia (Subscr. to: Artia, Ve Smeckach 30, 111 27 Prague 1, Czechoslovakia) Ed. Vladimir Havlicek. charts. illus. circ. 600. (back issues avail.) Indexed: Bull.Signal. Ref.Zh. GeoRef.

560 SZ ISSN 0080-7389
SCHWEIZERISCHE PALAEONTOLOGISCHE ABHANDLUNGEN/MEMOIRES SUISSE DE PALEONTOLOGIE. (Text in English, French, German, Italian) 1874. irreg. price varies. (Schweizerische Naturforschende Gesellschaft) Birkhaeuser Verlag, P.O. Box 133, CH-4010 Basel, Switzerland. Ed. B. Engesser. index. Indexed: Biol.Abstr. GeoRef.

560 US ISSN 0081-0266
SMITHSONIAN CONTRIBUTIONS TO PALEOBIOLOGY. 1969. irreg., no.60, 1986. Smithsonian Institution Press, 955 L'Enfant Plaza, Rm. 2100, Washington, DC 20560. TEL 202-287-3738. Ed. Barbara T. Spann. circ. 2,500. (reprint service avail. from UMI) Indexed: Biol.Abstr. GeoRef.

560 572 913 SA ISSN 0303-2515
SOUTH AFRICAN MUSEUM. ANNALS/SUID-AFRIKAANSE MUSEUM. ANNALE. (Text in English) 1898. irreg. price varies. South African Museum, Box 61, Cape Town 8000, South Africa. Ed. Elizabeth Louw. illus. circ. 450. (back issues avail.) Indexed: Biol.Abstr. Ocean.Abstr. Abstr.Anthropol. Aqua.Sci.& Fish.Abstr. GeoRef. Ind.S.A.Per. Sel.Water Res.Abstr. Zoo.Rec.

SPELEOLOGICAL SOCIETY OF JAPAN. JOURNAL. see *EARTH SCIENCES*

560 IT
STUDI E RICERCHE SUI GIACIMENTI TERZIARI DI BOLCA. (Text and summaries in English, French, Italian) 1969. irreg. L.30000. Museo Civico di Storia Naturale di Verona, Lungadige Porta Vittoria 9, 37129 Verona, Italy. circ. 600. (back issues avail.)

STUDI PER L'ECOLOGIA DEL QUATERNARIO. see *ANTHROPOLOGY*

TERTIARY RESEARCH SPECIAL PAPERS. see *EARTH SCIENCES — Geology*

TOHOKU UNIVERSITY. INSTITUTE OF GEOLOGY AND PALEONTOLOGY. CONTRIBUTIONS/TOHOKU DAIGAKU RIGAKUBU CHISHITSUGAKU KOSEIBUTSUGAKU KYOSHITSU KENKYU HOBUN HOKOKU. see *EARTH SCIENCES — Geology*

TOHOKU UNIVERSITY. INSTITUTE OF GEOLOGY AND PALEONTOLOGY. SCIENCE REPORTS. SECOND SERIES. see *EARTH SCIENCES — Geology*

565 NO ISSN 0085-7386
TRILOBITE NEWS. (Text in English) 1971. a., latest 1976. free. Universitet i Oslo, Paleontologiska Museum, Sarsgate 1, Oslo 5, Norway. Ed. D.L. Bruton. bk. rev. abstr. bibl. index. circ. 250. Indexed: Biol.Abstr. GeoRef.

560   IT
UNIVERSITA DEGLI STUDI DI FERRARA. ISTITUTO DI GEOLOGIA. ANNALI. SEZIONE 15. PALEONTOLOGIA UMANA E PALETNOLOGIA. (Text and summaries in English, French, Italian) 1959. irreg., vol.2, no.12, 1976. exchange basis. Universita degli Studi di Ferrara, Istituto di Geologia, C.So Ercole 1 d'Este 32, Ferrara, Italy. circ. 450.
  Formerly: Universita degli Studi di Ferrara. Istituto di Geologia, Paleontologia e Paleontologia Umana. Annali. Sezione 15. Paleontologia Umana e Paleontologia (ISSN 0071-4542)

UNIVERSITA DEGLI STUDI DI FERRARA. ISTITUTO DI GEOLOGIA. PUBBLICAZIONI. see *EARTH SCIENCES — Geology*

UNIVERSITAET HAMBURG. GEOLOGISCH-PALAEONTOLOGISCHES INSTITUT. MITTEILUNGEN. see *EARTH SCIENCES — Geology*

UNIVERSITAET STUTTGART. INSTITUT FUER GEOLOGIE UND PALAEONTOLOGIE ARBEITEN NEUE FOLGE. see *EARTH SCIENCES*

560   US   ISSN 0075-5044
UNIVERSITY OF KANSAS. PALEONTOLOGICAL CONTRIBUTIONS. ARTICLES. 1947. irreg., no.66, 1984. price varies. University of Kansas, Paleontological Institute, 121 Lindley Hall, Lawrence, KS 66045 TEL 913-864-3338. (Subscr. to: University of Kansas Libraries, Gifts & Exchange Dept., Lawrence, KS 66045) Ed. Roger L. Kaesler. abstr. bibl. circ. 1,500. (back issues avail.) Indexed: Biol.Abstr. Geo.Abstr.

560   US   ISSN 0278-9744
UNIVERSITY OF KANSAS. PALEONTOLOGICAL CONTRIBUTIONS. MONOGRAPHS. 1982. irreg. price varies. University of Kansas, Paleontological Institute, 121 Lindley Hall, Lawrence, KS 66045 TEL 913-864-3338. (Subscr. to: Exchange & Gifts Dept., University of Kansas Libraries, Lawrence, KS 66045) Ed. Roger L. Kaesler. abstr. bibl. circ. 700. (back issues avail.) Indexed: Biol.Abstr.

560   US   ISSN 0075-5052
UNIVERSITY OF KANSAS. PALEONTOLOGICAL CONTRIBUTIONS. PAPERS. 1965. irreg., no.117, 1986. price varies. University of Kansas, Paleontological Institute, 121 Lindley Hall, Lawrence, KS 66045 TEL 913-864-3338. (Subscr. to: University of Kansas Libraries, Exchange & Gifts Dept., Lawrence, KS 66045) Ed. Roger L. Kaesler. abstr. bibl. circ. 1,500. (back issues avail.) Indexed: Biol.Abstr. GeoRef.

560   US   ISSN 0041-9834
UNIVERSITY OF MICHIGAN. MUSEUM OF PALEONTOLOGY. CONTRIBUTIONS. 1924. irreg., vol.26, nos.7-13, 1983. price varies. University of Michigan, Museum of Paleontology, Museums Bldg., Ann Arbor, MI 48109. TEL 313-764-0489. Ed. Gerald R. Smith. circ. 500. Indexed: Biol.Abstr.

560   US   ISSN 0148-3838
UNIVERSITY OF MICHIGAN. MUSEUM OF PALEONTOLOGY. PAPERS ON PALEONTOLOGY. 1972. irreg., no.26, 1982. University of Michigan, Museum of Paleontology, Ann Arbor, MI 48109. TEL 313-764-0489. Indexed: GeoRef.

550   CS
USTREDNI USTAV GEOLOGICKY. ROZPRAVY. (Text in English or German; summaries in Czech and English) 1926. irreg. Ustredni Ustav Geologicky, Malostranske nam. 19, 118 21 Prague 1, Czechoslovakia (Subscr. to: Artia, Ve Smeckach 30, 111 27 Prague 1, Czechoslovakia) charts. illus. circ. 650. (back issues avail.) Indexed: Bull.Signal. Ref.Zh. GeoRef.

560   NE   ISSN 0083-4963
UTRECHT MICROPALEONTOLOGICAL BULLETINS. (Text in English) 1969. irreg., no.26, 1982. price varies. Rijksuniversiteit te Utrecht, Department of Stratigraphy and Paleontology, c/o T. van Schaik, Budapestlaan 4, 3584 CD Utrecht, Netherlands. Ed. C.W. Drooger. Indexed: GeoRef.

560 551   GW   ISSN 0373-9627
ZITTELIANA; Abhandlungen der Bayerischen Staatssammlung fuer Palaeontologie und historische Geologie. 1969. irreg. price varies. Bayerische Staatssammlung fuer Palaeontologie und Historische Geologie, Richard-Wagner-Strasse 10, 8000 Munich 2, W. Germany (B.R.D.) Ed. Dietrich Herm. Indexed: Biol.Abstr. GeoRef.

PALEONTOLOGY — Abstracting, Bibliographies, Statistics

AMERICAN ASSOCIATION OF STRATIGRAPHIC PALYNOLOGISTS. ABSTRACTS OF PAPERS PRESENTED AT THE ANNUAL MEETINGS. see *EARTH SCIENCES — Abstracting, Bibliographies, Statistics*

PAPER AND PULP

see also Packaging

ADVANCES IN DRYING. see *ENGINEERING — Mechanical Engineering*

ANNUAL BOOK OF A S T M STANDARDS. VOLUME 15.09. PAPER; PACKAGING; FLEXIBLE BARRIER MATERIALS; BUSINESS COPY PRODUCTS. see *ENGINEERING — Engineering Mechanics And Materials*

BENIBANA. see *AGRICULTURE — Crop Production And Soil*

676.2   UK   ISSN 0068-2330
BRITISH PAPER AND BOARD INDUSTRY FEDERATION. TECHNICAL ASSOCIATION. TECHNICAL PAPERS. 1960. a. price varies. Paper Industry Technical Association, Pira House, Randalls Rd., Leatherhead KT22 4RU, England. Ed. M. Marley. index.

676   CN   ISSN 0068-9505
CANADIAN PULP AND PAPER ASSOCIATION. PULP AND PAPER REPORT. a. free. Canadian Pulp and Paper Association, Sun Life Bldg., 23 floor, 1155 Metcalfe St., Montreal, Que. H3B 2X9, Canada. TEL 514-886-6621. circ. 5,000. Indexed: CS Ind.

676.1   CN
CANADIAN PULP AND PAPER ASSOCIATION. TECHNICAL SECTION. PROCEEDINGS. 1915. a. Can.$40 to non-members. Canadian Pulp and Paper Association, Sun Life Bldg., 23 floor, 1155 Metcalfe St., Montreal, Que. H3B 2X9, Canada. TEL 514-866-6621. index. circ. 100. Indexed: Abstr.Bull.Inst.Pap.Chem.

676   CN
CANADIAN PULP AND PAPER ASSOCIATION. WOODLANDS SECTION. PUBLICATIONS. 1927. irreg. ‡ Canadian Pulp and Paper Association, Sun Life Bldg., 23 floor, 1155 Metcalfe St., Montreal, Que. H3B 2X9. TEL 514-866-6621. Indexed: Abstr.Bull.Inst.Pap.Chem.

676   NE
HANDBOOK OF PAPER SCIENCE. 1980. irreg. price varies. Elsevier Science Publishers B.V., Box 211, 1000 AE Amsterdam, Netherlands.

INDUSTRIEGEWERKSCHAFT DRUCK UND PAPIER. SCHRIFTENREIHE FUER BETRIEBSRATE. see *PRINTING*

676   US   ISSN 0361-4719
INSTRUMENTATION IN THE PULP AND PAPER INDUSTRY. Includes: International I S A Pulp and Paper Instrumentation Symposium Proceedings. 1960. a. price varies. Instrument Society of America, 67 Alexander Dr., Box 12277, Research Triangle Park, NC 27709. TEL 919-549-8411. (reprint service avail. from UMI,ISI and publisher)

676 670   US   ISSN 0097-2509
INTERNATIONAL PULP & PAPER DIRECTORY. 1974. biennial. Miller Freeman Publications, Inc., 500 Howard St., San Francisco, CA 94105. TEL 415-397-1881. Ed. Vincent M. Ridley.

676   US   ISSN 0076-0277
LOCKWOOD'S DIRECTORY OF THE PAPER AND ALLIED TRADES. 1873. a. $95 (abridged edt. $80) Vance Publishing Corporation (New York), 122 E. 42nd St., New York, NY 10168. TEL 212-682-7777. Ed. S. Wolert. adv. index. circ. 4,600.

676   NE   ISSN 0077-1414
MONUMENTA CHARTAE PAPYRACEAE HISTORIAM ILLUSTRANTIA/COLLECTION OF WORKS AND DOCUMENTS ILLUSTRATING THE HISTORY OF PAPER. (Text mainly in English; occasionally in other languages) 1950. irreg., vol.14, 1977. price varies. Paper Publications Society, Universiteits-Bibliotheek, Singel 425, 1012 W P Amsterdam, Netherlands. Ed. J.S.G. Simmons. circ. 500.

676 686.2   UK   ISSN 0262-8600
P I R A ANNUAL REVIEW OF RESEARCH & SERVICES. 1977. a. membership. Paper, Printing & Packaging Industries Research Association, Randalls Rd., Leatherhead, Surrey KT22 7RU, England. illus. Indexed: Curr.Pack.Abstr.

676   UK
PAPER INDUSTRY TECHNICAL ASSOCIATION. FUNDAMENTAL RESEARCH INTERNATIONAL SYMPOSIA. 1958. quadrennial. price varies. Paper Industry Technical Association, Pira House, Randalls Rd., Leatherhead KT22 4RU, England. Indexed: Abstr.Bull.Inst.Pap.Chem.
  Formerly: British Paper and Board Industry Federation. Technical Association. Fundamental Research International Symposia (ISSN 0068-2322)

676   US
PAPER MERCHANT PERFORMANCE. 1935. a. $150. National Paper Trade Association, Inc., 111 Great Neck Rd., Ste. 603, Great Neck, NY 11021. TEL 516-829-3070. Ed. John S. LaRosa. charts. stat. circ. 2,500.

676   US
PAPER, PAPERBOARD, WOODPULP CAPACITY; fiber consumption. 1958. a. $275. American Paper Institute, Inc., 260 Madison Ave., New York, NY 10016. TEL 212-340-0600. circ. 2,500.

676   UK   ISSN 0302-4180
PAPER REVIEW OF THE YEAR. 1973. a. £16.80. Benn Publications Ltd., Sovereign Way, Tonbridge, Kent TN9 1RW, England. Ed. Martin Bayliss. index. circ. 8,437.

676 330   US
PAPER SALES CONVENTION NEWS. 1952. a. (in 3 eds.) Harcourt Brace Jovanovich, Inc., 7500 Old Oak Blvd., Cleveland, OH 44130 TEL 216-243-8100. (Subscr. address: 1 E. First St., Duluth, MN 55802) Ed. Roy Wirtzfeld. circ. 3,550.

PAPER YEAR BOOK. see *BUSINESS AND ECONOMICS — Trade And Industrial Directories*

676   UK   ISSN 0079-158X
PHILLIPS' PAPER TRADE DIRECTORY - EUROPE-MILLS OF THE WORLD. 1904. a. £65. Benn Business Information Services Ltd., P.O. Box 20, Sovereign Way, Tonbridge, Kent TN9 1RQ, England. adv. index. circ. 3,277.
  Incorporating: Papermakers' and Merchants' Directory of All Nations (ISSN 0078-9038)

POST'S PULP & PAPER DIRECTORY. see *BUSINESS AND ECONOMICS — Trade And Industrial Directories*

676   US
PULP & PAPER BUYERS GUIDE. a. $30. Miller Freeman Publications, Inc., 500 Howard St., San Francisco, CA 94105. TEL 415-397-1881. Ed. Ken L. Patrick. circ. 26,000. (also avail. in microfilm; reprint service avail. from UMI)

676   CN   ISSN 0708-501X
PULP & PAPER CANADA DIRECTORY. 1907. a. Can.$56($32) Southam Communications Ltd., 310 Victoria Ave., Suite 201, Westmount, P. Q. H3Z 2M9, Canada. TEL 514-487-2302. Ed. P. Williamson. adv. index. circ. 1,816. Indexed: Abstr.Bull.Inst.Pap.Chem.
  Former titles: Pulp and Paper Canada Business Directory (ISSN 0317-3550); Canada's Pulp and Paper Business Directory (ISSN 0079-7936)

676　　　　　　　　　CN　ISSN 0709-2563
PULP & PAPER CANADA'S ANNUAL & DIRECTORY. 1930. a. Can.$58($81) Southam Communications Limited, 1450 Don Mills Road, Don Mills, Ontario M3B 2X7, Canada. Ed. Peter N. Williamson. adv. index. circ. 1,800.
　　Former titles: Pulp and Paper Canada's Reference Manual and Buyers' Guide; Pulp and Paper Magazine of Canada's Reference Manual and Buyers' Guide (ISSN 0079-7952)

676　　　　　　　　　US　ISSN 0190-2172
PULP AND PAPER INDUSTRY TECHNICAL CONFERENCE. CONFERENCE RECORD. a. (I E E E, Industry Applications Society) Institute of Electrical and Electronics Engineers, Inc., 345 E. 47th St., New York, NY 10017 TEL 212-705-7900. (Subscr. address: 445 Hoes Ln., Piscataway, NJ 08854)
　　Formerly: Pulp and Paper Industry Technical Conference. Record (ISSN 0079-7944)

676　　　　　　　　　US
PULP & PAPER INTERNATIONAL FACTBOOK. 1986. biennial. $169. Miller Freeman Publications, Inc., 500 Howard St., San Francisco, CA 94105. TEL 415-397-1881. Ed. Carl P. Espe.

676　　　　　　　　　US
PULP & PAPER NORTH AMERICAN INDUSTRY FACTBOOK. 1980. biennial. $165. Miller Freeman Publications, Inc., 500 Howard St., San Francisco, CA 94105. TEL 415-397-1881. Ed. Willard E. Mies. circ. 600. (reprint service avail. from UMI)

676　　　　　　　　　US
PULP & PAPER PRICEBOOK. 1984. a. (plus q. supp.) $397. Miller Freeman Publications, Inc., 500 Howard St., San Francisco, CA 94105. TEL 415-397-1881. Ed. Willard E. Mies. (reprint service avail. from UMI)

676　　　　　　　　　CN　ISSN 0079-7960
PULP AND PAPER RESEARCH INSTITUTE OF CANADA. ANNUAL REPORT. 1968. a. free. ‡ Pulp and Paper Research Institute of Canada, 570 St. John's Road, Pointe Claire, Que. H9R 3J9, Canada. TEL 514-697-4110. circ. 2,500.

676　　　　　　　　　SW　ISSN 0348-2650
S T F I MEDDELANDE. SERIES A. (Text in Swedish; summaries in English) 1969. irreg., no.677, 1981. exchange basis. Svenska Traeforskningsinstitutet - Swedish Forest Products Research Laboratory, Box 5604, S-114 86 Stockholm, Sweden. illus. cum.index: 1969-1983. circ. 500. Indexed: Abstr.Bull.Inst.Pap.Chem. Forest.Abstr.　Forest Prod.Abstr.
　　Formerly: Svenska Traeforskningsinstitutet. Meddelande. Series A (ISSN 0085-6983)

676　　　　　　　　　US　ISSN 0081-2129
SOURCES OF SUPPLY/BUYERS GUIDE. 1924. a. $60. Advertisers and Publishers Service, Inc., Drawer 795, Park Ridge, IL 60068. TEL 312-823-3145. Ed. L.B. Cowan. adv. circ. 1,500.
　　Formerly: Source of Supply Directory.

STATISTICS OF PAPER, PAPERBOARD AND WOOD PULP. see *PAPER AND PULP — Abstracting, Bibliographies, Statistics*

SVENSK TRAEVARU- OCH PAPERSMASSETIDNING/SWEDISH TIMBER AND WOOD PULP JOURNAL. see *FORESTS AND FORESTRY — Lumber And Wood*

676　　　　　　　　　US
T A P P I TEST METHODS. 1926. irreg. $750 to non-members; members $502.50. ‡ Technical Association of the Pulp and Paper Industry, Inc., Technology Park/Atlanta, Box 105113, Atlanta, GA 30348. TEL 404-446-1400. index. (looseleaf format)
　　Former titles: T A P P I Standards and Provisional Methods; T A P P I Standards and Suggested Methods.

676　　　　　　　　　US
TECHNICAL ASSOCIATION OF THE PULP AND PAPER INDUSTRY. ANNUAL MEETING PROCEEDINGS. 1980. a. $69.95 to non-members; members $46.87. Technical Association of the Pulp and Paper Industry, Inc., Technology Park/Atlanta, Box 105113, Atlanta, GA 30348. TEL 404-446-1400.

676　　　　　　　　　US
TECHNICAL ASSOCIATION OF THE PULP AND PAPER INDUSTRY. COATING CONFERENCE. PROCEEDINGS. a. $64.95 to non-members; members $43.52. Technical Association of the Pulp and Paper Industry, Inc., Technology Park/Atlanta, Box 105113, Atlanta, GA 30348. TEL 404-446-1400.

TECHNICAL ASSOCIATION OF THE PULP AND PAPER INDUSTRY. CORRUGATED CONTAINERS CONFERENCE. PROCEEDINGS. see *PACKAGING*

676　　　　　　　　　US　ISSN 0091-7737
TECHNICAL ASSOCIATION OF THE PULP AND PAPER INDUSTRY. DIRECTORY. Running title: T A P P I Directory. 1931. a. $75. ‡ Technical Association of the Pulp and Paper Industry, Inc., Technology Park/Atlanta, Box 105113, Atlanta, GA 30348. TEL 404-446-1400. adv. circ. 22,000. Key Title: Directory - Technical Association of the Pulp and Paper Industry.

676　　　　　　　　　US
TECHNICAL ASSOCIATION OF THE PULP AND PAPER INDUSTRY. ENGINEERING CONFERENCE PROCEEDINGS. (In 3 books) a. $149.95 to non-members; members $100.47. Technical Association of the Pulp and Paper Industry, Inc., Technology Park/Atlanta, Box 105113, Atlanta, GA 30348. TEL 404-446-1400.

676　　　　　　　　　US
TECHNICAL ASSOCIATION OF THE PULP AND PAPER INDUSTRY. INTERNATIONAL PROCESS & MATERIALS QUALITY EVALUATION PROCEEDINGS. (Each year held jointly with a different TAPPI section) a. $69.95 to non-members; members $46.87. Technical Association of the Pulp and Paper Industry, Technology Park/Atlanta, Box 105113, Atlanta, GA 30348. TEL 404-446-1400. circ. 500. Indexed: Chem.Abstr.　Eng.Ind.
　　Formerly: Technical Association of the Pulp and Paper Industry. Testing Conference Proceedings.

676　　　　　　　　　US
TECHNICAL ASSOCIATION OF THE PULP AND PAPER INDUSTRY. PAPER FINISHING AND CONVERTING CONFERENCE. PROCEEDINGS. a. $64.95 to non-members; members $43.52. Technical Association of the Pulp and Paper Industry, Inc., Technology Park/Atlanta, Box 105113, Atlanta, GA 30348. TEL 404-446-1400. adv.

676　　　　　　　　　US
TECHNICAL ASSOCIATION OF THE PULP AND PAPER INDUSTRY. PAPERMAKERS CONFERENCE PROCEEDINGS. a. $49.95 to non-members; members $33.47. Technical Association of the Pulp and Paper Industry, Inc., Technology Park/Atlanta, Box 105113, Atlanta, GA 30348. TEL 404-394-6130.

TECHNICAL ASSOCIATION OF THE PULP AND PAPER INDUSTRY. PRINTING AND REPROGRAPHY CONFERENCE PROCEEDINGS. see *PRINTING*

676　　　　　　　　　US
TECHNICAL ASSOCIATION OF THE PULP AND PAPER INDUSTRY. PULPING CONFERENCE PROCEEDINGS. a. $139.95 to non-members; members $93.77. Technical Association of the Pulp and Paper Industry, Inc., Technology Park/Atlanta, Box 105113, Atlanta, GA 30348. TEL 404-446-1400.

676　　　　　　　　　US
TRANSPORT AND HANDLING IN THE PULP AND PAPER INDUSTRY; proceedings. 1975. irreg. (Pulp & Paper International Symposium) Miller Freeman Publications, Inc., 500 Howard St., San Francisco, CA 94105. TEL 415-397-1881. illus. index. (reprint service avail. from UMI)

676　　　　　　　　　US　ISSN 0083-7024
WALDEN'S A B C GUIDE AND PAPER PRODUCTION YEARBOOK. 1885. a. $77.50. Walden - Mott Corporation, 475 Kinderkamack Rd., Oradell, NJ 07649. TEL 201-261-2630. Ed. Michael Balbian. adv. index.

676　　　　　　　　　UK
WHO'S WHO IN CORRUGATED. a. £7. International Paper Board Industry, Binsted House, Devonshire Close, Devonshire St., London W1N 2DL, England. Ed. Kenneth C. Binsted.

676　　　　　　　　　US
WHO'S WHO IN PAPER DISTRIBUTION. 1903. a. $25. National Paper Trade Association, Inc., 111 Great Neck Rd., Ste. 603, Great Neck, NY 11021. TEL 516-829-3070. Ed. William H. Frohlich. adv. charts. stat. circ. 2,500.
　　Former titles: Who's Who in Paper Distribution and Factbook; Who's Who in Paper Distribution.

WOOD PULP AND FIBER STATISTICS. see *PAPER AND PULP — Abstracting, Bibliographies, Statistics*

PAPER AND PULP — Abstracting, Bibliographies, Statistics

338.4　　　　　　　　CN　ISSN 0316-4241
CANADIAN PULP AND PAPER ASSOCIATION. ANNUAL NEWSPRINT SUPPLEMENT. a. free. Canadian Pulp and Paper Association, Sun Life Building, 23rd Floor, 1155 Metcalfe St., Montreal, Que. H3B 2X9, Canada. TEL 514-866-6621. stat.

676　016　　　　　　　US　ISSN 0020-3033
INSTITUTE OF PAPER CHEMISTRY. ABSTRACT BULLETIN. 1930. m. price varies. Institute of Paper Chemistry, 1043 E. South River St., Box 1039, Appleton, WI 54912. TEL 414-734-9251. Ed. Francis J. Lynch. bk. rev. abstr. index. cum.index. circ. 800. (microfilm; reprint service avail. from IPC; back issues avail.) Indexed: Biol.Abstr. Anal.Abstr.　Forest.Abstr.　Forest Prod.Abstr. Graph.Arts Lit.Abstr.　Int.Packag.Abstr.　Paper & Bd.Abstr.
　●Also available online. Vendors: DIALOG.

676　016　　　　　　　US　ISSN 0073-9480
INSTITUTE OF PAPER CHEMISTRY. BIBLIOGRAPHIC SERIES. 1929. irreg., no.292, 1984. price varies. Institute of Paper Chemistry, 1043 E. South River St., Box 1039, Appleton, WI 54915. TEL 414-734-9251. Ed. Frederick Boye. bk. rev. circ. 600. Indexed: Forest.Abstr.　Forest Prod.Abstr.

676　　　　　　　　　NE　ISSN 0168-4361
NETHERLANDS. CENTRAAL BUREAU VOOR DE STATISTIEK. PRODUKTIESTATISTIEKEN: PAPIER- EN KARTONINDUSTRIE. a. fl.9.50. Centraal Bureau voor de Statistiek, Prinses Beatrixlaan 428, Voorburg, Netherlands (Orders to: Staatsuitgeverij, Christoffel Plantijnstraat, The Hague, Netherlands)
　　Formed by the merger of: Netherlands. Centraal Bureau voor de Statistiek. Produktiestatistiek van de Papierindustries & Netherlands. Centraal Bureau voor de Statistiek. Produktiestatistiek Strokartonindustrie.

676　　　　　　　　　US
NEWSPAPER AND NEWSPRINT FACTS AT A GLANCE. 1958. a. $2.50 per no. Newsprint Information Committee, 420 Lexington Ave., New York, NY 10017. TEL 212-697-5600. Ed. John C. Waugh. charts. illus. stat. circ. 10,000.

676　016　　　　　　　UK　ISSN 0307-0778
PAPER AND BOARD ABSTRACTS. 1965. m. $385 to non-members. (Paper & Board, Printing and Packaging Industries Research Association) Pergamon Press Ltd., Headington Hill Hall, Oxford OX3 0BW, England. Ed. Susan White. bk. rev. abstr. index. (also avail. in microfilm from UMI; reprint service avail. from UMI) Indexed: Curr.Cont.　World Text.Abstr.
　●Also available online. Vendors: Orbit Information Technologies, Pergamon Infoline.
　　Formerly (until 1976): Kenley Abstracts.

676　　　　　　　　　US　ISSN 0731-8863
STATISTICS OF PAPER, PAPERBOARD AND WOOD PULP. 1947. a. $250. American Paper Institute, Inc., 260 Madison Ave., New York, NY 10016. TEL 212-340-0600.
　　Former titles: Statistics of Paper and Paperboard (ISSN 0097-4730) & Paperboard Industry Statistics.

676 310   FR
STATISTIQUES DE L'INDUSTRIE FRANCAISE DES PATES. PAPIERS ET CARTONS. a. C.O.P.A.C.E.L., 154, Boulevard Haussmann, 75008 Paris, France. illus.
    Continues: Quelques Donnees Statistiques sur l'Industrie Francaise des Pates, Papiers, Cartons (ISSN 0481-0112)

676   US
WOOD PULP AND FIBER STATISTICS. 1936. a. $75. American Paper Institute, Inc., 260 Madison Ave., New York, NY 10016. TEL 212-340-0600.

PARAPSYCHOLOGY AND OCCULTISM

133   UK   ISSN 0141-0121
AQUARIAN ARROW. 1977. irreg. (approx. 3/yr.) £3($6) for 4 issues. Neopantheist Society, BCM-OPAL, London WC1N 3XX, England. Ed. Zachary Cox. adv. bk. rev. circ. 300. (back issues avail.)

133   US
BOOKS OF ORAL TRADITION. (Text in English, Hebrew) 1980. biennial. Quantal Publishing, Box 1598, Goleta, CA 93107. TEL 805-964-7293. Ed. William Cox. circ. 3,000. (back issues avail.)

CINCINNATI JOURNAL OF MAGIC. see *PHILOSOPHY*

133   US
ENCYCLOPEDIA OF OCCULTISM AND PARAPSYCHOLOGY. 1978. irreg., 2nd edt., 1984-85. $275. Gale Research Company, Book Tower, Detroit, MI 48226. TEL 313-961-2242. Ed. Leslie Shepard. Indexed: Child.Auth.& Illus.

132   FR   ISSN 0534-9168
INTERNATIONAL CONGRESS OF PSYCHOPATHOLOGICAL ART. PROGRAM. PROGRAMME. (Text in English, French and German) irreg. International Society of Art and Psychopathology, c/o Dr. C. Wiart, Clinique de la Faculte, 100 rue de la Sante, 75014 Paris, France.

INTERSTELLAR BULLETINS. see *PHILOSOPHY*

IO. see *ANTHROPOLOGY*

133   US
METASCIENCE ANNUAL; a new age journal of parapsychology. 1979. a. $25. MetaScience Foundation, Box 32, Kingston, RI 02881. Ed. Marc Seifer. adv. bk. rev. bibl. charts. illus. stat. index. circ. 1,500. (back issues avail.)
    Formerly: MetaScience Quarterly; Which superseded (1977-1978): Journal of Occult Studies.

133   UK
NEOMETAPHYSICAL DIGEST. 1952. biennial. £5($10) Society of Metaphysicians Ltd., Archers' Court, Stonestile Lane, the Ridge, Hastings, E.Sussex TN35 4PG, England. Ed. J.J. Williamson. bk. rev. circ. 60,000.
    Formerly: Metaphysical Digest.

133   US
NEWS NOVEL. 1969. irreg. Box 3232, Riverside, CA 92519. Ed. Darlene Wheeler.

133.91   US
NUERUOLOG; the journal of reality frontiers. 1975. irreg. $1.50. Network Publishing, Box 317, Berkeley, CA 94701. TEL 415-849-2665. Ed. Ted Schultz. bk. rev. abstr. bibl. charts. illus. tr.lit. circ. 1,500. (back issues avail.)

133   US
OCCULTISM UPDATE. (Supplement to the Encyclopedia of Occultism and Parapsychology) 1978. irreg., latest 2nd edt., 1986. $72. Gale Research Company, Book Tower, Detroit, MI 48226. TEL 313-961-2242. Ed. Leslie Shepard.

133   US   ISSN 0078-9437
PARAPSYCHOLOGICAL MONOGRAPHS. 1958. irreg., latest no.18. price varies. Parapsychology Foundation, 228 E. 71st St., New York, NY 10021. Indexed: Psychol.Abstr.

133   US
PARAPSYCHOLOGY FOUNDATION. PROCEEDINGS OF INTERNATIONAL CONFERENCES. 1953. a. price varies. Parapsychology Foundation, 228 E. 71st St., New York, NY 10021.

133.324   UK   ISSN 0079-4953
PREDICTION ANNUAL. a. £1.75. Link House Magazines Ltd., Link House, Dingwall Ave., Croydon CR9 2TA, England. Ed. Jo Logan. adv. bk. rev.

133.91   US   ISSN 0276-1610
PSYCHIC STUDIES. 1982. a., latest vol.4, 1979. price varies. Gordon and Breach Science Publishers, 50 West 23rd St., New York, NY 10010. TEL 212-206-8900. Ed. Stanley Krippner, Irene Hall.

133   IT
QUADERNI DI PARAPSICOLOGIA. (Text in Italian; summaries in English, Italian) a. L.30000($20) includes Bollettino. Centro Studi Parapsicologici (C.S.P.), Via L. Valeriani, 39, I-40134 Bologna, Italy. Ed. Piero Cassoli. bk. rev. circ. 450. (back issues avail.)

133.5   UK
RAPHAEL'S ASTROLOGICAL ALMANAC. 1819. a. £1.50. W. Foulsham & Co. Ltd., Yeovil Rd., Slough SL1 4JH, England.

133   US
RESEARCH FOR RELIGION & PARAPSYCHOLOGY. 1975. irreg. (1-2/yr.) $5. International Association for Religion & Parapsychology, 399 Sunset Dr., Encinitas, CA 92024.
    Formerly: International Association for Religion & Parapsychology Journal.

133   US   ISSN 0094-7172
RESEARCH IN PARAPSYCHOLOGY. 1972. a. price varies. (Parapsychological Association) Scarecrow Press, Inc., 52 Liberty St., Metuchen, NJ 08840. TEL 201-548-8600.
    Continues: Parapsychological Association. Proceedings.

133   UK   ISSN 0143-0181
REVELATION. 1972. irreg., (1-2/yr.) £2.80($4) for 4 issues. 2 Rose Cottage, Farm Rd., Ruardean Woodside, Ruardean, Gloucestershire, GL17 9XL, England. Ed. Peter Carman. adv. bk. rev. circ. 300.

133   FR   ISSN 0294-2623
REVUE DE PARAPSYCHOLOGIE. (Text in French; summaries occasionally in English) 1975. irreg. 120 F. Groupe d'Etude et de Recherche en Parapsychologie, 8 rue Octave Dubois, 95150 Taverny, France. Ed. Gisele Titeux. bk. rev. charts. circ. 1,000. (back issues avail.)

133   FR   ISSN 0484-8934
REVUE METAPSYCHIQUE. 1920. irreg. 40 F. per no. Institut Metapsychique International, 1 Place de Wagram, 75017 Paris, France. Ed. Hubert Larcher. bk. rev. circ. 500.

133   UK   ISSN 0081-1475
SOCIETY FOR PSYCHICAL RESEARCH. PROCEEDINGS. 1882. irreg. membership. Society for Psychical Research, 1 Adam and Eve Mews, London W8 6UG, England. Ed. John Beloff. Indexed: Br.Hum.Ind. Psychol.Abstr.

133   UK   ISSN 0143-5418
SUT ANUBIS. irreg. £5.75($10) Sut Anubis, Occultique, 73 Kettering Rd., Northampton NN1 4AW, England. adv. bk. rev. circ. 500.

133.4   US   ISSN 0085-8250
WITCHCRAFT DIGEST. (Supplement to W I C A Newsletter) 1970. a. $2 per no. (Witches International Craft Associates; Witches Liberation Movement) Hero Press, Ste. 1B, 153 West 80 St., New York, NY 10024. Ed. Leo Louis Martello. adv. bk. rev. circ. 3,000.
    Formerly: Witchcraft (ISSN 0014-2840)

133   US   ISSN 0741-6229
ZETETIC SCHOLAR. 1978. irreg. $18. Center for Scientific Anomalies Research, Box 1052, Ann Arbor, MI 48106 (Subscr. to: Department of Sociology, Eastern Michigan University, Ypsilanti, MI 48197) Ed. Marcello Truzzi. bk. rev. bibl. circ. 600. Indexed: Sociol.Abstr. Lang.& Lang.Behav.Abstr.

PATENTS, TRADEMARKS AND COPYRIGHTS

608.7   UK
ABSTRACTS AND ABRIDGEMENTS OF PATENT SPECIFICATIONS. 1883. w. price varies. Patent Office, Sales Branch, Orpington, Kent BR5 3RD, England. circ. 400.

346.73 608.7   US   ISSN 0361-3844
ATTORNEYS AND AGENTS REGISTERED TO PRACTICE BEFORE THE U.S. PATENT AND TRADEMARK OFFICE. irreg. $17. U.S. Patent and Trademark Office, Washington, DC 20231 TEL 703-557-1728. (Orders to: Supt. of Documents, Washington, DC 20402)
    Former titles: Attorneys and Agents Registered to Practice Before the U.S. Patent Office (ISSN 0092-5934); Roster of Attorneys and Agents Registered to Practice Before the U.S. Patent Office; Directory of Registered Patent Attorneys and Agents (ISSN 0565-9582)

608.7   AT
AUSTRALIA. DESIGNS OFFICE. ANNUAL RECORD OF DESIGNS OFFICE PROCEEDINGS. 1973. a. Aus.$25. Patent Office, Information Services Section, Scarborough House, Woden, A.C.T. 2606, Australia. circ. 100.
    Former titles: Australia. Designs Office. Registered Owners of Designs and Articles in Respect of Which Designs Have Been Registered & Australia. Designs Office. Registered Owners of Designs and Articles in Respect of Which Designs Have Been Registered Under the Designs Act & Australia. Designs Office. Registered Owners of Designs.

608.7   AT   ISSN 0311-2152
AUSTRALIA. PATENT OFFICE. ANNUAL REPORT OF ACTIVITIES. 1972/73. a. Aus.$4. Patent Office, Information Services Section, Scarborough House, Canberra, A.C.T. 2600, Australia. illus. circ. 500.
    Formerly: Australia. Patent Office. Report.

608.7   FR
B.O.P.I. STATISTIQUES. (Bulletin Officiel de la Propriete Industrielle) 1958. a. 50 F. each. Institut National de la Propriete Industrielle, 26 bis rue de Leningrad, 75800 Paris Cedex 08, France. index. circ. 1,200. (back issues avail.)

608.7   UK
CHARTERED INSTITUTE OF PATENTS AGENTS. REGISTER OF PATENT AGENTS. 1889. a. £2. Chartered Institute of Patents Agents, Staple Inn Buildings, High Holborn, London, WC1V 7PZ, England. adv. circ. 2,750.

347.7   US   ISSN 0069-9950
COPYRIGHT LAW SYMPOSIUM. 1950. irreg., no.25, 1980. price varies. (American Society of Composers, Authors, and Publishers) Columbia University Press, 562 W. 113th St., New York, NY 10025. TEL 212-678-6777. Indexed: Leg.Per. C.L.I. L.R.I.

340   UN   ISSN 0069-9969
COPYRIGHT LAWS AND TREATIES OF THE WORLD. SUPPLEMENTS. a. Unesco, 7-9 Place de Fontenoy, 75700 Paris, France. (Co-sponsor: World Intellectual Property Organization) (also avail. in looseleaf format)

340   US   ISSN 0070-3176
DECISIONS OF THE UNITED STATES COURTS INVOLVING COPYRIGHTS. (Subseries of U.S. Copyright Office. Bulletin) 1910. a. price varies. U.S. Library of Congress, Copyright Office, The Library of Congress, Washington, DC 20559 TEL 202-275-2051. (Orders to: Supt. of Documents, Washington, DC 20402) cum.index.

608.7   DK
DIREKTORAT UNDER FORANDRING. 1975. a. free. Direktoratet for Patent- og Varemaerkevaesenet - Danish Patents and Trademark Office, Nyropsgade 45, DK-1602 Copenhagen V, Denmark. Ed. P.L. Thoft. circ. 5,000.
    Formerly: Denmark. Direktoratet for Patent- og Varemaerkevaesenet. Aarsberetning.

608.7 GW ISSN 0170-9291
EUROPEAN PATENT OFFICE. ANNUAL REPORT. (Text in English, French and German) 1978. a. free. European Patent Office, Erhardtstrasse 27, D-8000 Munich 2, W. Germany (B.R.D.) circ. 5,000. (back issues avail.)

608.7 UK
EUROPEAN PATENTS HANDBOOK. irreg. Longman Professional, 21-27 Lamb's Conduit St., London WC1N 3NJ, England. (looseleaf format)

LA FRANCE DE L'INDUSTRIE ET SES SERVICES. see BUSINESS AND ECONOMICS — Trade And Industrial Directories

608.7 US ISSN 0083-3029
GENERAL INFORMATION CONCERNING TRADEMARKS. irreg. $1.50. U.S. Patent and Trademark Office, Washington, DC 20231 TEL 703-557-3158. (Orders to: Supt. of Documents, Washington, DC 20402)

608.7 UK ISSN 0072-5706
GREAT BRITAIN. DEPARTMENT OF TRADE. PATENTS, DESIGN AND TRADE MARKS (ANNUAL REPORT) a. H.M.S.O., P.O. Box 569, London SE1 9NH, England. (reprint service avail. from UMI)

GUIDE TO AVAILABLE TECHNOLOGIES; an annual guide to business opportunities in technology. see TECHNOLOGY: COMPREHENSIVE WORKS

HANDBOOK FOR LIBRARIES & OTHER ORGANIZATIONAL USERS WHICH COPY FROM SERIALS & SEPARATES; procedures for using the programs of the Copyright Clearance Center, Inc. see PUBLISHING AND BOOK TRADE

340 CN
HUGHES ON COPYRIGHT AND INDUSTRIAL DESIGN. a. $137.50. Butterworth & Co. (Canada) Ltd., 2265 Midland Avenue, Scarborough, Ont. M1P 4S1, Canada. TEL 416-292-1421. Ed. Roger T. Hughes. (looseleaf format)

608.7 US ISSN 0362-0719
INDEX OF PATENTS ISSUED FROM THE UNITED STATES PATENT AND TRADEMARK OFFICE. 1920. a. price varies. U.S. Patent and Trademark Office, Washington, DC 20231 TEL 703-557-3341. (Orders to: Supt. of Documents, Washington, DC 20402)
  Formerly: U.S. Patent Office. Index of Patents Issued from the United States Patent Office (ISSN 0083-3037)

608.7 US ISSN 0099-0809
INDEX OF TRADEMARKS ISSUED FROM THE U.S. PATENT AND TRADEMARK OFFICE. a. price varies. U.S. Patent and Trademark Office, Washington, DC 20231 TEL 703-557-3341. (Orders to: Supt. of Documents, Washington, DC 20402)
  Formerly: Index of Trademarks Issued from the United States Patent Office (ISSN 0083-3045)

608.7 US
INDEX TO THE U.S. PATENT CLASSIFICATION. a. U.S. Patent and Trademark Office, Washington, DC 20231.

INDUSTRIAL PROPERTY LAW. ANNUAL. see LAW

INFORMATION SOURCES. see COMPUTERS

340 AT
INSTITUTE OF PATENT ATTORNEYS OF AUSTRALIA. ANNUAL PROCEEDINGS. 1919. irreg., every 3-5 yrs. membership. Institute of Patent Attorneys of Australia, P.O. Box 18, Collins Street, Melbourne, Vic. 3000, Australia. Ed. R.J. Strickland. bk. rev. circ. 250.

608.7 US ISSN 0193-4864
INTELLECTUAL PROPERTY LAW REVIEW. 1969. a. $69.50. Clark Boardman Company, Ltd., 435 Hudson St., New York, NY 10014. Ed. Thomas E. Costner. index. Indexed: Leg.Per. C.L.I. L.R.I.
  Formerly: Patent Law Review (ISSN 0079-0168)

341.758 FR ISSN 0074-2899
INTERNATIONAL CONFEDERATION OF SOCIETIES OF AUTHORS AND COMPOSERS. irreg., no.186, 1976. International Confederation of Societies of Authors and Composers, 11 rue Keppler, 75116 Paris, France.

340 AU ISSN 0539-1512
INTERNATIONALE GESELLSCHAFT FUER URHEBERRECHT. YEARBOOK. (Text in English, French, German, Italian and Spanish) irreg., vol.5, 1984. Manzsche Verlags-und Universitaetsbuchhandlung, Kohlmarkt 16, 1014 Vienna 1, Austria. circ. 1,200.

608.7 US
LAW REPRINTS: PATENT, TRADEMARK & COPYRIGHT SERIES. 1977. irreg. $245. Congressional Information Service, Inc., 4520 East-West Hwy., Ste. 800, Bethesda, MD 20814. TEL 800-638-8380. Ed. Bart Sigerson. index.
  Former titles: B N A's Law Reprints: Patent, Trademark and Copyright Series (ISSN 0275-7001); Law Reprints, Patent, Trademark and Copyright Series.

340 608.7 JA
MOJI SHOHYOSHU. (Text in Japanese) 1985. a. (Benrishikai) Nihon Benrishi Kyodo Kumiai, Stanley Bldg. 3F, 5-3, 3-Chome, Kasumigaseki, Chiyoda-Ku, Tokyo 100, Japan. circ. 830.

340 NE
MONOGRAPHS ON INDUSTRIAL PROPERTY AND COPYRIGHT LAW. (Text in English) 1976. irreg. Martinus Nijhoff Publishers, Postbus 163, 8300 AD Dordrecht, Netherlands.

602.7 US ISSN 0272-8826
NEW TRADE NAMES. (Supplement to: Trade Names Dictionary) 1976. a., between edts. of Trade Names Dictionary. $220 for 2 yrs. Gale Research Company, Book Tower, Detroit, MI 48226. TEL 313-961-2242. Ed. Donna Wood.

608.7 CN ISSN 0079-015X
PATENT AND TRADEMARK INSTITUTE OF CANADA. ANNUAL PROCEEDINGS. 1928. a. membership. Patent and Trademark Institute of Canada, Box 1298, Sta. B, Ottawa, Ont. K1P 5R3, Canada. TEL 613-234-0516. circ. controlled.

608.7 US ISSN 0553-3864
PATENT LAW ANNUAL-SOUTHWESTERN LEGAL FOUNDATION. a. $55. Matthew Bender & Co., Inc., 235 E. 45th St., New York, NY 10017. TEL 212-661-5050. Ed. Virginia S. Cameron. Indexed: Leg.Per. C.L.I. L.R.I.

340 US ISSN 0192-8198
PATENT LAW HANDBOOK. a. $47.50. Clark Boardman Company, Ltd., 435 Hudson St., New York, NY 10014.

608.7 II
PATENT OFFICE TECHNICAL SOCIETY. JOURNAL. (Text in English) vol.10, 1976. irreg. Rs.15. Patent Office Technical Society, 214, Acharya Jagadish Bose Rd., Calcutta 700 017, India. Ed. N.R. Seth. adv. bk. rev. patents. stat. circ. 250. (also avail. in microfilm from WSH) Indexed: Leg.Per. SSCI. C.L.I.

608.7 PL ISSN 0208-550X
PROBLEMY PRAWA WYNALAZCZEGO I PATENTOWEGO. (Text in Polish; summaries in German and Polish) 1974. irreg. price varies. Uniwersytet Slaski w Katowicach, Ul. Bankowa 14, 40-007 Katowice, Poland.

608.7 UK
REGISTER OF PATENT AGENTS. 1889. a. £2. Chartered Institute of Patent Agents, Staple Inn Bldgs., High Holborn, London WC1V 7PZ, England. circ. 2,500.

608.7 DK ISSN 0107-590X
REGISTER OVER DANSKE PATENTER UDSTEDT. 1970. a. Kr.300. Direktoratet for Patent og Varemaerkevaesenet, Nyropsgade 45, 1602 Copenhagen K, Denmark.

608.7 UK ISSN 0080-1364
REPORTS OF PATENT, DESIGN, TRADE MARK AND OTHER CASES. 1884. irreg. £68.90. Patent Office, St. Mary Cray, Orpington, Kent, BR5 3RD, England. Ed. Michael Fysh. circ. 1,800.

602.7 IT
SIGLARIO ITALIANO/ITALIAN TRADE-MARKS. 1983. a. L.45000. Guida Monaci S.p.A., Via Francesco Crispi 10, 00187 Rome, Italy.

602.7 SW
SVENSKT VARUMAERKESARKIV/SWEDISH TRADEMARK ARCHIVE; computer-indexed microfiche archive including full information about registered trademarks and pending applications. 1976. a. (with updates weekly) Kr.4000 (minimum 2 yrs.); pending applications only Kr.1000/yr. Patent-och Registreringsverket - Royal Patent and Registration Office, Box 5055, S-102 42 Stockholm, Sweden.

608 SW
SWEDEN. PATENT- OCH REGISTERERINGSVERKET. AARSBERAETTELSE/SWEDEN. ROYAL PATENT AND REGISTRATION OFFICE. ANNUAL REPORT. (Text in English & Swedish) 1965. a. Kr.20. Patent- och Registreringsverket - Royal Patent and Registration Office, Box 5055, S-102 42 Stockholm, Sweden. pat. stat. circ. 3,000.

602.7 US
TRADE NAMES DICTIONARY. (Supplement: New Trade Names) 1976. irreg. $289 (2 vols.) Gale Research Company, Book Tower, Detroit, MI 48226. TEL 313-961-2242. Ed. Donna Wood.

608.7 US ISSN 0082-5786
TRADEMARK REGISTER OF THE UNITED STATES. 1958. a. $247. The Trademark Register, 1050 Connecticut Ave., Washington, DC 20036. TEL 202-429-6668. Ed. Cyril W. Sernak. cum.index: 1881-1986.

340 US ISSN 0090-2845
U.S. COPYRIGHT OFFICE. ANNUAL REPORT OF THE REGISTER OF COPYRIGHTS. 1910. a. price varies. U.S. Library of Congress, Copyright Office, Library of Congress, Washington, DC 20559 TEL 202-275-2051. (Orders to: Supt. of Documents, Washington, DC 20402) Key Title: Annual Report of the Register of Copyrights.

608.7 US ISSN 0083-3002
U.S. PATENT AND TRADEMARK OFFICE. ANNUAL REPORT OF THE COMMISSIONER OF PATENTS. 1837. a. price varies. U.S. Patent and Trademark Office, Washington, DC 20231 TEL 703-557-3341. (Orders to: Supt. of Documents, Washington, DC 20402)

608.7 US ISSN 0083-3010
U.S. PATENT AND TRADEMARK OFFICE. CLASSIFICATION BULLETINS. irreg. price varies. U.S. Patent and Trademark Office, Washington, DC 20231 TEL 703-557-3341. (Orders to: Supt. of Documents, Washington, DC 20402)

608.7 UK
UNITED STATES PATENTS ABSTRACTS. PART 1: CHEMICAL. w. $730. Derwent Publications Ltd., Rochdale House, 128 Theobalds Rd., London WC1X 8RP, England (Subscr. to: Derwent Inc., 6845 Elm St., Ste. 500, McLean VA 22101)
  Formerly: United States Patents Report. Part 1: Chemical.

608.7 UK
WORLD PATENTS ABSTRACTS JOURNALS. (In seven sections) 1975. w. price varies. Derwent Publications Ltd., Rochdale House, 128 Theobalds Rd., London WC1X 8RP, England (Subscr. to: Derwent Inc., 6845 Elm St., Ste. 500, McLean VA 22101)
  ●Also available online. Vendors: DIALOG, Orbit Information Technologies, Telesystemes - Questel.

PATENTS, TRADEMARKS AND COPYRIGHTS — Abstracting, Bibliographies, Statistics

ABSTRACTS AND ABRIDGEMENTS OF PATENT SPECIFICATIONS. see PATENTS, TRADEMARKS AND COPYRIGHTS

PEDIATRICS

608.7 016 UK
BELGIAN PATENTS ABSTRACTS. 1955. w. $730. Derwent Publications Ltd., Rochdale House, 128 Theobalds Rd., London WC1X 8RP, England (Subscr. to: Derwent Inc., 6845 Elm St., Ste. 500, McLean, VA 22101) abstr. illus.
Formerly: Belgian Patents Report (ISSN 0011-9121)

608.7 016 UK ISSN 0007-1609
BRITISH PATENTS ABSTRACTS. 1951. w. $885 for chemical, mechanical, electrical. Derwent Publications Ltd., Rochdale House, 128 Theobalds Rd., London WC1X 8RP, England (Subscr. to: Derwent Inc., 6845 Elm St., Ste. 500, McLean VA 22101) abstr. illus.

608.7 600 016 UK ISSN 0016-1098
FRENCH PATENTS ABSTRACTS. 1961. w. $645. Derwent Publications Ltd., Rochdale House, 128 Theobalds Rd., London WC1X 8RP, England (Subscr. to: Derwent Inc., 6845 Elm St., Ste. 500, McLean VA 22101) abstr. illus. Indexed: Nutr.Abstr.

608.7 600 016 UK ISSN 0016-8807
GERMAN PATENTS ABSTRACTS. (In two editions: Chemical and Non-Chemical) (Text in English) 1953. w. $350 (chemical); $480(non-chemical) Derwent Publications Ltd., Rochdale House, 128 Theobalds Rd., London WC1X 8RP, England. abstr. illus. pat.

608.7 310 UN ISSN 0377-0044
INDUSTRIAL PROPERTY, STATISTICS B/ PROPRIETE INDUSTRIELLE, STATISTIQUES B. (Text in English and French) a. 155 Fr. World Intellectual Property Organization (WIPO) - Organisation Mondiale de la Propriete Intellectuelle, Publication Section, 34 Chemin des Colombettes, 1211 Geneva 20, Switzerland.

608.7 016 US
N A S A PATENT ABSTRACTS BIBLIOGRAPHY: A CONTINUING BIBLIOGRAPHY. SECTION 1. ABSTRACTS. 1969. s-a. $11.50 per no. U.S. National Aeronautics and Space Administration, Scientific and Technical Information Facility, Box 8757, Baltimore-Washington International Airport, MD 21240 TEL 301-621-0153. (Orders to: NTIS, 5285 Port Royal Rd., Springfield, VA 22161) index.

608.7 016 US
N A S A PATENT ABSTRACTS BIBLIOGRAPHY: A CONTINUING BIBLIOGRAPHY. SECTION 2. INDEXES. 1969. s-a. $23 per no. U.S. National Aeronautics and Space Administration, Scientific and Technical Information Facility, Box 8757, Baltimore-Washington International Airport, MD 21240 TEL 301-621-0153. (Not avail. on subscription; single issues avail. from NTIS, 5285 Port Royal Rd., Springfield, VA 22161) index.

PEDIATRICS

see Medical Sciences—Pediatrics

PERFUMES AND COSMETICS

see Beauty Culture—Perfumes and Cosmetics

PERSONAL COMPUTERS

see Computers—Personal Computers

PERSONNEL MANAGEMENT

see Business and Economics—Personnel Management

PETROLEUM AND GAS

A A E C NUCLEAR NEWS. see ENERGY

A A P G STUDIES IN GEOLOGY SERIES. (American Association of Petroleum Geologists) see EARTH SCIENCES — Geology

A M P L A YEARBOOK. (Australian Mining and Petroleum Law Association Ltd.) see MINES AND MINING INDUSTRY

553 AT ISSN 0084-7534
A.P.E.A. JOURNAL. 1961. a. Aus.$80. Australian Petroleum Exploration Association, Box 3974, Sydney, N.S.W. 2001, Australia. Ed. L. Baigent. adv. circ. 1,500. Indexed: Chem.Abstr. Aus.Sci.Ind. GeoRef.

ABERDEEN PORT HANDBOOK. see BUSINESS AND ECONOMICS — Trade And Industrial Directories

ACTA UNIVERSITATIS DE ATTILA JOZSEF NOMINATAE. ACTA MINERALOGICA - PETROGRAPHICA. see MINES AND MINING INDUSTRY

665.5 PL
AKADEMIA GORNICZO-HUTNICZA IM. STANISLAWA STASZICA. ZESZYTY NAUKOWE. DRILLING OIL GAS. (Text in English and Polish; summaries in English, Polish, Russian) 1985. irreg., no.3, 1987. price varies. (Akademia Gorniczo-Hutnicza im. Stanislawa Staszica) Wydawnictwo A G H, Manifestu Lipcowego 16, 31-109 Krakow, Poland (Dist. by: Ars Polona, Krakowskie Przedmiescie 7, 00-068 Warsaw, Poland) Ed. Z. Kleczek. illus. circ. 550.

338.2 665.5 US ISSN 0065-5813
ALASKA PETROLEUM AND INDUSTRIAL DIRECTORY. 1958. biennial. $60. Manufacturers' News, Inc., 4 E. Huron St., Chicago, IL 60611. circ. 200.
Formerly (until 1970): Alaska Petroleum Directory.

665 US
ALASKA SUMMARY REPORT/INDEX. 1980. a. free. Outer Continental Shelf Information Program, Offshore Information Services, Minerals Management Service, 1951 Kidwell Dr., Vienna, VA 22180. TEL 703-285-2285. circ. 2,500.
Formed by the 1985 merger of: Arctic Summary Report & Bering Sea Summary Report & Alaska Index.

620 CN ISSN 0034-5180
ALBERTA RESEARCH COUNCIL. INFORMATION SERIES. 1947. irreg. price varies. Alberta Research Council, Publications Dept., P.O. Box 8330, Sta. F, Edmonton, Alta. T6H 5X2, Canada. TEL 403-450-5111. Indexed: Chem.Abstr. Eng.Ind.

665.74 531.64 CN ISSN 0229-8546
ALBERTA'S RESERVE OF GAS: COMPLETE LISTING. 1979. a. Can.$100. Alberta, Energy Resources Conservation Board, 640-5 Ave. SW, Calgary, Alberta T2P 3G4, Canada. (also avail. in microfiche)

665.5 GW
ALLGEMEINE GASTARIFE IN DER BUNDESREPUBLIK DEUTSCHLAND. 1970. a. price varies. (Verband des Deutschen Gas- und Wasserwerke) ZfGW-Verlag GmbH, Voltastr. 79, 6000 Frankfurt 90, W. Germany (B.R.D.) stat. circ. (controlled) (looseleaf format)

665.5 US ISSN 0272-8370
AMERICAN ASSOCIATION OF PETROLEUM LANDMEN. MEMBERSHIP DIRECTORY. 1955. a. $50. American Association of Petroleum Landmen, 1470 Continental Plaza, Fort Worth, TX 76102-5398. TEL 817-335-2275. Ed. Danna Brown. adv. illus. circ. 11,000.

665.7 US ISSN 0362-4994
AMERICAN GAS ASSOCIATION. OPERATING SECTION. PROCEEDINGS. 1965. a. $10. American Gas Association, 1515 Wilson Blvd., Arlington, VA 22209. TEL 703-841-8400. illus. Indexed: Chem.Abstr. Gas Abstr. GeoRef. Key Title: Operating Section Proceedings.

338.47 665.74 US
AMERICAN GAS ASSOCIATION RATE SERVICE. 1919. a. $175 to non-members; members $150. American Gas Association, Financial and Administrative Section Services, 1515 Wilson Blvd., Arlington, VA 22209. TEL 703-841-8400. Ed. Sheila Rana. circ. 500. (looseleaf format)

025.3 665.5 US ISSN 0193-5151
AMERICAN PETROLEUM INSTITUTE. CENTRAL ABSTRACTING AND INDEXING SERVICE. THESAURUS. 1964. a. $150 ($50 to non-profit organizations) American Petroleum Institute, Central Abstracting and Indexing Service, 156 William St., New York, NY 10038. TEL 212-587-9660. Key Title: Thesaurus - American Petroleum Institute.
Continues: American Petroleum Institute. Information Retrieval System, Subject Authority List.

AMERICAN PETROLEUM INSTITUTE. HEALTH AND ENVIRONMENTAL SCIENCES DEPARTMENT. RESEARCH REPORTS. see PUBLIC HEALTH AND SAFETY

665.5 US ISSN 0163-495X
AMERICAN PETROLEUM INSTITUTE. REFINING DEPARTMENT. PROCEEDINGS. 1931. a. price varies. American Petroleum Institute, Refining Department, 1220 L St., N.W., Washington, DC 20005. TEL 202-682-7000. Ed. David H. Orgel. circ. 1,500. Indexed: Chem.Abstr. Alt.Press Ind.
Formerly: American Petroleum Institute. Division of Refining. Proceedings. (ISSN 0569-6909)

665.7 US ISSN 0066-149X
ANALYSES OF NATURAL GASES OF THE UNITED STATES. (Subseries of: Information Circular) 1917. a. price varies. U.S. Bureau of Mines, Dept. of the Interior, 4900 La Salle Rd., Avondale, MD 20782. TEL 301-436-8538.

ANNUAL BOOK OF A S T M STANDARDS. VOLUME 05.01. PETROLEUM PRODUCTS AND LUBRICANTS (1) see ENGINEERING — Engineering Mechanics And Materials

ANNUAL BOOK OF A S T M STANDARDS. VOLUME 05.02. PETROLEUM PRODUCTS AND LUBRICANTS (2) see ENGINEERING — Engineering Mechanics And Materials

ANNUAL BOOK OF A S T M STANDARDS. VOLUME 05.03. PETROLEUM PRODUCTS AND LUBRICANTS (3); CATALYSTS. see ENGINEERING — Engineering Mechanics And Materials

ANNUAL BOOK OF A S T M STANDARDS. VOLUME 05.05. GASEOUS FUELS; COAL AND COKE. see ENGINEERING — Engineering Mechanics And Materials

665.7 UN ISSN 0066-3824
ANNUAL BULLETIN OF GAS STATISTICS FOR EUROPE/BULLETIN ANNUEL DE STATISTIQUES DE GAZ POUR L'EUROPE. (Text in English, French and Russian) 1955. a., latest vol.29, 1983. price varies. Economic Commission for Europe (ECE), Palais des Nations, 1211 Geneva 10, Switzerland (Or United Nations Publications, Rm. DC2-853, New York, NY 10017)

PETROLEUM AND GAS

665.5   US
ANNUAL REVIEW OF CALIFORNIA-ALASKA OIL AND GAS EXPLORATION. 1944. a. $40. Munger Oil Information Service, Inc., 9800 S. Sepulveda Blvd., Ste. 723, Box 45738, Los Angeles, CA 90045. TEL 213-776-3990. Ed. Averill H. Munger. circ. 300.
    Formerly: Annual Review of California Oil and Gas Exploration.

338.2   FR
ARAB OIL & GAS DIRECTORY. (Text in English) 1974. a. $215. Arab Petroleum Research Center, 7 av. Ingres, 75781 Paris Cedex 16, France. Ed. Nicolas Sarkis. adv. illus. stat. circ. 5,250.

557   622   US
ARIZONA. OIL AND GAS CONSERVATION COMMISSION. REPORT OF INVESTIGATION. irreg., no.4, 1974. Oil and Gas Conservation Commission (El Dorado), c/o Dept. of Commerce, 314 E. Oak St., El Dorado, AR 71730. TEL 501-862-4965. Ed. Jack N. Conley. bibl. illus. stat. circ. 200. Indexed: GeoRef.

665   US   ISSN 0273-5229
ARMSTRONG OIL DIRECTORIES: ROCKY MOUNTAIN AND CENTRAL UNITED STATES. 1961. a. $30. Oil Men's Association of America, c/o Alan Armstrong, Ed., 1606 South Jackson St., Amarillo, TX 79102. TEL 806-374-1818.
    Former titles: Armstrong Oil Directory: Central United States; Hank Seale Oil Directory: Central United States (ISSN 0073-0238)

665   US   ISSN 0273-4931
ARMSTRONG OIL DIRECTORY: LOUISIANA, MISSISSIPPI, ARKANSAS, TEXAS GULF COAST AND EAST TEXAS. Variant title (1980): Armstrong Oil Directories: Louisiana, Texas Gulf Coast, East Texas, Arkansas and Mississippi. 1958. a. $30. Oil Men's Association of America, c/o Alan Armstrong, Ed., 1606 South Jackson St., Amarillo, TX 79102. TEL 806-374-1818.
    Formerly: Hank Seale Oil Directory: Louisiana, Mississippi, Arkansas, Texas Gulf Coast and East Texas (ISSN 0073-0254)

665   US
ARMSTRONG OIL DIRECTORY: TEXAS INCLUDING SOUTHEAST NEW MEXICO. 1957. a. $30. Oil Men's Association of America, c/o Alan Armstrong, Ed., 1606 South Jackson St., Amarillo, TX 79102. TEL 806-374-1818.
    Formerly: Hank Seale Oil Directory: Texas Including Southeast New Mexico (ISSN 0073-0262)

665.5   338.7   US   ISSN 0748-4089
ASIA-PACIFIC/AFRICA-MIDDLE EAST PETROLEUM. 1979. a. $120 sold only as a 2 volume set with European Petroleum Directory. PennWell Publishing Co., Box 1260, Tulsa, OK 74101. TEL 918-835-3161. Ed. William R. Leek, Jr. adv.
    Formerly: Asia-Pacific Petroleum Directory (ISSN 0270-1235); Incorporating (as of 1985): Africa-Middle East Petroleum Directory (ISSN 0197-7830); Which superseded in part: Eastern Hemisphere Petroleum Directory (ISSN 0070-8224)

665.5   551   US
ATLANTIC SUMMARY REPORT/INDEX. 1980. a. Outer Continental Shelf Information Program, Offshore Information Services, Minerals Management Service, 1951 Kidwell Dr., Vienna, VA 22180. TEL 703-285-2285. circ. 2,500.
    Formed by the 1985 merger of: Atlantic Index; Mid-Atlantic Summary Report; Atlantic Summary Report; Which was formerly (until 1983): South Atlantic Summary Report.

665.5   550   AT   ISSN 0817-9263
AUSTRALIA. BUREAU OF MINERAL RESOURCES. GEOLOGY AND GEOPHYSICS. AUSTRALIAN PETROLEUM ACCUMULATIONS REPORT. 1986. irreg. price varies. Bureau of Mineral Resources, Geology and Geophysics, G.P.O. Box 378, Canberra, A.C.T. 2601, Australia.

AUSTRALIAN CONFERENCE ON CHEMICAL ENGINEERING. PROCEEDINGS. see ENGINEERING — Chemical Engineering

696   AT   ISSN 0727-3541
AUSTRALIAN GAS INDUSTRY DIRECTORY. a. Aus.$10. Australian Gas Association, G.P.O. Box 323, Canberra, A.C.T. 2601, Australia. Ed. Eric D. Storr.
    Former titles: Directory of the Australian Gas Industry (ISSN 0706-666X); Australian Gas Association. Directory.

553   AT   ISSN 0314-3171
AUSTRALIAN INSTITUTE OF PETROLEUM. ANNUAL REPORT. 1977. a. free. Australian Institute of Petroleum, Ltd., 227 Collins St., Melbourne, Vic. 3000, Australia.

338.47   US
AUTOMOTIVE FUEL ECONOMY PROGRAM. ANNUAL REPORT TO THE CONGRESS. a. U.S. Department of Transportation, National Highway Traffic Safety Administration, Washington, DC 20590. TEL 202-655-4000.

338.2   UK
B P STATISTICAL REVIEW OF WORLD ENERGY. a. British Petroleum Co. p.l.c., Britannic House, Moor Lane, London EC2Y 9BU, England (U.S. dist.: BP North America Inc., 620 Fifth Ave., New York, NY 10020) circ. 40,000.
    Formerly: Statistical Review of the World Oil Industry (ISSN 0081-5039)

BRITISH COLUMBIA. MINISTRY OF ENERGY, MINES AND PETROLEUM RESOURCES. ANNUAL REPORT. see MINES AND MINING INDUSTRY

BRITISH COLUMBIA. MINISTRY OF ENERGY, MINES AND PETROLEUM RESOURCES. BULLETIN. see EARTH SCIENCES — Geology

665.7   UK   ISSN 0072-0216
BRITISH GAS CORPORATION. REPORT AND ACCOUNTS. 1948/50. a. free. British Gas Corporation, Rivermill House, 152 Grosvenor Rd., London SW1V 3JL, England. Ed. Richard Batson. circ. 20,000. (also avail. in microfilm)
    Formerly: Gas Council (Great Britain) Report and Accounts.

665.5   UK
BRITISH PUMP MARKET. 1981. biennial. £33.50. C H W Roles & Associates Ltd., Rawplug House, London Rd., Kingston upon Thames, Surrey KT2 6NH, England. Ed. Richard R.S. Tomes. adv.

662.6   UK
BRITOIL. ANNUAL REPORT. 1983. a. Britoil PLC, 150 St. Vincent St., Glasgow, G2 5LJ, Scotland. circ. 50,000.

665.7   US   ISSN 0197-8098
BROWN'S DIRECTORY OF NORTH AMERICAN AND INTERNATIONAL GAS COMPANIES. 1887. a. $145. Harcourt Brace Jovanovich, Inc., 7500 Old Oak Blvd., Cleveland, OH 44130 TEL 216-243-8100. (Subscr. to: One E. First St., Duluth, MN 55802) Ed. Dean Hale. adv. circ. 962.
    Formerly (until 1978): Brown's Directory of North American Gas Companies (ISSN 0068-2888)

662   627   UK   ISSN 0305-0122
BULK CARRIER REGISTER. 1969. a. $150. Clarkson Research Studies Ltd., 12 Camomile St., London EC3A 7BP, England. adv.

665.5   US   ISSN 0362-1243
CALIFORNIA. DIVISION OF OIL AND GAS. ANNUAL REPORT OF THE STATE OIL AND GAS SUPERVISOR. 1915. a. free. Divison of Oil and Gas, 1416 9th St., Sacramento, CA 95814. Ed. Susan Hodgson. illus. circ. 2,200. Indexed: GeoRef.

338.2   CN
CANADA. ENERGY, MINES AND RESOURCES CANADA. INDIAN AND NORTHERN AFFAIRS. CANADA OIL AND GAS LANDS ADMINISTRATION ANNUAL REPORT (YEAR) (Editions in English and French) 1965. a. free. Energy, Mines and Resources Canada, Indian And Northern Affairs Canada, 355 River Road, Ottawa, Ont. K1A 0E4, Canada. TEL 613-997-0380. bibl. charts. illus. stat. circ. 4,000. (tabloid format)
    Formerly: Canada. Department of Indian and Northern Affairs. Oil and Gas Land and Exploration Section. Oil and Gas Activities. North of 60.

622.33   CN   ISSN 0317-4085
CANADA. ENERGY, MINES AND RESOURCES CANADA. INDIAN AND NORTHERN AFFAIRS. CANADA OIL AND GAS LANDS ADMINISTRATION RELEASED GEOPHYSICAL/GEOLOGICAL DATA. irreg. free. Indian and Northern Affairs, 355 River Road, Ottawa, Ont. K1A 0E4, Canada. TEL 613-997-0380.
    Formerly: Canada. Northern Natural Resources and Environment Branch. Oil and Mineral Division. North of 60: Oil and Gas Technical Reports; Supersedes: Canada. Northern Economic Development Branch. Oil and Gas Technical Reports- North of 60.

CANADIAN GAS ASSOCIATION. STATISTICAL SUMMARY OF THE CANADIAN GAS INDUSTRY. see ENERGY

CANADIAN GAS ASSOCIATION DIRECTORY; utilities, transmission & production companies. see ENERGY

CANADIAN GAS FACTS. see ENERGY

CANADIAN NATIONAL ENERGY FORUM PROCEEDINGS. see ENERGY

CANADIAN OIL & GAS HANDBOOK. see MINES AND MINING INDUSTRY

665.5   VE
COLECCION LA ALQUITRANA. 1975. irreg., no.5, 1976. Ministerio de Energia y Minas, Torre Norte, Centro Simon Bolivar, Caracas, Venezuela (Subscr. to: Ministerio de Energia y Minas, Biblioteca, Torre Oeste, Parque Central Piso 2, Caracas-Venezuela) bibl.

665.5   333.91   UY
COMISION DE INTEGRACION ELECTRICA REGIONAL. RECURSOS ENERGETICOS DE LOS PAISES DE LA C I E R. (Text in Castilian, Portuguese) 1968. irreg. Comision de Integracion Electrica Regional, Bulevar Artigas 996, Montevideo, Uruguay. index.

COMITE DE CONTROLE DE L'ELECTRICITE ET DU GAZ. RAPPORT ANNUEL. see ELECTRICITY AND ELECTRICAL ENGINEERING

665.5   US
COMPOSITE CATALOG OF OIL FIELD EQUIPMENT & SERVICES. 1929. biennial. Gulf Publishing Co., Box 2608, Houston, TX 77001. TEL 713-529-4301. Ed. Robert Rust. adv. tr.lit. index. circ. 20,000. (reprint service avail. from UMI)

665.7   DK
DANISH OFFSHORE GUIDE AND YEARBOOK. 1983. a. Kr.175. Bjoerndal & Gundestrup A-S, Oestre Havnevej, 6700 Esbjerg, Denmark. Ed. Kurt Bjoerndal. adv. illus. circ. 7,500.
    Former titles: Danish Offshore Guide & Westcoast Offshore Guide (ISSN 0108-9161)

622   IS
DELEK. ANNUAL REPORT. (Text in English and Hebrew) a. free. Delek, Israel Fuel Corporation, 6 Ahuzat Bayit St, Tel Aviv, Israel.

665.5   NE
DEVELOPMENTS IN PETROLEUM SCIENCE. irreg., vol.20, 1985. Elsevier Science Publishers B.V., Box 211, 1000 AE Amsterdam, Netherlands. Indexed: Chem.Abstr.

662   UR
DINAMIKA IZLUCHAYUSCHEGO GAZA. 1974. irreg. 0.51 Rub. Akademiya Nauk S.S.S.R., Vychislitel'nyi Tsentr, Ul. Vavilova, 40, Moscow V-333, Russian S.F.S.R., U.S.S.R.

DIRECTORY OF CERTIFIED APPLIANCES AND ACCESSORIES. see ENERGY

DIRECTORY OF ELECTRIC LIGHT AND POWER COMPANIES. see ELECTRICITY AND ELECTRICAL ENGINEERING

665.5   US
DIRECTORY OF GAS UTILITY COMPANIES. a. $25. Midwest Oil Register, Inc., Box 700597, Tulsa, OK 74170. TEL 918-742-9925.

PETROLEUM AND GAS

665.7 US
DIRECTORY OF MUNICIPAL NATURAL GAS SYSTEMS. a. $10. American Public Gas Association, Box 1426, Vienna, VA 22180. TEL 703-281-2910. Ed. Carole Curtis. adv. circ. 750.

655.5 658.8 US ISSN 0070-5993
DIRECTORY OF OIL MARKETING AND WHOLESALE DISTRIBUTORS. 1945. a. $25. Midwest Oil Register, Inc., Box 700597, Tulsa, OK 74170. TEL 918-742-9925.

665.5 US ISSN 0415-9764
DIRECTORY OF OIL WELL DRILLING CONTRACTORS. a. $40. Midwest Oil Register, Inc., Box 700597, Tulsa, OK 74170. TEL 918-742-9925.

665.5 US ISSN 0415-9772
DIRECTORY OF OIL WELL SUPPLY COMPANIES. a. $40. Midwest Oil Register, Inc., Box 700597, Tulsa, OK 74170. TEL 918-742-9925.

380 US
DIRECTORY OF PRODUCERS AND DRILLING CONTRACTORS: CALIFORNIA. 1945. a. $10. Midwest Oil Register, Inc., Box 700597, Tulsa, OK 74105. TEL 918-742-9925.

380 US
DIRECTORY OF PRODUCERS AND DRILLING CONTRACTORS: KANSAS. 1945. a. $10. Midwest Oil Register, Inc., Box 700597, Tulsa, OK 74170. TEL 918-742-9925.

380 US
DIRECTORY OF PRODUCERS AND DRILLING CONTRACTORS: LOUISIANA, ARKANSAS, FLORIDA, GEORGIA. 1945. a. $15. Midwest Oil Register, Inc., Box 700597, Tulsa, OK 74105. TEL 918-742-9925.

380 US
DIRECTORY OF PRODUCERS AND DRILLING CONTRACTORS: MICHIGAN, INDIANA, ILLINOIS, KENTUCKY. 1945. a. $10. Midwest Oil Register, Inc., Box 700597, Tulsa, OK 74170. TEL 918-742-9925.

380 US
DIRECTORY OF PRODUCERS AND DRILLING CONTRACTORS: OKLAHOMA. 1945. a. $20. Midwest Oil Register, Inc., Box 700597, Tulsa, OK 74170. TEL 918-742-9925.

380 US
DIRECTORY OF PRODUCERS AND DRILLING CONTRACTORS: ROCKY MOUNTAIN REGION, WILLISTON BASIN, FOUR CORNERS NEW MEXICO. 1945. a. $15. Midwest Oil Register, Inc., Box 700597, Tulsa, OK 74170. TEL 918-742-9925.

380 US
DIRECTORY OF PRODUCERS AND DRILLING CONTRACTORS: TEXAS. 1945. a. $30. Midwest Oil Register, Inc., Box 700597, Tulsa, OK 74170. TEL 918-742-9925.

665.5 SP
ENCICLOPEDIA NACIONAL DEL PETROLEO PETROLQUIMICA Y GAS. 1970. a. 8000 ptas.($55) Oilgas S.A., Paseo de la Habana, 48, 28036 Madrid, Spain. Ed. Carlos Martin. circ. 6,000.

665.7 IT ISSN 0071-0687
ENTE NAZIONALE IDROCARBURI. REPORT AND STATEMENT OF ACCOUNTS.* a. Ente Nazionale Idrocarburi, Piazzale Enrico Mattei 1, 00144 Rome, Italy.

665.5 US ISSN 0275-3871
EUROPEAN PETROLEUM DIRECTORY. 1979. a. $120 sold only as a 2 volume set with Asia-Pacific/Africa-Middle East Directory. Pennwell Publishing Co., Box 1260, Tulsa, OK 74101. TEL 918-835-3161. Ed. William R. Leek, Jr. adv.
  Supersedes in part: Eastern Hemisphere Petroleum Directory (ISSN 0070-8224)

665.5 GW ISSN 0342-6947
EUROPEAN PETROLEUM YEARBOOK/JAHRBUCH DER EUROPAEISCHEN ERDOELINDUSTRIE/ANNUAIRE EUROPEEN DU PETROLE. Variant title: A N E P. (Text in English, French and German) 1963. a. DM.158. Otto Vieth Verlag in Urban-Verlag Hamburg-Wien GmbH, P.O. Box 701606, 2000 Hamburg 70, W. Germany (B.R.D.) Ed. Thomas Vieth. adv. circ. 3,000.

FACTS & FIGURES; a comparative statistical analysis. see *ENERGY*

665.5 US
FEDERAL COAL MANAGEMENT REPORT. 1977. a. U.S. Department of the Interior, Bureau of Land Management, Washington, DC 20240. TEL 202-655-4000. circ. 1,800.

665.5 UK ISSN 0141-3228
FINANCIAL TIMES INTERNATIONAL YEAR BOOKS: OIL AND GAS. 1910. a. £54. Longman Group Ltd., Fourth Ave., Harlow, Essex CM19 5AA, England (Dist. in U.S. and Canada by: Longman Group USA Inc., 500 North Dearborn St., Chicago, IL 60610)
  Formerly: Oil and Petroleum Year Book.

668 UK ISSN 0141-3236
FINANCIAL TIMES INTERNATIONAL YEAR BOOKS: WHO'S WHO IN WORLD OIL AND GAS. a. £32. Longman Group Ltd., Fourth Ave., Harlow, Essex CM19 5AA, England (Dist. in U.S. and Canada by: Longman Group USA Inc., 500 North Dearborn St., Chicago, IL 60610)

FOREIGN TRADE REPORTS. BUNKER FUELS. see *BUSINESS AND ECONOMICS — International Commerce*

665.5 VE
FRENTE NACIONAL PRO-DEFENSA DEL PETROLEO VENEZOLANO. ACTUACIONES. 1970. irreg. $5 per no. Frente Nacional Pro Defensa del Petroleo Venezolano, Apto. 50514, Caracas 105, Venezuela. circ. 3,000.

662 AT ISSN 0072-0208
GAS AND FUEL CORPORATION OF VICTORIA. ANNUAL REPORT. a. free. ‡ Gas and Fuel Corporation of Victoria, 171 Flinders St., Melbourne 3000, Vic., Australia. circ. 9,500.

665.7 UK ISSN 0307-3084
GAS DIRECTORY AND WHO'S WHO. 1896. a. £45. Benn Business Information Services Ltd., P.O. Box 20, Sovereign Way, Tonbridge, Kent TN9 1RQ, England. adv. index. circ. 1,187.
  Former titles: Gas Directory and Undertakings of the World; Incorporating: Gas Journal Directory (ISSN 0072-0240); Gas Industry Directory (ISSN 0072-0232); Who's Who in the Gas Industry (ISSN 0083-9779)

665 US
GAS FACTS; a statistical record of the gas utility industry. 1946. a. $35 to non-members; members $25. American Gas Association, Department of Statistics, 1515 Wilson Blvd, Arlington, VA 22209. TEL 703-841-8400. circ. 3,000.

665.7 UK ISSN 0072-0259
GAS MARKETING POCKET BOOK AND DIARY. 1972. a. £3. Benn Publications Ltd., Sovereign Way, Tonbridge, Kent TN9 1RW, England. Ed. G. Battison. circ. 8,500.
  Formerly: Gas Services Pocket Book.

665.5 US ISSN 0096-8870
GAS PROCESSORS ASSOCIATION. ANNUAL CONVENTION. PROCEEDINGS.* Title varies: Natural Gas Processors Association. Annual Convention. Proceedings. 1921. a. price varies. Gas Processors Association, 6526 E. 60th, Tulsa, OK 74145-9202. TEL 918-582-5112. circ. 5,000. Indexed: Chem.Abstr. Fuel & Energy Abstr. Gas Abstr.

665.5 US ISSN 0016-4976
GAS SCOPE. 1964. irreg. free. Institute of Gas Technology, 3424 S. State St., Chicago, IL 60616. TEL 312-567-3650. Ed. Colleen Taylor Sen. illus. circ. 9,000.

662 FR ISSN 0072-0321
GAZ DE FRANCE. SECRETARIAT GENERAL. SCHEMA D'ORGANISATION PROFOR.* 1966. a. Gaz de France, Departement Profor, 5 Av. de Friedland, 75008 Paris, France.

338.8 531.6 UK
GREAT BRITAIN. DEPARTMENT OF ENERGY. DEVELOPMENT OF THE OIL AND GAS RESOURCES OF THE UNITED KINGDOM. a. Department of Energy, Thames House South, Millbank, London SW1P 4QJ, England (Avail. from: H.M.S.O., P.O. Box 276, London SW8 5DT, England) illus.

665.5 US
GUIA PETROLERA DE EQUIPOS SERVICIOS. 1980. every 18 mos. Pennwell Publishing Co., 1421 S. Sheridan Rd., Box 1260, Tulsa, OK 74101. TEL 918-835-3161. adv.
  Formerly: Guia del Equipo Petrolero.

GUIDE TO U S G S GEOLOGIC AND HYDROLOGIC MAPS. see *EARTH SCIENCES*

665 US
GULF OF MEXICO SUMARY REPORT/INDEX. 1980. a. free. Outer Continental Shelf Information Program, Offshore Information Services, Minerals Management Service, 1951 Kidwell Dr., Vienna, VA 22180. TEL 703-285-2285. circ. 2,500.
  Formed by the merger of: Gulf of Mexico Index & Gulf of Mexico Summary Report.

338.2 US ISSN 0073-2656
HISTORICAL STATISTICS OF THE GAS INDUSTRY. 1956. irreg. $15. American Gas Association, Department of Statistics, 1515 Wilson Blvd., Arlington, VA 22209. TEL 703-841-8400. circ. 1,000.

665.5 US
HYDROCARBON PROCESSING CATALOG AND DIRECTORY. 1929. a. Gulf Publishing Co., Box 2608, Houston, TX 77001. TEL 713-529-4301.
  Formerly: Hydrocarbon Processing Catalog.

665.5 US
ILLINOIS PETROLEUM. 1926. irreg., no.127, 1986. price varies. ‡ State Geological Survey, Natural Resources Bldg., 615 E. Peabody Dr., Champaign, IL 61820. TEL 217-344-1481. abstr. bibl. charts. illus. stat. circ. 3,100. Indexed: Geo.Abstr. GeoRef. Petrol.Abstr.

338.7 II
INDO-BURMA PETROLEUM COMPANY. ANNUAL REPORT. (Text in English) a. Indo-Burma Petroleum Company, Gillander House, Netaji Subhas Rd., Box 952, Calcutta 700 001, India. stat.

665.5 IT ISSN 0073-7275
INDUSTRIA DEL PETROLIO IN ITALIA. a. Direzione Generale delle Fonti di Energia e Industrie di Base, Via Molise 2, 00187 Rome, Italy. charts. stat.

665.5 338.2 MX
INDUSTRIA PETROLERA EN MEXICO. 1980. irreg. price varies. Instituto Nacional de Estadistica, Geografia e Informatica, Secretaria de Programacion y Presupuesto, Patriotismo 711 Torre "A" P.H., Col. San Juan Mixcoac, Deleg. Benito Juarez, 03910 Mexico, D.F., Mexico TEL 598-99-05. (Subscr. to: Rio Rhin No. 56, Col. Cuauhtemoc, 06500 Mexico, D.F., Mexico)

665.5 FR ISSN 0073-8360
INSTITUT FRANCAIS DU PETROLE. COLLECTION COLLOQUES ET SEMINAIRES. 1964. irreg., vol.44, 1986. price varies. Editions Technip, 27 rue Ginoux, 75737 Paris Cedex 15, France. circ. 1,250. Indexed: Bull.Signal. Chem.Abstr. Geophys.Abstr. Petrol.Abstr.

665.5 FR ISSN 0073-8379
INSTITUT FRANCAIS DU PETROLE. RAPPORT ANNUEL. 1963. a. free. Institut Francais du Petrole (IFP), 1 et 4 av. de Bois-Preau, B.P. No. 311, 92506 Rueil-Malmaison Cedex, France. circ. 8,000. Indexed: Ocean.Abstr. Petrol.Abstr.

665.5 551 IS ISSN 0073-8832
INSTITUTE FOR PETROLEUM RESEARCH AND GEOPHYSICS, HOLON, ISRAEL. REPORT. irreg. Institute for Petroleum Research and Geophysics, Box 1717, Holon, Israel.

665.5 UK
INSTITUTE OF ENERGY. NORTHERN IRELAND SECTION. YEAR BOOK. 1970. a. £2. Institute of Fuel, Northern Ireland Section, 3 Clarence St. W., Belfast, N. Ireland. Ed. F.R. McBride. circ. 1,200.
Formerly: Institute of Fuel. Northern Ireland Section. Year Book.

665.5 UK
INSTITUTE OF ENERGY. PAPERS OF THE NATIONAL CONVENTION. 1972. a. £12($29.50) Institute of Energy, 18 Devonshire St., London W1N 2AU, England.
Formerly: Institute of Fuel. Papers of the National Convention.

INSTITUTE OF ENERGY. REPORT AND ACCOUNTS. see ENERGY

662 US
INSTITUTE OF GAS TECHNOLOGY. ANNUAL REPORT. a. free. Institute of Gas Technology, 3424 S. State St., Chicago, IL 60616. TEL 312-567-3650. Ed. Colleen Taylor Sen. stat.
Formerly: Institute of Gas Technology. Director's Report.

665.5 622 553.28 PL ISSN 0032-6232
INSTYTUT NAFTOWY. PRACE. (Summaries in English, French, and Russian) 1950. irreg. (5-7/yr.) price varies. Wydawnictwo "Slask", Ul. Armii Czerwonej 51, 40-156 Katowice, Poland. (Co-sponsor: Ministerstwo Gornictwa i Energetyki) Ed. Jozef Gumulczynski. charts. illus. circ. 1,000. (also avail. in microfilm) Indexed: Chem.Abstr.

INTERNATIONAL BUSINESS OPPORTUNITIES. OIL & GAS IN AFRICA. see ENERGY

INTERNATIONAL BUSINESS OPPORTUNITIES. OIL & GAS IN THE MIDDLE EAST. see ENERGY

665.7 US
INTERNATIONAL CONFERENCE ON LIQUEFIED NATURAL GAS. PAPERS. (Papers in English, some in French; abstracts in English and French) 1968. irreg. $85 for 1986 edt. ‡ Institute of Gas Technology, 3424 South State St., Chicago, IL 60616. TEL 312-567-3650. (Co-sponsors: International Gas Union; International Institute of Refrigeration) Ed. Bonnie Feingold. Indexed: Chem.Abstr. Gas Abstr.
Formerly: International Conference on Liquefied Natural Gas. Proceedings (ISSN 0538-611X)

665.5 US ISSN 0736-5721
INTERNATIONAL GAS RESEARCH CONFERENCE. PROCEEDINGS. 1980. a. $59. (Gas Research Institute) Government Institutes, Inc., 966 Hungerford Dr., No. 24, Rockville, MD 20850. Indexed: Chem.Abstr.

338.39 FR
INTERNATIONAL GAS UNION. PROCEEDINGS OF WORLD GAS CONFERENCES. (Text in English and French) 1931. triennial, 1985, 16th, Munich. International Gas Union - Union Internationale de l'Industrie du Gaz, 62 rue de Courcelles, 75008 Paris, France. Ed. B. Goudal, Gen.Sec.
Formerly: International Gas Union. Proceedings of Conferences (ISSN 0074-6126)

665.5 US
INTERNATIONAL OIL AND GAS DEVELOPMENT YEARBOOK. 1930. a. price varies. International Oil Scouts Association, Box 272949, Houston, TX 77277-2949. circ. 1,500. (back issues avail.)

INTERNATIONAL OIL SCOUTS ASSOCIATION DIRECTORY. see BUSINESS AND ECONOMICS — Trade And Industrial Directories

665.5 US ISSN 0148-0375
INTERNATIONAL PETROLEUM ENCYCLOPEDIA. 1968. a. $75. PennWell Publishing Co., P.O. Box 1260, Tulsa, OK 74101. TEL 918-835-3161. Ed. John C. McCaslin. adv.

338.47 US
INTERSTATE OIL COMPACT COMMISSION ANNUAL REPORT. 1974. a. Interstate Oil Compact Commission, Box 53127, Oklahoma City, OK 73152. TEL 405-525-3556.

665.5 UR ISSN 0202-7429
ITOGI NAUKI I TEKHNIKI: RAZRABOTKA NEFTYANYKH I GAZOVYKH MESTOROZHDENII. irreg., latest vol.19, 1987. price varies. Vsesoyuznyi Institut Nauchno-Tekhnicheskoi Informatsii (VINITI), Baltiiskaya ul. 14, Moscow A-219, Russian S.F.S.R., U.S.S.R. (Subscr. to: Mezhdunarodnaya Kniga, Dimitrova ul. 39, 113095 Moscow, Russian S.F.S.R., U.S.S.R.)

665.5 NE
JAARBOEK VAN DE OPENBARE GASVOORZIENING. 1971. a. fl.30. Vereniging van Exploitanten van Gasbedrijven in Nederland, Postbus 137, 7300 AC Apeldoorn, Netherlands. (Co-sponsor: VEG-Gasinstituut N.V.) circ. 2,000.

665.5 JA
JAPAN PETROLEUM INDUSTRY YEARBOOK. (Text in English) 1983. a. $180. Japan International Consultants, Ltd., 2-5-19, Sekimae, Musahinoshi, Tokyo 180, Japan. Ed. John Victor Gano. circ. 500.

547 YU
JUGOPETROL, TRGOVINSKO PREDUZECE ZA PROMET NAFTE I NAFTINIH DERIVATA. BILTEN. 1972. irreg. Jugopetrol, 23. Oktobar 27, Novi Sad, Yugoslavia. Ed. Sava Vrbaski.

662 HU ISSN 0075-6962
KOSZEN ES KOOLAJ ANYAGISMERETI MONOGRAFIAK. 1964. irreg. price varies. (Magyar Tudomanyos Akademia) Akademiai Kiado, Publishing House of the Hungarian Academy of Sciences, P.O. Box 24, H-1363 Budapest, Hungary.

KYUSHU UNIVERSITY. DEPARTMENT OF GEOLOGY. SCIENCE REPORTS/KYUSHU DAIGAKU RIGAKUBU KENKYU HOKOKU CHISHITSUGAKU. see EARTH SCIENCES — Geology

665.7 338.39 US ISSN 0075-9759
L P-GAS MARKET FACTS; statistical handbook of the LP-gas industry. 1950. a. $6. ‡ National L P-Gas Association, Statistical and Market Research Committee, 1301 W. 22nd St., Oak Brook, IL 60521. Ed. W.H. Butterbaugh. index. circ. 2,000.

338.47 US ISSN 0539-2063
LEGAL REPORT OF OIL AND GAS CONSERVATION ACTIVITIES. a. Interstate Oil Compact Commission, Box 53127, Oklahoma City, OK 73152. TEL 405-525-3556.

662 627 UK ISSN 0305-1803
LIQUID GAS CARRIER REGISTER. 1966. a. $90. Clarkson Research Studies Ltd., 12 Camomile St., London EC3A 7BP, England.

665 HU
MAGYAR OLAJIPARI MUZEUM. EVKONYV. 1974. a. Magyar Olajipari Muzeum, Zalaegerszeg, Hungary. illus.

665.7 US ISSN 0085-3429
MICHIGAN'S OIL AND GAS FIELDS: ANNUAL STATISTICAL SUMMARY. 1964. a. $2. Department of Natural Resources, Geological Survey Division, Information Services Center, Box 30028, Lansing, MI 48909. TEL 517-373-1256.

353.9 US ISSN 0095-3024
MINNESOTA. DEPARTMENT OF REVENUE. PETROLEUM DIVISION. ANNUAL REPORT. 1973. a. Department of Revenue, Petroleum Division, Centennial Office Bldg., St. Paul, MN 55145. TEL 612-296-3781. Key Title: Annual Report - Petroleum Division.

665.5 MR
MOROCCO. MINISTERE DE L'ENERGIE ET DES MINES. ACTIVITE DU SECTEUR PETROLIER. (Text in French) 1956. irreg. $10. Direction des Mines et de la Geologie, Direction de l'Energie, Rabat, Morocco. stat.
Formerly: Morocco. Direction des Mines et de la Geologie. Activite du Secteur Petrolier.

655.5 US
N P N FACTBOOK. (National Petroleum News) a. $35. Hunter Publishing Co., Inc., 950 Lee St., Des Plaines, IL 60016. TEL 312-296-0770. stat.

NATIONAL STRIPPER WELL SURVEY. see ENERGY

NATURAL GAS ANNUAL. see ENERGY

665.5 UR
NEFTEGAZONOSNYE I PERSPEKTIVNYE KOMPLEKSY TSENTRAL'NYKH I VOSTOCHNYKH OBLASTEI RUSSKOI PLATFORMY. (Subseries of: Vsesoyuznyi Nauchno-Issledovatel'skii Geologorazvedochnyi Neftyanoi Institut. Trudy) irreg. 1.65 Rub. per issue. (Vsesoyuznyi Nauchno-Issledovatel'skii Geologorazvedochnyi Neftyanoi Institut) Izdatel'stvo Nedra, Tretyakovskii proezd, 1, Moscow K-12, Russian S.F.S.R., U.S.S.R. illus.

NEFTENA I VUGLISTNA GEOLOGIIA/ PETROLEUM AND COAL GEOLOGY. see EARTH SCIENCES — Geology

665.5 NO
NORSK PETROLEUMSFORENING. AARBOK/ NORWEGIAN PETROLEUM SOCIETY. YEARBOOK. (Text in Norwegian) 1979. a. (Norsk Petroleumsforening) Norwegian Information Publishers A-S, P.O. Box 873, Sentrum, Oslo 1, Norway.

665.5 UK ISSN 0265-5039
NORTH SEA OIL & GAS DIRECTORY. 1972. a. £39.95($65) Spearhead Publications Ltd., 55/59 Fife Rd., Kingston-upon-Thames, Surrey, KT1 1TA, England. Ed. Judith Patten. adv. circ. 3,500.

338.4 NO
NORWEGIAN OFFSHORE INDEX. (Text in English) 1974. a. contr. free circ. abroad. (Export Council of Norway) Selvig Publishing A-S, Box 9070 Vaterland, 0134 Oslo 1, Norway. (Co-sponsor: Federation of Norwegian Industries)

338.47 011 KU
O A P E C ENERGY BIBLIOGRAPHY. (Text in Arabic and English) 1977. a. free. Organization of Arab Petroleum Exporting Countries, P.O. Box 20501, Safat, Kuwait.

338.47 011 KU
O A P E C LIBRARY INDEX. (Text in Arabic) 1982. s-a. free. Organization of Arab Petroleum Exporting Countries, P.O. Box 20501, Safat, Kuwait.

338.47 KU
O A P E C LIBRARY PERIODICALS HOLDINGS. (Text in Arabic and English) 1977. irreg. $24. Organization of Arab Petroleum Exporting countries, P.O. Box 20501, Safat, Kuwait.

665.7 US
OFFSHORE CONTRACTORS AND EQUIPMENT WORLDWIDE DIRECTORY. 1969. a. $85. PennWell Publishing Co., Box 1260, Tulsa, OK 74101. TEL 918-835-3161. Ed. Robert M. Wilkerson. adv.
Former titles: Offshore Contractors and Equipment Directory (ISSN 0475-1310); Worldwide Offshore Contractors Directory (ISSN 0084-2575)

662 627 UK ISSN 0309-040X
OFFSHORE SERVICE VESSEL REGISTER. 1977. a. $150. Clarkson Research Studies Ltd., 12 Camomile St., London EC3A 7BP, England. adv.

OFFSHORE SERVICE VESSELS; guide to the American fleet. see TRANSPORTATION — Ships And Shipping

OFFSHORE TUGS; guide to the American fleet. see TRANSPORTATION — Ships And Shipping

330.9 665.5 KU
OIL AND ARAB COOPERATION. ANNUAL REVIEW. a. $10. Organization of Arab Petroleum Exporting Countries, Box 20501, Kuwait.
Formerly: Petroleum and Arab Economic Development.

338.2 US ISSN 0471-380X
OIL & GAS DIRECTORY. 1970/71. a. $40. ‡ Geophysical Directory, Inc., 2200 Welch Ave., Box 13508, Houston, TX 77019. TEL 713-529-8789. Ed. Claudia La Calli. adv. circ. 3,500.

338.47   US   ISSN 0747-2528
OIL & GAS PRODUCING INDUSTRY IN YOUR STATE. 1939. a. $23.50 (for 2 yrs; includes Petroleum Independent Magazine) ‡ (Independent Petroleum Association of America) Petroleum Independent Publishers, Inc., 1101 16th St., N.W., Washington, DC 20036. TEL 202-857-4775. Ed. Deborah Rowell. adv. charts. illus. stat. circ. 20,000.
Formerly: Oil Producing Industry in Your State.

665.5   UK
OIL AND OIL FIELD EQUIPMENT & SERVICE COMPANIES WORLDWIDE. 1985. a. £48. E. & F.N. Spon Ltd., 11 New Fetter Ln., London EC4P 4EE, England.
Formerly: Oil and Gas Industry (ISSN 0265-640X)

665.5   US   ISSN 0474-0114
OIL DIRECTORY OF CANADA. a. $20. Midwest Oil Register, Inc., Box 700597, Tulsa, OK 74170. TEL 918-742-9925.

665.5   US   ISSN 0472-7711
OIL DIRECTORY OF COMPANIES OUTSIDE THE U.S. AND CANADA. a. $20. Midwest Oil Register, Inc., Box 700597, Tulsa, OK 74170. TEL 918-742-9925.

665.5 338.2   US   ISSN 0471-3877
OIL DIRECTORY OF HOUSTON, TEXAS. a. $15. Midwest Oil Register, Inc., Box 700597, Tulsa, OK 74170. TEL 918-742-9925.

662   US
OIL PRICE DATABOOK. irreg., latest 1981. Oil Buyers' Guide, Box 998, Lakewood, NJ 08701. TEL 201-367-1600.

OIL SHALE SYMPOSIUM PROCEEDINGS. see MINES AND MINING INDUSTRY

OILS, LUBRICANTS, AND PETROLEUM PRODUCTS. see ENGINEERING — Hydraulic Engineering

338.47   DK   ISSN 0109-3916
OLIEBERETNING. 1979. a. free. Oliebranchens Faellesrepraesentation, Amaliegade 10, 1256 Copenhagen K, Denmark. illus.
Formerly: Oliebranchens Faellesrepraesentation. Beretning.

338.2   CN
ONTARIO. MINISTRY OF NATURAL RESOURCES. PETROLEUM RESOURCES LAB. DRILLING AND PRODUCTION REPORT, OIL AND NATURAL GAS. 1965. a. price varies. Ministry of Natural Resources, Petroleum Resources Lab, Parliament Bldgs., Toronto, Ont. M7A 1W3, Canada. TEL 416-965-2000. circ. 650.
Formerly: Ontario. Ministry of Natural Resources. Petroleum Resources Branch. Drilling and Production Report, Oil and Natural Gas (ISSN 0078-5059)

553   US   ISSN 0078-5741
OREGON. STATE DEPARTMENT OF GEOLOGY AND MINERAL INDUSTRIES. OIL AND GAS INVESTIGATIONS. 1963. irreg., no. 14, 1985. price varies. Department of Geology and Mineral Industries, 910 State Office Building, Portland, OR 97201. TEL 503-229-5580.

338.2 665.5   FR   ISSN 0474-6007
ORGANIZATION FOR ECONOMIC COOPERATION AND DEVELOPMENT. SPECIAL COMMITTEE FOR OIL. OIL STATISTICS. SUPPLY AND DISPOSAL. (Text in English and French) 1961. irreg. $13. Organization for Economic Cooperation and Development, 2 rue Andre Pascal, 75775 Paris 16, France (U. S. orders to: O.E.C.D. Publications and Information Center; 1750 Pennsylvania Ave., N. W., Washington, D. C. 20006) (also avail. in microfiche)

665.5   KU
ORGANIZATION OF ARAB PETROLEUM EXPORTING COUNTRIES. ANNUAL ENERGY REPORT. a. $4. Organization of Arab Petroleum Exporting Countries, Box 20501, Safat, Kuwait.

665.2 338.2   KU
ORGANIZATION OF ARAB PETROLEUM EXPORTING COUNTRIES. ANNUAL STATISTICAL REPORT. 1974. a. $12. Organization of Arab Petroleum Exporting Countries, Box 20501, Safat, Kuwait. circ. 1,500.

341.7   KU
ORGANIZATION OF ARAB PETROLEUM EXPORTING COUNTRIES. SECRETARY GENERAL'S ANNUAL REPORT. 1974. a. free. Organization of Arab Petroleum Exporting Countries, Box 20501, Safat, Kuwait. charts. stat. circ. 2,500.

338.2 665.5   AU
ORGANIZATION OF THE PETROLEUM EXPORTING COUNTRIES. ANNUAL REPORT. 1967. a. Organization of the Petroleum Exporting Countries, Public Information Department, Obere-Donaustr. 93, A-1020 Vienna, Austria.
Formerly: Organization of the Petroleum Exporting Countries. Annual Review and Record (ISSN 0474-6317)

338.2 665.5   AU   ISSN 0475-0608
ORGANIZATION OF THE PETROLEUM EXPORTING COUNTRIES. ANNUAL STATISTICAL BULLETIN. 1965. a. price varies. Organization of the Petroleum Exporting Countries, Public Information Department, Obere-Donaustr. 93, A-1020 Vienna, Austria.

665   US
PACIFIC SUMMARY REPORT/INDEX. 1980. a. free. Outer Continental Shelf Information Program, Offshore Information Services, Minerals Management Service, 1951 Kidwell Dr., Vienna, VA 22180. TEL 703-285-2285. circ. 2,500.
Formed by the merger of: Pacific Index & Pacific Summary Report.

665   PK   ISSN 0552-9115
PAKISTAN PETROLEUM LIMITED. ANNUAL REPORT. (Text in English) 1952. a. $6. (Pakistan Petroleum Ltd.) Pakistan Petroleum Ltd., PIDC House, Dr. Ziauddin Ahmad Rd., Karachi 4, Pakistan. Ed. Ahsan Halim. circ. 5,000.

665.5   BL
PETROBRAS. CONSOLIDATED REPORT. (Text in English) a. Petroleo Brasileiro S.A., Servico de Relacoes Publicas, Av. Republica do Chile, 65 S-2056, Rio de Janeiro RJ, Brazil. charts. illus. stat.

665.5   FR   ISSN 0069-6552
PETROLE (YEAR); activite de l'industrie petroliere. 1950. a. 615 F. Comite Professionnel du Petrole, 51 bd. de Courcelles, 75008 Paris, France.

665.5   BL
PETROLEO E GAS. irreg. Shell Brasil, S.A., Av. Rio Branco 109, Rio de Janeiro, Brazil. illus.

PETROLEUM AND CHEMICAL INDUSTRY CONFERENCE. RECORD OF CONFERENCE PAPERS. see ENGINEERING — Chemical Engineering

665.5   US
PETROLEUM EQUIPMENT DIRECTORY. 1955. a. $15. Petroleum Equipment Institute, Box 2380, Tulsa, OK 74101. TEL 918-743-9941. Ed. Robert N. Renkes. adv. circ. 3,000.

665.5 552   CH
PETROLEUM GEOLOGY OF TAIWAN/T'AIWAN SHIH YU TI CHIH. (Text in English) 1962. a. Chinese Petroleum Corporation, Exploration Division, 46 Chung Cheng Rd., Miaoli, Taiwan, Republic of China. Indexed: GeoRef.

665.5   US
PETROLEUM INDUSTRY IN ILLINOIS. (Subseries of: Illinois Petroleum) 1933. a. $1.25 per no. State Geological Survey, Natural Resources Bldg., 615 E. Peabody Dr., Champaign, IL 61820. TEL 217-344-1481. stat. (back issues avail.)

665.5   JA
PETROLEUM INDUSTRY IN JAPAN. (Text in English) 1955. a. membership. World Petroleum Congress, Japanese National Committee - Sekai Sekiyu Kaigi Nihon Kokunai Iinkai, Kasahara Bldg., 1-6-10 Uchi Kanda, Chiyoda-ku, Tokyo 101, Japan. stat.

665.5 918   US
PETROLEUM: LATIN AMERICAN INDUTRIAL REPORT. (Avail. for each of 22 Latin American countries) 1985. a. $435 per country report per industry covered. Aurora International, Box 9099, Bridgeport, CT 06601-2099. TEL 203-368-0579. Ed. Andres C. Aquino.

662   US
PETROLEUM MARKETER'S HANDBOOK. irreg. $69. Oil Buyer's Guide, Box 998, Lakewood, NJ 08701. TEL 201-367-1600.

PETROLEUM SOFTWARE DIRECTORY. see COMPUTERS — Software

665.54   US
PIPE LINE & PIPE LINE CONTRACTORS. a. $25. Midwest Oil Register, Inc., Box 700597, Tulsa, OK 74171. TEL 918-742-9925.

665.5   US
PIPE LINE ANNUAL DIRECTORY OF PIPELINES. 1928. a. $30. Oildom Publishing Co., 3314 Mercer St., Houston, TX 77027. TEL 713-622-0676. Ed. Oliver Klinger, Jr. adv. stat. circ. 13,200.

665.5   US
PIPELINE ANNUAL DIRECTORY. 1950. a. $30. Oildom Publishing Company, 3314 Mercer, Houston, TX 77027. TEL 713-622-0676. Ed. Oliver Klinger. adv. circ. 13,000.

665.5   US
PIPELINE CONTRACTORS DIRECTORY. a. $30. Oildom Publishing Co., 3314 Mercer, Houston, TX 77027. Ed. Oliver Klinger. adv.

553   UR
PRIRODNYI GAZ SIBIRI. 1969. irreg. Vsesoyuznyi Nauchno-Issledovatelskii Institut Prirodnykh Gazov, Tyumenskii Filial, Tyumen, Russian S.F.S.R., U.S.S.R. illus.

665.53   US
REFINING, CONSTRUCTION, PETROCHEMICAL & NATURAL GAS PROCESSING PLANTS OF THE WORLD. a. $30. Midwest Oil Register, Inc., Box 700597, Tulsa, OK 74170. TEL 918-742-9925.

665.5   US   ISSN 0190-8715
REPORTS ON RESEARCH ASSISTED BY THE PETROLEUM RESEARCH FUND. a. American Chemical Society, 1155 16th St., N.W., Washington, DC 20036. TEL 202-872-4600.
Formerly: American Chemical Society. Reports of Research Supported By The Petroleum Research Fund.

622.338   US   ISSN 0270-7527
RESUME (DENVER); a review of oil and gas activity in the United States. a. Petroleum Information Corp., 4100 E. Dry Creek Rd., Littleton, CO 80122. TEL 303-740-7100.

SASKATCHEWAN ENERGY & MINES. ANNUAL REPORT. see MINES AND MINING INDUSTRY

SASKATCHEWAN ENERGY AND MINES. MINERAL STATISTICS YEARBOOK. see MINES AND MINING INDUSTRY

553 665   CN
SASKATCHEWAN ENERGY & MINES. PETROLEUM AND NATURAL GAS RESERVOIR ANNUAL. 1963. a. Can.$60. ‡ Saskatchewan Energy & Mines, 1914 Hamilton St., Regina, Sask. S4P 4V4, Canada. TEL 306-787-2528.
Former titles: Saskatchewan Mineral Resources. Petroleum and Natural Gas Reservoir Annual (ISSN 0707-2562); Saskatchewan. Department of Mineral Resources. Petroleum and Natural Gas Reservoir Annual.

338.7   CN
SASKOIL. ANNUAL REPORT. 1974. a. free. Saskatchewan Oil and Gas Corporation, 1945 Hamilton St., Box 1550, Regina, Sask. S4P 3C4, Canada. TEL 306-781-8200. Ed.Bd. charts. illus. circ. 15,000.
Formerly: Saskatchewan Oil and Gas Corporation. Annual Report.

SCHEDULE OF WELLS DRILLED FOR OIL AND GAS IN ALBERTA. see ENERGY

665.5 UK
SCOTTISH PETROLEUM ANNUAL. 1982. a. £8.50($12) Aberdeen Petroleum Publishing Ltd., 37 Huntly St., Aberdeen AB1 1TH, Scotland. Ed. Ted Strachan. adv.

665.5 AU ISSN 0080-858X
SELECTED DOCUMENTS OF THE INTERNATIONAL PETROLEUM INDUSTRY. 1966. a. price varies. Organization of the Petroleum Exporting Countries, Public Information Department, Obere-Donaustr. 93, A-1020 Vienna, Austria.

665.5 FR
SOCIETE NATIONALE ELF AQUITAINE. RAPPORT ANNUEL. a. free. Societe Nationale Elf Aquitaine, Direction des Relations Publiques et de la Communication, Tour Elf, Cedex 45, 92078 Paris La Defense, France. charts. illus. stat.

665.5 622 US
SOCIETY OF PETROLEUM ENGINEERS. REPRINT SERIES. 1958. irreg. price varies. Society of Petroleum Engineers, Inc., Box 833836, Richardson, TX 75083-3836. TEL 214-659-3377. Ed. Jim McInnis. Indexed: Eng.Ind. Ocean.Abstr.
Formerly: Society of Petroleum Engineers of American Institute of Mining, Metallurgical and Petroleum Engineers. Petroleum Transactions Reprint Series (ISSN 0081-1688)

665.5 US ISSN 0081-1696
SOCIETY OF PETROLEUM ENGINEERS. TRANSACTIONS. 1925. a. $70 to non-members. Society of Petroleum Engineers, Inc., Box 833836, Richardson, TX 75083-3836. TEL 214-669-3377. Ed. Jim McInnis. charts. illus. index. circ. 5,000. (back issues avail.) Indexed: Chem.Abstr. Eng.Ind. Gas Abstr. GeoRef. Petrol.Abstr.
Formerly: Society of Petroleum Engineers of American Institute of Mining, Metallurgical and Petroleum Engineers. Transactions.

622.338 US ISSN 0081-1718
SOCIETY OF PROFESSIONAL WELL LOGGING ANALYSTS. S P W L A ANNUAL LOGGING SYMPOSIUM TRANSACTIONS. 1960. a. price varies. Society of Professional Well Log Analysts, 6001 Gulf Frwy, Ste. C 129, Houston, TX 77023. adv. bibl. charts. illus. circ. 2,500. (also avail. in microfiche) Indexed: GeoRef. Petrol.Abstr.

665.5 SP
SPAIN. MINISTERIO DE ECONOMIA Y HACIENDA. DELEGACION DEL GOBIERNO EN CAMPSA. MEMORIA. 1969. a. free. Ministerio de Economia y Hacienda, Delegacion del Gobierno en Campsa, Capitan Haya, 41, 28020 Madrid, Spain. Ed. F. Hevia. illus. circ. 2,000.
Petroleum industry and trade

665.7 NE ISSN 0081-5225
STATISTIEK VAN DE GASVOORZIENING IN NEDERLAND. 1953. a. fl.12.50. Centraal Bureau voor de Statistiek, Prinses Beatrixlaan 428, Voorburg, Netherlands (Orders to: Staatsuitgeverij, Christoffel Plantijnstraat, The Hague, Netherlands) circ. 375.

338.4 FR
STATISTIQUES DE L'INDUSTRIE GAZIERE EN FRANCE. irreg. Direction du Gaz, de l'Electricite et du Charbon, 3-5 Rue Barbet de Jouy, 75700 Paris, France. illus.
Continues: France. Direction du Gaz et de l'Electricite. Statistiques Officielles de l'Industrie Gaziere en France (ISSN 0429-3843)

STEAM-ELECTRIC PLANT FACTORS (1978) see *MINES AND MINING INDUSTRY*

STEELMAKING CONFERENCE: PROCEEDINGS. see *MINES AND MINING INDUSTRY*

STRATHCLYDE OIL REGISTER. see *BUSINESS AND ECONOMICS — Trade And Industrial Directories*

665.54 US
SYNTHETIC PIPELINE GAS SYMPOSIUM. PROCEEDINGS. vol.7, 1975. irreg. $50 for latest issue. American Gas Association, 1515 Wilson Blvd., Arlington, VA 22209. TEL 703-841-8400. (Co-sponsors: U.S. Energy Research; Development Administration; International Gas Union)
Pipes

662 627 UK ISSN 0305-179X
TANKER REGISTER. 1960. a. $150. Clarkson Research Studies Ltd., 12 Camomile St., London EC3A 7BP, England.

665.538 US
TEXAS. RAILROAD COMMISSION. OIL AND GAS DIVISION. ANNUAL REPORT. a. $12. Railroad Commission, Oil and Gas Publications, Drawer 12967, Capitol Station, Austin, TX 78711. TEL 512-463-7255.
Fuel

354 TR
TRINIDAD AND TOBAGO. MINISTRY OF ENERGY AND NATURAL RESOURCES. ANNUAL REPORT. 1964. a. free. Ministry of Energy and Natural Resources, Box 96, Port-of-Spain, Trinidad, W.I. illus. stat. circ. 500.
Former titles: Trinidad and Tobago. Ministry of Energy and Energy-Based Industries. Annual Report; Trinidad and Tobago. Ministry of Petroleum and Mines. Annual Report.

665.5 US ISSN 0082-8599
U S A OIL INDUSTRY DIRECTORY. 1962. a. $95. PennWell Publishing Co., Box 1260, Tulsa, OK 74101. TEL 918-835-3161. Ed. William R. Leek, Jr. adv.

665.5 US
U S A OILFIELD SERVICE, SUPPLY, AND MANUFACTURERS DIRECTORY. 1983. a. $85. PennWell Publishing Co., Box 1260, Tulsa, OK 74101. TEL 918-835-3161. Ed. Robert M. Wilkerson. adv.
Former titles: Oilfield Service, Supply, and Manufacturers Worldwide Directory (ISSN 0736-038X); Oilfield Service, Supply, and Manufacturers Directory.

665.5 US
U S CRUDE OIL, NATURAL GAS, AND NATURAL GAS LIQUIDS. a. $4.50. U.S. Energy Information Administration, 1000 Independence Ave., Washington, DC 20585 TEL 202-252-8800. (Subscr. to Supt. of Documents, Washington, DC 20402) charts.

552 TS
UNITED ARAB EMIRATES. MINISTRY OF PETROLEUM AND INDUSTRY. AKHBAR AL-PETROL WALL SINAA. irreg. Ministry of Petroleum and Industry, Abu Dhabi, United Arab Emirates. Ed. Muhammad al-Sitri.

UNITED KINGDOM OFFSHORE LEGISLATION GUIDE. see *LAW*

665.538 US
U.S. DEPARTMENT OF ENERGY. STRATEGIC PETROLEUM RESERVE OFFICE. ANNUAL REPORT. a. U.S. Department of Energy, Strategic Petroleum Reserve Office, Washington, DC 20545. TEL 202-252-5000.
Fuel

VENEZUELA. MINISTERIO DE ENERGIA Y MINAS. MEMORIA Y CUENTA. see *MINES AND MINING INDUSTRY*

338.2 VE
VENEZUELA. MINISTERIO DE ENERGIA Y MINAS. PETROLEO Y OTROS DATOS ESTADISTICOS. English edition: Venezuelan Petroleum Industry. Statistical Data. a. free. Ministerio de Energia y Minas, Oficina de Estudios Economicos Energeticos, Torre Norte, Caracas, Venezuela (Subscr. to: Ministerio de Energia y Minas, Biblioteca, Torre Oeste Piso 2, Parque Central, Caracas-Venezuela)
Formerly: Venezuela. Ministerio de Minas e Hidrocarburos. Oficina de Economia Petrolera. Petroleo y Otros Datos Estadisticos (ISSN 0083-5390)

665.54 UK
WORLD PIPELINES. 1983. a. £18. P.O. Box 21, Beaconsfield, Bucks HP9 1NS, England. Ed. John Tiratsoo.

665.5 US ISSN 0084-2583
WORLDWIDE PETROCHEMICAL DIRECTORY. 1962. a. $85. PennWell Publishing Co., Box 1260, Tulsa, OK 74101. TEL 918-835-3161. Ed. William R. Leek, Jr. adv.

665.73 US ISSN 0277-0962
WORLDWIDE REFINING AND GAS PROCESSING DIRECTORY. 1942. a. $65. PennWell Publishing Co., Box 1260, Tulsa, OK 74101. TEL 918-835-3161. Ed. William R. Leek, Jr. adv.

WORLDWIDE SYNTHETIC FUELS AND ALTERNATE ENERGY DIRECTORY. see *ENERGY*

PETROLEUM AND GAS —
Abstracting, Bibliographies, Statistics

665.5 016 US
A P I ABSTRACTS/LITERATURE. 1978. w. American Petroleum Institute, Central Abstracting and Indexing Service, 156 William St., New York, NY 10038. TEL 212-587-9660. Ed. E.H. Brenner. circ. 2,000.
●Also available online. Vendors: Orbit Information Technologies.
Former titles (1961-1977): Abstracts of Refining Literature (ISSN 0003-0422) 1954-1960: A.P.I. Technical Abstracts (ISSN 0096-5073); Incorporating: Abstracts of Air and Water Conservation Literature; Abstracts of Health and Environment Literature; Abstracts of Petroleum Refining and Petrochemicals Literature; Abstracts of Petroleum Substitutes Literature; Which was formerly titled: Abstracts of Petroleum Substitutes Literature and Patents (ISSN 0003-0414); and Abstracts of Transportation and Storage Literature; Which was formerly: Abstracts of Transportation and Storage Literature and Patents (ISSN 0003-0449)

665.5 US
A P I ABSTRACTS/OILFIELD CHEMICALS. 1981. m. $640. American Petroleum Institute, 156 William St., New York, NY 10038. TEL 212-587-9660. Ed. E.H. Brenner. pat. circ. 300. (back issues avail.)

665.5 016 US
A P I ABSTRACTS/PATENTS. 1978. w. $7,500. American Petroleum Institute, Central Abstracting and Indexing Service, 156 William St., New York, NY 10038. TEL 212-587-9660. Ed. E.H. Brenner. pat. circ. 2,000.
Supersedes (1971-1977): A P I Patent Alert; Formerly (1960-1971): American Petroleum Institute. Abstracts of Refining Patents (ISSN 0003-0430)

622.33 US ISSN 0273-1916
ALASKA. OIL AND GAS CONSERVATION COMMISSION. STATISTICAL REPORT. a. Oil and Gas Conservation Commission, 3001 Porcupine Dr., Anchorage, AK 99501. TEL 907-279-1433. illus. (microfiche)
Former titles: Alaska. Division of Oil and Gas Conservation. Statistical Report; Alaska. Department of Natural Resources. Division of Oil and Gas. Statistical Report (ISSN 0360-5558)

665.7 CN ISSN 0068-7103
CANADA. STATISTICS CANADA. CRUDE PETROLEUM AND NATURAL GAS INDUSTRY/INDUSTRIE DU PETROLE BRUT ET DU GAZ NATUREL. (Catalog 26-213) (Text in English and French) 1926. a. Can.$20($21) Statistics Canada, Communications Division, 3rd Floor, R.H. Coats Bldg., Ottawa, Ont. K1A 0T6, Canada TEL 613-993-7276. (Subscr. to: Publications Sales and Services, Ottawa, Ont. K1A 0T6, Canada) (also avail. in microform from MMI.)

665.5 CN ISSN 0527-5318
CANADA. STATISTICS CANADA. GAS UTILITIES (TRANSPORT AND DISTRIBUTION SYSTEMS) /SERVICES DE GAZ (RESEAUX DE TRANSPORT ET DE DISTRIBUTION) (Catalog 57-205) (Text in English and French) 1959. a. Can.$20($21) Statistics Canada, Communications Division, 3rd Floor, R.H. Coats Bldg., Ottawa, Ont. K1A 0T6, Canada TEL 613-993-7276. (Subscr. to: Publications Sales and Services, Ottawa, Ont. K1A 0T6, Canada) stat. (also avail. in microform from MML)

868 PETS

665.538 662 016   UK   ISSN 0140-6701
FUEL AND ENERGY ABSTRACTS; a summary of world literature on all technical and scientific aspects of fuel and power. 1960. bi-m. £153($275) (Institute of Fuel) Butterworth Scientific Ltd., P.O. Box 63, Westbury House, Bury St., Guildford, Surrey GU2 5BH, England TEL 0483-31261. (Subscr. address: Westbury Subscription Services, P.O. Box 101, Sevenoaks, Kent TN15 8PL, England) Ed. Stella Dutton. (back issues avail.) Indexed: Chem.Abstr. Anal.Abstr. Br.Ceram.Abstr. Fluidex.
 Formerly: Fuel Abstracts and Current Titles (ISSN 0016-2388)

665.7 016   US   ISSN 0016-4844
GAS ABSTRACTS. 1945. m. $125. Institute of Gas Technology, 3424 S. State St., Chicago, IL 60616. TEL 312-567-3650. Ed. J.L. Schaeffer. bk. rev. index. circ. 1,000. (also avail. in microform from UMI; reprint service avail. from UMI) Indexed: Chem.Abstr. Eng.Ind.

665.5   US
GUIDE TO PETROLEUM STATISTICAL INFORMATION. a. $50. American Petroleum Institute, Central Abstracting and Indexing Service, 156 William St., New York, NY 10038. TEL 212-587-9660.

665.5   II
INDIAN PETROLEUM AND PETROCHEMICALS STATISTICS. (Text in English) 1976. a. free. Ministry of Petroleum, Economics and Statistics Division, New Delhi 110001, India. stat. circ. controlled.
 Formerly: Indian Petroleum and Chemicals Statistics.

338.27   IO
INDONESIA OIL STATISTICS/STATISTIK PERMINYAKAN INDONESIA. (Text in English) 1971. q. with a. cumulation. Direktorat Jenderal Minyak Dan Gas Bumi, Programming & Reporting Division - Directorate General Oil and Gas, Jln. M.H. Thamrin No. 1, Jakarta 10110, Indonesia.

INDUSTRIA PETROLERA EN MEXICO. see PETROLEUM AND GAS

665.5 016   UK   ISSN 0309-4944
INTERNATIONAL PETROLEUM ABSTRACTS. 1973. q. $230. (Institute of Petroleum) John Wiley & Sons Ltd., Baffins Lane, Chichester, Sussex PO19 1UD, England. Ed. Gretchen E. Taylor.
 ●Also available online. Vendors: Pergamon Infoline.

665.5   LY   ISSN 0075-9260
LIBYA. CENSUS AND STATISTICAL OFFICE. REPORT OF THE ANNUAL SURVEY OF PETROLEUM MINING INDUSTRY. (Text in Arabic and English) 1965. a. free. Census and Statistical Department, Ministry of Planning, Tripoli, Libya.

665.5 016   UK   ISSN 0305-0513
OFFSHORE ABSTRACTS. 1974. bi-m. £110. Offshore Information Literature, 37B New Cavendish St., London W1M 8JR, England. Ed. G.E. Taylor. bk. rev. abstr. index. Indexed: BMT.

665.5   UK
OFFSHORE DRILLING REPORT (YEAR) 1982. a. £50. Petroleum Information Ltd., Norman House, 105-109 Strand, London WC2R 0BX, England. Ed. John Hartley. (back issues avail.)

665.5   UK
ONSHORE ACTIVITY REPORT (YEAR) 1982. a. £30. Petroleum Information Ltd., Norman House, 105-109 Strand, London WC2R 0BY, England. Ed. Timothy H. Shingler. (back issues avail.)

665.5 338.2   FR
ORGANIZATION FOR ECONOMIC COOPERATION AND DEVELOPMENT. ANNUAL OIL AND GAS STATISTICS/ STATISTIQUES ANNUELLES DU PETROLE ET DU GAZ NATUREL. (Text in English & French) 1970. a. $40. Organisation for Economic Cooperation and Development, 2 rue Andre-Pascal, 75775 Paris Cedex 16, France (U.S. orders to: O.E.C.D. Publications and Information Center, 1750 Pennsylvania Ave., N.W., Washington, DC 20006) charts. stat. (also avail. in microfiche; back issues avail.)
 Former titles: Organization for Economic Cooperation and Development. Annual Oil and Gas Statistics/Statistiques Annuelles des Hydrocarbures et du Gaz Naturel; Organization for Economic Cooperation and Development. Oil Statistics/ Statistiques Petrolieres; Organization for Economic Cooperation and Development. Provisional Oil Statistics/Statistiques Petrolieres Provisoires (ISSN 0029-7062)

665.5 016   US   ISSN 0031-6423
PETROLEUM ABSTRACTS. 1961. w. service basis. University of Tulsa, Information Services Division, 600 South College, Tulsa, OK 74104. TEL 918-592-6000. Ed. John L. Dowgray. illus. stat. index. cum.index. circ. 1,800. (also avail. in microform)
 ●Also available online. Vendors: Orbit Information Technologies.

665.5 016   US
PETROLEUM/ENERGY BUSINESS NEWS INDEX. 1975. m. $610. American Petroleum Institute, Central Abstracting and Indexing Service, 156 William St., New York, NY 10038. TEL 212-587-9660.

665.5 627   UK   ISSN 0265-3990
PIPELINES ABSTRACTS. 1984. bi-m. £99($163) B H R A Fluid Engineering, Cranfield, Bedford MK43 0AJ, England (Dist. in U.S. by: Learned Information Inc., 143 Old Marlton Pike, Medford, NJ 08055) bk. rev. abstr. index. cum.index.

310   US
STATISTICS FOR GAS UTILITIES IN PENNSYLVANIA. 1956. a. free. Department of Commerce, Bureau of Policy, Planning, & Systems Development, 474 Forum Bldg., Harrisburg, PA 17120. TEL 717-787-7532. charts. stat. circ. controlled.

PETS

636.8   AT
A C I YEAR BOOK. 1978. a. Aus.$3.50 per no. Australian Cat Federation, Inc., c/o Ms. J. Ruasack, 32 Tarrant St., Prospect, S.A. 5082, Australia. adv. circ. 1,000. (back issues avail)

179.3   SA   ISSN 0379-654X
ANIMAL ANTI-CRUELTY LEAGUE. CHAIRMAN'S REPORT. 1972. a. R.10 free. Animal Anti-Cruelty League, P.O. Box 49007, Rosettenville, Transvaal, South Africa.

636   UK
BARBARA WOODHOUSE ANIMAL ANNUAL. a. Grandreams Ltd., Jadwin Hse., 205/211 Kentish Town Rd., London, NW5 2JH, England.

636.7   US
BULL SHEET.* 1973. irreg. (4-5/yr.) Obedience Steward Club, c/o Delores Randazzo, 1869 82nd St., Brooklyn, NY 11214. circ. 75.

179.3   UK   ISSN 0263-1407
C J A AND H S A NEWSLETTER. 1979. a. Council of Justice to Animals and Humane Slaughter Association, 34 Blanche Lane, Potters Bar, Herts EN6 3PA, England.

636.8   US
CAT FANCIERS' ASSOCIATION. ANNUAL YEARBOOK. 1958. a. $24.95. Cat Fanciers Association, 1309 Allaire Ave., Ocean, NJ 07712. TEL 201-531-7095. Ed. Marna Fogarty. adv. bk. rev. circ. 7,000.

636.8   AT
CAT FANCIERS' MAGAZINE. 1971. irreg. Aus.$2. Cat Fanciers' Club of Tasmania, P.O. Box 114, North Hobart, Tas. 7002, Australia.

636   DK
DENMARK. STATENS HUSDYRBRUGSFORSOEG. AARSRAPPORT. 1974. a. free. Statens Husdyrbrugsforsoeg - National Institute of Animal Science, Rolighedsvej 25, 1958 Frederiksberg C, Denmark.

636.8   UK   ISSN 0070-7015
DOG WORLD ANNUAL. 1930. a. $18. M.J. Boulding, Ed. & Pub., 9 Tufton St., Ashford, Kent TN23 1QN, England. index.

636.7   CN
DOGS IN CANADA ANNUAL. a. Apex Publishers & Publicity Ltd., 43 Railside Rd., Don Mills, Ont. M3A 3L9, Canada. TEL 416-441-3228. Ed. Elizabeth M. Dunn. adv. circ. 60,000.

636.7 362.41   US
I G E NEWS. irreg. free. International Guiding Eyes, 13445 Glenoaks Blvd., Sylmar, CA 91342.
 Formerly: International Guiding Eyes. Newsletter.

636.7   UK
KENNEL CLUB YEARBOOK. (Published in three parts) a. £1 for each part. Kennel Club, 1 Clarges Street, Piccadilly, London, W1Y 8 AB, England. Ed. Charles Colborn. circ. 3,000.

636   AT
KENNEL CONTROL COUNCIL GAZETTE DOGS. 1935. m. Aus.$15. Kennel Control Council, Royal Showgrounds, Epsom Road, Ascot Vale, Vic. 3032, Australia. Ed. W.C. Kinsman. adv. bk. rev. circ. 25,000.

636.73   UK   ISSN 0260-5627
LABRADOR RETRIEVER CLUB OF WALES. YEARBOOK. 1980. a. £2. Labrador Retriever Club of Wales, c/o M. Williams, 6 Dan-y-Felin, Llantrisant, Pontyclun, Mid Glam CF7 8EH, Wales. adv. bk. rev. illus. circ. 500.

636.1   UK   ISSN 0077-4448
NATIONAL EQUINE (AND SMALLER ANIMALS) DEFENCE LEAGUE. ANNUAL REPORT. 1909. a. membership. National Equine Defence League, Oak Tree Farm, Wetheral Shields, Carlisle CA4 8JA, England. Ed. Frank E. Tebbutt. circ. 3,000.

614.7   US
ONE WORLD. 1981. irreg. $10 to non-members. Trans-Species Unlimited, Box 1553, Williamsport, PA 17703-1553. TEL 717-322-3252. Ed. Dr. George P. Cave. bk. rev. circ. 7,000. (back issues avail.)
 Animal rights

636   DK   ISSN 0106-6714
OPDRAETTERVEJVISEREN. vol.46, 1980. irreg. free. Dansk Kennel Klub, Parkvej 1, Jersie Strand, 2680 Solroed Strand, Denmark. illus.

PETS WELCOME; animal lovers' holiday guide. see TRAVEL AND TOURISM

636 179.3   UK
SCOTTISH ANTI-VIVISECTION SOCIETY. ANNUAL REPORT. a. Scottish Anti-Vivisection Society, 121 West Regent St., Glasgow G2 2SD, Scotland.

SCOTTISH SOCIETY FOR PREVENTION OF VIVISECTION. ANNUAL PICTORIAL REVIEW. see MEDICAL SCIENCES — Experimental Medicine, Laboratory Technique

636.7   US
SHELTIE PACESETTER TRADE SECRETS BOOK. 1982. quinquennial. $5.95. 28614 Quail Hill Dr., Rancho Palos Verdes, CA 90274. TEL 213-541-7820. Ed. Nancy Lee Marshall.
 Dogs

636.7   US   ISSN 0082-5441
TOURING WITH TOWSER. 1948. biennial. $1.50. Gaines Dog Care Center, 660 White Plains Rd., Tarrytown, NY 10591 TEL 914-333-8622. (Orders to: Box 8172, Kankakee, IL 60902) Ed. Tom O'Shea. circ. 22,500.

636.7 US
WHERE TO BUY, BOARD OR TRAIN A DOG. biennial. $1.50. Gaines Dog Care Center, 660 White Plains Rd., Tarrytown, NY 10591 TEL 914-333-8622. (Orders to: Gaines Kennel Directory, Box 8177, Kankakee, IL 60902)

636.7 AT ISSN 0312-3480
WORKING KELPIE COUNCIL. NATIONAL STUD BOOK. 1967. irreg. Aus.$6 to non members. Working Kelpie Council, P.O. Box 306, Castle Hill, N.S.W. 2154, Australia. Ed. B.M. Cooper. circ. 400.

636 GW
ZUCHTBUCH FUER DEUTSCHE SCHAEFERHUNDE. 1901. a. DM.36.90. Verein fuer Deutsche Schaeferhunde, Beim Schnarrbrunnen 4-6, 8900 Augsburg 1, W. Germany (B.R.D.) Ed.Bd. circ. 2,450.

PHARMACY AND PHARMACOLOGY

see also *Drug Abuse and Alcoholism*

ACCESSOIREX. see *MEDICAL SCIENCES*

615.1 370.58 US
ACCREDITED PROFESSIONAL PROGRAMS OF COLLEGES AND SCHOOLS OF PHARMACY. 1940. a. free. American Council on Pharmaceutical Education, 311 W. Superior St., Chicago, IL 60610. TEL 312-664-3575. Ed. Dr. Daniel A. Nona. circ. 10,000.
Formerly: Accredited Colleges of Pharmacy (ISSN 0065-7980)

615.78 US ISSN 0147-071X
ADVANCES IN BEHAVIORAL PHARMACOLOGY. 1977. irreg., vol.4, 1984. Academic Press, Inc., Orlando, FL 32887. TEL 305-345-2000. illus.

615 616.8 US ISSN 0065-2229
ADVANCES IN BIOCHEMICAL PSYCHOPHARMACOLOGY. 1969. irreg., vol.21, 1979. price varies. Raven Press, 1185 Ave. of the Americas, New York, NY 10036. TEL 212-575-0335. Eds. E. Costa, P. Greengard. Indexed: Biol.Abstr. Chem.Abstr. Curr.Cont. Ind.Med. Ind.Sci.Rev.

410 US ISSN 0190-4817
ADVANCES IN CANCER CHEMOTHERAPY. 1979. irreg. price varies. Marcel Dekker, Inc., 270 Madison Ave., New York, NY 10016. TEL 212-696-9000. Ed. Andre Rosowsky. Indexed: Biol.Abstr. Biotech.Abstr.

ADVANCES IN CLINICAL CHEMISTRY. see *BIOLOGY — Biological Chemistry*

ADVANCES IN CYTOPHARMACOLOGY. see *BIOLOGY — Cytology And Histology*

615.1 US ISSN 0065-2490
ADVANCES IN DRUG RESEARCH. 1964. irreg., vol.14, 1985. Academic Press Inc., Orlando, FL 32887. TEL 305-345-2000. Ed. B. Testa. index. Indexed: Biol.Abstr. Ind.Med. Biotech.Abstr. Ind.Vet. Vet.Bull.

615.7 US ISSN 0272-068X
ADVANCES IN HUMAN PSYCHOPHARMACOLOGY; a research annual. 1980. a. $28.75 to individuals; institutions $57.50. J A I Press Inc., 36 Sherwood Pl., Box 1678, Greenwich, CT 06836. TEL 203-661-7602. Eds. Graham D. Burrows, John S. Werry. Indexed: Chem.Abstr. Psychol.Abstr.

615 US ISSN 0065-3136
ADVANCES IN PHARMACEUTICAL SCIENCES. 1964. irreg., vol.5, 1982. Academic Press Inc., Orlando, FL 32887. TEL 305-345-6000. Eds. H.S. Bean, A.H. Beckett. index. Indexed: Biol.Abstr. I.P.A. Ind.Med. Biotech.Abstr.
●Also available online.

615.1 US ISSN 0065-3144
ADVANCES IN PHARMACOLOGY AND CHEMOTHERAPY. 1962. irreg., vol.20, 1984. Academic Press, Inc., Orlando, FL 32887. TEL 305-345-2000. Ed. S. Garattini. index. Indexed: Biol.Abstr. Chem.Abstr. Ind.Med. Sci.Cit.Ind. Biotech.Abstr. Ind.Vet. Ind.Sci.Rev. Vet.Bull.
Former titles: Advances in Pharmacology; Advances in Chemotherapy.

615.19 SZ ISSN 0253-2093
ADVANCES IN PHARMACOTHERAPY. (Text in English) 1981. irreg. price varies. S. Karger AG, Allschwilerstr. 10, CH-4009 Basel, Switzerland. Ed.Bd. Indexed: Biol.Abstr. Chem.Abstr.

ADVANCES IN STEROID BIOCHEMISTRY AND PHARMACOLOGY (YEAR) see *BIOLOGY — Biological Chemistry*

ALKALOIDS; chemistry and pharmacology. see *CHEMISTRY — Organic Chemistry*

615 US
AMERICAN ASSOCIATION OF COLLEGES OF PHARMACY. ANNUAL SURVEY OF FACULTY SALARIES. 1980. a. $15. American Association of Colleges of Pharmacy, Office of Educational Research and Development, 1426 Prince St., Alexnadria, VA 22314-2815. Ed. Richard P. Penna. circ. 1,600.

615.1 US ISSN 0364-7471
AMERICAN DRUGGIST BLUE BOOK. a. $25. Hearst Corp., American Druggist, 555 W. 57th St., New York, NY 10019. TEL 212-399-3262. circ. 69, 913.
Formerly: American Druggist Blue Price Book.

615 US
AMERICAN HOSPITAL FORMULARY SERVICE DRUG INFORMATION. 1959. 1 base vol. plus 3 supplements per yr. $55. American Society of Hospital Pharmacists, c/o Jean Rogers, Dir., Mkt. Svcs., 4630 Montgomery Ave., Bethesda, MD 20814. TEL 301-657-3000. Ed. Gerald K. McEvoy. (reprint service avail. from UMI)
●Also available online. Vendors: BRS, DIALOG, Mead Data Central.
Formerly (until 1984): American Hospital Formulary Service.

615.19 US
ANALYTICAL PROFILES OF DRUG SUBSTANCES. 1972. irreg., vol.15, 1986. Academic Press, Inc., Orlando, FL 32887. TEL 305-345-2000. Ed. Klaus Florey. Indexed: Chem.ASbstr.

615.1 FR ISSN 0066-2186
ANNALES MOREAU DE TOURS. 1962. irreg. price varies. Presses Universitaires de France, 108 bd. Saint Germain, 75279 Paris Cedex 6, France (Service des Periodiques, 12 rue Jean de Beauvais, 75005 Paris) (reprint service avail. from KTO)

615 FR ISSN 0396-0625
ANNUAIRE DES FOURNISSEURS DE LABORATOIRES PHARMACEUTIQUES ET COSMETIQUES. vol.2, 1976. a. Agence de Diffusion et de Publicite, 24 Place du General Catroux, 75017 Paris, France.
Continues: Annuaire des Fournisseurs de Laboratoires Pharmaceutiques (ISSN 0517-8991)

615.19 UK ISSN 0260-955X
ANNUAL REGISTER OF PHARMACEUTICAL CHEMISTS. 1869. a. £50. Pharmaceutical Society of Great Britain, 1 Lambeth High St., London SE1 7JN, England. index. circ. 1,000.

615.1 US ISSN 0065-7743
ANNUAL REPORTS IN MEDICINAL CHEMISTRY. 1966. irreg., vol.21, 1986. (American Chemical Society, Division of Medicinal Chemistry) Academic Press, Inc., Orlando, FL 32887. TEL 305-345-2000. Ed. Frank H. Clarke. Indexed: Biol.Abstr. Chem.Abstr. Curr.Cont. Sci.Cit.Ind. Dairy Sci.Abstr. Ind.Sci.Rev.

651 US ISSN 0743-9539
ANNUAL REVIEW OF CHRONOPHARMACOLOGY. 1984. a. $95. Pergamon Press, Inc., Journals Division, Maxwell House, Fairview Park, Elmsford, NY 10523 TEL 914-592-7700. (And Headington Hill Hall, Oxford, OX3 0BW, England) Ed. Dr. Michael Smolensky. adv. (also avail. in microform from MIM,UMI) Indexed: Curr.Cont.

615.1 US ISSN 0362-1642
ANNUAL REVIEW OF PHARMACOLOGY AND TOXICOLOGY. 1961. a. $31. Annual Reviews Inc., 4139 El Camino Way, Palo Alto, CA 94303-0897. TEL 415-493-4400. Eds. Robert George, Ronald Okun. bibl. index. cum.index. (back issues avail.; reprint service avail. from ISI) Indexed: Biol.Abstr. Chem.Abstr. Excerp.Med. Ind.Med. Psychol.Abstr. Sci.Cit.Ind. Biotech.Abstr. Helminthol.Abstr. Ind.Sci.Rev. Ind.Vet. M.M.R.I. Vet.Bull.
Formerly: Annual Review of Pharmacology (ISSN 0066-4251)

615.1 SZ ISSN 0066-4758
ANTIBIOTICS AND CHEMOTHERAPY. (Text in English) 1954. irreg. (approx. 1/yr.) price varies. S. Karger AG, Allschwilerstrasse 10, P.O. Box, CH-4009 Basel, Switzerland. Ed. H. Schoenfeld. (reprint service avail. from ISI) Indexed: Biol.Abstr. Chem.Abstr. Curr.Cont. Ind.Med.

615.1 GW ISSN 0066-5347
APOTHEKER - JAHRBUCH. 1915. a. price varies. (Deutscher Apotheker Verein) Wissenschaftliche Verlagsgesellschaft mbH, Postfach 40, 7000 Stuttgart 1, W. Germany (B.R.D.) Ed.Bd. adv. index. cum.index.

615.1 GR ISSN 0003-8148
ARCHEIA TES PHARMAKEUTIKES (ATHENS) (Text in English, French and Greek) 1932. irreg. Dr.150($3) Greek Pharmaceutical Society, Emm. Benakis 30, Athens 10678, Greece. Ed. N.H. Choulis. adv. bk. rev. bibl. charts. illus. index. circ. 1,000. Indexed: Biol.Abstr. Chem.Abstr.

615.1 SP
ARCHIVAS DE FARMACOLOGIA Y TOXICOLOGIA. 1949. irreg. Universidad Complutense de Madrid, Facultad de Medicina, Pabellon, Madrid 3, Spain.
Formerly (1949-1975): Spain. Consejo Superior de Investigaciones Cientificas. Instituto de Farmacologia Experimental. Archivos (ISSN 0024-9629)

615.9 US ISSN 0171-9750
ARCHIVES OF TOXICOLOGY. SUPPLEMENT. 1978. irreg., vol.10, 1987. price varies. Springer-Verlag, 175 Fifth Ave., New York, NY 10010 TEL 212-460-1500. (Also Berlin, Heidelberg, Tokyo and Vienna) (also avail. in microform from UMI; reprint service avail. from ISI) Indexed: Chem.Abstr. Ind.Med. Nutr.Abstr. Dent.Ind.

615 SP ISSN 0304-8616
ARCHIVOS DE FARMACOLOGIA Y TOXICOLOGIA. 1975. irreg. Universidad Complutense de Madrid, Departamento Coordinado de Farmacologia, Ciudad Universitaria, Madrid, Spain. Indexed: Biol.Abstr. Chem.Abstr. Excerp.Med. Ind.Med.

615.1 CN ISSN 0066-9555
ASSOCIATION OF FACULTIES OF PHARMACY OF CANADA. PROCEEDINGS. 1970. a. Can.$10 to non-members. Association of Faculties of Pharmacy, 1815 Alta Vista Drive, Ottawa, Ont. K1G 3Y6, Canada. circ. 200.
Formerly (until vol.26, 1969): Canadian Conference of Pharmaceutical Faculties. Proceedings.

615 SP ISSN 0210-3397
AVANCES EN TERAPEUTICA. 1969. a. 2900 ptas. (Universidad Autonoma de Barcelona) Salvat Editores, S.A., Mallorca 45, 08029 Barcelona, Spain. TEL 201-09-11. Eds. J. Laporte, J.A. Salva. charts. illus. circ. 1,500. Indexed: Chem.Abstr. Curr.Cont.

BRAUNSCHWEIGER VEROEFFENTLICHUNGEN ZUR GESCHICHTE DER PHARMAZIE. see *HISTORY — History Of Europe*

615   GW   ISSN 0722-7159
BRAUNSCHWEIGER VEROEFFENTLICHUNGEN ZUR GESCHICHTE DER PHARMAZIE UND NATURWISSENSCHAFTEN. 1957. irreg., vol.29, 1985. price varies. Deutscher Apotheker Verlag, Postfach 40, 7000 Stuttgart 1, W. Germany (B.R.D.) Ed. Wolfgang Schneider.
 Formerly: Technische Universitaet Braunschweig. Pharmaziegeschichtlichen Seminar. Veroeffentlichungen (ISSN 0068-0729)
 History

615   BL
BRAZIL. CONSELHO FEDERAL DE FARMACIA. RELATORIO. irreg. Conselho Federal de Farmacia, Brasilia, Brazil. illus.

615   UK
BRITISH PHARMACOLOGICAL SOCIETY. SYMPOSIA. 1973. irreg. (1-2/yr.) price varies. British Pharmacological Society, c/o Dr. G.N. Woodruff, Merck Sharp & Dohme Research Laboratories, Neuroscience Research Centre, Terlings Park, Eastwick Rd., Harlow, Essex CM20 2QR, England.

BRITISH PHARMACOPOEIA (VETERINARY) see *VETERINARY SCIENCE*

615.1   UK   ISSN 0068-2519
BRITISH SOCIETY FOR THE HISTORY OF PHARMACY. TRANSACTIONS. 1970. irreg. price varies. British Society for the History of Pharmacy, 36 York Place, Edinburgh EH1 3HU, Scotland. Ed. M.P. Earles.
 History

615.328   CN
CANADIAN SELF-MEDICATION. irreg. Can.$60. Canadian Pharmaceutical Association, 1785 Alta Vista Drive, Ottawa, Ont. K1G 3Y6, Canada.

615.1   UK   ISSN 0262-5881
CHEMIST & DRUGGIST DIRECTORY. 1868. a. £55. Benn Business Information Services Ltd., P.O. Box 20, Sovereign Way, Tonbridge, Kent TN9 1RQ, England. adv. circ. 3,000.

CHEMISTRY AND PHARMACOLOGY OF DRUGS. see *CHEMISTRY*

615   US   ISSN 0362-5664
CLINICAL NEUROPHARMACOLOGY. 1976. q. $85 to individuals; institutions $105. Raven Press, 1185 Ave. of the Americas, New York, NY 10036. TEL 212-575-0335. Ed. Harold L. Klawans. adv. charts. illus. index. circ. 3,500. (back issues avail) Indexed: Biol.Abstr. Chem.Abstr. Curr.Cont. Excerp.Med. Ind.Med. Sci.Cit.Ind. Ind.Sci.Rev.

615   CN   ISSN 0069-7966
COMPENDIUM OF PHARMACEUTICALS AND SPECIALTIES. French edition: Compendium des Produits et Specialites Pharmaceutiques (ISSN 0317-2813) (Text in English and French) 1960. a. Can.$74 for french edition; $62 for english edition. Canadian Pharmaceutical Association, 1785 Alta Vista Dr., Ottawa, Ont. K1G 3Y6, Canada. TEL 613-523-7877. Ed. C. Krogh. bk. rev. circ. 78,000.

COMPUTERTALK PHARMACY SYSTEMS BUYERS GUIDE. see *MEDICAL SCIENCES — Computer Applications*

615.9   SZ   ISSN 0254-8739
CONCEPTS IN TOXICOLOGY. (Text in English) 1984. irreg. 288 Fr. S. Karger AG, Allschwilerstrasse 10, P.O. Box, CH-4009 Basel, Switzerland. Ed. F. Homburger. Indexed: Biol.Abstr. Curr.Cont. Ind.Med.

CRITICAL REPORTS ON APPLIED CHEMISTRY. see *CHEMISTRY*

615   SP   ISSN 0210-6566
CUADERNOS DE HISTORIA DE LA FARMACIA. 1971. irreg. price varies. Universidad de Granada, Secretariado de Publicaciones, Antiguo Colegio Maximo de Cartujo, Granada, Spain. Ed. Jose L. Valverde.

CUBA. CENTRO DE INFORMACION Y DOCUMENTACION AGROPECUARIO. BOLETIN DE RESENAS. SERIE: PLANTAS MEDICINALES. see *BIOLOGY — Botany*

615.9   US
CURRENT ISSUES IN TOXICOLOGY. 1984. irreg. price varies. (International Life Science Institute) Springer-Verlag, 175 Fifth Ave., New York, NY 10010 TEL 212-460-1500. (Also Berlin, Heidelberg, Tokyo, Vienna) (reprint service avail. from ISI)

CURRENT TOPICS IN ENVIRONMENTAL AND TOXICOLOGICAL CHEMISTRY. see *CHEMISTRY*

615   DK   ISSN 0105-7480
DANSKE LAEGEMIDDELSTANDARDER. 1978. a. Kr.164. (Sundhedsstyrelsen, Farmaceutiske Laboratorium) Nyt Nordisk Forlag-Arnold Busck A-S, Koebmagergade 49, DK-1150 Copenhagen K, Denmark.

DE TEXTOS. see *SOCIOLOGY*

615   MX
DICCIONARIO DE ESPECIALIDADES FARMACEUTICAS. 1944. a. San Bernardino 17, Col.del Valle, 03100 Mexico, D.F., Mexico. adv. circ. 55,000.

615   BL
DICIONARIO DE ESPECIALIDADES FARMACEUTICAS. 1971. a. $70. Editora de Publicacoes Medicas Ltda (Subsidiary of: Editora de Publicacoes Cientificas Ltda.) Rua Major Suckow, 30 a 36, 20911 Rio de Janeiro RJ, Brazil. Ed. Jose Maria de Sousa e Melo. adv. circ. 55,000.

615   FR   ISSN 0419-1153
DICTIONNAIRE VIDAL. 1914. a. 530 F. Office de Vulgarisation Pharmaceutique (OVP), 11 rue Quentin Bauchart, 75008 Paris, France. circ. 180, 000.
 Supersedes: Dictionnaire de Specialites Pharmaceutiques.

615   BL   ISSN 0070-6612
DIRETORIO BRASILEIRO DA INDUSTRIA FARMACEUTICA. 1968. a. free. Associacao Brasileira da Industria Farmaceutica, Av. Beira Mar 262, CEP 20000 Rio de Janeiro, R J, Brazil. adv.

615.9   US
DRUG AND CHEMICAL TOXICOLOGY SERIES. 1984. irreg., vol.5, 1986. price varies. Marcel Dekker, Inc., 270 Madison Ave., New York, NY 10016. TEL 212-696-9000. Eds. F.J. DiCarlo, F.W. Oehme.

615 668.5   US   ISSN 0732-0760
DRUG AND COSMETIC CATALOG. 1931. a. $20. Harcourt Brace Jovanovich, Inc., 7500 Old Oak Blvd., Cleveland, OH 44130 TEL 216-243-8100. (Subscr. to: 1 E. First St., Duluth, MN 55802) Ed. Donald A. Davis. circ. 4,743.

615   JA   ISSN 0289-9922
DRUG APPROVAL AND LICENSING PROCEDURES IN JAPAN. (Text in English) 1973. a. $295. Yakugyo Jiho Co., Ltd., 2-36 Kanda Jimbo-cho, Chiyoda-ku, Tokyo 101, Japan.

615.19   US   ISSN 0884-2884
DRUG DESIGN AND DELIVERY. 1986. 1 vol. per yr., 4 nos. per yr. $220 to individuals; institutions $176. Harwood Academic Publishers, Box 786, Cooper Sta., New York, NY 10276 TEL 212-206-8900. (Subscr. to: Harwood Academic Publishers, P.O Box 197, London WC2E 9PX, England) Ed. Jack S. Morley.

615.19   GW   ISSN 0343-4842
DRUG DEVELOPMENT AND EVOLUTION. 1977. irreg. price varies. Gustav Fischer Verlag, Wollgrasweg 49, Postfach 720143, 7000 Stuttgart 70, W. Germany (B.R.D.) illus. Indexed: Chem.Abstr.

DRUG STORE MARKET GUIDE; a detailed distribution analysis of chain and wholesale drug store industry. see *BUSINESS AND ECONOMICS — Trade And Industrial Directories*

615.329   US
DRUG STORE NEWS REFERENCE FOR PHARMACY PRACTICE. 1960. a. $0.75. Lebhar-Friedman, Inc., 425 Park Ave., New York, NY 10022. TEL 212-371-9400. adv. circ. 56,537.

615.1   US   ISSN 0070-7376
DRUG TOPICS REDBOOK. 1897. a. $23. Medical Economics Co., 680 Kinderkamack Rd., Oradell, NJ 07649. TEL 201-262-3030. Ed. Valentine A. Caroinale. circ. 70,000. (also avail. in magnetic tape)

DRUG TRADE NAME CROSS REFERENCE LIST. see *PHARMACY AND PHARMACOLOGY — Abstracting, Bibliographies, Statistics*

615.7   US
DRUGS AND THE PHARMACEUTICAL SCIENCES. 1975. irreg., vol.25, 1984. price varies. Marcel Dekker, Inc., 270 Madison Ave., New York, NY 10016. TEL 212-696-9000. Ed. J. Swarbuck.

615   US   ISSN 0070-7392
DRUGS IN CURRENT USE AND NEW DRUGS. 1955. a. price varies. Springer Publishing Company, 536 Broadway, New York, NY 10012. TEL 212-431-4370. Ed. Dr. Walter Modell. circ. 1,880. (also avail. in microform from UMI; back issues avail.; reprint service avail. from UMI)

615   US   ISSN 0070-7406
DRUGS OF CHOICE. 1958. biennial. $56.95. C. V. Mosby Co., 11830 Westline Industrial Dr., St. Louis, MO 63146. TEL 314-872-8370. Ed. Dr. Walter Modell. Indexed: Chem.Abstr.

615.19   AT   ISSN 0157-9509
E T C H. (Ethical Tablet and Capsule Handbook); ethical tablet and capsule handbook. 1980. a. Aus.$9. P V P Publications Pty. Ltd., Box 278, Balgowlah, NSW 2093, Australia. circ. 8,500.

641.18   US
EDMUNDS PRESCRIPTION DRUG PRICES. 1981. a. $3.50 per vol. Edmund Publications Corp., 515 Hempstead Tpke., West Hempstead, NY 11552. TEL 516-292-0044. Ed. Michael Groher.

615   US   ISSN 0071-1446
ESSAYS IN TOXICOLOGY. 1969. irreg., vol.7, 1976. Academic Press, Inc., Orlando, FL 32887. TEL 305-345-2000. Ed. F.R. Blood. Indexed: Biol.Abstr.

614.35 614.28   UN   ISSN 0082-8335
ESTIMATED WORLD REQUIREMENTS OF NARCOTIC DRUGS. (Supplement avail.: Estimated World Requirements of Narcotic Drugs. Supplement) (Text in English, French and Spanish) 1946. a., latest 1986 (pub.1985) $9.50. International Narcotics Control Board - Organe International de Controle des Stupefiants, Vienna International Centre, P.O. Box 500, 1400 Vienna, Austria (Or United Nations Publications, Rm. LX-2300, New York, NY 10017)

614 016   US   ISSN 0429-9442
F D A CLINICAL EXPERIENCE ABSTRACTS. irreg., approx. m. U.S. Food and Drug Administration, 5600 Fisher's Lane, Rockville, MD 20857. TEL 301-443-1544.

F D A COMPLIANCE POLICY GUIDES. MANUAL. (U.S. Food and Drug Administration) see *FOOD AND FOOD INDUSTRIES*

615.1   US
FACTS AND COMPARISONS. 1947. m. with annual edt. $118. 111 West Port Plaza, St. Louis, MO 63146-3098. TEL 314-878-2515. Ed. Erwin K. Kastrup. index. (looseleaf format; also avail. in microfiche)
 Former titles: Drug Facts and Comparisons (ISSN 0277-9714); Facts and Comparisons (ISSN 0014-6617)

615.1   US   ISSN 0272-197X
FALCONER'S CURRENT DRUG HANDBOOK. a. W. B. Saunders Co., West Washington Square, Philadelphia, PA 91905. TEL 215-574-4700.

615.5   US   ISSN 0276-4318
FAMILY PHYSICIAN'S COMPENDIUM OF DRUG THERAPY. 1980. a. Biomedical Information Corp., 800 Second Ave, New York, NY 10017. TEL 212-599-3400.

615.1 SZ ISSN 0071-786X
FORTSCHRITTE DER
ARZNEIMITTELFORSCHUNG/PROGRESS IN
DRUG RESEARCH/PROGRES DES
RECHERCHES PHARMACEUTIQUES. (Text in
English, French and German) 1959. irreg. (1-2/yr.)
Birkhaeuser Verlag, P.O. Box 133, CH 4010 Basel,
Switzerland. Ed. Ernst Jucker. Indexed: Biol.Abstr.
Chem.Abstr. I.P.A. Ind.Med. Biotech.Abstr.
●Also available online.

615.19 JA ISSN 0434-0094
GIFU PHARMACEUTICAL UNIVERSITY.
ANNUAL PROCEEDINGS. (Text in Japanese)
1951. a. free. Gifu Pharmaceutical University, 5-6-1,
Mitahora-higashi, Gifu 502, Japan. Ed.Bd. Indexed:
Chem.Abstr.

615.19 US ISSN 0171-2004
HANDBOOK OF EXPERIMENTAL
PHARMACOLOGY. 1950. irreg., vol.81, 1986.
Springer-Verlag, 175 Fifth Ave., New York, NY
10010. TEL 212-460-1500. (reprint service avail.
from ISI) Indexed: Chem.Abstr.

HANDBOOK OF NATURAL TOXINS. see
MEDICAL SCIENCES

615.1 US ISSN 0073-1420
HAYES DRUGGIST DIRECTORY. 1912. a. $240.
Edward N. Hayes, Ed. & Pub., 4229 Birch St,
Newport Beach, CA 92660. TEL 714-756-9063.

615.9 FR
INCOMPATEX. 1984. a. 419 F. Societe d'Editions
Medico-Pharmaceutiques, 26 rue Lebrun, 75013
Paris, France. (looseleaf format)

615 SZ
INDEX NOMINUM. (Text in English, French and
German) 1956. biennial. 220 Fr. Societe Suisse de
Pharmacie, Marktgasse 52, 3011 Berne, Switzerland.

615.1 II ISSN 0073-6635
INDIAN PHARMACEUTICAL GUIDE. (Text in
English) 1963. a. $60. Pamposh Publications, 506
Ashok Bhawan, 93 Nehru Pl., New Delhi 110019,
India. Ed. Mohan C. Bazaz. adv. circ. 5,000.

615 SP
INDICE DE ACTUALIDAD FARMACOLOGICA.
1971. a. $150. Julio Garcia Peri, Ed., Sanchez
Pacheco 81-83, Madrid 2, Spain. adv. circ. 4,000.

615 IT ISSN 0073-7984
INFORMATORE FARMACEUTICO. 1940. a.
L.196000 includes subscr. to Notiziario Medico
Farmaceutico. Organizzazione Editoriale Medico-
Farmaceutica, Via Edolo 42, Box 10434, 20125
Milan, Italy (U.S. dist.: Drug Intelligence & Clinical
Pharmacy, Box 42435, Cincinnati OH 45242) Ed.
Dr. Lucio Marini.

615.1 NZ ISSN 0156-2703
INPHARMA; weekly reports from the current
international drug literature. 1975. w. $840. ADIS
Press, Ltd., Private Bag, Mairangi Bay, Auckland
10, New Zealand. Ed. Peter Louisson.

INTERNATIONAL CONGRESS ON CLINICAL
CHEMISTRY. ABSTRACTS. see *BIOLOGY —
Biological Chemistry*

INTERNATIONAL CONGRESS ON CLINICAL
CHEMISTRY. PAPERS. see *BIOLOGY —
Biological Chemistry*

615 US
INTERNATIONAL DIRECTORY OF
INVESTIGATORS IN
PSYCHOPHARMACOLOGY.* 1973. irreg. U.S.
Public Health Service, Alcohol, Drug Abuse &
Mental Health Administration, 5600 Fishers Lane,
Rm. 9-105, Rockville, MD 20852. TEL 301-496-
4000. (Co-sponsor: World Health Organization) Ed.
Alice A. Leeds. circ. 6,000.

300 614.35 UN
INTERNATIONAL NARCOTICS CONTROL
BOARD. COMPARATIVE STATEMENT OF
ESTIMATES AND STATISTICS ON NARCOTIC
DRUGS FOR (YEAR) (Text in English, French
and Spanish) a. $6. International Narcotics Control
Board - Organe International de Controle des
Stupefiants, Vienna International Centre, P.O. Box
500, 1400 Vienna, Austria (Or United Nations
Publications, Room LX-2300, New York, NY
10017)
Formerly: International Narcotics Control Board.
Comparative Statement of Estimates and Statistics
on Narcotic Drugs Furnished by Governments in
Accordance with the International Treaties.

615 UN ISSN 0257-3717
INTERNATIONAL NARCOTICS CONTROL
BOARD. REPORT FOR (YEAR) a. $5.
International Narcotics Control Board - Organe
International de Controle des Stupefiants, Vienna
International Centre, P.O. Box 500, 1400 Vienna,
Austria (Or United Nations Publications, Room LX-
2300, New York, NY 10017)
Former titles: United Nations. International
Narcotics Control Board. Annual Report; United
Nations. Permanent Central Opium Board. Report
of the Permanent Central Opium Board on its
Work; United Nations. Permanent Central Opium
Board. Report to the Economic and Social Council
on the Work of the Permanent Central Narcotics
(Opium) Board (ISSN 0082-8343)

614 UN
INTERNATIONAL NARCOTICS CONTROL
BOARD. STATISTICS ON NARCOTIC DRUGS
FOR (YEAR) (Text in English, French and
Spanish) 1968. a., latest 1984 (pub. 1985) $15.
International Narcotics Control Board - Organe
International de Controle des Stupefiants, Vienna
International Centre, P.O. Box 500, 1400 Vienna,
Austria (Or United Nations Publications, Room LX-
2300, New York, NY 10017)
Former titles: United Nations. International
Narcotics Control Board. Statistics on Narcotic
Drugs Furnished by Governments in Accordance
with the International Treaties; Until 1984: United
Nations. International Narcotics Control Board.
Statistics on Narcotic Drugs Furnished by
Governments in Accordance with the International
Treaties and Maximum Levels of Opium Stocks
(ISSN 0566-7658)

614 UN
INTERNATIONAL NARCOTICS CONTROL
BOARD. STATISTICS ON PSYCHOTROPIC
SUBSTANCES FOR (YEAR) (Text in English,
French and Spanish) 1977. a., latest 1984 (pub.
1985) $12.50. International Narcotics Control Board
- Organe International de Controle des Stupefiants,
Vienna International Centre, P.O. Box 500, 1400
Vienna, Austria (Or United Nations Publications,
Room LX-2300, New York, NY 10017)
Formerly: United Nations. International
Narcotics Control Board. Statistics on Psychotropic
Substances Furnished by Governments in
Accordance with the Convention of 1971 on
Psychotropic Substances (ISSN 0253-9403)

INTERNATIONAL SYMPOSIUM ON QUANTUM
BIOLOGY AND QUANTUM
PHARMACOLOGY. PROCEEDINGS. see
BIOLOGY

615.19 SZ ISSN 0301-3154
INTERNATIONAL SYMPOSIUM ON THE
PHARMACOLOGY OF
THERMOREGULATION. (Text in English) irreg.,
6th 1985, Jasper, Alberta. price varies. S. Karger
AG, Allschwilerstr. 10, P.O. Box, CH-4009 Basel,
Switzerland. (reprint service avail. from ISI)
Indexed: Biol.Abstr. Curr.Cont. Ind.Med.

615.1 GW ISSN 0074-9729
INTERNATIONALE GESELLSCHAFT FUER
GESCHICHTE DER PHARMAZIE.
VEROEFFENTLICHUNGEN. NEUE FOLGE.
(Text in English and German) 1953; N.S. irreg.,
vol.54, 1985. price varies. Wissenschaftliche
Verlagsgesellschaft mbH, Postfach 40, 7000
Stuttgart 1, W. Germany (B.R.D.) Ed. Wolfgang-
Hagen Hein.
History

615.5 US ISSN 0276-4342
INTERNIST'S COMPENDIUM OF DRUG
THERAPY. Spine title: Compendium of Drug
Therapy. 1980. a. Biomedical Information Corp.,
800 Second Ave, New York, NY 10017. TEL 212-
599-3400.

615 JA
JAPAN DRUG INDUSTRY REVIEW. (Text in
English) a. $88. Yakugyo Jiho Co., Ltd., 2-36
Kanda Jimbo-Cho, Chiyoda-ku, Tokyo 101, Japan.
Formerly (until 1976): Handbook of the Japan
Drug Industry.

615.1 UA ISSN 0085-2406
JOURNAL OF DRUG RESEARCH OF EGYPT.
Cover title: Journal of Drug Research. (Text in
English; summaries in Arabic and English.) 1968. a.
$12. National Organisation for Drug Control and
Research, Drug Research and Control Center, 6,
Abou-Hazem St., Pyramids Ave., Box 29, Cairo,
Egypt. Ed.Bd. bk. rev. illus. Indexed: Biol.Abstr.
Chem.Abstr. Excerp.Med. I.P.A. Nutr.Abstr.
Anal.Abstr. Mass Spectr.Bull.
●Also available online.

615.1 JA ISSN 0023-1657
KINKI UNIVERSITY. BULLETIN OF
PHARMACY/KINKI DAIGAKU
YAKUGAKUBU KIYO. 1959. irreg. Kinki
University, Faculty of Pharmaceutical Sciences, 321
Kowakae, Higashiosaka, Osaka, Japan. Ed. Shoji
Takemura. circ. 1,000. Indexed: Biol.Abstr.
Chem.Abstr. I.P.A.

615 DK ISSN 0106-1275
LAEGEFORENINGENS
MEDICINFORTEGNELSE. 1963. biennial.
Kr.250. Laegeforeningens Forlag, Esplanaden 8A/4,
1263 Copenhagen K, Denmark.

615 DK ISSN 0108-0687
LAEGEMIDDELFORBRUGET I DANMARK. 1981.
a. free. Dansk Laegemiddelstatistik, Marielundvej
32B, 2730 Herlev, Denmark. circ. 7,000.

LITHIUM THERAPY MONOGRAPHS. see
*MEDICAL SCIENCES — Radiology And Nuclear
Medicine*

615.19 AT
M I M S ANNUAL. 1977. a. Aus.$45. I M S
Publishing, 100 Alexander St., Crows Nest, NSW
2065, Australia. Ed. Leanne Wilkinson. adv. charts.
circ. 26,000.

615 SA ISSN 0076-8847
M I M S DESK REFERENCE. 1965. a. R.80 per no.
M.I.M.S. (Pty) Ltd., P.O. Box 2059, Pretoria 0001,
South Africa. Ed. Deo Botha. adv. index. circ. 9,
500.
Formerly: M I M S Reference Manual.

615 US ISSN 0085-3100
MARIO NEGRI INSTITUTE FOR
PHARMACOLOGICAL RESEARCH.
MONOGRAPHS. 1970. irreg., no.13, 1979. price
varies. Raven Press, 1185 Ave. of the Americas,
New York, NY 10036. TEL 212-575-0335. Ed.
Silvio Garattini. Indexed: Biol.Abstr. Chem.Abstr.
Curr.Cont.
*Proceedings of international biomedical symposia
covering pharmacological problems*

615 UK
MARTINDALE: THE EXTRA PHARMACOPOEIA.
1883. quinquennial; latest 1982. £69($130) per
copy. Pharmaceutical Society of Great Britain, 1
Lambeth High St., London SE1 7JN, England (Dist.
in U.S. by: Rittenhouse Book Distributors,
Philadelphia, PA 19406) Ed. James E. Reynolds.
index.
●Also available online. Vendors: Data-Star,
DIALOG.
Incorporating: Squires Companion.

615 US ISSN 0076-6054
MEDICINAL CHEMISTRY; series of monographs.
1963. irreg., vol.20, 1985. Academic Press Inc.,
Orlando, FL 32887. TEL 305-345-2000. Ed. George
de Stevens. Indexed: Biol.Abstr.

615 DK ISSN 0900-4858
MEDICINTAKST. 1955. irreg. Kr.75.
Sundhedsstyrelsen, St. Kongensgade 1, 1264
Copenhagen K, Denmark (Subscr. to: Danske
Boghendleres, Kommissionsanstalt, Sijangade 6,
2300 Copenhagen S, Denmark)

615   US   ISSN 0076-6518
MERCK INDEX: AN ENCYCLOPEDIA OF CHEMICALS AND DRUGS. 1889. irreg., 10th edt., 1983. $28.50. Merck and Co., Inc, Box 2000, Rahway, NJ 07065. TEL 201-574-5403. Ed. Martha Windholz.
● Also available online. Vendors: Telesystemes - Questel.

615.19   US   ISSN 0732-7218
MODERN METHODS IN PHARMACOLOGY. 1982. irreg. price varies. Alan R. Liss, Inc., 41 E. 11th St., New York, NY 10003. TEL 212-475-7700. Indexed: Biol.Abstr. Chem.Abstr.

615   US   ISSN 0098-6925
MODERN PHARMACOLOGY-TOXICOLOGY SERIES. 1973. irreg., vol.21, 1982. Marcel Dekker, Inc., 270 Madison Ave., New York, NY 10016. TEL 212-696-9000. Eds. W. Bousquet, R.F. Palmer. illus. Indexed: Chem.Abstr.
Formerly: Modern Pharmacology (ISSN 0092-0150)

MODERN PROBLEMS OF PHARMACOPSYCHIATRY. see *MEDICAL SCIENCES — Psychiatry And Neurology*

615.19   540   JA   ISSN 0369-5611
NAGOYA CITY UNIVERSITY. FACULTY OF PHARMACEUTICAL SCIENCE. ANNUAL REPORT/NAGOYA-SHIRITSU DAIGAKU YAKUGAKUBU KENKYU NEMPO. (Text in English or Japanese) vol.12, 1964. a. free. Nagoya City University, Faculty of Pharmaceutical Sciences, Tanabe-Dohri 3-1, Mizuho-Ku, Nagoya 467, Japan. Ed.Bd. bibl. circ. 400. Indexed: Biol.Abstr. Chem.Abstr.

615   US   ISSN 0077-3263
NATIONAL ASSOCIATION OF BOARDS OF PHARMACY. PROCEEDINGS. 1904. a. $15. National Association of Boards of Pharmacy, 1300 Higgins Rd., No. 103, Park Ridge, IL 60068-5743. TEL 312-698-6227. Ed. Fred T. Mahaffey. index. circ. 300. Indexed: I.P.A.
● Also available online.

NEPAL. DEPARTMENT OF MEDICINAL PLANTS. ANNUAL REPORT. see *BIOLOGY — Botany*

615.19   AT   ISSN 0818-4453
NON-PRESCRIPTION PRODUCTS GUIDE. a. Aus.$34.50. Australian Pharmaceutical Publishing Co. Ltd., 40 Burwood Rd., Hawthorn, Vic. 3122, Australia. Ed. J. Thomas. adv.

OCULAR THERAPEUTICS AND PHARMACOLOGY. see *MEDICAL SCIENCES — Ophthalmology And Optometry*

615   JA   ISSN 0387-480X
OSAKA UNIVERSITY. FACULTY OF PHARMACEUTICAL SCIENCES. MEMOIRS/ OSAKA DAIGAKU YAKUGAKUBU KIYO. (Text in English) 1970. a. exchange basis. Osaka University, Faculty of Pharmaceutical Sciences - Osaka Daigaku Yakugakubu, 1-6 Yamadaoka, Suita, Osaka 565, Japan. Ed. Chuzo Iwata. abstr. circ. 300.

615.1   US   ISSN 0272-7064
OSTEOPATHIC PHYSICIAN'S COMPENDIUM OF DRUG THERAPY. 1980. a. Biomedical Information Corp., 800 Second Ave, New York, NY 10017. TEL 212-599-3400.

615.19   US
P M A STATISTICAL FACTBOOK; pharmaceuticals, in-vivo diagnostic. irreg., once every 3 or 4 yrs. $15. Pharmaceutical Manufacturers Association, 1100 15th St. N.W., Washington, DC 20005. TEL 202-835-3400. Ed.Bd. charts. stat. circ. 500. (looseleaf format)
Formerly: Prescription Drug Industry Fact Book.

615   616.5   FR
PARAPHARMEX. a., with 16 supplements. 303 F. Societe d'Editions Medico-Pharmaceutiques, 26 rue le Brun, 75013 Paris, France. circ. 9,000 (controlled) (looseleaf format; also avail. in microfiche)

615   UK
PHARMA-PROGNOSIS INTERNATIONAL. 1980. a. $15,000. IMSWORLD Publications Ltd., 11-13 Melton St., London NW1 2EH, England.

615   UK
PHARMACEUTICAL CODEX. 1907. quinquennial. £33. Pharmaceutical Society of Great Britain, 1 Lambeth High St., London SE1 7JN, England. bibl. charts. illus. circ. 20,000.

615   US
PHARMACEUTICAL: LATIN AMERICAN INDUSTRIAL REPORT. (Avail. for each of 22 Latin American countries) 1985. a. $435 per country report per industry covered. Aurora International, Box 9099, Bridgeport, CT 06601-0209. TEL 203-368-0579. Ed. Andres C. Aquino.

PHARMACEUTICAL MANUFACTURERS OF JAPAN. see *BUSINESS AND ECONOMICS — Trade And Industrial Directories*

615   US
PHARMACEUTICAL MARKETERS DIRECTORY. 1977. a. $109. Fisher-Stevens Publications Group, 100 Campus Rd., Totowa, NJ 07512. TEL 201-890-1122. Ed. Marianne McCabe. adv. circ. 3,000.

PHARMACEUTICAL MEDICINE. see *MEDICAL SCIENCES*

615.1   DK   ISSN 0901-9936
PHARMACOLOGY AND TOXICOLOGY. SUPPLEMENTUM. (Text in English) 1947. irreg. free to subscribers. Munksgaard, Noerre Soegade 35, DK-1370 Copenhagen K, Denmark. Ed. Jens Schou. (reprint service avail. from ISI) Indexed: Biol.Abstr. Chem.Abstr. Curr.Cont. Excerp.Med. Ind.Med. Nutr.Abstr.
Formerly: Acta Pharmacologica et Toxicologica. Supplementum (ISSN 0065-1508)

615.19   340   US   ISSN 0149-1717
PHARMACY AND LAW DIGEST. 1965. a. $59.50. Facts and Comparisons, 111 W. Port Plaza, Ste. 423, St. Louis, MO 63146-3098. TEL 314-878-2515. Ed. Joseph L. Fink, III. (looseleaf format)

615.19   AT
PHARMACY GUILD OF AUSTRALIA. ANNUAL REPORT. 1975. a. Pharmacy Guild of Australia, Box 36, Deakin, ACT 2600, Australia. circ. 5,500.
Pharmacy Guild of Australia. National Report.

615.19   AT
PHARMACY GUILD OF AUSTRALIA. NATIONAL NEWSLETTER. 1976. irreg. Aus.$.20 to members. Pharmacy Guild of Australia, Box 36, Deakin, ACT 2600, Australia. Ed. Robert Davies. circ. 5,000. (back issues avail.)

615   GW   ISSN 0344-7154
PHARMAKOTHERAPIE. 1978. irreg. DM.24($12) per no. Dustri-Verlag Dr. Karl Feistle, Bahnhofstr. 9, 8024 Deisenhofen, W. Germany (B.R.D.) Indexed: Chem.Abstr. Excerp.Med.

615   II   ISSN 0379-556X
PHARMSTUDENT. (Text in English) 1952. a. $8. Pharmaceutical Society, c/o Department of Pharmaceutics, Banaras Hindu University, Varanasi 221005, India. Ed. J.K. Pandit. adv. circ. 600. Indexed: Chem.Abstr.

615.9   CN
POISON MANAGEMENT MANUAL. every 2-3 years. Can.$39. Canadian Pharmaceutical Association, 1785 Alta Vista Dr., Ottawa, Ont. K1G 3Y6. Ed. Carmen Krogh.

615.7   AT   ISSN 0818-4445
PRESCRIPTION PRODUCTS GUIDE. 1959. a. Aus.$59.50. Australian Pharmaceutical Publishing Co. Ltd, 40 Burwood Rd., Hawthorn, Vic. 3122, Australia. Ed. J. Thomas. circ. 5,000.
Formerly: Prescription Proprietaries Guide for Health Professionals.

615   SZ   ISSN 0079-6085
PROGRESS IN BIOCHEMICAL PHARMACOLOGY. (Text in English) 1965. irreg. (approx. 1/yr.) price varies. S. Karger AG, Allschwilerstrasse 10, P.O. Box, CH-4009 Basel, Switzerland. Ed. R. Paoletti. (reprint service avail. from ISI, back issues avail.) Indexed: Biol.Abstr. Chem.Abstr. Curr.Cont. Ind.Med.

615.9   US   ISSN 0079-6158
PROGRESS IN CHEMICAL TOXICOLOGY. 1963. irreg., vol.5, 1975. Academic Press, Inc, Orlando, FL 32887. TEL 305-345-2000. Ed. A. Stolman. index. Indexed: Biol.Abstr. Ind.Med.

PSYCHEDELIC MONOGRAPHS AND ESSAYS. see *PSYCHOLOGY*

615   US
PSYCHOPHARMACOLOGY SUPPLEMENTA. 1984. irreg., vol.3, 1986. price varies. Springer-Verlag, 175 Fifth Ave., New York, NY 10010 TEL 212-460-1500. (Also Berlin, Heidelberg, Tokyo, Vienna) (reprint service avail. from ISI)

615.1   GW   ISSN 0080-0899
REMEDIA HOECHST. 1900. biennial. free. Hoechst AG, Postfach 800320, 6230 Frankfurt 80, W. Germany (B.R.D.) circ. 130,000.

615   IT
REPERTORIO TERAPEUTICO; medicamenta-drugs international index. (Text in English and Italian) 1963. irreg., 7th edt. Organizzazione Editoriale Medico-Farmaceutica, Via Edolo 42, Box 10434, 20125 Milan, Italy (U.S. dist.: Drug Intelligence & Clinical Pharmacy, Box 42435, Cincinnati, OH 45242) Ed. Dr. Lucio Marini.

REVIEWS OF HEMATOLOGY. see *BIOLOGY*

REVIEWS OF PHYSIOLOGY, BIOCHEMISTRY AND EXPERIMENTAL PHARMACOLOGY. see *BIOLOGY — Physiology*

615   CR
REVISTA CIENCIAS FARMACEUTICAS.* (Text in Spanish; summaries in English & Spanish) 1976. a. Col.10($2) Colegio de Farmaceuticos de Costa Rica, Apdo. 396, San Jose, Costa Rica. Indexed: I.P.A.

615.1   BL   ISSN 0101-3793
REVISTA DE CIENCIAS FARMACEUTICAS. 1978. a. $30 or exchange basis. Universidade Estadual Paulista, Av. Vicente Ferreira 1278, Caixa Postal 630, 17.500 Marilia SP, Brazil. bibl. charts. circ. controlled. Indexed: Biol.Abstr. Chem.Abstr. Excerp.Med. I.P.A. Anal.Abstr.
● Also available online.
Formerly: Faculdade de Ciencias Farmaceuticas de Araraquara. Revista; Which superseded in part (1967-1978): Faculdade de Farmacia e Odontologia de Araraquara. Revista (ISSN 0014-6684)

615   IT   ISSN 0081-0703
S.I.S.F. DOCUMENTI. 1965. irreg. price varies. Societa Italiana di Scienze Farmaceutiche, Via Giorgio Jan 18, 20129 Milan, Italy.

615.19   SZ   ISSN 0256-730X
SAFETY EVALUATION AND REGULATION OF CHEMICALS. (Text in English) 1983. irreg. price varies. S. Karger AG, Allschwilerstrasse 10, P.O Box, CH-4009 Basel, Switzerland. Ed. F. Homburger. Indexed: Biol.Abstr. Curr.Cont. Ind.Med.

615   JA
SAIKIN NO SHINYAKU/NEW DRUGS IN JAPAN. 1950. a. 3500 Yen. Yakuji Nippo, Ltd., 1-11, Kanda Izumicho, Chiyoda-ku, Tokyo, 101, Japan. circ. 20,000. (back issues avail.)

615.19   JA   ISSN 0080-6064
SANKYO KENKYUSHO NEMPO/SANKYO RESEARCH LABORATORIES. ANNUAL REPORT. (Text in English and Japanese; summaries in English) 1946. a. free contr. circ. Sankyo Co., Ltd., Research Institute - Sankyo K.K. Sogo Kenkyusho, 1-2-58 Hiromachi, Shinagawa-ku, Tokyo 140, Japan. Ed. Yukichi Kishida. abstr. Indexed: Biol.Abstr. Chem.Abstr.

615   368.4   CN   ISSN 0707-0152
SASKATCHEWAN. PRESCRIPTION DRUG PLAN. ANNUAL REPORT. 1976. a. Prescription Drug Plan, Department of Health, 3475 Albert St., Regina., Sask., Canada. TEL 306-565-3317. circ. 1, 800.

615   US
SCHOOLS IN THE UNITED STATES AND CANADA OFFERING GRADUATE EDUCATION IN PHARMACOLOGY. 1963. biennial. free. American Society for Pharmacology and Experimental Therapeutics, 9650 Rockville Pike, Bethesda, MD 20814. Ed. Kay A. Croker.

615.19   GW
SEIBT PHARMA-TECHNIK. (Text in English, French and German) biennial. DM.74. Seibt Verlag, Pilgersheimer Str. 38, D-8000 Munich 90, W. Germany (B.R.D.)

615.9 340 US
SURVEY OF PHARMACY LAW. 1950. a. $20.
National Association of Boards of Pharmacy, 1300 Higgins Rd., No 103, Park Ridge, IL 60068. TEL 312-698-6227. Ed. Fred T. Mahaffey. stat. charts. circ. 20,000.

TAKEDA RESEARCH LABORATORIES. JOURNAL. see *BIOLOGY*

615 613 DK ISSN 0107-1181
TAL OG DATA, MEDICIN OG SUNDHEDSVAESEN/FACTS, MEDICINE AND HEALTH CARE, DENMARK. (Text in Danish and English) 1976. a. free. Foreningen af Danske Medicinfabrikker, Landemaerket 25, 1119 Copenhagen K, Denmark. illus. circ. 6,000.
Formerly: Tal og Data om Medicin.

615.9 FR
TAREX. 1969. a. 262 F. Societe d'Editions Medico-Pharmaceutiques (SEMP), 26 rue Lebrun, 75013 Paris, France. bk. rev. circ. 17,000(controlled) (looseleaf format)

615.9 US
TARGET ORGAN TOXICOLOGY SERIES. irreg. Raven Press, 1185 Ave. of the Americas, New York, NY 10036. TEL 212-575-0335. Ed. Robert L. Dixon.
Formerly: Target Organ Toxicity.
Toxicology

615 DK ISSN 0082-4003
THERIACA; samlinger til farmaciens og medicinens historie. (Text in Danish; summaries in English) 1956. irreg., no.22, 1982. price varies. Dansk Farmacihistorisk Selskab - Danish Society of the History of Pharmacy, Farmacilaboratorium, Universistetsparken 2, DK-2100 Copenhagen, Denmark.
History

615 US ISSN 0090-6816
U S A N AND THE U S P DICTIONARY OF DRUG NAMES. 1963. a. $60. ‡ United States Pharmacopeial Convention, Inc., 12601 Twinbrook Pkwy., Rockville, MD 20852. TEL 301-881-0666. Ed. Mary C. Griffiths.

615 DK ISSN 0108-948X
UNDERSOEGELSE OVER APOTEKERNES DRIFTSFORHOLD; regnskabsresultater fra apoteker. vol.9, 1944. a. Kr.35. Sundhedsstyrelsen, St. Kongensgade 1, 1264 Copenhagen K, Denmark. (Co-sponsor: Apotekerfonden)

615.1 US ISSN 0077-4235
U.S. FOOD AND DRUG ADMINISTRATION. NATIONAL DRUG CODE DIRECTORY. 1969. biennial. $32. U.S. Food and Drug Administration, Bureau of Drugs, 5600 Fisher's Lane, Rockville, MD 20857 TEL 301-443-1544. (Orders to: Supt. of Documents, Washington, DC 20402)

615.11
UNITED STATES PHARMACOPEIA - NATIONAL FORMULARY. 1820. irreg.; USP vol.20, 1980; NF vol.15, 1980. $165 includes annual supplements. United States Pharmacopeial Convention, Inc, 12601 Twinbrook Parkway, Rockville, MD 20852.
Formed by the 1980 merger of: National Formulary (ISSN 0084-6414) & United States Pharmacopeia; Which was formerly titled: Pharmacopeia of the United States of America (ISSN 0079-1407)

615 SP ISSN 0067-4176
UNIVERSIDAD DE BARCELONA. FACULTAD DE FARMACIA. MEMORIA.* biennial. price varies. Universidad de Barcelona, Facultad de Farmacia, Av. Jose Antonio 585, Barcelona 7, Spain.

615.19 BL
UNIVERSIDADE DE SAO PAULO. REVISTA DE FARMACIA E BIOQUIMICA. 1939. a. exchange basis. Universidade de Sao Paulo, Faculdade de Farmacia e Bioquimica, Conj. das Quimicas-Cid. Universitaria, Caixa Postal 30786, Sao Paulo, Brazil. bk. rev. circ. 1,000. (back issues avail.) Indexed: Chem.Abstr. I.P.A. Nutr.Abstr. Anal.Abstr. Helminthol.Abstr.
● Also available online.
Formerly: Universidade de Sao Paulo. Faculdade de Farmacia e Bioquimica. Revista; Supersedes in part (1939-1962): Universidade de Sao Paulo. Faculdade de Farmacia. Anais (ISSN 0365-2181)

615.329 547 BL ISSN 0080-0228
UNIVERSIDADE FEDERAL DE PERNAMBUCO. INSTITUTO DE ANTIBIOTICOS. REVISTA. (Text in Portuguese; summaries in English and Portuguese) 1958. irreg., latest vol.5, 1975. avail. on exchange. ‡ Universidade Federal de Pernambuco, Departamento de Antibioticos, Recife, Pernambuco, Brazil. bibl. charts. illus. circ. 800. Indexed: Chem.Abstr.

615.1 CS ISSN 0041-9087
UNIVERSITAS COMENIANA. ACTA PHARMACEUTICAE. (Text in English, German and Russian) 1958. 1-2 nos. per yr. exchange basis. (Univerzita Komenskeho, Farmaceuticka Fakulta) Slovenske Pedagogicke Nakladatelstvo, Sasinkova 5, 815 60 Bratislava, Czechoslovakia (Subscr. to: Univerzita Komenskeho, Farmaceuticka Fakulta, Ustredna Kniznica, Odbojarov 12, 880 34 Bratislava) Ed. Tomas Pardel. charts. illus. index. Indexed: Biol.Abstr. Chem.Abstr. I.P.A.
Formerly: Acta Facultatis Pharmaceuticae Bohemoslovenicae.

615.328 612.405 US ISSN 0083-6729
VITAMINS AND HORMONES: ADVANCES IN RESEARCH AND APPLICATIONS. 1943. irreg., latest vol.42, 1985. Academic Press, Inc (Subsidiary of: Harcourt Brace Jovanovich) Orlando, FL 32887. TEL 305-345-2000. Eds. R. Harris, K. Thimann. index. cum.index: vols.1-5, 1943-1947 in vol.6, 1948; vols.6-10, 1948-1952 in vol.11, 1953; vols.11-15, 1953-1957 in vol.16, 1958. Indexed: Biol.Abstr. Chem.Abstr. Excerp.Med. Ind.Med. Nutr.Abstr. Anim.Breed.Abstr. Biotech.Abstr. Dairy Sci.Abstr. Vet.Bull.

615 JA ISSN 0509-5832
WAKSMAN FOUNDATION OF JAPAN. REPORT. (Text in English) 1962. a. exchange basis. Waksman Foundation of Japan - Nihon Wakkusuman Zaidan, c/o Keio Daigaku Igakubu, 30-8 Daikyo-machi, Shinjuku-ku, Tokyo 106, Japan.

615.19 GW ISSN 0171-4449
WER UND WAS IN DER DEUTSCHEN PHARMAZEUTISCHEN-INDUSTRIE. 1978. biennial. DM.155. B. Behr's GmbH & Co., Averhoffstr. 10, 2000 Hamburg 76, W. Germany (B.R.D.)

615.19 NR ISSN 0303-691X
WEST AFRICAN JOURNAL OF PHARMACOLOGY AND DRUG RESEARCH. 1974. biennial. $10.60. (West African Society for Pharmacology) Literamed Publications Nigeria, Ltd., Oregun Village, P.M.B. 1068, Ikeja, Nigeria. Indexed: Biol.Abstr. Chem.Abstr. Excerp.Med. Ind.Med.

615.1 US ISSN 0083-8969
WESTERN PHARMACOLOGY SOCIETY. PROCEEDINGS. 1958. a. $14. Western Pharmacology Society, c/o Peter Lomax, Ed., Dept. of Pharmacology, U.C.L.A. School of Medicine, Los Angeles, CA 90024. TEL 213-825-6373. circ. 800. (also avail. in microform from UMI; reprint service avail. from UMI) Indexed: Biol.Abstr. Chem.Abstr. Curr.Cont. Excerp.Med. Ind.Med. Nutr.Abstr. Dairy Sci.Abstr.

615 UK
WORLD DIRECTORY OF PHARMACEUTICAL MANUFACTURERS. 1977. a. $200. IMSWORLD Publications Ltd., 11-13 Melton St., London NW1 2EH, England.
● Also available online.

615 UK
WORLD DRUG MARKET MANUAL. 1975. a. $5000. IMSWORLD Publications Ltd., 11-13 Melton St., London NW1 2EH, England.
● Also available online.

615 UK
WORLD LICENSE REVIEW. 1980. a. $750. IMSWORLD Publications Ltd., 11-13 Melton St., London NW1 3EH, England.
● Also available online.

615 JA
YAMANOUCHI SEIYAKU KENKYU HOKOKU/ YAMANOUCHI CENTRAL RESEARCH LABORATORIES. REPORT. (Text in English and Japanese) 1969. a. free. Yamanouchi Central Research Laboratories, 1-8, 1-Chome, Azusawa, Itabashi-ku, Tokyo 174, Japan. circ. 3,000.

615.1058 US ISSN 0084-3733
YEAR BOOK OF DRUG THERAPY. 1933. a. $44.95. Year Book Medical Publishers, Inc., 35 E. Wacker Dr., Chicago, IL 60601. TEL 312-726-9733. Ed. Leo Hollister, M.D. illus.
Formerly: Year Book of General Therapeutics (ISSN 0270-3866)

PHARMACY AND PHARMACOLOGY — Abstracting, Bibliographies, Statistics

615 016 US ISSN 0069-4770
CLIN-ALERT. 1962. 24/yr. $74.95. Science Editors, Inc., 149 Thierman Lane, Box 7185, Louisville, KY 40207. TEL 502-897-5310. Ed. Ramona Scheible. cum.index quarterly. (back issues avail.)
Consists of numbered abstracts of current reports dealing with adverse drug reactions, interactions, related therapeutic hazards

CONTAMINATION CONTROL ABSTRACTS. see *ENGINEERING — Abstracting, Bibliographies, Statistics*

CURRENT BIBLIOGRAPHIES ON SCIENCE & TECHNOLOGY: BIOLOGY, PHARMACY & FOOD SCIENCE. see *BIOLOGY — Abstracting, Bibliographies, Statistics*

615 US
DRUG TRADE NAME CROSS REFERENCE LIST. Cover title: X Ref - (Year) 1973. a. $50. American Society of Hospital Pharmacists, 4630 Montgomery Ave., Bethesda, MD 20814. TEL 301-657-3000. Ed. Dwight R. Tousignaut. (reprint service avail.) Indexed: I.P.A.

615.19 II
INDIAN CHEMICALS AND PHARMACEUTICALS STATISTICS. (Text in English) 1967. a. free. Ministry of Chemicals and Fertilizers, Economics and Statistics Division, New Delhi, India. stat. circ. controlled.

615 016 US ISSN 0020-8264
INTERNATIONAL PHARMACEUTICAL ABSTRACTS; key to the world's literature of pharmacy. 1964. s-m. $375. American Society of Hospital Pharmacists, c/o Jean Rogers, Dir., Mkt. Svcs., 4630 Montgomery Ave., Bethesda, MD 20814. TEL 301-657-3000. Ed. Dwight R. Tousignaut. index. circ. 1,200. (also avail. in microform from UMI; reprint service avail. from UMI) Indexed: Anal.Abstr. JAMA.
● Also available online. Vendors: BRS, DIALOG, European Space Agency.

615.19 UK ISSN 0264-2247
INTERNATIONAL PHARMACEUTICAL TECHNOLOGY & PRODUCT MANUFACTURE ABSTRACTS. 1983. q. £80($168) Childwall University Press Ltd., Box 78, London NW11 0PG, England. Ed.Bd.

615 016 US ISSN 0362-4439
PHARMACEUTICAL NEWS INDEX. (Hard copy ceased 1984) 1976. m. Data Courier, 620 S. Fifth St., Louisville, KY 40202. TEL 800-626-2823. Ed. Susan Baker. bibl. (looseleaf format; back issues avail.)
● Available only online. Vendors: DIALOG.

615.1 US ISSN 0031-7152
PHARMINDEX. 1958. m. $92 (renewal $71) Skyline Publishers, Inc., Box 1029 University Sta., Portland, OR 97207. TEL 503-228-6568. Ed. Frank D. Portash. mkt. tr.lit. index m. and a. Indexed: Chem.Abstr. I.P.A. Excerp.Med.

016 615.9 US ISSN 0140-5365
TOXICOLOGY ABSTRACTS. 1978. m. $445. Cambridge Scientific Abstracts, 5161 River Rd., Bethesda, MD 20816. TEL 301-951-1400. adv. bk. rev. index. (also avail. in magnetic tape) Indexed: Cal.Tiss.Abstr. Chemorec.Abstr. Oncol.Abstr.
● Also available online. Vendors: DIALOG.

PHILATELY

769.56 DK
A F A DANMARK FIREBLOKKE. irreg. Aarhus Frimaerkehandel, Bruunsgade 42, 8000 Arhus C, Denmark. illus.

769.56 DK
A F A DANMARK FRIMAERKEKATALOG. irreg. Aarhus Frimaerkehandel, Bruunsgade 42, 8000 Arhus C, Denmark. illus.

769.56 DK
A F A OESTEUROPA FRIMAERKEKATALOG. Title varies: Oesteuropa Frimaerkekatalog. irreg. Aarhus Frimaerkehandel, Bruunsgade 42, 8000 Aarhus C, Denmark. illus.
Supersedes in part: A F A Europe Frimaerkekatolog.

769.56 DK
A F A SKANDINAVIEN FRIMAERKEKATALOG. irreg. Aarhus Frimaerkehandel, Bruunsgade 42, 8000 Arhus C, Denmark. illus.

769.56 DK
A F A VESTEUROPA FRIMAERKEKATALOG. Title varies: Vesteuropa Frimaerkekatalog. 1974. irreg. Aarhus Frimaerkehandel, Bruunsgade 4, 8000 Aarhus C, Denmark. illus.
Supersedes in part: A F A Europa Frimaerkekatalog.

769.56 UK ISSN 0142-9868
AFRICA SINCE INDEPENDENCE STAMP CATALOGUE. (In three parts) 1980. irreg. price varies. Stanley Gibbons Publications Ltd., Unit 5 Parkside, Christchurch Rd., Ringwood, Hamps. BH24 3SH, England.

769.56 US
AMERICAN PHILATELIC CONGRESS. CONGRESS BOOK. 1935. a. $17.50 to non-members; members $15. American Philatelic Congress, c/o Mary Ann Owens, Sec.-Treas., Box 1164, Brooklyn, NY 11202-1164. Ed. Barbara Mueller. bk. rev. charts, illus. cum.index every 5 yrs. circ. 1,000.

769.56 AT ISSN 0155-8498
AUSTRALASIAN STAMP CATALOGUE. 1964. a. Aus.$9.95. Seven Seas Stamps Pty. Ltd., 62 Wingewarra St., Dubbo 2830, Australia. Ed. D.A. Foster. bk. rev. illus. circ. 40,000.

760 AT
AUSTRALIAN STAMP BULLETIN. 1979. irreg. free. Australia Post Headquarters, Stamps and Philatelic Branch, P.O. Box 302, Carlton South, Vic. 3053, Australia (Subscriptions to: Australian Stamp Bulletin, Locked Bag 8, South Melbourne, Vic. 3205, Australia) bk. rev. circ. 360,000.
Formerly: Philatelic Bulletin.

769.56 UK ISSN 0142-9760
AUSTRIA & HUNGARY STAMP CATALOGUE. 1979. irreg. price varies. Stanley Gibbons Publications Ltd., Unit 5 Parkside, Christchurch Rd., Ringwood, Hamps. BH24 3SH, England.

769.56 UK
BALE CATALOGUE OF ISRAEL POSTAGE STAMPS. 1969. a. price varies. Michael H. Bale, Ed. & Pub., 41 High St., Ilfracombe, England. adv. circ. 2,500.
Former titles: Bale Catalogue of Palestine and Israel Stamps (ISSN 0305-4039); Bale Catalogue of Israel Stamps (ISSN 0067-3048)

769.56 UK ISSN 0142-9779
BALKANS STAMP CATALOGUE. 1980. irreg. price varies. Stanley Gibbons Publications Ltd., Unit 5 Parkside, Christchurch Rd., Ringwood, Hamps. BH24 3SH, England.

769.56 GW ISSN 0005-4364
BALLON KURIER. 1952. a. free. Pestalozzi Kinder- und Jugenddorf Wahlwies, 7768 Stockach 14, W. Germany (B.R.D.) Ed. H.J. Scheer. adv. bk. rev. illus. circ. 3,000. (looseleaf format)

769.56 UK ISSN 0142-9787
BENELUX STAMP CATALOGUE. 1979. irreg. price varies. Stanley Gibbons Publications Ltd., Unit 5 Parkside, Christchurch Rd., Ringwood, Hamps. BH24 3SH, England.

737 UK ISSN 0142-9752
BRITISH COMMONWEALTH STAMP CATALOGUE. 1865. a. £17.50. Stanley Gibbons Publications Ltd., Unit 5 Parkside, Christchurch Rd., Ringwood, Hamps. BH24 3SH, England.

769.56 UK ISSN 0950-575X
BRITISH JOURNAL OF RUSSIAN PHILATELY. (Text in English; summaries occasionally in transliterated Russian) 1937. a. £8($12) membership. British Society of Russian Philately, c/o N.J.D. Ames, Freefolk Priory, Freefolk, Whitchurch, Hants RG28 7NL, England. Ed. R.L. Joseph. bk. rev. index. circ. 250 (controlled) Indexed: Stamp J.Ind.

769.56 UK
BRITISH PHILATELIC FEDERATION. CONGRESS HANDBOOK. irreg.? $7.50. (Practical Publishing Ltd.) Stamp News Ltd., 6 London St., London W2 1HR, England.

769.56 UK
BRITISH STAMP VALUES. 1979. a. £2.95. Link House Magazines Ltd., Link House, Dingwall Ave., Croydon CR9 2TA, England. Ed. Richard West.

769.56 NZ
CAMPBELL PATERSON'S LOOSE-LEAF COLOUR CATALOGUE OF NEW ZEALAND STAMPS (SPECIALISED) 1953. a. NZ.$59.75. Campbell Paterson Ltd., P.O. Box 5555, Auckland 1, New Zealand.

769.56 UK ISSN 0142-9876
CENTRAL AMERICA STAMP CATALOGUE. 1980. irreg. price varies. Stanley Gibbons Publications Ltd., Unit 5 Parkside, Christchurch Rd., Ringwood, Hamps. BH24 2SH, England.

769.56 UK ISSN 0142-9884
CENTRAL ASIA STAMP CATALOGUE. 1981. irreg. price varies. Stanley Gibbons Publications Ltd., Unit 5 Parkside, Christchurch Rd., Ringwood, Hamps. BH24 2SH, England.

769.56 CS
CESKOSLOVENSKO. Spine title: Katalog Ceskoslovenskych Znamek. irreg. 40 Kcs. (Postovni Filatelisticka Sluzba) Nakladatelstvi Dopravy a Spoju, Hybernska 5, 115 78 Prague 1, Czechoslovakia. illus.

769.56 UK ISSN 0142-5625
CHANNEL ISLANDS SPECIALISED CATALOGUE. 1979. irreg. price varies. Stanley Gibbons Publications Ltd., Unit 5 Parkside, Christchurch Rd., Ringwood, Hamps. BH24 3SH, England.

769.56 UK
CHANNEL ISLANDS STAMPS AND POSTAL HISTORY. 1979. irreg. £6. Stanley Gibbons Publications, 5 Parkside, Ringwood, Hampshire BH24 3SH, England. Ed. David Aggersberg.

769.56 UK ISSN 0142-9892
CHINA STAMP CATALOGUE. 1979. irreg. price varies. Stanley Gibbons Publications Ltd., Unit 5 Parkside, Chrishchurch Rd., Ringwood, Hamps. BH24 3SH, England.

769.56 UK
COLLECT BIRDS ON STAMPS. 1983. irreg. price varies. Stanley Gibbons Publications Ltd., Unit 5 Parkside, Christchurch Rd., Ringwood, Hamps. BH24 3SH, England.

769.56 UK
COLLECT CHANNEL ISLANDS AND ISLE OF MAN STAMPS. 1972. a. price varies. Stanley Gibbons Publications Ltd., Unit 5 Parkside, Christchurch Rd., Ringwood, Hamps. BH24 3SH, England.
Formerly (until 1984): Collect Channel Islands Stamps (ISSN 0306-5103)

769.56 990 AT ISSN 0727-4211
COLLECTION OF AUSTRALIAN STAMPS. 1981. a. Aus.$37.95. Australia Post, P.O. Box 302, Carlton South, Victoria 3053, Australia (Subscr. to: Philatelic Bureau, GPO Box 9988, Melbourne, VIC 3001, Australia) Ed. J. Monie. illus.

769.56 UK ISSN 0142-9795
CZECHOSLOVAKIA & POLAND STAMP CATALOGUE. 1980. irreg. price varies. Stanley Gibbons Publications Ltd., Unit 5 Parkside, Christchurch Rd., Ringwood, Hamps. BH24 3SH, England.

769.56 DK ISSN 0109-3371
D K; frimaerkatalog Danmark, med Groenland, Faeroeerne D V I, Island (Kongeriget) 1984. a. Kr.88. Saga, P.O. Box 82, 3520 Farum, Denmark (Orders to: Danske Boghendleres Kommissionsanstalt, Siljangade 6, 2300 Copenhagen S, Denmark) Ed. Tove Christensen. adv. illus. circ. 5,000.

759.56 US
DUCK STAMP DATA. base vol. plus update service. $12. U.S. Fish & Wildlife Service, Department of the Interior, Washington, DC 20246 TEL 202-653-7501. (Orders to: Supt. of Documents, Washington, DC 20402)

769.56 SW
EESTI FILATELIST/ESTONIAN PHILATELIST. (Text in English and German; summaries in English) a. Society of Estonian Philatelists in Sweden, Mandolingatan 17, S-421 45 Vastra Frolunda, Sweden. Ed. Elmar Ojaste. circ. 700. (back issues avail.)

769.56 UK
ELIZABETHAN CATALOGUE OF MODERN COMMONWEALTH STAMPS. 1965. a. price varies. ‡ Stanley Gibbons Publications Ltd., Unit 5 Parkside, Christchurch Rd., Ringwood, Hamps. BH24 3SH, England. illus.
Formerly: Elizabethan Stamp Catalogue (ISSN 0071-0024)

769.56 YU ISSN 0015-0967
FILATELIJA. (Text in Croatian) 1940. irreg. (2-3/yr.) $2.50 per no. Hrvatski Filatelisticki Savez, Habdeliceva 2, 41000 Zagreb, Yugoslavia. Ed. Velimir Ercegovic. adv. bk. rev. illus. index. circ. 4, 500.

796.56 DK ISSN 0108-0296
FILATELISTISK KATALOG-NOEGLE/PHILATELISTIC CATALOGUE KEY/PHILATELISTISCHER KATALOG-SCHLUESSEL. (Text in Danish, English, French and German) 1981. a. Kr.49. Kylling & Soen, Sankt Knuds Vej 10, 3000 Helsingoer, Denmark. Preben Kylling. adv. illus. circ. 5,000.

769.56 UK ISSN 0142-9809
FRANCE STAMP CATALOGUE. 1979. irreg. price varies. Stanley Gibbons Publications Ltd., Unit 5 Parkside, Christchurch Rd., Ringwood, Hamps. BH24 3SH, England.

769.56 UK ISSN 0142-9817
GERMANY STAMP CATALOGUE. 1979. irreg. price varies. Stanley Gibbons Publications Ltd., Unit 5 Parkside, Christchurch Rd., Ringwood, Hamps. BH24 3SH, England.

769.56 UK ISSN 0072-7229
GREAT BRITAIN SPECIALISED STAMP CATALOGUE. (Issued in 4 volumes) 1963. irreg. price varies. ‡ Stanley Gibbons Publications Ltd., Unit 5 Parkside, Christchurch Rd., Ringwood, Hamps. BH24 3SH, England. index.

760 AT
GREAT WALL. 1956. irreg. China Stamp Collector's Club of Australasia, c/o Norman S. Hale, Box H137, Australia Square, Sydney, N.S.W. 2000, Australia. Ed. S. R. Tyler.

769.56 GT ISSN 0046-6549
GUATEMALA FILATELICA. 1932. a. $6. ‡ Asociacion Filatelica de Guatemala, Apdo. Postal 39, Guatemala. Ed. Col. Romeo J. Routhier. adv. bk. rev. charts. illus. stat. circ. 500.

383.2 US ISSN 0072-9981
HANDBOOK ON U.S. LUMINESCENT STAMPS. 1970. irreg. (every 2-3 yrs.) latest, 1975. $4. ‡ Alfred G. Boerger, Ed. & Pub., Box 23822, Ft. Lauderdale, FL 33307. TEL 305-563-6590. adv. bk. rev. circ. 3,000.

769.56 US
HAWAIIAN PHILATELIST. 1978. irreg., approx. 6/yr. $9.95. Los Angeles Stamp Company, c/o Gretchen H. Mitchell, Box 1387, Los Angeles, CA 90078. TEL 213-467-2215. bk. rev.

769.56 SZ ISSN 0074-7343
INTERNATIONAL PHILATELIC FEDERATION. GENERAL ASSEMBLY. PROCES-VERBAL. 1973. irreg. (5-6/yr.) free to members. International Philatelic Federation - Federation Internationale de Philatelie, Via Cortivo 22c, CH-6976 Castagnola, Switzerland.

769.56 UK ISSN 0142-9825
ITALY & SWITZERLAND STAMP CATALOGUE. 1980. irreg. price varies. Stanley Gibbons Publications Ltd., Unit 5 Parkside, Christchurch Rd., Ringwood, Hamps. BH24 3SH, England.

769.56 UK ISSN 0142-9906
JAPAN & KOREA STAMP CATALOGUE. 1980. irreg. price varies. Stanley Gibbons Publications Ltd., Unit 5 Parkside, Christchurch Rd., Ringwood, Hamps. BH24 3SH, England.

769.56 GW ISSN 0076-7727
MICHEL-BRIEFMARKEN-KATALOGE. 1910. a. and irreg. price varies. Schwaneberger Verlag GmbH, Muthmannstr. 4, D-8000 Munich 45, W. Germany (B.R.D.)

769.56 UK ISSN 0142-9914
MIDDLE EAST STAMP CATALOGUE. 1980. irreg. price varies. Stanley Gibbons Publications Ltd., Unit 5 Parkside, Christchurch Rd., Ringwood, Hamps. BH24 3SH, England.

769.56 US ISSN 0076-9029
MINKUS AUSTRIA, SWITZERLAND, LICHTENSTEIN STAMP CATALOG. 1981. biennial. $4.25. Minkus Publications, Inc., 41 W. 25th St., New York, NY 10010. Ed. George Tlamsa.

769.56 US
MINKUS BELGIUM, NETHERLANDS, LUXEMBOURG COLONIES STAMP CATALOGUE. biennial. $5.75. Minkus Publications, Inc., 41 W. 25th St., New York, NY 10010. Ed. George A. Tlamsa.

769.56 US
MINKUS FRANCE, MONACO, ANDORRA STAMP CATALOG. biennial. $5.95. Minkus Publications, Inc., 41 W. 25th St., New York, NY 10010. Ed. Joseph Zollman.

769.56 US
MINKUS GREECE, TURKEY STAMP CATALOG. biennial. $4.75. Minkus Publications, Inc., 41 W. 25th St., New York, NY 10010. Ed. George A. Tlamsa.

769.56 US ISSN 0076-9053
MINKUS ITALY, SAN MARINO AND VATICAN STAMP CATALOG. 1961. biennial. $5.25. Minkus Publications, Inc., 41 W. 25th St., New York, NY 10010. Ed. George Tlamsa.

769.56 US ISSN 0076-9061
MINKUS NEW AMERICAN STAMP CATALOG. 1953. a. $9.95. Minkus Publications, Inc., 41 W. 25 St., New York, NY 10010. TEL 212-741-1334. Ed. Mark Rosenstein.

769.56 US ISSN 0076-907X
MINKUS NEW WORLD WIDE STAMP CATALOG. 1955. a. Minkus Publications, Inc., 41 W. 25 St., New York, NY 10010. TEL 212-741-1334.

769.56 US
MINKUS SCANDINAVIA, BALTIC COUNTRIES STAMP CATALOG. biennial. Minkus Publications, Inc., 141 W. 25th St., New York, NY 10010. Ed. Joseph Zollman.

769.56 US ISSN 0078-091X
NOBLE OFFICIAL CATALOG OF CANADA PRECANCELS. 1923. irreg., 13th ed., 1981. $3. Gilbert W. Noble, Ed. & Pub., Box 931, Winter Park, FL 32789. TEL 305-647-2431. circ. 2,000.

769.56 US ISSN 0078-0928
NOBLE OFFICIAL CATALOG OF UNITED STATES BUREAU PRECANCELS. 1926. irreg. $6. Gilbert W. Noble, Ed. & Pub., Box 931, Winter Park, FL 32789. circ. 1,000.

736 DK ISSN 0105-9106
NORDISK JULEMAERKE KATALOG; Nordic Christmas seal catalogue. 1977. biennial. Kronprinsensvej 43, DK-2000 Copenhagen F, Denmark.

769.56 PK ISSN 0078-8422
PAKISTAN POSTAGE STAMPS. (Text in English) 1960. irreg., latest 1966. Rs.1.50. Post Office Department, Karachi, Pakistan. adv. circ. 6,000.

769.55 AT ISSN 0155-6215
POCKET AUSTRALIAN STAMP CATALOGUE. 1970. a. Aus.$3.25. Seven Seas Stamps Pty. Ltd., 62 Wingewarra St., Dubbo, N.S.W. 2830, Australia. Ed. D. Foster. illus. circ. 35,000.

769.56 UK ISSN 0142-9833
PORTUGAL & SPAIN STAMP CATALOGUE. 1980. irreg. price varies. Stanley Gibbons Publications Ltd., Unit 5 Parkside, Christchurch Rd., Ringwood, Hamps. BH24 3SH, England.

769.56 NZ
POSTAGE STAMPS OF NEW ZEALAND. irreg. Royal Philatelic Society of New Zealand, Box 1269, Wellington, New Zealand.

769.56 UK ISSN 0140-8003
PRIVATE POST. 1977. a. £3. Cinderella Stamp Club, c/o L.N. Williams, Ed., 44 The Ridgeway, London NW11 8QS, England. bibl. illus. circ. 600. (back issues avail.)

769 SA
R.S.A. POSTAGE STAMP CATALOGUE. 1969. irreg. R.3.25. Arcade Stamp Shop, Investment Bldg., 97 Commissioner St., Johannesburg, South Africa. Eds. N. Dorn, C. Slagt. illus. circ. 3,000.

769.56 RH
RHODESIA STAMP CATALOGUE. 1971. a. Z.$9.75. Zimbabwe Stamp Co. (Pvt.) Ltd., Box 200, Harare, Zimbabwe. Ed. D.G. Pollard. illus. index. circ. 7,000.

769.56 NZ
ROYAL PHILATELIC SOCIETY OF NEW ZEALAND. ANNUAL REPORT. a. Royal Philatelic Society of New Zealand, Box 1269, Wellington, New Zealand. Ed. D.B. Tennant. adv.

769.56 UK ISSN 0142-9841
RUSSIA STAMP CATALOGUE. 1981. irreg. price varies. Stanley Gibbons Publications Ltd., Unit 5 Parkside, Christchurch Rd., Ringwood, Hamps. BH24 3SH, England.

769.56 UK ISSN 0142-985X
SCANDINAVIA STAMP CATALOGUE. 1980. irreg. price varies. Stanley Gibbons Publications Ltd., Unit 5 Parkside, Christchurch Rd., Ringwood, Hamps. BH24 3SH, England.

769.56 UK ISSN 0080-8164
SCOTTISH POSTMARK GROUP. HANDBOOK.* 1962. irreg. price varies. Scottish Postmark Group, David C. Jefferies, 11 Craigcrook Ave., Edinburgh EH4 3QE, Scotland.

769.56 US
SCOTT'S SPECIALIZED CATALOGUE OF U.S. STAMPS. 1923. a. Scott Publishing Company, Box 828, Sidney, OH 45365. Ed. William Cummings.

769.56 US
SCOTT'S STANDARD POSTAGE STAMP CATALOGUE. 1867. a. Scott Publishing Company, Box 828, Sidney, OH 45365. Ed. William Cummings.

769.56 UK ISSN 0142-9922
SOUTH AMERICA STAMP CATALOGUE. 1980. irreg. price varies. Stanley Gibbons Publications Ltd., Unit 5 Parkside, Christchurch Rd., Ringwood, Hamps. BH24 3SH, England.

769.56 UK ISSN 0142-9930
SOUTH-EAST ASIA STAMP CATALOGUE. 1981. irreg. price varies. Stanley Gibbons Publications Ltd., Unit 5 Parkside, Christchurch Rd., Ringwood, Hamps. BH24 3SH, England.

769.56 US
STAMP EXCHANGERS ANNUAL DIRECTORY. 1963. a. $3.50. Levine Publications, Box 3987, Trenton, NJ 08629. Ed. L. Jan Olssen. adv. bk. rev. charts. illus. circ. 5,872.

769.56 UK ISSN 0081-4210
STAMPS OF THE WORLD. (In two volumes) 1934. a. price varies. ‡ Stanley Gibbons Publications Ltd., Unit 5 Parkside, Christchurch Rd., Ringwood, Hamps. BH24 3SH, England.

769.56 UK ISSN 0144-249X
STANLEY GIBBONS POSTCARD CATALOGUE. 1980. irreg. £4.95. Stanley Gibbons Publications Ltd., Unit 5 Parkside, Christchurch Rd., Ringwood, Hamps. BH24 3SH, England.

769.56 US ISSN 0090-7286
TOPICAL NEW ISSUES. (Subseries of: American Topical Association. Topical Handbook) a. $7. American Topical Association, Inc., Box 630, Johnstown, PA 15907. illus.

769.56 US ISSN 0049-4135
TOPICAL STAMP HANDBOOKS. 1951. irreg., no.110, 1986. price varies. American Topical Association, Inc., Box 630, Johnstown, PA 15907. TEL 814-539-6301. Ed. Donald W. Smith. index, cum. index. every 5 yrs.

383.2 US
UNITED STATES POSTAGE STAMPS. 1927. irreg. $8.50. U.S. Postal Service, 475 l'Enfant Plaza West S.W., Washington, DC 20260 TEL 202-245-4000. (Orders to: Supt. Doc., Washington, DC 20402) Formerly (until 1970): Postage Stamps of the United States (ISSN 0079-4244)

769.56 UK ISSN 0142-9949
UNITED STATES STAMP CATALOGUE. 1981. irreg. price varies. Stanley Gibbons Publications Ltd., Unit 5 Parkside, Christchurch Rd., Ringwood, Hamps. BH24 3SH, England.

769.56 UK ISSN 0260-1265
YEARBOOK AND PHILATELIC SOCIETIES' DIRECTORY. a. (British Philatelic Federation) Stamp News Ltd., 6 London St., London W2 1HR, England.

769.56 RH
ZIMBABWE STAMP CATALOGUE. a. Zimbabwe Stamp Co. (Pvt.) Ltd., Box 200, Harare, Zimbabwe. Ed. D.G. Pollard.

769.56 US
7-1-71 AFFAIR CATALOG/HANDBOOK. 1976. a. $3.95. R E M Catalog, Box 985, Morrow, GA 30260-0985 TEL 404-961-4624. Ed. Roy E. Mooney. adv. bk. rev. circ. 300. (looseleaf format; back issues avail.)

PHILOSOPHY

see also Religions and Theology

100 370 GW ISSN 0065-0366
ABHANDLUNGEN ZUR PHILOSOPHIE, PSYCHOLOGIE UND PAEDAGOGIK. 1954. irreg., vol.205, 1986. price varies. Bouvier Verlag Herbert Grundmann, Am Hof 32, Postfach 1268, 5300 Bonn 1, W. Germany (B.R.D.)

100 HU ISSN 0324-6302
ACTA MARXISTICA LENINISTICA. FILOZOFIAI TANULMANYOK. (Text in Hungarian, occasionally German, Russian) 1962. irreg., vol.28, 1982. Kossuth Lajos Tudomanyegyetem, Egyetem Ter 1, 4010 Debrecen, Hungary. Ed. Istvan Konya.

140 HU ISSN 0324-6353
ACTA MARXISTICA LENINISTICA. TUDOMANYOS SZOCIALIZMUS TANULMANYOK. (Text in Hungarian, occasionally German, Russian) 1962. irreg., vol.29, 1983. Kossuth Lajos Tudomanyegyetem, Egyetem Ter 1, 4010 Debrecen, Hungary. Ed. Dezso Farkas.

PHILOSOPHY

100 200   IT   ISSN 0065-1540
ACTA PHILOSOPHICA ET THEOLOGICA. (Text in English, French, German, Italian, Rumanian, Spanish) 1958. irreg. price varies. Societa Accademica Romena, Foro Traiano 1a, 00187 Rome, Italy.

100   SW   ISSN 0283-2380
ACTA PHILOSOPHICA GOTHOBURGENSIA. a. Kr.125. University of Gothenburg, Department of Philosophy, P.O. Box 5096, S-402 22 Goeteborg, Sweden (Distr.in U.S by: Humanities Press Inc., 171 First Ave., Atlantic Highlands, NJ 07716-1289) Ed. Claes Aaberg.

100 370   PL   ISSN 0208-6107
ACTA UNIVERSITATIS LODZIENSIS: FOLIA PHILOSOPHICA. (Text in Polish; summaries in various languages) 1981. irreg. Uniwersytet Lodzki, Drukarnia Wojskowa, Ul. Gdanska 130, Lodz, Poland (Dist. by: Ars Polona-Ruch, Krakowskie Przedmiescie 7, Warsaw, Poland) Ed.Bd. Indexed: Math.R.
    Supersedes in part: Uniwersytet Lodzki. Zeszyty Naukowe. Seria 1: Nauki Humanistyczno-Spoleczne.

100   PL   ISSN 0208-564X
ACTA UNIVERSITATIS NICOLAI COPERNICI. FILOZOFIA. 1960. irreg. price varies. Uniwersytet Mikolaja Kopernika, Fosa Staromiejska 3, Torun, Poland (Dist.by Osrodek Rozpowszechniania Wydawnictw Naukowych PAN, Palac Kultury i Nauki, 00-901 Warsaw, Poland)
    Formerly: Uniwersytet Mikolaja Kopernika, Torun. Nauki Humanistyczno-Spoleczne. Filozofia (ISSN 0083-4475)

100   HU   ISSN 0231-2670
ACTA UNIVERSITATIS SZEGEDIENSIS DE ATTILA JOZSEF NOMINATAE. SECTION PHILOSOPHICA - FILOZOFIA. (Text in Hungarian; summaries in English or Russian) 1943. a. exchange basis. Attila Jozsef University, c/o E. Szabo, Exchange Librarian, Dugonics ter 13, P.O.B. 393, Szeged H-6701, Hungary (Subscr. to: Kultura, Box 149, H-1389 Budapest, Hungary) Ed. Laszlo Horuczi. circ. 500.
    Supersedes (as of 1959): Acta Universitatis Szegediensis. Sectio Philosophica (ISSN 0586-3724)

100   SA
AFRIQUE ET PHILOSOPHIE. (Text in French) 1976. a. 350 Fr.CFA. Faculte de Theologie Catholique de Kinshasa, Cercle Philosphique de Kinshasa, B.P. 1534, Kinshasa-Limete, Zaire. Ed. Kadioto Kabanda. adv. bk. rev. circ. 100.

100 301   IT
AGORA (RAVENNA) irreg. Angelo Longo Editore, Via Paolo Costa 33, P.O. Box 431, 48100 Ravenna, Italy.

100   CL   ISSN 0568-3939
AISTHESIS; revista chilena de investigaciones esteticas. 1966. a. $6.50. Pontificia Universidad Catolica de Chile, Instituto de Estetica, Diagonal Oriente 3.100, Santiago, Chile. Ed. Radoslav Ivelic. bibl. cum.index. circ. 1,000. Indexed: Hisp.Amer.Per.Ind.

ALEA. see *LITERATURE*

100   LH   ISSN 0149-2004
ALETHEIA; an international journal of philosophy. (Text in English, German) 1977. a. $14. Internationale Akademie der Philosophie, Obergass 75, FL-9494 Schaan, Lichtenstein. Ed. Josef Seifert. Indexed: Phil.Ind.

282 206   US   ISSN 0065-7638
AMERICAN CATHOLIC PHILOSOPHICAL ASSOCIATION. PROCEEDINGS. 1926. a. $12. American Catholic Philosophical Association, The Catholic University of America, 403 Administration Bldg., Washington, DC 20064. TEL 202-635-5518. Ed. Daniel O. Dahlstrom. adv. cum.index: vols.1-32, 1926-58. (also avail. in microfilm from UMI; reprint service avail. from UMI) Indexed: Cath.Ind. Curr.Cont. Arts & Hum.Cit.Ind. Phil.Ind.

AMERICAN PHILOSOPHICAL SOCIETY. MEMOIRS. see *HISTORY*

AMERICAN PHILOSOPHICAL SOCIETY. TRANSACTIONS. see *HISTORY*

106   US   ISSN 0065-9762
AMERICAN PHILOSOPHICAL SOCIETY. YEARBOOK. 1937. a. $10. American Philosophical Society, 104 S. Fifth St., Philadelphia, PA 19106. TEL 215-627-0706. Ed. Herman H. Goldstine. index. (also avail. in microform from UMI; reprint service avail. from UMI,ISI) Indexed: Hist.Abstr. Amer.Hist.& Life. GeoRef.

100   US
AMERICAN UNIVERSITY STUDIES. SERIES 5. PHILOSOPHY. 1983. irreg. Peter Lang Publishing, Inc., 62 West 45th St., New York, NY 10036. TEL 212-302-6740.

100   NE
ANALECTA CARTESIANA. (Text in French) 1981. irreg. price varies. Quadratures, Postbus 6463, 1005 EL Amsterdam, Netherlands.
    Formerly: Collectanea Cartesiana.

100   NE
ANALECTA HUSSERLIANA; yearbook of phenomenological research. (Text in English) 1971. irreg. price varies. D. Reidel Publishing Co., Box 17, 3300 AA Dordrecht, Netherlands (And 190 Old Derby St., Hingham, MA 02043) Ed. Anna-Teresa Tymieniecka.

891   II
ANANDA ACHARYA UNIVERSAL SERIES. (Text in English) 1978. irreg. price varies. Vishveshvaranand Vedic Research Institute, P.O. Sadhu Ashram, Hoshiarpur 146021, Punjab, India.

ANNALES D'ESTHETIQUE/CHRONIKA AISTHETIKES. see *ART*

100 301   PL   ISSN 0137-2025
ANNALES UNIVERSITATIS MARIAE CURIE-SKLODOWSKA. SECTIO I. PHILOSOPHIA-SOCIOLOGIA. (Text in English or Polish; summaries in English, French, German, Russian) 1976. a. price varies. Uniwersytet Marii Curie-Sklodowskiej, Plac Marii Curie-Sklodowskiej 5, 20-031 Lublin, Poland. Ed. Z. Cackowski. circ. 500.

100   IT
ANNUARIO FILOSOFICO (YEAR) a. L.50000. U. Mursia Editore spa, Via Tadino 29, 20124 Milano, Italy.

ANTICHITA CLASSICA E CRISTIANA. see *HISTORY*

104   US   ISSN 0066-5614
AQUINAS LECTURE SERIES. 1937. a. price varies. (Marquette University, Aristotelean Society) Marquette University Press, 1324 W. Wisconsin Ave., Milwaukee, WI 53233. TEL 414-224-1564. (back issues avail.)

170 300 340   GW   ISSN 0341-079X
ARCHIV FUER RECHTS- UND SOZIALPHILOSOPHIE. BEIHEFTE. (Text in English, French, German) irreg., vol.29, 1987. price varies. (Internationale Vereinigung fuer Rechts- und Sozialphilosophie) Franz Steiner Verlag Wiesbaden GmbH, Birkenwaldstr. 44, Postfach 347, D-7000 Stuttgart 1, W. Germany (B.R.D.)

100   GW   ISSN 0722-5679
ARCHIV FUER RECHTS UND SOZIALPHILOSOPHIE. SUPPLEMENTA. irreg., vol.1, part 4, 1983. price varies. (Internationale Vereinigung fuer Rechts und Sozialphilosophie) Franz Steiner Verlag Wiesbaden GmbH, Birkenwaldstr. 44, Postfach 347, D-7000 Stuttgart 1, W. Germany (B.R.D.)

180   FR   ISSN 0373-5478
ARCHIVES D'HISTOIRE DOCTRINALE ET LITTERAIRE DU MOYEN AGE. (Text in English, French, German and Latin) 1926. a. price varies. Librairie Philosophique J. Vrin, 6 Place de la Sorbonne, 75005 Paris, France. Ed.Bd. index. circ. 750. Indexed: M.L.A.

100   NE   ISSN 0066-6610
ARCHIVES INTERNATIONALES D'HISTOIRE DES IDEES/INTERNATIONAL ARCHIVES OF THE HISTORY OF IDEAS. (Text in English and French) 1963. irreg. price varies. Martinus Nijhoff Publishers, Postbus 163, 3300 AD Dordrecht, Netherlands. Eds. P. Dibon, R. Popkin.

100   SP
ARCHIVUM (OVIEDO) (Text in Spanish) 1950. a. 4, 500 ptas. Universidad Oviedo, Arias de Velsco, No.2, Oviedo, Spain.

109 309   PL   ISSN 0066-6874
ARCHIWUM HISTORII FILOZOFII I MYSLI SPOLECZNEJ. (Text in Polish; summaries in French, German, or Russian) 1954. a. price varies. (Polska Akademia Nauk, Instytut Filozofii i Socjologii) Ossolineum, Publishing House of the Polish Academy of Sciences, Rynek 9, Wroclaw, Poland. Ed. Andrzej Walicki.

100   UK
ARGUMENTS OF THE PHILOSOPHERS. irreg. price varies. Routledge & Kegan Paul PLC, 11 New Fetter Lane, London EC4P 4EE, England (U.S. address: 9 Park St., Boston, MA 02108)

149   US   ISSN 0304-1409
ATHEIST. (Issued as a supplement to the Truth Seeker) 1946. irreg. $9. (Atheist Association) Truth Seeker Co., Inc., Box 2832, San Diego, CA 92112. TEL 619-574-7600. Ed. James Hervey Johnson. circ. 500.

100   AT
AUSTRALASIAN JOURNAL OF PHILOSOPHY. MONOGRAPH SERIES. 1982. irreg. Aus.$12 per no. Australasian Association of Philosophy, Philosophy Department, La Trobe University, Bundoora, Vic. 3083, Australia. Ed. Brian Ellis. circ. 1,200.

AUSTRALASIAN STUDIES IN HISTORY AND PHILOSOPHY OF SCIENCE. see *SOCIAL SCIENCES: COMPREHENSIVE WORKS*

100 230   GW   ISSN 0067-5024
BEITRAEGE ZUR GESCHICHTE DER PHILOSOPHIE UND THEOLOGIE DES MITTELALTERS NEUE FOLGE. 1894; N.S. 1970. irreg. price varies. Aschendorffsche Verlagsbuchhandlung, Soester Str. 13, 4400 Muenster, W. Germany (B.R.D.) Eds. Ludwig Hoedl, Wolfgang Kluxen.

100 320   GE   ISSN 0232-2803
BEITRAEGE ZUR KRITIK DER BUERGERLICHEN IDEOLOGIE UND DES REVISIONISMUS. 1976. irreg., vol.11, 1983. Akademie-Verlag Berlin, Leipziger Str. 3-4, 1086 Berlin, E. Germany (D.D.R.)

105   FR   ISSN 0339-8498
BELISANE; bulletin de philosophie et d'histoire traditionnelles. 1977. q. 24 F. Claude Boumendil, Repro 2000, 11 rue Gutenberg, 06000 Nice, France. Eds. Claude Passet, Daniel Robert.

100 011   GW   ISSN 0173-1831
BIBLIOGRAPHIEN ZUR PHILOSOPHIE. (Text in English and German) 1979. irreg. price varies. Edition Gemini, Nonnenwerthstr. 66, D-5000 Koeln 41, W. Germany (B.R.D.) Ed. Gernot Gabel. circ. 200. (back issues avail.)

BIBLIOTECA DE ESTUDIOS PARAGUAYOS. see *HISTORY — History Of North And South America*

100   PO
BIBLIOTECA DE FILOSOFIA; filosofia e epistemologia. 1977. a. Esc.350($7) Regra do Jogo, Edicoes Lda., Rua Luz Soriano, 19 s/1 Esq., 1200 Lisboa, Portugal. Eds. Fernando Gil, Manuel Maria Carrilho.

100   BE   ISSN 0067-8430
BIBLIOTHEQUE PHILOSOPHIQUE DE LOUVAIN. (Text in Flemish, French) 1947. irreg. price varies. (Institut de Philosophie de Louvain) Editions Nauwelaerts, 148 Mechelstraat, 3000 Louvain, Belgium.

100   GW   ISSN 0344-1857
BONNER AKADEMISCHE REDEN. no.16, 1951. irreg., no.59, 1984. price varies. Bouvier Verlag Herbert Grundmann, Am Hof 32, Postfach 1268, 5300 Bonn 1, W. Germany (B.R.D.)

100   NE   ISSN 0524-112X
BOSTON COLLEGE STUDIES IN PHILOSOPHY. (Text in English) 1966. irreg. price varies. (Boston College, US) Martinus Nijhoff Publishers, Postbus 163, 3300 AD Dordrecht, Netherlands. Ed. J. Beinauer. Indexed: Phil.Ind. Rel.Ind.Two.

100 500   NE   ISSN 0068-0346
BOSTON STUDIES IN THE PHILOSOPHY OF
SCIENCE; Boston colloquium for the philosophy of
science. (Text in English) 1963. irreg. price varies.
D. Reidel Publishing Co., Box 17, 3300 AA
Dordrecht, Netherlands (And 190 Old Derby St.,
Hingham, MA 02043) Eds. Robert S. Cohen, Marx
W. Wartofsky. Indexed: Biol.Abstr. Math.R.

BOSTON UNIVERSITY STUDIES IN
PHILOSOPHY AND RELIGION. see
RELIGIONS AND THEOLOGY

101   US
BOWLING GREEN STUDIES IN APPLIED
PHILOSOPHY. 1979. a. Bowling Green State
University, Department of Philosophy, Bowling
Green, OH 43403. TEL 419-372-2110. Eds. Fred
D. Miller, Thomas W. Attig.

101   GW
BRENNESSEL; Jahresschrift fuer Philosophie und
verwandte Gebiete. 1974. a. Womm-Press, Mittelstr.
51, 4934 Horn - Bad Meinberg 1, W. Germany
(B.R.D.) Ed. H. Knauf. circ. 3,000.

180   BE   ISSN 0068-4023
BULLETIN DE PHILOSOPHIE MEDIEVALE. (Text
mainly in French; contributions in English, German,
Italian and Spanish) 1959. a. 800 Fr.($20)
International Society for the Study of Medieval
Philosophy - Societe Internationale pour l'Etude de
la Philosophie Medievale, College Thomas More, 1
Chemin d'Aristote, B-1348 Louvain-la-Neuve,
Belgium. Ed. C. Wenin. adv. circ. 1,000. (back
issues avail.) Indexed: Phil.Ind.
   Formerly (1959-1963): Societe Internationale
pour l'Etude de la Philosophie Medievale. Bulletin.

100   BE   ISSN 0008-0284
CAHIERS INTERNATIONAUX DE
SYMBOLISME. 1962. irreg. (3-4/yr.) 600 Fr. to
individuals; Fr. 1000 to institutions and libraries (for
3 issues) Universite de l'Etat a Mons, Centre
Interdisciplinaire d'Etudes Philosophique, 17 Place
Warocque, 7000 Mons, Belgium. bk. rev. circ. 1,200.
Indexed: M.L.A. Lang.& Lang.Behav.Abstr.

100   ZR
CAHIERS PHILOSOPHIQUES AFRICAINS/
AFRICAN PHILOSOPHICAL JOURNAL. (Text
in French) 1972. irreg. Z.$80. (Universite Nationale
du Zaire, Lubumbashi, Department de Philosophie)
Presses Universitaires de Lumumbashi, B. P. 1825,
Lubumbashi, Zaire. bk. rev. Indexed: CERDIC.

100   FR   ISSN 0763-1529
CAHIERS RAYMOND ABELLIO; recherche pour la
nouvelle gnose. 1983. a. 60 F. Media Pluriel, 228
rue de Courcelles, 75017 Paris, France. Ed. Rene
Chaminade. adv. circ. 1,000. (back issues avail.)

108   US
CENTER FOR PHILOSOPHIC EXCHANGE.
ANNUAL PROCEEDINGS. 1969. a. $22. Center
for Philosophic Exchange, State University College
at Brockport, Brockport, NY 14420. TEL 716-395-
2493. Ed. Jack Glickman. circ. 300.

100   IT   ISSN 0392-7334
CENTRO DI STUDI VICHIANI. BOLLETTINO.
1971. a. L.30000($7) Bibliopolis, Via Arangio Ruiz
83, 80122 Naples, Italy. Ed.Bd. Indexed: M.L.A.
Lang.& Lang.Behav.Abstr. Phil.Ind.

160   IT
CENTRO SUPERIORE DI LOGICA E SCIENZE
COMPARATE. QUADERNI. 1971. irreg., no.8,
1976. Centro Superiore di Logica e Scienze
Comparate, Via Belmeloro 3, 40126 Bologna, Italy.

100   CE   ISSN 0577-4772
CEYLON RATIONALIST AMBASSADOR. (Text in
English) 1967? a. Rs.5($1) Ceylon Rationalist
Association, 89 Pamankada Ln., Colombo 5, Sri
Lanka. Ed. Abraham T. Kovoor. circ. 3,000. (back
issues avail.)

110 133   US
CINCINNATI JOURNAL OF MAGIC. 1976. a.
$5.50. Black Moon Publishing, Box 1343,
Cincinnati, OH 45201. Eds. Louis Lindenschmidt,
Joe Bounds. bk. rev. circ. 1,000.
   Formerly: Cincinnati Journal of Ceremonial
Magic.

100   BL
COLECAO ECUMENISMO E HUMANISMO.
vol.33, 1984. irreg. Editora Paz e Terra S A, Rua
Sao Jose, 90-18 andar, Centro Rio de Janeiro, RJ,
Brazil.

100   SP   ISSN 0069-5076
COLECCION FILOSOFICA. 1963. irreg., no.47,
1986. price varies. (Universidad de Navarra,
Facultad de Filosofia y Letras) Ediciones
Universidad de Navarra, S.A., Apdo. 396, 31080
Pamplona, Spain.

COLLECTED WORKS OF ERASMUS. see
HUMANITIES: COMPREHENSIVE WORKS

100   CN
COLLECTION PHILOSOPHICA. 1972. irreg. price
varies. University of Ottawa Press, 603 Cumberland,
Ottawa, Ont., K1N 6N5, Canada. TEL 613-564-
2270. Ed. Guy Lafrance.

100   GE
COLLEGIUM PHILOSOPHICUM JENENSE. 1977.
irreg., vol.6, 1985. price varies. (Friedrich-Schiller-
Universitaet, Sektion Marxistisch-Leninistische
Philosophie) Hermann Boehlaus Nachfolger,
Meyerstr. 50a, 53 Weimar, E. Germany (D.D.R.)
(back issues avail.)

COMMENTS & CRITICISMS. see *PSYCHOLOGY*

100   AU   ISSN 0259-0670
CONCEPTUS-STUDIEN. 1984. irreg., no. 4, 1986.
price varies. Verband der Wissenschaftlichen
Gesellschaften Oesterreichs, Lindengasse 37, A-
1070 Vienna, Austria.

CONFERENCE ON EDITORIAL PROBLEMS:
UNIVERSITY OF TORONTO. see *LITERATURE*

100   GW   ISSN 0589-4069
CONSCIENTIA. 1968. irreg., vol.12, 1984. price
varies. Bouvier Verlag Herbert Grundmann, Am Hof
32, Postfach 1268, 5300 Bonn 1, W. Germany
(B.R.D.) Ed. Gerhard Funke.

100   US
CONSCIOUSNESS AND SELF-REGULATION:
ADVANCES IN RESEARCH. 1976. a. price
varies. Plenum Publishing Corp., 233 Spring St.,
New York, NY 10013. TEL 212-620-8047. Eds.
Gary Schwartz, David Shapiro.

108   US
CONTEMPORARY GERMAN PHILOSOPHY.
1982. a. $24.50. Pennsylvania State University
Press, 215 Wagner Bldg., University Park, PA
16802. TEL 814-865-1327. Ed.Bd.

100   US   ISSN 0414-7790
CONTEMPORARY PHILOSOPHY SERIES. irreg.
price varies. Cornell University Press, 124 Roberts
Pl., Ithaca, NY 14850. TEL 607-257-7000.

100   US   ISSN 0084-926X
CONTRIBUTIONS IN PHILOSOPHY. 1968. irreg.,
no.25, 1984. price varies. Greenwood Press, 88 Post
Rd. W., Box 5007, Westport, CT 06881. TEL 203-
226-3571.

CORONA. see *LITERATURE*

108   IT
CORPUS PHILOSOPHORUM MEDII AEVI. SERIE
I. CATALOGO DI MANOSCRITTI FILOSOFICI
NELLE BIBLIOTECHE ITALIANE. 1980. irreg.,
no.4, 1983. price varies. Casa Editrice Leo S.
Olschki, Casella Postale 66, 50100 Florence, Italy.

100   IT
CORPUS PHILOSOPHORUM MEDII AEVI. SERIE
II. STUDI E TESTI. 1980. irreg., no.4, 1983. price
varies. Casa Editrice Leo S. Olschki, Casella Postale
66, 50100 Florence, Italy.

CRITICAL REVIEW. see *LITERATURE*

149   US   ISSN 8756-1247
CRUCIBLE AND SCIENTIFIC ATHEIST. Variant
title: Crucible. 1964. irreg. $50 per 6 issues. De
Young Press, Spencer, IA 51301-7252. Ed. Mary de
Young. adv. bk. rev. circ. 2,500.
   Formerly: Scientific Atheist.

100   MX   ISSN 0185-2604
CUADERNOS DE CRITICA (MEXICO) 1977.
irreg., no.43, 1986. Universidad Nacional Autonoma
de Mexico, Instituto de Investigaciones Filosoficas,
Apdo. Postal 70-447, Mexico, D.F., Mexico (Orders
to: Direccion General De Fomento Editorial, Porto
Alegre No. 260, San Andres Tetepilco, 094 40,
Mexico, D.F., Mexico)

100   AG
CUADERNOS DE FILOSOFIA. no.23, 1975. irreg.
price varies. Universidad de Buenos Aires, Facultad
de Filosofia y Letras, Departamento de
Publicaciones, Marcelo T. de Alvear 2230, Codigo
1122, Buenos Aires, Argentina. Ed. Eugenie
Pucciarelli. bk. rev. abstr. bibl. index. circ. 1,500.
Indexed: Phil.Ind.

100   CL
CUADERNOS DE FILOSOFIA. (Text in Portuguese
and Spanish) 1970. irreg. $6. Universidad de
Concepcion, Departamento de Filosofia, Casilla
2092, Concepcion, Chile. bk. rev. circ. 500.

100   SP   ISSN 0210-4857
CUADERNOS SALMANTINOS DE FILOSOFIA.
1974. a. 650 ptas.($13) Universidad Pontificia de
Salamanca, Compania 1, Salamanca, Spain. Ed.
Saturnino Alvarez Turienzo.

CULTURA, HISTORIA Y FILOSOFIA. see
HISTORY — History Of Europe

DALLAS INSTITUTE OF HUMANITIES AND
CULTURE. INSTITUTE NEWSLETTER. see
HUMANITIES: COMPREHENSIVE WORKS

108 320   US
DANDELION. 1977. irreg. $4.50. Michael E.
Coughlin Ed. & Pub., 1985 Selby Ave., St. Paul,
MN 55104. TEL 612-646-8917. adv. bk. rev. circ.
400. (back issues avail.)

100   DK   ISSN 0070-2749
DANISH YEARBOOK OF PHILOSOPHY. (Text in
English) 1964. a. Kr.120. Museum Tusculanums
Forlag, Njalsgade 94, DK-2300 Copenhagen S,
Denmark. Ed.Bd. index. circ. 400. (reprint service
avail. from ISI) Indexed: Curr.Cont. Phil.Ind.

100   GW   ISSN 0070-3419
DENKEN, SCHAUEN, SINNEN. 1962. irreg. price
varies. Verlag Freies Geistesleben GmbH,
Haussmannstr. 76, 7000 Stuttgart, W. Germany
(B.R.D.) Indexed: Dm.

100   AT   ISSN 0084-9804
DIALECTIC. 1967. irreg. $3. ‡ Newcastle University
Philosophy Club, c/o Department of Philosophy,
Univ. of Newcastle, N.S.W. 2308, Australia. Ed.Bd.
circ. 225.

100   NE
DIALECTICS AND REVOLUTION. 1976. irreg.
price varies. B. R. Gruener B.V., Nieuwe
Herengracht 31, 1011 RM Amsterdam,
Netherlands.

160   IT
DIALETTICA. irreg. price varies. Edizioni Studium,
Via Cassiodoro 14, 00193 Rome, Italy.

100   MX   ISSN 0419-0890
DIANOIA; anuario de filosofia. 1955. a.
Mex.$550($12) Universidad Nacional Autonoma de
Mexico, Instituto de Investigaciones Filosoficas,
Torre Uno de Humanidades, 2 Piso, Ciudad
Universitaria, Coyoacan 04510, Mexico, D.F.,
Mexico. circ. 1,200. (back issues avail.) Indexed:
Hisp.Amer.Per.Ind. Phil.Ind.

100   SZ   ISSN 0070-4806
DIDEROT STUDIES. (Text in English and French)
1949. irreg., no.22, 1986. price varies. Librarie
Droz, 11 rue Massot, 1211 Geneva 12, Switzerland.
Eds. Otis Fellows, Diana Guiragossian. bk. rev.
Indexed: M.L.A.

105   GR
DIOTIMA; epitheoresis philosophikes ereunes/revue
de recherche philosophique/review of philosophical
research. (Text in English, French, or Greek) 1973.
irreg. $10. (Hellenic Society for Philosophical
Studies) Grigoris Publications, 71 Solonos St.,
Athens 143, Greece. Ed. L. Bargeliotes. adv. bk.
rev. Indexed: Phil.Ind.

100   US   ISSN 0070-508X
DIRECTORY OF AMERICAN PHILOSOPHERS.
1962. biennial. $47. Bowling Green State University,
Philosophy Documentation Center, Bowling Green,
OH 43403-0189. TEL 419-372-2419. Ed. Archie J.
Bahm. circ. 1,100.

DIVREI HA-AKADEMIA HA-LEUMIT HA-
YISRAELIT LEMADAIM. see *HISTORY*

100   UK   ISSN 0142-3371
EFRYDIAU ATHRONYDDOL. (Text in Welsh)
1938. a. £1.50. University of Wales Press, 6
Gwennyth St., Cathays, Cardiff CF2 4YD, Wales.
Ed. John Daniel. bk. rev. circ. 200.

ESCRITOS. see *LITERATURE*

108   SP
ESPASA UNIVERSITARIA. FILOSOFIA Y
PENSAMIENTO. irreg., no.13, 1983. Editorial
Espasa-Calpe, S.A., Carretera de Irun, Madrid 34,
Spain.

100   BE   ISSN 0071-1349
ESSAIS PHILOSOPHIQUES. no.5, 1950. irreg.,
no.10, 1985. price varies. Universite Catholique de
Louvain, Institut Superieur de Philosophie, 1
Chemin d'Aristote, 1348 Louvain-La-Neuve,
Belgium.

100   VE
ESTUDIOS FILOSOFICOS. 1974. irreg. $4 per no.
Universidad Simon Bolivar, Departamento de
Filosofia, Apdo. 80659, Caracas, Venezuela. (Co-
sponsor: Sociedad Venezolana de Filosofia) Ed.
Alberto Rosales. bibl.

ETHICS AND INTERNATIONAL AFFAIRS. see
POLITICAL SCIENCE — International Relations

100   AG   ISSN 0325-5387
ETHOS; revista de filosofia practica. 1973. a. $10.
Instituto de Filosofia Practica, Viamonte 1596, 1055
Buenos Aires, Argentina. Ed. Julio Guido Soaje
Ramos. bk. rev. bibl. circ. 500. Indexed: SSCI.

100   CN   ISSN 0708-319X
ETIENNE GILSON SERIES. 1979. irreg. price
varies. Pontifical Institute of Mediaeval Studies, 59
Queen's Park Crescent E., Toronto, Ont. M5S 2C4,
Canada. TEL 416-926-7144. circ. 500.

170   PL   ISSN 0014-2263
ETYKA. (Text in Polish; summaries in English and
Russian) 1966. a. price varies. (Polska Akademia
Nauk, Instytut Filozofii i Socjologii) Panstwowe
Wydawnictwo Naukowe, Miodowa 10, 00-251
Warsaw, Poland. Ed. Henryk Jankowski. bk. rev.
abstr. circ. 1,100. Indexed: Phil.Ind.

100 500   DK   ISSN 0106-6668
FILOSOFI OG VIDENSKABSTEORI PAA
ROSKILDE UNIVERSITETSCENTER. 1979.
biennial. Kr.100. Roskilde Universitetscenter,
Institut for Uddannelsesforskning, Medieforskning
og Videnskabsteori Institut VII, Postbox 260, 4000
Roskilde, Denmark. Ed. Arne Thing Mortensen. bk.
rev. circ. 300.

100   DK   ISSN 0106-0449
FILOSOFISKE STUDIER. 1978. a. free. Koebenhavns
Universitet, Filosofisk Institut - University of
Copenhagen, Koebmagergade 50, 1150 Copenhagen
K, Denmark. Ed.Bd. circ. 600.

197   UR
FILOSOFSKIE NAUKI. 1971. irreg. 0.95 Rub.
Kazakhskii Gosudarstvennyi Universitet, Ul. Lenina
18, Alma-Ata, Kazakh S.S.R., U.S.S.R. bibl.

100   PL
FILOZOFIA-LOGIKA. 1961. irreg. price varies.
Adam Mickiewicz University Press, Marchlewskiego
128, 61-874 Poznan, Poland. bk. rev.
Formerly: Uniwersytet im. Adama Mickiewicza w
Poznaniu. Wydzial Filozoficzno-Historyczny. Prace.
Seria Filozofia-Logika (ISSN 0083-4246)

100   HU   ISSN 0071-4992
FILOZOFIAI TANULMANYOK. 1964. irreg. price
varies. (Magyar Tudomanyos Akademia) Akademiai
Kiado, Publishing House of the Hungarian Academy
of Sciences, P.O. Box 24, H-1363 Budapest,
Hungary.

FRANCISCAN STUDIES. see *RELIGIONS AND
THEOLOGY — Roman Catholic*

100 301 335   GW   ISSN 0067-5911
FREIE UNIVERSITAET BERLIN. OSTEUROPA-
INSTITUT. PHILOSOPHISCHE UND
SOZIOLOGISCHE VEROEFFENTLICHUNGEN.
1959. irreg., vol.23, 1985. price varies. (Freie
Universitaet Berlin, Osteuropa-Institut) Verlag Otto
Harrassowitz, Taunusstr. 14, Postfach 2929, D-6200
Wiesbaden, W. Germany (B.R.D.) Eds. H. Lieber,
H. Buetow, T. Ahlberg. circ. 500.

100   DR
FUNDACION RODRIGUEZ DEMORIZI.
BOLETIN. 1978. irreg., latest 1981. (Fundacion
Rodriguez Demorizi) Editora Taller, Isabel la
Catolica 309, Apdo. de Correos 2190, Z-1, Santo
Domingo, Dominican Republic.

100 943   GE
G.W. LEIBNIZ: SAEMLICHE SCHRIFTEN UND
BRIEFE. (Text in French, German and Latin) 1950.
irreg., vol.3, 1986. (Akademie der Wissenschaften
der DDR) Akademie-Verlag Berlin, Leipziger Str.3-
4, 1086 Berlin, E. Germany (D.D.R.)

GESHER. see *RELIGIONS AND THEOLOGY —
Judaic*

100   II
GOKULDAS SANSKRIT SERIES. (Text in English
and Sanskrit) no.4, 1975. irreg., latest no.74, 1985.
Rs.25($4) Chaukhambha Orientalia, Gokul Bhawan,
K 37/109 Gopal Mandir Lane, Varanasi 221001,
India.

100   GW   ISSN 0072-9604
HAMBURGER STUDIEN ZUR PHILOSOPHIE.
1970. irreg., no.7, 1979. price varies. Verlag Helmut
Buske, Schlueterstr. 14, 2000 Hamburg 13, W.
Germany (B.R.D.)

100   US
HEGEL SOCIETY OF AMERICA.
PROCEEDINGS. 1968. biennial. $17.50. (Hegel
Society of America) State University of New York
Press, State University Plaza, Albany, NY 12246.

190   GW   ISSN 0073-1587
HEGEL-STUDIEN. 1955. irreg., vol.20, 1986. price
varies. (Deutsche Forschungsgemeinschaft, Hegel
Kommission) Bouvier Verlag Herbert Grundmann,
Am Hof 32, Postfach 1268, 5300 Bonn 1, W.
Germany (B.R.D.) Eds. F. Nicolin, O. Poeggeler.
Indexed: Curr.Cont. Arts & Hum.Cit.Ind.

140   GW   ISSN 0440-5927
HEGEL-STUDIEN BEIHEFTE. (Subseries of Hegel-
Studien. Beiheft) 1964. irreg., latest no.29, 1986.
free. Bouvier Verlag Herbert Grundmann, Am Hof
32, Postfach 1268, 5300 Bonn 1, W. Germany
(B.R.D.) Eds. F. Nicolini, O. Poeggeler. adv. bk.
rev. circ. 1,000.
Formerly: Internationale Vereinigung zur
Foerderung des Studiums der Hegelschen
Philosophie. Veroeffentlichung.

100   GW
HESTIA. 1960. biennial. price varies. Bouvier Verlag
Herbert Grundmann, Am Hof 32, Postfach 1268,
5300 Bonn 1, W. Germany (B.R.D.)

170 300   IT   ISSN 0018-4292
HOMINE. (Summaries in Italian and English) 1962.
irreg., latest nos.38-40. L.12000($8.50) per no.
(Centro di Ricerca per le Scienze Morali e Sociali)
Casa Editrice G. C. Sansoni Editore Nuova S.p.A.,
Via Benedetto Varchi 47, 50132 Florence, Italy. Ed.
Franco Lombardi. bk. rev. bibl. charts. illus. index.
cum.index. circ. 1,500.

100   NE   ISSN 0439-9714
HUSSERLIANA. (Text in German) 1950. irreg. price
varies. (Centre d'Archives Husserl, BE) Martinus
Nijhoff Publishers, Spuiboulevard 50, 3311 GR
Dordrecht, Netherlands.

HYPOMNEMATA; Untersuchungen zur Antike und
zu ihrem Nachleben. see *CLASSICAL STUDIES*

100   UK
IDEAS AND IDEOLOGIES. 1978. irreg. price varies.
Edward Arnold (Publishers) Ltd., 41 Bedford Sq.,
London WC1B 3DQ, England.

100   CK   ISSN 0019-140X
IDEAS Y VALORES. 1951. irreg., no.58, 1980.
exchange basis. Universidad Nacional de Colombia,
Facultad de Ciencias Humanas, Departamento de
Filosofia, Apdo. Aereo 14490, Ciudad Universitaria,
Bogota, Colombia. Dir. Ruben Sierra Mejia. bk. rev.
circ. 2,000.

100   FR   ISSN 0378-4789
INDEPENDENT JOURNAL OF PHILOSOPHY/
REVUE INDEPENDANTE DE PHILOSOPHIE;
unabhangige Zeitschrift feur Philosophie. (Text in
English, French and German) 1977. a. $22.50 to
individuals; $37.50 to institutions. George Elliott
Tucker, Ed. & Pub., 51 bd. de Vaugirard, 75015
Paris, France. adv. bk. rev. bibl. circ. 700. (back
issues avail.) Indexed: Phil.Ind.

100   II   ISSN 0376-4109
INDIAN PHILOSOPHICAL ANNUAL. 1967. a.
Rs.10 plus postage. University of Madras, Centre
for Advanced Study in Philosophy, Chepauk,
Triplicane P.O., Madras 600005, Tamil Nadu, India.
Ed. T.M.P. Mahadevan. circ. 300.

100   GE   ISSN 0138-242X
INFORMATIONSBULLETIN; aus dem
Philosophischen Leben der D.D.R. 1965. irreg.
M.5.40 per no. Zentralstelle fuer Philosophische
Information und Dokumentation, J.-Dieckmann-Str.
19-23, 1086 Berlin, E. Germany (D.D.R.) Ed. U.
Richter. circ. 600.
Formerly: Informationen aus dem
Philosophischen Leben in der D.D.R. (ISSN 0020-
0328)

100   PO
INSTITUTO NACIONAL DE INVESTIGACAO
CIENTIFICA. TEXTOS CLASSICOS. irreg.,
no.11, 1981. Instituto Nacional de Investigacao
Cientifica, Centro de Estudos Classicos y
Humanisticos, Coimbra, Portugal.

INTERNATIONAL COUNCIL FOR PHILOSOPHY
AND HUMANISTIC STUDIES. BULLETIN. see
HUMANITIES: COMPREHENSIVE WORKS

100   US   ISSN 0074-4603
INTERNATIONAL DIRECTORY OF
PHILOSOPHY AND PHILOSOPHERS. 1965.
quadrennial since 1978. $47. Bowling Green State
University, Philosophy Documentation Center,
Bowling Green, OH 43403-0189. TEL 419-372-
2419. Ed. Ramona Cormier et al. circ. 850.

190   NE   ISSN 0074-6258
INTERNATIONAL HUMANIST AND ETHICAL
UNION. PROCEEDINGS OF THE CONGRESS.
1952. irreg., 8th, 1982. Amsterdam. price varies.
International Humanist and Ethical Union,
Oudkerkhof 11, 3512 GH Utrecht, Netherlands.
circ. 1,500.

100   FR   ISSN 0074-6525
INTERNATIONAL INSTITUTE OF PHILOSOPHY.
ACTES. (Proceedings of annual meeting) (Text in
English, French or German) 1955. a., 22nd Berne,
1976. International Institute of Philosophy, 173 bd.
St. Germain, 75272 Paris, France.
Proceedings published in host country

100   DK   ISSN 0108-3104
INTERNATIONAL KIERKEGAARD
NEWSLETTER. 1979. a. free. Julia Watkin Ed. &
Pub., Stenagervej 15, 2900 Hellerup, Denmark. adv.
bk. rev. circ. 1,000. Indexed: Phil.Ind.

160   IT
INTERPRETAZIONI. irreg. price varies. Edizioni
Studium, Via Cassiodoro 14, 00193 Rome, Italy.

130   IC
INTERSTELLAR BULLETINS. 1966-1974; resumed
1979. irreg. Kr.120($1.25) (Felag Nyalssinna)
Bioradii Publications, Box 722, Reykjavik, Iceland.
Ed. Thorsteinn Gudjonsson. bk. rev. circ. 400.
(processed)
Formerly: Interstellar Communication (ISSN
0020-9740)

INTERVENTI CLASSENSI. see *LITERATURE*

160 510   UR   ISSN 0302-9085
ISSLEDOVANIA PO TEORII ALGORIFMOV I
MATEMATICHESKOI LOGIKE. 1973. irreg. 1.12
Rub. Akademiya Nauk S.S.S.R., Vychislitel'nyi
Tsentr, Ul. Vavilova, 40, Moscow V-333, Russian
S.F.S.R., U.S.S.R.

JAG. see POLITICAL SCIENCE

JAPAN ASSOCIATION FOR PHILOSOPHY OF SCIENCE. ANNALS. see SCIENCES: COMPREHENSIVE WORKS

JOURNAL OF OUR TIME. see LITERATURE

JOURNAL OF THE PHILOSOPHY OF SPORT. see SPORTS AND GAMES

100 GW
KATALOG PHILOSOPHIE. 1965. biennial. DM.31.30. Werbegemeinschaft Elwert and Meurer, Hauptstr. 101, 1000 Berlin 62, W. Germany (B.R.D.) adv.
Formerly: Jahreskatalog Philosophie (ISSN 0075-2916)

100 PL
KATOLICKI UNIWERSYTET LUBELSKI. WYDZIAL FILOZOFICZNY. ROZPRAWY. (Text in Polish; summaries in English, French or German) 1957. irreg. price varies. Katolicki Uniwersytet Lubelski, Towarzystwo Naukowe, Chopina 29, 20-023 Lublin, Poland. index. circ. 3,150.

KENNEDY INSTITUTE OF BIOETHICS. SCOPE NOTE. see MEDICAL SCIENCES

100 200 DK ISSN 0075-6032
KIERKEGAARDIANA. (Text in Danish, English, French and German; summaries in English) 1955. biennial. Kr.200($25) (Soren Kierkegaard Selskabet, Filosofisk Institut) C.A. Reitzels Forlag, Kobmagergade 50, 1150 Copenhagen K, Denmark. Ed.Bd. bk. rev. circ. 500.

100 US
KIERKEGAARD'S WRITINGS. 1978. a. price varies. Princeton University Press, 3175 Princeton Pike, Lawrenceville, NJ 08648. TEL 609-896-1344. (reprint service avail. from UMI)

100 AU ISSN 0259-0743
KLAGENFURTER BEITRAEGE ZUR PHILOSOPHIE. (Supplement avail.) 1979. irreg. price varies. Verband der Wissenschaftlichen Gesellschaften Oesterreichs, Lindengasse 37, A-1070 Vienna, Austria. Ed. Thomas Macho, Christof Subik.

100 GW ISSN 0454-448X
KOSMOSOPHIE. irreg., vol.4, 1977. price varies. (Paracelsus-Kommission) Franz Steiner Verlag Wiesbaden GmbH, Birkenwaldstr. 44, Postfach 347, D-7000 Stuttgart 1, W. Germany (B.R.D.) Ed. Kurt Goldammer.

100 GE ISSN 0138-3612
KRITIK DER BUERGERLICHEN IDEOLOGIE. 1971. irreg., vol.107, 1986. (Akademie der Wissenschaften der DDR) Akademie-Verlag Berlin, Leipziger Str. 3-4, 1086 Berlin, E. Germany (D.D.R.)

KUNGLIGA VITTERHETS-, HISTORIE- OCH ANTIKVITETS AKADEMIEN. HANDLINGAR. FILOLOGISK-FILOSOFISKA SERIEN/ROYAL ACADEMY OF LETTERS, HISTORY AND ANTIQUITIES. PROCEEDINGS. PHILOLOGICAL-PHILOSOPHICAL SERIES. see LINGUISTICS

LAW AND PHILOSOPHY LIBRARY. see LAW

100 DK ISSN 0106-8989
LIBER ACADEMIAE KIERKEGAARDIENSIS ANNUARIUS. (Text in Danish, English, German and Italian) 1980. irreg. Kr.122. C.A. Reitzels Forlag, Norregade 20, DK-1165 Copenhagen K, Denmark.

100 UK ISSN 0267-7091
LIBERTARIAN ALLIANCE. PHILOSOPHICAL NOTES. 1985. irreg. £5($10) Libertarian Alliance, 3 Langley Court, Covent Garden, London WC2E 9JY, England. Ed.Bd. adv. bk. rev. film rev. bibl. circ. 1,000. (back issues avail.)

100 200 UK
LIBRARY OF PHILOSOPHY AND RELIGION. irreg. price varies. Macmillan Press Ltd., 4 Little Essex St., London WC2R 3LF, England. Ed. Prof. John Hick.

100 SW
LIBRARY OF THEORIA. (Text in English) 1955. irreg., no.16, 1985. price varies. Liber Forlag, S-205 10, Malmo, Sweden. Ed.Bd.

100 SP
LIBROS DE INICIACION FILOSOFICA. 1982. irreg., no.9, 1986. price varies. (Universidad de Navarra, Facultad de Filosofia y Letras) Ediciones Universidad de Navarra, S.A., Apdo. 396, 31080 Pamplona, Spain.

100 US ISSN 0075-9554
LINDLEY LECTURE. 1961. a. $1.50. University of Kansas, Department of Philosophy, Lawrence, KS 66045. TEL 913-864-2700. Ed. A.C. Genova. circ. 600.

100 301.1 150 UR ISSN 0202-2001
LITUANISTIKA V S.S.S.R. FILOSOFIYA I PSIKHOLOGIYA; nauchno-referativnyi sbornik. (Text in Russian) 1977. a. 0.70 Rub. Akademiya Nauk Litovskoi S.S.R., Nauchno-Informatsionnyi Tsentr, Michurino g-ve 1/46, Vilnius, Lithuanian S.S.R., U.S.S.R. Ed. A. Balsys. circ. 300.

100 200 575 600 US
LIVE AND LET LIVE. 1977. irreg. (2-4/yr.) donations. Church of Eternal Life & Liberty, Inc., c/o Rev. Patrick A. Heller, Ed., 300 Frandor Ave., Lansing, MI 48912-5202. bk. rev. circ. 150.

100 UK ISSN 0307-2606
LOCKE NEWSLETTER. (Text in English, French, German and Italian) 1970. a. £4. Roland Hall, Ed. & Pub., Department of Philosophy, University of York, Heslington, York YO1 5DD, England. adv. bk. rev. circ. 600. Indexed: Phil.Ind.

101 US
LOVE. 1978. irreg. free. Box 9, Prospect Hill, NC 27314. Eds. Bob Love, Pat Warren. circ. 100.
Formerly: Love: The Journal of the Human Spirit.

100 GE
LUDWIG FEUERBACH: GESAMMELTE WERKE. 1967. irreg., vol.17, 1984. Akademie-Verlag Berlin, Leipziger Str. 3-4, 1086 Berlin, E. Germany (D.D.R.) Ed. Werner Schuffenhauer.

100 GW ISSN 0076-2776
MAINZER PHILOSOPHISCHE FORSCHUNGEN. 1966. irreg., vol.29, 1986. price varies. Bouvier Verlag Herbert Grundmann, Am Hof 32, Postfach 1268, 5300 Bonn 1, W. Germany (B.R.D.) Ed. Gerhard Funke.

106 806 UK
MANCHESTER MEMOIRS. 1785. a. £6.50. Manchester Literary and Philosophical Society, 14 Kennedy St., Manchester M2 4BY, England. Ed. A.L. Smyth. bk. rev. circ. 600. Indexed: Br.Hum.Ind. Hist.Abstr. Amer.Hist.& Life. GeoRef.
Formerly: Manchester Literary and Philosophical Society. Memoirs and Proceedings (ISSN 0076-3721)

100 US
MATERIAL FOR THOUGHT. 1970. irreg. $4.95 per no. Far West Editions, Box 549, San Francisco, CA 94101. TEL 415-586-4951. bk. rev. circ. 3,500.

180 US ISSN 0076-5856
MEDIAEVAL PHILOSOPHICAL TEXTS IN TRANSLATION. 1942. a. price varies. Marquette University Press, 1324 W. Wisconsin Ave., Milwaukee, WI 53233. TEL 414-224-1564.

100 PL ISSN 0076-5880
MEDIAEVALIA PHILOSOPHICA POLONORUM. (Text in French or German) 1957. a. price varies. (Polska Akademia Nauk, Instytut Filozofii i Socjologii) Ossolineum, Publishing House of the Polish Academy of Sciences, Rynek 9, 50-106 Wroclaw, Poland (Dist. by: Ars Polona-Ruch, Krakowskie Przedmiescie 7, Warsaw, Poland) Ed. W. Senko. Indexed: M.L.A.

109 IT
MEDIOEVO; rivista di storia della filosofia medievale. 1975. irreg. price varies. (Universita degli Studi di Padova, Centro per Ricerche di Filosofia Medievale) Editrice Antenore, Via Rusca 15, Padua 35100, Italy. Ed.Bd.

142 US
MEDITATION. irreg. Intergroup for Planetary Oneness, 17510 Sherman Way No. 212, Van Nuys, CA 91406. TEL 818-343-4998.

100 AU ISSN 0076-6720
METAPHYSISCHE RUNDSCHAU. irreg. Fuchtshallergasse 4/25, A-1090 Vienna, Austria.

100 US ISSN 0363-6550
MIDWEST STUDIES IN PHILOSOPHY. 1976. a. University of Minnesota Press, 2037 University Ave., S.E., Minneapolis, MN 55414. TEL 612-624-2516. Ed.Bd. Indexed: Phil.Ind.

100 500 US ISSN 0076-9258
MINNESOTA STUDIES IN THE PHILOSOPHY OF SCIENCE. 1956. irreg., vol.10, 1984. price varies. (Minnesota Center for Philosophy of Science) University of Minnesota Press, 2037 University Ave., S.E., Minneapolis, MN 55414. TEL 612-624-2516. Ed.Bd. index. Indexed: SSCI. ASCA.

180 930 GW
MISCELLANEA MEDIAEVALIA. 1962. irreg., vol.17, 1985. price varies. (Universitaet zu Koeln, Thomas-Institut) Walter de Gruyter und Co., Genthiner Str.13, 1000 Berlin 30, W. Germany (B.R.D.) (U.S. adress: Walter de Gruyter, Inc., 200 Saw Mill Rd., Hawthorne, N.Y. 10532) Ed. Albert Zimmermann. Indexed: M.L.A. Rel.Ind.Two.

MITZION TETZEH TORAH. M.T.T. see RELIGIONS AND THEOLOGY — Judaic

100 GW ISSN 0170-3013
MODERN GERMAN STUDIES. irreg., no.14, 1985. price varies. Bouvier Verlag Herbert Grundmann, Am Hof 32, Postfach 1268, 5300 Bonn 1, W. Germany (B.R.D.)

108 GW
MONOGRAPHIEN ZUR PHILOSOPHISCHEN FORSCHUNG. 1947. irreg., no.232, 1985. price varies. Verlag Anton Hain GmbH, Adelheidstr. 2, Postfach 1220, 6240 Koenigstein, W. Germany (B.R.D.) Ed. Georgi Schischkoff.

100 US ISSN 0068-4333
MONOGRAPHS IN PHILOSOPHY AND RELIGIOUS HISTORY. (Text in various languages) 1966. irreg. (approx. 25/yr); no.129, 1973. price varies. Lenox Hill Publishing and Distributing Corporation, 235 E. 44th St., New York, NY 10017. (back issues avail.)
Formerly: Burt Franklin Philosophy Monograph Series.

100 UK
NATIONAL SECULAR SOCIETY. ANNUAL REPORT. 1867. a. membership. National Secular Society, 702 Holloway Rd., London N19, England. Ed. T. Mullins.

100 500 UR
NEKOTORYE FILOSOFSKIE VOPROSY SOVREMENNOGO ESTESTVOZNANIYA. 1973. irreg. 0.66 Rub. (Leningradskii Universitet) Lenizdat, Fontanka 59, Leningrad, Russian S.F.S.R., U.S.S.R.

100 GW ISSN 0085-3917
NEUE HEFTE FUER PHILOSOPHIE. 1971. irreg., no.23, 1984. price varies. Vandenhoeck und Ruprecht, Theaterstr. 13, Postfach 37 53, 3400 Goettingen, W. Germany (B.R.D.) Ed.Bd. circ. 2, 200. Indexed: Phil.Ind.

120 US
NEW STUDIES IN PRACTICAL PHILOSOPHY. irreg. price varies. University of California Press, 2120 Berkeley Way, Berkeley, CA 94720. TEL 415-642-4247.

100 US ISSN 0733-9542
NEW VICO STUDIES. 1983. a. $15. Institute for Vico Studies, 69 Fifth Ave., Ste. 17A, New York, NY 10003. Eds. Giorgio Tagliacozzo, Donald Phillip Verene. bk. rev. circ. 750. Indexed: Phil.Ind.

PHILOSOPHY

100   GW   ISSN 0342-1422
NIETZSCHE-STUDIEN; internationales Jahrbuch fuer die Nietzsche-Forschung. (Text in English and German) a. price varies. Walter de Gruyter und Co., Genthiner Str. 13, 1000 Berlin 30, W. Germany (B.R.D.) (U.S. adress: Walter de Gruyter, Inc., 200 Saw Mill Rd., Hawthorne, N.Y. 10532) Indexed: M.L.A.

NIGHTSUN. see *LITERATURE*

100   NE
NIJHOFF INTERNATIONAL PHILOSOPHY SERIES. (Text in English) 1976. irreg. price varies. (AT) Martinus Nijhoff Publishers, Postbus 163, 3300 AD Dordrecht, Netherlands. Ed. Jan T.J. Srzednicki. Indexed: Math.R.
     Formerly: Melbourne International Philosophy Series.

NORSKE VIDENSKAPS-AKADEMI. HISTORISK-FILOSOFISK KLASSE. AVHANDLINGER TWO. see *HISTORY*

NUOVA UNIVERSALE STUDIUM. see *LITERATURE*

NUOVI ANNALI DELLA FACOLTA DI MAGISTERO DELL'UNIVERSITA DI MESSINA. see *HUMANITIES: COMPREHENSIVE WORKS*

100   DK   ISSN 0107-7384
ODENSE UNIVERSITY STUDIES IN PHILOSOPHY. (Text in Danish and English) 1972. irreg., no.7, 1986. price varies. Odense University Press, 36, Pjentedamsgade, DK-5000 Odense, Denmark. (back issues avail.)

OESTERREICHISCHE AKADEMIE DER WISSENSCHAFTEN. PHILOSOPHISCH-HISTORISCHE KLASSE. ANZEIGER. see *HISTORY — History Of Europe*

100 900   AU
OESTERREICHISCHE AKADEMIE DER WISSENSCHAFTEN. PHILOSOPHISCH-HISTORISCHE KLASSE. SITZUNGSBERICHTE. 1848. irreg. price varies. Verlag der Oesterreichischen Akademie der Wissenschaften, Dr. Ignaz Seipel Platz 2, A-1010 Vienna, Austria. charts. circ. 500.

OXFORD CLASSICAL AND PHILOSOPHICAL MONOGRAPHS. see *CLASSICAL STUDIES*

100 800   DK   ISSN 0109-4831
P S; tidsskrift for spontan satire, fjollet filosofi, funny fiction and lojerlig ligegyldighed. 1981. irreg. (3-4/yr.) Kr.52. Kreativ Filosofi Forening, Aakjaersvej 3, 6600 Vejen, Denmark. Ed. Bjarne Poulsen. adv. bk. rev. illus. circ. 200.
     Formerly: Philosophus (ISSN 0108-7460)

100   PK   ISSN 0078-8406
PAKISTAN PHILOSOPHICAL CONGRESS. PROCEEDINGS. (Text in English) 1954. a. $7. Pakistan Philosophical Congress, Department of Philosophy, University of the Punjab, New Campus, Lahore 20, Pakistan. Ed. Abdul Khaliq. circ. 900.

170   US   ISSN 0079-0249
PAUL ANTHONY BRICK LECTURES. 1960. irreg., no.9, 1973. price varies. University of Missouri Press, 200 Lewis Hall, Columbia, MO 65211. TEL 314-882-2121.

104   US   ISSN 0079-0257
PAUL CARUS LECTURES. 1925. irreg., no.16, 1986. price varies. (American Philosophical Association) Open Court Publishing Co. (Subsidiary of: Carus Corporation) Box 300, Peru, IL 61354. TEL 815-223-2520. index in each volume. (reprint service avail. from UMI)

PERSISTENCE OF VISION. see *MOTION PICTURES*

100   NE
PERSPEKTIVEN DER PHILOSOPHIE. NEUES JAHRBUCH. (Text in English, German) 1975. a. fl.105. Editions Rodopi B.V., Keizersgracht 302-304, 1016 Amsterdam, Netherlands. Ed.Bd. adv. bk. rev. circ. 500.

DIE PFORTE; Zeitschrift und Schriften fuer wertidealistische Philosophie und Kultur. see *LITERARY AND POLITICAL REVIEWS*

100   NE   ISSN 0079-1350
PHAENOMENOLOGICA. (Text in English, French, German) 1958. irreg. price varies. (Centre d'Archives Husserl, BE) Martinus Nijhoff Publishers, Postbus 163, 3300 AD Dordrecht, Netherlands. Ed. S. Ysseling. Indexed: Rel.Ind.Two.

100   US   ISSN 0885-3886
PHENOMENOLOGICAL INQUIRY; a review of philosophical ideas and trends. (Text mainly in English; occasionally in French, German) 1976. a. $10 to individuals; institutions $14. World Institute for Advanced Phenomenological Research and Learning, 348 Payson Rd., Belmont, MA 02178. TEL 617-489-3696. Ed. A.T. Tymieniecka. adv. bk. rev. bibl. circ. 1,000. (back issues avail.)
     Formerly (until 1985): Phenomenology Information Bulletin (ISSN 0278-8322)

100   NE
PHILOSOPHER'S INDEX. q. fl.205. D. Reidel Publishing Co., Box 17, 3300 AA Dordrecht, Netherlands (And 190 Old Derby St., Hingham, MA 02043) adv.

100   BE   ISSN 0079-1660
PHILOSOPHES CONTEMPORAINS. 1955, no.7. irreg. price varies. Universite Catholique de Louvain, Institut Superieur de Philosophie, 1 Chemin d'Aristote, 1348 Louvain-La-Neuve, Belgium.

100   BE   ISSN 0079-1679
PHILOSOPHES MEDIEVAUX. 1948. irreg., no.27, 1986. price varies. Universite Catholique de Louvain, Institut Superieur de Philosophie, 1 Chemin d'Aristote, 1348 Louvain-La-Neuve, Belgium.

105   GR
PHILOSOPHIA. (Text in English, French, German, or Greek) 1971. a. $20. Academy of Athens, Research Center for Greek Philosophy - Kentron Erevnis tes Hellenikes Philosophias, 14 Anagnostopoulou St., Athens 10673, Greece. Ed.Bd. bk. rev. circ. 600. Indexed: Bull.Signal. Phil.Ind.

180   NE   ISSN 0079-1687
PHILOSOPHIA ANTIQUA. 1946. irreg., vol.44, 1986. price varies. E. J. Brill, P.O. Box 9000, 2300 PA Leiden, Netherlands.

PHILOSOPHIA MATHEMATICA. see *MATHEMATICS*

530 146   GW   ISSN 0031-8027
PHILOSOPHIA NATURALIS; Archiv fuer Naturphilosophie und die philosophischen Grenzgebiete der exakten Wissenschaften und Wissenschaftsgeschichte. 1950. irreg., vol.21, 1983/84. DM.145. Verlag Anton Hain GmbH, Adelheidstr 2, Postfach 1220, 6240 Koenigstein, W. Germany (B.R.D.) Ed. Joseph Meurers. adv. bk. rev. bibl. index. circ. 1,000. Indexed: Math.R. Phil.Ind.

100   NE
PHILOSOPHIA SPINOZAE PERENNIS. 1976. irreg., no.4, 1979. price varies. Van Gorcum, Box 43, 9400 AA Assen, Netherlands. Ed. H.G. Hubbeling. bibl. index.

100   SJ   ISSN 0079-1695
PHILOSOPHICAL SOCIETY OF THE SUDAN. PROCEEDINGS OF THE ANNUAL CONFERENCE. (Text and summaries in Arabic and English) 1952. a. price varies. Philosophical Society of the Sudan, P.O. Box 526, Khartoum, Sudan.

100   NE
PHILOSOPHICAL STUDIES SERIES IN PHILOSOPHY. 1974. irreg. price varies. D. Reidel Publishing Co., Box 17, 3300 AA Dordrecht, Netherlands (And 190 Old Derby St., Hingham, MA 02043) Eds. Wilfrid Sellars, Keith Lehrer. Indexed: Math.R.

105   FR   ISSN 0182-7103
PHILOSOPHIE. 1972. a. 68 F. Universite de Toulouse II (le Mirail), Service des Publications, 56 rue du Taur, 31069 Toulouse Cedex, France. Ed. J.M. Gabaude.

181   GE   ISSN 0233-089X
PHILOSOPHIEHISTORISCHE TEXTE. 1955. irreg. price varies. Akademie-Verlag, Leipziger Str. 3-4, 1086 Berlin, E. Germany (D.D.R.)
     Formerly: Philosophische Studientexte (ISSN 0079-1717)

100   GW   ISSN 0175-6508
PHILOSOPHISCHE ABHANDLUNGEN. irreg., vol.53, 1985. price varies. Vittorio Klostermann, Frauenlobstr. 22, Postfach 900601, 6000 Frankfurt 90, W. Germany (B.R.D) Indexed: Math.R.

100   GW   ISSN 0031-8183
PHILOSOPHISCHES JAHRBUCH. 1888. a. DM.52. (Goerres-Gesellschaft) Karl Alber GmbH, Hermann-Herder-Str.4, 7800 Freiburg, W. Germany (B.R.D.) Ed.Bd. bk. rev. abstr. bibl. circ. 800. Indexed: Curr.Cont. Arts & Hum.Cit.Ind. Ind.Bk.Rev.Hum. Phil.Ind.

100 610   NE
PHILOSOPHY AND MEDICINE. (Text in English) 1975. irreg. price varies. D. Reidel Publishing Co., Postbus 17, 3300 AA Dordrecht, Netherlands (And 190 Old Derby St., Hingham, MA 02043) Eds. H. Tristram Engelhardt Jr., Stuart F. Spicker. Indexed: Biol.Abstr.

100 206   US   ISSN 0739-1218
PHILOSOPHY AND THE ARTS; a literary and philosophical review. 1975. a. $2.98. Philosophy and the Arts, Box 431, Jerome Ave. Sta., Bronx, NY 10468. TEL 212-654-3955. Ed. Daniel Manesse. bk. rev.
     Incorporating: Bertrand Russell Today.

100   US   ISSN 0742-2733
PHILOSOPHY IN CONTEXT. 1972. a. $4. Cleveland State University, Department of Philosophy, Cleveland, OH 44115. Ed. Richard M. Fox. adv. circ. 300. (back issues avail.) Indexed: Phil.Ind.

100   US   ISSN 0164-0771
PHILOSOPHY RESEARCH ARCHIVES; a bilingual journal of philosophy. (Text and summaries in English and French) 1976. a. $19 to individuals; institutions $39. Bowling Green State University, Philosophy Documentation Center, Bowling Green, OH 43403-0189. TEL 419-372-2419. (Co-sponsor: American Philosophical Association; Canadian Philosophical Association) Ed. Robert Turnbull. Indexed: Phil.Ind.

170   US
PHILOSPHY IN SCIENCE. a. $28 per no. Pachart Publishing House, 1130 San Lucas Cir., Tucson, AZ 85704. TEL 602-297-4797. Ed.Bd.

100   PL   ISSN 0079-4635
POZNANSKIE TOWARZYSTWO PRZYJACIOL NAUK. KOMISJA FILOZOFICZNA. PRACE. (Text in German, Polish; summaries in English, French, German, Russian) 1921. irreg., vol.14, 1983. price varies. Panstwowe Wydawnictwo Naukowe, Miodowa 10, 00-251 Warsaw, Poland (Dist. by: Ars Polona, Krakowskie Przedmiescie 7, 00-068 Warsaw, Poland)

PRAGMATICS AND DISCOURSE ANALYSIS. see *LINGUISTICS*

181.45   US   ISSN 0149-953X
PRANA YOGA LIFE. 1977. irreg. $3. Prana Yoga Ashram, Box 1037, Berkeley, CA 94701. TEL 415-549-2911. Ed. Swami Vignanananda. adv. bk. rev. illus. circ. 1,500. (back issues avail.)

105   BL
PRESENCA FILOSOFICA. (Text in Portuguese and French; occasionally in English) 1974. irreg. $25. Sociedade Brasileira de Filosofos Catolicos, Rua Benjamin Constant 23/420, 20.241-Rio de Janeiro-RJ, Brazil. Ed. Prof. Tarcisio Meirelles Padilha. bibl. circ. 2,000.

100   FR
PRESENCE DE GABRIEL MARCEL. CAHIER. 1978. a. 100 F. Presence de Gabriel Marcel, 9 ave Franklin-Roosevelt, 75008 Paris, France. Ed. Joel Bouessee. circ. 3,000.

100 001.3   GW
PROBLEMATA. 1971. irreg. price varies. Friedrich Frommann Verlag Guenther Holzboog GmbH und Co., Postfach 500460, Koenig-Karl-Str. 27, 7000 Stuttgart 50, W. Germany (B.R.D.) Ed. Guenther Holzboog. Indexed: Math.R.

160 RM
PROBLEME DE LOGICA. 1969. irreg., vol.9, 1986. (Academia de Stiinte Sociale si Politice) Editura Academiei Republicii Socialiste Rumania, Calea Victoriei 125, 79717 Bucharest, Rumania (Subscr. to: ARTEXIM, Str. Piata Scinteii 1, P.O. Box 33-16, 70055 Bucharest, Rumania)

100 US
PROBLEMS IN CONTEMPORARY PHILOSOPHY. 1986. irreg., vol.3, 1987. $39.95 per no. Edwin Mellen Press, Box 450, Lewiston, NY 10492.

100 NE
PROFILES; an international series on contemporary philosophers and logicians. 1979. irreg. price varies. D. Reidel Publishing Company, Box 17, 3300 AA Dordrecht, Netherlands (And 190 Old Derby St., Hingham, MA 02043) Eds. R.J. Bogdan, I. Niiniluoto. bibl. index. (back issues avail.)

100 IT
PUBBLICAZIONI DI VERIFICHE. irreg. price varies. Verifiche, Casella Postale 269, Trento, Italy.

PUBLICATIONS IN MEDIEVAL STUDIES. see HISTORY — History Of Europe

PURE LIFE SOCIETY. ANNUAL REPORT. see RELIGIONS AND THEOLOGY

100 IT
QUADERNI DI FILOSOFIA. 1978. irreg., no.3, 1980. price varies. (Universita degli Studi di Palermo, Istituto di Filosofia) Editrice Italo-Latino-Americana Palma, Via B. Castiglia 6, 90141 Palermo, Italy. Ed.Bd.

100 IT
QUADERNI DI VERIFICHE. irreg. price varies. Verifiche, Casella Postale 269, Trento, Italy. Ed. Franco Chiereghin. bibl.

QUAKER ENCOUNTERS. see RELIGIONS AND THEOLOGY — Other Denominations And Sects

294.54 200 IT
RASSEGNA DI LETTERATURA TOMISTICA. (Text mainly in French and Italian) 1969. a. price varies. Editrice Domenicana Italiana, Via L. Palmieri 19, 80133 Naples, Italy. Ed. P. Clementte Vansteenkiste OP. bk. rev. (back issues avail.)
Formerly: Bulletin Thomiste.

294.54 572 ZR
RECHERCHES PHILOSOPHIQUES AFRICAINES. (Text in French) 1917. a. $5. Faculte de Theologie Catholique de Kinshasa, Department de Philosophie et Religions Africaines, B.P. 1534, Kinshasa-Limete, Zaire. Ed. Tshiamalenga Ntumba. adv. bk. rev. circ. 1,500.
Formerly (until 1977): Recherches Philosophiques Africaines. Collection.

RELIGION AND SOCIETY. see RELIGIONS AND THEOLOGY

RENCONTRES INTERNATIONALES DE GENEVE. see SOCIAL SCIENCES: COMPREHENSIVE WORKS

160 PL ISSN 0137-2904
REPORTS ON MATHEMATICAL LOGIC. (Text in English; summaries in Polish) 1973. irreg., no.18, 1984. price varies. (Uniwersytet Jagiellonski) Panstwowe Wydawnictwo Naukowe, Ul.Miodowa 10, 00-251 Warsaw, Poland (Dist. by: Ars Polona, Krakowskie Przedmiescie 7, 00-068 Warsaw, Poland) (Co-sponsor: Uniwersytet Slaski w Katowicach) Ed. W.A. Pogorzelski. circ. 700. Indexed: Math.R. Ref.Zh. Phil.Ind.
Formerly: Uniwersytet Jagiellonski, Krakow. Zeszyty Naukowe. Prace z Logiki (ISSN 0083-4432)

100 US ISSN 0085-5553
RESEARCH IN PHENOMENOLOGY. 1971. a. $15 individuals; libraries $22.50. Humanities Press, Inc., 171 First Ave., Atlantic Highlands, NJ 07716. TEL 201-872-1441. Ed. John Sallis. adv. bk. rev. circ. 1,000. (back issues avail.) Indexed: Hum.Ind. Phil.Ind.

100 601 US ISSN 0161-7249
RESEARCH IN PHILOSOPHY AND TECHNOLOGY. (Supplement avail.: Jacques Ellul: A Comprehensive Bibliography) 1978. a. $26.25 to individuals; institutions $52.50. (Society for Philosophy and Technology) J A I Press Inc., Box 1678, 36 Sherwood Pl., Greenwich, CT 06836. TEL 203-661-7602. Eds. Paul T. Durbin, Carl Mitcham. bibl.

170 BE
RESEAUX; revue interdisciplinaire de philosophie morale et politique. 1965. irreg. (3-4/yr.) 600 Fr. to individuals; institutions and libraries Fr. 1000 (for 3 issues) Universite de l'Etat a Mons, Centre Interdisciplinaire d'Etudes Philosophique, 17 Place Warocque, B-7000 Mons, Belgium. Ed. Robert Joly. bk. rev. bibl. Indexed: Lang.& Lang.Behav.Abstr.
Formerly: Revue Universitaire de Science Morale (ISSN 0035-435X)

330 II ISSN 0258-1701
REVIEW JOURNAL OF PHILOSOPHY AND SOCIAL SCIENCE. (Text in English) biennial. Rs.70($10) Anu Prakashan, Shivaji Rd, Meerut 25001, India (Editorial office: Dr. Michael V. Belok, College of Education, Arizona State University, Tempe, AZ 85281) Ed. Michael V. Belok.

170 US
REVISIONS (NOTRE DAME) 1981. a. price varies. University of Notre Dame Press, Notre Dame, IN 46556. TEL 219-239-6346. Eds. Stanley Hauerwas, Alasdair MacIntyre.

100 CL ISSN 0034-8236
REVISTA DE FILOSOFIA. 1949. irreg. $10. Universidad de Chile, Departamento de Filosofia, Humanidades y Educacion, Avda. Larrain 9925-La Reina, Santiago de Chile, Chile. Dir. Jorge Avila. bk. rev. circ. 500.

100 CL
REVISTA PHILOSOPHICA. 1978. a. $10. (Universidad Catolica de Valparaiso, Instituto de Filosofia) Ediciones Universitarias de Valparaiso, Casilla 1415, Valparaiso, Chile. Ed. Juan Antonio Widow. bk. rev. circ. 300.
Formerly: Philosophica.

REVUE DE THEOLOGIE ET DE PHILOSOPHIE. CAHIERS. see RELIGIONS AND THEOLOGY

294.54 ZR
REVUE PHILOSOPHIQUE DE KINSHASA. (Text in French and English) 1977. a. $25. Faculte de Theologie Catholique de Kinshasa, Department de Philosophie et Religions Africaines, B.P. 1534, Kinshasa-Limete, Zaire. Ed. Tshiamalenga Ntumba. adv. bk. rev. circ. 1,500.

100 UK ISSN 0080-4436
ROYAL INSTITUTE OF PHILOSOPHY. LECTURES. 1968. a., latest vol.8, 1973. price varies. Macmillan Press Ltd., Little Essex St., London W.C.2, England. Indexed: Rel.Ind.Two.

100 IT
SAGGI FILOSOFICI. 1979. irreg., vol.4, 1983. price varies. Casa Editrice Leo S. Olschki, Casella Postale 66, 50100 Florence, Italy.

100 920 AU ISSN 0259-0794
SALZBURGER BEITRAEGE ZUR PARACELSUSFORSCHUNG. 1960. irreg., no.24, 1986. price varies. (Internationale Paracelsus-Gesellschaft) Verband der Wissenschaftlichen Gesellschaften Oesterreichs, Lindengasse 37, A-1070 Vienna, Austria.

100 AU ISSN 0080-5696
SALZBURGER JAHRBUCH FUER PHILOSOPHIE. 1957. a. price varies. Universitaetsverlag Anton Pustet, Bergstr. 12, Postfach 144, A-5021 Salzburg, Austria. Indexed: Phil.Ind.

100 AU ISSN 0080-5726
SALZBURGER STUDIEN ZUR PHILOSOPHIE. 1962. irreg. price varies. Universitaetsverlag Anton Pustet, Bergstr. 12, Postschliessfach 144, 5021 Salzburg, Austria.

100 GW ISSN 0080-6935
SCHOPENHAUER-JAHRBUCH. a. DM.45. (Schopenhauer Gesellschaft e.V.) Verlag Dr. Waldemar Kramer, Bornheimer Landwehr 57a, 6000 Frankfurt 60, W. Germany (B.R.D.) bk. rev. circ. 1,912. Indexed: Phil.Ind.

100 943 GE ISSN 0138-3418
SCHRIFTEN ZUR PHILOSOPHIE UND IHRER GESCHICHTE. 1976. irreg., vol.42, 1986. (Akademie der Wissenschaften der DDR) Akademie-Verlag DDR, Leipziger Str. 3-4, 1086 Berlin, E. Germany (D.D.R.)

200 US ISSN 0193-3396
SCIENCE AND NATURE; the annual of Marxist philosophy for natural scientists. 1978. a. $6.50 to individuals; institutions $15. 53 Hickory Hill Rd., Tappan, NY 10983. TEL 914-359-2283. Ed. Lester Talkington. adv. bk. rev. circ. 2,000. (back issues avail.) Indexed: Sociol.Abstr. Alt.Press Ind. Left Ind.

294 200 US
SELBST-VERWIRKLICHUNG: JAHRESHEFT. (Text in German) 1959. a. $2. Self-Realization Fellowship, Inc., 3880 San Rafael Ave., Los Angeles, CA 90065. TEL 213-225-2471. Ed. Jane Brush. illus. circ. 5,100.
Formerly (until 1969): Gemeinschaft der Selbst-Verwirklichung. Jahresheft (ISSN 0072-0577)

100 UK ISSN 0262-9356
SHARE IT; a magazine to celebrate & promote awareness of our true identity. 1979. irreg. £1 per no. c/o Anne Seward, Ed., Roots Church Ln., Playford, Ipswich IP6 9DS, England. bk. rev. illus.
Formerly: Nacton Newsletter.

SHAW ANNUAL. see LITERATURE

SOCIAL RESPONSIBILITY: BUSINESS, JOURNALISM, LAW, MEDICINE. see LAW

SOCIETY FOR RENAISSANCE STUDIES. OCCASIONAL PAPERS. see LITERATURE

100 CH
SOOCHOW UNIVERSITY. PHILOSOPHY DEPARTMENT. CHUAN-HSI LU. 1982. a. $12 per no. Soochow University, Philosophy Department, Wai Shuang Hsi, Shin Lin, Taipei, Taiwan, Republic of China. Ed. Ling-Ling Chao.

SOVIETICA. PUBLICATIONS AND MONOGRAPHS. see HISTORY — History Of Europe

100 GW
SPECULA. 1978. irreg. price varies. Friedrich Frommann Verlag Guenther Holzboog GmbH und Co., Postfach 500460, Koenig-Karl-Str. 27, 7000 Stuttgart 50, W. Germany (B.R.D.) Ed. Guenther Holzboog.

101 SW ISSN 0491-0877
STOCKHOLM STUDIES IN PHILOSOPHY. (Subseries of Acta Universitatis Stockholmiensis) (Text in English) 1957. irreg., latest no. 6. price varies. (Stockholms Universitet) Almqvist & Wiksell International, Box 62, S-101 20 Stockholm, Sweden. Eds. Harald Ofstad, Anders Wedberg. (back issues avail.)

100 IT
STUDI FILOSOFICI. 1978. a. price varies. (Istituto Universitario Orientale) Casa Editrice Leo. S. Olschki, Viuzzo del Pozzetto (Viale Europa), 50136 Florence, Italy.

STUDI URBINATI. SERIE B: LETTERATURA, STORIA, FILOSOFIA. see LITERATURE

100 IT ISSN 0081-6310
STUDIA ARISTOTELICA. 1958. irreg., no.11, 1984. price varies. (Universita degli Studi di Padova) Editrice Antenore, Via G. Rusca 15, 35100 Padua, Italy.

100 NE
STUDIA CARTESIANA. (Text in English and French) 1979. irreg. price varies. Quadratures, Postbus 6463, 1005 EL Amsterdam, Netherlands. Ed.Bd. bk. rev.

111.85 PL ISSN 0081-637X
STUDIA ESTETYCZNE. (Text in Polish; summaries in English and Russian) 1964. irreg., vol.17, 1981. price varies. (Polska Akademia Nauk, Instytut Filozofii i Socjologii) Panstwowe Wydawnictwo Naukowe, Ul. Miodowa 10, 00-251 Warsaw, Poland (Dist. by: Ars Polona, Krakowskie Przedmiescie 7, 00-068 Warsaw, Poland) Ed. Slaw Krzemien-Ojak. bk. rev. circ. 500.

PHILOSOPHY

100   GW   ISSN 0341-0765
STUDIA LEIBNITIANA. SONDERHEFTE. (Text in English and German) irreg., vol.15, 1987. price varies. (Gottfried Wilhelm Leibniz Gesellschaft, Hannover) Franz Steiner Verlag Wiesbaden GmbH, Birkenwaldstr. 44, Postfach 347, D-7000 Stuttgart 1, W. Germany (B.R.D.) Ed.Bd. Indexed: Math.R.

100   GW   ISSN 0303-5980
STUDIA LEIBNITIANA. SUPPLEMENTA. (Text in English, French, and German) irreg., vol.26, 1986. price varies. (Gottfried Wilhelm Leibniz Gesellschaft, Hannover) Franz Steiner Verlag Wiesbaden GmbH, Birkenwaldstr. 44, Postfach 347, D-7000 Stuttgart 1, W. Germany (B.R.D.) Ed.Bd. Indexed: Math.R.

100 200   SW
STUDIA PHILOSOPHIAE RELIGIONIS. (Text in English) 1975. irreg., no.12, 1984. price varies. Liber Forlag, S-205 10, Malmo, Sweden. Eds. Hans Hof, Hampus Lyttkens.

100   RM   ISSN 0578-5480
STUDIA UNIVERSITATIS "BABES-BOLYAI". PHILOSOPHIA. (Text in Rumanian; summaries in English, French, German, Russian) 1958. a. exchange basis. Universitatea "Babes-Bolyai", Biblioteca Centrala Universitara, Str. Clinicilor 2, Cluj-Napoca, Rumania. bk. rev. cum.index: 1956-1963; 1964-1970.
    Incorporates (since 1975): Studia Universitatis Babes-Bolyai. Psychologia-Pedagogia (ISSN 0578-5502) & Studia Universitatis Babes-Bolyai. Sociologia.

100   NE
STUDIEN ZUR ANTIKEN PHILOSOPHIE. 1971. irreg. price varies. B. R. Gruener B.V., Nieuwe Herengracht 31, 1011 RM Amsterdam, Netherlands. (back issues avail.)

100   GW   ISSN 0340-5958
STUDIEN ZUR FRANZOESISCHEN PHILOSOPHIE DES ZWANZIGSTEN JAHRHUNDERTS. irreg., vol.12, 1986. price varies. Bouvier Verlag Herbert Grundmann, Am Hof 32, Postfach 1268, 5300 Bonn 1, W. Germany (B.R.D.) Eds. V.V. Berning, H.R. Schlette.

109   GW
STUDIEN ZUR PHILOSOPHIE DES 18. JAHRHUNDERTS. 1976. irreg. price varies. Verlag Peter Lang GmbH, Hinter den Ulmen 19, D-6000 Frankfurt/Main 50, W. Germany (B.R.D.)

100 800   GW   ISSN 0081-735X
STUDIEN ZUR PHILOSOPHIE UND LITERATUR DES NEUNZEHNTEN JAHRHUNDERTS. 1968. irreg., vol.36, 1979. price varies. Vittorio Klostermann, Frauenlobstr. 22, 6000 Frankfurt 90, W. Germany (B.R.D.)

100   US
STUDIES IN ASIAN THOUGHT AND RELIGION. 1983. irreg., vol. 5, 1987. $39.95 per no. Edwin Mellen Press, Box 450, Lewiston, NY 14092.

108   US
STUDIES IN CONTEMPORARY GERMAN SOCIAL THOUGHT. irreg. (3-4/yr.) M I T Press, Book Division, 28 Carleton St., Cambridge, MA 02142. TEL 617-253-5242. Ed. Thomas McCarthy.

STUDIES IN LINGUISTICS AND PHILOSOPHY. see *PSYCHOLOGY*

STUDIES IN MARXISM. see *POLITICAL SCIENCE*

100   JA   ISSN 0081-8380
STUDIES IN PHILOSOPHY.* (Text in English, French and German) irreg. available on exchange only. Fukuoka University, Faculty of Literature, 11 Nanakuma, Fukuoka City, Japan.

100   GW   ISSN 0081-8399
STUDIES IN PHILOSOPHY. 1963. irreg. price varies. Walter de Gruyter & Co., Mouton Publishers, Postfach 110240, D-1000 Berlin 11, W. Germany (B.R.D.) (U.S. addr: Mouton Publishers, division of Walter de Gruyter, Inc., 200 Saw Mill River Rd., Hawthorne, NY 10532)

100   US   ISSN 0585-6965
STUDIES IN PHILOSOPHY & THE HISTORY OF PHILOSOPHY. 1961. irreg., vol.16, 1986. price varies. ‡ Catholic University of America Press, 620 Michigan Ave. N.E., Washington, DC 20064. TEL 202-635-5052. Ed. Jude P. Dougherty. (reprint service avail. from UMI) Indexed: Phil.Ind.

100 900   US
STUDIES IN THE HISTORY OF PHILOSOPHY. vol.5, 1987. irreg. $39.95 per no. Edwin Mellen Press, Box 450, Lewiston, NY 14092.

STUDIES IN THE LOGIC OF SCIENCE. see *SCIENCES: COMPREHENSIVE WORKS*

181 954 294   NE
STUDIES OF CLASSICAL INDIA. 1978. irreg. price varies. D. Reidel Publishing Co., Box 17, 3300 AA Dordrecht, Netherlands (And 190 Old Derby St., Hingham, MA 02043) Eds. B.K. Matilal, J.M. Masson.

100   FR
SURFACES (PARIS, 1978) 1978. irreg. Editions Jean-Michel Place, 12 rue Pierre et Marie Curie, 75005 Paris, France. Dir. Peter Hoy.

160   GW   ISSN 0082-0660
SYMBOLON; Jahrbuch fuer Symbolforschung. (Vols.1-7 published by Schwabe-Verlag, Basel) 1955; N.S. 1975. a. price varies. (Gesellschaft fuer Wissenschaftliche Symbolforschung) DuMont Buchverlag GmbH & Co. KG, Apostelnkloster 21-25, 5000 Koln 1, W. Germany (B.R.D.) Ed. Julius Schwabe. index. circ. 1,000.

109 160   NE   ISSN 0082-111X
SYNTHESE HISTORICAL LIBRARY; texts and studies in the history of logic and philosophy. 1969. irreg. price varies. D. Reidel Publishing Co., Postbus 17, 3300 AA Dordrecht, Netherlands (And 190 Old Derby St., Hingham, MA 02043) Ed.Bd. Indexed: Math.R.

109   NE   ISSN 0082-1128
SYNTHESE LIBRARY; monographs on epistemology, logic, methodology, philosophy of science and of knowledge, and the mathematical methods of social and behavioral sciences. 1959. irreg. price varies. D. Reidel Publishing Co., Postbus 17, 3300 AA Dordrecht, Netherlands (And 190 Old Derby St., Hingham, MA 02043) Ed. J. Hintikka. Indexed: Math.R.

100   US   ISSN 0271-2482
T A T JOURNAL. 1977. a. T A T Foundation, Box 236, Bellaire, OH 43906. Ed. Louis Khourey. adv. bk. rev. illus.

100   US   ISSN 0275-7656
TANNER LECTURES ON HUMAN VALUES. 1980. a. $20 price varies. University of Utah Press, Salt Lake City, UT 84112. TEL 801-581-6771. (Co-publisher: Cambridge University Press) Ed. Sterling M. McMurrin.

TEMPS DE LA REFLEXION. see *LITERATURE*

TEXAS TECH UNIVERSITY. GRADUATE STUDIES. see *HUMANITIES: COMPREHENSIVE WORKS*

250   GE   ISSN 0138-2144
THEMATISCHE INFORMATION PHILOSOPHIE. 1977. irreg. M.4.50 per no. Zentralstelle fuer Philosophische Information und Dokumentation, J.-Dieckmann-Str. 19-23, 1086 Berlin, E. Germany (D.D.R.) Ed. U. Richter. circ. 150.
    Formerly (1974-76): Sonderinformation Philosophie; 1965-1970: Informationen Philosophie.

100   SW   ISSN 0040-5825
THEORIA; a Swedish journal of philosophy. (Text in English) 1935. 3/yr. Kr.16. Swedish Council for Research in the Humanities and Social Sciences, Kungshuset i Lundagaard, S-223 50 Lund, Sweden. Ed.Bd. bk. rev. bibl. Indexed: Curr.Cont. Math.R. Psychol.Abstr. SSCI.

THEORY AND DECISION LIBRARY; an international series in the philosophy and methodology of the social and behavioral sciences. see *SOCIAL SCIENCES: COMPREHENSIVE WORKS*

THOUGHTS FOR ALL SEASONS; the magazine of epigrams. see *LITERATURE — Poetry*

110   DK   ISSN 0108-4712
TIDSSKRIFT FOR OPLYSNINGENS TIDSALDER. 1980. irreg. Kr.10 per no. (Foreningen for Transcendental Meditation i Danmark) Akademiet for Bevidsthedsudvikling, Dybesoevej 114, 4581 Roervig, Denmark. bk. rev. illus. circ. 4,500.

105   US
TOPICS IN PHILOSOPHY. 1975. irreg. price varies. University of California Press, 2120 Berkeley Way, Berkeley, CA 94720. TEL 415-642-4247.

100   GW
TOTOK: HANDBUCH DER GESCHICHTE DER PHILOSOPHIE. irreg., vol.5, 1986. price varies. Vittorio Klostermann, Frauenlobstr. 22, D-6000 Frankfurt 90, W. Germany(B.R.D.)

100   BL   ISSN 0101-3173
TRANS/FORM/ACAO; revista de filosofia. (Text in Portuguese; summaries in English and Portuguese) 1974-1975; resumed 1980. a. $30 or exchange basis. Universidade Estadual Paulista, Faculdade de Educacao, Filosofia, Ciencias Sociais e da Documentacao, Av. Vicente Ferreira 1278, Caixa Postal 603, 17.500 Marilia SP, Brazil. circ. 1,000. (back issues avail.) Indexed: Phil.Ind.

108 100   US
UNITY-AND-DIVERSITY WORLD DIRECTORY. 1965. a. $4. Unity-and-Diversity World Council, 1010 S. Flower St., Ste. 500, Los Angeles, CA 90015-1428. Ed.Bd. circ. 10,000.
    Former titles: Directory for a New World; Unity-in-Diversity Council Directory; International Cooperation Council. Directory (ISSN 0074-4239)

100   II   ISSN 0041-8218
UNIVERSALIST. 1968. irreg. (2-4/yr.) Rs.15.($2.) (World Jnana Sadhak Society) Jnana Sadhak Publishing House, Babupara-Mishralodge, Jalpaiguri 735101, West Bengal, India. Eds. Rajkishore Mollenhauer, B. Mollenhauer. bk. rev.

100   SP
UNIVERSIDAD DE DEUSTO. PUBLICACIONES. FILOSOFIA. 1977. irreg. Universidad Comercial de Deusto, Bilbao, Spain.

100   SP   ISSN 0008-7750
UNIVERSIDAD DE GRANADA. CATEDRA FRANCISCO SUAREZ. ANALES. (Text planned in English, French, German; summaries in Spanish) 1961. a. 400 ptas. Universidad de Granada, Catedra Francisco Suarez, Secretariado de Publicaciones, Hospital Real, Granada, Spain. Dir. Nicolas M. Lopez Calera.

100   UY
UNIVERSIDAD DE LA REPUBLICA. FACULTAD DE HUMANIDADES Y CIENCIAS. REVISTA. SERIE FILOSOFIA. irreg. exchange basis. Universidad de la Republica, Facultad de Humanidades y Ciencias, Seccion Revista, Tristan Narvaja 1674, Montevideo, Uruguay. Dir. Beatriz Martinez Osorio.
    Supersedes in part: Universidad de la Republica. Facultad de Humanidades y Ciencias. Revista.

110   SP   ISSN 0580-8650
UNIVERSIDAD DE MADRID. SEMINARIO DE METAFISICA. ANALES. 1966. a. 200 ptas. Universidad Complutense de Madrid, Catedra de Metafisica (Critica), Servicio de Publicaciones, Madrid, Spain. Ed. Sergio Rabade Romeo. adv. bk. rev. bibl. circ. 500. Indexed: Phil.Ind.

100   SP   ISSN 0213-2958
UNIVERSIDAD DE MURCIA. ANALES DE FILOLOGIA FRANCESA. 1985. a. ($600) Universidad de Murcia, Secretario de Publicaciones e Intercambio Cientifico, Santo Cristo, 1, 30001 Murcia, Spain. TEL 968 24 92 00.

100   SP   ISSN 0213-4365
UNIVERSIDAD DE MURCIA. ANALES DE FILOLOGIA HISPANICA. 1985. a. ($800) Universidad de Murcia, Secretariado de Publicaciones e Intercambio Cientifico, Santo Cristo, 1, 30001 Murcia, Spain. TEL 968 24 92 00.

100   SP   ISSN 0212-9698
UNIVERSIDAD DE MURCIA. ANALES DE FILOSOFIA. 1983. a. 1000 ptas. Universidad de Murcia, Secretariado de Publicaciones e Intercambio Cientifico, Santo Cristo, 1, 30001 Murcia, Spain. TEL 968 24 92 00. Ed. Eduardo Bello Reguera. circ. 300. (back issues avail.)

UNIVERSIDAD DE MURCIA. ANALES DE
FILOSOFIA Y CIENCIAS DE LA EDUCACION.
see EDUCATION

910   SP   ISSN 0213-5485
UNIVERSIDAD DE MURCIA. CUADERNOS DE
FILOLOGIA INGLESA. 1985. a. ($500)
Universidad de Murcia, Secretariado de
Publicaciones e Intercambio Cientifico, Santos
Cristo, 1, 30001 Murcia, Spain. TEL 968 24 92 00.

100 460   MX   ISSN 0185-2558
UNIVERSIDAD NACIONAL AUTONOMA DE
MEXICO. INSTITUTO DE INVESTIGACIONES
FILOSOFICAS. CUADERNOS. 1959. irreg., no.43,
1985. Universidad Nacional Autonoma de
Mexico, Instituto de Investigaciones Filosoficas, Apdo. Postal
70-447, Mexico, D.F., Mexico (Orders to: Direccion
General de Fomento Editorial, Porto Alegre No.
260, San Andres Tetepilco, 09440 Mexico, D.F.,
Mexico) circ. 2,000.

UNIVERSIDAD PONTIFICIA COMILLAS DE
MADRID. PUBLICACIONES. SERIE 1:
ESTUDIOS. see RELIGIONS AND THEOLOGY

100   IT
UNIVERSITA DEGLI STUDI DI FIRENZE.
ISTITUTO DI FILOSOFIA. ANNALI. 1979. a.
Casa Editrice Leo S. Olschki, Casella Postale 66,
50100 Florence, Italy. Ed. Francesco Adorno. circ.
1,000. (back issues avail.)

100   IT
UNIVERSITA DEGLI STUDI DI LECCE.
BOLLETTINO DI STORIA DELLA FILOSOFIA.
1973. a. Universita degli Studi di Lecce, Facolta di
Lettere e Filosofia, Via V.M. Stampacchia, 73100
Lecce, Italy. Ed. Prof. Giovanni Papuli.

100   IT   ISSN 0078-7779
UNIVERSITA DEGLI STUDI DI PADOVA.
SCUOLA DI PERFEZIONAMENTO IN
FILOSOFIA. PUBBLICAZIONI. 1963. irreg.
L.1000.($1.60) Casa Editrice Dott. Antonio Milani,
Via Jappelli 5, 35100 Padua, Italy.

UNIVERSITA DEGLI STUDI DI SIENA.
FACOLTA DI LETTERE E FILOSOFIA.
ANNALI. see LITERATURE

100   RM   ISSN 0379-7856
UNIVERSITATEA "AL. I. CUZA" DIN IASI.
ANALELE STIINTIFICE. SECTIUNEA 3B:
FILOZOFIE. (Text in Rumanian, English, French)
a. 35 lei. Universitatea "Al. I. Cuza" din Iasi, Calea
23 August, Nr. 11, Jassy, Rumania (Subscr. to:
ILEXIM, Str. 13 Decembrie Nr. 3, P.O. Box 136-
137, Bucharest, Rumania) Ed. Petru Ioan. circ. 550.
Formerly: Universitatea "Al. I. Cuza" din Iasi.
Analele Stiintifice. Sectiunea 3b: Stiinte Filozofice
(ISSN 0075-353X)

100 940 340   RM
UNIVERSITATEA BUCURESTI. ANALELE.
FILOZOFIE. ISTORIE. DREPT. (Text in various
languages with summaries) a. $10. Universitatea
Bucuresti, Bd. Gh. Gheorghiu-Dej Nr. G4,
Bucharest, Rumania.

100   BE   ISSN 0076-1273
UNIVERSITE CATHOLIQUE DE LOUVAIN.
INSTITUT SUPERIEUR DE PHILOSOPHIE.
COURS PUBLIES. 1964. irreg. price varies. 1
Chemin d'Aristote, 1348 Louvain-La-Neuve,
Belgium.

084   FR
UNIVERSITE DE BESANCON. CENTRE DE
DOCUMENTATION ET DE BIBLIOGRAPHIE
PHILOSOPHIQUES. TRAVAUX. 1973. irreg.
(Universite de Besancon, Centre de Documentation
et de Bibliographie Philosophiques) Societe
d'Edition "les Belles Lettres", 95, Boulevard Raspail,
75006 Paris, France. illus.

100   BE   ISSN 0771-4963
UNIVERSITE LIBRE DE BRUXELLES. INSTITUT
DE PHILOSOPHIE. ANNALES. 1969. a. Editions
de l'Universite de Bruxelles, Avenue P. Heger, 26-
C.P. 163, B-1050 Brussels, Belgium. bk. rev. bibl.
circ. 1,000. Indexed: Art & Archaeol.Tech.Abstr.

100   II
UNIVERSITY OF CALCUTTA. DEPARTMENT OF
PHILOSOPHY. JOURNAL. (Text in English)
1975. a. Rs.5. University of Calcutta, Department of
Philosophy, Asutosh Bldg., Calcutta 700073, India.

UNIVERSITY OF KANSAS. CENTER FOR EAST
ASIAN STUDIES. INTERNATIONAL STUDIES:
EAST ASIAN SERIES. REFERENCE SERIES.
see HISTORY — History Of Asia

UNIVERSITY OF KANSAS. CENTER FOR EAST
ASIAN STUDIES. INTERNATIONAL STUDIES:
EAST ASIAN SERIES. RESEARCH SERIES. see
HISTORY — History Of Asia

180   II   ISSN 0076-2253
UNIVERSITY OF MADRAS. PHILOSOPHICAL
SERIES.* irreg. University of Madras, Chepauk,
Triplicane, Madras 600005, Tamil Nadu, India.

700 500   UK   ISSN 0078-0251
UNIVERSITY OF NEWCASTLE-UPON-TYNE.
PHILOSOPHICAL SOCIETY. PROCEEDINGS.*
1964. irreg., vol.1, no.15, 1969. 5s.($0.60)
University of Newcastle-Upon-Tyne, Philosophical
Society, Armstrong Bldg., Queen Victoria Rd.,
Newcastle-Upon-Tyne NE1 7RU, England. Ed. J.A.
Richardson.

UNIVERSITY OF NOTRE DAME. STUDIES IN
THE PHILOSOPHY OF RELIGION. see
RELIGIONS AND THEOLOGY

105   SL
UNIVERSITY OF SIERRA LEONE. FOURAH BAY
COLLEGE. PHILOSOPHICAL SOCIETY.
JOURNAL. 1977. a. University of Sierra Leone,
Fourah Bay College, Philosophical Society,
Freetown, Sierra Leone.

501 500   NE
UNIVERSITY OF WESTERN ONTARIO SERIES
IN PHILOSOPHY OF SCIENCE. Variant title:
Western Ontario Series. 1972. irreg. price varies.
(University of Western Ontario, CN) D. Reidel
Publishing Co., Postbus 17, 3300 AA Dordrecht,
Netherlands (And 190 Old Derby St., Hingham,
WA 02043) Ed. R.E. Butts.

100   CS   ISSN 0231-7664
UNIVERZITA J. E. PURKYNE. FILOZOFICKA
FAKULTA. SBORNIK PRACI. B: RADA
FILOZOFICKA. irreg., approx. a. Univerzita J. E.
Purkyne, Filozoficka Fakulta, A. Novaka 1, 602 00
Brno, Czechoslovakia.

100   CS
UNIVERZITA KOMENSKEHO. FILOZOFICKA
FAKULTA. ZBORNIK: INFORMATIKA. (Text in
Slovak; summaries in English, German and Russian)
1973. a. exchange basis. Slovenske Pedagogicke
Nakladatelstvo, Sasinkova 5, 815 60 Bratislava,
Czechoslovakia. Ed. Emilia Chura.

UNIVERZITA KOMENSKEHO. FILOZOFICKA
FAKULTA. ZBORNIK: MARXIZMUS-
LENINIZMUS. see POLITICAL SCIENCE

100   CS   ISSN 0083-4181
UNIVERZITA KOMENSKEHO. FILOZOFICKA
FAKULTA. ZBORNIK: PHILOSOPHICA. (Text in
Czech or Slovak; summaries in German and
Russian) 1960. a. exchange basis. (Univerzita
Komenskeho, Filozoficka Fakulta) Slovenske
Pedagogicke Nakladatelstvo, Sasinkova 5, 815 60
Bratislava, Czechoslovakia. Ed. Lev Hanzel. circ.
700.

100 301   PL   ISSN 0072-0453
UNIWERSYTET GDANSKI. WYDZIAL
HUMANISTYCZNY. ZESZYTY NAUKOWE.
FILOZOFIA I SOCJOLOGIA. 1965. irreg. price
varies. Uniwersytet Gdanski, Ul. Czerwonej Armii
110, 81-824 Sopot, Poland (Dist. by: Ars Polona-
Ruch, Krakowskie Przedmiescie 7, Warsaw, Poland)

100   US
VAN LEER JERUSALEM FOUNDATION SERIES.
1975. irreg. price varies. Humanities Press, Inc., 171
First Ave., Atlantic Highlands, NJ 07716. TEL 201-
872-1441. Ed.Bd.

100   AU   ISSN 0083-999X
WIENER JAHRBUCH FUER PHILOSOPHIE. 1968.
a. price varies. Wilhelm Braumueller, Universitaets-
Verlagsbuchhandlung GmbH, Servitengasse 5, A-
1092 Vienna, Austria. Ed. Erich Heintel. bk. rev.
index. circ. 500.

181.4 954   AU   ISSN 0084-0084
WIENER ZEITSCHRIFT FUER DIE KUNDE
SUEDASIENS UND ARCHIV FUER INDISCHE
PHILOSPHIE. 1957. a. S.210. (Oesterreichische
Akademie der Wissenschaften, Kommission fuer
Sprachen und Kulturen Sued- und Ostasiens) Gerold
und Co., Graben 31, A-1011 Vienna, Austria (and
E. J. Brill, Antwerpener Str. 6-12, Leiden,
Netherlands) (Co-sponsor: Universitaet Wien.
Indologisches Institut) Eds. E. Frauwallner, G.
Oberhammer. Indexed: Numis.Lit.
   Formerl titles (until 1969): Wiener Zeitschrift
fuer Die Kunde Sued- und Ostasiens & Archiv fuer
Indische Philosophie.

100   NE   ISSN 0084-0106
WIJSGERIGE TEKSTEN EN STUDIES/
PHILOSOPHICAL TEXTS AND STUDIES. 1956.
irreg., no.23, 1975. price varies. ‡ (Rijksuniversiteit
te Utrecht - University of Utrecht) Van Gorcum,
Box 43, 9400 AA Assen, Netherlands (Dist. by
Humanities Press, Inc., 171 First Ave, Atlantic
Highlands, N.J. 07716) Eds. C.J. de Vogel, K.
Kuypers.

100   GW   ISSN 0175-6486
WISSENSCHAFT UND GEGENWART.
GEISTESWISSENSCHAFTLICHE REIHE. irreg.,
no.64, 1984. price varies. Vittorio Klostermann,
Frauenlobstr. 22, Postfach 900601, 6000 Frankfurt
90, W. Germany (B.R.D.)

574   US
WOODBRIDGE LECTURES, COLUMBIA
UNIVERSITY. no.4, 1972. irreg. Columbia
University Press, 562 W. 113th St., New York, NY
10025. TEL 212-678-6777.

181 891   II   ISSN 0084-1242
WOOLNER INDOLOGICAL SERIES. (Text in
English, Hindi and Sanskrit) 1960. irreg.; vol.21,
1976. price varies. Vishveshvaranand Vedic
Research Institute, P. O. Sadhu Ashram, Hoshiarpur
146021, Punjab, India. Ed. S. Bhaskaran Nair.

100   II
WORLD'S WISDOM SERIES. (Text in English)
1976. irreg. Oriental Publishers and Distributors,
1488, Pataudi House, Darya Ganj, New Delhi
110002, India.

709   PL
WYDZIAL FILOLOGICZNO-FILOZOFICZNEGO.
PRACE. (Text in Polish; summaries in English,
French, German) 1948. irreg. price varies.
Towarzystwo Naukowe w Toruniu, Ul. Wysoka 16,
87-100 Torun, Poland (Dist. by: Ars-Polona Ruch,
Krakowskie Przedmiescie 7, 00-068 Warsaw,
Poland)

YOGA LIFE. see PHYSICAL FITNESS AND
HYGIENE

YOKOHAMA NATIONAL UNIVERSITY.
HUMANITIES. SECTION 1: PHILOSOPHY
AND SOCIAL SCIENCES/YOKOHAMA
KOKURITSU DAIGAKU JIMBUN KIYO DAI-1-
RUI, TETSUGAKU, SHAKAI KAGAKU. see
SOCIAL SCIENCES: COMPREHENSIVE
WORKS

101   GW   ISSN 0514-2733
ZEITSCHRIFT FUER PHILOSOPHISCHE
FORSCHUNG. BEIHEFTE. 1950. irreg., no.43,
1984. price varies. Verlag Anton Hain GmbH,
Adelheidstr. 2, Postfach 1220, 6240 Koenigstein, W.
Germany (B.R.D.) Eds. H.M. Baumgartner, O.
Hoeffe.

PHILOSOPHY — Abstracting, Bibliographies, Statistics

ABSTRACTS OF BULGARIAN SCIENTIFIC
LITERATURE. PHILOSOPHY, SOCIOLOGY,
SCIENCE OF SCIENCES, PSYCHOLOGY AND
PEDAGOGICS. see EDUCATION — Abstracting,
Bibliographies, Statistics

100 016   VC   ISSN 0084-7836
BIBLIOGRAPHIA INTERNATIONALIS
SPIRITUALITATIS. (Text in various languages;
summaries in Latin) 1966. a. L.80000($55)
(Pontificio Istituto di Spiritualita) Edizioni del
Teresianum, Piazza S. Pancrazio 5-A, 00152 Rome,
Italy. circ. 650.

PHOTOGRAPHY

100   US   ISSN 0742-6887
BIBLIOGRAPHIES AND INDEXES IN PHILOSOPHY. irreg. price varies. Greenwood Press, 88 Post Rd. W., Box 5007, Westport, CT 06881. TEL 203-226-3571.

100   FR   ISSN 0080-4789
RUDOLF STEINER PUBLICATIONS. 1963. irreg. 69 F. (Rudolf Steiner Nachlassverwaltung) Librairie Fischbacher, 33 Rue de Seine, 75006 Paris, France. Ed. V. Rivierez.

PHOTOGRAPHY

see also Motion Pictures

770   070.49   DK   ISSN 0109-4440
AARETS PRESSEFOTO. a. Kr.10. Pressefotografforbundet, Gammel Strand 46, 1202 Copenhagen K, Denmark.

ACOUSTICAL IMAGING: RECENT ADVANCES IN VISUALIZATION AND CHARACTERIZATION. see *PHYSICS — Sound*

AERIAL ARCHAEOLOGY. see *ARCHAEOLOGY*

AILERON; a literary journal. see *LITERATURE*

770   FR   ISSN 0084-6481
ANNUAIRE DE LA PHOTOGRAPHIE PROFESSIONNELLE. 1966. a. 78 F. Confederation Francaise de la Photographie, 16 place Vendome, 75001 Paris, France. Ed. Antoine de Saisset. adv.

770   II
ANNUAL OF INDIAN PHOTOGRAPHY. 1978. a. Rs.12. Sooriya Publishing House, 52 Thaiyappa Mudali St, V.O.C. Nagar, Madras 600001, India.

770   IT
ANNUARIO FOTOGRAFICO. 1978. a. L.6500. Editrice Progresso s.r.l., Viale Piceno 14, 20129 Milan, Italy. Ed. G.R. Namias. adv. circ. 44,000.

779   US
ARCHIVE (TUCSON)* 1976. irreg., no.13, 1981. $20 for 4 nos. (University of Arizona, Center for Creative Photography) University of Arizona Library, Tucson, AZ 85721. TEL 602-621-7968. circ. 800.
    Formerly (1976-1981): Center for Creative Photography.

770   AT
AUSTRALIAN PHOTOGRAPHY PHOTO-DIRECTORY. 1951. a. Aus.$4.50 per no. Yaffa Publishing Group Pty. Ltd., 432-436 Elizabeth St., Surry Hills, N.S.W. 2010, Australia. adv. bk. rev. circ. 28,000.
    Formerly: Australian Photography Directory (ISSN 0067-2076)

770   US
BEST OF PHOTOJOURNALISM; newspaper and magazine pictures of the year. 1975. a. $14.95. (National Press Photographers Association) Running Press Book Publishers, 125 S. 22nd St., Philadelphia, PA 19103. TEL 215-567-5080. Ed. Cal Olsen. (back issues avail.)

770   UK   ISSN 0068-2217
BRITISH JOURNAL OF PHOTOGRAPHY ANNUAL. 1860. a. £6. Henry Greenwood & Co. Ltd., 28 Great James St., London WC1N 3HL, England (Dist. in U.S. by: Writer's Digest Books, 9933 Alliance Rd., Cincinnati, Ohio 45242) Ed. G.W. Crawley. adv. index. circ. 12,000. (also avail. in microfilm)

770   UK
CAMERA TEST. a. £3. Haymarket Publishing Ltd., 38-42 Hampton Rd., Teddington, Middx. TW11 0JE, England. illus.

CAMERART PHOTO TRADE DIRECTORY. see *BUSINESS AND ECONOMICS — Trade And Industrial Directories*

770   CN
CANADIAN DIRECTORY OF PROFESSIONAL PHOTOGRAPHY. 1980. a. Can.$10. (Professional Photographers of Canada) Craig Kelman & Associates Ltd., 17-399 Berry St., Winnipeg, MB R3J 1N6, Canada TEL 604-885-7798. (Subscr. addr.: c/o Oma Marler, 1811 McKenzie Rd., Abbotsford, B.C. V2S 3ZZ, Canada) Ed. Craig Kelman.

CHAMPAIGN COUNTY HISTORICAL ARCHIVES HISTORICAL PUBLICATIONS SERIES. see *HISTORY — History Of North And South America*

CHICAGO RENAISSANCE. see *LITERATURE*

770   SZ   ISSN 0573-0473
COMMITTEE OF THE PROFESSIONAL PHOTOGRAPHERS OF EUROPE. GENERAL ASSEMBLY. REPORT OF PROCEEDINGS.* a. Committee of the Professional Photographers of Europe, Hafnerstr. 24, Zuerich 5, Switzerland.

770   US
CONTEMPORARY PHOTOGRAPHERS. 1982. quinquennial. St. Martin's Press, Scholarly and Reference Division, 175 Fifth Ave., New York, NY 10010. TEL 212-674-5151. Ed.Bd.

CREATIVE BLACK BOOK. PORTFOLIO EDITION. see *ADVERTISING AND PUBLIC RELATIONS*

CREATIVE SOURCE AUSTRALIA; the wizards of Oz. see *ARTS AND HANDICRAFTS*

770   DK
DANISH PHOTOGRAPHY (YEAR) a. Selskabet for Dansk Fotografi - Society of Danish Photography, Danmarksgade 16, DK-4874 Gedser, Denmark. Ed. Niels Bjerre. adv. circ. 1,000.

DANSKE REKLAMEFOTOGRAFER. see *ADVERTISING AND PUBLIC RELATIONS*

770   US
DIRECTORY OF C E, PHOTOGRAPHY & MAJOR APPLIANCE RETAILERS & DISTRIBUTORS. 1987. a. $189. Chain Store Guide, 425 Park Ave., New York, NY 10022. TEL 212-371-9400.

DIRECTORY OF LIBRARY REPROGRAPHIC SERVICES. see *LIBRARY AND INFORMATION SCIENCES*

770   US   ISSN 0070-6140
DIRECTORY OF PROFESSIONAL PHOTOGRAPHY. 1938. a. $50. ‡ (Professional Photographers of America) P P of A Publications and Events, Inc., 1090 Executive Way, Des Plaines, IL 60018. TEL 312-299-8161. Ed. Alfred DeBat. adv. circ. 15,000.

770   UK
EUROPEAN PHOTOGRAPHY. 1981. a. £25. D & AD European Illustration, Nash House, 12 Carlton House Terrace, London SW1Y 5AH, England. Ed. Edward Booth-Clibborn. Indexed: Artbibl.

770   BE
FEDERATION NATIONALE DE LA PHOTOGRAPHIE PROFESIONELLE. ANNUAIRE. Short title: F.N.P.P. Annuaire. (Text in Flemish and English) a. (Nationale Federatie van Beroepsfotografie) Editions Publi-Contact, Ave. Hansen-Soulie 98, 1040 Brussels, Belgium. adv.

FIELD OF VISION. see *MOTION PICTURES*

770   IE   ISSN 0790-4940
FOCUS (DUBLIN) 1979. irreg. Irish Professional Photographers Association, Charnwood Photography, Unit 1, Dundrum Shopping Centre, Dublin 14, Ireland. Ed. Edward Moss. adv. bk. rev. illus. circ. 300.

770   SP
FOTO GALAXIS. (Text in English & Spanish) irreg. Galaxis, S.A., Zamora 46-48, Barcelona, Spain. illus.

770   DK   ISSN 0108-0016
FOTO-REVYEN. 1982. a. Kr.64.50. Bonnier Specialmagasiner, Noerre Farimagsgade 49, 1375 Copenhagen K, Denmark. illus.

526.982   MX
FOTOGRAMETRIA, FOTOINTERPRETACION Y GEODESIA. 1970. irreg. Mex.$250. Sociedad Mexicana de Fotogrametria, Fotointerpretacion y Geodesia, Apartado Postal 25-447, Mexico 13, D.F., Mexico. Ed. Alberto Aspe Rojas. adv. illus.

770   301.2   US
FRAME/WORK. 1976. irreg. (2-3/yr.) $15. Los Angeles Center for Photographic Studies, 814 S. Spring St., Los Angeles, CA 90014. TEL 213-623-9410. Ed. Howard Spector. adv. circ. 2,000.
    Formerly (until 1986): Obscura.

GADNEY'S GUIDE TO INTERNATIONAL CONTESTS, FESTIVALS & GRANTS IN FILM & VIDEO, PHOTOGRAPHY, TV-RADIO BROADCASTING, WRITING, POETRY, PLAYWRITING & JOURNALISM. see *MOTION PICTURES*

GRAPHIS POSTERS; international annual of poster art. see *ART*

770   FR
GUIDE D'ACHAT DE LA PHOTOGRAPHIE. 1981. a. Editions V. M., 116 bd. Malesherbes, 75017 Paris, France. Ed. Robert Monnier. adv. illus. circ. 45,000.
    Former titles: Guide d'Achat de la Photographie: 20 Objectifs pour Appareils Reflex 24 x 36; Guide d'Achat de la Photographie: 60 Objectifs pour Appareils Reflex 24 x 36.

778.1   UK   ISSN 0266-6960
INFORMATION MEDIA & TECHNOLOGY. 1967. 4/yr. £41. CIMTECH, P.O. Box 109, Hatfield Polytechnic, College Lane, Hatfield, Herts. AL10 9AB, England. Ed. B.J.S. Williams. adv. bk. rev. abstr. charts. illus. index. cum.index. circ. 1,100. (also avail. in microfiche) Indexed: LISA. Sci.Abstr. Inform.Sci.Abstr. C.I.S. Abstr. Consum.Ind. Graph.Arts Lit.Abstr.
    Former titles: Reprographics Quarterly (ISSN 0306-2880); (until 1984): N R C D Abstracts; N R C D Bulletin (ISSN 0027-6928)
    Reprography

770   US   ISSN 0024-063X
LEICA PHOTOGRAPHY. 1932. irreg. free to Leica owners. E. Leitz, Inc., Rockleigh, NJ 07647. TEL 201-767-1100. Ed. Helen Wright. bk. rev. charts. illus. index. circ. 55,000.

LIGHTWORKS. see *ART*

778.35   FR   ISSN 0076-6364
MEMOIRES DE PHOTO-INTERPRETATION. 1963. irreg., no.7, 1970. price varies. (Ecole Pratique des Hautes Etudes) Librairie Touzot, 38 rue Saint Sulpice, 75278 Paris Cedex 06, France. Indexed: GeoRef.

778.315   UK
MICROGRAPHICS AND OPTICAL STORAGE BUYER'S GUIDE. 1981. a. £10. G.G. Baker & Associates, c/o Alan Armstrong & Assoc. Ltd., 72 Park Rd., London NW1 4SH, England. adv. illus. circ. 1,000.
    Formerly: Micrographics Year Book (ISSN 0260-7069)

MIDLAND REVIEW. see *LITERATURE*

779.05   US
MODERN PHOTOGRAPHY'S PHOTO BUYING GUIDE. 1969. a. $4.95 per no. A B C Leisure Magazines, Inc, 825 Seventh Ave., New York, NY 10019. TEL 212-265-8360. Ed. Harold Martin. adv. illus. circ. 125,000.

770   UK   ISSN 0143-036X
NEW MAGIC LANTERN JOURNAL. 1978. irreg. £2.50 per issue. Magic Lantern Society of Great Britain, 36 Meon Rd., London W3 8AN, England. Ed. David Henry. bk. rev. illus. circ. 500.

NEW VIRGINIA REVIEW. see *LITERATURE*

770   DK   ISSN 0107-6329
OBJEKTIV. 1976. irreg. free to libraries. Dansk Fotohistorisk Selskab, c/o Flemming Berendt, Teglgaardsvej 649, 3050 Humlebaek, Denmark. illus.

P T N MASTER BUYING GUIDE & DIRECTORY. (Photographic Trade News) see *BUSINESS AND ECONOMICS — Trade And Industrial Directories*

PAN-EROTIC REVIEW. see *ART*

PHOTO, CINE, VIDEO BUYER'S GUIDE. see *COMMUNICATIONS — Radio And Television*

770.5 US ISSN 0093-1365
PHOTO INFORMATION ALMANAC. 1960. a. $2.95. A B C Leisure Magazines, Inc., Photographic Publishing Division, 825 Seventh Ave., New York, NY 10019. TEL 212-265-8360. Ed. Harold O. Martin. adv. illus. circ. 100,000.

771 US
PHOTO-LAB INDEX; cumulative formulary of standard recommended photographic procedures. 1939. a. (q. updates) $59.95 $24.50 for supplements. ‡ Morgan & Morgan Inc., 145 Palisade St, Dobbs Ferry, NY 10522. TEL 914-693-0023. Ed. Liliane Morgan. charts. index. cum.index. circ. 8,000. (looseleaf format)

770 US
PHOTOGRAPH COLLECTORS' RESOURCE DIRECTORY. biennial. $24.95. Photographic Arts Center, 127 E. 59 St., New York, NY 10022. TEL 212-620-3196. Ed. Peter H. Falk.

770 US ISSN 0147-247X
PHOTOGRAPHER'S MARKET. 1979. a. $16.95. F & W Publications, Inc., 9933 Alliance Rd., Cincinnati, OH 45242. TEL 513-984-0717. Ed. Connie Eidenier.

770 US
PHOTOGRAPHIC ART MARKET AUCTION PRICE RESULTS AND ANALYSIS. 1981. biennial. $69.50. Photographic Arts Center, 127 E. 59 St., New York, NY 10022. TEL 212-620-3196. Ed. Robert S. Persky. circ. 1,000.

770.62 US ISSN 0093-254X
PHOTOGRAPHIC HISTORICAL SOCIETY OF NEW YORK. MEMBERSHIP DIRECTORY. a. membership. Photographic Historical Society of New York, Box 1775, Grand Central Sta., New York, NY 10103. TEL 212-594-5056. illus. circ. 600.

770 US
PHOTOGRAPHIC TRADE NEWS MASTER BUYING GUIDE. (Not for sale to general public) 1937. a. $6 included with subscr. to Photographic Trade News. P T N Publishing Corp., 210 Crossways Park Dr., Woodbury, NY 11797. TEL 516-496-8000. adv. illus. circ. (controlled)

770 659 SZ ISSN 0079-1830
PHOTOGRAPHIS; international annual of advertising and editorial photography. (Text in English, French, German) 1966. a. 112 Fr.($59.50) B. Martin Pedersen Graphis Press Corp, 107 Dufourstrasse, 8008 Zurich, Switzerland (Dist. by Watson-Guptill Publications, P.O. Box 2014, Lakewood, NJ 08701) Ed. B. Martin Pedersen. index. circ. 12,500.

770 CN
PHOTOGRAPHY AT OPEN SPACE MONOGRAPHS. 1976. irreg. price varies. Photography at Open Space, P.O. Box 5207, Sta. B, Victoria, B.C. V8R 6N4, Canada. Ed. Tom Gore. bk. rev. circ. 500.

770 CN
PHOTOGRAPHY MONOGRAPH SERIES. 1978. irreg. Photography at Open Space, Box 5207, Sta. B, Victoria, B.C. V8R 6N4, Canada. Ed. Tom Gore. circ. 600.

770 UK
PHOTOGRAPHY REPORT. 1980. biennial. £160. Euromonitor Publications Ltd., 87-88 Turnmill St., London EC1M 5QU, England.

770 AT ISSN 0727-3967
PHOTOWORLD ANNUAL. 1979. a. Australian Hi-Fi Publications Pty. Ltd., Box 341, Mona Vale, N.S.W. 2103, Australia. Ed. Neil Sudbury.
Formerly: Photographic World Annual.

PIG IRON. see *LITERATURE*

770 380.1 AT
PROFESSIONAL AND INDUSTRIAL PHOTOGRAPHIC EQUIPMENT. 1971. a. Aus.$4. Yaffa Publishing Group Pty. Ltd., 432-436 Elizabeth St., Surry Hills, N.S.W. 2010, Australia. circ. 8,000.
Formerly: Australian Photography Professional and Industrial Catalogue.

PROFESSIONAL PHOTOGRAPHER DIRECTORY AND BUYER'S GUIDE. see *BUSINESS AND ECONOMICS — Trade And Industrial Directories*

770 US
PROFESSIONAL PHOTOGRAPHIC EQUIPMENT DIRECTORY AND BUYING GUIDE. 1975. a. $15. P T N Publishing Corp., 210 Crossways Park Dr., Woodbury, NY 11797. TEL 516-496-8000. adv. illus.

770 IT
PROFESSIONAL PHOTOGRAPHY. 1984. a. L.9000. Editrice Progresso s.r.l., Viale Piceno 14, 20129 Milan, Italy. bk. rev. illus. index. circ. 35,000.

SHOWCASE. see *CLOTHING TRADE — Fashions*

770 US ISSN 0081-5586
STILL: YALE PHOTOGRAPHY ANNUAL. 1970. irreg., latest no.3, 1973. price varies. Yale University, School of Art and Architecture, Department of Graphic Design, 180 York St., New Haven, CT 06520 TEL 203-436-0308. (Dist. by: George Wittenborn, Inc., 1018 Madison Ave., New York, N.Y. 10021)

770 US
STUDIES IN THE FINE ARTS: STUDIES IN PHOTOGRAPHY. irreg., vol.8, 1985. U M I Research Press, 300 N. Zeeb Rd., Ann Arbor, MI 48106. Ed. Diane Kirkpatrick.

770 FI ISSN 0356-8075
VALOKUVAUKSEN VUOSIKIRJA/FINNISH PHOTOGRAPHIC YEARBOOK/FINSK FOTOGRAFISK ARSBOK. (Text in English, Finnish and Swedish) 1972. a. Fmk.100($20) Suomen Valokuvataiteen Museon Saatio - Foundation of the Photographic Museum of Finland, Box 596, SF-00101 Helsinki 10, Finland. Ed. Ritva Keski-Korhonen. adv. illus. circ. 5,000.

770 US ISSN 0084-103X
WOLFMAN REPORT ON THE PHOTOGRAPHIC INDUSTRY IN THE UNITED STATES. 1958. a. $115 per no. A B C Leisure Magazines, Inc., 825 7th Ave., New York, NY 10019. TEL 212-265-8360. Ed. Lydia Wolfman. adv. circ. 9,000.

770 US ISSN 0197-3444
WORKSHOP ON COLOR AERIAL PHOTOGRAPHY IN THE PLANT SCIENCES. PROCEEDINGS. biennial. $30 to non-members; members $22. American Society for Photogrammetry and Remote Sensing, 210 Little Falls St., Falls Church, VA 22046. TEL 703-534-6617.

WRITERS' AND PHOTOGRAPHERS' MARKETING GUIDE; DIRECTORY OF AUSTRALIAN AND NEW ZEALAND LITERARY AND PHOTO MARKETS. see *PUBLISHING AND BOOK TRADE*

PHOTOGRAPHY — Abstracting, Bibliographies, Statistics

BRITISH CATALOGUE OF AUDIO-VISUAL MATERIALS. see *SOUND RECORDING AND REPRODUCTION — Abstracting, Bibliographies, Statistics*

770 016 UK ISSN 0031-8701
PHOTOGRAPHIC ABSTRACTS. 1921. 6/yr. £70. (Royal Photographic Society of Great Britain, Scientific and Technical Group) Pergamon Journals Ltd., Headington Hill Hall, Oxford, OX3 0BW, England. Ed. B.J. Smith. abstr. index. cum.index. circ. 250. (also avail. in microfiche; back issues avail.)
•Also available online. Vendors: Pergamon Infoline.

770 011 US
PHOTOGRAPHY MAGAZINE INDEX. 1984. a. Paragon Publishing, Box 53, Santa Rosa, CA 95402. TEL 707-527-8185. Ed. Stu Berger. index.

770 016 UR ISSN 0370-8063
REFERATIVNYI ZHURNAL. FOTOKINOTEKHNIKA. 1957. m. 27.60 Rub. 30 Rub. including index. Vsesoyuznyi Institut Nauchno-Tekhnicheskoi Informatsii (VINITI), Baltiiskaya ul., 14, Moscow A-219, Russian S.F.S.R., U.S.S.R. (Subscr. to: Mezhdunarodnaya Kniga, Dimitrova ul. 39, 113095 Moscow, Russian S.F.S.R., U.S.S.R.)

PHYSICAL CHEMISTRY

see *Chemistry — Physical Chemistry*

PHYSICAL FITNESS AND HYGIENE

see also *Medical Sciences; Nutrition and Dietetics; Public Health and Safety; Sports and Games*

ACTA MEDICA ET SOCIOLOGICA. see *SOCIOLOGY*

330 613 US ISSN 0731-2199
ADVANCES IN HEALTH ECONOMICS AND HEALTH SERVICES RESEARCH. 1979. a. $24.75 to individuals; institutions $49.50. J A I Press Inc., Box 1678, 36 Sherwood Pl., Greenwich, CT 06836. TEL 203-661-7602. Eds. Richard M. Scheffler, Louis F. Rossiter. Indexed: Abstr.Health Care Manage.Stud.
Formerly (until 1981): Research in Health Economics (ISSN 0197-0690)

ADVANCES IN HEALTH EDUCATION. see *EDUCATION — Teaching Methods And Curriculum*

613.7 649 US
ADVANCES IN MOTOR DEVELOPMENT RESEARCH. 1987. a. $47.50. A M S Press, Inc., 56 E. 13th St., New York, NY 10003. TEL 212-777-4700. Ed. Jane E. Clark. index. circ. 600. (back issues avail.)

ANGOLA. SECRETARIA PROVINCIAL DE SAUDE, TRABALHO. PREVIDENCIA E ASSISTENCIA. SINTESE DA ACTIVIDADE DOS SERVICOS E ORGANISMOS. see *PUBLIC ADMINISTRATION*

613 US ISSN 0278-4653
ANNUAL EDITIONS: HEALTH. 1975. a. $9.50. Dushkin Publishing Group, Inc., Sluice Dock, Guilford, CT 06437. TEL 203-453-4351. Ed. Ian Nielsen. illus.
Former titles (1980-1981): Readings in Health (ISSN 0730-8930); Annual Editions: Readings in Health (ISSN 0360-9766)

613.2 US
BETTER HOMES AND GARDENS LOW-CALORIE RECIPES. 1978. a. $2.50 per no. Meredith Corporation, Special Interest Publications, 1716 Locust St., Des Moines, IA 50336. TEL 515-284-3000. circ. 500,000.
Formerly: Diet and Exercise (ISSN 0163-0334)

613.7 US
CORPORATE FITNESS BUYER'S GUIDE. 1984. a. $25. Brentwood Publishing Corp. (Subsidiary of: Simon & Schuster, unit of Gulf & Western, Inc.) 1640 5th St., Santa Monica, CA 90401. TEL 213-395-0234. Ed. Martin H. Waldman. adv. tr.lit. circ. 19,500.
Formerly: Corporate Fitness and Recreation Buyer's Guide.

CURRENT TOPICS IN BIOENERGETICS. see *BIOLOGY — Biophysics*

613.7 UK ISSN 0143-5094
EUROPEAN MONOGRAPHS IN HEALTH EDUCATION RESEARCH. (Text in English, French, German) 1980. s-a. £5. Scottish Health Education Group, Woodburn House, Canaan Lane, Edinburgh EH10 4SG, Scotland. Ed. Dr. L. Baric.

613.7 641.1   US   ISSN 0748-3155
EXERCISE PHYSIOLOGY; current selected research. 1985. a. $67.50. A M S Press, Inc., 56 E. 13th St., New York, NY 10003. TEL 212-777-4700. Ed. Charles O. Dotson. index. circ. 600. (back issues avail.)

FIRST YEAR OF LIFE; a guide to your baby's growth and development month by month. see CHILDREN AND YOUTH — About

FLOWER ESSENCE SOCIETY NEWSLETTER. see BIOLOGY — Botany

613.7   SZ
FORSCHUNGSINSTITUT DER EIDGENOESSISCHEN TURN- UND SPORTSCHULE MAGGLINGEN. WISSENSCHAFTLICHE SCHRIFTENREIHE. no.7, 1976. irreg. Birkhaeuser Verlag, P.O. Box 133, CH-4010 Basel, Switzerland.

HANDBOOK OF PSYCHOLOGY AND HEALTH. see PSYCHOLOGY

HAWAII. DEPARTMENT OF HEALTH. RESEARCH AND STATISTICS OFFICE. R & S REPORT. see POPULATION STUDIES — Abstracting, Bibliographies, Statistics

613.7   UK
HEALTH AND BEAUTY NEWS. 1933. a. membership. Women's League of Health and Beauty, 18 Charing Cross Rd., London WC2H 0HR, England. TEL 01-240 8456. bk. rev. circ. 27,000.

613.7 610   US
HEALTH & MEDICAL HORIZONS. 1982. a. $19.95 to libraries. Macmillan Educational Company, 866 Third Ave., New York, NY 10022. Ed. Robert Famighetti. index.

613.7   US   ISSN 0276-606X
HEALTH OF KANSAS CHART BOOK. 1978. irreg. Department of Health and Environment, Topeka, KS 66620. TEL 913-862-9360.

613.7   US
HEALTH POLICY SERIES. 1981. a. Marcel Dekker, Inc., 270 Madison Ave., New York, NY 10016. TEL 212-696-9000. Ed. Milton I. Roemer. Indexed: Med.Care Rev.

613.7 200   US   ISSN 0276-4148
HIMALAYAN INTERNATIONAL INSTITUTE/ ELEANOR N. DANA LABORATORY. RESEARCH BULLETIN. 1980. a. $6. Himalayan International Institute of Yoga Science & Philosophy of the U.S.A., R.R. 1, Box 400, Honesdale, PA 18431. TEL 717-253-5551. charts. illus. stat. circ. 1,000.

613.7   US
HUMAN ECOLOGY. ANNUAL REPORT. a. New York State College of Human Ecology, Cornell University, Ithaca, NY 14853.

I C H P E R CONGRESS PROCEEDINGS. (International Council on Health, Physical Education and Recreation) see MEDICAL SCIENCES

I D E A INDUSTRY DIRECTORY. (International Dance-Exercise Association) see BUSINESS AND ECONOMICS — Trade And Industrial Directories

613 614   IT
INTERNATIONAL CONGRESS ON HYGIENE AND PREVENTIVE MEDICINE. PROCEEDINGS. (Text in English and French) irreg., 1983, Heidelberg. price varies. International Federation for Preventive and Social Medicine, Via Salaria 237, 00199 Rome, Italy. Ed. G.A. Canaperia.

613   US   ISSN 0363-0366
MEDICAL AND HEALTH ANNUAL. 1976. a. $23.95. Encyclopaedia Britannica, Inc., 310 S. Michigan Ave., Chicago, IL 60604. TEL 312-347-7000. Ed. Ellen Bernstein. index.

613   US
MEDICAL & HEALTH INFORMATION DIRECTORY. 1978. irreg., latest 3rd edt., 1986. $425 for 3 vol. set. Gale Research Company, Book Tower, Detroit, MI 48226. TEL 313-961-2242. Ed.Bd.

PSYCHOLOGY AND SOCIOLOGY OF SPORT; current selected research. see PSYCHOLOGY

PUERTO RICO. DEPARTMENT OF HEALTH. BOLETIN ESTADISTICO. see SOCIAL SERVICES AND WELFARE

PUERTO RICO. DEPARTMENT OF HEALTH. INFORME ANUAL DE FACILIDADES DE SALUD. see SOCIAL SERVICES AND WELFARE

PUERTO RICO. DEPARTMENT OF HEALTH. INFORME DEL REGISTRO DE PROFESIONALES DE LA SALUD. see SOCIAL SERVICES AND WELFARE

RECENT ADVANCES IN OBESITY RESEARCH. see MEDICAL SCIENCES

ROBERT WOOD JOHNSON FOUNDATION. ANNUAL REPORT. see MEDICAL SCIENCES

RX HOME CARE BUYER'S GUIDE. see HOSPITALS

SALUD PARA TODOS. see CHILDREN AND YOUTH — For

SOZIALMEDIZINISCHE UND PAEDAGOGISCHE JUGENDKUNDE. see MEDICAL SCIENCES

613.7 640.73   US
SPA & SAUNA BUYERS GUIDE. 1979. a. Harcourt Brace Jovanovich, Inc., 7500 Old Oak Blvd., Cleveland, OH 44130 TEL 216-243-8100. (Subscr. address: 1 E. First St., Duluth, MN 55802) Ed. Susan Kopicki. circ. 8,353.

613.7 360   US
STUDIES IN HEALTH AND HUMAN SERVICES. 1983. irreg., vol.9, 1986. $39.95 per no. Edwin Mellen Press, Box 450, Lewiston, NY 14092.

613.7 790.1   FI
STUDIES IN SPORT, PHYSICAL EDUCATION AND HEALTH. (Text in English and Finnish) 1971. irreg., no.9, 1976. exchange basis. Jyvaskylan Yliopisto - University of Jyvaskyla, Seminaarinkatu 15, 40100 Jyvaskyla 10, Finland. Ed. Paavo V. Komi. circ. 450.

SUMITOMO BULLETIN OF INDUSTRIAL HEALTH/SUMITOMO SANGYO EISEI. see INDUSTRIAL HEALTH AND SAFETY

TAL OG DATA, MEDICIN OG SUNDHEDSVAESEN/FACTS, MEDICINE AND HEALTH CARE, DENMARK. see PHARMACY AND PHARMACOLOGY

VOGUE BEAUTY & HEALTH GUIDE. see BEAUTY CULTURE

613.7   US
WASHINGTON. STATE HEALTH PLAN. 1980. a. $6.40. State Health Coordinating Council, Council Mail Stop ET-29, Olympia, WA 98504. TEL 206-753-9659. circ. 450.

WOMAN'S DAY 101 WAYS TO LOSE WEIGHT AND STAY HEALTHY. see NUTRITION AND DIETETICS

613.7 181.45   CN
YOGA LIFE. 1977. irreg. donations. Sivananda Yoga Vedanta Centre, Headquarters, Sivananda Ashram Yoga Camp, 8th, Val Morin, Que. J0T 2R0, Canada. Ed. Vishnu Devananda. illus. circ. 40,000.
Former titles: International Sivananda Yoga Life and Yoga Vacations (ISSN 0708-076X); International Yoga Life and Yoga Vacations (ISSN 0381-9043)

PHYSICAL FITNESS AND HYGIENE — Abstracting, Bibliographies, Statistics

A D F A AUDIO VISUAL CATALOGUE. (Alcohol and Drug Foundation, Australia) see LIBRARY AND INFORMATION SCIENCES — Abstracting, Bibliographies, Statistics

613 016   US
ABSTRACT NEWSLETTER: HEALTH PLANNING & HEALTH SERVICES RESEARCH. w. $89. U.S. National Technical Information Service, 5285 Port Royal Road, Springfield, VA 22161. TEL 703-487-4630. Ed. Linda J. LaGarde. index. (back issues avail.)
Former titles: Weekly Abstract Newsletter: Health Planning and Health Services Research; Weekly Government Abstracts. Health Planning and Health Services Research (ISSN 0199-9974); Weekly Government Abstracts. Health Planning (ISSN 0017-9086)

613.7 011.8 614.8   US   ISSN 0278-2340
B I H E P. (Bibliographic Index of Health Education Periodicals) 1981. q. $160. Indiana University, Center for Health & Safety Studies, HPER Bldg. Rm. 116, Indiana University, Bloomington, IN 47405. TEL 812-335-7975. Ed. William J. Bailey. bk. rev. circ. 500. (back issues avail.)

016 613.85   US   ISSN 0067-7361
BIBLIOGRAPHY ON SMOKING AND HEALTH. (Subseries of: Public Health Service Bibliography Series) 1967. a. free; limited distribution. U.S. Office on Smoking and Health, Technical Information Center, Park Bldg., Rm. 116, 5600 Fishers Ln., Rockville, MD 20857. TEL 301-443-1575. Ed. Donald R. Shopland. index.

614   UK   ISSN 0140-3273
HEALTH EDUCATION INDEX; and guide to voluntary social welfare organizations. 1967. 2/yr. B. Edsall & Co. Ltd., 124 Belgrave Rd., London SW1V 2BL, England. Ed. B. Edsall. adv. illus.

613.7 790 370   US   ISSN 0090-5119
HEALTH, PHYSICAL EDUCATION AND RECREATION MICROFORM PUBLICATIONS BULLETIN. 1949. s-a. free. ‡ Microform Publications, University of Oregon, College of Human Development and Performance, 1479 Moss St., Eugene, OR 97403. TEL 503-686-4117. Ed. Dr. Eric D. Zemper. cum.index: 1949-1986. circ. 2,630. (also avail. in microfiche)
Formerly: Health, Physical Education, and Recreation Microcard Bulletin (ISSN 0017-906X) Physical education

613.7 016   US   ISSN 0191-9202
PHYSICAL EDUCATION INDEX. 1978. q. $150. BenOak Publishing Company, Box 474, Cape Girardeau, MO 63701. TEL 314-334-8789. Ed. Ronald F. Kirby. bk. rev. index. (back issues avail.)

613 016   US
WELLNESS MEDIA: AN AUDIOVISUAL SOURCEBOOK. 1972. irreg. $50. (National Information Center for Educational Media) Access Innovations, Inc., Box 40130, Albuquerque, NM 87196. TEL 505-265-3591.
Formerly (until 1987): N I C E M Index to Health and Safety Education - Multimedia.

PHYSICS

see also Physics — Heat; Physics — Mechanics; Physics — Nuclear Energy; Physics — Optics; Physics — Sound

530   US   ISSN 0094-243X
A I P CONFERENCE PROCEEDINGS. 1970. irreg., no.151, 1986. American Institute of Physics, 335 E. 45th St., New York, NY 10017. TEL 212-661-9404. Ed. Rita G. Lerner. bibl. charts. illus. stat. (back issues avail.) Indexed: Biol.Abstr. C.P.I. Chem.Abstr. Math.R. Sci.Abstr. Sci.Cit.Ind. Phys.Abstr. GeoRef. Phys.Ber.

530   CH   ISSN 0304-5293
ACADEMIA SINICA. INSTITUTE OF PHYSICS. ANNUAL REPORT. 1970. a. exchange basis. Academia Sinica, Institute of Physics, Nankang, Taipei 115, Taiwan, Republic of China. Ed. E.K. Lin. circ. 500. Indexed: Biol.Abstr. Chem.Abstr. Met.Abstr. Sci.Abstr. World Alum.Abstr.

PHYSICS

530 US ISSN 0065-1559
ACTA PHYSICA AUSTRIACA. SUPPLEMENT. 1965. irreg., no.27, 1986. price varies. Springer-Verlag, 175 Fifth Ave., New York, NY 10010 TEL 212-460-1500. (Also Berlin, Heidelberg, Tokyo and Vienna) (also avail. in microform from UMI; reprint service avail. from ISI) Indexed: Math.R. Sci.Abstr. Phys.Abstr.

530 540 HU ISSN 0567-7947
ACTA PHYSICA ET CHIMICA DEBRECINA. (Text in English, German, Russian) 1962. irreg., vol.24, 1982. Kossuth Lajos Tudomanyegyetem, Egyetem Ter 1, H-4010 Debrecen 10, Hungary. Eds. R. Gaspar, S. Makleit. Indexed: Chem.Abstr.

530 HU ISSN 0231-4428
ACTA PHYSICA HUNGARICA. (Text in English, French, German or Russian) 1951. 8/yr. (in 2 vols., 4 nos./vol.) $52. (Magyar Tudomanyos Akademia) Akademiai Kiado, Publishing House of the Hungarian Academy of Sciences, P.O. Box 24, H-1363 Budapest, Hungary. Ed. Istvan Kovacs. adv. bk. rev. bibl. charts. illus. index. Indexed: Chem.Abstr. Curr.Cont. Math.R. Met.Abstr. Sci.Abstr. Sci.Cit.Ind. ASCA. Ind.Sci.Rev. Int.Aerosp.Abstr. Phys.Ber. Risk Abstr.
Formerly: Academia Scientiarum Hungarica. Acta Physica (ISSN 0001-6705)

530 370 PL ISSN 0208-6190
ACTA UNIVERSITATIS LODZIENSIS: FOLIA PHYSICA. (Text in Polish; summaries in various languages) irreg. Uniwersytet Lodzki, Drukarnia Wojskowa, Ul. Gdanska 130, Lodz, Poland (Dist by: Ars Polona-Ruch, Krakowskie Przedmiescie 7, Warsaw, Poland)

530 US
ADHESIVES D.A.T.A. BOOK. biennial. $150. D.A.T.A., Inc. (Subsidiary of: International Thomson Organization) 9889 Willow Creek Rd., Box 26875, San Diego, CA 92126. TEL 619-578-7600. Ed. Steven d'Adolf.

530 US
ADVANCES IN AEROSOL PHYSICS. irreg., vol.7, 1973. price varies. Halsted Press (Subsidiary of: John Wiley & Sons, Inc.) 605 Third Ave., New York, NY 10016. TEL 212-850-6000. Ed. V.A. Fedoseev.

530 541.3 US ISSN 0065-2385
ADVANCES IN CHEMICAL PHYSICS. 1958. irreg., vol.70, 1987. price varies. John Wiley & Sons, Inc., 605 Third Ave., New York, NY 10016. TEL 212-850-6000. Ed. I. Prigogine. Indexed: Biol.Abstr. Chem.Abstr. Sci.Cit.Ind. Ind.Sci.Rev. Mass Spectr.Bull.

ADVANCES IN ELECTRONICS AND ELECTRON PHYSICS. see *ELECTRICITY AND ELECTRICAL ENGINEERING*

538 US ISSN 0065-2873
ADVANCES IN MAGNETIC RESONANCE. 1965. irreg., vol.11, 1983. Academic Press, Inc., Orlando, FL 32887. TEL 305-345-2000. Ed. J.S. Waugh. index. Indexed: Sci.Cit.Ind. Ind.Sci.Rev.

ADVANCES IN MICROWAVES. see *ELECTRICITY AND ELECTRICAL ENGINEERING*

530 NE
ADVANCES IN SOLID STATE TECHNOLOGY. 1985. irreg. price varies. D. Reidel Publishing Company, Box 17, 3300 AA Dordrecht, Netherlands.

530 PL ISSN 0860-0260
AKADEMIA GORNICZO-HUTNICZA IM. STANISLAWA STASZICA. ZESZYTY NAUKOWE. FIZYKA. (Text in English and Polish; summaries in English, Polish, Russian) 1984. irreg., no.10, 1986. price varies. (Akademia Gorniczo-Hutnicza im. Stanislawa Staszica) Wydawnictwo A G H, Manifestu Lipcowego 16, 31-109 Krakow, Poland (Dist. by: Ars Polona, Krakowskie Przedmiescie 7, 00-068 Warsaw, Poland) Ed. Z. Kleczek. circ. 300.

530 PL ISSN 0208-8940
AKADEMIA ROLNICZA, POZNAN. ROCZNIKI. FIZYKA, CHEMIA. (Text in Polish; summaries in English and Russian) 1976. irreg. price varies. Akademia Rolnicza, Poznan, Ul. Wojska Polskiego 28, 60-637 Poznan, Poland. Indexed: Bibl. Agri.

AKADEMIE DER WISSENSCHAFTEN, GOETTINGEN. NACHRICHTEN 2. MATHEMATISCH-PHYSIKALISCHE KLASSE. see *MATHEMATICS*

AKADEMIE DER WISSENSCHAFTEN IN GOETTINGEN. ABHANDLUNGEN. MATHEMATISCH-PHYSIKALISCHE KLASSE. DRITTE FOLGE. see *MATHEMATICS*

AMERICAN CRYSTALLOGRAPHIC ASSOCIATION. PROGRAM & ABSTRACTS. see *CHEMISTRY — Crystallography*

530 FI ISSN 0066-2003
ANNALES ACADEMIAE SCIENTIARUM FENNICAE. SERIES A, VI: PHYSICA. (Text in English, French, German) 1957. irreg. price varies. Suomalainen Tiedeakatemia - Academia Scientiarum Fennica, Snellmanink. 9-11, 00170 Helsinki, Finland. Ed. Matti Punkkinen. cum.index: 1957-1972 in vol. 400. circ. 600. (also avail. in microform; back issues avail.) Indexed: Appl.Mech.R. Bull.Signal. Chem.Abstr. Ref.Zn. Sci.Abstr. GeoRef. Int.Aerosp.Abstr. Nucl.Sci.Abstr. Phys.Abstr. Phys.Ber.

530 PL ISSN 0137-6861
ANNALES UNIVERSITATIS MARIAE CURIE-SKLODOWSKA. SECTIO AAA. PHYSICA. (Text in English, French, Polish; summaries in English, Polish and Russian) 1978. a. price varies. Uniwersytet Marii Curie-Sklodowskiej, Plac Marii Curie-Sklodowskiej 5, 20-031 Lublin, Poland. Ed. Mieczyslaw Subotowicz. circ. 575. Indexed: Chem.Abstr.
Supersedes in part (after 1978): Annales Universitatis Mariae Curie-Sklodowska. Sectio AA. Physica et Chemica (ISSN 0137-1819)

ANNUAL REVIEW OF ASTRONOMY AND ASTROPHYSICS. see *ASTRONOMY*

531.14 US
ANNUAL SUMMARY OF PROGRESS IN GRAVITATION SCIENCES. 1974. a. membership. (Ensanian Physicochemical Institute) Minas Ensanian Corporation, Box 98, Eldred, PA 16731. TEL 814-225-3296. Ed. Minas Ensanian. adv. bk. rev. abstr. bibl. charts. illus. pat. stat. circ. 100(controlled)

530 620 US ISSN 0066-5509
APPLIED PHYSICS AND ENGINEERING. (Text in English) 1967. irreg., no.12, 1976. price varies. Springer-Verlag, 175 Fifth Ave., New York, NY 10010 TEL 212-460-1500. (Also Berlin, Heidelberg, Tokyo and Vienna) (reprint service avail. from ISI)

530 NO ISSN 0365-2459
ARKIV FOR DET FYSISKE SEMINAR I TRONDHEIM. (Text in English) 1953. bi-w. Kr.370($39) Instituut for Teoretisk Fysikk, N-7034 Trondheim NTH, Norway. circ. 160. Indexed: Phys.Abstr. Sci.Abstr.

ASTROPHYSICS AND SPACE SCIENCE LIBRARY; a series of books on the developments of space science and of general astronomy and astrophysics published in connection with the journal Space Science Reviews. see *ASTRONOMY*

530 NE
ATOMIC ENERGY LEVELS AND GROTRIAN DIAGRAMS. 1976. irreg., latest 1982. price varies. Elsevier Science Publishers B.V., Box 211, 1000 AE Amsterdam, Netherlands. Eds. S. Bashkin, J.O. Stoner.

AURORAL OBSERVATORY. MAGNETIC OBSERVATIONS. see *ASTRONOMY*

530 AT ISSN 0155-624X
AUSTRALIAN NATIONAL UNIVERSITY. RESEARCH SCHOOL OF PHYSICAL SCIENCES. ANNUAL REPORT. 1972. a. Australian National University, Research School of Advanced Sciences, G.P.O. Box 4, Canberra, A.C.T. 2601, Australia. Ed. J.H. Carver. circ. 500.

530 AT ISSN 0084-7518
AUSTRALIAN NATIONAL UNIVERSITY, CANBERRA. RESEARCH SCHOOL OF PHYSICAL SCIENCES. RESEARCH PAPER. irreg. free to qualified personnel. Australian National University, Research School of Physical Sciences, G.P.O. Box 4, Canberra, A.C.T. 2601, Australia.

530 GE ISSN 0323-5130
BEITRAEGE ZUR FORSCHUNGSTECHNOLOGIE; Schriftenreihe fuer Experimentalmethodik, Systemanalyse und Instumentierung in der Wissenschaftlichen, Medizinischen und technischen Forschung. (Text in German; summaries in English, German and Russian) 1975. irreg., vol.13, 1986. (Akademie der Wissenschaften der DDR) Akademie-Verlag Berlin, Leipziger Str.3-4, 1086 Berlin, E. Germany (D.D.R.)

530 PL ISSN 0137-5059
BIBLIOTEKA FIZYKI. 1974. irreg., vol.10, 1982. Panstwowe Wydawnictwo Naukowe, Ul. Miodowa 10, 00-251 Warsaw, Poland (Dist. by: Ars Polona, Krakowskie Przedmiescie 7, 00-068 Warsaw, Poland)

539 621.48 SZ ISSN 0304-2901
C E R N ANNUAL REPORT. French edition: C E R N Rapport Annuel (ISSN 0304-291X) (Former name of body: Conseil Europeen pour la Recherche Nucleaire) (Éditions in English and French) 1955. a. free. European Laboratory for Particle Physics, CH-1211 Geneva 23, Switzerland. circ. 7,000 combined. Indexed: INIS Atomind. Phys.Abstr.

539.7 SZ ISSN 0366-5690
C E R N-H E R A REPORTS. (Former name of body: Conseil Europeen pour la Recherche Nucleaire) 1969. irreg. free. European Laboratory for Particle Physics, CH-1211 Geneva 23, Switzerland. (also avail. in microfiche) Indexed: INIS Atomind. Phys.Abstr.

539 SZ ISSN 0007-8328
C E R N REPORTS. (Former name of body: Conseil Europeen pour la Recherche Nucleaire) 1955. irreg. free. European Laboratory for Particle Physics, CH-1211 Geneva 23, Switzerland. (also avail. in microfiche) Indexed: Chem.Abstr. INIS Atomind. Phys.Abstr.

539 SZ ISSN 0531-4283
C E R N SCHOOL OF PHYSICS. PROCEEDINGS. (Former name of body: Conseil Europeen pour la Recherche Nucleaire/European Organization for Nuclear Research) 1962. a. free. European Laboratory for Paricle Physics, CH-1211 Geneva 23, Switzerland. circ. 4,000. (also avail. in microfiche) Indexed: INIS Atomind. Phys.Abstr.

C.S.I.R.O. DIVISION OF MATERIALS SCIENCE. RESEARCH REPORT. see *CHEMISTRY — Inorganic Chemistry*

530 510 UK
CAMBRIDGE MONOGRAPHS ON MATHEMATICAL PHYSICS. irreg., no.7, 1982. $57.50 cloth; paper $27.95 latest vol. Cambridge University Press, Edinburgh Bldg., Shaftesbury Rd., Cambridge CB2 2RU, England (And 32 E. 57th St., New York NY 10022) Ed.Bd. Indexed: Math.R. Phys.Ber.

530 UK
CAMBRIDGE MONOGRAPHS ON PHYSICS. irreg. price varies. Cambridge University Press, Edinburgh Bldg., Shaftesbury Rd., Cambridge CB2 2RU, England (And 32 E. 57th St., New York NY 10022) Eds. M.W. Berry, C. Jordan.

530 UK
CAMBRIDGE SOLID STATE SCIENCE SERIES. irreg. price varies. Cambridge University Press, Edinburgh Bldg., Shaftesbury Rd., Cambridge CB2 2RU, England (And 32 E. 57th St., New York NY 10022) Ed.Bd.

530 US ISSN 0069-3294
CHICAGO LECTURES IN PHYSICS. 1963. irreg., vol.7, 1985. price varies. University of Chicago Press, 5801 S. Ellis Ave., Chicago, IL 60637. TEL 312-962-7700. (reprint service avail. from UMI,ISI)

530 510 FI ISSN 0069-6609
COMMENTATIONES PHYSICO-MATHEMATICAE. (Text in English and German) 1924. irreg. price varies. Finnish Society of Sciences and Letters, Snellmansgatan 9-11, SF-00170 Helsinki, Finland. Ed. Erik Spring. charts. illus. index. circ. 1,000 (approx.) Indexed: Bull.Signal. Chem.Abstr. Curr.Cont. Ref.Zh. Sci.Abstr. Sci.Cit.Ind. Ind.Sci.Rev. Phys.Ber. Zent.Math.

COMMENTS ON ASTROPHYSICS. see *ASTRONOMY*

COMMONWEALTH SCIENTIFIC AND INDUSTRIAL RESEARCH ORGANIZATION. DIVISION OF TEXTILE PHYSICS. ANNUAL REPORT. see *TEXTILE INDUSTRIES AND FABRICS*

530   US
COMPUTATIONAL MICROELECTRONICS. 1986. irreg. price varies. Springer-Verlag, 175 Fifth Ave., New York, NY 10160 TEL 212-460-1500. (Also Berlin, Heidelberg, Tokyo, Vienna) (reprint service avail. from ISI)

530   US   ISSN 0272-2488
CONTEMPORARY CONCEPTS IN PHYSICS. 1981. irreg. Harwood Academic Publisher GmbH, Box 786, Cooper Sta., New York, NY 10276. TEL 212-242-4464. Ed. Henry Primakoff. Indexed: Math.R.

530   US
CONTEMPORARY PHYSICS. 1986. irreg. price varies. Springer-Verlag, 175 Fifth Ave., New York, NY 10160 TEL 212-460-1500. (Also Berlin, Heidelberg, Tokyo, Vienna) (reprint service avail. from ISI)

530   NE   ISSN 0165-1854
CURRENT TOPICS IN MATERIALS SCIENCE. 1977. irreg., vol.12, 1986. price varies. Elsevier Science Publishers B.V., Box 211, 1006 AE Amsterdam, Netherlands. Ed. E. Kaldis. Indexed: Chem.Abstr.

530 540   US
DAHLEM WORKSHOP REPORTS. PHYSICAL AND CHEMICAL SCIENCES RESEARCH REPORT. irreg., vol.5, 1984. Springer-Verlag, 175 Fifth Ave., New York, NY 10010 TEL 212-460-1500. (Also Berlin, Heidelberg, Tokyo and Vienna)

530   DK   ISSN 0105-0907
DANMARKS TEKNISKE HOEJSKOLE. FYSISK LABORATORIUM 1. REPORT. No. 247, 1982. irreg. Danmarks Tekniske Hoejskole, Fysisk Laboratorium I, Lundtoftvej 100, Bygn. 309, 2800 Lyngby, Denmark. illus. circ. 100.

530 548   NE
DEFECTS IN SOLIDS. 1968. irreg.; vol.14, 1985. price varies. Elsevier Science Publishers B.V., Box 211, 1000 AE Amsterdam, Netherlands. Indexed: Phys.Ber.
Formerly: Defects in Crystalline Solids (ISSN 0070-3230)

530   DK   ISSN 0107-8348
DENMARK. FORSOEGSANLAEG RISOE. FYSIKAFDELINGEN. ANNUAL PROGRESS REPORT. 1970. a. Kr.48.80. G.E.C. GAD, Dansk og Udenlandsk Boghandel Aktieselskab, Vimmelskaftet 32, 1161 Copenhagen K, Denmark.

530   GW   ISSN 0420-0195
DEUTSCHE PHYSIKALISCHE GESELLSCHAFT. VERHANDLUNGEN. (Text and summaries in English and German) 1966. irreg., (4-8/yr.) membership. (Deutsche Physikalische Gesellschaft) Physik-Verlag GmbH, Postfach 1260/1280, D6940 Weinheim, W. Germany (B.R.D.) (U.S. adress: V C H Publishers, 220 East 23rd St., NY, NY, 10010-4606.) Ed. U. Poerschke. adv. circ. controlled.

DIRECTORY OF PHYSICS & ASTRONOMY STAFF (YEAR) see *EDUCATION — Higher Education*

DIRECTORY OF THE SOLAR INDUSTRY. see *BUSINESS AND ECONOMICS — Trade And Industrial Directories*

530   NE
DISLOCATIONS IN SOLIDS. 1978. irreg., vol.6, 1983. price varies. Elsevier Science Publishers B.V., Box 211, 1000 AE Amsterdam, Netherlands. Ed. F.R.N. Nabarro.

530 510 591   IS
DIVREI HA-AKADEMIA HA-LEUMIT HA-YISRAELIT LEMADAIM-HA-HATIVA LE-MADAEI HA-TEVA. (Text in Hebrew) 1966. irreg. $3 per no. Israel Academy of Sciences and Humanities, 43 Jabotinski St., P.O.B. 4040, 91040 Jerusalem, Israel. circ. 900. Indexed: Ind.Heb.Per.

530   IE   ISSN 0070-7414
DUBLIN INSTITUTE FOR ADVANCED STUDIES. COMMUNICATIONS. SERIES A. 1943. irreg., no.23, 1975. price varies. ‡ Dublin Institute for Advanced Studies, 10 Burlington Rd., Dublin 4, Ireland. Indexed: Math.R. Sci.Abstr. Phys.Ber.

ECLETICA QUIMICA; serie quimica. see *CHEMISTRY*

530   NE
ENRICO FERMI INTERNATIONAL SUMMER SCHOOL OF PHYSICS. 1976. irreg., vol.90, 1985. price varies. Elsevier Science Publishers B.V., Box 211, 1000 AE Amsterdam, Netherlands.

530   DK   ISSN 0106-407X
ENVIRONMENTAL RADIOACTIVITY IN DENMARK. 1961. a. Kr.61. Risoe National Laboratory, Box 49, DK-4000 Roskilde, Denmark (Subscr. to: G.E.C. Gad, Vimmelskaftet 32, DK-1161 Copenhagen K, Denmark). illus.
Formerly: Environmental Radioactivity at Risoe.

530   DK   ISSN 0108-0962
ENVIRONMENTAL RADIOACTIVITY IN GREENLAND. 1962. a. Kr.36.60. G.E.C. GAD, Dansk og Udenlandsk Boghandel Aktieselskab, Vimmelskaftet 32, 1161 Copenhagen K, Denmark. illus.

530   DK   ISSN 0107-9069
ENVIRONMENTAL RADIOACTIVITY IN THE FAROES. 1962. a. Kr.36.60. G.E.C. GAD, Dansk og Udenlandsk Boghandel Aktieselskab, Vimmelskaftet 32, 1161 Copenhagen K, Denmark.

530   GE
ERGEBNISSE DER PLASMAPHYSIK UND DER GASELEKTRONIK. SCHRIFTENREIHE. 1967. irreg. price varies. Akademie-Verlag, Leipziger Str. 3-4, 1086 Berlin, E. Germany (D.D.R.) Ed.Bd.

530   US   ISSN 0071-1438
ESSAYS IN PHYSICS. 1970. irreg., vol.6, 1976. Academic Press Inc., 111 Fifth Ave., New York, NY 10003. TEL 212-741-6800. Eds. G.K.T. Conn, G.N. Fowler. Indexed: Nucl.Sci.Abstr.

530   SZ
EUROPHYSICS CONFERENCE ABSTRACTS. a. 330 Fr. European Physical Society, Box 69, CH-1213 Petit-Lancy 2, Switzerland. Indexed: Phys.Ber.

530   PL   ISSN 0554-825X
FIZYKA. 1961. irreg., no.24, 1976. price varies. Adam Mickiewicz University Press, Marchlewskiego 128, 61-874 Poznan, Poland.
Formerly: Uniwersytet im. Adama Mickiewicza w Poznaniu. Wydzial Matematyki, Fizyki i Chemii. Seria Fizyka.

530   CS   ISSN 0323-0287
FOLIA FACULTATIS SCIENTIARUM NATURALIUM UNIVERSITATIS PURKYNIANAE BRUNENSIS: PHYSICA. vol.14, 1973. irreg (7-12/yr.) price varies. Universita J. E. Purkyne, Prirodovedecka Fakulta, Kotlarska 2, 611 37 Brno, Czechoslovakia. Indexed: Sci.Abstr.

530   FR
FRANCE. MINISTERE DE L'INDUSTRIE ET DE LA RECHERCHE. REPERTOIRE NATIONAL DES LABORATOIRES; LA RECHERCHE UNIVERSITAIRE; TOME 1: SCIENCES DE LA MATIERE. 1964. irreg. Documentation Francaise, 29-31 Quai Voltaire, 75340 Paris 07, France.
Formerly: France. Delegation Generale a la Recherche Scientifique et Technique. Repertoire National des Laboratoires; la Recherche Universitaire; Sciences Exactes et Naturelles. Tome 1: Physique (ISSN 0071-8572)

530   US   ISSN 0429-7725
FRONTIERS IN PHYSICS.* 1961. irreg., no.60, 1984. price varies. Benjamin-Cummings Publishing Co., Inc. (Subsidiary of: Addison-Wesley Publishing Co.) 1 Jacob Way, Reading, MA 01867. Ed. Richard W. Mixter. Indexed: Math.R.

530   NE
FUNDAMENTAL THEORIES OF PHYSICS; an international series of monographs on the fundamental theories of physics: their clarification, development and application. 1982. irreg. price varies. D. Reidel Publishing Co., Box 17, 3300 AA Dordrecht, Netherlands (And 190 Old Derby St., Hingham, MA 02043) Ed. Alwyn van der Merwe.

530   DK   ISSN 0109-6664
FYSIKTIPS. 1976. irreg. Kr.31.70. Danmarks Fysik og Kemilaererforening, Dyrlaege Jurgensens Gade 11, 3740 Svaneke, Denmark. illus.
Formerly: Gode Gamle Fysiktips.

530 378   US   ISSN 0147-1821
GRADUATE PROGRAMS: PHYSICS, ASTRONOMY, AND RELATED FIELDS. 1970. a. $20. American Institute of Physics, Dept. N/M, 335 E. 45th St., New York, NY 10017. TEL 516-349-7800. Ed. Lynn Pappas.

530   US
GRADUATE TEXTS IN CONTEMPORARY PHYSICS. 1986. irreg. price varies. Springer-Verlag, 175 Fifth Ave., New York, NY 10160 TEL 212-460-1500. (Also Berlin, Heidelberg, Tokyo, Vienna) (reprint service avail. from ISI)

535 540   US   ISSN 0072-8403
GUIDE TO FLUORESCENCE LITERATURE. 1967. irreg., vol.3, 1974. price varies. Plenum Publishing Corp., I.F.I.-Plenum Data Co., 233 Spring St., New York, NY 10013. TEL 212-741-6680. Ed. R.A. Passwater.

530   GE   ISSN 0073-2850
HOCHSCHULBUECHER FUER PHYSIK. 1953. irreg. price varies. VEB Deutscher Verlag der Wissenschaften, Postfach 1216, 1080 Berlin, E. Germany (D.D.R.) Eds. Robert Rompe, Ernst Schmutzer.

530   NE
LES HOUCHES SUMMER SCHOOL PROCEEDINGS. (Text in English and French) 1951. irreg., vol.41, 1986. price varies. Elsevier Science Publishers B.V., Box 211, 1000 AE Amsterdam, Netherlands.
Formerly: Ecole d'Ete de Physique Theorique. Les Houches.

510.78   US   ISSN 0085-2082
I B M RESEARCH SYMPOSIA SERIES. 1971. irreg. price varies. Plenum Publishing Corp., 233 Spring St., New York, NY 10013. TEL 212-620-8047.

530   UK   ISSN 0305-2346
INSTITUTE OF PHYSICS, LONDON. CONFERENCE SERIES. PROCEEDINGS. 1967. irreg., no.80, 1986. price varies. Institute of Physics, Techno House, Redcliffe Way, Bristol BS1 6NX, England (U.S. address: Heyden & Son Inc., U.S. address: Adam Hilger Ltd., P.O. Box 230, Accord, MA 02018) circ. 750. Indexed: Chem.Abstr. Sci.Cit.Ind. Phys.Ber.

530   RM
INSTITUTUL PEDAGOGIC ORADEA. LUCRARI STIINTIFICE: SERIA FIZICA. (Continues in part its Lucrari Stiintifice: Seria Matematica, Fizica, Chimie (1971-72), its Lucrari Stiintifice: Seria A and Seria B (1969-1970), and its Lucrari Stiintifice (1967-68)) (Text in Rumanian, occasionally in English or French; summaries in Rumanian, French or German) 1967. a. Institutul Pedagogic Oradea, Calea Armatei Rosii Nr. 5, Oradea, Rumania.

530   UN   ISSN 0304-7091
INTERNATIONAL CENTRE FOR THEORETICAL PHYSICS. ANNUAL REPORT. 1964. a. free. International Atomic Energy Agency, International Centre for Theoretical Physics, Strada Costiera 11, Box 586, Trieste 34100, Italy. Ed. A.M. Hamende. circ. 2,000.
Formerly (until 1965): International Centre for Theoretical Physics. Report (ISSN 0538-5415)

539.7   US   ISSN 0534-8676
INTERNATIONAL CONFERENCE ON ELECTRON AND ION BEAM SCIENCE AND TECHNOLOGY. ABSTRACTS.* irreg., 4th, 1970, Los Angeles. $10. Electrochemical Society, Box 2071, Princeton, NJ 08540. TEL 609-737-1902.

621.3   NE
INTERNATIONAL CONFERENCE ON STRUCTURAL MECHANICS IN REACTOR TECHNOLOGY. PROCEEDINGS. vol.3, 1975. irreg. price varies. Elsevier Science Publishers B.V., Box 211, 1000 AE Amsterdam, Netherlands.

538   US
INTERNATIONAL MAGNETICS CONFERENCE. DIGESTS OF THE INTERMAG CONFERENCE. a. price varies. (I E E E, Magnetics Society) Institute of Electrical and Electronics Engineers, Inc., 345 E. 47th St., New York, NY 10017 TEL 212-705-7900. (Subscr. address: 445 Hoes Ln., Piscataway, NJ 08854)
Former titles: Abstracts of the Intermag Conference & International Magnetics Conference. Digest (ISSN 0074-6843)

INTERNATIONAL MONOGRAPHS ON ADVANCED MATHEMATICS AND PHYSICS. see *MATHEMATICS*

530   US
INTERNATIONAL SCHOOL OF PHYSICS "ENRICO FERMI". ITALIAN PHYSICAL SOCIETY. PROCEEDINGS. 1959. irreg., vol.57, 1977. (Societa Italiana di Fisica, IT) Academic Press, Inc., Orlando, FL 32887. TEL 305-345-2000. Indexed: Chem.Abstr. Math.R.
Former titles: International School of Physics "Enrico Fermi." Proceedings; (1963-19??): International School of Physics "Ettore Majorana." Proceedings (ISSN 0074-7858)

530 531   UK   ISSN 0539-0133
INTERNATIONAL SERIES IN SOLID STATE PHYSICS. 1963. irreg., vol.7, 1970. price varies. Pergamon Press, Ltd., Headington Hill Hall, Oxford OX3 0BW, England (U.S. subscr. to: Maxwell House, Fairview Park, Elmsford, NY 10523) index.
Formerly: International Series of Monographs on Solid State Physics.

530   US
INTERNATIONAL SERIES OF MONOGRAPHS ON PHYSICS. irreg. price varies. Oxford University Press, 200 Madison Ave., New York, NY 10016 TEL 212-679-7300. (And Ely House, 37 Dover St., London W1X 4AH England) Ed.Bd. Indexed: Math.R.

533.5   NE
INTERNATIONAL SYMPOSIUM ON SURFACE PHYSICS. SOLID-VACUUM INTERFACE. PROCEEDINGS. irreg., 4th, 1976, Eindhoven. Elsevier Science Publishers B.V., Box 211, 1000 AE Amsterdam, Netherlands.

IOWA AGRICULTURE AND HOME ECONOMICS EXPERIMENT STATION. RESEARCH BULLETIN. see *AGRICULTURE*

530   IS   ISSN 0309-8710
ISRAEL PHYSICAL SOCIETY. ANNALS; conference proceedings. (Text in English) 1977. a. price varies. Israel Physical Society, P.O. Box 16105, Jerusalem 91 160, Israel (U.S. Distributor: American Institute of Physics, Marketing Services, 335 E. 45 St., New York, NY 10017) (Co-sponsors: American Institute of Physics, Technion - Israel Institute of Technology) Eds. R. Weil, C.G. Kuper. circ. 600. (back issues avail., reprint service avail. from ISI) Indexed: Chem.Abstr. Math.R. Sci.Abstr. Phys.Ber.

530   FI   ISSN 0075-465X
JYVASKYLAN YLIOPISTO. DEPARTMENT OF PHYSICS. RESEARCH REPORT. 1969. irreg., (5-6/yr.), latest no.6, 1985. exchange basis. University of Jyvaskyla, Department of Physics, Seminaarinkatu 15, SF-40100 Jyraskyla, Finland. circ. 130. (processed)

KONGELIGE DANSKE VIDENSKABERNES SELSKAB. MATEMATISK-FYSISKE MEDDELELSER. see *MATHEMATICS*

530   JA
KUMAMOTO UNIVERSITY. DEPARTMENT OF PHYSICS. PHYSICS REPORTS. 1973. biennial. free. Kumamoto University, Department of Physics - Kumamoto Daigaku Rigakubu Butsurikyoshitsu, Faculty of Science, 2-39-1 Kurokami, Kumamoto 860, Japan. Ed. Kunihide Okada. circ. 400. Indexed: GeoRef.

530 548   US   ISSN 0075-787X
LANDOLT-BOERNSTEIN, ZAHLENWERTE UND FUNKTIONEN AUS NATURWISSENSCHAFTEN UND TECHNIK. NEUE SERIE. GROUP 3: CRYSTAL PHYSICS. 1966. irreg., vol.19A, 1986. price varies. Springer-Verlag, 175 Fifth Ave., New York, NY 10010 TEL 212-460-1500. (Also Berlin, Heidelberg, Tokyo and Vienna) Ed. K.H. Hellwege. (reprint service avail. from ISI)

LAWRENCE BERKELEY LABORATORY. RESEARCH HIGHLIGHTS. see *SCIENCES: COMPREHENSIVE WORKS*

530   US   ISSN 0075-8450
LECTURE NOTES IN PHYSICS. 1969. irreg., vol.264, 1986. price varies. Springer-Verlag, 175 Fifth Ave., New York, NY 10010 TEL 212-460-1500. (also Berlin, Heidelberg, Vienna) (reprint service avail. from ISI) Indexed: Chem.Abstr. Ind.Sci.Rev. Phys.Ber.

MASS SPECTROMETRY. see *CHEMISTRY*

MATEMATICHESKAYA FIZIKA I FUNKTSIONAL'NYI ANALIZ. see *MATHEMATICS*

530   NE
MATERIALS PROCESSING: THEORY AND PRACTICES. 1980. irreg., vol.5, 1985. price varies. Elsevier Science Publishers B.V., Box 211, 1000 AE Amsterdam, Netherlands. Ed. F.F.Y. Wang.

530   NE
MATHEMATICAL APPROACHES TO GEOPHYSICS. 1983. irreg. price varies. D. Reidel Publishing Co., Box 17, 3300 AA Dordrecht, Netherlands (And 190 Old Derby St., Hingham, MA 02043) Indexed: Math.R.

MATHEMATICAL PHYSICS AND APPLIED MATHEMATICS. see *MATHEMATICS*

530   NE
MATHEMATICAL PHYSICS STUDIES. (Supplementary series to: Letters in Mathematical Physics) 1977. irreg. price varies. D. Reidel Publishing Co., Box 17, 3300 AA Dordrecht, Netherlands (And 190 Old Derby St., Hingham, MA 02043) Ed.Bd. Indexed: Math.R.

MEDICAL PHYSICS SERIES. see *MEDICAL SCIENCES*

METHODEN UND VERFAHREN DER MATHEMATISCHEN PHYSIK. see *MATHEMATICS*

530   US   ISSN 0076-695X
METHODS OF EXPERIMENTAL PHYSICS. 1959. irreg., vol.23, 1986. $80. Academic Press, Inc., Orlando, FL 32887. TEL 305-345-2000. Ed. L. Marton. Indexed: Chem.Abstr. Phys.Ber.

MONOGRAPHS IN PHYSICAL MEASUREMENT. see *ENGINEERING*

530 540   US
MONOGRAPHS ON THE PHYSICS AND CHEMISTRY OF MATERIALS. irreg. price varies. Oxford University Press, 200 Madison Ave., New York, NY 10016 TEL 212-679-7300. (And Ely House, 37 Dover St., London W1X 4AH, England) Ed.Bd.

530 541   FR   ISSN 0078-9771
MUSEUM NATIONAL D'HISTOIRE NATURELLE, PARIS. MEMOIRES. NOUVELLE SERIE. SERIE D. SCIENCES PHYSICO-CHIMIQUES. 1950. irreg. price varies. Museum National d'Histoire Naturelle, 38 rue Geoffroy Saint-Hilaire, 75005 Paris, France.

530   NE
N I K H E F. ANNUAL REPORT. 1946. a. Nationaal Instituut voor Kernfysica en Hoge-Energiefysica, Sectie-K - Institute for Nuclear Physics Research, Postbus 4395, 1009 AJ Amsterdam, Netherlands (Mailing address: Postbus 41882, 1009 DB Amsterdam, Netherlands) circ. 650.
Former titles: National Instituut voor Kernfysica en Hoge-Energiefysica; Instituut voor Kernphysisch Onderzoek. Annual Report.

530   JA   ISSN 0910-0717
NAGOYA UNIVERSITY. COSMIC-RAY RESEARCH LABORATORY. PROCEEDINGS/ MEIDAI UCHUSEN KENKYUSHITSU KIJI. (Text in Japanese) 1947. irreg. (1-2/yr.) exchange basis. ‡ Nagoya University, Cosmic-Ray Research Laboratory - Nagoya Daigaku Rigakubu Uchusen Boenkyo, Furo-cho, Chikusa-ku, Nagoya 464, Japan. cum.index: 1947-1986. Indexed: Chem.Abstr. Sci.Abstr.

530   JA
NAGOYA UNIVERSITY. COSMIC-RAY RESEARCH LABORATORY. REPORT. (Text in English) 1975. irreg. Nagoya University, Cosmic-Ray Research Laboratory, Chikus-Ku, Nagoya 464, Japan.

530.44   JA   ISSN 0547-1567
NAGOYA UNIVERSITY. INSTITUTE OF PLASMA PHYSICS. ANNUAL REVIEW/NAGOYA DAIGAKU PURAZUMA KENKYUSHO NENPO. (Text in English) 1960/61. a. exchange basis. Nagoya University, Institute of Plasma Physics - Nagoya Daigaku Purazuma Kenkyusho, Furo-cho, Chikusa-ku, Nagoya-shi 464, Japan.

530.44   JA
NAGOYA UNIVERSITY. INSTITUTE OF PLASMA PHYSICS. TECHNICAL REPORTS. (Text in English) 1969. irreg. exchange basis. Nagoya University, Institute of Plasma Physics - Nagoya Daigaku Purazuma Kenkyusho, Furo-cho, Chikusa-ku, Nagoya-shi 464, Japan.

530.07   NE
NEDERLANDSE CENTRALE ORGANISATIE VOOR TOEGEPAST-NATUURWETENSCHAPPELIJK ONDERZOEK. TECHNISCH-PHYSISCHE DIENST. ANNUAL REPORT. (Text in English) 1946. a. Nederlandse Centrale Organisatie voor Toegepast-Natuurwetenschappelijk Onderzoek, Technisch-Physische Dienst, Stieltjesweg 1, Delft, Netherlands. Ed.Bd. circ. 2,700.

530   UN   ISSN 0077-8907
NEW TRENDS IN PHYSICS TEACHING. (Text in English and French) 1968. irreg. price varies. Unesco, 7-9 Place de Fontenoy, 75700 Paris, France (Dist. in U.S. by: Bernan Associates-Unipub, 4611-F Assembly Dr., Lanham, MD 20706-4391)

539   JA
NIIGATA AIRGLOW OBSERVATORY. BULLETIN. (Text in English) 1972. a. on exchange basis. Niigata University, Faculty of Science, 8050 Igarashi Nino-cho, Niigata-shi 950-21, Japan.

530   JA
NIIGATA UNIVERSITY. FACULTY OF SCIENCE. SCIENCE REPORTS. SERIES B: PHYSICS. (Text in European languages) 1964. irreg. exchange basis. Niigata University, Faculty of Science - Niigata Daigaku Rigakubu, 8050 Igarashi Nino-cho, Niigata-shi 950-21, Japan.

539.7   NE
NIKHEF K BULLETIN. (Text in English) 1976. irreg. National Instituut voor Kernfysica en Hoge-Energiefysica, Sectie-K - Institute for Nuclear Physics Research, Box 4395, 1009 AJ Amsterdam, Netherlands. illus. circ. 150.
Formerly: I K O Newsletter.

530.4   US   ISSN 0078-0995
NON-METALLIC SOLIDS; a series of monographs. 1971. irreg., vol.3, 1972. Academic Press Inc., Orlando, FL 32887. TEL 305-345-2000. Eds. J.P. Roberts, P. Popper.

548   NE
NORTH-HOLLAND SERIES IN CRYSTAL GROWTH. irreg., vol.2, 1979. Elsevier Science Publishers B.V., Box 211, 1000 AE Amsterdam, Netherlands.

530 621   US
NUMERICAL FLUID MECHANICS AND HEAT TRANSFER REVIEW. 1986. irreg. price varies. Hemisphere Publishing Corporation, 79 Madison Ave., New York, NY 10016. TEL 212-725-1999. Ed. T.C. Chawla.

PHYSICS

530   US   ISSN 0078-6322
ORGANIZATION OF AMERICAN STATES. DEPARTMENT OF SCIENTIFIC AFFAIRS. SERIE DE FISICA: MONOGRAFIAS. (Subseries of Coleccion de Monografias Cientificas) (Text in Spanish) 1965. irreg., no.13, 1979. $3.50 per no. Organization of American States, Department of Publications, Washington, DC 20006. TEL 703-941-1617. circ. 3,000.

538.3   UR
PARAMAGNITNYI REZONANS. irreg. 0.58 Rub. per issue. Kazanskii Universitet, Ul. Lenina, 4/5, Kazan, Russian S.F.S.R., U.S.S.R. illus. Indexed: Chem.Abstr.

PEDAGOGICKA FAKULTA V OSTRAVE. MATEMATIKA, FYZIKA. see *MATHEMATICS*

530   UK   ISSN 0141-1594
PHASE TRANSITIONS. 1979. 4/yr. (in 1 vol., 4 nos./vol.) $268 academic $166. Gordon and Breach Science Publishers Ltd., P.O. Box 197, London WC2E 9PX, England. Ed. A.M. Glazer. adv. bk. rev. charts. illus. (also avail. in microform) Indexed: Chem.Abstr. Met.Abstr. Sci.Abstr. Phys.Ber. World Alum.Abstr.

530.07   II
PHYSICAL RESEARCH LABORATORY, AHMEDABAD: ANNUAL REPORT. (Text in English) 1954. a. ‡ Physical Research Laboratory, Ahmedabad-9, India. illus. circ. 250.

530   SZ
PHYSICS: A SERIES OF MONOGRAPHS & TRACTS. (Text in English) 1981. irreg. $88. Harwood Academic Publishers GmbH, Poststrasse 22, CH-7000 Chur, Switzerland. Ed. P.B. Burt. bk. rev.
Formerly: Quantum Mechanics and Nonlinear Waves.

530   CS
PHYSICS AND APPLICATIONS. (Text in English) a. price varies. (Slovenska Akademia Vied) Veda, Publishing House of the Slovak Academy of Sciences, Klemensova 19, 814 30 Bratislava, Czechoslovakia (Subscr. to: Slovart, Gottwaldovo nam. 6, 817 64 Bratislava) Ed. Mikulas Blazek. Indexed: Chem.Abstr.
Formerly: High Energy Particle Physics.

PHYSICS AND CHEMISTRY IN SPACE. see *CHEMISTRY*

530   US
PHYSICS IN COLLISION. 1982. a. price varies. Plenum Publishing Corp., 233 Spring St., New York, NY 10013. TEL 212-620-8047. Ed.Bd. Indexed: Chem.Abstr.

PHYSICS MANPOWER - EDUCATION AND EMPLOYMENT STATISTICS. see *EDUCATION — Higher Education*

530   US
PHYSICS NEWS. a. free. American Institute of Physics, 335 E. 45 St., New York, NY 10017. TEL 212-661-9404. Ed. Philip Shewe. (back issues avail.) Indexed: PMR.
Formerly: Physics (ISSN 0092-8437)

530   US   ISSN 0079-1970
PHYSICS OF THIN FILMS; ADVANCES IN RESEARCH AND DEVELOPMENT. 1963. irreg., vol.12, 1982. Academic Press, Inc., Orlando, FL 32887. TEL 305-345-2000. Eds. George Haas, R.E. Thun. index. Indexed: Chem.Abstr.

530   GE   ISSN 0079-1997
PHYSIKALISCH-CHEMISCHE TRENN- UND MESSMETHODEN. 1960. irreg. price varies. VEB Deutscher Verlag der Wissenschaften, Postfach 1216, 1080 Berlin, E. Germany (D.D.R.) Ed. Erich Krell.

530 621   UK   ISSN 0079-208X
PION APPLIED PHYSICS SERIES. 1970. irreg. price varies. Pion Ltd., 207 Brondesbury Park, London NW2 5JN, England (Dist. by: Methuen Inc., 29 W. 35th St., New York, NY 10001) Ed. H.J. Goldsmid.

530   PL
POLITECHNIKA GDANSKA. INSTYTUT FIZYKI. RAPORT. 1982. a. price varies. Politechnika Gdanska, Ul. Majakowskiego 11/12, 80-592 Gdansk 6, Poland.

530   PL   ISSN 0072-0364
POLITECHNIKA GDANSKA. ZESZYTY NAUKOWE. FIZYKA. 1967. irreg. price varies. Politechnika Gdanska, Majakowskiego 11/12, 81-952 Gdansk 6, Poland (Dist. by: Osrodek Rozpowszechniania Wydawnictw Naukowych Pan, Palac Kultury i Nauki, 00-901 Warsaw, Poland)

530   PL   ISSN 0137-2564
POLITECHNIKA LODZKA. ZESZYTY NAUKOWE. FIZYKA. (Text in Polish; summaries in English and Russian) 1973. irreg. price varies. Politechnika Lodzka, Ul. Zwirki 36, 90-924 Lodz, Poland (Dist. by: Ars Polona-Ruch, Krakowskie Przedmiescie 7, Warsaw, Poland) Ed. Jan Karniewicz. circ. 383. Indexed: Chem.Abstr.

POLITECHNIKA SLASKA. ZESZYTY NAUKOWE. MATEMATYKA-FIZYKA. see *MATHEMATICS*

530   PL
POLITECHNIKA WARSZAWSKA. INSTYTUT FIZYKI. PRACE. (Text in English, Polish and Russian) irreg., no.13, 1975. price varies. Politechnika Warszawska, Instytut Fizyki, Plac Jednosci Robotniczej 1, 00-661 Warsaw, Poland. Ed. Wlodzimierz Scislowski. Indexed: Chem.Abstr.

621   PL   ISSN 0137-625X
POLITECHNIKA WROCLAWSKA. INSTYTUT FIZYKI. PRACE NAUKOWE. KONFERENCJE. 1977. irreg., no.3, 1984. price varies. Politechnika Wroclawska, Wybrzeze Wyspianskiego 27, 50-370 Wroclaw, Poland (Dist. by: Ars Polona-Ruch, Krakowskie Przedmiescie 7, Warsaw, Poland) Ed. Jerzy Ciekot. Indexed: Sci.Abstr.

621 530   PL   ISSN 0370-0828
POLITECHNIKA WROCLAWSKA. INSTYTUT FIZYKI. PRACE NAUKOWE. MONOGRAFIE. (Text in Polish; summaries in English and Russian) 1972. irreg., no.8, 1983. price varies. Politechnika Wroclawska, Wybrzeze Wyspianskiego 27, 50-370 Wroclaw, Poland (Dist. by: Ars Polona-Ruch, Krakowskie Przedmiescie 7, Warsaw, Poland) Ed. Marian Kloza. Indexed: Sci.Abstr.

621   PL   ISSN 0324-9697
POLITECHNIKA WROCLAWSKA. INSTYTUT FIZYKI. PRACE NAUKOWE. STUDIA I MATERIALY. (Text in Polish; summaries in English and Russian) 1969. irreg., no.7, 1976. price varies. Politechnika Wroclawska, Wybrzeze Wyspianskiego 27, 50-370 Wroclaw, Poland (Dist. by: Ars Polona-Ruch, Krakowskie Przedmiescie 7, Warsaw, Poland) Ed. Marian Kloza. Indexed: Chem.Abstr.

POLITECHNIKA WROCLAWSKA. INSTYTUT MATEMATYKI. PRACE NAUKOWE. STUDIA I MATERIALY. see *MATHEMATICS*

530   US
POLYMER PHYSICS. 1977. irreg., vol.2, 1977. Academic Press, Inc., Orlando, FL 32887. TEL 305-345-2000. Ed. R.S. Stein.

530 510   PL   ISSN 0137-8996
POZNANSKIE TOWARZYSTWO PRZYJACIOL NAUK. KOMISJA MATEMATYCZNO-PRZYRODNICZA. PRACE. (Text in Polish; summaries in English and French) 1921. irreg., vol.11, 1979. price varies. (Poznanskie Towarzystwo Przyjaciol Nauk) Panstwowe Wydawnictwo Naulowe, Ul. Miodowa 10, Warsaw, Poland (Dist by Ars Polona-Ruch, Krakowskie Przedmiescie 7, Warsaw, Poland) Indexed: Chem.Abstr.

530   US   ISSN 0079-5216
PRINCETON SERIES IN PHYSICS. 1971. irreg. price varies. Princeton University Press, 3175 Princeton Pike, Lawrenceville, NJ 08648. TEL 609-896-1344. Eds. A.S. Wightman, J.J. Hopfield. (reprint service avail. from UMI) Indexed: Math.R.

530 551.5   UR
PROBLEMY FIZIKI ATMOSFERY. vol.15, 1978. irreg. 1.50 Rub. per no. Leningradskii Universitet, Universitetskaya Nab. 7/9, Leningrad B-164, Russian S.F.S.R., U.S.S.R. circ. 1,000. Indexed: Chem.Abstr. GeoRef.

PROGRESS IN NUCLEAR ENERGY (NEW SERIES) see *CHEMISTRY*

530   US
PROGRESS IN PHYSICS. 1981. irreg. Birkhauser Boston, Inc., 380 Green St., Cambridge, MA 02139. TEL 617-876-2333. Ed.Bd. Indexed: Chem.Abstr. Math.R.

530   US   ISSN 0079-6816
PROGRESS IN SURFACE SCIENCE. 1971. m. in 3 vols. $275 (annual bound volume $378) Pergamon Press, Inc., Journals Division, Maxwell House, Fairview Park, Elmsford, NY 10523 TEL 914-592-7700. (And Headington Hill Hall, Oxford OX3 0BW, England) Ed. Sydney G. Davison. (also avail. in microform from MIM,UMI) Indexed: Chem.Abstr. Curr.Cont. Met.Abstr. Sci.Abstr. Mass Spectr.Bull. Phys.Ber. World Alum.Abstr.

530 621   US   ISSN 0079-8193
PURE AND APPLIED PHYSICS; a series of monographs and textbooks. irreg., vol.43, 1986. Academic Press Inc., Orlando, FL 32887. TEL 305-345-2000. Eds. H.S.W. Massey, Keith A. Brueckner.

530 378   UK   ISSN 0308-9290
RESEARCH FIELDS IN PHYSICS AT UNITED KINGDOM UNIVERSITIES AND POLYTECHNICS. vol.7, 1984. every 2-3 yrs. £27.50. Institute of Physics, Techno House, Redcliffe Way, Bristol BS1 6NX, England (Distr. in U.S. by: Adam Hilger Ltd., P.O. Box 230, Accord, MA 02018)

RESEARCH IN SURFACE FORCES. see *CHEMISTRY — Physical Chemistry*

530   US
REVIEWS OF MODERN PHYSICS MONOGRAPHS. 1969. irreg., vol.2, 1971. Academic Press, Inc., Orlando, FL 32887. TEL 305-345-2000.

530.44   US   ISSN 0080-2050
REVIEWS OF PLASMA PHYSICS. (English translation of original Russian text) 1965. irreg., vol.10, 1986. price varies. Consultants Bureau (Subsidiary of: Plenum Publishing Corp.) 233 Spring St., New York, NY 10013. TEL 212-620-4332. Ed. M.A. Leontovich.

530.15   AG   ISSN 0080-2360
REVISTA DE MATEMATICA Y FISICA TEORICA. SERIE A. (Text in Spanish, French, German, Italian and English; summaries in English) 1940. a. $15. ‡ Universidad Nacional de Tucuman, Facultad de Ciencias Exactas y Tecnologia, Avda. Independencia 1700, Tucuman, Argentina. Ed. Raul Luccioni, Augusto Battig. bk. rev. index. circ. 1,000. Indexed: Math.R. Zent.Math.

530   DK   ISSN 0418-6435
RISOE-M. No. 233, 1965. irreg. free. Risoe National Laboratory, P.O. Box 49, DK-4000 Roskilde, Denmark. Indexed: Chem.Abstr.

SAGA UNIVERSITY. FACULTY OF SCIENCE AND ENGINEERING. REPORTS. see *ENGINEERING*

SAITAMA UNIVERSITY. SCIENCE REPORTS. SERIES A: MATHEMATICS. see *MATHEMATICS*

SCIENZE DELLA MATERIA. see *CHEMISTRY*

530   NE   ISSN 0080-8636
SELECTED TOPICS IN SOLID STATE PHYSICS. (Text in English) 1962. irreg., vol.17, 1985. price varies. Elsevier Science Publishers B.V., Box 211, 1000 AE Amsterdam, Netherlands. Ed. E.P. Wohlfarth.

SERIE DI MATEMATICA E FISICA. see *MATHEMATICS*

SERIE DI MATEMATICA E FISICA. PROBLEMI RISOLTI. see *MATHEMATICS*

530   510   JA
SHINSHU UNIVERSITY. FACULTY OF TEXTILE SCIENCE AND TECHNOLOGY. JOURNAL. SERIES F: PHYSICS AND MATHEMATICS. (Text in European languages; summaries in English) 1962. irreg. exchange basis. Shinshu University, Faculty of Textile Science and Technology - Shinshu Daigaku Sen'i Gakubu, 3-15-1 Tokida, Ueda, Nagano 386, Japan.

SMITHSONIAN CONTRIBUTIONS TO ASTROPHYSICS. see *ASTRONOMY*

SMITHSONIAN INSTITUTION. ASTROPHYSICAL OBSERVATORY. S A O SPECIAL REPORT. see *ASTRONOMY*

530   IT
SOCIETA ITALIANA DI FISICA. CONGRESSO NAZIONALE. a. Societa Italiana di Fisica, Dipartimento di Biologia, Via Trieste 75, Italy.

530   FR   ISSN 0081-1076
SOCIETE FRANCAISE DE PHYSIQUE. ANNUAIRE. 1913. triennial. 250 F. Societe Francaise de Physique, 33 rue Croulebarbe, 75013 Paris, France.

533.5   FR   ISSN 0223-4335
SOCIETE FRANCAISE DU VIDE. COMPTES RENDUS DES TRAVAUX DES CONGRES ET COLLOQUES. irreg. price varies. Societe Francaise du Vide, 19 rue du Renard, 75004 Paris, France.
Vacuum techniques

SOLAR TERRESTRIAL ENVIRONMENTAL RESEARCH IN JAPAN. see *EARTH SCIENCES — Geophysics*

530   US   ISSN 0081-1947
SOLID STATE PHYSICS; ADVANCES IN RESEARCH AND APPLICATIONS. 1955. irreg., vol.39, 1986. Academic Press, Inc., Orlando, FL 32887. TEL 305-345-2000. Ed.Bd. index. cum.index (subject): vols.1-10, 1955-1960, vol.11, 1960. Indexed: ASCA. GeoRef.

530   510   US   ISSN 0143-0416
SOVIET SCIENTIFIC REVIEWS. SECTION C: MATHEMATICAL PHYSICS REVIEWS. vol.2, 1981. 4/yr. (in 1 vol., 4 nos./vol.) $218 to individuals; academic price $134. Harwood Academic Publishers, 50 W. 23rd St., New York, NY 10010. Ed. S.P. Novikov. index. (back issues avail.)

530   US
SPRINGER PROCEEDINGS IN PHYSICS. 1984. irreg., latest 1986. price varies. Springer-Verlag, 175 Fifth Ave., New York, NY 10010 TEL 212-460-1500. (Also Berlin, Heidelberg, Tokyo, Vienna) (reprint service avail. from ISI)

530   540   US   ISSN 0172-6218
SPRINGER SERIES IN CHEMICAL PHYSICS. 1978. irreg., vol.46, 1986. price varies. Springer-Verlag, 175 Fifth Ave., New York, NY 10010 TEL 212-460-1500. (Also Berlin, Heidelberg, Tokyo and Vienna) Ed.Bd. (reprint service avail. from ISI) Indexed: Biol.Abstr. Chem.Abstr. Phys.Ber.

530   US   ISSN 0172-5726
SPRINGER SERIES IN COMPUTATIONAL PHYSICS. 1977. irreg., latest 1986. price varies. Springer-Verlag, 175 Fifth Ave., New York, NY 10010 TEL 212-460-1500. (Also Berlin, Heidelberg, Tokyo and Vienna) Ed. H. Cabannes. (reprint service avail. from ISI) Indexed: Math.R.

SPRINGER SERIES IN ELECTROPHYSICS. see *ELECTRICITY AND ELECTRICAL ENGINEERING*

530   US
SPRINGER SERIES IN MATERIALS SCIENCES. 1986. irreg. price varies. Springer-Verlag, 175 Fifth Ave., New York, NY 10160 TEL 212-460-1500. (Also Berlin, Heidelberg, Tokyo, Vienna) (reprint service avail. from ISI)

530   US
SPRINGER SERIES IN SURFACE SCIENCES. 1986. irreg. price varies. Springer-Verlag, 175 Fifth Ave., New York, NY 10160 TEL 212-460-1500. (Also Berlin, Heidelberg, Tokyo, Vienna) (reprint service avail. from ISI)

539   US   ISSN 0081-3869
SPRINGER TRACTS IN MODERN PHYSICS. (Text in English) 1964. irreg., vol.108, 1986. price varies. Springer-Verlag, 175 Fifth Ave., New York, NY 10010 TEL 212-460-1500. (Also Berlin, Heidelberg, Tokyo and Vienna) (reprint service avail. from ISI) Indexed: ASCA. Phys.Ber.
Continues: Ergebnisse der Exacten Naturwissenschaften.

STAATLICHE MATHEMATISCH-PHYSIKALISCHE SALONS, DRESDEN. VEROEFFENTLICHUNGEN. see *MATHEMATICS*

530   RM
STUDIA UNIVERSITATIS "BABES-BOLYAI". PHYSICA. (Text in Rumanian; summaries in English, French, German, Russian) 1959. a. exchange basis. Universitatea "Babes-Bolyai", Biblioteca Centrala Universitara, Str. Clinicilor Nr. 2, Cluj-Napoca, Rumania. Indexed: Chem.Abstr. Math.R.

530   NE   ISSN 0081-8542
STUDIES IN STATISTICAL MECHANICS. 1962. irreg., vol.12, 1985. price varies. Elsevier Science Publishers B.V., Box 211, 1000 AE Amsterdam, Netherlands. Eds. E.W. Montroll, J.L. Lebowitz.

STUDIES IN THE HISTORY OF MATHEMATICS AND PHYSICAL SCIENCES. see *MATHEMATICS*

541.345   NE   ISSN 0039-6028
SURFACE SCIENCE; a journal devoted to the physics and chemistry of interfaces. (Text in English, French or German; summaries in English) 1964. irreg. price varies. Elsevier Science Publishers B.V., Box 211, 1000 AE Amsterdam, Netherlands. Ed. Harry C. Gatos. adv. bk. rev. bibl. charts. illus. index. Indexed: Chem.Abstr. Curr.Cont. Met.Abstr. Sci.Abstr. ASCA. Br.Ceram.Abstr. Int.Aerosp.Abstr. INSPEC. Mass Spectr.Bull. Phys.Ber. World Alum.Abstr.

SYMPOSIA ON THEORETICAL PHYSICS AND MATHEMATICS. see *MATHEMATICS*

530   CH
TAIPEI. ACADEMIA SINICA. INSTITUTE OF PHYSICS. ANNUAL REPORT. a. Taiwan. Institute of Physics. Academica Sinica, Taipei, Taiwan 115, Republic of China. Indexed: Met.Abstr.

530   US
TECHNIQUES OF PHYSICS. 1973. irreg., vol.7, 1984. Academic Press Inc., Orlando, FL 32887. TEL 305-345-2000. Eds. N.H. March, H.N. Daglish.

530   NE
TECHNISCH FYSISCHE DIENST TNO-TH. JAARVERSLAG. (Toegepast-Natuurwetenschappelijk Onderzoek. Technisch Fysische Dienst) (Text in Dutch; summaries in English) 1946. a. Technisch Fysische Dienst TNO-TH - T N O Institute of Applied Physics, Stieltjesweg 1, Box 155, Delft, Netherlands. Ed.Bd. illus. circ. 2,500.

530   US   ISSN 0082-2590
TECHNISCHE PHYSIK IN EINZELDARSTELLUNGEN. 1948. irreg., vol.18, 1973. price varies. Springer-Verlag, 175 Fifth Ave., New York, NY 10010 TEL 212-460-1500. (also Berlin, Heidelberg, Tokyo and Vienna) (reprint service avail. from ISI)

TEKSTER FRA I M F U F A. (Institut for Studiet af Matematik og Fysik Samt Deres Funktioner i Undervisning Forskning og Anvendelse) see *MATHEMATICS*

530   US   ISSN 0172-5998
TEXTS AND MONOGRAPHS IN PHYSICS. 1976. irreg. Springer Verlag, 175 Fifth Ave., New York, NY 10010 TEL 212-460-1500. (And Berlin, Heidelberg, Tokyo and Vienna) Ed. W. Beiglboeck. (reprint service avail. from ISI) Indexed: Math.R.

530   621   US   ISSN 0303-4216
TOPICS IN APPLIED PHYSICS. 1974. irreg., vol.58, 1985. Springer-Verlag, 175 Fifth Ave., New York, NY 10010 TEL 212-460-1500. (Also Berlin, Heidelberg, Tokyo and Vienna) (reprint service avail. from ISI) Indexed: Biol.Abstr. ASCA. Phys.Ber.

530   US   ISSN 0342-6793
TOPICS IN CURRENT PHYSICS. 1976. irreg., vol.41, 1986. price varies. Springer-Verlag, 175 Fifth Ave., New York, NY 10010 TEL 212-460-1500. (Also Berlin, Heidelberg, Tokyo and Vienna) (reprint service avail. from ISI) Indexed: Chem.Abstr. Phys.Ber.

530   US
TRIESTE NOTES IN PHYSICS. 1986. irreg. price varies. Springer-Verlag, 175 Fifth Ave., New York, NY 10160 TEL 212-460-1500. (Also Berlin, Heidelberg, Tokyo, Vienna) (reprint service avail. from ISI)

530   CK
UNIVERSIDAD DE ANTIOQUIA. CUADERNOS. 1981. irreg. Universidad de Antioquia, Extension Cultural, Medellin, Colombia.

530   RM   ISSN 0041-9141
UNIVERSITATEA "AL. I. CUZA" DIN IASI. ANALELE STIINTIFICE. SECTIUNEA 1B: FIZICA. (Text in English, French, German, Italian, Rumanian or Russian) 1955. a. 35 lei. Universitatea "Al. I. Cuza" din Iasi, Calea 23 August Nr. 11, Jassy, Rumania (Subscr. to: ILEXIM, Str. 13 Decembrie Nr. 3, P.O. Box 136-137, Bucharest, Rumania) Ed. M. Sorohan. bk. rev. abstr. charts. illus. circ. 250. Indexed: Chem.Abstr. Math.R. Sci.Abstr.

UNIVERSITATEA DIN BRASOV. BULETINUL. SERIA C. STIINTE ALE NATURRI SI PEDAGOGIE. see *MATHEMATICS*

UNIVERSITATEA DIN CRAIOVA. ANALE. SERIA: MATEMATICA, FIZICA-CHIMIE. see *MATHEMATICS*

530   FR   ISSN 0069-4738
UNIVERSITE DE CLERMONT-FERRAND II. ANNALES SCIENTIFIQUES. SERIE PHYSIQUE. 1963. irreg. price varies. Universite de Clermont-Ferrand II, Unite d'Enseignement et de Recherche de Sciences Exactes et Naturelles, B.P. 45, 63170 Aubiere, France. circ. 250. (back issues avail.)

UNIVERSITEXTS. see *MATHEMATICS*

530   520   CN
UNIVERSITY OF BRITISH COLUMBIA, PHYSICS SOCIETY. JOURNAL. 1960. a. Can.$3 to non-members. University of British Columbia, Physics Society, Dept. of Physics, 6224 Agriculture Rd., Vancouver, B.C. V6T 2A6, Canada. TEL 604-228-2211. Ed. Patrick S.C. Bruskiewich. adv. circ. 150. (back issues avail.)

530   DK   ISSN 0106-7222
UNIVERSITY OF COPENHAGEN. PHYSICS LABORTORY II. REPORT. (Text in English) 1972. irreg. free. Koebenhavns Universitet, Physics Laboratory II, H.C. Oersted Institut, Copenhagen, Denmark. circ. 100.

530   NE   ISSN 0022-8141
UNIVERSITY OF LEIDEN. KAMERLINGH ONNES LABORATORY. COMMUNICATIONS. (Text in English; occasionally in French and German) 1885. a. free. Rijksuniversiteit te Leiden, Kamerlingh Onnes Laboratory, Nieuwsteeg 18, 2311 SB Leiden, Netherlands. Ed. M. Durieux. charts. illus. circ. 450. Indexed: Sci.Abstr.

530   PP   ISSN 0085-4735
UNIVERSITY OF PAPUA NEW GUINEA. DEPARTMENT OF PHYSICS. TECHNICAL PAPER. 1968. irreg. free. ‡ University of Papua New Guinea, Department of Physics, Box 4820, University P.O., Papua New Guinea. circ. 75.

530   JA   ISSN 0082-4798
UNIVERSITY OF TOKYO. INSTITUTE FOR SOLID STATE PHYSICS. TECHNICAL REPORT. SERIES A. (Text in English) 1959. irreg. (approx. 60/yr.) University of Tokyo, Institute for Solid State Physics - Tokyo Daigaku Bussei Kenkyusho, 7-22-1 Roppongi, Minato-ku, Tokyo 106, Japan.

PHYSICS — ABSTRACTING, BIBLIOGRAPHIES, STATISTICS

530   JA   ISSN 0082-4801
UNIVERSITY OF TOKYO. INSTITUTE FOR SOLID STATE PHYSICS. TECHNICAL REPORT. SERIES B. (Text in English) 1960. irreg. (approx. 1/yr.), no.15, 1973. University of Tokyo, Institute for Solid State Physics - Tokyo Daigaku Bussei Kenkyusho, 7-22-1 Roppongi, Minato-ku, Tokyo 106, Japan.

530   PL
UNIWERSYTET GDANSKI. WYDZIAL MATEMATYKI, FIZYKI, CHEMII. ZESZYTY NAUKOWE. FIZYKA. (Text in Polish; summaries in English) 1972. irreg. price varies. Uniwersytet Gdanski, Ul. Czerwonej Armii 110, 81-824 Sopot, Poland. illus.

530   613.7   PL   ISSN 0208-4872
UNIWERSYTET GDANSKI. WYDZIAL MATEMATYKI, FIZYKI I CHEMII. ZESZYTY NAUKOWE. PROBLEMY DYDAKTYKI FIZYKI. (Text in Polish; summaries in English and Russian) 1974. irreg. price varies. Uniwersytet Gdanski, Ul. Armii Czerwonej 110, 81-824 Sopot, Poland. Ed. Kazimierz Badziag.
    Formerly: Uniwersytet Gdanski. Zeszyty Naukowe Wydzialu Matematyki, Fizyki i Chemii. Problemy Dydaktyki.

530   PL   ISSN 0083-4335
UNIWERSYTET JAGIELLONSKI. ZESZYTY NAUKOWE. PRACE FIZYCZNE. (Text in English and Polish; summaries in English and Russian) 1963. irreg., vol.23, 1984. price varies. Panstwowe Wydawnictwo Naukowe, Miodowa 10, 00-251 Warsaw, Poland (Dist. by: Ars Polona, Krakowskie Przedmiescie 7, 00-068 Warsaw, Poland) Ed. Bronislaw Sredniawa. circ. 470. Indexed: Math.R.

530   SW   ISSN 0349-2699
UPPSALA IONOSPHERIC OBSERVATORY. SCIENTIFIC REPORTS. 1977. irreg. price varies. Uppsala Ionospheric Observatory, S-755 90 Uppsala, Sweden.

530   SW   ISSN 0349-2680
UPPSALA IONOSPHERIC OBSERVATORY. TECHNICAL REPORTS. 1978. irreg. price varies. Uppsala Ionospheric Observatory, S-755 90 Uppsala, Sweden.

500.9   540   530   320   GE
URANIA UNIVERSUM. 1955. a. M.15. Urania Verlag Leipzig, Salomonstrasse 26/28, PSF 969, DDR 7010 Leipzig, E. Germany (D.D.R.) Ed. Henry Heinig. circ. 60,000.

VICTORIA, BRITISH COLUMBIA. DOMINION ASTROPHYSICAL OBSERVATORY. PUBLICATIONS. see ASTRONOMY

530   UR   ISSN 0301-6919
VOPROSY FIZIKI TVERDOGO TELA. irreg. 2.30 Rub. Chelyabinskii Gosudarstvennyi Pedagogicheskii Institut, Chelyabinsk, Russian S.F.S.R., U.S.S.R. illus.

WHO'S WHO IN MECHANICAL ENGINEERING & MATERIALS SCIENCE. see
ENGINEERING — Mechanical Engineering

WISSENSCHAFTLICHE TASCHENBUECHER. REIHE MATHEMATIK, PHYSIK. see
MATHEMATICS

530   GE   ISSN 0138-127X
WISSENSCHAFTLICHE TASCHENBUECHER. REIHE TEXTE UND STUDIEN. 1970. irreg. price varies. Akademie-Verlag, Leipziger Str. 3-4, 1086 Berlin, E. Germany (D.D.R.)

530   PL   ISSN 0078-5385
WYZSZA SZKOLA PEDAGOGICZNA, OPOLE. ZESZYTY NAUKOWE. SERIA A. FIZYKA. (Text in Polish; summaries in English) 1963. irreg., vol.21, 1981. price varies; available on exchange. Wyzsza Szkola Pedagogiczna, Opole, Oleska 48, 45-052 Opole, Poland (Dist. by: Ars Polona-Ruch, Krakowskie Przedmiescie 7, Warsaw, Poland) Ed. Jozef Kusz. circ. 300. Indexed: Chem.Abstr. Math.R.

539.7   GE   ISSN 0323-8776
Z F I - MITTEILUNGEN. 1974. irreg., no.18, 1979. Akademie der Wissenschaften der DDR, Zentralinstitut fuer Isotopen- und Strahlenforschung, Permoserstr. 15, 705 Leipzig, E. Germany(D.D.R.) Ed. R. Schroeter. (also avail. in microfiche) Indexed: Biol.Abstr. Chem.Abstr. INIS Atomind.

530   PL   ISSN 0044-1597
ZAGADNIENIA DRGAN NIELINIOWYCH/ NONLINEAR VIBRATIONS PROBLEMS. (Text in English, Polish; summaries in English, Polish, Russian) 1960. irreg., vol.21, 1983. price varies. (Polska Akademia Nauk, Instytut Podstawowych Problemow Techniki) Panstwowe Wydawnictwo Naukowe, Ul. Miodowa 10, 00-251 Warsaw, Poland (Dist. by: Asr Polona, Krakowskie Przedmiescie 7, 00-068 Warsaw, Poland) abstr. bibl. charts. illus. index. circ. 300. Indexed: Sci.Abstr.

PHYSICS — Abstracting, Bibliographies, Statistics

530   016   US   ISSN 0163-1446
ABSTRACT NEWSLETTER: PHYSICS. w. $79. U.S. National Technical Information Service, 5285 Port Royal Rd., Springfield, VA 22161. TEL 703-487-4630. Ed. Linda J. LaGarde. index. (back issues avail.)
    Former titles: Weekly Abstract Newsletter: Physics; Weekly Government Abstracts. Physics.

ABSTRACTS OF BULGARIAN SCIENTIFIC LITERATURE. MATHEMATICAL AND PHYSICAL SCIENCES. see MATHEMATICS — Abstracting, Bibliographies, Statistics

534   016   UK   ISSN 0001-4974
ACOUSTICS ABSTRACTS. 1967. m. £175($295) Multi-Science Publishing Co. Ltd., 107 High St., Brentwood, Essex CM14 4RX, England. Ed. J. Scott. abstr. index. Indexed: Fluidex.
    Formerly: Acoustics and Ultrasonics Abstracts.

539.7   614   016   UK   ISSN 0305-7615
APPLIED HEALTH PHYSICS ABSTRACTS AND NOTES. 1975. q. $180. Nuclear Technology Publishing, Box 7, Ashford, Kent TN25 4NW, England. Ed. E.P. Goldfinch. circ. 1,000. (back issues avail.)

ASTRONOMY AND ASTROPHYSICS ABSTRACTS. see ASTRONOMY — Abstracting, Bibliographies, Statistics

535   016   UK   ISSN 0309-1813
ATOMIC ABSORPTION & EMISSION SPECTROMETRY ABSTRACTS. 1969. bi-m. £60($78) PRM Science & Technology Agency Ltd., 261a Finchley Rd., Hampstead, London NW3 6LU, England. Ed. Dr. J.D. Donaldson. index.
    Formerly: Atomic Absorption and Flame Emission Spectroscopy Abstracts (ISSN 0004-7074)

539   016   CN   ISSN 0067-0405
ATOMIC ENERGY OF CANADA. LIST OF PUBLICATIONS. 1952. irreg. free. Atomic Energy of Canada Ltd., Chalk River Nuclear Laboratories, Technical Information Branch, S.D.D.O., Sta. 14, Chalk River, Ont. K0J 1J0, Canada. TEL 613-687-5581.

539.7   016   AT
AUSTRALIA. ATOMIC ENERGY COMMISSION. RESEARCH ESTABLISHMENT. LIST OF REPORT PUBLICATIONS. irreg. Australian Atomic Energy Commission, Menai, N.S.W. 2234, Australia. illus.

530   016   BL   ISSN 0067-6640
BIBLIOGRAFIA BRASILEIRA DE FISICA. 1961. irreg. Cr.$600($25) Instituto Brasileiro de Informacao em Ciencia e Tecnologia, SCRN 708/709 Bloco B Loja 18E 30, 70740 Brasilia DF, Brazil. bk. rev. circ. 300.
    Supersedes in part: Bibliografia Brasileira de Matematica e Fisica.

539.7   016   UN
C I N D A; an index to the literature on microscopic neutron data. (Text in English; foreword in English, French, Russian & Spanish) 1965. a. price varies. International Atomic Energy Agency, Division of Publications, Wagramer Str. 5, Box 100, A-1400 Vienna, Austria (Dist. in U.S. by: Bernan Associates-Unipub, 4611-F Assembly Dr., Lanham, MD 20706-4391) (Co-sponsors U.S.A. National Nuclear Data Center; U.S.S.R. Nuclear Data Centre; N.E.A. Databank; IAEA Nuclear Data Section) circ. 1,500.

539.7   011   US
CUMULATIVE BIBLIOGRAPHY OF LITERATURE EXAMINED BY THE RADIATION SHIELDING INFORMATION CENTER. 1965. irreg. free. Oak Ridge National Laboratory, Radiation Shielding Information Center, Box X, Oak Ridge, TN 37830. TEL 615-574-6176. Ed. D.K. Trubey. circ. 200. (also avail. in microfiche; back issues avail.)

530   016   520   UK   ISSN 0011-3786
CURRENT PAPERS IN PHYSICS; containing about 78,000 titles of research articles from the world's physics journals. 1966. fortn. $230 to non-members. INSPEC, I.E.E., Station House, Nightingale Rd., Hitchin, Herts. SG5 1RJ, England (U.S. address: 445 Hoes Lane, Piscataway, NJ 08854) Indexed: Fluidex.

530   016   US   ISSN 0098-9819
CURRENT PHYSICS INDEX. 1975. q. $355. American Institute of Physics, 335 E. 45th St., New York, NY 10017. TEL 212-661-9404. bibl. cum.index. (back issues avail.)

532   016   GW   ISSN 0340-8388
DOKUMENTATION RHEOLOGIE/ DOCUMENTATION RHEOLOGY. (Text in English) 1954. a. price varies. Bundesanstalt fuer Materialpruefung, Unter den Eichen 87, 1000 Berlin 45, W. Germany (B.R.D.) (Co-sponsor: Deutsche Rheologische Gesellschaft) Ed. Edith Rudolph. bibl. index. circ. 500. (back issues avail.)
    ●Also available online. Vendors: INKA.
    Formerly: Deutsche Rheologische Gesellschaft. Berichte (ISSN 0012-0626)

539.7   016   UK   ISSN 0301-7575
ELECTRON SPIN RESONANCE SPECTROSCOPY ABSTRACTS. 1973. q. £45. PRM Science & Technology Agency Ltd., 261a Finchley Rd., Hampstead, London NW3 6LU, England.

539.7   015   EI
EURO ABSTRACTS SECTION I. EURATOM AND EEC RESEARCH. (Text in English) 1962. m. price varies. (European Atomic Energy Community) Office for Official Publications of the European Communities, P.O. Box 1003, L-2985 Luxembourg, Luxembourg (Dist. in U.S. by: European Community Information Service, 2100 M St., N.W., Ste. 707, Washington, DC 20037) abstr. pat. index. circ. 2,200. (also avail. in microform from UMI) Indexed: Anal.Abstr. Br.Ceram.Abstr.
    Former titles: Euro Abstracts (ISSN 0014-2352) & EURATOM Information.

539.7   016   SZ   ISSN 0304-2871
EUROPEAN ORGANIZATION FOR NUCLEAR RESEARCH. LISTE DES PUBLICATIONS SCIENTIFIQUES/LIST OF SCIENTIFIC PUBLICATIONS. (Former name of body: Conseil Europeen pour la Recherche Nucleaire) 1955. irreg. free. European Laboratory for Particle Physics, CH-1211 Geneva 23, Switzerland.
    Former titles: European Organization for Nuclear Research. Repertoire des Communications Scientifiques. Index of Scientific Publications (ISSN 0423-7781); European Organization for Nuclear Research. Repertoire des Publications Scientifiques. Index of Scientific Publications.

530   US   ISSN 0749-4823
GENERAL PHYSICS ADVANCE ABSTRACTS. 1985. s-m. $150 to non-members. American Institute of Physics, 335 East 45th St., New York, NY 10017. TEL 212-661-9404. Eds. Rosalind Nissim, Kathleen Bubbeo.

539.76 016   GW ISSN 0018-1447
HIGH ENERGY PHYSICS INDEX/
HOCHENERGIEPHYSIK-INDEX. (Text in
English; contents page in English and German)
1963. fortn. DM.385 incl. thesaurus and index.
(Deutsches Elektonen-Synchotron (DESY))
Fachinformationszentrum Energie, Physik,
Mathematik GmbH, D-7514 Eggenstein-
Leopoldshafen 2, W. Germany (B.R.D.) adv. bk.
rev. index. circ. 160.

016 621.48   UN ISSN 0534-7319
I A E A LIBRARY FILM CATALOG. 1962. irreg.
free. ‡ International Atomic Energy Agency,
Kaertner Ring 11, Wagramer Str. 5, Box 100, A-
1400 Vienna, Austria. index. circ. 5,500.

539.7 016   UN ISSN 0004-7139
I N I S ATOMINDEX. (Text in English; summaries
in English, French, Russian or Spanish) 1970. s-m.
S.4400 incl. indexes. International Atomic Energy
Agency, Wagramer Str. 5, Box 100, A-1400 Vienna,
Austria (Dist. in U.S. by: Bernan Associates-Unipub,
4611-F Assembly Dr., Lanham, MD 20706-4391)
bibl. s-a index. circ. 1,650. Indexed: Chem.Abstr.
Anal.Abstr. Mass Spectr.Bull.
●Also available online. Vendors: CISTI, European
Space Agency.
  Incorporates (as of June 1976): Nuclear Science
Abstracts (United States Energy Research and
Development Administration) (ISSN 0029-5612)

530   JA
J A E R I REPORT. (Text in English or Japanese)
1957. irreg. exchange. Japan Atomic Energy
Research Institute, Department of Technical
Information, Tokai-mura, Naka-gun, Ibaraki-ken
319-11, Japan.

535.58 016   US ISSN 0022-0264
JOURNAL OF CURRENT LASER ABSTRACTS.
1964. m. $360. PennWell Publishing Co., 119
Russell St., Box 1153, Littleton, MA 01460-0753.
TEL 617-486-9501. bk. rev. abstr. bibl. charts.
illus. pat. index. (back issues avail.)

530 668.4   UK ISSN 0950-4753
KEY ABSTRACTS - ADVANCED MATERIALS.
1987. m. $110 to non-members. INSPEC, I.E.E.,
Station House, Nightingale Rd., Hitchin, Herts. SG5
1RJ, England (U.S. addr.: 445 Hoes Lane,
Piscataway, NJ 08854) index.

535.84 535.58 016 UK ISSN 0309-5320
LASER RAMAN & INFRARED SPECTROSCOPY
ABSTRACTS. 1971. bi-m. £45. PRM Science &
Technology Agency Ltd., 261a Finchley Rd.,
Hampstead, London NW3 6LU, England. Ed. J.N.
Crosby. abstr.
  Formed by the merger of: Laser Raman
Spectroscopy Abstracts (ISSN 0047-410X) &
Infrared Spectroscopy Abstracts.

535.84 016   UK
MOESSBAUER SPECTROSCOPY ABSTRACTS.
1978. q. $92.56. PRM Science & Technology
Agency Ltd., 261a Finchley Rd., Hampstead,
London NW3 6LU, England.

539.7 016   UK ISSN 0047-9446
NEUTRON ACTIVATION ANALYSIS
ABSTRACTS. 1973. q. £45($78) PRM Science &
Technology Agency Ltd., 261A Finchley Rd.,
Hampstead, London NW3 6LU, England. Ed. J.
Silver. index.

543 539.7 016   UK ISSN 0048-1033
NUCLEAR MAGNETIC RESONANCE
SPECTROMETRY ABSTRACTS. 1971. bi-m. £60.
PRM Science & Technology Agency Ltd., 261A
Finchley Rd., Hampstead, London NW3 6LU,
England. Ed.Bd.

530 016   FR
P A S C A L EXPLORE. PART 11: PHYSIQUE
ATOMIQUE ET MOLECULAIRE. PLASMAS.
1985. 10/yr. 915 F. Centre National de la
Recherche Scientifique, Centre de Documentation
Scientifique et Technique, Service des
Abonnements, 26 rue Boyer, 75971 Paris 20,
France. Ed. C. Degen. abstr. index. cum.index. (also
avail. in microform from MIM)
  Supersedes (1961-1984): Bulletin Signaletique.
Part 165: Atomes et Molecules. Plasmas (ISSN
0398-9968); Bulletin Signaletique. Part 165: Atomes
et Molecules. Physiques des Fluides et Plasmas
(ISSN 0301-3359); Bulletin Signaletique. Part 165:
Physique Atomique et Moleculaire. Physique des
Fluides et des Plasmas; Supersedes in part: Bulletin
Signaletique. Part 160: Structure de la Matiere 1
(ISSN 0007-537X)

530 016   FR
P A S C A L EXPLORE. PART 12: ETAT
CONDENSE. 1985. 10/yr. 915 F. Centre National
de la Recherche Scientifique, Centre de
Documentation Scientifique et Technique, Service
des Abonnements, 26 rue Boyer, 75971 Paris 20,
France. abstr. index. cum.index. (also avail. in
microform from MIM)
  Supersedes (1961-1984): Bulletin Signaletique.
Part 160: Physique de l'Etat Condense (ISSN 0301-
3332); Which supersedes in part: Bulletin
Signaletique. Part 160: Structure de la Matiere I
(ISSN 0007-537X)

535 011   US
P A S C A L EXPLORE. PART 27: METHODES
DE FORMATION ET TRAITEMENT DES
IMAGES. 1985. 10/yr. 545 F. Centre National de
la Recherche Scientifique, Centre de Documentation
Scientifique et Technique, Service des
Abonnements, 26 rue Boyer, 75971 Paris 20,
France.
  Supersedes in part (1961-1984): Bulletin
Signaletique. Part 130: Physique Mathematique,
Optique, Acoustique, Mechanique, Chaleur (ISSN
0397-7757)

P A S C A L EXPLORE. PART 32: METROLOGIE
ET APPAREILLAGE EN PHYSIQUE ET
PHYSICOCHIMIE. see *METROLOGY AND
STANDARDIZATION — Abstracting,
Bibliographies, Statistics*

536 016   FR
P A S C A L THEMA. PART 230: ENERGIE. 1985.
10/yr. 1390 F. Centre National de la Recherche
Scientifique, Centre de Documentation
Scientifique et Technique, Service des Abonnements, 26 rue
Boyer, 75971 Paris 20, France. abstr. index.
cum.index. (also avail. in microform from MIM)
  Supersedes (1969-1984): Bulletin Signaletique.
Part 730: Combustibles. Energie (ISSN 0007-5647)

530 016   US ISSN 0048-4024
PHYSICAL REVIEW ABSTRACTS. 1970. s-m. $160.
(American Physical Society) American Institute of
Physics, 335 E 45th St., New York, NY 10017.
TEL 212-661-9404. Ed. M. Judd. abstr.

530 016   US ISSN 0094-0003
PHYSICAL REVIEW/INDEX. a. $40 to non-
members. American Institute of Physics, 335 E.
45th St., New York, NY 10017. TEL 212-661-9404.
Ed.Bd. (also avail. in microfiche)

530 016   UK ISSN 0036-8091
PHYSICS ABSTRACTS. Alternative title: INSPEC.
Section A. 1898. bi-m. $1765. INSPEC, I.E.E.,
Station House, Nightingale Rd., Hitchin, Herts. SG5
1RJ, England (U.S. address: 445 Hoes Lane,
Piscataway, NJ 08854) adv. abstr. index. cum.index
every 4 years. (also avail. in microform from MIM)
Indexed: Chem.Abstr. Br.Ceram.Abstr. Mass
Spectr.Bull.
●Also available online. Vendors: BRS, CEDOCAR,
CISTI, Data-Star, DIALOG, European Space
Agency, JICST, Orbit Information Technologies,
STN International, University of Tsukuba.

530 016   GW ISSN 0170-7434
PHYSICS BRIEFS/PHYSIKALISCHE BERICHTE;
an abstracting journal covering all fields of physics.
(Text in English) 1920. 24/yr. DM.3600($1550)
(Information Center for Energy, Physics,
Mathematics, GW) Physik-Verlag GmbH, Postfach
1260/1280, D-6940 Weinheim, W. Germany
(B.R.D.) TEL 212-661-9404. (U.S. addr.: V C H
Publishers, Inc., 220 East 23rd St., NY, NY, 10010-
4606.) (Co-sponsors: German Physical Society;
American Institute of Physics) bk. rev. abstr. index.
circ. 350. (also avail. in magnetic tape)
  Supersedes: Physikalische Berichte (ISSN 0031-
9260)

016 530   UK
POLAROGRAPHY ABSTRACTS. 1976/77. q. £45.
Science and Technology Agency, 787 High Rd.,
North Finchley, London N12 8JT, England.

530 016   UR ISSN 0034-2343
REFERATIVNYI ZHURNAL. FIZIKA. 1954. m. 751
Rub. including index. Vsesoyuznyi Institut
Nauchno-Tekhnicheskoi Informatsii (VINITI),
Baltiiskaya ul., 14, Moscow A-219, Russian
S.F.S.R., U.S.S.R. (Subscr. to: Mezhdunarodnaya
Kniga, Dimitrova ul. 39, 113095 Moscow, Russian
S.F.S.R., U.S.S.R.) Indexed: Chem.Abstr.

535   UR ISSN 0234-9647
REFERATIVNYI ZHURNAL. VOLOKONNO-
OPTICHESKIE SYSTEMY. 1987. m. 47 Rub. (56
Rub. with index) Vsesoyuznyi Institut Nauchno-
Tekhnicheskoi Informatsii (VINITI), Baltiiskaya ul.
14, Moscow A-219, Russian S.F.S.R., U.S.S.R.

621.483 016   UR ISSN 0034-2653
REFERATIVNYI ZHURNAL. YADERNYE
REAKTORY. 1958. m. 24.40 Rub. 25 Rub.
including index. Vsesoyuznyi Institut Nauchno-
Tekhnicheskoi Informatsii (VINITI), Baltiiskaya ul.,
14, Moscow A-219, Russian S.F.S.R., U.S.S.R
(Subscr. to: Mezhdunarodnaya Kniga, Moscow G-
200, Russian S.F.S.R., U.S.S.R.) Indexed:
Chem.Abstr.

530 016   US ISSN 0735-0791
RELIABILITY PHYSICS. Represents: International
Reliability Physics Symposium. Proceedings. a. (I E
E E, Electron Devices Society and Reliability
Society) Institute of Electrical and Electronics
Engineers, Inc., 345 E. 47th St., New York, NY
10017 TEL 212-705-7900. (Subscr. address: 445
Hoes Ln., Piscataway, NJ 08854) Indexed:
Chem.Abstr.
  Former titles: Reliability Physics Symposium.
Proceedings; Reliability Physics Symposium.
Presentation Abstracts; Reliability Physics
Symposium Abstracts (ISSN 0080-0821)

532 540 016   US ISSN 0035-452X
RHEOLOGY ABSTRACTS; a survey of world
literature. 1958. q. $115. (British Society of
Rheology) Pergamon Press, Inc., Journals Division,
Maxwell House, Fairview Park, Elmsford, NY
10523 TEL 914-592-7700. (And Headington Hill
Hall, Oxford OX3 0BW, England) Ed. Stephen T.E.
Aldhouse. adv. bk. rev. abstr. circ. 1,300. (also avail.
in microform from MIM,UMI) Indexed: Biol.Abstr.
Br.Ceram.Abstr. RAPRA.

535.84 016   UK ISSN 0036-1178
S.D.C. BULLETIN. 1963. irreg. £5. Scientific
Documentation Centre Ltd., Halbeath House,
Dunfermline, Fife KY12 0TZ, Scotland. Ed. P.S.
Davison. bk. rev. abstr. bibl. index.
  Formerly: Spectra Index and S.D.C. Bulletin.
Spectroscopy

SOLID-LIQUID FLOW ABSTRACTS. see
*ENGINEERING — Abstracting, Bibliographies,
Statistics*

531 016   US
SOLID STATE ABSTRACTS JOURNAL; an abstract
journal involving the physics, metallurgy,
crystallography, chemistry and device technology of
solids. 1957. bi-m. $550. Cambridge Scientific
Abstracts, 5161 River Rd., Bethesda, MD 20816.
TEL 301-951-1400. Ed. Pamela J. Eilers. adv. bk.
rev. abstr. index; cum.index. circ. 2,800. (also avail.
in microfilm) Indexed: Chem.Abstr. Cal.Tiss.Abstr.
Chemorec.Abstr. Oncol.Abstr.
●Also available online. Vendors: DIALOG.

Formerly: Solid State Abstracts (ISSN 0038-108X); Incorporating: Science Research Abstracts Journal. Laser and Electro-Optic Reviews; Quantum Electronics; Unconventional Energy Sources & Science Research Abstracts Journal. Superconductivity; Magnetohydrodynamics and Plasmas; Theoretical Physics (ISSN 0361-3321); Which was formerly: Science Research Abstracts, Part A. MHD and Plasmas; Superconductivity and Research; and Theoretical Physics; Which was formed by the merger of: Theoretical Physics Journal (ISSN 0049-3678) Magnetohydrodynamics and Plasmas (ISSN 0047-5505)

530.41 016   US   ISSN 0081-1963
SOLID STATE PHYSICS LITERATURE GUIDES. 1970. irreg. price varies. Plenum Publishing Corp., I.F.I.--Plenum Data Co., 233 Spring St., New York, NY 10013. TEL 212-620-8047.

530 016   UK   ISSN 0049-2639
SURFACE WAVE ABSTRACTS. 1971. q. £85($150) Multi-Science Publishing Co. Ltd., 107 High St., Brentwood, Essex CM14 4RX, England. Ed. J. Scott. bk. rev. abstr. bibl. index.

311   DK
UNIVERSITY OF COPENHAGEN. INSTITUTE OF MATHEMATICAL STATISTICS. ANNUAL REPORT. (Text in English) a. Koebenhavns Universitet, Institut for Matematisk Statistik, 5 Universitetsparken, 2100 Copenhagen OE, Denmark.

533.5 016   US   ISSN 0042-207X
VACUUM; the international journal and abstracting service for vacuum science and technology. 1951. m. $205. (British Vacuum Council, UK) Pergamon Press, Inc., Journals Division, Maxwell House, Fairview Park, Elmsford, NY 10523 TEL 914-592-7700. (and Headington Hill Hall, Oxford OX3 0BW, Eng) Ed. J.S. Colligon. adv. bk. rev. abstr. illus. index. circ. 1,500. (also avail. in microform from MIM,UMI) Indexed: Appl.Mech.Rev. A.S.& T.Ind. Br.Tech.Ind. Chem.Abstr. Curr.Cont. Eng.Ind. Met.Abstr. Sci.Abstr. Anal.Abstr. Art & Archaeol.Tech.Abstr. Fluidex. ISMEC. Mass Spectr.Bull. Phys.Ber. World Alum.Abstr.

553 016   UK   ISSN 0309-5312
X-RAY DIFFRACTION ABSTRACTS. 1973. q. £45. PRM Science and Technology Agency Ltd., 261A Finchley Rd., Hampstead, London NW3 6LU, England. abstr. bibl.

ZIDIS. see *BUSINESS AND ECONOMICS — Abstracting, Bibliographies, Statistics*

PHYSICS — Heat

621.59 536.56   US   ISSN 0065-2482
ADVANCES IN CRYOGENIC ENGINEERING. Represents: Cryogenic Engineering Conference Proceedings. Even-numbered vols. represent: International Cryogenic Materials Conferences. 1960. irreg. price varies. Plenum Publishing Corp., 233 Spring St., New York, NY 10013. TEL 212-620-8047. Indexed: Chem.Abstr.

536.2   US   ISSN 0065-2717
ADVANCES IN HEAT TRANSFER. (Supplements avail.) 1964. irreg., vol.17, 1985. Academic Press, Inc., Orlando, FL 32887. TEL 305-345-2000. Ed. Thomas F. Irvine, Jr. index. Indexed: Appl.Mech.Rev. GeoRef.

536   UR   ISSN 0082-4089
AKADEMIYA NAUK LITOVSKOI S.S.R. SILUMINE FIZIKA/THERMOPHYSICS/TEPLOFIZIKA. (Text in Russian; summaries in English and Lithuanian) 1968. a. price varies. (Institute of Physical and Technical Problems of Energetics) Izdatel'stvo Mokslas, Zvaigzdziu 23, Vilnius 232050, Lithuanian S.S.R., U.S.S.R. Ed. A. Zukauskas.

536 621   US   ISSN 0066-1538
ANALYTICAL CALORIMETRY. Represents: American Chemical Society Symposium on Analytical Calorimetry. 1968. irreg. price varies. Plenum Publishing Corp., 233 Spring St., New York, NY 10013. TEL 212-620-8047.

536   US
COMBUSTION; an international series. 1986. irreg. price varies. Hemisphere Publishing Corporation, 79 Madison Ave., New York, NY 10016. TEL 212-725-1999. Ed. Norman Chigier.

COMITE INTERNATIONAL DES POIDS ET MESURES. COMITE CONSULTATIF DE THERMOMETRIE. RAPPORTS ET ANNEXES. see *METROLOGY AND STANDARDIZATION*

536   UK   ISSN 0143-3598
FOULING PREVENTION RESEARCH DIGEST. 1979. q. $120. Heat Transfer and Fluid Flow Service, AERE Harwell, Oxon OX11 0RA, England (Distr. by: Lavis Marketing, 73 Lime Walk, Oxford OX3 7AD, England) Ed. Pascale Hicklin. adv. index. circ. 400. (back issues avail.) Indexed: Dairy Sci.Abstr.

536 697   UK
H M T: THE SCIENCE AND APPLICATION OF HEAT MASS TRANSFER; reports, reviews & computer programs. 1977. irreg., vol.6, 1982. Pergamon Press, Ltd., Headington Hill Hall, Oxford OX3 0BW, England (U.S. subscr. to: Maxwell House, Fairview Park, Elmsford, NY 10523) Ed. D. Brian Spalding.

536 535 600   JA   ISSN 0386-8044
INFRARED SOCIETY OF JAPAN. PROCEEDING. (Text and summaries in Japanese) a. 2000 Yen. Kyoto Institute of Technology, Department of Electronics, Matsugasaki, Sakyo-ku, Goshokaido-choh, Kyoto 606, Japan. Ed. Suteo Tsutsumi. circ. 1,000. Indexed: Sci.Abstr.

536.7 551.5   US
INTERNATIONAL CONFERENCE ON ATMOSPHERIC ELECTRICITY. PUBLICATION. 1974. irreg., 7th, 1984. $30. American Meteorological Society, 45 Beacon St., Boston, MA 02108. TEL 617-227-2425.

536 540   JA   ISSN 0074-3178
INTERNATIONAL CONFERENCE ON LOW TEMPERATURE PHYSICS. REPORTS.* 1949. biennial, 12th, 1970, Kyoto. (Intl. Union of Pure and Applied Physics) Inquire: Institute for Solid State Physics, University of Tokyo, 7-21-1 Ropong, Minato-Ku, Tokyo, Japan.
Reports published in host country

536.56   US   ISSN 0538-7051
INTERNATIONAL CRYOGENICS MONOGRAPH SERIES. 1964. irreg. price varies. Plenum Publishing Corp., 233 Spring St., New York, NY 10013. TEL 212-620-8047. Eds. K. Timmerhaus, A.F. Clark.

INTERNATIONAL SERIES IN HEAT AND MASS TRANSFER. see *ENGINEERING*

KYOTO UNIVERSITY. RESEARCH REACTOR INSTITUTE. ANNUAL REPORTS. see *CHEMISTRY — Inorganic Chemistry*

536   JA   ISSN 0439-3538
LOW TEMPERATURE SCIENCE. SERIES A. PHYSICAL SCIENCE. (From No. 1-10 (1952-1956) Series A and B issued in one vol.) (Text in Japanese; summaries in English) 1952. a. exchange basis. Hokkaido University, Institute of Low Temperature Science, North 19, West 8, Kita-ku, Sapporo 060, Japan. Ed. Seiiti Kinosita. circ. 600. Indexed: Sci.Abstr.
Formerly: Hokkaido University. Institute of Low Temperature Science. Series A. Physical Science (ISSN 0073-2931)

536.56   NE   ISSN 0079-6417
PROGRESS IN LOW TEMPERATURE PHYSICS. 1955. irreg., vol.8, 1982. price varies. Elsevier Science Publishers B.V., P.O. Box 211, 1000 AE Amsterdam, Netherlands. Ed. C.J. Gorter.
Cryogenics

536   US   ISSN 0091-9322
TEMPERATURE: ITS MEASUREMENT AND CONTROL IN SCIENCE AND INDUSTRY. Variant title: American Institute of Physics. Symposium on Temperature. Proceedings. irreg., approx. every 10 years. price varies. Instrument Society of America, 67 Alexander Dr., Box 12277, Research Triangle Park, NC 27709. TEL 919-549-8411. (reprint service avail. from UMI, ISI and publisher)

536   UR
TEPLOPROVODNOST' I DIFFUZIYA. 1969. irreg. 0.54 Rub. Politehniskais Instituts, Riga, Ul. Lenina, 1, Riga, Latvian S.S.R., U.S.S.R. illus.

532 536   UR
VOPROSY GIDRODINAMIKI I TEPLOOBMENA V KRIOGENNYKH SISTEMAKH. 1970. irreg. 0.85 Rub. Akademiya Nauk Ukrainskoi S.S.R., Fiziko-Tekhnicheskii Institut Nizkikh Temperatur, Pr. Lenina 47, Kharkov, Ukrainian S.S.R., U.S.S.R. illus.

PHYSICS — Mechanics

530 620.1   US   ISSN 0065-2156
ADVANCES IN APPLIED MECHANICS. (Supplements avail: Rarefied Gas Dynamics) 1948. irreg., vol.24, 1984. Academic Press, Inc., Orlando, FL 32887. TEL 305-345-2000. Ed. Chia-Shun Yih. index. Indexed: Appl.Mech.Rev. Math.R. Sci.Cit.Ind.

532   US   ISSN 0066-4189
ANNUAL REVIEW OF FLUID MECHANICS. 1969. a. $32. Annual Reviews Inc., 4139 El Camino Way, Palo Alto, CA 94306. TEL 415-493-4400. Eds. Milton Van Dyke, John L. Lumley. bibl. charts. illus. index; cum.index. (back issues avail.; reprint service avail. from ISI) Indexed: Appl.Mech.Rev. Biol.Abstr. Chem.Abstr. Curr.Cont. Ocean.Abstr. Sci.Abstr. Sci.Cit.Ind. Fluidex. GeoRef. Int.Aerosp.Abstr. Ind.Sci.Rev. M.M.R.I. Nucl.Sci.Abstr. Phys.Ber. Sel.Water Res.Abstr. T.C.E.A.
Rheology

APPLIED MATHEMATICS AND MECHANICS; an international series of monographs. see *MATHEMATICS*

531   BU   ISSN 0204-7594
BIOMEKHANIKA/BIOMECHANICS. (Text in Bulgarian and Russian; summaries in English and Russian) 1974. irreg. 2 lv. per no. (Bulgarska Akademiia na Naukite, Tsentralna Laboratoriia po Biomekhanika) Publishing House of the Bulgarian Academy of Sciences, Acad. G. Bonchev St., Bldg. 6, 1113 Sofia, Bulgaria (Dist. by: Hemus, 6, Rouski Blvd., 1000 Sofia, Bulgaria) Ed. G. Brankov. bibl. illus. circ. 470. Indexed: Biol.Abstr.

531 510   UK
CAMBRIDGE MONOGRAPHS ON MECHANICS AND APPLIED MATHEMATICS. irreg. price varies. Cambridge University Press, Edinburgh Bldg., Shaftesbury Rd., Cambridge CB2 2RU, England (And 32 E. 57th St., New York NY 10022) Eds. G.K. Batchelor, J.W. Miles. Indexed: Math.R.

533   UR
CHISLENNYE METODY V DINAMIKE RAZREZHENNYKH GAZOV. 1973. irreg. 0.73 Rub. Akademiya Nauk S.S.S.R., Laboratoriya Teorii Protsessov Perenosa, Leninskii prospekt, 14, Moscow V-71, Russian S.F.S.R., U.S.S.R. illus. Indexed: Chem.Abstr.

D C A M M REPORT. (Danish Center for Applied Mathematics and Mechanics) see *MATHEMATICS*

533   SZ   ISSN 0084-5744
EIDGENOESSISCHE TECHNISCHE HOCHSCHULE ZUERICH. MITTEILUNGEN. AERODYNAMIK. (Text in English, French and German) no.9, 1949. irreg., no.32, 1963. price varies. (Swiss Federal Institute of Technology) E T H Zurich, Ramistr 101, 8092 Zurich, Switzerland.

531   UR
FIZICHESKAYA MEKHANIKA. 1974. irreg. vol.3, 1978. 1.80 Rub. per no. Leningradskii Universitet, Universitetskaya Nab. 7/9, Leningrad B-164, Russian S.F.S.R., U.S.S.R. abstr. bibl. charts. circ. 2,000. Indexed: Chem.Abstr.

FIZIKO-KHIMICHESKA MEKHANIKA/PHYSICO-CHEMICAL MECHANICS. see *CHEMISTRY — Physical Chemistry*

532   PL   ISSN 0137-6462
FLUID DYNAMICS TRANSACTIONS. (Text in English) irreg., vol.11, 1983. price varies. (Polska Akademia Nauk, Instytut Podstawowych Problemow Techniki) Panstwowe Wydawnictwo Naukowe, Miodowa 10, 00-251 Warsaw, Poland (Dist. by: Ars Polona, Krakowskie Przedmiescie 7, 00-068 Warsaw, Poland) Ed.Bd. circ. 250.

MATHEMATISCHE FORSCHUNG. SCHRIFTENREIHE. see *MATHEMATICS*

531   NE
MECHANICS: DYNAMICAL SYSTEMS. (Text in English) 1974. irreg. price varies. Martinus Nijhoff Publishers, Box 163, 3300 AD Dordrecht, Netherlands. bibl.

531   NE
MECHANICS OF ELASTIC AND INELASTIC SOLIDS. (Text in English) irreg. price varies. Martinus Nijhoff Publishers, Postbus 163, 3300 AD Dordrecht, Netherlands.

531   UR   ISSN 0321-1975
MEKHANIKA TVERDOGO TELA; respublikanskii mezhvedomstvennyi sbornik nauchnykh trudov. (Text in Russian) 1969. a. (Akademiya Nauk Ukrainskoi S.S.R, Institut Prikladnoi Matematiki i Mekhaniki) Izdatel'stvo Naukova Dumka, c/o Yu.A. Khramov, Dir, Ul. Repina, 3, Kiev 252 601, Ukrainian S.S.R., U.S.S.R. (Subscr. to: Mezhdunarodnaya Kniga, Moscow, G-200, Russian S.F.S.R., U.S.S.R.) Ed. P.V. Kharlamov. Indexed: Math.R. Met.Abstr. Sci.Abstr. World Alum.Abstr.

533   GW   ISSN 0374-1257
MITTEILUNGEN AUS DEM MAX-PLANCK-INSTITUT FUER STROEMUNGSFORSCHUNG. 1950. irreg no.81, 1986. price varies. Max-Planck-Institut fuer Stroemungsforschung, Bunsenstr. 10, 3400 Goettingen, W. Germany (B.R.D.) Ed. E.A. Mueller. circ. 300. Indexed: Appl.Mech.Rev.
Formerly: Mitteilungen aus dem Max-Planck-Institut fuer Stroemungsforschung und der Aerodynamischen Versuchsansalt (ISSN 0076-5678)

530 540   NE
PHYSICS AND CHEMISTRY OF MATERIALS WITH LOW-DIMENSIONAL STRUCTURES. (Text in English) 1976. irreg. price varies. D. Reidel Publishing Co., Box 17, 3300 AA Dordrecht, Netherlands (And 190 Old Derby St., Hingham, MA 02043) Ed. E. Mooser. Indexed: Chem.Abstr.
Formerly: Physics and Chemistry of Materials with Layered Structures.

531   PL   ISSN 0372-9486
POLITECHNIKA KRAKOWSKA. ZESZYTY NAUKOWE. MECHANIKA. (Text in Polish; summaries in English, French, German, Russian) 1956. irreg. price varies. Politechnika Krakowska, Ul. Warszawska 24, 31-155 Krakow, Poland (Dist. by: Ars Polona-Ruch, Krakowskie Przedmiescie 7, 00-068 Warsaw, Poland) bibl. charts. illus. circ. 200. Indexed: Math.R.

531   PL   ISSN 0079-4538
POLITECHNIKA POZNANSKA. ZESZYTY NAUKOWE. MECHANIKA. (Text in Polish; summaries in English and Russian) 1958. irreg. price varies. Politechnika Poznanska, Pl. Curie-Sklodowskiej 5, Poznan, Poland. Ed. Czeslaw Cempel. circ. 150.

POLITECHNIKA WROCLAWSKA. INSTYTUT MATERIALOZNAWSTWA I MECHANIKI TECHNICZNEJ. PRACE NAUKOWE. KONFERENCJE. see *ENGINEERING — Mechanical Engineering*

531   PL   ISSN 0324-9565
POLITECHNIKA WROCLAWSKA. INSTYTUT MATERIALOZNAWSTWA I MECHANIKI TECHNICZNEJ. PRACE NAUKOWE. MONOGRAFIE. (Text in Polish; summaries in English and Russian) 1969. irreg., no.18, 1986. price varies. Politechnika Wroclawska, Wybrzeze Wyspianskiego 27, 50-370 Wroclaw, Poland (Dist. by: Ars Polona-Ruch, Krakowskie Przedmiescie 7, Warsaw, Poland) Ed. Jerzy Ciekot.

531   PL   ISSN 0370-0917
POLITECHNIKA WROCLAWSKA. INSTYTUT MATERIALOZNAWSTWA I MECHANIKI TECHNICZNEJ. PRACE NAUKOWE. STUDIA I MATERIALY. (Text in Polish; summaries in English and Russian) 1970. irreg., no.26, 1983. price varies. Politechnika Wroclawska, Wybrzeze Wyspianskiego 27, 50-370 Wroclaw, Poland (Dist. by: Ars Polona-Ruch, Krakowskie Przedmiescie 7, Warsaw, Poland) Ed. Marian Kloza. Indexed: Chem.Abstr.

621.3   PL   ISSN 0324-9395
POLITECHNIKA WROCLAWSKA. INSTYTUT TECHNIKI CIEPLNEJ I MECHANIKI PLYNOW. PRACE NAUKOWE. KONFERENCJE. (Text in Polish and English) 1974. irreg., no.4, 1986. price varies. Politechnika Wroclawska, Wybrzeze Wyspianskiego 27, 50-370 Wroclaw, Poland (Dist. by: Ars Polona-Ruch, Krakowskie Przedmiescie 7, Warsaw, Poland) Ed. Jery Ciekot. circ. 575.

621.3   PL   ISSN 0324-9387
POLITECHNIKA WROCLAWSKA. INSTYTUT TECHNIKI CIEPLNEJ I MECHANIKI PLYNOW. PRACE NAUKOWE. MONOGRAFIE. (Text in Polish; summaries in English and Russian) 1970. irreg., no.11, 1985. price varies. Politechnika Wroclawska, Wybrzeze Wyspianskiego 27, 50-370 Wroclaw, Poland (Dist. by: Ars Polona-Ruch, Krakowskie Przedmiescie 7, Warsaw, Poland) Ed. Jerzy Ciekot.

621.3   PL   ISSN 0324-9409
POLITECHNIKA WROCLAWSKA. INSTYTUT TECHNIKI CIEPLNEJ I MECHANIKI PLYNOW. PRACE NAUKOWE. STUDIA I MATERIALY. (Text in Polish; summaries in English and Russian) 1970. irreg., no.13, 1987. price varies. Politechnika Wroclawska, Wybrzeze Wyspianskiego 27, 50-370 Wroclaw, Poland (Dist. by: Ars Polona-Ruch, Krakowskie Przedmiescie 7, Warsaw, Poland) Ed. Jeny Ciekot.

531 620.1   PL   ISSN 0079-3337
POLSKA AKADEMIA NAUK. ODDZIAL W KRAKOWIE. KOMISJA MECHANIKI STOSOWANEJ. PRACE: MECHANIKA. (Text in English and Polish; summaries in English and Russian) 1966. irreg., no.12, 1986. price varies. Ossolineum, Publishing House of the Polish Academy of Sciences, Rynek 9, Wroclaw, Poland (Dist. by: Ars Polona-Ruch, Krakowskie Przedmiescie 7, Warsaw, Poland) Ed. Roman Ciesielski.
Formerly: Polska Akademia Nauk. Komisja Nauk Technicznych. Prace.

671   UR
PRIKLADNAYA MEKHANIKA I PRIBOROSTROENIE. 1973. irreg. 1.07 Rub. (Leningradskii Universitet) Lenizdat, Fontanka, 59, Leningrad, Russian S.F.S.R., U.S.S.R. illus.

PROBLEMY ISTORII MATEMATIKI I MEKHANIKI. see *MATHEMATICS*

532   US   ISSN 0035-4538
RHEOLOGY BULLETIN. 1937. irreg. membership. Society of Rheology, Center for Composite Materials, University of Delaware, Newark, DE 19716. TEL 302-451-2328. Ed. A.B. Metzner.

531   FR   ISSN 0081-0835
SOCIETE D'ERGONOMIE DE LANGUE FRANCAISE. ACTES DU CONGRES. 1963. irreg. Societe d'Ergonomie de la Langue Francaise, Faculte de Medecine de Caen, Laboratoire de Physiologie, CHU Cote de Nacre, 14032 Caen, France.

531   NE
STUDIES IN APPLIED MECHANICS. 1979. irreg., vol.12, 1985. price varies. Elsevier Science Publishers B.V., Box 211, 1000 AE Amsterdam, Netherlands. Indexed: Sci.Abstr.

532   US   ISSN 0082-0849
SYMPOSIUM ON NAVAL HYDRODYNAMICS. PROCEEDINGS. 1956. biennial. price varies. U.S. Department of the Navy, Office of Naval Research, 800 North Quincy, Arlington, VA 22217. TEL 202-545-6700.

T & A M REPORT. (Department of Theoretical and Applied Mechanics) see *ENGINEERING — Engineering Mechanics And Materials*

VOPROSY GIDRODINAMIKI I TEPLOOBMENA V KRIOGENNYKH SISTEMAKH. see *PHYSICS — Heat*

PHYSICS — Nuclear Energy

A E. see *ENERGY*

539   CN   ISSN 0067-0367
A E C L REPORT SERIES. (Text in English; abstracts in English and French) 1952. irreg. price varies. Atomic Energy of Canada Ltd., Chalk River Nuclear Laboratories, Technical Information Branch, S.D.D.O., Sta. 14, Chalk River, Ont. K0J 1J0, Canada. TEL 613-687-5581. cum.index. Indexed: Chem.Abstr. INIS Atomind.

539.7   FI   ISSN 0355-2721
ACTA POLYTECHNICA SCANDINAVICA. APPLIED PHYSICS SERIES. (Text and summaries in English) irreg. (4-5yr.) Fmk.130. Teknillisten Tieteiden Akatemia - Finnish Academy of Technical Sciences, Kansakoulukatu 10 A, SF-00100 Helsinki 10, Finland. Ed. Mauri Luukkala. index; cum.index (1958-1985) circ. 250. (also avail. in microfilm from UMI; back issues avail.; reprint service avail. from UMI) Indexed: Chem.Abstr. Curr.Cont. Met.Abstr. Sci.Abstr. ASCA. World Alum.Abstr.
Formerly: Acta Polytechnica Scandinavica. Physics Including Nucleonics Series (ISSN 0001-6888)

539   US   ISSN 0065-2199
ADVANCES IN ATOMIC AND MOLECULAR PHYSICS. 1965. irreg., vol.22, 1986. Academic Press, Inc., Orlando, FL 32887. TEL 305-345-2000. Ed. D.R. Bates. index. Indexed: Chem.Abstr. Sci.Cit.Ind. Ind.Sci.Rev. Mass Spectr.Bull. Phys.Ber.

539   US   ISSN 0065-2970
ADVANCES IN NUCLEAR PHYSICS. 1968. irreg. price varies. Plenum Publishing Corp., 233 Spring St., New York, NY 10013. TEL 212-620-8047. Eds. J.W. Negele, E. Vogt. Indexed: Sci.Cit.Ind. ASCA. Ind.Sci.Rev. Phys.Ber.

539 621.48   US   ISSN 0065-2989
ADVANCES IN NUCLEAR SCIENCE AND TECHNOLOGY. 1962. irreg., vol.9, 1976. Academic Press, Inc., Orlando, FL 32887. TEL 305-345-2000. Eds. E.J. Henley, H. Kouts. index. Indexed: Chem.Abstr.

539 570   IO
ALMANAK NUKLIR BIOLOGI DAN KIMIA.* Short title: Almanak NUBIKA. 1974. a. $14. National Atomic Energy Agency, Pusat Nuklir, Biologi dan Kimia, P.O.B. 85 KBY, Jakarta South, Indonesia. illus.

539   US
AMERICAN NUCLEAR SOCIETY. PROCEEDINGS OF THE EXECUTIVE CONFERENCE. irreg., latest 1983. price varies. American Nuclear Society, 555 N. Kensington Ave., La Grange Park, IL 60525. TEL 312-352-6611.

539   US
AMERICAN NUCLEAR SOCIETY. PROCEEDINGS OF THE NATIONAL TOPICAL MEETING. irreg. price varies. American Nuclear Society, 555 N. Kensington Ave., La Grange Park, IL 60525. TEL 312-352-6611.

539   US
AMERICAN NUCLEAR SOCIETY. PROCEEDINGS OF THE PACIFIC BASIN CONFERENCE ON NUCLEAR POWER DEVELOPMENT. 1976. irreg., 5th, 1985. price varies. American Nuclear Society, 555 N. Kensington Ave., La Grange Park, IL 60525. TEL 312-352-6611. (reprint service avail.)

621.48   FR   ISSN 0066-2593
ANNUAIRE DE L'ACTIVITE NUCLEAIRE FRANCAISE. 1962. irreg. 90 F. Groupe Intersyndical de l'Industrie Nucleaire (GIIN), Forum Atomique Francais, 15 rue Beaujon, 75008 Paris, France. circ. 3,000.
Formerly: Annuaire Bilingue de l'Industrie Nucleaire Francaise.

PHYSICS — NUCLEAR ENERGY

539   US   ISSN 0163-8998
ANNUAL REVIEW OF NUCLEAR AND PARTICLE SCIENCE. 1952. a. $34. Annual Reviews Inc., 4139 El Camino Way, Palo Alto, CA 94306. TEL 415-493-4400. Ed. J.D. Jackson. bibl. index. cum.index. (back issues avail.; reprint service avail. from ISI) Indexed: Biol.Abstr. Chem.Abstr. Curr.Cont. Sci.Abstr. Sci.Cit.Ind. GeoRef. M.M.R.I. Nucl.Sci.Abstr. Phys.Ber.
    Formerly (until 1978): Annual Review of Nuclear Science (ISSN 0066-4243)

539.7   US
ARIZONA RADIATION REVIEW.* 1981. irreg. Radiation Regulatory Agency, 4814 S. 40th St., Phoenix, AZ 85040. Ed. Cindy Osborne. circ. 6,000. (tabloid format; back issues avail.)
    Formerly: Radiation Review.

539.7   PH   ISSN 0115-3757
ATOMEDIA. (Text in English) 1976. biennial. Philippine Atomic Energy Commission, Don Marianos Marcas Ave., Diliman, Quezon City, Philippines. Ed. Remedios A. Savellano. circ. 2,000. (back issues avail.)

539   CN   ISSN 0067-0383
ATOMIC ENERGY OF CANADA. ANNUAL REPORT. 1952/53. a. free. Atomic Energy of Canada Ltd., Chalk River Nuclear Laboratories, Technical Information Branch, S.D.D.O., Sta. 14, Chalk River, Ont. K0J 1J0, Canada. TEL 613-687-5581. Indexed: INIS Atomind.

539.7   JA
ATOMIC ENERGY POCKETBOOK. (Text in Japanese) 1964. a. 4200 Yen. Japan Atomic Industrial Forum, Inc. - Nihon Genshiryoku Sangyo Kaigi, Toshin Bldg. 1-1-13, Shimbashi, Minato-ku, Tokyo 105, Japan.

539.7   US   ISSN 0090-6360
ATOMIC PHYSICS. Represents: International Conference on Atomic Physics. Proceedings. 1969. irreg. price varies. Plenum Publishing Corp., 233 Spring St., New York, NY 10013. TEL 212-620-8047. illus. Indexed: Chem.Abstr.

539 621.48   AT   ISSN 0067-1657
AUSTRALIA. ATOMIC ENERGY COMMISSION. RESEARCH ESTABLISHMENT. A A E C/E. 1958. irreg. $2.20 restricted distribution. Australian Atomic Energy Commission, Menai, N.S.W. 2234, Australia. index. cum.index: 1958-1981. (also avail. in microfiche) Indexed: INIS Atomind. Nucl.Sci.Abstr.

539 621.48   AT
AUSTRALIA. ATOMIC ENERGY COMMISSION. RESEARCH ESTABLISHMENT. A A E C/IP. 1975. irreg. Aus.$2. Australian Atomic Energy Commission, Menai, N.S.W. 2234, Australia. circ. controlled. (also avail. in microfiche) Indexed: INIS Atomind.

539 621.48   AT   ISSN 0067-1665
AUSTRALIA. ATOMIC ENERGY COMMISSION. RESEARCH ESTABLISHMENT. A A E C/M. 1959. irreg. $2.20 restricted distribution. Australian Atomic Energy Commission, Menai, N.S.W. 2234, Australia. index. cum.index: 1959-1981. Indexed: Biol.Abstr. INIS Atomind. Nucl.Sci.Abstr.

539.7   US
BENCHMARK PAPERS IN NUCLEAR PHYSICS. (Each vol. has distinctive title) 1976. irreg., vol.2, 1976. price varies. Van Nostrand Reinhold Company, 7625 Empire Dr., Florence, KY 41042. TEL 606-525-6600. illus. index.

539   II
BHABHA ATOMIC RESEARCH CENTRE. NUCLEAR PHYSICS DIVISION. ANNUAL REPORT. 1971. a. $5. Bhabha Atomic Research Centre, Trombay, Bombay 400085, India. circ. controlled. Indexed: Chem.Abstr. Nucl.Sci.Abstr.

539.7   US   ISSN 0092-1548
BROOKHAVEN HIGHLIGHTS. 1971. a. Brookhaven National Laboratory, Upton, NY 11973 TEL 516-282-2123. (Orders to: National Technical Information Service, 5285 Port Royal Rd., Springfield, VA 22151) Eds. J.B. Horner Kuper, Ken Ryan. illus. (also avail. in microfiche)

539.7   US
BROOKHAVEN LECTURE SERIES. no.83, 1969. irreg., no.145, 1977. Brookhaven National Laboratory, Upton, NY 11973 TEL 516-282-2123. (Orders to: National Technical Information Service, 5285 Port Royal Rd., Springfield, VA 22151) (back issues avail.) Indexed: Biol.Abstr.

539.7   EI
BUREAU EURISOTOP. CAHIERS D'INFORMATION. (Texts available in Dutch, English, French, German or Italian) 1963. irreg., latest issue 1975. free. Bureau Eurisotop, Rue de la Loi 200, 1049 Brussels, Belgium. circ. controlled. Indexed: INIS Atomind. Nucl.Sci.Abstr.

539.7   EI
BUREAU EURISOTOP. INFORMATIONS TECHNICO-ECONOMIQUES. (Texts available in Dutch, English, French, German or Italian) 1963. irreg., latest issue 1975. free. Bureau Eurisotop, Rue de la Loi 200, 1049 Brussels, Belgium. circ. controlled. Indexed: INIS Atomind. Nucl.Sci.Abstr.

539.7   JA
BUYERS' GUIDE: NUCLEAR INDUSTRY IN JAPAN. (Text in English) 1961. irreg. 2500 Yen. Japan Atomic Industrial Forum, Inc., Toshin Bldg., 1-1-13, Shimbashi, Minato-ku, Tokyo 105, Japan.

C E G B ABSTRACTS. (Central Electricity Generating Board) see *ELECTRICITY AND ELECTRICAL ENGINEERING — Abstracting, Bibliographies, Statistics*

C E R N ANNUAL REPORT. see *PHYSICS*

C E R N-H E R A REPORTS. see *PHYSICS*

C E R N REPORTS. see *PHYSICS*

C E R N SCHOOL OF PHYSICS. PROCEEDINGS. see *PHYSICS*

539   CN
CANADIAN NUCLEAR ASSOCIATION. ANNUAL INTERNATIONAL CONFERENCE PROCEEDINGS. 1961. a. Canadian Nuclear Association, c/o D.T. Waechter, 111 Elizabeth St., 11th Fl., Toronto, Ont. M5G 1P7, Canada. TEL 416-977-6152. circ. 150.
    Former titles (until 1984): Canadian Nuclear Association. Annual International Conference. Summaries (ISSN 0706-1293); Canadian Nuclear Association. Annual Meeting; Canadian Conference on Uranium and Atomic Energy. Proceedings (ISSN 0068-8517)

539   CN   ISSN 0227-1907
CANADIAN NUCLEAR SOCIETY. ANNUAL CONFERENCE PROCEEDINGS. (Text in English) 1980. a. Canadian Nuclear Society, c/o D.T. Waechter, 111 Elizabeth St., 11th Fl., Toronto, Ont. M5G 1P7, Canada. TEL 416-977-6152. Indexed: Chem.Abstr.

539   CN   ISSN 0227-0129
CANADIAN NUCLEAR SOCIETY. ANNUAL CONFERENCE SUMMARIES. French edition: Societe Nucleaire Canadienne. Sommaires du Congres. (Editions in English and French) 1981. a. Canadian Nuclear Society, c/o D.T. Waechter, 111 Elizabeth St., 11th Floor, Toronto, Ont. M5G 1P7, Canada. TEL 416-977-6152.
    Formerly: Canadian Nuclear Society. Transactions (ISSN 0226-7470)

539.7   EI
COMMISSION OF THE EUROPEAN COMMUNITIES. OPERATION OF NUCLEAR POWER STATIONS. 1982. a. price varies. Office for Official Publications of the European Communities, P.O. Box 1003, L-2985 Luxembourg, Luxembourg (Dist. in the U.S. by: European Communities Information Service, 2100 M St., N.W., Suite 707, Washington, DC 20037)

539 621   US   ISSN 0069-8644
CONFERENCE ON REMOTE SYSTEMS TECHNOLOGY. PROCEEDINGS. 1951. a. $48. American Nuclear Society, 555 N. Kensington Ave., La Grange Park, IL 60525. TEL 312-352-6611. circ. 500. (reprint service avail.) Indexed: Biol.Abstr. Chem.Abstr. Sci.Abstr.

CUMULATIVE BIBLIOGRAPHY OF LITERATURE EXAMINED BY THE RADIATION SHIELDING INFORMATION CENTER. see *PHYSICS — Abstracting, Bibliographies, Statistics*

539 621.48   DK   ISSN 0106-2840
DENMARK. FORSOEGSANSLAEG RISOE. RISOE-R. (Text in English) 1957. irreg., no.455, 1981. price varies. Forsoegsanslaeg Risoe - Risoe National Laboratory, DK-4000 Roskilde, Denmark. circ. 300.
    Formerly: Denmark. Atomenergikomissionens Forsoegsanslaeg, Risoe. Risoe Report (ISSN 0418-6443)

ENVIRONMENTAL COALITION ON NUCLEAR POWER NEWSLETTER. see *ENERGY*

539 621.48   FR   ISSN 0071-8467
FRANCE. COMMISSARIAT A L'ENERGIE ATOMIQUE. ANNUAL REPORT. 1945. a. free. Commissariat a l'Energie Atomique, 29-33 rue de la Federation, 75015 Paris, France. circ. 20,000. Indexed: GeoRef.

539.7   JA
HANDBOOK OF NUCLEAR SAFEGUARDS. (Text in Japanese) 1984. a. 4800 Yen. Japan Atomic Industrial Forum, Inc., Toshin Bldg., 1-1-13, Shimbashi, Minato-ku, Tokyo 105, Japan.

539.721   US
HAWAII CONFERENCE ON HIGH ENERGY PHYSICS. 1972. biennial. price varies. (University of Hawaii, High Energy Physics Group) University of Hawaii Press, 2840 Kolowalu St., Honolulu, HI 96822. TEL 808-948-8697. (reprint service avail. from UMI,ISI)
    Formerly: Hawaii Topical Conference in Particle Physics. Proceedings (ISSN 0073-1153)

539.7   UN
I A E A TECHNICAL DOCUMENTS SERIES. (Text in English) 1966. irreg. free. International Atomic Energy Agency, Wagramer Strasse 5, Box 100, A-1400 Vienna, Austria. circ. 200. (also avail. in microfiche)

621.3 621.3   US
I E E E CONFERENCE ON HUMAN FACTORS AND NUCLEAR SAFETY. CONFERENCE RECORD. Variant title: I E E E Conference on Human Factors and Power Plants. 1979. irreg., 3rd 1985. price varies. (I E E E, Power Engineering Society) Institute of Electrical and Electronics Engineers, Inc., 345 E. 47th St., New York, NY 10017 TEL 212-705-7900. (Subscr. address: 445 Hoes Lane, Piscataway, NJ 08854)
    Formerly (1979-1981): I E E E Standards Workshop on Human Factors and Nuclear Safety. Conference Record.

I N I S REFERENCE SERIES. see *LIBRARY AND INFORMATION SCIENCES*

539   II   ISSN 0073-618X
INDIA. DEPARTMENT OF ATOMIC ENERGY. ANNUAL REPORT. (Text in English and Hindi) 1963. a. free. Department of Atomic Energy, Publications Officer, Chhatrapati Shivaji Maharaj Marg, Bombay 400039, India. circ. 4,100.

539.7   SP   ISSN 0081-3397
INFORMES J.E.N. (Text in Spanish; summaries in English and Spanish) 1956. irreg., 40-50/yr. price varies. (Centro de Investigaciones Energeticas, Medioambientales y Tecnologicas, Junta de Energia Nuclear) Ministerio de Industria, Avda. Complutense, 28040 Madrid, Spain. bk. rev. circ. 300. (back issues avail.) Indexed: Chem.Abstr. Nucl.Sci.Abstr.

539.7   FR
INSTITUT DES SCIENCES NUCLEAIRES GRENOBLE. RAPPORT. (Text in French; summaries in English) 1970. biennial. free. Institut des Sciences Nucleaires Grenoble, 53 av. des Martyrs, 38026 Grenoble Cedex, France. TEL 76-47-66-36. circ. 500. (back issues avail.) Indexed: INIS Atomind.
    Formerly (until 1981): Universite Scientifique et Medical de Grenoble. Institut des Sciences Nucleaires. Rapport Annuel (ISSN 0399-127X)

539 621.48   US   ISSN 0073-9472
INSTITUTE OF NUCLEAR MATERIALS MANAGEMENT. PROCEEDINGS OF ANNUAL MEETING. 1960. a. $50. Institute of Nuclear Materials Management, Inc., 60 Revere Dr., Ste. 500, Northbrook, IL 60062-1563. TEL 312-480-9573.

530   RM
INSTITUTUL DE FIZICA ATOMICA. SESIUNEA STIINTIFICA ANUALA DE COMUNICARI; PROGRAM SI REZUMATE. a. Institutul de Fizica Atomica, Soseaua Magurele, Bucharest, Rumania.

539.7 621.48   UN   ISSN 0085-2023
INTERNATIONAL ATOMIC ENERGY AGENCY. ANNUAL REPORT. (Report of Board of Governors to General Conference) (Editions in English, French, Russian, Spanish) 1958. a. free. International Atomic Energy Agency, Wagramer Str. 5, Box 100, A-1400 Vienna, Austria. circ. 4,600.

INTERNATIONAL ATOMIC ENERGY AGENCY. LEGAL SERIES. see *LAW*

539 621.48   UN
INTERNATIONAL ATOMIC ENERGY AGENCY. NUCLEAR POWER REACTORS IN THE WORLD. (Text in English) a. price varies. International Atomic Energy Agency, Wagramer Str. 5, Box 100, A-1400 Vienna, Austria (Dist. in U.S. by: Bernan Associates-Unipub, 4611-F Assembly Dr., Lanham, MD 20706-4391)
   Formerly: International Atomic Energy Agency. Power Reactors in Member States.

539 621.48   UN   ISSN 0074-1876
INTERNATIONAL ATOMIC ENERGY AGENCY. PANEL PROCEEDINGS SERIES. (Text in English, French or Spanish) 1960. irreg. price varies. International Atomic Energy Agency, Wagramer Str. 5, Box 100, A-1400 Vienna, Austria (Dist. in U.S. by: Bernan Associates-Unipub, 4611-F Assembly Dr., Lanham, MD 20706-4391) Indexed: Excerp.Med.

539 621.48   UN   ISSN 0074-1884
INTERNATIONAL ATOMIC ENERGY AGENCY. PROCEEDINGS SERIES. (Text in English, French, Russian and Spanish) 1959. irreg. price varies. International Atomic Energy Agency, Wagramer Str. 5, Box 100, A-1400 Vienna, Austria (Dist. in U.S. by: Bernan Associates-Unipub, 4611-F Assembly Dr., Lanham, MD 20706-4391) Indexed: Biol.Abstr. Excerp.Med.

539 621.48   UN   ISSN 0074-1906
INTERNATIONAL ATOMIC ENERGY AGENCY. TECHNICAL DIRECTORIES. (Text in English) 1959. irreg. price varies. International Atomic Energy Agency, Wagramer Str. 5, Box 100, A-1400 Vienna, Austria (Dist. in U.S. by: Bernan Associates-Unipub, 4611-F Assembly Dr., Lanham, MD 20706-4391)

539 621.48   UN   ISSN 0074-1914
INTERNATIONAL ATOMIC ENERGY AGENCY. TECHNICAL REPORT SERIES. (Text mainly in English; some in French, Russian or Spanish) 1960. irreg. price varies. International Atomic Energy Agency, Wagramer Str. 5, Box 100, A-1400 Vienna, Austria (Dist. in U.S. by: Bernan Associates-Unipub, 4611-F Assembly Dr., Lanham, MD 20706-4391) Indexed: Biol.Abstr. Ocean.Abstr. Pollut.Abstr. Soils & Fert.

539.722   II   ISSN 0074-3046
INTERNATIONAL CONFERENCE ON COSMIC RAYS. (PROCEEDINGS) biennial, 18th, 1983, India. $120. Tata Institute of Fundamental Research, c/o Prof. P.V. Ramana Murthy, Colaba, Bombay 5, India.
   Proceedings published in host country

539.75   US
INTERNATIONAL CONFERENCE ON THE PHYSICS OF ELECTRONIC AND ATOMIC COLLISIONS. ABSTRACTS OF CONTRIBUTED PAPERS AND INVITED PAPERS. Variant titles: Electronic and Atomic Collisions. Physics of Electronic and Atomic Collisions. (Publisher varies for each conference; 7th, 10th, 11th, 12th pub. by North Holland) 1958. irreg., 13th, 1983, Berlin. $150. International Union of Pure and Applied Physics, Commission on Atomic and Molecular Physics and Spectroscopy, c/o John S. Risley, Sec., Department of Physics, North Carolina State University, Raleigh, NC 27695-8202. TEL 919-737-2521. circ. 1,500. Indexed: Phys.Abstr.
   Formerly: International Conference on the Physics of Electronic and Atomic Collisions. Papers (ISSN 0074-333X)

INTERNATIONAL DIRECTORY OF NUCLEAR UTILITIES. see *ENERGY*

539.7   US
INTERSOCIETY ENERGY CONVERSION CONFERENCE. PROCEEDINGS. Variant title: I E C E C. (In 3 vols.) a. price varies. American Nuclear Society, 555 N. Kensington Ave., La Grange Park, IL 60525 TEL 312-352-6611. (And American Institute of Chemical Engineers, 345 E. 47th St., New York, NY 10017) (reprint service avail.) Indexed: Chem.Abstr. API Abstr.

621.48   IS   ISSN 0333-5771
ISRAEL. ATOMIC ENERGY COMMISSION. ANNUAL REPORT. a. exchange basis. Israel Atomic Energy Commission, Soreq Nuclear Research Centre, Yavne 70600, Israel.

621.48   IS   ISSN 0075-0980
ISRAEL. ATOMIC ENERGY COMMISSION. IA-REPORTS. (Text in English or Hebrew, with English abstracts) 1958. irreg., latest issue 1986. exchange basis. ‡ Israel Atomic Energy Commission, Soreq Nuclear Research Centre, Yavne, Israel 70600. Indexed: Chem.Abstr.

539.7   JA
J A E R I REPORTS. LIST. (Text in English or Japanese) a. Japan Atomic Energy Research Institute, Department of Technical Information, Tokai-mura, Naka-gun, Ibaraki-ken 319-11, Japan.

523.01   US
J I L A DATA CENTER. REPORT. 1965. irreg. free. Joint Institute for Laboratory Astrophysics, University of Colorado, Boulder, CO 80309. TEL 303-492-7801. Ed. Jean W. Gallagher. Indexed: Chem.Abstr.
   Formerly: J I L A Information Center. Report (ISSN 0449-1343)

539 621.48   JA   ISSN 0449-4830
JAPAN ATOMIC ENERGY COMMISSION. ANNUAL REPORT/GENSHIRYOKU NENPO. (Text in English) 1961. a. exchange basis. Japan Atomic Energy Commission - Genshiryoku Iinkai, 2-2-1 Kasumigaseki, Chiyoda-ku, Tokyo 100, Japan. Ed.Bd. circ. 300.

539.7   EI
JOINT NUCLEAR RESEARCH CENTER, ISPRA, ITALY. ANNUAL REPORT. a. Commission of the European Communities, Luxembourg, Luxembourg (Dist. in the U.S. by: European Community Information Service, 2100 M St., N.W., Ste. 707 Washington, DC 20037)

539 621.48   GW   ISSN 0171-3191
KERNFORSCHUNGSZENTRUM KARLSRUHE. ERGEBNISBERICHT UEBER FORSCHUNG UND ENTWICKLUNG. 1970. a. DM.50. Kernforschungszentrum Karlsruhe GmbH, Weberstr. 5, Postfach 3640, 7500 Karlsruhe, W. Germany (B.R.D.) illus. circ. 1,000. Indexed: Chem.Abstr.
   Formerly: Gesellschaft fuer Kernforschung. Bericht ueber Forschungs- und Entwicklungsarbeiten.

539.7   JA   ISSN 0386-0752
KYOTO UNIVERSITY. INSTITUTE OF ATOMIC ENERGY. RESEARCH ACTIVITIES. (Text in English) 1968. a. Kyoto University, Institute of Atomic Energy - Kyoto Daigaku Genshi Enerugi Kenkyusho, Gokasho, Uji 611, Japan. Ed.Bd.

539.7   JA
KYOTO UNIVERSITY. INSTITUTE OF ATOMIC ENERGY. TECHNICAL REPORTS/KYOTO DAIGAKU GENSHI ENERUGI KENKYUSHO KENKYU HOKOKU. (Text in English) 1951. irreg. Kyoto University, Institute of Atomic Energy - Kyoto Daigaku Genshi Enerugi Kenkyusho, Gokasho, Uji 611, Japan.

KYOTO UNIVERSITY. RESEARCH REACTOR INSTITUTE. ANNUAL REPORTS. see *CHEMISTRY — Inorganic Chemistry*

539   US   ISSN 0075-7888
LANDOLT-BOERNSTEIN, ZAHLENWERTE UND FUNKTIONEN AUS NATURWISSENSCHAFTEN UND TECHNIK. NEUE SERIE. GROUP 1: NUCLEAR PHYSICS/LANDOLT-BOERNSTEIN NUMERICAL DATA AND FUNCTIONAL RELATIONSHIPS IN SCIENCE AND TECHNOLOGY. NEW SERIES. 1961. irreg. price varies. Springer-Verlag, 175 Fifth Ave., New York, NY 10010 TEL 212-460-1500. (Also Berlin, Heidelberg, Vienna) (reprint service avail. from ISI)

539   US   ISSN 0075-7918
LANDOLT-BOERNSTEIN, ZAHLENWERTE UND FUNKTIONEN AUS NATURWISSENSCHAFTEN UND TECHNIK. NEUE SERIE. GROUP 2: ATOMIC PHYSICS. 1965. irreg., vol.17B, 1986. price varies. Springer-Verlag, 175 Fifth Ave., New York, NY 10010 TEL 212-460-1500. (Also Berlin, Heidelberg, Tokyo and Vienna) (reprint service avail. from ISI)

539.733   US
MICHIGAN STATE UNIVERSITY. NATIONAL SUPERCONDUCTING CYCLOTRON LABORATORY (PUBLICATION) no.21, 1964. irreg., no.38, 1982. Michigan State University, Superconducting Cyclotron Laboratory, East Lansing, MI 48824. TEL 517-355-9671. circ. 300.
   Formerly: Michigan State University. Department of Physics. Cyclotron Project (Publication) (ISSN 0076-8146)

539.7   SZ   ISSN 0259-9805
MUON CATALYZED FUSION. 1986. a. 305 Fr. J.C. Baltzer AG, Scientific Publishing Company, Wettsteinplatz 10, CH-4058 Basel, Switzerland. Eds. L.I. Ponomarev, C. Petitjean.

539.7   US   ISSN 0078-088X
N M R (Nuclear Magnetic Resonance); basic principles and progress. (Text mainly in English, occasionally in German) 1969. irreg., vol.20, 1982. price varies. Springer - Verlag, 175 Fifth Ave., New York, NY 10010 TEL 212-460-1500. (And Berlin, Heidelberg, Tokyo and Vienna) Ed. E. Fluck. illus. (reprint service avail. from ISI)

539   JA
N S R A MEMO. (Text in Japanese) 1966. irreg. exchange basis. Nuclear Safety Research Association - Genshiryoku Anzen Kenkyu Kyokai, 1-2-2 Uchisaiwai-cho, Chiyoda-ku, Tokyo 100, Japan. abstr.

539 621.48   JA
NIHON UNIVERSITY. ATOMIC ENERGY RESEARCH INSTITUTE. ANNUAL REPORT. (Text in English) 1968. a. exchange basis. Nihon University, Atomic Energy Research Institute, 1-8 Kanda Surugadai, Chiyoda-ku, Tokyo 101, Japan. circ. 280.

539.7   JA
NUCLEAR ALMANAC/GENSHIRYOKU NENKAN. (Text in Japanese) 1957. a. 5600 Yen. Japan Atomic Industrial Forum, Inc. - Nihon Genshiryoku Sangyo Kaigi, Toshin Bldg., 1-1-13 Shimbashi, Minato-ku, Tokyo 105, Japan.

539   CN   ISSN 0383-8536
NUCLEAR CANADA. YEARBOOK. (Includes: Canadian Nuclear Industry Buyer's Guide) 1976. a. Canadian Nuclear Association, c/o D.T. Waechter, 111 Elizabeth St., 11th Fl., Toronto, Ont. M5G 1P7, Canada. TEL 416-977-6152. circ. 2,500.

539.7   UN
NUCLEAR DATA NEWSLETTER. (Text in English) 1979. irreg. free. International Atomic Energy Agency, Wagramer Strasse 5, Box 100, A-1400 Vienna, Austria. circ. 2,300.

PHYSICS — NUCLEAR ENERGY

621.48   US   ISSN 0029-5574
NUCLEAR NEWS BUYERS GUIDE. Variant title: Nuclear News Industry Report. 1969. a. $64 or with subscr. to Nuclear News. American Nuclear Society, 555 N. Kensington Ave., La Grange Park, IL 60525. TEL 312-352-6611. Ed. Jon Payne. adv. circ. 15,000.

539.7   US
NUCLEAR PHYSICS MONOGRAPHS. 1978. irreg. price varies. Plenum Publishing Corp., 233 Spring St., New York, NY 10013. TEL 212-620-8047. Eds. Erich W. Vogt, John W. Negele.

539.7   JA
NUCLEAR POWER PLANTS IN THE WORLD/ GENSHIRYOKU HATSUDENSYO. (Text in English) 1962. a. 2500 Yen. Japan Atomic Industrial Forum, Inc. - Nihon Genshiryoku Sangyo Kaigi, Toshin Bldg., 1-1-13 Shimbashi, Minato-ku, Tokyo 105, Japan.

539   621   US
NUCLEAR SCIENCE TECHNOLOGY MONOGRAPH SERIES. 1966. irreg. American Nuclear Society, 555 N. Kensington Ave., La Grange Park, IL 60525. TEL 312-352-6611. (Co-sponsors: U.S. Department of Energy; U.S. Nuclear Regulatory Commission) bk. rev. circ. 1,000. Indexed: Biol.Abstr.
Formerly: A E C/A N S Monographs (ISSN 0065-9487)

539.7   630   615.842   PH
NUCLEUS. (Text in English) 1960. a. P.20($20) Radioisotope Society of the Philippines, c/o Philippine Atomic Energy Commission, Don Mariano Marcos Avenue, Diliman, Quezon City, Philippines. Ed. Aida D. Davila Eugenio. circ. 500.

539.7   DK
O O A - SAERTRYK. 1974. irreg., no.25, 1985. Organisationen til Oplysning Om Atomkraft, Ryesgade 19, 2200 Copenhagen, Denmark.

539   621.48   FR   ISSN 0078-625X
ORGANIZATION FOR ECONOMIC COOPERATION AND DEVELOPMENT. NUCLEAR ENERGY AGENCY. ACTIVITY REPORT. (Was European Nuclear Energy Agency until 1972 when Japan became first non-European member.) (English and French Editions) 1958. a. free. Organization for Economic Cooperation and Development, Nuclear Energy Agency, 38 bd. Suchet, 75016 Paris, France (U.S. subscr. to: O.E.C.D. Publications and Information Center, 1750 Pennsylvania Ave. N.W., Washington, DC 20006) charts. illus. stat. circ. 3,500. (also avail. in microfiche)

539   621.381   FR
ORGANIZATION FOR ECONOMIC COOPERATION AND DEVELOPMENT. NUCLEAR ENERGY AGENCY. SUMMARY OF NUCLEAR POWER AND FUEL CYCLE DATA IN O E C D MEMBER COUNTRIES. (Editions in English and French) 1983. a. free. Organization for Economic Cooperation and Development, Nuclear Energy Agency, 38 bd. Suchet, 75016 Paris, France.

539   JA   ISSN 0473-4580
OSAKA UNIVERSITY. LABORATORY OF NUCLEAR STUDIES. ANNUAL REPORT. (Text in English) 1962. a. exchange basis. Osaka University, Laboratory of Nuclear Studies, 1-1 Machikanayama-cho, Toyonaka, Osaka 560, Japan. Ed.Bd.

539.7   660   JA
P N C REVIEW. (Text in English) a. Power Reactor and Nuclear Fuel Development Corporation, 9-13, 1-Chome, Akasaka, Minato-Ku, Tokyo 107, Japan.

539.7   JA
PEOPLES IN ATOMS. (Text in Japanese) 1977. a. 5200 Yen. Japan Atomic Industrial Forum, Inc., Toshin Bldg., 1-1-13, Shimbashi, Minato-ku, Tokyo 105, Japan.

539.7   PH   ISSN 0553-9978
PHILIPPINE ATOMIC ENERGY COMMISSION. ANNUAL REPORT. a. free. ‡ Philippine Atomic Energy Commission, Don Mariano Marcos Ave., Diliman, Quezon City, Phillipines. illus. circ. 1,000. Indexed: Biol.Abstr.

539   PH   ISSN 0079-1490
PHILIPPINES NUCLEAR JOURNAL. 1966. irreg. $10. ‡ Philippine Atomic Energy Commission, Don Mariano Marcos Ave., Diliman, Quezon City, Philippines. Ed. Carlito R. Aleta. circ. 2,000. Indexed: Biol.Abstr.

539.7   544.6   US   ISSN 0079-6565
PROGRESS IN NUCLEAR MAGNETIC RESONANCE SPECTROSCOPY. Variant title: Progress in Nuclear Magnetic Resonance Spectroscopy of Cyclopentadienyl Compounds. 1966. 4/yr. plus a. bound vol. $145 (annual bound volume $138) Pergamon Press, Inc., Journals Division, Maxwell House, Fairview Park, Elmsford, NY 10523 TEL 914-592-7700. (And: Headington Hill Hall, Oxford OX3 0BW, England) Ed. L.H. Sutcliffe. index. (also avail. in microform from MIM,UMI) Indexed: Chem.Abstr. Curr.Cont. Met.Abstr. Sci.Abstr. World Alum.Abstr.

539   JA   ISSN 0289-842X
RIKEN. ACCELERATOR PROGRESS REPORT. (Text in English) 1967. a. 5000 Yen. Institute of Physical and Chemical Research, Cyclotron Laboratory - Rikagaku Kenkyusho, 2-1 Hirosawa, Wako 351-01, Japan.
Former titles: I P C R Accelerator Progress Report; I P C R Cyclotron Progress Report.

539   JA
RIKEN. CYCLOTRON REPORT. (Text in European languages) 1970. irreg. Institute of Physical and Chemical Research, Cyclotron Laboratory - Rikagaku Kenkyusho, 2-1 Hirosawa, Wako 351-01, Japan.
Formerly: I P C R Cyclotron Report.

539   621.48   JA
RIKKYO UNIVERSITY. INSTITUTE FOR ATOMIC ENERGY. REPORT. (Text in English and Japanese) 1966. irreg. exchange basis. Rikkyo University, Institute for Atomic Energy, 10 Matsukoshi, Sajima, Yokosuka-shi 240-01, Japan. circ. 100.

539.7   SZ
S I N NEWSLETTER. (Included in: Schweizerisches Institut fuer Nuklearforschung. Jahresbericht) (Text in English) a. Schweizerisches Institut fuer Nuklearforschung, CH-5234 Villigen, Switzerland. Indexed: Sci.Abstr.
Formerly: S I N Physics Report.

539.7   SZ
SCHWEIZERISCHES INSTITUT FUER NUKLEARFORSCHUNG. JAHRESBERICHT. (Includes: S I N Newsletter) (Text mostly in German) a. Schweizerisches Institut fuer Nuklearforschung, CH-5234 Villigen, Switzerland.

539   CN
T R I U M F ANNUAL REPORT SCIENTIFIC ACTIVITIES. (Tri-University Meson Facility) 1967. a. free. T R I U M F, 4004 Wesbrook Mall, Vancouver, B.C. V6T 2A3, Canada. TEL 604-228-4711. Ed. Dr. George A. Ludgate. Indexed: Nucl.Sci.Abstr.
Formerly (until 1980): T R I U M F Annual Report (ISSN 0082-6367)

539   CN
T R I U M F FINANCIAL AND ADMINISTRATIVE ANNUAL REPORT. (Tri-University Meson Facility) 1980. a. free. T R I U M F, 4004 Wesbrook Mall, Vancouver, B.C. V6T 2A3, Canada. TEL 604-228-4711. Ed. Geroge A. Ludgate.

539.7   614   GW
UEBERSETZUNGEN - KERNTECHNISCHE REGELN. English edition: Translations - Safety Codes and Guides. 1974. irreg. DM.20. Gesellschaft fuer Reaktorsicherheit, Schwertnergasse 1, 5000 Cologne 1, W. Germany (B.R.D.) circ. 300. (reprint service avail. from ISI)

539   621.48   UK   ISSN 0082-7940
UNITED KINGDOM ATOMIC ENERGY AUTHORITY. ANNUAL REPORT. 1954. a. price varies. H.M.S.O., P.O.B. 569, London SE1 9NH, England. (reprint service avail. from UMI)

UNITED NATIONS DISARMAMENT YEARBOOK. see *MILITARY*

UNITED NATIONS ECONOMIC AND SOCIAL COUNCIL. DISARMAMENT STUDY SERIES. see *MILITARY*

539.7   US
U.S. NUCLEAR REGULATORY COMMISSION. WATER REACTOR SAFETY RESEARCH INFORMATION MEETING. PROCEEDINGS. irreg., vol.4, 1984. U.S. Nuclear Regulatory Commission, Office of Nuclear Regulatory Research, Washington, DC 20555.

539.7   540   CN
UNIVERSITE LAVAL. CENTRE DE RECHERCHES SUR LES ATOMES ET LES MOLECULES. RAPPORT ANNUEL; physics and chemistry of atoms and molecules. (Text in French) 1968. a. free. Universite Laval, Centre de Recherches sur les Atomes et les Molecules, Quebec, Que. G1K 7P4, Canada. TEL 418-656-3120. Ed. J.A. Herman. circ. controlled.

539.7   CN
UNIVERSITY OF ALBERTA. NUCLEAR RESEARCH CENTRE. PROGRESS REPORT. 1969. a. free. University of Alberta, Nuclear Research Centre, Edmonton, Alta. T6G 2N5, Canada. TEL 403-432-3637. circ. 300. (back issues avail.)

539   JA
UNIVERSITY OF TOKYO. INSTITUTE FOR NUCLEAR STUDY. ANNUAL REPORT. (Text in English) 1960. a. exchange basis. University of Tokyo, Institute for Nuclear Study - Tokyo Daigaku Genshikaku Kenkyusho, 3-2-1 Midori-cho Tanashi-shi, Tokyo 188, Japan. abstr.

539   JA   ISSN 0495-7814
UNIVERSITY OF TOKYO. INSTITUTE FOR NUCLEAR STUDY. INS-J. (Text in English) 1957. irreg. exchange basis. University of Tokyo, Institute for Nuclear Study - Tokyo Daigaku Genshikaku Kenkyusho, 3-2-1 Midori-cho Tanashi-shi, Tokyo 188, Japan. Indexed: Chem.Abstr.

539   JA
UNIVERSITY OF TOKYO. INSTITUTE FOR NUCLEAR STUDY. INS-PH. (Text in Japanese) 1969. irreg. exchange basis. University of Tokyo, Institute for Nuclear Study - Tokyo Daigaku Genshikaku Kenkyusho, 3-2-1 Midori-cho Tanashi-shi, Tokyo 188, Japan.

539   JA   ISSN 0563-7848
UNIVERSITY OF TOKYO. INSTITUTE FOR NUCLEAR STUDY. INS-PT. (Text in Japanese; summaries in English) 1957. irreg. exchange basis. University of Tokyo, Institute for Nuclear Study - Tokyo Daigaku Genshikaku Kenkyusho, 3-2-1 Midori-cho Tanashi-shi, Tokyo 188, Japan.

539   JA
UNIVERSITY OF TOKYO. INSTITUTE FOR NUCLEAR STUDY. INS-TCH. (Text in Japanese; summaries in English) 1967. irreg. exchange basis. University of Tokyo, Institute for Nuclear Study - Tokyo Daigaku Genshikaku Kenkyusho, 3-2-1 Midori-cho Tanashi-shi, Tokyo 188, Japan.

539   JA
UNIVERSITY OF TOKYO. INSTITUTE FOR NUCLEAR STUDY. INS-TEC. (Text in Japanese; summaries in English) 1971. irreg. exchange basis. University of Tokyo, Institute for Nuclear Study - Tokyo Daigaku Genshikaku Kenkyusho, 3-2-1 Midori-cho Tanashi-shi, Tokyo 188, Japan.

539   JA   ISSN 0563-7872
UNIVERSITY OF TOKYO. INSTITUTE FOR NUCLEAR STUDY. INS-TH. (Text in Japanese; summaries in English) 1954. irreg. exchange basis. University of Tokyo, Institute for Nuclear Study - Tokyo Daigaku Genshikaku Kenkyusho, 3-2-1 Midori-cho Tanashi-shi, Tokyo 188, Japan.

539   JA   ISSN 0563-7880
UNIVERSITY OF TOKYO. INSTITUTE FOR NUCLEAR STUDY. INS-TL. (Text in Japanese; summaries in English) 1954. irreg. exchange basis. University of Tokyo, Institute for Nuclear Study - Tokyo Daigaku Genshikaku Kenkyusho, 3-2-1 Midori-cho Tanashi-shi, Tokyo 188, Japan. Indexed: Chem.Abstr.

539 JA
UNIVERSITY OF TOKYO. INSTITUTE FOR NUCLEAR STUDY. INS-TS. (Text in Japanese; summaries in English) 1967. irreg. exchange basis. University of Tokyo, Institute for Nuclear Study - Tokyo Daigaku Genshikaku Kenkyusho, 3-2-1 Midori-cho Tanashi-shi, Tokyo 188, Japan.

539 JA ISSN 0495-7822
UNIVERSITY OF TOKYO. INSTITUTE FOR NUCLEAR STUDY. REPORT. (Text in English) 1959. irreg. exchange basis. University of Tokyo, Institute for Nuclear Study - Tokyo Daigaku Genshikaku Kenkyusho, 3-2-1 Midori-cho Tanashi-shi, Tokyo 188, Japan.

539.7 UK
WORLD NUCLEAR DIRECTORY. 1961. irreg., 7th edt., 1985. £120. Longman Group Ltd., Fourth Ave., Harlow, Essex CM19 5AA, England (Dist. in U.S. and Canada by Gale Research Co. Ltd., Book Tower, Detroit, MI 48226)
Formerly: Nuclear Research Index.

WORLDWIDE REPORT: NUCLEAR DEVELOPMENT AND PROLIFERATION. see MILITARY

338.4 US
WORLDWIDE URANIUM PRODUCER PROFILES. 1973; N.S. 1977. irreg. Nuclear Assurance Corporation, 5720 Peachtree Pkwy., Norcross, GA 30092. TEL 404-447-1144.
Formerly: Nuclear Industry Status (ISSN 0092-9751)

PHYSICS — Optics

535.8 541 HU ISSN 0065-0412
ABSORPTION SPECTRA IN THE ULTRAVIOLET AND VISIBLE REGION. (Text in English) 1959. irreg. vol.24, 1982. price varies. (Magyar Tudomanyos Akademia) Akademiai Kiado, Publishing House of the Hungarian Academy of Sciences, P.O. Box 24, H-1363 Budapest, Hungary (Distr. in U.S. by Robert E. Krieger Publishing Co. Inc., 645 New York Ave., Huntington, N.Y. 11743) Ed. Laszlo Lang.

578 535 UK ISSN 0065-3012
ADVANCES IN OPTICAL AND ELECTRON MICROSCOPY. 1966. irreg., vol.10, 1987. price varies. Academic Press Inc. (London) Ltd., 24-28 Oval Rd., London NW1 7DX, England (and 111 Fifth Ave., New York, N.Y. 10003) Eds. V.E. Cosslett, R. Barer. Indexed: Biol.Abstr. GeoRef.

535.84 UK ISSN 0306-1353
ANNUAL REPORTS ON ANALYTICAL ATOMIC SPECTROSCOPY. 1971. a. price varies. Royal Society of Chemistry, Burlington House, London W1V 0BN, England (Subscr. to: Distribution Centre, Blackhorse Rd., Letchworth, Herts SG6 1HN, England) Eds. M.S. Cresser, L. Ebdon. bibl. charts. illus. Indexed: Biol.Abstr.

535 US ISSN 0066-4103
ANNUAL REPORTS ON N M R SPECTROSCOPY. 1968. a., vol.17, 1986. $100. Academic Press Inc., Orlando, FL 32887. TEL 305-345-2000. Ed. G.A. Webb. Indexed: Chem.Abstr.
Formerly: Annual Review of N M R Spectroscopy (ISSN 0066-4235)

535 681 US ISSN 0066-5495
APPLIED OPTICS. SUPPLEMENT. 1962. irreg., no.3, 1969. price varies. (Optical Society of America, Inc.) American Institute of Physics, 335 E. 45th St., New York, NY 10017. TEL 212-661-9404. Eds. K.E. Shuler, W.R. Bennet, Jr. (also avail. in microfiche) Indexed: Phys.Abstr.

535 US
BENCHMARK PAPERS IN OPTICS. (Each vol. has distinctive title) 1975. irreg., vol.3, 1977. price varies. Van Nostrand Reinhold Company, 7625 Empire Dr., Florence, KY 41042. TEL 606-525-6600. illus. index.

COMITE INTERNATIONAL DES POIDS ET MESURES. COMITE CONSULTATIF DE PHOTOMETRIE ET RADIOMETRIE.(RAPPORT ET ANNEXES) see METROLOGY AND STANDARDIZATION

535 SZ ISSN 0084-5752
EIDGENOESSISCHE TECHNISCHE HOCHSCHULE ZUERICH. MITTEILUNGEN. PHOTOELASTIZITAET. 1943. irreg., no.10, 1965. (Swiss Federal Institute of Technology) E T H Zentrum, Ramistr. 101, 8001 Zurich, Switzerland.

ELECTRON MICROSCOPY SOCIETY OF SOUTHERN AFRICA. PROCEEDINGS/ ELEKTRONMIKROSKOPIEVERENIGING VAN SUIDELIKE AFRIKA. VERRIGTINGS. see BIOLOGY — Microscopy

535.58 US
HOLOGRAPHY DIRECTORY. 1979. irreg. $30. Museum of Holography, Information Services, 11 Mercer St., New York, NY 10013. Ed. Ian Lancaster.

INFRARED SOCIETY OF JAPAN. PROCEEDING. see PHYSICS — Heat

535.58 US ISSN 0190-4132
INTERNATIONAL CONFERENCE OF LASERS. PROCEEDINGS. 1979. a. $95. (Society for Optical & Quantum Electronics) S T S Press, Box 245, McLean, VA 22101. TEL 703-642-5835. Ed. C.P. Wang. circ. 350. Indexed: Chem.abstr.

535 HU ISSN 0237-2215
INTERNATIONAL SYMPOSIUM OF THE TECHNICAL COMMITTEE ON PHOTON-DETECTORS. (Text in English) 1980. biennial, latest 11th, Weimar, DDR, 1984. $41. Orszagos Muszaki Informacios Kozpont es Konyvtar (O.M.I.K.K.) - National Technical Information Centre and Library, Muzeum u. 17, H-1428 Budapest, Hungary. (Co-sponsor: International Measurement Convederation (IMEKO)) Ed. J. Schanda. circ. 150. (also avail. in microfiche; back issues avail.) Indexed: Chem.Abstr.

535 681.1 GW ISSN 0075-272X
JAHRBUCH FUER OPTIK UND FEINMECHANIK. 1954. a. DM.38. Fachverlag Schiele und Schoen GmbH, Markgrafenstr. 11, 1000 Berlin 61, W. Germany (B.R.D.) Ed. Dionys Hacman. adv. circ. 5,000.

535 658.8 US ISSN 8755-1616
LASER FOCUS/ELECTRO OPTICS BUYERS' GUIDE. 1966. a. $65 domestic; foreign $90. PennWell Publishing Company, 119 Russell St., Box 1153, Littleton, MA 01460-0753. Ed. Nancy Ferrell. adv. circ. 41,000.
Former titles: Laser Focus Buyers' Guide (ISSN 0075-8027); Until 1970: Laser Marketers' and Buyers' Guide.

535 US
MAGNETIC RESONANCE ANNUAL. a. Raven Press, 1185 Ave. of the Americas, New York, NY 10036. Ed. Herbert Y. Dressel.

535 338.47 US ISSN 0191-0647
OPTICAL INDUSTRY AND SYSTEMS PURCHASING DIRECTORY. 1954. a. $86. Laurin Publishing Co., Inc., Box 1146, Berkshire Common, Pittsfield, MA 01202. TEL 413-499-0514. Ed. T.C. Laurin. adv. circ. 20,000.
Supersedes (1963-1978): Optical Industry and Systems Directory (ISSN 0078-5474)

621.381 535 US
OPTICAL MEMORY REPORT. a. Rothchild Consultants, 256 Laguna Honda Blvd., San Francisco, CA 94116-1496.

535 621 US ISSN 0078-5482
OPTICAL PHYSICS AND ENGINEERING. 1967. irreg. price varies. Plenum Publishing Corp., 233 Spring St., New York, NY 10013. TEL 212-620-8047. Ed. William L. Wolfe.

535 US ISSN 0078-5504
OPTICS AND SPECTROSCOPY. SUPPLEMENT. (English translation of Russian language editions) 1966. irreg., no.4, 1970. $25. (Optical Society of America, Inc.) American Institute of Physics, 335 E. 45th St., New York, NY 10017. TEL 212-661-9404.

PROGRESS IN NUCLEAR MAGNETIC RESONANCE SPECTROSCOPY. see PHYSICS — Nuclear Energy

535 NE ISSN 0079-6638
PROGRESS IN OPTICS. 1961. irreg, vol.22, 1985. price varies. Elsevier Science Publishers B.V., Box 211, 1000 AE Amsterdam, Netherlands. Ed. E. Wolf. index. cum.index: vols.1-15. Indexed: ASCA. Phys.Ber.

REFERATIVNYI ZHURNAL. VOLOKONNO-OPTICHESKIE SYSTEMY. see PHYSICS — Abstracting, Bibliographies, Statistics

SPECTROSCOPIC PROPERTIES OF INORGANIC & ORGANOMETALLIC COMPOUNDS. see CHEMISTRY

535 US ISSN 0342-4111
SPRINGER SERIES IN OPTICAL SCIENCES. 1976. irreg., vol.51, 1986. price varies. Springer Verlag, 175 Fifth Ave., New York, NY 10010 TEL 212-460-1500. (And Berlin, Heidelberg, Tokyo and Vienna) (reprint service avail. from ISI) Indexed: Chem.Abstr. Phys.Ber.

535 UR
USPEKHI FORONIKI. vol.6, 1977. irreg. 1.83 Rub. per no. Leningradskii Universitet, Universitetskaya Nab. 7/9, Leningrad B-164, Russian S.F.S.R., U.S.S.R. bibl. circ. 705. Indexed: Chem.Abstr.

535 US ISSN 0888-5974
WHO'S WHO IN PHYSICS & OPTICS. 1979. biennial. $545. Research Publications, Inc. (Woodbridge), 12 Lunar Dr., Drawer AB, Woodbridge, CT 06525. TEL 203-297-2600.

617.7 GW
WISSENSCHAFTLICHE VEREINIGUNG FUER AUGENOPTIK UND OPTOMETRIE. FACHVORTRAEGE DES WVAO - JAHRESKONGRESSES. 1952. a. price varies. Wissenschaftliche Vereinigung fuer Augenoptik und Optometrie e.V., Adam-Karrillon-Str. 32, 6500 Mainz, W. Germany (B.R.D.) Ed. Hartmut Glaser. adv.
Formerly: Wissenschaftliche Vereinigung der Augenoptiker. Fachvortraege der Jahrestagungen (ISSN 0084-1005)

535 GW ISSN 0044-2054
ZEISS INFORMATION. (German and English editions) 1953. irreg. free. Carl Zeiss, Postfach 1369/1380, 7082 Oberkochen, W. Germany (B.R.D.) Ed. Wolfgang Pfeiffer. charts. illus. index. circ. 80,000. Indexed: Biol.Abstr. Chem.Abstr. Met.Abstr. Sci.Abstr. World Alum.Abstr.

PHYSICS — Sound

see also Sound Recording and Reproduction

534 774 US ISSN 0270-5117
ACOUSTICAL IMAGING: RECENT ADVANCES IN VISUALIZATION AND CHARACTERIZATION. Represents: International Symposium on Acoustical Imaging. Proceedings. 1969. irreg., vol.15, 1985. price varies. Plenum Publishing Corp., 233 Spring St., New York, NY 10013. TEL 212-620-8047. Indexed: Biol.Abstr. Chem.Abstr.
Formerly (until 1977): Acoustical Holography (ISSN 0065-0870)

534 DK ISSN 0105-614X
AKADEMIET FOR DE TEKNISKE VIDENSKABER. LYDTEKNISK INSTITUT. RAPPORT. no.31, 1982. irreg. free. Akademiet for de Tekniske Videnskaber, Lydteknisk Institut - Danish Acoustical Institute, Building 356, Akademivej, DK-2800 Lyngby, Denmark. illus.

534 PL ISSN 0554-8039
AKUSTYKA. 1972. irreg., no.2, 1976. price varies. Uniwersytet im. Adama Mickiewicza w Poznaniu, Wieniawskiego 1, 61-712 Poznan, Poland (Dist. by: Ars Polona, Krakowskie Przedmiescie 7, 00-068 Warsaw, Poland)
Formerly: Uniwersytet im. Adama Mickiewicza w Poznaniu. Wydzial Matematyki, Fizyki i Chemii. Prace. Seria Akustyka.

PHYSIOLOGY

AMERICAN INSTITUTE OF ULTRASOUND IN MEDICINE. ANNUAL SCIENTIFIC CONFERENCE. PROCEEDINGS. see *MEDICAL SCIENCES*

534　　　　　US
BENCHMARK PAPERS IN ACOUSTICS. (Each vol. has distinctive title) 1972. irreg., vol.20, 1985. price varies. Van Nostrand Reinhold Company, 7625 Empire Dr., Florence, KY 41042. TEL 606-525-6600. Ed. R.B. Lindsay. illus. index.

534　　　DK　ISSN 0105-2853
DANMARKS TEKNISKE HOEJSKOLE. LABORATORIET FOR AKUSTIK. PUBLIKATION. irreg. price varies. Danmarks Tekniske Hoejskole, Laboratoriet for Akustik, Bygn 352, 2800 Lyngby, Denmark. illus.

534　　　SW　ISSN 0349-2710
E I S C A T TECHNICAL NOTE. (Text in English) irreg. European Incoherent Scatter Scientific Association, Box 705, S-981 27 Kiruna, Sweden.

534　　　　　SW
EUROPEAN INCOHERENT SCATTER SCIENTIFIC ASSOCIATION. ANNUAL REPORT. (Text in English) a. European Incoherent Scatter Scientific Association, Box 705, S-981 27 Kiruna, Sweden.

534　　　　　UK
EUROPEAN SOLID STATE DEVICE RESEARCH CONFERENCE. SOLID STATE DEVICES. (Published in host country: UK, France or W. Germany) a., latest UK, 1983. Institute of Physics, Techno House, Redcliffe Way, Bristol BS1 6NX, England.

FREQUENCY CONTROL SYMPOSIUM. see *ELECTRICITY AND ELECTRICAL ENGINEERING*

534　　　　　UK
HANDBOOK OF NOISE AND VIBRATION CONTROL. vol.5, 1979. irreg. £48. Trade & Technical Press Ltd., Crown House, Morden, Surrey, SM4 5EW, England.

534　　　CN　ISSN 0074-400X
INTERNATIONAL CONFERENCE ON ACOUSTICS. REPORTS. 1953. irreg., 11th. 1983, Paris, France. International Commission on Acoustics, c/o Dr. E.A.W. Shaw, Division de Physique, Conseil National de Recherches, Ottawa, Ont. K1A 0R6, Canada. TEL 613-966-5845.

INTERVAL; exploring the sonic spectrum. see *MUSIC*

534　　　US　ISSN 0079-1873
PHYSICAL ACOUSTICS: PRINCIPLES AND METHODS. 1964. irreg., vol.17, 1984. Academic Press Inc., Orlando, FL 32887. TEL 305-345-2000. Ed. W.P. Mason.

534　　　　　UR
PROBLEMY DIFRAKTSII I RASPROSTRANENIYA VOLN/PROBLEMS OF DIFFRACTION AND SPREADING OF WAVES. vol.15, 1977. irreg. 1.69 Rub. per no. Leningradskii Universitet, Universitetskaya Nab. 7/9, Leningrad B-164, Russian S.F.S.R., U.S.S.R. abstr. bibl. circ. 900.

534　　　DK　ISSN 0105-3027
TECHNICAL UNIVERSITY OF DENMARK. ACOUSTICS LABORATORY REPORT. no.34, 1982. irreg. price varies. Danmarks Tekniske Hoejskole, Laboratoriet for Akustik, Bygning 352, 2800 Lyngby, Denmark. illus.

534　　　UR　ISSN 0369-6367
ULTRAGARSAS/ULTRASOUND. (Text in Russian; summaries in English and Lithuanian) 1969. a. price varies. Izdatel'stvo Mokslas, Zvaigzdziu 23, Vilnius 232050, Lithuanian S.S.R., U.S.S.R. (Co-sponsor: Ministerstvo Vysshego Obrazovaniya Litovskoi S.S.R.) Ed. V. Domarkas. circ. 500.

620.2　534　　US　ISSN 0090-5607
ULTRASONICS SYMPOSIUM. PROCEEDINGS. a. price varies. (I E E E, Ultrasonics, Ferroelectrics, and Frequency Control Society) Institute of Electrical and Electronics Engineers, Inc., 345 E. 47th St., New York, NY 10017 TEL 212-705-7900. (Subscr. address: 445 Hoes Ln., Piscataway, NJ 08854) Indexed: Chem.Abstr. Key Title: Proceedings - Ultrasonics Symposium.

PHYSIOLOGY

see *Biology—Physiology*

PLASTICS

668.4　　　　　CK
ACOPLASTICOS. 1957. a. Asociacion Colombiana de Industrias Plasticas Acoplasticos, Carrera 10a, No. 27-27, Interior 134 Of. 901 (Edificio Bachue), Apdo. 29844, Bogota, Colombia. adv.

668.3　　　JA　ISSN 0001-8201
ADHESION SOCIETY OF JAPAN. JOURNAL/NIHON SETCHAKU KYOKAISHI. (Text in English and Japanese) 1965. irreg., 6-8/yr. Adhesion Society of Japan - Nihon Setchaku Kyokai, c/o Osaka-furitsu Kogyo Gijutsu Kenkyusho, Enokojima, Nishi-ku, Osaka 550, Japan. Ed. Kazumune Nakao. adv. bk. rev. abstr. charts. illus. pat. index.

ADVANCES IN URETHANE SCIENCE AND TECHNOLOGY. see *CHEMISTRY — Organic Chemistry*

ANNUAL BOOK OF A S T M STANDARDS. VOLUME 04.09. WOOD. see *ENGINEERING — Engineering Mechanics And Materials*

ANNUAL BOOK OF A S T M STANDARDS. VOLUME 08.01. PLASTICS (1): C 177 TO D 1600. see *ENGINEERING — Engineering Mechanics And Materials*

ANNUAL BOOK OF A S T M STANDARDS. VOLUME 08.02. PLASTICS (2): D 1601 TO D 3099. see *ENGINEERING — Engineering Mechanics And Materials*

ANNUAL BOOK OF A S T M STANDARDS. VOLUME 08.04. PLASTIC PIPE AND BUILDING PRODUCTS. see *ENGINEERING — Engineering Mechanics And Materials*

668.4　　　　　MX
ANUARIO LATINOAMERICANO DE LOS PLASTICOS. 1973. a. $25. Anuarios Latinoamericanos, S.A. de C.V., Colima No. 436, Piso 2, Mexico 7, DF, Mexico. Ed. Roberto J. Marquez. adv. circ. 7,000.
Formerly: Directorio Nacional de la Industria de los Plasticos y Proveedores (Year)

ASSOCIATION FRANCAISE DES INGENIEURS DU CAOUTCHOUC ET DES PLASTIQUES. ANNUAIRE. see *RUBBER*

BENCHMARK PAPERS IN POLYMER CHEMISTRY. see *CHEMISTRY*

668.4　　　CN　ISSN 0068-9459
CANADIAN PLASTICS DIRECTORY AND BUYER'S GUIDE. 1959. a. Can.$25. Southam Communications Ltd., 1450 Don Mills Rd., Don Mills, Ont. M3B 2X7, Canada. TEL 416-445-6641.

668.4　677　　UK　ISSN 0268-0491
CARBON & HIGH PERFORMANCE FIBRES DIRECTORY. 1981. biennial. £29.50($49.50) Pammac Directories Ltd., Loudwater House, London Rd., Loudwater, High Wycombe HP10 9TL, England. Ed. D. Pamington. adv. (back issues avail.)

CONFERENCE OF ELECTRICAL ENGINEERING PROBLEMS IN THE RUBBER AND PLASTICS INDUSTRIES. I E E E CONFERENCE RECORD. see *RUBBER*

668.4　　　　　US
CONFERENCE ON CONTINGENCY PLANNING FOR PLASTICS. PROCEEDINGS. 1974. a. $125. (Business Communications Co., Inc.) Plastics Publishing Co., 25 Var Zant St., Norwalk, CT 06855. Ed. Louis Naturman. circ. 1,000. (also avail. in microfilm; microfiche; back issues avail.)

668.4　　　FR　ISSN 0071-9056
FRANCE PLASTIQUES. 1949. a. 266 F. Creations, Editions et Productions Publicitaires, 1 Place d'Estienne d'Orves, 75009 Paris, France. Ed. Georges Prieux. adv. circ. 5,000.

668.4　　　SZ　ISSN 0073-0084
HANDBUCH DER INTERNATIONALEN KUNSTSTOFFINDUSTRIE/INTERNATIONAL PLASTICS DIRECTORY/MANUEL INTERNATIONAL DES PLASTIQUES. (Text and index in English, French and German) 1958. every 10 yrs. 300 Fr. Verlag fuer Internationale Wirtschaftsliteratur GmbH, Box 108, CH-8047 Zurich, Switzerland. Ed. Walter Hirt. index.

668.4　　　　　II
HINDUSTAN LATEX. VARSHIKA RIPORTA/HINDUSTAN LATEX. ANNUAL REPORTS. (Text in Hindi and English) 11 edt., 1976/77. a. Varikkat House, TC 4/485, Kowdiar, Trivandrum 695003, India. stat.

668.4　　　US　ISSN 0579-5400
INTERNATIONAL CELLULAR PLASTICS CONFERENCE. PROCEEDINGS. irreg., no.2, 1968. price varies. Society of Plastics Industry, Inc., 355 Lexington Ave., New York, NY 10017. TEL 212-573-9400. circ. 1,000.

668.4　540　　UK　ISSN 0307-174X
INTERNATIONAL POLYMER SCIENCE AND TECHNOLOGY. 1974. m. £342($527) R A P R A Technology Ltd., Shawbury, Shrewsbury SY4 4NR, England. abstr. annual index to translations. circ. 350. (back issues avail.) Indexed: Excerp.Med. Art & Archaeol.Tech.Abstr. Fluidex.

668.4　547　　　US
INTERNATIONAL PROGRESS IN URETHANES. 1976. irreg. price varies. Technomic Publishing Co., Inc., 851 New Holland Ave., Box 3535, Lancaster, PA 17604. TEL 717-291-5609. Ed.Bd. Indexed: Chem.Abstr.

668.4　　　GW　ISSN 0075-7276
KUNSTSTOFF-INDUSTRIE UND IHRE HELFER. a. DM.38. Industrieschau-Verlagsgesellschaft, Berliner Allee 8, 6100 Darmstadt, W. Germany (B.R.D.)

668.4　　　GW　ISSN 0075-7292
KUNSTSTOFFE IM LEBENSMITTELVERKEHR. 1962. irreg., no.35, 1986. DM.118. (Bundesgesundheitsamt, Kunststoff-Kommission) Carl Heymanns Verlag KG, Luxemburgerstr. 449, 5000 Cologne 41, W. Germany (B.R.D.)

668.4　　　　　GW
KUNSTSTOFFPRODUKTE. a. Verlag Hoppenstedt & Co., Havelstr. 9, P.O. Box 4006, 6100 Darmstadt 1, W. Germany (B.R.D.)

660.2　　　US　ISSN 0085-3518
MODERN PLASTICS ENCYCLOPEDIA. (Special October issue of: Modern Plastics) 1925. a. McGraw-Hill Publications Co., 1221 Ave. of the Americas, New York, NY 10020. Ed. Joan Agranoff. adv. circ. 48,700.

668.4　　　　　US
MONOGRAPHS ON PLASTICS SERIES. 1972. irreg., vol.1, pt.2, 1973. price varies. Marcel Dekker, Inc., 270 Madison Avenue, New York, NY 10016. TEL 212-696-9000. Ed. M. Frisch.

668.4　630　　　US
NATIONAL AGRICULTURAL PLASTICS ASSOCIATION. PROCEEDINGS. 1960. irreg., 19th, 1986. price varies. National Agricultural Plastics Association, c/o H. Carl Hoefer, Jr., Exec. Sec., Box 767, Manchester, MO 63011. TEL 314-394-9292. circ. 400.

NEW TRADE NAMES IN THE RUBBER AND PLASTICS INDUSTRIES. see *RUBBER*

668.4 US
NORTH CAROLINA PLASTICS PROCESSORS AND PRODUCERS. biennial? $10. North Carolina State University, School of Engineering, Industrial Extension Service, Box 7902, Raleigh, NC 27695-7902. TEL 919-737-2358. Ed. Paul Cowgill.

668.4 SW
P K L PLASTER. 1969. biennial. Kr.100. Plast- och Kemikalieleverantoerers Foerening, Box 5512, S-114 85 Stockholm, Sweden.

668.4 UK
PLASTIC INDUSTRY DIRECTORY. irreg. Maclaren Publishers Ltd., Maclaren House, 19 Scarbrook Rd., Croydon CR9 1QH, England.

PLASTICHEM. see *ENGINEERING — Chemical Engineering*

668.4 MX
PLASTICOS Y RESINAS (ANNUAL) 1964. a. Mex.$2000($25) Litoimpresores, S.A., Espana 396, 09880 Mexico, D.F., Mexico. Ed. Cesar Macazaga. adv.

668.4 CN
PLASTICS BUSINESS GREENBOOK. a. Can.$50. Kerrwil Publications Ltd., 501 Oakdale Rd., Downsview, Ont. M3N 1W7, Canada. TEL 416-746-7360. Ed. Karen Berlenbach.

668.4 US
PLASTICS COMPOUNDING REDBOOK. 1981. a. $20. Harcourt Brace Jovanovich, Inc., 7500 Old Oak Blvd., Cleveland, OH 44130 TEL 216-243-8100. (Subscr. to: 1 E. First St., Duluth, MN 55802) Ed. Mary C. McMurrer. adv. charts. illus. circ. 14,000. (back issues avail.)

668.4 US
PLASTICS D.A.T.A. BOOK; thermoplastics and thermosets. 8th edt., 1987. a. $175. D.A.T.A., Inc. (Subsidiary of: International Thomson Organization) 9889 Willow Creek Rd., Box 26875, San Diego, CA 92126. TEL 619-578-7600.

668 US
PLASTICS: LATIN AMERICAN INDUSTRIAL REPORT. (Avail. for each of 22 Latin American countries) 1985. a. $435 per country report per industry covered. Aurora International, Box 9099, Bridgeport, CT 06601-2099. TEL 203-368-0579. Ed. Andres C. Aquino.

668.4 US
PLASTICS TECHNOLOGY. PLASTICS MANUFACTURING HANDBOOK AND BUYERS GUIDE. 1967. a. included in subscr. to Plastics Technology. Bill Communications, Inc., 633 Third Ave., New York, NY 10017. TEL 212-986-4800. Ed. Matthew H. Naitove. adv. charts. illus. tr.lit. index. circ. 40,000. (reprint service avail. from UMI)

668.4 IS
PLASTIKA BE-ISRAEL/ISRAEL PLASTICS.* (Text in Hebrew; summaries in English) 1971. irreg., 3-4/yr. $6. (Israel Plastics Society) Zimet Advertising and Publishing Co., 5 Mane St., Tel Aviv 64168, Israel. (Co-sponsor: Israel Plastics Manufacturers Association) Ed. I.G. Zewi. adv. bk. rev. circ. controlled. (back issues avail.) Indexed: Chem.Abstr.
Formerly: Polimerim ve-Homarim Plastiyim/Polymers and Plastic Materials.

668.4 PL ISSN 0370-0879
POLITECHNIKA WROCLAWSKA. INSTYTUT TECHNOLOGIII ORGANICZNEJ I TWORZYW SZTUCZNYCH. PRACE NAUKOWE. STUDIA I MATERIALY. (Text in Polish; summaries in English and Russian) 1971. irreg., no.17, 1977. price varies. Politechnika Wroclawska, Wybrzeze Wyspianskiego 27, 50-370 Wroclaw, Poland (Dist. by: Ars Polona-Ruch, Krakowskie Przedmiescie 7, Warsaw, Poland) Ed. Marian Kloza. Indexed: Chem.Abstr.

668.4 US ISSN 0171-709X
POLYMERS-PROPERTIES AND APPLICATIONS. 1952. irreg., vol.12, 1986. price varies. Springer-Verlag, 175 Fifth Ave., New York, NY 10010 TEL 212-460-1500. (Also Berlin, Heidelberg, Tokyo and Vienna) Ed. K.A. Wolf. (reprint service avail. from ISI)
Formerly (until vol.15, 1970): Chemie, Physik und Technologie der Kunststoffe in Einzeldarstellungen (ISSN 0069-3073)

668.4 UK ISSN 0306-3607
REINFORCED PLASTICS CONGRESS. 1958. biennial. £25. ‡ British Plastics Federation, 5 Belgrave Sq., London SW1X 8PH, England. Ed. W. Rouse. circ. 1,000.
Formerly: International Reinforced Plastics Conference. Papers and Proceedings. (ISSN 0074-7661)

RUBBER RESEARCH INSTITUTE OF SRI LANKA. JOURNAL. see *RUBBER*

RUBBICANA-EUROPE (YEAR) see *RUBBER*

660 US
SOCIETY OF PLASTICS ENGINEERS MONOGRAPHS. 1973. irreg., unnumbered, latest, 1984. price varies. John Wiley & Sons, Inc., 605 Third Ave., New York, NY 10016. TEL 212-850-6000.

668.4 US
SOCIETY OF THE PLASTICS INDUSTRY. REINFORCED PLASTICS COMPOSITES INSTITUTE. ANNUAL TECHNICAL CONFERENCE. PREPRINT. 1946. a. $75. Society of the Plastics Industry, 355 Lexington Ave., New York, NY 10017. Ed. J. McDermott. circ. 3,000. Indexed: Chem.Abstr.
Formerly: Society of the Plastics Industry. Reinforced Plastics Composites Institute. Annual Technical Conference. Proceedings.

668.4 US
SOCIETY OF THE PLASTICS INDUSTRY. URETHANE DIVISION. CONFERENCE PROCEEDINGS. 1979. irreg. price varies. Technomic Publishing Co., Inc., 851 New Holland Ave., Box 3535, Lancaster, PA 17604. TEL 717-291-5609.

668.4 US
STRUCTURAL FOAM CONFERENCE. PROCEEDINGS. vol.3, 1975. irreg. (Society of the Plastics Industry) Technomic Publishing Co. Inc., 851 New Holland Ave., Box 3535, Lancaster, PA 17604. TEL 717-291-5609.

SYNDICAT GENERAL DES COMMERCES ET INDUSTRIES DU CAOUTCHOUC ET DES PLASTIQUES. GUIDE. see *BUSINESS AND ECONOMICS — Trade And Industrial Directories*

668.4 658.78 US
U S FOAMED PLASTICS MARKETS AND DIRECTORY. Title varies: International Foamed Plastic Markets and Directory. 1963. a. $40. Technomic Publishing Co. Inc., 851 New Holland Ave., Box 3535, Lancaster, PA 17604. TEL 717-291-5609. Ed. M. Kohudic. circ. 8,000.
Formerly: United States Foamed Plastic Markets and Directory (ISSN 0083-0968)

668.4 US ISSN 0149-1342
URETHANE ABSTRACTS. 1971. m. $115. Technomic Publishing Co., Inc., 851 Holland Ave., Box 3535, Lancaster, PA 17604. TEL 717-291-5609. Ed.Bd. circ. 210.

668.4 540 US ISSN 0888-5958
WHO'S WHO IN CHEMISTRY & PLASTICS. 1979. biennial. $545. Research Publications, Inc. (Woodbridge), 12 Lunar Dr., Drawe AB, Woodbridge, CT 06525. TEL 203-297-2600.

668.4 US
WORLD PLASTICS. 1979. a. price on request. S R I International, World Petrochemicals Program, 333 Ravenswood Ave., Menlo Park, CA 94025. TEL 415-326-6200.

PLASTICS — Abstracting, Bibliographies, Statistics

KEY ABSTRACTS - ADVANCED MATERIALS. see *PHYSICS — Abstracting, Bibliographies, Statistics*

R A P R A ABSTRACTS. see *RUBBER — Abstracting, Bibliographies, Statistics*

POETRY

see *Literature — Poetry*

POLITICAL SCIENCE

see also *Political Science — Civil Rights; Political Science — International Relations; Public Administration*

321 US ISSN 0066-1228
A C A INDEX; analysis of voting records of members of U. S. Congress. 1960. a. contributions of $15 or more. Americans for Constitutional Action, 955 l'Enfant Plaza North, S.W., Washington, DC 20024. TEL 202-484-5525. cum.index: 1955 (Senate); 1957(House of Representatives) circ. 5,000.

350 US
A I RECOMMENDS.* irreg. Associated Industries of New York State, Inc., 152 Washington Ave., Albany, NY 12210.

320 US ISSN 0094-7954
A P S A DEPARTMENTAL SERVICES PROGRAM SURVEY OF DEPARTMENTS. 1971/72. a. $20. American Political Science Association, 1527 New Hampshire Ave., N.W., Washington, DC 20036. stat. circ. 650.

320.07 US
A P S A DIRECTORY OF DEPARTMENT CHAIRPERSONS. 1972. a. $20. American Political Science Association, 1527 New Hampshire Ave., N.W., Washington, DC 20036. TEL 202-483-2512. circ. 650.
Formerly: A P S A Directory of Department Chairmen (ISSN 0092-8658)

320 DK ISSN 0901-5213
AARHUS UNIVERSITET. INSTITUT FOR STATSKUNDSKAB. ARBEJDSPAPIR. irreg. Aarhus Universitet, Institut for Statskundskab - University of Aarhus, Institute of Political Science, Universitetsparken, DK-8000 Aarhus C, Denmark.

320 US ISSN 0195-914X
ABRAHAM LINCOLN ASSOCIATION. PAPERS. 1979. a. $15. Abraham Lincoln Association, Old State Capitol, Springfield, IL 62701. Ed. Marilyn H. Immel. circ. 360 (controlled)

320 300 VE
ACADEMIA DE CIENCIAS POLITICAS Y SOCIALES. BOLETIN. 1937. irreg. Academia de Ciencias Politicas y Sociales, Ciudad Universitaria, Caracas, Venezuela. bibl.

320 AG
ACADEMIA NACIONAL DE CIENCIAS MORALES Y POLITICAS. ANALES. 1972. a. Academia Nacional de Ciencias Morales y Politicas, Avda. Alvear 1711-P.B. (1014), Buenos Aires, Argentina.

320 US ISSN 0065-0684
ACADEMY OF POLITICAL SCIENCE. PROCEEDINGS. 1910. irreg., approx. 2/yr. membership. Academy of Political Science, 2852 Broadway, New York, NY 10025. TEL 212-866-6752. index. circ. 11,000. (also avail. in microform from UMI; reprint service avail. from UMI) Indexed: Curr.Cont. P.A.I.S. SSCI. Soc.Sci.Ind. A.B.C.Pol.Sci. High.Educ.Curr.Aware.Bull.

ACTA FACULTATIS POLITICO-JURIDICAE UNIVERSITATIS SCIENTIARUM BUDAPESTIENSIS DE ROLANDO EOTVOS NOMINATAE. see *LAW*

ACTA UNIVERSITATIS DE ATTILA JOZSEF NOMINATAE. ACTA IURIDICA ET POLITICA. see *LAW*

320 PL ISSN 0137-6667
ACTA UNIVERSITATIS NICOLAI COPERNICI. NAUKI POLITYCZNE. 1967. irreg. price varies. Uniwersytet Mikolaja Kopernika, Fosa Staromiejska 3, Torun, Poland (Dist. by Osrodek Rozpowszechniania Wydawnictw Naukowych PAN, Palac Kultury i Nauki, 00-901 Warsaw, Poland)

320.531　　　　　　HU　ISSN 0563-0657
ACTA UNIVERSITATIS SZEGEDIENSIS DE
ATTILA JOZSEF NOMINATAE. SECTIO
SCIENTIAE SOCIALISMI. TUDOMANYOS
SZOCIALIZMUS. (Subseries of: Acta Universitatis
Szegediensis de Attila Jozsef Nominatae. Sectio
Scientiae Socialismi. ISSN 0230-3558) (Text in
Hungarian, Russian; summaries in French and
Russian) 1961. a. exchange basis. Attila Jozsef
University, c/o E. Szabo, Exchange Librarian,
Dugonics ter 13, P.O.B. 393, Szeged H-6701,
Hungary (Subscr. to: Kultura, Box 149, H-1389
Budapest, Hungary) Ed. Laszlo J. Nagy. circ. 300.
　　Marxism

329　　　　　　　　AT　ISSN 0311-2527
ACTION REPORT.* 1972. irreg. Australia Party,
Victorian Branch, 23 Ringwood Rd., Ringwood, Vic.
3134, Australia.
　　Supersedes: Australia Party. Victorian Branch.
Report.

328 973　　　　　　　US
ADVANCE LOCATOR FOR CAPITOL HILL.
Variant title: C.S.D. Advance Locator. 1963. a. $12.
Congressional Staff Directory Ltd., Box 62, Mt.
Vernon, VA 22121. TEL 703-765-3400.

320　　　　　　　　　US
ADVANCES IN POLITICAL SCIENCE. 1982. irreg.
$29.95. Sage Publications, Inc., 2111 W. Hillcrest
Dr., Newbury Park, CA 91320. TEL 805-499-0721.
Ed. Richard L. Merritt.

AFRICA REVIEW. see BUSINESS AND
ECONOMICS — Economic Situation And
Conditions

320 350　　　　　　SA　ISSN 0304-615X
AFRICANUS. (Text in English and Afrikaans) 1972.
a. R.3. University of South Africa, Department of
Development Administration and Politics, Box 392,
Pretoria 0001, South Africa. Ed. R.J. Cornwell. adv.
bk. rev. charts. stat. circ. 330. (back issues avail.)
Indexed: Curr.Cont.Africa. Ind.S.A.Per.

949.65　　　　　　　US　ISSN 0002-4651
ALBANIA REPORT. 1970. irreg., no.63, 1985.
contributions. (Albanian Affairs Study Group)
Gamma Publishing Co., Box 206, Church Street
Sta., New York, NY 10008. TEL 718-633-0530. Ed.
Jack Shulman. circ. 3,000.

322.4　　　　　　　　FR
ALBANIAN RESISTANCE. vol.25, 1978. irreg.
National Democratic Committee for a Free Albania,
18 bis rue Brunel, 75017 Paris, France. (processed)

324　　　　　　　　　US　ISSN 0065-678X
AMERICA VOTES; handbook of contemporary
American election statistics. 1956. biennial.
Congressional Quarterly Inc., 1414 22nd St., N.W.,
Washington, DC 20037. TEL 202-887-8500. Ed.
Richard M. Scammon.

335　　　　　　　　　US　ISSN 0084-6368
AMERICAN INSTITUTE FOR MARXIST
STUDIES. OCCASIONAL PAPERS. 1966. irreg.,
no.24, 1982. American Institute for Marxist Studies,
85 E. 4th St., New York, NY 10003.

320　　　　　　　　　US
AMERICAN JEWISH COMMITTEE. DOMESTIC
AFFAIRS DEPARTMENT. PERTINENT
PAPERS. At head of title: Our Stake in the Urban
Condition. 1978. irreg., approx. 2/yr. $0.25 per no.
American Jewish Committee, Domestic Affairs
Department, 165 E. 56th St., New York, NY
10022. TEL 212-751-4000. circ. 3,000.

323　　　　　　　　　US　ISSN 0066-1236
AMERICANS FOR CONSTITUTIONAL ACTION.
REPORT. 1961. a. contributions of $15 or more.
Americans for Constitutional Action, 955 l'Enfant
Plaza N., S.W., Washington, DC 20024. TEL 202-
484-5525. circ. 5,000.

320　　　　　　　　　GW　ISSN 0072-9426
ANALYSEN. 1965. irreg. price varies. (Hochschule
fuer Wirtschaft und Politik, Hamburg) Leske Verlag
und Budrich GmbH, Gerhart-Hauptmann-Str.27,
Postfach 300406, 5090 Leverkusen 3, W. Germany
(B.R.D.)

328　　　　　　　　　BE　ISSN 0066-1589
ANCIENS PAYS ET ASSEMBLEES D'ETATS.
(Text in language of contributor) 1950. irreg. price
varies. (International Committee of Historical
Sciences, Commission for the History of State
Assemblies) Editions Nauwelaerts, 148
Mechelsestraat, 3000 Louvain, Belgium.

320　　　　　　　　　FR　ISSN 0066-2356
ANNEE POLITIQUE. 1876; N.S. 1944. a. $38.54.
(Presses Universitaires de France) Editions du
Moniteur, 17 rue d'Uzes, 75002 Paris, France.

320 960　　　　　　SG　ISSN 0066-2364
ANNEE POLITIQUE AFRICAINE. 1964. a. 17.500
Fr.CFA. Societe Africaine d'Edition, B.P. 1877,
Dakar, Senegal (And 32, rue de l'Echiquier, Paris,
France) Ed.Bd.
　　Formed by the 1981 merger of: Annee Politique
Africaine & Economie Africaine.

320　　　　　　　　　SZ　ISSN 0066-2372
ANNEE POLITIQUE SUISSE/SCHWEIZERISCHE
POLITIK IM JAHRE. (Text in German and
French) 1965. a. 30 Fr. Universitaet Bern,
Forschungszentrum fuer Schweizerische Politik -
Universite de Berne, Centre de Recherche de
Politique Suisse, Neubrueck Str. 10, 3012 Berne,
Switzerland. Eds. Peter Gigl, Hans Hirtzer. index.
circ. 1,500.

320　　　　　　　　　CN　ISSN 0706-1021
ANNUAIRE FRANCO-ONTARIEN. 1978. a.
Conseil des Affaires Franco-Ontariennes, 900 Bay
St., 4th floor, Mowat Block, Toronto, Ont. M7A
1C2, Canada.
　　Formerly: Bottin des Organismes Franco-
Ontariens (ISSN 0707-3356)

320　　　　　　　　　SZ　ISSN 0066-3727
ANNUAIRE SUISSE DE SCIENCE POLITIQUE/
SCHWEIZERISCHES JAHRBUCH FUER
POLITISCHE WISSENSCHAFT/SWISS
POLITICAL SCIENCE YEARBOOK. (Text in
English, French and German) 1961. a. price varies.
(Forschungsstelle fuer Politische Wissenschaft) Paul
Haupt AG, Falkenplatz 14, CH-3001 Berne,
Switzerland. Ed. G. Schmid. Indexed: Hist.Abstr.
A.B.C.Pol.Sci.　Amer.Hist.& Life.

320.4
ANNUAL EDITIONS: AMERICAN
GOVERNMENT. 1971. a. 9.50. Dushkin
Publishing Group, Inc., Sluice Dock, Guilford, CT
06437. TEL 203-453-4351. Ed. Ian Nielsen. illus.
　　Formerly: Annual Editions: Readings in
American Government (ISSN 0090-547X)

320　　　　　　　　　US
ANNUAL EDITIONS: COMPARATIVE POLITICS.
a. $9.50. Dushkin Publishing Group Inc., Sluice
Duck, Guilford, CT 06437. TEL 203-453-4351.

320　　　　　　　　　UK　ISSN 0066-4057
ANNUAL REGISTER WORLD EVENTS. 1758. a.
£40. Longman Group Ltd., Fourth Ave., Harlow,
Essex CM19 5AA, England (Distr. in U.S. and
Canada by: Gale Research Co. Ltd., Book Tower,
Detroit, MI 48226) Ed. H.V. Hodson. index.

320　　　　　　　　　US　ISSN 0748-8599
ANNUAL REVIEW OF POLITICAL SCIENCE.
1985. a. price varies. Ablex Publishing Corp., 355
Chestnut St., Norwood, NJ 07648. TEL 201-767-
8450. Ed. Samuel Long.

320　　　　　　　　　MX
ANUARIO POLITICO DE AMERICA LATINA.
1974. a. Universidad Nacional Autonoma de
Mexico, Facultad de Ciencias Politicas y Sociales,
Ciudad Universitaria, Mexico 20, D.F., Mexico.

ARABIAN STUDIES. see HISTORY — History Of
The Near East

ASIA & PACIFIC REVIEW. see BUSINESS AND
ECONOMICS — Economic Situation And
Conditions

320　　　　　　　　　SA
ASSOCIATION FOR RURAL ADVANCEMENT.
REPORTS. (Text in English and Zulu) 1980. irreg.
free. Association for Rural Advancement, Box 2517,
Pietermaritzburg 3200, South Africa. Ed. Marie
Dyer. circ. 1,400. (looseleaf format; back issues
avail.)

320　　　　　　　　　US
AT THE POLLS SERIES. irreg. price varies.
(American Enterprise Institute for Public Policy
Research) Duke University Press, 6697 College Sta.,
Durham, NC 27708. TEL 919-684-2173. Ed.
Howard R. Penniman.

320.51 329.9　　　AT　ISSN 0004-9654
AUSTRALIAN LIBERAL. 1957. irreg. Aus.$2.50.
Liberal Party of Australia, Federal Secretariat, Box
21, Queen Victoria Terrace, A.C.T. 2600, Australia.
Ed. Graham Howard. adv. bk. rev. circ. 50,000.

320.531　　　　　　AT　ISSN 0310-8252
AUSTRALIAN MARXIST REVIEW. 1972. irreg. (3-
4/yr.) Aus.$6. Socialist Party of Australia, 65
Campbell St., Surry Hills, NSW 2010, Australia. Ed.
P.D. Symon. bibl. circ. 1,000.

320　　　　　　　　　AT
AUSTRALIAN NATIONAL UNIVERSITY,
CANBERRA. RESEARCH SCHOOL OF SOCIAL
SCIENCES. DEPARTMENT OF POLITICAL
SCIENCE. OCCASIONAL PAPERS. 1965. irreg.,
no.19, 1986. price varies. Australian National
University, Department of Political Science, Box 4,
Canberra, A.C.T. 2600, Australia (Dist. in U.S. by
International Scholarly Book Services, Box 4347,
Portland, Ore. 97208) circ. 625.
　　Formerly: Australian National University,
Canberra. Department of Political Science.
Occasional Paper. (ISSN 0067-2033)

320　　　　　　　　　BG
BANGLADESH POLITICAL STUDIES. (Text in
English or Bengali) 1978. a. Tk.35. University of
Chittagong, Department of Political Science,
Chittagong, Bangladesh. Ed. B.P. Barua. adv. bk.
rev. circ. 1,000.

320　　　　　　　　　GW　ISSN 0522-6643
BEITRAEGE ZUR GESCHICHTE DES
PARLEMENTARISMUS UND DER
POLITISCHEN PARTEIEN. 1952. irreg., vol.67,
1980. price varies. Droste-Verlag GmbH, Pressehaus
Am Martin-Luther-Platz, Postfach 1122, 4000
Duesseldorf 1, W. Germany (B.R.D.)

BEITRAEGE ZUR KRITIK DER
BUERGERLICHEN IDEOLOGIE UND DES
REVISIONISMUS. see PHILOSOPHY

BEITRAEGE ZUR ZEITGESCHICHTE. see
HISTORY

320　　　　　　　　　US　ISSN 0067-5717
BENJAMIN F. FAIRLESS LECTURES. 1964. a.
(Carnegie-Mellon University) Columbia University
Press, 562 W. 113th St., New York, NY 10025.
TEL 212-678-6777.

320 943.8　　　　　　PL
BIBLIOTEKA POLONIJNA/POLONIA LIBRARY.
1960. irreg., vol.17, 1986. price varies. (Polska
Akademia Nauk, Komitet Badania Polonii
Zagranicznej) Ossolineum, Publishing House of the
Polish Academy of Sciences, Rynek 9, Wroclaw,
Poland. Ed. Wiktor Szczerba.
　　Formerly (until 1977): Problemy Polonii
Zagranicznej (ISSN 0079-5798)

320　　　　　　　　　US
BLACK POLITICAL STUDIES. irreg. latest no. 2.
Borgo Press, Box 2845, San Bernardino, CA 92406.
TEL 714-884-5813.

320 972　　　　　　　US
BORDER ISSUES AND PUBLIC POLICY.
RESEARCH PAPERS. 1982. irreg., latest no.23,
1985. $4 per no. University of Texas at El Paso,
Center for Inter-American and Border Studies,
Publications Program, El Paso, TX 79968-0605.

320 972　　　　　　　US
BORDER PERSPECTIVES. RESEARCH PAPERS.
1983. irreg., latest no.10, 1985. $4 per no.
University of Texas at El Paso, Center for Inter-
American and Border Studies, Publications Program,
El Paso, TX 79968-0605.

320 800　　　　　　US　ISSN 0278-9752
BORGO POLITICAL SCENARIOS. 1982. irreg.,
approx. a. $19.95 (hardcover); $9.95 (paperback) per
no. Borgo Press, Box 2845, San Bernardino, CA
92406. TEL 714-884-5813.

BORGO REFERENCE LIBRARY. see HISTORY

POLITICAL SCIENCE

320 301 US
BRITISH POLITICAL SOCIOLOGY YEARBOOK. 1974. a. Halsted Press (Subsidiary of: John Wiley & Sons, Inc.) 605 Third Ave., New York, NY 10016. TEL 212-850-6000. Ed. Ivor Crewe.

C C I A BACKGROUND INFORMATION. (World Council of Churches, Commission on International Affairs) see RELIGIONS AND THEOLOGY

320 327 BE
C E P S WORKING DOCUMENTS (POLITICAL) (Text in English) 1983. bi-m. 200 Fr. per no. Centre for European Policy Studies, 33 rue Ducale, 1000 Brussels, Belgium. Ed. Helen Bloom. (back issues avail.)

320 CU
C I A C. a. Movimiento Cubano por la Paz, Linea No. 556, Vedado, Havana, Cuba.

322.4 PO
CADERNOS POLITICOS DE EDUCACAO POPULAR. no.4, 1975. irreg. $15. Iniciativas Editoriais, Av. Rio de Janeiro 6, Lisbon, Lisbon 5.

320 BE ISSN 0575-0571
CAHIERS DE BRUGES/BRUGES QUARTERLY. (Text in French or English; summary in other language) 1951. irreg. (College d'Europe) Uitgeverij de Tempel, 41 Tempelhof, Bruges, Belgium. Indexed: Hist.Abstr. Amer.Hist.& Life.

320 FR ISSN 0068-5194
CAHIERS NEPALAIS. 1969. irreg. price varies. Editions du C N R S, 295 rue St. Jacques, 75005 Paris, France.

320 US ISSN 0084-8271
CALIFORNIA GOVERNMENT & POLITICS ANNUAL. 1970. a. $5.95. California Journal, Inc., 1714 Capitol Ave., Sacramento, CA 95814. TEL 916-444-2840. Ed. Thomas R. Hoeber. circ. 7,000. (also avail. in microfilm)

320 UK ISSN 0575-6871
CAMBRIDGE STUDIES IN THE HISTORY AND THEORY OF POLITICS. 1967. irreg. price varies. Cambridge University Press, Edinburgh Bldg., Shaftesbury Rd., Cambridge CB2 2RU, England (And 32 E. 57th St., New York NY 10022) Ed.Bd.

320 US
CAMPAIGN GUIDE FOR CORPORATIONS AND LABOR ORGANIZATIONS. irreg. Federal Election Commission, Washington, DC 20463. TEL 202-376-5140.

320 US
CAMPAIGN GUIDE FOR NON-CONNECTED COMMITTEES. irreg. Federal Election Commission, Washington, DC 20463. TEL 202-376-5140.

CANADA. PRIVACY COMMISSIONER. ANNUAL REPORT. see COMPUTERS — Computer Security

971 327 US ISSN 0045-4257
CANADA TODAY/D'AUJOURD'HUI (WASHINGTON) 1970. 4-6/yr. free. ‡ Canadian Embassy, Public Affairs Division, 1771 N St., N.W., Washington, DC 20036. TEL 202-785-1400. Ed. Judith C. Webster. bk. rev. bibl. illus. circ. 100,000.

320 CN ISSN 0068-8835
CANADIAN GOVERNMENT SERIES. 1947. irreg. price varies. University of Toronto Press, Front Campus, Toronto, Ont. M5S 1A6, Canada TEL 613-667-7791. (and 33 East Tupper St., Buffalo, N.Y. 14203) Ed. C.B. Macpherson.

320 301 CN ISSN 0380-9420
CANADIAN JOURNAL OF POLITICAL & SOCIAL THEORY/REVUE CANADIENNE DE THEORIE POLITIQUE ET SOCIALE. (Text in English & French) 1977. triennial. Can.$15($17) individuals; Can.$25($27) libraries; Can. $10 ($12) students. Arthur & Marilouise Kroker, Ed. & Pub., Concordia University, Department of Political Science, 7141 Sherbrooke St. W., Montreal, Que. H4B 1R6, Canada. TEL 514-841-2112. Ed. Arthur Kroker. adv. bk. rev. film rev. index. circ. 2,000. (back issues avail.) Indexed: Sociol.Abstr. A.B.C.Pol.Sci. Alt.Press Ind. CMI. Can.Ind. Int.Polit.Sci.Abstr. Lang.& Lang.Behav.Abstr.

328 CN ISSN 0315-6168
CANADIAN PARLIAMENTARY GUIDE. a. price varies. P. G. Normandin, P.O. Box 3453, Sta. C, Ottawa, Ont. K1Y 4J6, Canada.

320 CN
CANADIAN POLITICAL SCIENCE ASSOCIATION. UPDATING THESES IN CANADIAN POLITICAL SCIENCE, COMPLETED AND IN PROGRESS. (Includes biennial supplements) 1970. biennial. Can.$45 (or free with subscr. to Journal of Political Science) Canadian Political Science Association, 12 Henderson Ave., University of Ottawa, Ottawa, Ont. K1N 6N5, Canada. circ. 2,000.

330.122 320.531 IT ISSN 0391-1934
CAPITALISMO E SOCIALISMO. (Numbers not published consecutively) 1975. irreg., no.15, 1983. price varies. Liguori Editore s.r.l., Via Mezzocannone 19, 80134 Naples, Italy. TEL 081/20 6077. Ed. Bruno Jossa.

320 US
CARIBBEAN-AMERICAN STUDIES. irreg., latest no.2. Borgo Press, Box 2845, San Bernardino, CA 92406. TEL 714-884-5813.

320 UK
CASEBOOK SERIES ON EUROPEAN POLITICS AND SOCIETY. 1981. irreg. (Center for European Studies. Harvard University) George Allen & Unwin (Publishers) Ltd., 40 Museum St., London W.C.1., England (U.S. addr.: Allen & Unwin Inc., 8 Winchester Place, Winchester, MA 01890)

320 US
CENTER FOR THE STUDY OF THE PRESIDENCY. PROCEEDINGS. 1971. irreg., vol.5, 1984. membership. Center for the Study of the Presidency, 208 E. 75th St., New York, NY 10021. TEL 212-249-1200. Ed. R. Gordon Hoxie. circ. 10,000. (also avail. in microform from UMI; reprint service avail. from UMI) Indexed: Abstr.Mil.Bibl.

320 PR
CENTRO DE ESTUDIOS DE LA REALIDAD PUERTORRIQUENA. CUADERNOS. no.5, 1982. irreg. Ediciones Huracan, Inc., Avda. Gonzalez 1003, Santa Rica, Rio Piedras, PR 00925.

CENTRO DE ESTUDIOS PUBLICOS. DOCUMENTO DE TRABAJO. see BUSINESS AND ECONOMICS — Economic Situation And Conditions

329.3 320 331.11 AT ISSN 0159-8872
CHALLENGE (PETERSHAM NORTH) 1976. irreg. (approx. bi-m.) Aus.$15. (Labor Party Left Steering Committee) Challenge Publications Pty. Ltd., P.O. Box N100, Petersham North, N.S.W. 2049, Australia. Ed. Les Carr. adv. bk. rev. circ. 3,000. (tabloid format; back issues avail.)

951 310 US ISSN 0190-602X
CHINA FACTS AND FIGURES ANNUAL. 1978. a. price varies. Academic International Press, Box 1111, Gulf Breeze, FL 32561. Ed. John L. Scherer. (back issues avail.)

320 301 355 US
CHINA REPORT: POLITICAL, SOCIOLOGICAL, AND MILITARY AFFAIRS. irreg. (approx. 90/yr.) $5 per no. U.S. Joint Publications Research Service, 1000 N. Glebe Rd., Arlington, VA 22201 TEL 703-487-4630. (Orders to: NTIS, Springfield, VA 22161)

320 US ISSN 8756-0844
CHINA RIGHTS ANNALS; human rights conditions in the People's Republic of China. 1979. irreg. $35. (Society for the Protection of East Asians' Human Rights) M.E. Sharpe, Inc., Box 1212, Cathedral Sta., New York, NY 10025. Ed. James D. Seymour. bk. rev. circ. 800. (also avail. in microfiche) Indexed: HR Rep.
Formerly (until 1984): S P E A H R Head (ISSN 0196-7428)

320 BE
CHRISTIAN DEMOCRATIC STUDY AND DOCUMENTATION CENTER. CAHIERS D'ETUDES. 1968. irreg. Christian Democratic World Union, 16 rue de la Victoire, Boite 1, 1060 Brussels, Belgium.
Formerly: International Christian Democratic Study and Documentation Center. Cahiers d'Etudes (ISSN 0538-5539)

CHRISTIAN PRISONERS IN THE U.S.S.R. see RELIGIONS AND THEOLOGY

320 SZ
CHRONICLE OF PARLIAMENTARY ELECTIONS AND DEVELOPMENTS. (Editions in French and English) 1967. a. 30 Fr. Inter-Parliamentary Union, International Center for Parliamentary Documentation - Union Interparlementaire, Place du Petit-Saconnex, 1209 Geneva, Switzerland.
Formerly (until vol.12, 1978): Chronicle of Parliamentary Elections (ISSN 0074-1043)

CIVILIAN CONGRESS; persons holding military office in Congress. see LAW

320 US
CLASS, STATE AND DEVELOPMENT. irreg. $28 cloth; $14 paper. Sage Publications, Inc., 2111 W. Hilllcrest Dr., Newbury Park, CA 91320. TEL 805-499-0721. Ed. Dale L. Johnson.

320 SZ ISSN 0069-4533
CLASSIQUES DE LA PENSEE POLITIQUE. 1965. irreg., no.13, 1983. price varies. Librarie Droz, 11 rue Massot, 1211 Geneva 12, Switzerland. circ. 1,000.

320 BL
COLECAO CAMINHOS BRASILEIROS. irreg. Edicoes Tiempo Brasileiro Ltda, Rua Bispo Coutinho 61, C.P. 16099, ZC-01 Laranjeiras, Rio de Janeiro, Brazil. Dir. Carlos Chagas Filho.

320 BL
COLECAO TENDENCIAS. irreg., vol.3, 1982. Edicoes Graal Ltda., Rua Hermenegildo de Barroa, 31-A, 20241 Gloria, Rio de Janeiro RJ, Brazil.

320 330 PO
COLECCAO HORIZONTE UNIVERSITARIO. no.30, 1982. irreg., no.40, 1984. Livros Horizonte, Lda., Rua das Chagas, 17, Lisbon 2, Portugal.

320 UY
COLECCION CIEN TEMAS BASICOS. no.18, 1976. irreg. Editorial Medina s.r.l., Montevideo, Uruguay.

320 CR
COLECCION CUADERNOS CEDAL. 1974. irreg. Centro de Estudios CEDAL, Apdo. 874, San Jose, Costa Rica. Ed. Alberto Baeza Flores.

320 ES
COLECCION DEBATE. 1983. irreg. (Universidad Centroamericana Jose Simeon Canas) U C A Editores, Autopista Sur, Jardines de Guadalupe, Apdo. Postal 668, San Salvador, El Salvador. circ. 1,300.

320 DR
COLECCION ESTUDIOS POLITICOS. irreg. Publicaciones ONAP, Edif. de Oficinas Gubernamentales, Av. Mexico esq. Leopoldo Navarro, Santo Domingo, Dominican Republic. circ. 750.

320 SP
COLECCION IBERICA. 1976. irreg. Editorial Anagrama, S.A., Calle Pedro de la Creu, 58, 08034 Barcelona, Spain.

320 VE
COLECCION MONOGRAFIAS POLITICAS.* 1978. irreg. Editorial Juridica Venezolana, Edif. Galipan, Av. Francisco de Miranda, Piso 3, Apdo. 17598, Caracas 1015-A, Venezuela.

320 SP
COLECCION VIERA Y CLAVIJO.* 1982. a. Universidad de la Laguna, Cabildo Insular de Gran Canaria, Avda de la Universidad s/n, La Laguna, Tenerife, Islas Canarias, Spain.

320.531 FR
COMBAT CULTUREL. 1975. irreg. price varies. Editions Syros, 1 rue de Varenne, 75006 Paris, France. illus.

POLITICAL SCIENCE

322.4   CK
COMITE DE ACCION INTERAMERICANA DE COLOMBIA. BOLETIN. irreg. Comite de Accion Interamericana de Colombia, Cra. 7 No.32-33, Of. 1601, Apdo. Aereo 10598, Bogota, Colombia.

330 320   EI
COMMISSION OF THE EUROPEAN COMMUNITIES. STUDIES: SOCIAL POLICY SERIES. (Text in Dutch, English, French, German or Italian) 1963. irreg. Office for Official Publications of the European Communities, P.O. Box 1003, L-2985, Luxembourg, Luxembourg (Dist. in the U.S. by European Community Information Service, 2100 M St., N.W., Ste. No. 707, Washington, DC 20037)
    Formerly: Commission of the European Communities. Etudes: Serie Politique Sociale (ISSN 0069-6730)

329.9   FR
COMMUNIST PROGRAM. (Text in English) 1975. irreg. 30 F.($4) (International Communist Party) Editions Programme, 20 rue Jean Bouton, 75012 Paris, France. Ed. Saro. bk. rev. bibl. charts. circ. 2, 400.
    Communism

320.532   FR
COMMUNISTES FRANCAIS ET L'EUROPE. 1978. irreg. Parti Communiste Francais, 2 Place du Colonel Fabien, 75019 Paris, France.

320 350   US
CONGRESS AND THE NATION. 1965. every 4 yrs. Congressional Quarterly Inc., 1414 22nd St., N.W., Washington, DC 20037. TEL 202-887-8500.

329.9   II   ISSN 0376-5776
CONGRESS MARCHES AHEAD. (Text in English) 1970. irreg. price varies. All India Congress Committee, Publications Department, 5 Dr. Rajendra Prasad Rd., New Delhi 110001, India.

320   US
CONGRESSIONAL ROLL CALL (YEAR); a chronology and analysis of votes in the House and Senate, 99th Congress, first session. 1972. a. $15.95 paperback. Congressional Quarterly, Inc., 1414 22nd St., N.W., Washington, DC 20037-9982. TEL 202-887-8500. charts. (back issues avail.)

CONGRESSIONAL STAFF DIRECTORY. see *PUBLIC ADMINISTRATION*

322.4   HO
CONSEJO CENTRAL EJECUTIVO DEL PARTIDO LIBERAL DE HONDURAS. MEMORIA. irreg. Partido Liberal, Consejo Central Ejecutivo, Tegucigalpa, Honduras.

CONTEMPORARY CHINA PAPERS. see *HISTORY — History Of Asia*

320   US   ISSN 0147-1066
CONTRIBUTIONS IN POLITICAL SCIENCE. 1978. irreg., no.106, 1984. price varies. Greenwood Press, 88 Post Rd. W., Box 5007, CT 06881. TEL 203-226-3571. Ed. Bernard K. Johnpoll.

CONTRIBUTIONS TO POLITICAL ECONOMY. see *BUSINESS AND ECONOMICS — Economic Situation And Conditions*

320   CK   ISSN 0120-4165
CONTROVERSIA. 1972. irreg. Col.$2000($50) Centro de Investigacion y Educacion Popular, Carrera 5, No.33A-08, Apdo. Aereo 25916, Bogota, Colombia. Ed. Alejandro Angulo. stat. circ. 2,000. (also avail. in microfiche)
    Formerly (until 1975): Anali-C I A S.

320   US   ISSN 0196-2809
COUNTRIES OF THE WORLD AND THEIR LEADERS YEARBOOK. 1974. irreg., latest 1987. $120 (2 vols.) Gale Research Company, Book Tower, Detroit, MI 48226. TEL 313-961-2242. Ed. Frank E. Bair.
    Formerly: Countries of the World.

320   CU
CRITERIOS. a. Ministerio de Cultura, 17 y H, Vedado, Havana, Cuba.

320   AG
CUADERNOS DE ESTUDIOS LATINOAMERICANOS. no.2, 1974. irreg. Universidad Nacional del Nordeste, Instituto de Letras, Resistencia, Chaco, Argentina. Dir. Alfredo Veirave.

320.531   US
CURRENT DIGEST OF THE SOVIET PRESS. ANNUAL INDEX. 1976. a. $16. Current Digest of the Soviet Press, 1480 West Lane Ave., Columbus, OH 43221. TEL 614-292-4234. Ed. Robert S. Ehlers.

320.531   US
CURRENT SOVIET POLICIES. 1953. every 5 years; latest vol.9, 1986 (27th C P S U Congress) $29. Current Digest of the Soviet Press, 1480 West Lane Ave., Columbus, OH 43221. TEL 614-422-4234. Ed. Robert S. Ehlers.

DANDELION. see *PHILOSOPHY*

DAYAN CENTER FOR MIDDLE EASTERN AND AFRICAN STUDIES. BULLETIN. see *GENERAL INTEREST PERIODICALS — Israel*

320   PE
DEBATE SOCIALISTA. 1977. irreg. Mosca Azul Editores, Conquistadores 1130, Lima 27, Peru. Ed. Mirko Lauer. circ. 2,000.

354   BU
DIRECTORY OF KEY BULGARIAN GOVERNMENT AND PARTY OFFICIALS. irreg. American Embassy (in Bulgaria), 1, Aleksandur Stamboliiski Blvd., Sofia, Bulgaria.

320.531   UK
DOCUMENTS IN SOCIALIST HISTORY. no.2, 1974. irreg. (Bertrand Russell Peace Foundation) Spokesman Books, Bertrand Russell House, Gamble St., Nottingham, England.

320 900   US
DOCUMENTS OF REVOLUTION. irreg. price varies. Cornell University Press, 124 Roberts Place, Ithaca, NY 14850. TEL 607-257-7000.

320   UK   ISSN 0070-7007
DOD'S PARLIAMENTARY COMPANION. 1832. a. £60. Dod's Parliamentary Companion Ltd., Elm Cottage, Chilsham Lane, Herstmonceux, Hailsham, E. Sussex BN27 4QQ, England. Ed. J Berwick Smith. adv. bk. rev. index. circ. 4,500. (also avail. in microform from UMI; reprint service avail. from UMI)

320 350.6   US
DOING BUSINESS WITH THE FEDERAL GOVERNMENT: A PROCUREMENT GUIDE. 1980. a. Northeast-Midwest Institute, Publications Office, 218 D. St., S.E., Washington, DC 20003. TEL 202-544-5200.
    Formerly: Guide to Federal Procurement (ISSN 0276-9891)

320 940   GW   ISSN 0070-7031
DOKUMENTE ZUR DEUTSCHLANDPOLITIK. (In five series) 1961. irreg., Vol.5, no.1, 1984. price varies. (Bundesminister fuer Innerdeutsche Beziehungen) Alfred Metzner Verlag, Zeppelinallee 43, D-6000 Frankfurt/Main 97, W. Germany (B.R.D.) Eds. Karl Dietrich Bracher, Hans-Adolf Jacobsen.

320 940   GW   ISSN 0341-3276
DOKUMENTE ZUR DEUTSCHLANDPOLITIK. BEIHEFTE. 1975. irreg. price varies. (Bundesministerium fuer Innerdeutsche Beziehungen) Alfred Metzner Verlag, Zeppelinallee 43, D-6000 Frankfurt/Main 97, W. Germany (B.R.D.) Eds. K.D. Bracher, H.A. Jacobsen.

DOMOVA POKLADNICA. see *LITERATURE*

320 614.7   US
DUKE PRESS GLOBAL ISSUES SERIES. 1983. irreg. price varies. Duke University Press, 6697 College Sta., Durham, NC 27708. TEL 919-684-2173. Eds. James E. Harf, B. Thomas Trout.

320   US
DUKE PRESS POLICY STUDIES. 1981. irreg. Duke University Press, 6697 College Sta., Durham, NC 27708.

320 301   US
EAST EUROPE REPORT. irreg. (approx. 200/yr.) $5 per no. U.S. Joint Publications Research Service, 1000 N. Glebe Rd., Arlington, VA 22201 TEL 703-487-4630. (Orders to: NTIS, Springfield, VA 22161)

335.83   UK
THE EGOIST; an individualist review. 1963. irreg. £1.70 for four nos. S.E. Parker, Ed. & Pub., 19 St. Stephen's Gardens, London W2 5QU, England. adv. bk. rev. circ. 175.
    Formerly: Ego; Incorporating: Minus One (ISSN 0026-5721)

320   IS
EINUNIM BIBIKORET HAMEDINA. a. State Comptrollers Office, P.O. Box 1081, Jerusalem 91 000, Israel.

ENLIGHTENMENT AND DISSENT. see *HISTORY*

ENVIO. see *HISTORY — History Of North And South America*

320   US
ESSAYS FOR THE THIRD CENTURY. 1978. irreg., latest 1983. price varies. University Press of Kentucky, Lexington, KY 40506-0024. TEL 606-257-2951. Ed. Vincent Davis. (reprint service avail. from UMI)

328   PN   ISSN 0250-4316
ESTADISTICA PANAMENA. SITUACION POLITICA, ADMINISTRATIVA Y JUSTICIA. SECCION 611. ESTADISTICA ELECTORAL. 1960. quadriennial. Bol.$0.75. Direccion de Estadistica y Censo, Contraloria General, Apartado 5213, Panama 5, Panama. circ. 2,000.
    Formerly: Estadistica Panamena. Estadistica Electoral (ISSN 0078-897X)

320   UK
EUROPEAN SOCIALIST THOUGHT SERIES. 1974. irreg., no.11, 1983. Spokesman Books, Bertrand Russell House, Gamble St., Nottingham, England.

320 970   US
EXECUTIVE BIO-PICTORIAL DIRECTORY. 1981. a. $39.95. Braddock Communications, Inc., 1001 Connecticut Ave., N.W., Ste. 216, Washington, DC 20036. TEL 202-296-1317. Ed. Stuart Carson.

328 364 360   US   ISSN 0071-9560
F C L ACTION. 1955. irreg. membership. Friends Committee on Legislation of California, 926 J St., Rm. 707, Sacramento, CA 95814. TEL 916-443-3734. Ed. Ed Klingelhofer. circ. 750.

320   UK   ISSN 0305-3555
FABIAN RESEARCH SERIES. 1931. irreg. £15($20) Fabian Society, 11 Dartmouth St., London SW1H 9BN, England. circ. 7,000.

320   UK   ISSN 0071-3570
FABIAN SOCIETY. ANNUAL REPORT. 1891. a. £0.50. Fabian Society, 11 Dartmouth St., London, SW1H 9BN, England.
    Formerly: Annual Report on Work of Fabian Society.

320   UK
FACT PAPER ON SOUTHERN AFRICA. 1976. irreg. £0.50. International Defense and Aid Fund for Southern Africa, Canon Collins House, 64 Essex Rd., London N18LR, England.

FACTS ON FILE. YEARBOOK. see *HISTORY — Abstracting, Bibliographies, Statistics*

320   US   ISSN 0195-749X
FEDERAL REGULATORY DIRECTORY. quadrennial. Congressional Quarterly Inc., 1414 22nd St. N.W., Washington, DC 20037. TEL 202-887-8500.

328   US
FEDERAL STAFF DIRECTORY. 1982. a. $45. Congressional Staff Directory Ltd., Box 62, Mount Vernon, VA 22121. TEL 703-765-3400. Eds. Charles B. Brownson, Anna L. Brownson.

FINLAND; books and publications in politics, political history and international relations. see *HISTORY — History Of Europe*

POLITICAL SCIENCE

320 011   FI   ISSN 0355-2195
FINLAND. TILASTOKESKUS. VALTIOLLISET VAALIT. TASAVALLAN PRESIDENTIN VAALIT VALISIJAMIESTEN. (Text in English, Finnish, Swedish) 1926. irreg. (approx. every 6 yrs.) Fmk.20. Tilastokeskus - Central Statistical Office of Finland, Annankatu 44, SF-00101 Helsinki 10, Finland (Subscr. to: Government Printing Center, Box 516, SF-00101 Helsinki, Finland)

FLINDERS JOURNAL OF HISTORY AND POLITICS. see *HISTORY — History Of Australasia And Other Areas*

FOCUS ON POLITICS. see *HISTORY*

320   AU
FOEDERALISMUS-STUDIEN. 1977. irreg., vol.2, 1978. price varies. Hermann Boehlaus Nachf., c/o Dr. Karl Lueger, Ring 12, A-1010 Vienna, Austria. Ed.Bd. circ. 650.

320   DK   ISSN 0108-3279
FORUM; et aabent venstresocialistik debatblad. 1982. irreg. (5-6/yr.) Kr.85. Aurikelvej 18, 2500 Valby, Denmark. illus. Indexed: Abstr.Engl.Stud.
 Formerly: V S R Kommunikation (ISSN 0108-4232)

320 900   AU
FORVM. 1954. irreg. (approx. 6/yr.) S.150($12) Gerhard Oberschlick, Ed. & Pub., Museumstr. 5, A-1070 Vienna, Austria. adv. bk. rev. index. circ. 34,000. (back issues avail.) Indexed: Hist.Abstr. Amer.Hist.& Life.

320   US
FORWARD (OAKLAND); journal of Socialist thought. 1978. Getting Together Publications, Box 29293, Oakland, CA 94604. Ed.Bd.

320.531   FR
FRANCE DES POINTS CHAUDS. Short title: Points Chauds. irreg. price varies. Editions Syros, 1 rue de Varenne, 75006 Paris, France.

327   FR   ISSN 0082-5409
FRANCE-IBERIE RECHERCHE. ETUDES ET DOCUMENTS. 1970. irreg. price varies. Universite de Toulouse II (le Mirail), Institut d'Etudes Hispaniques, Hispanoamericaines, 5 Allees Antonio Machado, 31058 Toulouse, France.

327   US   ISSN 0488-728X
FREE ALBANIAN/SHQIPTARI I LIRE. (Text in English and Albanian) 1957. irreg. (1-2/yr.) donation. Free Albania Committee, 150 Fifth Ave., New York, NY 10011. TEL 212-691-9797. Ed.Bd. bk. rev. illus. circ. 1,000. (tabloid format)

FREIE UNIVERSITAET BERLIN. OSTEUROPA-INSTITUT. BERICHTE. see *HUMANITIES: COMPREHENSIVE WORKS*

FREIE UNIVERSITAET BERLIN. OSTEUROPA-INSTITUT. ERZIEHUNGSWISSENSCHAFTLICHE VEROEFFENTLICHUNGEN. see *EDUCATION*

FREIE UNIVERSITAET BERLIN. OSTEUROPA-INSTITUT. PHILOSOPHISCHE UND SOZIOLOGISCHE VEROEFFENTLICHUNGEN. see *PHILOSOPHY*

322.4   GW
FRIEDEN. 1981. a. Lamuv Verlag GmbH, Martinstr. 7, 5303 Bornheim 3, W. Germany (B.R.D.) Eds. A. Meyer, K. Rabe. circ. 30,000. (back issues avail.)

320 300   US   ISSN 0161-3340
GENERAL SOCIAL SURVEYS. 1972. a. National Opinion Research Center, 1155 E. 60th St., Chicago, IL 60637. TEL 312-962-1213.

320   US   ISSN 0736-7163
GEORGETOWN UNIVERSITY CENTER FOR STRATEGIC AND INTERNATIONAL STUDIES. SIGNIFICANT ISSUES SERIES. 1979. irreg., vol.7, 1985. price varies ($6.95 to $12.95) Georgetown University, Center for Strategic and International Studies, 1800 K St. N.W., Ste. 400, Washington, DC 20006. TEL 202-775-3119. Ed. Amos A. Jordan. circ. 1,500.

320   SW
GOETEBORG STUDIES IN POLITICS. irreg. price varies. Liber Forlag, S-205 10, Malmo, Sweden. Ed. Joergen Westerstaahl.
 Formerly: Studier i Politik/Studies in Politics.

300   II   ISSN 0436-1326
GOKHALE INSTITUTE MIMEOGRAPH SERIES. 1967. irreg. price varies. Gokhale Institute of Politics and Economics, Pune 411004, India.

320 330   II   ISSN 0072-4912
GOKHALE INSTITUTE OF POLITICS AND ECONOMICS. STUDIES. (Text in English) irreg., 1975, no.64. price varies. Gokhale Institute of Politics and Economics, Pune 411004, India (Dist. by: Orient Longman Ltd., Nicol Rd., Ballard Estate, Bombay 400038, India)

320 800 301   US   ISSN 0270-7497
GREAT ISSUES OF THE DAY. 1981. irreg., approx. 2/yr. $17.95 (hardcover); $8.95 (paperback) per no. Borgo Press, Box 2845, San Bernardino, CA 92406. TEL 714-884-5813.

320   US
GREENWOOD HISTORICAL ENCYCLOPEDIA OF THE WORLD'S POLITICAL PARTIES. 1982. irreg. price varies. Greenwood Press, Box 5007, 88 Post Rd. West, Westport, CT 06881. TEL 203-226-3571.
 Formerly: Greenwood Encyclopedia of the World's Political Parties.

320.5   US   ISSN 8756-0208
GUIDE TO THE AMERICAN LEFT; directory and bibliography. 1979. a. $24.95. Laird Wilcox, Box 2047, Olathe, KS 66061. TEL 913-829-0609. bibl. circ. 700. Indexed: P.A.I.S. Vert.File Ind.
 Formerly: Directory of the American Left; Supersedes (1969-1970): Guide to the American Left (ISSN 0017-5315)

320   US   ISSN 8756-0216
GUIDE TO THE AMERICAN RIGHT; directory and bibliography. 1978. a. $24.95. Laird Wilcox, Box 2047, Olathe, KS 66061. TEL 913-829-0609. circ. 1,800. Indexed: P.A.I.S. Vert.File Ind.
 Formerly: Directory of the American Right.

320   US
GUIDE TO U.S. GOVERNMENT DIRECTORIES. 1981. irreg., vol.2, 1985. $60.50. Oryx Press, 2214 N. Central at Encanto, Phoenix, AZ 85004-1483. TEL 602-254-6156. Ed. Donna Rae Larson. (back issues avail.)

956.940 296   SA   ISSN 0017-6354
HABINYAN. (Text in English) irreg., (approx. 4/yr.) membership. Ichud Habonim S.A., Zionist Centre, 84 de Villiers St., Johannesburg, South Africa. circ. 1,500.
 Supersedes in part: Kol Hatnua.
Zionism

320 301   SZ   ISSN 0073-182X
HELVETIA POLITICA; Schriften des Forschungszentrums fuer Geschichte und Soziologie der schweizerischen Politik. (Text in French, German or Italian) 1966. irreg. price varies. ‡ Francke Verlag, Postfach, CH-3000 Berne 26, Switzerland. Ed.Bd.

322.4   GW   ISSN 0722-8252
HIMMEL & ERDE; international revue. 1981. irreg. Verlag Roter Funke, Goethestr. 22, D-2800 Bremen 1, W. Germany (B.R.D.) Ed. Klaus Mecking. (back issues avail.)

HISTORIC DOCUMENTS. see *HISTORY — History Of North And South America*

HITOTSUBASHI JOURNAL OF LAW AND POLITICS. see *LAW*

320   UK   ISSN 0142-7377
HULL PAPERS IN POLITICS. 1978. irreg. price varies. University of Hull, Department of Politics, Hull, England. Ed. Dr. Philip Norton.

HUMAN RESOURCES ABSTRACTS; an international information service. see *ABSTRACTING AND INDEXING SERVICES*

320   DK   ISSN 0106-4177
HVEM, HVAD, HVOR. 1982. a. Kr.78. Bibliotekscentralen, Telegrafvej 5, DK-2750 Ballerup, Denmark.

320   SZ
I P Z INFORMATION. REIHE S: SUBVERSION. 1971. irreg., no.17, 1978. price varies. Institut fuer Politologische Zeitfragen, Postfach 2720, 8023 Zurich, Switzerland.

I S H I OCCASIONAL PAPERS IN SOCIAL CHANGE. (Institute for the Study of Human Issues) see *SOCIOLOGY*

320.531   AU
I U S Y BULLETIN. 1971. irreg. free. International Union of Socialist Youth, Neustiftgasse, A-1070 Vienna, Austria. Ed. Htun Aung. illus.
 Formerly: I U S Y Survey (ISSN 0019-0888)
Socialism

320   PE
IDEOLOGIA Y POLITICA. (Text in Castellano) 1973. irreg., latest no.2. price varies. (Instituto de Estudios Peruanos) I E P Ediciones, Horacio Urteaga 694 (Campo de Marte), Lima 11, Peru. (back issues avail.)

ILLINOIS GOVERNMENT RESEARCH. see *PUBLIC ADMINISTRATION*

320 301 800   IT
INDAGINI E PROSPETTIVE. irreg. Angelo Longo Editore, Via Paolo Costa 33, P.O. Box 431, 48100 Ravenna, Italy.

320   FR   ISSN 0073-7836
INFORMATHEQUE.* irreg. price varies. Entreprise Moderne d'Edition, 17 rue Vieta, 75017 Paris, France (Subscr. Address: 9 rue du Roussillon-Zone Industrielle, 91220 Bretigny-sur-Orge, France)

300   AU   ISSN 0083-6125
INFORMATIONEN ZU AKTUELLEN FRAGEN DER SOZIAL- UND WIRTSCHAFTPOLITIK. 1962. irreg. price varies. ‡ Verein fuer Sozial- und Wirtschaftsforschung, Renngasse 12, A-1010 Vienna, Austria. Ed.Bd. circ. 1,000.

320   FR   ISSN 0073-7925
INFORMATIONS ET ETUDES SOCIALISTES.* 1971. irreg. 20 F. Institut d'Etudes Socialistes, Paris, 25 rue du Louvre, Paris 1er, France.

340   PE
INFORMES. no.8, 1982. irreg. Instituto de Promocion y Educacion Popular, Av. Pardo 130, Chimbote, Peru.

INSTITUT DES HAUTES ETUDES DE L'AMERIQUE LATINE. COLLECTION DES TRAVAUX ET MEMOIRES. see *HISTORY — History Of North And South America*

INSTITUT ZA MEDJUNARODNU POLITIKU I PRIVREDU. GODISNIJAK. see *POLITICAL SCIENCE — International Relations*

320 340   IT
INSTITUTE OF EUROPEAN STUDIES. ANNALI I S E. (Text in English, French, Italian; summaries in Italian) 1979. a. L.25000($15) Institute of European Studies, Via Poli 29, I-00187 Rome, Italy. Ed. Michele Formica. bk. rev. circ. 3,500. (back issues avail.)

320   SI   ISSN 0377-5437
INSTITUTE OF SOUTHEAST ASIAN STUDIES. ANNUAL REVIEW. (Text in English) 1974. a. price varies. Institute of Southeast Asian Studies, Heng Mui Keng Terrace, Pasir Panjang, Singapore 0511, Singapore.

320   SI
INSTITUTE OF SOUTHEAST ASIAN STUDIES. MONOGRAPHS SERIES. (Text in English) 1973. irreg., no.73, 1987. price varies. Institute of Southeast Asian Studies, Heng Mui Keng Terrace, Pasir Panjang, Singapore 0511, Singapore.

320   AG   ISSN 0074-0063
INSTITUTO DE CIENCIA POLITICA RAFAEL BIELSA. ANUARIO. 1968. a. Arg.$75($8) Universidad Nacional de Rosario, Instituto de Ciencia Politica Rafael Bielsa, Facultad de Ciencia Politica y Relaciones Internacionales, Division Publicaciones, Cordoba 2020, Rosario, Argentina. Ed. Alberto Dominguez.

320 330.9 US ISSN 0730-2355
INTELLECTUAL ACTIVIST. 1979. irreg., latest vol.4. $44. Intellectual Activist, Inc., 131 Fifth Ave., Ste. 101, New York, NY 10003. TEL 212-982-8357. Ed. Peter Schwartz. bk. rev. (back issues avail.)

322.44 IS
INTER. (Text in English) a. Tel Aviv University, Jaffee Center for Strategic Studies, Ramat Aviv, Tel Aviv 69 978, Israel.

INTERNATIONAL JOURNAL OF GROUP TENSIONS. see *PSYCHOLOGY*

320 CN
INTERNATIONAL POLITICAL SCIENCE ASSOCIATION. WORLD CONGRESS. 1951. triennial, 12th, 1982 Rio de Janeiro; 13th, 1985 Paris, France. price varies. International Political Science Association, c/o University of Ottawa, Ottawa, Ont. K1N 6N5, Canada. TEL 613-564-5818. (also avail. in microfiche)
 Formerly: International Political Science Association. World Conference. Proceedings (ISSN 0074-7467)

INTERNATIONAL YEAR BOOK AND STATESMEN'S WHO'S WHO. see *SOCIAL SCIENCES: COMPREHENSIVE WORKS*

320 US
INTERNATIONAL YEARBOOK FOR STUDIES OF LEADERS AND LEADERSHIP. a. Northern Illinois University Press, DeKalb, IL 60115. TEL 815-753-1826. bibl.

320 US
INTERNATIONAL YEARBOOK OF ORGANIZATIONAL DEMOCRACY. 1982. a. John Wiley & Sons, Inc., 605 Third Ave., New York, NY 10016. TEL 212-850-6000. Ed. B. Wilbert.

320 SZ ISSN 0579-8337
INTER-PARLIAMENTARY UNION. SERIES: "REPORTS AND DOCUMENTS". 1965. irreg., no.13, 1986. price varies. Inter-Parliamentary Union, Place du Petit-Saconnex, 1209 Geneva, Switzerland.

320 US ISSN 0074-1078
INTER-UNIVERSITY CONSORTIUM FOR POLITICAL AND SOCIAL RESEARCH. ANNUAL REPORT. 1963. a. free. Inter-University Consortium for Political and Social Research, Box 1248, Ann Arbor, MI 48106. TEL 313-764-2570.

320 352 310 US
IOWA OFFICIAL REGISTER. 1892. biennial. free. Secretary of State of Iowa, State Capitol Bldg., Des Moines, IA 50319 TEL 515-281-5866. (Subscr. to: State Printing Office, Grimes State Office Building, Des Moines, IA 50319) Ed. Tamara Rood. illus.

320 IE ISSN 0790-7184
IRISH POLITICAL STUDIES. a. £9. Political Studies Association of Ireland, Social Sciences Research Centre, University College Galway, Ireland. Eds. P. Arthur, M. Laver.

IRODALOM - SZOCIALIZMUS. see *LITERATURE*

320 IT
ISTITUTO GRAMSCI PIEMONTESE. MATERIALI.* vol.2, 1976. irreg. (Istituto Gramsci Piemontese) T. Musolini Editore, Via Rubiana 47, 10139 Turin, Italy.

051 US ISSN 0021-390X
JAG. 1962. irreg. (9-10/yr.) free. Jag, Inc., 10 E. Charles, Oelwein, IA 50662. TEL 319-283-3491. Ed. Dr. R.S. Jaggard. circ. 1,250. (processed; back issues avail.) Indexed: Leg.Per. C.L.I.

328.54 II ISSN 0448-2433
JAMMU AND KASHMIR. LEGISLATIVE COUNCIL. COMMITTEE ON PRIVILEGES. REPORT. (Text in English) irreg. Legislative Council, Comittee on Privileges, Srinagar, Jammu and Kashmir, India.

320.532 JA ISSN 0007-4683
JAPANESE COMMUNIST PARTY. CENTRAL COMMITTEE. BULLETIN: INFORMATION FOR ABROAD. (Text in English) 1961. irreg. $60. Japanese Communist Party, Sendagaya 4-26-7, Shibuya-ku, Tokyo, Japan. adv. illus.

JERUSALEM INSTITUTE FOR ISRAEL STUDIES. DISCUSSION PAPERS. see *HUMANITIES: COMPREHENSIVE WORKS*

320 327 IS ISSN 0334-2786
JERUSALEM PAPERS ON PEACE PROBLEMS. (Text and summaries in English) 1974. irreg. price varies. Leonard Davis Institute for International Relations, Truman Building, Mt. Scopus, Jerusalem 91905, Israel (Subscr. to: The Leonard Davis Institute, Hebrew University, 91904 Jerusalem, Israel) Ed. Gabriel Sheffer. circ. 250. (back issues avail.)

323.1 947 296 IS ISSN 0021-6895
JEWS AND THE JEWISH PEOPLE; excerpts from the Soviet press. 1961. irreg. (2-4/yr.) $10 per vol. Hebrew University, Center for Research and Documentation of East-European Jewry, Givat Ram, Jerusalem 91 904, Israel. Ed. Y. Ingerman. circ. 500.

JOHNS HOPKINS UNIVERSITY STUDIES IN HISTORICAL AND POLITICAL SCIENCE. see *HISTORY*

954.9 320 PK
JOURNAL OF POLITICAL SCIENCE. (Text in English) 1971. a. Rps.80($4) Government College, Department of Political Science, Lahore, Pakistan (Subscr: No-F.G.4, Wahdat Colony, Lahore-16, Pakistan) Eds. Hameed A.K. Rai. adv. bk. rev. circ. 200. Indexed: A.B.C.Pol.Sci.
 Formerly: Journal of History and Political Science.

320 US
JOURNAL OF SOCIAL AND POLITICAL STUDIES MONOGRAPH SERIES. (Former name of council: Council on American Affairs) 1957. irreg., unnumbered. Council for Social and Economic Studies, 1133 13 St., N.W., Comm. 2, Washington, DC 20005. TEL 202-789-0231.

329.9 DK ISSN 0109-890X
K T. 1982. irreg. Kr.15 per no. Kommunistisk Arbejderparti, Studiestraede 24, 1455 Copenhagen K, Denmark. Eds. Philip Arctander, Kari Soenshagen. bk. rev. illus. circ. 1,000.
 Formerly: Kommunistisk Tidsskrift (ISSN 0105-1903)

320 370 574 530 US
KETTERING REPORT. 1961. biennial. free. Charles F. Kettering Foundation, 5335 Far Hills Ave., Dayton, OH 45429. TEL 513-434-7300. Ddr. Robert E. Daley. circ. 5,000.
 Formerly: Charles F. Kettering Foundation. Annual Report (ISSN 0069-2735)

KOBLENZER GEOGRAPHISCHES KOLLOQUIUM. see *GEOGRAPHY*

322.4 GW
KOELNER FRIEDENS-ANZEIGER; Zeitung aus der Koelner Friedensbewegung. 1981. irreg. DM.25($10) students DM.10. Koelner Friedensforum, Roonstr. 71, D-5000 Cologne 1, W. Germany (B.R.D.) Ed.Bd. circ. 5,000. (back issues avail.)

320.532 UR
KOMMUNISTICHESKAYA PARTIYA SOVETSKOGO SOYUZA. VYSSHAYA PARTIINAYA SHKOLA. UCHENYE ZAPISKI. 1973. irreg. 1.14 Rub. Izdatel'stvo Mysl', Leninskii Prospekt 15, 117071 Moscow B-71, Russian S.F.S.R., U.S.S.R.

320 330 KO
KOREA POLICY SERIES.* no.16, 1973. irreg. Korean Overseas Information Service, Seoul, S. Korea.

KOREAN AFFAIRS REPORT. see *BUSINESS AND ECONOMICS — Economic Situation And Conditions*

L A W G LETTER. (Latin American Working Group) see *LITERARY AND POLITICAL REVIEWS*

329 US ISSN 0882-116X
L F L REPORTS. 1981. irreg. donations. Libertarians for Life, 13424 Hathaway Dr., Wheaton, MD 20906. TEL 301-460-4141. Ed. Glen Garvin. bk. rev. circ. 1,000. (back issues avail.)

LATIN AMERICA & CARIBBEAN REVIEW. see *BUSINESS AND ECONOMICS — Economic Situation And Conditions*

LAW AND POLITICAL REVIEW. see *LAW*

320 016 US ISSN 0733-2998
LEFT INDEX; a quarterly index to periodicals of the left. 1982. q. $35 to individuals; $55 institutions. Reference and Research Services, 511 Lincoln St., Santa Cruz, CA 95060. Ed. Joan Nordquist. (back issues avail.)

322.4 UK ISSN 0267-7121
LIBERTARIAN ALLIANCE. BACKGROUND BRIEFINGS. 1985. irreg. £5($10) Libertarian Alliance, 3 Langley Court, Covent Garden, London WC2E 9JY, England. Ed.Bd. adv. bk. rev. bibl. film rev. circ. 1,000. (back issues avail.)

323.4 UK ISSN 0267-677X
LIBERTARIAN ALLIANCE. CULTURAL NOTES. 1983. irreg. £5($10) Libertarian Alliance, 3 Langley Court, Covent Garden, London WC2E 9JY, England. Ed.Bd. adv. bk. rev. bibl. film rev. circ. 1, 000. (back issues avail.)

332.4 UK ISSN 0267-6761
LIBERTARIAN ALLIANCE. FOREIGN POLICY PERSPECTIVES. 1983. irreg. £5($10) Libertarian Alliance, 3 Langley Court, Covent Garden, London WC2E 9JY, England. Ed.Bd. adv. bk. rev. bibl. film rev. circ. 1,000. (back issues avail.)

332.4 UK ISSN 0267-7156
LIBERTARIAN ALLIANCE. PERSONAL PERSPECTIVES. 1984. irreg. £5($10) Libertarian Alliance, 3 Langley Court, Covent Garden, London WC2E 9JY, England. Ed.Bd. adv. bk. rev. bibl. film rev. circ. 1,000. (back issues avail.)

322.4 UK ISSN 0267-7059
LIBERTARIAN ALLIANCE. POLITICAL NOTES. 1979. irreg. £5($10) Libertarian Alliance, 3 Langley Court, Covent Garden, London WC2E 9JY, England. Ed.Bd. adv. bk. rev. bibl. film rev. circ. 1, 000. (back issues avail.)

300 320 UK ISSN 0267-7067
LIBERTARIAN ALLIANCE. SCIENTIFIC NOTES. 1985. irreg. £5($10) Libertarian Alliance, 3 Langley Court, Covent Garden, London WC2E 9JY, England. Ed.Bd. adv. bk. rev. film rev. bibl. circ. 1, 000. (back issues avail.)

320 UK ISSN 0267-7180
LIBERTARIAN ALLIANCE. STUDY GUIDES. 1985. irreg. £5($10) Libertarian Alliance, 3 Langley Court, Covent Garden, London WC2E 9JY, England.

322.4 UK
LIBERTARIAN ALLIANCE. TACTICAL NOTES. 1985. irreg. £5($10) Libertarian Alliance, 3 Langley Court, Covent Garden, London WC2E 9JY, England. Ed.Bd. adv. bk. rev. bibl. film rev. circ. 1, 000. (back issues avail.)

322.4 UK
LIBERTARIAN ALLIANCE. WORLD REPORTS. 1985. irreg. £5($10) Libertarian Alliance, 3 Langley Court, Covent Garden, London WC2E 9JY, England. Ed.Bd. adv. bk. rev. bibl. film rev. circ. 1, 000. (back issues avail.)
 Formerly (until 1985): Liberation Alliance. International Reports.

322.4 UK ISSN 0267-6788
LIBERTARIAN NEWS. 1982. irreg. £5($10) Libertarian Alliance, 3 Langley Court, Covent Garden, London WC2E 9JY, England. Ed.Bd. adv. bk. rev. bibl. film rev. circ. 1,000. (back issues avail.)

322.4 UK ISSN 0267-6796
LIBERTARIAN REPRINTS. 1979. irreg. £5($10) Libertarian Alliance, 3 Langley Court, Covent Garden, London WC2E 9JY, Englnad. Ed.Bd. adv. bk. rev. bibl. film rev. circ. 1,000. (back issues avail.)

320 LH
LIECHTENSTEIN POLITISCHE SCHRIFTEN. 1972. irreg. $13. Verlag der Liechtensteinischen Akademischen Gesellschaft, Am Schragen Weg 2, Postfach 44, FL-9490 Vaduz, Liechtenstein. circ. 1, 000.

POLITICAL SCIENCE

320 IS ISSN 0334-3952
MAASEF. (Text in Hebrew) 1971. a. Institute for the Study of the Jewish Labour Party, Givat Haviva, D.N Menashe 37 850, Israel.

335 HU ISSN 0076-2415
MAGYAR MUNKASMOZGALMI MUZEUM. EVKONYV. 1967/68. biennial. 90 Ft. Muzsak Kozmuvelodesi Kiado, 1139 Kartacs ul. 24-26, Budapest, Hungary. Ed.Bd.

320 UG
MAKERERE POLITICAL REVIEW.* 1971. irreg. Makerere Political Society, Political Science Department, Makerere University, Kampala, Uganda. Ed. Amos Danson Twino. bibl.

320.531 CE
MAKSVADAYA. (Text in Sinhalese) 1970. irreg. Naba Sama Samaja Party, 17 Barracks Lane, Kew Rd., Colombo 2, Sri Lanka. Ed. Vickamabahu Karanarathne. adv. bk. rev. circ. 500.

320 MW ISSN 0076-3225
MALAWI. MINISTRY OF LOCAL GOVERNMENT. ANNUAL REPORT. a. K.0.50. Government Printer, Box 37, Zomba, Malawi.

320 914 UK ISSN 0542-4550
MALTA YEARBOOK. a. $10. New Product Newsletter Co. Ltd., 1A Chesterfield St., London W.1., England.

320 US
MARINE AFFAIRS JOURNAL. 1973. a. University of Rhode Island, Marine Advisory Service, Marine Affairs Program, Narragansett Bay Campus, Narragansett, RI 02882. TEL 401-792-6498. charts. circ. 300. Indexed: Ocean.Abstr.

MARXISM AND THE MASS MEDIA; towards a basic bibliography. see COMMUNICATIONS

MARXISTISCHE STUDIEN. see SOCIAL SCIENCES: COMPREHENSIVE WORKS

320 AT ISSN 0085-3224
MELBOURNE JOURNAL OF POLITICS. 1968. a. Aus.$7. ‡ University of Melbourne, Political Science Society, Parkville, Vic. 3052, Australia. Ed.Bd. adv. bk. rev. circ. 1,000. (back issues avail.) Indexed: Aus.P.A.I.S.

320 AT
MELBOURNE POLITICS MONOGRAPHS. 1973. a. Aus.$8.95. ‡ University of Melbourne, Department of Political Science, Parkville 3052, Victoria, Australia. Ed.Bd. adv. bk. rev. bibl. circ. 1,000.

949.3 BE ISSN 0025-908X
MEMO FROM BELGIUM. (Editions in Dutch, English, French, German, Italian, Spanish) 1960. irreg. (4-6/yr.) free. Ministere des Affaires Etrangeres, 2 rue des Quatre Bras, 1000 Brussels, Belgium (For English edition, inquire: Consulate General de Belgique, Information Officer, 50 Rockefeller Plaza, Suite 1104, New York, New York) charts. illus. circ. 3,000. Indexed: P.A.I.S.

320 US
MISSOURI ANNUAL CAMPAIGN FINANCE REPORT. 1979. a. free. Office of the Secretary of State, Campaign Reporting Division, Box 1370, Jefferson City, MO 65102. TEL 314-751-3077. circ. 2,500.

MONASH PAPERS ON SOUTHEAST ASIA. see HISTORY — History Of Asia

MONGOLIA REPORT. see BUSINESS AND ECONOMICS — Economic Situation And Conditions

320 AT ISSN 0077-2143
MUNICIPAL ASSOCIATION OF VICTORIA. MINUTES OF PROCEEDINGS OF ANNUAL SESSION. 1879. a. free; available to member councils. ‡ Municipal Association of Victoria, 468 St. Kilda Rd., Melbourne, Vic. 3004, Australia. Ed. Ian R. Pawsey. index. circ. 4,000.

808.8 UK
NATIONAL AWAMI PARTY OF BANGLADESH (IN GREAT BRITAIN). BULLETIN.* irreg., no.5, 1973. National Awami Party of Bangla Desh, 86 Oakleigh Road, London N.11, England. Ed. Fazlul Huq.

352 AT ISSN 0085-3682
NATIONAL CIVIC COUNCIL. FACTS. 1959. irreg., no.4, 1982. Aus.$8. National Civic Council, 254 Queen St., Melbourne, Vic. 3000, Australia. Ed. Peter W. Taylor. adv. circ. 7,000.

NATIONAL DIRECTORY OF CORPORATE PUBLIC AFFAIRS. see BUSINESS AND ECONOMICS

NATIONAL DIRECTORY OF STATE AGENCIES. see BUSINESS AND ECONOMICS — Trade And Industrial Directories

329 US ISSN 0077-5282
NATIONAL PARTY PLATFORMS. SUPPLEMENT. (Sixth edition covers 1840-1976; supplement in 1982 covers 1980) 1961. irreg. latest 1982. price varies. University of Illinois Press, 54 E. Gregory Dr., Champaign, IL 61820. TEL 217-333-0950. Ed. Donald B. Johnson.

960 338 CX ISSN 0028-050X
NATIONS NOUVELLES. (Text in French) N.S. 1966. irreg. 3500 Fr.CFA. Organisation Commune Africaine et Mauricienne (OCAM), B.P. 965, Bangui, Central African Republic. Ed. Pierre Debato. adv. bibl. charts. illus. stat. circ. 700.

329 PL ISSN 0137-141X
NAUKI POLITYCZNE. 1974. irreg. price varies. Adam Mickiewicz University Press, Marchlewskiego 128, 61-874 Poznan, Poland.

320 GW ISSN 0176-604X
NEUE POLITISCHE LITERATUR. BEIHEFTE; Forschungsberichte zur internationalen Literatur. (Supplement to: Neue Politische Literatur (ISSN-0028-3320)) irreg., vol.3, 1986. price varies. Franz Steiner Verlag Wiesbaden GmbH, Birkenwaldstr. 44, Postfach 347, 7000 Stuttgart 1, W. Germany (B.R.D.)

320 330 UK
NEW AFRICAN YEARBOOK: EAST AND SOUTH. a. £14.95($29.95). I.C. Publications Ltd., P.O. Box 261, 69 Gt. Queen St., London WC2B 5BN, England. Ed. Alan Rake. adv. circ. 10,000.
Supersedes in part: New African Yearbook (ISSN 0308-1699)

320 330 UK
NEW AFRICAN YEARBOOK: WEST AND CENTRAL. 1977. a. £14.95($29.95) I.C. Publications Ltd., P.O. Box 261, 69 Gt Queen St., London WC2B 5BN, England. Ed. Alan Rake. adv. bk. rev. illus. stat. circ. 10,000. (back issues avail.)
Supersedes in part: New African Yearbook (ISSN 0308-1699)

320 DK ISSN 0108-1829
NEW UNITED NATIONS PUBLICATIONS. 1982. irreg. (5-6/yr.) free. F N S Informationskontor for de Nordiske Lande - United Nations Information Centre for the Nordic Countries, H.C. Andersens Boulevard 37, 1553 Copenhagen V, Denmark.
Formerly: United Nations Publications.

NEW ZEALAND SLAVONIC JOURNAL. see HUMANITIES: COMPREHENSIVE WORKS

952 US
NEWSLETTER OF RESEARCH ON JAPANESE POLITICS. 1969. a. $4.25. ‡ Brigham Young University, Asian Studies Program, Kennedy Center for International Studies-745 SWKT, Provo, UT 84602. TEL 801-378-3303. Ed. Lee W. Farnsworth. bk. rev. bibl. circ. 200. (tabloid format; back issues avail.)

320 US ISSN 0078-0979
NOMOS. 1958. a. price varies. (American Society for Political and Legal Philosophy) New York University Press, Washington Square, New York, NY 10003. TEL 212-598-2886. Eds. J. Roland Pennock, John W. Chapman.

320 CR
NOTICIAS DE GUATEMALA. irreg. Apartado Postal 463, San Juan de Tibas, Costa Rica. Indexed: HR Rep.

OBLASTNI MUZEUM V GOTTWALDOVE. ZPRAVY. see HISTORY — History Of Europe

OCCASIONAL PAPERS IN ILLINOIS POLITICS. see PUBLIC ADMINISTRATION

ODENSE UNIVERSITET. INSTITUT FOR OFFENTLIG OEKONOMI OG POLITIK. OCCASIONAL PAPER. see BUSINESS AND ECONOMICS

320 AU ISSN 0170-0847
OESTERREICHISCHES JAHRBUCH FUER POLITIK. a. price varies. Verlag fuer Geschichte und Politik, Neulinggasse 26, A-1030 Vienna, Austria. Eds. Andreas Khol, Gunter Ofner, Alfred Stirnmann.

ONE FAMILY. see SOCIAL SERVICES AND WELFARE

320 338 UK
P S I: REPORT SERIES. 1933. irreg. £55 (includes Discussion Papers; Studies in European Politics; Policy Studies. Policy Studies Institute, 100 Park Village East, London NW1, England.
Formerly: P E P (ISSN 0030-7947)

PAKISTAN. NATIONAL ASSEMBLY. DEBATES. OFFICIAL REPORT. see PUBLIC ADMINISTRATION

329 BE
PANORAMA DEMOCRATE CHRETIEN. (Text in French) 1968. irreg. Christian Democratic International, 16 rue de la Victoire, Boite 1, 1060 Brussels, Belgium.
Formerly: International Christian Democratic Study and Documentation Center. Informations (ISSN 0538-5555)

322 AT
PARLIAMENTARY HANDBOOK OF THE COMMONWEALTH OF AUSTRALIA. 1915. irreg., approx every 3 yrs. price varies. Australian Government Publishing Service, Box 84, Canberra, A.C.T. 2601, Australia. illus. circ. 2,000.
Former titles: Australian Parliamentary Handbook; Parliamentary Handbook of the Commonwealth of Australia.

329.9 CK
PARTIDO COMUNISTA DE COLOMBIA. DOCUMENTOS. 1975. irreg. Editorial 8 de Junio, Apdo. 51694, Medellin, Colombia.

329.9 SP
PARTIDO SOCIALISTA POPULAR. CONGRESO. (ACTAS)* no.3, 1976. irreg. Tucar Ediciones S.A., Eduardo Dato 21, Madrid 10, Spain.

320 PE
PARTIDO SOCIALISTA REVOLUCIONARIO. INFORMES. 1977. irreg. Partido Socialista Revolucionario, Pontevedra 173 - Surco, Lima, Peru. Ed. Francisco Moncloa.

320 CN ISSN 0553-4283
PEACE RESEARCH REVIEWS. 1967. irreg. $20 for 6 nos. Peace Research Institute-Dundas, 25 Dundana Ave., Dundas, Ont. L9H 4E5, Canada. Eds. Alan Newcombe, Hanna Newcombe. circ. 500. Indexed: A.B.C.Pol.Sci. Abstr.Mil.Bibl.

322.4 SJ
PEOPLE'S VOICE. (Text in English) irreg., vol.2, no.7, 1980. Tigray People's Liberation Front, Foreign Relations Bureau, Box 8177, Khartoum, Sudan.

001.45 960 US
PERSPECTIVES ON SOUTHERN AFRICA. irreg., no.34, 1982. price varies. University of California Press, 2120 Berkeley Way, Berkeley, CA 94720. TEL 415-642-4247.

PHILIPPINES YEARBOOK OF THE FOOKIEN TIMES. see BUSINESS AND ECONOMICS — Banking And Finance

320 US
PITTSBURGH SERIES IN POLICY & INSTITUTIONAL STUDIES. 1983. irreg. price varies. University of Pittsburgh Press, 127 N. Bellefield Ave., Pittsburgh, PA 15260. Ed. Bert A. Rockman.

322.4 US
PLANET EARTH.* a. $25. Planetary Citizens, 325 9th St., San Francisco, CA 94103. Ed. Carol J. Anderer.

POLITICAL SCIENCE

329   FR
LE POING ET LA ROSE. 1970. irreg. Parti Socialiste, 10 rue de Solferino, 75333 Paris Cedex 07, France. Ed. Lionel Jospin.
    Formerly: Bulletin Socialiste (ISSN 0068-4155)

320   US   ISSN 0160-2675
POLICY GRANTS DIRECTORY. 1977. irreg. $4 to individuals; institutions $8. Policy Studies Organization, University of Illinois, 361 Lincoln Hall, Urbana, IL 61801. TEL 217-359-8541. Eds. Stuart Nagel, Marian Neef. bibl. charts. stat. index. circ. 2,400. (reprint service avail. from ISI)

320 070.5   US   ISSN 0272-0671
POLICY PUBLISHERS AND ASSOCIATIONS DIRECTORY. 1980. irreg. $4 to individuals; institutions $8. Policy Studies Organization, University of Illinois at Urbana-Champaign, 361 Lincoln Hall, Urbana, IL 61801. TEL 217-359-8541. Eds. Stuart Nagel, Kathleen Burkholder. (reprint service avail. from ISI)

320   US   ISSN 0270-1200
POLICY RESEARCH CENTERS DIRECTORY. 1978. irreg. $4 to individuals; institutions $8. Policy Studies Organization, University of Illinois, 361 Lincoln Hall, Urbana, IL 61801. TEL 217-359-8541. Eds. Stuart Nagel, Marian Neef. bibl. charts. stat. index. circ. 2,400. (reprint service avail. from ISI)

309.2   US   ISSN 0362-6016
POLICY STUDIES DIRECTORY. 1972. irreg. $4 to individuals; institutions $8. Policy Studies Organization, University of Illinois at Urbana-Champaign, 361 Lincoln Hall, Urbana, IL 61801. TEL 217-359-8541. Eds. Stuart Nagel, Marian Neef. bibl. charts. stat. index. circ. 2,400. (reprint service avail. from ISI)

309.2   US   ISSN 0275-4002
POLICY STUDIES PERSONNEL DIRECTORY. 1979. irreg. $4 to individuals; institutions $8. Policy Studies Organization, 361 Lincoln Hall, University of Illinois, Urbana, IL 61801. TEL 217-359-8541. Eds. Stuart Nagel, Nancy Munshaw. bibl. charts. stat. index. circ. 2,400. (reprint service avail. from ISI)

320   PL   ISSN 0208-7375
POLISH POLITICAL SCIENCE. (Text in English) 1967. a. price varies. (Polskie Towarzystwo Nauk Politycznych) Ossolineum, Publishing House of the Polish Academy of Sciences, Rynek 9, Wroclaw, Poland (Dist. by: Ars Polona-Ruch, Krakowskie Przedmiescie 7, Warsaw, Poland) Ed. Longin Pastusiak. circ. 700.
    Formerly (until 1981): Polish Round Table (ISSN 0079-3000)

320   VE
POLITEIA. 1972. a. price varies. Universidad Central de Venezuela, Instituto de Estudios Politicos, Caracas, Venezuela (Subscr. to: Servicio de Distribucion y Venta, Biblioteca Central, Universidad Central, Caracas, Venezuela) bk. rev. circ. 2,000.

320   SI   ISSN 0217-7587
POLITEIA. (Text in English) 1971. a. S.$2.50. National University of Singapore, Political Science Society, c/o Department of Political Science, Kent Ridge, Singapore 0511, Singapore. Ed. Leong Sook Mei. adv. bk. rev. circ. 2,000.
    Formerly: University of Singapore Political Science Society. Journal.

320   UY   ISSN 0079-3027
POLITICA.* irreg. Editorial Arca, Colonia 1263, Montevideo, Uruguay.

POLITICAL ANTHROPOLOGY. see *SOCIOLOGY*

320   GE
POLITICAL DOCUMENTS OF THE GERMAN DEMOCRATIC REPUBLIC. (Text in English) 1974. irreg. Panorama DDR - Auslandspresseagentur GmbH, Wilhelm-Pieck-Str. 49, 1054 Berlin, E. Germany (D.D.R.)

POLITICAL ECONOMY OF WORLD-SYSTEMS ANNUALS. see *BUSINESS AND ECONOMICS — Economic Systems And Theories, Economic History*

320 309   US
POLITICAL HANDBOOK OF THE WORLD. 1928. a. $49.95. (State University of New York at Binghamton, Center for Social Analysis) McGraw-Hill Book Co., 1221 Ave. of the Americas, New York, NY 10020. TEL 212-512-2000. Ed. Arthur S. Banks. circ. 7,000.
    Formerly: Political Handbook and Atlas of the World (ISSN 0079-3035)

320   UK
POLITICAL PARTIES OF THE WORLD. 1980. triennial. £48($90) Longman Group Ltd., Fourth Ave., Harlow, Essex CM19 5AA, England. Ed. Alan J. Day.

320 301   US   ISSN 0198-8719
POLITICAL POWER AND SOCIAL THEORY; a research annual. 1980. a. $23.75 to individuals; institutions $47.50. J A I Press Inc., Box 1678, 36 Sherwood Pl., Greenwich, CT 06836. TEL 203-661-7602. Ed. Maurice Zeitlin. Indexed: Amer.Bibl.Slavic & E.Eur.Stud. Lang.& Lang.Behav.Abstr.

POLITICAL SCIENCE ABSTRACTS. see *POLITICAL SCIENCE — Abstracting, Bibliographies, Statistics*

320   US   ISSN 0190-521X
POLITICAL SCIENCE DISCUSSION PAPERS. 1969. irreg. Kent State University, Department of Political Science, Kent, OH 44242-0001. TEL 216-672-2060. Ed. Joyce Baugh.

320   US   ISSN 0091-3715
POLITICAL SCIENCE REVIEWER; an annual review of books. 1971. a. $10. Intercollegiate Studies Institute, Inc., 14 S. Bryn Mawr Ave., Bryn Mawr, PA 19010. TEL 215-525-7501. Ed. George W. Carey. adv. bk. rev. circ. 2,000. (also avail. in microform from BLH,UMI; back issues avail.) Indexed: Bk.Rev.Ind.

329.9   UK   ISSN 0144-0918
POLITICS AND POWER. 1980. irreg. £5.95. Routledge & Kegan Paul PLC, 11 New Fetter Lane, London EC4P 4EE, England (U.S. address: Routledge Journals, 9 Park St., Boston MA 02108) Ed.Bd. adv. bk. rev. circ. 2,000.

320   US
POLITICS IN AMERICA. 1981. biennial. Congressional Quarterly Inc., 1414 22nd St., N.W., Washington, DC 20037. TEL 202-887-8500. Ed. Alan Ehrenhalt.

320   AU
POLITISCHE BILDUNG. irreg. S.24 per no. (Bundesministerium fuer Unterricht und Kunst) Verlag fuer Geschichte und Politik, Neulinggasse 26, A-1030 Vienna, Austria. Ed.Bd.

325   CN
PRINCE EDWARD ISLAND. CIVIL SERVICE COMMISSION. ANNUAL REPORT. 1963. a. free. ‡ Civil Service Commission, P.O. Box 2000, Charlottetown, Prince Edward Island, Canada. TEL 902-368-4185. circ. 125.

320   SZ
PRO UND KONTRA. 1982. irreg. 8 Fr. Schweizerische Arbeitsgemeinschaft fuer Demokratie, Feldeggstr. 65, Postfach 387, 8034 Zurich, Switzerland. circ. 3,000. (back issues avail.)

329.9   UK
PROBLEMS OF COMMUNISM. 1974. irreg. £4 for 3 issues. British & Irish Communist Organisation, 10 Athol St., Belfast BT12 4GX, Northern Ireland. Ed. Jack Lane. circ. 750. Indexed: Curr.Cont. P.A.I.S. SSCI. Soc.Sci.Ind. A.B.C.Pol.Sci. Ind.U.S.Gov.Per.

335   II
PROBLEMS OF NATIONAL LIBERATION. (Text in English) 1974. irreg. Rs.3. Ranadhir Dasgupta, 10 Bondel Rd., Calcutta 700019, India. Eds. Satyendra Narayan Mazumdar, Narahari Kaviraj. adv. bk. rev. circ. 1,000.
    Communism

320.52   CN
PROGRESSIVE CONSERVATIVE ASSOCIATION OF ALBERTA. PROGRESS BULLETIN. irreg. (4-5/yr.) free. Progressive Conservative Association of Alberta, No. 32, 9912-106th St., Edmonton, Alta. T5K 1C5, Canada. TEL 403-262-7931.

320   US   ISSN 0275-9322
PUBLIC EYE; a journal of social and political issues concerning repression in America. 1977. irreg., approx. 4/yr. $8 to individuals; institutions $15. Citizens in Defense of Civil Liberties, 343 S. Dearborn, No. 918, Chicago, IL 60604. Ed. Chip Berlet. bk. rev. illus. circ. 7,000. (also avail. in microfilm; back issues avail.) Indexed: Alt.Press Ind. HR Rep.

320   UY
PURIFICACION. 1977. irreg. Instituto Nacional de Investigaciones Historicas y Geopoliticas, Avda. 18 de Julio 2226, Montevideo, Uruguay. Ed. J.J. Scapusio.

320   IT
QUADERNI DEL SALVEMINI. vol. 16/17, 1975. irreg. price varies. Movimento Gaetano Salvemini, Via di Torre Argentina 18, 00186 Rome, Italy. Ed.Bd.

QUADERNI FIORENTINI PER LA STORIA DEL PENSIERO GIURIDICO MODERNO. see *LAW*

320   IT
QUADERNI SICILIANI. 1973. irreg. L.300. (Partito Comunista Italiano) Di Modica, Via M. Stabile 216, 90141 Sicily, Italy. illus.

320 330   II
R.B.R.R. KALE MEMORIAL LECTURES. 1937. a; none published 1947 or 1970. price varies. Gokhale Institute of Politics and Economics, Pune 411004, India (Dist. by: Orient Longman, Ltd., Nicol Rd., Ballard Estate, Bombay 400038, India)

320 327   US   ISSN 0079-9491
RADNER LECTURES. irreg., no.7, 1976. Columbia University Press, 562 W. 113th St., New York, NY 10025. TEL 212-678-6777.

320   GO   ISSN 0486-106X
REALITES GABONAISES. (Text in French) 1960. irreg. (3-4/yr.) 1000 Fr.CFA($44.12) Institut Pedagogique National, B.P. 813, Libreville, Gabon. Ed. M. A. Bouanga. illus. Indexed: Curr.Cont.Africa.

320.532   CN
REBEL YOUTH. 1970. irreg. Can.$5. Socialist Perpectives for Youth, 24 Cecil St., Toronto, Ont., Canada. Ed. Olga Lazavidis. adv. bk. rev. circ. 3, 000.
    Former titles: Young Worker (ISSN 0382-4047) & Young Communist (ISSN 0382-4039)

RECHTS- UND STAATSWISSENSCHAFTEN. see *LAW*

RECHTSWISSENSCHAFT UND SOZIALPOLITIK. see *LAW*

320 362.971   CN
REPERTOIRE ADMINISTRATIF.* no.2, 1975. irreg. Can.$6. Editeur Officiel du Quebec, 1283 Bd. Charest ouest, Quebec G1N 2C9, Canada. TEL 413-643-3895. adv. circ. 3,000.
    Formerly: Collection l'Etat et le Citoyen.

320   IE
REPSOL PAMPHLETS. irreg, no.7, 1971. Republican Educational Department, 30 Gardiner Place, Dublin 1, Ireland. Ed.Bd. charts.

329   US   ISSN 0363-9290
REPUBLICAN ALMANAC. biennial. $25. Republican National Committee, Political/Research Division, 310 First St., S.E., Washington, DC 20003. TEL 202-863-8500. illus.

320   UK   ISSN 0144-7548
REPUBLICAN ENGLISHMAN. 1979. irreg. Republican Party of England, 44 Water St., Accrington, Lancs. BB5 6QZ, England. Ed. Thomas Smith. bk. rev. circ. 50.

RESEARCH IN POLITICAL ECONOMY; an annual compilation of research. see *BUSINESS AND ECONOMICS — Economic Systems And Theories, Economic History*

RESEARCH IN SOCIAL PROBLEMS AND PUBLIC POLICY; a research annual. see *SOCIOLOGY*

RESEAUX; revue interdisciplinaire de philosophie morale et politique. see *PHILOSOPHY*

POLITICAL SCIENCE

320   US
RESOURCE RECOVERY YEAR BOOK. 1982. biennial. $315 to individuals; institutions $435. Governmental Advisory Associates, Inc., 177 E. 87 St., New York, NY 10128. TEL 212-410-4165. Ed. Robert Gould. circ. 500.

320   AG   ISSN 0034-7019
REVISTA ARGENTINA DE CIENCIA POLITICA.* vol.2, 1961. irreg. Asociacion Argentina de Ciencia Politica, Solis 443, Buenos Aires, Argentina. bk. rev.

320   AG
REVISTA ARGENTINA DE POLITICA. 1958. irreg. Editorial Norte, Cuenca 1818, Buenos Aires, Argentina. Ed. S. W. Medraho.

320.531   US   ISSN 0193-3612
REVOLUTION. Spanish edition: Revolucion (ISSN 0193-3493) 1973. irreg., approx. 2/yr. $14 to individuals; libraries $20. (Revolutionary Communist Party, Central Committee) R C P Publications, Inc., Box 3486, Merchandise Mart, Chicago, IL 60654. TEL 312-663-5920. bk. rev. index. circ. 5,000. (also avail. in microfilm from UMI; reprint service avail. from UMI)
Marxism

322   PO
RISCO. 1985. irreg. (?) Fernando Jorge de Azevedo, Edicoes, Rua Antonio Maria Cardoso, 68, 1er piso a/c CNC, Lisbon, Portugal. Dir. Joao Carlos Espada. circ. 3,000.

320.532   CN   ISSN 0047-6110
ROAD OF THE PARTY. 1970. irreg. Can.$20. Communist Party of Canada (Marxist - Leninist), Central Committee, Box 666, Station C, Montreal, Que., Canada TEL 416-252-3658. (Subscr. to: National Publications Centre, Box 727, Adelaide Station, Toronto, Ont. M5C 2J8, Canada) Ed. Hardial S. Bains. charts. illus.
Formerly (until 1980): Mass Line.
Communism

320   350   II
ROLE OF STATE LEGISLATURES IN THE FREEDOM STRUGGLE. 1976. irreg. Rs.30. Indian Council of Historical Research, 35 Ferozeshah Rd., New Delhi 110001, India (Distributed by: People's Publishing House Ltd., Rani Jhansi Rd., New Delhi 110005, India)

320   US
S C A FREE SPEECH YEARBOOK. 1960. a. $6. Speech Communication Association, 5105 Blacklick Rd., No. E, Annandale, VA 22003. TEL 703-750-0533. Ed. Stephen Smith. (reprint service avail. from UMI) Indexed: ASCA.
Formerly: Freedom of Speech Yearbook (ISSN 0071-9366)

329.9   DK   ISSN 0902-1612
S F. STATUS. 1975. a. Kr.55. Socialistiske Perspektiver Forlag, Silkeborgvej 13, 8000 Aarhus C, Denmark. Eds. Aage Frandsen, Lars Kjargaard. illus. circ. 650.
Former titles: Socialistisk Folkeparti. Status (ISSN 0108-7908) & S F Status.

320   DK   ISSN 0108-2655
S T S DEBAT. 1982. irreg. (4-5/yr.) free. (Sammenslutningen af Tvaerpolitiske Studenterorganisationer) Jens Baggesensvej 98, 8200 Aarhus N, Denmark. illus.
Formerly: S T S Information (ISSN 0105-5003)

329   AT
S.Y.A. INTERNAL BULLETIN. 1970. irreg. Socialist Youth Alliance, c/o Col. Moynard, 6 Uther St., Surry Hills, N.S.W. 2010, Australia.

SAGE SERIES ON AFRICAN MODERNIZATION AND DEVELOPMENT. see *BUSINESS AND ECONOMICS* — *International Development And Assistance*

320   US
SAGE YEARBOOKS IN POLITICS AND PUBLIC POLICY. 1975. a. $14.95 softcover; hardcover $29.95. (Policy Studies Organization) Sage Publications, Inc., 2111 W. Hillcrest Dr., Newbury Park, CA 91320 TEL 805-499-0721. (And Sage Publications, Ltd., 28 Banner St., London EC1Y 8QE, England) Ed. Stuart S. Nagel. bibl. charts. illus. stat. (back issues avail.)

SAMISDAT; Stimmen aus den "anderen Russland". see *HISTORY* — *History Of Europe*

320   SZ
ST. GALLER STUDIEN ZUR POLITIKWISSENSCHAFT. 1975. irreg., no.10, 1982. price varies. Paul Haupt AG, Falkenplatz 14, CH-3001 Berne, Switzerland.

320   US
SCHOOL OF INTERNATIONAL STUDIES. PUBLICATIONS ON RUSSIA AND EASTERN EUROPE. 1969. irreg., no.10, 1982. price varies. (University of Washington, School of International Studies) University of Washington Press, Seattle, WA 98105. TEL 206-543-4050.
Formerly: Publications on Russia and Eastern Europe (ISSN 0079-7790)

SCHOULER LECTURES IN HISTORY AND POLITICAL SCIENCE. see *HISTORY*

SCHRIFTENREIHE DAS ANDERE DEUTSCHLAND. see *HISTORY* — *History Of Europe*

320   UK
SCOTTISH GOVERNMENT YEARBOOK. 1976. a. £7.95. Unit for the Study of Government in Scotland, 31 Buccleuch Place, Edinburgh EH8 9JT, Scotland. Ed. David McCrone. adv. bk. rev. bibl. stat. circ. 900. (back issues avail.)

320   FR   ISSN 0080-8938
SERIE AFRIQUE NOIRE. 1970. irreg. price varies. (Institut d'Etudes Politiques de Bordeaux) Editions A. Pedone, 13 rue Soufflot, 75005 Paris, France.

SERIE NOVAS PERSPECTIVAS. see *HISTORY* — *History Of North And South America*

320   FR   ISSN 0586-9889
SERIE VIE LOCALE. 1969. irreg. price varies. (Institut d'Etudes Politiques de Bordeaux, Centre d'Etude et de Recherche sur la Vie Locale) Editions A. Pedone, 13 rue Soufflot, 75005 Paris, France.

320   CU
SERVI-GUIA OPINA. a. Instituto de la Demanda Interna, M 17 y 19, Vedado, Apdo. Postal 4104, Havana, Cuba.

SHVUT; Jewish problems in the USSR and Eastern Europe. see *ETHNIC INTERESTS*

320   DK   ISSN 0108-7266
SIKKERHED OG NEDRUSTNING.* 1983. a. Kr.60. (Sikkerhed og Nedrustning Udvalg) Forlaget Europa, Kompaniestraede 33, 1208 Copenhagen K, Denmark.
Formerly: Sikkerheds og Nedrustningspolitiske Udvalg. Aarsbereting.

SIR GEORGE EARLE MEMORIAL LECTURE ON INDUSTRY AND GOVERNMENT. see *BUSINESS AND ECONOMICS*

SLOVAK PRESS DIGEST. see *ETHNIC INTERESTS*

SLOVANSKE STUDIE. see *HISTORY* — *History Of Europe*

320.531   US
SOCIAL DEMOCRAT.* 1972. irreg. $2. Young Social Democrats, 181 Hudson St., No. 3A, New York, NY 10013-1804. adv. bk. rev. circ. 1,500.
Socialism

335   UK   ISSN 0081-0606
SOCIALIST REGISTER; a survey of movements and ideas. 1964. a. price varies. Merlin Press Ltd., 3 Manchester Rd, London E14 9BD, England. Ed.Bd. bk. rev. circ. 6,000.

320.531   BU   ISSN 0204-9619
SOFIISKI UNIVERSITET. KATEDRA PO NAUCHEN KOMUNIZM. GODISHNIK. (Text in Bulgarian) irreg., vol.72, 1979. 2.36 lv. Sofiiski Universitet, Katedra po Nauchen Komunizm., Sofia, Bulgaria. Ed. S. Petrov. circ. 550.
Formerly: Sofiiski Universitet. Ideologicheski Katedri. Godishnik.
Marxism

SOOCHOW JOURNAL OF POLITICAL SCIENCE & SOCIOLOGY. see *SOCIAL SCIENCES: COMPREHENSIVE WORKS*

SOUTHEAST ASIA REPORT. see *BUSINESS AND ECONOMICS* — *Economic Situation And Conditions*

320   900   AT   ISSN 0158-6041
SOUTH EAST ASIAN MONOGRAPH SERIES. 1976. irreg. Aus.$3. James Cook University of North Queensland, Centre for South East Asian Studies Committee, Townsville, Qld. 4811, Australia. Ed. Bob Hering. adv. bk. rev. circ. 350.

320.531   US   ISSN 0038-6596
SPARTACIST. (Supplement to Workers Vanguard) 1964. irreg. $0.50 per no.; included in subscr. to Workers Vanguard. (Spartacist League) Spartacist Publishing Co., Box 1377, New York, NY 10116. TEL 212-732-7861. Ed.Bd. Indexed: Alt.Press Ind.
Marxism

320   US   ISSN 0584-9365
SPOTLIGHT ON AFRICA. 1966. a. $10. American-African Affairs Association, 1735 DeSales St., N.W., Washington, DC 20036. Ed. J.A. Parker. bk. rev. circ. 1,500.

320   SZ   ISSN 0081-4105
STAAT UND POLITIK. 1966. irreg., vol.31, 1985. price varies. Paul Haupt AG, Falkenplatz 14, 3001 Berne, Switzerland. Ed. Richard Reich.

STAT A PRAVO. see *LAW*

STATE GOVERNMENT; guide to current issues and activities. see *PUBLIC ADMINISTRATION*

320   NR
STATESMAN. 1973. a. £N1($3.40) Political Science Student Association, Political Science Students Association, University of Ibadan, Department of Political Science, Ibadan, Nigeria. Ed. Doji Ajayi. adv. bk. rev. bibl. circ. 500.

320   UK   ISSN 0081-4601
STATESMAN'S YEAR BOOK; statistical and historical annual of the states of the world. 1864. a. £13.75. Macmillan Press Ltd. (Subsidiary of: Macmillan Publishers Ltd.) Little Essex St., London WC2R 3LF, England. Ed. John Paxton. index. circ. 35,000.

320   SW   ISSN 0346-6620
STOCKHOLM STUDIES IN POLITICS. (Text in Swedish or English; summaries in English) 1971. irreg. price varies. University of Stockholm, Department of Political Science - Stockholms Universitet. Statsvetenskapliga Institutionen, S-106 91, Stockholm, Sweden.

STOKVIS STUDIES IN HISTORICAL CHRONOLOGY & THOUGHT. see *HISTORY*

320   US
STUDIES IN AMERICAN POLITICAL DEVELOPMENT. 1986. a. price varies. Yale University Press, 92A Yale Sta., New Haven, CT 06520. TEL 203-432-4969. Eds. Karen Orren, Stephen Skowronek.

STUDIES IN DEFENSE POLICY. see *MILITARY*

320   II
STUDIES IN ELECTORAL POLITICS IN THE INDIAN STATES. (Text in English) irreg. Manohar Book Service, 2 Daryaganj, Ansari Rd., Panna Bhawan, Delhi 110006, India. Eds. Myron Weiner, John Osgood Field. charts, stat.

320   338   UK
STUDIES IN EUROPEAN POLITICS. 1979. irreg. £55 (subscription also includes P S I Report Series; Discussion Papers; Policy Studies) Policy Studies Institute, 100 Park Village East, London NW1, England.

320   US   ISSN 0273-1231
STUDIES IN FREEDOM. 1981. irreg. price varies. (Freedom House) Greenwood Press, Box 5007, 88 Post Rd. West, Westport, CT 06881. TEL 203-226-3571.

320   US   ISSN 0081-7996
STUDIES IN HISTORICAL AND POLITICAL SCIENCE. EXTRA VOLUMES. irreg., vol.15, 1968. (Johns Hopkins University) Bergman Publishers, Inc., 224 W. 20th St., New York, NY 10011. TEL 212-685-9074.

320 US ISSN 0081-802X
STUDIES IN INTERNATIONAL AFFAIRS
(BALTIMORE) 1967. irreg, no.26, 1975. price
varies. (Washington Center of Foreign Policy
Research) Johns Hopkins University Press, 710 W.
40th St., Ste. 275, Baltimore, MD 21211. TEL 301-
338-6900. (reprint service avail. from UMI)

320 US
STUDIES IN INTERNATIONAL AND
COMPARATIVE POLITICS. Variant title: Studies
in Comparative Politics Series. 1973. irreg., no.16,
1985. price varies. A B C-Clio, 2040 Alameda
Padre Serra, Box 4397, Santa Barbara, CA 93140-
4397. TEL 805-963-4221. Ed. Peter H. Merkl.

320.531 US
STUDIES IN MARXISM. 1977. irreg. (Marxist
Educational Press) M E P Publications, University
of Minnesota, 215 Ford Hall, 224 Church St., S.E.,
Minneapolis, MN 55455. TEL 612-872-9897. Ed.
William L. Rowe. adv. circ. 1,500.

320 US
STUDIES IN SOCIAL AND POLITICAL THEORY.
1986. $39.95 per no. Edwin Mellen Press, Box 450,
Lewiston, NY 14092.

320 330 CN
STUDIES IN THE POLITICAL ECONOMY OF
CANADA. 1970. irreg. price varies. University of
Toronto Press, Front Campus, Toronto, Ont. M5S
1A6, Canada TEL 613-667-7791. (U.S. address: 33
E. Tupper St., Buffalo, NY 14203)

320 355 CN ISSN 0081-8690
STUDIES IN THE STRUCTURE OF POWER:
DECISION MAKING IN CANADA. 1964. irreg.
price varies. (Social Science Research Council of
Canada) University of Toronto Press, Front
Campus, Toronto, Ont. M5S 1A6, Canada TEL
613-667-7791. (and 33 East Tupper St., Buffalo,
N.Y. 14023) Ed. John Meisel.

STUDIES ON FASCISM AND HITLERITE
CRIMES. see HISTORY — History Of Europe

320 UK ISSN 0585-7694
STUDY CENTRE FOR YUGOSLAV AFFAIRS.
REVIEW. 1960. irreg. price varies. Study Centre for
Yugoslav Affairs, 4 Audley Square, S. Audley St.,
London W1Y 5DR, England. Ed. Desimir Tochitch.
adv. bk. rev. bibl. circ. 3,000.

SUB-SAHARAN AFRICA REPORT. see BUSINESS
AND ECONOMICS — Economic Situation And
Conditions

320 US ISSN 0146-2156
SUMMARY OF CONGRESS. Variant title:
Congressional Summary. 1976. biennial. subscription
contained in price for Taylor's Encyclopedia of
Government Officials. Political Research, Inc.,
Tegoland at Bent Tree, 16850 Dallas Parkway,
Dallas, TX 75248. TEL 214-931-8827.

SURMACH. see MILITARY

320.531 YU ISSN 0350-0144
SURVEY SARAJEVO; periodical for social studies.
Cover title: Survey. (Text in English) 1974. a. 4500
din.($15) Univerzitet u Sarajevu - University of
Sarajevo, Obala 7/III, Room 202, P.O. Box 265,
71000 Sarajevo, Yugoslavia. Ed. Radovan
Milanovic. bk. rev. bibl.

328 SW
SWEDEN. RIKSDAGEN. FOERTECKNING
OEVER RIKSDAGENS LEDAMOETER. a.
Kr.15. Riksdagen, Riksdagens Tryckeriexpedition, S-
100 12 Stockholm, Sweden.

320 SW
SWEDEN. RIKSDAGEN. RIKSDAGEN AARSBOK.
a. Fritzes Bokhandel, Box 16356, S-103 27
Stockholm, Sweden.
  Continues: Sweden. Riksdagen. Riksdag.

320 AU
TANGENTE. bi-m. S.45. Ring Freiheitlicher Jugend,
Kaerntnerstrasse 28, Mezzanin, A-1010 Vienna,
Austria. Ed. Karl Sevelda. adv.

320 MX
TEMAS NACIONALES. 1975. irreg. Mex.$25($2.50)
Instituto de Estudios Politicos Economicos y
Sociales, Insurgentes Norte, 59, Mexico, D.F.,
Mexico. charts.

320 IT ISSN 0392-2154
TEORIE E OGGETTI. 1978. irreg., no.26, 1986. price
varies. Liguori Editore s.r.l., Via Mezzocannone 19,
80134 Naples, Italy. TEL 081/20 6077. Eds.
Roberto Esposito, Giancarlo Mazzacurati.

320 VE
TESTIMONIOS VIOLENTOS. irreg., no.6, 1982.
Universidad Central de Venezuela, Facultad de
Ciencias Economicas y Sociales, Division de
Publicaciones, Caracas, Venezuela.

320 920 UK ISSN 0082-4399
TIMES GUIDE TO THE HOUSE OF COMMONS;
complete survey of Parliament after a General
Election. 1880. irreg. price varies. Times Books
Ltd., 16 Golden Square, London W1R 4BN,
England. Ed. Alan Wood. index. circ. 7,500.

320 327 GW
TUDUV-STUDIE. REIHE
POLITIKWISSENSCHAFTEN. 1983. irreg. price
varies. Tuduv Verlagsgesellschaft mbH,
Gabelsbergerstr. 15, 8000 Munich 2, W. Germany
(B.R.D.)

320 US ISSN 0082-6774
TULANE STUDIES IN POLITICAL SCIENCE.
1954. irreg., vol.15, 1975. price varies per vol.
Tulane University, Department of Political Science,
New Orleans, LA 70118. TEL 504-865-5166. circ.
500.

320 310 US ISSN 0148-7760
U.S.S.R. FACTS & FIGURES ANNUAL. 1977. a.
price varies. Academic International Press, Box
1111, Gulf Breeze, FL 32561. Ed. John L. Scherer.
(back issues avail.)

320.532 IS
U.S.S.R. OVERVIEW. (Text in English) a.
International Centre of Contemporary Research,
Rehov Harav Agan 24, Jerusalem 91 006, Israel.

320.253 301 US
U S S R REPORT: POLITICAL AND
SOCIOLOGICAL AFFAIRS. 1969. irreg., approx.
60/yr. $5 per no. U.S. Joint Publications Research
Service, 1000 N. Glebe Rd., Arlington, VA 22201
TEL 703-487-4630. (Orders to: NTIS, Springfield,
VA 22161)
  Formerly: Translations on U S S R Political and
Sociological Affairs.

U S S R REPORT: PROBLEMS OF THE FAR
EAST. see POLITICAL SCIENCE — International
Relations

320.253 US
U S S R REPORT: TRANSLATIONS FROM
"KOMMUNIST". 1966. irreg. (approx. 20/yr.) $5
per no. U.S. Joint Publications Research Service,
1000 N. Glebe Rd., Arlington, VA 22201 TEL 703-
487-4630. (Orders to: NTIS, Springfield, VA 22161)
  Formerly: Translations from "Kommunist".

U S S R REPORT: U S A. ECONOMICS,
POLITICS, IDEOLOGY. see BUSINESS AND
ECONOMICS — Economic Situation And
Conditions

320.531 US
U S S R TODAY. 1981. triennial. $15. Current Digest
of the Soviet Press, 1480 West Lane Ave.,
Columbus, OH 43221. TEL 614-292-4234. Eds.
Fred C. Schulze, Gordon Livermore.

UMEAA STUDIES IN POLITICS AND PUBLIC
ADMINISTRATION. see PUBLIC
ADMINISTRATION

320 MY
UNITED MALAYS NATIONAL ORGANISATION.
PENVATA. irreg. United Malays National
Organisation, J1. T. Ab. Rahman, Bangunan
UMNO, Kuala Lumpur, Malaysia.

UNITED NATIONS DISARMAMENT
YEARBOOK. see MILITARY

UNITED NATIONS ECONOMIC AND SOCIAL
COUNCIL. DISARMAMENT STUDY SERIES.
see MILITARY

320 US ISSN 0082-9447
U.S. BUREAU OF THE CENSUS.
CONGRESSIONAL DISTRICT DATA BOOK.
(Series PHC80-4) 1961. irreg. price varies. U.S.
Bureau of the Census, Customer Services,
Washington, DC 20233 TEL 301-763-4100. (Orders
to: Supt. of Documents, Washington, DC 20402)
(also avail. in microfiche)

320 US
U.S. CONGRESS. CONGRESSIONAL
DIRECTORY. 1857. a. avail. in 3 different edts.
U.S. Government Printing Office, Superintendent of
Documents, Washington, DC 20402. TEL 202-275-
2051. Ed. Larry Kennedy. circ. 100,000. (also avail.
in microform from UMI)

320 US
U.S. DEPARTMENT OF JUSTICE. OFFICE OF
LEGAL COUNSEL. OPINIONS. a. $15. U.S.
Department of Justice, Office of Legal Counsel,
Washington, DC 20530. Ed. Margaret C. Love.

U.S. DEPARTMENT OF STATE. OFFICE OF THE
GEOGRAPHER. GEOGRAPHIC NOTES. see
GEOGRAPHY

320 US
U.S. FEDERAL ELECTION COMMISSION.
ANNUAL REPORT. 1975. a. price varies. Federal
Election Commission, Washington, DC 20463 TEL
202-523-4089. (Orders to: Supt. of Documents,
Washington, DC 20402) Ed. Louise D. Wides.
charts. illus. stat. circ. 1,800. (also avail. in
microfilm; back issues avail.)

327.73 US ISSN 0270-370X
UNITED STATES FOREIGN POLICY; a report of
the Secretary of State. 1969. a. U.S. Department of
State, 2201 C St. N.W., Washington, DC 20520.
TEL 202-634-3600.

UNITED STATES GOVERNMENT MANUAL
(1973) see PUBLIC ADMINISTRATION

320 US
UNITED STATES POLITICAL SCIENCE
DOCUMENTS. 1975. a. $300. University of
Pittsburgh, NASA Industrial Applications Center,
823 William Pitt Union, Pittsburgh, PA 15260. TEL
412-648-7000. Ed. Dr. Paul A. McWilliams. circ.
300.
●Also available online. Vendors: DIALOG.

320 IT
UNIVERSITA DEGLI STUDI DI TRIESTE.
FACOLTA DI SCIENZE POLITICHE.
PUBBLICAZIONI. 1975. irreg., no.20, 1981. price
varies. Casa Editrice Dott. A. Giuffre, Via B.
Arsizio 40, 20151 Milan, Italy. bibl.

320 970 FR ISSN 0399-0443
UNIVERSITE DE BORDEAUX III. CENTRE DE
RECHERCHES SUR L'AMERIQUE
ANGLOPHONE. ANNALES. N.S. 1976. a. 80
F.($6) per no. Maison des Sciences de l'Homme
d'Aquitaine, Esplanade des Antilles, Domaine
Universitaire, 33405 Talence Cedex, France. Ed.
J.F. Beranger. adv. circ. 200.

327 301 US ISSN 0068-6093
UNIVERSITY OF CALIFORNIA, BERKELEY.
INSTITUTE OF INTERNATIONAL STUDIES.
RESEARCH SERIES. 1961. irreg. (2-3/yr.) price
varies. University of California, Berkeley, Institute
of International Studies, 215 Moses Hall, Berkeley,
CA 94720. TEL 415-642-7189. Ed. Paul M.
Gilchrist. Indexed: GeoRef.

320 UK ISSN 0305-8646
UNIVERSITY OF GLASGOW. INSTITUTE OF
LATIN AMERICAN STUDIES. OCCASIONAL
PAPERS. (Text in English) 1971. irreg. University
of Glasgow, Institute of Latin American Studies,
Glasgow GL2 8QH, Scotland. Ed.Bd. bibl.

320   US
UNIVERSITY OF TEXAS, AUSTIN. LYNDON B. JOHNSON SCHOOL OF PUBLIC AFFAIRS. POLICY RESEARCH PROJECT REPORT SERIES. 1971. irreg., no.56, 1983. University of Texas at Austin, Lyndon B. Johnson School of Public Affairs, Drawer Y, Austin, TX 78713-7450. TEL 512-471-4962. charts. stat.
   Former titles: University of Texas, Austin. Lyndon B. Johnson School of Public Affairs. Policy Research Project Report & University of Texas, Austin. Lyndon B. Johnson School of Public Affairs. Seminar Research Report.

320.5322   335.43   CS
UNIVERZITA KOMENSKEHO. FILOZOFICKA FAKULTA. ZBORNIK: MARXIZMUS-LENINIZMUS. (Text in Slovak. contents page and summaries in English and Russian) 1962. irreg., approx. a. exchange basis. Slovenske Pedagogicke Nakladatelstvo, Sasinkova 5, 815 60 Bratislava, Czechoslovakia.

320.53   CS
UNIVERZITA KOMENSKEHO. USTAV MARXIZMU-LENINIZMU. ZBORNIK: DEJINY ROBOTNICKEHO HNUTIA. (Text in Slovak; summaries in English, German, Russian) 1972. irreg. price varies. Univerzita Komenskeho, Ustav Marxizmu-Leninizmu, Safarikovo nam. 12, Bratislava, Czechoslovakia.

146.3   320.53   CS
UNIVERZITA KOMENSKEHO. USTAV MARXIZMU-LENINIZMU. ZBORNIK: MARXISTICKA FILOZOFIA. (Supersedes in part the Institute's Zbornik and continues its vol. numbering) (Text in Slovak; summaries in English, German, Russian) 1970. irreg. price varies. Univerzita Komenskeho, Ustav Marxizmu-Leninizmu, Safarikovo nam. 12, Bratislava, Czechoslovakia.

320   PL   ISSN 0208-4732
UNIWERSYTET GDANSKI. WYDZIAL HUMANISTYCZNY. ZESZYTY NAUKOWE. NAUKI POLITYCZNE. 1972. irreg. price varies. Uniwersytet Gdanski, Ul. Armii Czerwonej 110, 81-824 Sopot, Poland. Ed. Kazimierz Podoski.

320   PL   ISSN 0137-2378
UNIWERSYTET JAGIELLONSKI. ZESZYTY NAUKOWE. PRACE Z NAUK POLITYCZNYCH. (Text in Polish; summaries English or Russian) 1971. irreg., vol.21, 1984. price varies. Panstwowe Wydawnictwo Naukowe, Miodowa 10, 00-251 Warsaw, Poland (Dist. by: Ars Polona, Krakowskie Przedmiescie 7, 00-068 Warsaw, Poland) Ed. P. Sarnecki. circ. 420.

320   PL   ISSN 0208-5437
UNIWERSYTET SLASKI W KATOWICACH. PRACE Z NAUK SPOLECZNYCH. (Text in Polish; summaries in English and Russian) 1975. irreg. price varies. Uniwersytet Slaski w Katowicach, Ul. Bankowa 14, 40-007 Katowice, Poland.

URANIA UNIVERSUM. see PHYSICS

320   340   GW   ISSN 0083-5676
VERFASSUNG UND VERFASSUNGSWIRKLICHKEIT. 1966. irreg., vol.12, 1978. price varies. Duncker und Humblot GmbH, Dietrich-Schaefer-Weg 9, 1000 Berlin 41, W. Germany (B.R.D.) Eds. Ferdinand A. Hermens, Werner Kaltefleiter. adv. bk. rev.

VIDEO OUT DISTRIBUTION CATALOGUE. see ART

959.7   UK
VIETNAM/SOUTH EAST ASIA INTERNATIONAL. 1963. a. £5($12) for individuals; £7 ($15) for institutions. International Confederation for Disarmament and Peace, 6 Endsleigh St., London W.C. 1, England. Ed. Peggy Duff. bk. rev. circ. 1,000.
   Former titles: Vietnam International; Vietnam International Information Bulletin (ISSN 0042-5745)

320   UR
VOPROSY KRITIKI BURZUAZNOI POLITIKI I IDEOLOGII. SBORNIK NAUCHNYKH TRUDOV. (Text in Russian) vol.3, 1977. a. 0.42 Rub. per issue. Latviiskii Gosudarstvennyi Universitet, Kafedra Nauchnogo Kommunizma, Bulvar Raynisa, 19, Riga, Latvian S.S.R., U.S.S.R. Indexed: Nutr.Abstr.
   Marxism

320   US
W R I NEWSLETTER. irreg., latest no.5. membership. Western Review Institute, Box 806, Chino, CA 91708.

320   JA   ISSN 0511-196X
WASEDA POLITICAL STUDIES. (Text in English) 1957. irreg. Waseda University, Graduate Division of Political Science, Totsuka-machi, Shinjuku-ku, Tokyo 160, Japan.

WEST EUROPE REPORT. see BUSINESS AND ECONOMICS — Economic Situation And Conditions

051   US   ISSN 0512-5804
WHAT THEY SAID. 1969. a. $35. Monitor Book Co., Inc., 9441 Wilshire Blvd., Box 3668, Beverly Hills, CA 90212. TEL 213-271-5558. Eds. Alan F. Pater, Jason R. Pater.

WHO'S WHO IN AMERICAN POLITICS. see BIOGRAPHY

320   364   917.306   156   US
WILCOX REPORT NEWSLETTER. 1970. irreg. $15. Laird Wilcox, Box 1832, Olathe, KS 66061. TEL 913-829-0609. circ. 285. (back issues avail.)
   Formerly: Wilcox Report (ISSN 0049-7630)

320   IS
WORLD ZIONIST ORGANIZATION. ZIONIST CONGRESS. KONGRES HA-TSIYONI. HAHLATOT. (Text in Hebrew) irreg. World Zionist Organization, Jerusalem, Israel.

WOYTINSKY LECTURES. see PUBLIC ADMINISTRATION

320   US   ISSN 0084-3490
YALE STUDIES IN POLITICAL SCIENCE. 1954. irreg., no.31, 1982. price varies. Yale University Press, 92A Yale Sta., New Haven, CT 06520. TEL 203-432-0940.

320.531   340   US   ISSN 0887-9117
YEARBOOK ON SOCIALIST LEGAL SYSTEMS. a. Transnational Publishers, Inc., Box 7282, Ardsley-on-Hudson, Dobbs Ferry, NY 10503.

369.4   UK   ISSN 0513-5982
YOUNG FABIAN PAMPHLET. 1961. irreg., no.50, 1982. £15($20) Fabian Society, 11 Dartmouth St., London SW1H 9BN, England. Ed.Bd. charts, stat. circ. 4,000.

Z PROBLEMATYKI PRAWA PRACY I POLITYKI SOCJALNEJ. see LAW

956.940   UK   ISSN 0084-5531
ZIONIST YEAR BOOK. 1951/52. a. £2($15) Zionist Federation of Great Britain and Northern Ireland, Balfour House, 741 High Rd., London N12 0BQ, England. Ed. Helen Hill. adv. bk. rev. index. circ. 1, 350.

ZUR POLITIK UND ZEITGESCHICHTE. see HISTORY

POLITICAL SCIENCE — Abstracting, Bibliographies, Statistics

320   016   US   ISSN 0001-0456
A B C POL SCI; a bibliography of contents: political science and government. 1969. 6/yr. (including indexes) price varies. A B C-Clio, 2040 Alameda Padre Serra, Box 4397, Santa Barbara, CA 93140-4397. TEL 805-963-4221. Ed. Lloyd W. Garrison. index. circ. 1,500.

A M T I D: APPLICATION OF MODERN TECHNOLOGY TO INTERNATIONAL DEVELOPMENT. see TECHNOLOGY: COMPREHENSIVE WORKS — Abstracting, Bibliographies, Statistics

ALTERNATIVE PRESS INDEX; an index to alternative and radical publications. see LITERARY AND POLITICAL REVIEWS — Abstracting, Bibliographies, Statistics

335   016   US   ISSN 0065-8650
AMERICAN INSTITUTE FOR MARXIST STUDIES. BIBLIOGRAPHIC SERIES. 1965. irreg., latest no.16. American Institute for Marxist Studies, 85 E. 4th St., New York, NY 10003.

320   AG   ISSN 0325-3147
ARGENTINA. CONGRESO. BIBLIOTECA. SERIE BIBLIOGRAFICA. irreg., no.3, 1982. Congreso, Biblioteca, Subdireccion de Referencia Legislativa, Buenos Aires, Argentina.

BIBLIOGRAPHIES AND INDEXES IN LAW AND POLITICAL SCIENCE. see LAW — Abstracting, Bibliographies, Statistics

320   016   GW   ISSN 0067-8015
BIBLIOTHECA IBERO-AMERICANA. 1959. irreg. price varies. (Ibero-Amerikanisches Institut, Berlin) Colloquium Verlag, Unter den Eichen 93, 1000 Berlin 45, W. Germany (B.R.D.) Ed. Wilhelm Stegmann. circ. 1,000.

320   DK   ISSN 0107-0452
COPENHAGEN POLITICAL STUDIES ABSTRACTS. 1982. a. free. University of Copenhagen, Institute of Political Studies - Koebenhavns Universitet, Rosenborggade 15/2, 1130 Copenhagen K, Denmark. Ed.Bd. bk. rev. circ. 500.
   Formerly: C P S A.

972.91   016   US   ISSN 0361-4441
CUBAN STUDIES/ESTUDIOS CUBANOS; scholarly multidisciplinary journal devoted entirely to Cuba. (As of 1986, subseries of Pitt Latin American Series) (Text in English or Spanish) 1970. a. price varies. University of Pittsburgh Press, 127 N. Bellefield Ave., Pittsburgh, PA 15260. Ed. Carmelo Mesa-Lago. adv. bk. rev. abstr. bibl. circ. 600. (back issues avail.) Indexed: Hist.Abstr. A.B.C.Pol.Sci. Amer.Bibl.Slavic & E.Eur.Stud. Amer.Hist.& Life. Hisp.Amer.Per.Ind.
   Formerly: Cuban Studies Newsletter/Boletin de Estudios Cubanos (ISSN 0011-2631)

015   US   ISSN 0011-3425
CURRENT DIGEST OF THE SOVIET PRESS. 1949. w. $540 to institutions. Current Digest of the Soviet Press, 1480 West Lane Ave., Columbus, OH 43221. TEL 614-292-4234. Ed. Fred C. Schulze. bk. rev. abstr. charts. illus. index. circ. 1,000. (also avail. in microfiche; microfilm; back issues avail.) Indexed: P.A.I.S. Int.Polit.Sci.Abstr.
   ●Also available online. Vendors: DIALOG, Mead Data Central.
   Incorporating: Current Abstracts of the Soviet Press (ISSN 0011-3166)

DOCUMENTATIEBLAD: THE ABSTRACTS JOURNAL OF THE AFRICAN STUDIES CENTRE LEIDEN. see HISTORY — Abstracting, Bibliographies, Statistics

015   327   II   ISSN 0419-5345
DOCUMENTATION ON ASIA. 1960. a. Rs.100($30) Indian Council of World Affairs, Library, Sapru House, Barakhamba Rd., New Delhi 110001, India. Eds. V. Machwe, Ashok Jambhakar.

314   320   FI
FINLAND. TILASTOKESKUS. VALTIOLLISET VAALIT. KANSANEDUSTAJAIN VAALIT/ FINLAND. STATISTIKCENTRALEN. STATLIGA VAL. RIDSDAGSMANNAVALEN/ FINLAND. CENTRAL STATISTICAL OFFICE. NATIONAL ELECTIONS. PARLIAMENTARY ELECTIONS. (Section XXIX A of Official Statistics of Finland) (Text in Finnish, Swedish and English) 1909. irreg. Fmk.32. Tilastokeskus, Annankatu 44, SF-00100 Helsinki 10, Finland (Subscr. to: Government Printing Centre, Box 516, SF-00100 Helsinki 10, Finland)
   Formerly: Finland. Tilastokeskus. Kansanedustajain Vaalit (ISSN 0355-2209)

FINLAND. TILASTOKESKUS. VALTIOLLISET VAALIT. TASAVALLAN PRESIDENTIN VAALIT VALISIJAMIESTEN. see POLITICAL SCIENCE

POLITICAL SCIENCE — CIVIL RIGHTS

327 015   UN   ISSN 0072-0658
GENERAL CATALOGUE OF UNESCO AND UNESCO-SPONSORED PUBLICATIONS. (Text in English and French) 1964. irreg. 8 F. Unesco, 7-9 Place de Fontenoy, 75700 Paris, France (Dist. in U.S. by: Bernan Associates-Unipub, 4611-F Assembly Dr., Lanham, MD 20706-4391)

HISTORICAL ABSTRACTS. PART A: MODERN HISTORY ABSTRACTS, 1450-1914. see *HISTORY — Abstracting, Bibliographies, Statistics*

HISTORICAL ABSTRACTS. PART B: TWENTIETH CENTURY ABSTRACTS, 1914 TO THE PRESENT. see *HISTORY — Abstracting, Bibliographies, Statistics*

323.4   US   ISSN 0098-0579
HUMAN RIGHTS ORGANIZATIONS & PERIODICALS DIRECTORY. 1973. irreg. $22. Meiklejohn Civil Liberties Institute, 1715 Francisco St., Berkeley, CA 94703. TEL 415-848-0599. Ed. David Christiano. bibl. circ. 1,000.

I C U I S JUSTICE MINISTRIES. (Institute on the Church in Urban Industrial Society) see *RELIGIONS AND THEOLOGY — Abstracting, Bibliographies, Statistics*

327 320   US   ISSN 0272-3875
INDEX: FOREIGN BROADCAST INFORMATION SERVICE DAILY REPORTS: ASIA AND PACIFIC. 1978. m. (plus annual cum.) $175. NewsBank, Inc., 58 Pine St., New Canaan, CT 06840. TEL 203-966-1100. Ed. Gwen Sloan. (back issues avail.)

327 320   US   ISSN 0271-1761
INDEX: FOREIGN BROADCAST INFORMATION SERVICE DAILY REPORTS: CHINA. 1975. m. (plus annual cum.) $175. NewsBank, Inc., 58 Pine St., New Canaan, CT 06840. Ed. Gwen Sloan. (back issues avail.)
Formerly: Index: Foreign Broadcast Information Service Daily Reports: People's Republic of China.

327 320   US   ISSN 0731-4116
INDEX: FOREIGN BROADCAST INFORMATION SERVICE DAILY REPORTS: EASTERN EUROPE. 1978. m. (plus annual cum.) $175. NewsBank, Inc., 58 Pine St., New Canaan, CT 06840. Ed. Gwen Sloan. (back issues avail.)

327 320   US   ISSN 0278-1360
INDEX: FOREIGN BROADCAST INFORMATION SERVICE DAILY REPORTS: LATIN AMERICA. 1978. m. (plus annual cum.) $175. NewsBank, Inc., 58 Pine St., New Canaan, CT 06840. Ed. Gwen Sloan. (back issues avail.)

327 320   US
INDEX: FOREIGN BROADCAST INFORMATION SERVICE DAILY REPORTS: MIDDLE EAST AND AFRICA. 1980. m. (plus annual cum.) $175. NewsBank, Inc., 58 Pine St., New Canaan, CT 06840. Ed. Gwen Sloan. (back issues avail.)
Formerly: Index: Foreign Broadcast Information Service Daily Reports: Middle East and North Africa (ISSN 0736-3427)

327 320   US   ISSN 0731-3233
INDEX: FOREIGN BROADCAST INFORMATION SERVICE DAILY REPORTS: SOUTH ASIA. 1980. m. (plus annual cum.) $175. NewsBank, Inc., 58 Pine St., New Canaan, CT 06840. Ed. Gwen Sloan. (back issues avail.)
Formerly: Index: Foreign Broadcast Information Service Daily Reports: Sub-Saharan Africa.

327 320   US   ISSN 0731-3276
INDEX: FOREIGN BROADCAST INFORMATION SERVICE DAILY REPORTS: SOVIET UNION. 1977. m. (plus annual cum.) $175. NewsBank, Inc., 58 Pine St., New Canaan, CT 06840. Ed. Gwen Sloan. (back issues avail.)

327 320   US
INDEX: FOREIGN BROADCAST INFORMATION SERVICE DAILY REPORTS: WESTERN EUROPE. 1978. m. (plus annual cum.) $175. NewsBank, Inc., 58 Pine St., New Canaan, CT 06840. Ed. Gwen Sloan. (back issues avail.)

341.13   UN   ISSN 0082-8157
INDEX TO PROCEEDINGS OF THE GENERAL ASSEMBLY OF THE UNITED NATIONS. (Issued as subseries of Official Records. Supplements) 1946. a. price varies. (United Nations, General Assembly) United Nations Publications, Room DC2-853, New York, NY 10017 (Or Distribution and Sales Section, Palais des Nations, CH-1211 Geneva 10, Switzerland)
Formerly: Resolutions of the General Assembly of the United Nations (ISSN 0082-8211)

INDIA AND WORLD AFFAIRS: AN ANNUAL BIBLIOGRAPHY. see *HISTORY — Abstracting, Bibliographies, Statistics*

320 016.32   US   ISSN 0085-2058
INTERNATIONAL BIBLIOGRAPHY OF THE SOCIAL SCIENCES. POLITICAL SCIENCE. Title page also reads: International Bibliography of Political Science. 1953. a. $110. Methuen Inc., 29 W. 35th St., New York, NY 10001-2291.

320   FR   ISSN 0020-8345
INTERNATIONAL POLITICAL SCIENCE ABSTRACTS/DOCUMENTATION POLITIQUE INTERNATIONALE. (Abstracts in English and French) 1951. bi-m. 1135 Fr.($170) to institutions; individuals $50. International Political Science Association, 27 rue Saint-Guillaume, 75341 Paris, Cedex 07, France. Ed. Serge Hurtig. adv. index. circ. 1,500. Indexed: E.I.

JOURNALS OF DISSENT AND SOCIAL CHANGE; a bibliography of titles in the California State University, Sacramento, library. see *SOCIOLOGY — Abstracting, Bibliographies, Statistics*

LEFT INDEX; a quarterly index to periodicals of the left. see *POLITICAL SCIENCE*

324   NE   ISSN 0168-4884
NETHERLANDS. CENTRAAL BUREAU VOOR DE STATISTIEK. STATISTIEK DER VERKIEZINGEN. GEMEENTERADEN. ELECTION STATISTICS. MUNICIPAL COUNCILS. (Text in Dutch and English) 1946. irreg. fl.22.50. Centraal Bureau voor de Statistiek, Prinses Beatrixlaan 428, Voorburg, Netherlands (Orders to: Staatsuitgeverij, Christoffel Plantijnstraat, The Hague, Netherlands)

324   NE   ISSN 0168-5686
NETHERLANDS. CENTRAAL BUREAU VOOR DE STATISTIEK. STATISTIEK DER VERKIEZINGEN. TWEEDE KAMER DER STATEN-GENERAAL. ELECTION STATISTICS. SECOND CHAMBER OF THE STATES-GENERAL. (Text in Dutch and English) 1946. irreg. fl.18.50. Centraal Bureau voor de Statistiek, Prinses Beatrixlaan 428, Voorburg, Netherlands (Orders to: Staatsuitgeverij, Christoffel Plantijnstraat, The Hague, Netherlands)

341.1 016   CN   ISSN 0031-3599
PEACE RESEARCH ABSTRACTS JOURNAL. 1964. m. $180. Peace Research Institute-Dundas, 25 Dundana Ave., Dundas, Ont. L9H 4E5, Canada. TEL 416-628-2356. Eds. Dr. Hanna Newcombe, Dr. Alan Newcombe. abstr. index. circ. 400. Indexed: Abstr.Mil.Bibl.

475   US
POLITICAL SCIENCE ABSTRACTS. a. $350. I F I Plenum Data Company (Subsidiary of: Subsidiary of: Plenum Publishing Corporation.) 233 Spring St., New York, NY 10013. TEL 212-741-6680.
Formerly: Universal Reference System: Political Science, Government, and Public Policy Series. Annual Supplement.

320 011   UK   ISSN 0307-9201
SAGE RACE RELATIONS ABSTRACTS. 1976. q. £34 to individuals; institutions £78. (Institute of Race Relations) Sage Publications Ltd., 28 Banner St., London EC1Y 8QE, England. Ed. Lou Kushnick. adv. bibl. index. (back issues avail.)

015   SI
SINGAPORE NATIONAL PRINTERS. PUBLICATIONS CATALOGUE. (Text in English) 1973. irreg, latest 1984. free. Singapore National Printers Ltd., 303 Upper Serangoon Road, Box 485, Singapore 13, Singapore. circ. 600.
Supersedes: Singapore. Catalogue of Government Publications.

327 011   SA
SOUTH AFRICAN INSTITUTE OF INTERNATIONAL AFFAIRS. BIBLIOGRAPHICAL SERIES/SUID-AFRIKAANSE INSTITUUT VAN INTERNASIONALE AANGELEENTHEDE. BIBLIOGRAFIESE REEKS. 1976. a. price varies. South African Institute of International Affairs, Box 31596, Braamfontein, 2017 Transvaal, South Africa

U.S. DEPARTMENT OF STATE. LIBRARY. COMMERCIAL LIBRARY PROGRAM. PUBLICATIONS LIST. see *LIBRARY AND INFORMATION SCIENCES — Abstracting, Bibliographies, Statistics*

327 016   US
WAR - PEACE BIBLIOGRAPHY SERIES. 1973. irreg., no.18, 1984. price varies. (California State University, Los Angeles, Center for the Study of Armament and Disarmanent) A B C-Clio, 2040 Alameda Padre Serra, Box 4397, Santa Barbara, CA 93140-4397. TEL 805-963-4221. Ed. Richard Dean Burns.

ZIONIST LiTERATURE. see *PUBLISHING AND BOOK TRADE — Abstracting, Bibliographies, Statistics*

POLITICAL SCIENCE — Civil Rights

323.4   CN   ISSN 0441-4128
AFFIRMATION. 1979. q. free. Ontario Human Rights Commission, Ministry of Labour, Suite M159A Ave., Macdonald Block, Queens's Park, Toronto, Ont. M7A 1A2, Canada. TEL 416-965-6841. Ed. W.G. Plaut. bk. rev. circ. 10,000.
Formerly (until 1981): Human Relations.

323.4   US   ISSN 0742-1044
ALETHEIA. 1983. irreg., no.2, 1984. free. (American Black and Ethnic Helsinki Monitoring Group) Black Employees of the Library of Congress, 6100 East View, Kenwood Park, Washington, DC 20034 (And 1412 Arcadia Ave., Capitol Heights, MD 20743) (Co-sponsor: Ethnic Employees of the Library of Congress)

AMNESTY INTERNATIONAL REPORT. see *POLITICAL SCIENCE — International Relations*

ANNEE AFRICAINE. see *LAW — International Law*

323.4   UK
ANTI-APARTHEID MOVEMENT. ANNUAL REPORT OF ACTIVITIES AND DEVELOPMENTS. a. Anti-Apartheid Movement, 13 Mandela St., London NW1, England. circ. 17,500.

323.4   UK
ANTI-SLAVERY REPORTER. 1840. a. £2. Anti-Slavery Society, 180 Brixton Rd., London, SW9 6AT, England. Ed. Alan Whittaker. adv. bk. rev. circ. 1,200.

BATTERED WOMEN'S DIRECTORY. see *WOMEN'S INTERESTS*

323.4   US
BILL OF RIGHTS JOURNAL. 1952. a. $15. National Emergency Civil Liberties Committee, 175 Fifth Ave., Rm. 814, New York, NY 10010. TEL 212-673-2040. Ed. Edith Tiger. (also avail. in microform from UMI; reprint service avail. from UMI) Indexed: Leg.Per. Alt.Press Ind. C.L.I. L.R.I.

BLACK POSITION. see *LITERATURE — Poetry*

323.4   UK   ISSN 0262-3781
BRIEFING PAPER ON SOUTHERN AFRICA. (Avail. only as supplement to: Focus on Political Repression in Southern Africa) 1981. irreg. International Defence and Aid Fund for Southern Africa (IDAFSA), I D A F Research, Information and Publications Department, Canon Collins House, 64 Essex Rd., London N1 8LR, England. Ed.Bd. Indexed: HR Rep.

CAHIERS DE L'AVENIR DE LA BRETAGNE. see *HISTORY*

POLITICAL SCIENCE — CIVIL RIGHTS

CANADA. INFORMATION COMMISSIONER. ANNUAL REPORT. see *LAW — International Law*

CHINA RIGHTS ANNALS; human rights conditions in the People's Republic of China. see *POLITICAL SCIENCE*

341.48   FR
COUNCIL OF EUROPE. STANDING COMMITTEE ON THE EUROPEAN CONVENTION ON ESTABLISHMENT (INDIVIDUALS). PERIODICAL REPORT. 1971. irreg. Council of Europe, Publication Section, 67006 Strasbourg, France (Dist. in U.S. by Manhattan Publishing Co., Box 650, Croton-on-Hudson, N.Y. 10520)

323.4   US
CUBAN AMERICAN NATIONAL FOUNDATION. PUBLICATION. irreg. no.21, 1987. Cuban American National Foundation, 1000 Thomas Jefferson St., N.W., Ste. 601, Washington, DC 20007. TEL 202-265-2822.

323.4   US
CUBAN UPDATE. irreg. Cuban American National Foundation, 1000 Thomas Jefferson St., N.W., Ste. 601, Washington, DC 20007.

DOCUMENTS OF UKRAINIAN SAMVYDAV. see *ETHNIC INTERESTS*

323.4   US
EQUAL EMPLOYMENT OPPORTUNITY. ANNUAL PROGRAM. a. Office of Equal Employment Opportunity and Contract Compliance, 271 Church St., New York, NY 10013. TEL 212-553-6845.

323.4   NE   ISSN 0071-2701
EUROPEAN CONVENTION ON HUMAN RIGHTS. YEARBOOK. 1959. a., except 1964. price varies. (Council of Europe, FR) Martinus Nijhoff, Postbus 163, 3300 AD Dordrecht, Netherlands.

323.4   GW   ISSN 0073-3903
EUROPEAN COURT OF HUMAN RIGHTS. PUBLICATIONS. SERIES A: JUDGMENTS AND DECISIONS/COUR EUROPEENNE DES DROITS DE L'HOMME. PUBLICATIONS. SERIE A: ARRETS ET DECISIONS. (Text in English and French) 1961. irreg., vol.105, 1986. Carl Heymanns Verlag KG, Luxemburgerstr. 449, 5000 Cologne 41, W. Germany (B.R.D.)

323   GW   ISSN 0073-3911
EUROPEAN COURT OF HUMAN RIGHTS. PUBLICATIONS. SERIES B: PLEADINGS, ORAL ARGUMENTS AND DOCUMENTS/ COUR EUROPEENNE DES DROITS DE L'HOMME. PUBLICATIONS. SERIE B: MEMOIRES, PLAIDOIRIES ET DOCUMENTS. (Text in English and French) 1961. irreg., vol.54, 1986. price varies. Carl Heymanns Verlag KG, Luxemburgerstr. 449, 5000 Cologne 41, W. Germany (B.R.D.)

323.4   US
FACT SHEETS ON INSTITUTIONAL RACISM; minority outlook on current issues. 1973. irreg., latest Nov. 1984. $2.95 per copy. ‡ Council on Interracial Books for Children, Inc., 1841 Broadway, Rm. 500, New York, NY 10023. TEL 212-757-5339. bibl. illus.
Supersedes: Viewpoint; Minority Outlook on Current Issues.

323.4   US
FACT SHEETS ON INSTITUTIONAL SEXISM. 1973. irreg., latest Apr. 1986. $2.95 per copy. Council on Interracial Books for Children, Inc., 1841 Broadway, New York, NY 10023. TEL 212-757-5339.

322.4   US
FIGHT THE RIGHT. 1981. irreg. free. Center for Constitutional Rights, 853 Broadway, New York, NY 10003. TEL 212-685-9038. illus. Indexed: Alt.Press Ind.

323.4   US   ISSN 0732-6610
FREEDOM IN THE WORLD; political rights and civil liberties. 1978. a. (Freedom House) Greenwood Press, 88 Post Road West, Box 5007, Westport, CT 06881. TEL 203-226-3571. Indexed: HR Rep.

323.4   052   301.2   AT
GAY INFORMATION; a journal of Gay studies. 1980. irreg. Aus.$22 to individuals; institutions $50. Gay Information Service, P.O. Box 943, Darlinghurst, NSW 2010, Australia. Ed.Bd. adv. bk. rev. abstr. bibl. illus. circ. 1,000. (back issues avail.) Indexed: Alt.Press Ind.

HOLOCAUST STUDIES ANNUAL. see *HISTORY — History Of Europe*

HOMOSEXUAL INFORMATION CENTER. NEWSLETTER. see *HOMOSEXUALITY*

323.4   CN
HUMAN RIGHTS ACT OF BRITISH COLUMBIA. 1976. a. free. Council of Human Rights, Parliament Bldg., Victoria, B.C. V8X 5Z8, Canada. TEL 604-389-3877.
Supersedes: British Columbia. Human Rights Commission. Annual Report (ISSN 0706-5426)

HUMAN RIGHTS ORGANIZATIONS & PERIODICALS DIRECTORY. see *POLITICAL SCIENCE — Abstracting, Bibliographies, Statistics*

I J A. RESEARCH REPORTS. (Institute of Jewish Affairs) see *ETHNIC INTERESTS*

I W G I A DOCUMENTS; documentation of oppression of ethnic groups in various countries. (International Work Group for Indigenous Affairs) see *ANTHROPOLOGY*

I W G I A NEWSLETTER. (International Work Group for Indigenous Affairs) see *ANTHROPOLOGY*

323   US   ISSN 0074-0764
INTER-AMERICAN COMMISSION OF WOMEN. SPECIAL ASSEMBLY. FINAL ACT/COMISION INTERAMERICANA DE MUJERES. ASAMBLEA EXTRAORDINARIA. ACTA FINAL. 1963, 3rd. biennial. price varies. Organization of American States, 17th and Constitution Aves. N.W., Washington, DC 20006. TEL 703-941-1617. circ. 3,000.

323.4   SZ
INTERNATIONAL DOCUMENTATION ON MACEDONIA. (Text in English and French) 1979. irreg., vol.13, 1982. 120 Fr.($60) Case Postale 37, 1292 Chambesy, Geneva, Switzerland. Ed. Theodore D. Dimitrov. bibl. charts. illus. index. (back issues avail.)

301.45   968   UN   ISSN 0538-8333
INTERNATIONAL LABOUR OFFICE. SPECIAL REPORT OF THE DIRECTOR-GENERAL ON THE APPLICATION OF THE DECLARATION CONCERNING THE POLICY OF APARTHEID OF THE REPUBLIC OF SOUTH AFRICA. 1965. a. price varies. International Labour Office - Bureau International du Travail, Publications Sales Service, CH-1211 Geneva 22, Switzerland (U.S. Distributor: I L O Branch Office, 1750 New York Ave. N.W., Washington, DC 20006) (also avail. in microform)

323.4   US   ISSN 0363-9347
INTERNATIONAL LEAGUE FOR HUMAN RIGHTS. ANNUAL REPORT. 1950. a. $20 includes subscription to Human Rights Bulletin. ‡ International League for Human Rights, 432 Park Ave. S., Ste. 1103, New York, NY 10016. TEL 212-972-9554. Ed. Felice Gaer. circ. controlled. (also avail. in microform)
Formerly: International League for the Rights of Man. Annual Report.

320.56   331.88   CS
INTERNATIONAL TRADE UNION CONFERENCE FOR ACTION AGAINST APARTHEID. RESOLUTION. (Text in English) 1977. irreg., 2nd 1977, Geneva; 4th, 1983. free. World Federation of Trade Unions, Vinohradska 10, 121 47 Prague 2, Czechoslovakia. illus. circ. 3,000.

320   US
IOWA CIVIL RIGHTS COMMISSION. ANNUAL REPORT. no.8, 1975. a. Civil Rights Commission, 211 E. Maple St., Des Moines, IA 50319. TEL 515-281-4121. circ. 800.

323.4   US
IOWA CIVIL RIGHTS COMMISSION. CASE REPORTS. 1977. a. Iowa Civil Rights Commission, 211 E. Maple St., 2nd Fl., Des Moines, IA 50319. Ed. Ione Shadduck. circ. 500.

323   341   IS   ISSN 0333-5925
ISRAEL YEARBOOK ON HUMAN RIGHTS. (Text in English) 1971. a. $12. ‡ Tel Aviv University, Faculty of Law, Ramat Aviv, Tel Aviv, Israel. Ed. Dr. Yoram Dinstein. bk. rev. circ. 1,500. Indexed: A.B.C.Pol.Sci. HR Rep.

JEWS OF THE SOVIET UNION. see *RELIGIONS AND THEOLOGY — Judaic*

KATALLAGETE. see *RELIGIONS AND THEOLOGY*

LIBERTARIAN ALLIANCE. CULTURAL NOTES. see *POLITICAL SCIENCE*

323.4   CN   ISSN 0383-5588
MANITOBA. HUMAN RIGHTS COMMISSION. ANNUAL REPORT. 1974. a. free. Human Rights Commission, 1007-330 Portage Ave., Winnipeg, Man. R3C 0C4, Canada. TEL 204-945-3007. illus. circ. 6,000.

323.4   US
MARTIN LUTHER KING, JR. CENTER FOR NON-VIOLENT SOCIAL CHANGE NEWSLETTER. 1973. irreg. donations. Martin Luther King, Jr. Center for Non-Violent Social Change, 449 Auburn Ave., N.E., Atlanta, GA 30312. TEL 404-524-1956. Ed. Hilda R. Tompkins. illus. circ. 30,000.
Formerly: Martin Luther King, Jr. Center for Social Change Newsletter.

323.4   US
MICHIGAN. CIVIL RIGHTS COMMISSION. ANNUAL REPORT. 1964. a. free. Department of Civil Rights, 303 W. Kalamazoo, 4th Fl., Lansing, MI 48913. TEL 517-334-6079. Ed. James H. Horn II. circ. 2,000.
Former titles (until 1972): Civil Rights in Michigan; Until 1970: Michigan. Civil Rights Commission. Report (ISSN 0076-7875)

323   US   ISSN 0076-9118
MINNESOTA. DEPARTMENT OF HUMAN RIGHTS. BIENNIAL REPORT. 1967/68. biennial. free. Department of Human Rights, 500 Bremer Tower, 7th & Minnesota, St. Paul, MN 55101. TEL 612-296-5663. circ. 1,000.

323.4   UK   ISSN 0260-6402
MINORITY RIGHTS GROUP. NEWSLETTER. 1978. irreg. (4-5/yr.) Minority Rights Group, 29 Craven St., London WC2N 5NG, England.

MINORITY RIGHTS GROUP. REPORTS. see *SOCIOLOGY*

323.4   US
NEW YORK (STATE). DIVISION OF HUMAN RIGHTS. ANNUAL REPORT. 1946. a. free. Division of Human Rights, 55 W. 125th St., New York, NY 10027. TEL 212-870-8400. Ed. Don Zirkel. circ. 3,000.
Former titles: State of Human Rights in New York; New York (State). Division of Human Rights. Annual Report.

323.4   US   ISSN 0270-2282
NORTH AMERICAN HUMAN RIGHTS DIRECTORY; directory of groups in the United States and Canada active in international human rights. 1980. irreg, latest, 2nd ed. $30. Garrett Park Press, Box 190F, Garrett Park, MD 20896. TEL 301-946-2553. Eds. Laurie S. Wiseberg, Harry M. Scoble.
Formerly: Human Rights Directory (ISSN 0197-8101)

320.532   919.7   US
OF HUMAN RIGHTS. 1977. a. free. Of Human Rights, Inc., Box 2160-Hoya Sta., Georgetown University, Washington, DC 20057. TEL 202-342-1586. circ. 10,000. (back issues avail.)

323.4   CN   ISSN 0702-0538
ONTARIO. HUMAN RIGHTS COMMISSION. ANNUAL REPORT. 1962. a. Human Rights Commission, 400 University Ave., Toronto, Ont. M7A 1T7, Canada. TEL 416-965-6841. Ed. Canon B.C. Purcell. circ. 10,000.

323.4   CN
OPERATION LIBERTE. 1978. irreg. Can.$25. Ligue des Droits et Libertes, 1825 de Champlain, Montreal, Que. H2L 2S9, Canada. TEL 514-527-8551. bk. rev. circ. 1,500. (back issues avail.)

POLITICAL SCIENCE — INTERNATIONAL RELATIONS

323.4 US ISSN 0032-9177
PROBE (SANTA BARBARA) 1968. irreg. donations.
‡ Box 13390 UCSB, Santa Barbara, CA 93107. Ed.
Perry Adams. adv. bk. rev. illus. circ. 15,000.
(tabloid format)
Formerly: Argo.

SIBYL-CHILD. see *WOMEN'S INTERESTS*

SPARTACUS INTERNATIONAL GAY GUIDE. see
TRAVEL AND TOURISM

323 US ISSN 0148-6985
STATE OF BLACK AMERICA. 1975. a. price varies.
(National Urban League) Transaction Books,
Rutgers University, New Brunswick, NJ 08903. Ed.
James D. Williams.

STUDIES IN HUMAN RIGHTS. see *POLITICAL
SCIENCE — International Relations*

323.4 US
STUDIES IN LAW AND SOCIAL CHANGE. irreg.,
latest 1986. Meiklejohn Civil Liberties Institute, Box
673, Berkeley, CA 94701. TEL 415-848-0599. Eds.
Ann Fagan Ginger, David Christiano.

301.45 SA ISSN 0081-9778
SURVEY OF RACE RELATIONS IN SOUTH
AFRICA. 1948. a. South African Institute of Race
Relations, 68 de Korte St., Box 97, Johannesburg,
South Africa. circ. 6,000. Indexed: HR Rep.
Formerly: Race Relations Survey.

SURVIVAL INTERNATIONAL REVIEW. see
ANTHROPOLOGY

323 FR ISSN 0082-7770
UNION PROFESSIONNELLE FEMININE.
ANNUAIRE.* 1964. a. Federation Francaise des
Clubs de Femmes de Carrieres Liberales et
Commerciales et de Professions Diverses, c/o Mme.
Kraemer-Bach, 75 rue de Longchamp, Paris 16e,
France.

323.4 US ISSN 0082-9641
U.S. COMMISSION ON CIVIL RIGHTS.
CLEARINGHOUSE PUBLICATIONS. 1965. irreg.
limited numbers of copies available free from the
Commission. U.S. Commission on Civil Rights,
1121 Vermont Ave. N.W., Washington, DC 20425
TEL 202-254-6697. (Orders to: Supt. of Documents,
Washington, DC 20402;, Or up to 50 copies avail.
free from U.S. Commission on Civil Rights)

U.S. EQUAL EMPLOYMENT OPPORTUNITY
COMMISSION. ANNUAL REPORT. see
*BUSINESS AND ECONOMICS — Labor And
Industrial Relations*

323.4 AT
VICTORIA. EQUAL OPPORTUNITY BOARD.
ANNUAL REPORT. 1979. a. Aus.$5.80. Equal
Opportunity Board, 356 Collins St., Melbourne
3000, Australia.

323.4 US ISSN 0083-8594
WEST VIRGINIA. HUMAN RIGHTS
COMMISSION. REPORT. 1961. free. Human
Rights Commission, 215 Professional Bldg., 1036
Quarrier St., Charleston, WV 25301. TEL 304-348-
2616. circ. 1,000.

323.4 UN ISSN 0084-4098
YEARBOOK ON HUMAN RIGHTS. (Editions in
English and French) 1946. irreg., latest 1979. price
varies. United Nations Publications, Room DC2-
853, New York, NY 10017 (Or Distribution and
Sales Section, CH-1211 Geneva 10, Switzerland)
(also avail. in microfiche)

POLITICAL SCIENCE — International Relations

see also *Law — International Law*

320 FR
A D U K. (Adresar Ukraintsiv u Vilnomu Sviti) 1973.
irreg. Premiere Imprimerie Ukrainienne en France,
3, rue du Sabot, 75006 Paris, France. illus.

A J M E NEWS. (Americans for Justice in the Middle
East) see *HISTORY — History Of The Near East*

327 US
AID MEMO. irreg. (8-12/yr) $0.75 per no. Center for
International Policy, 236 Massachusetts Ave., N.E.,
Ste. 505, Washington, DC 20002.

ALTERNATIVE TRADING NEWS. see *BUSINESS
AND ECONOMICS — International Development
And Assistance*

327 GW
AMERICAN-GERMAN STUDIES/DEUTSCH-
AMERIKANISCHE STUDIEN. (Text and
summaries in English, German) 1985. irreg. price
varies. Verlag H.-D. Heinz, Steiermaerkerstr. 132,
7000 Stuttgart 30, W. Germany (B.R.D.) Ed.Bd. bk.
rev. circ. 400. (back issues avail.) Indexed: M.L.A.

327 296 US
AMERICAN JEWISH ALTERNATIVES TO
ZIONISM. REPORT. 1968. irreg. (3-4/yr.)
(American Jewish Alternatives to Zionism, Inc.)
Maple Leaf Press, c/o Elmer Berger, Ed., 133 E. 73
St., No. 404, New York, NY 10021. TEL 212-628-
2727. bk. rev. circ. 1,000.

327 JA ISSN 0387-2815
AMERICAN REVIEW. (Text in Japanese and
English; summaries in English) 1967. a. $15 per no.
Japanese Association for American Studies,
University of Tokyo, Center for American Studies,
8-1, 3-chome, Komaba, Meguro-ku, Tokyo 153,
Japan. Ed. Takashi Hirano. bibl. circ. 1,000.

323 UK
AMNESTY INTERNATIONAL REPORT. 1962. a.
£5. Amnesty International, 1 Easton St., London
WC1X 8DJ, England. Indexed: HR Rep.
Formerly: Amnesty International Annual Report
(ISSN 0569-9495)

327 BE ISSN 0066-2135
ANNALES D'ETUDES INTERNATIONALES.
English edition: Annals of International Studies.
1970. a. 600 Fr. (Universite de Geneve, Institut
Universitaire de Hautes Etudes Internationales, SZ
- University of Geneva. Graduate Institute of
International Studies) Etablissements Emile
Bruylant, 67 rue de la Regence, 1000 Brussels,
Belgium. Indexed: Hist.Abstr. P.A.I.S. Amer.Hist.&
Life.

327 FR ISSN 0066-295X
ANNUAIRE DIPLOMATIQUE ET CONSULAIRE
DE LA REPUBLIQUE FRANCAISE. 1879. a. 482
F. Ministere des Affaires Etrangeres, Direction du
Personnel et de l'Administration Generale, 23 rue
de La Perouse, 75016 Paris, France (Subscr. to:
l'Imprimerie Nationale, 27, rue de la Convention,
75015 Paris, France) adv. circ. 2,900.

327 CN ISSN 0384-1103
ANNUAL CANADIAN-AMERICAN SEMINAR.
PROCEEDINGS. (Each issue has distinctive title)
1961. a. Can.$20. University of Windsor, Centre for
Canadian-American Studies, 401 Sunset Ave.,
Windsor, Ont. N9B 3P4, Canada. TEL 519-253-
4232. Ed. Dr. James Chacko. circ. 2,000.
Former titles: Institute for Canadian-American
Relations (Papers) & Seminar on Canadian-
American Relations (Papers) (ISSN 0080-8814)

327 900 US
ANNUAL REGISTER. a. $95. Gale Research Co.,
Book Tower, Detroit, MI 48226. TEL 313-961-
2242. Ed. H.U. Hodson. (back issues avail.)

341.13 327 US ISSN 0066-4340
ANNUAL REVIEW OF UNITED NATIONS
AFFAIRS. 1949. a. price varies. Oceana
Publications, Inc., Dobbs Ferry, NY 10522. TEL
914-693-1320. Ed. William A. Landskron. index.
cum.index in 1965-66 vol.

327 IT
ANNUARIO DIPLOMATICO DELLA
REPUBBLICA ITALIANA. 1963. a. Ministero
degli Affari Esteri, Rome, Italy. circ. 1,500.
Formerly: Annuario Diplomatico del Regno
d'Italia.

320.9 JA
ASIAN PARLIAMENTARIANS' UNION.
CENTRAL SECRETARIAT. REPORT ON
MEETING OF APU SECRETARIES-GENERAL
IN TOKYO.* 1972. a. Asian Parliamentarians'
Union, TBR Bldg., Room 807, 2-10-2 Nagata-cho,
Chiyoda-ku, Tokyo, Japan.

327 AT ISSN 0519-5950
AUSTRALIA. DEPARTMENT OF FOREIGN
AFFAIRS. SELECT DOCUMENTS ON
INTERNATIONAL AFFAIRS; international
treaties and conventions. irreg. price varies.
Department of Foreign Affairs, Canberra, A.C.T.
2600, Australia.
Incorporating: Australia. Department of Foreign
Affairs. International Treaties and Conventions
(ISSN 0084-7135)

361 AT ISSN 0810-0055
AUSTRALIA NEW ZEALAND FOUNDATION.
ANNUAL REPORT (YEAR); promoting friendship
across the Tasman. a. free. (Australia New Zealand
Foundation) Australian Government Publishing
Service, P.O. Box 70E, Queen Victoria Terrace,
Canberra, A.C.T. 2600, Australia.

327 AT
AUSTRALIAN-AMERICAN NEWS N.S.W.
ANNUAL EDITION. irreg. Aus.$50 per no.
Australian-American Association, N.S.W. Division,
39-41 Lower Fort St., Sydney, N.S.W. 2000,
Australia. Ed. T. Padley. adv. illus.

327 AT
AUSTRALIA'S OVERSEAS DEVELOPMENT
ASSISTANCE. BUDGET PAPER. 1973. a. price
varies. Department of the Treasury, G.P.O. Box 84,
Canberra, A.C.T. 2601, Australia.
Former titles: Australia's Overseas Development
Assistance (ISSN 0312-9217) & Australia's External
Aid (ISSN 0310-6152)

327 CN ISSN 0708-0859
B.C. PEACE NEWS. 1978. irreg. subscription price
included in membership. B.C. Peace Council, 712-
207 West Hastings St., Vancouver, B.C. V6B 1H7,
Canada. TEL 604-685-9958. Ed.Bd. bk. rev. circ.
500.
Formerly: B.C. News (ISSN 0708-0840)

327 341 UK
BAILRIGG PAPERS ON INTERNATIONAL
SECURITY. 1980. irreg. University of Lancaster,
Centre for the Study of Arms Control and
International Security, Bailrigg, Lancaster LA1 4YR,
England.

341.13 UN ISSN 0067-4419
BASIC FACTS ABOUT THE UNITED NATIONS.
irreg. $2.75. United Nations Publications, Room
DC2-853, New York, NY 10017 (Or Distribution
and Sales Section, Palais des Nations, CH-1211
Geneva 10, Switzerland)

338.9 GW ISSN 0170-1916
BOCHUMER MATERIALEN ZUR
ENTWICKLUNGSFORSCHUNG UND
ENTWICKLUNGSPOLITIK. 1976. irreg. price
varies. (Ruhr-Universitaet, Bochum, Institut fuer
Entwicklungsforschung und Entwicklungspolitik) K.
Thienemanns Verlag, Edition Erdmann, Blumenstr.
36, 7000 Stuttgart, W. Germany (B.R.D.) Indexed:
Rural Recreat.Tour.Abstr. World Agri.Econ.&
Rural Sociol.Abstr.

327 338.9 GW ISSN 0572-6654
BOCHUMER SCHRIFTEN ZUR
ENTWICKLUNGSFORSCHUNG UND
ENTWICKLUNGSPOLITIK. 1968. irreg. price
varies. (Ruhr-Universitaet, Bochum, Institut fuer
Entwicklungsforschung und Entwicklungspolitik) K.
Thienemanns Verlag, Edition Erdmann, Blumenstr.
36, 700 Stuttgart 1, W. Germany (B.R.D.) circ. 1,
000.

327 UK ISSN 0307-2061
BRITISH NATIONAL ASSOCIATION FOR
SOVIET AND EAST EUROPEAN STUDIES.
INFORMATION BULLETIN. 1975. a.
membership. British National Association for Soviet
and East European Studies, University of Glasgow,
29 Bute Gardens, Glasgow G12 8RS, Scotland. Ed.
D. Matko. bk. rev. bibl. circ. 2,000.

327 GW ISSN 0435-7183
BUNDESINSTITUT FUER
OSTWISSENSCHAFTLICHE UND
INTERNATIONALE STUDIEN. BERICHTE.
1967. irreg. DM.30. Bundesinstitut fuer
Ostwissenschaftliche und Internationale Studien,
Lindenborn Str. 22, 5000 Cologne, W. Germany
(B.R.D.) bibl. circ. 1,100.

POLITICAL SCIENCE — INTERNATIONAL RELATIONS

C E P S WORKING DOCUMENTS (POLITICAL) (Centre for European Policy Studies) see *POLITICAL SCIENCE*

327   US   ISSN 0730-9058
C W/P S SPECIAL STUDIES. 1977. irreg., no.7, 1983. $2.50 per no. Center for War-Peace Studies, 218 E. 18th St., New York, NY 10003. TEL 212-475-1077. Ed. Richard Hudson.
Formerly: C W/P S Study.

327   FR   ISSN 0084-8220
CAHIERS AMITIE FRANCO-VIETNAMIENNE.* a. Association d'Amitie Franco-Vietnamienne, 37, rue Ballu, 75009 Paris, France. bibl. charts. illus.

CAHIERS DE BRUGES/BRUGES QUARTERLY. see *POLITICAL SCIENCE*

327   US
CALIFORNIA STATE UNIVERSITY, LOS ANGELES. CENTER FOR THE STUDY OF ARMAMENT AND DISARMAMENT. OCCASIONAL PAPERS SERIES. 1972. irreg., no.14, 1985. $3.95 per no. California State University, Los Angeles, Center for the Study of Armament and Disarmament, 5151 State University Dr., Los Angeles, CA 90032. Ed. Udo Heyn. circ. 300. Indexed: Vert.File Ind.

327   US
CAMPAIGN AGAINST U.S. INTERVENTION; legislative update. irreg., (every 4-6 wks.) $20. Coalition for a New Foreign Policy, 712 G St., S.E., Washington, DC 20003-2852. TEL 202-546-8400.
Formerly: Legislative Update.

327   CN
CANADA. DEPARTMENT OF EXTERNAL AFFAIRS. REFERENCE PAPERS. irreg. Department of External Affairs, External Information Programs Division, Ottawa, Ont. K1A 0G2, Canada. TEL 613-996-9134.

327   CN
CANADA. DEPARTMENT OF EXTERNAL AFFAIRS. STATEMENTS AND SPEECHES. 1945. irreg. free. Department of External Affairs, External Information Programs Division, Ottawa, Ont. K1A 0G2, Canada. TEL 613-996-9134. circ. 4, 000.

327   CN   ISSN 0068-7685
CANADA IN WORLD AFFAIRS. irreg. Canadian Institute of International Affairs, 15 King's College Circle, Toronto, Ont. M5S 2V9, Canada. TEL 416-979-1851.

327   CN   ISSN 0317-5693
CANADIAN COMMISSION FOR UNESCO. ANNUAL REPORT. (Text in English and French) 1958. a. free. ‡ Canadian Commission for Unesco, Box 1047, Ottawa, Ont. K1P 5V8, Canada. TEL 613-237-3400. circ. 3,500.

327   CN
CANADIAN FOREIGN RELATIONS. (Text in English and French) a. Department of External Affairs, Domestic Information Division, Ottawa, Ont. K1A 0G2, Canada. TEL 613-996-9134. illus.

CANADO-AMERICAIN. see *ETHNIC INTERESTS*

327   CN   ISSN 0383-2848
CARLETON UNIVERSITY, OTTAWA. NORMAN PATERSON SCHOOL OF INTERNATIONAL AFFAIRS. BIBLIOGRAPHY SERIES. 1975. irreg. (1-2/yr) Can.$6 per no. Carleton University, Norman Paterson School of International Affairs, Ottawa, Ont. K1S 5B6, Canada. TEL 613-564-2695. Ed. Rede Widstrand. circ. 600.

327.172   US   ISSN 0094-3029
CARNEGIE ENDOWMENT FOR INTERNATIONAL PEACE. FINANCIAL REPORT. irreg. Carnegie Endowment for International Peace, 11 Dupont Circle, N.W., Washington, DC 20036. TEL 202-797-6400. (reprint service avail. from UMI) Key Title: Financial Report - Carnegie Endowment for International Peace.

327   US
CARNEGIE ENDOWMENT FOR INTERNATIONAL PEACE IN THE 1970'S. 1979. irreg. free. Carnegie Endowment for International Peace, 11 Dupont Circle N.W., Washington, DC 20036. TEL 202-797-6400. circ. controlled. (reprint service avail. from UMI)
Supersedes (1911-1979): Carnegie Endowment for International Peace Report (ISSN 0069-0643); Which was formerly: Carnegie Endowment for International Peace. Annual Report.

327   US   ISSN 0732-0078
CENTER FOR PEACE AND CONFLICT STUDIES. OCCASIONAL PAPERS. 1981. irreg. price varies. Wayne State University, Center for Peace and Conflict Studies, Detroit, MI 48202. TEL 313-577-3453.

327   US   ISSN 0740-0004
CENTRAL AMERICA AND THE CARIBBEAN: DEVELOPMENT ASSISTANCE ABROAD. a. American Council of Voluntary Agencies for Foreign Service, Inc., Technical Assistance Information Clearing House, 200 Park Ave. So., New York, NY 10003. Eds. Florence M. Lowenstein, Roger B. McClanahan.

CENTRAL ASIAN COLLECTANEA. see *BIBLIOGRAPHIES*

327   US   ISSN 0145-9686
CLEMENTS' ENCYCLOPEDIA OF WORLD GOVERNMENTS. 1974. biennial. $340 (includes Clements' International Report, Updates and Matching Supplement Organizer) Political Research, Inc., Tegoland at Bent Tree, 16850 Dallas Parkway, Dallas, TX 75248. TEL 214-931-8827. Ed. John Clements.

COMMONWEALTH INSTITUTE, LONDON. ANNUAL REPORT. see *GEOGRAPHY*

341.1   US   ISSN 0010-955X
COSMOPOLITAN CONTACT.* (Text in various languages) 1962. irreg. $4. ‡ (Planetary Legion for Peace - PLP) Pantheon Press-General Enterprises, Box 89300, Honolulu, HI 96830-9300. Ed. Romulus Rexner. adv. bk. rev. illus. circ. 1,500. (processed; back issues avail.)

COUNCIL OF EUROPE. COMMITTEE OF INDEPENDENT EXPERTS ON THE EUROPEAN SOCIAL CHARTER. CONCLUSIONS. see *SOCIAL SERVICES AND WELFARE*

327.73   US   ISSN 0192-236X
COUNCIL ON FOREIGN RELATIONS. ANNUAL REPORT. a. Council on Foreign Relations, Inc., 58 E. 68th St., New York, NY 10021. TEL 212-734-0400. (reprint service avail. from UMI)
Formerly: Council on Foreign Relations. President's Report (ISSN 0093-4615)

327   US   ISSN 0743-0388
CURRENT ISSUES (ARLINGTON) 1977. a. $8. Close Up Foundation, 1235 Jefferson Davis Hwy., Arlington, VA 22202. TEL 703-892-5400. Ed. Patricia Bandy. charts. illus. stat. circ. 36,000.

327   DK   ISSN 0900-2871
DANSKE SELSKAB. NYT; oplysning om Danmark og kulturelt samvirke med andre nationer. 1983. irreg., (4-5/yr.) free. Danske Selskab, 2 Kultorvet, 1175 Copenhagen K, Denmark. Ed. Per Himmelstrup. circ. 1,000.

327   UK   ISSN 0070-2900
DAVID DAVIES MEMORIAL INSTITUTE OF INTERNATIONAL STUDIES, LONDON. ANNUAL MEMORIAL LECTURE. 1954. a. £1. David Davies Memorial Institute of International Studies, 2 Chadwick St., London SW1P 2EP, England. Ed. Sheila Harden.

DEFENSE FOREIGN AFFAIRS HANDBOOK; political, economic & defense data on every country in the world. see *MILITARY*

327   GW   ISSN 0080-7125
DEUTSCH-AUSLAENDISCHE BEZIEHUNGEN. SCHRIFTENREIHE. 1961. irreg. price varies. (Institut fuer Auslandsbeziehungen, Stuttgart) K. Thienemanns Verlag, Edition Erdmann, Blumenstr. 36, 7000 Stuttgart 1, W. Germany (B.R.D.) circ. 3, 000.

327   AU
DIALOGO; Austria-America Latina. (Text in Portuguese, Spanish) 1982. a. free. Oesterreichisches Lateinamerika-Institut, Schmerlingplatz 8, 1010 Vienna, Austria. Ed.Bd. adv. circ. 3,000. (back issues avail.)

DIGEST OF WORLD EVENTS. see *HISTORY*

327   UK
DIPLOMATIC & CONSULAR YEAR BOOK. 1978. a. £14.95($25) Diplomatic & Consular Year Book International Ltd., 11-13 Cricklewood Lane, London NW2 1ET, England. Ed. Kim O'Brien. adv. bk. rev. circ. 5,000.

327   CN   ISSN 0486-4514
DIPLOMATIC CORPS AND CONSULAR AND OTHER REPRESENTATIVES IN CANADA/ CORPS DIPLOMATIQUE ET REPRESENTANTS CONSULAIRES ET AUTRES AU CANADA. (Text in English and French) 1969. irreg. Can.$2.75. Department of External Affairs, Ottawa, Ont. K1A 0G2, Canada. TEL 613-996-9134.

327   NP
DIPLOMATIC LIST AND LIST OF REPRESENTATIVES OF UNITED NATIONS AND ITS SPECIALIZED AGENCIES AND OTHER MISSIONS. (Text in English) a. Protocol Division, Ministry of Foreign Affairs, Kathmandu, Nepal.

327   UK
DIPLOMATIC SERVICE LIST. a. price varies. Her Majesty's Stationery Office, Box 276, London SW8 5DT, England. circ. 3,000.

327   UY
DOCUMENTACION INTERNACIONAL. no.2, 1982. irreg. Fundacion de Cultura Universitaria, Montevideo, Uruguay.

327   US
DUKE UNIVERSITY. CENTER FOR INTERNATIONAL STUDIES. PUBLICATIONS. 1956. irreg. price varies. Duke University Press, Center for International Studies, 6697 College Sta., Durham, NC 27708. TEL 919-684-2173.
Formerly: Duke University. Commonwealth-Studies Center. Publications (ISSN 0070-7473)

327   NE   ISSN 0423-6645
E A A S NEWSLETTER. (Text in English) 1955. biennial. fl.16.50. (European Association for American Studies) Amerika Instituut, University of Amsterdam, Jodenbreestr., 1011 N Amsterdam, Netherlands. Ed. Pierre Michel. adv. circ. 3,000. Indexed: Hist.Abstr. Amer.Hist.& Life.

327   UK
E L T S A NEWSLETTER. 1974. irreg., (3-4/yr.) £2.50. End Loans to Southern Africa, 134 Wrottesley Rd., London NW10 5XR, England. Ed. Rev. David A. Haslam. circ. 1,000. (looseleaf format) Indexed: HR Rep.

327   US   ISSN 0070-8100
EAST EUROPE MONOGRAPHS. 1969. irreg., no.4, 1974. price varies. (Studiengesellschaft fuer Fragen Mittel- und Osteuropaeischer Partnerschaft, GW) Park College, Governmental Research Bureau, Kansas City, MO 64152. TEL 816-741-2000. Eds. Jerzy Hauptmann, Gotthold Rhode.

327   NE
EAST-WEST PERSPECTIVES. (Text in English) 1976. irreg. price varies. (East-West Foundation) Martinus Nijhoff Publishers, Postbus 163, 3300 AD Dordrecht, Netherlands. Ed.Bd. charts. stat.

327 170   US
ETHICS AND INTERNATIONAL AFFAIRS. 1987. a. $20. Carnegie Council on Ethics and International Affairs, 170 E. 64th St., New York, NY 10021. TEL 212-838-4120. Ed. Robert J. Myers.

327 016   EI   ISSN 0071-2213
ETUDES UNIVERSITAIRES SUR L'INTEGRATION EUROPEENNE/UNIVERSITY STUDIES ON EUROPEAN INTEGRATION. (Editions in English and French) 1963. irreg. price varies. (European Community Institute for University Studies) Commission of the European Communities, 200, rue de la Loi, B-1049 Brussels, Belgium. Ed. Anne-Marie Nantermoz. circ. 4,000.

POLITICAL SCIENCE — INTERNATIONAL RELATIONS

327 341   GW   ISSN 0071-2329
EUROPAEISCHE SCHRIFTEN. 1963. irreg. (Institut fuer Europaeische Politik, Bonn) Europa Union Verlag GmbH, Bachstr. 32, 5300 Bonn 1, W. Germany (B.R.D.) Ed. Wolfgang Wessels.

341.13   UN
EVERYONE'S UNITED NATIONS. 1948. irreg., latest no.10. $14.95. United Nations Publications, Room DC2-853, New York, NY 10017 (Or Distribution and Sales Section, Palais des Nations, CH-1211 Geneva 10, Switzerland)
    Formerly (until 1979): Everyman's United Nations (ISSN 0071-3244)

327   US
EXECUTIVE MEMORANDUM. (Topic varies per issue) 1982. irreg. price varies. Heritage Foundation, 214 Massachusetts Ave., N.E., Washington, DC 20002. TEL 202-546-4400. (looseleaf format; also avail. in microfiche; back issues avail.)

FILMOTECA ULTRAMARINA PORTUGUESA. BOLETIM. see *HISTORY*

FIRST HAND INFORMATION. see *HISTORY — History Of Europe*

327   US   ISSN 0071-7320
FOREIGN CONSULAR OFFICES IN THE UNITED STATES. (Subseries of U. S. Dept. of State. Department and Foreign Service Series) 1932. a. U.S. Department of State, 2201 C St. N.W., Washington, DC 20520 TEL 202-655-4000. (Orders to Supt. of Documents, Washington, DC 20402)

327   US
FOREIGN POLICY RESEARCH INSTITUTE. ANNUAL REPORT. 1957. a. Foreign Policy Research Institute, 3508 Market St., Suite 350, Philadelphia, PA 19104. TEL 215-382-0685.

327   US   ISSN 0071-7355
FOREIGN RELATIONS OF THE UNITED STATES. 1861. irreg. price varies. U.S. Department of State, Bureau of Public Affairs, Office of the Historian, Washington, DC 20520 TEL 202-655-4000. (Orders to Supt. of Documents, Washington, DC 20402)

354   FR
FRANCE. MEDIATEUR. RAPPORT ANNUEL DU MEDIATEUR. 1973. a. Direction des Journaux Officiels, 26 rue Desaix, 75015 Paris, France.

327   FR
FRANCE. MINISTERE DES RELATIONS EXTERIEURES. SOUS-DIRECTIONS DES ETUDES ET DEVELOPPEMENT. ETUDES ET DOCUMENTS. irreg. Ministere des Relations Exterieures, Sous-Direction des Etudes du Developpement, Service de la Cooperation et du Developpement, 20 rue Monsieur, 75700 Paris, France. circ. 500.
    Former titles: France. Ministere de la Cooperation. Sous-Direction des Etudes de Developpement. Etudes et Documents; France. Ministere de la Cooperation. Services des Etudes et Questions Internationales. Etudes et Documents (ISSN 0247-4468)

327   FR   ISSN 0071-8181
FRANCE-ALLEMAGNE. 1967. irreg., approximately 3/yr. free. Internationale Union of Mayors, Mairie de Paris, 75196 Paris, France.

327   II
GANDHI PEACE FOUNDATION LECTURES. irreg. Radakrishna Indraprastha Estate, Nehru House, 221/3 Deen Royal Upadhyaya Marg, New Delhi 110002, India.

GERMANY (FEDERAL REPUBLIC, 1949-). DEUTSCHER BUNDESTAG. WISSENSCHAFTLICHE DIENSTE. MATERIALIEN. see *BIBLIOGRAPHIES*

327   US   ISSN 0730-9112
GLOBAL REPORT; progress toward a world of peace with justice. 1977. irreg. $20. Center for War-Peace Studies, 218 E. 18th St., New York, NY 10003. TEL 212-475-1077. Ed. Richard Hudson. circ. 2,300.

GLOBAL RISK ASSESSMENTS; issues, concepts and applications. see *BUSINESS AND ECONOMICS — International Commerce*

327   UK   ISSN 0072-6397
GREAT BRITAIN. FOREIGN AND COMMONWEALTH OFFICE. TREATY SERIES. 1892. irreg. H.M.S.O., Box 569, London SE1 9NH, England. (reprint service avail. from UMI)

327.73   US   ISSN 0072-727X
GREAT DECISIONS. 1955. a. $7. Foreign Policy Association, 205 Lexington Ave., New York, NY 10016. TEL 212-481-8450. Ed. Nancy Hoepli. circ. 80,000. (reprint service avail. from UMI) Indexed: Abstr.Mil.Bibl.

327   US   ISSN 0194-3790
HANDBOOK OF THE NATIONS. 1979. irreg., latest 6th edt., 1986. $78. Gale Research Company, Book Tower, Detroit, MI 48226. TEL 313-961-2242.
    A reprint of the CIA's World Factbook

341   327   US   ISSN 0073-0734
HARVARD UNIVERSITY. CENTER FOR INTERNATIONAL AFFAIRS. ANNUAL REPORT. 1961 (1958-1960) a. free. Harvard University, Center for International Affairs, 1737 Cambridge St., Cambridge, MA 02138. TEL 617-495-4420. Ed. Theresa Leary. circ. 3,000.

327   YU
HRONIKA MEDJUNARODNIH DOGADJAJA/ CHRONICLE OF INTERNATIONAL EVENTS. (Text in Serbocroation) 1964. a. 3800 din. Institut za Medjunarodnu Politiku i Privredu - Institute of International Politics and Economics, Makedonska 25, Box 750, Belgrade, Yugoslavia. Ed. Kosara Grujovic.

327   US   ISSN 0073-3776
HUDSON INSTITUTE. REPORT TO THE MEMBERS.* 1962. a. free. Hudson Institute, Box 26919, Indianapolis, IN 46226-0919. circ. 4,500.

I C M E NEWS. (International Committee for Museums of Ethnography) see *GEOGRAPHY*

INDEX: FOREIGN BROADCAST INFORMATION SERVICE DAILY REPORTS: ASIA AND PACIFIC. see *POLITICAL SCIENCE — Abstracting, Bibliographies, Statistics*

INDEX: FOREIGN BROADCAST INFORMATION SERVICE DAILY REPORTS: CHINA. see *POLITICAL SCIENCE — Abstracting, Bibliographies, Statistics*

INDEX: FOREIGN BROADCAST INFORMATION SERVICE DAILY REPORTS: EASTERN EUROPE. see *POLITICAL SCIENCE — Abstracting, Bibliographies, Statistics*

INDEX: FOREIGN BROADCAST INFORMATION SERVICE DAILY REPORTS: LATIN AMERICA. see *POLITICAL SCIENCE — Abstracting, Bibliographies, Statistics*

INDEX: FOREIGN BROADCAST INFORMATION SERVICE DAILY REPORTS: MIDDLE EAST AND AFRICA. see *POLITICAL SCIENCE — Abstracting, Bibliographies, Statistics*

INDEX: FOREIGN BROADCAST INFORMATION SERVICE DAILY REPORTS: SOUTH ASIA. see *POLITICAL SCIENCE — Abstracting, Bibliographies, Statistics*

INDEX: FOREIGN BROADCAST INFORMATION SERVICE DAILY REPORTS: SOVIET UNION. see *POLITICAL SCIENCE — Abstracting, Bibliographies, Statistics*

INDEX: FOREIGN BROADCAST INFORMATION SERVICE DAILY REPORTS: WESTERN EUROPE. see *POLITICAL SCIENCE — Abstracting, Bibliographies, Statistics*

327   016   US   ISSN 0193-905X
INDEX TO INTERNATIONAL PUBLIC OPINION. 1980. a. price varies. (Survey Research Consultants International, Inc.) Greenwood Press, 88 Post Rd. W., Box 5007, Westport, CT 06881 TEL 203-226-3511. (Orders in Eastern Hemisphere to: Macmillan, 4 Little Essex St., London WC2R 3LF, England) Eds. Elizabeth Hann Hastings, Philip K. Hastings.

327   II
INDIAN FOREIGN POLICY ANNUAL SURVEY. irreg. Sterling Publishers Pvt. Ltd., L-10 Green Park Extn., New Delhi 110 016, India. Ed. Shri Ram Sharma. circ. 1,100.

327   954   II   ISSN 0537-2704
INDIAN YEARBOOK OF INTERNATIONAL AFFAIRS. 1952-1968; N.S. 1973. a. Indian Study Group of International Affairs, University of Madras, Chepauk, Triplicane P.O., Madras 600005, Tamil Nadu, India. bk. rev. index.
    Law and international relations

980   GW   ISSN 0073-8948
INSTITUT FUER IBEROAMERIKA-KUNDE. SCHRIFTENREIHE. (Text in German; occasionally Spanish) 1963. irreg., no. 28, 1977. price varies. K. Thienemanns Verlag, Edition Erdmann, Blumenstr. 36, 7000 Stuttgart, W. Germany (B.R.D.)

327   YU
INSTITUT ZA MEDJUNARODNU POLITIKU I PRIVREDU. GODISNIJAK. a. 1200 din. Institut za Medjunarodnu Politiku i Privredu - Institute of International Politics and Economics, Makedonska 25, Box 750, Belgrade, Yugoslavia. Ed. Vatroslav Vekaric.

327   BL
INSTITUTO CULTURAL ITALO-BRASILEIRO. CADERNO. no.8, 1972. irreg. Instituto Cultural Italo-Brasileiro, Rua Frei Caneca 1071, Sao Paulo, Brazil.

327   NE   ISSN 0579-8108
INTERNATIONAL CONFERENCE ON WORLD POLITICS. CONFERENCE PAPERS.* irreg. International Conference on World Politics, Secretariat, P.O. Box 9058, The Hague, Netherlands.

327   US
INTERNATIONAL LEADERSHIP. 1987. irreg. membership. American Center for International Leadership, 522 Franklin St., Columbus, IN 47201. TEL 812-376-3456. Ed. Lynn Sanborne.

327   JA
INTERNATIONAL RELATIONS COMMITTEE. NEW ENERGY FOUNDATION. ANNUAL REPORT ON INTERNATIONAL RELATIONS. a. International Relations Committee, New Energy Foundation, N. 10 Mori-building, 1-18, Toranomon, 1-chome, Minato-ku, Tokyo 105, Japan.

327   900   NE
INTERNATIONAL STRAITS OF THE WORLD. 1978. irreg. price varies. Martinus Nijhoff Publishers, Postbus 163, 3300 AD Dordrecht, Netherlands.

327   GW
INTERNATIONALE POLITIK UND WIRTSCHAFT. irreg., vol.50, 1987. price varies. (Deutsche Gesellschaft fuer Auswaertige Politik) R. Oldenbourg Verlag GmbH, Rosenheimer Str. 145, 8000 Munich 80, W. Germany (B.R.D.)

INTERNATIONALES RECHT UND DIPLOMATIE. see *LAW — International Law*

320   SZ   ISSN 0074-1051
INTER-PARLIAMENTARY UNION. CONFERENCE PROCEEDINGS/UNION INTERPARLEMENTAIRE. COMPTES RENDUS DES CONFERENCES. (Text in English and French) 1897. a. 20 Fr. for vol. 1; 45 francs for vol. 2. Inter-Parliamentary Union - Union Interparlementaire, Place du Petit Saconnex, 1209 Geneva, Switzerland. circ. 800.

327   338.91   IE   ISSN 0332-1460
IRISH STUDIES IN INTERNATIONAL AFFAIRS. 1979. a. £6. Royal Irish Academy, 19 Dawson St., Dublin 2, Ireland. Ed. J. Bradley. (back issues avail.)

327   DK   ISSN 0108-3783
ISRAELSKE AMBASSADE. INFORMATION. 1980. irreg. free. Israelske Ambassade, Trondhjems Plads 4, 2100 Copenhagen OE, Denmark.

327   SI
ISSUES IN SOUTHEAST ASIAN SECURITY. 1983. irreg., latest no. 5, 1985. price varies. Institute of Southeast Asian Studies, Heng Mui Keng Terrace, Pasir Panjang, Singapore 0511, Singapore.

327   US   ISSN 0075-2142
JACOB BLAUSTEIN LECTURES IN INTERNATIONAL AFFAIRS. 1967. irreg., no.2, 1971. Columbia University Press, 562 W. 113th St., New York, NY 10025. TEL 212-678-6777.

JERUSALEM PAPERS ON PEACE PROBLEMS. see POLITICAL SCIENCE

327   TZ
JOURNAL OF INTERNATIONAL RELATIONS. 1976. irreg. (3-4/yr.) $1.50 per no. International Relations Association, University of Dar es Salaam, Dar es Salaam, Tanzania. Ed. Mzirai Kangero. circ. 300.
    Formerly (until no.2, 1978): International Relations Association. Journal.

327   956.94   LE
KATIB AL-FILASTINI. (Text in Arabic) 1978. irreg. £L150. Ittihad al-Amm lil-Kuttab wa-al-Sahafiyin al-Filastiniyin, Box 3075, Beirut, Lebanon.

KOELNER FRIEDENS-ANZEIGER; Zeitung aus der Koelner Friedensbewegung. see POLITICAL SCIENCE

327   KO
KOREAN JOURNAL OF INTERNATIONAL RELATIONS. 1963. irreg. Korean Association of International Relations, c/o Graduate School of Public Administration, Seoul National University, 119 Tongsung-Dong, Chongno-Ku, Seoul, S. Korea.

951.9   SW   ISSN 0023-4079
KOREANSK JOURNAL. (Text in Swedish; summaries in English) 1950. irreg. (4-6/yr.) Kr.25($5.) Swedish-Korean Society, Box 3259, S-103 65 Stockholm 3, Sweden. Eds. Aake J. Ek, Lennart V. Toernqvist. adv. bk. rev. abstr. art rev. film rev. illus. play rev. stat. tr.lit. circ. 4,500.

327   US   ISSN 0736-4148
LATIN AMERICA AND CARIBBEAN CONTEMPORARY RECORD. 1981. a. $255. Holmes & Meier Publishers, Inc., 30 Irving Pl., New York, NY 10003. TEL 212-254-4100. Ed. Abraham F. Lowenthal. adv. bk. rev. bibl. charts. illus. stat. index.

327   LO   ISSN 0460-2099
LESOTHO. MINISTRY OF FOREIGN AFFAIRS. DIPLOMATIC AND CONSULAR LIST. a. Ministry of Foreign Affairs, Maseru, Lesotho.

354   LB
LIBERIA. MINISTRY OF FOREIGN AFFAIRS. ANNUAL REPORT. a. Ministry of Foreign Affairs, Monrovia, Liberia.

227   YU
LISTE DES MEMBRES DU CORPS DIPLOMATIQUE A BEOGRAD. (Text in French) 1946. a. Savezni Sekretarijat za Inostrane Poslove - Federal Secretariat for Foreign Affairs, Belgrade, Yugoslavia. circ. 1,000.

327   HU   ISSN 0541-9220
MAGYAR KULPOLITIKAI EVKONYV. 1968. a. $7.20. Kulugymininiszterium, 1525 Budapest, Pf. 62, Hungary.

327   IT
MANUALI DI POLITICA INTERNAZIONALE. irreg. price varies. Istituto per gli Studi di Politica Internazionale, Via Clerica, 5, 20100 Milan, Italy.

MATERIALIEN ZUM INTERNATIONALEN KULTURAUSTAUSCH/STUDIES IN INTERNATIONAL CULTURAL RELATIONS. see ORIENTAL STUDIES

327   MF   ISSN 0085-3194
MAURITIUS DIRECTORY OF THE DIPLOMATIC CORPS. 1969. a. Rs.30. (Ministry of External Affairs, Tourism and Immigration) Government Printing Office, Port Louis, Mauritius (Subscr. to: Government Printing Office, Elizabeth II Ave., Port Louis, Mauritius) circ. 400.

MIDDLE EAST: ABSTRACTS AND INDEX. see ABSTRACTING AND INDEXING SERVICES

327   US   ISSN 0733-5350
MIDDLE EAST ANNUAL. 1981. a. $47. G.K. Hall & Co., 70 Lincoln St., Boston, MA 02111. Ed. David H. Partington.

MIDDLE EAST CONTEMPORARY SURVEY. see HISTORY — History Of The Near East

327   US   ISSN 0077-0582
MONOGRAPH SERIES IN WORLD AFFAIRS. 1963. irreg., approx. 4/yr. $24. University of Denver, Graduate School of International Studies, c/o Karen A. Feste, Ed., Denver, CO 80208. TEL 303-871-2555. adv. circ. 1,000. Indexed: SSCI.

355   BE
N A T O AND THE WARSAW PACT - FORCE COMPARISONS/O T A N ET LE PACTE DE VARSOVIE - COMPARISON DES FORCES EN PRESENCE. 1982. biennial. North Atlantic Treaty Organization, Information Service, 1110 Brussels, Belgium (U.S. address: Distribution Officer, Bureau of Public Affairs, Dept. of State, Washington, DC 20520)

355   BE
N A T O BASIC DOCUMENTS/O T A N DOCUMENTS FONDAMENTAUX. 1975. irreg. North Atlantic Treaty Organization, Information Service, 1110 Brussels, Belgium (U.S. address: Distribution Officer, Bureau of Public Affairs, Dept. of State, Washington, DC 20520)

355   BE
N A T O FINAL COMMUNIQUES/O T A N COMMUNIQUES FINALS. (Annual supplements avail.) 1970. quinquennial. North Atlantic Treaty Organization, Information Service, 1110 Brussels, Belgium (U.S. Address: Distribution Officer, Bureau of Public Affairs, Dpet. of State, Washington, DC 20520)

355   BE   ISSN 0549-7175
N A T O HANDBOOK. French edt.: Manuel de l' O T A N. (Editions in various languages) 1952. a. (English and French editions); irreg. (other languages) free. North Atlantic Treaty Organization, Information Service, 1110 Brussels, Belgium, Belgium (U.S. address: Distribution Officer, Bureau of Public Affairs, Dept. of State, Washington, DC 20520)

327   NO   ISSN 0800-0018
N U P I NOTAT. (Text in English and Norwegian) irreg. no.290, 1983. Kr.250 incl. N U P I Rapport. Norsk Utenrikspolitisk Institutt - Norwegian Institute of International Affairs, Postboks 8159, Dep., 0033 Oslo 1, Norway. Indexed: Abstr.Mil.Bibl.

327   NO   ISSN 0800-000X
N U P I RAPPORT. (Text in English and Norwegian) irreg., no.82, 1983. Kr.250 incl. N U P I Notat. Norsk Utenrikspolitisk Institutt - Norwegian Institute of International Affairs, Postboks 8159, Dep., 0033 Oslo 1, Norway.

327   NZ   ISSN 0111-5251
NEW ZEALAND. MINISTRY OF FOREIGN AFFAIRS. PROJECT PROFILES; New Zealand bilateral aid programme. 1980. a. free. Ministry of Foreign Affairs, External Aid Division, c/o Information Officer, Private Bag, Wellington, New Zealand. circ. 3,000.

327.931   NZ
NEW ZEALAND. MINISTRY OF FOREIGN AFFAIRS. REPORT. (Subseries of: New Zealand. Ministry of Foreign Affairs. Publication) a. price varies. Ministry of Foreign Affairs, Wellington, New Zealand (Subscr. address: Government Bookshop, Private Bag, Wellington, New Zealand)

341.23   NZ   ISSN 0110-1951
NEW ZEALAND. MINISTRY OF FOREIGN AFFAIRS. UNITED NATIONS HANDBOOK. a. NZ.$10. Ministry of Foreign Affairs, Wellington, New Zealand.
    Continues: New Zealand. Department of External Affairs. United Nations and Specialised Agencies Handbook.

916.69   NR   ISSN 0078-0685
NIGERIA YEAR BOOK. (Text in English) 1952. a. Daily Time of Nigeria, P.O. Box 139, Lagos, Nigeria. adv.

327   NR   ISSN 0078-0731
NIGERIAN INSTITUTE OF INTERNATIONAL AFFAIRS. LECTURE SERIES. (Text in English) 1969. irreg. price varies. Nigerian Institute of International Affairs, G.P.O. 1727, Lagos, Nigeria.

327   NR   ISSN 0331-6254
NIGERIAN INSTITUTE OF INTERNATIONAL AFFAIRS. MONOGRAPH SERIES. (Text in English) 1979. irreg. Nigerian Institute of International Affairs, G.P.O. Box 1727, Kofo Aboyomi Rd., Victoria Island, Lagos, Nigeria (U.S. dist.: First Western Corp., 6323 Beachway Dr., Falls Church, VA 22044) charts. stat. (back issues avail.)

301.29   NO
NORGE-AMERIKA FORENINGEN. YEARBOOK. 1945. a. free. Norway-America Association, Drammensvn. 20C, 0255 Oslo 2, Norway. Ed. Bjorn Heimar. adv. bk. rev. illus. circ. 2,000.
    Continues: Norge-Amerika Foreningen. Report.

327   NO   ISSN 0332-7299
NORSK UTENRIKSPOLITISK AARBOK. (Subseries of: Utenrikspolitiske Skrifter) 1974. a. Kr.165. Norsk Utenrikspolitisk Institutt - Norwegian Institute of International Affairs, Postboks 8159, Dep., 0033 Oslo 1, Norway. stat. circ. 1,300.

355   BE
NORTH ATLANTIC TREATY ORGANIZATION. FACTS AND FIGURES/ALLIANCE ATLANTIQUE. STRUCTURE, FAITS ET CHIFFRES. 1957. irreg. North Atlantic Treaty Organization, Information Service, 1110 Brussels, Belgium (U.S. Address: Distribution Officer, Bureau of Public Affairs, Dept. of State, Washington, DC 20520)

329   BE
ORGANISATION INTERNATIONALE ET RELATIONS INTERNATIONALES. 1975. a. 2809 Fr. (Centre de Recherches sur les Institutions Internationales) Etablissements Emile Bruylant, 67 rue de la Regence, 1000 Brussels, Belgium.

341.18   US
ORGANIZATION OF AMERICAN STATES. GENERAL ASSEMBLY. ACTAS Y DOCUMENTOS. irreg. price varies. Organization of American States, Department of Publications, Washington, DC 20006. TEL 703-941-1617. circ. 2,000.

327   FI   ISSN 0355-1849
PAASIKIVI-SOCIETY. MIMEOGRAPH SERIES. (Text mostly in Finnish) irreg., no.33, 1982. (Finnish Institute of International Affairs) Ulkopoliittinen Instituutti, Pursimiehenkatu 8, SF-00150 Helsinki, Finland. (processed)

327   UK
PAN-EUROPEAN ASSOCIATIONS; a directory of multi-national organisations in Europe. 1983. irreg. £40($120) C.B.D. Research Ltd., 15 Wickham Rd., Beckenham, Kent BR3 2JS, England. Ed. C.A.P. Henderson. circ. 2,000.

341.1   AT   ISSN 0031-3564
PEACE PLANS. (Text in English and German) 1964. irreg. Aus.$1 per microfiche. ‡ Libertarian Microfiche Publishing, 7 Oxley St, Berrima, N.S.W. 2577, Australia. Ed. John M. Zube. bk. rev. bibl. index; cum.index. circ. 150. (microfiche)

327   US
PHILADELPHIA POLICY PAPERS. 1964. irreg. price varies. ‡ Foreign Policy Research Institute, 3508 Market St., Suite 350, Philadelphia, PA 19104. TEL 215-382-0685. Ed. Adam Garfinkle. circ. 2, 000.
    Former titles: Foreign Policy Research Institute. Monograph Series; Foreign Policy Research Institute. Research Monograph Series (ISSN 0553-5743)

327   950   PH
PHILIPPINES CHINESE HISTORICAL ASSOCIATION. ANNALS. (Text in English) vol.5, 1975. a. P.25($6) Philippine Chinese Historical Association, Box 3131, Manila, Philippines. Ed. Gideon Hsu. bibl.

327   US
PHOENIX (DUMONT) 1984. irreg. (approx. 4/yr.) $10. Phoenix Publications, Box 132, Dumont, NJ 07628. TEL 201-385-8225. Ed. Pierre Papazian. bk. rev. circ. 1,000.

320   BL
POLITICA E ESTRATEGIA. 1983. q. $30. Sociedade Brasileira de Cultura, Alameda Eduardo Prado, 705, C.P. 30004, 01218 Sao Paulo, Brazil. Ed. Antonio Carlos Pereira. adv. circ. 2,300.

POLITICAL SCIENCE — INTERNATIONAL RELATIONS

POLITICS OF LIBERATION SERIES. see
HISTORY — History Of Europe

PRINCETON UNIVERSITY. CENTER OF
INTERNATIONAL STUDIES POLICY
MEMORANDUM. see *LAW — International Law*

341 327   US ISSN 0555-1501
PRINCETON UNIVERSITY. CENTER OF
INTERNATIONAL STUDIES. RESEARCH
MONOGRAPH SERIES. 1959. irreg., no.49, 1985.
price varies. Princeton University, Center of
International Studies, Corwin Hall, Princeton, NJ
08544. TEL 609-452-4851. (back issues avail.;
reprint service avail. from UMI)

327   US
PRINCETON UNIVERSITY. CENTER OF
INTERNATIONAL STUDIES. WORLD ORDER
STUDIES PROGRAM: OCCASIONAL PAPER.
1975. irreg., no.14, 1985. price varies. Princeton
University, Center of International Studies, Corwin
Hall, Princeton, NJ 08544. TEL 609-924-7911.
(reprint service avail. from UMI)

RADNER LECTURES. see *POLITICAL SCIENCE*

327   FR ISSN 0080-0333
RECUEIL DES INSTRUCTIONS DONNEES AUX
AMBASSADEURS ET MINISTRES DE
FRANCE. irreg., vol.29, 1970. price varies. Editions
du C N R S, 295 rue St. Jacques, 75005 Paris,
France.

327   US ISSN 0748-0571
REPORT OF A VANTAGE CONFERENCE. 1973.
irreg., no.12, 1986. free. Stanley Foundation, 420 E.
Third St., Muscatine, IA 52761. TEL 319-264-1500.
circ. 10,000.
 Formerly: Vantage Conference Report (ISSN
0145-8833)

327   US
REPORT ON THE SITUATION ON HUMAN
RIGHTS IN THE REPUBLIC OF GUATEMALA.
1962. irreg., latest 1983. $6. Inter-American
Commission on Human Rights, 1889 F. St. N.W.,
Ste. 820E, Washington, DC 20006 TEL 202-789-
6000. (Orders to: General Secretariat, Organization
of American States, Office of Publications,
Washington, DC 20006)

RUHR-UNIVERSITAET. INSTITUT ZUR
GESCHICHTE DER ARBEITERBEWEGUNG.
MITTEILUNGSBLATT. see *LABOR UNIONS*

327   SW ISSN 0348-2626
S A R E C REPORT. (Text in English) 1972. irreg. 2-
5/yr. Swedish Agency for Research Cooperation
with Developing Countries - Styrelsen foer U-
Landsforskning, S-105 25 Stockholm, Sweden. bibl.
illus. circ. 4,000.
 Formerly: S I D A Development Studies.

327 341.37 UK ISSN 0267-2537
S I P R I CHEMICAL & BIOLOGICAL WARFARE
STUDIES. irreg. (Stockholm International Peace
Research Institute (S.I.P.R.I.), SW) Oxford
University Press, Walton St., Oxford OX2 6DP,
England.

327   UK
S I P R I YEARBOOK: WORLD ARMAMENTS
AND DISARMAMENT. 1969. a. £28. (Stockholm
International Peace Research Institute (S.I.P.R.I.),
SW) Oxford University Press, Walton St., Oxford
OX2 6DP, England. Ed. Henry Hardy. circ. 3,500.
 Formerly: World Armaments and Disarmament:
S I P R I Yearbook (ISSN 0347-2205)

327   US ISSN 0094-0658
SAGE INTERNATIONAL YEARBOOK OF
FOREIGN POLICY STUDIES. 1973. a. $29.95 for
hardcover; softcover $14.95. Sage Publications, Inc.,
2111 W. Hillcrest Dr., Newbury Park, CA 91320
TEL 805-499-0721. (And Sage Publications, Ltd.,
28 Banner St., London EC1Y 8QE, England) Ed.
Patrick McGowan. (back issues avail.)

327   SZ
SCHWEIZERISCHE GESELLSCHAFT FUER
AUSSENPOLITIK. SCHRIFTENREIHE. 1972.
irreg., no.10, 1984. price varies. Paul Haupt AG,
Falkenplatz 14, CH-3001 Berne, Switzerland.

351   SG
SENEGAL. LISTE DU CORPS DIPLOMATIQUE.
irreg. Imprimerie Nationale, Rufisque, Senegal.
 Continues: Senegal. Service du Protocole. Liste
Diplomatique et Consulaire.

327   FR ISSN 0080-8903
SENNACIECA REVUO. (Text in Esperanto) 1952. a.
$8. Sennacieca Asocio Tutmonda, 67 av. Gambetta,
75020 Paris, France. bk. rev.

327   BL
SERIE CAPISTRANO DE ABREU. 1982. a. Colegio
Pedro II, Secretaria de Ensino, Campo de Sao
Cristovao, 177 CEP 20291, Rio de Janeiro, Brazil.

327   SA
SOUTH AFRICAN INSTITUTE OF
INTERNATIONAL AFFAIRS. BIENNIAL
REPORT OF THE NATIONAL CHAIRMAN.
1978. biennial. R.2. South African Institute of
International Affairs, Box 31596, Braamfontein,
2017 Transvaal, South Africa.
 Former titles (until 1984): South African Institute
of International Affairs. Report of the National
Chairman; South African Institute of International
Affairs. Biennial Council Report; Supersedes (1966-
1977): South African Institute of International
Affairs. Annual Report (ISSN 0081-2439)

327   SA
SOUTH AFRICAN INSTITUTE OF
INTERNATIONAL AFFAIRS. OCCASIONAL
PAPERS. irreg. price varies. South African Institute
of International Affairs, Box 31596, Braamfontein,
2017 Transvaal, South Africa.

327   SA
SOUTH AFRICAN INSTITUTE OF
INTERNATIONAL AFFAIRS. SPECIAL
STUDIES. 1977. irreg. price varies. South African
Institute of International Affairs, Box 31596,
Braamfontein, 2017 Transvaal, South Africa.

327   NL
SOUTH PACIFIC COMMISSION. ANNUAL
REPORT. (Text in English and French) 1948. a.
free. South Pacific Commission, B.P. D5, Noumea,
Cedex, New Caledonia. Indexed: Field Crop Abstr.
Herb.Abstr.
 Formerly: South Pacific Commission. South
Pacific Report (ISSN 0081-2854)

327   US
SOVIET-EAST EUROPEAN SURVEY; selected
research and analysis from Radio Free Europe-
Radio Liberty. 1985. a. price varies. Duke
University Press, 6697 College Sta., Durham, NC
27708. TEL 919-684-2173. Ed. Vojtech Mastny.

327   US
SOVIET FOREIGN POLICY TODAY; reports and
commentaries from the Soviet press. 1983. triennial.
2nd ed. $18. Current Digest of the Soviet Press,
1480 West Lane Ave., Columbus, OH 43221. TEL
614-292-4234. Ed. Gordon Livermore.
 Formerly: Soviet Foreign Policy.

320   US ISSN 0145-8841
STANLEY FOUNDATION. POLICY PAPER. 1972.
irreg., no.37, 1986. free. Stanley Foundation, 420 E.
Third St., Muscatine, IA 52761. TEL 319-264-1500.
circ. 18,000. Indexed: Abstr.Mil.Bibl.
 Formerly: Stanley Foundation. Occasional Paper.

327   UK ISSN 0459-7230
STRATEGIC SURVEY. 1967. a. £8($14)
International Institute for Strategic Studies, 23
Tavistock St., London WC2E 7NQ, England (U.S.
dist.: Marketing International, Inc., 1120
Connecticut Ave., N.W., Ste. 940, Washington, DC
20036) charts. circ. 15,000.

327   US ISSN 0748-9641
STRATEGY FOR PEACE U.S. FOREIGN POLICY
CONFERENCE. REPORT. 1960. a. free. ‡ Stanley
Foundation, 420 E. Third St., Muscatine, IA 52761.
TEL 319-264-1500. circ. 22,000.
 Formerly: Strategy for Peace Conference. Report
(ISSN 0081-5942)

323.4   US ISSN 0146-3586
STUDIES IN HUMAN RIGHTS. 1975. irreg. price
varies. Greenwood Press, 88 Post Rd. W., Box
5007, Westport, CT 06881. TEL 203-226-3571. Ed.
George W. Shepherd.

327   US
STUDIES IN INTERNATIONAL AFFAIRS
(COLUMBIA) 1961. irreg., latest 1979. University
of South Carolina, Institute of International Studies,
Columbia, SC 29208. TEL 803-777-8180. Ed.
Donald J. Pachala. (back issues avail.)

327   BE
STUDIES IN INTERNATIONAL RELATIONS.
1973. irreg., no.5, 1986. Leuven University Press,
Krakenstraat 3, B-3000 Louvain, Belgium.

327   US
SURVEY OF INTERNATIONAL AFFAIRS. irreg.
price varies. (Royal Institute of International Affairs,
UK) Oxford University Press, 200 Madison Ave.,
New York, NY 10016 TEL 212-679-7300. (And
Ely House, 37 Dover St., London W1X 4AH,
England)

SURVEY OF PRESS FREEDOM IN LATIN
AMERICA. see *JOURNALISM*

327   SW ISSN 0346-5578
SVERIGE-E G. Variant title: Sverige-Europeiska
Gemenskaperna. 1973. a. (Utrikesdepartementet -
Ministry of Foreign Affairs) Allmaenna Foerlaget,
Box 5227, 102 45 Stockholm, Sweden.

327   IS
TEL-AVIV UNIVERSITY. DAVID HOROWITZ
INSTITUTE FOR THE RESEARCH OF
DEVELOPING COUNTRIES. ANNUAL
REPORT. (Text in English) a. Tel-Aviv University,
David Horowitz Institute for the Research of
Developing Countries, Tel-Aviv, Israel.

327   IS
TEL-AVIV UNIVERSITY. DAVID HOROWITZ
INSTITUTE FOR THE RESEARCH OF
DEVELOPING COUNTRIES. RESEARCH
REPORTS AND PAPERS. (Text in Hebrew &
English) 1972. irreg. Tel-Aviv University, David
Horowitz Institute for the Research of Developing
Countries, Tel-Aviv, Israel. circ. 250. (looseleaf
format)

327   TH
THAILAND. MINISTRY OF FOREIGN AFFAIRS.
NEWS BULLETIN. no. 9, 1977. irreg. Ministry of
Foreign Affairs, Department of Information,
Bangkok, Thailand. circ. 7,500.

949.2   NE ISSN 0023-3412
TRACTATENBLAD VAN HET KONINKRIJK DER
NEDERLANDEN. (Text in Dutch; occasionally in
English, French) 1951. 200/yr. (approx.) (Ministerie
van Buitenlandse Zaken) Staatsuitgeverij, Chr.
Plantijnstraat 2, 2515 TZ The Hague, Netherlands.
index. circ. 500. Indexed: Key to Econ.Sci.
Treaties

327   GW ISSN 0344-9823
TRANSNATIONAL. irreg. DM.8 per no. Europa
Union Verlag GmbH, Bachstr. 32, Postfach 15 29,
5300 Bonn 1, W. Germany (B.R.D.) Ed. Walter
Boehm.

327   US
TRIANGLE PAPERS. 1973. irreg., approx. a. price
varies. (Trilateral Commission) New York
University Press, Washington Square, New York,
NY 10003. TEL 212-598-2886. Ed.Bd. circ. 3,000.
(back issues avail.)

TUDUV-STUDIE. REIHE
POLITIKWISSENSCHAFTEN. see *POLITICAL
SCIENCE*

366   US ISSN 0041-4611
TWENTIETH CENTURY FUND. NEWSLETTER.
1949. irreg., (approx. 3/yr.) free. Twentieth Century
Fund, 41 E. 70th St., New York, NY 10021. TEL
212-535-4441. Ed. Beverly Goldberg. circ. 10,
000(approx.) Indexed: Vert.File Ind.

327   UN
U N I T A R PEACEFUL SETTLEMENT SERIES.
(Editions in English and French) 1971. irreg. price
varies. United Nations Institute for Training and
Research, Publications Office, 801 United Nations
Plaza, New York, NY 10017 (Order from: United
Nations Publications Sales, DC 2 Room 874, New
York, NY 10017; or Distribution and Sales Section,
Palais des Nations, CH 1211 Geneva 10,
Switzerland) bk. rev.

POLITICAL SCIENCE — INTERNATIONAL RELATIONS 919

327 UN
U N I T A R REGIONAL STUDIES. 1972. irreg. price varies. United Nations Institute for Training and Research, Publications Office, 801 United Nations Plaza, New York, NY 10017 (Order from: United Nations Publications Sales, DC 2 Room 874, New York, NY 10017; or Distribution and Sales Section, Palais des Nations, CH 1211 Geneva 10, Switzerland) bk. rev.

327 UN
U N STUDIES. 1982. irreg. Heritage Foundation, 214 Massachusetts Ave., N.E., Washington, DC 20002. TEL 202-546-4400. (looseleaf format; also avail. in microfiche; back issues avail.)

U S - JAPAN RELATIONS. see *HISTORY*

327 US
U S RELATIONS WITH LATIN AMERICAN NATIONS. 1982. a. $19.95. Documentary Publications, 106 Kenan St., Chapel Hill, NC 27514-3922.

327   330.9   320   US
U S S R REPORT: PROBLEMS OF THE FAR EAST. irreg., (approx. 5/yr.) $5 per no. U.S. Joint Publications Research Service, 1000 N. Glebe Rd., Arlington, VA 22201 TEL 703-487-4630. (Orders to: NTIS, Springfield, VA 22161)
  Formerly: Problems of the Far East.
  Translations of articles by Soviet writers on Soviet relations with China and other Asian countries, and on economic and political conditions in China and Asia

U S S R REPORT: WORLD ECONOMY AND INTERNATIOAL RELATIONS. see *BUSINESS AND ECONOMICS*

327 UN ISSN 0082-7509
UNESCO. RECORDS OF THE GENERAL CONFERENCE. PROCEEDINGS. (Text in English, French, Russian and Spanish) irreg., 23rd session, 1986. price varies. Unesco, 7-9 Place de Fontenoy, 75700 Paris, France (Dist. in U.S. by: Bernan Associates-Unipub, 4611-F Assembly Dr., Lanham, MD 20706-4391)

327 UN ISSN 0082-7517
UNESCO. RECORDS OF THE GENERAL CONFERENCE. RESOLUTIONS. (Text in Arabic, English, French, Spanish and Russian) irreg., 23rd session, 1986. price varies. Unesco, 7-9 Place de Fontenoy, 75700 Paris, France (Dist. in U.S. by: Bernan Associates-Unipub, 4611-F Assembly Dr., Lanham, MD 20706-4391)

327 UN ISSN 0082-7525
UNESCO. REPORT OF THE DIRECTOR-GENERAL ON THE ACTIVITIES OF THE ORGANIZATION. (Text in Arabic, English, French, Spanish and Russian) 1959. biennial. price varies. Unesco, 7-9 Place de Fontenoy, 75700 Paris, France (Dist. in U.S. by: Bernan Associates-Unipub, 4611-F Assembly Dr., Lanham, MD 20706-4391)

327 US ISSN 0250-779X
UNESCO YEARBOOK ON PEACE AND CONFLICT STUDIES. 1981. a. $30. (United Nations Educational, Scientific and Cultural Organization) Greenwood Press, 88 Post Rd. W., Westport, CT 06881. TEL 203-226-3571. Ed. Hylke Tromp. Indexed: GeoRef.

341.13 UN ISSN 0082-8084
UNITED NATIONS. ECONOMIC AND SOCIAL COUNCIL. INDEX TO PROCEEDINGS. 1946. a.; latest 1985. $15. United Nations Publications, Room DC2-853, New York, NY 10017 (Or Distribution and Sales Section, Palais des Nations, CH-1211 Geneva 10, Switzerland) (also avail. in microfiche)

341.13 UN ISSN 0082-8092
UNITED NATIONS. ECONOMIC AND SOCIAL COUNCIL. OFFICIAL RECORDS. irreg. price varies. United Nations Publications, Room DC2-853, New York, NY 10017 (Or Distribution and Sales Section, Palais des Nations, CH-1211 Geneva 10, Switzerland) (also avail. in microfiche)

341.13 UN ISSN 0082-8408
UNITED NATIONS. SECURITY COUNCIL. INDEX TO PROCEEDINGS. 1946. a. $9.50. (United Nations Security Council) United Nations Publications, Room DC2-853, New York, NY 10017 (Or Distribution and Sales Section, Palais des Nations, CH-1211 Geneva 10, Switzerland) (also avail. in microfiche)

341.13 UN ISSN 0082-8416
UNITED NATIONS. SECURITY COUNCIL. OFFICIAL RECORDS. irreg. price varies. United Nations Publications, Room DC2-853, New York, NY 10017 (Or Distribution and Sales Section, Palais des Nations, CH-1211 Geneva 10, Switzerland) (also avail. in microfiche)

341.13 UN ISSN 0082-8483
UNITED NATIONS. TRADE AND DEVELOPMENT BOARD. OFFICIAL RECORDS. SUPPLEMENTS. 1965. irreg. price varies. United Nations Conference on Trade and Development, Palais des Nations (UNCTAD), 1211 Geneva 10, Switzerland (Or United Nations Publications, Room LX-2300, New York, NY 10017) (also avail. in microfiche)

341.13 UN ISSN 0082-8491
UNITED NATIONS. TRUSTEESHIP COUNCIL. INDEX TO PROCEEDINGS. 1953. a. $5. United Nations Publications, Room DC2-853, New York, NY 10017 (Or Distribution and Sales Section, Palais des Nations, CH-1211 Geneva 10, Switzerland) (also avail. in microfiche)

341.13 UN ISSN 0082-8505
UNITED NATIONS. TRUSTEESHIP COUNCIL. OFFICIAL RECORDS. (Meetings not yet published) irreg., 39th session, 1972. price varies. United Nations Publications, Room DC2-853, New York, NY 10017 (Or Distribution and Sales Section, Palais des Nations, CH-1211 Geneva 10, Switzerland) (also avail. in microfiche)

341.13 UN ISSN 0082-8513
UNITED NATIONS. TRUSTEESHIP COUNCIL. OFFICIAL RECORDS. SUPPLEMENTS. irreg. price varies. United Nations Publications, Room DC2-853, New York, NY 10017 (Or Distribution and Sales Section, Palais des Nations, CH-1211 Geneva 10, Switzerland) (also avail. in microfiche)

341.13 UN ISSN 0082-8521
UNITED NATIONS. YEARBOOK. 1946/47. a., latest, vol.36, 1982. $75. United Nations Publications, Room DC2-853, New York, NY 10017 (Or Distribution and Sales Section, Palais des Nations, CH-1200 Geneva 10, Switzerland) index. (also avail. in microfiche)

327 AT
UNITED NATIONS GENERAL ASSEMBLY: REPORT OF THE AUSTRALIAN DELEGATION. 1946. a. price varies. Australian Government Publishing Service, G.P.O. Box 84, Canberra, A.C.T. 2601, Australia.
  Formerly: Australian Mission to the United Nations. United Nations General Assembly. Australian Delegation. Report.

327 UN
UNITED NATIONS INSTITUTE FOR TRAINING AND RESEARCH. REPORT OF THE EXECUTIVE DIRECTOR. a.; latest, 1984. $1.50 (1972) United Nations Institute for Training and Research, Publications Office, 801 United Nations Plaza, New York, NY 10017 (Order from: United Nations Publications Sales, DC 2 Room 874, New York, NY 10017; or Distribution and Sales Section, Palais des Nations, CH 1211 Geneva 10, Switzerland)

341.13 US ISSN 0743-9180
UNITED NATIONS ISSUES CONFERENCE. REPORT. 1970. a. free. Stanley Foundation, 420 E. Third St., Muscatine, IA 52761. TEL 319-264-1500. circ. 8,000.
  Former titles: Conference on United Nations Procedures. Report (ISSN 0069-8601); Conference on Organization and Procedures of the United Nations Report.

341.13 US ISSN 0748-433X
UNITED NATIONS OF THE NEXT DECADE CONFERENCE. REPORT. 1965. a. free. Stanley Foundation, 420 E. Third St., Muscatine, IA 52761. TEL 319-264-1500. circ. 22,000.

358 US ISSN 0082-8688
U.S. AIR FORCE ACADEMY ASSEMBLY. PROCEEDINGS. 1959. a. free to qualified personnel. United States Air Force Academy, Dept. of Political Science, Colorado Springs, CO 80840 TEL 303-472-2270. (Orders to: Supt. of Documents, Washington, DC 20402) (Co-Sponsor: Columbia University American Assembly Program)

327 US
U.S. DEPARTMENT OF STATE. BUREAU OF PUBLIC AFFAIRS. CURRENT POLICY. irreg., no.646, 1984. U.S. Department of State, Bureau of Public Affairs, 2201 C St. N.W., Washington, DC 20520.

327 US ISSN 0083-0038
U.S. DEPARTMENT OF STATE. DEPARTMENT AND FOREIGN SERVICE SERIES. 1948. irreg. price varies. U.S. Department of State, Bureau of Public Affairs, 2201 C St. N.W., Washington, DC 20520 TEL 202-632-1394. (Orders to Supt. of Documents, Washington, DC 20402)

327 US ISSN 0083-0054
U.S. DEPARTMENT OF STATE. EAST ASIAN AND PACIFIC SERIES. 1932. irreg., no.214, 1975. U.S. Department of State, Bureau of Public Affairs, Washington, DC 20250 TEL 202-655-4000. (Orders to: Supt. of Documents, Washington, DC 20402)
  Formerly: Far Eastern Series (ISSN 0083-0089)

327   382   US ISSN 0083-0097
U.S. DEPARTMENT OF STATE. GENERAL FOREIGN POLICY SERIES. 1948. irreg. price varies. U.S. Department of State, Bureau of Public Affairs, 2201 C St. N.W., Washington, DC 20520 TEL 202-632-1394. (Orders to Supt. of Documents, Washington, DC 20402)

327 US ISSN 0083-0143
U.S. DEPARTMENT OF STATE. INTER-AMERICAN SERIES. 1929. irreg. price varies. U.S. Department of State, Bureau of Public Affairs, 2201 C St., N.W., Washington, DC 20520 TEL 202-632-1394. (Orders to Supt. of Documents, Washington, DC 20402)

327 US ISSN 0083-0119
U.S. DEPARTMENT OF STATE. INTERNATIONAL INFORMATION AND CULTURAL SERIES. 1948. irreg. price varies. U.S. Department of State, Bureau of Public Affairs, 2201 C St. N.W., Washington, DC 20520 TEL 202-632-1394. (Orders to Supt. of Documents, Washington, DC 20402)

327 US ISSN 0083-0127
U.S. DEPARTMENT OF STATE. INTERNATIONAL ORGANIZATION AND CONFERENCE SERIES. 1959. irreg. price varies. U.S. Department of State, Bureau of Public Affairs, 2201 C St.N.W., Washington, DC 20520 TEL 202-632-1394. (Orders to Supt. of Documents, Washington, DC 20402)

327 US ISSN 0083-0135
U.S. DEPARTMENT OF STATE. INTERNATIONAL ORGANIZATION SERIES. 1968. irreg. price varies. U.S. Department of State, Bureau of Public Affairs, 2201 C St.N.W., Washington, DC 20520 TEL 202-632-1394. (Orders to Supt. of Documents, Washington, DC 20402)

327 US ISSN 0083-3088
U.S. PEACE CORPS. ANNUAL REPORT. 1962. a. free. U.S. Peace Corps, 806 Connecticut Ave., N.W., Washington, DC 20526. TEL 202-254-5010.

327 US
UNITED STATES & THE WORLD: FOREIGN PERSPECTIVES. 1975. irreg., latest 1979. price varies. University of Chicago Press, 5801 S. Ellis Ave., Chicago, IL 60037. TEL 312-962-7700. Ed. Akira Iriye. adv. bk. rev. (reprint service avail. from UMI,ISI)

327 US ISSN 0083-0208
UNITED STATES PARTICIPATION IN THE UNITED NATIONS; report by the President to Congress. (Subseries of its International Organization and Conference Series) 1948. a. U.S. Department of State, Bureau of International Organization Affairs, 2201 C St., N.W., Washington, DC 20520 TEL 202-632-1394. (Orders to: Supt. of Documents, Washington, DC 20402)

327   CN   ISSN 0083-3681
UNIVERS POLITIQUE; RELATIONS
INTERNATIONALES. 1968. a. price varies.
Editions Richelieu, 142 rue Saint Pierre, C.P. 216,
St. Jean-sur-Richelieu, Quebec J3B 6Z4, Canada.
Ed. Jean Meyriat.

327.2   CL
UNIVERSIDAD DE GUAYAQUIL. ESCUELA DE
DIPLOMACIA. REVISTA. 1973. irreg.
Universidad de Guayaquil, Escuela de Diplomacia,
Calle Chile 900, Apdo. 471, Guayaquil, Chile.

UNIVERSIDAD DE PANAMA. FACULTAD DE
DERECHO Y CIENCIAS POLITICAS.
CUADERNOS. see *LAW*

327   GW   ISSN 0341-3233
UNIVERSITAET HAMBURG. INSTITUT FUER
INTERNATIONALE ANGELEGENHEITEN.
VEROEFFENTLICHUNGEN. 1975. irreg., vol. 11,
1983. price varies. Nomos Verlagsgesellschaft mbH
und Co. KG, Waldseestr. 3-5, Postfach 610, 7570
Baden Baden, W. Germany (B.R.D.) Indexed: Rural
Recreat.Tour.Abstr. World Agri.Econ.& Rural
Sociol.Abstr.

UNIVERSITAET HAMBURG. INSTITUT FUER
INTERNATIONALE ANGELEGENHEITEN.
WERKHEFTE. see *LAW — International Law*

327.73   BE   ISSN 0076-1206
UNIVERSITE CATHOLIQUE DE LOUVAIN.
CENTRE D'ETUDES POLITIQUES. WORKING
GROUP "AMERICAN FOREIGN POLICY."
CAHIER.* 1969. irreg. Universite Catholique de
Louvain, Centre d'Etudes Politiques, 1348 Louvain-
la-Neuve, Belgium (Dist. in U.S. by: Humanities
Press, Inc., 171 First Ave., Atlantic Highlands, NJ
07716)

320   US   ISSN 0731-6321
UNIVERSITY OF CALIFORNIA, BERKELEY.
INSTITUTE OF INTERNATIONAL STUDIES.
POLICY PAPERS IN INTERNATIONAL
AFFAIRS. 1977. 2-3/yr. price varies. University of
California, Berkeley, Institute of International
Studies, 215 Moses Hall, Berkeley, CA 94720. TEL
415-642-7189. Ed. Paul M. Gilchrist.

327   US   ISSN 0085-6452
UNIVERSITY OF SOUTH CAROLINA.
INSTITUTE OF INTERNATIONAL STUDIES.
ESSAY SERIES. 1967. irreg., no.9, 1979. $2 per
no. ‡ Columbia, SC 29208. TEL 803-777-7461. circ.
200. (back issues avail.)

327   NO
UTENRIKSPOLITISKE SKRIFTER/NORWEGIAN
FOREIGN POLICY STUDIES. (Text in English
and Norwegian) irreg. Norsk Utenrikspolitisk
Institutt - Norwegian Institute of International
Affairs, Postboks 8159, Dep., 0033 Oslo 1, Norway.

332.6   US   ISSN 0278-937X
WASHINGTON PAPERS. 1972. irreg. Praeger
Publishers (Subsidiary of: Greenwood Press, Inc.)
521 Fifth Ave., New York, NY 10175. TEL 212-
599-8400. Ed. Walter Laqueur. (back issues avail.)
Indexed: A.B.C.Pol.Sci.

327   CN
WELLESLEY PAPERS. 1973. irreg. price varies. ‡
Canadian Institute of International Affairs, 15
King's College Circle, Toronto, Ont. M5S 2V9,
Canada. TEL 416-979-1851. Ed.Bd. bibl.

327   US   ISSN 0277-1527
WORLD FACTBOOK. a. U.S. Central Intelligence
Agency, Washington, DC 20505. TEL 703-351-
7676.
Formerly: National Basic Intelligence Factbook
(ISSN 0098-2091)

341.37   US
WORLD TREATY INDEX. 1975. irreg., 2nd, 1984. ‡
A B C-Clio, 2040 Alameda Padre Serra, Box 4397,
Santa Barbara, CA 93140-4397. TEL 805-963-4221.
Ed. Peter H. Rohn.

327   355   US
WORLDWIDE REPORT: ARMS CONTROL. irreg.
(approx. 100/yr.) $5 per no. U.S. Joint Publications
Research Service, 1000 N. Glebe Rd., Arlington,
VA 22201 TEL 703-487-4630. (Orders to: NTIS,
Springfield, VA 22161)

327.471   FI   ISSN 0355-0079
YEARBOOK OF FINNISH FOREIGN POLICY.
(Text in English) 1973. a. Fmk.60($12)
Ulkopoliittinen Instituutti - Finnish Institute of
International Affairs, Pursimiehenkatu 8, SF-00150
Helsinki, Finland. Ed. Kari Mottola. Indexed:
A.B.C.Pol.Sci. Int.Polit.Sci.Abstr.

327   BE   ISSN 0084-3806
YEARBOOK OF INTERNATIONAL CONGRESS
PROCEEDINGS. (Text in English; index in
French) 1969. irreg. 960 Fr. Union of International
Associations, Rue Washington 40, 1050 Bruxelles,
Belgium.

327   BE   ISSN 0084-3814
YEARBOOK OF INTERNATIONAL
ORGANIZATIONS. French edition: Annuaire des
Organisations Internationales. (Text in English;
index in English and French) 1949. biennial. 2300
Fr.($168) Union of International Associations, Rue
Washington 40, 1050 Bruxelles, Belgium.

327 301   BE   ISSN 0304-0089
YEARBOOK OF WORLD PROBLEMS AND
HUMAN POTENTIAL. 1976. irreg. 2300 Fr.
Union of International Associations, Rue
Washington 40, 1050 Brussels, Belgium. (Co-
sponsor: Mankind 2000) bibl.

327 335   US   ISSN 0084-4101
YEARBOOK ON INTERNATIONAL
COMMUNIST AFFAIRS; parties and revolutionary
movements. 1966. a. $49.95. (Hoover Institution on
War, Revolution and Peace) Hoover Institution
Press, Stanford University, Stanford, CA 94305.
TEL 415-723-3373. Ed. Richard F. Staar. index.
circ. 2,000. (back issues avail.)

327   FI   ISSN 0781-2442
YHDISTYNEIDEN KANSAKUNTIEN
YLEISKOKOUS (YEAR) (Text in Finnish;
occasionally in English) 1957. a. Fmk.49.
Ulkoasiainministerio - Ministry for Foreign Affairs,
PL 276, 00171 Helsinki, Finland. circ. 1,000.
Formerly: Suomen Osallistuminen Yhdistyneiden
Kansakuntien Toimintaan (ISSN 0081-9441)

YOUR UNITED NATIONS; official guidebook. see
HISTORY

327 338.9   US   ISSN 0427-8968
YUGOSLAV FACTS AND VIEWS. Title varies:
Facts & Views. (Text in English) 1948. irreg. free.
Yugoslav Press and Cultural Center, 767 Third
Ave., New York, NY 10017. TEL 212-838-2306.
circ. 2,000. (back issues avail.)

POPULATION STUDIES

see also Birth Control

304   US   ISSN 0741-2150
AMERICAN UNIVERSITY STUDIES. SERIES 16.
ECONOMICS. 1984. irreg. Peter Lang Publishing,
Inc., 62 W. 45th St., New York, NY 10036. TEL
212-302-6740. Ed. Jay Wilson.

312   FR   ISSN 0066-2062
ANNALES DE DEMOGRAPHIE HISTORIQUE.
(Text in English and French) 1970. a. $35. (Societe
de Demographie Historique) Ecole des Hautes
Etudes en Sciences Sociales, 131 bd. St. Michel,
75005 Paris, France. Indexed: Hist.Abstr.
Amer.Hist.& Life. Popul.Ind.

312   FR
ANNUAIRE DES CENTRES DE RECHERCHE
DEMOGRAPHIQUE/DIRECTORY OF
DEMOGRAPHIC RESEARCH CENTERS. 1974.
irreg., 2nd 1980. free. Committee for International
Cooperation in National Research in Demography,
27 rue du Commandeur, 75675 Paris Cedex 14,
France.

312   UK   ISSN 0066-3964
ANNUAL ESTIMATES OF THE POPULATION
OF SCOTLAND. 1958. a. £1.25. Her Majesty's
Stationery Office (H.M.S.O.), P.O. Box 569,
London SE1 9NH, England. (Co-sponsor: General
Register Office, Scotland) circ. 600.

ARKANSAS. BUREAU OF VITAL STATISTICS.
ANNUAL REPORT OF BIRTHS, DEATHS,
MARRIAGES AND DIVORCES AS REPORTED
TO THE BUREAU OF VITAL STATISTICS. see
*POPULATION STUDIES — Abstracting,
Bibliographies, Statistics*

ARKANSAS VITAL STATISTICS. see
*POPULATION STUDIES — Abstracting,
Bibliographies, Statistics*

301.3   UN   ISSN 0066-8451
ASIAN POPULATION STUDIES SERIES. (Text in
English) 1967. irreg. price varies. United Nations
Economic and Social Commission for Asia and the
Pacific, United Nations Bldg., Rajadamnern Ave.,
Bangkok 10200, Thailand (Dist. by: United Nations
Publications, Room LX-2300, New York, NY
10017; or Distribution and Sales Section, Palais des
Nations, CH-1 211 Geneva 10, Switzerland)
Indexed: Popul.Ind.

AUSTRALIA. BUREAU OF STATISTICS. SOUTH
AUSTRALIAN OFFICE. BIRTHS, SOUTH
AUSTRALIA. see *POPULATION STUDIES —
Abstracting, Bibliographies, Statistics*

AUSTRALIA. BUREAU OF STATISTICS. SOUTH
AUSTRALIAN OFFICE. DEATHS, SOUTH
AUSTRALIA. see *POPULATION STUDIES —
Abstracting, Bibliographies, Statistics*

AUSTRALIA. BUREAU OF STATISTICS. SOUTH
AUSTRALIAN OFFICE. DIVORCES, SOUTH
AUSTRALIA. see *POPULATION STUDIES —
Abstracting, Bibliographies, Statistics*

AUSTRALIA. BUREAU OF STATISTICS.
TASMANIAN OFFICE. DIVORCES
TASMANIA. see *POPULATION STUDIES —
Abstracting, Bibliographies, Statistics*

312   AT
AUSTRALIAN INSTITUTE OF FAMILY STUDIES.
ANNUAL REPORT. 1981. a. Australian Institute
of Family Studies, Board of Management, 766
Elizabeth St., Melbourne, Vic. 3000, Australia. Ed.
M. Davis. circ. 1,000.

AUSTRALIAN NATIONAL UNIVERSITY.
CANBERRA. DEPARTMENT OF
DEMOGRAPHY. FAMILY AND FERTILITY
CHANGE. see *SOCIOLOGY*

301.32   AT
AUSTRALIAN NATIONAL UNIVERSITY,
CANBERRA. DEPARTMENT OF
DEMOGRAPHY. STUDIES IN MIGRATION
AND URBANIZATION. 1975. irreg. Aus.$5.95.
Australian National University, Department of
Demography, Canberra, A.C.T. 2600, Australia.

AUSTRIA. STATISTISCHES ZENTRALAMT. DIE
NATUERLICHE
BEVOELKERUNGSBEWEGUNG. see
*POPULATION STUDIES — Abstracting,
Bibliographies, Statistics*

312   II
BARODA REPORTER. (Text in English) 1960. a.
free. Population Research Centre, Maharajah
Sayajirao University of Baroda, Faculty of Science,
Baroda 2, India. Ed. M.M. Gandotra. adv. bk. rev.
abstr. bibl. charts. illus. stat. circ. 500. (record)

312   BE
BELGIUM. CENTRE D'ETUDE DE LA
POPULATION ET DE LA FAMILLE. ANNUAL
REPORT. a. Centre d'Etude de la Population et de
la Famille - Population and Family Study Centre,
Manhattan Center, Toren H2, Kruisvaartenstraat 3,
1000 Brussels, Belgium.

312   BE
BELGIUM. CENTRE D'ETUDE DE LA
POPULATION ET DE LA FAMILLE.
DOSSIERS. (Text in French) irreg. (Ministere de la
Sante Publique et de la Famille, Centre d'Etude de
la Population et de la Famille) Editions Labor, Rue
Royale 342, 1030 Brussels, Belgium.

POPULATION STUDIES

312   GW ISSN 0072-1867
BEVOELKERUNGSSTRUKTUR UND WIRTSCHAFTSKRAFT DER BUNDESLAENDER. a. DM.19.50. (Statistisches Bundesamt) W. Kohlhammer-Verlag GmbH, Abt. Veroeffentlichungen des Statistischen Bundesamtes, Philipp-Reis-Str. 3, Postfach 421120, 6500 Mainz 42, W. Germany (B.R.D.)

CANADA. IMMIGRATION AND DEMOGRAPHIC POLICY GROUP. IMMIGRATION STATISTICS. see *POPULATION STUDIES — Abstracting, Bibliographies, Statistics*

CENTRE FOR URBAN AND COMMUNITY STUDIES. MAJOR REPORT SERIES. see *HOUSING AND URBAN PLANNING*

CENTRE FOR URBAN AND COMMUNITY STUDIES. RESEARCH PAPERS. see *HOUSING AND URBAN PLANNING*

312   UN
CENTRO LATINOAMERICANO DE DEMOGRAFIA. SERIE OI: PUBLICACIONES CONJUNTAS CON INSTITUCIONES NACIONALES DE PAISES DE AMERICA LATINA. 1967. irreg. $6. United Nations, Centro Latinoamericano de Demografia - United Nations. Regional Centre, Casilla 91, Santiago, Chile. stat.

COLOMBIA. DEPARTAMENTO ADMINISTRATIVO NACIONAL DE ESTADISTICA. ANUARIO DEMOGRAFICO. see *POPULATION STUDIES — Abstracting, Bibliographies, Statistics*

312   FR
COMITE INTERNATIONAL DE COOPERATION DANS LES RECHERCHES NATIONALES EN DEMOGRAPHIE. ACTES DES SEMINAIRES. 1973. irreg. Committee for International Cooperation in National Research in Demography, 27 rue du Commandeur, 75675 Paris Cedex 14, France.

312   AG
CONSEJO LATINOAMERICANO DE CIENCIAS SOCIALES. SERIE POBLACION. INFORME DE INVESTIGACION. 1973. irreg. price varies. Consejo Latinoamericano de Ciencias Sociales, Callao 875, 1023 Buenos Aires, Argentina.

312   US ISSN 0082-9471
CURRENT POPULATION REPORTS. (In 8 major series) 1947. irreg. price varies. U.S. Bureau of the Census, Customer Services, Washington, DC 20233 TEL 301-763-4100. (Orders to: Supt. of Documents, Washington, DC 20402) Indexed: Curr.Lit.Fam.Plan.

CURRENT POPULATION REPORTS: CONSUMER INCOME. see *BUSINESS AND ECONOMICS — Macroeconomics*

312   US
CURRENT POPULATION REPORTS: FARM POPULATION. (Series P-27) 1945. irreg. price varies. U.S. Bureau of the Census, Customer Services, Washington, DC 20402 TEL 301-763-4100. (Orders to: Supt. of Documents, Washington, DC 20402)

312   US
CURRENT POPULATION REPORTS: LOCAL POPULATION ESTIMATES. (Series P-26) 1969. irreg. U.S. Bureau of the Census, Customer Services, Washington, DC 20233 TEL 301-763-4100. (Orders to: Supt. of Documents, Washington, DC 20402)
Formerly: Current Population Reports: Federal-State Cooperative Program for Population Estimates (ISSN 0565-0917)

301   US ISSN 0363-6836
CURRENT POPULATION REPORTS: POPULATION CHARACTERISTICS. (Series P-20; 6 titles in series) 1946. irreg. U.S. Bureau of the Census, Data User Services Division, Customer Services, Washington, DC 20233 TEL 202-783-3238. (Subscriptions to: Supt. of Documents, Washington, DC 20402)

312   US
CURRENT POPULATION REPORTS: POPULATION CHARACTERISTICS. GEOGRAPHIC MOBILITY. (Series P-20) 1948. a. price varies. U.S. Bureau of the Census, Customer Services, Washington, DC 20233 TEL 301-763-4100. (Orders to: Supt. of Documents, Washington, DC 20402)
Formerly: Current Population Reports: Population Characteristics. Mobility of the Population of the United States (ISSN 0076-986X)

312   US
CURRENT POPULATION REPORTS: POPULATION CHARACTERISTICS. HOUSEHOLD AND FAMILY CHARACTERISTICS. (Series P-20) a. price varies. U.S. Bureau of the Census, Customer Services, Washington, DC 20233 TEL 301-763-4100. (Orders to: Supt. of Documents, Washington, DC 20402)

312   US
CURRENT POPULATION REPORTS: POPULATION CHARACTERISTICS. MARITAL STATUS AND LIVING ARRANGEMENTS. (Series P-20) a. price varies. U.S. Bureau of the Census, Customer Services Dept., Washington, DC 20233 TEL 301-763-4100. (Orders to: Supt. of Documents, Washington, DC 20402)
Formerly: Current Population Reports: Population Characteristics. Marital Status and Family Status (ISSN 0082-9501)

312   US
CURRENT POPULATION REPORTS: POPULATION CHARACTERISTICS. SCHOOL ENROLLMENT: SOCIAL AND ECONOMIC CHARACTERISTICS OF STUDENTS. (Series P-20) a. price varies. U.S. Bureau of the Census, Customer Services, Washington, DC 20233 TEL 301-763-4100. (Orders to: Supt. of Documents, Washington, DC 20402)
Formerly: U.S. Bureau of the Census. Current Population Reports: School Enrollment: October (Year) (ISSN 0082-9528)

312   US
CURRENT POPULATION REPORTS: POPULATION CHARACTERISTICS. SOCIAL AND ECONOMIC CHARACTERISTICS OF THE BLACK POPULATION. (Series P-20) irreg. price varies. U.S. Bureau of the Census, Customer Services, Washington, DC 20233 TEL 301-763-4100. (Orders to: Supt. of Documents, Washington, DC 20402) Indexed: Rehabil.Lit.
Formerly: U.S. Bureau of the Census. Current Population Reports: Negro Population (ISSN 0082-951X)

312   US
CURRENT POPULATION REPORTS: POPULATION ESTIMATES AND PROJECTIONS. (Series P-25) 1947. m. (plus a. issue) U.S. Bureau of the Census, Customer Services, Washington, DC 20402 TEL 301-763-4100. (Orders to: Supt. of Documents, Washington, DC 20402)

312   US ISSN 0071-1616
CURRENT POPULATION REPORTS: POPULATION ESTIMATES AND PROJECTIONS. ESTIMATES OF THE POPULATION OF THE UNITED STATES AND COMPONENTS OF POPULATION CHANGE. (Series P-25) a. price varies. U.S. Bureau of the Census, Customer Services, Washington, DC 20233 TEL 301-763-4100. (Orders to: Supt. of Documents, Washington, DC 20402)

312   US
CURRENT POPULATION REPORTS: POPULATION ESTIMATES AND PROJECTIONS. ESTIMATES OF THE POPULATION OF THE UNITED STATES BY AGE, RACE AND SEX. (Series P-25) a. price varies. U.S. Bureau of the Census, Customer Services, Washington, DC 20233 TEL 301-763-4100. (Orders to: Supt. of Documents, Washington, DC 20402) Indexed: Rehabil.Lit.
Formerly: Current Population Reports, P-25: Population Estimates and Projections. Estimates of the Population of the United States by Age, Color, and Sex (ISSN 0071-1624)

312   US
CURRENT POPULATION REPORTS: SPECIAL CENSUSES. (Series P-28) irreg. U.S. Bureau of the Census, Customer Services, Washington, DC 20233 TEL 301-763-4100. (Orders to: Supt. of Documents, Washington, DC 20402)

312   US ISSN 0498-8485
CURRENT POPULATION REPORTS: SPECIAL STUDIES. (Series P-23) 1949. irreg. U.S. Bureau of the Census, Customer Services, Washington, DC 20233 TEL 301-763-4100. (Orders to: Supt. of Documents, Washington, DC 20402)

DEMOGRAFSKA STATISTIKA. see *POPULATION STUDIES — Abstracting, Bibliographies, Statistics*

312   US
DEMOGRAPHIC GUIDE TO ARIZONA (YEAR) 1967. a. free. ‡ Department of Economic Security, Population Statistics Unit, Box 6123-045Z, Phoenix, AZ 85005. TEL 602-255-5984. Ed. David H. Lillie. circ. 2,000.
Formerly: Population Estimates of Arizona (ISSN 0079-3906)

312   UN
DEMOGRAPHIC HANDBOOK FOR AFRICA/GUIDE DEMOGRAPHIE DE L'AFRIQUE. (Text in English and French) irreg.; latest 1978. United Nations Economic Commission for Africa, Box 3001, Addis Ababa, Ethiopia.

910   US ISSN 0275-9594
DEMOGRAPHIC MONOGRAPHS. vol.9, 1969. a. price varies. Gordon and Breach Science Publishers, 50 West 23rd St., New York, NY 10010. TEL 212-206-8900. Ed.Bd.

312   UN ISSN 0082-8041
DEMOGRAPHIC YEARBOOK. (Text in English and French) 1949. a., latest 1983. price varies. United Nations, Department of Economic and Social Affairs, Secretariat, New York, NY 10017 (Dist. by: United Nations Sales Section, Room A-3315, New York, NY; or Palais des Nations, CH-1211 Geneva 10, Switzerland)

312   CM ISSN 0151-1408
DEMOGRAPHIE AFRICAINE: BULLETIN DE LIAISON. (Supplement avail.: Groupe de Demographie Africaine. Etudes et Documents) 1979. a. free. Institut de Formation et de Recherche en Demographie (I F O R D), Yaounde, Cameroon. Indexed: Popul.Ind.
Formerly: Demographie en Afrique d'Expression Francaise: Bulletin de Liaison.

312   FR ISSN 0070-3354
DEMOGRAPHIE ET SCIENCES HUMAINES. 1970. irreg. (Institut National d'Etudes Demographiques) Presses Universitaires de France, 108 bd. Saint Germain, 75279 Paris Cedex 6, France (Service des Periodiques, 12 rue Jean de Beauvais, 75005 Paris) (reprint service avail. from KTO)

312   FR ISSN 0070-3362
DEMOGRAPHIE ET SOCIETES. 1960. irreg. price varies. (Ecole Pratique des Hautes Etudes, Centre de Recherches Historiques) Librairie Touzot, 38 rue Saint Sulpice, 75278 Paris Cedex 06, France.

DENMARK. DANMARKS STATISTIK. BEFOLKNINGENS BEVAEGELSER/VITAL STATISTICS. see *POPULATION STUDIES — Abstracting, Bibliographies, Statistics*

DENMARK. DANMARKS STATISTIK. FAERDSELSUHELD/ROAD TRAFFIC ACCIDENTS. see *POPULATION STUDIES — Abstracting, Bibliographies, Statistics*

301.32   DK ISSN 0900-2510
DENMARK. MINISTERIET FOR GROENLAND. STATISTIKE MEDDELELSER. 1960. a. free. Ministeriet for Groenland, Statistisk Kontor, Hausergade 3, 1128 Copenhagen K, Denmark. circ. 700.
Former titles (until 1984): Denmark. Ministeriet for Groenland. Statistisk Kontor. Meddelelser (ISSN 0106-2891); Denmark. Ministeriet for Groenland. Oekonomisk-Statistisk Kontor. Meddelelser.

POPULATION STUDIES

325.1 US ISSN 0277-724X
DIRECTORY OF NONPROFIT IMMIGRATION COUNSELING AGENCIES. a. U.S. Immigration and Naturalization Service, 425 I St. N.W., Washington, DC 20536. TEL 202-724-7796.

312 BE
DOSSIERS DE DEMOGRAPHIE DE LA BELGIQUE. 1975. irreg. 325 Fr. (Societe Belge de Demographie) Editions Derouaux, 10, Place St.-Jacques, Liege, Belgium. (looseleaf format)

312 US ISSN 0191-3905
DRAPER FUND REPORT. 1965. irreg. free. Population Crisis Committee, 1120 Nineteenth St., N.W., Ste. 550, Washington, DC 20036. TEL 202-659-1833. charts. illus. stat. circ. 55,000. Indexed: Nutr.Abstr. P.A.I.S.
Former titles: Draper World Population Fund Report; (until 1975): Victor-Bostrom Fund Report.

325 US
EAST-WEST POPULATION INSTITUTE. PAPERS. 1970. irreg. $12. (East-West Population Institute) Center for Cultural and Technical Interchange Between East and West, Inc., 1777 East-West Rd., Honolulu, HI 96848. TEL 808-944-7391. Ed. Sandra E. Ward. circ. 900.
Former titles: East-West Center. Papers; East-West Population Institute. Working Papers (ISSN 0732-0531)

312 CN ISSN 0703-8763
EDMONTON AREA SERIES REPORT. 1977. irreg. free. Population Research Laboratory, Department of Sociology, University of Alberta, Edmonton, Alb. T6G 2H4, Canada. TEL 403-432-4659. (reprint service avail. from MML)

325 DK ISSN 0900-7679
EMIGRANTEN. 1985. a. Kr.95. Dansk Udvandrerhistorisk Selskab, Postboks 1731, DK-9100 Aalborg, Denmark.

312 DK ISSN 0108-5557
FAROERNE OG GROENLAND. 1984. irreg., 9-10/yr. Kr.28.69. Danmarks Statistik, Sejroegade 11, 2100 Copenhagen OE, Denmark. circ. 1,250. (back issues avail.)

FIJI. BUREAU OF STATISTICS. FIJI FERTILITY SURVEY. see POPULATION STUDIES — Abstracting, Bibliographies, Statistics

FIJI. BUREAU OF STATISTICS. POPULATION OF FIJI; monograph for the U N World population. see POPULATION STUDIES — Abstracting, Bibliographies, Statistics

310 FR ISSN 0071-8823
FRANCE. INSTITUT NATIONAL D'ETUDES DEMOGRAPHIQUES. CAHIERS DE TRAVAUX ET DOCUMENTS. 1946. irreg., no.107, 1983. price varies. Institut National d'Etudes Demographiques, 27 rue du Commandeur, 75675 Paris Cedex 14, France. Ed. G. Calot.

FRANCE. INSTITUT NATIONAL DE LA STATISTIQUE ET DES ETUDES ECONOMIQUES. COLLECTIONS. SERIE D, DEMOGRAPHIE ET EMPLOI. see POPULATION STUDIES — Abstracting, Bibliographies, Statistics

GEORGIA VITAL STATISTICS DATA BOOK. see POPULATION STUDIES — Abstracting, Bibliographies, Statistics

312 GH
GHANA POPULATION STUDIES. 1969. irreg., no.8, 1977. price varies. University of Ghana, Institute of Statistical, Social and Economic Research, Legon, Ghana.

301.426 SW
GOETEBORGS UNIVERSITET. DEMOGRAPHIC RESEARCH INSTITUTE. REPORTS. no.14, 1974. irreg. Goeteborgs Universitet, Demographic Research Institute, Viktoriagatan 13, S-411 25 Goeteborg, Sweden (Dist. by: Almqvist & Wiksell International, 26 Gamla Brogatan, S-111 20 Stockholm, Sweden).

312 610 UK ISSN 0072-6400
GREAT BRITAIN. GENERAL REGISTER OFFICE. STUDIES ON MEDICAL AND POPULATION SUBJECTS. 1948. irreg. price varies. H.M.S.O., Box 569, London SE1 9NH, England. (reprint service avail. from UMI)

312 UK
GREAT BRITAIN. OFFICE OF POPULATION CENSUSES AND SURVEYS. POPULATION ESTIMATES: ENGLAND AND WALES. a. H.M.S.O., Box 569, London SE1 9NH, England.

314 DK ISSN 0105-0885
GROENLANDS BEFOLKNING/KALATDLIT NUNANE INUIT. (Text in Danish and Eskimo) 1976. a. free. Ministeriet for Groenland, Copenhagen, Denmark. circ. 600.

312 UN
GUIDE TO SOURCES OF INTERNATIONAL POPULATION ASSISTANCE. (Text in English, French and Spanish) 1976. triennial. $12 per issue. United Nations Fund for Population Activities, 220 E. 42nd St., New York, NY 10017. circ. 2,500. (also avail. in microfilm)

HAWAII. DEPARTMENT OF HEALTH. RESEARCH AND STATISTICS OFFICE. R & S REPORT. see POPULATION STUDIES — Abstracting, Bibliographies, Statistics

312 HU ISSN 0134-0050
HISTORISCH-DEMOGRAPHISCHE MITTEILUNGEN/COMMUNICATIONS DE DEMOGRAPHIE HISTORIQUE. (Text in French and German) 1971. irreg. Eotvos Lorand Tudomanyegyetem, Allam es Jogtudomanyi Kar, Statisztikai Tanszek, Egyetem ter 1-3, Budapest 5, Hungary. Ed. Jozsef Kovacsics. bk. rev. Indexed: Popul.Ind.

312 UK
HUMAN LIFE MATTERS. irreg. Human Life Council, Humanae Vitae House, Chapel Brae, Braemar, Aberdeenshire AB3 5YS, Scotland. Ed. Sara Brown.

HUNGARY. KOZPONTI STATISZTIKAI HIVATAL. DEMOGRAFIAI EVKONYV. see POPULATION STUDIES — Abstracting, Bibliographies, Statistics

312 BE
I U S S P PAPERS/U I E S P DOCUMENTS DE L'UNION. 1974. irreg. $5. International Union for the Scientific Study of Population, 34 rue des Augustins, 4000 Liege, Belgium. bibl. charts. illus. stats. (back issues avail.)

325.1 US ISSN 0749-5951
IMMIGRANT COMMUNITIES & ETHNIC MINORITIES IN THE UNITED STATES & CANADA. 1984. irreg., no.2, 1986. price varies. A M S Press, Inc., 56 E. 13th St., New York, NY 10003. TEL 212-777-4700. (back issues avail.)

IMMIGRATION AND NATIONALITY LAW REVIEW. see LAW

325.1 CN
IMMIGRATION LAW REPORTER. N.S. m. Carswell Legal Publications, 2330 Midland Ave., Agincourt, Ont. M1S 1P7, Canada. TEL 416-291-8421. Ed. Cecil L. Rotenberg.

325 US ISSN 0275-634X
IN DEFENSE OF THE ALIEN. 1978. a. $14.95. Center for Migration Studies, 209 Flagg Pl., Staten Island, NY 10304-1148. TEL 718-351-8800. Ed. Lydio F. Tomasi. circ. 750.

INDIA. MINISTRY OF HOME AFFAIRS. VITAL STATISTICS DIVISION. CAUSES OF DEATH; A SURVEY. see POPULATION STUDIES — Abstracting, Bibliographies, Statistics

INDIA. MINISTRY OF HOME AFFAIRS. VITAL STATISTICS DIVISION. SAMPLE REGISTRATION BULLETIN. see POPULATION STUDIES — Abstracting, Bibliographies, Statistics

INDIAN HEALTH TRENDS AND SERVICES. see PUBLIC HEALTH AND SAFETY

613.9 US
INDUCED ABORTION: A WORLD REVIEW. 1973. irreg., 6th edt. 1986. $10. Alan Guttmacher Institute, 111 Fifth Ave., New York, NY 10003. Eds. Christopher Tietze, Stanley K. Henshaw. charts. circ. 17,000. (reprint service avail. from UMI)

312 BL ISSN 0100-7173
INFORME DEMOGRAFICO. 1980. irreg. $8. Fundacao Sistema Estadual de Analise de Dados, Av. Casper Libero, 464, 01033 Sao Paulo, Brazil. circ. 500.

312 II ISSN 0070-3311
INSTITUTE OF ECONOMIC GROWTH, DELHI. CENSUS STUDIES. (Text in English) 1969. irreg. Rs.30. Institute of Economic Growth, Delhi, Univeristy of Delhi, Delhi 110007, India.

312 II
INSTITUTE OF ECONOMIC RESEARCH. PUBLICATIONS ON DEMOGRAPHY. (Text in English) irreg. price varies. Institute of Economic Research, Director, Vidyagiri, Dharwar 580004, Karnataka, India.

312 IS ISSN 0333-9874
INTEGRATED RURAL DEVELOPMENT. PUBLICATIONS. (Text in English) irreg. free. Settlement Study Center, P.O. Box 2355, Rehovot 76 120, Israel. TEL 08-474111.

325 SZ
INTERGOVERNMENTAL COMMITTEE FOR MIGRATION. REVIEW OF ACHIEVEMENTS. (Editions in English, French and Spanish) 1969. a. free. Intergovernmental Committee for Migration, 17 Route des Morillons, Case Postale 71, CH-1211 Geneva 19, Switzerland. circ. 5,000.
Formerly: Intergovernmental Committee for European Migration. Review of Achievements.

312 BE ISSN 0255-0849
INTERNATIONAL BIBLIOGRAPHY OF HISTORICAL DEMOGRAPHY/BIBLIOGRAPHIE INTERNATIONALE DE LA DEMOGRAPHIE HISTORIQUE. (Text in English and French) 1978. a. $10. International Union for the Scientific Study of Population, 34 rue des Augustins, 4000 Liege, Belgium. Ed.Bd. bibl. index. circ. 4,000. (back issues avail.) Indexed: Popul.Ind.

301.32 II
INTERNATIONAL INSTITUTE FOR POPULATION SCIENCES. DIRECTOR'S REPORT. (Text in English) 1956/57. a. free. International Institute for Population Sciences, Govandi Station Rd., Deonar, Bombay 400088, India. Dir. K. Srinivasan. circ. 800.
Former titles: International Institute for Population Studies. Annual Report & Demographic Training and Research Centre. Annual Report & International Institute for Population Studies. Director's Report.

325 CN ISSN 0383-2767
INTERNATIONAL NEWSLETTER ON MIGRATION. 1971. irreg. University of Waterloo, Waterloo, Ont. N2L 3GI, Canada. TEL 519-885-1211.
Formerly: International Migration Newsletter (ISSN 0383-2759)

312 BE ISSN 0074-9338
INTERNATIONAL POPULATION CONFERENCE. PROCEEDINGS. French edition: Congres International de la Population. Proceedings (ISSN 0254-5217) quadriennial. International Union for the Scientific Study of Population, 34 rue des Augustins, 4000 Liege, Belgium. Indexed: Popul.Ind.

312 US
INTERNATIONAL POPULATION DATA. irreg. U.S. Bureau of the Census, Customer Services, Washington, DC 20233 TEL 301-763-4100. (Orders to: Supt. of Documents, Washington, DC 20402)
Former titles: Current Population Reports: International Population Data; Current Population Reports: International Population Reports (ISSN 0082-9498)

301.32 US ISSN 0363-5155
INVENTORY OF POPULATION PROJECTS IN DEVELOPING COUNTRIES AROUND THE WORLD. 1975. a. $12. United Nations Fund for Population Activities, 220 E. 42 St., New York, NY 10017. circ. 2,500. (also avail. in microfilm)

ISRAEL. CENTRAL BUREAU OF STATISTICS.
CAUSES OF DEATH. see *POPULATION
STUDIES — Abstracting, Bibliographies, Statistics*

ISRAEL. CENTRAL BUREAU OF STATISTICS.
SUICIDES AND ATTEMPTED SUICIDES. see
*POPULATION STUDIES — Abstracting,
Bibliographies, Statistics*

ITALY. ISTITUTO CENTRALE DI STATISTICA.
ANNUARIO DI STATISTICHE
DEMOGRAFICHE. see *POPULATION
STUDIES — Abstracting, Bibliographies, Statistics*

JAHRBUCH FUER FRAENKISCHE
LANDESFORSCHUNG. see *HISTORY — History
Of Europe*

312   JA
JAPAN. INSTITUTE OF POPULATION
PROBLEMS. ANNUAL REPORT. 1977. a.
Ministry of Health & Welfare, Institute of
Population Problems, 2-2, 1-chome, Kasumigaseki,
Chiyoda-ku, Tokyo, Japan.

325   US
JOHNS HOPKINS UNIVERSITY. POPULATION
INFORMATION PROGRAM. POPULATION
REPORTS. ARABIC EDITION. 1973. irreg.,
vol.14, 1986. free to qualified personnel. Johns
Hopkins University, Population Information
Program, 624 N. Broadway, Baltimore, MD 21205.
TEL 301-955-8200. Ed. Ward Rinehart. bibl.
charts. illus. stat. circ. controlled. (looseleaf
format; back issues avail.) Indexed: Popul.Ind.
 Formerly: George Washington University.
Population Information Program. Population
Reports.

312   US
KANSAS. DEPARTMENT OF HEALTH AND
ENVIRONMENT. ANNUAL SUMMARY OF
VITAL STATISTICS. a. Department of Health and
Environment, Topeka, KS 66620. TEL 913-862-
9360. stat.

312   KO
KOREA (REPUBLIC). ECONOMIC PLANNING
BOARD. YEARBOOK OF MIGRATION
STATISTICS. (Text in English & Korean) 1970. a.
National Bureau of Statistics, Economic Planning
Board, Gyeongun-Dong, Jongo-Gu, Seoul, S. Korea.
Ed. Myong Hyun Sohn. circ. 200.

LATIN AMERICAN INTEGRATION PROCESS IN
(YEAR) see *POPULATION STUDIES —
Abstracting, Bibliographies, Statistics*

301.426   IO
LEMBAGA KELUARGA BERENTJANA
NASIONAL.* 1969/1970. a. Sekretariat
Pemerintah Daerah, Propinsi Djawa Tengah,
Lamporan, Indonesia. charts. stat.

LIBYA. CENSUS AND STATISTICAL OFFICE.
GENERAL POPULATION CENSUS. see
*POPULATION STUDIES — Abstracting,
Bibliographies, Statistics*

312   UK ISSN 0260-8405
LINCOLNSHIRE POPULATION. 1979. a. £0.30.
Lincolnshire County Council, County Planning
Office, Newland, Lincoln LN1 1YG, England. illus.
charts.

MALTA. CENTRAL OFFICE OF STATISTICS.
DEMOGRAPHIC REVIEW. see *POPULATION
STUDIES — Abstracting, Bibliographies, Statistics*

325   FI
MIGRATION INSTITUTE. MIGRATION
STUDIES. (Includes three series: A (Finnish); B
(Swedish); C (English)) 1974. irreg. price varies.
Migration Institute, Piispankatu 3, 20500 Turku 50,
Finland. Dir. Olavi Koivukangas. bk. rev. charts.
stat. circ. 1,000.
 Formerly: Institute for Migration, Turku.
Migration Studies (ISSN 0356-780X)

301.3   SZ ISSN 0544-1188
MIGRATION TODAY. (Editions in English, French
and Spanish) 1963. irreg., (approx. 3/yr.) free.
World Council of Churches, Commission on Inter-
Church Aid, Refugee and World Service, Migration
Desk, 150 Route de Ferney, 1211 Geneva 20,
Switzerland. Ed. Andre Jacques. bk. rev. circ. 4,000.
Indexed: P.A.I.S. Abstr.Musl.Rel. C.I.J.E.
CERDIC. HR Rep.

312   US ISSN 0734-032X
MISSOURI POPULATION ESTIMATES; by county,
by age, by sex. a. free. Department of Health,
Center for Health Statistics, Box 570, Jefferson
City, MO 65102. TEL 314-751-8074. Ed. Garland
Land.

312   US ISSN 0077-0930
MONOGRAPHS IN POPULATION BIOLOGY.
1967. irreg., latest, no.20. price varies. Princeton
University Press, 3175 Princeton Pike,
Lawrenceville, NJ 08648. TEL 609-896-1344. Ed.
R.M. May. (reprint service avail. from UMI)
Indexed: Biol.Abstr. Ind.Med.

MOUVEMENT NATUREL DE LA POPULATION
DE LA GRECE. see *POPULATION STUDIES —
Abstracting, Bibliographies, Statistics*

MOVIMIENTO NATURAL DE LA POBLACION
DE ESPANA. see *POPULATION STUDIES —
Abstracting, Bibliographies, Statistics*

312   NE
NEDERLANDS INTERUNIVERSITAIR
DEMOGRAFISCH INSTITUUT.
PUBLICATIONS. (Text in English) 1976. irreg.
price varies. (Nederlands Interuniversitair
Demografisch Instituut - Netherlands Interuniversity
Demographic Institute) Martinus Nijhoff Publishers,
Postbus 163, 3300 AD Dordrecht, Netherlands.
(Co-sponsor: Population and Family Study Centre)

312   NE
NEDERLANDS INTERUNIVERSITAIR
DEMOGRAFISCH INSTITUUT. WORKING
PAPERS. (Text in English) 1973. irreg. free.
Nederlands Interuniversitair Demografisch Instituut
- Netherlands Interuniversity Demographic Institute,
Lange Houtstraat 19, 2511 CV The Hague,
Netherlands. circ. 125.

NETHERLANDS. CENTRAAL BUREAU VOOR
DE STATISTIEK. JAARSTATISTIEK VAN DE
BEVOLKING. POPULATION STATISTICS. see
*POPULATION STUDIES — Abstracting,
Bibliographies, Statistics*

NEW ZEALAND. DEPARTMENT OF
STATISTICS. POPULATION CENSUS: AGES,
MARITAL STATUS AND FERTILITY. see
*POPULATION STUDIES — Abstracting,
Bibliographies, Statistics*

NEW ZEALAND. DEPARTMENT OF
STATISTICS. POPULATION CENSUS:
BIRTHPLACES AND ETHNIC ORIGIN. see
*POPULATION STUDIES — Abstracting,
Bibliographies, Statistics*

NEW ZEALAND. DEPARTMENT OF
STATISTICS. POPULATION CENSUS:
DWELLINGS. see *POPULATION STUDIES —
Abstracting, Bibliographies, Statistics*

NEW ZEALAND. DEPARTMENT OF
STATISTICS. POPULATION CENSUS:
EDUCATION AND TRAINING. see
*POPULATION STUDIES — Abstracting,
Bibliographies, Statistics*

NEW ZEALAND. DEPARTMENT OF
STATISTICS. POPULATION CENSUS:
GENERAL REPORT. see *POPULATION
STUDIES — Abstracting, Bibliographies, Statistics*

NEW ZEALAND. DEPARTMENT OF
STATISTICS. POPULATION CENSUS:
HOUSEHOLDS AND FAMILIES. see
*POPULATION STUDIES — Abstracting,
Bibliographies, Statistics*

NEW ZEALAND. DEPARTMENT OF
STATISTICS. POPULATION CENSUS:
INCOMES AND SOCIAL SECURITY
BENEFITS. see *POPULATION STUDIES —
Abstracting, Bibliographies, Statistics*

NEW ZEALAND. DEPARTMENT OF
STATISTICS. POPULATION CENSUS: LABOUR
FORCE. see *POPULATION STUDIES —
Abstracting, Bibliographies, Statistics*

NEW ZEALAND. DEPARTMENT OF
STATISTICS. POPULATION CENSUS: MAORI
POPULATION AND DWELLINGS. see
*POPULATION STUDIES — Abstracting,
Bibliographies, Statistics*

NEW ZEALAND. DEPARTMENT OF
STATISTICS. POPULATION CENSUS:
PROVISIONAL STATISTICS SERIES.
BULLETIN ONE. LOCAL AUTHORITY AREAS.
see *POPULATION STUDIES — Abstracting,
Bibliographies, Statistics*

NEW ZEALAND. DEPARTMENT OF
STATISTICS. POPULATION CENSUS:
RELIGIOUS PROFESSIONS. see *POPULATION
STUDIES — Abstracting, Bibliographies, Statistics*

312   NQ
NICARAGUA. INSTITUTO NACIONAL DE
ESTADISTICAS Y CENSOS. BOLETIN
DEMOGRAFICO. no.2, 1978. irreg. C.$15($4) per
no. Instituto Nacional de Estadisticos y Census,
Apdo. Postal 4031, Managua, Nicaragua. stat.
 Formerly: Nicaragua. Oficina Ejectiva de
Encuestos y Censos. Boletin Demografico.

NORSK VILTFORSKNING. MEDDELESER. see
BIOLOGY

312   CN
NORTHERN ONTARIO DIRECTORY; information
guide to unincorporated communities & Indian
reserves. 1979. biennial. Can.$3.50. Ministry of
Northern Development and Mines, Information
Service Branch, 10 Wellesley St. E., 9th Floor,
Toronto, Ont. M4Y 1G2, Canada. TEL 416-965-
7577. Ed. Peter Overton. circ. 10,000.

301.32   MG
NY MPONIN'I MADAGASIKARA. (Text in French
or Malagasy) 1975. irreg. Direction de la Recherche
Scientifique et Technique, Section de Demographie,
B.P. 4096, Antananarivo, Malagasy Republic.

OWNER OCCUPIED HOUSING STATISTICS
FROM HOMESTEAD REBATE AND INCOME
TAX DATA MATCH. see *HOUSING AND
URBAN PLANNING*

PENNSYLVANIA VITAL STATISTICS. see
*POPULATION STUDIES — Abstracting,
Bibliographies, Statistics*

325.1   PH
PHILIPPINES. MINISTRY OF HUMAN
SETTLEMENTS. ANNUAL REPORT. a. Ministry
of Human Settlements, Agustin I Bldg., Emerald
Ave., Pasig, Metro Manilla, Philippines.

PHILIPPINES. NATIONAL CENSUS AND
STATISTICS OFFICE. SOCIAL INDICATOR. see
*POPULATION STUDIES — Abstracting,
Bibliographies, Statistics*

312   UR ISSN 0203-9699
POLUTEHNILINE INSTITUUT TALLINN.
NARODONASELENIE I RABOCHAYA SILA.
(Subseries of Its Toimetised) (Text in Russian;
summaries in English or German) irreg. price varies.
Polutehniline Instituut Tallinn, Ehitajate tee 5,
Tallinn, Estonian S.S.R., U.S.S.R.

301.32 312   CS
POPULACNI ZPRAVY. 1976. irreg., (1-2/yr.) free.
Federalni Ministerstvo Prace a Socialnich Veci -
Federal Ministry of Labour and Social Affairs,
Palackeho nam. 4, 12801 Prague 2, Czechoslovakia.
Ed. Vladimir Marik. circ. 1,600. Indexed: Popul.Ind.

312   US
POPULATION; briefing papers on issues of national
and international importance in the population field.
1976. irreg. free. Population Crisis Committee, 1120
Nineteenth St., N.W., Washington, DC 20036. TEL
202-659-1833. charts. stat. Indexed:
Curr.Lit.Fam.Plan.

312   NE ISSN 0169-1422
POPULATION AND FAMILY IN THE LOW
COUNTRIES. (Text in English) 1976. irreg. fl.30
per vol. Nederlands Interuniversitair Demografisch
Instituut - Netherlands Interuniversity Demographic
Institute, Lange Houtstr. 19, 2511 Cv The Hague,
Netherlands. (Co-sponsor: Centrum voor
Bevolkings- en Gezinsstudien - Population and
Family Study Centre) Ed.Bd.

POPULATION AND FAMILY PLANNING
PROGRAMS. see *POPULATION STUDIES —
Abstracting, Bibliographies, Statistics*

325 UN ISSN 0251-7604
POPULATION BULLETIN OF THE UNITED
NATIONS. (Text in English, French, Spanish)
1948. irreg. price varies. United Nations
Publications, Sales Section, Rm. DC2-0853, New
York, NY 10017. TEL 212-754-8302.

312 PP ISSN 0079-3868
POPULATION CENSUS OF PAPUA NEW
GUINEA. POPULATION CHARACTERISTICS
BULLETIN SERIES. 1966. irreg., latest issue, 1980.
free. National Statistical Office, P.O. Wards Strip,
Papua New Guinea. Ed. J.J. Shadlow. circ. 842.

312 US ISSN 0361-7858
POPULATION COUNCIL ANNUAL REPORT.
1952. a. free. Population Council, One Dag
Hammarskjold Plaza, New York, NY 10017. TEL
212-644-1300. Ed. Robert Heidel. (reprint service
avail. from UMI) Indexed: Biol.Abstr.

POPULATION GROWTH OF IRAN. see
*POPULATION STUDIES — Abstracting,
Bibliographies, Statistics*

301.32 TH
POPULATION NEWSLETTER. 1969. irreg. (3-4/yr.)
free. Chulalongkorn University, Institute of
Population Studies, Bangkok 10500, Thailand. bk.
rev. circ. 1,000. (tabloid format) Indexed:
Abstr.Hyg.

POPULATION OF THE MUNICIPALITIES OF
THE NETHERLANDS. see *POPULATION
STUDIES — Abstracting, Bibliographies, Statistics*

POPULATION REPORTS. see *POPULATION
STUDIES — Abstracting, Bibliographies, Statistics*

312 917.602 US ISSN 0191-913X
POPULATION RESEARCH CENTER PAPERS.
1979. irreg. $4 per no. University of Texas,
Population Research Center, Main Bldg. 1800,
Austin, TX 78712-1088. TEL 512-471-5514.

312 CN ISSN 0317-2473
POPULATION RESEARCH LABORATORY.
DISCUSSION PAPER SERIES. 1973. irreg. free.
Population Research Laboratory, Department of
Sociology, University of Alberta, Edmonton, Alb.
T6G 2H4. TEL 403-432-4659. (reprint service avail.
from MML)

312 CN ISSN 0317-3100
POPULATION RESEARCH LABORATORY.
POPULATION REPRINT SERIES. 1972. irreg.
free. Population Research Laboratory, Department
of Sociology, University of Alberta, Edmonton, Alb.
T6G 2H4, Canada. TEL 403-432-4659. (reprint
service avail. from MML)

312 UN ISSN 0082-805X
POPULATION STUDIES. (Editions in English,
French and Spanish) 1948. irreg., latest no.97, 1985.
price varies. (United Nations, Department of
Economic and Social Affairs) United Nations
Publications, Room DC2-853, New York, NY
10017. Indexed: Nutr.Abstr. Geo.Abstr.

312 US ISSN 0736-7716
POPULATION TRENDS AND PUBLIC POLICY.
1980. irreg. membership. Population Reference
Bureau, Inc., 777 14th St. N.W., Washington, DC
20005. TEL 202-785-4664. circ. 6,000. Indexed:
Popul.Ind.

PORTUGAL. INSTITUTO NACIONAL DE
ESTATISTICA. CENTRO DE ESTUDOS
DEMOGRAFICOS. CADERNO. see
*POPULATION STUDIES — Abstracting,
Bibliographies, Statistics*

PORTUGAL. INSTITUTO NACIONAL DE
ESTATISTICA. CENTRO DE ESTUDOS
DEMOGRAFICOS. REVISTA. see *POPULATION
STUDIES — Abstracting, Bibliographies, Statistics*

PORTUGAL. INSTITUTO NACIONAL DE
ESTATISTICA. ESTATISTICAS
DEMOGRAFICAS. CONTINENTE, ACORES E
MADEIRA. see *POPULATION STUDIES —
Abstracting, Bibliographies, Statistics*

312 301.32 PL ISSN 0079-7189
PRZESZLOSC DEMOGRAFICZNA POLSKI;
materialy i studia. (Text in Polish; summaries in
English) 1967. irreg., no.14, 1983. price varies.
(Polska Akademia Nauk, Komitet Nauk
Demograficznych) Panstwowe Wydawnictwo
Naukowe, Ul. Miodowa 10, 00-251 Warsaw, Poland
(Dist. by: Ars Polona, Krakowskie Przedmiescie 7,
00-068 Warsaw, Poland) Ed. E. Vidrose. bibl. circ.
300. Indexed: Popul.Ind.

312 FR
RAPPORT SUR LA SITUATION
DEMOGRAPHIQUE DE LA FRANCE. 1970. a.
Institut National d'Etudes Demographiques, 27 rue
du Commandeur, 75675 Paris Cedex 14, France.
Ed. G. Calot. bk. rev. stat. circ. 2,000.

325.2 UN ISSN 0253-1445
REFUGEE ABSTRACTS. (Text in English, French)
1982. q. $20 to individuals, $30 to libraries. United
Nations High Commissioner for Refugees, Centre
for Documentation on Refugees (CDR), Palais des
Nations, 1211 Geneva 10, Switzerland. Ed. Hans
Thoolen. bk. rev. abstr. circ. 1,650. (also avail. in
magnetic tape; back issues avail.) Indexed: HR Rep.

REPRODUCTIONS. see *BIOLOGY*

325 NE ISSN 0080-1623
RESEARCH GROUP FOR EUROPEAN
MIGRATION PROBLEMS. PUBLICATIONS.
1951. irreg. price varies. Martinus Nijhoff
Publishers, Postbus 163, 3300 AD Dordrecht,
Netherlands. Ed. G. Beyer.

301.32 330 US ISSN 0163-7878
RESEARCH IN POPULATION ECONOMICS; an
annual compilation of research. 1978. a. $26.25 to
individuals; institutions $52.50. J A I Press Inc.,
Box 1678, 36 Sherwood Pl., Greenwich, CT 06836-
1678. TEL 203-661-7602. Ed. Paul Schultz.
Indexed: Curr.Cont. Popul.Ind.

301.426 US
RESEARCH MONOGRAPHS ON HUMAN
POPULATION. irreg. price varies. Oxford
University Press, 200 Madison Ave., New York,
NY 10016 TEL 212-679-7300. (And Ely House, 37
Dover St., London W1X 4AH, England) Ed. G.
Aimsworth Harrison.

312 AT ISSN 0727-6982
REVIEW OF AUSTRALIA'S DEMOGRAPHIC
TRENDS. 1981. a. (Department of Immigration and
Ethnic Affairs) Australian Government Publishing
Service, Canberra, Australia. circ. 5,000.

RHODE ISLAND. DEPARTMENT OF HEALTH.
VITAL STATISTICS. see *POPULATION
STUDIES — Abstracting, Bibliographies, Statistics*

312 325 KO
SEOUL NATIONAL UNIVERSITY. POPULATION
AND DEVELOPMENT STUDIES CENTER.
BULLETIN. (Text in English; summaries in
Korean) 1972. a. 1000 Won($6) Seoul National
University, Population and Development Studies
Center, Gwan-ak Gu, Seoul 151, S. Korea. Ed. Dr.
Tai Hwan Kwon. bk. rev. bibl. circ. 500.

312 FR
SOCIO-ECONOMIC DIFFERENTIAL
MORTALITY IN INDUSTRIALIZED
SOCIETIES. 1980. a. free. International
Cooperation in National Research in Demography,
27 rue du Commander, 75675 Paris Cedex 14,
France.

SOUTH CAROLINA VITAL AND MORBIDITY
STATISTICS. see *POPULATION STUDIES —
Abstracting, Bibliographies, Statistics*

325 US
SPECTRUM (ST. PAUL) 1975. irreg., latest 1984. $5
to individuals; institutions $8. University of
Minnesota, Immigration History Research Center,
826 Berry St., St. Paul, MN 55114. TEL 612-627-
4208. Ed. Stephanie Cain Van D'Elden. bk. rev.
illus. circ. 500. (back issues avail.)

STATISTICAL REPORTS OF CHANGWAT. see
GEOGRAPHY

312 630 IO ISSN 0126-2912
STATISTICAL YEAR BOOK OF INDONESIA.
(Text in English, Indonesian) 1976. a. $18. Central
Bureau of Statistics, Jl. Dr Sutomo 8, Jakarta Pusat,
Indonesia. circ. 1,500.

STATISTISCHES JAHRBUCH DER STADT
NUERNBERG. see *STATISTICS*

301.3 PL
STUDIA POLONIJNE. (Text in Polish; summaries in
English) 1976. irreg. price varies. Katolicki
Uniwersytet Lubelski, Towarzystwo Naukowe,
Chopina 29, 20-023 Lublin, Poland. index. circ. 3,
125.

312 301.32 US
STUDIES IN POPULATION. 1974. irreg., no.40,
1986. Academic Press, Inc., Orlando, FL 32887.
TEL 305-345-2000. Ed. H.H. Winsborough.
Indexed: Math.R.

312 US ISSN 0147-1104
STUDIES IN POPULATION AND URBAN
DEMOGRAPHY. 1975. irreg. price varies.
Greenwood Press, 88 Post Rd. W., Box 5007,
Westport, CT 06881. TEL 203-226-3571. Ed.
Kingsley Davis.

312 US
STUDIES IN SOCIAL AND ECONOMIC
DEMOGRAPHY. 1978. irreg. Duke University
Press, 6697 College Sta., Durham, NC 27708. TEL
919-684-2173.

SWEDEN. STATISTISKA CENTRALBYRAAN.
BEFOLKNINGSFOERAENDRINGAR. see
*POPULATION STUDIES — Abstracting,
Bibliographies, Statistics*

SWEDEN. STATISTISKA CENTRALBYRAAN.
FOLKMAENGD. see *POPULATION
STUDIES — Abstracting, Bibliographies, Statistics*

TEXAS VITAL STATISTICS. see *POPULATION
STUDIES — Abstracting, Bibliographies, Statistics*

312 JA
TOCHIGI-KEN NO JINKO/POPULATION IN
TOCHIGI PREFECTURE. a. free. Tochigi
Prefecture, Tochigi-Ken, Kikaku-Bu, 1-20, 1-Chome,
Hanawada, Utsunomiya-Shi 320, Japan. Ed.
Mashamitsu Sakakibara. circ. 500. (back issues
avail.)

312 TU
TURKISH JOURNAL OF POPULATION STUDIES.
a. TL.1000($4) Hacettepe University, Institute of
Population Studies, Ankara, Turkey. Ed. Ergul
Tuncbilek.

312 UN ISSN 0503-3934
UNITED NATIONS. REGIONAL CENTRE FOR
DEMOGRAPHIC TRAINING AND RESEARCH
IN LATIN AMERICA. SERIE A/CENTRO
LATINOAMERICANO DE DEMOGRAFIA.
SERIE A: INFORMES SOBRE
INVESTIGACIONES REALIZADAS. (1986
Catalog Available) 1962. irreg. $6 per no. United
Nations, Centro Latinoamericano de Demografia -
United Nations. Regional Center for Demographic
Training and Research in Latin America, Casilla 91,
Santiago, Chile. stat. circ. 400.

312 UN ISSN 0503-3942
UNITED NATIONS. REGIONAL CENTRE FOR
DEMOGRAPHIC TRAINING AND RESEARCH
IN LATIN AMERICA. SERIE C/CENTRO
LATINOAMERICANO DE DEMOGRAFIA.
SERIE C: INFORMES SOBRE
INVESTIGACIONES REALIZADAS POR LOS
ALUMNOS DEL CENTRO. (1986 Catalog
available) 1963. irreg. $6 per no. United Nations,
Centro Latinoamericano de Demografia, Casilla 91,
Santiago, Chile. stat. circ. 400.

312 UN ISSN 0503-3950
UNITED NATIONS. REGIONAL CENTRE FOR
DEMOGRAPHIC TRAINING AND RESEARCH
IN LATIN AMERICA. SERIE D/CENTRO
LATINOAMERICANO DE DEMOGRAFIA.
SERIE D: TRADUCCIONES, ESTUDIOS,
CONFERENCIAS Y OTROS TRABAJOS
PREPARADOS POR PROFESORES Y
EXPERTOS VISITANTES. (1986 Catalog
available) 1962. irreg. $6 per no. United Nations,
Centro Latinoamericano de Demografia, Casilla 91,
Santiago, Chile. circ. 400.

312   UN
UNITED NATIONS. REGIONAL CENTRE FOR DEMOGRAPHIC TRAINING AND RESEARCH IN LATIN AMERICA. SERIE E/CENTRO LATINOAMERICANO DE DEMOGRAFIA. SERIE E: LIBROS. 1967. irreg. price varies. United Nations, Centro Latinoamericano de Demografia - United Nations. Regional Centre for Demographic Training and Research in Latin America, Casilla 91, Santiago, Chile. stat. circ. 400.

312   US   ISSN 0082-9390
U.S. BUREAU OF THE CENSUS. CENSUS OF POPULATION. (Issued in several series) 1790. decennial. price varies. U.S. Bureau of the Census, Customer Services, Washington, DC 20233 TEL 301-763-4100. (Orders to: Supt. of Documents, Washington, DC 20402)

325   US   ISSN 0083-1220
U.S. IMMIGRATION AND NATURALIZATION SERVICE. ADMINISTRATIVE DECISIONS UNDER IMMIGRATION AND NATIONALITY LAWS. 1940. irreg. price varies. U.S. Immigration and Naturalization Service, c/o Charles J. Gentry, Board of Immigration Appeals, Washington, DC 20530 TEL 202-724-7796. (Orders to: Supt. of Documents, Washington, DC 20402)

325   US   ISSN 0083-1239
U.S. IMMIGRATION AND NATURALIZATION SERVICE. ADMINISTRATIVE DECISIONS UNDER IMMIGRATION AND NATIONALITY LAWS. INTERIM DECISIONS OF THE DEPARTMENT OF JUSTICE. irreg. $4.25 per year. U.S. Immigration and Naturalization Service, c/o Charles J. Gentry, Board of Immigration Appeals, Washington, DC 20530 TEL 202-724-7796. (Orders to: Supt. of Documents, Washington, DC 20402)

325   US   ISSN 0083-1247
U.S. IMMIGRATION AND NATURALIZATION SERVICE. ANNUAL REPORT. 1892. a. price varies. U.S. Immigration and Naturalization Service., 425 I St. N.W., Washington, DC 20536 TEL 202-724-7796. (Orders to: Supt. of Documents, Washington, DC 20402)

301.32   US
U.S. INTERAGENCY COMMITTEE ON POPULATION RESEARCH. INVENTORY AND ANALYSIS OF FEDERAL POPULATION RESEARCH. 1970/71. a. free. U.S. Department of Health and Human Services, NICHD, NIH, Bldg. 31, Rm. 2A47, Bethesda, MD 20892. TEL 301-472-9093. Ed. George Lewerenz. circ. 5,000.
Former titles: U.S. Center for Population Research. Inventory of Federal Population Research; U.S. National Institute of Child Health and Human Development. Center for Population Research. Federal Program in Population Research.

U.S. NATIONAL CENTER FOR HEALTH STATISTICS. VITAL AND HEALTH STATISTICS. SERIES 1. PROGRAMS AND COLLECTION PROCEDURES. see *PUBLIC HEALTH AND SAFETY*

U.S. NATIONAL CENTER FOR HEALTH STATISTICS. VITAL AND HEALTH STATISTICS. SERIES 2. DATA EVALUATION AND METHODS RESEARCH. see *PUBLIC HEALTH AND SAFETY*

U.S. NATIONAL CENTER FOR HEALTH STATISTICS. VITAL AND HEALTH STATISTICS. SERIES 3. ANALYTICAL STUDIES. see *PUBLIC HEALTH AND SAFETY*

U.S. NATIONAL CENTER FOR HEALTH STATISTICS. VITAL AND HEALTH STATISTICS. SERIES 4. DOCUMENTS AND COMMITTEE REPORT. see *PUBLIC HEALTH AND SAFETY*

U.S. NATIONAL CENTER FOR HEALTH STATISTICS. VITAL AND HEALTH STATISTICS. SERIES 20. DATA ON MORTALITY. see *PUBLIC HEALTH AND SAFETY*

U.S. NATIONAL CENTER FOR HEALTH STATISTICS. VITAL AND HEALTH STATISTICS. SERIES 21. DATA ON NATALITY, MARRIAGE, AND DIVORCE. see *PUBLIC HEALTH AND SAFETY*

312   US
U.S. NATIONAL CENTER FOR HEALTH STATISTICS. VITAL AND HEALTH STATISTICS. SERIES 23: DATA FROM THE NATIONAL SURVEY OF FAMILY GROWTH. 1976. irreg. U.S. National Center for Health Statistics, 3700 East-West Highway, Hyattsville, MD 20782. TEL 301-436-8500. Indexed: Popul.Ind.

UNIVERSITY OF DAR ES SALAAM. BUREAU OF RESOURCE ASSESSMENT AND LAND USE PLANNING. ANNUAL REPORT. see *ENVIRONMENTAL STUDIES*

UNIVERSITY OF DAR ES SALAAM. BUREAU OF RESOURCE ASSESSMENT AND LAND USE PLANNING. RESEARCH PAPER. see *ENVIRONMENTAL STUDIES*

UNIVERSITY OF DAR ES SALAAM. BUREAU OF RESOURCE ASSESSMENT AND LAND USE PLANNING. RESEARCH REPORT. see *ENVIRONMENTAL STUDIES*

312 301.2   NR
UNIVERSITY OF LAGOS. HUMAN RESOURCES RESEARCH UNIT. MONOGRAPH. no.2, 1974. irreg. (University of Lagos, Human Resources Research Unit) Lagos University Press, P.O. Box 132, Akoka, Yaba, Lagos, Nigeria.

301.32   US
UNIVERSITY OF MICHIGAN. POPULATION STUDIES CENTER. REPORT. 1961. irreg., latest 1982/1984. University of Michigan, Population Studies Center, Ann Arbor, MI 48104. TEL 313-763-7275. Ed. Kathleen Duke. circ. 500.
Formerly: University of Michigan. Population Studies Center. Annual Report.

301.3   US   ISSN 0084-0734
UNIVERSITY OF WISCONSIN, MADISON. APPLIED POPULATION LABORATORY. POPULATION NOTES. 1961. irreg., no.10, 1980. University of Wisconsin-Madison, Applied Population Laboratory, Department of Rural Sociology, 316 Agricultural Hall, Madison, WI 53706. TEL 608-262-1515. circ. 800.

301.3   US   ISSN 0084-0742
UNIVERSITY OF WISCONSIN, MADISON. APPLIED POPULATION LABORATORY. POPULATION SERIES. 1961. irreg., no. 70-14, 1980. price varies. University of Wisconsin-Madison, Applied Population Laboratory, Department of Rural Sociology, 316 Agricultural Hall, Madison, WI 53706. TEL 608-262-1515. circ. 500.

312   US
UNIVERSITY OF WISCONSIN, MADISON. APPLIED POPULATION LABORATORY. TECHNICAL SERIES. 1977. irreg., no. 70-5, 1979. University of Wisconsin-Madison, Applied Population Laboratory, Department of Rural Sociology, 316 Agricultural Hall, Madison, WI 53706. TEL 608-262-1515.

URUGUAY. DIRECCION GENERAL DE ESTADISTICA Y CENSOS. ESTADISTICAS VITALES. see *POPULATION STUDIES — Abstracting, Bibliographies, Statistics*

UTAH VITAL STATISTICS ANNUAL REPORT. see *POPULATION STUDIES — Abstracting, Bibliographies, Statistics*

VANUATU. BUREAU OF STATISTICS. CENSUS OF POPULATION AND HOUSING. VILA AND SANTO, FINAL RESULTS: PART 2: POPULATION DATA/RECENSEMENT DE LA POPULATION ET DE L'HABITAT, VILA ET LUGANVILLE, RESULTANTS DEFINITIFS: 2EME PARTIE: DONNEES SUR LA POPULATION. see *POPULATION STUDIES — Abstracting, Bibliographies, Statistics*

VANUATU. NATIONAL PLANNING AND STATISTICS OFFICE. CENSUS OF POPULATION (YEAR). BASE TABLES/TABLES DE BASE. see *POPULATION STUDIES — Abstracting, Bibliographies, Statistics*

VITAL STATISTICS OF THE UNITED STATES. see *PUBLIC HEALTH AND SAFETY*

312   US
WASHINGTON (STATE) OFFICE OF FINANCIAL MANAGEMENT. POLICY ANALYSIS AND FORECASTING. POPULATION TRENDS. 1968. a. free. State Office of Financial Management, Policy Analysis and Forecasting, Insurance Blvd., Olympia, WA 98504 TEL 206-753-4549. (Dist. by: State Library, Olympia WA 98504) circ. 2,000. (also avail. in microfiche)
Former titles: Washington (State) Office of Financial Management. Forecasting and Support Division. Population Trends & Washington (State) Office of Program Planning and Fiscal Management. Population and Enrollment Section. Population Trends (ISSN 0083-7482); Before 1970: Washington (State) Planning and Community Affairs Agency. Population Series.

312   US   ISSN 0091-5254
WISCONSIN POPULATION PROJECTIONS. 1969. irreg., 3rd edt., 1975. $5. Department of Administration, Bureau of Program Management, Madison, WI 53702 TEL 608-266-1694. (Order from: Document Sales Unit, 202 S. Thornton Ave., Madison, WI 53702) stat.

WORLD FERTILITY SURVEY. ANNUAL REPORTS. see *POPULATION STUDIES — Abstracting, Bibliographies, Statistics*

WORLD FERTILITY SURVEY. BASIC DOCUMENTATION. see *POPULATION STUDIES — Abstracting, Bibliographies, Statistics*

WORLD FERTILITY SURVEY. COUNTRY REPORTS. see *POPULATION STUDIES — Abstracting, Bibliographies, Statistics*

WORLD FERTILITY SURVEY. OCCASIONAL PAPERS. see *POPULATION STUDIES — Abstracting, Bibliographies, Statistics*

WORLD FERTILITY SURVEY. SCIENTIFIC REPORTS. see *POPULATION STUDIES — Abstracting, Bibliographies, Statistics*

WORLD FERTILITY SURVEY. SUMMARIES OF COUNTRY REPORTS. see *POPULATION STUDIES — Abstracting, Bibliographies, Statistics*

WORLD FERTILITY SURVEY. TECHNICAL BULLETINS. see *POPULATION STUDIES — Abstracting, Bibliographies, Statistics*

312   US   ISSN 0085-8315
WORLD POPULATION DATA SHEET. 1962. a. $2. Population Reference Bureau, Inc., 777 14th St. N.W., Washington, DC 20005. TEL 202-639-8040. Ed. Carl Haub. stat. circ. 130,000. (wall chart format)

312   FI   ISSN 0506-3590
YEARBOOK OF POPULATION RESEARCH IN FINLAND/VAESTOENTUTKIMUKSEN VUOSIKIRJA. (Text in English) 1946. a. Fmk.85. Vaestontutkimuslaitos - Population Research Institute, Kalevankatu 16, 00100 Helsinki 10, Finland. Ed. Jarl Lindgren. bk. rev. bibl. circ. 800. Indexed: Popul.Ind.

ZAMBIA. CENTRAL STATISTICAL OFFICE. MIGRATION STATISTICS. see *POPULATION STUDIES — Abstracting, Bibliographies, Statistics*

325   ZA   ISSN 0084-4802
ZAMBIA. IMMIGRATION DEPARTMENT. REPORT. 1964. a. 10 n. Government Printer, Box 136, Lusaka, Zambia.

POPULATION STUDIES — Abstracting, Bibliographies, Statistics

312   US   ISSN 0066-0752
AMERICAN STATISTICAL ASSOCIATION. SOCIAL STATISTICS SECTION. PROCEEDINGS. 1958. a. $23 to non-members; members $18. American Statistical Association, 806 15th St., N.W., Ste. 640, Washington, DC 20005. TEL 202-393-3253. (also avail. in microform from UMI)

POPULATION STUDIES — ABSTRACTING, BIBLIOGRAPHIES, STATISTICS

318   AG
ARGENTINA. INSTITUTO NACIONAL DE ESTADISTICA Y CENSOS. ANUARIO ESTADISTICO. 1973. a. $60. Instituto Nacional de Estadistica y Censos, Hipolito Yrigoyen 250, Buenos Aires, Argentina.

312   US   ISSN 0094-3576
ARKANSAS. BUREAU OF VITAL STATISTICS. ANNUAL REPORT OF BIRTHS, DEATHS, MARRIAGES AND DIVORCES AS REPORTED TO THE BUREAU OF VITAL STATISTICS. Variant title: Arkansas Vital Statistics Report. a. free. Bureau of Vital Statistics, Little Rock, AR 72201. TEL 501-661-2336. illus. stat. Key Title: Annual Report of Births, Deaths, Marriages and Divorces as Reported to the Bureau of Vital Statistics (Little Rock)

312.097   US   ISSN 0364-0728
ARKANSAS VITAL STATISTICS. 1970. a. free. Division of Health Statistics and Epidemiology, 4815 W. Markham St., Little Rock, AR 72201. TEL 501-661-2368. circ. 750.

312   AT   ISSN 0067-0766
AUSTRALIA. BUREAU OF STATISTICS. CAUSES OF DEATH, AUSTRALIA. 1962. a. Aus.$2.30. Australian Bureau of Statistics, Box 10, Belconnen, A.C.T. 2616, Australia. circ. 1,000.

312   AT
AUSTRALIA. BUREAU OF STATISTICS. QUEENSLAND OFFICE. ESTIMATED RESIDENT POPULATION AND AREAS FOR EACH LOCAL AUTHORITY AREA, QUEENSLAND. a. free. Australian Bureau of Statistics, Queensland Office, 313 Adelaide St., Brisbane, Queensland 4000, Australia. stat. circ. 2, 500. (processed)
    Formerly: Australia. Bureau of Statistics. Queensland Office. Population Estimates and Areas for Local Authority Areas.

312   AT   ISSN 0067-088X
AUSTRALIA. BUREAU OF STATISTICS. SOUTH AUSTRALIAN OFFICE. BIRTHS, SOUTH AUSTRALIA. 1969. a. free. Australian Bureau of Statistics, South Australian Office, Box 2272, G.P.O., Adelaide, S.A. 5001, Australia.

312   AT   ISSN 0067-0898
AUSTRALIA. BUREAU OF STATISTICS. SOUTH AUSTRALIAN OFFICE. DEATHS, SOUTH AUSTRALIA. 1969. a. free. Australian Bureau of Statistics, South Australian Office, Box 2272, G.P.O., Adelaide, S.A. 5001, Australia.

312   AT   ISSN 0067-0901
AUSTRALIA. BUREAU OF STATISTICS. SOUTH AUSTRALIAN OFFICE. DIVORCES, SOUTH AUSTRALIA. 1947. a. free. Australian Bureau of Statistics, South Australian Office, Box 2272, G.P.O., Adelaide, S.A. 5001, Australia.

301   AT   ISSN 0705-5773
AUSTRALIA. BUREAU OF STATISTICS. TASMANIAN OFFICE. DIVORCES TASMANIA. 1979. a. Australian Bureau of Statistics, Tasmanian Office, Box 66 A, G.P.O., Hobart, Tasmania 7001, Australia.

312   AT
AUSTRALIA. BUREAU OF STATISTICS. VICTORIAN OFFICE. ESTIMATED RESIDENT POPULATION IN LOCAL GOVERNMENT AREAS, VICTORIA. 1955. a. free. Australian Bureau of Statistics, Victorian Office, Box 2796Y, G.P.O., Melbourne, Vic. 3001, Australia. circ. 3,000.
    Former titles: Australia. Bureau of Statistics. Victorian Office. Estimated Population in Local Government Areas, Victoria (ISSN 0705-6257); Australia. Bureau of Statistics. Victorian Office. Estimated Population and Dwellings by Local Government Areas.

312   AU
AUSTRIA. STATISTISCHES ZENTRALAMT. DEMOGRAPHISCHES JAHRBUCH OESTERREICHS. (Subseries of its Beitraege zur Oesterreichischen Statistik) 1951. a. S.340. Oesterreichisches Statistisches Zentralamt, Hintere Zollamtsstr. 2b, 1033 Vienna, Austria.

312   AU   ISSN 0067-2335
AUSTRIA. STATISTISCHES ZENTRALAMT. DIE NATUERLICHE BEVOELKERUNGSBEWEGUNG. (Subseries of: Beitraege zur Oesterreichischen Statistik) 1951. a. S.180. Oesterreichisches Statistisches Zentralamt, Hintere Zollamtsstr. 2b, 1003 Vienna, Austria. circ. 450.

BARBADOS. REGISTRATION OFFICE. REPORT ON VITAL STATISTICS & REGISTRATIONS. see *PUBLIC ADMINISTRATION — Abstracting, Bibliographies, Statistics*

312   DK   ISSN 0108-8076
BEFOLKNINGEN I KOMMUNERNE / POPULATIONS OF MUNICIPALITIES. 1971. a. Kr.77.87. Danmarks Statistik, Sejroegade 11, 2100 Copenhagen OE, Denmark. TEL 01-29-82-22. stats. (back issues avail.)
    Formerly: Denmark. Danmarks Statistik. Befolkningen i de Enkelte Kommuner.

309   BE
BELGIUM. INSTITUT NATIONAL DE STATISTIQUE. BEVOLKINGSSTATISTIEKEN. irreg. 290 Fr. Institut National de Statistique - Nationaal Instituut voor de Statistiek, Leuvenseweg 44, 1000 Brussels, Belgium.

312.2   BE
BELGIUM. INSTITUT NATIONAL DE STATISTIQUE. STATISTIQUES DES CAUSES DE DECES. irreg. 430 Fr. per no. Institut National de Statistique, 44 rue de Louvain, 1000 Brussels, Belgium.

312   PL   ISSN 0067-7795
BIBLIOTEKA WIADOMOSCI STATYSTYCZNYCH. 1967. irreg., vol.33, 1983. Glowny Urzad Statystyczny, Al. Niepodleglosci 208, Warsaw, Poland.

312   CN
CANADA. IMMIGRATION AND DEMOGRAPHIC POLICY GROUP. IMMIGRATION STATISTICS. (Text in English and French) a. Employment and Immigration Canada, Regional Library, P.O. Box 7500, Station A, Montreal, Quebec H3C 3L4, Canada. TEL 613-995-8131.
    Formerly: Canada. Immigration Division. Immigration Statistics (ISSN 0576-2286)

312   CN   ISSN 0380-7533
CANADA. STATISTICS CANADA. CAUSES OF DEATH, PROVINCES BY SEX AND CANADA BY SEX AND AGE/CAUSES DE DECES, PAR PROVINCES SELON LE SEXE ET LE CANADA SELON LE SEXE ET L'AGE. (Catalogue 84-203) (Text in English and French) 1965. a. Can.$35($36.50) Statistics Canada, Communications Division, 3rd Floor, R.H. Coats Bldg., Ottawa, Ont. K1A 0T6, Canada TEL 613-993-7276. (Subscr. to: Publications Sales and Services, Ottawa, Ont. K1A 0T6, Canada) (also avail. in microform from MML)

CANADA. STATISTICS CANADA. FAMILY INCOMES (CENSUS FAMILIES) /REVENUS DES FAMILLE (FAMILLES DE RECENSEMENT) see *BUSINESS AND ECONOMICS — Abstracting, Bibliographies, Statistics*

317   CU
CENSO DE POBLACION Y VIVIENDAS. (Issued from 1972 as a number of Anuario Estadistico de Cuba) a. free. Comite Estatal de Estadisticas, Direccion de Informacion y Relaciones Internacionales, Centro de Informacion Cientifico-Tecnico, Av.Tercera no.4410, Municipio de Playa, Havana, Cuba. charts. stat.

312   CK
COLOMBIA. DEPARTAMENTO ADMINISTRATIVO NACIONAL DE ESTADISTICA. ANUARIO DEMOGRAFICO. a. Departamento Administrativo Nacional de Estadistica, Banco Nacional de Datos, Apdo Nacional 80043, Bogota D.E., Colombia.

314   IT   ISSN 0010-4957
COMUNE DI ROMA. UFFICIO DI STATISTICA E CENSIMENTO. BOLLETTINO STATISTICO. 1877. irreg., latest no.8, 1968. L.1500. Comune di Roma, Ufficio di Statistica e Censimento, Via della Greca 5, 00186 Rome, Italy. circ. 650.

312.8   CY   ISSN 0590-4846
CYPRUS. DEPARTMENT OF STATISTICS AND RESEARCH. DEMOGRAPHIC REPORT. (Text in English and Greek) 1963. a. cyprus pounds 3. Department of Statistics and Research, Ministry of Finance, Nicosia, Cyprus.

310   CY
CYPRUS. DEPARTMENT OF STATISTICS AND RESEARCH. DEMOGRAPHIC SURVEY. (YEAR) (Text in English) 1980. irreg. £C5. Ministry of Finance, Department of Statistics and Research, Nicosia, Cyprus.
    Formerly: Cyprus. Department of Statistics and Research. Multi-Round Dempographic Survey. Main Report.

310   CY
CYPRUS. DEPARTMENT OF STATISTICS AND RESEARCH. MULTI-ROUND DEMOGRAPHIC SURVEY. MIGRATION IN CYPRUS. (Text in English) 1980. irreg. cyprus pounds 1.50. Ministry of Finance, Department of Statistics and Research, Nicosia, Cyprus.

310   CY
CYPRUS. DEPARTMENT OF STATISTICS AND RESEARCH. MULTI-ROUND DEMOGRAPHIC SURVEY. SUMMARY OF MAIN DEMOGRAPHIC CHARACTERISTICS. (Text in English) 1980. irreg. cyprus pounds 0.50. Ministry of Finance, Department of Statistics and Research, Nicosia, Cyprus.

CYPRUS. DEPARTMENT OF STATISTICS AND RESEARCH. TOURISM, MIGRATION AND TRAVEL STATISTICS. see *TRAVEL AND TOURISM — Abstracting, Bibliographies, Statistics*

312   YU   ISSN 0084-4357
DEMOGRAFSKA STATISTIKA. 1956. a. 100 din.($11.11) Savezni Zavod za Statistiku, Kneza Milosa 20, Belgrade, Yugoslavia. circ. 600.
    Formerly: Yugoslavia. Savezni Zavod za Statistuku. Vitalna Statistika.

312   DK   ISSN 0070-3478
DENMARK. DANMARKS STATISTIK. BEFOLKNINGENS BEVAEGELSER/VITAL STATISTICS. (Text in Danish; notes in English) 1931/33. a. Kr.60.66. Danmarks Statistik, Sejroegade 11, 2100 Copenhagen OE, Denmark.

614 388.312 314   DK   ISSN 0070-3516
DENMARK. DANMARKS STATISTIK. FAERDSELSUHELD/ROAD TRAFFIC ACCIDENTS. (Text in Danish, notes in English) 1930. a. Kr.43.44. Danmarks Statistik, Sejroegade 11, 2100 Copenhagen OE, Denmark.

312 310   PN   ISSN 0379-4237
ESTADISTICA PANAMENA. SITUACION DEMOGRAFICA. SECCION 221. ESTADISTICAS VITALES. 1957. a. Bl.1.00. Direccion de Estadistica y Censo, Contraloria General, Apartado 5213, Panama 5, Panama. circ. 1, 800.

325.7287   PN   ISSN 0378-4975
ESTADISTICA PANAMENA. SITUACION DEMOGRAFICA. SECCION 231. MIGRACION INTERNACIONAL. 1970. a. Bl.0.75. Direccion de Estadistica y Censo, Contraloria General, Apdo. Postal 5213, Panama 5, Panama. circ. 1,000.

312   FJ
FIJI. BUREAU OF STATISTICS. FIJI FERTILITY SURVEY. 1974. irreg. $2.50. Bureau of Statistics, Box 2221, Suva, Fiji.

312   FJ
FIJI. BUREAU OF STATISTICS. POPULATION OF FIJI; monograph for the U N World population. 1974. irreg. free. Bureau of Statistics, Box 2221, Suva, Fiji.

POPULATION STUDIES — ABSTRACTING, BIBLIOGRAPHIES, STATISTICS

312   FI
FINLAND. TILASTOKESKUS. KUOLLEISUUS. KUOLLEISUUS- JA ELOONJAAMISTAULUJA/ FINLAND. STATISTIKCENTRALEN. DOEDLIGHET. DOEDLIGHETS- OCH LIVSLAENGDSTABELLER/FINLAND. CENTRAL STATISTICAL OFFICE. MORTALITY. LIFE TABLES. (Text in English, Finnish and Swedish) 1924. irreg. Tilastokeskus, Annankatu 44, SF-00100 Helsinki 10, Finland (Subscr. to: Government Printing Centre, Box 516, SF-00100 Helsinki 10, Finland)
    Formerly: Finland. Tilastokeskus. Kuolleisuus- Ja Eloonjaamistauluja (ISSN 0355-2128)

312   FI
FINLAND. TILASTOKESKUS. VAESTO/ FINLAND. STATISTIKCENTRALEN. BEFOLKNING/FINLAND. CENTRAL STATISTICAL OFFICE. POPULATION. (Section VIA of Official Statistics of Finland) (Text in English, Finnish and Swedish) 1871. a. Fmk.136. Tilastokeskus, Annankatu 44, SF-00100 Helsinki 10, Finland (Subscr. to: Government Printing Centre, Box 516, SF-00100 Helsinki 10, Finland)
    Formerly: Finland. Tilastokeskus. Vaestonmuutokset (ISSN 0430-5612)

312   FI
FINLAND. TILASTOKESKUS. VAESTO- JA ASUNTOLASKENTA/FINLAND. STATISTIKCENTRALEN. FOLK- OCH BOSTADSRAEKNINGEN/FINLAND. CENTRAL STATISTICAL OFFICE. POPULATION AND HOUSING CENSUS. (Section VI C of Official Statistics of Finland) (Text in English, Finnish and Swedish) 1950. irreg. (every 5 years), latest 1980. price varies. Tilastokeskus, Annankatu 44, SF-00100 Helsinki 10, Finland (Subscr. to: Government Printing Centre, Box 516, SF-00100 Helsinki 10, Finland)
    Formerly: Finland. Tilastokeskus. Vaestolaskenta (ISSN 0355-2136)

310   US
FLORIDA VITAL STATISTICS. 1935. a. Department of Health & Rehabilitative Services, Office of Vital Statistics, Public Health Statistics & Records Registration Section, Box 210, Jacksonville, FL 32231. TEL 904-354-3961. circ. 600.

312 331   FR   ISSN 0533-0807
FRANCE. INSTITUT NATIONAL DE LA STATISTIQUE ET DES ETUDES ECONOMIQUES. COLLECTIONS. SERIE D, DEMOGRAPHIE ET EMPLOI. (Text in French; summaries in English and Spanish) 1969. irreg. 690 F. for 10 nos. Institut National de la Statistique et des Etudes Economiques, 18 bd. A. Pinard, 75675 Paris, France. circ. 2,400. Indexed: P.A.I.S.For.Lang.Ind.

325   FR   ISSN 0071-903X
FRANCE. OFFICE NATIONAL D'IMMIGRATION. STATISTIQUES DE L'IMMIGRATION. 1967. a. Office National d'Immigration, Service de l'Information et des relations Publiques, 44 rue Bargue, 75732 Paris Cedex 15, France.

312   US
GEORGIA DESCRIPTIONS IN DATA. 1982. a. $7.50. State Data Center, Office of Planning and Budget, 270 Washington St., S.W., Atlanta, GA 30334. Eds. Tom Wagner, Robin Kirkpatrick. circ. 1,500.
    Supersedes: Georgia. State Data Center. City Population Estimates (ISSN 0362-3904)

312   US
GEORGIA VITAL STATISTICS DATA BOOK. 1947. a. ‡ Department of Human Resources, Division of Public Health, Ste. 200, 878 Peachtree St., N.E., Atlanta, GA 30309. TEL 404-894-6482. Ed. Michael R. Lavoie. circ. 600. (also avail. in microfiche)
    Former titles: Georgia Vital and Health Statistics (ISSN 0362-0665); Georgia Vital Morbidity Statistics (ISSN 0072-1379)

312   GW   ISSN 0072-1794
GERMANY (FEDERAL REPUBLIC, 1949-). STATISTISCHES BUNDESAMT. FACHSERIE 1, BEVOELKERUNG UND ERWERBSTAETIGKEIT, REIHE 1: GEBIET UND BEVOELKERUNG. 1959. a. price varies. W. Kohlhammer-Verlag GmbH, Abt. Veroeffentlichungen des Statistischen Bundesamtes, Philipp-Reis-Str. 3, Postfach 421120, 6500 Mainz 42, W. Germany (B.R.D.)

312   GW
GERMANY (FEDERAL REPUBLIC, 1949-). STATISTISCHES BUNDESAMT. FACHSERIE 1, BEVOELKERUNG UND ERWERBSTAETIGKEIT, REIHE 3: HAUSHAELTE UND FAMILIEN. 1969. irreg. DM.15. W. Kohlhammer-Verlag GmbH, Abt. Veroeffentlichungen des Statistischen Bundesamtes, Philipp-Reis-Str. 3, Postfach 421120, 6500 Mainz 42, W. Germany (B.R.D.)

016   BE
GEZINSWETENSCHAPPELIJKE DOCUMENTATIE; Jaarboek. 1976. a. 1.390 Fr. University Press Leuven, Krakenstraat 3, 3000 Leuven, Belgium. Ed.Bd. circ. 800.
    Formerly (1983): Gezinssociologische Documentatie.

312   US   ISSN 0093-3481
HAWAII. DEPARTMENT OF HEALTH. RESEARCH AND STATISTICS OFFICE. R & S REPORT. 1973. irreg. free. Department of Health, Research and Statistics Office, Box 3378, Honolulu, HI 96801. TEL 808-548-6454. stat. Key Title: R & S Report (Honolulu)

312   HU   ISSN 0073-4020
HUNGARY. KOZPONTI STATISZTIKAI HIVATAL. DEMOGRAFIAI EVKONYV. 1965. a. 250 Ft. Statisztikai Kiado Vallalat, Kaszasdulo u. 2, P.O.B.99, 1300 Budapest 3, Hungary.

312   BE
I P D WORKING PAPERS. (Text in English) 1975. irreg. $4.50 per no. Vrije Universiteit Brussel, Interuniversity Programme in Demography, Pleinlaan 2, 1050 Brussels, Belgium. Ed. R. Lesthaeghe. bibl. charts. stat. circ. 200. Indexed: Popul.Ind.
    Formerly (until 1983): Demografie.

312.2   II
INDIA. MINISTRY OF HOME AFFAIRS. VITAL STATISTICS DIVISION. CAUSES OF DEATH; A SURVEY. (Text in English) a. Ministry of Home Affairs, Vital Statistics Division, Registrar General, West Block No. 1, R. K. Puram, New Delhi 110066, India. stat.

312   II
INDIA. MINISTRY OF HOME AFFAIRS. VITAL STATISTICS DIVISION. SAMPLE REGISTRATION BULLETIN. (Text in English) 1964/65. biennial. Ministry of Home Affairs, Vital Statistics Division, Registrar General, West Block No. 1, R. K. Puram, New Delhi 110066, India. charts. stat. (processed)
    Absorbed: India. Office of the Registrar General. Newsletter (ISSN 0537-0035)

312   IS   ISSN 0075-0999
ISRAEL. CENTRAL BUREAU OF STATISTICS. CAUSES OF DEATH. (Subseries of its Special Series) (Text in Hebrew and English) 1950. irreg. price varies. Central Bureau of Statistics, Box 13015, Jerusalem, Israel.

312   IS
ISRAEL. CENTRAL BUREAU OF STATISTICS. SUICIDES AND ATTEMPTED SUICIDES. (Text in Hebrew and English) 1968? irreg., latest issue 1976. $4 price varies. Central Bureau of Statistics, Box 13015, Jerusalem, Israel.

310   IS   ISSN 0075-1111
ISRAEL. CENTRAL BUREAU OF STATISTICS. VITAL STATISTICS. (Subseries of its Special Series) (Text in English and Hebrew) 1965/66 (pub. 1969) irreg., latest issue no. 745, 1981. price varies. Central Bureau of Statistics, Box 13015, Jerusalem, Israel.

325 331   IT   ISSN 0390-6450
ITALY. ISTITUTO CENTRALE DI STATISTICA. ANNUARIO DI STATISTICHE DEL LAVORO. 1959. a. L.8000. Istituto Centrale di Statistica, Via Cesare Balbo 16, 00100 Rome, Italy. circ. 1,350.
    Formerly: Annuario di Statistiche del Lavoro e dell'Emigrazione (ISSN 0075-1693)

312   IT   ISSN 0075-1685
ITALY. ISTITUTO CENTRALE DI STATISTICA. ANNUARIO DI STATISTICHE DEMOGRAFICHE. (Published in: two vols.) a. L.10000 per vol. Istituto Centrale di Statistica, Via Cesare Balbo 16, 00100 Rome, Italy. circ. 1,200.

315 312   KO
KOREA (REPUBLIC). POPULATION & HOUSING CENSUS REPORT. 1960. quinquennial. 17,400 Won. National Bureau of Statistics, Economic Planning Board, 90 Gyeongun-Dong, Jongro-Gu, Seoul, S. Korea. Ed. Myong Hyun Sohn. circ. 1,500.

325.1   AG
LATIN AMERICAN INTEGRATION PROCESS IN (YEAR) (Text in English) 1972. a. $20. Institute for Latin-American Integration - Instituto para la Integracion de America Latina, Esmeralda 130, piso 18, Casilla 39, Suc. 1, 1401, Buenos Aires, Argentina. circ. 1,500.

312   LY   ISSN 0075-9236
LIBYA. CENSUS AND STATISTICAL OFFICE. GENERAL POPULATION CENSUS. (Text in Arabic and English) 1954. decennial. free. Census and Statistical Department, Ministry of Planning, Tripoli, Libya.

312   LU   ISSN 0076-1613
LUXEMBOURG. SERVICE CENTRAL DE LA STATISTIQUE ET DES ETUDES ECONOMIQUES. COLLECTION RP: RECENSEMENTS DE LA POPULATION. 1962. irreg. price varies. Service Central de la Statistique et des Etudes Economiques, 19-21 Boulevard Royal, B.P. 304, 2013 Luxembourg, Luxembourg.

312   US
MAINE. VITAL STATISTICS. 1892. a. $7. Department of Human Services, Office of Health Planning and Development, 151 Capitol St., Sta. 11, Augusta, ME 04333 TEL 207-289-3001. (Subscr. to : Data Division, Augusta, ME 04333) Ed. Ellen M. Naor. circ. 500.
    Former titles: Maine. Department of Human Services. Bureau of Health Planning and Development. Vital Statistics & Maine. Division of Research and Vital Records. Annual Statistical Report.

310 312   MW   ISSN 0076-3276
MALAWI. NATIONAL STATISTICAL OFFICE. HOUSEHOLD INCOME AND EXPENDITURE SURVEY. 1968. irreg. K.8.50($9.50) ‡ National Statistical Office, Box 333, Zomba, Malawi.

312   MW   ISSN 0076-3306
MALAWI. NATIONAL STATISTICAL OFFICE. POPULATION CENSUS FINAL REPORT. 1966. irreg. (probably every 10 yrs) K.7.50($10.20) ‡ National Statistical Office, Box 333, Zomba, Malawi.

312   MY
MALAYSIA. DEPARTMENT OF STATISTICS. VITAL STATISTICS: PENINSULAR MALAYSIA. (Text in English & Malay) 1964. a, latest 1976. Department of Statistics - Jabatan Perangkaan, Jalan Young, Kuala Lumpur 10-01, Malaysia. stat. circ. 800. (processed)

312   MM   ISSN 0076-3470
MALTA. CENTRAL OFFICE OF STATISTICS. DEMOGRAPHIC REVIEW. a. Central Office of Statistics, Auberge d'Italie, Valletta, Malta (Subscr. to: Information Division, Auberge de Castille, Valletta, Malta)

312.2   NZ   ISSN 0548-9911
MORTALITY AND DEMOGRAPHIC DATA. a. price varies. National Health Statistics Centre, Private Bag 2, Upper Willis St., Wellington, New Zealand. circ. controlled.

POPULATION STUDIES — ABSTRACTING, BIBLIOGRAPHIES, STATISTICS

312   GR   ISSN 0077-6114
MOUVEMENT NATUREL DE LA POPULATION DE LA GRECE. (Text in Greek and French) 1956. a., latest 1981. $7. National Statistical Service, Publications and Information Division, 14-16 Lycourgou St., Athens 10166, Greece.

325   SP   ISSN 0077-1767
MOVIMIENTO NATURAL DE LA POBLACION DE ESPANA. 1961. a. price varies. Instituto Nacional de Estadistica, P de la Castellana, 183, Madrid 16, Spain.

312   614   NE   ISSN 0168-4000
NETHERLANDS. CENTRAAL BUREAU VOOR DE STATISTIEK. JAARSTATISTIEK VAN DE BEVOLKING. POPULATION STATISTICS. (Supplement to Maandstatistiek van Bevolking en Volksgezonheid) 1971. a. fl.30.50. Centraal Bureau voor de Statistiek, Prinses Beatrixlaan 428, Voorburg, Netherlands (Orders to: Staatsuitgeverij, Christoffel Plantijnstraat, The Hague, Netherlands) circ. 1,000.
    Formerly: Netherlands. Centraal Bureau voor de Statistiek. Jaaroverzicht Bevolking en Bevolking en Volksgezondheid. Population and Health Statistics.

312   US   ISSN 0095-5523
NEW HAMPSHIRE VITAL STATISTICS. 1880. a. Bureau of Vital Records and Health Statistics, Division of Public Health Services, Concord, NH 03301. TEL 603-271-4651. Ed. Charles Sirc. circ. 350.

312.097   US   ISSN 0091-9187
NEW JERSEY. OFFICE OF DEMOGRAPHIC AND ECONOMIC ANALYSIS. POPULATION ESTIMATES FOR NEW JERSEY. (Report year ends July 1) a. Department of Labor, Division of Planning & Research, Office of Demographic and Economic Analysis, CN-388, Trenton, NJ 08625-0388. TEL 609-292-0076.

312   NZ   ISSN 0112-9155
NEW ZEALAND. DEPARTMENT OF STATISTICS. DEMOGRAPHIC TRENDS BULLETIN. a. NZ.$20.90. Department of Statistics, Private Bag, Wellington, New Zealand (Subscr. to: Government Printing Office, Publications, Private Bag, Wellington, New Zealand)
    Formerly: New Zealand. Department of Statistics. Population and Migration. Part A: Population (ISSN 0110-375X); Supersedes in part: New Zealand. Department of Statistics. Population and Migration; New Zealand. Department of Statistics. Statistical Report of Population, Migration and Building. (ISSN 0077-9903)

312   NZ   ISSN 0112-6709
NEW ZEALAND. DEPARTMENT OF STATISTICS. EXTERNAL MIGRATION STATISTICS. a. NZ.$7.15. Department of Statistics, Private Bag, Wellington, New Zealand (Subscr to: Government Printing Office, Publications, Private Bag, Wellington, New Zealand)
    Formerly: New Zealand. Department of Statistics. Population and Migration. Part B: External Migration (ISSN 0110-3768); Supersedes in part: New Zealand. Department of Statistics. Population and Migration.

312   NZ
NEW ZEALAND. DEPARTMENT OF STATISTICS. POPULATION CENSUS: AGES, MARITAL STATUS AND FERTILITY. quinquennial, 1981, issued 1983. NZ.$12. Department of Statistics, Private Bag, Wellington, New Zealand (Subscr. to: Government Printing Office, Publications, Private Bag, Wellington, New Zealand)
    Formerly: New Zealand. Department of Statistics. Population Census: Ages and Marital Status (ISSN 0077-9687)

312   NZ
NEW ZEALAND. DEPARTMENT OF STATISTICS. POPULATION CENSUS: BIRTHPLACES AND ETHNIC ORIGIN. quinquennial, 1981, issued 1983. NZ.$9. Department of Statistics, Private Bag, Wellington, New Zealand (Subscr. to: Government Printing Office Publications, Private Bag, Wellington, New Zealand)
    Formerly: New Zealand. Department of Statistics. Population Census: Race (ISSN 0077-9776)

312   NZ   ISSN 0077-9695
NEW ZEALAND. DEPARTMENT OF STATISTICS. POPULATION CENSUS: DWELLINGS. quinquennial, 1981, issued 1983. NZ.$6. Department of Statistics, Private Bag, Wellington, New Zealand (Subscr. to: Government Printing Office, Publications, Private Bag, Wellington, New Zealand)

312   NZ
NEW ZEALAND. DEPARTMENT OF STATISTICS. POPULATION CENSUS: EDUCATION AND TRAINING. quinquennial, 1981 issued 1984. NZ.$6.60. Department of Statistics, Private Bag, Wellington, New Zealand (Subscr. to: Government Printing Office, Publications, Private Bag, Wellington, New Zealand)
    Formerly: New Zealand. Department of Statistics. Population Census: Education (ISSN 0077-9709)

312   NZ   ISSN 0077-9717
NEW ZEALAND. DEPARTMENT OF STATISTICS. POPULATION CENSUS: GENERAL REPORT. quinquennial, 1981 issued 1985. NZ.$15. Department of Statistics, Private Bag, Wellington, New Zealand (Subscr. to: Government Printing Office, Publications, Private Bag, Wellington, New Zealand)

312   NZ
NEW ZEALAND. DEPARTMENT OF STATISTICS. POPULATION CENSUS: HOUSEHOLDS AND FAMILIES. quinquennial, 1981, issued 1984. NZ.$9.90. Department of Statistics, Private Bag, Wellington, New Zealand (Subscr. to: Government Printing Office, Publications, Private Bag, Wellington, New Zealand)
    Formerly: New Zealand. Department of Statistics. Population Census: Households (ISSN 0077-9725)

312   NZ
NEW ZEALAND. DEPARTMENT OF STATISTICS. POPULATION CENSUS: INCOMES AND SOCIAL SECURITY BENEFITS. quinquennial, 1981, issued 1983. NZ.$8.80. Department of Statistics, Private Bag, Wellington, New Zealand (Subscr. to: Government Printing Office, Publications, Private Bag. Wellington, New Zealand)
    Formerly: New Zealand. Department of Statistics. Population Census: Incomes (ISSN 0077-9733)

310   312   NZ   ISSN 0110-8700
NEW ZEALAND. DEPARTMENT OF STATISTICS. POPULATION CENSUS: INTERNAL MIGRATION. 1971. quinquennial, 1981, issued 1984. NZ.$15.40. Department of Statistics, Private Bag, Wellington, New Zealand (Subscr. to: Government Printing Office, Publications, Private Bag, Wellington, New Zealand)

312   NZ
NEW ZEALAND. DEPARTMENT OF STATISTICS. POPULATION CENSUS: LABOUR FORCE. quinquennial, 1981, issued 1983. NZ.$13.20. Department of Statistics, Private Bag, Wellington, New Zealand (Subscr. to: Government Printing Office, Publications, Private Bag. Wellington, New Zealand)
    Formerly: New Zealand. Department of Statistics. Population Census: Industries and Occupations (ISSN 0077-9741)

312   NZ
NEW ZEALAND. DEPARTMENT OF STATISTICS. POPULATION CENSUS. LOCATION AND INCREASE OF POPULATION. PART A: POPULATION SIZE AND DISTRIBUTION. quinquennial, 1981. NZ.$5. Department of Statistics, Private Bag, Wellington, New Zealand (Subscr. to: Government Printing Office, Publications, Private Bag. Wellington, New Zealand)
    Supersedes in part: New Zealand. Department of Statistics. Population Census: Increase and Location of Population (ISSN 0077-9792)

312   NZ
NEW ZEALAND. DEPARTMENT OF STATISTICS. POPULATION CENSUS. LOCATION AND INCREASE OF POPULATION. PART B: POPULATION DENSITY. quinquennial, 1981 issued 1982. NZ.$6.60. Department of Statistics, Private Bag, Wellington, New Zealand (Subscr. to: Government Printing Office, Publications, Private Bag, Wellington, New Zealand)
    Supersedes in part: New Zealand. Department of Statistics. Population Census: Increase and Location of Population (ISSN 0077-9792)

312   NZ
NEW ZEALAND. DEPARTMENT OF STATISTICS. POPULATION CENSUS: MAORI POPULATION AND DWELLINGS. quinquennial, 1981, issued 1982. NZ.$13.20. Department of Statistics, Private Bag, Wellington, New Zealand (Subscr. to: Government Printing Office, Publications, Private Bag, Wellington, New Zealand)

312   NZ
NEW ZEALAND. DEPARTMENT OF STATISTICS. POPULATION CENSUS: PROVISIONAL STATISTICS SERIES. BULLETIN ONE. LOCAL AUTHORITY AREAS. quinquennial. NZ.$5.50. Department of Statistics, Private Bag, Wellington, New Zealand (Subscr. to: Government Printing Office, Publications, Private Bag, Wellington, New Zealand)
    Former titles: New Zealand. Department of Statistics. Population Census: Provisional Population and Dwelling Statistics; New Zealand. Department of Statistics. Population Census: Provisional Report on Population and Dwellings (ISSN 0077-9768)

312   NZ   ISSN 0077-9784
NEW ZEALAND. DEPARTMENT OF STATISTICS. POPULATION CENSUS: RELIGIOUS PROFESSIONS. quinquennial, 1981, issued 1983. NZ.$6.60. Department of Statistics, Private Bag, Wellington, New Zealand (Subscr. to: Government Printing Office, Publications, Private Bag, Wellington, New Zealand)

312   US
NORTH CAROLINA. DIVISION OF HEALTH SERVICES. STATE CENTER FOR HEALTH STATISTICS. NORTH CAROLINA VITAL STATISTICS. 1916. a. free. ‡ Department of Human Resources, Division of Health Services, Box 2091, Raleigh, NC 27602. TEL 919-733-4534.
    Formerly: North Carolina. Division of Health Services. Public Health Statistics Branch. North Carolina Vital Statistics (ISSN 0078-1371)

312   NO   ISSN 0550-7170
NORWAY. STATISTISK SENTRALBYRAA. FOLKEMENGDEN ETTER ALDER OG EKTESKAPELIG STATUS/POPULATION BY AGE AND MARITAL STATUS. (Subseries of its Norges Offisielle Statistikk) (Text in English and Norwegian) a. Kr.50. Statistisk Sentralbyraa, Box 8131 Dep., 0033 Oslo 1, Norway. circ. 2,200.

312   NO   ISSN 0332-8015
NORWAY. STATISTISK SENTRALBYRAA. FRAMSKRIVING AV FOLKEMENGDEN: REGIONALE TALL/POPULATION PROJECTIONS: REGIONAL FIGURES. (Subseries of its Norges Offisielle Statistikk) irreg. Kr.35. Statistisk Sentralbyraa, Box 8131 Dep., 0033 Oslo 1, Norway. circ. 2,750.

312   US
OKLAHOMA POPULATION ESTIMATES. 1967. a. free. Employment Security Commission, Office of Economic Analysis, 213 Will Rogers Bldg., Oklahoma City, OK 73105. Ed. Roger Jacks. charts. stat. circ. 850.

312   US
PENNSYLVANIA VITAL STATISTICS. 1951. a. free. Department of Health, State Health Data Center, Box 90, Harrisburg, PA 17108. TEL 717-783-2548. circ. 1,000.
    Formerly: Pennsylvania Natality and Mortality Statistics.

312   PH
PHILIPPINES. NATIONAL CENSUS AND STATISTICS OFFICE. SOCIAL INDICATOR. Short title: Social Indicators of the Philippines. a, latest 1974. P.7($3) National Census and Statistics Office, Ramon Magsaysay Blvd., Manila, Philippines. Ed. Tito A. Mijares. charts. stat.

315   PH   ISSN 0554-0186
PHILIPPINES. NATIONAL CENSUS AND STATISTICS OFFICE. VITAL STATISTICAL REPORT. a, latest 1974. P.18($6) National Census and Statistics Office, Ramon Magsaysay Blvd., Box 779, Manila, Philippines.

315 312   PH
PHILIPPINES. NATIONAL CENSUS AND STATISTICS OFFICE. YEARBOOK. Short title: Philippine Yearbook. (Text in English) 1940. biennial. P.100($35) National Census and Statistics Office, Ramon Magsaysay Blvd., Box 779, Manila, Philippines. Ed.Bd.

317.3   US   ISSN 0079-2403
POCKET DATA BOOK, USA. 1967. irreg. price varies. U.S. Bureau of the Census, Customer Service, Washington, DC 20233 TEL 301-763-4100. (Orders to: Supt. of Documents, Washington, DC 20402) (also avail. in microform)

312   PL   ISSN 0079-2616
POLAND. GLOWNY URZAD STATYSTYCZNY. ROCZNIK DEMOGRAFICZNY. (Subseries of its: Statystyka Polski) (Text in Polish; summaries in English and Russian) 1968. a. 85 Zl. Glowny Urzad Statystyczny, Al. Niepodlegosci 208, 00-925 Warsaw, Poland.

301.426 613.9   US   ISSN 0161-0902
POPULATION AND FAMILY PLANNING PROGRAMS. 1969. irreg., 12th edt., 1985. $7. Population Council, One Dag Hammarskjold Plaza, New York, NY 10017. TEL 212-644-1300. Ed. Dorothy L. Nortman. charts. (reprint service avail. from UMI)
Planned parenthood

312   IR
POPULATION GROWTH OF IRAN. 1974. irreg. Statistical Centre, Dr. Fatemi Ave, Teheran 14144, Iran. charts. stat.

301.42   US   ISSN 0032-4701
POPULATION INDEX. 1935. q. $60. (Population Association of America) Princeton University, Office of Population Research, 21 Prospect Ave., Princeton, NJ 08544. TEL 609-452-4949. Ed. Richard Hankinson. adv. abstr. bibl. charts. index. cum.index. circ. 4,600. (also avail. in microfilm from UMI; reprint service avail. from UMI) Indexed: Curr.Cont. P.A.I.S. SSCI. Curr.Lit.Fam.Plan. E.I.

312   NE   ISSN 0168-3853
POPULATION OF THE MUNICIPALITIES OF THE NETHERLANDS. (Text in Dutch and English) 1944/46. a. fl.15. Centraal Bureau voor de Statistiek, Prinses Beatrixlaan 428, Voorburg, Netherlands (Orders to: Staatsuitgeverij, Christoffel Plantijnstraat, The Hague, Netherlands)

301.32   US   ISSN 0145-9643
POPULATION REPORTS. 1973. irreg. free. Department of Health, Research and Statistics Office, Box 3378, Honolulu, HI 96801. TEL 808-548-6454. Indexed: Curr.Lit.Fam.Plan. Sage Fam.Stud.Abstr.
Supersedes (as of 1973): Population Mobility in Hawaii (ISSN 0094-0348)

312   PO   ISSN 0379-7007
PORTUGAL. INSTITUTO NACIONAL DE ESTATISTICA. CENTRO DE ESTUDOS DEMOGRAFICOS. CADERNO. (Text in French or Portuguese) 1976. irreg. Instituto Nacional de Estatistica, 1078 Lisbon Codex, Portugal (Orders to: Imprensa Nacional, Casa da Moeda, Direccao Comercial, rua D. Francisco Manuel de Melo 5, 1000 Lisbon, Portugal) charts.

312   PO   ISSN 0079-4082
PORTUGAL. INSTITUTO NACIONAL DE ESTATISTICA. CENTRO DE ESTUDOS DEMOGRAFICOS. REVISTA. (Text in Portuguese) 1945. irreg. Instituto Nacional de Estatistica, 1078 Lisbon Codex, Portugal (Orders to: Imprensa Nacional, Casa da Moeda, Direccao Comercial, rua D. Francisco Manuel de Melo 5, 1000 Lisbon, Portugal) Indexed: Popul.Ind.

312   PO
PORTUGAL. INSTITUTO NACIONAL DE ESTATISTICA. ESTATISTICAS DEMOGRAFICAS. CONTINENTE, ACORES E MADEIRA. (Text in French and Portuguese) 1887. a. Esc.1000. Instituto Nacional de Estatistica, Av. Antonio Jose de Almeida, 1078 Lisbon Codex, Portugal (Orders to: Imprensa Nacional, Casa da Moeda, Direccao Comercial, rua D. Francisco Manuel de Melo 5,1000 Lisbon, Portugal)
Former titles: Portugal. Instituto Nacional de Estatistica. Estatisticas Demograficas Continente e Ilhas Adjacentes (ISSN 0377-2284); Portugal. Instituto Nacional de Estatistica. Estatisticas Demograficas; Portugal. Instituto Nacional de Estatistica. Anuario Demografico. (ISSN 0079-4104)

312   PR   ISSN 0555-6511
PUERTO RICO. DIVISION OF DEMOGRAPHIC REGISTRY AND VITAL STATISTICS. ANNUAL VITAL STATISTICS REPORT. (Text in English and Spanish) 1970. a. Department of Health, Office of Statistics Analysis and Information Control, Stop 19 Ponce de Leon Ave., San Juan, PR 00901.

312   US
RHODE ISLAND. DEPARTMENT OF HEALTH. VITAL STATISTICS. a. free. Department of Health, 101 Health Bldg., Davis St., Providence, RI 02908. TEL 401-277-2231.

312   UK   ISSN 0080-7869
SCOTLAND. REGISTRAR GENERAL. ANNUAL REPORT. 1855. a. price varies. H.M.S.O., P.O. Box 569, London SE1 9NH, England. (reprint service avail. from UMI)

016 312   NE   ISSN 0167-4757
SELECTED ANNOTATED BIBLIOGRAPHY OF POPULATION STUDIES IN THE NETHERLANDS. (Text in English) 1975. a. fl.6.50 in the Netherlands; other countries free. Nederlands Interuniversitair Demografisch Instituut - Netherlands Interuniversity Demographic Institute, Lange Houtstraat 19, 2511 CV The Hague, Netherlands. (Co-sponsor: Netherlands Demographic Society) Ed. T.J. Augenbroe-Siebenga. circ. 750. Indexed: Popul.Ind.
Formerly (1970-1973): Bibliografie van in Nederland verschenen demografische Studies.

312 316   SA
SOUTH AFRICA. CENTRAL STATISTICAL SERVICE. DEATH OF BLACKS. (Text in Afrikaans and English) a., latest 1983. Central Statistical Service, Private Bag X44, Pretoria 0001, South Africa. stat.
Formerly: South Africa. Department of Statistics. Report on Bantu Deaths in Selected Magisterial Districts/Verslag oor Bantoesterfgevalle in Uitgesoekte Landdrosdistrikte.

312   SA
SOUTH AFRICA. CENTRAL STATISTICAL SERVICE. REPORT ON BIRTHS: WHITE, COLOURED AND ASIANS. (Report No. 07-01) a., latest 1984. Central Statistical Service, Private Bag X44, Pretoria 0001, South Africa (Orders to: Government Printer, Bosman St., Private Bag X85, Pretoria 0001, South Africa)
Former titles: South Africa. Department of Statistics. Report on Births: White, Colored and Asians; South Africa. Department of Statistics. Report on Births.

312.5   SA
SOUTH AFRICA. CENTRAL STATISTICAL SERVICE. REPORT ON MARRIAGES AND DIVORCES: SOUTH AFRICA. (Report No. 07-02) 1972. a., latest 1984. Central Statistical Service, Private Bag X44, Pretoria 0001, South Africa (Orders to: Government Printer, Bosman St., Private Bag X85, Pretoria 0001, South Africa)
Formerly: South Africa. Department of Statistics. Report on Marriages and Divorces: South Africa.

301.32 916.804   SA
SOUTH AFRICA. CENTRAL STATISTICAL SERVICE. TOURISM AND MIGRATION. (Report No. 19-01) a., latest 1984. Central Statistical Service, Private Bag X44, Pretoria 0001, South Africa (Orders to: Government Printer, Bosman St., Private Bag X85, Pretoria 0001, South Africa)
Formerly: South Africa. Department of Statistics. Tourism and Migration.

312   US   ISSN 0094-6338
SOUTH CAROLINA VITAL AND MORBIDITY STATISTICS. 1972. a. Department of Health and Environmental Control, Office of Vital Records and Public Health Statistics, 2600 Bull St., Columbia, SC 29201. TEL 803-734-4860. circ. 400. (also avail. in microfiche)

317 312   JM
STATISTICAL INSTITUTE OF JAMAICA. DEMOGRAPHIC STATISTICS. 1971. a.,latest issue, 1983. Jam.$8. Statistical Institute of Jamaica, 9 Swallowfield Road, Kingston 5, Jamaica. stat. (back issues avail.)
Formerly: Jamaica. Department of Statistics. Demographic Statistics.

STATISTICAL SUMMARY OF THAILAND. see *AGRICULTURE — Abstracting, Bibliographies, Statistics*

315 312   TH
SURVEY OF MIGRATION IN BANGKOK METROPOLIS. (Text in English and Thai) 1974. irreg. National Statistical Office, Larn Luang Rd., Bangkok, Thailand. charts. stat.

312   SW   ISSN 0082-0156
SWEDEN. STATISTISKA CENTRALBYRAAN. BEFOLKNINGSFOERAENDRINGAR. (Text in Swedish; summaries in English) 1911. a. price varies. Distribution, S-701 89 Oerebro, Sweden. circ. 1,600.

312   SW   ISSN 0082-0164
SWEDEN. STATISTISKA CENTRALBYRAAN. FOLKMAENGD. (Text in English; summaries in English) 1910. a, 3 vols. Kr.170. Statistiska Centralbyraan, Distribution, S-701 89 Oerebro, Sweden. circ. 2,700.

312   SW   ISSN 0082-0245
SWEDEN. STATISTISKA CENTRALBYRAAN. STATISTISKA MEDDELANDEN. SUBGROUP BE (POPULATION) (Text in Swedish; table heads and summaries in English) 1963 N.S. irreg. Kr.290. Statistiska Centralbyraan, Distribution, S-701 89 Oerebro, Sweden. circ. 1,700. Indexed: Popul.Ind.

312.5   SZ
SWITZERLAND. BUNDESAMT FUER STATISTIK. HEIRATEN, LEBENDGEBORENE UND GESTORBENE IN DEN GEMEINDEN/ MARIAGES, NAISSANCES ET DECES DANS LES COMMUNES. 1971. a. 12 Fr. Bundesamt fuer Statistik, Hallwylstr. 15, 3003 Berne, Switzerland. stat. circ. 750.

312   US   ISSN 0495-257X
TEXAS VITAL STATISTICS. 1973. a. Department of Health, 1100 W. 49th St., Austin, TX 78756. TEL 512-458-7111.

312 016   US
U.S. BUREAU OF THE CENSUS. CENSUS CATALOG AND GUIDE. 1946. a. price varies. U.S. Bureau of the Census, Customer Services, Washington, DC 20233 TEL 301-763-4100. (Orders to: Supt. of Documents, Washington, DC 20402)
Formerly: U.S. Bureau of the Census. Bureau of the Census Catalog (ISSN 0007-618X)

U.S. NATIONAL CENTER FOR HEALTH STATISTICS. CATALOG OF PUBLICATIONS. see *PUBLIC HEALTH AND SAFETY — Abstracting, Bibliographies, Statistics*

314 312   IT
UNIVERSITA DEGLI STUDI DI PADOVA. FACOLTA DI SCIENZE STATISTICHE, DEMOGRAFICHE ED ATTUARIALI. SERIE ESTRATTI. 1969. irreg., no.204, 1980. (Universita degli Studi di Padova, Facolta di Scienze Statistiche, Demografiche ed Attuariali) C L E U P, Via G. Prati, 19, 35100 Padua, Italy. bibl.

314 312   IT
UNIVERSITA DEGLI STUDI DI PADOVA. FACOLTA DI SCIENZE STATISTICHE, DEMOGRAFICHE ED ATTUARIALI. SERIE PUBBLICAZIONI. 1971. irreg., no.16, 1981. (Universita degli Studi di Padova, Facolta di Scienze Statistiche, Demografiche ed Attuariali) C L E U P, Via G. Prati, 19, 35100 Padua, Italy.

930 POSTAL AFFAIRS

312 UY
URUGUAY. DIRECCION GENERAL DE ESTADISTICA Y CENSOS. ESTADISTICAS VITALES. (Suspended 1974-1977; volume for 1978 contains 1975 statistics) 1961; N.S. 1978. irreg. Direccion General de Estadistica y Censos, Montevideo, Uruguay.

312.5 US
UTAH MARRIAGE AND DIVORCE ANNUAL REPORT. a. $10. Department of Health, Bureau of Policy Analysis, Box 16700, Salt Lake City, UT 84116-0700. TEL 801-538-6310.

614 US ISSN 0500-7720
UTAH VITAL STATISTICS ANNUAL REPORT. a. $10. Department of Health, Bureau of Policy Analysis, Box 16700, Salt Lake City, UT 84116-0700. TEL 801-538-6310. stat.

312 NN
VANUATU. BUREAU OF STATISTICS. CENSUS OF POPULATION AND HOUSING. VILA AND SANTO, FINAL RESULTS: PART 2: POPULATION DATA/RECENESMENT DE LA POPULATION ET DE L'HABITAT, VILA ET LUGANVILLE, RESULTANTS DEFINITIFS: 2EME PARTIE: DONNEES SUR LA POPULATION. (Text in English, French) 1972 ed., 1978. irreg. free. Condominium Bureau of Statistics, Port Vila, Vanuatu. stat. circ. 400.

312 NN
VANUATU. NATIONAL PLANNING AND STATISTICS OFFICE. CENSUS OF POPULATION (YEAR). BASE TABLES/TABLES DE BASE. (Text in English and French) 1972. irreg. $100. Informations Department, Statistics Division, NP 50, Port-Vila, Vanuatu. stat. circ. 300.
Formerly (until 1983): Vanuatu. Condominium Bureau of Statistics. Census of Population and Housing, Vila and Santo, Preliminary Results/Recensement de la Population et de l'Habitat, Port Vila et Luganville, Resultats Preliniares.

312 US ISSN 0161-8695
VITAL STATISTICS OF IOWA. 1975. a. free. Department of Health, Statistical Services, Des Moines, IA 50319. TEL 515-281-4945. Ed. Michael Dare. stat. circ. 400. (also avail. in microfiche)
Formed by the merger of: Iowa Summary of Vital Statistics (ISSN 0090-5143) & Iowa Detailed Report of Vital Statistics (ISSN 0362-9473)

310 CN
VITAL STATISTICS OF THE PROVINCE OF BRITISH COLUMBIA. 1944. a. free. Ministry of Health, Division of Vital Statistics, Victoria, B.C., Canada. TEL 604-387-4827. Ed. A. Harvey Hersom. circ. 700.

312 NE
WORLD FERTILITY SURVEY. ANNUAL REPORTS. 1975. a. International Statistical Institute, 428 Prinses Beatrixlaan, Box 950, 2270 AZ Voorburg, Netherlands. Indexed: Biol.Abstr.
Former Titles: World Fertility Survey. Progress Reports; Fertility Survey. Report.

312 NE
WORLD FERTILITY SURVEY. BASIC DOCUMENTATION. (Editions in Arabic, English, French and Spanish) irreg. (6-8/yr) free. International Statistical Institute, Prinses Beatrixlaan 428, Box 950, 2270 AZ Voorburg, Netherlands.

321 NE
WORLD FERTILITY SURVEY. COUNTRY REPORTS. (Editions in Arabic, English, French, and Spanish) 1976. irreg. price varies. International Statistical Institute, Prinses Beatrixlaan 428, Box 950, 2270 AZ Voorburg, Netherlands. stat. Indexed: Biol.Abstr.

312 NE
WORLD FERTILITY SURVEY. OCCASIONAL PAPERS. 1973. irreg. free. International Statistical Institute, Prinses Beatrixlaan 428, Box 950, 2270 AZ Voorburg, Netherlands.

312 NE
WORLD FERTILITY SURVEY. SCIENTIFIC REPORTS. 1977. irreg. free. International Statistical Institute, Prinses Beatrixlaan 428, Box 950, 2270 AZ Voorburg, Netherlands. Indexed: Biol.Abstr. Popul.Ind.

312 NE
WORLD FERTILITY SURVEY. SUMMARIES OF COUNTRY REPORTS. (Editions in Arabic, English and French) 1977. irreg. International Statistical Institute, Box 950, 2270 AZ Voorburg, Netherlands. Indexed: Popul.Ind.
Formerly: World Fertility Survey. Summaries.

312 NE
WORLD FERTILITY SURVEY. TECHNICAL BULLETINS. 1977. irreg. free. International Statistical Institute, Prinses Beatrixlaan 428, Box 950, 2270 AZ Voorburg, Netherlands. stat. Indexed: Popul.Ind.

316 325 ZA ISSN 0084-4543
ZAMBIA. CENTRAL STATISTICAL OFFICE. MIGRATION STATISTICS. Title varies: Zambia. Central Statistical Office. Migration Statistics: Immigrants and Visitors. 1965. a. K.1.50. Central Statistical Office, P.O. Box 31908, Lusaka, Zambia.

316 312 ZA ISSN 0084-456X
ZAMBIA. CENTRAL STATISTICAL OFFICE. VITAL STATISTICS. Variant title: Zambia. Central Statistical Office. Registered Births, Marriages and Deaths (Vital Statistics) 1965. a, latest 1975. K.0.20. Central Statistical Office, P.O. Box 31908, Lusaka, Zambia.

POSTAL AFFAIRS

see Communications—Postal Affairs

POULTRY AND LIVESTOCK

see Agriculture—Poultry and Livestock

PRINTING

760 US ISSN 0275-9470
A I G A GRAPHIC DESIGN U S A. 1980. a. membership. (American Institute of Graphic Arts) Watson-Guptill Publications, Inc., One Astor Plaza, New York, NY 10036. TEL 212-764-7300. (Co-publisher: Watson-Guptil) Ed. C. Ray Smith.
Supersedes: A I G A Best Books Show & Communication Graphics & Covers & Insides.

686.2 US
A T F NEWSLETTER. 1978. a. $2 per no. American Typecasting Fellowship, Box 263, Terra Alta, WV 26764. TEL 304-789-2300. Ed. Richard L. Hopkins. adv. bk. rev. circ. 400.

686.2 US ISSN 0276-5519
AMERICAN REGISTER OF PRINTING AND GRAPHIC ARTS SERVICES. 1981. a. $20. In-Register, Inc., 1485 Bayshore Blvd., San Francisco, CA 94124. TEL 415-467-8760. Ed. Richard Michaels. adv. charts. circ. 50,000.

686.2 US
ANNUAL GUIDE TO RIBBONS AND TONER; product overview and industry directory. a. Datek Information Services, Box 68, Newtonville, MA 02160. TEL 617-893-9130. Ed. Frank A. Stefansson.

BIBLIOTHECA HUNGARICA ANTIQUA. see PUBLISHING AND BOOK TRADE

BOGVENNEN. see PUBLISHING AND BOOK TRADE

686.2 FR ISSN 0572-7529
BUREAU INTERNATIONAL DES SOCIETES GERANT LES DROITS D'ENREGISTREMENT ET DE REPRODUCTION MECANIQUE. BULLETIN. irreg. International Bureau of the Societies Administering the Rights of Mechanical Recording and Reproduction, 12 rue Ballu, 75009 Paris, France.

CAMBRIDGE AUTHORS' AND PUBLISHERS' GUIDES. see PUBLISHING AND BOOK TRADE

CATALOGO DELLA GRAFICA ITALIANA. see ART

760 FR
COURRIER TECHNIQUE ARTS GRAPHIQUES. irreg., no.26, 1975. Kodak-Pathe, Division Marches et Graphiques, 8 et 14 rue Villiot, 75580 Paris Cedex 12, France. Ed. Claude Vimeux.

686.2 GW
DRUCK-SACHEN; Informationsdienst der deutschen Druckindustrie. a. Bundesverband Druck E.V., Biebricher Allee 79, 6200 Wiesbaden, W. Germany (B.R.D.) Ed. Peter Klemm.

686.2 070.5 US
ELECTRONIC PRINTING SYSTEMS: DIRECTIONS IN DIGITAL IMAGING. CONFERENCE PROCEEDINGS. (In 2 vols.) 1984. a. $95 per vol. Dunn Technology, Inc., 1855 E. Vista Way, No.1, Vista, CA 92084-3316. Ed. S. Thomas Dunn. (back issues avail.)

686.2 676.3 US ISSN 0741-7160
EXPORT GRAFICAS U S A; with an international buyer's guide and directory. (Text in Spanish) 1980. a. $25 includes Artes Graficas U S A. Graphic Arts Trade Journals International, Inc., Box 81, Farmingdale, NY 11735. TEL 516-694-4842. Ed. Lydia Miura. adv. circ. 9,519. Indexed: Graph.Arts Lit.Abstr.

FACTOTUM. see LIBRARY AND INFORMATION SCIENCES

655.255 US ISSN 0015-2803
FIRST TO FINAL. 1957. irreg. ‡ Proofreaders Club of New York, 38-15 149 St, Flushing, NY 11354. Ed. Allan Treshan. (back issues avail.)

686.2 US ISSN 0428-5670
FLEXOGRAPHIC TECHNICAL ASSOCIATION. REPORT OF THE PROCEEDINGS: ANNUAL MEETING AND TECHNICAL FORUM. 1959. a. membership. Flexographic Technical Association, 95 W. 19th St., Huntington Station, NY 11746. illus. circ. 1,200. Key Title: Report of the Proceedings. Annual Meeting and Technical Forum.

686.2 GW
FOGRA-LITERATUR-PROFIL. 1975. irreg. (4-6/yr) DM.500 to individuals; members DM. 200. Deutsche Forschungsgesellschaft fuer Druck- und Reproduktionstechnik e.V. (FOGRA), Postfach 800469, Streitfeldstr. 19, 8000 Munich 80, W. Germany(B.R.D.)

760 AU ISSN 0016-3562
G L V MITTEILUNGEN. (Graphische Lehr- und Versuchsanstalt) 1959. irreg. (1-2/yr.) free. Hoehere Graphische Bundes Lehr und Versuchsanstalt, Leyserstr. 6, A-1140 Vienna, Austria. Ed. Dr. Wilhelm Mutschlechner. bk. rev. charts. illus. index. circ. 500.

686.232 US ISSN 0534-0489
G R I NEWSLETTER.* 1962. irreg. (3-4/yr.) membership only. ‡ Gravure Research Institute, 60 E. 42nd St., No. 1545, New York, NY 10165-0169. Ed. Harvey F. George. bk. rev. charts. illus. pat. stat. cum.index. circ. 600 (controlled) (back issues avail.) Indexed: Graph.Arts Lit.Abstr.

686.2 DK ISSN 0109-0879
GRAFISKE FUNKTIONAERER. 1981. irreg. membership. Grafiske Funktionaerers Landsforening, Christian IX's Gade 7, 1111 Copenhagen K, Denmark. illus.
Former titles: Grafiske Funktionaerers Landsforening. Orientering (ISSN 0109-0860); Grafiske Funktionaerers Landsforening. Medlemsblad (ISSN 0105-9041)

655 US ISSN 0147-1651
GRAPHIC ARTS GREEN BOOK; directory of graphic arts operating firms in Illinois, Indiana, Michigan and Wisconsin. 1970. a. $65. A.F. Lewis Co. Inc., 15 Spinning Wheel Rd., Hinsdale, IL 60521 TEL 312-323-9777. (And 79 Madison Ave., New York, NY 10016) Eds. Bill Curran, Linda Kubista. adv. index. circ. 10,000.
Formerly: Graphic Arts Trade Directory and Register (ISSN 0072-5498)

PRINTING — ABSTRACTING, BIBLIOGRAPHIES, STATISTICS

760   US   ISSN 0096-1159
GRAPHIC ARTS TECHNICAL FOUNDATION. RESEARCH PROJECT REPORT. 1947. irreg (6-8/yr.) $7.50 to non-members; members $3.75. ‡ Graphic Arts Technical Foundation, 4615 Forbes Ave, Pittsburgh, PA 15213. TEL 412-621-6941. Indexed: Graph.Arts Lit.Abstr.
     Formerly (until no.101., Apr. 1974): Graphic Arts Technical Foundation. Research Progress Report.

GRAPHIS ANNUAL; international annual of advertising and editorial graphics. see *ART*

763   AU   ISSN 0075-2266
GRAPHISCHE UNTERNEHMUNGEN OESTERREICHS. JAHRBUCH. 1930. a. S.215. Hauptverband der Graphischen Unternehmungen Oesterreichs, Gruenangergasse 4, A-1010 Vienna, Austria. adv. circ. 950.

686.2   FR
GUTENBERG; annuaire des industries graphiques. 1936. a. 350 F. Editions Technorama, 31 Place Saint Ferdinand, 75017 Paris, France. Ed. R. Baschet. circ. 2,500.

943 655   GW   ISSN 0072-9094
GUTENBERG-JAHRBUCH. 1926. a. DM.80. (International Association Past and Present of Printing Arts) Gutenberg-Gesellschaft e.V., Liebfrauenplatz 5, 6500 Mainz, W. Germany (B.R.D.) Ed. Hans-Joachim Koppitz. adv. bk. rev. circ. 2,000. Indexed: M.L.A.

686.2   GW   ISSN 0073-0173
HANDBUCH FUER DIE DRUCKINDUSTRIE BERLIN. 1946. a. DM.10. Kupijai und Prochnow, Verlag und Druckerei, Bluecherstr. 22, 1000 Berlin 61, W. Germany (B.R.D.)

686.2   GW
HANDSATZLETTER; Monografien der modernen Typographie. 1967. irreg. free. Johannes Wagner Schriftgiesserei und Messinglinienfabrik, Theodor-Heuss-Strasse 49, Postfach 227, 8070 Ingolstadt, W. Germany (B.R.D.) Ed. M. Droese. circ. 7,000.

760   GW
IMPRIMATUR. NEUE FOLGE. irreg., vol.12, 1987. price varies. Verlag Otto Harrassowitz, Taunusstr. 14, Postfach 2929, D-6200 Wiesbaden 1, W. Germany (B.R.D.) Indexed: M.L.A.
     Formerly: Imprimatur; Jahrbuch fuer Buecherfreunde. Neue Folge (ISSN 0073-5620)

INDIAN & EASTERN NEWSPAPER SOCIETY PRESS HANDBOOK. see *JOURNALISM*

686.2   GW   ISSN 0170-3463
INDUSTRIEGEWERKSCHAFT DRUCK UND PAPIER. SCHRIFTENREIHE FUER BETRIEBSRATE. 1969. irreg. exchange basis. Industriegewerkschaft Druck und Papier, Friedrichstr. 15, Postfach 1282, 7000 Stuttgart 1, W. Germany (B.R.D.) Ed.Bd. charts. illus.

INTERNATIONAL DIRECTORY OF PRIVATE PRESSES. see *BUSINESS AND ECONOMICS — Trade And Industrial Directories*

ISRAEL BOOK TRADE DIRECTORY; a guide to publishers, printers and ancillary book trade services in Israel. see *PUBLISHING AND BOOK TRADE*

655   JA   ISSN 0546-0719
JAPAN PRINTING ART ANNUAL/NIHON INSATSU NENKAN. 1957. a. Japan Printing News Co., Ltd. - Nippon Insatsu Shinbunsha, 1-16-8 Shintomi, Chuo-ku, Tokyo 104, Japan. adv. circ. 4,500.

686.221   JA
JAPAN TYPOGRAPHY ANNUAL/NIHON TAIPOGURAFI NENKAN. (Text in Japanese; title and captions for plates in English) 1974. a. $30. (Japan Typography Association) Nihon Taipogurafi Kyokai) Gurafikkusha, Box 102, 1-9-12 Kudan Kita, Chiyoda-ku, Tokyo, Japan (Overseas Distributor: Orion Books, Export Dept., 1-58 Kanda Jimbocho, Chiyoda-ku, Tokyo 101, Japan) illus.
     Continues: Nihon Retaringu Nenkan.

686.2   US
LASERS IN GRAPHICS: ELECTRONIC PUBLISHING IN THE 80'S. CONFERENCE PROCEEDINGS. (In 2 vols.) 1979. a. $95 per vol. Dunn Technology, Inc., 1855 E. Vista Way, No. 1, Vista, CA 92084-3316. Ed. S. Thomas Dunn. circ. 1,000. (back issues avail.) Indexed: Graph.Arts Lit.Abstr.

760   DK
LEVERANDOERHAANDBOGEN (HELLERUP); for virksom- heder i den grafiske branche. a. Grafiske Haandboger, Hellerupvej 66, 2900 Hellerup, Denmark. adv. circ. 3,300.

760   FR
MATERIEL GRAPHIQUE.* 1958. a. 180 F. Societe des Editions de l' Imprimerie Nouvelle, 53 guai Seine 19e, Paris, France. Ed. M. Mauduit. circ. 6,000.

P I R A ANNUAL REVIEW OF RESEARCH & SERVICES. (Paper, Printing & Packaging Industries Research Association) see *PAPER AND PULP*

POLONIA TYPOGRAPHICA SAECULI SEDECIMI. see *ART*

760   NE   ISSN 0032-7476
PRENT 190; new circle of collectors of modern graphic art. 1965. a. fl.725. Gerlach en Co. B. V., Art Section, Schiphol-Center, Amsterdam, Netherlands. Ed. L. Gans. circ. 1,500.

686.2   UK
PRINTERS YEARBOOK. 1982. a. £40. ‡ British Printing Industries Federation, 11 Bedford Row, London, WC1R 4DX, England. adv. index. circ. 3,200.
     Former titles: Printing Industries Annual (ISSN 0308-1443); British Federation of Master Printers. Master Printers Annual (ISSN 0068-1989)

665.1   UK   ISSN 0079-5321
PRINTING HISTORICAL SOCIETY. JOURNAL. 1965. a. membership. Printing Historical Society, St. Bride Institute, Bride Lane, Fleet St, London E.C.4, England. Ed. James Mosley. circ. 1,000. Indexed: Br.Hum.Ind.

655   US   ISSN 0193-3949
PRINTING TRADES BLUE BOOK. DELAWARE VALLEY-OHIO EDITION; directory of graphic arts operating firms and suppliers in Ohio, Pennsylvania, Delaware, Maryland, District of Columbia, and its Virginia suburbs. 1979. biennial. $67.65. A.F. Lewis Co. Inc. (New York), 79 Madison Ave., New York, NY 10016. TEL 212-679-0770. adv. index. circ. 6,000.

655   US   ISSN 0079-5348
PRINTING TRADES BLUE BOOK. NEW YORK EDITION; directory of graphic arts operating firms and suppliers in metropolitan New York and New Jersey. 1910. a. $67.65. A.F. Lewis Co. Inc. (New York), 79 Madison Ave., New York, NY 10016. TEL 212-679-0770. adv. index. circ. 6,000.

655   US   ISSN 0079-5356
PRINTING TRADES BLUE BOOK. NORTHEASTERN EDITION; directory of graphic arts operating firms and suppliers in New England and upstate New York. 1962/63. biennial. $67.95. A.F. Lewis, Inc. (New York), 79 Madison Ave., New York, NY 10016. TEL 212-679-0770. adv. index. circ. 6,000.

655   US   ISSN 0079-5364
PRINTING TRADES BLUE BOOK. SOUTHEASTERN EDITION; directory of graphic arts operating firms and suppliers in Virginia (except D.C. suburbs), W. Virginia, North Carolina, South Carolina, Georgia, Florida, Kentucky, Tennessee, Alabama, Mississippi, and Louisiana. 1961/62. biennial. $67.65. A.F. Lewis Co. Inc. (New York), 79 Madison Ave., New York, NY 10016. adv. index. circ. 6,000.

655   UK   ISSN 0079-5372
PRINTING TRADES DIRECTORY. 1960. a. £60. Benn Business Information Services Ltd., P.O. Box 20, Sovereign Way, Tonbridge, Kent TN9 1RQ, England. adv. index. circ. 2,500.

760 659.1   DK
PRODUKTIONSHAANDBOGEN; grafisk produktion - reklamevirksomhed. a. Grafiske Haandboger, Hellerupvej 66, 2900 Hellerup, Denmark. adv. circ. 5,051.

655   FR   ISSN 0066-3638
QUATRE MILLE IMPRIMERIES FRANCAISES.* 1960. a. 248.30 F. Societe des Editions de l' Imprimerie Nouvelle, 53 guai Seine 19e, Paris, France.
     Before 1966: Quatre Mille Imprimeries.

686.2   UK
SCOTTISH DECORATORS' YEAR BOOK AND REVIEW. a. Scottish Decorators' Federation, 249 W. George St., Glasgow G2 4RB, Scotland. Ed. I.W.S. Brown. adv. circ. 500.
     Formerly: Scottish Decorators' Review.

760   US   ISSN 0082-2299
T A G A PROCEEDINGS; technical papers presented at annual meeting. 1949. a. $55. Technical Association of the Graphic Arts, Rochester Institute of Technology, T & E Center, Box 9887, Rochester, NY 14623-0887. Ed. Michael H. Bruno. index. cum.index: 1949-1985. circ. 1,000. (back issues avail.) Indexed: Abstr.Bull.Inst.Pap.Chem. Graph.Arts Lit.Abstr.

676 686.2   US
TECHNICAL ASSOCIATION OF THE PULP AND PAPER INDUSTRY. PRINTING AND REPROGRAPHY CONFERENCE PROCEEDINGS. biennial. $49.95 to non-members; members $33.47. Technical Association of the Pulp and Paper Industry, Inc., Technology Park/Atlanta, Box 105113, Atlanta, GA 30348. TEL 404-446-1400.

686.2   US
TYPOGRAPHY 7. 1980. a. $35. (Type Directors Club of New York) Watson-Guptill Publications, One Astor Plaza, New York, NY 10036. TEL 212-363-5679. circ. 20,000.
     Formerly: Typography (ISSN 0275-6870)

686.2   US
UNITED STATES TRADE SHOW TIMES. (Separate editions for each trade show) 1965. irreg. free. Fichera Publications, Inc., 777 S. State Rd. 7, Margate, FL 33068. TEL 305-971-4360. adv. circ. 10,000.

686.2   GW   ISSN 0724-9586
WOLFENBUETTLER SCHRIFTEN ZUR GESCHICHTE DES BUCHWESENS. 1977. irreg., vol.13, 1987. price varies. Verlag Otto Harrassowitz, Taunusstr. 14, Postfach 2929, D-6200 Wiesbaden, W. Germany (B.R.D.) Ed. Paul Raabe.

PRINTING — Abstracting, Bibliographies, Statistics

016 686.2   NE
ANNUAL BIBLIOGRAPHY OF THE HISTORY OF THE PRINTED BOOK AND LIBRARY. Variant title: A B H B. (Text in English) 1973. a. price varies. Martinus Nijhoff Publishers, Postbus 163, 3300 AD Dordrecht, Netherlands. Ed. H.D.L. Vervliet.

686.2 070   CN   ISSN 0575-9412
CANADA. STATISTICS CANADA. PRINTING, PUBLISHING AND ALLIED INDUSTRIES. (Catalogue 36-203) (Text in English and French) 1920. a. Can.$20($21) Statistics Canada, Communications Division, 3rd Floor, R.H. Coats Bldg., Ottawa, Ont. K1A 0T6, Canada TEL 613-993-7276. (Subscr. to: Publications Sales and Services, Ottawa, Ont. K1A 0T6, Canada)

760 016   US   ISSN 0017-3282
GRAPHIC ARTS ABSTRACTS. 1947. m. $40 to non-members. ‡ Graphic Arts Technical Foundation, 4615 Forbes Ave., Pittsburgh, PA 15213. TEL 412-621-6941. Ed. Diana Lammert. bk. rev. index. circ. 6,500. (also avail. in microfilm from UMI; reprint service avail. from UMI) Indexed: Abstr.Bull.Inst.Pap.Chem. Graph.Arts Lit.Abstr.

686.2 016 UR ISSN 0320-5223
REFERATIVNYI ZHURNAL. EKONOMIKA, ORGANIZATSIYA, TEKHNOLOGIYA I OBORUDOVANIE POLIGRAFICHESKOGO PROIZVODSTVA. 1975. m. 46.20 Rub. Vsesoyuznyi Institut Nauchno-Tekhnicheskoi Informatsii (VINITI), Baltiiskaya ul. 14, Moscow A-219, Russian S.F.S.R., U.S.S.R. (Subscr. to: Mezhdunarodnaya Kniga, Dimitrova ul. 39, 113095 Moscow, Russian S.F.S.R., U.S.S.R.)

PRINTING — Computer Applications

see also Computers — Computer Graphics

PRODUCTION OF GOODS AND SERVICES

see Business and Economics — Production of Goods and Services

PROTESTANTISM

see Religions and Theology — Protestant

PSYCHIATRY AND NEUROLOGY

see Medical Sciences — Psychiatry and Neurology

PSYCHOLOGY

see also Medical Sciences — Psychiatry and Neurology

370.15 DK ISSN 0105-2861
AARHUS UNIVERSITET. PSYKOLOGISK SKRIFTSERI. (Text in Danish; summaries in English) irreg. (Aarhus Universitet, Psykologisk Institut) Bibliotekscentralen, Telegrafvej 5, DK-2750 Ballerup, Denmark. Indexed: Psychol.Abstr.

150 US
ACADEMIC PRESS SERIES IN COGNITION AND PERCEPTION. 1973. irreg., unnumbered, latest 1986. price varies. Academic Press, Inc., Orlando, FL 32887. TEL 305-345-2000. Eds. Edward C. Carterette, Morton P. Friedman.

155 SW ISSN 0065-1605
ACTA PSYCHOLOGICA - GOTHOBURGENSIA.*
(Text in English) 1956. irreg. price varies. Goeteborgs Universitet, Department of Psychology, Fack, S-400 20 Goeteborg 14, Sweden. Ed. John Elmgren.

370.15 150 PL ISSN 0208-6093
ACTA UNIVERSITATIS LODZIENSIS: FOLIA PAEDAGOGICA ET PSYCHOLOGICA. (Text in German and Polish; summaries in English and German) 1980. irreg. Uniwersytet Lodzki, Drukarnia Wojskowa, Ul. Gdanska 130, Lodz, Poland. charts.
Educational

370.15 150 HU ISSN 0324-7260
ACTA UNIVERSITATIS SZEGEDIENSIS DE ATTILA JOZSEF NOMINATAE. SECTIO PAEDAGOGICA ET PSYCHOLOGICA. (Text in English or Hungarian) 1956. a. exchange basis. Attila Jozsef University, c/o E. Szabo, Exchange Librarian, Dugonics ter 13, P.O.B. 393, Szeged H-6701, Hungary (Subscr. to: Kultura, Box 149, H-1389 Budapest, Hungary) Ed. Lajos Duro. circ. 300. Indexed: M.L.A.
Educational

155 US ISSN 0748-8572
ADVANCES IN APPLIED DEVELOPMENTAL PSYCHOLOGY. 1985. a. price varies. Ablex Publishing Corp., 355 Chestnut St., Norwood, NJ 07648. TEL 201-767-8450. Ed. Irving Sigel.

150 301.1 US
ADVANCES IN APPLIED SOCIAL PSYCHOLOGY. 1980. irreg., vol.3, 1986. Lawrence Erlbaum Associates, Inc., 365 Broadway, Hillsdale, NJ 07642. Eds. M.J. Saks, L. Saxe. (back issues avail.) Indexed: Curr.Cont. Psychol.Abstr.

155 US
ADVANCES IN BEHAVIORAL BIOLOGY. irreg. price varies. Plenum Publishing Corp., 233 Spring St., New York, NY 10013. TEL 212-620-8047.

152.8 330.9 US ISSN 0890-0159
ADVANCES IN BEHAVIORAL ECONOMICS. 1986. irreg. price varies. Ablex Publishing Corp., 355 Chestnut St., Norwood, NJ 07648. TEL 201-767-8450. Eds. Leonard Green, John Kagel.

155 618.92 US ISSN 0065-2407
ADVANCES IN CHILD DEVELOPMENT AND BEHAVIOR. 1963. irreg., vol.19, 1985. Academic Press, Inc., Orlando, FL 32887. TEL 305-345-2000. Eds. Hanye W. Reese. L. P. Lipsitt. index. Indexed: Biol.Abstr. Ind.Med. SSCI.

155 US ISSN 0276-9913
ADVANCES IN DESCRIPTIVE PSYCHOLOGY. 1981. a. $26.25 to individuals; institutions $52.50. (Society for Descriptive Psychology) J A I Press Inc., Box 1678, 36 Sherwood Pl., Greenwich, CT 06836. TEL 203-661-7602. Eds. Keith E. Davis, Thomas O. Mitchell. Indexed: Psychol.Abstr.

155 US ISSN 0275-3049
ADVANCES IN DEVELOPMENTAL PSYCHOLOGY. 1981. irreg., vol.5, 1986. Lawrence Erlbaum Associates, Inc., 365 Broadway, Hillsdale, NJ 07642. TEL 201-666-4110. Ed.Bd. bibl. charts. illus. (back issues avail.) Indexed: Curr.Cont. Psychol.Abstr.

150 614.7 US
ADVANCES IN ENVIRONMENTAL PSYCHOLOGY. 1978. irreg., vol.6, 1986. Lawrence Erlbaum Associates, Inc., 365 Broadway, Hillsdale, NJ 07642. TEL 201-666-4110. Ed.Bd. (back issues avail.) Indexed: Curr.Cont. Psych.Abstr.

ADVANCES IN EXPERIMENTAL SOCIAL PSYCHOLOGY. see SOCIOLOGY

301.1 US ISSN 0270-9228
ADVANCES IN FAMILY INTERVENTION, ASSESSMENT AND THEORY; a research annual. 1980. a. $23.75 to individuals; institutions $47.50. J A I Press Inc., Box 1678, 36 Sherwood Pl., Greenwich, CT 06836. TEL 203-661-7602. Ed. John P. Vincent. Indexed: Psychol.Abstr.

155.937 616.89 US ISSN 0747-6353
ADVANCES IN FORENSIC PSYCHOLOGY AND PSYCHIATRY. 1984. a. price varies. Ablex Publishing Corp., 355 Chestnut St., Norwood, NJ 07648. TEL 201-767-8450. Ed. Robert W. Rieber.

ADVANCES IN HEALTH EDUCATION. see EDUCATION — Teaching Methods And Curriculum

ADVANCES IN INFANCY RESEARCH. see MEDICAL SCIENCES — Pediatrics

150 US ISSN 0163-5379
ADVANCES IN INSTRUCTIONAL PSYCHOLOGY. 1978. irreg., vol.3, 1986. Lawrence Erlbaum Associates, Inc., 365 Broadway, Hillsdale, NJ 07642. TEL 201-666-4110. Ed. Robert Glaser. illus. (back issues avail.) Indexed: Curr.Cont. Psych.Abstr.

ADVANCES IN LEARNING AND BEHAVIORAL DISABILITIES. see CHILDREN AND YOUTH — About

614.58 US
ADVANCES IN MOTIVATION AND ACHIEVEMENT. 1984. a. $23.75 to individuals; institutions $47.50. J A I Press Inc., Box 1678, 36 Sherwood Pl., Greenwich, CT 06836. TEL 203-661-7602. Eds. David E. Bartz, Martin L. Maehr.

155 US ISSN 8755-0032
ADVANCES IN NEURAL AND BEHAVIORAL DEVELOPMENT. 1985. a. price varies. Ablex Publishing Corp., 355 Chestnut St., Norwood, NJ 07648. TEL 201-767-8450. Ed. Richard N. Aslin.

150 616.8 US ISSN 0278-2367
ADVANCES IN PERSONALITY ASSESSMENT. 1982. irreg., vol.6, 1986. Lawrence Erlbaum Associates, Inc., 365 Broadway, Box 237, Hillsdale, NJ 07642. TEL 201-666-4110. Eds. Charles D. Spielberger, James N. Butcher. (back issues avail.) Indexed: Curr.Cont. Psychol.Abstr.

370.15 US ISSN 0270-3920
ADVANCES IN SCHOOL PSYCHOLOGY. 1981. irreg., latest vol.5. Lawrence Erlbaum Associates, Inc., 365 Broadway, Box 237, Hillsdale, NJ 07642. TEL 201-666-4110. Ed. Thomas R. Kratochwill. (back issues avail.) Indexed: Curr.Cont. Psych.Abstr.

157 US
ADVANCES IN TEST ANXIETY RESEARCH. 1982. irreg., vol.3, 1985. Lawrence Erlbaum Associates, Inc., 365 Broadway, Box 237, Hillsdale, NJ 07642. TEL 201-666-4110. Ed.Bd. (back issues avail.)

152.8 371.3 US ISSN 0278-2359
ADVANCES IN THE PSYCHOLOGY OF HUMAN INTELLIGENCE. 1982. irreg., vol.3, 1986. Lawrence Erlbaum Associates, Inc., 365 Broadway, Box 237, Hillsdale, NJ 07642. TEL 201-666-4110. Ed. Robert J. Sternberg. (back issues avail.) Indexed: Curr.Cont. Psych.Abstr.

150 US ISSN 0065-3454
ADVANCES IN THE STUDY OF BEHAVIOR. 1965. irreg., vol. 16, 1986. Academic Press, Inc., Orlando, FL 32887. TEL 305-345-2000. Ed.Bd. index. Indexed: Biol.Abstr. Sci.Cit.Ind. Dairy Sci.Abstr. Ind.Sci.Rev.

150 301.16 US
ADVANCES IN THE STUDY OF COMMUNICATION AND AFFECT. 1974. irreg. price varies. Plenum Publishing Corp., 233 Spring St., New York, NY 10013. TEL 212-620-8047.

157 US
AMERICAN ASSOCIATION OF SUICIDOLOGY. PROCEEDINGS OF THE ANNUAL MEETING. 8th., 1975. a. price varies. American Association of Suicidology, 2459 S. Ash, Denver, CO 80222. TEL 303-692-0985. Ed. Dr. Roni Cohen-Sandler. circ. 1, 000. (looseleaf format; back issues avail.)

614.58 614.58 US ISSN 0730-7128
AMERICAN ASSOCIATION ON MENTAL DEFICIENCY. MONOGRAPHS. 1973. irreg. price varies. American Association on Mental Deficiency, 1719 Kalorama Rd., N.W., Washington, DC 20009. TEL 202-387-1968. Ed. Michael J. Begab.

616.89
AMERICAN GROUP PSYCHOTHERAPY MONOGRAPH SERIES. 1984. irreg., no.4 in prep. price varies. International Universities Press, Inc., 59 Boston Post Rd., Box 1524, Madison, CT 06443-1524. TEL 203-245-4000. Ed. Dr. Robert Dies.

150 US ISSN 0065-9843
AMERICAN PSYCHOANALYTIC ASSOCIATION. JOURNAL. MONOGRAPH. 1953. irreg., no.4, 1971. International Universities Press, Inc., 59 Boston Post Rd., Box 1524, Madison, CT 06443-1524. TEL 203-245-4000. Indexed: Biol.Abstr. SSCI.

150.19 US
AMERICAN PSYCHOANALYTIC ASSOCIATION. WORKSHOP SERIES. 1985. irreg. price varies. International Universities Press, Inc., 59 Boston Post Rd., Box 1524, Madison, CT 06443-1524. TEL 203-245-4000. Ed. Arnold Rothstein.

AMERICAN PSYCHOLOGICAL ASSOCIATION. DIRECTORY. see BIOGRAPHY

AMERICAN PSYCHOLOGICAL ASSOCIATION. MEMBERSHIP REGISTER. see BIOGRAPHY

362.29 US ISSN 0740-0454
AMERICAN UNIVERSITY STUDIES. SERIES 8. PSYCHOLOGY. 1983. irreg. Peter Lang Publishing, Inc., 62 W. 45th. St., New York, NY 10036. TEL 212-302-6740. Ed. Jay Wilson.

PSYCHOLOGY

AMSTERDAM STUDIES IN THE THEORY AND HISTORY OF LINGUISTIC SCIENCE. SERIES 2: CLASSICS IN PSYCHOLINGUISTICS. see *LINGUISTICS*

301.1 150   IO
ANDA; majalah psikologi populer. irreg. Yayasan Bina Psikologi, c/o Mulyono & Associates, Gedung Pant Trisula, Jalan Menteng Raya 35, Box 3216, Jakarta, Indonesia.

155.4   US
ANNALS OF CHILD DEVELOPMENT. 1984. a. $23.75 to individuals; institutions $47.50. J A I Press Inc., Box 1678, Greenwich, CT 06830. TEL 203-661-7602. Ed. Grover J. Whitehurst.

152.8   US
ANNALS OF THEORETICAL PSYCHOLOGY. 1984. irreg. Plenum Publishing Corp., 233 Spring St., New York, NY 10013. TEL 212-670-8047.

370.15   US
ANNUAL EDITIONS: EDUCATIONAL PSYCHOLOGY. 1981. a. $9.50. Dushkin Publishing Group, Inc., Sluice Dock, Guilford, CT 06437. Ed. Ian Neilsen.

ANNUAL EDITIONS: HUMAN SEXUALITY. see *BIOLOGY*

158.105   US   ISSN 0198-912X
ANNUAL EDITIONS: PERSONAL GROWTH AND BEHAVIOR. Cover title: Annual Editions: Personal Growth and Adjustment. 1975. a. $9.50. Dushkin Publishing Group, Inc., Sluice Dock, Guilford, CT 06437. TEL 203-453-4351. Ed. Ian Nielsen. illus. index. (back issues avail.)
Formerly: Annual Editions: Readings in Personality and Adjustment (ISSN 0361-3836)

150   US   ISSN 0272-3794
ANNUAL EDITIONS: PSYCHOLOGY. 1971. a. $9.50. Dushkin Publishing Group, Inc., Sluice Dock, Guilford, CT 06437. TEL 203-453-4351. Ed. Ian Nielsen.
Formerly: Annual Editions: Readings in Psychology (ISSN 0197-0542)

ANNUAL EDITIONS: READINGS IN HUMAN DEVELOPMENT. see *BIOLOGY — Physiology*

150   US   ISSN 0092-5055
ANNUAL OF PSYCHOANALYSIS. 1973. a. price varies. (Chicago Institute for Psychoanalysis) International Universities Press, Inc., 59 Boston Post Rd., Box 1524, Madison, CT 06443-1524. TEL 203-245-4000. Indexed: Biol.Abstr. Psychol.Abstr. Psychoanal.Abstr.

370   JA   ISSN 0452-9650
ANNUAL REPORT OF EDUCATIONAL PSYCHOLOGY IN JAPAN/KYOIKU SHINRIGAKU NEMPO. 1961. a. 1600 Yen. Japanese Association of Educational Psychology - Nihon Kyoiku-shinri Gakkai, c/o Faculty of Education, University of Tokyo, 7-3-1 Hongo, Bunkyo-ku, Tokyo 113, Japan.

150   US   ISSN 0066-4308
ANNUAL REVIEW OF PSYCHOLOGY. 1950. a. $31. Annual Reviews Inc., 4139 El Camino Way, Palo Alto, CA 94306. TEL 415-493-4400. Eds. Lyman W. Porter, Mark R. Rosenzweig. bibl. index. cum.index. (back issues avail.; reprint service avail. from ISI) Indexed: Biol.Abstr. Chem.Abstr. Curr.Cont. Excerp.Med. Ind.Med. Psychol.Abstr. SSCI. Sci.Cit.Ind. Soc.Sci.Ind. Adol.Ment.Hlth.Abstr. Child Devel.Abstr. DSH Abstr. Ind.Sci.Rev. Lang.& Lang.Behav.Abstr. M.M.R.I.

ANUARIO DE SOCIOLOGIA Y PSICOLOGIA JURIDICAS. see *LAW*

APPLIED SOCIAL PSYCHOLOGY ANNUAL. see *SOCIOLOGY*

ARCHIV FUER RELIGIONSPSYCHOLOGIE. see *RELIGIONS AND THEOLOGY*

ATTI DELLO PSICODRAMMA. see *THEATER*

152   CK   ISSN 0120-3797
AVANCES EN PSICOLOGIA CLINICA LATINOAMERICANA. 1982. a. $7. Foundation for the Advancement of Psychology, Apdo. 92621, Bogota, Colombia. Ed. Ruben Ardila. adv. bk. rev. bibl. illus. stat. circ. 2,500. Indexed: Biol.Abstr. Curr.Cont. Psychol.Abstr.

BASIC CONCEPTS IN EDUCATIONAL PSYCHOLOGY SERIES. see *EDUCATION*

150   US
BASIC CONCEPTS IN PSYCHOLOGY SERIES. irreg. price varies. Brooks-Cole Publishing Co., 555 Abrego St., Monterey, CA 93940. TEL 408-373-0728.

157   GW
BEITRAEGE ZUR INDIVIDUALPSYCHOLOGIE. 1978. irreg., no.7, 1986. price varies. Ernst Reinhardt GmbH und Co., Verlag, Kemnatenstr. 46, 8000 Munich 19, W. Germany (B.R.D.)

155.4   GW   ISSN 0340-0123
BEITRAEGE ZUR PSYCHODIAGNOSTIK DES KINDES. 1972. irreg., no.7, 1984. price varies. Ernst Reinhardt GmbH und Co., Verlag, Kemnatenstr. 46, 8000 Munich 19, W. Germany (B.R.D.) Eds. G. Biermann, M. Kos.

614.58   GW   ISSN 0173-0967
BEITRAEGE ZUR PSYCHOLOGIE UND SOZIOLOGIE DES KRANKEN MENSCHEN. 1974. irreg., no.6, 1986. price varies. Ernst Reinhardt GmbH und Co., Verlag, Kemnatenstr. 46, 8000 Munich 19, W. Germany (B.R.D.) Eds. G. Biermann, J. von Troschke.

150   US
BEITRAEGE ZUR PSYCHOPATHOLOGIE. irreg., vol.4, 1983. Springer-Verlag, 175 Fifth Ave., New York, NY 10010 TEL 212-460-1500. (And Berlin, Heidelberg, Tokyo and Vienna)

155.2   GW   ISSN 0067-5210
BEITRAEGE ZUR SEXUALFORSCHUNG. 1952. irreg., vol.63, 1987. price varies. (Deutsche Gesellschaft fuer Sexualforschung) Ferdinand Enke Verlag, Postfach 1304, 7000 Stuttgart 1, W. Germany (B.R.D.) Ed.Bd. Indexed: Biol.Abstr. Excerp.Med. Ind.Med.

BIBLIOGRAPHIES IN THE HISTORY OF PSYCHOLOGY AND PSYCHIATRY. see *PSYCHOLOGY — Abstracting, Bibliographies, Statistics*

BIBLIOGRAPHY OF EDUCATION THESES IN AUSTRALIA. see *EDUCATION — Abstracting, Bibliographies, Statistics*

150 610   US   ISSN 0094-0895
BIOFEEDBACK SOCIETY OF AMERICA. PROCEEDINGS OF THE ANNUAL MEETING. (Former name of organization: Biofeedback Research Society) 1972. a. $30 to non-members; members $15. Biofeedback Society of America, 10200 W. 44th Ave., Ste. 304, Wheat Ridge, CO 80033. TEL 303-422-8436. Ed. Francine Butler. adv. circ. 2,000.

150   UK   ISSN 0309-7773
BRITISH PSYCHOLOGICAL SOCIETY. ANNUAL REPORT. a. free. British Psychological Society, St. Andrew's House, 48 Princess Rd. East, Leicester LE1 7DR, England. circ. 12,500.

364   UK
BRITISH PSYCHOLOGICAL SOCIETY. DIVISION OF CRIMINOLOGICAL & LEGAL PSYCHOLOGY. OCCASIONAL PAPERS. 1981. irreg. British Psychological Society, Division of Criminological and Legal Psychology, St. Andrews House, 48 Princess Rd. E., Leicester LE1 7DR, England. Ed.Bd. circ. 250.

150   CN   ISSN 0068-9211
CANADIAN MENTAL HEALTH ASSOCIATION. ANNUAL REPORT/ASSOCIATION CANADIENNE POUR LA SANTE MENTALE. RAPPORT ANNUEL. 1926. a. free. Canadian Mental Health Association, 2160 Yonge St., Toronto, Ont. M4S 2Z3, Canada. TEL 416-484-7750. Indexed: Curr.Cont.

150.19 155.4   US
CARNEGIE-MELLON SYMPOSIA ON COGNITION. Also known as: Carnegie Symposium on Cognition. 1974. irreg., 19th 1985. Lawrence Erlbaum Associates, Inc., 365 Broadway, Box 237, Hillsdale, NJ 07642. TEL 201-666-4110. Indexed: Curr.Cont. Psychol.Abstr.

CASE ANALYSIS IN SOCIAL SCIENCE AND SOCIAL THERAPY. see *SOCIAL SCIENCES: COMPREHENSIVE WORKS*

CHILD BEHAVIOR AND DEVELOPMENT. see *MEDICAL SCIENCES — Pediatrics*

155.4   SZ   ISSN 0251-2467
CHILD HEALTH AND DEVELOPMENT. (Text in English and French) irreg. price varies. S. Karger AG, P.O. Box, CH-4009 Basel, Switzerland. Ed. M. Manciaux. Indexed: Biol.Abstr.

CHILD STUDY JOURNAL MONOGRAPH. see *EDUCATION*

150 130   CH
CHINESE JOURNAL OF PSYCHOLOGY. (Text in Chinese and English) 1958. a. $5. Chinese Psychological Association, c/o Department of Psychology, National Taiwan University, Taipei, Taiwan, Republic of China. Ed. Jong-Tsun Huang. adv. circ. 200. (back issues avail.) Indexed: Biol.Abstr. Curr.Cont. Psychol.Abstr. SSCI. ASCA.
Formerly: Acta Psychologica Taiwanica (ISSN 0065-1613)

150.19   US
CLASSICS IN PSYCHOANALYSIS. 1984. irreg., no. 6 in prep. price varies. (Chicago Institute for Psychoanaiysis) International Universities Press, Inc., 59 Boston Post Rd., Box 1524, Madison, CT 06443-1524. TEL 203-245-4000. Ed. Dr. George Pollock.

COGNITION AND LITERACY. see *EDUCATION*

301.1   US   ISSN 0732-1295
COGNITIVE SCIENCE SERIES (CAMBRIDGE) irreg., vol.8, 1985. Harvard University Press, 79 Garden St., Cambridge, MA 02138. TEL 617-495-2600.

150   US
COGNITIVE SCIENCE SERIES (HILLSDALE) 1981. irreg. Lawrence Erlbaum Associates, Inc., 365 Broadway, Box 237, Hillsdale, NJ 07642. TEL 201-666-4110. Eds. Donald A. Norman, Roger Schank. bibl. charts. illus. Indexed: Curr.Cont. Psychol.Abstr.

COLLECTION PSYCHOLOGIE ET PEDAGOGIE DE LA MUSIQUE. see *MUSIC*

156 109   US   ISSN 0267-9469
COMMENTS & CRITICISMS. 1983. irreg. Prytaneum Press, 1015 Bryan, Amarilld, TX 79102. TEL 806-372-7888. Ed. Don D. Davis. bk. rev. circ. 500.

150.9   FR
CONFLUENTS PSYCHANALYTIQUES. 1980. irreg. Societe d'Edition les Belles Lettres, 95 bd. Raspail, 75006 Paris, France.

155.937   US
CONNECTICUT HOSPICE NEWSLETTER. irreg. 61 Burban Dr., Branford, CT 06405. TEL 203-481-6231.

616.89   BL
CONTRIBUICOES EM PSICOLOGIA, PSIQUIATRIA E PSICANALISE. irreg. Editora Campus Ltda. (Subsidiary of: Elsevier North-Holland, Inc) Rua Barao de Itapagipe 55, Rio Comprido, 20261 Rio de Janeiro RJ, Brazil.

150   US   ISSN 0736-2714
CONTRIBUTIONS IN PSYCHOLOGY. 1983. irreg. price varies. Greenwood Press, 88 Post Rd. W., Box 5007, Westport, CT 06881. TEL 203-226-3571. bibl. index.

155.4 US
CONTRIBUTIONS TO RESIDENTIAL TREATMENT. 1957. a. $15. American Association of Children's Residential Centers, 440 First St., N.W., Ste. 310, Washington, DC 20001. TEL 202-638-1604. Ed. Claudia C. Waller. circ. 200. (back issues avail.)

150 CL
CUADERNOS DE PSICOLOGIA.* 1972. irreg. Universidad de Chile, Departamento de Psicologia, Av. Bernardo O'Higgins 1058, Casilla 10-D, Santiago, Chile. illus.

155.4 US
CULTURAL CONTEXT OF INFANCY. 1987. irreg. price varies. Ablex Publishing Corp., 355 Chestnut St., Norwood, NJ 07648. TEL 201-767-8450. Ed. J. Kevin Nugent.

150 US ISSN 0070-2145
CURRENT TOPICS IN CLINICAL AND COMMUNITY PSYCHOLOGY. 1969. irreg., vol.3, 1971. Academic Press, Inc., Orlando, FL 32887. TEL 305-345-2000. Ed. C.D. Spielberger.

150 US ISSN 8755-0040
CURRENT TOPICS IN HUMAN INTELLIGENCE. 1985. irreg. price varies. Ablex Publishing Corp., 355 Chestnut St., Norwood, NJ 07648. TEL 201-767-8450. Ed. Douglas Detterman.

370.15 150 US
CURRENT TOPICS IN LEARNING DISABILITIES. 1983. irreg. price varies. Ablex Publishing Corp., 355 Chestnut St., Norwood, NJ 07648. TEL 201-767-8450. Eds. James McKinney, Lynne Feagans.

DANMARKS LAERERHOESKOLE. INSTITUT FOR PAEDAGOGIK OG PSYKOLOGI. TESTSAMLING. see EDUCATION

150 301 US
DEATH AND DYING A TO Z. base vol. plus q. supplements. $69. Croner Publications, Inc., 211-05 Jamaica Ave., Queens Village, NY 11428. TEL 718-464-0866.

618.92 US
DEVELOPMENTAL & BEHAVIORAL PEDIATRICS: SELECTED TOPICS. 1987. irreg. price varies. Plenum Publishing Corp., 233 Spring St., New York, NY 10013. TEL 212-620-8047.

157 US
DEVELOPMENTS IN CLINICAL PSYCHOLOGY. 1984. irreg. price varies. Ablex Publishing Corp., 355 Chestnut St., Norwood, NJ 07648. TEL 201-767-8450. Ed. Glenn R. Caddy.

DIRECTORY FOR EXCEPTIONAL CHILDREN; a listing of educational and training facilities. see EDUCATION — Special Education And Rehabilitation

DIRECTORY OF BEHAVIORAL GRADUATE STUDY. see EDUCATION — Guides To Schools And Colleges

150 301 370 US ISSN 0731-8081
DIRECTORY OF UNPUBLISHED EXPERIMENTAL MENTAL MEASURES. 1974. irreg., vol.4, 1985. Human Sciences Press, Inc., 72 Fifth Ave., New York, NY 10011. Ed. Bert A. Goldman. (reprint service avail. from ISI,UMI)

616.891 FR ISSN 0012-477X
DOCUMENTS ET DEBATS.* 1970. irreg. (4-5/yr.) membership. Association Psychanalytique de France, 24 Place Dauphine, 75006 Paris, France. Ed. Dr. G. Rosolato. bk. rev. abstr. bibl. circ. 200. (processed)
Psychoanalysis

E R I C CLEARINGHOUSE ON TESTS, MEASUREMENT, AND EVALUATION. T M E REPORT SERIES. see EDUCATION

370 150 SW ISSN 0070-9263
EDUCATIONAL AND PSYCHOLOGICAL INTERACTIONS. (Text in English) 1964. irreg. free. Malmoe School of Education, Box 23501, S-200 45 Malmoe, Sweden. Ed. Aake Bjerstedt. Indexed: Psychol.Abstr. Child Devel.Abstr. Sociol.Abstr.

158 UR
EKSPERIMENTAL'NAYA I PRIKLADNAYA PSIKHOLOGIYA. vol.8, 1977. irreg. 0.80 Rub. per issue. Leningradskii Universitet, Universitetskaya Nab. 7/9, Leningrad B-164, Russian S.F.S.R., U.S.S.R. circ. 5,150.

150 UR
EKSPERIMENTAL'NOE ISSLEDOVANIE LICHNOSTI I TEMPERAMENTA. (Subseries of: Permskii Gosudarstvennyi Pedagogicheskii Institut. Uchenye Zapiski) irreg. 0.50 Rub. Permskii Gosudarstvennyi Pedagogicheskii Institut, Perm, Russian S.F.S.R., U.S.S.R. illus.

150 US
EMOTION; theory, research and experience. 1980. irreg., vol.3, 1985. Academic Press Inc., 111 Fifth Ave., New York, NY 10003. TEL 212-741-6800.

150.19 US
EMPIRICAL STUDIES OF PSYCHOANALYTIC THEORIES, 1 & 2. 1983. biennial. $29.95 per no. Analytic Press, Inc., 365 Broadway, Hillsdale, NJ 07642. TEL 201-666-4110. Ed. Joseph Masling.

616.89 US
ENCOUNTERER. 1971. irreg. $5 for 20 nos. Golden Gate Foundation for Group Treatment, Box 1141, Vallejo, CA 94590. Ed. Dr. F.H. Ernst.

301.15 US
EUROPEAN MONOGRAPHS IN SOCIAL PSYCHOLOGY. 1971. irreg., no.35, 1985. $49.50. (European Association of Experimental Social Psychology) Academic Press Inc., Orlando, FL 32887. TEL 305-345-2000. Eds. R. Eiser, K. Scherer. Indexed: Psychol.Abstr.

301.1 150 FR
FACTUELLES.* 1977. irreg. Editions Copernic, 14 rue d'Armorique, 75015 Paris, France. Dir. Alain de Benoist.

155.937 US
FOUNDATION OF THANATOLOGY SERIES.* irreg. price varies. Charles C. Thomas, Publisher, 2600 South First St., Springfield, IL 62717.

GAY COUNSELLING. see HOMOSEXUALITY

GENESIS OF BEHAVIOR. see MEDICAL SCIENCES — Psychiatry And Neurology

150.5 IT
GIORNALE ITALIANO DI PSICOLOGIA. QUADERNI. no.2, 1977. irreg. Societa Editrice il Mulino, Via Santo Stefano 6, 40125 Bologna, Italy.

150 378 US
GRADUATE STUDY IN PSYCHOLOGY AND ASSOCIATED FIELDS. 17th edt., 1984. a. $18.50 to non-members; members $14.50. American Psychological Association, Committee on Graduate Education & Training, Educational Affairs Office, 1200 17th St., N.W., Washington, DC 20036. Ed. Jan Woodring. circ. 15,000. Indexed: Psychol.Abstr.
Formerly (until 1983): Graduate Study in Psychology (ISSN 0072-5277)

150 US ISSN 0093-4763
GROUPS: A JOURNAL OF GROUP DYNAMICS AND PSYCHOTHERAPY. vol.5, 1974. a. $7. Association of Medical Group Psychoanalysts, c/o David Weisselberger, M.D., Ed., 185 E. 85 St., New York, NY 10028. TEL 212-534-5836. circ. controlled. Indexed: Excerp.Med. Psychol.Abstr.
Formerly: Journal of Psychoanalysis in Groups (ISSN 0022-3964)

150 GW ISSN 0085-1302
GRUPPENPSYCHOTHERAPIE UND GRUPPENDYNAMIK. BEIHEFTE. 1972. irreg., no.19, 1984. price varies. Vandenhoeck und Ruprecht, Theaterstr. 13, Postfach 37 53, 3400 Goettingen, W. Germany (B.R.D.) Ed. A. Heigl-Evers. circ. 1,900.

155.4 613.7 US
HANDBOOK OF PSYCHOLOGY AND HEALTH. 1982. irreg., vol.4, 1984. Lawrence Erlbaum Associates, Inc., 365 Broadway, Hillsdale, NJ 07642. TEL 201-666-4110. Eds. Andrew Baum, Jerome E. Singer. (back issues avail.) Indexed: Curr.Cont. Psychol.Abstr.

150 UK ISSN 0266-4771
HARVEST. 1954. a. £8($18) Analytical Psychology Club, 37 York Street Chambers, York St., London W1H 1DE, England. Ed. Joel Ryce-Menuhin. bk. rev.

150 CN ISSN 0085-1493
HERE AND NOW; a brief of news from the IPR. (Text and summaries in French) 1969. irreg. contr. free circ. Institute of Psychological Research, Inc., 34 Fleury St. W., Montreal 357, P.Q., Canada. TEL 514-382-3000. Ed. Jean-Marc Chevrier. adv. bk. rev. circ. 2,000.

150.19 US ISSN 0734-9831
HISTORY OF PSYCHOANALYSIS. 1984. irreg. (Chicago Institute for Psychoanalysis) International Universities Press, Inc., 59 Boston Post Rd., Box 1524, Madison, CT 06443-1524. TEL 203-245-4000. Ed. Dr. George H. Pollock. Indexed: Psychol.Abstr.

155 US
HUMAN BEHAVIOR AND ENVIRONMENT. 1976. irreg. price varies. Plenum Publishing Corp., 233 Spring St., New York, NY 10013. TEL 212-620-8047. Ed. Irwin Altman. Indexed: Psychol.Abstr.

155 US
HUMAN DEVELOPMENT (NORWOOD) 1986. irreg. price varies. Ablex Publishing Corp., 355 Chestnut St., Norwood, NJ 07648. TEL 201-767-8450. Ed. Sidney Strauss.

301.1 US ISSN 0163-5182
HUMAN FACTORS SOCIETY ANNUAL MEETING. PROCEEDINGS. 1972. a. $35. Human Factors Society, Box 1369, Santa Monica, CA 90406. TEL 213-394-9793. (also avail. in microform from UMI; reprint service avail. from UMI) Indexed: Int.Aerosp.Abstr.
Formerly: Human Factors Society. Proceedings of the Annual Meeting (ISSN 0363-9797)

370.15 155.5 301 US ISSN 0885-1174
HUMAN STRESS CURRENT ADVANCES IN RESEARCH. 1986. a. $57.50. A M S Press, Inc., 56 E. 13th St., New York, NY 10003. TEL 212-777-4700. Ed. James H. Humphrey. index. circ. 600. (back issues avail.)

HYMAN BLUMBERG SYMPOSIUM SERIES. see EDUCATION

150 IT
INCONSCIO E CULTURA. (Numbers not published consecutively) 1978. irreg., no.11, 1986. price varies. Liguori Editore s.r.l., Via Mezzocannone 19, 80134 Naples, Italy. TEL 081/20 6077. Ed. Aldo Carotenuto.

150 UK ISSN 0073-9561
INSTITUTE OF PSYCHOPHYSICAL RESEARCH. PROCEEDINGS. 1968. irreg. £7.95($18.95) per vol. Institute of Psychophysical Research, 118 Banbury Rd., Oxford OX2 6JU, England. Ed.Bd. circ. 2,500. (back issues avail.)

370 150 RM
INSTITUTUL PEDAGOGIC ORADEA. LUCRARI STIINTIFICE: SERIA PEDAGOGIE, PSIHOLOGIE, METODICA. (Continues in part its Lucrari Stiintifice: Seria Istorie, Stiinte Sociale, Pedagogie (1971-72), its Lucrari Stiintifice: Seria A and Seria B (1969-70), and its Lucrari Stiintifice (1967-68).) (Text in Rumanian, occasionally in English or French; summaries in English, French, German or Rumanian) 1967. irreg. Institutul Pedagogic Oradea, Calea Armatei Rosii Nr. 5, Oradea, Rumania.

150 NE
INTERNATIONAL ASSOCIATION FOR CROSS-CULTURAL PSYCHOLOGY. INTERNATIONAL CONFERENCE. SELECTED PAPERS. irreg., 6th, 1984, Acapulco, Mexico. Swets Publishing Service (Subsidiary of: Swets en Zeitlinger B.V.) Heereweg 347, 2161 CA Lisse, Netherlands (Dist. in the U.S. and Canada by: Hogrefe International, Inc., 525 Eglinton Ave. East, Toronto, Ont., Canada M4P 1N5)

150 BE ISSN 0074-1574
INTERNATIONAL ASSOCIATION OF APPLIED PSYCHOLOGY. PROCEEDINGS OF CONGRESS.* 1920. irreg., 1971, 17th, Liege. Editest, 16 rue de Chambery, 1040 Brussels, Belgium (Inquire: Prof. R. Piret, 47 rue Cesar Franck, 4000 Liege, Belgium)
Proceedings published in host country

137 US ISSN 0534-9044
INTERNATIONAL CONGRESS OF GRAPHOANALYSTS. PROCEEDINGS. 1929. a. International Graphoanalysis Society, 111 N. Canal St., Chicago, IL 60606. TEL 312-930-9446. Ed. V. Peter Ferrara. circ. 5,000.

150 NE ISSN 0085-2112
INTERNATIONAL CONGRESS OF PSYCHOLOGY. PROCEEDINGS. quadrennial; 1984, 23rd, Mexico. (International Union of Psychological Science) North-Holland (Subsidiary of: Elsevier Science Publishers B.V.) P.O. Box 211, 1000 AE Amsterdam, Netherlands.
Published by host national organization: Great Britain, 1969; Japan, 1972; France, 1976; German Democratic Republic, 1980.

301.1 320 US ISSN 0047-0732
INTERNATIONAL JOURNAL OF GROUP TENSIONS. 1971. a. $20 to individuals; institutions $28. International Organization for the Study of Group Tensions, 240 E. 76th St., New York, NY 10021. Ed. Benjamin B. Wolman. adv. bk. rev. bibl. index. circ. 600. (also avail. in microform from UMI; reprint service avail. from UMI) Indexed: Psychol.Abstr. SSCI.

150 BE
INTERNATIONAL LEAGUE OF SOCIETIES FOR PERSONS WITH MENTAL HANDICAP. WORLD CONGRESS PROCEEDINGS. (Text in English, French, German and Spanish) irreg., 7th, 1978, Vienna. International League of Societies for the Mentally Handicapped, 248 Av. Louise, Bte. 17, B-1050 Brussels, Belgium. Ed. P.J. Renoir.
Formerly: International League of Societies for the Mentally Handicapped. World Congress Proceedings (ISSN 0074-6754)

150 UK ISSN 0074-8137
INTERNATIONAL SERIES IN EXPERIMENTAL PSYCHOLOGY. 1964. irreg., vol.26, 1983. price varies. Pergamon Press, Ltd., Headington Hill Hall, Oxford OX3 OBW, England (U.S. subscr. to: Maxwell House, Fairview Park, Elmsford, NY 10523) Indexed: Math.R.

150 GW ISSN 0075-2363
JAHRBUCH DER PSYCHOANALYSE; Beitraege zur Theorie und Praxis. 1964. irreg., vol.13, 1981. price varies. Friedrich Frommann Verlag Guenther Holzboog GmbH und Co., Postfach 500460, Koenig-Karl-Str. 27, 7000 Stuttgart 50, W. Germany (B.R.D.) Ed.Bd. adv. circ. 1,000. Indexed: Psychol.Abstr.

150 GW ISSN 0075-2924
JAHRESKATALOG PSYCHOLOGIE. a. DM.29.80. Werbegemeinschaft Elwert und Meurer, Hauptstr. 101, 1000 Berlin 62, W. Germany (B.R.D.) adv.

JAPANESE BULLETIN OF ART THERAPY. see *ART*

150 UK ISSN 0143-1218
JOURNAL OF BIODYNAMIC PSYCHOLOGY. 1980. a. £3. Biodynamic Psychology Publications, Boyesen Institute for Biodynamic Psychology, Centre Ave., Acton, London W.3, England. Ed. Courtney Young. adv. bk. rev. circ. 1,000.

616.89 200 US ISSN 0886-5477
JOURNAL OF PASTORAL PSYCHOTHERAPY. 1986. a. $24 to individuals; institutions $32; libraries $42. Haworth Press, Inc., 28 E. 22nd St., New York, NY 10010-6194. Ed. Harold T. Kriesel. (also avail. in microfiche)

JYVASKYLA STUDIES IN EDUCATION, PSYCHOLOGY AND SOCIAL RESEARCH. see *EDUCATION*

616.89 GW ISSN 0343-9429
KLINISCHE PSYCHOLOGIE UND PSYCHOPATHOLOGIE. 1978. irreg., no.37, 1985. price varies. Ferdinand Enke Verlag, Postfach 1304, D 7000 Stuttgart 1, W. Germany (B.R.D.) Ed. H. Remschmidt.

LAW AND PSYCHOLOGY REVIEW. see *LAW*

150 US
LEHR- UND FORSCHUNGSTEXTE PSYCHOLOGIE/LECTURE NOTES IN PSYCHOLOGY. (Text in German) 1981. irreg., vol.11, 1984. Springer-Verlag, 175 Fifth Ave., New York, NY 10010 TEL 212-460-1500. (And Berlin, Heidelberg, Tokyo and Vienna) Ed.Bd.

301.1 150 UK ISSN 0267-7172
LIBERTARIAN ALLIANCE. PSYCHOLOGICAL NOTES. 1985. irreg. £5($10) Libertarian Alliance, 3 Langley Court, Covent Garden, London WC2E 9JY, England.

156 US
LIBRARY OF ANALYTICAL PSYCHOLOGY SERIES. 1973. irreg. vol.7, 1986. (Society of Analytical Psychology) Academic Press Inc., Orlando, FL 32887. TEL 305-345-2000. Ed. K. Lambert.

301.1 US
LIMERENCE FORUM; open forum and research instrument. 1982. irreg. price varies. c/o Randall Tennor, Ed., Rd. 2, Box 251, Millsboro, DE 19966.

LITUANISTIKA V S.S.S.R. FILOSOFIYA I PSIKHOLOGIYA; nauchno-referativnyi sbornik. see *PHILOSOPHY*

MATHEMATICS EDUCATION LIBRARY. see *EDUCATION*

155.4 US
MENTAL HEALTH IN CHILDREN. 1975. irreg. $39.95. P J D Publications Ltd., Box 966, Westbury, NY 11590. TEL 516-626-0650. Ed. Dr. D. V. Siva Sankar. (back issues avail.)

151.22 371.26 US ISSN 0076-6461
MENTAL MEASUREMENTS YEARBOOK. 1938. irreg., every 3-5 yrs. price varies. Buros Institute of Mental Measurements, 135 Bancroft, University of Nebraska-Lincoln, Lincoln, NE 68588-0348 (Dist. by: University of Nebraska Press, 901 N. 17th St., Lincoln, NE 68588-0520)
●Also available online.

155.4 US ISSN 0076-9266
MINNESOTA SYMPOSIA ON CHILD PSYCHOLOGY. 1966. a. (University of Minnesota, Institute of Child Development) Lawrence Erlbaum Associates, Inc., 365 Broadway, Box 237, Hillsdale, NJ 07642. TEL 201-666-4110. (back issues avail.) Indexed: Biol.Abstr. Curr.Cont. Psych.Abstr. SSCI.

150 130 SP ISSN 0077-0469
MONOGRAFIAS DE PSICOLOGIA, NORMAL Y PATOLOGICA. 1945. irreg. price varies. Espasa-Calpe, S. A., Carretera de Irun, km. 12,200, Apdo. 547, 28049 Madrid, Spain. Ed. Jose Germain.

150 PL ISSN 0077-0515
MONOGRAFIE PSYCHOLOGICZNE. (Text in Polish; summaries in English and Russian) 1968. irreg., vol.50, 1985. price varies. (Polska Akademia Nauk, Komitet Nauk Psychologicznych) Ossolineum, Publishing House of the Polish Academy of Sciences, Rynek 9, 50-106 Wroclaw, Poland (Dist. by: Ars Polona-Ruch, Krakowskie Przedmiescie 7, Warsaw, Poland) Ed. Tadeusz Tomaszewski. Indexed: Math.R.

150 FR ISSN 0077-071X
MONOGRAPHIES FRANCAISES DE PSYCHOLOGIE. 1959. irreg., no.27, 1974. price varies. Editions du C N R S, 295 rue St. Jacques, 75005 Paris, France. Indexed: Psychol.Abstr.

MONOGRAPHS ON INFANCY. see *MEDICAL SCIENCES — Pediatrics*

MUSIKPSYCHOLOGIE. see *MUSIC*

150 US ISSN 0271-7557
NAROPA INSTITUTE JOURNAL OF PSYCHOLOGY. 1980. irreg. $10. (Naropa Institute) Nalanda Press, 2130 Arapahoe Ave., Boulder, CO 80302. TEL 303-444-2373. Ed. Dr. Edward M. Podvall. bk. rev. circ. 2,000. (back issues avail.) Indexed: Psychol.Abstr.

NATIONAL GUILD OF CATHOLIC PSYCHIATRISTS. BULLETIN. see *MEDICAL SCIENCES — Psychiatry And Neurology*

150.19 US ISSN 0077-5339
NATIONAL PSYCHOLOGICAL ASSOCIATION FOR PSYCHOANALYSIS. BULLETIN. 1950. a. National Psychological Association for Psychoanalysis, Inc., 150 W. 13 St., New York, NY 10011. TEL 212-924-7440. circ. 7,000.

159 US ISSN 0070-2099
NEBRASKA SYMPOSIUM ON MOTIVATION (PUBLICATION) (Subseries of Research in Motivation Series) 1953. a. price varies. (University of Nebraska, Department of Psychology) University of Nebraska Press, 901 N. 17 St., Lincoln, NE 68588-0520. TEL 402-472-3581. index. cum.index: 1953-1958. (back issues avail.) Indexed: Ind.Med. Psychol.Abstr. SSCI.

NEW BABYLON: STUDIES IN THE SOCIAL SCIENCES. see *SOCIOLOGY*

370.15 150 US
NEW JERSEY JOURNAL OF SCHOOL PSYCHOLOGY. 1982. a. $5.95 to non-members; libraries $10. New Jersey Association of School Psychologists, c/o Howard Kaplan, Ed., 538 Andria Ave., No. 276, South Somerville, NJ 08876. Indexed: Psychol.Abstr.

150 US ISSN 0077-9008
NEW YORK PSYCHOANALYTIC INSTITUTE. KRIS STUDY GROUP. MONOGRAPHS. 1965. irreg., no.7, 1984. price varies. International Universities Press, Inc., 59 Boston Post Rd., Box 1524, Madison, CT 06443-1524. TEL 203-245-4000. Ed. Dr. Edward Joseph. Indexed: Biol.Abstr.

150 DK ISSN 0029-1463
NORDISK PSYKOLOGI. (Text in Danish, Norwegian, Swedish; occasionally in English; summaries in English) 1949. irreg. (4-6/yr.) Kr.300. Akademisk Forlag, Store Kannikestraede 8, P.O. Box 54, 1002 Copenhagen K, Denmark. Ed. Per Schultz Joergensen. adv. bk. rev. bibl. charts. illus. stat. index. circ. 7,000. Indexed: Biol.Abstr. Chem.Abstr. Psychol.Abstr. SSCI.

370.15 150 DK ISSN 0900-8772
NORDISK PSYKOLOGISK LITTERATUR. a. Kr.150. Bibliotekscentralen, Telegrafvej 5, DK-2750 Ballerup, Denmark.

ODENSE UNIVERSITY STUDIES IN PSYCHIATRY AND MEDICAL PSYCHOLOGY. see *MEDICAL SCIENCES — Psychiatry And Neurology*

614.58 US
OKLAHOMA DEPARTMENT OF MENTAL HEALTH. ANNUAL REPORT.* a. Department of Mental Health, Box 53277 Capitol Sta., Oklahoma City, OK 73105. TEL 405-521-0044. Ed. R. Brown. circ. 1,000.
Formerly: Mental Health Care in Oklahoma. Annual Report.

301.1 309 US
ONTARIO SYMPOSIA ON PERSONALITY AND SOCIAL COGNITION. 1981. a. Lawrence Erlbaum Associates, Inc., 365 Broadway, Hillsdale, NJ 07642. TEL 201-666-4110. Ed.Bd. index. Indexed: Curr.Cont. Psych.Abstr.

150 US
ORGANIZATIONAL AND OCCUPATIONAL PSYCHOLOGY. 1979. irreg., vol.17, 1986. Academic Press Inc., Orlando, FL 32887. TEL 305-345-2000. Ed. P. Warr.

150 II
OSMANIA UNIVERSITY. DEPARTMENT OF PSYCHOLOGY. RESEARCH BULLETIN. (Text in English) 1965. irreg. Osmania University, Department of Psychology, Hyderabad 500007, Andhra Pradesh, India. Ed. Shalini Bhogle. bk. rev. bibl. charts. stat. circ. controlled. Indexed: Psychol.Abstr.

150 US
P S C P TIMES. 1971. irreg. (6-8/yr.) $5. Philadelphia Society of Clinical Psychologists, Box 27014, Philadelphia, PA 19118. TEL 215-836-9196. Eds. Lita L. Schwartz, Frank A. Melone. circ. 200.

150 US ISSN 0079-0931
PERSONALITY AND PSYCHOPATHOLOGY; a series of texts, monographs and treatises. 1967. irreg., vol.35, 1986. Academic Press Inc., Orlando, FL 32887. TEL 305-345-2000. Ed. Brenden Maher. Indexed: Chem.Abstr.

301.1 150 CK ISSN 0120-3878
PERSPECTIVAS EN PSICOLOGIA. (Editions available in English and Spanish) 1982. a. Col.$400($6) Fundacion Universidad de Manizales, Facultad de Psicologia, Apdo. Aereo 868, Manizales, Colombia. Ed.Bd. bk. rev. circ. 1,000. Indexed: Psychol.Abstr.

PERSPECTIVES IN LAW AND PSYCHOLOGY. see LAW

PRAGMATICS AND DISCOURSE ANALYSIS. see LINGUISTICS

150 616.89 GW ISSN 0085-5073
PRAXIS DER KINDERPSYCHOLOGIE UND KINDERPSYCHIATRIE. BEIHEFTE. 1958. irreg. price varies. Vandenhoeck und Ruprecht, Theaterstr. 13, 3400 Goettingen, W. Germany (B.R.D.) Ed. Annemarie Duehrssen. Indexed: Ind.Med. Psychol.Abstr. SSCI. Lang.& Lang.Behav.Abstr.

158.7 US ISSN 0277-4178
PROBLEMS OF INDUSTRIAL PSYCHIATRIC MEDICINE SERIES. irreg., vol.11, 1985. prices varies. Human Sciences Press, Inc., 72 Fifth Ave., New York, NY 10011-8004. TEL 212-243-6000. Ed. Sherman N. Keiffer.

616.8 US ISSN 0099-037X
PROGRESS IN BEHAVIOR MODIFICATION. 1975. a., vol.20, 1986. $49.50. Academic Press, Inc., Orlando, FL 32887. TEL 305-345-2000. Ed. M. Hersen. Indexed: Ind.Med. SSCI. Adol.Ment.Hlth.Abstr.

155 US ISSN 0079-6255
PROGRESS IN EXPERIMENTAL PERSONALITY RESEARCH. 1964. irreg., vol.13, 1984. price varies. Academic Press, Inc Orlando, FL 32887. TEL 305-345-2000. Ed. B. Maher. Indexed: Biol.Abstr. Ind.Med.

131 US
PROGRESS IN PSYCHOBIOLOGY AND PHYSIOLOGICAL PSYCHOLOGY. 1967. irreg., vol.11, 1985. Academic Press, Inc, Orlando, FL 32887. TEL 305-345-2745. Eds. Eliot Stellar, James M. Sprague.
    Former titles: Psychobiology and Physiological Psychology; Until vol.6: Progress in Physiological Psychology (ISSN 0079-6670)

150 IT ISSN 0392-209X
PSICHIATRIA E CULTURA. 1979. irreg., no.7, 1984. Liguori Editore s.r.l., Via Mezzocannone 19, 80134 Naples, Italy. TEL 081/20 6077. Eds. Raffaello Vizioli, Antonio De Rosa.

158 UR
PSIKHOLOGICHESKIE ISSLEDOVANIYA. no.6, 1976. irreg. Moskovskii Universitet, Leninskie Gory, Moscow V-234, Russian S.F.S.R., U.S.S.R. circ. 5, 500.

150.19 200 615.7 US ISSN 0892-371X
PSYCHEDELIC MONOGRAPHS AND ESSAYS. 1985. a. $8. P M & E, Inc., 624 N.E. 12th Ave., No. 1, Ft. Lauderdale, FL 33301. TEL 305-763-8436. Ed. Thomas Lyttle. adv. bk. rev. circ. 10,000. (back issues avail.)

155.4 US ISSN 0079-7308
PSYCHOANALYTIC STUDY OF THE CHILD. 1945. a. price varies. Yale University Press, 92A Yale Sta., New Haven, CT 06520. TEL 203-432-0940. Ed. Albert J. Solnit, M.D. Indexed: Biol.Abstr. Educ.Ind. Excerp.Med. Ind.Med. Psychol.Abstr. SSCI. Psychoanal.Abstr.

150 NE ISSN 0079-7324
PSYCHOLOGEN ADRESBOEK. 1960. a. fl.15. Nederlands Instituut van Psychologen - Netherlands Psychological Association, Nicolaas Maesstraat 120, Postbus 5362, 1007 AJ Amsterdam, Netherlands. adv. circ. 6,000.

370.15 CS
PSYCHOLOGIA A SKOLA. 1972. irreg., approx. 2/yr. price varies. Slovenske Pedagogicke Nakladatelstvo, Sasinkova 5, 815 60 Bratislava, Czechoslovakia.

150 370 PL
PSYCHOLOGIA-PEDAGOGIKA. 1961. irreg. price varies. Adam Mickiewicz University Press, Marchlewskiego 128, 61-874 Poznan, Poland. bk. rev. Indexed: Psychol.Abstr.
    Formerly: Uniwersytet im. Adama Mickiewicza w Poznaniu. Wydzial Historyczny. Prace. Seria Psychologia-Pedagogika (ISSN 0083-4254)

150 GW
PSYCHOLOGIA UNIVERSALIS FORSCHUNGSERGEBNISSE AUS DEM GESAMTGEBIET DER PSYCHOLOGIE. 1952. irreg., no.47, 1985. price varies. Verlag Anton Hain GmbH, Adelheidstr. 2, Postfach 1220, 6240 Koenigstein, W. Germany (B.R.D.) Ed. Bd. Indexed: Psychol.Abstr.

150 SA
PSYCHOLOGICAL INSTITUTE OF THE REPUBLIC OF SOUTH AFRICA. PROCEEDINGS/SIELKUNDIGE INSTITUUT VAN DIE REPUBLIEK VAN SUID-AFRIKA. VERRIGTINGS. (Text in Afrikaans and English) 1962. a. Psychological Institute of the Republic of South Africa, Box 2729, Pretoria, South Africa.

616.89 US ISSN 0048-5748
PSYCHOLOGICAL ISSUES. 1959. irreg., no.56, 1986. price varies. International Universities Press, Inc., 59 Boston Post Rd., Box 1524, Madison, CT 06443-1524. TEL 203-245-4000. Ed. Herbert Schlesinger. illus. circ. 1,000. Indexed: Ind.Med. Psychol.Abstr. SSCI.

150 US ISSN 0079-7359
PSYCHOLOGICAL ISSUES. MONOGRAPH. irreg., no.55, 1983. price varies. International Universities Press, Inc., 59 Boston Post Rd., Box 1524, Madison, CT 06443-1524. TEL 203-245-4000. Ed. Herbert J. Schlesinger. Indexed: Biol.Abstr.

150 SW ISSN 0555-5620
PSYCHOLOGICAL RESEARCH BULLETIN. (Text in English) 1961. irreg, no.1-3, 1985. $15 incl. irreg. Monograph Series. Lunds Universitet, Department of Psychology, Paradisgatan 5 P, 22350 Lund, Sweden. TEL 046-10 87 55. Ed. G. Smith. bibl. charts. circ. 600. Indexed: Psychol.Abstr.

158.7 PL ISSN 0208-5569
PSYCHOLOGICZNE PROBLEMY FUNKCJONOWANIA CZLOWIEKA W SYTUACJI PRACY. (Text in Polish; summaries in English and Russian) 1980. irreg. price varies. Uniwersytet Slaski w Katowicach, Ul. Bankowa 14, 40-007 Katowice, Poland.

150 GW ISSN 0079-7405
PSYCHOLOGIE UND PERSON. 1961. irreg., no.25, 1985. price varies. Ernst Reinhardt, GmbH und Co., Verlag, Kemnatenstr. 46, 8000 Munich 19, W. Germany (B.R.D.)

370.15 301 613.7 US ISSN 0885-7423
PSYCHOLOGY AND SOCIOLOGY OF SPORT; current research interest 1986. a. $57.50. A M S Press, Inc., 56 E. 13th St., New York, NY 10003. TEL 212-777-4700. Ed. Lee Vander Veldon. index. circ. 550. (back issues avail.)

152.5 US ISSN 0079-7421
PSYCHOLOGY OF LEARNING AND MOTIVATION: ADVANCES IN RESEARCH AND THEORY. 1967. irreg., vol.20, 1986. $39.50. Academic Press, Inc Orlando, FL 32887. TEL 305-345-2000. Ed. G. H. Bower. Indexed: Educ.Ind. SSCI.

150 DK ISSN 0107-3060
PSYKOLOGISK LABORATORIUM. FORSKNINGSRAPPORT. (Text in Danish; summaries in English) 1983. irreg. free. University of Copenhagen, Department of Psychology, Njalsgade 94, 2300 Copenhagen S, Denmark. Ed. Benny Karpauschof. circ. 200.

150 HU ISSN 0079-7456
PSZICHOLOGIA A GYAKORLATBAN. 1963. irreg., vol.45, 1985. price varies. (Magyar Tudomanyos Akademia) Akademiai Kiado, Publishing House of the Hungarian Academy of Sciences, P.O. Box 24, H-1363 Budapest, Hungary.

150 HU ISSN 0079-7464
PSZICHOLOGIAI TANULMANYOK. (Text in Hungarian; summaries in English and German) 1958. irreg., vol.15, 1979. price varies. (Magyar Tudomanyos Akademia) Akademiai Kiado, Publishing House of the Hungarian Academy of Sciences, P.O. Box 24, H-1363 Budapest, Hungary. Indexed: Psychol.Abstr.

150 US
PUBLICATIONS FOR THE ADVANCEMENT OF THEORY AND HISTORY IN PSYCHOLOGY. 1980. irreg. price varies. Ablex Publishing Corp., 355 Chestnut St., Norwood, NJ 07648. Ed. David Bakan.

150 NZ ISSN 0079-7731
PUBLICATIONS IN PSYCHOLOGY. 1952. irreg., no.29, 1983. exchange basis. ‡ Victoria University of Wellington, Department of Psychology, Private Bag, Wellington, New Zealand. Eds. A.R. Forbes, M.J. White. circ. 100. Indexed: Psychol.Abstr.

157 US
RESEARCH IN CLINICAL PSYCHOLOGY. irreg., vol.14, 1985. U M I Research Press, 300 N. Zeeb Rd., Ann Arbor, MI 48106. Ed. Peter Nathan.

RESEARCH IN COMMUNITY AND MENTAL HEALTH; an annual compilation of research. see PUBLIC HEALTH AND SAFETY

301.18 US ISSN 0191-3085
RESEARCH IN ORGANIZATIONAL BEHAVIOR; an annual series of analytical essays and critical reviews. 1979. a. $28.75 to individuals; institutions $57.50. J A I Press Inc., 36 Sherwood Pl., Box 1678, Greenwich, CT 06836-1678. TEL 203-661-7602. Eds. Barry M. Staw, L.L. Cummings. Indexed: Psychol.Abstr. SSCI. ASCA.

616.8 US
REVIEW OF BEHAVIOR THERAPY: THEORY & PRACTICE. 1973. biennial. price varies. Guilford Publications, Inc., 200 Park Ave. S., New York, NY 10003. TEL 212-674-1900. Ed.Bd. (back issues avail.) Indexed: Biol.Abstr. Psychol.Abstr.
    Formerly: Annual Review of Behavior Therapy: Theory & Practice (ISSN 0091-6595)

302.05 US ISSN 0270-1987
REVIEW OF PERSONALITY AND SOCIAL PSYCHOLOGY. 1980? a. $29.95 cloth; $14.95 paper. (Society for Personality and Social Psychology) Sage Publications, Inc., 2111 W. Hillcrest Dr., Newbury Park, CA 91320. TEL 805-499-0721.

616.89 BL
REVISTA DE PSICANALISE INTEGRAL. 1978. a. $4. (International Society of Analytical Trilogy) Proton Editora Ltda., Av. Reboucas 3115, Sao Paulo, Brazil. Ed. Marc Andre R. Keppe. circ. 1, 500.
    Formerly: Analytical Trilogy.

157 BL ISSN 0048-7740
REVISTA DE PSICOLOGIA NORMAL E PATOLOGICA. (Suspended publication 1976-1979) N.S. 1979. irreg. Pontificia Universidade Catolica de Sao Paulo, Faculdade de Psicologia, Rua Monte Alegre 984, Sao Paulo, Brazil.

150 BE ISSN 0085-1078
RIJKSUNIVERSITEIT TE GENT. LABORATORIUM VOOR EXPERIMENTELE, DIFFERENTIELE EN GENETISCHE PSYCHOLOGIE. MEDEDELINGEN EN WERKDOCUMENTEN. (Text in Dutch, English or French) 1961. irreg. $10 per no. ‡ Rijksuniversiteit te Gent, Laboratorium voor Experimentele, Differentiele en Genetische Psychologie, H. Dunantlaan 2, 9000 Ghent, Belgium. (Co-sponsor: Centrum voor Ontwikkelingspsychologie) Ed. W. De Coster. circ. 500.

150   US   ISSN 0277-4240
RUTGERS PROFESSIONAL PSYCHOLOGY
  REVIEW. 1982. irreg., approx. a. $29.95.
  Transaction Books, Rutgers University, New
  Brunswick, NJ 08903. TEL 201-932-2280. Ed.
  Donald R. Peterson.

614.58   US
SAGE SERIES IN COMMUNITY MENTAL
  HEALTH. 1981. irreg. $29.95 cloth; $14.95 paper.
  Sage Publications, Inc., 2111 W. Hillcrest Dr.,
  Newbury Park, CA 91320. TEL 805-499-0721. Ed.
  Lonnie R. Snowden. bibl.
    Formerly: Sage Annual Reviews of Community
  Mental Health.

150   301.2   US
SAGE SERIES IN CROSS CULTURAL RESEARCH
  AND METHODOLOGY. 1977. irreg. $29.95 cloth;
  paper $14.95. Sage Publications, Inc., 2111 W.
  Hillcrest Dr., Newbury Park, CA 91320. TEL 805-
  499-0721. (And Sage Publications, Ltd., 28 Banner
  St., London EC1Y 8QE, England) Eds. Walter J.
  Lonner, John W. Berry.
    Formerly: Cross Cultural Research and
  Methodology Series.

SELF-HELP GROUP DIRECTORY. see SOCIAL
  SERVICES AND WELFARE

150   360   US
SELF HELP REPORTER NEWSLETTER. 1977.
  irreg. $10. National Self Help Clearinghouse, 33 W.
  42 St., New York, NY 10036. TEL 212-840-1259.
  Ed. Audrey Gartner. bk. rev. circ. 1,000.

150   361   US   ISSN 0146-0846
SERIES IN CLINICAL AND COMMUNITY
  PSYCHOLOGY. 1974. irreg., unnumbered, latest
  1983. price varies. Hemisphere Publishing
  Corporation, 79 Madison Ave., New York, NY
  10016. Eds. Charles D. Spielberger, Irwin G.
  Sarason. bibl. charts. illus. index. (back issues
  avail.) Indexed: Psychol.Abstr.
    Formerly: Series in Clinical Psychology.

155.937   US   ISSN 0275-3510
SERIES IN DEATH EDUCATION, AGING, AND
  HEALTH CARE. 1979. irreg., unnumbered, latest
  1984. price varies. Hemisphere Publishing
  Corporation, 79 Madison Ave., New York, NY
  10016. Ed. Hannelore Wass. bibl. charts. illus.
  index. (back issues avail.)

301.1   150   UK
SOCIAL PSYCHOLOGY OF LANGUAGE. 1982.
  irreg. Edward Arnold (Publishers) Ltd., 41 Bedford
  Square, London WC1B 3DQ, England.

150   US   ISSN 0362-0522
SPRING (DALLAS); an annual of archetypal
  psychology and Jungian thought. 1941. a. $15 to
  individuals; institutions $20. Spring Publications,
  Inc., Box 222069, Dallas, TX 75222. TEL 214-943-
  4093. Ed. James Hillman. adv. circ. 1,800. (back
  issues avail.) Indexed: Psychol.Abstr. PMR.

155   US
SPRINGER SERIES IN COGNITIVE
  DEVELOPMENT. 1982. irreg., latest 1986.
  Springer-Verlag, 175 Fifth Ave., New York, NY
  10010 TEL 212-460-1500. (Also Berlin, Heidelberg,
  Tokyo and Vienna)

301.1   150   US
SPRINGER SERIES IN SOCIAL PSYCHOLOGY.
  irreg. Springer-Verlag, 175 Fifth Ave., New York,
  NY 10010 TEL 212-460-1500. (Also Berlin,
  Heidelberg, Tokyo and Vienna) Ed. R.F. Kidd.

150   SW   ISSN 0345-0139
STOCKHOLMS UNIVERSITET. PSYKOLOGISKA
  INSTITUTIONEN. REPORT SERIES. (Text in
  English) 1954. irreg., approx. 20/yr. $1. Stockholms
  Universitet, Psykologiska Institutionen, S-106 91
  Stockholm, Sweden. Ed.Bd. index. circ. 500.
  Indexed: Psychol.Abstr.

152   SW   ISSN 0345-021X
STOCKHOLMS UNIVERSITET. PSYKOLOGISKA
  INSTITUTIONEN. REPORTS. SUPPLEMENT
  SERIES. (Text in English) 1970. irreg., approx. 5/
  yr. free. Stockholms Universitet, Psykologiska
  Institutionen, S-106 91 Stockholm, Sweden. Ed.Bd.
  index. circ. 500. Indexed: Psychol.Abstr.

150   US   ISSN 0364-1112
STRESS AND ANXIETY. (Subseries of: Series in
  Clinical and Community Psychology) 1975. irreg.,
  vol.9, 1985. price varies. Hemisphere Publishing
  Corporation, 79 Madison Ave., New York, NY
  10016. Eds. C.D. Spielberger, I.G. Sarason. bibl.
  charts. illus. index. (back issues avail.) Indexed:
  Psychol.Abstr.

STUDIA PSYCHOLOGICA ET PAEDAGOGICA.
  see EDUCATION

155.4   AU   ISSN 0255-6715
STUDIEN ZUR KINDERPSYCHOANALYSE. 1981.
  a. S.160. (Oesterreichische Studiengesellschaft fuer
  Kinderpsychoanalyse) Verband der
  Wissenschaftlichen Gesellschaft Oesterreichs,
  Lindengasse 37, A-1070 Vienna, Austria.

155.4   AU   ISSN 0255-6715
STUDIEN ZUR KINDERPSYCHOANALYSE.
  JAHRBUCH. 1981. a. S.160. (Oesterreichische
  Studiengesellschaft fuer Kinderpsychoanalyse)
  Verband der Wissenschaftlichen Gesellschaft
  Oesterreichs, Lindengasse 37, A-1070 Vienna,
  Austria.

STUDIENHEFTE PSYCHOLOGIE IN
  ERZIEHUNG UND UNTERRICHT. see
  EDUCATION — Higher Education

370.15   GW   ISSN 0173-0975
STUDIENREIHE PAEDAGOGISCHE
  PSYCHOLOGIE. 1978. irreg. price varies. Ernst
  Reinhardt GmbH und Co., Verlag, Kemnatenstr. 46,
  8000 Munich 19, W. Germany (B.R.D.) Ed. R.
  Dieterich.
    Educational

STUDIES IN EDUCATION AND PSYCHOLOGY.
  see EDUCATION

150   410 100   NE
STUDIES IN LINGUISTICS AND PHILOSOPHY.
  1978. irreg. price varies. D. Reidel Publishing Co.,
  Box 17, 3300 AA Dordrecht, Netherlands (And 190
  Old Derby St., Hingham, MA 02043) Ed.Bd.
  Indexed: Math.R.
    Formerly: Synthese Language Library.

STUDIES IN THE LEARNING SCIENCES. see
  EDUCATION

STUDIES IN THEORETICAL
  PSYCHOLINGUISTICS. see LINGUISTICS

152.8   US
STUDYING ORGANIZATIONS: INNOVATIONS
  IN METHODOLOGY. vol. 1-6, 1982. irreg. $9.95
  paper; cloth $18.95. Sage Publications, Inc., 2111
  W. Hillcrest Dr., Newbury Park, CA 91320. TEL
  805-499-0721. (Co-sponsor: American Psychological
  Association (Division 14)) (back issues avail.)

375   371.3   US   ISSN 0361-025X
TESTS IN PRINT. 1961. irreg., no.3, 1983. price
  varies. Buros Institute of Mental Measurements, 135
  Bancroft, University of Nebraska-Lincoln, Lincoln,
  NE 68588-0348 (Dist. by: University of Nebraska
  Press, 901 N. 17th St., Lincoln, NE 68588-0520)

THANATOLOGY ABSTRACTS. see
  PSYCHOLOGY — Abstracting, Bibliographies,
  Statistics

614.58   US
THEORETICAL ISSUES IN COGNITIVE
  SCIENCE. 1986. irreg. price varies. Ablex
  Publishing Corp., 355 Chestnut St., Norwood, NJ
  07648. TEL 201-767-8450. Ed. Zenon Pylyshyn.

THEORIA; a Swedish journal of philosophy. see
  PHILOSOPHY

150   US
THEORIEN DER PSYCHOLOGIE. vol.6, 1983.
  irreg. Springer-Verlag, 175 Fifth Ave., New York,
  NY 10010. TEL 212-460-1500. Ed. E. Scheerer.

155   618.92   US
THEORY AND RESEARCH IN BEHAVIORAL
  PEDIATRICS. 1982. irreg. price varies. Plenum
  Publishing Corp., 233 Spring St., New York, NY
  10013. TEL 202-620-8047. Ed.Bd.

150   JA   ISSN 0040-8743
TOHOKU PSYCHOLOGICA FOLIA. (Text in
  European languages) 1933. a. exchange basis. ‡
  Tohoku University, Department of Psychology,
  Faculty of Arts & Letters, Kawauchi, Sendai 980,
  Japan. Ed. Kinya Maruyama. charts. illus. index.
  circ. 800. Indexed: Biol.Abstr. Curr.Cont.
  Psychol.Abstr. Child Devel.Abstr.

155   US
TOPICS IN COGNITIVE DEVELOPMENT. 1977.
  irreg. price varies. (Jean Piaget Society) Plenum
  Publishing Corp., 233 Spring St., New York, NY
  10013. TEL 212-620-8047. Ed. Marilyn H. Appel.

150   US   ISSN 0161-7648
TOWSON STATE UNIVERSITY JOURNAL OF
  PSYCHOLOGY. 1977. irreg., vol.2, 1978. free. (Psi
  Chi, National Honor Society in Psychology)
  Towson State University, Department of
  Psychology, Towson, MD 21204. TEL 301-321-
  2634. circ. 700. Indexed: Psychol.Abstr.

614.58   US
TRANSITIONS IN MENTAL RETARDATION.
  1984. a. price varies. Ablex Publishing Corp., 355
  Chestnut St., Norwood, NJ 07648. TEL 201-767-
  8450. Eds. James Mulick, Richard Antonak.

137.7   FR   ISSN 0041-2864
TRIBUNE GRAPHOLOGIQUE; l'annuaire de la
  graphologie. 1950. a. 8 F. Institut International de
  Recherches Graphologiques, Pave du Roy, 77780
  Bourron Marlotte, France. Ed. H. Ostrach. adv. bk.
  rev. bibl. charts. circ. 1,000. (tabloid format)

150   FI   ISSN 0356-8741
TURUN YLIOPISTO. PSYKOLOGIAN
  TUTKIMUKSIA. 1969. irreg. price varies. Turun
  Yliopisto, Psykologian Laitos - University of Turku,
  Dept. of Psycholigy, Arwidssonink 1, SF-20500
  Turku 50, Finland. Ed. Kirsti Lagerspetz. circ. 500.
    Supersedes in part: Turun Yliopisto. Psykologian
  Laitos. Reports (ISSN 0082-7037)

U S S R REPORT: LIFE SCIENCES, BIOMEDICAL
  AND BEHAVIORAL SCIENCES. see MEDICAL
  SCIENCES

370.15   SP   ISSN 0212-9728
UNIVERSIDAD DE MURCIA. ANALES DE
  PSICOLOGIA. 1984. a. ($1000) Universidad de
  Murcia, Secretariado de Publicaciones e Intercambio
  Cientifico, Santo Cristo, 1, 30001 Murcia, Spain.
  TEL 968 24 92 00.

150   NO   ISSN 0333-4325
UNIVERSITY OF BERGEN. INSTITUTE OF
  PSYCHOLOGY. PSYCHOLOGICAL REPORT
  SERIES. (Text in English, Norwegian) 1968. irreg.
  (6-10/yr.) Universitetet i Bergen, Psykologisk
  Institutt, Box 25, 5014 Bergen-U, Norway. Ed. Tore
  Helstrup. charts. stat.
    Formerly: University of Bergen. Institute of
  Psychology. Report.

150   301   NZ   ISSN 0069-3774
UNIVERSITY OF CANTERBURY. DEPARTMENT
  OF PSYCHOLOGY AND SOCIOLOGY.
  RESEARCH PROJECTS. 1956. irreg., 2-3/yr.;
  no.24, 1975. price varies. University of Canterbury,
  Department of Psychology, Christchurch, New
  Zealand. Ed. B.G. Stacey. circ. 250 (approx.)
  Indexed: Psychol.Abstr.

150   FI   ISSN 0359-0216
UNIVERSITY OF TURKU. PSYCHOLOGICAL
  RESEARCH REPORTS. (Text in English) 1963.
  irreg., no.61, 1984. price varies. Turun Yliopisto,
  Psykologian Laitos - University of Turku,
  Department of Psychology, Arwidssonink 1, SF-
  20500 Turku 50, Finland. Ed. Kirsti Lagerspetz.
  circ. 500.
    Supersedes in part: Turun Yliopisto. Psykologian
  Laitos. Reports (ISSN 0082-7037)

370.15   CS   ISSN 0068-2705
UNIVERZITA J.E. PURKYNE. FILOZOFICKA
  FAKULTA. SBORNIK PRACI. I: RADA
  PEDAGOGICKA - PSYCHOLOGICKA. irreg.,
  approx. a. Univerzita J.E. Purkyne, Filozoficka
  Fakulta, A. Novaka 1, 602 00 Brno,
  Czechoslovakia. Indexed: Psychol.Abstr.

PSYCHOLOGY — ABSTRACTING, BIBLIOGRAPHIES, STATISTICS

150   CS   ISSN 0083-419X
UNIVERZITA KOMENSKEHO. FILOZOFICKA FAKULTA. ZBORNIK: PSYCHOLOGICA. (Text in Slovak; summaries in English, German and Russian) 1961. a. exchange basis. Univerzita Komenskeho, Filozoficka Fakulta, Gondova 2, 806 01 Bratislava, Czechoslovakia. Ed. Tomas Pardel. circ. 400. Indexed: Psychol.Abstr.

370.14 150   PL   ISSN 0208-4562
UNIWERSYTET GDANSKI. WYDZIAL HUMANISTYCZNY. ZESZYTY NAUKOWE. PSYCHOLOGIA. (Text in Polish; summaries in English, Russian) 1978. irreg. price varies. Uniwersytet Gdanski, Ul. Armii Czerwonej 110, 81-824 Sopot, Poland (Dist. by: Ars Polona-Ruch, Krakowskie Przedmiescie 7, 00-680 Warsaw, Poland)

150 370   PL   ISSN 0083-4408
UNIWERSYTET JAGIELLONSKI. ZESZYTY NAUKOWE. PRACE PSYCHOLOGICZNO-PEDAGOGICZNE. 1957. irreg., vol.34, 1983. price varies. Panstwowe Wydawnictwo Naukowe, Miodowa 10, 00-251 Warsaw, Poland (Dist. by: Ars Polona, Krakowskie Przedmiescie 7, 00-068 Warsaw, Poland) Ed. Maria Susulowska. illus.

301.1 150 364   US
VIOLENCE AND VICTIMS. 1986. q. $28 to individuals; institutions $54. (University of New Hampshire, Family Research Laboratory) Springer Publishing Company, 536 Broadway, New York, NY 10012. TEL 212-431-4370. Ed. Angela Browne. adv. bk. rev.

150 616.8   US   ISSN 0083-8977
W P S PROFESSIONAL HANDBOOK SERIES. 1965. irreg. price varies. Western Psychological Services, 12031 Wilshire Blvd, Los Angeles, CA 90025. TEL 213-478-2061. Ed. Nancy Sundquist.

614.58 616.8   GW   ISSN 0173-3524
WERKSTATTSCHRIFTEN ZUR SOZIALPSYCHIATRIE. 1973. irreg. Psychiatrie-Verlag GmbH, Celsiusstr. 112, D-5300 Bonn 1, W. Germany (B.R.D.) Ed.Bd. adv. bk. rev. circ. 800.

WILCOX REPORT NEWSLETTER. see *POLITICAL SCIENCE*

WORLD COUNCIL FOR GIFTED AND TALENTED CHILDREN. YEARBOOK. see *EDUCATION — Special Education And Rehabilitation*

150.19   GW   ISSN 0344-8274
WUNDERBLOCK; Zeitschrift fuer Psychoanalyse. 1978. irreg. DM.55. Verlag der Wunderblock, Konstanzer Strasse 11, D-1000 Berlin 31, West Germany (B.R.D.) adv. bk. rev. (back issues avail.)

150   PL   ISSN 0208-9564
WYZSZA SZKOLA PEDAGOGICZNA, OPOLE. ZESZYTY NAUKOWE. SERIA A. PSYCHOLOGIA. (Text in Polish; summaries in English) 1979. irreg., vol. 2, 1980. price varies; avail. on exchange basis. Wyzsza Szkola Pedagogiczna, Opole, Oleska 48, 45-052 Opole, Poland (Dist. by: Ars Polona-Ruch, Krakowskie Przedmiescie 7, Warsaw, Poland)

ZEITSCHRIFT FUER PSYCHOSOMATISCHE MEDIZIN UND PSYCHOANALYSE. BEIHEFTE. see *MEDICAL SCIENCES — Psychiatry And Neurology*

PSYCHOLOGY — Abstracting, Bibliographies, Statistics

310 150   JA
BEHAVIORMETRIKA. (Text mainly in English) 1974. a. price varies. (Behaviormetric Society of Japan) Japan Publications Trading Co., Ltd., Box 5030, Tokyo International, Tokyo 100-31, Japan (Or 1255 Howard St., San Francisco, CA 94103) Ed. Chikio Hayashi. Indexed: Psychol.Abstr. J.Cont.Quant.Meth. Lang.& Lang.Behav.Abstr.

BENCHMARK PAPERS IN BEHAVIOR. see *BIOLOGY — Zoology*

016 150   AG   ISSN 0523-1698
BIBLIOGRAFIA ARGENTINA DE PSICOLOGIA.* irreg., nos. 5-6, 1970. Ministerio de Cultura y Educacion, Direccion de Bibliotecos, 538 Calle 7, La Plata, Argentina.

150 011   US   ISSN 0360-277X
BIBLIOGRAPHIC GUIDE TO PSYCHOLOGY. (Text in various languages) a. price varies. G. K. Hall & Co., 70 Lincoln St., Boston, MA 02111. TEL 617-423-3990.
Formerly: Psychology Book Guide.

301.1 016   GW   ISSN 0303-5999
BIBLIOGRAPHIE DER DEUTSCHSPRACHIGEN PSYCHOLOGISCHEN LITERATUR. a. DM.238 (approx.) Vittorio Klostermann, Frauenlobstr. 22, Postfach 900601, D-6000 Frankfurt 90, W. Germany (B.R.D.) Ed. J. Dambauer.

150   US   ISSN 0742-681X
BIBLIOGRAPHIES AND INDEXES IN PSYCHOLOGY. 1984. irreg. price varies. Greenwood Press (Subsidiary of: Congressional Information Service, Inc.) 88 Post Rd. W., Box 5007, Westport, CT 06881. TEL 203-226-3571.

616.89 150   US
BIBLIOGRAPHIES IN THE HISTORY OF PSYCHOLOGY AND PSYCHIATRY. 1982. irreg. Kraus International Publications, One Water St., White Plains, NY 10601. TEL 914-761-9600. Ed. Robert H. Wozniak.

150 016   CN   ISSN 0705-5870
GERMAN JOURNAL OF PSYCHOLOGY; a quarterly of abstracts and review articles. (Text in English) 1977. q. Can.$65($48) for institutions; Can.$39($29) for individuals. (International Union of Psychological Science) C.J. Hogrefe, Inc., 12-14 Bruce Park Ave., Toronto, Ontario M4P 2S3, Canada. TEL 416-482-6339. Ed. K. Pawlik. adv. bk. rev. abstr. tr.lit. circ. 2,000. Indexed: Psychol.Abstr.

150   US   ISSN 0073-5884
INDEX OF PSYCHOANALYTIC WRITINGS. no.14, 1966. irreg. International Universities Press, Inc., 59 Boston Post Rd., Box 1524, Madison, CT 06443-1524. TEL 203-245-4000. Ed. Alexander Grinstein.

150 016   II   ISSN 0250-9679
INDIAN PSYCHOLOGICAL ABSTRACTS. (Text in English) 1972. q. Rs.20($6) to individuals; institutions Rs. 30 ($8) Indian Council of Social Science Research, 35 Ferozshah Rd., New Delhi 110002, India (Subscr. to: Behavioural Sciences Centre, 32 Netaji Subhash Marg, New Delhi 110002, India) (Co-sponsor: Indian Psychological Association) Ed. Udai Pareek. adv. bk. rev. abstr. circ. 600. (back issues avail.)

P A S C A L EXPLORE. PART 65: PSYCHOLOGIE. PSYCHOPATHOLOGIE. PSYCHIATRIE. see *MEDICAL SCIENCES — Abstracting, Bibliographies, Statistics*

150.19   US
PSYCHOANALYTIC ABSTRACTS. 1985. q. $30 to individuals; institutions $50. American Psychological Association, Division of Psychoanalysis, One Plaka Ct., Old Brookville, NY 11545. Ed. Edward S. Penzer.

150 016   US   ISSN 0033-2887
PSYCHOLOGICAL ABSTRACTS. 1927. m. $750 to institutions & non-members; members $375. American Psychological Association, 1200 17th St., N.W., Washington, DC 20036. TEL 202-955-7600. Ed. Lois Granick. adv. abstr. cum.index. circ. 4,000. (also avail. in microform from MIM,UMI; reprint service avail. from UMI) Indexed: Ergon.Abstr. JAMA. Popul.Ind.
●Also available online. Vendors: BRS, DIMDI, Data-Star, DIALOG, Orbit Information Technologies.

152 573   US   ISSN 0272-0582
PSYCHOLOGICAL CINEMA REGISTER; films and video in the behavioral sciences. Abbreviated title: P C R. 1944. a.? Pennsylvania State University, Audio-Visual Services, University Park, PA 16802. TEL 814-865-6314. circ. 9,000.

150 016   US   ISSN 0273-3579
PSYCHOLOGY INFORMATION GUIDE SERIES. 1979. irreg., vol.6, 1980. $62. Gale Research Company, Book Tower, Detroit, MI 48226. TEL 313-961-2242. Eds. Sydney Schultz, Duane Schultz.

150   US   ISSN 0271-7506
PSYCSCAN: APPLIED PSYCHOLOGY. q. $25 to non-members; members $12.50; institutions $50. American Psychological Association, 1200 17th St., N.W., Washington, DC 20036. TEL 202-955-7600. circ. 2,500.

157   US   ISSN 0197-1484
PSYCSCAN: CLINICAL PSYCHOLOGY. q. $25 to non-members; members $12.50; institutions $50. American Psychological Association, 1200 17th St. N.W., Washington, DC 20036. TEL 202-955-7600. Ed. Lois Granick. circ. 7,000. (back issues avail.)

150   US   ISSN 0197-1492
PSYCSCAN: DEVELOPMENTAL PSYCHOLOGY. q. $25 to non-members; members $12.50; institutions $50. American Psychological Association, 1200 17th St., N.W., Washington, DC 20036. TEL 202-955-7600. circ. 3,000.

155   US
PSYCSCAN: LEARNING AND COMMUNICATION DISORDERS AND MENTAL RETARDATION. q. $25 to non-members; members $12.50; institutions $50. American Psychological Association, 1200 17th St., N.W., Washington, DC 20036. TEL 202-955-7600. circ. 8,000.
Formerly: Psycscan: Learning Disabilities/Mental Retardation (ISSN 0730-1928)

155.937   US
THANATOLOGY ABSTRACTS. biennial. $17 per no. Foundation of Thanatology, Foundation Book & Periodical Division, Box 1191, Brooklyn, NY 11202-1202. (also avail. in microform from UMI; back issues avail.)
Formerly: Funeral Service Abstracts.

PUBLIC ADMINISTRATION

see also *Public Administration—Municipal Government; Housing and Urban Planning; Social Services and Welfare*

350   TS
ABU DHABI. DEPARTMENT OF PLANNING. STATISTICAL ABSTRACT AND YEARBOOK. a. Department of Planning, Abu Dhabi, United Arab Emirates.

350   TS
ABU DHABI OFFICAL GAZETTE. (Text in Arabic and English) irreg. Council of Ministers Secretariat, Box 516, Abu Dhabi, United Arab Emirates.

350   BG
ADMINISTRATIVE AFFAIRS IN BANGLADESH. 1979. a. $5. University of Dacca, Center for Administrative Studies, Room No. 4036, Arts Faculty Bldg., Dacca 2, Bangladesh.

ADVANCE LOCATOR FOR CAPITOL HILL. see *POLITICAL SCIENCE*

AFRICANUS. see *POLITICAL SCIENCE*

350   US
ALABAMA COUNTY DATA BOOK. a. $5. Department of Economic and Community Affairs, State Capitol, Montgomery, AL 36130. TEL 205-284-8910. charts. stat.

353.9   US   ISSN 0095-3865
ALASKA. LEGISLATURE. BUDGET AND AUDIT COMMITTEE. ANNUAL REPORT. 1965. a. free. Legislative Budget and Audit Committee, Pouch W, Juneau, AK 99811. circ. 200. Key Title: Annual Report - State of Alaska, Legislative Budget and Audit Committee.

353.9   US   ISSN 0363-5376
ALASKA. OFFICE OF OMBUDSMAN. REPORT OF THE OMBUDSMAN. 1975. a. Office of Ombudsman, Pouch WO, Juneau, AK 99801. TEL 907-465-4970. circ. 2,000. Key Title: Report of the Ombudsman (Juneau)

PUBLIC ADMINISTRATION

353.9 US ISSN 0092-1858
ALASKA BLUE BOOK. 1973. biennial. $7.50. Department of Education, Division of State Libraries, Box G, Juneau, AK 99811. TEL 907-465-2910. illus. stat. circ. controlled.

363.6 CN
ALBERTA. DEPARTMENT OF UTILITIES. ANNUAL REPORT. 1974. a. free. Department of Transportation and Utilities, 12323 Stony Plain Rd., 7th Fl., Edmonton, Alta. T5N 3Y9, Canada. TEL 403-427-3021. circ. 450.
Former titles (until 1986): Alberta. Department of Utilities and Telecommunications. Annual Report; (until 1981): Alberta. Department of Utilities and Telephones. Annual Report; Alberta. Utilities Division. Annual Report (ISSN 0381-2294)

AMERICAN PUBLIC WORKS ASSOCIATION. DIRECTORY. see *TECHNOLOGY: COMPREHENSIVE WORKS*

350 US
AMERICAN SOCIETY FOR PUBLIC ADMINISTRATION. SECTION ON INTERNATIONAL AND COMPARATIVE ADMINISTRATION. OCCASIONAL PAPERS. 1974. irreg., latest 1985. $3 per no. American Society for Public Administration, Section on International and Comparative Administration, 1120 G St., N.W., Washington, DC 20005. Ed. Prof. Louis A. Picard. circ. 550. (back issues avail.; reprint service avail from KTO)

354 AO
ANGOLA. SECRETARIA PROVINCIAL DE SAUDE, TRABALHO. PREVIDENCIA E ASSISTENCIA. SINTESE DA ACTIVIDADE DOS SERVICOS E ORGANISMOS.* 1963. irreg, (approx. 1/yr.) free. Secretaria Provincial de Saude, Trabalho, Previdencia e Assistencia, Luanda, Angola. circ. controlled. (tabloid format)

350 US ISSN 0278-4289
ANNALS OF PUBLIC ADMINISTRATION. 1982. irreg., vol.5, 1983. price varies. Marcel Dekker, Inc., 270 Madison Ave., New York, NY 10016. TEL 212-696-9000. Ed. Jack Rabin.

351 ML ISSN 0066-2453
ANNUAIRE ADMINISTRATIF DE LA REPUBLIQUE DU MALI. 1964. a. Chambre de Commerce et d'Industrie du Mali, B.P. 46, Bamako, Mali. circ. 100.

350 BE ISSN 0066-2461
ANNUAIRE ADMINISTRATIF ET JUDICIAIRE DE BELGIQUE/ADMINISTRATIEF EN GERECHTELIJK JAARBOEK VOOR BELGIE. 1869. a. 5.150 Fr. Etablessements Emile Bruylant, 67 rue de la Regence, 1000 Brussels, Belgium. circ. 4,400.

916.7 GO
ANNUAIRE NATIONAL OFFICIEL DE LA REPUBLIQUE GABONAISE. 1973. a. 5000 Fr.CFA. Agence Havas Gabon, B.P. 213, Libreville, Gabon. adv. illus. stat. circ. 5,000.

350 UK
ANNUAL CATALOGUE OF GOVERNMENT PUBLICATIONS. a. Her Majesty's Stationery Office, Box 276, London SW8 5DT, England. circ. 6,600.

350 US
ANNUAL EDITIONS: STATE & LOCAL GOVERNMENT. 1978. a. Dushkin Publishing Group, Inc., Sluice Dock, Guilford, CT 06437. TEL 203-453-4351. Ed. Ian Nielsen.

350 US ISSN 0731-339X
ANNUAL GUIDE TO PUBLIC POLICY EXPERTS. a. $5.95. Heritage Foundation, Inc., 214 Massachusetts Ave., Washington, DC 20002. Eds. Cathrine Ludwig, Robert Huberty.

350 IT ISSN 0084-6619
ANNUARIO AMMINISTRATIVO ITALIANO/ ITALIAN ADMINISTRATIVE DIRECTORY. a. L.120000. Guida Monaci, Via Francesco Crispi 10, 00187 Rome, Italy.

350 UK ISSN 0261-6793
ARABIAN GOVERNMENT AND PUBLIC SERVICES. 1981. a. £47($95) Beacon Publications PLC., York House, Newton Close, Park Farm, Wellingborough, Northamptonshire NN8 3UW, England. Ed. Shahrukh Husain. adv. bk. rev. circ. 8,000.

350 AG ISSN 0301-7818
ARGENTINA. BIBLIOTECA DEL CONGRESO. BOLETIN LEGISLATIVO. 1976. irreg. Biblioteca del Congreso, Buenos Aires, Argentina.

333.7 AG ISSN 0302-5705
ARGENTINA. SERVICIO NACIONAL DE PARQUES NACIONAL. ANALES. 1945. irreg. 25000p. Servicio Nacional de Parques Nacionales, Santa Fe 690, Buenos Aires, Argentina. illus. circ. 4,000.
Continues: Argentina. Direccion General de Parques Nacionales. Anales de Parques Nacionales (ISSN 0518-4614)

350 US
ARKANSAS STATE DIRECTORY. 1973. biennial. $6. Heritage Publishing Co. (North Little Rock), 2401 Wildwood Dr., Box 9067, North Little Rock, AR 72119. TEL 501-835-9111. adv. circ. 4,000.

350 UK ISSN 0305-2044
ASSOCIATION OF COUNTY COUNCILS. YEARBOOK. a. £2. Association of County Councils, Eaton House, 66A Eaton Square, London, SW1W 9BH, England. adv. circ. 5,000.

336.94 AT ISSN 0705-0550
AUSTRALIA. BUREAU OF STATISTICS. COMMONWEALTH GOVERNMENT FINANCE. a. Aus.$2.90. Australian Bureau of Statistics, P.O. Box 10, Belconnen, A.C.T. 2616, Australia. illus. stat. circ. 1,000.

350 AT
AUSTRALIA. PUBLIC SERVICE BOARD. ANNUAL REPORT. 1924. a. price varies. Australian Government Publishing Service, G.P.O. Box 84, Canberra, A.C.T. 2601, Australia. circ. 4,500.

350 GW ISSN 0082-1888
B A T: TASCHENBUCH FUER DEN OEFFENTLICHEN DIENST. 1965. a. DM.54.80. Walhalla- und Praetoria-Verlag Georg Zwichenpflug, Dolomitenstr. 1, Postfach 301, 8400 Regensburg 1, W. Germany (B.R.D.) Ed. Manfred Petin.
Formerly: Taschenbuch fuer den Oeffentilichen Dienst.

350 US
BACKGROUNDER UPDATES. 1977. irreg., no. 33. $1. Heritage Foundation, Inc., 214 Massachusetts Ave., N.E., Washington, DC 20002. TEL 202-546-4400. (looseleaf format; also avail. in microfiche; back issues avail.)

348 US ISSN 0092-0959
BALDWIN'S OHIO LEGISLATIVE SERVICE. 1971. m. $210. Banks-Baldwin Law Publishing Co., University Center, Box 1974, Cleveland, OH 44106. TEL 216-721-7373. circ. 5,000.

351 BG
BANGLADESH. MINISTRY OF FOREIGN AFFAIRS. LIST OF THE DIPLOMATIC CORPS AND OTHER FOREIGN REPRESENTATIVES. (Text in English) Tk.5.75. Ministry of Foreign Affairs, Dacca, Bangladesh.

352 GW ISSN 0067-4702
BAYERISCHES BEAMTEN-JAHRBUCH (YEAR) 1968. a. DM.65. (Bayerischer Beamtenbund) Walhalla-und-Praetoria-Verlag, Dolomitenstr. 1, Postfach 301, 8400 Regensburg 1, W. Germany (B. R. D.) Ed. Dieter Kattenbeck.

354 NR
BENDEL STATE. MINISTRY OF INFORMATION, SOCIAL DEVELOPMENT AND SPORTS. ESTIMATE. a. £N5. Ministry of Information, Social Development and Sports, Printing and Stationery Division, P.M.B. 1099, Benin City, Nigeria (Orders to Bendel State Government Printer, Government Press, Benin City, Nigeria)
Formerly: Bendel State. Ministry of Home Affairs and Information. Mid-Western State Estimates.

350 BE ISSN 0005-8777
BENELUX PUBLIKATIEBLAD/BULLETIN BENELUX. (Supplement to: Textes de Base Benelux/Basic Benelux Texts) (Text in Dutch and French) 1958. irreg., approx. 8/yr. 1.60 Fr. per no. B E N E L U X Economic Union, Rue de la Regence 39, 1000 Brussels, Belgium. (looseleaf format)

353.002 US ISSN 0882-1593
BLACK ELECTED OFFICIALS; a national roster. 1970. a. $29.50. (Joint Center for Political Studies) Bernan-Unipub, Government and International Agency Publications Service, 4611-F Assembly Dr., Lanham, MD 20706-4391. TEL 301-459-7666. stat. index. circ. 5,000.
Formerly: National Roster of Black Elected Officials (ISSN 0092-2935)

350 US
BLUE SKY NEWS. a. free. North American Securities Administrators Association, Inc., 2930 S.W. Wanamaker Dr., Ste. 5, Topeka, KS 66614. circ. 300.

351 US ISSN 0068-0125
BOOK OF THE STATES. 1935. biennial. $42.50. Council of State Governments, Box 11910, Iron Works Pike, Lexington, KY 40578. TEL 606-252-2291. Ed. Deborah Gona. index. circ. 11,000.

350 FR
BOTTIN ADMINISTRATIF. 1943. a. $81. Societe Didot Bottin, 28 rue du Docteur Finlay, 75738 Paris Cedex 15, France.

353.002 US ISSN 0363-6275
BRADDOCK'S FEDERAL-STATE-LOCAL GOVERNMENT DIRECTORY. 1975. a. $49.95. Braddock Communications, Inc., 1001 Connecticut Ave., N.W., Ste. 216, Washington, DC 20036. TEL 202-296-1317. Ed. Stuart Carson.

350 BL
BRAZIL. CAMARA DOS DEPUTADOS. ALMANAQUE DOS FUNCIONARIOS DE SECRETARIA. 1952. biennial. free. Camara dos Deputados, Centro de Documentacao e Informacao, Anexo 2, 70160 Brasilia DF, Brazil. circ. controlled.

631.6 BL ISSN 0101-5680
BRAZIL. DEPARTAMENTO NACIONAL DE OBRAS CONTRA AS SECAS. RELATORIO. Cover title: Relatoria D N O C S. 1945. a. free. Departamento Nacional de Obras Contra as Secas, Av. Duque de Caixias 1700, Fortaleza-Ceara 60000, Brazil. bk. rev. charts. illus. stat. circ. controlled. (processed) Indexed: Biol.Abstr.

352 657 BL
BRAZIL. INSPETORIA-GERAL DE FINANCAS. BALANCOS GERAIS DA UNIAO.* 1972. a. free. Inspetoria-Geral de Financas, Esplanada dos Ministerios, Brasilia D.F., Brazil.

363.6 AU ISSN 0520-9048
BRENNSTOFFSTATISTIK DER WAERMEKRAFTWERKE FUER DIE OEFFENTLICHE ELEKTRIZITAETSVERSORGUNG IN OESTERREICH. (Issued in cooperation with Osterreichische Elektrizitaetswirtschafts-A.G.) 1955. a. Bundesministerium fuer Handel, Gewerbe und Industrie, Am Hof 6a, A-1010 Vienna, Austria. circ. 900.

350 CN ISSN 0007-0513
BRITISH COLUMBIA GOVERNMENT NEWS. 1953. irreg., 8-10/yr. free. Ministry of the Provincial Secretary, Parliament Buildings, Victoria, B.C. V8V 1X4, Canada. TEL 604-873-3455. Ed. J.A.D. Stuart. circ. 110,000. (tabloid format)

354.666 LB
BUDGET OF THE GOVERNMENT OF LIBERIA.* 1960. a. Bureau of the Budget, Monrovia, Liberia.

363.6 FR ISSN 0154-0033
BULLETIN OFFICIEL DU MINISTERE DE L'ENVIRONNEMENT ET DU CADRE DE VIE ET DU MINISTERE DES TRANSPORTS. irreg. 288 F. France. Direction des Journaux Officiels, 26 rue Desaix, 75732 Paris, France. (Co-sponsor: Ministere des Transports)

C I S FEDERAL REGISTER INDEX. (Congressional Information Service, Inc.) see *ABSTRACTING AND INDEXING SERVICES*

PUBLIC ADMINISTRATION

CALIFORNIA. OFFICE OF ADMINISTRATIVE LAW. ANNIVERSARY REPORT. see *LAW*

300 978 350   US   ISSN 0068-5615
CALIFORNIA HANDBOOK; a comprehensive guide to sources of current information and action. 1969. irreg., 5th edt. 1987. $30. California Institute of Public Affairs, Box 10, Claremont, CA 91711. TEL 714-624-5212. Ed. Thaddeus C. Trzyna. index. circ. 2,500.

320   US
CALIFORNIA JOURNAL ALMANAC OF STATE GOVERNMENT AND POLITICS. 1975. biennial. $5.95. California Journal, Inc., 1714 Capitol Ave., Sacramento, CA 95814. TEL 916-444-2840. Ed. Thomas R. Hoeber. charts. illus. stat.

328 920   US   ISSN 0068-6530
CALIFORNIANS IN CONGRESS. 1955. biennial. free. (California Congressional Recognition Program) Claremont McKenna College, Department of Political Science, Pitzer Hall, Claremont, CA 91711. TEL 714-621-8000. Eds. Alan Heslop, Florence Adams. circ. 2,500. (back issues avail.)

CAMERA DEI DEPUTATI. BOLLETTINO DI INFORMAZIONI COSTITUZIONALI E PARLAMENTARI. see *LAW*

350   US
CAMPAIGN GUIDE FOR CONGRESSIONAL CANDIDATE AND COMMITTEES. irreg. Federal Election Commission, Washington, DC 20463. TEL 202-523-4089.

350   US
CAMPAIGN GUIDE FOR PARTY COMMITTEES. irreg. Federal Election Commission, Washington, DC 20463. TEL 202-523-4089.

350   CN   ISSN 0382-1161
CANADA. COMMISSIONER OF OFFICIAL LANGUAGES. ANNUAL REPORT. (Text in English and French) 1971. a. Office of the Commissioner of Official Languages, 110 O'Connor St., Ottawa, Ont. K1A 0T8, Canada. TEL 613-995-7717. Ed.Bd. circ. 11,000.

350   CN
CANADA. DEPARTMENT OF CONSUMER & CORPORATE AFFAIRS. ANNUAL REPORT. (Text in English & French) 1968. a. free. Department of Consumer & Corporate Affairs, Ottawa, Ont. K1A 0C9, Canada. TEL 613-997-3284. charts. stat. circ. 2,000.

CANADA. LAW REFORM COMMISSION. ANNUAL REPORT. see *LAW*

537   CN   ISSN 0825-0170
CANADA. NATIONAL ENERGY BOARD. INFORMATION BULLETINS. 1984. irreg. National Energy Board, Ottawa, Ont. K1A 0E5, Canada. TEL 613-998-7192. circ. controlled.
   Formerly (until 1983): Canada. National Energy Board. Staff Papers.

350   CN
CANADA. NATIONAL ENERGY BOARD. REPORTS TO THE GOVERNOR IN COUNCIL. 1960. irreg. National Energy Board, 473 Albert St., Ottawa, Ont. K1A 0E5, Canada. TEL 613-998-7192. circ. controlled.

350.722   CN
CANADA. TREASURY BOARD SECRETARIAT. ESTIMATES. PART I: GOVERNMENT EXPENDITURES PLAN/CANADA. CONSEIL DU TRESOR. BUDGET DES DEPENSES. PARTIE I: PLAN DE DEPENSES DU GOUVERNEMENT. (Text in English and French) 1977. a. Can.$15. Treasury Board, Ottawa, Ont. K1A 0R5, Canada. TEL 613-997-2560. charts. stat.
   Formerly: Canada. Treasury Board Secretariat. Federal Expenditure Plan (ISSN 0706-6007)

354   CN
CANADA. TREASURY BOARD SECRETARIAT. ESTIMATES. PART II: ESTIMATES/CANADA. CONSEIL DU TRESOR. BUDGET DES DEPENSES. PARTIE II: BUDGET DES DEPENSES. a. Can.$15. Treasury Board, Ottawa, Ont. K1A 0R5, Canada. TEL 613-997-2560. stat.

309.1   SG
CARTE D'IDENTITE DU SENEGAL. 1971. a. free. Ministere de l'Information et de Telecommunications, Direction de l'Information, 58 Bd. de la Republique, Dakar, Senegal. illus. stat.

328   CJ   ISSN 0300-4740
CAYMAN ISLANDS. LEGISLATIVE ASSEMBLY. MINUTES. 1966. irreg. price varies. Legislative Assembly, Box 890, Grand Cayman, Cayman Islands, B.W.I. (processed)

350   FR
CENTRE NATIONAL DE LA RECHERCHE SCIENTIFIQUE. ANNUAIRE EUROPEEN D'ADMINISTRATION PUBLIQUE. a. (Universite de Droit, d'Economie et des Sciences d'Aix-Marseille, Centre de Recherches Administratives) Editions du C N R S, 295 rue St. Jacques, 75005 Paris, France.

350   JA
CHINA DIRECTORY. (Text in English and Japanese) 1971. a. 15,000 Yen($80) Radiopress, Inc, Fuji Television Bldg, 3-1 Kawada- cho, Shinjuku-ku, Tokyo 162, Japan. bk. rev. Indices in Chinese and Pinyin. circ. 2,500.

350   US
CITIZEN'S GUIDE TO LOCAL GOVERNMENT. a. $25. Washington Research Council, 906 South Columbia, Ste. 350, Olympia, WA 98501. TEL 206-357-6643.

350   US
CIVIL SERVICE NEWS. irreg. free. ‡ U.S. Office of Personnel Management, News Unit, 1900 E St., Room 5F10, Washington, DC 20415. TEL 202-655-4000. (processed)
   Formerly: Civil Service News Releases (ISSN 0009-8019)

350   UK   ISSN 0302-329X
CIVIL SERVICE YEAR BOOK. a. £4. Civil Service Department, Whitehall, London S.W.1, England (Avail. from H.M.S.O., c/o Liaison Officer, Atlantic House, Holborn Viaduct, London EC1P 1BN, England)
   Formerly: British Imperial Calendar and Civil Service List.

350 340   US
CODE OF MARYLAND REGULATIONS. Short title: C O M A R. 1976. a. $500. Division of State Documents, Box 802, Annapolis, MD 21404. TEL 301-974-2486. Ed. Robert J. Colborn, Jr. circ. 300.
●Also available online.

350   CK
COLOMBIA. DEPARTAMENTO ADMINISTRATIVO NACIONAL DE ESTADISTICA. DIVISION POLITICO-ADMINISTRATIVA. 1953. irreg. Departamento Administrativo Nacional de Estadistica, Banco Nacional de Datos, Centro Administrativo Nacional, Apdo. Aereo 80043, Avenida Eldorado, Bogota, Colombia. illus.

350   RE
COMMENTAIRES DES PRINCIPALES DECISIONS DU TRIBUNAL ADMINISTRATIF DE LA REUNION. (Subseries of: Dossiers du Centre d'Etudes) 1974. a. 100 F. Centre Universitaire de la Reunion, Centre d'Etudes Administratives, 24, 26 av. de la Victoire, Saint-Denis, Reunion. circ. 150.

354.94   AT
COMMONWEALTH GOVERNMENT DIRECTORY. 1973. irreg. price varies. Australian Government Publishing Service, G.P.O. Box 84, Canberra, A.C.T. 2601, Australia.
   Formerly: Australian Government Directory.

350   AT
COMMONWEALTH OF AUSTRALIA GAZETTE: PERIODIC. irreg. Australian Government Publishing Service, G.P.O. Box 84, Canberra, A.C.T. 2601, Australia.

350   AT
COMMONWEALTH OF AUSTRALIA GAZETTE: SPECIAL. irreg. Australian Government Publishing Service, G.P.O. Box 84, Canberra A.C.T. 2601, Australia.

350   MW
COMMONWEALTH PARLIAMENTARY ASSOCIATION. MALAWI BRANCH. CONFERENCE. REPORT OF PROCEEDINGS. a., 12th, 1980. Commonwealth Parliamentary Association, Malawi Branch, c/o Parliament of Malawi, Box 80, Zomba, Malawi.

350   MW
COMMONWEALTH PARLIAMENTARY ASSOCIATION. MALAWI BRANCH. EXECUTIVE COMMITTEE. ANNUAL REPORT. (Text in English) a. Commonwealth Parliamentary Association, Malawi Branch, c/o Parliament of Malawi, Box 80, Zomba, Malawi.

CONGRESS AND THE NATION. see *POLITICAL SCIENCE*

350 336   TT
CONGRESS OF MICRONESIA. JOINT COMMITTEE ON PROGRAM AND BUDGET PLANNING. PUBLIC HEARINGS ON HIGH COMMISSIONER'S PRELIMINARY BUDGET. (Text in English) a. Congress of Micronesia, Joint Committee on Program and Budget Planning, Capitol Hill, Saipan 96950, Mariana Islands.

CONGRESS OF MICRONESIA. SENATE. JOURNAL. see *LAW*

350   US   ISSN 0069-892X
CONGRESSIONAL RECORD DIGEST AND TALLY OF ROLL CALL VOTES. 1961. irreg., (8-9/yr.) free to contributors. Americans for Constitutional Action, 955 l'Enfant Plaza North, S.W., Suite 1000, Washington, DC 20024. TEL 202-484-5525. circ. 5,000.

350 973   US   ISSN 0069-8938
CONGRESSIONAL STAFF DIRECTORY. 1959. a. $45. Congressional Staff Directory Ltd., Box 62, Mount Vernon, VA 22121. TEL 703-765-3400. Ed. Charles Brownson.

350.6   US
CONSOLIDATED FEDERAL FUNDS REPORT. 1981. a. price varies. U.S. Bureau of the Census, Washington, DC 20233. (Co-sponsor: Office of Management and Budget) circ. 7,000.

350   US
CONTEMPORARY GOVERNMENT SERIES. irreg. price varies. Houghton Mifflin Co., One Beacon St., Boston, MA 02107. TEL 617-725-5000.

011   UK   ISSN 0070-1211
COUNCILS, COMMITTEES AND BOARDS; a handbook of advisory, consultative, executive and similar bodies in British public life. 1970. biennial, latest no.6, 1984. £48($130) ‡ C.B.D. Research Ltd., 15 Wickham Rd., Beckenham, Kent BR3 2JS, England (Dist. in U.S. by: Gale Research Co., Penobscot Bldg., Detroit, MI 48226) Ed. L. Sellar. index. circ. 2,000.

350   US
CURRENT GOVERNMENTS REPORTS. (Published in several series, avail. separately) a? U.S. Bureau of the Census, Customer Services, Washington, DC 20233. TEL 301-763-4100.

350 331   US
CURRENT GOVERNMENTS REPORTS: COUNTY EMPLOYMENT. (Series GE-4) a. price varies. U.S. Bureau of the Census, Customer Services, Washington, DC 20233. TEL 301-763-4100. (also avail. in microfiche)

CURRENT GOVERNMENTS REPORTS: FINANCES OF EMPLOYEE RETIREMENT SYSTEMS OF STATE AND LOCAL GOVERNMENTS. see *BUSINESS AND ECONOMICS — Public Finance, Taxation*

353.9   US
D E S ACTIVITIES REPORT. 1973. a. Department of Economic Security, Box 6123, Phoenix, AZ 85005. TEL 602-255-4791. illus.
   Formerly: Arizona. Department of Economic Security. Annual Report (ISSN 0094-0712)

350   DK   ISSN 0105-4554
DANSKE STATSLAAN. 1924. a. Kr.40. Finansministeriet - Ministry of Finance, Copenhagen, Denmark (Orders to: Danske Boghandleres Kommissionsanstalt, Siljangade 6, 2300 Copenhagen S, Denmark) circ. 2,000.

PUBLIC ADMINISTRATION 941

350 340 SJ
DEMOCRATIC REPUBLIC OF THE SUDAN
GAZETTE. LEGISLATIVE SUPPLEMENT.
Variant title: Democratic Republic of the Sudan
Gazette. Special Legislative Supplement. Arabic
edition: Mulhaq al-Tashri lil-Jaridah al-Rasmiyah li-
Jumhuriyat al-Sudan al-Dimuqratiyah. irreg.
Attorney General, Attorney General's Chambers,
Box 302, Khartoum, Sudan.

350 DK ISSN 0108-979X
DENMARK. INDENRIGSMINISTERIET.
INDENRIGSMINISTERIETS AFGOERELSER
OG UDTALELSER OM KOMMUNALE
FORHOLD. 1981. a. free. Indenrigsministeriet,
Christiansborg Slotsplads 1, 1218 Copenhagen K,
Denmark.

352 GW ISSN 0070-4423
DEUTSCHES BEAMTEN-JAHRBUCH;
BUNDESAUSGABE. 1968. a. DM.65. (Deutscher
Beamtenbund) Walhalla-und Praetoria-Verlag,
Dolomitenstr. 1, Postf. 301, 8400 Regensburg 1, W.
Germany (B.R.D.) Eds. Erich Sayn, Karl-August
Weber. bk. rev.

350 PH ISSN 0115-7000
DEVELOPMENT ADMINISTRATION JOURNAL.
(Text in English) 1981. biennial. Mindanao State
University, University Research Center, P.O. Box
5594, Iligan City, Philippines.

350 US
DIALOGUES IN PUBLIC POLICY. Variant title:
Brookings Dialogues in Public Policy. 1982. irreg.,
no.11, 1985. price varies. Brookings Institution,
1775 Massachusetts Ave., N.W., Washington, DC
20036. TEL 202-797-6258.

350 GT
DIARIO DE CENTRO AMERICA. 1880. irreg. $54.
18 Calle No. 6-72, Zona 1, Guatemala. Ed. Luis
Mendizabal R. adv. bk. rev. circ. 10,000.
 Formerly: Guatemalteco.
Official organ of the Republic of Guatemala

034 350 FR
DICTIONNAIRE DES COMMUNES
(LAVAUZELLE ET CIE) quadrennial. 133 F. per
no. Editions Charles Lavauzelle, Le Prouet, B.P. 8,
87350 Panazol, France.

362 US
DIRECTORY OF NEBRASKA SERVICES. 1983? a.
free. Department of Public Institutions, Box 94728,
Lincoln, NE 68509. TEL 402-471-4567. Ed. Ronald
L. Jensen. circ. 1,500.
 Formerly: D P I Yellow Pages (ISSN 0360-4357)

352 US
DIRECTORY OF NEW MEXICO MUNICIPAL
OFFICIALS. a. $25. ‡ New Mexico Municipal
League, 1229 Paseo de Peralta, Box 846, Santa Fe,
NM 87504-0846. TEL 505-982-5573. Ed. William
F. Fulginiti. adv. circ. 1,400.
 Formerly: Directory of Municipal Officials of
New Mexico (ISSN 0070-5888)

350 US
DIRECTORY OF OKLAHOMA. 1907. biennial. $6.
Department of Libraries, 200 N.E. 18th St.,
Oklahoma City, OK 72105. Ed. Patricia Lester.
circ. 7,500.

352 US
DIRECTORY OF REGIONAL COUNCILS. 1969. a.
$35 to members; non-members $45. ‡ National
Association of Regional Councils, 1700 K St. N.W.,
Washington, DC 20006. TEL 202-457-0710. Ed.
Carole Anne Boileau. adv. circ. 2,000.
 Former titles: National Association of Regional
Councils. Directory (ISSN 0095-1455) & Regional
Council Directory (ISSN 0190-2334); Directory of
Regional Councils (ISSN 0070-6205)

353.9 US ISSN 0440-4947
DIRECTORY OF STATE, COUNTY, AND
FEDERAL OFFICIALS. 1964. a. price varies.
Legislative Reference Bureau, State Capitol,
Honolulu, HI 96813. TEL 808-548-6237.

DIRECTORY OF STATE ENVIRONMENT
AGENCIES. see *ENVIRONMENTAL STUDIES*

350 US
DIRECTORY OF TENNESSEE MUNICIPAL
OFFICIALS. a. $25. University of Tennessee,
Institute for Public Service, Municipal Technical
Advisory Service, 891 20th St., Knoxville, TN
37996-4400. TEL 615-974-1009.

DOING BUSINESS WITH THE FEDERAL
GOVERNMENT: A PROCUREMENT GUIDE.
see *POLITICAL SCIENCE*

354.729 DR
DOMINICAN REPUBLIC. OFICINA NACIONAL
DE PRESUPUESTO. EJECUCION
PRESUPUESTARIA. INFORME.* a. Oficina
Nacional de Presupuesto, Santo Domingo,
Dominican Republic. charts. stat.
 Formerly: Dominican Republic. Oficina Nacional
de Presupuesto. Ejecucion del Presupuesto.

354 DR
DOMINICAN REPUBLIC SECRETARIA DE
ESTADO DE OBRAS PUBLICAS Y
COMUNICACIONES. OPC. 1972. irreg. free. ‡
Secretaria de Estado de Obras Publicas y
Comunicaciones, c/o Director General de
Programacion y Proyectos, Santo Domingo,
Dominican Republic. adv. index. circ. 1,000.
 Formerly: Dominican Republic. Secretaria de
Obras Publicas y Comunicaciones. Estadistica (ISSN
0070-7066)

350 DK ISSN 0108-9900
E D B - KURSUSKATALOG; oversigt over
brugerorienterede edb-kurser for medarbejdere i den
offentlige forvaltning. 1983. a. Kr.20. Forvaltningens
Edb-Kursusudvalg, Administrationsdepartentet -
Ministry of Finance, Department of Administration,
Holmens Kanal 20/3, 1060 Copenhagen K,
Denmark (Orders to: Danske Boghandleres
Kommissionsanstalt, Siljangade 6, 2300 Copenhagen
S, Denmark) circ. 2,000.

350 US
ECONOMIC INDICATORS (CHARLESTON) 1981.
quinquennial. West Virginia Research League, Inc.,
1107 Charleston National Plaza, Charleston, WV
25301. TEL 304-346-9451. Ed. Sarah F. Roach.
Indexed: Mag.Ind.

350 CK
ENCUENTRO NACIONAL DE
INVESTIGADORES EN ADMINISTRACION.
MEMORIAS. no.3, 1983. irreg. Universidad de
Antioquia, Facultad de Ciencias Economicas, Apdo.
Aereo 1226, Medellin, Colombia. (Co-sponsor:
Facultad de Administracion de Empresas)

351 US ISSN 0092-8380
ENCYCLOPEDIA OF GOVERNMENTAL
ADVISORY ORGANIZATIONS. 1973. irreg., 5th
edt. 1985. $435. Gale Research Company, Book
Tower, Detroit, MI 48226. TEL 313-961-2242. Ed.
Denise A. Allard.

350 US
ESSAYS IN PUBLIC WORKS HISTORY. 1976.
irreg., no. 13, 1982. $15. Public Works Historical
Society, 1313 E. 60th St., Chicago, IL 60637. TEL
312-667-2200. Ed. Howard Rosen.

354 PN ISSN 0378-2603
ESTADISTICA PANAMENA. SITUACION
ECONOMICA. SECCION 342. CUENTAS
NACIONALES. 1950. a. Bl.0.75. Direccion de
Estadistica y Censo, Contraloria General, Apartado
5213, Panama 5, Panama. circ. 2,200.

ETHICS AND PUBLIC POLICY CENTER.
NEWSLETTER. see *ETHNIC INTERESTS*

352 FR
EUROPEAN CONFERENCE OF LOCAL AND
REGIONAL AUTHORITIES. OFFICIAL
REPORTS OF DEBATES. (Reports of 1st-3rd
Sessions never published) 1962. a. $18. European
Conference of Local and Regional Authorities,
Publications Section, Strasbourg, France (Dist. in
U.S. by Manhattan Publishing Co., P.O.Box 650
Croton on Hudson, New York, N.Y. 10520)
(Affiliate: Council of Europe) bk. rev.
 Formerly: European Conference of Local
Authorities. Official Reports of Debates (ISSN
0071-2620)

352 FR
EUROPEAN CONFERENCE OF LOCAL AND
REGIONAL AUTHORITIES. TEXTS ADOPTED.
(For 1st and 2nd Sessions, Documents and Texts
Adopted issued in one vol.) 1957. a. $5. European
Conference of Local and Regional Authorities,
Publications Section, Strasbourg, France (Dist. in
U.S. by Manhattan Publishing Co., P.O.Box 650,
Croton on Hudson, New York, N.Y. 10520) bk. rev.
 Formerly: European Conference of Local
Authorities. Texts Adopted (ISSN 0071-2639)

350 II ISSN 0085-1795
F M U OCCASIONAL LECTURES. no.2, 1971.
irreg. price varies. Indian Institute of Public
Administration, Financial Management Unit,
Indraprastha Estate, Ring Rd., New Delhi 110002,
India.

351 US ISSN 0071-4127
FEDERAL EMPLOYEES ALMANAC. 1954. a.
$3.95 per no. Federal Employees News Digest, Inc.,
Box 7528, Falls Church, VA 22046. TEL 703-533-
3031. Ed. Joseph Young. circ. 100.

FEDERAL REGULATORY DIRECTORY. see
POLITICAL SCIENCE

FEDERAL STAFF DIRECTORY. see *POLITICAL
SCIENCE*

350 US ISSN 0734-4651
FEDERAL/STATE EXECUTIVE DIRECTORY. a.
$99. Carroll Publishing Company, 1058 Thomas
Jefferson St., N.W., Washington, DC 20007. TEL
202-333-8620. Ed. Nancy Cahill.

350 FJ
FIJI TODAY. a. free. Department of Information,
Government Bldgs., Suva, Fiji.
 Formerly: Fiji Information.

353.9 US ISSN 0095-5175
FLORIDA. OFFICE OF THE GOVERNOR.
BUDGET IN BRIEF. (Formerly issued by Florida.
Department of Administration) a. Office of the
Governor, The Capitol, Tallahassee, FL 32301. TEL
904-488-1234. Key Title: Budget in Brief - State of
Florida.

350 DK ISSN 0107-9670
FOLKETINGETS HAANDBOG. 1956. irreg. Kr.98
per no. (Folketing, Praesidium) J.H. Schultz Forlag,
Moentergade 21, 1116 Copenhagen, Denmark. Ed.
Kristian Hvidt. illus. circ. 3,000.

944 338.9 FR ISSN 0071-8491
FRANCE. COMMISSION NATIONALE DE
L'AMENAGEMENT DU TERRITOIRE.
RAPPORT. 1964. irreg., no.2, 1971. Documentation
Francaise, 29/31 Quai Voltaire, 75340 Paris Cedex
07, France.

350 FR ISSN 0071-8513
FRANCE. CONSEIL NATIONAL DE LA
COMPTABILITE. RAPPORT D'ACTIVITE. 1962.
irreg., no.8, 1975. price varies. Conseil National de
la Comptabilite, c/o Imprimerie Nationale,
Etablissement de Douai. Route d'Auby, 59128
Flers-en-Escrebieux, France.

363.6 FR
FRANCE. MINISTERE DE L'ENVIRONMENT ET
DU CADRE DE VIE. INSPECTION GENERALE
DE L'EQUIPEMENT. a. Direction des Journaux
Officiels, 26 rue Desaix, 75732 Paris Cedex 15,
France.

001.4 GW
GERMANY (FEDERAL REPUBLIC, 1949-).
BUNDESMINISTERIUM FUER FORSCHUNG
UND TECHNOLOGIE, BUNDESBERICHT
FORSCHUNG.* 1979. irreg. free. Verlag Dr.
Heger, Goethestrasse 54, 53 Bonn-Bad Godesberg,
W. Germany (B.R.D.) Indexed: Nutr.Abstr.
 Formerly: Germany (Federal Republic, 1949-).
Bundesministerium fuer Bildung und Wissenschaft.
Forschungsbericht der Bundesregierung.

354 GW
GERMANY (FEDERAL REPUBLIC, 1949-).
PRESSE- UND INFORMATIONSAMT
BULLETIN ARCHIVE SUPPLEMENT. (Text in
English) 1974. irreg. Presse und Informationsamt -
Press and Information Office, Welckerstr. 11, 5300
Bonn, W. Germany (B.R.D.)

PUBLIC ADMINISTRATION

350   UK   ISSN 0140-5764
GOVERNMENT AND MUNICIPAL
CONTRACTORS. 1935. a. £30. Sell's Publications
Ltd., 55 High St., Epsom, Surrey KT19 8DW,
England. adv. bk. rev. circ. 5,000.
    Former titles: Sell's Government and Municipal
Contractors Register (ISSN 0072-5129);
Government and Municipal Contractors Register.

350   SI
GOVERNMENT AND PUBLIC
ADMINISTRATION SOCIETY. JOURNAL. (Text
in Chinese and English) a. not for sale. Government
and Public Administration Society, Nanyang
University, Singapore, Singapore.

353   US   ISSN 0072-5153
GOVERNMENT CONTRACTS MONOGRAPHS.
1961. irreg., no.12, 1979. price varies. ‡ George
Washington University, Government Contracts
Program, 801 22nd St., N.W., T-412, Washington,
DC 20052.

350   MF
GOVERNMENT GAZETTE OF MAURITIUS. (Text
in English) irreg., no.34, 1981. Government Printing
Office, Elizabeth II Ave., Port Louis, Mauritius.
index.

350   MF
GOVERNMENT GAZETTE OF MAURITIUS.
LEGAL SUPPLEMENT. ACT. (Text in English)
irreg., no.2, 1981. Government Printing Office,
Elizabeth II Ave., Port Louis, Mauritius.

350   MF
GOVERNMENT GAZETTE OF MAURITIUS.
LEGAL SUPPLEMENT. GOVERNMENT
NOTICE. (Text in English) irreg., no.84, 1981.
Government Printing Office, Elizabeth II Ave., Port
Louis, Mauritius.

350   MF
GOVERNMENT GAZETTE OF MAURITIUS.
LEGAL SUPPLEMENT. PROCLAMATION.
(Text in English) irreg., no.3, 1981. Government
Printing Office, Elizabeth II Ave., Port Louis,
Mauritius.

350   MF
GOVERNMENT GAZETTE OF MAURITIUS.
SPECIAL LEGAL SUPPLEMENT. A BILL. (Text
in English) irreg., no.7, 1981. Government Printing
Office, Elizabeth II Ave., Port Louis, Mauritius.

350   US   ISSN 0072-517X
GOVERNMENT IN HAWAII; a handbook of
financial statistics. 1954. a. $3. Tax Foundation of
Hawaii, 220 S. King, Ste. 680, Honolulu, HI 96813.
Ed. Lowell L. Kalapa. circ. 3,500. Indexed: Vert.File
Ind.

354.54   II
GOVERNMENT OF ANDHRA PRADESH.
REPORT.* (Text in English) a. Office of the
Comptroller and Auditor-General, Director of
Printing and Stationery, Hyderabad, Andhra
Pradesh, India.
    Continues: Government of Andhra Pradesh.
Audit Report.

363.6   US   ISSN 0737-5255
GOVERNMENT PROGRAMS AND PROJECTS
DIRECTORY. irreg. $135. Gale Research
Company, Book Tower, Detroit, MI 48226. Ed.
Anthony T. Kruzas, Kay Gill.

350   US   ISSN 0072-520X
GOVERNMENTAL RESEARCH ASSOCIATION
DIRECTORY; directory of organizations and
individuals professionally engaged in governmental
research and related activities. 1938. biennial. $25.
Governmental Research Association, Inc., 24
Province St., Boston, MA 02108. TEL 617-720-
1000. index. circ. 700.

350   US
GOVERNORS OF OKLAHOMA. 1967. quadrennial.
Department of Libraries, 200 N.E. 18th St.,
Oklahoma City, OK 73105. circ. 5,000.

350   US
GRADUATE PROGRAMS IN PUBLIC AFFAIRS
AND PUBLIC ADMINISTRATION. Variant titles:
Directory: Graduate Programs in Public Affairs and
Public Administrator. Programs in Public Affairs
and Administration. 1972. biennial. $12.50. National
Association of Schools of Public Affairs and
Administration, 1120 G. St., N.W., Ste. 520,
Washington, DC 20005. TEL 202-628-8961. Ed.
Alfred M. Zuck. circ. 1,500. Indexed: C.I.J.E.
    Formerly: Graduate School Programs in Public
Affairs and Public Administration (ISSN 0094-6648)

GRADUATE SCHOOL JOURNAL. see
*EDUCATION — School Organization And
Administration*

351.1   UK   ISSN 0307-9589
GREAT BRITAIN. CIVIL SERVICE
DEPARTMENT. REPORT. 1969. irreg., 3rd, 1973.
price varies. Civil Service Department, Whitehall,
London SW1A 2AZ, England (Avail. from
H.M.S.O., c/o Liaison Officer, Atlantic House,
Holborn Viaduct, London EC1P 1BN, England)
stat.

GREAT BRITAIN. DEPARTMENT OF THE
ENVIRONMENT. STATISTICS FOR TOWN
AND COUNTRY PLANNING. SERIES 1. see
HOUSING AND URBAN PLANNING

GREAT BRITAIN. DEPARTMENT OF THE
ENVIRONMENT. STATISTICS FOR TOWN
AND COUNTRY PLANNING. SERIES 2. see
HOUSING AND URBAN PLANNING

350   UK   ISSN 0072-7032
GREAT BRITAIN. PUBLIC WORKS LOAN
BOARD. REPORT. 1875. a. £4.75. Public Works
Loan Board, Royex House, London EC2V 7LR,
England (Avail. from: H.M.S.O., P.O. Box 276,
London SW8 5DT, England) circ. 500.

352   300   UK   ISSN 0072-7350
GREATER LONDON PAPERS; problems of
government of greater London. 1961. irreg., latest
1976. price varies. London School of Economics
and Political Science, Houghton St., Aldwych,
London WC2A 2AE, England.

353.9   US   ISSN 0072-8454
GUIDE TO GOVERNMENT IN HAWAII. 1961.
irreg., 8th edt., 1984. $3. Legislative Reference
Bureau, State Capitol, Honolulu, HI 96813. TEL
808-548-6237.

353.9   US   ISSN 0091-0716
GUIDE TO NEBRASKA STATE AGENCIES.
(Supplement to: Nebraska State Publications
Checklist) 1973. a. included in subscr. to Nebraska
State Publications Checklist. Nebraska Publications
Clearinghouse, 1420 P St., NE, Lincoln, NE 68508.
Ed. Karen Lusk. circ. 200. (also avail. in microfiche)

HANDAKTEN FUER DIE STANDESAMTLICHE
ARBEIT. see *LAW*

350   336   US
HAWAII. LEGISLATIVE AUDITOR. SPECIAL
REPORTS. 1965. irreg., 3-5/yr. free. ‡ Office of the
Auditor, State Capitol, Honolulu, HI 96813. TEL
808-548-2450. charts. stat.

350   US   ISSN 0073-1277
HAWAII. LEGISLATIVE REFERENCE BUREAU.
REPORT. 1951. irreg. price varies. Legislative
Reference Bureau, State Capitol, Honolulu, HI
96813. TEL 808-548-6237.

350   US   ISSN 0272-1155
HERITAGE LECTURES. 1980. irreg., no.80, 1986.
price varies. Heritage Foundation, Inc., 214
Massachusetts Ave., NE, Washington, DC 20002.
TEL 202-546-4400. index. (also avail. in microfiche;
back issues avail.)

350   331   BE
HOGE RAAD VOOR DE MIDDENSTAND.
JAARVERSLAG. (Text in Dutch) 1982. a. Hoge
Raad voor de Middenstand, Liefdadigheidsstraat 24,
1040 Brussels, Belgium.

350   HO
HONDURAS. CONGRESO NACIONAL.
BOLETIN. irreg., no.18, 1982. Congreso Nacional,
Oficina de Boletines y Publicaciones, Tegucigalpa,
Honduras.

350   US   ISSN 0073-3873
HUMAN RESOURCES RESEARCH
ORGANIZATION. PROFESSIONAL PAPERS.
1966. irreg. free. Human Resources Research
Organization, 1100 S. Washington St., Alexandria,
VA 22314. (also avail. in microform from NTI)
Indexed: Psychol.Abstr.

353   US   ISSN 0195-7783
ILLINOIS GOVERNMENT RESEARCH. 1959.
irreg., approx. 2/yr. free. University of Illinois,
Institute of Government & Public Affairs, 1201 W.
Nevada St., Urbana, IL 61801. TEL 217-333-3340.
Ed. Anna J. Merritt. circ. 1,200.
    Formerly: Illinois Government. (ISSN 0073-4837)

INDEX TO COLORADO STATE PUBLICATIONS.
see *BIBLIOGRAPHIES*

INDEX TO THE CODE OF FEDERAL
REGULATIONS. see *ABSTRACTING AND
INDEXING SERVICES*

350   II   ISSN 0073-6171
INDIA. CENTRAL VIGILANCE COMMISSION.
REPORT. (Text in English and Hindi) 1965. a. free.
Central Vigilance Commission, No.3, Dr. Rajendra
Prasad Road, New Delhi, India. circ. controlled.

354   II
INDIA. DEPARTMENT OF ECONOMIC
AFFAIRS. BUDGET DIVISION. KEY TO THE
BUDGET DOCUMENTS. (Text in English) a.
Department of Economic Affairs, Budget Division,
New Delhi, India.

INDIA. DEPARTMENT OF POWER. REPORT. see
ENERGY

354   II   ISSN 0445-6831
INDIA. PARLIAMENT. PUBLIC ACCOUNTS
COMMITTEE. REPORT ON THE ACCOUNTS.
(Each report covers various agencies of the
government.) (Text in English) 1947/48. a.
Parliament, Public Accounts Committee, Lok Sabha
Secretariat, New Delhi, India.

351.1   II   ISSN 0073-6236
INDIA. UNION PUBLIC SERVICE COMMISSION
REPORT. (Report year ends Mar. 31) (Text in
English) 1951. a. Union Public Service Commission,
Minto Rd., New Delhi, India.

350   IO
INDONESIA. DEPARTEMEN PENERANGAN.
SIARAN UMUM. irreg. Department of
Information, Direktorat Publikasi, Jl. Merdeka Barat
7, Jakarta, Indonesia.

350   IE   ISSN 0073-9596
INSTITUTE OF PUBLIC ADMINISTRATION,
DUBLIN. ADMINISTRATION YEARBOOK
AND DIARY. (Text mainly in English; some Irish)
1967. a. £18. Institute of Public Administration, 57-
61 Lansdowne Rd, Dublin 4, Ireland. Ed. I.
MacAulay. adv. circ. 8,500.

350   IE   ISSN 0073-9588
INSTITUTE OF PUBLIC ADMINISTRATION,
DUBLIN. ANNUAL REPORT. (Text mainly in
English; some Irish) 1958. a. free. Institute of Public
Administration, 57-61 Lansdowne Road, Dublin 4,
Ireland. Ed. Jim O'Donnell. circ. 2,000.

354   SJ   ISSN 0073-9618
INSTITUTE OF PUBLIC ADMINISTRATION,
KHARTOUM. OCCASIONAL PAPERS. 1964.
irreg. Institute of Public Administration, P.O. Box
1492, Khartoum, Sudan.

354   SJ   ISSN 0073-9626
INSTITUTE OF PUBLIC ADMINISTRATION,
KHARTOUM. PROCEEDINGS OF THE
ANNUAL ROUND TABLE CONFERENCE.
(Text in Arabic or English) 1959. irreg. Institute of
Public Administration, P.O. Box 1492, Khartoum,
Sudan.

350   CR   ISSN 0073-9944
INSTITUTO CENTROAMERICANO DE
ADMINISTRACION PUBLICA. SERIE 100.
ASPECTOS HUMANOS DE LA
ADMINISTRACION. 1965. irreg. price varies.
Instituto Centroamericano de Administracion
Publica, Apartado 10025, San Jose, Costa Rica.

PUBLIC ADMINISTRATION 943

350 CR ISSN 0073-9952
INSTITUTO CENTROAMERICANO DE ADMINISTRACION PUBLICA. SERIE 200. CIENCIA DE LA ADMINISTRACION. 1960. irreg. price varies. Instituto Centroamericano de Administracion Publica, Apartado 10025, San Jose, Costa Rica.

350 CR ISSN 0073-9960
INSTITUTO CENTROAMERICANO DE ADMINISTRACION PUBLICA. SERIE 300: INVESTIGACION. 1968. irreg. price varies. Instituto Centroamericano de Administracion Publica, Apartado 10025, San Jose, Costa Rica.

350 CR ISSN 0073-9979
INSTITUTO CENTROAMERICANO DE ADMINISTRACION PUBLICA. SERIE 400: ECONOMIA Y FINANZAS. 1968. irreg. price varies. Instituto Centroamericano de Administracion Publica, Apartado 10025, San Jose, Costa Rica.

350 CR ISSN 0073-9995
INSTITUTO CENTROAMERICANO DE ADMINISTRACION PUBLICA. SERIE 600: INFORMES DE SEMINARIOS. 1964. irreg. price varies. Instituto Centroamericano de Administracion Publica, Apartado 10025, San Jose, Costa Rica.

350 CR ISSN 0074-0004
INSTITUTO CENTROAMERICANO DE ADMINISTRACION PUBLICA. SERIE 700: MATERIALES DE INFORMACION. 1966. irreg. free. Instituto Centroamericano de Administracion Publica, Apartado 10025, San Jose, Costa Rica.

350 CR ISSN 0074-0012
INSTITUTO CENTROAMERICANO DE ADMINISTRACION PUBLICA. SERIE 800: METODOLOGIA DE LA ADMINISTRACION. 1964. irreg. price varies. Instituto Centroamericano de Administracion Publica, Apartado 10025, San Jose, Costa Rica.

350 CR ISSN 0074-0020
INSTITUTO CENTROAMERICANO DE ADMINISTRACION PUBLICA. SERIE 900: MISCELANEAS. 1965. irreg. price varies. Instituto Centroamericano de Administracion Publica, Apartado 10025, San Jose, Costa Rica.

350 BE ISSN 0074-6479
INTERNATIONAL INSTITUTE OF ADMINISTRATIVE SCIENCES. REPORTS OF THE INTERNATIONAL CONGRESS. 1910. triennial since 1947; 19th, 1983, West Berlin. price varies. International Institute of Administrative Sciences, 1 rue Defacqz, Bte.11, 1050 Brussels, Belgium.

INTERNATIONAL SECURITY DIRECTORY; world defense, police & fire hqs., security companies, their products and supplies. see *CRIMINOLOGY AND LAW ENFORCEMENT — Security*

350 IT ISSN 0074-9435
INTERNATIONAL UNION OF LATIN NOTARIES. PROCEEDINGS OF CONGRESS. 1948. biennial. Intl. Union of Latin Notaries, Notario Gallavresi, Via Senato n.37, Milan, Italy. adv. bk. rev.
1971, 11th, Athens

350 US ISSN 0074-106X
INTER-UNIVERSITY CASE PROGRAM. CASE STUDY. (Title varies: I C P Case Series; at head of title: Cases in Public Administration and Policy Information) 1951. irreg. price varies. Inter-University Case Program, Inc., Box 229, Syracuse, NY 13210. Ed. E.A. Bock.

350 IQ
IRAQ. MINISTRY OF INFORMATION. INFORMATION SERIES. irreg., no.72, 1977. Ministry of Information, Baghdad, Iraq.

350 IQ
IRAQ GOVERNMENT GAZETTE. (Editions in Arabic and English) 1922. w. (English edt.) irreg. (Arabic edt.) Ministry of Information, Baghdad, Iraq. circ. 4,000 (Arabic edt.) 450 (English edt.)

350 IE
IRELAND. PUBLIC SERVICE ADVISORY COUNCIL. REPORT. 1975. a. £1.85. Government Publications Sales Office, Sun Alliance House, Molesworth St., Dublin 2, Ireland.

350 IS
ISRAEL. COMMISSIONER FOR COMPLAINTS FROM THE PUBLIC (OMBUDSMAN) ANNUAL REPORT. (Editions in Hebrew, occasionally in English) 1972. a. free. Commissioner for Complaints from the Public, Jerusalem, Israel. circ. 2,000.

354 IV
IVORY COAST. DIRECTION DU BUDGET SPECIAL D'INVESTISSEMENT ET D'EQUIPMENT. RAPPORT DE PRESENTATION DU BUDGET SPECIAL D'INVESTISSEMENT ET D'EQUIPMENT.* irreg. Direction du Budget Special d'Investissement et d'Equipement, Abidjan, Ivory Coast. stat.

350 IS ISSN 0021-3705
J N F ILLUSTRATED. (Editions in English, French, German and Spanish) 1927. a. Jewish National Fund, Box 183, Jerusalem, Israel. Ed. Lenny Labensohn. charts. illus. circ. 30,000.

350 JA
JAPANESE SOCIETY FOR PUBLIC ADMINISTRATION. ANNALS/NIPPON GYOSEI KENKYU NENPO. (Text in Japanese) a. Japanese Society for Public Administration - Nippon Gyosei Gakkai, c/o Faculty of Law, University of Tokyo, Motofuji-cho, Bunkyo-ku, Tokyo 113, Japan. bibl.

350 FT
JOURNAL OFFICIEL DE LA REPUBLIQUE DE DJIBOUTI. (Text in French) 1977. irreg. 5720 Fr.CFA. Secretaire General du Gouvernement, Djibouti, Djibouti (Subscr. to: Impr. Administrative, B.P. 268, Djibouti, Djibouti) adv.

JUDICIAL STAFF DIRECTORY. see *LAW*

350 KE ISSN 0075-5761
K I A OCCASIONAL PAPERS. 1968. irreg., latest no. 4. price varies. Kenya Institute of Administration, P.O. Lower Kabete, Nairobi, Kenya. Ed. H.K.M. Wacirah.

352 NR
KADUNA STATE. MINISTRY OF WORKS. REPORT.* 1960/61. a. price varies. Ministry of Works, Kaduna, Nigeria.
Formerly: North-Central State. Ministry of Works. Report (ISSN 0078-1762)

354.669 NR
KANO STATE OF NIGERIA GAZETTE. 1967. irreg. free. Government Printing Press, P.O. Box 469, Kano, Nigeria. circ. 3,500.
Continues: Northern Nigeria Gazette.

354 II
KARNATAKA. DEPARTMENT OF TOURISM. ANNUAL REPORT. (Text in English) 1975. a. Department of Information and Tourism, 5 Infantry Rd., Bangalore, India.

338.9 KE
KENYA. MINISTRY OF FINANCE AND PLANNING. BUDGET SPEECH BY MINISTER FOR FINANCE AND PLANNING. (Text in English) a. Ministry of Finance and Planning, Box 30007, Nairobi, Kenya (Orders to: Government Printing and Stationery Department, Box 30128, Nairobi, Kenya)
Former titles: Kenya. Ministry of Finance and Economic Planning. Budget Speech; Kenya. Ministry of Finance. Speech Delivered to the National Assembly, Presenting the Budget.

354 KE
KENYA. MINISTRY OF FINANCE AND PLANNING. PLAN IMPLEMENTATION REPORT. 1973. irreg. Ministry of Finance and Planning, Box 30007, Nairobi, Kenya (Orders to: Government Printing and Stationery Department, Box 30128, Nairobi, Kenya)

350 KE
KENYA. OFFICE OF THE DISTRICT COMMISSIONER. ANNUAL REPORT. a. Office of the District Commissioner, South Nyanza District, P.O. Box 1, Homa Bay, Kenya.

350 KE ISSN 0075-5931
KENYA. PUBLIC ACCOUNTS COMMITTEE. ANNUAL REPORT. a., latest 1980/81. EAs.20. Government Printing and Stationery Department, Box 30128, Nairobi, Kenya.

350 KE
KENYA GAZETTE SUPPLEMENT. (Issued in 3 parts: Acts, Bills and Legislative Supplement) (Text in English) irreg. Government Printing and Stationery Department, Box 30128, Nairobi, Kenya. index.

354 KE ISSN 0065-1966
KENYA INSTITUTE OF ADMINISTRATION. JOURNAL. 1965. a. EAs.7.50. Kenya Institute of Administration, P.O. Lower Kabete, Nairobi, Kenya. Ed. H.K.M. Wacirah.
Formerly: Administration in Kenya.

350 DK ISSN 0085-2589
KONGELIG DANSK HOF- OG STATSKALENDER; STATSHAANDBOG FOR KONGERIGET DANMARK. 1734. a. price varies. J.H. Schultz Forlag, Moentergade 21, DK-1116 Copenhagen K, Denmark. Eds. Herluf Nielsen, Morten Estrup. adv. circ. 2,000.

350 US
LANE STUDIES IN REGIONAL GOVERNMENT. irreg. price varies. University of California Press, 2120 Berkeley Way, Berkeley, CA 94720. TEL 415-642-4247.

350 LB
LIBERIA. INSTITUTE OF PUBLIC ADMINISTRATION. ANNUAL REPORT. 1973. a. free. Institute of Public Administration, Monrovia, Liberia. circ. 200.

354 LB
LIBERIA. MINISTRY OF ACTION FOR DEVELOPMENT AND PROGRESS. ANNUAL REPORT. a. Ministry of Action for Development and Progress, Monrovia, Liberia.

354 LB ISSN 0304-7326
LIBERIA. MINISTRY OF PUBLIC WORKS. ANNUAL REPORT. (Text in English) a. Ministry of Public Works, Monrovia, Liberia.

350 LB
LIBERIA. OFFICE OF NATIONAL PLANNING. ANNUAL REPORT TO THE PRESIDENT ON THE OPERATION AND ACTIVITIES. 1961. a. Office of National Planning, Monrovia, Liberia.
Formerly: Liberia. Bureau of Economic Research and Statistics. Annual Report to the President on the Operation and Activities.

340 352 AT ISSN 0076-0242
LOCAL GOVERNMENT REPORTS OF AUSTRALIA. 1911. irreg. Aus.$105. Law Book Co. Ltd., 44-50 Waterloo Rd., North Ryde, N.S.W. 2112, Australia. Ed. Kenneth Gifford.

350 UK ISSN 0307-0441
LOCAL GOVERNMENT TRENDS. 1974. a. £18. Chartered Institute of Public Finance and Accountancy, 3 Robert St., London WC2N 6BH, England. (back issues avail.)

350 US
M A P A ANNUAL REPORT. a. free. Omaha-Council Bluffs Metropolitan Area Planning Agency, 2222 Cuming St., Omaha, NE 68102-4328. circ. 1,000.

350 US
M T A S MUNICIPAL TECHNICAL REPORT. 1973. irreg., no.30, 1984. $1. University of Tennessee, Municipal Technical Advisory Service, 891 20th St., Knoxville, TN 37996-4400. TEL 615-974-1008. circ. 300.
Formerly: University of Tennessee. Institute for Public Service. M T A S Municipal Technical Report.

MAINE REGISTER: STATE YEARBOOK AND LEGISLATIVE MANUAL. see *PUBLIC ADMINISTRATION — Municipal Government*

350 MW
MALAWI. ECONOMIC PLANNING DIVISION. MID-YEAR ECONOMIC REVIEW. (Text in English) 1971. a. Government Printer, Box 37, Zomba, Malawi.

350 MW
MALAWI GAZETTE SUPPLEMENT CONTAINING ACTS. (Text in English) irreg. Government Printer, Box 37, Zomba, Malawi.

PUBLIC ADMINISTRATION

350 MW
MALAWI GAZETTE SUPPLEMENT CONTAINING BILLS. (Text in English) irreg. Government Printer, Box 37, Zomba, Malawi.

350 MW
MALAWI GAZETTE SUPPLEMENT CONTAINING REGULATIONS, RULES, ETC. (Text in English) irreg. Government Printer, Box 37, Zomba, Malawi.

350 MW
MALAWI GOVERNMENT DIRECTORY. (Text in English) a. Government Printer, Box 37, Zomba, Malawi.

363.6 AT
MANPOWER SERVICES GUIDE. 1980. a. free. Australian Government Publishing Service, Box 84, Canberra, ACT 2600, Australia. circ. 100,000.

141 310 US ISSN 0094-4491
MARYLAND MANUAL. Title varies: Manual-State of Maryland. 1898. biennial. $10. State Archives, Hall of Records Commission, 350 Rowe Blvd., Annapolis, MD 21401. TEL 301-269-3914. Ed. Gregory A. Stiverson. charts. illus. stat. index. circ. 8,500. (back issues avail.)

MASSACHUSETTS TAXPAYERS FOUNDATION. STATE BUDGET TRENDS. see BUSINESS AND ECONOMICS — Economic Situation And Conditions

350 MF
MAURITIUS. LEGISLATIVE ASSEMBLY. DEBATES. (Text in English) irreg., latest 4th session, no. 9, 1980. Government Printing Office, Elizabeth II Ave., Port Louis, Mauritius.

350 MF ISSN 0076-5503
MAURITIUS. LEGISLATIVE ASSEMBLY. SESSIONAL PAPER. irreg., latest 1972. price varies. Government Printing Office, Elizabeth II Ave., Port Louis, Mauritius.

MAURITIUS. MINISTRY OF WORKS AND INTERNAL COMMUNICATIONS. REPORT. see TRANSPORTATION

350 MF
MAURITIUS. OMBUDSMAN. REPORT. (Text in English) a., latest 1980. Government Printing Office, Elizabeth II Ave., Port Louis, Mauritius.

350 MF
MAURITIUS. PUBLIC SERVICE COMMISSION. REPORT. (Text in English) triennial, latest 1976/78. Government Printing Office, Elizabeth II Ave., Port Louis, Mauritius.

352 US ISSN 0076-7115
METROPOLITAN WASHINGTON COUNCIL OF GOVERNMENTS. REGIONAL DIRECTORY. 1962. a. $5. Metropolitan Washington Council of Governments, 1875 Eye St. N.W., Washington, DC 20006. TEL 202-223-6800.

350 US ISSN 0076-7956
MICHIGAN GOVERNMENTAL STUDIES. irreg., no.59, 1968. price varies. ‡ University of Michigan, Institute of Public Policy Studies, 1516 Rackham Bldg., Ann Arbor, MI 48104. TEL 313-764-1817.

MICHIGAN STATE EMPLOYEES' RETIREMENT SYSTEM FINANCIAL AND STATISTICAL REPORT. see BUSINESS AND ECONOMICS — Labor And Industrial Relations

340 US
MINNESOTA GUIDEBOOK TO STATE AGENCY SERVICES. 1977. quadrennial. $15. Department of Administration, Documents Division, 117 University Ave., St. Paul, MN 55155. TEL 612-297-3000. Ed. Robin PanLener. index. circ. 11,250.

MINNESOTA RULES. see LAW

MINNESOTA RULES. SUPPLEMENT. see LAW

350 GW
MITTEILUNGEN DER FACHHOCHSCHULE DES BUNDES. 1979. biennial. free. Fachhochschule des Bundes fuer Oeffentliche Verwaltung Mitteilungen, Bernhard-Feilchenfeld-Str. 9, 5000 Koln 51, W. Germany (B.R.D.) Ed.Bd. bk. rev. circ. 900. (back issues avail.)

350 US ISSN 0093-8246
MONTANA. DEPARTMENT OF BUSINESS REGULATION. ANNUAL REPORT. a. Department of Business Regulation, 805 N. Main, Helena, MT 59601. TEL 406-449-3163. Key Title: Annual Report of the Department of Business Regulation (Helena)

353.9 US ISSN 0090-4325
MONTANA. OFFICE OF THE LEGISLATIVE AUDITOR. DEPARTMENT OF INSTITUTIONS REIMBURSEMENTS PROGRAM; REPORT ON AUDIT. (Report year ends June 30) biennial. Office of the Legislative Auditor, State Capitol, Rm. 135, Helena, MT 59620. TEL 406-444-3122.

MONTANA. OFFICE OF THE LEGISLATIVE AUDITOR. STATE OF MONTANA BOARD OF INVESTMENTS. REPORT ON EXAMINATION OF FINANCIAL STATEMENTS. see BUSINESS AND ECONOMICS — Investments

350 UK ISSN 0077-4456
N A L G O ANNUAL REPORT. 1906. a. National and Local Government Officers Association, Nalgo House, 1 Mabledon Place, London WC1H 9AJ, England. Ed. John D. Daly.

NATIONAL ARCHIVES OF ZAMBIA. CALENDARS OF THE DISTRICT NOTEBOOKS. see HISTORY — History Of Africa

353.008 US
NATIONAL ASSOCIATION OF REGULATORY UTILITY COMMISSIONERS. ANNUAL REPORT ON UTILITY AND CARRIER REGULATION. a. $50. National Association of Regulatory Utility Commissioners, 1102 Interstate Commerce Commission Bldg., Box 684, Washington, DC 20044. TEL 202-898-2200.

NATIONAL CIVIL SERVICE LEAGUE. ANNUAL REPORT. see BUSINESS AND ECONOMICS — Labor And Industrial Relations

336.782 US
NEBRASKA. DEPARTMENT OF ADMINISTRATIVE SERVICES. ANNUAL FISCAL REPORT. Cover title: State of Nebraska Annual Fiscal Report. 1966. a. free. ‡ State Department of Administrative Services, Lincoln, NE 68509. TEL 402-471-3593. illus. stat. circ. 350.
Former titles: Nebraska. Accounting Division. Annual Fiscal Report & Nebraska. Accounting Division. Annual Report of Receipts and Disbursements (ISSN 0090-628X)

353.9 US
NEVADA. OFFICE OF LEGISLATIVE AUDITOR. BIENNIAL REPORT. (Subseries of Nevada. Legislative Counsel Bureau. Bulletin) 1974. biennial. Office of Legislative Auditor, Carson City, NV 89710. TEL 702-885-5622. stat.
Formerly: Nevada. Office of Fiscal Analyst. Annual Report (ISSN 0092-6841)

NEW SOUTH WALES. DEPARTMENT OF AGRICULTURE. ANNUAL REPORT. see AGRICULTURE

352 US
NEW YORK (STATE) DEPARTMENT OF STATE. MANUAL FOR THE USE OF THE LEGISLATURE OF THE STATE OF NEW YORK; New York State Legislative manual. 1827. biennial. $15. Department of State, Division of Information Services, 162 Washington Ave., Albany, NY 12231. Dir. Maureen L. Bigness. circ. 15,500.

350 US
NEW YORK (STATE) LEGISLATIVE COMMISSION ON EXPENDITURE REVIEW. PROGRAM AUDITS. 1971. irreg. free. Legislative Commission on Expenditure Review, 111 Washington Ave., Albany, NY 12210. Dir. Bernard P. Geizer. circ. 1,000.

350 US
NEW YORK RED BOOK. 1895. biennial. $45. Williams Press Inc., Box 4025, Patroon Sta., Albany, NY 12204. TEL 518-434-1141. Ed. George A. Mitchell. circ. 15,000.

353.9 US
NEW YORK SEA GRANT INSTITUTE. ANNUAL REPORT. 1973. a. State University of New York at Albany, 411 State St., Albany, NY 12246. TEL 518-457-3300. (Co-publisher: Cornell University) Ed. Bruce M. Kantrowitz. adv. bk. rev. illus. circ. 1, 500.
Formerly: New York State Sea Grant Program. Annual Report (ISSN 0360-3326)

353.97 US
NEW YORK STATE. STATE SCIENCE SERVICE. BIENNIAL REPORT. biennial. (State Science Service) University of the State of New York Press, Albany, NY 12230.

338.9 US ISSN 0077-9423
NEW YORK STATE URBAN DEVELOPMENT CORPORATION. ANNUAL REPORT. 1969-1975; resumed 1977. a. free. Urban Development Corporation, 1515 Broadway, New York, NY 10036. TEL 212-930-9000. circ. controlled.

354 NZ
NEW ZEALAND. DEPARTMENT OF MAORI AFFAIRS. ANNUAL REPORT. 1930. a. price varies. Department of Maori Affairs, Private Bag, Wellington, New Zealand. Ed. Andrew Robb. circ. 5,000.
Formerly: New Zealand. Department of Maori Affairs. Report.

350 NZ ISSN 0111-0470
NEW ZEALAND PLANNING COUNCIL. PLANNING PAPER. no.5, 1980. irreg. New Zealand Planning Council, Box 5066, Wellington, New Zealand. circ. 2,000.

350 US
NORTH CAROLINA. SECRETARY OF STATE. DIRECTORY OF STATE AND COUNTY OFFICIALS. 1936. a. free. Secretary of State, 300 N. Salisbury St., Raleigh, NC 27611. TEL 919-733-7355. Ed. John L. Cheney, Jr.

353.9 US
NORTH CAROLINA. STATE GOALS AND POLICY BOARD. ANNUAL REPORT. 1972. a. Department of Administration, State Goals and Policy Board, 116 W. Jones St., Raleigh, NC 27611. TEL 919-733-4131. Ed. Doris I. Gupton. stat. circ. 3,000.
Formerly: North Carolina. Council on State Goals and Policy. Annual Report (ISSN 0093-9730)

350 US
NORTH CAROLINA MANUAL. 1901. biennial. Secretary of State, 300 N. Salisbury St., Raleigh, NC 27611. TEL 919-733-7355. Ed. John L. Cheney, Jr. circ. 4,500(controlled)

NORTHEAST REGIONAL SCIENCE REVIEW. see HOUSING AND URBAN PLANNING

323 UK
NORTHERN IRELAND. COMMISSIONER FOR COMPLAINTS. ANNUAL REPORT. 1970. a. price varies. H.M.S.O., Progressive House, 33 Wellington Place, Belfast BT1 6HN, N. Ireland (Orders to H.M. Stationery Office, Chichester House, Chichester St., Belfast, Northern Ireland) circ. 170.

354 CN
NOVA SCOTIA. DEPARTMENT OF DEVELOPMENT. ANNUAL REPORT. 1971. a. free. Department of Development, Box 519, Halifax, N.S. B3J 2R7, Canada. TEL 902-424-8920. Ed. Carole MacDonald. circ. 300 (controlled)

354.716 CN
NOVA SCOTIA. OFFICE OF THE OMBUDSMAN. ANNUAL REPORT. 1971. a. free. Office of the Ombudsman, Halifax, Nova Scotia, Canada. TEL 902-424-6780. Ed. W. Andrew MacKay. circ. 1,000.

350 US
OCCASIONAL PAPERS IN ILLINOIS POLITICS. 1981. irreg. free. Institute of Government and Public Affairs, 1201 W. Nevada St., Urbana, IL 61801. TEL 217-333-3340. Ed. Anna J. Merritt.

PUBLIC ADMINISTRATION 945

350 US
OHIO STATE UNIVERSITY. SCHOOL OF PUBLIC ADMINISTRATION. WORKING PAPER SERIES. 1972. irreg. free. Ohio State University, Administrative Science Research, 1775 College Rd., Columbus, OH 42310. TEL 614-422-8696. circ. controlled.

350 US
OKLAHOMA STATE AGENCIES, BOARDS, COMMISSIONS, COURTS, INSTITUTIONS, LEGISLATURE AND OFFICERS. 1953. a. Department of Libraries, Legislative Reference Division, 200 N.E. 18th St., Oklahoma City, OK 73105. circ. 1,000.

350 CN ISSN 0318-0743
ONTARIO. PROVINCIAL-MUNICIPAL AFFAIRS SECRETARIAT. MUNICIPAL DIRECTORY. (Text in English and French) 1948. a. Can.$4. Ministry of Municipal Affairs, Provincial-Municipal Affairs Secretariat, 777 Bay St., 13th Fl., Toronto, Ont. M5G 2E5, Canada. charts. stat. index.

350 US
OREGON BLUE BOOK. 1904. biennial. $6 per no. Secretary of State, 136 State Capitol, Salem, OR 97310. TEL 503-378-4139. Ed. Tom Bryson. circ. 25,000.

354 TH ISSN 0475-2015
ORGANIZATIONAL DIRECTORY OF THE GOVERNMENT OF THAILAND. (Text in English and Thai) irreg. Translation & Secretarial Office, 56 Suan Luang I St., Pathum Wan, Bangkok, Thailand.

354.669 NR
OYO STATE. ESTIMATES INCLUDING BUDGET SPEECH AND MEMORANDUM. Short title: Oyo State of Nigeria Estimates. a. £N40. Government Printer, Ibadan, Nigeria.
Formerly: Western State. Estimates Including Budget Speech and Memorandum.

340.05 NR
OYO STATE OF NIGERIA GAZETTE. (Supplements accompany some numbers) irreg. £N12. Government Printer, Ibadan, Nigeria.
Formerly: Western State. Gazette.

350 PK ISSN 0078-8333
PAKISTAN. NATIONAL ASSEMBLY. DEBATES. OFFICIAL REPORT. (Text in English) 1962. irreg. Rs.0.50. National Assembly, Islamabad, Pakistan (Order from: Manager of Publications, Government of Pakistan, 2nd Floor, Ahmad Chamber, Tariq Rd., P.E.C.H.S., Karachi 29, Pakistan)

350 PN
PANAMA. TRIBUNAL ELECTORAL. MEMORIA. irreg. Tribunal Electoral, Panama, Panama.

350 US ISSN 0078-9151
PAPERS IN PUBLIC ADMINISTRATION. 1962. irreg., no.33, 1977. price varies. ‡ Arizona State University, Center for Public Affairs, Tempe, AZ 85281. TEL 602-965-3926. Ed. Richard A. Eribes. index. circ. 750.
Supersedes (as of 1970): Arizona State University. Governmental Finance Institute. Proceedings (ISSN 0072-5196)

350 US ISSN 0078-916X
PAPERS IN PUBLIC ADMINISTRATION.* 1948. irreg., no.47, 1965. price varies. ‡ University of Michigan, Institute of Public Policy Studies, 1516 Rackham Bldg., Ann Arbor, MI 48104.

354 PP ISSN 0078-9399
PAPUA NEW GUINEA. PUBLIC SERVICE BOARD. REPORT. a. price varies. Government Printer, Box 2150, Konedobu, Papua New Guinea.

350 UK
PARLIAMENTARY YEAR BOOK. 1979. a. £14.95($27) Blake's Houses of Parliament Year Book International Ltd., 11-13 Cricklewwod Lane, London NW2 1ET, England. Ed. Kim O'Brien. adv. bk. rev. circ. 2,500.

350 920 BL
PERFIS PARLAMENTARES. 1977. irreg. Camara dos Deputados, Brasilia, Brazil. circ. 2,000.

350 PH
PHILIPPINES. DEPARTMENT OF PUBLIC INFORMATION. POLICY STATEMENTS. irreg., no.13, 1977. Department of Public Information, c/o Bureau of National and Foreign Information, U P L Building, Box 3396, Intramuros, Manila, Philippines.

350 020.6 PH
PHILIPPINES. GOVERNMENT PRINTING OFFICE. ITEMIZATION OF PERSONAL SERVICES AND ORGANIZATIONAL CHARTS. a. Government Printing Office, Boston St., Port Area, Manila, Philippines.

352.7 NE ISSN 0304-176X
PLANNING AND ADMINISTRATION. 1967. 2/yr. fl.57 to members; members fl.57. International Union of Local Authorities, Wassenaarseweg 41, 2596 CG The Hague, Netherlands.
Formerly (until 1974): Studies in Comparative Local Government.

350 US ISSN 0163-108X
POLICY STUDIES REVIEW ANNUAL. 1977. a. $40. Sage Publications, Inc., 2111 W. Hillcrest Dr., Newbury Park, CA 91320 TEL 805-499-0721. (And Sage Publications, Ltd., 28 Banner St., London EC1Y 8QE, England) Ed.Bd. bibl.

353 US ISSN 0362-4765
POLITICAL SCIENCE UTILIZATION DIRECTORY. 1975. irreg. $4 to individuals; institutions $8. Policy Studies Organization, University of Illinois, 361 Lincoln Hall, Urbana, IL 61801. TEL 217-359-8541. Eds. Stuart Nagel, Marian Neef. bibl. charts. stat. index. circ. 2,400. (reprint service avail. from ISI)

POPULATION TRENDS AND PUBLIC POLICY. see POPULATION STUDIES

350.6 PO
PORTUGAL. MINISTERIO DO ULTRAMAR. RELATORIO DAS ACTIVIDADES. 1969. a. Ministerio do Ultramar, Agencia-Geral do Ultramar, Lisbon 3, Portugal.

PRINCE EDWARD ISLAND. DEPARTMENT OF COMMUNITY AND CULTURAL AFFAIRS. ANNUAL REPORT. see ENVIRONMENTAL STUDIES

330 CN
PRINCE EDWARD ISLAND. DEPARTMENT OF INDUSTRY. ANNUAL REPORT. 1950. a. free. Department of Industry, P.O. Box 2000, Charlottetown, P.E.I. C1A 7N8, Canada. TEL 902-368-4240. stat. circ. 200.
Formerly: Prince Edward Island. Department of Industry and Commerce. Annual Commerce.

338.9 380 CN ISSN 0079-5151
PRINCE EDWARD ISLAND. PUBLIC UTILITIES COMMISSION. ANNUAL REPORT. 1961. a. free. Public Utilities Commission, Box 577, Charlottetown, P.E.I. C1A 7L1, Canada. TEL 902-892-3501. circ. 325.

352 CN ISSN 0381-7962
PUBLIC EMPLOYEES JOURNAL/JOURNAL DES EMPLOYES PUBLICS. 1969. a. New Brunswick Public Employees Association, Box 95, 238 King St., Fredericton, N.B., Canada. TEL 506-458-8440. illus.
Supersedes: Civil Service Digest (ISSN 0578-3828)

350 UK
PUBLIC GENERAL ACTS & GENERAL SYNOD MEASURES. a. price varies. H.M.S.O., Box 569, Cornwall House, London SE1 9NH, England.

353.03 973 US ISSN 0079-7626
PUBLIC PAPERS OF THE PRESIDENTS OF THE UNITED STATES. a. price varies. U.S. Office of the Federal Register, National Archives and Records Administration, Washington, DC 20408 TEL 202-523-5240. (Orders to: Supt. of Documents, Washington, DC 20402)

354.9 NZ
PUBLIC SECTOR RESEARCH PAPERS. 1979. irreg. NZ.$20. New Zealand Institute of Public Administration, Box 5032, Lambton Quay, Wellington, New Zealand.

PUBLIC UTILITIES LAW ANTHOLOGY. see LAW

PUBLIC WORKS HISTORICAL SOCIETY NEWSLETTER. see HISTORY — History Of North And South America

350 SZ ISSN 0080-7249
PUBLICUS; Schweizer Jahrbuch des Oeffentlichen Lebens. (Text in French and German) 1958. a. 53 Fr. ‡ Schwabe und Co. AG, Steinentorstr. 13, 4010 Basel, Switzerland. Ed. Hans Reimann. adv. index. circ. 4,500.

350 PR
PUERTO RICO. OFICINA DE PRESUPUESTO Y GERENCIA. BOLETIN DE PRESUPUESTO Y GERENCIA. 1952. irreg. (approx. 4-6/yr.) free. Oficina de Presupuesto y Gerencia - Puerto Rico. Office of Budget and Management, Cruz 254, Apto. 3228, San Juan, PR 00904. bk. rev. bibl. illus. stat. cum.index: 1952-1984. circ. 3,000.
Formerly: Puerto Rico. Negociado del Presupuesto. Boletin de Gerencia Administrativa.

354 AT
QUEENSLAND. LAND ADMINISTRATION COMMISSION. ANNUAL REPORT. a. Queensland. Government Printer, Brisbane, Australia. illus. stat.

350 DK ISSN 0107-8747
RASP; tidsskrift for administration, samfundsoekonomi & planlaegning. 1981. irreg. Kr.45 per no. (Aalborg Universitetscenter) Aalborg Universitetsforlag, Aalborg, Denmark.

350 SW
REGISTER OVER GAELLANDE S F S-FOERFATTNINGAR. irreg (approx. every 4 yrs.) Kr.175. Allmaenna Foerlaget, Box 5227, 102 45 Stockholm, Sweden.

350 SP
RENTA NACIONAL DE ESPANA; y su distribucion provincial (year) no.10, 1976. irreg. Banco de Bilbao, Servicio de Estudios, Apartado 21, Bilbao, Spain. charts. stat.

350 RE
REPERTOIRE DES TEXTES LEGISLATIFS ET REGLEMENTAIRES ET DES REPONSES AUX QUESTIONS ECRITES CONCERNANT LA REUNION. 1975. a. 100 F. Centre Universitaire de la Reunion, Center d'Etudes Administratives, 24, 26 av. de la Victoire, Saint-Denis, Reunion. circ. 150.

350 FR
REPERTOIRE PERMANENT DE L'ADMINISTRATION FRANCAISE. 1945. a. Documentation Francaise, 29-31 Quai Voltaire, 75340 Paris, France. circ. 10,000. (also avail. in microfiche)
Formerly: France. Delegation Generale a la Recherche Scientifique et Technique. Repertoire Permanent de l'Administration Publique (ISSN 0080-1186).

350 SE
REPUBLIC OF SEYCHELLES OFFICIAL GAZETTE. (Text in English) irreg. SRl.151.20. Government Printing Office, c/o Seychelles National Bookshop, Albert St., Victoria, Seychelles. adv. circ. 800.
Supersedes: Seychelles Government Gazette.

350 658 US
RESEARCH IN PUBLIC POLICY AND MANAGEMENT. 1978. a. $21.25 to individuals; institutions $42.50. (Association for Public Policy Analysis Management) J A I Press Inc., Box 1678, 36 Sherwood Pl., Greenwich, CT 06836. TEL 203-661-7602. Ed. John Crecine.

ROLE OF STATE LEGISLATURES IN THE FREEDOM STRUGGLE. see POLITICAL SCIENCE

353.9 US
ROSTER-CALIFORNIA STATE, COUNTY, CITY AND TOWNSHIP OFFICIALS STATE OFFICIALS OF THE UNITED STATES. Variant title: California Roster. a. $6.70. Office of Procurement, Dept. of General Services Publications, Box 1015, N. Highlands, CA 95660. TEL 916-445-3441. Ed. Melissa Warren. circ. 25,000.

PUBLIC ADMINISTRATION

351   RW
RWANDA. DIRECTION GENERALE DE LA STATISTIQUE. RAPPORT ANNUEL. a. Direction Generale de la Statistique, B.P. 46, Kigali, Rwanda.
    Formerly: Rwanda. Direction Generale de la Documentation et de la Statistique. Rapport Annuel (ISSN 0080-5033)

SAIGAI NO JITTAI TO SHOBO NO GENKYO/ ANNUAL REPORT OF FIRE AND DISASTER PREVENTION. see *FIRE PREVENTION*

350   US
SALARY AND FRINGE BENEFITS SURVEY OF TENNESSEE MUNICIPALITIES. a. $15. University of Tennessee, Institute for Public Service, Municipal Technical Advisory Service, 891 20th St., Knoxville, TN 37996-4400. TEL 615-974-1009.

350   BL
SAO PAULO, BRAZIL (STATE). DEPARTAMENTO DE EDIFICIOS E OBRAS PUBLICAS. RELATORIO DE ATIVIDADES. irreg. Departamento de Edificios e Obras Publicas, Sao Paulo, Brazil. stat.

338 381   CN   ISSN 0080-6498
SASKATCHEWAN. DEPARTMENT OF INDUSTRY AND COMMERCE. REPORT FOR THE FISCAL YEAR.* 1957. a. free. Government Printing Co., 2005 8th St., Regina, Sask. S4P 3V7, Canada. TEL 306-566-9393.

350   GW
SCHRIFTEN ZUR OEFFENTLICHEN VERWALTUNG UND OEFFENTLICHEN WIRTSCHAFT. (Text in German; summaries in English, French and Russian) 1974. irreg. price varies. Nomos Verlagsgesellschaft mbH und Co. Kg., Postfach 610, 7570 Baden-Baden, W. Germany (B.R.D.) Eds. P. Eichhorn, P. Friedrich.

350   UK   ISSN 0305-6562
SCOTLANDS REGIONS. 1933. a. £2. William Culross & Son Ltd., Queen Street, Coupar Angus, Perthshire, Scotland.
    Incorporating: County and Municipal Year Book for Scotland (ISSN 0070-1300)

350   SG
SENEGAL. SECRETARIAT GENERAL DU GOUVERNMENT. DIRECTION DES ARCHIVES. RAPPORT ANNUEL. (Text in French) 1976. a. Secretariat General de la Presidence de la Republique, Direction des Archives, Immeuble Administratif, Dakar, Senegal. Ed. Saliou Mbaye.

SEYCHELLES. OFFICE OF THE PRESIDENT. BUDGET ADDRESS. see *BUSINESS AND ECONOMICS — Public Finance, Taxation*

350   SI   ISSN 0129-3109
SINGAPORE GOVERNMENT DIRECTORY. 1960. biennial. $7.00. Ministry of Communications and Information, Fourth Storey, Government Offices, St. Andrew's Rd., Singapore 0617, Singapore. circ. 8,000.

350   YU   ISSN 0037-7147
SLUZBEN VESNIK NA SOCIJALISTICKA REPUBLIKA MAKEDONIJA. (Text in Macedonian) 1945. irreg. 380 din. Socijalisticki Savez Radnog Naroda SR Makedonije, 29 Noemvri 10a, Skopje, Yugoslavia. Ed. Petar Janevski.

350   US
SOURCE BOOK OF AMERICAN STATE LEGISLATION. 1976. a. $10. American Legislative Exchange Council, 214 Massachusetts Ave., N.E., Ste. 400, Washington, DC 20002. TEL 202-547-4646. Eds. Sen. James Butcher, Brian Young. circ. 7,500.

350   US   ISSN 0362-3475
SOUTHEAST MICHIGAN COUNCIL OF GOVERNMENTS. ANNUAL REPORT. 1970. a. Southeast Michigan Council of Governments, 800 Book Bldg., Detroit, MI 48226. TEL 313-961-4266. illus. circ. 11,000. Key Title: Annual Report - Southeast Michigan Council of Governments.

350   SX
SOUTH WEST AFRICA ADMINISTRATION: WHITE PAPER ON THE ACTIVITIES OF THE DIFFERENT BRANCHES. 1974. irreg. $0.75. Administration, Private Bag 13186, Windhoek, Namibia.

354   SP
SPAIN. MINISTERIO DE HACIENDA. SUBDIRECCION GENERAL DE ORGANIZACION E INFORMACION. ESTADISTICA DE LA INFORMACION AL PUBLICO.* (Text in English, French, German and Spanish) 1971/73. irreg. free. Ministerio de Hacienda, Servicio de Publicaciones, Madrid (8), Spain.

363.6   SP
SPAIN. MINISTERIO DE LA VIVIENDA. SERIE 3: VIVIENDA. 1974 (no. 1010) irreg. Ministerio de la Vivienda, Secretaria General Tecnica, Madrid, Spain.

350   SP
SPAIN. SERVICIO CENTRAL DE PUBLICACIONES DEL MINISTERIO DE RELACIONES CON LAS CORTES Y DE LA SECRETARIA DE ESTADO. irreg. price varies. (Ministerio de Relaciones con las Cortes y de la Secretaria de Estado, Servicio Central de Publicaciones) Spain. Boletin Oficial del Estado, Trafalgar, 29, 28010 Madrid, Spain.
    Formerly: Spain. Servicio Central de Publicaciones de la Presidencia del Gobierno. Coleccion Informe.

350   US   ISSN 0561-8630
STATE ADMINISTRATIVE OFFICIALS (CLASSIFIED BY FUNCTIONS) (Supplements Book of the States) 1957. biennial. $22.50. Council of State Governments, Box 11910, Iron Works Pike, Lexington, KY 40578. TEL 606-252-2291.
    Formerly: Administrative Officials Classified by Functions (ISSN 0191-9458)

350   US
STATE DIRECTORY OF KENTUCKY. 1965. a. $11 to individuals; $10 libraries. Directories, Inc., Box 187, Pewee Valley, KY 40056. Ed. Mary McKay Wright. circ. 4,500.

350   US
STATE ELECTIVE OFFICIALS AND THE LEGISLATURES. (Supplements Book of the States) biennial. $22.50. Council of State Governments, Box 11910, Iron Works Pike, Lexington, KY 40578. TEL 606-252-2291.

350 320   US
STATE GOVERNMENT; guide to current issues and activities. 1985. a. Congressional Quarterly, Inc., 1414 22nd St., N.W., Washington, DC 20037. TEL 202-887-8500. Ed. Thad L. Beyle.

350   US
STATE INFORMATION BOOK. 1973. biennial. $69.95. Infax Corporation, 10502 Grosvenor Pl., Rockville, MD 20852. TEL 301-493-9438. Ed. Gerry Jones. circ. 3,000.

350   US   ISSN 0195-6639
STATE LEGISLATIVE LEADERSHIP, COMMITTEES AND STAFF. (Supplements Book of States) biennial. $22.50. Council of State Governments, Box 11910, Iron Works Pike, Lexington, KY 40578. TEL 606-252-2291.
    Formerly: Principal Legislative Staff Offices.

350   US
STATE LEGISLATIVE REPORT. irreg., (10-12/yr.) $30. National Conference of State Legislatures, 1050 17th St., Ste. 2100, Denver, CO 80265. TEL 303-623-7800.

350   UK
STRATHCLYDE REGIONAL COUNCIL. ANNUAL REPORT & FINANCIAL STATEMENT. 1980. a. free. Strathclyde Regional Council, Public Relations Department, 20 India St., Glasgow G2 4PF, Scotland. Ed. Robert Calderwood. circ. 10,000.
    Formerly: Strathclyde's Budget (ISSN 0260-8065)

354.624   SJ
SUDAN. MINISTRY OF FINANCE AND NATIONAL ECONOMY. ANNUAL BUDGET SPEECH, PROPOSALS FOR THE GENERAL BUDGET AND THE DEVELOPMENT BUDGET. a. Ministry of Finance and National Economy, Box 298, Khartoum, Sudan.

354.624   SJ
SUDAN. MINISTRY OF FINANCE AND NATIONAL ECONOMY. GENERAL BUDGET: REVIEW, PRESENTATION AND ANALYSIS. irreg. Ministry of Finance and National Economy, Box 298, Khartoum, Sudan.

350   SJ
SUDAN JOURNAL OF ADMINISTRATION AND DEVELOPMENT. (Text in Arabic or English) 1965. a. Institute of Public Administration, Box 1492, Khartoum, Sudan.

353.9   US   ISSN 0070-1157
SUGGESTED STATE LEGISLATION. 1941. a., latest vol.45. $25. Council of State Governments, Box 11910, Iron Works Pike, Lexington, KY 40578. TEL 606-252-2291. cum.index. circ. 5,500. Indexed: Leg.Per. C.L.I.

350   US
SUMMARY OF PUBLIC ACTS OF INTEREST TO MUNICIPAL OFFICIALS. a. $10. University of Tennessee, Institute for Public Service, Municipal Technical Advisory Service, 891 20th St., Knoxville, TN 37996-4400. TEL 615-974-1009.

354   SQ
SWAZILAND. MINISTRY OF FINANCE. RECURRENT ESTIMATES OF PUBLIC EXPENDITURE. (Report year ends Mar. 31.) a. Ministry of Finance Office, Box 443, Mbabane, Swaziland.
    Formerly: Swaziland. Central Statistical Office. Recurrent Estimates of Public Expenditure.

350 015   GW   ISSN 0082-1829
TASCHENBUCH DES OEFFENTLICHEN LEBENS; Bundesrepublik Deutschland. 1950. a. DM.94.20 price varies. Festland-Verlag Gmbh, Postfach 200561, Basteistr. 88, D-5300 Bonn 2, W. Germany (B.R.D.) Ed. Heinz H. Hey. adv. circ. 15,000.

350   US   ISSN 0082-2183
TAYLOR'S ENCYCLOPEDIA OF GOVERNMENT OFFICIALS. FEDERAL AND STATE. (Cum. supplement avail.) 1967. biennial. $395 (includes monthly World of Politics plus full service) Political Research, Inc., Tegoland at Bent Tree, 16850 Dallas Parkway, Dallas, TX 75248. TEL 214-931-8827. Ed. John Clements. index.

353.9   US
TEXAS. LEGISLATIVE REFERENCE LIBRARY. CHIEF ELECTED AND ADMINISTRATIVE OFFICIALS. 1971/73. biennial. free. Legislative Reference Library, Box 12488-Capitol Station, Austin, TX 78711. TEL 512-463-1252. Ed. Sally Reynolds.

350.6   US   ISSN 0363-7530
TEXAS STATE DIRECTORY. 1940. a. $21.95. Texas State Directory, Inc., Box 12186, Capitol Sta., Austin, TX 78711. TEL 512-477-5698. Ed. Julie F. Sayers. adv. circ. 7,000.

354   NZ
TOTALISATOR AGENCY BOARD. ANNUAL REPORT. 1951. a. free. Totalisator Agency Board, 304 Lambton Quay, Wellington, New Zealand. Ed. R.H. Pope. illus. circ. 1,300.

350 320   SW
UMEAA STUDIES IN POLITICS AND PUBLIC ADMINISTRATION. (Text in English or Swedish; summaries in English) 1978. irreg., no.9, 1984. price varies. Liber Forlag, S-205 10, Malmo, Sweden. Ed. Sten Berglund.

350   CN   ISSN 0082-7762
UNION OF NOVA SCOTIA MUNICIPALITIES. PROCEEDINGS OF THE ANNUAL CONVENTION. 1906. biennial. free. ‡ Union of Nova Scotia Municipalities, Suite 132, 136 Roy Bldg., 1657 Barrington St., Halifax, N.S. B3J 2A1, Canada. TEL 902-423-8331. circ. 1,200.

333   US   ISSN 0082-9110
U.S. BUREAU OF LAND MANAGEMENT. PUBLIC LAND STATISTICS. 1816. a. U.S. Bureau of Land Management, Division of Record Systems, U.S. Dept. of the Interior, Washington, DC 20240 TEL 303-236-6638. (Orders to: Supt. of Documents, Washington, DC 20402) Ed. L.I. Anderson. circ. 4,000. (also avail. in microfiche) Key Title: Public Land Statistics.

352 US ISSN 0082-9358
U.S. BUREAU OF THE CENSUS. CENSUS OF GOVERNMENTS. 1850. quinquennial since 1957. price varies. U.S. Bureau of the Census, Customer Services Dept., Washington, DC 20233 TEL 301-763-4100. (Orders to: Supt. of Documents, Washington, DC 20402) (also avail. in microform)
Covers finance, taxes and employment

350 US ISSN 0190-9797
U.S. CIVIL SERVICE COMMISSION. ANNUAL REPORT. 1884. a. U.S. Office of Personnel Management, 1900 E Street, N.W., Washington, DC 20415 TEL 202-655-4000. (Orders to Supt. of Documents, Government Printing Office, Washington, DC 20402) charts. illus. stat. circ. 3,000 (controlled)

355.03 US ISSN 0091-6919
U.S. DEPARTMENT OF DEFENSE. DEFENSE DEPARTMENT REPORT; a statement by the Secretary of Defense to the Congress on the budget and defense programs. 1968. a. price varies. U.S. Department of Defense, The Pentagon, Washington, DC 20301 TEL 202-545-6700. (Orders to: Supt. of Documents, Washington, DC 20402) (also avail. in microfiche) Indexed: C.I.S.Ind. Key Title: Statement of Secretary of Defense Before the House Armed Services Committee on the Defense Budget and Program.

U.S. LIBRARY OF CONGRESS. CONGRESSIONAL RESEARCH SERVICE. DIGEST OF PUBLIC GENERAL BILLS AND RESOLUTIONS. see *LAW*

U.S. NATIONAL PARK SERVICE. ANNUAL REPORT TO CONGRESS ON THE FEDERAL ARCHEOLOGICAL PROGRAM. see *ARCHAEOLOGY*

328.73 US ISSN 0095-2109
U.S. OFFICE OF TECHNOLOGY ASSESSMENT ANNUAL REPORT TO THE CONGRESS. 1974. a. U.S. Office of Technology Assessment, Washington, DC 20510 TEL 202-224-8713. (Subscr. to: Supt. of Documents, U.S. Government Printing Office, Washington, DC 20402) circ. 3,000. Key Title: Annual Report to the Congress by the Office of Technology Assessment.

353 US ISSN 0092-1904
UNITED STATES GOVERNMENT MANUAL (1973) 1934. a. $15. U.S. Office of the Federal Register, National Archives and Records Administration, Washington, DC 20408 TEL 202-523-5240. (Orders to: Supt. of Documents, Washington, DC 20402) (also avail. in microform from UMI)
Former titles (1948-1973): United States Government Organization Manual (ISSN 0083-1174); (1934-1948): United States Government Manual (1973-1981)

UNIVERSIDAD DE SEVILLA. INSTITUTO GARCIA OVIEDO. PUBLICACIONES. see *LAW*

350 AG
UNIVERSIDAD NACIONAL DEL LITORAL. FACULTAD DE CIENCIAS DE LA ADMINISTRACION. REVISTA. 1969. a. Universidad Nacional del Litoral, Facultad de Ciencias de la Administracion, 25 de Mayo, 1783, Santa Fe, Argentina.

350 US
UNIVERSITY OF CALIFORNIA, SANTA BARBARA. URBAN ECONOMICS PROGRAM. RESEARCH REPORTS IN PUBLIC POLICY. no.2, 1975. irreg. University of California, Santa Barbara, Urban Economics Program, Santa Barbara, CA 93106. TEL 805-961-2311.

350 US ISSN 0194-2670
UNIVERSITY OF NEW MEXICO. DIVISION OF GOVERNMENT RESEARCH. MONOGRAPH SERIES. 1946. irreg., vol.86, 1981. free. University of New Mexico, Institute for Applied Research Services, Division of Government Research, Albuquerque, NM 87131. TEL 505-277-3305. Ed. Robert U. Anderson. bk. rev. abstr. circ. 600.

350 US
UNIVERSITY OF TEXAS AT AUSTIN. INSTITUTE OF LATIN AMERICAN STUDIES. TECHNICAL PAPERS SERIES. 1976. irreg., no.46, 1985. free. University of Texas at Austin, Institute of Latin American Studies, Sid W. Richardson Hall, Room 1.310, Austin, TX 78712. TEL 512-471-5551. Ed. Alfred H. Saulniers. stat. circ. 800 (controlled) (back issues avail.)

350 US
UNIVERSITY OF TEXAS, AUSTIN. LYNDON B. JOHNSON SCHOOL OF PUBLIC AFFAIRS. WORKING PAPER SERIES. vol.5, 1976. irreg. University of Texas at Austin, Lyndon B. Johnson School of Public Affairs, Austin, TX 78713-7450. TEL 512-471-4962.

350 PH
UNIVERSITY OF THE PHILIPPINES. COLLEGE OF PUBLIC ADMINISTRATION. PUBLIC ADMINISTRATION AND SPECIAL STUDIES SERIES. (Text in English) a. price varies. University of the Philippines, College of Public Administration, Box 474, Manila, Philippines.

350 UY
URUGUAY. CONSEJO DE ESTADO. DIARIO DE SESSIONES. 1974. irreg. Consejo de Estado, Montevideo, Uruguay.

350 AU
DIE VERWALTUNG DER STADT WIEN. 1863. a. S.200. Statistisches Amt der Stadt Wien, Volksgartenstr. 3, 1016 Vienna, Austria (Subscr. to: Jugend und Volk Verlagsgesellschaft mbH, Tiefer Graben 7-9, A-1010 Vienna, Austria) illus. index. circ. 400. (back issues avail.)

363.6 AG
VIALIDAD ARGENTINA. 1974. irreg. Arg.$8. Direccion Nacional de Vialidad, Avenida Maipu 3, Buenos Aires, Argentina. stat.

350 360 AT ISSN 0727-5803
VICTORIAN CONSULTATIVE COMMITTEE ON SOCIAL DEVELOPMENT. ANNUAL REVIEW. 1979. a. Victoria Consultative Committee on Social Development, 290 Wellington St., Collingwood, Vic. 3066, Australia. circ. 150. (back issues avail.)

350 AT ISSN 0158-1589
VICTORIAN GOVERNMENT DIRECTORY. 1971. a. Aus.$3. Department of the Premier, 1 Treasury Place, Melbourne, Vic. 3000, Australia.
Formerly: Victoria, Australia. Directory of Government Departments and Authorities (ISSN 0310-8546)

VIE DES AFFAIRES; bulletin consacre a l'analyse du avis emis par les dirigeants d'entreprise a l'egard du droit economique et des politiques gouvernementales. see *BUSINESS AND ECONOMICS — Management*

350 VI
VIRGIN ISLANDS OF THE UNITED STATES BLUE BOOK. 1981. biennial. $5. Division of Libraries, Museums of Archaelogical Services, Department of Conservation and Cultural Affairs, P.O. Box 390, St. Thomas, U.S. Virgin Islands 00801 TEL 809-774-3407. Ed. Jeannette B. Allis.
Formerly: Virgin Island Blue Book.

350 US
WASHINGTON (STATE). JOINT BOARD OF LEGISLATIVE ETHICS. ANNUAL REPORT. a. Joint Board of Legislative Ethics, 101 Senate Office Bldg., Olympia, WA 98504.

328.797 US ISSN 0091-8253
WASHINGTON (STATE) LEGISLATURE. PICTORIAL DIRECTORY. 1909. irreg., published each distinct legislation session. free. Legislature, Olympia, WA 98504. TEL 206-786-7550. illus. circ. 19,000. Key Title: Pictorial Directory - Washington State Legislature.

350 US ISSN 0192-060X
WASHINGTON REPRESENTATIVES. 1977. a. $50. Columbia Books, Inc., 1350 New York Ave., Ste. 207, Washington, DC 20005. TEL 202-737-3777. Eds. Arthur Close, John Gregg.
Formerly (until 1979): Directory of Washington Representatives of American Associations and Industry (ISSN 0147-216X)

350 US
WE THE PEOPLE. vol.2, 1986. irreg. Commission on the Bicentennial of the United States Constitution, 736 Jackson Pl., N.W., Washington, DC 20503.

350 US
WEST VIRGINIA. LEGISLATURE. COMMISSION ON SPECIAL INVESTIGATIONS. REPORT TO THE WEST VIRGINIA LEGISLATURE. 1981. a. free. Legislature, Charleston, WV 25305. TEL 304-348-2345. Ed. Henry F. Bernhards. circ. 300.
Formerly: West Virginia. Legislature. Purchasing Practices and Procedures Commission. Report to the West Virginia Legislature.

350 US
WHO IS WHO IN THE OKLAHOMA LEGISLATURE. 1963. biennial. free. Department of Libraries, 200 N. E. 18 St., Oklahoma City, OK 73105. TEL 405-521-2502. circ. 4,500.

336 US ISSN 0085-8226
WISCONSIN. DEPARTMENT OF ADMINISTRATION. ANNUAL FISCAL REPORT. 1950. a. free. Department of Administration, Bureau of Financial Operations, Box 7864, Madison, WI 53707. TEL 608-266-1694. Ed. George R. Natzke. circ. 1,000.

350 US
WISCONSIN. STATE ELECTIONS BOARD. ANNUAL REPORT. 1975. biennial. State Elections Board, 132 E. Wilson St., Ste. 300, Madison, WI 53702. TEL 608-266-8005. circ. 100.

350 US
WISCONSIN BLUE BOOK. biennial. $6.30. Department of Administration, Document Sales, 202 S. Thornton Ave., Box 7840, Madison, WI 53707. TEL 608-266-3358.

350.6 US ISSN 0276-900X
WORLDWIDE GOVERNMENT DIRECTORY.* 1981. a. $250. Lambert Publications, Inc., Box 21008, Washington, DC 20009-0508. TEL 202-332-0973. Ed. Bart Stevens. adv. circ. 2,000.

350 US ISSN 0084-263X
WOYTINSKY LECTURES. 1967. irreg., no.3, 1972. price varies. ‡ University of Michigan, Institute of Public Policy Studies, 1516 Rackham Bldg., Ann Arbor, MI 48104. TEL 313-764-1817.

350 US ISSN 0094-3924
WYOMING. STATE OF WYOMING ANNUAL REPORT. 1973. a. Department of Administration and Fiscal Control, Research and Statistics Division, 302 Emerson Bldg., Cheyenne, WY 82002. TEL 307-777-7504. stat. circ. controlled.

350 US
WYOMING DATA HANDBOOK. biennial. Department of Administration and Fiscal Control, Research and Statistics Division, 302 Emerson Bldg., Cheyenne, WY 82002. TEL 307-777-7504. charts. stat. circ. 1,300.

ZAMBIA. CENTRAL STATISTICAL OFFICE. NATIONAL ACCOUNTS. see *BUSINESS AND ECONOMICS — Public Finance, Taxation*

342 ZA
ZAMBIA. COMMISSION FOR INVESTIGATIONS. ANNUAL REPORT. 1975. a. K.2.50. Commission for Investigations, Old Bank of Zambia Bldg., 3rd Fl., P.O. Box 50494, Ridgeway, Lusaka, Zambia (Orders to: Government Printer, Box 136, Lusaka, Zambia) circ. 500.

350 US ISSN 0164-0356
50 STATE LEGISLATIVE REVIEW. 1977. biennial. price included in subscription to Taylor's Encyclopedia of Government Officials, Federal and State. Political Research, Inc., Tegoland at Bent Tree, 16850 Dallas Parkway, Dallas, TX 75248. TEL 214-931-8827.

PUBLIC ADMINISTRATION —
Abstracting, Bibliographies, Statistics

A B C POL SCI; a bibliography of contents: political science and government. see *POLITICAL SCIENCE — Abstracting, Bibliographies, Statistics*

PUBLIC ADMINISTRATION — ABSTRACTING, BIBLIOGRAPHIES, STATISTICS

350 016   AT   ISSN 0727-8926
A P A I S: AUSTRALIAN PUBLIC AFFAIRS INFORMATION SERVICE; subject index to current literature. 1945. 11/yr. Aus.$90 (Aus.$39 for annual cum.) National Library of Australia, Sales and Subscriptions Section, Canberra, A.C.T. 2600, Australia. index. circ. 1,000.
    Formerly: Australian Public Affairs Information Service (ISSN 0005-0075)

350   SW   ISSN 0065-020X
AARSBOK FOER SVERIGES KUMMUNER. (Text in Swedish; summaries in English) 1918. a. Kr.90. Statistics Distribution, Distribution, S-701 89 Oerebro, Sweden. circ. 3,500.

350 016   US
ABSTRACT NEWSLETTER: ADMINISTRATION AND MANAGEMENT. 1974. w. $89. U.S. National Technical Information Service, 5285 Port Royal Rd., Springfield, VA 22161. TEL 703-487-4630. Ed. Linda J. LaGarde. index. (back issues avail.)
    Former titles: Weekly Abstract Newsletter: Administration and Management; Weekly Government Abstracts. Administration and Management; Weekly Government Abstracts. Administration (ISSN 0364-7986)

350 016   US
ABSTRACT NEWSLETTER: PROBLEM-SOLVING INFORMATION FOR STATE AND LOCAL GOVERNMENTS. w. $79. U.S. National Technical Information Service, 5285 Port Royal Rd., Springfield, VA 22161. TEL 703-487-4630. Ed. Linda J. LaGarde. index. (back issues avail.)
    Former titles: Weekly Abstract Newsletter: Problem-Solving Information for State and Local Governments; Weekly Government Abstracts. Problem-Solving Information for State and Local Governments (ISSN 0364-6459); Weekly Government Abstracts. Problem Solving Technology for State and Local Governments.

312   US   ISSN 0095-3431
ALABAMA'S VITAL EVENTS. 1971. a. $10. Department of Public Health, Bureau of Vital Statistics, Montgomery, AL 36130. TEL 205-261-5041. Ed. Dale Quinney. illus. circ. 450. (also avail. in microfiche)

350   US   ISSN 0568-8442
ALASKA. STATE LIBRARY, JUNEAU. STATE AND LOCAL PUBLICATIONS RECEIVED-ALASKA. (Limited Edt.) 1965. irreg. $5. Department of Education, Division of State Libraries, Box G, Juneau, AK 99811. TEL 907-465-2942. (Affiliate: Alaska State Library) Ed. Mike Mitchell. illus. index. circ. controlled.

316   AO   ISSN 0066-5193
ANGOLA. DIRECCAO DOS SERVICOS DE ESTATISTICA. ANUARIO ESTATISTICO. 1933. a. Esc.100. Direccao dos Servicos de Estatistica, C.P. 1215, Luanda, Angola. circ. 1,000.

316   AO
ANGOLA. DIRECCAO DOS SERVICOS DE ESTATISTICA. INFORMACOES ESTATISTICAS. 1970. a. free. Direccao dos Servicos de Estatistica, Ministerio do Planeamento e Coordenacao Economica, C. P. 1215, Luanda, Angola. stat. circ. 7,000.

350   IT   ISSN 0390-654X
ANNUARIO DI CONTABILITA NAZIONALE TOMO 1. a. L.7500. Istituto Centrale di Statistica, Via Cesare Balbo 16, 00100 Rome, Italy.

350   IT   ISSN 0390-6531
ANNUARIO DI CONTABILITA NAZIONALE TOMO 2. a. L.7000. Istituto Centrale di Statistica, Via Cesare Balbo 16, 00100 Rome, Italy.

350 319.4   AT
AUSTRALIA. BUREAU OF STATISTICS. ADOPTIONS. 1979. a. Australian Bureau of Statistics, Ground Floor, Wing 5, Cameron Offices, Belconnen, A.C.T. 2617, Australia

350 319.4   AT
AUSTRALIA. BUREAU OF STATISTICS. APPARENT CONSUMPTION OF FOODSTUFFS AND NUTRIENTS. 1948. a. free. Australian Bureau of Statistics, Ground Floor, Wing 5, Belconnen, A.C.T. 2617, Australia. circ. 2,000. (processed)

350 319.4   AT
AUSTRALIA. BUREAU OF STATISTICS. APPARENT CONSUMPTION OF SELECTED FOODSTUFFS, PRELIMINARY. 1978. a. Australian Bureau of Statistics, Ground Floor, Wing 5, Cameron Offices, Belconnen, A.C.T. 2617, Australia.

350 319.4   AT
AUSTRALIA. BUREAU OF STATISTICS. BIRTHS. 1968. a. Australian Bureau of Statistics, Ground Floor, Wing 5, Cameron Offices, Belconnen, A.C.T. 2617, Australia.

350 319.4   AT
AUSTRALIA. BUREAU OF STATISTICS. CATALOGUE OF PUBLICATIONS. a. free. Australian Bureau of Statistics, Ground Floor, Wing 5, Belconnen, A.C.T. 2617, Australia. circ. 8,000.

350 319.4   AT
AUSTRALIA. BUREAU OF STATISTICS. CHILD IN CARE. 1982. a. Australian Bureau of Statistics, Ground Floor, Wing 5, Cameron Offices, Belconnen, A.C.T. 2617, Australia.

350 319.4   AT
AUSTRALIA. BUREAU OF STATISTICS. DEATHS. a. free. Australian Bureau of Statistics, Ground Floor, Wing 5, Belconnen, A.C.T. 2617, Australia. illus. circ. 1,000.

350 319.4   AT
AUSTRALIA. BUREAU OF STATISTICS. DIVORCES. 1960. a. Australian Bureau of Statistics, Ground Floor, Wing 5, Cameron Offices, Belconnen. A.C.T. 2617, Australia.

350 319.4   AT
AUSTRALIA. BUREAU OF STATISTICS. ESTIMATED RESIDENT POPULATION SEX AND AGE: STATES AND TERRITORIES OF AUSTRALIA. 1968. a. Australian Bureau of Statistics, Ground Floor, Wing 5, Cameron Offices, Belconnen, A.C.T. 2617, Australia.

350 319.4   AT
AUSTRALIA. BUREAU OF STATISTICS. MARRIAGES. 1967. a. Australian Bureau of Statistics, Ground Floor, Wing 5, Cameron Offices, Belconnen, A.C.T. 2617, Australia.

350 319.4   AT
AUSTRALIA. BUREAU OF STATISTICS. NATIONAL SCHOOLS STATISTICS COLLECTION. a. Australian Bureau of Statistics, Ground Floor, Wing 5, Cameron Offices, Belconnen, A.C.T.2617, Australia.
    Formed by the merger of: National Schools Collection: Government Schools & Non-Government Schools.

350 319.4   AT
AUSTRALIA. BUREAU OF STATISTICS. NATIONAL SCHOOLS STATISTICS COLLECTION. PRELIMINARY. 1984. a. Australian Bureau of Statistics, Ground Floor, Wing 5, Cameron Offices, Belconnen, A.C.T. 2617, Australia.

350 319.4   AT
AUSTRALIA. BUREAU OF STATISTICS. PERINATAL DEATHS. 1973. a. Australian Bureau of Statistics, Ground Floor, Wing 5, Cameron Offices, Belconnen, A.C.T. 2617, Australia.

350 319.4   AT
AUSTRALIA. BUREAU OF STATISTICS. PROJECTIONS OF THE POPULATION. 1955. irreg. Australian Bureau of Statistics, Ground Floor, Wing 5, Cameron Offices, Belconnen, A.C.T. 2617, Australia.

350 319.4   AT   ISSN 0571-964X
AUSTRALIA. BUREAU OF STATISTICS. SEASONALLY ADJUSTED INDICATORS. 1967. a. price on request. Australian Bureau of Statistics, Ground Floor, Wing 5, Cameron Offices, Belconnen, A.C.T. 2617, Australia. circ. 1,500.

350 319.4   AT   ISSN 0705-0496
AUSTRALIA. BUREAU OF STATISTICS. SOCIAL INDICATORS. (Supplement available) 1976. irreg. price on request. Australian Bureau of Statistics, Ground Floor, Wing 5, Belconnen, A.C.T. 2617, Australia. charts. stat. circ. 5,500.

350 319.4   AT
AUSTRALIA. BUREAU OF STATISTICS. TECHNICAL PAPERS. irreg. Aus.$1.00. Australian Bureau of Statistics, Ground Floor, Wing 5, Cameron Offices, Belconnen, A.C.T. 2617, Australia.

350 319.4   AT
AUSTRALIA. BUREAU OF STATISTICS. TERTIARY EDUCATION. 1983. a. Aus.$1.80. Australian Bureau of Statistics, Ground Floor, Wing 5, Cameron Offices, Belconnen, A.C.T. 2617, Australia.

994 319   AT
AUSTRALIA. BUREAU OF STATISTICS. WESTERN AUSTRALIAN OFFICE. LOCAL GOVERNMENT, WESTERN AUSTRALIA. 1960. a. Aus.$1.90. Australian Bureau of Statistics, Western Australian Office, 1-3 St. George's Terrace, Perth, W.A. 6000, Australia. index. circ. 800.
    Formerly: Australia. Bureau of Statistics. Western Australian Office. Abstract of Statistics of Local Government Areas. (ISSN 0067-124X)

312   BB
BARBADOS. REGISTRATION OFFICE. REPORT ON VITAL STATISTICS & REGISTRATIONS. a., latest edt. 1981. free. Registration Office, Bridgetown, Barbados, W. Indies. stat. circ. 100.

310 350   BO
BOLIVIA. INSTITUTO NACIONAL DE ESTADISTICA. ESTADISTICAS REGIONALES DEPARTAMENTALES. 1976. a. $5. Instituto Nacional de Estadistica, Casilla de Correo No. 6129, La Paz, Bolivia.

310   BL
BRAZIL. SERVICO SOCIAL DO COMERCIO. ANUARIO ESTATISTICO. 1962. a. free. Servico Social do Comercio, Assessoria de Divulgacao e Promocao Institucional, Rua Voluntarios da Patria 169, 22270 Rio de Janeiro, Brazil. stat.

350   FR   ISSN 0293-9614
BULLETIN SIGNALETIQUE D'INFORMATION ADMINISTRATIVE. 1982. m. 875 F. Documentation Francaise, 29-31 quai Voltaire, 75340 Paris Cedex 07, France (Subscr. to: Documentation Francaise, 124 rue Henri Barbusse, 93308 Aubervilliers) (also avail. in microfilm; back issues avail) Indexed: P.A.I.S.For.Lang.Ind.
•Also available online. Vendors: European Space Agency.

328 016   US   ISSN 0007-8514
C I S INDEX. 1970. m. (with q. and a. cumulations) price varies. Congressional Information Service, Inc., 4520 East-West Hwy., Ste. 800, Bethesda, MD 20814. TEL 301-654-1550. Ed. Bernard Hayden. abstr. index. cum.index: 1970-74; 1975-78; 1979-82. (reprint service avail.)
•Also available online. Vendors: Orbit Information Technologies.

350 011   US
C S I CONGRESSIONAL RECORD ABSTRACTS: ENERGY EDITION. d. following session of Congress. $495. Capitol Services, Inc., NSA, 5161 River Rd., Bethesda, MD 20816.

351 317   CN   ISSN 0527-5148
CANADA. STATISTICS CANADA. FEDERAL GOVERNMENT EMPLOYMENT IN METROPOLITAN AREAS/EMPLOI DANS L'ADMINISTRATION FEDERALE REGIONS METROPOLITAINES. (Catalogue 72-205) (Text in English and French) 1968. a. Can.$20($21) Statistics Canada, Communications Division, 3rd Floor, R.H. Coats Bldg., Ottawa, Ont. K1A 0T6, Canada TEL 613-993-7276. (Subscr. to: Publications Sales and Services, Ottawa, Ont. K1A 0T6, Canada) (also avail. in microform from MML)

336.71   CN   ISSN 0703-2749
CANADA. STATISTICS CANADA. LOCAL GOVERNMENT FINANCE: REVENUE AND EXPENDITURE, ASSETS AND LIABILITIES, ACTUAL/FINANCES PUBLIQUES LOCALES: REVENUS ET DEPENSES, ACTIF ET PASSIF, CHIFFRES REELS. (Catalogue 68-204) (Text in English and French) 1944. a. Can.$20($21) Statistics Canada, Communications Division, 3rd Floor, R.H. Coats Bldg., Ottawa, Ont. K1A 0T6, Canada TEL 613-993-7276. (Subscr. to: Publications Sales and Services, Ottawa, Ont. K1A 0T6, Canada) (also avail. in microform from MML)

350 658 US
CASES IN PUBLIC POLICY AND
MANAGEMENT; an annotated bibliography. 1978.
irreg., 4th edt., 1984. $10 per no. Boston University,
Public Policy and Management Program for
Educational Development, 621 Commonwealth
Ave., Boston, MA 02215. TEL 617-353-4748. Ed.
Paul Dryfoos. bk. rev. circ. 2,000. (back issues
avail.)

350 UK ISSN 0260-9762
CHARTERED INSTITUTE OF PUBLIC FINANCE
AND ACCOUNTANCY. LOCAL
GOVERNMENT COMPARATIVE STATISTICS.
1981. a. £18. Chartered Institute of Public Finance
and Accountancy, 3 Robert St., London WC2N
6BH, England.

350 UK ISSN 0260-8642
CHARTERED INSTITUTE OF PUBLIC FINANCE
AND ACCOUNTANCY. PLANNING AND
DEVELOPMENT STATISTICS. ACTUALS. 1978.
a. £14. Chartered Institute of Public Finance and
Accountancy, 3 Robert St., London WC2N 6BH,
England. (back issues avail.)
  Supersedes in part: Chartered Institute of Public
Finance and Accountancy. Planning Estimates
Statistics. Actuals (ISSN 0307-8329)

350 UK
CHARTERED INSTITUTE OF PUBLIC FINANCE
AND ACCOUNTANCY. PLANNING AND
DEVELOPMENT STATISTICS. ESTIMATES.
1976. a. £14. Chartered Institute of Public Finance
and Accountancy, 3 Robert St., London WC2N
6BH, England. (back issues avail.)
  Supersedes in part: Chartered Institute of Public
Finance and Accountancy. Planning Estimates
Statistics. Actuals (ISSN 0307-8329)

350 UK ISSN 0260-7603
CHARTERED INSTITUTE OF PUBLIC FINANCE
AND ACCOUNTANCY. WASTE COLLECTION
STATISTICS. ACTUALS. 1977. a. £14. Chartered
Institute of Public Finance and Accountancy, 3
Robert St., London WC2N 6BH, England. (back
issues avail.)

350 628 UK ISSN 0140-0150
CHARTERED INSTITUTE OF PUBLIC FINANCE
AND ACCOUNTANCY. WASTE DISPOSAL
STATISTICS. ACTUALS. 1981. a. £10. Chartered
Institute of Public Finance and Accountancy, 3
Robert St., London WC2N 6BH, England.

350 628 UK ISSN 0140-0142
CHARTERED INSTITUTE OF PUBLIC FINANCE
AND ACCOUNTANCY. WASTE DISPOSAL
STATISTICS. ESTIMATES. 1981. a. £10.
Chartered Institute of Public Finance and
Accountancy, 3 Robert St., London WC2N 6BH,
England.

015 US
CHECKLIST OF VERMONT STATE
PUBLICATIONS. 1970. irreg., 1985 edt. in prep.
free. Department of Libraries, Law and Documents
Unit, c/o State Office Bldg. Post Office, Montpelier,
VT 05602. TEL 802-828-3268. circ. 350.
  Formerly: Checklist of Available Vermont State
Publications.

350 IT ISSN 0390-6574
CONTI DEGLI ITALIANI. a. L.3000. Istituto
Centrale di Statistica, Via Cesare Balbo 16, 00100
Rome, Italy.

352 DK ISSN 0106-9802
DENMARK. DANMARKS STATISTIK.
KOMMUNALE FINANSER /LOCAL
GOVERNMENT FINANCE. (Text in Danish and
English) 1981. a. Kr.68.85. Danmarks Statistik,
Sejroegade 11, 2100 Copenhagen OE, Denmark.
  Formerly: Denmark. Danmarks Statistik.
Kommunale Finanser for Regnskabsaaret.

350 DK ISSN 0108-8173
DENMARK. DANMARKS STATISTIK.
NATIONALREGNSKABSSTATISTIK /
NATIONAL ACCOUNTS STATISTICS. (Text in
Danish and English) 1983. a. Kr.77.87. Danmarks
Statistik, Sejroegade 11, 2100 Copenhagen OE,
Denmark.

350 DK ISSN 0107-0371
DENMARK. DANMARKS STATISTIK. VALGENE
TIL DE KOMMUNALE OG
AMTSKOMMUNALE RAAD. 1971. irreg.
Danmarks Statistik, Sejroegade 11, 2100
Copenhagen OE, Denmark.
  Formerly: Denmark. Danmarks Statistik. Valgene
til de Kommunale Raad.

314 352 FI ISSN 0355-2217
FINLAND. TILASTOKESKUS.
KUNNALLISVAALIT/FINLAND.
STATISTIKCENTRALEN.
KOMMUNALVALEN/FINLAND. CENTRAL
STATISTICAL OFFICE. MUNICIPAL
ELECTIONS. (Section XXIX B of Official
Statistics of Finland) (Text in English, Finnish and
Swedish) 1931. irreg; latest 1984. Fmk.65.
Tilastokeskus, Annankatu 44, SF-00100 Helsinki 10,
Finland (Subscr. to: Government Printing Centre,
Box 516, SF-00100 Helsinki 10, Finland)

INDEX TO CURRENT URBAN DOCUMENTS. see
HOUSING AND URBAN PLANNING —
Abstracting, Bibliographies, Statistics

352 DK ISSN 0105-7456
KOMMUNAL LITTERATUR. 1972. a. Kr.284.15.
Bibliotekscentralen, Tempovej 7-11, DK-2750
Ballerup, Denmark. Ed. Boerge Kristiansen.

314.21 UK ISSN 0308-0900
LONDON FACTS AND FIGURES. (Subseries of:
Greater London Council. Publication) 1972. irreg.
£3 to non-London local government. Greater
London Council, Intelligence Unit, County Hall,
London SE1 7PB, England. circ. 1,000.

371.82 US ISSN 0097-9325
NEBRASKA STATISTICAL HANDBOOK. biennial.
$6. Department of Economic Development,
Division of Research, Box 94666, Lincoln, NE
68509. TEL 402-471-3111. Ed. Shirley Kling. circ.
1,000.

324 NE ISSN 0168-5732
NETHERLANDS. CENTRAAL BUREAU VOOR
DE STATISTIEK. STATISTIEK DER
VERKIEZINGEN. PROVINCIALE STATEN.
ELECTION STATISTICS. PROVINCIAL
COUNCILS. (Text in Dutch and English) 1946.
irreg. fl.18.50. Centraal Bureau voor de Statistiek,
Prinses Beatrixlaan 428, Voorburg, Netherlands
(Orders to: Staatsuitgeverij, Christoffel
Plantijnstraat, The Hague, Netherlands)

352 NZ ISSN 0110-3466
NEW ZEALAND. DEPARTMENT OF
STATISTICS. LOCAL AUTHORITY
STATISTICS. a. NZ.$15.40. Department of
Statistics, Private Bag, Wellington, New Zealand
(Subscr. to: Government Printing Office,
Publications, Private Bag, Wellington, New Zealand)

328 NO ISSN 0332-8023
NORWAY. STATISTISK SENTRALBYRAA.
KOMMUNE OG FYLKESTINGS VALGET/
MUNICIPAL AND COUNTY ELECTIONS.
(Subseries of its Norges Offisielle Statistikk) (Text
in English and Norwegian) 1902. quadrennial.
Kr.30. Statistisk Sentralbyraa, Box 8131 Dep., 0033
Oslo 1, Norway. circ. 2,300.
  Formerly: Norway. Statistisk Sentralbyraa.
Kommunevalget/Municipal Elections.

350 NO
NORWAY. STATISTISK SENTRALBYRAA.
STORTINGSVALG/PARLIAMENTARY
ELECTIONS. (Subseries of its Norges Offisiele
Statistikk) 1894. quadrennial. price varies. Statistisk
Sentralbyraa, Box 8131-Dep., 0033 Oslo 1, Norway.
circ. 2,300.

380 US ISSN 0091-0546
OREGON. PUBLIC UTILITY COMMISSIONER.
STATISTICS OF ELECTRIC, GAS, STEAM
HEAT, TELEPHONE, TELEGRAPH AND
WATER COMPANIES. 1970. a. $7.50. Public
Utility Commissioner, Labor & Industries Bldg.,
Salem, OR 97310. TEL 503-378-5849. stat. circ.
350.

PARLIAMENTARY YEAR BOOK. see PUBLIC
ADMINISTRATION

PERSONNEL LITERATURE. see BUSINESS AND
ECONOMICS — Abstracting, Bibliographies,
Statistics

350 016 UK ISSN 0140-4768
RURAL DEVELOPMENT ABSTRACTS. 1978. q.
£62($106) C.A.B. International, Farnham House,
Farnham Royal, Slough SL2 3BN, England (U.S.
subscr. to: C.A.B. International, North American
Office, 845 N. Park Ave., Tucson, AR 85719) circ.
500. (also avail. in microfiche; back issues avail.)
Indexed: E.I.
●Also available online. Vendors: BRS, CISTI,
DIMDI, DIALOG, European Space Agency.

350 US ISSN 0094-6958
SAGE PUBLIC ADMINISTRATION ABSTRACTS.
1974. q. $55 to individuals; institutions $110. Sage
Publications, Inc., 2111 W. Hillcrest Dr., Newbury
Park, CA 91320 TEL 805-499-0721. (And Sage
Publications, Ltd., 28 Banner St., London EC1Y
8QE, England) Ed.Bd. adv. index. (back issues
avail.)

350 SI ISSN 0129-9786
SINGAPORE. DEPARTMENT OF STATISTICS.
REPORT ON THE SURVEY OF SERVICES.
biennial. S.11.70. Department of Statistics, Maxwell
Road PO Box 3010, Singapore 1, Singapore.

352 SA
SOUTH AFRICA. CENTRAL STATISTICAL
SERVICES. LOCAL GOVERNMENT
STATISTICS. (Report No. 13-03, in 2 vols.) a.,
latest 1980/1981. Central Statistical Department,
Private Bag X44, Pretoria 0001, South Africa
(Orders to: Government Printer, Bosman St.,
Private Bag X85, Pretoria 0001, South Africa)
  Formerly: South Africa. Department of Statistics.
Local Government Statistics.

352 SA
SOUTH AFRICA. CENTRAL STATISTICAL
SERVICES. STATISTICS OF
ADMINISTRATION BOARDS. (Report No. 13-
13) a., latest 1981/82. Central Statistical Board,
Private Bag X44, Pretoria 0001, South Africa
(Orders to: Government Printer, Bosman St.,
Private Bag X85, Pretoria 0001, South Africa)
  Former titles: South Africa. Department of
Statistics. Statistics of Administration Boards; (until
1977): South Africa. Department of Statistics.
Statistics of Bantu Affairs Administration Boards.

350 SA ISSN 0379-6078
SOUTH AFRICA. GOVERNMENT GAZETTE
INDEX. 1979. q. (annual cum.) R.40. State Library,
Box 397, Pretoria 0001, South Africa. circ. 600.
(also avail. in microfiche; back issues avail.)

353.9 US
STATISTICAL REVIEW OF GOVERNMENT IN
UTAH. 1958. a. $10. Utah Foundation, 308
Continental Bank Bldg., Salt Lake City, UT 84101.
TEL 801-364-1837. Ed. Allan J. Witt. circ. 1,000.

350 IT ISSN 0075-1820
STATISTICHE DEI BILANCI DELLE
AMMINISTRAZIONI REGIONALI,
PROVINCIALI E COMUNALI. biennial. L.8000.
Istituto Centrale di Statistica, Via Cesare Balbo 16,
00100 Rome, Italy.

350 IT
STATISTICHE SULLA PUBBLICA
AMMINISTRAZIONE. irreg. L.12000. Istituto
Centrale di Statistica, Via Cesare Balbo 16, 00100
Rome, Italy.

314 DK ISSN 0107-6744
STATISTISK TIAARS-OVERSIGT FOR
KOEBENHAVNS KOMMUNE. English edition:
Statistical Ten-Year Review of the Municipality of
Copenhagen. 1981. biennial. Kr.15. Statistisk
Kontor, Vester Voldgade 87, 1552 Copenhagen V,
Denmark. illus.

350 SA ISSN 0257-5418
TRANSKEI GOVERNMENT GAZETTE INDEX.
1982. a. R.7.50. State Library, P.O. Box 397,
Pretoria 0001, South Africa. (Co-sponsor: University
of the Witwatersrand) Ed. Shelagh de Wet.
  Formerly: Transkei Official Gazette (ISSN 0257-
540X)

U.S. BUREAU OF THE CENSUS. CENSUS
CATALOG AND GUIDE. see POPULATION
STUDIES — Abstracting, Bibliographies, Statistics

PUBLIC ADMINISTRATION — MUNICIPAL GOVERNMENT

350 011 US
U.S. GENERAL SERVICES ADMINISTRATION. PUBLICATIONS. 1979. a. U.S. General Services Administration, General Services Bldg., 18th & F Sts. N.W., Washington, DC 20405 (Orders to: Supt. of Documents, Washington, DC 20402)

350 614.7 011 UK
URBAN ABSTRACTS. 1974. every 4 wks. £70. Research Library, London Residuary Body, County Hall, Rm. 514, London SE1 7PB, England (Subscr. to: Technical Communications, 100 High Ave., Stevenage, Herts. SG6 3RR, England) Ed. Susan Biggs. circ. 1,600. (back issues avail.)
●Also available online. Vendors: European Space Agency, Pergamon Infoline, Scicon Ltd.
Formerly issued as two parts: Urban Abstracts Series 1: Policy; Urban Abstracts Series 2: Technical; Which superseded in part: Urban Abstracts (ISSN 0305-103X)

352 US ISSN 0300-6859
URBAN AFFAIRS ABSTRACTS. 1971. w. with s-a. and a. cumulations. $275. National League of Cities, 1301 Pennsylvania Ave., N.W., Washington, DC 20004. TEL 202-626-3210. Ed. Nancy Minter. abstr. bibl. index. circ. 400. (processed)

312 350 US ISSN 0511-6775
WEST VIRGINIA STATISTICAL HANDBOOK. 1955. irreg. $4.50 per no. West Virginia University, Bureau of Business Research, Box 6025, Morgantown, WV 26506-6025. TEL 304-293-0111. Ed. Stanley J. Kloc. stat. Indexed: P.A.I.S.

350.6 US
WESTERN GOVERNMENT DIRECTORIES. 1954. biennial. $12. Mirror-Free Press Inc., Box 13279, Sacramento, CA 95813. TEL 916-448-0312. Ed. Richard Fowler. adv. circ. 34,000.

350 314 YU
YUGOSLAVIA. SAVEZNI ZAVOD ZA STATISTIKU. KOMUNALNI FONDOVI U GRADSKIM NASELJIMA. (Subseries of: Yugoslavia. Savezni Zavod za Statistiku. Statisticki Bilten) irreg. 4 din. Savezni Zavod za Statistiku, Kneza Milosa 20, Belgrade, Yugoslavia.

350 316 ZA
ZAMBIA. CENTRAL STATISTICAL OFFICE. FINANCIAL STATISTICS OF GOVERNMENT SECTOR (ECONOMIC AND FUNCTIONAL ANALYSIS) 1964. a. K.5. Central Statistical Office, P.O. Box 31908, Lusaka, Zambia.
Formerly: Zambia. Central Statistical Office. Government Sector Accounts (Economic and Functional Analysis) (ISSN 0084-4527)

PUBLIC ADMINISTRATION — Municipal Government

see also Housing and Urban Planning

352 AT
ADELAIDE CITY COUNCIL MUNICIPAL REFERENCE BOOK. 1911. irreg. free. Adelaide City Council, Town Hall, King William St., Adelaide, S.A. 5000, Australia. circ. 2,000.
Formerly: Adelaide City Council Municipal Yearbook (ISSN 0084-5922)

352 US
ALASKA MUNICIPAL OFFICIALS DIRECTORY. 1958. a. $13. Alaska Municipal League, 105 Municipal Way, Ste. 301, Juneau, AK 99801.

352 DK ISSN 0105-8509
AMSTKOMMUNERNES OEKONOMI; budget. 1978. a. Kr.75. Amstraadforeningen i Danmark, Landemarket 10, DK-1119 Copenhagen K, Denmark. illus. circ. 1,800.
Formerly: Oekonomisk Oversigt for Amtskommunerne.

352.008 MF ISSN 0304-6451
ASSOCIATION OF URBAN AUTHORITIES. ANNUAL BULLETIN. Added title: Local Government in Mauritius. (Text in English and French) 1962. a. Association of Urban Authorities, City Hall, Port Louis, Mauritius. circ. 200.

352 FR
BOTTIN COMMUNES. 1978. a. $85. Societe Didot Bottin, 28 rue du Docteur Finlay, 75738 Paris Cedex 15, France.

352 310 CN
BRITISH COLUMBIA LIST; of official personnel in Federal, Provincial and Municipal Governments in the Province of British Columbia. 1978. biennial. Can.$38. B and C List (1982) Ltd., 301-1177 W. Broadway, Vancouver, B.C. V6H 1G3, Canada. TEL 604-732-4646. Ed. Marilyn Krygier. adv. circ. 15,000.

352 370 US
C G R B BULLETIN. 1913. irreg., 8-18/yr. $35. Citizens' Governmental Research Bureau, 125 E. Wells St., Rm. 616, Milwaukee, WI 53202-3580. TEL 414-276-8240. Ed. Jean B. Tyler. charts. stat. circ. 1,500.
Milwaukee region

352 US
CALIFORNIA ROSTER; California state, city and township officials; state officials of the U S; directory of state services. a. price varies. Secretary of State, 1230 J St., Sacramento, CA 95814 TEL 916-445-6375. (Subscr. to: Department of General Services, Publications Unit, Box 1015, North Highlands, CA 95660) Ed. Melissa Warren. circ. 10, 000.

352 UK ISSN 0266-9013
CHARTERED INSTITUTE OF PUBLIC FINANCE AND ACCOUNTANCY. BLOCK GRANT STATISTICS. 1984. a. £14. Chartered Institute of Public Finance and Accountancy, 3 Robert St., London WC2N 6BH, England.

330 US ISSN 0009-756X
CITIZENS' BUSINESS. 1910. irreg. $6 for 2 yrs. to non-members. Pennsylvania Economy League, Eastern Division, 1211 Chestnut St., Ste. 600, Philadelphia, PA 19107-4103. TEL 215-864-9562. stat. circ. 3,000. (processed)

352 US
CITIZENS UNION FOUNDATION. OCCASIONAL PAPER SERIES. 1977. irreg. Citizens Union Foundation, Inc., 198 Broadway, New York, NY 10038. TEL 212-227-0342.
Formerly: Citizens Union Research Foundation. Occasional Paper Studies.

352 AT
CITY OF PERTH. LORD MAYOR'S REPORT. 1970. a. City of Perth, Perth, W.A., Australia. Ed. Michael A. Michael. illus. stat. circ. 2,500.
Formerly: City of Perth. Annual Report.

352 IT
COMPENDIO DATI; patrimoniali, economici, finanziari, tecnici, produttivi e del personale. 1976. a. L.80000. Confederazione Italiana dei Servizi Pubblici degli Enti Locali, Piazza Cola di Rienzo n.80/a, I-00192 Rome, Italy.

COMPENSATION (WASHINGTON); an annual report on local government executive salaries and fringe benefits. see *BUSINESS AND ECONOMICS — Personnel Management*

352 IT
CONFEDERAZIONE ITALIANA DEI SERVIZI PUBBLICI DEGLI ENTI LOCALI. ANNUARIO. 1961? a. L.80000. Confederazione Italiana dei Servizi Pubblici degli Enti Locali, Piazza Cola di Rienzo, 80, 00192 Rome, Italy. stat.

350 FR
COUNCIL OF EUROPE. STEERING COMMITTEE ON REGIONAL AND MUNICIPAL MATTERS. STUDY SERIES: LOCAL AND REGIONAL AUTHORITIES IN EUROPE. 1972. irreg. price varies. Council of Europe, Steering Committee on Regional and Municipal Matters, Publications Section, 67006 Strasbourg, France (Dist. in U.S. by Manhattan Publishing Co., 225 Lafayette St., New York, NY 10012) Ed.Bd. charts. stat.
Formerly: Council of Europe. Committee on Cooperation in Municipal and Regional Matters. Study Series: Local and Regional Authorities in Europe.

352 US ISSN 0011-3727
CURRENT MUNICIPAL PROBLEMS. Annual cumulation (ISSN 0161-5122) 1959. q. (plus a. cum.) $99. Callaghan & Co., 3201 Old Glenview Rd., Wilmette, IL 60091. TEL 312-256-7000. Ed. Byron S. Matthews. bk. rev. charts. cum.index. circ. 761. (also avail. in microfiche from UMI) Indexed: SSCI. C.L.I. L.R.I. Sel.Water Res.Abstr.

DALLAS INSTITUTE OF HUMANITIES AND CULTURE. INSTITUTE NEWSLETTER. see *HUMANITIES: COMPREHENSIVE WORKS*

352 US ISSN 0090-1989
DIRECTORY: NORTH DAKOTA CITY OFFICIALS. 27th edt. 1978. biennial. $8. North Dakota League of Cities, Box 2235, Bismarck, ND 58502. TEL 701-223-3518. Ed. Robert E. Johnson. adv.

917.63 US ISSN 0092-0614
DIRECTORY OF LOUISIANA CITIES, TOWNS AND VILLAGES. irreg. $2. Department of Transportation and Development, Box 94245, Capitol Station, Baton Rouge, LA 70804. TEL 504-379-1109.

352 US
DIRECTORY OF MINNESOTA CITY OFFICIALS. 1986. a. $16.65. League of Minnesota Cities, 183 University Ave. E., St. Paul, MN 55101-2526. TEL 612-227-5600. Ed. Jean Mehle. circ. 3,000.
Formerly: Directory of Minnesota Municipal Officials.

352 US
DIRECTORY OF NORTH CAROLINA MUNICIPAL OFFICIALS. a. $20. ‡ North Carolina League of Municipalities, Box 3069, 215 N. Dawson St., Raleigh, NC 27602. TEL 919-834-1311. Ed. Margot F. Christensen. circ. 675.

DIRECTORY OF RESEARCH & DEVELOPMENT CONTRACTORS. see *SCIENCES: COMPREHENSIVE WORKS*

352 IT ISSN 0012-4737
DOCUMENTI DI VITA COMUNALE.* 1961. irreg., (approx. 3/yr.) free. Sindacato di Mogliano, Piazza Caduti 1, 31021 Magliano Veneto, Treviso, Italy. Ed. Dir. Giuseppe Marton. adv. bk. rev. abstr. illus. stat. tr.lit. circ. 5,500 (controlled)

352 614.8 360 US ISSN 0273-4435
FEDERAL FUNDING GUIDE. 1976. a. (with q. supplements) $139.95. Government Information Services, 1611 N. Kent St., Ste. 508, Arlington, VA 22209. TEL 703-528-1082. Eds. Charles J. Edwards, Jan Balkin.
Formerly: Federal Funding Guide for Local Governments (ISSN 0362-4285)

352 BL
FUNDACAO DE ASSISTENCIA AOS MUNICIPIOS DO ESTADO DO PARANA. BOLETIM INFORMATIVO. 1975. irreg. free. Fundacao de Assistencia aos Municipios, Rua Voluntarios da Patria 547, Curitiba, Parana, Brazil.

352 AU ISSN 0016-609X
GEMEINDEBOTE. 1963. irreg., 4-6/yr. free. Marktgemeinde Hinterbruehl. Gemeindeamt, Hauptstr. 66, A-2371 Hinterbruehl, Austria. Ed. G. Tartarotti. stat. circ. 1,200.

352 GW ISSN 0016-6200
GEMEINSAMES AMTSBLATT DES LANDES BADEN-WUERTTEMBERG. 1953. irreg., approx. 40/yr. DM.66. Innenministerium, Dorotheenstr. 6, Postfach 277, 7000 Stuttgart 1, W. Germany (B.R.D.) Ed. H. Luetze. bk. rev. index.

352 GW ISSN 0342-3557
GESETZ UND VERORDNUNGSBLATT FUER DAS LAND HESSEN. 1945. DM.68. (Staatskanzlei) Verlag Dr. Max Gehlen GmbH und Co. KG, Daimlerstr. 12, Postfach 2463, 6380 Bad Homburg, W. Germany (B.R.D.) index. circ. 8,000.

352 606 US ISSN 0883-8690
GOVERNMENT ASSISTANCE ALMANAC. 1985. biennial. $23.45. Foggy Bottom Publications, Box 57150, West End Station, Washington, DC 20037. TEL 202-448-4600. Ed. J. Robert Dumouchel. stats. index.

352 336   UK   ISSN 0308-1745
GREAT BRITAIN. DEPARTMENT OF THE
ENVIRONMENT. LOCAL GOVERNMENT
FINANCIAL STATISTICS: ENGLAND AND
WALES. (Joint publication with the Welsh Office)
a. price varies. H.M.S.O., Box 569, London SE1
9NH, England. stat.

GREEK GOLDEN GUIDE. see *BUSINESS AND
ECONOMICS — Trade And Industrial Directories*

323   US   ISSN 0073-1137
HAWAII. OFFICE OF THE OMBUDSMAN.
REPORT. 1971. a. free. Office of the Ombudsman,
Kekuanaoa Bldg., 4th Fl., 465 S. King St., Honolulu,
HI 96813. TEL 808-548-7811. Ed. Wayne Matsuo.
circ. controlled.

HERNE IN ZAHLEN.
JAHRESVEROEFFENTLICHUNGEN. see
*BUSINESS AND ECONOMICS — Abstracting,
Bibliographies, Statistics*

352   SP
INSTITUTO DE ESTUDIOS DE
ADMINISTRACION LOCAL. CATEDRA
CALVO SOTELO. CONFERENCIAS.* 1974.
irreg. Instituto de Estudios de Administracion Local,
Catedra Calvo Sotelo, Joaguin Garcia Morato 7,
Madrid 10, Spain.

IOWA OFFICIAL REGISTER. see *POLITICAL
SCIENCE*

336   IS
ISRAEL. KNESSET. HA-VA'ADA LE-INYANEI
BIKORET HA-MEDINA. SIKUMEHA VE-
HATSA 'OTEHA SHEL HA-VA'ADA LE-
INYANEI BIKORET HA-MEDINA LE-DIN VE-
KHESHBON SHEL MEVAKER HA-MEDINA.
1973. a. Knesset, State Control Committee,
Jerusalem, Israel. Ed. Aharon Berkner. circ.
controlled. (processed)

ITALIAN GOLDEN GUIDE. see *BUSINESS AND
ECONOMICS — Trade And Industrial Directories*

352   AU   ISSN 0022-7552
KAERNTNER GEMEINDEBLATT. 1926. irreg.,
(approx. 15/yr.) S.790. (Amt der Kaerntner
Landesregierung) Kaertner Druck- und Verlags-
Gesellschaft mbH, Viktringer Ring 28, A-9010
Klagenfurt, Austria. bk. rev. stat. index. (also avail.
in microform)

352   DK   ISSN 0900-1484
KOMMUNAL AARBOG. 1930. a. Kr.447.75. Ferslew
Tryk, Overgaden n. Vandet 17, 1414 Copenhagen,
Denmark.

352   DK   ISSN 0107-5098
KOMMUNAL BUDGETREDEGOERELSE. 1980. a.
Kr.130. (Kommunernes Landsforening) Forlaget
Kommuneinformation, Sommerstedgade 7, DK-1718
Copenhagen V, Denmark.

352   AU   ISSN 0023-7884
LANDESGESETZBLATT FUER DAS LAND
SALZBURG. 1945. irreg. S.400. Bundesland
Salzburg, Chiemseehof, A-5010 Salzburg, Austria.
index. circ. 2,000. (looseleaf format)

354   LB   ISSN 0304-730X
LIBERIA. MINISTRY OF LOCAL
GOVERNMENT, RURAL DEVELOPMENT &
URBAN RECONSTRUCTION. ANNUAL
REPORT.* (Report year ends Sept. 30) 1972. a.
Ministry of Rural Development, P.O. Box 9030,
Monrovia, Liberia.
    Continues the publication with the same title
issued by the Ministry under its earlier name: Dept.
of Internal Affairs.

352   FR
LOCAL AND REGIONAL AUTHORITIES IN
EUROPE. STUDY SERIES. (Text in English or
French) 1972. 2-3/yr. price varies. Council of
Europe, Activities of the Steering Committee for
Regional and Municipal Matters, Publications
Section, 67000 Strasbourg, France (Dist. in U.S. by:
Manhattan Publishing Co., 80 Brook St., Box 650,
Croton, NY 10520)

352   UK   ISSN 0267-2022
LOCAL GOVERNMENT ADMINISTRATORS'
OFFICIAL SOURCE BOOK. 1985. a. £19.95.
Millbank Publications, 25 Catherine St., London
WC2B 5JW, England. Ed. K.J. Allen. adv. circ. 3,
000.

352   UK   ISSN 0305-0130
LOCAL GOVERNMENT COMPANION. 1974. a.
£11. Parliamentary Research Services, 18 Lincoln
Green, Chichester, West Sussex PO19 4DN,
England. Eds. F.W.S. Craig, E.P. Craig.

352   JA   ISSN 0288-7622
LOCAL GOVERNMENT REVIEW IN JAPAN.
(Text in English) 1973. a. free. General Center for
Local Autonomy - Jichi Sogo Center, 8th Fl.,
Toranomon Bldg., 1-7-1, Nishi-Shimbashi, Minato-
ku, Tokyo 105, Japan. circ. 600.
    Formerly: Local Government Review (ISSN
0449-0193)

352 350   US
MAINE REGISTER: STATE YEARBOOK AND
LEGISLATIVE MANUAL. 1822. a. $69. Tower
Publishing Company, 34 Diamond St., Box 7220,
Portland, ME 04112. TEL 207-774-9813. adv.
index. circ. 1,000. (back issues avail.)

352   US   ISSN 0361-2090
MASSACHUSETTS MUNICIPAL DIRECTORY.
(Supplement to: Municipal Forum) 1964/1965. a.
$18. Massachusetts Municipal Association, 60
Temple Place, Boston, MA 02111. TEL 617-426-
7272. Ed. Noni Flanagan. adv. bk. rev. circ. 4,200.

351   CN   ISSN 0076-7093
METROPOLITAN TORONTO. 1954. irreg., latest
1975. free. Municipality of Metropolitan Toronto,
Clerk's Dept., Toronto, Ont. M5H 2N1, Canada.
TEL 416-947-8016.

350   US   ISSN 0026-9980
MONTANA LEAGUE OF CITIES & TOWNS.
NEWSLETTER. no.139, 1975. irreg. (3-4/yr.) free.
Montana League of Cities & Towns, Box 1704,
Helena, MT 59624. TEL 406-442-8768. adv. illus.
circ. 1,200.
    Formerly: Montana Municipal League.
Newsletter.

352   AT   ISSN 0085-3585
MUNICIPAL ASSOCIATION OF TASMANIA.
SESSION. MINUTES OF PROCEEDINGS. 1916.
a. free. ‡ Municipal Association of Tasmania, 176a
Macquarie St., Hobart, Tas. 7000, Australia. Ed.
L.R. Armsby. index. circ 200 (controlled)

352.16   US   ISSN 0077-2151
MUNICIPAL INDEX; purchasing guide for city
officials and consulting engineers. 1924. a. $37.50.
Communication Channels, Inc., 6255 Barfield Rd.,
Atlanta, GA 30328. TEL 404-256-9800. Ed.
Barbara Katinsky. adv. circ. 40,000.

352   US   ISSN 0077-2186
MUNICIPAL YEAR BOOK. 1922. a. $46. ‡
International City Management Association, 1120 G
St., N.W., Washington, DC 20005. TEL 202-626-
4600. Ed. J.B. Yowell. bk. rev. circ. 14,000.
    Formerly: City Manager Yearbook.

352   UK
MUNICIPAL YEAR BOOK. 1897. a. £49. Municipal
Publications Ltd., 178-202 Great Portland St.,
London W1N 6NH, England. Ed. W.A.C. Roope.
adv. circ. 6,000.

352   US   ISSN 0276-489X
MUNICIPAL YEAR BOOK DIRECTORIES. 1981.
a. $19.75. International City Management
Association, 1120 G. St., N.W., Ste. 300,
Washington, DC 20005. TEL 202-626-4600. Ed.
Mary A. Schellinger.

352   CN
NATIONAL ASSEMBLY GUIDEBOOK. 1985. irreg.
Can.$49.95. Corpus Information Service, Division of
Southam Communications Ltd., 1450 Don Mills
Road, Don Mills, Ont. M3B 2X7, Canada. TEL
416-445-6641. Ed. Derry McDonell.

352   US
NATIONAL MUNICIPAL POLICY. 1951. a. $10 to
non-members. ‡ National League of Cities, 1301
Pennsylvania Ave., N.W., Washington, DC 20004.
TEL 202-626-3030. index.

352   CN   ISSN 0381-7970
NEW BRUNSWICK PUBLIC EMPLOYEES
ASSOCIATION. NEWS LETTER. 1970. irreg.
New Brunswick Public Employees Association, Box
95, 238 King St., Fredericton, N.B., Canada. TEL
506-458-8440. Key Title: News Letter - New
Brunswick Public Employees Association.

352   UK
NEW LOCAL GOVERNMENT SERIES. no. 13,
1975. irreg. George Allen & Unwin (Publishers)
Ltd., 40 Museum St., London W.C.1, England (U.S.
addr.: Allen & Unwin Inc., 8 Winchester Place,
Winchester, MA 01890)

352.12   US   ISSN 0094-7547
NEW YORK (CITY) MAYOR. SCHEDULES
SUPPORTING THE EXECUTIVE BUDGET.
irreg. Office of the Mayor, City Hall, New York,
NY 10007. TEL 212-566-5700. Key Title:
Schedules Supporting the Executive Budget.

383   SA
OFFICIAL SOUTH AFRICAN MUNICIPAL
YEARBOOK/AMPTELIKE SUID-AFRIKAANSE
MUNISIPALE JAARBOEK; official South Africa.
(Text in Afrikaans and English) 1909. a. R.49.50.
(South African Association of Municipal
Employees) Melton Publications (Pty.) Ltd., P.O.
Box 84248, Greenside 2034, South Africa. Ed. Del
Kevan. circ. 3,000.
    Formerly: Municipal Yearbook.

ONTARIO. PROVINCIAL-MUNICIPAL AFFAIRS
SECRETARIAT. MUNICIPAL DIRECTORY. see
PUBLIC ADMINISTRATION

352   CN
OTTAWA GUIDEBOOK. 1987. irreg. Can.$69.95.
Corpus Information Services, Division of Southam
Communications Ltd., 1450 Don Mills Road, Don
Mills, Ont. M3B 2X7, Canada. TEL 416-445-6641.
Ed. Derry McDonell.

352 361.6   UK
PUBLIC AUTHORITIES DIRECTORY. 1975. a.
£30. L.G.C. Communications, 122 Minories,
London EC3N 1NT, England. Ed. Geoffrey Smith.
adv. circ. 1,000.

628   US   ISSN 0163-9730
PUBLIC WORKS MANUAL; and catalog file. 1977.
a. $20. Public Works Journal Corporation, 200 S.
Broad St., Ridgewood, NJ 07451. TEL 201-445-
5800. Ed. E.B. Rodie. adv. circ. 44,000. (reprint
service avail. from UMI)
    Formed by the merger of: Environmental Wastes
Control Manual (ISSN 0071-0946); Street and
Highway Manual (ISSN 0081-5977); Water Works
Manual (ISSN 0083-7717)

352   CN
QUEEN'S PARK GUIDEBOOK. 1985. irreg.
Can.$49.95. Corpus Information Services, Division
of Southam Communications Ltd., 1450 Don Mills
Road, Don Mills, Ont. M3B 2X7, Canada. Ed.
Derry McDonnel.

352   US
RESEARCH IN URBAN ECONOMICS. 1981. a.
$24.75 to individuals; institutions $49.50. J A I
Press Inc., Box 1678, 36 Sherwood Pl., Greenwich,
CT 06836. TEL 203-661-7602. Ed. J. Vernon
Henderson.

352   US
SALARIES AND WAGES FOR MICHIGAN
MUNICIPALITIES OVER 1,000 POPULATION.
1942. a. $40. Michigan Municipal League, 1675
Green Rd., Box 1487, Ann Arbor, MI 48106. TEL
313-662-3246.
    Formed by the merger of: Salaries and Wages for
Michigan Municipalities over 4,000 Population;
Which was formerly titled: Salaries, Wages, and
Fringe Benefits in Michigan Municipalities over 4,
000 Population (ISSN 0080-5548) & Salaries and
Wages for Michigan Municipalities under 4,000
Population. Which was formerly titled: Salaries and
Wages for Michigan Villages and Cities 1,000-4,000
Population; Salaries, Wages and Fringe Benefits for
Michigan Villages and Cities 1,000-4,000 Population
(ISSN 0077-216X).

352   CN   ISSN 0581-8435
SASKATCHEWAN MUNICIPAL DIRECTORY.
1909. a. Can.$10. Saskatchewan Urban Affairs, 2151
Scarth St., Regina, Sask. S4P 3V7, Canada. TEL
306-787-2664. Ed. Irene Rau. circ. 6,500.

952   PUBLIC FINANCE, TAXATION

352   YU   ISSN 0037-7104
SLUZBENE NOVINE OPCINE KARLOVAC. 1964. irreg. 150 din. Skupstina Opcine Karlovac, Banjavciceva 9, Karlovac, Yugoslavia. Ed. Vladimir Funduk.

352   YU   ISSN 0037-7120
SLUZBENI GLASNIK OPCINE ROVINJ. (Text in Italian and Serbo-Croatian) 1964. irreg. 30 din. Skupstina Opcine Rovinj, Ul. Matteotti 1/1, Rovinj, Yugoslavia. Ed. Marija Matosovic.

352   US
STATE MUNICIPAL LEAGUE DIRECTORY. a. $25. National League of Cities, 1301 Pennsylvania Ave., N.W., Washington, DC 20004. TEL 202-626-3000.

352   US
UNIVERSITY OF ALASKA. COOPERATIVE EXTENSION SERVICE. LOCAL GOVERNMENT HI-LITES. 1972. irreg. University of Alaska, Cooperative Extension Service, Fairbanks, AK 99701. TEL 907-278-3141. (Co-sponsor: U.S. Department of Agriculture) Ed. A. Nakazawa.

352   PH
UNIVERSITY OF THE PHILIPPINES. COLLEGE OF PUBLIC ADMINISTRATION. LOCAL GOVERNMENT STUDIES. (Text in English) 1962. irreg. University of the Philippines, College of Public Administration, Local Government Center, Box 474, Manila, Philippines.

URBAN INSTITUTE. ANNUAL REPORT. see HOUSING AND URBAN PLANNING

URBAN INSTITUTE. POLICY AND RESEARCH REPORT. see HOUSING AND URBAN PLANNING

PUBLIC FINANCE, TAXATION

see Business and Economics — Public Finance, Taxation

PUBLIC HEALTH AND SAFETY

see also Birth Control; Fire Prevention; Funerals

614   UN
A F R O TECHNICAL PAPERS. 1970. irreg., 2-4/yr. World Health Organization, Regional Office for Africa - Organisation Mondiale de la Sante. Bureau Regionale de l'Afrique, B.P. No.6, Brazzaville, Congo. Indexed: Rural Recreat.Tour.Abstr. World Agri.Econ.& Rural Sociol.Abstr.

614   UN
A F R O TECHNICAL REPORT SERIES. REPORTS OF MEETINGS OF EXPERT COMMITTEES. 1976. irreg., 3-4/yr. World Health Organization, Regional Office for Africa - Organisation Mondiale de la Sante. Bureau Regional de l'Afrique, P.O. Box 6, Brazzaville, Congo.

614.8   US   ISSN 0148-6039
ACCIDENT FACTS. a. National Safety Council, 444 N. Michigan Ave., Chicago, IL 60611. TEL 312-527-4800.

614.8 310   US
ADVANCES IN RISK ANALYSIS. 1983. irreg. (Society for Risk Analysis) Plenum Press, 233 Spring St., New York, NY 10013. TEL 212-620-8000. Ed.Bd. (back issues avail.)

614   GW   ISSN 0172-2131
AKADEMIE FUER OEFFENTLICHES GESUNDHEITSWESEN. SCHRIFTENREIHE. 1973. irreg. price varies. Akademie fuer Oeffentliches Gesundheitswesen, Auf'm Hennekamp 70, 4000 Duesseldorf 1, W. Germany (B.R.D.)
Formerly: Akademie fuer Staatsmedizin, Duesseldorf. Jahrbuch (ISSN 0065-5392)

614   DK   ISSN 0107-7619
AKTIVITETEN I SYGEHUSVAESENET. 1979. a. Kr.25. Sundhedsstyrelsen, St. Kongensgade 1, 1264 Copenhagen, Denmark (Subscr. to: Statens Informationtjeneste, Bredgade 20, 1260 Copenhagen K, Denmark)

ALBERTA. DEPARTMENT OF SOCIAL SERVICES AND COMMUNITY HEALTH. ANNUAL REPORT. see SOCIAL SERVICES AND WELFARE

614 360   CN   ISSN 0707-1434
ALBERTA. HEALTH AND SOCIAL SERVICES DISCIPLINES COMMITTEE. ANNUAL REPORT. 1977. a. free. Health and Social Services Disciplines Committee, Alberta Social Services and Community Health, South Tower, Seventh St. Plaza, 10030-107th St., Edmonton, Alba. T5J 3E4, Canada. TEL 403-427-6904. Ed. Raymond W. Pong. circ. 800.

AMERICAN HOSPITAL ASSOCIATION. GUIDE TO THE HEALTH CARE FIELD. see HOSPITALS — Abstracting, Bibliographies, Statistics

614 600   US
AMERICAN PETROLEUM INSTITUTE. HEALTH AND ENVIRONMENTAL SCIENCES DEPARTMENT. RESEARCH REPORTS. irreg. price varies. American Petroleum Institute, Health and Environmental Sciences Department, 1220 L St., N.W., Washington, DC 20005.
Former titles: American Petroleum Institute. Medicine and Biological Science Department. Medical Research Reports; American Petroleum Institute. Committee of Medicine and Environmental Health. Medical Research Reports.

628   US   ISSN 0066-068X
AMERICAN SOCIETY OF SANITARY ENGINEERING. YEAR BOOK. 1906. a. $10 each per 2 part book. American Society of Sanitary Engineering, c/o Gael H. Dunn, Ed., Box 40362, Bay Village, OH 44140. TEL 216-835-3040. adv. cum.index 1906-1950; 1951-1963; 1963-1970. circ. 2,700.
Sanitary engineering

614   IT
ANNALI DI STUDI GIURIDICI E SOCIO-ECONOMICI SUI SERVIZII SANITARI NAZIONALE E REGIONALE. 1975. irreg. Maria Ragno, Via Crescenzio 43, Rome, Italy.

628   US
ANNUAL CONFERENCE ON ACTIVATED SLUDGE PROCESS CONTROL. PROCEEDINGS. 1981. a. Arthur Technology, Inc., Box 1236, Fond du Lac, WI 54935-6836. Ed. Robert M. Arthur.

614   US   ISSN 0163-7525
ANNUAL REVIEW OF PUBLIC HEALTH. 1980. a. $31. Annual Reviews Inc., 4139 El Camino Way, Palo Alto, CA 94306. TEL 415-493-4400. Ed. Lester Breslow. bibl. index. cum.index. (back issues avail.; reprint service avail. from ISI) Indexed: Curr.Cont. Ind.Med. SSCI. Abstr.Hyg. Adol.Ment.Hlth.Abstr. CINAHL. Risk Abstr.

628   IT
ANNUARIO SANITARIO. a. L.85000. Guida Monaci, Via F. Crispi 10, 00187 Rome, Italy. Ed. Alberto Zapponini.

353.9   US   ISSN 0362-1421
ARIZONA. DEPARTMENT OF HEALTH SERVICES. ANNUAL REPORT. 1974. a. free. Department of Health Services, 1740 W. Adams St., Phoenix, AZ 85007. TEL 602-255-1000. illus. Key Title: Annual Report of the Arizona Department of Health Services.

628   US
ARIZONA RADIATION REGULATORY AGENCY. ANNUAL REPORT.* 1981. a. Radiation Regulatory Agency, 4814 S. 40th St., Phoenix, AZ 85040.

614   UK   ISSN 0140-4563
ASSOCIATION OF NATIONAL HEALTH SERVICE SUPPLIES OFFICERS. REFERENCE BOOK & BUYER'S GUIDE. a. £30. Sterling Publications Ltd., 86-88 Edgware Rd., London, W2 2YW, England. adv.

614   AT
AUSTRALIA. DEPARTMENT OF HEALTH. ANNUAL REPORT. 1954. a. Department of Health, Box 100, Woden, A.C.T. 2606, Australia. illus. circ. 2,500.

614   AT   ISSN 0067-2165
AUSTRALIAN STUDIES IN HEALTH SERVICE ADMINISTRATION. 1968. irreg., nos. 51-54, 1984. Aus.$45. University of New South Wales, School of Health Administration, P.O. Box 1, Kensington, N.S.W. 2033, Australia. Ed. C. Grant. circ. 300.

B I H E P. (Bibliographic Index of Health Education Periodicals) see PHYSICAL FITNESS AND HYGIENE — Abstracting, Bibliographies, Statistics

614.5   US
B M F T RISIKO- UND SICHERHEITSFORSCHUNG. 1982. irreg. (Bundesministerium fuer Forschung und Technologie, GW) Springer-Verlag, 175 Fifth Ave., New York, NY 10010 TEL 212-460-1500. (Also Berlin, Tokyo and Vienna) Indexed: Chem.Abstr.

610   BB
BARBADOS. MINISTRY OF HEALTH AND COMMUNITY SERVICES. CHIEF MEDICAL OFFICER. ANNUAL REPORT. 1972. a. free. Ministry of Health and Community Services, Bridgetown, Barbados, W. Indies. Ed. Dr. L. Harney. charts. illus. stat. circ. 300.
Formerly: Barbados. Ministry of Health and Welfare. Chief Medical Officer. Annual Report.

614   SA
BE SAFE AT HOME/WEES VEILIG TUIS. (Text in Afrikaans and English) a. Medical Association of South Africa, Medical House, Central Square, Pinelands 7405, South Africa. adv.

614 613   GE   ISSN 0067-5083
BEITRAEGE ZUR HYGIENE UND EPIDEMIOLOGIE. 1943. irreg., vol. 25, 1981. price varies. Johann Ambrosius Barth Verlag, Salomonstr. 18b, DDR-7010 Leipzig, E. Germany (D.D.R.) (Orders to: Buchexport, Leninstr. 16, DDR-7010 Leipzig, E. Germany (D.D.R.)) Eds. H. Habs, H. Rische. (back issues avail.) Indexed: Excerp.Med. Ind.Med.

BELGIUM. MINISTERE DE LA SANTE PUBLIQUE ET DE LA FAMILLE. RAPPORT ANNUEL. see SOCIAL SERVICES AND WELFARE

BELGIUM. MINISTERIE VAN VOLKSGEZONDHEID EN VAN HET GEZIN. CENTRUM VOOR BEVOLKINGS- EN GEZINSSTUDIES. TECHNISCH RAPPORT. see SOCIAL SERVICES AND WELFARE

BIOMEDICAL ENGINEERING AND HEALTH SYSTEMS: A WILEY-INTERSCIENCE SERIES. see MEDICAL SCIENCES

628   VE
BOLETIN DE SALUD PUBLICA. 1941. a. Ministerio de Sanidad y Asistencia Social, Direccion de Salud Publica, Caracas, Venezuela. (Co-sponsor: Venezuela. Oficina de los Servicios Regionales de Salud) Ed.Bd. charts. illus.
Supersedes: Uruguay. Consejo de Salud Publica. Boletin.

614   MX
BOLETIN EPIDEMIOLOGICO. 1973. a. free. Instituto Mexicano del Seguro Social, Subdireccion General Medica, Jefatura de Servicios de Medicina Preventiva, Passeo de la Reforma 476, Colonia Juarez, Mexico, D.F., Mexico. stat. circ. 500.
Formerly: Boletin Epidemiologico Anual.
Epidemiology

614   BS
BOTSWANA. MINISTRY OF HEALTH. REPORT. 1973. a. Ministry of Health, Gaborone, Botswana.
Formerly: Botswana. Department of Health. Report.

BRITISH COLUMBIA. MEDICAL SERVICES PLAN. PRACTITIONERS' NEWSLETTER. see MEDICAL SCIENCES

PUBLIC HEALTH AND SAFETY

614.8   CN   ISSN 0706-4810
BRITISH COLUMBIA. MINISTRY OF HEALTH. ANNUAL REPORT. 1975. a. free. Ministry of Health, Victoria, B.C., Canada. TEL 604-386-3166. circ. 1,500.
    Formerly: British Columbia. Department of Health. Annual Report (ISSN 0701-5372)

614 360   CN   ISSN 0068-7456
CANADA. DEPARTMENT OF NATIONAL HEALTH AND WELFARE. ANNUAL REPORT. (Text in English and French) 1944. a. free. Department of National Health and Welfare, Ottawa, Ont. K1A 0K9, Canada. TEL 613-996-4650. circ. 10,000. Indexed: Med. Care Rev.

CANADIAN MENTAL HEALTH ASSOCIATION. ANNUAL REPORT/ASSOCIATION CANADIENNE POUR LA SANTE MENTALE. RAPPORT ANNUEL. see *PSYCHOLOGY*

614   FR   ISSN 0069-2603
CHAMBRE SYNDICALE NATIONALE DES ENTREPRISES ET INDUSTRIES DE L'HYGIENE PUBLIQUE. ANNUAIRE. 1963. biennial. 50 F. Chambre Syndicale Nationale des Entreprises et Industries de l'Hygiene Publique, 10 rue Washington, 75008 Paris, France.

614.8   UK   ISSN 0266-9552
CHARTERED INSTITUTE OF PUBLIC FINANCE AND ACCOUNTANCY. ENVIRONMENTAL HEALTH STATISTICS. ACTUALS. 1984. a. £14. Chartered Institute of Public Finance and Accountancy, 3 Robert St., London WC2N 6BH, England.

CHEMICAL INDUSTRY INSTITUTE OF TOXICOLOGY SERIES. see *INDUSTRIAL HEALTH AND SAFETY*

613.62   EI
COMMISSION OF THE EUROPEAN COMMUNITIES. ANNUAL REPORTS ON THE PROGRESS OF RESEARCH WORK PROMOTED BY THE ECSC. French edition: Commission des Communautes Europeennes. Rapports Annuels sur l'Etat des Travaux de Recherches Encouragees par la CECA. 1967. a. Commission of the European Communities, Service de Renseignment et de Diffusion des Documents, Rue de la Loi 200, 1049 Brussels, Belgium. circ. controlled.

614   BL
COMPANHIA ESTADUAL DE TECNOLOGIA DE SANEAMENTO BASICO E DE DEFESA DO MEIO AMBIENTE. DIRECTORIA RELATORIA ANUAL. 1974. a. Companhia Estadual de Tecnologia de Saneamento Basico e Defesa do Meio Ambiente, Avda. Prof. Frederico Hermann Filho 345, CEP 05459, Sao Paulo, Brazil. illus. circ. 2, 000.

628   US   ISSN 0069-8474
CONFERENCE OF STATE SANITARY ENGINEERS. REPORT OF PROCEEDINGS. 1920. a. U.S. Public Health Service, Department of Health, Education and Welfare, Washington, DC 20201. TEL 202-245-6761.

614   US
CONTEMPORARY COMMUNITY HEALTH SERIES. irreg. price varies. University of Pittsburgh Press, 127 N. Bellefield Ave., Pittsburgh, PA 15260. TEL 412-624-4110.

614.49   SZ   ISSN 0377-3574
CONTRIBUTIONS TO EPIDEMIOLOGY AND BIOSTATISTICS. (Text in English) 1977. irreg., approx. a. price varies. S. Karger AG, Allschwilerstrasse 10, P.O. Box, CH-4009 Basel, Switzerland. Ed. M. Davies. (reprint service avail. from ISI) Indexed: Biol.Abstr.

353.9   US   ISSN 0095-6422
DELAWARE. DEPARTMENT OF HEALTH AND SOCIAL SERVICE. ANNUAL REPORT. a. Department of Health and Social Services, 1901 N. Dupont Hwy., New Castle, DE 09720. illus. Key Title: Annual Report - Department of Health and Social Services.

DENMARK. DANMARKS STATISTIK. FAERDSELSUHELD/ROAD TRAFFIC ACCIDENTS. see *POPULATION STUDIES — Abstracting, Bibliographies, Statistics*

DIRECTORY OF SOCIAL AND HEALTH AGENCIES OF NEW YORK CITY. see *SOCIAL SERVICES AND WELFARE*

614   DK   ISSN 0108-5646
DOEDSAARSAGERNE/CAUSES OF DEATH IN DENMARK. (Text in Danish and English) 1980. a. Kr.25. Sundhedsstyrelsen, St. Kongensgade 1, 1264 Copenhagen K, Denmark (Orders to: Danske Boghandleres Kommissionsanstalt, Siljangade 6, 2300 Copenhagen S, Denmark)
    Formerly: Doedsaarsagerne i Kongeriget Danmark.

628   SP
EDUCACION SANITARIA. 1983. irreg., no.3, 1986. price varies. (Universidad de Navarra, Facultad de Medicina) Ediciones Universidad de Navarra, S.A., Apdo. 396, 31080 Pamplona, Spain.

614   HU   ISSN 0073-4012
EGESZSEGNEVELES SZAKKONYVTARA. 1967. irreg. price varies. Medicina Kiado, Beloiannisz u. 8, 1054 Budapest, Hungary.

614.8   614.86   US
EMERGENCY RESPONSE GUIDEBOOK. a. U.S. Department of Transportation, Materials Transportation Bureau, Washington, DC 20590.

ENVIRONMENTAL RADIATION SURVEILLANCE IN WASHINGTON STATE. ANNUAL REPORT. see *ENVIRONMENTAL STUDIES*

614.49   US   ISSN 0193-936X
EPIDEMIOLOGIC REVIEWS. 1979. a. $10. Johns Hopkins Hospital, 600 N. Wolfe St., Baltimore, MD 21205. TEL 301-955-3286. Eds. Neal Nathanson, Leon Gordis. Indexed: Excerp.Med. Ind.Med. Sci.Cit.Ind. Abstr.Hyg. Helminthol.Abstr. Ind.Sci.Rev. Ind.Vet. Vet.Bull. Trop.Dis.Bull.

ESTIMATED WORLD REQUIREMENTS OF NARCOTIC DRUGS. see *PHARMACY AND PHARMACOLOGY*

614.8   UN   ISSN 0250-8710
EURO REPORTS AND STUDIES. French edition (ISSN 0250-8400); Russian edition (ISSN 0250-8729) (Editions in English, French and Russian) 1980. irreg. World Health Organization, Regional Office for Europe, Scherfigsvej 8, 2100 Copenhagen 0, Denmark. Indexed: Biol.Abstr. Curr.Cont. Abstr.Hyg. ERIC.

614.7   EI
EUROPEAN ATOMIC ENERGY COMMUNITY. CONTAMINATION RADIOACTIVE DES DENREES ALIMENTAIRES DANS LES PAYS DE LA COMMUNAUTE. (Multilingual text in Dutch, French, German and Italian) 1965. a. price varies. Office for Official Publications of the European Communities, P.O. Box 1003, L-2985 Luxembourg, Luxembourg (Dist. in U.S. by: European Community Information Service, 2100 M St., N.W., Ste. 707, Washington, D.C. 20037)

614.7   EI
EUROPEAN ATOMIC ENERGY COMMUNITY. RESULTATS DES MESURES DE LA RADIOACTIVITE AMBIANTE DANS LES PAYS DE LA COMMUNAUTE: AIR-RETOMBEE-EAUX. (Editions also in Dutch, German and Italian) 1965. a. price varies. Office for Official Publications of the European Communities, P.O. Box 1003, L-2985 Luxembourg, Luxembourg (Dist. in U.S. by: European Community Information Service, 2100 M St., N.W., Ste. 707, Washington, D.C. 20037)

FACTS AND ADVICE FOR AIRLINE PASSENGERS. see *TRANSPORTATION — Air Transport*

FEDERAL FUNDING GUIDE. see *PUBLIC ADMINISTRATION — Municipal Government*

614   US   ISSN 0278-1808
FOCAL POINTS. Variant title: Health Education Focal Points. 1975-1981; resumed 1983. irreg., approx. 6/yr. U.S. Centers for Disease Control, Center for Health Promotion and Education, 1600 Clifton Rd., Atlanta, GA 30333. TEL 404-329-3311. Indexed: Rehabil.Lit.

614   FR
FRANCE. MINISTERE DE LA SANTE ET DE LA SECURITE SOCIALE. ANNUAIRE DES STATISTIQUES SANITAIRES ET SOCIALES. 1971. a. price varies. Documentation Francaise, 29-31 Quai Voltaire, 75340 Paris, France. (Co-sponsor: Ministere de la Sante)
    Supersedes: France. Ministere de la Sante et de la Securite Sociale. Tableaux Statistiques "Sante et Securite Sociale; France. Ministere de la Sante. Tableaux Sante et Securite Sociale; France. Ministere de la Sante Publique et de la Securite Sociale. Annuaire Statistique de la Sante et de l'Action Sociale (ISSN 0071-8866)

614   FR
FRANCE. MINISTERE DE LA SANTE ET DE LA SECURITE SOCIALE. NOTES D'INFORMATION. 1969. irreg., no. 145, 1980. free. Ministere de la Sante et de la Securite Sociale, Service de Press, 8 Ave. de Segur, 75700 Paris, France.
    Former titles: France. Ministere de la Sante. Note d'Information (ISSN 0071-8882); Before 1969: France. Ministere des Affaires Sociales. Information Actualites.

FREEDOM OF INFORMATION FACT SHEETS. see *LAW*

614.8   614.7   JA   ISSN 0287-1254
FUKUOKA-KEN EISEI KOGAI SENTA NENPO/ FUKUOKA ENVIRONMENTAL RESEARCH CENTER. ANNUAL REPORT. 1974. a. free. Fukuoka-Ken Eisei Senta - Fukuoka Environmental Research Center, Fukuoka 818-01, Japan. Ed.Bd. circ. 500. (back issues avail.)

614 362.11   UK   ISSN 0072-6036
GREAT BRITAIN. DEPARTMENT OF HEALTH AND SOCIAL SECURITY. HOSPITAL IN-PATIENT INQUIRY. 1960. irreg. price varies. H.M.S.O., P.O. Box 569, London SE1 9NH, England. (reprint service avail. from UMI)

614   UK   ISSN 0072-6087
GREAT BRITAIN. DEPARTMENT OF HEALTH AND SOCIAL SECURITY. ON THE STATE OF THE PUBLIC HEALTH. (Annual Report of the Chief Medical Officer of the Department of Health and Social Security) 1921. a. price varies. H.M.S.O., P.O. Box 569, London SE1 9NH, England. (reprint service avail. from UMI)

614   UK   ISSN 0080-7877
GREAT BRITAIN. SCOTTISH HEALTH SERVICES PLANNING COUNCIL. ANNUAL REPORT. 1974. a. £3.50. Scottish Health Service Planning Council, St. Andrews House, Regent Rd., Edinburgh, Scotland (Avail. from: H.M.S.O., c/o Liaison Officer, Atlantic House, Holborn Viaduct, London EC1P 1BN, England) Ed. W.S. Garquhak. circ. 100.

HAWAII. DEPARTMENT OF HEALTH. MENTAL HEALTH SERVICES FOR CHILDREN AND YOUTH; children's MH services branch. see *SOCIAL SERVICES AND WELFARE*

614   UK
HEALTH AND PERSONAL SOCIAL SERVICES STATISTICS. a. H.M.S.O., P.O. Box 569, London SE1 9NH, England. (reprint service avail. from UMI)
    Formerly: Digest of Health Statistics for England and Wales (ISSN 0070-4849)

614 360   CN
HEALTH AND SOCIAL SERVICE MANPOWER IN ALBERTA. 1978. a. free. Health and Social Services Disciplines Committee, Alberta Social Services and Community Health, South Tower, Seventh St. Plaza, 10030-107th St., Edmonton, Alba. T5J 3E4, Canada. TEL 403-427-6904. Ed. Raymond W. Pong. circ. 800.

614 610 340   US
HEALTH LAW BULLETIN. 1958. irreg. University of North Carolina at Chapel Hill, Institute of Government, Chapel Hill, NC 27514. TEL 919-966-4119. Ed. Anne M. Dellinger. bibl.

HEALTH ORGANIZATIONS OF THE U.S., CANADA AND THE WORLD; a directory of voluntary associations, professional societies and other groups concerned with health and related fields. see *MEDICAL SCIENCES*

PUBLIC HEALTH AND SAFETY

614   UK
HEALTH SERVICES. 1982. irreg. Pergamon Press Ltd., Headington Hall, Oxford OX3 0BW, England. Ed. Jill Turner.
Formerly: Times Health Supplement.

HEALTH SERVICES LAW VICTORIA. see *LAW*

658 658   US   ISSN 0361-0195
HEALTH SYSTEMS MANAGEMENT. 1974. irreg., no.18, 1985. S P Medical & Scientific Books (Subsidiary of: Spectrum Publications, Inc.) 175-20 Wexford Terrace, Jamaica, NY 11432. TEL 718-658-0888. Ed. Dr. Samuel Levey.

I E E E CONFERENCE ON HUMAN FACTORS AND NUCLEAR SAFETY. CONFERENCE RECORD. see *PHYSICS — Nuclear Energy*

610.6   IT
I.F.P.S.M. NEWS. (Text in English and French) irreg. International Federation for Preventive and Social Medicine, Via Salaria 237, 00199 Rome, Italy.
Formerly: I.F.H.P.M. News.

613 310   US   ISSN 0885-9914
INDIAN HEALTH TRENDS AND SERVICES. 1969. irreg. free. U.S. Public Health Service, Resources and Services Administration, 5600 Fishers Ln., Rm. 6A-30, Rockville, MD 20857 TEL 202-545-6700. (Orders to: Supt. of Documents, Washington, DC 20402) stat. circ. 15,000.

614   JA
INSTITUTE OF PUBLIC HEALTH. ANNUAL REPORT/KOKURITSU KOSHU EISEI-IN NENPO. (Text in Japanese) 1948. a. Institute of Public Health - Kokuritsu Koshu Eisei-in, 4-6-1 Shiroganedai, Minato-ku, Tokyo 108, Japan.

614.8   UK
INSTITUTION OF PUBLIC HEALTH ENGINEERS YEARBOOK. a. Sterling Publications Ltd., 86-88 Edgware Rd., London W2 2YW, England. Ed. R.E. Beardsall.
Supersedes (as of 1982): Institution of Public Health Engineers Data Book.

616.988   PO   ISSN 0303-7762
INSTITUTO DE HIGIENE E MEDICINA TROPICAL. ANAIS. (Text and summaries in English, French and Portuguese) 1943. irreg. price varies. Instituto de Higiene e Medicina Tropical, Centro de Documentacao e Informacao Cientifica, Rua da Junqueira, 96, Lisbon 3, Portugal. bk. rev. circ. 1,000. Indexed: Biol.Abstr. Excerp.Med. Ind.Med. Abstr.Hyg. Helminthol.Abstr. Ind.Vet. Rev.Appl.Entomol. Vet.Bull. Trop.Dis.Bull.
Formerly: Lisbon. Escola Nacional de Saude de Medicina Tropical. Anais (ISSN 0075-9767)
Tropical medicine

614   MX
INSTITUTO MEXICANO DEL SEGURO SOCIAL. BOLETIN ESTADISTICO. 1972. a. free. Instituto Mexicano del Seguro Social, Subdireccion General Medica, Jefatura de Servicios de Medicina Preventiva, Passeo de la Reforma 476, Colonia Juarez, Mexico, D.F., Mexico. circ. 500.

614   MX
INSTITUTO MEXICANO DEL SEGURO SOCIAL. BOLETIN SOBRE MORBILIDAD HOSPITALARIA. 1982. a. free. Instituto Mexicano del Seguro Social, Subdireccion General Medica, Jefatura de Servicios de Medicina Preventiva, Passeo de la Reforma 476, Colonia Juarez, Mexico, D.F., Mexico. circ. 500.

614   MX
INSTITUTO MEXICANO DEL SEGURO SOCIAL. BOLETIN SOBRE MORTALIDAD. 1977. a. free. Instituto Mexicano del Seguro Social, Subdireccion General Medica, Jefatura de Servicios de Medicina Preventiva, Passeo de la Reforma 476, Colonia Juarez, Mexico, D.F., Mexico. circ. 500.

614   MX
INSTITUTO MEXICANO DEL SEGURO SOCIAL. BOLETIN SOBRE MOTIVOS DE CONSULTA. 1980. a. free. Instituto Mexicano del Seguro Social, Subdireccion General Medica, Jefatura de Servicios de Medicina Preventiva, Passeo de la Reforma 476, Colonia Juarez, Mexico, D.F., Mexico. circ. 500.

614   BE   ISSN 0378-892X
INSTITUUT VOOR HYGIENE EN EPIDEMIOLOGIE. RESEAU SOUFRE-FUMEE/ZWAVEL-ROOK MEETNET. Short titles: Reseau Soufre-Fumee; Zwavel-Rook Meetnet. (Text in Dutch and French) 1968. a. $5. Instituut voor Hygiene en Epidemiologie, Juliette Wytsmanstraat 14, 1050 Brussels, Belgium. charts. stat. circ. 600.
Epidemiology

INSTYTUT BADAN JADROWYCH. ZAKLAD RADIOBIOLOGII I OCHRONY ZDROWIA. PRACE DOSWIADCZAINE. see *MEDICAL SCIENCES — Radiology And Nuclear Medicine*

614   UN   ISSN 0074-1892
INTERNATIONAL ATOMIC ENERGY AGENCY. SAFETY SERIES. (Text in English, French, Russian or Spanish) 1960. irreg. price varies. International Atomic Energy Agency, Wagramer Str. 5, Box 100, A-1400 Vienna, Austria (Dist. in U.S. by: Bernan Associates-Unipub, 4611-F Assembly Dr., Lanham, MD 20706-4391) Indexed: Biol.Abstr. Pollut.Abstr.

INTERNATIONAL CONGRESS ON HYGIENE AND PREVENTIVE MEDICINE. PROCEEDINGS. see *PHYSICAL FITNESS AND HYGIENE*

INTERNATIONAL NARCOTICS CONTROL BOARD. COMPARATIVE STATEMENT OF ESTIMATES AND STATISTICS ON NARCOTIC DRUGS FOR (YEAR) see *PHARMACY AND PHARMACOLOGY*

INTERNATIONAL NARCOTICS CONTROL BOARD. REPORT FOR (YEAR) see *PHARMACY AND PHARMACOLOGY*

INTERNATIONAL NARCOTICS CONTROL BOARD. STATISTICS ON NARCOTIC DRUGS FOR (YEAR) see *PHARMACY AND PHARMACOLOGY*

INTERNATIONAL NARCOTICS CONTROL BOARD. STATISTICS ON PSYCHOTROPIC SUBSTANCES FOR (YEAR) see *PHARMACY AND PHARMACOLOGY*

INTERNATIONAL SECURITY DIRECTORY; world defense, police & fire hqs., security companies, their products and supplies. see *CRIMINOLOGY AND LAW ENFORCEMENT — Security*

INTERNATIONAL UNION OF SCHOOL AND UNIVERSITY HEALTH AND MEDICINE. CONGRESS REPORTS. see *EDUCATION*

614   UN   ISSN 0449-122X
JOINT F A O/W H O CODEX ALIMENTARIUS COMMISSION. REPORT OF THE SESSION. (Editions in English, French, Spanish) 1963. irreg., (approx. biennial) free. Food and Agriculture Organization of the United Nations, Distribution and Sales Section, Via delle Terme di Caracalla, 00100 Rome, Italy (Dist. in U.S. by: Bernan Associates-Unipub, 4611-F Assembly Drive, Lanham, MD 20706-4391)

614   US   ISSN 0075-4668
KAISER FOUNDATION MEDICAL CARE PROGRAM. ANNUAL REPORT. 1960. a. free. ‡ Kaiser Foundation Medical Care Program, Public Affairs, 27th Fl., Ordway Bldg., Kaiser Center, Oakland, CA 94666. TEL 415-428-5000. Ed. D.A. Scannell. circ. 24,000.

614.8   JA
KOKUTETSU CHUO HOKEN KANRIJOHO; health control. (Text and summaries in English, Japanese) 1955. a. free. Japanese National Railways, Central Health Institute, 2-1 Yoyogi, Shibuyaku, Tokyo 151, Japan. circ. 1,000. (back issues avail.)

614   NE
KONINKLIJK INSTITUUT VOOR DE TROPEN. DEPARTMENT OF TROPICAL HYGIENE. ANNUAL REPORT. (Text in English) a. Koninklijk Instituut voor de Tropen, Department of Tropical Hygiene, Mauritskade 63, 1092 AD Amsterdam, Netherlands. Eds. J.W.L. Kleevens, A. van Amerongen-Woudstra.

614   NE   ISSN 0075-6954
KOSTEN EN FINANCIERING VAN DE GEZONDHEIDZORG IN NEDERLAND/COST OF HEALTH CARE IN THE NETHERLANDS. (Text in Dutch and English) 1953. irreg. fl.14.40. Centraal Bureau voor de Statistiek, Prinses Beatrixlaan 428, Voorburg, Netherlands (Orders to: Staatsuitgeverij, Christoffel Plantijnstraat, The Hague, Netherlands)

614   IS   ISSN 0301-4843
KUPAT-HOLIM YEARBOOK. (Editions in English and Hebrew) 1971. a. free. Kupat Holim, Health Insurance Institution of Histadrut, 101 Arlosoroff St., Tel Aviv, Israel. Indexed: Biol.Abstr. Chem.Abstr.

614.83   US   ISSN 0277-9196
LAURISTON S. TAYLOR LECTURE SERIES. 1977. a. price varies. National Council on Radiation Protection and Measurements, 7910 Woodmont Ave., Ste. 1016, Bethesda, MD 20814. TEL 301-657-2652. Ed. W. Roger Ney.

614   LB
LIBERIA. MINISTRY OF HEALTH AND SOCIAL WELFARE. ANNUAL REPORT.* a., latest 1975. Ministry of Health and Social Welfare, Monrovia, Liberia.

614   FI   ISSN 0355-6654
LIIKENNETURVA. REPORTS. 1965. irreg., no. 19, 1977. Liikenneturva - Central Organization for Traffic Safety in Finland, Iso Robertinkatu 20, 00120 Helsinki 12, Finland. circ. 200.

362.1   ZA
LUSAKA. MEDICAL OFFICER OF HEALTH. ANNUAL REPORT. 1966. a. free. Health and Welfare Department, Medical Officer of Health, Public Health Department, Box 789, Lusaka, Zambia. stat. circ. 300.

MAISONS D'ENFANTS ET D'ADOLESCENTS DE FRANCE. ALBUM-ANNUAIRE NATIONAL; publication documentaire illustree des etablissements de vacances, de repos, de soins, de cure et de prevention pour enfants et adolescents. see *CHILDREN AND YOUTH — About*

614   CN   ISSN 0383-3925
MANITOBA. HEALTH SERVICES COMMISSION. ANNUAL REPORT. 1971. a. free. Health Services Commission, Box 925, 599 Empress St., Winnipeg, Man. R3C 2T6, Canada. TEL 204-786-7101.

353.9   US
MASSACHUSETTS. DEPARTMENT OF PUBLIC HEALTH. ANNUAL REPORT. 1870. a. free. Department of Public Health, 150 Tremont St., Boston, MA 02111. TEL 617-727-2700. Ed. Pearl K. Russo. illus. circ. 4,000.

614   MF
MAURITIUS. MINISTRY OF HEALTH. ANNUAL REPORT. (Text in English) a. Government Printing Office, Elizabeth II Ave., Port Louis, Mauritius.

614   US
MENTAL HEALTH DIRECTORY.* 1971. a. $5. U.S. Public Health Service, Alcohol, Drug Abuse & Mental Health Administration, 5600 Fishers Lane, Rockville, MD 20857 (Orders to: Supt. of Documents, Washington, DC 20402)

MENTAL HEALTH STATISTICS FOR ILLINOIS. see *SOCIAL SERVICES AND WELFARE*

MISSOURI. DIVISION OF HIGHWAY SAFETY. HIGHWAY SAFETY PLAN. see *TRANSPORTATION — Roads And Traffic*

614   UY
MORBILIDAD. irreg. Ministerio de Salud Publica, Departamento de Estadistica, Montevideo, Uruguay. stat.

614.862   US
MOTOR VEHICLE SAFETY; a report on activities under the National Traffic and Motor Vehicle Safety Act of 1966. 1966. a. U.S. National Highway Traffic Safety Administration, 400 Seventh St., N.W., Washington, DC 20590. (Prepared with: U.S. Federal Highway Administration)

PUBLIC HEALTH AND SAFETY

614.83 US
N C R P COMMENTARY. 1982. irreg. price varies. National Council on Radiation Protection and Measurements, 7910 Woodmont Ave., Ste. 1016, Bethesda, MD 20814. TEL 301-657-2652. Ed. W. Roger Ney.

614.8 355.23 US ISSN 0083-209X
N C R P REPORT. 1931. irreg., no.86, 1986. price varies. National Council on Radiation Protection and Measurements, 7910 Woodmont Ave., Ste. 1016, Bethesda, MD 20814. TEL 301-657-2652. Ed. W. Roger Ney. Indexed: Biol.Abstr. GeoRef.

614.83 US
N C R P SYMPOSIUM PROCEEDINGS. 1982. irreg. $20. National Council on Radiation Protection and Measurements, 7910 Woodmont Ave., Ste. 1016, Bethesda, MD 20814. TEL 301-657-2652. Ed. W. Roger Ney.

614.8 US
N E I S S DATA HIGHLIGHTS. (National Electronic Injury Surveillance System) 1973. a. free. (U.S. Consumer Product Safety Commission) U.S. National Injury Information Clearinghouse, 5401 Westbard Ave., Washington, DC 20207. TEL 202-492-6424. charts. index. circ. 3,000.
Formerly: N E I S S News (ISSN 0364-6475)
Safety education

614.8 374 JA ISSN 0287-9549
NARA WOMEN'S UNIVERSITY. HEALTH ADMINISTRATION CENTER. ARCHIVES OF HEALTH CARE/NARA JOSHIDAIGAKU HOKEN SENTA NENPO. (Text in Japanese; summaries in English) 1978. a. Nara Women's University, Health Administration Center, Kita-Uoya-Higashi, Nara-Shi 630, Japan. Ed. Kimihiro Yamamoto. circ. 500.

628 380.1 UK
NATIONAL ASSOCIATION OF WASTE DISPOSAL CONTRACTORS. TRADE DIRECTORY. 1968. a. £7.50 to non-members. National Association of Waste Disposal Contractors, Suite 26/29, Wheatsheaf House, 4 Carmelite St., London EC4Y 0BY, England. Ed. Alec Paris. circ. 1,500.

614.8 II
NATIONAL CONFERENCE ON SAFETY. PROCEEDINGS. 1970. a. Rs.10. National Safety Council, Central Labour Institute Bldg., Sion, Bombay 22, India. Ed. A.A. Krishnan. charts. circ. 2,000.

614.83 355.23 US ISSN 0195-7740
NATIONAL COUNCIL ON RADIATION PROTECTION AND MEASUREMENTS. PROCEEDINGS OF THE ANNUAL MEETING. 15th, 1979. a. price varies. National Council on Radiation Protection and Measurements, 7910 Woodmont Ave., Ste. 1016, Bethesda, MD 20814. TEL 301-657-2652.

614.8 US
NATIONAL HEALTH CARE EXPENDITURES STUDY. DATA PREVIEW. 1980. irreg. free. U.S. Department of Health and Human Services, National Center for Health Services, Research and Health Care Technology Assessment, 3-50 Park Bldg., Rockville, MD 20857. Ed. Daniel C. Walder. circ. 6,500.

614 JA ISSN 0077-5002
NATIONAL INSTITUTE OF HYGIENIC SCIENCES. BULLETIN/EISEI SHIKENJO HOKOKU. (Text in Japanese; summaries in English) 1886. a. National Institute of Hygienic Sciences - Kokuritsu Eisei Shikenjo, 1-18-1 Kamiyoga, Setagaya-ku, Tokyo 158, Japan. Ed. Hironori Takemaka. circ. 1,000. Indexed: Biol.Abstr. Chem.Abstr. Excerp.Med. Ind.Med. Dairy Sci.Abstr. Food Sci.& Tech.Abstr. Rev.Plant Path. Trop.Dis.Bull.

NETHERLANDS. CENTRAAL BUREAU VOOR DE STATISTIEK. JAARSTATISTIEK VAN DE BEVOLKING. POPULATION STATISTICS. see *POPULATION STUDIES — Abstracting, Bibliographies, Statistics*

614.05 NE
NETHERLANDS. RIJKSINSTITUUT VOOR DE VOLKSGEZONDHEID. MEDEDELINGEN. irreg. Rijksinstituut voor de Volksgezondheid, Utrecht, Netherlands. illus.

614 CN
NEW BRUNSWICK. DEPARTMENT OF HEALTH. ANNUAL REPORT; New Brunswick people and health. (Text in English and French) 1918. a. free. Department of Health, Box 6000, Fredericton, N.B. E3B 5H1, Canada. TEL 506-453-2536. David Gibbs. stat. circ. 700.

614 US
NEW YORK (STATE). DEPARTMENT OF HEALTH. MONOGRAPH. 1969. irreg., no.19, 1982. Department of Health, Office of Health Communications, Albany, NY 12237. charts. stat. (back issues avail.)

614 US
NEW YORK (STATE). HEALTH PLANNING COMMISSION, ADMINISTRATIVE PROGRAM FOR HEALTH PLANNING AND DEVELOPMENT. a. Health Planning Commission, Empire State Plaza, Tower Bldg. Rm. 1683, Albany, NY 12237.

353.9 US ISSN 0361-4018
NEW YORK STATE MEDICAL CARE FACILITIES FINANCE AGENCY. ANNUAL REPORT. 1974. a. Medical Care Facilities Finance Agency, 3 Park Ave., New York, NY 10016. TEL 212-686-9700. charts. illus. Key Title: Annual Report - New York State Medical Care Facilities Finance Agency.

614 NZ ISSN 0548-944X
NEW ZEALAND. DEPARTMENT OF HEALTH. SPECIAL REPORT SERIES. 1960. irreg. price varies. Department of Health, Private Bag 2, Upper Willis St., Wellington, New Zealand. circ. 300. (back issues avail.) Indexed: Biol.Abstr.

614 NZ
NEW ZEALAND HEALTH STATISTICS REPORT. a. Department of Health, National Health Statistics Centre, Private Bag 2, Upper Willis St., Wellington, New Zealand.

NOVA SCOTIA. DEPARTMENT OF PUBLIC HEALTH. NUTRITION DIVISION. ANNUAL REPORT. see *NUTRITION AND DIETETICS*

NUCLEAR POWER SAFETY REPORT. see *ENERGY*

PERSPECTIVE. CLEVELAND FOUNDATION OCCASIONAL PAPER. see *SOCIAL SERVICES AND WELFARE*

614 UN ISSN 0587-5943
PESTICIDE RESIDUES IN FOOD. 1966. a. price varies. Food and Agriculture Organization of the United Nations, Distribution and Sales Section, Via delle Terme di Caracalla, I-00100 Rome, Italy.
Formerly: Codex Committee on Pesticide Residues. Report on the Meeting.

628 PL
POLITECHNIKA SLASKA. ZESZYTY NAUKOWE. INZYNIERIA SRODOWISKA. (Text in Polish; summaries in English and Russian) 1960. irreg. price varies. Politechnika Slaska, W. Pstrowskiego 7, 44-100 Gliwice, Poland (Dist. by: Ars Polona, Krakowskie Przedmiescie 7, 00-068 Warsaw, Poland) Ed. Waclaw Kusznik. circ. 300.
Formerly (until vol.25, 1985): Politechnika Slaska. Zeszyty Naukowe. Inzynieria Sanitarna (ISSN 0072-4696)

627 628 PL ISSN 0084-2869
POLITECHNIKA WROCLAWSKA. INSTYTUT INZYNIERII OCHRONY SRODOWSKA. PRACE NAUKOWE. MONOGRAFIE. (Text in Polish; summaries in English, French, German, Russian) 1969. irreg., no.25, 1986. price varies. Politechnika Wroclawska, Wybrzeze Wyspianskiego 27, 50-370 Wroclaw, Poland (Dist. by: Ars Polona-Ruch, Krakowskie Przedmiescie 7, Warsaw, Poland) Ed. Jerzy Ciekot.

628 US ISSN 0090-516X
POLLUTION TECHNOLOGY REVIEW. 1973. irreg., no.143, 1986. price varies. Noyes Data Corporation, Noyes Bldg., Mill Road at Grand Ave., Park Ridge, NJ 07656. TEL 201-391-8484.
Formerly: Pollution Control Review (ISSN 0079-3116)

628 PL ISSN 0079-3477
POLSKA AKADEMIA NAUK. KOMITET GOSPODARKI WODNEJ. PRACE I STUDIA. 1956. irreg., vol.11, 1972. price varies. Panstwowe Wydawnictwo Naukowe, Ul. Miodowa 10, 00-251 Warsaw, Poland (Dist. by: Ars Polona, Krakowskie Przedmiescie 7, 00-068 Warsaw, Poland)

628 UR ISSN 0203-9702
POLUTEHNILINE INSTITUUT TALLINN. NEUSTANOVIVSHEESYA DVIZHENIYA ZHIDKOSTI V TRUBAKH. (Subseries of its Toimetised) (Text in Russian; summaries in English or German) irreg. price varies. Polutehniline Instituut Tallinn, Ehitajate tee 5, Tallinn, Estonian S.S.R., U.S.S.R.

354 614 CN
PRINCE EDWARD ISLAND. DEPARTMENT OF HEALTH AND SOCIAL SERVICES. ANNUAL REPORT. a. Department of Health and Social Services, Box 2000, Charlottetown, P.E.I. C1A 7N8, Canada. TEL 902-892-5471. Ed. Rick Callaghan. circ. 350.
Formerly: Prince Edward Island. Department of Health. Annual Report (ISSN 0317-4530)

614 JA
PUBLIC CLEANSING SERVICES IN TOKYO/ SEISO JIGYO GAIYO. (Text in English) 1965. a. exchange basis. Bureau of Public Cleansing - Tokyo-to Seiso-kyoku Somu-bu, 3-8-1 Marunouchi, Chiyoda-ku, Tokyo 100, Japan. Ed.Bd. circ. 500.
Formerly: Public Cleansing Service in Tokyo.

614 UG
PUBLIC HEALTH AND HYGIENE.* vol.4, 1972. a. Public Health Inspectors' Association, Box 46, Kampala, Uganda. Ed. Wazarwahi Bwengye. adv. bibl. illus.

PUBLIC HEALTH IN EUROPE. see *MEDICAL SCIENCES*

PUBLIC HEALTH LABORATORY SERVICE BOARD. ANNUAL REPORT. see *MEDICAL SCIENCES — Communicable Diseases*

614 US ISSN 0079-7596
PUBLIC HEALTH MONOGRAPH.* no.3, 1951. irreg. U.S. Public Health Service, Dept. of Health Education and Welfare, Bethesda, MD 20014. TEL 301-444-6656. Indexed: Biol.Abstr. Ind.Med.
Continues: Public Health Technical Monograph.

614 UN ISSN 0555-6015
PUBLIC HEALTH PAPERS. French edition: Cahiers de Sante Publique. Russian edition: Tetradi Obshchestvennogo Zdravookhranenia. Spanish edition: Cuadernos de Salud Publica. (Editions in Arabic, English, Russian, Spanish) 1959. irreg., no.82, 1986. World Health Organization - Organisation Mondiale de la Sante, Distribution and Sales Service, 20 Avenue Appia, CH-1211 Geneva 27, Switzerland. TEL 91-21-11. circ. 12,000. Indexed: Biol.Abstr. Excerp.Med. Ind.Med. Abstr.Hyg. Med. Care Rev. Rural Recreat.Tour.Abstr. World Agri.Econ.& Rural Sociol.Abstr.

628 310 PR
PUERTO RICO. STATISTICS, ANALYSIS AND CONTROL OF INFORMATION. ANNUAL VITAL STATISTICS REPORT. (Text in English and Spanish) 1974. a. Department of Health, Office of Statistics Analysis and Information Control, Stop 18 Ponce de Leon Ave., San Juan, PR 00901. Ed. Ruth M. Gonzalez. charts. stat. circ. 1,500. (back issues avail.)
Sanitary engineering

RAUMPLANUNG UND UMWELTSCHUTZ IM KANTON ZURICH. see *HOUSING AND URBAN PLANNING*

614 CK
REGISTRO DE ORGANISMOS DE SALUD. 1976. a. Departamento Administrativo Nacional de Estadistica, Banco Nacional de Datos, Apdo. Aereo 80043, Bogota, D.E., Colombia.

614 UN ISSN 0085-5529
REPORT ON THE WORLD HEALTH SITUATION. (Editions in Arabic, Chinese, English, French, Russian, Spanish) 1959. every 6 yrs. World Health Organization - Organisation Mondiale de la Sante, Distribution and Sales, 20 Avenue Appia, CH-1211 Geneva 27, Switzerland. TEL 91-21-11. circ. 6,200.

616.89 150   US   ISSN 0192-0812
RESEARCH IN COMMUNITY AND MENTAL
HEALTH; an annual compilation of research. 1979.
a. $23.75 to individuals; institutions $47.50. J A I
Press Inc., Box 1678, 36 Sherwood Pl., Greenwich,
CT 06836. TEL 203-661-7602. Ed. Roberta G.
Simmons. Indexed: Psychol.Abstr.

RESEARCH IN THE SOCIOLOGY OF HEALTH
CARE; a research annual. see *MEDICAL
SCIENCES*

RESEAU AUTOMATIQUE BELGE DE LA
POLLUTION ATMOSPHERIQUE. see *MEDICAL
SCIENCES*

362.2   US   ISSN 0094-291X
RHODE ISLAND. DEPARTMENT OF MENTAL
HEALTH, RETARDATION AND HOSPITALS.
MENTAL HEALTH, RETARDATION AND
HOSPITALS. 1971. a. free. Department of Mental
Health, Retardation and Hospitals, Aime J. Forand
Bldgs., 600 New London Ave., Cranston, RI 02920.
TEL 401-464-1000. Key Title: Mental Health,
Retardation and Hospitals (Cranston)

614   RW
RWANDA. MINISTERE DE LA SANTE
PUBLIQUE. RAPPORT ANNUEL. a. Ministere de
la Sante Publique, B.P. 84, Kigali, Rwanda. circ.
200.

SAFETY SCIENCE ABSTRACTS JOURNAL. see
ABSTRACTING AND INDEXING SERVICES

628   JA
SAITAMA-KEN EISEI TOKEI NENPO/ANNUAL
REPORT OF PUBLIC HEALTH, SAITAMA
PREFECTURE. (Text in Japanese) 1950. a. free.
Saitama Prefecture, Saitama-Ken, Eisei-Bu, 15-1, 3-
Chome, Takasago, Urawa-Shi 336, Japan.

362.1   UK
SCOTTISH HEALTH SERVICES. irreg. H.M.S.O.
(Edinburgh), 13a Castle St., Edinburgh EH2 3AR,
Scotland. (reprint service avail. from UMI)

SHONI NO HOKEN/HEALTH FOR CHILDREN.
see *CHILDREN AND YOUTH — About*

614.8   DK   ISSN 0108-6650
SIKKERHED. (Supplement to: Socialpaedagogernes
Landsforbund. T R Information) 1981. irreg. free.
Socialpaedagogernes Landsforbund,
Brolaeggerstraede 9/st, 1211 Copenhagen K,
Denmark. illus.

614   SI   ISSN 0129-7457
SINGAPORE COMMUNITY HEALTH BULLETIN.
(Text in English) 1967. a. free. (Ministry of Health)
Ministry of Health and Ministry of the
Environment, 55 Cuppage Rd., 09-00 Cuppage
Centre, Singapore 0922, Singapore. (Co-sponsor:
Singapore Ministry of Environment; Training and
Health Education Department) Ed. Dr. Luisa Lee.
circ. controlled. Indexed: Excerp.Med.
Formerly: Singapore Public Health Bulletin.

614   DK   ISSN 0900-1980
SOCIAL ADMINISTRATION; lovsamling for
praktikere og tilstudiebrug. 1984. a. Kr.195.20.
Forlag for Social og Sundhedssektor, Albertslund,
Denmark.

614   DK   ISSN 0900-2030
SOCIAL SIKRING; lovsamling for praktikere og til
studier. 1984. a. Kr.195.20. Forlag for Social og
Sundhedssektor, Albertslund, Denmark.

610   TH
SOUTHEAST ASIAN REGIONAL SEMINAR ON
TROPICAL MEDICINE & PUBLIC HEALTH.
PROCEEDINGS. (Text in English) irreg. Southeast
Asian Ministers of Education Organisation,
Regional Tropical Medicine & Public Health Project,
Tropmed Central Office, 420/6 Rajvithi Rd.,
Bangkok 10400, Thailand. circ. 450.

STUDIES ON CURRENT HEALTH PROBLEMS.
see *MEDICAL SCIENCES*

614   DK   ISSN 0105-5151
SUNDHEDSSTYRELSEN. AARSBERETNING.
1843. a. free. Sundhedsstyrelsen, St. Kongensgade 1,
1264 Copenhagen K, Denmark.

SUNDHEDSSTYRELSEN VITALSTATISTIK. see
STATISTICS

614   SW   ISSN 0346-8445
SWEDEN. SJUKVAARDENS OCH
SOCIALVAARDENS PLANERINGS- OCH
RATIONALISERINGSINSTITUT. S P R I
INFORMERAR. Short title: S P R I Informerar.
1968. irreg. (8-10/yr.) free. Sjukvaardens och
Socialvaardens Planerings- och
Rationaliseringsinstitut - Swedish Planning and
Rationalization Institute of the Health and Social
Services, Box 27310, S-102 54 Stockholm, Sweden.

614   SW   ISSN 0082-0113
SWEDEN. SJUKVAARDENS OCH
SOCIALVAARDENS PLANERINGS- OCH
RATIONALISERINGSINSTITUT. S P R I RAAD.
Short title: S P R I Raad. (Text in Swedish;
summaries in English) 1968. irreg. price varies.
Sjukvaardens och Socialvaardens Planerings- och
Rationaliseringsinstitut - Swedish Planning and
Rationalization Institute of the Health and Social
Services, Box 27310, S-102 54 Stockholm, Sweden.

614   SW   ISSN 0586-1691
SWEDEN. SJUKVAARDENS OCH
SOCIALVAARDENS PLANERINGS-OCH
RATIONALISERINGSINSTITUT. S P R I
RAPPORT. Short title: S P R I Rapport. (Text in
Swedish; summaries in English) 1968. irreg. price
varies. Sjukvaardens och Socialvaardens Planerings-
och Rationaliseringsinstitut - Swedish Planning and
Rationalization Institute of the Health and Social
Services, Box 27310, S-102 54 Stockholm, Sweden.
Indexed: Abstr.Health Care Manage.Stud.

614   SW   ISSN 0303-6553
SWEDEN. SJUKVAARDENS OCH
SOCIALVAARDENS PLANERINGS-OCH
RATIONALISERINGSINSTITUT. S P R I RAAD
1. Short titles: S P R I Raad 1. (Text in Swedish;
summaries in English) 1972. irreg. price varies.
Sjukvaardens och Socialvaardens Planerings- och
Rationaliseringsinstitut - Swedish Planning and
Rationalization Institute of the Health and Social
Services, Box 27310, S 102 54 Stockholm, Sweden.

614   SW   ISSN 0303-6545
SWEDEN. SJUKVAARDENS OCH
SOCIALVAARDENS PLANERINGS-OCH
RATIONALISERINGSINSTITUT. S P R I RAAD
4. Short title: S P R I Raad 4. (Text in Swedish;
summaries in English) 1971. irreg. price varies.
Sjukvaardens och Socialvaardens Planerings- och
Rationaliseringsinstitut - Swedish Planning and
Rationalization Institute of the Health and Social
Services, Box 27310, S 102 54 Stockholm, Sweden.

614   SW   ISSN 0303-6510
SWEDEN. SJUKVAARDENS OCH
SOCIALVAARDENS PLANERINGS- OCH
RATIONALISERINGSINSTITUT. S P R I RAAD
5. Short title: S P R I Raad 5. (Text in Swedish;
summaries in English) 1969. irreg. price varies.
Sjukvaardens och Socialvaardens Planerings-och
Rationaliseringinstitut - Swedish Planning and
Rationalization Institute of the Health and Social
Services, Box 27310, S 102 54 Stockholm, Sweden.

614   SW   ISSN 0303-6529
SWEDEN. SJUKVAARDENS OCH
SOCIALVAARDENS PLANERINGS- OCH
RATIONALISERINGSINSTITUT. S P R I RAAD
6. Short titles: S P R I Raad 6. (Text in Swedish;
summaries in English) 1971. irreg. price varies.
Sjukvaardens och Socialvaardens Planerings-och
Rationaliseringsinstitut - Swedish Planning and
Rationalization Institute of the Health and Social
Services, Box 27310, S 102 54 Stockholm, Sweden.

614   SW   ISSN 0303-6537
SWEDEN. SJUKVAARDENS OCH
SOCIALVAARDENS PLANERINGS- OCH
RATIONALISERINGSINSTITUT. S P R I RAAD
7. Short title: S P R I Raad 7. (Text in Swedish;
summaries in English) 1971. irreg. price varies.
Sjukvaardens och Socialvaardens Planerings-och
Rationaliseringsinstitut - Swedish Planning and
Rationalization Institute of the Health and Social
Services, Box 27310, S 102 54 Stockholm, Sweden.

614   SW   ISSN 0082-0105
SWEDEN. SJUKVAARDENS OCH
SOCIALVAARDENS PLANERINGS- OCH
RATIONALISERINGSINSTITUT. S P R I
SPECIFIKATIONER. Short title: S P R I
Specifikationer. (Text in Swedish; titles in English)
1968. irreg. price varies. Sjukvaardens och
Socialvaardens Planerings- och
Rationaliseringsinstitut - Swedish Planning and
Rationalization Institute of the Health and Social
Services, Box 27310, S-102 54 Stockholm, Sweden.

614   US   ISSN 0163-1667
TEXAS. DEPARTMENT OF HEALTH
RESOURCES. BIENNIAL REPORT. biennial.
Department of Health, 1100 W. 49th St., Austin,
TX 78756. TEL 512-458-7111. Key Title: Biennial
Report - Texas Department of Health Resources.

TOKYO METROPOLITAN RESEARCH
LABORATORY OF PUBLIC HEALTH,
ANNUAL REPORT/TOKYO-TORITSU EISEI
KENKYUSHO KENKYU NENPO. see *MEDICAL
SCIENCES*

614   TO   ISSN 0082-4895
TONGA. MINISTER OF HEALTH. REPORT. (Text
in English and Tongan) 1951. a. price varies. ‡
Government Printer, Nuku-Alofa, Tongatapu, Tonga
Islands.

614   JA
TOYAMA PREFECTURE. ANNUAL REPORT OF
PUBLIC HEALTH/TOYAMA-KEN EISEI TOKEI
NENPO. (Text in Japanese) 1949. a. free. Welfare
Department - Toyama-ken Kosei-bu, 1-7
Shinsogawa, Toyama 930, Japan. circ. 400.

614.8   US   ISSN 0275-844X
TRACE ANALYSIS. 1981. irreg., vol.4, 1985. $65.
Academic Press, Inc., Orlando, FL 32887. TEL
305-345-2000. Ed. James F. Lawrence.

TRACE SUBSTANCES IN ENVIRONMENTAL
HEALTH. see *ENVIRONMENTAL STUDIES*

UEBERSETZUNGEN - KERNTECHNISCHE
REGELN. see *PHYSICS — Nuclear Energy*

312   US   ISSN 0090-1156
U.S. CENTER FOR DISEASE CONTROL.
BRUCELLOSIS SURVEILLANCE: ANNUAL
SUMMARY. a. U.S. Center for Disease Control,
1600 Clifton Rd., NE, Atlanta, GA 30333. TEL
404-329-3311. illus. Key Title: Brucellosis
Surveillance; Annual Summary.

615.9   US   ISSN 0098-6623
U.S. CENTER FOR DISEASE CONTROL.
FOODBORNE & WATERBORNE DISEASE
OUTBREAKS. ANNUAL SUMMARY. a. U.S.
Center for Disease Control, 1600 Clifton Rd., NE,
Atlanta, GA 30333. TEL 404-329-3311. Key Title:
Foodborne & Waterborne Disease Outbreaks.
Annual Summary.
  Continues: U.S. Center for Disease Control.
Foodborne Outbreaks; Annual Summary.

614   US
U.S. CENTER FOR DISEASE CONTROL.
SALMONELLA SURVEILLANCE. ANNUAL
SUMMARY. 1962. a. free. ‡ U.S. Center for
Disease Control, Bureau of Epidemiology. Bacterial
Disease Division, 1600 Clifton Rd., NE, Atlanta,
GA 30333. TEL 404-329-3311. charts. stat. circ. 3,
000.

U.S. CENTERS FOR DISEASE CONTROL.
ABORTION SURVEILLANCE. ANNUAL
SUMMARY. see *BIRTH CONTROL*

U.S. CENTERS FOR DISEASE CONTROL.
DIPHTHERIA SURVEILLANCE REPORT. see
MEDICAL SCIENCES — Communicable Diseases

U.S. CENTERS FOR DISEASE CONTROL.
LEPROSY SURVEILLANCE REPORT. see
MEDICAL SCIENCES — Communicable Diseases

U.S. CENTERS FOR DISEASE CONTROL.
LISTERIOSIS SURVEILLANCE REPORT. see
MEDICAL SCIENCES — Communicable Diseases

U.S. CENTERS FOR DISEASE CONTROL.
MALARIA SURVEILLANCE REPORT. see
MEDICAL SCIENCES — Communicable Diseases

PUBLIC HEALTH AND SAFETY

628 US
U.S. DEFENSE LOGISTICS AGENCY. D O D HAZARDOUS MATERIALS INFORMATION SYSTEM: HAZARDOUS ITEM LISTING. irreg., base. vol. plus updates. $75. U.S. Defense Logistics Agency, Cameron Station, Alexandria, VA 22314 TEL 703-545-6700. (Orders to: Supt. of Documents, Washington, DC 20402) (microfiche)

312 US
U.S. NATIONAL CENTER FOR HEALTH STATISTICS. ADVANCE DATA FROM VITAL AND HEALTH STATISTICS. no.47, 1979. irreg., no.95, 1984. U.S. National Center for Health Statistics, 3700 East-West Highway, Hyattsville, MD 20782. TEL 301-436-8500. Indexed: Nutr.Abstr.

312 US ISSN 0083-2014
U.S. NATIONAL CENTER FOR HEALTH STATISTICS. VITAL AND HEALTH STATISTICS. SERIES 1. PROGRAMS AND COLLECTION PROCEDURES. 1963. irreg. price varies. U.S. National Center for Health Statistics, Scientific and Technical Information Branch, 3700 East-West Highway, Hyattsville, MD 20782. TEL 301-436-8500. Indexed: Excerp.Med.

312 US ISSN 0083-2057
U.S. NATIONAL CENTER FOR HEALTH STATISTICS. VITAL AND HEALTH STATISTICS. SERIES 2. DATA EVALUATION AND METHODS RESEARCH. 1963. irreg. price varies. U.S. National Center for Health Statistics, Scientific and Technical Information Branch, 3700 East-West Highway, Hyattsville, MD 20782. TEL 301-436-8500. Indexed: Excerp.Med. Popul.Ind.

312 US ISSN 0083-2065
U.S. NATIONAL CENTER FOR HEALTH STATISTICS. VITAL AND HEALTH STATISTICS. SERIES 3. ANALYTICAL STUDIES. 1964. irreg. price varies. U.S. National Center for Health Statistics, Scientific and Technical Information Branch, 3700 East-West Highway, Hyattsville, MD 20782. TEL 301-436-8500. Indexed: Excerp.Med.

312 US ISSN 0083-2073
U.S. NATIONAL CENTER FOR HEALTH STATISTICS. VITAL AND HEALTH STATISTICS. SERIES 4. DOCUMENTS AND COMMITTEE REPORT. 1965. irreg. price varies. U.S. National Center for Health Statistics, Scientific and Technical Information Branch, 3700 East-West Highway, Hyattsville, MD 20782. TEL 301-436-8500. Indexed: Excerp.Med.

614 US ISSN 0083-1972
U.S. NATIONAL CENTER FOR HEALTH STATISTICS. VITAL AND HEALTH STATISTICS. SERIES 10. DATA FROM THE HEALTH INTERVIEW SURVEY. 1963. irreg. price varies. U. S. National Center for Health Statistics, Scientific and Technical Information Branch, 3700 East-West Highway, Hyattsville, MD 20782. TEL 301-436-8500. Indexed: Excerp.Med.

614 US
U.S. NATIONAL CENTER FOR HEALTH STATISTICS. VITAL AND HEALTH STATISTICS. SERIES 11. DATA FROM THE HEALTH AND NUTRITION EXAMINATION SURVEY. 1964. irreg. price varies. U. S. National Center for Health Statistics, Scientific and Technical Information Branch, 3700 East-West Highway, Hyattsville, MD 20782. TEL 301-436-8500. Indexed: Excerp.Med.
Formerly: U.S. National Center for Health Statistics. Vital and Health Statistics. Series 11. Data from the Health Examination Survey (ISSN 0083-1980)

362 US
U.S. NATIONAL CENTER FOR HEALTH STATISTICS. VITAL AND HEALTH STATISTICS. SERIES 13. DATA ON HEALTH RESOURCES UTILIZATION. 1966. irreg. price varies. U.S. National Center for Health Statistics, Scientific and Technical Information Branch, 3700 East-West Highway, Hyattsville, MD 20782. TEL 301-436-8500. Indexed: Excerp.Med.
Incorporating: U.S. National Center for Health Care Statistics. Vital and Health Statistics. Series 12. Data from the Institutional Population Surveys (ISSN 0083-1964); Formerly: U.S. National Center for Health Care Statistics. Vital and Health Statistics. Series 13. Data from the Hospital Discharge Survey (ISSN 0083-2006)

614 US ISSN 0083-1999
U.S. NATIONAL CENTER FOR HEALTH STATISTICS. VITAL AND HEALTH STATISTICS. SERIES 14. DATA ON HEALTH RESOURCES: MANPOWER AND FACILITIES. 1968. irreg. price varies. U.S. National Center for Health Statistics, Scientific and Technical Information Branch, 3700 East-West Highway, Hyattsville, MD 20782. TEL 301-436-8500. Indexed: Excerp.Med.

312 US ISSN 0083-2022
U.S. NATIONAL CENTER FOR HEALTH STATISTICS. VITAL AND HEALTH STATISTICS. SERIES 20. DATA ON MORTALITY. 1965. irreg. price varies. U.S. National Center for Health Statistics, Scientific and Technical Information Branch, 3700 East-West Highway, Hyattsville, MD 20782. TEL 301-436-8500. Indexed: Excerp.Med.
Incorporating in part: U.S. National Center for Health Statistics. Vital and Health Statistics. Series 22. Data on Natality and Mortality Surveys (ISSN 0083-2049)

312 US ISSN 0083-2030
U.S. NATIONAL CENTER FOR HEALTH STATISTICS. VITAL AND HEALTH STATISTICS. SERIES 21. DATA ON NATALITY, MARRIAGE, AND DIVORCE. 1964. irreg. price varies. U.S. National Center for Health Statistics, Scientific and Technical Information Branch, 3700 East-West Highway, Hyattsville, MD 20782. TEL 301-436-8500. Indexed: Excerp.Med. Popul.Ind.
Incorporating in part: U.S. National Center for Health Statistics. Vital and Health Statistics. Series 22. Data on Natality and Mortality Surveys (ISSN 0083-2049)

628 GT
UNIVERSIDAD DE SAN CARLOS. FACULTAD DE INGENERIA. ESCUELA REGIONAL DE INGENIERIA SANITARIA. CARTA PERIODICA. 1966. irreg. Universidad de San Carlos de Guatemala, Escuela Regional de Ingenieria Sanitaria, Ciudad Universitaria, Zona 12, Guatemala. Ed. Arturo Acajabon Mendoza. bibl. charts. illus.
Formerly: Brujula.

UNIVERSITY OF DELAWARE DISASTER RESEARCH CENTER. REPORT SERIES. see SOCIAL SERVICES AND WELFARE

614 UN
VACCINATION CERTIFICATE REQUIREMENTS AND HEALTH ADVICE FOR INTERNATIONAL TRAVEL/CERTIFICATS DE VACCINATION EXIGES ET CONSEILS D'HYGIENE POUR LES VOYAGES INTERNATIONAUX. (Editions in English, French, German) a. World Health Organization - Organisation Mondiale de la Sante, Distribution and Sales, 20 Avenue Appia, CH-1211 Geneva 27, Switzerland. TEL 91-21-11. circ. 15,000.
Former titles: Vaccination Certificate Requirements for International Travel and Health Advice to Travellers/Certificate de Vaccination Exiges dans les Voyages Internationaux et Conseils d'Hygiene a l'Intention des Voyageurs & Vaccination Certificate Requirements for International Travel (ISSN 0512-3011)

VERKEHRSPSYCHOLOGISCHER INFORMATIONSDIENST. see TRANSPORTATION — Roads And Traffic

614 US
VITAL AND HEALTH STATISTICS MONOGRAPHS. 1960? irreg. American Public Health Association, 1015 15th St., N.W., Washington, DC 20005 TEL 202-789-5600. (Dist. by: Harvard University Press, 79 Garden St., Cambridge, MA 02138) Indexed: Excerp.Med.

614.109 US ISSN 0083-6710
VITAL STATISTICS OF THE UNITED STATES. 1937. a. price varies. U.S. National Center for Health Statistics, 3700 East-West Highway, Hyattsville, MD 20782. TEL 301-436-8500.

W H O OFFSET PUBLICATIONS. (World Health Organization) see PUBLIC HEALTH AND SAFETY — Abstracting, Bibliographies, Statistics

W H O TECHNICAL REPORT SERIES. (World Health Organization) see MEDICAL SCIENCES

WISCONSIN. DEPARTMENT OF NATURAL RESOURCES. ANNUAL WATER QUALITY REPORT TO CONGRESS. see ENVIRONMENTAL STUDIES

614.85 SW
WORKING ENVIRONMENT; arbetsmiljoe international. (Text in English) 1977. a. free. Foereningen foer Arbetarskydd - Swedish Work Environment Association, Kungsholms Hamnplan 3, S-112 20 Stockholm, Sweden. Ed. Bertil Delin. adv. illus. circ. 20,000. Indexed: Biol.Dig. C.I.S. Abstr. Ergon.Abstr.

614 UN
WORLD HEALTH ORGANIZATION. HANDBOOK OF RESOLUTIONS AND DECISIONS OF THE WORLD HEALTH ASSEMBLY AND THE EXECUTIVE BOARD. (Editions in Arabic, Chinese, English, French, Russian, Spanish) 1948. biennial. World Health Organization - Organisation Mondiale de la Sante, Distribution and Sales, 20 Avenue Appia, CH-1211 Geneva 27, Switzerland. TEL 91-21-11. circ. 8,000.
Formerly: World Health Organization. World Health Assembly and the Executive Board. Handbook of Resolutions and Decisions. (ISSN 0301-0740)

614 UN ISSN 0512-3038
WORLD HEALTH ORGANIZATION. MONOGRAPH SERIES. 1951. irreg. World Health Organization - Organisation Mondiale de la Sante, Distribution and Sales, 20 Avenue Appia, CH-1211 Geneva 27, Switzerland. TEL 91-21-11. circ. 9,000. Indexed: Biol.Abstr. Excerp.Med. Ind.Med. Rev.Appl.Entomol.

614 UN
WORLD HEALTH ORGANIZATION. REGIONAL OFFICE FOR AFRICA. REPORT OF THE REGIONAL COMMITTEE. 1959. a. ‡ World Health Organization, Regional Office for Africa - Organisation Mondiale de la Sante. Bureau Regional de l'Afrique, B.P. No. 6, Brazzaville, Congo.
Formerly: World Health Organization. Regional Office for Africa. Report of the Regional Committee. Minutes of the Plenary Session (ISSN 0512-3070)

614 UN ISSN 0510-8837
WORLD HEALTH ORGANIZATION. REGIONAL OFFICE FOR AFRICA. REPORT OF THE REGIONAL DIRECTOR. 1951. a. World Health Organization, Regional Office for Africa - Organisation Mondiale de la Sante. Bureau Regional de l'Afrique, B.P. No. 6, Brazzaville, Congo.

614 UN
WORLD HEALTH ORGANIZATION. REGIONAL OFFICE FOR THE EASTERN MEDITERRANEAN. BIENNIAL REPORT OF THE REGIONAL DIRECTOR. 1950. biennial. free to qualified personnel. World Health Organization, Regional Office for the Eastern Mediterranean, P.O. Box 1517, Alexandria, Egypt. circ. 3,000.
Formerly (until 1979): World Health Organization. Regional Office for the Eastern Mediterranean. Annual Report of the Regional Director (ISSN 0512-3089)

PUBLIC HEALTH AND SAFETY — ABSTRACTING, BIBLIOGRAPHIES, STATISTICS

614   UN   ISSN 0512-4921
WORLD HEALTH ORGANIZATION. REGIONAL OFFICE FOR THE WESTERN PACIFIC. ANNUAL REPORT OF THE REGIONAL DIRECTOR TO THE REGIONAL COMMITTEE FOR THE WESTERN PACIFIC. a. World Health Organization, Regional Office for the Western Pacific, P.O. Box 2932, Manila, Philippines.

WORLD HEALTH ORGANIZATION. REGIONAL OFFICE FOR THE WESTERN PACIFIC. REPORT ON THE REGIONAL SEMINAR ON THE ROLE OF THE HOSPITAL IN THE PUBLIC HEALTH PROGRAMME. see *HOSPITALS*

614   UN   ISSN 0085-8285
WORLD HEALTH ORGANIZATION. WORK OF W H O; biennial report of the director-general to the World Health Assembly and to the United Nations. (Editions in Arabic, Chinese, English, French, Russian, Spanish) 1948. biennial. World Health Organization - Organisation Mondiale de la Sante, Distribution and Sales, 20 Avenue Appia, CH-1211 Geneva 27, Switzerland. TEL 91-21-11. circ. 8,000.

614.4   US
WORLDWIDE REPORT: EPIDEMIOLOGY. irreg. (approx. 30/yr.) $5 per no. U.S. Joint Publications Research Service, 1000 N. Glebe Rd., Arlington, VA 22201 TEL 703-487-4630. (Orders to: NTIS, Springfield, VA 22161)
Former titles: World Epidemiology Review; Epidemiology Reports from the World Press.

614.8   US
WYOMING. CHARACTERISTICS OF OCCUPATIONAL INJURIES AND ILLNESSES. 1978. a. Department of Labor and Statistics, Herschler Building, Cheyenne, WY 82002. TEL 307-777-7261.

WYOMING. DEPARTMENT OF HEALTH AND SOCIAL SERVICES. ANNUAL REPORT. see *SOCIAL SERVICES AND WELFARE*

628   JA   ISSN 0912-2826
YOKOHAMA CITY INSTITUTE OF HEALTH. ANNUAL REPORT. (Text in Japanese; summaries in English) 1962. a. Yokohama City Institute of Health, 2-17, 1-chome, Takigashira, Isogo-Ku, Yokohama-Shi 235, Japan. circ. 300.

614.44 610   GW   ISSN 0174-3015
ZENTRALBLATT FUER BAKTERIOLOGIE, PARASITENKUNDE, INFEKTIONSKRANKHEITEN UND HYGIENE. SERIES B: KRANKENHAUSHYGIENE-PRAEVENTIVE MEDIZIN-BETRIEBSHYGIENE. irreg., 6 nos. per vol. DM.320 separately; DM 284 with originale abt a. Gustav Fischer Verlag, Wollgrasweg 49, Postfach 720143, 7000 Stuttgart 70, W. Germany (B.R.D.) Ed. M. Knorr. circ. 1, 200. Indexed: Biol.Abstr. Excerp.Med. Ind.Med. Nutr.Abstr. Dent.Ind. Helminthol.Abstr.
Formerly: Zentralblatt fuer Bakteriologie, Parasitenkunde, Infektionskrankheiten und Hygiene. Orginale Reihe B: Hygiene - Praventive Medizin.

614   DK   ISSN 0107-6663
ZONETERAPI OG SUNDHED.* 1981. irreg., (2-4/yr.) Kr.30 free to libraries. Landsforeningen til Zoneterapiens Fremme, c/o Jorn Steen, Ed., Rulkehojen 40, 5260 Odense S., Denmark. illus.

PUBLIC HEALTH AND SAFETY —
Abstracting, Bibliographies, Statistics

312   BE   ISSN 0522-7690
ANNUAIRE STATISTIQUE DE LA SANTE PUBLIQUE/STATISTISCH JAARBOEK VAN VOLKSGEZONDHEID. (Text in Dutch) 1950. a. free. Ministere de la Sante Publique et de la Famille, Centre de Traitement de l'Information - Ministerie van Volksgezondheid en van het Gezin, Cite Administrative de l'Etat, Quartier Vesale, 1010 Brussels, Belgium. illus. stat.

APPLIED HEALTH PHYSICS ABSTRACTS AND NOTES. see *PHYSICS — Abstracting, Bibliographies, Statistics*

614 318   AG
ARGENTINA. SECRETARIA DE ESTADO DE SALUD PUBLICA. PROGRAMA NACIONAL DE ESTADISTICAS DE SALUD. vol. 6, 1976. irreg. Secretaria de Estado de Salud Publica, Alsina 301, Buenos Aires, Argentina.

614.86   BE   ISSN 0067-5504
BELGIUM. INSTITUT NATIONAL DE STATISTIQUE. STATISTIQUE DES ACCIDENTS DE LA CIRCULATION SUR LA VOIE PUBLIQUE. (Text in Dutch and French) 1954. a. 290 Fr. Institut National de Statistique, 44 rue de Louvain, 1000 Brussels, Belgium.
Formerly: Belgium. Institut National de Statistique. Statistique des Accidents de Roulage (ISSN 0067-5512)

310   BE
BELGIUM. MINISTERE DE LA SANTE PUBLIQUE ET DE LA FAMILLE. PREMIERS ET PRINCIPAUX RESULTATS STATISTIQUES DE L'ENQUETE DANS LES ETABLISSEMENTS DE SOINS/EERSTE EN VOORNAAMSTE STATISTISCHE UITKOMSTEN VAN DE ENQUETE IN DE VERZORGINGSINSTELLINGEN. (Text in Dutch and French) 1962. a. free. Ministere de la Sante Publique et de la Famille, Administration des Etablissements de Soins-Service d'Etudes - Ministerie van Volksgezondheid en van het Gezin, Bestuur voor de Verzorgingsinstellingen Studiedienst, Cite Administrative de l'Etat, Quartier Vesale, 1010 Brussels, Belgium. circ. 1,500.

361.6 016   CN
CANADA. DEPARTMENT OF NATIONAL HEALTH AND WELFARE. LIBRARY. ACQUISITIONS. (Text in English and French) 1947. irreg. Department of National Health and Welfare., Library, Ottawa, Ont., Canada. TEL 613-996-4650.

614   UK   ISSN 0263-2969
CHARTERED INSTITUTE OF PUBLIC FINANCE AND ACCOUNTANCY. CEMETERIES & CREMATORIA STATISTICS. ACTUALS. 1981. a. £14. Chartered Institute of Public Finance and Accountancy, 3 Robert St., London WC2N 6BH, England. (back issues avail.)
Former titles: Chartered Institute of Public Finance and Accountancy. Crematoria Statistics. Actuals (ISSN 0534-2104) & Chartered Institute of Public Finance and Accountancy. Cemeteries Statistics. Actuals (ISSN 0260-9959)

CHARTERED INSTITUTE OF PUBLIC FINANCE AND ACCOUNTANCY. WASTE DISPOSAL STATISTICS. ACTUALS. see *PUBLIC ADMINISTRATION — Abstracting, Bibliographies, Statistics*

CHARTERED INSTITUTE OF PUBLIC FINANCE AND ACCOUNTANCY. WASTE DISPOSAL STATISTICS. ESTIMATES. see *PUBLIC ADMINISTRATION — Abstracting, Bibliographies, Statistics*

614   CL
CHILE. INSTITUTO NACIONAL DE ESTADISTICAS. ESTADISTICAS DE SALUD; recursos y atenciones. 1965. a. $9. Instituto Nacional de Estadisticas, Av. Bulnes 418, Casilla 498, Correo 3-Santiago, Chile.

614   NE
COMPENDIUM GEZONDHEIDSSTATISTIEK NEDERLAND/COMPENDIUM HEALTH STATISTICS OF THE NETHERLANDS. (Text in Dutch and English) 1974. irreg. fl.55. Centraal Bureau voor de Statistiek, Prinses Beatrixlaan 428, Voorburg, Netherlands (Orders to: Staatsuitgeverij, Christoffel Plantijnstraat, The Hague, Netherlands) (Co-sponsor: Ministry of Public Health and Environmental Hygiene) circ. 2,000.

610   JA
EISEI TOKEI KARA MITA AICHI-KEN NO SUGATA. 1985. a. Aichi-Ken Eisei-Bu Somu-Ka, 1-2, 3-chome, Sannomaru, Naka-ku, Nagoya-shi, Japan. circ. 200.

614 016   NE   ISSN 0014-4215
EXCERPTA MEDICA. SECTION 17: PUBLIC HEALTH, SOCIAL MEDICINE & HYGIENE. 1955. 20/yr. fl.960. Elsevier Science Publishers B.V., Box 211, 1000 AE Amsterdam, Netherlands. adv. bk. rev. abstr. index. cum.index. Indexed: Chem.Abstr. Excerp.Med. Popul.Ind.
●Also available online. Vendors: BRS, DIALOG.

EXCERPTA MEDICA. SECTION 35: OCCUPATIONAL HEALTH AND INDUSTRIAL MEDICINE. see *MEDICAL SCIENCES — Abstracting, Bibliographies, Statistics*

EXCERPTA MEDICA. SECTION 46: ENVIRONMENTAL HEALTH AND POLLUTION CONTROL. see *ENVIRONMENTAL STUDIES — Abstracting, Bibliographies, Statistics*

614 312   GW   ISSN 0072-1840
GERMANY (FEDERAL REPUBLIC, 1949-). STATISTISCHES BUNDESAMT. FACHSERIE 12, GESUNDHEITSWESEN, REIHE 1: AUSGEWAEHLTE ZAHLEN FUER DAS GESUNDHEITSWESEN. 1959. a. DM.12. W. Kohlhammer-Verlag GmbH, Abt. Veroeffentlichungen des Statistischen Bundesamtes, Philipp-Reis-Str. 3, Postfach 421120, 6500 Mainz 42, W. Germany (B.R.D.)

GREECE. NATIONAL STATISTICAL SERVICE. SOCIAL WELFARE AND HEALTH STATISTICS. see *SOCIAL SERVICES AND WELFARE — Abstracting, Bibliographies, Statistics*

614   UN   ISSN 0085-1450
HEALTH PHYSICS RESEARCH ABSTRACTS. (Text in English) 1967. irreg. free. International Atomic Energy Agency, Wagramer Str. 5, Box 100, A-1400 Vienna, Austria. circ. 600.

HEALTH SERVICE ABSTRACTS. see *SOCIAL SERVICES AND WELFARE — Abstracting, Bibliographies, Statistics*

312 614 360   US   ISSN 0362-9279
IDAHO. DEPARTMENT OF HEALTH AND WELFARE. ANNUAL SUMMARY OF VITAL STATISTICS. Cover title: Vital Statistics, Idaho. 1946. a. $6.50. Department of Health and Welfare, Vital Statistics Unit, Statehouse, Boise, ID 83720. TEL 208-334-5976. Ed. Janet Wick. circ. 800. Key Title: Annual Summary of Vital Statistics (Boise)

614   IT   ISSN 0075-1758
ITALY. ISTITUTO CENTRALE DI STATISTICA. ANNUARIO DI STATISTICHE SANITARIE. 1962. a. L.18000. Istituto Centrale di Statistica, Via Cesare Balbo 16, 00100 Rome, Italy. circ. 1,150.

JAPAN. MINISTRY OF HEALTH AND WELFARE. STATISTICS AND INFORMATION DEPARTMENT. REPORT ON BASIC SURVEY OF HEALTH AND WELFARE ADMINISTRATION. see *SOCIAL SERVICES AND WELFARE — Abstracting, Bibliographies, Statistics*

628 360   JA
JAPAN. MINISTRY OF HEALTH AND WELFARE. STATISTICS AND INFORMATION DEPARTMENT. STATISTICAL HANDBOOK ON HEALTH AND SOCIAL WELFARE. a. 1.800 Yen. Ministry of Health and Welfare, Statistics and Information Department, 7-3 Ichigaya-Honmura cho, Shinjuku-ku, Tokyo 162, Japan (Order from: Health & Welfare Statistics Association, c/o Mezon Azabu, 5-13-14 Roppongi, Minato-ku, Tokyo, Japan)
Sanitary engineering

628 315   JA
JAPAN. MINISTRY OF HEALTH AND WELFARE. STATISTICS AND INFORMATION DEPARTMENT. STATISTICAL REPORT ON PUBLIC HEALTH SERVICES. a. 3.000 Yen. Ministry of Health and Welfare, Statistics and Information Department, 7-3 Ichigaya-Honmura cho, Shinjuku-ku, Tokyo 162, Japan (Order from: Health & Welfare Statistics and Association, c/o Mezon Azabu, 5-13-14 Roppongi, Minato-ku, Tokyo, Japan)
Sanitary engineering

614.1 US
KENTUCKY. CABINET FOR HUMAN RESOURCES. VITAL STATISTICS REPORT. 1911. a. free. Cabinet for Human Resources, Division of Hfealth Policy & Resource Development, 275 E. Main St., Frankfort, KY 40621. TEL 502-564-2336. circ. 3,000. Key Title: Kentucky Annual Vital Statistics Report.
Former titles: Kentucky. Department for Human Resources. Selected Vital Statistics and Planning Data (ISSN 0145-5990) & Kentucky Vital Statistics (ISSN 0098-6739); Kentucky Vital Statistics Report.

628 UK ISSN 0264-6714
KEY STATISTICAL INDICATORS FOR NATIONAL HEALTH SERVICE MANAGEMENT IN WALES. 1983. a. £2. Welsh Office, Economic and Statistical Services Division, New Crown Buildings, Cathays Park, Cardiff CF1 3NQ, Wales. Ed. S.M. Stansfield. stat. circ. 800. (back issues avail.)

614 310 CN
MANITOBA. HEALTH SERVICES COMMISSION. ANNUAL STATISTICS. 1971. a. free. Health Services Commission, Box 925, 599 Empress St., Winnipeg, Man. R3C 2T6, Canada. TEL 204-786-7101.
Formerly: Manitoba. Health Services Commission. Statistical Supplement to the Annual Report (ISSN 0383-3933)

614 016 US ISSN 0025-7087
MEDICAL CARE REVIEW. 1944. s-a. $32.50. ‡ (Foundation of the American College of Healthcare Executives) Health Administration Press, 1021 E. Huron St., Ann Arbor, MI 48104-9990 TEL 313-764-1380. (Subscr. to: Order Processing Center, 1951 Cornell, Melrose Park, IL 60160) Ed. Roice D. Luke. bibl. index. circ. 1,300. (also avail. in microform from UMI; reprint service avail. from UMI) Indexed: I.P.A. Hosp.Lit.Ind. Abstr.Health Care Manage.Stud. Med.Care.Res.
Formerly: Public Health Economics and Medical Care Abstracts.

614 310 US ISSN 0539-7413
MICHIGAN HEALTH STATISTICS. 1898. a. $11. Department of Public Health, Office of State Registrar and Center for Health Statistics, 3500 N. Logan St., Lansing, MI 48909. TEL 517-373-1390. Ed. Janet Eyster. illus. circ. 350. (also avail. in microfiche)
Continues: Michigan Public Health Statistics.

312 US ISSN 0094-5641
MINNESOTA HEALTH STATISTICS. 1950. a. free. Department of Health, Center for Health Statistics, 717 Delaware St., S.E., Minneapolis, MN 55440. TEL 612-296-5353. Ed. Paul D. Gunderson. circ. 900.

312 US ISSN 0098-1974
MISSOURI VITAL STATISTICS. a. free. Department of Health, Center for Health Statistics, Box 570, Jefferson City, MO 65102. TEL 314-751-8074. Ed. Garland Land. circ. 900. (also avail. in microfiche)

614 US ISSN 0077-1198
MONTANA VITAL STATISTICS. 1954. a. free. ‡ Department of Health and Environmental Sciences, Bureau of Records & Statistics, Helena, MT 59620. TEL 406-444-2614. Ed. John C. Wilson. circ. 850.
Former titles: Montana. State Department of Health. Annual Statistical Supplement (ISSN 0097-9120) & Montana State Board of Health. Annual Statistical Supplement (ISSN 0097-9112)

NORTH CAROLINA. DIVISION OF HEALTH SERVICES. STATE CENTER FOR HEALTH STATISTICS. NORTH CAROLINA VITAL STATISTICS. see *POPULATION STUDIES — Abstracting, Bibliographies, Statistics*

312.267 US ISSN 0085-428X
NORTH CAROLINA COMMUNICABLE DISEASE MORBIDITY STATISTICS. 1918. a. free. ‡ Department of Human Resources, Division of Health Services, P.O. Box 2091, Raleigh, NC 27602. stat.

373 NO ISSN 0332-7906
NORWAY. STATISTISK SENTRALBYRAA. HELSESTATISTIKK/HEALTH STATISTICS. (Subseries of its Norges Offisielle Statistikk) (Text in Norwegian; summaries in English) a. Kr.45. Statistisk Sentralbyraa, Box 8131-Dep., 0033 Oslo 1, Norway. circ. 2,000.

312 US ISSN 0098-5651
OKLAHOMA HEALTH STATISTICS. a. free. Department of Health, Public Health Statistics Division, Box 53551, Oklahoma City, OK 73105. TEL 405-271-5600. illus.
Formerly (1943-1971): Public Health Statistics, State of Oklahoma (ISSN 0099-118X)

312 614 US
OREGON PUBLIC HEALTH STATISTICS REPORT. Cover title: Oregon State Health Division, Vital Statistics Annual Report. Variant title: Oregon Vital Statistics. 1960. a. $3. ‡ State Health Division, c/o State Office, 1400 S.W. Fifth Ave., Portland, OR 97201. TEL 503-229-5897. stat. circ. 600.

614 314 PL ISSN 0079-2748
POLAND. GLOWNY URZAD STATYSTYCZNY. ROCZNIK STATYSTYCZNY OCHRONY ZDROWIA. YEARBOOK OF PUBLIC HEALTH STATISTICS. (Issued in its Seria Roczniki Branzowe. Branch Yearbooks) irreg., latest 1985. Glowny Urzad Statystyczny, Al. Niepodleglosci 208, 00-925 Warsaw, Poland.

614 US ISSN 0079-7588
PUBLIC HEALTH CONFERENCE ON RECORDS AND STATISTICS. PROCEEDINGS. 2nd, 1950. a. U.S. National Center for Health Statistics, 3700 East-West Highway, Hyattsville, MD 20782. TEL 301-436-8500.

614.84 016 UR ISSN 0202-9898
REFERATIVNYI ZHURNAL. POZHARNAYA OKHRANA. 1971. m. 63.80 Rub. 66 Rub. including index. Vsesoyuznyi Institut Nauchno-Tekhnicheskoi Informatsii (VINITI), Baltiiskaya ul., 14, Moscow A-219, Russian S.F.S.R., U.S.S.R. (Subscr. to: Mezhdunarodnaya Kniga, Dimitrova ul. 39, 113095 Moscow, Russian S.F.S.R., U.S.S.R.)

614.8 016 CN ISSN 0824-8672
SALUS; low cost rural health care and health manpower training: an annotated bibliography with special emphasis on developing countries. 1975. a. Can.$10. International Development Research Centre, Box 8500, Ottawa, Ont. K1G 3H9, Canada. TEL 613-236-6163. Ed. Rosanna M. Bechtel. circ. 2,500.

368.384 IT ISSN 0075-188X
STATISTICA DEGLI INCIDENTI STRADALI. a. L.7000. Istituto Centrale di Statistica, Via Cesare Balbo 16, 00100 Rome, Italy.

614 NZ ISSN 0550-824X
TRENDS IN HEALTH AND HEALTH SERVICES. biennial. price varies. National Health Statistics Centre, Private Bag 2, Upper Willis St., Wellington, New Zealand. circ. controlled.

317 016 US ISSN 0278-4912
U.S. NATIONAL CENTER FOR HEALTH STATISTICS. CATALOG OF PUBLICATIONS. biennial. free. U.S. Department of Health, Education and Welfare, U.S. National Center for Health Statistics, 3700 East-West Highway, Hyattsville, MD 20782. TEL 301-436-8500.
Formerly: U.S. National Center for Health Statistics. Current Listing and Topical Index to the Vital and Health Statistics Series (ISSN 0092-7287)

614 UN
W H O OFFSET PUBLICATIONS. (Text in English and French; some in Arabic, Chinese, Russian and Spanish) 1973. irreg. World Health Organization - Organisation Mondiale de la Sante, Distribution and Sales, 20 Ave Appia, CH-1211 Geneva 27, Switzerland. TEL 91-21-11. bibl. circ. 10, 000(combined) Indexed: Biol.Abstr. Ind.Med. Abstr.Hyg. Dent.Ind. Trop.Dis.Bull.

628 016 US ISSN 0083-761X
WASTE MANAGEMENT RESEARCH ABSTRACTS. (Text in English, French, Russian and Spanish) 1965. irreg. free. International Atomic Energy Agency, Wagramer Str. 5, Box 100, A-1400 Vienna, Austria. circ. 650.

614 UN ISSN 0250-3794
WORLD HEALTH STATISTICS ANNUAL. (Text in English, French) a. World Health Organization - Organisation Mondiale de la Sante, Distribution and Sales, 20 Ave. Appia, CH-1211 Geneva 27, Switzerland. TEL 91-21-11. circ. 4,800.
Formerly (until 1965): Annual Epidemiological and Vital Statistics.

614 UN ISSN 0379-8070
WORLD HEALTH STATISTICS QUARTERLY. (Text in English and French) 1947. q. $45. World Health Organization - Organisation Mondiale de la Sante, Distribution and Sales, 20 Ave. Appia, CH-1211 Geneva 27, Switzerland. TEL 91-21-11. stat. circ. 5,000. Indexed: Excerp.Med. Ind.Med. Abstr.Hyg. Child Devel.Abstr. Dent.Ind. Popul.Ind. Trop.Dis.Bull.
Former titles, until 1967: World Health Statistics Report (ISSN 0043-8510); 1947-1967: Epidemiological and Vital Statistics Report.

PUBLISHING AND BOOK TRADE

see also *Bibliographies; Journalism; Patents, Trademarks and Copyrights; Printing*

070.5 US ISSN 0065-0005
A B BOOKMAN'S YEARBOOK; specialist book trade annual. 1949. a. $10. Specialist Book World, Box AB, Clifton, NJ 07015. TEL 201-772-0020. Ed. Jacob L. Chernofsky. adv. bk. rev. index. cum.index: 10 year periods. circ. 10,000.

070.5 US ISSN 0065-0048
A B C OF BOOK TRADE. 1966. quinquennial. $10. A B Bookman Publications, Inc., Box AB, Clifton, NJ 07015. TEL 201-772-0020. Ed. Jacob L. Chernofsky.

070.5 AT
A B P A DIRECTORY OF MEMBERS. a. Aus.$9. Australian Book Publishers Association, 161 Clarence St., Sydney, N.S.W. 2000, Australia.

658.8 GW ISSN 0065-2032
ADRESSBUCH FUER DEN DEUTSCHSPRACHIGEN BUCHHANDEL. 1839. a. DM.131. Buchhaendler-Vereinigung GmbH, Grosser Hirschgraben 17-21, Postfach 100442, 6000 Frankfurt 1, W. Germany (B.R.D.) adv. circ. 4,000.

070.5 UK
AFRICAN BOOK WORLD AND PRESS: A DIRECTORY. 1977. triennial. price varies. Hans Zell Publishers (Subsidiary of: K.G. Saur Ltd.) Box 56, 52 St. Giles, Oxford OX1 3EL, England (Dist. in U.S. by: K.G. Saur Inc., 175 Fifth Ave., New York, NY 10010) Ed. Hans M. Zell. adv. circ. 1, 500.

070.5 US ISSN 0065-759X
AMERICAN BOOK TRADE DIRECTORY. 1915. a. $149.95. (Jaques Cattell Press) R.R. Bowker Company, Database Publishing Group, 245 W. 17th St., New York, NY 10011. TEL 800-521-8110. index.

090.75 US
AMERICAN INSTITUTE FOR CONSERVATION OF HISTORIC AND ARTISTIC WORKS. BOOK & PAPER GROUP ANNUAL. 1982. a. American Institute for Conservation of Historic and Artistic Works, Book and Paper Group, 3545 Williamsburg Ln., N.W., Washington, DC 20008.
Formerly: American Institute for Conservation of Historic and Artistic Works. Postprints.

AMERICAN SOCIETY OF BOOKPLATE COLLECTORS AND DESIGNERS. YEAR BOOK. see *HOBBIES*

655.5 UK ISSN 0066-3913
ANNUAL DIRECTORY OF BOOKSELLERS IN THE BRITISH ISLES SPECIALISING IN ANTIQUARIAN AND OUT-OF-PRINT BOOKS. 1970. a. Stoate & Bishop Ltd., St. James Sq., Cheltenham GL50 3PU, England.

070.5 GW ISSN 0066-4596
ANSCHRIFTEN DEUTSCHER VERLAGE UND AUSLAENDISCHER VERLAGE MIT DEUTSCHEN AUSLIEFERUNGEN. 1950. a. DM.57.40. Verlag der Schillerbuchhandlung Hans Banger, Guldenbachstr. 1, D-5000 Koeln 41, W. Germany (B.R.D.)

017.8 US ISSN 0197-0364
ANTIQUARIAN TRADE LIST ANNUAL. a. Pergamon Press, Inc., Maxwell House, Fairview Park, Elmsford, NY 10523. TEL 914-592-7700. (microfiche)

PUBLISHING AND BOOK TRADE

070.5　　　　II　　ISSN 0066-8362
ASIAN BOOK TRADE DIRECTORY.* (Prepared with the assistance of UNESCO) (Text in English) 1964. irreg., 2nd edt., 1967. Rs.25($4) Nirmala Sadanand Publishers, 35 C Tardeo Rd., Bombay 400034, India. Ed. Sadanand Bhatkal.
　　Formerly: Directory of Asian Book Trade.

070　　　　　　US
ASSEMBLING ANNUAL. 1970. a. $10. (Participation Projects Foundation) Assembling Press, Rutgers University, Mason Gross School of the Arts, Visual Arts Department, 358 George St., New Brunswick, NJ 08903. Ed. Charles Doria. illus. circ. 1,000. (also avail. in microfilm from UMI; back issues avail.)
　　Formerly: Assembling (ISSN 0161-8318)

070.5　　　　　US　　ISSN 0276-5349
ASSOCIATION OF AMERICAN PUBLISHERS. ANNUAL REPORT. a. Association of American Publishers, 220 E. 23rd St., New York, NY 10010. TEL 212-689-8920. Key Title: Annual Report-Association of American Publishers.

071　　　　　　US　　ISSN 0147-0310
ASSOCIATION OF AMERICAN PUBLISHERS. EXHIBITS DIRECTORY. 1967. a. $65 to non-members; members $37.50. Association of American Publishers, 220 E. 23rd St., New York, NY 10010. TEL 212-689-8920. Ed. Ray George. circ. 700.
　　Continues: Directory of Exhibit Opportunities.

070.5　　　　　US　　ISSN 0739-3024
ASSOCIATION OF AMERICAN UNIVERSITY PRESSES DIRECTORY. 1960/61. a. $11. (Association of American University Presses, Inc.) American University Press Services, Inc., One Park Ave., Rm. 1102, New York, NY 10016. TEL 212-889-6040. index. circ. (controlled)

658.8　　　　　AT
AUSTRALIAN BOOKSELLERS. 1977. a. Aus.$30. D.W. Thorpe Pty Ltd., 20-24 Stokes St., Port Melbourne 3207, Australia. Ed. Penny Somma. circ. 4,000.

020 940 090　　　GE　　ISSN 0067-5091
BEITRAEGE ZUR INKUNABELKUNDE. DRITTE FOLGE. 1965. irreg., vol. 8, 1983. price varies. (Deutsche Staatsbibliothek) Akademie-Verlag, Leipziger Strasse 3-4, 108 Berlin, E. Germany (D.D.R.)

741.6　　　　　US
BEST IN COVERS AND POSTERS. 1975. a. $19.50. R C Publications, Inc., 104 Fifth Ave., 9th Fl., New York, NY 10011 TEL 301-229-9040. (Subscr. to: 6400 Goldsboro Rd., Bethesda, MD 20817) illus.
　　Formed by the 1977 merger of: Best in Covers (ISSN 0361-2066) & Best in Posters (ISSN 0360-8085)

070.5 809　　　BE
BIBLIOLOGIA. 1983. irreg. N.V. Brepols I.G.P., Rue Baron Frans du Four 8, B-2300 Turnhout, Belgium.

090 070.5 686　　HU　　ISSN 0067-8007
BIBLIOTHECA HUNGARICA ANTIQUA. 1960. irreg., vol.12, 1983. price varies. (Magyar Tudomanyos Akademia) Akademiai Kiado, Publishing House of the Hungarian Academy of Sciences, P.O. Box 24, H-1363 Budapest, Hungary.

011 020　　　UK　　ISSN 0006-193X
BIBLIOTHECK; a Scottish journal of bibliography and allied topics. 1956. 3/yr. (plus annual supplement) £7.50($15.50) to individuals; £9.50($20) to institutions. Library Association, Scottish Group, Edinburgh University Library, George Square, Edinburgh EH8 9LJ, Scotland. Ed. H. Wright. adv. bk. rev. bibl. cum.index: 1956-1970. circ. 300. Indexed: Abstr.Engl.Stud. LISA. M.L.A.

070.5　　　　　DK　　ISSN 0107-5187
BOG OG BAAND. 1980. a. Kr.235.30. Bibliotekscentralen, Tempovej 7-11, DK-2750 Ballerup, Denmark.

658.8　　　　　DK　　ISSN 0006-5749
BOGVENNEN. 1893. a. Kr.100. (Forening for Boghaandverk) Christian Ejlers Forlag A-S, Brolaeggerstraede 4, 1018 Copenhagen K, Denmark. TEL 01-12 21 14. Ed.Bd. bk. rev. illus. index. cum.index every 3 years. circ. 3,500.

070.5　　　　　UK　　ISSN 0068-0095
BOOK AUCTION RECORDS. 1902. a. £54. Wm. Dawson & Sons Ltd., Cannon House, Folkestone, Kent CT19 5EE, England. Ed. Wendy Y. Heath. adv. cum.index every 5 years.
　　A priced and annotated annual record of books auctioned world wide

020.75　　　　　US
BOOK COLLECTORS' HANDBOOK OF VALUES. irreg. price varies. G. P. Putnam's Sons, 200 Madison Ave., New York, NY 10016. TEL 212-576-8900.

070.5 001.3　　　US　　ISSN 0094-9426
BOOK FORUM. 1974. irreg. (approx. Q) $12 to individuals; institutions $20. Hudson River Press, 38 E. 76th St., New York, NY 10021 TEL 212-861-8328. (Subscr. to: Box 126, Rhinecliff, NY 12574) Ed. Marshall Hayes. adv. bk. rev. bibl. index. circ. 5,200. (back issues avail.) Indexed: Curr.Cont. M.L.A. Amer.Hum.Ind. Arts & Hum.Cit.Ind. Bk.Rev.Ind. Amer.Bibl.Slavic & E.Eur.Stud. Abstr.Engl.Stud.

658.8　　　　　US　　ISSN 0160-970X
BOOK INDUSTRY TRENDS. Represents: Book Industry Study Group. Research Report. 1977. a. $150. Book Industry Study Group, Inc., 160 Fifth Ave., New York, NY 10010. TEL 212-929-1393. Ed. John P. Dessauer.

658.8　　　　　UK
BOOK MARKETS IN THE AMERICAS, AFRICA, ASIA AND AUSTRALASIA. 1984. irreg. £95. Euromonitor Publications Ltd., 87-88 Turnmill St., London EC1M 5QU, England.

070.5 658.8　　　UK
BOOK MARKETS IN WESTERN AND EASTERN EUROPE. 1978. irreg. £95($165) Euromonitor Publications Ltd., 87-88 Turnmill St., London EC1M 5QU, England. charts. stat.

070.5 658.8　　　UK
BOOK PUBLISHERS. 1984. irreg. £125($150) Jordan & Sons Ltd., Jordan House, 47 Brunswick Place, London N1 6EE, England.

070.5　　　　　UK　　ISSN 0142-7628
BOOK REPORT. 1975. a. £135($275) Euromonitor Publications Ltd., 87-88 Turnmill St., London EC1M 5QU, England. (back issues avail.)

028.1　　　　　US　　ISSN 0145-627X
BOOK TALK. 1971. irreg. (5/yr.) $7.50. New Mexico Book League, 8632 Horacio Pl., N.E., Albuquerque, NM 87111. TEL 505-299-8940. Ed. Carol A. Myers. adv. bk. rev. circ. 500. (back issues avail.)

070.025　　　　CN　　ISSN 0700-5296
BOOK TRADE IN CANADA/INDUSTRIE DU LIVRE AU CANADA. (Text in English and French) 1975. a. $27.50. Ampersand Communications Services Inc., R.R.1, Caledon, Ont. L0N 1C0, Canada. TEL 519-927-3321. Ed. Eunice A. Thorne. circ. 2,000.
　　Formerly (until 1976): Book Publishers in Canada.

070.5　　　　　UK　　ISSN 0143-0270
BOOKDEALERS IN INDIA, PAKISTAN AND SRI LANKA. 1977. triennial. $7.50. Europa Publications Ltd., 18 Bedford Sq., London WC1B 3JN, England.

070.5　　　　　US　　ISSN 0068-0133
BOOKMAN'S GUIDE TO AMERICANA. 1960. irreg., 9th ed., 1986. price varies. Scarecrow Press, Inc., 52 Liberty St., Box 4167, Metuchen, NJ 08840. TEL 201-548-8600. circ. 3,000.

070.5　　　　　US　　ISSN 0068-0141
BOOKMAN'S PRICE INDEX; guide to the values of rare and other out-of-print books. 1964. irreg., vol.33, 1986. $170 per vol. Gale Research Company, Book Tower, Detroit, MI 48226. TEL 313-961-2242. Ed. Daniel F. McGrath.

BOOKMARK; diary and directory for readers and writers, libraries and librarians, publishers and booksellers. see LIBRARY AND INFORMATION SCIENCES

BOOKS AND LIBRARIES AT THE UNIVERSITY OF KANSAS. see LIBRARY AND INFORMATION SCIENCES

070.5　　　　　CN
BOOKS FOR EVERYBODY. a. Key Publishers Co. Ltd., 56 The Esplanade, Ste. 213, Toronto, Ont. M5E 1A7, Canada. TEL 416-364-3333. Ed. Pat Skinner. adv. circ. 210,000.

070.5 658.8　　　UK　　ISSN 0141-917X
BOOKSELLERS ASSOCIATION OF GREAT BRITAIN AND IRELAND. CHARTER GROUP. ECONOMIC SURVEY. a. Booksellers Association Service House Limited, 154 Buckingham Palace Rd., London SW1W 9TZ, England.

070.5　　　　　UK
BOOKSELLERS ASSOCIATION OF GREAT BRITAIN AND IRELAND. DIRECTORY OF MEMBERS. a. Booksellers Association Service House Limited, 154 Buckingham Palace Rd., London SW1W 9TZ, England. index.
　　Formerly: Booksellers Association of Great Britain and Ireland. List of Members (ISSN 0068-0249)

655　　　　　UK　　ISSN 0068-0257
BOOKSELLERS ASSOCIATION OF GREAT BRITAIN AND IRELAND. TRADE REFERENCE BOOK. 1969. irreg., Apr. 1984. Booksellers Association Service House Limited, 154 Buckingham Palace Rd., London SW1W 9TZ, England.

BOWKER ANNUAL; of library and book trade information. see LIBRARY AND INFORMATION SCIENCES

070.5　　　　　UK　　ISSN 0302-2846
BRITISH BOOK DESIGN & PRODUCTION. 1946. a. Trust Book, Book House, 45 East Hill, Wandsworth, London SW18 2QZ, England. illus.
　　Continues: British Book Production.

070.5　　　　　GW　　ISSN 0068-3051
BUCH UND BUCHHANDEL IN ZAHLEN. 1952. a. price varies. Boersenverein des Deutschen Buchhandels, Gr. Hirschgraben 17-21, 6000 Frankfurt, W. Germany (B.R.D.) Ed. Dr. Horst Machill.

070.5　　　　　GW　　ISSN 0170-5105
BUCHHANDELSGESCHICHTE. ZWEITE FOLGE; Aufsaetze, Rezensionen und Berichte zur Geschichte des Buchwesens. 1979. irreg., (approx. 4/yr) DM.35.40. (Historische Kommission des Boersenvereins des Deutschen Buchhandels e.V.) Buchhaendler-Vereinigung GmbH, Gr. Hirschgraben 17-21, D-6000 Frankfurt 1, W. Germany (B.R.D.) bk. rev.

686　　　　　GW　　ISSN 0724-7001
BUCHWISSENSCHAFTLICHE BEITRAEGE AUS DEM DEUTSCHEN BUCHARCHIV MUENCHEN. 1950. irreg., no.17, 1986. price varies. (Deutsches Bucharchiv, Muenchen) Verlag Otto Harrassowitz, Taunusstr. 14, Postfach 2929, 6200 Wiesbaden 1, W. Germany (B.R.D.) Ed. Ludwig Delp.
　　Formerly: Buchwissenschaftliche Beitraege (ISSN 0407-5439)

091　　　　　ET
BULLETIN OF ETHIOPIAN MANUSCRIPTS. (Text in English or Ethiopian) a. Ethiopian Manuscript Microfilm Library, Box 30274, Addis Ababa, Ethiopia.

BUREAU INTERNATIONAL DES SOCIETES GERANT LES DROITS D'ENREGISTREMENT ET DE REPRODUCTION MECANIQUE. BULLETIN. see PRINTING

658.8　　　　　US　　ISSN 0732-6599
BUY BOOKS WHERE, SELL BOOKS WHERE; a directory of out of print book dealers and their author-subject specialties. 1978. a. $25. Ruth E. Robinson Books, Rt. 7, Box 162A, Morgantown, WV 26505. TEL 304-594-3140. Eds. Ruth E. Robinson, Daryush Farudi. adv. circ. 3,000.
　　Booksellers

028.5　　　　　US
C B C FEATURES; containing news of the children's book world. 1945. irreg. (every 8 mos.) $25. Children's Book Council, Inc., 67 Irving Pl., New York, NY 10003. TEL 212-254-2666. Ed. Jeanette Brod. bibl. circ. 40,000. Indexed: Child.Lit.Abstr.
　　Formerly: Calendar (ISSN 0008-0721)

070.5 686   UK
CAMBRIDGE AUTHORS' AND PUBLISHERS'
GUIDES. 1951. irreg. price varies. Cambridge
University Press, Edinburgh Bldg., Shaftesbury Rd.,
Cambridge CB2 2RU, England (And: 32 E. 57th
St., New York, NY 10022)
   Formerly: Cambridge Authors' and Printers'
Guides (ISSN 0068-6603)

070.5   UK
CARFAX NEWS. 1981. irreg. Carfax Publishing Co.,
Box 25, Abingdon, Oxfordshire OX14 3UE,
England.

070.5   UK
CASSELL AND PUBLISHERS ASSOCIATION
DIRECTORY OF PUBLISHING IN GREAT
BRITAIN, THE COMMONWEALTH, IRELAND,
SOUTH AFRICA AND PAKISTAN. 1960. a.
£17.95. Cassell Ltd., 1 St. Anne's Rd., Eastbourne,
E. Sussex BN21 3UN, England. Ed. Jane Deam.
adv. index. circ. 5,000.
   Former titles: Cassell's Directory of Publishing in
Great Britain, The Commonwealth, Ireland, South
Africa and Pakistan (ISSN 0308-7018); Cassell's
Directory of Publishing in Great Britain, The
Commonwealth, Ireland and South Africa (ISSN
0069-097X)

CATHOLIC TRUTH. see RELIGIONS AND
THEOLOGY — Roman Catholic

070.5   BE
CERCLE BELGE DE LA LIBRAIRIE. ANNUAIRE.
1926. a. 1060 Fr. Cercle Belge de la Librairie (CBL)
, 35 rue de la Chasse Royale, 1160 Brussels,
Belgium.

070.5   FR
CEUX QUI FONT L'EDITION. 1977. biennial. 490
F. Publications Professionnelles Francaises, 15
Square de Vergennes, 75015 Paris, France.
(Affiliate: France Expansion)

070.5   US   ISSN 0069-3472
CHILDREN'S BOOKS: AWARDS AND PRIZES.
1969. irreg. $50. ‡ Children's Book Council, Inc., 67
Irving Pl., New York, NY 10003. TEL 212-254-
2666. index. circ. 6,000.

028.5   UK   ISSN 0266-4232
CHILDREN'S BOOKS OF THE YEAR. 1971. a.
Trust Book, Book House, 45 East Hill, Wandsworth,
London SW18 2QZ, England.

CHILDREN'S BOOKS OF THE YEAR (YEAR) see
CHILDREN AND YOUTH — For

070.5   US
CHILDREN'S BOOKS: ONE HUNDRED TITLES
FOR READING AND SHARING. 1980. a. $2.
New York Public Library, Office of Branch
Libraries, 455 Fifth Ave., New York, NY 10016.
TEL 212-340-0892.
   Former titles: Children's Books and Recordings:
Suggested as Holiday Gifts; Children's Books:
Suggested as Holiday Gifts (ISSN 0069-3502)

CHRISTIAN LIBRARIAN. see LIBRARY AND
INFORMATION SCIENCES

COMPUTER BOOKBASE; reference guide to
microcomputer books. see COMPUTERS —
Microcomputers

070.5 792   SA   ISSN 0250-2003
CONTACTS. (Text in English) 1978. a. free.
Limelight Publishing Co. Pty. Ltd., P.O. Box 2768,
Randburg 2125, South Africa. TEL 011-793-7231.
Ed. Melanie Engelbrecht. adv. index. circ. 5,000.
(back issues avail.)

CONTEMPORARY JAPANESE BOOKS. see
BIBLIOGRAPHIES

CUMULATIVE BOOK INDEX; a world list of books
in the English Language. see BIBLIOGRAPHIES

070.5   GE   ISSN 0459-004X
DEUTSCHE BUECHEREI. JAHRBUCH. 1965. a.
Deutsche Buecherei, Deutscher Platz, 7010 Leipzig,
E. Germany (D.D.R.) bibl. illus. index.

DEUTSCHES BUECHERVERZEICHNIS. see
LIBRARY AND INFORMATION SCIENCES

070.5   GW
DEUTSCHES VERLAGSREGISTER; Verlage mit
ihrem periodischen Schrifttum. 1970. irreg. DM.41.
Stamm Verlag GmbH, Goldammerweg 16, 4300
Essen 1, W. Germany (B.R.D.) Ed. Willy Stamm.
adv. bibl. circ. 2,000.

070.5   UK
DIRECTORY OF BOOK PUBLISHERS AND
WHOLESALERS. a. Booksellers Association
Service House Limited, 154 Buckingham Palace
Rd., London SW1W 9TZ, England.
   Formerly: Directory of Book Publishers,
Wholesalers and Their Terms.

020.75   US
DIRECTORY OF EDITORIAL RESOURCES. 1981.
biennial. $11.50. Editorial Experts, Inc., 85 S. Bragg
St., Ste. 400, Alexandria, VA 22312. TEL 703-642-
3040. Eds. Betsy Colgan, Eleanor Johnson.

DIRECTORY OF FLORIDA WRITERS. see
ADVERTISING AND PUBLIC RELATIONS

DIRECTORY OF POETRY PUBLISHERS. see
LITERATURE — Poetry

658.8   UK
DIRECTORY OF SPECIALIST BOOKDEALERS IN
THE UK HANDLING MAINLY NEW BOOKS.
1978. triennial. £12. Peter Marcan Publications, 31
Rowliff Rd., High Wycombe, Bucks, England. adv.
circ. 1,000.
   Formerly: Directory of Specialist Bookdealers.

051   US
DONNELLEY-DIRECTORY RECORD. 1970. irreg.
free. Donnelley Directory (New York), 287
Bowman Ave., Purchase, NY 10577. TEL 914-933-
6718. Ed. T. Taraba. circ. 3,000.
   House organ

ELECTRONIC PRINTING SYSTEMS:
DIRECTIONS IN DIGITAL IMAGING.
CONFERENCE PROCEEDINGS. see PRINTING

ENTERTAINMENT, PUBLISHING AND THE
ARTS HANDBOOK. see
COMMUNICATIONS — Radio And Television

070.5   UK   ISSN 0071-2523
EUROPEAN BOOKDEALERS; a directory of dealers
in secondhand and antiquarian books on the
continent of Europe. (Text in English, French and
German) 1966. biennial. $40. Europa Publications
Ltd., 18 Bedford Sq., London WC1B 3JN, England.

FACHLITERATUR ZUM BUCH- UND
BIBLIOTHEKSWESEN/INTERNATIONAL
BIBLIOGRAPHY OF THE BOOK TRADE AND
LIBRARIANSHIP. see LIBRARY AND
INFORMATION SCIENCES

070.5   AG
FEDERACION ARGENTINA DE PERIODISTAS.
GACETA.* 1970. a. Federacion Argentina de
Periodistas, Lavalle 1464, Buenos Aires, Argentina.
illus.

070.5   DK   ISSN 0109-405X
FORLAGSVEJVISER. 1984. a. Kr.238.80.
Bibliotekscentralen, Tempovej 7-11, 2750 Ballerup,
Denmark.

655   FR   ISSN 0078-9666
FRANCE. IMPRIMERIE NATIONALE.
ANNUAIRE. 1962. a. Imprimerie Nationale,
S.E.V.P.O., 39 rue de la Convention, 75732 Paris
Cedex 15, France.

070.5 380   CN   ISSN 0226-9031
FREELANCE EDITORS' ASSOCIATION OF
CANADA. DIRECTORY OF MEMBERS. (Text
in English and French) 1980. a. Can.$10. Freelance
Editors' Association of Canada - Association
Canadienne des Pigistes de l'Edition, 34 Ross St.,
Ste. 200, Toronto, Ont. M5T 1Z9, Canada. TEL
416-593-4692. Ed. Catherine Cragg. circ. 1,200.

070.5 371.42 659.1
658   US
FREELANCERS OF NORTH AMERICA. 1984. a.
$37.95. Research Associates International, Author
Aid, 340 E. 52nd St., New York, NY 10022 TEL
212-758-4213. Ed. Leonie Rosenstiel. adv.

FRIENDS OF THE NATIONAL LIBRARIES.
ANNUAL REPORT. see LIBRARY AND
INFORMATION SCIENCES

655   SY   ISSN 0072-0690
GENERAL DIRECTORY OF THE PRESS AND
PERIODICALS IN JORDAN AND KUWAIT.* a.
$15. Syrian Documentation Papers, P.O. Box 2712,
Damascus, Syria.

655   SY   ISSN 0072-0704
GENERAL DIRECTORY OF THE PRESS AND
PERIODICALS IN SYRIA.* a. $15. Syrian
Documentation Papers, P.O. Box 2712, Damascus,
Syria.

070.5   GE   ISSN 0067-5040
GESCHICHTE DES BUCHWESENS. BEITRAEGE.
1965. irreg. M.20. (Boersenverein der Deutschen
Buchhaendler, Historische Kommission) VEB
Fachbuchverlag, Postfach 67, DDR-7031 Leipzig, E.
Germany (D.D.R.)

028.1 028.5   UK
THE GOOD BOOK GUIDE TO CHILDREN'S
BOOKS. a. $8.50. Braithwaite & Taylor Ltd., 91
Great Russell St., London WC1B 3PS, England. Ed.
Peter Braithwaite. bk. rev.

070.5   CN
GRANT FUNDING AND SMALL BUSINESS AID
PROGRAMS FEDERAL AND PROVINCIAL; a
guide for the Canadian magazine industry. irreg.
Can.$4.50 to non-members; members Can.$3.75.
Canadian Periodical Publishers' Association, 2
Stewart St., Toronto, Ont. M5V 1H6, Canada. TEL
416-362-2546.

070.5   BL
GUIA DAS EDITORAS BRASILEIRAS. 1978. irreg.
Sindicato Nacional dos Editores de Livros, Av. Rio
Branco 37, s/1503/06, 20097 Rio de Janeiro R.J.,
Brazil.

658.8   BL
GUIA DAS LIVRARIAS E PONTOS DE VENDA
DE LIVROS NO BRASIL. 1976. irreg. Sindicato
Nacional dos Editores de Livros, Av. Rio Branco
37, s/1503/06, 20097 Rio de Janeiro R.J., Brazil.

070.5   SP   ISSN 0072-7903
GUIA DE EDITORES Y DE LIBREROS DE
ESPANA. 1950. irreg. price varies. Instituto
Nacional del Libro Espanol, Santiago Rusinol 8,
Madrid 3, Spain.

070.5   FR
GUIDE A L'USAGE DES AMATEURS DE
LIVRES. 1930. a. price varies. Syndicut du Livre
Ancien et des Metiers Annexes, 14 av. de
Friedland, 75008 Paris, France.
   Former titles: Guide du Livre Ancien et du Livre
d'Occasion & Syndicat National de la Librairie
Ancienne et Moderne. Repertoire (ISSN 0080-1100)

GUIDE TO MICROFORMS IN PRINT. AUTHOR,
TITLE. see BIBLIOGRAPHIES

070.5   JA
GUIDE TO PUBLISHERS AND RELATED
INDUSTRIES IN JAPAN. (Text in English) 1970.
biennial. free. Publishers Association for Cultural
Exchange, 1-2-1 Sarugaku-cho, Chiyoda-ku, Tokyo
101, Japan. Ed. Hiroyasu Ochiai.

090.75   BE
GULDEN PASSER/COMPAS D'OR. (Text in Dutch,
English, French, and German) 1923. a. 500 Fr.($13)
Vereeniging der Antwerpsche Bibliophielen -
Antwerp Bibliophile Society, Museum Plantin-
Moretus, Vrijdammarkt 22, B-2000 Antwerp,
Belgium. Eds. Francine de Nave, Marius de
Schepper. bk. rev. circ. 1,000.

HAIKU REVIEW. see LITERATURE — Poetry

070.5   US
HANDBOOK FOR LIBRARIES & OTHER
ORGANIZATIONAL USERS WHICH COPY
FROM SERIALS & SEPARATES; procedures for
using the programs of the Copyright Clearance
Center, Inc. 1978. irreg. free. Copyright Clearance
Center, Inc., 27 Congress St., Salem, MA 01970.
TEL 617-744-3350.

PUBLISHING AND BOOK TRADE

655　　　　　　GW　ISSN 0073-0165
HANDBUCH FUER DEN WERBENDEN BUCH- UND ZEITSCHRIFTENHANDEL. 1939. a. DM.20. Bundesverband des Werbenden Buch- und Zeitschriftenhandels e.V., Akazienstr. 10, 5000 Cologne 71, W. Germany (B.R.D.)

HANDSATZLETTER; Monografien der modernen Typographie. see *PRINTING*

029　070.5　　　　GW　ISSN 0342-4634
I S B N REVIEW. (International Standard Book Number) (Text in English, French and German) 1977. a. price varies. (International I S B N Agency) Staatsbibliothek Preussischer Kulturbesitz, Potsdamer Str. 33, Postfach 1407, 1000 Berlin 30, W. Germany (B.R.D) Ed. H. Walravens. adv. circ. 250. Indexed: Nutr.Abstr.

070　　　　　　　US
INDEX TO WHO'S WHO BOOKS. a. $60. Marquis Who's Who, 3002 Glenview Rd., Wilmette, IL 60091. TEL 312-441-2387.
Formerly: Index to All Books.

028.1　970.1　　　CN　ISSN 0709-9010
INDIAN BOOK REVIEW DIGEST. 1977. a. LITIR Database, c/o Department of English, University of Alberta, Edmonton, Alta. T6G 2E5, Canada. TEL 403-432-3258. Ed. Brahma Chandhuri.

020　027.7　　　　US　ISSN 0019-6800
INDIANA UNIVERSITY BOOKMAN. 1956. irreg. $10. Indiana University, Lilly Library, Bloomington, IN 47405. TEL 812-335-2452. Ed. William R. Cagle. circ. 500 (controlled) (also avail. in microform from UMI) Indexed: M.L.A.
Supersedes: Indiana Quarterly for Bookmen.

INFORMATION SOURCES. see *COMPUTERS*

070.5　　　　　　US
INTERNAL PUBLICATIONS DIRECTORY. (Vol.5 of Working Press of the Nation) 1946. a. $115. National Research Bureau, Inc., 310 S. Michigan Ave., Chicago, IL 60604. TEL 312-663-5580. Ed. Nancy Veatch. bk. rev. index.
Formerly: Gebbie House Magazine Directory (ISSN 0072-0526)

655.5　070.5　　　DK　ISSN 0538-7159
INTERNATIONAL DIRECTORY OF ANTIQUARIAN BOOKSELLERS/REPERTOIRE INTERNATIONAL DE LA LIBRAIRIE ANCIENNE. (Text in English and French) 1951-52. irreg., latest 1986. $35. International League of Antiquarian Booksellers, Box 2184, DK 1017 Copenhagen K, Denmark. Eds. Hans Bagger, Heinz Pummer. adv. circ. 1,800.

070.5　　　　　　US
INTERNATIONAL I S B N PUBLISHERS' DIRECTORY. a. $149.95. (International ISBN Agency, Berlin) R.R. Bowker Company, 245 W. 17th St., New York, NY 10011. TEL 212-916-1600.

070.5　　　　　　US　ISSN 0074-6827
INTERNATIONAL LITERARY MARKET PLACE. Variant title (1975-76, 1977-78): European Literary Market Place. 1966. a. $110. R.R. Bowker Company, Database Publishing Group, 245 W. 17th St.., New York, NY 10011. TEL 800-521-8110. index.

070.5　　　　　　SZ　ISSN 0074-7556
INTERNATIONAL PUBLISHERS ASSOCIATION. PROCEEDINGS OF CONGRESS. 1896. quadrennial, 22nd, 1984, Mexico City. 60 Fr. International Publishers Association - Union Internationale des Editeurs (Internationale Verleger-Union), Ave. Miremont 3, 1206 Geneva, Switzerland. circ. 1,100.

070.5　　　　　　IS　ISSN 0333-6018
ISRAEL BOOK TRADE DIRECTORY; a guide to publishers, printers and ancillary book trade services in Israel. (Text in English) 1967. biennial. Israel Export Institute, Book and Printing Center, Industry House, 29 Hamered St., P.O. Box 50084, Tel Aviv, Israel. circ. 3,000.
Former titles: Israel Book Trades Directory: a Select List; Publishers and Printers of Israel; a Select List (ISSN 0079-7820)

070.5　　　　　　IT　ISSN 0075-1677
ITALY. ISTITUTO CENTRALE DI STATISTICA. ANNUARIO DELLE STATISTICHE CULTURALI. a. L.5000. Istituto Centrale di Statistica, Via Cesare Balbo 16, 00100 Rome, Italy. circ. 1,200.

JAHRBUCH DER AUKTIONSPREISE FUER BUECHER, HANDSCHRIFTEN UND AUTOGRAPHEN; Ergebnisse der Auktionen in Deutschland, Holland, Oesterreich und der Schweiz. see *MUSEUMS AND ART GALLERIES*

070.5　　　　　　JA　ISSN 0287-9530
JAPAN DIRECTORY OF PROFESSIONAL ASSOCIATIONS. (Text in English) 1984. triennial. $150. Intercontinental Marketing KK, Japan Publications Guide Service, Wako 5 Bldg., 1-19-8 Kakigaracho Nihonbashi, Chuoku Tokyo 103, Japan (Subscr. to: Japan Publications Guide Service, CPO Box 971, Tokyo 100-91, Japan) Ed. Warren E. Ball. adv. stat. tr.lit. circ. 2,000.

070.5　　　　　　IS
KATALOG SEFARIM KELALI. (Text in Hebrew) 1973. biennial. $70. (Eddy Levy Scientific and Commercial Programming Co.Ltd) Book Publishers Association of Israel, c/o Eddie Levy, Goldberg 1, Tel Aviv 65784, Israel. Ed. Zwi Steiner. adv. bk. rev. circ. 3,000.

KLEIO. see *HISTORY*

070.5　015　　　　KO　ISSN 0075-6881
KOREAN PUBLICATIONS YEARBOOK/ HAN'QUK CH'ULP AN YON'GAM. 1963. a. 30000 Won($40) Korean Publishers Association, 105-2 Sagan-Dong, Chongno-Ku, Seoul, S. Korea. TEL 735-2701. circ. 2,500. (back issues avail.)

070.5　　　　　　BE
LIJSTENBOEK. 1929. a. 450 Fr.($8) Vereniging ter Bevordering van het Vlaamse Boekwezen - Association of Publishers of Dutch Language Books, Frankrijklei 93, B-2000 Antwerp, Belgium. index. circ. 1,500.

LITERARY AGENTS OF NORTH AMERICA MARKETPLACE. see *LITERATURE*

070.5　　　　　　US　ISSN 0161-2905
LITERARY MARKET PLACE; the directory of American book publishing. 1940. a. $85. R.R. Bowker Company, Database Publishing Group, 245 W. 17th St., New York, NY 10011. TEL 800-521-8110. index.
Formed by the 1972 merger of: Literary Market Place (ISSN 0075-9899); Names and Numbers.

070.5　　　　　　PO
LIVRARIA FIGUEIRINHAS CATALOGO. 1898. a. free. Livraria Editora Figueirinhas Lda., Praca da Liberdade 66-68, Porto, Portugal. circ. 5,000.

MAGAZINE INDEX. see *ABSTRACTING AND INDEXING SERVICES*

070.5　　　　　　US　ISSN 0000-0434
MAGAZINE INDUSTRY MARKET PLACE; the directory of American periodical publishing. Short title: M I M P. 1980. a. $69.95. R.R. Bowker Company, Database Publishing Group, 245 W. 17th St., New York, NY 10011. TEL 800-521-8110. adv.

MAGILL'S LITERARY ANNUAL. see *LITERATURE*

MEDIA PERSONNEL DIRECTORY. see *JOURNALISM*

070.5　　　　　　US
NATIONAL NEWSLETTERS, DIRECTORY AND REPORTING SERVICES; a reference guide to national and international services, financial services, association bulletins, and training and educational services. (In 8 parts) 1966. irreg., latest 3rd edt., 1986. $140. Gale Research Company, Book Tower, Detroit, MI 48226. TEL 313-961-2242. Eds. Brigitte T. Darnay, John Nimchuk.
Formerly: National Directory of Newsletters and Reporting Services (ISSN 0547-6232)

070.5　　　　　　CN　ISSN 0077-5347
NATIONAL PUBLISHING DIRECTORY.* 1964-65. biennial. Prestige Books of Canada, 99 Vaugham Rd., Toronto, Ont., Canada.

686.3　　　　　　UK　ISSN 0261-5363
NEW BOOKBINDER. 1981. a. £15 to individuals. (Designer Bookbinders) Carfax Publishing Co., P.O. Box 25, Abingdon, Oxfordshire OX14 3UE, England (Distr. in U.S. by: Carfax Publishing Co., 85 Ash St., Hopkinton, MA 01748) Ed.Bd. adv. bk. rev. circ. 800. (back issues avail.)

NEWSPAPER PUBLISHERS HANDBOOK. see *JOURNALISM*

NOTABLE CHILDREN'S TRADE BOOKS IN THE FIELD OF SOCIAL STUDIES. see *SOCIAL SCIENCES: COMPREHENSIVE WORKS — Abstracting, Bibliographies, Statistics*

070.5　　　　　　US　ISSN 0078-2882
O.P. MARKET. (Out of Print) 1948. a. $10. (Antiquarian Bookman) A B Bookman Publications, Box AB, Clifton, NJ 07015. TEL 201-772-0020. Ed. Jacob L. Chernofsky. adv. bk. rev. circ. 10,000.
Out-of-print market

070.5　　　　　　AU　ISSN 0078-3455
DAS OESTERREICHISCHE BUCH. 1947. a. Hauptverband des oesterreichischen Buchhandels, Gruenangergasse 4, A-1010 Vienna, Austria.

070.5　　　　　　DK　ISSN 0107-380X
OPLAGSBULLETIN. 1932. a. Kr.54 per no. (free to libraries) Dansk Oplagskontrol - Danish Bureau of Circulations, Frederiksbergade 5, 1459 Copenhagen K, Denmark. circ. 2,200.

070.5　　　　　　UK　ISSN 0078-7159
OVERSEAS NEWSPAPERS AND PERIODICALS. (Issued in 2 vols., Vol. 1: Markets in Europe; Vol. 2: Markets outside Europe) 1952. biennial. £17($50) per vol. New Product Newsletter Co. Ltd., 1A Chesterfield St., London W.1, England. Ed. H.R. Vaughan. adv. circ. 5,000. (also avail. in microfilm from UMI)

070.5　　　　　　US　ISSN 0737-7843
PERIODICAL TITLE ABBREVIATIONS; covering periodical title abbreviations in science, the social sciences, the humanities, law, medicine, religion, library science, engineering, education, business, art, and many other fields. (In 3 Vols: Vol.1, by Abbreviation; Vol.2, by Title; Vol.3, New Abbrev.) 1969. irreg., 5th edt., 1986. vol.1, $155; vol.2, $155; vol.3, $125. Gale Research Company, Book Tower, Detroit, MI 48226. TEL 313-961-2242. Ed. Leland G. Alkire, Jr.

POLICY PUBLISHERS AND ASSOCIATIONS DIRECTORY. see *POLITICAL SCIENCE*

PRESSE-PORTRAETS; das Angebot des Pressehandels. see *BIBLIOGRAPHIES*

070　　　　　　　AU
PRESSEHANDBUCH (YEAR) 1953. a. S.780. Verband Oesterreichischer Zeitungsherausgeber und Zeitungsverleger, Schreyvogelgasse 3, A-1010 Vienna, Austria. adv. bk. rev. mkt. tr.lit. index. circ. 2,000.
Formerly: Oesterreichs Presse, Werbung, Graphik (ISSN 0030-0004)

070.5　　　　　　US
PRINTING & PUBLISHING: LATIN AMERICAN INDUSTRIAL REPORT. (Avail. for each of 22 Latin American countries) 1985. a. $435 per country report per industry covered. Aurora International, Box 9099, Bridgeport, CT 06601-2099. TEL 203-368-0579. Ed. Andres C. Aquino.

070.5　　　　　　CH
PUBLICATIONS YEARBOOK, REPUBLIC OF CHINA; including catalogs of books and records. 1977. a. China Publishing Company, Box 337, Taipei, Taiwan, Republic of China.

PUBLISHERS' CATALOGS ANNUAL. see *BIBLIOGRAPHIES*

PUBLISHERS, DISTRIBUTORS AND WHOLESALERS OF THE UNITED STATES. see *BUSINESS AND ECONOMICS — Trade And Industrial Directories*

070.5　　　　　　UK　ISSN 0079-7839
PUBLISHERS IN THE UNITED KINGDOM AND THEIR ADDRESSES. 1946. a. £5.50. J. Whitaker & Sons Ltd., 12 Dyott St., London WC1A 1DF, England.

655 FR
REPERTOIRE INTERNATIONAL DES EDITEURS ET DIFFUSEURS DE LANGUE FRANCAISE. a. 295.10 F. Editions du Cercle de la Librairie, 35 rue Gregoire de Tours, 75279 Paris Cedex 06, France. circ. 5,000.
Formerly: Livre de Langue Francaise - Repertoire des Editeurs (ISSN 0076-0110)

070.5 CN
RIGHTS CANADA. 1976. a. Canadian Book Publishers Council, 45 Charles St. E., Toronto, Ont. M4Y 1S2, Canada. adv. illus. circ. 4,000.

070.5 740 SZ ISSN 0080-6838
SCHOENSTE SCHWEIZER BUECHER. (Text in English, French and German) 1943. a. free. Schweizerischer Buchhaendler- und Verleger-Verband, Box 408, CH-8034 Zurich, Switzerland. (Co-sponsor: Eidgenoessisches Departement des Innern) bk. rev.

070.5 GE
DIE SCHOENSTEN BUECHER DER DEUTSCHEN DEMOKRATISCHEN REPUBLIK. 1963. a. M.5. VEB Fachbuchverlag, Postfach 67, DDR-7031 Leipzig, E. Germany (D.D.R.)
Formerly: Spiegel Deutscher Buchkunst (ISSN 0081-3702)
Report on the year's best books

070.5 SZ ISSN 0080-7230
SCHWEIZER BUCHHANDELS-ADRESSBUCH. 1965/66. a. price varies. Schweizerischer Buchhaendler- und Verleger-Verband, P.O.B. 408, CH-8034 Zurich, Switzerland.

070.5 UK
SHEPPARD'S BOOK DEALERS IN BRITISH ISLES. 1951. biennial. £18($40) Europa Publications Ltd., 18 Bedford Sq., London WC1B 3JN, England.
Formerly: Directory of Dealers in Secondhand and Antiquarian Books in the British Isles (ISSN 0070-5411)

070.5 UK
SHEPPARD'S BOOKDEALERS IN NORTH AMERICA. 1956. biennial. £18($40) Europa Publications Ltd., 18 Bedford Sq., London WC1B 3JN, England. index. circ. 4,000.
Formerly: Bookdealers in North America (ISSN 0068-0109)

070.5 SI ISSN 0080-9659
SINGAPORE BOOK WORLD. (Text in Chinese, English and Malay) 1970. a. $20. National Book Development Council of Singapore, NBDCS Secretariat, Bukit Merah Branch Library, Bukit Merah Central, Singapore 0315. Ed.Bd. adv. bk. rev. circ. 1,000. (back issues avail.) Indexed: Lib.Sci.Abstr.

020.75 MX
SISTEMA NACIONAL DE ARCHIVOS. INVENTARIOS. irreg. Archivo General de la Nacion, Tacuba No. 8, Mexico 1, D.F., Mexico.

655 090 FR ISSN 0081-0878
SOCIETE DES FRANCS-BIBLIOPHILES. ANNUAIRE. 1948. a. membership. 39 rue Raynouard, 75016 Paris, France.

070.5 US
SOCIETY OF SCHOLARLY PUBLISHING. PROCEEDINGS OF ANNUAL MEETINGS. 1979. a. price varies. Society for Scholarly Publishing, 2000 Florida Ave., N.W., Washington, DC 20009. TEL 202-328-3555. circ. 500.
Formerly: S S P Proceedings (ISSN 0196-6146)

SOLANUS; international journal for Russian & East European bibliographic, library & publishing studies. see *LIBRARY AND INFORMATION SCIENCES*

STUDIA O KSIAZCE. see *LIBRARY AND INFORMATION SCIENCES*

079.7 CU
U P E C. irreg. Union de Periodistas de Cuba, Calle 23, No. 452, Havana, Cuba. illus.

U S REAL ESTATE REGISTER. see *ADVERTISING AND PUBLIC RELATIONS*

070.5 UN
UNESCO. STUDIES ON BOOKS AND READING. (Text in English; occasionally in Arabic, French, Spanish and Russian) irreg. free. Unesco, Division for Book Promotion, Audiovisual Archives and International Exchanges, 7 place de Fontenoy, 7500 Paris, France. charts. circ. 2,500.

020 US ISSN 0275-9616
U.S. LIBRARY OF CONGRESS. MANUSCRIPT DIVISION. ACQUISITIONS. 1979. a. free to libraries. U.S. Library of Congress, Washington, DC 20540.

070.5 016 US ISSN 0083-4807
USED BOOK PRICE GUIDE. 1962. quinquennial supplement. $79 for supplement. ‡ Price Guide Publishers, Box 525, Kenmore, WA 98028-0525. Ed. Mildred S. Mandeville.

VERBREITUNGSDATEN DER SCHWEIZER PRESSE. see *ADVERTISING AND PUBLIC RELATIONS*

070.5 NE
VERENIGDE NEDERLANDSE UITGEVERSBEDRIJVEN. ANNUAL REPORT. a. Verenigde Nederlandse Uitgeversbedrijven, 5-25 Ceylonpoort, 2037 AA Haarlem, Netherlands.

070.5 GW ISSN 0170-7213
WHO'S WHO AT THE FRANKFURT BOOK FAIR; an International Publishers' Guide. 1969. a. price varies. (Frankfurt Book Fair) K.G. Saur Verlag KG, Poessenbacherstr. 12 B, Postfach 711009, 8000 Munich 71, W. Germany (B.R.D.) (U.S. and Canadian subscr. to: K.G. Saur Inc., 175 Fifth Ave., New York, N.Y. 10010) adv. (reprint service avail. from UMI, ISI)

070.5 UK ISSN 0084-2664
WRITERS' AND ARTISTS' YEARBOOK; a directory for writers, artists, playwrights, writers for film, radio and television, photographers and composers. 1907. a. £5.95. A. & C. Black (Publishers) Ltd., 35 Bedford Row, London WC1R 4JH, England. index.

070.5 AT ISSN 0084-2680
WRITERS' AND PHOTOGRAPHERS' MARKETING GUIDE; DIRECTORY OF AUSTRALIAN AND NEW ZEALAND LITERARY AND PHOTO MARKETS. 1945. biennial. Aus.$7.50. Australian Writers' Professional Service, Box 28, Collins St. P.O., Melbourne, Vic. 3001, Australia. Ed. G.R. Pittaway.

070.5 US ISSN 0084-2710
WRITER'S HANDBOOK. 1936. a. $25.95. Writer, Inc., 120 Boylston St., Boston, MA 02116. TEL 617-423-3157. Ed. Sylvia K. Burack. (reprint service avail. from UMI, BLH)

070.5 808 US
WRITERS INK. 1975. irreg. (2-4/yr.) $6 per no. (Alliance of New York Writers and Publishers, Inc.) Writers Ink Press, 194 Soundview Dr., Rocky Point, NY 11778 TEL 516-744-7058. Eds. David B. Axelrod, Joan C. Hand. bk. rev. film rev. play rev. illus. circ. 2,000.

070.5 US ISSN 0084-2729
WRITER'S MARKET. 1926. a. $21.95. F & W Publications, Inc., 9933 Alliance Rd., Cincinnati, OH 45242. TEL 513-984-0717. Ed. Becky Williams. index. (reprint service avail. from UMI)

070.5 800 US ISSN 0084-2737
WRITER'S YEARBOOK. 1930. a. $2.95. F & W Publications, Inc., 9933 Alliance Rd., Cincinnati, OH 45242. TEL 513-984-0717. Ed. Bill Brohaugh. adv. circ. 75,000. (also avail. in microform from UMI; reprint service avail. from UMI)

5001 HARD TO FIND PUBLISHERS. see *LIBRARY AND INFORMATION SCIENCES*

PUBLISHING AND BOOK TRADE —
Abstracting, Bibliographies, Statistics

070 015 US ISSN 0091-9357
AMERICAN BOOK PRICES CURRENT. a. price varies. Bancroft-Parkman, Inc., Box 236, Washington, CT 06793. TEL 212-237-7715.

070 015 US
AMERICAN BOOK PRICES CURRENT. FOUR YEAR INDEX. quadrennial. price varies. Bancroft-Parkman, Inc., Box 236, Washington, CT 06793. TEL 212-737-2715.
Formerly: American Book Prices Current. Five Year Index.

655 011 US ISSN 0002-7707
AMERICAN BOOK PUBLISHING RECORD/B P R; arranged by subject according to the Dewey Decimal Classification and indexed by author and title. 1960. m. with a. & 5-yr. cumulations. $70 for m.; $119.95 for a. cum.; $199 for 5-yr. cum. R.R. Bowker Company, Database Publishing Group, 245 W. 17th St., New York, NY 10011. TEL 800-521-8110. index. cum.index. circ. 7,345. Indexed: Abstr.Bull.Inst.Pap.Chem.

070.5 010 AE ISSN 0066-5630
ARAB BOOK ANNUAL/AL-KITAB AL-ARABI FI AAM. (Text in Arabic; summary in English) 1961. a. £E1800($8.70) Societe Nationale d'Edition et de Diffusion, 3 bd. Zirout Youcef, Algiers, Algeria.

070.5 US ISSN 8755-9633
BEST BOOKS BY CONSENSUS (YEAR) 1981. a. $5.75. Info Digest, 9302 Parkside, Box 165, Morton Grove, IL 60053. Ed. Chung I. Park. circ. 450. (back issues avail.)
Supersedes (after 1982): Best Sellers and Best Choices (Year) (ISSN 0275-0945)

070.5 BL
BIBLIOGRAPHIA BRASILIANA. irreg. $150. Livraria Kosmos Editora, S.A., Rua do Rosario 135-137, Rio de Janeiro ZC 00, Brazil.

BIBLIOGRAPHY NEWSLETTER. see *LIBRARY AND INFORMATION SCIENCES — Abstracting, Bibliographies, Statistics*

028.5 016 US ISSN 0147-250X
BIBLIOGRAPHY OF BOOKS FOR CHILDREN. 1935. quadrennial. $8.50 to members; non-members $10. Association for Childhood Education International, 11141 Georgia Ave., Ste. 200, Wheaton, MD 20902. TEL 301-942-2443. Ed. Sylvia Sunderlin. adv. bk. rev. (reprint service avail. from UMI)

BOOK REPORT. see *PUBLISHING AND BOOK TRADE*

028.1 011 US ISSN 0006-7326
BOOK REVIEW DIGEST; an index to reviews of current books. 1905. m., except Feb. and July (quarterly and annual cumulations) service basis. H.W. Wilson Co., 950 University Ave., Bronx, NY 10452. TEL 212-588-8400. Ed. Martha Mooney. bk. rev. cum.index 1905-1974.
●Also available online. Vendors: Wilsonline.

070.5 015 AU
BUECHER (YEAR); Das Lesemazin fuer Sie. 1949. a. Hauptverband des Oesterreichischen Buchhandels, Gruenangergasse 4, A-1010 Vienna, Austria. adv. bk. rev.
Former titles: Buecher fuer Alle (ISSN 0067-0634) & Aus der Schatzkammer der Buecher.

070.5 US ISSN 0198-8433
CALIFORNIA ACADEMIC LIBRARIES LIST OF SERIALS. Short title: C A L L S. (Available online through UC MELVYL Online Catalog) 1976. a. $220 ($155 for microfiche only) University of California, Division of Library Automation, 186 University Hall, Berkeley, CA 94720 TEL 415-642-9485. (Subscr. address: CLASS, 1415 Koll Circle, Ste. 101, San Jose, CA 95112) Ed. Teresa Montgomery. circ. 300. (microfiche)

CANADA. STATISTICS CANADA. PRINTING, PUBLISHING AND ALLIED INDUSTRIES. see *PRINTING — Abstracting, Bibliographies, Statistics*

070.5 AG
CATALOGO COLECTIVO DE PUBLICACIONES PERIODICAS EXISTENTES EN BIBLIOTECAS CIENTIFICAS Y TECNICAS ARGENTINA. 1942; 2nd edt. 1962. irreg., suppl. 1972, 1981. $80. Consejo Nacional de Investigaciones Cientificas y Tecnicas, Moreno 433, 1091 Buenos Aires, Argentina.

015 IT
CATALOGO DEI LIBRI IN COMMERCIO/ ITALIAN BOOKS IN PRINT. 1970. biennial. price varies. (Associazione Italiana Editori) Editrice Bibliografica s.r.l., Viale Vittorio Veneto 24, 20124 Milan, Italy (Dist. in U.S., Canada and Latin America by: R.R. Bowker Co., Box 1807, Ann Arbor, MI 48106) circ. 3,000. (also avail. in magnetic tape; back issues avail.)
Formerly: Catalogo dei Libri Italiani in Commercio (ISSN 0069-1054)

028.5 016 UK ISSN 0306-2015
CHILDREN'S LITERATURE ABSTRACTS. 1973. q. £11($17) International Federation of Library Associations, Children's Section, Tan-y-capel, Bont Dolgadfan, Llanbrynmair, Powys SY19 7BB, Wales. Ed. Colin Ray. abstr. index. circ. 500. (also avail. in microform from MIM)

070.5 015 GW
DEUTSCHE BIBLIOGRAPHIE. FUENFJAHRES-VERZEICHNIS. 1945/1950. irreg. price varies. (Deutsche Bibliothek) Buchhaendler-Vereinigung GmbH, Gr. Hirschgraben 17-21, 6000 Frankfurt 1, W. Germany (B.R.D.) bibl. index.

070.5 015 SP ISSN 0210-6833
DIPUTACIO PROVINCIAL. BIBLIOTECA CATALUNYA CATALEG LA PRODUCCION EDITORIAL BARCELONESA. 1949/1950. a. Diputacio Provincial, Biblioteca de Catalunya, Carme, 47, 08002 Barcelona, Spain.
Formerly (until 1978): Universidad de Barcelona. Biblioteca Central. Catalogos de la Production Editorial Barcelona (ISSN 0067-4141)

808 US ISSN 0095-6414
DIRECTORY OF SMALL MAGAZINE/PRESS EDITORS AND PUBLISHERS. 1970. a. $15.95. Dustbooks, Box 100, Paradise, CA 95969. TEL 916-877-6110. Ed. Len Fulton.

070.5 944 US
FRENCH XX BIBLIOGRAPHY. (Text in English, French) a., latest vol.38, 1987. $76. Associated University Presses, 440 Forsgate Dr., Cranbury, NJ 08512. (Co-sponsor: Susquehanna University Press) Ed. Douglas W. Alden. (back issues avail.)

016 028 GW
FREUDE MIT BUECHERN. 1951. a. DM.3. Verlag Buecherschiff Walter Reutin, Rheinstr. 122, Postfach 210947, 7500 Karlsruhe 21, W. Germany (B.R.D.) Ed. H. Bode. bk. rev. circ. 5,000.

015 PK
ILMI A'INO. (Text in Sindhi) a. Rs.2. University of Sind, Institute of Sindhology, Jamshoro, Hyderabad 6, Pakistan.
List of books and periodicals, publishers, cultural and literary organizations in Sind

070.5 011 SA ISSN 0379-0584
INDEX TO SOUTH AFRICAN PERIODICALS/ REPERTORIUM VAN SUID-AFRIKAANSE TYDSKRIFARTIKELS. (Text in Afrikaans and English) 1940. a. R.35. Johannesburg Public Library, Market Square, Johannesburg 2001, South Africa. circ. 300. (microfiche; back issues avail.)

070.5 016 GW
INTERNATIONAL BOOKS IN PRINT; English-language titles published outside the USA and Great Britain. 1979. a. price varies. K. G. Saur Verlag KG, Poessenbacherstr. 12 B, Postfach 711009, 8000 Munich 71, W. Germany (B.R.D.) (U.S. and Canadian subscr. to: K.G. Saur Inc., 185 Fifth Ave., New York, N.Y. 10010) (reprint service avail. from UMI, ISI)

070.5 016 US
INTERNATIONAL DIRECTORY OF CHILDREN'S LITERATURE. 1973. biennial. $29.95. George Kurian Reference Books, Box 519, Baldwin Place, NY 10505. Ed. Mary Beth Dunhouse. bk. rev. circ. 3,500.
Formerly: Children's Literary Almanac (ISSN 0093-0431)

070 US ISSN 0092-3974
INTERNATIONAL DIRECTORY OF LITTLE MAGAZINES AND SMALL PRESSES. 1965. a. $20.95. Dustbooks, Box 100, Paradise, CA 95969. TEL 916-877-6110. Ed. Len Fulton. adv. circ. 10,000.
Formerly: Directory of Little Magazines, Small Presses and Underground Newspapers (ISSN 0084-9979)

070.5 GW ISSN 0074-9877
INTERNATIONALES VERLAGSADRESSBUCH/ PUBLISHERS' INTERNATIONAL DIRECTORY. 1962. a (formerly irreg., 13th edt. 1986) price varies. K. G. Saur Verlag KG, Poessenbacherstr. 12 B, Postfach 711009, 8000 Munich 71, W. Germany (B.R.D.) (U.S. and Canadian subscr. to: K.G. Saur Inc., 175 Fifth Ave., New York, N.Y. 10010) Ed. Barbara Vessel. adv. (reprint service avail. from UMI, ISI)

655 020 011 IT ISSN 0391-5972
ISTITUTO CENTRALE PER LA PATOLOGIA DEL LIBRO "ALFONSO GALLO." BOLLETTINO. (Suspended with vol. 31, 1972 resumed in 1978, with vol. 32, 1973/74) (Text in Italian; summaries in English) 1939. a. L.15000. Istituto Centrale per la Patologia del Libro "Alfonso Gallo.", Via Milano 76, 00184 Rome, Italy. Ed.Bd. adv. bk. rev. bibl. charts. illus. cum.index. circ. 500. Indexed: Biol.Abstr. Lib.Lit. Abstr.Bull.Inst.Pap.Chem. Lib.Sci.Abstr. Rev.Appl.Entomol.
Formerly: Istituto di Patologia del Libro "Alfonso Gallo." Bollettino (ISSN 0020-403X)

090.75 011 IT
LIBRI RARI; collezione di ristampe con nuovi apparati. 1977. irreg., latest 1985. price varies. Edizioni Il Polifilo, Via Borgonuovo 2, 20121 Milan, Italy.

028.1 016 US
REFERENCE SOURCES. 1977. a. $75. Pierian Press, Box 1808, Ann Arbor, MI 48106. TEL 313-434-5530. Ed. C. Edward Wall. (back issues avail.)
Supersedes (1973-1979): Reference Book Review Index.

070.5 PL ISSN 0511-1196
RUCH WYDAWNICZY W LICZBACH/POLISH PUBLISHING IN FIGURES. 1955. a. 130 Zl. Biblioteka Narodowa, Instytut Bibliograficzny, Ul. Hankiewicz 1, 00-973 Warsaw, Poland TEL 48-22-22-46-21. (Dist. by: Ars Polona-Ruch, ul. Krakowskie Przedmiescie 7, 00-068 Warsaw, Poland) Ed. Krystyna Bankowska-Bober. circ. 400.

686 GE ISSN 0232-5616
SAECHSISCHE LANDESBIBLIOTHEK. BIBLIOGRAPHIE ILLUSTRIERTE BUECHER DER DEUTSCHEN DEMOKRATISCHEN REPUBLIK. (Text in German) 1973. a. Saechsische Landesbibliothek, Marienalle 12, 8060 Dresden, E. Germany (D.D.R) Eds. E. Stimmel, Hans-Joachim Kunz.

808 016 US
SMALL PRESS RECORD OF BOOKS IN PRINT. 1969. a. $31.95. Dustbooks, Box 100, Paradise, CA 95969. TEL 916-877-6110. Ed. Len Fulton. adv.

020 296 016 US ISSN 0039-3568
STUDIES IN BIBLIOGRAPHY AND BOOKLORE; devoted to research in the field of Jewish bibliography. (Text in English, Hebrew and other languages) 1953. irreg. price varies. Hebrew Union College - Jewish Institutional of Religion, Library, 3101 Clifton Ave., Cincinnati, OH 45220. TEL 513-221-1875. Ed.Bd. bk. rev. bibl. cum.index: vols. 1-16. circ. 1,100. Indexed: Hist.Abstr. Amer.Hist. & Life. Ind.Jew.Per.

015 CN
SUBJECT GUIDE TO CANADIAN BOOKS IN PRINT. 1973. a. University of Toronto Press., Toronto, Ont., Canada. TEL 613-667-7791.

070.5 015 SQ ISSN 0378-7710
SWAZILAND NATIONAL BIBLIOGRAPHY. (Volume published in 1977 covers 1973-1976) 1977. triennial. $12.50. University of Swaziland Library, Research and Publications Committee, Private Bag, Kwaluseni, Swaziland. Ed.Bd. circ. 300.

070.5 070 US
U S PROGRESSIVE PERIODICALS DIRECTORY. 1981. irreg. $8. Progressive Education, Box 120574, Nashville, TN 37212. Ed. Craig T. Canan. circ. 1, 500.
Formerly: U S Progressive Periodicals Directory Update.

UNIVERSITY MICROFILMS INTERNATIONAL NEWSLETTER. see *LIBRARY AND INFORMATION SCIENCES — Abstracting, Bibliographies, Statistics*

011 UK ISSN 0140-4229
WHITAKER'S CUMULATIVE BOOK LIST. 1924. a. £37. J. Whitaker & Sons Ltd., 12 Dyott St., London WC1A 1DF, England.

296 016 IS ISSN 0044-4774
ZIONIST LITERATURE. (Text in English and Hebrew) 1936. bi-m. free. ‡ World Zionist Organization, Central Zionist Archives, Box 92, Jerusalem 91000, Israel. Ed. Ms. H.A. Abrahami. circ. 1,250.

PUBLISHING AND BOOK TRADE — Computer Applications

070.3 US ISSN 0740-4085
COMPUTER PUBLISHERS & PUBLICATIONS; an international directory. 1984. biennial. $149.95. Communications Trends, Inc., 2 East Ave., Larchmont, NY 10538. TEL 914-833-0600. Ed. Frederick Evan. adv. bk. rev.

ELECTRONIC PUBLISHING ABSTRACTS. see *COMPUTERS — Abstracting, Bibliographies, Statistics*

070.5 US
HUMAN RESOURCES INFORMATION NETWORK UPDATE. 1984. irreg. free. The Bureau of National Affairs, Inc., 1231 25th St., N.W., Washington, DC 20037. TEL 202-452-4200.

070.5 025 US
PLUS; Plus System newsletter. 1987. irreg. free. R.R. Bowker Company, Electronic Publishing Division, 245 W. 17th St., New York, NY 10011-0418. TEL 800-323-3288. Ed. Martin Brooks.

RADIO AND TELEVISION

see *Communications — Radio and Television*

RADIOLOGY AND NUCLEAR MEDICINE

see *Medical Sciences — Radiology and Nuclear Medicine*

RAILROADS

see *Transportation — Railroads*

REAL ESTATE

see also *Architecture; Building and Construction; Business and Economics — Investments; Housing and Urban Planning*

333 368 US ISSN 0569-7840
A S A MONOGRAPH. 1969. irreg., no.8, 1979. $5. American Society of Appraisers, Box 17265, Washington, DC 20041. TEL 703-620-3838.

ALBERTA INSURANCE REPORT. see
INSURANCE

333.332   CN   ISSN 0003-7079
APPRAISAL INSTITUTE DIGEST. vol.4, 1970. irreg., 5-6/yr. included in Canadian Appraiser. Appraisal Institute of Canada, 309-93 Lombard Ave., Winnipeg, Man. R3B 3B1, Canada. TEL 204-942-0751. Ed. T.J. Gifford. charts. illus. circ. 8,200.

526.9   CN   ISSN 0318-2126
ASSOCIATION OF NEW BRUNSWICK LAND SURVEYORS. ANNUAL REPORT. 1955. a. Association of New Brunswick Land Surveyors, P.O. Box 22, Fredericton, New Brunswick E3B 4Y2, Canada. TEL 506-457-1847. adv. circ. 150 (controlled)

333.33   658   US   ISSN 0738-2170
B O M A EXPERIENCE EXCHANGE REPORT; income/expense analysis for office buildings. 1920. a. $195. Building Owners and Managers Association International, 1250 Eye St., N.W., Ste. 200, Washington, DC 20005. TEL 202-289-7000. Ed. J. Kenneth Sugarman. circ. 8,000. (back issues avail.)

333.33   US
BLACK'S GUIDE TO THE OFFICE SPACE MARKET. CONNECTICUT/NEW YORK SUBURBS. 1976. a. $39.95. Black's Guide, Inc. (Subsidiary of: McGraw-Hill Informations Systems Company) 620 Shrewsbury Ave., Box 2090, Red Bank, NJ 07701. TEL 201-842-6060. Ed. David G. Hanson. adv.

333.33   US
BLACK'S GUIDE TO THE OFFICE SPACE MARKET. NORTHERN NEW JERSEY. 1976. a. $59.95. Black' Guide, Inc. (Subsidiary of: McGraw-Hill Information Systems Company) 620 Shrewsbury Ave., Box 2090, Red Bank, NJ 07701. TEL 201-842-6060. Ed. David G. Hanson. adv.

333.33   US
BLACK'S GUIDE TO THE OFFICE SPACE MARKET. PHILADELPHIA AND SUBURBS. 1976. a. $39.95. Black's Guide, Inc. (Subsidiary of: McGraw-Hill Information Systems Company) 620 Shrewsbury Ave., Box 2090, Red Bank, NJ 07701. TEL 201-842-6060. Ed. David G. Hanson. adv.

333.33   US
BLACK'S GUIDE TO THE OFFICE SPACE MARKET. WASHINGTON/BALTIMORE. 1976. a. $59.95. Black's Guide, Inc. (Subsidiary of: McGraw-Hill Information Systems Company) 620 Shrewsbury Ave., Box 2090, Red Bank, NJ 07701. TEL 201-842-6060. Ed. David G. Hanson. adv.

333.3   690   UK   ISSN 0262-8155
BUILDING SOCIETIES ASSOCIATION. REPORT OF THE COUNCIL. 1942. a. £3. Building Societies Association, 3 Savile Row, London W1X 1AF, England.

333.3   332   UK   ISSN 0266-4828
BUILDING SOCIETY FACTBOOK (YEAR) 1980. a. £5. Building Societies Association, 3 Savile Row, London W1X 1AF, England.
   Formerly: Building Societies in (Year) (ISSN 0261-6408)

333.33   690   UK
C A L U S RESEARCH REPORTS. (Centre for Advanced Land Use Studies) 1975. irreg., no.15, 1985. price varies. College of Estate Management, Whiteknights, Reading RG6 2AW, England.

333.33   CJ
CAYMAN ISLANDS REAL ESTATE REVIEW. 1977. a. free. Cayman Free Press Ltd., Special Publications Division, Box 1365, Grand Cayman, Cayman Islands, British W.I. TEL 809-949-5111. adv. circ. 20,000.

333   658.7   US   ISSN 0732-5983
DIRECTORY OF MAJOR MALLS; lists existing and planned shopping centers in the United States and Canada over 250,000 sq. ft. of gross leasable area. 1977. a. $250. M J J T M Publications Corp., Box 2, Suffern, NY 10901. TEL 914-357-7690. Ed. Murray Shor. adv.

DIRECTORY OF PROPERTY INVESTORS AND DEVELOPERS. see *BUSINESS AND ECONOMICS — Investments*

333.33   US   ISSN 0277-9986
DIRECTORY OF REAL ESTATE INVESTORS. 1982. a. $115. Whole World Publishing, Inc., 400 Lake Cook Rd., Ste. 207, Deerfield, IL 60015. TEL 312-945-8050. Ed. William J. Feinberg. adv. circ. 4, 500.

333.33   US   ISSN 0070-704X
DOLLARS AND CENTS OF SHOPPING CENTERS. 1961. triennial. $124. ‡ Urban Land Institute, 1090 Vermont Ave., N.W., Ste. 300, Washington, DC 20005. TEL 202-289-8500. Ed. Frank Spink. (reprint service avail. from UMI)

333.33   US   ISSN 0160-9629
E-R-C DIRECTORY; employee relocation real estate services. 1964. a. $20. Employee Relocation Council, 1720 N St., N.W., Washington, DC 20036. TEL 202-857-0857. Ed. Jerry Holloman. circ. 16, 000.
   Formerly: E R E A C Directory (ISSN 0071-0113)

333.33   DK   ISSN 0108-2698
EJENDOMSINFORMATION; bolig og oekonomi. 1981. irreg. Ejendomsmaeglernes Datacentrum-Gruppen i Koege Bugt, c/o Greve Strand Distribution, Vesterbjerg 52, 2670 Greve Strand, Denmark. illus.

333   US   ISSN 0191-2208
EXPENSE ANALYSIS: CONDOMINIUMS, COOPERATIVES AND PLANNED UNIT DEVELOPMENTS. a. $62. Institute of Real Estate Management, 430 N. Michigan Ave., Chicago, IL 60611. TEL 312-661-1930. Ed. Kenneth Anderson.
   Supersedes in part: Income-Expense Analysis. Apartments, Condominiums and Cooperatives (ISSN 0161-5262)

333.3   332.6   UK   ISSN 0260-8812
FORECAST OF SHOP RENTS. 1977. a. free. Hillier Parker May & Rowden, 77 Grosvenor St., London W1A 2BT, England. Ed. Dr. R.K. Schiller. charts. stat. index. circ. 2,800.

333.33   910   910   US   ISSN 0884-4089
GREENER PASTURES GAZETTE; the newsletter dedicated to the search for countryside Edens where the good life still exists. 1985. irreg. $3 per no. Relocation Research, Box 864, Bend, OR 97709. TEL 503-388-0079. Ed. William L. Seavey. bk. rev. index. circ. 300. (back issues avail.)

HOW TO BUY AND SELL BUSINESS OPPORTUNITIES. see *BUSINESS AND ECONOMICS — Investments*

690   333   US   ISSN 0194-1941
INCOME-EXPENSE ANALYSIS: CONVENTIONAL APARTMENTS. 1954. a. $45. Institute of Real Estate Management, 430 N. Michigan Ave., Chicago, IL 60611. TEL 312-661-1930. Ed. Kenneth Anderson.
   Formerly: Income-Expense Analysis: Apartments; Supersedes in part: Income-Expense Analysis. Apartments, Condominiums and Cooperatives (ISSN 0161-5262); Until 1973: Apartment Building Income-Expense Analysis (ISSN 0084-6651)

333   US
INCOME-EXPENSE ANALYSIS: OFFICE BUILDINGS, DOWNTOWN AND SUBURBAN. 1976. a. $79. Institute of Real Estate Management, 430 N. Michigan Ave., Chicago, IL 60611. TEL 312-661-1930. Ed. Kenneth Anderson.
   Supersedes: Income-Expense Analysis: Suburban Office Buildings.

333.33   US   ISSN 0730-0131
INDUSTRIAL REAL ESTATE MARKET SURVEY. 1980. a. $75. Society of Industrial and Office Realtors, 777 14th St., N.W., Washington, DC 20005. TEL 202-383-1150. Ed. Jeanne R. Smith. circ. 3,000.

333.33   UK
KEMPS PROPERTY INDUSTRY YEARBOOK. 1974. a. $45. Kemps Group (Printers & Publishers) Ltd., 1-5 Bath St., London EC1V 9QA, England.
   Formerly: Kemps Estate Agents Yearbook and Directory.

333.33   FR   ISSN 0024-5674
LOCATIONS VACANCES. a. 20 F. Editions Indicateur Bertrand, 11 et 13 rue du Louvre, 75001 Paris, France. adv. bk. rev.
   Advertisements for the renting of vacation homes, etc. in France and elsewhere

333.33   US
MANAGING THE NATION'S PUBLIC LANDS. 1980. a. U.S. Department of the Interior, Bureau of Land Management, Washington, DC 20240.

333.33   US
MARKET PROFILES. 1986. a. Urban Land Institute, 1090 Vermont Ave., N.W., Washington, DC 20005. TEL 202-289-8500. Ed. J. Thomas Black. charts. illus. stat.

333.33   690   US   ISSN 0732-815X
MEANS SQUARE FOOT COSTS; residential, commercial, industrial, institutional. 1980. a. $45.95. R.S. Means Company, Inc., 100 Construction Plaza, Kingston, MA 02364. Ed. William D. Mahoney. circ. 14,000. (also avail. in microform)
   Formerly: Appraisal Manual (ISSN 0272-0051)

333.33   CN
METROTRENDS. 1958. a. Can.$25. Real Estate Board of Greater Vancouver, 1101 W. Broadway, Vancouver, B.C. V6H 1G2, Canada. TEL 604-736-4551. stat. circ. 1,000. (looseleaf format)
   Formerly (until 1984): Real Estate Trends in Metropolitan Vancouver (ISSN 0085-5405)

333.33   917   CN   ISSN 0713-8369
MOVING TO & AROUND ALBERTA. a. Can.$4.95. Moving Publications Ltd., Box 272, Station C, Winnipeg, Man. R3M 3S7, Canada. TEL 204-837-5348.

333.33   917   CN   ISSN 0228-7153
MOVING TO & AROUND MARITIMES & NEWFOUNDLAND. biennial. Can.$4.95. Moving Publications Ltd., Box 272, Sta. C, Winnipeg, Man. R3M 3S7, Canada. TEL 204-837-5348.

333.33   917   CN   ISSN 0715-8114
MOVING TO & AROUND SOUTHWESTERN ONTARIO. biennial. Can.$4.95. Moving Publications Ltd., Box 272, Sta. C, Winnipeg, Man. R3M 3S7, Canada. TEL 204-837-5348.

333.33   917   CN   ISSN 0715-7053
MOVING TO & AROUND WINNIPEG & MANITOBA. biennial. Can.$4.95. Moving Publications Ltd., Box 272, Sta. C, Winnipeg, Man. R3M 3S7, Canada. TEL 204-837-5348.

333.33   917   CN   ISSN 0229-5040
MOVING TO DALLAS/FORT WORTH. a. Can.$4.95. Moving Publications Ltd., Box 272, Station C, Winnipeg, Man. R3M 3S7, Canada. TEL 204-837-5348.

333.33   917   CN   ISSN 0713-4819
MOVING TO DENVER. a. Can.$4.95. Moving Publications Ltd., Box 272, Station C, Winnipeg, Man. R3M 3S7, Canada. TEL 204-837-5348.

333.33   917.13   CN   ISSN 0226-7837
MOVING TO OTTAWA/HULL. (Text in English and French) 1978. a. Moving Publications Ltd., Box 272, Station C, Winnipeg, Man. R3M 3S7, Canada. TEL 204-837-5348. illus.

333.33   917.124   CN   ISSN 0225-5383
MOVING TO SASKATCHEWAN. 1980. biennial. Can.$4.95. Moving Publications Ltd., Box 272, Station C, Winnipeg, Man. R3M 3S7, Canada. TEL 204-837-5348. illus.

333.33   917   CN
MOVING TO THE SAN FRANCISCO BAY AND GREATER SACRAMENTO. a. Can.$4.95. Moving Publications Ltd., Box 272, Station C, Winnipeg, Man. R3M 3S7, Canada. TEL 204-837-5348.
   Formerly: Moving to San Fransisco and the Bay Area (ISSN 0714-7295)

333.33   917.11   CN   ISSN 0226-7276
MOVING TO VANCOUVER & B.C. 1977. a. Moving Publications Ltd., Box 272, Station C, Winnipeg, Man. R3M 3S7, Canada. TEL 204-837-5348. illus.
   Formerly: Moving to Vancouver/Victoria (ISSN 0702-9187)

333.33 US
NATIONAL REAL ESTATE INVESTOR
DIRECTORY. a. $29.95 included in subscr. to
National Real Estate Investor. Communication
Channels, Inc., 6255 Barfield Rd., Atlanta, GA
30328. TEL 404-256-9800. Ed. Barbara Katinsky.
adv. circ. 28,000. (also avail. in microfilm)

333.3
NATIONAL ROSTER OF REALTORS
DIRECTORY. 1962. a. $50 to qualified personell. ‡
(National Association of Realtors) Stamats
Communications Inc., 427 Sixth Ave., S.E., Cedar
Rapids, IA 52406. TEL 319-364-6032. Ed. Evelyn
Oldridge. adv. illus. circ. 10,000.
Formerly: National Roster of Realtors (ISSN
0090-1741)

333.33 UK ISSN 0078-3048
OCCASIONAL PAPERS IN ESTATE
MANAGEMENT. 1966. irreg., no.11, 1978. price
varies. College of Estate Management,
Whiteknights, Reading RG6 2AW, England.

OLD-HOUSE JOURNAL CATALOG. see
BUILDING AND CONSTRUCTION

333.33 US
PREVIEWS GUIDE TO THE WORLD'S FINE
REAL ESTATE. 1935. a. plus supps. $18. Previews
Inc. (Subsidiary of: Allstate Enterprises, Inc.) 51
Weaver St., Greenwich, CT 06830. TEL 203-622-
8600. adv. circ. 20,000.

333.33 CN
PRINCE EDWARD ISLAND. LAND
DEVELOPMENT CORPORATION. ANNUAL
REPORT. 1971. a. Land Development Corporation,
Charlottetown, P.E.1., Canada. TEL 902-892-4137.
illus.

333.33 US
PRIVATE ISLAND "INVENTORY".* 1975. a., (plus
irreg. supplements) $20. Private Islands Unlimited,
Box 22775, Ft. Lauderdale, FL 33335-2775. Ed.
Donald C. Ward. adv. circ. 5,000.

333.33 HK
PROPERTY REVIEW; a summary of supply,
vacancies, rentals and purchase prices. (Text in
English) 1975. a. Rating and Valuation Department,
500 Hennessy Road, 26th Floor, Hennessy Centre,
Causeway Bay, Hong Kong. circ. 1,000.

333.33 UK ISSN 0305-5752
PROPERTY STUDIES IN THE U.K. AND
OVERSEAS. 1974. irreg., no.9, 1984. price varies.
College of Estate Management, Whiteknights,
Reading RG6 2AW, England. Eds. A.W. Davidson,
J.E. Leonard.

333.33 US
R E I S REPORT: INDUSTRIAL MARKET
SERVICE. 1980. irreg. price varies. R E I S
Reports, Inc., 250 W. 57th St., Ste. 1701, New
York, NY 10107. TEL 212-247-4433. Ed. Lloyd
Lynford.

332.6 333.33 US ISSN 0095-1374
R.E.I.T. FACT BOOK. 1974. a. $15. National
Association of Real Estate Investment Trusts, 1101
17th St., N.W., Washington, DC 20036. TEL 202-
785-8717. Ed. Michael E. Dunbar. illus. circ. 3,500.

RAND MCNALLY PLACES RATED ALMANAC.
see HOUSING AND URBAN PLANNING

347.2 CN
REAL ESTATE DEVELOPMENT ANNUAL. 1965.
a. Can.$45. Maclean-Hunter Ltd., Business
Publication Division, Maclean-Hunter Bldg., 777
Bay St., Toronto, Ont. M5W 1A7, Canada. TEL
416-596-5760. Ed. John Fennell. adv. circ. 10,206.
Formerly: Canadian Real Estate Annual (ISSN
0068-9564)

333.3 US ISSN 0098-8936
REAL ESTATE DIRECTORY OF MANHATTAN.
a. $495. Real Estate Data, Inc., 475 Fifth Ave., Ste.
1901, New York, NY 10017. TEL 212-532-2705.
Formerly: Real Estate Directory of the Borough
of Manhattan.

333.33 US
REAL ESTATE FOR PROFESSIONAL
PRACTITIONERS: A WILEY SERIES. 1973.
irreg., latest 1986. price varies. John Wiley & Sons,
Inc., 605 Third Ave., New York, NY 10016. TEL
212-850-6000. Ed. D. Clurman.

333.33 AT
REAL ESTATE INSTITUTE OF QUEENSLAND.
ANNUAL REPORT. no.62, 1981. a. Real Estate
Institute of Queensland, 88 Brunswick St., Fortitude
Valley, Qld. 4006, Australia. circ. 1,000.

333.33 US ISSN 0079-9890
REAL ESTATE REPORTS. 1966. irreg., no.36, 1982.
price varies. University of Connecticut, Center for
Real Estate & Urban Economic Studies, U-41, Rm.
426, 368 Fairfield Rd., Storrs, CT 06268. TEL 203-
486-3227. Ed. Judith B. Paesani. circ. 500. (also
avail. in microfiche; Braille)

333.33 US
REAL ESTATE TAX ANALYST. 1985. irreg. $78.
Federal Research Press, 210 Lincoln St., Ste. 700,
Boston, MA 02111-2491. TEL 800-682-5759. Ed.
Lewis R. Kaster.

333 US ISSN 0090-399X
REALTY BLUEBOOK. 1966. a. $22. Professional
Publishing Corp., 122 Paul Dr., San Rafael, CA
94903. TEL 415-472-1964. Ed. R.W. de Heer. circ.
100,000.

333.33 US ISSN 0731-7999
RESEARCH IN REAL ESTATE. 1981. a. $24.75 to
individuals; institutions $49.50. J A I Press Inc.,
Box 1678, 36 Sherwood Pl., Greenwich, CT 06836.
TEL 203-661-7602. Ed. C.F. Sirmans.

333.33 US
RETAIL TENANT DIRECTORY. 1978. a. $250.
National Mall Monitor, (Subsidiary of: Maclean
Hunter Media) 2535 Landmark Dr., No. 207,
Clearwater, FL 33519. Ed. Donna Wetmore. circ. 2,
000.

STATE OF FLORIDA LAND DEVELOPMENT
GUIDE. see HOUSING AND URBAN
PLANNING

STRUCTURING FOREIGN INVESTMENT IN U.S.
REAL ESTATE. see LAW

333.33 690 UK
STUDIES IN CONSTRUCTION ECONOMY. 1978.
irreg., no.3, 1981. price varies. College of Estate
Management, Whiteknights, Reading RG6 2AW,
England.

333.33 DK
TYPEHUS REVYEN. a. Bonniers Specialmagasiner,
Noerre Farimagsgade 49, 1375 Copenhagen K,
Denmark. adv. circ. 15,000.

U S REAL ESTATE REGISTER. see
ADVERTISING AND PUBLIC RELATIONS

U.S. FEDERAL HOME LOAN BANK BOARD.
REPORT. see BUSINESS AND ECONOMICS —
Banking And Finance

U.S. FEDERAL HOME LOAN BANK BOARD.
TRENDS IN THE SAVINGS AND LOAN
FIELD. see BUSINESS AND ECONOMICS —
Banking And Finance

333.33 US ISSN 0068-5968
UNIVERSITY OF CALIFORNIA, BERKELEY.
CENTER FOR REAL ESTATE AND URBAN
ECONOMICS. REPRINT SERIES. 1948. irreg.,
latest no.50. price varies. ‡ University of California,
Berkeley, Center for Real Estate and Urban
Economics, 156 Barrows Hall, Berkeley, CA 94720.

333.3 US
UNIVERSITY OF CALIFORNIA, BERKELEY.
CENTER FOR REAL ESTATE AND URBAN
ECONOMICS. WORKING PAPER. 1950. irreg.,
no.87-123, 1984. price varies. ‡ University of
California, Berkeley, Center for Real Estate and
Urban Economics, 156 Barrows Hall, Berkeley, CA
94720.
Formerly: University of California, Berkeley.
Center for Real Estate and Urban Economics.
Research Report (ISSN 0068-5976)

333.33 US
UNIVERSITY OF CONNECTICUT. CENTER FOR
REAL ESTATE AND URBAN ECONOMIC
STUDIES. ANNUAL REPORT. 1965. a.
University of Connecticut, Center for Real Estate
and Urban Economic Studies, U-41, Rm. 426, 368
Fairfield Rd., Storrs, CT 06268. TEL 203-486-3227.

333.33 US ISSN 0069-9047
UNIVERSITY OF CONNECTICUT. CENTER FOR
REAL ESTATE AND URBAN ECONOMIC
STUDIES. GENERAL SERIES. 1968. irreg., no.18,
1985. price varies. ‡ University of Connecticut,
Center for Real Estate and Urban Economic
Studies, U-41, Rm. 426, 368 Fairfield Rd., Storrs,
CT 06268. TEL 203-486-3227. Ed. Judith B.
Paesani. circ. 300.

333 US
UNIVERSITY OF CONNECTICUT. CENTER FOR
REAL ESTATE AND URBAN ECONOMIC
STUDIES. WORKING PAPER. 1970. irreg., no.4,
1977. free. University of Connecticut, Center for
Real Estate and Urban Economic Studies, U-41,
Rm. 426, 368 Fairfield Rd., Storrs, CT 06268. TEL
203-486-3227. Ed. Judith B. Paesani.

333.33 US ISSN 0511-8719
WHERE TO RETIRE ON A SMALL INCOME.
biennial. $4.95. Harian Publications, One Vernon
Ave., Floral Park, NY 11001. TEL 516-437-3440.
Ed. Norman D. Ford. charts. illus.

REAL ESTATE — Abstracting, Bibliographies, Statistics

333 010 368 US
BIBLIOGRAPHY OF APPRAISAL LITERATURE.
1974. irreg. $30. American Society of Appraisers,
Box 17265, Washington, DC 20041. TEL 703-620-
3838. Ed. Dexter D. MacBride.

333.33 314 DK ISSN 0070-3508
DENMARK. DANMARKS STATISTIK.
EJENDOMSSALG/SALES OF REAL
PROPERTY. (Text in Danish; notes in English)
1845/49. a. Kr.34.43. Danmarks Statistik,
Sejroegade, 2100 Copenhagen OE, Denmark.

333.33 SA
SOUTH AFRICA. CENTRAL STATISTICAL
SERVICE. TRANSFERS OF RURAL
IMMOVABLE PROPERTY. (Report No. 06-02) a.,
latest 1986. Central Statistical Service, Private Bag
X44, Pretoria 0001, South Africa.
Formerly: South Africa. Department of Statistics.
Transfers of Rural Immovable Property.

333.34 314 SP
SPAIN. INSTITUTO NACIONAL DE
ESTADISTICA. LA RENTA NACIONAL EN
(YEAR) Y SU DISTRIBUTION. a. 1700 ptas.
Instituto Nacional de Estadistica, P de la Castellana,
183, Madrid 16, Spain.
Formerly: Spain. Instituto Nacional de
Estadistica. Informe sobre la Distribucion de las
Rentas (ISSN 0081-3370)

RELIGIONS AND THEOLOGY

see also Religions and Theology—Islamic;
Religions and Theology—Judaic;
Religions and Theology—Oriental;
Religions and Theology—Protestant;
Religions and Theology—Roman
Catholic; Religions and Theology—Other
Denominations and Sects

268 US ISSN 0277-1071
A A R ACADEMY SERIES. 1974. irreg. (American
Academy of Religion) Scholars Press, Box 1608,
Decatur, GA 30031-1608. Ed. Carl Raschke.
Formerly: A A R Dissertation Series.

200 US ISSN 0084-6287
A A R STUDIES IN RELIGION. 1970. irreg., no.34,
1984. (American Academy of Religion) Scholars
Press, Box 1608, Decatur, GA 30031-1608. Eds.
Charley Hardwick, James Duke.

200   US
A T L A BIBLIOGRAPHY SERIES. no.17, 1987. irreg. price varies. (American Theological Library Association) Scarecrow Press, Inc., 52 Liberty St., Box 4167, Metuchen, NJ 08840. TEL 201-548-8600. Ed. Kenneth E. Rowe.

200   US
A T L A MONOGRAPH SERIES. no.22, 1985. irreg. (American Theological Library Association) Scarecrow Press, Inc., 52 Liberty St., Box 4167, Metuchen, NJ 08840. TEL 201-548-8600. Ed. Dr. Kenneth E. Rowe.

255   NO   ISSN 0400-227X
AARBOK FOR DEN NORSKE KIRKE. 1951. a. Kr.55. Verbum Kirkeraadet, Underhaugsveien 15, Oslo 3, Norway. Ed. Gunnar Roedahl. stat. index. circ. 3,500.

200   DK   ISSN 0901-4497
AARHUS UNIVERSITET. TEOLOGISKE FAKULTET. BIBLIOGRAFI. a. free. Aarhus Universitet, Teologiske Fakultet, Nordre Ringgade 1, DK-Aarhus 8000 C, Denmark.

ABINGDON CLERGY INCOME TAX GUIDE. see BUSINESS AND ECONOMICS — Public Finance, Taxation

200   DK   ISSN 0065-1354
ACTA JUTLANDICA. 1985. irreg. Bibliotekscentralen, Telegrafvej 5, DK-2750 Ballerup, Denmark.

ACTA PHILOSOPHICA ET THEOLOGICA. see PHILOSOPHY

200   NE   ISSN 0065-1672
ACTA THEOLOGICA DANICA. (Text in English and German) 1958. irreg., vol.19, 1986. price varies. E. J. Brill, P.O. Box 9000, 2300 PA Leiden, Netherlands.

200   US   ISSN 0272-7250
ALBANIAN CATHOLIC BULLETIN/BULETINI KATOLIK SHQIPTAR. (Text in Albanian and English) 1980. a. donations. Albanian Catholic Information Center, Box 1217 University, Santa Clara, CA 95053. Ed. Gjon Sinishta. bk. rev. circ. 1,500. (back issues avail.)

200   UK
ALCUIN. 1897. a. $18. Alcuin Club, 5 St. Andrew St., London EC4A 3AB, England. bk. rev.

266   KE
ALL AFRICA CONFERENCE OF CHURCHES. REFUGEE DEPARTMENT. PROGRESS REPORT. a., latest 1974. All Africa Conference of Churches, Refugee Department, Pioneer House, Government Rd., Box 20301, Nairobi, Kenya.

266   KE
ALL AFRICA CONFERENCE OF CHURCHES. REFUGEE DEPARTMENT. PROJECT LIST. a., latest 1977. All Africa Conference of Churches, Refugee Department, Pioneer House, Government Rd., Box 20301, Nairobi, Kenya.

ALLE BOERNS JUL. see CHILDREN AND YOUTH — For

ALLIANCE REVIEW. see EDUCATION

200   800   DK   ISSN 0900-1573
ALMANAK FOR TEOLOGI OG LITTERATUR. 1985. a. Kr.138. Forlaget Anis, Aarhus, Denmark. bk. rev.

240   SP
ALMANAQUE MISAL. a. 424 ptas.($3.50) Editorial Sal Terrae, Guevara 20, Santander, Spain.

200   US
AMERICAN ACADEMY OF RELIGION. ANNUAL MEETING. a. Scholars Press, Box 1608, Decatur, GA 30031-1608. (Co-sponsor: Society of Biblical Literature)

291.2   US   ISSN 0740-0446
AMERICAN UNIVERSITY STUDIES. SERIES 7. THEOLOGY AND RELIGION. 1984. irreg. Peter Lang Publishing, Inc., 62 W. 45th St., New York, NY 10036. TEL 212-302-6740. Ed. Jay Wilson.

200   NE   ISSN 0169-0272
AMSTERDAM STUDIES IN THEOLOGY. 1979. irreg. Editions Rodopi B.V., Keizersgracht 302-304, 1016 EX Amsterdam, Netherlands.

809   AU
ANALECTA CARTUSIANA; review for Carthusian history and spirituality. (Text in various languages) 1970. irreg., no.113, 1986. DM.65 per no. Universitaet Salzburg, Institut fuer Englische Sprache, Akademiestr. 24, A-5020 Salzburg, Austria. Ed. James Hogg. circ. 300. (back issues avail) Indexed: M.L.A.

200   FR   ISSN 0066-2860
ANNUAIRE DES INSTITUTS DE RELIGIEUSES EN FRANCE. 1959. irreg., latest 1980. 50 F. Service National des Vocations Francais, 106 rue du Bac, 75341 Paris, France.

200   US   ISSN 0735-0864
ANSELM STUDIES; an occasional journal. 1983. irreg. $35. Kraus International Publications (Subsidiary of: Kraus-Thomson Organization Ltd.) One Water St., White Plains, NY 10601. TEL 914-761-9600.

200   GW
ARBEITEN ZUR GESCHICHTE DES PIETISMUS. 1979. irreg. Vandenhoeck & Ruprecht, Robert-Bosch-Breite 6, Postfach 3753, D-3400 Goettingen, W. Germany (B.R.D.) Ed.Bd.

200   GW
ARBEITEN ZUR KIRCHLICHEN ZEITGESCHICHTE. REIHE B; Darstellung. 1975. irreg. Vandenhoeck & Ruprecht, Robert-Bosch-Breite 6, Postfach 3753, D-3400 Goettingen, W. Germany (B.R.D.) Ed.Bd.

200   GW
ARBEITEN ZUR PASTORALTHEOLOGIE. 1962. irreg. (Verlagsbuchhandlung) Vandenhoeck & Ruprecht, Robert-Bosch-Breite 6, Postfach 3753, D-3400 Goettingen, W. Germany (B.R.D.) Ed.Bd.

200   GW   ISSN 0066-5711
ARBEITEN ZUR THEOLOGIE. REIHE 1. 1960. irreg., vol.69, 1984. price varies. Calwer Verlag, Scharnhauser Str.44, 7000 Stuttgart 70, W. Germany (B.R.D.)

243   GW   ISSN 0066-6386
ARCHIV FUER LITURGIEWISSENSCHAFT. 1950. a. DM.208. (Abt-Herwegen-Institut fuer Liturgische und Monastische Forschung) Verlag Friedrich Pustet, Gutenbergstr. 8, 8400 Regensburg 1, W. Germany (B.R.D.) Ed. Emmanuel v. Severus. bk. rev. circ. 800. Indexed: CERDIC. New Test.Abstr. Rel.Ind.One.

209   GW   ISSN 0066-6432
ARCHIV FUER MITTELRHEINISCHE KIRCHENGESCHICHTE. 1949. a. DM.48. Gesellschaft fuer Mittelrheinische Kirchengeschichte, Jesuitenstr. 13, 5500 Trier, W. Germany (B.R.D.) Indexed: Bibl.Cart.

200   150   GW   ISSN 0084-6724
ARCHIV FUER RELIGIONSPSYCHOLOGIE. vol.4, 1929. irreg., vol.15, 1982. price varies. (Internationale Gesellschaft fuer Religionspsychologie) Vandenhoeck und Ruprecht, Theaterstr. 13, Postfach 37 53, 3400 Goettingen, W. Germany (B.R.D.) Eds. K. Krenn, Wilhelm Keilbach.

209   GW   ISSN 0066-6491
ARCHIV FUER SCHLESISCHE KIRCHENGESCHICHTE. 1949. a. DM.25. (Institut fuer Ostdeutsche Kirchen- und Kulturgeschichte) Verlag August Lax, Postfach 10 08 65, 3200 Hildesheim, W. Germany (B.R.D.) circ. 900. (reprint service avail. from CIP) Indexed: Numis.Lit.

291.64   US
ARCHIVE FOR REFORMATION HISTORY. LITERATURE REVIEW/ARCHIV FUER REFORMATIONSGESCHICHTE. LITERATURBERICHT. 1972. a. $24. American Society for Reformation Research, 6477 San Bonita, St. Louis, MO 63105.

260   IT   ISSN 0066-6688
ARCHIVIO ITALIANO PER LA STORIA DELLA PIETA. (Text in language of contributor) 1951. irreg., vol. 7, 1980. price varies. Edizioni di Storia e Letteratura, Via Lancellotti 18, 00186 Rome, Italy. Ed. Romana Guarnieri.

200   949.5   GR
ARISTOTELION PANEPISTEMION THESSALONIKES. THEOLOGIKE SCHOLE. EPISTEMONIKE EPETERIS. 1953. a. Theologike Schole Panepistemiou Thessalonikes, Serron 39, Triandria, Salonika, Greece. Indexed: Chem.Abstr.

200   DK   ISSN 0107-4520
ARKEN-TRYK. no.15, 1982. irreg. price varies. (Teologiske Fakultet) Forlaget Arken, Koebmagegade 44-46, 1150 Copenhagen K, Denmark.

ARMARIUM CODICUM INSIGNIUM. see HISTORY — History Of Europe

200   060   FR   ISSN 0066-8907
ASSOCIATION DES AMIS DE PIERRE TEILHARD DE CHARDIN. BULLETIN. 1966. a. Association des Amis de Pierre Teilhard de Chardin, 38 rue Geoffroy-Saint-Hilaire, 75005 Paris, France. bibl.

378   US
ASSOCIATION FOR PROFESSIONAL EDUCATION FOR MINISTRY. REPORT OF THE BIENNIAL MEETING. 1950. biennial. $10. Association for Professional Education for Ministry, c/o Oliver Williams, Pres., University of Notre Dame, Notre Dame, IN 46556 TEL 219-239-5000. (Orders to: Joseph Kelly, Treas., St. Bernard's Seminary, 2260 Lake Ave., Rochester, NY 14612) Ed. Gaylord Noyce. circ. 400.
Missions

230   IT
ASSOCIATION INTERNATIONALE D'ETUDES PATRISTIQUES. BULLETIN D'INFORMATION ET DE LIAISON. (Text in English, French) 1968. irreg., 1-2/yr. 30 F. per no. for libraries only. (International Association for Patristic Studies - Association Internationale d'Etudes Patristiques) Brepols Publisher, c/o A. Di Berardino, Sec. Gen., Institutum Patristicum Augustinianum, Via S. Uffizio, 25, 00193 Rome, Italy (Subscr. to: B. Gain, 7, av. Aumont, 60500 Chantilly, France) Ed. A. di Berardino. bk. rev. bibl. circ. 800.

268   US   ISSN 0362-1472
ASSOCIATION OF THEOLOGICAL SCHOOLS IN THE UNITED STATES AND CANADA. BULLETIN. 1937. biennial. $5. Association of Theological Schools, Box 130, Vandalia, OH 45377. TEL 513-898-4654. Ed. David Schuler. circ. 2,000.
Formerly: American Association of Theological Schools in the United States and Canada. Bulletin (ISSN 0065-7360)

268   US
ASSOCIATION OF THEOLOGICAL SCHOOLS IN THE UNITED STATES AND CANADA. DIRECTORY. 1918. a. $3.50. Association of Theological Schools, Box 130, Vandalia, OH 45377. TEL 513-898-4654. Ed. Jill Scott Norton.
Formerly: American Association of Theological Schools in the United States and Canada. Directory (ISSN 0065-7379)

ATHEIST. see PHILOSOPHY

220   AT   ISSN 0045-0308
AUSTRALIAN BIBLICAL REVIEW. 1951. a. Aus.$4.50($5.50) Fellowship for Biblical Studies, c/o Queen's College, University of Melbourne, Parkville, Vic. 3052, Australia. Eds. E.F. Osborn, N.M. Watson. bk. rev. circ. 350-400. Indexed: Old Test.Abstr. CERDIC. New Test.Abstr. Rel.Ind.One. Rel.& Theol.Abstr.

200   283   AT   ISSN 0812-0811
AUSTRALIAN LECTIONARY (YEAR) 1978. a. Aus.$2. Anglican Information Office, 1st Floor, St. Andrews House, Sydney Square, N.S.W. 2000, Australia. Ed. Gilbert Sinden. circ. 13,000. (back issues avail.)

297.89   CN   ISSN 0708-5052
BAHA'I STUDIES. 1976. irreg. Can.$4 per no. Association for Baha'i Studies, 34 Copernicus St., Ottawa, Ont. K1N 7K4, Canada. TEL 613-233-1903. Ed.Bd. circ. 2,000.

RELIGIONS AND THEOLOGY

297.89 IS ISSN 0045-1320
BAHA'I WORLD. (Text primarily in English; occasional articles in French, German and Persian) 1925. irreg., vol.17, 1982. price varies. Baha'i World Centre, Box 155, Haifa 31-001, Israel (U.S. dist.: Baha'i Publishing Trust, 415 Linden Ave., Wilmette, Illinois 60091) Ed. Roger White. circ. 15,000.

970 001 US ISSN 0067-3129
BAMPTON LECTURES IN AMERICA. 1949. irreg., no.20, 1978. price varies. Columbia University Press, 562 W. 113th St., New York, NY 10025. TEL 212-678-6777.

BEITRAEGE ZUR GESCHICHTE DER PHILOSOPHIE UND THEOLOGIE DES MITTELALTERS NEUE FOLGE. see *PHILOSOPHY*

266 GW ISSN 0342-1341
BEITRAEGE ZUR GESCHICHTE DES ALTEN MOENCHTUMS UND DES BENEDIKTINERORDENS. 1912. irreg. price varies. Aschendorffsche Verlagsbuchhandlung, Soester Str. 13, 4400 Muenster, W. Germany (B.R.D.) Ed. Emmanuel v. Severus.

230 GW ISSN 0067-5172
BEITRAEGE ZUR OEKUMENISCHEN THEOLOGIE. 1967. irreg., vol.18, 1981. price varies. Ferdinand Schoeningh, Juehenplatz 1, 4790 Paderborn, W. Germany (B.R.D.) Ed. Heinrich Fries. circ. 500.

260 GW
BERCKERS KATOLISCHER TASCHENKALENDER. 1955. a. DM.8.50. Verlag Butzon und Bercker, Hoogeweg 71, Postfach 215, 4178 Kevelaer, W. Germany (B.R.D.) circ. 20,000.
Former titles: Berckers Taschenkalender; Berckers Katholischer Taschenkalender.

200 GW ISSN 0174-2477
BERLINER ISLAMSTUDIEN. 1981. irreg., vol.4, 1986. price varies. (Institut fuer Islamwissenschaft der Freien Universitaet Berlin) Franz Steiner Verlag Wiesbaden GmbH, Birkenwaldstr. 44, Postfach 347, D-7000 Stuttgart 1, W. Germany (B.R.D.) Ed.Bd.

220 GW
BIBEL IM JAHR(YEAR) 1964. a. DM.6.80. Katholisches Bibelwerk e.V., Silberburgstr. 121, 7000 Stuttgart 1, W. Germany (B.R.D.) Ed. P.G. Mueller. adv. bk. rev. illus. index.

220 US ISSN 0067-6535
BIBLICAL RESEARCH. 1956. a. $5. (Chicago Society of Biblical Research) Franciscan Publishers, Franciscan Center, Pulaski, WI 54162. TEL 312-241-7800. Ed. Robert Boling. index. circ. 700. (also avail. in microform from UMI; back issues avail.) Indexed: Old Test.Abstr. CERDIC. New Test.Abstr. Rel.Ind.One.

200 US ISSN 0277-0474
BIBLICAL SCHOLARSHIP IN NORTH AMERICA. irreg. (Society of Biblical Literature) Scholars Press, Box 1608, Decatur, GA 30031-1608. Ed. Kent Harold Richards.

BIBLIOGRAFIA TEOLOGICA COMENTADA DEL AREA IBEROAMERICANA. see *BIBLIOGRAPHIES*

200 SP ISSN 0067-740X
BIBLIOTECA DE TEOLOGIA. 1964. irreg., no.16, 1983. price varies. (Universidad de Navarra, Facultad de Teologia) Ediciones Universidad de Navarra, S.A., Apdo. 396, 31080 Pamplona, Spain.

200 SW
BIBLIOTECA THEOLOGIAE PRACTICAE. (Text in Swedish; summaries in English or German) 1957. irreg., no. 40, 1983. price varies. Liber Forlag, S-205 10, Malmo, Sweden. Eds. Carl-Gustaf Andren, Aake Andren.

209 PL ISSN 0519-8658
BIBLIOTEKA PISARZY REFORMACYJNYCH. (Text in Latin and Polish) 1958. irreg., vol.15, 1982. price varies. (Polska Akademia Nauk, Instytut Filozofii i Socjologii) Panstwowe Wydawnictwo Naukowe, Ul. Miodowa 10, 00-251 Warsaw, Poland (Dist. by: Ars Polona, Krakowskie Przedmiescie 7, 00-068 Warsaw, Poland) Ed. L. Szczucki. circ. 350.

BIBLIOTHECA DISSIDENTIUM. see *BIBLIOGRAPHIES*

200 BE
BIBLIOTHECA EPHEMERIDUM THEOLOGICARUM LOVANIENSIUM. vol.31, 1972. irreg, vol.77, 1987. Leuven University Press, Krakenstraat 3, B-3000 Louvain, Belgium. Indexed: Rel.Ind.Two.

200 NE
BIBLIOTHECA HUMANISTICA & REFORMATORICA. (Text in English, French or German) 1971. irreg., vol.37, 1986. price varies. De Graaf Publishers, Box 6, 2420 AA Nieuwkoop, Netherlands.

220 SZ ISSN 0582-1673
BIBLISCHE BEITRAEGE. 1961. irreg., no.13, 1977. price varies. (Schweizerisches Katholisches Bibelwerk) Verlag S K B, c/o Pierre Casetti, Ed., Pfisternweg 5, CH-6015 Reussbuehl, Switzerland. adv. illus. circ. 1,750.

220 GW ISSN 0523-5154
BIBLISCHE UNTERSUCHUNGEN. 1967. irreg., vol.17, 1986. price varies. Verlag Friedrich Pustet, Gutenbergstr. 8, 8400 Regensburg 1, W. Germany (B.R.D.) Eds. Jost Eckert, Josef Hainz. circ. 800.

220 GW
BIBLISCHES SEMINAR. 1967. irreg. price varies. Calwer Verlag, Scharnhauser Str. 44, 7000 Stuttgart 70, W. Germany (B.R.D.)

270 940 GW
BLAETTER FUER WUERTTEMBERGISCHE KIRCHENGESCHICHTE. 1895. a. DM.60. Verein fuer Wuerttembergische Kirchengeschichte, Gaensheidestr. 4, Postfach 92, 7000 Stuttgart 1, W. Germany (B.R.D.) Eds. Gerhard Schaefer, Martin Brecht. bk. rev. index. Indexed: Hist.Abstr. Amer.Hist.& Life.

200 100 US
BOSTON UNIVERSITY STUDIES IN PHILOSOPHY AND RELIGION. 1980. irreg. University of Notre Dame Press, Notre Dame, IN 46556. TEL 219-239-6346. Ed. Leroy S. Rouner. Indexed: Rel.Ind.Two.

200 GW ISSN 0068-0443
BOTSCHAFT DES ALTEN TESTAMENTS; Erlauterungen Alttestamentlicher Schriften. 1958. irreg., vol.7/8, 1980. price varies. Calwer Verlag, Scharnhauser Str. 44, 7000 Stuttgart 70, W. Germany (B.R.D.)

207 268.8 US ISSN 0068-2721
BROADMAN COMMENTS; INTERNATIONAL SUNDAY SCHOOL LESSONS. 1945. a. or q. $5.95. Broadman Press, 127 Ninth Ave. N., Nashville, TN 37234. TEL 615-251-2000. Ed. Donald F. Ackland. circ. 14,500.

200 SZ
C C I A BACKGROUND INFORMATION. 1975. irreg., (approx. 2/yr.) $20. World Council of Churches, Commission on International Affairs, 150 Route de Ferney, Box 66, 1211 Geneva 20, Switzerland. Ed. Erich Weingaertner. circ. 2,000.

200 CN
CAHIERS DE RECHERCHE ETHIQUE. (Text in French) 1977. irreg. price varies. Editions Fides, 5710 Ave. Decelles, Montreal, Que. H3S 2C5, Canada. TEL 514-735-6406. Indexed: CERDIC.

220 GW
CALWER THEOLOGISCHE MONOGRAPHIEN. REIHE A: BIBELWISSENSCHAFT. 1972. irreg., no.14, 1984. price varies. Calwer Verlag, Scharnhauser Str. 44, 7000 Stuttgart 70, W. Germany (B.R.D.) Eds. Peter Stuhlmacher, Claus Westermann.

230 GW
CALWER THEOLOGISCHE MONOGRAPHIEN. REIHE B: SYSTEMATISCHE THEOLOGIE UND KIRCHENGESCHICHTE. 1973. irreg., no.9, 1985. price varies. Calwer Verlag, Scharnhauser Str. 44, 7000 Stuttgart 70, W. Germany (B.R.D.) Ed.Bd.

200 GW
CALWER THEOLOGISCHE MONOGRAPHIEN. REIHE C: PRAKTISCHE THEOLOGIE UND MISSIONSWISSENSCHAFT. 1973. irreg., vol.12, 1985. price varies. Calwer Verlag, Scharnhauser Str. 44, 7000 Stuttgart 70, W. Germany (B.R.D.) Eds. S.H. Buekle, M. Seitz.

277.1 CN ISSN 0701-4309
CANADIAN COUNCIL OF CHURCHES. RECORD OF PROCEEDINGS. 1944. triennial. Canadian Council of Churches - Conseil Canadien des Eglises, 40 St. Clair Ave., East, Toronto. Ont. M4T 1M9, Canada. TEL 416-921-4152.

220 CN ISSN 0068-970X
CANADIAN SOCIETY OF BIBLICAL STUDIES. BULLETIN/SOCIETE CANADIENNE DES ETUDES BIBLIQUES. BULLETIN. (Not issued 1960-1963) 1935. a. included in membership fee. Canadian Society of Biblical Studies, c/o Memorial University of Newfoundland, Dept. of Religious Studies, St. John's, Nfld. A1C 5S7, Canada. TEL 709-737-8166. Ed. Dr. D.J. Hawkin. circ. 220.

260 GW
CARITAS-KALENDER. 1924. a. DM.5.80. (Deutscher Caritasverband) Lambertus-Verlag GmbH, Woelflinstr. 4, Postfach 1026, 7800 Freiburg, W. Germany (B.R.D.) Ed. Peter Gralla. adv. circ. 70,000.

CARL NEWELL JACKSON LECTURES. see *FOLKLORE*

222 US
CATHOLIC BIBLE QUARTERLY MONOGRAPH SERIES. 1971. irreg. price varies. Catholic Biblical Association of America, Catholic University of America, Washington, DC 20064. TEL 202-635-5519. Ed.Bd. circ. 1,000. Indexed: Cath.Ind. Old Test.Abstr. Rel.Per. New Test.Abstr.

CATHOLIC HEALTH ASSOCIATION OF THE UNITED STATES. GUIDEBOOK. see *HOSPITALS*

CENTRE; Bible data bank. see *HUMANITIES: COMPREHENSIVE WORKS — Computer Applications*

CENTRO CAMUNO DI STUDI PREISTORICI. BOLLETTINO. see *ARCHAEOLOGY*

CENTRO CAMUNO DI STUDI PREISTORICI. SYMPOSIA. see *ART*

200 MW
CHANCELLOR COLLEGE. DEPARTMENT OF RELIGIOUS STUDIES. STAFF SEMINAR PAPER. no.4, 1979. irreg. Chancellor College, Department of Religious Studies, Box 280, Zomba, Malawi.

200 US
CHICAGO HISTORY OF AMERICAN RELIGION. 1973. irreg., latest 1981. price varies. University of Chicago Press, 5801 S. Ellis Ave., Chicago, IL 60637. TEL 312-962-7600. Ed. Martin E. Marty. adv. bk. rev. (reprint service avail. from UMI,ISI)

CHRISTIAN CHAMBER OF COMMERCE. CLASSIFIED MEMBERSHIP DIRECTORY. see *ADVERTISING AND PUBLIC RELATIONS*

275 PH ISSN 0045-6810
CHRISTIAN INSTITUTE FOR ETHNIC STUDIES IN ASIA. BULLETIN.* vol.4, 1970. 2-3/yr. Christian Institute for Ethnic Studies in Asia, Box 3167, Manila, Philippines. Eds. Alex J. Grant, Rufino Tima. bk. rev. bibl. charts.

320.532 US
CHRISTIAN PRISONERS IN THE U.S.S.R. 1981. a. (Society for the Study of Religion Under Communism) Keston College, U.S.A., Box 1310, Framingham, MA 01701 TEL 617-822-2965. (And: Keston College, Heathfield Rd., Keston, Kent BR2 6BA, England)
Formerly: Soviet Christian Prisoner List (ISSN 0278-1018)

207 US
CHRISTIAN RESEARCH JOURNAL. 1975. triennial. $7.50. Christian Research Institute, Box 500, San Juan Capistrano, CA 92693-0500. TEL 714-855-9926. Ed. Elliot Miller. adv. bk. rev. bibl. circ. 10,000.
Former titles: Forward (San Juan Capistrano) & Christian Research Institute. Newsletter (ISSN 0045-6845)

RELIGIONS AND THEOLOGY

200   MW
CHRISTIAN SERVICE COMMITTEE OF THE CHURCHES IN MALAWI. ANNUAL REPORT. (Text in English) a. free. Christian Service Committee of the Churches in Malawi, Box 51294, Limbe, Malawi.

268   UK
CHURCH POCKET BOOK AND DIARY. a. price varies. Society for Promoting Christian Knowledge, c/o Mrs. Cazz Colmer, Holy Trinity Church, Marylebone Rd., London NW1 4DU, England. circ. 6,000.
    Formerly: Churchman's Pocket Book and Diary (ISSN 0069-4029)

200 900   BE
CLAIRLIEU: TIJDSCHRIFT GEWIJD AAN DE GESCHIEDENIS DER KRUISHEREN. (Editions in Dutch, English, French and German) 1943. a. 350 Fr. Geschiedkundige Kring "Clairlieu", Catharinadal 3, 3590 Achel, Belgium. Ed. A. Ramaekers. bk. rev. Indexed: Hist.Abstr. Amer.Hist.& Life.

200   AG
COLECCION AMANECE. no.4, 1976. irreg. Editora Patria Grande, Casilla de Correo 5, Buenos Aires 1408, Argentina.

200   SP   ISSN 0069-505X
COLECCION CANONICA. 1959. irreg., no.89, 1986. price varies. (Universidad de Navarra, Facultad de Derecho Canonico) Ediciones Universidad de Navarra, S.A., Apdo. 396, 31080 Pamplona, Spain.
    Canon law

200   CK
COLECCION COMUNICACION.* 1977. irreg. Ediciones Paulinas, Apdo. 100282, Bogota, Colombia.

262.9   SP   ISSN 0210-0711
COLECTANEA DE JURISPRUDENCIA CANONICA. 1974. a. 850 ptas.($22) Universidad Pontificia de Salamanca, Calle Compania 1, Salamanca, Spain. Ed. Juan Luis Acebal.
    Canon law

369.4   UY
CONFEDERACION LATINOAMERICANA DE ASOCIACIONES CRISTIANAS DE JOVENES. CARTA. (Editions in English and Spanish) irreg. free. Confederacion Latinoamericana de Asociaciones Cristianas de Jovenes, Casilla 172, Montevideo, Uruguay.
    Formerly: Federacion Sudamericana de Asociaciones Cristianas de Jovenes. Noticias (ISSN 0428-1039)

200   SW   ISSN 0069-8946
CONIECTANEA BIBLICA. NEW TESTAMENT SERIES. (Text in English and French) 1966. irreg., no.14, 1985. price varies. Liber Forlag, S-205 10, Malmo, Sweden. Eds. Birger Gerhardsson, Lars Hartman.
    Continues: Acta Seminarii Neotestamentici Upsaliensis & Coniectanea Neotestamentica.

200   SW   ISSN 0069-8954
CONIECTANEA BIBLICA. OLD TESTAMENT SERIES. 1967. irreg., no.23, 1984. price varies. Liber Forlag, S-205 10, Malmo, Sweden. Eds. Tryggve Mettinger, Helmer Ringgren.

200   US
CONSULTATION ON CHURCH UNION. DIGEST. 1962. irreg., approx. every 18 mos., latest issue 1984. price varies. Consultation on Church Union, Research Park, 151 Wall St., Princeton, NJ 08540-1514. Ed. Gerald F. Moede.
    Former titles: Consultation on Church Union. Official Record (ISSN 0272-8958); Consultation on Church. Digest (ISSN 0589-4867)

200   US   ISSN 0196-7053
CONTRIBUTIONS TO THE STUDY OF RELIGION. 1981. irreg. price varies. Greenwood Press, 88 Post Rd. W., Box 5007, Westport, CT 06881. TEL 203-226-3571. Ed. Henry W. Bowden.

200   NE
COPTIC STUDIES. 1978. irreg. price varies. E.J. Brill, P.O. Box 9000, 2300 PA Leiden, Netherlands. Ed. M. Krause.

COURTENAY LIBRARY OF REFORMATION CLASSICS. see HISTORY — History Of Europe

COURTENAY REFORMATION FACSIMILES. see HISTORY — History Of Europe

COURTENAY STUDIES IN REFORMATION THEOLOGY. see HISTORY — History Of Europe

200   US   ISSN 0738-6001
CREATION/EVOLUTION. irreg. $9 for 4 issues. American Humanist Association, 7 Harwood Dr., Box 146, Amherst, NY 14226-0146. TEL 716-839-5080. Ed. Frederick Edwords. bk. rev. bibl. circ. 1,500. (back issues avail.)

200   CR
CUADERNOS D E I. 1980. irreg., no.5, 1981. Departamento Ecumenico de Investigaciones, Apdo. 339, S. Pedro Montes de Oca, San Jose, Costa Rica.

200   PE
CUADERNOS DE TEOLOGIA ACTUAL, CIENCIAS SOCIALES Y REALIDAD NACIONAL.* 1977. irreg. Centro de Proyeccion Cristiana, Javier Prado Oeste 595, Lima, Peru.

270   GW   ISSN 0070-2234
CUSANUS-GESELLSCHAFT. BUCHREIHE. 1964. irreg. price varies. Aschendorffsche Verlagsbuchhandlung, Soester Str. 13, 4400 Muenster, W. Germany (B.R.D.) Ed.Bd.

200   DK   ISSN 0900-1581
DAGDRYP; daglig bibellaesning. 1984. a. Kr.10. Bibliotekscentralen, Telegrafvej 5, DK-2750 Ballerup, Denmark.

220   DK   ISSN 0109-5846
DANSKE BIBELSELSKABS AARBOG. 1966. a. Kr.35. Danske Bibelselskab, Frederiksborggade 50, 1360 Copenhagen K, Denmark.
    Formerly: Danske Bibelselskabs Aarsberetning.

200   US   ISSN 0193-6883
DENOMINATIONS IN AMERICA. 1985. irreg. price varies. Greenwood Press, 88 Post Rd. W., Box 5007, Westport, CT 06881. TEL 203-226-3571. Ed. Harry Bowden.

200   US
DIRECTORY OF CHURCHES AND SYNAGOGUES. 1934. a. $10. Council of Churches of the City of New York, 475 Riverside Dr., New York, NY 10115. TEL 212-749-1214. Ed. Rev. Leland Gartrell. adv. circ. 2,500.

200   US
DIRECTORY OF DEPARTMENTS AND PROGRAMS OF RELIGIOUS STUDIES IN NORTH AMERICA. 1978. a. price varies. Council on the Study of Religion, Mercer University, Macon, GA 31207. TEL 912-741-2376. Ed. Watson E. Mills.

200   GW
DIREKTORIUM FUER DAS BISTUM MUENSTER. a. DM.8.50. Verlag Regensberg, Daimlerweg 58, Postfach 6748, 4400 Muenster, W. Germany (B.R.D.).

200   CN   ISSN 0318-0123
DONUM DEI. French edition (ISSN 0318-0131) (Editions in English and French) 1958. a. price varies. ‡ Canadian Religious Conference, 324 Laurier E, Ottawa, Ont. K1N 6P6, Canada. TEL 613-236-0824. Ed. Albert Landry. circ. 8,000(both edts.)

DOUAI MAGAZINE. see COLLEGE AND ALUMNI

200 947   BU   ISSN 0323-9578
DUKHOVNA AKADEMIYA SV. KLIMENT OKHRIDSKI. GODISHNIK. 1923. a. Sinodalno Izdatelstvo, Ul. Sveta Sofia 2, Sofia, Bulgaria (Subscr. to: Hemus Foreign Trade Co., 6 Ruski Blvd., 1000 Sofia, Bulgaria)
    Formerly: Sofia. Universitet. Bogoslovski Fakultet. Godishnik.

248.83   GW   ISSN 0012-7981
E S G - NACHRICHTEN. 1953. irreg., 7-8/yr. DM.25. (Evangelische Studentengemeinde in der Bundesrepublik Deutschland und Berlin (West)) Alektor-Verlag, Kniebisstr. 29, 7000 Stuttgart 1, W. Germany (B.R.D.) Ed. Ekkehard Pohlmann. adv. bk. rev. circ. 800. (processed)

200   FR   ISSN 0070-8860
ECRITS LIBRES. 1955. irreg., no.16, 1973. 63 F. Librairie Fischbacher, 33 rue de Seine, 75006 Paris, France.

200   SP
ENSENANZA DE LA RELIGION. 1982. irreg., no.2, 1986. price varies. (Universidad de Navarra, Facultad de Teologia) Ediciones Universidad de Navarra, S.A., Apdo. 396, 31080 Pamplona, Spain.

200 901   US
EPOCHE; journal of the history of religions at U.C.L.A. 1972. a. $6. University of California, Los Angeles, Graduate Student Association, 301 Kerchoff Hall, 308 Westwood Plaza, Los Angeles, CA 90024 (Subscr. to: Dept. of History, Los Angeles, CA 90024) Ed. Rick Talbott. cum.index: 1972-82. circ. 850. (back issues avail.)

ETUDES GREGORIENNES; revue de musicologie religieuse. see MUSIC

200 950   NE   ISSN 0531-1950
ETUDES PRELIMINAIRES AUX RELIGIONS ORIENTALES DANS L'EMPIRE ROMAIN. 1961. irreg., vol. 105, 1985. price varies. E. J. Brill, P.O. Box 9000, 2300 PA Leiden, Netherlands. Indexed: Rel.Ind.Two.

200 060   FR   ISSN 0082-2612
ETUDES TEILHARDIENNES/TEILHARDIAN STUDIES. 1969. irreg. price varies. Editions du Seuil, 27 rue Jacob, 75261 Paris Cedex 06, France. Ed. J.P. DeMoulin. Indexed: Rel.Ind.One.

255   US   ISSN 0362-0867
EXPLOR. 1975. a. free. Garrett-Evangelical Theological Seminary, c/o T. Thomas Nustad, 2121 Sheridan Rd., Evanston, IL 60201. Ed. S. Dean McBride. illus. circ. 6,500. Indexed: Old Test.Abstr. Rel.Ind.One.

200   US
FACT BOOK ON THEOLOGICAL EDUCATION. 1971. a. $15. Association of Theological Schools, Box 130, Vandalia, OH 45377. TEL 513-898-4654. Ed. Marvin J. Taylor. circ. 700.

200   SZ   ISSN 0512-2589
FAITH AND ORDER PAPERS. 1949; N.S. irreg., no.134, 1984. price varies. World Council of Churches, 150 Route de Ferney, CH-1211 Geneva 20, Switzerland (Dist. in the U.S. by: World Council of Churches Distribution Center, Rt 111 & Sharadin Road, P.O. Box 346, Kutztown, PA 19530-0346) cum.index: 1910-70. Indexed: Rel.Ind.Two.

200   IT
FILOSOFIA DELLA RELIGIONE. TESTI E STUDI. 1977. irreg., latest no.3. price varies. Paideia Editrice, Via Corsica 130, 25125 Brescia, Italy.

200   UK
FOR CHRIST AND PEACE. 1951. irreg. $10. Loverseed Press, 141 Woolacombe Rd., Blackheath, London SE3, England. circ. 1,500.

200   GW
FORSCHUNGEN ZUR KIRCHEN- UND DOGMENGESCHICHTE. 1954. irreg. Vandenhoeck & Ruprecht, Robert-Bosch-Breite 6, Postfach 3753, D-3400 Goettingen, W. Germany (B.R.D.)

200   GW
FORSCHUNGEN ZUR RELIGION UND LITERATUR DES ALTEN UND NEUEN TESTAMENTS. 1930. irreg. Vandenhoeck & Ruprecht, Robert-Bosch-Breite 6, Postfach 3753, D-3400 Goettingen, W. Germany (B.R.D.) Eds. Wolfgang Schrage, Rudolf Smend.

FRANKFURTER KIRCHLICHES JAHRBUCH. see HISTORY — History Of Europe

200   US
GENERAL CONVENTION OF THE NEW JERUSALEM. JOURNAL. 1817. a. $10. General Convention of the New Jerusalem, 48 Sargent St., Newton, MA 02158. Ed. Ethelwyn Worden. circ. 500.

RELIGIONS AND THEOLOGY

271   IT   ISSN 0072-4548
GIOVENTU PASSIONISTA/PASSIONIST YOUTH; rivista di formazione e d'informazione passionista. (Text in various languages; summaries in English) 1955. irreg., no. 3, 1960. $3. Edizioni E C O, 64048 S. Gabriele (Teramo), Italy. Ed. P. Natale Cavatassi.

200   GW   ISSN 0179-3551
GLAUBE UND LERNEN; Zeitschrift fuer theologische Urteilsbildung. a. DM.29.80 (students DM.19.80) Vandenhoeck & Ruprecht, Postfach 3753, Theaterstr. 13, D-3400 Goettingen, W. Germany (B.R.D.) Ed.Bd.

200   400   GE   ISSN 0232-2900
GRIECHISCHEN CHRISTLICHEN SCHRIFTSTELLER DER ERSTEN JAHRHUNDERTE. (Text in Greek and Latin) 1953. irreg., latest 1985. (Akademie der Wissenschaften der DDR) Akademie-Verlag Berlin, Leipziger Str. 3-4, 1086 Berlin, E. Germany (D.D.R.)

268   260   US
GUIDE TO CHRISTIAN CAMPS & CONFERENCE CENTERS. 1981. a. $9.95. Christian Camping International, Box 646, Wheaton, IL 60189. TEL 312-462-0300. Ed. Charlyene Wall. adv. circ. 9,000.
Former titles: Guide to Christian Camps; Christian Camping International Directory (ISSN 0069-3855); Before 1969: Christian Camp and Conference Association. International Directory.

200   GW   ISSN 0017-5730
GUSTAV-ADOLF-BLATT. 1955. irreg. (1-4/yr.) DM.5. (Evangelische Kirche in Deutschland) Gustav-Adolf-Werk, Olgastr. 8, 3500 Kassel 1, W. Germany (B.R.D.) Ed. Dr. Fritz Heinrich Ryssel. bk. rev. circ. 25,000.

268   US   ISSN 0072-9787
HANDBOOK OF DENOMINATIONS IN THE U.S. quinquennial. $10.95. Abingdon, 201 8th Ave. S, Box 801, Nashville, TN 37202. TEL 615-749-6347.

266   UK
HAPPY DAY DIARY. 1928. a. 50p. ‡ Lord's Day Observance Society, 5 Victory Ave., Morden, Surrey SM4 6DL, England. Ed. J.G. Roberts. circ. 45,000.

HARVARD SEMITIC MONOGRAPHS. see *LINGUISTICS*

201   US   ISSN 0073-0726
HARVARD THEOLOGICAL STUDIES. 1916. irreg., no.34, 1982. price varies. Harvard Divinity School, 45 Francis Ave., Cambridge, MA 02138.

200   US
HERMENEUTICS: STUDIES IN THE HISTORY OF RELIGION. irreg. price varies. University of California Press, 2120 Berkeley Way, Berkeley, CA 94720. TEL 415-642-4247.

200   GW   ISSN 0440-7180
HERMENEUTISCHE UNTERSUCHUNGEN ZUR THEOLOGIE. (Text in English, German) irreg., latest vol.23, 1985. J.C.B. Mohr (Paul Siebeck), Wilhelmstr. 18, Postfach 20 40, D-7400 Tuebingen, W. Germany (B.R.D.) Ed.Bd.

HIMALAYAN INTERNATIONAL INSTITUTE/ ELEANOR N. DANA LABORATORY. RESEARCH BULLETIN. see *PHYSICAL FITNESS AND HYGIENE*

HISTORIANS OF EARLY MODERN EUROPE. see *HISTORY — History Of Europe*

200   933   IS
HOLY PLACES OF PALESTINE. (Text in various languages) 1970. irreg. Franciscan Printing Press, Box 14064, Jerusalem 91140, Israel.

220   US   ISSN 0195-9085
HORIZONS IN BIBLICAL THEOLOGY. 1979. a. $12 to individuals; institutions $15; students $8. Pittsburgh Theological Seminary, 616 N. Highland Ave., Pittsburgh, PA 15206. TEL 412-362-5610. Eds. G. Coates,, D. Gowan. adv. bk. rev. circ. 300. (back issues avail.) Indexed: Old Test.Abstr. New Test.Abstr. Rel.Ind.One. Rel.& Theol.Abstr.

200   JA   ISSN 0073-3938
HUMANITIES, CHRISTIANITY AND CULTURE. (Text in English, French German, Japanese; summaries in English and Japanese) 1964. approx. a. 400 Yen per no. International Christian University, Institute for the Study of Christianity and Culture - Kokusai Kirisutokyo Daigaku Kirisutokyo to Bunka Kenkyujo, 3-10-2 Osawa, Mitaka, Tokyo 181, Japan. Ed. Koichi Namiki. circ. 560.
Formerly: International Christian University. Publications IV-B. Christianity and Culture.

200   NE
ICONOGRAPHY OF RELIGIONS. irreg. price varies. (Rijksuniversiteit te Groningen, Institute of Religious Iconography) E. J. Brill, P.O. Box 9000, 2300 PA Leiden, Netherlands. Ed.Bd.

200   US   ISSN 0363-5058
IN COMMON. 1971. irreg. $2. ‡ Consultation on Church Union, Research Park, 151 Wall St., Princeton, NJ 08540-1514. Ed. David W. Taylor. circ. 10,000.

200   200   GW
INSTITUT FUER EUROPAEISCHE GESCHICHTE, MAINZ. VEROEFFENTLICHUNGEN. ABTEILUNG UNIVERSALGESCHICHTE UND ABTEILUNG FUER ABENDLAENDISCHE RELIGIONSGESCHICHTE. (Text in English, French, and German) irreg., vol.124, 1987. price varies. Franz Steiner Verlag Wiesbaden GmbH, Birkenwaldstr. 44, Postfach 347, D-7000 Stuttgart 1, W. Germany (B.R.D.) Eds. K.O. von Aretin, P. Manns.
Formerly: Institut fuer Europaeische Geschichte, Mainz. Veroeffentlichungen. Abteilung Universitaetsgeschichte und Abteilung fuer Abendlaendische Religionsphilosophie (ISSN 0537-7919)

200   200   GW
INSTITUT FUER EUROPAEISCHE GESCHICHTE, MAINZ. VORTRAEGE. ABTEILUNG UNIVERSALGESCHICHTE UND ABTEILUNG FUER ABENDLAENDISCHE RELIGIONSGESCHICHTE. (Text in English, French, and German) irreg., vol.79, 1984. price varies. Franz Steiner Verlag Wiesbaden GmbH, Birkenwaldstr. 44, Postfach 347, D-7000 Stuttgart 1, W. Germany (B.R.D.) Eds. K.O. von Aretin, P. Manns.
Formerly: Institut fuer Europaeische Geschichte, Mainz. Vortraege. Abteilung Universalgeschichte und Abteilung fuer Abendlaendische Religionsphilosophie (ISSN 0537-7927)

200   MX
INSTITUTO SUPERIOR DE ESTUDIOS ECLESIASTICOS. LIBRO ANUAL. vol.9, 1980. a. Instituto Superior de Estudios Eclesiasticos, Victoria 21, Mexico 22, D.F., Mexico. bk. rev. Indexed: New Test.Abstr.

200   UY
INSTITUTO TEOLOGICO DEL URUGUAY. CUADERNOS. no.4, 1978. irreg. Instituto Teologico del Uruguay, Av. de Octubre 3060, Montevideo, Uruguay.

INSTRUMENTA LEXICOLOGIA LATINA. SERIES A & B. see *CLASSICAL STUDIES*

367   US
INTERNATIONAL ASSOCIATION OF LIBERAL RELIGIOUS WOMEN. NEWSLETTER.* 1949. a. membership. International Association of Liberal Religious Women, c/o Tina Jas, Sec., 43 Coolidge Ave., Lexington, MA 02173 (Edit. address: Havikhorst 17hs, Amsterdam 1083 TM, Netherlands) Ed. Gusta Greve.
Former titles: International Union of Liberal Christian Women. Newsletter; International League of Liberal Christian Women. Newsletter (ISSN 0074-6746)

200   CH   ISSN 0074-297X
INTERNATIONAL CONFERENCE FOR THE SOCIOLOGY OF RELIGION. 1948. biennial, 18th, 1985, Leuven-louvain-la-Neuve. 35 Fr. International Conference for the Sociology of Religion, 10 Terreaux, 1003 Lausanne, Switzerland. bk. rev.

268   US
INTERNATIONAL LESSON ANNUAL; commentary and teaching suggestions on the International Sunday School lessons. a. $7.50. Abingdon, 201 Eighth Ave. S., Box 801, Nashville, TN 37202. TEL 615-749-6347. Ed. Horace R. Weaver.

200   IE   ISSN 0332-4427
IRISH BIBLICAL ASSOCIATION. PROCEEDINGS. 1976. a. £16. Irish Biblical Association, Trinity College, Dublin 2, Ireland. Ed.Bd. adv. circ. 250. (back issues avail.) Indexed: Old Test.Abstr. New Test.Abstr.

270   GW   ISSN 0075-2541
JAHRBUCH FUER ANTIKE UND CHRISTENTUM. 1958. a. price varies. (Universitaet Bonn, Franz Joseph Doelger-Institut) Aschendorffsche Verlagsbuchhandlung, Soester Str. 13, Postfach 1124, 4400 Muenster, W. Germany (B.R.D.) bk. rev. Indexed: Br.Archaeol.Abstr. New Test.Abstr. RILA.

270   GW   ISSN 0075-2568
JAHRBUCH FUER BERLIN-BRANDENBURGISCHE KIRCHENGESCHICHTE. vol.55, 1985. a. DM.28. (Arbeitsgemeinschaft fuer Berlin-Brandenburgische Kirchengeschichte) Wichern-Verlag GmbH, Abt. CZV-Verlag, Bachstr. 1-2, 1000 Berlin 21, W. Germany (B.R.D.) circ. 850.
Supersedes: Jahrbuch fuer Brandenburgische Kirchengeschichte.

JAHRBUCH FUER CHRISTLICHE SOZIALWISSENSCHAFTEN. see *SOCIOLOGY*

264   245   GW   ISSN 0075-2681
JAHRBUCH FUER LITURGIK UND HYMNOLOGIE. 1955. a. price varies. (International Fellowship of Research in Hymnology - Internationale Arbeitsgemeinschaft fuer Hymnologie) Johannes Stauda Verlag GmbH, Heinrich-Schuetz-Allee 33, 3500 Kassel-Wilhelmshoehe, W. Germany (B.R.D.) Ed.Bd. bk. rev. circ. 1,000. Indexed: CERDIC. RILM.

270   GW   ISSN 0075-2762
JAHRBUCH FUER SCHLESISCHE KIRCHENGESCHICHTE. 1882. a. DM.34. (Verein fuer Schlesische Kirchengeschichte e.V.) Verlag Unser Weg, Meesenring 15, 2400 Luebeck 1, W. Germany (B.R.D.) Ed. Dietrich Meyer. bk. rev.

260   GW
JAHRBUCH MISSION. 1969. a. DM.6.80. (Verband Evangelischer Missionskonferenzen) Missionshilfe Verlag, Mittelweg 143, 2000 Hamburg 13, W. Germany (B.R.D.) Ed. Joachim Wietzke. bk. rev. circ. 10,000.
Formerly: Evangelische Mission Jahrbuch (ISSN 0531-4798)
Missions

200   UK   ISSN 0143-5108
JOURNAL FOR THE STUDY OF THE NEW TESTAMENT. SUPPLEMENT SERIES. irreg. price varies. J S O T Press, 343 Fulwood Rd., University of Sheffield, Sheffield S10 3BP, England. Indexed: New Test.Abstr.

221   UK   ISSN 0309-0787
JOURNAL FOR THE STUDY OF THE OLD TESTAMENT. SUPPLEMENT SERIES. irreg. price varies. J S O T Press, 343 Fulwood Rd., University of Sheffield, Sheffield S10 3BP, England. Ed.Bd. Indexed: Old Test.Abstr.

JOURNAL OF COMPARATIVE SOCIOLOGY & RELIGION. see *SOCIOLOGY*

JOURNAL OF PASTORAL PSYCHOTHERAPY. see *PSYCHOLOGY*

377.8   US   ISSN 0160-7774
JOURNAL OF SUPERVISION AND TRAINING IN MINISTRY. 1978. irreg., vol.8, 1986. $10. Association for Clinical Pastoral Education, North Central Region, Box 6777, Chicago, IL 60680. TEL 312-942-5572. (Co-sponsor: American Association of Pastoral Counselors. Central Region) Ed. George Fitchett. adv. bk. rev. circ. 1,000. Indexed: Rel.Per. Rel.Ind.One.

KACIC. see *HISTORY — History Of Europe*

KANON. see *LAW*

261   US   ISSN 0022-9288
KATALLAGETE. 1965. irreg. $10 for 4 issues. Katallagete, Inc., Box 2307, College Sta., Berea, KY 40404. TEL 606-986-8218. Ed. James Y. Holloway. bk. rev. illus. circ. 4,500. (also avail. in microform from UMI) Indexed: Rel.Per. CERDIC. Rel.Ind.One.

KIERKEGAARDIANA. see *PHILOSOPHY*

200   GW
KIRCHE UND KONFESSION. 1962. irreg. (Konfessionskundliche Institut des Ev. Bundes) Vandenhoeck & Ruprecht, Robert-Bosch-Breite 6, Postfach 3753, D-3400 Goettingen, W. Germany (B.R.D.)

KIRCHE UND RECHT. see *LAW*

200   DK   ISSN 0107-9824
KIRKEFONDETS AARBOG. 1929. a. Kr.50. Kirkefondet, Valby Tingsted 7, 2500 Valby, Denmark. adv. illus. circ. 6,000.
Formerly: Koebenhavnske Kirkefondets Aarbog.

209   DK   ISSN 0450-3171
KIRKEHISTORISKE SAMLINGER. (Text in Danish, English, German and Swedish) 1849. a. Kr.105. (Selskabet for Danmarks Kirkehistorie) Akademisk Forlag, Store Kannikestraede 8, P.O. Box 54, 1002 Copenhagen K, Denmark (Orders to: Danske Boghandleres Kommissionsanstalt, Siljangade 6, 2300 Copenhagen S, Denmark)

200   DK   ISSN 0105-4821
KOEBENHAVNS UNIVERSITET. INSTITUT FOR RELIGIONSHISTORIE. SKRIFTER. 1976. irreg. Koebenhavns Universitet, Institut for Religionshistorie, Copenhagen, Denmark.

200   DK   ISSN 0107-7902
KOSMOS. Esperanto edition: Kosmo (ISSN 0107-7953); German edition (ISSN 0107-7937); Swedish edition (ISSN 0107-7910) (Text in English; editions in Esperanto, Danish, German and Swedish) 1978. irreg. Kr.40. Martinus Institut, Mariendalsvej 94, Copenhagen F, Denmark. bk. rev. Indexed: Chem.Abstr.
Formerly: Contact with the Martinus Institute of Spiritual Science.

200   SW   ISSN 0085-2619
KYRKOHISTORISK AARSSKRIFT. (Text in Swedish and English; summaries in English, German and French) 1900. a. Kr.75. Svenska Kyrkohistoriska Foereningen, Box 1604, S-751 46, Sweden. Ed. Harry Lenhammar. adv. bk. rev. circ. 1,000. Indexed: Hist.Abstr. Amer.Hist.& Life.

200   US   ISSN 0075-8531
LECTURES ON THE HISTORY OF RELIGIONS. NEW SERIES. no.9, 1971. irreg., no.11, 1977. Columbia University Press, 562 W. 113th St., New York, NY 10025. TEL 212-678-6777.

266.025   UK   ISSN 0075-8809
LEPROSY MISSION, LONDON. ANNUAL REPORT. 1874. a. free. ‡ Leprosy Mission, 50 Portland Place, London W1N 3DG, England. Ed. U. Sadie. circ. 9,000.
Formerly: Mission to Lepers, London. Annual Report.
Missions

LIBRARY OF PHILOSOPHY AND RELIGION. see *PHILOSOPHY*

200 800   US   ISSN 0732-1929
LITERATURE AND BELIEF. 1981. a. $4. Brigham Young University, College of Humanities, Center for the Study of Christian Values in Literature, Jesse Knight Bldg., Provo, UT 84602. TEL 801-378-2304. Ed. Jay Fox. bk. rev. circ. 1,000. Indexed: M.L.A. Abstr.Engl.Stud. LCR.

200   GW   ISSN 0076-0048
LITURGIEWISSENSCHAFTLICHE QUELLEN UND FORSCHUNGEN. 1919. irreg. price varies. Aschendorffsche Verlagsbuchhandlung, Soester Str. 13, 4400 Muenster, W. Germany (B.R.D.) Ed. W. Heckenbach.

LIVE AND LET LIVE. see *PHILOSOPHY*

200 060   PH   ISSN 0076-0471
LOGOS; a series of monographs in scripture, theology, philosophy. (Text in English) 1966. irreg., no.14, 1985. price varies. Loyola School of Theology, Ateneo de Manila University, Box 4082, Manila, Philippines. Ed. Joseph L. Roche. circ. 500. Indexed: Chr.Per.Ind.

274   PO   ISSN 0076-1508
LUSITANIA SACRA. 1956. a. 140 esc. Centro de Estudos de Historia Eclesiastica, Campo dos Martires da Patria, 45, Lisbon-1, Portugal. Ed. Isaias da Rosa Pereira. Indexed: Hist.Abstr. Amer.Hist.& Life.

200 020   US   ISSN 0076-4434
MARIAN LIBRARY STUDIES. NEW SERIES. (Text in language of author) 1951; N.S. 1969. a. $10. University of Dayton, Marian Library, Dayton, OH 45469-0001. TEL 513-229-4214. Ed. Theodore Koehler. circ. 200. Indexed: Cath.Ind. CERDIC. New Test.Abstr.

200   MM
MELITA THEOLOGICA. (Text in English and Italian) 1946. a. $8. Mater Admirabilis College, Faculty of Theology, Tal-Virtu', Rabat, Malta. (Co-sponsor: Theological Students' Association) adv. bk. rev. index. circ. 1,000. Indexed: Old Test. Abstr. New Test.Abstr. Rel.& Theol.Abstr.

200   IT
MEMORIE DOMENICANE. 1884; N.S. 1970. a. price varies. Centro Riviste della Provincia Romana dei Frati Predicatori, Piazza S. Domenico 1, 51100 Pistoia, Italy. Ed. Eugenio Marino. bk. rev. bibl. circ. 400. (tabloid format) Indexed: CERDIC. RILA.

267 270   ZA   ISSN 0076-8901
MINDOLO NEWS LETTER. 1961. irreg., no.33, 1970. K.2($3) donation. (Mindolo Ecumenical Foundation) Mission Press, Ndola, P.O. Box 1493, Kitwe, Zambia. Ed. Jonathan C. Phiri. adv. circ. 4, 000 (approx.)

266   UK
MISSIONS TO SEAMEN ANNUAL REPORT. 1856. a. free. Missions to Seamen, St. Michael Paternoster Royal, College Hill, London EC4R 2RL, England. Ed. Gillian Ennis. index.
Formerly: Missions to Seamen Handbook (ISSN 0076-9401)
Missions

266   GW   ISSN 0076-941X
MISSIONSWISSENSCHAFTLICHE ABHANDLUNGEN UND TEXTE/ETUDES ET DOCUMENTS MISSIONNAIRES/MISSION STUDIES AND DOCUMENTS. 1917. irreg. price varies. (Internationales Institut fuer Missionswissenschaftliche Forschungen) Aschendorffsche Verlagsbuchhandlung, Soester Str. 13, 4400 Muenster, W. Germany (B.R.D.)
Missions

266   GW   ISSN 0076-9428
MISSIONSWISSENSCHAFTLICHE FORSCHUNGEN. 1962. irreg. price varies. Guetersloher Verlagshaus Gerd Mohn, Koenigstr. 23-25, Postfach 1343, 4830 Guetersloh, W. Germany (B.R.D.)
Missions

200   GW
MODELLE FUER DEN RELIGIONSUNTERRICHT. Short title: M.R.U. 1975. irreg., no.8, 1979. price varies. (Religionspaedagogische Projektentwicklung in Baden und Wuerttemberg) Calwer Verlag, Scharnhauser Str. 44, 7000 Stuttgart 70, W. Germany (B.R.D.) (Co-publisher: Koesel-Verlag) Eds. Klaus Dessecker, Gerhard Martin.

200   GW
NADEZHDA; khristianskoye chtenie. (Text and summaries in Russian) 1978. a. DM.20. Possev-Verlag, Flurscheideweg 15, D-6230 Frankfurt am Main 80, W. Germany (B.R.D.) circ. 2,000. (back issues avail.)

200   NE
NAG HAMMADI STUDIES. 1971. irreg., vol.29, 1985. price varies. E.J. Brill, P.O. Box 9000, 2300 PA Leiden, Netherlands. Ed.Bd.

200 952   JA   ISSN 0386-720X
NANZAN INSTITUTE FOR RELIGION AND CULTURE. BULLETIN. (Text In English) 1977. a. free. Nanzan Institute for Religion and Culture, 18 Yamazato-cho, Showa-ku, 466 Nagoya, Japan. TEL 052-832-3111. Ed. Jan Van Bragt. circ. 1,200. (back issues avail.)

220   NE   ISSN 0077-8842
NEW TESTAMENT TOOLS AND STUDIES. 1960. irreg., vol.10, 1980. price varies. E.J. Brill, P.O. Box 9000, 2300 PA Leiden, Netherlands. Ed. Bruce M. Metzger.

200   NE
NISABA. 1973. irreg., vol.15, 1986. price varies. E.J. Brill, P.O. Box 9000, 2300 PA Leiden, Netherlands.

200   SW   ISSN 0085-4212
NORDISK EKUMENISK AARSBOK. (Text in Danish, Norwegian and Swedish) 1972. biennial, latest 84-85. Kr.70. Nordiska Ekumeniska Institutet - Nordic Ecumenical Institute, Box 438, S-751 06 Uppsala, Sweden. Ed. Kjell Ove Nilsson. adv. bk. rev. illus. index. circ. 1,000. Indexed: CERDIC.

225   NE
NOVUM TESTAMENTUM. SUPPLEMENTS. 1958. irreg., vol.55, 1985. price varies. E.J. Brill, P.O. Box 9000, 2300 PA Leiden, Netherlands. Ed.Bd. Indexed: Rel.Ind.One.

200   NE
NUMEN SUPPLEMENTS. 1954. irreg., vol.48, 1986. price varies. E.J. Brill, P.O. Box 9000, 2300 PA Leiden, Netherlands. Indexed: Rel.Ind.Two.
Formerly: Studies in the History of Religions (ISSN 0585-7260)

266   DK   ISSN 0108-8297
NYE AAR; kirkelig forening for den indre mission i Danmark. 1906. a. Kr.50. (Kirkelig Forening) Lohse, Fredericia, Denmark. Ed. Verner Andersen. adv. illus.

200 947   US   ISSN 0731-5465
OCCASIONAL PAPERS ON RELIGION IN EASTERN EUROPE. 1981. irreg. (approx. 6-8/yr) $35. (Christian Associated for Relationships with Eastern Europe) Princeton Theological Seminary, c/o Rosemont College, Rosemont, PA 19010. TEL 215-527-0200. Ed. Paul Mojzes. bk. rev. circ. 700. (looseleaf format; back issues avail.)

200   SA
OLD TESTAMENT ESSAYS. (Text in English and German; summaries in English) 1983. a. R.8. Old Testament Essays, Department of Old Testament, P.O. Box 392, 0001 Pretoria, South Africa. Ed. J.J. Burden. circ. 300. (back issues avail.) Indexed: Old Test.Abstr.

200   GW   ISSN 0340-6407
ORIENS CHRISTIANUS; Hefte fuer die Kunde des christlichen Orients. 1911. a. DM.80 (approx.) Verlag Otto Harrassowitz, Taunusstr. 14, Postfach 2929, 6200 Wiesbaden 1, W. Germany (B.R.D.) Ed. Julius Assfalg, Hubert Kanfholt. adv. bk. rev. circ. 400. (back issues avail.) Indexed: Rel.Ind.One.

221   NE
OUDTESTAMENTISCHE STUDIEN. (Text in English and German) 1942. irreg., vol.23, 1984. price varies. E.J. Brill, P.O. Box 9000, 2300 PA Leiden, Netherlands. Ed. A.S. van der Woude. Indexed: Old Test.Abstr.

201   US   ISSN 0078-7272
OXFORD THEOLOGICAL MONOGRAPHS. irreg. Oxford University Press, 200 Madison Ave., New York, NY 10016 TEL 212-679-7300. (And: Ely House, 37 Dover St., London W1X 4AH, England) Ed.Bd.

200   US
PERE MARQUETTE THEOLOGY LECTURE SERIES. 1969. a. $7.95. Marquette University Press, 1324 W. Wisconsin Ave., Milwaukee, WI 53233. TEL 414-224-1564.

PHILOSOPHY AND THE ARTS; a literary and philosophical review. see *PHILOSOPHY*

207 268.8   US   ISSN 0079-2543
POINTS FOR EMPHASIS; INTERNATIONAL
SUNDAY SCHOOL LESSONS IN POCKET
SIZE. (Large type edition also avail.) 1917. a. $2.95
(large type edt. $3.95) Broadman Press, 127 Ninth
Ave. N., Nashville, TN 37234. TEL 615-251-2000.
Ed. William J. Fallis. circ. 46,000.

200   YU   ISSN 0032-700X
PRAVOSLAVNO MISAO. (Text in Serbo-Croatian)
1959. a. 100 din.($5) Udruzenje Pravoslavnog
Svestenstva SFR Jugoslavije, Glavni Savez,
Francuska 31-1, Belgrade, Yugoslavia. Ed. Dusan
Strbac. bk. rev. circ. 1,600.
    Cyrillic alphabet

281   CS   ISSN 0079-4937
PRAVOSLAVNY THEOLOGICKY SBORNIK. (Text
in Czech or Slovak) 1967. irreg., no.4, 1974. 52
Kcs.($7) Pravoslavna Cirkev Ceskoslovenska, V
jame 6, 110 00 Prague 1, Czechoslovakia. adv. circ.
3,000.

200   CN   ISSN 0079-4996
PRESBYTERIAN CHURCH IN CANADA.
GENERAL ASSEMBLY. ACTS AND
PROCEEDINGS. a. Can.$7. Presbyterian Church
in Canada, General Assembly, 50 Wynford Dr.,
Don Mills, Ont. M3C IJ7, Canada. TEL 416-441-
1111.

200   NE
PROBLEME DER AEGYPTOLOGIE. 1953. irreg.
price varies. E.J. Brill, P.O. Box 9000, 2300 PA
Leiden, Netherlands. Ed. W. Helck.

220   NE   ISSN 0079-7197
PSEUDEPIGRAPHA VETERIS TESTAMENTI
GRAECE. 1964. irreg., vol.4, 1977. price varies.
(Rijksuniversiteit te Leiden) E.J. Brill, P.O. Box
9000, 2300 PA Leiden, Netherlands.

PSYCHEDELIC MONOGRAPHS AND ESSAYS.
see *PSYCHOLOGY*

297   MY   ISSN 0552-6426
PURE LIFE SOCIETY. ANNUAL REPORT. 1953.
a. membership. Pure Life Society, Batu 6, Jalan
Puchong, Jalan Kelang Lama P.O., Kuala Lumpur,
Malaysia.

200 933   IS
QUADERNI DE "LA TERRA SANTA". (Text in
various languages) 1963. irreg. Franciscan Printing
Press, Box 14064, Jerusalem 91140, Israel.

260   GW   ISSN 0079-9084
QUELLEN UND FORSCHUNGEN ZUR
WUERTTEMBERGISCHEN
KIRCHENGESCHICHTE. 1967. irreg., vol.7, 1981.
Calwer Verlag, Scharnhauser Str. 44, 7000 Stuttgart
70, W. Germany (B.R.D.) Eds. Martin Brecht,
Gerhard Schaefer.

240   CN   ISSN 0079-9351
R.M. BUCKE MEMORIAL SOCIETY FOR THE
STUDY OF RELIGIOUS EXPERIENCE.
PROCEEDINGS OF THE CONFERENCE. 1965.
irreg., vol.7, 1974. price varies. R.M. Bucke
Memorial Society, 1033 Pine Ave. W., Montreal,
Que. H3A 1A1, Canada. Ed. Raymond H. Prince.
circ. 300. (back issues avail.)

RASSEGNA DI LETTERATURA TOMISTICA. see
PHILOSOPHY

262.9 200   FR
RECHERCHES INSTITUTIONNELLES. (In 4
Series: Droit et Eglises; Institutions et Histoire;
Culture et Religion; Recherche Documentaire) irreg.
Universite de Strasbourg II, Centre de Recherche et
de Documentation des Institutions Chretiennes, 9
Place de l'Universite, 67084 Strasbourg Cedex,
France. Eds. J. Schlick, M. Zimmerman. circ. 2,000.

266   US
REFUGEES AMONG US- UNREACHED
PEOPLES. 1979. a. $9.95. Missions Advanced
Research and Communications Center, 919 W.
Huntington Dr., Monrovia, CA 91016. TEL 818-
303-8811. Eds. Edward R. Dayton, Samuel Wilson.
circ. 600.
    Formerly: Unreached Peoples.

200   GW
REGULAE BENEDICTI STUDIA. ANNUARIUM
INTERNATIONALE. (Text in English, French and
German) 1972. a. price varies. Eos Verlag, Erzabtei
St. Ottilien, D-8917 St. Ottilien, W. Germany
(B.R.D) Eds. B. Jaspert, E. Manning.

RELIGIOESE GRAPHIK; Blaetter fuer Freunde
Christlicher Gebrauchsgraphik. see *ART*

290 200   GW   ISSN 0080-0848
RELIGION AND REASON; METHOD AND
THEORY IN THE STUDY AND
INTERPRETATION OF RELIGION. 1972. irreg.
price varies. Walter de Gruyter & Co., Mouton
Publishers, Postfach 110240, D-1000 Berlin 11, W.
Germany (B.R.D.) (U.S. addr.: Mouton Publishers,
division of Walter de Gruyter, Inc., 200 Saw Mill
River Road, Hawthorne, NY 10532) Ed. J.D.J.
Waardenburg.

200 100   GW
RELIGION AND SOCIETY. 1976. irreg. price varies.
Walter de Gruyter & Co., Mouton Publishers,
Postfach 110240, D-1000 Berlin 11, W. Germany
(B.R.D.) (U.S. addr.: Mouton Publishers, division of
Walter de Gruyter, Inc., 200 Saw Mill River Road,
Hawthorne, NY 10532) Eds. J.D.J. Waardenburg, L.
Laeyendecker.

200   FR   ISSN 0080-0864
RELIGION ET SCIENCES DE L'HOMME. 1971.
irreg. price varies. Editions du Centurion, 17 rue du
Babylone, Paris 75007, France.

200 060   AU
RELIGION, WISSENSCHAFT, KULTUR.
SCHRIFTENREIHE. 1950. a. Verlag Herold,
Freyung 6, A-1010 Vienna, Austria.
    Formerly: Religion, Wissenschaft, Kultur.
Jahrbuch (ISSN 0080-0872)

200 301   IT   ISSN 0391-853X
RELIGIONE E SOCIETA. 1977. irreg. price varies.
Edizioni Studium, Via Cassiodoro 14, 00193 Rome,
Italy.

200   GW
RELIGIONSPAEDAGOGISCHE PRAXIS. Short
title: R P P. 1971. irreg., vol.20, 1977. price varies.
Calwer Verlag, Scharnhauser Str. 44, 7000 Stuttgart
70, W. Germany (B.R.D.) (Co-publisher: Koesel-
Verlag) Eds. Horst Klaus Berg, Wolfgang Langer.
(back issues avail.)

RELIGIOUS AND INSPIRATIONAL BOOKS AND
SERIALS IN PRINT. see *BIBLIOGRAPHIES*

200   US
RESEARCH IN MINISTRY; an index to Doctor of
Ministry project reports and theses. 1983. a. $40.
American Theological Library Association, 5600 S.
Woodlawn Ave., Chicago, IL 60637. TEL 312-386-
0461. Ed. Thomas J. Davis. abstr. circ. 145.
(looseleaf format; back issues avail.)

230 100   SZ   ISSN 0250-6971
REVUE DE THEOLOGIE ET DE PHILOSOPHIE.
CAHIERS. 1977. irreg. (approx. 1/yr.) Revue de
Theologie et de Philosophie, Chemin des Cedres, 7,
CH-1004 Lausanne, Switzerland. Indexed: New
Test.Abstr. Rel.Ind.One.

209   IT
RIVISTA DI STORIA E LETTERATURA
RELIGIOSA. BIBLIOTECA; studi e testi. 1967.
irreg., no.7, 1984. price varies. Casa Editrice Leo S.
Olschki, Casella Postale 66, 50100 Florence, Italy.
Indexed: Arts & Hum.Cit.Ind.

ROEMISCHE HISTORISCHE MITTEILUNGEN.
see *HISTORY — History Of Europe*

220   SP
SAGRADA BIBLIA. 1976. irreg., no.8, 1986. price
varies. (Universidad de Navarra, Facultad de
Teologia) Ediciones Universidad de Navarra, S.A.,
Apdo. 396, 31080 Pamplona, Spain.
    Bible

250   AU   ISSN 0036-3162
ST. POELTNER DIOEZESANBLATT. 1785. irreg.
(at least 12/yr.) S.400. Bischoefliches Ordinariat
Sanct Poelten, Domplatz 1, A-3100 St. Poelten,
Austria. Ed. Dr. Heinrich Fasching. bk. rev. bibl.
charts. circ. 800.

200   US   ISSN 0082-4208
ST. THOMAS MORE LECTURES. 1964. irreg., no.3,
1969. price varies. Yale University Press, 92A Yale
Station, New Haven, CT 06520. TEL 203-432-0940.

200   CN   ISSN 0709-616X
SALT. 1979. a. Can.$15. Alberta Teachers'
Association, Religious Studies and Moral Education
Council, 11010 142nd St., Edmonton, Alta. T5N
2R1, Canada. Ed. Rose Marie Hague. bk. rev. circ.
242.

200   UK   ISSN 0264-5572
SCOTTISH CHURCH HISTORY SOCIETY.
RECORDS. 1923. a. £5($10) Scottish Church
History Society, Grange Manse, 51 Portland Rd.,
Kilmarnock, Ayrshire KA1 2EQ, Scotland. Ed.
James Kirk. bibl. index. circ. 260. (back issues
avail.)

200   FI   ISSN 0582-3226
SCRIPTA INSTITUTI DONNERIANI ABOENSIS.
(Text in English, French, German) 1967. triennial.
Fmk.100. Donner Institute for Research in Religious
and Cultural History, Gezeliusgatan 2, P.O. Box 70,
SF-20501 Aabo/Turku, Finland (Subscr. to:
Almqvist & Wiksell International, Box 62, S-10120
Stockholm, Sweden) Tore Ahlbaeck. circ. 250.
Indexed: Arts & Hum.Cit.Ind.

220   UK
SCRIPTURE EXAMINATION MATERIAL AND
ANNUAL SCRIPTURE PROJECT. a. £1. National
Christian Education Council, Robert Denholm
House, Nutfield, Redhill, Surrey RH1 4HW,
England. Ed. C. Jamieson. circ. 16,800.

SELBST-VERWIRKLICHUNG: JAHRESHEFT. see
PHILOSOPHY

200   FR   ISSN 0075-4544
SIR MOSES MONTEFIORE COLLECTIONS DES
JUIFS CELEBRES. Title varies: Juifs Celebres.
1969. irreg. 35 F. Librairie du Centre
Communautaire, 19 bd. Poissonniere, 75002 Paris,
France. circ. 10,000.

225   UK   ISSN 0081-1432
SOCIETY FOR NEW TESTAMENT STUDIES.
MONOGRAPH SERIES. 1965. irreg., no.51, 1984.
$29.50 for latest vol. Cambridge University Press,
Edinburgh Bldg., Shaftesbury Rd., Cambridge CB2
2RU, England (And: 32 E. 57th St. , New York NY
10022) Ed. R. Wilson. index.

221   UK
SOCIETY FOR OLD TESTAMENT STUDIES.
MONOGRAPHS. 1972. irreg., no.6, 1979. $21.95
for latest vol. Cambridge University Press,
Edinburgh Bldg., Shaftesbury Rd., Cambridge CB2
2RU, England (And: 32 E. 57th St., New York, NY
10022)

200   US
SOCIETY FOR THE SCIENTIFIC STUDY OF
RELIGION. MONOGRAPH SERIES. no.4, 1984.
irreg. Society for the Scientific Study of Religion,
Marist Hall, Rm. 108, Catholic University of
America, Washington, DC 20064.

220   US   ISSN 0145-2711
SOCIETY OF BIBLICAL LITERATURE. SEMINAR
PAPERS (YEAR) a. $15. (Society of Biblical
Literature) Scholars Press, Box 1608, Decatur, GA
30031-1608. Ed. Kent H. Richards. (back issues
avail.) Indexed: Rel.Ind.One.

200   US   ISSN 0732-4928
SOCIETY OF CHRISTIAN ETHICS. ANNUAL.
1975. a. $12. Georgetown University Press,
Intercultural Center, Georgetown University,
Washington, DC 20057. Ed. Diane Yeager. adv.
circ. 850. (also avail. in microfilm)

230   SZ   ISSN 0067-4907
SONDERBAENDE ZUR THEOLOGISCHEN
ZEITSCHRIFT. 1966. irreg., no.10, 1981. price
varies. Friedrich Reinhardt Verlag, Missionsstr. 36,
CH-4012 Basel, Switzerland (Dist. by: Albert J.
Phiebig Books, Box 352, White Plains, NY 10602)
Ed. B. Reicke. circ. 1,000.
    Formerly: Beihefte zur Theologischen Zeitschrift.

200   027.7   MW
SOURCES FOR THE STUDY OF RELIGION IN
MALAWI. (Text in English) 1979. irreg., latest
no.11, 1984. $2.50 per no. University of Malawi,
Chancellor College, Department of Religion, P.O.
Box 280, Zomba, Malawi. Ed. J.C. Chakanza. circ.
200.

200   808.81   US
SPIRIT WINGS. 1986. a. $5. Broken Streets, 57
Morningside Dr., E., Bristol, CT 06010. Ed. Ron
Grossman. adv. circ. 125. (back issues avail.)

200   IT
SPIRITUALITA CRISTIANA. 1981. irreg. price
varies. Edizioni Studium, Via Cassiodoro 14, 00193
Rome, Italy.

268.8   US   ISSN 0081-4245
STANDARD LESSON COMMENTARY;
International Sunday School lessons. 1954. a. $9.50
casebound; $7.95 kivar. ‡ Standard Publishing, 8121
Hamilton Ave., Cincinnati, OH 45231. TEL 513-
931-4050. Ed. James Fehl. circ. 180,000.

200   DK   ISSN 0108-2884
STORE GLAEDE. 1973. a. Kr.10. Nyt Liv
Folkekirkeligt Forbund for Evangelisation i
Danmark, Rosenvej 1, 4340 Toelloese, Denmark.
illus.

220   NE
STUDIA AD CORPUS HELLENISTICUM NOVI
TESTAMENTI. (Text in English, French and
German) 1970. irreg., vol.6, 1980. price varies. E.J.
Brill, P.O. Box 9000, 2300 PA Leiden, Netherlands.
Ed.Bd.

268   IT
STUDIA EPHEMERIDIS AUGUSTINIANUM.
1967. irreg. Institutum Patristicum Augustinianum,
Via S. Uffizio, 25, 00193 Rome, Italy. (back issues
avail.)

220   NE
STUDIA IN VETERIS TESTAMENTI
PSEUDEPIGRAPHA. 1970. irreg., vol.8, 1985.
price varies. E.J. Brill, P.O. Box 9000, 2300 PA
Leiden, Netherlands. Eds. A.M. Denis, M. de
Jonge.

100   GW   ISSN 0081-6663
STUDIA IRENICA. (Text in English and German)
1968. irreg., no.19, 1971. Gertenberg Verlag,
Rathausstr. 18, Postfach 390, 3200 Hildesheim, W.
Germany (B.R.D.) Ed. Axel Hilmar Swinne.
   Before 1971: Frankfurt am Main. Universitaet.
Institut fuer Wissenschaftliche Irenik. Schriften.

STUDIA PHILOSOPHIAE RELIGIONIS. see
PHILOSOPHY

200   NE   ISSN 0585-5500
STUDIA POST-BIBLICA. 1959. irreg., vol.36, 1986.
price varies. E.J. Brill, P.O. Box 9000, 2300 PA
Leiden, Netherlands.

266   SP
STUDIA SILENSIA. (Text in English, French,
German, Portuguese and Spanish) 1975. a. price
varies. Abadia de Santo Domingo de Silos, E-09610,
Libreria de la Abadia, Burgos, Spain. Ed. Clemente
de la Serna. illus. stat. tr.lit. index. cum.index. circ.
1,500. (back issues avail.)

200   GW
STUDIEN ZUR KIRCHENGESCHICHTE
NIEDERSACHSENS. 1919. irreg. Vandenhoeck &
Ruprecht, Robert-Bosch-Breite 6, Postfach 3753, D-
3400 Goettingen, W. Germany (B.R.D.) Ed. Hans
W. Krummede.

200   GW
STUDIEN ZUR THEOLOGIE UND
GEISTESGESCHICHTE DES 19.
JAHRHUNDERTS. 1972. irreg. Vandenhoeck &
Ruprecht, Robert-Bosch-Breite 6, Postfach 3753, D-
3400 Goettingen, W. Germany (B.R.D.) Ed.Bd.

200   GW
STUDIEN ZUR UMWELT DES NEUEN
TESTAMENTS. 1968. irreg. Vandenhoeck &
Ruprecht, Robert-Bosch-Breite 6, Postfach 3753, D-
3400 Goettingen, W. Germany (B.R.D.) Ed.Bd.

200   US
STUDIES IN AMERICAN RELIGION. 1980. irreg.,
vol.22, 1986. $39.95 per no. Edwin Mellen Press,
Box 450, Lewiston, NY 14092. Ed. Herbert
Richardson. bibl. index.

STUDIES IN ART AND RELIGIOUS
INTERPRETATION. see ART

222   US
STUDIES IN BIBLE AND EARLY
CHRISTIANITY. 1982. irreg., vol.8, 1986. $39.95
per no. Edwin Mellen Press, Box 450, Lewiston,
NY 14092.

200   IS
STUDIES IN BIBLE AND EXEGESIS. 1980. irreg.
Bar Ilan University Press, Ramat Gan 52 100,
Israel.

200   NE
STUDIES IN GREEK AND ROMAN RELIGION.
1980. irreg., vol.3, 1986. price varies. E.J. Brill, P.O.
Box 9000, 2300 PA Leiden, Netherlands. Ed. H.S.
Versnel.

200   NE   ISSN 0585-6914
STUDIES IN MEDIEVAL AND REFORMATION
THOUGHT. 1966. irreg., vol. 37, 1986. price varies.
E.J. Brill, P.O. Box 9000, 2300 PA Leiden,
Netherlands. Ed. H.A. Oberman. (back issues avail.)

200   US
STUDIES IN RELIGION AND SOCIETY. 1981.
irreg., vol.17,, 1987. $39.95 per no. Edwin Mellen
Press, Box 450, Lewiston, NY 14092. Indexed:
Rel.Ind.Two.

230   NE   ISSN 0081-8607
STUDIES IN THE HISTORY OF CHRISTIAN
THOUGHT. 1966. irreg., vol.36, 1986. price varies.
E.J. Brill, P.O. Box 9000, 2300 PA Leiden,
Netherlands. Ed. Heiko A. Oberman.

200   301.412   US
STUDIES IN WOMEN AND RELIGION. 1979.
irreg., vol.21, 1986. $39.95 per no. Edwin Mellen
Press, Box 450, Lewiston, NY 14092.

200   NE
STUDIES ON RELIGION IN AFRICA. 1970. irreg.,
vol.5, 1984. price varies. E.J. Brill, P.O. Box 9000,
2300 PA Leiden, Netherlands. bibl.

220   IS   ISSN 0081-8909
STUDIUM BIBLICUM FRANCISCANUM.
ANALECTA. (Language of text varies) 1962. irreg.
price varies. Franciscan Printing Press, Box 14064,
91140 Jerusalem, Israel. circ. 1,000.

220   IS   ISSN 0081-8917
STUDIUM BIBLICUM FRANCISCANUM.
COLLECTIO MAIOR. (Text in various languages)
1941. irreg. price varies. Franciscan Printing Press,
P.O.B. 14064, 91140 Jerusalem, Israel. circ. 1,000.

220   IS   ISSN 0081-8925
STUDIUM BIBLICUM FRANCISCANUM.
COLLECTIO MINOR. (Text in various languages)
1961. irreg., no.33, 1984. price varies. Franciscan
Printing Press, P.O.B. 14064, 91140 Jerusalem,
Israel. circ. 1,000.

220   IS   ISSN 0081-8933
STUDIUM BIBLICUM FRANCISCANUM. LIBER
ANNUUS. (Text in various languages) 1951. a.
price varies. Franciscan Printing Press, Box 14064,
91140 Jerusalem, Israel. circ. 1,200. Indexed: RILA.

200   CU
SU VOZ. a. Iglesia Presbiteriana, 24 No. 171st 13 y
15, Vedado, Habana 4, Havana, Cuba.

209   BE
SUBSIDA HAGIOGRAPHICA. irreg., no.71, 1986.
Societe des Bollandistes, 24 bd. Saint-Michel, 1040
Brussels, Belgium.

260   US
SUCCESSFUL WRITERS AND EDITORS
GUIDEBOOK.* 1977. irreg. $10.95. ‡ (Christian
Writers Institute) Creation House, 190 N.
Westmonte Dr., Altamonte Spring, FL 32714-3342.
Ed. Robert Walker.
   Formerly: Handbook for Christian Writers (ISSN
0069-391X)

RELIGIONS AND THEOLOGY   973

220   SW
SVENSK EXEGETISK AARSBOK. (Text in English
or Swedish) 1936. a. (Uppsala Exegetiska Saellskap)
Liber Forlag, S-205 10, Malmo, Sweden. bk. rev.
illus. Indexed: Old Test.Abstr. New Test.Abstr.

268.8   US   ISSN 0082-1713
TARBELL'S TEACHER'S GUIDE; to the
International Sunday School Lessons. 1905. a.
$7.95. Fleming H. Revell Co., 184 Central Ave.,
Old Tappan, NJ 07675. TEL 201-768-8060. Ed.
William P. Barker.

TASCHENBUCH FUER LITURGIE
KIRCHENMUSIK UND MUSIKERZIEHUNG.
see MUSIC

200   FI   ISSN 0497-1817
TEMENOS (TURKU) (Text in English, French,
German) 1965. a. Fmk.110. Finnish Society for the
Study of Comparative Religion, Henrikinkatu 3,
20500 Turku, Finland. Ed. Lauri Honko. circ. 250.
Indexed: Arts & Hum.Cit.Ind.

200   465   GE   ISSN 0082-3589
TEXTE UND UNTERSUCHUNGEN ZUR
GESCHICHTE DER ALTCHRISTLICHEN
LITERATUR. 1952. irreg., vol.132, 1984. price
varies. (Akademie der Wissenschaften der DDR,
Zentralinstitut fuer Alte Geschichte und
Archaeologie) Akademie-Verlag, Leipziger Str. 3-4,
1086 Berlin, E. Germany (D.D.R.)

200   US
TEXTS AND STUDIES IN RELIGION. 1977. irreg.,
vol.29, 1987. $39.95 per no. Edwin Mellen Press,
Box 450, Lewiston, NY 14092.

220   IS   ISSN 0082-3767
TEXTUS. (Text in English; summaries in Hebrew)
1960. approx. a. $6. (Hebrew University of
Jerusalem, Bible Project) Magnes Press, The Hebrew
University, Jerusalem, Israel. cum.index 1960-1966.

200   GW   ISSN 0082-3775
TEXTUS PATRISTICI ET LITURGICI. 1964. irreg.
price varies. (Institutum Liturgicum Ratisbonense)
Verlag Friedrich Pustet, Gutenbergstr. 8, 8400
Regensburg 1, W. Germany (B.R.D.) Ed. Klaus
Gamber. circ. 1,000.

200   US   ISSN 0362-0603
THEOLOGICAL MARKINGS. 1971. a. free to
qualified personnel. United Theological Seminary of
the Twin Cities, 3000 Fifth St. N.W., New
Brighton, MN 55112. TEL 612-633-4311. Ed.
Eugene C. Jaberg. bk. rev. circ. 1,550. Indexed:
Rel.Ind.One.

230   GW
THEOLOGIE UND DIENST. 1973. irreg., latest
no.30. price varies. (Prediger- und Missionsseminar
St. Chrischona) Brunnen-Verlag GmbH, Gottlieb-
Daimler-str. 22, Postfach 5205, 6300 Giessen 1, W.
Germany (B.R.D.) Ed.Bd. circ. 3,000.

230   SZ   ISSN 0082-3902
THEOLOGISCHE DISSERTATIONEN. (Editions in
English and German; summaries in English or
German) 1969. irreg., no.17, 1986. price varies.
(Universitaet Basel, Theologische Fakultaet)
Friedrich Reinhardt Verlag, Missionsstr. 36, CH-
4012 Basel, Switzerland (Dist. by: Albert J. Phiebig
Books, Box 352, White Plains, NY 10602) Ed. Bo
Reicke.

THEOLOGY AND SCIENTIFIC CULTURE. see
SCIENCES: COMPREHENSIVE WORKS

200   US
THREE MINUTES A DAY; reflections for each day
of the year. 1949. irreg. $5 per no. Christophers,
Inc., 12 E. 48th St., New York, NY 10017. TEL
212-759-4050. Ed. Joseph R. Thomas.

200   US
TORONTO STUDIES IN THEOLOGY. 1978. irreg.,
vol.28, 1987. $39.95 per no. Edwin Mellen Press,
Box 450, Lewiston, NY 14092.

200   BE
TRADUCTIONS HEBRAIQUES DES EVANGILES.
1982. irreg. N.V. Brepols I.G.P., Rue Baron du Four
8, B-2300 Turnhout, Belgium.

200   US   ISSN 0742-2393
TRINITY UNIVERSITY MONOGRAPH SERIES IN RELIGION. 1972. irreg., (approx. every 18 mos.) Trinity University Press, 715 Stadium Dr., San Antonio, TX 78284. TEL 512-736-7619. Ed. William O. Walker, Jr.

200   GW
TUDUV-STUDIE. REIHE RELIGIONSWISSENSCHAFTEN. 1975. irreg. price varies. Tuduv Verlagsgesellschaft mbH, Gabelsbergerstr. 15, 8000 Munich 2, W. Germany (B.R.D.)

207   UK   ISSN 0082-7118
TYNDALE BULLETIN. 1956. a. £5.95. Inter-Varsity Press, Norton St., Nottingham NG7 3HR, England. Ed. M.J. Harris. bk. rev. circ. 600. (back issues avail.) Indexed: Old Test.Abstr. New Test.Abstr. Rel.& Theol.Abstr. Rel.Ind.One.

200   FR   ISSN 0396-2393
UNION DES SUPERIEURES MAJEURS DE FRANCE. ANNUAIRE. 1975. a. Union des Superieures Majeures des Instituts Religieux de France, 10 rue Jean-Bart, 75006 Paris, France.

266   UK
UNITED SOCIETY FOR THE PROPAGATION OF THE GOSPEL. YEARBOOK. 1704. a. United Society for the Propagation of the Gospel, 15 Tufton St., London SW1P 3QQ, England.
Formerly: United Society for the Propagation of the Gospel. Annual Report/Review (ISSN 0144-9508)
Missions

200   US
UNIVERSAL LIFE - THE INNER RELIGION. 1985. irreg. Box 3549, Woodbridge, CT 06525. Ed. Kathleen Scott.
Formerly: Homebringing Mission of Jesus Christ.

200   SP   ISSN 0078-8759
UNIVERSIDAD DE NAVARRA. FACULTAD DE DERECHO CANONICO. MANUALES: DERECHO CANONICO. 1973. irreg., no.6, 1984. price varies. Ediciones Universidad de Navarra, S.A., Apdo. 396, 31080 Pamplona, Spain.
Canon law

200   CK
UNIVERSIDAD JAVERIANA. FACULTAD DE TEOLOGIA. COLECCION PROFESORES. irreg. Col.400 price varies. Pontificia Universidad Javeriana, Facultad de Teologia, Apdo. Aereo 54-953, Bogota, D.E. 2, Colombia.

200 100   SP
UNIVERSIDAD PONTIFICIA COMILLAS DE MADRID. PUBLICACIONES. SERIE 1: ESTUDIOS. Theology section (ISSN 0211-2752); Philosophy section (ISSN 0211-2779); Canon section (ISSN 0211-2760) 1975. irreg., no.32, 1984. Universidad Pontificia Comillas de Madrid, Comision de Publicaciones, E-28049 Madrid, Spain. Ed. Antonio Vargas-Machuca.

230   AU   ISSN 0579-7780
UNIVERSITAET INNSBRUCK. THEOLOGISCHE FAKULTAET. STUDIEN UND ARBEITEN. (Subseries of: Universitaet Innsbruck. Veroeffentlichungen) 1968. irreg., vol.10, 1974. price varies. Oesterreichische Kommissionsbuchhandlung, Maximilianstrasse 17, A-6020 Innsbruck, Austria. Ed. Hans Bernhard Meyer.

266   GW   ISSN 0077-197X
UNIVERSITAET MUENSTER. INSTITUT FUER MISSIONSWISSENSCHAFT. VEROEFFENTLICHUNGEN. 1949. irreg. price varies. Aschendorffsche Verlagsbuchhandlung, Soester Str. 13, 4400 Muenster, W. Germany (B.R.D.) Ed. Josef Glazik.
Missions

UNIVERSITE SAINT-JOSEPH. FACULTE DES LETTRES ET DES SCIENCES HUMAINES. RECHERCHE. SERIE B: ORIENT CHRETIEN. see *ORIENTAL STUDIES*

UNIVERSITY OF DAYTON REVIEW. see *LITERARY AND POLITICAL REVIEWS*

200 100   US
UNIVERSITY OF NOTRE DAME. STUDIES IN THE PHILOSOPHY OF RELIGION. 1979. irreg. University of Notre Dame Press, Notre Dame, IN 46556. TEL 219-239-6346. Ed. Frederick Crosson.

200 930   IT   ISSN 0391-8564
VERBA SENIORUM. irreg. price varies. Edizioni Studium, Via Cassiodoro 14, 00193 Rome, Italy.

221   NE   ISSN 0083-5889
VETUS TESTAMENTUM. SUPPLEMENTS. 1953. irreg., vol.38, 1986. price varies. (International Organization for the Study of the Old Testament) E.J. Brill, P.O. Box 9000, 2300 PA Leiden, Netherlands.

200   NE   ISSN 0169-5606
VISIBLE RELIGION; annual for religious iconography. (Text in English, French and German) 1982. a. price varies. (State University Groningen, Institute for Religious Iconography) E.J. Brill, P.O. Box 9000, 2300 PA Leiden, Netherlands. Ed. H.G. Kippenberg. circ. 200.

200   CN   ISSN 0507-1690
VITA EVANGELICA. French edition (ISSN 0315-5048) (Editions in English and French) 1965. irreg., no.12, 1984. price varies. ‡ Canadian Religious Conference, 324 Laurier E., Ottawa, Ont. K1N 6P6, Canada. TEL 613-236-0824. Ed. Albert Landry. circ. 3,500 (French edt.); 3,500 (English edt.)

200   GW   ISSN 0083-6923
VORREFORMATIONSGESCHICHTLICHE FORSCHUNGEN. 1902. irreg. price varies. Aschendorffsche Verlagsbuchhandlung, Soester Str. 13, 4400 Muenster, W. Germany (B.R.D.) Ed. Erwin Iserloh.

200   UK   ISSN 0263-6786
VOX EVANGELICA. 1959. a. £3.95($10.85) (London Bible College) Paternoster Press Ltd., Paternoster House, 3 Mount Radford Crescent, Exeter, Devon EX2 4JW, England. Ed. Harold H. Rowdon. circ. 600. (tabloid format; back issues avail.) Indexed: Old Test.Abstr. CERDIC.

230   GW
WESTFALIA SACRA; Quellen und Forschungen zur Kirchengeschichte Westfalens. 1948. irreg. price varies. Aschendorffsche Verlagsbuchhandlung, Soester Str. 13, 4400 Muenster, W. Germany (B.R.D.) Ed. Alois Schroeer.

222   GW
WISSENSCHAFTLICHE UNTERSUCHUNGEN ZUM NEUEN TESTAMENT. (Text in English and German) 1950. irreg. price varies. Verlag J.C.B. Mohr (Paul Siebeck), Wilhelmstr. 18, Postfach 2040, 7400 Tuebingen, W. Germany (B.R.D.) Ed. Martin Hengel, Otfried Hofius.

200   SZ   ISSN 0084-1676
WORLD COUNCIL OF CHURCHES. GENERAL ASSEMBLY. ASSEMBLY-REPORTS. (Text in English) 1948. irreg., 6th, 1983. price varies. World Council of Churches, 150 Route de Ferney, CH-1211 Geneva 20, Switzerland (Dist. in the U.S. by: World Council of Churches Distribution Center, Rt 111 & Sharadin Road, P.O. Box 346, Kutztown, PA 19530-0346)

200   SZ   ISSN 0084-1684
WORLD COUNCIL OF CHURCHES. MINUTES AND REPORTS OF THE CENTRAL COMMITTEE MEETING. (Text in English, German, French and Spanish) 1948. approx. a., 37th, 1985. price varies. World Council of Churches, 150 Route de Ferney, CH-1211 Geneva 20, Switzerland (Dist. in the U.S. by: World Council of Churches Distribution Center, Rt 222 & Sharadin Road, P.O. Box 346, Kutztown, PA 19530-0346)

WORLD'S WISDOM SERIES. see *PHILOSOPHY*

200   US   ISSN 0084-3407
YALE PUBLICATIONS IN RELIGION. a. price varies. Yale University Press, 92A Yale Sta., New Haven, CT 06520. TEL 203-432-0940.

200   US   ISSN 0084-3644
YEARBOOK OF AMERICAN AND CANADIAN CHURCHES. 1916. a. $15.95. Abingdon, 201 Eighth Ave., So., Box 801, Nashville, TN 37202. TEL 615-749-6347. Ed. Constant H. Jacquet, Jr.
Formerly: Yearbook of American Churches.

260   US   ISSN 0084-4128
YEARBOOKS IN CHRISTIAN EDUCATION. 1969. a. price varies. (Lutheran Church in America, Board of Publication) Fortress Press, 2900 Queen Lane, Philadelphia, PA 19129. TEL 215-848-6800.

200   UK   ISSN 0085-8374
YORK JOURNAL OF CONVOCATION. 1856. irreg. £2.50. (Convocation of York) Church Information Office, Church House, Westminster, London SW1, England. Ed. Canon R.J. Graham. circ. 400 (controlled)

267.5   US   ISSN 0084-4306
YOUNG WOMEN'S CHRISTIAN ASSOCIATION OF THE UNITED STATES OF AMERICA. THE PRINTOUT. a. membership. Young Women's Christian Association of the United States of America, National Board, 726 Broadway, New York, NY 10003. TEL 212-614-2700. Ed.Bd.
Formerly: Tallies and Trends: Annual Statistical Report.

200   GW
ZEITSCHRIFT FUER DIE ALTTESTAMENTLICHE WISSENSCHAFT. BEIHEFTE. (Text in English and German) irreg., no.166, 1986. price varies. Walter de Gruyter und Co., Genthiner Str. 13, 1000 Berlin 30, W. Germany (B.R.D.) (U.S. adress: Walter de Gruyter, Inc., 200 Saw Mill Rd., Hawthorne, N.Y. 10532) Ed. Otto Kaiser. bibl. Indexed: Rel.& Theol.Abstr.

200   NE
ZEITSCHRIFT FUER RELIGIONS- UND GEISTESGESCHICHTE. BEIHEFTE. 1955. irreg., vol.30, 1986. price varies. E.J. Brill, P.O. Box 9000, 2300 PA Leiden, Netherlands. Indexed: Rel.& Theol.Abstr. Rel.Ind.One.

250   US   ISSN 0084-5558
ZONDERVAN PASTOR'S ANNUAL. 1966. a. Zondervan Publishing House, 1415 Lake Dr. S.E., Grand Rapids, MI 49506. TEL 616-698-6900. Ed. T.T. Crabtree. circ. 14,000. (reprint service avail. from UMI)

RELIGIONS AND THEOLOGY —
Abstracting, Bibliographies, Statistics

250 016   US   ISSN 0733-2599
ABSTRACTS OF RESEARCH IN PASTORAL CARE AND COUNSELING. 1972. a. $25. Joint Council on Research in Pastoral Care and Counseling, c/o Mary Fran Hughes-McIntyre, Box 5184, Richmond, VA 23220. TEL 804-353-3439. adv. bk. rev. circ. 400. (back issues avail.)
Formerly: Pastoral Care and Counseling Abstracts.

200 314   VC
ANNUARIUM STATISTICUM ECCLESIAE/ STATISTIQUE DE L'EGLISE/STATISTICAL YEARBOOK OF THE CHURCH. (Text in Latin, English and French) 1969. a. L.40000. (Segretaria di Stato, Ufficio Centrale di Statistica della Chiesa) Libreria Editrice Vaticana, Vatican City, Italy. charts. stat.
Formerly: Raccolta di Tavole Statistiche.

271   VC   ISSN 0570-7242
ARCHIVUM BIBLIOGRAPHICUM CARMELITANUM. (Text in Latin and modern languages) 1956. a. L.26000($12) Edizioni del Teresianum, Piazza S. Pancrazio 5-A, 00152 Rome, Italy. Ed. Father Simeon de la Sagrada Familia, O.C.D. circ. 400.

280.4 016   US   ISSN 0066-8710
ASSOCIATED CHURCH PRESS. DIRECTORY. 1947. a. $20 ($6 to libraries) (Associated Church Press) Associated Church Press, Box 306, Geneva, IL 60134. TEL 312-232-1055. Ed. Donald F. Hetzler. adv. circ. 600.
Listing of Protestant and other religious publications in the United States and Canada

282   IT
BIBLIOGRAFIA MISSIONARIA. 1935. a. $20. Pontificia Universita Urbaniana, Pontificia Biblioteca Missionaria della S.C. per l'Evangelizzazione dei Popoli, Via Urbano VIII, 16, 000165 Rome, Italy. Ed. Willi Henkel. bk. rev. circ. 5,000.

255 011 920 IT
BIBLIOGRAPHIA FRANCISCANA. (Annual supplement to Collectanea Franciscana) (Text in Latin) 1931. a. price varies. Frati Minori Cappuccini, Istituto Storico, Casella Postale 9091, Circonv. Occidentale 6850 (GRA km 65), 00163 Rome, Italy. circ. 800.

296 016 US ISSN 0067-6853
BIBLIOGRAPHICA JUDAICA. 1969. irreg., no.9, 1985. Library of Hebrew Union College-Jewish Institute of Religion, 3101 Clifton Ave., Cincinnati, OH 45220. TEL 513-221-1875. Ed. Herbert C. Zafren.

200 US ISSN 0742-6836
BIBLIOGRAPHIES AND INDEXES IN RELIGIOUS STUDIES. 1984. irreg. price varies. Greenwood Press (Subsidiary of: Congressional Information Service, Inc.) 88 Post Rd. W., Box 5007, Westport, CT 06881. TEL 203-226-3571. Ed. Gary E. Gorman.

282 011 US ISSN 0008-8285
CATHOLIC PERIODICAL AND LITERATURE INDEX. 1930. bi-m. with biennial cum. (service basis) Catholic Library Association, 461 W. Lancaster Ave., Haverford, PA 19041. TEL 215-649-5250. Ed. Natalie A. Logan. bk. rev. abstr. bibl. circ. 1,500. (also avail. in microfilm from UMI)
  Former titles: Catholic Periodical Index (ISSN 0363-6895); Guide to Catholic Literature (ISSN 0145-191X)

280 016 US ISSN 0069-3871
CHRISTIAN PERIODICAL INDEX; an index to subjects, authors and book reviews. 1959. q. plus annual. $60 (including annual) Association of Christian Librarians Inc., Cedarville College Library, Cedarville, OH 45314. Ed. Douglas J. Butler. circ. 450. (reprint service avail. from UMI)

200 US ISSN 0883-1440
CURRENT CHRISTIAN ABSTRACTS. 1985. m. $36. Box 7596, Columbia, MO 65205. Eds. Betty Gibb, Sue Job. circ. 500.

016.2 US ISSN 0270-2347
CURRENT CHRISTIAN BOOKS. 1975. a. $54.95. (Christian Booksellers Association) C B A Service Corporation, Box 200, Colorado Springs, CO 80901. TEL 303-576-7880. Ed. Cherie Rayburn. circ. 2, 700. (also avail. in microfiche)
  Incorporating: Current Christian Books. Authors and Titles (ISSN 0098-5554) & Current Christian Books. Titles, Authors, and Publishers (ISSN 0098-5562)

220 016 VC ISSN 0392-7423
ELENCHUS BIBLIOGRAPHICUS BIBLICUS. a. $85. (Pontificio Istituto Biblico) Biblical Institute Press, Piazza della Pilotta 35, 00187 Rome, Italy. Ed. Robert North S.J.
  Bible

016 200 320 US ISSN 0161-6072
I C U I S JUSTICE MINISTRIES. 1978. irreg. $8 to individuals; institutions $12. Institute on the Church in Urban Industrial Society, 5700 S. Woodlawn Ave., Chicago, IL 60637. TEL 312-643-7111. Ed. Clinton Stockwell, Dick Simpson. bk. rev. bibl. circ. 300. Indexed: Rel.Ind.One.
  Supersedes (1970-1978): I C U I S Abstract Service.

294.3 II
INDEX INTERNATIONALIS INDICUS. 1970. triennial. price varies. Centre for Asian Dokumentation, P.O. Box 11215, K-15, Cit Bldg., Christopher Rd., Calcutta 700014, India (Distr. by: Verlag Otto Harrassowitz, Taunusstr. 14, P.O. Box 2929, 6200 Wiesbaden 1, W. Germany (B.R.D.)) Ed. S. Chaudhuri. adv. circ. 500.

296 016 IS ISSN 0073-5817
INDEX OF ARTICLES ON JEWISH STUDIES/ RESHIMAT MA'AMARIM BE-MADA'E HA-YAHADUT. (Text in various languages) 1969. biennial. $20 single issue; $25 double issue. ‡ Jewish National and University Library, Box 503, Jerusalem, Israel. circ. 1,200.

289 016 US ISSN 0073-5981
INDEX TO PERIODICALS OF THE CHURCH OF JESUS CHRIST OF LATTER-DAY SAINTS. CUMULATIVE EDITION. 1961. a. $5 yearly; $10.00 cum. 1961-1970. Church of Jesus Christ of Latter-day Saints, 50 E. North Temple St., Salt Lake City, UT 84150 TEL 801-531-2531. (Subscr. to: Salt Lake Distribution Center, 1999 West 1700 South, Salt Lake City, UT 84104) index. circ. 5,000.

016 200 NE
INTERNATIONAL BIBLIOGRAPHY OF THE HISTORY OF RELIGIONS/BIBLIOGRAPHIE INTERNATIONAL DE L'HISTOIRE DES RELIGIONS. 1954. a. price varies. E.J. Brill, P.O. Box 9000, 2300 PA Leiden, Netherlands.

297 GW ISSN 0724-2263
ISLAMIC BOOK REVIEW INDEX. (Text in English) 1982. a. DM.60($29) Wolfgang H. Behn, Ed. & Pub., Rosenheimer Str. 5, D-1000 Berlin 30, W. Germany (B.R.D.) bk. rev. circ. 500. (back issues avail.)

016 282 NE
KATHOLIEK DOCUMENTATIE CENTRUM. BIBLIOGRAFIEEN. irreg. price varies. Katholiek Documentatie Centrum, Erasmuslaan 36, 6525 GG Nijmegen, Netherlands.

284 ZA
LUTHERAN CHURCH OF CENTRAL AFRICA. STATISTICAL REPORT. (Text in English) a. Lutheran Church of Central Africa, Box CH 195, Lusaka, Zambia.

220 016 US ISSN 0028-6877
NEW TESTAMENT ABSTRACTS; a record of current literature. 1956. 3/yr. $24. Weston School of Theology, 3 Phillips Place, Cambridge, MA 02138 TEL 617-492-1960. (Subscr. to: Catholic Biblical Association of America, Catholic University of America, Washington, DC 20064) Ed. D.J. Harrington. adv. bk. rev. abstr. index; cum.index: vols. 1-15 (1956-1970) circ. 2,150. (back issues avail) Indexed: Int.Z.Bibelwiiss.

016 260 FR
OECUMENE; international bibliography indexed by computer. (Text and summaries in English, French, German, Italian and Spanish) 1977. biennial. 260 F.($20) Universite de Strasbourg II, Centre de Recherche et de Documentation des Institutions Chretiennes, 9 Place de l'Universite, 67084 Strasbourg Cedex, France. bk. rev. circ. 1,000. (back issues avail.)

220 US ISSN 0364-8591
OLD TESTAMENT ABSTRACTS. 1978. 3/yr. $14. Catholic Biblical Association of America, Catholic University of America, Washington, DC 20064. TEL 202-635-5519. Ed. Bruce Vawter, C.M. circ. 20,000.

200 016 US ISSN 0149-8428
RELIGION INDEX ONE: PERIODICALS. 1949. s-a. plus a. cum. $285. American Theological Library Association, Religion Indexes, 5600 S. Woodlawn Ave., Chicago, IL 60637. TEL 312-947-9417. circ. 1,200.
  ●Also available online. Vendors: BRS, DIALOG.
  Formerly: Index to Religious Periodical Literature (ISSN 0019-4107)

200 US ISSN 0149-8436
RELIGION INDEX TWO: MULTI-AUTHOR WORKS. 1976. a. $177. American Theological Library Association, Religion Indexes, 5600 S. Woodlawn Ave., Chicago, IL 60637. TEL 312-947-9417. Ed. Erica Treesh. circ. 1,000.
  ●Also available online. Vendors: BRS, DIALOG.

200 016 US ISSN 0034-4044
RELIGIOUS & THEOLOGICAL ABSTRACTS. 1958. q. $23.25 to individuals; institutions $46.50. Religious & Theological Abstracts Inc., Box 215, Myerstown, PA 17067. TEL 717-866-6734. Ed. J.C. Christman. abstr. index. circ. 1,100. (also avail. in microfiche; back issues avail.)

200 UK ISSN 0081-1440
SOCIETY FOR OLD TESTAMENT STUDY. BOOK LIST. 1946. a. £12($12) ‡ Society for Old Testament Study, c/o M. E. J. Richardson, Middle Eastern Studies, University of Manchester, Manchester M13 9PL, England. Ed. G. Auld. adv. bk. rev. index. circ. 1,500.

STUDIES IN BIBLIOGRAPHY AND BOOKLORE; devoted to research in the field of Jewish bibliography. see *PUBLISHING AND BOOK TRADE — Abstracting, Bibliographies, Statistics*

200 016 UK
THEOLOGICAL AND RELIGIOUS BIBLIOGRAPHIES. 1972. irreg. £2. Theological Abstracting and Bibliographical Services, 33 Mayfield Grove, Harrogate, North Yorkshire HG1 5HD, England. Ed. G.P. Cornish. bk. rev. circ. 150. (also avail. in microfilm)
  Formerly (until vol.3, 1981): Theological and Religious Index (ISSN 0306-087X)

200 US
TOPICS IN RELIGION: A BIBLIOGRAPHIC SERIES. irreg. price varies. Greenwood Press, 88 Post Rd. W., Box 5007, Westport, CT 06881. TEL 203-226-3571. Ed. Gary E. Gorman.

ZIONIST LITERATURE. see *PUBLISHING AND BOOK TRADE — Abstracting, Bibliographies, Statistics*

RELIGIONS AND THEOLOGY — Islamic

268 NR ISSN 0065-468X
AHMADU BELLO UNIVERSITY. CENTRE OF ISLAMIC LEGAL STUDIES. JOURNAL. 1966. irreg., vol.5, 1974. Ahmadu Bello University, Centre of Islamic Legal Studies, P.M.B. 1013, Zaria, Nigeria (Overseas orders to: Wiley & Sons Ltd., Lincoln's Inn Archway, Carey St., London W.C. 2, England)

ANNALES ISLAMOLOGIQUES. see *ORIENTAL STUDIES*

297 NE
ASFAR. 1977. irreg. price varies. Rijksuniversiteit te Leiden, Documentatiebureau Islam-Christendom, Theologisch Instituut, Rapenburg 59, Leiden, Netherlands.

956 297 GW ISSN 0170-3102
BIBLIOTHECA ISLAMICA. (Text in English and German) irreg., vol.32, 1987. price varies. (Deutsche Morgenlaendische Gesellschaft) Franz Steiner Verlag Wiesbaden GmbH, Birkenwaldstr. 44, Postfach 347, D-7000 Stuttgart 1, W. Germany (B.R.D.) Ed.Bd.

297 956 UA ISSN 0259-7373
BULLETIN CRITIQUE DES ANNALES ISLAMOLOGIQUES. 1986. a. Institut Francais d'Archeologie Orientale du Caire, 37 rue El Sheikh Aly Youssef, Mounira, Cairo, Egypt. circ. 800.

FREIBURGER ISLAMSTUDIEN. see *ORIENTAL STUDIES*

297 PK
HAMDARD FOUNDATION. REPORT. 1980. biennial. free. Hamdard Foundation, Nazimabad, Karachi 8, Pakistan. circ. 2,000.

JUSUR; the U C L A journal of Middle Eastern studies. see *HISTORY — History Of The Near East*

297 PK ISSN 0541-5462
M.I.I. SERIES.* 1966. irreg. Muslim Intellectuals' International, Box 5294, Karachi, Pakistan.

297 LE
RISALEH AL-ISLAMIYAH. irreg. £L1.50 per no. Box 155063, Beirut, Lebanon.

297 SI ISSN 0559-2674
SEDAR; journal of Islamic studies. 1968. biennial. S.$2. ‡ University of Singapore, Muslim Society, Yusof Ishak House, Clementi Rd., Kent Ridge, Singapore 5, Singapore. Ed. M. Dzulfighar Mohd. adv. bibl.

297 400 LE
UNIVERSITE SAINT-JOSEPH. FACULTE DES LETTRES ET DES SCIENCES HUMAINES. RECHERCHE. SERIE A: LANGUE ARABE ET PENSEE ISLAMIQUE. (Previously published by its Institut des Lettres Orientales in 4 series) 1956; N.S. 1971. irreg. price varies. Dar el-Mashreq S.A.R.L., 2 rue Huvelin, Box 946, Beirut, Lebanon (Subscr. to: Librairie Orientale, Box 946, Beirut, Lebanon)

200 PK ISSN 0084-2052
WORLD MUSLIM CONFERENCE. PROCEEDINGS. (Published in: Muslim World) (Text in English) biennial. World Muslim Congress - Motamar al-Alam al-Islami, 224, Sharafabad, Karachi 0511, Pakistan.

297 PK ISSN 0084-2060
WORLD MUSLIM GAZETTEER. (Text in English) 1964. quinquennial. $35. World Muslim Congress - Motamar Al-Alam al-Islami, 224, Sharafabad, Karachi 0511, Pakistan. Ed. Inamullah Khan.

297 GW ISSN 0040-8646
WUDD; dedicated to the cause of Islam. 1970. a. DM.2. Hadayatullah Huebsch, Wickerer Str. 12, 6000 Frankfurt 1, W. Germany (B.R.D.) adv. bk. rev. charts.
Formerly: Toern.

RELIGIONS AND THEOLOGY — Judaic

see also Ethnic Interests

296 US ISSN 0065-6798
AMERICAN ACADEMY FOR JEWISH RESEARCH. PROCEEDINGS OF THE A A J R. 1929. a. $20. American Academy for Jewish Research, 3080 Broadway, New York, NY 10027. TEL 212-678-8864. Ed. Isaac E. Barzilay. circ. 400.

296 US ISSN 0065-8987
AMERICAN JEWISH YEAR BOOK. 1899. a. $25.95. (American Jewish Committee) Jewish Publication Society, 1930 Chestnut, Philadelphia, PA 19103 TEL 215-564-5925. Ed. David Singer. index. circ. 5,000. (also avail. in microform) Indexed: Amer.Bibl.Slavic & E.Eur.Stud.

296 NE ISSN 0066-5681
ARBEITEN ZUR GESCHICHTE DES ANTIKEN JUDENTUMS UND DES URCHRISTENTUMS. 1961. irreg., no.15, 1978. price varies. (Institutum Iudaicum, Tuebingen, GW) E.J. Brill, P.O. Box 9000, 2300 PA Leiden, Netherlands.

296 NE
ARBEITEN ZUR LITERATUR UND GESCHICHTE DES HELLENISTISCHEN JUDENTUMS. (Text in German) irreg., vol.19, 1986. price varies. E.J. Brill, P.O. Box 9000, 2300 PA Leiden, Netherlands.

ARBEITSINFORMATIONEN UEBER STUDIENPROJEKTE AUF DEM GEBIET DER GESCHICHTE DES DEUTSCHEN JUDENTUMS UND DES ANTISEMITISMUS. see HISTORY — History Of Europe

296 US ISSN 0067-2742
B.G. RUDOLPH LECTURES IN JUDAIC STUDIES. 1963. a. free. Syracuse University, Department of Religion, Jewish Studies Program, Syracuse, NY 13244-1170. TEL 315-423-3861. Ed. Alan L. Berger. circ. 7,500.

296 IS
BAOR HATORAH. (Text in English and Hebrew) a. Association of Religious Academians, P.O. Box 5749, Jerusalem 91 047, Israel. TEL 02-223702. Ed. Elena Cohen.

296 300 IS ISSN 0067-4109
BAR-ILAN: ANNUAL OF BAR-ILAN UNIVERSITY. (Text in Hebrew; summaries in English) 1963. a. $20. Bar-Ilan University, Ramat-Gan, Israel. Ed.Bd. Indexed: Ind.Heb.Per.

296 IS ISSN 0334-1380
BARKAI. 1984. a. IS.10($8) Mifal Rabanim Ubnei Torah, P.O. Box 7524, Jerusalem, Israel. TEL 02-248113. Ed. Rabbi Shaul Yisraeli. circ. 2,000.

296 IS
BASHAVIL HAREFUAH. a. $3. Laniado Hospital, Netanya 42 150, Israel. TEL 053-21666. Ed. Rabbi Schwartz.

296 IS
BEER-SHEVA. (Text in Hebrew; summaries in English) 1973. a. Ben-Gurion University of the Negev, Box 2053, Beersheva, Israel. Ed.Bd. illus. circ. 1,000.

296.68 US
B'KITZUR/BRIEFS. vol.3, 1973. irreg., 2-3/yr. free. (Solomon Schechter Day School Association) United Synagogue of America, Commission on Jewish Education, 155 Fifth Ave., New York, NY 10010. TEL 212-260-8450. Ed. Meir Efrati. bk. rev. stat. circ. 2,000.

CANADIAN JEWISH ARCHIVES (NEW SERIES) see ETHNIC INTERESTS

296 US ISSN 0069-1607
CENTRAL CONFERENCE OF AMERICAN RABBIS. YEARBOOK. 1890. a. $17.50. ‡ (Central Conference of American Rabbis) C C A R Press, 21 E. 40th St., 14th Fl., New York, NY 10016. TEL 212-684-4990. Ed. Elliot L. Stevens. cum.index: 1951-1970. circ. 1,500. Indexed: Rel.Ind.Two.

296 SP
COLECCION SENDA ABIERTA. SERIE 2 (AZUL): JUDAISMO. 1974. irreg. 150 ptas. (Centro de Estudios Judeo-Cristianos) Studium Ediciones, Bailen 19, Madrid 13, Spain.

COLLECTION FRANCO-JUDAICA. see ETHNIC INTERESTS

296 NE
COMPENDIA RERUM IUDAICARUM AD NOVUM TESTAMENTUM. sect.1, no.2, 1976. irreg. price varies. Van Gorcum, Box 43, 9400 AA Assen, Netherlands.

CONFERENCE OF PRESIDENTS OF MAJOR AMERICAN JEWISH ORGANIZATIONS. ANNUAL REPORT. see ETHNIC INTERESTS

CONTEMPORARY JEWRY; a journal of sociological inquiry. see ETHNIC INTERESTS

DISPERSION Y UNIDAD. see HISTORY — History Of The Near East

296 IS ISSN 0303-7819
ENCYCLOPAEDIA JUDAICA YEAR BOOK. (Text in English) 1973. a. Keter Publishing House Ltd., Givat Shaul Industrial Area, Box 7145, Jerusalem, Israel (U.S. orders to: Keter Inc., 440 Park Ave. South, New York, NY 10016)

296 NE
ETUDES SUR LE JUDAISME MEDIEVAL. 1968. irreg., vol.12, 1985. price varies. E.J. Brill, P.O. Box 9000, 2300 PA Leiden, Netherlands. Ed. G. Vajda.

FRANKFURTER JUDAISTISCHE BEITRAEGE. see ETHNIC INTERESTS

296 US ISSN 0016-9145
GESHER. (Text in English and Hebrew) a. $5. (Yeshiva University, Student Organization of Yeshiva) Rabbi Isaac Elchanan Theological Seminary, 500 W. 185th St., New York, NY 10033. TEL 212-960-5277. Ed.Bd.

296 US ISSN 0017-6532
HADOROM.* (Text in English; contents page in English) 1957. a. $10. Rabbinical Council of America, 275 Seventh Ave., New York, NY 10001. Ed. Rabbi Gdalia Schwartz. bk. rev. circ. 1,300.

HA-MESIVTA. see LAW

HARVARD JUDAIC MONOGRAPHS. see ETHNIC INTERESTS

HEBREW UNION COLLEGE ANNUAL. see ETHNIC INTERESTS

HEBREW UNION COLLEGE ANNUAL SUPPLEMENTS. see ETHNIC INTERESTS

296.67 US ISSN 0732-0914
HERITAGE (WALTHAM) 1968. biennial, no.2, 1981. $50 to members. ‡ American Jewish Historical Society, 2 Thornton Rd., Waltham, MA 02154. TEL 617-891-8110. Ed. Bernard Wax. circ. 3,800.
Former titles (until 1984): American Jewish Historical Society. Report; (until 1976): American Jewish Historical Society. News (ISSN 0065-8944)

296 US ISSN 0075-3726
JEWISH BOOK ANNUAL. (Text in English, Hebrew and Yiddish) 1942. a. $25. J W B Jewish Book Coucil of America, 15 E. 26th St., New York, NY 10010. TEL 212-532-4949. Ed. Jacob Kabakoff. bk. rev. circ. 1,200. Indexed: Ind.Heb.Per. Amer.Bibl.Slavic & E.Eur.Stud.

909 UK ISSN 0306-7998
JEWISH HISTORICAL SOCIETY OF ENGLAND. ANNUAL REPORT AND ACCOUNTS FOR THE SESSION. 1890. a. membership. Jewish Historical Society of England, Mocatta Library & Museum, University College, 33 Seymour Place, London W1H 5AP, England.
Continues: Jewish Historical Society of England. Report and Balance Sheet.

296 UK
JEWISH HISTORICAL SOCIETY OF ENGLAND. TRANSACTIONS. biennial. membership. Jewish Historical Society of England, Mocatta Library & Museum, University College, 33 Seymour Place, London W1H 5AP, England.

JEWISH LANGUAGE REVIEW. see LINGUISTICS

296 NE
JEWISH LAW ANNUAL. 1978. a. price varies. E.J. Brill, P.O. Box 9000, 2300 PA Leiden, Netherlands. Ed. Bernard S. Jackson. Indexed: Old Test.Abstr.

296 US
JEWISH PROCLAIMER. 1981. irreg. $15 donation. National Center for Understanding Judaism, Box 651, Woodmoor Station, Silver Spring, MD 20901. Ed. Ash Gerecht. circ. 6,000.

296 UK ISSN 0075-3769
JEWISH YEAR BOOK. 1896. a. £2($16.50) Jewish Chronicle Publications, 25 Furnival St, London EC4A 1JT, England. Ed. Roger Japhet. adv. bk. rev. circ. 5,000. (also avail. in microform)

296 IS ISSN 0334-0953
JEWS OF THE SOVIET UNION. 1978. irreg. (Israel Public Council for Soviet Jewry, Scientist Committee) Magnes Press University, The Hebrew University, Jerusalem 91 904, Israel. Ed. David Prital.

JOURNAL OF JEWISH ART. see ART

JOURNAL OF JEWISH MUSIC AND LITURGY. see MUSIC

296 US
KEREM SHLOMO. (Text in Hebrew) 1977. irreg., 10-12/yr. $15. Bobover Congregation, 1577 48th St., Brooklyn, NY 11219. TEL 718-438-2018. Ed. Shmerel Zitronenbaum. bibl. index. circ. 2,500. (back issues avail.)

KOSHER DIRECTORY. see ETHNIC INTERESTS

296 UK ISSN 0075-8744
LEO BAECK INSTITUTE. YEAR BOOK. 1956. a. £12. Secker & Warburg, 54 Poland St., London W1V 3DF, England (Dist. in U.S. by: Leo Baeck Institute, 129 E. 73rd St., New York, NY 10021) Ed. Arnold Paucker. bk. rev. index, cum.index: vols.1-20, pub. in 1982. circ. 2,500. Indexed: Hist.Abstr. Amer.Hist.& Life. Amer.Bibl.Slavic & E.Eur.Stud.

296 US
LIBRARY OF JEWISH LAW AND ETHICS. irreg., vol.4, 1977. price varies. Ktav Publishing House, 900 Jefferson St., No. 6249, Hoboken, NJ 07030-7205. TEL 201-963-9524.

296 IS
MAGAL. irreg. Bar Ilan University Press, Ramat Gan 52 100, Israel.

296 IS ISSN 0541-5632
MITZION TETZEH TORAH. M.T.T. 1968. irreg., (approx. 2/yr.) price varies. Mitzion Tetzeh Torah, Ltd., Box 29435, 9 Derech Haifa Rd., Tel-Aviv, Israel. Ed. G. Rachaman. adv. bk. rev. circ. 1,000.

MUSICA JUDAICA. see *MUSIC*

296 IS ISSN 0048-0460
NIV HAMIDRASHIA. (Text in English and Hebrew) 1963. irreg. $7 per no. Friends of the Midrashia, Israel, 3, Achuzath Bayeth St., Tel Aviv, Israel. Eds. Israel Sadan, Alexander Carlebach. adv. bk. rev. circ. 5,000. Indexed: Ind.Heb.Per.

296 US ISSN 0079-936X
RABBINICAL ASSEMBLY, NEW YORK. PROCEEDINGS. (Text in English with some Hebrew and Yiddish) 1927. a. (suspended 1970-1973) $7.50. Rabbinical Assembly, 3080 Broadway, New York, NY 10027. TEL 212-678-8060. Ed. Jules Harlow. cum.index: 1927-1968. circ. 1,400.

SEMITIC STUDY SERIES. see *ORIENTAL STUDIES*

SHVUT; Jewish problems in the USSR and Eastern Europe. see *ETHNIC INTERESTS*

296 US ISSN 0196-2183
SOLOMON GOLDMAN LECTURES; perspectives in Jewish learning. 1977. irreg. $5 paperback; $7 hardback. Spertus College of Judaica Press, 618 S. Michigan Ave., Chicago, IL 60605. TEL 312-922-9012. Ed. N. Stampfer. circ. 500.
Supersedes: Perspectives in Jewish Learning (ISSN 0079-1016)

SOURCES OF CONTEMPORARY JEWISH THOUGHT/MEKEVOT. see *LITERARY AND POLITICAL REVIEWS*

296 IT
STORIA DELL'EBRAISMO IN ITALIA. 1980. irreg., vol.6, 1985. price varies. Casa Editrice Leo S. Olschki, Casella Postale 66, 50100 Florence, Italy.

296 NE ISSN 0081-6914
STUDIA SEMITICA NEERLANDICA. 1956. irreg., no.17, 1975. price varies. Van Gorcum, Box 43, 9400 AA Assen, Netherlands.

296 US ISSN 0081-7511
STUDIES IN AMERICAN JEWISH HISTORY. 1951. irreg., no.5, 1968. price varies. ‡ American Jewish Historical Society, 2 Thornton Rd., Waltham, MA 02154. TEL 617-891-8110. index. circ. 1,000.

296.68 IS ISSN 0333-9661
STUDIES IN JEWISH EDUCATION. 1983. a. Hebrew University, Samuel Mendel Melton Centre for Jewish Education in Jerusalem, Mount Scopus, Jerusalem 91 905, Israel. circ. 1,000.

296 US ISSN 0884-6952
STUDIES IN JUDAICA & THE HOLOCAUST. 1985. irreg., latest no.3. $19.95 cloth; 9.95 paper. Borgo Press, Box 2845, San Bernardino, CA 92406. TEL 714-884-5813.

296 NE
STUDIES IN JUDAISM IN LATE ANTIQUITY. 1973. irreg., vol.37, 1984. price varies. E.J. Brill, P.O. Box 9000, 2300 PA Leiden, Netherlands.

296 NE
STUDIES IN JUDAISM IN MODERN TIMES. 1978. irreg., vol.7, 1986. price varies. E.J. Brill, P.O. Box 9000, 2300 PA Leiden, Netherlands. Ed. J. Neusner.

296 NE
STUDIES ON THE TEXTS OF THE DESERT OF JUDAH. 1957. irreg., vol.8, 1975. price varies. E.J. Brill, P.O. Box 9000, 2300 PA Leiden, Netherlands. Ed. J. van der Ploeg.

296 GW
TEXTE UND STUDIEN ZUM ANTIKEN JUDENTUM. English Edition: Texts and Studies in Medieval and Early Modern Judaism. (Text in English, French and German) 1981. irreg. price varies. Verlag J.C.B. Mohr (Paul Siebeck), Wilhelmstr. 18, Postfach 2040, 7400 Tuebingen, W. Germany (B.R.D.) Eds. Martin Hengel, Peter Schaefer.

296 NE ISSN 0082-3899
THEOKRATIA; JAHRBUCH DES INSTITUTUM JUDAICUM DELITZSCHIANUM. 1967-69. a. price varies. (Institutum Judaicum Delitzschianum) E.J. Brill, P.O. Box 9000, 2300 PA Leiden, Netherlands.

296.8 US ISSN 0363-3810
UNION OF AMERICAN HEBREW CONGREGATIONS. STATE OF OUR UNION. biennial. Union of American Hebrew Congregations, 838 Fifth Ave., New York, NY 10021. TEL 212-249-0100.

296 US ISSN 0041-8153
UNITED SYNAGOGUE REVIEW. 1943. biennial. $3. United Synagogue of America, 155 Fifth Ave., New York, NY 10010. TEL 212-533-7800. Ed. Ruth M. Perry. adv. bk. rev. illus. circ. 250,000. (also avail. in microform from UMI)

296 US
VOICE OF JUDAISM. 1960. irreg. free. National Jewish Information Service, 5174 W. 8th St., Los Angeles, CA 90036. TEL 213-936-6033. Ed. Rabbi Moshe M. Maggal.

956.940 IS
WORD AND DEED. (Text in English) irreg. World Zionist Organization, Youth and Hechalutz Department, Box 92, Jerusalem, Israel.

WORKING PAPERS IN YIDDISH AND EAST EUROPEAN JEWISH STUDIES/IN GANG FUN ARBET: YIDISH UN MIZRAKH EYROPEISHE YIDISHE SHTUDIES. see *ETHNIC INTERESTS*

296 IS ISSN 0084-2516
WORLD ZIONIST ORGANIZATION. GENERAL COUNCIL. ADDRESSES, DEBATES, RESOLUTIONS.* (Text in English) a. World Zionist Organization, Box 92, Jerusalem, Israel.

296 IS
YAD VASHEM STUDIES. (Text in English and Hebrew) 1957. irreg., vol.14, 1981. price varies. Yad Vashem Martyr's and Heroes Remembrance Authority, Box 3477, Jerusalem, Israel. Ed. Livia Rothkirchen. bk. rev. index. cum.index: 1957-67. circ. 1,500.
Formerly (until 1976): Yad Vashem Studies on the European Jewish Catastrophe and Resistance (ISSN 0084-3296)

296 US ISSN 0084-3369
YALE JUDAICA SERIES. 1948. irreg., no.23, 1982. price varies. Yale University Press, 92A Yale Sta., New Haven, CT 06520. TEL 203-432-0940.

296 US ISSN 0044-0256
YAVNEH STUDIES.* 1967. irreg. membership. Yavneh, 66-05 108 St., Forest Hills, NY 11375. Ed.Bd. circ. 4,000. (processed)
Topics in Jewish philososphy intended for a college audience

296 IS
YEARBOOK OF RELIGIOUS ZIONISM. (Text in English and Hebrew) a. IS.15($10) Misilot, P.O. Box 7524, Jerusalem, Israel. TEL 02-248113.

YESHIVA UNIVERSITY SEPHARDIC BULLETIN. see *ETHNIC INTERESTS*

YIDDISH LITERARY AND LINGUISTIC PERIODICALS AND MISCELLANIES; a selective annotated bibliography. see *LINGUISTICS*

RELIGIONS AND THEOLOGY — Oriental

299 301.15 IO
ATMA JAYA RESEARCH CENTRE. SOCIO-RELIGIOUS RESEARCH REPORT/PUSAT PENELITIAN ATMA JAYA. LAPORAN PENELITIAN KEAGAMAAN. 1977. irreg. Atma Jaya Research Centre - Pusat Penelitian Atma Jaya, Jalan Jenderal Sudirman 49a, Box 2639, Jakarta 10001, Indonesia.

294.3 US
BLIND DONKEY. 1975. irreg. $10 for 4 issues. Diamond Sangha, Inc., 2119 Kaloa Way, Honolulu, HI 96822. bk. rev. circ. 400.

BOOKS AND ARTICLES ON ORIENTAL SUBJECTS PUBLISHED IN JAPAN. see *HISTORY — History Of Asia*

BRAHMAVIDYA. see *ORIENTAL STUDIES*

294.3 II
BUDDHIST STUDIES. (Text in English, Hindi and Sanskrit) 1974. a. Rs.10. University of Delhi, Department of Buddhist Studies, Delhi 110007, India. Ed. Kewal Krishan Mittal. bk. rev.

294.3 US ISSN 0097-7209
CRYSTAL MIRROR; annual of Tibetan Buddhism. 1971. irreg., latest vol.7. (Tibetan Nyingma Meditation Center) Dharma Publishing, 2425 Hillside Ave., Berkeley, CA 94704. TEL 415-548-5407. illus.

294.6 II
GURU NANAK COMMEMORATIVE LECTURES. (Text in English) 1970. a. Punjabi University, Publication Bureau, Patiala 1470002, India. Ed. Taran Singh. circ. 1,100.

INDEX INTERNATIONALIS INDICUS. see *RELIGIONS AND THEOLOGY — Abstracting, Bibliographies, Statistics*

294.3 JA
INSTITUTE FOR THE COMPREHENSIVE STUDY OF LOTUS SUTRA. JOURNAL/HOKKE BUNKA KENKYU. (Text in English or Japanese) 1975. a. 3000 Yen. Rissho University, Institute for the Comprehensive Study of Lotus Sutra - Rissho Daigaku Hokekyo Bunka Kenkyujo, 4-2-16 Osaki, Shinagawa-ku, Tokyo 141, Japan. Ed. Zuiryu Nakamura. bk. rev. illus.

299.51 US
JOURNAL OF CHINESE RELIGIONS. 1975. a. $10 to individuals; institutions $10. Society for the Study of Chinese Religions, c/o Rodney L. Taylor, Ed., Department of Religious Studies, University of Colorado, Boulder, CO 80309. TEL 303-492-0111. bk. rev. circ. 125.
Formerly (until 1982): Society for the Study of Chinese Religions. Bulletin.

294.592 AT ISSN 0706-6449
JOURNAL OF STUDIES IN THE BHAGAVADGITA. 1981. irreg. Aus.$10 to individuals; Aus.$15 to institutions. University of Sydney, Department of Religious Studies, Sydney, N.S.W. 2006, Australia. Ed.Bd. bk. rev. circ. 100. (back issues avail.) Indexed: Rel.Per. Rel.Ind.One.

PATROLOGIA SYRIACA ET ORIENTALIS. see *RELIGIONS AND THEOLOGY — Roman Catholic*

294 II ISSN 0554-9906
PRAKIT JAIN INSTITUTE RESEARCH PUBLICATION SERIES. (Text in English and Hindi) 1964. irreg. price varies. Bihar Research Institute of Prakit, Jainology, and Ahimsa, Vaishali, India. Ed. G.C. Choudhary.

294.5 II
SIDDHA VANI. (Text in English or Hindi) 1972. a. Rs.6($1.50) Siddha Yoga Dham, S-174 Panch Shila Park, New Delhi 110017, India. Ed. Janak Nanda. adv. illus. circ. 2,000.

297 II
SRI AUROBINDO. ARCHIVES AND RESEARCH. 1977. biennial. Rs.40($7.50) Sri Aurobindo Ashram Trust, Pondicherry 605002, India. Ed. H. Patel.

290 GW ISSN 0340-6792
STUDIES IN ORIENTAL RELIGIONS. (Text in English and German) 1976. irreg., vol.14, 1986. price varies. Verlag Otto Harrassowitz, Taunusstr. 14, Postfach 2929, 6200 Wiesbaden 1, W. Germany (B.R.D.) Eds. W. Heissig, H.J. Klimkeit.

STUDIES OF CLASSICAL INDIA. see *PHILOSOPHY*

299 US
SYRACUSE UNIVERSITY. FOREIGN AND COMPARATIVE STUDIES. SOUTH ASIAN SPECIAL PUBLICATIONS. 1976. irreg., no.4, 1983. price varies. Syracuse University, Foreign and Comparative Studies, 724 Comstock Ave., Syracuse, NY 13244. TEL 315-423-2552. Ed. Robert N. Kearney.

294 TH ISSN 0084-1781
WORLD FELLOWSHIP OF BUDDHISTS. BOOK
SERIES. 1965. irreg., latest issue 1977. price varies.
World Fellowship of Buddhists, 33 Sukhumvit Rd.,
Bangkok 10-100, Thailand.

294.3 SI
YOUNG BUDDHIST. (Text in Chinese, English) a.
Singapore Buddhist Youth Organisations Joint
Celebrations Committee, 83 Silat Road, Singapore
3, Singapore. illus.

299.56 NE
ZEN EXTRA. 1981. a. price varies. Stichting
Theresiahoeve, Dominicanenstr. 24, 5453 JN
Langenboom, Netherlands. Ed. Judith Bossert. adv.

RELIGIONS AND THEOLOGY —
Protestant

268 US ISSN 0149-998X
ADULT PLANBOOK; resources for adult Christian
education in United Methodist Churches. 1959. a.
free. (United Methodist Church) United Methodist
Publishing House, Graded Press, 201 Eighth Ave.
S., Nashville, TN 37203. TEL 615-749-6417. Ed.
John P. Gilbert. bk. rev. circ. 200,000.
Formerly: United Methodist Church (United
States) Division of Education. Adult Planbook
(ISSN 0082-7983)

286 US ISSN 0091-9381
AMERICAN BAPTIST CHURCHES IN THE U.S.A.
DIRECTORY. 1971. a. $5. American Baptist
Churches in the U.S.A., Box 851, Valley Forge, PA
19482-0851. TEL 215-768-2000. Ed. Robert C.
Campbell. circ. 6,000.
Supersedes in part: American Baptist Convention.
Directory (ISSN 0096-3380); American Baptist
Convention. Yearbook.

286 US ISSN 0092-3478
AMERICAN BAPTIST CHURCHES IN THE U.S.A.
YEARBOOK. 1907. a. $5. American Baptist
Churches in the U.S.A., Box 851, Valley Forge, PA
19482-0851. TEL 215-768-2000. Ed. Robert C.
Campbell. illus. circ. 3,500. Key Title: Yearbook of
the American Baptist Churches in the U.S.A.

286 US ISSN 0066-1708
ANDREWS UNIVERSITY. MONOGRAPHS. 1966.
irreg., 1983, vol.13. price varies. Andrews University
Press, Berrien Springs, MI 49104. TEL 616-471-
3392. Ed. Robert E. Firth. adv. bk. rev.

283 CN
ANGLICAN CHURCH OF CANADA. GENERAL
SYNOD. JOURNAL. 1894. triennial. Anglican
Church of Canada, General Synod, 600 Jarvis St.,
Toronto, Ont. M4Y 2J6, Canada. TEL 416-924-
9192. circ. 450.
Formerly (until 1980): Anglican Chiurch of
Canada. General Synod. Journal of Proceedings
(ISSN 0380-2469)

266 CN ISSN 0317-8765
ANGLICAN YEAR BOOK. 1900. a. Can.$17.95.
(Anglican Church of Canada) Anglican Book
Centre, 600 Jarvis St., Toronto, Ont. M4Y 2J6,
Canada. TEL 416-924-9192. Ed. B. Lloyd. adv. stat.
circ. 1,000.

284 FR ISSN 0066-362X
ANNUAIRE PROTESTANT; LA FRANCE
PROTESTANTE ET LES EGLISES DE LANGUE
FRANCAISE. 1922, 40th ed. a. 84 F. (Centrale du
Livre Protestant) Librairie Fischbacher, 33 rue de
Seine, 75006 Paris, France.

AUSTRALIAN LECTIONARY (YEAR) see
RELIGIONS AND THEOLOGY

266 US ISSN 0091-2743
BAPTIST MISSIONARY ASSOCIATION OF
AMERICA. DIRECTORY AND HANDBOOK.
1961. a. free. Baptist News Service, Box 97,
Jacksonville, TX 75766. TEL 214-586-8617. Eds.
Leon Gaylor, James C. Blaylock. circ. 5,000. Key
Title: Directory and Handbook - Baptist Missionary
Association of America.
Missions

266 UK ISSN 0067-4060
BAPTIST MISSIONARY SOCIETY, LONDON.
ANNUAL REPORT. 1792. a. free. Baptist
Missionary Society, 93 Gloucester Place, London,
W1H 4AA, England. circ. 7,000.
Missions

266.6 UK ISSN 0067-4079
BAPTIST MISSIONARY SOCIETY, LONDON.
OFFICIAL REPORT AND DIRECTORY OF
MISSIONARIES. 1793. a. free. Baptist Missionary
Society, 93 Gloucester Place, London W1H 4AA,
England. circ. 6,000.
Missions

286.1 UK ISSN 0302-3184
BAPTIST UNION DIRECTORY. 1861. a. £4.20.
Baptist Union of Great Britain and Ireland, 4,
Southampton Row, London WC1B 4AB, England.
Ed. B. Green. adv. circ. 2,500.

286 UK ISSN 0067-4087
BAPTIST UNION OF WESTERN CANADA.
YEARBOOK. 1907. a. Can.$9. Baptist Union of
Western Canada, 838 11th Ave., S.W., Ste. 202,
Calgary, Albt. T2R 0E5, Canada. TEL 403-243-
6880. Ed. D.N. Moffat. circ. 700 (controlled) (also
avail. in microfilm)

286 US ISSN 0067-4095
BAPTIST WORLD ALLIANCE. CONGRESS
REPORTS. 1905. quinquennial; 15th, Los Angeles,
1985 (published in 1986) $11.50. Baptist World
Alliance, 6733 Curran St., McLean, VA 22101-
3804. TEL 703-790-8980. Ed. John Mannen Wilkes.
circ. 15,000.

286 CN
BAPTIST YEARBOOK. a. Baptist Convention of
Ontario and Quebec, 217 St. George St., Toronto,
Ont. M5R 2M2, Canada. Ed. Rev. Philip Karpetz.
circ. 1,500.

284 NE
BIBLIOTHECA UNITARIORUM. 1983. irreg., latest
no.1, 1983. price varies. De Graaf Publishers,
Postbus 6, 2420 AA Nieuwkoop, Netherlands. Ed.
Robert Dan.

BLACK MINISTRIES. see ETHNIC INTERESTS

283 GW ISSN 0341-9452
BLAETTER FUER PFAELZISCHE
KIRCHENGESCHICHTE UND RELIGIOESE
VOLKSKUNDE. 1925. a. DM.40. Verein fuer
Pfaelzische Kirchengeschichte, Herzogstr. 8, 6660
Zweibruecken, W. Germany (B.R.D.) (Subscr. to:
Herzogstr. 8, D-6660 Zweibruecken, W. Germany
(B.R.D.)) bk. rev. index. (back issues avail.)

267 UK
C W M REPORT. 1795. biennial. £1. Council for
World Mission, 11 Carteret St., London SW1H
9DL, England. circ. 15,000.
Formerly: Congregational Council for World
Mission. Annual Report (ISSN 0069-8857)
Missions

CHRISTIAN LIBRARIAN. see LIBRARY AND
INFORMATION SCIENCES

250 UK
CHRISTIAN YEAR. 1987. a. £4.95. Methodist
Publishing House, Wellington Rd., Wimbledon,
London SW19 8EU, England. circ. 25,000.

200 UK
CHURCH ARMY. FRONT LINE. 1981. a. Church
Army, Independents Rd., Blackheath, London SE3
9LG, England. illus.
Formerly: Church Army. Centenary News.

283 UK ISSN 0069-3987
CHURCH OF ENGLAND YEARBOOK. 1882. a.
£12.50. C I O Publishing, Church House, Dean's
Yard, London SW1P 3NZ, England. Ed. Mrs. Jo
Linzey. adv. bk. rev. circ. 3,000.

285.241 UK ISSN 0069-3995
CHURCH OF SCOTLAND. YEARBOOK. 1885. a.
£7.50. Saint Andrew Press, 121 George St.,
Edinburgh EH2 4YN, Scotland. Ed. Rev. Andrew
Herron. adv. index. circ. 2,500.

268 UK
DAILY WATCHWORDS; the Moravian textbook
with almanack. 1722. a. £1.30. Moravian Union
Inc., Moravian Book Room, 5 Muswell Hill, London
N.10 3TJ, England. Ed. J.M. Cooper. circ. 5,000.

DEUTSCHER HUGENOTTEN-VEREIN E.V.
GESCHICHTSBLAETTER. see HISTORY —
History Of Europe

DOOPSGEZINDE BIJDRAGEN. see HISTORY —
History Of Europe

284 CN ISSN 0702-844X
END-TIME NEWS. 1970. irreg. Solbrekken
Evangelistic Association, Box 2424, Edmonton,
Alta., Canada. TEL 403-483-4040. illus.
Formerly: Edmonton Revival Centre. News
(ISSN 0702-8458)

284 US
EPISCOPAL CLERICAL DIRECTORY. biennial.
Church Hymnal Corporation, 800 Second Ave.,
New York, NY 10017.

280 FR ISSN 0071-1330
ESPRIT ET LIBERTE; Protestantisme liberal. 1956.
irreg., no.24, 1973. 45 F. Librairie Fischbacher, 33
rue de Seine, 75006 Paris, France. Indexed: Canon
Law Abstr.

286.1 CN ISSN 0317-266X
EVANGELICAL BAPTIST CHURCHES IN
CANADA. FELLOWSHIP YEARBOOK. 1959. a.
Fellowship of Evangelical Baptist Churches in
Canada, 3034 Bayview Ave., Willowdale, Ont. M2N
6J5, Canada. TEL 416-223-8696. illus. Key Title:
Fellowship Yearbook.
Formerly: Missions Digest and Year Book (ISSN
0544-439X)

266 GW
EVANGELISCH-LUTHERISCH MISSIONSWERK
IN NIEDERSACHSEN. JAHRBUCH (YEAR)
1954. a. DM.4. (Evangelisch-Lutherisch
Missionswerk in Niedersachsen) Missionshandlung
Hermannsburg, Harmsstr. 2-6, D-3102
Hermannsburg, W. Germany (B.R.D.) Ed. Reinhart
Mueller. circ. 4,500. (back issues avail.)
Formerly (until 1979): Die Hermannsburger
Mission im Jahre (Year)

284 FR
FEDERATION PROTESTANTE DE FRANCE.
ANNUAIRE. 1952. a. 180 F. Federation
Protestante de France, c/o J. R. Graff, Ed., 47 rue
de Clichy, 75009 Paris, France.
Formerly: France Prostestante (ISSN 0071-9064)

266 285 AT ISSN 0016-2108
FRONTIER NEWS. 1930. a. free. Uniting Church,
Frontier Services, 123 Clarence St., Sydney, N.S.W.
2000, Australia. Ed. Gray Birch. bk. rev. charts.
illus. stat. circ. 17,500. (tabloid format)
Missions

GESELLSCHAFT FUER DIE GESCHICHTE DES
PROTESTANTISMUS IN OESTERREICH.
JAHRBUCH. see HISTORY — History Of Europe

GESELLSCHAFT FUER NIEDERSAECHSISCHE
KIRCHENGESCHICHTE. JAHRBUCH. see
HISTORY — History Of Europe

HISTORICAL INTELLIGENCER. see HISTORY

200 UK
HISTORICAL SOCIETY OF THE CHURCH IN
WALES. JOURNAL. 1946. a. £2. Historical
Society of the Church in Wales, c/o Owen W.
Jones, The Vicarage, Builth Wells, Brec, Wales. Ed.
Canon David Walker. charts. stat. Indexed:
Br.Archaeol.Abstr.

940 200 UK
HISTORICAL SOCIETY OF THE PRESBYTERIAN
CHURCH OF WALES. JOURNAL. (Text in
English and Welsh) 1916. a. 50p. Historical Society
of the Presbyterian Church of Wales, The Manse,
Caradog Rd., Aberystwyth, Dyfed, Wales. Ed. Rev.
Gomer M. Roberts. bk. rev. circ. 600.

286 UK ISSN 0261-1325
I S ANNUAL. 1980. a. £1. Inter-School Christian
Fellowship, 130 City Rd., London EC1V 2NJ,
England. Ed. Tricia Williams. adv. bk. rev. illus.
circ. 2,000.

RELIGIONS AND THEOLOGY — PROTESTANT

284 GW
IMMER GRUEN. 1911. a. DM.6.20. Quell Verlag Stuttgart, Fuertbachstr. 12A, Postfach 897, 7000 Stuttgart 1, W. Germany (B.R.D.) Ed. Johannes Burdinski. circ. 25,000.

284 IO
INDONESIA. DIRECTORATE GENERAL OF PROTESTANT AFFAIRS. ANNUAL REPORT/ INDONESIA. DIREKTORAT JENDERAL BIMBINGAN MASYARAKAT KRISTEN/ PROTESTAN LAPORAN TAHUNAN. (Text in Indonesian) a. Directorate General of Protestant Affairs, Jalan Moh. Husni Thamrin, Jakarta, Indonesia.

286 CN ISSN 0383-6061
INTERCOM. 1968. irreg. Fellowship of Evangelical Baptist Churches in Canada, 3034 Bayview Ave., Willowdale, Ont. M2N 6J5, Canada. TEL 416-223-8696.

286.0415 UK ISSN 0075-0727
IRISH BAPTIST HISTORICAL SOCIETY. JOURNAL. 1969. a. £3($5.50) Baptist Union of Ireland, 3 Fitzwilliam St., Belfast BT9 6AW, Northern Ireland. TEL 023-669157. Ed. Joshua Thompson. bk. rev. cum.index: vols.1-15 in prep. circ. 250.

274 GW ISSN 0075-6210
KIRCHLICHES JAHRBUCH FUER DIE EVANGELISCHE KIRCHE IN DEUTSCHLAND. a. price varies. Guetersloher Verlagshaus Gerd Mohn, Koenigstr. 23-25, Postfach 1343, 4830 Guetersloh, W. Germany (B.R.D.)

284 GW
KONSTANZER GROSSDRUCKKALENDER. 1934. a. DM.8. Christliche Verlagsanstalt GmbH, Zasiusstrasse 8, D-7750 Konstanz, W. Germany (B.R.D.) Eds. Liselore Loeffler, Wilhelm Schott. bk. rev.

284 GW ISSN 0174-1764
L F B DOCUMENTATION. REPORT. 1978. irreg. DM.22($10) (Lutheran World Federation-Geneva) Kreuz Verlag Zeitschriften GmbH, Breitwiesenstr. 30, 7000 Stuttgart 80, W. Germany (B.R.D.) circ. 3, 500.

266.6 LB
LIBERIA BAPTIST MISSIONARY AND EDUCATIONAL CONVENTION. YEARBOOK. (Text in English) a. Liberia Baptist Missionary and Educational Convention, Bentol City, Liberia. illus.

284 GW
LIBFRAUEN KALENDER. 1983. a. DM.3.50. Birken Verlag, 8055 Hallbergmoos-Girbeneck, W. Germany (B.R.D.) Ed. Franz Habock.

284 US
LUTHERAN ANNUAL. 1910. a. $4.95 paper, $6.95 spiral. ‡ (Lutheran Church-Missouri Synod) Concordia Publishing House, 1333 S. Kirkwood Rd., St. Louis, MO 63122. TEL 314-664-7000. Ed. Jack Gerber. adv. circ. 30,000.

284 US
LUTHERAN CHURCH IN AMERICA. YEARBOOK. 1961. a. $4.50. Board of Publication on Lutheran Church in America, 2900 Queen Lane, Philadelphia, PA 19129. TEL 215-846-6800. Ed. R.T. Swanson. adv. circ. 15,000.
Formerly: American Lutheran Church. Yearbook (ISSN 0569-6348)

284 AT ISSN 0726-4305
LUTHERAN CHURCH OF AUSTRALIA. YEARBOOK. 1967. a. Aus.$6. Lutheran Publishing House, 205 Halifax St., Adelaide, S.A. 5000, Australia. Ed. K.J. Schmidt.
Formed by the merger of: Australian Lutheran Almanac & Lutheran Almanac.

284 CN ISSN 0316-800X
LUTHERAN CHURCHES IN CANADA. DIRECTORY. 1954. a. Can.$3.50. ‡ Lutheran Council in Canada, 25 Old York Mills Rd., Willowdale, Ont. M2P 1B5, Canada. TEL 416-488-9430. Ed. Lawrence Likness. adv. circ. 1,500.

284.1 US ISSN 0076-1540
LUTHERAN WORLD FEDERATION. PROCEEDINGS OF THE ASSEMBLY. irreg., 1970, 5th, Evian-Les-Bains, France. Augsburg Publishing House, 426 South 5th St., Minneapolis, MN 55415. TEL 612-330-3300. Indexed: Rel.Ind.One.

284 GW
LUTHERJAHRBUCH. 1919. a. DM.25. (Luther-Gesellschaft) Vandenhoeck und Ruprecht, Postfach 3753, 3400 Goettingen, W. Germany (B.R.D.) Ed. Helmar Junghans.

289 UK
METHODIST CONFERENCE. MINUTES AND YEARBOOK. 1932. a. £7. Methodist Publishing House, Wellington Rd., Wimbledon, London SW19 8EU, England. circ. 6,000.

691 UK
METHODIST DIARIES. 1850. a. Methodist Publishing House, Wellington Rd., Wimbledon, London SW19 8EU, England. circ. 8,000.

287 SW ISSN 0543-6206
METODISTKYRKANS I SVERIGE. AARSBOK. 1896. a. Kr.35. (Metodistkyrkans i Sverige - United Methodist Church in Sweden) Foerlaget Sanctus, Box 5020, 102 41 Stockholm, Sweden. Rev. Lars Collin. stat. circ. 400.

266 284 US ISSN 0093-8130
MISSION HANDBOOK: NORTH AMERICAN PROTESTANT MINISTRIES OVERSEAS. 1951. triennial. Missions Advanced Research and Communication Center, (Subsidiary of: World Vision International) 919 W. Huntington Dr., Monrovia, CA 91016. TEL 818-303-8811. Ed. Samuel Wilson. index.
Formerly: North American Protestant Ministries Overseas (ISSN 0078-1339)
Missions

266 UK ISSN 0077-3557
NATIONAL BIBLE SOCIETY OF SCOTLAND. ANNUAL REPORT. (Supplement to: Word at Work) 1860. a. free. National Bible Society of Scotland, 7 Hampton Terrace, Edinburgh EH12 5XU, Scotland. Ed. Colin S. Hay. circ. 1,000.

260 US
NATIONAL COUNCIL OF THE CHURCHES OF CHRIST IN THE U.S.A. TRIENNIAL REPORT. 1946. triennial. (National Council of the Churches of Christ in the U.S.A.) National Council of Churches, News and Information Office, 475 Riverside Dr., Rm. 850, New York, NY 10115. TEL 212-870-2227. Ed. Martin Bailey. circ. 2,000.

268 UK ISSN 0079-0117
PARTNERS IN LEARNING. 1968. a. £5. Methodist Church, Division of Education and Youth, 2 Chester House, Pages Lane, London N10 1PR, England (And: National Christian Education Council, Robert Denholm House, Nutfield, Redhill RH1 4HW Surrey, England) (Co-sponsor: Joint Publications Board) Ed. Wilfred Tooley. circ. 24, 000.

280 370 US ISSN 0162-5381
PLANBOOK FOR LEADERS OF CHILDREN. a. (United Methodist Church, Board of Discipleship) Graded Press, 201 Eighth Ave. S., Box 801, Nashville, TN 37202. TEL 615-749-6421. Ed. Mary Frances Pope.

205 US
R E S MISSION BULLETIN. 1981. irreg., approx. q. $5. Reformed Ecumenical Synod, 1677 Gentian Dr., S.E., Grand Rapids, MI 49508. TEL 616-455-1126. Paul G. Schrotenboer. circ. 700.
Formerly: R E S World Diaconal Bulletin.

284 GW ISSN 0171-3469
REFORMATIONSGESCHICHTLICHE STUDIEN UND TEXTE. 1906. irreg., vol.123, 1985. price varies. Aschendorffsche Verlagsbuchhandlung, Soester Str. 13, 4400 Muenster, W. Germany (B.R.D.) Ed. Erwin Iserloh.

280 US ISSN 0080-0481
REFORMED CHURCH OF AMERICA. HISTORICAL SERIES. no.2, 1970. irreg. Wm. B. Eerdmans Publishing Co., 255 Jefferson Ave., S.E., Grand Rapids, MI 49503. TEL 616-459-4591.

267 UK ISSN 0260-0617
SCOTTISH EPISCOPAL CHURCH YEARBOOK. 1879. a. £2.50. ‡ Scottish Episcopal Church, 21 Grosvenor Crescent, Edinburgh EH12 5EE, Scotland. index. circ. 800.

261 SZ ISSN 0559-4065
SEMINAR OF AFRICAN CHRISTIAN STUDENTS IN EUROPE. REPORT.* (Each vol. also has a distinctive title) a. Seminar of African Christian Students in Europe, John Knox House, Chemins des Crets, Grand Saconnex, Geneva, Switzerland.

286 SA
SOUTH AFRICAN BAPTIST HANDBOOK. 1985. a. R.8.50($6.50) Baptist Union of Southern Africa, P.O. Box 1085, Roodepoort 1725, South Africa (Subscr.to: Baptist Publishing House, P.O. Box 50, Roodepoort 1725. South Africa) Ed. E.A. Hermanson. circ. 1,200. (back issues avail.)

286 US ISSN 0146-0196
SOUTH CAROLINA BAPTIST HISTORICAL SOCIETY JOURNAL. 1975. a. $3. South Carolina Baptist Historical Society, Furman University Library, Greenville, SC 29613. TEL 803-294-2194. Ed. J. Glenwood Clayton. circ. 200. (back issues avail.)

286 016 US ISSN 0081-3001
SOUTHERN BAPTIST CONVENTION. ANNUAL. 1845. a. $7.50. Southern Baptist Convention, 901 Commerce, Nashville, TN 37203. TEL 615-244-2355. Ed. Martin Bradley. subject index cumulated irregularly, 1953 (1845-1953), 1965 (1954-1965) circ. 35,000. (also avail. in microfilm)

286 016 US ISSN 0081-301X
SOUTHERN BAPTIST CONVENTION. HISTORICAL COMMISSION. MICROFILM CATALOGUE. 1954. a. $8. Southern Baptist Convention, Historical Commission, 901 Commerce St., Ste. 400, Nashville, TN 37203-3620. TEL 615-244-0344. Ed. Lynn E. May, Jr. adv. circ. 1,500.

284 AU
STUDIEN UND TEXTE ZUR KIRCHENGESCHICHTE UND GESCHICHTE. (Consists of two series) 1975. irreg., vol.4 (series 1), vol.3 (series 2), 1979. price varies. Hermann Boehlaus Nachf., c/o Dr. Karl Lueger, Ring 12, A-1010 Vienna, Austria. Ed. Peter Barton. circ. 800. (back issues avail.) Indexed: Rel.Ind.Two.

285.834 US
SUMMER SERVICE OPPORTUNITIES. 1970. a. free. United Church of Christ, Board for Homeland Ministries, Voluntary Service Office, 132 W. 31st St., New York, NY 10001. TEL 212-239-8700. Ed. Carl A. Bade. circ. 6,000.

284 UK ISSN 0082-6588
TRINITARIAN BIBLE SOCIETY. ANNUAL REPORT. 1831. a. 50p. ‡ Trinitarian Bible Society, 217 Kingston Rd., London SW19 3NN, England.

267 UK
UNITARIAN AND FREE CHRISTIAN CHURCHES. HANDBOOK AND DIRECTORY OF THE GENERAL ASSEMBLY. 1890. a (directory); quinquennial (handbook) £5. General Assembly of Unitarian Free Christian Churches, Essex Hall, 1-6 Essex St., Strand, London, WC2R 3HY, England. Ed. Christine Hayhurst. circ. 850.
Formerly: Unitarian and Free Christian Churches. Yearbook of the General Assembly (ISSN 0082-7797)

288 UK ISSN 0082-7800
UNITARIAN HISTORICAL SOCIETY, LONDON. TRANSACTIONS. 1917. a. £4 to institutions. Unitarian Historical Society, c/o Hon. Treasurer, 58 Stoneygate Court, London Rd., Leicester LE2 2AJ, England. Ed. Rev. H.J. McLachlan. adv. bk. rev. index every 4 years. circ. 325. Indexed: Br.Hum.Ind.

266 US ISSN 0082-7827
UNITARIAN UNIVERSALIST DIRECTORY. 1961. a. $15. Unitarian Universalist Association, 25 Beacon St., Boston, MA 02108. TEL 617-742-2100. Ed. Rev. Mark W. Harris. adv. circ. 2,500. (also avail. in microform from UMI)

RELIGIONS AND THEOLOGY — ROMAN CATHOLIC

288 900   US
UNITARIAN UNIVERSALIST HISTORICAL
SOCIETY. PROCEEDINGS. 1925. a. or biennal;
latest vol.20, 1984/86. $8 per part (2 parts per vol.)
Unitarian Universalist Historical Society, c/o
Conrad Wright, Harvard Divinity School, Andover
Hall, Cambridge, MA 02138. TEL 617-495-5750.
Ed. Richard Myers. bk. rev. circ. 400.
   Formerly: Unitarian Historical Society.
Proceedings (ISSN 0082-7819)

286   CN   ISSN 0082-7843
UNITED BAPTIST CONVENTION OF THE
ATLANTIC PROVINCES. YEARBOOK. 1963. a.
price varies. United Baptist Convention of the
Atlantic Provinces, 1655 Manawagonish Rd., Saint
John, N.B. E2M 3Y2, Canada. TEL 506-674-2006.
Ed. Eugene M. Thompson. index. circ. 2,200.

200   CN   ISSN 0082-786X
UNITED CHURCH OF CANADA. COMMITTEE
ON ARCHIVES. BULLETIN. RECORDS AND
PROCEEDINGS. 1948. a. United Church of
Canada, Committee on Archives, Victoria
University, 73 Queen's Park Cres., Toronto, Ont.
M5S 1K7, Canada. TEL 416-585-4563. bk. rev. circ.
800. Indexed: Hist.Abstr. Amer.Hist.& Life.

200   CN   ISSN 0082-7878
UNITED CHURCH OF CANADA. GENERAL
COUNCIL. RECORD OF PROCEEDINGS. 1925.
biennial. United Church of Canada, General
Council, 85 St. Clair Ave. E., Toronto, Ont. M4T
1M8, Canada. TEL 416-925-5931. circ. 4,000.

200   CN   ISSN 0082-7886
UNITED CHURCH OF CANADA. YEAR BOOK.
1925. a. United Church of Canada, 85 St. Clair
Ave. E., Toronto, Ont. M4T 1M8, Canada. TEL
416-925-5931. circ. 4,000.

285.241   UK   ISSN 0082-7908
UNITED FREE CHURCH OF SCOTLAND.
HANDBOOK. 1930. biennial. £1.25. United Free
Church of Scotland, 11 Newton Place, Glasgow G3
7PR, Scotland. Ed. E.S. Nicoll. bk. rev. circ. 600.

287   US   ISSN 0160-0885
UNITED METHODIST CHURCH. CURRICULUM
PLANS. 1941. a. $6. United Methodist Church,
General Board of Discipleship, Curriculum
Resources Committee, Box 801, Nashville, TN
37202. TEL 615-749-6000. Ed. Dal Joon Won. circ.
500. Key Title: Curriculum Plans.

287   US   ISSN 0503-3551
UNITED METHODIST CHURCH. GENERAL
MINUTES OF THE ANNUAL CONFERENCES.
1968. a. $9 paperbound; $13 clothbound. (United
Methodist Church, General Council on Finance and
Administration) Parthenon Press, 1200 Davis St.,
Evanston, IL 60201. TEL 312-869-3345. Ed. Daniel
A. Nielsen. illus. circ. 2,500. Key Title: General
Minutes of the Annual Conferences of the United
Methodist Church.

287.6   US   ISSN 0503-356X
UNITED METHODIST DIRECTORY. irreg. $4.95.
United Methodist Publishing House, 201 8th Ave.
S., Nashville, TN 37203. TEL 615-749-6000.

285   US   ISSN 0082-8548
UNITED PRESBYTERIAN CHURCH IN THE
UNITED STATES OF AMERICA. MINUTES OF
THE GENERAL ASSEMBLY. a. $4. United
Presbyterian Church in the U.S.A., 475 Riverside
Dr., Rm. 1201, New York, NY 10027. TEL 212-
870-2515. circ. 16,000.

285   UK
UNITED REFORMED CHURCH IN THE UNITED
KINGDOM. UNITED REFORMED CHURCH
YEAR BOOK. 1973. a. £6.50. ‡ United Reformed
Church in the United Kingdom, 86 Tavistock Pl.,
London WC1H 9RT, England. Ed. Sheila Lowden,
Cyril Lowden. adv. circ. 2,000.
   Formerly: Congregational Church in England and
Wales. Congregational Year book (ISSN 0069-8849)

285   UK
UNITED REFORMED CHURCH POCKET DIARY.
a. £1.30. United Reformed Church, 86 Tavistock
Pl., London WC1H 9RT, England.

285   UK
UNITED REFORMED CHURCH, YORKSHIRE
PROVINCE, PROVINCIAL HANDBOOK. 1973.
a. £0.90. United Reformed Church (Yorkshire
Province), 43 Hunslet Ln., Leeds LS10 1JW,
England. Ed. J.E.M. Gilbey. circ. 450.

286   US   ISSN 0083-6311
VIRGINIA BAPTIST REGISTER. 1962. a. $4.50 to
non-members. Virginia Baptist Historical Society,
Box 34, Univ. of Richmond, VA 23173. TEL 804-
289-8437. Ed. John S. Moore. bk. rev. cum.index
every 5 yrs. circ. 750. (also avail. in microfilm)
   Early Virginia Baptist history

280 370   US   ISSN 0512-9575
YOUTH PLANBOOK. a. (United Methodist Church,
Board of Discipleship) Graded Press, 201 Eighth
Ave. S., Box 801, Nashville, TN 37202. TEL 615-
749-6421. Ed. Sharilyn Adair.

284   GW   ISSN 0342-4316
ZEITSCHRIFT FUER BAYERISCHE
KIRCHENGESCHICHTE. 1926. a. DM.15. Verein
fuer Bayerische Kirchengeschichte, Veilhofstr. 28,
D-8500 Nuremburg 20, W. Germany (B.R.D.) Ed.
Horst Weigelt. bk. rev. circ. 800.

RELIGIONS AND THEOLOGY — Roman Catholic

271   US   ISSN 0567-6630
ACADEMY OF AMERICAN FRANCISCAN
HISTORY. BIBLIOGRAPHICAL SERIES. 1953.
irreg., no.4, vol.1, 1978. $17.50. Academy of
American Franciscan History, Box 34440, West
Bethesda, MD 20817. TEL 301-365-1763.

271   US   ISSN 0065-0633
ACADEMY OF AMERICAN FRANCISCAN
HISTORY. DOCUMENTARY SERIES. 1951.
irreg., vol.11, 1979. price varies. Academy of
American Franciscan History, Box 34440, West
Bethesda, MD 20817. TEL 301-365-1763.
   History

271   US   ISSN 0065-0641
ACADEMY OF AMERICAN FRANCISCAN
HISTORY. MONOGRAPH SERIES. 1953. irreg.,
vol.13, 1981. price varies. Academy of American
Franciscan History, Box 34440, West Bethesda, MD
20817. TEL 301-365-1763.

271   US   ISSN 0065-065X
ACADEMY OF AMERICAN FRANCISCAN
HISTORY. PROPAGANDA FIDE SERIES. 1966.
irreg., vol.8, 1980. $40. Academy of American
Franciscan History, Box 34440, West Bethesda, MD
20817. TEL 301-365-1763. Eds. Mathias Kiemen,
Alexander Wyse. index.
   History

ACTA MEDIAEVALIA. see *HISTORY — History
Of Europe*

270   VC   ISSN 0065-1443
ACTA NUNTIATURAE GALLICAE. 1961. irreg.
price varies. (Pontificia Universita Gregoriana,
Facolta di Storia Ecclesiastica) Gregorian University
Press, Piazza della Pilotta, 35, 00187 Rome, Italy.
(Co-sponsor Ecole Francaise de Rome) Ed. Pierre
Blet, S.J. circ. 1,000.

282   IT   ISSN 0001-642X
ACTA ORDINIS SANCTI AUGUSTINI;
commentarium officiale. (Text in Latin and various
languages) 1956. a. L.5500. Order of Saint
Augustine, Economato Generale, Via S. Uffizio 25,
00193 Rome, Italy. circ. 500. (back issues avail.)

282   CN   ISSN 0316-473X
ALBERTA CATHOLIC DIRECTORY. 1920. a.
Can.$6. Western Catholic Reporter, 10562 - 109th
St., Edmonton, Alta, T5H 3B2, Canada. Ed. E.
Abele. adv. circ. 1,500.
   Missions

ALLGEMEINER CAECILIEN-VERBAND.
SCHRIFTENREIHE. see *MUSIC*

200   PE
AMERICA LATINA. BOLETIN. no.15, Feb., 1978.
irreg. Movimiento Internacional de Estudiantes
Catolicos, Centro de Documentacion, Apartado
3564, Lima 100, Peru. illus.

AMERICAN CATHOLIC PHILOSOPHICAL
ASSOCIATION. PROCEEDINGS. see
PHILOSOPHY

282   IT   ISSN 0066-135X
ANALECTA BIBLICA. (Texts in various languages)
1952. irreg., no.109. price varies. (Pontificio Istituto
Biblico) Biblical Institute Press, Piazza della Pilotta
35, I-00187 Rome, Italy. Ed. P. Karl Ploetz, SJ.
circ. 300.

270 282   VC   ISSN 0066-1376
ANALECTA GREGORIANA. (Text in various
languages) 1930. irreg., latest vol.212. price varies.
(Pontificia Universita Gregoriana) Gregorian
University Press, Piazza della Pilotta, 35, 00187
Rome, Italy. Ed. Angel Anton.

282   BE   ISSN 0066-1414
ANALECTA VATICANO-BELGICA. DEUXIEME
SERIE. SECTION A: NONCIATURE DE
FLANDRE.* 1924. irreg. price varies. Institut
Historique Belge de Rome, c/o Archives Generales
du Royaume, 2-6 rue de Ruysbroeck, B-1000
Brussels, Belgium. circ. controlled.

274   BE   ISSN 0066-1422
ANALECTA VATICANO-BELGICA. DEUXIEME
SERIE. SECTION B: NONCIATURE DE
COLOGNE.* 1956. irreg. price varies. Institut
Historique Belge de Rome, c/o Archives Generales
du Royaume, 2-6 rue de Ruysbroeck, B-1000
Brussels, Belgium. circ. controlled.

282   BE   ISSN 0066-1430
ANALECTA VATICANO-BELGICA. DEUXIEME
SERIE. SECTION C: NONCIATURE DE
BRUXELLES.* 1956. irreg. price varies. Institut
Historique Belge de Rome, c/o Archives Generales
du Royaume, 2-6 rue de Ruysbroeck, B-1000
Brussels, Belgium. circ. controlled.

282   BE   ISSN 0066-1449
ANALECTA VATICANO-BELGICA. PREMIERE
SERIE: DOCUMENTS RELATIFS AUX
ANCIENS DIOCESES DE CAMBRAI, LIEGE,
THEROUANNE ET TOURNAI.* 1906. irreg.
price varies. Institut Historique Belge de Rome, c/o
Archives Generales du Royaume, 2-6 Rue de
Ruysbroeck, B-1000 Brussels, Belgium. circ.
controlled.

282   FR   ISSN 0066-2488
ANNUAIRE CATHOLIQUE DE FRANCE. 1950.
biennial. 340 F. Publicat, 17 bd. Poissonniere, 75002
Paris, France. adv.

282.675   ZR
ANNUAIRE DE L'EGLISE CATHOLIQUE AU
ZAIRE. a. Edition du Secretariat-General, Kinshasa-
Combe, Zaire. illus.

282   FR
ANNUAIRE DU DIOCESE DE LYON. 1826. a. 90
F. Archeveche de Lyon, 1 Place de Fourviere,
69321 Lyon Cedex 05, France.
   Formerly (until 1972): Ordo et Annuaire de
l'Archdiocese de Lyon.

266   IT   ISSN 0066-4464
ANNUARIO CATTOLICO D'ITALIA. 1956.
biennial. L.130000. Editoriale Italiana, Via Vigliena
10, Rome, Italy. index. circ. 8,000.

282   US
ARCHDIOCESE OF CINCINNATI DIRECTORY
AND BUYER'S GUIDE. 1959. a. $12. Catholic
Telegraph, 100 E. Eighth St., Cincinnati, OH
45202. TEL 513-421-3131. Ed. James Stackpoole.
adv. stat. circ. 3,000.

282   VC   ISSN 0066-6785
ARCHIVUM HISTORIAE PONTIFICAE. (Text in
English, French, German, Italian, Latin or Spanish;
summaries in Latin) 1963. a. $50. (Pontificia
Universita Gregoriana, Facolta di Storia
Ecclesiastica) Gregorian University Press, Piazza
della Pilotta, 35, 00187 Rome, Italy. Ed. Paulius
Rabikauskas, S.J. adv. bk. rev. bibl. circ. 750. (back
issues avail.)

282   CL
ARZOBISPADO DE SANTIAGO. VICARIA DE LA
SOLIDARIDAD. ESTUDIOS. 1978. irreg.
Arzobispado de Santiago, Vicaria de la Solidaridad,
Plaza de Armas 444, Casilla 30D, Santiago, Chile.

RELIGIONS AND THEOLOGY — ROMAN CATHOLIC

282 US ISSN 0094-5323
AUGUSTINIAN STUDIES. (Text in various languages) 1970. a. $15. (Villanova University, Augustinian Institute) Villanova University Press, c/o B.A. Paparella, Villanova, PA 19085. TEL 215-645-7500. Ed. Russell D. DeSimone. bk. rev. circ. 300. Indexed: Cath.Ind. Phil.Ind.

271 UK ISSN 0522-8883
BENEDICTINE YEARBOOK. 1863. a. $2. English Congregation of the Order of Saint Benedict, Ampleforth Abbey, York Y06 4EN, England. Ed. Rev. J. Gordon Beattie. adv. circ. 4,000.
Supersedes: Benedictine Almanach.

282 IT
LA BIBBIA NELLA STORIA. 1984. irreg. Centro Editoriale Dehoniano, Via Nosadella 6, I-40123 Bologna, Italy. Ed.Bd.

282 VC
BIBLICA ET ORIENTALIA. 1928. irreg., no.41, 1986. price varies. (Pontificio Istituto Biblico) Biblical Institute Press, Piazza della Pilotta 35, 00187 Rome, Italy.

282 VC
BIBLIOTECA APOSTOLICA VATICANA. CATALOGHI DI MANOSCRITTI. 1902. irreg., no.42, 1978. price varies. Biblioteca Apostolica Vaticana, 00120 Vatican City.

282 VC
BIBLIOTECA APOSTOLICA VATICANA. CATALOGHI DI MOSTRE. 1904. irreg., no.18, 1977. price varies. Biblioteca Apostolica Vaticana, 00120 Vatican City.

282 VC
BIBLIOTECA APOSTOLICA VATICANA. ILLUSTRAZIONI DI CODICI. CODICI VATICANI. SERIES MAJOR. 1902. irreg., no. 37, 1975. price varies. Biblioteca Apostolica Vaticana, 00120 Vatican City.

282 VC
BIBLIOTECA APOSTOLICA VATICANA. ILLUSTRAZIONI DI CODICI. CODICI VATICANI. SERIES MINOR. 1910. irreg., no. 4, 1978. price varies. Biblioteca Apostolica Vaticana, 00120 Vatican City.

282 VC
BIBLIOTECA APOSTOLICA VATICANA. STUDI E TESTI. 1900. irreg., no.283, 1979. price varies. Biblioteca Apostolica Vaticana, 00120 Vatican City.

282 IT
BIBLIOTHECA INSTITUTI HISTORICI SOCIETATIS IESU. 1941. irreg., latest no.45, 1986. Institutum Historicum Societatis Iesu - Jesuit Historical Institute, Via dei Penitenzieri 20, 00193 Rome, Italy. (back issues avail.)

200 IT ISSN 0067-8163
BIBLIOTHECA SERAPHICO-CAPUCCINA. (Multilingual text) 1932. irreg., no.33, 1986. price varies. Frati Minori Cappuccini, Istituto Storico, Cas. Post. 9091, Circonv. Occidentale 6850 (GRA km 65), 00163 Rome, Italy. index. circ. 500.

200 BE ISSN 0067-8279
BIBLIOTHEQUE DE LA REVUE D'HISTOIRE ECCLESIASTIQUE. (Text in Dutch, English, French and Italian) 1928. irreg. Universite Catholique de Louvain, Bureau de la Revue d'Histoire Ecclesiastique, Bibliotheque, 1348 Louvain-la-Neuve, Louvain, Belgium.

282 BO
BOLIVIA: GUIA ECLESIASTICA. 1977. irreg. Conferencia Episcopal Boliviana, Secretaria General, Casilla 2309, La Paz, Bolivia. illus.
Formerly: Guia de la Iglesia.

282 UK ISSN 0262-6896
C A S NEWSLETTER. 1980. a. Catholic Archives Society, c/o M.A. Kuhn-Regnier, St. Peter's Grange, Prinknash Abbey, Cranham, Gloucester GL4 8EX, England.

285 PH
CARDINAL BEA STUDIES. Short title: C B S. 1970. irreg., no.7, 1977. Cardinal Bea Institute for Ecumenical Studies, Box 4082, Manila, Philippines. Ed. Pedro S. de Achutegui, S.J. circ. 750.

282 US ISSN 0069-1208
CATHOLIC ALMANAC. 1904. a. $13.95. Our Sunday Visitor, Inc., 200 Noll Plaza, Huntington, IN 46750. TEL 219-356-8400. Eds. Rev. Felician A. Fox, Rose A. Avalon. index.
Formerly: National Catholic Almanac.

282 UK ISSN 0261-4316
CATHOLIC ARCHIVES. 1981. a. £2. Catholic Archives Society, c/o R.M. Gard, Ed., 21 Larchwood Ave., North Gosforth, Newcastle-upon-Tyne NE13 6PY, England. circ. 350. Indexed: CERDIC.

282 US ISSN 0069-1216
CATHOLIC CENTRAL UNION OF AMERICA. PROCEEDINGS. 1855. a. $3. Catholic Central Union of America, 3835 Westminster Place, St. Louis, MO 63108. TEL 314-371-0889. Ed. Harvey J. Johnson. circ. 1,250. (also avail. in microfilm)

267 UK ISSN 0069-1224
CATHOLIC DIRECTORY. 1837. a. £8.95. Associated Catholic Publications (1912) Ltd., 33-39 Bowling Green Lane, London EC1R 0AB, England. Ed. Rev. David Morris. adv.

282 US
CATHOLIC DIRECTORY (SAN DIEGO) 1936. a. $8. Roman Catholic Diocese of San Diego, Box 81869, San Diego, CA 92138. TEL 619-574-6393. Ed. Bill Finley. adv. circ. 30,000.

282 US
CATHOLIC DIRECTORY (SAN FRANCISCO); Marin, San Francisco and San Mateo Counties. a. $11. Archdiocese of San Francisco, 441 Church St., San Francisco, CA 94114. TEL 415-565-3630. Ed. Maury Welsh. adv. stat.

267 UK ISSN 0306-5677
CATHOLIC DIRECTORY FOR SCOTLAND. 1828. a. £10. John S. Burns and Sons, 25 Finlas St., Possilpark, Glasgow, G22 5DS, Scotland.
Formerly: Catholic Directory for the Clergy and Laity in Scotland (ISSN 0069-1232)

282 UK
CATHOLIC DIRECTORY OF ENGLAND AND WALES. 1839. a. £12.50. Associated Catholic Newspapers Ltd., 33-39 Bowling Green Lane, London, EC1R 0AB, England. Ed. D. Norris. adv.

282 SA
CATHOLIC DIRECTORY OF SOUTHERN AFRICA. 1906. biennial. R.20. Southern African Catholic Bishops' Conference, 140 Visagie St., Pretoria 0001, South Africa. TEL 012-323 6458. adv. stat. index. circ. 1,500.

282 US
CATHOLIC DIRECTORY OF THE ARCHDIOCESE OF BALTIMORE. 1921. a. $9. Cathedral Foundation, 320 Cathedral St., Baltimore, MD 21201. TEL 301-547-5314. adv. circ. 1,700.
Formerly: Archdiocese of Baltimore. Directory.

282 377.8 UK
CATHOLIC EDUCATION. 1978. biennial. £4. Catholic Education Council for England and Wales, 41 Cromwell Rd., London SW7 2DJ, England. Ed. R.F. Cunningham.

CATHOLIC HEALTH ASSOCIATION OF CANADA. DIRECTORY. see *MEDICAL SCIENCES*

282 US
CATHOLIC TELEPHONE GUIDE. a. $22. Catholic News Publishing Co.,Inc., 210 N. Ave., New Rochelle, NY 10801. TEL 914-632-1220.

282 US ISSN 0069-1267
CATHOLIC THEOLOGICAL SOCIETY OF AMERICA. PROCEEDINGS. 1946. a. $7.50. ‡ Catholic Theological Society of America, Bellarmine College, 2001 Newburg Rd., Louisville, KY 40205. Ed. George Kilcourse. index. cum.index. circ. 1,600. (also avail. in microform from UMI; reprint service avail. from UMI) Indexed: Cath.Ind. CERDIC. New Test.Abstr.

282 UK ISSN 0411-275X
CATHOLIC TRUTH. 1896. a. £1($2.40) ‡ Incorporated Catholic Truth Society, 38/40 Eccleston Square, London SW1V 1PD, England. Ed. David Murphy. adv. bk. rev. bibl. circ. 35, 000(controlled)
Incorporating: Catholic Book Notes.

282 FR
CATHOLICISME HIER, AUJOURD'HUI, DEMAIN. 1935. irreg., (approx. 3/yr.) 131 F.($22) per vol. Letouzey et Ane Editeurs, 87 bd. Raspail, 75006 Paris, France. Ed.Bd.

282 UK ISSN 0263-466X
CHRISTIAN BRETHREN REVIEW. 1963. irreg. £7.50($20.60) (Christian Brethren Reseach Fellowship) Paternoster Press, 3 Mount Radford Crescent, Exeter EX2 4JW, England (U.S. subscr. addr.: Box 11127, Birmingham, Alabama 35201) Ed. H.H. Rowdon. adv. bk. rev. circ. 800. (back issues avail.)

282 US ISSN 0197-0348
CHRONICLE OF THE CATHOLIC CHURCH IN LITHUANIA. 1972. irreg. $12. Lithuanian Catholic Religious Aid, 351 Highland Blvd., Brooklyn, NY 11207. TEL 718-647-2434. Eds. Marian Skabeikis, Rev. Casimir Pugevicus. illus. circ. 6,500. (back issues avail.)

282 VC ISSN 0578-4182
CLARETIANUM; commentaria theologica. (Text in various European languages) 1961. a. L.25000($20) Institutum Theologiae Vitae Religiosae, Largo Lorenzo Mossa 4, 00165 Rome, Italy. Ed. Bruno Proietti. bk. rev. bibl. circ. 300. Indexed: CERDIC. Canon Law Abstr.
Formerly: Theologica.

282 IT
CODICE DEL VATICANO II. 1984. irreg. Centro Editoriale Dehoniano, Via Nosadella 6, I-40123 Bologna, Italy.

282 BL
COLECAO FE E REALIDADE. no.3, 1977. irreg. S Leopoldo, Rua Euclides da Cunha 241, 11165 Santos, SP, Brazil.

282 SP
COLECCION HISTORIA DE LA IGLESIA. 1971. irreg., no.15, 1986. price varies. (Universidad de Navarra, Departamento de Historia de la Iglesia) Ediciones Universidad de Navarra, S.A., Apdo. 396, 31080 Pamplona, Spain.

282 SP
COLECCION TEOLOGICA. 1970. irreg., no.49, 1986. price varies. (Universidad de Navarra, Facultad de Teologia) Ediciones Universidad de Navarra, S.A., Apdo. 396, 31080 Pamplona, Spain.

282 SP
COLEGIO MAYOR P. FELIPE SCIO. PUBLICACIONES. 1975. irreg. price varies. Ediciones Calasancias, Paseo de Canalejas 75, Apdo. 206, Salamanca, Spain.

282 IT ISSN 0069-5254
COLLANA RICCIANA. FONTI. 1963. irreg., no.12, 1975. price varies. Casa Editrice Leo S. Olschki, Casella Postale 66, 50100 Florence, Italy. Ed. P. di Agresti. circ. 1,000.

282 GW ISSN 0070-0320
CORPUS CATHOLICORUM. 1919. irreg. price varies. Aschendorffsche Verlagsbuchhandlung, Soester Str. 13, 4400 Muenster, W. Germany (B.R.D.) Ed. Erwin Iserloh.

282 BE
CORPUS CHRISTIANORUM. CONTINUATIO MEDIAEVALIS. 1966. irreg., (2-3/yr.) (Abbey of Steenbrugge) N.V. Brepols I.G.P., Rue Baron Francois du Four 8, B-2300 Turnhout, Belgium. Ed.Bd.

282 BE
CORPUS CHRISTIANORUM. SERIES APOCRYPHORUM. 1983. irreg. (Association pour l'Etude de la Litterature Apocrypha Chretienne) N.V. Brepols I.G.P., Rue Baron Frans du Four 8, B-2300 Turnhout, Belgium.

RELIGIONS AND THEOLOGY — ROMAN CATHOLIC

200   BE
CORPUS CHRISTIANORUM. SERIES GRAECA. 1977. irreg., (2-3/yr.) (Centrum voor Hellenisme en Kristendom, Leuven) N.V. Brepols I.G.P., Rue Baron Francois du Four 8, B-2300 Turnhout, Belgium. (Co-publisher: Leuven University Press)

282   BE
CORPUS CHRISTIANORUM. SERIES LATINA. 1952. irreg., (6-7/yr.) (Abbey of Steenbrugge) N.V. Brepols I.G.P., Rue Baron Francois du Four 8, B-2300 Turnhout, Belgium. Ed.Bd.

282   PE
CUADERNOS DE ESTUDIO. 1979. irreg. $40 (includes subscr. to: Testimonios (en Historieta), Cuadernos de Capacitacion and Cuadernos Populares) Comision Evangelica Latinoamericana de Educacion Cristiana, Av. General Garzon 2267, Lima 11, Peru.

282   CK
CUADERNOS DE TEOLOGIA Y PASTORAL.* irreg. Ediciones Paulinas, Apdo. 100282, Bogota, Colombia.

282   CR
D E I CUADERNOS. irreg., no.6, 1982. Departamento Ecumenico de Investigaciones, Apdo. 339, S. Pedro Montes de Oca, San Jose, Costa Rica.

282   CN
DIOCESE DE SAINT-JEAN-LONGUEUIL. ANNUAIRE. a. Can.$5. Eglise Catholique, Diocese de Saint-Jean-Longueuil, C.P. 40, Boulevard Ste-Foy, Longueuil, PQ J4K 4X8, Canada. TEL 514-679-1100. circ. 900. (looseleaf format)

282   AU
DIOEZESE LINZ. JAHRBUCH. a. S.70($4) Harrachstr. 5, A-4020 Linz, Austria. Ed. Wolfgang Katzboeck. adv. bk. rev. circ. 30,000. (back issues avail.)

282   AU
DIOZESE GURK. JAHRBUCH/KRSKE SKOFIJE. ZBORNIK. (Text in German, Slovenian) 1979. a. S.50($3) Bischoefliches Gurker Ordinariat, Marianneng. 2, A-9020 Klagenfurt, Austria. Ed.Bd. bk. rev. circ. 7,000. (back issues avail.)

282   MG
EGLISE CATHOLIQUE A MADAGASCAR. Cover title: Annuaire de l'Eglise Catholique a Madagascar. (Text in French or Malagasy) a. Impr. Catholique, 127, Arabe Lenine Vladimir, Antananarivo, Malagasy Republic.

200   DR
EME EME; estudios Dominicanos. 1972. irreg. RD.$0.50 single issue. Universidad Catolica Madre y Maestra, Centro de Estudios Dominicanos, Santiago de los Caballeros, Dominican Republic. Ed. Frank Moya Pons. index. circ. 2,000. Indexed: Hist.Abstr. Amer.Hist.& Life.

282   UK
ENGLISH BENEDICTINE CONGREGATION. ORDO. 1885. a. £0.80. Ampleforth Abbey, York YO6 4EN, England. Ed. Rev. V. Wace. circ. 1,400.

282   US   ISSN 0014-8814
FATHERS OF THE CHURCH. 1947. irreg., vol.75, 1987. price varies. Catholic University of America Press, 620 Michigan Ave. N.E., Washington, DC 20064. TEL 202-635-5052.

282   US   ISSN 0275-6145
FIRST CATHOLIC SLOVAK UNION OF AMERICA. MINUTES OF ANNUAL MEETING. a. First Catholic Slovak Union of America, 3289 E. 55th St., Cleveland, OH 44127. TEL 216-341-3355. Key Title: Minutes of the Annual Meeting of the First Catholic Slovak Union of the United States of America and Canada.

282   IT
FONTI E STUDI PER LA STORIA DEL SANTO A PADOVA. (Text in English or Italian) 1976. irreg. L.40000. Neri Pozza Editore, Via Gazzolle 6, 36100 Vicenza, Italy. Ed. Antonino Poppi. bibl. illus.

FRAENKISCHER HAUSKALENDER UND CARITASKALENDER. see *BIOGRAPHY*

271.3   US   ISSN 0080-5459
FRANCISCAN STUDIES. 1941. a. $16. Franciscan Institute, St. Bonaventure University, Drawer F, St. Bonaventure, NY 14778. TEL 716-375-2105. Ed. Rev. Conrad L. Harkins, O.F.M. (also avail. in microform from UMI; reprint service avail. from UMI) Indexed: Cath.Ind. M.L.A. CERDIC. Phil.Ind. Rel.Ind.Two.

GRADUATE SCHOOL GUIDE. see *EDUCATION — Guides To Schools And Colleges*

282   US
GUIDE TO RELIGIOUS MINISTRIES FOR CATHOLIC MEN AND WOMEN. 1979. a. $5. Catholic News Publishing Co., Inc., 210 N. Ave., New Rochelle, NY 10801. TEL 914-632-1220. Ed. Victor L. Ridder, Jr. adv. tr.lit. circ. 30,000.
   Formerly: Guide to Religious Careers for Catholic Men and Women.

282   HK   ISSN 0073-3210
HONG KONG CATHOLIC CHURCH DIRECTORY/HSIANG-KANG T'IEN CHU CHIAO SHOU T'SE. (Text in Chinese and English) 1954. a. $2.50. Catholic Truth Society, Catholic Diocese Centre, Box 2984, Hong Kong, Hong Kong. Ed. Louis Lee. adv. circ. 3,000.

200 230   FR
INSTITUT CATHOLIQUE DE PARIS. ANNUAIRE. a. Institut Catholique de Paris, 21, rue d'Assas, 75270 Paris Cedex 06, France.

282   IT   ISSN 0074-5782
INTERNATIONAL EUCHARIST CONGRESS. PROCEEDINGS.* irreg., 1968, 39th, Bogota. Luis Cardinal Goncha, c/o Cardinal James K. Knox, Via del Pozzeto 160, Rome, Italy.

282   UK   ISSN 0075-0735
IRISH CATHOLIC DIRECTORY. 1838. a. £7.95. (Roman Catholic Church in All Ireland) Associated Catholic Publications (1912) Ltd., 33-39 Bowling Green Lane, London EC1R 0AB, England. adv. index.

282   IT
ISTITUTO DI SCIENZE RELIGIOSE IN TRENTO. PUBBLICAZIONI. 1981. irreg. Centro Editoriale Dehoniano, Via Nosadella 6, I-40123 Bologna, Italy. Ed.Bd.

282   AU
JAHRBUCH DER ERZDIOESE VON WIEN. a. (Erzbischoefliches Pastoralamt Wien) Wiener Dom-Verlag GmbH, Strozzigasse 8, Postfach 321, 1081 Wien, Austria. Ed. Johannes Pesl. adv. illus.
   Formerly: Jahrbuch fuer die Kirche von Wien.

200   US
KALENDAR JEDNOTA. (Text in Slovak) 1897. a. First Catholic Slovak Union, 3289 E. 55th St., Cleveland, OH 44127 TEL 216-341-3355. (Subscr. addr.: Jednota Printery, Box 150, Middletown, PA 17057) Ed. Joseph C. Krajsa. Indexed: Hist.Abstr. Amer.Hist.& Life.
   Formerly: Jednota Kalendar.

282   PL   ISSN 0860-410X
KALENDARZ SLOWA BOZEGO. 1979. a. Ksieza Werbisci, Ostrobramska 90, 04-118 Warsaw 44, Poland. Ed. Marek Grzech. circ. 200,000. (back issues avail.)

282   NE
KATHOLIEK DOCUMENTATIE CENTRUM. ARCHIEVEN. 1973. irreg. price varies. Katholiek Documentatie Centrum, Erasmuslaan 36, 6525 GG Nijmegen, Netherlands.

282   NE
KATHOLIEK DOCUMENTATIE CENTRUM. JAARBOEK. (Summaries in English and French) 1971. a. price varies. Katholiek Documentatie Centrum, Erasmuslaan 36, 6525 GG Nijmegen, Netherlands. (Co-sponsor: Archief voor de Geschiedenis van de Katholieke Kerk in Nederland) Indexed: CERDIC.

282   NE
KATHOLIEK DOCUMENTATIE CENTRUM. PUBLICATIES. 1971. irreg., vol.11, 1983. price varies. Katholiek Documentatie Centrum, Erasmuslaan 36, 6525 GG Nijmegen, Netherlands. (back issues avail.)

200   GW   ISSN 0170-7302
KATHOLISCHES LEBEN UND KIRCHENREFORM IM ZEITALTER DER GLAUBENSSPALTUNG. 1927. irreg. price varies. Aschendorffsche Verlagsbuchhandlung, Soester Str. 13, 4400 Muenster, W. Germany (B.R.D.) Ed. Erwin Iserloh.

201   PL
KATOLICKI UNIWERSYTET LUBELSKI. WYDZIAL TEOLOGICZNO-KANONICZNY. ROZPRAWY. (Text in Polish; summaries in English or French) 1947. irreg. price varies. Katolicki Uniwersytet Lubelski, Towarzystwo Naukowe, Chopina 29, 20-023 Lublin, Poland. index. circ. 3, 150.

KLEINE CHORZEITUNG; Mitteilungsblatt fuer die katholischen Kirchenchoere. see *MUSIC*

282   GW
LESEPLAN JAHRESLOSUNG. a. DM.1. Katholisches Bibelwerk e.V., Silberburgstr. 121, 7000 Stuttgart 1, W. Germany (B.R.D.)

282   LO
LESOTHO CATHOLIC DIRECTORY. 1977. irreg. latest 1985. $5. (Lesotho Catholic Bishops Conference) Mazenod Printing Works Pty. Ltd., Box 39, Mazenod 160, Lesotho. Ed. F. Mairot. circ. 300.

282   UK
LIVERPOOL CATHOLIC DIRECTORY. 1928. a. £1. Catholic Pictorial Ltd., Media House, 34 Stafford St., Liverpool L3 8LX, England. Ed. Rev. Paul Thompson. adv. circ. 9,000.

282   US   ISSN 0464-9680
MARIAN STUDIES. (Represents: Proceedings of society's annual convention) 1950. a. $10 domestic; foreign $12. Mariological Society of America, Marian Library, University of Dayton, Dayton, OH 45469-0001. TEL 513-229-4214. Ed. Theodore A. Loehler. adv. bibl. cum.index.

282   PL   ISSN 0076-5244
MATERIALY ZRODLOWE DO DZIEJOW KOSCIOLA W POLSCE. 1965. irreg. price varies. Towarzystwo Naukowe Katolickiego Uniwersytetu Lubelskiego, Al. Raclawickie 14, Lublin, Poland (Dist. by: Ars Polona-Ruch, Krakowskie Przedmiescie 7, Warsaw, Poland) (Co-sponsor: Instytut Geografii Historycznej Kosciola w Polsce przy K.U.L.) Ed. Jerzy Kloczowski. circ. 1,000.

266 282   US
MISSION HANDBOOK. 1950. a. $1.50. United States Catholic Mission Association, 1233 Lawrence St., N.E., Washington, DC 20017. TEL 202-832-3112. Ed. Sr. Mary Godfrey. circ. 1,500.
   Former titles: United States Catholic Mission and Association. Handbook; United States Catholic Mission Council. Handbook; United States Catholic Missionary Personnel Overseas (ISSN 0082-9560) *Missions*

255   CN
MONASTIC STUDIES. 1963. a. $20. Benedictine Priory of Montreal, 1475 Pine Ave., Montreal, Que. H3G 1B3, Canada. TEL 514-849-2728. Ed. Laurence Freeman. bk. rev. circ. 2,500. (also avail. in microform from UMI) Indexed: Cath.Ind.

200   IT   ISSN 0077-1449
MONUMENTA HISTORICA ORDINIS MINORUM CAPUCCINORUM. (Text in Italian and Latin) 1937. irreg., no.17, 1985. price varies. Frati Minori Cappuccini, Istituto Storico, Cas. Post. 9091, Circonv. Occidentale 6850 (GRA km 65), 00163 Rome, Italy. Ed. Mariano d'Alatri. index. circ. 500.

282   IT
MONUMENTA HISTORICA SOCIETATIS IESU. irreg., latest vol.129. Institutum Historicum Societatis Iesu - Jesuit Historical Institute, Via dei Penitenzieri 20, 00193 Rome, Italy. (back issues avail.)

282   VC   ISSN 0077-1457
MONUMENTA IURIS CANONICI. (Series A: Corpus Glossatorum; Series B: Corpus Collectionum; Series C: Subsidia) 1969. irreg. price varies. Biblioteca Apostolica Vaticana, c/o F. Werlen, Economo, 00120 Vatican City, Italy.

282   GW   ISSN 0077-2011
MUENSTERSCHWARZACHER STUDIEN. 1965. irreg. price varies. (Benediktinerabtei Muensterschwarzach) Vier-Tuerme-Verlag, 8711 Muensterschwarzach, W. Germany (B.R.D.) Ed. Pirmin Hugger. adv. bk. rev.

NATIONAL DIRECTORY OF CATHOLIC HIGHER EDUCATION. see *EDUCATION — Guides To Schools And Colleges*

NATIONAL GUILD OF CATHOLIC PSYCHIATRISTS. BULLETIN. see *MEDICAL SCIENCES — Psychiatry And Neurology*

282   US
NOTRE DAME STUDIES IN AMERICAN CATHOLICISM. 1979. irreg. University of Notre Dame Press, Notre Dame, IN 46556. TEL 219-239-6346. bibl.

282   IT   ISSN 0078-253X
NOVARIEN. 1967. irreg. price varies. Associazione di Storia Ecclesiastica Novarese, Presso Archivio Storico Diocesano, Palazzo Vescovile, I-28100 Novara, Italy. Ed. Angelo L. Stoppa. bk. rev. circ. 1,000.

270   239   AU
OESTERREICHISCHE AKADEMIE DER WISSENSCHAFTEN. KOMMISSION ZUR HERAUSGABE DES CORPUS DER LATEINISCHEN KIRCHENVAETER. VEROEFFENTLICHUNGEN. irreg. Verlag der Oesterreichischen Akademie der Wissenschaften, Ignaz Seipel-Platz 2, A-1010 Vienna, Austria.

282   US
OFFICIAL WISCONSIN PASTORAL HANDBOOK. 1962. a. $10 to qualified personnel. ‡ (Milwaukee Catholic Press Apostolate) Catholic Herald, 3501 S. Lake Dr., Box 1572, Milwaukee, WI 53201. adv. circ. 2,300(controlled)

ORIENTALIA CHRISTIANA ANALECTA. see *ORIENTAL STUDIES*

PAEPSTE UND PAPSTTUM. see *HISTORY — History Of Europe*

200   CL
PANORAMA DE LA TEOLOGIA LATINOAMERICANA. 1974. a. $8. Universidad Catolica de Chile, Seminario Latinoamericano de Documentacon, Casilla 114 D, Santiago, Chile. circ. 3,000.

282   299   BE
PATROLOGIA SYRIACA ET ORIENTALIS. 1983. irreg. N.V. Brepols I.G.P., Rue Baron Frans du Four 8, B-2300 Turnhout, Belgium.

267   SZ   ISSN 0079-0281
PAX ROMANA. Represents: International Catholic Movement for Intellectual Cultural Affairs. Proceedings of the Plenary Assembly. quadrennial, latest 1983. $10. International Catholic Movement for Intellectual and Cultural Affairs - Pax Romana, General Secretariat, B.P. 85, 37-39 Rue de Vermont, CH-1211 Geneva 20-CIC, Switzerland (Subscr. to: Mouvement International des Intellectuels CAtholiques, Pax Romana, 1701 Fribourg, Switzerland) circ. 600.

255   IT
PICENUM SERAPHICUM. (Text in Italian) irreg. L.3500. Biblioteca Francescana, Conto Corrente Postale 15/27009, Falconara M. 60015, Italy.

282   FR
POINT THEOLOGIQUE. irreg. 3141 Fr. Editions Beauchesne, 72 rue des Saints Peres, 75007 Paris, France. Ed. Charles Kannengiesser. Indexed: Rel.Ind.Two.

270   VC
PONTIFICIA UNIVERSITA GREGORIANA. DOCUMENTA MISSIONALIA. (Multi-language text) 1964. irreg. price varies. Gregorian University Press, Piazza della Pilotta, 35, Italy. Ed. Mariasusai Dhavamony.

270   VC   ISSN 0080-3979
PONTIFICIA UNIVERSITA GREGORIANA. MISCELLANEA HISTORIAE PONTIFICIAE. (Multi-language text) 1939. irreg., latest, vol.52. price varies. Gregorian University Press, Piazza della Pilotta, 35, 00187 Rome, Italy. Ed. Vincenzo Monachino.

266   VC   ISSN 0080-3987
PONTIFICIA UNIVERSITA GREGORIANA. STUDIA MISSIONALIA. (Multi-language text) 1943. a. $40. Gregorian University Press, Piazza della Pilotta, 35, 00187 Rome, Italy. Ed. Mariasusai Dhavamony. Indexed: Cath.Ind. Rel.Ind.One.

282   GW   ISSN 0172-0929
PRIESTERJAHRHEFT. 1926. a. free. Bonifatiuswerk der Deutschen Katholiken e.V., Kamp 22, 4790 Paderborn, W. Germany (B.R.D.) Ed. Georg Walf. circ. 22,000 (controlled)

282   BE
PROBLEMES D'HISTOIRE DU CHRISTIANISME. (Text in French) 1970/71. a. price varies. (Universite Libre de Bruxelles, Institut d'Histoire du Christianisme et de la Pensee Laique) Editions de l'Universite de Bruxelles, Avenue P. Heger, 26-C.P. 163, B-1050 Brussels, Belgium. Indexed: CERDIC.

282   BE
REVUE THEOLOGIQUE DE LOUVAIN. CAHIERS. (Text in French) 1980. irreg., vol.2, 1980. (Universite Catholique de Louvain, Facultes de Theologie et de Droit Canonique) Editions Peeters s.p.r.l., Bondgenotenlaan 153, B-3000 Louvain, Belgium. Indexed: Old Test.Abstr. CERDIC.

200   US   ISSN 0080-5432
SAINT BONAVENTURE UNIVERSITY. FRANCISCAN INSTITUTE. PHILOSOPHY SERIES. 1944. irreg., no.16, 1972. price varies. Franciscan Institute, St. Bonaventure University, St. Bonaventure, NY 14778. TEL 716-375-2105. Ed. Rev. George H. Marcil, O.F.M.

200   US   ISSN 0080-5440
SAINT BONAVENTURE UNIVERSITY. FRANCISCAN INSTITUTE. TEXT SERIES. 1951. irreg., no.16, 1972. price varies. Franciscan Institute, St. Bonaventure University, St. Bonaventure, NY 14778. TEL 716-375-2105. Ed. Rev. George H. Marcil, O.F.M.

200   CN   ISSN 0085-6134
SLOVENSKI JEZUITI V KANADE. YEAR BOOK. (Text in Slovak; summaries in English) 1954. a. contr. free circ. Slovak Jesuit Fathers in Canada, Box 600, Cambridge, Ont. N1R 5W3, Canada. TEL 519-621-8491. Ed. Rev. Vincent Danco. adv. bk. rev. illus. stat. circ. 8,000.

282   GW
SPEYER. DIOEZESE. DIREKTORIUM SPIRENSE-OFFIZIUM UND MESSFEIER. 1824. a. DM.10. Bischoefliches Ordinariat Speyer, Pfaffengasse 16, 6720 Speyer, W. Germany (B.R.D.) Ed. Domvikar Otto Georgens. circ. 2,500.

940   AU   ISSN 0081-5594
STILLE SCHAR. 1953. a. S.45. (Emporer Charles League for Peace Among the Nations) Gebetsliga, Zisterzienserstift, A-3180 Lilienfeld, NO, Austria. circ. 5,000.

230   GW   ISSN 0081-7295
STUDIEN ZUR GESCHICHTE DER KATHOLISCHEN MORALTHEOLOGIE. vol.3, 1955. irreg., vol.28, 1986. price varies. Verlag Friedrich Pustet, Gutenbergstr. 8, 8400 Regensburg 1, W. Germany (B.R.D.) Ed. Johannes Gruendel. circ. 500.

255   IT   ISSN 0562-4649
SUBSIDIA SCIENTIFICA FRANCISCALIA. (Text in French, German, Italian and Latin) 1962. irreg., no.6, 1978. price varies. Frati Minori Cappuccini, Istituto Storico, Casella Postale 9091, Circonv. Occidentale 6850 (GRA km 65), 00163 Rome, Italy. index. circ. 500.

200   CL   ISSN 0069-3596
UNIVERSIDAD CATOLICA DE CHILE. FACULTAD DE TEOLOGIA. ANALES. 1940. irreg. Universidad Catolica de Chile, Facultad de Teologia, Jose Batile y Ordonez 3300, Casilla 114-D, Santiago, Chile. cum.index: 1940-1969. circ. 500. Indexed: Bull.Sign. Cath.Ind.

282   BE
UNIVERSITE CATHOLIQUE DE LOUVAIN. FACULTES DE THEOLOGIE ET DE DROIT CANONIQUE. COLLECTION DES DISSERTATIONS PRESENTEES POUR L'OBTENTION DU GRADE DE MAITRE A LA FACULTE DE THEOLOGIE OU A LA FACULTE DE DROIT CANONIQUE. 1841. irreg. (series quarto, vol. 5, 1985) Universite Catholique de Louvain, Facultes de Theologie et de Droit Canonique, Grand-Place 45, 1348 Louvain-la-Neuve, Belgium.
Formerly: Universite Catholique de Louvain. Facultes de Theologie et de Droit Canonique. Dissertationes ad Gradum Magistri in Facultate Theologica Vel in Facultate Iuris Canonici Consequendum Conscriptae.

200   BE   ISSN 0076-1230
UNIVERSITE CATHOLIQUE DE LOUVAIN. FACULTES DE THEOLOGIE ET DE DROIT CANONIQUE. TRAVAUX DE DOCTORAT EN THEOLOGIE ET EN DROIT CANONIQUE. NOUVELLE SERIE. 1969. irreg., vol. 11, 1985. exchange basis. Universite Catholique de Louvain, Facultes de Theologie et de Droit Canonique, Grand-Place 45, 1348 Louvain-la-Neuve, Belgium. circ. 120.

268   US   ISSN 0070-3052
UNIVERSITY OF DAYTON. SCHOOL OF EDUCATION. WORKSHOP PROCEEDINGS. 1970. irreg., latest issue, 1971. $3.25. University of Dayton, School of Education, Dayton, OH 45469. TEL 513-229-3146. Ed. Louis J. Faerber.
Catholic education: elementary and secondary

264   US   ISSN 0076-003X
UNIVERSITY OF NOTRE DAME. DEPARTMENT OF THEOLOGY. LITURGICAL STUDIES. 1955. irreg., no.11, 1977. price varies. ‡ University of Notre Dame Press, Notre Dame, IN 46556. TEL 219-239-6346. Indexed: Cath.Ind.

282   US   ISSN 0193-9211
WORD & SPIRIT. 1979. a. price varies. (St. Scholastica Priory) St. Bede's Publications, Box 545, Rt. 32, Petersham, MA 01366. TEL 617-724-3407. Ed.Bd. circ. 300. (also avail. in microform from UMI; back issues avail.) Indexed: Cath.Ind. CERDIC. ERIC. Rel.& Theol.Abstr.

282   947   US
WORLD LITHUANIAN ROMAN CATHOLIC DIRECTORY. 1975. biennial. $10. Lithuanian R.C. Priests' League, 351 Highland Blvd., Brooklyn, NY 11207. TEL 718-827-1350. Ed. Victor Dabusis. adv. stat. circ. 1,000.

RELIGIONS AND THEOLOGY — Other Denominations And Sects

200   GW
ALT-KATHOLISCHES JAHRBUCH. 1901. a. DM.6. Katholisches Bistum der Alt-Katholiken in Deutschland, Gregor-Mendel-Str. 28, 5300 Bonn 1, W. Germany (B.R.D.) circ. 6,000.

281.9   GR
ANALECTA VLATADON. irreg., latest no.49. price varies. Patriarchal Institute for Patristic Studies, Heptapyrgiou 64, 546 34 Thessaloniki, Greece.

200   FR   ISSN 0083-6184
ASSEMBLEES DE DIEU DE FRANCE. ANNUAIRE.* 1958. a. 8 F. Viens et Vois, 10 rue de Sentier, 75002 Paris, France.

281.9   GR
ATHENISIN ETHNIKON KAI KAPODISTRAKION PANEPISTEMION. THEOLOGIKE SCHOLE. EPISTEMONIKE EPETERIS. (Text in English, French and Greek) 1935. a. Athenisin Ethnikon kai Kapodistrakion, Theologike Schole, Odos Panepistimiou, Athens 143, Greece.

297.88   US   ISSN 0005-2388
AWAKENER; a journal devoted to Meher Baba. 1953. a. $12. (Universal Spiritual League of America, Inc.) Awakener Press, 938 18th St., Hermosa Beach, CA 90254. TEL 213-379-2656. Ed. Filis Frederick. bk. rev. illus. circ. 1,000. (back issues avail.) Indexed: New Per.Ind.

RELIGIONS AND THEOLOGY — OTHER DENOMINATIONS AND SECTS

289.6   CN
CANADIAN QUAKER HISTORY NEWSLETTER. 1972. irreg., (2-3/yr.) Canadian Friends Historical Association, 60 Lowther Ave., Toronto, Ont. M5R 1C7, Canada. Eds. Kathleen Hertzberg, Jane Zavitz. circ. 150.

275.93   TH
CHRISTIAN DIRECTORY. (Text in English and Thai) a. B.75. Suthep Chaviwan, Box 1405, Bangkok, Thailand. illus.

267   UK
CHRISTIAN ENDEAVOUR PROGRAMME BOOK. 1896. a. £2.25 for each edt. ‡ Christian Endeavour Union of Great Britain and Ireland, 18 Leam Terrace, Royal Leamington Spa, Warwickshire CV31 1BB, England. Ed. Olive Woodham. adv. bk. rev. circ. 1,700.
    Former titles: Christian Endeavour Topic Book; Christian Endeavour Year Book (ISSN 0069-3863)
Missions

281.9   GR
CHRISTIAN LITERATURE. irreg., latest vol.2. price varies. Patriarchal Institute for Patristic Studies, Heptapyrgiou 64, 546 34 Thessaloniki, Greece.

281.9   BE   ISSN 0070-0398
CORPUS SCRIPTORUM CHRISTIANORUM ORIENTALIUM: AETHIOPICA. (Text in Ethiopian) 1904. irreg., latest no.78, 1985. price varies. (Universitatis Catholicae Lovaniensis) Editions Peeters s.p.r.l., Bondgenotenlaan 153, B-3000 Louvain, Belgium. (Co-sponsor: Catholic University of America) bk. rev.

281.9   BE   ISSN 0070-0401
CORPUS SCRIPTORUM CHRISTIANORUM ORIENTALIUM: ARABICA. (Text in Arabic) 1903. irreg., latest no.45, 1985. price varies. (Universitatis Catholicae Lovaniensis) Editions Peeters s.p.r.l., Bondgenotenlaan 153, B-3000 Louvain, Belgium. (Co-sponsor: Catholic University of America) bk. rev.

281.9   BE   ISSN 0070-041X
CORPUS SCRIPTORUM CHRISTIANORUM ORIENTALIUM: ARMENIACA. (Text in Armenian) 1953. irreg., no.14, 1984. price varies. (Universitatis Catholicae Lovaniensis) Editions Peeters s.p.r.l., Bondgenotenlaan 153, B-3000 Louvain, Belgium. (Co-sponsor: Catholic University of America) bk. rev.

281.9   BE   ISSN 0070-0428
CORPUS SCRIPTORUM CHRISTIANORUM ORIENTALIUM: COPTICA. (Text in Coptic) 1906. irreg., no.42, 1980. price varies. (Universitatis Catholicae Lovaniensis) Editions Peeters s.p.r.l., Bondgenotenlaan 153, B-3000 Louvain, Belgium. (Co-sponsor: Catholic University of America) bk. rev.

281.9   BE   ISSN 0070-0436
CORPUS SCRIPTORUM CHRISTIANORUM ORIENTALIUM: IBERICA. (Text in Georgian) 1950. irreg., latest no.20, 1984. price varies. (Universitatis Catholicae Lovaniensis) Editions Peeters s.p.r.l., Bondgenotenlaan 153, B-3000 Louvain, Belgium. (Co-sponsor: Catholic University of America) bk. rev.

281.9   BE   ISSN 0070-0444
CORPUS SCRIPTORUM CHRISTIANORUM ORIENTALIUM: SUBSIDIA. (Text in English, French and German) 1950. irreg., no.73, 1985. price varies. (Universitatis Catholicae Lovaniensis) Editions Peeters s.p.r.l., Bondgenotenlaan 153, B-3000 Louvain, Belgium. (Co-sponsor: Catholic University of America) bk. rev.

281.9   BE   ISSN 0070-0452
CORPUS SCRIPTORUM CHRISTIANORUM ORIENTALIUM: SYRIACA. 1903. irreg., no.202, 1985. price varies. (Universitatis Catholicae Lovaniensis) Editions Peeters s.p.r.l., Bondgenotenlaan, B-3000 Louvain, Belgium. (Co-sponsor: Catholic University of America) bk. rev.

242.2   US   ISSN 0092-7147
DAILY BREAD; a devotional guide for every day of the year. 1969. a. $7.50. (Reorganized Church of Jesus Christ of Latter Day Saints) Herald Publishing House, 3225 S. Noland Rd., Box HH, Independence, MO 64055. TEL 816-252-5010. Ed. Richard Brown. circ. 12,000.

289.3   US   ISSN 0093-786X
DESERET NEWS CHURCH ALMANAC. 1974. a. $4.75. Deseret News Publishing Co., Box 1257, Salt Lake City, UT 84110. TEL 801-237-2141. Ed. Dell Van Orden. illus. circ. 10,000.

289.9   US
ECK MATA JOURNAL. 1976. a. $3.95. Eckankar Publications, Box 27300, Minneapolis, MN 55427-0300. Ed. Suzanne Vlcek. circ. 20,000.
    Formerly: Eck News.

267   UK   ISSN 0071-9587
FRIENDS HISTORICAL SOCIETY. JOURNAL. 1903. a. £4($6) to individuals; £6($9) to institutions. Friends Historical Society, Friends House, Euston Rd., London NW1 2BJ, England. Ed. Gerald A.J. Hodgett. adv. bk. rev. circ. 500. Indexed: Br.Hum.Ind. Hist.Abstr. Amer.Hist.& Life.

200   UK   ISSN 0072-0666
GENERAL CONFERENCE OF THE NEW CHURCH. YEARBOOK. 1789. a. ‡ General Conference of the New Church, c/o G.S. Kuphal, Ed., 20 Red Barn Rd., Brightlingsea, Golchester, Essex CO7 0SH, England. circ. 500.

GREEK ORTHODOX CALENDAR. see *ETHNIC INTERESTS*

299   UK
HEATHEN. 1971. irreg. membership. Pagan Movement, Can y Lloer, Ffarmers, Llanwrda, Dyfed, Wales. adv. circ. 300.

261   US   ISSN 0073-9456
INSTITUTE OF MENNONITE STUDIES SERIES. 1961. irreg. price varies. ‡ (Associated Mennonite Biblical Seminaries) Faith and Life Press, 724 Main St., Box 347, Newton, KS 67114. TEL 316-283-5100. Ed. Maynard Shelly.

299   US   ISSN 0886-6910
ISKCON REVIEW; academic perspectives on the Hare Krishna movement. 1985. a. $6. Institute for Vaishnaya Studies, c/o Steven J. Gelberg, 41 West Allens Lane, Philadelphia, PA 19119. TEL 215-242-6578. bk. rev. circ. 1,200. (back issues avail.)

200   CN
ISSUE. 1974? irreg. free. United Church of Canada, 85 St. Clair Ave. E., Toronto, Ont. M4T 1M8, Canada. TEL 416-925-5931. Ed.Bd. illus. Indexed: Curr.Cont.Africa.

289   NE
JAARBOEK VAN DE CHRISTELIJKE GEREFORMEERDE KERKEN IN NEDERLAND. 1909. a. (Christelijke Gereformeerde Kerk) D.J. van Brummen, Buyten 2 Schipperheyn, Amsterdam, Netherlands. adv.

289.9   US   ISSN 0075-3602
JEHOVAH'S WITNESSES YEARBOOK. Variant title: Yearbook of Jehovah's Witnesses. (Text in various European languages) 1927. a. $1. (Jehovah's Witnesses, Governing Body) Watchtower Bible and Tract Society of New York, Inc., 25 Columbia Hts., Brooklyn, NY 11201. TEL 718-625-3600. index. circ. 1,000,000.
    Report of international preaching

289.3   US   ISSN 0094-7342
JOURNAL OF MORMON HISTORY. 1974. a. $7.50. Mormon History Association, Box 7010, University Sta., Provo, UT 84602. Ed. Dean May. circ. 1,000. Indexed: CERDIC.

289.3   US   ISSN 0094-5633
MEASURING MORMONISM. 1974. a. $3. Association for the Study of Sociology, Inc., 3646 East 3580 South, Salt Lake City, UT 84109 TEL 801-581-6153. (Or: Glenn M. Vernon, Ed., University of Utah, Department of Sociology, Salt Lake City, UT 84112)

290   US   ISSN 0076-6429
MENNONITE HISTORY SERIES. vol.2, 1966. irreg. ‡ (Mennonite Church, General Conference, Commission on Education) Faith and Life Press, 724 Main St., Newton, KS 67114. TEL 316-283-5100. Ed. Maynard Shelly.

289.7   US
MENNONITE YEARBOOK AND DIRECTORY. 1905. biennial. $7.95. Mennonite Publishing House, 616 Walnut Ave., Scottdale, PA 15683. TEL 412-887-8500. Ed. James E. Horsch.

281.9   FR   ISSN 0026-0266
MESSAGER DE L'EXARCHAT DU PATRIARCHE RUSSE EN EUROPE OCCIDENTALE. (Text in French and Russian) 1950. a. 90 F. (Union des Associations Culturelles de l'Eglise Orthodoxe) Exarchat du Patriarche de Moscou, 26 rue Preclet, 75015 Paris, France. Ed.Bd. bk. rev. bibl. illus. cum.index. circ. 700. Indexed: CERDIC.

281   US
MODERN ORTHODOX SAINTS. 1971. irreg., vol.8, 1985. price varies. Institute for Byzantine and Modern Greek Studies, 115 Gilbert Rd., Belmont, MA 02178. TEL 617-484-6595. Ed. Constantine Cavarnos. bibl. illus. index. circ. 1,000.

200   BG
NATIONAL COUNCIL OF CHURCHES, BANGLADESH. ANNUAL REPORT. (Text in English and Bengali) a. National Council of Churches, Bangladesh, 395, New Eskaton Rd., Dacca 2, Bangladesh. stat.

200   US   ISSN 0145-7950
ORTHODOX CHURCH IN AMERICA. YEARBOOK AND CHURCH DIRECTORY. a. $10. Orthodox Church in America, Box 675, Syosset, NY 11791. TEL 516-922-0550. charts. illus. stat. circ. 3,000. Key Title: Yearbook and Church Directory of the Orthodox Church in America.
    Supersedes: Russian Orthodox Greek-Catholic Church of America. Yearbook (ISSN 0095-2257); Russian Orthodox Greek Catholic Church of America. Yearbook and Church Directory (ISSN 0557-532X)

281.9   GR
PATRIARCHAL INSTITUTE FOR PATRISTIC STUDIES. THEOLOGICAL STUDIES. irreg., latest no.5. price varies. Patriarchal Institute for Patristic Studies, Heptapyrgiou 64, 546 34 Thessaloniki, Greece. Ed. P.C. Christou.

289.6 100   UK
QUAKER ENCOUNTERS. 1978. irreg., vol.3, 1978. William Sessions Ltd., Ebor Press, York YO3 9HS, England.

QUAKER PEACE & SERVICE. ANNUAL REPORT. see *SOCIAL SERVICES AND WELFARE*

289.6   US   ISSN 0033-5088
QUAKER RELIGIOUS THOUGHT. 1959. irreg., (approx. 2/yr.) $12 for 4 nos. Quaker Theological Discussion Group, Rte. 4, Box 471-A, Easton, PA 18042. Ed. Dean Freiday. bk. rev. circ. 500. Indexed: CERDIC.

289   US   ISSN 0586-7282
SALT LAKE CITY MESSENGER. 1964. irreg., no.62, 1985. free. Utah Lighthouse Ministry, 1350 South West Temple St., Box 1884, Salt Lake City, UT 84110. TEL 801-485-8894. Ed. Jerald Tanner. adv. circ. 13,500. (looseleaf format)

267.15   UK   ISSN 0080-567X
SALVATION ARMY YEAR BOOK. 1906. a. £2.95 paperback; £5.95 hardback. ‡ (Salvation Army) Salvationist Publishing and Supplies, Ltd., Judd St., Kings Cross, London WC1H 9NN, England. index. circ. 11,000.

SHARE IT; a magazine to celebrate & promote awareness of our true identity. see *PHILOSOPHY*

200   US   ISSN 0160-0354
SPIRITUAL COMMUNITY GUIDE; the new consciousness source book. 1972. irreg;. no.6, 1985. $8.95. Arcline Publications, Box 1550, Pomona, CA 91769. TEL 714-623-1738. Ed. Parmatma Singh Khalsa. circ. 20,000.

280   US   ISSN 0081-7538
STUDIES IN ANABAPTIST AND MENNONITE HISTORY. 1929. irreg., no.27, 1984. price varies. (Mennonite Historical Society) Mennonite Publishing House, Herald Press, 616 Walnut Ave., Scottdale, PA 15683. TEL 412-887-8500.

STUDIES IN ASIAN THOUGHT AND RELIGION. see *PHILOSOPHY*

289 US
STUDIES IN EVANGELICALISM. 1980. irreg., no.8, 1986. Scarecrow Press, Inc., 52 Liberty St., Box 4167, Metuchen, NJ 08840. Eds. Kenneth E. Rowe, Donald W. Dayton.

658.32 US ISSN 0360-9782
UNITED CHURCH OF CHRIST. PENSION BOARDS (ANNUAL REPORT) 1967. a. free. United Church of Christ, Pension Boards, 132 W. 31st St., New York, NY 10001. TEL 212-239-8700. Ed. Edmund Tortora. circ. 15,000. Key Title: Pension Boards.

294.37 US
WHEEL SERIES. 1973. irreg., no.3, 1982. Four Seasons Foundation, Box 31190, San Francisco, CA 94131 (Dist. by: Subco, Box 10233, Eugene, OR 97440) Ed. Donald Allen. circ. 3,000.

RESPIRATORY DISEASES

see Medical Sciences — Respiratory Diseases

RHEUMATOLOGY

see Medical Sciences — Rheumatology

ROADS AND TRAFFIC

see Transportation — Roads and Traffic

ROMAN CATHOLICISM

see Religions and Theology — Roman Catholic

RUBBER

ANNUAL BOOK OF A S T M STANDARDS. VOLUME 09.01. RUBBER, NATURAL AND SYNTHETIC--GENERAL TEST METHODS; CARBON BLACK. see ENGINEERING — Engineering Mechanics And Materials

ANNUAL BOOK OF A S T M STANDARDS. VOLUME 09.02. RUBBER PRODUCTS, INDUSTRIAL--SPECIFICATIONS AND RELATED TEST METHODS; GASKETS; TIRES. see ENGINEERING — Engineering Mechanics And Materials

678 IT ISSN 0066-4499
ANNUARIO DELL'INDUSTRIA ITALIANA DELLA GOMMA/YEARBOOK OF THE ITALIAN RUBBER INDUSTRY. (Text in English, French, German and Spanish) 1962. a. L.60000. (Associazione Nazionale fra le Industrie della Gomma) Gesto s.r.l., Via C. Battisti, 21, 20122 Milan, Italy. Ed. Enzo Belli-Nicoletti. adv.

678 668 FR ISSN 0066-9229
ASSOCIATION FRANCAISE DES INGENIEURS DU CAOUTCHOUC ET DES PLASTIQUES. ANNUAIRE. 1956. biennial. membership. Association Francaise des Ingenieurs du Caoutchouc et des Plastiques, 60 rue Auber, 94408 Vitry-Seine, France. adv. bk. rev.

678.2 UK ISSN 0266-397X
B.R.M.A. DIRECTORY RUBBER AND POLYURETHANE. (Text in English, French, German and Spanish) 1967. triennial. £12. British Rubber Manufacturers' Association Ltd., 90-91 Tottenham Court Rd., London W1P 0BR, England. circ. 1,000.
Formerly: British Rubber Industry Directory.

678.2 US
BLUE BOOK OF MATERIALS, COMPOUNDING INGREDIENTS AND MACHINERY FOR RUBBER. 1936. a. $63. Lippincott & Peto, Inc., 1867 W. Market St., Akron, OH 44313. TEL 216-864-2122. Ed. Don R. Smith. adv. circ. 4,500. (reprint service avail. from UMI)

678 668.4 US ISSN 0272-4685
CONFERENCE OF ELECTRICAL ENGINEERING PROBLEMS IN THE RUBBER AND PLASTICS INDUSTRIES. I E E E CONFERENCE RECORD. a. (I E E E, Industry Applications Society) Institute of Electrical and Electronics Engineers, Inc., 345 E. 47th St., New York, NY 10017 TEL 212-705-7900. (Subscr. address: 445 Hoes Lane, Piscataway, NJ 08854)
Former titles: Electrical Engineering Problems in the Rubber and Plastics Industry Technical Conference. Record (ISSN 0732-295X); Rubber and Plastics Industry Technical Conference. Record (ISSN 0080-4762)

338.476 AG ISSN 0533-4500
GUIA DE LA INDUSTRIA DEL CAUCHO. 1970. biennial. Arg.$3000($32) or exchange basis. Federacion Argentina de la Industria del Caucho, Av. Leandro N. Alem 1067, Piso 16, 1001 Buenos Aires, Argentina. Ed. Antonio C. Castro. circ. 3, 000.

678 MX
GUIA DE LA INDUSTRIA: HULERA. 1968. a. Editorial Cosmos, Espana No. 396, 09880 Mexico, D.F., Mexico. Ed. Cesar Macazaga O. adv. circ. 5, 000.

678 SZ ISSN 0073-0076
HANDBUCH DER INTERNATIONALEN KAUTSCHUKINDUSTRIE/INTERNATIONAL RUBBER DIRECTORY/MANUEL INTERNATIONAL DE CAOUTCHOUC. (Text in English, French, German) 1955. every 5 yrs. 300 Fr. Verlag fuer Internationale Wirtschaftsliteratur GmbH, Box 108, CH-8047 Zurich, Switzerland. Ed. Walter Hirt.

338.476 MX
HULERA. 1963. a. Mex.$2000($25) Litoimpresores, S.A., Espana 396, 09880 Mexico, D.F., Mexico. Ed. Cesar Macazaga. adv.
Formerley: Metalmecanica.

678 II ISSN 0073-6651
INDIAN RUBBER STATISTICS. (Text in English) 1958. a. price varies. Rubber Board, Box 280, Kottayam 686001, Kerala, India.

678 US ISSN 0146-3977
INTERNATIONAL INSTITUTE OF SYNTHETIC RUBBER PRODUCERS. ANNUAL MEETING PROCEEDINGS. 1961. a. $100. International Institute of Synthetic Rubber Producers, 2077 S. Gessner Rd., Ste. 133, Houston, TX 77063. Ed. R.J. Killian. circ. 350. Indexed: Chem.Abstr.

678 UK
INTERNATIONAL RUBBER FORUM. a. £20($40) International Rubber Study Group, Brettenham House, 5-6 Lancaster Place, London WC2E 7ET, England.

678 UK ISSN 0074-7823
INTERNATIONAL RUBBER STUDY GROUP. SUMMARY OF PROCEEDINGS OF THE GROUP MEETINGS AND ASSEMBLIES. a. £20($40) International Rubber Study Group, Brettenham House, 5-6 Lancaster Place, London WC2E 7ET, England.

678.2 MY ISSN 0126-8309
MALAYSIAN RUBBER PRODUCERS' COUNCIL. ANNUAL REPORT/MAJLIS PENGELUAR-PENGELUAR GETAH MALAYSIA. LAPURAN TAHUNAN. (Text in Malay and English) 1951. a. M.$10. Malaysian Rubber Producers' Council - Majlis Penguluar-Pengeluar Getah Malaysia, P.O. Box 12688, 50786 Kuala Lumpur, Malaysia. stat. circ. 600.
Formerly: Rubber Producers' Council of Malaysia. Annual Report.

MODERN TIRE DEALER PRODUCTS CATALOG. see TRANSPORTATION

678 668.4 UK ISSN 0077-8869
NEW TRADE NAMES IN THE RUBBER AND PLASTICS INDUSTRIES. 1926. a. £41. R A P R A Technology Ltd., Shawbury, Shrewsbury, Shropshire, England. circ. 500.
●Also available online. Vendors: Pergamon Infoline.

678 CE
R R I S L BULLETIN. (Text in English) irreg. Rubber Research Institute of Sri Lanka, Dartonfield, Agalawatta, Sri Lanka. Indexed: Biol.Abstr. Hort.Abstr. Plant Breed Abstr. Sri Lanka Sci.Ind. Rev.Plant Path.
Supersedes: R R I C Bulletin.

338.476 US
RUBBER DIRECTORY AND BUYERS GUIDE (YEAR); a directory of rubber product manufacturers and rubber industry suppliers in North America. Short title: Rubbicana (Year) 1978. a. $60. (Rubber and Plastic News) Crain Communications, Inc. (Akron), 34 N. Hawkins Ave., Akron, OH 44313. TEL 216-836-9180. Ed. Edward Noga. circ. 16,500. (back issues avail.)

338 US
RUBBER: LATIN AMERICAN INDUSTRIAL REPORT. (Avail. for each of 22 Latin American countries) 1985. a. $435 per country report per industry covered. Aurora International, Box 9099, Bridgeport, CT 06601-2099. TEL 203-368-0579. Ed. Andres C. Aquino.

678 US ISSN 0361-0640
RUBBER RED BOOK; directory of the rubber industry. 1936. a. $49.50. Communication Channels, Inc., 6255 Barfield Rd., Atlanta, GA 30328. TEL 404-256-9800. Ed. Barbara Katinsky. circ. 5,600.

633.895 MY ISSN 0126-8279
RUBBER RESEARCH INSTITUTE OF MALAYSIA. ANNUAL REPORT. a. M.$25($15) Rubber Research Institute of Malaysia - Institut Penyelidikan Getah Tanah Malaysia, Box 10150, Kuala Lumpur 01-02, Malaysia. circ. 1,700. Indexed: Biol.Abstr. Hort.Abstr. Rev.Plant Path.
Formerly (until 1973): Kuala Lumpur. Rubber Research Institute of Malaya. Annual Report.

633.895 MY ISSN 0126-5849
RUBBER RESEARCH INSTITUTE OF MALAYSIA. PLANTERS CONFERENCE PROCEEDINGS. biennial. M.$35($21) Rubber Research Institute of Malaysia - Institut Penyelidikan Getah Tanah Malaysia, Box 10150, Kuala Lumpur 01-02, Malaysia. charts. illus. circ. 2,000. Indexed: Chem.Abstr.

678 CE
RUBBER RESEARCH INSTITUTE OF SRI LANKA. ANNUAL REVIEW. (Text in English) a. Rubber Research Institute of Sri Lanka, Dartonfield, Agalawatta, Sri Lanka. Indexed: Biol.Abstr. Hort.Abstr. Rev.Plant Path. Weed Abstr.
Supersedes: Rubber Research Institute of Ceylon. Annual Review.

678 668.4 CE
RUBBER RESEARCH INSTITUTE OF SRI LANKA. JOURNAL. (Text in English) vol.53, 1976. irreg. $10. ‡ Rubber Research Institute of Sri Lanka, Dartonfield, Agalawatta, Sri Lanka. Ed. Dr. O.S. Peries. adv. bk. rev. charts. illus. circ. 2,500. Indexed: Biol.Abstr. Chem.Abstr. Abstr.Trop.Agri. Hort.Abstr. RAPRA. Soils & Fert. Trop.Abstr. Plant Breed.Abstr. Sri Lanka Sci.Ind. Rural Recreat.Tour.Abstr. Rev.Plant Path. World Agri.Econ.& Rural Sociol.Abstr.
Formerly (until 1976): Rubber Research Institute of Sri Lanka. Quarterly Journal (ISSN 0035-9521)

678 US
RUBBER WORLD BLUE BOOK. 1935. a. $65. Lippincott & Peto, 1867 W. Market St., Akron, OH 44313. TEL 212-864-2122. (reprint service avail. from UMI)

678.2 UK
RUBBICANA-EUROPE (YEAR) biennial. £60. Crain Communications Ltd., 20-22 Bedford Row, London WC1R 4EW, England.

SYNDICAT GENERAL DES COMMERCES ET INDUSTRIES DU CAOUTCHOUC ET DES PLASTIQUES. GUIDE. see BUSINESS AND ECONOMICS — Trade And Industrial Directories

986 RUBBER — ABSTRACTING, BIBLIOGRAPHIES, STATISTICS

678.32 US ISSN 0082-4496
TIRE AND RIM ASSOCIATION. STANDARDS YEAR BOOK. 1927. a. price varies. ‡ Tire and Rim Association, Inc., 3200 W. Market St., Akron, OH 44313. TEL 216-836-5553. circ. 5,000.

678.2 629.286 AT
TYRE AND RIM ASSOCIATION OF AUSTRALIA STANDARDS MANUAL. 1958. a. Aus.$17. Tyre and Rim Association of Australia, 1/795 Glenferrie Rd., Hawthorn, Vic. 3122, Australia. circ. 1,700.

678.2 US ISSN 0083-5218
VANDERBILT RUBBER HANDBOOK. 1968. irreg. R.T. Vanderbilt Co., Inc., 30 Winfield St., Norwalk, CT 06855. TEL 203-853-1400. Ed. Robert O. Babbit. index.
A source of technical information for those directly connected with the compounding and processing of rubber and synthetic elastomers in their dry form

678 GW ISSN 0083-694X
VULKANISEUR - JAHRBUCH. 1952. a. DM.5. Bielefelder Verlagsanstalt KG, Niederwall 53, Postfach 1140, 4800 Bielefeld, W. Germany (B.R.D.) adv. circ. 5,000.

678 UK
WORLD RUBBER STATISTICS HANDBOOK. every 5 yrs. International Rubber Study Group, Brettenham House, 5/6 Lancaster Place, London WC2E 7ET, England.

RUBBER — Abstracting, Bibliographies, Statistics

382 318 BL ISSN 0572-5534
BRAZIL. SUPERINTENDENCIA DA BORRACHA. ANNUARIO ESTATISTICO. MERCADO ESTRANGEIRO. 1966? a. Superintendencia da Borracha, Avda. Almirante Barroso 81, Caixa Postal 610, Rio de Janeiro RJ, Brazil. charts.

678.2 CN ISSN 0300-0214
CANADA. STATISTICS CANADA. RUBBER PRODUCTS INDUSTRIES. (Catalogue 33-206) (Text in English and French) 1919. a. Can.$20($21) Statistics Canada, Communications Division, 3rd Floor, R.H. Coats Bldg., Ottawa, Ont. K1A 0T6, Canada TEL 613-993-7276. (Subscr. to: Publications Sales and Services, Ottawa, Ont. K1A 0T6, Canada)

678 668.4 016 UK ISSN 0033-6750
R A P R A ABSTRACTS. 1923. m. £495($735) R A P R A Technology Ltd., Shawbury, Shrewsbury SY4 4NR, England. Ed. C. Green. adv. bk. rev. abstr, stat. index. circ. 700. Indexed: Art & Archaeol.Tech.Abstr. World Text.Abstr.
●Also available online. Vendors: Orbit Information Technologies, Pergamon Infoline.

SCHOOL ORGANIZATION AND ADMINISTRATION

see Education — School Organization and Administration

SCIENCES: COMPREHENSIVE WORKS

508.1 US ISSN 0271-2229
A A A S PUBLICATION. irreg. American Association for the Advancement of Science, 1333 H St., N.W., Washington, DC 20005. TEL 202-326-6450. Indexed: GeoRef.
Formerly: A A A S Miscellaneous Publication.

A A E C NUCLEAR NEWS. see ENERGY

500 919.8 550 AT
A N A R E REPORT. (Australian National Antarctic Research Expeditions) 1950. irreg. free. Department of Science, Antarctic Division, Channel Highway, Kingston, Tas. 7150, Australia. Ed. S.A. Potter. circ. 400. (back issues avail.) Indexed: GeoRef.
Formerly: A N A R E Scientific Report.

500 AT ISSN 0729-6533
A N A R E RESEARCH NOTES. (Australian National Antarctic Research Expeditions) 1982. irreg. free. Australian National Antarctic Research Expeditions, Department of Science, Antarctic Division, Channel Highway, Kingston, Tas. 7150, Australia. Ed. S.A. Potter. circ. 400. (back issues avail.)

500 AT ISSN 0312-8059
A N Z A A S CONGRESS PAPERS. 1970. a. price varies. (Australian and New Zealand Association for the Advancement of Science) University of New South Wales Library, Box 1, Kensington, N.S.W. 2033, Australia. Ed. Peter Dobrovits. (microfiche) Indexed: Chem.Abstr. Aus. P.A.I.S. Aus.Sci.Ind.

500 GW ISSN 0343-7051
ABHANDLUNGEN AUS DEM GEBIET DER AUSLANDSKUNDE. SERIES B & C. (Text in English and German) irreg., vol.74, 1975. price varies. (Universitaet Hamburg, Seminar fuer Kultur und Geschichte Indiens) Franz Steiner Verlag Wiesbaden GmbH, Birkenwaldstr. 44, Postfach 347, D-7000 Stuttgart 1, W. Germany (B.R.D.) Indexed: Excerp.Med.

500 DR
ACADEMIA DE CIENCIAS DE LA REPUBLICA DOMINICANA. ANUARIO. (Text in English, French and Spanish; summaries in Spanish) 1975. a. $15. Academia de Ciencias de la Republica Dominicana, Calle las Damas 112, Esquina el Conde, Apdo. 932, Santo Domingo, Dominican Republic.

500 FI ISSN 0356-6927
ACADEMIA SCIENTIARUM FENNICA. YEARBOOK/SUOMALAINEN TIEDEAKATEMIA. VUOSIKIRJA. (Text in Finnish or English; summaries in English) 1977. a. Suomalainen Tiedeakatemia - Academia Scientiarum Fennica, Snellmaninkatu 9-11, 00170 Helsinki 1, Finland. Ed. Aarne Nyyssonen. index. circ. 1,300. (back issues avail.; reprint service avail. from UMI) Indexed: Biol.Abstr. Ref.Zh.
Supersedes (from 1977): Academia Scientiarum Fennica. Proceedings/Sitzungsberichte (ISSN 0065-0501)

500 BE
ACADEMIAE ANALECTA. MEDEDELINGEN VAN DE KONINKLIJKE ACADEMIE VOOR WETENSCHAPPEN, LETTEREN EN SCHONE KUNSTEN VAN BELGIE. SERIES 1: KLASSE DER WETENSCHAPPEN. (Text in Dutch and English; summaries in English) 1938. irreg. price varies. Koninklijke Academie voor Wetenschappen, Letteren en Schone Kunsten van Belgie, 1 Hertogsstraat, B-1000 Bruxelles, Belgium (Subscr.to: Brepols Publishers, Baron Frans du Foursstraat, B-2300 Turnhout, Belgium) Ed. G. Verbeke. circ. 1, 000. (back issues avail.)

500 FR ISSN 0065-0552
ACADEMIE DES SCIENCES. ANNUAIRE. 1917. a. (Academie des Sciences) Centrale des Revues Dunod-Gauthiers Villars, 23 quai Conti, 75006 Paris, France.

500 FR ISSN 0065-0560
ACADEMIE DES SCIENCES. INDEX BIOGRAPHIQUE DES MEMBRES ET CORRESPONDANTS. 1939. irreg. Centrale des Revues Dunod Gauthier-Villars, 23 Quai de Conti, 75006 Paris, France.

509 GW ISSN 0366-8258
ACADEMIE INTERNATIONALE D'HISTOIRE DES SCIENCES. COLLECTION DES TRAVAUX. (Text in English, French, German) irreg., vol.23, 1976. irreg. price varies. Franz Steiner Verlag Wiesbaden GmbH, Birkenwaldstr. 44, Postfach 347, D-7000 Stuttgart 1, W. Germany (B.R.D.) Indexed: Math.R.

500 060 PL ISSN 0079-3159
ACADEMIE POLONAISE DES SCIENCES. CENTRE SCIENTIFIQUE, PARIS. CONFERENCES. (Text in French) 1953. irreg., no.132, 1982. price varies. (Polska Akademia Nauk, Centre Scientifique, Paris, FR) Panstwowe Wydawnictwo Naukowe, Ul. Miodowa 10, 00-251 Warsaw, Poland (Dist. by: Ars Polona, Krakowskie Przedmiescie 7, 00-068 Warsaw, Poland) Ed. L. Kasprzyk.

ACADEMIE ROYALE DES SCIENCES, DES LETTRES ET DES BEAUX-ARTS DE BELGIQUE. ANNUAIRE. see HUMANITIES: COMPREHENSIVE WORKS

500 BE
ACADEMIE ROYALE DES SCIENCES, DES LETTRES ET DES BEAUX ARTS DE BELGIQUE. CLASSE DES SCIENCES. MEMOIRES. 1904. irreg. price varies. Academie Royale des Sciences, des Lettres et des Beaux Arts de Belgique., Classe des Sciences, Palais des Academies, 1 rue Ducale, 1000 Bussels, Belgium (Subscr. to: Office International des Periodiques, 114 Ave. Brand Withloch, 1040 Brussels, Belgium) Ed.Bd. circ. 500.

ACADEMIE SERBE DES SCIENCES ET DES ARTS. CLASSE DES SCIENCES MATHEMATIQUES ET NATURELLES. BULLETIN. SCIENCES MATHEMATIQUES. see MATHEMATICS

500 US ISSN 0096-7750
ACADEMY OF NATURAL SCIENCES OF PHILADELPHIA. MONOGRAPHS. 1935. irreg., no.22, 1983. price varies. Academy of Natural Sciences of Philadelphia, 19th St. and the Parkway, Philadelphia, PA 19103. TEL 215-299-1050. Ed. K. Elaine Hoagland. bibl. charts. illus. stat. (back issues avail.) Indexed: Biol.Abstr. GeoRef.

500 US ISSN 0097-3157
ACADEMY OF NATURAL SCIENCES OF PHILADELPHIA. PROCEEDINGS; original research in systematics, evolution & ecology. 1842. a. $26. Academy of Natural Sciences of Philadelphia, 19th St. and the Parkway, Philadelphia, PA 19103. Ed. K. Elaine Hoagland. bibl. charts. illus. stat. (back issues avail.) Indexed: Biol.Abstr. Curr.Cont. Excerp.Med. Geo.Abstr. GeoRef.

500 US ISSN 0097-3254
ACADEMY OF NATURAL SCIENCES OF PHILADELPHIA. SPECIAL PUBLICATIONS. 1922. irreg., no.15, 1985. price varies. Academy of Natural Sciences of Philadelphia, 19th St. and the Parkway, Philadelphia, PA 19103. TEL 215-299-1050. Ed. K. Elaine Hoagland. bibl. charts. illus. stat. (back issues avail.) Indexed: Biol.Abstr. GeoRef.

500.2 510 IT ISSN 0373-3033
ACCADEMIA DELLE SCIENZE DI TORINO. MEMORIE. PART 1. CLASSE DI SCIENZE FISICHE, MATEMATICHE E NATURALI. 1977. irreg., 1-4/yr. price varies. Accademia delle Scienze di Torino, Via Maria Vittoria 3, 10123 Turin, Italy (Subscr. to: Bottega d'Erasmo, via G. Ferrari 9, 10124 Turin, Italy) Ed. Vittorio Cirilli. charts. illus. circ. 500. Indexed: Biol.Abstr.

500 IT ISSN 0392-2219
ACCADEMIA LIGURE DI SCIENZE E LETTERE. ATTI. (Text in English, French and Italian) 1890. a. L.7000($12) Accademia Ligure di Scienze e Lettere, Via Balbi 10, Palazzo Reale, 16126 Genoa, Italy. Ed. Pietro Scotti. circ. 500. Indexed: Biol.Abstr. Chem.Abstr. Math.R. Sci.Abstr. GeoRef.

500 IT ISSN 0065-0765
ACCADEMIA PATAVINA DI SCIENZE LETTERE ED ARTI. COLLANA ACCADEMICA. 1966. irreg., no.6, 1975. price varies. Accademia Patavina di Scienze Lettere ed Arti, Via Accademia 7, 35100 Padua, Italy.

500 060 IT ISSN 0065-0781
ACCADEMIA TOSCANA DI SCIENZE E LETTERE LA COLOMBARIA. STUDI. 1953. irreg., vol.80, 1986. price varies. Casa Editrice Leo S. Olschki, Casella Postale 66, 50100 Florence, Italy. circ. 1,000.

ACTA ACADEMIAE ABOENSIS, SERIES B: MATHEMATICA ET PHYSICA. see MATHEMATICS

500 919 998 DK ISSN 0065-1028
ACTA ARCTICA. (Text in English, French and German) 1943. irreg., (every 3-5/yr.) price varies. (Arktisk Institut) C.A. Reitzels Forlag, Norregade 20, DK-1165 Copenhagen K, Denmark. Ed. Helge Larsen. (back issues avail.) Indexed: Biol.Abstr.

SCIENCES: COMPREHENSIVE WORKS

500.9 610   GE   ISSN 0001-5857
ACTA HISTORICA LEOPOLDINA. (Supplements avail.) 1963. irreg., vol.16, 1986. price varies. (Deutsche Akademie der Naturforscher Leopoldina, Archiv fuer Geschichte der Naturforschung und Medizin) Johann Ambrosius Barth Verlag, Salomonstr. 18b, DDR-7010 Leipzig, E. Germany (D.D.R.) (Orders to: Buchexport, Leninstr. 16, DDR-7010 Leipzig, E. Germany (D.D.R.)) Ed. Dr. G. Uschmann. bibl. charts. illus. circ. 1,200. Indexed: Biol.Abstr. Math.R.
History

500 600   DK   ISSN 0065-1311
ACTA HISTORICA SCIENTIARUM NATURALIUM ET MEDICINALIUM. (Text in Danish, English, or German) 1942. irreg., no.32, 1979. price varies. C. A. Reitzels Forlag, Norregade 20, DK-1165 Copenhagen K, Denmark. (back issues avail.) Indexed: Ind.Med. GeoRef.

500 600   MX   ISSN 0567-7785
ACTA MEXICANA DE CIENCIA Y TECNOLOGIA. (Text in English or Spanish) 1967. irreg., vol.14, 1980. Instituto Politecnico Nacional, Comision de Operacion y Fomento de Actividades Academicas, Apdo. Postal 42-161, Mexico 17, D.F., Mexico. bibl. charts. illus. index. circ. 1,000. Indexed: Biol.Abstr. Math.R. Sci.Abstr.

ACTA REGIAE SOCIETATIS SCIENTIARUM ET LITTERARUM GOTHOBURGENSIS. INTERDISCIPLINARIA. see *HUMANITIES: COMPREHENSIVE WORKS*

500   SW
ACTA UNIVERSITATIS UPSALIENSIS. (Text in several languages) 1773. irreg. price varies. (Kungliga Vetenskaps-Societeten - Royal Society of Sciences of Uppsala) Almqvist & Wiksell International, Box 62, S-101 20 Stockholm, Sweden. bibl. charts. illus. index. Indexed: M.L.A. GeoRef.
Formerly (until 1968): Nova Act Regiae Societatis Scientiarum Upsaliensis (ISSN 0029-5000)

ADVANCES IN X-RAY ANALYSIS. see *TECHNOLOGY: COMPREHENSIVE WORKS*

500   GE   ISSN 0304-2154
AKADEMIE DER WISSENSCHAFTEN DER DDR. JAHRBUCH. 1950. a. price varies. Akademie-Verlag, Leipziger Strasse 3-4, 1086 Berlin, E. Germany (D.D.R.) Ed. W. Scheler.
Formerly: Akademie der Wissenschaften. Berlin. Jahrbuch (ISSN 0065-5066)

500   GE   ISSN 0138-4112
AKADEMIE DER WISSENSCHAFTEN DER DDR. STUDIEN DER GESCHICHTE. 1975. irreg., vol.12, 1986. (Akademie der Wissenschaften der DDR) Akademie-Verlag Berlin, Leipziger Str. 3-4, 1086 Berlin, E. Germany (D.D.R.)

500   GW   ISSN 0084-6082
AKADEMIE DER WISSENSCHAFTEN, GOETTINGEN. JAHRBUCH. 1939. a. price varies. Vandenhoeck und Ruprecht, Theaterstr. 13, Postfach 37 53, 3400 Goettingen, W. Germany (B.R.D.) Indexed: GeoRef.

001.3 500   GW   ISSN 0084-6104
AKADEMIE DER WISSENSCHAFTEN UND DER LITERATUR, MAINZ. JAHRBUCH. a. price varies. Franz Steiner Verlag Wiesbaden GmbH, Birkenwaldstr. 44, Postfach 347, D-7000 Stuttgart 1, W. Germany (B.R.D.) Indexed: GeoRef.

510 500   GW   ISSN 0002-2993
AKADEMIE DER WISSENSCHAFTEN UND DER LITERATUR, MAINZ. MATHEMATISCH-NATURWISSENSCHAFTLICHE KLASSE. ABHANDLUNGEN. (Text in English, French and German) 1950. irreg. price varies. (Mathematisch-Naturwissenschaftliche Klasse) Franz Steiner Verlag Wiesbaden GmbH, Birkenwaldstr. 44, Postfach 347, D-7000 Stuttgart 1, W. Germany (B.R.D.) abstr. charts. illus. index. Indexed: Biol.Abstr. Chem.Abstr. GeoRef.

500   GW   ISSN 0065-5538
AKADEMISCHE VORTRAEGE UND ABHANDLUNGEN. 1946. irreg., no.46, 1979. price varies. Bouvier Verlag Herbert Grundmann, Am Hof 32, Postfach 1268, 5300 Bonn 1, W. Germany (B.R.D.)

ALBERTA RESEARCH COUNCIL. ANNUAL REPORT. see *TECHNOLOGY: COMPREHENSIVE WORKS*

500   CN
ALBERTA RESEARCH COUNCIL. ATMOSPHERIC SCIENCES REPORTS. irreg. price varies. Alberta Research Council, Publications Department, P.O. Box 8330, Sta. F, Edmonton, Alta. T6H 5X2, Canada. TEL 403-450-5111.
Formerly: Alberta Research Council. Hail Studies Reports (ISSN 0080-1542)

ALBERTA RESEARCH COUNCIL. REPORTS. see *TECHNOLOGY: COMPREHENSIVE WORKS*

500.9 370   CN   ISSN 0701-1024
ALBERTA SCIENCE EDUCATION JOURNAL. 1962. a. Can.$20. Alberta Teachers' Association, Science Council, 11010 142nd St., Edmonton, Alta. T5N 2R1, Canada. TEL 403-453-2411. Ed. Gary Gay. bk. rev. charts. circ. 823.
Formerly: S C A T Bulletin (ISSN 0036-1100)

500.9   GW
ALPENINSTITUT. SCHRIFTENREIHE. (Text in French, German and Italian) 1974. irreg. price varies. (Alpeninstitut fuer Umweltforschung und Entwicklungsplanung in der GFL) Nelles Verlag, Schleissheimer Str. 371 b, 8000 Munich 45, W. Germany (B.R.D.) Ed. Walter Danz.
Natural history

500   US   ISSN 0361-7874
AMERICAN ASSOCIATION FOR THE ADVANCEMENT OF SCIENCE. HANDBOOK; OFFICERS, ORGANIZATION, ACTIVITIES. a. $3. American Association for the Advancement of Science, 1333 H St., N.W., Washington, DC 20005. TEL 202-326-6450.

500   US   ISSN 0361-1833
AMERICAN ASSOCIATION FOR THE ADVANCEMENT OF SCIENCE. MEETING PROGRAM. 1972. a. $7. American Association for the Advancement of Science, 1333 H St., N.W., Washington, DC 20005. TEL 202-326-6450. Ed. Arthur Herschman. adv. index. circ. 8,000. Indexed: GeoRef. Key Title: Annual Meeting - American Association for the Advancement of Science.

620 616   US   ISSN 0065-7964
AMERICAN COUNCIL OF INDEPENDENT LABORATORIES. DIRECTORY. 1937. biennial. $5. American Council of Independent Laboratories, Inc., 1725 K St. N.W., Washington, DC 20006. TEL 202-887-5872. Ed. Joseph O'Neil. circ. 7,000.

AMERICAN MEN AND WOMEN OF SCIENCE. PHYSICAL AND BIOLOGICAL SCIENCES. see *BIOGRAPHY*

500.9   US   ISSN 0003-0082
AMERICAN MUSEUM NOVITATES. 1921. irreg. price varies. American Museum of Natural History, Central Park W. at 79th St., New York, NY 10024. TEL 212-873-1300. Ed. Brenda Jones. circ. 1,500. Indexed: Biol.Abstr. Bull.Signal. GeoRef. Key Word Ind.Wildl.Res. Zoo.Rec.

AMERICAN MUSEUM OF NATURAL HISTORY. ANNUAL REPORT. see *MUSEUMS AND ART GALLERIES*

500.3 069   US   ISSN 0003-0090
AMERICAN MUSEUM OF NATURAL HISTORY. BULLETIN. 1881. irreg. price varies. American Museum of Natural History, Central Park W. and 79th St., New York, NY 10024. TEL 212-873-1300. Ed. Brenda Jones. circ. 1,500. (also avail. in microform from UMI; reprint service avail. from UMI) Indexed: Biol.Abstr. Bull.Signal. Sci.Cit.Ind. Geo.Abstr. GeoRef. Zoo.Rec.

AMERICAN PHILOSOPHICAL SOCIETY. MEMOIRS. see *HISTORY*

AMERICAN PHILOSOPHICAL SOCIETY. TRANSACTIONS. see *HISTORY*

500   SP   ISSN 0374-5880
ANALES DE LA UNIVERSIDAD HISPALENSE. SERIE: CIENCIAS. 1967. irreg., latest no.25. pric varies. Universidad de Sevilla, San Fernando 4, Seville, Spain. charts. illus.

300 500 610   SP   ISSN 0210-7678
ANALES DE LA UNIVERSIDAD HISPALENSE. SERIE: FILOSOFIA Y LETRAS. 1969. irreg. (3-4/ yr.); latest no.88. price varies per no. Universidad de Sevilla, San Fernando 4, Seville, Spain. Indexed: Biol.Abstr. Hist.Abstr. Amer.Hist.& Life.
Formerly: Universidad Hispalense. Anales. Series: Filosofia y Letras, Derecho, Medicina, Ciencias y Veterinaria (ISSN 0041-8552)

500   FR
ANNUAIRE DES FOURNISSEURS DE LABORATOIRES DE RECHERCHES. 1967. a. Agence de Diffusion et de Publicite, 24 Place du General Catroux, 75017 Paris, France. Ed. Raymond Mery. adv. circ. 3,500.

500   US   ISSN 0084-6600
ANNUAL REVIEW OF MATERIALS SCIENCE. 1971. a. $64. Annual Reviews Inc., 4139 El Camino Way, Palo Alto, CA 94306. TEL 415-493-4400. Ed. Robert A. Huggins. bibl. index. cum.index. (back issues avail.; reprint service avail. from ISI) Indexed: Chem.Abstr. Curr.Cont. Sci.Abstr. Int.Aerosp.Abstr. Ind.Sci.Rev. M.M.R.I. Nucl.Sci.Abstr. Phys.Ber.

500   IC
ARBOK VISINDAFELAGS ISLENDINGA. 1975. irreg. Visindafelag Islendinga - Societas Scientiarum Islandica (Icelandic Scientific Society), Haskolabokasafn, 101 Reykjavik, Iceland.

509.798   US
ARCTIC SCIENCE CONFERENCE. PROCEEDINGS. 1950. a. price varies. American Association for the Advancement of Science, Arctic Division, Box 80271, Fairbanks, AK 99708. circ. 600. Indexed: Biol.Abstr. GeoRef.
Former titles: Alaska Science Conference. Proceedings (ISSN 0084-6120); (1951-1969): Science in Alaska (ISSN 0191-2151)

500 600   UK
ASLIB DIRECTORY OF INFORMATION SOURCES IN THE UNITED KINGDOM. VOLUME 1: SCIENCE, TECHNOLOGY AND COMMERCE. 1928. irreg. (approx. every 2 yrs.) £46($85.50) Aslib, Association for Information Management, Information House, 26-27 Boswell St., London WC1N 3JZ, England (Distr. in U.S. by: Learned Information Inc., 143 Old Marlton Pike, Medford, NJ 08055) Ed. Ellen M. Codlin.

500 600   SA   ISSN 0373-4250
ASSOCIATED SCIENTIFIC AND TECHNICAL SOCIETIES OF SOUTH AFRICA. ANNUAL PROCEEDINGS. (Text in English) a. free. Associated Scientific and Technical Societies of South Africa, Kelvin House, 2 Hollard St., Johannesburg, South Africa. circ. 22,000. (back issues avail.) Indexed: Biol.Abstr. Sci.Abstr.

500   CN   ISSN 0066-8842
ASSOCIATION CANADIENNE-FRANCAISE POUR L'AVANCEMENT DES SCIENCES. ANNALES. 1935. a. Can.$12. Association Canadienne-Francaise pour l'Avancement des Sciences, C. P. 6060, Montreal, Que. H3C 3A7, Canada. TEL 514-342-1411. circ. 4,000. Indexed: Biol.Abstr. Arct.Bibl. GeoRef.

500.9   ML
ASSOCIATION DES NATURALISTES DU MALI. BULLETIN. a. Association des Naturalistes du Mali, B.P. 1746, Bamako, Mali.

500.9   DK   ISSN 0067-0227
ATLANTIDE REPORT. SCIENTIFIC RESULTS OF THE DANISH EXPEDITION TO THE COASTS OF TROPICAL WEST AFRICA. (Text in English and French) 1950. irreg. price varies. (Koebenhavns Universitet) Scandinavian Science Press Ltd., Langasen 4, Ganlose, 2760 Malov, Denmark. (Co-sponsor: British Museum) Eds. Joergen Knudsen, Torben Wolff. Indexed: Biol.Abstr.

500   US   ISSN 0077-5630
ATOLL RESEARCH BULLETIN. 1951. irreg. Smithsonian Institution Press, 955 L'Enfant Plaza, Rm. 2100, Washington, DC 20560. TEL 202-287-3738. Ed. F.R. Fosberg. (reprint service avail. from UMI) Indexed: Biol.Abstr. Ocean.Abstr. Field Crop Abstr. Geo.Abstr. GeoRef. Herb.Abstr.

500　　　　　　　AT　ISSN 0067-1568
AUSTRALIAN ACADEMY OF SCIENCE.
  REPORTS. 1957. irreg. Aus.$9.95 per no.
  Australian Academy of Science, P.O. Box 783,
  Canberra, A.C.T. 2601, Australia. circ. 1,500.

500　　　　　　　AT　ISSN 0067-1584
AUSTRALIAN ACADEMY OF SCIENCE. YEAR
  BOOK. 1956. a. Aus.$25. Australian Academy of
  Science, P.O. Box 783, Canberra, A.C.T. 2601,
  Australia. index. circ. 1,500.

500　　　　　　　AU　ISSN 0300-2772
AUSTRIA. BUNDESMINISTERIUM FUER
  WISSENSCHAFT UND FORSCHUNG.
  BERICHT DER BUNDESREGIERUNG AN DEN
  NATIONALRAT. 1968. a. free. Bundesministerium
  fuer Wissenschaft und Forschung, 1 Minoritenplatz
  5, A-1014 Vienna, Austria. stat. Key Title: Bericht
  der Bundesregierung an den Nationalrat.

500　　　　　　　CN
B.C. RESEARCH. ANNUAL REPORT. 1944/45. a.
  free. British Columbia Research Council, 3650
  Wesbrook Mall, Vancouver, B.C. V6S 2L2, Canada.
  TEL 604-224-4331. circ. 2,000.
  Formerly: British Columbia Research Council.
  Annual Report (ISSN 0068-1652)

B.C. SCIENCE TEACHER. see EDUCATION —
  Teaching Methods And Curriculum

500　　　　　　　BG
BANGLADESH SCIENCE CONFERENCE.
  PROCEEDINGS. a. (Bangladesh Association for
  the Advancement of Science) University of Dacca,
  Ramna, Dacca 2, Bangladesh.

500.9　　　　　　IQ
BASRAH NATURAL HISTORY MUSEUM.
  BULLETIN. (Text in English; summaries in Arabic
  and English) 1974. irreg. exchange basis. Basrah
  Natural History Museum, University of Basrah,
  Basrah, Iraq. Ed. Khalaf al-Robaae. abstr. bibl.
  index. Indexed: Biol.Abstr.

500.9　　　　　　IQ
BASRAH NATURAL HISTORY MUSEUM.
  PUBLICATION. 1976. irreg. exchange basis. Basrah
  Natural History Museum, University of Basrah,
  Basrah, Iraq. Ed. Khalaf al Robaae. Indexed:
  Biol.Abstr.

500　　　　　　　GW　ISSN 0084-6090
BAYERISCHE AKADEMIE DER
  WISSENSCHAFTEN. JAHRBUCH. 1912. a. price
  varies. C. H. Beck'sche Verlagsbuchhandlung,
  Wilhelmstr. 9, 8000 Munich 40, W. Germany
  (B.R.D.) index. Indexed: Biol.Abstr. GeoRef.

500.9　　　　　　GW　ISSN 0005-6995
BAYERISCHE AKADEMIE DER
  WISSENSCHAFTEN. MATHEMATISCH-
  NATURWISSENSCHAFTLICHE KLASSE.
  ABHANDLUNGEN. 1929. N.S. no.1. biennial.
  Bayerische Akademie der Wissenschaften,
  Marstallplatz 8, 8000 Munich 22, W. Germany
  (B.R.D.) Indexed: Appl.Mech.Rev. Biol.Abstr.
  Chem.Abstr. Math.R. GeoRef.

500 510　　　　GW　ISSN 0340-7586
BAYERISCHE AKADEMIE DER
  WISSENSCHAFTEN. MATHEMATISCH-
  NATURWISSENSCHAFTLICHE KLASSE.
  SITZUNGBERICHTE. 1871. a. (plus offprints)
  price varies. Bayerische Akademie der
  Wissenschaften, Marstallplatz 8, 8000 Munich 22,
  W. Germany (B.R.D.) Indexed: Biol.Abstr. Math.R.
  GeoRef.

BAYERISCHE AKADEMIE DER
  WISSENSCHAFTEN. PHILOSOPHISCH-
  HISTORISCHE KLASSE. ABHANDLUNGEN.
  see HUMANITIES: COMPREHENSIVE WORKS

BAYERISCHE AKADEMIE DER
  WISSENSCHAFTEN. PHILOSOPHISCH-
  HISTORISCHE KLASSE. SITZUNGSBERICHTE.
  see HUMANITIES: COMPREHENSIVE WORKS

500　　　　　　　GE　ISSN 0232-1556
BEITRAEGE ZUR ALEXANDER-VON
  HUMBOLDT-FORSCHUNG. 1968. irreg., vol.8,
  1986. Akademie-Verlag Berlin, Leipziger Str. 3-4,
  1086 Berlin, E. Germany (D.D.R.)

500　　　　　　　GW　ISSN 0522-6570
BEITRAEGE ZUR GESCHICHTE DER
  WISSENSCHAFT UND DER TECHNIK. 1961.
  irreg., vol.20, 1986. price varies. (Deutsche
  Gesellschaft fuer Geschichte der Medizin,
  Naturwissenschaft und Technik e.V.) Franz Steiner
  Verlag Wiesbaden GmbH, Birkenwaldstr. 44,
  Postfach 347, D-7000 Stuttgart 1, W. Germany
  (B.R.D.) illus.
  History

500　　　　　　　BE　ISSN 0067-5407
BELGIUM. NATIONAAL FONDS VOOR
  WETENSCHAPPELIJK ONDERZOEK.
  JAARVERSLAG/BELGIUM. FONDS
  NATIONAL DE LA RECHERCHE
  SCIENTIFIQUE. RAPPORT ANNUEL. (Text in
  Dutch or French) 1928. a. Nationaal Fonds voor
  Wetenschappelijk Onderzoek - Fond National de la
  Recherche Scientifique, Egmontstraat 5, B-1050
  Brussels, Belgium. (back isssues avail.)

507　　　　　　　BE
BELGIUM. NATIONAAL FONDS VOOR
  WETENSCHAPPELIJK ONDERZOEK. LIJST
  DER KREDIETGENIETERS/BELGIUM. FONDS
  NATIONAL DE LA RECHERCHE
  SCIENTIFIQUE. LISTES DES BENEFICIAIRES
  D'UNE SUBVENTION. (Text in Dutch or French;
  summaries in English) 1928. a. Nationaal Fonds
  voor Wetenschappelijk Onderzoek - Fond National
  de la Recherche Scientifique, Egmontstraat 5, B-
  1050 Brussels, Belgium. circ. 2,100.

500　　　　　　　IS
BEN-GURION UNIVERSITY OF THE NEGEV.
  THE INSTITUTES FOR APPLIED RESEARCH.
  SCIENTIFIC ACTIVITIES. (Text in English)
  1973/74. irreg. free. Ben-Gurion University of the
  Negev, The Institutes for Applied Research, P.O.
  Box 1025, Beer-Sheva 84110, Israel. Ed. Dorot
  Imber. circ. 1,500. Indexed: Field Crop Abstr.
  Herb.Abstr. Hort.Abstr.
  Formerly: Ben-Gurion University of the Negev.
  Research and Development Authority. Applied
  Research Institute. Scientific Activities; Which
  superseded: Negev Institute for Arid Zone Research,
  Beer-Sheva, Israel. Report for Year (ISSN 0077-
  6467)

500.9　　　　　　GW　ISSN 0067-5806
BERICHTE DES VEREINS NATUR UND HEIMAT
  UND DES NATURHISTORISCHEN MUSEUMS
  ZU LUEBECK. 1959. irreg., (every 2-3/yrs.)
  DM.25. Naturhistorisches Museum zu Luebeck,
  Muehlendamm 1, 2400 Luebeck, W. Germany
  (B.R.D.) Eds. M. Diehl, G. Studnitz.

500　　　　　　　US　ISSN 0145-0379
BERKELEY PAPERS IN HISTORY OF SCIENCE.
  1977. irreg., latest no.9, 1984. price varies.
  University of California, Berkeley, Office for
  History of Science and Technology, 470 Stephens
  Hall, Berkeley, CA 94720. TEL 415-642-4581. Ed.
  J.L. Heilbron. circ. 1,000. Indexed: Math.R.

500　　　　　　　GW　ISSN 0171-3302
BERLINER WISSENSCHAFTLICHER
  GESELLSCHAFT. JAHRBUCH. 1978. a. price
  varies. (Berliner Wissenschaftlicher Gesellschaft,
  e.V.) Duncker & Humblot GmbH, Dietrich-
  Schaefer-Weg 9, 1000 Berlin 41, W. Germany
  (B.R.D.)

500.9　　　　　　US　ISSN 0005-9439
BERNICE P. BISHOP MUSEUM BULLETIN. 1922.
  irreg. price varies. Bishop Museum Press, Box
  19000-A, Honolulu, HI 96817. Indexed: Biol.Abstr.
  GeoRef.

500.9 572　　　　US　ISSN 0067-6160
BERNICE PAUAHI BISHOP MUSEUM,
  HONOLULU. OCCASIONAL PAPERS. 1898. a.
  $35. Bishop Museum Press, Box 19000-A,
  Honolulu, HI 96817. Indexed: Biol.Abstr. GeoRef.

500.9 572　　　　US　ISSN 0067-6179
BERNICE PAUAHI BISHOP MUSEUM,
  HONOLULU. SPECIAL PUBLICATIONS. 1892.
  irreg. price varies. Bishop Museum Press, Box
  19000-A, Honolulu, HI 96817. Indexed: Biol.Abstr.

500　　　　　　　CK
BIBLIOTECA JOSE JERONIMO TRIANA
  (SERIAL) (Text in English and Spanish) 1983.
  irreg. $10 or exchange basis. Universidad de
  Colombia, Instituto de Ciencias Naturales, Apdo.
  7495, Bogota, D.E., Colombia. Eds. Pedro M. Ruiz
  C., Santiago Diaz-Piedrahita. circ. 1,000.

500　　　　　　　FR　ISSN 0072-7520
BIBLIOTHEQUE UNIVERSITAIRE, GRENOBLE.
  PUBLICATIONS. 1969. irreg. price varies.
  Bibliotheque Universitaire, Grenoble, Saint-Martin-
  d'Heres, 38401 Grenoble, France.

500　　　　　　　GW　ISSN 0523-8226
BOETHIUS; Texte und Abhandlugen zur Geschichte
  der exakten Wissenschaften. 1962. irreg., vol.17,
  1987. price varies. Franz Steiner Verlag Wiesbaden
  GmbH, Birkenwaldstr. 44, Postfach 347, D-7000
  Stuttgart 1, W. Germany (B.R.D.) Ed.Bd. illus.
  History

500　　　　　　　TU
BOGAZICI UNIVERSITY JOURNAL: SCIENCES.
  (Text in English or Turkish) 1973. a. $10. Bogazici
  Universitesi, Box 2, Istanbul, Turkey.

BOSTON STUDIES IN THE PHILOSOPHY OF
  SCIENCE; Boston colloquium for the philosophy of
  science. see PHILOSOPHY

500　　　　　　　GW
BRAUNSCHWEIGISCHE WISSENSCHAFTLICHE
  GESELLSCHAFT. ABHANDLUNGEN. 1949.
  irreg. price varies. Verlag Erich Goltze GmbH und
  Co. KG, Stresemannstr. 28, 3400 Goettingen, W.
  Germany (B.R.D.) Ed. K.H. Olsen. Indexed:
  Biol.Abstr. Math.R. GeoRef.

500 600　　　　BL
BRAZIL. CONSELHO NACIONAL DE
  DESENVOLVIMENTO CIENTIFICO E
  TECNOLOGICO. BOLETIM.* vol. 2, 1977. irreg.
  Conselho Nacional de Desenvolvimento Cientifico e
  Tecnologico, Edificio CNPQ, Av. W3 Norte, Q.
  507/B, CP 11-1142, 70740 Brasilia D.F., Brazil.

500　　　　　　　BL
BRAZIL. CONSELHO NACIONAL DE
  DESENVOLVIMENTO CIENTIFICO E
  TECNOLOGICO. PROGRAMA DO TROPICA
  SEMI-ARIDO (PUBLICACION) irreg. Conselho
  Nacional de Desenvolvimento Cientifico e
  Tecnologico, Programa do Tropico Semi-Arido, Av.
  W-3 Norte Q-507-B, 11-1142 Brasilia, Brazil. Ed.
  Domingos Carvalho da Silva. charts. stat.

500　　　　　　　BL
BRAZIL. CONSELHO NACIONAL DE
  DESENVOLVIMENTO CIENTIFICO E
  TECNOLOGICO. RELATORIO DE
  ATIVIDADES.* 1975. irreg. Conselho Nacional de
  Desenvolvimento Cientifico e Tecnologico, Edificio
  CNPQ, Av. W3 Norte, Q. 507/B, CP 11-1142,
  70740 Brasilia D.F., Brazil.

500　　　　　　　CR　ISSN 0304-3711
BRENESIA. (Text in various languages; summaries in
  Spanish; abstracts in English) 1972. irreg., approx. s-
  a. $6. Museo Nacional de Costa Rica,
  Departamento de Historia Natural, Box 749, San
  Jose, Costa Rica. Ed. Luis Diego Gomez P. circ. 1,
  000. (tabloid format) Indexed: Biol.Abstr. Zoo.Rec.
  GeoRef. Rev.Appl.Entomol. Rev.Plant Path.

502　　　　　　　UK　ISSN 0068-1040
BRISTOL NATURALISTS' SOCIETY.
  PROCEEDINGS. 1862. a. £2. Bristol Naturalists'
  Society, City Museum, Bristol BS8 1RL, England.
  Ed. A.E. Frey. adv. circ. 750. (also avail. in
  microform from UMI; reprint service avail. from
  UMI) Indexed: Br.Hum.Ind. GeoRef.

509　　　　　　　UK　ISSN 0141-3325
BRITISH ANTARCTIC SURVEY. ANNUAL
  REPORT. a. British Antarctic Survey, Madingley
  Rd., Cambridge CB3 OET, England.

500.1 560　　　　FR　ISSN 0373-2061
BULLETIN SCIENTIFIQUE DE BOURGOGNE.
  1931. biennial. 100 F. Societe des Sciences
  Naturelles de Dijon, Faculte de Sciences,
  Departement de Biologie, 6 bd. Gabriel, F 21100-
  Dijon, France (Subscr. address: Librairie de
  l'Universite, 17 rue de la Liberte, 21014 Dijon,
  France) (Co-sponsor: Universite de Dijon) Dir. J.P.
  Henry. bk. rev. circ. 400. Indexed: Bull.Signal.
  GeoRef.

500 600　　　　　　　BE　ISSN 0069-2026
C R I C RAPPORT DE RECHERCHE. (Text in Dutch, English and French) 1962. irreg. 200 Fr. Centre National de Recherches Scientifiques et Techniques pour l'Industrie Cimentiere, 46 rue Cesar Franck, B-1050 Brussels, Belgium.

500 600　　　　　　　SA　ISSN 0370-8454
C S I R ANNUAL REPORT. 1945. a. free. Council for Scientific and Industrial Research, Publishing Division, Box 395, Pretoria 0001, South Africa. circ. 3,000(English edt.); 2,500(Afrikaans edt.)

500　　　　　　　　　GH
C S I R HANDBOOK. 1970. irreg. Council for Scientific and Industrial Research, Box M32, Accra, Ghana. (back issues avail.)

068　　　　　　　　　AT　ISSN 0157-7204
C S I R O DIRECTORY. 1951. a. Aus.$3. Commonwealth for Scientific and Industrial Research Organisation, 314 Albert St., East Melbourne, Vic. 3002, Australia.

500 600　　　　　　　AT　ISSN 0069-7192
C S I R O FILM CATALOGUE. irreg. free. Commonwealth for Scientific and Industrial Research Organisation, 314 Albert St., E. Melbourne 3002, Vic., Australia.

500 600　　　　　　　SA　ISSN 0081-2390
C S I R O ORGANISATION AND ACTIVITIES. irreg. free. Council for Scientific and Industrial Research Organisation, Publishing Division, Box 395, Pretoria 0001, South Africa. Ed. P. Pretorius. circ. 2,500 English edt.; 2,500 Afrikaans edt.

574 550　　　　　　　US　ISSN 0068-5461
CALIFORNIA ACADEMY OF SCIENCES. OCCASIONAL PAPERS. 1890. irreg., no.146, 1986. $20 (includes Proceedings) California Academy of Sciences, Golden Gate Park, San Francisco, CA 94118. TEL 415-750-7116. Ed. Daphne Fautin. charts. illus. circ. 1,000. (also avail. in microform from UMI; microfiche; back issues avail.; reprint service avail. from UMI) Indexed: Biol.Abstr. Ocean.Abstr. GeoRef. Rev.Appl.Entomol. Zoo.Rec.

500 060　　　　　　　US　ISSN 0068-547X
CALIFORNIA ACADEMY OF SCIENCES. PROCEEDINGS. 1854. irreg. (3-8/yr.), vol.44, 1986. price varies per no.; annual subscr. with Occasional Papers $20. California Academy of Sciences, Golden Gate Park, San Francisco, CA 94118. TEL 415-750-7116. Ed. Daphne Fautin. index in each vol. circ. 1,000. (also avail. in microform from UMI; reprint service avail. from UMI) Indexed: Biol.Abstr. Ocean.Abstr. GeoRef. Key Word Ind.Wildl.Res. Rev.Appl.Entomol. Zoo.Rec.

354　　　　　　　　　CN
CANADA. MINISTRY OF STATE FOR SCIENCE AND TECHNOLOGY. ANNUAL REPORT/RAPPORT ANNUEL. 1971/72. a. Ministry of State for Science and Technology, Ottawa, Canada. TEL 613-997-0028. circ. 3,000.

500 026　　　　　　　CN　ISSN 0703-0320
CANADA INSTITUTE FOR SCIENTIFIC AND TECHNICAL INFORMATION. ANNUAL REPORT/INSTITUT CANADIEN DE L'INFORMATION SCIENTIFIQUE ET TECHNIQUE. RAPPORT ANNUEL. a. free. (National Research Council of Canada) C.I.S.T.I. Publications, Ottawa, Ont. K1A 0S2, Canada. TEL 613-993-3854. circ. 4,000.
Formerly: National Science Library of Canada. Annual Report (ISSN 0077-5576)

500　　　　　　　　　US　ISSN 0069-066X
CARNEGIE INSTITUTION OF WASHINGTON. YEAR BOOK. 1903. a. $7. Carnegie Institution of Washington, 1530 P St., N.W., Washington, DC 20005. TEL 202-387-6400. Ed. R. Bowers. bibl. illus. circ. 500. Indexed: Biol.Abstr. Chem.Abstr. GeoRef.

500.9 574 572 560　US　ISSN 0097-4463
CARNEGIE MUSEUM OF NATURAL HISTORY. ANNALS OF (THE) CARNEGIE MUSEUM. 1901. irreg., vol.55, 1986. $35 to individuals; institutions $65. ‡ Carnegie Museum of Natural History, 4400 Forbes Ave., Pittsburgh, PA 15213. TEL 412-622-3280. Eds. John Carter, Leonard Krishtalka. charts. illus. index. circ. 800. (back issues avail.) Indexed: Biol.Abstr. GeoRef. Zoo.Rec. Key Title: Annals of the Carnegie Museum.

500 574 572 560　US　ISSN 0145-9058
CARNEGIE MUSEUM OF NATURAL HISTORY. BULLETIN. 1976. irreg., no.26, 1986. price varies. Carnegie Museum of Natural History, 4400 Forbes Ave., Pittsburgh, PA 15213. TEL 412-622-3280. Eds. John Carter, Leonard Krishtalka. bibl. charts. illus. index. circ. (controlled) (back issues avail.) Indexed: Biol.Abstr. GeoRef.

500.9　　　　　　　　US　ISSN 0145-9031
CARNEGIE MUSEUM OF NATURAL HISTORY. SPECIAL PUBLICATION. 1975. irreg., no.12, 1986. price varies. Carnegie Museum of Natural History, 4400 Forbes Ave., Pittsburgh, PA 15213. (back issues avail.) Indexed: Biol.Abstr.

500　　　　　　　　　UK　ISSN 0069-0945
CASS LIBRARY OF SCIENCE CLASSICS. 1967. irreg., no.23, 1971. price varies. Frank Cass & Co. Ltd., Gainsborough House, 11 Gainsborough Rd., London E11 1RS, England (Dist. in U.S. by: Biblio Distribution Center, 81 Adams Dr., Totowa, N.J. 07512)

500　　　　　　　　　DK　ISSN 0107-9786
CENTRALE VIDENSKABSETISKE KOMITE. BERETNING/CENTRAL SCIENTIFIC-ETHICAL COMMITTEE OF DENMARK. REPORT. 1982. a. free. Centrale Videnskabsetiske Komite, Forskningssekretariatet, Copenhagen, Denmark.

CENTRE NATIONAL DE DOCUMENTATION SCIENTIFIQUE ET TECHNIQUE. RAPPORT D'ACTIVITE. see TECHNOLOGY: COMPREHENSIVE WORKS

500　　　　　　　　　FR
CENTRE NATIONAL DE LA RECHERCHE SCIENTIFIQUE. COLLOQUES INTERNATIONAUX. SCIENCES MATHEMATIQUES, PHYSIQUES, CHIMIQUES, BIOLOGIQUES ET MEDICALES. no.8, 1949. irreg. Editions du C N R S, 295 rue St. Jacques, 75005 Paris, France. Indexed: Biol.Abstr.
Formerly: Centre National de la Recherche Scientifique. Colloques Internationaux. Sciences Mathematiques, Physico-Chimiques, Biologiques et Naturelles (ISSN 0071-8300)

500　　　　　　　　　FR　ISSN 0071-8327
CENTRE NATIONAL DE LA RECHERCHE SCIENTIFIQUE. RAPPORT D'ACTIVITE. 1958/59. a. free. (Centre National de la Recherche Scientifique) Editions du C N R S, 295 rue St. Jacques, 75005 Paris, France. Indexed: GeoRef.

500　　　　　　　　　CS　ISSN 0069-228X
CESKOSLOVENSKA AKADEMIE VED. ROZPRAVY. M P V: RADA MATEMATICKYCH A PRIRODNICH VED. 1891. irreg., vol.85, 1975. price varies. Academia, Publishing House of the Czechoslovak Academy of Sciences, Vodickova 40, 112 29 Prague 1, Czechoslovakia. circ. 1,000. Indexed: Biol.Abstr. Math.R. GeoRef.

500 600　　　　　　　CE
CEYLON INSTITUTE OF SCIENTIFIC & INDUSTRIAL RESEARCH. ANNUAL REPORT. 1956. a. $25. Ceylon Institute of Scientific & Industrial Research, 363 Bauddhaloka Mawatha, Box 787, Colombo 7, Sri Lanka. circ. 300.

500 600　　　　　　　US
CHECKPOINT (WASHINGTON); newsletter from the frontiers of a future civilized world order. 1965. irreg., latest vol.11, no.1, 1984. donation. War Control Planners Inc., Box 19127, Washington, DC 20036. TEL 202-785-0708. Ed. Howard G. Kurtz. bk. rev. illus. circ. 3,000.

500　　　　　　　　　US　ISSN 0009-3491
CHICAGO ACADEMY OF SCIENCES. BULLETIN. 1883. irreg., latest vol.12, no.1, 1980. price varies. Chicago Academy of Sciences, 2001 N. Clark St., Chicago, IL 60614. TEL 312-549-0606. Ed. Paul G. Heltne. charts. illus. bibl. circ. 1,019. (also avail. in microform from UMI; reprint service avail. from UMI) Indexed: Biol.Abstr.

500 600　　　　　　　US
CHINA REPORT: SCIENCE AND TECHNOLOGY. irreg. (approx. 50/yr.) $5 per no. U.S. Joint Publications Research Service, 1000 N. Glebe Rd., Arlington, VA 22201 TEL 703-487-4630. (Orders to: NTIS, Springfield, VA 22161)

951 500　　　　　　　US　ISSN 0361-9001
CHINESE SCIENCE. 1975. irreg. (1-2/yr.) $12 for 4 nos. History and Sociology of Science, University of Pennsylvania, Philadelphia, PA 19104. TEL 215-898-7454. Ed. N. Sivin. adv. bk. rev. circ. 350.

500 600　　　　　　　JA　ISSN 0578-2228
CHUO UNIVERSITY. FACULTY OF SCIENCE AND ENGINEERING. BULLETIN/CHUO DAIGAKU RIKOGAKUBU KIYO. (Summaries and some articles in English) a. Chuo University, Faculty of Science and Engineering, 1-13-27 Kasuga, Bunkyo-ku, Tokyo 112, Japan. illus.

500 600　　　　　　　BL　ISSN 0084-8794
CIENCIA. (Text in Portuguese; summaries in English) vol.1, no.2, 1980. irreg. avail. on exchange. Centro Academico Piraja da Silva, Faculdade de Ciencias Medicas e Biologicas de Botucatu, C.P. 102, Rubiao-Junior, Botucatu, S.P., Brazil.

CIENCIAS TECNICAS FISICAS Y MATEMATICAS. see TECHNOLOGY: COMPREHENSIVE WORKS

580 590 579　　　　　AT
CLEMATIS. 1962. a. Aus.$0.50. Bairnsdale Field Naturalists' Club, 13 Turnbull St., Bairnsdale, Vic. 3550, Australia. Ed. Ronald S. Yeates. circ. controlled.

500　　　　　　　　　SP
COLECCION CIENCIAS, HUMANIDADES E INGENIERIA. irreg. (approx. 4/yr.) price varies. Colegio de Ingenieros de Caminos, Canales y Puertos, Almagro, 42, 28010 Madrid, Spain.

500　　　　　　　　　CK
COLECCION: DOCUMENTOS E HISTORIA DE LA CIENCIA EN COLOMBIA. irreg. Fondo Colombiano de Investigaciones Cientificas, Apdo. Aereo 29828, Bogota, Colombia.

500　　　　　　　　　NZ　ISSN 0112-2479
COLLECTED PAPERS FROM THE JOURNAL OF THE ROYAL SOCIETY OF NEW ZEALAND. 1984. irreg. price varies. Royal Society of New Zealand, Private Bag, Wellington 1, New Zealand. Ed. Carolyn M. King.

500　　　　　　　　　US　ISSN 0096-2279
COLORADO-WYOMING ACADEMY OF SCIENCES JOURNAL.* 1929. a. $5. Colorado-Wyoming Academy of Science., c/o Dept. of Environmental, Populations and Organismic Biology, University of Colorado, Boulder, CO 80302. Ed.Bd. abstr. circ. 300. Indexed: Biol.Abstr. GeoRef.

500　　　　　　　　　UK　ISSN 0069-6277
COLSTON RESEARCH SOCIETY, BRISTOL, ENGLAND. PROCEEDINGS OF THE SYMPOSIUM. COLSTON RESEARCH PAPERS. 1948. a. price varies. John Wright Journals, Techno House, Redcliffe Way, Bristol BS1 6NX, England. Indexed: Biol.Abstr.

500　　　　　　　　　FR
COMITE DES TRAVAUX HISTORIQUES ET SCIENTIFIQUES. SECTION DES SCIENCES. BULLETIN. 1956. irreg. price varies. Comite des Travaux Historiques et Scientifiques, 3-5 bd. Pasteur, 75015 Paris, France. Indexed: Math.R.

500　　　　　　　　　FR
COMITE DES TRAVAUX HISTORIQUES ET SCIENTIFIQUES. SECTION DES SCIENCES. COMPTES RENDUS DU CONGRES NATIONAL DES SOCIETES SAVANTES. 1961. a. price varies. Comite des Travaux Historiques et Scientifiques, 3-5 bd. Pasteur, 75015 Paris, France.

SCIENCES: COMPREHENSIVE WORKS

500 600   CN   ISSN 0074-9540
CONGRES INTERNATIONAL D'HISTOIRE DES SCIENCES. ACTES. 1947. quadrennial. International Union of the History & Philosophy of Science, c/o William R. Shea, Dept. of Philosophy, McGill University, Montreal, Que. H3A 1G5, Canada. TEL 514-392-4311.

001.3 500   US   ISSN 0069-8970
CONNECTICUT ACADEMY OF ARTS AND SCIENCES. MEMOIRS. 1801. irreg., vol.20, 1982. Archon Books (Subsidiary of: Shoe String Press, Inc.) 925 Sherman Ave., Box 4327, Hamden, CT 06514. TEL 203-248-6307. Ed. Catherine Skinner. illus. Indexed: Biol.Abstr.

CONNECTICUT ACADEMY OF ARTS AND SCIENCES. TRANSACTIONS. see *HUMANITIES: COMPREHENSIVE WORKS*

001 502   AG
CONSEJO NACIONAL DE INVESTIGACIONES CIENTIFICAS Y TECNICAS. INFORME SOBRE UN AÑO DE LABOR. irreg. Consejo Nacional de Investigaciones Cientificas y Tecnicas, Rivadavia 1917, 1033 Buenos Aires, Argentina. illus.

550   US   ISSN 0459-8113
CONTRIBUTIONS IN SCIENCE. (Text in English; occasional summaries in Spanish) 1957. irreg., no.367, 1985. Natural History Museum of Los Angeles County, 900 Exposition Blvd., Los Angeles, CA 90007. TEL 213-744-3330. Ed. Robin A. Simpson. circ. 2,000. Indexed: Biol.Abstr. Ocean.Abstr. Zoo.Rec. GeoRef.
    Formerly: Natural History Museum of Los Angeles County. Contributions in Science (ISSN 0076-0900); Incorporating (after 1978): Science Bulletin (ISSN 0076-0935)

500 600   UR   ISSN 0130-3252
CONTRIBUTIONS TO THE HISTORY OF NATURAL SCIENCES AND TECHNOLOGY IN THE BALTIC/IZ ISTORII ESTESTVOZNANIYA I TEKHNIKI PRIBALTIKI. (Text in Russian; contents in English) 1968. a. or biennial. 1.60 Rub. (Akademiya Nauk Latviiskoi S.S.R.) Izdatel'stvo Zinatne, Turgeneva iela, 19, Riga, Latvian S.S.R., U.S.S.R. Ed. P. Valeskalns. bk. rev. circ. 1,000. Indexed: Bull.Signal. Chem.Abstr. Ref.Zh.
    Formerly: Contributions to the History of Science and Technology in Baltics. (ISSN 0069-9713)

500   FR
COURRIER DU C N R S SUPPLEMENT. 1973. irreg., approx. 2-3/yr. 20 F. (Centre National de la Recherche Scientifique) Editions du C N R S, 295 rue St. Jacques, 75005 Paris, France.

500   US   ISSN 0070-1416
CRANBROOK INSTITUTE OF SCIENCE, BLOOMFIELD HILLS, MICHIGAN. BULLETIN. (Each bulletin has a distinctive title) 1931. irreg., no.59, 1985. price varies. ‡ Cranbrook Institute of Science, Box 801, Bloomfield Hills, MI 48013. TEL 313-645-3256. Dir. Robert West. adv. bk. rev. (reprint service avail. from UMI) Indexed: Biol.Abstr.

500.9   UK   ISSN 0309-8656
CROYDON NATURAL HISTORY & SCIENTIFIC SOCIETY. PROCEEDINGS AND TRANSACTIONS. 1871. irreg. (approx. 3-4/yr.) £5 (includes the Society's Bulletin) Croydon Natural History and Scientific Society Ltd., 96A Brighton Rd., South Croydon, Surrey CR2 6AD, England. Ed. F.G. Peake. charts. illus. cum.index. circ. 1, 000. Indexed: Br.Geol.Lit. Br.Archaeol.Abstr.

CUADERNOS VALENCIANOS DE HISTORIA DE LA MEDICINA Y DE LA CIENCIA. see *MEDICAL SCIENCES*

500   US
CURRENT CONTENTS ADDRESS DIRECTORY-SCIENCE & TECHNOLOGY. (Includes Author Index, Organizational Index, Geographical Index) 1985. a. $345. Institute for Scientific Information, 3501 Market St., Philadelphia, PA 19104 TEL 215-386-0100. (And 132 High St., Uxbridge, Middlesex, UB8 1DP, England)
    Supersedes in part (after 1985): Current Bibliographic Directory of the Arts and Sciences; Which was formerly (1970-1978): I S I's Who Is Publishing in Science (ISSN 0360-8174); 1966-1970: International Directory of Research and Development Scientists (ISSN 0190-6003)

500   JA
CURRENT SCIENCE AND TECHNOLOGY RESEARCH IN JAPAN. (Text in English) 1980. biennial. 30.000 Yen. Japan Information Center of Science and Technology - Nihon Kagaku Gijutsu Joho Senta, 5-2 Nagata-cho, 2-Chome, Chiyoda-Ku, Tokyo 100, Japan. index. circ. 1,500. (back issues avail.)

500   US   ISSN 0732-4383
CURRENT TOPICS IN CHINESE SCIENCE. a. Gordon and Breach Science Publishers, Inc., 50 W. 23rd St., New York, NY 10010. TEL 212-206-8900. Indexed: Biol.Abstr.

500   US   ISSN 0275-9098
CURRENT TOPICS OF CONTEMPORARY THOUGHT. 1973. a., latest vol.3, 1985. price varies. Gordon and Breach Science Publishers, 50 West 23rd Street, New York, NY 10010. TEL 212-206-8900. Eds. Rubin Gotesky, Ervin Laszlo.

500 330 630   NZ   ISSN 0110-5221
D S I R DISCUSSION PAPER. 1978. irreg. price varies. (Department of Scientific and Industrial Research) Science Information Publishing Center, P.O. Box 9741, Wellington, New Zealand. bibl. charts. illus. stat. (back issues avail.)

DAEDALUS. see *MUSEUMS AND ART GALLERIES*

500.9   DK   ISSN 0373-3874
DANSK NATURHISTORISK FORENING. VIDENSKABELIGE MEDDELELSER. 1968. a. Kr.350. Dansk Naturhistorisk Forening, Universitetsparken 15, 2100 Copenhagen OE, Denmark. Ed. Ole Tendal. illus. circ. 1,060. Indexed: Bio.Abstr. Zoo.Rec.
    Formerly: Dansk Naturhistorisk Forening i Koebenhavn. Videnskabelige Meddelelser.

500.9   US   ISSN 0084-9650
DELAWARE MUSEUM OF NATURAL HISTORY. MONOGRAPH SERIES. 1970. irreg., latest no.4, 1982. price varies. Delaware Museum of Natural History, Box 3937, Greenville, DE 19807. TEL 302-658-9111. Indexed: Biol.Abstr.

500.9   US   ISSN 0084-9669
DELAWARE MUSEUM OF NATURAL HISTORY. REPRODUCTION SERIES. 1968. irreg., no.1, 1968. price varies. Delaware Museum of Natural History, Box 3937, Greenville, DE 19807. TEL 302-658-9111. Indexed: Biol.Abstr.

500   DK
DENMARK. PLANLAEGNINGSRAADET FOR FORSKNINGEN DANDOK-STATENS 6 FORSKNINGSRAED. BERETNING. 1974. biennial. free. Forskningssekretariatet, Holmens Kanal 7, Copenhagen, Denmark. circ. 1,200.
    Formerly: Denmark. Planlægningsraadet for Forskingen-Statens 6 Forskningsraed. Beretning (ISSN 0105-452X)

500   GW   ISSN 0070-3974
DEUTSCHE FORSCHUNGSGEMEINSCHAFT. DENKSCHRIFTEN ZUR LAGE DER DEUTSCHEN WISSENSCHAFT. 1957. irreg. price varies. V C H Verlagsgesellschaft mbH, Postfach 1260/1280, 6940 Weinheim, W. Germany (B.R.D.) (U.S. adress: 220 East 23rd. St., NY, NY, 10010-4606) bk. rev.

500   GW   ISSN 0070-3982
DEUTSCHE FORSCHUNGSGEMEINSCHAFT. FORSCHUNGSBERICHTE. 1957. irreg. price varies. V C H Verlagsgesellschaft mbH, Postfach 1260/1280, 6940 Weinheim, W. Germany (B.R.D.) (U.S. adress: 220 East 23rd St., NY, NY, 10010-4606.)

500   GW   ISSN 0070-3990
DEUTSCHE FORSCHUNGSGEMEINSCHAFT. KOMMISSIONENMITTEILUNGEN. 1964. irreg. price varies. V C H Verlagsgesellschaft mbH, Postfach 1260/1280, D-6940 Weinheim, W. Germany (B.R.D.) (U.S. adress: 220 East 23rd St., NY NY 10010-4606.) bk. rev. Indexed: Chem.Abstr. GeoRef.

500   GW   ISSN 0418-842X
DEUTSCHE FORSCHUNGSGEMEINSCHAFT. MEXIKO-PROJEKT; eine deutsch-mexikanische interdisziplinaere Regionalforschung im Becken von Puebla-Tlaxcala. (Text in German and Spanish) irreg., vol.19, 1984. price varies. Franz Steiner Verlag Wiesbaden GmbH, Birkenwaldstr. 44, Postfach 347, D-7000 Stuttgart 1, W. Germany (B.R.D.) Ed. Wilhelm Lauer. Indexed: GeoRef.

DEVONSHIRE ASSOCIATION FOR THE ADVANCEMENT OF SCIENCE, LITERATURE AND ART. REPORT AND TRANSACTIONS. see *ART*

500   AT   ISSN 0727-6753
DIRECTORY OF C S I R O RESEARCH PROGRAMS. a. Aus.$30. C.S.I.R.O., 314 Albert St., East Melbourne, Vic. 3002, Australia. Ed. Elizabeth Odgers. index.

500   UK   ISSN 0309-5339
DIRECTORY OF EUROPEAN ASSOCIATIONS. PART 2: NATIONAL LEARNED, SCIENTIFIC & TECHNICAL SOCIETIES. 1975. irreg., latest no.3, 1984. £52.50($95) C.B.D. Research Ltd., 15 Wickham Rd., Beckenham, Kent BR3 2JS, England (Dist. in U.S. by: Gale Research Co., Penobscot Bldg., Detroit, MI 48226) Ed. R.W. Adams. circ. 4, 000.

500   CN   ISSN 0316-0297
DIRECTORY OF FEDERALLY SUPPORTED RESEARCH IN UNIVERSITIES/REPERTOIRE DE LA RECHERCHE DANS LES UNIVERSITES SUBVENTIONNEE PAR LE GOUVERNEMENT FEDERAL. 1972/73. a. Can.$77. (National Research Council of Canada) C.I.S.T.I. Publications, Ottawa, Ont. K1A 0S2, Canada. TEL 613-993-3736. circ. 300.
● Also available online. Vendors: CISTI.

500   RH
DIRECTORY OF ORGANIZATIONS CONCERNED WITH SCIENTIFIC RESEARCH AND TECHNICAL SERVICES IN ZIMBABWE. 1959. triennial, latest 1979. Scientific Liaison Office, Box 8510, Causeway, Zimbabwe.
    Formerly: Directory of Organizations Concerned with Scientific Research and Technical Services in Rhodesia.

500 352   US
DIRECTORY OF RESEARCH & DEVELOPMENT CONTRACTORS. 1971. a. $15. Government Data Publications, 1120 Connecticut Ave., N.W., Washington, DC 20036.

500 026   IS
DIRECTORY OF RESEARCH INSTITUTES IN ISRAEL. (Text in English; indexes in English and Hebrew) 1982. irreg. $40. National Center of Scientific and Technological Information, Box 20125, Tel-Aviv, Israel. Ed. G. Gilat. index. circ. 300.

500   US   ISSN 0070-6256
DIRECTORY OF SCIENCE RESOURCES FOR MARYLAND. 1963. irreg., latest 1980/81. $7. Department of Economic and Community Development, Business Directories, 45 Calvert St., Annapolis, MD 21401. TEL 301-269-2041. Ed. Marilyn Corbett. adv.

500 060   IS   ISSN 0334-2824
DIRECTORY OF SCIENTIFIC AND TECHNICAL ASSOCIATIONS IN ISRAEL. (Guides to Sources of Information Series, No. 2) (Text in English and Hebrew) 1962. irreg., 3rd edt. 1978. $25. National Center of Scientific and Technological Information, Box 20125, Tel-Aviv, Israel.
    Formerly: Directory of Scientific and Technical Associations and Institutes in Israel (ISSN 0070-6264)

500   UK   ISSN 0070-6272
DIRECTORY OF SCIENTIFIC DIRECTORIES. irreg., 4th edt., 1985. £80. ‡ Longman Group Ltd., Fourth Ave., Harlow, Essex CM19 5AA, England (Dist. in U.S. and Canada by: Gale Research Co. Ltd., Book Tower, Detroit, MI 48226)

500   NR   ISSN 0070-6280
DIRECTORY OF SCIENTIFIC RESEARCH IN NIGERIA. 1968. a. Science Association of Nigeria, Box 4039, Ibadan, Nigeria.

500 600   PK
DIRECTORY OF THE SCIENTISTS, TECHNOLOGISTS, AND ENGINEERS OF THE P C S I R. (Text in English) 1972. a. Pakistan Council of Scientific and Industrial Research, Publications Branch, 39 Garden Rd., Karachi 0310, Pakistan. circ. controlled.

500   SW   ISSN 0347-5719
DOCUMENTA. 1972. irreg., (3-5/yr.) Kungliga Vetenskapsakademien - Royal Swedish Academy of Sciences, Box 50005, S-104 05 Stockholm, Sweden. bibl. illus.

DOCUMENTS HISTORIQUES DES SCIENCES. see *HISTORY — History Of Europe*

500.9   IT   ISSN 0417-9927
DORIANA. (Supplement to its Annali) (Text and summaries in English, French, German, Italian and Spanish) 1949. irreg., no.250, 1983. exchange basis only. Museo Civico di Storia Naturale "G. Doria", Via Brigata Liguria 9, 16121 Genoa, Italy. Indexed: Biol.Abstr. Entomol.Abstr. Bull.Signal. Rev.Appl.Entomol. Zoo.Rec.
Natural history

500.9 913   UK   ISSN 0070-7112
DORSET NATURAL HISTORY AND ARCHAEOLOGICAL SOCIETY. PROCEEDINGS. 1877. a. £10. Dorset County Museum, Dorchester, Dorset, England. Ed. J.C. Chaplin. circ. 2,000. Indexed: Br.Hum.Ind. Br.Geol.Lit. Br.Archaeol.Abstr. Numis.Lit.

500   US
DREXEL FACULTY PUBLICATION. 1978. a. free. ‡ Drexel University, Office of Sponsored Projects, 32nd & Market Sts., Philadelphia, PA 19104. TEL 215-895-2499. Ed. Dr. Kenneth N. Geller. circ. 200.
Supersedes (1971-1978): Drexel Research Conference. Summary Report (ISSN 0085-0071)

500   SZ
ECOLE POLYTECHNIQUE FEDERALE DE LAUSANNE. PUBLICATION. no.120, 1971. irreg. Ecole Polytechnique Federale de Lausanne, 33 Ave. de Cour, 1007 Lausanne, Switzerland.

500 060   US   ISSN 0196-9110
ENCYCLIA. 1924. a. $12. Utah Academy of Sciences, Arts, and Letters, c/o Jean Anne Waterstradt, Ed., 3128 JKHB Brigham Young University, Provo, UT 84602. TEL 801-378-3385. circ. 1,000. Indexed: Chem.Abstr. M.L.A. Math R. Sociol.Abstr. Arts & Hum.Cit.Index. Excerp.Bot. Field Crop Abstr. GeoRef. Herb.Abstr. Hort.Abstr. Lang.& Lang.Behav.Abstr. Rev.Plant Path.
Formerly (until vol.54, 1977): Utah Academy of Science, Arts, and Letters. Proceedings (ISSN 0083-4823)

500.9   US
ENTOMOLOGY OF THE CALIFORNIA CHANNEL ISLANDS. 1985. irreg. $20. Santa Barbara Museum of Natural History, 2559 Puesta del Sol Rd., Santa Barbara, CA 93105. TEL 805-682-4711. Eds. Arnold Menke, Douglass Miller.

500 600   NE
EPISTEME; a series in the foundational methodological, philosophical, psychological, sociological and political aspects of the sciences, pure and applied. (Text in English) 1975. irreg. price varies. D. Reidel Publishing Co., Box 17, 3300 AA Dordrecht, Netherlands (And 190 Old Derby St., Hingham, MA 02043) Ed. Mario Bunge. Indexed: Math.R.

500   GW   ISSN 0340-8833
ERNST-MACH-INSTITUT, FREIBURG. BERICHT. irreg. Ernst-Mach Institut, Eckerstr. 4, 7800 Freiburg, W. Germany (B.R.D.)
Formerly: Ernst-Mach-Institut, Freiburg. Wissenschaftlicher Bericht (ISSN 0071-1217)

500 600   US
EUROPE-LATIN AMERICA REPORT: SCIENCE AND TECHNOLOGY. irreg. (approx. 40/yr.) $5 per no. U.S. Joint Publications Research Service, 1000 N. Glebe Rd., Arlington, VA 22201 TEL 703-487-4630. (Orders to: NTIS, Springfield, VA 22161)

500 600   UK
EUROPEAN RESEARCH CENTRES; a directory of organizations in science, technology, agriculture and medicine. triennial, 6th edt., 1985. £195. Longman Group Ltd., Fourth Ave., Harlow, Essex CM19 5AA, England (Dist. in U.S. & Canada by: Gale Research Co. Ltd., Book Tower, Detroit, MI 48226)

500 600   UK
EUROPEAN SOURCES OF SCIENTIFIC AND TECHNICAL INFORMATION. triennial, 6th edt., 1985. £105. Longman Group Ltd., Fourth Ave., Harlow, Essex CM19 5AA, England (Dist. in U.S. & Canada by: Gale Research Co. Ltd., Book Tower, Detroit, MI 48226)

500 600   SZ   ISSN 0071-335X
EXPERIENTIA. SUPPLEMENTUM. (Text in English, French and German) 1953. irreg., latest 1985. price varies. Birkhaeuser Verlag, P.O. Box 133, CH-4010 Basel, Switzerland. Indexed: Biol.Abstr. Chem.Abstr. Ind.Med.

FILOSOFI OG VIDENSKABSTEORI PAA ROSKILDE UNIVERSITETSCENTER. see *PHILOSOPHY*

500 600   US
FOCUS ON SCI-TECH. 1972. irreg. Carnegie Library of Pittsburgh, Science and Technology Department, 4400 Forbes Ave., Pittsburgh, PA 15213. TEL 412-622-3141. bk. rev. bibl. circ. 500(controlled)

910   CS
FOLIA FACULTATIS SCIENTIARUM NATURALIUM UNIVERSITATIS PURKYNIANAE BRUNENSIS: GEOGRAPHIA. irreg., (7-12/yr.) price varies. Universita J. E. Purkyne, Prirodovedecka Fakulta, Kotlarska 2, 611 37 Brno, Czechoslovakia.

500 333.78 639.9   UK   ISSN 0309-7560
FORTH NATURALIST AND HISTORIAN. 1976. a. £3($6) Forth Naturalist and Historian Editorial Board, University of Stirling, Stirling FK9 4LA, Scotland. Ed. L. Corbett. cum.index (vol.1-5) circ. 500. Indexed: Biol.Abstr. Aqua.Sci.& Fish.Abstr. Zoo.Rec.

500   FR   ISSN 0071-8319
FRANCE. CENTRE NATIONAL DE LA RECHERCHE SCIENTIFIQUE. COLLOQUES NATIONAUX. irreg., no.933, 1975. Editions du C N R S, 295 rue St. Jacques, 75005 Paris, France.

500 949.3   BE   ISSN 0251-2408
DE FRANSE NEDERLANDEN/PAYS-BAS FRANCAIS. 1976. a. 1.100 Fr. Stichting Ons Erfdeel, Murissonstraat 260, B-8530 Rekkem, Belgium. Ed. Jozef Deleu. circ. 2,000.

629.13   FA   ISSN 0085-0896
FRODSKAPARRIT; ANNALES SOCIETATIS SCIENTIARUM FAEROENSIS. (Text mainly in Faroese: summaries in English and occasionally in other languages) 1952. a. price varies. (Mentunargrunnr Foeroya Loegt ngs) Foeroya Frodskaparfelag, DK-3800 Torshavn, Faeroe Islands. Ed.Bd. index. circ. 1,000.

500   FA   ISSN 0429-7539
FRODSKAPARRIT; ANNALES SOCIETATIS SCIENTIARUM FAERONSIS. SUPPLEMENTA. (Text and summaries in Danish, Faroese or English) 1954. irreg. Foeroya Frodskaparfelag, DK-3800 Torshavn, Faeroe Islands. index. Indexed: M.L.A.

500   JA   ISSN 0071-9781
FUKUI UNIVERSITY. FACULTY OF EDUCATION. MEMOIRS. SERIES 2: NATURAL SCIENCE. (Text in English or Japanese) 1961. irreg. Fukui University, Faculty of Education - Fukui Daigaku Kyoikugakubu, 3-9-1 Bunkyo, Fukui-shi 910, Japan.

060   AG
FUNDACION BARILOCHE. MEMORIA ANUAL. a. Fundacion Bariloche, Casilla de Correo 138, San Carlos de Bariloche - Rio Negro, Argentina.

GDANSKIE TOWARZYSTWO NAUKOWE. WYDZIAL 3. NAUK MATEMATYCZNO-PRZYRODNICZYCH. ROZPRAWY. see *MATHEMATICS*

500 001.4   US   ISSN 0072-0798
GENERAL SYSTEMS YEARBOOK. 1956. a. $32 to non-members. (Society for General Systems Research) University of Louisville, Systems Science Institute, Louisville, KY 40292. TEL 502-588-5555. bk. rev. circ. 2,000. (back issues avail.)

007   GW
GERMANY (FEDERAL REPUBLIC, 1949-). BUNDESMINISTERIUM FUER FORSCHUNG UND TECHNOLOGIE. B M F T FOERDERUNGSKATALOG. 1971. a. DM.30. Bundesministerium fuer Forschung und Technologie, Heinemannstr. 2, Bonn 2, W. Germany (B.R.D.) circ. 4,000.

500.9   GW   ISSN 0037-5942
GESELLSCHAFT NATURFORSCHENDER FREUNDE ZU BERLIN. SITZUNGSBERICHTE. NEUE FOLGE. 1961. a. price varies. Duncker und Humblot GmbH, Dietrich-Schaefer-Weg 9, 1000 Berlin 41, W. Germany (B.R.D.) Ed. Hildegard Struebing.
Natural history

GLASGOW NATURALIST. see *BIOLOGY*

500   SW   ISSN 0348-6788
GOTHENBURG STUDIES IN THE HISTORY OF SCIENCE AND IDEAS. (Subseries of Acta Universitatis Gothoburgensis) 1979. irreg., vol.7, 1985. price varies; also exchange basis. Acta Universitatis Gothoburgensis, Box 5096, S-402 22 Goeteborg, Sweden (Dist. in U.S., Canada, and Mexico by: Humanities Press, Inc., 171 First Ave., Atlantic Highlands, NJ 07716) Eds. Sven-Eric Liedman, Henrik Sandblad.

500   UK   ISSN 0072-5919
GREAT BRITAIN. DEPARTMENT OF EDUCATION AND SCIENCE. SCIENCE POLICY STUDIES. 1967. irreg. price varies. H.M.S.O., Box 569, London SE1 9NH, England. (Co-sponsor: Department of Education and Science)

500   IC
GREINAR; collection of miscellaneous papers. 1935. irreg., latest no.6, 1977. price varies. Visindafelag Islendinga - Societas Scientiarum Islandica (Icelandic Scientific Society), Haskolabokasafn, 101 Reykjavik, Iceland. circ. 1,000.

500 100 200   GW
GRENZFRAGEN. 1972. irreg., vol.7, 1978. (Goerres-Gesellschaft) Karl Alber GmbH, Hermann Herder Str. 4, 7800 Freiburg, W. Germany (B.R.D.) Ed. Norbert A. Luyten.

500   GW
GRUNDLAGEN DER EXAKTEN NATURWISSENSCHAFTEN. (Text in English, German) 1980. irreg. price varies. Bibliographisches Institut, Dudenstr. 6, Box 311, D-6800 Mannheim 1, W. Germany (B.R.D.) Ed. Peter Mittelstaedt.

500.9   JA   ISSN 0017-5668
GUNMA UNIVERSITY. FACULTY OF EDUCATION. SCIENCE REPORTS. (Text in English and Japanese; summaries in English) 1950. a. exchange basis. Gunma University, Faculty of Education, Gunma University Library, 4-2, Aramaki, Maebashi, Gunma, Japan. Ed.Bd. Indexed: Biol.Abstr.

500 600   TU   ISSN 0072-9221
HACETTEPE FEN VE MUHENDISLIK BILIMLERI DERGISI. (Text in Turkish; summaries in English, French and German) 1971. a. TL.10($0.75) University of Hacettepe, Faculty of Science and Engineering, Ankara, Turkey. Ed. Alaattin Kutsal.

500   US   ISSN 0073-1595
HEIDELBERG SCIENCE LIBRARY. 1967. irreg.; unnumbered after vol.22; latest 1983. Springer-Verlag, 175 Fifth Ave, New York, NY 10010 TEL 212-460-1500. (Also Berlin, Heidelberg, Vienna) (reprint service avail. from ISI) Indexed: Biol.Abstr.

500   US   ISSN 0371-0165
HEIDELBERGER AKADEMIE DER WISSENSCHAFTEN. MATHEMATISCH-NATURWISSENSCHAFTLICHE KLASSE. SITZUNGSBERICHTE. 1948. irreg., latest 1984. price varies. Springer-Verlag, 175 Fifth Ave, New York, NY 10010 TEL 212-460-1500. (Also Berlin, Heidelberg, Tokyo and Vienna) (reprint service avail. from ISI) Indexed: Nutr.Abstr.

SCIENCES: COMPREHENSIVE WORKS

500   US   ISSN 0073-1633
HEIDELBERGER ARBEITSBUECHER. 1971. irreg., no.10, 1976. price varies. Springer-Verlag, 175 Fifth Ave., New York, NY 10010 TEL 212-460-1500. (Also Berlin, Heidelberg, Vienna) (reprint service avail. from ISI)

500   US   ISSN 0073-1641
HEIDELBERGER JAHRBUECHER. 1957. a. price varies. (Universitaets-Gesellschaft Heidelberg, GW) Springer-Verlag, 175 Fifth Ave., New York, NY 10010 TEL 212-460-1500. (Also Berlin, Heidelberg, Tokyo and Vienna) Ed. H.Schipperges. (reprint service avail. from ISI) Indexed: Biol.Abstr. Hist.Abstr. Amer.Hist.& Life.

500   US   ISSN 0073-1684
HEIDELBERGER TASCHENBUECHER. 1964. irreg., no.243, 1986. price varies. Springer-Verlag, 175 Fifth Ave., New York, NY 10010 TEL 212-460-1500. (Also Berlin, Heidelberg, Tokyo and Vienna) (reprint service avail. from ISI) Indexed: Biol.Abstr.

500   FR   ISSN 0073-2362
HISTOIRE DE LA PENSEE. 1960. irreg. price varies. Editions Hermann, 293 rue Lecourbe, 75015 Paris, France.

509   JA
HISTORIA SCIENTIARUM. (Text in English) 1962. a. 3,000 Yen. History of Science Society of Japan - Nippon Kagakushi Gakkai, c/o Tokyo Institute of Technology, O-okayama, Meguro-ku, Tokyo 152, Japan. Indexed: Hist.Abstr. Math.R. Amer.Hist.& Life.
    Formerly (until 1980): Japanese Studies in the History of Science (ISSN 0090-0176)

500   SP   ISSN 0073-2494
HISTORIA Y FILOSOFIA DE LA CIENCIA. SERIE MAYOR. ENCUADERNADA. 1938. irreg. price varies. Espasa-Calpe, S.A., Carretera de Irun 12200, Apartado 547, Madrid 34, Spain.

500   SP   ISSN 0073-2508
HISTORIA Y FILOSOFIA DE LA CIENCIA. SERIE MENOR. RUSTICA. 1938. irreg. price varies. Espasa-Calpe, S.A., Carretera de Irun 12200, Apartado 547, Madrid 34, Spain.

500   GW   ISSN 0073-2532
HISTORIAE SCIENTIARUM ELEMENTA. (Text in English, German and Latin) 1962. irreg., vol.5, 1973. price varies. (Werner Fritsch Verlag) Theodor Ackermann, Ludwigstr. 7, 8000 Munich 22, W. Germany (B.R.D.) Ed. Werner Fritsch.

500   AT
HISTORICAL RECORDS OF AUSTRALIAN SCIENCE. 1966. a. Aus.$22.50. Australian Academy of Science, P.O. Box 783, Canberra, A.C.T. 2601, Australia. index. circ. 1,000.
    Formerly: Australian Academy of Science. Records (ISSN 0067-155X)

500   US
HISTORICAL STUDIES IN THE PHYSICAL SCIENCES. 1977. irreg. price varies. Johns Hopkins University Press, 701 W. 40th St., Ste. 275, Baltimore, MD 21211. TEL 301-338-6987. (reprint service avail. from UMI)

500   BE
HISTORISCHE DOCUMENTEN VAN DE WETENSCHAPPEN. (Editions in Dutch and French) 1966. irreg. price varies. Belgisch Komitee voor de Geschiedenis der Wetenschappen, Centrale Bibliotheek van de Univ., Rozier 9, 9000 Ghent, Belgium.

700 500   JA   ISSN 0073-2788
HITOTSUBASHI JOURNAL OF ARTS AND SCIENCES. (Text in English, French or German) 1960. a. Hitotsubashi University, Hitotsubashi Academy, 2-1 Naka, Kunitachi, Tokyo 186, Japan. Ed. T. Ogura. cum.index. circ. 900. Indexed: M.L.A. Math.R.

500   US   ISSN 0075-0344
I A S BULLETIN. 1967. irreg. Iowa Academy of Science, Sci. 3538, University of Northern Iowa, Cedar Falls, IA 50614. TEL 319-273-2021.

I A T U L QUARTERLY. (International Association of Technological Universities Libraries) see *LIBRARY AND INFORMATION SCIENCES*

500   US   ISSN 0196-7703
IDAHO MUSEUM OF NATURAL HISTORY. OCCASIONAL PAPERS. 1958. irreg. price varies. ‡ Idaho Museum of Natural History, Idaho State University, Box 8096, Pocatello, ID 83209. TEL 208-236-0211. Ed. Barry L. Keller. circ. 500. (reprint service avail. from UMI)
    Formerly: Idaho State University Museum. Occasional Papers (ISSN 0073-4551)

500.9   US   ISSN 0073-4918
ILLINOIS. NATURAL HISTORY SURVEY. BULLETIN. 1876. irreg., vol.33, no.4, 1985. ‡ Department of Energy and Natural Resources, Natural History Survey Division, Natural Resources Bldg., 607 E. Peabody Dr., Champaign, IL 61820. TEL 217-333-6880. bibl. illus. Indexed: Biol.Abstr. Wild Life Rev. Zoo.Rec.

500.9   US   ISSN 0073-4926
ILLINOIS. NATURAL HISTORY SURVEY. CIRCULAR. 1918. irreg., no.55, 1980. free. ‡ Department of Energy and Natural Resources, Natural History Survey Division, Natural Resources Bldg., 607 E. Peabody Dr., Champaign, IL 61820. TEL 217-333-6880. Ed. Robert M. Zewadski. Indexed: Biol.Abstr. Zoo.Rec.

500   US   ISSN 0162-1939
ILLINOIS. STATE MUSEUM. GUIDEBOOKLET SERIES. 1977. irreg., no.5, 1980. Illinois State Museum, Springfield, IL 62706. TEL 217-782-7386.

500   US   ISSN 0095-2893
ILLINOIS. STATE MUSEUM. INVENTORY OF THE COLLECTIONS. 1969. irreg., no.1, pt.5, 1986. free. Illinois State Museum, Springfield, IL 62706. TEL 217-782-7386.

500   US   ISSN 0360-0297
ILLINOIS. STATE MUSEUM. POPULAR SCIENCE SERIES. 1939. irreg., vol.9, 1978. price varies. Illinois State Museum, Spring and Edwards Sts., Springfield, IL 62706. TEL 217-782-7386. illus. Indexed: GeoRef. Key Title: Popular Science Series.

557 970 570   US   ISSN 0445-3395
ILLINOIS. STATE MUSEUM. SCIENTIFIC PAPERS SERIES. 1940. irreg., vol.21, 1985. price varies. Illinois State Museum, Springfield, IL 62706. TEL 217-782-7386. illus.

200   AU
IMPULSE AUS WISSENSCHAFT UND FORSCHUNG. 1986. a. DM.30. Resch Verlag, Maxmillianstr. 8, A-6010 Innsbruck, Austria. Ed. Andreas Resch. circ. 1,000.

500 600   II   ISSN 0085-1779
INDIA. DEPARTMENT OF SCIENCE & TECHNOLOGY. ANNUAL REPORT. (Text in English) 1969. a. Ministry of Science and Technology, Department of Science & Technology, New Delhi 110 016, India. charts. stat.
    Formerly: India. Committe on Science and Technology. Annual Report.

INDIAN NATIONAL SCIENCE ACADEMY. BIOGRAPHICAL MEMOIRS OF FELLOWS. see *BIOGRAPHY*

500   II   ISSN 0378-6242
INDIAN NATIONAL SCIENCE ACADEMY. BULLETIN. 1952. irreg. price varies per issue. Indian National Science Academy, Bahadur Shah Zafar Marg, New Delhi 110002, India. abstr. charts. illus. circ. 600(approx.) Indexed: Sci.Abstr. GeoRef.
    Continues: National Institute of Sciences of India. Bulletin (ISSN 0027-9528)

500   II
INDIAN NATIONAL SCIENCE ACADEMY. MONOGRAPHS. 1960. irreg. price varies. Indian National Science Academy, Bahadur Zafar Marg, New Delhi 110002, India.
    Continues: National Institute of Sciences of India. N I S I Monographs (ISSN 0470-1380)

500   II   ISSN 0073-6600
INDIAN NATIONAL SCIENCE ACADEMY. PROCEEDINGS. (Text in English) 1935; in separate pts. since 1955. Parts A (Physical Sciences) and B (Biological Sciences) published in alternate months. Rs.120($40) Indian National Science Academy, Bahadur Shah Zafar Marg, New Delhi 110002, India. index. circ. 1,000. Indexed: Biol.Abstr. Excerp.Med. Chem.Abstr. Met.Abstr. Math.R. Sci.Abstr. Nutr.Abstr. Sci.Abstr. GeoRef.
    Formerly: National Institute of Sciences of India. Proceedings.

500   II
INDIAN NATIONAL SCIENCE ACADEMY. TRANSACTIONS. irreg. price varies. Indian National Science Academy, Bahadur Shah Zafar Marg, New Delhi 110002, India.

500   II   ISSN 0073-6619
INDIAN NATIONAL SCIENCE ACADEMY. YEAR BOOK. (Text in English) 1960. a. Rs.15($5) Indian National Science Academy, Bahadur Shah Zafar Marg, New Delhi 110002, India. circ. 1,000. Indexed: Biol.Abstr.
    Formerly: National Institute of Sciences of India, Calcutta. Year Book; Continues: National Institute of Sciences of India. Yearbook (ISSN 0547-7573)

500 600   II   ISSN 0085-1817
INDIAN SCIENCE CONGRESS ASSOCIATION. PROCEEDINGS. (Text in English) 1914. a. Rs.200. Indian Science Congress Association, 14 Dr. Biresh Guha St., Calcutta 700017, India. index. circ. 5,000. Indexed: Biol.Abstr.

500   US   ISSN 0073-6759
INDIANA ACADEMY OF SCIENCE. MONOGRAPH. 1969. irreg. price varies. Indiana Academy of Science, 140 N. Senate Ave., Indianapolis, IN 46204. TEL 317-232-3686. Ed. William R. Eberly. Indexed: Biol.Abstr.

500   US   ISSN 0073-6767
INDIANA ACADEMY OF SCIENCE. PROCEEDINGS. 1891. a. $12. Indiana Academy of Science, 140 N. Senate Ave., Indianapolis, IN 46204. Ed. Donald R. Winslow. cum.index: vols.1-90, 1891-1980. Indexed: Biol.Abstr. Chem.Abstr. GeoRef. Vet.Bull.

500   IO   ISSN 0126-0812
INDONESIA. NATIONAL SCIENTIFIC DOCUMENTATION CENTER. ANNUAL REPORT/INDONESIA. PUSAT DOKUMENTASI ILMIAH NASIONAL. LAPORAN TAHUNAN. a. National Scientific Documentation Center, Jl. Jenderal Gatot Subroto, Box 3065/Jkt., Jakarta, Indonesia.

605   IR
INFORMATIONS ET NOUVEAUTES TECHNIQUES/ETTELA'AT VA TAZEHA-YE FANNI. (Text in French, Persian) 1961. irreg. free. Centre Francais d'Information Technique et Industrielle, 62 Forsat Ave., Shahreza Ave., Box 11-1555, Teheran, Iran. Eds. Aleksandr Gerigoriyans, Bahman Shahparast. circ. 800.

060   PL   ISSN 0537-667X
INFORMATOR NAUKI POLSKIEJ. 1958. a. 1950($92.86) Centrum Informacji Naukowej, Technicznej i Ekonomicznej, Redakcja Informatora Nauki Polskiej, P.O. Box 355, 00-950 Warsaw, Poland. (Co-sponsor: Urzad Postepu Naukowo-Technicznego i Wdrozen) Ed. Mieczyslaw Stanczak.

001.3   FR   ISSN 0073-8190
INSTITUT DE FRANCE. ANNUAIRE. 1796. a. membership. Institut de France, 23 Quai de Conti, 75006 Paris, France.

500   II   ISSN 0073-8336
INSTITUT FRANCAIS DE PONDICHERY. SECTION SCIENTIFIQUE ET TECHNIQUE. TRAVAUX. (Text and summaries in English, French) 1957. irreg., (approx. 2/yr.) price varies. Institut Francais de Pondichery, Box 33, Pondichery 605001, India. Ed. P. Legris. index. circ. 1,000. Indexed: Biol.Abstr. Bull.Signal. Forest.Abstr. Forest Prod.Abstr.

SCIENCES: COMPREHENSIVE WORKS

500 060   II   ISSN 0073-8344
INSTITUT FRANCAIS DE PONDICHERY. SECTION SCIENTIFIQUE ET TECHNIQUE. TRAVAUX. HORS SERIE. (Text in English and French) 1957. irreg. price varies. Institut Francais de Pondichery, Box 33, Pondichery 605001, India. Ed. P. Legris. index. circ. 1,200-1,500. Indexed: Biol.Abstr. Bull.Signal.

500   RW
INSTITUT NATIONAL DE RECHERCHE SCIENTIFIQUE. RAPPORT POUR L'ANNEE. a. Institut National de Recherche Scientifique, BP 218, Butare, Rwanda.

500 600   AO   ISSN 0074-0098
INSTITUTO DE INVESTIGACAO CIENTIFICA DE ANGOLA. MEMORIAS E TRABALHOS. (Text in Portuguese; summaries in English, French, German) 1960. irreg., no.8, 1971. price varies. Instituto de Investigacao Cientifica de Angola, Departamento de Documentacao e Informacao, Box 3244, Luanda, Angola. abstr. (also avail. in microform)

500 600   AO   ISSN 0003-343X
INSTITUTO DE INVESTIGACAO CIENTIFICA DE ANGOLA. RELATORIOS E COMMUNICACOES. 1962. irreg., no.25, 1973. Instituto de Investigacao Cientifica de Angola, Departamento de Documentacao e Informacao, Box 3244, Luanda, Angola.

500   DR   ISSN 0378-956X
INSTITUTO TECNOLOGICO DE SANTO DOMINGO. DOCUMENTOS. 1976. irreg., no.6, 1981. free. Instituto Tecnologico de Santo Domingo, Apdo. Postal 249-2, Santo Domingo, Dominican Republic.

INTER-AMERICAN COUNCIL FOR EDUCATION, SCIENCE, AND CULTURE. FINAL REPORT. see *EDUCATION*

909 500   US   ISSN 0534-8803
INTERNATIONAL CONFERENCE ON SCIENCE AND WORLD AFFAIRS. PROCEEDINGS.* a. International Conference on Science and World Affairs, 935 E. 60th St., Chicago, IL 60637.

500   NE   ISSN 0074-3402
INTERNATIONAL CONGRESS FOR LOGIC, METHODOLOGY AND PHILOSOPHY OF SCIENCE. PROCEEDINGS. 1960. quadrennial, 6th, 1980. Hannover. Elsevier Science Publishers B.V., Box 211, 1000 AE Amsterdam, Netherlands.

500   FR   ISSN 0074-4387
INTERNATIONAL COUNCIL OF SCIENTIFIC UNIONS. YEAR BOOK. 1954. a. free. International Council of Scientific Unions - Conseil International des Unions Scientifiques, 51 bd. de Montmorency, Paris 75016, France. Eds. F.W.G. Baker, P.A. Bahmani Fard. index. circ. 4,000.

500   US   ISSN 0883-0185
INTERNATIONAL REVIEWS IN IMMUNOLOGY. 1986. 4/yr. (in 1 vol.) $160 for individuals; academic institutions $128; corporations $160. Gordon & Breach Science Publishers, Box 786, Cooper Station, New York, NY 10276 TEL 212-206-8900. (Subscr. to: Box 197, London, WC2E 9PX, England) Ed. Heinz Kohler.

500.9   IQ
IRAQ NATURAL HISTORY MUSEUM. BULLETIN. (Text in English; summaries in Arabic and English) 1961. irreg. ID.2500 per no. Iraq Natural History Museum, University of Baghdad, Bab al-Muadham, Baghdad, Iraq. Ed. Munir K. Bunni. (back issues avail.) Indexed: Biol.Abstr. Zoo.Rec.
Former titles: Iraq Natural History Research Center and Museum. Bulletin; Iraq Natural History Museum. Bulletin (ISSN 0021-0897)

574   IQ
IRAQ NATURAL HISTORY MUSEUM. PUBLICATION. (Text in English; summaries in English and Arabic) 1950. irreg. ID.2000 per no. Iraq Natural History Museum, University of Baghdad, Bab al-Muadham, Baghdad, Iraq. Ed. Munir K. Bunni. Indexed: Biol.Abstr. Zoo.Rec.
Former titles: Iraq Natural History Research Centre and Museum. Publications; Iraq Natural History Museum. Publication (ISSN 0085-2260)

ISLE OF MAN NATURAL HISTORY AND ANTIQUARIAN SOCIETY. PROCEEDINGS. see *HISTORY*

500   IS   ISSN 0080-7753
ISRAEL. NATIONAL COUNCIL FOR RESEARCH AND DEVELOPMENT. SCIENTIFIC RESEARCH IN ISRAEL. 1968. irreg., 7th edt., 1986. $25. National Council for Research and Development, P.O.B. 801, 8a Hornkania St., Jerusalem 91000, Israel. TEL 663203. Ed. Larry Lester. circ. 3,000.

500 600   IS   ISSN 0578-9230
ISRAEL ACADEMY OF SCIENCES AND HUMANITIES. SECTION OF HUMANITIES. PROCEEDINGS. (Supersedes in part the Academy's Proceedings) (Text in English and French) 1966. irreg. $3 per no. Israel Academy of Sciences and Humanities, Box 4040, Jerusalem 91040, Israel. circ. 500. (back issues avail.) Indexed: Ind.Heb.Per.

500   IS   ISSN 0333-6190
ISRAEL ACADEMY OF SCIENCES AND HUMANITIES. SECTION OF SCIENCES. PROCEEDINGS. (Text in English) 1963. irreg. Israel Academy of Sciences and Humanities, 43 Jabotinski St., P.O. Box 4040, 91040 Jerusalem, Israel. circ. 900. (back issues avail.) Indexed: Ind.Heb.Per.

500   IT
ISTITUTO COMELIANA DI LUGANO. COLLECTIO MONOGRAPHICA MINOR. 1976. irreg., vol.4, 1978. L.10000. Giardini Editori e Stampatori, Via Santa Bibbiana 28, 56100 Pisa, Italy.

500   IT   ISSN 0075-1499
ISTITUTO E MUSEO DI STORIA DELLA SCIENZA. BIBLIOTECA. 1957. irreg., no.8, 1970. price varies. Casa Editrice Leo S. Olschki, Casella Postale 66, 50100 Florence, Italy. Ed. Paolo Galluzzi. circ. 1,000.

500   IT   ISSN 0021-2504
ISTITUTO LOMBARDO ACCADEMIA DI SCIENZE E LETTERE. RENDICONTI. A. vol.107, 1973. a. price varies. Istituto Lombardo Accademia di Scienze e Lettere, Via Borgonuovo 25, 20121 Milan, Italy. Indexed: Appl.Mech.Rev. Chem.Abstr. M.L.A. Math.R. GeoRef.

IWATE UNIVERSITY. FACULTY OF EDUCATION. ANNUAL REPORT. see *LITERATURE*

500   GE
J.C. POGGENDORFF: BIOGRAPHISCH-LITERARISCHES HANDWOERTERBUCH DER EXAKTEN NATURWISSENSCHAFTEN. Vol.7, 1955. irreg., latest 1986. (Saechsische Akademie der Wissenschaften zu Leipzig) Akademie-Verlag Berlin, Leipziger Str. 3-4, 1086 Berlin, E. Germany (D.D.R.)

500   JA
J S P S ANNUAL REPORT/NIPPON GAKUJUTSU SHINKOKAI. a. Japan Society for the Promotion of Science, 2-1-2 Hitotsubashi, Chiyoda-ku, Tokyo 101, Japan.

JAHRBUCH FUER BIOTECHNOLOGIE. see *BIOLOGY — Biophysics*

500   GW   ISSN 0173-7600
JAHRBUCH FUER REGIONALWISSENSCHAFT. 1980. a. price varies. Vandenhoeck und Ruprecht, Theaterstr. 13, Postfach 37 53, D-3400 Goettingen, W. Germany (B.R.D.) Ed.Bd. circ. 350.

501   JA   ISSN 0453-0691
JAPAN ASSOCIATION FOR PHILOSOPHY OF SCIENCE. ANNALS. (Text in English) 1954. a. 2400 Yen. Japan Association for Philosophy of Science - Kagaku Kisoron Gakkai, c/o Institute of Statistical Mathematics, 4-6-7 Minami Azabu, Minato-ku, Tokyo 106, Japan. Indexed: Biol.Abstr. Math.R. Psychol.Abstr. Sci.Abstr.

500 600   US
JAPAN REPORT: SCIENCE AND TECHNOLOGY. irreg., (approx. 40/yr.) $5 per no. U.S. Joint Publications Research Service, 1000 N. Glebe Rd., Arlington, VA 22201 TEL 703-487-4630. (Orders to: NTIS, Springfield, VA 22161)

500   GW
JOACHIM-JUNGLUS-GESELLSCHAFT DER WISSENSCHAFTEN, HAMBURG. VEROEFFENTLICHUNGEN. 1957. irreg. Vandenhoeck & Ruprecht, Robert-Bosch-Breite 6, Postfach 3753, D-3400 Goettingen, W. Germany (B.R.D.)

500   AU   ISSN 0259-0689
JOHANNES-KEPLER-UNIVERSITAET LINZ. DISSERTATIONEN. 1974. irreg., no.61, 1986. price varies. (Johannes-Kepler-Universitaet Linz) Verband der Wissenschaftlichen Gesellschaften Oesterreichs, Lindengasse 37, A-1070 Vienna, Austria.
Formerly: Johannes-Kepler-Hochschule Linz. Dissertationen.

500   JA   ISSN 0075-4307
JOURNAL OF NATURAL SCIENCE. (Text in English or Japanese) vol.2, 1952. a. avail. on exchange basis. Tokushima University, Faculty of Education - Tokushima Daigaku Kyoiku Gakubu, Kyoiku-gakubu, Tokushima, Japan.

500   TU   ISSN 0022-4057
JOURNAL OF PURE AND APPLIED SCIENCES/ TEMEL VE UYGULAMALI BILMLER DERGISI. Title varies: M E T U Journal of Pure and Applied Sciences. (Text in English and Turkish) 1968. irreg., (approx. 3/yr.) TL.60($5) (Turk Tarih Kurumu Basimevi) Middle East Technical University, Public Relations and Publications Office, Ismet Inonu Bulvari, Ankara, Turkey. Ed. Dogan Altinbilek. bk. rev. abstr. bibl. charts. illus. index. circ. 500. Indexed: Appl.Mech.Rev. Chem.Abstr. Curr.Cont. Math.R. Sci.Cit.Ind. GeoRef.

500   JA   ISSN 0302-0479
KANAZAWA UNIVERSITY. COLLEGE OF LIBERAL ARTS. ANNALS OF SCIENCE/ KANAZAWA DAIGAKU KYOYOBU RONSHU, SHIZENGAKU- HEN. (Text in English or Japanese) 1965. a. Kanazawa University, College of Liberal Arts - Kanazawa Daigaku Kyoyobu, Kanazawa 920, Japan. illus. Indexed: Biol.Abstr. Math.R.

500   JA
KANAZAWA UNIVERSITY. FACULTY OF EDUCATION. BULLETIN: NATURAL SCIENCE/KANAZAWA DAIGAKU KYOIKUGAKUBU KIYO, SHIZENGAKU-HEN. (Text in Japanese; summaries and some articles in English) 1952. irreg. Kanazawa University, Faculty of Education - Kanazawa Daigaku Kyoikugakubu, 1-1 Marunouchi, Kanazawa 920, Japan. Indexed: Biol.Abstr. GeoRef.

500   II   ISSN 0075-5168
KARNATAK UNIVERSITY, DHARWAD, INDIA. JOURNAL. SCIENCE. (Text in English) 1956. a. Rs.8($4) Karnatak University, Director, Prasaranga, Dharwad 580003, Karnataka, India. Ed. M.I. Savadatti. circ. 250. Indexed: Biol.Abstr. Chem.Abstr. Math.R. Entomol.Abstr. GeoRef.

620   JA   ISSN 0286-4215
KEIO SCIENCE AND TECHNOLOGY REPORTS. (Text in English, French and German) 1948. irreg. exchange only. Keio University, Faculty of Science and Technology - Keio Gijuku Daigaku Rikogakubu, Matsushita Memorial Library, 3-14-1, Hiyoshi, Kohoku-ku, Yokohama 223, Japan. Ed. Yasuji Ohtsuka. charts. illus. stat. circ. 1,000. Indexed: Chem.Abstr. Math.R. JCT. Phys.Abstr.
Former titles: Keio Engineering Reports; Keio University. Fujihara Memorial Faculty of Engineering. Proceedings. (ISSN 0016-2507)

500 600   KE
KENYA NATIONAL ACADEMY FOR ADVANCEMENT OF ARTS AND SCIENCES. NEWSLETTER. Short title: K N A A S News. 1977. a. Kenya National Academy for Advancement of Arts and Sciences, Box 47288, Nairobi, Kenya. Ed. Francis Inganji.

500 700   KE
KENYA NATIONAL ACADEMY OF SCIENCES. ANNUAL REPORT. (Text in English) a. Kenya National Academy of Science, Box 47288, Nairobi, Kenya.
Formerly: Kenya National Academy for Advancement of Arts and Sciences. Annual Report.

KENYA PAST AND PRESENT. see *HISTORY — History Of Africa*

SCIENCES: COMPREHENSIVE WORKS

500 SU ISSN 0735-9799
KING SAUD UNIVERSITY. COLLEGE OF SCIENCE. JOURNAL. (Text in English; summaries in Arabic) 1969. a. $10. King Saud University, College of Science, Libraries, P.O. Box 22480, Riyadh, Saudi Arabia. Ed. M. Abdel-Rahman. charts. illus. circ. 3,000.
Formerly: University of Riyadh. Faculty of Sciences. Bulletin.

500.9 913 US ISSN 0075-6245
KIRTLANDIA. 1967. irreg., no.41, 1985. price varies. ‡ Cleveland Museum of Natural History, Wade Oval, University Circle, Cleveland, OH 44106. TEL 216-231-4600. Ed. David Brose. circ. 850. Indexed: Biol.Abstr. GeoRef. Zoo.Rec.

500 JA ISSN 0450-609X
KOBE UNIVERSITY OF MERCANTILE MARINE. REVIEW. PART 2. MARITIME STUDIES, AND SCIENCE AND ENGINEERING. (Text in Japanese, Abstracts in English) 1953. a. Kobe University of Mercantile Marine, 5-1-1 Fukae-Minami-machi, Higashinada-ku, Kobe 658, Japan.
Formerly (until 1980): Kobe University of Mercantile Marine. Review. Part 2. Navigation, Marine Engineering, Nuclear Engineering and Scientific Section.

001.3 500 NO ISSN 0368-6302
KONGELIGE NORSKE VIDENSKABERS SELSKAB. 1926. a. Kr.60. (Royal Norwegian Society of Sciences and Letters) Norwegian University Press, Kolstadgt. 1, Box 2959-Toeyen, 0608 Oslo 6, Norway (U.S. address: Publications Expediting Inc., 200 Meacham Ave., Elmont, NY 11003) Ed. Olaf I. Roenning. Indexed: Biol.Abstr. Math.R. Sci.Abstr.
Formerly: Kongelige Norske Videnskabers Selskab. Forhandlinger.

001.3 500 NO ISSN 0368-6310
KONGELIGE NORSKE VIDENSKABERS SELSKAB. SKRIFTER/ROYAL NORWEGIAN SOCIETY OF SCIENCES. PUBLICATIONS. (Text in English) 1791. irreg. price varies. (Royal Norwegian Society of Sciences and Letters) Norwegian University Press, Kolstadgt. 1, Box 2959-Toeyen, 0608 Oslo 6, Norway (U.S. address: Publications Expediting Inc., 200 Meacham Ave., Elmont, NY 11003) Ed. Olaf I. Roenning. charts. illus. stat. Indexed: Biol.Abstr. Chem.Abstr. Math.R. Sci.Abstr.

500 NE ISSN 0065-5503
KONINKLIJKE NEDERLANDSE AKADEMIE VAN WETENSCHAPPEN. AFDELING NATUURKUNDE, VERHANDELINGEN. EERSTE REEKS. (Text in Dutch, English, French and German) 1893. irreg., vol.32, 1984. price varies. ‡ North Holland Publishing Company, Box 211, 1000 AE Amsterdam, Netherlands. Ed. F.C. Bos. adv. bk. rev. circ. 1,000.

500 NE ISSN 0065-552X
KONINKLIJKE NEDERLANDSE AKADEMIE VAN WETENSCHAPPEN. AFDELING NATUURKUNDE. VERHANDELINGEN. TWEEDE REEKS. (Text in English, French, German and Dutch) 1893. irreg., vol.85, 1985. price varies. ‡ Elsevier Science Publishers B.V., Box 211, 1000 AE Amsterdam, Netherlands. Ed. A.M. Verheggen. adv. bk. rev. circ. 1,000.

500 HU ISSN 0075-6946
KORUNK TUDOMANYA. 1964. irreg. price varies. (Magyar Tudomanyos Akademia) Akademiai Kiado, Publishing House of the Hungarian Academy of Sciences, Box 24, H-1363 Budapest, Hungary.

500 BE
KTEMATA. (Text in French) 1974. irreg., latest no.9, 1986. price varies. Editions Peeters s.p.r.l., Bondgenotenlaan, B-3000 Louvain, Belgium.

500 060 SW ISSN 0081-9956
KUNGL VETENSKAPSAKADEMIEN. BIDRAG TILL KUNGLIGA VETENSKAPSAKADEMIENS HISTORIA. 1963. irreg., vol.17, 1985. price varies. Kungliga Vetenskapsakademien - Royal Swedish Academy of Sciences, Box 50005, S-104 05 Stockholm, Sweden.

500 KU ISSN 0250-4065
KUWAIT INSTITUTE FOR SCIENTIFIC RESEARCH. ANNUAL RESEARCH REPORT. 1977. a. free. Kuwait Institute for Scientific Research, P.O. Box 24885, Safat, Kuwait. Ed.Bd. circ. 2,000. (back issues avail.) Indexed: Chem.Abstr.

505 605 JA ISSN 0911-0305
KYOTO INSTITUTE OF TECHNOLOGY. FACULTY OF ENGINEERING AND DESIGN. MEMOIRS. (Text in English and European languages) 1952. a. exchange basis. Kyoto Institute of Technology, Faculty of Engineering and Design - Kyoto Kogei Sen'i Daigaku, Kogeigakubu, Matsugasaki, Sakyoku, Kyoto 606, Japan. circ. 820. Indexed: Chem.Abstr. Math.R. Sci.Abstr.
Formerly: Kyoto Technical University. Faculty of Industrial Arts. Memoirs: Science and Technology (ISSN 0453-0047)

500 JA
KYOTO PREFECTURAL UNIVERSITY. SCIENTIFIC REPORTS: NATURAL SCIENCE AND LIVING SCIENCE/KYOTO-FURITSU DAIGAKU GAKUJUTSU HOKOKU RIGAKU SEIKATSUKAGAKU. (Text in Japanese; summaries in English) 1952. irreg., no.27, 1976. avail. on exchange. Kyoto Prefectural University - Kyoto-furitsu Daigaku, Shimogamo Hangi-cho, Sakyo-ku, Kyoto 606, Japan. Ed. Z. Hayashino. Indexed: Math.R. C.I.S. Abstr.
Formerly: Kyoto Prefectural University. Scientific Reports: Natural Science, Domestic Science and Social Welfare (ISSN 0075-739X)

KYUSHU INSTITUTE OF TECHNOLOGY. BULLETIN: MATHEMATICS, NATURAL SCIENCE/KYUSHU KOGYO DAIGAKU KENKYU HOKOKU, SHIZENKAGAKU. see *MATHEMATICS*

LASER. see *TECHNOLOGY: COMPREHENSIVE WORKS*

500 539 US ISSN 0091-9489
LAWRENCE BERKELEY LABORATORY. RESEARCH HIGHLIGHTS. 1967. a. free. University of California, Berkeley, Lawrence Berkeley Laboratory, Public Information Department, Berkeley, CA 94720. TEL 415-486-5771. circ. 12,500. (back issues avail.)

500 UK
LEEDS PHILOSOPHICAL AND LITERARY SOCIETY. PROCEEDINGS. SCIENTIFIC. 1925. a. price varies. Leeds Philosophical and Literary Society, Central Museum, Calverley St., Leeds 2, England. Ed. P.R.J. Burch. charts. index. circ. 650. Indexed: Biol.Abstr. Br.Hum.Ind. Sci.Abstr. GeoRef.

500 GE ISSN 0323-4444
LEOPOLDINA; Mitteilungen der Deutschen Akademie der Naturforscher Leopoldina, Reihe 3. (Reihe 1: 1859-1922; Reihe 2: 1926-1930) (Text in English, German) 1955. a. exchange basis. Deutsche Akademie der Naturforscher Leopoldina, August-Bebel-Str. 50a, 4010 Halle/S., E. Germany (D.D.R.) Ed. Georg Uschmann. bk. rev. circ. 1,500. Indexed: GeoRef.

500 US ISSN 0075-9104
LIBRARY OF EXACT PHILOSOPHY. Short title: L E P. (Text in English and German) 1970. irreg., no.13, 1981. Springer-Verlag, 175 Fifth Ave., New York, NY 10010 TEL 212-460-1500. (Also Berlin, Heidelberg, Tokyo and Vienna) Ed. M. Bunge. (reprint service avail. from ISI)

LOS ANGELES COUNCIL OF ENGINEERS & SCIENTISTS. PROCEEDINGS SERIES. see *ENGINEERING*

500 US
LOUISIANA ACADEMY OF SCIENCES. PROCEEDINGS. 1932. a. $15. Louisiana Academy of Sciences, c/o Dr. Brad Mc Pherson, Department of Biology, Centenary College, Shreveport, LA 71104. Ed. Robert Kolinsky. circ. 400. (back issues avail.) Indexed: Biol.Abstr. Chem.Abstr. Zoo.Rec.

509 016 SW ISSN 0076-163X
LYCHNOS-BIBLIOTEK. STUDIES OCH KAELLSKRIFTER UDGIVNA AV LAERDOMSHISTORISKA SAMFUNDET. STUDIES AND SOURCES PUBLISHED BY THE SWEDISH HISTORY OF SCIENCE SOCIETY. 1936. irreg. price varies. (Laerdomshistoriska Samfundet - Swedish History of Science Society) Almqvist & Wiksell International, Box 62, S-101 20 Stockholm, Sweden. Ed. Sten Lindroth. index. Indexed: Hist.Abstr. Amer.Hist.& Life.

509 SW ISSN 0076-1648
LYCHNOS-LAERDOMSHISTORISKA SAMFUNDETS AARSBOK. ANNUAL OF THE SWEDISH HISTORY OF SCIENCE SOCIETY. 1936. a. price varies. (Laerdomshistoriska Samfundet) Almqvist & Wiksell International, Box 62, S-101 20 Stockholm, Sweden. Ed. Sten Lindroth. bk. rev. index.

505.8 US ISSN 0076-2016
MCGRAW-HILL YEARBOOK OF SCIENCE AND TECHNOLOGY. 1962. a. $50. McGraw-Hill Book Co., 1221 Ave. of the Americas, New York, NY 10020. TEL 212-512-2000. Ed. Sybil Parker.

500 SX
MADOQUA. (Text and Summaries in Afrikaans, English and German) 1969. irreg. (3-4/yr.) R.15. Department of Agriculture and Nature Conservation, Private Bag 13306, Windhoek 9000, South West Africa. Ed. E. Joubert. circ. 750. (back issues avail.) Indexed: Biol.Abstr. Curr.Tit.Ocean. Field Crop Abstr. Herb.Abstr. Ind.Vet. Ind.S.A.Per. Vet.Bull.
Supersedes (as of vol.9, no.1, Jan. 1975): Madoqua. Series 1 & Madoqua. Series 2 & Namib Desert Research Station. Scientific Papers.

500 II ISSN 0085-2945
MADRAS. GOVERNMENT MUSEUM. BULLETIN. NEW SERIES. (Text in English) 1931. irreg. price varies. Government Museum, Madras, Director of Museums, Pantheon Road, Egmore, Madras 600008, India.

500 001.3 YU
MAKEDONSKA AKADEMIJA NA NAUKITE I UMETNOSTITE. LETOPIS. 1969. a. Makedonska Akademija na Naukite i Umetnostite, Bulevar Krste Misrkov bb, Box 428, Skopje, Yugoslavia. Ed. Krum Tomovski.

507 UG
MAKERERE UNIVERSITY. SCIENCE FACULTY. HANDBOOK. irreg. Makerere University, Science Faculty, Box 7062, Kampala, Uganda. Ed. A.J. Lutalo. circ. 1,000.

500 MW
MALAWI JOURNAL OF SCIENCE. 1972. a. 25p. Association for the Advancement of Science of Malawi, Box 280, Zomba, Malawi. adv. bk. rev. circ. 1,000.

500 MY ISSN 0301-0554
MALAYSIAN JOURNAL OF SCIENCE/JERNAL SAINS MALAYSIA. (Text in English) 1971. a. $6. University of Malaya, Faculty of Science, Lembah Pantai, Kuala Lumpur 22-11, Malaysia. Ed. Dr. Yong Hoi Sen. adv. bk. rev. circ. 1,000. Indexed: Biol.Abstr. Chem.Abstr.

500 913 581 551 GW
MARSCHENRAT ZUR FOERDERUNG DER FORSCHUNG IM KUESTENGEBIET DER NORDSEE. NACHRICHTEN. 1962. a. free. Marschenrat zur Foerderung der Forschung im Kuestengebiet der Nordsee, Viktoriastr. 26, 2940 Wilhelmshaven 1, W. Germany (B.R.D.) Ed.Bd. circ. 1,200.

500 GE ISSN 0233-173X
MAURITIANA (ALTENBURG) 1958. biennial. price varies. Naturkundliches Museum "Mauritianum", Postfach 216, 74 Altenburg, E. Germany (D.D.R.) Eds. Norbert Hoeser. circ. 800.
Formerly: Naturkundliches Museum "Mauritianum" Altenburg. Abhandlungen und Berichte (ISSN 0065-6631)

MAWDSLEY MEMOIRS. see *GEOGRAPHY*

SCIENCES: COMPREHENSIVE WORKS

500   GW   ISSN 0341-0218
MAX-PLANCK-GESELLSCHAFT. JAHRBUCH. 1951. a. price varies. Vandenhoeck & Ruprecht Verlagsbuchhandlung, Theaterstr. 13, Postfach 77, 3400 Goettingen, W. Germany (B.R.D.) Eds. Ulrike Emrich, Robert Gerwin. bk. rev. index. circ. 4,000. (back issues avail.) Indexed: Biol.Abstr.

500   GW   ISSN 0076-5635
MAX-PLANCK-GESELLSCHAFT ZUR FOERDERUNG DER WISSENSCHAFTEN. JAHRBUCH. 1951. a. DM.84. Max-Planck-Gesellschaft zur Foerderung der Wissenschaften, Residenzstr. 1A, 8000 Munich 2, W. Germany (B.R.D.) Eds. U. Emrich, R. Gerwin.

500   GW   ISSN 0341-7778
MAX-PLANCK-GESELLSCHAFT ZUR FOERDERUNG DER WISSENSCHAFTEN BERICHTE UND MITTEILUNGEN. 1952. irreg. ‡ Max-Planck-Gesellschaft zur Foerderung der Wissenschaften., Residenzstr. 1a, Postfach 647, 8000 Munich 2, W. Germany (B.R.D.) Ed.Bd. bibl. charts. illus. circ. 6,000.
Formerly: Max-Planck-Gesellschaft zur Foerderung der Wissenschaften Mitteilungen (ISSN 0025-6102)

500   NE
METHODS AND PHENOMENA; their applications in science and technology. 1975. irreg., vol.7, 1984. price varies. Elsevier Science Publishers B.V., Box 211, 1000 AE Amsterdam, Netherlands. Eds. S.P. Wolsky, A.W. Czanderna.

500.9   UK   ISSN 0144-0497
MIDDLE THAMES NATURALIST. 1948. a. avail. in U.K. only. Middle Thames Natural History Society, c/o J.K. Letts, 113 Holtspur Top Lane, Beaconsfield, Bucks HP9 1DT, England. Ed. M. Taylor. adv. circ. 450.
Natural history

500   US
MIDWEST RESEARCH INSTITUTE. ANNUAL REPORT. 1945. a. Midwest Research Institute, 425 Volker Blvd., Kansas City, MO 64110. TEL 816-753-7600. circ. 13,000.

959 398   PH   ISSN 0115-7329
MINDANAO STATE UNIVERSITY. U R C PROFESSIONAL PAPERS. 1981. irreg. Mindanao State University, University Research Center, P.O. Box 5594, Iligan City 8801, Philippines.

MINNESOTA STUDIES IN THE PHILOSOPHY OF SCIENCE. see *PHILOSOPHY*

500 600   PL   ISSN 0077-054X
MONOGRAFIE Z DZIEJOW NAUKI I TECHNIKI. (Text in Polish and French; summaries in English, French, German and Russian) 1957. irreg., vol.134, 1986. price varies. (Polska Akademia Nauk, Zaklad Historii Nauki i Techniki) Ossolineum, Publishing House of the Polish Academy of Sciences, Rynek 9, 50-106 Wroclaw, Poland (Dist. by: Ars Polona-Ruch, Krakowskie Przedmiescie 7, Warsaw, Poland) Ed. B. Suchodolski. Indexed: Math.R.

500 574   US
MONTANA ACADEMY OF SCIENCES. PROCEEDINGS. 1942. a. $7.50. Montana Academy of Sciences, Department of Microbiology, University of Montana, Missoula, MT 59812. TEL 406-243-0211. Ed. John F. Tibbs. bibl. charts. illus. stat. circ. 550. (back issues avail.) Indexed: Biol.Abstr. GeoRef.

MUNICH ROUND UP. see *LITERATURE*

500.9   IT   ISSN 0365-4389
MUSEO CIVICO DI STORIA NATURALE "GIACOMO DORIA," GENOA. ANNALI. (Text in English, French, German, Italian and Spanish) 1870. biennial. exchange only. Museo Civico di Storia Naturale "G. Doria", Via Brigata Liguria 9, 16121 Genoa, Italy. Indexed: Biol.Abstr. Bull.Signal. Entomol.Abstr. Rev.Appl.Entomol. Zoo.Rec.

500   IT   ISSN 0392-0062
MUSEO CIVICO DI STORIA NATURALE, VERONA. BOLLETINO. (Issued in 3 Parts: Biologica, Abiologica & Preistorica) (Text in English, French, German and Italian; summaries in English, French and German) 1946. a. exchange basis. Museo Civico di Storia Naturale, Verona, Lungadige Porta Vittoria Nr. 9, 37129 Verona, Italy. Ed.Bd. circ. 600. (back issues avail.) Indexed: Biol.Abstr. Zoo.Rec. GeoRef.
Supersedes in part (since 1974): Museo Civico di Storia Naturale, Verona. Memorie (ISSN 0085-767X)

500.9   AG
MUSEO MUNICIPAL DE HISTORIA NATURAL DE SAN RAFAEL. REVISTA. 1956. irreg. price varies. Museo Municipal de Historia Natural de San Rafael, Parque Mariano Moreno, 5600 San Rafael, Mendoza, Argentina. Ed. Humberto A. Lagiglia. bk. rev. charts. illus. index. circ. 1,500. Indexed: Biol.Abstr.
Former titles: Museo de Historia Natural de San Rafael. Revista; Museo de Historia Natural de San Rafael. Revista Cientifica de Investigaciones (ISSN 0027-3902)

500.9 069   UY
MUSEO NACIONAL DE HISTORIA NATURAL. ANALES. 1894; N.S. 1925. irreg; 1974, latest issue. free on exchange. Museo Nacional de Historia Natural, Casilla de Correo 399, Montevideo, Uruguay. circ. 1,200. Indexed: Biol.Abstr.
Formerly: Montevideo. Museo de Historia Natural. Anales.

500   BL   ISSN 0077-2240
MUSEU PARAENSE EMILIO GOELDI. PUBLICACOES AVULSAS. 1964. irreg., no.39, 1984. Conselho Nacional de Desenvolvimento Cientifico e Tecnologico, Museu Paraense Emilio Goeldi, Caixa Postal 399, Belem, Para, Brazil. Ed. Mario Ferreira Simoes. bibl. illus. circ. 1,000. Indexed: Biol.Abstr. GeoRef.

500.9   FR   ISSN 0078-9720
MUSEUM NATIONAL D'HISTOIRE NATURELLE, PARIS. ANNUAIRE. 1939. a. Museum National d'Histoire Naturelle, 38 rue Geoffroy Saint-Hilaire, 75005 Paris, France. Indexed: Biol.Abstr.

500.9   FR   ISSN 0078-9739
MUSEUM NATIONAL D'HISTOIRE NATURELLE, PARIS. ARCHIVES. (Text in English and French) 1802. irreg. price varies. Museum National d'Histoire Naturelle, 38 rue Geoffroy Saint-Hilaire, 75005 Paris, France. Indexed: Biol.Abstr. GeoRef.

500.9   FR
MUSEUM NATIONAL D'HISTOIRE NATURELLE, PARIS. GRANDS NATURALISTES FRANCAIS. 1952. irreg. price varies. Museum National d'Histoire Naturelle, 38 rue Geoffroy Saint-Hilaire, 75005 Paris, France. Dir. Roger Heim. illus.

N A T O ADVANCED SCIENCE INSTITUTE SERIES. C: MATHEMATICAL AND PHYSICAL SCIENCES. see *MATHEMATICS*

500   NO   ISSN 0800-4412
N D R E PUBLICATIONS. (Text and summaries in English) 1953. irreg., no.72, 1979. Forsvarets Forskningsinstitutt - Norwegian Defence Research Establishment, Box 25, N-2007 Kjeller, Norway. circ. (controlled)
Formerly: Norway. Forsvaret forskningsinstitutt. N D R E Report (ISSN 0085-4301)

500   CH
N S C REVIEW. (Text in English) 1965. a. free. National Science Council of the Republic of China, 2 Canton St., Taipei, Taiwan 107, Republic of China.

500   CH
N S C SPECIAL PUBLICATION. 1978. irreg. National Science Council of the Republic of China, 2 Canton St., Taipei, Taiwan 107, Republic of China.

500   CH   ISSN 0252-8177
N S C SYMPOSIUM SERIES. 1979. irreg. National Science Council of the Republic of China, 2 Canton St, Taipei, Taiwan 107, Republic of China. Indexed: Biol.Abstr.

500.9   GE
N T M GESCHICHTE DER NATURWISSENSCHAFTEN, TECHNIK UND MEDIZIN. SCHRIFTENREIHE. 1960. irreg., (approx. 2/yr.) M.33.40 per vol. Akademische Verlagsgesellschaft Geest and Portig K.G., Sternwartenstr. 8, 701 Leipzig, E. Germany (D.D.R.) Ed.Bd. adv. bk. rev. bibl. charts. illus. index.
Former titles: Geschichte der Naturwissenschaften, Technik und Medizin. Schriftenreihe (ISSN 0036-6978); Zeitschrift fuer Geschichte der Naturwissenschaften, der Technik und der Medizin.

NATIONAL ACADEMY OF SCIENCES. BIOGRAPHICAL MEMOIRS. see *BIOGRAPHY*

500   US   ISSN 0739-361X
NATIONAL ASSOCIATION OF ACADEMIES OF SCIENCE. DIRECTORY AND PROCEEDINGS. 1977. a. $15. National Association of Academies of Science, Department of Biology, Lafayette College, Easton, PA 18042 TEL 215-250-5464. (Order from: Allen Press, Inc., 1041 New Hampshire St., Box 368, Lawrence, KS 66044) (Affiliate: American Association for the Advancement of Science) Ed. Dr. S.K. Majumdar. circ. 500. (back issues avail.) Indexed: ERIC.
Formerly: Association of Academies of Science. Directory and Proceedings.

500   JA   ISSN 0386-555X
NATIONAL INSTITUTE OF POLAR RESEARCH. MEMOIRS. SERIES F: LOGISTICS. (Text and abstracts in English) 1964. irreg., no.4, 1982. exchange basis. National Institute of Polar Research - Kokuritsu Kyokuchi Kenkyujo, 9-10, Kaga, 1-chome, Itabashi-ku, Tokyo 173, Japan. Ed. Tatsuro Matsuda. circ. 1,000. Indexed: Curr.Antarc.Lit.
Supersedes: Japanese Antarctic Research Expedition, 1956-1962. Scientific Reports. Series F: Logistic (ISSN 0075-3408)

500   SA   ISSN 0067-9194
NATIONAL MUSEUM, BLOEMFONTEIN. MEMOIRS. (Text in Afrikaans and English) 1952. irreg., no.21, 1986. price varies; dist. to institutions usually on exchange basis. National Museum, Bloemfontein, Box 266, Bloemfontein 9300, South Africa. TEL 051-79609. abstr.bibl.charts.illus.stat. (back issues avail.)

500   SA   ISSN 0067-9208
NATIONAL MUSEUM, BLOEMFONTEIN. RESEARCHE/NASIONALE MUSEUM BLOEMFONTEIN. NAVORSINGE. (Text in Afrikaans or English) 1952. irreg., vol.5, no.11, 1986. price varies; dist. to institutions usually on exchange basis. National Museum Bloemfontein - Nasionale Museum Bloemfontein, Box 266, Bloemfontein 9300, South Africa. TEL 051-79609. abstr. bibl. charts. illus. stat. circ. 1,000. (back issues avail.) Indexed: Biol.Abstr.

500.9   CN   ISSN 0704-576X
NATIONAL MUSEUM OF NATURAL SCIENCES. SYLLOGEUS. (Text in English and French) 1972. irreg. free. National Museums of Canada, National Museum of Natural Sciences, Ottawa, Ont. K1A 0M8, Canada. TEL 613-996-3102. circ. 1,000. (back issues avail.) Indexed: Biol.Abstr.

507   US
NATIONAL PATTERNS OF SCIENCE AND TECHNOLOGY. a. U.S. National Science Foundation, 1800 G St., N.W., Washington, DC 20550. TEL 202-634-4622.
Formerly: National Patterns of R. & D. Resources; Funds & Manpower in the United States (ISSN 0093-8572)

500   CN
NATIONAL RESEARCH COUNCIL OF CANADA. N R C ANNUAL REPORT/RAPPORT ANNUEL DU C N R C. (Text in English & French) 1916. a. free. ‡ National Research Council of Canada, Public Relations and Information Services, M-58, Ottawa K1A 0R6, Ontario, Canada. TEL 613-993-9101. Ed. Joan Powers Rickerd. circ. 10,000.
Formerly: National Research Council of Canada. Report of the President/Rapport du President.

354.415 IE
NATIONAL SCIENCE COUNCIL (IRELAND).
PROGRESS REPORT. 1972. irreg. £0.15.
Government Publications Sales Office, Sun Alliance
House, Molesworth St., Dublin 2, Ireland. circ. 1,
200.

500 IE ISSN 0085-3836
NATIONAL SCIENCE COUNCIL (IRELAND).
REGISTER OF SCIENTIFIC RESEARCH
PERSONNEL. 1968. irreg. £32.5. Government
Publications Sales Office, Sun Alliance House,
Molesworth St., Dublin 2, Ireland. Eds. Diarmuid
Murphy, Donal O. Brolchain. circ. 800. (tabloid
format)

500 CH
NATIONAL SCIENCE COUNCIL OF THE
REPUBLIC OF CHINA. ANNUAL REPORT.
(Text in Chinese) 1963. a. free. National Science
Council of the Republic of China, 2 Canton St.,
Taipei, Taiwan 107, Republic of China.

500 JA ISSN 0082-4755
NATIONAL SCIENCE MUSEUM. MEMOIRS.
(Text in English and Japanese; summaries in
English) 1968. a. avail. on exchange basis only.
National Science Museum - Kokuritsu Kagaku
Hakubutsukan, 7-20 Ueno Park, Daito-ku, Tokyo
110, Japan. Ed.Bd. circ. 1,000(controlled) Indexed:
Biol.Abstr. GeoRef.

500.9 AU ISSN 0028-0607
NATUR UND LAND. vol.56, 1970. irreg. (4-6/yr.)
S.140. Oesterreichischer Naturschutzbund, Postfach
910, A-6040 Innsbruck, Austria. (Co-sponsor:
Oesterreichische Gesellschaft fuer Natur- und
Umweltschutz) Ed. Walter Kofler. bk. rev. charts.
illus. stat. index. circ. 3,500. Indexed: Biol.Abstr.
Ecol.Abstr. Environ.Abstr.

505 US ISSN 0076-0943
NATURAL HISTORY MUSEUM OF LOS
ANGELES COUNTY. SCIENCE SERIES. 1930.
irreg. no.31, 1985. Natural History Museum of Los
Angeles County, 900 Exposition Blvd., Los Angeles,
CA 90007. bk. rev. circ. 5,000. Indexed: Biol.Abstr.

NATURAL SCIENCES AND ENGINEERING
RESEARCH COUNCIL OF CANADA. LIST OF
SCHOLARSHIPS AND GRANTS IN AID OF
RESEARCH/CONSEIL DE RECHERCHES EN
SCIENCES NATURELLES ET EN GENIE DU
CANADA. LISTE DES BOURSES ET
SUBVENTIONS DE RECHERCHE. see
EDUCATION — Higher Education

NATURAL SCIENCES AND ENGINEERING
RESEARCH COUNCIL OF CANADA. REPORT
OF THE PRESIDENT/CONSEIL DE
RECHERCHES EN SCIENCES NATURELLES
ET EN GENIE DU CANADA. RAPPORT DU
PRESIDENT. see EDUCATION — Higher
Education

500 SZ ISSN 0077-6122
NATURFORSCHENDE GESELLSCHAFT IN
BASEL. VERHANDLUNGEN/SOCIETY FOR
NATURAL SCIENCES, BASEL.
PROCEEDINGS. 1854. irreg. (approx. 1/yr.) price
varies. Birkhaeuser Verlag, P.O. Box 133, CH-4010
Basel, Switzerland. Ed. H. Schaefer. Indexed:
Biol.Abstr. GeoRef.

500 SZ ISSN 0077-6130
NATURFORSCHENDE GESELLSCHAFT IN
BERN. MITTEILUNGEN. (Text in German;
summaries in English and French) 1843. a. 30 Fr.
Naturforschende Gesellschaft in Bern, Stadt-und
Universitaetsbibliothek, Muenstergasse 61, CH-3000
Berne 7, Switzerland. Ed. H. Hutzli. adv. cum.index:
1944-1968 in no.26 (1969) circ. 1,400. Indexed:
Biol.Abstr. GeoRef. VITIS.

500.9 SZ
NATURHISTORISCHES MUSEUM BERN.
JAHRBUCH. 1965. triennial. 60 Fr.
Naturhistorisches Museum, Bernastr. 15, CH-3005
Berne, Switzerland. Ed. Marcel Guentert. illus. circ.
500. (back issues avail.)

500.9 AU ISSN 0083-6133
NATURHISTORISCHES MUSEUM IN WIEN.
ANNALEN. (Text in English, French & German;
summaries in English, French, German, Italian &
Spanish) 1886. a. price varies. Naturhistorisches
Museum in Wien, Burgring 7, P.F.417, A-1014
Vienna, Austria. bk. rev. index. circ. 1,100. (back
issues avail.) Indexed: Biol.Abstr. GeoRef.
Rev.Appl.Entomol.

509 AU
NATURHISTORISCHES MUSEUM IN WIEN.
NEUE DENKSCHRIFTEN. 1976. irreg. price
varies. Ferdinand Berger & Soehne OHG, Wienerstr.
80, A-3580 Horn, Austria. Eds. Ortwin Schultz,
Friedrich Bachmayer.

500.9 AU ISSN 0505-5164
NATURHISTORISCHES MUSEUM IN WIEN.
VEROEFFENTLICHUNGEN. NEUE FOLGE.
1958. irreg. price varies. Naturhistorisches Museum
in Wien, Burgring 7, P.F. 417, A-1014 Vienna,
Austria. Indexed: GeoRef.

500 AU ISSN 0470-3901
NATURKUNDLICHES JAHRBUCH DER STADT
LINZ. 1955. a. S.290. Naturkundliche Station,
Roseggerstr. 22, A-4020 Linz, Austria. Ed. Gerhard
Pfitzner. illus. circ. 500.

500 DK ISSN 0109-2995
NATURLIGVIS; fra data til viden, forskningshistorier.
1983. a. free. Koebenhavns Universitet,
Naturvidenskablige Fakultet, Jagtvej 155B, 2200
Copenhagen N, Denmark. illus.

500 GW ISSN 0077-6157
NATURWISSENSCHAFTLICHE RUNDSCHAU.
BUECHER DER ZEITSCHRIFT. 1966. irreg. price
varies; special rate for subscribers of
"Naturwissenschaftliche Rundschau".
Wissenschaftliche Verlagsgesellschaft mbH, Postfach
40, 7000 Stuttgart 1, W. Germany (B.R.D.)

500 GW ISSN 0077-6165
NATURWISSENSCHAFTLICHER VEREIN FUER
SCHLESWIG-HOLSTEIN. SCHRIFTEN. 1870.
irreg. price varies. Lipsius & Tischer, Holstenstr. 40,
2300 Kiel, W. Germany (B.R.D.) Ed. Dr. Heinz
Klug. bk. rev. circ. 150. Indexed: Biol.Abstr.
GeoRef.

500.9 AU
NATURWISSENSCHAFTLICHER VEREIN FUER
STEIERMARK. MITTEILUNGEN. 1863. a. S.200.
Naturwissenschaftlicher Verein fuer Steiermark,
Universitaetsbibliothek, Universitaetsplatz 3, A-8010
Graz, Austria. Eds. J.Gepp, T. Teich. bk. rev.
charts. illus. index. cum.index. (back issues avail.)
Indexed: Biol.Abstr. GeoRef. VITIS.

500 PL ISSN 0077-6181
NAUKA DLA WSZYSTKICH. 1966. irreg. price
varies. (Polska Akademia Nauk, Oddzial w
Krakowie) Ossolineum, Publishing House of the
Polish Academy of Sciences, Rynek 9, 50-106
Wroclaw, Poland (Dist. by Ars: Polona, Krakowskie
Przedmiescie 7, 00-068 Warsaw, Poland) Ed.
Zygmunt Czerny.

500 UR
NAUKA SEGODNYA. 1973. a. 0.80 Rub.
Izdatel'stvo Znanie, Novaya pl., 3-4, 101835
Moscow, Russian S.F.S.R., U.S.S.R. Ed. E. Etingof.

500 US
NAUKOVE TOVARYSTVO IMENI
SHEVCHENKA. PROCEEDINGS OF THE
SECTION OF MATHEMATICS AND PHYSICS.
(Text in English and Ukrainian) vol.6, 1964. irreg.
$2 per copy. ‡ Shevchenko Scientific Society, 63
Fourth Ave., New York, NY 10003. TEL 212-929-
7622. circ. 500.
    Supersedes in part its: Proceedings of the Section
of Mathematics, Natural Science and Medicine
(ISSN 0470-5017)

500 US ISSN 0077-6343
NEBRASKA ACADEMY OF SCIENCES.
PROCEEDINGS. a. $1.50. Nebraska Academy of
Sciences, 306 Morrill Hall, 14th & U Sts., Lincoln,
NE 68588. Ed. A.W. Zechmann. Indexed:
Biol.Abstr. GeoRef. VITIS.

500 US ISSN 0077-6351
NEBRASKA ACADEMY OF SCIENCES.
TRANSACTIONS. 1970/71. a. Nebraska Academy
of Sciences, 306 Morrill Hall, 14th & U Sts.,
Lincoln, NE 68588. Eds. Brent B. Nickal, T. Mylan
Stout. Indexed: Biol.Abstr. GeoRef. VITIS.

NEKOTORYE FILOSOFSKIE VOPROSY
SOVREMENNOGO ESTESTVOZNANIYA. see
PHILOSOPHY

500 US ISSN 0085-3887
NEMOURIA: OCCASIONAL PAPERS OF THE
DELAWARE MUSEUM OF NATURAL
HISTORY. 1970. irreg., no.29, 1985. price varies.
Delaware Museum of Natural History, Box 3937,
Greenville, DE 19807. TEL 302-658-9111. Eds. J.E.
DuPont, D.M. Niles. Indexed: Biol.Abstr. M.L.A.

500 GW
NEUE MUENCHNER BEITRAEGE ZUR
GESCHICHTE DER MEDIZIN UND
NATURWISSENSCHAFTEN.
NATURWISSENSCHAFTSHISTORISCHE
REIHE. 1969. irreg., vol.6, 1979. price varies.
(Werner Fritsch Verlag) Theodor Ackermann,
Ludwigstr. 7, 8000 Munich 22, W. Germany
(B.R.D.) Eds. Friedrich Klemm, Christa Habrich.
index.

500.9 US ISSN 0077-7900
NEVADA. STATE MUSEUM, CARSON CITY.
NATURAL HISTORY PUBLICATIONS. 1962.
irreg., no.4, 1980. price varies. Nevada State
Museum, Department of Anthropology, Capitol
Complex, Carson City, NV 89710. TEL 702-885-
4217. Ed. J. Scott Miller. circ. 1,000.

500 US ISSN 0028-5463
NEW JERSEY ACADEMY OF SCIENCE.
NEWSLETTER. 1966. irreg. membership. New
Jersey Academy of Science, Box B, Rutgers
University, Piscataway, NJ 08854. TEL 201-463-
0511. Ed. Charles Roman. bk. rev. circ. 700.

500 US ISSN 0077-8923
NEW YORK ACADEMY OF SCIENCES.
ANNALS. 1877. irreg. price varies. New York
Academy of Sciences, 2 E. 63rd St., New York, NY
10021. TEL 212-838-0230. Ed. Bill Boland. bibl.
charts. illus. index. cum.index: 1960-74. circ. 1,
000. (also avail. in microfilm; back issues avail.;
reprint service avail. from UMI) Indexed:
Biol.Abstr. Chem.Abstr. Excerp.Med. Ind.Med.
M.L.A. Math.R. Nutr.Abstr. Psychol.Abstr.
Sci.Cit.Ind. Abstr.Health Care Manage.Stud.
Anim.Breed.Abstr. Biotech.Abstr. C.I.S. Asbtr.
Dairy Sci.Abstr. Dent.Ind. Field Crop Abstr.
GeoRef. Helminthol.Abstr. Herb.Abstr.
Hort.Abstr. Ind.Vet. Int.Aerosp.Abstr. Soils &
Fert. Vet.Bull. Weed Abstr.

500 US ISSN 0028-7113
NEW YORK ACADEMY OF SCIENCES.
TRANSACTIONS. 1881. irreg. New York
Academy of Sciences, 2 E. 63rd St., New York, NY
10021. Ed. Bill Boland. (also avail. in microform
from UMI; back issues avail.; reprint service avail.
from UMI) Indexed: Biol.Abstr. Chem.Abstr.
Math.R. Helminthol.Abstr. Ind.Vet. Vet.Bull.

500 US
NEW YORK STATE MUSEUM. BULLETIN. 1887.
irreg., no.458, 1986. price varies. New York State
Museum, 3140 Cultural Education Center, Albany,
NY 12230. illus. Indexed: Biol.Abstr. GeoRef.
Rev.Appl.Entomol.

500 US
NEW YORK STATE MUSEUM. CIRCULAR. 1928.
irreg., no.49, 1981. price varies. New York State
Museum, 3140 Cultural Education Center, Albany,
NY 12230. charts. illus. Indexed: Biol.Abstr.
GeoRef.
    Formerly: New York State Museum and Science
Service. Circular.

500 US
NEW YORK STATE MUSEUM. LEAFLET. Variant
title: Educational Leaflet. 1949. irreg., no.26, 1986.
price varies. New York State Museum, 3140
Cultural Education Center, Albany, NY 12230.
charts. illus. Indexed: Biol.Abstr.

SCIENCES: COMPREHENSIVE WORKS

500 US
NEW YORK STATE MUSEUM. MEMOIR. 1889. irreg., no.22, 1976. New York State Museum, 3140 Cultural Education Center, Albany, NY 12230. charts. illus. Indexed: Biol.Abstr. GeoRef.
Formerly: New York State Museum and Science Service. Memoir.

500 NZ ISSN 0077-9601
NEW ZEALAND. DEPARTMENT OF SCIENTIFIC AND INDUSTRIAL RESEARCH. ANNUAL REPORT. 1927. a. price varies. Government printing Office, Private Bag, Wellington, New Zealand. Indexed: Anim.Breed.Abstr. Rev.Appl.Entomol.

500 NZ ISSN 0077-961X
NEW ZEALAND. DEPARTMENT OF SCIENTIFIC AND INDUSTRIAL RESEARCH. BULLETIN. 1927. irreg, no.238, 1986. price varies. Department of Scientific and Industrial Research, Science Information Publishing Centre, Box 9741, Wellington, New Zealand. charts. illus. (back issues avail.) Indexed: Biol.Abstr. GeoRef. Petrol.Abstr. Rev.Appl.Entomol.

500 NZ ISSN 0077-9636
NEW ZEALAND. DEPARTMENT OF SCIENTIFIC AND INDUSTRIAL RESEARCH. INFORMATION SERIES. 1948. irreg, no.161, 1985. price varies. Department of Scientific and Industrial Research, Science Information Publishing Centre, Box 9741, Wellington, New Zealand. charts. illus. (back issues avail.) Indexed: Biol.Abstr. Chem.Abstr. GeoRef.

500 JA ISSN 0078-0944
NODA INSTITUTE FOR SCIENTIFIC RESEARCH. REPORT/NODA SANGYO KAGAKU KENKYUSHO KENKYU HOKOKU. (Text in English) 1957. a. free or exchange. Noda Institute for Scientific Research - Noda Sangyo Kagaku Kenkyusho, 399 Noda, Noda-shi, Chiba-ken 278, Japan. Ed. Narimasa Saito. bk. rev. circ. 1,000. Indexed: Biol.Abstr. Chem.Abstr. Rev.Plant Path. VITIS.

500 UK
NONLINEAR SCIENCE: THEORY AND APPLICATIONS. 1985. irreg. price varies. Manchester University Press, Oxoford Rd., Manchester M13 9PL, England. TEL 061-273 5539. Ed. A.V. Holden.

NORDICANA. see ANTHROPOLOGY

500 NO ISSN 0078-1231
NORGES TEKNISK-NATURVITENSKAPELIGE FORSKNINGSRAAD. AARSBERETNING. 1947/48. a. free. Norges Teknisk-Naturvitenskapelige Forskningsraad - Royal Norwegian Council for Scientific and Industrial Research, Sognsveinen 72, Taasen, Oslo 8, Norway. circ. 5,000.

500 510 NO
NORSKE VIDENSKAPS-AKADEMI. NATURVIDENSKAPELIG KLASSE. SKRIFTER. (Text in several languages) 1925. irreg. price varies. (Norwegian Academy of Sciences and Letters) Norwegian University Press, Kolstadgt. 1, Box 2959-Toeyen, 0608 Oslo 6, Norway (U.S. address: Publications Expediting Inc., 200 Meacham Ave., Elmont, NY 11003) abstr. bibl. circ. 1,000. Indexed: Appl.Mech.Rev. Biol.Abstr. Chem.Abstr. Math.R. Sci.Abstr.
Formerly: Norske Videnskaps-Akademi. Matematisk-Naturvidenkapelig Klasse. Skrifter (ISSN 0029-2338)

500 US
NORTH DAKOTA ACADEMY OF SCIENCE. PROCEEDINGS. 1947. a. $5 per vol. North Dakota Academy of Science, Box 8123, University Station, Grand Forks, ND 58202. TEL 701-777-2786. Ed. A. William Johnson. circ. 750. Indexed: Biol.Abstr. Chem.Abstr. GeoRef.

500 UK ISSN 0144-0586
NORTHAMPTONSHIRE NATURAL HISTORY SOCIETY AND FIELD CLUB JOURNAL. 1880. a. £2. Northamptonshire Natural History Society and Field Club, c/o S.V.F. Leleux, Treas., 34 Broadway, Northampton NN1 4SF, England. Ed. C.A. Robinson. charts. illus. circ. 500. (back issues avail.) Indexed: Br.Archaeol.Abstr. Geo.Abstr. GeoRef.

500.9 US ISSN 0029-4608
NOTULAE NATURAE. 1939. irreg., nos. 463-464, 1986. price varies. Academy of Natural Sciences of Philadelphia, 19th St. and the Parkway, Philadelphia, PA 19103. TEL 215-299-1050. Ed. K. Elaine Hoagland. abstr. bibl. charts. illus. stat. (back issues avail.) Indexed: Biol.Abstr. Chem.Abstr. Key Title: Notulae Naturae of the Academy of Natural Sciences of Philadelphia.

510 GE
NOVA ACTA LEOPOLDINA. (Text in English and German) 1670. irreg., no.264, 1986. price varies. (Deutsche Akademie der Naturforscher Leopoldina) Johann Ambrosius Barth Verlag, Salomonstr. 18b, Postfach 109, DDR-7010 Leipzig, E. Germany (D.D.R.) (Orders to: Buchexport, Leninstr. 16, DDR-7010 Leipzig, E. Germany (D.D.R.)) Ed. Prof. J.H. Scharf. charts. illus. stat. (back issues avail.) Indexed: Biol.Abstr. Chem.Abstr. Math.R. GeoRef.

NOVA SCOTIA RESEARCH FOUNDATION CORPORATION. ANNUAL REPORT. see TECHNOLOGY: COMPREHENSIVE WORKS

500 CN ISSN 0078-2521
NOVA SCOTIAN INSTITUTE OF SCIENCE. PROCEEDINGS. 1862. irreg. Can.$30. Nova Scotian Institute of Science, Science Library, Dalhousie University, Halifax, N.S. B3H 4J3, Canada. TEL 902-424-2331. Ed. A. Taylor. circ. 600. (also avail. in microfilm from CLA) Indexed: Biol.Abstr. GeoRef.

500 GW ISSN 0172-732X
O L B G INFO; Mitteilungsblatt der Online-Benutzergruppe in der D G D. irreg., (approx. 4/yr.) DM.40 to non-members. Deutsche Gesellschaft fuer Dokumentation e.V., Westendstr. 19, D-6000 Frankfurt, W. Germany (B.R.D.) (back issues avail.)
Formerly: Online Info.

500 600 FR ISSN 0071-9013
O.R.S.T.O.M. INSTITUT FRANCAIS DE RECHERCHE POUR LE DEVELOPEMENT EN COOPERATION. RAPPORT D'ACTIVITE. (Office de la Recherche Scientifique et Technique en Cooperation) irreg. O R S T O M, Institut Francais de Recherche Scientifique pour le Developpement en Cooperation, 70/74 Route d'Aulnay, 93140 Bondy, France.

500 GW ISSN 0078-2920
OBERHESSISCHE GESELLSCHAFT FUER NATUR- UND HEILKUNDE, GIESSEN. BERICHTE. a. Wilhelm Schmitz Verlag, Kattenbachstr. 5, D-6300 Lahn-Wissmer, W. Germany (B.R.D.) (And: Postfach 111108, D-6300 Giessen, W. Germany (B.R.D.)) Ed. Ruediger Knapp. circ. 600. Indexed: GeoRef. VITIS.

001.3 500 AU ISSN 0378-8644
OESTERREICHISCHE AKADEMIE DER WISSENSCHAFTEN. ALMANACH. 1851. a. price varies. Verlag der Oesterreichischen Akademie der Wissenschaften, Dr. Ignaz Seipel-Platz 2, A-1010 Vienna, Austria. Indexed: GeoRef.

OESTERREICHISCHE AKADEMIE DER WISSENSCHAFTEN, VIENNA. MATHEMATISCH-NATURWISSENSCHAFTLICHE KLASSE. DENKSCHRIFTEN. see MATHEMATICS

500 CU
OFICINA NACIONAL DE INVENCIONES, INFORMACION TECNICA Y MARCOS. BOLETIN. Short title: O N I I T E M. Boletin. irreg. Academia de Ciencias, 13 No. 409, esq. a F, Vedado, Havana, Cuba.

500 FR ISSN 0078-5601
ORDRE DES GEOMETRES-EXPERTS. ANNUAIRE. 1956. a. 800 F. (Ordre des Geometres-Experts) Publi-Topex, 13 rue Leon Cogniet, 75017 Paris, France. Ed. Helene Alvares-Correa. adv. bk. rev. circ. 3,000.

500 600 NR ISSN 0474-6171
ORGANIZATION OF AFRICAN UNITY. SCIENTIFIC TECHNICAL AND RESEARCH COMMISSION. PUBLICATION. 1951. irreg. Organization of African Unity, Scientific Technical and Research Commission, P.M.B. 2359, Lagos, Nigeria.

500 US
ORGANIZATION OF AMERICAN STATES. DEPARTMENT OF SCIENTIFIC AFFAIRS. REPORT OF ACTIVITIES. 1963. irreg. Organization of American States, Department of Publications, Washington, DC 20006. TEL 703-941-1617.
Formerly: Pan American Union. Department of Scientific Affairs. Report of Activities. (ISSN 0553-0334)

500 574 US
ORGANIZATION OF AMERICAN STATES. GENERAL SECRETARIAT. PROGRAM OF SCIENTIFIC MONOGRAPHS. (Text in Spanish and Portuguese) 1965. irreg. (5-7/yr.) $3.50 per no. Organization of American States, General Secretariat, Office of Sales & Promotion, 1889 F St., N.W., Washington, DC 20006. TEL 202-789-3338. Ed. Eva V. Chesneau. circ. 10,000. (back issues avail.) Indexed: Biol.Abstr. Chem.Abstr.

500 PL ISSN 0078-6500
ORGANON. (Text in English, French, German and Russian) 1963. a. price varies. (Polska Akademia Nauk, Zaklad Historii Nauki i Techniki) Panstwowe Wydawnictwo Naukowe, Middowa 10, 00-251 Warsaw, Poland (Dist. by: Ars Polona, Krakowskie Przedmiescie 7, 00-068 Warsaw, Poland) Ed. Bogdan Suchodolski. bibl. illus. circ. 660.

500.9 JA ISSN 0078-6675
OSAKA MUSEUM OF NATURAL HISTORY. BULLETIN/OSAKA-SHIRITSU SHIZENSHI HAKUBUTSUKAN KENKYU HOKOKU. (Text in English or Japanese; summaries of Japanese articles in English) 1954. a. avail. on exchange basis only. Osaka Museum of Natural History - Osaka-shiritsu Shizenshi Hakubutsukan, Nagai Park, Higashisumiyoshi-Ku, Osaka 546, Japan. Ed. Yasuhiko Shibata. circ. 1,000. Indexed: Biol.Abstr. GeoRef.

500.9 JA ISSN 0078-6683
OSAKA MUSEUM OF NATURAL HISTORY. OCCASIONAL PAPERS/SHIZENSHI KENKYU. (Text in English or Japanese; summaries in English) 1968. irreg., (1-3/yr.) avail. on exchange basis only. Osaka Museum of Natural History - Osaka-shiritsu Shizenshi Hakubutsukan, Nagai Park, Higashisumiyoshi-Ku, Osaka 546, Japan. Ed. Yasuhiko Shibata. circ. 1,000. Indexed: Biol.Abstr. GeoRef. Rev.Appl.Entomol.

500 900 US ISSN 0369-7827
OSIRIS; a research journal devoted to the history of science and its cultural influences. 1936. a. $29. History of Science Society, Inc., 215 South 34th St., Philadelphia, PA 19104-6310 (Subscr. address: Box 529, Canton, MA 02021) Ed. Arnold Thackray. adv. circ. 1,000. (back issues avail.)

500 GW ISSN 0340-4781
OSNABRUECKER NATURWISSENSCHAFTLICHE MITTEILUNGEN. (Text in German; summaries in English and German) 1873. a. DM.15. Naturwissenschaftlicher Verein Osnabrueck, Am Schoelerberg 8, 4500 Osnabrueck, W. Germany (B.R.D.) (Co-sponsor: Naturwissentschaftliches Museum Osnabrueck) Ed.Bd. bk. rev. illus. stat. circ. 900. Indexed: GeoRef. Numis.Lit.

500 US
PACIFIC SCIENCE ASSOCIATION. CONGRESS AND INTER-CONGRESS PROCEEDINGS. (Proceedings published by host country.) 1920. biennial. ‡ Box 17801, Honolulu, HI 96817. TEL 808-847-3511.
Formerly: Pacific Science Association. Congress Proceedings (ISSN 0078-7647)

PACT. see ARCHAEOLOGY

500 PK
PAKISTAN ASSOCIATION FOR THE ADVANCEMENT OF SCIENCE. ANNUAL REPORT. (Text in English) a. Rs.5($2) Pakistan Association for the Advancement of Science, 6-B Gulberg II, Lahore 11, Pakistan.

500 PK ISSN 0078-8430
PAKISTAN SCIENCE CONFERENCE. PROCEEDINGS. (Text in English) a. Rs.100($30) Pakistan Association for the Advancement of Science, 6-B Gulberg II, Lahore 11, Pakistan. index. Indexed: Biol.Abstr. GeoRef.

SCIENCES: COMPREHENSIVE WORKS

500   PP   ISSN 0085-4700
PAPUA AND NEW GUINEA SCIENTIFIC SOCIETY. TRANSACTIONS. 1960. a. Papua & New Guinea Scientific Society, c/o Office of the Dean of Science, University of Papua New Guinea, Box 320, Papua New Guinea.

500.9   FR   ISSN 0180-961X
PARC NATIONAL DE LA VANOISE. TRAVAUX SCIENTIFIQUES. (Text in French; summaries in English, German and Italian) 1970. a. 70 F. Ministere de l'Environnement, Direction de la Protection de la Nature, Parc National de la Vanoise, B.P. 705, 73007 Chambery, France. circ. 1,000.

500.9   US   ISSN 0079-032X
PEABODY MUSEUM OF NATURAL HISTORY. BULLETIN. 1926. irreg., no.42, 1986. price varies. Peabody Museum of Natural History, Yale University, 170 Whitney Ave., Box 6666, New Haven, CT 06511-8161. TEL 203-432-3786. Eds. John Ostrom, Zelda Edelson. circ. 500. (back issues avail.) Indexed: Biol.Abstr. GeoRef. Key Title: Bulletin - Peabody Museum of Natural History.
    Supersedes (in 1967): Bulletin of Bingham Oceanographic Collection.

500.9   US   ISSN 0079-0338
PEABODY MUSEUM OF NATURAL HISTORY. SPECIAL PUBLICATION. 1961. irreg., no. 4, 1982. price varies. Peabody Museum of Natural History, Yale University, 170 Whitney, Box 6666, New Haven, CT 06511-8161. TEL 203-432-3786.

PETERSON'S GRADUATE PROGRAMS IN THE PHYSICAL SCIENCES AND MATHEMATICS (YEAR) see *EDUCATION — Guides To Schools And Colleges*

500   PH   ISSN 0079-1466
PHILIPPINE SCIENTIST. (Text in English) 1964. a. P.80($8) (University of San Carlos) San Carlos Publications, P.O. Box 182, Cebu City 6401, Philippines. Ed. Joseph Baumgartner. circ. 180. (back issues avail.) Indexed: Biol.Abstr. Ind.Phil.Per.

500   PH
PHILIPPINES. NATIONAL SCIENCE & TECHNOLOGY AUTHORITY. ANNUAL REPORT. Short title: N S T A Annual Report. a. National Science & Technology Authority, Information Division, Box 3596, Manila, Philippines. charts. illus.
    Formerly: Phillipines. National Science Development Board. Annual Report.

500 919   NO
POLAR RESEARCH. 1982. irreg., 2-3/yr. Kr.80($27) (Norwegian Polar Research Institute) University Press, P.O. Box 2959, Toeyen, 0969 Oslo 6, Norway. Ed. Annemor Brekke. circ. 300. Indexed: Curr.Cont.

500   PL   ISSN 0137-6225
POLITECHNIKA WROCLAWSKA. BIBLIOTEKA GLOWNA I OSRODEK INFORMACJI NAUKOWO-TECHNICZNEJ. PRACE NAUKOWE. STUDIA I MATERIALY. (Text in Polish; summaries in English and Russian) 1974. irreg., no.2, 1977. price varies. Politechnika Wroclawska, Wybrzeze Wyspianskiego 27, 50-370 Wroclaw, Poland (Dist. by: Ars Polona-Ruch, Krakowskie Przedmiescie 7, Warsaw, Poland) Ed. Jerzy Ciekot. circ. 965.

POLITECNICA; revista de informacion tecnico - cientifica. see *ENGINEERING*

001.3 500   UK   ISSN 0079-371X
POLSKIE TOWARZYSTWO NAUKOWE NA OBCZYZNIE. ROCZNIK. 1951. a. £2. ‡ Polish Society of Arts and Sciences Abroad, 20 Princes Gate, London, S.W.7, England. Ed. B. Helczynski. circ. 600.

500.9   US   ISSN 0079-4295
POSTILLA. 1950. irreg., no.197, 1986. price varies. Peabody Museum of Natural History, Yale University, 170 Whitney, Box 6666, New Haven, CT 06511-8161. TEL 203-432-3786. Eds. John Ostrom, Zelda Edelson. index. circ. 500. (back issues avail.) Indexed: Biol.Abstr. GeoRef.

500   SA   ISSN 0079-4341
POTCHEFSTROOM UNIVERSITY FOR CHRISTIAN HIGHER EDUCATION. WETENSKAPLIKE BYDRAES. REEKS B: NATUURWETENSKAPPE. SERIES. irreg. free. Potchefstroom University for Christian Higher Education, Potchefstroom, South Africa. Indexed: Biol.Abstr.

PRAJNAN. see *EDUCATION — Teaching Methods And Curriculum*

PROBABLE LEVELS OF R & D EXPENDITURES: FORECAST AND ANALYSIS. see *TECHNOLOGY: COMPREHENSIVE WORKS*

500   GW
PROBLEME DER KUESTENFORSCHUNG IM SUEDLICHEN NORDSEEGEBIET. 1940. irreg., vol.16, 1986. (Niedersechsiches Landesinstitut fuer Marschen und Kuestenforschung) Verlag A. Lax, Kreuzstr. 21, Postfach 10 08 05, D-3200 Hildesheim, W. Germany (B.R.D.)

500   II   ISSN 0556-1906
PROGRESS OF SCIENCE IN INDIA. 1951. irreg. price varies. Indian National Science Academy, Bahadur Zafar Marg, New Delhi 110002, India.

500 300   AO
PUBLICACOES CULTURAIS DA COMPANHIA. (Alternating series: biology, geology, climatology, history, archaeology and ethnology) (Text in English, French and Portuguese) irreg. Museu de Dundo, Dundo, Luanda, Angola.

500   US   ISSN 0079-7685
PUBLICATIONS IN MEDIEVAL SCIENCE. 1952. irreg. price varies. ‡ University of Wisconsin Press, 114 N. Murray St., Madison, WI 53715. TEL 608-262-4952. (reprint service avail. from UMI)

500   HU   ISSN 0133-2929
PUBLICATIONS OF THE TECHNICAL UNIVERSITY FOR HEAVY INDUSTRY. SERIES D: NATURAL SCIENCES. (Text in English, German, Russian) irreg., vol.35, no.1, 1982. Nehezipari Muszaki Egyetem, Miskolc, Hungary. bibl. index. circ. 500.

500   IT
QUADERNI DI SCIENZA. 1959. irreg., no.5, 1976. Giardini Editori e Stampatori, Via Santa Bibbiana 28, 56100 Pisa, Italy.

QUEEN VICTORIA MUSEUM AND ART GALLERY. LAUNCESTON, TASMANIA. RECORDS. see *MUSEUMS AND ART GALLERIES*

081 500 600   US
RAND REPORT SERIES. irreg. Rand Corporation, 1700 Main St., Santa Monica, CA 90406. TEL 213-393-0411. Indexed: Geo.Abstr. Med.Care Rev. Popul.Ind.
    Former titles: Rand Paper Series (ISSN 0092-2803) & Rand Corporation. Paper.

507 370   IS   ISSN 0034-3609
REHOVOT. (Text in English) 1959. a. free. Weizmann Institute of Science, Rehovot, Israel. Ed. Rinna Samuel. illus. circ. 19,000.

500 600   SA   ISSN 0081-2412
REPORT TO S C A R ON SOUTH AFRICAN ANTARCTIC RESEARCH ACTIVITIES. (Scientific Committee for Antarctic Research) 1963. a. free. Council for Scientific and Industrial Research, South African Scientific Committee for Antartic Research, Box 395, Pretoria 0001, South Africa. circ. 300.

500   US   ISSN 0080-1461
RESEARCH AND DEVELOPMENT DIRECTORY. (Title var:es: Unique 3-in-1 Research & Development Directory) 1959. a. $15. Government Data Publications, 1120 Connecticut Ave., N.W., Washington, DC 20036. Ed. Siegfried Lobel.

500   IE   ISSN 0085-5545
RESEARCH AND DEVELOPMENT IN IRELAND. 1967. irreg. £2.45. Government Publications Sales Office, Sun Alliance House, Molesworth St., Dublin 2, Ireland. Ed. Diarmuid Murphy.

500 007   US   ISSN 0080-1518
RESEARCH CENTERS DIRECTORY; a guide to approximately 9,200 university-related & other non-profit research organizations. 1962. irreg., (approx. every 14 months), latest 11th edt., 1986. $355. Gale Research Company, Book Tower, Detroit, MI 48226. TEL 313-961-2242. Ed. Mary Michelle Watkins. index. circ. 2,500.

001.3 500 600   GW
RHEINISCH-WESTFAELISCHE AKADEMIE DER WISSENSCHAFTEN. VORTRAEGE NATUR-INGENIEUR-UND WIRTSCHAFTSWISSENSCHAFTEN. 1950. irreg. Westdeutscher Verlag GmbH (Opladen), Reuschenberger Str. 55, Postfach 300620, 5090 Leverkusen 3 - Opladen, W. Germany (B.R.D.) Indexed: Biol.Abstr. Chem.Abstr. GeoRef.
    Former titles: Rheinisch-Westfaelische Akademie der Wissenschaften. Veroeffentichungen (ISSN 0066-5754); (1950-1970): Arbeitsgemeinschaft fuer Forschung des Landes Nordrhein-Westfalen. Veroeffentlichungen.

500   IC
RIT OCCASIONAL PAPERS. (Text usually in English) 1923. irreg., latest no.44, 1985. price varies. Visindafelag Islendinga - Societas Scientiarum Islandica (Icelandic Scientific Society), Haskolabokasafn, 101 Reykjavik, Iceland. circ. 1,000.

500   UK
ROYAL INSTITUTION OF GREAT BRITAIN. PROCEEDINGS. 1851. a. Royal Institution of Great Britain, 21 Albemarle St., London W1X 4BS, England. Indexed: Br.Hum.Ind. Chem.Abstr. Sci.Abstr. Br.Ceram.Abstr. Br.Archaeol.Abstr.

500   UK
ROYAL INSTITUTION OF GREAT BRITAIN. RECORD. 1799. a. £3. Royal Institution of Great Britain, 21 Albemarle St., London W1X 4BS, England. circ. 3,000(controlled)
    Formerly: Royal Institution of Great Britain. Annual Report.

500   CN   ISSN 0080-4517
ROYAL SOCIETY OF CANADA. PROCEEDINGS. (Bound volume available: Proceedings and Transactions (ISSN 0316-4616)) (Text in English and French) 1882; N.S. vol.21, 1983. a. Can.$6.75. Royal Society of Canada, 344 Wellington St., Ottawa, Ont. K1A ON4, Canada. TEL 613-992-3468. Ed. Prof. John M. Robson. (back issues avail., reprint service avail. from UMI) Indexed: Math.R. GeoRef.

500   CN   ISSN 0316-4616
ROYAL SOCIETY OF CANADA. PROCEEDINGS AND TRANSACTIONS. (Bound volume includes Proceedings (ISSN 0080-4517) and Transactions (ISSN 0035-9122)) 1882; N.S. vol.21, 1983. a. Can.$26.25. Royal Society of Canada, 344 Wellington St., Ottawa, Ont. K1A ON4, Canada. TEL 613-992-3468. Ed. Prof. John M. Robson. (also avail. in microform from UMI; reprint service avail. from UMI) Indexed: Can.Ind.

500   CN   ISSN 0035-9122
ROYAL SOCIETY OF CANADA. TRANSACTIONS. (Bound volume available: Proceedings and Transactions (ISSN 0316-4616)) (Text in English and French) 1882; N.S. vol.21, 1983. a. Can.$13.50. Royal Society of Canada, 344 Wellington St., Ottawa, Ont. K1A ON4, Canada. TEL 613-992-3468. Ed. Prof. John M. Robson. bibl. charts. illus. cum.index 1882-1957 (in several vols) circ. 1,400. (also avail. in microform from MML; reprint service avail. from UMI) Indexed: Biol.Abstr. Chem.Abstr. Eng.Ind. Math.R. Met.Abstr. Sci.Abstr. Can.Ind. GeoRef. Hort.Abstr. Petrol.Abstr. Rev.Plant Path.

500   UK   ISSN 0080-4576
ROYAL SOCIETY OF EDINBURGH. YEAR BOOK. 1941. a. £7.50($17.50) Royal Society of Edinburgh, 22-24 George St., Edinburgh EH2 2PQ, Scotland. Ed. E.A. Ingpen. circ. 1,500.

ROYAL SOCIETY OF LONDON. PHILOSOPHICAL TRANSACTIONS. SERIES A. MATHEMATICAL AND PHYSICAL SCIENCES. see *MATHEMATICS*

ROYAL SOCIETY OF LONDON. PROCEEDINGS. SERIES A. MATHEMATICAL AND PHYSICAL SCIENCES. see *MATHEMATICS*

506   UK   ISSN 0080-4673
ROYAL SOCIETY OF LONDON. YEAR BOOK. 1898. a. £10.50. Royal Society of London, 6 Carlton House Terrace, London SW1Y 5AG, England. circ. 1,400. (reprint service avail. from ISI)

500   500   NZ   ISSN 0370-6559
ROYAL SOCIETY OF NEW ZEALAND. BULLETIN SERIES. 1910. irreg. Royal Society of New Zealand, Private Bag, Wellington, New Zealand. circ. 300.
  Formerly: Royal Society of New Zealand. Bulletin.

500   NZ   ISSN 0111-3895
ROYAL SOCIETY OF NEW ZEALAND. MISCELLANEOUS SERIES. irreg. Royal Society of New Zealand, Private Bag, Wellington, New Zealand.

506   AT   ISSN 0080-469X
ROYAL SOCIETY OF QUEENSLAND, ST. LUCIA. PROCEEDINGS. 1884. a. Aus.$20. Royal Society of Queensland, Chemistry Dept., University of Queensland, St. Lucia, Queensland 4067, Australia. Ed. E.D. McKenzie. circ. 640. Indexed: Nutr.Abstr. Field Crop Abstr. Forest.Abstr. Forest Prod.Abstr. GeoRef. Herb.Abstr. Hort.Abstr. Rev.Appl.Entomol. Rev.Plant Path. Soils & Fert.

500   SA   ISSN 0035-919X
ROYAL SOCIETY OF SOUTH AFRICA. TRANSACTIONS. 1877. irreg. (1-2/yr.) price varies. Royal Society of South Africa, University of Cape Town, Rondebosch 7700, South Africa. Ed. A.W. Sloan. bibl. charts. illus. cum.index: 1878-1909, 1909-1955. circ. 700. (also avail. in microfilm from UMI) Indexed: Biol.Abstr. Chem.Abstr. Curr.Cont. Excerp.Med. Math.R. Sci.Abstr. S.A.Waterabstr. Geo.Abstr. Ind.S.A.Per. Sel.Water Res.Abstr.

500   AT   ISSN 0085-5812
ROYAL SOCIETY OF SOUTH AUSTRALIA. TRANSACTIONS. 1878. a. Aus.$30. Royal Society of South Australia Inc., S.A. Museum, North Terrace, Adelaide, S.A. 5000, Australia. Ed. M. Davies. index. circ. 800. Indexed: Anim.Behav.Abstr. Aqua.Sci.& Fish.Abstr. Biol.Abstr. Ecol.Abstr. Entomol.Abstr. Microbol.Abstr. Mineral.Abstr. Zoo.Rec. Abstr.Anthropol. Field Crop Abstr. GeoRef. Herb.Abstr. Rev.Plant Path. Soils & Fert.

506   AT   ISSN 0080-4703
ROYAL SOCIETY OF TASMANIA, HOBART. PAPERS AND PROCEEDINGS. 1848. a. Aus.$15. Royal Society of Tasmania, Box 1166M, Hobart, Tasmania 7001, Australia. Ed. M.R. Banks. circ. 600. Indexed: Biol.Abstr. Math.R. GeoRef. VITIS.

991.1 570   MY   ISSN 0036-2131
SABAH SOCIETY. JOURNAL. 1961. irreg., latest vol.8, 1985. M.13 per no. Sabah Society - Pertubuhan Sabah, P.O. Box 10547, 88806 Kota Kinabalu, Sabah, Malaysia. Ed. Patricia Regis. bk. rev. circ. 165. (tabloid format) Indexed: E.I.
  Natural history

500   GE   ISSN 0080-5262
SAECHSISCHE AKADEMIE DER WISSENSCHAFTEN, LEIPZIG. JAHRBUCH. 1955 (covering 1949-53) irreg., latest 1984 (covering 1981-82) price varies. Akademie-Verlag, Leipziger Str. 3-4, 108 Berlin, E. Germany (D.D.R.) Ed. Gerald Wiemers.

500   510   GE   ISSN 0365-6470
SAECHSISCHE AKADEMIE DER WISSENSCHAFTEN, LEIPZIG. MATHEMATISCH-NATURWISSENSCHAFTLICHE KLASSE. ABHANDLUNGEN. 1896. irreg., vol.56, 1985. price varies. Akademie-Verlag, Leipziger Str. 3-4, 1086 Berlin, E. Germany (D.D.R.) Indexed: Math.R.

510   500   GE   ISSN 0080-5270
SAECHSISCHE AKADEMIE DER WISSENSCHAFTEN, LEIPZIG. MATHEMATISCH-NATURWISSENSCHAFTLICHE KLASSE. SITZUNGSBERICHTE. 1896. irreg., vol.124, 1983. price varies. Akademie-Verlag, Leipziger Str. 3-4, 1086 Berlin, E. Germany (D.D.R.) Indexed: GeoRef.

500   IS
SAMUEL NEAMAN INSTITUTE FOR ADVANCED STUDIES IN SCIENCE AND TECHNOLOGY. ANNUAL REPORT. (Text in English) 1978. a. Technion - Israel Institute of Technology, Samuel Neaman Institute for Advanced Studies in Science and Technology, Technion City, Haifa 32 000, Isreal.

500.9 500   US   ISSN 0080-5920
SAN DIEGO SOCIETY OF NATURAL HISTORY. MEMOIRS. 1931. irreg. price varies. San Diego Society of Natural History, Box 1390, Balboa Park, San Diego, CA 92112. TEL 619-232-3821. index. circ. 750. Indexed: Biol.Abstr. Ecol.Abstr. GeoRef.

500.9   US   ISSN 0080-5947
SAN DIEGO SOCIETY OF NATURAL HISTORY. TRANSACTIONS. 1905. irreg. price varies. San Diego Society of Natural History, Box 1390, Balboa Park, San Diego, CA 92112. TEL 619-232-3821. (Co-sponosr: Museum of Natural History Library) (back issues avail.) Indexed: Biol.Abstr. Ecol.Abstr. Geo.Abstr. GeoRef. Zoo.Rec.
  Incorporating: San Diego Society of Natural History. Occasional Papers (ISSN 0080-5939)

500   SZ   ISSN 0080-6056
SANKT GALLISCHE NATURWISSENSCHAFTLICHE GESELLSCHAFT. BERICHT UEBER DIE TAETIGKEIT. 1860. irreg., vol.79, 1969. approx. $4. Sankt Gallische Naturwissenschaftliche Gesellschaft, St. Gallen, Switzerland. Ed. Dr. Oskar Keller.

SANTA BARBARA MUSEUM OF NATURAL HISTORY. OCCASIONAL PAPERS. see
MUSEUMS AND ART GALLERIES

500   CN   ISSN 0080-6587
SASKATCHEWAN RESEARCH COUNCIL. ANNUAL REPORT. 1947. a. free. Saskatchewan Research Council Library, 30 Campus Dr., Saskatoon, Sask. S7N 0X1, Canada. TEL 306-664-5400. Indexed: GeoRef.

500   SZ
SCHWEIZERISCHE NATURFORSCHENDE GESELLSCHAFT. DENKSCHRIFTEN. (Text in English, French and German) 1829. irreg. price varies. (Schweizerische Naturforschende Gesellschaft) Birkhaeuser Verlag, P.O. Box 133, Basel CH-4010, Switzerland. Ed. H. Schaefer. Indexed: Biol.Abstr. GeoRef.

500   SZ
SCHWEIZERISCHER WISSENSCHAFTSRAT. JAHRESBERICHT/CONSEIL SUISSE DE LA SCIENCE. RAPPORT ANNUEL. (Text in French, German) 1965. a. free. Schweizerischer Wissenschaftsrat, Wildhainweg 9, Postfach 2732, 3001 Berne, Switzerland.

500   600   UK   ISSN 0261-7005
SCIENCE AND ENGINEERING RESEARCH COUNCIL. REPORT. 1965/66. a. price varies. Science and Engineering Research Council, Polaris House, North Star Ave., Swindon SN2 1ET, England. Ed. John Litt. illus. circ. 4,000.
  Formerly: Great Britain. Science Research Council. Report (ISSN 0072-7148)

500   600   KO
SCIENCE AND TECHNOLOGY.* (Text in Korean and English; summaries in English) 1955. irreg. exchange basis. Korea University, College of Science and Engineering, 1 Anam-Dong, Seoul 132, S. Korea.
  Formerly: Goryo Daehakgyo Nonmunjip Science.

SCIENCE AND TECHNOLOGY (PITTSBURGH); a purchase guide for branch and public libraries. see
LIBRARY AND INFORMATION SCIENCES

500   600   UK
SCIENCE AND TECHNOLOGY IN CHINA. 1984. triennial. £49($110) Longman Group Ltd., Fourth Ave., Harlow, Essex CM19 5AA, England. Ed. Alan M. Anderson.

500   600   UK
SCIENCE AND TECHNOLOGY IN JAPAN. 1984. triennial. £49($110) Longman Group Ltd., Fourth Ave., Harlow, Essex CM19 5AA, England. Ed. Alan M. Anderson.

500   600   UK
SCIENCE AND TECHNOLOGY IN LATIN AMERICA. triennial. £49($110) Longman Group Ltd., Fourth Ave., Harlow, Essex CM19 5AA, England.

500   600   UK
SCIENCE AND TECHNOLOGY IN THE MIDDLE EAST. 1982. triennial. £49. Longman Group Ltd., Fourth Ave., Harlow, Essex CM19 5AA, England.

500   UK   ISSN 0300-3361
SCIENCE CHELSEA. 1965. irreg., vol.8, 1979. £0.50($1.50) Chelsea College, Students Union, Manresa Rd., London SW3 6LX, England. Ed. P. Ansell. adv. bk. rev. bibl. charts. illus. index. circ. 1,000.

500   US   ISSN 0161-3170
SCIENCE CITATION INDEX JOURNAL CITATION REPORT. Short title: SCI-J C R. (Includes Journal Ranking, Reference Data, and Source Data Packages) 1975. a. $275 (incl. in subscr. to Science Citation Index) Institute for Scientific Information, 3501 Market St., Philadelphia, PA 19104 TEL 215-386-0100. (And: 132 High St., Uxbridge, Middlesex, UB8 1DP, England)
  Formerly: I S I Journal Citation Reports.

500   JA   ISSN 0448-4703
SCIENCE COUNCIL OF JAPAN. ANNUAL REPORT. (Text·in English) 1950. triennial. exchange basis. Science Council of Japan - Nihon Gakujutsu Kaigi, 7-22-34 Roppongi, Minato-ku, Tokyo 106, Japan. Indexed: GeoRef.

SCIENCE EDUCATION IN ZAMBIA. see
EDUCATION

500   US
SCIENCE, MEDICINE AND TECHNOLOGY IN EAST ASIA. 1981. a. $6 paperbound; hardcover $9. Center for Chinese Studies, University of Michigan, 104 Lane Hall, Ann Arbor, MI 48109. TEL 313-764-1817. Ed. Nathan Sivin.

500   US
SCIENCE MUSEUM OF MINNESOTA. MONOGRAPH. 1972. irreg. Science Museum of Minnesota, 30 E. 10th St., St. Paul, MN 55101. TEL 612-221-9488. Ed. Bruce R. Erickson. Indexed: Biol.Abstr. GeoRef.

500   US   ISSN 0161-4452
SCIENCE MUSEUM OF MINNESOTA. SCIENTIFIC PUBLICATIONS, NEW SERIES. 1966. irreg. $0.55. Science Museum of Minnesota, 30 E. 10th St., St. Paul, MN 55101. TEL 612-221-9488. Ed. Bruce R. Erickson. Indexed: Biol.Abstr. GeoRef. Key Title: Scientific Publications of the Science Museum of Minnesota.
  Supersedes: Science Museum of Minnesota. Scientific Bulletin; Formerly: Science Museum of Minnesota. Scientific Publications (ISSN 0080-5521)

500   AT
SCIENCE MUSEUM OF VICTORIA. MONOGRAPHS. 1977. irreg. price varies. Science Museum of Victoria, 304-328 Swanston St., Melbourne, Vic. 3000, Australia.

371.3 500   JM
SCIENCE NOTES AND NEWS. irreg. Association of Science Teachers of Jamaica, c/o Honorary Secretary, Olive Baxter, 46 Paddington Terrace, Kingston 6, Jamaica, W.I.
  Study and teaching

500   FR   ISSN 0080-7540
SCIENCE NOUVELLE.* No.8, 1970. irreg. price varies. Editions R. Laffont, 6 Place Saint-Sulpice, 75006 Paris, France.
  Formerly (until 1970): Jeune Science.

500   UN   ISSN 0080-7591
SCIENCE POLICY STUDIES AND DOCUMENTS. (Text in English or French) 1965. irreg., no.61, 1985. price varies. Unesco, 7-9 Place de Fontenoy, 75700 Paris, France (Dist. in U.S. by: Bernan Associates-Unipub, 4611-F Assembly Dr., Lanham, MD 20706-4391)

SCIENCES: COMPREHENSIVE WORKS

500   AT
SCIENCE TEACHERS ASSOCIATION OF QUEENSLAND. NEWSLETTER. 1961. irreg. Aus.$2 each issue. Science Teachers Association of Queensland, c/o Alan Cook, Education Dept., University of Queensland, St. Lucia, Qld. 4067, Australia. Ed. Alan Cook. adv. bk. rev. circ. 700.

SCIENCE YEAR. see ENCYCLOPEDIAS AND GENERAL ALMANACS

500 600   JA
SCIENTIFIC AND TECHNICAL INFORMATION IN FOREIGN COUNTRIES/KAIGAKI KAGAKU GIJUTSU JOHO SHIRYO. (Text in Japanese) irreg. Science and Technology Agency, Planning Bureau - Kagaku Gijutsu-cho Keikaku-kyoku, 2-2-1 Kasumigaseki, Chiyoda-ku, Tokyo 100, Japan.

500 600   SA   ISSN 0080-7710
SCIENTIFIC AND TECHNICAL SOCIETIES IN SOUTH AFRICA/WETENSKAPLIKE EN TEGNIESE VERENIGINGS IN SUID-AFRIKA. irreg. price varies. Council for Scientific and Industrial Research, Publishing Division, Box 395, Pretoria 0001, South Africa. circ. 800.

500 600   CN   ISSN 0586-7746
SCIENTIFIC AND TECHNICAL SOCIETIES OF CANADA/SOCIETES SCIENTIFIQUES ET TECHNIQUES DU CANADA. 1968. biennial. Can.$12. (National Research Council of Canada) C.I.S.T.I. Publications, Ottawa, Ont. K1A 0S2, Canada. TEL 613-993-3736. circ. 675.

505   HK   ISSN 0586-5751
SCIENTIFIC DIRECTORY OF HONG KONG. 1968. quadrennial; latest 1978. HK.$35. Government Information Services, Beaconsfield House, Queen's Rd., Central, Victoria, Hong Kong, Hong Kong.

500 600   SA   ISSN 0080-7761
SCIENTIFIC RESEARCH ORGANIZATIONS IN SOUTH AFRICA/WETENSKAPLIKE NAVORSINGSORGANISASIES IN SUID-AFRIKA. irreg. price varies. Council for Scientific and Industrial Research, Publishing Division, Box 395, Pretoria 0001, South Africa. circ. 800.

910   CS
SCRIPTA FACULTATIS SCIENTIARUM NATURALIUM UNIVERSITATIS PURKYNIANAE BRUNENSIS: GEOGRAPHIA. (Text in English, French, German and Russian) 1971. irreg., (1-2/yr.) 13 Kcs. per no. Universita J.E. Purkyne, Prirodovedecka Fakulta, Kotlarska 2, 611 37 Brno, Czechoslovakia. Ed. Jindrich Stelcl. charts. illus. maps.
Formerly (until 1970): Universita J. E. Purkyne. Prirodovedecka Fakulta. Spisy.

500.9   UK   ISSN 0080-9241
SHERBORN FUND FACSIMILES. (Text mainly in English; occasionally in other European languages) 1959. irreg., no.4, 1973. price varies. Society for the History of Natural History, c/o British Museum (Natural History), Cromwell Rd., London SW7 5BD, England.

500   JA
SHIMANE UNIVERSITY. FACULTY OF SCIENCE. MEMOIRS. (Text in English and Japanese) 1966. a. Shimane University, Faculty of Science, 1060 Nishikawatsu-cho, Matsue-shi, Shimane-ken, Japan. Ed.Bd. circ. 600. Indexed: Biol.Abstr. Math.R.

SHIVAJI UNIVERSITY, KOLHAPUR, INDIA. JOURNAL. HUMANITIES AND SCIENCES. see HUMANITIES: COMPREHENSIVE WORKS

505   JA   ISSN 0583-0923
SHIZUOKA UNIVERSITY. FACULTY OF SCIENCE. REPORTS/SHIZUOKA DAIGAKU RIGAKUBU KENKYU HOKOKU. (Text in European languages) 1965. a. exchange basis. Shizuoka University, Faculty of Science - Shizuoka Daigaku Rigakubu, 836 Oya, Shizuoka-shi 422, Japan. Ed.Bd. circ. 400. Indexed: Biol.Abstr. Math.R. GeoRef.

500.9   TH
SIAM SOCIETY. NATURAL HISTORY BULLETIN. 1913. a. B.300($15) Siam Society, 131 Soi Asoke, Sukhumvit Rd., Bangkok, Thailand. Ed.Bd. bk. rev. (back issues avail.) Indexed: Biol.Abstr. Hist.Abstr. Amer.Hist.& Life.

506   US   ISSN 0080-9578
SIGMA ZETAN. 1927. a. free to members. Sigma Zeta, c/o George W. Welker, Ed., Ball State University, Muncie, IN 47306. TEL 317-288-7542. circ. 1,200.

500   ET
SINET: PROCEEDINGS OF ANNUAL PROGRAMMES REVIEW CONFERENCE. (Text in English) 1978. a. Addis Ababa University, Faculty of Science, Box 1176, Addis Ababa, Ethiopia.

500.9 331.11   SI
SINGAPORE. MINISTRY OF SCIENCE AND TECHNOLOGY. NATIONAL SURVEY OF SCIENTIFIC MANPOWER. (Text in English) 1974. a. Ministry of Science and Technology, Singapore, Singapore.

500   SI
SINGAPORE. SCIENCE COUNCIL. ANNUAL REPORTS.* 1972. a. Science Council, Singapore, Singapore. charts. illus. stat.

500   US   ISSN 0081-0339
SMITHSONIAN OPPORTUNITIES FOR RESEARCH AND STUDY IN HISTORY ART SCIENCE. Title varies: Smithsonian Research Opportunities. 1964. biennial. free. ‡ Smithsonian Institution, Washington, DC 20560. TEL 202-357-1300. index.
Formerly: Smithsonian Institution Opportunities for Research and Advanced Study.

500   AG
SOCIEDAD CIENTIFICA ARGENTINA. CICLO DE CONFERENCIAS. irreg. Sociedad Cientifica Argentina, Comision de Cursos y Conferencias, Av. Santa Fe 1145, Buenos Aires, Argentina. illus.

509   MX
SOCIEDAD MEXICANA DE HISTORIA DE LA CIENCIA Y DE LA TECNOLOGIA. ANALES. 1969. irreg. $8. Sociedad Mexicana de Historia de la Ciencia y de la Tecnologia, Av. Dr. Vertiz 724, Mexico 12, D.F., Mexico. Ed. Enrique Beltran. illus. Indexed: Hist.Abstr. Amer.Hist.& Life.

500   IT   ISSN 0391-609X
SOCIETA E LA SCIENZA. 1977. irreg., no.8, 1986. price varies. Liguori Editore s.r.l., Via Mezzocannone 19, 80134 Naples, Italy. TEL 081/20 6077. Ed. Felice Ippolito. Indexed: Math.R.

500   IT
SOCIETA ITALIANA PER IL PROGRESSO DELLE SCIENZE. ATTI DELLA RIUNIONE.* 1907. irreg. Societa Italiana per Il Progresso delle Scienze, 202 viale Reg. Margherita, Rome, Italy.

500.9   FR   ISSN 0753-4655
SOCIETE D'HISTOIRE NATURELLE DU DOUBS. BULLETIN. (Text in French; summaries occasionally in English) 1899; N.S. 1968. a. membership. Societe d'Histoire Naturelle du Doubs, Institut des Sciences Naturelles, Place Leclerc, 25030 Besancon Cedex, France. Ed. Bernard Bonnet. adv. bk. rev. bibl. charts. cum.index. circ. 500. Indexed: Biol.Abstr. VITIS.
Former titles (until 1968): Federation des Societes d'Histoire Naturelle de Franche-Comte. Bulletin (ISSN 0014-9357); Societe d'Histoire Naturelle du Doubs. Bulletin.
Natural history

500 800   PL   ISSN 0459-6854
SOCIETE DES SCIENCES ET DES LETTRES DE LODZ. BULLETIN. (Text in English, French, German, Russian) 1950. a. 50 Zl. per no. Lodzkie Towarzystwo Naukowe - Society of Arts and Sciences of Lodz, Piotrkowska 179, 90-447 Lodz, Poland (Dist. by: Ars Polona-Ruch, Krakowskie Przedmiescie 7, 00-068 Warsaw, Poland) Ed. Jozef Matuszewski. bibl. illus. circ. 500. Indexed: Biol.Abstr. Math.R. GeoRef.

500.9   FR
SOCIETE DES SCIENCES PHYSIQUES ET NATURELLES DE BORDEAUX. MEMOIRES. 1854. irreg., latest 1975/76. price varies. Bibliotheque Interuniversitaire de Bordeaux, Section des Sciences, Ancien Chemin Bernos, 33-Talence, France.

500.1   SZ   ISSN 0037-9611
SOCIETE VAUDOISE DES SCIENCES NATURELLES. MEMOIRES. (Text in French; summaries in English, French and German) 1920. irreg. price varies. Societe Vaudoise des Sciences Naturelles, Palais de Rumine, 1005 Lausanne, Switzerland. adv. bibl. charts. illus. maps. index. Indexed: Biol.Abstr. Chem.Abstr. GeoRef.

500   US
SOCIETY FOR GENERAL SYSTEMS RESEARCH. PROCEEDINGS. 1956. a. $45. (Society for General Systems Research) University of Louisville, Systems Science Institute, Louisville, KY 40292. TEL 502-588-5555.

301 500   NE
SOCIOLOGY OF THE SCIENCES. YEARBOOK. (Text in English) 1977. a. price varies. D. Reidel Publishing Co., Box 17, 3300 AA Dordrecht, Netherlands (And: 190 Old Derby St., Hingham, MA 02043) Ed. R.D. Whitley.
Formerly: Sociology of the Sciences.

SOCIOLOGY OF THE SCIENCES MONOGRAPHS. see SOCIOLOGY

SOMERSET ARCHAEOLOGY AND NATURAL HISTORY. see ARCHAEOLOGY

SOOCHOW JOURNAL OF MATHEMATICS. see MATHEMATICS

509   II
SOURCE MATERIALS ON THE HISTORY OF SCIENCE IN INDIA. irreg. price varies. Indian National Science Academy, Bahadur Zafar Marg, New Delhi 110002, India.

500 600   SA   ISSN 0081-2455
SOUTH AFRICAN JOURNAL OF ANTARCTIC RESEARCH. 1971. a. free. Council for Scientific and Industrial Research, South African Scientific Committee for Antarctic Research, Box 395, Pretoria 0001, South Africa. Ed. P.R. Condy. circ. 500. Indexed: Biol.Abstr. Chem.Abstr. Sci.Abstr. Geo.Abstr. GeoRef. Ind.S.A.Per.

500   US   ISSN 0096-414X
SOUTH CAROLINA ACADEMY OF SCIENCE. BULLETIN. 1935. a. $10. South Carolina Academy of Science, c/o John L. Safko, Treas., Dept. of Physics & Astronomy, University of South Carolina, Columbia, SC 29208. TEL 803-777-6466. Ed. G.T. Cowley. index. circ. 1,000. (back issues avail.) Indexed: Biol.Abstr.

500   US
SOUTH DAKOTA ACADEMY OF SCIENCE. PROCEEDINGS. 1916. a. $11.25. ‡ South Dakota Academy of Science, University of South Dakota, HCR 531, Box 97, Pierre, SD 57501. TEL 605-677-5011. Ed. Carroll Hanten. charts. illus. circ. 350(controlled) Indexed: Chem.Abstr. Geo.Abstr. GeoRef.

500   CE   ISSN 0081-3745
SPOLIA ZEYLANICA/BULLETIN OF THE NATIONAL MUSEUMS OF SRI LANKA. (Text in English) 1904. a. price varies. Department of National Museums, Box 854, Sir Marcus Fernando Mawatha, Colombo 7, Sri Lanka. Indexed: Biol.Abstr. GeoRef.

500   US   ISSN 0171-1873
SPRINGER SERIES IN SOLID STATE SCIENCES. 1978. irreg., vol.68, 1986. price varies. Springer-Verlag, 175 Fifth Ave., New York, NY 10010 TEL 212-460-1500. (Also Berlin, Heidelberg, Tokyo and Vienna) Ed.Bd. (reprint service avail. from ISI) Indexed: Chem.Abstr. Phys.Ber.

500   US   ISSN 0172-7389
SPRINGER SERIES IN SYNERGETICS. vol.32, 1986. irreg. Springer-Verlag, 175 Fifth Ave., New York, NY 10010 TEL 212-460-1500. (Also Berlin and Heidelberg) Ed. H.Haken. Indexed: Chem.Abstr.

500 US ISSN 0081-3877
SPRINGER TRACTS IN NATURAL
PHILOSOPHY. 1964. irreg., vol.30, 1985. price
varies. Springer-Verlag, 175 Fifth Ave., New York,
NY 10010 TEL 212-460-1500. (Also Berlin,
Heidelberg, Tokyo and Vienna) Ed. B.D. Coleman.
circ. 2,000. (reprint service avail. from ISI) Indexed:
Math.R.
  Continues: Ergebnisse der Angewandten
Mathematik.

500 CE
SRI LANKA ASSOCIATION FOR THE
ADVANCEMENT OF SCIENCE.
PROCEEDINGS. (Text in English) 1945. a. Sri
Lanka Association for the Advancement of Science,
Vidya Mawatha, Colombo 7, Sri Lanka. Ed. Ms.
C.L.M. Nethsingha. circ. 2,000. Indexed: Biol.Abstr.
GeoRef. Sri Lanka Sci.Ind.

500 YU ISSN 0081-4024
SRPSKA AKADEMIJA NAUKA I UMETNOSTI.
ODELJENJE PRIRODNO-MATEMATICKIH
NAUKA. POSEBNA IZDANJA. (Text in Serbo-
Croatian; summaries in English, French, German or
Russian) 1950. irreg., no.39, 1972. price varies.
Srpska Akademija Nauka i Umetnosti, Knez
Mihailova 35, 11001 Belgrade, Yugoslavia (Dist. by:
Prosveta, Terazije 16, Belgrade, Yugoslavia) circ.
500. Indexed: Biol.Abstr. Chem.Abstr. GeoRef.
Ref.Zh.

060 500 YU
SRPSKA AKADEMIJA NAUKA I UMETNOSTI.
POVREMENA IZDANJA. irreg. Srpska Akademija
Nauka i Umetnosti, Knez Mihailova 35, 11001
Belgrade, Yugoslavia.

SRPSKA AKADEMIJA NAUKA I UMETNOSTI
SPOMENICA. see HUMANITIES:
COMPREHENSIVE WORKS

500 600 GW
STIFTERVERBAND FUER DIE DEUTSCHE
WISSENSCHAFT. TAETIGKEITSBERICHT.
1950. a. membership. ‡ Stifterverband fuer die
Deutsche Wissenschaft, Brucker Holt 56, 4300
Essen, W. Germany (B.R.D.) circ. 10,000.
Supersedes: Stifterverband fuer die Deutsche
Wissenschaft. Jahrbuch (ISSN 0081-5551)

500.9 BE
STUDIA ALGOLIGICA LOVANIENSIA. (Text in
French) 1974. irreg. price varies. Editions Peeters
s.p.r.l., Bondgenotenlaan, B-3000 Leuven, Belgium.

500 PL ISSN 0081-6590
STUDIA I MATERIALY Z DZIEJOW NAUKI
POLSKIEJ. SERIA C. HISTORIA NAUK
MATEMATYCZNYCH, FIZYKO-
CHEMICZNYCH I GEOLOGICZNO-
GEOGRAFICZNYCH. (Text in Polish; summaries
in Russian and French) 1957. irreg., vol.29, 1981.
price varies. (Polska Akademia Nauk, Zaklad
Historii Nauki, Oswiaty i Techniki) Panstwowe
Wydawnictwo Naukowe, Ul. Miodowa 10, 00-251
Warsaw, Poland (Dist. by: Ars Polona, Krakowskie
Przedmiescie 7, 00-068 Warsaw, Poland) Ed. E.
Olszewski. bibl. illus. circ. 210.

500 PL ISSN 0081-6612
STUDIA I MATERIALY Z DZIEJOW NAUKI
POLSKIEJ. SERIA E. ZAGADNIENIA
OGOLNE. (Text in Polish; summaries in English,
Russian and French) 1967. irreg., no.7, 1983. price
varies. (Polska Akademia Nauk, Zaklad Historii
Nauki, Oswiaty i Techniki) Panstwowe
Wydawnictwo Naukowe, Ul. Miodowa 10, 00-251
Warsaw, Poland (Dist. by: Ars Polona, Krakowskie
Przedmiescie 7, 00-068 Warsaw, Poland) Ed. B.
Jaczewski. index. circ. 260.

500 GW
STUDIA SPINOZANA; an international &
interdisciplinary series. 1985. a. DM.48($19.80)
Walther & Walther, Richard-Wagner Strasse 19, D-
3000 Hannover, W. Germany (B.R.D.) (Distr. in
U.S. by: Dr. Douglas J. Den Uyl, Bellarmine
College, Newburg Rd., Louisville, KY 40205)

500 GE ISSN 0081-7384
STUDIENBUECHEREI. 1970. irreg. price varies.
VEB Deutscher Verlag der Wissenschaften, Postfach
1216, 1080 Berlin, E. Germany (D.D.R.)

501 US ISSN 0081-8577
STUDIES IN THE FOUNDATIONS,
METHODOLOGY AND PHILOSOPHY OF
SCIENCE. 1967. irreg., no.4, 1971. price varies.
Springer-Verlag, 175 Fifth Ave., New York, NY
10010 TEL 212-460-1500. (Also Berlin, Heidelberg,
Tokyo and Vienna) Ed. M. Bunge. (reprint service
avail. from ISI)

509 NE
STUDIES IN THE HISTORY OF MODERN
SCIENCE. 1977. irreg. price varies. D. Reidel
Publishing Co., Box 17, 3300 AA Dordrecht,
Netherlands (And: 190 Old Derby St., Hingham,
MA 02043) Ed.Bd. Indexed: Math.R.

501 160 US
STUDIES IN THE LOGIC OF SCIENCE. 1971.
irreg. price varies. University of California Press,
2120 Berkeley Way, Berkeley, CA 94720. TEL 415-
642-4247.

500 US
STUDIES IN THE NATURAL SCIENCES. 1973.
irreg. price varies. (University of Miami, Center for
Theoretical Studies) Plenum Publishing Corp., 233
Spring St., New York, NY 10013. TEL 212-620-
8047. Indexed: Chem.Abstr.

354 SJ
SUDAN. NATIONAL COUNCIL FOR RESEARCH.
SCIENCE POLICY AND ANNUAL REPORT.
(Text in English) a., latest 1975/76. exchange basis.
National Council for Research, Box 2404,
Khartoum, Sudan.

SUDAN RESEARCH INFORMATION BULLETIN.
see HUMANITIES: COMPREHENSIVE WORKS

SUDHOFFS ARCHIV. BEIHEFTE. see MEDICAL
SCIENCES

500 600 PL ISSN 0082-1241
SZCZECINSKIE TOWARZYSTWO NAUKOWE.
SPRAWOZDANIA. 1960. irreg. price varies.
Szczecinskie Towarzystwo Naukowe, Rycerska 3,
70-537 Szczecin, Poland.

500 PL ISSN 0137-5326
SZKICE LEGNICKIE. vol.12, 1984. irreg. price
varies. (Legnickie Towarzystwo Przyjaciol Nauk)
Ossolineum, Publishing House of the Polish
Academy of Sciences, Rynek 9, Wroclaw, Poland
(Dist. by: Ars Polona-Ruch, Krakowskie
Przedmiescie 7, Warsaw, Poland) Ed. Tadeusz
Guminski.

500.9 NZ ISSN 0496-8026
TANE. 1948. a. NZ.$13 for institutions. Auckland
University Field Club, c/o Botany Department,
University of Auckland, Private Bag, Auckland,
New Zealand. Ed. Michael Morris. illus. circ. 250.
Indexed: Biol.Abstr.

500 TZ
TANZANIA JOURNAL OF SCIENCE. (Text in
English) 1975. a. $10. University of Dar es Salaam,
Faculty of Science, Box 35065, Dar es Salaam,
Tanzania. Ed. J.R. Mainoya. bk. rev. Indexed:
Chem.Abstr.
  Formerly: University of Dar es Salam. University
Science Journal (ISSN 0250-5592)

500 FI ISSN 0358-5069
TECHNICAL RESEARCH CENTRE OF
FINLAND. PUBLICATIONS. (Text in English)
1981. irreg. Valtion Teknillinen Tutkimuskeskus,
Vuorimiehentie 5, 02150 Espoo 15, Finland.
Indexed: Biol.Abstr. Chem.Abstr.

600 US
TECHNOCRACY. INFORMATION BRIEFS. irreg.
Technocracy, Inc., Continental Headquarters,
Savannah, OH 44874. TEL 419-962-4712.

TEXAS TECH UNIVERSITY. MUSEUM. SPECIAL
PUBLICATIONS. see MUSEUMS AND ART
GALLERIES

500 200 US
THEOLOGY AND SCIENTIFIC CULTURE. no.3,
1982. irreg. Oxford University Press, Inc., 200
Madison Ave., New York, NY 10016. bibl. index.

THOMAS SAY FOUNDATION MONOGRAPHS.
see BIOLOGY — Entomology

509 RM
TIBISCUS. SERIA STIINTELE NATURII. (Text in
Romanian; summaries in German) a. Muzeul
Banatului, Piata Huniade Nr.1, Timisoara, Rumania.

500 JA ISSN 0387-9844
TOKYO METROPOLITAN UNIVERSITY.
ANNUAL REPORT OF RESEARCH ON THE
OGASAWARA (BONIN) ISLANDS. (Text in
Japanese) 1977. a. free. Tokyo Metropolitan
University, Ogasawara Research Committee, 2-1-1,
Fukasawa, Setagaya-Ku 158, Tokyo, Japan. Ed.
Mikio Ono. circ. 800. (back issues avail.)

TOKYO UNIVERSITY OF FISHERIES. REPORT/
TOKYO SUISAN DAIGAKU RONSHU. see FISH
AND FISHERIES

TOPIC; a journal of the liberal arts. see
HUMANITIES: COMPREHENSIVE WORKS

500.9 UK ISSN 0082-5344
TORQUAY NATURAL HISTORY SOCIETY.
TRANSACTIONS AND PROCEEDINGS. 1909.
a. £2. Torquay Natural History Society, The
Museum, Babbacombe Road, Torquay TQ1 1HG,
England. Ed. J. Mason-Martin. circ. 700. Indexed:
Br.Archaeol.Abstr.

500 PL ISSN 0371-375X
TOWARZYSTWO NAUKOWE W TORUNIU.
SPRAWOZDANIA. 1949. a. price varies.
Towarzystwo Naukowe w Toruniu - Torun Scientific
Society, Ul. Wysoka 16, 87-100 Torun, Poland
(Subscr. to: Ars Polona-Ruch, Krakowskie
Przedmiescie 7, Warsaw, Poland) circ. 700.

500.9 SA ISSN 0041-1752
TRANSVAAL MUSEUM. ANNALS/TRANSVAAL
MUSEUM ANNALE. (Text in Afrikaans, English,
French and German) 1908. irreg., vol.34, 1986.
price varies. Transvaal Museum, Box 413, Pretoria,
South Africa. Ed. Dr. Dippenaar. illus. index. circ.
350. (tabloid format; back issues avail.) Indexed:
Biol.Abstr. Zoo.Rec. GeoRef. Ind.S.A.Per.

500 CR ISSN 0069-2107
TROPICAL SCIENCE CENTER, COSTA RICA.
OCCASIONAL PAPER. 1963. irreg., latest 1987.
price varies. Tropical Science Center, Calle 1, No.
442, Apdo. 2959, San Jose, Costa Rica. Ed. Joseph
A. Tosi. circ. 250. Indexed: Chem.Abstr.

501 HU ISSN 0082-6707
TUDOMANYSZERVEZESI FUZETEK. 1965. irreg.
price varies. (Magyar Tudomanyos Akademia)
Akademiai Kiado, Publishing House of the
Hungarian Academy of Sciences, Box 24, H-1363
Budapest, Hungary.

509 609 HU ISSN 0082-6715
TUDOMANYTORTENETI TANULMANYOK.
1961. irreg. price varies. (Magyar Tudomanyos
Akademia) Akademiai Kiado, Publishing House of
the Hungarian Academy of Sciences, Box 24, H-
1363 Budapest, Hungary.

500 FI ISSN 0082-7002
TURUN YLIOPISTO. JULKAISUJA. SARJA A. I.
ASTRONOMICA-CHEMICA-PHYSICA-
MATHEMATICA. (Latin title: Annales
Universitatis Turkuensis) (Text in English, Finnish,
French and German) 1922. irreg. price varies. Turun
Yliopisto - University of Turku, SF-20500 Turku 50,
Finland (Dist. by: Akateeminen Kirjakauppa, SF-
00100 Helsinki 10, Finland) Indexed: Sci.Abstr.

TURUN YLIOPISTO. JULKAISUJA. SARJA C.
SCRIPTA LINGUA FENNICA EDITA. see
HUMANITIES: COMPREHENSIVE WORKS

500 300 001.3 PH
U P RESEARCH MONITOR. 1978. a. free.
University of the Philippines, N S T A Intergrated
Research Program "A", P N B Bldg. U.P. Campus,
Diliman, Quezon City, Philippines. Ed. Lourdes B.
Alba. circ. 1,000. (back issues avail.)

500 600 US
U S S R REPORT: SCIENCE AND TECHNOLOGY
POLICY. irreg. (approx. 30/yr.) $5 per no. U.S.
Joint Publications Research Service, 1000 N. Glebe
Rd., Arlington, VA 22201 TEL 703-487-4630.
(Orders to: NTIS, Springfield, VA 22161)

SCIENCES: COMPREHENSIVE WORKS

500.9   GW   ISSN 0068-0885
UEBERSEE-MUSEUM, BREMEN. VEROEFFENTLICHUNGEN. REIHE A: NATURWISSENSCHAFTEN. 1949. irreg., vol.7, 1985. price varies. Uebersee-Museum, Bremen, Bahnhofsplatz 13, 2800 Bremen, W. Germany (B.R.D.)

UNION LIST OF SCIENTIFIC AND TECHNICAL PERIODICALS IN ZAMBIA. see *BIBLIOGRAPHIES*

338.973   US
U.S. NATIONAL SCIENCE FOUNDATION. FEDERAL FUNDS FOR RESEARCH DEVELOPMENT. (Subseries of: U.S. National Science Foundation. Surveys of Science Resource Series) a. U.S. National Science Foundation, 1800 G St., N.W., Washington, DC 20550. TEL 202-634-4622.
    Former titles: U.S. National Science Foundation. Federal Funds for Research, Development, and other Scientific Activities (ISSN 0198-8700); U.S. National Science Foundation. Federal Funds for Science (ISSN 0083-2359)

U.S. NATIONAL SCIENCE FOUNDATION. GUIDE TO PROGRAMS. see *EDUCATION — School Organization And Administration*

500 600   US   ISSN 0083-2405
U.S. NATIONAL SCIENCE FOUNDATION. SURVEYS OF SCIENCE RESOURCES SERIES. irreg. price varies. U.S. National Science Foundation, 1800 G St., N.W., Washington, DC 20550. TEL 202-634-4622.

500   IS
UNITED STATES-ISRAEL BINATIONAL SCIENCE FOUNDATION. ANNUAL REPORT. (Text in English) 1974. a. United States - Israel Binational Science Foundation, P.O. Box 7677, Jerusalem 91076, Israel.

500   FR   ISSN 0083-3673
UNIVERS HISTORIQUE. 1970. irreg. price varies. Editions du Seuil, 27 rue Jacob, 75261 Paris Cedex 06, France. Eds. Jacques Julliard, Michel Winock.

500   SP   ISSN 0075-7721
UNIVERSIDAD DE LA LAGUNA. FACULTAD DE CIENCIAS. ANALES. a., latest no.9. 150 ptas. Universidad de la Laguna, Secretariado de Publicaciones, Laguna, Canary Islands, Spain.

500   SP   ISSN 0213-5469
UNIVERSIDAD DE MURCIA. ANALES DE CIENCIAS. 1930. irreg., latest vol.44, 1986. ($750) Universidad de Murcia, Secretariado de Publicaciones e Intercambio Cientifico, Santo Cristo, 1, 30001 Murcia, Spain. TEL 968 24 92 00.
    Former titles (1954-1984): Universidad de Murcia. Anales de Ciencias (ISSN 0463-9847); (1930-1954): Universidad de Murcia. Anales de Ciencias.

500   PY
UNIVERSIDAD NACIONAL DE ASUNCION. INSTITUTO DE CIENCIAS. MEMORIA. irreg. Universidad Nacional de Asuncion, Asuncion, Paraguay.

500   PO   ISSN 0066-8079
UNIVERSIDADE DE LISBOA. FACULDADE DE CIENCIAS. INSTITUTO BOTANICO. ARTIGO DE DIVULGACAO. irreg. price varies. Universidade de Lisboa, Faculdade de Ciencias, Instituto Botanico, Lisbon 2, Portugal.

500   BL   ISSN 0102-597X
UNIVERSIDADE FEDERAL DO RIO GRANDE DO SUL. INSTITUTO DE BIOCIENCIAS. BOLETIM. (Text in Portuguese; summaries occasionally in English) 1954. irreg., no.40, 1986. exchange. ‡ Universidade Federal do Rio Grande do Sul, Instituto de Biociencias, Biblioteca- Av. Paulo Gama, s/n, 90040 Porto Alegre, RS, Brazil. Ed.Bd. index. circ. 1,000. Indexed: Biol.Abstr. Chem.Abstr.
    Former titles (until 1977): Universidade Federal do Rio Grande do Sul. Instituto Central de Biociencias. Boletim (ISSN 0101-0972); Until 1970: Universidade do Rio Grande do Sul. Instituto de Ciencias Naturais. Boletim (ISSN 0079-4058)

001.3 500   GW   ISSN 0512-1523
UNIVERSITAET FRANKFURT. WISSENSCHAFTLICHE GESELLSCHAFT. SITZUNGSBERICHTE. 1962. irreg., vol.23, 1986. price varies. (Wissenschaftliche Gesellschaft) Franz Steiner Verlag Wiesbaden GmbH, Birkenwaldstr. 44, Postfach 347, D-7000 Stuttgart 1, W. Germany (B.R.D.)

500   AU   ISSN 0259-0700
UNIVERSITAET SALZBURG. DISSERTATIONEN. 1970. irreg., no.22, 1986. price varies. (Universitaet Salzburg) Verband der Wissenschaftlichen Gesellschaften Oesterreichs, Lindengasse 37, A-1070 Vienna, Austria.

500   AU   ISSN 0379-1424
UNIVERSITAET WIEN. DISSERTATIONEN. 1967. irreg., no.179, 1986. price varies. Verband der Wissenschaftlichen Gesellschaften Oesterreichs, Lindengasse 37, A-1070 Vienna, Austria.

500   RM
UNIVERSITATEA BUCURESTI. ANALELE. STIINTELE NATURII. (Text in English, French, or Rumanian) a. $10. Universitatea Bucuresti, Bd. 6h. Gheorghi-Dej Nr. 64, Bucharest, Rumania. Indexed: Biol.Abstr.

500.2   AE   ISSN 0002-533X
UNIVERSITE D'ALGER. PUBLICATIONS SCIENTIFIQUES. SERIE B: SCIENCES PHYSIQUES.* 1954. irreg. 15 F. per no. Universite d'Alger, 2 rue Didouche-Mourad, Algiers, Algeria. charts.

500 510   MG
UNIVERSITE DE MADAGASCAR. ETABLISSEMENT D'ENSEIGNEMENT SUPERIEUR DES SCIENCES. ANNALES: SERIE SCIENCES DE LA NATURE ET MATHEMATIQUES. (Text in French) no.4, 1966. a. Universite de Madagascar, Etablissement d'Enseignement Superieur des Sciences, B.P. 138, Antananarivo, Malagasy Republic.

500   FR   ISSN 0078-9887
UNIVERSITE DE PARIS. FACULTE DES LETTRES ET SCIENCES HUMAINES. PUBLICATIONS. SERIE ACTA. 1970. irreg. price varies. Presses Universitaires de France, 108 bd. Saint Germain, 75279 Paris Cedex 6, France (Service des Periodiques, 12 rue Jean de Beauvais, 75005 Paris) (reprint service avail. from KTO)

505   CM   ISSN 0566-201X
UNIVERSITE DE YAOUNDE. FACULTE DES SCIENCES. ANNALES. 1968. irreg. free. Universite de Yaounde, Faculte des Sciences, Box 337, Yaounde, Cameroon (Dist. by: Service Central des Bibliotheques, Services des Publications, B.P. 1312, Yaounde, Cameroon) illus.
    Continues: Universite Federale du Cameroun. Faculte des Sciences. Annales.

550 919.8   US   ISSN 0069-6145
UNIVERSITY OF COLORADO. INSTITUTE OF ARCTIC AND ALPINE RESEARCH. OCCASIONAL PAPERS. 1971. irreg. price varies. University of Colorado, Institute of Arctic and Alpine Research, Boulder, CO 80309. TEL 303-492-6387. Ed. Kathleen A. Salzberg. circ. 200. (also avail. in microfiche from NTI) Indexed: Biol.Abstr. Geo.Abstr.

UNIVERSITY OF KANSAS. MUSEUM OF NATURAL HISTORY. MISCELLANEOUS PUBLICATIONS. see *BIOLOGY*

UNIVERSITY OF KANSAS. MUSEUM OF NATURAL HISTORY. MONOGRAPHS. see *BIOLOGY*

574 500.9   US   ISSN 0091-7958
UNIVERSITY OF KANSAS. MUSEUM OF NATURAL HISTORY. OCCASIONAL PAPERS. 1971. irreg., no.121, 1986. ‡ University of Kansas, Museum of Natural History, Lawrence, KS 66045. Ed. Joseph T. Collins. circ. 1,500. Indexed: Biol.Abstr. GeoRef.

UNIVERSITY OF KANSAS. MUSEUM OF NATURAL HISTORY. PUBLIC EDUCATION SERIES. see *BIOLOGY*

UNIVERSITY OF KANSAS. MUSEUM OF NATURAL HISTORY. SPECIAL PUBLICATIONS. see *BIOLOGY*

500   US   ISSN 0022-8850
UNIVERSITY OF KANSAS SCIENCE BULLETIN. 1902. irreg., (approx. 5/yr.) $20 per vol. ‡ University of Kansas, Lawrence, KS 66045. TEL 913-864-3347. Ed. William L. Bloom. circ. 900. Indexed: Biol.Abstr. Chem.Abstr. Zoo.Rec. GeoRef. Rev.Appl.Entomol.

500   NR   ISSN 0075-7713
UNIVERSITY OF LAGOS. SCIENTIFIC MONOGRAPH SERIES. 1971. irreg. price varies. (University of Lagos) Lagos University Press, P.O. 132, Akoka, Yaba, Lagos, Nigeria.

500   US   ISSN 0077-796X
UNIVERSITY OF NEVADA. DESERT RESEARCH INSTITUTE. TECHNICAL REPORT. 1966. irreg. price varies. University of Nevada, Desert Research Institute, Social Sciences Center, Box 60220, Reno, NV 89506. TEL 702-673-7303. circ. 750. Indexed: Abstr.Anthropol.

500   II   ISSN 0551-4932
UNIVERSITY OF POONA SCIENCE AND TECHNOLOGY. JOURNAL. (Text in English) 1952. biennial. exchange basis. University of Poona, Ganeshkhind, Pune-411007, India. Ed. B.K. Kale. circ. 300. Indexed: Chem.Abstr. Math.R. Field Crop Abstr. GeoRef. Herb.Abstr. Rev.Plant Path. Soils & Fert. VITIS.

500   GH   ISSN 0075-7225
UNIVERSITY OF SCIENCE AND TECHNOLOGY. JOURNAL. 1955. irreg., approx. a. University of Science and Technology, Kumasi, Ghana. Ed. A.B.K. Dadzle. bk. rev. circ. 500.
    Nos. 1-6 issued as: Kumasitech.

500   PK   ISSN 0080-9624
UNIVERSITY OF SIND. RESEARCH JOURNAL. SCIENCE SERIES. (Text in English) 1965. a. Rs.25($4) University of Sind, Faculty of Science, Jamshoro, Hyderabad 6, Pakistan.

500   JA   ISSN 0040-8964
UNIVERSITY OF TOKYO. COLLEGE OF GENERAL EDUCATION. SCIENTIFIC PAPERS/TOKYO DAIGAKU KYOYOGAKUBU SHIZENKAGAKU KIYO. (Text in European languages) 1951. a. exchange basis. University of Tokyo, College of General Education - Tokyo Daigaku Kyoyogakubu, 865 Komaba, Meguro-ku, Tokyo 153, Japan. Ed.Bd. charts. illus. index. circ. 460. Indexed: Appl.Mech.Rev. Biol.Abstr. Chem.Abstr. Math.R. Sci.Abstr. GeoRef. Plant Breed.Abstr.

UNIVERSITY OF WESTERN ONTARIO SERIES IN PHILOSOPHY OF SCIENCE. see *PHILOSOPHY*

500   PL
UNIWERSYTET GDANSKI. ZESZYTY NAUKOWE. ROZPRAWY I MONOGRAFIE. 1978. irreg. price varies. Uniwersytet Gdanski, Ul. Czerwonej Armii 110, 81-824 Sopot, Poland.

500   II   ISSN 0083-5013
UTTAR PRADESH, INDIA. SCIENTIFIC RESEARCH COMMITTEE MONOGRAPH SERIES. (Text in English) irreg. price varies. Scientific Research Committee, Uttar Pradesh, Chhattar Manzil Palace, Lucknow, Uttar Pradesh, India.

500 600   GW   ISSN 0083-5080
VADEMECUM DEUTSCHER LEHR- UND FORSCHUNGSSTAETTEN. (Vademecum of German Universities and Research Center) 1954. irreg., latest 1985. DM.290. Verlag Dr. Josef Raabe KG, Rotebuehlstr. 77, 7000 Stuttgart 1, W. Germany (B.R.D.) adv.

500   US   ISSN 0083-5846
VERSTAENDLICHE WISSENSCHAFT. (Issues not numbered consecutively) (Text in German) 1952. irreg., vol.116, 1981. price varies. Springer-Verlag, 175 Fifth Ave., New York, NY 10010 TEL 212-460-1500. (Also Berlin, Heidelberg, Tokyo and Vienna) (reprint service avail. from ISI) Indexed: Biol.Abstr.

500 620   JA   ISSN 0369-1950
WASEDA UNIVERSITY. SCHOOL OF SCIENCE AND ENGINEERING. MEMOIRS/WASEDA DAIGAKU RIKOGAKUBU KIYO. (Text in English) 1922. a. free. Waseda University, School of Science and Engineering - Waseda Daigaku Rikogakubu, 4-170 Nishiokubo, Shinjuku-ku, Tokyo 160, Japan. Ed. Fusao Hayama. Indexed: Chem.Abstr. Math.R. Met.Abstr. Sci.Abstr. JCT. World Alum.Abstr.

500 620   JA   ISSN 0285-4333
WASEDA UNIVERSITY. SCIENCE AND ENGINEERING RESEARCH LABORATORY. REPORT. (Text in English) 1973. irreg. Waseda University, Science and Engineering Research Laboratory - Waseda Daigaku Rikogaku Kenkyusho, 17 Kikui-cho, Shinjuku-ku, Tokyo 162, Japan.

500 600   IS   ISSN 0083-7849
WEIZMANN INSTITUTE OF SCIENCE, REHOVOT, ISRAEL. SCIENTIFIC ACTIVITIES. (Text in English) 1953. a. Weizmann Institute of Science, Rehovot, Israel. circ. 3,000.

500   UK   ISSN 0083-7989
WENNER GREN CENTER INTERNATIONAL SYMPOSIUM SERIES. 1962. irreg. price varies. Macmillan Press Ltd., 4 Little Essex St., London WC2R 3LF, England. Indexed: Biol.Abstr. Chem.Abstr.

500.9   GW
WESTFAELISCHEN MUSEUM FUER NATURKUNDE. ABHANDLUNGEN. 1930. irreg., 2-4/yr. price varies. ‡ Westfaelisches Museum fuer Naturkunde zu Muenster in Westfalen, Sentruper Str. 285, 4400 Muenster, W. Germany (B.R.D.) charts. illus. index. Indexed: Biol.Abstr.
Formerly: Landesmuseum fuer Naturkunde zu Muenster in Westfalen. Abhandlungen (ISSN 0023-7906)
Natural history

500 600   US
WHO KNOWS: A GUIDE TO WASHINGTON EXPERTS. 1978. irreg. (approx. every 18 mos.) $125. Washington Researchers Publishing (Subsidiary of: Washington Researchers, Ltd.) 2612 P St., N.W., Washington, DC 20007. TEL 202-333-3499. Ed.Bd.
Former titles: Who Knows: the Directory of Experts; (until 1986): Researcher's Guide to Washington.

WHO'S WHO IN INDIAN SCIENCE. see BIOGRAPHY

500 600   US   ISSN 0887-5901
WHO'S WHO IN TECHNOLOGY. 1979. biennial. $545. Research Publications, Inc. (Woodbridge), 12 Lunar Dr., Drawer AB, Woodbridge, CT 06525. TEL 203-297-2600.

WILTSHIRE ARCHAEOLOGICAL AND NATURAL HISTORY MAGAZINE (1982) see ARCHAEOLOGY

WILTSHIRE ARCHAEOLOGICAL AND NATURAL HISTORY SOCIETY. ANNUAL REPORT (1983) see ARCHAEOLOGY

WISSENSCHAFTEN IN DER D.D.R. see HISTORY — History Of Europe

500   YU   ISSN 0350-0012
WISSENSCHAFTLICHE MITTEILUNGEN DES BOSNISCH-HERZEGOWINISCHEN LANDESMUSEUMS. NATURWISSENSCHAFT. (Text in German) no.5, 1975. irreg. Zemaljski Muzej Bosne i Hercegovine, Vojvode Putnika 7, Sarajevo, Yugoslavia. Ed. Zeljka Bjelcic.

WOMEN AND MINORITIES IN SCIENCE AND ENGINEERING. see ENGINEERING

500   PL   ISSN 0084-3024
WROCLAWSKIE TOWARZYSTWO NAUKOWE. PRACE. SERIA B. NAUKI SCISLE. (Text in Polish; summaries in English, French, and German) 1947. irreg., no.209, 1986. price varies. Ossolineum, Publishing House of the Polish Academy of Sciences, Rynek 9, Wroclaw, Poland. Ed. J. Kolbuszewski.

500   PL   ISSN 0371-4756
WROCLAWSKIE TOWARZYSTWO NAUKOWE. SPRAWOZDANIA. SERIA A. irreg., vol.39, 1986. price varies. Ossolineum, Publishing House of the Polish Academy of Sciences, Rynek 9, Wroclaw, Poland (Dist. by: Ars Polona-Ruch, Krakowskie Przedmiescie 7, Warsaw, Poland) Ed. A. Galos.

500   US   ISSN 0084-3113
WYKEHAM SCIENCE SERIES. 1969. irreg., no.58, 1981. Taylor & Francis, Inc., 242 Cherry St., Philadelphia, PA 19106. TEL 800-821-8312. (reprint service avail. from UMI)

500   US   ISSN 0096-3291
YEARBOOK OF SCIENCE AND THE FUTURE. 1969. a. $24.95. Encyclopaedia Britannica, Inc., 310 S. Michigan Ave., Chicago, IL 60604. TEL 312-347-7000. Ed. David Calhoun. index.
Formerly: Britannica Yearbook of Science and the Future (ISSN 0068-1199)

500   JA   ISSN 0085-8366
YOKOHAMA NATIONAL UNIVERSITY. SCIENCE REPORTS. SECTION 1: MATHEMATICS, PHYSICS, CHEMISTRY/ YOKOHAMA KOKURITSU DAIGAKU RIKA KIYO, DAI-1-RUI, SUGAKU, BUTSURIGAKU, KAGAKU. (Text in European languages) 1952. a. exchange basis only. Yokohama National University, Faculty of Education - Yokohama Kokuritsu Daigaku Kyoikugakubu, Tokiwadai 156, Hodogaya-ku, Yokohama 240, Japan. Indexed: Math.R. Met.Abstr. Sci.Abstr. JCT.

500   JA
YOKOSUKA CITY MUSEUM. SCIENCE REPORT. (Text and summaries in English and Japanese) 1956. irreg. $5. 95 Fukadadai, Yokosuka, Kanagawa 238, Japan. Ed. N. Onba. circ. 1,000. (back issues avail.) Indexed: Biol.Abstr.

500   ZA   ISSN 0084-4950
ZAMBIA. NATIONAL COUNCIL FOR SCIENTIFIC RESEARCH. ANNUAL REPORT. 1968. a., latest 1980. National Council for Scientific Research, Box CH 158, Chelston, Lusaka, Zambia.

500 600   ZA
ZAMBIA JOURNAL OF SCIENCE AND TECHNOLOGY. (Text in English) 1976. a. $6 per no. National Council for Scientific Research, P.O. Box CH.158, Chelston, Lusaka, Zambia. Ed.Bd. circ. 300. (back issues avail.)

500   YU   ISSN 0581-7528
ZEMALJSKI MUZEJ BOSNE I HERCEGOVINE. GLASNIK. PRIRODNE NAUKE. (Summaries in English, French or German) 1969 N.S. a. Zemaljski Muzej Bosne i Hercegovine, Vojvode Putnika 7, Sarajevo, Yugoslavia. Ed. Zeljka Bjelic. illus.
Continues: Glasnik Zemaljskog Muzeja u Sarajevu.

500   RH
ZIMBABWE SCIENTIFIC ASSOCIATION. TRANSACTION. (Text in English) 1901. irreg. Z.$10. Zimbawe Scientific Association, Box 8351, Causeway, Harare, Zimbabwe. Ed. Glyn A. Vale. circ. 550. (back issues avail.) Indexed: Biol.Abstr. Sci.Abstr. GeoRef. Ind.S.A.Per. Soils & Fert.
Formerly: Rhodesia Scientific Association. Transaction.

SCIENCES: COMPREHENSIVE WORKS — Abstracting, Bibliographies, Statistics

500 016   SW   ISSN 0001-3676
ABSTRACTS OF UPPSALA DISSERTATIONS IN SCIENCE. 1961. 20/yr. price varies. Almqvist and Wiksell International, Box 62, S-101 20 Stockholm, Sweden. index. Indexed: Biol.Abstr. Chem.Abstr. Sci.Abstr.

APPLIED SCIENCE AND TECHNOLOGY INDEX; a cumulative subject index to English language periodicals in the fields of aeronautics and space science, automation, chemistry, construction, earth sciences, electricity and electronics, etc. see ENGINEERING — Abstracting, Bibliographies, Statistics

013   US   ISSN 0084-7712
BATTELLE MEMORIAL INSTITUTE. PUBLISHED PAPERS AND ARTICLES. 1970. a. free to qualified personnel. Battelle Memorial Institute, Corporate Communications Office, Attn: James R. Hunkler, 505 King Ave., Columbus, OH 43201. TEL 614-424-6424. circ. 1,000. (processed; reprint service avail. from UMI)

500 015   SZ   ISSN 0067-6829
BIBLIOGRAPHIA SCIENTIAE NATURALIS HELVETICA. (Text in French, German) 1927. a. price varies. Bibliotheque Nationale Suisse, Hallwylstrasse 15, 3003 Berne, Switzerland. Ed. Anton Caflisch. circ. 700(controlled) (back issues avail.) Indexed: GeoRef.

500 600   US
BIBLIOGRAPHIES OF THE HISTORY OF SCIENCE AND TECHNOLOGY. 1982. a. price varies. Garland Publishing Inc., 136 Madison Ave., New York, NY 10016. TEL 212-686-7492. Eds. Robert Multhauf, Ellen Wells. circ. 375.

500 016   II
BIBLIOGRAPHY OF DOCTORAL DISSERTATIONS; NATURAL AND APPLIED SCIENCES. (Text in English) a. Rs.90. Association of Indian Universities, A.I.U. House, 16 Kotla Marg., New Delhi 110 002, India.

016   CC
CHINESE SCIENCE ABSTRACTS. (Text in English) m. $10 per no. Science Press, 137 Chaoyangmennei St., Beijing, Peoples Republic of China. Ed.Bd.

500 016   UK   ISSN 0309-8591
CROYDON BIBLIOGRAPHIES FOR REGIONAL SURVEY. 1968. irreg. included in subscription for the Proceedings of the Croydon Natural History & Scientific Society. Croydon Natural History & Scientific Society Ltd., 96a Brighton Rd., South Croydon, Surrey CR2 6AD, England. Ed. P.W. Sowan. bibl. circ. 850.

CURRENT BIOTECHNOLOGY ABSTRACTS. see BIOLOGY — Abstracting, Bibliographies, Statistics

500 020 015   UK   ISSN 0267-1948
CURRENT RESEARCH IN BRITAIN. PHYSICAL SCIENCES. 1980. a. £59. British Library, Document Supply Centre, Boston Spa, Wetherby, West Yorkshire LS23 7BQ, England. Ed. A. Young.
Formerly: Research in British Universities Polytechnics and Colleges. Vol.1: Physical Sciences (ISSN 0142-2472)

500 016   JA
DIRECTORY OF JAPANESE SCIENTIFIC PERIODICALS. (Text in English and Japanese) quinquennial, latest 1984. 7400 Yen. National Diet Library - Kokuritsu Kokkai Toshokan, 1-10-1 Nagata-cho, Chiyoda-ku, Tokyo 100, Japan.

016   PK
DIRECTORY OF SCIENTIFIC PERIODICALS OF PAKISTAN. irreg. Rs.5($1) Pakistan Scientific and Technological Information Centre, Quaid-i-Azam University Campus, Box 1217, Islamabad, Pakistan. Dir. Aejaz Ahmed Malik. circ. 500. (also avail. in microfilm)

500 016   II   ISSN 0376-8554
DIRECTORY OF SCIENTIFIC RESEARCH IN INDIAN UNIVERSITIES. a. Rs.35. (University Grants Commission) Indian National Scientific Documentation Centre, Hillside Rd., New Delhi 110012, India. (Co-sponsor: Council of Scientific and Industrial Research)

311   FI   ISSN 0355-2233
FINLAND. TILASTOKESKUS. TUTKIMUSTOIMINTA/FINLAND. STATISTIKCENTRALEN. FORSKNINGSVERKSAMHETEN/FINLAND. CENTRAL STATISTICAL OFFICE. RESEARCH ACTIVITY. (Section XXXVIII of Official Statistics of Finland) (Text in English, Finnish and Swedish) 1974. biennial. Fmk.30. Tilastokeskus, Annankatu 44, SF-00100 Helsinki 10, Finland (Subscr. to: Government Printing Centre, Box 516, SF-00100 Helsinki 10, Finland)

500 011　　　　US　ISSN 0190-3241
FUTURE SURVEY; a monthly abstract of books, articles and reports concerning trends, forecasts and ideas about the future. (Supplement avail.: Future Survey Annual) 1979. m. $49 to individuals; libraries $75. World Future Society, 4916 St. Elmo Ave., Bethesda, MD 20814. TEL 301-656-8274. Ed. Michael Marien. index. circ. 2,000. (back issues avail.; reprint service avail. from UMI) Indexed: Pers.Lit.
　Formerly: Public Policy Book Forecast (ISSN 0197-9035)

016 500　　　US　ISSN 0162-1963
GENERAL SCIENCE INDEX. 1978. m. (except Jun. & Dec.); cumulated annually. service basis. H.W. Wilson Co., 950 University Ave., Bronx, NY 10452. TEL 212-588-8400. Ed. Joyce Howard. (avail.on CD-ROM)
　●Also available online. Vendors: Wilsonline.

016 500　　　　GH
GHANA SCIENCE ABSTRACTS. (Text in English) q. Council for Scientific and Industrial Research, Box M32, Accra, Ghana. Ed. J.A. Villars. abstr. bibl. Indexed: Nutr.Abstr. Field Crop Abstr. Herb.Abstr.

GUIDE TO AMERICAN SCIENTIFIC AND TECHNICAL DIRECTORIES. see TECHNOLOGY: COMPREHENSIVE WORKS — Abstracting, Bibliographies, Statistics

500 600　　　HU　ISSN 0237-0808
HUNGARIAN R AND D ABSTRACTS. SCIENCE AND TECHNOLOGY. 1985. q. $50. Orszagos Muszaki Informacios Kozpont es Konyvtar (O.M.I.K.K.) - National Technical Information Centre and Library, Muzeum u. 17, Box 12, 1428 Budapest, Hungary. Indexed: World Text.Abstr.
　Supersedes: Hungarian Technical Abstracts (ISSN 0018-7771)

500　　　　HU　ISSN 0302-2226
HUNGARY. KOZPONTI STATISZTIKAI HIVATAL. TUDOMANYOS KUTATAS ES FEOLESZTES. a. 110 Ft. Statisztikai Kiado Vallalat, Kazasdulo u. 2, Box 99, 1033 Budapest 3, Hungary (Subscr. to: Kultura, Box 149, H-1389 Budapest, Hungary)

INDEX DOCUMENTATION-ECONOMIE-SCIENCE-TECHNIQUE. see BUSINESS AND ECONOMICS — Abstracting, Bibliographies, Statistics

011　　　　US　ISSN 0360-0661
INDEX TO SCIENTIFIC REVIEWS. Short title: I S R. (Permuterm Subject Index, Source Index, Corporate Index, and Research-Front Specialty Index) 1974. s-a.(annual cumulation) $575 to main libraries; departmental libraries $250. Institute for Scientific Information, 3501 Market St., Philadelphia, PA 19104 TEL 215-386-0100. (And 132 High St., Uxbridge, Middlesex, UB8 1DP, England) (also avail. in magnetic tape)

500 600　　　SP
INDEX TO SPANISH SCIENCE AND TECHNOLOGY. English edition of: Indice Espanol de Sciencia y Tecnologia. s-a. 2500 ptas. Instituto de Informacion y Documentacion en Ciencia y Tecnologia (ICYT), Joaquin Costa 22, 28002 Madrid, Spain.

500 600　　　II
INDIA. DEPARTMENT OF SCIENCE AND TECHNOLOGY. RESEARCH AND DEVELOPMENT STATISTICS. 1973. a. Rs.50. Department of Science and Technology, New Mehrauli Rd., New Delhi 110016, India. Ed. A.R. Rajeswari. charts. stat. circ. 1,000.
　Formerly: National Committee on Science and Technology. Research and Development Statistics.

500 016　　　II　ISSN 0019-6339
INDIAN SCIENCE ABSTRACTS. 1965. m. Rs.100($60) Indian National Scientific Documentation Centre, Hillside Rd., New Delhi 110012, India. Ed. A. Krishnan. abstr. index. circ. 800. Indexed: Chem.Abstr. Nutr.Abstr. Anim.Breed.Abstr. Field Crop Abstr. Herb.Abstr. Hort.Abstr. Plant Breed.Abstr.

500 010　　　AO　ISSN 0074-008X
INSTITUTO DE INVESTIGACAO CIENTIFICA DE ANGOLA. BIBLIOGRAFICAS TEMATICAS. 1969. irreg., 1973, no.19. free to qualified personnel. Instituto de Investigacao Cientifica de Angola, Departamento de Documentacao e Informacao, Box 3244, Luanda, Angola. Indexed: Trop.Abstr.

500　　　　JA
JAPANESE PERIODICALS INDEX. SCIENCE AND TECHNOLOGY/ZASSHI KIJI SAKUIN. KAGAKU GIJUTSU-HEN. (Text in Japanese and European languages) 1950. q. 20.000 Yen. Kinokuniya-Shoten - National Diet Library, 1-10-1 Nagata-cho, Chiyoda-ku, Tokyo 100, Japan. circ. 840.

500.9 016　　　SZ
KEY WORD INDEX OF WILDLIFE RESEARCH. (Text in English or German) 1974. a. 70. Swiss Wildlife Information Service, University of Zurich, Strickhofstr. 39, CH-8057 Zurich, Switzerland. Ed. Rolf Anderegg. circ. 700.

500 016　　　KO　ISSN 0023-4052
KOREAN SCIENTIFIC ABSTRACTS. 1969. bi-m. $30. ‡ Korea Institute for Economics and Technology, P.O.B. 205, 206-9 Cheongryangri-Dong, Dongdaimun-Ku, S. Korea. abstr. index. circ. 700. (reprint service avail. from UMI) Indexed: Nutr.Abstr. Anim.Breed.Abstr. BMT. Br.Ceram.Abstr. Forest.Abstr. Forest Prod.Abstr. Graph.Arts Lit.Abstr. Plant Breed.Abstr.

500　　　　US　ISSN 0090-5232
L C SCIENCE TRACER BULLET. 1972. irreg. free. U.S. Library of Congress, Science and Technology Division, Washington, DC 20540. TEL 202-287-5580.

500 015　　　TH　ISSN 0125-4537
LIST OF SCIENTIFIC AND TECHNICAL LITERATURE RELATING TO THAILAND. (Text in English) 1964. irreg. $2 per no. (Thai National Documentation Centre) Thailand Institute of Scientific and Technological Research, 196 Phahonyothin Road, Bangkhen, Bangkok 10900, Thailand. circ. 500.

500 015　　　HU　ISSN 0133-8862
MAGYAR TUDOMANYOS AKADEMIA KONVYTARANAK KIADVANYAI. (Text in Hungarian; summaries in English, French, German & Russian) 1956. irreg., 4-6/yr. exchange basis. Magyar Tudomanyos Akademia Konyvtara, Akademia u. 2, P.O. Box 7, 1054 Budapest V, Hungary. Ed. Istvan Rejto.

500 015　　　NZ　ISSN 0111-672X
NEW ZEALAND SCIENCE ABSTRACTS. 1980. q. NZ.$75. Department of Scientific and Industrial Research, Science Information Publishing Centre, Box 9741, Wellington, New Zealand. Ed. E. Saul. (back issues avail.) Indexed: Ind.Vet. Vet.Bull.

OUTSTANDING SCIENCE TRADE BOOKS FOR CHILDREN. see CHILDREN AND YOUTH — Abstracting, Bibliographies, Statistics

500 016　　　PK　ISSN 0031-0085
PAKISTAN SCIENCE ABSTRACTS. (Text in English) 1961. q. Rps.35($14) Pakistan Scientific and Technological Information Centre, Quaid-i-Azam University Campus, Box 1217, Islamabad, Pakistan. Ed. Ghulam Hamid Khan. abstr. pat. index. circ. 500(approx.) (also avail. in microfilm)

500 016　　　PH　ISSN 0115-8724
PHILIPPINE SCIENCE AND TECHNOLOGY ABSTRACTS BIBLIOGRAPHY. 1960. bi-m. $24. National Science Development Board, Scientific Library and Documentation Division, Box 3596, Manila, Philippines. abstr. index. circ. 1,000. (also avail. in microfilm) Indexed: Biol.Abstr.
　Formed by the merger of: Philippine Abstracts (ISSN 0031-7438) & Philippine Science Index.

500 016　　　RM　ISSN 0035-8096
RUMANIAN SCIENTIFIC ABSTRACTS. 1973. m. 200 lei. Academia de Stiinte Sociale si Politice, Intrarea Ministerului, nr. 2, Sectorul 1, Postal nr. 1, Casuta Postala 1-702, Bucharest, Rumania (Subscr. to: ILEXIM, Str. 13 Decembrie Nr. 3, P.O. Box 136-137, Bucharest, Rumania) Ed. Cristina Krikorian. bk. rev. abstr. index. circ. 1,000. Indexed: Appl.Mech.Rev. Bull.Signal. Ref.Zh. Field Crop Abstr. Herb.Abstr.

500 016　　　US　ISSN 0036-827X
SCIENCE CITATION INDEX. Short title: S C I. (Includes Source Index, Citation Index, Permuterm Subject Index, and Corporate Index) 1955. 6/yr. (plus annual cum.) $6200. Institute for Scientific Information, 3501 Market St., Phildadelphia, PA 19104 TEL 215-386-0100. (And 132 High St., Uxbridge, Middlesex, UB8 1DP, England) 10 yr. cum.index: 1955-1964; 5 yr. cum.index: 1965-1969, 1970-1974, 1976-1979, 1980-1984. (also avail. in magnetic tape)
　●Also available online. Vendors: BRS, CISTI, Data-Star, DIALOG.

500　　　　US
SCIENCE INDICATORS. 1973. biennial. National Science Foundation, 1800 G St., N.W., Rm. 533, Washington, DC 20550. TEL 202-634-4622. Ed. Carlos Kruytbosch. bibl. charts. stat. index. circ. 10,000.

500 600 016　　　US　ISSN 0000-054X
SCIENTIFIC AND TECHNICAL BOOKS AND SERIALS IN PRINT. 1972. a. $175. R.R. Bowker Company, Database Publishing Group, 245 W. 17th St., New York, NY 10011. TEL 800-521-8110. (avail. online)
　Formerly (until 1977): Scientific and Technical Books in Print (ISSN 0000-0248)

500 016　　　TH　ISSN 0125-4529
SCIENTIFIC SERIALS IN THAI LIBRARIES. (Text and summaries in English) 1968. a. B.450($36) Thailand Institute of Scientific and Technological Research, 196 Phahonyothin Rd., Bang Khen, Bangkok 10900, Thailand. Indexed: Biol.Abstr.

500 600 016　　　US　ISSN 0037-1343
SELECTED RAND ABSTRACTS; a quarterly guide to publications of the Rand Corporation. 1963. q. $15 to individuals; free to agencies of the government, academic and public libraries and to non-profit research organizations. ‡ Rand Corporation, Publications Dept., 1700 Main St., Santa Monica, CA 90406-2138. TEL 213-393-0411. abstr. index. circ. 6,000. Indexed: Abstr.Mil.Bibl. Fluidex. Rehabil.Lit.
　Formerly (1946-1962): Rand Corporation. Index of Selected Publications (ISSN 0485-9790)

016 500　　　CE
SRI LANKA SCIENCE INDEX. (Text in English) 1977. q. $7 exchange basis. (Sri Lanka Scientific and Technical Information Centre) Natural Resources, Energy and Science Authority, 47/5 Maitland Place, Colombo 7, Sri Lanka.

500　　　　SJ
SUDAN SCIENCE ABSTRACTS. 1980. a. National Council for Research, National Documentation Centre, Box 2404, Khartoum, Sudan.

500 600 016　　　US　ISSN 0040-0890
TECHNICAL BOOK REVIEW INDEX. 1935. m.(Sep.-Jun.) $45. J A A D Publishing Co., 427 Wimer Dr., Pittsburgh, PA 15237. Ed. Albert F. Kamper. adv. bk. rev. index. circ. 1,500. (also avail. in microform from UMI; reprint service avail. from UMI) Indexed: Chem.Abstr.

500 011　　　TU
TURKISH DISSERTATION INDEX. (Text in English) 1977. a. exchange basis. Turkish Scientific and Technical Documentation Centre - Turkiye Bilimsel ve Teknik Dokumantasyon, Ataturk Bulvari 221, Kavaklidere, Ankara, Turkey. Ed. Filiz Yucel. abstr. circ. 2,500.

310 500　　　UN
UNESCO. STATISTICS ON SCIENCE AND TECHNOLOGY/STATISTIQUES RELATIVES AUX SCIENCE ET A LA TECHNOLOGIE/ ESTADISTICAS RELATIVAS A LA CIENCIA Y A LA TECNOLOGIA. (Text in English, French and Spanish) a., latest no.11, 1981. Unesco, Division of Statistics on Science and Technology, Office of Statistics, 7-9 Place de Fontenoy, 75700 Paris, France.

500 016   CN   ISSN 0082-7657
UNION LIST OF SCIENTIFIC SERIALS IN CANADIAN LIBRARIES/CATALOGUE COLLECTIF DES PUBLICATIONS SCIENTIFIQUES DANS LES BIBLIOTHEQUES CANADIENNES. 1957. biennial; 11th, 1985. Can.$185 hardbound; Can.$150 softbound; Can.$20 microfiche. (National Research Council of Canada) C.I.S.T.I. Publications, Ottawa, Ont. K1A 0S2, Canada. TEL 613-993-3736. circ. 1,000. (also avail. in microfiche)
●Also available online. Vendors: CISTI.

500   ZA
ZAMBIA. NATIONAL COUNCIL FOR SCIENTIFIC RESEARCH. N C S R BIBLIOGRAPHY. Short title: N C S R Bibliography. 1976. irreg., latest 1979. K.1.50. National Council for Scientific Research, Box CH 158, Chelston, Lusaka, Zambia.

500 016   ZA
ZAMBIA SCIENCE ABSTRACTS. 1977. a. K.5. National Council for Scientific Research, Box CH 158, Chelston, Lusaka, Zambia. Ed. W.C. Mushipi.

500 016   RH
ZIMBABWE RESEARCH INDEX; register of current research in Zimbabwe. 1971. a. exchange basis. Scientific Liaison Office, Box 8510, Causeway, Zimbabwe (Orders to: Government Printer, Box 8062, Causeway, Zimbabwe) (Co-sponsor: University of Zimbabwe) index. circ. 500 (controlled) (processed) Indexed: Anim.Breed.Abstr.
Formerly: Rhodesia Research Index.

SCIENCES: COMPREHENSIVE WORKS — Computer Applications

500   US   ISSN 0888-2231
APPLICATIONS OF COMPUTER SCIENCE SERIES. 1986. irreg. Computer Science Press, Inc., 1803 Research Blvd., Ste. 500, Rockville, MD 20850. TEL 301-251-9050. Ed. Arthur D. Friedman. (back issues avail.)

001.6 539.7   SZ   ISSN 0304-2898
C E R N SCHOOL OF COMPUTING. PROCEEDINGS. (Former name of body: Conseil Europeen pour la Recherche Nucleaire) 1970. biennial. European Laboratory for Particle Physics, CH-1211 Geneva 23, Switzerland. (also avail. in microfiche) Indexed: INIS Atomind.

621.381 500   AT   ISSN 0816-6013
COMMONWEALTH SCIENTIFIC AND INDUSTRIAL RESEARCH ORGANIZATION. DIVISION OF GEOMECHANICS. GEOMECHANICS COMPUTER PROGRAMS. 1972. irreg. Aus.$10 per no. C.S.I.R.O., Division of Geomechanics, Box 54, Mount Waverley, Vic. 3149, Australia.

550 001.6   US
COMPUTER METHODS IN THE GEOSCIENCES. 1982. irreg., vol.3, 1984. price varies. Van Nostrand Reinhold Company, 7625 Empire Dr., Florence, KY 41042. TEL 606-525-6600. Ed. D.F. Merriam. illus. index.

651.8 540 574.192   US
COMPUTERS IN CHEMICAL AND BIOCHEMICAL RESEARCH. 1972. irreg., vol.2, 1974. Academic Press Inc., Orlando, FL 32887. TEL 305-345-2000. Eds. Charles E. Klapfenstein, Charles L. Wilkins. Indexed: Biol.Abstr.

621.3   UK   ISSN 0266-1616
INSPEC MATTERS. 1974. q. free. INSPEC, I.E.E., Station House, Nightingale Rd., Hitchin, Herts. SG5 1RJ, England (U.S. address: 445 Hoes Lane, Piscataway, NJ 08854) Indexed: Br.Ceram.Abstr. Graph.Arts Lit.Abstr.

621.3   UK
INSPEC THESAURUS. biennial. $75. INSPEC, I.E.E., Station House, Nightingale Rd., Hitchin, Herts. SG5 1RJ, England (U.S. address: 445 Hoes Lane, Piscataway, NJ 08854)

INTERNATIONAL SCIENTIFIC SOFTWARE DIRECTORY. see COMPUTERS — Software

913   UK   ISSN 0586-9668
SCIENCE AND ARCHAEOLOGY. 1970. a. £5. Research Centre for Computer Archaeology, Computer Centre, Blackheath Lane, Stafford ST18 0AD, England (Subscr. address: 88 Caverswall Rd., Weston Coyney, Stoke-on-Trent, Staffordshire ST3 6PL, England) (Co-sponsor: North Staffordshire Polytechnic) Ed. J.D. Wilcock. adv. bk. rev. bibl. charts. illus. circ. 250. (also avail. in microfiche) Indexed: Br.Archaeol.Abstr. Art & Archaeol.Tech.Abstr.

SECURITY

see Criminology and Law Enforcement — Security

SHIPS AND SHIPPING

see Transportation — Ships and Shipping

SHOES AND BOOTS

see also Leather and Fur Industries

685.31 380.1   US
AMERICAN SHOEMAKING DIRECTORY. a. $23. Shoe Trades Publishing Co., 56 Creighton St., Cambridge, MA 02140. TEL 617-482-2387. circ. 2,000. (back issues avail.)

CANADIAN FOOTWEAR & LEATHER DIRECTORY. see BUSINESS AND ECONOMICS — Trade And Industrial Directories

685.31 658.8   US   ISSN 0069-2387
CHAIN SHOE STORES AND LEASED SHOE DEPARTMENT OPERATORS.* 1962. a. $3.50 (free with subscr. to Leather and Shoes) Nickerson & Collins Co., Rumpf Publishing Division, 850 Busse Hwy., Park Ridge, IL 60068-5980. index.

CLOTHING AND FOOTWEAR INSTITUTE YEAR BOOK AND MEMBERSHIP REGISTER. see CLOTHING TRADE

338   US   ISSN 0095-1048
FOOTWEAR MANUAL. (Subscription includes Quarterly Report) 1975. a. plus q. supplements. $200 to libraries; non-members $400; members $100. Footwear Industries of America, 3700 Market St., Philadelphia, PA 19104. Ed. Elisabeth Forest. stat. circ. 300.
Supersedes: Facts and Figures on Footwear (ISSN 0362-3890)

338.4   US   ISSN 0429-0208
FOOTWEAR NEWS FACT BOOK. 1954. irreg. free. Footwear News, 7 E. 12th St., New York, NY 10003. TEL 212-741-4000. illus.

LEATHER & FOOTWEARS/KAWA TO HAKIMONO. see LEATHER AND FUR INDUSTRIES

685.31 380.1   US
SHOE FACTORY BUYERS GUIDE; directory of suppliers to the shoe manufacturing industry. a. $17. Shoe Trades Publishing Co., 56 Creighton St., Cambridge, MA 02140. TEL 617-492-2387. adv. circ. 200. (back issues avail.)

684.3   UK   ISSN 0080-9349
SHOE TRADES DIRECTORY. 1948. a. £27.50. New Century Publishing Co. Ltd., 84-88 Great Eastern Street, London EC2A 3ED, England. adv.
Incorporating: Shoe Retailers Manual (ISSN 0140-5578)

SHOES AND BOOTS — Abstracting, Bibliographies, Statistics

310 685   UK   ISSN 0308-9398
FOOTWEAR INDUSTRY STATISTICAL REVIEW. 1972. a. £25. British Footwear Manufacturers Federation, 72 Dean St., London W1V 5HB, England. circ. 400.

SMALL BUSINESS

see Business and Economics — Small Business

SOCIAL SCIENCES: COMPREHENSIVE WORKS

300 370   US   ISSN 0044-9687
A T S S BULLETIN. vol.39, 1971. irreg., 5-6/yr. membership. Association of Teachers of Social Studies in the City of New York, c/o Bell Sigelalis Pres., John Dewey High School, 50 Avenue X, Brooklyn, NY 11223. Ed. William McGinn. adv. bk. rev. bibl. circ. 1,200.

300   FI
AABO AKADEMI. STATSVETENSKAPLIGA FAKULTETEN. MEDDELANDEN. (Text in English, French and Swedish) 1956. irreg. free. Aabo Akademi, Statsvetenskapliga - Swedish University of Aabo, Faculty of Social Sciences, Domkyrkotorget 3, 20500 Aabo 50, Finland. Ed. Lauri Karvonen. circ. 150.
Formed by the merger (from Jan 1979) of: Aabo Akademi. Statsvetenskapliga Fakulteten. Meddelanden. Serie A (ISSN 0355-4031) & Aabo Akademi. Statsvetenskapliga Fakulteten. Meddelanden. Serie B (ISSN 0355-4465)

ACADEMIA DE CIENCIAS POLITICAS Y SOCIALES. BOLETIN. see POLITICAL SCIENCE

300   AT
ACADEMY OF THE SOCIAL SCIENCES IN AUSTRALIA. ANNUAL REPORT. 1971. a. membership. Academy of the Social Sciences in Australia, G.P.O. Box 1956, Canberra, A.C.T. 2601, Australia. TEL 062-491788. circ. 500(AP)

300 610   US   ISSN 0275-5742
ADVANCES IN MEDICAL SOCIAL SCIENCE: HEALTH AND ILLNESS AS VIEWED BY ANTHROPOLOGY, GEOGRAPHY, HISTORY, PSYCHOLOGY AND SOCIOLOGY. irreg., latest vol.2, 1984. Gordon and Breach Science Publishers, 50 W. 23rd St., New York, NY 10010. TEL 212-206-8900. Ed. Julio L. Ruffini.

AFRICA IN THE MODERN WORLD. see HISTORY — History Of Africa

300   US
AFRICAN - AMERICAN ISSUES CENTER DISCUSSION PAPERS. 1984. irreg., no.13, 1986. Boston University, African Studies Center, 270 Bay State Rd., Boston, MA 02215. TEL 617-353-3673.

300 960   US
AFRICAN RESEARCH STUDIES. 1958. irreg., no.15, 1984. Boston University, African Studies Center, 270 Bay State Rd., Boston, MA 02215. TEL 617-353-3673.

300 910.03   US   ISSN 0882-5297
AFRO-AMERICAN CULTURE AND SOCIETY MONOGRAPH SERIES. Variant title: C A A S Monograph Series. 1980. irreg., vol.6 in prep. price varies. University of California, Los Angeles, Center for Afro-American Studies, 3111 Campbell Hall, 401 S. Hilgard Ave., Los Angeles, CA 90024.

SOCIAL SCIENCES: COMPREHENSIVE WORKS

300　330.1　　　PL
AKADEMIA ROLNICZA W SZCZECINIE.
ZESZYTY NAUKOWE. NAUK SPOLECZNYCH
I EKONOMICZNYCH. 1976. irreg., no. 112, 1984.
price varies. Akademia Rolnicza, Janosika 8, 71-424
Szczecin, Poland. Ed. Prof. Mieczyslaw Jasnowski.
bk. rev. Indexed: Chem.Abstr.　Nutr.Abstr.　Field
Crop Abstr.

300　　　　GE　ISSN 0138-1059
AKADEMIE DER WISSENSCHAFTEN DER DDR.
ABHANDLUNGEN. ABTEILUNG
MATHEMATIK, NATURWISSENSCHAFTEN,
TECHNIK. 1975. irreg. price varies. Akademie-
Verlag, Leipziger Str. 3-4, 1086 Berlin, E. Germany
(D.D.R.) Indexed: Biol.Abstr.　Chem.Abstr.
Math.R.

300　　　　YU　ISSN 0350-0039
AKADEMIJA NAUKA I UMJETNOSTI BOSNE I
HERCEGOVINE. ODELJENJE DRUSTVENIH
NAUKA. RADOVI. vol.17, 1974. irreg. price
varies. Akademija Nauka i Umjetnosti Bosne i
Hercegovine, Odeljenje Drustvenih Nauka, Ul. 6.
novembra br. 7, P.O. Box ol-54, 7100 Sarajevo,
Yugoslavia. Hamdija Cemerlic. circ. 800.

300　　　　CN　ISSN 0702-9659
ALBERTA. ALBERTA CULTURE. ANNUAL
REPORT. 1975. a. free. Alberta Culture, 10004-104
Ave., Edmonton, Albt. T5J 0K5, Canada. TEL 403-
427-6530. Ed. Mary Layman. circ. 800.

300　　　　GW
ALLENSBACHER BERICHTE. 1949. irreg. (2-3/
month) DM.70. (Institut fuer Demoskopie
Allensbach) Verlag fuer Demoskopie, Radolfzeller
Str. 8, 7753 Allensbach, W. Germany (B.R.D.) Eds.
Elisabeth Noelle-Neumann, Edgar Piel. circ. 500.
(back issues avail.)

300　572　　　CN　ISSN 0702-8865
ALTERNATE ROUTES; a critical review. 1977. a.
Can.$4.50. c/o Department of Sociology/
Anthropology, Carleton University, Ottawa, Ont.
K1S 5B6, Canada. TEL 613-231-7177. Ed.Bd. adv.
circ. 300. Indexed: Sociol.Abstr.　Lang.&
Lang.Behav.Abstr.

306　　　　US　ISSN 0740-0489
AMERICAN UNIVERSITY STUDIES. SERIES 11.
ANTHROPOLOGY AND SOCIOLOGY. 1984.
irreg. Peter Lang Publishing, Inc., 62 W. 45th St.,
New York, NY 10036. TEL 212-302-6740. Ed. Jay
Wilson.

300　　　　FI　ISSN 0066-2011
ANNALES ACADEMIAE SCIENTIARUM
FENNICAE. SERIES B. (Text in English, French,
German) 1909. irreg. price varies. Suomalainen
Tiedeakatemia - Academia Scientiarum Fennica,
Snellmanink. 9-11, 00170 Helsinki, Finland. Ed.
Yrjo Blomstedt. cum.index (1909-1968 in vol. 150)
circ. 600. (back issues avail.; reprint service avail.
from UMI) Indexed: Abstr.Engl.Stud.　Bull.Signal.
Hist.Abstr.　Psychol.Abstr.　Lang.&
Lang.Behav.Abstr.

300　　　　FR　ISSN 0066-2607
ANNUAIRE DE L'AFRIQUE DU NORD. 1962. a.
price varies. Editions du C N R S, 295 rue St.
Jacques, 75005 Paris, France. Indexed:
Curr.Cont.Africa.

300　　　　FR　ISSN 0397-8249
ANNUAIRE DE L'U R S S ET DES PAYS
SOCIALISTES EUROPEENS. 1965. every 18
months. 350 Fr. (Centre de Recherches sur l'URSS
et les Pays de l'Est) Librairie Istra, 15 rue des Juifs,
67001 Strasbourg Cedex, France.
Formerly: Annuaire de l'U.R.S.S. (ISSN 0066-
2704)

969.005　　　FR　ISSN 0247-400X
ANNUAIRE DES PAYS DE L'OCEAN INDIEN.
(Text in French; summaries in English) 1974. a. 305
F. (Centre National de la Recherche Scientifique,
Centre d'Etudes et de Recherches sur les Societes
de l'Ocean Indien) Presses Universitaires d'Aix-
Marseille, 3 Av. Robert Schuman, 13621 Aix en
Provence, France. (Co-sponsor: Universite d'Aix-
Marseille III (Universite de Droit d'Economie et des
Sciences)) Eds. L. Favoreu, J. Benoit. bk. rev. illus.
circ. 800. Indexed: Curr.Cont.Africa.

300　986.1　　　CK　ISSN 0066-5045
ANUARIO COLOMBIANO DE HISTORIA
SOCIAL Y DE LA CULTURA. 1963. irreg.
exchange basis. Universidad Nacional de Colombia,
Facultad de Ciencias Humanas, Departamento de
Historia, Apartado Aereo 14490, Ciudad
Universitaria, Bogota, D.E., Colombia. Ed. Jaime
Jaramillo Uribe. circ. 5,000.

300　　　　SP　ISSN 0570-4324
ANUARIO IBEROAMERICANO; hechos y
documentos. 1962. a. 600 ptas.($8.50) Centro
Iberoamericano de Cooperacion, Departamento de
Documentacion Iberoamericana, Avda. Reyes
Catolicas 3, Ciudad Universitaria, Madrid 3, Spain.
(back issues avail.)

339.47　330.9　　　AU
ARBEITSGEMEINSCHAFT FUER
LEBENSNIVEAUVERGLEICHE.
SCHRIFTENREIHE. Variant title: Was Heisst Gut
Leben? (Text in German; summaries in English)
1972. irreg. free. Arbeitsgemeinschaft fuer
Lebensniveauvergleiche, Postfach 149, A-1131
Vienna, Austria. TEL (222)63 42 21. Ed. Lore
Scheer. bibl.　charts. circ. 2,000.

ARCHIWUM HISTORII FILOZOFII I MYSLI
SPOLECZNEJ. see PHILOSOPHY

300　610　　　UK
ASLIB DIRECTORY OF INFORMATION
SOURCES IN THE UNITED KINGDOM.
VOLUME 2: SOCIAL SCIENCES, MEDICINE
AND THE HUMANITIES. 1928. irreg. (approx.
every 2 yrs.) £60($109) Aslib, Association for
Information Management, Information House, 26-27
Boswell St., London WC1N 3J2, England (Distr. in
U.S. by: Learned Information Inc., 143 Old Marlton
Pike, Medford, NJ 08055) Ed. Ellen M. Codlin.
index.

ASPECTS OF GREEK AND ROMAN LIFE. see
CLASSICAL STUDIES

300　　　　VE
ATLANTIDA. 1974. irreg. free to qualified personnel.
Universidad Simon Bolivar, Division de Sociales y
Humanidades, Valle de Sartenejas, Caracas,
Venezuela. circ. 1,000.

509　150　　　NE
AUSTRALASIAN STUDIES IN HISTORY AND
PHILOSOPHY OF SCIENCE. 1982. irreg. price
varies. D. Reidel Publishing Co., Box 17, 3300 AA
Dordrecht, Netherlands (And 190 Old Derby St.,
Hingham, MA 02043) Ed. R.W. Home.
Formerly: Australasian Studies in History and
Philosophy.

300　　　　AT　ISSN 0157-6232
AUSTRALIAN NATIONAL UNIVERSITY.
DEVELOPMENT STUDIES CENTRE.
DEMOGRAPHY TEACHING NOTES. irreg.
Aus.$10.65. Australian National University,
National Centre for Development Studies, Canberra,
A.C.T. 2601, Australia. TEL 062-493-897.

300　　　　AT　ISSN 0157-5767
AUSTRALIAN NATIONAL UNIVERSITY.
DEVELOPMENT STUDIES CENTRE.
MONOGRAPH. 1975. irreg., no.33, 1984. price
varies. Australian National University, National
Centre for Development Studies, Canberra, A.C.T.
2600, Australia. TEL 062-493-897. circ. 700.
Indexed: Sociol.Abstr.　Rural Recreat.Tour.Abstr.
World Agri.Econ.& Rural Sociol.Abstr.

300　　　　AT　ISSN 0155-9060
AUSTRALIAN NATIONAL UNIVERSITY.
DEVELOPMENT STUDIES CENTRE. PACIFIC
RESEARCH MONOGRAPH. irreg. price varies.
Australian National University, Development
Studies Centre, Canberra, A.C.T. 2601, Australia.
TEL 062-493897.

300　　　　AT　ISSN 0814-1266
AUSTRALIAN NATIONAL UNIVERSITY.
DEVELOPMENT STUDIES CENTRE.
WORKING PAPERS. irreg. free. Australian
National University, Development Studies Centre,
Canberra, A.C.T. 2601, Australia. TEL 062-493897.
Indexed: Geo.Abstr.　Rural Recreat.Tour.Abstr.
World Agri.Econ.& Rural Sociol.Abstr.

BAR-ILAN: ANNUAL OF BAR-ILAN
UNIVERSITY. see RELIGIONS AND
THEOLOGY — Judaic

300　　　　GE
BEITRAEGE ZUR GESCHICHTE THUERINGENS.
1968. irreg. DM.1.80. (Museen der Stadt Erfurt)
Sed-Bezirksleitung Erfurt, Erfurt, E. Germany
(D.D.R.) Ed. Horst H. Mueller. illus.

BIBLIOGRAPHY OF EDUCATION THESES IN
AUSTRALIA. see EDUCATION — Abstracting,
Bibliographies, Statistics

300　　　　PY
BIBLIOTECA CLASICOS COLORADOS. 1975.
irreg. Instituto Colorado de Cultura, Asuncion,
Paraguay.

300　　　　AG
BIBLIOTECA DE CIENCIAS SOCIALES. irreg.,
no.2, 1982. Consejo Latinoamericano de Ciencias
Sociales, Centro Internacional de Formacion de
Ciencias Ambientales, Av. Callao 873, Buenos
Aires, Argentina. Ed. Mario R. dos Santos.

300　　　　AG
BIBLIOTECA DE ECONOMIA, POLITICA,
SOCIEDAD. SERIE MAYOR.* irreg. Editorial
Paidos, Defensa 599, Buenos Aires, 1065,
Argentina.

300　　　　AG
BIBLIOTECA DE ECONOMIA, POLITICA,
SOCIEDAD. SERIE MENOR.* vol.6, 1976. irreg.
Editorial Paidos, Defensa 599, Buenos Aires, 1065,
Argentina.

500　001.3　　　FI　ISSN 0067-8481
BIDRAG TILL KAENNEDOM AV FINLANDS
NATUR OCH FOLK. (Text in Finnish or Swedish)
1858. irreg. price varies. Finnish Society of Sciences
and Letters, Snellmansgatan 9-11, SF-00170
Helsinki 17, Finland. Ed. Paul Fogelberg. circ. 700.

300　　　　TU
BOGAZICI UNIVERSITY JOURNAL:
MANAGEMENT, ECONOMIC AND SOCIAL
SCIENCES/BOGAZICI UNIVERSITESI
DERGISI: EY ONETICILIK, EKONOMI, VE
SOSYAL BILIMLER. (Text in English or Turkish)
1973. a. $10. Bogazici Universitesi, Box 2, Istanbul,
Turkey. bibl.　stat.
Formerly: Bogazici University Journal: Social
Sciences.

300　960　　　US
BOSTON UNIVERSITY PAPERS ON AFRICA.
1964. irreg., no.7, 1982. Boston University, African
Studies Center, 270 Bay State Rd., Boston, MA
02215. TEL 617-353-3673.

300　　　　US
BROOKINGS REPRINT SERIES. 1954? irreg. $20.
Brookings Institution, 1775 Massachusetts Ave.,
N.W., Washington, DC 20036. TEL 202-797-6258.
Former titles: Brookings Pamphlet Series;
Brookings Institution. Reprint (ISSN 0068-2810);
Brookings Research Report Series (ISSN 0068-
2829)

300　920　　　II
BUILDERS OF INDIAN ANTHROPOLOGY. (Text
in English) 1978. irreg. Rs.12. N.K. Bose Memorial
Foundation, B-8/9 Bara Gambhir Singh, Gauriganj,
Varanasi 221001, India. Ed. Surajit Sinha. circ. 500.

BULLETIN ECONOMIQUE ET SOCIAL DU
MAROC. see BUSINESS AND ECONOMICS

BURT FRANKLIN AMERICAN CLASSICS IN
HISTORY AND SOCIAL SCIENCES. see
HISTORY — History Of North And South
America

BURT FRANKLIN ESSAYS IN HISTORY,
ECONOMICS, AND SOCIAL SCIENCES. see
HISTORY

300　910.03　　　US　ISSN 0882-5300
C A A S SPECIAL PUBLICATION SERIES. 1977.
irreg., vol.7 in prep. price varies. University of
California, Los Angeles, Center for Afro-American
Studies, 3111 Campbell Hall, 401 S. Hilgard Ave.,
Los Angeles, CA 90024.

SOCIAL SCIENCES: COMPREHENSIVE WORKS

300   SZ   ISSN 0008-0497
CAHIERS VILFREDO PARETO; revue Europeenne des Sciences sociales. Variant title: R E S S. (Text in English, French, German and Italian) 1963. irreg. price varies. Librarie Droz, 11 rue Massot, 1211 Geneva 12, Switzerland. Ed. Giovanni Busino. bk. rev. circ. 2,000. Indexed: SSCI.

CALIFORNIA HANDBOOK; a comprehensive guide to sources of current information and action. see *PUBLIC ADMINISTRATION*

CAMBRIDGE COMMONWEALTH SERIES. see *HISTORY*

300   MQ
CARBET; revue Martiniquaise de sciences sociales. triennial. Editions Desormeaux, Rue Galieni, 97200 Fort de France, Martinique. Ed. Emile Desormeaux.

300   US   ISSN 0149-6948
CASE ANALYSIS IN SOCIAL SCIENCE AND SOCIAL THERAPY. 1978. irreg., approx. 1/yr., 4 nos. per vol. $20 to individuals; institutions $30. Progresiv Publishr, 401 E. 32nd St., Rm. 1002, Chicago, IL 60616. TEL 312-225-9181. Ed. Kenneth H. Ives. bk. rev. charts. stat. circ. 100. (back issues avail.) Indexed: Psychol.Abstr. Sociol.Abstr. Soc.Work.Res.& Abstr.

300   US   ISSN 0008-7661
CATALYST (PETERBOROUGH) 1965. irreg. Can.$10. Department of Sociology, S U N Y, Amherst, NY 14226. Ed. E. Porvell. adv. bk. rev. circ. 2,000. (also avail. in microfilm from UMI; reprint service avail. from UMI) Indexed: Hist.Abstr. Sociol.Abstr. Amer.Hist.& Life. Int.Bibl.Soc.Sci.

300   CV
CENTRO DE ESTUDOS DE CABO VERDE. REVISTA: SERIE DE CIENCIAS HUMANAS. Short title: Serie de Ciencias Humanas. (At head of title, 1973- : Junta de Investigacoes do Ultramar) (Summaries in English) 1973. irreg. Centro de Estudos de Cabo Verde, Praia, Sao Tiago, Cape Verde Islands. bibl. stat.

300   UY
CENTRO DE INFORMACIONES Y ESTUDIOS DEL URUGUAY. CUADERNOS. 1976. irreg. price varies. Centro de Informaciones y Estudios de Uruguay, J. Paullier 1174, Casilla de Correo 10587, Montevideo, Uruguay. circ. 150.

300   CS   ISSN 0069-2298
CESKOSLOVENSKA AKADEMIE VED. ROZPRAVY. S V: RADA SPOLECENSKYCH VED. 1891. irreg., vol.85, 1975. irreg. Academia, Publishing House of the Czechoslovak Academy of Sciences, Vodickova 40, 112 29 Prague 1, Czechoslovakia. circ. 1,000. Indexed: Numis.LIt.

300 614.7   UK   ISSN 0144-9877
CHELMER WORKING PAPERS IN ENVIRONMENTAL PLANNING. 1979. irreg. Chelmer Institute of Higher Education, Faculty of Social Sciences, Department of Planning, Victoria Rd. S., Chelmsford, Essex CM1 1LL, England. Ed. David Crouch. Indexed: Geo.Abstr.

300   KO
CHIN-TAN SOCIETY. CHIN-TAN HAK-PO. (Summaries in English) 1940. a. Chin-Tan Society, c/o National Museum of Korea, Seoul, S. Korea. Ed. Yi Pyeng-do. bibl. Indexed: Hist.Abstr. Amer.Hist.& Life.

300   BL
CIENCIAS SOCIAS HOJE (YEAR) irreg. (Associacao Nacional de Pos-Graduacao e Pesquisa en Ciencias Sociais) Cortez Editora, Rua Bartira, 387, 05009 Sao Paulo, SP, Brazil. Ed.Bd.

300   SX
CIMBEBASIA. SERIES B: CULTURAL HISTORY. (Text in English; summaries in French or German) 1962. irreg., vol.4, no.1, 1985. price varies. State Museum, Box 1203, Windhoek, Southwest Africa. Ed. J. Kinahan. charts. illus. circ. 400. (back issues avail.) Indexed: Ind.S.A.Per.

300   SX
CIMBEBASIA MEMOIRS. (Text primarily in English; summaries in French or German) 1967. irreg., latest, no.6, 1985. price varies. State Museum, Box 1203, Windhoek, Southwest Africa. Eds. H. Rust, J. Kinahan. circ. 400.

300   GW   ISSN 0069-4290
CIVILISATIONS ET SOCIETES. 1965. irreg., no.63, 1979. price varies. (Ecole des Hautes Etudes en Sciences Sociales, Centre de Recherches Historiques, FR) Walter de Gruyter & Co., Mouton Publishers, Postfach 110240, D-1000 Berlin 11, W. Germany (B.R.D.) (U.S. address: Mouton Publishers, division of Walter de Gruyter, Inc., 200 Saw Mill River Rd., Hawthorne, NY 10532)

CIVILIZATION AND SOCIETY: STUDIES IN SOCIAL, ECONOMIC AND CULTURAL HISTORY. see *HISTORY*

300   CL
COLECCION FE E HISTORIA. 1977. irreg. Instituto Latinoamericano de Doctrinas y Estudios Sociales, Departamento de Publicaciones, Almirante Barroso 6, Casilla 1446 Correo 21, Santiago, Chile.

COLOQUIO DE ESTUDOS LUSO BRASILEIROS. ANAIS. see *LINGUISTICS*

300   FI   ISSN 0355-256X
COMMENTATIONES SCIENTIARUM SOCIALIUM. (Text in English) 1972. irreg. price varies. Finnish Society of Sciences and Letters, Snellmansgatan 9-11, SF-000170 Helsinki 17, Finland. Ed. Leif Nordberg. circ. 900.

300   EI
COMMISSION OF THE EUROPEAN COMMUNITIES. REPORT ON THE SOCIAL SITUATION. (Published with its General Report on the Activities of the Communities) (Editions also in Dutch, French, German, Italian) 1968. a. price varies. Office for Official Publications of the European Communities, P.O. Box 1003, L-2985 Luxembourg, Luxembourg (Dist. in U.S. by European Communities Information Service, 2100 M St., N.W., Suite 707, Washington D.C. 20037)
    Formerly: Commission of the European Communities. Expose sur l'Evolution Sociale dans la Communaute (ISSN 0531-3724)

300   US   ISSN 0147-4642
COMMUNICATION YEARBOOK. 1977. a. $44.95. (International Communication Association) Transaction Books, Rutgers University, New Brunswick, NJ 08903. TEL 201-932-2280. Ed. Michael Burgoon.

301 410   UK   ISSN 0143-7704
COMMUNITY STUDIES SERIES. 1980. irreg. price varies. Centre for English Cultural Tradition and Language, Division of Continuing Education, University of Sheffield, Sheffield S10 2TN, England. Ed. J.D.A. Widdowson. bk. rev. circ. 1,000.

300   CK
CONGRESO INTERNACIONAL DE VIVIENDA POPULAR. no.3, 1974. irreg.? Col.$90. (Servicio Latino-Americano y Asiatico de Vivienda Popular) Centro de Investigacion y Educacion Popular, Carrera 5 No.33A-08, Apdo. Aereo 25916, Bogota, Colombia.

300 360   US
CONTEMPORARY EVALUATION RESEARCH. 1979. irreg. $28 cloth; paper $14. Sage Publications, Inc., 2111 W. Hillcrest Dr., Newbury Park, CA 91320 TEL 805-499-0721. (And Sage Publications, Ltd., 28 Banner St., London EC1Y 8QE, England) Eds. Howard E. Freeman, Richard A. Berk.

300   BL
CONTRIBUICOES EM CIENCIAS SOCIAIS. irreg. Editora Campus Ltda (Subsidiary of: Elsevier North-Holland, Inc) Rua Barao de Itapagipe 55, Rio Comprido, 20261 Rio de Janeiro RJ, Brazil.

300   TZ
COUNCIL FOR THE SOCIAL SCIENCES IN EAST AFRICA. SOCIAL SCIENCE CONFERENCE. PROCEEDINGS. a. EAs.200($29) Council for the Social Sciences in East Africa, Social Science Conference, University of Dar-es-Salaam, Faculty of Arts and Social Science, Box 35091, Dar-es-Salaam, Tanzania. charts. stat.

CRIME, LAW, AND DEVIANCE SERIES. see *CRIMINOLOGY AND LAW ENFORCEMENT*

300   PE
CRITICA ANDINA. 1978. irreg. $12 (to individuals; $18 to institutions) Instituto de Estudios Sociales, Director de Publicaciones, Casilla Postal 790, Cusco, Peru. Dir. Marco Villasante. adv. bk. rev. circ. 2,000.

300   AG   ISSN 0325-9676
CRITICA Y UTOPIA. 1979. irreg., no.5, 1981. Consejo Latinoamericano de Ciencias Sociales, Callao 875, 1023 Buenos Aires, Argentina. Indexed: P.A.I.S.For.Lang.Ind.

300   PE
CUADERNOS DE SOCIEDAD Y POLITICA. 1976. irreg. Cuadernos de Sociedad y Cultura, Apartado 11154, Correo Santa Beatriz, Lima, Peru.

CULTURES DU CANADA FRANCAIS. see *HISTORY — History Of North And South America*

300 001.3   US
CURRENT CONTENTS ADDRESS DIRECTORY-SOCIAL SCIENCES/ARTS & HUMANITIES. (Includes Author Index, Organizational Index, Geographical Index) 1985. a. $195. Institute for Scientific Information, 3501 Market St., Philadelphia, PA 19104 TEL 215-386-0100. (And 132 High St., Uxbridge, Middlesex, UB8 1DP, England)
    Formerly (until 1985): Current Bibliographic Directory of the Arts and Sciencies.

CURRENT RESEARCH IN BRITISH STUDIES BY AMERICAN AND CANADIAN SCHOLARS. see *HUMANITIES: COMPREHENSIVE WORKS*

DATA BOOK OF SOCIAL STUDIES MATERIALS AND RESOURCES. see *EDUCATION — Teaching Methods And Curriculum*

300   AG
DAVID Y GOLIATH. 1970. irreg. $12. Consejo Latinoamericano de Ciencias Sociales, Callao 875, 1023 Buenos Aires, Argentina. Ed.Bd. bibl. circ. 2, 000.
    Formerly: C L A C S O Boletin (ISSN 0325-0431)

300 900 400   II   ISSN 0045-9801
DECCAN COLLEGE. POSTGRADUATE & RESEARCH INSTITUTE. BULLETIN. (Text in English) a. $30. Deccan College, Postgraduate & Research Institute, Poona 411006, India. bk. rev. circ. 500. (back issues avail.) Indexed: GeoRef.

E S R C STUDENTSHIP HANDBOOK; postgraduate studentships in the social sciences. (Economic and Social Research Council) see *EDUCATION — Guides To Schools And Colleges*

300   KE   ISSN 0424-0928
EAST AFRICAN STUDIES. 1953. irreg. (Makerere University, Makerere Institute of Social Research, UG) East African Publishing House, Box 30571, Lusaka Close, off Lusaka Rd., Nairobi, Kenya. charts.

EAST ASIAN SOCIAL SCIENCE MONOGRAPHS. see *HISTORY — History Of Asia*

300   SP
EDICIONES PENINSULA. SERIE UNIVERSITARIA. HISTORIA, CIENCIA, SOCIEDAD. 1966. irreg. Ediciones Peninsula, Provenza 278, Barcelona 8, Spain.

ENCYCLOPAEDIA AFRICANA. INFORMATION REPORT. see *HISTORY — History Of Africa*

300   SP
ENSAYOS - PLANETA DE ECONOMIA Y CIENCIAS SOCIALES.* no. 22, 1977. irreg. Cupsa Editorial, Paseo de la Habana 136, Madrid 16, Spain. Ed. Rafael Martinez Cortina.

ESSAYS ON THE ECONOMY AND SOCIETY OF THE SUDAN. see *BUSINESS AND ECONOMICS — Economic Situation And Conditions*

300   AT
ETHOS ANNUAL. (Supplement to: Ethos Papers) 1971. a. Victorian Association of Social Studies Teachers, Box 91, Balaclava, Vic. 3183, Australia. adv. circ. 1,500.
    Supersedes in part: Ethos.

300   GW   ISSN 0071-271X
EUROPEAN COORDINATION CENTRE FOR
RESEARCH AND DOCUMENTATION IN
SOCIAL SCIENCES. PUBLICATIONS. 1971.
irreg. price varies. Walter de Gruyter & Co.,
Mouton Publishers, Postfach 110240, D-1000 Berlin
11, W. Germany (B.R.D.) (U.S. addr.: Mouton
Publishers, division of Walter de Gruyter, Inc., 200
Saw Mill River Road, Hawthorne, NY 10532)

300   US   ISSN 0364-7390
EVALUATION STUDIES REVIEW ANNUAL.
1976. a. $59.95. Sage Publications, Inc., 2111 W.
Hillcrest Dr., Newbury Park, CA 91320 TEL 805-
499-0721. (And: Sage Publications, Ltd., 28 Banner
St., London EC1Y 8QE, England) Ed.Bd. (back
issues avail.)

300 301   UK
EXPLORATIONS IN URBAN ANALYSIS. 1978.
irreg. price varies. Edward Arnold (Publishers) Ltd.,
41 Bedford Square, London WC1B 3DQ, England.

368.4   FI   ISSN 0430-5205
FINLAND. KANSANELAKELAITOS.
JULKAISUJA. SARJA A. (Text in Finnish and
English; summaries in English) 1967. irreg., no.
A22, 1985. Kansanelakelaitos - Social Insurance
Institution of Finland, Research Institute for Social
Security, P.O. Box 78, SF 00381 Helsinki 38,
Finland. bibl.

610 368   FI   ISSN 0355-4848
FINLAND. KANSANELAKELAITOS.
JULKAISUJA. SARJA E. (Text in English and
Finnish) 1967. irreg., no.E128, 1986.
Kansanelakelaitos - Social Insurance Institution of
Finland, Research Institute for Social Security, P.O.
Box 78, SF-00381 Helsinki 38, Finland.

610 368.4   FI   ISSN 0355-4821
FINLAND. KANSANELAKELAITOS.
JULKAISUJA. SARJA M. (Summaries in English)
1967. irreg., no.M58, 1986. Kansanelakelaitos -
Social Insurance Institution of Finland, Research
Institute for Social Security, P.O. Box 78, SF-00381
Helsinki 38, Finland.

FLORIDA STATE UNIVERSITY. CENTER FOR
YUGOSLAV-AMERICAN STUDIES,
RESEARCH, AND EXCHANGES.
PROCEEDINGS AND REPORTS OF
SEMINARS AND RESEARCH. see *HISTORY —
History Of Europe*

301 945   IT   ISSN 0544-1374
FONDAZIONE GIANGIACOMO FELTRINELLI.
ANNALI. 1958. a. price varies. Fondazione
Giangiacomo Feltrinelli, Via Romagnosi 3, 20121
Milan, Italy. bk. rev. circ. 3,000.

300 060 370   US   ISSN 0071-7274
FORD FOUNDATION ANNUAL REPORT. a. free.
Ford Foundation, Office of Reports, c/o Carolee
Iltis, 320 E. 43rd St., New York, NY 10017. TEL
212-573-5000.

300   FR
FRANCE. MINISTERE DE L'INDUSTRIE ET DE
LA RECHERCHE. REPERTOIRE NATIONAL
DES LABORATOIRES; LA RECHERCHE
UNIVERSITAIRE. TOME 3: SCIENCES
HUMAINES ET SOCIALES. 1966. irreg.
Documentation Francaise, 29-31 Quai Voltaire,
75340 Paris 07, France.
    Formerly: France. Delegation Generale a la
Recherche Scientifique et Technique. Repertoire
National des Laboratoires; la Recherche
Universitaire; Sciences Exactes et Naturelles. Tome
3: Chimie (ISSN 0071-8556)

300   BL
FUNDACAO JOAQUIM NABUCO. SERIE
MONOGRAFIAS. 1975. irreg., no.26, 0982. $2.50
per no. (Fundacao Joaquim Nabuco) Editora
Massangana, Rua Dois Irmaos, 15 Apipucos Recife,
Brazil.
    Formerly: Instituto Joaquim Nabuco de Pesquisas
Sociais. Serie Monografias.

GENERAL SOCIAL SURVEYS. see *POLITICAL
SCIENCE*

300   GW
GESELLSCHAFT, RECHT, WIRTSCHAFT. 1978.
irreg., vol.14, 1985. price varies. Bibliographisches
Institut, Dudenstr. 6, Postfach 311, 6800 Mannheim
1, W. Germany (B.R.D.) Ed.Bd. Indexed: Math.R.

301   SW   ISSN 0072-5099
GOETEBORGS UNIVERSITET. SOCIOLOGISKA
INSTITUTIONEN. FORSKNINGS-RAPPORT.
(Text in Swedish; summaries in English) 1964. irreg.
price varies. Goeteborgs Universitet, Sociologiska
Institutionen, Karl Johansgatan 27, S-414 59
Goeteborg, Sweden.

300   UK
GREAT BRITAIN. ECONOMIC & SOCIAL
RESEARCH COUNCIL. BURSARY
HANDBOOK. 1969. a. free. Economic & Social
Research Council, Postgraduate Training Division,
160 Great Portland St., London W1N 6DT,
England. circ. 2,000.
    Formerly: Great Britain. Social Science Research
Council. Bursary Scheme.

300   UK   ISSN 0266-2043
GREAT BRITAIN. ECONOMIC AND SOCIAL
RESEARCH COUNCIL. REPORT. 1966/67. a.
Economic and Social Research Council, 160 Gt.
Portland St., London W1N 6BA, England.
    Formerly (until Jan. 1984): Great Britain. Social
Science Research Council. Report (ISSN 0081-
0444)

300   UK   ISSN 0266-2159
GREAT BRITAIN. ECONOMIC AND SOCIAL
RESEARCH COUNCIL. RESEARCH
SUPPORTED BY THE ECONOMIC AND
SOCIAL RESEARCH COUNCIL. 1967. a. £7.50.
Economic and Social Research Council, 160 Gt.
Portland St., London W1N 6BA, England. index.
circ. 1,500.
    Formerly (until Jan. 1984): Great Britain. Social
Science Research Council. Research Supported by
the Social Science Research Council (ISSN 0583-
6948)

300   UK
GREAT BRITAIN. ECONOMIC & SOCIAL
RESEARCH COUNCIL. STUDENTSHIP
HANDBOOK. 1966. a. free. Economic & Social
Research Council, Postgraduate Training Division,
160 Great Portland St., London W1N 6DT,
England.
    Formerly: Great Britain. Social Science Research
Council. Studentship Handbook.

331.2   UK
GREAT BRITAIN. GOVERNMENT ACTUARY.
OCCUPATIONAL PENSION BOARD. ANNUAL
REPORT. irreg. price varies. H.M.S.O., Box 569,
London SE1 9NH, England. (reprint service avail.
from UMI)

300   GW
GRUNDRISS DER SOZIALWISSENSCHAFT. 1953.
irreg. Vandenhoeck & Ruprecht, Robert-Bosch-
Breite 6, Postfach 3753, D-3400 Goettingen, W.
Germany (B.R.D.)

HARRY S. TRUMAN RESEARCH INSTITUTE
FOR THE ADVANCEMENT OF PEACE.
REPRINT SERIES. see *BIBLIOGRAPHIES*

300   IS   ISSN 0333-6964
HEBREW UNIVERSITY OF JERUSALEM.
AUTHORITY FOR RESEARCH AND
DEVELOPMENT. CURRENT RESEARCH. (Vol.
1: Research; Vol. 2: Publications) (Text in English)
1964/65. a. Hebrew University of Jerusalem,
Jerusalem, Israel. Ed. S. Glatzer. author index. circ.
controlled.
    Formed by the merger of: Hebrew University of
Jerusalem. Authority for Research and
Development. Research Report: Humanities, Social
Sciences, Law, Education, Social Work, Library
(ISSN 0075-3645) & Hebrew University of
Jerusalem. Authority for Research and
Development. Research Report. Science and
Agriculture (ISSN 0075-3653) & Hebrew University
of Jerusalem. Authority for Research Report.
Medicine, Pharmacy, Dental Medicine (ISSN 0075-
3637)

300   JA   ISSN 0073-280X
HITOTSUBASHI JOURNAL OF SOCIAL STUDIES.
1960. a. Hitotsubashi University, Hitotsubashi
Academy, 2-1 Naka, Kunitachi, Tokyo 186, Japan.
Ed. S. Honda. circ. 900. Indexed: P.A.I.S. SSCI.

300 001.3   SA
HUMAN SCIENCES RESEARCH COUNCIL.
ANNUAL REPORT. (Text in Afrikaans and
English) 1969/70. a. free. ‡ Human Sciences
Research Council, Private Bag X41, Pretoria 0001,
South Africa. circ. 1,400.

HUMAN SETTLEMENT ISSUES. see *HOUSING
AND URBAN PLANNING*

300   PP
I A S E R DISCUSSION PAPERS. 1976. irreg. price
varies. Institute of Applied Social & Economic
Research, Box 5854, Boroko, Papua New Guinea.
Indexed: Rural Recreat.Tour.Abstr. World
Agri.Econ. & Rural Sociol.Abstr.

300   PP
I A S E R MONOGRAPHS. 1976. irreg. price varies.
Institute of Applied Social & Economic Research,
Box 5854, Boroko, Papua New Guinea. Indexed:
Geo.Abstr.

300   PP
I A S E R SPECIAL PUBLICATIONS. 1981. irreg.
K.10 for 6 nos. Institute of Applied Social and
Economic Research of Papua New Guinea, Box
5854, Boroko, Papua New Guinea. Ed. Jim Robbins.
circ. 300.

300   US
I S E R OCCASIONAL PAPERS. 1970. irreg., no.16,
1985. $2 per no. University of Alaska, Institute of
Social and Economic Research, 3211 Providence
Dr., Anchorage, AK 99508-4614. TEL 907-786-
7710. Ed. Ronald Crowe. bibl.
    Formerly: I S E G R Occasional Papers.

I S E R RESEARCH NOTES. (Institute of Social and
Economic Research) see *BUSINESS AND
ECONOMICS*

300   NR
IBADAN SOCIAL SCIENCES SERIES. irreg., no.7,
1976. Ibadan University Press, University of Ibadan,
Ibadan, Nigeria.

INDEX TO INTERNATIONAL PUBLIC OPINION.
see *POLITICAL SCIENCE — International
Relations*

300   II
INDIAN COUNCIL OF SOCIAL RESEARCH.
ANNUAL REPORT. (Editions in English and
Hindi) 1970. a. free. Indian Council of Social
Science Research, 35 Ferozshah Rd., New Delhi
110001, India. circ. 1,200 (both edts.) (back issues
avail.)

300   II   ISSN 0073-6694
INDIAN STATISTICAL INSTITUTE.
ECONOMETRIC AND SOCIAL SCIENCES
SERIES. RESEARCH MONOGRAPHS. irreg.
Statistical Publishing Society, 204/1 Barrackpore
Trunk Rd., Calcutta 700035, India. Ed. C. R. Rao.

300   AU   ISSN 0046-9696
INSTITUT FUER GESELLSCHAFTSPOLITIK.
MITTEILUNGEN. 1970. irreg. M.80. Sensen-
Verlag Ernst Schwarcz, Sensengasse 4, A-1090
Vienna, Austria. Ed. Dorothea Broessler. adv. circ.
3,000.

300   JA   ISSN 0563-8186
INSTITUTE FOR COMPARATIVE STUDIES OF
CULTURE. ANNALS. (Text in Japanese) 1955. a.
2500 Yen. Institute for Comparative Studies of
Culture, c/o Tokyo Woman's Christian University,
2-6-1 Zempukuji, Suginami-ku, Tokyo 167, Japan.
title index. circ. 600.
    Formerly: Institute for Comparative Studies of
Culture. Publications.

INSTITUTE OF SOCIAL AND ECONOMIC
RESEARCH. REPORTS. see *BUSINESS AND
ECONOMICS*

300   SI
INSTITUTE OF SOUTHEAST ASIAN STUDIES.
FIELD REPORTS SERIES. (Text in English) 1973.
irreg., no.15, 1987. price varies. Institute of
Southeast Asian Studies, Heng Mui Keng Terrace,
Pasir Panjang, Singapore 0511, Singapore.

300   CK
INSTITUTO COLOMBIANO DE CULTURA.
GACETA; revista internacional de cultura. 1976.
irreg. $3 per no. Instituto Colombiano de Cultura,
Carrera 3-A no. 18-24, Apdo. Aereo 29665, Bogota,
Colombia. Ed. Gloria Zea de Uribe.

300   RM
INSTITUTUL PEDAGOGIC ORADEA. LUCRARI
STIINTIFICE: SERIA STIINTE SOCIALE.
(Continues in part its Lucrari Stiintifice: Seria
Istorie, Stiinte Sociale, Pedagogie (1971-1972), its
Lucrari Stiintifice: Seria A and Seria B (1969-1970),
and its Lucrari Stiintifice (1967-68).) (Text in
Rumanian, occasionally in English or French;
summaries in English, French, German or
Rumanian) 1973. a. Institutul Pedagogic Oradea,
Calea Armatei Roseii Nr. 5, Oradea, Rumania.

300   NG   ISSN 0534-4751
INTER-AFRICAN CONFERENCE ON SOCIAL
SCIENCE MEETING.* 1955. irreg. (Commission
for Technical Co-Operation in Africa South of the
Sahara) Maison de l'Afrique, B.P. 878, Niamey,
Niger.

INTER-AMERICAN ECONOMIC AND SOCIAL
COUNCIL. FINAL REPORT OF THE ANNUAL
MEETING AT THE MINISTERIAL LEVEL. see
HISTORY — History Of North And South
America

INTERNATIONAL CONFERENCE OF
ORIENTALISTS IN JAPAN. TRANSACTIONS.
see HISTORY

300   GW   ISSN 0074-8404
INTERNATIONAL SOCIAL SCIENCE COUNCIL.
PUBLICATIONS. irreg. price varies. Walter de
Gruyter & Co., Mouton Publishers, Postfach
110240, D-1000 Berlin 11, W. Germany (B.R.D.)
(U.S. addr.: Mouton Publishers, Division of Walter
de Gruyter, Inc. 200 Saw Mill River Road,
Hawthorne, NY 10532)

INTERNATIONAL STUDIES IN SOCIOLOGY
AND SOCIAL ANTHROPOLOGY. see
SOCIOLOGY

300 320   UK   ISSN 0074-9621
INTERNATIONAL YEAR BOOK AND
STATESMEN'S WHO'S WHO. 1953. a. £80.
Thomas Skinner Directories, Windsor Court, East
Grinstead House, East Grinstead, West Sussex
RH19 1XB, England. adv. index. circ. 3,000.

300   UK
INTERNATIONAL YEARBOOK OF
ORGANIZATION STUDIES. 1980. a. Routledge &
Kegan Paul PLC, 11 New Fetter Lane, London
EC4P 4EE, England (U.S. orders to: 9 Park St.,
Boston, MA 02108) Ed. David Dunkerley.

300   US   ISSN 0362-8736
INTER-UNIVERSITY CONSORTIUM FOR
POLITICAL AND SOCIAL RESEARCH. GUIDE
TO RESOURCES AND SERVICES. 1962. a. free.
Inter-University Consortium for Political and Social
Research, Box 1248, Ann Arbor, MI 48106. TEL
313-764-2570.

IRISH ECONOMIC AND SOCIAL HISTORY. see
HISTORY — History Of Europe

ISTITUTO GIAPPONESE DI CULTURA, ROME.
ANNUARIO. see HISTORY — History Of Europe

IWATE MEDICAL UNIVERSITY SCHOOL OF
LIBERAL ARTS & SCIENCES. ANNUAL
REPORT. see HUMANITIES:
COMPREHENSIVE WORKS

IWATE UNIVERSITY. FACULTY OF
EDUCATION. ANNUAL REPORT. see
LITERATURE

JAHRBUCH FUER SOZIOLOGIE UND
SOZIALPOLITIK. see SOCIOLOGY

JERUSALEM INSTITUTE FOR ISRAEL STUDIES.
DISCUSSION PAPERS. see HUMANITIES:
COMPREHENSIVE WORKS

300   US
JOURNAL OF INDO-EUROPEAN STUDIES
MONOGRAPH SERIES. irreg., latest no.5.
Institute for the Study of Man, Inc., 1133 13th St.,
N.W., Ste. Comm. 2, Washington, DC 20005. TEL
202-789-0231.

300   JA   ISSN 0388-0508
JOURNAL OF INTERCULTURAL STUDIES. (Text
in English) 1974. a. 2500 Yen($25) Kansai
University of Foreign Studies, Intercultural Research
Institute, 16-1 Kitakatahoko-Cho, Hirakata City,
Osaka 573, Japan. Ed. Haruo Kozu. adv. bk. rev.
charts. illus. circ. 1,000. Indexed: Lang.&
Lang.Behav.Abstr.

300   JA
JOURNAL OF SOCIAL SCIENCES. (Text in
English) no.16, 1978. a. International Christian
University, Social Science Research Institute -
Kokusai Kiristokyo Daigaku, 3-10-2 Osawa, Mitaka,
Tokyo 181, Japan. Eds. Toshiki Mogami, Tadashi
Fujita. bk. rev.

300   JA
JOURNAL OF SOCIAL SCIENCES AND
HUMANITIES/JIMBUN GAKUHO. 1944. a.
Tokyo Metropolitan University, The Faculty of
Social Sciences and Humanities - Tokyo-toritsu
Daigaku Jinbun Gakubu, 1-1-1 Yakumo, Meguro-ku,
Tokyo 152, Japan. circ. 650. Indexed: Hist.Abstr.
Amer.Hist.& Life.

KALYANI; journal of humanities and social sciences
of the University of Kelaniya. see HUMANITIES:
COMPREHENSIVE WORKS

300   II   ISSN 0075-5176
KARNATAK UNIVERSITY, DHARWAD, INDIA.
JOURNAL. SOCIAL SCIENCES. (Text in English)
1965. a. Rs.8($4) Karnatak University, Director,
Prasaranga, Dharwad 580003, Karnataka, India. Ed.
K. Chandrasekharaiah. circ. 500.

300   PL
KATOLICKI UNIWERSYTET LUBELSKI.
WYDZIAL NAUK SPOLECZNYCH.
ROZPRAWY. (Text in Polish; summaries in English
or French) 1947. irreg. price varies. Katolicki
Uniwersytet Lubelski, Towarzystwo Naukowe,
Chopina 29, 20-023 Lublin, Poland. index. circ. 1,
025.

KOBE UNIVERSITY OF MERCANTILE MARINE.
REVIEW. PART 1. STUDIES IN HUMANITIES
AND SOCIAL SCIENCE. see HUMANITIES:
COMPREHENSIVE WORKS

KULTUR UND GESELLSCHAFT; Neue historische
Forschungen. see HISTORY

KYUSHU INSTITUTE OF TECHNOLOGY.
BULLETIN: HUMANITIES, SOCIAL
SCIENCES/KYUSHU KOGYO DAIGAKU
KENKYU HOKOKU, JINBUN-SHAKAI-
KAGAKU. see HUMANITIES:
COMPREHENSIVE WORKS

300 001.3   US
LATIN AMERICAN MONOGRAPH AND
DOCUMENT SERIES. irreg. University of
Pittsburgh, Center for Latin American Studies, 4-E-
04 Forbes Quadrangle, Pittsburgh, PA 15260.

970   US   ISSN 0075-8108
LATIN AMERICAN MONOGRAPHS. 1965. irreg.,
no.26, 1984. price varies. (University of Florida,
Center for Latin American Studies) University
Presses of Florida, 15 N. W. 15 St., Gainesville, FL
32603. TEL 904-392-1351. Ed.Bd. Indexed: SSCI.

300   US
LATINOAMERICA. no.17, 1985. a. Universidad
Nacional Autonoma de Mexico, Centro
Coordinador y Difusor de Estudios
Latinoamericanos, P.B. de la Torre I de
Humanidades, Ciudad Universitaria C.P. 04510,
Mexico, D.F., Mexico. Ed. Elsa Cecilia Frost. circ.
1,000.

LAW & INEQUALITY; a journal of theory and
practice. see LAW

LAW AND PSYCHOLOGY REVIEW. see LAW

966.6 300   US
LIBERIAN STUDIES MONOGRAPH SERIES.
1972. irreg., no.8, 1985. price varies. Institute for
Liberian Studies, 4719 Chester Ave., Philadelphia,
PA 19143. charts. illus.

966.6 300   US
LIBERIAN STUDIES RESEARCH WORKING
PAPERS. 1971. irreg., no.7, 1980. price varies.
Institute for Liberian Studies, 4719 Chester Ave.,
Philadelphia, PA 19143. bibl.

LIBERTARIAN ALLIANCE. SCIENTIFIC NOTES.
see POLITICAL SCIENCE

LIBRARY OF LAW AND CONTEMPORARY
PROBLEMS. see LAW

300   MY
M C D S OCCASIONAL PAPER SERIES. (Text in
English) 1974. irreg., latest no. 6. exchange basis.
Malaysian Centre for Development Studies, Prime
Minister's Department, Government Complex,
Block K 11 & K 12, Jalan Duta, Kuala Lumpur,
Malaysia. Ed. Engku M. Anuar.

300   CN   ISSN 0821-6452
MCGILL STUDIES IN INTERNATIONAL
DEVELOPMENT. 1975. irreg. $2.50 per copy.
McGill University, Centre for Developing-Area
Studies, 3715 Peel St., Montreal, Que. H3A 1X1,
Canada. TEL 514-392-5327. Ed. Rosalind E. Boyd.
circ. 400.
 Formerly: McGill University, Montreal. Centre
for Developing-Area Studies. Working Papers (ISSN
0384-059X)

300   CN   ISSN 0076-1893
MCGILL UNIVERSITY, MONTREAL. CENTRE
FOR DEVELOPING-AREA STUDIES. ANNUAL
REPORT. 1967/68. a. $3 per copy. McGill
University, Centre for Developing-Area Studies,
3715 Peel St., Montreal, Que. H3A 1X1, Canada.
TEL 514-392-5321.

300   CN   ISSN 0702-8431
MCGILL UNIVERSITY, MONTREAL. CENTRE
FOR DEVELOPING-AREA STUDIES.
OCCASIONAL MONOGRAPH SERIES. 1969.
irreg., no.21, 1986. price varies. McGill University,
Centre for Developing-Area Studies, 3715 Peel St.,
Montreal, Que. H3A 1X1, Canada. TEL 514-392-
5327. Ed. Rosalind Boyd. circ. 1,000.
 Formerly: McGill University, Montreal. Centre
for Developing-Area Studies. Occasional Paper
Series (ISSN 0076-1907)

MAISON FRANCO-JAPONAISE. BULLETIN. see
ORIENTAL STUDIES

300   MW
MALAWI JOURNAL OF SOCIAL SCIENCE. 1972.
a., latest vol.9, 1982. $7. University of Malawi,
Faculty of Social Science, Box 280, Zomba, Malawi.
Ed.Bd. bk. rev. circ. 500. (back issues avail.)
 Formerly: Chancellor College. Journal of Social
Science (ISSN 0302-3060)

MAN IN SOUTHEAST ASIA. see
ANTHROPOLOGY

300   CE
MARGA INSTITUTE. PROGRESS REPORT. (Text
in English) 1973. irreg., no.3, 1979. Marga Institute
(Sri Lanka Centre for Development Studies), Box
601, 61 Isipathana Mawatha, Colombo 5, Sri Lanka.
circ. 2,000.

300 320.531   GW   ISSN 0171-3698
MARXISTISCHE STUDIEN. 1978. biennial.
DM.32($11) Institut fuer Marxistische Studien und
Forschungen, Liebigstr. 6, D-6000 Frankfurt/M.-1,
W. Germany (B.R.D.) Ed.Bd. circ. 3,000. (back
issues avail.)

MASTER'S THESES IN THE ARTS AND SOCIAL
SCIENCES. see ART

MAX-PLANCK-GESELLSCHAFT. JAHRBUCH. see
SCIENCES: COMPREHENSIVE WORKS

SOCIAL SCIENCES: COMPREHENSIVE WORKS

300   GW   ISSN 0076-6828
METHODS AND MODELS IN THE SOCIAL SCIENCES. 1971. irreg. price varies. Walter de Gruyter & Co., Mouton Publishers, Postfach 110240, D-1000 Berlin 11, W. Germany (B.R.D.) (U.S. addr.: Mouton Publishers, division of Walter de Gruyter, Inc., 200 Saw Mill River Road, Hawthorne, NY 10532)

300   VI
MICROSTATE STUDIES. 1977. a. College of the Virgin Islands, Caribbean Research Institute, St. Thomas, VI 00801. Ed. Norwell Harrigan. circ. 200.

300   US
MIDDLE STATES COUNCIL FOR THE SOCIAL STUDIES. JOURNAL. 1978. a. $5. Middle States Council for the Social Studies, Rider College, Box 6400, Lawrenceville, NJ 08648. TEL 609-896-5176. Eds. Albert Nissman, David Pierfy. adv. bk. rev. circ. 750. (back issues avail.; reprint service avail. from UMI)
    Supersedes (1903-1978): Middle States Council for the Social Studies. Proceedings.

300   SP
MISION CIENTIFICA ESPANOLA EN HISPANOAMERICA. MEMORIAS. vol.3, 1976. irreg. Direccion General de Relaciones Culturales, Madrid, Spain.

301.15   331.1   US
MONOGRAPHS IN ORGANIZATIONAL BEHAVIOUR AND INDUSTRIAL RELATIONS. 1983. irreg., vol.4, 1985. J A I Press Inc., Box 1678, 36 Sherwood Pl., Greenwich, CT 06836. TEL 203-661-7602. Ed. Samuel B. Bacharach. bibl. index.

300   US
MONOGRAPHS ON SCIENCE, TECHNOLOGY, AND SOCIETY. irreg. price varies. Oxford University Press, 200 Madison Ave., New York, NY 10016 TEL 212-679-7300. (And Ely House, 37 Dover St., London W1X 4AH, England) Ed. Sir Alec Merrison.

MUSEE ROYAL DE L'AFRIQUE CENTRALE. ANNALES. SERIE IN 8. SCIENCES HUMAINES/KONINKLIJK MUSEUM VOOR MIDDEN-AFRIKA. ANNALEN. REEKS IN 8. MENSELIJKE WETENSCHAPPEN. see *HUMANITIES: COMPREHENSIVE WORKS*

300   330   NR
N I S E R OCCASIONAL PAPERS. irreg. price varies. Nigerian Institute of Social and Economic Research, P.M.B. 5, University of Ibadan, Ibadan, Nigeria. TEL 01-410935.

300   UN
NAMIBIA STUDIES SERIES. (Text in English) 1978. irreg. free. United Nations Institute for Namibia, Publications Section, P.O. Box 33811, Lusaka, Zambia. TEL 216468. Ed. N.K. Duggal. bibl. charts. illus. stat. circ. 2,000. (back issues avail.)

300   US   ISSN 0077-4049
NATIONAL COUNCIL FOR THE SOCIAL STUDIES. BULLETINS. 1964. irreg. price varies. National Council for the Social Studies, 3501 Newark St., N.W., Washington, DC 20016. TEL 202-966-7840. Indexed: Curr.Cont. SSCI.

300   US   ISSN 0085-3712
NATIONAL COUNCIL FOR THE SOCIAL STUDIES. HOW TO DO IT SERIES. irreg. $1.75 per no. National Council for the Social Studies, 3501 Newark St., N.W., Washington, DC 20016. TEL 202-966-7840.

300   UK   ISSN 0077-491X
NATIONAL INSTITUTE OF ECONOMIC AND SOCIAL RESEARCH. ANNUAL REPORT. 1941. a. free. National Institute of Economic and Social Research, 2 Dean Trench St., Smith Sq., London SW1P 3HE, England. circ. 2,000.

NATIONAL INSTITUTE OF ECONOMIC AND SOCIAL RESEARCH, LONDON. ECONOMIC AND SOCIAL STUDIES. see *BUSINESS AND ECONOMICS*

300   US   ISSN 0077-5274
NATIONAL OPINION RESEARCH CENTER. REPORT. 1941. irreg., no.131, 1983. ‡ National Opinion Research Center, 1155 E. 60th St., Chicago, IL 60637. TEL 312-962-1213. Ed. Susan Campbell.

300   CH   ISSN 0077-5835
NATIONAL TAIWAN UNIVERSITY. COLLEGE OF LAW. JOURNAL OF SOCIAL SCIENCE. (Text in Chinese or English) 1950. irreg., no.34, 1986. NT.$180. National Taiwan University, College of Law, Taipei, Taiwan, Republic of China.

300   NZ   ISSN 0112-2339
NEW ZEALAND. DEPARTMENT OF SCIENTIFIC AND INDUSTRIAL RESEARCH. SOCIAL SCIENCE SERIES. 1984. irreg., no.2, 1986. price varies. Department of Scientific and Industrial Research, Scientific Information Publishing Centre, P.O. Box 9741, Wellington, New Zealand.

NEW ZEALAND SLAVONIC JOURNAL. see *HUMANITIES: COMPREHENSIVE WORKS*

300   330   NR   ISSN 0078-074X
NIGERIAN INSTITUTE OF SOCIAL AND ECONOMIC RESEARCH. ANNUAL REPORT. 1954. a. free. Nigerian Institute of Social and Economic Research, Private Mail Bag 5, University of Ibadan, Ibadan, Nigeria. TEL 01-410935.
    Formerly: West African Institute of Social and Economic Research. Annual Report.

300   US   ISSN 0196-1063
NORTHERN SOCIAL SCIENCE REVIEW. 1976. a. free. Northern State College, Social Science Department, S. Jay St., Aberdeen, SD 57401. Ed. Bd. circ. 400.

OCCASIONAL PAPERS IN ECONOMIC AND SOCIAL HISTORY. see *BUSINESS AND ECONOMICS — Economic Systems And Theories, Economic History*

300   AU
OESTERREICHISCHE AKADEMIE DER WISSENSCHAFTEN. KOMMISSION FUER SOZIAL- UND WIRTSCHAFTWISSENSCHAFTEN. VEROEFFENTLICHUNGEN. (Subseries of its Philosophisch-Historische Klasse. Sitzungsberichte) 1973. irreg. price varies. Verlag der Oesterreichischen Akademie der Wissenschaften, Dr. Ignaz Seipel-Platz 2, 1010 Vienna, Austria. circ. 500.

300   JA   ISSN 0386-8176
OGASAWARA RESEARCH COMMITTEE. PUBLICATIONS. (Text in Japanese; summaries in English) 1978. irreg. free. Tokyo Metropolitan University, Ogasawara Research Committee, Fukasawa 2-1-1, Setagaya-Ku, Tokyo 158, Japan. Ed. Mikio Ono. circ. 800. (back issues avail.)

300   CN   ISSN 0475-0209
ONE WORLD. 1966. irreg. (1-2/yr.) Can.$20. Alberta Teachers' Association, Social Studies Council, 11010 142nd St., Edmonton, Alta. T5N 2R1, Canada. Ed. Ron Carswell. bk. rev. circ. 1,114. Indexed: Can.Educ.Ind. Rel.Ind.One.

300   US   ISSN 0370-1093
OREGON ACADEMY OF SCIENCE. PROCEEDINGS. 1943. a. $8. Oregon Academy of Science, c/o Donald Unger, Sci-Tech Div., Kerr Library, Oregon State University, Corvallis, OR 97331. TEL 503-754-4592. Eds. Clade Curran, John Mairs. circ. 200. Indexed: Biol.Abstr. Chem.Abstr.

320   338   UK
P S I DISCUSSION PAPERS. 1980. irreg. £55 (subscription also includes Report Series; Studies in European Politics; Policy Studies) Policy Studies Institute, 100 Park Village East, London NW1, England.

P S I: REPORT SERIES. (Policy Studies Institute) see *POLITICAL SCIENCE*

300   CH
PAPERS IN SOCIAL SCIENCES. no.80, 1980. irreg. Academia Sinica, Institute of Three Principles of the People, Nankang, Taipei, Taiwan, Republic of China.

300   BL   ISSN 0101-3459
PERSPECTIVAS; revista de ciencias sociais. (Text in Portuguese; summaries in English and Portuguese) 1976-1977; resumed 1980. a. $30 or exchange basis. Universidade Estadual Paulista, Av. Vicente Ferreira 1278, Caixa Postal 603, 17.500 Marilia SP, Brazil. bk. rev. bibl. circ. 1,000. Indexed: Bull.Signal. Sociol.Abstr. Abstr.Anthropol. Lang.& Lang.Behav.Abstr.

300   PL   ISSN 0574-9077
POLITECHNIKA CZESTOCHOWSKA. ZESZYTY NAUKOWE. NAUKI SPOLECZNO-EKONOMICZNE. (Text in Polish; summaries in English and Russian) 1964. irreg. Politechnika Czestochowska, Ul. Deglera 31, 42-200 Czestochowa, Poland (Dist. by: Ars Polona-Ruch, Krakowskie Przedmiescie 7, Warsaw, Poland) Ed. Mieczyslaw Stanczyk.

300   PL
POLITECHNIKA GDANSKA. INSTYTUT NAUK SPOLECZNYCH. RAPORT. 1982. a. price varies. Politechnika Gdanska, Ul. Majakowskiego 11/12, 80-592 Gdansk 6, Poland.

300   330   PL   ISSN 0137-2599
POLITECHNIKA LODZKA. ZESZYTY NAUKOWE. ORGANIZACJA I ZARZADZANIE. (Text in Polish; summaries in English and Russian) 1975. irreg. price varies. Politechnika Lodzka, Ul. Zworki 36, 90-924 Lodz, Poland (Dist. by: Ars Polona-Ruch, Krakowkie Przedmiescie 7, Warsaw, Poland) Ed. Jerzy Nowakowski. circ. 210.

300   PL   ISSN 0072-4718
POLITECHNIKA SLASKA. ZESZYTY NAUKOWE. NAUKI SPOLECZNE. (Text in Polish; summaries in English, and Russian) 1964. irreg. price varies. Politechnika Slaska, W. Pstrowskiego 7, 44-100 Gliwice, Poland (Dist by: Ars Polona, Krakowskie Przedmiescie 7, 00-068 Warsaw, Poland) Ed. Malgorzata Nizio-Baron.

300   PL   ISSN 0860-3200
POLITECHNIKA WROCLAWSKA. INSTYTUT NAUK EKONOMICZNO-SPOLECZNYCH. PRACE NAUKOWE. KONFERENCJE. 1986. irreg. price varies. Politechnika Wroclawska, Wybrzeze Wyspianskiego 27, 50-370 Wroclaw, Poland. Ed. Jerzy Ciekot.

300   PL   ISSN 0239-3204
POLITECHNIKA WROCLAWSKA. INSTYTUT NAUK EKONOMICZNO-SPOLECZNYCH. PRACE NAUKOWE. MONOGRAFIE. (Text in Polish; summaries in English and Russian) 1971. irreg., no.22, 1985. price varies. Politechnika Wroclawska, Wybrzeze Wyspianskiego 27, 50-370 Wroclaw, Poland (Dist. by: Ars Polona-Ruch, Krakowskie Przedmiescie 7, Warsaw, Poland) Ed. Jerzy Ciekot.
    Formerly: Politechnika Wroclawska. Instytut Nauk Spolecznych. Prace Naukowe. Monografie (ISSN 0324-9506)

300   PL   ISSN 0239-3212
POLITECHNIKA WROCLAWSKA. INSTYTUT NAUK EKONOMICZNO-SPOLECZNYCH. PRACE NAUKOWE. STUDIA I MATERIALY. (Text in Polish; summaries in English and Russian) 1969. irreg., no.10, 1979. price varies. Politechnika Wroclawska, Wybrzeze Wyspianskiego 27, 50-370 Wroclaw, Poland (Dist. by: Ars Polona-Ruch, Krakowskie Przedmiescie 7, Warsaw, Poland) Ed. Marian Kloza.
    Formerly: Politechnika Wroclawska. Instytut Nauk Spolecznych. Prace Naukowe. Studia i Materialy (ISSN 0324-9514)

300   PE
PONTIFICIA UNIVERSIDAD CATOLICA. REVISTA. N.S. 1977. irreg. $7.50. Pontificia Universidad Catolica, Ave. Bolivar s/n, Pueblo Libre, Apdo. 1761, Lima 21, Peru. Ed. Gerardo Alarco. bk. rev.

300   PE
PONTIFICIA UNIVERSIDAD CATOLICA DEL PERU. DEPARTAMENTO DE CIENCIAS SOCIALES. SERIE: EDICIONES PREVIAS. no.5, 1975. irreg. Pontificia Universidad Catolica del Peru, Departamento de Ciencias Sociales, Fondo Editorial, Apdo. 1761, Lima 100, Peru.

300 VC ISSN 0080-3960
PONTIFICIA UNIVERSITA GREGORIANA.
ISTITUTO DI SCIENZE SOCIALI STUDIA
SOCIALIA. 1955. irreg. price varies. Pontificia
Universita Gregoriana, School of Social Sciences,
Piazza della Pilotta 4, 00187 Rome, Italy. Ed. Sergi
Bernal Restrepo, SJ. circ. 200.

300 PL ISSN 0079-4716
POZNANSKIE TOWARZYSTWO PRZYJACIOL
NAUK. KOMISJA NAUK SPOLECZNYCH.
PRACE. (Text in Polish; summaries in English,
French, German, Russian) 1922. irreg., vol.22, 1981.
price varies. (Poznanskie Towarzystwo Przyjaciol
Nauk) Panstwowe Wydawnictwo Naukowe,
Ul.Miodowa 10, Warsaw, Poland (Dist. by Ars
Polona-Ruch, Krakowskie Przedmiescie 7, Warsaw,
Poland) Ed. Wojciech R. Rzepka.

300 YU ISSN 0032-7271
PREGLED; casopis za drustvena pitanja. 1910. a.
6000 din.($20) Univerzitet u Sarajevu, Vojvode
Stepe obala 7/111, 71000 Sarajevo, Yugoslavia. Ed.
Radovan Milanovic.

300 UR ISSN 0079-5763
PROBLEMS OF THE CONTEMPORARY
WORLD/PROBLEMES DU MONDE
CONTEMPORAIN/PROBLEMAS DEL MUNDO
CONTEMPORANEO. (Text in English, French,
Spanish) 1969. irreg. available on exchange.
Akademiya Nauk S.S.S.R., Leninskii prospekt, 14,
Moscow V-71, Russian S.F.S.R., U.S.S.R. Ed. I.
Grigulevich. circ. 750. Indexed: Math.R.

300 FR ISSN 0079-7448
PSYCHOTHEQUE.* 1969. irreg. 19.95 F. Editions
Jean Pierre Delarge (Subsidiary of: Editions
Universitaires B G) 77 rue de Vaugirard, 75006
Paris, France.

300 US
PUBLIC POLICY STUDIES IN THE SOUTH; a
selected research guide. 1975. a. $6. Southern
Center for Studies in Public Policy, Clark College,
Atlanta, GA 30314. TEL 404-681-3080.

PUBLICACOES CULTURAIS DA COMPANHIA.
see SCIENCES: COMPREHENSIVE WORKS

300 954 572 FR ISSN 0339-1744
PURUSHARTHA. 1975. irreg. price varies. (Centre
d'Etudes de l'Inde et de l'Asie du Sud) Editions de
l'Ecole des Hautes Etudes en Sciences Sociales, 131
bd. Saint Michel, 75005 Paris, France (Dist. by:
Centre Interinstitutionnel pour la Diffusion de
Publications en Science Humaines, 131 bd. Saint
Michel, 75005 Paris, France) adv. circ. 500.

300 US ISSN 0149-192X
QUANTITATIVE APPLICATIONS IN THE
SOCIAL SCIENCES. 1976. irreg., no.25, 1982. $6
per no. Sage Publications, Inc., 2111 W. Hillcrest
Dr., Newbury Park, CA 91320 TEL 805-499-0721.
(And Sage Publications, Ltd., 28 Banner St.,
London EC1Y 8QE, England) Eds. John L.
Sullivan, Richard G. Niemi. (back issues avail.)

327 US
R F. 1972. irreg. free. Rockefeller Foundation, 1133
Ave. of the Americas, New York, NY 10036. TEL
212-869-8500. Ed. Henry Romney. bk. rev. illus.
circ. 35,000. Indexed: P.A.I.S. Curr.Lit.Fam.Plan.
Formerly: R F Illustrated (ISSN 0090-9599)

300 II
RECENT TRENDS IN SOCIAL SCIENCES. 1975.
irreg. Rs.24($5) Anu Prakashan, Shivaji Rd., Meerut
25001, India. Ed. Dr. Ram Nath Sharma. adv. bk.
rev.

300 FR ISSN 0557-6989
RECHERCHES ANGLAISES ET AMERICAINES.
a. price varies. Universite de Strasbourg II, Service
des Periodiques, 22 rue Descartes, 67084
Strasbourg, France. Ed. A. Bleikasten. Indexed:
M.L.A. Abstr.Engl.Stud.

RECHERCHES D'HISTOIRE ET DE SCIENCES
SOCIALES/STUDIES IN HISTORY AND THE
SOCIAL SCIENCES. see HISTORY

300 US ISSN 0730-3335
REFERENCE SOURCES FOR THE SOCIAL
SCIENCES AND HUMANITIES. 1982. irreg.
price varies. Greenwood Press, Box 5007, 88 Post
Rd. West, Westport, CT 06881. TEL 203-226-3571.
Ed. Raymond G. McInnis.

300 100 SZ
RENCONTRES INTERNATIONALES DE
GENEVE. 1947. biennial. 39 Fr. Editions de la
Baconniere S.A., Box 185, CH-2017 Boudry,
Switzerland.

300 UN ISSN 0080-1348
REPORTS AND PAPERS IN THE SOCIAL
SCIENCES. (Editions in English and French) 1955.
irreg., no.55, 1984. price varies. Unesco, 7-9 Place
de Fontenoy, 75700 Paris, France (Dist. in U.S. by:
Bernan Associates-Unipub, 4611-F Assembly Dr.,
Lanham, MD 20706-4391)

RESEARCH JOURNAL: HUMANITIES AND
SOCIAL SCIENCES. see HUMANITIES:
COMPREHENSIVE WORKS

REVIEW JOURNAL OF PHILOSOPHY AND
SOCIAL SCIENCE. see PHILOSOPHY

300 FR ISSN 0336-1578
REVUE DES SCIENCES SOCIALES DE LA
FRANCE DE L'EST. 1971? a. price varies.
Universite de Strasbourg II, 22 rue Descartes, 67084
Strasbourg, France. Ed. Freddy Raphael.

300 PL
ROCZNIKI NAUK SPOLECZNYCH. (Text in
Polish; summaries in English) 1949. a. price varies.
Katolicki Uniwersytet Lubelski, Towarzystwo
Naukowe, Chopina 29, 20-023 Lublin, Poland. circ.
820.

RUSSIAN SERIES ON SOCIAL HISTORY. see
HISTORY — History Of Asia

300 SX
S.W.A. SCIENTIFIC SOCIETY. JOURNAL. Title
varies: South West Africa Scientific Society Journal.
(Text in English, Afrikaans or German) 1925. a.
membership. S.W.A. Scientific Society, Box 67,
Windhoek 9000, South West Africa/Namibia. Ed.
A. Henrichsen. adv. bk. rev. illus.

301 US
SAGE LIBRARY OF SOCIAL RESEARCH. 1973.
irreg. (14-24/yr.) $29 for hardcover; soft $14.50.
Sage Publications, Inc., 2111 W. Hillcrest Dr.,
Newbury Park, CA 91320 TEL 805-499-0721. (And
Sage Publications, Ltd., 28 Banner St., London
EC1Y 8QE, England)

300 330 UK
SCOTTISH ECONOMIC AND SOCIAL HISTORY.
1981. a. £2. University of Glasgow, Department of
Scottish History, Glasgow G12 8RT, Scotland. Eds.
R.M. Mitchison, H. Fraser. bk. rev. circ. 400.

SCRIPTA HIEROSOLYMITANA. see
HUMANITIES: COMPREHENSIVE WORKS

300 620 JA
SENDAI NATIONAL COLLEGE OF
TECHNOLOGY. RESEARCH REPORTS. (Text in
Japanese; summaries in English) 1972. a. free.
Sendai National College of Technology, 5-2,
Nagata-Cho 2-Chome, Chiyoda-Ku, Tokyo 100,
Japan. TEL 03-581-6411. charts. index. circ. 270.
Formerly: Sendai Radio Technical College.
Research Reports (ISSN 0386-4243)

300 JA
SHIMANE UNIVERSITY. FACULTY OF LAW
AND LITERATURE. MEMOIRS/SHIMANE
DAIGAKU HOBUNGAKUBU KIYO.
BUNDAKUKAHEN. (Text in Japanese and
English) 1973. a. Shimane University, Faculty of
Law and Literature, 1060 Nishikawatsu-cho,
Matsue-shi, Shimane-ken, Japan. Ed.Bd. circ. 400.

300 370 SP
SISTEMA DE INDICADORES SOCIO-
ECONOMICOS Y EDUCATIVOS DE LA O E I.
1980. a. 24000 ptas.($240) Organizacion de Estados
Iberoamericanos (OEI), Ciudad Universitaria, 28040
Madrid, Spain. circ. 1,000.
Formerly: Educacion en Iberoamerica: Sistema de
Indicadores Socio Economicos y Educativos.

300 900 NE ISSN 0081-0401
SOCIAAL-HISTORISCHE STUDIEN. (Text in
Dutch; summaries in English or French) 1959.
irreg., no.9, 1980. price varies. (International
Institute for Social History) Van Gorcum, Box 43,
9400 AA Assen, Netherlands.

300 JA ISSN 0559-698X
SOCIAL DEVELOPMENT RESEARCH
INSTITUTE. ORGANIZATION AND
ACTIVITIES. (Text in English) irreg. free. Social
Development Research Institute - Shakai Hosho
Kenkyusho, 3-3-4 Kasumigaseki, Chiyoda-ku, Tokyo
100, Japan.

300 CN
SOCIAL SCIENCE FEDERATION OF CANADA.
ANNUAL REPORT. (Text in English and French)
a. free. Social Science Federation of Canada, 151
Slater St., Ste. 415, Ottawa K1P 5H3, Canada. TEL
613-238-6112. circ. 600.
Formerly: Social Science Research Council of
Canada. Report (ISSN 0081-0452)

309.1 KO
SOCIAL SCIENCE JOURNAL. (Text in English)
1973. a. $5. Korean National Commission for
UNESCO, Box Central 64, Seoul, S. Korea. (Co-
sponsor: Korean Social Science Research Council)
bibl. stat. Indexed: Psychol.Abstr.

330 II
SOCIAL SCIENCES RESEARCH SERIES. (Text in
English) 1975. irreg., no.5, 1985) price varies.
Indian Institute of Geography, 120/A Nehru Nagar
East, Secunderabad 500026, Andhra Pradesh, India.
Ed. B.N. Chaturuedi. circ. 1,000.
Supersedes: Wealth and Welfare of Andhra
Pradesh Series (ISSN 0083-7776)

300 CN
SOCIAL SCIENCES SYMPOSIUM SERIES. irreg.
University of Calgary, Faculty of Social Sciences,
Calgary, Alta. T2N 1N4, Canada.

300 NR ISSN 0081-0487
SOCIAL SCIENTIST.* 1965. a. University of Ife,
Economics Society, Ile-Ife, Nigeria. Indexed:
Geo.Abstr.

300 301 UK
SOCIAL STRUCTURE AND SOCIAL CHANGE.
1977. irreg. price varies. Edward Arnold
(Publishers) Ltd., 41 Bedford Square, London
WC1B 3DQ, England.

SOCIAL STUDIES AUDIOVISUALS: A
TEACHER'S SOURCEBOOK. (National
Information Center for Educational Media) see
EDUCATION — Teaching Methods And
Curriculum

300 FR ISSN 0081-0894
SOCIETE DES OCEANISTES. PUBLICATIONS.
1951. irreg. price varies. Societe des Oceanistes,
Musee de l'Homme, 75116 Paris, France. bk. rev.
circ. 500.

300 320 CH
SOOCHOW JOURNAL OF POLITICAL SCIENCE
& SOCIOLOGY. 1977. a. $15 per no. Soochow
University, Wai Shuang Hsi, Shih Lin, Taipei,
Taiwan, Republic of China.
Formerly: Soochow Journal of Social and
Political Sciences.

SOZIAL- UND WIRTSCHAFTSHISTORISCHE
STUDIEN. see BUSINESS AND
ECONOMICS — Economic Systems And
Theories, Economic History

300 SZ
SOZIOOEKONOMISCHE FORSCHUNGEN. 1974.
irreg., no.19, 1985. price varies. Paul Haupt AG,
Falkenplatz 14, CH-3001 Berne, Switzerland.

300 YU ISSN 0081-394X
SRPSKA AKADEMIJA NAUKA I UMETNOSTI.
ODELJENJE DRUSTVENIH NAUKA. GLAS.
(Text in Serbo-Croatian; summaries in English,
French, German or Russian) 1951. irreg. price
varies. Srpska Akademija Nauka i Umetnosti, Knez
Mihailova 35, 11001 Belgrade, Yugoslavia (Dist. by:
Prosveta, Terazije 16, Belgrade, Yugoslavia) circ. 1,
000. Indexed: Hist.Abstr. Amer.Hist.& Life. Art &
Archaeol.Tech.Abstr. Int.Aerosp.Abstr.

300 YU ISSN 0081-3982
SRPSKA AKADEMIJA NAUKA I UMETNOSTI. ODELJENJE DRUSTVENIH NAUKA. POSEBNA IZDANJA. (Text in Serbo-Croatian; summaries in English, French, German or Russian) N.S. 1949. irreg. price varies. Srpska Akademija Nauka i Umetnosti, Knez Mihailova 35, 11001 Belgrade, Yugoslavia (Dist. by: Prosveta, Terazije 16, Belgrade, Yugoslavia) circ. 1,000. Indexed: Hist.Abstr.

300 913 720 YU ISSN 0081-4059
SRPSKA AKADEMIJA NAUKA I UMETNOSTI. ODELJENJE DRUSTVENIH NAUKA. SPOMENIK. (Text in Serbo-Croatian; summaries in English, French, German or Russian) N.S. 1950. irreg. price varies. Srpska Akademija Nauka i Umetnosti, Knez Mihailova 35, 11001 Belgrade, Yugoslavia (Dist. by: Prosveta, Terazije 16, Belgrade, Yugoslavia) circ. 1,000.

SRPSKA AKADEMIJA NAUKA I UMETNOSTI SPOMENICA. see *HUMANITIES: COMPREHENSIVE WORKS*

300 943.8 PL ISSN 0081-6574
STUDIA I MATERIALY Z DZIEJOW NAUKI POLSKIEJ. SERIA A. HISTORIA NAUK SPOLECZNYCH. (Text in Polish; summaries in English, French, Russian) 1957. irreg., vol.16, 1984. price varies. (Polska Akademia Nauk, Zaklad Historii Nauki, Oswiaty i Techniki) Panstwowe Wydawnictwo Naukowe, Ul. Miodowa 10, 00-251 Warsaw, Poland (Dist. by: Ars Polona, Krakowskie Przedmiescie 7, 00-068 Warsaw, Poland) Ed. E. Olszewski. illus. circ. 320.

STUDIES IN EUROPEAN POLITICS. see *POLITICAL SCIENCE*

STUDIES IN ORIENTAL CULTURE. see *HISTORY — History Of Asia*

300 301 UK
STUDIES IN SOCIAL AND DEMOGRAPHIC HISTORY. 1980. irreg. price varies. Edward Arnold (Publishers) Ltd., 41 Bedford Square, London WC1B 3DQ, England.

STUDIES IN SOCIAL EXPERIMENTATION. see *SOCIOLOGY*

300 NE
STUDIES IN SOCIAL HISTORY. (Text in English) 1976. irreg. price varies. (International Institute for Social History) Martinus Nijhoff Publishers, Postbus 163, 3300 AD Dordrecht, Netherlands.

300 US
STUDIES IN THE HISTORY OF SCIENCE. vol.5, 1979. irreg. Burt Franklin & Co., Inc., 235 E. 44th St., New York, NY 10017. TEL 212-687-5250. Ed. L. Pearce Williams.

300 GW ISSN 0081-8674
STUDIES IN THE SOCIAL SCIENCES. 1966. irreg. price varies. Walter de Gruyter & Co., Mouton Publishers, Postfach 110240, D-1000 Berlin 11, W. Germany (B.R.D.) (U.S. addr.: Mouton Publishers, division of Walter de Gruyter, Inc., 200 Saw Mill River Road, Hawthorne, NY 10532)

300 SJ
SUDAN. ECONOMIC AND SOCIAL RESEARCH COUNCIL. BULLETIN. irreg. Economic and Social Research Council, Box 1166, Khartoum, Sudan.

300 SJ
SUDAN. ECONOMIC AND SOCIAL RESEARCH COUNCIL. OCCASIONAL PAPER. irreg., no.7, 1976. Economic and Social Research Council, 1 Box 1166, Khartoum, Sudan. bibl.

300 SJ
SUDAN. ECONOMIC AND SOCIAL RESEARCH COUNCIL. RESEARCH REPORT. irreg., no.3, 1978. Economic and Social Research Council, Box 1166, Khartoum, Sudan.

SUDAN RESEARCH INFORMATION BULLETIN. see *HUMANITIES: COMPREHENSIVE WORKS*

SYNTHESE LIBRARY; monographs on epistemology, logic, methodology, philosophy of science and of knowledge, and the mathematical methods of social and behavioral sciences. see *PHILOSOPHY*

960 US
SYRACUSE UNIVERSITY. FOREIGN AND COMPARATIVE STUDIES. AFRICAN SERIES. (Former name of issuing body: Maxwell School of Citizenship and Public Affairs) 1971. irreg., vol.42, 1986. price varies. ‡ Syracuse University, Foreign and Comparative Studies, 724 Comstock Ave., Syracuse, NY 13244. TEL 315-423-2552. Ed. Minion K.C. Morrison. Indexed: Geo.Abstr.
 Formerly (until vol.25, 1976): Syracuse University. Program of East African Studies. Eastern African Series.

300 PL ISSN 0082-1292
SZCZECINSKIE TOWARZYSTWO NAUKOWE. WYDZIAL NAUK SPOLECZNYCH. (Text in Polish; summaries in English, German or Russian) 1959. irreg., vol.36, 1984. price varies. Panstwowe Wydawnictwo Naukowe, Ul. Miodowa 10, 00-251 Warsaw, Poland (Dist. by: Ars Polona, Krakowskie Przedmiescie 7, 00-068 Warsaw, Poland) Ed. H. Lesinski. circ. 400.
 Formerly: Szczecinskie Towarzystwo Naukowe. Wydzial Nauk Spolecznych. Prace (ISSN 0082-1284)

300 SZ ISSN 0080-7427
T.M. (Tatsachen und Meinungen) 1968. irreg., no.55, 1986. price varies. (Schweizerisches Ost-Institut - Swiss Eastern Institute) Verlag SOI, Jubilaeumsstr. 41, CH-3000 Berne 6, Switzerland. Ed. Peter Sager.

300 HU ISSN 0082-1748
TARSADALOMTUDOMANYI KISMONOGRAFIAK. 1961. irreg. price varies. (Magyar Tudomanyos Akademia) Akademiai Kiado, Publishing House of the Hungarian Academy of Sciences, Box 24, H-1363 Budapest, Hungary.

300 NE
THEORY AND DECISION LIBRARY; an international series in the philosophy and methodology of the social and behavioral sciences. (Text in English) 1973. irreg. price varies. D. Reidel Publishing Co., Box 17, 3300 AA Dordrecht, Netherlands (And 190 Old Derby St., Hingham, MA 02043) Eds. Gerald Eberlein, Werner Leinfellner. Indexed: Psychol.Abstr.

TOPIC; a journal of the liberal arts. see *HUMANITIES: COMPREHENSIVE WORKS*

300 GY
TRANSITION. a. University of Guyana, Faculty of Social Sciences and the Institute of Development Studies, Georgetown, Guyana.

300 SZ ISSN 0082-6022
TRAVAUX DE DROIT, D'ECONOMIQUE DE SOCIOLOGIE ET DE SCIENCES POLITIQUES. (Text in English and French) 1963. irreg., no.151, 1986. price varies. Librarie Droz, 11 rue Massot, 1211 Geneva, Switzerland. Ed. G. Busino. circ. 1, 000.

300 GW
TUDUV-STUDIEN. REIHE SOZIALWISSENSCHAFTEN. 1976. irreg. price varies. Tuduv Verlagsgesellschaft mbH, Gabelsbergerstr. 15, 8000 Munich 2, W. Germany (B.R.D.) adv.

U P RESEARCH MONITOR. (University of the Philippines) see *SCIENCES: COMPREHENSIVE WORKS*

300 UN
UNITED NATIONS INSTITUTE FOR NAMIBIA. OCCASIONAL PAPERS. (Text in English) 1985. irreg. free. United Nations Institute for Namibia, Publications Section, P.O. Box 33811, Lusaka, Zambia. TEL 216468. Ed. N.K. Duggal. bibl. charts. illus. stat. circ. 2,000.

300 UN
UNITED NATIONS RESEARCH INSTITUTE FOR SOCIAL DEVELOPMENT. REPORT. 1963. irreg. United Nations Research Institute for Social Development (UNRISD), Reference Centre, Palais des Nations, CH-1211 Geneva 10, Switzerland. circ. 3,000. Indexed: Geo.Abstr.

300 CK
UNIVERSIDAD DE ANTIOQUIA. DEBATES NACIONALES. 1981. irreg. Universidad de Antioquia, Extension Cultural, Medellin, Colombia. Ed. Dr. Alberto Santofimio Botero.

300 PR
UNIVERSIDAD INTERAMERICANA DE PUERTO RICO. DEPARTAMENTO DE CIENCIAS SOCIALES. REVISTA ANALES. 1980. a. $6. (Universidad Interamericana, Departamento de Ciencias Sociales) Antillian College Press, San German, Puerto Rico. Ed. Hector Feliciano. bk. rev. circ. 2,000. Indexed: Sociol.Abstr.

300 CK ISSN 0502-949X
UNIVERSIDAD NACIONAL DE COLOMBIA. DIRECCION DE DIVULGACION CULTURAL. REVISTA. 1968. irreg. exchange basis. Universidad Nacional de Colombia, Direccion de Divulgacion Cultural, Apartado Aereo 14490, Bogota, D.E., Colombia. circ. 5,000.

300 CL
UNIVERSIDAD TECNICA DEL ESTADO. REVISTA. 1970. irreg. $4. Universidad Tecnica del Estado, Avda. Ecuador 3469, Correo 2, Santiago, Chile. illus.

500 BL
UNIVERSIDADE DO AMAZONAS. CENTRO DE PESQUISAS SOCIO-ECONOMICAS. BOLETIM TECNICO INFORMATIVO.* irreg. Universidade do Amazonas, Centro de Pesquisas Socio-Economicas, Rua Jose Paranagua 200, C P 348, 69000 Manaus, AM, Brazil.

300 100 BL ISSN 0041-8870
UNIVERSIDADE FEDERAL DO CEARA. DEPARTAMENTO DE CIENCIAS SOCIAIS E FILOSOFIA. DOCUMENTOS. (Text in English, Portuguese; summaries in English) 1967. irreg., vol.8, no.2, 1977. Cr.$5.($6.) (Universidade Federal do Ceara, Departamento de Ciencias Sociais e Filosofia) Imprensa Universitaria do Ceara, 2762 Avda. da Universidade, C.P. 1257, Fortaleza BR Ceara, Brazil. Ed. Paulo Elpidio De Menezes Neto. adv. bk. rev. circ. 2,000.

300 BE ISSN 0076-1214
UNIVERSITE CATHOLIQUE DE LOUVAIN. ECOLE DES SCIENCES POLITIQUES ET SOCIALES. COLLECTION.* (Text in Flemish, French) 1894. irreg. price varies. 1348 Louvain-la-Neuve, Belgium.

300 330 BE ISSN 0076-1303
UNIVERSITE CATHOLIQUE DE LOUVAIN. INSTITUT DE RECHERCHES ECONOMIQUES, POLITIQUES ET SOCIALES. PUBLICATIONS.* irreg. price varies. Editions Nauwelaerts, 148 Mechelsestraat, 3000 Louvain, Belgium. Ed. Dupriez.

301.3 FR ISSN 0065-4949
UNIVERSITE D'AIX-MARSEILLE I. CENTRE D'ETUDES DES SOCIETES MEDITERRANEENNES. CAHIERS. 1966. a. Universite d'Aix-Marseille I (Universite de Provence), Centre d'Etudes des Societes Mediterraneennes, Service des Publications, 13621 Aix en Provence, France.

300 HT
UNIVERSITE D'ETAT. FACULTE D'ETHNOLOGIE. REVUE. 1958. irreg. Universite de l'Etat, Faculte d'Ethnologie, Place des Heros de l'Independance, Angle Ave., Magloire Ambroise, Et Rue St. Honore, Port-au-Prince, Haiti.
 Formerly: Universite d'Etat. Faculte d'Ethnologie. Centre de Recherches en Sciences Humaines et Sociales. Revue.

UNIVERSITE DE DAKAR. FACULTE DES LETTRES ET SCIENCES HUMAINES. ANNALES. see *LITERATURE*

UNIVERSITE DE DROIT, ECONOMIE ET DE SCIENCES SOCIALES DE PARIS. TRAVAUX DU SEMINAIRE DE RECHERCHES SUR LES FAITS ELECTORAUX DE MONSIEUR LE PROFESSEUR ROBERT VILLERS. see *LAW*

300 400 FR ISSN 0078-9895
UNIVERSITE DE PARIS. FACULTE DES LETTRES ET SCIENCES HUMAINES. PUBLICATIONS. SERIE RECHERCHES. 1961. irreg. price varies. Presses Universitaires de France, 108 bd. Saint Germain, 75279 Paris Cedex 6, France (Service des Periodiques, 12 rue Jean de Beauvais, 75005 Paris) (reprint service avail. from KTO)

300 FR ISSN 0563-9727
UNIVERSITE DES SCIENCES SOCIALES DE TOULOUSE. ANNALES. 1953. a. 130 F. Universite de Toulouse I (Sciences Sociales), Place Anatole France, 31042 Toulouse, France.

300 SA
UNIVERSITY OF DURBAN-WESTVILLE. INSTITUTE FOR SOCIAL AND ECONOMIC RESEARCH. ANNUAL REPORT. 1973. a. free. University of Durban-Westville, Institute for Social and Economic Research, Private Bag X54001, Durban 4000, South Africa. Ed. J.F. Butler-Adam. circ. 800.

300 900 US ISSN 0071-6197
UNIVERSITY OF FLORIDA MONOGRAPHS. SOCIAL SCIENCES. 1959. irreg. price varies. University Presses of Florida, 15 N.W. 15 St, Gainesville, FL 32603. TEL 904-392-1351. Ed.Bd.

300 GH
UNIVERSITY OF GHANA. INSTITUTE OF STATISTICAL, SOCIAL AND ECONOMIC RESEARCH. DISCUSSION PAPERS. (Text in English) 1977. irreg., no.14, 1984. University of Ghana, Institute of Statistical, Social and Economic Research, Box 74, Legon, Ghana.

UNIVERSITY OF HONG KONG. CENTRE OF ASIAN STUDIES. OCCASIONAL PAPERS AND MONOGRAPHS. see ORIENTAL STUDIES

UNIVERSITY OF KHARTOUM. DEVELOPMENT STUDIES AND RESEARCH CENTRE. DISCUSSION PAPERS. see BUSINESS AND ECONOMICS — International Development And Assistance

300 UK ISSN 0308-6119
UNIVERSITY OF LONDON. CONTEMPORARY CHINA INSTITUTE. RESEARCH NOTES AND STUDIES. 1976. irreg. price varies. University of London, School of Oriental and African Studies, Malet St., London WC1E 7HP, England. (Co-sponsor: Contermporary China Institute)

325.3 UK ISSN 0076-0781
UNIVERSITY OF LONDON. INSTITUTE OF COMMONWEALTH STUDIES. ANNUAL REPORT. 1949. a. free. University of London, Institute of Commonwealth Studies, 27-28 Russell Sq., London WC1B 5DS, England.

300 UK ISSN 0076-0773
UNIVERSITY OF LONDON. INSTITUTE OF COMMONWEALTH STUDIES. COLLECTED SEMINAR PAPERS. 1967. irreg., no.35, 1985. price varies. University of London, Institute of Commonwealth Studies, 27-28 Russell Sq., London WC1B 5DS, England. circ. 400.

300.7 KE
UNIVERSITY OF NAIROBI. INSTITUTE FOR DEVELOPMENT STUDIES. RESEARCH AND PUBLICATIONS. 1969. a. free. University of Nairobi, Institute for Development Studies, Box 30197, Nairobi, Kenya. circ. 2,000 (approx.)

300 SA
UNIVERSITY OF NATAL. CENTRE FOR APPLIED SOCIAL RESEARCH. ANNUAL REPORT. 1958/59. a. free. University of Natal, Centre for Applied Social Research, Durban, South Africa. Ed. L. Schlemmer. circ. 150.
Formerly: University of Natal. Institute for Social Research. Annual Report (ISSN 0070-7759)

300 US
UNIVERSITY OF NEW MEXICO. LATIN AMERICAN INSTITUTE. RESEARCH PAPER SERIES. 1979. irreg., latest no.17. University of New Mexico, Latin American Institute, 801 Yale N.E., Albuquerque, NM 87131. bibl. charts. stats. cum.index. circ. 800.

300 US
UNIVERSITY OF NORTH CAROLINA, CHAPEL HILL. INSTITUTE FOR RESEARCH IN SOCIAL SCIENCE. TECHNICAL PAPERS. 1977. irreg., no.7, 1983. I R S S Publications, Manning Hall 026A, Chapel Hill, NC 27514. TEL 919-962-2211. Ed. Angell Beza.

300 US
UNIVERSITY OF NORTH CAROLINA, CHAPEL HILL. INSTITUTE FOR RESEARCH IN SOCIAL SCIENCE. WORKING PAPERS IN METHODOLOGY. 1967. irreg., no.10, 1978. I R S S Publications, Manning Hall 026A, Chapel Hill, NC 27514. Ed. Angell Beza.

300 001.3 US
UNIVERSITY OF PITTSBURGH. CENTER FOR INTERNATIONAL STUDIES. LATIN AMERICAN REPRINT SERIES. (Text in English or Spanish) 1970. irreg., no.19, 1983. free. University of Pittsburgh, Center for Latin American Studies, U C I S, 4E04 Forbes Quadrangle, Pittsburgh, PA 15260. TEL 412-624-5563. Dir. Robert D. Drennan. circ. 650.
Formerly: University of Pittsburgh. Center for International Studies: Latin American Studies. Occasional Papers (ISSN 0075-8140)

UNIVERSITY OF SIND. RESEARCH JOURNAL. ARTS SERIES: HUMANITIES AND SOCIAL SCIENCES. see ART

300 BB
UNIVERSITY OF THE WEST INDIES. INSTITUTE OF SOCIAL AND ECONOMIC RESEARCH. OCCASIONAL PAPERS. 1975. irreg., no.17, 1983. University of the West Indies, Institute of Social and Economic Research (Eastern Caribbean), P.O. Box 64, Bridgetown, Barbados, W. Indies. circ. 500.

300 TR
UNIVERSITY OF THE WEST INDIES, TRINIDAD. INSTITUTE OF SOCIAL & ECONOMIC RESEARCH. OCCASIONAL PAPERS: GENERAL SERIES. 1977. irreg. price varies. University of the West Indies, Institute of Social & Economic Research, St. Augustine, Trinidad, West Indies. Ed. Jack Harewood. charts. stat. circ. 220. (back issues avail.)

300 JA ISSN 0563-8054
UNIVERSITY OF TOKYO. INSTITUTE OF SOCIAL SCIENCE. ANNALS. (Text in English) 1953. a. free to research and educational institutions. ‡ University of Tokyo, Institute of Social Science, 7-3-1 Hongo, Bunkyo-ku, Tokyo 113, Japan. circ. 200.
Formerly: Social Science Abstracts.

300 UK ISSN 0307-0042
UNIVERSITY OF WALES. BOARD OF CELTIC STUDIES. SOCIAL SCIENCE MONOGRAPHS. 1975. irreg. price varies. (Board of Celtic Studies) University of Wales Press, 6 Gwennyth St., Cathays, Cardiff CF2 4YD, Wales. Ed. Harold Carter.

300 AT
UNIVERSITY OF WESTERN AUSTRALIA. REPORT ON RESEARCH. 1950. a. University of Western Australia, Nedlands, W.A. 6009, Australia. Ed. M. Chesterton. circ. 1,500.

301.4 US
UNIVERSITY OF WISCONSIN, MADISON. INSTITUTE FOR RESEARCH ON POVERTY. DISCUSSION PAPER SERIES. 1967. irreg., no.820, 1986. $25. University of Wisconsin-Madison, Institute for Research on Poverty, 3412 Social Science Bldg., 1180 Observatory Dr., Madison, WI 53706. TEL 608-262-6358.

301.4 US
UNIVERSITY OF WISCONSIN, MADISON. INSTITUTE FOR RESEARCH ON POVERTY. MONOGRAPH SERIES. 1970. irreg., no.53, 1985. (University of Wisconsin-Madison, Institute for Research on Poverty) Academic Press, Inc., 3412 Social Science Bldg., 1180 Observatory Dr., Madison, WI 53706. TEL 305-345-2000.

301.45 US ISSN 0084-0769
UNIVERSITY OF WISCONSIN, MADISON. INSTITUTE FOR RESEARCH ON POVERTY. REPRINT SERIES. 1966. irreg., no.549, 1986. $20. University of Wisconsin-Madison, Institute for Research on Poverty, 3412 Social Sciences Bldg., 1180 Observatory Drive, Madison, WI 53706. TEL 608-262-6358.

301.4 US
UNIVERSITY OF WISCONSIN, MADISON. INSTITUTE FOR RESEARCH ON POVERTY. SPECIAL REPORT SERIES. 1966. irreg., no.42, 1986. price varies. University of Wisconsin-Madison, Institute for Research on Poverty, 3412 Social Science Bldg., 1180 Observatory Dr., Madison, WI 53706. TEL 608-262-6358.

300 ZA ISSN 0084-5108
UNIVERSITY OF ZAMBIA. INSTITUTE FOR AFRICAN STUDIES. COMMUNICATION. 1966. a. $5. University of Zambia, Box 32379, Lusaka, Zambia (Dist. by: Humanities Press, Inc., 171 First Ave., Atlantic Highlands, NJ 07016) Ed.Bd. circ. 750.

URBAN HISTORY YEARBOOK. see HISTORY — History Of Europe

VIDEO OUT DISTRIBUTION CATALOGUE. see ART

330 300 GW ISSN 0341-0846
VIERTELJAHRSCHRIFT FUER SOZIAL- UND WIRTSCHAFTSGESCHICHTE. BEIHEFTE. irreg., vol.81, 1987. price varies. Franz Steiner Verlag Wiesbaden GmbH, Birkenwaldstr. 44, Postfach 347, D-7000 Stuttgart 1, W. Germany (B.R.D.) Ed.Bd.

VIETNAMESE STUDIES. see HISTORY — History Of Asia

300 US
VIRGINIA SOCIAL SCIENCE JOURNAL. 1966. a. $12. Virginia Social Science Association, c/o Dr. Barbara B. Knight, Dept. of Public Affairs, George Mason University, 4400 University Dr., Fairfax, VA 22030. circ. 300. (back issues avail.)

300 060 FR ISSN 0083-6672
VISTI IZ SARSELIU. (Text in Ukrainian) 1963. irreg., no.28, 1986. $2. Societe Scientifique Sevcenko, 29, rue des Bauves, 95200 Sarcelles, France. Ed. Athanas Figol. circ. 1,000.

300 GW ISSN 0173-1955
VON DEUTSCHLAND NACH AMERIKA. irreg., vol.2, 1981. price varies. Franz Steiner Verlag Wiesbaden GmbH, Birkenwaldstr. 44, Postfach 347, D-7000 Stuttgart 1, W. Germany (B.R.D.) Ed. Guenter Moltmann.

300 US ISSN 0081-8682
WEST GEORGIA COLLEGE STUDIES IN THE SOCIAL SCIENCES. 1962. a. $4. West Georgia College, School of Arts and Sciences, Carrollton, GA 30118-0001. TEL 404-836-6449. Ed. Robert Claxton. adv. bk. rev. bibl. circ. 500.

300 960 US
WORKING PAPERS IN AFRICAN STUDIES. 1976. irreg., no.113, 1986. Boston University, African Studies Center, 270 Bay State Rd., Boston, MA 02215. TEL 617-353-3673.

300 US ISSN 0084-3326
YALE FASTBACKS. 1970. irreg., no.27, 1983. price varies. Yale University Press, 92A Yale Sta., New Haven, CT 06520. TEL 203-432-0940.

950 US ISSN 0513-4501
YALE SOUTHEAST ASIA STUDIES. MONOGRAPH SERIES. 1961. irreg., no.27, 1985. Yale University, Council on Southeast Asia Studies, Box 13A, 85 Trumbull St., New Haven, CT 06520. TEL 203-436-8897. Ed. M.K. Mansfield. adv. (reprint service avail. from UMI)

300 UK
YEARBOOK OF SOCIAL POLICY IN BRITAIN. a. £16.95. Routledge & Kegan Paul PLC, 11 New Fetter Lane, London EC4P 4EE, England (U.S. orders: 9 Park St., Boston, MA 02108) Ed. K. Jones.
Formerly: Yearbook of Social Studies.

300 US ISSN 0084-4209
YIVO ANNUAL OF JEWISH SOCIAL SCIENCE. 1946. irreg., vol.18, 1976. $18. Y I V O Institute for Jewish Research, 1048 Fifth Ave., New York, NY 10028. TEL 212-535-6700. Ed.Bd. index. circ. 2,000. Indexed: Hist.Abstr. SSCI. Amer.Hist.& Life. Lang.& Lang.Behav.Abstr.

300   US   ISSN 0084-4217
YIVO BLETER/YIVO PAGES. (Text in Yiddish; summaries in English) 1931. irreg., vol.46, 1975. $15. Y I V O Institute for Jewish Research, 1048 Fifth Ave., New York, NY 10028. TEL 212-535-6700. Ed.Bd. bk. rev. circ. 1,500. Indexed: Hist.Abstr. Amer.Hist.& Life.

100 300   JA   ISSN 0513-5621
YOKOHAMA NATIONAL UNIVERSITY. HUMANITIES. SECTION 1: PHILOSOPHY AND SOCIAL SCIENCES/YOKOHAMA KOKURITSU DAIGAKU JIMBUN KIYO DAI-1-RUI, TETSUGAKU, SHAKAI KAGAKU.* (Text in Japanese; summaries in English) 1953. a. Yokohama National University, Department of Sociology, 156 Tokiwadi, Hodogaya-ku, Yokohama 240, Japan.

300   YU   ISSN 0044-1937
ZBORNIK ZA DRUSTVENE NAUKE. (Text in Serbo-Croatian) 1915. a. Matica Srpska, Matice Srpske 1, Novi Sad, Yugoslavia. Ed. Miladen Stojanov.
Cyrillic alphabet

SOCIAL SCIENCES: COMPREHENSIVE WORKS —
Abstracting, Bibliographies, Statistics

300 314   BE   ISSN 0067-5563
BELGIUM. INSTITUT NATIONAL DE STATISTIQUE. STATISTIQUES SOCIALES. (Text in Dutch and French) 1970. irreg. (1-4/yr.) 290 Fr. Institut National de Statistique, 44 rue de Louvain, 1000 Brussels, Belgium. Indexed: P.A.I.S.For.Lang.Ind.

300 016   US
BIBLIOGRAPHIE COURANTE D'ARTICLES DE PERIODIQUES POSTERIEURS A 1944 SUR LES PROBLEMES POLITIQUES, ECONOMIQUES ET SOCIAUX/INDEX TO POST-1944 PERIODICAL ARTICLES ON POLITICAL, ECONOMIC AND SOCIAL PROBLEMS. 1968. a. (Fondation Nationale des Sciences Politiques, FR) G.K. Hall & Co., 70 Lincoln St., Boston, MA 02111. TEL 617-423-3990.

300 054.1   FR
BIBLIOGRAPHIE DES TRAVAUX EN LANGUE FRANCAISE SUR L'AFRIQUE AU SUD DU SAHARA, SCIENCES HUMAINES ET SOCIALES. a. Centre d'Etudes Africaines, 54 bd. Raspail, 75006 Paris, France.

300   BE
BIBLIOGRAPHIE ETHNOGRAPHIQUE DE L'AFRIQUE SUD-SAHARIENNE; sciences humaines et sociales. 1932. a., latest 1984 (covers 1980) 1200 Fr. Musee Royal de l'Afrique Centrale, 13 Steenweg op Leuven, B-1980 Tervuren, Belgium.
Formerly (until 1962): Bibliographie Ethnographique du Congo Belge et des Regions Avoisinantes.

300 016   II
BIBLIOGRAPHY OF DOCTORAL DISSERTATIONS: SOCIAL SCIENCES AND HUMANITIES. (Text in English) 1974. a. Rs.90. Association of Indian Universities, Deen Dayal Upadhyay Marg, New Delhi 110 002, India. circ. 500.

CURRENT DIGEST OF THE SOVIET PRESS. see *POLITICAL SCIENCE — Abstracting, Bibliographies, Statistics*

300 020 015   UK   ISSN 0267-1964
CURRENT RESEARCH IN BRITAIN. SOCIAL SCIENCES. 1980. a. £46. British Library, Document Supply Centre, Boston Spa, Wetherby, West Yorkshire LS23 7BQ, England. Ed. A. Young.
Formerly: Research in British Universities Polytechnics and Colleges. Vol.3: Social Sciences (ISSN 0143-0742)

DISSERTATION ABSTRACTS INTERNATIONAL. SECTION A: HUMANITIES AND SOCIAL SCIENCES. see *HUMANITIES: COMPREHENSIVE WORKS — Abstracting, Bibliographies, Statistics*

300 016   BO
EXTENSION BIBLIOGRAFICA. 1974. irreg., no.10, 1984. price varies. Centro de Investigaciones Sociales, Casilla 6931 - C.C., La Paz, Bolivia.

314   FI
FINLAND. TILASTOKESKUS. TILASTOLLISIA TIEDONANTOJA. KULTTUURITILASTO/FINLAND. STATISTIKCENTRALEN. STATISTISKA MEDDELANDEN KULTURSTATISTIK/FINLAND. CENTRAL STATISTICAL OFFICE. STATISTICAL SURVEYS. CULTURAL STATISTICS. (Text in English, Finnish and Swedish) 1978. irreg., latest 1981. Fmk.150. Tilastokeskus, Annankatu 44, SF-00100 Helsinki 10, Finland (Subscr. to: Government Printing Centre, Box 516, SF-00101 Helsinki 10, Finland)

300 016   US
FUTURE - ABSTRACTS.* 1975. m. $110 individuals; $295 corporations. Futuremics, Inc., 1629 K St., N.W., Ste. 5129 L, Washington, DC 20006. Eds. Kent Myers, Sandra Lauffer. bk. rev. film rev. abstr. bibl. charts. stat. index. circ. 500. (cards; back issues avail.)

300 016   US
GUIDE TO ALTERNATIVE PERIODICALS. 1980. a. price varies. New Pages Press, 4426 S. Belsay Rd., Grand Blanc, MI 48439. TEL 313-742-9583. Ed. Casey Hill. adv. illus.

300 011   TH   ISSN 0125-5827
INDEX TO THAI PERIODICAL LITERATURE. (Text in Thai) 1964. a. $14. National Institute of Development Administration, Library and Information Center, Klongjan, Bangkapi, Bangkok 10240, Thailand. index. circ. 200.

016.3091   II
INDIA. MINISTRY OF EDUCATION AND SOCIAL WELFARE. DEPARTMENT OF SOCIAL WELFARE. DOCUMENTATION SERVICE BULLETIN. 1968. a. free. ‡ Ministry of Education and Social Welfare, Department of Social Welfare, Shastri Bhavan, New Delhi 110001, India. circ. controlled.

JAPAN. MINISTRY OF HEALTH AND WELFARE. STATISTICS AND INFORMATION DEPARTMENT. REPORT ON SURVEY OF SOCIO-ECONOMIC ASPECTS ON VITAL EVENTS. see *BUSINESS AND ECONOMICS — Abstracting, Bibliographies, Statistics*

JAPANESE PERIODICALS INDEX. HUMANITIES AND SOCIAL SCIENCE SECTION/ZASSHI KIJI SAKUIN. JIMBUN SHAKAI-HEN. see *HUMANITIES: COMPREHENSIVE WORKS — Abstracting, Bibliographies, Statistics*

300 016   UK   ISSN 0076-051X
LONDON BIBLIOGRAPHY OF THE SOCIAL SCIENCES. 1931. a. price varies. (British Library of Political and Economic Science) Mansell Publishing Ltd., 6 All Saints St., London N1 9RL, England (Dist. in U.S. by: H.W. Wilson Co., 950 University Ave., Bronx, NY 10452)

300   NE   ISSN 0168-5988
NETHERLANDS. CENTRAAL BUREAU VOOR DE STATISTIEK. BIBLIOGRAFIE VAN REGIONALE ONDERZOEKINGEN OP SOCIAALWETENSCHAPPELIJK TERREIN. BIBLIOGRAPHY OF REGIONAL STUDIES IN THE SOCIAL SCIENCES. (Text in Dutch and English) 1945. a., 1981 latest supplement. fl.14.40. Centraal Bureau voor de Statistiek, Prinses Beatrixlaan 428, Voorburg, Netherlands (Orders to: Staatsuitgeverij, Christoffel Plantijnstraat, The Hague, Netherlands)

300 310   NR
NIGERIA. FEDERAL OFFICE OF STATISTICS. SOCIAL STATISTICS IN NIGERIA. a. £N2. Federal Office of Statistics, P.M.B. 12528, Lagos, Nigeria.

800 011 300   US
NOTABLE CHILDREN'S TRADE BOOKS IN THE FIELD OF SOCIAL STUDIES. 1971. a. (National Council for the Social Studies, Joint Committee Project) Children's Book Council, Inc., 67 Irving Pl., New York, NY 10003. TEL 212-254-2666. Ed. Jeanette Brod.
Grades K-8

P A I S BULLETIN. (Public Affairs Information Service, Inc.) see *BUSINESS AND ECONOMICS — Abstracting, Bibliographies, Statistics*

016 300   US   ISSN 0091-3707
SOCIAL SCIENCES CITATION INDEX. Short title: S S C. (Includes Source Index, Citation Index, Permuterm Subject Index, and Corporate Index.) 1969. 3/yr. (including annual cum.) $3100. Institute for Scientific Information, 3501 Market St., Philadelphia, PA 19104 TEL 215-386-0100. (And 132 High St., Uxbridge, Middlesex, UB8 1DP, England) 5-yr. cum.index: 1966-1970; 1971-1975; 1976-1980; 1981-1985.
●Also available online. Vendors: BRS, CISTI, DIALOG.

300   US   ISSN 0161-3162
SOCIAL SCIENCES CITATION INDEX JOURNAL CITATION REPORTS. Short title: SSCI-J C R. (Includes Journal Ranking, Reference Data, and Soruce Data Packages) 1977. a. $275 (included in subscr. to Social Sciences Citation Index) Institute for Scientific Information, 3501 Market St., Philadelphia, PA 19104 TEL 215-386-0100. (And 132 High St., Uxbridge, Middlesex., UB8 1DP, England)
Formerly: I S I Journal Citation Reports.

300 016   US   ISSN 0094-4920
SOCIAL SCIENCES INDEX; an author and subject index to periodicals in the fields of anthropology, area studies, economics, environmental science, geography, law and criminology, medical sciences, political science, psychology, public administration, sociology and related subjects. 1974. q. (annual cumulations) service basis. ‡ H. W. Wilson Co., 950 University Ave., Bronx, NY 10452. TEL 212-588-8400. Ed. Joseph Bloomfield. (avail. on CD-ROM)
●Also available online. Vendors: Wilsonline.
Supersedes in part: Social Sciences and Humanities Index (ISSN 0037-7899)

972   US
SYRACUSE UNIVERSITY. FOREIGN AND COMPARATIVE STUDIES. LATIN AMERICAN SERIES. (Former name of issuing body: Maxwell School of Citizenship and Public Affairs) 1980. irreg., no.8, 1986. price varies. Syracuse University, Foreign and Comparative Studies, 724 Comstock Ave., Syracuse, NY 13244. TEL 315-423-2552. Ed. Rolena Adorno.

950   US
SYRACUSE UNIVERSITY. FOREIGN AND COMPARATIVE STUDIES. SOUTH ASIAN SERIES. (Former name of issuing body: Maxwell School of Citizenship and Public Affairs) 1976. irreg., no.11, 1986. price varies. Syracuse University, Foreign and Comparative Studies, 724 Comstock Ave., Syracuse, NY 13244. TEL 315-423-2552. Ed. Robert N. Kearney.

011   II
UNION CATALOGUE OF SOCIAL SCIENCE PERIODICALS/SERIALS. (Text in English) 1973. irreg. Rs.1530($460) (Indian Council of Social Science Research) Social Science Documentation Centre, 35 Ferozshah Rd., New Delhi 110001, India. Ed. S.P. Agrawal. bibl. index. circ. 1,000.
Formerly: I C S S R Union Catalogue of Social Science Periodicals/Serials.

016   US   ISSN 0565-0828
U.S. BUREAU OF THE CENSUS. CENSUS BUREAU METHODOLOGICAL RESEARCH; an annotated list of papers and reports. irreg. U.S. Bureau of the Census, Customer Services, Washington, DC 20233 TEL 301-763-4100. (Orders to: Supt. of Documents, Washington, DC 20402)
Key Title: Census Bureau Methodological Research.

300 015   JM
UNIVERSITY OF THE WEST INDIES. INSTITUTE OF SOCIAL AND ECONOMIC RESEARCH. OCCASIONAL BIBLIOGRAPHY SERIES. 1974. irreg. University of the West Indies, Institute of Social and Economic Research, Mona 7, Kingston, Jamaica.

SOCIAL SERVICES AND WELFARE

300 US ISSN 0734-9033
WHOLE AGAIN RESOURCE GUIDE; periodical and resource directory. 1982. irreg., 2nd edt. 1987. $24.95. SourceNet, Box 6767, Santa Barbara, CA 93160. TEL 805-964-6066. Ed. Tim Ryan. bk. rev. bibl. illus. index. circ. 5,000. (back issues avail.)
Incorporating: International Guide to Psi-Periodicals (ISSN 0277-9870)

300 016 UN
WORLD DIRECTORY OF SOCIAL SCIENCE INSTITUTIONS. (Text in English and French) 1970. irreg., latest 1985. Unesco, 7 Place de Fontenoy, 75700 Paris, France (Dist. in U.S. by: Bernan Associates-Unipub, 4611-F Assembly Dr., Lanham, MD 20706)
Formerly: World Index of Social Science Institutions.

300 UN ISSN 0084-1870
WORLD LIST OF SOCIAL SCIENCE PERIODICALS. (Text in English and French) irreg. Unesco, 7-9 Place de Fontenoy, 75700 Paris, France (Dist. in U.S. by: Bernan Associates-Unipub, 4611-F Assembly Dr., Lanham, MD 20706-4391)

SOCIAL SERVICES AND WELFARE

see also Blind; Deaf; Drug Abuse and Alcoholism; Public Health and Safety

360 614 CN ISSN 0381-4327
ALBERTA. DEPARTMENT OF SOCIAL SERVICES AND COMMUNITY HEALTH. ANNUAL REPORT. 1972. a. free. Social Services and Community Health, Seventh St. Plaza, 10030 107th St., Edmonton. Alta. T5J 3E4, Canada. TEL 403-427-4801. Ed. John Gibson. circ. 1,200.
Formerly: Alberta. Department of Health and Social Development. Annual Report (ISSN 0084-6163)

ALBERTA. HEALTH AND SOCIAL SERVICES DISCIPLINES COMMITTEE. ANNUAL REPORT. see PUBLIC HEALTH AND SAFETY

362.41 US ISSN 0065-8359
AMERICAN FOUNDATION FOR THE BLIND. ANNUAL REPORT. 1923. a. free. American Foundation for the Blind, Inc., 15 W. 16 St, New York, NY 10011. TEL 212-620-2000. (also avail. in microfiche; reprint service avail. from UMI)

361.7 US ISSN 0071-9617
AMERICAN FRIENDS SERVICE COMMITTEE. ANNUAL REPORT. 1917. a. free to contributors. American Friends Service Committee, 1501 Cherry St., Philadelphia, PA 19102.

361.7 US
AMERICAN HUMANE ASSOCIATION ANNUAL REPORT. 1952. a., 1974. American Humane Association, 9725 E. Hampden Ave., Denver, CO 80231. TEL 303-695-0811. Ed. Carol Moulton. circ. 3,000.
Formerly: American Humane Association. National Humane Report (ISSN 0065-8596)

361.6 US ISSN 0163-8300
AMERICAN PUBLIC WELFARE ASSOCIATION. W - MEMO. 1961. irreg. (20-25/yr) $50. American Public Welfare Association, 1125 15th St. N.W., Washington, DC 20005. TEL 202-293-7550. (looseleaf format)

361 US
AMERICAN RED CROSS. ANNUAL REPORT. 1901. a. free. American National Red Cross, 17th and D Sts., N.W., Washington, DC 20006. Ed. Betty Wagner. circ. 30,000.
Formerly: American National Red Cross. Annual Report (ISSN 0080-0384)

360 368.4 US ISSN 0191-118X
ANALYSIS OF WORKERS' COMPENSATION LAWS. a. $12. Chamber of Commerce of the U.S., 1615 H St., N.W., Washington, DC 20062. TEL 202-659-6000.
Formerly: Analysis of Workmen's Compensation Laws (ISSN 0577-5183)

ANNUAIRE H L M. (Habitations a Loyer Modere) see HOUSING AND URBAN PLANNING

309.1 US ISSN 0272-4464
ANNUAL EDITIONS: SOCIAL PROBLEMS. 1973. a. $9.50. Dushkin Publishing Group, Inc., Guilford, CT 06437. TEL 203-453-4351. Ed. Ian Nielsen. illus. Indexed: Soc.Sci.Ind. Lang.& Lang.Behav.Abstr.
Formerly: Annual Editions: Readings in Social Problems (ISSN 0094-9183)

360 US ISSN 0197-2251
ANNUAL REVIEW OF REHABILITATION. 1980. a. price varies. Springer Publishing Company, 536 Broadway, New York, NY 10012. TEL 212-431-4370. Eds. E.L. Pan, S.S. Newman. circ. 417. Indexed: Ind.Med. Psychol.Abstr.

353.9 610 US
ARKANSAS. DIVISION OF REHABILITATION SERVICES. ANNUAL REPORT. 1940. a. Division of Rehabilitation Services, Box 3781, Little Rock, AR 72203. TEL 501-371-2411. illus. stat. circ. 1,000.
Rehabilitation

362.41 US ISSN 0067-9186
ASSOCIATION FOR EDUCATION AND REHABILITATION OF THE BLIND AND VISUALLY IMPAIRED. YEARBOOK. 1964. a. $15.50 domestic; foreign $17.50 (free to members) Association for Education and Rehabilitation of the Blind and Visually Impaired, 206 N. Washington St., Ste. 320, Alexandria, VA 22314. TEL 703-548-1884. Ed. Teresa DeFerrari. circ. 6,000.
Incorporates (1976-1982): Blindness, Visual Impairment, Deaf-Blindness; Which was formerly (until 1983): Blindness.

AUSTRALIA NEW ZEALAND FOUNDATION. ANNUAL REPORT (YEAR); promoting friendship across the Tasman. see POLITICAL SCIENCE — International Relations

368.4 AT
AUSTRALIAN SUPERANNUATION AND EMPLOYEE BENEFITS GUIDE. 1972. irreg., approx. 10/yr. Aus.$388. C C H Australia Ltd., Box 230, North Ryde, N.S.W. 2113, Australia.
Formerly: Australian Superannuation and Employee Benefits Planning in Action (ISSN 0310-1347)

362.7 AU
AUSTRIA. STATISTISCHES ZENTRALAMT. JUGENDWOHLFAHRTSPFLEGE. vol.327, 1972. a. S.65. Hintere Zollamtstr. 2b, A-1033 Vienna, Austria.

361 UK ISSN 0260-082X
B A A F DISCUSSION SERIES. irreg. British Agencies for Adoption & Fostering, 11 Southwark St., London SE1 1RQ, England.

362.7 UK ISSN 0260-3888
B A A F NEWS. 1981. irreg. British Agencies for Adoption & Fostering, 11 Southwark St., London SE1 1RQ, England.
Formerly: A B A F A News.

361 UK
B A A F PRACTICE SERIES. irreg. British Agencies for Adoption and Fostering, 11 Southwark St., London SE1 1RQ, England.

361 UK
B A A F RESEARCH SERIES. irreg. British Agencies for Adoption & Fostering, 11 Southwark St., London SE1 1RQ, England.

371.3 360 IO
BALAI PENDIDIKAN DAN LATIHAN TENAGA SOCIAL. LAPORAN. a. Balai Pendidikan dan Latihan Tenaga Sosial, Jl. Laksamana Laut R.E. Martadinata 112, Badung, Indonesia.
Study and teaching

360 614 BE
BELGIUM. MINISTERE DE LA SANTE PUBLIQUE ET DE LA FAMILLE. RAPPORT ANNUEL. (Text in Dutch and French) 1954. a. Ministere de la Sante Publique et de la Famille, Cite Administrative de l'Etat, Bibliotheque, Quartier Vesale, 1010 Brussels, Belgium. charts. stat.

613.62 360 BE
BELGIUM. MINISTERIE VAN VOLKSGEZONDHEID EN VAN HET GEZIN. CENTRUM VOOR BEVOLKINGS- EN GEZINSSTUDIES. TECHNISCH RAPPORT. (Text in Dutch) no.6, 1975. irreg. Ministerie van Volksgezondheid en van het Gezin, Hotel Lendi-Manhattan Center, Rue des Croisades 3, 1000 Brussels, Belgium. charts. stat.

360 BL
BEMFAM.* vol.10, 1976. irreg. Sociedade Civil Bem-Estar Familiar no Brasil, Rua das Laranjeiras 308, 20000 Rio de Janeiro, Brazil. Ed. Walter Rodrigues.

360 DK ISSN 0108-8351
BISTANDSHAANDBOGEN; opslagsbog for medarbejdere i social- og sundhedssektoren. 1983. a. Kr.341.60 to individuals; institutions KR.290.35. Forlag for Social- og Sundhedssektor, Vaerkstedsgaarden 7, 2620 Albertslund, Copenhagen. illus.

361.8 US
BLACK PAPERS. irreg. New York Urban League, 218 W. 40th St., New York, NY 10018. TEL 212-730-5200.

360 GW ISSN 0067-9178
BLICK HINTER DIE FASSADE; Aspekte moderner Sozialarbeit. 1961. a. DM.90. Kodex-Verlag GmbH, Eugenstr. 16, 7000 Stuttgart 1, W. Germany (B.R.D.)

361.6 BL
BRASILIA. FUNDACAO DO SERVICO SOCIAL DO DISTRITO FEDERAL. RELATORIO ANUAL DAS ATIVIDADES. a. Fundacao do Servico Social do Distrito Federal, Brasilia, Brazil.

360 BL
BRAZIL. SERVICO SOCIAL DO COMERCIO. ADMINISTRACAO REGIONAL DO ESTADO DE SAO PAULO. RELATORIA ANNUAL. 1958. a. free. Servico Social do Comercio, Administracao Regional do Estado de Sao Paulo, Rua Dr. Vila Nova, 228, Sao Paulo, Brazil. illus. circ. 2,000.

361 UK
BRITISH ASSOCIATION OF SOCIAL WORKERS. ANNUAL REPORT. 1970. a. £2. British Association of Social Workers, 16 Kent St., Birmingham B5 6RD, England. adv. bk. rev. bibl. tr.lit. circ. 14,000.

361 CN
BRITISH COLUMBIA. MINISTRY OF SOCIAL SERVICES AND HOUSING. SERVICES FOR PEOPLE. ANNUAL REPORT (YEAR) 1945. a. free. Ministry of Social Services and Housing, Parliament Buildings, Victoria, British Columbia V8V 1X4, Canada. TEL 604-387-4421. circ. 1,200.
Former titles: British Columbia. Ministry of Human Resources. Services for People (ISSN 0317-4670); British Columbia. Department of Human Resources. Annual Report (ISSN 0068-1466)

360 US
CALIFORNIA STATE PLAN FOR REHABILITATION FACILITIES. a. Health and Welfare Agency, Department of Rehabilitation, 830 K St. Mall, Sacramento, CA 95814.

CANADA. DEPARTMENT OF NATIONAL HEALTH AND WELFARE. ANNUAL REPORT. see PUBLIC HEALTH AND SAFETY

300 CN ISSN 0068-8584
CANADIAN COUNCIL ON SOCIAL DEVELOPMENT. ANNUAL REPORT/RAPPORT ANNUEL. (Text in English and French) 1920. a. membership. Canadian Council on Social Development, 55 Parkdale Ave., Box 3505, Station C, Ottawa, Ont. K1Y 4G1, Canada. TEL 613-728-1865. circ. 6,000.

360 CN
CANADIAN FACT BOOK ON POVERTY/DONNEES DE BASE SUR LA PAUVRETE AU CANADA. 1975. irreg. Can.$7.95. Canadian Council on Social Development, 55 Parkdale Ave., Box 3505, Station C, Ottawa, Ont. K1Y 4G1, Canada.

CANADIAN NATIONAL INSTITUTE FOR THE BLIND. NATIONAL ANNUAL REPORT. see BLIND

SOCIAL SERVICES AND WELFARE

362.4   CN   ISSN 0068-9424
CANADIAN PARAPLEGIC ASSOCIATION. ANNUAL REPORT. 1946. a. free. ‡ Canadian Paraplegic Association, National Office, 520 Sutherland Drive, Toronto, Ont. M4G 3V9, Canada. TEL 416-422-5640. Ed. Peter Bernauer. circ. 5,000.
Rehabilitation

CANADIAN PERSPECTIVE. see *BUSINESS AND ECONOMICS* — *Labor And Industrial Relations*

361.5   CN   ISSN 0068-9572
CANADIAN RED CROSS SOCIETY. ANNUAL REPORT. (Text in English and French) 1914. a. free. ‡ Canadian Red Cross Society, National Headquarters, 95 Wellesley St. E., Toronto, Ont. M4Y 1H6, Canada. TEL 416-923-6692. circ. 60,000.

360   CN
CANADIAN SOCIAL WORK REVIEW. (Text in English and French) 1974. a. Can.$18($22) (Can.$9 for students) Canadian Association of Schools of Social Work, 55 Parkdale Ave., Ottawa, Ont. K1Y 1E5, Canada. TEL 613-563-1217. Eds. Shankar A. Yelaja and Robert Mayer. adv. bk. rev. circ. 350.
Supersedes (in 1983): Canadian Journal of Social Work Education (ISSN 0316-8565)

361   GW   ISSN 0069-0570
CARITAS; JAHRBUCH DES DEUTSCHEN CARITASVERBANDES. 1968. a. DM.12.80($4) Deutscher Caritasverband, Karlstr. 40, 7800 Freiburg, W. Germany (B.R.D.)

361   US
CATHOLIC RELIEF SERVICES. ANNUAL REPORT. a. Catholic Relief Services, 1011 First Ave., New York, NY 10022. TEL 212-838-4700.

360   UK   ISSN 0590-9783
CHARITIES DIGEST. 1882. a. £7.65. Family Welfare Association, 501-505 Kingsland Rd., London E8 4AU, England. Ed.Bd. adv. circ. 6,000.

CHARTERED INSTITUTE OF PUBLIC FINANCE AND ACCOUNTANCY. PROBATION. ESTIMATES. see *SOCIAL SERVICES AND WELFARE* — *Abstracting, Bibliographies, Statistics*

360   UK   ISSN 0140-8291
CHARTERED INSTITUTE OF PUBLIC FINANCE AND ACCOUNTANCY. PROBATION STATISTICS. ACTUALS. 1984. a. £10. Chartered Institute of Public Finance and Accountancy, 3 Robert St., London WC2N 6BH, England.

362.7   US
CHILD WELFARE LEAGUE OF AMERICA. DIRECTORY OF MEMBER AND ASSOCIATE AGENCIES. a. $14. Child Welfare League of America, Inc., 440 First St., Ste. 310, Washington, DC 20001. TEL 202-638-2952.
Former titles: Child Welfare League of America. Directory of Member And Associate Agencies Listing; Child Welfare League of America. Directory of Member Agencies and Associates (ISSN 0529-1674)

360   SP
COLECCION CUADERNOS DE TRABAJO SOCIAL. 1973. irreg., no.4, 1974. price varies. (Universidad de Navarra, Escuela de Asistentes Sociales) Ediciones Universidad de Navarra, S.A., Apdo. 396, 31080 Pamplona, Spain.

COLLEGES AND UNIVERSITIES WITH ACCREDITED UNDERGRADUATE SOCIAL WORK PROGRAMS. see *EDUCATION* — *Higher Education*

361.8   US
COMMUNITY RESOURCES DIRECTORY. 1984. a. $115. Gale Research Company, Book Tower, Detroit, MI 48226. Ed. Harriet Clyde Kipps.

309.2   UK   ISSN 0307-6067
COMMUNITY WORK. 1974. irreg. price varies. Routledge & Kegan Paul PLC, 11 New Fetter Lane, London EC4P 4EE, England (U.S. orders to: 9 Park St., Boston, MA 02108)

CONSUMERS AFFAIRS COUNCIL OF TASMANIA. ANNUAL REPORT. see *CONSUMER EDUCATION AND PROTECTION*

CONTEMPORARY EVALUATION RESEARCH. see *SOCIAL SCIENCES: COMPREHENSIVE WORKS*

361.7 380   US   ISSN 0197-937X
CORPORATE 500: THE DIRECTORY OF CORPORATE PHILANTHROPY. 1980. a. $20-Public Management Institute, 358 Brannan St., San Francisco, CA 94107 TEL 415-896-1900. (Subscr. to: Gale Research Co., Book Tower, Detroit, MI 48226) Ed. Kenneth Gilman. circ. 2,000.

360   UN   ISSN 0538-8295
COST OF SOCIAL SECURITY. irreg. price varies. International Labour Office - Bureau International du Travail, Publications Sales Service, CH-1211 Geneva 22, Switzerland (U.S. distributors: I L O Branch Office, 1750 New York Ave. N.W., Washington, DC 20006)

360 327   FR
COUNCIL OF EUROPE. COMMITTEE OF INDEPENDENT EXPERTS ON THE EUROPEAN SOCIAL CHARTER. CONCLUSIONS. (Text in English; French edition also available) 1970. biennial. price varies. Council of Europe, Publications Section, 67006 Strasbourg, France (Dist. in U.S. by: Manhattan Publishing Co., Box 650, Croton-on-Hudson, N.Y. 10520)

CRIMINAL INJURIES COMPENSATION. see *LAW*

360   BL
CRITICA SOCIAL. 1974. irreg. Universidade Catolica de Minas Gerais, Escola de Servico Social, Av. Dom Jose Gaspar 500, Belo Horizonte 30000, Minas Gerais, Brazil.

361   CY   ISSN 0070-2404
CYPRUS. DEPARTMENT OF SOCIAL WELFARE SERVICES. ANNUAL REPORT. (Text in Greek; summaries in English avail.) 1952. a. free. Department of Social Welfare Services, c/o Director, Nicosia, Cyprus.

DELAWARE. DEPARTMENT OF HEALTH AND SOCIAL SERVICE. ANNUAL REPORT. see *PUBLIC HEALTH AND SAFETY*

360   DK   ISSN 0583-712X
DENMARK. SOCIALFORSKNINGSINSTITUTT. PUBLIKATION. 1985. irreg. Kr.60. (Socialforskningsinstitutt) Bibliotekscentralen, Telegrafvej 5, DK-2750 Ballerup, Denmark.

361   DK   ISSN 0081-0584
DENMARK. SOCIALFORSKNINGSINSTITUTTET. BERETNING OM SOCIALFORSKNINGSINSTITUTTETS VIRKSOMHED. Cover title: Denmark. Socialforskningsinstituttet. Socialforskningsinstituttets Virksomhed. 1960. a. price varies. Socialforskningsinstituttet - Danish National Institute of Social Research, Borgergade 28, DK-1300 Copenhagen K, Denmark.

301   DK
DENMARK. SOCIALFORSKNINGSINSTITUTTET. MEDDELELSER. 1972. irreg., no.46, 1986. price varies. Socialforskningsinstituttet - Danish National Institute of Social Research, Borgergade 28, DK-1300 Copenhagen K, Denmark.

301   DK
DENMARK. SOCIALFORSKNINGSINSTITUTTET. PJECER. 1973. irreg., no.16, 1985. price varies. Socialforskningsinstituttet - Danish National Institute of Social Research, 28 Borgergade, DK-1300 Copenhagen K, Denmark.

301   DK
DENMARK. SOCIALFORSKNINGSINSTITUTTET. PUBLIKATIONER. (Text in Danish; summaries in English) 1960. irreg., no.153, 1986. price varies. Socialforskningsinstituttet - Danish National Institute of Social Research, Borgergade 28, DK-1300 Copenhagen K, Denmark.

301   DK
DENMARK. SOCIALFORSKNINGSINSTITUTTET. SMAATRYK. 1973. irreg., no.13, 1985. Socialforskningsinstituttet - Danish National Institute of Social Research, Borgergade 28, DK-1300 Copenhagen K, Denmark.

301   DK
DENMARK. SOCIALFORSKNINGSINSTITUTTET. STUDIER. (Text in Danish; summaries occasionally in English) 1962. irreg., no.52, 1986. price varies. Socialforskningsinstituttet - Danish National Institute of Social Research, Borgergade 28, DK-1300 Copenhagen K, Denmark.

361.7   US
DIRECTORY. DIOCESAN AGENCIES OF CATHOLIC CHARITIES AND CATHOLIC CHARITIES U S A MEMBER INSTITUTIONS. UNITED STATES, PUERTO RICO AND CANADA. a. $10. Catholic Charities U S A, 1319 F. St., N.W., Washington, DC 20004. TEL 202-639-8400.
Former titles: Directory. Diocesan Agencies of Catholic Charities and NCCC Member Institutions. United States, Puerto Rico and Canada; Directory. Diocesan Agencies of Catholic Charities. United States, Puerto Rico and Canada (ISSN 0091-1003)

360   UK   ISSN 0309-4413
DIRECTORY FOR DISABLED PEOPLE. 1977. irreg. £12.50. Woodhead-Faulkner (Publishers) Ltd., Fitzwilliam House, 32 Trumpington St., Cambridge CB2, England. Eds. Ann Darnbrough, Derek Kinrade. (back issues avail.)

360   UK
DIRECTORY OF AIDS FOR DISABLED AND ELDERLY PEOPLE. 1986. irreg. £14.95. Woodhead-Faulkner (Publishers) Ltd., Fitzwilliam House, 32 Trumpington St., Cambridge CB2 1QY, England.

362   UK   ISSN 0070-5268
DIRECTORY OF CHURCH OF ENGLAND SOCIAL SERVICES. 1950. biennial. 65p. Church of England, Board for Social Responsibility, Church House, Deans Yard, London, SW1P 3NZ, England. Ed. Alison Webster. circ. 1,000. (also avail. in microfiche)
Formerly: Directory of Church of England Moral and Social Welfare Work.

360   US
DIRECTORY OF COMMUNITY RESOURCES AND SERVICES. 1943. a. $35. United Way of the Texas Gulf Coast, 1010 Waugh Dr., Box 13668, Houston, TX 77219. TEL 713-525-8596. Ed. Valerie D. Cook. index. circ. 1,800. (looseleaf format)

361.6   CN   ISSN 0315-0631
DIRECTORY OF COMMUNITY SERVICES IN METROPOLITAN TORONTO. 1938. a. Can.$40. Community Information Centre of Metropolitan Toronto, 34 King St. E., Third Floor, Toronto, Ont. M5C 1E5, Canada. TEL 416-863-1941. Ed. Stephen MacDonald. circ. 6,000.

361.6   CN   ISSN 0319-258X
DIRECTORY OF COMMUNITY SERVICES OF GREATER MONTREAL; welfare-health-recreation. (Text in English and French) 1956. biennial. Can.$20. Information and Referral Centre of Greater Montreal Foundation, 1800 Dorchester Blvd. W., Montreal H3H 2H2, Canada. TEL 514-931-2292. Ed.Bd. circ. 3,500.
Formerly: Directory of Health, Welfare and Recreation Services of Greater Montreal (ISSN 0070-5640)

360   US
DIRECTORY OF FEDERAL AID FOR HEALTH AND ALLIED FIELDS. irreg. Ready Reference Press, Box 5879, Santa Monica, CA 90405.

362.6   US
DIRECTORY OF FEDERAL AID FOR THE AGING. irreg. Ready Reference Press, Box 5879, Santa Monica, CA 90405.

362.4 371   US
DIRECTORY OF FEDERAL AID FOR THE HANDICAPPED. irreg. Ready Reference Press, Box 5879, Santa Monica, CA 90405.

360   UK   ISSN 0070-5624
DIRECTORY OF GRANT-MAKING TRUSTS. 1968. biennial. £46. Charities Aid Foundation, 48 Pembury Rd., Tonbridge TN9 2JD, Kent, England. Ed. Anne Villemur. circ. 3,500.

SOCIAL SERVICES AND WELFARE

361.7 US ISSN 0161-2638
DIRECTORY OF JEWISH FEDERATIONS, WELFARE FUNDS AND COMMUNITY COUNCILS. 1936. a. $10. ‡ Council of Jewish Federations, Inc., 730 Broadway, 2nd Fl., New York, NY 10003. index. circ. 1,000.
Formerly: Jewish Federations, Welfare Funds and Community Councils Directory (ISSN 0075-3734)

DIRECTORY OF NEBRASKA SERVICES. see *PUBLIC ADMINISTRATION*

360 US
DIRECTORY OF NURSING HOME FACILITIES. 1982. irreg. $125. Oryx Press, 2214 N. Central at Encanto, Ste. 103, Phoenix, AZ 85004. TEL 602-254-6156. Ed. Sam Mongeau.

362.8 US ISSN 0362-7179
DIRECTORY OF SERVICES FOR MIGRANT FAMILIES/DIRECTORIO DE SERVICIOS PARA FAMILIAS MIGRANTES. (Text in English and Spanish) 1975. irreg. Office of Education, Migrant Education Section, Springfield, IL 62777. TEL 217-782-4321.

361.8 AT
DIRECTORY OF SHELTERED WORKSHOPS, ACTIVITY CENTRES AND OTHER VOCATIONAL REHABILITATION FACILITIES IN N.S.W AND A.C.T. 1970. a. Aus.$5. Association of Rehabilitation Facilities, 17/4 Selems Parade, Revesby, NSW 2212, Australia. Ed. Robert A. Brooks. circ. 800.

360 614 US ISSN 0085-0012
DIRECTORY OF SOCIAL AND HEALTH AGENCIES OF NEW YORK CITY. 1883. biennial. $24. (Community Council of Greater New York) Columbia University Press, 562 W. 113th St., New York, NY 10025. TEL 212-678-6777. Eds. Rowena McDade, William James Smith. circ. 7,000.

362.1 AT ISSN 0812-4663
DISABILITY AIDS DIRECTORY. 1984. biennial. Mount Eagle Publications Pty. Ltd., P.O. Box 84, Heidelberg, Victoria 3084, Australia. Ed. Kennith Lloyd Jones. adv. bibl. index. circ. 10,000.

362.6 DK ISSN 0107-8275
E G V INFORMATION. no.16, 1981. irreg. price varies. Ensomme Gamles Vaern, Tingskiftevej 2, 2900 Hellerup, Denmark.

360 NE
E I S S YEARBOOK/E I S S ANNUAIRE. (Text in English and French) a. price varies. (European Institute for Social Security) Kluwer Law and Taxation Publishers, Box 23, 7400 GA Deventer, Netherlands. illus.

361 US ISSN 0071-0237
ENCYCLOPEDIA OF SOCIAL WORK. 1929. irreg., approx. every 10 yrs., no.18, 1986. $75 (includes supplement) National Association of Social Workers, Publications Department, 7981 Eastern Ave., Silver Spring, MD 20910. TEL 301-565-0333. Ed. Anne Minahan. circ. 25,000. Indexed: Abstr.Soc.Work.
Formerly: Social Work Year Book.

360 IS
ETGAR (TEL AVIV) 1975. irreg. free. Havaad Hapoale, Rehov Arlozorov 93, Tel Aviv, Israel. TEL 03-431458. Ed. Karmi Patael.

360 917.306 US ISSN 0737-1411
ETHNIC AMERICAN VOLUNTARY ORGANIZATIONS. 1983. irreg. price varies. Greenwood Press, 88 Post Rd. W., Box 5007, Westport, CT 06881. TEL 203-226-3571.

F C L ACTION. (Friends Committee on Legislation of California) see *POLITICAL SCIENCE*

360 NE
FACT SHEET ON THE NETHERLANDS. (Text in Dutch, English, French, German and Spanish) irreg. Ministerie van Welzijn Volksgezondheid en Cultuur, Steenvoordelaan 370, Rijswijk (Z.H.), Netherlands.

FEDERAL FUNDING GUIDE. see *PUBLIC ADMINISTRATION — Municipal Government*

360 FI ISSN 0071-5336
FINLAND. SOSIAALI- JA TERVEYSMINISTERIO. TUKIMUSOSASTO. SOSIAALISIA ERIKOISTUTKIMUKSIA/FINLAND. MINISTRY OF SOCIAL AFFAIRS AND HEALTH. RESEARCH DEPARTMENT. SPECIAL SOCIAL STUDIES. (Section XXXII of Official Statistics of Finland) (Text in Finnish, summaries in English and Swedish) 1921. irreg. (4-6/yr.), latest no.119, 1986. price varies. Ministry of Social Affairs and Health, Research Department - Sosiaali- ja Terveysministerio. Tukimusosasto, Haapaniemenkatu 5, Box 303, SF-00171 Helsinki 17, Finland (Subscr. to: Government Printing Centre, Box 516, SF-00101 Helsinki 10, Finland) circ. 550.

360 FI ISSN 0355-4759
FINLAND. SOSIAALIHALLITUS. HUOLTOAPU/FINLAND. NATIONAL BOARD OF SOCIAL WELFARE. HOMEHELP/FINLAND. SOCIALSTYRELSEN. SOCIALHJAELP. (Text in English, Finnish and Swedish) 1969. biennial. Fmk.25. Sosiaalihallitus, Siltaarenkatu 18 C, SF-00530 Helsinki, Finland (Subscr.to: Government Printing Center, Box 516, SF- 00101, Helsinki, Finland) Ed. Kyllikki Korpi. circ. 1,000.

360 FI ISSN 0355-4767
FINLAND. SOSIAALIHALLITUS. KODINHOITOAPU/FINLAND. NATIONAL BOARD OF SOCIAL WELFARE. SOCIAL ASSISTANCE/FINLAND. SOCIALSTYRELSEN. HEMVAARDSHJAELP. (Text in English, Finnish and Swedish) 1971. biennial. Fmk.21. Sosiaalihallitus, Siltaarenkatu 18 C, SF-00530 Helsinki, Finland (Subscr.to: Government Printing Center, Box 516, SF-00101, Helsinki, Finland) Ed. Kyllikki Korpi. circ. 1,200.

360 FI ISSN 0071-5328
FINLAND. SOSIAALIHALLITUS. SOSIAALIHUOLTOTILASTON VUOSIKIRJA/FINLAND. NATIONAL BOARD OF SOCIAL WELFARE. YEARBOOK OF SOCIAL WELFARE STATISTICS/FINLAND. SOCIALSTYRELSEN. SOCIALVAARDSSTATISTISK AARSBOK. (Section XXI B of Official Statistics of Finland) (Text in English, Finnish and Swedish) 1959. a. Fmk.40. Sosiaalihallitus, Siltaarenkatu 18 C, Helsinki, Finland. Ed. Kyllikki Korpi. circ. 1,100.

353.9 US
FLORIDA. DEPARTMENT OF CORRECTIONS. ANNUAL REPORT. a. Department of Corrections, 1311 Winewood Blvd., Tallahassee, FL 32301. TEL 904-488-5021. stat.
Formerly: Florida. Division of Corrections. Financial Report (ISSN 0094-6435)

360 GW ISSN 0071-7835
FORTBILDUNG UND PRAXIS. (Supplement to: Wege zur Sozialversicherung) 1949. irreg. price varies. Asgard-Verlag Dr. Werner Hippe KG, Einsteinstr. 10, Postfach 3080, 5205 St. Augustin 3, W. Germany (B.R.D.)

FRAENKISCHER HAUSKALENDER UND CARITASKALENDER. see *BIOGRAPHY*

360 FR ISSN 0184-6469
FRANCE. CAISSE NATIONALE DES ALLOCATIONS FAMILIALES. STATISTIQUES PRESTATIONS DE LOGEMENT. a. Caisse Nationale des Allocations Familiales, 23 rue Daviel, 75634 Paris Cedex 13, France.

352 BL
FUNDACAO DE ASSISTENCIA AOS MUNICIPIOS DO ESTADO DO PARANA. BOLETIM DOS MUNICIPIOS. 1972. irreg. free. Fundacao de Assistencia aos Municipios, Rua Voluntarios da Patria 547, Curitiba, Parana, Brazil.

GAY COUNSELLING. see *HOMOSEXUALITY*

360 US ISSN 0745-5070
GERIATRIC GUIDE TO PERTINENT PUBLICATIONS. 1979. a. $14.95. D R S Geriatric Publishing Co., 7435 S.E. 71st St., Mercer Island, WA 98040. TEL 206-232-9689. Ed. Frances Greer.

361.73 US
GIVING U.S.A. ANNUAL REPORT; a compilation of facts and trends on American philanthropy for the year. 1956. a. $30. ‡ American Association of Fund-Raising Counsel, Inc., 25 W. 43rd St., New York, NY 10036. TEL 212-354-5799. Ed. Lawrence A. Clancy. circ. 18,000.

361 UK ISSN 0143-7429
GLASGOW DIRECTORY OF VOLUNTARY ORGANIZATIONS. 1980. irreg. £2. Glasgow Council for Voluntary Services, 11 Queens Cres., Glasgow G4 9AS, Scotland. Ed. Sheena Vassie. adv. illus. circ. 800.

360 JM
GRACE, KENNEDY FOUNDATION. ANNUAL REPORT. 1984. a. free. (Grace, Kennedy Foundation) 64 Harbour St., Kingston, Jamaica, W. Indies TEL 809-922-3440-9. (Subscr. to: 1 St. Lucia Crescent, Kingston 5, Jamaica, W. Indies) Ed. Marjorie Humphreys. circ. 500. (back issues avail.)

GREAT BRITAIN. DEPARTMENT OF HEALTH AND SOCIAL SECURITY. HEALTH BUILDING NOTES. see *HOSPITALS*

GREAT BRITAIN. DEPARTMENT OF HEALTH AND SOCIAL SECURITY. HEALTH EQUIPMENT NOTES. see *HOSPITALS*

GREAT BRITAIN. DEPARTMENT OF HEALTH AND SOCIAL SECURITY. HOSPITAL IN-PATIENT INQUIRY. see *PUBLIC HEALTH AND SAFETY*

368.4 UK
GREAT BRITAIN. DEPARTMENT OF HEALTH AND SOCIAL SECURITY. SOCIAL SECURITY STATISTICS. 1973. a. price varies. H.M.S.O., Box 569, London SE1 9NH, England. illus. stat. (reprint service avail. from UMI)

GREAT BRITAIN. DEPARTMENT OF HEALTH AND SOCIAL SECURITY. STATISTICAL AND RESEARCH REPORT SERIES. see *HOSPITALS*

362 UK ISSN 0072-8756
GUIDE TO THE SOCIAL SERVICES. 1882. a. £7.65. ‡ Family Welfare Association, 501-505 Kingsland Rd., London E8 4AU, England. Ed.Bd. circ. 9,000.

362.7 DK
HAANBOG FOR BOERNE- OG UNGDOMINSTITUTIONER. DOEGNINSTITUTIONER. triennial. Kroghs Forlag A-S, Kr. Hansens Vej 3, 7100 Vejle, Denmark. Ed. Finn Suenson. adv. circ. 3,000.
Formerly: Haandbog for Boerne- og Ungdominstitutioner.

HANDICAPPED FUNDING DIRECTORY; a guide to sources of funding in the United States for handicapped programs & services. see *EDUCATION — Special Education And Rehabilitation*

362.7 US ISSN 0362-6296
HAWAII. DEPARTMENT OF HEALTH. MENTAL HEALTH SERVICES FOR CHILDREN AND YOUTH; children's MH services branch. 1970. a. Department of Health, Mental Health Division, Children's Mental Health Services Branch, 3627 Kilauea Ave., Rm. 101, Honolulu, HI 96816. TEL 808-548-6335. stat. circ. 300. Key Title: Mental Health Services for Children and Youth.

HAWAII. DEPARTMENT OF HEALTH. WAIMANO TRAINING SCHOOL AND HOSPITAL DIVISION (REPORT) see *HOSPITALS*

362 618.92 US
HAWAII. FAMILY HEALTH SERVICES DIVISION. CRIPPLED CHILDREN SERVICES BRANCH. REPORT. a. free. Department of Health, Family Health Services Division, Box 3378, Honolulu, HI 96801. TEL 808-847-1662.
Formerly: Hawaii. Children's Health Services Division. Crippled Children Branch Report (ISSN 0073-1013)

HEALTH AND SOCIAL SERVICE MANPOWER IN ALBERTA. see *PUBLIC HEALTH AND SAFETY*

SOCIAL SERVICES AND WELFARE

360 US ISSN 0361-4468
HEALTH, UNITED STATES. a. price varies. U.S. National Center for Health Statistics, Scientific and Technical Information Branch, 3700 East-West Highway, Hyattsville, MD 20782. TEL 301-436-8500. (Co-sponsor: U.S. National Center for Health Services Research)

362 UK ISSN 0260-5295
HOME CARE SERVICES, DAY CARE ESTABLISHMENTS, DAY SERVICES - SCOTLAND. 1976. a. Social Work Services Group, Statistics Branch, 43 Jeffrey St., Rm. 424, Edinburgh EH1 1DN, Scotland.
Supersedes in part (1971-1975): Scottish Social Work Statistics (ISSN 0307-9597)

360 US
HOME CARE SERVICES IN NEW YORK STATE. Variant title: Directory of Home Care Services in New York. 1979. irreg. Office of Health Systems Management, Department of Health, Tower Bldg., Gov. Nelson A. Rockefeller Empire State Plaza, Albany, NY 12237.

361.6 HO
HONDURAS. SECRETARIA DE TRABAJO Y PREVISION SOCIAL. BOLETIN DE ESTADISTICAS LABORALES. 1973. a. Ministerio de Trabajo y Prevision Social, Planificacion Sectorial y Estadistica Laboreal, Tegucigalpa, Honduras.

360 UK
HOW TO LIVE IN BRITAIN. 1952. a. price varies. Macmillan Overseas Ltd., Houndmills, Basingstoke RG21 2XS, England.

360 US
HUMAN SERVICES DIRECTORY; health and social agencies in Greater Cleveland. 1946. biennial. $10. Federation for Community Planning, 1001 Huron Rd, Cleveland, OH 44115. TEL 216-781-2944. circ. 5,000.
Formerly: Health and Welfare Directory.

360 PR ISSN 0441-4144
HUMANIDAD. 1967. a. $2. Universidad de Puerto Rico, Escuela Graduada de Trabajo Social, Rio Piedras, PR 00931. Ed. Josef R. de Caraballo. bibl. cum.index: vols.1-8, 1967-1974. circ. 2,000.

361 AU ISSN 0098-8278
I A S S W DIRECTORY; MEMBER SCHOOLS AND ASSOCIATIONS. biennial. $6. International Association of Schools of Social Work, Freytaggasse 32, A-1210 Vienna, Austria. circ. 1,000. Key Title: I A S S W Directory.
Continues: International Association of Schools of Social Work. Directory of Members and Constitution.

I P C POVERTY RESEARCH SERIES. (Institute of Philippine Culture) see SOCIOLOGY

362.7 II
INDIAN COUNCIL FOR CHILD WELFARE. ANNUAL REPORT. (Text in English) a. Indian Council for Child Welfare, 4 Deen Dayal Upadhyaya Marg, New Delhi 110002, India.

360 CN ISSN 0827-4789
INITIATIVE. (Text in English, French) 1985. irreg. (4-5/yr.) free. Canadian Council on Social Development, 55 Parkdale Ave., Box 3505, Sta. C, Ottawa, Ont. K1Y 4G1, Canada. Ed. Bill McIntosh. circ. 9,000.

961 SG
INSTITUT FONDAMENTAL D'AFRIQUE NOIRE. RAPPORT ANNUEL. a. Institut Fondamental d'Afrique Noire, B.P. 206, Dakar, Senegal.

361 US
INSTITUTION ANALYSIS. 1977. irreg., no.38, 1986. price varies. Heritage Foundation, 214 Massachusetts Ave., N.E., Washington, DC 20002.

362.7 371.9 UY
INSTITUTO INTERAMERICANO DEL NINO. EDUCACION ESPECIAL. INFORMES TECNICOS. irreg. Instituto Interamericano del Nino, Avda. 8 de Octubre No. 2904, Montevideo, Uruguay.

362.7 310 UY
INSTITUTO INTERAMERICANO DEL NINO. ESTADISTICA E INFORMATICA. INFORMES TECNICOS. irreg. Instituto Interamericano del Nino, Avda. 8 de Octubre No. 2904, Montevideo, Uruguay.

362.7 UY
INSTITUTO INTERAMERICANO DEL NINO. REGISTRO CIVIL. INFORMES TECNICOS. irreg. Instituto Interamericano del Nino, Avda. 8 de Octubre No. 2904, Montevideo, Urugay.

362.7 UY
INSTITUTO INTERAMERICANO DEL NINO. SERVICIO SOCIAL. INFORMES TECNICOS. irreg. Instituto Interamericano del Nino, Avda. 8 de Octubre no. 2904, Montevideo, Uruguay. circ. 600.
Formerly: Instituto Interamericano del Nino. Publicaciones sobre Servicio Social.

362.7 UY
INTERAMERICAN CHILDREN'S INSTITUTE. REPORT OF THE GENERAL DIRECTOR. a. Instituto Interamericano del Nino, Avda. 8 de Octubre no. 2904, Montevideo, Uruguay. illus.

361.77 SZ
INTERNATIONAL COMMITTEE OF THE RED CROSS. ANNUAL REPORT/RAPPORT D'ACTIVITE/INFORME DE ACTIVIDAD/ TAETIGKEITSBERICHT. (Text in Arabic, English, French, German and Spanish) a. 12 Fr. International Committee of the Red Cross, 17 Avenue de la Paix, 1202 Geneva, Switzerland.
Red Cross

361 US ISSN 0074-2961
INTERNATIONAL CONFERENCE OF SOCIAL WORK. CONFERENCE PROCEEDINGS. biennial, 18th San Juan, P.R., 1976. (International Council on Social Welfare) Columbia University Press, 562 W. 113th St., New York, NY 10025. TEL 212-678-6777.

INTERNATIONAL DIRECTORY OF PRISONERS' AID AGENCIES. see CRIMINOLOGY AND LAW ENFORCEMENT

361 US ISSN 0538-9461
INTERNATIONAL RESCUE COMMITTEE ANNUAL REPORT. a. free. International Rescue Committee, 386 Park Avenue South, New York, NY 10016. TEL 212-679-0010.

360 UK
INTERNATIONAL WHO'S WHO IN COMMUNITY SERVICE. 1974. irreg. Melrose Press Ltd., 3 Regal Lane, Soham, Ely, Cambs. CB7 5BA, England.

362.7 UK
INVALID CHILDREN'S AID NATIONWIDE YEAR BOOK. a. free. Invalid Children's Aid Association, 198 City Rd., London EC1V 2PH, England. Ed. Miranda de Grey. adv. circ. 3,000.
Formerly: Invalid Children's Aid Association Year Book.

360 US ISSN 0148-6802
INVEST YOURSELF. 1944. a. $2. ‡ Commission on Voluntary Service & Action, 475 Riverside Drive, New York, NY 10027 (Subscr. to: Invest Yourself Circulation Office, Peltoma Rd., Haddonfield, NJ 08033) circ. 10,000.

360 IE
IRELAND. DEPARTMENT OF SOCIAL WELFARE. STATISTICAL INFORMATION ON SOCIAL WELFARE. a. £1.40 free. Department of Social Welfare, c/o Secretary, Dublin 2, Ireland.

362 IS ISSN 0075-1014
ISRAEL. CENTRAL BUREAU OF STATISTICS. DIAGNOSTIC STATISTICS OF HOSPITALIZED PATIENTS. (Subseries of its Special Series) (Text in English and Hebrew) 1950. irreg. price varies. Central Bureau of Statistics, Box 13015, Jerusalem, Israel.

ISRAEL SOCIETY FOR REHABILITATION OF THE DISABLED. ANNUAL. see
EDUCATION — Special Education And Rehabilitation

360 CN
ISSUES IN CANADIAN SOCIAL POLICY/ POLITIQUE SOCIALE AU CANADA. (Editions in English and French) 1982. biennial. Can.$12.95. Canadian Council on Social Development, 55 Parkdale Ave., Box 3505, Station C, Ottawa, Ont. K1Y 4G1, Canada.

361 JA
JAPANESE REPORT TO THE INTERNATIONAL COUNCIL ON SOCIAL WELFARE. 1954. a. free. International Council on Social Welfare, Japanese National Committee, 3-3-4 Kasumigaseki, Chiyoda-ku, Tokyo, Japan.
Formerly: International Conference of Social Work. Japanese National Committee. Progress Report (ISSN 0538-6039)

360 296 US ISSN 0021-6712
JEWISH SOCIAL WORK FORUM. 1964. a. $4. Yeshiva University, Wurzweiler School of Social Work, Alumni Association, 2495 Amsterdam Ave., New York, NY 10033. TEL 212-790-0241. Ed. Norman Linzer. adv. bk. rev. charts. circ. 950. Indexed: Sociol.Abstr. Lang.& Lang.Behav.Abstr.

JOURNAL OF TEACHING IN SOCIAL WORK; innovations in instruction, training and educational practice. see EDUCATION — Teaching Methods And Curriculum

360 364.7 CN ISSN 0225-4115
JUSTICE - DIRECTORY OF SERVICES/JUSTICE - REPERTOIRE DES SERVICES. (Text in English and French) 1980. a. Can.$15. Canadian Criminal Justice Association - Association Canadienne de Justice Penale, 55 Parkdale Ave., Ottawa, Ont. K1Y 1E5, Canada. TEL 613-725-3715. circ. 800.
Formerly: Directory of Correctional Services in Canada /Repertoire des Services de Correction du Canada (ISSN 0070-5381)

362.7 US
KENTUCKY. DEPARTMENT OF HUMAN RESOURCES. ANNUAL REPORT. a. Department for Human Resources, Frankfort, KY 40601. TEL 502-564-2336.
Incorporating: Kentucky. Department of Child Welfare. Annual Report.

360 KE ISSN 0075-594X
KENYA. PUBLIC SERVICE COMMISSION. ANNUAL REPORT. a. EAs.3. Government Printing and Stationery Department, Box 30128, Nairobi, Kenya.

360 KE
KENYA NATIONAL COUNCIL OF SOCIAL SERVICES. ANNUAL REPORT. (Text in English) a. Kenya National Council of Social Services, Box 47628, Nairobi, Kenya.

KETTERING REPORT. see POLITICAL SCIENCE

360 DK ISSN 0900-274X
KOEBENHAVNS UNIVERSITET. INSTITUT FOR SAMFUNDSFAG OG FORVALTNING. FORSKNINGRAPPORT. 1984. irreg. free. University of Copenhagen, Institut of Political Studies, Rosenborggade 15, DK-1130 Copenhagen K, Demark. illus.

KOSTEN EN FINANCIERING VAN DE GEZONDHEIDZORG IN NEDERLAND/COST OF HEALTH CARE IN THE NETHERLANDS. see PUBLIC HEALTH AND SAFETY

354 LB
LIBERIA. GENERAL SERVICES AGENCY. ANNUAL REPORT. a. General Services Agency, Box 9027, Monrovia, Liberia. stat.

354 LB
LIBERIA. MINISTRY OF LABOUR, YOUTH & SPORTS. ANNUAL REPORT.* (Text in English) a. Ministry of Labour, Youth & Sports, Camp Johnson Rd., Monrovia, Liberia. stat.

361.6 US ISSN 0362-8868
LOUISIANA. HEALTH AND HUMAN RESOURCES ADMINISTRATION COMPREHENSIVE ANNUAL SERVICES PROGRAM PLAN FOR SOCIAL SERVICES UNDER TITLE 20. a. Health and Human Resources Administration, Baton Rouge, LA 70804. TEL 504-342-6711. illus. stat. Key Title: Comprehensive Annual Services Program Plan for Social Services Under Title 20.

SOCIAL SERVICES AND WELFARE 1019

344 US ISSN 0092-9476
MARYLAND. DEPARTMENT OF HUMAN RESOURCES. INFORMATION PAMPHLET.* irreg., latest no.60. Department of Human Resources, Social Services Administration, 1100 N. Eutaw St., Baltimore, MD 21201. Key Title: Information Pamphlet - Department of Employment and Social Services (Baltimore)

368.4 MF
MAURITIUS. MINISTRY OF SOCIAL SECURITY, NATIONAL SOLIDARITE AND REFORM INSTITUTIONS. 1962. a. Rs.25. Ministry of Social Security, National Solidarity and Reform Institution, Astor Court, Lislet Geoffroy St., Port Louis, Mauritius (Orders to: Government Printing Office, Elizabeth II Ave., Port Louis, Mauritius) Ed.Bd. circ. 300.
Former titles: Mauritius. Ministry for Employment and Social Security and National Solidarite; Until 1982: Mauritius. Ministry of Social Security. Annual Report (ISSN 0076-5538)

360 610 US ISSN 0098-3616
MEDICAID RECIPIENT CHARACTERISTICS AND UNITS OF SELECTED MEDICAL SERVICES. (NCSS Report B-4 Supplement) a. U.S. National Center for Social Statistics, U.S. Dept. of Health, Education and Human Services, 330 Independence Ave., S.W., Washington, DC 20201. TEL 301-436-7900.

362 US ISSN 0076-6453
MENTAL HEALTH STATISTICS FOR ILLINOIS. 1930. a. free. ‡ Department of Mental Health and Developmental Disabilities, 401 S. Spring St., Springfield, IL 62706. TEL 217-782-2753. circ. 1, 100.
Formerly: Illinois. Department of Mental Health. Administrator's Data Manual.

353.9 US
MISSOURI. DIVISION OF YOUTH SERVICES. ANNUAL REPORT. 1949. a. 1. Department of Social Services, Division of Youth Services, Broadway State Office Bldg., Box 447, Jefferson City, MO 65101. TEL 314-751-3324. Ed. Connie Chadwick. illus. stat. circ. 500.
Formerly: Missouri. State Board of Training Schools. Annual Report (ISSN 0098-0110)

N A A C P ANNUAL REPORT. (National Association for the Advancement of Colored People) see SOCIOLOGY

360 II ISSN 0253-6757
N I H F W TECHNICAL REPORTS. 1978. irreg. free. National Institute of Health and Family Welfare, New Mehrauli Rd., Munirka, New Delhi 110 067, India. circ. 3,000.

361.8 US
N R A G PAPERS. 1976. irreg., vol.4, 1984. Northern Rockies Action Group, Inc., 9 Placer St., Helena, MT 59601. Ed. Linda Wood. illus. circ. 400 (controlled)

360 UK
NATIONAL ASSOCIATION OF ALMSHOUSES. YEARBOOK AND STATEMENT OF ACCOUNTS. a. 30p. per no. National Association of Almshouses, Wokingham, Berkshire RG11 5RU, England. Ed.Bd. stat.

361.6 US
NATIONAL CONFERENCE OF STATE SOCIAL SECURITY ADMINISTRATORS. PROCEEDINGS.* 1952. a. National Conference of State Social Security Administrators, c/o Social Security Division, Employees Retirement System of Georgia, Two Northside 75, Ste. 400, Atlanta, GA 30318. circ. controlled.

360 UK
NATIONAL COUNCIL FOR VOLUNTARY ORGANIZATIONS. ANNUAL REPORT. irreg., latest 1983/84. free. National Council for Voluntary Organisations, 26 Bedford Sq., London WC1B 3HU, England. circ. 6,000.
Formerly: National Council of Social Service. Annual Report (ISSN 0077-409X)

360 UK ISSN 0077-4774
NATIONAL INSTITUTE SOCIAL SERVICES LIBRARY. 1964. irreg., no.30, 1976. price varies. (National Institute for Social Work) George Allen & Unwin (Publishers) Ltd., 40 Museum St., London WC1, England (U.S. addr.: Allen & Unwin Inc., 8 Winchester Place, Winchester, MA 01890)
Formerly: National Institute for Social Work Training Series.

360 US
NATIONAL PRO-LIFE JOURNAL. 1976. irreg. Pro-Life Publications, Box 172, Fairfax, VA 22030. Ed. Audree Ryberg.

362.7 UK ISSN 0077-5754
NATIONAL SOCIETY FOR PREVENTION OF CRUELTY TO CHILDREN. ANNUAL REPORT. 1885. a. ‡ National Society for the Prevention of Cruelty to Children, 67 Saffron Hill, London EC1N 8RS, England. circ. 10,000.

360 US
NEBRASKA. DEPARTMENT OF SOCIAL SERVICES. ANNUAL REPORT. no.38, 1974. a. Department of Social Services, Research and Finance Division, Box 95026, 301 Centennial Mall So., Lincoln, NE 68509. Ed. Beverly Kellison. charts. stat. circ. 500.
Formerly: Nebraska. Department of Public Welfare. Annual Report.

NEPAL FAMILY PLANNING AND MATERNAL CHILD HEALTH BOARD. ANNUAL REPORT. see BIRTH CONTROL

NETHERLANDS. CENTRAAL BUREAU VOOR DE STATISTIEK. DIAGNOSESTATISTIEK BEDRIJFSVERENIGINGEN (OMSLAGLEDEN). SOCIAL INSURANCE SICKNESS STATISTICS. see INSURANCE

353.9 US ISSN 0090-077X
NEW JERSEY. DEVELOPMENTAL DISABILITIES COUNCIL. ANNUAL REPORT. 1971. a. free. ‡ Developmental Disabilities Council, 108-110 N. Broad St., CN 700, Trenton, NJ 08625. TEL 609-292-3745. Ed. Virginia Persing. circ. 3,000.
Supersedes: New Jersey Mental Retardation Planning Board. Annual Report.

NEW MEXICO. VETERANS' SERVICE COMMISSION. REPORT. see MILITARY

361 US
NEW YORK (STATE) ASSEMBLY. STANDING COMMITTEE ON CHILDREN AND FAMILIES. ANNUAL REPORT. a. State Assembly, Room 422, State Capitol, Albany, NY 12248. TEL 518-455-5474.

NEW YORK (STATE). ASSEMBLY. STANDING COMMITTEE ON VETERANS' AFFAIRS. ANNUAL REPORT. see MILITARY

361 US ISSN 0363-9835
NEW YORK (STATE). DEPARTMENT OF SOCIAL SERVICES. ANNUAL REPORT. 1974. a. Department of Social Services, 40 N. Pearl St., Albany, NY 12243.
Formerly: New York (State). Board of Social Welfare. Annual Report (ISSN 0363-9843)

362.974 US ISSN 0090-4716
NEW YORK (STATE) DEPARTMENT OF SOCIAL SERVICES. BUREAU OF DATA MANAGEMENT AND ANALYSIS. PROGRAM ANALYSIS REPORT. 1954. irreg., no.65, 1980. free. ‡ Department of Social Services, 40 N. Pearl St., Albany, NY 12243.
Formerly: New York (State) Department of Social Services. Bureau of Research. Program Analysis Report.

362.974 US ISSN 0162-6302
NEW YORK (STATE) DEPARTMENT OF SOCIAL SERVICES. BUREAU OF DATA MANAGEMENT AND ANALYSIS. PROGRAM BRIEF. 1961. irreg. free. ‡ Department of Social Services, 40 N. Pearl St., Albany, NY 12243. Ed. Herbert Altrasso. illus.
Formerly: New York (State) Department of Social Services. Bureau of Research. Program Brief. (ISSN 0361-6436)

362.4 US
NEW YORK (STATE). OFFICE OF ADVOCATE FOR THE DISABLED. ANNUAL REPORT. 1980. a. free. Office of Advocate for the Disabled, One Empire State Plaza, Albany, NY 12223. circ. 3, 000.

361.8 US
NEW YORK URBAN LEAGUE. ANNUAL REPORT. a. New York Urban League, 218 W. 40th St., New York, NY 10018. TEL 212-730-5200.
Formerly: Urban League of Greater New York. Annual Report.

361 NZ ISSN 0080-0392
NEW ZEALAND RED CROSS SOCIETY. REPORT. 1931. a. free. New Zealand Red Cross Society Inc., Box 12-140, Wellington North, New Zealand.

361 CN ISSN 0078-0294
NEWFOUNDLAND. DEPARTMENT OF SOCIAL SERVICES. ANNUAL REPORT. 1950/51. a. free. Department of Social Services, P.O. Box 4750, Confederation Bldg., West Block, St. John's, Newfoundland A1C 5T7, Canada. TEL 709-576-3607. Ed.Bd. circ. 300.

360 AU
NIEDEROESTERREICHISCHE SOZIALHILFE UND JUGENDWOHLFAHRTSPFLEGE. 1974. a. free. Amt der Niederoesterreichischen Landesregierung, Abteilung R 2-Statistik, Suedstadtzentrum 4/4, A-2344 Maria Enzersdorf, Austria. Ed. Herwig Schoen.

362.4 NR ISSN 0078-0804
NIGERIAN NATIONAL ADVISORY COUNCIL FOR THE BLIND. ANNUAL REPORT. 1961/62. a. Nigerian National Advisory Council for the Blind, c/o Federal Ministry of Information, Lagos, Nigeria.

361.6 US ISSN 0095-4942
NORTH CAROLINA. DEPARTMENT OF HUMAN RESOURCES. ANNUAL PLAN OF WORK. a. $10.75. Department of Human Resources, 325 N. Salisbury St., Raleigh, NC 27611. TEL 919-733-4471. Key Title: Annual Plan of Work - Department of Human Resources.

360 US
OKLAHOMA. DEPARTMENT OF HUMAN SERVICES. ANNUAL REPORT. 1936. a. free. Commission for Human Services, Department of Human Services, Box 25352, Oklahoma City, OK 73125. TEL 405-521-2778. Ed. Robert Fulton. charts. stat.
Formerly (until 1979): Oklahoma. Department of Institutions, Social and Rehabilitative Services. Annual Report (ISSN 0078-4362)

360 US
OKLAHOMA. DEPARTMENT OF HUMAN SERVICES. ANNUAL STATISTICAL REPORT. 1983. a. free. Commission for Human Services, Department of Human Services, Box 25352, Oklahoma City, OK 73125. TEL 405-521-2778.

OLD AGE: A REGISTER OF SOCIAL RESEARCH. see GERONTOLOGY AND GERIATRICS

362.8 320 US
ONE FAMILY.* irreg. $5. Planetary Citizens, 325 9th St., San Francisco, CA 94103. Ed. Carol J. Anderer.

362 CN
ONTARIO. MINISTRY OF COMMUNITY AND SOCIAL SERVICES. SOCIAL ASSISTANCE REVIEW BOARD. ANNUAL REPORT OF THE CHAIRMAN. (Report Year Ends Mar. 31) a. Can.$1. Ministry of Community and Social Services, Toronto, Ont., Canada. TEL 416-965-7825. illus.

362.734 US
ORPHAN VOYAGE. ADOPTION SERIES. 1983. irreg. membership. Orphan Voyage, 2141 Road 2300, Cedaredge, CO 81413. TEL 303-856-3937. Ed. Jean M. Paton. bibl. circ. 500. (back issues avail.)
Formerly: Orphan Voyage. Log.

362.6 US
PENNSYLVANIA. ADMINISTRATION ON AGING. STATE PLAN ON AGING. 1979. a. Department of Aging, 401 Finance Bldg., Harrisburg, PA 17120. TEL 717-255-2790.

SOCIAL SERVICES AND WELFARE

361.6   US
PENNSYLVANIA. DEVELOPMENTAL DISABILITIES PLANNING COUNCIL. PENNSYLVANIA STATE PLAN. 1977. a. Developmental Disabilities Planning Council, Health & Welfare Bldg., Harrisburg, PA 17120. Ed. Janeen DuChane. circ. 2,000.

362.6   UK   ISSN 0140-6647
PENSION FUNDS & THEIR ADVISERS. 1978. a. £39.50. A.P. Information Services Ltd., 33 Ashbourne Ave., London NW11 0DU, England TEL 01-458-1607. (Distr. in U.S. by: Money Market Directories Inc., 300 Eastmarket St., Charlottesville, VA 22901) Ed. Alan Philipp. circ. 3,500.

361.73   US
PEOPLE IN PHILANTHROPHY; a guide to philanthropic leaders, major donors, and funding connections. a. $187. Taft Corporation, 5125 MacArthur Blvd., N.W., Washington, DC 20016. TEL 800-424-3761.

361   US
PERSPECTIVE. CLEVELAND FOUNDATION OCCASIONAL PAPER. 1975. irreg. free. Cleveland Foundation, 1400 Hanna Bldg., Cleveland, OH 44115. TEL 216-861-3810. Ed. Dennis J. Dooley. charts. illus. circ. 6,500.
    Former titles: Cleveland Foundation Perspective; Cleveland Foundation Quarterly.

360   DK   ISSN 0108-0857
PLEJEHJEMSHAANDBOGEN; opslagsbog for medarbejdere i den sociale sektor. 1982. a. Kr.341. Forlag for Social- og Sundhedssektor, Vaerkstedsgaarden 7, 2620 Albertslund, Denmark.

POLICY NOTES. see BUSINESS AND ECONOMICS — International Development And Assistance

360   US
POLICY STUDIES IN EMPLOYMENT AND WELFARE. 1969. irreg., no.39, 1983. price varies. Johns Hopkins University Press, 710 W. 40th St., Ste. 275, Baltimore, MD 21211. TEL 301-338-6900. (reprint service avail. from UMI)

POLLING. see MEDICAL SCIENCES

301.44   US
POVERTY IN SOUTH DAKOTA.* a. ‡ Economic Opportunity Office, Community Service Block Grant Program, State Government Operations, Office of the Governor, 500 E. Capitol Ave., Pierre, SD 57501. TEL 605-224-8280. Ed. George J. Mauer. illus. stat.
    Formerly (until 1975): Annual Causes and Conditions of Poverty in South Dakota (ISSN 0091-0724)

PUBLIC AUTHORITIES DIRECTORY. see PUBLIC ADMINISTRATION — Municipal Government

360   US   ISSN 0163-8297
PUBLIC WELFARE DIRECTORY. 1940. a. $60. American Public Welfare Association, 1125 15th St. N.W., Washington, DC 20005. TEL 202-293-7550. Ed. Amy Weinstein. circ. 5,000.

360   613   US
PUERTO RICO. DEPARTMENT OF HEALTH. BOLETIN ESTADISTICO. (Text in Spanish) 1979. irreg. free. Department of Health, Box 9342, Santurce, PR 00908. TEL 809-721-4050. circ. 500.

360   613   US
PUERTO RICO. DEPARTMENT OF HEALTH. INFORME ANUAL DE FACILIDADES DE SALUD. (Text in Spanish) 1979. a. free. Department of Health, Box 9342, Santurce, PR 00908. TEL 809-721-4050. circ. 500.

360   613   US
PUERTO RICO. DEPARTMENT OF HEALTH. INFORME DEL REGISTRO DE PROFESIONALES DE LA SALUD. (Text in Spanish) 1979. biennial. free. Department of Health, Box 9342, Santurce, PR 00908. TEL 809-721-4050. circ. 500.

362   UK   ISSN 0260-9584
QUAKER PEACE & SERVICE. ANNUAL REPORT. 1927. a. free. Quaker Peace and Service, Friends House, Euston Road, London NW1 2BJ, England. Ed. Grace Crookall-Greening. illus.
    Formerly: Friends Service Council. Annual Report (ISSN 0071-9609)

360   CN   ISSN 0318-4854
QUEBEC (PROVINCE). CURATELLE PUBLIQUE. RAPPORT ANNUEL DU CURATEUR PUBLIC.* a. (Curatelle Publique) Editeur Officiel du Quebec, 1283 Bd. Charest Ouest, Quebec, P.Q. G1N 2C9, Canada. TEL 413-643-3895.
    Formerly: Quebec (Province). Curatelle Publique du Quebec. Rapport Annuel.

RALPH H. BLANCHARD MEMORIAL ENDOWMENT SERIES. see INSURANCE

REFUGEE ABSTRACTS. see POPULATION STUDIES

361   US   ISSN 0091-2859
REGIONAL INSTITUTE OF SOCIAL WELFARE RESEARCH. ANNUAL REPORT. 1968. a. free. 468 N. Milledge Ave., Box 152, Athens, GA 30603. TEL 404-542-7614. Key Title: Annual Report - Regional Institute of Social Welfare Research.

360   GW
REGIONAL PLANNING. 1971. irreg., vol.12, 1983. price varies. (United Nations Research Institute for Social Development, UN) Walter de Gruyter & Co., Mouton Publishers, Postfach 110240, D-1000 Berlin 11, W. Germany (B.R.D.) (U.S. addr: Mouton Publishers, division of Walter de Gruyter, Inc., 200 Saw Mill River Road, Hawthorne, NY 10532) bibl.

REPERTOIRE ADMINISTRATIF. see POLITICAL SCIENCE

360   PR   ISSN 0034-8937
REVISTA DE SERVICIO SOCIAL. 1940. irreg. Facultad de la Escuela de Trabajo Social, Apdo. 6679, Santurce, PR 00914. adv. bk. rev. bibl. charts. illus. index. circ. 1,000.

REVUE DU TRAVAIL. see BUSINESS AND ECONOMICS — Labor And Industrial Relations

ROSTER OF AFRICA SOCIAL SCIENTISTS. see BUSINESS AND ECONOMICS — International Development And Assistance

179.3   UK
ROYAL HUMANE SOCIETY. ANNUAL REPORT. 1774. a. free. ‡ (Royal Humane Society) Blackfords Truro Cornwall, Brettenham House, Lancaster Place, London WC2E 7EP, England. Ed. Maj. A.J. Dickinson. circ. 800.

361.8   US
ST. PAUL URBAN LEAGUE. ANNUAL REPORT. 1924. a. free. St. Paul Urban League, 401 Selby Ave., St. Paul, MN 55102. TEL 612-224-5771. Ed. L.G. Lambert. circ. 3,000. (tabloid format)

360   CN
SASKATCHEWAN. DEPARTMENT OF SOCIAL SERVICES. ANNUAL REPORT. 1915. a. free. Department of Social Services, Regina, Sask., Canada. TEL 306-787-3494. illus.
    Formerly: Saskatchewan. Department of Social Welfare. Annual Report (ISSN 0708-3882)

362.7   US
SAVE THE CHILDREN. ANNUAL REPORT. a. Save the Children Federation, 54 Wilton Rd., Box 950, Westport, CT 06881. TEL 203-226-7272.

SCHOOLS OF SOCIAL WORK WITH ACCREDITED MASTER'S DEGREE PROGRAMS. see EDUCATION — Higher Education

301.3   GW   ISSN 0080-7133
SCHRIFTENREIHE FUER LAENDLICHE SOZIALFRAGEN. 1951. irreg., no.95, 1985. price varies. Agrarsoziale Gesellschaft e.V., Kurze Geismarstr. 23/25, 3400 Goettingen, W. Germany (B.R.D.) index.

361.8   614.58   US   ISSN 0740-7548
SELF-HELP GROUP DIRECTORY. 1981. a. $15. New Jersey Self-Help Clearinghouse, St. Clare's-Riverside Medical Center, Pocono Rd., Denville, NJ 07834. TEL 201-625-7101. Ed. Abigail Meese. circ. 2,000.
    Formerly: Self-Help Group Sourcebook.

SELF HELP REPORTER NEWSLETTER. see PSYCHOLOGY

SERIES IN CLINICAL AND COMMUNITY PSYCHOLOGY. see PSYCHOLOGY

360   JA
SHAKAI FUKUSHI NO DOKO. 1957. a. 320 Yen. National Council of Social Welfare - Zenkoku Shakai Fukushi Kyogikai, 3-3-4 Kasumigaseki, Chiyoda-ku, Tokyo, Japan. Ed. Yoshiyuki Kobayashi. circ. 3,000.

SOCIAL SECURITY HANDBOOK. see INSURANCE

360   US
SOCIAL SERVICE DELIVERY SYSTEMS; an international annual. 1975. irreg. $29.95 cloth; $14.95 paper. Sage Publications, Inc., 2111 W. Hillcrest Dr., Newbury Park, CA 91320 TEL 805-499-0721. (And Sage Publications, Ltd., 28 Banner St., London EC1Y 8QE, England) Ed.Bd.

360   US
SOCIAL SERVICE ORGANIZATIONS AND AGENCIES DIRECTORY. 1982. irreg. $130. Gale Research Company, Book Tower, Detroit, MI 48034. TEL 313-961-2242. Ed. Anthony T. Kruzas.

361.6   CN
SOCIAL SERVICES FOR NOVA SCOTIANS. 1973. a. Can.$12. Department of Social Services, Box 696, Halifax, Nova Scotia B3J 2T7, Canada. TEL 902-424-4455. Ed. Allan Clark. illus. stat. circ. 1,000.
    Formerly: Social Services in Nova Scotia (ISSN 0317-4336); Continues: Welfare Services in Nova Scotia.

362   US   ISSN 0094-1220
SOCIAL SERVICES IN NORTH DAKOTA; biennial report. 1973. biennial. Department of Human Services, State Capitol, Bismark, ND 58505.

360   UK   ISSN 0307-093X
SOCIAL SERVICES YEARBOOK. 1972. a. £25.50. (Association of County Councils) Councils and Education Press (Subsidiary of: Longman Group Ltd.) Westgate House, The High, Harlow, Essex CM20 1NE, England. (Co-sponsor: Association of Metropolitan Authorities) Ed. Susan Higgins. adv.

SOCIAL WELFARE LAW. see LAW

360   JA
SOCIAL WELFARE SERVICES IN JAPAN. 1960. a. 2000 Yen. International Council on Social Welfare, Japanese National Committee, 3-3-4 Kasumigaseki, Chiyoda-ku, Tokyo, Japan.

360   US   ISSN 0081-055X
SOCIAL WORK AND SOCIAL ISSUES. 1969. irreg., no.5, 1977. Columbia University Press, 562 W. 113th St., New York, NY 10025. TEL 212-678-6777.

360   AG   ISSN 0037-8569
SOCIEDAD ESPANOLA DE SOCORROS MUTUOS Y BENEFICENCIA. BOLETIN.* 1968. irreg. (4-5/yr.) free. Sociedad Espanola de Socorros Mutuos y Beneficencia, Rodriquez No. 545, Tandil, Buenos Aires, Argentina. Ed. Ernesto Enrique Reclusa. circ. 2,000. (looseleaf format)

360   IS   ISSN 0334-4029
SOCIETY AND WELFARE/HEVRA U-REVAHA; quarterly for social work. (Text in Hebrew and English) 1978. irreg. IS.20($15) Ministry of Labour and Social Affairs, Box 1260, Jerusalem, Israel. TEL 02-719081. Ed. Dr. Shimon Spiro. bk. rev.

SOCIAL SERVICES AND WELFARE 1021

361   US   ISSN 0740-4549
SOURCE BOOK: SOCIAL AND HEALTH SERVICES IN THE GREATER NEW YORK AREA. 1984. irreg. (Services Agency Inventory System) Bernan-Unipub, Government and International Agency Publications Service, 4611-F Assembly Dr., Lanham, MD 20706-4391. TEL 301-459-7666. (Co-sponsors: City of New York Human Resources Administration; Community Council of Greater New York) Ed. Nancy Lecyn-Kirby.

SOUTH AFRICAN MEDICAL AND DENTAL COUNCIL. REGISTER OF SUPPLEMENTARY HEALTH SERVICES PROFESSIONS. see *MEDICAL SCIENCES*

360   US
SPRINGER SERIES ON SOCIAL WORK. irreg., vol.9, 1986. price varies. Springer Publishing Company, 536 Broadway, New York, NY 10012. Ed. Albert Roberts, D.S.W.

361   US   ISSN 0091-7192
STATISTICS ON SOCIAL WORK EDUCATION IN THE UNITED STATES. 1952. a. $7.50. ‡ Council on Social Work Education, 111 Eighth Ave., Ste. 501, New York, NY 10011. TEL 212-242-3800. circ. 1,400.
   Formerly: Statistics on Social Work Education (ISSN 0081-5217)

362.8   UK
STUDENT WELFARE MANUAL. 1970. a. £10. National Union of Students, 461 Holloway Rd., London N7 6LJ, England. circ. 3,000.

363 378   GW
STUDIENSTIFTUNG. JAHRESBERICHT. 1970. a. free. Studienstiftung des Deutschen Volkes, Koblenzer Str. 77, 5300 Bonn 1, W. Germany (B.R.D.) Ed. Klaus H. Kohrs. illus. stat. circ. 23,000.

STUDIES IN HEALTH AND HUMAN SERVICES. see *PHYSICAL FITNESS AND HYGIENE*

360   UK
STUDIES IN SOCIAL POLICY AND WELFARE. no.6, 1978. irreg. £8. Heinemann Educational Books Ltd., 22 Bedford Square, London WC1B 3HH, England. Ed. Robert Pinker. bibl.

360   US   ISSN 8755-5360
STUDIES IN SOCIAL WELFARE POLICIES AND PROGRAMS. 1985. irreg. price varies. Greenwood Press, 88 Post Rd. W., Box 5007, Westport, CT 06881. TEL 203-226-3571.

SUMMARY INFORMATION ON MASTER OF SOCIAL WORK PROGRAMS. see *EDUCATION — Higher Education*

SUMMER SERVICE OPPORTUNITIES. see *RELIGIONS AND THEOLOGY — Protestant*

360   SW   ISSN 0346-6019
SWEDEN. SOCIALSTYRELSEN. FOERFATTNINGSSAMLING: SOCIAL. 1976. irreg., approx. 5/yr. Kr.75. Socialstyrelsen - National Board of Health and Welfare, 106 30 Stockholm, Sweden. index. (looseleaf format)
   Supersedes in part (1883-1976): Sweden. Medicinalvaesendet. Foerfattningssamling (ISSN 0346-5837)

360   SW   ISSN 0346-5799
SWEDEN. SOCIALSTYRELSEN. REDOVISAR. 1974, no.36. irreg. (10-15/yr.) price varies. (National Board of Health and Welfare) Allmaenna Foerlaget, Box 5227, Stockholm, Sweden. charts. circ. 2,000.

360   GW   ISSN 0281-6881
SWEDEN SJUKVAARDENS OCH SOCIALVAARDENS PLANERINGS OCH RATIONALISERINGSINS. 1968. irreg. Sjukvaardens och Socialvaardens Planeringsinstitut - Swedish Planning and Rationalization Institute of the Health and Social Services, Box 27310, S-102 54 Stockholm, Sweden.

360   US   ISSN 0732-8958
TAFT CORPORATE GIVING DIRECTORY. (Section of: Taft Corporate Information System) 1981. a. $267. Taft Group, 5130 MacArthur Blvd., Washington, DC 20016. TEL 202-966-7086.
   Formerly: Taft Corporate Directory.

360   US   ISSN 0730-6237
TAFT FOUNDATION REPORTER. (Section of: Taft Foundation Information System) 1971. a. $287. Taft Group, 5130 MacArthur Blvd., Washington, DC 20016. TEL 202-966-7086.

362
TEXAS. DEPARTMENT ON AGING. BIENNIAL REPORT. biennial. Department on Aging, Box 12786, Capitol Station, Austin, TX 78711. TEL 512-444-2727.
   Former titles: Texas. Department on Aging. Annual Report; Texas. Governor's Committee on Aging. Biennial Report (ISSN 0082-3058)

360   IS
TZAADIM. irreg. Association for the Advancement of the Mentally Handicapped, P.O.B. 24003, Tel Aviv, Israel. TEL 03-492222.

360   US   ISSN 0082-8556
U S O ANNUAL REPORT. a. free. ‡ United Service Organizations, Inc., 601 Indiana Ave., Washington, DC 20004. TEL 202-783-8121. Ed. Patricia Elgin. circ. 15,000.

361.8   US
UNITED COMMUNITY PLANNING CORPORATION. REPORT.* irreg., no.161, 1979. United Community Planning Corporation, 60 State St., 6th Fl., Boston, MA 02109-1803.

360   UN   ISSN 0252-452X
UNITED NATIONS ECONOMIC AND SOCIAL COMMISSION FOR ASIA AND THE PACIFIC. SOCIAL DEVELOPMENT DIVISION. SOCIAL WORK EDUCATION AND DEVELOPMENT. 1966. irreg. United Nations Economic and Social Commission for Asia and the Pacific, Social Development Division, United Nations Bldg., Rajadamnern Ave., Bangkok 2, Thailand.
   Formerly: United Nations Economic and Social Commission for Asia and the Pacific. Social Development Division. Social Work Training and Teaching Materials Newsletter (ISSN 0085-7513)

361.6   US   ISSN 0190-373X
U.S. COMMUNITY SERVICES ADMINISTRATION. ANNUAL REPORT OF COMMUNITY SERVICES ADMINISTRATION. 1976. a. U.S. Community Services Administration, Washington, DC 20506. TEL 202-655-4000. Key Title: Annual Report of Community Services Administration.
   Formerly: U.S. Office of Economic Opportunity. Annual Report.

353.007   US   ISSN 0091-6242
U.S. GENERAL SERVICES ADMINISTRATION. MANAGEMENT REPORT. a. U.S. General Services Administration, General Services Bldg., Eighteenth & F Sts., N.W., Washington, DC 20405. TEL 202-343-4511. stat. Key Title: Management Report - General Services Administration.

360   US   ISSN 0566-0327
U.S. SOCIAL SECURITY ADMINISTRATION. O R S I P NOTES. 1978. irreg. U.S. Department of Health, Education, and Welfare, U.S. Social Security Administration, Office of Research, Statistics and International Policy, Universal North Bldg., Rm. 1120, 1875 Connecticut Ave., N.W., Washington, DC 20009. TEL 202-673-5579. stat. circ. 3,443. Indexed: Ind.U.S.Gov.Per.
   Formerly (until 1985): U.S. Social Security Administration. Research and Statistics Notes.

362   CN
UNITED WAY OF CANADA. DIRECTORY OF MEMBERS.* (Text in English and French) 1963. a. Can.$3.50. ‡ United Way of Canada, 600-150 Kent, Ottawa, Ont. K1P 5P4, Canada. TEL 613-236-7041. index. cum.index. (processed)
   Formerly: Directory of Canadian Community Funds and Councils (ISSN 0084-9863)

361   US
UNIVERSITY OF DELAWARE DISASTER RESEARCH CENTER. REPORT SERIES. 1968. irreg. University of Delaware, Disaster Research Center, Newark, DE 19716. TEL 302-451-6618.
   Formerly: Ohio State University. Disaster Research Center. Report Series (ISSN 0078-4133)

360   US   ISSN 0272-9016
UNIVERSITY OF SOUTHERN CALIFORNIA. SCHOOL OF SOCIAL WORK. SOCIAL WORK PAPERS. 1953. irreg. $6.75 per no. University of Southern California, School of Social Work, University Park, Los Angeles, CA 90089. TEL 213-743-2711. Ed.Bd. circ. 3,000. Indexed: ERIC. Lang.& Lang.Behav.Abstr. Soc.Work Res.& Abstr. Key Title: Social Work Papers of the School of Social Work, University of Southern California.
   Formerly: University of Southern California. School of Social Work. Social Work Papers of the Faculty, Alumni and Students.

362.4   DK   ISSN 0900-2863
VANFOERES JUL. 1958. a. Kr.20. Landsforeningen af Vanfoere, Hans Knudsen Plads 1A, 2100 Copenhagen OE, Denmark. illus.

361.6   VE
VENEZUELA. MINISTERIO DE SANIDAD Y ASISTENCIA SOCIAL. MEMORIA Y CUENTA. 1936. a. Ministerio de Sanidad y Asistencia Social, Oficina de Publicaciones, Biblioteca y Archivo, Centro Simon Bolivar, Edificio Sur, Caracas, Venezuela. Ed. Manuel Boet. circ. 3,000.

368   AU
VERBAND DER VERSICHERUNGSUNTERNEHMUNGEN OESTERREICHS. GESCHAEFTSBERICHT. 1956. a. free. Verband der Versicherungsunternehmungen Oesterreichs, Schwarzenbergplatz 7, A-1030 Vienna, Austria. Ed. Gregor Kozak. circ. 750.
   Formerly: Verband der Versicherungsunternehmungen Oesterreichs. Bericht ueber das Geschaeftsjahr (ISSN 0083-5501)

360   UK   ISSN 0083-601X
VICTORIA LEAGUE FOR COMMONWEALTH FRIENDSHIP. ANNUAL REPORT. 1901. a. membership. ‡ Victoria League, 18 Northumberland Ave., London WC2N 5BJ, England.

VICTORIAN CONSULTATIVE COMMITTEE ON SOCIAL DEVELOPMENT. ANNUAL REVIEW. see *PUBLIC ADMINISTRATION*

360   UK
VOLUNTARY AGENCIES. 1928. a. £5.25. National Council for Voluntary Organisations, Bedford Square Press, 26 Bedford Sq., London WC1B 3HU, England.
   Former titles: Voluntary Organisations & Voluntary Social Services (ISSN 0083-6907)

361.7   US
WASHINGTON (STATE). ATTORNEY GENERAL'S OFFICE. CHARITABLE TRUST DIRECTORY. 1967. a. $5. Attorney General's Office, Olympia, WA 98504. TEL 206-753-6299. Ed. Jeanette Dieckman. circ. 375.
   Formerly: Washington (State). Attorney General's Office. Directory of Charitable Organizations and Trusts Registered with the Office of Attorney General (ISSN 0093-6693)

354   AT
WESTERN AUSTRALIA. DEPARTMENT FOR COMMUNITY SERVICES. ANNUAL REPORT. 1973. a. Department for Community Services, 81 St. Georges Terrace, Perth, W.A. 6000, Australia. stat. circ. 600.
   Formerly: Western Australia. Department for Community Welfare. Annual Report.

360   US
WHEREVER THEY GO. 1965? irreg., 3-4/yr. free. United Service Organizations Inc., 601 Indiana Ave., Washington, DC 20004. TEL 202-783-8121. illus. circ. 15,000. (tabloid format; also avail. in microform from UMI)

361.7   UK
WILL TO CHARITY: CHARITIES' STORY BOOK. no.4, 1974. a. £3. Will to Charity Ltd., 84 Claverton St., London SW1V 3AX, England. Ed. Erroll Christie. adv. illus. circ. 24,000.

369.4   UK   ISSN 0052-2678
WORLD COUNCIL OF YOUNG MEN'S SERVICE CLUBS. MINUTES OF THE GENERAL MEETING. 1962. a. free. ‡ World Council of Young Men's Service Clubs, Polton Rd., Loanhead EH20 9DB, England. circ. 500. (processed)

362   FR   ISSN 0084-2044
WORLD MOVEMENT OF MOTHERS. REPORTS OF MEETINGS. irreg., 9th, 1971, Strasbourg. World Movement of Mothers, c/o M. de Vaublanc, Secretaire Generale, 56 rue de Passy, 75016 Paris, France.

362.8   US   ISSN 0197-5439
WORLD REFUGEE SURVEY. 1958. a. $6. United States Committee for Refugees, 815 15th St., No. 610, Washington, DC 20005. TEL 202-667-0782. Ed. Virginia Hamilton. bk. rev. charts. illus. stat. circ. 20,000. Indexed: HR Rep. Refug.Abstr.
   Formerly: World Refugee Survey Report (ISSN 0162-9832)

301.4   FR
WORLD UNION FOR THE SAFEGUARD OF YOUTH. CONFERENCE PROCEEDINGS.* (Editions in English and French) 1960. triennial, 5th, 1972, Paris. World Union for the Safeguard of Youth, 28 Place Saint-Georges, 75442 Paris Cedex 9, France.
   Formerly: World Union of Organizations for the Safeguard of Youth (ISSN 0084-2400)

WORLD'S WOMAN'S CHRISTIAN TEMPERANCE UNION. TRIENNIAL REPORT. see *DRUG ABUSE AND ALCOHOLISM*

353.9 614   US   ISSN 0098-6984
WYOMING. DEPARTMENT OF HEALTH AND SOCIAL SERVICES. ANNUAL REPORT. a. Department of Health and Social Services, 117 Hathaway Bldg., Cheyenne, WY 82002-0710. TEL 307-777-7656. Key Title: Annual Report of the Health and Social Services.

267.3   US   ISSN 0084-4292
Y M C A YEARBOOK AND OFFICIAL ROSTER. 1877. a. $30. ‡ Young Men's Christian Association of the U S A, National Council, 101 N. Wacker Dr., Chicago, IL 60606-1718. Ed. Stanley Haidl. circ. 2,000.

360   US
YOUR (YEAR) GUIDE TO SOCIAL SECURITY BENEFITS. 1982. a. $15.95 hardbound; paperbound $7.95. Facts on File, Inc., 460 Park Ave. S., New York, NY 10016. TEL 212-683-2244. Ed. Leona G. Rubin.

362.7   UK
YOUTH SERVICES GUIDE. 1982. a. free. N U S Marketing, University of London Union, Malet St., London WC1, England. Ed. John Faircloth. circ. 5, 000.

362.7   US   ISSN 0196-9668
YOUTH-SERVING ORGANIZATIONS DIRECTORY. 1978. irreg., latest 2nd edt., 1980. $75. Gale Research Company, Book Tower, Detroit, MI 48226. TEL 313-961-2242.

360 309.1   ZA   ISSN 0084-4608
ZAMBIA. DEPARTMENT OF COMMUNITY DEVELOPMENT. REPORT. 1964. irreg., (approx. a.), latest 1975. 10 n. Government Printer, Box 136, Lusaka, Zambia.

360   ZA   ISSN 0084-4667
ZAMBIA. DEPARTMENT OF SOCIAL WELFARE. REPORT. 1964. a. Government Printer, Box 136, Lusaka, Zambia.

360   ZA   ISSN 0081-0533
ZAMBIA. DEPARTMENT OF SOCIAL WELFARE. SOCIAL WELFARE RESEARCH MONOGRAPHS. a. price varies. Government Printer, Box 136, Lusaka, Zambia.

360   ZA   ISSN 0084-5035
ZAMBIA. PUBLIC SERVICE COMMISSION. REPORT. 1964. a. 10 n. Government Printer, Box 136, Lusaka, Zambia.

ZEITSCHRIFTENBIBLIOGRAPHIE GERONTOLOGIE. see *GERONTOLOGY AND GERIATRICS*

SOCIAL SERVICES AND WELFARE — Abstracting, Bibliographies, Statistics

361 314   AU
AUSTRIA. STATISTISCHES ZENTRALAMT. OEFFENTLICHE FUERSORGE. vol.360, 1974. a. S.55. Hintere Zollamtsstr. 2b, 1033 Vienna, Austria. circ. 400.

300 016   BL   ISSN 0067-6608
BIBLIOGRAFIA BRASILEIRA DE CIENCIAS SOCIAIS. 1954. a. Cr.$600($25) Instituto Brasileiro de Informacao em Ciencia e Tecnologia, SCRN 708/709 Bloco B Loja 18E 30, 70740 Brasilia DF, Brazil. bk. rev. circ. 300.
   Supersedes: Bibliografia Economico-Social.

CANADA. DEPARTMENT OF NATIONAL HEALTH AND WELFARE. LIBRARY. ACQUISITIONS. see *PUBLIC HEALTH AND SAFETY — Abstracting, Bibliographies, Statistics*

CANADA. STATISTICS CANADA. LIST OF CANADIAN HOSPITALS AND SPECIAL CARE FACILITIES/LISTE DES HOPITAUX CANADIENS ET DES ETABLISSEMENTS DE SOINS SPECIAUX. see *HOSPITALS — Abstracting, Bibliographies, Statistics*

360   UK
CHARITY STATISTICS. 1978. a. £18.50. Charities Aid Foundation, 48 Pembury Rd., Tonbridge, Kent TN9 2JD, England. Ed. J. McQuillan. circ. 2,000.

360   UK   ISSN 0144-610X
CHARTERED INSTITUTE OF PUBLIC FINANCE AND ACCOUNTANCY. PERSONAL SOCIAL SERVICES ESTIMATE STATISTICS. 1974. a. £14. Chartered Institute of Public Finance and Accountancy, 3 Robert St., London WC2N 6BH, England. (back issues avail.)

310 360   UK   ISSN 0309-653X
CHARTERED INSTITUTE OF PUBLIC FINANCE AND ACCOUNTANCY. PERSONAL SOCIAL SERVICES STATISTICS. ACTUALS. 1949/50. a. £14. Chartered Institute of Public Finance and Accountancy, 3 Robert St., London WC2N 6BH, England. stat. (back issues avail.)
   Formerly: Chartered Institute of Public Finance and Accountancy. Local Health and Social Services Statistics (ISSN 0307-0506)

360   UK   ISSN 0264-6544
CHARTERED INSTITUTE OF PUBLIC FINANCE AND ACCOUNTANCY. PROBATION. ESTIMATES. 1983. a. £11. Chartered Institute of Public Finance and Accountancy, 3 Robert St., London WC2N 6BH, England.

360   UK   ISSN 0144-5081
COMMUNITY SERVICE STATISTICS: SCOTLAND. 1980. a. Social Work Services Group, 43 Jeffry St., Edinburgh EH1 1DN, England.

010 060   US
COMSEARCH: BROAD TOPICS. 1982. a. $38. Foundation Center, 79 Fifth Ave., New York, NY 10003. TEL 212-620-4230.
   Incorporating: International Philanthropy.

010 060   US
COMSEARCH: GEOGRAPHICS. (Avail. for 19 areas) 1980. a. $30. Foundation Center, 79 Fifth Ave., New York, NY 10003. TEL 212-620-4230.

010 060   US
COMSEARCH: SUBJECTS. 1972. a. $18. Foundation Center, 79 Fifth Ave., New York, NY 10003. TEL 212-620-4230. (also avail. in microfiche)
   Formerly: Comsearch Printouts: Subjects; Supersedes in part: Comsearch Printouts; Supersedes (since 1977): Foundation Grants Index; Subjects on Microfiche (ISSN 0090-1601)

361.6 318   DR
DOMINICAN REPUBLIC. SECRETARIA DE SANIDAD Y ASISTENCIA PUBLICA. CUADROS ESTADISTICOS. irreg. Secretaria de Sanidad y Asistencia Publica, Ciudad Trujillo, Dominican Republic.

318   PN   ISSN 0378-262X
ESTADISTICA PANAMENA. SITUACION SOCIAL. SECCION 431. ASISTENCIA SOCIAL. 1957. a. Bl.0.75. Direccion de Estadistica y Censo, Contraloria General, Apartado 5213, Panama 5, Panama. circ. 1,100.

362   US
FLORIDA. DEPARTMENT OF HEALTH AND REHABILITATIVE SERVICES. ANNUAL STATISTICAL REPORT. a. Department of Health and Rehabilitative Services, 1317 Winewood Blvd., Tallahassee, FL 32302. TEL 904-488-1234.
   Formerly: Florida. Division of Family Services. Annual Statistical Report (ISSN 0093-6715)

010 060   US   ISSN 0190-3357
FOUNDATION CENTER. ANNUAL REPORT. 1956. a. free. Foundation Center, 79 Fifth Ave., New York, NY 10003. TEL 212-620-4230.
   Formerly: Foundation Center. Report (ISSN 0548-7269)

010 060   US   ISSN 0730-1677
FOUNDATION CENTER NATIONAL DATA BOOK. 1975. a. $60. Foundation Center, 79 Fifth Ave., New York, NY 10003. TEL 212-620-4230. Key Title: National Data Book.
   ●Also available online. Vendors: DIALOG.

010 060   US   ISSN 0071-8092
FOUNDATION DIRECTORY. (Supplement avail.) 1960. biennial. $85. ‡ Foundation Center, 79 Fifth Ave., New York, NY 10003. TEL 212-620-4230. charts. stat. index. circ. 8,000. Indexed: ERIC.
   ●Also available online. Vendors: DIALOG.
   Supersedes: American Foundations and their Fields.

010 060   US
FOUNDATION DIRECTORY SUPPLEMENT. 1982. biennial. $30. Foundation Center, 79 Fifth Ave., New York, NY 10003. TEL 212-620-4230.

010 060   US
FOUNDATION GRANTS INDEX. 1970. a. $46. Foundation Center, 79 Fifth Ave., New York, NY 10003. TEL 212-620-4230.
   ●Also available online. Vendors: DIALOG.

361.73   US
FOUNDATION GRANTS TO INDIVIDUALS. 1977. biennial. $18. Foundation Center, 79 Fifth Ave., New York, NY 10003. TEL 212-620-4230.

361.73   US
FOUNDATIONS TODAY: CURRENT FACTS AND FIGURES ON PRIVATE FOUNDATIONS. a. $2.50. Foundation Center, 79 Fifth Ave., New York, NY 10003. TEL 212-620-4230.

362.8   FR   ISSN 0181-0804
FRANCE. CAISSE NATIONALE DES ALLOCATIONS FAMILIALES. STATISTIQUES ACTION SOCIALE. a. Caisse Nationale des Allocations Familiales, 23 rue Daviel, 75634 Paris Cedex 13, France. charts. stat.
   Formerly: France. Caisse Nationale des Allocations Familiales. Action Sociale.

362.5   FR   ISSN 0182-1598
FRANCE. CAISSE NATIONALE DES ALLOCATIONS FAMILIALES. STATISTIQUES PRESTATIONS FAMILIALES. RESULTATS GENERAUX: RECETTES, DEPENSES, BENEFICIAIRES. a. Caisse Nationale des Allocations Familiales, 23 rue Daviel, 75634 Paris Cedex 13, France. charts. stat.
   Formerly: France. Caisse Nationale des Allocations Familiales. Prestations Familiales. Resultats Generaux: Recettes, Depenses, Beneficiaires.

362 314   GW   ISSN 0072-3754
GERMANY (FEDERAL REPUBLIC, 1949-). STATISTISCHES BUNDESAMT. FACHSERIE 13, REIHE 2: SOZIALHILFE; REIHE 3: KRIEGSOPFERFUERSORGE. a. price varies. W. Kohlhammer-Verlag GmbH, Abt. Veroeffentlichungen des Statistischen Bundesamtes, Philipp-Reis-Str. 3, Postfach 421120, 6500 Mainz 42, W. Germany (B.R.D.).

362 314   GW   ISSN 0072-3762
GERMANY (FEDERAL REPUBLIC, 1949-).
STATISTISCHES BUNDESAMT. FACHSERIE
13, SOZIALLEISTUNGEN, REIHE 6:
JUGENDHILFE. a. price varies. W. Kohlhammer-
Verlag GmbH, Abt. Veroeffentlichungen des
Statistischen Bundesamtes, Philipp-Reis-Str. 3,
Postfach 421120, 6500 Mainz 42, W. Germany
(B.R.D.)

360   GR   ISSN 0253-9454
GREECE. NATIONAL STATISTICAL SERVICE.
SOCIAL WELFARE AND HEALTH
STATISTICS. (Text in English and Greek) 1967. a.,
latest 1983. $7. National Statistical Service,
Publications and Information Division, 14-16
Lycourgou St., 10166 Athens, Greece.

360 614   UK
HEALTH SERVICE ABSTRACTS. 1974. m. £20.50.
Department of Health and Social Security, Library,
Rm. A111, Alexander Fleming House, Elephant and
Castle, London SE1 6BY, England (Subscr. addr.:
P.O. Box 21, Stanmore, Middlesex HA7 1AY,
England) Ed. I.M.M. Cameron.
  Incorporating (as of May 1985): Hospital
Abstracts (ISSN 0018-5507) & Current Literature
on Health Services (ISSN 0141-0571) & Current
Literature on General Medical Practice.

IDAHO. DEPARTMENT OF HEALTH AND
WELFARE. ANNUAL SUMMARY OF VITAL
STATISTICS. see *PUBLIC HEALTH AND
SAFETY — Abstracting, Bibliographies, Statistics*

360 628   JA
JAPAN. MINISTRY OF HEALTH AND
WELFARE. STATISTICS AND INFORMATION
DEPARTMENT. REPORT ON BASIC SURVEY
OF HEALTH AND WELFARE
ADMINISTRATION. a. 3000 Yen. Ministry of
Health and Welfare, Statistics and Information
Department, 7-3 Ichigaya-Honmura cho, Shinjuku-
ku, Tokyo 162, Japan (Order from: Health &
Welfare Statistics Association, c/o Mezon Azabu, 5-
13-14 Roppongi, Minato-ku, Tokyo, Japan)

360 315   JA
JAPAN. MINISTRY OF HEALTH AND
WELFARE. STATISTICS AND INFORMATION
DEPARTMENT. REPORT ON SURVEY OF
LIVELIHOOD AID SERVICES. a. 2600 Yen.
Ministry of Health and Welfare, Statistics and
Information Department, 7-3 Ichigaya-Honmura
cho, Shinjuku-ku, Tokyo 162, Japan (Order from:
Health & Welfare Statistics Association, c/o Mezon
Azabu, 5-13-14 Roppongi, Minato-ku, Tokyo,
Japan)

360 315   JA
JAPAN. MINISTRY OF HEALTH AND
WELFARE. STATISTICS AND INFORMATION
DEPARTMENT. REPORT ON SURVEY OF
SOCIAL WELFARE FACILITIES. a. 3000 Yen.
Ministry of Health and Welfare, Statistics and
Information Department, 7-3 Ichigaya-Honmura
cho, Shinjuku-ku, Tokyo 162, Japan (Order from:
Health & Welfare Statistics Association, c/o Mezon
Azabu, 5-13-14 Roppongi, Minato-ku, Tokyo,
Japan)

JAPAN. MINISTRY OF HEALTH AND
WELFARE. STATISTICS AND INFORMATION
DEPARTMENT. STATISTICAL HANDBOOK
ON HEALTH AND SOCIAL WELFARE. see
*PUBLIC HEALTH AND SAFETY — Abstracting,
Bibliographies, Statistics*

360 315   JA
JAPAN. MINISTRY OF HEALTH AND
WELFARE. STATISTICS AND INFORMATION
DEPARTMENT. STATISTICAL REPORT ON
SOCIAL WELFARE SERVICES. a. 3.000 Yen.
Ministry of Health and Welfare, Statistics and
Information Department, 7-3 Ichigaya-Honmura
cho, Shinjuku-ku, Tokyo 162, Japan (Order from:
Health & Welfare Statistics Association, c/o Mezon
Azabu, 5-13-14 Roppongi, minato-ku, Tokyo, Japan)

361   US   ISSN 0093-7835
MICHIGAN. DEPARTMENT OF SOCIAL
SERVICES. PROGRAM STATISTICS. (Report
year Ends Sept. 30) a. Department of Social
Services, Box 30037, 300 S. Capitol Ave., Lansing,
MI 48909. TEL 517-373-2005. Key Title: Program
Statistics - Michigan Department of Social Services.
Supersedes: Michigan. Department of Social
Services. Public Assistance Statistics (ISSN 0093-
6774)

360 336   NE   ISSN 0168-4086
NETHERLANDS. CENTRAAL BUREAU VOOR
DE STATISTIEK. STATISTIEK VAN DE
ALGEMENE BIJSTAND. STATISTICS OF
PUBLIC ASSISTANCE. (Text in Dutch and
English) 1965. a. fl.10.25. Centraal Bureau voor de
Statistiek, Prinses Beatrixlaan 428, Voorburg,
Netherlands (Orders to: Staatsuitgeverij, Christoffel
Plantijnstraat, The Hague, Netherlands)

362   NE
NETHERLANDS. CENTRAAL BUREAU VOOR
DE STATISTIEK. STATISTIEK VAN DE
BEJAARDENOORDEN. HOMES FOR THE
AGED. (Text in Dutch and English) 1950. a.
fl.25.30. Centraal Bureau voor de Statistiek, Prinses
Beatrixlaan 428, Voorburg, Netherlands (Orders to:
Staatsuitgeverij, Christoffel Plantijnstraat, The
Hague, Netherlands)

SALUS; low cost rural health care and health
manpower training: an annotated bibliography with
special emphasis on developing countries. see
*PUBLIC HEALTH AND SAFETY — Abstracting,
Bibliographies, Statistics*

360 315   CH
SOCIAL AFFAIRS STATISTICS OF TAIWAN/
CHUNG-HUA MIN KUO TAI-WAN SHENG
SHE HUI SHIH YEH TUNG CHI. (Text in
English and Chinese) a. Department of Social
Affairs, Nan-Tou Hsien, Taiwan, Republic of China.
stat.

362 016   US   ISSN 0148-0847
SOCIAL WORK RESEARCH AND ABSTRACTS.
1965. q. $55 to non-members; institutions $75.
National Association of Social Workers, Publications
Department, 7981 Eastern Ave., Silver Spring, MD
20910 TEL 301-565-0333. Ed. Eileen Gambrill. adv.
index. circ. 5,000. (also avail. in microform from
UMI; reprint service avail. from UMI) Indexed:
Psychol.Abstr. SSCI. Sociol.Abstr.
Soc.Work.Res.& Abstr. Adol.Ment.Hlth.Abstr.
ASCA. Abstr.Health Care Manage.Stud.
Crim.Just.Abstr. CLOA. Hosp.Lit.Ind. Lang.&
Lang.Behav.Abstr. Med.Care Rev. Rehabil.Lit.
Sage Pub.Admin.Abstr.
  Formerly: Abstracts for Social Workers (ISSN
0001-3412)

360 310   US   ISSN 0099-2305
SOUTH DAKOTA. STATE DEPARTMENT OF
PUBLIC WELFARE. RESEARCH AND
STATISTICS ANNUAL REPORT. a. State
Department of Public Welfare, Division of Research
and Statistics, Office Bldg. No. One, Pierre, SD
57501. stat. Key Title: Research and Statistics
Annual Report.

360 314   SW   ISSN 0082-0326
SWEDEN. STATISTISKA CENTRALBYRAAN.
STATISTISKA MEDDELANDEN. SUBGROUP S
(SOCIAL WELFARE STATISTICS) (Text in
Swedish; table heads and summaries in English)
1963 N.S. irreg. Kr.320. Statistiska Centralbyraan,
Distribution, S-701 89 Oerebro, Sweden. circ. 1,300.

360 016   US   ISSN 0278-0143
U.S. DEPARTMENT OF HEALTH AND HUMAN
SERVICES. PUBLICATION CATALOG. irreg.,
latest 1975, next 1978. free. U.S. Department of
Health, Education and Welfare, 330 Independence
Ave. S.W., Washington, DC 20201. TEL 202-655-
4000. Indexed: CINHAL.
  Formerly: U.S. Department of Health, Education
and Welfare. Catalog of Publications (ISSN 0275-
8210)

362.5   US   ISSN 0360-4594
U.S. FOOD AND NUTRITION SERVICE. FOOD
AND NUTRITION PROGRAMS. a. U.S.
Department of Agriculture, Food and Nutrition
Service, Alexandria, VA 22302. TEL 202-447-8046.
Key Title: Food and Nutrition Programs.

SOCIOLOGY

see also *Folklore; Social Sciences:
Comprehensive Works; Social Services
and Welfare*

301   SA
A S S A PROCEEDINGS. 1973. irreg. R.4($4)
Association for Sociology in Southern Africa, Dept.
of Sociology, University of Cape Town, Rondebosch
7700, South Africa. Ed. Ken Jubber. circ. 300.

301   US
ACCENT ON LIVING BUYER'S GUIDE. 1977.
biennial. $10. Cheever Publishing, Inc., Box 700,
Bloomington, IL 61702. TEL 309-378-2961. Ed.
Raymond Cheever. adv. circ. 20,000. (back issues
avail.)

614   BU   ISSN 0515-2925
ACTA MEDICA ET SOCIOLOGICA. 1962. irreg.,
6th, 1972, Varna; last 9th, 1983, Barcelona, Spain.
International Medical Association for the Study of
Living Conditions and Health, c/o J. de Castro, Bd.
D. Nestorov 15, BG-1431 Sofia, Bulgaria.

301   IT   ISSN 0065-1656
ACTA SCIENTIARUM SOCIALIUM. (Text in
English, French, German, Italian, Rumanian,
Spanish) 1959. irreg. price varies. Societa
Accademica Romena, Foro Traiano 1a, 00187
Rome, Italy.

301   MX
ACTA SOCIOLOGICA. SERIE PROMOCION
SOCIAL.* 1969. a. Universidad Nacional
Autonoma de Mexico, Facultad de Ciencias
Politicas y Sociales, Centro de Estudios del
Desarrollo, Ciudad Universitaria, Villa Obregon,
Mexico 20, D.F., Mexico. Ed. Ricardo Pozas
Arciniega. bibl. illus.

301 370   PL
ACTA UNIVERSITATIS LODZIENSIS: FOLIA
SOCIOLOGICA. (Text in Polish; summaries in
various languages) irreg. Uniwersytet Lodzki,
Drukarnia Wojskowa, Ul. Gdanska 130, Lodz,
Poland (Dist. by: Ars Polona-Ruch, Krakowskie
Przedmiescie 7, Warsaw, Poland)

ADVANCES IN APPLIED SOCIAL
PSYCHOLOGY. see *PSYCHOLOGY*

301.15   US   ISSN 0065-2601
ADVANCES IN EXPERIMENTAL SOCIAL
PSYCHOLOGY. 1964. irreg., vol.19, 1986.
Academic Press, Inc., Orlando, FL 32887. TEL
305-345-2000. Ed. Leonard Berkowitz. index.
Indexed: Biol.Abstr. SSCI.

ADVANCES IN FAMILY INTERVENTION,
ASSESSMENT AND THEORY; a research annual.
see *PSYCHOLOGY*

301   US
ADVANCES IN GROUP PROCESSES. 1984. a.
$24.75 to individuals; institutions $49.50. J A I
Press Inc., 36 Sherwood Pl., Box 1678, Greenwich,
CT 06836-1678. TEL 203-661-7602. Ed. Edward J.
Lawler.

ADVANCES IN THE STUDY OF
COMMUNICATION AND AFFECT. see
PSYCHOLOGY

AGORA (RAVENNA) see *PHILOSOPHY*

301.4 338.1   GW   ISSN 0065-437X
AGRARSOZIALE GESELLSCHAFT.
GESCHAEFTS- UND ARBEITSBERICHT. 1950/
51. a. free. Agrarsoziale Gesellschaft e.V., Kurze
Geismarstr. 23/25, 3400 Goettingen, W. Germany
(B.R.D.)
  Until 1968: Agrarsoziale Gesellschaft.
Arbeitsbericht.

301.4   GW   ISSN 0170-7671
AGRARSOZIALE GESELLSCHAFT. KLEINE
REIHE. 1970. irreg., no.28, 1987. price varies.
Agrarsoziale Gesellschaft e.V., Kurze Geismarstr.
23/25, 3400 Goettingen, W. Germany (B.R.D.)
Indexed: Rural Recreat.Tour.Abstr. World
Agri.Econ.& Rural Sociol.Abstr.

SOCIOLOGY

301.4 GW ISSN 0344-5712
AGRARSOZIALE GESELLSCHAFT. MATERIALSAMMLUNG. 1953. irreg., no.176, 1986. price varies. Agrarsoziale Gesellschaft e.V., Kurze Geismarstr. 23/25, 3400 Goettingen, W. Germany (B.R.D.) Indexed: Geo.Abstr.

301.15 GW
ALLENSBACHER JAHRBUCH DER DEMOSKOPIE. 1947. irreg. price varies. (Institut fuer Demoskopie, Allensbach) Verlag fuer Demoskopie, Radolfzeller Str. 8, 7753 Allensbach, W. Germany (B.R.D.) Ed. E. Noelle. adv. bk. rev. circ. 3,000.
Former title: Jahrbuch der Oeffentlichen Meinung (ISSN 0075-2347)

334 UK
ALTERNATIVE COMMUNITIES MAGAZINE. 1979. irreg. £6.64 for 12 nos. The Teachers, York Place, Bangor, Gwynedd LL57 1HE, Wales. Ed. Michele Bland. adv. bk. rev. illus. circ. 800. (back issues avail.)
Incorporating: International Journal of Alternative Communities.

301 PE ISSN 0065-6763
AMERICA - PROBLEMA. 1968. irreg., latest no.11. price varies. (Instituto de Estudios Peruanos) I E P Ediciones, Horacio Urteaga 694 (Campo de Marte), Lima 11, Peru.

301.4 US
AMERICAN CULTURAL HERITAGE SERIES. a. $18.39. Burt Franklin & Company, 235 E. 44 St., New York, NY 10017. TEL 212-687-5250. Ed. Jack Salzman.

301 US ISSN 0065-8197
AMERICAN ETHNOLOGICAL SOCIETY. MONOGRAPHS. 1940. irreg., vol.55, 1973. price varies. (American Ethnological Society) West Publishing Co., Box 3526, St. Paul, MN 55165 TEL 612-288-2500. (Vols. before 1972 dist. by: University of Washington Press, Seattle, WA 98105)

301 US
AMERICAN SOCIOLOGICAL ASSOCIATION. PROCEEDINGS OF ANNUAL MEETING. a. $2.50. American Sociological Association, 1722 N St., N.W., Washington, DC 20036. TEL 202-833-3410. (reprint service avail. from UMI)

AMERICAN UNIVERSITY STUDIES. SERIES 16. ECONOMICS. see POPULATION STUDIES

301 SP ISSN 0066-1473
ANALES DE MORAL SOCIAL Y ECONOMICA. 1962. irreg. 125 ptas. Centro de Estudios Sociales de la Santa Cruz del Valle de los Caidos, Madrid, Spain (Distr. by: Aguilar, S.A. de Publicaciones, Juan Bravo 38, Madrid 6, Spain)

301 PL
ANALIZY I PROBY TECHNIK BADAWCZYCH W SOCJOLOGII. (Text in Polish; summaries in English and Russian) irreg., vol.6, 1986. price varies. (Polska Akademia Nauk, Instytut Filozofii i Socjologii) Ossolineum, Publishing House of the Polish Academy of Sciences, Rynek 9, Wroclaw, Poland (Dist. by: Ars Polona-Ruch, Krakowskie Przedmiescie 7, Warsaw, Poland) Eds. Z. Gostkowski, J. Lutynski.

ANCIENT GREEK CITIES REPORT. see HOUSING AND URBAN PLANNING

ANNALES UNIVERSITATIS MARIAE CURIE-SKLODOWSKA. SECTIO I. PHILOSOPHIA-SOCIOLOGIA. see PHILOSOPHY

301 FR ISSN 0066-2399
ANNEE SOCIOLOGIQUE. 1896. a. 270 F. Presses Universitaires de France, 108 bd. Saint Germain, 75279 Paris Cedex 6, France (Service des Periodiques, 12 rue Jean de Beauvais, 75005 Paris) (reprint service avail. from KTO) Indexed: CERDIC. Lang.& Lang.Behav.Abstr.

ANNUAL EDITIONS: HUMAN SEXUALITY. see BIOLOGY

306.8 US ISSN 0272-7897
ANNUAL EDITIONS: MARRIAGE AND FAMILY. 1974. a. $9.50. Dushkin Publishing Group, Inc., Sluice Dock, Guilford, CT 06437. TEL 203-453-4351. Ed. Ian Nielsen. illus.
Formerly: Annual Editions: Readings in Marriage and Family (ISSN 0095-6155)

301 US ISSN 0277-9315
ANNUAL EDITIONS: SOCIOLOGY. 1972. a. $9.50. Dushkin Publishing Group, Inc., Sluice Dock, Guilford, CT 06437. TEL 203-453-4351. Ed. Ian Nielsen. illus. index. (back issues avail.) Indexed: Soc.Sci.Ind.
Formerly: Annual Editions: Readings in Sociology (ISSN 0090-4236)

301.364 US ISSN 0160-9815
ANNUAL EDITIONS: URBAN SOCIETY; an annual editions reader. 1978. biennial. $9.95. Dushkin Publishing Group, Inc., Sluice Dock, Guilford, CT 06437. TEL 203-453-4351. index. (back issues avail.)
Formerly: Focus: Urban Society.

301 US ISSN 0360-0572
ANNUAL REVIEW OF SOCIOLOGY. 1975. a. $31. Annual Reviews Inc., 4139 El Camino Way, Palo Alto, CA 94306. TEL 415-493-4400. Ed. W. Richard Scott. bibl. cum.index. (back issues avail.; reprint service avail. from ISI) Indexed: Biol.Abstr. Curr.Cont. Psychol.Abstr. SSCI. Soc.Sci.Ind. Amer.Bibl.Slavic & E.Eur.Stud. Lang.& Lang.Behav.Abstr.

ANUARIO DE SOCIOLOGIA Y PSICOLOGIA JURIDICAS. see LAW

309.1 US ISSN 0503-5422
APPALACHIAN REGIONAL COMMISSION. ANNUAL REPORT. 1965. a. free. U.S. Appalachian Regional Commission, 1666 Connecticut Ave. N.W., Washington, DC 20235. TEL 202-673-7835. Ed. Elise F. Kendrick. circ. 3,000. (back issues available) Indexed: P.A.I.S.

301.1 150 US ISSN 0196-4151
APPLIED SOCIAL PSYCHOLOGY ANNUAL. a. $29.95 cloth; $14.95 paper. (Society for the Psychological Study of Social Issues) Sage Publications, Inc., 2111 W. Hillcrest Dr., Newbury Park, CA 91320. TEL 805-944-0721. Indexed: Psychol.Abstr.

ASPECTS OF FRANCE. see ETHNIC INTERESTS

ATMA JAYA RESEARCH CENTRE. SOCIO-MEDICAL RESEARCH REPORT/PUSAT PENELITIAN ATMA JAYA. PENELITIAN TENTANG KEBUTUHAN KESEHATAN MASYARAKAT DAN SISTEM PELEYANAN KESEHATAN DI KECAMATAN PENJARINGAN. see MEDICAL SCIENCES

ATMA JAYA RESEARCH CENTRE. SOCIO-RELIGIOUS RESEARCH REPORT/PUSAT PENELITIAN ATMA JAYA. LAPORAN PENELITIAN KEAGAMAAN. see RELIGIONS AND THEOLOGY — Oriental

301 AT
AUSTRALIAN NATIONAL UNIVERSITY. CANBERRA. DEPARTMENT OF DEMOGRAPHY. FAMILY AND FERTILITY CHANGE. 1977. irreg. Aus.$9.50. Australian National University, Department of Demography, P.O. Box 4, Canberra, A.C.T. 2600, Australia.

301.4 BG ISSN 0070-8178
BANGLADESH RESEARCH AND EVALUATION CENTRE. REPORT.* (Text in English) a. Bangladesh Research and Evaluation Centre, 16 B, Rd. No. 7, Dhanmondi, Bangladesh.

301 GW
BEITRAEGE ZUR MITTELSTANDSFORSCHUNG. 1974. irreg., no.95, 1983. price varies. (Institut fuer Mittelstandsforschung) Verlag Metzler-Poeschel, P.O. Box 7, D-7408 Kusterdinger, W. Germany (B.R.D.) Eds. M. Ernst Kamp, F. Klein-Blenkers.

BEITRAEGE ZUR PSYCHOLOGIE UND SOZIOLOGIE DES KRANKEN MENSCHEN. see PSYCHOLOGY

301 US ISSN 0067-5830
BERKELEY JOURNAL OF SOCIOLOGY; critical review. 1955. a. $6 to individuals; institutions $12. University of California, Berkeley, Sociology Department, 410 Barrows Hall, Berkeley, CA 94720 TEL 415-642-2771. (Subscr. to: 458 A Barrows Hall, Berkeley, CA 94720) Ed.Bd. adv. bk. rev. index. circ. 1,500. (back issues avail.) Indexed: Sociol.Abstr. Amer.Bibl.Slavic & E.Eur.Stud. Alt.Press Ind. Lang.& Lang.Behav.Abstr.
Formerly (vols.1-4, 1955-58): Berkeley Publications in Society and Institutions.

301 SZ ISSN 0067-6136
BERNER BEITRAEGE ZUR SOZIOLOGIE. 1959. irreg., vol.18, 1977. price varies. (Universitaet Bern, Institut fuer Soziologie und Sozio-Oekonomische Entwicklungsfragen) Paul Haupt AG, Falkenplatz 14, CH-3001 Berne, Switzerland.

301.2 PL ISSN 0067-7655
BIBLIOTEKA ETNOGRAFII POLSKIEJ. (Text in English or Polish; summaries in English, French or German) 1958. a. price varies. (Polska Akademia Nauk, Instytut Historii Kultury Materialnej) Ossolineum, Publishing House of the Polish Academy of Sciences, Rynek 9, 50-106 Wroclaw, Poland (Dist. by: Ars Polona-Ruch, Krakowskie Przedmiescie 7, Warsaw, Poland) Ed. Maria Frankowska.

BIHAR RESEARCH SOCIETY. JOURNAL. see HISTORY — History Of The Near East

301 GW ISSN 0068-0044
BONNER BEITRAEGE ZUR SOZIOLOGIE. 1964. irreg., no.20, 1982. price varies. (Rheinische Friedrich-Wilhelms-Universitaet, Institut fuer Soziologie) Ferdinand Enke Verlag, Postfach 1304, 7000 Stuttgart 1, W. Germany (B.R.D.) Ed. G. Eisermann.

BRITISH POLITICAL SOCIOLOGY YEARBOOK. see POLITICAL SCIENCE

BULLETIN OF TIBETOLOGY. see HISTORY — History Of Asia

301 374 UK
C C E T S W REPORTING. 1978. irreg. free. Central Council for Education and Training in Social Work, Derbyshire House, St. Chad's St., London WC1H 8AD, England. Ed. Ed Pritchard. illus. circ. controlled.
Supersedes (after no.3, 1979): C C E T S W News (ISSN 0142-2693); Which was formerly (until 1978): C C E T S W Bulletin.

301.35 301.364 BL
CADERNOS DE ESTUDOS RURAIS E URBANOS. 1968. a. Cr.$15000($15) Centro de Estudos Rurais e Urbanos, Cidade Unversitaria, Caixa Postal 8105, Sao Paulo, Brazil. Eds. Maria Queiroz, Olga Moraes von Simson. bk. rev. bibl. circ. 1,300.

368.4 FR
CAISSES CENTRALES DE MUTUALITE SOCIALE AGRICOLE. STATISTIQUES. (First part: Resultats d'Ensemble; second part: Resultats Detailles) 1969. a. 75 F. Union des Caisses Centrales de la Mutualite Agricole, 8-10 rue d'Astorg, 75380 Paris Cedex 8, France. stat.

301 UK ISSN 0068-6727
CAMBRIDGE PAPERS IN SOCIOLOGY. 1970. irreg., no.5, 1975. $32.50 for latest vol. Cambridge University Press, Edinburgh Bldg., Shaftesbury Rd., Cambridge CB2 2RU, England (and 32 E. 57 St., New York NY 10022) Eds. R.M. Blackburn, J.H. Goldthorpe. index.

301 UK ISSN 0068-6808
CAMBRIDGE STUDIES IN SOCIOLOGY. 1968. irreg., no.10, 1978. price varies. Cambridge University Press, Edinburgh Bldg., Shaftesbury Rd., Cambridge CB2 2RU, England (and 32 E. 57 St., New York, NY 10022) Eds. R.M. Blackburn, J.H. Goldthorpe. index.

CANADIAN JOURNAL OF LAW AND SOCIETY. see LAW

CANADIAN JOURNAL OF POLITICAL & SOCIAL THEORY/REVUE CANADIENNE DE THEORIE POLITIQUE ET SOCIALE. see POLITICAL SCIENCE

CASE ANALYSIS IN SOCIAL SCIENCE AND SOCIAL THERAPY. see *SOCIAL SCIENCES: COMPREHENSIVE WORKS*

CENTRE D'ETUDES ETHNOLOGIQUES. PUBLICATIONS. SERIE 2: MEMOIRES ET MONOGRAPHIES. see *ANTHROPOLOGY*

CENTRE D'ETUDES ETHNOLOGIQUES BANDUNDU. PUBLICATIONS. see *ANTHROPOLOGY*

301.45   SA
CENTRE FOR INTERGROUP STUDIES. ANNUAL REPORT. Variant title: Abe Bailey Institute of Inter-Racial Studies. Annual Report. (Text in English) 1968. a. free. University of Cape Town, Centre for Intergroup Studies, Rondebosch, South Africa. Ed. Prof. H.W. van der Merwe. bibl. circ. 2,200 (controlled)

CENTRE FOR URBAN AND COMMUNITY STUDIES. BIBLIOGRAPHIC SERIES. see *HOUSING AND URBAN PLANNING*

CENTRE FOR URBAN AND COMMUNITY STUDIES. MAJOR REPORT SERIES. see *HOUSING AND URBAN PLANNING*

CENTRE FOR URBAN AND COMMUNITY STUDIES. RESEARCH PAPERS. see *HOUSING AND URBAN PLANNING*

301   330.9   BO
CENTRO DE ESTUDIOS DE LA REALIDAD ECONOMICA Y SOCIAL. SERIE COCHABAMBA. irreg., no.6, 1985. Centro de Estudios de la Realidad Economica y Social, Casilla 10018, La Paz, Bolivia. TEL (tel.) 321643.

CENTRO DE ESTUDIOS DE LA REALIDAD ECONOMICA Y SOCIAL. SERIE ESTUDIOS REGIONALES. see *BUSINESS AND ECONOMICS — Economic Situation And Conditions*

301.35   330.9   BO
CENTRO DE ESTUDIOS DE LA REALIDAD ECONOMICA Y SOCIAL. SERIE ESTUDIOS URBANOS. irreg., no.9, 1982. Centro de Estudios de la Realidad Economica y Social, Casilla 10018, La Paz, Bolivia.

301   330.9   BO
CENTRO DE ESTUDIOS DE LA REALIDAD ECONOMICA Y SOCIAL. SERIE MOVIMIENTOS SOCIALES. irreg., no.3, 1985. Centro de Estudios de la Realidad Economica y Social, Casilla 10018, La Paz, Bolivia. TEL (tel.) 321643.

301.364   AG   ISSN 0326-1417
CENTRO DE ESTUDIOS URBANOS Y REGIONALES. CUADERNOS. 1982. irreg. Ediciones C E U R, Av. Corrientes 2835, Piso 7 A, 1193 Buenos Aires, Argentina. TEL 961-8159-2355. circ. 500.

301.364   AG
CENTRO DE ESTUDIOS URBANOS Y REGIONALES. INFORMES DE INVESTIGACION. 1985. irreg. Ediciones C E U R, Av. Corrientes 2835, Piso 7 A, 1193 Buenos Aires, Argentina. TEL 961-8159-2355. circ. 500.

CHINA REPORT: POLITICAL, SOCIOLOGICAL, AND MILITARY AFFAIRS. see *POLITICAL SCIENCE*

301   US
CITY AND SOCIETY. 1977. irreg., vol.6, 1982. $25 cloth; $12.50 paper. Sage Publications, Inc., 2111 W. Hillcrest Dr., Newbury Park, CA 91320 TEL 805-499-0721. (And Sage Publications, Ltd., 28 Banner St., London EC1Y 8QE, England) Ed. Gerald Suttles.

CIVILIAN CONGRESS; persons holding military office in Congress. see *LAW*

301   US
CLINICAL SOCIOLOGY REVIEW. vol.2, 1984. a. price varies. (Clinical Sociology Association) Brunner-Mazel, Inc., 19 Union Sq. W., New York, NY 10003. TEL 212-924-3344. Ed. David Kellen. bk. rev. circ. 500-600. Indexed: Psychol.Abstr.

301   SP
COLECCION FUNDACION F O E S S A. SERIE ESTUDIOS. 1969. irreg. (Fundacion Fomento de Estudios Sociales y Sociologia Aplicada) Euramerica, S.A., Mateo Inurria, 15, Madrid-16, Spain. bibl. charts.

301   US   ISSN 0195-6310
COMPARATIVE SOCIAL RESEARCH. 1978. a. $21.25 to individuals; institutions $42.50. J A I Press Inc., Box 1678, 36 Sherwood Pl., Greenwich, CT 06836. TEL 203-661-7602. Ed. Richard A. Tomasson. Indexed: Lang.& Lang.Behav.Abstr.
Formerly (until vol.2): Comparative Studies in Sociology (ISSN 0164-1247)

301.3   US   ISSN 0069-9055
CONNECTICUT URBAN RESEARCH REPORT. 1963. irreg., no.26, 1979. price varies. University of Connecticut, Institute of Urban Research, Storrs, CT 06268. TEL 203-486-4518. Ed. Morton Tenzer.

CONNEXIONS; address book of alternative projects. see *LITERARY AND POLITICAL REVIEWS*

301   UK   ISSN 0069-942X
CONTEMPORARY ISSUES SERIES. 1969. a. Peter Owen Ltd., 73 Kenway Rd., London SW5 0RE, England (Dist. in U.S. by: Humanities Press Inc., 450 Park Ave. So., New York, NY 10010)

301.15   US
CONTEMPORARY STUDIES IN APPLIED BEHAVIORAL SCIENCE. 1983. irreg., vol.3, 1985. $22.50 to individuals; institutions $45. J A I Press Inc., Box 1678, 36 Sherwood Pl., Greenwich, CT 06836. Ed. Louis A. Zurcher. bibl. index.

301   US
CONTEMPORARY STUDIES IN SOCIOLOGY.* irreg., vol.2, 1983. J A I Press, Box 1678, Greenwich, CT 06836-1678. Ed. John Clark.

301   IT   ISSN 0391-1926
CONTRIBUTI DI SOCIOLOGIA. (Numbers not published consecutively) 1973. irreg., no.69, 1986. price varies. Liguori Editore s.r.l., Via Mezzocannone 19, 80134 Naples, Italy. TEL 081/20 6077. Ed. Franco Ferrarotti.

301   IT   ISSN 0391-3171
CONTRIBUTI DI SOCIOLOGIA. READINGS. 1978. irreg., no.10, 1983. price varies. Liguori Editore s.r.l., Via Mezzocannone 19, 80134 Naples, Italy. TEL 081/20 6077. Ed. Franco Ferrarotti.

301.4   US   ISSN 0147-1023
CONTRIBUTIONS IN FAMILY STUDIES. 1977. irreg., no.8, 1984. price varies. Greenwood Press, 88 Post Rd. W., Box 5007, Westport, CT 06881. TEL 203-226-3571. Ed. Carol V. R. George.

301.4   US   ISSN 0147-1031
CONTRIBUTIONS IN INTERCULTURAL AND COMPARATIVE STUDIES. 1976. irreg. price varies. Greenwood Press, 88 Post Rd. W., Box 5007, Westport, CT 06881. TEL 203-226-3571. Ed. Ann M. Pescatello.

301   US   ISSN 0084-9278
CONTRIBUTIONS IN SOCIOLOGY. 1970. irreg. price varies. Greenwood Press, 88 Post Rd. W., Box 5007, Westport, CT 06881. TEL 203-226-3571. Ed. Don Martindale.

301.5   410   GW
CONTRIBUTIONS TO THE SOCIOLOGY OF LANGUAGE. 1972. irreg., vol.45, 1986. price varies. Walter de Gruyter & Co., Mouton Publishers, Postfach 110240, D-1000 Berlin 11, W. Germany (B.R.D.) (U.S. addr.: Mouton Publishers, division of Walter de Gruyter, Inc., 200 Saw Mill River Road, Hawthorne, NY 10532) Ed. Joshua A. Fishman.

CONTRIBUTIONS TO THE STUDY OF POPULAR CULTURE. see *ANTHROPOLOGY*

301   PY
CUADERNOS B P D. SERIE: SOCIAL. 1982. irreg. Banco Paraguayo de Datos, Casilla de Correo 1140, McArthur 250, Asuncion, Paraguay.

CUADERNOS C I P C A (SERIE POPULAR) (Centro de Investigacion y Promocion del Campesinado) see *EDUCATION — Adult Education*

301   SP   ISSN 0302-7724
CUADERNOS DE REALIDADES SOCIALES. no. 4, May 1974. irreg. 400 ptas.($11) Instituto de Sociologia Aplicada, Claudio Coello 141, Madrid, Spain. bk. rev. bibl. circ. 1,000.

301   IT   ISSN 0392-2111
CULTURA E MASS MEDIA. 1979. irreg., no.9, 1985. price varies. Liguori Editore s.r.l., Via Mezzocannone 19, 80134 Naples, Italy. TEL 081/20 6077. Ed. Alberto Abruzzese.

301   US   ISSN 0278-1204
CURRENT PERSPECTIVES IN SOCIAL THEORY; a research annual. 1980. a. $23.75 to individuals; institutions $47.50. J A I Press Inc., Box 1678, 36 Sherwood Pl., Greenwich, CT 06836. TEL 203-661-7602. Ed. Scott G. McNall. Indexed: SSCI. Lang.& Lang.Behav.Abstr.

361   US   ISSN 0164-1875
D R C BOOK & MONOGRAPH SERIES. 1968. irreg. University of Delaware, Disaster Research Center, Newark, DE 19716. TEL 302-451-6618.
Formerly: Ohio State University. Disaster Research Center. D R C - T R (ISSN 0078-4109)

361   US   ISSN 0164-1867
D R C HISTORICAL AND COMPARATIVE DISASTERS SERIES. 1977. irreg. University of Delaware, Disaster Research Center, Newark, DE 19716. TEL 302-451-6618.

301.2   UR
DAGESTANSKII ETNOGRAFICHESKII SBORNIK. 1974. irreg. 1.49 Rub. Akademiya Nauk S.S.S.R., Dagestanskii Filial, Institut Istorii, Yazyka i Literatury, Ul. Gadzhieva, 45, Makhachkala, Dagestan Autonomous S.S.R., U.S.S.R. illus.

301   301.412   615.7   BO
DE TEXTOS. irreg., no.10, 1985. price varies. Centro de Investigaciones Sociales, Casilla 6931 - Correo Central, La Paz, Bolivia.

DEATH AND DYING A TO Z. see *PSYCHOLOGY*

301   PE
DEBATES EN SOCIOLOGIA. 1977. a. $6.50. (Pontificia Universidad Catolica del Peru, Departamento de Ciencias Sociales) Fondo Editorial, Apdo. 1761, Lima 100, Peru. Ed. Gonzalo Portocarrero. charts. illus.

DENMARK. SOCIALFORSKNINGSINSTITUTTET. MEDDELELSER. see *SOCIAL SERVICES AND WELFARE*

DENMARK. SOCIALFORSKNINGSINSTITUTTET. PJECER. see *SOCIAL SERVICES AND WELFARE*

DENMARK. SOCIALFORSKNINGSINSTITUTTET. PUBLIKATIONER. see *SOCIAL SERVICES AND WELFARE*

DENMARK. SOCIALFORSKNINGSINSTITUTTET. SMAATRYK. see *SOCIAL SERVICES AND WELFARE*

DENMARK. SOCIALFORSKNINGSINSTITUTTET. STUDIER. see *SOCIAL SERVICES AND WELFARE*

301   II
DIBRUGARH UNIVERSITY. CENTRE FOR SOCIOLOGICAL STUDY OF THE FRONTIER REGION. NORTH EASTERN RESEARCH BULLETIN. 1970. a. Rs.5. Dibrugarh University, Centre for Sociological Study of Frontier Region, Dept. of Sociology, Rajabheta, Dibrugarh, Assam, India. Ed. S.M. Dubey. bk. rev. bibl. circ. 500.

DIRECTORY OF UNPUBLISHED EXPERIMENTAL MENTAL MEASURES. see *PSYCHOLOGY*

301.428   US   ISSN 0012-4230
DIVORCE CHATS. 1961. irreg. membership. ‡ United States Divorce Reform, Inc., Box 243, Kenwood, CA 95452. TEL 707-833-2550. Ed. George Partis. bk. rev. circ. 1,500. (processed)

301.4   BO
DOCUMENTOS INSTITUCIONALES OFICIALES. 1972. irreg., no.25, 1985. price varies. Centro de Investigaciones Sociales, Casilla 6931 - C.C., La Paz, Bolivia.

SOCIOLOGY

301.2   US
DUBLIN SEMINAR FOR NEW ENGLAND FOLKLIFE. ANNUAL PROCEEDINGS. 1976. a. $7. (Dublin Seminar for New England Folklife) Boston University Scholarly Publications, 985 Commonwealth Ave., Boston, MA 02215. TEL 617-353-4106. Ed. Peter Benes. adv. bibl. charts. illus. index. circ. 1,500. (back issues avail.)

EAST EUROPE REPORT. see *POLITICAL SCIENCE*

301   UK
EDINBURGH STUDIES IN SOCIOLOGY. irreg. (approx. 2 vols./yr.) price varies. Macmillan Press Ltd., 4 Little Essex St., London WC2R 3LF, England. Ed.Bd.

301   NE
ERASMUS UNIVERSITEIT, ROTTERDAM. CENTRUM VOOR MAATSCHAPPIJGESCHIEDENIS. MEDEDELINGEN/INFORMATION BULLETIN. 1978. irreg., no.7, 1979. Erasmus Universiteit, Rotterdam, Centrum voor Maatschappijgeschiedenis, Postbus 1738, Rotterdam, Netherlands.

309   BO
ESTUDIOS DE POBLACION Y DESARROLLO. 1974. irreg., no.29, 1985. price varies. Centro de Investigaciones Sociales, Casilla 6931 - C.C., La Paz, Bolivia.

301   BO
ESTUDIOS DE RECURSOS HUMANOS. 1978. irreg., no.10, 1985. Centro de Investigaciones Sociales, Casilla 6931 - C.C., La Paz, Bolivia.

301.4   BO
ESTUDIOS DE SOCIOLOGIA FAMILIAR. 1975. irreg., no.7, 1985. Centro de Investigaciones Sociales, Casilla 6931 - C.C., La Paz, Bolivia.

301   MX
ESTUDIOS FRONTERIZOS MEXICO - ESTADOS UNIDOS. 1984. irreg. CEFNOMEX, Abelardo L. Rodriguez No. 21, Zona del Rio, Tijuana, Baja California 22320, Mexico.

301.364   BO
ESTUDIOS URBANOS. 1973. irreg., no.6, 1979. price varies. Centro de Investigaciones Sociales, Casilla 6931 - C.C., La Paz, Bolivia.

301 960   SG
ETUDES SENEGALAISES. 1949. irreg. Institut Fondamental d'Afrique Noire, Centre de Saint-Louis de Senegal, Universite de Dakar, B.P. 206, Dakar, Senegal. illus.

301   FR   ISSN 0531-2663
EUROPEAN ASPECTS, SOCIAL STUDIES SERIES; a collection of studies relating to European integration. 1959. irreg. Council of Europe, Publications Section, 67000 Strasbourg, France (Dist. in U.S. by: Manhattan Publishing Co., Box 650, Croton-on-Hudson, N.Y. 10520)

EVALUATION COMMENT; the journal of educational evaluation. see *EDUCATION*

EXPLORATIONS IN URBAN ANALYSIS. see *SOCIAL SCIENCES: COMPREHENSIVE WORKS*

F A O ECONOMIC AND SOCIAL DEVELOPMENT PAPER. (Food and Agriculture Organization of the United Nations) see *BUSINESS AND ECONOMICS*

FACT SHEETS ON INSTITUTIONAL RACISM; minority outlook on current issues. see *POLITICAL SCIENCE — Civil Rights*

301.4   US   ISSN 0734-2926
FAMILY STUDIES REVIEW YEARBOOK. 1983. a. $59.95. Sage Publications, Inc., 2111 W. Hilllcrest Dr., Newbury Park, CA 91320 TEL 805-499-0721. (Subscr. to: Box 5024, Beverly Hills, CA 90210) Eds. Brent C. Miller, David H. Olson.

309 310   FI
FINLAND. STATISTIKCENTRALEN. STATISTISKA MEDDELANDEN. LEVNADSFOERHAALANDEN I FINLAND/ FINLAND. CENTRAL STATISTICAL OFFICE. LIVING CONDITIONS IN FINLAND. 1980. irreg. Fmk.89. Tilastokeskus, Annankatu 44, SF-00100 Helsinki 10, Finland.

309 310   FI
FINLAND. TILASTOKESKUS. TILASTOLLISIA TIEDONANTOJA. NAISTEN ASEMA/ FINLAND. STATISTIKCENTRALEEN. STATISTISKA MEDDELANDEN. KVINNORNAS STAELLNING/FINLAND. CENTRAL STATISTICAL OFFICE. STATISTICAL SURVEYS. POSITION OF WOMEN. (Text in English, Finnish, Swedish) 1980. irreg. Fmk.60. Central Statistical Office, P.O. Box 504, SF-00101 Helsinki, Finland.

FRAME/WORK. see *PHOTOGRAPHY*

FREIE UNIVERSITAET BERLIN. OSTEUROPA-INSTITUT. PHILOSOPHISCHE UND SOZIOLOGISCHE VEROEFFENTLICHUNGEN. see *PHILOSOPHY*

301 330   BL
FUNDACAO CENTRO DE PESQUISAS ECONOMICAS E SOCIAIS DO PIAUI. RELATORIO DE ATIVIDADES. Cover title: Fundacao Centro de Pesquisas Economicas e Sociais do Piaui. Atividades C E P R O. irreg. Fundacao Centro de Pesquisas Economicas e Sociais do Piaui, Av. Miguel Rosa 3190/S, Caixa Postal 429, 6400 Teresina-Piaui, Brazil.

301   BL
FUNDACAO JOAQUIM NABUCO. SERIE CURSOS E CONFERENCIAS. 1974. irreg., no.23, 1985. (Fundacao Joaquim Nabuco) Editora Massangana, Rua Dois Irmaos, 15 Apipucos Recife, Brazil.
Formerly: Instituto Joaquim Nabuco de Pesquisas Sociais. Serie Cursos e Conferencias.

301   BL
FUNDACAO JOAQUIM NABUCO. SERIE DOCUMENTOS. 1975. irreg., no.27, 1985. (Fundacao Joaquim Nabuco) Editora Massangana, Rua Dois Irmaos, 15 Apipucos Recife, Brazil.
Formerly: Instituto Joaquim Nabuco de Pesquisas Sociais. Serie Documentos.

301   BL
FUNDACAO JOAQUIM NABUCO. SERIE ESTUDOS E PESQUISAS. 1974. irreg., no.37, 1985. (Fundacao Joaquim Nabuco) Editora Massangana, Rua Dois Irmaos, 15 Apipucos Recife, Brazil. Indexed: Rural Recreat.Tour.Abstr. World Agri.Econ.& Rural Sociol.Abstr.
Formerly: Instituto Joaquim Nabuco de Pesquisas Sociais. Serie Estudos e Pesquisas.

301   AG
FUNDACION BARILOCHE. DESARROLLOS SINERGICOS. PUBLICACIONES. irreg. Fundacion Bariloche, Desarrollos Sinergicos, Casilla de Correo 138, 8400 San Carlos de Bariloche - Rio Negro, Argentina.
Former titles: Fundacion Bariloche. Departamento de Sociologia. Publicaciones & Fundacion Bariloche. Departamento de Sociologia. Documentos de Trabajo (ISSN 0071-9838)

GAY COUNSELLING. see *HOMOSEXUALITY*

GAY INFORMATION; a journal of Gay studies. see *POLITICAL SCIENCE — Civil Rights*

GENERAL SOCIAL SURVEYS. see *POLITICAL SCIENCE*

GEOGRAFIA URBANA. see *GEOGRAPHY*

301   SW   ISSN 0072-5102
GOETEBORGS UNIVERSITET. SOCIOLOGISKA INSTITUTIONEN. MONOGRAFIER. (Text in Swedish; summaries in English) 1968. irreg., no.33, 1984. price varies. Goteborgs Universitet, Sociologiska Institutionen, Karl Johansgatan 27, S-414 59 Goeteborg, Sweden.

301   PL   ISSN 0072-5013
GORNOSLASKIE STUDIA SOCJOLOGICZNE. 1963. irreg. Slaski Instytut Naukowy, Ul. Francuska 12, Katowice, Poland (Dist. by: Ars Polona-Ruch, Krakowskie Przedmiescie 7, Warsaw, Poland)

GRADUATE SCHOOL JOURNAL. see *EDUCATION — School Organization And Administration*

301   UK   ISSN 0072-5765
GREAT BRITAIN. CENTRAL STATISTICAL OFFICE. SOCIAL TRENDS. 1970. a. Central Statistical Office, Great George St., London SW1P 3AQ, England (Avail. from: Open University Educational Enterprises Ltd., 12 Cofferidge Close, Stony Stratford, Milton Keynes MK11 1BY, England) charts. stat.

GREAT BRITAIN. DEPARTMENT OF THE ENVIRONMENT. REPORT ON RESEARCH AND DEVELOPMENT. see *ENVIRONMENTAL STUDIES*

GREAT ISSUES OF THE DAY. see *POLITICAL SCIENCE*

301   US   ISSN 0091-7052
GUIDE TO GRADUATE DEPARTMENTS OF SOCIOLOGY. a. $10. American Sociological Association, 1722 N St., N.W., Washington, DC 20036. TEL 202-833-3410. (reprint service avail. from UMI)

301 900 330 398   US   ISSN 0146-5414
HARVEST BOOK SERIES. 1966. irreg. $15. Harvest Publishers, Box 9503 N. Berkeley Station, 1521 Shattuck Ave., Berkeley, CA 94709. Ed. William Brady. adv. bk. rev. circ. 1,500. (back issues avail.) Indexed: Alt.Press.Ind.

301   GW   ISSN 0073-1676
HEIDELBERGER SOCIOLOGICA. 1962. irreg. price varies. (Universitaet Heidelberg, Institut fuer Soziologie und Ethnologie) Verlag J.C.B. Mohr (Paul Siebeck), Wilhelmstr. 18, Postfach 2040, 7400 Tuebingen, W. Germany (B.R.D.) Ed. W.E. Muehlmann.

301   US   ISSN 0073-1986
HERITAGE OF SOCIOLOGY. 1964. irreg., no.43, 1984. price varies. University of Chicago Press, 5801 S. Ellis Ave., Chicago, IL 60637. TEL 312-962-7700. Ed. Morris Janowitz. (reprint service avail. from UMI,ISI)

301   FR   ISSN 0563-9743
HOMO. (Text in French; summaries in English) 1953. a. 55 F. Universite de Toulouse II (le Mirail), 56 rue du Taur, 31069 Toulouse Cedex, France. Ed. J.P. Martineau. Indexed: Biol.Abstr. SSCI.

301   SP
HOMO SOCIOLOGICUS. 1974. irreg. Ediciones Peninsula, Provenza 278, Barcelona-8, Spain.

HONG KONG SOCIAL AND ECONOMIC TRENDS. see *BUSINESS AND ECONOMICS — Economic Situation And Conditions*

HUMAN RESOURCES ABSTRACTS; an international information service. see *ABSTRACTING AND INDEXING SERVICES*

HUMAN STRESS CURRENT ADVANCES IN RESEARCH. see *PSYCHOLOGY*

301   DK   ISSN 0105-0532
I E F INFORMATION.* no.18, 1981. irreg. Koebenhavns Universitet, Institut for Europaeisk Folkelivsforskning, Frue Plads, 1168 Copenhagen K, Denmark. illus.

I L P E S CUADERNOS. (Instituto Latinamericano de Planificacion Economica y Social) see *BUSINESS AND ECONOMICS — Macroeconomics*

301.2 991.4   PH   ISSN 0073-9537
I P C MONOGRAPHS. (Text in English) irreg. price varies. Ateneo de Manila University, Institute of Philippine Culture, Box 154, Manila, Philippines. Ed. Alfonso De Guzman II.

301.2 991.4   PH   ISSN 0073-9545
I P C PAPERS. (Text in English) irreg., latest no.15. price varies. Ateneo de Manila University, Institute of Philippine Culture, Box 154, Manila, Philippines.

309 PH
I P C POVERTY RESEARCH SERIES. irreg. Ateneo de Manila University, Institute of Philippine Culture, Box 154, Manila, Philippines.

301 BL
I P E A RELATORIOS DE PESQUISA. 1971. irreg. price varies. Instituto de Planejamento Economico e Social, Caixa Postal 2672, Rio de Janeiro, Brazil.

301 AT
I R S A ITEMS. (Text in English; occasionally summaries in Spanish) 1977. a. membership. International Rural Sociology Association, c/o Dept. of Sociology, Michigan State University, East Lansing, MI 48824. Ed. Harry Schwarzweller. bk. rev. circ. 1,700. (tabloid format)

301 320 US
I S H I OCCASIONAL PAPERS IN SOCIAL CHANGE. 1976. irreg., no.6, 1982. price varies. Institute for the Study of Human Issues, 210 S. 13th St., Philadelphia, PA 19104. TEL 215-732-9729. Ed. J.M. Jutkowitz. circ. 1,000. (also avail. in microform from UMI)

IN THE MAKING; directory of radical cooperation. see BUSINESS AND ECONOMICS — Cooperatives

INDAGINI E PROSPETTIVE. see POLITICAL SCIENCE

INSTITUT ZA KRIMINOLOSKA I SOCIOLOSKA ISTRAZIVANJA. ZBORNIK. see CRIMINOLOGY AND LAW ENFORCEMENT

INSTITUTE OF DEVELOPMENT STUDIES. ANNUAL REPORT. see BUSINESS AND ECONOMICS — International Development And Assistance

301.45 UK
INSTITUTE OF RACE RELATIONS. ANNUAL REPORT. 1974/75. a. Institute of Race Relations, 2-6 Leeke St., London WC1X 9HS, England.

301 NE
INSTITUTE OF SOCIAL STUDIES, THE HAGUE. RESEARCH REPORT SERIES. (Text in English) 1977. irreg. price varies. Martinus Nijhoff, Box 269, 2501 AX The Hague, Netherlands. Indexed: Rural Recreat.Tour.Abstr. World Agri.Econ.& Rural Sociol.Abstr.

INSTITUTE ON PLURALISM AND GROUP IDENTITY. WORKING PAPER SERIES. see ETHNIC INTERESTS

301.35 PE
INSTITUTO DE ESTUDIOS ANDINOS. CUADERNOS. 1978. irreg. Instituto de Estudios Andinos, Apartado 289, Huancayo, Peru. illus.

309 PE
INSTITUTO DE ESTUDIOS PERUANOS. COLECCION MINIMA. 1973. irreg., latest no.14. price varies. I E P Ediciones, Horacio Urteaga 694 (Campo de Marte), Lima 11, Peru.

309 PE
INSTITUTO DE ESTUDIOS PERUANOS. ESTUDIOS DE LA SOCIEDAD RURAL. 1967. irreg., latest no.10. price varies. I E P Ediciones, Horacio Urteaga 694 (Campo de Marte), Lima 11, Peru.

301 340 UY
INSTITUTO INTERAMERICANO DEL NINO. JURIDICO SOCIAL. INFORMES TECNICOS. irreg. Instituto Interamericano del Nino, Avda. 8 de Octubre No. 2904, Montevideo, Uruguay.

362.7 FR ISSN 0538-5490
INTERNATIONAL CHILDREN'S CENTRE. PARIS. REPORT OF THE DIRECTOR-GENERAL TO THE EXECUTIVE BOARD. irreg. International Children's Centre, Chateau de Longchamp, Bois de Boulogne, 75016 Paris, France.

616.8 362 FR ISSN 0534-8021
INTERNATIONAL CHILDREN'S CENTRE. PARIS. TRAVAUX ET DOCUMENTS. 1950. irreg. International Children's Centre, Chateau de Longchamp, Bois de Boulogne, 75016 Paris, France.

INTERNATIONAL CONFERENCE FOR THE SOCIOLOGY OF RELIGION. see RELIGIONS AND THEOLOGY

INTERNATIONAL JOURNAL OF GROUP TENSIONS. see PSYCHOLOGY

301 NE ISSN 0074-8684
INTERNATIONAL STUDIES IN SOCIOLOGY AND SOCIAL ANTHROPOLOGY. 1963. irreg., vol.45, 1986. price varies. E.J. Brill, P.O. Box 9000, 2300 PA Leiden, Netherlands. Ed. K. Ishwaran.

IRISH JOURNAL OF AGRICULTURAL ECONOMICS AND RURAL SOCIOLOGY. see AGRICULTURE — Agricultural Economics

261 GW ISSN 0075-2584
JAHRBUCH FUER CHRISTLICHE SOZIALWISSENSCHAFTEN. Title varies: Jahrbuch des Instituts fuer Christliche Sozialwissenschaften. 1960. a. DM.48. (Universitaet Muenster, Institut fuer Christliche Sozialwissenschaften) Verlag Regensberg, Daimlerweg 58, Postfach 6748/6749, 4400 Muenster, W. Germany (B.R.D.) Indexed: CERDIC.

301 GE ISSN 0138-435X
JAHRBUCH FUER SOZIOLOGIE UND SOZIALPOLITIK. (Text in German; summaries English, French and Russian) 1980. a. (Akademie der Wissenschaften der DDR) Akademie-Verlag DDR, Leipziger Str. 3-4, 1086 Berlin, E. Germany (D.D.R.)

301 572 MY
JERNAL ANTROPOLOJI DAN SOSIOLOJI. (Text in English and Malay) 1972. a. M.$3. National University of Malaysia, Persatuan Kajimanusia Dan Kajimasharakat - Universiti Kebangsaan Malaysia, Bangi, Kajang, Selangor, Malaysia. bk. rev. bibl.

301.3 IS
JERUSALEM URBAN STUDIES. (Text in English) 1970. irreg. $2. Hebrew University of Jerusalem, Institute of Urban & Regional Studies, Jerusalem, Israel. Eds. Arieh Shahar, Erik Cohen. charts. circ. 1,000.

301 200 CN ISSN 0709-3519
JOURNAL OF COMPARATIVE SOCIOLOGY & RELIGION. 1973. a. $50. Canada Sociological Research Centre, P.O. Box 7305, Ottawa K1N 6N5, Canada. Ed. Amarjit S. Sethi. adv. bk. rev. circ. 1,000. (back issues avail.)

301 NR
KANO STUDIES; journal of Saharan and Sudanic research. 1973. a. (Abdullahi Bayero College) Oxford University Press (Nigerian Branch), P.M.B. 5095, Oxford House, Iddo Gate, Ibadan, Nigeria. Ed. John E. Lavers. adv. bk. rev. Indexed: M.L.A.

334 IS ISSN 0334-2182
KIBBUTZ (TEL AVIV); interdisciplinary research review. (Text in English, Hebrew) 1973. a. price varies. Federation of Kibbutz Movements, Box 303, Tel Aviv 61-000, Israel. Eds. Shimon Shur, Henry Near. circ. 1,250. Indexed: Lang.& Lang.Behav.Abstr.

301 US ISSN 0278-1557
KNOWLEDGE AND SOCIETY; studies in the sociology of culture past and present. 1978. irreg., vol.5, 1985. $23.75 to individuals; institutions $47.50. J A I Press Inc., Box 1678, 36 Sherwood Pl., Greenwich, CT 06836. TEL 203-661-7602. Eds. Hernrika Kuklick, Elizabeth Long. Indexed: Lang.& Lang.Behav.Abstr.
Formerly: Research in Sociology of Knowledge, Science and Art (ISSN 0163-0180)

301 DK ISSN 0900-9922
KOBENHAVNS UNIVERSITET. SOCIOLOGISK INSTITUT. AFHANDLING. 1981. irreg. Kobenhavns Universitet, Sociologisk Institut, Njalsgade 94, 2300 Copenhagen S, Denmark.

301 DK ISSN 0900-9876
KOBENHAVNS UNIVERSITET. SOCIOLOGISK INSTITUT. ARBEJDSPAPIR. irreg. Kr.5. Kobenhavns Universitet, Sociologisk Institut, Njalsgade 94, 2300 Copenhagen S, Denmark.

301 AT
LA TROBE SOCIOLOGY PAPERS. 1973. irreg. La Trobe University, Department of Sociology, School of Social Sciences, Bundoora, Vic. 3083, Australia. circ. 300.

LAENDERMONOGRAPHIEN. see GEOGRAPHY

301 340 US
LAW, STATE AND SOCIETY. 1979. irreg., no.13, 1985. Academic Press Inc., Orlando, FL 32887. TEL 305-345-2000. Ed.Bd.

LEGON FAMILY RESEARCH PAPERS. see ANTHROPOLOGY

301 UK ISSN 0267-7113
LIBERTARIAN ALLIANCE. SOCIOLOGICAL NOTES. 1985. irreg. £5($10) Libertarian Alliance, 3 Langley Court, Covent Garden, London WC2E 9JY, England.

LIMERENCE FORUM; open forum and research instrument. see PSYCHOLOGY

301.2 PL ISSN 0076-1435
LUD. (Text in Polish; summaries in English and German) 1895. a. price varies. Polskie Towarzystwo Ludoznawcze, Ul. Szewska 36, 50-139 Wroclaw, Poland (Dist. by: Ars Polona, Krakowskie Przedmiescie 7, Warsaw, Poland) Ed. Jozef Burszta. bk. rev. index. circ. 800.

309 NE ISSN 0168-2857
MAANDBLAD AKTIVITEITENSEKTOR. 1980. a. fl.79. Vuga Uitgeverij BV, Box 16400, 2500 BK The Hague, Netherlands. Ed. Rene Wagemaker. adv. bk. rev. circ. 5,500.
Incorporates: Ligament.

301 RH
MAMBO OCCASIONAL PAPERS. SOCIO-ECONOMIC SERIES. 1974. irreg.; latest no.20, 1985. Mambo Press, Box 779, Gwelo, Zimbabwe.

MAN AND SOCIETY/MANUSIA DAN MASYARAKAT. see ANTHROPOLOGY

301 GW
VON MANN ZU MANN. 1980. irreg. DM.3($30) Stiftung Aktiv gegen Sexismus, Marburgerstr. 9, 6000 Frankfurt 90, W. Germany (B.R.D.) Ed. Rudi Gerharz.

301 US ISSN 0743-7528
MATERIAL CULTURE DIRECTORIES. irreg. price varies. Greenwood Press, 88 Post Rd. W., Box 5007, Westport, CT 06881. TEL 203-226-3571.

301.2 GW ISSN 0543-4726
DER MENSCH ALS SOZIALES UND PERSONALES WESEN. 1963. irreg., vol.7, 1987. price varies. Ferdinand Enke Verlag, Postfach 1304, D 7000 Stuttgart 1, W. Germany (B.R.D) Ed. G. Wurzbacher.

301.45 UK ISSN 0305-6252
MINORITY RIGHTS GROUP. REPORTS. 1970. irreg., (approx. 5/yr.) £7.50($15) Minority Rights Group, 29 Craven St., London WC2N 5NT, England (Orders to: 35 Claremont Ave. 4S, New York, NY 10027.) Ed. Ben Whitaker. bibl. illus. stat. circ. 1,500. (also avail. in microfiche) Indexed: HR Rep.

301 BO
MONOGRAFIAS DE POBLACION Y DESARROLLO. 1974. irreg., no.23, 1985. price varies. Centro de Investigaciones Sociales, Casilla 6931 - C.C., La Paz, Bolivia.

301 BO
MONOGRAFIAS DE RECURSOS HUMANOS. 1978. irreg., no.4, 1985. price varies. Centro de Investigaciones Sociales, Casilla 6931 - C.C., La Paz, Bolivia.

301.4 BO
MONOGRAFIAS DE SOCIOLOGIA FAMILIAR. 1974. irreg., no.9, 1984. price varies. Centro de Investigaciones Sociales, Casilla 6931 - C.C., La Paz, Bolivia.

SOCIOLOGY

301 572   NE
MONOGRAPHS AND THEORETICAL STUDIES IN SOCIOLOGY AND ANTHROPOLOGY IN HONOUR OF NELS ANDERSON. 1972. irreg., vol.22, 1986. price varies. E.J. Brill, P.O. Box 9000, 2300 PA Leiden, Netherlands. Ed. L. Ishwaran.

MUSIK UND GESELLSCHAFT. see *MUSIC*

301   US   ISSN 0077-3212
N A A C P ANNUAL REPORT.* 1910. a. $1. National Association for the Advancement of Colored People, 4805 Mt. Hope Dr., Baltimore, MD 21215-3297. circ. 5,000. (also avail. in microform from BLH)

309.1   US   ISSN 0077-5266
NATIONAL OPINION RESEARCH CENTER. NEWSLETTER. 1967. irreg., no.9, 1974. free. ‡ National Opinion Research Center, c/o Susan Campbell, 1155 E. 60th St., Chicago, IL 60637. TEL 312-962-1213. Ed. Susan Campbell. circ. 800.

301   CH   ISSN 0077-5851
NATIONAL TAIWAN UNIVERSITY JOURNAL OF SOCIOLOGY/TAI-WAN TA HSUEH SHE HUI HSUEH K'AN. (Text in Chinese and English) 1963. a. $2.50. ‡ National Taiwan University, Department of Sociology, 21 Hsu-Chow Road, Taipei, Taiwan 100, Republic of China. Ed. Albert R. O'Hara. bk. rev. circ. 300. Indexed: Lang.& Lang.Behav.Abstr.

572 301.2   HU   ISSN 0541-9522
NEPI KULTURA-NEPI TARSADALOM. (Text in Hungarian; summaries in German) 1968. irreg., vol.13, 1983. (Magyar Tudomanyos Akademia, Neprajzi Kutato Csoport) Akademiai Kiado, Publishing House of the Hungarian Academy of Sciences, Box 24, H-1363 Budapest, Hungary. abstr. bibl. illus.

301   NE
NETHERLANDS. SOCIAAL EN CULTUREEL PLANBUREAU. SOCIAL AND CULTURAL REPORT. (Text in English) 1975. biennial. Sociaal en Cultureel Planbureau - Social and Cultural Planning Office, J.C. van Markenlaan 3, Rijswijk, Netherlands. charts. stat. circ. 1,000.

300 150   GW   ISSN 0077-801X
NEW BABYLON: STUDIES IN THE SOCIAL SCIENCES. irreg. price varies. Walter de Gruyter und Co., Postfach 110240, D-1000 Berlin 11, W. Germany (B.R.D.) (U.S. adress: Walter de Gruyter, Inc., 200 Saw Mill Rd., Hawthorne, N.Y. 10532)

301 051   US   ISSN 0081-8291
NEW YORK UNIVERSITY. STUDIES IN NEAR EASTERN CIVILIZATION. 1968. irreg., approx. a., latest no.12. New York University Press, Bobst Library, 70 Washington Sq. So., New York, NY 10012. Ed. Bayly Winder.

NORWAY. STATISTISK SENTRALBYRAA. ARTIKLER/ARTICLES. see *BUSINESS AND ECONOMICS — Economic Systems And Theories, Economic History*

314 330.9   NO   ISSN 0085-4344
NORWAY. STATISTISK SENTRALBYRAA. SAMFUNNSOEKONOMISKE STUDIER/ SOCIAL ECONOMIC STUDIES. (Text in Norwegian; summaries in English) 1954. irreg. price varies. Statistisk Sentralbyraa, Box 8131 Dep., 0033 Oslo 1, Norway. circ. 2,000.

ONTARIO SYMPOSIA ON PERSONALITY AND SOCIAL COGNITION. see *PSYCHOLOGY*

301 572   CN
P.E.I. COMMUNITY STUDIES. (Prince Edward Island) 1974. a. price varies. University of Prince Edward Island, Department of Sociology and Anthropology, Charlottetown, P.E.I. C1A 4P3, Canada. Ed. Satadal Das Gupta. circ. controlled.

301   IS
PAPERS IN SOCIOLOGY. 1972. a. $3. Hebrew University of Jerusalem, Department of Sociology, Givat Ram Campus, Jerusalem, Israel (Subscr. to: Jerusalem Academic Press, Box 2390, Jerusalem, Israel) abstr. (back issues avail.)

PAPERS ON EUROPEAN AND MEDITERRANEAN SOCIETIES. see *ANTHROPOLOGY*

PERSPECTIVES ON THE AMERICAN SOUTH. see *HISTORY — History Of North And South America*

301   PE   ISSN 0079-1075
PERU - PROBLEMA. 1969. irreg., no.21, 1984. price varies. (Instituto de Estudios Peruanos) I E P Ediciones, Horacio Urteaga 694 (Campo de Marte), Lima 11, Peru. Ed. Jose Matos Mar. bk. rev.

301   US
PHENOMENOLOGY AND THE HUMAN SCIENCES. 1976. irreg. $7. University of Oklahoma, Center for the Study of Phenomenology, Dale Hall Tower, Dayton, OK 73019. Ed. D. Lawrence Wieder. (back issues avail.) Indexed: Curr.Cont.
Formerly: Annals of Phenomenological Sociology (ISSN 0363-647X)

301 330   UK   ISSN 0141-2779
PLANNING FOR SOCIAL CHANGE. 1979. a. $3000. Henley Centre for Forecasting, 2 Tudor St., Blackfriars, London EC4Y 0AA, England. Ed. R.J. Tyrrell.

POLITICA E ESTRATEGIA. see *POLITICAL SCIENCE — International Relations*

320   US   ISSN 0732-1228
POLITICAL ANTHROPOLOGY. 1980. a. price varies. Transaction Books, Rutgers University, New Brunswick, NJ 08903. TEL 201-932-2280. Ed. Myron J. Aronoff.

POLITICAL POWER AND SOCIAL THEORY; a research annual. see *POLITICAL SCIENCE*

301   PL   ISSN 0079-3442
POLSKA AKADEMIA NAUK. ODDZIAL W KRAKOWIE. KOMISJA SOCJOLOGICZNA. PRACE. (Text in Polish; summaries in English, French, Russian) 1963. irreg., no.48, 1984. price varies. Ossolineum, Publishing House of the Polish Academy of Sciences, Rynek 9, 50-106 Wroclaw, Poland (Dist. by: Ars Polona-Ruch, Krakowskie Przedmiescie 7, Warsaw, Poland)

301   PL   ISSN 0079-3620
POLSKA 2000. 1970. irreg., 3-4 per year. price varies. (Polska Akademia Nauk, Komitet Badan i Prognoz "Polska 2000") Ossolineum, Publishing House of the Polish Academy of Sciences, Rynek 9, Wroclaw, Poland (Dist. by: Ars Polona-Ruch, Krakowskie Przedmiescie 7, Warsaw, Poland) Ed. Antoni Rajkiewicz. circ. 2,000.

301   US
POPULAR CULTURE ASSOCIATION. NEWSLETTER AND POPULAR CULTURE METHODS. 1971. irreg. membership. (Popular Culture Association) Bowling Green State University, Popular Culture Center, Bowling Green, OH 43403. TEL 409-372-2981. Ed. Michael T. Marsden. adv. circ. 2,500. (also avail. in microform from UMI; reprint service avail. from UMI)
Incorporating: Popular Culture Association Newsletter (ISSN 0048-4822)

301   PO   ISSN 0870-6506
PORTUGAL. INSTITUTO NACIONAL DE ESTATISTICA. ESTATISTICAS DE SEGURANCA SOCIAL, ASSOCIACOES SINDICAIS E PATRONAIS. CONTINENTE, ACORES E MADEIRA. (Text in French and Portuguese) 1938. a. Esc.840. Instituto Nacional de Estatistica, Av. Antonio Jose de Almeida, 1078 Lisbon Codex, Portugal (Orders to: Imprensa Nacional, Casa da Moeda, Direccao Comercial, rua D. Francisco Manuel de Melo 5, 1000 Lisbon, Portugal)
Formerly: Portugal. Instituto Nacional de Estatistica. Estatisticas das Organizacoes Sindicais (ISSN 0079-4163)

PSYCHOLOGY AND SOCIOLOGY OF SPORT; current selected research. see *PSYCHOLOGY*

301.45   US
PUBLICATIONS ON ETHNICITY AND NATIONALITY. 1979. irreg., vol.3, 1981. University of Washington Press, Seattle, WA 98105. TEL 206-543-4050.

301   IT   ISSN 0391-8521
QUALITA DELLA VITA. 1978. irreg., no.10, 1985. price varies. Edizioni Studium, Via Cassiodoro 14, 00193 Rome, Italy.

301   CN
QUEBEC (PROVINCE). CONSEIL DES AFFAIRES SOCIALES ET DE LA FAMILLE. RAPPORT ANNUEL.* a. (Conseil des Affaires Sociales et de la Famille) Editeur Officiel du Quebec, 1283 Bd. Charest Ouest, Quebec, P.Q. G1N 2C9, Canada. TEL 413-643-3895.
Formerly: Quebec (Province). Family and Social Affairs Council. Annual Report.

RELIGIONE E SOCIETA. see *RELIGIONS AND THEOLOGY*

RESEARCH; contributions to interdisciplinary anthropology. see *ANTHROPOLOGY*

RESEARCH IN LAW, DEVIANCE AND SOCIAL CONTROL. see *LAW*

301   US   ISSN 0732-1317
RESEARCH IN PUBLIC POLICY ANALYSIS AND MANAGEMENT. irreg. $20 to individuals; institutions $40. (Association for Public Policy Analysis Management) J A I Press Inc., 36 Sherwood Pl., Box 1678, Greenwich, CT 06836-1678. TEL 203-661-7602. Ed. John P. Crecine.

305.8   US   ISSN 0195-7449
RESEARCH IN RACE AND ETHNIC RELATIONS; a research annual. 1979. a. $23.75 to individuals; institutions $47.50. J A I Press Inc., Box 1678, 36 Sherwood Pl., Greenwich, CT 06836. TEL 203-661-7602. Eds. Cora Bagley Marrett, Cheryl B. Leggon. adv. bk. rev. Indexed: Psychol.Abstr. Lang.& Lang.Behav.Abstr.
Race relations

301   US
RESEARCH IN RURAL SOCIOLOGY AND DEVELOPMENT. 1984. a. J A I Press Inc., 36 Sherwood Pl., Greenwich, CT 06830. Ed. Harry K. Schwarzweller.

301.24   US   ISSN 0163-786X
RESEARCH IN SOCIAL MOVEMENTS, CONFLICTS AND CHANGE. 1978. a. $23.75 to individuals; institutions $47.50. J A I Press Inc., Box 1678, 36 Sherwood Pl., Greenwich, CT 06836. TEL 203-661-7602. Ed. Louis Kriesberg. Indexed: Lang.& Lang.Behav.Abstr.

301.07   US   ISSN 0196-1152
RESEARCH IN SOCIAL PROBLEMS AND PUBLIC POLICY; a research annual. 1979. a. $23.75 to individuals; institutions $47.50. J A I Press Inc., Box 1285, 36 Sherwood Pl., Greenwich, CT 06836. TEL 203-661-7602. Eds. Michael Lewis, JoAnn L. Miller. Indexed: Psychol.Abstr. Lang.& Lang.Behav.Abstr.

305.5   US   ISSN 0276-5624
RESEARCH IN SOCIAL STRATIFICATION AND MOBILITY; a research annual. 1981. a. $23.75 to individuals; institutions $47.50. J A I Press Inc., Box 1678, 36 Sherwood Pl., Greenwich, CT 06836-1678. TEL 203-661-7602. Ed. Robert V. Robinson. Indexed: Lang.& Lang.Behav.Abstr.

301   US   ISSN 0272-2801
RESEARCH IN THE INTERWEAVE OF SOCIAL ROLES; a research annual. 1980. a. $23.75 to individuals; institutions $47.50. J A I Press Inc., Box 1678, 36 Sherwood Pl., Greenwich, CT 06836. TEL 203-661-7602. Ed. Helen Z. Lopata. Indexed: Psychol.Abstr.

301.15   US
RESEARCH IN THE INTERWEAVE OF SOCIAL ROLES: FRIENDSHIP. 1981. a. J A I Press Inc., 36 Sherwood Pl., Box 1678, Greenwich, CT 06836-1678. TEL 203-661-7602. Indexed: Lang.& Lang.Behav.Abstr.
Formerly: Research in the Interweave of Social Roles: Women and Men.

RESEARCH IN THE SOCIOLOGY OF HEALTH CARE; a research annual. see *MEDICAL SCIENCES*

301.34   US   ISSN 0733-558X
RESEARCH IN THE SOCIOLOGY OF ORGANIZATIONS. 1982. a. $23.75. to individuals; institutions $47.50. J A I Press Inc., 36 Sherwood Pl., Box 1678, Greenwich, CT 06836-1678. TEL 203-661-7602. Ed. Samuel B. Bacharach. Indexed: Lang.& Lang.Behav.Abstr.

RESEARCH IN THE SOCIOLOGY OF WORK. see
*BUSINESS AND ECONOMICS — Labor And
Industrial Relations*

301   YU   ISSN 0350-154X
REVIJA ZA SOCIOLOGIJU/SOCIOLOGICAL
REVIEW. (Text in Serbocroatian; summaries in
English) 1971. irreg. 800 din.($8) Sociolosko
Drustvo Hrvatske - Croatian Sociological
Association, Filozofski fakultet, Odsjek za
Sociologiju, Djure Salaja 3, 41000 Zagreb,
Yugoslavia. Ed. Ognjen Caldarovic. adv. bk. rev.
bibl. circ. 1,000. Indexed: Lang.& Lang.Behav.Abstr.

301   CK
REVISTA DE SOCIOLOGIA. vol.9, 1977. a.
Universidad Pontificia Bolivariana, Facultad de
Sociologia, Avda. la Playa 40-88, Apartado Aereo
1178, Medellin, Colombia. bibl. charts. stat.

RIJKSUNIVERSITEIT TE LEIDEN. INSTITUUT
VOOR CULTURELE ANTROPOLOGIE EN
SOCIOLOGIE DER NIET-WESTERSE VOLKEN.
PUBLICATIE. see *ANTHROPOLOGY*

301.2   IT   ISSN 0085-5731
RIVISTA DI ETNOGRAFIA.* 1946. a. L.5000. Via
Alfrado Rocco No. 98, Naples, Italy. Ed. Giovanni
Tucci.

301   PL   ISSN 0080-3731
ROCZNIKI SOCJOLOGII WSI. STUDIA I
MATERIALY. (Text in Polish; summaries in
English and Russian) 1962. a. price varies. (Polska
Akademia Nauk, Instytut Filozofii i Socjologii)
Ossolineum, Publishing House of the Polish
Academy of Sciences, Rynek 9, Wroclaw, Poland
(Dist. by: Ars Polona-Ruch, Krakowskie
Przedmiescie 7, Warsaw, Poland) Ed. F. Mleczko.
bk. rev. circ. 500.

301   DK   ISSN 0108-2205
ROSKILDE UNIVERSITETSCENTER. INSTITUT
FOR SAMFUNDSOEKONOMI OG
PLANLAEGNING. ARBEJDSPAPIR. 1981. irreg.,
no.2, 1987. free. Roskilde Universitetscenter,
Institut for Samfundsoekonomi og Planlaegning,
Institut VIII, Postbox 260, 4000 Roskilde, Denmark.

301   US   ISSN 0197-9272
SAGE ANNUAL REVIEWS OF STUDIES IN
DEVIANCE. 1977. irreg., vol.7, 1983. $29.95 for
hardcover; softcover $14.95. Sage Publications, Inc.,
2111 W. Hillcrest Dr., Newbury Park, CA 91320
TEL 805-499-0721. (And Sage Publications, Ltd.,
28 Banner St., London EC1Y 8QE, England) Eds.
Edward Sagarin, Charles Winick. (back issues avail.)

301   US
SAGE STUDIES IN INTERNATIONAL
SOCIOLOGY. 1976. irreg. $15 for softcover;
hardcover $40. (International Sociological
Association) Sage Publications, Inc., 2111 W.
Hillcrest Dr., Newbury Park, CA 91320 TEL 805-
499-0721. (And Sage Publications, Ltd., 28 Banner
St., London EC1Y 8QE, England) bibl. charts.
stat.

SAMISKE SAMLINGER. see *ANTHROPOLOGY*

301   GW
SCHRIFTEN ZUR MITTELSTANDSFORSCHUNG.
1962, N.S. 1984. irreg., no.85, 1981. price varies.
(Institut fuer Mittelstandsforschung) C.E. Poeschel
Verlag, Postfach 529, Kernerstr. 43, 7000 Stuttgart
1, W. Germany (B.R.D.) Eds. Horst Albach,
Herbert Hax.

SLOVANSKE STUDIE. see *HISTORY — History Of
Europe*

301.2   KE
SOCIAL PERSPECTIVES. irreg. Central Bureau of
Statistics, Social Statistics Section, Ministry of
Finance & Planning, Box 30266, Nairobi, Kenya
(Orders to: Central Bureau of Statistics, Box 30266,
Nairobi, Kenya) charts. stat.

301.2   US   ISSN 0737-6871
SOCIAL PROCESS IN HAWAII. 1935. a. price
varies. (University of Hawaii at Manoa, Department
of Sociology) University of Hawaii Press, 2840
Kolowalu St., Honolulu, HI 96822. TEL 808-948-
8943. Eds. Michael Weinstein, Kiyoshi Ikeda. bk.
rev. circ. 850.

SOCIAL PSYCHOLOGY OF LANGUAGE. see
PSYCHOLOGY

301.15   SZ
SOCIAL STRATEGIES; monographs on sociology
and social policy/monographien zur Soziologie und
Gesellschaftspolitik. (Text in English, French and
German) 1975. irreg., no.17, 1985. price varies.
Social Strategies Publishers Co-Operative Society,
Parkweg 12, CH-4051 Basel, Switzerland. Ed. Paul
Trappe. adv. bk. rev. circ. 2,000.

SOCIAL STRUCTURE AND SOCIAL CHANGE.
see *SOCIAL SCIENCES: COMPREHENSIVE
WORKS*

301   UY   ISSN 0081-0649
SOCIEDAD URUGUAYA.* irreg. Editorial Arca,
Colonia 1263, Montevideo, Uruguay.

SOCIO-ECONOMIC REVIEW OF PUNJAB. see
*BUSINESS AND ECONOMICS — Economic
Situation And Conditions*

301   IT
SOCIOLOGIA. no.4, 1975. irreg. Societa Editrice
Napoletana s.r.l., Corso Umberto I 34, 80138
Naples, Italy. Ed. Aurelio Paolinelli. Indexed:
Lang.& Lang.Behav.Abstr.

301   BL   ISSN 0081-1742
SOCIOLOGIA II. (Subseries of: Sao Paulo, Brazil
(City) Universidade. Faculdade de Filosofia,
Ciencias e Letras. Boletim) 1958. irreg.
Universidade de Sao Paulo, Faculdade de Filosofia,
Letras e Ciencias Humanas, Cidade Universitaria,
"Armando de Salles Oliveira", Caixa Postal 8105,
Sao Paulo, Brazil.

301.01   US   ISSN 0081-1750
SOCIOLOGICAL METHODOLOGY. 1969. a. price
varies. American Sociological Association, 1722 N.
St. N.W., Washington, DC 20036. (also avail. in
microform from UMI; back issues avail.; reprint
service avail. from UMI) Indexed: Lang.&
Lang.Behav.Abstr.

301   DK
SOCIOLOGICAL MICROJOURNAL. (Text in
English, French and German) 1967. a. Kr.55($8)
Erik Manniche and Kaare Svalastoga, Eds. & Pubs.,
22 Linneagade, 1361 Copenhagen K, Denmark. (back
issues avail.)

301 572   US
SOCIOLOGICAL OBSERVATIONS. 1977. irreg.,
vol.15, 1983. $28 cloth; $14 paper. Sage
Publications, Inc., 2111 W. Hillcrest Dr., Newbury
Park, CA 91320 TEL 805-499-0721. (And Sage
Publications, Ltd., 28 Banner St., London EC1Y
8QE, England) Ed. John M. Johnson. (back issues
avail.)

301   US   ISSN 0163-8505
SOCIOLOGICAL PRACTICE. 1976. irreg., approx.
1/yr., 2 nos. per vol. $16 to individuals; $30
institutions. Progresiv Publishr, 401 E. 32nd St.,
Suite 1002, Chicago, IL 60616. Ed. Kenneth Ives.
bk. rev. stat. circ. 200. (also avail. in microform
from UMI; reprint service avail. from UMI)
Indexed: Sociol.Abstr. Lang.& Lang.Behav.Abstr.
    Formerly (1976-1977): S P: Sociological Practice
(ISSN 0360-845X)

301   UK   ISSN 0081-1769
SOCIOLOGICAL REVIEW. MONOGRAPH. 1958.
irreg., no.28, 1980. price varies. University of Keele,
Keele, Staffordshire ST5 5BG, England. Eds. R.
Frankenberg, W.M. Williams. Indexed: Curr.Cont.
Ind.Med. SSCI. ASCA. Lang.& Lang.Behav.Abstr.

301   FR
SOCIOLOGIE PERMANENTE. 1978. irreg. Editions
du Seuil, 27 rue Jacob, 75261 Paris Cedex 6,
France. Dir. Alain Touraine.

301   BE
SOCIOLOGISCHE VERKENNINGEN. no.2, 1972.
irreg., no.10, 1986. Leuven University Press,
Krakenstraat 3, B-3000 Louvain, Belgium.

301   NR   ISSN 0081-1807
SOCIOLOGIST.* 1968. a. University of Ibadan,
Sociological Society, Ibadan, Nigeria.

301   US
SOCIOLOGY OF MUSIC SERIES. 1983. irreg., no.4,
1984. Pendragon Press, Rt. 1, Box 159, Stuyvesant,
NY 12173-9720. TEL 518-828-3008.

SOCIOLOGY OF THE SCIENCES. YEARBOOK.
see *SCIENCES: COMPREHENSIVE WORKS*

301 500   NE
SOCIOLOGY OF THE SCIENCES
MONOGRAPHS. 1982. irreg. price varies. D.
Reidel Publishing Co., Box 17, 3300 AA Dordrecht,
Netherlands (And 190 Old Derby St., Hingham,
MA 02043)

301   UR
SOTSIOLOGIYA KUL'TURY. 1974. a. 1.40 Rub.
(Nauchno-Issledovatel'skii Institut Kul'tury, Otdel
Sotsiologicheskikh Issledovanii) Izdatel'stvo
Sovetskaya Rossiya, Proezd Sapunova 13/15,
Moscow K-12, Russian S.F.S.R., U.S.S.R.
    Formerly: Nauchno-Issledovatel'skii Institut
Kul'tury. Trudy.

SOUTH ASIA: JOURNAL OF SOUTH ASIAN
STUDIES. see *HISTORY — History Of Asia*

301   GW   ISSN 0340-9201
SOZIALISATION UND KOMMUNIKATION. 1974.
irreg., no.9, 1980. price varies. (Universitaet
Erlangen-Nuernberg) Ferdinand Enke Verlag,
Ruedigerstr. 14, 7000 Stuttgart 30, W. Germany
(B.R.D.) Indexed: Biol.Abstr.

301   GE   ISSN 0020-0395
SOZIOLOGISCHE FORSCHUNG IN DER D.D.R.
INFORMATIONEN. 1965. irreg. M.3.20 per issue.
Akademie fuer Gesellschaftswissenschaften beim ZK
der SED, Zentralstelle fuer Soziologische
Information und Dokumentation, Johannes-
Dieckmann-Str. 19-23, 1086 Berlin, E. Germany
(D.D.R.) Ed. Gerda Correns. circ. 750.

301   GW   ISSN 0081-3265
SOZIOLOGISCHE GEGENWARTSFRAGEN.
NEUE FOLGE. 1957. irreg., no.45, 1982. price
varies. Ferdinand Enke Verlag, Postfach 1304, 7000
Stuttgart 1, W. Germany (B.R.D.) Ed.Bd.

SPAIN. INSTITUTO NACIONAL DE
INVESTIGACIONES AGRARIAS. ANALES.
SERIE: ECONOMIA Y SOCIOLOGIA
AGRARIAS. see *AGRICULTURE — Agricultural
Economics*

301 333.7   AT
SPEAK. 1969. a. Aus.$0.10. c/o Audrey Windram,
Ed., Conrad St., Longwood, S.A. 5153, Australia.

309   IT
STRATIFICAZIONE E CLASSI SOCIALI IN
ITALIA. QUADERNI DI RICERCA. 1976. irreg.
(Fondazione Giovanni Agnelli) Editoriale Valentino,
Via G. Giancosa 38, 10125 Turin, Italy.

301   US   ISSN 0884-870X
STRESS IN MODERN SOCIETY. 1984. irreg., latest
vol.3. $32.50. A M S Press, Inc., 56 E. 13th St.,
New York, NY 10003. TEL 212-777-4700.

STUDIA ANTHROPONYMICA SCANDINAVICA;
tidskrift foer nordisk personnamnsforskning. see
GENEALOGY AND HERALDRY

STUDIEN ZUR LITERATUR- UND
SOZIALGESCHICHTE SPANIENS UND
LATEINAMERIKAS. see *LITERATURE*

301   US   ISSN 0730-9139
STUDIES IN LATIN AMERICAN POPULAR
CULTURE. 1982. a. $15 to individuals; institutions
$30. c/o Charles M. Tatum, Department of Foreign
Languages, New Mexico State University, Box 3-L,
Las Cruces, NM 88003. TEL 505-646-2942. Eds.
Harold E. Hinds, Jr., Charles M. Tatum. adv. bk.
rev. circ. 500. Indexed: M.L.A. Hisp.Amer.Per.Ind.

STUDIES IN SOCIAL AND DEMOGRAPHIC
HISTORY. see *SOCIAL SCIENCES:
COMPREHENSIVE WORKS*

301   US
STUDIES IN SOCIAL DISCONTINUITY. 1974.
irreg., no.51, 1985. Academic Press, Inc., Orlando,
FL 32887. TEL 305-345-2000. Eds. C. Tilly, E.
Shorter.

STUDIES IN SOCIAL ECONOMICS. see
BUSINESS AND ECONOMICS

SOCIOLOGY

300 301 US
STUDIES IN SOCIAL EXPERIMENTATION. 1975. irreg., no.6, 1981. price varies. Brookings Institution, 1775 Massachusetts Ave. N.W., Washington, DC 20036. TEL 202-797-6258.

301 US ISSN 0081-8518
STUDIES IN SOCIAL LIFE.* 1953. irreg. price varies. Kluwer Nijhoff Publishing, 101 Philip Dr., Assinippi Pk., Norwell, MA 02061 (Foreign distr.: Kluwer Academic Publishers Group, Distribution Center, Box 322, 3300 AH Dordrecht, Netherlands) Ed. G. Beyer. Indexed: SSCI.

301 AT ISSN 0156-4420
STUDIES IN SOCIETY. 1978. irreg. price varies. George Allen & Unwin Australia Pty. Ltd., 8 Napier St, N. Sydney 2060, Australia. Ed. Ronald Wild. bibl.

301 II
STUDIES IN SOCIOLOGY. Variant title: Rajasthan University Studies in Sociology. (Text in English and Hindi) vol.4, 1973. a. Rs.1 per copy. University of Rajasthan, Gandhi Nagar, Jaipur 302004, India. Ed. T.K.N. Unnithan.

301 II
STUDIES IN SOCIOLOGY AND SOCIAL ANTHROPOLOGY. (Text in English) 1978. irreg. price varies. Hindustan Publishing Corp., 6-U.B. Jawahar Nagar, Delhi 110007, India. Ed. M.N. Srinivas.

301.1 US ISSN 0163-2396
STUDIES IN SYMBOLIC INTERACTION; an annual compilation of research. 1978. a. $23.75 to individuals; institutions $47.50. J A I Press Inc., Box 1678, 36 Sherwood Pl., Greenwich, CT 06836. TEL 203-661-7602. Ed. Norman K. Denzin. illus. Indexed: Psychol.Abstr. Lang.& Lang.Behav.Abstr.

309 960 ZA
STUDIES IN ZAMBIAN SOCIETY. 1978. irreg., no.3, 1978. price varies. University of Zambia, School of Humanities and Social Sciences, Committee on Student Publications, Box 2379, Lusaka, Zambia. Ed. L.M. van den Berg. circ. 1,000.

301 NE ISSN 0081-8771
STUDIES OF DEVELOPING COUNTRIES. (Text mainly in English) 1963. irreg., no.25, 1979. price varies. Van Gorcum, P.O. Box 43, 9400 AA Assen, Netherlands (Dist. by: Humanities Press, Inc., 171 First Ave., Atlantic Highlands, NJ 07716)
Formerly: Non-European Societies.

STUDIES OF ISRAELI SOCIETY. see *ETHNIC INTERESTS*

STUDIES OF URBAN SOCIETY. see *HOUSING AND URBAN PLANNING*

301 US ISSN 0039-4394
SUBTERRANEAN SOCIOLOGY NEWSLETTER. 1967-1980; resumed 1987. irreg., latest 1980. $3. Subterranean Sociological Association, Dept. of Sociology, Eastern Michigan University, Ypsilanti, MI 48197. TEL 313-487-1849. Ed. Marcello Truzzi. bk. rev. bibl. circ. 600(controlled) (processed)

301 HU ISSN 0082-1322
SZOCIOLOGIAI TANULMANYOK. 1966. irreg., vol.28, 1986. price varies. (Magyar Tudomanyos Akademia) Akademiai Kiado, Publishing House of the Hungarian Academy of Sciences, P.O. Box 24, H-1363 Budapest, Hungary.

301.16 AG
TALLER DE CULTURA Y MEDIOS DE COMUNICACION. DOCUMENTOS DE TRABAJO. 1983. irreg. Centro de Participacion Politica, Taller de Cultura, H. Yrigoyen 1419, Buenos Aires, Argentina.

TECHNIK UND GESELLSCHAFT. see *TECHNOLOGY: COMPREHENSIVE WORKS*

301 IS
TEL AVIV-YAFO. CENTER FOR ECONOMIC AND SOCIAL RESEARCH. RESEARCH AND SURVEYS SERIES/TEL-AVIV-YAFO. HA-MERKAZ LE-MEKHKAR KALKALI VE-KHEVRATI. MEKHKARIM VE-SEKARIM. (Text in English and Hebrew) 1963, no. 12. irreg. Center for Economic and Social Research, Tel Aviv-Jaffa Municipality, Malkhei Israel Square, Tel Aviv, Israel. Ed. H. Har-Paz. circ. 600.
Formerly: Tel Aviv-Yafo. Research and Statistical Department. Special Surveys (ISSN 0082-2639)

301.451 TU ISSN 0082-6898
TURKISH REVIEW OF ETHNOGRAPHY/TURK ETNOGRAFYA DERGISI. 1956. a. price varies. Directorate General of Antiquities and Museums, Department for Research Publications, Ankara, Turkey.
Formerly: Turk Tarih-Arkeologya ve Etnografya Dergisi.

TWENTIETH CENTURY FUND. NEWSLETTER. see *POLITICAL SCIENCE — International Relations*

U S S R REPORT: LIFE SCIENCES, BIOMEDICAL AND BEHAVIORAL SCIENCES. see *MEDICAL SCIENCES*

U S S R REPORT: POLITICAL AND SOCIOLOGICAL AFFAIRS. see *POLITICAL SCIENCE*

301 GW ISSN 0170-2416
UEBERSEE-MUSEUM, BREMEN. VEROEFFENTLICHUNGEN. REIHE E: HUMAN-OEKOLOGIE. 1978. irreg., vol.3, 1980. price varies. Uebersee-Museum, Bremen, Bahnhofsplatz 13, 2800 Bremen, W. Germany(B.R.D.) Indexed: Biol.Abstr.

301 PR
UNIVERSIDAD DE PUERTO RICO. CENTRO DE INVESTIGACIONES SOCIALES. INFORME ANUAL. (Text in Spanish) 1974/75. a. free. Universidad de Puerto Rico, Centro de Investigaciones Sociales, Rio Piedras, PR 00931. Ed. Wenceslao Serra Deliz. bk. rev. bibl. circ. 1,000.

UNIVERSIDADE DE SAO PAULO. INSTITUTO DE ESTUDOS BRASILEIROS. PUBLICACOES. see *GEOGRAPHY*

UNIVERSIDADE DE SAO PAULO. INSTITUTO DE ESTUDOS BRASILEIROS. REVISTA. see *GEOGRAPHY*

572 301 FR ISSN 0249-5635
UNIVERSITE DE BORDEAUX II. CAHIERS ETHNOLOGIQUES. 1972. a. 60 F. (Universite de Bordeaux II, Centre d'Etudes et de Recherches Ethnologiques) Presses Universitaires de Bordeaux, 3 place de la Victoire, 33000 Bordeaux, France. circ. 400.
Formerly: Universite de Bordeaux II. Centre d'Etudes et de Recherchers Ethnologiques. Cahiers.

UNIVERSITE NATIONALE DE COTE D'IVOIRE. ANNALES. SERIE F: ETHNOSOCIOLOGIE. see *ANTHROPOLOGY*

301.18 US
UNIVERSITY ASSOCIATES, INC. ANNUAL; developing human resources. 1972. a. $26.95 paperbound; $65.95 looseleaf. University Associates, Inc., 8517 Production Ave., San Diego, CA 92121. TEL 619-578-5900. Ed. J. William Pfeiffer. circ. 9,000.
Former titles: Annual Handbook for Group Facilitators; Developing Human Resources (ISSN 0732-037X); Annual for Group Facilitators; Annual Handbook for Group Facilitators (ISSN 0094-601X)

330 US
UNIVERSITY OF ALASKA. INSTITUTE OF SOCIAL AND ECONOMIC RESEARCH. RESEARCH SUMMARY. 1980. irreg., no.33, 1987. free. University of Alaska, Institute of Social and Economic Research, 3211 Providence Dr., Anchorage, AK 99508. TEL 907-786-7710. Ed. Linda Leask. bk. rev. charts. stat. circ. 1,900. (also avail. in microfiche; back issues avail.)

301 NZ
UNIVERSITY OF AUCKLAND. DEPARTMENT OF SOCIOLOGY. PAPERS IN COMPARATIVE SOCIOLOGY. 1974. irreg., no.7, 1977. price varies. University of Auckland, Department of Sociology, Private Bag, Auckland, New Zealand. Ed. Ian Carter. circ. 100.

UNIVERSITY OF BIRMINGHAM. CENTRE FOR URBAN AND REGIONAL STUDIES. OCCASIONAL PAPERS. see *HOUSING AND URBAN PLANNING*

UNIVERSITY OF BIRMINGHAM. CENTRE FOR URBAN AND REGIONAL STUDIES. RESEARCH MEMORANDUM. see *HOUSING AND URBAN PLANNING*

UNIVERSITY OF BIRMINGHAM. CENTRE FOR URBAN AND REGIONAL STUDIES. URBAN AND REGIONAL STUDIES. see *HOUSING AND URBAN PLANNING*

UNIVERSITY OF BIRMINGHAM. CENTRE FOR URBAN AND REGIONAL STUDIES. WORKING PAPER. see *HOUSING AND URBAN PLANNING*

UNIVERSITY OF CALIFORNIA, BERKELEY. INSTITUTE OF INTERNATIONAL STUDIES. RESEARCH SERIES. see *POLITICAL SCIENCE*

UNIVERSITY OF CANTERBURY. DEPARTMENT OF PSYCHOLOGY AND SOCIOLOGY. RESEARCH PROJECTS. see *PSYCHOLOGY*

301 GH
UNIVERSITY OF GHANA. DEPARTMENT OF SOCIOLOGY. CURRENT RESEARCH REPORT SERIES. no.2, 1972. irreg. University of Ghana, Department of Sociology, Legon, Ghana.

UNIVERSITY OF LAGOS. HUMAN RESOURCES RESEARCH UNIT. MONOGRAPH. see *POPULATION STUDIES*

301 330 JM
UNIVERSITY OF THE WEST INDIES. INSTITUTE OF SOCIAL AND ECONOMIC RESEARCH. WORKING PAPERS. no.7, 1975. irreg. University of the West Indies, Institute of Social and Economic Research, Mona, Kingston 7, Jamaica.

UNIVERZITA J. E. PURKYNE. FILOZOFICKA FAKULTA. SBORNIK PRACI. G: RADA SOCIALNEVEDNA. see *BUSINESS AND ECONOMICS — Economic Systems And Theories, Economic History*

URBANIZACION, MIGRACIONES Y CAMBIOS EN LA SOCIEDAD PERUANA. see *ANTHROPOLOGY*

301 UK
V E S NEWSLETTER. no.12, 1981. irreg., (3-4/yr.) Voluntary Euthanasia Society, 13 Prince of Wales Terrace, London W8 5PG, England.
Former titles: Exit; Exit News; Right to Die.

VIOLENCE AND VICTIMS. see *PSYCHOLOGY*

301 IT
VITTORIO BACCELLI MAGAZINE. biennial. L.10000. Vittorio Baccelli, Ed. & Pub., C.P. 132, 55100 Lucca, Italy.

338.91 301.412 US
W I D FORUM. 1984. irreg., no.5, 1985. Michigan State University, Office of Women in International Development, 202 International Center, E. Lansing, MI 48824-1035. TEL 517-353-5040. Ed. Rita S. Gallin. circ. 250.

WARSAW AGRICULTURAL UNIVERSITY. S G G W - A R. ANNALS. AGRICULTURAL ECONOMICS AND RURAL SOCIOLOGY. see *AGRICULTURE — Agricultural Economics*

301 US
WINGED MERCURY MISSIVE. 1981. irreg. $5. Winged Mercury Networking, 6020 Piedmont Pl., Lynchburg, VA 24502. Ed. Gary Smith. bk. rev. circ. 288.

301　　　　　　GE　ISSN 0138-5755
WISSENSCHAFT UND GESELLSCHAFT. 1973. irreg., latest vol.23, 1985. (Akademie der Wissenschaften der DDR) Akademie-Verlag Berlin, Leipziger Str. 3-4, 1086 Berlin, E. Germany (D.D.R.)

WISSENSCHAFTLICHE PAPERBACKS; Sozial- und Wirtschaftsgeschichte. see *BUSINESS AND ECONOMICS — Economic Systems And Theories, Economic History*

301.34　　　　　　TR
WORKING PAPERS ON CARIBBEAN SOCIETY. SERIES A: NEW PERSPECTIVES IN THEORY AND ANALYSIS. 1978. irreg. $2. University of the West Indies, Department of Sociology, St. Augustine, Trinidad and Tobago.

301.34　　　　　　TR
WORKING PAPERS ON CARIBBEAN SOCIETY. SERIES C: RESEARCH FINDINGS. irreg. University of the West Indies, Department of Sociology, St. Augustine, Trinidad and Tobago.

WORKING PAPERS ON WOMEN IN INTERNATIONAL DEVELOPMENT. see *BUSINESS AND ECONOMICS — International Development And Assistance*

WORLDWATCH PAPERS. see *ENVIRONMENTAL STUDIES*

YEARBOOK OF WORLD PROBLEMS AND HUMAN POTENTIAL. see *POLITICAL SCIENCE — International Relations*

Z PROBLEMATYKI PRAWA PRACY I POLITYKI SOCJALNEJ. see *LAW*

301　　　　　　FR
200 GROUPES FRANCAIS D'AFRIQUE NOIRE.* 1980. a. 1300 F. Ediafric-la Documentation Africaine, 57 Ave. d'Iena, 75016 Paris, France.

301　　　　　　FR
500 PREMIERES ENTREPRISES D'AFRIQUE NOIRE.* 1977. a. 990 F. Ediafric-la Documentation Africaine, 57 Ave. d'Iena, 75016 Paris, France.

SOCIOLOGY — Abstracting, Bibliographies, Statistics

301 011　　　US　ISSN 0740-8978
AMERICAN PUBLIC OPINION INDEX. 1983 (for 1981) a. $125. Opinion Research Service, Box 70205, Louisville, KY 40270. TEL 502-456-5320. Ed. D.A. Gilbert. (also avail. in microfiche)

301　　　　　　NE
BIBLIOGRAFIE NEDERLANDSE SOCIOLOGIE. 1972. a. fl.45.00. Rijksuniversiteit te Utrecht, Bureau Bibliografie Nederlandse Sociologie, Heidelberglaan 2, Postbus 80140, Utrecht, Netherlands. Ed.Bd. circ. 200.

301　　　US　ISSN 0742-6895
BIBLIOGRAPHIES AND INDEXES IN SOCIOLOGY. 1984. irreg. price varies. Greenwood Press, 88 Post Rd. W., Box 5007, Westport, CT 06881. TEL 203-226-3571.

301 016　　　FR　ISSN 0007-5566
BULLETIN SIGNALETIQUE. PART 521: SOCIOLOGIE - ETHNOLOGIE. 1947. q. 375 F. Centre National de la Recherche Scientifique, Centre de Documentation Sciences Humaines, 54 bd. Raspail, 75260 Paris Cedex, France. cum.index. Indexed: E.I. Popul.Ind.
●Also available online. Vendors: European Space Agency.

300 150 370　　　US　ISSN 0092-6361
CURRENT CONTENTS/SOCIAL & BEHAVIORAL SCIENCES. Short title: C C/S & B S. (Includes Author Index and Address Directory, Current Book Contents and Title Word Index) 1969. w. $283. Institute for Scientific Information, 3501 Market St., Philadelphia, PA 19104 TEL 215-386-0100. (And 132 High St., Uxbridge, Middlesex, UB8 1DP, England) Indexed: SSCI. Compumath. E.I. Ind.Sci.Rev. Popul.Ind.
Formerly: C C-B S E/Current Contents, Behavioral, Social and Educational Sciences (ISSN 0011-3387)

301 016　　　GR　ISSN 0013-2934
EKISTIC INDEX. s-a. $120. Athens Center of Ekistics, 24, Strat. Syndesmou St., Box 3471, Athens 10210, Greece. Ed. P. Psomopoulos. index. cum.index. (back issues avail.)

318　　　PN　ISSN 0378-6765
ESTADISTICA PANAMENA. SITUACION SOCIAL. SECCION 451. ACCIDENTES DE TRANSITO. 1958. a. Bl.0.75. Direccion de Estadistica y Censo, Contraloria General, Apartado 5213, Panama 5, Panama. circ. 850.

309　　　　　　FR
FRANCE. INSTITUT NATIONAL DE LA STATISTIQUE ET DES ETUDES ECONOMIQUES. SERIE M: MENAGES. 1968. a. 635 F. Institut National de la Statistique et des Etudes Economiques, 18 bd. A. Pinard, 75675 Paris 14, France.

I C S S R JOURNAL OF ABSTRACTS AND REVIEWS: SOCIOLOGY & SOCIAL ANTHROPOLOGY. (Indian Council of Social Science Research) see *ANTHROPOLOGY — Abstracting, Bibliographies, Statistics*

301 016.3　　　US　ISSN 0085-2066
INTERNATIONAL BIBLIOGRAPHY OF THE SOCIAL SCIENCES. SOCIOLOGY. Title page also reads: International Bibliography of Sociology. a. $110. Methuen Inc., 29 W. 35th St., New York, NY 10001-2291.

301.4 016　　　US　ISSN 0094-7814
INVENTORY OF MARRIAGE AND FAMILY LITERATURE. 1974. a. $99.95 hardcover; paper $49.95. Sage Publications, Inc., 2111 W. Hillcrest Dr., Newbury Park, CA 91320. TEL 805-499-0721. Eds. David H. Olson, Roxanne Markoff.
Formerly: International Bibliography of Research in Marriage and the Family (ISSN 0095-4551)

301.4 322.4 016　　　US
JOURNALS OF DISSENT AND SOCIAL CHANGE; a bibliography of titles in the California State University, Sacramento, library. 1969. irreg., 6th edt., 1986; suppl. 1983. $20. ‡ California State University, Sacramento, Library, 2000 Jedsmith Dr., Sacramento, CA 95819 TEL 916-278-6634. (Order from: University Bookstore, California State University, Sacramento, 6000 J St., Sacramento, CA 95819) Ed. John Liberty. circ. controlled. (processed)

NOTES AND ABSTRACTS IN AMERICAN AND INTERNATIONAL EDUCATION. see *EDUCATION — Abstracting, Bibliographies, Statistics*

PEACE RESEARCH ABSTRACTS JOURNAL. see *POLITICAL SCIENCE — Abstracting, Bibliographies, Statistics*

309 330.9 016　　　JM
S E C I N ABSTRACTS. JOURNAL. 1982. biennial. $20. (Socio-Economic Information Network, Planning Institute of Jamaica) Documentation Center, 39-41 Barbados Ave., Kingston 5, Jamaica. circ. 150.
Formerly: S E C I N Abstracts.

301 016　　　US　ISSN 0164-0283
SAGE FAMILY STUDIES ABSTRACTS. 1979. q. $55 to individuals; institutions $110. Sage Publications, Inc., 2111 W. Hillcrest Dr., Newbury Park, CA 91320 TEL 805-499-0721. (And Sage Publications, Ltd., 28 Banner St., London EC1Y 8QE, England)

312 301　　　　　　NZ
SOCIAL TRENDS IN NEW ZEALAND. 1977. irreg. NZ.$4.50. Department of Statistics, Private Bag, Wellington, New Zealand.

301 016　　　US　ISSN 0038-0202
SOCIOLOGICAL ABSTRACTS. (Also avail. on CD-ROM) 1953. 5/yr. $264 (annual index $48) Sociological Abstracts, Inc., Box 22206, San Diego, CA 92122. TEL 619-565-6603. (Co-sponsor: International Sociological Association) Ed. Leo P. Chall. adv. abstr. index. cum.index: vols.1-10, 11-15. circ. 2,000. (back issues avail.) Indexed: Popul.Ind.
●Also available online. Vendors: BRS, Data-Star, DIALOG.

SOCIOLOGY OF EDUCATION ABSTRACTS. see *EDUCATION — Abstracting, Bibliographies, Statistics*

WORLD AGRICULTURAL ECONOMICS AND RURAL SOCIOLOGY ABSTRACTS; abstracts of world literature. see *AGRICULTURE — Abstracting, Bibliographies, Statistics*

SOFTWARE

see *Computers — Software*

SOUND

see *Physics — Sound*

SOUND RECORDING AND REPRODUCTION

see also *Music*

534　　　AT　ISSN 0310-8902
AUSTRALIAN HI-FI ANNUAL. 1971. a. Australian Hi-Fi Publications Pty. Ltd., P.O. Box 341, Mona Vale, N.S.W. 2103, Australia. Ed. Greg Borrowman. Indexed: Pinpointer.

338.4 780　　　　　　US
BILLBOARD'S AUDIO/VIDEO/TAPE SOURCEBOOK. Variant title: Audio/Video/Tape Directory. a. $27. Billboard Directories, 1515 Broadway, 39th Fl., New York, NY 10036. TEL 212-764-7300. (also avail. in microfilm)
Formerly: Billboard International Tape Directory (ISSN 0090-645X)

621.389　　　US　ISSN 0160-7790
BILLBOARD'S INTERNATIONAL RECORDING EQUIPMENT & STUDIO DIRECTORY. a. $27. Billboard Directories, 1515 Broadway, 39th Fl., New York, NY 10036. TEL 212-764-7300.
Formerly: Billboard International Directory of Recording Studios.

780　　　　　　US
BILLBOARD'S INTERNATIONAL RECORDING STUDIO AND EQUIPMENT DIRECTORY. 1968. a. $27. Billboard Directories, 1515 Broadway, New York, NY 10026 (And 9000 Sunset Blvd., Los Angeles, CA 90069) (also avail. in microfilm from KTO)
Former titles: International Recording Studio and Equipment Directory; International Recording Equipment and Studio Directory; International Recording Studio and Equipment Directory; International Directory of Recording Studios (ISSN 0067-8627)

253　　　US　ISSN 0192-334X
DISCOGRAPHIES. 1979. irreg. price varies. Greenwood Press, 88 Post Rd. W., Box 5007, Westport, CT 06881. TEL 203-226-3571. Ed. Michael Gray.

DOWN HOME MUSIC NEWSLETTER. see *MUSIC*

621.389　　　UK　ISSN 0262-0812
GRAMOPHONE SPOKEN WORD & MISCELLANEOUS CATALOGUE. 1960. a. £3.30($5.94) General Gramophone Publications Ltd., 177/179 Kenton Rd., Harrow, Middx HA3 0HA, England. circ. 3,000.

621.389　　　　　　AG
GUIA DE AUDIO. a. $2.50. Editorial Fotografia Universal, Muniz 1327/49, Buenos Aires, Argentina.

789.91 621.389　　　　　　UK
GUIDE TO A P R S MEMBER STUDIOS. 1981. a. membership. Association of Professional Recording Studios, 163 A High St., Rickmansworth WD3 1AY, England. Ed. P. Vaughan. adv. circ. 10,000.
Formerly: Recording in Great Britain.

SOUND RECORDING AND REPRODUCTION — ABSTRACTING, BIBLIOGRAPHIES, STATISTICS

621.389   DK   ISSN 0108-4658
HI-FI AND VIDEO REVYEN. a. Kr.84.50. Bonniers Specialmagasiner, Noerre Farimagsgade 49, 1375 Copenhagen K, Denmark. adv. circ. 28,000.
    Formerly: Hi-Fi Revyen.

016.789   II   ISSN 0302-6744
INDIAN RECORDS. (Text in English) irreg. Gramophone Company of India, Calcutta, India. bibl.

PAUL'S RECORD MAGAZINE. see *MUSIC*

621.389   AT   ISSN 0819-0216
STEREO BUYER'S GUIDE. AUDIO YEARBOOK. 1971. a. Australian Hi-Fi Publications Pty. Ltd., Box 341, Mona Vale, N.S.W. 2103, Australia. Ed. Don Norris.
    Formerly: Stereo Buyer's Guide. Manual (ISSN 0312-0058)

621.389   AT   ISSN 0819-0208
STEREO BUYER'S GUIDE. C D PLAYERS, CASSETTES DECKS AND TURNTABLES. 1971. a. Australian Hi-Fi Publications Pty. Ltd., Box 341, Mona Vale, N.S.W. 2103, Australia. Ed. Don Norris.
    Former titles: Stereo Buyer's Guide. Turntables and Compact Disc Players & Stereo Buyer's Guide. Turntables (ISSN 0312-0066)

621.387   AT   ISSN 0819-0194
STEREO BUYER'S GUIDE. LOUDSPEAKERS, AMPLIFIERS AND TUNERS. 1971. a. Australian Hi-Fi Publications Pty. Ltd., Box 341, Mona Vale, N.S.W. 2103, Australia. Ed. Don Norris.
    Former Titles: Stereo Buyer's Guide. Amplifiers, FM Tuners and Receivers (ISSN 0727-4459) & Stereo Buyer's Guide. Amplifiers.

621.389   US
STEREO REVIEW'S CAR STEREO BUYERS GUIDE. 1984. a. $3.95. C B S Magazines, Stereo Review Department, 1515 Broadway, New York, NY 10036. TEL 212-719-6000. Ed. William Burton. adv. circ. 225,000.

338.4   US
STEREO REVIEW'S STEREO BUYERS GUIDE. 1957. a. $3.95. C B S Magazines, Stereo Review Department, 1515 Broadway, New York, NY 10036. TEL 212-719-6000. Ed. William Burton. adv. circ. 200,000.
    Former titles: Stereo Directory and Buying Guide (ISSN 0090-6786); Stereo/Hi-Fi Directory (ISSN 0081-5470)

681.6   621.3   US
STEREO REVIEW'S TAPE RECORDING & BUYING GUIDE. 1965. a. $3.95. C B S Magazines, Stereo Review Department, 1515 Broadway, New York, NY 10036. TEL 212-719-6000. Ed. William Burton. adv. circ. 150,000.
    Former titles: Tape Recording and Buying Guide (ISSN 0093-996X); Tape Recorder Annual.

STEREO REVIEW'S VIDEO BUYERS GUIDE. see *COMMUNICATIONS — Radio And Television*

621.389   UK
STUDIO SOUND'S PRO-AUDIO DIRECTORY. 1981. a. £13($25) Link House Magazines Ltd., Link House, Dingwall Ave., Croydon CR9 2TA, England. Ed. Sally Baker. illus.
    Former titles: Studio Sound's Pro-Audio Yearbook (ISSN 0260-8537) & Pro-Audio Yearbook.

789.9   UK
WHICH HI-FI? 1969. a. £3. Haymarket Publishing Ltd., 38-42 Hampton Rd., Teddington, Middx. TW11 0JE, England. Ed. Gareth Renowden.
    Incorporating: Hi-Fi Annual and Test; Formerly: Hi-Fi Sound Annual (ISSN 0073-2044)

SOUND RECORDING AND REPRODUCTION — Abstracting, Bibliographies, Statistics

621.389   770   370   UK
BRITISH CATALOGUE OF AUDIO-VISUAL MATERIALS. Variant title: A V M A R C. 1979. irreg., latest 1983. £12.50. British Library, Bibliographic Services, 2 Sheraton St., London W1V 4BH, England. TEL 01-323-7220. (back issues avail.)
    ●Also available online.

620   011   US
DIRECTORY OF SPOKEN-WORD AUDIO-CASSETTES. 1972. biennial. $24.50. Jeffrey Norton Publishers, Inc., On-the-Green, Cuilford, CT 06437. Ed. Gerald McKee. bk. rev.
    Former titles (until 1982): Audio-Cassette Directory; (until 1979): Directory of Spoken-Voice Audio-Cassettes.

MUSIC, BOOKS ON MUSIC AND SOUND RECORDINGS. see *MUSIC — Abstracting, Bibliographies, Statistics*

SPECIAL EDUCATION AND REHABILITATION

see *Education — Special Education and Rehabilitation*

SPORTS AND GAMES

see also *Medical Sciences — Sports Medicine; Sports and Games — Ball Games; Sports and Games — Bicycles and Motorcycles; Sports and Games — Boats and Boating; Sports and Games — Horses and Horsemanship; Sports and Games — Outdoor Life*

796.4   US   ISSN 0361-4654
A A U JUNIOR OLYMPIC HANDBOOK. a. Amateur Athletic Union of the United States, 3400 W. 86th St., Indianapolis, IN 46268. TEL 317-872-2900. illus.

796   SW
AARETS BANDY. a. Kr.299. Stroembergs Idrottsboecker, Vittangigatan 27, Vaellingby, Stockholm, Sweden.

796   SW   ISSN 0567-4573
AARETS IDROTT. a. Kr.314. Stroembergs Idrottsboecker, Vittangigatan 27, Vaellingby, Stockholm, Sweden.

796.9   SW
AARETS ISHOCKEY. a. Kr.299. (Svenska Ishockeyfoerbundet) Stroembergs Idrottsboecker, Vittangigatan 27, Vaellingby, Stockholm, Sweden. illus.

796   FR   ISSN 0065-0579
ACADEMIE DES SPORTS, PARIS. ANNUAIRE. 1965. irreg. (Academie des Sports, Paris) Editions Person, 34 rue de Penthievre, 75008 Paris, France. Ed. Baron J. de Nervo. adv.

790   CS
ALBUM SLAVNYCH SPORTOVCOV. irreg, vol.4, 1976. price varies. Sport, Publishing House of the Central Committee of the Slovak Physical Culture Organization, Fucikova 14, 893 44 Bratislava, Czechoslovakia. illus.

796   UK   ISSN 0065-6690
AMATEUR ATHLETIC ASSOCIATION. HANDBOOK.* 1925. a. £2.50. (Amateur Athletic Association) BAAB AAA, 5 Church Rd., Great Bookham, Leatherhead, Surrey KT23 3PM, England. Ed. M.A. Farrell. adv. circ. 4,500.

796   US   ISSN 0091-3405
AMATEUR ATHLETIC UNION OF THE UNITED STATES. OFFICIAL HANDBOOK OF THE A A U CODE. Cover title: A A U Code. 1888. a. $10. Amateur Athletic Union of the United States, 3400 W. 86th St., Indianapolis, IN 46268. TEL 317-872-2900. illus. Key Title: Official Handbook of the A.A.U. Code.

796   US   ISSN 0516-8635
AMATEUR HOCKEY ASSOCIATION OF THE UNITED STATES. OFFICIAL GUIDE. a. $2.50. Amateur Hockey Association of the United States, c/o Hal Trumble, Exec.Dir., 2997 Broadmoor Valley Rd., Colorado Springs, CO 80906.

796   US
AMATEUR HOCKEY ASSOCIATION OF THE UNITED STATES. RULE BOOK. biennial. $5. Amateur Hockey Association of the United States, c/o Hal Trumble, Exec Dir., 2997 Broadmoor Valley Rd., Colorado Springs, CO 80906. TEL 303-576-4990.

796.962   US   ISSN 0516-866X
AMATEUR SKATING UNION OF THE UNITED STATES. OFFICAL HANDBOOK. 1930. quadrennial. $6. Amateur Skating Union of the United States, 1033 Shady Ln., Glen Ellyn, IL 60137. TEL 312-469-2107. circ. 1,500. (looseleaf format)

797.21   UK
AMATEUR SWIMMING ASSOCIATION HANDBOOK. 1905. a. Amateur Swimming Association, Harold Fern House, Derby Square, Loughborough, Leics. LE11 0AL, England. Ed. A. Williams. circ. 3,700.

797   910.09   US
AMERICA'S CUP CHALLENGE AND GUIDE TO AUSTRALIA. 1986. irreg. C D M Communications, Inc., 100 Fifth Ave., New York, NY 10011. TEL 212-243-0773. Ed. Stephen A. Sochia.

790.1   US
AMUSEMENT RIDES & GAMES BUYERS' GUIDE. a. $3.50. Billboard Publications, Inc., Amusement Business Group, 1515 Broadway, New York, NY 10036. TEL 212-764-7300. Ed. Paul Curran.

790.1   FR
ANNEE SPORTIVE U.S.M.T. a. membership. Union Sportive Metropolitaine des Transports, 159 Bd de la Villette, Paris 10, France. adv.

796   FR
ATHLERAMA (TODAY) 1962. a. Federation Francaise d'Athletisme, 10 rue Faubourg Poissonniere, 75480 Paris Cedex 10, France. TEL 47 70 80 81. circ. 5,000.
    Formerly (until 1982): Athletisme Francais (ISSN 0067-012X)

ATLANTIC CITY ACTION. see *BUSINESS AND ECONOMICS — Investments*

793   US   ISSN 0092-6256
AURORA A F X ROAD RACING HANDBOOK. 1973. a. $4.95. Auto World, Inc., 701 N. Keyser Ave., Scranton, PA 18508. TEL 717-346-7495. Ed. Oscar Koveleski. circ. 40,000.

793   AT
AUSTRALIAN CHESS LORE. 1981. irreg. price varies. A.C.L. Partnership, 3 Roger Pitt St., Modbury Heights, S.A. 5092, Australia. circ. 200. (back issues avail.)

796.345   UK   ISSN 0262-1940
BADMINTON ASSOCIATION OF ENGLAND. ANNUAL HANDBOOK. 1900. a. £2. Badminton Association of England, National Badminton Centre, Bradwell Rd., Loughton Lodge, Milton Keynes MK8 9LA, England. Ed. G.C. Lamb. adv. index. circ. 8,000.
    Formerly: Badminton Association of England. Official Handbook (ISSN 0067-2882)

796.345   IE
BADMINTON IRELAND. 1977. a. (Badminton Union of Ireland) Sean Graham, 22 Moore St., Dublin 1, Ireland. illus.
    Formerly: Irish Badminton Handbook.

SPORTS AND GAMES

796.345   DK   ISSN 0107-766X
BADMINTON REVY. 1973. a. Kr.30. B E H O, c/o
Danske Boghendleres Kommissionsanstalt,
Siljangade 6, 2300 Copenhagen S, Denmark. illus.
   Formerly: Badminton Jul.

796.345   UK
BADMINTON SPORTING DIARY. 1954. a. Frank
Smythson Ltd., 54 New Bond St., London W1Y
ODE, England. Ed. R. O'Connell. circ. 3,
000(controlled)

785.06   US
BATON TWIRLING HANDBOOK. Cover title: A A
U Official Handbook: Baton Twirling. irreg., latest
1985. $3.50. Amateur Athletic Union of the United
States, 3400 W. 86th St., Indianapolis, IN 46268.
TEL 317-872-2900. illus.
   Formerly: Baton Twirling Rules and Regulations
(ISSN 0361-221X)

796.082   US   ISSN 0067-6292
BEST SPORTS STORIES. 1944. a. $9.95 softcover;
hardcover $14.95. Sporting News Publishing Co.,
Attn: Richard Water, Pres., 1212 N. Lindbergh
Blvd., St. Louis, MO 63132. TEL 314-997-7111.

371.7   US
BLUE BOOK OF COLLEGE ATHLETICS. 1930. a.
$14. Rohrich Corp., 903 E. Tallmadge Ave., Akron,
OH 44310-3592. TEL 216-633-1711. Ed. A.W.
Tinker. circ. 6,000.

799.202   US
BLUE BOOK OF GUN VALUES. 1981. a. $14.95.
Investment Rarities, Inc., One Appletree Sq.,
Minneapolis, MN 55408. Ed. Steven P. Fjestad.
circ. 17,000.
   Formerly: Barry Fain's Private Blue Book of Gun
Values.

371.7   US
BLUE BOOK OF JUNIOR & COMMUNITY
COLLEGE ATHLETICS. 1958. a. $12. Rohrich
Corp., 903 E. Tallmadge Ave., Akron, OH 44310-
3592. TEL 216-633-1711. Ed. A.W. Tinker. circ. 2,
500.
   Formerly: Blue Book of Junior College Athletics
(ISSN 0520-2973)

790.1   UK
BOB WILSON'S T V SPORTS ANNUAL. 1979. a.
£1.95. Brown Watson Ltd., 44 Hill St., London
W1X 84B, England.

790   US
BOSTON MARATHON. 1979. a. $2. Boston Phoenix,
Inc., 100 Massachusetts Ave., Boston, MA 02115.
TEL 617-536-5390. Ed. Tory Carlson. adv. circ.
116,800.

796.815   UK
BOXING NEWS ANNUAL. 1945. a. £3.95. R & D
Publications Ltd., 30-34 Langham St., London W1N
5LB, England. Ed. Harry Mullan. adv. circ. 6,000.

796.41   US   ISSN 0160-3280
BOYS GYMNASTICS RULEBOOK. a. $3.00.
National Federation of State High School
Associations, 11724 Plaza Circle, Box 20626,
Kansas City, MO 64195. TEL 816-464-5400.

796   UK   ISSN 0068-1938
BRITISH CYCLING FEDERATION. HANDBOOK.
1959. a. £2. British Cycling Federation, 16 Upper
Woburn Place, London WC1H 0QE, England. Ed.
L.A. Unwin. adv. circ. 8,500.
   Formerly: British Cycling Federation. Racing
Handbook.

790.1   UK
BRITISH OLYMPIC ASSOCIATION YEAR BOOK
AND DIARY. a. Welbecson Ltd., 3 Thomas St.,
Hull, Humberside HU9 1EJ, England.

790.1   GW   ISSN 0723-9297
BUDO UND TRANSKULTURELLE
BEWEGUNGSFORSCHUNG. 1983. irreg., vol.10,
1986. price varies. Verlag Ingrid Czwalina,
Reesenbuettler Redder 75, D-2070 Ahrensburg, W.
Germany (B.R.D.) Ed. Dr. Horst Tiwald.

796   GW
BUNDESINSTITUT FUER
SPORTWISSENSCHAFT. BERICHTE UND
ASPEKTE (YEAR) 1973. biennial. Bundesinstitut
fuer Sportwissenschaft, Carl-Diem-Weg 4, 5000
Cologne 41, W. Germany (B.R.D.) TEL 02 21/49
79-0. illus. circ. 2,000.

790.1   AT
C A M S MANUAL OF MOTOR SPORT. 1959. a.
Aus.$10. Confederation of Australian Motor Sport,
National Council of C A M S, P.O. Box 441,
Camberwell, Vic. 3124, Australia. Ed. John A.
Keeffe. adv. circ. 10,000.

796.5   UK   ISSN 0068-5267
CAIRNGORM CLUB JOURNAL. 1889. biennial,
no.99, 1983. £1. Cairngorm Club, c/o Secretary
R.C. Shirreffs, 18 Bon-Accord Square, Aberdeen
AB9 1YE, Scotland. Ed. A.D. Chessell. adv. bk.
rev. index. circ. 420.

CANADIAN SPORTING GOODS &
PLAYTHINGS. DIRECTORY. see BUSINESS
AND ECONOMICS — Trade And Industrial
Directories

CELEBRITY DIRECTORY; how to reach movie, tv
stars and other celebrities. see MOTION
PICTURES

798   AG   ISSN 0008-8986
CENTAUROS; revista de polo, turf, equitacion, pato y
troto. 1955. irreg., vol.40, 1978. Arg.$15. San
Martin 66, Buenos Aires, Argentina. Eds. Jorge
Oliva & Manuel Caramelo Gomex. Indexed: SSCI.

CHARTERED INSTITUTE OF PUBLIC FINANCE
AND ACCOUNTANCY. EDUCATION
STATISTICS. UNIT COSTS. see EDUCATION —
Abstracting, Bibliographies, Statistics

796.41   UK
CHASEFORM JUMPING ANNUAL. a. £14.
Raceform Ltd., 2 York Rd., London SW11 3PZ,
England.

796   US   ISSN 0084-8891
COLORADO SKI AND WINTER RECREATION
STATISTICS. 1968. a. $25. University of Colorado,
Graduate School of Business Administration,
Boulder, CO 80309. TEL 303-492-8227. Ed. Karen
Duea. circ. 200.

790.1   US
COMPLETE SPORTS BASEBALL SPECIAL. a.
Lexington Library, Inc., 355 Lexington Ave., New
York, NY 10017. TEL 212-391-1400. Eds. Stephen
Ciacciarelli, Thomas Walsh. adv. charts. illus.
   Formerly: Complete Sports.

382   BL
CONFEDERACAO BRASILEIRA DE FUTEBOL.
RELATORIO. a. Confederacao Brasileira de
Desportos, Rua da Alfandega, 70, Rio de Janeiro,
Brazil. illus.
   Formerly (after 1983): Confederacao Brasileira de
Desportos. Relatorio.

CORD SPORTFACTS GUNS GUIDE. see HOBBIES

688.76   US   ISSN 0736-0703
COST OF DOING BUSINESS FOR RETAIL
SPORTING GOODS STORES. 1968. biennial. $30.
National Sporting Goods Association, 1699 Wall
St., Mt. Prospect, IL 60056. TEL 312-439-4000.

790.1   DK
DANSK IDRAETS-FORBUND. AARBOG. a. Dansk
Idraets-Forbund, Idraettens Hus, 2605 Broendby,
Denmark. adv. circ. 13,800.

613.7 790.1   GE   ISSN 0457-3919
DEUTSCHE HOCHSCHULE FUER
KOERPERKULTUR. WISSENSCHAFTLICHE
ZEITSCHRIFT. (Summaries in English, French,
German and Russian) 1959. a. M.57.90 per no.
Deutsche Hochschule fuer Koerperkultur Leipzig,
Friedrich Ludwig Jahn Allee 59, 701 Leipzig, E.
Germany (D.D.R.) Ed. Karl-Heinz Bauersfeld. bk.
rev. illus. index. (tabloid format)

796   GW   ISSN 0075-2401
DEUTSCHER TURNER-BUND. JAHRBUCH DER
TURNKUNST. 1906. a. DM.15. Bernecker Verlag,
Unter dem Schoenberg 1, D-3508 Melsungen, W.
Germany (B.R.D.) (Subscr. to: Deutscher Turner-
Bund (D.T.B.), Otto-Fleck-Schneise 8, D-6000
Frankfurt/M 71, W. Germany (B.R.D.)) adv.

796   GW   ISSN 0173-0843
DOKUMENTE ZUM HOCHSCHULSPORT. 1976.
irreg., (vol.18, 1985) price varies. (Freie Universitaet
Berlin, Zentraleinrichtung Hochschulsport) Verlag
Ingrid Czwalina, Reesenbuettler Redder 75, 2070
Ahrensburg, W. Germany (B.R.D.)

790.1   IT
EUROSKI. 1967. a. L.4500. Ideapiu S.r.l., Via Durini
3, 20122 Milan, Italy. Ed. Paolo De Michele. adv.
circ. 26,000.

FEDERATION EQUESTRE FRANCAISE. GUIDE
OFFICIEL DU CAVALIER. see SPORTS AND
GAMES — Horses And Horsemanship

799.3   CN   ISSN 0226-773X
FEDERATION OF CANADIAN ARCHERS.
RULES BOOK. (Editions in English and French)
1984. irreg. Can.$10. Federation of Canadian
Archers, 333 River Rd., Vanier, Ont. K1L 8H9,
Canada. TEL 613-748-5604.

796.355   US
FIELD HOCKEY RULEBOOK. a. $2.50. National
Federation of State High School Associations,
11724 Plaza Circle, Box 20626, Kansas City, MO
64195. TEL 816-464-5400. Ed. Kristy R. Parnell.

796   FR   ISSN 0071-9102
FRANCE-SPORTS. (Text in French; summaries in
English, German, Italian and Spanish) 1954.
biennial. 135 F. Creations, Editions et Productions
Publicitaires, 1 Place d'Estienne d'Orves, 75009
Paris, France. Ed. Georges Prieux. adv. circ. 8,500.

790.1   GW
FUNBOARD; surf spezial. 1983. irreg. (1-2/yr.)
DM.10 per no. Delius Klasing Verlag, Siekerwall 21,
Postfach 48 09, D-4800 Bielefeld 1, W. Germany
(B.R.D.) circ. 67,800(controlled)

796.41   US
GIRLS GYMNASTICS RULES AND MANUAL. a.
$3.00. National Federation of State High School
Associations, 11724 Plaza Circle, Box 20626,
Kansas City, MO 64195. TEL 816-464-5400.
   Former titles: Girls Gymnastics Rules (ISSN
0270-2029); Incorporating: Girls Gymnastics
Manual.

796   US   ISSN 0072-4955
GOLF GUIDE. 1963. a. $2. Snibbe Books, 1115
Ponce de Leon, Clearwater, FL 33516. TEL 813-
586-1779. Ed. Joseph Gambatese.

GUIDA DELLO SCIATORE. see TRAVEL AND
TOURISM

796   AU   ISSN 0072-9698
HANDBALL UND FAUSTBALL IN
OESTERREICH. irreg. Oesterreichischer Handball-
und Faustball-Bund, Hauslabgasse 24, A-1050
Vienna, Austria. Ed. Friedrich Duschka.

796   UK   ISSN 0073-0416
HARPERS GUIDE TO SPORTS TRADE. 1948. a.
£48. Harpers Sports & Leisure, 2 Silverdale Rd.,
Bushey, Watford, Herts. WD2 2L2, England. Ed.
M. Johnson. adv. circ. 3,600.

796   US   ISSN 0278-4955
HOCKEY GUIDE. 1967. a. $9.95. Sporting News
Publishing Co., 1212 N. Lindbergh Blvd., St Louis,
MO 63132. TEL 314-997-7111. Ed. Larry Wigge.
illus. stat. circ. 4,000.
   Former titles: Pro and Amateur Hockey Guide
(ISSN 0090-0818); Pro and Senior Hockey Guide
(ISSN 0079-550X)

796   UK   ISSN 0073-3164
HOMING WORLD STUD BOOK. 1938. a. £2.00.
Royal Pigeon Racing Association, British Homing
World, 26 High St., Welshpool, Powys SY21 7JP,
Wales. Ed. John R. Thomas. adv.

796   SZ
I S U CONSTITUTION. (Text in English) biennial;
latest issue 1986. 8 Fr. International Skating Union,
Postfach, 7270 Davos-Platz, Switzerland.

SPORTS AND GAMES

796   SZ
I S U REGULATIONS. (Text in English) biennial; latest issue 1986. 20 Fr. International Skating Union, Postfach, 7270 Davos-Platz, Switzerland.

796.962   US   ISSN 0732-8117
ICE HOCKEY RULE BOOK. a. $2.50. National Federation of State High School Associations, 11724 Plaza Circle, Box 20626, Kansas City, MO 64195. TEL 816-464-5400. Ed. Richard G. Fawcett.

790.1   DK   ISSN 0900-8632
IDRAETSHISTORISK AARBOG. a. (Dansk Idraetshistorisk Forening) Bibliotekscnetralen, Telegrafvej 5, DK-2750 ballerup, Denmark.

790.1   DK   ISSN 0900-7008
IDRAETTENS FORSKNINGSRAAD. FORSKNINGSOVERSIGT. a. Kr.47.50. (Idraettens Forskningsraad) Bibliotekscentralen, Telegrafvej 5, DK-2750 Ballerup, Denmark.

797.21   UK
INSTITUTE OF SWIMMING TEACHERS & COACHES DIRECTORY OF MEMBERSHIP. 1982. biennial. £12.50 to non-members. Institute of Swimming Teachers & Coaches, Lantern House, 38 Leicester Road, Loughborough, England. Ed. B.W. Relf. circ. 8,000.

371.7   RM
INSTITUTUL PEDAGOGIC ORADEA. LUCRARI STIINTIFICE SERIA EDUCATIE FIZICA SI SPORT. (Continues in part its Lucrari Stiintifice: Seria Educatie Fizica, Biologie, Stiinte Medicale (1971-72), its Lucrari Stiintifice: Seria A and Seria B (1969-70), and its Lucrari Stiintifice (1967-68)) (Text in Rumanian, occasionally in English or French; summaries in Rumanian, English or German) 1967. a. Institutul Pedagogic Oradea, Calea Armatei Rosii Nr. 5, Oradea, Rumania.

796   UK   ISSN 0074-137X
INTERNATIONAL ARCHERY FEDERATION. BULLETIN OFFICIEL. (Text in English and French) biennial., no.26, 1974. price varies. International Archery Federation, 46 The Balk, Walton, Wakefield, England. Ed. Mrs. I. K. Frith. adv.

796 371   JA   ISSN 0074-1728
INTERNATIONAL ASSOCIATION OF PHYSICAL EDUCATION AND SPORTS FOR GIRLS AND WOMEN. PROCEEDINGS OF THE INTERNATIONAL CONGRESS. (Proceedings publihsed by host countries) irreg., 6th, 1969, Tokyo. Japan Association of Physical Education for Women and Girls, 6-102 O.M.Y.C., 3-1 Jinen-cho Yoyogi, Shibuya-ku, Tokyo, Japan. circ. contr.circ.

790.1   UK
INTERNATIONAL ATHLETICS GUIDE. 1983. a. $13.95. Tantivy Press, 136-148 Tooley St., London SE1 2TT, England (Dist. in U.S. by: New York Zoetrope Inc., 838 Broadway, New York, NY 10003) Ed. Mel Watman. adv. bk. rev.
Formerly: International Running Guide.

796.345   UK   ISSN 0255-4437
INTERNATIONAL BADMINTON FEDERATION. ANNUAL STATUTE BOOK. 1935. a. £5. International Badminton Federation, 24 Winchcombe House, Winchcombe St., Cheltenham, Glos. GL52 2NA, England. index. circ. 2,000.
Formerly: International Badminton Federation. Annual Handbook (ISSN 0074-1981)

796.35   US
INTERNATIONAL FIELD HOCKEY RULES. a. International Hockey Federation, USFHA National Office, 1750 E. Boulder, Colorado Springs, CO 80909. TEL 303-578-4567.
Formerly: Official Field Hockey Rules for School Girls (ISSN 0362-3270)

796   GR   ISSN 0074-7181
INTERNATIONAL OLYMPIC ACADEMY. REPORT OF THE SESSIONS. (Since 1968 issued in separate English, French and Greek vols.) 1961. a., 13th, 1973, Olympia, Greece. $5 for non-qualified personnel. Hellenic Olympic Committee, 4 Kapsali St., Athens 138, Greece. cum.index: 1961-69. circ. 9,000. Indexed: Sportsearch.

796   FR   ISSN 0074-7645
INTERNATIONAL REFERENCE ANNUAL FOR BUILDING AND EQUIPMENT OF SPORTS, TOURISM, RECREATION INSTALLATIONS. 1970. a. price varies. Techno-Loisirs, 3 rue Sivel, Paris 14, France. adv. circ. 10,000.

796   SZ   ISSN 0539-0168
INTERNATIONAL SKATING UNION. ICE DANCING REGULATIONS. biennial. 16 Fr. International Skating Union, Postfach, 7270 Davos-Platz, Switzerland.

796   SZ   ISSN 0535-2479
INTERNATIONAL SKATING UNION. MINUTES OF CONGRESS. (Text in English) biennial, latest 1986, Velden. 10 Fr. International Skating Union, Postfach, 7270 Davos-Platz, Switzerland.

796.72   IE
IRISH MOTORSPORT YEARBOOK; cars, rallys, racing, trials & karts. a. Sean Graham, 22/23 Moore St., Dublin 1, Ireland. illus.
Automobile racing

JOURNAL OF MAGIC HISTORY. see *THEATER*

796   US   ISSN 0094-8705
JOURNAL OF THE PHILOSOPHY OF SPORT. 1974. a. $10 to individuals; institutions $15. (Philosophic Society for the Study of Sport) Human Kinetics Publishers, Inc., 1607 N. Market, Box 5076, Champaign, IL 61820. TEL 217-351-5076. Ed. Klaus V. Meier. bk. rev. bibl. circ. 385. (back issues avail.) Indexed: Phil.Ind. Sportsearch.

796   FI   ISSN 0075-4684
KALASTUSPAIKKAOPAS. 1966. irreg. (approx. biennial) Fmk.45. Kalatalouden Keskusliitto - Federation of Finnish Fisheries Associations (Centralfoerbundet foer Fiskerihushaallning, Koydenpunojankatu 7 B 23, 00180 Helsinki 18, Finland. Ed.Bd. adv. index. circ. 4,000.

796   MY   ISSN 0085-2481
KARATE INTERNATIONAL ANNUAL. (Text in Chinese and English) 1971. a. M.$3.50($1.50) ‡ (Karate Association of Malaysia) Karate Budokan International Inc., No. 5, Jalan Taman (7/6), Petaling Jaya 46050, Malaysia. Ed. Chew Choo Soot. adv. bk. rev. charts. illus. circ. 20,000.

790.1   US
LET'S MAKE IT OFFICIAL. a. $2. National Federation of State High School Associations, 11724 Plaza Circle, Box 20626, Kansas City, MO 64195. TEL 816-464-5400.

354   CN
MANITOBA LOTTERIES FOUNDATION. ANNUAL REPORT. (Report year ends Mar. 31) 1971/72. a. Manitoba Lotteries Foundation, 830 Empress St., Winnipeg, Man. R3G 3H3, Canada. TEL 204-945-2670. illus. stat. circ. 500.
Formerly: Manitoba. Lotteries Commission. Annual Report (ISSN 0703-0827)

790.1   CK
MERIDIANO DEPORTIVO. 1975. irreg. c/o Efrain Tobon, Apdo. Aereo 8275, Medellin, Colombia.

796.41   US   ISSN 0363-9282
N A G W S GUIDE. GYMNASTICS. 1963/65. $8.95. American Alliance for Health, Physical Education, Recreation and Dance, National Association for Girls and Women in Sport, 1900 Association Dr., Reston, VA 22091. TEL 703-476-3481. circ. 5,000. Indexed: ERIC.
Formerly: Gymnastics Guide.

796   US   ISSN 0077-3336
N A I A HANDBOOK. 1959. a. $7.50. National Association of Intercollegiate Athletics, 1221 Baltimore St., Kansas City, MO 64105. TEL 816-842-5050. Ed. Jefferson Farris. (reprint service avail. from UMI)

796   US   ISSN 0077-3344
N A I A OFFICIAL RECORDS BOOK. 1958. a. $10. National Association of Intercollegiate Athletics, 1221 Baltimore, Kansas City, MO 64105. TEL 816-842-5050. Ed. Charles Eppler. index. circ. 2,500. (reprint service avail. from UMI)

790.1   US
N C A A DIRECTORY. 1976. a. $6. National Collegiate Athletic Association, Box 1906, Mission, KS 66201. TEL 913-384-3220. circ. 2,500.

797.21   US   ISSN 0736-5128
N C A A MEN'S & WOMEN'S SWIMMING AND DIVING RULES. 1925. a. $3. National Collegiate Athletic Association, Box 1906, Mission, KS 66201. TEL 913-384-3220. circ. 8,200.
Former titles: N C A A Swimming (ISSN 0272-8095) & Official National Collegiate Athletic Association Swimming Guide.

796   US   ISSN 0735-9195
N C A A MEN'S ICE HOCKEY RULES AND INTERPRETATIONS. 1926. a. $3. National Collegiate Athletic Association, Box 1906, Mission, KS 66201. TEL 913-384-3220. circ. 10,000.
Formerly: Official National Collegiate Athletic Association Ice Hockey Guide.

790.1   US   ISSN 0734-0508
N C A A MEN'S WATER POLO RULES. 1970. a. $3. National Collegiate Athletic Association, Box 1906, Mission, KS 66222. TEL 913-384-3220.
Former titles: N C A A Water Polo Rules (ISSN 0271-860X) & Official National Collegiate Athletic Association Water Polo Rules.

796   CN   ISSN 0079-5569
N.H.L. PRO HOCKEY. 1969. a. Can.$4.50. ‡ PaperJacks Ltd., 330 Steelcase Rd. E., Markham, Ont. L3R 2M1, Canada. TEL 416-475-1261. Ed. James Proudfoot. index. circ. 20,000.

796   US   ISSN 0077-3794
NATIONAL COLLEGIATE ATHLETIC ASSOCIATION. ANNUAL REPORTS. 1966. a. $8. National Collegiate Athletic Association, Box 1906, Mission, KS 66201. TEL 913-384-3220. circ. 2,500.

796   US   ISSN 0077-3808
NATIONAL COLLEGIATE ATHLETIC ASSOCIATION. CONVENTION PROCEEDINGS. 1906; 1967 as independent title. a. $12. National Collegiate Athletic Association, Box 1906, Mission, KS 66201. TEL 913-384-3220. circ. 2,500.

796   US   ISSN 0077-3816
NATIONAL COLLEGIATE ATHLETIC ASSOCIATION. MANUAL. Cover title: N C A A Manual. 1906; 1966 as independent title. a. $8. National Collegiate Athletic Association, Box 1906, Mission, KS 66201. TEL 913-384-3220. circ. 7,500.

796.06   US   ISSN 0094-4459
NATIONAL COLLEGIATE ATHLETIC ASSOCIATION. PROCEEDINGS OF THE SPECIAL CONVENTION. 1973. irreg. National Collegiate Athletic Association, Box 1906, Mission, KS 66201. TEL 913-384-3220. Key Title: Proceedings of the Special Convention of the National Collegiate Athletic Association.

790.1   US   ISSN 0736-511X
NATIONAL COLLEGIATE ATHLETIC ASSOCIATION WRESTLING RULES. 1927. a. $3. National Collegiate Athletic Association, Box 1906, Mission, KS 66201. TEL 913-384-3220. Ed. David Adams. circ. 10,000.
Formerly: Official National Collegiate Athletic Association Wrestling Guide.

796   US   ISSN 0190-4329
NATIONAL COLLEGIATE CHAMPIONSHIPS. 1954. a. $8. National Collegiate Athletic Association, Box 1906, Mission, KS 66201. TEL 913-384-3220. circ. 2,700.
Formerly: National Collegiate Championships Record Book (ISSN 0148-9798)

796   US   ISSN 0547-616X
NATIONAL DIRECTORY OF COLLEGE ATHLETICS (MEN'S EDITION) 1968. a. $14. (National Association of Collegiate Directors of Athletics) Ray Franks Publishing Ranch, Box 7068, Amarillo, TX 79109. TEL 806-355-6417.

796   US
NATIONAL DIRECTORY OF COLLEGE ATHLETICS (WOMEN) 1973. a. $10. Ray Franks Publishing Ranch, Box 7068, Amarillo, TX 79109. TEL 806-355-6417. Ed. Ray Franks. illus.
Formerly: National Directory of Women's Athletics (ISSN 0092-5489)

SPORTS AND GAMES

790.1   US
NATIONAL FEDERATION HANDBOOK. a. $2. National Federation of State High School Associations, 11724 Plaza Circle, Box 20626, Kansas City, MO 64195. TEL 816-464-5400.

790.1   US
NATIONAL HIGH SCHOOL SPORTS RECORD BOOK. a. $3.95. National Federation of State High School Associations, 11724 Plaza Circle, Box 20626, Kansas City, MO 64195. TEL 816-464-5400. Ed. Bruce Howard.

796.9   CN
NATIONAL HOCKEY LEAGUE. OFFICIAL RULE BOOK. 1931. a. $3.50. National Hockey League, 960 Sun Life Bldg., Montreal H3B 2W2, Canada. TEL 514-871-9220. Ed. Brian O'Neill. illus.

790.025   US   ISSN 0276-5276
NATIONAL RECREATIONAL, SPORTING AND HOBBY ORGANIZATIONS OF THE UNITED STATES. 1981. a. $30. Columbia Books, Inc., 1350 New York Ave., Ste. 207, Washington, DC 20005. TEL 202-737-3777. Eds. Craig Colgate Jr., Regina Germain.

796.72   US
NATIONAL SPEEDWAY DIRECTORY. 1975. a. $7.50. Slideways Pubications, Box 448, Comstock Park, MI 49321. Eds. Allan E. Brown, Ross Ferguson. adv. stat. circ. 12,000.
     Formerly: Midwest Auto Racing Guide.

688.76   US
NATIONAL SPORTING GOODS ASSOCIATION BUYING GUIDE. 1967. a. $15 membership. National Sporting Goods Association, Lake Center Plaza Bldg., 1699 Wall St., Mt. Prospect, IL 60056. TEL 312-439-4000. adv. circ. 20,000.

790.1   US   ISSN 0739-6074
NATIONWIDE DIRECTORY OF SPORTING GOODS BUYERS. a. $102. Salesman's Guide, Inc., 1140 Broadway, New York, NY 10001. TEL 212-684-2985. index.

794.1   US   ISSN 0168-7697
NEW IN CHESS YEARBOOK. every 10 months. Albert Henderson, Inc., 2423 Noble Station, Bridgeport, CT 06608.

790.1   US
NEW JERSEY. CASINO CONTROL COMMISSION. ANNUAL REPORT. 1979. a. Casino Control Commission, Attn: Carol Kokotajlo, Public Information Ass't, Box CN 208, Trenton, NJ 08625. TEL 609-530-4901. Ed. Thomas P. Flynn. circ. 1,500.

796.962   US
NEW YORK RANGERS YEARBOOK; official guide and records. 1926. a. $4 per copy. New York Rangers Hockey Club, Madison Square Garden, 4 Pennsylvania Plaza, New York, NY 10001. TEL 212-563-8000. Eds. Vince Casey, Bonnie Murman. adv. illus. stat.
     Formerly: New York Rangers Blue Book.

790.1   DK   ISSN 0900-0283
NORMTALSUNDERSOEGELSE FOR SPORTSBRANCHEN. 1983. a. Kr.305. Danmarks Sportshandler-Forening, Konsulenttjeneste, Naverland 34, 2600 Glosrup, Denmark. illus.

796   970   980   US   ISSN 0093-6235
NORTH AMERICAN SOCIETY FOR SPORT HISTORY. PROCEEDINGS. 1973. a. membership. North American Society for Sport History, c/o Ronald A. Smith, 101 White Bldg., Penn State University, University Park, PA 16802. adv. circ. 1,000. Indexed: Popul.Ind.

796   US
NORTHERN CALIFORNIA GOLF ASSOCIATION. BLUE BOOK. 1961. a. $10 to non-members. Northern California Golf Association, Box NCGA, Pebble Beach, CA 93953. TEL 408-625-4653. Ed. Ted Blofsky, Jr. adv. circ. 95,000.

790   CN
NOVA SCOTIA. DEPARTMENT OF RECREATION. ANNUAL REPORT. 1974. a. Department of Recreation, 5151 George St., Box 864, Halifax, N.S. B3J 2V2, Canada. TEL 902-424-7624. illus.

790.1   UK
OLEANDER GAMES AND PASTIMES SERIES. a. Oleander Press, 17 Stansgate Ave., Cambridge CB2 2QZ, England (U.S. address: 210 Fifth Ave., New York, NY 10010)

790.1   CN   ISSN 0702-7842
ONTARIO. MINISTERE DES AFFAIRES CULTURELLES ET DES LOIS DE L'ONTARIO. RAPPORT ANNUEL. 1983. a. Ministry of Tourism and Recreation, Parliament Bldgs., Toronto, Ont. M7A 2R9, Canada. TEL 416-965-2506. circ. 10,000.

794.1   IT
QUADERNI DI SCACCHI: I GRANDI GIOCATORI. 1975. irreg. L.2500. Mursia Editore, Via Tadino 29, Milan, Italy. illus.

790.1   DK   ISSN 0107-3052
RACE WALKING WORLD STATISTICS. 1962. a. $5. Association of Track and Field Statisticians, Buelowsvej 40, 1870 Frederiksberg C, Denmark. Ed. Palle Lassen. illus. circ. 400.

796   UK
RACEFORM FLAT ANNUAL. 1899. a. £15. Raceform Ltd., 2 York Road, London SW11 3PZ, England. Ed. D. Corbett. adv. circ. 11,000.
     Formerly: Raceform Up-to-Date Form Book Annual (ISSN 0081-377X)

796   UK
RACING AND FOOTBALL OUTLOOK: FOOTBALL ANNUAL. 1935. a. £1.20. Webster's Publications Ltd., Onslow House, 60-66 Saffron Hill, London EC1N 8AY, England. circ. 75,000.

796   UK
RACING AND FOOTBALL OUTLOOK: JUMPING ANNUAL. 1968. a. £1. Webster's Publications Ltd., Onslow House, 60-66 Saffron Hill, London EC1N 8AY, England. circ. 28,000.

796   UK   ISSN 0079-9424
RACING AND FOOTBALL OUTLOOK: RACING ANNUAL. 1909. a. £1. Webster's Publications Ltd., Onslow House, 60-66 Saffron Hill, London EC1N 8AY, England. circ. 40,000.
     Formerly: Racing and Football Racing Annual.

790.1   658   UK   ISSN 0144-624X
RECREATION MANAGEMENT HANDBOOK. 1975. biennial. £19.50. E. & F.N. Spon Ltd., 11 New Fetter Lane, London EC4P 4EE, England. circ. 2,500.
     Formerly: Recreation Management Yearbook (ISSN 0306-3062)

790.1   UK   ISSN 0267-2103
RECREATION MANAGERS' ASSOCIATION OF GREAT BRITAIN YEAR BOOK. 1982. a. £9.95. Millbank Publications, 25 Catherine St., London WC2B 5JW, England. TEL 01-379-3036. Ed. K.J. Allen. circ. 2,500.

796   FR   ISSN 0080-1135
REPERTOIRE GENERAL DES CLUBS SPORTIFS DE FRANCE.* 1962. irreg. Editions du Forum, 13 rue Giacierre, Paris 13e, France.

796   CN
RINGETTE CANADA. OFFICIAL RULES (YEARS) (Text in English and French) 1965. a. Can.$2. Ringette Canada Publications, Tower C, 6th floor, 333 River Rd., Vanier, Ont. K1L 8H9, Canada. TEL 613-748-5655. Ed. D. MacQuarrie. adv. circ. 10,000. (back issues avail.)
     Formerly: Ontario Ringette Association. Official Rules.

796   UK   ISSN 0080-4282
ROYAL CALEDONIAN CURLING CLUB. ANNUAL. 1838. a. £1.50. Royal Caledonian Curling Club, 2 Coates Crescent, Edinburgh EH3 7AN, Scotland. Ed. J.M. Artken. adv. circ. 4,500.

796.72   UK
ROYAL SCOTTISH AUTOMOBILE CLUB OFFICIAL HANDBOOK. 1907. a. £5. Royal Scottish Automobile Club, 11 Blythswood Sq., Glasgow G2 4AG, Scotland. Ed. Jonathan Lord. adv. circ. 5,000.

796   UK   ISSN 0080-4819
RUFF'S GUIDE TO THE TURF AND THE SPORTING LIFE ANNUAL. 1842. a. £20. Mirror Group Newspapers Ltd., Sporting Life, 9 New Fetter Lane, London EC4A 1AR, England. Ed. Ken Oliver. adv.

799.202   US   ISSN 0080-9365
SHOOTER'S BIBLE. 1928. a. $13.95. Stoeger Publishing Co., 55 Ruta Ct., S. Hackensack, NJ 07405. TEL 201-440-2700.

790.1   UK
SMALL SIDE TEAM GAMES AND POTTED SPORTS. 1935. irreg. £0.55 per no. Ministry of Defense, Army Sport Control Board, Clayton Barracks, Aldershot, England.

790.1   UK   ISSN 0560-6152
SOCIETY OF ARCHER-ANTIQUARIES. JOURNAL. 1958. a. membership. ‡ Society of Archer-Antiquaries, c/o J. Osborne, 236 Bexley Lane, Sidcup, Kent DA14 4JH, England. Ed. E. McEwen. bk. rev. charts. illus. circ. controlled.

SPA DATA AND REFERENCE ANNUAL. see *BUILDING AND CONSTRUCTION*

790.1   DK   ISSN 0109-2146
SPORT; aarhusiansk idraet paa mange led i tekst og billeder. 1983. a. Kr.49.50. Fioltryk, Rudolfgaardsvej 3, 8260 Viby J., Denmark. illus.

790.1   DK   ISSN 0109-159X
SPORT PAA BORNHOLM. 1983. a. Kr.58.50. Bornholmerens Forlag, c/o Colbergs Boghandel, Store Torv 9, 3700 Roenne, Denmark. Eds. Lasse Kofoed, Holger Larsen. illus.

793   NE   ISSN 0077-6777
SPORTACCOMMODATIE IN NEDERLAND/ SPORTS: PUBLIC ACCOMMODATION. (Text in Dutch and English) 1959. irreg. price varies. Centraal Bureau voor de Statistiek, Prinses Beatrixlaan 428, Voorburg, Netherlands (Orders to: Staatsuitgeverij, Christoffel Plantijnstraat, The Hague, Netherlands)

790.1   US
SPORTS AND RECREATIONAL PROGRAMS OF THE NATION'S UNIVERSITIES AND COLLEGES. 1958. quinquennial. $4. National Collegiate Athletic Association, Box 1906, Mission, KS 66201. TEL 913-384-3220. circ. 3,000.

790.1   US
SPORTS MARKET PLACE. 1980. a. $115. Sportsguide, Inc., Box 1417, Princeton, NJ 08542. TEL 609-921-8599. Ed. Richard A. Lipsey. adv. index. circ. 1,500.
     Formerly: Sportsguide (ISSN 0277-0296)

SPORTS TRADER BUYER'S GUIDE. see *BUSINESS AND ECONOMICS — Marketing And Purchasing*

790.1   KE
SPORTSWORLD. (Text in English) 1980. irreg. (approx. m.) Hivona International Ltd., Box 48423, Nairobi, Kenya.

790.1   NE
SPORTWETENSCHAPPELIJKE ONDERZOEKINGEN. 1978. irreg. price varies. Uitgeverij de Vriesebosch, Jacobijnestraat 5, 2011 TG Haarlem, Netherlands. illus. circ. 1,500.

796   GW   ISSN 0342-457X
SPORTWISSENSCHAFT UND SPORTPRAXIS. 1970. irreg.,(vol.58, 1986) price varies. Verlag Ingrid Czwalina, Reesenbuettler Redder 75, 2070 Ahrensburg, W. Germany (B.R.D.) Ed. Clemens Czwalina.
     Formerly: Schriftenreihe fuer Sportwissenschaft und Sportpraxis (ISSN 0080-7141)

796   GW   ISSN 0340-0956
SPORTWISSENSCHAFTLICHE DISSERTATIONEN. 1975. irreg.,(vol.28,1985) price varies. Verlag Ingrid Czwalina, Reesenbuettler Redder 75, 2070 Ahrensburg, W. Germany (B.R.D.) Eds. Clemens Czwalina, Eike Jost.

636.596   UK
SQUILLS INTERNATIONAL PIGEON RACING YEAR BOOK. 1951. a. Racing Pigeon Publishing Co. Ltd., 19 Doughty St., London WC1N 2PT, England. adv.

SPORTS AND GAMES — ABSTRACTING, BIBLIOGRAPHIES, STATISTICS

790.1 613.7   GW
STADION;* Internationale Zeitschrift fuer Geschichte des Sports und der Koerperkultur. (Text in English, French, German, Greek, Italian and Russian; summaries in English, French and German) 1975. irreg., 1-2/yr. DM.69.50. (Institut fuer Sportgeschichte der Deutschen Sorthochschule, Koeln) Verlag Hans Richarz, Postfach 1165, 5205 St. Augustin, W. Germany (B.R.D.) Eds. Wolfgang Decker, Manfred Laemmer. adv. bk. rev. circ. 400. (back issues avail.) Indexed: Hist. Abstr.
    Incorporates: Arena.

STUDIES IN SPORT, PHYSICAL EDUCATION AND HEALTH. see *PHYSICAL FITNESS AND HYGIENE*

793   US
STUDY OF FINANCIAL RESULTS AND REPORTING TRENDS IN THE GAMING INDUSTRY. 1981. a. $35. Laventhol & Horwath, 1845 Walnut St., Philadelphia, PA 19103. TEL 215-299-1600. charts. circ. 4,000.

797   US   ISSN 0276-6582
SURFBOARD. (Text in English, French and Spanish) 1963. a. $12.95. Box 9024, La Jolla, CA 92038. Ed. Stephen M. Shaw. adv. circ. 10,000.
    Formerly: Surfboard Builder's Yearbook (ISSN 0081-9611)

797.21   US
SWIMMING AND DIVING AND WATER POLO RULEBOOK. a. $2.50. National Federation of State High School Associations, 11724 Plaza Circle, Box 20626, Kansas City, MO 64195. TEL 816-464-5400.
    Formerly: Swimming and Diving Rules (ISSN 0163-2884) & Swimming and Diving Case Book (ISSN 0145-3831); Supersedes: Swimming Rules.

688.76   CH
T S M A SPORTS EQUIPMENT. (Text in English) a. $40. China Economic News Service, 561 Chungsiao East Rd., Sec. 4, 5th floor, Taipei 105, Taiwan, Republic of China.
    Formerly: Taiwan Sporting Goods.

790   KO
TAEHAN CHEYKHOE. CHEYUK CHONGSO. 1973. irreg. Korea Amateur Sports Association, 19 Mugyodong, Seoul, S. Korea. Ed.Bd. illus.

688.76   FR
TECHNO-LOISIRS; guide international annuel de la construction et de l'equipment pour le sport et les loisirs. (Text in various European languages and Esperanto) 1971. biennial. 50 F.($10) Editions Techno-Loisirs, 3 rue Sivel, 75014 Paris, France. Ed. Georges Caille. adv. bk. rev. play rev. bibl. illus. patents. stat. tr.lit. index. circ. 10,000. (also avail. in magnetic tape)

796.86   US
U S F A RULE BOOK: U S & INTERNATIONAL RULES. irreg. $10. United States Fencing Association, Inc., 1750 E. Boulder St., Colorado Springs, CO 80909.
    Formerly: Fencing Rules for Competitions.

796.342   US
U S T A COLLEGE TENNIS GUIDE. 1976. biennial. $3.50. United States Tennis Association, Center for Education and Recreational Tennis, 729 Alexander Rd., Princeton, NJ 08540. TEL 609-452-2580. circ. 5,000.

799.202 799.2   US
UNIFORM HUNTER CASUALTY REPORT. 1961. a. free. Commission of Game and Inland Fisheries, 4010 W. Broad St., Richmond, VA 23230. TEL 804-257-1000. Ed. Capt. Herb Foster. stat. cum.index. circ. 500. (looseleaf format; back issues avail.)

796.42   US
UNITED STATES CROSS-COUNTRY COACHES ASSOCIATION. ANNUAL BUSINESS MEETING. MINUTES. a. free. United States Cross-Country Coaches Association, c/o Ken O'Brien, Sec., Boyden Gym, University of Massachusetts, Amherst, MA 01003. TEL 413-545-2759.
    Supersedes: United States Cross-Country Coaches Association. Proceedings; Which was formerly: United States Cross-Country and Distance Running Coaches Association. Proceedings (ISSN 0082-9706)

790.1   UK
WELSH AMATEUR SWIMMING ASSOCIATION. HANDBOOK. 1897. every 4 yrs. £4. Welsh Amateur Swimming Association, National Sports Centre for Wales, Sophia Gardens, Cardiff CF1 9SW, Wales. adv. circ. 500. (looseleaf format)

796.815
WHO'S WHO IN KARATE AND THE OTHER MARTIAL ARTS AND DIRECTORY OF BLACK BELTS.* a. Who's Who in Karate, Box 490, Grimesland, NC 27837-0490. Ed. Jerri Harris.

790.1   UK
WOMEN'S SQUASH RACKETS ASSOCIATION. HANDBOOK. 1934. a. £1. ‡ Women's Squash Rackets Association, 345 Upper Richmond Rd. W., Sheen, London SW14 8QN, England. Ed. Christina Myers. adv. circ. 3,500.

796.9   US   ISSN 0095-7240
WORLD ALMANAC GUIDE TO PRO HOCKEY. irreg. $1.95. Bantam Books, Inc., 666 Fifth Ave., New York, NY 10019. TEL 212-765-6500. illus.

790.1   US
WRESTLING MANUAL AND CASE BOOK. biennial. $2.50. National Federation of State High School Associations, 11724 Plaza Circle, Box 20626, Kansas City, MO 64195. TEL 816-464-5400.
    Supersedes: Wrestling Officials Manual.

790.1   US
WRESTLING RULEBOOK. a. $2.50. National Federation of State High School Associations, 11724 Plaza Circle, Box 20626, Kansas City, MO 64195. TEL 816-464-5400.

794.1   UK
YEAR BOOK OF CHESS. 1919. a. £4. British Chess Federation, 9A Grand Parade, St. Leonards-on-Sea, East Sussex TN38 0DD, England. Ed. B. Concannon. adv. circ. 1,500.

ZAMBIA. MINISTRY OF YOUTH AND SPORT. DEPARTMENT OF YOUTH DEVELOPMENT. ANNUAL REPORT. see *CHILDREN AND YOUTH — About*

796   ZA   ISSN 0084-506X
ZAMBIA. SPORTS DIRECTORATE. REPORT. 1968. a., latest 1973. 35 n. Government Printer, P.O. Box 136, Lusaka, Zambia.

SPORTS AND GAMES — Abstracting, Bibliographies, Statistics

796.93   US
BIBLIOGRAPHY OF SKIING STUDIES. biennial. $15. University of Colorado, Graduate School of Business Administration, Campus Box 420, Boulder, CO 80309. TEL 303-492-8227. Ed. C.R. Goeldner. circ. 200.

797   FR   ISSN 0067-8260
BIBLIOTHEQUE DE LA MER. 1970. irreg. price varies. Tchou Editeur, 6 rue du Mail, 75002 Paris, France.

796.95 310   US   ISSN 0163-7207
BOATING REGISTRATION STATISTICS. a. $20. National Marine Manufacturers Association, 353 Lexington Ave., New York, NY 10016 TEL 212-684-6622. (Or 401 N. Michigan Ave., Chicago, IL 60611) stat.

796.95   US
BOATING STATISTICS. 1960. a. free. U.S. Coast Guard, Commandant G-BP, 2100 Second St., S.W., Washington, DC 20593. TEL 202-426-1830. stat. circ. 7,000. (back issues avail. to 1974)
    Formerly: U.S. Coast Guard Boating Statistics (ISSN 0565-1530)

338.4   CN   ISSN 0575-979X
CANADA. STATISTICS CANADA. SPORTING GOODS AND TOY INDUSTRIES/ FABRICATION D'ARTICLES DE SPORT ET DE JOUETS. (Catalogue 47-204) (Text in English & French) 1925. a. Can.$20($21) Statistics Canada, Communications Division, 3rd Floor, R.H. Coats Bldg., Ottawa, Ont. K1A 0T6, Canada TEL 613-993-7276. (Subscr. to: Publications Sales and Services, Ottawa, Ont. K1A 0T6, Canada) (also avail. in microform from MML)

790.1   UK   ISSN 0142-1484
CHARTERED INSTITUTE OF PUBLIC FINANCE AND ACCOUNTANCY. CHARGES FOR LEISURE SERVICES. 1978. a. £10. Chartered Institute of Public Finance and Accountancy, 3 Robert St., London WC2N 6BH, England. (back issues avail.)

790.1   UK   ISSN 0141-187X
CHARTERED INSTITUTE OF PUBLIC FINANCE AND ACCOUNTANCY. LEISURE AND RECREATION STATISTICS. ESTIMATES. 1977. a. £14. Chartered Institute of Public Finance and Accountancy, 3 Robert St., London WC2N 6BH, England. stat. (back issues avail.)
    Formerly: Chartered Institute of Public Finance and Accountancy. Leisure Estimate Statistics.

790.1   UK   ISSN 0266-9560
CHARTERED INSTITUTE OF PUBLIC FINANCE AND ACCOUNTANCY. LEISURE USAGE. ACTUALS. 1983. a. £11. Chartered Institute of Public Finance and Accountancy, 3 Robert St., London WC2N 6BH, England.

796.41   DK   ISSN 0107-4547
D A FI TAL. 1978. a. Kr.60. Dansk Athletik Forbund, Idraettens Hus, Broenby Stadion 20, 2600 Glostrup, Denmark. illus.
    Formerly: Dansk Athletik Forbund. Statistik.

796.397   US
DAGUERREOTYPES. 1934. irreg., latest 1981. $14.95 hardcover; paperback $9.95. Sporting News Publishing Co., 1212 N. Lindbergh, St. Louis, MO 63132. TEL 314-997-7111. Ed. Paul MacFarlane.

HEALTH, PHYSICAL EDUCATION AND RECREATION MICROFORM PUBLICATIONS BULLETIN. see *PHYSICAL FITNESS AND HYGIENE — Abstracting, Bibliographies, Statistics*

629.227   NE   ISSN 0168-5864
NETHERLANDS. CENTRAAL BUREAU VOOR DE STATISTIEK. PRODUKTIESTATISTIEKEN: RIJWIEL- EN MOTORRIJWIELINDUSTRIE. (Text in Dutch; summaries in English) a. fl.12.45. Centraal Bureau voor de Statistiek, Prinses Beatrixlaan 428, Voorburg, Netherlands (Orders to: Staatsuitgeverij, Christoffel Plantijnstraat, The Hague, Netherlands)

790 314   NE   ISSN 0168-4248
NETHERLANDS. CENTRAAL BUREAU VOOR DE STATISTIEK. STATISTIEK VAN DE INKOMSTEN EN UITGAVEN DER OVERHEID VOOR CULTUUR EN RECREATIE. STATISTICS OF GOVERNMENT EXPENDITURE ON CULTURE AND RECREATION. (Text in Dutch and English) 1964. a. fl.25.25. Centraal Bureau voor de Statistiek, Prinses Beatrixlaan 428, Voorburg, Netherlands (Orders to: Staatsuitgeverij, Christoffel Plantijnstraat, The Hague, Netherlands)
    Formerly: Netherlands.Centraal Bureau voor de Statistiek. Statistiek van de Uitgaven der Overheid voor Cultuur en Recreatie (ISSN 0077-7196)

796.42   DK   ISSN 0108-3821
RACE WALKING WORLD STATISTICS - WOMEN. 1978. a. $4. Association of Track and Field Statisticians, Buelowsvej 40, 1870 Frederiksberg C, Denmark. Ed. Palle Lassen. illus. circ. 400.
    Formerly: Women's Race-Walking.

SPORT FISHERY ABSTRACTS; an abstracting service for fishery research and management. see *FISH AND FISHERIES — Abstracting, Bibliographies, Statistics*

SPORTS AND GAMES — BALL GAMES

688.76 US
SPORTING GOODS MARKET. 1973. a. $115. National Sporting Goods Association, 1699 Wall St., Mt. Prospect, IL 60056. TEL 312-439-4000. Ed. Thomas B. Doyle. (also avail. in microform; back issues avail.)

SPORTS DOCUMENTATION CENTRE. SERIAL. see EDUCATION — Abstracting, Bibliographies, Statistics

790.1 US
SPORTS, GAMES, AND PASTIMES INFORMATION GUIDE SERIES. 1979. irreg., vol.10, 1980. $62. Gale Research Company, Book Tower, Detroit, MI 48226. TEL 313-961-2242. Ed. Ronald Ziegler. (back issues avail.)

790.1 016 US ISSN 0883-1580
SPORTS PERIODICALS INDEX.* 1985. m. with a. cum. $245. National Information Systems, Inc., c/o N.R.C., 2750 S. State, Ann Arbor, MI 48104-6738. Ed. Grant Elderidge.

798.4 UK
STATISTICAL RECORD. 1971. q. (plus annual no.) Weatherbys, Sanders Rd., Wellingborough, Northants., England. adv. stat. circ. 1,000.

799 310 US
U.S. FISH AND WILDLIFE SERVICE. NATIONAL SURVEY OF HUNTING, FISHING AND WILDLIFE-ASSOCIATED RECREATION. 1955. irreg., 6th, 1982. U.S. Fish and Wildlife Service, Washington, DC 20240. TEL 303-226-9403. charts. illus. stat.

WILDLIFE REVIEW (FORT COLLINS); an abstracting service for wildlife management. see CONSERVATION — Abstracting, Bibliographies, Statistics

SPORTS AND GAMES — Ball Games

796.323 US ISSN 0733-0448
A C C BASKETBALL HANDBOOK. (Atlantic Coast Conference) 1974. a. $6. U M I Publications, Inc., Box 30036, Charlotte, NC 28230. TEL 704-374-0420. Ed. Ivan Mothershead. adv. circ. 100,000. (back issues avail.)

796 SW ISSN 0567-4565
AARETS FOTBOLL. a. Kr.314. Stroembergs Idrottsboecker, Vittangigatan 27, Vaellingby, Stockholm, Sweden.

796.334 IT
AGENDA DELLO SPORT. 1975. a. L.15000. Longega Maurizio, Ed. & Pub., Via Cesare De Fabritiis, 133, I-00136 Rome, Italy. adv. bk. rev. circ. 1,986.

794.6 CN
ALBERTA GOLF GUIDE. a. Can.$2.95. Sylvester Publications Ltd., 6430 Golden West Ave., Ste. 201, Red Deer, Alta. T4P 1A6, Canada. Ed. Donald C. Sylvester. adv. circ. 15,000. (back issues avail.)
Formerly: Golf Courses of Alberta.

796.3 SZ
ALMANACCO CALCISTICO SVIZZERO. (Text in Italian) 1950. a. 20 Fr. (Giornale del Popolo) Armando Libotte, Casella Postale, 6976 Castagnola, Switzerland. Ed.Bd. adv. stat. circ. 2,000.

796.357 US ISSN 0065-6739
AMATEUR SOFTBALL ASSOCIATION OF AMERICA. OFFICIAL GUIDE AND RULE BOOK. 1933. a. $2.50. Amateur Softball Association of America, 2801 N.E. 50th St., Oklahoma City, OK 73111. TEL 405-424-5266.

796.33 FR
ANNEE DU FOOTBALL. 1973. a. price varies. Editions Calmann-Levy, 3 rue Auber, 75009 Paris, France. Ed. Jacques Thibert. illus.

796.33 FR
ANNEE DU RUGBY. 1973. a. price varies. Editions Calmann-Levy, 3 rue Auber, 75009 Paris, France. Ed. Christian Montaignac. illus.

796.342 FR
ANNEE DU TENNIS. 1979. a. price varies. Editions Calmann-Levy, 3 rue Auber, 75009 Paris, France. Ed.Bd. illus.

796.342 IT
ANNUARIO ILLUSTRATO DEL TENNIS. 1979. a. L.6000($15.50) D M K Editrice s.r.l., Via Boscovich 14, 20124 Milan, Italy. adv. illus. circ. 70,000.

796.334 UK ISSN 0263-0354
ASSOCIATION OF FOOTBALL STATISTICIANS. ANNUAL. 1981. a. £6.50. Association of Football Statisticians, c/o R.J. Spiller, Ed., 22 Bretons, Basildon, Essex, England. adv. bk. rev. circ. 1,200.

796 AT ISSN 0084-7291
AUSTRALIAN CRICKET YEARBOOK. 1970. a. Aus.$3.50. Modern Magazines (Holdings) Ltd., Ryrie House, 15 Boundary St., Rushcutter's Bay, N.S.W. 2011, Australia.

796 GW
BADMINTON. 1970. a. DM.6.90. (Deutscher Badminton Verband) Oskar Klokow, Verlag und Versandbuchhandlung, Kalandstr. 19, 2400 Luebeck, W. Germany (B.R.D.) Ed. Oskar Klokow. stat.

796.357 US ISSN 0270-4218
BASEBALL CASE BOOK. a. $2.50. National Federation of State High School Associations, 11724 Plaza Circle, Box 20626, Kansas City, MO 64195. TEL 816-464-5400.

796.357 US
BASEBALL FORECAST (YEAR) a. Lexington Library, Inc., 355 Lexington Ave., New York, NY 10017. TEL 212-391-1400. Eds. Stephen Ciacciarelli, Thomas Walsh. adv. charts. illus.

796.3 US ISSN 0067-4273
BASEBALL GUIDE. 1965. a. $2. Snibbe Books, 1115 Ponce de Leon, Clearwater, FL 33516. TEL 813-586-1779. Ed. Mike Tierney. circ. 500,000.

796.357 US
BASEBALL HISTORICAL REVIEW. 1981. irreg. $4. Society for American Baseball Research, Inc., Box 1010, Cooperstown, NY 13326. Ed. L. Robert Davids.

796.357 US
BASEBALL ILLUSTRATED (YEAR) a. Lexington Library, Inc., 355 Lexington Ave., New York, NY 10017. TEL 212-391-1400. Eds. Stephen Ciacciarelli, Thomas Walsh. adv. charts. illus.

796.357 US
BASEBALL PREVIEW (YEAR) a. Lexington Library, Inc., 355 Lexington Ave., New York, NY 10017. TEL 212-491-1400. Eds. Stephen Ciacciarelli, Thomas Walsh. adv. charts. illus.
Formerly: Saga's Baseball Special.

796.357 US ISSN 0734-6891
BASEBALL RESEARCH JOURNAL. 1972. a. $6. Society for American Baseball Research, Inc., Box 1010, Cooperstown, NY 13326. Ed. Clifford Kachline. Indexed: Hist.Abstr. Amer.Hist.& Life.

796.357 US
BASEBALL RULEBOOK. a. $2.50. National Federation of State High School Associations, 11724 Plaza Circle, Box 20626, Kansas City, MO 64195. TEL 816-464-5400.

796.357 US
BASEBALL UMPIRES MANUAL. biennial. $2.50. National Federation of State High School Associations, 11724 Plaza Circle, Box 20626, Kansas City, MO 64195. TEL 816-464-5400.

796.323 US
BASKETBALL ANNUAL (YEAR) a. Lexington Library, Inc., 355 Lexington Ave., New York, NY 10017. TEL 212-391-1400. Eds. Stephen Ciacciarelli, Thomas Walsh. adv. charts. illus.

796.32 US ISSN 0525-4663
BASKETBALL CASE BOOK. a. $2.50. National Federation of State High School Associations, 11724 Plaza Circle, Box 20626, Kansas City, MO 64195. TEL 816-464-5400. adv. illus. circ. 300,000.

796.323 US
BASKETBALL FORECAST (YEAR) a. Lexington Library, Inc., 355 Lexington Ave., New York, NY 10017. TEL 212-391-1400. Eds. Stephen Ciacciarelli, Thomas Walsh. adv. charts. illus.

796.323 US
BASKETBALL HANDBOOK. biennial. $2.50. National Federation of State High School Associations, 11724 Plaza Circle, Box 20626, Kansas City, MO 64195. TEL 816-464-5400.

796.323 US ISSN 0270-4226
BASKETBALL OFFICIALS MANUAL. biennial. $2.50. National Federation of State High School Associations, 11724 Plaza Circle, Box 20626, Kansas City, MO 64195. TEL 816-464-5400.

796.323 US
BASKETBALL - SIMPLIFIED & ILLUSTRATED RULES. a. $2.50. National Federation of State High School Associations, 11724 Plaza Circle, Box 20626, Kansas City, MO 64195. TEL 816-464-5400.
Formerly: Basketball Rulebook.

796.323 US
BASKETBALL STATISTICIANS' MANUAL. a. $2.75. National Collegiate Athletic Association, Box 1906, Mission, KS 66201. TEL 913-384-3220. stat.

796.357 US ISSN 0731-812X
BATTER PERFORMANCE HANDBOOK. 1980. a. $3.75. Research Analysis Publications, Box 49213, Los Angeles, CA 90049. Ed. Ronald H. Lewis. adv. charts. stat. circ. 5,500.

794.6 UK
BEDFORDSHIRE COUNTY BOWLING ASSOCIATION. HANDBOOK. a. 50p. A.A. Wharton, 47 Aspen Ave., Bedford, England. adv. circ. 1,400.

796.342 GW ISSN 0723-1407
BEITRAEGE ZUR THEORIE UND PRAXIS DES TENNISUNTERRICHTS UND -TRAININGS. irreg.,(vol. 10,1986) price varies. (Deutscher Tennis Bund Sportwissenschaftlicher Beirat) Verlag Ingrid Czwalina, Reesenbuettler Redder 75, D-2070 Ahrensburg, W. Germany (B.R.D.)

796.357 UK
BENSON AND HEDGES CRICKET YEAR. 1981. a. £14.95. Pelham Books Ltd., 27 Wrights Lane, London W8 5TZ, England. Ed. David Lemmon.

796.332 378.198 US
BIG TEN FOOTBALL YEARBOOK. a. $6. Big Ten Intercollegiate Conference, 1111 Plaza Dr., Ste. 600, Schaumburg, IL 60173-4990. TEL 312-885-3933. charts. illus. stat.

796.357 US
BOOK OF BASEBALL RECORDS. a. $11.95. Seymour Siwoff, Ed. & Pub., 500 Fifth Ave., New York, NY 10036. TEL 212-869-1530.

796.357 US ISSN 0739-4667
BOOK ON STARTING PITCHERS. 1983. a. $18. Research Analysis Publications, Box 49213, Los Angeles, CA 90049. Ed. Ronald H. Lewis.

796.342 DK ISSN 0109-6761
BORDTENNIS AARBOGEN. 1982. a. Kr.30. Dansk Bord-Tennis Union, Ydraettens Hus, 2605 Broendby, Denmark. Torben Snowman. adv. illus. circ. 3,000.

794.6 658.8 US ISSN 0068-0559
BOWLING AND BILLIARD BUYERS GUIDE. Title varies: Bowling Buyers Guide. 1961. a. $10. National Bowlers Journal, Inc., 875 N. Michigan Ave., Ste. 3734, Chicago, IL 60611. Ed. Ernest H. Ahlborn.

794.6 CN
BRITISH COLUMBIA GUIDE. 1987. a. Can.$2.95. Sylvester Publications Ltd., 6430 Golden West Ave., Ste. 201, Red Deer, Alta. T4P 1A6, Canada.

796.323 US
C B A MEDIA GUIDE/YEARBOOK. a. Continential Basketball Association, 425 S. Cherry St., Ste. 230, Denver, CO 80222. TEL 303-331-0404. Ed. Colleen Miller. adv. circ. 5,000.

SPORTS AND GAMES — BALL GAMES

796.352 CN ISSN 0316-8131
CANADIAN AND PROVINCIAL GOLF RECORDS. 1972. a. Royal Canadian Golf Association, Golf House, R.R. 2, Oakville, Ont. L6J 4Z3, Canada. TEL 416-844-1800. circ. 1,500.
Formerly: Royal Canadian Golf Association. National Tournament Records (ISSN 0316-8212) *Golf*

796.352 CN ISSN 0084-8565
CANADIAN LADIES' GOLF ASSOCIATION. YEAR BOOK. (Text in English & French) 1947. a. Can.$1.50. Canadian Ladies' Golf Association, 333 River Rd., Ottawa, Ontario, KIL 8B9, Canada. TEL 613-748-5642. Ed. Leonard Murphy. adv. bk. rev. illus. stat. index. circ. 10,000.

796.332 CN
CANADIAN PRO FOOTBALL. a. Can.$4.95. PaperJacks Ltd., 330 Steelcase Rd. E., Markham, Ont. L3R 2Ml, Canada. TEL 416-475-1261. Ed. Terry Jones. illus. stat.

796.325 CN
CANADIAN VOLLEYBALL ANNUAL AND RULE BOOK. a. $4.50. Canadian Volleyball Association, 333 River Rd., Vanier, Ont. K1L 8H9, Canada. TEL 613-748-5681. circ. 12,000.

796.357 UK
CLUB CRICKET CONFERENCE OFFICIAL HANDBOOK. 1915. a. £20. Club Cricket Conference, 353 West Barnes Lane, New Malden, Surrey KT3 6JF, England. Ed. Derek Annetts.

796.334 UK ISSN 0260-8804
CLYDESDALE BANK SCOTTISH FOOTBALL LEAGUE REVIEW. 1980. a. £3. Scottish Football League, 188 West Regent St., Glasgow G2 4RY, Scotland. Ed. James Farry. adv. illus. circ. 20,000.

796.332 US ISSN 0733-2823
COLLEGE FOOTBALL YEARBOOK. a. $3.50. Sporting News Publishing Co., 1212 N. Lindbergh Blvd., St. Louis, MO 63166. adv.

796.357 US
COMPLETE BASEBALL RECORD BOOK. Variant title: Sporting News Official Baseball Record Book. 1949. a. $12.95. Sporting News Publishing Co., 1212 N. Lindbergh Blvd., Box 56, St. Louis, MO 63132. TEL 314-997-7111. Ed. Craig Carter. (processed)
Former titles (until 1985): Official Baseball Record Book (ISSN 0078-4605); One for the Book.

796.33 US ISSN 0361-2988
COMPLETE HANDBOOK OF PRO FOOTBALL. (Subseries of: Signet Books) 1975. a. $3.95. New American Library (New York), 1633 Broadway, New York, NY 10019. TEL 212-397-8000. Ed. Zander Hollander. illus.

796.332 US
COMPLETE SPORTS PRO FOOTBALL SPECIAL. a. Lexington Library, Inc., 355 Lexington Ave., New York, NY 10017. Eds. Stephen Ciacciarelli, Thomas Walsh. adv. charts. illus.

796.358 AT ISSN 0310-9356
CRICKET QUADRANT. 1973. irreg. Aus.$0.40 per no. Australian Cricket Society, A.C.T. Branch, 91 Gouger St., Torrens, A.C.T. 2607, Australia. Ed. Julian Oakley.

796.332 US
DALLAS COWBOYS OUTLOOK. 1967. a. $4.21. Sports Communications, Inc., P.O. Box 95, Waco, TX 76703. TEL 817-752-4351. Ed. Dave Campbell. adv. circ. 55,622.

796.352 DK ISSN 0109-5994
DANSK GOLFHAANDBOG. 1984. a. Kr.30. Dansk Golf Union, c/o Release, Hollufgaard Moelle, 5220 Odense SOE. illus.
Formerly: Dansk Golfkalender.

796.3 UK
EVENING TIMES WEE RED BOOK; the football annual. 1930? a. 50p. George Outram & Co. Ltd., 195 Albion St., Glasgow G1 1HP, Scotland. Ed. George McKechnie. adv. circ. 40,000.

796.357 CN
EXPO'S BASEBALL YEARBOOK. 1969. a. Can.$3.50. Montreal Baseball Club Ltd., Box 500, Sta. M, Montreal, Que. H1V 3P2, Canada. TEL 514-253-3434. Eds. Richard Griffin, Monique Giroux. adv. circ. 50,000.
Formerly: Expo's Baseball Magazine.

796 FR ISSN 0071-4267
FEDERATION INTERNATIONALE DE RUGBY AMATEUR. ANNUAIRE. 1965. a. International Amateur Rugby Federation, 7 Cite d'Antin, 75009 Paris, France.

796.332 DK
FODBOLD JUL. a. Bonniers Soecialmagasiner, Noerre Farimagsgade 49, 1375 Copenhagen K, Denmark. adv. circ. 25,000.

796.334 DK ISSN 0901-1595
FODBOLD POSTER BLADET. 1985. irreg. Kr.29.50 per issue. Bibliotekscentralen, Telegrafvej 5, DK-2750 Ballerup, Denmark.

796 DK ISSN 0108-5077
FODBOLDENS AARSREVY. 1982. a. Kr.38.50. Bonnier Specialmagasiner, Noerre Farimagsgade 49, 1375 Copenhagen K, Denmark. illus. circ. 29,500.

796.332 UK ISSN 0071-724X
FOOTBALL ASSOCIATION YEAR BOOK. 1979. a. £3.95. Pelham Books Ltd., 27 Wrights Lane, London W8 5TZ, England. adv. Indexed: Br.Hum.Ind.

796.332 US ISSN 0163-6200
FOOTBALL CASE BOOK. a. $2.50. National Federation of State High School Associations, 11724 Plaza Circle, Box 20626, Kansas City, MO 64195. TEL 816-464-5400.

796.334 UK
FOOTBALL CHAMPIONS. a. £1.50. Purnell Books (Subsidiary of: Macdonald & Co. (Publishers) Ltd.) 3rd Fl., Greater London House, Hampstead Rd., London NW1 7QX, England.

796.332 US
FOOTBALL FORECAST (YEAR) a. Lexington Library, Inc., 355 Lexington Ave., New York, NY 10017. TEL 212-391-1400. Eds. Stephen Ciacciarelli, Thomas Walsh. adv. charts. illus.

796.3 US ISSN 0069-5548
FOOTBALL GUIDE. 1963. a. $2. Snibbe Books, 1115 Ponce de Leon, Clearwater, FL 33516. TEL 813-586-1779. Ed. Mike Tierney. circ. 1,000,0000.
Formerly: College and Pro Football Guide.

796.332 US
FOOTBALL HANDBOOK. biennial. $2.50. National Federation of State High School Associations, 11724 Plaza Circle, Box 20626, Kansas City, MO 64195. TEL 816-464-5400.

796.332 US
FOOTBALL OFFICIALS MANUAL. biennial. $2.50. National Federation of State High School Associations, 11724 Plaza Circle, Box 20626, Kansas City, MO 64195. TEL 816-464-5400.
Formerly: Football Officials Handbook.

796.332 US ISSN 0071-7258
FOOTBALL REGISTER. 1966. a. $9.95. Sporting News Publishing Co., 1212 N. Lindbergh Blvd., St. Louis, MO 63132 TEL 314-997-7111. (Orders to: Box 56, St. Louis, MO 63166) Ed. Howard M. Balzer.

796.332 US
FOOTBALL ROUNDUP. no.12, 1971. a. $2.25. ǂ Lopez Publications, Inc., 23 W. 26th St., New York, NY 10010. Ed. Herbert M. Furlow. adv. charts. illus. stat. circ. 179,000.

796.332 US
FOOTBALL RULEBOOK. a. $2.50. National Federation of State High School Associations, 11724 Plaza Circle, Box 20626, Kansas City, MO 64195. TEL 816-464-5400.

796.332 US
FOOTBALL RULES - SIMPLIFIED AND ILLUSTRATED. a. $2.50. National Federation of State High School Associations, 11724 Plaza Circle, Box 20626, Kansas City, MO 64195. TEL 816-464-5400.

796.332 US
FOOTBALL STATISTICIAN'S MANUAL. a. $2.75. National Collegiate Athletic Association, Box 1906, Mission, KS 66201. TEL 913-384-3220. stat.

796 GW ISSN 0017-1735
GOLF. 1961. a. DM.96. Jahr Verlag GmbH & Co., Burchardstr. 14, D-2000 Hamburg 1, W. Germany (B.R.D.) Ed. Gunter Marks. adv. bk. rev. circ. 10, 500.
Formerly: Where to Golf in Europe (ISSN 0083-9213)

GOLF COURSE BUILDERS OF AMERICA DIRECTORY. see *BUILDING AND CONSTRUCTION*

658 US ISSN 0436-1474
GOLF COURSE SUPERINTENDENTS ASSOCIATION OF AMERICA. MEMBERSHIP DIRECTORY; who's who in golf course management. Spine title: G C S A A Membership Directory. a. $100 to non-members. Golf Course Superintendents Association of America, 1617 St. Andrews Drive, Lawrence, KS 66046. TEL 913-841-2240. Ed. Clay Loyd. circ. 7,000. Key Title: Membership Directory of the Golf Course Superintendents Association of America.

796.352 US ISSN 0072-4947
GOLF COURSE SUPERINTENDENTS ASSOCIATION OF AMERICA. PROCEEDINGS OF THE INTERNATIONAL CONFERENCE AND SHOW. a. $20 to non-members. Golf Course Superintendents Association of America, 1617 St. Andrews Drive, Lawrence, KS 66046. TEL 913-841-2240. Ed. Clay Loyd. circ. 4,500.

796.352 FR
GOLF EN FRANCE; guide des terrains de golf francais. 1969. a. 55 F. Editions Person, 34 rue de Penthievre, 75008 Paris, France.

796 UK ISSN 0072-4963
GOLF RULES ILLUSTRATED. 1969. quadrennial. £4.75. (Royal and Ancient Golf Club of St. Andrews) Munro-Barr Publications Ltd., 1 Park Circus, Glasgow G3 6AS, Scotland. Ed. Percy Huggins.

796.352 UK ISSN 0263-4066
GOLF - WHERE TO PLAY AND WHERE TO STAY. 1977. a. £4. McMillan Martin Ltd., Charles Roe House, Chestergate, Macclesfield, Cheshire SK11 6DL, England. adv. stat. index. circ. 10,000.

796 UK ISSN 0072-498X
GOLFER'S HANDBOOK. 1897. a. £20($30) McMillan Press Ltd., 4 Little Essex St., London, England. Ed. Laurence Viney. adv. circ. 10,000.

796.352 UK
GOLFING YEAR. 1948. a. £3.50. (English Golf Union) Creative Press (Reading) Ltd., Portman Rd., Reading, Berks., England. Ed. K. Wright. adv. bk. rev. circ. 2,500.

796.3 UK ISSN 0085-1566
HOCKEY ASSOCIATION. OFFICIAL HANDBOOK. 1900. a. £1. Hockey Association, 16 Upper Woburn Place, London WC1H 0QD, England. Ed. S.A. Catton. adv. index. cum. index. circ. 1,100.

796 920 US ISSN 0090-2292
HOCKEY REGISTER. 1972. a. $9.95. Sporting News Publishing Co., 1212 N. Lindbergh Blvd., St. Louis, MO 63132. TEL 314-997-7111. Eds. Larry Wigge, Frank Polnaszek. illus. stat.

796 US ISSN 0731-8162
INSIDERS BASEBALL FACT-BOOK. 1976. a. $10. Research Analysis Publications, Box 49213, Los Angeles, CA 90049. Ed. Ronald H. Lewis. charts. stat. circ. 4,000.

796.357 US ISSN 0731-8146
INSIDERS BASEBALL FACT-BOOK EXTRA. 1982. a. $8. Research Analysis Publications, Box 49213, Los Angeles, CA 90049. Ed. Ronald H. Lewis. circ. 4,000.

SPORTS AND GAMES — BALL GAMES

793   **GW**
INTERNATIONAL BASKETBALL FEDERATION. OFFICIAL REPORT OF THE WORLD CONGRESS. 1932. irreg., 1986, 13th, Montreal. International Basketball Federation, Postfach 700607, D-8000 Munich 70, W. Germany (B.R.D.) circ. 300.
Formerly: International Amateur Basketball Federation. Official Report of the World Congress (ISSN 0534-6622)

796.332   **UK**   **ISSN 0074-610X**
INTERNATIONAL FOOTBALL BOOK. 1959. a. £6.95. Souvenir Press Ltd., 43 Great Russell St., London WC1B 3PA, England. Ed. Gordon Hallam. circ. 7,000.

796.357   **US**
INTERNATIONAL SOFTBALL CONGRESS (YEAR) OFFICIAL YEARBOOK AND GUIDE. 1953. a. $2. International Softball Congress, 6007 E. Hillcrest Circle, Anaheim Hills, CA 92807. TEL 714-998-5694. Ed. Milt Stark. adv. circ. 10,000.

IO. see *ANTHROPOLOGY*

796.334   **UK**
KENNY DALGLISH SOCCER ANNUAL. 1979. a. £1.95. Brown Watson Ltd., 44 Hill St., London, W1X 84B, England.

796.357   **US**   **ISSN 0075-6385**
KNOTTY PROBLEMS OF BASEBALL. 1950. irreg. $5. Sporting News Publishing Co., P.O. Box 56, St. Louis, MO 63166. TEL 314-997-7111. Ed. Larry Wigge. (reprint service avail. from UMI)

796.352   **UK**
LADY GOLFER'S HANDBOOK. 1894. a. £2. Ladies Golf Union, 12 the Links, St. Andrews, Fife, Scotland. adv. circ. 3,000.

796.332   **US**
LINDY'S S.E.C. FOOTBALL ANNUAL. 1982. a. $3.95 per no. D M D Publications, 2151 Highland Ave. S., Ste. 208, Birmingham, AL 35205. TEL 205-933-1227. Ed. Lindy Davis Jr. adv. circ. 135,000.

796.357   **US**
MINOR LEAGUE BASEBALL STARS. 1978. irreg. $5. Society for American Baseball Research, Inc., Box 1010, Cooperstown, NY 13326. Ed. L. Robert Davids.

796.355   **US**
N A G W S GUIDE. FIELD HOCKEY. 1950/52. biennial. $3.95. American Alliance for Health, Physical Education, Recreation, and Dance, National Association for Girls and Women in Sport, 1900 Association Dr., Reston, VA 22091. TEL 703-476-3481. circ. 15,000. Indexed: ERIC.
Supersedes in part: Field Hockey-Lacrosse Guide (ISSN 0065-7026)

796.33   **US**   **ISSN 0163-4747**
N A G W S GUIDE. SOCCER. 1927. a. $3.95. American Alliance for Health, Physical Education, Recreation, and Dance, National Association for Girls and Women in Sport, 1900 Association Dr., Reston, VA 22091. TEL 703-476-3481. illus. circ. 9,000.
Supersedes: N A G W S Guide. Soccer, Speedball, Flag Football (ISSN 0145-6601)

796.4   **US**   **ISSN 0363-2504**
N A G W S GUIDE. SOFTBALL. 1938. biennial. $3.95. American Alliance for Health, Physical Education, Recreation, and Dance, National Association for Girls and Women in Sport, 1900 Association Dr., Reston, VA 22091. TEL 703-476-3481. circ. 23,000. Indexed: ERIC.

796.342   **US**   **ISSN 0272-863X**
N A G W S GUIDE. TENNIS. 1938. biennial. $4.50. American Alliance for Health, Physical Education, Recreation, and Dance, National Association for Girls and Women in Sport, 1900 Association Dr., Reston, VA 22091. TEL 703-476-3481. circ. 13,000. Indexed: ERIC.
Supersedes in part: Tennis-Badminton-Squash Guide (ISSN 0065-7042); Tennis-Badminton Guide.

796.325   **US**
N A G W S GUIDE. VOLLEYBALL. 1938. biennial. $5.50. American Alliance for Health, Physical Education, Recreation, and Dance, National Association for Girls and Women in Sport, 1900 Association Dr., Reston, VA 22091. TEL 703-476-3481. circ. 17,000. Indexed: ERIC.
Formerly: Volleyball Guide (ISSN 0065-7050)

796   **US**   **ISSN 0736-5209**
N C A A BASEBALL RULES. 1974. a. $3. National Collegiate Athletic Association, Box 1906, Mission, KS 66201. TEL 913-384-3220.
Former titles: N C A A Baseball Annual Guide; Official National Collegiate Athletic Association Baseball Guide (ISSN 0466-1478)

796.323   **US**   **ISSN 0276-1017**
N C A A BASKETBALL. 1923. a. $5. National Collegiate Athletic Association, Box 1906, Mission, KS 66201. TEL 913-384-3220. circ. 12,000.
Incorporates: N C A A Basketball Records; Formerly (until 1980): Official National Collegiate Athletic Association Basketball Guide.

796.33   **US**   **ISSN 0735-5475**
N C A A FOOTBALL. 1969. a. $5. National Collegiate Athletic Association, Box 1906, Mission, KS 66201. TEL 913-384-3220. illus. stat. circ. 4,000.
Incorporates: N C A A Football Guide; Former titles: N C A A Football Records; College Football Modern Record Book (ISSN 0092-881X)

796.32   **US**
N C A A MEN'S BASKETBALL RULES AND INTERPRETATIONS. 1967. a. $3. National Collegiate Athletic Association, Box 1906, Mission, KS 66201. TEL 913-384-3220. illus. circ. 25,000.
Former titles: N C A A Basketball Rules and Interpretations; Official National Collegiate Athletic Association Basketball Rules and Interpretations (ISSN 0163-2817); Official National Collegiate Athletic Association Basketball Rules (ISSN 0094-5234)

796.32   **US**
N C A A MEN'S ILLUSTRATED BASKETBALL RULES. a. $3. National Collegiate Athletic Association, Box 1906, Mission, KS 66601. TEL 913-384-3220.
Former titles: N C A A Illustrated Men's Rules (ISSN 0736-5179) & N C A A Illustrated Basketball Rules (ISSN 0272-5754)

796   **US**   **ISSN 0736-7775**
N C A A MEN'S LACROSSE RULES. a. $3. National Collegiate Athletic Association, Box 1906, Mission, KS 66201. TEL 913-384-3220.
Former titles: N C A A Lacrosse Guide (ISSN 0732-9059) & Official N C A A Lacrosse Guide.

796.334   **US**   **ISSN 0735-0368**
N C A A MEN'S SOCCER RULES. 1927. a. $3. National Collegiate Athletic Association, Box 1906, Mission, KS 66201. TEL 913-384-3220. circ. 11,700.
Formerly: Official National Collegiate Athletic Association Soccer Guide.

796.332   **US**
N F L PREVIEW (YEAR) a. Lexington Library, Inc., 355 Lexington Ave., New York, NY 10017. TEL 212-391-1400. Eds. Stephen Ciacciarelli, Thomas Walsh. adv. charts. illus.

796.33   **US**   **ISSN 0736-5160**
NATIONAL COLLEGIATE ATHLETIC ASSOCIATION FOOTBALL RULES & INTERPRETATIONS. Cover title: N C A A Football Rules & Interpretations. 1961. a. $3. National Collegiate Athletic Association, Box 1906, Mission, KS 66201. TEL 913-384-3220. Ed. David Nelson. circ. 24,000.
Formerly: Official National Collegiate Athletic Association Football Rules and Interpretations (ISSN 0094-5226)

796.9   **CN**
NATIONAL HOCKEY LEAGUE. GUIDE. 1947. a. $16.95. National Hockey League, 960 Sun Life Building, Montreal, Quebec H3B 2W2, Canada. TEL 514-871-9220. Ed. Gary Meagher.

796.357   **US**   **ISSN 0734-6905**
NATIONAL PASTIME. 1982. a. $7. Society for American Baseball Research, Inc., 18 Virginia Ave., Saugerties, NY 12477 TEL 914-246-9241. (Subscr. to: Box 1010, Cooperstown, NY 13326) Ed. John Thorn. adv. circ. 8,000.

796.323   **US**
NATIONAL WHEELCHAIR BASKETBALL ASSOCIATION. DIRECTORY. 1960. a. $50. National Wheelchair Basketball Association, 110 Seaton Bldg., University of Kentucky, Lexington, KY 40506. Ed. Stan Labanowich. circ. 350.

796.332   **US**
NEW YORK JETS OFFICIAL YEARBOOK. 1971. a. $2 per copy. (New York Jets Football Club Inc.) Football Publications Inc., 4100 Palisade Ave., Union City, NJ 07087. Ed. Frank Ramos. charts. illus. stat. circ. 60,000.

796.323   **US**
NEW YORK KNICKS YEARBOOK; official guide and record book. 1957. a. $5 per copy. (New York Knickerbockers Basketball Club) Madison Square Garden Corporation (Subsidiary of: Gulf & Western) 4 Pennsylvania Plaza, New York, NY 10001. TEL 212-563-8000. Eds. John Cirillo, Carl Martin. charts. illus. stat.

796.357   **US**   **ISSN 0078-3838**
OFFICIAL BASEBALL GUIDE. 1942. a. $9.95. Sporting News Publishing Co., 1212 N. Lindbergh Blvd., St. Louis, MO 63132. TEL 314-997-7111.

796.357   **US**   **ISSN 0162-542X**
OFFICIAL BASEBALL REGISTER. 1940. a. $9.95. Sporting News Publishing Co., 1212 N. Lindbergh Blvd., St. Louis, MO 63132. TEL 314-997-7111. cum.index: 1940-1973.
Formerly: Baseball Register (ISSN 0067-4281)

796.357   **US**   **ISSN 0078-3846**
OFFICIAL BASEBALL RULES. 1950. a. $2.50. Sporting News Publishing Co., 1212 N. Lindbergh Blvd., St. Louis, MO 63132. TEL 314-997-7111.

796.3   **US**
OFFICIAL LAWN BOWLS ALMANAC. 1964. irreg. $1 to non-members. American Lawn Bowls Association, 445 Surfview Dr., Pacific Palisades, CA 90272. TEL 213-454-2775.
Former titles (until 1984): Official Lawn Bowls Handbook (ISSN 0065-9053); Lawn Bowler's Handbook.

796.3   **US**   **ISSN 0078-3862**
OFFICIAL NATIONAL BASKETBALL ASSOCIATION GUIDE. 1958. a. $9.95. Sporting News Publishing Co., 1212 N. Lindbergh Blvd., St. Louis, MO 63132. TEL 314-997-7111. Ed. Mike Douchant.

796.323   **US**   **ISSN 0277-559X**
OFFICIAL READ-EASY BASKETBALL RULES. 1973. a. $1.50. National Collegiate Athletic Association, Box 1906, Mission, KS 66201. TEL 913-384-3220. illus. circ. 5,200.

796.358   **PK**
PAKISTAN BOOK OF CRICKET. (Text in English) 1976. a. Rs.10. Q. Ahmed, Pub., Third Floor, Spencers Bldg., I.I. Chundrigar Rd., G.P.O. Box 3721, Karachi, Pakistan. charts. illus.

796.357   **US**   **ISSN 0731-8138**
PITCHER PERFORMANCE HANDBOOK. 1965. a. $3. ‡ Research Analysis Publications, Box 49213, Los Angeles, CA 90049. Ed. Ronald H. Lewis. adv. charts. stat. circ. 8,000.

796.358   **UK**   **ISSN 0079-2314**
PLAYFAIR CRICKET ANNUAL. a. £1.75. Queen Anne Press Ltd., Greater London House, Hampstead Rd., London NW1 7QX, England. Ed. Bill Frindall. circ. 60,000.

796.3   **UK**   **ISSN 0079-2322**
PLAYFAIR FOOTBALL ANNUAL. 1948. a. £1.95. Queen Anne Press Ltd., Greater London House, Hampstead Rd., London NW1 7QX, England. Ed. P. Dunk. circ. 40,000.

796.333   **SA**
PLAYFAIR S.A. RUGBY YEARBOOK. (Text in Afrikaans and English) a. R.1.20. Promco (Pty) Ltd., 1202 Radio City, Tulbagh Square, Cape Town 8001, South Africa. Ed. L. Van Wyck. adv.

796.357   US
PONY BASEBALL. BLUE BOOK. 1959. triennial. $4. ‡ Pony Baseball, Inc., Box 225, Washington, PA 15301. TEL 412-225-1060. Eds. Roy Gillespie, Abraham Key. circ. 14,000.
Formerly: Boys Baseball. Blue Book (ISSN 0068-0575)

796.352   US
PRIVATE COUNTRY CLUB GUEST POLICY DIRECTORY. 1976. a. $25. Pazdur Publishing Co., 2171 Campus Dr., Irvine, CA 92715. TEL 714-752-6474. Ed. Edward F. Pazdur. adv. circ. 100,000.
Supersedes (1976-1979): Golf and Country Club Guest Policy Directory.

796.322   US
PRO BASKETBALL ILLUSTRATED (YEAR) a. Lexington Library, Inc., 355 Lexington Ave., New York, NY 10017. TEL 212-391-1400. Eds. Stephen Ciacciarelli, Thomas Walsh. charts. illus.

796.3305   US   ISSN 0079-5526
PRO FOOTBALL (LOS ANGELES) 1960. a. $2.95. Petersen Publishing Co., 8490 Sunset Blvd., Los Angeles, CA 90069. TEL 213-657-5100.
Formerly: Petersen's Pro Football Annual (ISSN 0079-1156)

796.332   US
PRO FOOTBALL ILLUSTRATED (YEAR) a. Lexington Library, Inc., 355 Lexington Ave., New York, NY 10017. Ed. David J. Elrich. adv.

RACING AND FOOTBALL OUTLOOK: FOOTBALL ANNUAL. see *SPORTS AND GAMES*

RACING AND FOOTBALL OUTLOOK: JUMPING ANNUAL. see *SPORTS AND GAMES*

RACING AND FOOTBALL OUTLOOK: RACING ANNUAL. see *SPORTS AND GAMES*

796.3   UK   ISSN 0080-4088
ROTHMANS FOOTBALL YEARBOOK. 1970. a. £10.95 (paperback); £14.95(hardcover) (Rothmans (U.K.) Ltd.) Queen Anne Press Ltd., Greater London House, Hampstead Rd., London NW1 7QX, England. Ed. Peter Dunk. adv. circ. 40,000.

796.333   UK   ISSN 0262-4745
ROTHMANS RUGBY LEAGUE YEARBOOK. 1981. a. £14.95. Queen Anne Press, 3rd Fl., Greater London House, London NW1 7QX, England. Eds. David Howes, Raymond Fletcher. illus. circ. 13,000.

796.333   UK
RUGBY ANNUAL FOR WALES. 1968. a. £2.50. Welsh Brewers Ltd., Maesycoed Rd., Cardiff CF4 4UW, Wales. Ed. Arwyn Owen. adv.

796.3   UK   ISSN 0080-4827
RUGBY FOOTBALL LEAGUE OFFICIAL GUIDE. a. Rugby Football League, 180 Chapeltown Road, Leeds LS7 4HT, England.

796.357   US
S A B R REVIEW OF BOOKS. a. $6. Society for American Baseball Research, Inc., Box 1010, Cooperstown, NY 13326. Ed. Paul Adomites.

796.352   UK
SCOTLAND HOME OF GOLF. 1970. a. £1.10. Pastime Publications Ltd., 15 Dublin Street Lane South, Edinburgh EH1 3PX, Scotland. adv.

796.334   US   ISSN 0731-9541
SOCCER RULEBOOK. a. $2.50. National Federation of State High School Associations, 11724 Plaza Circle, Box 20626, Kansas City, MO 64195. TEL 816-464-5400.
Formerly: National Federation of State High School Associations. Soccer Rules (ISSN 0163-4763)

796.3   UK   ISSN 0081-038X
SOCCER YEAR BOOK FOR NORTHERN IRELAND. 1966. a. £1.50. Howard Publications, 39 Boucher Rd., Belfast BT12 6UT, Northern Ireland. Ed. Malcolm Brodie.

796.357   US   ISSN 0732-2844
SOFTBALL RULE BOOK. a. $2.50. National Federation of State High School Associations, 11724 Plaza Circle, Box 20626, Kansas City, MO 64195. TEL 816-464-5400. Ed. Bradley A. Rumble.
Formerly: National Federation of State High School Associations. Softball Rules (ISSN 0146-8286)

796.357   US   ISSN 0275-0732
SPORTING NEWS BASEBALL YEARBOOK. a. $3.50. Sporting News Publishing Co., 1212 N. Lindbergh Blvd., St. Louis, MO 63132. adv.

796.323   US   ISSN 0739-3067
SPORTING NEWS OFFICIAL N B A REGISTER. a. $9.95. Sporting News Publishing Co., 1212 N. Lindbergh Blvd., St. Louis, MO 63132. TEL 314-997-7111. Ed. Mike Douchant. (back issues avail.)
Formerly: Sporting News National Basketball Association Register (ISSN 0271-8170)

796.323   US   ISSN 0733-6047
SPORTING NEWS PRO-COLLEGE BASKETBALL YEARBOOK. a. $3.50. Sporting News Publishing Co., 1212 N. Lindbergh Blvd., St. Louis, MO 63132 TEL 314-997-7111. (Box 44, St. Louis, MO 63166) Ed. Mike Douchant. adv.

796.332   US   ISSN 0732-1902
SPORTING NEWS PRO FOOTBALL GUIDE. 1970. a. $9.95. Sporting News Publishing Co., 1212 N. Lindbergh Blvd., St. Louis, MO 63132 TEL 314-997-7111. (Subscr. to: Box 44, St. Louis, MO 63166) Ed.Bd. (back issues avail.)
Formerly: Sporting News' National Football Guide (ISSN 0081-3788)

796.332   US   ISSN 0276-2307
SPORTING NEWS PRO FOOTBALL YEARBOOK. a. $3.50. Sporting News Publishing Co., 1212 N. Lindbergh Blvd., St. Louis, MO 63132 TEL 314-997-7111. (Subscr. to: Box 44, St. Louis, MO 63166) Ed. Howard Balzer. adv.

796.332   US   ISSN 0275-4487
SPORTING NEWS SUPER BOWL BOOK. a. $9.95. Sporting News Publishing Co., 1212 N. Lindbergh Blvd., St. Louis, MO 63132 TEL 314-997-7111. (Subscr. to: Box 44, St. Louis, MO 63166) Ed. Bob McCoy. (back issues avail.)

796.332   US
SPORTS QUARTERLY - FOOTBALL PROS. 1962. a. $2 newsstand sales only. Lopez Publications, Inc., 23 W. 26th St., New York, NY 10010. Ed. Herbert M. Furlow. adv. circ. 228,000.

796   UK
SQUASH RACKETS ASSOCIATION. ANNUAL. 1930. a. £7.95. Squash Rackets Association, Francis House, Francis St, London SW1P 1DE, England. Ed. Larry Halpin. adv. circ. 8,700.
Formerly: Squash Rackets Association. Handbook (ISSN 0081-3885)

796.257   US   ISSN 0161-2018
STREET & SMITH'S OFFICIAL YEARBOOK: BASEBALL. 1941. a. $2.95 not avail. by subscription. Conde Nast Publications Inc., Street & Smith's Division, 350 Madison Ave., New York, NY 10017. Ed. Gerard Kavanagh. adv. circ. 445, 000.
Formerly: Street and Smith's Baseball Yearbook (ISSN 0491-1520)

796.32   US   ISSN 0149-7103
STREET & SMITH'S OFFICIAL YEARBOOK: BASKETBALL. a. $2.95. Conde Nast Publications Inc., Street & Smith's Division, 350 Madison Ave., New York, NY 10017. Ed. Jim O'Brien. adv. illus. circ. 410,000.
Formerly: Street and Smith's College and Pro Official Basketball Yearbook (ISSN 0092-511X)

796.33   US   ISSN 0091-9977
STREET & SMITH'S OFFICIAL YEARBOOK: COLLEGE FOOTBALL. a. $2.95. Conde Nast Publications Inc., Street and Smith's Division, 350 Madison Ave., New York, NY 10017. Ed. Gerard Kavanagh. adv. illus. circ. 450,000.

796.33   US   ISSN 0092-3214
STREET & SMITH'S OFFICIAL YEARBOOK: PRO FOOTBALL. a. $2.95. Conde Nast Publications Inc., Street & Smith's Division, 350 Madison Ave., New York, NY 10017. Ed. Gerard Kavanagh. adv. illus. circ. 475,000. (reprint service avail. from UMI) Key Title: Street and Smith's Official Yearbook. Pro Football.

796.342   UK
TENNIS GREAT BRITAIN. 1980. a. £5.95. Lawn Tennis Association, Barons Court, London W14 9EG, England. Ed. David Irvine. adv. circ. 13,000.
Formerly: Lawn Tennis Association Handbook.

796.332   UK
TOPICAL TIMES FOOTBALL BOOK. 1959. a. £2.05. D.C. Thomson & Co. Ltd., 185 Fleet St., London EC4A 2HS, England.

796.342   US
TOURNAMENT TIMES. (Text mainly in English; occasionally in Greek, Spanish) 1978. irreg., approx. 5/yr. $8. Western Tennis Publishing, Box 4577, Santa Fe, NM 87502. TEL 505-471-3378. Ed. Bob Raedisch. (back issues avail.)

796   SZ   ISSN 0570-2070
UNION OF EUROPEAN FOOTBALL ASSOCIATIONS. HANDBOOK OF U E F A. (Text in English, French and German) 1959. irreg. 100 Fr. for base vol., Fr. 30 for updates (3 yrs.) Union of European Football Associations - Union des Associations Europeennes de Football, 33 Jupiter Strasse, Case Postale 16, 3000 Berne 15, Switzerland. Ed. U. Rudolph Rothenbuehler. bk. rev. circ. 2,500.

796.342   US   ISSN 0083-1557
UNITED STATES LAWN TENNIS ASSOCIATION. YEARBOOK. 1937. a. $9. Harold O. Zimman, Inc., 156 Broad St., Lynn, MA 01901. TEL 617-598-9432. Ed. Adam Scharff. adv. circ. 15,000.

796.353   US   ISSN 0083-3118
UNITED STATES POLO ASSOCIATION. YEARBOOK. 1890. a. $25. (United States Polo Association) Kelmscott Press, 120 Mill St., Lexington, KY 40507-1207. Ed. Lou Ann Koop. adv. circ. 2,400.

796.343   US   ISSN 0083-3398
UNITED STATES SQUASH RACQUETS ASSOCIATION. OFFICIAL YEAR BOOK. 1925. a. $6. United States Squash Racquets Association, 211 Ford Rd., Bala-Cynwyd, PA 19004. TEL 215-667-4006. Ed. Darwin P. Kingsley, III. adv. index. circ. 10,000.

796.325   US   ISSN 0083-3592
UNITED STATES VOLLEYBALL ASSOCIATION. OFFICIAL VOLLEYBALL GUIDE AND RULE BOOK. 1920. a. $5.50. ‡ United States Volleyball Association, Sales Office, 1750 E. Boulder St., Colorado Springs, CO 80909. TEL 303-632-5551. adv. index. circ. 25,000. (also avail. in microfiche)

796.325   US
VOLLEYBALL CASE BOOK. biennial. $2.50. National Federation of State High School Associations, 11724 Plaza Circle, Box 20626, Kansas City, MO 64185. TEL 816-464-5400.

796.325   US
VOLLEYBALL RULEBOOK. a. $2.50. National Federation of State High School Associations, 11724 Plaza Circle, Box 20626, Kansas City, MO 64195. TEL 816-464-5400.

WEEDS TREES & TURF GOLF DAILY. see *GARDENING AND HORTICULTURE*

794.6   US   ISSN 0361-3976
WOMEN'S INTERNATIONAL BOWLING CONGRESS. PLAYING RULES. a. Women's International Bowling Congress, Inc., 5301 S. 76th St., Greendale, WI 53129. TEL 414-421-9000. Ed. Sharon Bergman. illus. Key Title: Playing Rules.

796.342   UK
WORLD OF TENNIS. 1969. a. £9.95. (International Tennis Federation) William Collins & Sons Ltd., 8 Grafton St., London W1X 4PA, England. Ed. John Barrett. adv. index. circ. 6,500.

SPORTS AND GAMES — BOATS AND BOATING   1041

796.334   UK
WORLD SOCCER STARS ANNUAL. 1983. a. £2.50. World International Publishing Ltd., Gt. Ducie St., Manchester, England. Ed. Mae Broadley. adv.

SPORTS AND GAMES — Bicycles And Motorcycles

388.347   796.7   IT
ALMANACCO LA MOTO. 1976. a. Edigamma s.r.l., Piazza dei Sanniti 9, 00185 Rome, Italy. Ed. Renato Circi. adv. circ. 90,000.

796.6   FR
ANNEE DU CYCLISME. 1974. a. price varies. Editions Calmann-Levy, 3 rue Auber, 75009 Paris, France. illus.

796.6   US
BICYCLE DEALER SHOWCASE BUYERS GUIDE. 1921. a. $20. Harcourt Brace Jovanovich, Inc., 7500 Old Oak Blvd., Cleveland, OH 44130 TEL 216-243-8100. (Subscr. address: 1 E. First St., Duluth, MN 55802) Ed. Molly Ingram. adv. circ. 10,148. (also avail. in microform from UMI)

BOTTIN AUTO-CYCLE-MOTO. see TRANSPORTATION — Automobiles

629.227   796.7   US
CHILTON'S MOTORCYCLE REPAIR MANUAL; from 1945 to 1981. 1974. irreg. price varies. Chilton Book Co., Automotive Editorial Department, Chilton Way, Radnor, PA 19089.

629.2   US   ISSN 0272-8923
CYCLE STREET AND TOURING GUIDE. 1980. a. $2.95. C B S, Inc.Publishing Co., Cycle (Subsidiary of: C B S, Inc.) 1515 Broadway, New York, NY 10036. illus.

796.7   US
CYCLE WORLD BUYER'S GUIDE. a. C B S Publications, Cycle World, 1515 Broadway, New York, NY 10036. TEL 212-975-7855. adv.

796   US   ISSN 0270-2746
CYCLE WORLD TEST ANNUAL AND BUYERS GUIDE. 1971. a. $3.50. C B S Magazines (Subsidiary of: C B S, Inc.) 1515 Broadway, New York, NY 10036. TEL 212-719-6000. Ed. Paul Dean. adv. bk. rev. charts. illus. tr.lit.
Formerly: Cycle World Road Test Annual.

796.6   DK   ISSN 0107-7805
CYKLE-JUL. vol.5, 1936. a. Kr.32.50. B E H O, c/o Danske Boghendleres Kommissionsanstalt, Siljangade 6, 2300 Copenhagen S, Denmark. illus.
Formerly: Cyclen.

796   US
EXPLORE MINNESOTA BIKING. triennial. Office of Tourism, 375 Jackson St., Ste. 205, St. Paul, MN 55101. circ. 80,000.

796   SZ   ISSN 0071-4283
FEDERATION INTERNATIONALE MOTOCYCLISTE. ANNUAIRE. (Including International Motorcycle Sporting Calendar) (Text in English and French) 1912. a. 20 Fr. International Motorcycle Federation, 19 Chemin William-Barbey, 1292 Chambesy-Geneva, Switzerland.

388.347   UK
GLASS'S MOTOR CYCLE CHECK BOOK. a. £8. Glass's Guide Service Ltd., Elgin House, St. George's Ave., Weybridge, Surrey KT13 0BX, England. adv.

796   JA   ISSN 0446-6667
JAPAN'S BICYCLE GUIDE. (Text in English) 1951. a. exchange basis. Japan Bicycle Industry Association, 1-9-3 Akasaka, Tokyo 107, Japan. adv. stat.

796.7   DK   ISSN 0107-0606
M C REVYEN. (Text in Danish) a. Bonniers Specialmagasiner, Noerre Farimagsgade 49, 1375 Copenhagen K, Denmark. Ed. Fl. Haslund.

388.347   UK
MOTOCOURSE. 1976. a. £18.95. Hazleton Publishing, 3 Richmond Hill, Richmond, Surrey TW10 6RE, England. Ed. Peter Clifford. adv.

796.75   FR   ISSN 0077-1570
MOTOCYCLO CATALOGUE; guide technique du cycle et du motocycle. 1951. a. 144 F. Editions S.O.S.P., 59-61 Avenue de la Grande Armee, 75782 Paris Cedex 16, France. Ed. C. L. Lavaud. index.

796   UK   ISSN 0306-4867
MOTOR CYCLE AND CYCLE TRADER YEAR BOOK. 1970. a. £6.90. Wheatland Journals Ltd., Penn House, Penn Place, Rickmansworth, Herts WD3 1SN, England. Ed. Robert Fairbairn. circ. 5,000.

796.75   US   ISSN 0077-1678
MOTORCYCLE BUYER'S GUIDE. 1970. a. $2.95. Petersen Publishing Co., 8490 Sunset Blvd., Los Angeles, CA 90069. TEL 213-854-2222.

388.347   640.73   US
MOTORCYCLE DEALERNEWS BUYERS GUIDE. a. $12. Harcourt Brace Jovanovich, Inc., 7500 Old Oak Blvd., Cleveland, OH 44130 TEL 216-243-8100. (Subscr. address: 1 E. First St., Duluth, MN 55802) Ed. Linda Dean. circ. 14,201.

796.7   JA
MOTORCYCLE JAPAN; annual guide to Japan's motorcycle industry. (Text in English) 1983. a. $30.40. Automotive Herald Co., Ltd., 3rd Shinto Bldg., 21-1 Shinbashi 5-chome, Minato-ku, Tokyo 105, Japan (U.S. address: Japan American Automotive Systems, Inc., 2424 W. Morse Ave., Chicago, IL 60645) Ed. M. Sakurazawa. circ. 8,000.

MOTORCYCLE PRODUCT NEWS TRADE DIRECTORY. see BUSINESS AND ECONOMICS — Trade And Industrial Directories

V K G JAHRBUCH; Mitgliederverzeichnis. (Verband der Kraftfahrzeugteile- und Zweiradgrosshaendler e.V.) see TRANSPORTATION — Automobiles

SPORTS AND GAMES — Boats And Boating

796   UK   ISSN 0144-1396
A Y R S AIRS. 1956. irreg. £12.50($20) Amateur Yacht Research Society, 10 Boringdon Terrace, Turnchapel, Plymouth PL9 9TQ, England. Ed. J. Morwood. bk. rev. circ. 1,400.

797.1   ISSN 0065-9797
AMERICAN POWER BOAT ASSOCIATION. A P B A RULE BOOK. (In 4 vols: Parts 1-3 Racing Rules: Part 4 Racing Records, Commissions, Membership Directory) 1903. a. $3 ea. part to non-members. American Power Boat Association, 17640 E. Nine Mile Rd., E. Detroit, MI 48021. TEL 313-773-9700. index.

797   FR   ISSN 0758-6639
ANNUAIRE NAUTISME. 1963. a. 140 F.($24) Editions de Chabassol, 30 rue de Gramont, 75002 Paris, France. Ed. B. Laloup. adv.

797.1   IT
ANNUARIO DELLA NAUTICA. a. Nautica Editrice, Via Tevere 44, 00198 Rome, Italy. adv. illus.

797.1   DK
BAAD - REVYEN. a. Bonniers Specialmagasiner, Noerre Farimagsgade 49, 1375 Copenhagen K, Denmark. adv. circ. 22,500.

796.95   UK
BLAKES BOATING HOLIDAY BOOKS. a. free. Blakes Holidays Ltd., Wroxham, Norwich NR12 8DH, England. Ed. T.E. Howes. adv. circ. 30,000.

BLAKES BOATING HOLIDAYS. see TRAVEL AND TOURISM

381.45   US   ISSN 0520-2949
BLUE BOOK, INBOARD/OUTDRIVE BOAT TRADE-IN GUIDE. (Each edt. covers an 8 or 9 year period) 26th edt., 1986. a. (in 2 vols.) $8.95 per vol. Intertec Publishing Corp., Abos Book Division, 9221 Quivira Rd., Overland Park, Kansas City, KS 66212. TEL 913-888-4664. (reprint service avail. from UMI)

387.2   380.1   US   ISSN 0006-5366
BOAT & MOTOR DEALER. (Annual Market Manual avail.) 1959. m. (plus a. supplement) $20. Van Zevern Publications, Inc., 3949 Oakton St., Skokie, IL 60076. TEL 312-982-1810. Ed. George P. Van Zevern. adv. bk. rev. circ. 28,000.

796.95   US
BOAT & MOTOR DEALER'S MARKET. 1969. a. $10. Van Zevern Publications, Inc., 3949 Oakton St., Skokie, IL 60076. TEL 312-982-1810. Ed. George Van Zevern. adv. bk. rev. circ. 28,000.

797   UK   ISSN 0067-933X
BOAT WORLD. 1964. a. £7.65. Transport Press, Quadrant House, Sutton, Surrey SM2 5AS, England. adv. bk. rev. circ. 10,000.

796.95   US
BOATING ALMANAC, VOL. 1 - RHODE ISLAND, MASSACHUSETTS, MAINE, NEW HAMPSHIRE. 1961. a. $8.50. Boating Almanac Co., Inc., 203 McKinsey Rd., Severna Park, MD 21146. TEL 301-647-0084. Ed. Peter A. Geis. adv. charts.

796.95   US
BOATING ALMANAC, VOL. 2 - LONG ISLAND, CONNECTICUT, RHODE ISLAND, SOUTHERN MASSACHUSETTS. 1961. a. $8.50. Boating Almanac Co., Inc., 203 McKinsey Rd., Severna Park, MD 21146. TEL 301-647-0084. Ed. Peter A. Geis. adv. charts.

796.95   US
BOATING ALMANAC, VOL. 3 - NEW JERSEY, DELAWARE BAY, HUDSON RIVER, LAKE CHAMPLAIN, ERIE CANAL. 1961. a. $8.50. Boating Almanac Co., Inc., 203 McKinsey Rd., Severna Park, MD 21146. TEL 301-647-0084. Ed. Peter A. Geis. adv. charts.

796.95   US
BOATING ALMANAC, VOL. 4 - CHESAPEAKE BAY, DELAWARE, MARYLAND, DISTRICT OF COLUMBIA, VIRGINIA. 1961. a. $8.50. Boating Almanac Co., Inc., 603 McKinsey Rd., Severna Park, MD 21146. TEL 301-647-0084. Ed. Peter A. Geis. adv. charts.

797   UK   ISSN 0309-1252
BRISTOW'S BOOK OF YACHTS. 1963. a. £3.95. Navigator Publishing Ltd., Moorhouse Farmhouse, Lower Kingston, Ringwood, Hants, England. Ed. Philip Bristow. circ. 5,000.
Formed by the merger of: Bristow's Book of Motor Cruisers & Bristow's Book of Sailing Cruisers.

797.123   UK   ISSN 0068-2446
BRITISH ROWING ALMANACK. 1861. a. £6 to non-members. Amateur Rowing Association, 6 Lower Mall, London W6 9DJ, England. Ed. Keith L. Osborne. bk. rev. index.

797   UK   ISSN 0068-290X
BROWN'S NAUTICAL ALMANAC. 1858. a. £29. Brown, Son and Ferguson Ltd., 4-10 Darnley St., Glasgow G41 2SD, Scotland. Eds. T. Nigel Brown, Capt. A.N. Cockroft. adv. circ. 18,000.

796.95   UK
CRUISING ASSOCIATION YEARBOOK. 1909. a. membership. Cruising Association, Ivory House, St. Katharine Dock, London E1 9AT, England. circ. 5,000.

796.95   UK
DEBRETT'S REGISTER OF YACHTS.* 1983. biennial. £40. Debrett's Peerage Ltd., 73-77 Britannia Rd., Fulham, London SW6 2JR, England. circ. 5,000.

FACOLTA DI SCIENZE NAUTICHE. ANNALI. see TRANSPORTATION — Ships And Shipping

797   FR   ISSN 0071-4194
FEDERATION FRANCAISE DE NATATION. ANNUAIRE. 1921. a. 185 F. Federation Francaise de Natation, 148 Av. Gambetta, 75020 Paris, France.

623.8   FI   ISSN 0356-7753
FINNISH BOATBUILDING INDUSTRY. (Text in: English, German, French) 1971. irreg. free. Suomen Vene- ja Moottoriyhdistys - Finnish Boat and Motor Association, Mariankatu 26 B 19, 00170 Helsinki 17, Finland.

SPORTS AND GAMES — HORSES AND HORSEMANSHIP

797.14 US
I C Y R A/N A DIRECTORY. a. free. Intercollegiate Yacht Racing Association of North America, 8893 Melinda Ct., Milan, MI 48160. Ed. George H. Griswold. circ. 400.

796.95 GW
INTERNATIONALES BODENSEE-JAHRBUCH DER SPORTSCHIFFAHRT. 1959. a. DM.16. Druck & Verlagshaus Hermann Daniel GmbH & Co. KG, Gruenewaldstr. 15, D-7460 Balingen 1, W. Germany (B.R.D.) circ. 10,000.

796.95 GW
INTERNATIONALES BODENSEE REGATTA PROGRAMM. 1959. a. DM.14. (Bodensee-Segler-Verband) Druck & Verlagshaus Hermann Daniel GmbH & Co. KH, Gruenewaldstr. 15, D-7460 Balingen 1, W. Germany (B.R.D.) circ. 8,000.

797 GW ISSN 0075-627X
KLASINGS BOOTSMARKT INTERNATIONAL; YACHTEN UND BOOTE ZUBEHOER, AUSRUESTUNG, MOTOREN. 1968. a. DM.19.80. Verlag Delius, Klasing und Co., Siekerwall 21, Postfach 4809, 4800 Bielefeld, W. Germany (B.R.D.) Ed. Kai Krueger. adv.

797 US ISSN 0075-8272
LAZY MAN'S GUIDE TO HOLIDAYS AFLOAT. 1966. a. £1. Boat Enquiries Ltd., 43 Botley Rd., Oxford OX2 0PT, England. Ed. Alan Macdonald. adv. bk. rev. circ. 120,000.

797.14 US ISSN 0076-0455
LOG OF THE STAR CLASS; official rule book. 1922. a. $5 membership. ‡ International Star Class Yacht Racing Association, 1545 Waukegan Rd., Glenview, IL 60025. Ed. Jane Lawrence. adv. circ. 4,000.

797 AT
MIRROR CLASS ASSOCIATION OF AUSTRALIA. YEARBOOK. 1969/70. a. Aus.$20. Mirror Class Association of Australia, 47 Gowrie St., South Oakleigh, Vic. 3167, Australia, Australia. Ed. W. Dooley. adv. circ. 400.
Supersedes in Part: Mirror Class Association of Australia. Constitution-Rules of Measurement.

797.1 US
N M M A CERTIFICATION HANDBOOK. 1956. a. National Marine Manufacturers Association, 353 Lexington Ave., New York, NY 10016 TEL 212-684-6622. (Or 401 N. Michigan Ave., Chicago, IL 60611) index.
Former titles: B I A Certification Handbook (ISSN 0067-9402); Boating Industry Associations Engineering Manual of Recommended Practices.

797.1 SZ
OEFFENTLICHE SCHIFFAHRT AUF DEN SCHWEIZER SEEN. 1976. irreg. Birkhaeuser Verlag, P.O. Box 133, CH-4010 Basel, Switzerland.

797.1 US ISSN 0193-3515
PACIFIC BOATING ALMANAC. NORTHERN CALIFORNIA & NEVADA. 1965. a. $11.95. Western Marine Enterprises, Inc., 4051 Glencoe, No. 14, Marina Del Rey, CA 90292. TEL 213-306-2094. Ed. Capt. William Berssen. illus.
Formerly: Sea Boating Almanac. Northern California and Nevada (ISSN 0363-7700)

797.9 US ISSN 0276-8771
PACIFIC BOATING ALMANAC. OREGON, WASHINGTON, BRITISH COLUMBIA & SOUTHEASTERN ALASKA. a. $11.95. Western Marine Enterprises, Inc., 4051 Glencoe, No. 14, Marina Del Rey, CA 90292. TEL 213-306-2094. Ed. Capt. William Berssen. illus.
Former titles: Pacific Almanac. Pacific Northwest and Alaska (ISSN 0148-1177) & Sea Boating Almanac. Pacific Northwest and Alaska (ISSN 0363-7999)

797.1 US ISSN 0193-3507
PACIFIC BOATING ALMANAC. SOUTHERN CALIFORNIA, ARIZONA, BAJA. a. $11.95. Western Marine Enterprises, Inc., 4051 Glencoe, No. 14, Marina Del Rey, CA 90292. TEL 213-306-2094. Ed. Capt. William Berssen. illus.
Formerly: Sea Boating Almanac. Southern California, Arizona, Baja (ISSN 0363-6712)

796.95 UK ISSN 0485-5175
ROVING COMMISSIONS; anthology of cruising logs. 1960. a. price varies. Royal Cruising Club, c/o C. Gorer, Lime Tree Cottage, The Middleway, Andover Down, Hants. SP11 6LS, England. Ed. Robin Bryer. bk. rev. circ. 1,000.

797.124 US ISSN 0148-8732
SAILBOAT & EQUIPMENT DIRECTORY. 1967. a. $3.95. Sail Publications, Inc., Charlestown Navy Yard, 100 First Ave., Charlestown, MA 02129-2097. TEL 617-241-9500. Ed. Keith Taylor. adv. bk. rev. illus. circ. 85,000.
Formerly (1967-1970): Sailboat Directory (ISSN 0581-3115)

623.82 UK ISSN 0143-1153
SELL'S MARINE MARKET. 1979. a. £9. Sell's Publications Ltd., 55 High St., Epsom, Surrey KT19 8DW, England.

796.95 US ISSN 0749-9361
SHOWBOAT CENTENNIALS NEWSLETTER. 1979. irreg., no.18, 1986. free. 76 Glen Dr., Worthington, OH 43085. TEL 614-431-9422. Ed. Donald T. McDaniel. circ. 100. (looseleaf format)

797.1 UK
SOLENT YEARBOOK; solent cruising & racing association year book. 1910. a. £2.50. (Solent Cruising & Racing Association) Isle of Wight County Press Ltd., 29 High Street, Newport, Isle of Wight PO30 1ST, England. Ed. R.L. Bradbeer. adv. charts. circ. 5,000.

796.95 US
STANDARDS AND RECOMMENDED PRACTICES FOR SMALL CRAFT. 1965. base vol. plus a. supplement. $100 for base vol.; supplements $20. American Boat & Yacht Council, Inc., Box 806, Amittyville, NY 11701. TEL 516-598-0550. Ed. G. James Lippmann. circ. 3,000. (looseleaf format)

796.9 US
WATERWAY GUIDE; the yachtsman's Bible. (Separate Northern, Southern, and Mid-Atlantic Editions) 1947. a. $16.95 per edition. ‡ (Whitney Communications) Waterway Guide, 850 Third Ave., New York, NY 10022. TEL 212-715-2600. Ed. Queene Hooper. adv. charts. illus. circ. 15,000.

796.7 AT
YACHTING ASSOCIATION OF WESTERN AUSTRALIA. YEAR BOOK. 1984. a. (Yachting Association of Western Australia) Wescolour Press, 340 High St., East Freemantle, W.A. 6158, Australia. circ. 5,000.

797.1 BE ISSN 0084-3237
YACHTING BELGE; revue annuelle et illustree des sports nautiques. 1962. a. 250 Fr. Editions EREL, 16 St. Sebastiaanstraat, 8400 Oostende, Belgium. Ed. M. Lanoye. adv. bk. rev. circ. 10,000.

796.95 UK
YACHTING WORLD DIARY. a. £5.90. Dataday Ltd., Dataday House, 8 Alexandra Rd., London SW19 7JZ, England.

797.1 US ISSN 0094-8136
YACHTING YEAR BOOK OF NORTHERN CALIFORNIA. 1922. a. $7.95. Pacific Inter-Club Yacht Association of Northern California, Publication Office, 391 Miller Ave., Ste. 103, Mill Valley, CA 94941. TEL 415-388-8327. Ed. Burnett Tregoning. adv. illus. circ. 10,000.

797.1 US
YACHTING'S BOAT BUYERS GUIDE. 1959. a. $3.95. C B S Magazines, Yachting Department, One Park Ave., New York, NY 10016. TEL 212-719-6000. Ed. Roy Hataway. adv. index. circ. 100,000.
Formerly: Boat Owners Buyers Guide (ISSN 0067-9321)

796.95 GW
YACHTLOGBUCH. 1979. a. DM.9.80. (Deutscher Boots) Christians & Reim Verlag GmbH, Dammtor Str. 30, 2000 Hamburg 36, W. Germany (B.R.D.) circ. 15,000.

769.95 910.202 US
YACHTSMAN'S GUIDE TO THE BAHAMAS. 1950. a. $14.95. Tropic Isle Publishers, Inc., 14038 W. Dixie Hwy., Box 610935, N. Miami, FL 33161. TEL 305-893-4277. Ed. Meredith Helleberg Fields. adv. circ. 15,000.

797.14 US ISSN 0084-3261
YACHTSMAN'S GUIDE TO THE CARIBBEAN. 1964. irreg., latest issue 1975. $6.75. Seaport Publishing Co., c/o Ed. Clifford M. Montague, 843 Delray Ave., Grand Rapids, MI 49506. TEL 616-949-0048. index.

797.14 US ISSN 0084-327X
YACHTSMAN'S GUIDE TO THE GREAT LAKES. 1956. a. $11.95. Seaway Publishing Co., 18-22 S. Elm ST., Zeeland, MI 49464. TEL 616-772-2132. adv. index. circ. 5,000.

796.95 US ISSN 0162-7635
YACHTSMAN'S GUIDE TO THE GREATER ANTILLES. 1982. a. $9.95. Tropic Isle Publishers, Inc., 14038 W. Dixie Hwy., Box 610935, N. Miami, FL 33161. TEL 305-893-4277. Ed. Harry Kline.

SPORTS AND GAMES — Horses And Horsemanship

636.1 CN
AGENDA AMERICAN ALMANAC (YEAR) 1985. a. Can.$9.95. Club Jockey du Quebec, 14 Pagnuelo St., Outremont, P.Q. H2V 3B9, Canada. Ed. Rene Benoit. bk. rev. circ. 8,000.
Formerly: American Racehorse Owners & Breeders Almanac.

798 US
APPALOOSA HORSE; STUD BOOK AND REGISTRY.* irreg., vol. 15, 1973. price varies. Appaloosa Horse Club Inc., Box 8403, Moscow, ID 83843. TEL 208-882-5578.

798 UK
ARAB HORSE STUD BOOK. 1919. a. price varies. Arab Horse Society, Goddards Green, Cranbrook, Kent TN17 3LP, England. circ. 1,000. (tabloid format)

798.2 AT
ARABIAN STUDS AND STALLIONS MAGAZINE; Australia's leading Arabian magazine. 1974. a. Aus.$15. (Horse World Publications) H.C. & J.A. Vink Publishers, P.O. Box 55, Cleveland, Qld. 4163, Australia. Ed. Herman C. Vink. adv. bk. rev. circ. 10,000. (back issues avail.)

798.4 AT ISSN 0084-7402
AUSTRALIAN HORSE RACING ANNUAL.* 1969. a. $7 per issue. Playfair Publishing Group, Box 52, Northbridge, N.S.W. 2063, Australia.

636.1 UK
BLOODSTOCK SALES REVIEW AND STUD REGISTER. 1966. a. £18. David Colman, Ed. & Pub., Walnut Tree Farmhouse, Bacton, Stowmarket, Suffolk, England. adv.

798 UK ISSN 0144-7203
BRITISH EQUESTRIAN DIRECTORY. 1979. a. £10.50($16.50) Equestrian Management Consultants Ltd., Wothersome Grange, Bramham, Wetherby, Yorks LS23 6LY, England. Ed. Antony Wakeham. adv. circ. 5,000.

798 UK
BRITISH HORSE SOCIETY DIARY. a. Welbecson Ltd., Strawberry Street, Hull, Humberside, HU9 1EX, England. circ. (controlled)

798 UK
BRITISH HORSE SOCIETY YEAR BOOK & EVENT GUIDE. 1983. a. £1.80. Welbecson Ltd., Strawberry St., Hull, Humberside, HU9 1EX, England. adv. circ. 42,000.

636.1 CN ISSN 0382-5795
CANADIAN HACKNEY STUD BOOK. 1905. irreg. Canadian Hackney Society, c/o Canadian National Live Stock Records, Ottawa, Ont., Canada. TEL 613-731-7110. illus.

796.42 UK
CHASERS AND HURDLERS. 1975. a. £52. Portway Press Ltd., Timeform House, Northgate, Halifax, West Yorkshire HX1 1XE, England.

636.1 UK
CLYDESDALE STUD BOOK. 1877. a. £5.50. Clydesdale Society of Great Britain and Ireland, 24 Beresford Terrace, Ayr, Ayrshire, Scotland. Ed. Robert S. Gilmour. circ. 300.

SPORTS AND GAMES — OUTDOOR LIFE

796　　　　　UK　　ISSN 0419-3806
DIRECTORY OF THE TURF. 1961. a. £28($55)
Pacemaker Publications, Albert Bridge House,
Albert Bridge Rd., London SW11 4PL, England
(Subscr. addr.: 20 Oxford Rd., Newbury, Berkshire
RG13 1PA, England) Ed. Martin Pickering. adv.
circ. 5,500.

798　　　　　BE
FATES HIPPIQUES BELGES; revue annuelle
illustree du sport equestre sur le galop, trot,
jumping, elevage, dressage, tourisme equestre. 1957.
a. 250 Fr. Editions E R E L, 16 St. Sebastiaanstraat,
8400 Oostende, Belgium. Ed. M. Lanoye. adv. bk.
rev. circ. 10,000.

798　　　　　FR
FEDERATION EQUESTRE FRANCAISE. GUIDE
OFFICIEL DU CAVALIER.* irreg. (Federation
Equestre Francaise) Editions Bastin-Lavauzelle, 164
Fg. Saint-Honore, 75008 Paris, France.
　Formerly: Federation Francaise des Sports
Equestres. Annuaire Officiel (ISSN 0071-4232)

636.1　　　　　SP　　ISSN 0085-1337
GUIA DE LOS CABALLOS VERIFICADAS EN
ESPANA. 1875. a. 1000 ptas. Sociedad de Fomento
de la Cria Caballar de Espana, 6, Fernanflor,
Madrid, Spain. circ. 2,000.

636.1　　　　　UK
HACKNEY HORSE SOCIETY YEAR BOOK. a. £6.
Hackney Horse Society, 34 Stockton, Nr.
Warminster, Wiltshire, England.

636.1　　　　　UK
HACKNEY STUD BOOK. quadrennial. £15. Hackney
Horse Society, 34 Stockton, Nr. Warminster,
Wiltshire, England.

798.2　　　　　US
HORSE ACTION. 1979. a. $3.95. Rich Publishing,
Inc., Box 555, Temecula, CA 92390. TEL 714-676-
5712. adv. circ. 61,100.

791.8　　　　　US
HORSE & RIDER ALL-WESTERN YEARBOOK.
1973. a. $3.95. ‡ Rich Publishing, Inc., Box 555,
Temecula, CA 92390. TEL 714-676-5712. Ed. Ray
Rich. adv. bk. rev. illus. circ. 75,000.

636.1　　　　　US
HORSE CARE. 1979. a. $3.95. Rich Publishing, Inc.,
41919 Moreno, Temecula, CA 92390. TEL 714-
676-5712. adv.

798.2　　　　　DK　　ISSN 0109-4777
HORSE HOLIDAYS IN W. EUROPE. (Text in
Danish, English, French and German) 1984. a.
Kr.49.95. Active Holiday Guidebooks, Graested,
Denmark. Ed. Janet L. Self. illus. circ. 2,000.

636.1　　　　　US
HORSE INDUSTRY DIRECTORY. 1972. a. $5.
American Horse Council, Inc., 1700 K St, N.W.,
No.300, Washington, DC 20006. TEL 202-296-
4031. Ed. Michael J. Nolan.

636.1　　　　　US
HORSE LOVER'S. 1936. a. $3.95. Rich Publishing,
Inc., Box 555, Temecula, CA 92390. adv. circ. 65,
000.

798　　336　　　US
HORSE OWNERS AND BREEDERS TAX
MANUAL. 1975. a. $90. American Horse Council,
Inc., 1700 K St., N.W., Washington, DC 20006.
circ. 4,300. (looseleaf format; back issues avail.)

798　　　　　UK
HORSE RACING QUIZ BOOK. a. £1.50. Raceform
Ltd., 2 York Rd., London SW11 3PZ, England.

636.1　　　　　US
HORSE WOMEN. 1978. a. $3.95. Rich Publishing,
Inc., 41919 Moreno, Box 555, Temecula, CA
92390. TEL 714-676-5712. Ed. Laurie Gudiero.
adv.

798　　　　　IE
IRISH SHOWJUMPING ANNUAL. 1978. a. Ree
Enterprises, 22 Moore St, Dublin 1, Ireland. illus.

354　　　　　CN　　ISSN 0317-7262
MANITOBA. HORSE RACING COMMISSION.
ANNUAL REPORT. a. free. Horse Racing
Commission, P.O. Box 40, Sta. A, Winnipeg, Man.
R3K 1Z9, Canada. TEL 204-885-7770. stat.

798　　　　　US
NATIONAL CUTTING HORSE ASSOCIATION.
RULE BOOK. 1946. a. $30. National Cutting
Horse Association, Box 12155, Fort Worth, TX
76121. TEL 817-244-6188. Ed. Zack T. Wood, Jr.
circ. 13,500.

798　　　　　FR　　ISSN 0078-7035
OU MONTER A CHEVAL. 1964. a. 55 F. price
varies. ‡ Guides Equestres, 5 rue Alexandre
Cabanel, 75012 Paris, France. Eds. Agnes
Lamoureux, Caroline Elgosi. adv. circ. 8,000.

798.2　　　　　UK
PONY CLUB ANNUAL. a. £1.95. Purnel! Books
(Subsidiary of: Mcdonald & Co. (Publishers) Ltd.)
3rd Fl., Greater London House, Hampstead Rd.,
London NW1 7QX, England. Ed. S. Hook.

798.2　　　　　UK
PONY MAGAZINE ANNUAL. a. £1.75. Purnell
Books (Subsidiary of: Macdonald & Co. (Publishers)
Ltd.) 3rd Fl., Greater London House, Hampstead
Rd., London NW1 7QX, England. Ed. S. Hook.

798　　　　　UK　　ISSN 0081-3761
RACEFORM "HORSES IN TRAINING". 1891. a.
£9. Raceform Ltd., 2 York Road, London SW11
3PZ, England. Ed. L. Bell. adv. circ. 13,000.
　Formerly: Sporting Chronicle "Horses in
Training".

798　　　　　UK　　ISSN 0079-9408
RACEHORSES. 1948. a. £52. Portway Press Ltd.,
Timeform House, Northgate, Halifax, Yorkshire
HX1 1XE, England. Ed. J.D. Newton. adv. circ. 9,
000.

791.8　　　　　SA
RAND SHOW GUIDE; equestrian catalogue and
arena programme. (Text in Afrikaans and English)
a. R.1. Witwatersrand Agricultural Society, Box
31777, Braamfontein, Johannesburg 2000, South
Africa. Ed. J. Kleynhans. adv.

636.1　　　　　UK
REGISTER OF NON-THOROUGHBRED MARES.
1974. a. £10. Weatherby's, Sanders Rd.,
Wellingborough, Northants. NN8 4BX, England.

798.2　　　　　UK
RIDING HANDBOOK. 1982. a. £5.95. Beacon
Publications PLC, York House, Newton Close, Park
Farm, Wellingborough, Northamptonshire NN8
3UW, England. Eds. Linda Burgess, Lesley Eccles.

636.1　　　　　UK
SHETLAND PONY STUD-BOOK SOCIETY
MAGAZINE. 1968. a. £1. D.M. Patterson, Ed. &
Pub., 8 Whinfield Rd., Montrose, Angus, England.
adv. circ. 1,500.

798　　　　　UK
SHIRE HORSE SHOW CATALOGUE. 1897. a. £1.
National Shire Horse Society, East of England
Showground, Peterborough PE2 0XE, England. Ed.
Roy W. Bird. adv. circ. 3,000.

636.1　　　　　UK
SHIRE HORSE STUD BOOK. a. £5. Shire Horse
Society, East of England Showground, Peterborough
PE2 0XE, England.

798　　　　　AT
SOUTH AUSTRALIAN RACEHORSE. 1964. irreg.
Bloodhorse Breeder's Association of Australia,
South Australian Division, Box 1695, G.P.O.
Adelaide, SA 5001, Australia. Ed. P. Duncan.

636.1　　　　　UK
STALLION REVIEW. 1912. a. £8. Thoroughbred
Publishers Ltd., 26 Charing Cross Road, London
WC2H 0DJ, England. adv. illus. circ. 6,000.
(processed)

636.1　　　　　DK　　ISSN 0107-3818
STAMBOG. a. Kr.73.20. (Dansk Varmblod, Dansk
Rideheste Avlsforbund) Landsudvalget for Hesteavl,
Vesterbrogade 6D, 1620 Copenhagen V, Denmark.
illus.
　Formerly: Dansk Sportsheste Avlsforbunds
Stambog.

636.1　　　　　DK　　ISSN 0900-5846
STAMBOG OVER SHETLAND PONYER. a. Kr.65.
Bibliotekscentralen, Telegrafvej 5, DK-2750
Ballerup, Denmark.

798　　　　　AT　　ISSN 0311-8215
STUD AND STABLE. 1971. irreg. Aus.$0.10.
Percival Publishing Co. Pty. Ltd., 862 Elizabeth St.,
Waterloo, NSW 2017, Australia.
　Formerly: Australasian Stud and Stable (ISSN
0310-6403)

636.1　　　　　UK
SUFFOLK STUD BOOK. 1880. a. £10. Suffolk Horse
Society, 6 Church St., Woodbridge, Suffolk,
England. Ed. Philip Ryder-Davies. adv. circ. 350.

798.2　　　　　US
TACK 'N TOGS BOOK; directory for retailers of
supplies for horse and rider. 1971. a. $10. ‡ Miller
Publishing Co., 12400 Whitewater Dr., Ste. 160,
Box 2400, Minnetonka, MN 55343. TEL 612-931-
0211. Ed. Dan DeWeese. adv. charts. stat. tr.lit.
circ. 22,023 (controlled) (reprint service avail. from
UMI)

636.1　　　　　AT　　ISSN 0311-8347
THOROUGHBRED BREEDERS' HANDBOOK;
stallion pedigrees for Australia and New Zealand.
1975. irreg. (3-4/yr.) Aus.$15. Libra Books Pty.
Ltd., GPO Box 10, Hobart, Tas. 7001, Australia.
Ed. B.M. Wicks. circ. 2,000. (back issues avail)

798　　　　　US　　ISSN 0082-4240
THOROUGHBRED RACING ASSOCIATIONS.
DIRECTORY AND RECORD BOOK. 1955. a.
free; limited distribution. ‡ Thoroughbred Racing
Associations, 300 Marcus Ave., Suite 2W4, Lake
Success, NY 11040. Ed. Christopher N. Scherf. circ.
3,000.

798　　　　　US　　ISSN 0083-3509
TROTTING AND PACING GUIDE; official
handbook of harness racing. 1947. a. $7.50. United
States Trotting Association, 750 Michigan Ave,
Columbus, OH 43215. TEL 614-224-2291. Ed. John
Pawlak. index. circ. 7,000.

798　　　　　US
U S E T NEWS. 1956. irreg. (5-6/yr.) membership.
United States Equestrian Team, c/o Bill Landsman
Associates, 17 E. 45th St., New York, NY 10017.
TEL 212-370-4160. Ed. Bill Landsman. circ. 15,000.

798　　　　　US
U S T A SIRES AND DAMS; the register. 1948. a.
$60. United States Trotting Association, 750
Michigan Ave, Columbus, OH 43215. TEL 614-
224-2291. Ed. David Carr. index. circ. 9,000.
　Formerly: Sires and Dams (ISSN 0083-3495)

798　　　　　US　　ISSN 0083-3517
U S T A YEAR BOOK. 1939. a. $10. United States
Trotting Association, 750 Michigan Ave, Columbus,
OH 43215. TEL 614-224-2291. Ed. David Carr.
index. circ. 8,000.

798　　　　　UK
WELSH PONY AND COB SOCIETY JOURNAL.
1962. a. membership. Welsh Pony and Cob Society,
c/o T.E. Roberts, Ed., 6 Chalybeate St.,
Aberystwyth, Dyfed, Wales. adv. circ. 6,000.

SPORTS AND GAMES — Outdoor Life

796.5　910.202　　　US
A A A CAMPBOOKS. a. membership. American
Automobile Association, 8111 Gatehouse Rd., Falls
Church, VA 22047. adv. circ. 3,501,300.

796.5　910　　　GW
A D A C - CAMPINGFUEHRER. BAND 1:
SUEDEUROPA. 1951. a. DM.19.80. ADAC Verlag
GmbH, Am Westpark 8, D-8000 Munich 70,
Postfach 70 01 26, W. Germany (B.R.D.) Ed. H.
Nitschke. adv. circ. 240,000.
　Supersedes in part: Internationaler
Campingfuehrer (ISSN 0074-9753)

796.5　910　　　GW
A D A C - CAMPINGFUEHRER. BAND 2:
DEUTSCHLAND, MITTELEUROPA,
NORDEUROPA. 1952. a. DM.19.80. ADAC
Verlag GmbH, Am Westpark 8, 8 Munich 70,
Postfach 70 01 26, West Germany (B.R.D.) adv.
circ. 60,000.
　Formerly: A D A C - Campingfuehrer. Band 2:
Deutschland, Mittel- und Nordeuropa.

SPORTS AND GAMES — OUTDOOR LIFE

796.52   US   ISSN 0065-082X
ACCIDENTS IN NORTH AMERICAN MOUNTAINEERING. 1948. a. $4. American Alpine Club, 113 E. 90 St., New York, NY 10128. TEL 212-722-1628. Ed. John E. Williamson. circ. 8,000. (reprint service avail. from UMI)
    Formerly: Accidents in American Mountaineering.

799.1   IT
AGEVOLAZIONI E VANTAGGI PER I PESCATORI FEDERATI. a. Federazione Italiana Pesca Sportiva, Viale Tiziano 70, Rome, Italy. Ed. Claudio Blasi. adv. circ. 800,000.

ALAN ROGERS' GOOD CAMPS GUIDE FOR FRANCE. see *TRAVEL AND TOURISM*

ALAN ROGERS' SELECTED SITES FOR CARAVANNING AND CAMPING IN EUROPE. see *TRAVEL AND TOURISM*

354.9   US   ISSN 0362-6962
ALASKA. DIVISION OF GAME. ANNUAL REPORT OF SURVEY - INVENTORY ACTIVITIES. 1970. a. Department of Fish and Game, Game Division, Box 3-2000, Juneau, AK 99802. TEL 907-465-4190. Ed. Barbara Townsend. illus. circ. 350. Key Title: Annual Report of Survey - Inventory Activities.

799   CN   ISSN 0318-4943
ALBERTA FISHING GUIDE. 1972. a. Can.$3.95. Barry Mitchell Publications Ltd., 3728-44 Ave., Red Deer, Alta. T4N 3H5, Canada. Ed. Ann Mitchell. adv. illus. circ. 30,000.

796.5   IT
ALMANACCO ROULOTTE. 1977. a. Edigamma s.r.l., Piazza dei Sanniti 9, 00185 Rome, Italy. Ed. Renato Circi.

799.31   US   ISSN 0065-6747
AMATEUR TRAPSHOOTING ASSOCIATION. OFFICIAL TRAPSHOOTING RULES. 1923. a. membership. Amateur Trapshooting Association, 601 W. National Rd., Vandalia, OH 45377-0458. TEL 513-898-4638. index. circ. 75,000.

796.52   US   ISSN 0065-6925
AMERICAN ALPINE JOURNAL. 1929. a. $14. American Alpine Club, 113 E. 90 St., New York, NY 10128. TEL 212-722-1628. Ed. H. Adams Carter. bk. rev. index. circ. 5,000. (also avail. in microform from UMI; reprint service avail. from UMI) Indexed: GeoRef.

799.1   UK
ANGLERS MAIL ANNUAL. 1975. a. £3.25. I P C Magazines Ltd., Fleetway Annuals, Kings Reach Tower, Stamford St., London SE1, England. Ed. J. Ingham. circ. 30,000.

799.1   UK
ANGLING GUIDE. 1970. irreg. £0.70. Department of Agriculture, Press Office, Upper Newtownards Rd., Belfast BT4 3SB, N. Ireland. adv. circ. 12,000.

796.42   AT
ANNUAL ALMANAC OF RECORDS AND RESULTS. 1958. a. Aus.$3. Australian Athletic Union, P.O. Box 254, Moonee Ponds, Vic. 3039, Australia. adv. circ. 4,000.

796.93   UK
ARMY SKI ASSOCIATION. YEAR BOOK. a. Combined Service Publications Ltd., Box 4, Farnborough, Hants, GU14 7LR, England. adv.

796   US
ASSOCIATION OF INDEPENDENT CAMPS. BUYERS GUIDE AND CAMP DIRECTORY. 1959. a. $7.50. (Association of Independent Camps) Camp Consulting Services, Ltd., 14 Wesley Court, Huntington, NY 11743. Ed. Joanna W. Howe. adv. circ. 3,000.
    Formerly: Association of Private Camps. Buyers Guide and Camp Directory (ISSN 0519-1505)

796.5 296   US
ASSOCIATION OF JEWISH SPONSORED CAMPS. CAMP DIRECTORY. a. Association of Jewish Sponsored Camps, 130 E. 59th St., New York, NY 10022. TEL 212-751-0477. circ. 100.

796.9   UK
AUDI/DAILY MAIL SKIER'S HOLIDAY GUIDE. 1971. a. £9.95. Ocean Publications Ltd., 34 Buckingham Palace Rd., London SW1W 0RE, England. Ed. David Ross. adv. illus. circ. 6,000.
    Former titles: Daily Mail Skier's Holiday Guide (ISSN 0309-5134); Peter Stuyvesant Travel Ski Guide.

796   AT
AUSTRALIAN LADIES GOLF UNION. OFFICIAL YEARBOOK. 1932. a. Aus.$3.50. Australian Ladies Golf Union, Mrs. K. D. Brown, Executive Director, 22 McKay Rd., Rowville, Vic. 3178, Australia. Ed. Dorothy Brown. adv. circ. 16,000.

796.93   AT   ISSN 0084-7593
AUSTRALIAN SKI YEARBOOK. 1928. a. Aus.$4.50 per no. Australian Ski Publications, 31 Coventry St., South Melbourne, Vic. 3205, Australia. Ed. Barry White. adv. bk. rev. circ. 15,000.

797   FR
AVIRON. 1886. irreg. (10-12/yr.) 140 F. Federation Francaise des Societes d'Aviron, 7 rue Lafayette, 75009 Paris, France. Ed. J. Rodenfuser. adv. illus. circ. 5,000. Indexed: Sportsearch.

799.1   US
B A S S FISHING GUIDE. 1974. a. $1.95 per no. (Bass Anglers Sportsman Society) B A S S Publications, Box 17900, One Bell Rd., Montgomery, AL 36141. Ed. Bob Cobb. circ. 125,000.

799.1   US
B A S S MASTER FISHING ANNUAL. 1973. a. $1.95 per no. (Bass Anglers Sportsman Society) B A S S Publications, Box 17900, One Bell Rd., Montgomery, AL 36141. Ed. Bob Cobb. circ. 125,000.

796   UK
B F S S REFERENCE BOOK. 1978. a. £8. British Field Sports Society, 59 Kennington Rd., London SE1 7PZ, England. Ed. Charles Roberts. adv. bk. rev. illus. circ. 60,000.
    Formerly: British Field Sports Society. Annual Journal.

799.2   UK   ISSN 0067-2947
BAILY'S HUNTING DIRECTORY. 1897. a. £18. J.A. Allen & Co. Ltd., 1 Lower Grosvenor Place, Buckingham Palace Road, London, SW1W OEL, England. Ed. Christine Berry. adv. bk. rev. circ. 1,750.

799.1   US
BASS AND FRESHWATER FISHING. 1979. a. $2.70. Times Mirror Magazines, Inc., 380 Madison Ave., New York, NY 10017. TEL 212-687-3000. Ed. Vin T. Sparano. circ. 150,000. (reprint service avail. from UMI)
    Former titles: Southern Fishing by Outdoor Life & Outdoor Life's Guide to Fishing the South.

796.5   GW   ISSN 0179-1419
BERG (YEAR); Alpenvereins-Jahrbuch. 1869. a. DM.19.80. Deutscher Alpenverein, Praterinsel 5, 8000 Munich 22, W. Germany (B.R.D.) (Co-sponsor: Oesterreichischer Alpenverein) index. Indexed: GeoRef.

BIRD WATCH. see *BIOLOGY — Ornithology*

799.2   US
BOW & ARROW MAGAZINE'S BOWHUNTER'S ANNUAL. Spine title: Bowhunter's Annual. 1975. a. $2.95. Gallant-Charger Publishing Company, Inc., 34249 Camino Capistrano, Box HH, Capistrano Beach, CA 92624. TEL 714-493-2101. Ed. Jack Lewis. adv. bk. rev. circ. 104,000.

796.522   CN   ISSN 0045-2998
BRITISH COLUMBIA MOUNTAINEER. 1917. biennial. Can.$3. British Columbia Mountaineering Club, Box 2674, Vancouver, B.C. V6B 3W8, Canada. TEL 604-687-3333. Ed. M.C. Feller. adv. bk. rev. circ. 500.

381.45   US   ISSN 0362-6180
BUYERS' GUIDE FOR THE MASS ENTERTAINMENT INDUSTRY. a. $15. Billboard Publications, Inc., Amusement Business Division, Box 24970, Nashville, TN 37202 TEL 615-748-8100. (Or 2160 Patterson St., Cincinnati, OH 45214) illus.
    Formerly: Amusement Equipment Buyers Guide; Incorporating: Facility Manager's Buyer's Guide & A B's Guide to Souvenirs and Novelties.

CALIFORNIA - NEVADA CAMPBOOK. see *TRAVEL AND TOURISM*

796.5 670   US
CAMP DIRECTORS PURCHASING GUIDE. 1964. a. $8.95. Klevens Publications, Inc., 7600 Ave. V, Littlerock, CA 93543. TEL 805-944-4111. Ed. John Keller. adv. bk. rev. circ. 14,736. (back issues avail.)

796.5   UK
CAMPING AND CARAVANNING IN BRITAIN. a. £5.95 to non-members. Automobile Association, Fanum House, Basingstoke, Hants RG21 2EA, England. adv.
    Formerly: Camping and Caravanning U.K.

CAMPING CARAVANNING AND SPORTS EQUIPMENT TRADES DIRECTORY. see *BUSINESS AND ECONOMICS — Trade And Industrial Directories*

796.54   UK
CAMPING CLUB HANDBOOK AND SITES LIST; camping sites yearbook. 1920. biennial. membership. Camping and Caravanning Club, 11 Lower Grosvenor Place, London SW1W 0EY, England. Ed. Valerie Kelly. circ. 90,000.
    Formerly: Camping Club of Great Britain and Ireland. Year Book with List of Camp Sites (ISSN 0068-6956)

796.5 910.202   IT
CAMPITUR: CAMPING, CARAVANING, VILLAGGI TURISTICI. 1973. a. L.4000. C P M Editrice s.a.s., Via Carducci 21, 20123 Milan, Italy. Ed. Ernesto Cavallini. adv. circ. 30,000.

796.52   CN   ISSN 0068-8207
CANADIAN ALPINE JOURNAL. 1907. a. price varies. Alpine Club of Canada, P.O. Box 91880, West Vancouver, BC V7V 4S4, Canada. TEL 403-762-4481. Ed. Moira Irvine. bk. rev. index; cum.index: 1907-1966. circ. 4,000. Indexed: GeoRef. Sportsearch.

796.5   AT
CARAVAN CAMPING DIRECTORY. a. membership. National Roads and Motorists Association, 151 Clarence T., Sydney, N.S.W. 2000, Australia.

796.5   SA
CARAVAN PARK, CAMPING & BACKPACKING GUIDE TO SOUTHERN AFRICAN/ WOONWAPARK, KAMPER AND VOETSLAANGIDS VIR SUIDER-AFRIKA. (Text in Afrikaans and English) a. Erudita Publications (Pty) Ltd., Cnr. 11th Ave. & Main Rd., P.O. Box 29159, Melville, Johannesburg 2109, South Africa.

CATALOGUE OF CANADIAN RECREATION AND LEISURE RESEARCH. see *TRAVEL AND TOURISM*

711   UK
CONGRESS IN PARK AND RECREATION ADMINISTRATION. REPORTS. triennial. International Federation of Park and Recreation Administration, c/o J.S. Thornton, Sec. Gen., The Grotto, Lower Basildon, Reading, Berkshire RG8 9NE, England.
    Formerly: World Congress in Public Park Administration. Reports (ISSN 0510-8225)

333.7   US   ISSN 0092-5764
CONNECTICUT WALK BOOK. 1937. irreg. $9.95. Connecticut Forest and Park Association, Meriden Rd., Rt. 66, Middletown, CT 06457. TEL 203-289-3637. illus.

799.2   US   ISSN 0092-8216
CORD SPORTFACTS: HUNTING. a. $2.50. Cord Communications Corp., 130 W. 42nd St., New York, NY 10036. TEL 212-840-0660. adv. illus. circ. 100,000.

D C C - CARAVAN MODELLFUEHRER. (Deutscher Camping Club e.V.) see *TRANSPORTATION — Automobiles*

D C C - TOURISTIK SERVICE. (Deutscher Camping Club e.V.) see *TRAVEL AND TOURISM*

779.2   US
DEER AND BIG GAME. 1977. a. $2.75. Times Mirror Magazines, Inc., 380 Madison Ave., New York, NY 10017. TEL 212-687-3000. Ed. Vin T. Sparano. adv. illus. circ. 150,000. (reprint service avail. from UMI)
Former titles: Midwest Fishing by Outdoor Life & Outdoor Life's Guide to Fishing the Midwest.

799.2   US
DEER HUNTING (LOS ANGELES) Cover title: Petersen's Complete Guide to Deer Hunting. 1977. a. Petersen Publishing Co., 8490 Sunset Blvd., Los Angeles, CA 90069. TEL 213-854-2222.

796.54   CN   ISSN 0316-1226
DIRECTORY OF ACCREDITED CAMPS.* (Text in English and French) 1973. a. free. Quebec Camping Association, 8775 Lacordaire, Montreal, Que. W1R 2A9, Canada.

796.5 296   US
DIRECTORY OF JEWISH RESIDENT SUMMER CAMPS. irreg. J W B, 15 E. 26th St., New York, NY 10010. TEL 212-532-4949.

796.93   UK   ISSN 0070-718X
DOWNHILL ONLY JOURNAL. 1936. a. free to members. Downhill Only Club, c/o D.F. Ryan, Brigadir, Lodwick, Monxton, Hants SP11 8AW, England. adv. bk. rev. index. circ. 1,700.

DUCK STAMP DATA. see *PHILATELY*

EASTERN CANADA CAMPBOOK. see *TRAVEL AND TOURISM*

796.93 330   US   ISSN 0147-4243
ECONOMIC ANALYSIS OF NORTH AMERICAN SKI AREAS. Variant title: N S A A Economic Analysis of North American Ski Areas. 1971. a. $50. (National Skiing Areas Association, Business Research Division) University of Colorado, Graduate School of Business Administration, Boulder, CO 80309. TEL 303-492-8227.
Supersedes (1971): N S A A Economics of the Skiing Industry.

796.5   GW   ISSN 0071-2272
EUROPA CAMPING UND CARAVANING. INTERNATIONALER FUEHRER. (Text in English, French and German) 1959. a. DM.18. Drei Brunnen Verlag, Postfach 1124, 7000 Stuttgart 1, W. Germany (B.R.D.) Ed. Heinz Dieter Schmoll.

EXPLORE MINNESOTA CAMPGROUNDS. see *TRAVEL AND TOURISM*

EXPLORE MINNESOTA CANOEING, BACKPACKING & HIKING. see *TRAVEL AND TOURISM*

EXPLORE MINNESOTA ON SKIS. see *TRAVEL AND TOURISM*

796   AT
EXTRA COVER. 1971. a. Aus.$0.20. (Australian Cricket Society) Thomas W. Williams & Associates Pty. Ltd., 254 George St., Sydney, NSW 2000, Australia.

799.17   US   ISSN 0163-5468
FIELD & STREAM BASS FISHING ANNUAL. Short title: Bass Fishing. 1977. a. $2.50 newsstand sales only. C B S Magazines, Consumer Publishing Group, 1515 Broadway, New York, NY 10036. TEL 212-719-6000. Ed. Glenn Sapir. circ. 200,000.

799   US
FIELD AND STREAM DEER HUNTER'S GUIDE ANNUAL. Short title: Deer Hunting. 1978. a. $2.50 newsstand sales only. C B S Magazines, Consumer Publishing Group, 1515 Broadway, New York, NY 10036. TEL 212-719-6000. Ed. Glenn Sapir. circ. 250,000.
Formerly: Field and Stream Deer Hunting Annual.

799.1   US   ISSN 0362-6385
FIELD & STREAM FISHING ANNUAL. Short title: Fishing. 1976. a. $2.50 newstand sales only. C B S Magazines, Consumer Publishing Group, 1515 Broadway, New York, NY 10036. TEL 212-719-6000. Ed. Glenn Sapir. illus. circ. 250,000.

799.2   US   ISSN 0361-3011
FIELD & STREAM HUNTING ANNUAL. Short title: Hunting Annual. 1975. a. $2.50 newsstand sales only. C B S Magazines, Consumer Publishing Group, 1515 Broadway, New York, NY 10036. TEL 212-719-6000. Ed. Glenn Sapir. illus. circ. 250, 000.

799.1   US
FISHERIES AND WILDLIFE RESEARCH. 1958. a. U.S. Fish and Wildlife Service, Washington, DC 20240 TEL 303-226-9403. (Orders to: Supt. Doc., Washington, DC 20402) illus.
Former titles: Sport Fishery and Wildlife Research (ISSN 0362-0700); U.S. Fish and Wildlife Service. Progress in Sport Fishery Research (ISSN 0079-6794)

799.1   US
FISHING AND BOATING ILLUSTRATED. a. $3.50. Gallant Publishing Co., Inc., 34249 Camino Capistrano, Capistrano Beach, CA 92624. TEL 714-493-2101. illus. (reprint service avail.)
Formerly: Bob Zwirz' Fishing Annual (ISSN 0363-5538)

799.1   UK   ISSN 0261-7943
FISHING HANDBOOK. 1981. a. £5.95. Beacon Publications PLC, York House, Newton Close, Park Farm, Wellingborough, Northamptonshire NN8 3UW, England. Ed. Sean Greaves.

799.1   US   ISSN 0164-0941
FISHING IN MARYLAND; with Delaware and Virginia coverage. 1953. a. $5.95. Fishing in Maryland, Inc., Box 201, Phoenix, MD 21131. TEL 301-243-3413. illus.
Supersedes in part: Fishing in the Mid-Atlantic; Fishing in Maryland and Virginia (ISSN 0363-8898)

799.1   US
FISHING IN NEW JERSEY. irreg. Fishing in Maryland, Inc., 10 Shanney Brook Ct., Box 201, Phoenix, MD 21131. TEL 301-243-3413.
Supersedes in part: Fishing in the Mid-Atlantic (ISSN 0363-552X)

796.5   GW   ISSN 0071-7711
FORSCHUNGSSTELLE FUER JAGDKUNDE UND WILDSCHADENVERHUETUNG. SCHRIFTENREIHE. 1960. irreg., no. 8, 1978. price varies. Verlag Paul Parey (Hamburg), Spitalerstr. 12, 2000 Hamburg 1, W. Germany (B.R.D) Ed.Bd. bibl. illus. index. (reprint service avail. from ISI)

FRANCE-SPORTS. see *SPORTS AND GAMES*

796.93   AU
FUER DIE SICHERHEIT IM BERGLAND. 1972. a. S.150. Oesterreichisches Kuratorium fuer Alpine Sicherheit, Prinz Eugen Str. 12, A-1040 Vienna, Austria. Ed. Eduard Rabofsky. circ. 3,000.

070.5 310   CN   ISSN 0318-9422
GOLD BOOK OF SNOWMOBILE DATA AND USED PRICES. a. Can.$9.95. Sanford Evans Communications Ltd., 1077 St. James St., Winnipeg, Man. R3C 3B1, Canada. TEL 204-775-0201. Ed. Gary Henry.

GOLDEN LIST OF BEACHES; indicates which beaches are likely to be polluted and which are believed to be free from sewage pollution. see *ENVIRONMENTAL STUDIES*

GOOD CAMPS GUIDE. see *TRAVEL AND TOURISM*

641.9477   US
GREAT LAKES CAMPBOOK. a. membership. American Automobile Association, 8111 Gatehouse Rd., Falls Church, VA 22047. TEL 703-222-6000. illus. circ. 302,000.
Formerly (until 1980): Great Lakes Camping.

GUIA QUATRO RODAS. CAMPING. see *TRAVEL AND TOURISM*

796 914.5   IT   ISSN 0072-792X
GUIDA CAMPING D'ITALIA. 1958. a. L.11000. Federazione Italiana del Campeggio e del Caravanning, Casella Postale 23, 50041 Calenzano (Florence), Italy. adv.

796   CN   ISSN 0705-8314
GUIDE DU CAMPING. 1961. a. Can.$1($2) per no. Association des Terrains de Camping du Quebec, 8775 Bd. Lacordaire, Ville St. Leonard, Que. H1R 2A9, Canada. TEL 514-323-1604. Dir. Huguette Brunet-Chalifoux. illus.
Formerly: Guide Camping (ISSN 0383-2368)

796.5   FR
GUIDE OFFICIEL CAMPING - CARAVANING. a. 142 F. (Federation Francaise de Camping et de Caravaning) Ediregie, B.P. 379, 75869 Paris Cedex 18, France. adv. circ. 135,000.

GUIDE TO CARAVAN AND CAMPING HOLIDAYS. see *TRAVEL AND TOURISM*

799.2   US
GUIDE TO HUNTING IN FLORIDA. 1979. a. $11.95. Florida Wildlife Federation, Box 15917, W. Palm Beach, FL 33416. TEL 305-439-3499. Ed. Diane Geans. adv. circ. 5,000.

799.2   US
GUN WORLD ANNUAL. 1973. a. $3.50. Gallant-Charger Publishing, Inc., 34249 Camino Capistrano, Capistrano Beach, CA 92624. TEL 714-493-2101. Ed. Jack Lewis. adv. bk. rev. illus. circ. 130,000. (also avail. in microfilm from UMI)
Formerly: Gun World Hunting Guide (ISSN 0362-4749)

919.4 796.74   AT   ISSN 0085-1477
HERALD CARAVANNING GUIDE. 1931. a. Aus.$1 ea. Herald Travel Bureau, Newspaper House, 247 Collins St., Melbourne, Vic. 3000, Australia. Ed. D. H. Day.

796.552   II
HIMALAYAN JOURNAL. (Text in English) 1928. a. Rs.100. (Himalayan Club) Oxford University Press, Oxford House, Apollo Bunder, Box 31, Bombay 400001, India. Ed. Soli S. Mehta. adv. bk. rev. charts. illus. index. circ. 1,500. (tabloid format) Indexed: Helminthol.Abstr.

799.2   GW
HIRSCHMANNBRIEF. 1961. a. $5. Verein Hirschmann e.V., Schriftfuehrer, Dr. Wolf-Eberhard Barth, 3424 Oderhaus Post St. Andreasberg, W. Germany (B.R.D.) circ. 550.

796.5   NE
HOLLAND CAMPING. 1965. a. fl.12.50. Holland Post, Postbus 335, 6800 AH Arnhem, Netherlands. adv. circ. 15,000.
Formerly: Camping Benelux.

HOSTELING HOLIDAYS. see *TRAVEL AND TOURISM*

799.2   US
HUNTING ANNUAL. 1980. a. $6.95. Petersen Publishing Co., 8490 Sunset Blvd., Los Angeles, CA 90069. TEL 213-854-2222. adv. circ. 110,000.

799.2   US
HUNTING GUNS BY OUTDOOR LIFE & JIM CARMICHEL. 1984. a. $2.75. Times Mirror Magazines, Inc., 380 Madison Ave., New York, NY 10017. TEL 212-687-3000. Ed. Vin T. Sparano. adv.

799.1   US
I W F A YEARBOOK. 1955. a. membership. International Women's Fishing Association, Drawer 3125, Palm Beach, FL 33480. Ed. Scotty Homes. adv. circ. 400.

INTERNATIONAL ATHLETICS GUIDE. see *SPORTS AND GAMES*

796.5   GW   ISSN 0074-7122
INTERNATIONAL NATURIST GUIDE/ INTERNATIONALER FKK-REISEFUEHRER/ GUIDE NATURISTE INTERNATIONALE. a. DM.6.80. (International Naturist Federation) Richard Danehl's Verlag, Postfach 500344, 2000 Hamburg 50, W. Germany (B.R.D.) adv.

797　　　　　　AT
IT. 1968. irreg. Aus.$0.10 per no. Canberra Bushwalking Club, Box 160, Canberra City, A.C.T. 2601, Australia.

799.2　　　　　　UK
LAKESCENE - GUIDE TO HUNTING IN LAKELAND. 1975. a. £2.50. Border Press Agency Ltd., 12 Lonsdale St., Carlisle, Cumbria CA1 1DD, England. Ed. John Barker. adv.

333.7　　　　　　US
LAND AND WATER CONSERVATION FUND GRANTS MANUAL. 1965. irreg. $45. U.S. National Park Service, U.S. Department of the Interior, Washington, DC 20240 TEL 202-343-1100. (Orders to: Supt. of Documents, Washington. DC 20402) (looseleaf format)
　　Formerly: U.S. Bureau of Outdoor Recreation. Recreation Grants-in-Aid Manual.

796.5　　　　　　CN
LEISUREWHEELS CAMPGROUND DIRECTORY. 1971. a. Can.$2.75. Tall Taylor Publishing Ltd., Box 40, Irricana, Alta. T0M 1B0, Canada. TEL 403-935-4688. adv. circ. 10,000.

799.2　891.87　641.5　CS　ISSN 0541-8836
MAGAZIN POLOVNIKA. a. 25 Kcs. Priroda, Krizkova 9, 815 34 Bratislava, Czechoslovakia. illus.

MIDEASTERN CAMPBOOK. see TRAVEL AND TOURISM

796.552　　　　　　SA
MOUNTAIN CLUB OF SOUTH AFRICA. JOURNAL. (Text in Afrikaans and English) 1894. a. R.7.50. Mountain Club of South Africa, 97 Hatfield St., Cape Town 8001, South Africa. Ed. P.D. Attenborough. adv. bk. rev. circ. 2,500.

796.42　　　　US　ISSN 0736-7783
N C A A MEN'S & WOMEN'S CROSS COUNTRY AND TRACK & FIELD RULES. 1922. a. $3. National Collegiate Athletic Association, Box 1906, Mission, KS 66201. TEL 913-384-3220. circ. 10,000.
　　Formerly: Official National Collegiate Athletic Association Track and Field Guide (ISSN 0196-9358)

796.93　　　　　　US
N C A A MEN'S AND WOMEN'S SKIING RULES. 1963. a. $4. National Collegiate Athletic Association, Box 1906, Mission, KS 66202. TEL 913-384-3220. Ed. Mary Ellen Cloninger. circ. 1,000.
　　Former titles: N C A A Skiing Rules; Until 1980: Official National Collegiate Athletic Association Skiing Rules; National Collegiate Athletic Association. Official Skiing Rules (ISSN 0469-8592)

799.31　　　　US　ISSN 0077-5738
NATIONAL SKEET SHOOTING ASSOCIATION. RECORDS ANNUAL. 1947. a. $9. National Skeet Shooting Association, Box 680007, San Antonio, TX 78268. TEL 512-688-3371. Ed. Phil Murray. adv. index. circ. 18,000.

354　　　　　　NE
NETHERLANDS. MINISTERIE VAN CULTUUR, RECREATIE EN MAATSCHAPPELIJK WERK. OPENLUCHTRECREATIE. (Summaries in English and French) irreg. Ministerie van Landbouw en Visserij Hoofddirectie Natuurbehoud en Openluchtrecreatie, Postbus 20401, 2500 EK The Hague, Netherlands. illus.

796.93　　　　　　US
NEW ENGLAND SKIERS' GUIDE.* 1983. a. $2.95 per no. New England Skier's Guide, Inc., 2 Bentley Ave., Poultney, VT 05764. TEL 802-287-9090. Ed. Gary Black, Jr. adv. circ. 100,000.

688.7　　　　US　ISSN 0163-5905
NORDIC.* a. (Nordic Skiing) Nordic Skico, 30 Sturgis Rd., Bronxville, NY 10708-5016.

NORSK FISKARALMANAKK. see FISH AND FISHERIES

NORTH CENTRAL CAMPBOOK. see TRAVEL AND TOURISM

NORTHWESTERN CAMPBOOK; including location maps. see TRAVEL AND TOURISM

796　　　　AU　ISSN 0029-8840
OESTERREICHISCHER ALPENVEREIN. AKADEMISCHE SEKTION GRAZ. MITTEILUNGEN. 1892. a. membership. Oesterreichischer Alpenverein, Akademische Sektion Graz, Rechbauerstr. 12, A-8010 Graz, Austria. Eds. G. Zellinger. adv. bk. rev. illus. circ. 1,200.

799.06　　　　CN　ISSN 0700-9909
OUTDOOR CREST. 1975. irreg. free. Toronto Sportsmen's Association, 17 Mill St., Willowdale, Ont. M2P 1B3, Canada. TEL 416-233-3297. Ed. Peter Edwards. illus. circ. 1,200.
　　Formerly: Outdoor Crest Newsletter (ISSN 0700-9895)

796.54　　　　　　US
PARENTS' GUIDE TO ACCREDITED CAMPS. 1952. a. $8.95 or with subscr. to Camping Magazine. ‡ American Camping Association, Bradford Woods, Martinsville, IN 46151. TEL 317-342-8456. Ed. Glenn T. Job. index. circ. 28,000.
　　Formed by the merger of: Parents' Guide to Accredited Camps. West Edition & Parents' Guide to Accredited Camps. South Edition & Parents' Guide to Accredited Camps. Northeast Edition & Parents' Guide to Accredited Camps. Midwest Edition.

797.173　914.2　　UK
PETER STUYVESENT TRAVEL WATERSKI GUIDE. 1983. a. £5.95. Ocean Publications Ltd., 34 Buckingham Palace Rd., London SW1W 0RE, England. Ed. Melanie Wood. adv.

797.172　914.2　　UK
PETER STUYVESENT TRAVEL WINDSURF GUIDE. 1982. a. £5.95. Ocean Publications Ltd., 34 Buckingham Palace Rd., London SW1W 0RE, England. Ed. Melanie Wood. adv.

910.2　　　　　　UK
PRACTICAL CAMPER'S SITES GUIDE. 1966. a. £3. Haymarket Publishing Ltd., 38-42 Hampton Rd., Teddington, Middx. TW11 0JE, England.
　　Formerly: Camping Sites in Britain and France (ISSN 0068-6980)

PSYCHOLOGY AND SOCIOLOGY OF SPORT; current selected research. see PSYCHOLOGY

796.54　　　　US　ISSN 0733-8309
RAND MCNALLY CAMPGROUND AND TRAILER PARK GUIDE. EASTERN. a. Rand McNally & Co., 8255 N. Central Park, Box 728, Skokie, IL 60076. TEL 312-673-9100.
　　Supersedes in part: Rand McNally Campground and Trailer Park Guide (ISSN 0079-9610); Rand McNally Guidebook to Campgrounds & Rand McNally Travel Trailer Guide (ISSN 0079-9645)

796.5　　　　US　ISSN 0079-9629
RAND MCNALLY NATIONAL PARK GUIDE. a. Rand McNally & Co., 8255 N. Central Park, Box 728, Skokie, IL 60076. Ed. Michael Frome.

790　　　　　　US
RECREATION AND OUTDOOR LIFE DIRECTORY; a guide to national and international organizations. 1979. irreg., 2nd edt., 1983. $140. Gale Research Company, Book Tower, Detroit, MI 48226. TEL 313-961-2242. Ed. Paul Wasserman.

796.522　　　AT　ISSN 0816-2425
ROCK. 1978-1980; Resumed in 1983. a. Aus.$4.25. Wild Publications Pty. Ltd., P.O. Box 415, Prahran, Vic. 3181, Australia. Ed. Chris Baxter. adv. circ. 2,750.

799.1　　　　　　UK
SCOTLAND FOR FISHING. 1970. a. £1.10. Pastime Publications Ltd., 15 Dublin Street Lane South, Edinburgh EH1 3PX, Scotland. adv.

796.522　　　UK　ISSN 0080-813X
SCOTTISH MOUNTAINEERING CLUB. JOURNAL.* 1890. a. £1.30. (Scottish Mountaineering Club) West Col Productions, Goring-on-Thames, Reading, Berks RG8 9AA, England. Ed. W.D. Brooker. adv. bk. rev.

799.2　　　　　　UK
SHOOTING HANDBOOK. 1980. a. $9.95. Beacon Publications PLC, York House, Newton Close, Park Farm, Wellingborough, Northamptonshire NN8 3UW, England. Ed. John Humphreys. adv.

796.93　914.2　　　UK
SKI HOLIDAYS SCOTLAND. 1983. a. free. Scottish Tourist Board, 23 Ravelston Terrace, Edinburgh EH4 3EU, Scotland. circ. 40,000.

796.93　　　　US　ISSN 0161-1054
SKI X-C. (Cross-country) 1978. a. $3.95. C B S Magazines, Outdoor Adventure Group, 1515 Broadway, New York, NY 10036. TEL 212-719-6000. adv. circ. 160,000.

796.93　　　　US　ISSN 0730-2150
SKIERS DIRECTORY. 1971. a. $3.95. C B S Magazines, Skiing Magazine Department, 1515 Broadway, New York, NY 10036. TEL 212-503-3920. Ed. William Grout. adv.

796.95　　　　　　CN
SNOWMOBILE SPORTS ANNUAL. 1974. a. Leisure Sports Publications, 1255 Yonge St., Toronto, Ont. M4T 1W6, Canada. TEL 416-922-7197. Ed. Reg Fife. adv. illus. Indexed: Sportsearch.

SOUTH CENTRAL CAMPBOOK. see TRAVEL AND TOURISM

799　　　　　　US
SOUTHEASTERN ASSOCIATION OF FISH AND WILDLIFE AGENCIES. PROCEEDINGS. 1947. a. $8. Southeastern Association of Fish and Wildlife Agencies, c/o Joe L. Herring, Sec.-Treas., Box 15570, Baton Rouge, LA 70895. cum.index: vols. 1-15 (1947-61) (back issues avail.) Indexed: Biol.Abstr.
　　Formerly: Southeastern Association of Game and Fish Commissioners. Proceedings of the Annual Conference (ISSN 0081-2943)

SOUTHEASTERN CAMPBOOK. see TRAVEL AND TOURISM

799　　　　US　ISSN 0081-2986
SOUTHERN ANGLER'S AND HUNTER'S GUIDE. 1961. a. $6.95. Southern Angler's Guide Publications, Box 2188, Hot Springs, AR 71914. TEL 501-623-8437. Ed. Don J. Fuelsch. adv. bk. rev. circ. 30,000.

SOUTHWESTERN CAMPBOOK. see TRAVEL AND TOURISM

799.1　　　　　　SW
SPORTFISKAREN. a. Kr.135. Sveriges Sportfiske och Fiskevaardsfoerbund, Box 11501, 100 61 Stockholm 14, Sweden. Ed. Jerry Pettersson. adv. bk. rev. illus. circ. 44,000.
　　Former titles: Svenskt Fiske; Fiske.

799.1　　　　US　ISSN 0742-0609
SPORTS AFIELD BASS. 1977. a. $2.50. Hearst Magazines, Sports Afield, 250 W. 55th St., New York, NY 10019. TEL 212-262-8830. Ed. Fred Kesting. adv. (also avail. in microfiche from BLH)

799.2　　　　US　ISSN 0160-1830
SPORTS AFIELD DEER. a. $2.50. Hearst Magazines, Sports Afield, 250 W. 55th St., New York, NY 10019. TEL 212-262-8830. Ed. Fred Kesting. circ. 250,000. (also avail. in microfiche from BLH)

799.1　　　　US　ISSN 0742-0587
SPORTS AFIELD FISHING. 1938. a. $2.50. Hearst Magazines, Sports Afield, 250 W. 55th St., New York, NY 10019. TEL 212-262-8830. Ed. Fred Kesting. (also avail. in microfiche from BLH)
　　Formerly: Sports Afield Fishing Annual (ISSN 0742-0587)

799.1　　　　US　ISSN 0742-0595
SPORTS AFIELD FISHING SECRETS. 1977. a. $2.50. Hearst Magazines, Sports Afield, 250 W. 55th St., New York, NY 10019. TEL 212-262-8830. Ed. Fred Kesting. adv. (also avail. in microfiche from BLH)

799.2　　　　US　ISSN 0276-8895
SPORTS AFIELD HUNTING ANNUAL. 1977. a. $2.50. Hearst Magazines, Sports Afield, 250 W. 55th St., New York, NY 10019. TEL 212-262-8830. Ed. Fred Kesting. adv.

799　　　　　US　ISSN 0270-3513
SPORTSMANS BOOK OF U.S. RECORDS. 1980. a. New York Outdoor Guide, 328 E. Main St., Rochester, NY 14604. Ed. Joseph Glogan.

796.172 GW
SURF KATALOG; Windsurfing. 1985. a. F.Ch. Heel Verlag, Koenigswinterer Strasse 528-536, 5300 Bonn 3 (Oberkassel), W. Germany (B.R.D.) Eds. H. Pohle, I. Riemann. circ. 10,000.

797 AT ISSN 0157-2938
TASMANIAN TRAMP. 1933. biennial. price varies. Hobart Walking Club, G.P.O. Box 753h, Hobart, Tas. 7001, Australia. Ed.Bd. adv. cum.index: 1933-1963; 1966-1979. circ. 1,000.

796.5 US ISSN 0049-3481
TETON. 1969. a. $1.95. Teton Magazine, Box 1903, Jackson Hole, WY 83001. TEL 307-733-9220. Ed. Gene Downer. adv. bk. rev. illus. circ. 20,000.

917.13 796.5 CN ISSN 0380-6197
THUNDER BAY CAMPING GUIDE.* 1972. irreg. Amethyst Holdings Ltd., 1126 Rolend St., Thunder Bay, Ont. P7B 5M4, Canada. TEL 807-623-4424. illus.

799.1 US
TIM KELLEY'S FISHING GUIDE; official Colorado-Wyoming fishing guide. 1954. biennial. $9.95. Hart Publications, Inc., 1900 Grant St., Ste. 400, Box 1917, Denver, CO 80201. TEL 303-837-1917. Ed. Dick Prouty. adv. charts. illus. circ. 20,000.
Formerly: Official Colorado-Wyoming Fishing Guide.

796.42 US
TRACK AND FIELD CASE BOOK. biennial. $2.50. National Federation of State High School Associations, 11724 Plaza Circle, Box 20626, Kansas City, MO 64195. TEL 816-464-5400. Ed. Thomas E. Frederick.

796.42 US
TRACK AND FIELD OFFICIALS MANUAL. biennial. $2.50. National Federation of State High School Associations, 11724 Plaza Circle, Box 20626, Kansas City, MO 64195. TEL 816-464-5400. Eds. Thomas Frederick, Richard Schindler.

796.42 US
TRACK AND FIELD RULEBOOK. a. $2.50. National Federation of State High School Associations, 11724 Plaza Circle, Box 20626, Kansas City, MO 64195. TEL 816-464-5400.
Formerly: Track and Field Rules and Records.

796 US
TRAIL BLAZER'S ALMANAC. 1934. a. per no. Trail Blazer's Publishing Co., 206 W. Fourth St., Kewanee, IL 61443. TEL 309-852-2602. Ed. Wm. H. Harper. adv. circ. 1,100,000(controlled)

917 US
TRAILER LIFE'S RECREATIONAL VEHICLE CAMPGROUND AND SERVICES DIRECTORY. Running title: R V Campground & Services Guide. 1971. a. $11.95. T L Enterprises, Inc., 29901 Agoura Rd., Agoura, CA 91301. TEL 213-991-4980. adv. illus. circ. 375,000.
Former titles: Good Sam Club's Recreational Vehicle Owners Directory (ISSN 0090-3256); Trailer Life's Recreational Vehicle Campground and Services Guide (ISSN 0093-4283)

UNIFORM HUNTER CASUALTY REPORT. see SPORTS AND GAMES

U.S. FISH AND WILDLIFE SERVICE. NATIONAL SURVEY OF HUNTING, FISHING AND WILDLIFE-ASSOCIATED RECREATION. see SPORTS AND GAMES — Abstracting, Bibliographies, Statistics

719.32 333.7 US
U.S. NATIONAL PARK SERVICE. RESEARCH REPORTS BY SERVICE PERSONNEL. 5-10 reports per year. U.S. National Park Service, Interior Bldg., Washington, DC 20240 TEL 202-343-1100. (Order from NTIS, Springfield, VA 22161)

796 AT
WALK. 1949. a. Aus.$1. Melbourne Bushwalkers, G.P.O. Box 1751q, Melbourne, Vic. 3001, Australia.

796 AT
THE WALKER. 1929. a. Aus.$3 per no. Melbourne Amateur Walking and Touring Club, G.P.O. Box 2446v, Melbourne, Vic. 3001, Australia. Ed. Graeme Wheeler. adv. bk. rev. circ. 3,000.
Formerly: Melbourne Walker.

WHEELERS R V RESORT AND CAMPGROUND GUIDE: NORTH AMERICAN EDITION. see TRAVEL AND TOURISM

799.1 UK
WHERE TO FISH. vol.79, 1984. biennial. £11.95. Thomas Harmsworth Publishing, 13 Nicosia Rd., London SW18 3RN, England. Ed. D.A. Orton. adv.

796.93 US ISSN 0163-9684
WHITE BOOK OF SKI AREAS. U S AND CANADA. 1976. a. $12.95. (Subaru of America, Inc.) Inter-Ski Services, Inc., Box 3635, Georgetown Station, Washington, DC 20007. TEL 202-342-0886. Ed. Robert G. Enzel. circ. 13,000.
Formerly: White Book of U S Ski Areas (ISSN 0145-6075)

917.59 US
WOODALL'S CAMPGROUND DIRECTORY. ARIZONA/NEW MEXICO EDITION. a. $3.95. Woodall Publishing Co., 500 Hyacinth Pl., Highland Park, IL 60035. TEL 312-433-4550.
Formerly: Woodall's Campground Directory. Arizona Edition (ISSN 0162-7384)

917.59 US ISSN 0163-5328
WOODALL'S CAMPGROUND DIRECTORY. ARKANSAS/MISSOURI EDITION. a. $3.95. Woodall Publishing Co., 500 Hyacinth Pl, Highland Park, IL 60035. TEL 312-433-4550.

917.59 US
WOODALL'S CAMPGROUND DIRECTORY. CALIFORNIA/NEVADA/MEXICO DIRECTORY. a. $3.95. Woodall Publishing Co., 500 Hyacinth Pl., Highland Park, IL 60035. TEL 312-433-4550.
Formerly: Woodall's Campground Directory. California Edition (ISSN 0162-7392)

917.59 US ISSN 0163-5344
WOODALL'S CAMPGROUND DIRECTORY. COLORADO EDITION. a. $3.95. Woodall Publishing Co., 500 Hyacinth Pl., Highland Park, IL 60035. TEL 312-433-4550.

917.59 US
WOODALL'S CAMPGROUND DIRECTORY. DELAWARE/MARYLAND/VIRGINIA/DISTRICT OF COLUMBIA EDITION. a. $3.95. Woodall Publishing Co., 500 Hyacinth Pl., Highland Park, IL 60035. TEL 312-433-4550.

917.59 US ISSN 0162-7406
WOODALL'S CAMPGROUND DIRECTORY. EASTERN EDITION. a. $7.95. Woodall Publishing Co., 500 Hyacinth Pl., Highland Park, IL 60035. TEL 312-433-4550.
Which was formerly titled: Woodall's Trailering Parks and Campgrounds (ISSN 0084-1110); Supersedes in part: Woodall's Campground Directory (ISSN 0362-3823)

917.59 US
WOODALL'S CAMPGROUND DIRECTORY. FLORIDA EDITION. 1973. a. $3.95. Woodall Publishing Co., 500 Hyacinth Place, Highland Park, IL 60035. TEL 312-433-4550. adv. illus.
Formerly: Woodall's Campground Directory. Florida Campgrounds Edition (ISSN 0090-5151)

917.59 US
WOODALL'S CAMPGROUND DIRECTORY. IDAHO/OREGON/WASHINGTON/BRITISH COLUMBIA EDITION. a. $3.95. Woodall Publishing Co., 500 Hyacinth Pl., Highland Park, IL 60035. TEL 312-433-4550.
Formerly: Woodall's Campground Directory. Idaho/Oregon/Washington Edition (ISSN 0163-2493)

917.59 US ISSN 0163-2485
WOODALL'S CAMPGROUND DIRECTORY. ILLINOIS/INDIANA EDITION. a. $3.95. Woodall Publishing Co., 500 Hyacinth Pl., Highland Park, IL 60035. TEL 312-433-4550.

917.59 US ISSN 0163-5336
WOODALL'S CAMPGROUND DIRECTORY. KENTUCKY/TENNESSEE EDITION. a. $3.95. Woodall Publishing Co., 500 Hyacinth Pl., Highland Park, IL 60035. TEL 312-433-4550.

917.59 US ISSN 0163-0121
WOODALL'S CAMPGROUND DIRECTORY. MICHIGAN EDITION. a. $3.95. Woodall Publishing Co., 500 Hyacinth Pl., Highland Park, IL 60035. TEL 312-433-4550.

917.59 US
WOODALL'S CAMPGROUND DIRECTORY. MINNESOTA/WISCONSIN EDITION. a. $3.95. Woodall Publishing Co., 500 Hyacinth Pl., Highland Park, IL 60035. TEL 312-433-4550.
Formerly: Woodall's Campground Directory. Wisconsin Edition (ISSN 0163-0105)

917.59 US ISSN 0163-0083
WOODALL'S CAMPGROUND DIRECTORY: NEW ENGLAND STATES EDITION. a. $3.95. Woodall Publishing Co., 500 Hyacinth Pl., Highland Park, IL 60035. TEL 312-433-4550.

917.59 US
WOODALL'S CAMPGROUND DIRECTORY. NEW JERSEY/OHIO/PENNSYLVANIA EDITIONS. a. $3.95. Woodall Publishing Co., 500 Hyacinth Pl., Highland Park, IL 60035. TEL 312-433-4550.
Formerly: Woodall's Campground Directory. Ohio/Pennsylvania Editions (ISSN 0163-1950)

917.59 US
WOODALL'S CAMPGROUND DIRECTORY. NEW YORK EDITION. a. $3.95. Woodall Publishing Co., 500 Hyacinth Pl., Highland Park, IL 60035. TEL 312-433-4550.
Formerly: Woodall's Campground Directory. New Jersey/New York Edition (ISSN 0163-0113)

917.59 US
WOODALL'S CAMPGROUND DIRECTORY. NORTH AMERICAN EDITION. a. $12.95. Woodall Publishing Co., 500 Hyacinth Pl., Highland Park, IL 60035. TEL 312-433-4550.
Former titles: Woodall's Campground Directory. North American/Canadian Edition (ISSN 0146-1362); Woodall's Campground Directory. North American Edition; Which superseded in part: Woodall's Campground Directory (ISSN 0362-3823) ; Which was formerly titled: Woodall's Trailering Parks and Campgrounds (ISSN 0084-1110)

917.59 US ISSN 0163-5352
WOODALL'S CAMPGROUND DIRECTORY. NORTH CAROLINA/SOUTH CAROLINA EDITION. a. $3.95. Woodall Publishing Co., 500 Hyacinth Pl., Highland Park, IL 60035. TEL 312-433-4550.

917.59 US ISSN 0163-240X
WOODALL'S CAMPGROUND DIRECTORY. ONTARIO EDITION. a. $3.95. Woodall Publishing Co., 500 Hyacinth Pl., Highland Park, IL 60035. TEL 312-433-4550.

917.59 US
WOODALL'S CAMPGROUND DIRECTORY. TEXAS/MEXICO EDITION. a. $3.95. Woodall Publishing Co., 500 Hyacinth Pl., Highland Park, IL 60035. TEL 312-433-4550.
Formerly: Woodall's Campground Directory. Texas Edition (ISSN 0162-7376)

917.59 US ISSN 0162-7414
WOODALL'S CAMPGROUND DIRECTORY. WESTERN EDITION. a. $7.95. Woodall Publishing Co., 500 Hyacinth Pl., Highland Park, IL 60035. TEL 312-433-4550.
Supersedes in part: Woodall's Campground Directory (ISSN 0362-3823)

796.5 US ISSN 0742-3977
WOODALL'S TENTING DIRECTORY. 1984. a. Woodall Publishing Co., 500 Hyacinth Pl., Highland Park, IL 60035. TEL 312-433-4550. adv. tr.lit. circ. 170,000.

WORLD RECORD GAME FISHES. see FISH AND FISHERIES

STATISTICS

see also specific subjects

STATISTICS

310 DK ISSN 0107-7120
AARHUS KOMMUNES STATISTISKE KONTOR. INFORMATION. 1970. irreg., (approx. 75/yr.) free. Aarhus Kommunes Statistiske Kontor, Raadhuset, 8100 Aarhus C, Denmark. (looseleaf format)

ADVANCES IN RISK ANALYSIS. see PUBLIC HEALTH AND SAFETY

ADVANCES IN STATISTICAL ANALYSIS AND STATISTICAL COMPUTING. see COMPUTERS

318 MX
AGENDA ESTADISTICA. a. Secretaria de Programacion y Presupuesto, Articulo 123 No. 88, Mexico 1, D.F., Mexico (Orders to: Direccion General de Estudios del Territorio Nacional, Balderas 71, Col. Centro, Mexico 1, D.F., Mexico)

AGRICULTURAL STATISTICS OF GREECE. see AGRICULTURE — Abstracting, Bibliographies, Statistics

ALABAMA'S VITAL EVENTS. see PUBLIC ADMINISTRATION — Abstracting, Bibliographies, Statistics

ALBERTA ECONOMIC ACCOUNTS. see BUSINESS AND ECONOMICS — Abstracting, Bibliographies, Statistics

311 CN
ALIGARH JOURNAL OF STATISTICS. 1981. a. Rs.50($20) Aligarh Muslim University, Department of Statistics, Aligarh 202001, India. Ed.Bd. circ. 300.

AMERICAN STATISTICAL ASSOCIATION. SECTION ON STATISTICAL EDUCATION. PROCEEDINGS. see EDUCATION

310 US ISSN 0149-9963
AMERICAN STATISTICAL ASSOCIATION. STATISTICAL COMPUTING SECTION. PROCEEDINGS (OF THE ANNUAL MEETING) 1976. a. $16 to non-members; members $11. American Statistical Association, 806 15th St. N.W., Washington, DC 20005. TEL 202-393-3253. stat.

311 US
AMERICAN STATISTICAL ASSOCIATION. SURVEY RESEARCH METHODS. PROCEEDINGS. 1978. a. $29 to non-members; members $24. American Statistical Association, 806 15th St. N.W., Washington, DC 20005. TEL 202-393-3253.
Formerly: American Statistical Association. Statistical Section. Proceedings.

016 US ISSN 0091-1658
AMERICAN STATISTICS INDEX; a comprehensive guide and index to the statistical publications of the U.S. Government. 1974. m. (with q. and a. cumulations) price varies. Congressional Information Service, Inc., 4520 East-West Hwy., Bethesda, MD 20814. TEL 301-654-1550. Ed. Daniel Coyle. abstr. stat. index. cum.index: 1980-84. (reprint service avail.) Indexed: Noise Pollut.Publ.Abstr. Popul.Ind. •Also available online. Vendors: DIALOG, Orbit Information Technologies.

ANGOLA. DIRECCAO DOS SERVICOS DE ESTATISTICA. ANUARIO ESTATISTICO. see PUBLIC ADMINISTRATION — Abstracting, Bibliographies, Statistics

ANGOLA. DIRECCAO DOS SERVICOS DE ESTATISTICA. INFORMACOES ESTATISTICAS. see PUBLIC ADMINISTRATION — Abstracting, Bibliographies, Statistics

ANNUAIRE DES STATISTIQUES DU COMMERCE EXTERIEUR DU TOGO. see BUSINESS AND ECONOMICS — Abstracting, Bibliographies, Statistics

317 CN ISSN 0066-3018
ANNUAIRE DU QUEBEC.* 1914. a. (Bureau of Statistics) Editeur Officiel du Quebec, 1283 Bd. Charest Ouest, Quebec G1N 2C9, Canada. TEL 418-643-3895. index. circ. 6,000.

316.6 DM
ANNUAIRE STATISTIQUE DE BENIN. a., latest 1975. 2000 Fr.CFA. Institut National de la Statistique et de l'Analyse Economique, B.P. 323, Cotonou, Benin.
Formerly: Annuaire Statistique du Dahomey.

314 BE ISSN 0066-3646
ANNUAIRE STATISTIQUE DE LA BELGIQUE. (Text in Dutch and French) 1870. a. 1035 Fr. Institut National de Statistique, 44 rue de Louvain, 1000 Brussels, Belgium.
Formerly (until 1960): Annuaire Statistique de la Belgique et du Congo Belge.

314 FR ISSN 0066-3654
ANNUAIRE STATISTIQUE DE LA FRANCE. 1876. a. 460 F.($96) Institut National de la Statistique et des Etudes Economiques, 18 bd A. Pinard, 75675 Paris 14, France. circ. 3,000.

316 TI ISSN 0066-3689
ANNUAIRE STATISTIQUE DE LA TUNISIE. a. Institut National de la Statistique, 70 rue Echcham, Tunis, Tunisia.

316 MR ISSN 0066-3719
ANNUAIRE STATISTIQUE DU MAROC. (Text in Arabic and French) a. DH.110. Direction de la Statistique, B.P. 178, Rabat, Morocco. (also avail. in microfiche)
Incorporating: Morocco. Direction de la Statistique. Statistiques Retrospectives & Parc Automobile du Maroc.

316.6 TG
ANNUAIRE STATISTIQUE DU TOGO. 1966. a., latest 1981/82. 4000 Fr.CFA. Direction de la Statistique, Boite Postale 118, Lome, Togo. illus. stat.

310 UK
ANNUAL ABSTRACT OF STATISTICS. a. price varies. H.M.S.O., Box 276, London, SW8 5DT, England. circ. 5,500.

ANNUAL BULLETIN OF ELECTRIC ENERGY STATISTICS FOR EUROPE. see ELECTRICITY AND ELECTRICAL ENGINEERING — Abstracting, Bibliographies, Statistics

ANNUAL BULLETIN OF STEEL STATISTICS FOR EUROPE. see METALLURGY — Abstracting, Bibliographies, Statistics

ANNUAL RETURNS OF PRODUCTION FROM QUARRIES AND MINERAL PRODUCTION STATISTICS. see MINES AND MINING INDUSTRY — Abstracting, Bibliographies, Statistics

310 MY ISSN 0080-6439
ANNUAL STATISTICAL BULLETIN SARAWAK. Variant title: Sarawak. Department of Statistics. Annual Statistical Bulletin. Variant title: Sarawak Annual Bulletin of Statistics. (Text in English) 1964. a. M.$5. Department of Statistics, Federal Complex, Jalan Simpang Tiga, Kuching, Sarawak, Malaysia.

314 IT ISSN 0066-4545
ANNUARIO STATISTICO ITALIANO. a. L.11000. Istituto Centrale di Statistica, Via Cesare Balbo 16, 00100 Rome, Italy. circ. 4,700.

ANNUARIUM STATISTICUM ECCLESIAE/ STATISTIQUE DE L'EGLISE/STATISTICAL YEARBOOK OF THE CHURCH. see RELIGIONS AND THEOLOGY — Abstracting, Bibliographies, Statistics

ANUARIO DE ESTADISTICAS ESTATALES. see GEOGRAPHY

317 CU ISSN 0574-6132
ANUARIO ESTADISTICO DE CUBA. English edition: Statistical Yearbook Compendium of the Republic of Cuba. 1952. a. free. Comite Estatal de Estadisticas, Centro de Informacion Cientifico-Tecnica, Gaveta Postal 6016, Havana, Cuba, Cuba. circ. 1,000.

314 SP ISSN 0066-5177
ANUARIO ESTADISTICO DE ESPANA. (In two editions: Edicion Extensa and Edicion Manual) 1912. a. Instituto Nacional de Estadistica, P de la Castellana, 183, Madrid 16, Spain.

318 PY
ANUARIO ESTADISTICO DEL PARAGUAY. 1886. a. exchange basis. Direccion General de Estadistica y Censos, Humaita 463, Asuncion, Paraguay (Subscr. to: Casilla de Correo 1118, Asuncion, Paraguay) Ed. Jose Diaz de Bedoya. circ. 1,500.

ANUARIO ESTADISTICO DE ENERGIA ELECTRICA. see ENERGY — Abstracting, Bibliographies, Statistics

318 BL ISSN 0100-1299
ANUARIO ESTADISTICO DO BRASIL/ STATISTICAL YEARBOOK OF BRAZIL. 1916. a. $50 price varies. Fundacao Instituto Brasileiro de Geografia e Estatistica, Centro de Servicos Graficos, Av. Brasil 15671, CEP 21241 Rio de Janeiro, Brazil. bk. rev. circ. 9,000. (back issues avail.)

318 BL ISSN 0100-8730
ANUARIO ESTADISTICO DO ESTADO DE SAO PAULO. 1979. a. $22. Fundacao Sistema Estadual de Analise de Dados, Av. Casper Libero, 464, 01033 Sao Paulo, Brazil. charts. circ. 1,200.

318 BL
ANUARIO ESTADISTICO DO RIO GRANDE DE SUL. 1972. a. Cr.$90. Fundacao de Economia e Estatistica, Rua Gen. Vitorino 77-2 andar, C.P. 2356, 90.000 Porto Alegre, RS, Brazil.

310 GW ISSN 0066-5673
ARBEITEN ZUR ANGEWANDTEN STATISTIK. 1967. irreg., vol. 27, 1986. price varies. Physica-Verlag GmbH und Co., Tiergartenstr. 17, Postfach 105280, D-6900 Heidelberg 1, W. Germany (B.R.D.) Ed.Bd. Indexed: Math.R.
Formerly: Berlin. Freie Universitaet. Institut fuer Statistik und Versicherungsmathematik. Berichte (ISSN 0067-5865)

314 GW ISSN 0072-162X
DAS ARBEITSGEBIET DER BUNDESSTATISTIK. (Editions in English, French and German) irreg. DM.29.40. (Statistisches Bundesamt) W. Kohlhammer-Verlag GmbH, Abt. Veroeffentlichungen des Statistischen Bundesamtes, Philipp-Reis-Str. 3, Postfach 421120, 6500 Mainz 42, W. Germany (B.R.D.)

318 AG
ARGENTINA. CENTRAL DE ESTADISTICAS NACIONALES. INFORME. 1976. irreg. $110. Central de Estadisticas Nacionales, Av. De Mayo 953, 1084 Buenos Aires, Argentina. Ed. Carlos A. Canto Yoy. circ. 500.

318 AG
ARGENTINA. COMISION NACIONAL DE VALORES. INFORMACION ESTADISTICA. irreg. Comision Nacional de Valores, 215 Hippolito Yrigoyen, Buenos Aires, Argentina.

ARGENTINA. INSTITUTO NACIONAL DE ESTADISTICA Y CENSOS. ANUARIO ESTADISTICO. see POPULATION STUDIES — Abstracting, Bibliographies, Statistics

ARIZONA STATISTICAL REVIEW. see BUSINESS AND ECONOMICS — Abstracting, Bibliographies, Statistics

AUSTRALIA. AIR TRANSPORT STATISTICS. AIRPORT TRAFFIC DATA. see TRANSPORTATION — Abstracting, Bibliographies, Statistics

AUSTRALIA. AIR TRANSPORT STATISTICS. AUSTRALIAN AIR DISTANCES. see TRANSPORTATION — Abstracting, Bibliographies, Statistics

AUSTRALIA. AIR TRANSPORT STATISTICS. FLIGHT CREW LICENCES. see TRANSPORTATION — Abstracting, Bibliographies, Statistics

AUSTRALIA. AUSTRALIAN BUREAU OF STATISTICS. TASMANIAN OFFICE. MINING TASMANIA. see MINES AND MINING INDUSTRY — Abstracting, Bibliographies, Statistics

AUSTRALIA. BUREAU OF STATISTICS. ADOPTIONS. see PUBLIC ADMINISTRATION — Abstracting, Bibliographies, Statistics

AUSTRALIA. BUREAU OF STATISTICS.
APPARENT CONSUMPTION OF FOODSTUFFS
AND NUTRIENTS. see *PUBLIC
ADMINISTRATION — Abstracting,
Bibliographies, Statistics*

AUSTRALIA. BUREAU OF STATISTICS.
APPARENT CONSUMPTION OF SELECTED
FOODSTUFFS, PRELIMINARY. see *PUBLIC
ADMINISTRATION — Abstracting,
Bibliographies, Statistics*

319   AT ISSN 0067-1754
AUSTRALIA. BUREAU OF STATISTICS.
AUSTRALIAN CAPITAL TERRITORY.
STATISTICAL SUMMARY. 1963. a. Aus.$5.80.
Australian Bureau of Statistics, P.O. Box 10,
Belconnen, A.C.T. 2616, Australia. circ. 1,000.

AUSTRALIA. BUREAU OF STATISTICS. BIRTHS.
see *PUBLIC ADMINISTRATION — Abstracting,
Bibliographies, Statistics*

AUSTRALIA. BUREAU OF STATISTICS.
CATALOGUE OF PUBLICATIONS. see *PUBLIC
ADMINISTRATION — Abstracting,
Bibliographies, Statistics*

AUSTRALIA. BUREAU OF STATISTICS. CHILD
IN CARE. see *PUBLIC ADMINISTRATION —
Abstracting, Bibliographies, Statistics*

AUSTRALIA. BUREAU OF STATISTICS.
DEATHS. see *PUBLIC ADMINISTRATION —
Abstracting, Bibliographies, Statistics*

AUSTRALIA. BUREAU OF STATISTICS.
DIVORCES. see *PUBLIC ADMINISTRATION —
Abstracting, Bibliographies, Statistics*

AUSTRALIA. BUREAU OF STATISTICS.
ESTIMATED RESIDENT POPULATION SEX
AND AGE: STATES AND TERRITORIES OF
AUSTRALIA. see *PUBLIC
ADMINISTRATION — Abstracting,
Bibliographies, Statistics*

AUSTRALIA. BUREAU OF STATISTICS.
GOVERNMENT FINANCIAL ESTIMATES,
AUSTRALIA. see *BUSINESS AND
ECONOMICS — Abstracting, Bibliographies,
Statistics*

319   AT
AUSTRALIA. BUREAU OF STATISTICS. LIST OF
PUBLICATIONS TO BE RELEASED. 1982. a.
free. Australian Bureau of Statistics, P.O. Box 10,
Belconnen, A.C.T. 2614, Australia. stat. circ. 40,
000.

AUSTRALIA. BUREAU OF STATISTICS.
MARRIAGES. see *PUBLIC
ADMINISTRATION — Abstracting,
Bibliographies, Statistics*

AUSTRALIA. BUREAU OF STATISTICS.
NATIONAL SCHOOLS STATISTICS
COLLECTION. see *PUBLIC
ADMINISTRATION — Abstracting,
Bibliographies, Statistics*

AUSTRALIA. BUREAU OF STATISTICS.
NATIONAL SCHOOLS STATISTICS
COLLECTION. PRELIMINARY. see *PUBLIC
ADMINISTRATION — Abstracting,
Bibliographies, Statistics*

319   AT ISSN 0067-0855
AUSTRALIA. BUREAU OF STATISTICS.
NORTHERN TERRITORY STATISTICAL
SUMMARY. 1960. a. Aus.$5.80. Australian Bureau
of Statistics, Box 10, Belconnen, A.C.T. 2616,
Australia. circ. 1,000.

AUSTRALIA. BUREAU OF STATISTICS.
PERINATAL DEATHS. see *PUBLIC
ADMINISTRATION — Abstracting,
Bibliographies, Statistics*

319   AT ISSN 0705-0488
AUSTRALIA. BUREAU OF STATISTICS. POCKET
YEAR BOOK, AUSTRALIA. 1913. a. Aus.$3.90.
Australian Bureau of Statistics, Box 10, Belconnen,
A.C.T. 2616, Australia. circ. 2,000.
 Formerly: Australia. Bureau of Statistics. Pocket
Compendium of Australian Statistics (ISSN 0079-
239X)

AUSTRALIA. BUREAU OF STATISTICS.
PROJECTIONS OF THE POPULATION. see
*PUBLIC ADMINISTRATION — Abstracting,
Bibliographies, Statistics*

AUSTRALIA. BUREAU OF STATISTICS.
QUEENSLAND OFFICE. ESTIMATED
RESIDENT POPULATION AND AREAS FOR
EACH LOCAL AUTHORITY AREA,
QUEENSLAND. see *POPULATION STUDIES —
Abstracting, Bibliographies, Statistics*

AUSTRALIA. BUREAU OF STATISTICS.
SEASONALLY ADJUSTED INDICATORS. see
*PUBLIC ADMINISTRATION — Abstracting,
Bibliographies, Statistics*

AUSTRALIA. BUREAU OF STATISTICS. SOCIAL
INDICATORS. see *PUBLIC
ADMINISTRATION — Abstracting,
Bibliographies, Statistics*

AUSTRALIA. BUREAU OF STATISTICS. STATE
AND LOCAL GOVERNMENT FINANCE,
AUSTRALIA. see *BUSINESS AND
ECONOMICS — Abstracting, Bibliographies,
Statistics*

319   AT ISSN 0314-1640
AUSTRALIA. BUREAU OF STATISTICS.
TASMANIAN OFFICE. POCKET YEAR BOOK
OF TASMANIA. 1913. a. Aus.$3.20. Australian
Bureau of Statistics, Tasmanian Office, G.P.O. Box
66A, Hobart, Tas. 7001, Australia. circ. 3,300.

AUSTRALIA. BUREAU OF STATISTICS.
TECHNICAL PAPERS. see *PUBLIC
ADMINISTRATION — Abstracting,
Bibliographies, Statistics*

AUSTRALIA. BUREAU OF STATISTICS.
TERTIARY EDUCATION. see *PUBLIC
ADMINISTRATION — Abstracting,
Bibliographies, Statistics*

994 319   AT ISSN 0067-1207
AUSTRALIA. BUREAU OF STATISTICS.
VICTORIAN OFFICE. VICTORIAN POCKET
YEARBOOK. 1956. a. Aus.$3.10. Australian
Bureau of Statistics, Victorian Office, Box 2796Y,
G.P.O. Melbourne, Victoria 3001, Australia. adv.
bk. rev. index. circ. 1,200.

994 319   AT ISSN 0067-1223
AUSTRALIA. BUREAU OF STATISTICS.
VICTORIAN OFFICE. VICTORIAN
YEARBOOK. 1873. a. Aus.$27. Australian Bureau
of Statistics, Victorian Office, Box 2796Y, G.P.O.
Melbourne, Victoria 3001, Australia. adv. bk. rev.
bibl. index. circ. 1,000.

319   AT
AUSTRALIA. BUREAU OF STATISTICS. YEAR
BOOK AUSTRALIA. 1908. a. Aus.$35.30.
Australian Bureau of Statistics, Box 10, Belconnen,
A.C.T. 2616, Australia. circ. 15,000.
 Former titles: Official Year Book of Australia
(ISSN 0312-4746); Official Year Book of the
Commonwealth of Australia (ISSN 0078-3927)

AUSTRALIA. NON-GOVERNMENT RAILWAYS
STATISTICS. see *TRANSPORTATION —
Abstracting, Bibliographies, Statistics*

319.4   AT
AUSTRALIA AT A GLANCE. 1971. a. free.
Australian Bureau of Statistics, P.O. Box 10,
Belconnen, A.C.T. 2616, Australia.

319.4   AT
AUSTRALIAN CAPITAL TERRITORY AT A
GLANCE. 1984. a. free. Australian Bureau of
Statistics, P.O. Box 10, Belconnen, ACT 2616,
Australia.

AUSTRALIAN ENERGY STATISTICS. see
ENERGY — Abstracting, Bibliographies, Statistics

AUSTRALIAN TRANSPORT INFORMATION
DIRECTORY. see *TRANSPORTATION*

AUSTRIA. STATISTISCHES ZENTRALAMT.
INDUSTRIE UND GEWERBESTATISTIK PART
1. see *BUSINESS AND ECONOMICS —
Abstracting, Bibliographies, Statistics*

310   AU
AUSTRIA. STATISTISCHES ZENTRALAMT.
MIKROZENSUS; JAHRESERGEBNISSE.
(Subseries of its Beitraege zur Oesterreichischen
Statistik) 1969. a. S.80. Hintere Zollamtsstr. 2b,
1033 Vienna, Austria. stat. circ. 500.

310   AU
AUSTRIA. STATISTISCHES ZENTRALAMT.
STATISTISCHE NACHRICHTEN. 1974. a. S.1,
060. Oesterreichisches Statistisches Zentralamt,
Hintere Zollamtstr. 2b, 1033 Vienna, Austria.
Indexed: P.A.I.S.For.Lang.Ind.

318   BF
BAHAMAS. DEPARTMENT OF STATISTICS.
STATISTICAL ABSTRACT. 1969. a. $6.
Department of Statistics, Box N 3904, Nassau,
Bahamas.

318   BL
BAHIA, BRAZIL (STATE). CENTRO DE
ESTATISTICA E INFORMACOES. ANUARIO
ESTATISTICO. (Former name of issuing body:
Centro de Planejamento e Estudos) 1972. a. free.
Centro de Estatistica e Informacoes, Ave. Luiz
Viana Filjo, s/n, Caixa Postal 928, 40000 Salvador-
Bahia, Brazil.

BANGLADESH BANK. STATISTICS
DEPARTMENT. ANNUAL BALANCE OF
PAYMENTS. see *BUSINESS AND
ECONOMICS — Abstracting, Bibliographies,
Statistics*

BAPTIST YEARBOOK. see *RELIGIONS AND
THEOLOGY — Protestant*

310   DK ISSN 0107-5071
BEFOLKNINGEN I KOEBENHAVN I JANUAR.
(Subseries: Tal fre Koebenhavns Statistike Kontor)
1977. a. Kr.10. Statistik Kontor, Vester Voldgade
87, 1552 Copenhagen V, Denmark (Subscr.to:
Danske Boghendleres Kommissionsanstalt,
Siljangade 6-8, 2300 Copenhagen S, Denmark)
 Formerly: Befolkningen i Januar.

314   AU ISSN 0067-2319
BEITRAEGE ZUR OESTERREICHISCHEN
STATISTIK. 1953. irreg. price varies.
Oesterreichisches Statistisches Zentralamt, Hintere
Zollamtsstr. 2b, 1033 Vienna, Austria.

314.93   BE
BELGIUM. INSTITUT NATIONAL DE
STATISTIQUE. ANNUAIRE DE STATISTIQUES
REGIONALES. 1976. a. 415 Fr. Institut National
de Statistique, 44 rue de Louvain, 1000 Brussels,
Belgium. charts. stat.

314   BE ISSN 0067-5431
BELGIUM. INSTITUT NATIONAL DE
STATISTIQUE. ANNUAIRE STATISTIQUE DE
POCHE. (Text in Dutch and French) 1965. a. 145
Fr. Institut National de Statistique, 44 rue de
Louvain, 1000 Brussels, Belgium.

310   BE
BELGIUM. INSTITUT NATIONAL DE
STATISTIQUE. ETUDES STATISTIQUES. irreg.,
nos. 58-61, 1980. 175 Fr. per no. Institut National
de Statistique, 44 rue de Louvain, 1000 Brussels,
Belgium. Indexed: P.A.I.S.For.Lang.Ind.

BELGIUM. INSTITUT NATIONAL DE
STATISTIQUE. STATISTIQUE DE LA
NAVIGATION INTERIEURE. see
*TRANSPORTATION — Abstracting,
Bibliographies, Statistics*

BELGIUM. INSTITUT NATIONAL DE
STATISTIQUE. STATISTIQUE DES
ACCIDENTS DE LA CIRCULATION SUR LA
VOIE PUBLIQUE. see *PUBLIC HEALTH AND
SAFETY — Abstracting, Bibliographies, Statistics*

BELGIUM. INSTITUT NATIONAL DE
STATISTIQUE. STATISTIQUE DES VEHICULES
A MOTEUR NEUFS MIS EN CIRCULATION.
see *TRANSPORTATION — Abstracting,
Bibliographies, Statistics*

BELGIUM. INSTITUT NATIONAL DE
STATISTIQUE. STATISTIQUE DU TOURISME
ET DE L'HOTELLERIE. see *TRAVEL AND
TOURISM — Abstracting, Bibliographies, Statistics*

1050 STATISTICS

BELGIUM. INSTITUT NATIONAL DE STATISTIQUE. STATISTIQUES DE LA CONSTRUCTION ET DU LOGEMENT. see *BUILDING AND CONSTRUCTION — Abstracting, Bibliographies, Statistics*

BELGIUM. MINISTERE DE L'EDUCATION NATIONALE ET DE LA CULTURE FRANCAISE. ANNUAIRE STATISTIQUE DE L'ENSEIGNEMENT. see *EDUCATION — Abstracting, Bibliographies, Statistics*

BELGIUM. MINISTERE DE LA SANTE PUBLIQUE ET DE LA FAMILLE. PREMIERS ET PRINCIPAUX RESULTATS STATISTIQUES DE L'ENQUETE DANS LES ETABLISSEMENTS DE SOINS/EERSTE EN VOORNAAMSTE STATISTISCHE UITKOMSTEN VAN DE ENQUETE IN DE VERZORGINGSINSTELLINGEN. see *PUBLIC HEALTH AND SAFETY — Abstracting, Bibliographies, Statistics*

BIBLIOGRAPHY OF ECONOMIC AND STATISTICAL PUBLICATIONS ON TANZANIA. see *BUSINESS AND ECONOMICS — Abstracting, Bibliographies, Statistics*

BILDUNG IM ZAHLENSPIEGEL. see *EDUCATION — Abstracting, Bibliographies, Statistics*

BLUE BOOK OF FOOD STORE OPERATORS & WHOLESALERS. see *FOOD AND FOOD INDUSTRIES — Abstracting, Bibliographies, Statistics*

BOLIVIA. INSTITUTO NACIONAL DE ESTADISTICA. ANUARIO DE COMERCIO EXTERIOR. see *BUSINESS AND ECONOMICS — Abstracting, Bibliographies, Statistics*

BOLIVIA. INSTITUTO NACIONAL DE ESTADISTICA. ANUARIO DE ESTADISTICAS INDUSTRIALES. see *BUSINESS AND ECONOMICS — Abstracting, Bibliographies, Statistics*

BOLIVIA. INSTITUTO NACIONAL DE ESTADISTICA. ESTADISTICAS REGIONALES DEPARTAMENTALES. see *PUBLIC ADMINISTRATION — Abstracting, Bibliographies, Statistics*

318   BO
BOLIVIA EN CIFRAS. 1972. a. Instituto Nacional de Estadistica, Casilla de Correo No. 6129, La Paz, Bolivia.

BOOK OF THE STATES. see *PUBLIC ADMINISTRATION*

BRAZIL. COMISSAO DE FINANCIAMENTO DA PRODUCAO. ANUARIO ESTATISTICO. see *BUSINESS AND ECONOMICS — Abstracting, Bibliographies, Statistics*

BRAZIL. SERVICO SOCIAL DO COMERCIO. ANUARIO ESTATISTICO. see *PUBLIC ADMINISTRATION — Abstracting, Bibliographies, Statistics*

BRITISH COLUMBIA LIST; of official personnel in Federal, Provincial and Municipal Governments in the Province of British Columbia. see *PUBLIC ADMINISTRATION — Municipal Government*

BRITISH VIRGIN ISLANDS. STATISTICS OFFICE. BALANCE OF PAYMENTS. see *BUSINESS AND ECONOMICS — Abstracting, Bibliographies, Statistics*

BRITISH VIRGIN ISLANDS. STATISTICS OFFICE. NATIONAL INCOME AND EXPENDITURE. see *BUSINESS AND ECONOMICS — Abstracting, Bibliographies, Statistics*

947 314   HU   ISSN 0521-4882
BUDAPEST STATISZTIKAI EVKONYVE. a. 170 Ft. (Kozponti Statisztikai Hivatal) Statisztikai Kiado Vallalat, Kaszasdulo u. 2, Box 99, 1300 Budapest 3, Hungary (Subscr. to: Kultura, Box 149, H-1389 Budapest, Hungary)

947 314   HU   ISSN 0438-2242
BUDAPEST STATISZTIKAI ZSEBKONYVE. a. 50 Ft. (Kozponti Statisztikai Hivatal) Statisztikai Kiado Vallalat, Kaszasdulo u. 2, Box 99, 1300 Budapest 3, Hungary (Subscr. to: Kultura, Box 149, H-1389 Budapest, Hungary) circ. 1,600.

316 316   BD
BURUNDI. DEPARTEMENT DES ETUDES ET STATISTIQUES. BULLETIN ANNUAIRE. a. 1100 Fr.CFA. Departement des Etudes et Statistiques, B.P. 156, Bujumbura, Burundi.

319   TR
C.S.O. STATISTICAL BULLETINS. 1972. irreg. free. Central Statistical Office, P.O. Box 98, 23 Park St., Port-of-Spain, Trinidad, W.I. (Orders to: Government Printing Office, 48 St. Vincent St., Port of Spain, Trinidad, W.I.)

312   US
CALIFORNIA COUNTY FACT BOOK.* 1960. a. $10.60. County Supervisors Association of California, 1100 K St., Ste. 101, Sacramento, CA 95814. TEL 916-441-4011. charts. stat. circ. 1,000.

CALIFORNIA WORK INJURIES AND ILLNESSES. see *INDUSTRIAL HEALTH AND SAFETY — Abstracting, Bibliographies, Statistics*

316   CM
CAMEROON. PROVINCIAL STATISTICAL SERVICE OF THE SOUTH WEST. ANNUAL STATISTICAL REPORT, SOUTH WEST PROVINCE. a. Service Provincial de la Statistique du Sud-Ouest, Box 93, Buea, Cameroon.

CAMEROUN. DIRECTION DE LA STATISTIQUE ET DE LA COMPTABILITE NATIONALE. NOTE ANNUELLE DE STATISTIQUE. see *BUSINESS AND ECONOMICS — Abstracting, Bibliographies, Statistics*

CANADA. STATISTICS CANADA. AGGREGATE PRODUCTIVITY MEASURES/MESURES GLOBALES DE PRODUCTIVITE. see *BUSINESS AND ECONOMICS — Abstracting, Bibliographies, Statistics*

CANADA. STATISTICS CANADA. AIR PASSENGER ORIGIN AND DESTINATION. CANADA-UNITED STATES REPORT/ORIGINE ET DESTINATION DES PASSAGERS AERIENS. RAPPORT SUR LE TRAFIC CANADA-ETAT UNIS. see *TRANSPORTATION — Abstracting, Bibliographies, Statistics*

354.71   CN   ISSN 0703-2633
CANADA. STATISTICS CANADA. ANNUAL REPORT/RAPPORT ANNUEL. (Catalogue 11-201) (Text in English and French) 1919. a. free. Statistics Canada, Communications Division, 3rd Floor, R.H. Coats Bldg., Ottawa, Ont. K1A 0T6, Canada TEL 613-993-7276. (Subscr. to: Publications Sales and Services, Ottawa, Ont. K1A 0T6, Canada) (also avail. in microform from MML)

CANADA. STATISTICS CANADA. AVIATION STATISTICS CENTRE. SERVICE BULLETIN/BULLETIN DE SERVICE DU CENTRE DES STATISTIQUES DE L'AVIATION. see *TRANSPORTATION — Abstracting, Bibliographies, Statistics*

CANADA. STATISTICS CANADA. BUILDING PERMITS. ANNUAL SUMMARY/PERMIS DE BATIR. see *BUILDING AND CONSTRUCTION — Abstracting, Bibliographies, Statistics*

CANADA. STATISTICS CANADA. CABLE TELEVISION/TELEDISTRIBUTION. see *COMMUNICATIONS — Abstracting, Bibliographies, Statistics*

CANADA. STATISTICS CANADA. CANADA'S MINERAL PRODUCTION: PRELIMINARY ESTIMATE/PRODUCTION MINERALE DU CANADA, CALCUL PRELIMINAIRE. see *MINES AND MINING INDUSTRY — Abstracting, Bibliographies, Statistics*

CANADA. STATISTICS CANADA. CANE AND BEET SUGAR PROCESSORS/TRAITEMENT DU SUCRE DE CANNE ET DE BETTERAVES. see *FOOD AND FOOD INDUSTRIES — Abstracting, Bibliographies, Statistics*

CANADA. STATISTICS CANADA. CARPET, MAT AND RUG INDUSTRY/INDUSTRIE DES TAPIS, DES CARPETTES ET DE LA MOQUETTE. see *TEXTILE INDUSTRIES AND FABRICS — Abstracting, Bibliographies, Statistics*

CANADA. STATISTICS CANADA. CAUSES OF DEATH, PROVINCES BY SEX AND CANADA BY SEX AND AGE/CAUSES DE DECES, PAR PROVINCES SELON LE SEXE ET LE CANADA SELON LE SEXE ET L'AGE. see *POPULATION STUDIES — Abstracting, Bibliographies, Statistics*

CANADA. STATISTICS CANADA. COAL MINES/MINES DE CHARBON. see *MINES AND MINING INDUSTRY — Abstracting, Bibliographies, Statistics*

CANADA. STATISTICS CANADA. COASTWISE SHIPPING STATISTICS. see *TRANSPORTATION — Abstracting, Bibliographies, Statistics*

CANADA. STATISTICS CANADA. COMMUNICATIONS AND ENERGY WIRE AND CABLE INDUSTRY/INDUSTRIE DES FILS ET CABLES ELECTRIQUES ET DE COMMUNICATIONS. see *ELECTRICITY AND ELECTRICAL ENGINEERING*

CANADA. STATISTICS CANADA. COMMUNICATIONS AND OTHER ELECTRONIC INDUSTRIES/INDUSTRIES DE L'EQUIPEMENT ET D'AUTRE MATERIEL ELECTRONIQUE. see *COMMUNICATIONS — Abstracting, Bibliographies, Statistics*

CANADA. STATISTICS CANADA. COMMUNICATIONS SERVICE BULLETIN/COMMUNICATIONS-BULLETIN DE SERVICE. see *COMMUNICATIONS — Abstracting, Bibliographies, Statistics*

CANADA. STATISTICS CANADA. CONSOLIDATED GOVERNMENT FINANCE: FISCAL YEAR ENDED NEAREST TO DECEMBER 31/FINANCES PUBLIQUES CONSOLIDEES: ANNEE FINANCIERE TERMINEE LE PLUS PRES DE 31 DECEMBRE. see *BUSINESS AND ECONOMICS — Abstracting, Bibliographies, Statistics*

CANADA. STATISTICS CANADA. CONSTRUCTION IN CANADA/CONSTRUCTION AU CANADA. see *BUILDING AND CONSTRUCTION — Abstracting, Bibliographies, Statistics*

CANADA. STATISTICS CANADA. CONTROL AND SALE OF ALCOHOLIC BEVERAGES IN CANADA/CONTROLE ET LA VENTE DES BOISSONS ALCOOLIQUES AU CANADA/CONTROLE ET LA VENTE DES BOISSONS ALCOOLIQUES AU CANADA. see *BEVERAGES — Abstracting, Bibliographies, Statistics*

CANADA. STATISTICS CANADA. CORPORATION FINANCIAL STATISTICS. see *BUSINESS AND ECONOMICS — Abstracting, Bibliographies, Statistics*

CANADA. STATISTICS CANADA. CORPORATION TAXATION STATISTICS. see *BUSINESS AND ECONOMICS — Abstracting, Bibliographies, Statistics*

CANADA. STATISTICS CANADA. CREDIT UNIONS. see *BUSINESS AND ECONOMICS — Abstracting, Bibliographies, Statistics*

CANADA. STATISTICS CANADA. CRUDE PETROLEUM AND NATURAL GAS INDUSTRY/INDUSTRIE DU PETROLE BRUT ET DU GAZ NATUREL. see *PETROLEUM AND GAS — Abstracting, Bibliographies, Statistics*

CANADA. STATISTICS CANADA. DIRECT SELLING IN CANADA/VENTE DIRECTE AU CANADA. see *BUSINESS AND ECONOMICS — Abstracting, Bibliographies, Statistics*

CANADA. STATISTICS CANADA. EDUCATION IN CANADA/EDUCATION AU CANADA. see *EDUCATION — Abstracting, Bibliographies, Statistics*

STATISTICS 1051

CANADA. STATISTICS CANADA. ELECTRIC POWER STATISTICS VOLUME 1: ANNUAL ELECTRIC POWER SURVEY OF CAPABILITY AND LOAD/STATISTIQUE DE L'ENERGIE ELECTRIQUE. VOLUME 1: ENQUETE ANNUELLE SUR LA PUISSANCE MAXIMALE ET SUR LA CHARGE DES RESEAUX. see *ELECTRICITY AND ELECTRICAL ENGINEERING* — *Abstracting, Bibliographies, Statistics*

CANADA. STATISTICS CANADA. ELECTRICAL CONTRACTING INDUSTRY/ ENTREPRENEURS D'INSTALLATIONS ELECTRIQUES. see *ELECTRICITY AND ELECTRICAL ENGINEERING* — *Abstracting, Bibliographies, Statistics*

CANADA. STATISTICS CANADA. ELEMENTARY-SECONDARY SCHOOL ENROLLMENT/EFFECTIFS DES ECOLES PRIMAIRES ET SECONDAIRES. see *EDUCATION* — *Abstracting, Bibliographies, Statistics*

CANADA. STATISTICS CANADA. ENROLLMENT IN COMMUNITY COLLEGES/ EFFECTIFS DES COLLEGES COMMUNAUTAIRES. see *EDUCATION* — *Abstracting, Bibliographies, Statistics*

CANADA. STATISTICS CANADA. EXPORTS-MERCHANDISE TRADE/EXPORTATIONS-COMMERCE DE MERCHANDISES. see *BUSINESS AND ECONOMICS* — *Abstracting, Bibliographies, Statistics*

CANADA. STATISTICS CANADA. FAMILY INCOMES (CENSUS FAMILIES) /REVENUS DES FAMILLE (FAMILLES DE RECENSEMENT) see *BUSINESS AND ECONOMICS* — *Abstracting, Bibliographies, Statistics*

CANADA. STATISTICS CANADA. FARM NET INCOME/REVENU NET AGRICOLE. see *AGRICULTURE* — *Abstracting, Bibliographies, Statistics*

CANADA. STATISTICS CANADA. FEDERAL GOVERNMENT EMPLOYMENT IN METROPOLITAN AREAS/EMPLOI DANS L'ADMINISTRATION FEDERALE REGIONS METROPOLITAINES. see *PUBLIC ADMINISTRATION* — *Abstracting, Bibliographies, Statistics*

CANADA. STATISTICS CANADA. FEDERAL GOVERNMENT FINANCE: REVENUE AND EXPENDITURE, ASSETS AND LIABILITIES/ FINANCES PUBLIQUES FEDERALES: RECETTES AND DEPENSES, ACTIF ET PASSIF. see *BUSINESS AND ECONOMICS* — *Abstracting, Bibliographies, Statistics*

CANADA. STATISTICS CANADA. FINANCIAL STATISTICS OF EDUCATION/STATISTIQUES FINANCIERES DE L'EDUCATION. see *EDUCATION* — *Abstracting, Bibliographies, Statistics*

CANADA. STATISTICS CANADA. FISH PRODUCTS INDUSTRY/INDUSTRIE DE LA TRANSFORMATION DU POISSON. see *FISH AND FISHERIES* — *Abstracting, Bibliographies, Statistics*

CANADA. STATISTICS CANADA. FLOUR AND BREAKFAST CEREAL PRODUCTS INDUSTRY/MEUNERIE ET FABRICATION DE CEREALES DE TABLE. see *FOOD AND FOOD INDUSTRIES* — *Abstracting, Bibliographies, Statistics*

CANADA. STATISTICS CANADA. FRUIT AND VEGETABLE PROCESSING INDUSTRIES/ PREPARATION DE FRUITS ET DE LEGUMES. see *FOOD AND FOOD INDUSTRIES* — *Abstracting, Bibliographies, Statistics*

CANADA. STATISTICS CANADA. FRUIT AND VEGETABLE PRODUCTION/PRODUCTION DE FRUITS ET DE LEGUMES. see *AGRICULTURE* — *Abstracting, Bibliographies, Statistics*

CANADA. STATISTICS CANADA. GAS UTILITIES (TRANSPORT AND DISTRIBUTION SYSTEMS) /SERVICES DE GAZ (RESEAUX DE TRANSPORT ET DE DISTRIBUTION) see *PETROLEUM AND GAS* — *Abstracting, Bibliographies, Statistics*

CANADA. STATISTICS CANADA. GENERAL REVIEW OF THE MINERAL INDUSTRIES/ REVUE GENERALE SUR LES INDUSTRIES MINERALES; mines, quarries and oil wells/mines, carrieres et puits de petrole. see *MINES AND MINING INDUSTRY* — *Abstracting, Bibliographies, Statistics*

CANADA. STATISTICS CANADA. GLASS AND GLASS PRODUCTS INDUSTRIES/INDUSTRIES DU VERRE ET D'ARTICLES EN VERRE. see *CERAMICS, GLASS AND POTTERY* — *Abstracting, Bibliographies, Statistics*

CANADA. STATISTICS CANADA. HIGHWAY, ROAD, STREET AND BRIDGE CONTRACTING INDUSTRY/ ENTREPRENEURS DE GRANDE ROUTE, CHEMIN, RUE ET PONT. see *ENGINEERING* — *Abstracting, Bibliographies, Statistics*

CANADA. STATISTICS CANADA. HISTORICAL LABOUR FORCE STATISTICS, ACTUAL DATA, SEASONAL FACTORS, SEASONALLY ADJUSTED DATA/STATISTIQUES CHRONOLOGIQUES SUR LA POPULATION ACTIVE, CHIFFRES REELS, FACTEURS SAISONNIERS ET DONNEES DESAISONNALISEES. see *BUSINESS AND ECONOMICS* — *Abstracting, Bibliographies, Statistics*

CANADA. STATISTICS CANADA. HOMICIDE IN CANADA: A STATISTICAL PERSPECTIVE/ L'HOMICIDE AU CANADA: PERSPECTIVE STATISTIQUE. see *CRIMINOLOGY AND LAW ENFORCEMENT* — *Abstracting, Bibliographies, Statistics*

CANADA. STATISTICS CANADA. HONEY PRODUCTION AND VALUE, PRODUCTION FORECAST/PRODUCTION ET VALEUR DU MIEL, PROVISION DE LA PRODUCTION. see *AGRICULTURE* — *Abstracting, Bibliographies, Statistics*

CANADA. STATISTICS CANADA. HOUSEHOLD FACILITIES AND EQUIPMENT/ L'EQUIPMENT MENAGER. see *HOME ECONOMICS* — *Abstracting, Bibliographies, Statistics*

CANADA. STATISTICS CANADA. IMPORTS-MERCHANDISE TRADE/IMPORTATIONS-COMMERCE DE MARCHANDISES. see *BUSINESS AND ECONOMICS* — *Abstracting, Bibliographies, Statistics*

CANADA. STATISTICS CANADA. INDEX OF FARM PRODUCTION/INDICE DE LA PRODUCTION AGRICOLE. see *AGRICULTURE* — *Abstracting, Bibliographies, Statistics*

CANADA. STATISTICS CANADA. JEWELLERY AND PRECIOUS METAL INDUSTRIES/ INDUSTRIES DE LA BIJOUTERIE ET DE L'ORFEVRERIE. see *JEWELRY, CLOCKS AND WATCHES* — *Abstracting, Bibliographies, Statistics*

CANADA. STATISTICS CANADA. LIST OF CANADIAN HOSPITALS AND SPECIAL CARE FACILITIES/LISTE DES HOPITAUX CANADIENS ET DES ETABLISSEMENTS DE SOINS SPECIAUX. see *HOSPITALS* — *Abstracting, Bibliographies, Statistics*

310   CN   ISSN 0228-5134
CANADA. STATISTICS CANADA. LISTING OF SUPPLEMENTARY DOCUMENTS. (Catalogue 11-207) (Text in English and French) 1980. a. Can.$5($6) Statistics Canada, Communications Division, 3rd Floor, R.H. Coats Bldg., Ottawa, Ont. K1A 0T6, Canada TEL 613-993-7276. (Subscr. to: Publications Sales and Services, Ottawa, Ont. K1A 0T6, Canada)

CANADA. STATISTICS CANADA. LIVESTOCK AND ANIMAL PRODUCTS STATISTICS/ STATISTIQUE DU BETAIL ET DES PRODUITS ANIMAUX. see *AGRICULTURE* — *Abstracting, Bibliographies, Statistics*

CANADA. STATISTICS CANADA. LOCAL GOVERNMENT FINANCE: REVENUE AND EXPENDITURE, ASSETS AND LIABILITIES, ACTUAL/FINANCES PUBLIQUES LOCALES: REVENUS ET DEPENSES, ACTIF ET PASSIF, CHIFFRES REELS. see *PUBLIC ADMINISTRATION* — *Abstracting, Bibliographies, Statistics*

CANADA. STATISTICS CANADA. MANUFACTURING INDUSTRIES OF CANADA: SUB-PROVINCIAL AREAS/ INDUSTRIES MANUFACTURES DU CANADA: NIVEAU INFRAPROVINCIAL/ INDUSTRIES MANUFACTURIERES DU CANADA: NIVEAU INFRAPROVINCIAL. see *BUSINESS AND ECONOMICS* — *Abstracting, Bibliographies, Statistics*

CANADA. STATISTICS CANADA. MARKET RESEARCH HANDBOOK. see *BUSINESS AND ECONOMICS* — *Abstracting, Bibliographies, Statistics*

CANADA. STATISTICS CANADA. MECHANICAL CONTRACTING INDUSTRY/ LES ENTREPRENEURS D'INSTALLATIONS MECANIQUES. see *ENGINEERING* — *Abstracting, Bibliographies, Statistics*

CANADA. STATISTICS CANADA. MEN'S CLOTHING INDUSTRIES/INDUSTRIE DES VETEMENTS POUR HOMMES. see *CLOTHING TRADE* — *Abstracting, Bibliographies, Statistics*

CANADA. STATISTICS CANADA. MISCELLANEOUS CLOTHING INDUSTRIES/ INDUSTRIES DIVERSES DE L'HABILLEMENT. see *CLOTHING TRADE* — *Abstracting, Bibliographies, Statistics*

CANADA. STATISTICS CANADA. MISCELLANEOUS FOOD PROCESSORS/ TRAITMENT DES PRODUITS ALIMENTAIRES DIVERS. see *FOOD AND FOOD INDUSTRIES* — *Abstracting, Bibliographies, Statistics*

CANADA. STATISTICS CANADA. MISCELLANEOUS MANUFACTURING INDUSTRIES/INDUSTRIES MANUFACTURIERES DIVERSES. see *BUSINESS AND ECONOMICS* — *Abstracting, Bibliographies, Statistics*

CANADA. STATISTICS CANADA. MOTION PICTURE THEATRES AND FILM DISTRIBUTORS/CINEMAS ET DISTRIBUTEURS DE FILMS. see *MOTION PICTURES* — *Abstracting, Bibliographies, Statistics*

CANADA. STATISTICS CANADA. NON-RESIDENTIAL GENERAL BUILDING CONTRACTING INDUSTRY/INDUSTRIE DES ENTREPRISES GENERALES EN CONSTRUCTION NON DOMICILIAIRE. see *BUILDING AND CONSTRUCTION* — *Abstracting, Bibliographies, Statistics*

CANADA. STATISTICS CANADA. ORNAMENTAL AND ARCHITECTURAL METAL PRODUCTS INDUSTRY/INDUSTRIE DES PRODUITS METALLIQUES D'ORNEMENT ET D'ARCHITECTURE. see *METALLURGY* — *Abstracting, Bibliographies, Statistics*

CANADA. STATISTICS CANADA. PASSENGER BUS AND URBAN TRANSIT STATISTICS/ STATISTIQUE DU TRANSPORT DES VOYAGEURS PAR AUTOBUS ET DU TRANSPORT URBAIN. see *TRANSPORTATION* — *Abstracting, Bibliographies, Statistics*

CANADA. STATISTICS CANADA. PENSION PLANS IN CANADA/REGIMES DE PENSIONS AU CANADA. see *INSURANCE* — *Abstracting, Bibliographies, Statistics*

1052 STATISTICS

CANADA. STATISTICS CANADA. PRINTING, PUBLISHING AND ALLIED INDUSTRIES. see *PRINTING — Abstracting, Bibliographies, Statistics*

CANADA. STATISTICS CANADA. PRIVATE AND PUBLIC INVESTMENT IN CANADA. INTENTIONS/INVESTISSEMENTS PRIVES ET PUBLICS AU CANADA. PERSPECTIVES. see *BUSINESS AND ECONOMICS — Abstracting, Bibliographies, Statistics*

CANADA. STATISTICS CANADA. PRIVATE AND PUBLIC INVESTMENT IN CANADA. REVISED INTENTIONS/INVESTISSEMENTS PRIVES ET PUBLICS AU CANADA. PERSPECTIVE REVISEE. see *BUSINESS AND ECONOMICS — Abstracting, Bibliographies, Statistics*

CANADA. STATISTICS CANADA. PRODUCTION AND VALUE OF MAPLE PRODUCTS/PRODUCTION ET VALEUR DES PRODUITS DE L'ERABLE. see *AGRICULTURE — Abstracting, Bibliographies, Statistics*

CANADA. STATISTICS CANADA. PRODUCTION OF POULTRY AND EGGS/PRODUCTION DE VOLAILLE ET OEUFS. see *AGRICULTURE — Abstracting, Bibliographies, Statistics*

CANADA. STATISTICS CANADA. PRODUCTS SHIPPED BY CANADIAN MANUFACTURERS/PRODUITS LIVRES PAR LES FABRICANTS CANADIENS. see *BUSINESS AND ECONOMICS — Abstracting, Bibliographies, Statistics*

CANADA. STATISTICS CANADA. PROVINCIAL GOVERNMENT ENTERPRISE FINANCE: INCOME AND EXPENDITURE, ASSETS, LIABILITIES AND NET WORTH/REVENUS ET DEPENSES, ACTIF, PASSIF ET VALEUR NETTE. see *BUSINESS AND ECONOMICS — Abstracting, Bibliographies, Statistics*

CANADA. STATISTICS CANADA. PROVINCIAL GOVERNMENT FINANCE: ASSETS, LIABILITIES, SOURCE AND APPLICATION OF FUNDS. see *BUSINESS AND ECONOMICS — Abstracting, Bibliographies, Statistics*

CANADA. STATISTICS CANADA. PULP AND PAPER MILLS/USINES DE PATES ET PAPIERS. see *FORESTS AND FORESTRY — Abstracting, Bibliographies, Statistics*

CANADA. STATISTICS CANADA. RADIO AND TELEVISION BROADCASTING/RADIODIFFUSION ET TELEVISION. see *COMMUNICATIONS — Abstracting, Bibliographies, Statistics*

CANADA. STATISTICS CANADA. REPORT ON FUR FARMS/RAPPORT SUR LES FERMES A FOURRURE. see *LEATHER AND FUR INDUSTRIES — Abstracting, Bibliographies, Statistics*

CANADA. STATISTICS CANADA. RETAIL CHAIN AND DEPARTMENT STORES. see *BUSINESS AND ECONOMICS — Abstracting, Bibliographies, Statistics*

CANADA. STATISTICS CANADA. ROAD MOTOR VEHICLES-FUEL SALES/VEHICULES AUTOMOBILES-VENTES DE CARBURANTS. see *TRANSPORTATION — Abstracting, Bibliographies, Statistics*

CANADA. STATISTICS CANADA. ROAD MOTOR VEHICLES-REGISTRATIONS/VEHICULES AUTOMOBILES-IMMATRICULATIONS. see *TRANSPORTATION — Abstracting, Bibliographies, Statistics*

CANADA. STATISTICS CANADA. RUBBER PRODUCTS INDUSTRIES. see *RUBBER — Abstracting, Bibliographies, Statistics*

CANADA. STATISTICS CANADA. SALARIES AND QUALIFICATIONS OF TEACHERS IN PUBLIC, ELEMENTARY AND SECONDARY SCHOOLS/TRAITEMENTS ET QUALIFICATIONS DES ENSEIGNANTS DES ECOLES PUBLIQUES, PRIMAIRES ET SECONDAIRES. see *EDUCATION — Abstracting, Bibliographies, Statistics*

CANADA. STATISTICS CANADA. SAWMILL, PLANING MILL AND SHINGLE MILL PRODUCTS INDUSTRIES/INDUSTRIES DES PRODUITS DE SCIERIES ET D'ATALIERS DE RABOTAGE. see *FORESTS AND FORESTRY — Abstracting, Bibliographies, Statistics*

CANADA. STATISTICS CANADA. SCIENTIFIC AND PROFESSIONAL EQUIPMENT INDUSTRIES/FABRICATION DE MATERIEL SCIENTIFIQUE ET PROFESSIONNEL. see *INSTRUMENTS — Abstracting, Bibliographies, Statistics*

CANADA. STATISTICS CANADA. SHORN WOOL PRODUCTION/PRODUCTION DE LAINE TONDUE. see *AGRICULTURE — Abstracting, Bibliographies, Statistics*

CANADA. STATISTICS CANADA. SPORTING GOODS AND TOY INDUSTRIES/FABRICATION D'ARTICLES DE SPORT ET DE JOUETS. see *SPORTS AND GAMES — Abstracting, Bibliographies, Statistics*

CANADA. STATISTICS CANADA. SURFACE AND MARINE TRANSPORT. SERVICE BULLETIN/BULLETIN DE SERVICE TRANSPORTS TERRESTRE ET MARITIMES. see *TRANSPORTATION — Abstracting, Bibliographies, Statistics*

CANADA. STATISTICS CANADA. SURGICAL PROCEDURES AND TREATMENTS/INTERVENTIONS CHIRURGICALES ET TRAITEMENTS; a report on the surgical operations and non-surgical procedures performed on in-patients in Canadian hospitals/un rapport sur les interventions chirurgicales et les actes non chirurgicaux, effectues sur les malades hospitalises dans les hopitaux Canadiens. see *MEDICAL SCIENCES — Abstracting, Bibliographies, Statistics*

CANADA. STATISTICS CANADA. SURVEY OF CANADIAN NURSERY TRADES INDUSTRY/ENQUETE SUR L'INDUSTRIE DES PEPINIERES CANADIENNES. see *GARDENING AND HORTICULTURE — Abstracting, Bibliographies, Statistics*

CANADA. STATISTICS CANADA. SYSTEM OF NATIONAL ACCOUNTS, CANADA'S INTERNATIONAL INVESTMENT POSITION/SYSTEME DE COMPTABILITE NATIONALE BILAN CANADIEN DES INVESTISSEMENTS INTERNATIONAUX. see *BUSINESS AND ECONOMICS — Abstracting, Bibliographies, Statistics*

CANADA. STATISTICS CANADA. TELECOMMUNICATIONS STATISTICS/STATISTIQUE DES TELECOMMUNICATIONS. see *COMMUNICATIONS — Abstracting, Bibliographies, Statistics*

CANADA. STATISTICS CANADA. TOBACCO PRODUCTS INDUSTRIES/INDUSTRIE DU TABAC. see *TOBACCO — Abstracting, Bibliographies, Statistics*

CANADA. STATISTICS CANADA. TRAVEL BETWEEN CANADA AND OTHER COUNTRIES/VOYAGES ENTRE LE CANADA ET LES AUTRES PAYS. see *TRAVEL AND TOURISM — Abstracting, Bibliographies, Statistics*

CANADA. STATISTICS CANADA. TRUSTEED PENSION PLANS-FINANCIAL STATISTICS/REGIMES DE PENSIONS EN FIDUCIE STATISTIQUE FINANCIERE. see *BUSINESS AND ECONOMICS — Abstracting, Bibliographies, Statistics*

CANADA. STATISTICS CANADA. VEGETABLE OIL MILLS/MOULINS A HUILE VEGETALE. see *FOOD AND FOOD INDUSTRIES — Abstracting, Bibliographies, Statistics*

CANADA. STATISTICS CANADA. VENDING MACHINE OPERATORS/EXPLOITANTS DE DISTRIBUTEURS AUTOMATIQUES. see *BUSINESS AND ECONOMICS — Abstracting, Bibliographies, Statistics*

CANADA. STATISTICS CANADA. WATER TRANSPORTATION/TRANSPORT PAR EAU. see *TRANSPORTATION — Abstracting, Bibliographies, Statistics*

CANADA. STATISTICS CANADA. WIRE AND WIRE PRODUCTS INDUSTRIES/INDUSTRIES DU FIL METALLIQUE ET DE SES PRODUITS. see *METALLURGY — Abstracting, Bibliographies, Statistics*

CANADA. STATISTICS CANADA. WOMEN'S AND CHILDREN'S CLOTHING INDUSTRIES/INDUSTRIES DES VETEMENTS POUR DAMES ET POUR ENFANTS. see *CLOTHING TRADE — Abstracting, Bibliographies, Statistics*

CANADA. STATISTICS CANADA. WOOL PRODUCTION AND SUPPLY/PRODUCTION ET STOCKS DE LAINE. see *TEXTILE INDUSTRIES AND FABRICS — Abstracting, Bibliographies, Statistics*

310　　　　CN　　ISSN 0832-655X
CANADIAN STATISTICS INDEX. (Text in English, French) 1986. q. (plus a. cumulation) Can.$225. Micromedia Ltd., 158 Pearl St., Toronto, Ont. M5H 1L3, Canada. TEL 416-593-5211. Ed. Rosemary McClelland. (back issues avail.)

CAPITAL EXPENDITURE AND DEBT FINANCING STATISTICS. see *BUSINESS AND ECONOMICS — Abstracting, Bibliographies, Statistics*

310　338.9　　　　JA
CATALOGUE OF STATISTICAL MATERIALS OF DEVELOPING COUNTRIES. (Text in English & Japanese) biennial. 1700 Yen. Institute of Developing Economies - Ajia Keizai Kenkyusho, 42 Ichigaya-Hommuracho, Shinjuku-ku, Tokyo 162, Japan.

CENSO DE POBLACION Y VIVIENDAS. see *POPULATION STUDIES — Abstracting, Bibliographies, Statistics*

CENSUS OF PRIVATE NON-PROFIT MAKING INSTITUTIONS IN FIJI. A REPORT. see *BUSINESS AND ECONOMICS — Abstracting, Bibliographies, Statistics*

CENTRE D'ENQUETES STATISTIQUES DE CAEN. ENQUETE ANNUELLE D'ENTREPRISE: INDUSTRIES DIVERSES. see *BUSINESS AND ECONOMICS — Abstracting, Bibliographies, Statistics*

CHARITY STATISTICS. see *SOCIAL SERVICES AND WELFARE — Abstracting, Bibliographies, Statistics*

CHARTERED INSTITUTE OF PUBLIC FINANCE AND ACCOUNTANCY. CEMETERIES & CREMATORIA STATISTICS. ACTUALS. see *PUBLIC HEALTH AND SAFETY — Abstracting, Bibliographies, Statistics*

CHARTERED INSTITUTE OF PUBLIC FINANCE AND ACCOUNTANCY. CHARGES FOR LEISURE SERVICES. see *SPORTS AND GAMES — Abstracting, Bibliographies, Statistics*

CHARTERED INSTITUTE OF PUBLIC FINANCE AND ACCOUNTANCY. EDUCATION ESTIMATES STATISTICS. see *EDUCATION — Abstracting, Bibliographies, Statistics*

CHARTERED INSTITUTE OF PUBLIC FINANCE AND ACCOUNTANCY. EDUCATION STATISTICS. ACTUALS. see *EDUCATION — Abstracting, Bibliographies, Statistics*

CHARTERED INSTITUTE OF PUBLIC FINANCE AND ACCOUNTANCY. FINANCIAL GENERAL & RATING STATISTICS. see *BUSINESS AND ECONOMICS — Abstracting, Bibliographies, Statistics*

STATISTICS 1053

CHARTERED INSTITUTE OF PUBLIC FINANCE AND ACCOUNTANCY. FIRE SERVICE STATISTICS. ACTUALS. see *FIRE PREVENTION* — *Abstracting, Bibliographies, Statistics*

CHARTERED INSTITUTE OF PUBLIC FINANCE AND ACCOUNTANCY. FIRE SERVICE STATISTICS. ESTIMATES. see *FIRE PREVENTION* — *Abstracting, Bibliographies, Statistics*

CHARTERED INSTITUTE OF PUBLIC FINANCE AND ACCOUNTANCY. HIGHWAYS AND TRANSPORTATION. ACTUALS. see *TRANSPORTATION* — *Abstracting, Bibliographies, Statistics*

CHARTERED INSTITUTE OF PUBLIC FINANCE AND ACCOUNTANCY. HIGHWAYS AND TRANSPORTATION STATISTICS. ESTIMATES. see *TRANSPORTATION* — *Abstracting, Bibliographies, Statistics*

CHARTERED INSTITUTE OF PUBLIC FINANCE AND ACCOUNTANCY. HOMELESSNESS STATISTICS. see *HOUSING AND URBAN PLANNING* — *Abstracting, Bibliographies, Statistics*

CHARTERED INSTITUTE OF PUBLIC FINANCE AND ACCOUNTANCY. HOUSING MAINTENANCE & MANAGEMENT. ACTUALS STATISTICS. see *HOUSING AND URBAN PLANNING* — *Abstracting, Bibliographies, Statistics*

CHARTERED INSTITUTE OF PUBLIC FINANCE AND ACCOUNTANCY. HOUSING REVENUE ACCOUNTS. ACTUALS STATISTICS. see *HOUSING AND URBAN PLANNING* — *Abstracting, Bibliographies, Statistics*

CHARTERED INSTITUTE OF PUBLIC FINANCE AND ACCOUNTANCY. HOUSING REVENUE ACCOUNT ESTIMATE STATISTICS. see *HOUSING AND URBAN PLANNING* — *Abstracting, Bibliographies, Statistics*

CHARTERED INSTITUTE OF PUBLIC FINANCE AND ACCOUNTANCY. HOUSING RENTS. STATISTICS. see *HOUSING AND URBAN PLANNING* — *Abstracting, Bibliographies, Statistics*

CHARTERED INSTITUTE OF PUBLIC FINANCE AND ACCOUNTANCY. LEISURE AND RECREATION STATISTICS. ESTIMATES. see *SPORTS AND GAMES* — *Abstracting, Bibliographies, Statistics*

CHARTERED INSTITUTE OF PUBLIC FINANCE AND ACCOUNTANCY. LEISURE USAGE. ACTUALS. see *SPORTS AND GAMES* — *Abstracting, Bibliographies, Statistics*

CHARTERED INSTITUTE OF PUBLIC FINANCE AND ACCOUNTANCY. LOCAL AUTHORITY AIRPORTS. ACCOUNTS AND STATISTICS. ACTUALS STATISTICS. see *TRANSPORTATION* — *Abstracting, Bibliographies, Statistics*

CHARTERED INSTITUTE OF PUBLIC FINANCE AND ACCOUNTANCY. LOCAL GOVERNMENT COMPARATIVE STATISTICS. see *PUBLIC ADMINISTRATION* — *Abstracting, Bibliographies, Statistics*

CHARTERED INSTITUTE OF PUBLIC FINANCE AND ACCOUNTANCY. PERSONAL SOCIAL SERVICES ESTIMATE STATISTICS. see *SOCIAL SERVICES AND WELFARE* — *Abstracting, Bibliographies, Statistics*

CHARTERED INSTITUTE OF PUBLIC FINANCE AND ACCOUNTANCY. PERSONAL SOCIAL SERVICES STATISTICS. ACTUALS. see *SOCIAL SERVICES AND WELFARE* — *Abstracting, Bibliographies, Statistics*

CHARTERED INSTITUTE OF PUBLIC FINANCE AND ACCOUNTANCY. PLANNING AND DEVELOPMENT STATISTICS. ACTUALS. see *PUBLIC ADMINISTRATION* — *Abstracting, Bibliographies, Statistics*

CHARTERED INSTITUTE OF PUBLIC FINANCE AND ACCOUNTANCY. PLANNING AND DEVELOPMENT STATISTICS. ESTIMATES. see *PUBLIC ADMINISTRATION* — *Abstracting, Bibliographies, Statistics*

CHARTERED INSTITUTE OF PUBLIC FINANCE AND ACCOUNTANCY. POLICE STATISTICS. ACTUALS. see *CRIMINOLOGY AND LAW ENFORCEMENT* — *Abstracting, Bibliographies, Statistics*

CHARTERED INSTITUTE OF PUBLIC FINANCE AND ACCOUNTANCY. POLICE STATISTICS. ESTIMATES. see *CRIMINOLOGY AND LAW ENFORCEMENT* — *Abstracting, Bibliographies, Statistics*

CHARTERED INSTITUTE OF PUBLIC FINANCE AND ACCOUNTANCY. PUBLIC LIBRARY STATISTICS. ACTUALS. see *LIBRARY AND INFORMATION SCIENCES* — *Abstracting, Bibliographies, Statistics*

CHARTERED INSTITUTE OF PUBLIC FINANCE AND ACCOUNTANCY. PUBLIC LIBRARY STATISTICS. ESTIMATES. see *LIBRARY AND INFORMATION SCIENCES* — *Abstracting, Bibliographies, Statistics*

CHARTERED INSTITUTE OF PUBLIC FINANCE AND ACCOUNTANCY. RATE COLLECTION STATISTICS. ACTUALS. see *BUSINESS AND ECONOMICS* — *Abstracting, Bibliographies, Statistics*

CHARTERED INSTITUTE OF PUBLIC FINANCE AND ACCOUNTANCY. SCHOOL MEALS STATISTICS. see *EDUCATION* — *Abstracting, Bibliographies, Statistics*

CHARTERED INSTITUTE OF PUBLIC FINANCE AND ACCOUNTANCY. WASTE COLLECTION STATISTICS. ACTUALS. see *PUBLIC ADMINISTRATION* — *Abstracting, Bibliographies, Statistics*

CHARTERED INSTITUTE OF PUBLIC FINANCE AND ACCOUNTANCY. WASTE DISPOSAL STATISTICS. ACTUALS. see *PUBLIC ADMINISTRATION* — *Abstracting, Bibliographies, Statistics*

CHARTERED INSTITUTE OF PUBLIC FINANCE AND ACCOUNTANCY. WASTE DISPOSAL STATISTICS. ESTIMATES. see *PUBLIC ADMINISTRATION* — *Abstracting, Bibliographies, Statistics*

CHARTERED INSTITUTE OF PUBLIC FINANCE AND ACCOUNTANCY. WATER SERVICES CHARGES STATISTICS. see *WATER RESOURCES* — *Abstracting, Bibliographies, Statistics*

318 CL
CHILE. INSTITUTO NACIONAL DE ESTADISTICAS. COMPENDIO ESTADISTICO. 1971. a. $10. Instituto Nacional de Estadisticas, Av. Bulnes 418, Casilla 498, Correo 3-Santiago, Chile. stat.

318 CL
CHILE. INSTITUTO NACIONAL DE ESTADISTICAS. SERIES ESTADISTICAS. 1981. quinquiennial. $20. Instituto Nacional de Estadisticas, Av. Bulnes 418, Casilla 498, Correo 3-Santiago, Chile.
Formerly: Chile. Instituto Nacional de Estadisticas. Anuario Estadistico.

CHINA FACTS AND FIGURES ANNUAL. see *POLITICAL SCIENCE*

339 318 CR
CIFRAS DE CUENTAS NACIONALES. 1968. a. free. Banco Central de Costa Rica, Departamento de Investigaciones y Estadistica, Apdo. 10058, San Jose, Costa Rica. charts. stat. circ. 300.

318 CK
COLOMBIA. DEPARTAMENTO ADMINISTRATIVO NACIONAL DE ESTADISTICA. ANUARIO DE JUSTICIA.* a. Departamento Administrativo Nacional de Estadistica, Centro Administrativo Nacional-Avda. El Dorado, Apdo. Aereo 80043, Bogota, Colombia.
Formerly: Colombia. Departamento Administrativo Nacional de Estadistica. Anuario General de Estadistica - Justicia.

318 CK
COLOMBIA. DEPARTAMENTO ADMINISTRATIVO NACIONAL DE ESTADISTICA. ESTADISTICAS HISTORICAS. irreg. Departamento Administrativo Nacional de Estadistica, Apartado Aereo 80043, Avda. Eldovado, Bogota, Colombia.

COLUMBIA. DEPARTAMENTO ADMINISTRATIVO NACIONAL DE ESTADISTICA. ANUARIO GENERAL DE ESTADISTICA - TRANSPORTES Y COMUNICACIONES. see *TRANSPORTATION* — *Abstracting, Bibliographies, Statistics*

310 IO
COMMUNICATION STATISTICS. (Text in Indonesian) 1965. a. $1. Central Bureau of Statistics, Jl. Dr Sutomo No. 8, Jakarta Pusat, Indonesia. circ. 151.

COMMUNITY SERVICE STATISTICS: SCOTLAND. see *SOCIAL SERVICES AND WELFARE* — *Abstracting, Bibliographies, Statistics*

COMPANHIA PARANAENSE DE ENERGIA. INFORME ESTATISTICO ANUAL. see *ENERGY* — *Abstracting, Bibliographies, Statistics*

COMPENDIO ESTADISTICO CENTROAMERICANO. see *BUSINESS AND ECONOMICS* — *Abstracting, Bibliographies, Statistics*

314 IT ISSN 0069-7958
COMPENDIO STATISTICO ITALIANO. a. L.8000. Istituto Centrale di Statistica, Via Cesare Balbo 16, 00100 Rome, Italy. circ. 12,250.
Formerly: Compendio Statistico (ISSN 0390-640X)

COMPENDIUM OF NEW ZEALAND FARM PRODUCTION STATISTICS. see *AGRICULTURE* — *Abstracting, Bibliographies, Statistics*

314 GR ISSN 0069-8245
CONCISE STATISTICAL YEARBOOK OF GREECE. (Text in English and Greek) 1962. a., latest 1983/84. $5. National Statistical Service, Publications and Information Division, 14-16 Lycourgou St., 10166 Athens, Greece.

COST AND PRODUCTION SURVEY REPORT. see *MEDICAL SCIENCES*

310 CR ISSN 0589-8544
COSTA RICA. DIRECCION GENERAL DE ESTADISTICA Y CENSOS. INVENTARIO DE LAS ESTADISTICAS NACIONALES. 1964. irreg., latest 1970. exchange basis. Direccion General de Estadistica y Censos, San Jose, Costa Rica.

CUBA EN CIFRAS. see *BUSINESS AND ECONOMICS* — *Abstracting, Bibliographies, Statistics*

CURRENT INDEX TO STATISTICS; applications-methods-theory. see *ABSTRACTING AND INDEXING SERVICES*

CURRENT INDUSTRIAL REPORTS: FATS AND OILS. OILSEED CRUSHINGS. see *FOOD AND FOOD INDUSTRIES* — *Abstracting, Bibliographies, Statistics*

CURRENT INDUSTRIAL REPORTS: FATS AND OILS. PRODUCTION, CONSUMPTION, AND FACTORY AND WAREHOUSE STOCKS. see *FOOD AND FOOD INDUSTRIES* — *Abstracting, Bibliographies, Statistics*

1054   STATISTICS

CURRENT INDUSTRIAL REPORTS: FINISHED FABRICS. PRODUCTION, INVENTORIES, AND UNFILLED ORDERS. see *TEXTILE INDUSTRIES AND FABRICS* — *Abstracting, Bibliographies, Statistics*

310   CY
CYPRUS. DEPARTMENT OF STATISTICS AND RESEARCH. CENSUS OF COTTAGE INDUSTRY. (Text in English) 1967. irreg. cyprus pounds 2. Ministry of Finance, Department of Statistics and Research, Nicosia, Cyprus.

CYPRUS. DEPARTMENT OF STATISTICS AND RESEARCH. CENSUS OF INDUSTRIAL PRODUCTION. see *BUSINESS AND ECONOMICS* — *Abstracting, Bibliographies, Statistics*

CYPRUS. DEPARTMENT OF STATISTICS AND RESEARCH. CENSUS OF POULTRY. see *AGRICULTURE* — *Abstracting, Bibliographies, Statistics*

CYPRUS. DEPARTMENT OF STATISTICS AND RESEARCH. CRIMINAL STATISTICS. see *CRIMINOLOGY AND LAW ENFORCEMENT* — *Abstracting, Bibliographies, Statistics*

CYPRUS. DEPARTMENT OF STATISTICS AND RESEARCH. DEMOGRAPHIC SURVEY. (YEAR) see *POPULATION STUDIES* — *Abstracting, Bibliographies, Statistics*

310   CY
CYPRUS. DEPARTMENT OF STATISTICS AND RESEARCH. FUNCTIONS AND SERVICES. (Text in English) 1981. irreg. cyprus Pounds 0.25. Ministry of Finance, Department of Statistics and Research, Nicosia, Cyprus.

CYPRUS. DEPARTMENT OF STATISTICS AND RESEARCH. HOUSEHOLD EXPENDITURE SURVEY. see *BUSINESS AND ECONOMICS* — *Abstracting, Bibliographies, Statistics*

CYPRUS. DEPARTMENT OF STATISTICS AND RESEARCH. MULTI-ROUND DEMOGRAPHIC SURVEY. MIGRATION IN CYPRUS. see *POPULATION STUDIES* — *Abstracting, Bibliographies, Statistics*

CYPRUS. DEPARTMENT OF STATISTICS AND RESEARCH. MULTI-ROUND DEMOGRAPHIC SURVEY. SUMMARY OF MAIN DEMOGRAPHIC CHARACTERISTICS. see *POPULATION STUDIES* — *Abstracting, Bibliographies, Statistics*

310   CY
CYPRUS. DEPARTMENT OF STATISTICS AND RESEARCH. QUESTIONNAIRES FOR CENSUSES AND SURVEYS. (Text in Greek and English) 1982. irreg. cyprus pounds 3. Ministry of Finance, Department of Statistics and Research, Nicosia, Cyprus.

312   CY   ISSN 0253-875X
CYPRUS. DEPARTMENT OF STATISTICS AND RESEARCH. STATISTICAL ABSTRACT. (Text in English) 1955. a. cyprus pounds 6. Department of Statistics and Research, Ministry of Finance, Nicosia, Cyprus.

314   CY
CYPRUS. DEPARTMENT OF STATISTICS AND RESEARCH. STATISTICAL POCKET BOOK. (Text in English) 1978. irreg. cyprus pounds 0.25. Department of Statistics and Research, Ministry of Finance, Nicosia, Cyprus.

314.37 947   CS   ISSN 0070-248X
CZECHOSLOVAKIA. FEDERALNI STATISTICKY URAD. STATISTICKA ROCENKA. (Text in Czech; summaries in English and Russian) 1957. approx. a. $20 per no. Statni Nakladatelstvi Technicke Literatury, Spalena 51, 113 02 Prague 1, Czechoslovakia. circ. 13,300.

314.8   DK   ISSN 0107-7139
DANMARK I TAL. English edition: Data on Denmark. 1981. a. free. Danmarks Statistik, Sejroegade 11, 2100 Copenhagen OE, Denmark. illus.

314   DK   ISSN 0070-3567
DENMARK. DANMARKS STATISTIK. STATISTISK AARBOG/STATISTICAL YEARBOOK. (Text in Danish; notes in English) 1896. a. Kr.98.36. Danmarks Statistik, Sejroegade 11, 2100 Copenhagen OE, Denmark. cum.index: 1769-1972.

314   DK   ISSN 0070-3583
DENMARK. DANMARKS STATISTIK. STATISTISK TIARS-OVERSIGT/STATISTICAL TEN-YEAR REVIEW. 1961. a. Kr.45.08. Danmarks Statistik, Sejroegade 11, 2100 Copenhagen OE, Denmark.

314   DK   ISSN 0039-0682
DENMARK. DANMARKS STATISTIK. STATISTISKE UNDERSOGELSER. 1958. irreg. price varies. Danmarks Statistik, Sejroegade 11, 2100 Copenhagen OE, Denmark.

310   DK   ISSN 0109-8314
DENMARK. DANMARKS STATISTIK. VEJVISER I STATISTIKEN. 1984. irreg. Danmarks Statistik, Sejroegade 11, 2100 Copenhagen OE, Denmark.

310   DK   ISSN 0106-9039
DENMARK. NORDISK STATISTISK SEKRETARIAT. TEKNISKE RAPPORTER. (Text in Scandinavian Languages) 1968. irreg., no.40, 1986. Nordisk Statistisk Sekretariat, Postbox 2550, DK-2100 Copenhagen OE, Denmark.

310   GW
DIE DIENSTSTELLEN DES FREISTAATES BAYERN IN DEN KREISFREIEN STAEDTEN UND LANDKREISEN. 1980. a. DM.18. Neuhauser Str. 51, 8000 Munich 2, W. Germany (B.R.D.) Ed.Bd.

310   UK   ISSN 0262-8295
DIGEST OF WELSH STATISTICS. 1954. a. £5. Welsh Office, Economic and Statistical Services Division, New Crown Bldg., Cathays Park, Cardiff CF1 3NQ, Wales. Ed. E. Swires-Hennessy. stat. circ. 800.

310   US   ISSN 0278-405X
DIRECTORY OF STATISTICIANS. triennial. $40. American Statistical Association, 806 15 St., N.W., Washington, DC 20005. TEL 202-393-3253.
   Formerly: Statisticians and Others in Allied Professions (ISSN 0081-508X)

310   GW
DUESSELDORF. STATISTISCHES JAHRBUCH. a. Amt fuer Statistik, Duesseldorf, W. Germany (B.R.D.)

314   GW   ISSN 0418-1263
DUESSELDORF IN ZAHLEN. 1902. a. DM.20. Landeshauptstadt, Amt fuer Statistik und Wahlen, Postfach 1120, 4000 Duesseldorf 1, W. Germany (B.R.D.) stat. circ. 570. (looseleaf format)

EDUCATION STATISTICS, NEW YORK STATE; prepared especially for members of the Legislature. see *EDUCATION* — *Abstracting, Bibliographies, Statistics*

315.6   UA
EGYPT. CENTRAL AGENCY FOR PUBLIC MOBILISATION AND STATISTICS. STATISTICAL YEARBOOK. (Text in Arabic and English) 1961. a. £E14. Central Agency for Public Mobilisation and Statistics, Box 2086, Nasr City, Cairo, Egypt.
   Formerly: Statistical Handbook of Egypt.

318   ES   ISSN 0080-5661
EL SALVADOR. DIRECCION GENERAL DE ESTADISTICA Y CENSOS. ANUARIO ESTADISTICO. a. free or exchange basis. Direccion General de Estadistica y Censos, 1 Calle Poniente y 43 Avenida Norte, San Salvador, El Salvador.

318   ES
EL SALVADOR EN CIFRAS. biennial. free or exchange basis. Direccion General de Estadistica y Censos, 1 Calle Poniente y 43 Avenida Sur, San Salvador, El Salvador.

ESTABLECIMIENTOS MANUFACTURERAS EN PUERTO RICO. see *BUSINESS AND ECONOMICS* — *Abstracting, Bibliographies, Statistics*

319   PN
ESTADISTICA PANAMENA. BOLETIN. 1963. irreg., no.979, 1985. Direccion de Estadistica y Censo, Apdo. 5213, Panama 5, Panama.

ESTADISTICA PANAMENA. SITUACION CULTURAL. SECCION 511. EDUCACION. see *EDUCATION* — *Abstracting, Bibliographies, Statistics*

ESTADISTICA PANAMENA. SITUACION DEMOGRAFICA. SECCION 221. ESTADISTICAS VITALES. see *POPULATION STUDIES* — *Abstracting, Bibliographies, Statistics*

ESTADISTICA PANAMENA. SITUACION ECONOMICA. SECCION 312. PRODUCCION PECUARIA. see *AGRICULTURE* — *Abstracting, Bibliographies, Statistics*

ESTADISTICA PANAMENA. SITUACION ECONOMICA. SECCION 312. SUPERFICIE SEMBRADA Y COSECHA DE ARROZ, MAIZ Y FRIJOL DE BEJUCO. see *AGRICULTURE* — *Abstracting, Bibliographies, Statistics*

ESTADISTICA PANAMENA. SITUACION ECONOMICA. SECCION 312. SUPERFICIE SEMBRADA Y COSECHA DE CAFE, TABACO Y CANA DE AZUCAR. see *AGRICULTURE* — *Abstracting, Bibliographies, Statistics*

ESTADISTICA PANAMENA. SITUACION ECONOMICA. SECCION 323. INDICE DE VOLUMEN FISICO DE LA PRODUCCION INDUSTRIAL. see *BUSINESS AND ECONOMICS* — *Abstracting, Bibliographies, Statistics*

ESTADISTICA PANAMENA. SITUACION ECONOMICA. SECCION 331-COMERCIO. ANUARIO DE COMERCIO EXTERIOR. see *BUSINESS AND ECONOMICS* — *Abstracting, Bibliographies, Statistics*

ESTADISTICA PANAMENA. SITUACION ECONOMICA. SECCION 331. COMERCIO EXTERIOR (PRELIMINARY REPORT) see *BUSINESS AND ECONOMICS* — *Abstracting, Bibliographies, Statistics*

ESTADISTICA PANAMENA. SITUACION ECONOMICA. SECCION 343-344. HACIENDA PUBLICA Y FINANZAS. see *BUSINESS AND ECONOMICS* — *Abstracting, Bibliographies, Statistics*

ESTADISTICA PANAMENA. SITUACION ECONOMICA. SECCION 351. PRECIOS PAGADOS POR EL PRODUCTOR AGROPECUARIO. see *AGRICULTURE* — *Abstracting, Bibliographies, Statistics*

ESTADISTICA PANAMENA. SITUACION ECONOMICA. SECCION 352. HOJA DE BALANCE DE ALIMENTOS. see *BUSINESS AND ECONOMICS* — *Abstracting, Bibliographies, Statistics*

ESTADISTICA PANAMENA. SITUACION POLITICA, ADMINISTRATIVA Y JUSTICIA. SECCION 631. JUSTICIA. see *LAW* — *Abstracting, Bibliographies, Statistics*

ESTADISTICA PANAMENA. SITUACION SOCIAL. SECCION 431. ASISTENCIA SOCIAL. see *SOCIAL SERVICES AND WELFARE* — *Abstracting, Bibliographies, Statistics*

ESTADISTICA PANAMENA. SITUACION SOCIAL. SECCION 451. ACCIDENTES DE TRANSITO. see *SOCIOLOGY* — *Abstracting, Bibliographies, Statistics*

ETESIA STATISTIKE. EREVNA TOU KARKINOU/ANNUAL STATISTICAL SURVEY OF CANCER. see *MEDICAL SCIENCES* — *Cancer*

EXPORT STATISTICS OF AFGHANISTAN/ IHSA'IYAH-I AMUAL-I SADIRATI-I AFGHANISTAN. see *BUSINESS AND ECONOMICS* — *Abstracting, Bibliographies, Statistics*

EXTERNAL TRADE STATISTICS OF GAMBIA. see *BUSINESS AND ECONOMICS* — *Abstracting, Bibliographies, Statistics*

315.4 II
FACTS ABOUT HARYANA. 1967. irreg. Director of Public Relations, Chandigarh, India. stat. circ. 3,000.

315 IS
FAMILY EXPENDITURE SURVEY. (Text in English and Hebrew) 1969. irreg. price varies. Central Bureau of Statistics, Box 13015, Hakirya Romems, Jerusalem, Israel. stat. (back issues avail.)

FARM BUSINESS STATISTICS FOR SOUTH EAST ENGLAND. see *AGRICULTURE — Abstracting, Bibliographies, Statistics*

FERTILISER ASSOCIATION OF INDIA. FERTILISER STATISTICS. see *AGRICULTURE — Abstracting, Bibliographies, Statistics*

FIJI. BUREAU OF STATISTICS. CENSUS OF DISTRIBUTION AND SERVICES. see *BUSINESS AND ECONOMICS — Abstracting, Bibliographies, Statistics*

310 US
FINANCES OF THE PUBLIC SCHOOL SYSTEMS. a. U.S. Bureau of the Census, Government Division, Washington, DC 20233. TEL 301-763-7664. (back issues avail.)

FINANCIAL STATISTICS OF SELECTED ELECTRIC UTILITIES. see *ENERGY — Abstracting, Bibliographies, Statistics*

FINLAND. STATISTIKCENTRALEN. STATISTISKA MEDDELANDEN. LEVNADSFOERHAALANDEN I FINLAND/ FINLAND. CENTRAL STATISTICAL OFFICE. LIVING CONDITIONS IN FINLAND. see *SOCIOLOGY*

311 FI ISSN 0355-2063
FINLAND. TILASTOKESKUS. KASIKIRJOJA/ FINLAND. STATISTIKCENTRALEN. HANDBOECKER/FINLAND. CENTRAL STATISTICAL OFFICE. HANDBOOKS. (Text in Finnish and sometimes in Swedish and English) 1971. irreg. price varies. Tilastokeskus, Annankatu 44, SF-00100 Helsinki 10, Finland (Subscr. to: Government Printing Centre, Box 516, SF-00100 Helsinki 10, Finland)

FINLAND. TILASTOKESKUS. TILASTOLLISIA TIEDONANTOJA. NAISTEN ASEMA/ FINLAND. STATISTIKCENTRALEEN. STATISTISKA MEDDELANDEN. KVINNORNAS STAELLNING/FINLAND. CENTRAL STATISTICAL OFFICE. STATISTICAL SURVEYS. POSITION OF WOMEN. see *SOCIOLOGY*

314 FI ISSN 0357-0614
FINLAND. TILASTOKESKUS. VALTION TILASTOJULKAISUT/FINLAND. STATISTIKCENTRALEN. STATENS STATISTISKA PUBLIKATIONER/FINLAND. CENTRAL STATISTICAL OFFICE. GOVERNMENT STATISTICS. (Text in English, Finnish and Swedish) 1978. a. Fmk.105. Tilastokeskus, Annankatu 44, SF-00100 Helsinki 10, Finland (Subscr. to: Government Printing Centre, Box 516, SF-00101 Helsinki, Finland)

310 GW
FLENSBURGER STATISTISCHE BLAETTER. 1975. irreg. (2-4/yr.) free. Stadt FLensburg, Der Magistrat, Amt fuer Stadtentwicklung und Statistik, Postfach 2742, 2390 Flensburg, W. Germany (B.R.D.) circ. 500.

310 GW
FLENSBURGER ZAHLENSPIEGEL (YEAR) 1951. a. DM.9. Stadt Flensburg, Der Magistrat, Amt fuer Stadtentwicklung u. Statistik, Postfach 2742, 2390 Flensburg, W. Germany (B.R.D.) circ. 500.

318 US ISSN 0071-6022
FLORIDA STATISTICAL ABSTRACT. Variant title: Florida Statistical Abstracts Annual. 1967. a. $19.95 pap.; $27.95 cloth. (University of Florida, Bureau of Economic and Business Research) University Presses of Florida, 15 N.W. 15th St., Gainesville, FL 32603. TEL 904-392-1351. Ed. Anne Shoemyen. circ. 3,700.

FLORIDA VITAL STATISTICS. see *POPULATION STUDIES — Abstracting, Bibliographies, Statistics*

310 US
FOUNDATION 500. 1974. a. $40. (Foundation Research Service) Douglas M. Lawson Associates, 39 E. 51st St., 4th Fl., New York, NY 10022. Ed. David M. Lawson. circ. 2,500.

FRANCE. INSTITUT NATIONAL DE LA STATISTIQUE ET DES ETUDES ECONOMIQUES. COLLECTIONS. SERIE R, REGIONS. see *BUSINESS AND ECONOMICS — Abstracting, Bibliographies, Statistics*

FRANCE. MINISTERE DE L'INDUSTRIE, DES P & T ET DU TOURISME. ENQUETE ANNUELLE D'ENTREPRISE. see *BUSINESS AND ECONOMICS — Abstracting, Bibliographies, Statistics*

314 GW ISSN 0071-9218
FRANKFURT AM MAIN. STATISTISCHES AMT UND WAHLAMT. STATISTISCHES JAHRBUCH. 1951. a. DM.16. Statistisches Amt und Wahlamt, Kurt Schumacherstr. 41, 6000 Frankfurt 1, W. Germany (B.R.D.) circ. 1,300.

FROZEN FISHERY PRODUCTS. ANNUAL SUMMARY. see *FISH AND FISHERIES — Abstracting, Bibliographies, Statistics*

310 GW
FULDA. STATISTISCHER BERICHT. 1974. a. free. Magistrat der Stadt Fulda, Abt. 103, Postfach 1020, D-6400 Fulda, W. Germany (B.R.D.) circ. 600.

GAMBIA. CENTRAL STATISTICS DEPARTMENT. EDUCATION STATISTICS. see *EDUCATION — Abstracting, Bibliographies, Statistics*

GAMBIA. CENTRAL STATISTICS DEPARTMENT. TOURIST STATISTICS. see *TRAVEL AND TOURISM — Abstracting, Bibliographies, Statistics*

GEORGIA DESCRIPTIONS IN DATA. see *POPULATION STUDIES — Abstracting, Bibliographies, Statistics*

GEORGIA STATISTICAL ABSTRACT. see *BUSINESS AND ECONOMICS — Abstracting, Bibliographies, Statistics*

GERIATRIC LENGTH OF STAY BY DIAGNOSIS AND OPERATION, UNITED STATES. see *HOSPITALS*

GERMANY (FEDERAL REPUBLIC, 1949-). BUNDESANSTALT FUER ARBEIT. BERUFSBERATUNG. ERGEBNISSE DER BERUFSBERATUNGSSTATISTIK. see *BUSINESS AND ECONOMICS — Abstracting, Bibliographies, Statistics*

GERMANY (FEDERAL REPUBLIC, 1949-). STATISTISCHES BUNDESAMT. FACHSERIE 7, AUSSENHANDEL, REIHE 2: AUSSENHANDEL NACH WAREN UND LAENDERN (SPEZIALHANDEL) see *BUSINESS AND ECONOMICS — Abstracting, Bibliographies, Statistics*

GERMANY (FEDERAL REPUBLIC, 1949-). STATISTISCHES BUNDESAMT. FACHSERIE 7, AUSSENHANDEL, REIHE 7: SONDERBEITRAEGE. see *BUSINESS AND ECONOMICS — Abstracting, Bibliographies, Statistics*

GERMANY (FEDERAL REPUBLIC, 1949-). STATISTISCHES BUNDESAMT. FACHSERIE 5, BAUTAETIGKEIT UND WOHNUNGEN, REIHE 1: BAUTAETIGKEIT. see *BUILDING AND CONSTRUCTION — Abstracting, Bibliographies, Statistics*

GERMANY (FEDERAL REPUBLIC, 1949-). STATISTISCHES BUNDESAMT. FACHSERIE 5, BAUTAETIGKEIT UND WOHNUNGEN, REIHE 2: BEWILLIGUNGEN IM SOZIALEN WOHNUNGSBAU. see *BUILDING AND CONSTRUCTION — Abstracting, Bibliographies, Statistics*

GERMANY (FEDERAL REPUBLIC, 1949-). STATISTISCHES BUNDESAMT. FACHSERIE 6, HANDEL, GASTGEWERBE, REISEVERKEHR; REIHE 3: EINZELHANDEL. see *BUSINESS AND ECONOMICS — Abstracting, Bibliographies, Statistics*

GERMANY (FEDERAL REPUBLIC, 1949-). STATISTISCHES BUNDESAMT. FACHSERIE 6, HANDEL, GASTGEWERBE, REISEVERKEHR; REIHE 5: WAHRENVERKEHR MIT BERLIN (WEST) see *BUSINESS AND ECONOMICS — Abstracting, Bibliographies, Statistics*

GERMANY (FEDERAL REPUBLIC, 1949-). STATISTISCHES BUNDESAMT. FACHSERIE 3, LAND- UND FORTSTWIRTSCHAFT, FISCHEREI; REIHE 2: BETRIEBS-, ARBEITS- UND EINKOMMENSVERHAELTNISSE. see *AGRICULTURE — Abstracting, Bibliographies, Statistics*

GERMANY (FEDERAL REPUBLIC, 1949-). STATISTISCHES BUNDESAMT. FACHSERIE 4, PRODUZIERENDES GEWERBE, REIHE 3.1: PRODUKTION GEWERBE DES IN- UND AUSLANDES. see *BUSINESS AND ECONOMICS — Abstracting, Bibliographies, Statistics*

GERMANY (FEDERAL REPUBLIC, 1949-). STATISTISCHES BUNDESAMT. FACHSERIE 8, VERKEHR, REIHE 3.3: HAUSHAELTE UND FAMILIEN. see *TRANSPORTATION — Abstracting, Bibliographies, Statistics*

GERMANY (FEDERAL REPUBLIC, 1949-). STATISTISCHES BUNDESAMT. FACHSERIE 11: BILDUNG UND KULTUR. see *EDUCATION — Abstracting, Bibliographies, Statistics*

GERMANY (FEDERAL REPUBLIC, 1949-). STATISTISCHES BUNDESAMT. FACHSERIE 12, GESUNDHEITSWESEN, REIHE 1: AUSGEWAEHLTE ZAHLEN FUER DAS GESUNDHEITSWESEN. see *PUBLIC HEALTH AND SAFETY — Abstracting, Bibliographies, Statistics*

GERMANY (FEDERAL REPUBLIC, 1949-). STATISTISCHES BUNDESAMT. FACHSERIE 16, LOEHNE UND GEHAELTER, REIHE 5.2: TARIFLOEHNE UND GEHAELTER DES AUSLANDES. see *BUSINESS AND ECONOMICS — Abstracting, Bibliographies, Statistics*

GERMANY (FEDERAL REPUBLIC, 1949-). STATISTISCHES BUNDESAMT. FACHSERIE 17, PREISE, REIHE 1: PREISE UND PREISINDIZES FUER DIE LAND- UND FORSTWIRTSCHAFT. see *AGRICULTURE — Abstracting, Bibliographies, Statistics*

GERMANY (FEDERAL REPUBLIC, 1949-). STATISTISCHES BUNDESAMT. FACHSERIE 17, PREISE, REIHE 9: PREISE FUER VERKEHRSLEISTUNGEN. see *TRANSPORTATION — Abstracting, Bibliographies, Statistics*

GERMANY (FEDERAL REPUBLIC, 1949-). STATISTISCHES BUNDESAMT. FACHSERIE 10. RECHTSPFLEGE. see *LAW — Abstracting, Bibliographies, Statistics*

318 GW
GERMANY (FEDERAL REPUBLIC, 1949-). STATISTISCHES BUNDESAMT. LAENDERBERICHTE. (Subseries of its Allgemeine Statistik des Auslandes; avail. for approx. 30 countries) irreg. DM.568.80. W. Kohlhammer-Verlag GmbH, Abt. Veroeffentlichungen des Statistischen Bundesamtes, Philipp-Reis-Str. 3, Postfach 421120, 6500 Mainz 42, W. Germany (B.R.D.)

GERMANY (FEDERAL REPUBLIC, 1949-) STATISTISCHES BUNDESAMT. WARENVERZEICHNIS FUER DIE AUSSENHANDELSSTATISTIK. see *BUSINESS AND ECONOMICS — Abstracting, Bibliographies, Statistics*

310 GW ISSN 0072-4114
GERMANY (FEDERAL REPUBLIC, 1949-)
STATISTISCHES BUNDESAMT.
ZAHLENKOMPASS/STATISTICAL COMPASS/
BOUSSOLE DES CHIFFRES/COMPAS DE
CIFRAS. (Editions in English, French, German and
Spanish) a. DM.3. W. Kohlhammer-Verlag GmbH,
Abt. Veroeffentlichungen des Statistischen
Bundesamtes, Philipp-Reis-Str. 3, Postfach 421120,
6500 Mainz 42, W. Germany (B.R.D.)

GHANA. CENTRAL BUREAU OF STATISTICS.
ECONOMIC SURVEY. see *BUSINESS AND
ECONOMICS* — *Abstracting, Bibliographies,
Statistics*

316 MF
GLANURES. (Text in English and French) a. free.
Ministry of Information and Broadcasting,
Government Centre, 6th Fl., Port Louis, Mauritius.
circ. 5,000.

310 SW ISSN 0072-5110
GOETEBORGS UNIVERSITET. STATISTISKA
INSTITUTIONEN. SKRIFTSERIE.
PUBLICATIONS. (Text in English or Swedish)
1954. irreg., no.16, 1974. price varies. Fack, S-104
05 Stockholm, Sweden. Ed. Anders Klevmarken.

318.1 BL
GOIAS, BRAZIL. SECRETARIA DO
PLANEJAMENTO E COORDENACAO.
BOLETIM ESTADISTICO. (Includes comparative
data for previous years) Secretaria do Planejamento
e Coordenacao, Goiania, Brazil.
 Continues: Goias, Brazil. Departamento Estadual
de Estatistica. Boletim Estatistico.

314 UK ISSN 0072-5730
GREAT BRITAIN. CENTRAL STATISTICAL
OFFICE. ANNUAL ABSTRACT OF
STATISTICS. 1948. a. £17.50. Central Statistical
Office, Great George St., London SW1P 3AQ,
England (Avail. from: Open University Educational
Enterprises Ltd., 12 Cofferidge Close, Stony
Stratford, Milton Keynes MK11 1BY England)

314 UK ISSN 0261-1791
GREAT BRITAIN. CENTRAL STATISTICAL
OFFICE. GUIDE TO OFFICIAL STATISTICS.
1976. biennial. £25. Central Statistical Office, Great
George St., London SW1P 3AQ, England (Avail.
from: Open University Educational Enterprises Ltd.,
12 Cofferidge Close, Stony Stratford, Milton Keynes
MK11 1BY, England)

314 UK ISSN 0261-1783
GREAT BRITAIN. CENTRAL STATISTICAL
OFFICE. REGIONAL TRENDS. 1965. a. £16.95.
Central Statistical Office, Great George St., London
SW1P 3AQ, England (Avail. from: Open University
Educational Enterprises Ltd., 12 Cofferidge Close,
Stony Stratford, Milton Keynes MK11 1BY
England) charts. stat.
 Former titles: Great Britain. Central Statistical
Office. Regional Statistics (ISSN 0308-146X); Great
Britain. Central Statistical Office Abstracts of
Regional Statistics (ISSN 0072-5749)

311 UK ISSN 0072-5757
GREAT BRITAIN. CENTRAL STATISTICAL
OFFICE. RESEARCH SERIES. 1968. irreg. price
varies. Central Statistical Office, Great George St.,
London SW1P 3AQ, England (Avail. from: Open
University Educational Enterprises Ltd., 12
Cofferidge Close, Stony Stratford, Milton Keynes
MK11 1BY, England)

311 UK ISSN 0081-8313
GREAT BRITAIN. CENTRAL STATISTICAL
OFFICE. STUDIES IN OFFICIAL STATISTICS.
irreg. price varies. Central Statistical Office, Great
George St., London SW1P 3AQ, England (Avail.
from: Open University Educational Enterprises Ltd.,
12 Cofferidge Close, Stony Stratford, Milton Keynes
MK11 1BY, England)

GREAT BRITAIN. HOME OFFICE. STATISTICS
OF THE MISUSE OF DRUGS IN THE UNITED
KINGDOM, SUPPLEMENTARY TABLES. see
MEDICAL SCIENCES — *Abstracting,
Bibliographies, Statistics*

GREECE. NATIONAL STATISTICAL SERVICE.
ANNUAL STATISTICAL SURVEY OF MINES,
QUARRIES AND SALTERNS. see *MINES AND
MINING INDUSTRY* — *Abstracting,
Bibliographies, Statistics*

GREECE. NATIONAL STATISTICAL SERVICE.
LABOUR FORCE SURVEY. see *BUSINESS AND
ECONOMICS* — *Abstracting, Bibliographies,
Statistics*

GREECE. NATIONAL STATISTICAL SERVICE.
RESULTS OF SEA FISHERY SURVEY BY
MOTOR VESSELS. see *FISH AND
FISHERIES* — *Abstracting, Bibliographies,
Statistics*

GREECE. NATIONAL STATISTICAL SERVICE.
SHIPPING STATISTICS. see
TRANSPORTATION — *Abstracting,
Bibliographies, Statistics*

GREECE. NATIONAL STATISTICAL SERVICE.
SOCIAL WELFARE AND HEALTH
STATISTICS. see *SOCIAL SERVICES AND
WELFARE* — *Abstracting, Bibliographies, Statistics*

GREECE. NATIONAL STATISTICAL SERVICE.
STATISTICS ON CIVIL, CRIMINAL AND
REFORMATORY JUSTICE. see *CRIMINOLOGY
AND LAW ENFORCEMENT* — *Abstracting,
Bibliographies, Statistics*

GREECE. NATIONAL STATISTICAL SERVICE.
STATISTICS ON THE DECLARED INCOME
OF LEGAL ENTITIES AND ITS TAXATION.
see *BUSINESS AND ECONOMICS* —
Abstracting, Bibliographies, Statistics

GREECE. NATIONAL STATISTICAL SERVICE.
STATISTICS ON THE DECLARED INCOME
OF PHYSICAL PERSONS AND ITS
TAXATION. see *BUSINESS AND
ECONOMICS* — *Abstracting, Bibliographies,
Statistics*

GREECE. NATIONAL STATISTICAL SERVICE.
TRANSPORT AND COMMUNICATION
STATISTICS. see *TRANSPORTATION* —
Abstracting, Bibliographies, Statistics

310 DK ISSN 0106-2875
GREENLAND IN FIGURES. (Text in English) 1978.
irreg., no.3 1984. free. Ministeriet for Groenland,
Statistisk Kontor, Hausergade 3, DK 1128
Copenhagen K, Denmark. circ. 4,000. (back issues
avail)

310 DK ISSN 0106-0899
GROENLAND I TAL. 1975. a. free. Ministeriet for
Groenland, Statistisk Kontor, Hausergade 3, 1128
Copenhagen K, Denmark. circ. 2,000.

318 GT
GUATEMALA. DIRECCION GENERAL DE
ESTADISTICA. ENCUESTA DE LA
INDUSTRIA MANUFACTURERA FABRIL.
Variant title: Encuesta Industrial. 1972. a. Direccion
General de Estadistica, Departamento de Estudios
Especiales y Estadisticas Continuas, Ministerio de
Economia, 8A Calle No. 9-55, Zona 1, Guatemala.
 Formerly: Guatemala. Direccion General de
Estadistica. Departamento de Estudios Especiales y
Estadisticas Continuas. Produccion, Venta y Otros
Ingresos de la Encuesta Anual de la Industria
Manufacturera Fabril.

318 GT
GUATEMALA. INSTITUTO NACIONAL DE
ESTADISTICA. ANUARIO ESTADISTICO.
(Former name of issuing body: Direccion General
de Estadistica) 1970. a. $10. ‡ Instituto Nacional de
Estadistica, Ministerio de Economia, 8A Calle no.
9-55, Zona 1, Guatemala, Guatemala. charts. illus.
 Formerly: Guatemala en Cifras.

317.281 GT ISSN 0017-5048
GUATEMALA. INSTITUTO NACIONAL DE
ESTADISTICA. BOLETIN ESTADISTICO.
(Former name of issuing body: Direccion General
de Estadistica) 1967. a. $8. ‡ Instituto Nacional de
Estadistica, Ministerio de Economia, 8A Calle no.
9-55, Zona 1, Guatemala, Guatemala. charts. mkt.
circ. 2,500.

310 GT
GUATEMALA. INSTITUTO NACIONAL DE
ESTADISTICA. INFORMADOR ESTADISTICO.
(Former name of issuing body: Direccion General
de Estadistica) irreg. Instituto Nacional de
Estadistica, Ministerio de Economia, 8A Calle No.
9-55, Zona 1, Guatemala, Guatemala. charts.

310 US
GUIDE TO U S GOVERNMENT STATISTICS. a.
$215. Documents Index, Inc., Box 195, McLean,
VA 22101. TEL 703-356-2434. Eds. Donna
Andriot, Jay Andriot.

317.29 HT ISSN 0017-6788
HAITI. INSTITUT HAITIEN DE STATISTIQUE.
BULLETIN TRIMESTRIEL DE STATISTIQUE.
1952. a., with q. supplement. free. Institut Haitien
de Statistique et d'Informatique, Departement des
Finances et des Affaires Economique, Blvd. Harry
Truman, Port-au-Prince, Haiti, W. Indies. Dir.
Jacques Vilgrain. charts. mkt. stat. circ. 500.

315 II ISSN 0072-9728
HANDBOOK OF BASIC STATISTICS OF
MAHARASHTRA STATE. (Editions in English
and Marathi) 1960. a. Rs.3.90. Directorate of
Economics and Statistics, D.D. Bldg, Old Custom
House, Bombay 400023, India. Ed. S. M. Vidwans.

HANDBUCH DER OESTERREICHISCHEN
SOZIALVERSICHERUNG. see *INSURANCE* —
Abstracting, Bibliographies, Statistics

310 DK ISSN 0106-8490
HANDELSHOEJSKOLEN I AARHUS.
SKRIFTSERIE. no.3, 1982. irreg. price varies.
Aarhus Graduate School of Management,
Department of Information Science, Fuglesangsalle
4, 8210 Aarhus V, Denmark. Ed. Kai Kristensen.
illus.

310 FI ISSN 0356-9489
HELSINGIN KAUPUNGIN TILASTOLLINEN
VUOSIKIRJA. (Text in Finnish and Swedish) 1908.
a. Fmk.90. Helsingin Kaupungin Tilastokeskus,
Helsingfors Stads Statistikcentral - City of Helsinki,
Statistical Centre, Toolontorinkatu 2 B, 00260
Helsinki 26, Finland. Ed. Pirkko-Leena Tuovinen.
stat. circ. 1,200. (back issues avail.)

HIGHER EDUCATION ABSTRACTS; abstracts of
periodical literature, monographs and conference
papers on college students, faculty and
administration. see *EDUCATION* — *Higher
Education*

317 US ISSN 0073-2664
HISTORICAL STATISTICS OF THE UNITED
STATES. 1949. irreg. price varies. U. S. Bureau of
the Census, Customer Services, Washington, DC
20233 TEL 301-763-4100. (Orders to: Supt. of
Documents, Washington, DC 20402)

318 HO
HONDURAS EN CIFRAS. 1965. a. free. Banco
Central de Honduras, Departamento de Estudios
Economicos, 1a calle, 6a y 7a avenida, Tegucigalpa,
D.C., Honduras.

315 HK
HONG KONG. ANNUAL DIGEST OF
STATISTICS. (Text in English) 1978. a. HK.$90.
Census and Statistics Department, Kai Tak
Commercial Bldg., 317 Des Voeux Rd., Central,
Hong Kong, Hong Kong (Subscr. to: Director of
Information Service, Information Services
Department, Beaconsfield House, Queens Rd.,
Central, Hong Kong, Hong Kong) charts. stat.

HONG KONG. ESTIMATES OF GROSS
DOMESTIC PRODUCT. see *BUSINESS AND
ECONOMICS* — *Abstracting, Bibliographies,
Statistics*

315 HK
HONG KONG IN FIGURES. 1976. a. free. Census
and Statistics Department, Kai Tak Commercial
Bldg., 317 Des Voeux Rd., Hong Kong, Hong Kong.

HOSPITAL STATISTICS (YEAR) see
HOSPITALS — *Abstracting, Bibliographies,
Statistics*

310 HU ISSN 0441-4713
HUNGARY. KOZPONTI STATISZTIKAI
HIVATAL. NEMZETKOZI STATISZTIKAI
EVKONYV. irreg. 220 Ft. Statisztikai Kiado
Vallalat, Kaszasdulo u. 2, P.O. Box 99, 1300
Budapest 3, Hungary (Subscr. to: Kultura, Box 149,
H-1389 Budapest, Hungary)

314　　　　　　　HU　ISSN 0073-4039
HUNGARY. KOZPONTI STATISZTIKAI
HIVATAL. STATISZTIKAI EVKONYV. (Text in
Hungarian, English, Russian) 1871. a. 264 Ft.
Statisztikai Kiado Vallalat, Kaszasdulo u. 2, P.O.
Box 99, 1300 Budapest 3, Hungary (Subscr. to:
Kultura, Box 149, H-1389 Budapest, Hungary)

947 314　　　　　HU　ISSN 0303-5344
HUNGARY. KOZPONTI STATISZTIKAI
HIVATAL. TERULETI STATISZTIKAI
EVKONYV. a. 140 Ft. Statisztikai Kiado Vallalat,
Kaszasdulo u. 2, P.O.B.99, 1300 Budapest 3,
Hungary (Subscr. to: Kultura, Box 149, H-1389
Budapest, Hungary)

319.4 333.91 330.9　AT　ISSN 0729-5030
HUNTER VALLEY RESEARCH FOUNDATION.
WORKING PAPERS. 1969. irreg. Hunter Valley
Research Foundation, P.O. Box 23, Tighes Hill,
NSW 2297, Australia. Ed. W.E.J. Paradice. charts.
stats. (back issues avail.)

IDAHO. DEPARTMENT OF HEALTH AND
WELFARE. ANNUAL SUMMARY OF VITAL
STATISTICS. see *PUBLIC HEALTH AND
SAFETY — Abstracting, Bibliographies, Statistics*

IMPORTS STATISTICS OF AFGHANISTAN/
IHSA'IYAH-I AMUAL-I VARIDATI-I
AFGHANISTAN. see *BUSINESS AND
ECONOMICS — Abstracting, Bibliographies,
Statistics*

310　　　　　　US　ISSN 0737-4461
INDEX TO INTERNATIONAL STATISTICS. 1983.
m. (with q. and a. cumulations) $995. Congressional
Information Service, Inc., 4520 East-West Hwy.,
Ste. 800, Bethesda, MD 20814. TEL 301-654-1550.
Ed. Polly A. Bosch. abstr. index. cum.index. (back
issues avail.; reprint service avail.)

315　　　　　　　II
INDIA. CENTRAL STATISTICAL
ORGANIZATION. ANNUAL REPORT. (Text in
English) 1949/50. a. price varies. Central Statistical
Organization, Sardar Patel Bhavan, Sansad Marg,
New Delhi 110001, India. adv. circ. 400.
　Formerly: India. Central Statistical Organization.
Sample Surveys of Current Interest in India. Report
(ISSN 0073-6163)

315.4　　　　　II　ISSN 0019-4174
INDIA. CENTRAL STATISTICAL
ORGANIZATION. MONTHLY ABSTRACT OF
STATISTICS. (Text in English and Hindi) 1948. m.
Rs.48($17.28) per no. Central Statistical
Organization, Sardar Patel Bhavan, Sansad Marg,
New Delhi 1, India. bk. rev. charts. circ. 650.

315　　　　　　II　ISSN 0073-6155
INDIA. CENTRAL STATISTICAL
ORGANIZATION. STATISTICAL ABSTRACT.
(Text in English) 1951. a. Rs.253.50($91.26) Central
Statistical Organization, Sardar Patel Bhavan,
Sansad Marg, New Delhi 110001, India.

INDIA. DEPARTMENT OF RURAL
DEVELOPMENT. ADMINISTRATIVE
INTELLIGENCE DIVISION. PROGRESS
REPORT ON SMALL FARMERS
DEVELOPMENT AGENCY PROGRAMME. see
AGRICULTURE — Agricultural Economics

INDIA. DEPARTMENT OF RURAL
DEVELOPMENT. ADMINISTRATIVE
INTELLIGENCE DIVISION. SOME SPECIAL
PROGRAMMES OF RURAL DEVELOPMENT;
STATISTICS. see *AGRICULTURE — Agricultural
Economics*

INDIAN PETROLEUM AND PETROCHEMICALS
STATISTICS. see *PETROLEUM AND GAS —
Abstracting, Bibliographies, Statistics*

310 001.6　　　　II　ISSN 0250-9636
INDIAN SOCIETY OF STATISTICS AND
OPERATIONS RESEARCH. JOURNAL. (Text in
English) 1980. a. Rs.70 to Indian libraries; US$35 to
foreign libraries. Indian Society of Statistics and
Operations Research, M.S. College, Department of
Mathematics, P.O. Box 65, Saharanpur 247001,
India. Eds. S.U. Khan, P.L. Maggu. adv. bk. rev.
abstr. bibl. stat. index. circ. 1,000. (back issues
avail.) Indexed: Math.R.　Zent.Math.

310　　　　　　　II　ISSN 0073-6686
INDIAN STATISTICAL INSTITUTE. ANNUAL
REPORT. 1932/1933. a. ‡ 203 Barrackpore Trunk
Rd., Calcutta 700035, India. circ. 2,000.

310　　　　　　　II
INDIAN STATISTICAL INSTITUTE. LECTURE
NOTES. 1961. irreg. price varies. Macmillan
Company of India Ltd., c/o Indian Statistical
Institute, 203 Barrackpore Trunk Rd., Calcutta
700035, India. (also avail. in microfilm)
　Formerly: Indian Statistical Institute. Research
and Training School. Publications.

310 519　　　　II　ISSN 0073-6716
INDIAN STATISTICAL INSTITUTE. STATISTICS
AND PROBABILITY SERIES. RESEARCH
MONOGRAPHS. irreg. Statistical Publishing
Society, 204/1 Barrackpore Trunk Rd., Calcutta
700035, India. Ed. R. R. Rao.

310　　　　　　　II　ISSN 0073-6724
INDIAN STATISTICAL SERIES. irreg, 1970, nos.
24, 25. price varies. Indian Statistical Institute, 203
Barrackpore Trunk Rd., Calcutta 700035, India.

INDICE DO BRASIL/BRAZILIAN INDEX
YEARBOOK. see *BUSINESS AND
ECONOMICS — Economic Situation And
Conditions*

310　　　　　　　IO
INDONESIA. SOCIAL WELFARE INDICATORS.
(Text in English, Indonesian) 1972. a. $5. Central
Bureau of Statistics, Jl. Dr. Sutomo No. 8, Jakarta
Pusat, Indonesia.

INDONESIA OIL STATISTICS/STATISTIK
PERMINYAKAN INDONESIA. see
*PETROLEUM AND GAS — Abstracting,
Bibliographies, Statistics*

INDONESIA STATISTICS. see *BUSINESS AND
ECONOMICS — Abstracting, Bibliographies,
Statistics*

INDONESIA TOURIST STATISTICS. see *TRAVEL
AND TOURISM — Abstracting, Bibliographies,
Statistics*

INFORMATIONS RECENTES SUR LES
COMPTES NATIONAUX DES PAYS EN
DEVELOPPMENT/LATEST INFORMATION
ON NATIONAL ACCOUNTS OF
DEVELOPING COUNTRIES. see *BUSINESS
AND ECONOMICS — Abstracting, Bibliographies,
Statistics*

314　　　　　　　AU
INNSBRUCK. STATISTISCHES JAHRBUCH. 1952.
a. S.125. Stadtmagistrat Innsbruck, A-6020
Innsbruck, Austria. index. circ. 500.

INSTITUTO INTERAMERICANO DEL NINO.
ESTADISTICA E INFORMATICA. INFORMES
TECNICOS. see *SOCIAL SERVICES AND
WELFARE*

INTERNATIONAL COMMISSION FOR THE
CONSERVATION OF ATLANTIC TUNAS.
STATISTICAL BULLETIN. see *FISH AND
FISHERIES — Abstracting, Bibliographies,
Statistics*

INTERNATIONAL COTTON INDUSTRY
STATISTICS. see *TEXTILE INDUSTRIES AND
FABRICS — Abstracting, Bibliographies, Statistics*

INTERNATIONAL COTTON-SYSTEM FIBRE
CONSUMPTION STATISTICS. see *TEXTILE
INDUSTRIES AND FABRICS — Abstracting,
Bibliographies, Statistics*

INTERNATIONAL MONETARY FUND.
GOVERNMENT FINANCE STATISTICS
YEARBOOK. see *BUSINESS AND
ECONOMICS — Abstracting, Bibliographies,
Statistics*

310　　　　　　　NE
INTERNATIONAL STATISTICAL INSTITUTE.
BULLETIN. 1885. biennial. fl.150. International
Statistical Institute, Prinses Beatrixlaan 428, Box
950, 2270 AZ Voorburg, Netherlands.

310　　　　　　NE　ISSN 0074-8609
INTERNATIONAL STATISTICAL INSTITUTE.
BULLETIN. PROCEEDINGS OF THE
BIENNIAL SESSIONS. (Edited by local organizing
committees in the respective host country) (Text in
English, French) 1895. biennial, 45th, 1985, Madrid.
price varies. International Statistical Institute,
Prinses Beatrixlaan 428, Box 950, 2270 AZ
Voorburg, Netherlands. Indexed: Math.R.
Stat.Theor.Meth.Abstr.

310　　　　　　　NE
INTERNATIONAL STATISTICAL INSTITUTE.
COMPARATIVE STUDIES. CROSS-NATIONAL
SUMMARIES AND E C E REPORTS. 1980. irreg.
free. International Statistical Institute, Prinses
Beatrixlaan 428, Box 950, 2270 AZ Voorburg,
Netherlands.
　Formerly: International Statistical Institute.
Comparative Studies. Cross-National Summaries.

310　　　　　　　NE
INTERNATIONAL STATISTICAL INSTITUTE.
PROCEEDINGS OF SPECIALIZED MEETINGS.
irreg. price varies. International Statistical Institute,
Prinses Beatrixlaan 428, Box 950, 2270 AZ
Voorburg, Netherlands.

INTERNATIONAL TEXTILE MACHINERY
SHIPMENT STATISTICS. see *TEXTILE
INDUSTRIES AND FABRICS — Abstracting,
Bibliographies, Statistics*

310　　　　　　　GW
INTERNATIONALE WIRTSCHAFTSZAHLEN/
INTERNATIONAL ECONOMIC INDICATORS.
(Text in English, German) 1980. a. DM.9.80.
(Institut der Deutschen Wirtschaft) Deutscher
Instituts Verlag GmbH, Gustav-Heinemann-Ufer 84-
88, Postfach 51 06 70, D-5000 Cologne 51, W.
Germany (B.R.D.) Ed. Joerg Beyfuss. circ. 5,000.

IOWA OFFICIAL REGISTER. see *POLITICAL
SCIENCE*

IOWA STATE UNIVERSITY. STATISTICAL
LABORATORY. ANNUAL REPORT. see
*MATHEMATICS — Abstracting, Bibliographies,
Statistics*

IRAN YEARBOOK; a complete directory and
encyclopedia of facts, data and statistics on Iran. see
HISTORY — History Of The Near East

315　　　　　　　IQ
IRAQ. CENTRAL STATISTICAL
ORGANIZATION. ANNUAL ABSTRACT OF
STATISTICS. (Text in Arabic and English) a.
ID.2($6) Central Statistical Organization,
Publication and Public Relations Department,
Baghdad, Iraq. stat. circ. 2,000.

319　　　　　　　IQ
IRAQ. CENTRAL STATISTICAL
ORGANIZATION. STATISTICAL POCKET
BOOK. a. ID.250. Central Statistical Organization,
Baghdad, Iraq. stat.

314　　　　　　IE　ISSN 0075-062X
IRELAND (EIRE) CENTRAL STATISTICS
OFFICE. TUARASCAIL AR STAIDREAMH
BEATHA. REPORT ON VITAL STATISTICS.
1864. a. £6.70. Central Statstics Office, Ardee Rd.,
Dublin 8, Ireland (Subscr. to: Government
Publication Office, Trade and Postal Sales, Bishop
St., Dublin 8, Ireland) circ. 800.

ISRAEL. CENTRAL BUREAU OF STATISTICS.
STAFF IN UNIVERSITIES. see *EDUCATION —
Abstracting, Bibliographies, Statistics*

315.69　　　　　IS　ISSN 0081-4679
ISRAEL. CENTRAL BUREAU OF STATISTICS.
STATISTICAL ABSTRACT OF ISRAEL/
SHENATON STATISTI LE-YISRAEL. (Text in
English and Hebrew) 1949/50. a., latest issue no.
35, 1984. $27. Central Bureau of Statistics, Box
13015, Jerusalem, Israel.

ISRAEL. CENTRAL BUREAU OF STATISTICS.
VITAL STATISTICS. see *POPULATION
STUDIES — Abstracting, Bibliographies, Statistics*

ITALY. ISTITUTO CENTRALE DI STATISTICA.
ANNUARIO DI STATISTICHE INDUSTRIALI.
see *BUSINESS AND ECONOMICS —
Abstracting, Bibliographies, Statistics*

1058 STATISTICS

ITALY. ISTITUTO CENTRALE DI STATISTICA. ANNUARIO STATISTICO DEL COMMERCIO INTERNO E DEL TURISMO. see BUSINESS AND ECONOMICS — Abstracting, Bibliographies, Statistics

ITALY. ISTITUTO CENTRALE DI STATISTICA. ANNUARIO STATISTICO DELLA NAVIGAZIONE MARITTIMA. see TRANSPORTATION — Abstracting, Bibliographies, Statistics

314 IT ISSN 0390-6434
ITALY. ISTITUTO CENTRALE DI STATISTICA. BOLLETINO MENSILE DI STATISTICA. SUPPLEMENTI. irreg. price varies. Istituto Centrale di Statistica, Via Cesare Balbo 16, 00100 Rome, Italy.

ITALY. ISTITUTO CENTRALE DI STATISTICA. STATISTICA ANNUALE DEL COMMERCIO CON L'ESTERO. TOMO 1. see BUSINESS AND ECONOMICS — Abstracting, Bibliographies, Statistics

ITALY. ISTITUTO CENTRALE DI STATISTICA. STATISTICA ANNUALE DEL COMMERCIO CON L'ESTERO. TOMO 2. see BUSINESS AND ECONOMICS — Abstracting, Bibliographies, Statistics

314 NE
JAARBOEK EINDHOVEN. 1967. a. Gemeentebestuur, Stadhuis, Eindhoven, Netherlands. Ed.Bd. stat. illus. index. circ. 500.

JAPAN. MINISTRY OF HEALTH AND WELFARE. STATISTICS AND INFORMATION DEPARTMENT. REPORT ON BASIC SURVEY OF HEALTH AND WELFARE ADMINISTRATION. see SOCIAL SERVICES AND WELFARE — Abstracting, Bibliographies, Statistics

JAPAN. MINISTRY OF HEALTH AND WELFARE. STATISTICS AND INFORMATION DEPARTMENT. REPORT ON OCCUPATIONAL STATISTICS ON VITAL EVENTS. see OCCUPATIONS AND CAREERS — Abstracting, Bibliographies, Statistics

JAPAN. MINISTRY OF HEALTH AND WELFARE. STATISTICS AND INFORMATION DEPARTMENT. REPORT ON SURVEY OF LIVELIHOOD AID SERVICES. see SOCIAL SERVICES AND WELFARE — Abstracting, Bibliographies, Statistics

JAPAN. MINISTRY OF HEALTH AND WELFARE. STATISTICS AND INFORMATION DEPARTMENT. REPORT ON SURVEY OF NATIONAL MEDICAL CARE INSURANCE SERVICES. see INSURANCE — Abstracting, Bibliographies, Statistics

JAPAN. MINISTRY OF HEALTH AND WELFARE. STATISTICS AND INFORMATION DEPARTMENT. REPORT ON SURVEY OF SOCIO-ECONOMIC ASPECTS ON VITAL EVENTS. see BUSINESS AND ECONOMICS — Abstracting, Bibliographies, Statistics

JAPAN. MINISTRY OF HEALTH AND WELFARE. STATISTICS AND INFORMATION DEPARTMENT. REPORT ON SURVEY OF SOCIAL WELFARE FACILITIES. see SOCIAL SERVICES AND WELFARE — Abstracting, Bibliographies, Statistics

JAPAN. MINISTRY OF HEALTH AND WELFARE. STATISTICS AND INFORMATION DEPARTMENT. STATISTICAL HANDBOOK ON HEALTH AND SOCIAL WELFARE. see PUBLIC HEALTH AND SAFETY — Abstracting, Bibliographies, Statistics

JAPAN. MINISTRY OF HEALTH AND WELFARE. STATISTICS AND INFORMATION DEPARTMENT. STATISTICS ON ACTIVITIES OF HEALTH CENTERS. see MEDICAL SCIENCES — Abstracting, Bibliographies, Statistics

JAPAN. MINISTRY OF HEALTH AND WELFARE. STATISTICS AND INFORMATION DEPARTMENT. STATISTICAL REPORT ON COMMUNICABLE DISEASES. see MEDICAL SCIENCES — Abstracting, Bibliographies, Statistics

JAPAN. MINISTRY OF HEALTH AND WELFARE. STATISTICS AND INFORMATION DEPARTMENT. STATISTICAL REPORT ON FOOD POISONINGS. see MEDICAL SCIENCES — Abstracting, Bibliographies, Statistics

JAPAN. MINISTRY OF HEALTH AND WELFARE. STATISTICS AND INFORMATION DEPARTMENT. STATISTICAL REPORT ON PUBLIC HEALTH SERVICES. see PUBLIC HEALTH AND SAFETY — Abstracting, Bibliographies, Statistics

JAPAN. MINISTRY OF HEALTH AND WELFARE. STATISTICS AND INFORMATION DEPARTMENT. STATISTICAL REPORT ON SOCIAL WELFARE SERVICES. see SOCIAL SERVICES AND WELFARE — Abstracting, Bibliographies, Statistics

312 JA ISSN 0075-3270
JAPAN. MINISTRY OF HEALTH AND WELFARE. STATISTICS AND INFORMATION DEPARTMENT. VITAL STATISTICS. Alternate title: Vital Statistics Japan. 1899. a. (in 3 vols.) 24700 Yen. Ministry of Health and Welfare, Statistics and Information Department, 7-3 Ichigaya-Honmura cho, Shinjuku-ku, Tokyo 162, Japan (Order from: Health & Welfare Statistics Association, c/o Mezon Azabu, 5-13-14, Roppongi, Minato-ku, Tokyo, Japan)

JAPAN. STATISTICS BUREAU. ANNUAL REPORT ON FAMILY INCOME AND EXPENDITURE SURVEY. see HOME ECONOMICS — Abstracting, Bibliographies, Statistics

JAPAN. STATISTICS BUREAU. EMPLOYMENT STATUS SURVEY. see BUSINESS AND ECONOMICS — Abstracting, Bibliographies, Statistics

315 JA ISSN 0389-9004
JAPAN STATISTICAL YEARBOOK. (Text in English and Japanese) 1949. a. 11.500 Yen. Statistics Bureau - Management and Coordination Agency, 19-1 Wakamatsu-cho, Shinjuku-ku, Tokyo 162, Japan (Subscr. to: Government Publications Service Centre, 1-2-1 Kasumigaseki, Chiyoda-Ku, Tokyo 100, Japan) circ. 800.

315 JO ISSN 0075-4013
JORDAN. DEPARTMENT OF STATISTICS. ANNUAL STATISTICAL YEARBOOK. (Text in Arabic and English) 1950. a. $20 incl. its External Trade Statistics. Department of Statistics, Amman, Jordan.

310 GW
JUSTIZ IN ZAHLEN. 1980. a. Justizministerium NW Duesseldorf, Martin-Luther-Platz 40, 4000 Duesseldorf 1, W. Germany (B.R.D.) circ. 10,000.

316 NR
KADUNA STATE STATISTICAL YEARBOOK. 1975. a. Ministry of Economic Planning and Rural Development, Economic Planning Division, P.M. Bag 2032, Kaduna, Nigeria.
 Continues: North Central State Statistical Yearbook.

316.69 NR
KANO STATE STATISTICAL YEAR BOOK. 1970. a. price varies. Statistics Division, P.M.B. 3291, Kano, Nigeria. Ed.Bd. bk. rev. stat.
 Continues: Northern Nigeria. Ministry of Economic Planning. Statistical Year Book.

KENTUCKY. CABINET FOR HUMAN RESOURCES. VITAL STATISTICS REPORT. see PUBLIC HEALTH AND SAFETY — Abstracting, Bibliographies, Statistics

KENYA. CENTRAL BUREAU OF STATISTICS. AGRICULTURAL CENSUS (LARGE FARM AREAS) see AGRICULTURE — Abstracting, Bibliographies, Statistics

KENYA. CENTRAL BUREAU OF STATISTICS. EMPLOYMENT AND EARNINGS IN THE MODERN SECTOR. see BUSINESS AND ECONOMICS — Abstracting, Bibliographies, Statistics

KNITSTATS; a yearly statistical bulletin for the hosiery and knitwear industry. see TEXTILE INDUSTRIES AND FABRICS — Abstracting, Bibliographies, Statistics

310 DK ISSN 0106-3839
KOBENHAVNS STATISTISKE AARBOG; for Koebenhavn og Frederiksberg samt Hovedstadsregionen. (Text in Danish and English) 1919. a. Kr.50. Statistisk Kontor - Copenhagen Statistical Office, Vester Voldgade 87, 1552 Copenhagen V, Denmark (Subscr. to: Danske Boghandleres Kommissionsanstalt, Siljangade 6-8, 2300 Copenhagen S, Denmark) Ed. Erik Daugaard Bentzen. circ. 3,000.

310 GW ISSN 0177-6355
KOELNER STATISTISCHE NACHRICHTEN. 1979. irreg. price varies. Amt fuer Statistik und Einwohnerwesen, Johannisstr. 72-80, D-5000 Cologne 1, W. Germany (B.R.D.)
 Formed by the merger of: Koelner Monatszahlen (ISSN 0023-2645) & Statistische Mitteilungen der Stadt Koeln.

KOREA (REPUBLIC). POPULATION & HOUSING CENSUS REPORT. see POPULATION STUDIES — Abstracting, Bibliographies, Statistics

315 KO ISSN 0081-4806
KOREA STATISTICAL KOREA/TONGGYE SUCHUP. (Text in English) 1962. a. 5,220 Won. National Bureau of Statistics, Economic Planning Board, Gyeongun-Dong, Jongro-Gu, Seoul, S. Korea. Ed. Myong Hyun Sohn. circ. 700.

315 KO ISSN 0075-6873
KOREA STATISTICAL YEARBOOK/HANGUK TONGGYE YONGAM. (Text in Korean and English) 1952. a. 13,920 Won. National Bureau of Statistics, Economic Planning Board, Gyeongun-Dong, Jongro-Gu, Seoul, S. Korea. Ed. Myong Hyun Sohn. circ. 500.

314 GW
KREFELD. AMT FUER STATISTIK UND STADTENTWICKLUNG. STATISTISCHES JAHRBUCH. 1926. a. DM.10. Amt fuer Statistik und Stadtentwicklung, Konrad-Adenauer-Platz 17, D-4150 Krefeld, W. Germany (B.R.D.) Ed.Bd. bk. rev. circ. 450.

315.367 KU
KUWAIT. CENTRAL STATISTICAL OFFICE. ANNUAL STATISTICAL ABSTRACT. (Text in Arabic and English) 1965. a. Central Statistical Office, P.O. Box 26188, Safat 13122, Kuwait. circ. 450.
 Supersedes (until 1980): Kuwait. Central Statistical Office. Monthly Digest of Statistics (ISSN 0023-5768)

315 LE ISSN 0075-8388
LEBANON. DIRECTION CENTRALE DE LA STATISTIQUE. RECUEIL DE STATISTIQUES LIBANAISES.* (Text in Arabic and French) 1963. a. free. Direction Centrale de la Statistique, Ministere du Plan, Beirut, Lebanon.

310 US
LECTURE NOTES IN STATISTICS. 1980. irreg., vol.40, 1986. price varies. Springer-Verlag, 175 Fifth Ave., New York, NY 10010 TEL 212-460-1500. (Also Berlin, Heidelberg, Tokyo and Vienna) Ed.Bd. (reprint service avail. from ISI)

LENGTH OF STAY BY DIAGNOSIS, CANADA. see HOSPITALS

LENGTH OF STAY BY DIAGNOSIS, UNITED STATES. see HOSPITALS

LENGTH OF STAY BY DIAGNOSIS, UNITED STATES, NORTH CENTRAL REGION. see HOSPITALS

LENGTH OF STAY BY DIAGNOSIS, UNITED STATES, NORTHEASTERN REGION. see HOSPITALS

LENGTH OF STAY BY DIAGNOSIS, UNITED STATES, SOUTHERN REGION. see HOSPITALS

LENGTH OF STAY BY DIAGNOSIS, UNITED STATES, WESTERN REGION. see *HOSPITALS*

LENGTH OF STAY BY OPERATION, CANADA. see *HOSPITALS*

LENGTH OF STAY BY OPERATION, UNITED STATES. see *HOSPITALS*

LENGTH OF STAY BY OPERATION, UNITED STATES, NORTH CENTRAL REGION. see *HOSPITALS*

LENGTH OF STAY BY OPERATION, UNITED STATES, NORTHEASTERN REGION. see *HOSPITALS*

LENGTH OF STAY BY OPERATION, UNITED STATES, SOUTHERN REGION. see *HOSPITALS*

LENGTH OF STAY BY OPERATION, UNITED STATES, WESTERN REGION. see *HOSPITALS*

309   DK   ISSN 0900-2499
LEVEVILKAAR I DANMARK/LIVING CONDITIONS IN DENMARK, COMPENDIUM OF STATISTICS; statistisk oversigt. (Text in Danish and English) 1976. quadrennial. Kr.97. Danmarks Statistik, Sejroegade 11, 2100 Copenhagen OE, Denmark (Subscr. to: Danske Boghendleres Kommissionsanstalt, Siljangade 6, 2300 Copenhagen S, Denmark)

315   LY   ISSN 0075-9287
LIBYA. CENSUS AND STATISTICAL OFFICE. STATISTICAL ABSTRACT. (Text in Arabic and English) 1958. a. free. Census and Statistical Department, Ministry of Planning, Tripoli, Libya.

LONDON FACTS AND FIGURES. see *PUBLIC ADMINISTRATION — Abstracting, Bibliographies, Statistics*

LUXEMBOURG. SERVICE CENTRAL DE LA STATISTIQUE ET DES ETUDES ECONOMIQUES. ANNUAIRE STATISTIQUE. see *BUSINESS AND ECONOMICS — Abstracting, Bibliographies, Statistics*

LUXEMBOURG. SERVICE CENTRAL DE LA STATISTIQUE ET DES ETUDES ECONOMIQUES. ANNUAIRE STATISTIQUE RETROSPECTIF. see *BUSINESS AND ECONOMICS — Abstracting, Bibliographies, Statistics*

LUXEMBOURG. SERVICE CENTRAL DE LA STATISTIQUE ET DES ETUDES ECONOMIQUES. COLLECTION D ET M: DEFINITIONS ET METHODES. see *BUSINESS AND ECONOMICS — Abstracting, Bibliographies, Statistics*

310   MH
MACAO. REPARTICAO DOS SERVICOS DE ESTATISTICA. ANUARIO DE ESTATISTICA. (Text in Chinese, English and Portuguese) a. free. Reparticao dos Servicos de Estatistica, Box 471, Macao. circ. 500.

MACAO. REPARTICAO DOS SERVICOS DE ESTATISTICA. ANUARIO DO COMERCIO EXTERNO. see *BUSINESS AND ECONOMICS — International Commerce*

314   HU   ISSN 0133-5847
MAGYAR STATISZTIKAI ZSEBKONYV. English edition: Statistical Pocket Book of Hungary. German edition: Taschenbuch Ungarus (ISSN 0139-4231); Russian edition: Vengerski Statisticheski Spravochnik (ISSN 0505-1975) 1933. a. 35 Ft. (Kozponti Statisztikai Hivatal) Statisztikai Kiado Vallalat, Kaszasdulo u. 2, P.O.B.99, 1300 Budapest 3, Hungary (Subscr. to: Kultura, Box 149, H-1389 Budapest, Hungary)

310   HU   ISSN 0230-5828
MAGYARORSZAG. English edition: Hungary. French edition: Hongrie (ISSN 0230-5747); German edition: Ungarn (ISSN 0230-5909); Russian edition: Vengria v Godu (ISSN 0230-5925) a. 15 Ft. (Kozponti Statisztikai Hivatal) Statisztikai Kiado Vallalat, Kaszasdulo u. 2, Box 99, 1300 Budapest 3, Hungary (Subscr. to: Kultura, Box 149, H-1389 Budapest, Hungary) Indexed: PROMT.

MALAGASY REPUBLIC. INSTITUT NATIONAL DE LA STATISTIQUE ET DE LA RECHERCHE ECONOMIQUE. RECENSEMENT INDUSTRIEL. see *BUSINESS AND ECONOMICS — Abstracting, Bibliographies, Statistics*

MALAWI. NATIONAL STATISTICAL OFFICE. HOUSEHOLD INCOME AND EXPENDITURE SURVEY. see *POPULATION STUDIES — Abstracting, Bibliographies, Statistics*

310   MW   ISSN 0076-3284
MALAWI. NATIONAL STATISTICAL OFFICE. NATIONAL ACCOUNTS REPORT. 1967. a. K.5.50($3.90) ‡ National Statistical Office, P.O. Box 333, Zomba, Malawi.

316   MW
MALAWI STATISTICAL YEARBOOK. 1965. a. (after 1972) K.8.50. ‡ National Statistical Office, Box 333, Zomba, Malawi.
Supersedes: Malawi. National Statistical Office. Compendium of Statistics (ISSN 0076-3268)

MALAYSIA. DEPARTMENT OF MINES. STATISTICS RELATING TO THE MINING INDUSTRY OF MALAYSIA. see *MINES AND MINING INDUSTRY — Abstracting, Bibliographies, Statistics*

315.95   MY   ISSN 0542-3570
MALAYSIA. DEPARTMENT OF STATISTICS. ANNUAL BULLETIN OF STATISTICS. (Text in English) 1964. a, latest 1977. M.$3. Department of Statistics - Jabatan Perangkaan, Jalan Young, Kuala Lumpur 10-01, Malaysia.

MALAYSIA. DEPARTMENT OF STATISTICS. VITAL STATISTICS: PENINSULAR MALAYSIA. see *POPULATION STUDIES — Abstracting, Bibliographies, Statistics*

314   MM   ISSN 0081-4733
MALTA. CENTRAL OFFICE OF STATISTICS. ANNUAL ABSTRACT OF STATISTICS. a. L.75. Central Office of Statistics, Auberge d'Italie, Valletta, Malta (Subscr. to: Information Division, Auberge de Castille, Vallette, Malta)

MANITOBA. HEALTH SERVICES COMMISSION. ANNUAL STATISTICS. see *PUBLIC HEALTH AND SAFETY — Abstracting, Bibliographies, Statistics*

MASSACHUSETTS TAXPAYERS FOUNDATION. STATE BUDGET TRENDS. see *BUSINESS AND ECONOMICS — Economic Situation And Conditions*

MAURITIUS. CENTRAL STATISTICAL OFFICE. INTERNATIONAL TRAVEL AND TOURISM. see *TRAVEL AND TOURISM — Abstracting, Bibliographies, Statistics*

316.982   MF
MAURITIUS. CENTRAL STATISTICAL OFFICE. STATISTICAL SUMMARY. 1978. a. Rs.20. Central Statistical Office, Rose Hill, Mauritius (Orders to: G.P.O., Elizabeth II, Port Louis, Mauritius)

METAL STATISTICS (YEARS) see *METALLURGY — Abstracting, Bibliographies, Statistics*

MEXICO. DIRECCION GENERAL DE ESTADISTICA. ESTADISTICA INDUSTRIAL ANUAL. see *BUSINESS AND ECONOMICS — Abstracting, Bibliographies, Statistics*

310   MX
MEXICO STATISTICAL DATA. (Text in English) 1980. a. free. Banco Nacional de Mexico, S.N.C., Department of Economic Research, Madero 21, Piso 2, 06000 Mexico, D.F., Mexico. circ. 6,000.

317   US   ISSN 0076-8308
MICHIGAN STATISTICAL ABSTRACT. 1955. a. $20. Wayne State University, Bureau of Business Research, Detroit, MI 48202. TEL 313-577-4213. Ed. David I. Verway. circ. 1,800. (also avail. in microform)

318   BL
MINAS GERAIS, BRAZIL. DEPARTAMENTO DE ESTRADAS DE RODAGEM. SERVICO DE TRANSITO. ESTATISTICA DE TRAFEGO E ACIDENTES. 1969. a. free. Departamento de Estradas de Rodagem, Servico de Transito, Av. Andradas, 1120, 30000 Belo Horizonte, Brazil. stat. circ. 1,000.
Formerly: Minas Gerais, Brazil. Departamento de Estradas de Rodagem. Servico de Transito. Estatistica de Trafego.

310 382   MJ
MONTSERRAT. STATISTICS OFFICE. OVERSEAS TRADE REPORT. irreg. Statistics Office, Plymouth, Monserrat.

MORTALITY AND DEMOGRAPHIC DATA. see *POPULATION STUDIES — Abstracting, Bibliographies, Statistics*

MUSIC U S A. see *MUSIC*

310   UR
NARODNOE KHOZYAISTVO ALTAISKOGO KRAYA. 1967. a. (Tsentral'noe Statisticheskoe Upravlenie) Izdatel'stvo Statistika, Altaiskoe Otdelenie, Barnaul, Russian S.F.S.R., U.S.S.R. stat. circ. 5,000.

NEBRASKA STATISTICAL HANDBOOK. see *PUBLIC ADMINISTRATION — Abstracting, Bibliographies, Statistics*

634.9   NE
NEDERLANDSE BOSSTATISTIEK. 1952. irreg., latest 1971 (covers 1964-68) fl.9. Centraal Bureau voor de Statistiek, Prinses Beatrixlaan 428, Voorburg, Netherlands (Orders to: Staatsuitgeverij, Christoffel Plantijnstraat, The Hague, Netherlands) circ. 650.

315.49   NP
NEPAL. CENTRAL BUREAU OF STATISTICS. STATISTICAL POCKET BOOK. (Text in English) 1974. irreg. Rs.3.50. Central Bureau of Statistics, Kathmandu, Nepal. illus. circ. 2,000.

NETHERLANDS. CENTRAAL BUREAU VOOR DE STATISTIEK. PER LEERLING BESCHIKBAAR GESTELDE BEDRAGEN VOOR HET LAGER ONDERWIJS. AMOUNTS PER PUPIL PROVIDED FOR PRIMARY EDUCATION. see *EDUCATION — Abstracting, Bibliographies, Statistics*

314   NE
NETHERLANDS. CENTRAAL BUREAU VOOR DE STATISTIEK. REGIONAAL STATISTISCH ZAKBOEK. a. Centraal Bureau voor de Statistiek, Prinses Beatrixlaan 428, Voorburg, Netherlands (Orders to: Staatsuitgeverij, Christoffel Plantijnstraat, The Hague, Netherlands)

310   NE
NETHERLANDS. CENTRAAL BUREAU VOOR DE STATISTIEK. STATISTICAL STUDIES. 1953. irreg. price varies. Centraal Bureau voor de Statistiek, Prinses Beatrixlaan 428, Voorburg, Netherlands (Orders to: Staatsuitgeverij, Christoffel Plantijnstraat, The Hague, Netherlands)

NETHERLANDS. CENTRAAL BUREAU VOOR DE STATISTIEK. STATISTIEK VAN DE INVESTERINGEN IN VASTE ACTIVA IN DE NIJVERHEID. STATISTICS ON FIXED CAPITAL FORMATION IN INDUSTRY. see *BUSINESS AND ECONOMICS — Abstracting, Bibliographies, Statistics*

310   NE   ISSN 0166-9680
NETHERLANDS. CENTRAAL BUREAU VOOR DE STATISTIEK. STATISTISCH BULLETIN. irreg. fl.55. Centraal Bureau voor de Statistiek, Prinses Beatrixlaan 428, Voorburg, Netherlands (Orders to: Staatsuitgeverij, Christoffel Plantijnstraat, The Hague, Netherlands) circ. 3,500.

310   NE   ISSN 0168-3705
NETHERLANDS. CENTRAAL BUREAU VOOR DE STATISTIEK. STATISTISCH ZAKBOEK. POCKET YEARBOOK. (Text in Dutch and English) 1944-46. a. fl.20.50. Centraal Bureau voor de Statistiek, Prinses Beatrixlaan 428, Voorburg, Netherlands (Orders to: Staatsuitgeverij, Christoffel Plantijnstraat, The Hague, Netherlands)

STATISTICS

NETHERLANDS. CENTRAAL BUREAU VOOR DE STATISTIEK. STATISTISCHE ONDERZOEKINGEN. see *BUSINESS AND ECONOMICS — Abstracting, Bibliographies, Statistics*

314   NE
NETHERLANDS. CENTRALE COMMISSIE VOOR DE STATISTIEK. JAARVERSLAG. 1899. a. Centrale Commissie voor de Statistiek, The Hague, Netherlands. Ed. W.F.M. de Vries. circ. 900.

NEW HAMPSHIRE VITAL STATISTICS. see *POPULATION STUDIES — Abstracting, Bibliographies, Statistics*

317   US   ISSN 0077-8575
NEW MEXICO STATISTICAL ABSTRACT. 1970. biennial. $15. University of New Mexico, Bureau of Business and Economic Research, Albuquerque, NM 87131. TEL 505-277-2216. circ. 450.

319.4   AT   ISSN 0725-5039
NEW SOUTH WALES IN BRIEF. 1977. a. free. Australian Bureau of Statistics, New South Wales Office, 3rd Floor, St. Andrews House, Sydney Square, Sydney, NSW 2000, Australia.

319   AT   ISSN 0085-4441
NEW SOUTH WALES YEAR BOOK. 1906. a. 30.70 softcover, Aus.$35.70 hardcover. Australian Bureau of Statistics, N.S.W. Office, St. Andrews House, Sydney Square, George St., Sydney, N.S.W. 2000, Australia.

317   US
NEW YORK (STATE). ROCKEFELLER INSTITUTE OF GOVERNMENT. NEW YORK STATE STATISTICAL YEARBOOK. 1967. a. $20. Nelson A. Rockefeller Institute of Government, 411 State St., Albany, NY 12203. Ed. Susan Lenz. index. circ. 5,000.
     Formerly: New York (State) Division of the Budget. New York State Statistical Yearbook (ISSN 0077-9334)

319   NZ   ISSN 0077-9652
NEW ZEALAND. DEPARTMENT OF STATISTICS. ANNUAL REPORT OF THE GOVERNMENT STATISTICIAN. a. NZ.$1.81. Department of Statistics, Private Bag, Wellington, New Zealand (Subscr. to: Government Printing Office, Publications, Private Bag, Wellington, New Zealand)

NEW ZEALAND. DEPARTMENT OF STATISTICS. DEMOGRAPHIC TRENDS BULLETIN. see *POPULATION STUDIES — Abstracting, Bibliographies, Statistics*

NEW ZEALAND. DEPARTMENT OF STATISTICS. EXTERNAL MIGRATION STATISTICS. see *POPULATION STUDIES — Abstracting, Bibliographies, Statistics*

NEW ZEALAND. DEPARTMENT OF STATISTICS. LOCAL AUTHORITY STATISTICS. see *PUBLIC ADMINISTRATION — Abstracting, Bibliographies, Statistics*

NEW ZEALAND. DEPARTMENT OF STATISTICS. POPULATION CENSUS: INTERNAL MIGRATION. see *POPULATION STUDIES — Abstracting, Bibliographies, Statistics*

NEW ZEALAND. DEPARTMENT OF STATISTICS. POPULATION CENSUS. LOCATION AND INCREASE OF POPULATION. PART A: POPULATION SIZE AND DISTRIBUTION. see *POPULATION STUDIES — Abstracting, Bibliographies, Statistics*

NEW ZEALAND. DEPARTMENT OF STATISTICS. POPULATION CENSUS. LOCATION AND INCREASE OF POPULATION. PART B: POPULATION DENSITY. see *POPULATION STUDIES — Abstracting, Bibliographies, Statistics*

319   NZ   ISSN 0110-4586
NEW ZEALAND. DEPARTMENT OF STATISTICS. VITAL STATISTICS. a. NZ.$14.85. Department of Statistics, Private Bag, Wellington, New Zealand (Subscr. to: Government Printing Office, Publications, Private Bag, Wellington, New Zealand)

NEW ZEALAND. NATIONAL HEALTH STATISTICS CENTRE. FETAL AND INFANT DEATHS. see *MEDICAL SCIENCES — Abstracting, Bibliographies, Statistics*

NEW ZEALAND CENSUS OF TRANSPORT, STORAGE & COMMUNICATION. see *TRANSPORTATION — Abstracting, Bibliographies, Statistics*

316   NR   ISSN 0078-0626
NIGERIA. FEDERAL OFFICE OF STATISTICS. ANNUAL ABSTRACT OF STATISTICS. (Text in English) a. Federal Office of Statistics, P.M.B. 12528, Nigeria.

NIGERIA. FEDERAL OFFICE OF STATISTICS. BUILDING AND CONSTRUCTION SURVEY. see *BUILDING AND CONSTRUCTION — Abstracting, Bibliographies, Statistics*

NIGERIA. FEDERAL OFFICE OF STATISTICS. INDUSTRIAL SURVEY. see *BUSINESS AND ECONOMICS — Abstracting, Bibliographies, Statistics*

NIGERIA. FEDERAL OFFICE OF STATISTICS. REPORT ON RURAL CONSUMER SURVEY. see *BUSINESS AND ECONOMICS — Abstracting, Bibliographies, Statistics*

NIGERIA. FEDERAL OFFICE OF STATISTICS. REPORT ON RURAL ECONOMIC SURVEY. see *BUSINESS AND ECONOMICS — Abstracting, Bibliographies, Statistics*

NIGERIA. FEDERAL OFFICE OF STATISTICS. REPORT ON RURAL HOUSEHOLD SURVEY. see *HOUSING AND URBAN PLANNING — Abstracting, Bibliographies, Statistics*

NIGERIA. FEDERAL OFFICE OF STATISTICS. REPORT ON URBAN CONSUMER SURVEY. see *BUSINESS AND ECONOMICS — Abstracting, Bibliographies, Statistics*

NIGERIA. FEDERAL OFFICE OF STATISTICS. REPORT ON URBAN HOUSEHOLD SURVEY. see *HOUSING AND URBAN PLANNING — Abstracting, Bibliographies, Statistics*

NIGERIA. FEDERAL OFFICE OF STATISTICS. SOCIAL STATISTICS IN NIGERIA. see *SOCIAL SCIENCES: COMPREHENSIVE WORKS — Abstracting, Bibliographies, Statistics*

314   DK   ISSN 0078-1088
NORDISK STATISTISK AARSBOK/YEARBOOK OF NORDIC STATISTICS. (Subseries of: Nordisk Utredningsserie) (Text in English and Swedish) 1962. a. Nordic Council of Ministers, Nordic Statistical Secretariat, Store Strandstraede 18, DK-1255 Copenhagen, Denmark. Ed. Harry de Sharengrad.

314   DK   ISSN 0332-6527
NORDISK STATISTISK SKRIFTSERIE/ STATISTICAL REPORTS OF THE NORDIC COUNTRIES. (Text in Scandinavian languages; editions occasionally in English) 1954. irreg., no.47, 1986. price varies. Nordisk Statistisk Sekretariat - Nordic Statistical Secretariat, Postbox 2550, DK-2100 Copenhagen OE, Denmark. circ. 3,000.

310   DK   ISSN 0078-1096
NORDISKE SJEFSSTATISTIKERMOETE/ MEETING OF THE CHIEF STATISTICIANS OF THE NORDIC COUNTRIES. (Forms also part of: Nordisk Statistisk Skriftserie) (Text in Danish, English, Norwegian and Swedish) 1967. triennial, latest 1984. Kr.70. Nordisk Statistisk Sekretariat, Postbox 2550, DK-2100 Copenhagen OE, Denmark. circ. 1,250.
     Formerly: Nordiske Statistiske Chefsmoede.

NORTH DAKOTA. JUDICIAL CONFERENCE. ANNUAL REPORT. see *LAW — Abstracting, Bibliographies, Statistics*

319.4   AT   ISSN 0815-3809
NORTHERN TERRITORY AT A GLANCE. 1983. a. free. Australian Bureau of Statistics, Northern Territory Office, 7th floor, MLC Building, 81 Smith Street, Darwin, N.T. 5790, Australia.

NORWAY. STATISTISK SENTRALBYRAA. ARBEIDSMARKEDSTATISTIKK/LABOUR MARKET STATISTICS. see *BUSINESS AND ECONOMICS — Abstracting, Bibliographies, Statistics*

NORWAY. STATISTISK SENTRALBYRAA. ELEKTRISITESSTATISTIKK/ELECTRICITY STATISTICS. see *ENERGY — Abstracting, Bibliographies, Statistics*

NORWAY. STATISTISK SENTRALBYRAA. FISKERISITESSTATISTIKK/FISHERY STATISTICS. see *FISH AND FISHERIES — Abstracting, Bibliographies, Statistics*

NORWAY. STATISTISK SENTRALBYRAA. FOLKEMENGDEN ETTER ALDER OG EKTESKAPELIG STATUS/POPULATION BY AGE AND MARITAL STATUS. see *POPULATION STUDIES — Abstracting, Bibliographies, Statistics*

NORWAY. STATISTISK SENTRALBYRAA. FRAMSKRIVING AV FOLKEMENGDEN: REGIONALE TALL/POPULATION PROJECTIONS: REGIONAL FIGURES. see *POPULATION STUDIES — Abstracting, Bibliographies, Statistics*

NORWAY. STATISTISK SENTRALBYRAA. HELSEPERSONELLSTATISTIKK. see *MEDICAL SCIENCES — Abstracting, Bibliographies, Statistics*

NORWAY. STATISTISK SENTRALBYRAA. HELSESTATISTIKK/HEALTH STATISTICS. see *PUBLIC HEALTH AND SAFETY — Abstracting, Bibliographies, Statistics*

NORWAY. STATISTISK SENTRALBYRAA. INDUSTRISTATISTIKK/INDUSTRIAL STATISTICS. VOL.1. see *BUSINESS AND ECONOMICS — Abstracting, Bibliographies, Statistics*

NORWAY. STATISTISK SENTRALBYRAA. INDUSTRISTATISTIKK/INDUSTRIAL STATISTICS. VOL.2. see *BUSINESS AND ECONOMICS — Abstracting, Bibliographies, Statistics*

NORWAY. STATISTISK SENTRALBYRAA. JORDBRUKSSTATISTIKK/AGRICULTURAL STATISTICS. see *AGRICULTURE — Abstracting, Bibliographies, Statistics*

NORWAY. STATISTISK SENTRALBYRAA. KOMMUNE OG FYLKESTINGS VALGET/ MUNICIPAL AND COUNTY ELECTIONS. see *PUBLIC ADMINISTRATION — Abstracting, Bibliographies, Statistics*

NORWAY. STATISTISK SENTRALBYRAA. KREDITTMARKED STATISTIKK/CREDIT MARKET STATISTICS. see *BUSINESS AND ECONOMICS — Abstracting, Bibliographies, Statistics*

NORWAY. STATISTISK SENTRALBYRAA. KRIMINALSTATISTIKK/CRIMINAL STATISTICS. see *CRIMINOLOGY AND LAW ENFORCEMENT — Abstracting, Bibliographies, Statistics*

NORWAY. STATISTISK SENTRALBYRAA. LOENNSSTATISTIKK/WAGE STATISTICS. see *BUSINESS AND ECONOMICS — Abstracting, Bibliographies, Statistics*

NORWAY. STATISTISK SENTRALBYRAA. NASJONALREGNSKAP/NATIONAL ACCOUNTS. see *BUSINESS AND ECONOMICS — Abstracting, Bibliographies, Statistics*

NORWAY. STATISTISK SENTRALBYRAA. OEKONOMISK UTSYN/ECONOMIC SURVEY. see *BUSINESS AND ECONOMICS — Abstracting, Bibliographies, Statistics*

NORWAY. STATISTISK SENTRALBYRAA. REISELIVSTATISKK/STATISTICS ON TRAVEL. see *TRAVEL AND TOURISM — Abstracting, Bibliographies, Statistics*

NORWAY. STATISTISK SENTRALBYRAA. SAMFERDSELSSTATISTIKK/TRANSPORT AND COMMUNICATION STATISTICS. see *TRANSPORTATION — Abstracting, Bibliographies, Statistics*

NORWAY. STATISTISK SENTRALBYRAA. SIVILRETTSSTATISTIKK/CIVIL JUDICIAL STATISTICS. see *CRIMINOLOGY AND LAW ENFORCEMENT — Abstracting, Bibliographies, Statistics*

NORWAY. STATISTISK SENTRALBYRAA. SKOGSTATSTIKK/FORESTRY STATISTICS. see *FORESTS AND FORESTRY — Abstracting, Bibliographies, Statistics*

314   NO   ISSN 0078-1932
NORWAY. STATISTISK SENTRALBYRAA. STATISTISK AARBOK/STATISTICAL YEARBOOK. (Subseries of its Norges Offisielle Statistikk) (Text in Norwegian and English) 1880. a. Kr.50. Statistisk Sentralbyraa, Box 8131 Dep., 0033 Oslo 1, Norway. circ. 43,000.

NORWAY. STATISTISK SENTRALBYRAA. STORTINGSVALG/PARLIAMENTARY ELECTIONS. see *PUBLIC ADMINISTRATION — Abstracting, Bibliographies, Statistics*

NORWAY. STATISTISK SENTRALBYRAA. UTDANNINGSSTATISTIKK: EDUCATIONAL STATISTICS. see *EDUCATION — Abstracting, Bibliographies, Statistics*

NORWAY. STATISTISK SENTRALBYRAA. UTENRIKSHANDEL/EXTERNAL TRADE. see *BUSINESS AND ECONOMICS — Abstracting, Bibliographies, Statistics*

NORWAY. STATISTISK SENTRALBYRAA. VAREHANDELSSTATISTIKK/WHOLESALE AND RETAIL TRADE STATISTICS. see *BUSINESS AND ECONOMICS — Abstracting, Bibliographies, Statistics*

310   330.9   AQ
O E C S ANNUAL DIGEST OF STATISTICS. 1984. a. EC$10($3.77) Organisation of Eastern Caribbean States, Economic Affairs Secretariat, P.O. Box 822, St. John's, Antigua, W.I. TEL 809-462-1530/3500. stat. circ. 350.

310   531.64   AQ
O E C S ENERGY BULLETIN. 1983. a. EC$25($9.43) Organisation of Eastern Caribbean States, Economic Affairs Secretariat, P.O. Box 822, St. John's, Antigua, W.I. TEL 809-462-1530/3500. charts. stat. circ. 350.

310   330.9   AQ
O E C S NATIONAL ACCOUNT DIGEST. 1985. a. EC$10($3.77) Organisation of Eastern Caribbean States, Economic Affairs Secretariat, P.O. Box 822, St. John's, Antigua, W.I. TEL 809-462-1530/3500. charts. stat. circ. 350.

310   330.9   AQ
O E C S STATISTICAL POCKET DIGEST. 1983. a. free. Organisation of Eastern Caribbean States, Economic Affairs Secretariat, P.O. Box 822, St. John's, Antigua, W.I. TEL 809-462-1530/3500. stat. circ. 1,500.

310   330.9   AQ
O E C S TRADE DIGEST. 1984. a. EC$10($3.77) Organisation of Eastern Caribbean States, Economic Affairs Secretariat, P.O. Box 822, St. John's, Antigua, W.I. TEL 809-462-1530/3500. stat. circ. 350.

OCCUPATIONAL DISEASE IN CALIFORNIA. see *INDUSTRIAL HEALTH AND SAFETY — Abstracting, Bibliographies, Statistics*

317   CN
ONTARIO STATISTICS. 1964. a. price varies. Ministry of Treasury and Economics, Statistical Service Branch, Toronto M7A 1Z1, Ont., Canada. TEL 416-965-7171. Ed. Shashi N. Sharma. circ. 6,000.
Formerly: Ontario Statistical Review (ISSN 0078-5113)

OREGON PUBLIC HEALTH STATISTICS REPORT. see *PUBLIC HEALTH AND SAFETY — Abstracting, Bibliographies, Statistics*

PAKISTAN INSTITUTE OF DEVELOPMENT ECONOMICS. STATISTICAL PAPERS. see *BUSINESS AND ECONOMICS — Abstracting, Bibliographies, Statistics*

315   PK   ISSN 0078-8473
PAKISTAN STATISTICAL ASSOCIATION. PROCEEDINGS. (Text in English) a. Rs.2. Pakistan Statistical Association, Institute of Statistics, University of the Punjab, Lahore, Pakistan.

318   PN   ISSN 0078-8996
PANAMA EN CIFRAS. 1953. a. Bl.0.75. Direccion de Estadistica y Censo, Contraloria General, Apartado 5213, Panama 5, Panama. circ. 8,000.

PAPUA NEW GUINEA. BUREAU OF STATISTICS. STATISTICAL BULLETIN: NATIONAL ACCOUNTS STATISTICS. see *BUSINESS AND ECONOMICS — Abstracting, Bibliographies, Statistics*

PAPUA NEW GUINEA. BUREAU OF STATISTICS. STATISTICAL BULLETIN: SURVEY OF RETAIL SALES AND SELECTED SERVICES. see *BUSINESS AND ECONOMICS — Abstracting, Bibliographies, Statistics*

PAPUA NEW GUINEA. NATIONAL STATISTICAL OFFICE. HOUSEHOLD EXPENDITURE SURVEY. PRELIMINARY BULLETIN. see *HOME ECONOMICS — Abstracting, Bibliographies, Statistics*

319.5   PP
PAPUA NEW GUINEA. NATIONAL STATISTICAL OFFICE. SUMMARY OF STATISTICS. (Text in English) 1970/71. a. National Statistical Office, P.O. Wards Strip, Papua New Guinea. illus. circ. 1,093.

PAPUA NEW GUINEA. NATIONAL STATISTICAL OFFICE. WORKER'S COMPENSATION CLAIMS. see *INSURANCE — Abstracting, Bibliographies, Statistics*

PEDIATRIC LENGTH OF STAY BY DIAGNOSIS AND OPERATION, UNITED STATES. see *HOSPITALS*

338.4   US   ISSN 0476-1103
PENNSYLVANIA STATISTICAL ABSTRACT. 1958. a. $15. Department of Commerce, Bureau of Policy, Planning & Systems Development, 474 Forum Bldg., Harrisburg, PA 17120 TEL 717-948-6336. (Orders to: Penn State University at Harrisburg, Middletown, PA 17057) stat.

PERSONALE- OG OEKONOMISTIK FOR SYGEHUSVAESENET. see *HOSPITALS*

315   PH
PHILIPPINES. NATIONAL CENSUS AND STATISTICS OFFICE. SPECIAL REPORT. 1970. irreg., no. 5, 1975. National Census and Statistics Office, Ramon Magsaysay Blvd., Box 779, Manila, Philippines.

PHILIPPINES. NATIONAL CENSUS AND STATISTICS OFFICE. VITAL STATISTICAL REPORT. see *POPULATION STUDIES — Abstracting, Bibliographies, Statistics*

319   AT   ISSN 0079-2446
POCKET YEAR BOOK OF SOUTH AUSTRALIA. 1917. a. Aus.$3.20. Australian Bureau of Statistics, South Australian Office, Box 2272 G.P.O., Adelaide, S.A. 5001, Australia.

319   AT   ISSN 0159-9321
POCKET YEARBOOK OF NEW SOUTH WALES. 1913. a. Aus.$3.50. Australian Bureau of Statistics, N.S.W. Office, St. Andrews House, Sydney Square, George St., Sydney, N.S.W. 2000, Australia.

314   PL   ISSN 0079-2608
POLAND. GLOWNY URZAD STATYSTYCZNY. MALY ROCZNIK STATYSTYCZNY. CONCISE STATISTICAL YEARBOOK. (Editions in English, French, German, Polish and Russian) 1958. a. 30 Zl. Glowny Urzad Statystyczny, Al. Niepodleglosci 208, 00-925 Warsaw, Poland.

314.38   PL
POLAND. GLOWNY URZAD STATYSTYCZNY. MALY ROCZNIK STATYSTYKI MIEDZYNARODOWEJ. (Subseries of its: Seria Statystyka Miedzynarodowa) 1972. irreg., latest 1986. 125 Zl. Glowny Urzad Statystyczny, Departament Wydawaictw, Al. Niepodleglosci 208, Warsaw, Poland. illus. stat.

314   PL   ISSN 0079-2756
POLAND. GLOWNY URZAD STATYSTYCZNY. ROCZNIK STATYSTYCZNY POWIATOW. STATISTICAL YEARBOOK OF COUNTIES. (Subseries of its: Statystyka Polski) 1970. a. 40 Zl. Glowny Urzad Statystyczny, Al. Niepodleglosci 208, 00-925 Warsaw, Poland.

314   PL   ISSN 0079-2780
POLAND. GLOWNY URZAD STATYSTYCZNY. ROCZNIK STATYSTYCZNY. STATISTICAL YEARBOOK. (Text in Polish; summaries in English and Russian) 1921. a. Glowny Urzad Statystyczny, Al. Niepodleglosci 208, 00-925 Warsaw, Poland.

310   PL   ISSN 0079-273X
POLAND. GLOWNY URZAD STATYSTYCZNY. ROCZNIK STATYSTYKI MIEDZYNARODOWEJ. YEARBOOK OF INTERNATIONAL STATISTICS. irreg., latest 1985. Glowny Urzad Statystyczny, Al. Niepodleglosci 208, 00-925 Warsaw, Poland.

311   PL
POLAND. GLOWNY URZAD STATYSTYCZNY. STATYSTYKA POLSKI. STUDIA I PRACE STATYSTYCZNE. (Text in Polish; summaries in English and Russian) 1966. irreg., latest 1986. Glowny Urzad Statystyczny, Al. Niepodleglosci 208, 00-925 Warsaw, Poland.
Formerly: Poland. Glowny Urzad Statystyczny. Studia i Prace Statystyczne (ISSN 0079-2845)

310   PL   ISSN 0079-2829
POLAND. GLOWNY URZAD STATYSTYCZNY. ZESZYTY METODYCZNE. 1966. irreg., latest 1986. price varies. Glowny Urzad Statystyczny, Al. Niepodleglosci 208, 00-925 Warsaw, Poland (Dist. by: Ars Polona-Ruch, Ul. Krakowskie Przedmiescie 7, Warsaw, Poland)

POPULATION GROWTH OF IRAN. see *POPULATION STUDIES — Abstracting, Bibliographies, Statistics*

314   PO
PORTUGAL. INSTITUTO NACIONAL DE ESTATISTICA. ANUARIO ESTATISTICO. CONTINENTE, ACORES E MADEIRA. (Text in French and Portuguese) 1875. a. Esc.1500. Instituto Nacional de Estatistica, Av. Antonio Jose de Almeida, 1078 Lisbon Codex, Portugal (Orders to: Imprensa Nacional, Casa da Moeda, Direccao Comercial, rua D. Francisco Manuel de Melo 5, 1000 Lisbon, Portugal)
Formerly: Portugal. Instituto Nacional de Estatistica. Anuario Estatistico (ISSN 0079-4112)

314   PO   ISSN 0378-3227
PORTUGAL. INSTITUTO NACIONAL DE ESTATISTICA. SERIE ESTATISTICAS REGIONAIS. 1970. irreg. Instituto Nacional de Estatistica, Av. Antonio Jose de Almeida, 1078 Lisbon Codex, Portugal (Orders to: Imprensa Nacional, Casa da Moeda, Direccao Comercial, rua D. Francisco Manuel de Melo 5, 1000 Lisbon, Portugal) stat. circ. controlled.

PORTUGAL. INSTITUTO NACIONAL DE ESTATISTICA. SERVICOS CENTRAIS. ESTATISTICAS DAS SOCIEDADES: CONTINENTE, ACORES E MADEIRA. see *BUSINESS AND ECONOMICS — Abstracting, Bibliographies, Statistics*

PORTUGAL. INSTITUTO NACIONAL DE ESTATISTICA. SERVICOS CENTRAIS. ESTATISTICAS DOS TRANSPORTES E COMMUNICACOES: CONTINENTE, ACORES E MADEIRA. see *TRANSPORTATION — Abstracting, Bibliographies, Statistics*

STATISTICS

314   PO   ISSN 0377-2470
PORTUGAL (YEAR) (Editions in English and Portuguese) 1969. a. Esc.120. Instituto Nacional de Estatistica, Av. Antonio Jose de Almeida, 1078 Lisbon Codex, Portugal.
    Formerly (until 1977): Portugal. Instituto Nacional de Estatistica. Servicos Centrais. Sinopse de Dados Estatisticos: Continente e Ilhas Adjacentes.

POULTRY MARKET STATISTICS. see *AGRICULTURE — Abstracting, Bibliographies, Statistics*

PRODUCCION AGRICOLA - PERIODO DE VERANO. see *AGRICULTURE — Abstracting, Bibliographies, Statistics*

310   CY
PROFILES OF EARNINGS IN CYPRUS; BY EDUCATION, OCCUPATION, EXPERIENCE, AGE, SEX AND SECTOR. (Text in English) 1979. irreg. £C0.50. Ministry of Finance, Department of Statistics and Research, Nicosia, Cyprus.

PUERTO RICO. DIVISION OF DEMOGRAPHIC REGISTRY AND VITAL STATISTICS. ANNUAL VITAL STATISTICS REPORT. see *POPULATION STUDIES — Abstracting, Bibliographies, Statistics*

PUERTO RICO. STATISTICS, ANALYSIS AND CONTROL OF INFORMATION. ANNUAL VITAL STATISTICS REPORT. see *PUBLIC HEALTH AND SAFETY*

QATAR YEARBOOK. see *HISTORY — History Of The Near East*

319   AT   ISSN 0085-5316
QUEENSLAND POCKET YEARBOOK. 1950. a. Aus.$3.50. Australian Bureau of Statistics, Queensland Office, 313 Adelaide St., Brisbane, Qld. 4000, Australia. index. circ. 2,500.

319   AT   ISSN 0085-5359
QUEENSLAND YEARBOOK. 1937. a. Aus.$22.70. Australian Bureau of Statistics, Queensland Office, 313 Adelaide St., Brisbane, Qld. 4000, Australia. index. circ. 2,500.

RACE WALKING WORLD STATISTICS. see *SPORTS AND GAMES*

RAJASTHAN, INDIA. DIRECTORATE OF ECONOMICS AND STATISTICS. BASIC STATISTICS. see *BUSINESS AND ECONOMICS — Abstracting, Bibliographies, Statistics*

310   UK   ISSN 0482-1319
REGISTER OF REGISTRARS. 1953. a. including cum.supplements. Extel Financial Ltd., 37-45 Paul St., London EC2A 4PB, England.

REPORT ON PASSENGER ROAD TRANSPORT IN ZAMBIA. see *TRANSPORTATION — Abstracting, Bibliographies, Statistics*

318   BL
RESENHA ESTATISTICA DO RIO GRANDE DO SUL. 1977. a. Cr$10. Fundacao de Economia e Estatistica, Rua Gen. Vitorino, 77-2 andar, C.P. 2355, 90.000 Porto Alegre RS, Brazil.

318   BL
REVISTA DO SEITE. 1980. irreg. Cr.$15.00($5) Fundacao de Economia e Estatistica, Rua Gen. Vitorino 77, C.P. 2355, 90.000 Porto Alegre, Brazil. Ed. Roberto La Rocca. (also avail. in microform)
    Formerly: Rio Grande do Sul, Brazil. Fundacao de Economia e Estatistica. Boletim Estatistico do Seite.

RHODE ISLAND. DEPARTMENT OF EDUCATION. (YEAR) STATISTICAL TABLES. see *EDUCATION — Abstracting, Bibliographies, Statistics*

314   IT   ISSN 0035-7960
ROMA E PROVINCIA ATTRAVERSO LA STATISTICA; dati mensili e annuali. 1956. a. L.800. per no. Camera di Commercio Industria Artigianato e Agricoltura di Roma, Via De'Burro 147, 00186 Rome, Italy. Ed. Dr. Leonida Attili. bk. rev. charts. stat. index; cum.index. circ. controlled.

314   DK   ISSN 0105-8339
ROSKILDE KOMMUNE. STATISTIKKEN. 1970. a. free. Roskilde Kommune, Udviklingsafdelingen, Stoeden 3/3, 4000 Roskilde, Denmark. circ. 425.

315   MY   ISSN 0080-5203
SABAH. DEPARTMENT OF STATISTICS. ANNUAL BULLETIN OF STATISTICS/SABAH. JABATAN PERANGKAAN. SIARAN PERANGKAAN TAHUNAN. 1964. a, latest 1981. M.$6. Department of Statistics, Federal Bldg., 1st fl., Jalan Mat Salleh, Kota Kinabalu, Sabah, Malaysia. circ. 465.

311   II   ISSN 0581-4790
SAMVADADHVAM. (Text in Bengali, English and Hindi) 1956. irreg. ‡ Indian Statistical Institute, 203 Barrackpore Trunk Rd., Calcutta 700035, India. Ed. Bd. bk. rev. bibl. charts. illus. stat. circ. 2,500 (controlled)

318   AG
SANTIAGO DEL ESTERO. DIRECCION GENERAL DE INVESTIGACIONES ESTADISTICA Y CENSOS. ESTADISTICAS SOCIALES. a. free. Direccion General de Investigaciones Estadistica y Censos, Palacio de los Tribunales, Santiago del Estero, Argentina. Dir. Jose Humberto Alegre. stat.

319   MY   ISSN 0080-6447
SARAWAK VITAL STATISTICS. (Text in English) 1966. a., latest 1976. M.$2. ‡ Department of Statistics, Federal Complex, Jalan Simpang Tiga, Kuching, Sarawak, Malaysia.

319   SU
SAUDI ARABIA. CENTRAL DEPARTMENT OF STATISTICS. STATISTICAL YEARBOOK. (Text in Arabic and English) 1965. a. sR.30. Central Department of Statistics, Box 3735, Riyadh 11118, Saudi Arabia.

SAUDI ARABIA. MINISTRY OF EDUCATION. EDUCATIONAL STATISTICS. see *EDUCATION — Abstracting, Bibliographies, Statistics*

SCOTLAND. REGISTRAR GENERAL. ANNUAL REPORT. see *POPULATION STUDIES — Abstracting, Bibliographies, Statistics*

314   UK
SCOTTISH ABSTRACT OF STATISTICS. 1971. a. £13.50. Scottish Office, New St. Andre'w House, rm.5/52, Edinburgh EH1 3SX, Scotland. circ. 850.
    Superseded in 1971: Digest of Scottish Statistics.

310   SE
SEYCHELLES. DEPARTMENT OF FINANCE. NATIONAL ACCOUNTS. a. R.5. Department of Finance, Statistics Division, P.O. Box 206, Independence House, Victoria, Republic of Seychelles.

310   SE
SEYCHELLES. DEPARTMENT OF FINANCE. STATISTICS DIVISION. STATISTICAL ABSTRACT. 1977. a. 60 Fr. Department of Finance, Statistics Division, P.O. Box 206, Victoria, Mahe, Seychelles. circ. 250.

SEYCHELLES. DEPARTMENT OF FINANCE. VISITOR SURVEY. see *TRAVEL AND TOURISM — Abstracting, Bibliographies, Statistics*

316   SE
SEYCHELLES. PRESIDENT'S OFFICE. STATISTICS DIVISION. CENSUS. irreg., latest 1977. Rs.80. President's Office, Department of Finance, Statistics Division, Box 206, Mahe, Seychelles.

SEYCHELLES. PRESIDENT'S OFFICE. STATISTICS DIVISION. HOUSEHOLD EXPENDITURE SURVEY. see *BUSINESS AND ECONOMICS — Abstracting, Bibliographies, Statistics*

SEYCHELLES. PRESIDENT'S OFFICE. STATISTICS DIVISION. MIGRATION AND TOURISM STATISTICS. see *TRAVEL AND TOURISM — Abstracting, Bibliographies, Statistics*

SEYCHELLES. PRESIDENT'S OFFICE. STATISTICS DIVISION. STATISTICAL ABSTRACT. see *BUSINESS AND ECONOMICS — Abstracting, Bibliographies, Statistics*

316   SL
SIERRA LEONE. CENTRAL STATISTICS OFFICE. ANNUAL STATISTICAL DIGEST. 1969? a. Le.8. Central Statistics Office, Tower Hill, Freetown, Sierra Leone.

310   SL   ISSN 0080-9535
SIERRA LEONE IN FIGURES. a. free. Bank of Sierra Leone, P.O. Box 30, Freetown, Sierra Leone.

SINGAPORE. DEPARTMENT OF STATISTICS. REPORT ON THE CENSUS OF WHOLESALE, RETAIL TRADES, RESTAURANTS & HOTELS. see *HOTELS AND RESTAURANTS — Abstracting, Bibliographies, Statistics*

SINGAPORE. DEPARTMENT OF STATISTICS. REPORT ON THE SURVEY OF SERVICES. see *PUBLIC ADMINISTRATION — Abstracting, Bibliographies, Statistics*

315   SI   ISSN 0583-3655
SINGAPORE YEARBOOK OF STATISTICS. a. S.$6.20. Department of Statistics, Maxwell Road PO Box 3010, Singapore 9050, Singapore.

SINOPSE ESTATISTICA DO BRASIL/ STATISTICAL ABSTRACT OF BRAZIL. see *BUSINESS AND ECONOMICS — Abstracting, Bibliographies, Statistics*

SOCIAL TRENDS IN NEW ZEALAND. see *SOCIOLOGY — Abstracting, Bibliographies, Statistics*

316   SO
SOMALIA IN FIGURES. triennial. Ministry of National Planning, Direction of Statistics, P.O. Box 1742, Mogadisho, Somalia.

310   SA
SOUTH AFRICA. CENTRAL STATISTICAL SERVICE. ANNUAL REPORT. a. Central Statistical Service, Private Bag X44, Pretoria 0001, South Africa. stat.
    Formerly: South Africa. Department of Statistics. Annual Report of the Statistics Advisory Council and of the Secretary of Statistics.

SOUTH AFRICA. CENTRAL STATISTICAL SERVICE. BUILDING PLANS PASSED AND BUILDINGS COMPLETED. see *BUILDING AND CONSTRUCTION — Abstracting, Bibliographies, Statistics*

SOUTH AFRICA. CENTRAL STATISTICAL SERVICE. CENSUS OF ELECTRICITY, GAS AND STEAM. see *ENERGY — Abstracting, Bibliographies, Statistics*

SOUTH AFRICA. CENTRAL STATISTICAL SERVICE. CENSUS OF TOWNSHIP DEVELOPERS/SENSUS VAN DORPSONTWIKKELAARS. see *HOUSING AND URBAN PLANNING — Abstracting, Bibliographies, Statistics*

SOUTH AFRICA. CENTRAL STATISTICAL SERVICE. DEATH OF BLACKS. see *POPULATION STUDIES — Abstracting, Bibliographies, Statistics*

SOUTH AFRICA. CENTRAL STATISTICAL SERVICE. EDUCATION: ASIAN. see *EDUCATION — Abstracting, Bibliographies, Statistics*

SOUTH AFRICA. CENTRAL STATISTICAL SERVICE. EDUCATION: WHITES. see *EDUCATION — Abstracting, Bibliographies, Statistics*

SOUTH AFRICA. CENTRAL STATISTICAL SERVICE. LABOUR STATISTICS: WAGE RATES, EARNINGS AND AVERAGE HOURS WORKED IN THE PRINTING AND NEWSPAPER INDUSTRY, ENGINEERING INDUSTRY, BUILDING INDUSTRY AND COMMERCE. see *BUSINESS AND ECONOMICS — Abstracting, Bibliographies, Statistics*

SOUTH AFRICA. CENTRAL STATISTICAL
SERVICE. MINING: FINANCIAL STATISTICS.
see *MINES AND MINING INDUSTRY —
Abstracting, Bibliographies, Statistics*

SOUTH AFRICA. CENTRAL STATISTICAL
SERVICE. REPORT ON BIRTHS: WHITE,
COLOURED AND ASIANS. see *POPULATION
STUDIES — Abstracting, Bibliographies, Statistics*

SOUTH AFRICA. CENTRAL STATISTICAL
SERVICE. REPORT ON MARRIAGES AND
DIVORCES: SOUTH AFRICA. see
*POPULATION STUDIES — Abstracting,
Bibliographies, Statistics*

SOUTH AFRICA. CENTRAL STATISTICAL
SERVICE. REPORT ON PRICES. see *BUSINESS
AND ECONOMICS — Abstracting, Bibliographies,
Statistics*

SOUTH AFRICA. CENTRAL STATISTICAL
SERVICE. ROAD TRAFFIC ACCIDENTS. see
*TRANSPORTATION — Abstracting,
Bibliographies, Statistics*

316   SA
SOUTH AFRICA. CENTRAL STATISTICAL
SERVICE. STATISTICAL NEWS RELEASES.
(Comprised of 63 series (P1-P30)) irreg. free.
Central Statistical Service, Private Bag X44, Pretoria
0001, South Africa.
 Formerly: South Africa. Department of Statistics.
Statistical News Releases.

SOUTH AFRICA. CENTRAL STATISTICAL
SERVICE. STATISTICS OF HOUSES AND
DOMESTIC SERVANTS AND OF FLATS. see
*HOUSING AND URBAN PLANNING —
Abstracting, Bibliographies, Statistics*

SOUTH AFRICA. CENTRAL STATISTICAL
SERVICE. STATISTICS OF MOTOR AND
OTHER VEHICLES. see *TRANSPORTATION —
Abstracting, Bibliographies, Statistics*

SOUTH AFRICA. CENTRAL STATISTICAL
SERVICE. STATISTICS OF NEW VEHICLES
REGISTERED. see *TRANSPORTATION —
Abstracting, Bibliographies, Statistics*

SOUTH AFRICA. CENTRAL STATISTICAL
SERVICE. SURVEY OF THE ACCOUNTS OF
COMPANIES. PART 1. SECONDARY AND
TERTIARY INDUSTRIES. see *BUSINESS AND
ECONOMICS — Abstracting, Bibliographies,
Statistics*

SOUTH AFRICA. CENTRAL STATISTICAL
SERVICE. SURVEY OF THE ACCOUNTS OF
COMPANIES. PART 2. MINING. see *BUSINESS
AND ECONOMICS — Abstracting, Bibliographies,
Statistics*

SOUTH AFRICA. CENTRAL STATISTICAL
SERVICE. TOURISM AND MIGRATION. see
*POPULATION STUDIES — Abstracting,
Bibliographies, Statistics*

SOUTH AFRICA. CENTRAL STATISTICAL
SERVICE. TRANSFERS OF RURAL
IMMOVABLE PROPERTY. see *REAL
ESTATE — Abstracting, Bibliographies, Statistics*

SOUTH AFRICA. CENTRAL STATISTICAL
SERVICES. LOCAL GOVERNMENT
STATISTICS. see *PUBLIC
ADMINISTRATION — Abstracting,
Bibliographies, Statistics*

SOUTH AFRICA. CENTRAL STATISTICAL
SERVICES. STATISTICS OF
ADMINISTRATION BOARDS. see *PUBLIC
ADMINISTRATION — Abstracting,
Bibliographies, Statistics*

SOUTH AFRICA. DEPARTMENT OF
AGRICULTURE AND FISHERIES. DIVISION
OF ECONOMIC SERVICES. ABSTRACT OF
AGRICULTURAL STATISTICS. see
*AGRICULTURE — Abstracting, Bibliographies,
Statistics*

SOUTH AFRICA. OFFICIAL YEARBOOK OF THE
REPUBLIC OF SOUTH AFRICA. see
HISTORY — Abstracting, Bibliographies, Statistics

316 SA ISSN 0081-2544
SOUTH AFRICAN STATISTICS. (Text in Afrikaans
and English) 1968. biennial, latest 1986. R.12.85.
Central Statistical Service, Private Bag X44, Pretoria
0001, South Africa (Orders to: Government Printer,
Bosman St., Private Bag X85, Pretoria 0001, South
Africa)
 Until 1966: South Africa. Department of
Statistics. Statistical Year Book.

319 AT ISSN 0085-6428
SOUTH AUSTRALIAN YEARBOOK. 1966. a.
Aus.$29.90. Australian Bureau of Statistics, South
Australian Office, Box 2272, Adelaide, S.A. 5001,
Australia.

317.57 US
SOUTH CAROLINA STATISTICAL ABSTRACT.
1972. a. $16. Budget and Control Board, Division of
Research and Statistical Services, Attn: Vivian
Stalvey, 1000 Assembly St., Rembert C. Dennis
Bldg., Rm. 337, Columbia, SC 29201. TEL 803-734-
3796. Ed. Billie R. Howell. stat. circ. 1,200. (also
avail. in microfiche)

SOUTH DAKOTA. STATE DEPARTMENT OF
PUBLIC WELFARE. RESEARCH AND
STATISTICS ANNUAL REPORT. see *SOCIAL
SERVICES AND WELFARE — Abstracting,
Bibliographies, Statistics*

310 NL
SOUTH PACIFIC COMMISSION. STATISTICAL
BULLETIN. (Text in English or French) 1973.
irreg., no. 15, 1978. free. South Pacific Commission,
B.P. D5, Noumea, Cedex, New Caledonia.

SOVIET ARMED FORCES REVIEW ANNUAL. see
MILITARY

314 SP ISSN 0014-1151
SPAIN. INSTITUTO NACIONAL DE
ESTADISTICA. ESTADISTICA ESPAÑOLA.
irreg. 600 ptas. Instituto Nacional de Estadistica, P
de la Castellana, 183, Madrid 16, Spain. bk. rev.
bibl. charts. illus. stat. circ. 1,000.

310 US ISSN 0172-7397
SPRINGER SERIES IN STATISTICS. 1979. irreg.,
latest 1986. price varies. Springer-Verlag, 175 Fifth
Ave., New York, NY 10010 TEL 212-460-1500.
(Also Berlin, Heidelberg, Tokyo and Vienna) Ed.Bd.
(reprint service avail. from ISI) Indexed: Math.R.

310 GW
STADT REMSCHEID STATISTISCHES
JAHRBUCH. 1949. a. Amt fuer Stadtentwicklung
und Statistik, Hindenburgstr. 52-58, D-5630
Remscheid, W. Germany (B.R.D.) Ed. Hoffmann.
circ. 450. (back issues avail.)

314 IC ISSN 0081-4652
STATISTICAL ABSTRACT OF ICELAND. 1930.
irreg., latest 1984. $30. ‡ Hagstofa Islands -
Statistical Bureau of Iceland, Hverfisgata 8-10, IS-
101 Reykjavik, Iceland. Ed. H. Snorrason. circ. 2,
500.

314 IE ISSN 0081-4660
STATISTICAL ABSTRACT OF IRELAND. 1931. a.
£12.50. Central Statistics Office, Earlsfort Terrace,
Dublin 4, Ireland (Subscr. to: Government
Publication Office, Trade and Postal Sales, Bishop
St., Dublin 8, Ireland) circ. 2,000.

315 II ISSN 0081-4709
STATISTICAL ABSTRACT OF MAHARASHTRA
STATE. (Text in English) a. Rs.20.50. Directorate
of Economics and Statistics, D.D. Bldg., Old
Custom House, Bombay 400023, India.

310 II ISSN 0081-4717
STATISTICAL ABSTRACT OF RAJASTHAN. (Text
in English) 1958. a. Rs.10. Directorate of
Economics and Statistics, Krishi Bhawan, Jaipur,
Rajasthan, India.

315 CE
STATISTICAL ABSTRACT OF THE
DEMOCRATIC SOCIALIST REPUBLIC OF SRI
LANKA. (Text in English, Sinhala and Tamil)
1949. irreg. price varies. Department of Census and
Statistics, Ministry of Plan Implementation, Box
563, Colombo 7, Sri Lanka (Order from:
Superintendent, Government Publications Bureau,
Colombo, Sri Lanka) index. circ. 1,820.
 Continues: Statistical Abstract of Ceylon (ISSN
0081-4636)

319 CJ
STATISTICAL ABSTRACT OF THE
GOVERNMENT OF THE CAYMAN ISLANDS.
1975. a. $15. Department of Finance &
Development, Statistics Unit, Grand Cayman Island,
Cayman Islands, B.W.I. Gov. Statistician Roy C.
Woods.

317.3 US ISSN 0081-4741
STATISTICAL ABSTRACT OF THE UNITED
STATES. 1878. a. price varies. U.S. Bureau of the
Census, Customer Services, Washington, DC 20233
TEL 301-763-4100. (Orders to: Supt. of Documents,
Washington, DC 20402) (also avail. in microfiche;
microform from UMI; reprint service avail. from
UMI)

311 IE ISSN 0081-4776
STATISTICAL AND SOCIAL INQUIRY SOCIETY
OF IRELAND. JOURNAL. 1846. a. £5. Statistical
and Social Inquiry Society of Ireland, c/o Economic
and Social Research Institute, 4 Burlington Road,
Dublin 4, Ireland. Ed. Kieran A. Kennedy.
cum.index: 1847-1947. circ. 700. Indexed: P.A.I.S.
Rural Recreat.Tour.Abstr. World Agri.Econ.&
Rural Sociol.Abstr.

310 TH
STATISTICAL BUDGET AND ACTIVITIES IN
THAILAND. (Text in Thai) 1966. a. National
Statistical Office, Kurng Kasem Road, Bangkok
Metropolis 10100, Thailand.

315 JA ISSN 0081-4792
STATISTICAL HANDBOOK OF JAPAN. (Text in
English) 1958. a. 1200 Yen. Statistics Bureau -
Management and Coordination Agency, 19-1
Wakamatsu-cho, Shinjuku-ku, Tokyo 162, Japan
(Subscr. to: Government Publications Service
Centre, 1-2-1 Kasumigaseki, Chiyoda-ku, Tokyo
100, Japan)

315 II
STATISTICAL HANDBOOK OF TAMIL NADU.
(Text in English) 1969. a. Rs.6. Director of
Statistics, Madras 600006, India (Subscr. to:
Government Publication Depot, 166 Anna Rd.,
Madras 600002, India)

315 TH ISSN 0081-4822
STATISTICAL HANDBOOK OF THAILAND. (Text
in English) 1964. irreg. price varies. National
Statistical Office, Larn Luang Rd., Bangkok,
Thailand. circ. 1,000.

316.67 GH
STATISTICAL HANDBOOK OF THE REPUBLIC
OF GHANA. a. NC.1.70. Information Services
Department, Box 745, Accra, Ghana.

310 AF
STATISTICAL INFORMATION OF
AFGHANISTAN/MA'LUMAT-I IHSA'IVI-I
AFGHANISTAN. (Text in Persian or Pushto) no.
3, 1975/1976. irreg. Central Statistical Office,
Nader Shah Minah, Block No. 4, Box 2002, Kabul,
Afghanistan. stat.

STATISTICAL INSTITUTE OF JAMAICA.
DEMOGRAPHIC STATISTICS. see
*POPULATION STUDIES — Abstracting,
Bibliographies, Statistics*

STATISTICAL INSTITUTE OF JAMAICA.
MONETARY STATISTICS REPORT. see
*BUSINESS AND ECONOMICS — Abstracting,
Bibliographies, Statistics*

STATISTICAL INSTITUTE OF JAMAICA.
NATIONAL INCOME AND PRODUCT. see
*BUSINESS AND ECONOMICS — Abstracting,
Bibliographies, Statistics*

319 JM
STATISTICAL INSTITUTE OF JAMAICA.
POCKETBOOK OF STATISTICS. 1978. a.
Jam.$10. Statistical Institute of Jamaica, 9
Swallowfield Rd., Kingston 5, Jamaica.
 Formerly: Jamaica. Department of Statistics.
Pocketbook of Statistics.

1064 STATISTICS

317 JM
STATISTICAL INSTITUTE OF JAMAICA.
STATISTICAL ABSTRACT. 1972. a. (published 9
months after year to which it relates) Jam.$21.
Statistical Institute of Jamaica, 9 Swallowfield Rd,
Kingston 5, Jamaica. circ. 1,000.
  Former titles: Jamaica. Department of Statistics.
Statistical Abstract & Jamaica. Department of
Statistics. Annual Abstract of Statistics (ISSN 0075-
2983)

310 JA ISSN 0561-922X
STATISTICAL NOTES OF JAPAN.* (Text in
English) 1953. a. free. International Statistical
Affairs Division, Statistical Standards Department,
Management and Coordination Agency, 19-1
Wakamatsu-Cho, Shinjuku-Ku, Tokyo, Japan. circ.
500.

STATISTICAL OFFICE OF THE EUROPEAN
  COMMUNITIES. GAS PRICES. see ENERGY

STATISTICAL OFFICE OF THE EUROPEAN
  COMMUNITIES. IRON AND STEEL.
  YEARBOOK. see METALLURGY — Abstracting,
  Bibliographies, Statistics

315 II ISSN 0081-5012
STATISTICAL POCKET BOOK: INDIA. (Text in
English) 1956. a. Rs.45($15.50) Central Statistical
Organization, Sardar Patel Bhavan, Sansad Marg,
New Delhi 110001, India.
  Formerly: Statistical Pocket Book of the Indian
Union.

315.8 AF
STATISTICAL POCKET-BOOK OF
AFGHANISTAN. 1972. irreg. Department of
Statistics, Kabul, Afghanistan. illus.

315 CE
STATISTICAL POCKET BOOK OF THE
DEMOCRATIC SOCIALIST REPUBLIC OF SRI
LANKA. (Text in English, Sinhala and Tamil)
1966. a. price varies. Department of Census and
Statistics, Plan Implementation, Box 563, Colombo
7, Sri Lanka (Order from: Superintendent,
Government Publications Bureau, Colombo, Sri
Lanka) circ. 3,450. (back issues avail.)
  Former titles: Statistical Pocket Book of Sri
Lanka; Which continues: Statistical Pocket Book of
Ceylon (ISSN 0585-1777)

319 TU
STATISTICAL POCKET BOOK OF TURKEY/
TURKIYE ISTATISTIK CEP YILLIGI. (Subseries
of its Yayin) (Text in English and Turkish) 1938.
biennial. State Institute of Statistics - Devlet
Istatistik Enstitusu, Necatibey Caddesi 114, Ankara,
Turkey.

310 BG
STATISTICAL POCKETBOOK OF BANGLADESH.
(Text in English) 1978. a. Tk.50 uS.$10 per no.
Bangladesh Bureau of Statistics, Secretariat, Dacca
2, Bangladesh. charts. stat. circ. 5,000.
  Formerly: Statistical Pocket Book of Bangladesh.

315.98 IO ISSN 0126-3595
STATISTICAL POCKETBOOK OF INDONESIA/
BUKU SAKU STATISTIK INDONESIA.
(Subseries of its Statistik Tahunan) (Text in English
and Indonesian) 1940. a. Central Bureau of
Statistics - Biro Pusat Statistik, Jalan Dr. Sutomo 8,
Box 3, Jakarta, Indonesia.
  Continues: Statistik Indonesia.

317 US
STATISTICAL PROFILE OF IOWA. a. free. Iowa
Department of Economic Development, 200 E.
Grand Ave., Des Moines, IA 50309. TEL 515-281-
3925. index.

310 US ISSN 0278-694X
STATISTICAL REFERENCE INDEX. 1980. m.
(with q. and a. cumulations) price varies.
Congressional Information Service, Inc., 4520 East-
West Hwy., Ste. 800, Bethesda, MD 20814. TEL
301-654-1550. Ed. Lynn K. Marble. stat. index.
cum.index: 1980-85. (back issues avail.)

STATISTICAL REVIEW OF GOVERNMENT IN
  UTAH. see PUBLIC ADMINISTRATION —
  Abstracting, Bibliographies, Statistics

310 US ISSN 0732-6971
STATISTICAL SERVICES DIRECTORY. 1982. a.
$200. Gale Research Company, Book Tower,
Detroit, MI 48226.

STATISTICAL THEORY AND METHOD
  ABSTRACTS. see ABSTRACTING AND
  INDEXING SERVICES

300.8 UN ISSN 0252-3655
STATISTICAL YEARBOOK FOR ASIA AND THE
PACIFIC/ANNUAIRE STATISTIQUE POUR
L'ASIE ET LE PACIFIQUE. (Text in English and
French) 1968. a. price varies. United Nations
Economic and Social Commission for Asia and the
Pacific, United Nations Bldg., Rajadamnern Ave.,
Bangkok 10200, Thailand (Dist. by United Nations
Publications, Room DC2-0853, New York, NY
10017; or Distribution and Sales Section, Palais des
Nations, CH-1211 Geneva 10, Switzerland)
  Formerly: Statistical Yearbook for Asia and the
Far East (ISSN 0085-6711)

318 UN
STATISTICAL YEARBOOK FOR LATIN
AMERICA/ANUARIO ESTADISTICO DE
AMERICA LATINA. (Text in English and
Spanish) a. price varies. Comision Economica para
America Latina (CEPAL), Casilla 179-D, Santiago,
Chile (Subscr. to: United Nations Publications, Sales
Section, Rm. DC2-0853, New York, NY 10017; or
Distribution and Sales Section, Palais des Nations,
1211 Geneva 10, Switzerland) charts. (back issues
avail.) Indexed: P.A.I.S.
  Formerly: Statistical Bulletin for Latin America
(ISSN 0041-6401)

315 BG ISSN 0302-2374
STATISTICAL YEARBOOK OF BANGLADESH.
(Text in English) 1964. a. Tk.150($30) Bangladesh
Bureau of Statistics, Secretariat, Dacca 2,
Bangladesh.
  Formerly: Statistical Digest of Bangladesh.

310 HK ISSN 0255-6766
STATISTICAL YEARBOOK OF CHINA. (Text in
English) 1981. a. $68. Economic Information &
Agency, 342 Hennessy Rd., 10th Fl., Hong Kong,
Hong Kong (U.S. and Europe subscr. to: Oxford
University Press, 200 Madison Ave., New York,
NY 10016) (back issues avail.)

314 GR ISSN 0081-5071
STATISTICAL YEARBOOK OF GREECE. (Text in
English and Greek) a., latest 1985. $20. National
Statistical Service, Publications and Information
Division, 14-16 Lycourgou St., 10166 Athens,
Greece.

319 IR
STATISTICAL YEARBOOK OF IRAN. (Edition in
Farsi) 1967. a. Statistical Centre, Dr. Fatemi Ave,
Teheran 14144, Iran. charts. illus. stat.

317.292 JM
STATISTICAL YEARBOOK OF JAMAICA. 1973. a.
Jam.$87. Statistical Institute of Jamaica, 9
Swallowfield Rd, Kingston 5, Jamaica. illus.

310 LH
STATISTICAL YEARBOOK OF LIECHTENSTEIN/
STATISTISCHES JAHRBUCH FUERSTENTUM
LIECHTENSTEIN. 1977. a. free. Office of
National Economy of the Principality of
Liechtenstein, Vaduz FL-9490, Liechtenstein.
Ed.Bd. circ. 1,200. (back issues avail.)

315 TH
STATISTICAL YEARBOOK OF THAILAND. (Text
in English and Thai) 1909. a. price varies. National
Statistical Office, Larn Luang Rd., Bangkok,
Thailand. circ. 1,000.

STATISTICAL YEARBOOK OF THE REPUBLIC
  OF CHINA. see BUSINESS AND
  ECONOMICS — Abstracting, Bibliographies,
  Statistics

314 GE ISSN 0433-6844
STATISTICHES TASCHENBUCH DER DDR.
(Editions in Arabic, English, French, German,
Russian, and Spanish) a. M.6.50. (Staatliche
Zentralverwaltung fuer Statistik) Staatsverlag der
DDR, Otto-Grotewohl-Str. 17, 1086 Berlin, E.
Germany(D.D.R.)

314 BU
STATISTICHESKI GODISHNIK NA NARODNA
REPUBLIKA BULGARIA. 1909. a. 7.28 lv.
Ministerstvo na Informatsiiata i Suobshteniiata,
Komitet za Socialna Informacia v N.R. Bulgaria, Ul.
Panaiot Volov 2, 1504 Sofia, Bulgaria. stat. circ. 2,
000.

314 BU
STATISTICHESKI SPRAVOCHNIK. 1959. a. 0.90 lv.
Ministerstvo na Informatsiiata i Suobshteniiata, 18,
Ul. Graf Ignatiev, Sofia, Bulgaria. (Co-sponsor:
Tsentralno Statistichesko Upravlenie) stat. circ. 5,
500.

STATISTICS - ASIA & AUSTRALASIA: SOURCES
  FOR MARKET RESEARCH. see
  BIBLIOGRAPHIES

STATISTICS OF ROAD TRAFFIC ACCIDENTS IN
  JAPAN. see TRANSPORTATION — Abstracting,
  Bibliographies, Statistics

STATISTICS OF SOUTHERN COLLEGE AND
  UNIVERSITY LIBRARIES. see LIBRARY AND
  INFORMATION SCIENCES — Abstracting,
  Bibliographies, Statistics

STATISTICS OF WORLD TRADE IN STEEL. see
  METALLURGY — Abstracting, Bibliographies,
  Statistics

STATISTICS ON ALCOHOL AND DRUG USE IN
  CANADA AND OTHER COUNTRIES. see
  DRUG ABUSE AND ALCOHOLISM —
  Abstracting, Bibliographies, Statistics

STATISTICS ON WORLD TRADE IN
  ENGINEERING PRODUCTS. BULLETIN. see
  METALLURGY — Abstracting, Bibliographies,
  Statistics

310 016 US ISSN 0585-198X
STATISTICS SOURCES; a subject guide to data on
industrial, business, social, educational, financial and
other topics for the U.S. and selected foreign
countries. irreg., 10th edt., 1986. $270. Gale
Research Company, Book Tower, Detroit, MI
48226. TEL 313-961-2242. Eds. Jacqueline
Wasserman O'Brien, Steven R. Wasserman.

310 DK ISSN 0106-2344
STATISTIK FOR HOVEDSTADSREGIONEN/
STATISTICAL YEARBOOK FOR THE
COPENHAGEN REGION. English edition:
Statistical Ten-Year Review of the Municipality of
Copenhagen. (Text in Danish and English) 1977. a.
Kr.10. Hovedstadsraadet, Kogelandevej 3, 2500
Copenhagen K, Denmark. Ed. P.J. Nielsen. illus.
circ. 2,500.

STATISTIQUE CRIMINELLE DE LA BELGIQUE.
  see CRIMINOLOGY AND LAW
  ENFORCEMENT — Abstracting, Bibliographies,
  Statistics

STATISTIQUES DE L'INDUSTRIE GAZIERE. see
  ENERGY — Abstracting, Bibliographies, Statistics

STATISTIQUES DU COMMERCE EXTERIEUR
  DE MADAGASCAR. see BUSINESS AND
  ECONOMICS — Abstracting, Bibliographies,
  Statistics

310 GW
STATISTISCHE KURZINFORMATION. 1982. irreg.
DM.2 per no. Statistisches Amt, Roemerstr. 10,
5100 Aachen, W. Germany (B.R.D.) circ. 350.
(back issues avail.)

STATISTISCHE STUDIEN. see BUSINESS AND
  ECONOMICS — Abstracting, Bibliographies,
  Statistics

314 AU ISSN 0081-5314
STATISTISCHES HANDBUCH FUER DIE
REPUBLIK OESTERREICH. 1882. a. $69. ‡
(Oesterreichisches Statistisches Zentralamt)
Oesterreichische Staatsdruckerei, Vienna, Austria.
adv. circ. 2,700.

314 GW ISSN 0081-5322
STATISTISCHES JAHRBUCH BERLIN. 1945. a.
DM.55. (Statistisches Landesamt) Kulturbuch-Verlag
GmbH, Passauer Str. 4, 1000 Berlin 30, W.
Germany (B.R.D.)
  Supersedes: Berlin in Zahlen.

314   GE
STATISTISCHES JAHRBUCH DER D D R. 1956. a. M.60. (Staatliche Zentralverwaltung fuer Statistik) Staatsverlag der DDR, Otto-Grotewohl-Str. 17, 1086 Berlin, E. Germany (D.D.R.) stat.

314   SZ   ISSN 0081-5330
STATISTISCHES JAHRBUCH DER SCHWEIZ/ ANNUAIRE STATISTIQUE DE LA SUISSE. 1891. a. price varies. (Statistisches Amt.) Birkhaeuser Verlag, P.O. Box 133, CH-4010 Basel, Switzerland.

314   GW
STATISTISCHES JAHRBUCH DER STADT AUGSBURG. 1953. irreg. DM.28. Amt fuer Stadtentwicklung und Statistik, Schmiedberg 6, 8900 Augsburg 22, W. Germany (B.R.D.) circ. 400.

310 312 352.7 330.9   GW
STATISTISCHES JAHRBUCH DER STADT NUERNBERG. 1977. a. DM.30. Amt fuer Stadtforschung und Statistik, Unschlittplatz 7a, 8500 Nuremberg 1, W. Germany (B.R.D.) stats. circ. 700. (back issues avail.)

310   AU
STATISTISCHES JAHRBUCH DER STADT WIEN. 1883. a. S.400. Statistisches Amt der Stadt Wien, Volksgartenstr. 3, A-1016 Vienna, Austria (Subscr. to: Jugend und Volk Verlagsgesellschaft m.b.H., Tiefer Graben 7-9, A-1010 Vienna, Austria) adv. charts. circ. 800. (back issues avail., index)

314   GW   ISSN 0081-5357
STATISTISCHES JAHRBUCH FUER DIE BUNDESREPUBLIK DEUTSCHLAND. 1952. a. DM.106. (Statistisches Bundesamt) W. Kohlhammer-Verlag GmbH, Abt. Veroeffentlichungen des Statistischen Bundesamtes, Philipp-Reis-Str. 3, Postfach 421120, 6500 Mainz 42, W. Germany (B.R.D.)

310   GW   ISSN 0077-2062
STATISTISCHES JAHRBUCH MUENCHEN. 1969. a. DM.25. Amt fuer Statistik und Datenanalyse, Tal 30, 8000 Munich 2, W. Germany (B.R.D.) Ed. Egon Dheus.

310   GW
STATISTISCHES LANDESAMT HAMBURG. DATEN UND INFORMATIONEN FALTBLATT. 1977. a. free. Statistisches Landesamt Hamburg, Steckelhorn 12, D-2000 Hamburg 11, W. Germany (B.R.D.) circ. 40,000.

310   AU
STATISTISCHES TASCHENBUCH DER STADT WIEN. 1884. a. S.60. Statistisches Amt der Stadt Wien, Volksgartenstr. 3, A-1016 Vienna, Austria (Subscr. to: Jugend und Volk Verlagsgesellschaft m.b.H., Tiefer Graben 7-9, A-1010 Vienna, Austria) adv. charts. stats. index. circ. 1,500. (back issues avail.)

310   SW   ISSN 0081-5381
STATISTISK AARSBOK FOER SVERIGE. 1914. a. Kr.230. Statistiska Centralbyraan, Distribution, S-701 89 Oerebro, Sweden. circ. 12,300.

STATISTISK TIAARS-OVERSIGT FOR KOEBENHAVNS KOMMUNE. see *PUBLIC ADMINISTRATION — Abstracting, Bibliographies, Statistics*

314   GW   ISSN 0072-3967
STUDIES ON STATISTICS. (Text in English) 1957. irreg. price varies. (Statistisches Bundesamt) W. Kohlhammer-Verlag GmbH, Abt. Veroeffentlichungen des Statistischen Bundesamtes, Philipp-Reis-Str. 3, Postfach 421120, 6500 Mainz 42, W. Germany (B.R.D.)

SUBJECT INDEX TO SOURCES OF COMPARATIVE INTERNATIONAL STATISTICS. see *ABSTRACTING AND INDEXING SERVICES*

310   SJ
SUDAN. DEPARTMENT OF STATISTICS. STATISTICAL YEARBOOK. (Text in English) 1973. a. Department of Statistics, Box 700, Khartoum, Sudan.

310 614.8   DK   ISSN 0107-749X
SUNDHEDSSTYRELSEN VITALSTATISTIK. 1983. a. Kr.30. Sundhedsstyrelsen, St. Kongensgade 1, 1264 Copenhagen K, Denmark.

314   FI   ISSN 0081-5063
SUOMEN TILASTOLLINEN VUOSIKIRJA/ STATISTISK AARSBOK FOER FINLAND/ STATISTICAL YEARBOOK OF FINLAND. (Text in English, Finnish and Swedish) 1879. a. Fmk.215. Tilastokeskus, Annankatu 44, SF-00100 Helsinki 10, Finland (Subscr. to: Government Printing Centre, Box 516, SF-00100 Helsinki 10, Finland) circ. 5, 000.

318   SR
SURINAM. ALGEMEEN BUREAU VOOR DE STATISTIEK. NATIONALE REKENINGEN. (Subseries of: Suriname in Cijfers) irreg. Algemeen Bureau voor de Statistiek, Paramaribo, Surinam.

314   GW
SURVEY OF GERMAN FEDERAL STATISTICS/ APERCU DE LA STATISTIQUE FEDERALE ALLEMANDE. (Editions in English and French) 1957. irreg. DM.15.80. (Statistisches Bundesamt) W. Kohlhammer-Verlag GmbH, Abt. Veroeffentlichungen des Statistischen Bundesamtes, Philipp-Reis-Str. 3, Postfach 421120, 6500 Mainz 42, W. Germany (B.R.D.)
    Formerly (1957-1970): Germany (Federal Republic, 1949-). Statistisches Bundesamt Arbeiten (ISSN 0072-1611)

310   US   ISSN 0737-545X
SURVEYS, POLLS, CENSUSES AND FORECASTS DIRECTORY. a. $230. Gale Research Company, Book Tower, Detroit, MI 48226.

316   SQ   ISSN 0586-1357
SWAZILAND. CENTRAL STATISTICAL OFFICE. ANNUAL STATISTICAL BULLETIN. 1966. a. e.2. Central Statistical Office, Box 456, Mbabane, Swaziland. illus. circ. 800.

316   SQ
SWAZILAND. CENTRAL STATISTICAL OFFICE. ANNUAL SURVEY OF SWAZI NATION LAND. 1972/73. a. free. Central Statistical Office, Box 456, Mbabane, Swaziland. stat. circ. 500.

SWAZILAND. CENTRAL STATISTICAL OFFICE. CENSUS OF INDUSTRIES. see *BUSINESS AND ECONOMICS — Abstracting, Bibliographies, Statistics*

SWAZILAND. CENTRAL STATISTICAL OFFICE. EDUCATION STATISTICS. see *EDUCATION — Abstracting, Bibliographies, Statistics*

SWAZILAND. CENTRAL STATISTICAL OFFICE. TIMBER STATISTICS. see *FORESTS AND FORESTRY — Abstracting, Bibliographies, Statistics*

SWEDEN. LUFTFARTSVERKET. AARSBOK. see *TRANSPORTATION — Abstracting, Bibliographies, Statistics*

309   SW
SWEDEN. STATISTISKA CENTRALBYRAAN. LEVNADSFOERHAALLANDEN AARSBOK/ LIVING CONDITIONS YEARBOOK. (Subseries of: Sweden. Statistiska Centralbyraan. Sveriges Officiella Statistik) (Text in English and Swedish) 1975. irreg. Statistiska Centralbyraan, Distribution, S-701 89 Oerebro, Sweden. illus.

314   SW   ISSN 0082-0229
SWEDEN. STATISTISKA CENTRALBYRAAN. MEDDELANDEN I SAMORDNINGSFRAAGOR. 1966. irreg. Statistiska Centralbyraan, Distribution, S-701 89 Oerebro, Sweden.

SWEDEN. STATISTISKA CENTRALBYRAAN. STATISTISKA MEDDELANDEN. SUBGROUP BO (HOUSING AND CONSTRUCTION) see *BUILDING AND CONSTRUCTION — Abstracting, Bibliographies, Statistics*

314   SW   ISSN 0082-0350
SWEDEN. STATISTISKA CENTRALBYRAAN. URVAL SKRIFTSERIES/SELECTION SERIES. (Text in Swedish; summaries in English) 1969. irreg. price varies. Statistiska Centralbyraan, Distribution, S-701 89 Oerebro, Sweden. circ. 750.

314   SW   ISSN 0280-7610
SWEDEN. STATISTISKA CENTRALBYRAANS BIBLIOTEK. STATISTIK FRAN ENSKILDA LAENDER. 1983. a. Kr.80. Statistiska Centralbyraan, Biblioteket, S-115 81 Stockholm, Sweden. circ. 100.

SWITZERLAND. BUNDESAMT FUER STATISTIK. HEIRATEN, LEBENDGEBORENE UND GESTORBENE IN DEN GEMEINDEN/ MARIAGES, NAISSANCES ET DECES DANS LES COMMUNES. see *POPULATION STUDIES — Abstracting, Bibliographies, Statistics*

SWITZERLAND. BUNDESAMT FUER STATISTIK. SCHUELERSTATISTIK/STATISTIQUE DES ELEVES. see *EDUCATION — Abstracting, Bibliographies, Statistics*

SWITZERLAND. DIRECTORATE GENERAL OF CUSTOMS. ANNUAL REPORT. see *BUSINESS AND ECONOMICS — Abstracting, Bibliographies, Statistics*

SWITZERLAND. DIRECTORATE GENERAL OF CUSTOMS. ANNUAL STATISTICS. see *BUSINESS AND ECONOMICS — Abstracting, Bibliographies, Statistics*

315   SY   ISSN 0081-4725
SYRIA. CENTRAL BUREAU OF STATISTICS. STATISTICAL ABSTRACT. (Text in Arabic, English) 1948. a. $50. ‡ Central Bureau of Statistics, Damascus, Syria.

310   II   ISSN 0082-1578
TAMIL NADU. DEPARTMENT OF STATISTICS. ANNUAL STATISTICAL ABSTRACT. (Text in English) 1954/55. a. Rs.11. Director of Statistics, Madras 600006, India (Subscr. to: Government Publication Depot, 166 Anna Rd., Madras 600002, India)

312.8   TZ
TANZANIA. BUREAU OF STATISTICS. MIGRATION STATISTICS. 1968. irreg., latest 1970 (pub. in 1972) Bureau of Statistics, Box 796, Dar es Salaam, Tanzania (Orders to: Government Publications Agency, Box 1801, Dar es Salaam, Tanzania)

331 316   TZ
TANZANIA. BUREAU OF STATISTICS. SURVEY OF EMPLOYMENT. 1961. irreg., (approx. a.) Bureau of Statistics, P.O. Box 796, Dar es Salaam, Tanzania (Orders to: Government Publications Agency, Box 1801, Dar es Salaam, Tanzania)
    Formerly (1961-1977, covers through 1973/74): Tanzania. Bureau of Statistics. Employment and Earnings (ISSN 0049-2973)

TANZANIA. BUREAU OF STATISTICS. SURVEY OF INDUSTRIAL PRODUCTION. see *BUSINESS AND ECONOMICS — Abstracting, Bibliographies, Statistics*

TAX BURDEN ON TOBACCO. see *TOBACCO — Abstracting, Bibliographies, Statistics*

317   US   ISSN 0082-2760
TENNESSEE STATISTICAL ABSTRACT. 1969. a. $22.95. University of Tennessee, Center for Business and Economic Research, Knoxville, TN 37916. TEL 615-974-5441. Ed. Betty B. Vickers. circ. 1,400.

TEXAS BLUE BOOK OF LIFE INSURANCE STATISTICS. see *INSURANCE*

310   TH
THAILAND. NATIONAL STATISTICAL OFFICE. ANNUAL REPORT. (Text in Thai) 1963. a. National Statistical Office, Krung Kasem Road, Bangkok, Thailand. Ed.Bd.

315   TH
THAILAND. NATIONAL STATISTICAL OFFICE. RESEARCH PAPER. 1975. irreg. National Statistical Office, Larn Luang Rd., Bangkok, Thailand.

THAILAND. NATIONAL STATISTICAL OFFICE. STATISTICAL BIBLIOGRAPHY. see *BIBLIOGRAPHIES*

TOURISM AND MIGRATION STATISTICS. see *TRAVEL AND TOURISM — Abstracting, Bibliographies, Statistics*

STATISTICS

TRADING STANDARDS AND CONSUMER PROTECTION STATISTICS. ACTUALS. see *BUSINESS AND ECONOMICS — Abstracting, Bibliographies, Statistics*

310 US
TREASURY ALASKA. Represents: Alaska. Department of Revenue. Treasury Division. Annual Financial Report. a. Department of Revenue, Treasury Division, Pouch SB, Juneau, AK 99811. TEL 907-465-2350.

311 TR ISSN 0082-6502
TRINIDAD AND TOBAGO. CENTRAL STATISTICAL OFFICE. ANNUAL STATISTICAL DIGEST. 1951. a., latest no. 31, 1984. T.T.$5. Central Statistical Office, P.O. Box 98, 23 Park St., Port-of-Spain, Trinidad, W.I. (Orders to: Government Printer, 48 St. Vincent St., Port-of-Spain, Trinidad, W.I.)

TRINIDAD AND TOBAGO. CENTRAL STATISTICAL OFFICE. BUSINESS SURVEYS. see *BUSINESS AND ECONOMICS — Abstracting, Bibliographies, Statistics*

312.8 TR
TRINIDAD AND TOBAGO. CENTRAL STATISTICAL OFFICE. ESTIMATED INTERNAL MIGRATION. BULLETIN. 1974. a. Central Statistical Office, P.O. Box 98, 23 Park St., Port-of-Spain, Trinidad, W.I. (Orders to: Government Printing Office, 48 St. Vincent St., Port of Spain, Trinidad, W.I.)

317 TR
TRINIDAD AND TOBAGO. CENTRAL STATISTICAL OFFICE. POCKET DIGEST. 1973. a. free. Central Statistical Office, P.O. Box 98, 23 Park St., Port-of-Spain, Trinidad, W.I. (Orders to: Government Printing Office, 48 St. Vincent St., Port-of-Spain, Trinidad, W.I.)

312 TR ISSN 0082-6553
TRINIDAD AND TOBAGO. CENTRAL STATISTICAL OFFICE. POPULATION AND VITAL STATISTICS; REPORT. 1953. a. T.T.$4. Central Statistical Office, P.O. Box 98, 23 Park St., Port-of-Spain, Trinidad, W.I. (Subscr. to: Government Printery, 48 St. Vincent St., Port-of-Spain, Trinidad, W.I.)

310 TR
TRINIDAD AND TOBAGO. CENTRAL STATISTICAL OFFICE. STAFF PAPERS. 1967. irreg. free. Central Statistical Office, P.O. Box 98, 23 Park St., Port-of-Spain, Trinidad, W.I. (Orders to Government Printing Office, 48 St. Vincent St., Port-of-Spain, Trinidad, W.I.)

301 GW ISSN 0722-494X
TUEXENIA. 1928. irreg. price varies. ‡ Floristisch-Soziologische Arbeitsgemeinschaft, Wilhelm-Weber-Str. 2, 3400 Goettingen, W. Germany (B.R.D.) Ed. H. Dierschke. bk. rev. circ. 1,400. Indexed: Biol.Abstr.
 Formerly (until 1980): Floristisch-Soziologische Arbeitsgemeinschaft. Mitteilungen (ISSN 0373-7632)

315 TU ISSN 0082-691X
TURKIYE ISTATISTIK YILLIGI/STATISTICAL YEARBOOK OF TURKEY. (Subseries of its Yayin) 1962. biennial. exchange basis. State Institute of Statistics, Necatibey Caddesi 114, Ankara, Turkey.

U.S.S.R. FACTS & FIGURES ANNUAL. see *POLITICAL SCIENCE*

310 060 UN ISSN 0082-7533
UNESCO STATISTICAL REPORTS AND STUDIES. (Editions in English and French) 1955. irreg., no.27, 1982. price varies. Unesco, 7-9 Place de Fontenoy, 75700 Paris, France (Dist. in U.S. by: Bernan Associates-Unipub, 4611-F Assembly Dr., Lanham, MD 20706-4391)

310 UN ISSN 0082-7541
UNESCO STATISTICAL YEARBOOK. (Text in English, French and Spanish) 1952. a., latest 1985. price varies. Unesco, 7-9 Place de Fontenoy, 75700 Paris, France (Dist. in U.S. by: Bernan Associates-Unipub, 4611-F Assembly Dr., Lanham, MD 20706-4391)

UNION LABOR IN CALIFORNIA. see *BUSINESS AND ECONOMICS — Labor And Industrial Relations*

310 UN ISSN 0082-8459
UNITED NATIONS. STATISTICAL YEARBOOK. (Text in English and French) 1949. a., latest 1982. $60. (United Nations Statistical Office) United Nations Publications, Room DC2-853, New York, NY 10017 (Or Distribution and Sales Section, Palais des Nations, CH-1211 Geneva 10, Switzerland) (also avail. in microfiche)

316 UN
UNITED NATIONS ECONOMIC COMMISSION FOR AFRICA. STATISTICAL NEWSLETTER. (Text in English) irreg. United Nations Economic Commission for Africa, Box 3001, Addis Ababa, Ethiopia.

317 US ISSN 0082-9455
U.S. BUREAU OF THE CENSUS. COUNTY AND CITY DATA BOOK. 1944. irreg. price varies. U.S. Bureau of the Census, Customer Services, Washington, DC 20233 TEL 301-763-4100. (Orders to: Supt. of Documents, Washington, DC 20402) (also avail. in microfiche)

317.3 US ISSN 0276-6566
U.S. BUREAU OF THE CENSUS. STATE AND METROPOLITAN AREA DATA BOOK. irreg. price varies. U.S. Bureau of the Census, Customer Services, Washington, DC 20233 TEL 301-763-4100. (Orders to: Supt of Documents, Washington, DC 20402) (also avail. in microfiche)

310 US ISSN 0082-9544
U.S. BUREAU OF THE CENSUS. TECHNICAL PAPER. 1953. irreg., no.54, 1985. price varies. U.S. Bureau of the Census, Customer Services, Washington, DC 20233 TEL 301-763-4100. (Orders to: Supt. of Documents, Washington, DC 20402) Key Title: Technical Paper - U.S. Department of Commerce, Social and Economics Statistics Administration, Bureau of the Census.

310 US ISSN 0082-9552
U.S. BUREAU OF THE CENSUS. WORKING PAPERS. 1954. irreg. U.S. Bureau of the Census, Customer Services, Washington, DC 20233. TEL 301-763-4100.

U.S. DEPARTMENT OF HOUSING AND URBAN DEVELOPMENT. STATISTICAL YEARBOOK. see *HOUSING AND URBAN PLANNING — Abstracting, Bibliographies, Statistics*

U.S. DEPARTMENT OF TRANSPORTATION. NATIONAL TRANSPORTATION STATISTICS. ANNUAL; a supplement to the summary of national transportation statistics. see *ENERGY — Abstracting, Bibliographies, Statistics*

U.S. FISH AND WILDLIFE SERVICE. NATIONAL SURVEY OF HUNTING, FISHING AND WILDLIFE-ASSOCIATED RECREATION. see *SPORTS AND GAMES — Abstracting, Bibliographies, Statistics*

UNIVERSIDADE FEDERAL DO RIO DE JANEIRO. INSTITUTO DE MATEMATICA. MEMORIAS DE MATEMATICA. see *MATHEMATICS — Abstracting, Bibliographies, Statistics*

314 DK ISSN 0105-9645
UNIVERSITETETS STATISTISKE INSTITUT. RESEARCH REPORT. no.76, 1981. irreg. Universitetets Statistiske Institut, Studiestraede 6, DK-1455 Copenhagen K, Denmark.
 Formerly: Koebenhavns Universitet. Statistiske Institut. Afhandlinger. Graa Serie.

310 DK ISSN 0900-0526
UNIVERSITY OF COPENHAGEN. STATISTICAL RESEARCH UNIT. RESEARCH REPORT. 1984. irreg. free. Koebenhavns Universitet, Statistical Research Unit - University of Copenhagen, Blegdamsvej 3, DK-2200 Copenhagen N, Denmark. Ed. Per Kragh Andersen. circ. 200.
 Formerly: Danish Medical Research Council. Statistical Research Unit. Research Report.

310 US ISSN 0078-1495
UNIVERSITY OF NORTH CAROLINA, CHAPEL HILL. INSTITUTE OF STATISTICS. MIMEO SERIES. 1947. irreg., approx. 3/mo. price varies. University of North Carolina at Chapel Hill, Department of Statistics, Chapel Hill, NC 27514. TEL 919-962-2307. cum.index.

310 UK
UNIVERSITY OF WARWICK BUSINESS INFORMATION SERVICE. OCCASIONAL REVIEW. 1980. irreg. University of Warwick Information Service, University of Warwick Library, Coventry CV4 7AL, England (Distr. in U.S. and Canada by: Addor Associates Inc., 115 Roseville Rd., P.O. Box 2128, Westport, CT 06880, U.S.A.)
 Formerly: Warwick Statistics Service. Occasional Review (ISSN 0144-6738)

UTAH MARRIAGE AND DIVORCE ANNUAL REPORT. see *POPULATION STUDIES — Abstracting, Bibliographies, Statistics*

UTAH STATISTICAL ABSTRACT. see *BUSINESS AND ECONOMICS — Abstracting, Bibliographies, Statistics*

VANUATU. NATIONAL PLANNING AND STATISTICS OFFICE. OVERSEAS SHIPPING AND AIRCRAFT STATISTICS/STATISTIQUES DE NAVIGATION MARITIME ET AERIENNE INTERNATIONALES. see *TRANSPORTATION — Abstracting, Bibliographies, Statistics*

VENEZUELA. MINISTERIO DE ENERGIA Y MINAS. APENDICE ESTADISTICO. see *ENERGY — Abstracting, Bibliographies, Statistics*

VITAL STATISTICS OF IOWA. see *POPULATION STUDIES — Abstracting, Bibliographies, Statistics*

VITAL STATISTICS OF THE PROVINCE OF BRITISH COLUMBIA. see *POPULATION STUDIES — Abstracting, Bibliographies, Statistics*

310 UR
VOPROSY STATISTIKI. (Subseries of: Latviiskii Gosudartstvennyi Universitet. Zinatniskie Raksti) irreg. 0.90 Rub. Latviiskii Gosudarstvennyi Universitet, Kafedra Statistiki i Planirovaniya Narodnogo Khozyaistva S.S.S.R., Bulvar Raynisa 19, Riga, Latvian S.S.R., U.S.S.R.

WASHINGTON (STATE). DEPARTMENT OF NATURAL RESOURCES. ANNUAL FIRE STATISTICS. see *FORESTS AND FORESTRY — Abstracting, Bibliographies, Statistics*

WATER TRANSPORT STATISTICS OF INDIA. see *TRANSPORTATION — Abstracting, Bibliographies, Statistics*

WEST BENGAL. ANNUAL FINANCIAL STATEMENT (BUDGET) see *BUSINESS AND ECONOMICS — Abstracting, Bibliographies, Statistics*

WEST BENGAL. BUREAU OF APPLIED ECONOMICS AND STATISTICS. STATISTICAL HANDBOOK. see *BUSINESS AND ECONOMICS — Abstracting, Bibliographies, Statistics*

WISCONSIN. DIVISION OF CORRECTIONS. OFFICE OF INFORMATION MANAGEMENT. ADMISSIONS TO JUVENILE INSTITUTIONS. see *CRIMINOLOGY AND LAW ENFORCEMENT — Abstracting, Bibliographies, Statistics*

WORLD MINERAL STATISTICS; world production, exports and imports. see *MINES AND MINING INDUSTRY — Abstracting, Bibliographies, Statistics*

379 US ISSN 0093-5530
WYOMING. DIVISION OF PLANNING, EVALUATION AND INFORMATION SERVICES. STATISTICAL REPORT SERIES. 1973. a. free. Division of Planning, Evaluation and Information Services, Cheyenne, WY 82001. TEL 307-777-6267. stat. Key Title: Statistical Report Series (Cheyenne)

315.6   YE
YEMEN. CENTRAL STATISTICAL OFFICE. STATISTICAL YEARBOOK. (Text in Arabic and English) 1971. a. 20 rials. Central Statistical Office, Sana'a, Yemen. illus.

ZAMBIA. CENTRAL STATISTICAL OFFICE. AGRICULTURAL AND PASTORAL PRODUCTION (COMMERCIAL FARMS) see AGRICULTURE — Abstracting, Bibliographies, Statistics

ZAMBIA. CENTRAL STATISTICAL OFFICE. AGRICULTURAL AND PASTORAL PRODUCTION (NON-COMMERCIAL) see AGRICULTURE — Abstracting, Bibliographies, Statistics

316   ZA   ISSN 0084-4551
ZAMBIA. CENTRAL STATISTICAL OFFICE. STATISTICAL YEAR BOOK. 1967. a. K.3. Central Statistical Office, P.O. Box 31908, Lusaka, Zambia.

ZAMBIA. CENTRAL STATISTICAL OFFICE. VITAL STATISTICS. see POPULATION STUDIES — Abstracting, Bibliographies, Statistics

ZIMBABWE. CENTRAL STATISTICAL OFFICE. CENSUS OF PRODUCTION. see BUSINESS AND ECONOMICS — Abstracting, Bibliographies, Statistics

ZIMBABWE. CENTRAL STATISTICAL OFFICE. INCOME TAX STATISTICS; analysis of assessments and loss statements. see BUSINESS AND ECONOMICS — Abstracting, Bibliographies, Statistics

SURGERY

see Medical Sciences — Surgery

TAXATION

see Business and Economics — Public Finance, Taxation

TEACHING METHODS AND CURRICULUM

see Education — Teaching Methods and Curriculum

TECHNOLOGY: COMPREHENSIVE WORKS

668.3   UK   ISSN 0305-3199
ADHESIVES DIRECTORY. (Text in English, French, German and Italian) 1966. a. £6.25. Wheatland Journals Ltd., Penn House, Penn Place, Rickmansworth, Herts. WD3 1SN, England. adv. charts. circ. 2,000.

ADVANCES IN ENVIRONMENTAL SCIENCE AND ENGINEERING. see ENVIRONMENTAL STUDIES

600   US   ISSN 0890-2771
ADVANCES IN HIGH-TECH MATERIALS; data file III. 1987. a. $390. Technical Insights, Inc., 52 N. Dean St., Englewood, NJ 07631 TEL 201-568-4744. (Subscr. to: Box 1304, Fort Lee, NJ 07024) bibl. pat. stat.

600   US   ISSN 0890-2763
ADVANCES IN R & D; data file IV. 1987. a. $415. Technical Insights, Inc., 52 N. Dean St., Englewood, NJ 07631 TEL 201-568-4744. (Subscr. to: Box 1304, Fort Lee, NJ 07024) bibl. pat. stat.

600   001.6   621.381   US   ISSN 0890-2755
ADVANCES IN SENSOR TECHNOLOGY. 1987. a. $400 (foreign $435) Technical Insights, Inc., 32 N. Dean St., Englewood, NJ 07631 TEL 201-568-4744. (Subscr. to: Box 1304, Ft. Lee, NJ 07024) bk. rev. bibl. charts. pat. stat. (back issues avail.)

669   620.1   US   ISSN 0069-8490
ADVANCES IN X-RAY ANALYSIS. Represents: Annual Conference on Applications of X-Ray Analysis. Proceedings. 1960. a. price varies. (University of Denver, Denver Research Institute) Plenum Publishing Corp., 233 Spring St., New York, NY 10013. TEL 212-620-8047. Ed.Bd. Indexed: Biol.Abstr. Chem.Abstr. Br.Ceram.Abstr. GeoRef.

AEROSPACE TESTING SEMINAR. PROCEEDINGS. see AERONAUTICS AND SPACE FLIGHT

600   CN   ISSN 0080-1526
ALBERTA RESEARCH COUNCIL. ANNUAL REPORT. 1919. a. free. Alberta Research Council, Publications Department, P.O. Box 8330, Sta. F, Edmonton, Alta. T6H 5X2, Canada. TEL 403-450-5111. Indexed: GeoRef.

ALBERTA RESEARCH COUNCIL. ATMOSPHERIC SCIENCES REPORTS. see SCIENCES: COMPREHENSIVE WORKS

600   CN
ALBERTA RESEARCH COUNCIL. REPORTS. 1919. irreg. price varies. Alberta Research Council, Publications Dept., P.O. Box 8330, Sta. F, Edmonton, Alta. T6H 5X2, Canada. TEL 403-450-5111. Indexed: GeoRef.
    Formerly: Research Council of Alberta. Report (ISSN 0080-1607)

600   378   II   ISSN 0065-6623
ALTECH. 1950. a. on exchange basis. (Anna University) Alagappa Chettiar College of Technology, Madras 600025, Tamil Nadu, India. Ed. G.S. Laddha. circ. 1,000. Indexed: Chem.Abstr.

AMERICAN COUNCIL OF INDEPENDENT LABORATORIES. DIRECTORY. see SCIENCES: COMPREHENSIVE WORKS

AMERICAN PETROLEUM INSTITUTE. HEALTH AND ENVIRONMENTAL SCIENCES DEPARTMENT. RESEARCH REPORTS. see PUBLIC HEALTH AND SAFETY

AMERICAN POWER CONFERENCE. PROCEEDINGS. see ENERGY

350   600   US   ISSN 0360-6899
AMERICAN PUBLIC WORKS ASSOCIATION. DIRECTORY. biennial. price varies. American Public Works Association, 1313 E. 60th St, Chicago, IL 60637.
    Former titles, 1959-1968: American Public Works Association. Yearbook (ISSN 0096-025X); Public Works Engineers' Yearbook.

600   US   ISSN 8755-9978
ANNUAL REPORT ON HIGH-TECH MATERIALS; the year that was; the year to come. 1984. a. $295. Technical Insights, Inc., 32 N. Dean St., Englewood, NJ 07631 TEL 201-568-4744. (Subscr. to: Box 1304, Fort Lee, NJ 07024) bibl. charts. pat. stat. circ. 270.

600   US   ISSN 0739-6325
ANNUAL REPORT ON RESEARCH AND DEVELOPMENT; the year that was; the year to come. 1984. a. $320. Technical Insights, Inc., 32 N. Dean St., Englewood, NJ 07631 TEL 201-568-4744. (Subscr. to: Box 1304, Fort Lee, NJ 07024) Ed. Robert L. Davidson. bibl. charts. pat. stat. circ. 265. (back issues avail.)

600   AG   ISSN 0325-6278
ARGENTINA. INSTITUTO NACIONAL DE TECNOLOGIA INDUSTRIA. BOLETIN TECNICO. 1967. irreg. Instituto Nacional de Tecnologia Industrial, Leandro N. Alem 1067, Casilla de Correo 1359, 1001 Buenos Aires, Argentina. Ed.Bd. charts. circ. 500.

600   TH   ISSN 0572-4198
ASIAN INSTITUTE OF TECHNOLOGY. RESEARCH SUMMARY. 1962. a. free. Asian Institute of Technology, c/o Academic Secretary, P.O. Box 2754, Bangkok, Thailand. circ. 1,000. (microfiche) Indexed: GeoRef.

ASLIB DIRECTORY OF INFORMATION SOURCES IN THE UNITED KINGDOM. VOLUME 1: SCIENCE, TECHNOLOGY AND COMMERCE. see SCIENCES: COMPREHENSIVE WORKS

ASSOCIATED SCIENTIFIC AND TECHNICAL SOCIETIES OF SOUTH AFRICA. ANNUAL PROCEEDINGS. see SCIENCES: COMPREHENSIVE WORKS

600   620   US
ASSOCIATION FOR INTEGRATED MANUFACTURING TECHNOLOGY. PROCEEDINGS. no.5, 1968. a. price varies. Association for Integrated Manufacturing Technology, Box 1235, Beloit, WI 53511. TEL 608-364-7949.

600   FR   ISSN 0066-9288
ASSOCIATION FRANCAISE DES EXPERTS DE LA COOPERATION TECHNIQUE INTERNATIONALE. ANNUAIRE. 1965. a. $2. Association Francaise des Experts de la Cooperation Technique Internationale, 6 rue de Marignan, 75008 Paris, France.

607   CN
B C I T ANNUAL REPORT. 1975. irreg. British Columbia Institute of Technology, 3700 Willingdon Ave., Burnaby, B.C., Canada. TEL 604-434-5734. Ed. Mary Bacon. illus.
    Former titles: B C I T: The Career Campus (ISSN 0707-3291); British Columbia Institute of Technology. Annual Report (ISSN 0381-260X)

600   510   US
BALSKRISHNAN - NEUSTADT SERIES. irreg. price varies. Holt, Rinehart and Winston, Inc., 383 Madison Ave., New York, NY 10017. TEL 212-688-9100.

BIBLIOGRAPHIC GUIDE TO TECHNOLOGY. see BIBLIOGRAPHIES

BIOTECHNOLOGY IN AGRICULUTURE AND FORESTRY. see AGRICULTURE

600   US   ISSN 0067-9127
BLAETTER FUER TECHNIKGESCHICHTE. 1932. irreg. (Technisches Museum fuer Industrie und Gewerbe, Forschungsinstitut fuer Technikgeschichte, AU) Springer Verlag, 175 Fifth Ave., New York, NY 10010. Indexed: Hist.Abstr. Amer.Hist.& Life.

BOMBAY TECHNOLOGIST. see CHEMISTRY

BRAZIL. CONSELHO NACIONAL DE DESENVOLVIMENTO CIENTIFICO E TECNOLOGICO. BOLETIM. see SCIENCES: COMPREHENSIVE WORKS

600   UK   ISSN 0140-766X
BRITISH ELECTROTECHNICAL APPROVALS BOARD. ANNUAL LIST OF APPROVED ELECTROTECHNICAL EQUIPMENT. 1966. a. free. B E A B, Mark House, the Green, 9-11 Queen's Rd., Hersham, Walton-on-Thames, Surrey KT12 5NA, England. circ. 10,000.

600   PL   ISSN 0068-4597
BYDGOSKIE TOWARZYSTWO NAUKOWE. WYDZIAL NAUK TECHNICZNYCH. PRACE. SERIA Z: (PRACE ZBIOROWE) 1966. irreg. price varies. Bydgoskie Towarzystwo Naukowe, Jezuicka 4, Bydgoszcz, Poland (Dist. by Ars Polona-Ruch, Krakowskie Przedmiescie 7, Warsaw, Poland)

C R C CRITICAL REVIEWS IN BIOTECHNOLOGY. see BIOLOGY

C R I C RAPPORT DE RECHERCHE. (Centre National de Recherches Scientifiques et Techniques pour l'Industrie Cimentiere) see SCIENCES: COMPREHENSIVE WORKS

C S I R ANNUAL REPORT. (Council for Scientific and Industrial Research) see SCIENCES: COMPREHENSIVE WORKS

TECHNOLOGY: COMPREHENSIVE WORKS

C S I R O DIRECTORY. (Commonwealth for Scientific and Industrial Research Organisation) see *SCIENCES: COMPREHENSIVE WORKS*

C S I R O FILM CATALOGUE. (Commonwealth for Scientific and Industrial Research Organisation) see *SCIENCES: COMPREHENSIVE WORKS*

C S I R O ORGANISATION AND ACTIVITIES. (Council for Scientific and Industrial Research Organisation) see *SCIENCES: COMPREHENSIVE WORKS*

CANADA. MINISTRY OF STATE FOR SCIENCE AND TECHNOLOGY. ANNUAL REPORT/ RAPPORT ANNUEL. see *SCIENCES: COMPREHENSIVE WORKS*

600   CN
CANADA. NATIONAL RESEARCH COUNCIL. PUBLICATIONS/CANADA. CONSEIL NATIONAL DE RECHERCHES. PUBLICATIONS. 1936. irreg. Can.$28. National Research Council, CISTI Publications - Conseil National de Recherches, Ottawa, Ont. K1A 0S2, Canada. TEL 613-993-3736. circ. 400.

CENTRE NATIONAL D'ART ET DE CULTURE GEORGES POMPIDOU. ANNUAIRE DES CONCEPTEURS. see *ART*

600 500   BE   ISSN 0069-1968
CENTRE NATIONAL DE DOCUMENTATION SCIENTIFIQUE ET TECHNIQUE. RAPPORT D'ACTIVITE. 1964. biennial. contr. free circ. ‡ Centre National de Documentation Scientifique et Technique - National Center for Scientific and Technical Documentation, 4, Bd. de l'Empereur, B-1000 Brussels, Belgium. Dir. A. Cockx. index. circ. 1,000. Indexed: Bull.Signal.

600   CS   ISSN 0069-2301
CESKOSLOVENSKA AKADEMIE VED. ROZPRAVY. T V: RADA TECHNICKYCH VED. 1891. irreg., vol. 85, 1975. price varies. Academia, Publishing House of the Czechoslovak Academy of Sciences, Vodickova 40, 112 29 Prague 1, Czechoslovakia. circ. 1,000.

CEYLON INSTITUTE OF SCIENTIFIC & INDUSTRIAL RESEARCH. ANNUAL REPORT. see *SCIENCES: COMPREHENSIVE WORKS*

CHECKPOINT (WASHINGTON); newsletter from the frontiers of a future civilized world order. see *SCIENCES: COMPREHENSIVE WORKS*

CHINA REPORT: SCIENCE AND TECHNOLOGY. see *SCIENCES: COMPREHENSIVE WORKS*

CHUBU INSTITUTE OF TECHNOLOGY. MEMOIRS/CHUBU KOGYO DAIGAKU. KIYO. see *ENGINEERING*

CHUO UNIVERSITY. FACULTY OF SCIENCE AND ENGINEERING. BULLETIN/CHUO DAIGAKU RIKOGAKUBU KIYO. see *SCIENCES: COMPREHENSIVE WORKS*

600 500   CU   ISSN 0253-7397
CIENCIAS TECNICAS FISICAS Y MATEMATICAS. 1981. irreg. exchange basis. Academia de Ciencias de Cuba, Apartado 2291, Zona 2, Havana, Cuba. Ed. Jose Altshuler. circ. 1, 250. Indexed: Sci.Abstr.

600   SP
COLECCION TECNOLOGIA Y SOCIEDAD. 1978. irreg. price varies. Editorial Gustavo Gili, S.A., Rosellon 87-89, Barcelona 29, Spain.

600   CL
COMITE DE INVESTIGACIONES TECNOLOGICAS DE CHILE. biennial. Comite de Investigaciones Tecnologicas de Chile, Avda. Santa Maria 6500, Casilla 667, Santiago, Chile. illus.

600   AT   ISSN 0069-7184
COMMONWEALTH SCIENTIFIC AND INDUSTRIAL RESEARCH ORGANIZATION. ANNUAL REPORT. 1948. a. Aus.$3. C.S.I.R.O., 314 Albert St., E. Melbourne 3002, Victoria, Australia. Indexed: Biol.Abstr. GeoRef.

CONFERENCE ON SPACE SIMULATION. PROCEEDINGS. see *AERONAUTICS AND SPACE FLIGHT*

600   US
CONFERENCE ON U S TECHNOLOGY POLICY. PROCEEDINGS. Variant title: I E E E Conference on U S Technology Policy. Proceedings. 1977. biennial. price varies. (I E E E, Technical Activities Board) Institute of Electrical and Electronics Engineers, Inc., 345 E. 47th St., New York, NY 10017 TEL 212-705-7900. (Subscr. to: IEEE Service Center, 445 Hoes Lane, Piscataway, NJ 08854) (Co-sponsor: IEEE, United States Activities Board)
  Formerly (1977-1979): Conference on U S Technological Policy. Proceedings.

600   CR   ISSN 0253-2492
CONSEJO NACIONAL DE INVESTIGACIONES CIENTIFICAS Y TECNOLOGICAS, COSTA RICA. INFORME ANUAL. 1975. a. free. Consejo Nacional de Investigaciones Cientificas y Tecnologicas, Departamento de Informacion y Documentacion, Apdo. 10318, San Jose, Costa Rica. circ. 1,000.

CONTRIBUTIONS TO THE HISTORY OF NATURAL SCIENCES AND TECHNOLOGY IN THE BALTIC/IZ ISTORII ESTESTVOZNANIYA I TEKHNIKI PRIBALTIKI. see *SCIENCES: COMPREHENSIVE WORKS*

600   US   ISSN 0887-1930
CORPORATE TECHNOLOGY DIRECTORY. 1986. a. $750. Corporate Technology Information Services, Inc., Two Laurel Ave., Box 281, Wellesley Hills, MA 02181. TEL 617-235-5330. Ed. Charles T. Peers, Jr. circ. 2,000.

600   DK   ISSN 0107-5403
D D V - ANALYSEN. 1981. a. Kr.200. Danske Vedligeholdelsesforening, c/o Danmarks Tekniske Hoejskole, Bybning 301, 2800 Lyngby, Denmark. illus.

600 340   GW   ISSN 0723-7685
D I N. CATALOG OF TECHNICAL RULES. (Text in English, German) 1926. a. DM.220($90) (Deutsches Institut fuer Normung (DIN)) Beuth Verlag GmbH, Burggrafenstr. 6, D-1000 Berlin 30, W. Germany (B.R.D.) (North American subscr. to: IPS International Service, Hingam, MA 02043 U.S.A.) circ. 11,000.

DAEDALUS. see *MUSEUMS AND ART GALLERIES*

007   US
DIRECTORY OF AMERICAN RESEARCH AND TECHNOLOGY. biennial. $185. (Jaques Cattell Press) R. R. Bowker Company, Database Publishing Group, 245 W. 17th St., New York, NY 10011. TEL 800-521-8110.
• Also available online. Vendors: Pergamon Infoline.
  Formerly (until 1986): Industrial Research Laboratories of the United States (ISSN 0073-7623)

DIRECTORY OF FEDERAL LABORATORIES. see *BUSINESS AND ECONOMICS — Trade And Industrial Directories*

DIRECTORY OF PUBLIC HIGH TECHNOLOGY CORPORATIONS. see *BUSINESS AND ECONOMICS — Trade And Industrial Directories*

DIRECTORY OF SCIENTIFIC AND TECHNICAL ASSOCIATIONS IN ISRAEL. see *SCIENCES: COMPREHENSIVE WORKS*

DIRECTORY OF THE SCIENTISTS, TECHNOLOGISTS, AND ENGINEERS OF THE P C S I R. (Pakistan Council of Scientific and Industrial Research) see *SCIENCES: COMPREHENSIVE WORKS*

600   DK   ISSN 0108-6707
DRIFTSTEKNIKERBOGEN. 1974. a. Kr.85. Danmarks Tekniske Hoejskole, Driftsteknisk Institut, Bygn. 423, DK-2800 Lyngby, Denmark. illus. circ. 300.
  Formerly: Driftsteknikerdag.

620   FR
ECOLE NATIONALE SUPERIEURE DE TECHNIQUES AVANCEES CENTRE D'EDITION ET DE DOCUMENTATION. RAPPORT D'ACTIVITE SUR LES RECHERCHES. 1972. a. free. Ecole Nationale Superieure de Techniques Avancees, Centre d'Edition et de Documentation, 32, Boulevard Victor, 75015 Paris, France.

600   NE   ISSN 0167-9708
EINDHOVEN UNIVERSITY OF TECHNOLOGY. RESEARCH REPORTS. Variant title: E U T Reports. (Text in Dutch and English) 1968. irreg. exchange. Eindhoven University of Technology, Postbus 513, 5600 MB Eindhoven, Netherlands. Ed.Bd. circ. 200. Indexed: INSPEC.

600   US
EMERGING TECHNOLOGIES. irreg., latest no.18. Technical Insights, Inc., Box 1304, Fort Lee, NJ 07024. charts. illus.

ENVIRONMENTAL SCIENCE AND TECHNOLOGY: A WILEY-INTERSCIENCE SERIES OF TEXTS AND MONOGRAPHS. see *ENVIRONMENTAL STUDIES*

EUROPE-LATIN AMERICA REPORT: SCIENCE AND TECHNOLOGY. see *SCIENCES: COMPREHENSIVE WORKS*

EUROPEAN RESEARCH CENTRES; a directory of organizations in science, technology, agriculture and medicine. see *SCIENCES: COMPREHENSIVE WORKS*

EUROPEAN SOURCES OF SCIENTIFIC AND TECHNICAL INFORMATION. see *SCIENCES: COMPREHENSIVE WORKS*

EXPERIENTIA. SUPPLEMENTUM. see *SCIENCES: COMPREHENSIVE WORKS*

600   DK   ISSN 0108-9048
F A T - BLADET. no.45, 1983. irreg. (2-4/yr.) membership. Foreningen af Teleteknikere, Rolfsvej 37/2, 2000 Copenhagen F, Denmark.
  Formerly: Foreningen af Teleteknikere.

600   US   ISSN 0172-5203
FACHBERICHTE MESSEN - STEUERN - REGELN. 1977. irreg., vol.10, 1983. price varies. Springer-Verlag, 175 Fifth Ave., New York, NY 10010 TEL 212-460-1500. (Also Berlin, Heidelberg, Tokyo and Vienna) (reprint service avail. from ISI)

600 500   UK   ISSN 0071-4097
FAWLEY FOUNDATION LECTURES. (No publication in 1985) 1954. a. £1. University of Southampton, Highfield, Southampton SO9 5NH, England. Ed. N.C. Hollingdale. circ. 3,500.

600   US
FIBER OPTICS TECHNICAL DIRECTORY. 1984. a. price varies. I S A Services, Inc., Box 12277, 67 Alexander Dr., Research Triangle Park, NC 27709. Ed. William M. Rowe. adv. tr.lit. circ. 10,000. (reprint service avail.)

FOCUS ON SCI-TECH. see *SCIENCES: COMPREHENSIVE WORKS*

600   US   ISSN 0161-5319
FRONTIERS OF POWER TECHNOLOGY CONFERENCE. PROCEEDINGS. 6th, 1973. irreg, latest 1979. price varies. Oklahoma State University, College of Engineering, Engineering Extension, 512 Engineering North, Stillwater, OK 74078. TEL 405-624-5276.

600   GW   ISSN 0071-9749
FUEHRER DURCH DIE TECHNISCHE LITERATUR; Katalog technischer Werke fuer Studium und Praxis. 1900. a. DM.21. Fr. Weidemanns Buchhandlung (H.Witt), Georgstr. 11, Postfach 6406, D 3 Hannover 1, W. Germany (B.R.D.) Eds. K. Deichmann, H. Knigge. adv. circ. 20,000.

600   JA
FUKUI UNIVERSITY. FACULTY OF EDUCATION. MEMOIRS. SERIES 5: APPLIED SCIENCE AND TECHNOLOGY. (Text in Japanese; summmaries in English and Japanese) 1964. a. Fukui University, Faculty of Education, 9-1, 3-chome, Bunkyo, Fukui 910, Japan.

600   US
G A T F TECHNICAL SERVICES REPORT. 1967. irreg. $7.50 to non-members; members $3.75. ‡ Graphic Arts Technical Foundation, 4615 Forbes Ave., Pittsburgh, PA 15213. TEL 412-621-6941. circ. controlled. Indexed: Graph.Arts Lit.Abstr.

TECHNOLOGY: COMPREHENSIVE WORKS

GERMANY (FEDERAL REPUBLIC, 1949-). BUNDESMINISTERIUM FUER FORSCHUNG UND TECHNOLOGIE. B M F T FOERDERUNGSKATALOG. see *SCIENCES: COMPREHENSIVE WORKS*

600   US
GOVERNMENT RESEARCH DIRECTORY. 1980. irreg., 4th edt., 1986. $350. Gale Research Company, Book Tower, Detroit, MI 48226. TEL 313-961-2242. Eds. Kay Gill, Susan E. Tufts.
 Formerly: Government Research Centers Directory (ISSN 0270-4811)

600   608.7   US
GUIDE TO AVAILABLE TECHNOLOGIES; an annual guide to business opportunities in technology. 1985. a. $150. Techni Research Associates, Inc., Willow Grove Plaza, York & Davisville Rds., Willow Grove, PA 19090. TEL 215-657-1753. Ed. L.F. Schiffman.

GUNMA UNIVERSITY, FACULTY OF EDUCATION. ANNUAL REPORT: ART, TECHNOLOGY, HEALTH & PHYSICAL EDUCATION, AND SCIENCE OF HUMAN LIVING SERIES. see *ART*

600   JA
HAKODATE TECHNICAL COLLEGE. RESEARCH REPORTS/HAKODATE KOGYO KOTO SENMON GAKKO KIYO. (Text in Japanese: summaries in English) 1967. a. Hakodate Technical College - Hakodate Kogyo Koto Senmon Gakko, 226 Tokura-cho, 2 Hakodate 042, Japan. illus. Indexed: Chem.Abstr.

HEALTH CARE INSTRUMENTATION; the information journal of current medical technology. see *INSTRUMENTS*

HEIDELBERGER ARBEITSBUECHER. see *SCIENCES: COMPREHENSIVE WORKS*

HEIDELBERGER JAHRBUECHER. see *SCIENCES: COMPREHENSIVE WORKS*

HEIDELBERGER TASCHENBUECHER. see *SCIENCES: COMPREHENSIVE WORKS*

600   UK   ISSN 0307-5451
HISTORY OF TECHNOLOGY. 1976. a. price varies. Mansell Publishing Ltd., 6 All Saints St., London N1 9RL, England (Dist. in U.S. by: H. W. Wilson Co., 950 University Ave., Bronx, NY 10452) Ed. Norman Smith. Indexed: Hist.Abstr. Amer.Hist.& Life. Br.Archaeol.Abstr.

670   HK
HONG KONG INDUSTRIAL PRODUCTS DIRECTORY/HSIANG-KANG KUNG YEH CHIH PIN NIEN CHIEN. (Text in Chinese and English) 1974. irreg. HK.$50.00. Hsiang-Kang Kung i Chih Pin Chang Fa Chan Hsieh Hui., Handicrafts Manufacturers Development Association, P.O. Box K-880, Chiu-Lung, Kowloon, Hong Kong. illus.

745.2   AU   ISSN 0018-7224
HUMAN INDUSTRIAL DESIGN. (Text in German) 1968. irreg. Verlag Dr. Herta Ranner, Zeismannsbrunngasse 1, A-1070 Vienna, Austria. Ed. H. Ranner. adv. bk. rev.

600   US
I E E E CONFERENCE ON DECISION AND CONTROL. PROCEEDINGS. a. price varies. (I E E E, Control Systems Society) Institute of Electrical and Electronics Engineers, Inc., 345 E. 47th St., New York, NY 10017 TEL 212-705-7900. (Subscr. address: 445 Hoes Lane, Piscataway, NJ 08854)
 Formerly (until 1982): I E E E Conference on Decision and Control, Including the Symposium on Adaptive Processes. Proceedings (ISSN 0191-2216); Incorporating (as of 1970): Symposium on Adaptive Processes.

600   US
I F U. (Text in German) vol.51, 1980. irreg. (Universitaet Stuttgart, Institut fuer Umformtechnik, GW) Springer-Verlag, 175 Fifth Ave., New York, NY 10010 TEL 212-460-1500. (Also Berlin, Heidelberg, Tokyo and Vienna) Ed. K. Lange. (reprint service avail. from ISI)

620   IE
I I R S OCCASIONAL REPORT SERIES. 1975. irreg. Institute for Industrial Research and Standards, Ballymun Rd., Dublin 9, Ireland. bibl. charts.

INDIA. DEPARTMENT OF SCIENCE & TECHNOLOGY. ANNUAL REPORT. see *SCIENCES: COMPREHENSIVE WORKS*

354.54   II
INDIA. DEPARTMENT OF SCIENCE AND TECHNOLOGY. REPORT. (Text in English) 1971/72. a. free. ‡ Department of Science and Technology, Technology Bhavan, New Mehrauli Rd., New Delhi 110029, India.

600   II   ISSN 0073-6503
INDIAN INSTITUTE OF TECHNOLOGY, BOMBAY. SERIES.* (Text in English) 1968. irreg., no.3, 1980. price varies. Indian Institute of Technology, Bombay, Powai, Bombay, India.

600   II   ISSN 0073-6511
INDIAN INSTITUTE OF TECHNOLOGY, MADRAS. ANNUAL REPORT. (Text in English) 1960. a. Indian Institute of Technology, Madras, The Registrar, Madras 600036, India.

600   GW   ISSN 0073-7739
INDUSTRIE ET ARTISANAT. 1965. irreg., no.5, 1968. price varies. (Ecole des Hautes Etudes en Sciences Sociales, Centre de Recherches Historiques, FR) Walter de Gruyter & Co., Mouton Publishers, Postfach 110240, D-1000 Berlin 11, W. Germany (B.R.D.) (U.S. address: Mouton Publishers, division of Walter de Gruyter, Inc., 200 Saw Mill River Rd., Hawthorne, NY 10532)

INFRARED SOCIETY OF JAPAN. PROCEEDING. see *PHYSICS — Heat*

INSTITUT FUER DEN WISSENSCHAFTLICHEN FILM. PUBLIKATIONEN ZU WISSENSCHAFTLICHEN FILMEN. SEKTION TECHNISCHE WISSENSCHAFTEN, NATURWISSENSCHAFTEN. see *MOTION PICTURES*

658   US
INTERNATIONAL TRENDS IN MANUFACTURING TECHNOLOGY. 1983. irreg., latest 1986. Springer-Verlag, 175 Fifth Ave., New York, NY 10010. TEL 212-460-1500. (Co-publisher: I F S (Publications) Ltd.) Ed.Bd.

ISRAEL. INSTITUTE FOR TECHNOLOGY AND STORAGE OF AGRICULTURAL PRODUCTS. SCIENTIFIC ACTIVITIES. see *AGRICULTURE*

ISRAEL ACADEMY OF SCIENCES AND HUMANITIES. SECTION OF HUMANITIES. PROCEEDINGS. see *SCIENCES: COMPREHENSIVE WORKS*

607   JA   ISSN 0441-0734
JAPAN. GOVERNMENT INDUSTRIAL DEVELOPMENT LABORATORY, HOKKAIDO. REPORTS/HOKKAIDO KOGYO KAIHATSU SHIKENJO HOKOKU. 1966. irreg. Government Industrial Development Laboratory, Hokkaido - Hokkaido Kogyo Kaihatsu Shikenjo, 41-2 Higashi-tsukisamu, Toyohira-ku, Sapporo 061-01, Hokkaido, Japan. Indexed: Chem.Abstr.

600   JA
JAPAN. GOVERNMENT INDUSTRIAL DEVELOPMENT LABORATORY, HOKKAIDO. TECHNICAL DATA/HOKKAIDO KOGYO KAIHATSU SHIKENJO GIJUTSU. 1961. irreg. Government Industrial Development Laboratory, Hokkaido - Hokkaido Kogyo Kaihatsu Shikenjo, 41-2 Higashi-tsukisamu, Toyohira-ku, Sapporo 06101, Hokkaido, Japan. charts.

JAPAN REPORT: SCIENCE AND TECHNOLOGY. see *SCIENCES: COMPREHENSIVE WORKS*

600   US
JOHNS HOPKINS STUDIES IN THE HISTORY OF TECHNOLOGY. 1967; N.S. 1978. irreg. price varies. Johns Hopkins University Press, 701 W. 40th St., Ste. 275, Baltimore, MD 21218. TEL 301-338-6900. (reprint service avail. from UMI)

JOURNAL OF PURE AND APPLIED SCIENCES/TEMEL VE UYGULAMALI BILMLER DERGISI. see *SCIENCES: COMPREHENSIVE WORKS*

620   JA   ISSN 0453-2198
KANSAI UNIVERSITY TECHNOLOGY REPORTS/KANSAI DAIGAKU KOGAKU KENKYU HOKOKU. (Text in English) 1959. a. exchange basis. Kansai University, Faculty of Engineering - Kansai University Kogakubu, 3-3-35 Yamate-cho, Suita 564, Osaka, Japan. Katsutaro Katsuta. bk. rev. Indexed: Chem.Abstr. Math.R. Sci.Abstr. Geo.Ref. JCT.

600   US
KENTUCKY MANUFACTURING DEVELOPMENTS. a. Department of Economic Development, Capitol Plaza Tower, Frankfort, KY 40601. TEL 502-564-7140. Ed. Evelyn Wise.
 Formerly (1954-1972): Manufacturing Developments in Kentucky.

KENYA NATIONAL ACADEMY FOR ADVANCEMENT OF ARTS AND SCIENCES. NEWSLETTER. see *SCIENCES: COMPREHENSIVE WORKS*

KORUNK TUDOMANYA. see *SCIENCES: COMPREHENSIVE WORKS*

600   KO
KWAHAK KISUL YORAM/HANDBOOK OF SCIENCE AND TECHNOLOGY. 1970. a. Ministry of Science and Technology, Seoul, S. Korea. circ. 1,500.

KYOTO INSTITUTE OF TECHNOLOGY. FACULTY OF ENGINEERING AND DESIGN. MEMOIRS. see *SCIENCES: COMPREHENSIVE WORKS*

600   US   ISSN 0075-7926
LANDOLT-BOERNSTEIN, ZAHLENWERTE UND FUNKTIONEN AUS NATURWISSENSCHAFTEN UND TECHNIK. NEUE SERIE. GROUP 4: MACROSCOPIC AND TECHNICAL PROPERTIES OF MATTER. 1974. irreg., vol.4, 1980. Springer-Verlag, 175 Fifth Ave., New York, NY 10010 TEL 212-460-1500. (Also Berlin, Heidelberg, Tokyo and Vienna) Ed. K.H. Hellwege. (reprint service avail. from ISI)

600   UK
LASER. 1966. irreg. £0.30 per no. ‡ 26 Selwood Rd., Addiscombe, Croydon CR0 7JR, Surrey, England. Ed.Bd. adv. bk. rev. bibl. charts. illus. circ. 100.

658.5   GW   ISSN 0024-0702
LEISTUNG.* 1950. irreg. DM.3.50. per no. Daco-Verlag Guenter Blaese, Richard Wagner Str. 10, 7000 Stuttgart 1, W. Germany (B.R.D.) Ed. Guenter Blaese. illus.

LICENSING LAW HANDBOOK. see *LAW*

LIVE AND LET LIVE. see *PHILOSOPHY*

600   PL   ISSN 0076-0439
LODZKIE TOWARZYSTWO NAUKOWE. WYDZIAL V. NAUK TECHNICZNYCH. PRACE. 1963. irreg., 1963. price varies. Panstwowe Wydawnictwo Naukowe, Ul. Miodowa 10, 00-251 Warsaw, Poland (Dist. by: Ars Polona, Krakowskie Przedmiescie 7, 00-068 Warsaw, Poland)

600   FR
M I D I S T RAPPORT D'ACTIVITE (YEAR) a. Ministere de la Recherche et de la Technologie, Mission Interministerielle de l'Information Scientifique et Technique, 9 rue Georges Pitard, 75015 Paris, France.

MCGRAW-HILL YEARBOOK OF SCIENCE AND TECHNOLOGY. see *SCIENCES: COMPREHENSIVE WORKS*

600   US
MARYLAND HIGH-TECH DIRECTORY. 1986. biennial. $25. Department of Economic and Community Development, Business Directories, 45 Calvert St., Annapolis, MD 21401. TEL 301-269-2041. Ed. Marilyn Corbett. circ. 4,000.

TECHNOLOGY: COMPREHENSIVE WORKS

607 FR ISSN 0071-9005
MEMOIRES O.R.S.T.O.M. 1961. irreg. price varies. O R S T O M, Institut Francais de Recherche Scientifique pour le Developpement en Cooperation, 70-74 Route d'Aulnay, 93140 Bondy, France. Indexed: Biol.Abstr.

600 JA
METROPOLITAN COLLEGE OF TECHNOLOGY, TOKYO. MEMOIRS/TOKYO-TORITSU KOKA TANKI DAIGAKU KENKYU HOKOKU. (Text in Japanese or English) 1973. a. Metropolitan Technical College - Tokyo-toritsu Koka Tanki Daigaku Gakujutsu Kenkyu Un'Eikai, 6-6 Asahigaoka Hino, Tokyo 191, Japan. Ed.Bd. circ. controlled.

670 JA ISSN 0540-469X
MITSUBISHI TECHNICAL BULLETIN. (Text in English) 1962. irreg. exchange basis. Mitsubishi Heavy Industries, Ltd., Technical Administration Dept., 2-5-1 Marunouchi, Chiyoda-ku, Tokyo 100, Japan. circ. 1,600. Indexed: Sci.Abstr.

600 020 HU ISSN 0324-7341
MODSZERTANI KIADVANYOK/METHODS OF INFORMATION AND DOCUMENTATION. (Text in Hungarian; summaries in English, German, Russian) 1966. irreg., no.44, 1976. price varies. O.M.I.K.K. Technoinform, Muzeum u. 17, P.O. Box 12, 1428 Budapest, Hungary.

MONOGRAFIE Z DZIEJOW NAUKI I TECHNIKI. see *SCIENCES: COMPREHENSIVE WORKS*

MONOGRAPHS ON SCIENCE, TECHNOLOGY, AND SOCIETY. see *SOCIAL SCIENCES: COMPREHENSIVE WORKS*

600 US
MOTOROLA TECHNICAL DISCLOSURE BULLETIN. 1980. irreg. free. Motorola, Inc., Patent Department, 1303 E. Algonquin Rd., Schaumburg, IL 60196. TEL 312-397-8000. circ. 600. Indexed: Sci.Abstr.

600 NE
N A T O ADVANCED SCIENCE INSTITUTES SERIES E: APPLIED SCIENCES. (Text in English) 1974. irreg. price varies. (North Atlantic Treaty Organization) Martinus Nijhoff Publishers, Postbus 163, 3300 AD Dordrecht, Netherlands. Indexed: Biol.Abstr. Chem.Abstr. Math.R. GeoRef.
Formerly: N A T O Advanced Study Institute Series E: Applied Sciences.

NARODNI TECHNICKE MUZEUM. CATALOGUES OF COLLECTIONS. see *MUSEUMS AND ART GALLERIES*

600 CS ISSN 0035-9378
NARODNI TECHNICKE MUZEUM. ROZPRAVY. (Text in Czech; summaries in English, German) 1962. irreg., (approx. 4/yr.) exchange basis only. Narodni Technicke Muzeum, Kostelni 42, 170 78 Prague 7, Czechoslovakia. bibl. illus. Indexed: Numis.Lit.

600 620 KO
NATIONAL INDUSTRIAL RESEARCH INSTITUTE. REPORT. (Text in Korean; summaries in English) 1948. a. free. National Industrial Research Institute, 199 Dongsoong-dong, Chongno-ku, Seoul, S. Korea. illus.

NEWCOMEN SOCIETY FOR THE STUDY OF THE HISTORY OF ENGINEERING AND TECHNOLOGY. TRANSACTIONS. see *ENGINEERING*

NORGES TEKNISK-NATURVITENSKAPELIGE FORSKNINGSRAAD. AARSBERETNING. see *SCIENCES: COMPREHENSIVE WORKS*

600 CN
NOVA SCOTIA RESEARCH FOUNDATION CORPORATION. ANNUAL REPORT. a. Nova Scotia Research Foundation Corporation, 100 Fenwick St., Box 790, Dartmouth, N.S. B2Y 3Z7, Canada. TEL 902-424-8670. Ed.Bd.

600 FR ISSN 0071-9021
O.R.S.T.O.M. INITIATIONS DOCUMENTATIONS TECHNIQUES. (Office de la Recherche Scientifique et Technique Outre-Mer) 1962. irreg. price varies. O R S T O M, Institut Francais de Recherche Scientifique pour le Developpement en Cooperation, 70-74 Route d'Aulnay, 93140 Bondy, France.

O.R.S.T.O.M. INSTITUT FRANCAIS DE RECHERCHE POUR LE DEVELOPEMENT EN COOPERATION. RAPPORT D'ACTIVITE. (Office de la Recherche Scientifique et Technique en Cooperation) see *SCIENCES: COMPREHENSIVE WORKS*

600 BL
OPEMA EM RITMO DE BRASIL JOVEM. 1968. irreg. free. (Ministerio dos Transportes, Operacao Maua) Assessoria de Relacoes Publicas, Editora, Promocoes e Publicidade Ltda., Av. Beira Mar 406, Grupo 906, Rio de Janeiro, Brazil. adv. illus. stat. circ. 60,000.

ORGANIZATION OF AFRICAN UNITY. SCIENTIFIC TECHNICAL AND RESEARCH COMMISSION. PUBLICATION. see *SCIENCES: COMPREHENSIVE WORKS*

607 JA ISSN 0369-0369
OSAKA UNIVERSITY. INSTITUTE OF SCIENTIFIC AND INDUSTRIAL RESEARCH. MEMOIRS/OSAKA DAIGAKU SANGYO KAGAKU KENKYUSHO KIYO. (Text in European languages) 1941. a. exchange basis. Osaka University, Institute of Scientific and Industrial Research - Osaka Daigaku Sangyo Kagaku Kenkyusho, Mihoga-oka, Ibaraki, Osaka 567, Japan. Ed.Bd. circ. 750. Indexed: Chem.Abstr.

600 PK
P A S T I C TRANSLATIONS. 1957. irreg., latest 1982. Rs.10($4) Pakistan Scientific and Technological Information Centre, Quaid-i-Azam University Campus, Box No.1217, Islamabad, Pakistan. index issued separately. circ. 500. (also avail. in microfilm)
Formerly: P A N S D O C Translations (ISSN 0078-8368)

600 PL ISSN 0137-138X
POLITECHNIKA KRAKOWSKA. ZESZYTY NAUKOWE. PODSTAWOWE NAUKI TECHNICZNE. (Text in Polish; summaries in English, French, German and Russian) 1968. irreg. price varies. Politechnika Krakowska, Ul. Warszawska 24, 31-155 Krakow, Poland (Dist. by Ars Polona-Ruch, Krakowskie Przedmiescie 7, 00-068 Warsaw, Poland) bibl. charts. illus. circ. 200.

620 US ISSN 0360-2273
POPULAR MECHANICS DO-IT-YOURSELF YEARBOOK. a. Hearst Magazines, Popular Mechanics, 224 W. 57th St., New York, NY 10019. illus.

PRAJNAN. see *EDUCATION — Teaching Methods And Curriculum*

607 US
PROBABLE LEVELS OF R & D EXPENDITURES: FORECAST AND ANALYSIS. 1960? a. free. ‡ Battelle Memorial Institute, Columbus Division, 505 King Ave., Columbus, OH 43201. TEL 614-424-6424. charts. stat. circ. controlled.

PRODUCTS FINISHING DIRECTORY. see *PAINTS AND PROTECTIVE COATINGS*

RAND REPORT SERIES. see *SCIENCES: COMPREHENSIVE WORKS*

600 CN
REPERTOIRE DES BASES DE DONNEES SCIENTIFIQUES ET TECHNIQUES AU CANADA/DIRECTORY OF CANADIAN SCIENTIFIC AND TECHNICAL DATABASES. 1984. triennial. Can.$10. (National Research Council of Canada) CISTI Publications, Ottawa, Ont. K1A 0S2, Canada. TEL 613-993-3736. circ. 700.

REPORT TO S C A R ON SOUTH AFRICAN ANTARCTIC RESEARCH ACTIVITIES. (Scientific Committee for Antarctic Research) see *SCIENCES: COMPREHENSIVE WORKS*

600 II
RESEARCH & DEVELOPMENT IN INDUSTRY. 1976. a. Rs.50. Department of Science and Technology, New Mehrauli Rd., New Delhi 110016, India. Ed. A.R. Rajeswari. circ. 1,000.

RESEARCH IN PHILOSOPHY AND TECHNOLOGY. see *PHILOSOPHY*

600 US
RESEARCH ON TECHNOLOGICAL INNOVATION, MANAGEMENT AND POLICY. 1983. a. $23.75 to individuals, institutions $49.50. J A I Press Inc., 36 Sherwood Place, Greenwich, CT 06830. Ed. Richard S. Rosenbloom.

667.2 UK
REVIEW OF PROGRESS IN COLORATION AND RELATED TOPICS. 1970. a. £7. Society of Dyers and Colourists, Box 244, Perkin House, Bradford, Yorkshire BD1 2JB, England. Ed. J.D. Watson. circ. 4,200. (also avail. in microfilm) Indexed: Chem.Abstr. Abstr.Bull.Inst.Pap.Chem. Art & Archaeol.Tech.Abstr. Text.Tech.Dig. World Text.Abstr.

RHEINISCH-WESTFAELISCHE AKADEMIE DER WISSENSCHAFTEN. VORTRAEGE NATUR-INGENIEUR-UND WIRTSCHAFTSWISSENSCHAFTEN. see *SCIENCES: COMPREHENSIVE WORKS*

600 SW
S T U INVESTIGATION. irreg., no.214, 1981. Styrelsen foer Teknisk Utveckling, Information Section - National Swedish Board for Technical Development, Stockholm, Sweden. (Co-sponsor: Swedish State Power Board)

SAMUEL NEAMAN INSTITUTE FOR ADVANCED STUDIES IN SCIENCE AND TECHNOLOGY. ANNUAL REPORT. see *SCIENCES: COMPREHENSIVE WORKS*

SASKATCHEWAN RESEARCH COUNCIL. ANNUAL REPORT. see *SCIENCES: COMPREHENSIVE WORKS*

SCIENCE AND ENGINEERING RESEARCH COUNCIL. REPORT. see *SCIENCES: COMPREHENSIVE WORKS*

SCIENCE AND TECHNOLOGY. see *SCIENCES: COMPREHENSIVE WORKS*

SCIENCE AND TECHNOLOGY IN CHINA. see *SCIENCES: COMPREHENSIVE WORKS*

SCIENCE AND TECHNOLOGY IN JAPAN. see *SCIENCES: COMPREHENSIVE WORKS*

SCIENCE AND TECHNOLOGY IN LATIN AMERICA. see *SCIENCES: COMPREHENSIVE WORKS*

SCIENCE AND TECHNOLOGY IN THE MIDDLE EAST. see *SCIENCES: COMPREHENSIVE WORKS*

SCIENCE, MEDICINE AND TECHNOLOGY IN EAST ASIA. see *SCIENCES: COMPREHENSIVE WORKS*

SCIENTIFIC AND TECHNICAL INFORMATION IN FOREIGN COUNTRIES/KAIGAKI KAGAKU GIJUTSU JOHO SHIRYO. see *SCIENCES: COMPREHENSIVE WORKS*

SCIENTIFIC AND TECHNICAL SOCIETIES IN SOUTH AFRICA/WETENSKAPLIKE EN TEGNIESE VERENIGINGS IN SUID-AFRIKA. see *SCIENCES: COMPREHENSIVE WORKS*

SCIENTIFIC AND TECHNICAL SOCIETIES OF CANADA/SOCIETES SCIENTIFIQUES ET TECHNIQUES DU CANADA. see *SCIENCES: COMPREHENSIVE WORKS*

SCIENTIFIC RESEARCH ORGANIZATIONS IN SOUTH AFRICA/WETENSKAPLIKE NAVORSINGSORGANISASIES IN SUID-AFRIKA. see *SCIENCES: COMPREHENSIVE WORKS*

TECHNOLOGY: COMPREHENSIVE WORKS

600 607   US   ISSN 0080-830X
SCRIPPS CLINIC AND RESEARCH
FOUNDATION. ANNUAL REPORT. 1924. a.
free. Scripps Clinic and Research Foundation, 10666
N. Torrey Pines Rd., La Jolla, CA 92037. TEL 619-
455-9100. circ. 5,000.

600   US   ISSN 0081-1491
SOCIETY FOR THE HISTORY OF
TECHNOLOGY. MONOGRAPH SERIES. 1962.
irreg., latest issue no. 8. (Society for the History of
Technology) M I T Press, c/o Alex Roland, Sec.,
Department of History, Duke University, Durham,
NC 27706 TEL 919-684-2758. (Subscr. to: Science
Editor, M I T Press, 28 Carleton St., Cambridge,
MA 02142)

600   US   ISSN 0081-1629
SOCIETY OF LOGISTICS ENGINEERS.
PROCEEDINGS. Variant title: International
Logistics Symposium Proceedings. 1966. a. price
varies. Society of Logistics Engineers, 125 W. Park
Loop, Ste. 201, Huntsville, AL 35806-1705. TEL
205-837-1092. (reprint service avail. from UMI)

SOUTH AFRICAN JOURNAL OF ANTARCTIC
RESEARCH. see *SCIENCES: COMPREHENSIVE
WORKS*

600   NL   ISSN 0081-2862
SOUTH PACIFIC COMMISSION. TECHNICAL
PAPER. (Text in English or French) 1949. irreg.,
no.178, 1979. price varies. South Pacific
Commission, B.P. D5, Noumea, Cedex, New
Caledonia. Indexed: Rev.Plant Path.

600   NE   ISSN 0168-468X
SPEUR- EN ONTWIKKELINGSWERK IN
NEDERLAND/RESEARCH AND
DEVELOPMENT ACTIVITIES IN THE
NETHERLANDS. (Text in Dutch and English)
1959. a. fl.24.75. Centraal Bureau voor de Statistiek,
Prinses Beatrixlaan 428, Voorburg, Netherlands
(Orders to: Staatsuitgeverij, Christoffel
Plantijnstraat, The Hague, Netherlands)

600   US   ISSN 0148-2203
SPINOFF. a. U.S. National Aeronautics and Space
Administration, Office of Space and Terrestrial
Applications, Box 8756, Baltimore-Washington
International Airport, MD 21240 TEL 202-755-
2320. (Orders to: Supt. of Documents, Washington,
DC 20402) illus. Indexed: Ind.How to Do It.

600   YU   ISSN 0081-3974
SRPSKA AKADEMIJA NAUKA I UMETNOSTI.
ODELJENJE TEHNICKIH NAUKA. GLAS. (Text
in Serbocroatian; summaries in English, French,
German or Russian) N.S. 1949. irreg. price varies.
Srpska Akademija Nauka i Umetnosti, Knez
Mihailova 35, 11001 Belgrade, Yugoslavia (Dist. by:
Prosveta, Terazije 16, Belgrade, Yugoslavia) circ.
500. Indexed: Chem.Abstr. Met.Abstr. Sci.Abstr.
Art & Archaeol.Tech.Abstr. World Alum.Abstr.

600   YU   ISSN 0081-4040
SRPSKA AKADEMIJA NAUKA I UMETNOSTI.
ODELJENJE TEHNICKIH NAUKA. POSEBNA
IZDANJA. (Text in Serbocroatian; summaries in
English, French, German or Russian) 1950. irreg.
price varies. Srpska Akademija Nauka i Umetnosti,
Knez Mihailova 35, 11001 Belgrade, Yugoslavia
(Dist. by: Prosveta, Terazije 16, Belgrade,
Yugoslavia) circ. 600. Indexed: Ref.Zh.

600   PL   ISSN 0081-6604
STUDIA I MATERIALY Z DZIEJOW NAUKI
POLSKIEJ. SERIA D. HISTORIA TECHNIKI I
NAUK TECHNICZNYCH. (Text in Polish;
summaries in English and French) 1958. irreg., no.9,
1978. price varies. (Polska Akademia Nauk, Zaklad
Historii Nauki, Oswiaty i Techniki) Panstwowe
Wydawnictwo Naukowe, Ul. Miodowa 10, 00-251
Warsaw, Poland (Dist. by: Ars Polona, Krakowskie
Przedmiescie 7, 00-068 Warsaw, Poland) Ed. E.
Olszewski. circ. 240.

STUDIA I MATERIALY Z DZIEJOW NAUKI
POLSKIEJ. SERIA E. ZAGADNIENIA
OGOLNE. see *SCIENCES: COMPREHENSIVE
WORKS*

600   US
STUDIES IN APPLIED REGIONAL SCIENCE.*
1976. irreg. price varies. Kluwer Nijhoff Publishing,
101 Philip Dr., Assinippi Park, Norwell, MA 02061
(Foreign distr: Kluwer Academic Publishers Group,
Distribution Center, P.O. Box 322, 3300 AH
Dordrecht, Netherlands) Ed. P. Nijkamp. charts.

620   SW
SWEDEN. STATENS JAERNVAEGARS
HUVUDKONTOR. GEOTEKNIK OCH
INGENJOERGEOLOGI. MEDDELANDEN.
(Text in Swedish; summaries in English) 1917.
irreg., no.45, 1985. price varies. Statens
Jaernvaegars Huvudkontor - State Railways Head
Office, Geotechnical Department, S-105 50
Stockholm, Sweden. circ. 650.
    Former titles: Sweden. Statens Jaernvaegars
Centralfoervaltning. Geoteknik och
Ingenjoergeologi. Meddelanden; Sweden. Statens
Jaernvaegars Centralfoervaltning. Geotekniska
Kontoret. Meddelanden.

600 330   SA   ISSN 0040-0955
T.I. (Technical Information for Industry) (Text in
Afrikaans and English) 1963. irreg. free. ‡ Council
for Scientific and Industrial Research, Technical
Information Service, Box 395, Pretoria 0001, South
Africa. Ed. E.L. Burger. charts. illus. index. circ. 8,
000. Indexed: Ind.S.A.Per.

600 370   US
TECHNICAL, TRADE & BUSINESS SCHOOL
DATA HANDBOOK. 1984. a. (in 4 vols.) $67.50.
Orchard House, Inc., Balls Hill Rd., Concord, MA
01742. Ed. Louis Mazzari. circ. 3,000. (also avail. in
microform)

600 301   GW
TECHNIK UND GESELLSCHAFT. 1982. a. price
varies. Campus Verlag, Myliusstr. 15, 6000
Frankfurt 1, W. Germany (B.R.D.) Ed. Gotthard
Bechmann. circ. 1,500.

600   GW   ISSN 0082-2361
TECHNIKGESCHICHTE IN
EINZELDARSTELLUNGEN. 1967. irreg. price
varies. (Verein Deutscher Ingenieure) V D I-Verlag
GmbH, Graf Recke Str. 84, Postfach 1139, 4000
Duesseldorf 1, W. Germany (B.R.D.) circ. 200.

600   IS
TECHNION - ISRAEL INSTITUTE OF
TECHNOLOGY. PRESIDENT'S REPORT. (Text
in English) 1975. a. free to qualified personnel.
Technion - Israel Institute of Technology, Division
of Public Affairs, Haifa 3200, Israel. Ed. Harvey L.
Brown. circ. 30,000. Indexed: Sci.Abstr.
    Formerly: Israel Institute of Technology.
President's Report and Reports of Other Officers
(ISSN 0072-9329)

600   FR   ISSN 0082-2469
TECHNIQUES D'AUJOURD'HUI. 1970. irreg. price
varies. Larousse, 17 rue du Montparnasse, 75280
Paris Cedex 06, France.

605   JA
TECHNIQUES INDUSTRIELLES DU JAPON.
(Text in French) 1959. a. 2,000 Yen. Societe-
Franco-Japonaise des Techniques Industrielles -
Nichifutsu Kogyo Gijyutsukai, 2-3 Kanda Surugadai,
Chiyoda-ku, Tokyo 101, Japan.

600   GT
TECHNOLOGICAL MONOGRAPHS. (Text in
Spanish; summaries in English) 1977. a. $15.
Instituto Centro Americano de Investigacion y
Tecnologia Industrial, Avda. la Reforma 4-47, Zona
10, Apdo. Postal 1552, Guatemala, Guatemala.
charts.

600   US
TECHNOLOGY FOR CHINA. 1986. a. $35 (free to
qualified personnel) Johnston International
Publishing Corporation, 386 Park Ave. S., New
York, NY 10016.

TECHNOLOGY TRANSFER SOCIETY.
INTERNATIONAL SYMPOSIUM
PROCEEDINGS. see *BUSINESS AND
ECONOMICS — Management*

TEKNISKA NOMENKLATURCENTRALEN
PUBLIKATIONER. see *LINGUISTICS*

600   MY
TEKNOLOGI. (Text in English and Malay) 1977.
irreg.? $4. University of Technology Malaysia,
Research & Consultancy Unit - Universiti Teknologi
Malaysia, Fakulti Kejuruteraan Letrik, Jalan
Gurney, 54100 Kuala Lumpur, Malaysia. Ed.
Mohamed Amin bin Alias. circ. 500.

600   DK   ISSN 0107-3761
TEKNOLOGI OG EFFEKTIVITET; orientering og
aarsberetning. 1981. a. free. Teknologistyrelsen,
Tagensvej 135, 2200 Copenhagen N, Denmark.

TELECOMMUNICATIONS SYSTEMS AND
SERVICES DIRECTORY; an international
descriptive guide to approximately 2,000
telecommunications organizations, systems, and
services. see *COMMUNICATIONS*

600 330   HU   ISSN 0521-4602
TEMADOKUMENTACIOS KIADVANYOK/
THEMATICAL REVIEWS. 1959. irreg., no.132,
1981. price varies. Orszagos Muszaki Informacios
Kozpont es Konyvtar (O.M.I.K.K.) - National
Technical Information Centre and Library, Muzeum
u. 17, Box 12, 1428 Budapest, Hungary.

605   JA   ISSN 0495-8055
TOKYO INSTITUTE OF TECHNOLOGY.
RESEARCH LABORATORY OF RESOURCES
UTILIZATION. REPORT/SHIGEN KAGUKU
KENKYUSHO. (Text in English) a. Tokyo Institute
of Technology, Research Laboratory of Resources
Utilization - Tokyo Kogyo Daigaku. Shigen Kagaku
Kenkyusho, 2-2-1 Okayama, Meguro-ku, Tokyo
145, Japan. Indexed: Sci.Abstr.

600   JA   ISSN 0082-4747
TOKYO METROPOLITAN UNIVERSITY.
FACULTY OF TECHNOLOGY. MEMOIRS/
TOKYO-TORITSU DAIGAKU KOGAKUBU
HOKOKU. (Text in English) 1951. a. free. Tokyo
Metropolitan University, Faculty of Technology -
Tokyo-toritsu Daigaku Kogakubu, 2-1-1 Fukazawa,
Setagaya-ku, Tokyo 158, Japan. Ed. Yoichi Higashi.
Indexed: Chem.Abstr. Met.Abstr. Sci.Abstr. JCT.
World Alum.Abstr.

TREATISE ON MATERIALS SCIENCE &
TECHNOLOGY. see *ENGINEERING —
Engineering Mechanics And Materials*

600   UK
TREVITHICK SOCIETY. OCCASIONAL
PUBLICATION. 1974. irreg., no.3, 1984. £3.
Trevithick Society, c/o Mr. E.W.A. Edmonds, Sec.,
Newlands, Tarrandean Lane, Perranwell Station,
Truro, Cornwall TR3 7NW, England. TEL (0872)
863931. circ. 1,000.

TUDOMANYTORTENETI TANULMANYOK. see
SCIENCES: COMPREHENSIVE WORKS

U S S R REPORT: SCIENCE AND TECHNOLOGY
POLICY. see *SCIENCES: COMPREHENSIVE
WORKS*

UNION LIST OF SCIENTIFIC AND TECHNICAL
PERIODICALS IN ZAMBIA. see
BIBLIOGRAPHIES

607   US
U.S. FEDERAL AVIATION ADMINISTRATION.
SYSTEMS RESEARCH AND DEVELOPMENT.
REPORT FAA-RD. 1958. irreg. price varies;
announcements of new titles in FAA NEWS. U.S.
Federal Aviation Administration, Systems Research
and Development Service, 800 Independence Ave.
S.W., Washington, DC 20591 TEL 202-655-4000.
(Order from: National Technical Information
Service, 5285 Port Royal Rd., Springfield, VA
22151)

U.S. NATIONAL AERONAUTICS AND SPACE
ADMINISTRATION. RESEARCH AND
TECHNOLOGY OPERATING PLAN (RTOP)
SUMMARY. see *AERONAUTICS AND SPACE
FLIGHT*

338 600   US   ISSN 0083-2383
U.S. NATIONAL SCIENCE FOUNDATION.
RESEARCH AND DEVELOPMENT IN
INDUSTRY. (Subseries of: U.S. National Science
Foundation. Surveys of Science Resource Series) a.
U.S. National Science Foundation, 1800 G St.,
N.W., Washington, DC 20550. TEL 202-634-4622.

1072 TECHNOLOGY: COMPREHENSIVE WORKS — ABSTRACTING, BIBLIOGRAPHIES, STATISTICS

600 378 CK
UNIVERSIDAD TECNOLOGICA DEL CHOCO. REVISTA. 1976. irreg. Universidad Tecnologica del Choco, Difusion Cultural, Carrera 2 no. 25-22, Quibdo, Choco, Colombia. Ed. Giorgio M. Manzini.

600 II
UNIVERSITY OF RAJASTHAN. STUDIES IN ENGINEERING AND TECHNOLOGY. 1967. irreg. University of Rajasthan, Gandhi Nagar, Jaipur 302004, India.

UNIVERSITY OF SCIENCE AND TECHNOLOGY. JOURNAL. see SCIENCES: COMPREHENSIVE WORKS

620 JA ISSN 0040-9006
UNIVERSITY OF TOKYO. INSTITUTE OF INDUSTRIAL SCIENCE. REPORT/TOKYO DAIGAKU SEISAN GIJUTSU KENKYUSHO HOKOKU. (Text mainly in Japanese, occasionally English, French or German) 1950. irreg. (6-8/yr.) free. University of Tokyo, Institute of Industrial Science - Tokyo Daigaku Seisan Gijutsu Kenkyusho, 7-22-1 Roppongi, Minato-ku, Tokyo 106, Japan. Ed. Prof. Egami. charts. circ. 900. Indexed: Chem.Abstr. Eng.Ind. Met.Abstr. Sci.Abstr. JCT.

600 FI ISSN 0357-9387
V T T SYMPOSIUM. (Text in official language of symposium) 1981. irreg. price varies. Valtion Teknillinen Tutkimuskeskus - Technical Research Centre of Finland, Vuorimiehentie 5, 02150 Espoo 15, Finland.

VADEMECUM DEUTSCHER LEHR- UND FORSCHUNGSSTAETTEN. (Vademecum of German Universities and Research Center) see SCIENCES: COMPREHENSIVE WORKS

600 FI ISSN 0358-5085
VALTION TEKNILLINEN TUTKIMUSKESKUS. TIEDOTTEITA/STATENS TEKNISKA FORSKNINGSCENTRAL. MEDDELANDEN/ TECHNICAL RESEARCH CENTRE OF FINLAND. RESEARCH NOTES. (Text in English, Finnish or Swedish) 1981. irreg. Valtion Teknillinen Tutkimuskeskus, Vuorimiehentie 5, 02150 Espoo 15, Finland.

600 FI ISSN 0358-5077
VALTION TEKNILLINEN TUTKIMUSKESKUS. TUTKIMUKSIA/STATENS TEKNISKA FORSKNINGSCENTRAL. FORSKNINGSRAPPORTER/TECHNICAL RESEARCH CENTRE OF FINLAND. RESEARCH REPORTS. (Text in English, Finnish or Swedish) 1981. irreg. Valtion Teknillinen Tutkimuskeskus, Vuorimiehentie 5, 02150 Espoo 15, Finland. Indexed: Biol.Abstr. Chem.Abstr.

WEIZMANN INSTITUTE OF SCIENCE, REHOVOT, ISRAEL. SCIENTIFIC ACTIVITIES. see SCIENCES: COMPREHENSIVE WORKS

WHERE AMERICA'S LARGE FOUNDATIONS MAKE THEIR GRANTS; who gets them and how much each receives. see HUMANITIES: COMPREHENSIVE WORKS

WHO KNOWS: A GUIDE TO WASHINGTON EXPERTS. see SCIENCES: COMPREHENSIVE WORKS

WHO'S WHO IN BIOTECHNOLOGY. see BIOLOGY

WHO'S WHO IN INDIAN ENGINEERING AND INDUSTRY. see BIOGRAPHY

WHO'S WHO IN TECHNOLOGY. see SCIENCES: COMPREHENSIVE WORKS

600 US ISSN 0084-3121
WYKEHAM TECHNOLOGICAL SERIES. (Issues not numbered consecutively) 1969. irreg., no.5, 1975. Taylor & Francis, Inc., 242 Cherry St., Philadelphia, PA 19106. TEL 800-821-8312. (reprint service avail. from UMI)

605 JA
YAMAGUCHI UNIVERSITY. FACULTY OF ENGINEERING. TECHNOLOGY REPORTS. (Text in English) 1972. a. exchange basis. Yamaguchi University, Faculty of Engineering - Yamaguchi Daigaku Kogakubu, Tokiwadai, Ube-shi 755, Japan. Indexed: Chem.Abstr. Sci.Abstr. JCT.

ZAMBIA JOURNAL OF SCIENCE AND TECHNOLOGY. see SCIENCES: COMPREHENSIVE WORKS

TECHNOLOGY: COMPREHENSIVE WORKS — Abstracting, Bibliographies, Statistics

600 327 US
A M T I D: APPLICATION OF MODERN TECHNOLOGY TO INTERNATIONAL DEVELOPMENT. irreg. U.S. Agency for International Development, Office of Public Affairs, Washington, DC 20523 (Orders to: NTIS, 5285 Port Royal Rd., Springfield, VA 22161) (Co-sponsor: U.S. National Technical Information Service)

600 016 US
ABSTRACT NEWSLETTER: GOVERNMENT INVENTIONS FOR LICENSING. w. $205. U.S. National Technical Information Service, 5285 Port Royal Rd., Springfield, VA 22161. TEL 703-487-4630. Ed. Linda J. LaGarde. index. (back issues avail.)
Former titles: Weekly Abstract Newsletter: Government Inventions for Licensing; Weekly Government Abstracts. Government Inventions for Licensing (ISSN 0364-6491)

600 016 US
ABSTRACT NEWSLETTER: MANUFACTURING TECHNOLOGY. w. $125. U.S. National Technical Information Service, 5285 Port Royal Rd., Springfield, VA 22161. TEL 703-487-4630. index.

ABSTRACT NEWSLETTER: URBAN AND REGIONAL TECHNOLOGY AND DEVELOPMENT. see HOUSING AND URBAN PLANNING — Abstracting, Bibliographies, Statistics

600 318 AG
ARGENTINA. INSTITUTO DE ASUNTOS TECNICOS. ESTADISTICAS. 1974. irreg. Instituto de Asuntos Tecnicos, Direccion de Estadistica, Palacio Municipal, Cordoba, Argentina. charts.

605 016 SP
ASOCIACION ESPANOLA DE PRENSA TECNICA. CATALOGO DE PUBLICACIONES ASOCIADAS. 1965. a. $10. Asociacion Espanola de Prensa Tecnica, Balmes 200, 2, 08006 Barcelona, Spain. adv. illus. circ. 12,000.

600 900 GE ISSN 0323-4355
BIBLIOGRAPHIE GESCHICHTE DER TECHNIK. (Text in German) 1971. a. DM.90. (Saechsische Landesbibliothek) Marienalle 12, 8060 Dresden, E. Germany (D.D.R) Eds. Michael Letocha, Peter Hesse. bk. rev. circ. 200.

BIBLIOGRAPHIES OF THE HISTORY OF SCIENCE AND TECHNOLOGY. see SCIENCES: COMPREHENSIVE WORKS — Abstracting, Bibliographies, Statistics

CURRENT BIBLIOGRAPHIES ON SCIENCE AND TECHNOLOGY: MECHANICAL ENGINEERING & CONSTRUCTION ENGINEERING. see METALLURGY — Abstracting, Bibliographies, Statistics

600 016 UK ISSN 0260-6593
CURRENT TECHNOLOGY INDEX. 1962. m. (plus a. cumulation) £260($592) Library Association Publishing Ltd., 7 Ridgmount St., London WC1E 7AE, England. Ed. T.J. Edwards. cum.index. (also avail. in microfilm; magnetic tape) Indexed: BMT. Fluidex.
Formerly: British Technology Index (ISSN 0007-1889)

600 016 CS
DEJINY VYROBNICH SIL. irreg. exchange basis. Narodni Technicke Muzeum, Kostelni 42, 170 78 Prague 7, Czechoslovakia.

500 600 016 US ISSN 0419-4217
DISSERTATION ABSTRACTS INTERNATIONAL. SECTION B: PHYSICAL SCIENCES AND ENGINEERING. 1938. m. $155. University Microfilms International, 300 N. Zeeb Rd., Ann Arbor, MI 48106. TEL 313-761-4700. abstr. index. circ. 2,000(combined) (also avail. in microfiche from UMI; reprint service avail. from UMI) Indexed: Biol.Abstr. Chem.Abstr. Eng.Ind. Nutr.Abstr. Psychol.Abstr. Abstr.Bull.Inst.Pap.Chem. API Abstr. Forest.Abstr. Forest Prod.Abstr. Food Sci.& Tech.Abstr. Geotech.Abstr. Helminthol.Abstr. Key Word Ind. Wildl.Res. Music Ind. Mass Spectr.Bull. RAPRA. Vet.Bull.
Formerly: Dissertation Abstracts.

FLUID SEALING ABSTRACTS. see ENGINEERING — Abstracting, Bibliographies, Statistics

FRENCH PATENTS ABSTRACTS. see PATENTS, TRADEMARKS AND COPYRIGHTS — Abstracting, Bibliographies, Statistics

GERMAN PATENTS ABSTRACTS. see PATENTS, TRADEMARKS AND COPYRIGHTS — Abstracting, Bibliographies, Statistics

600 500 016 US ISSN 0094-4505
GUIDE TO AMERICAN SCIENTIFIC AND TECHNICAL DIRECTORIES. 1972. triennial. $55. Todd Publications, Box 92, Lenox Hill Sta., New York, NY 10021. Ed. Barry T. Klein.

HUNGARIAN R AND D ABSTRACTS. SCIENCE AND TECHNOLOGY. see SCIENCES: COMPREHENSIVE WORKS — Abstracting, Bibliographies, Statistics

INDEX DOCUMENTATION-ECONOMIE-SCIENCE-TECHNIQUE. see BUSINESS AND ECONOMICS — Abstracting, Bibliographies, Statistics

INDEX TO SPANISH SCIENCE AND TECHNOLOGY. see SCIENCES: COMPREHENSIVE WORKS — Abstracting, Bibliographies, Statistics

INDIA. DEPARTMENT OF SCIENCE AND TECHNOLOGY. RESEARCH AND DEVELOPMENT STATISTICS. see SCIENCES: COMPREHENSIVE WORKS — Abstracting, Bibliographies, Statistics

600 016 II
INDIAN INSTITUTE OF TECHNOLOGY, MADRAS. PH.D. DISSERTATION ABSTRACTS. (Text in English) a. Indian Institute of Technology, Madras, The Registrar, Madras 600036, India.

600 016 TZ ISSN 0251-2459
INDUSTRIAL ABSTRACTS FOR TANZANIA. 1981. q. Library Services Board, National Documentation Centre, P.O. Box 9283, Dar es Salaam, Tanzania.

KOREAN SCIENTIFIC ABSTRACTS. see SCIENCES: COMPREHENSIVE WORKS — Abstracting, Bibliographies, Statistics

016 600 PK
LISTS OF P A S T I C BIBLIOGRAPHIES. (Text in English) 1957 (latest 1978) a. Rs.10($4) Pakistan Scientific and Technological Information Centre, Quaid-i-Azam University, Box 217, Islamabad, Pakistan. Ed. Mumtaz Begum. circ. 500. (also avail. in microfilm)
Formerly: Lists of P A N S Doc Bibliographies (ISSN 0078-835X)

600 016 CS
NARODNI TECHNICKE MUZEUM. BIBLIOGRAFIE. PRAMENY. (Text in Czech and German) 1970. irreg. exchange basis. Narodni Technicke Muzeum, Kostelni 42, 170 78 Prague 7, Czechoslovakia.

600 330 016   PL   ISSN 0032-3004
POLISH TECHNICAL AND ECONOMIC
ABSTRACTS. (Editions in English, French,
German and Russian) 1951. q. $26. Instytut
Informacji Naukowej, Technicznej i Ekonomicznej,
Al. Niepodleglosci 188, 00-931 Warsaw, Poland
(Dist. by: Ars Polona - Ruch, Krakowskie
Przedmiescie 7, Warsaw, Poland) Ed. E. Zwolanski.
adv. abstr. index. circ. 1,500. Indexed: Chem.Abstr.
RAPRA. Fluidex. Plant Breed.Abstr.
   Formerly: Polish Technical Abstracts.

600   UK
PRODUCTIVITY INSIGHTS. 1982. q. £40. John
Russell Associates Ltd., 28 Princess Way,
Camberley, Surrey GU15 3SP, England. Ed. A.J.
Dalton. bk. rev. circ. 90.
   Incorporating: Abstracts on Productivity,
Technology and Training (ISSN 0265-0940)

600   UR
REFERATIVNYI ZHURNAL. TEKHNICHESKAYA
ESTETIKA I ERGONOMIKA. 1987. fortn. 26.40
Rub. includes index. Vsesoyuznyi Institut Nauchno-
Tekhnicheskoi Informatsii (VINITI), Baltiiskaya ul.
14, A-219 Moscow, Russian S.F.S.R., U.S.S.R.

SCIENTIFIC AND TECHNICAL BOOKS AND
SERIALS IN PRINT. see SCIENCES:
COMPREHENSIVE WORKS — Abstracting,
Bibliographies, Statistics

SCIENTIFIC SERIALS IN THAI LIBRARIES. see
SCIENCES: COMPREHENSIVE WORKS —
Abstracting, Bibliographies, Statistics

SELECTED RAND ABSTRACTS; a quarterly guide
to publications of the Rand Corporation. see
SCIENCES: COMPREHENSIVE WORKS —
Abstracting, Bibliographies, Statistics

TECHNICAL BOOK REVIEW INDEX. see
SCIENCES: COMPREHENSIVE WORKS —
Abstracting, Bibliographies, Statistics

TECHNICAL EDUCATION ABSTRACTS. see
EDUCATION — Abstracting, Bibliographies,
Statistics

TRIBOS - TRIBOLOGY ABSTRACTS. see
ENGINEERING — Abstracting, Bibliographies,
Statistics

TELEPHONE AND TELEGRAPH

see Communications — Telephone and
Telegraph

TEXTILE INDUSTRIES AND FABRICS

see also Cleaning and Dyeing; Clothing
Trade

667 338.4   II   ISSN 0075-4005
AHMEDABAD TEXTILE INDUSTRY'S
RESEARCH ASSOCIATION. JOINT
TECHNOLOGICAL CONFERENCES.
PROCEEDINGS. (Text in English) 1960. a. $7.
Ahmedabad Textile Industry's Research Association,
Polytechnic P.O., Ahmedabad 380015, India. circ.
1,000. Indexed: Text.Tech.Dig. World Text.Abstr.

677   SP
ALGODON HACE SUS CUENTAS. 1956. biennial.
1300 ptas. Asociacion Industrial Textil de Proceso
Algodoner (A I T P A), Gran Via, 670, 08010
Barcelona, Spain. stat. circ. 500.

677   II
ALL INDIA HANDLOOM EXPORTERS GUIDE.
irreg. $10 per no. c/o S. Narayanan, 11-B
Ramachandra Iyer St., Madras 600017, India.

ALL INDIA TEXTILES DIRECTORY. see
BUSINESS AND ECONOMICS — Trade And
Industrial Directories

ALL PAKISTAN TEXTILE MILLS ASSOCIATION.
CHAIRMAN'S REVIEW. see BUSINESS AND
ECONOMICS — Production Of Goods And
Services

677.028   US   ISSN 0040-490X
AMERICAN ASSOCIATION OF TEXTILE
CHEMISTS AND COLORISTS. BUYER'S
GUIDE. (Special (July) issue of: Textile Chemist
and Colorist) 1969. a. $60 to non-members;
members $30. American Association of Textile
Chemists and Colorists, P.O. Box 12215, Research
Triangle Park, NC 27709. TEL 919-549-8141. Ed.
Jack Kissiah. adv. circ. 10,500.
   Formerly: American Association of Textile
Chemists and Colorists. Products Buyer's Guide
(ISSN 0065-7352)

677.028   US   ISSN 0192-4699
AMERICAN ASSOCIATION OF TEXTILE
CHEMISTS AND COLORISTS. NATIONAL
TECHNICAL CONFERENCE. BOOK OF
PAPERS. 1974. a. $56 to non-members; members
$30. American Association of Textile Chemists and
Colorists, Box 12215, Research Triangle Park, NC
27709. TEL 919-549-8141. (back issues avail.)
Indexed: Chem.Abstr. Eng.Ind. Tex.Techn.Dig.
World Text.Abstr. Key Title: Book of Papers,
National Technical Conference.

677.028   US
AMERICAN ASSOCIATION OF TEXTILE
CHEMISTS AND COLORISTS. TECHNICAL
MANUAL. 1924. a. $34 to members; $63 non-
members. American Association of Textile Chemists
and Colorists, Box 12215, Research Triangle Park,
NC 27709. TEL 919-549-8141. circ. 2,000.

ANNUAL BOOK OF A S T M STANDARDS.
VOLUME 07.01. TEXTILES--YARN, FABRICS,
AND GENERAL TEST METHODS. see
ENGINEERING — Engineering Mechanics And
Materials

ANNUAL BOOK OF A S T M STANDARDS.
VOLUME 07.02. TEXTILES--FIBERS, ZIPPERS.
see ENGINEERING — Engineering Mechanics
And Materials

677   IT
ANNUARIO DELL'INDUSTRIA ITALIANA
DELLA MAGLIERIA E DELLA
CALZETTERIA. (Text in English, French,
German, Italian and Spanish) 1970. a. L.75000.
(Italian Association of Knitwear Producers) Gesto
s.r.l., Via Cesare Battisti 21, 20122 Milan, Italy.
adv.

APPAREL BUYERS GUIDE YEAR BOOK. see
BUSINESS AND ECONOMICS — Trade And
Industrial Directories

646   US   ISSN 0275-8873
APPAREL PLANT WAGES SURVEY.* a. $62.50 to
non-members; members $18. American Apparel
Manufacturers Association, 2500 Wilson Blvd., Ste.
301, Arlington, VA 22201-3816.
   Supersedes in part: Apparel Plant Wages and
Personnel Policies (ISSN 0084-6678)

677   BE   ISSN 0571-1924
ARTES TEXTILES: BIJRAGEN TOT DE
GESCHIEDENIS VAN DE TAPIJT. (Text in
Dutch) 1953. irreg. Vereniging voor de
Geschiedenis van de Textiele Kunsten, Centrum
Voor de Geschiedenis van de Tapijtkunst, Frans de
Coninckstr. 17, 9218 Ledeberg, Belgium. bk. rev.
bibl. Indexed: RILA.

677.2   SP   ISSN 0571-3609
ASOCIACION DE INVESTIGACION TEXTIL
ALGODONERA. COLECCION DE MANUALES
TECNICOS. irreg. Asociacion de Investigacion
Textil Algodonera, Gran via de les Corts Catalanes
670, 08010 Barcelona, Spain. illus.
   Cotton

677.2   SP
ASOCIACION DE INVESTIGACION TEXTIL
ALGODONERA. ESTUDIOS Y DOCUMENTOS.
no.2, 1976. irreg. Asociacion de Investigacion Textil
Algodonera, Gran via de les Corts Catalanes 670,
08010 Barcelona, Spain.
   Cotton

677   II   ISSN 0084-8859
C.T.T.S. ANNUAL. (Text and summaries in English)
1949. a. College of Textile Technology, Serampore,
Students Union, Serampore, West Bengal, India. Ed.
S.C. Ukil.

CANADIAN TEXTILE DIRECTORY. see
BUSINESS AND ECONOMICS — Trade And
Industrial Directories

CARBON & HIGH PERFORMANCE FIBRES
DIRECTORY. see PLASTICS

677   US
CARPET AND RUG INSTITUTE. DIRECTORY.
1950. a. $15. Carpet and Rug Institute, Box 2048,
Dalton, GA 30720. TEL 404-278-3176. Ed. Truett
Lomax.
   Formerly: Carpet and Rug Institute. Directory
and Report (ISSN 0069-0740)

677   UK   ISSN 0069-0767
CARPET ANNUAL. 1931. a. £45. Benn Business
Information Services Ltd., P.O. Box 20, Sovereign
Way, Tonbridge, Kent TN9 1RQ, England. adv.
circ. 1,300.

677   US   ISSN 0095-6457
CARPET SPECIFIER'S HANDBOOK. 1974. irreg.,
3rd edt., 1979. $15. Carpet and Rug Institute, Box
2048, Dalton, GA 30720. TEL 404-278-3176. illus.

CATALOGUE BIENNALE INTERNATIONALE
DE LAUSANNE. see ART

677   US
CLARK'S DIRECTORY OF SOUTHERN TEXTILE
MILLS. a. $23.50. Billian Publishing Co., 2100
Powers Ferry Rd., Ste. 125, Atlanta, GA 30339.
TEL 404-955-5656.

677.3   AT   ISSN 0312-5211
COMMONWEALTH SCIENTIFIC AND
INDUSTRIAL RESEARCH ORGANIZATION. C
S I R O TEXTILE NEWS. 1954. irreg. free.
C.S.I.R.O., Division of Textile Industry, Box 21,
Belmont, Vic. 3216, Australia. Ed. W.S. Boston.
circ. 800. Indexed: World Text.Abstr.
   Formerly: Commonwealth Scientific and
Industrial Research Organization. Wool Research
Laboratories. C S I R O Wool Textile News.

677 530   AT
COMMONWEALTH SCIENTIFIC AND
INDUSTRIAL RESEARCH ORGANIZATION.
DIVISION OF TEXTILE PHYSICS. ANNUAL
REPORT. 1970/71. a. free. C.S.I.R.O., Division of
Textile Physics, 338 Blaxland Rd., Ryde, N.S.W.
2112, Australia. circ. 700.

677.21   US   ISSN 0070-0673
COTTON INTERNATIONAL. 1914. a. $17. Meister
Publishing Co., 37841 Euclid Ave., Willoughby, OH
44094. TEL 216-942-2000. Ed. William Spencer.
circ. 10,788. Indexed: Text.Tech.Dig.
   Formerly: Cotton Trade Journal International.

677 382   DK   ISSN 0109-8586
DANSK TEXTIL EXPORTGUIDE/DANISH
TEXTILE EXPORT GUIDE. 1983. biennial. free.
Textilindustrien, Postboks 300, 7400 Herning,
Denmark. Ed. Lena Brogaard.

677   US   ISSN 0363-5252
DAVISON'S SALESMAN'S BOOK. 1910. a. $45.
Davison Publishing Co., Inc., Box 477, Ridgewood,
NJ 07451. TEL 201-445-3135. Ed. Bruce W. Nealy.

677   US   ISSN 0070-2951
DAVISON'S TEXTILE BLUE BOOK. 1866. a. $90.
Davison Publishing Co., Inc., Box 477, Ridgewood,
NJ 07451. TEL 201-445-3135. Ed. Bruce W. Nealy.

677   US
DAVISON'S TEXTILE BUYER'S GUIDE. 1934. a.
$40. Davison Publishing Co., Inc., Box 477,
Ridgewood, NJ 07451. TEL 201-445-3135. Ed.
Bruce W. Nealy.

DESIGN FROM SCANDINAVIA; a Scandinavian
production in furniture, textiles, illumination, arts
and crafts and industrial design. see INTERIOR
DESIGN AND DECORATION — Furniture And
House Furnishings

TEXTILE INDUSTRIES AND FABRICS

677.3 GW
DEUTSCHES WOLLFORSCHUNGSINSTITUT. VORTRAEGE. 1953. irreg. DM.10. Deutsches Wollforschungsinstitut, Technische Hochschule Aachen, Veltmanplatz 8, 5100 Aachen, W. Germany (B.R.D.)
Wool

677 620 SP
DIRECTORY OF THE SPANISH COTTON-SYSTEM TEXTILE ENTERPRISES/ DIRECTORIO EMPRESAS TEXTILES DE PROCESO ALGODONERO/DIRECTORI EMPRESES TEXTILS DE PROCES COTONER/ DIRECTOIRE ENTREPRISES TEXTILES DE PROCESSUS COTONNIER. (Text in English, French, Portuguese, Spanish) a. 3000 ptas.($22) Asociacion Industrial Textil de Proceso Algodonero (A.I.T.P.A.), Gran Via de les Corts Catalanes, 670, 08010 Barcelona, Spain. TEL 318 92 00.

380.1 II
DIRECTORY OF WOOL, HOSIERY AND FABRICS. (Text in English) 1950. a. Rs.50. Commerce Publications Limited, NKM International House, 178 Backbay Reclamation, Bombay 400020, India. Ed. Vadilal Dagli.
Formerly: India and Pakistan Wool, Hosiery and Fabrics.

E N I ANNUAL REPORT. (Ente Nazionale Idrocarburi) see *ENERGY*

677 US ISSN 0080-6811
EMBROIDERY DIRECTORY. 1947. a. $5. Schiffli Lace and Embroidery Manufacturers Association, 512 23 St., Union City, NJ 07087. TEL 201-863-7300. Ed. I. Leonard Seiler. adv. circ. 2,000.
Former titles: Schiffli Digest and Directory; Schiffli Directory.

677 US
EMBROIDERY NEWS. 1955. irreg. (6-8/yr.) free to qualified personnel. Schiffli Lace and Embroidery Manufacturers Association, Inc., 512 23rd St., Union City, NJ 07087. TEL 201-863-7300. Ed. I. Leonard Seiler. adv. bk. rev. circ. 850.

677 687
FAIRCHILD'S TEXTILE & APPAREL FINANCIAL DIRECTORY. 1974. a. $50. Fairchild Books (Subsidiary of: Fairchild Publications Inc.) 7 E. 12th St., New York, NY 10003. TEL 212-741-4280. Ed. Robert Benjamin. circ. 1,500. (back issues avail.)

677 US ISSN 0071-4682
FIBER SCIENCE SERIES. 1970. irreg., vol.8, 1979. price varies. Marcel Dekker, Inc., 270 Madison Ave., New York, NY 10016. TEL 212-696-9000. Ed. L. Rebenfeld.

338.4 II ISSN 0436-7316
HANDBOOK OF THE INDIAN COTTON TEXTILE INDUSTRY. (Text in English) a. Rs.15. Cotton Textiles Export Promotion Council, Engineering Centre 9, 4 Mathew Rd., Bombay, India.

677 II
HISTORIC TEXTILES OF INDIA. (Text in English) 1972. irreg., vol.4, 1980. $80. Calico Museum of Textiles, Sarabhai Foundation, The Retreat, Shahibag, Ahmedabad 380 004, India. Ed. John Irwin. circ. 500.

677 US
I N D A ASSOCIATION OF THE NONWOVEN FABRICS INDUSTRY. TECHNICAL SYMPOSIUM PAPERS. (Former name of issuing body: International Nonwovens and Disposables Association) 1973. a. price varies. I N D A Association of the Nonwoven Fabrics Industry, 1700 Broadway, 25th Fl., New York, NY 10019. TEL 212-582-8401.

677 SZ
I T M F DIRECTORY. biennial. free. ‡ International Textile Manufacturers Federation, Am Schanzengraben 29, Postfach, 8039 Zurich, Switzerland. Ed. Herwig M. Strolz.
Formerly: I F C A T I Directory (ISSN 0445-0698)

677 UK ISSN 0073-604X
INDEX TO TEXTILE AUXILIARIES. 1967. biennial. £10. World Textiles Publications Ltd, 76 Kirkgate, Bradford, W. Yorkshire BD1 1TB, England.
Published for the International Dyer

381 II
INDIA. TEXTILES COMMITTEE. CONSUMER PURCHASES OF TEXTILES. (Text in English) 1969. m. (plus a.) Rs.700 (Rs. 300 for a. edt. only) Textiles Committee, 406 Kakad Chambers, 79 Dr. Annie Besant Rd., Worli, Bombay 400018, India. charts. stat. circ. 200.

677.13 676.14 II ISSN 0073-6562
INDIAN JUTE MILLS ASSOCIATION. ANNUAL SUMMARY OF JUTE AND GUNNY STATISTICS. (Annual supplement to "Monthly Summary") (Text in English) 1955. a. Rs.25 per copy. Indian Jute Mills Association, Royal Exchange, 6 Netaji Subhas Rd., Calcutta 1, India. circ. 400.

677 676 II ISSN 0073-6570
INDIAN JUTE MILLS ASSOCIATION. LOOM AND SPINDLE STATISTICS. 1941. biennial. Rs.5. Indian Jute Mills Association, Royal Exchange, 6 Netaji Subhas Rd., Calcutta 1, India. circ. 500.

677 II ISSN 0537-2666
INDIAN TEXTILE ANNUAL & DIRECTORY. (Text in English) 1965. a. $10. Eastland Publications (Private) Ltd., 44 Chittaranjan Ave., Calcutta 12, India. Ed. J.R. Dutta. adv. bk. rev. charts. illus. pat. circ. 5,000.

677 US ISSN 0019-8307
INDUSTRIAL FABRIC PRODUCTS REVIEW BUYER'S GUIDE. 1976. a. $25. Industrial Fabrics Association International, 345 Cedar Bldg., Ste. 450, St. Paul, MN 55101. TEL 612-222-2508. Ed. Roger Barr. adv. circ. 6,000.

677 US
INTERIOR TEXTILES NATIONAL BUYERS GUIDE. 1954. a. $10. Columbia Communications, Inc., 370 Lexington Ave., New York, NY 10017. TEL 212-532-9290. Ed. Mark Richards. adv. bk. rev. circ. 18,000(controlled)
Formerly: Curtain, Drapery and Bedspread National Buyers Guide (ISSN 0084-9502)

667 338.4 US ISSN 0095-683X
INTERNATIONAL DIRECTORY OF THE NONWOVEN FABRICS INDUSTRY. 1970. biennial. price varies. I N D A Association of the Nonwoven Fabrics Industry, 1700 Broadway, 25th Fl., New York, NY 10019. TEL 212-582-8401. Ed. J.G. Nestos.
Formerly: Directory for the Nonwoven Fabrics and Disposable Soft Goods Industries (ISSN 0070-5020)

667 677 IT ISSN 0074-5898
INTERNATIONAL FEDERATION OF ASSOCIATIONS OF TEXTILE CHEMISTS AND COLORISTS. REPORTS OF CONGRESS. irreg., 11th, 1978, Italy. Associazione Italiana di Chimica Tessile e Coloristica, Via Borgonnovo 11, I-20121 Milano, Italy.

677 SZ
INTERNATIONAL PRODUCTION COST COMPARISON. 1979. biennial. 50 Fr. International Textile Manufacturers Federation, Am Schanzengraben 29, Postfach, 8039 Zurich, Switzerland.

677 UK ISSN 0074-9087
INTERNATIONAL TEXTILE MACHINERY. 1967. a. £5. World Textiles Publications, 76 Kirkgate, Bradford, W. Yorkshire BD1 1TB, England. Ed. Eugene P. Dempsey.
Supersedes: Textile Recorder Annual and Machinery Review.

677 SZ
INTERNATIONAL TEXTILE MANUFACTURING. 1960. a. 50 Fr. International Textile Manufacturers Federation, Am Schanzengraben 29, Postfach, 8039 Zurich, Switzerland. Ed: World Text.Abstr.
Supersedes: Cotton and Allied Textile Industries (ISSN 0574-2315)

677 UR
KALININSKII NAUCHNO-ISSLEDOVATEL'SKII INSTITUT TEKSTIL'NOI PROMYSHLENNOSTI. NAUCHNO-ISSLEDOVATEL'SKIE TRUDY. 1971. irreg. 0.67 Rub. Kalininskii Nauchno-Issledovatel'skii Institut Tekstil'noi Promyshlennosti, Kalinin, Russian S.F.S.R., U.S.S.R. illus.

677 338.4 US ISSN 0085-2562
KNITTING TIMES YEARBOOK. a. $15. National Knitwear and Sportswear Association, 386 Park Ave. So., New York, NY 10016. TEL 212-683-7520.

677 US
LATIN AMERICAN TEXTILE INDUSTRY DIRECTORY. (Text in English, Portuguese, Spanish) 1985. a. $150 per m. Aurora International, Box 9099, Bridgeport, CT 06601-2099. TEL 203-368-0579. Ed. Andres C. Aquino. adv.

338.4 JA
MAN-MADE FIBERS OF JAPAN. (Text in English) a. $27. Japan Chemical Fibres Association, No. 3 Nihonbashi-Muromachi 3-chome, Chuo-ku, Tokyo 103, Japan. illus.

677 US
MILL REPORT. 1976. irreg. Platt Saco Lowell, Drawer 2327, Greenville, SC 29602. TEL 803-859-3211. charts. illus.

NATIONAL COTTONSEED PRODUCTS ASSOCIATION. TRADING RULES. see *ENGINEERING* — Chemical Engineering

677 TZ
NATIONAL TEXTILE CORPORATION. ANNUAL REPORT AND ACCOUNTS. (Text in English) 1974. a. National Textile Corporation, Administrative and Welfare Office, Box 9531, Dar es Salaam, Tanzania. adv. circ. 500.

NECKWEAR INDUSTRY DIRECTORY. see *CLOTHING TRADE*

338.1 NZ ISSN 0110-1242
NEW ZEALAND WOOL BOARD. STATISTICAL HANDBOOK. 1972. a. free. New Zealand Wool Board, Private Bag, Wellington, New Zealand. stat. circ. 1,600.
Formerly (until 1977): Statistical Analysis of New Zealand Wool Production and Disposal.

677.028 658 US
NYLON FILAMENT & POLYESTER FILAMENT GROWTH. 1983. triennial. $9,800. Statistikon Corp., 81 Peach Tree Dr., Box 246, E. Norwich, NY 11732. TEL 516-922-0882. Ed. Jordan P. Yale.

PAKISTAN CENTRAL COTTON COMMITTEE. AGRICULTURAL SURVEY REPORT. see *AGRICULTURE* — Crop Production And Soil

PAKISTAN CENTRAL COTTON COMMITTEE. TECHNOLOGICAL BULLETIN. SERIES A. see *AGRICULTURE* — Crop Production And Soil

PAKISTAN CENTRAL COTTON COMMITTEE. TECHNOLOGICAL BULLETIN. SERIES B. see *AGRICULTURE* — Crop Production And Soil

677 US
PLATT SACO LOWELL REPLACEMENT PARTS NEWS. vol.17, 1976. irreg. free to customers. Platt Saco Lowell, Replacement Parts Center, Box 327, Greenville, SC 29602. TEL 803-859-3211. Ed. L.H. Irby. illus. circ. 3,000. (tabloid format)

677 PL ISSN 0076-0331
POLITECHNIKA LODZKA. ZESZYTY NAUKOWE. WLOKIENNICTWO. (Text in Polish; summaries in English and Russian) 1954. irreg. price varies. Politechnika Lodzka, Ul. Zwirki 36, 90-924 Lodz, Poland (Dist. by: Ars Polona-Ruch, Krakowskie Przedmiescie 7, Warsaw, Poland) Ed. Witold Zurek. circ. 263. Indexed: Chem.Abstr. World Text.Abstr. Text.Tech.Dig.

677.2 IT
RAPPORTO SULLA INDUSTRIA COTONIERA ITALIANA. (Supplement to: Industria Cotoniera) a. free. Istituto per Assistenza e Servizi alle Aziende Tessili s.r.l. (I.A.S.A.T.), 1 via Borgonuovo 11, Milan, Italy.

677.3   SA   ISSN 0081-2560
S A W T R I TECHNICAL REPORT. 1952. irreg. $7 per copy. South African Wool and Textile Research Institute, Box 1124, Port Elizabeth 6000, South Africa. Ed. P. Horn. circ. 250. Indexed: World Text.Abstr. Text.Tech.Dig.
Wool

SERICULTURAL EXPERIMENT STATION. ANNUAL REPORT/SANSHI SHIKENJO, NEMPO. see *AGRICULTURE*

677   IT
LA SETA. (Text in English, Italian; summaries in English, French, Italian) 1931. a. free. Stazione Sperimentale per la Seta, Via G. Colombo 81, 20133 Milan, Italy. TEL 02 235047. Ed. Alberto Girelli. bk. rev. abstr. bibl. charts. illus. stat. circ. 1,000. (back issues avail.)

SHINSHU UNIVERSITY. FACULTY OF TEXTILE SCIENCE AND TECHNOLOGY. JOURNAL. SERIES A: BIOLOGY. see *BIOLOGY*

SHINSHU UNIVERSITY. FACULTY OF TEXTILE SCIENCE AND TECHNOLOGY. JOURNAL. SERIES C: CHEMISTRY. see *ENGINEERING — Chemical Engineering*

SHINSHU UNIVERSITY. FACULTY OF TEXTILE SCIENCE AND TECHNOLOGY. JOURNAL. SERIES D: ARTS. see *ART*

677   UK   ISSN 0306-5154
SHIRLEY INSTITUTE PUBLICATIONS. S: SERIES. 1972. irreg. price varies. Shirley Institute, Manchester M20 8RX, England.

SHUTTLE CRAFT GUILD. MONOGRAPHS. see *HOME ECONOMICS*

677.3   SA   ISSN 0560-9941
SOUTH AFRICAN WOOL AND TEXTILE RESEARCH INSTITUTE. ANNUAL REPORT. (Text in Afrikaans and English) 1954. a. free. South African Wool and Textile Research Institute, Box 1124, Port Elizabeth 6000, South Africa. Ed. P. Horn. bibl. charts. illus. circ. 1,200.
Wool

677   FR   ISSN 0082-1047
SYNDICAT GENERAL DE L'INDUSTRIE COTONNIERE FRANCAISE. ANNUAIRE. 1970. a. free. (Syndicat General de l'Industrie Cotonniere Francaise et Textiles Allies) Service de Presse Edition Information, 3 Av. Ruysdael, 75367 Paris Cedex 08, France. adv.

677   GW
TASCHENBUCH DER TEXTILEN RAUMAUSSTATTUNG. a. DM.42. Fachverlag Schiele und Schoen GmbH, Markgrafenstr. 11, 1000 Berlin 61, W. Germany (B.R.D.) Ed. Wilhelm Artz.

677   GW   ISSN 0082-1837
TASCHENBUCH DES TEXTILEINZELHANDELS. 1962. a. Deutscher Fachverlag GmbH, Schumannstr. 27, Postfach 100606, 6000 Frankfurt 1, W. Germany (B.R.D.)

677   GW   ISSN 0082-1896
TASCHENBUCH FUER DIE TEXTIL-INDUSTRIE. 1951. a. DM.39.50. Fachverlag Schiele und Schoen GmbH, Markgrafenstr. 11, 1000 Berlin 61, W. Germany (B.R.D.) Eds. M. Malthes, W. Lang. adv. circ. 5,000.

TEXINFORM; information index for the textile industry. see *BUSINESS AND ECONOMICS — Trade And Industrial Directories*

338.4   US   ISSN 0092-3540
TEXSCOPE: U S A TEXTILE INDUSTRY OVERVIEW. 1974. irreg., latest 1983. Werner Management Consultants, Inc., 111 W. 40th St., New York, NY 10018. TEL 212-730-1280. Ed. Mary Scannapield. stat. circ. controlled. Key Title: Texscope (New York)

677   GW   ISSN 0082-3627
TEXTIL-INDUSTRIE UND IHRE HELFER. 1957. a. DM.38. Industrieschau-Verlagsgesellschaft, Berliner Allee 8, 6000 Darmstadt, W. Germany (B.R.D.)

677   AT
TEXTILE AND APPAREL INDEX OF AUSTRALIA. 1950. biennial. Aus.$20. Textile Index of Australia, 9 Sterland Ave., North Manly, NSW 2100, Australia.

338.47   FR   ISSN 0474-6023
TEXTILE INDUSTRY IN O.E.C.D. COUNTRIES. (Only avail. on microfiche since 1986) 1953. irreg. $9. Organization for Economic Cooperation and Development, 2 rue Andre Pascal, 75775 Paris 16, France (U.S. orders to: O.E.C.D. Publications and Information Center, 1750 Pennsylvania Ave., N.W., Washington, DC 20006) (also avail. in microfiche)

677   US   ISSN 0094-9884
TEXTILE INDUSTRY TECHNICAL CONFERENCE (PUBLICATION) Variant title: Annual Textile Industry Technical Conference (Publication) a. (I E E E, Industry Applications Society) Institute of Electrical and Electronics Engineers, Inc., 345 E. 47th St., New York, NY 10017 TEL 212-705-7900. (Subscr. address: 445 Hoes Lane, Piscataway, NJ 08854)
Textile Industry Technical Conference. Record (ISSN 0082-3651)

677   UK
TEXTILE INSTITUTE. ANNUAL CONFERENCE. a. Textile Institute, 10 Blackfriars St., Manchester M3 5DR, England. Ed. P.W. Harrison. bibl. charts. illus. stat. Indexed: World Text.Abstr.

677   UK
TEXTILE INSTITUTE. ANNUAL REPORT. 1965. a. Textile Institute, 10 Blackfriars St., Manchester M3 5DR, England.

677   JA   ISSN 0082-366X
TEXTILE JAPAN/TEKISUTAIRU JAPAN. (Text in English) 1957. a. $12. Nihon Sen'i Shinbun Co., Ltd., 3-9 Hongo, Nihonbashi, Chuo-ku, Tokyo 103, Japan. Ed.Bd.

677 700   US   ISSN 0083-7407
TEXTILE MUSEUM JOURNAL. 1962. a. $35 membership. Textile Museum, 2320 S. St. N.W., Washington, DC 20008. TEL 202-667-0441. Ed. Patricia Fiske. circ. 3,000. Indexed: Art Ind. Art & Archaeol.Tech.Abstr. World Text.Abstr.
Supersedes: Workshop Notes Washington, D.C. Textile Museum.

677   NE
TEXTILE SCIENCE AND TECHNOLOGY. 1975. irreg., vol.7, 1985. price varies. Elsevier Science Publishers B.V., Box 211, 1000 AE Amsterdam, Netherlands.

677   US   ISSN 0495-369X
TEXTILE WORLD BUYER'S GUIDE/FACT FILE; McGraw-Hill's international textile magazine. (Special issue of Textile World) a. $15. McGraw-Hill Publications Co., 1221 Ave. of Americas, New York, NY 10020 (Subscr. to: Box 532, Hightstown, NJ 08520) Ed. Laurence A. Christiansen, Jr. adv. circ. controlled. (also avail. in microfilm from UMI)

677   US
TEXTILES: LATIN AMERICAN INDUSTRIAL REPORT. (Avail. for each of 22 Latin American countries) 1985. a. $435 per country report per industry covered. Aurora International, Box 9099, Bridgeport, CT 06601-2099. TEL 203-368-0579.

UNCOVERINGS; research papers. see *HISTORY — History Of North And South America*

677.3   NZ   ISSN 0112-2908
WOOL RESEARCH ORGANISATION OF NEW ZEALAND COMMUNICATIONS. 1967. irreg. NZ.$20. Wool Research Organisation of New Zealand, Private Bag, Christchurch, New Zealand.

677.3   NZ   ISSN 0112-2851
WOOL RESEARCH ORGANISATION OF NEW ZEALAND REPORTS. 1970. irreg. NZ.$20. Wool Research Organisation of New Zealand, Private Bag, Christchurch, New Zealand. TEL (3) 252-421.

677.3   NZ   ISSN 0112-2932
WOOL RESEARCH ORGANISATION OF NEW ZEALAND TECHNICAL PAPERS. 1969. irreg. price varies. Wool Research Organisation of New Zealand (Inc.), Private Bag, Christchurch, New Zealand. TEL 3-252-421. Ed. L.F. Story. bibl. stat. circ. 150. Indexed: Chem.Abstr. Text.Tech.Dig. World Text.Abstr.
Formerly (until vol. 4, Feb. 1980): Technical Papers on New Zealand Wool (ISSN 0111-0950)

677.3   AT   ISSN 0084-1218
WOOL REVIEW. 1938. a. free. ‡ National Council of Wool Selling Brokers of Australia, 1st Floor, Wool Exchange House, 530 Little Collins St., Melbourne 3000, Australia.

677.3   UK
WOOL SCIENCE REVIEW. 1948. irreg. free. International Wool Secretariat, Development Centre, Valley Drive, Ikley, West Yorkshire LS29 8PB, England. circ. 3,000. Indexed: Chem.Abstr. World Text.Abstr.

TEXTILE INDUSTRIES AND FABRICS — Abstracting, Bibliographies, Statistics

677   AT   ISSN 0311-9882
AUSTRALIAN WOOL SALE STATISTICS. STATISTICAL ANALYSIS. PART A & B. (Issued in Two Parts) 1972. a. free. Australian Wool Corporation, Box 4867, Melbourne, Vic. 3001, Australia. Ed. C.A.F. Faden. circ. 700.
Former titles: Australian Wool (ISSN 0067-222X) ; Australian Wool Corporation. Statistical Analysis (ISSN 0084-764X)

677   CN   ISSN 0527-4893
CANADA. STATISTICS CANADA. CARPET, MAT AND RUG INDUSTRY/INDUSTRIE DES TAPIS, DES CARPETTES ET DE LA MOQUETTE. (Catalogue 34-221) (Text in English and French) 1960. a. Can.$20($21) Statistics Canada, Communications Division, 3rd Floor, R.H. Coats Bldg., Ottawa, Ont. K1A 0T6, Canada TEL 613-993-7276. (Subscr. to: Publications Sales and Services, Ottawa, Ont. K1A 0T6, Canada) (also avail. in microform from MML)

338.4   CN   ISSN 0300-0265
CANADA. STATISTICS CANADA. WOOL PRODUCTION AND SUPPLY/PRODUCTION ET STOCKS DE LAINE. (Catalogue 23-205) (Text in English & French) 1939. a. Can.$15($16) Statistics Canada, Communications Division, 3rd Floor, R.H. Coats Bldg., Ottawa, Ont. K1A 0T6, Canada TEL 613-993-7276. (Subscr. to: Publications Sales and Services, Ottawa, Ont. K1A 0T6, Canada) (also avail. in microform from MML)

677 310   US
CURRENT INDUSTRIAL REPORTS: FINISHED FABRICS. PRODUCTION, INVENTORIES, AND UNFILLED ORDERS. (Series M-22-A) m. (plus a. issue) $15. U.S. Bureau of the Census, Customer Services (Publications), Washington, DC 20233 TEL 301-763-4100. (Subscr. to: Supt. of Documents, Washington, DC 20402)
Formerly: Current Industrial Reports: Woven Fabrics. Production, Inventories, and Unfilled Orders (ISSN 0145-5028)

677.2 314   IT   ISSN 0423-7269
EUROPEAN COTTON INDUSTRY STATISTICS. 1958. a. Istituto per Assistenza e Servizi alle Aziende Tessili s.r.l. (I.A.S.A.T.), Via Borgonuovo 11, 20121 Milan, Italy.

338.4 677   II
INDIAN COTTON TEXTILE INDUSTRY; ANNUAL STATISTICAL BULLETIN. (Text in English) 1968. a. Southern India Mills' Association, Coimbatore, India. circ. 500.

677.2   SZ   ISSN 0538-6829
INTERNATIONAL COTTON INDUSTRY STATISTICS. 1958. a. 70 Fr. ‡ International Textile Manufacturers Federation, Am Schanzengraben 29, Postfach, 8039 Zurich, Switzerland. charts. stat. (MI) Indexed: World Text.Abstr.

677.2   SZ
INTERNATIONAL COTTON-SYSTEM FIBRE
CONSUMPTION STATISTICS. 1974. a. 20 Fr.
International Textile Manufacturers Federation, Am
Schanzengraben 29, Postfach, 8039 Zurich,
Switzerland. charts. stat. (MI) Indexed: World
Text.Abstr.

677   FR   ISSN 0074-7599
INTERNATIONAL RAYON AND SYNTHETIC
FIBRES COMMITTEE. STATISTICAL
YEARBOOK. 1965. a. 75 Fr. ‡ International Rayon
and Synthetic Fibres Committee, 29 rue de
Courcelles, 75008 Paris, France. circ. 3,500.

677.2   SZ
INTERNATIONAL TEXTILE MACHINERY
SHIPMENT STATISTICS. 1974. a. 100 Fr.
International Textile Manufacturers Federation, Am
Schanzengraben 29, Postfach, 8039 Zurich,
Switzerland. charts. stat.
    Formerly: International Cotton Industry
Statistics. Supplement.

677 338.1   JA   ISSN 0447-5321
JAPAN COTTON STATISTICS AND RELATED
DATA. 1953. a. $12. Japan Cotton Traders'
Association - Nihon Menka Kyokai, Box Osaka
Central 951, 1-8-2 Utsubu-Honmachi, Nishiku,
Osaka, Japan.

677.3 310   UK   ISSN 0260-8855
KNITSTATS; a yearly statistical bulletin for the
hosiery and knitwear industry. 1976. a. £20. Hatra,
7 Gregory Boulevard, Nottingham NG7 6LD,
England. Ed. J.A. Smirfitt. index. circ. 700. (back
issues avail.) Indexed: World Text.Abstr.

677.39   II
SILK IN INDIA. biennial. Central Silk Board, United
Mansions, 2nd Fl., 39 M.G. Road, Bangalore 560
001, India. stat.

677 016   UK   ISSN 0260-4256
TEXTILE DIGEST. 1970. m. $72. Shirley Institute,
Manchester M2Q 8RX, England.
    Formerly: Digest of English-Language Textile
Literature (ISSN 0306-1639)

677 016.677   US   ISSN 0040-5191
TEXTILE TECHNOLOGY DIGEST. 1944. m. $300.
Institute of Textile Technology, Charlottesville, VA
22902. TEL 804-296-5511. Ed. Phil Lawrence. bk.
rev. abstr. pat. tr.lit. tr.mk. index. circ. 1,000.
(also avail. in microform from UMI) Indexed:
Abstr.Bull.Inst.Pap.Chem. World Text.Abstr.
●Also available online. Vendors: DIALOG.

677 016   UK   ISSN 0043-9118
WORLD TEXTILE ABSTRACTS. 1969. s-m. $324.
Shirley Institute, Manchester M20 8RX, England.
Ed. B.C. Wedgbury. bk. rev. index. (back issues
avail) Indexed: Appl.Mech.Rev. Anim.Breed.Abstr.
Abstr.Bull.Inst.Pap.Chem. Anal.Abstr.
Ergon.Abstr.
●Also available online. Vendors: DIALOG,
Pergamon Infoline.
    Supersedes: Shirley Institute Summary of Current
Literature; Textile Abstracts.

THEATER

see also Dance

A M S STUDIES IN THE RENAISSANCE. see
LITERATURE

ADVANCEMENT 2: LITERATURE, MEDIA
ARTS, OPERA-MUSICAL THEATRE, VISUAL
ARTS. see *LITERATURE*

791   PL   ISSN 0065-6526
ALMANACH SCENY POLSKIEJ. 1959/60. a. 200
Zl. (Polska Akademia Nauk, Instytut Sztuki)
Wydawnictwa Artystyczne i Filmowe, Ul. Pulawska
61, Warsaw, Poland TEL 048-22-45-53-01. (Dist.
by: Ars Polona-Ruch, Krakowskie Przedmiescie 7,
Warsaw, Poland) Ed. Kazimierz Andrzej Wysinski.
circ. 1,500.

ALPHA. see *LITERATURE*

792   US
ALPHA PSI OMEGA: PLAYBILL. 1927. a. free
contr. circ. Alpha Psi Omega National Theatre
Honorary, Eastern Illinois University, Charleston,
IL 61920. TEL 217-581-2021. (Co-Sponsor: Delta
Psi Omega) Ed. Dr. D.P Garner. bk. rev. play rev.
illus. stat. circ. 7,000.

ANGLICA GERMANICA: SERIES 2. see
LINGUISTICS

792   FR   ISSN 0066-3026
ANNUAIRE DU SPECTACLE. (Comprised of Four
Volumes) 1956, 11th edt. a. 60 F. per volume;
complete collection 220 F. Editions Raoult, 17
Faubourg Montmartre, 75009 Paris, France.

792   IT   ISSN 0066-6661
ARCHIVIO DEL TEATRO ITALIANO. 1968. irreg;
latest issue, 1982. price varies. Edizioni Il Polifilo,
Via Borgonuovo 2, 20121 Milan, Italy. Ed.
Giovanni Macchia.

792   UK   ISSN 0143-8131
ARTISTES AND THEIR AGENTS. a. £7.95. John
Offord (Publications) Ltd., 12 The Avenue,
Eastbourne, East Sussex BN21 3YA, England.

ASOCIACION ARGENTINA DE ACTORES.
MEMORIA Y BALANCE. see *LABOR UNIONS*

792   IS   ISSN 0334-5963
ASSAPH. SECTION C. STUDIES IN THE
THEATRE. (Text in English) 1984. a. $6 to
individuals; institutions $10. Tel-Aviv University,
Faculty of Visual and Performing Arts, Department
of Theatre Arts, Ramat Aviv, 69 978 Tel Aviv,
Israel. Ed. Avraham Oz. circ. 1,500. (back issues
avail.)

792 150   IT
ATTI DELLO PSICODRAMMA. (Text in Italian;
summaries in English) 1975. a. L.30000 for 2 years.
Astrolabio-Ubaldini, Via Lungara 3, 00165 Rome,
Italy. (Co-sponsor: Associazione Ricerche sullo
Psicodramma Analitico di Roma) Ed. Ottavio
Rosati. adv. illus. circ. 5,000. Indexed:
Psychol.Abstr.

792.02   BG
BAHUBACANA. (Text in Bengali) 1978. irreg. Tk.3.
Bahubacana Natyagoshthi, 11/2 Jaynag Rd., Bakshi
Bazar, Dacca 1, Bangladesh. play rev.

792   CN
BEHIND THE SCENES. 1986. every 18 months.
Can.$8.95. PACT Communications Centre, 64
Charles Street East, Toronto, Ont. M4Y 1T1. TEL
416-968-3033. illus.

BERNARD SHAW SOCIETY JOURNAL. see
LITERATURE

792   US
BEST PLAYS OF ... (YEAR) 1920. a. $17.95. Dodd,
Mead & Co., Inc., 79 Madison Ave., New York,
NY 10013. TEL 212-685-6464. Ed. Otis L.
Guernsey, Jr. play rev. illus. tr.lit. circ. 2,500.
(back issues avail.)

792   US   ISSN 0360-2788
BIBLIOGRAPHIC GUIDE TO THEATRE ARTS. a.
G. K. Hall & Co., 70 Lincoln St., Boston, MA
02111. TEL 617-423-3990.

792 380   UK   ISSN 0142-5218
BRITISH ALTERNATIVE THEATRE
DIRECTORY. 1979. a. £7.95. John Offord
(Publications) Ltd., 12 The Avenue, Eastbourne,
East Sussex BN21 3YA, England. Ed. Catherine
Itzin.

792 380   UK   ISSN 0306-4107
BRITISH THEATRE DIRECTORY. 1972. a. £13.95.
John Offord (Publications) Ltd., 12 The Avenue,
Eastbourne, East Sussex BN21 3YA, England. Ed.
John Offord. adv.

CANADA COUNCIL ANNUAL REPORT AND
SUPPLEMENT/RAPPORT ANNUEL DU
CONSEIL DES ARTS DU CANADA ET SON
SUPPLEMENT. see *ART*

792   CN
CANADA ON STAGE: THE NATIONAL
THEATRE YEARBOOK. 1974. a. Can.$19.95.
PACT Communications Centre, Faculty of
Administrative Studies, c/o Carla Wittes, Projects
Manager, 64 Charles St. East, Toronto, Ont. M4Y
1T1, Canada. TEL 416-968-3033. illus. index.
    Formerly: Canada on Stage: Canadian Theatre
Review Yearbook (ISSN 0380-9455)

792   CN
CANADIAN THEATRE REVIEW. 1974. a. Can.$10
to individuals; Can. $15 to libraries. University of
Toronto Press, Journals Management Department,
63A St. George Street, Toronto, Ont. M5S 1A6,
Canada. adv. bk. rev. illus. index. circ. 10,000.
    Formerly: Canadian Theatre Review Yearbook
(ISSN 0316-1323)

658 791   US   ISSN 0090-2985
CARNIVAL & CIRCUS BOOKING GUIDE. 1972. a.
$3.50. Billboard Publications Inc., Amusement
Business Division, Box 24970, Nashville, TN 37202.
TEL 615-748-8100. Ed. Steve Rogers. adv. abstr.
stat. circ. 12,000. (also avail. in microform)

790.2   US
CAVALCADE OF ACTS & ATTRACTIONS. 1973.
a. $18. Billboard Publications, Inc., Amusement
Business Division, Box 24970, Nashville, TN 37202.
TEL 615-748-8100. illus.
    Formerly: Cavalcade and Directory of Acts and
Attractions (ISSN 0090-2993)

792   US   ISSN 0069-1372
CELEBRITY SERVICE INTERNATIONAL
CONTACT BOOK; trade directory/entertainment
industry. a. $25. Celebrity Service, Inc., 1780
Broadway, Ste. 300, New York, NY 10019. TEL
212-757-7979. Ed. Donnali Shor. adv.

CENTRE CULTUREL FRANCAIS DE YAOUNDE.
PROGRAMME SAISON. see *ART*

CINEGUIA; annuario espanol del espectaculo y
audiovisuales. see *MOTION PICTURES*

CINEMA AND SOCIETY. see *MOTION
PICTURES*

792 800   US   ISSN 0748-237X
CLIPPER STUDIES IN THE AMERICAN
THEATER. 1985. irreg., (approx. 2/yr.) $19.95
hardcover per no.; paperback $9.95 per no. Borgo
Press, Box 2845, San Bernardino, CA 92406. TEL
714-884-5813.

792   BL
COLECAO TEATRO. no.2, 1974. irreg. Universidade
Federal do Rio Grande do Sul, Porto Alegre, Brazil.
bibl.

792   IT
COLLANA DEL TEATRO DI ROMA. 1977. irreg.
Officina Edizioni, Passeggiata di Ripetta 25, 00186
Rome, Italy.

792   US
COMPLETE CATALOGUE OF PLAYS (YEAR)
1936. a. Dramatists Play Service, Inc., 440 Park
Ave. S., New York, NY 10016. TEL 212-683-8960.
Ed. F. Andrew Leslie. adv. circ. 35,000.

CONNECTICUT POETRY REVIEW. see
LITERATURE — Poetry

CONTACTS. see *PUBLISHING AND BOOK
TRADE*

792 780.65   AT
CONTACTS & FACILITIES; in the entertainment
industry. 1963. a. Aus.$20. Showcast Publications
Pty. Ltd, Box 141, Spit Junction, N.S.W. 2088,
Australia.

CONTEMPORARY THEATRE, FILM &
TELEVISION. see *BIOGRAPHY*

792   US   ISSN 0163-3821
CONTRIBUTIONS IN DRAMA AND THEATRE
STUDIES. 1979. irreg. price varies. Greenwood
Press, 88 Post Rd. W., Box 5007, Westport, CT
06881. TEL 203-226-3571. Ed. Joseph Donohue.

800   UK
CORNISH PLAY SERIES. 1970. irreg. Lodeneck
Press Ltd., 17 Duke St., Padstow, Cornwall, United
Kingdom. circ. 1,500.

792 920   CN   ISSN 0315-3290
CREATIVE CANADA. 1971. irreg. (University of
Victoria, McPherson Library) University of Toronto
Press, Front Campus, Toronto, Ont. M5S 1A6,
Canada. TEL 613-667-7791. Indexed: Child.Auth.&
Illus. Perf.Arts Biog.Master Ind.

792   GW   ISSN 0070-4431
DEUTSCHES BUEHNEN-JAHRBUCH;
Theatergeschichtliches Jahr- und Adressbuch. 1889.
a. DM.52. (Genossenschaft Deutscher
Buehnenangehoeriger) Buehnenschriften-Vertriebs-
Gesellschaft, Feldbrunnenstr. 74, 2000 Hamburg 13,
W. Germany (B.R.D.) adv.

791.53   UK
DIRECTORY OF PROFESSIONAL PUPPETEERS.
1976. biennial. £2.50. Puppet Centre Trust,
Battersea Arts Centre, Lavender Hill, London SW11
5TJ, England. Ed.Bd. illus. circ. 2,000. (back issues
avail.)
  Puppets

DIRECTORY OF THE ARTS. see *ART*

842 792   FR
DOCUMENTATION THEATRALE; fiches
analytiques. 1974. a. 10 F. Universite de Paris X
(Paris-Nanterre), Centre d'Etudes Theatrales, 200
Av. de la Republique, 92001 Nanterre Cedex,
France (Orders to: Librairie de Coupe-Papier, 19
rue de l'Odeon, 75006 Paris, France) (Co-sponsor:
Centre de Recherches Historiques de l'Ecole des
Hautes Etudes en Sciences Sociales) Eds. Jacqueline
Jomaron, Bernard Faivre. bk. rev. abstr. bibl. film
rev. play rev. index.

800   US   ISSN 0733-1606
DRAMATISTS SOURCEBOOK. 1982. a. $10.95.
Theatre Communications Group, 355 Lexington
Ave., New York, NY 10017. TEL 212-697-5230.
Ed. M. Elizabeth Osborn. index. circ. 5,000.

792   UK   ISSN 0141-1179
DRAMAU'R BYD. (Text in Welsh) 1969. irreg. price
varies. (Welsh Arts Council) University of Wales
Press, 6 Gwennyth St., Cathays, Cardiff CF2 4YD,
Wales. Ed. William R. Lewis.

792 370 793.3   UK   ISSN 0260-311X
EDUCATIONAL DRAMA ASSOCIATION.
NEWSLETTER. 1980. irreg. Educational Drama
Association, c/o S. Demmery, Lee's Barn Field
Assarts, Minster Lovell, Oxfordshire OX8 5NQ,
England. Ed. Mrs. A. Tucker.

EDWARDIAN STUDIES. see *LITERATURE*

792   US
EMPIRICAL RESEARCH IN THEATRE ANNUAL.
1971-1975; reestablished 1980. a. $10. Bowling
Green State University, Center for Communications
Research, 315 South Hall, Bowling Green, OH
43403. TEL 419-372-2531. (Co-sponsor: Speech
Communication Association, Theatre Division) Ed.
Briant Hamor Lee. bk. rev. circ. 500. (also avail. in
microform from UMI; reprint service avail. from
UMI) Indexed: Curr.Cont. Sociol.Abstr. Arts &
Hum.Cit.Ind. Lang.& Lang.Behav.Abstr.
   Formerly: Empirical Research in Theatre (ISSN
0361-2767)

ENCORE. see *LITERATURE*

ENJOYING THE ARTS. see *DANCE*

ENTERTAINMENT, PUBLISHING AND THE
ARTS HANDBOOK. see
COMMUNICATIONS — Radio And Television

792 780   US
ESSAYS ON ASIAN THEATER, MUSIC AND
DANCE. vol.3, 1974. irreg. price varies. Asia
Society, 725 Park Ave., New York, NY 10021. TEL
212-288-6400.

ETUDES CINEMATOGRAPHIQUES. see *MOTION
PICTURES*

800   IT
EVENTO TEATRALE. SEZIONE: AUTORI
ITALIANI DEL NOVECENTO.* 1976. irreg.
Edizioni Abete, Via Prenestina, 685, Rome, Italy.

792   US
EXPERIMENT THEATRE; "one minute" poetic
drama. irreg. $4.50. Experiment Press, 6565 N.E.
Windermere Rd., Seattle, WA 98105. Ed. Carol Ely
Harper.

FACE TO FACE WITH TALENT. see
COMMUNICATIONS — Radio And Television

FACILITIES DIRECTORY/REPERTOIRE DES
SALLES DE SPECTACLE. see *DANCE*

301.415   792.026   US
FEMALE IMPERSONATOR NEWS.* 1973. irreg.
(10-12/yr.) $25. Neptune Productions, 2412 Hwy.
71, Apt. 2C, Spring Lake Hts., NJ 07762. Ed. Betty
Johnson. film rev. play rev. bibl. circ. 10,000.
(tabloid format)

792   UK   ISSN 0016-4283
GAMBIT; an international drama magazine. 1963.
irreg. £6 for 2 issues. John Calder (Publishers) Ltd.,
18 Brewer St., London W1R 4AS, England. Eds.
John Calder, Tony Dunn. adv. bk. rev. illus. play
rev. circ. 1,500. Indexed: Abstr.Engl.Stud.
Ind.Bk.Rev.Hum.
  Plays

792   FR   ISSN 0072-8063
GUIDE DU SHOW-BUSINESS; GUIDE
PROFESSIONNEL DU SPECTACLE. 1963. a.
600 F. Societe d'Editions Radio-Phono, 11 rue Jean
Bologne, 75016 Paris, France. Dir. Sabine Gay. adv.

800   CN
HALLOWEEN; an occasional theatrical letter. no.2,
1976. irreg. University of Western Ontario,
Department of English, London, Ontario, Canada.
TEL 519-885-1211. Ed. James Reaney.

HISPANIC AMERICAN ARTS; all you want or must
know, about everything, in all the fields of Hispanic
American arts. see *ART*

792 407   US
ILLINOIS SPEECH AND THEATRE
ASSOCIATION. JOURNAL. a. $2. Illinois Speech
and Theatre Association, Bradley University, Peoria,
IL 62650. TEL 217-581-2016. Ed. Frank E.
Parcells. adv. circ. 650. (back issues avail.) Indexed:
ERIC.

800 792   UK   ISSN 0260-7964
IRISH DRAMA SELECTIONS. 1982. irreg. price
varies. Colin Smythe Ltd., Box 6, Gerrards Cross,
Buckinghamshire SL9 8XA, England (Pub. in U.S.
by: Catholic University of America Press, 620
Michigan Ave. N.E., Washington, DC 20064) Eds.
Ann Saddlemyer, Joseph Ronsley.

792   IT
ISTITUZIONI CULTURALI PIEMONTESI.
PUBBLICAZIONI. 1976. irreg. (Istituzioni Culturali
Piemontesi) Cassa di Risparmio di Torino, Via XX
Settembre 31, Turin, Italy.

792   BE
J E B THEATRE. irreg. (2-3/yr.) Direction Generale
de la Jeunesse et des Loisirs, Galerie Ravenstein 78,
1000 Brussels, Belgium.

820   AU
JACOBEAN DRAMA STUDIES. (Text in English)
1972. irreg., no.100, 1986. S.245. Universitaet
Salzburg, Institut fuer Englische Sprache,
Akademiestr. 24, A-5020 Salzburg, Austria. Ed.
James Hogg. circ. 300. Indexed: M.L.A.

JOURNAL OF BECKETT STUDIES. see
LITERATURE

793.8   US   ISSN 0192-9917
JOURNAL OF MAGIC HISTORY. 1979. irreg.,
approx. 3/yr. $14. Timsco, Box 7149, Toledo, OH
43615. TEL 419-841-2659. Ed. Steven S. Tigner.
bk. rev. film rev. play rev. bibl. charts. illus.
index. circ. 250. Indexed: Hist.Abstr. Amer.Hist.&
Life.

LEEDS MEDIEVAL STUDIES. see *LITERATURE*

792   UK   ISSN 0263-2322
LONDON THEATRE INDEX (YEAR) 1981. a.
£5($10) London Theatre Record, 4 Cross Deep
Gardens, Twickenham, Middx. TW1 4QU, England.
Ed. Ian Herber. adv.

792   US   ISSN 0025-3928
MARQUEE. 1969. q. (plus special annual issue) $20.
Theatre Historical Society of America, 624 Wynne
Rd., Springfield, PA 19064 (Subscr. to: 249 Grattan
St., San Francisco, CA 94117) Eds. Irvin R. Glazer,
Robert Headley, Jr. bk. rev. illus. index. cum.index:
1970-1979. circ. 1,200. (also avail. in microform
from UMI; back issues avail.) Indexed: Avery Ind.
  History

792.02   US   ISSN 0731-3403
MEDIEVAL AND RENAISSANCE DRAMA IN
ENGLAND; an annual gathering of research,
criticism, and reviews. 1984. a. $49.50 hardbound.
A M S Press, Inc., 56 E. 13th St., New York, NY
10003. TEL 212-777-4700. Ed. J. Leeds Barroll, III.
bk. rev. (back issues avail.)

791.53   GW   ISSN 0076-6216
MEISTER DES PUPPENSPIELS. (Text generally in
German; occasionally in Dutch, English and other
languages) 1959. irreg. price varies. Deutsches
Institut fuer Puppenspiel, HAttingerstr. 467, 4630
Bochum, W. Germany (B.R.D.) Ed. Dr. Juergen
Kluender.

MISSOURI SPEECH JOURNAL. see
COMMUNICATIONS

MUSICA, IMMAGINE, TEATRO. see *MUSIC*

NATIONAL ASSOCIATION OF THEATRE
NURSES. ANNUAL CONGRESS HANDBOOK.
see *MEDICAL SCIENCES* — Nurses And
Nursing

792   NE   ISSN 0077-6688
NETHERLANDS. CENTRAAL BUREAU VOOR
DE STATISTIEK. BEZOEK AAN
VERMAKELIJKHEIDSINSTELLINGEN.
ATTENDANCE AT PUBLIC
ENTERTAINMENTS. (Text in Dutch and English)
1940/41. a. fl.6. Centraal Bureau voor de Statistiek,
Prinses Beatrixlaan 428, Voorburg, Netherlands
(Orders to: Staatsuitgeverij, Christoffel
Plantijnstraat, The Hague, Netherlands)

792   NE   ISSN 0168-3519
NETHERLANDS. CENTRAAL BUREAU VOOR
DE STATISTIEK. MUZIEK EN THEATER.
fl.23.95. Centraal Bureau voor de Statistiek, Prinses
Beatrixlaan 428, Voorburg, Netherlands (Orders to:
Staatsuitgeverij, Christoffel Plantijnstraat, The
Hague, Netherlands)
   Formerly: Netherlands. Centraal Bureau voor de
Statistiek. Statistiek van het Gesubsidieerde Toneel.

NEUE WEGE; Kulturzeitschrift junger Menschen. see
CHILDREN AND YOUTH — For

NEW PLAYS U S A. see *LITERATURE*

792 384.55   US
NEW YORK CASTING/SURVIVAL GUIDE; and
datebook. 1980. a. $15. Peter Glenn Publications,
Inc., 17 E. 48th St., New York, NY 10017. TEL
212-688-7940. Ed. Chip Brill. adv.

792   US   ISSN 0028-7784
NEW YORK THEATRE CRITICS' REVIEWS. 1940.
irreg. (18-20/yr.) $90. Proscenium Publications, 4
Park Ave., New York, NY 10016. TEL 212-532-
2570. Eds. Joan Marlowe, Betty Blake. index.
cum.index: 1940-1972; 1973-1985. (looseleaf format)
Indexed: Curr.Cont. Arts & Hum.Cit.Ind.

792   US
NEW YORK TIMES THEATRE REVIEWS. 1870.
biennial. Times Books (Subsidiary of: Random
House, Inc.) 201 E. 50th St., New York, NY
10022-7703. TEL 212-751-2600. illus.

OFFICIAL DIRECTORY OF FESTIVALS, SPORTS
& SPECIAL EVENTS. see *BUSINESS AND
ECONOMICS* — Marketing And Purchasing

792   US
ON-STAGE STUDIES. 1976. a. $3.50. (Colorado
Shakespeare Festival) University of Colorado,
Department of Theatre and Dance, Box 261,
Boulder, CO 80309-0261. TEL 303-492-7355. Ed.
Martin Cobin. circ. 500.
   Formerly: Colorado Shakespeare Festival Annual
(ISSN 0198-831X)

792 910.03   US
OVERTURE; a Black theatre annual. 1981. a. $5. Audience Development Committee, Box 30, Manhattanville Station, New York, NY 10027. Ed. A. Peter Bailey.

800 792   UK   ISSN 0141-1152
OXFORD THEATRE TEXTS. 1972. irreg. price varies. Colin Smythe Ltd., Box 6, Gerrards Cross, Buckinghamshire SL9 8XA, England (Dist. in U.S. by: Humanities Press, 171 First Ave., Atlantic Highlands, NJ 07716) illus.

792 016   US   ISSN 0360-3814
PERFORMING ARTS RESOURCES. 1974. a. membership. Theatre Library Association, 111 Amsterdam Ave., New York, NY 10023. Ed. Barbara Naomi Cohen. circ. 500. Indexed: M.L.A.

792   UK
PLATFORM (LONDON); new perspectives on theatre today. 1979. irreg. £3.25 to individuals; £5.50 to institutions. c/o University of Essex, Department of Literature, Colchester CO4 3SQ, England. Ed.Bd. adv. bk. rev. illus. circ. 1,500.

822   UK   ISSN 0554-3045
PLAYS. A CLASSIFIED GUIDE TO PLAY SELECTION. 1951. a. £2.20($6) Stacey Publications, 1 Hawthorndene Road, Hayes, Bromley, Kent, England. Ed. Roy Stacey. adv. bibl.

800   US
PLAYS & PLAYWRIGHTS. 1985. biennial. $29.95 free. International Society of Dramatists, Box 1310, Miami, FL 33153. TEL 305-756-8313. Ed. A. Delaplaine. circ. 5,600.

800   US   ISSN 0736-0711
PLAYS IN PROCESS. 1980. a. $60. Theatre Communications Group, 355 Lexington Ave., New York, NY 10017. TEL 212-697-5230. Ed. James Leverett. circ. 400. (back issues avail.)

792   US   ISSN 0033-1007
PROLOGUE (MEDFORD) 1945. irreg., (3-4/yr.) free. Tufts University, Department of Drama & Dance, Medford, MA 02155. TEL 617-381-3524. Ed. Downing Cless. play progr. circ. 5,000. Indexed: Amer.Bibl.Slavic & E.Eur.Stud.

792.02   AU   ISSN 0259-0786
QUELLEN ZUR THEATERGESCHICHTE. 1975. irreg., no.3, 1981. price varies. Verband der Wissenschaftlichen Gesellschaften Oesterreichs, Lindengasse 37, A-1070 Vienna, Austria. Ed. Otto Schindler.

792 809   US   ISSN 0486-3739
RENAISSANCE DRAMA. 1967. a. $24.95. Northwestern University Press, 1735 Benson Ave., Evanston, IL 60201. TEL 312-492-5313. Ed. Mary Beth Rose. circ. 1,000. Indexed: Curr.Cont. M.L.A. Arts & Hum.Cit.Ind.

792   US   ISSN 0098-647X
RESEARCH OPPORTUNITIES IN RENAISSANCE DRAMA. 1956. a. free. Modern Language Association of America, Conference on Research Opportunities in Renaissance Drama, c/o David M. Bergeron, Ed., Department of English, University of Kansas, Lawrence, KS 66045. TEL 913-866-2700. adv. bk. rev. play rev. bibl. illus. circ. 1,700. Indexed: M.L.A.

792   UK
SADLER'S WELLS THEATRE PROGRAMME. irreg. £0.70. Sadler's Wells Trust Ltd., Rosebery Ave., London EC1R 4TN, England. adv. bk. rev. bibl. illus. circ. 9,000. (back issues avail.)

792   NE
SCENARIUM; Nederlandse reeks voor theaterwetenschap. 1977. a. fl.25. Nederlands Theater Instituut, Herengracht 166-8, 1016 BP Amsterdam, Netherlands. (Co-sponsor: Theatermuseum Te Amsterdam) Ed.Bd. circ. 1,000.

729   GW   ISSN 0342-4553
SCHAUSPIELFUEHRER; der Inhalt der wichtigsten Theaterstuecke aus aller Welt. 1953. triennial. DM.128 per vol. (Universitaet Wien, Institut fuer Theaterwissenschaft, AU) Anton Hiersemann Verlag, Rosenberger. 113, Postfach 723, 7000 Stuttgart 1, W. Germany (B.R.D.) Ed. Margret Dietrich.

792   SZ
SCHWEIZERISCHE GESELLSCHAFT FUER THEATERKULTUR. JAHRBUECHER. 1928. a. price varies. Schweizerische Gesellschaft fuer Theaterkultur - Swiss Association for Theatre Research, c/o Lydia Benz-Burger, Herenholzweg 33, 8906 Bonstetten, Switzerland.

792   SZ
SCHWEIZERISCHE GESELLSCHAFT FUER THEATERKULTUR. SCHRIFTEN. 1928. irreg., no.16, 1982. Schweizerische Gesellschaft fuer Theaterkultur - Swiss Association for Theatre Research, c/o Lydia Benz-Burger, Herenholzweg 33, 8906 Bonstetten, Switzerland.

SHAVIAN. see LITERATURE

SHOWCALL. see MUSIC

792   AT
SHOWCAST DIRECTORY. 1963. a. Aus.$70. Showcast Publications Pty. Ltd., Box 141, Spit Junction, N.S.W. 2088, Australia.
 Formerly: Showcast General Directory.
 Directory of actors and actresses

792   US
SIMON'S DIRECTORY OF THEATRICAL MATERIALS, SERVICES AND INFORMATION. 1955. irreg. price varies. Package Publicity Service, Inc., 27 W. 24th St., Rm. 402, New York, NY 10010. Ed. Avivah Simon. adv. bk. rev. circ. 10,000.

792   DK   ISSN 0106-665X
SKUESPILREGISTER. 1979. a. Kr.122.35. Bibliotekscentralen, Tempovej 7-11, DK-2750 Ballerup, Denmark.

SO AND SO MAGAZINE. see LITERATURE — Poetry

792   CN
SPONSORS' HANDBOOK FOR THE 80'S/GUIDE DU COMMANDITAIRE POUR LES ANNEES 80. (Editions in English and French) 1975. irreg., latest August, 1983. Can.$10. Canada Council, Touring Office, Box 1047, 99 Metcalfe St., Ottawa, Ont. K1P 5V8, Canada. TEL 613-598-4342.
 Formerly: Sponsors' Handbook for Touring Attractions.

792   ZA
STAGE. (Text in English) 1956. irreg. price varies. Lusaka Theatre Club (Co-Op) Ltd., Box 30615, Lusaka, Zambia. Ed. Mase Mulondiwa. adv. bk. rev. play rev. circ. 300(controlled)

792 380   US
STAGE MANAGERS DIRECTORY. 1983. a. $10. Broadway Press, 120 Duane St., Ste. 407, New York, NY 10007. TEL 212-693-0570. Eds. Cathy B. Blaser, David K. Rodger. circ. 1,000.
 Formerly: Stage Managers' Association Directory.

792 791.43   IE
STAGECAST-IRISH STAGE AND SCREEN DIRECTORY. 1962. biennial. $9. Stagecast Publications, 15 Eaton Square, Monkstown, Dublin County, Ireland. Ed. Derek Young. adv. illus. stat. circ. 500. (back issues avail.)

792   CN   ISSN 0085-6770
STRATFORD FESTIVAL; souvenir book. (Includes: Stratford Festival Story) 1953. a. Can.$10. ‡ Stratford Shakespearean Festival Foundation of Canada, Box 520, Stratford, Ont. N5A 6V2, Canada. TEL 519-271-4040.

792 800   UK
STRATFORD-UPON-AVON STUDIES. 1961. irreg. price varies. Edward Arnold (Publishers) Ltd., 41 Bedford Square, London WC1B 3DQ, England.

890   SW
STRINDBERGIANA. (Text in Swedish) 1985. a. $20. Strinbergssallskapet, Drottninggatan 85, 11160 Stockholm, Sweden. Ed. Anita Persson.

792   US   ISSN 0081-6051
STUBS (METRO N.Y.); the seating plan guide for New York theatres, music halls, sports stadia. 1967. irreg. $6.95. Stubs Communications Co., 234 W. 44th St., New York, NY 10036. TEL 212-398-8370. Ed. Ronald S. Lee. adv. circ. 30,000.

792   PL   ISSN 0208-404X
STUDIA I MATERIALY DO DZIEJOW TEATRU POLSKIEGO. 1957. irreg., vol.17, 1985. price varies. (Polska Akademia Nauk, Instytut Sztuki) Ossolineum, Publishing House of the Polish Academy of Sciences, Rynek 9, Wroclaw, Poland (Dist. by: Ars Polona-Ruch, Krakowskie Przedmiescie 7, Warsaw, Poland)
 Formerly: Studia i Materialy z Dziejow Teatru Polskiego (ISSN 0081-6647)

792 800   US   ISSN 0886-7097
STUDIES IN AMERICAN DRAMA, 1945-PRESENT. 1986. a. $8 (foreign $10) c/o J. Madison Davis, Bus. Mgr., Humanities Div., Pennsylvania State Univ., Behrend College, Erie, PA 16563. TEL 814-898-6108. Eds. Philip C. Kolin, Colby H. Kullman. play rev. bibl. illus. circ. 315. (back issues avail.)

792   RM   ISSN 0039-3991
STUDII SI CERCETARI DE ISTORIA ARTEI. SERIA TEATRU-MUZICA-CINEMATOGRAFIE. (Summaries in English, French, German and Russian) 1954. a. 35 lei($45) (Academia de Stiinte Sociale si Politice) Editura Academiei Republicii Socialiste Rumania, Calea Victoriei 125, 79717 Bucharest, Rumania (Subscr. to: ROMPRESFILATELIA, Calea Grivitei 64-66, P.O. Box 12-201, 78104 Bucharest, Rumania) Ed. Mihnea Gheorghiu. bk. rev. illus. index. Indexed: RILM.
 History

STUDII SI CERCETARI DE ISTORIA ARTEI. SERIA TEATRU, MUZICA, CINEMATOGRAFIE/STUDIES AND RESEARCH IN ART HISTORY. SERIES: THEATRE, MUSIC, CINEMATOGRAPHY. see MOTION PICTURES

792   SZ
SZENE SCHWEIZ/SCENE SUISSE/SCENA SVIZZERA. 1973. a. 25 Fr. Schweizerische Gesellschaft fuer Theaterkultur - Swiss Association for Theatre Research, c/o Lydia Benz-Burger, Herenholzweg 33, 8906 Bonstetten, Switzerland.

792.926   US
T V SWINGERS. 1974. a. $8 per no. Neptune Productions, Box N, Belmar, NJ 07719. TEL 201-449-0299. Ed. Betty Johnson. circ. 10,000.

792   UK   ISSN 0306-9389
TABS. (Text in English; summaries in French and German) 1937. irreg. free. Rank Strand Ltd., Box 51, Great West Rd., Brentford, Middx. TW8 9HR, England. Ed. Richard Harris. bk. rev. charts. illus. circ. 14,000. Indexed: Br.Tech.Ind.

792   DK   ISSN 0901-0106
TEATER FOR BOERN OG UNGE. a. Kr.15. (Tatercentrum i Danmark) Bibliotekscentralen, Telegrafvej 5, DK-2750 Ballerup, Denmark.

792   DK   ISSN 0106-7672
TEATER I DANMARK/THEATRE IN DENMARK. (Text in Danish and English) no.16, 1980. a. Kr.110.65. (Dansk I T I Center - Danish Centre of I T I) Bibliotekscentralen, Tempovej 7-11, DK-2750 Ballerup, Denmark. illus.

792   DK   ISSN 0107-248X
TEATERRAADETS INDSTILLING. 1976. a. free. Ministry of Culture, Danish Theater Council, Frederiksborggade 20/3, 1360 Copenhagen K, Denmark.

792   DK   ISSN 0109-3363
TEATERSEMINAR. 1982. a. Kr.45. Danmarks Teaterforeninger, Frederiksborggade 20/3 m.f., 1360 Copenhagen K, Denmark.

792   IT
TEATRO. irreg. Angelo Longo Editore, Via Paolo Costa 33, P.O. Box 431, 48100 Ravenna, Italy.

792   GW
THEATERPAEDAGOGISCHE BIBLIOTHEK. 1983. irreg., vol.4, 1985. Florian Noetzel Verlag, Heinrichshofen Buecher, Valoisstrasse 11, 2940 Wilhelmshaven, W. Germany (B.R.D.) (Dist. in U.S. by: C.F. Peters Corp., 373 Park Ave. S., New York, NY 10016) Ed. Georg Immelmann, Rudolf Lichtenhan.

792.02 US
THEATRE AND DRAMATIC STUDIES. 1981.
irreg., vol.34, 1986. U M I Research Press, 300 N.
Zeeb Rd., Ann Arbor, MI 48106. Ed. Oscar
Brockett.

792 792 US
THEATRE ANGELS. a. $150. Leo Shull Publications,
1501 Broadway, New York, NY 10036. TEL 212-
354-7600.

792 US ISSN 0082-3821
THEATRE ANNUAL. 1942. a. price varies.
University of Akron, College of Fine Arts and
Applied Arts, c/o Wallace Sterling, Ed.,
Department of Music, Theatre and Dance, Akron,
OH 44325. TEL 216-375-6846. circ. 350. Indexed:
Curr.Cont. M.L.A. Arts & Hum.Cit.Ind.
Abstr.Engl.Stud.

842 FR
THEATRE D'AUJOURD'HUI. 1976. irreg. price
varies. Editons Klincksieck, 11 rue de Lille, 75005
Paris, France.

792 US ISSN 0271-3136
THEATRE DIRECTORY; the annual contact
resource of theatres and related organizations. 1972.
a. $4.95. Theatre Communications Group, 355
Lexington Ave., New York, NY 10017. TEL 212-
697-5230. Ed. John Istel. circ. 5,000.

792 US ISSN 0733-2033
THEATRE HISTORY STUDIES. 1981. a. $6. Mid-
America Theatre Association, c/o Ron Engle, Ed.,
Theatre Arts Department, University of North
Dakota, Box 8182, Grand Forks, ND 58202. TEL
701-777-3446. (Co-sponsor: University of North
Dakota) adv. bk. rev. circ. 700.

792 UK ISSN 0309-8036
THEATRE PAPERS. no.10, 1978. a. Dartington
College of Arts, Department of Theatre, Devon,
England. Ed. Peter Hulton. circ. 4,000.

792 US ISSN 0361-7947
THEATRE PROFILES; an illustrated reference guide
to nonprofit professional theatres in the United
States. 1973. biennial. $18.95. Theatre
Communications Group, 355 Lexington Ave., New
York, NY 10017. TEL 212-697-5230. Ed. Laura
Ross. illus. (back issues avail.)

792 US ISSN 0082-3848
THEATRE STUDENT SERIES. 1968. irreg. price
varies. ‡ Rosen Publishing Group, 29 E. 21st St.,
New York, NY 10010. TEL 212-777-3017. Ed.
Ruth C. Rosen. index from 1968.

792.02 US ISSN 0362-0964
THEATRE STUDIES. 1955. a. $4 to individuals;
institutions $6. ‡ Ohio State University, Theatre
Research Institute, 1089 Drake Union, 1849
Cannon Drive, Columbus, OH 43210. TEL 614-
422-5821. Ed.Bd. bk. rev. bibl. illus. cum.index
vols. 1-20 in vol. 20 (1973-74) circ. 1,200. (also
avail. in microfilm; back issues avail.) Indexed:
Curr.Cont. M.L.A. G.Perf.Arts. Amer.Hum.Ind.
Arts & Hum.Cit.Ind. Abstr.Engl.Stud. T.D.S.I.
G.Perf.Arts.

792.0973 US ISSN 0082-3856
THEATRE WORLD. a. $25. Crown Publishers, Inc.,
One Park Ave., New York, NY 10016. TEL 212-
532-9200. Ed. John Willis.

792 UK ISSN 0263-676X
THEMES IN DRAMA. 1979. a. $32 to individuals;
institutions $55. Cambridge University Press,
Edinburgh Bldg., Shaftesbury Rd., Cambridge CB2
2RU, England (And 32 E. 57th St., New York, NY
10022) Ed. James Redmond. (back issues avail.)

792 CN
TOUR ORGANIZERS' HANDBOOK/GUIDE DU
DIRECTEUR DE TOURNEES DE
SPECTACLES. (Text in English and French) 1977.
irreg., latest May, 1981. Can.$10. Canada Council,
Touring Office, Box 1047, 99 Metcalfe St., Ottawa,
Ont. K1P 5V8, Canada. TEL 613-598-4342.

790.2 CN
TOURING ARTISTS DIRECTORY OF THE
PERFORMING ARTS IN CANADA
(BIENNIAL)/REPERTOIRE DES ARTISITES ET
COMPAGNIES DE TOURNEE AU CANADA.
(Text in English and French) 1975. biennial, latest
1986. Can.$25. Canada Council, Touring Office,
Box 1047, 99 Metcalfe St., Ottawa, Ont. K1P 5V8,
Canada. TEL 613-598-4342. index.

790.2 CN ISSN 0715-755X
TOURING ARTISTS' DIRECTORY OF THE
PERFORMING ARTS IN CANADA (YEAR)/
REPERTOIRE DES ARTISTES ET
COMPAGNIES DE TOURNEES AU CANADA
(YEAR) 1975. a. Can.$25. Touring Office of the
Canada Council - Office des tournees du Conseil
des arts du Canada, Ottawa, Ont., Canada. TEL
613-598-4342. circ. 4,000.
Formerly: Tournees de Spectacles (ISSN 0317-
5979)

792 SP
UNIVERSIDAD DE MURCIA. CATEDRA DE
TEATRO. CUADERNOS. 1978. irreg. Universidad
de Murcia, Catedra de Teatro, Santo Cristo 1,
Murcia, Spain. circ. 2,000.

792.07 TZ
UNIVERSITY OF DAR ES SALAAM. THEATRE
ARTS DEPARTMENT. ANNUAL REPORT. a.
University of Dar es Salaam, Theatre Arts
Department, Box 35091, Dar es Salaam, Tanzania.

792 UR ISSN 0507-3952
VOPROSY TEATRA; sbornik statei i materialov.
1965. a. 1.45 Rub. Vserossiiskoe Teatral'noe
Obshchestvo, Ul. Gorkogo, 16, Moscow, Russian
S.F.S.R., U.S.S.R. (Co-sponsor: Institut Istorii
Iskusstv) bibl. illus.

800 US ISSN 0147-4502
WEST COAST PLAYS. 1977. a. $25. California
Theatre Council, Box 48320, Los Angeles, CA
90048-0320. TEL 213-874-3163. Ed. Robert
Hurwitt. adv. bk. rev. circ. 1,500.

792 AU
WIENER FORSCHUNGEN ZUR THEATER UND
MEDIENWISSENSCHAFT. 1972. irreg. price
varies. (Universitaet Wien, Institut fuer
Theaterwissenschaft) Wilhelm Braumueller,
Universitaets-Verlagsbuchhandlung GmbH,
Servitengasse 5, A-1092 Vienna, Austria. Ed.
Margaret Dietrich. index. circ. 1,000.
Formerly: Vienna. Universitaet. Institut fuer
Theaterwissenschaft. Wissenschaftliche Reihe (ISSN
0083-6176)

792 AU ISSN 0377-0745
WIENER GESELLSCHAFT FUER
THEATERFORSCHUNG. JAHRBUCH. 1944.
irreg., no.27, 1986. price varies. (Wiener
Gesellschaft fuer Theaterforschung) Verband der
Wissenschaftlichen Gesellschaften Oesterreichs,
Lindengasse 37, A-1070 Vienna, Austria. Ed. Otto
G. Schindler. circ. 500.

WINTERFARE. see LITERATURE

THEATER — Abstracting, Bibliographies, Statistics

800 792.8 US ISSN 0742-6933
BIBLIOGRAPHIES AND INDEXES IN THE
PERFORMING ARTS. 1984. irreg. price varies.
Greenwood Press, 88 Post Rd. W., Box 5007,
Westport, CT 06881. TEL 203-226-3571.

011 US
PERFORMING ARTS BIOGRAPHY MASTER
INDEX. 1979. irreg. $170. Gale Research
Company, Book Tower, Detroit, MI 48226. TEL
313-961-2242. Eds. Barbara McNeil, Miranda
Herbert.
Formerly: Theatre, Film, and Television
Biographies Master Index.

792 016 CN
PLAYWRIGHTS UNION OF CANADA
CATALOGUE OF CANADIAN PLAYS. 1977. a.
free. Playwrights Union of Canada, 8 York St., 6th
Floor, Toronto, Ont. M5J 1R2, Canada. TEL 416-
947-0201. Ed. Winston Smith. illus. circ. 10,000.
Formerly: Directory of Canadian Plays and
Playwrights (ISSN 0707-5456)

792 US
THEATRE/DRAMA ABSTRACTS. 1974. 3/yr. (plus
annual cumulation) $33 (with Speech
Communication Abstracts, $50) Theatre, Drama and
Speech Information Center, 1 Erin Court, Pleasant
Hill, CA 94523. Ed. Paul T. Adalian Jr. index. circ.
600. (processed)
Supersedes in part (1975): Theatre/Drama and
Speech Index (ISSN 0094-7822)

THEORY OF COMPUTING

see Computers—Theory of Computing

TOBACCO

679.7 FR
ANNALES DU TABAC. 1963. a. free to qualified
personnel. Societe d'Exploitation Industrielle des
Tabacs et Allumettes, 53 Quai d'Orsay, 75340 Paris,
France. Ed. C. Joigny. bibl. circ. 1,100. Indexed:
Chem.Abstr. Excerp.Med. Field Crop Abstr.
Herb.Abstr. Plant Breed.Absrt. Soils & Fert.
Weed Abstr.

350 679.7 AT ISSN 0404-181X
AUSTRALIA. DEPARTMENT OF PRIMARY
INDUSTRY. TOBACCO INDUSTRY TRUST.
ACCOUNT ANNUAL REPORT. 1956. a. free.
Department of Primary Industry, Field Crop
Division, Edmund Barton Bldg., Broughton St.,
Barton, A.C.T. 2600, Australia.

679.73 GW ISSN 0173-783X
BEITRAEGE ZUR TABAKFORSCHUNG
INTERNATIONAL. (Text in English and German;
summaries in English, French and German) 1961.
irreg. free. Verband der Cigarettenindustrie,
Harvestehuder Weg 88, D-2000 Hamburg 13, W.
Germany (B.R.D.) Ed. Bd. illus. circ. 1,100. (also
avail. in microfilm from UMI) Indexed: Biol.Abstr.
Chem.Abstr. Curr.Cont. Excerp.Med. Sci.Cit.Ind.
Anal.Abstr. Field Crop Abstr. Helminthol.Abstr.
Herb.Abstr.
Formerly (until 1978): Beitraege zur
Tabakforschung (ISSN 0005-819X)

633.71 II
CENTRAL TOBACCO RESEARCH INSTITUTE
AND ITS REGIONAL RESEARCH STATIONS.
ANNUAL REPORT. (Text in English) 1967. a.
exchange basis. Central Tobacco Research Institute,
Rajahmundry 533104, India. Ed.Bd. charts. stat.
circ. 150.
Incorporating: Tobacco Research Institute.
Annual Report; Tobacco Research Station, Hunsur,
Report; Wrapper and Hookah Tobacco Research
Station Report.

COUNCIL FOR TOBACCO RESEARCH--U.S.A.
REPORT. see MEDICAL SCIENCES

DUTY & TAX-FREE SHOP WORLD GUIDE
SERIES. VOL. 3: BEST "N" MOST IN
CIGARETTES, CIGARS AND TOBACCO. see
BUSINESS AND ECONOMICS — International
Commerce

679.7 FR
FEDERATION DES DEBITANTS DE TABAC DE
L'ILE-DE-FRANCE. ANNUAIRE OFFICIEL.
1952. a. Societe Pym, 27 rue Hermel, 75018 Paris,
France. adv. bk. rev. annual index.

679.7 II
INDIA. TOBACCO BOARD. ANNUAL REPORT.
1975. a. Tobacco Board, Box 451, Lakshmipuram,
Guntur 522007, India.

TOBACCO — ABSTRACTING, BIBLIOGRAPHIES, STATISTICS

679.7　　　　　　　　BL
INSTITUTO BAHIANO DO FUMO. BOLETIM INFORMATIVO: COMERCIO EXTERIOR - ESPORTACAO DE FUMO EM FOLHAS. irreg. Instituto Bahiano do Fumo, Rua de Belgica, 2, Edificio Roosevelt, Salvador-Bahia, Brazil.

633.71　　　　　　　　IT
ISTITUTO SPERIMENTALE PER IL TABACCO. ANNALI. (Summaries in English) 1973. a. free. Istituto Sperimentale per il Tabacco, Via P. Vitiello 66, 84018 Scafati, Italy. Ed. Emanuel Marcelli. circ. 1,000. (back issues avail.) Indexed: Biol.Abstr. Field Crop Abstr. Herb.Abstr. Plant Breed.Abstr.

679.7　658.8　　　　　MF
MAURITIUS. TOBACCO BOARD. ANNUAL REPORT. 1932. a. free. Tobacco Board, Plaine Lauzun, Mauritius. Ed.Bd. charts. circ. 325. Indexed: Tob.Abstr.

633.71　　　　　　　　NR
NIGERIAN TOBACCO COMPANY. ANNUAL REPORT AND ACCOUNTS. 1964. a. free. Nigerian Tobacco Company Ltd., Corporate Affairs Department, Western House, 8/10 Broad St., P.O. Box 137, Nigeria. Ed. Irene Ubah. circ. 50,000.
　Formerly: Nigerian Tobacco Company. Report (ISSN 0078-0820)

633.71　633.71　　　　US
NORTH CAROLINA TOBACCO REPORT. 1950. a. free. Department of Agriculture, Box 27647, Raleigh, NC 27611. Ed. John H. Cyrus. charts. stat. circ. 6,000. (back issues avail.)

679.7　　　　　US　ISSN 0363-8480
RECENT ADVANCES IN TOBACCO SCIENCE. 1975. a. $6. Tobacco Chemists' Research Conference, c/o Tobacco Literature Service, 2314 D.H. Hill Library, Raleigh, NC 27695-7111. TEL 919-737-2836. circ. 600. Indexed: Chem.Abstr.

658.8　679.7　　　　　AT
SMOKING HABITS OF AUSTRALIANS. 1973. a. Aus.$87.50. Roy Morgan Research Centre Pty. Ltd., Box 2282U, Melbourne, Vic. 3001, Australia.

338.1　　　　　　　　SA
SOUTH AFRICA. TOBACCO BOARD. ANNUAL REPORT/JAARVERSLAG. 1939/40. a. $0.95. Tobacco Board, Box 26100, Arcadia, Pretoria 0007, South Africa. Ed.Bd. stat. circ. 1,000.
　Continues: South Africa. Tobacco Industry Control Board. Report.

679.7　　　　　US　ISSN 0082-4593
TOBACCO ASSOCIATES. ANNUAL REPORT. 1948. a. free. Tobacco Associates, Inc., 1306 Annapolis Dr., Ste. 102, Raleigh, NC 27605. TEL 919-821-7670. cum.index: 1948-1972. circ. 7,500.

679　918　　　　　　US
TOBACCO: LATIN AMERICAN INDUSTRIAL REPORT. (Avail. for each of 22 Latin American countries) 1985. a. $435 per country report per industry covered. Aurora International, Box 9099, Bridgeport, CT 06601-2099. TEL 203-368-0579. Ed. Andres C. Aquino.

633.71　　　　　　　　US
TOBACCO REPRINT SERIES. 1954. irreg. free to qualified personnel. Tobacco Literature Service, North Carolina State University, Box 7111, 2314 D.H. Hill Library, Raleigh, NC 27695. TEL 919-737-2836. charts. illus. circ. 150(controlled) (tabloid format)

679.7　　　　　US　ISSN 0082-4623
TOBACCO SCIENCE YEARBOOK.* 1958. a. $20. Lockwood Trade Journal Co., Inc., 130 W. 42nd St., New York, NY 10036-7802. index. (reprint service avail. from UMI)

658.8　　　　　　　　UK
TOBACCO TRADE MARKETING DIRECTORY. a. $22. International Trade Publications Ltd., Queensway House, 2 Queensway, Redhill, Surrey RH1 1QS, England.
　Incorporating: Tobacco Directory and Diary (ISSN 0264-5394) & Tobacco Trade Year Book and Diary (ISSN 0082-4631) & Smoker's Handbook (ISSN 0081-0355)

658.8　679.7　　　　US　ISSN 0083-3479
UNITED STATES TOBACCO AND CANDY JOURNAL SUPPLIER DIRECTORY. 1963. a. $10. B M T Publications, Inc., 254 W. 31st St., New York, NY 10001. TEL 212-594-4120. Ed. Jerry Sullivan. adv. index. circ. 5,000.
　Formerly: United States Tobacco Journal Supplier Directory.

679.7　　　　　UK　ISSN 0084-2273
WORLD TOBACCO DIRECTORY. (Text in English; summaries in French, German, Spanish) 1938. a. $78. International Trade Publications Ltd., Queensway House, 2 Queensway, Redhill, Surrey RH1 1QS, England. adv.

679.7　　　　　　　　RH
ZIMBABWE. TOBACCO RESEARCH BOARD. ANNUAL REPORT AND ACCOUNTS. 1954/55. a. free. ‡ Tobacco Research Board, Box 1909, Harare, Zimbabwe. circ. 660.
　Formerly: Zimbabwe-Rhodesia. Tobacco Research Board. Annual Report and Accounts (ISSN 0080-2875)

TOBACCO — Abstracting, Bibliographies, Statistics

338.4　　　　　CN　ISSN 0300-0249
CANADA. STATISTICS CANADA. TOBACCO PRODUCTS INDUSTRIES/INDUSTRIE DU TABAC. (Catalogue 32-225) (Text in English, French) 1918. a. Can.$20($21) Statistics Canada, Communications Division, 3rd Floor, R.H. Coats Bldg., Ottawa, Ont. K1A 0T6, Canada TEL 613-993-7276. (Subscr. to: Publications Sales and Services, Ottawa, Ont. K1A 0T6, Canada) (also avail. in microform from MML)

658.8　336　310　　US　ISSN 0563-6191
TAX BURDEN ON TOBACCO. 1966. a. Tobacco Institute, 1875 I St.,N.W., Washington, DC 20006. TEL 202-457-4800. stat. circ. 2,500.

633.71　016　　　　US　ISSN 0040-8298
TOBACCO ABSTRACTS; world literature on Nicotiana. 1957. bi-m. $15. Tobacco Literature Service, 2314 D. H. Hill Library, North Carolina State University, Raleigh, NC 27695-7111. TEL 919-737-2836. Ed. Pamela E. Puryear. abstr. index. circ. 500. Indexed: Field Crop Abstr. Herb.Abstr. Plant Breed.Abstr.

679.7　016　　　　UK　ISSN 0563-6140
TOBACCO BIBLIOGRAPHY. 1955. s-m. £162.75. ‡ Imperial Tobacco Ltd., P.O. Box 244, Hartcliffe, Bristol BS99 7UJ, England. TEL 0272-781111. Ed.Bd. bibl. circ. 80.

633.71　679.7　317　　US
U.S. AGRICULTURAL MARKETING SERVICE. ANNUAL REPORT ON TOBACCO STATISTICS. (Subseries of U.S.D.A. Statistical Bulletin) a. $2. U.S. Agricultural Marketing Service, Washington, DC 20250. TEL 202-447-3489. stat. (tabloid format)

TRADE AND INDUSTRIAL DIRECTORIES

see Business and Economics—Trade and Industrial Directories

TRANSPORTATION

see also Transportation—Air Transport; Transportation—Automobiles; Transportation—Computer Applications; Transportation—Railroads; Transportation—Roads and Traffic; Transportation—Ships and Shipping; Transportation—Trucks and Trucking

380.5　　　　　CN　ISSN 0702-7702
ALBERTA TRANSPORTATION. ANNUAL REPORT. 1975. a. Alberta Transportation, Public Communications Office, Main floor, Twin Atria, 4999-98 Ave., Edmonton, Alta. T6B 2X3, Canada. TEL 403-427-7674. circ. 600. (also avail. in microfiche from MML)
　Formerly: Alberta. Department of Transportation. Annual Report (ISSN 0318-4757)

388.322　　　　US　ISSN 0278-1565
AMERICAN BUS ASSOCIATION. REPORT. 1927. a. American Bus Association, 1025 Connecticut Ave., N.W., Washington, DC 20036. TEL 202-293-5890. stat.
　Former titles: American Bus Association. Annual Report (ISSN 0738-2685); Incorporating (as of 1977): Bus Facts (ISSN 0734-5917)

380.5　　　　　FR　ISSN 0066-3549
ANNUAIRE NATIONAL DES TRANSPORTS. 1948. a. 470 F. Editions Louis Johanet, 68 rue Boursault, 75017 Paris, France. adv.

380.5　　　　　UN　ISSN 0066-3859
ANNUAL BULLETIN OF TRANSPORT STATISTICS FOR EUROPE. (Text in English, French and Russian) 1950. a., latest vol.35, 1983. price varies. Economic Commission for Europe (ECE), Palais des Nations, 1211 Geneva 10, Switzerland (Or United Nations Publications, Rm. DC2-853, New York, NY 10017)

380.5　　　　　　　　SP
ANO DEL TRANSPORTE. 1976. a. 1000 ptas. Edisport S.L., Isaac Peral 12, Madrid, Spain. illus.

380.52　　　　　　　BL
ANUARIO ESTATISTICO DOS TRANSPORTES. 1970. a. free. Empresa Brasileira de Planejamento de Transportes, G E I P O T, San Quadro 3 LoteA, 70,040 Brasilia, DF, Brazil. circ. 1,000.

380.1　　　　　　　　UK
ARABIAN TRANSPORT GUIDE. a. $65. Beacon Publications PLC, York House, Newton Close, Park Farm, Wellingborough, Northamptonshire NN8 3UW, England.

380.5　388.3　　　　　AT
AUSTRALIAN ROAD RESEARCH BOARD. RESEARCH REPORT. 1975. irreg. Aus.$12 per no. Australian Road Research Board, 500 Burwood Rd., Vermont South, Vic. 3133, Australia. circ. 350. (back issues avail.)

380.5　388.3　　　　AT　ISSN 0572-144X
AUSTRALIAN ROAD RESEARCH BOARD. SPECIAL REPORT. 1966. irreg. Aus.$30($20) per copy. Australian Road Research Board, 500 Burwood Highway, Vermont South, Vic. 3150, Australia. TEL 03-235-1555. circ. 350. (also avail. in microfiche; back issues avail.)

380.5　388.3　　　　AT　ISSN 0313-895X
AUSTRALIAN ROAD RESEARCH BOARD. TECHNICAL MANUAL. 1977. irreg. Aus.$10($7) per copy. Australian Road Reseach Board, 500 Burwood Highway, Vermont South, Vic. 350, Australia. circ. 350. (also avail. in microfiche; back issues avail.)

380.5　　　　　AT　ISSN 0311-628X
AUSTRALIAN TRANSPORT. 1973/74. a. price varies. Australian Government Publishing Service, G.P.O. Box 84, Canberra, A.C.T. 2601, Australia. charts. illus. stat.
　Formerly: Australia. Department of Civil Aviation. Civil Aviation Report (ISSN 0572-0400)

380.5　310　　　　AT　ISSN 0811-3688
AUSTRALIAN TRANSPORT INFORMATION DIRECTORY. 1982. a. Aus.$3.90. (Bureau of Transport Economics) Australian Government Publishing Service (Griffith), 109 Canberra Ave, Griffith, ACT 2603, Australia (Subscr. to: Mail Order Sales, GPO Box 84, Canberra, ACT 2601, Australia) Ed.Bd. circ. 400. (back issues avail.)
　●Also available online. Vendors: Bureau of Transport Economics.

380.52　001.6　　　US　ISSN 0739-9022
AUTOMATED MATERIALS HANDLING AND STORAGE.* 1983. a. (plus m. updates) $140. Auerbach Publishers, Inc., One Penn Plaza, New York, NY 10119. TEL 609-662-2070.

B I C-CODE. (Bureau International des Containers-Code) see *PACKAGING*

380.5 US
BATTERY COUNCIL INTERNATIONAL. CONVENTION MINUTES. 1975. a. $15. Battery Council International, 111 E. Wacker Dr., Chicago, IL 60601. TEL 312-644-6610. abstr. charts. illus. stat. circ. 750.

380.52 UK
BRITAIN'S FREIGHT-FORWARDING INDUSTRY. 1986. irreg. £95($150) Jordan & Sons Ltd., Jordan House, 47 Brunswick House, London N1 6EE, England.

380.52 387 UK
BULK HANDLING & TRANSPORT. 1977. biennial. price varies. C. S. Publications Ltd., 54 Cheam Common Rd., Worcester Park, Surrey KT4 8RJ, England. Ed. Patrick Finley. circ. 2,000.

388.322 US
BUS GARAGE INDEX. 1967. a. $12. Friendship Publications, Inc., Spokane, WA 99210-1472. Ed. William A. Luke. circ. 2,000.

338.3 US ISSN 0363-3764
BUS RIDE: BUS INDUSTRY DIRECTORY. Spine title: Bus Industry Directory. 1972. a. $40. Friendship Publications, Inc., Box 1472, Spokane, WA 99210-1472. TEL 509-328-9181. Ed. William A. Luke. adv. circ. 1,500.

380.5 CN ISSN 0068-9912
CANADA. TRANSPORT COMMISSION. ANNUAL REPORT. (Text in English and French) 1968. a. free. Canadian Transport Commission, 275 Slater St., Ottawa, Ont. K1A 0N9, Canada TEL 819-997-4035. (Subscr. to: Supply and Services Canada, Publications Division, Ottawa, Ont. K1A 0S9, Canada) circ. 7,500.

380.5 384 CN
CANADIAN NATIONAL ANNUAL REPORT. (Editions in English and French) 1923. a. free. Canadian National Railways, Corporate Communications, P.O. Box 8100, Montreal, Que H3C 3N4, Canada. Ed. D.E. Todd. circ. 35,000. (also avail. in microfiche)

711.7 II ISSN 0069-1690
CENTRAL ROAD RESEARCH INSTITUTE, NEW DELHI. ROAD RESEARCH PAPER. (Text in English) 1956. irreg., no.178, 1982. free. Central Road Research Institute, P.O. Central Road Research Institute, New Delhi 110020, India. (Affiliate: Council of Scientific and Industrial Research) circ. controlled. Indexed: Chem.Abstr. Eng.Ind.

380.5 NR
CHARTERED INSTITUTE OF TRANSPORT. ANNUAL. 1959. a. Chartered Institute of Transport, Nigerian Ports Authority, 51 Herbert Macauley St., Ebuke-metta, Lagos, Nigeria. adv.

380.5 UK ISSN 0306-9559
CHARTERED INSTITUTE OF TRANSPORT. HANDBOOK. 1930. a. free. Chartered Institute of Transport, 80 Portland Place, London W1N 4DP, England. Ed. L.F. Aldridge. circ. 5,000.

380.5 US
CHICAGO AREA TRANSPORTATION STUDY. ANNUAL REPORT. irreg., latest 1981. Chicago Area Transportation Study, 300 W. Adams St., Chicago, IL 60606. TEL 312-793-7433. charts. illus.

380.5 UK
COMMERCIAL VEHICLE & BUYER'S GUIDE. 1981. a. £12.95. Kogan Page Ltd., 120 Pentonville Rd., London N1 9JN, England. Ed. Christopher Mann. adv. illus. charts.
Former titles: Commercial Vehicle and P S V Buyer's Guide (ISSN 0261-0450); Shell Commercial Vehicle and P S V Buyer's Guide; Commercial Vehicle Buyer's Guide (ISSN 0141-5743)

385 EI
COMMISSION OF THE EUROPEAN COMMUNITIES. EUROPA TRANSPORT. ANNUAL REPORT. (Supplement to: C E C Documentation Bulletin) 1980. a. $4. Commission of the European Communities, Directorate-General for Transport, 200, rue de la Loi, 1049 Brussels, Belgium. circ. 3,500.

388 US ISSN 0069-9039
CONNECTICUT MASTER TRANSPORTATION PLAN. 1971. a. Department of Transportation (Conndot), c/o Director of Planning, Bureau of Planning & Research, 24 Wolcott Hill Rd., Wethersfield, CT 06109. TEL 203-566-5114. circ. 1,000.
Incorporating (as of 1973): Connecticut Highway Needs Report.

380.52 380.1 GW
CONTAINER CONTACTS. 1971. a. DM.33. K.O. Storck Verlag, Stahltwiete 7, 2000 Hamburg 50, W. Germany (B.R.D.) Ed. H. Meder.

658.7 UK ISSN 0305-7402
CONTAINERISATION INTERNATIONAL YEARBOOK. 1968. a. £67. National Magazine Co. Ltd., 72 Broadwick St., London W1V 2BP, England. Ed. Mark Lambert. adv. illus. circ. 2,500.

CUMBRIA & NORTH LANCASHIRE INDUSTRY AND BUILDING INDUSTRY YEAR BOOK. see *BUSINESS AND ECONOMICS*

629.2 DK
D V BOGEN. 1960. a. Danske Vognmaend Hovedorganisationen, Gammeltorv 18, 1457 Copenhagen K, Denmark. cum.index: 1960-1981 in no. 22.
Formerly: L D V Bogen.

380.52 DK ISSN 0900-1999
DANMARKS TRANSPORT. TIDENDES DESTINATIONREGISTER. 1985. a. Kr.58.55. Forlaget Erik Larsen A-S, Soendervangen 47, 34600 Birkeroed, Denmark.

380.5 US
DATA RESOURCES TRANSPORTATION REVIEW. a. Data Resources, 24 Hartwell Ave., Lexington, MA 02173. TEL 617-863-5100.

380.5 GW ISSN 0070-4210
DEUTSCHE KRAFTFAHRTFORSCHUNG UND STRASSENVERKEHRSTECHNIK. 1938. irreg. (Verein Deutscher Ingenieure) V D I-Verlag GmbH, Graf Recke Str. 84, Postfach 1139, 4000 Duesseldorf 1, W. Germany (B.R.D.) circ. 500.

380.5 GW
DEUTSCHE VERKEHRSWISSENSCHAFTLICHE GESELLSCHAFT. SCHRIFTENREIHE. REIHE A. DOKUMENTATION. 1965. a. DM.39. Deutsche Verkehrswissenschaftliche Gesellschaft, Bruederstr. 53, 5060 Bergisch Gladbach 1, W. Germany (B.R.D.) Ed. K. Thielen. bk. rev. circ. 1,800.

380.5 NE
DEVELOPMENTS IN TRANSPORT STUDIES. 1980. irreg. price varies. Martinus Nijhoff, Spuiboulevard 50, 3311 GR Dordrecht, Netherlands.

380.5 US ISSN 0270-8264
DIRECTORY OF RESEARCH, DEVELOPMENT AND DEMONSTRATION PROJECTS. a. U.S. Urban Mass Transportation Administration, 400 Seventh St. S.W., Washington, DC 20590. TEL 202-246-4043. illus.
Former titles: Improving Urban Mobility (ISSN 0270-8248) & Directory of Research, Development, and Demonstrations.

380.5 US
DWIGHT'S TRUCK EQUIPMENT MANUAL. 1963. a. free to qualified personnel. Dwight Publishing Company, 4782 N. Cumberland Blvd., Milwaukee, WI 53211. Ed. Roth D. Row. adv. circ. 4,500.
Formerly: Dwight's Special Truck Equipment Manual.

380.5 NE
E W SPECIAL; transport en verpakking. no.2, 1976. irreg. fl.1 per no. B. V. Uitgeversmaatschappij Bonaventura, Box 152, Amsterdam, Netherlands. Ed. J. Folkerstma.

380.5 FR
ENQUETE PERMANENTE SUR L'UTILISATION DES VEHICULES DE TRANSPORT EN COMMUN DE PERSONNES EN (YEAR) 1979. a. Observatoire Economique et Statistique des Transports, 55 rue Brillat-Savarin, 75658 Paris Cedex 13, France. Ed. Yves Jacquin. circ. 1,000.

380.5 001.5 PN ISSN 0378-7389
ESTADISTICA PANAMENA. SITUACION ECONOMICA. SECCION 333 Y 334. TRANSPORTE Y COMUNICACIONES. 1958. a. Bl.0.75. Direccion de Estadistica y Censo, Contraloria General, Apartado 5213, Panama 5, Panama. circ. 1,200.

380.5 SZ ISSN 0071-3120
EUROPEAN PASSENGER TRAIN TIMETABLE CONFERENCE MINUTES. (Text in French, German, Italian and Russian) 1923. a. membership. Chemins de Fer Federaux Suisses - Swiss Federal Railways, Hochschulstr. 6, CH-3030 Berne, Switzerland. circ. 550 (controlled)

380.52 UK
F T A YEARBOOK. 1963. a. membership. Freight Transport Association Ltd., Hermes House, St. Johns Rd., Tunbridge Wells TN4 9UZ, England. adv. circ. 21,000.

388.3 US ISSN 0092-0177
FLORIDA. DIVISION OF MOTOR VEHICLES. TAGS AND REVENUE. 1928. a. free. Department of Highway Safety and Motor Vehicles, Division of Administrative Services, Neil Kirkman Building, Tallahassee, FL 32304. TEL 904-488-6084. circ. 1,000.

388 UK ISSN 0071-9471
FREIGHT INDUSTRY YEARBOOK; classified reference and guide for transport vehicle manufacturers, operators and users. 1950. a. £25. Guardian Communications Ltd., Third Floor, Abany House, Hurst St., Birmingham B5 4BD, England. Ed. E.M. Gibbins. adv.
Formerly: Goods Vehicle Year Book.

388 UK
GLASS'S COMMERCIAL VEHICLE CHECK BOOK. a. £10. Glass's Guide Service Ltd., Elgin House, St. George's Ave., Weybridge, Surrey KT13 0BX, England. adv.

380.5 GW ISSN 0073-019X
HANDBUCH OEFFENTLICHER VERKEHRSBETRIEBE. 1952. biennial. price varies. (Verband Oeffentlicher Verkehrsbetriebe) Erich Schmidt Verlag GmbH (Bielefeld), Viktoriastr. 44A, Postfach 7330, 4800 Bielefeld 1, W. Germany (B.R.D.) adv.

658.7 US
HANDLING & SHIPPING MANAGEMENTS PRESIDENTIAL ISSUE. a. $10. Penton Publishing, 1100 Superior Ave., Cleveland, OH 44114. TEL 216-696-7000. Ed. Art Eddy. adv. illus. (reprint service avail. from UMI)
Formerly: Handling and Shipping. Presidential Issue.

380.5 387 FR
INSTITUT MEDITERRANEEN DES TRANSPORTS MARITIMES. (Text in French; Summaries in English) 1984. a. 100 Fr.($14) Edisud, La Calade, RN 7, 13090 Aix-en-Provence, France. bk. rev. (back issues avail.)

388 PL
INSTYTUT TRANSPORTU SAMOCHODOWEGO. ZESZYTY NAUKOWE. (Text in Polish; summaries in English and Russian) 1962. irreg. (approx. 4-6/yr.) Instytut Transportu Samochodowego, Stalingradzka 40, Warsaw, Poland. bk. rev. illus. stat. pat. circ. controlled.

385.1 BE ISSN 0378-1968
INTERNATIONAL STATISTICAL HANDBOOK OF URBAN PUBLIC TRANSPORT/RECUEIL INTERNATIONAL DE STATISTIQUES DES TRANSPORTS PUBLICS URBAINS/ INTERNATIONALES STATISTIK-HANDBUCH FUER DEN OEFFENTLICHEN STADTVERKEHR. 1964. quinquennial. 4500 Fr.($105) International Union of Public Transport, Av. de l'Uruguay 19, B-1050 Brussels, Belgium.
Supersedes: International Union of Public Transport. Transports Publics dans les Principales Villes du Monde (ISSN 0539-113X)

INTERNATIONAL SYMPOSIUM ON THE AERODYNAMICS AND VENTILATION OF VEHICLE TUNNELS. PROCEEDINGS. see *ENGINEERING — Civil Engineering*

INTERNATIONAL TRANSPORT WORKERS'
FEDERATION REPORT ON ACTIVITIES. see
LABOR UNIONS

386   BE   ISSN 0074-9311
INTERNATIONAL UNION FOR INLAND
NAVIGATION. ANNUAL REPORT. (Editions in
English, French, and German) 1953. a. free.
International Union for Inland Navigation - Union
Internationale de la Navigation Fluviale, 19 rue de
la Presse, 1000 Brussels, Belgium.

380.5   BE
INTERNATIONAL UNION OF PUBLIC
TRANSPORT. PROCEEDINGS OF THE
INTERNATIONAL CONGRESS. biennial. $15.
International Union of Public Transport, Av. de
l'Uruguay 19, B-1050 Brussels, Belgium.
    Formerly: International Union of Public
Transport. Reports and Proceedings of the
International Congress (ISSN 0074-9494)

380.5   BE
INTERNATIONAL UNION OF PUBLIC
TRANSPORT. TECHNICAL REPORTS OF THE
CONGRESSES. French edition: Union
Internationale des Transports Publics. Rapports
Techniques des Congres Internationaux. German
edition: Internationaler Verband fuer Oeffentliches
Verkehrswesen. Technische Berichte zu den
Internationalen Kongressen. (Editions in English,
French, and German) 1885. biennial. price varies.
International Union of Public Transport, Av. de
l'Uruguay 19, B-1050 Brussels, Belgium. adv. circ.
18,000.

380.5   UR   ISSN 0134-7799
ITOGI NAUKI I TEKHNIKI: ORGANIZATSIYA
UPRAVLENIYA TRANSPORTOM (VINITI).
irreg., vol.6, 1987. price varies. Vsesoyuznyi Institut
Nauchno-Tekhnicheskoi Informatsii (VINITI),
Baltiiskaya ul. 14, Moscow 121200, Russian
S.F.S.R., U.S.S.R.

380.52   UR   ISSN 0202-7909
ITOGI NAUKI I TEKHNIKI: PROMYSHLENNYI
TRANSPORT. irreg., latest vol.11, 1986. price
varies. Vsesoyuznyi Institut Nauchno-Tekhnicheskoi
Informatsii (VINITI), Baltiiskaya ul. 14, Moscow A-
219, Russian S.F.S.R., U.S.S.R. (Subscr. to:
Mezhdunarodnaya Kniga, Dimitrova ul. 39, 113095
Moscow, Russian S.F.S.R., U.S.S.R.)

380.5   UK
JANE'S URBAN TRANSPORT SYSTEMS. 1982. a.
£48.50($110) Jane's Publishing Co., 238 City Rd.,
London EC1V 2PU, England (Subscr.to: Jane's
Publishing Inc., 20 Park Plaza, Boston, MA 02116)
Eds. Chris Bushen, Peter Storham. adv. index.

380.5   PK   ISSN 0075-5109
KARACHI PORT TRUST. YEAR BOOK OF
INFORMATION, PORT OF KARACHI,
PAKISTAN. (Text in English) 1961. a. Rs.45.
Karachi Port Trust, Kafil Ahmed, Karachi, Pakistan.

380.52   DK   ISSN 0108-8335
KRAKS TRANSPORTKATALOG. 1973. a. Kr.135.
Kraks Legat, Nytorv 17, DK-1450 Copenhagen K,
Denmark. adv. circ. 9,000.

LAMY TRANSPORT. see *LAW — International Law*

LIBERIA. MINISTRY OF COMMERCE,
INDUSTRY AND TRANSPORTATION.
ANNUAL REPORT. see *BUSINESS AND
ECONOMICS — Production Of Goods And
Services*

388.322   UK   ISSN 0076-0013
LITTLE RED BOOK, CLASSIFIED TO ALL
PUBLIC TRANSPORT FLEET OWNERS AND
OPERATORS AND VEHICLE
MANUFACTURERS. 1899. a. price varies. Ian
Allan Ltd., Coombelands House, Addlestone,
Weybridge, Surrey KT15 0HY, England. Ed.
Stephen Morris. adv. circ. 2,250. (reprint service
avail. from UMI)
    Formerly: Passenger Transport Year Book.

MALAWI. NAITONAL STATISTICAL OFFICE.
TRANSPORT STATISTICS. see
*TRANSPORTATION — Abstracting,
Bibliographies, Statistics*

     MF   ISSN 0076-5554
MAURITIUS. MINISTRY OF WORKS AND
INTERNAL COMMUNICATIONS. REPORT. a.
price varies. Government Printing
Office, Elizabeth II Ave., Port Louis, Mauritius.

380.5   US
MODERN TIRE DEALER PRODUCTS
CATALOG. 1972. a. $10. ‡ Bill Communications
Inc., 110 N. Miller Rd., Akron, OH 44313. TEL
216-867-4401. Ed. David Burkhardt. adv. circ. 33,
000(controlled) (reprint service avail. from UMI)

380.5   NZ
MOTOR INDUSTRY YEAR BOOK. 1947. a.
NZ.$23. New Zealand Motor Trade Federation, Box
390, Wellington, New Zealand. Ed. R.C. Morpeth.
adv. circ. 1,000.

381.41   US   ISSN 0094-2790
MOVEMENT OF CALIFORNIA FRUITS AND
VEGETABLES BY RAIL, TRUCK, AND AIR. a.
$4. Federal-State Market News Service, 1220 N St.,
Sacramento, CA 95814. stat.

380.5   US
N F T A ANNUAL REPORT. 1967. a. free. Niagara
Frontier Transportation Authority, Public Relations
Director, 181 Ellicott St., Buffalo, NY 14205. TEL
716-855-7300. circ. 500.

380.5   NE
N I W O MEDEDELINGEN. irreg. Nederlandsche
Internationale Wegvervoer Organisatie, Postbus 104,
2280 AC Rijswijk, Netherlands. adv. circ. 2,
500(controlled)

380.5   US   ISSN 0547-5554
NATIONAL COOPERATIVE HIGHWAY
RESEARCH PROGRAM RESEARCH RESULTS
DIGEST. irreg., no.145, 1985. price varies. National
Research Council, Transportation Research Board,
2101 Constitution Ave., N.W., Washington, DC
20418. TEL 202-334-2934.

380.5   US
NATIONAL COOPERATIVE TRANSIT
RESEARCH AND DEVELOPMENT PROGRAM.
MISCELLANEOUS PUBLICATIONS. irreg., latest
1985. price varies. National Research Council,
Transportation Research Board, 2101 Constitution
Ave., N.W., Washington, DC 20418. TEL 202-334-
2934.

380.5   US
NATIONAL COOPERATIVE TRANSIT
RESEARCH AND DEVELOPMENT PROGRAM.
RESEARCH RESULTS DIGEST. irreg., latest
no.4, 1985. price varies. National Research Council,
Transportation Research Board, 2101 Constitution
Ave., N.W., Washington, DC 20418. TEL 202-334-
2934.

380.5   US
NATIONAL COOPERATIVE TRANSIT
RESEARCH & DEVELOPMENT PROGRAM.
SUMMARY OF PROGRESS THROUGH (YEAR)
1964. a. National Cooperative Transit Research &
Development Program, Transportation Research
Board, 2101 Constitution Ave., N.W., Washington,
DC 20418. Helen Mack. circ. 4,000. (also avail. in
microfiche)
    Formerly: National Cooperative Transit Research
and Development Program. Summary of Progress.

380.5   US   ISSN 0732-4839
NATIONAL COOPERATIVE TRANSIT
RESEARCH AND DEVELOPMENT PROGRAM
REPORT. irreg., no.12, 1985. price varies. National
Research Council, Transportation Research Board,
2101 Constitution Ave., N.W., Washington DC
20418. TEL 202-334-2934.

380.5   US   ISSN 0732-1856
NATIONAL COOPERATIVE TRANSIT
RESEARCH AND DEVELOPMENT PROGRAM
SYNTHESIS OF TRANSIT PRACTICE. irreg.,
no.6, 1985. price varies. National Research Council,
Transportation Research Board, 2101 Constitution
Ave., N.W., Washington, DC 20418. TEL 202-334-
2934.

NATIONAL INSTITUTE FOR TRANSPORT AND
ROAD RESEARCH. ANNUAL REPORT/
NASIONALE INSTITUUT VIR VERVOER- EN
PADNAVORSING. JAARVERSLAG. see
TRANSPORTATION — Roads And Traffic

380.5   US   ISSN 0148-849X
NATIONAL RESEARCH COUNCIL.
TRANSPORTATION RESEARCH BOARD.
BIBLIOGRAPHY. no.62, 1984. irreg. price varies.
National Research Council, Transportation Research
Board, 2101 Constitution Ave., N.W., Washington,
DC 20418. TEL 202-334-2934. bibl.

387   623.89   AT   ISSN 0077-6262
NAVIGATION. 1959. a. $4. Australian Institute of
Navigation, Box 2250 G.P.O, Sydney, N.S.W,
Australia. Ed. S. Cohen. adv. bk. rev. circ. 600.
Indexed: Int.Aerosp.Abstr.

388   387   NE   ISSN 0168-5074
NETHERLANDS. CENTRAAL BUREAU VOOR
DE STATISTIEK. STATISTIEK VAN HET
PERSONENVERVOER. STATISTICS OF
PASSENGER TRANSPORT. (Text in Dutch and
English) 1943. a. fl.14.10. Centraal Bureau voor de
Statistiek, Prinses Beatrixlaan 428, Voorburg,
Netherlands (Orders to: Staatsuitgeverij, Christoffel
Plantijnstraat, The Hague, Netherlands)

380.5   US
NEW JERSEY. DEPARTMENT OF
TRANSPORTATION. ANNUAL REPORT. 1894.
a. free. Department of Transportation, 1035
Parkway Ave., CN 600, Trenton, NJ 08625. charts.
illus.
    Former titles (1975-1977): New Jersey.
Department of Transportation. Highlight of
Activities; 1970-1974: New Jersey. Department of
Transportation. Report of Operations (ISSN 0085-
395X); Until 1970: New Jersey. Department of
Transportation. Annual Report.

380   NZ   ISSN 0110-3458
NEW ZEALAND. DEPARTMENT OF
STATISTICS. TRANSPORT STATISTICS. a.
NZ.$7.15. Department of Statistics, Private Bag,
Wellington, New Zealand (Subscr. to: Government
Printing Office, Publications, Private Bag,
Wellington, New Zealand)

380.5   614.86   NZ
NEW ZEALAND. MINISTRY OF TRANSPORT.
TRAFFIC RESEARCH CIRCULAR. 1974. irreg.
Ministry of Transport, Private Bag, Wellington, New
Zealand.

380.5   388.413   NZ   ISSN 0110-6872
NEW ZEALAND. MINISTRY OF TRANSPORT.
TRAFFIC RESEARCH REPORT. 1974. irreg.
Ministry of Transport, Private Bag, Wellington, New
Zealand. circ. 700.

380.5   330   DK   ISSN 0359-7601
NORDISK KOMITE FOR
TRANSPORTOEKONOMISK FORSKNING.
PUBLIKATION. (Text in Danish or Swedish)
irreg., no.41, 1983. free. Nordisk Komite for
Transportoekonomisk Forskning, Ministeriet for
Offentlige Arbejder, Planlaegningsafdelingen,
Frederikholms Kanal 27, DK-1220 Copenhagen K,
Denmark.

380.5   US
NORTHWESTERN UNIVERSITY.
TRANSPORTATION CENTER. PUBLICATIONS
LIST. 1978. a. free. Northwestern University,
Transportation Center, 1936 Sheridan Rd.,
Evanston, IL 60201. TEL 312-492-7287. circ. 2,500.

380.5   II   ISSN 0079-2381
POCKET BOOK OF TRANSPORT STATISTICS OF
INDIA. 1968. a. $12.96. Ministry of Shipping and
Transport, Transport Research Division, I D A
Bldg, Jamnagar House, Shahjahan Rd., New Delhi
110011, India (Orders to: Controller of Publications,
Civil Lines, Delhi 110006, India)
    Formerly: India Transport Statistics.

380.5   PL   ISSN 0860-0783
POLITECHNIKA KRAKOWSKA. ZESZYTY
NAUKOWE. TRANSPORT. (Text in Polish;
summaries in English, French, German and Russian)
1977. irreg. price varies. Politechnika Krakowska,
Ul. Warszawska 24, 31-155 Krakow, Poland (Dist.
by: Ars Polona-Ruch, Krakowskie Przedmiescie 7,
00-068 Warsaw, Poland) bibl. charts. illus. circ.
200.

380.5 PL ISSN 0209-3324
POLITECHNIKA SLASKA. ZESZYTY NAUKOWE. TRANSPORT. 1983. irreg. Politechnika Slaska, W. Pstrowskiego 7, 44-100 Gliwice, Poland (Dist. by: Ars Polona, Krakowskie Przedmiescie 7, 00-068 Warsaw, Poland) Ed. Barbara Maciejna.

387 US ISSN 0085-5030
PORT OF NEW ORLEANS ANNUAL DIRECTORY. 1969. a. free to qualified personnel. Port of New Orleans, 2 Canal St., Box 60046, New Orleans, LA 70160. TEL 504-528-3249. Ed. Russ Greenbaum. adv. bk. rev. charts. illus. stat. circ. 18,000 (controlled)

380.5 JA
PROBLEMS OF TRANSPORTATION IN JAPAN. (Text in English) 1975. irreg. Institute of Transportation Economics - Un'Yu Chosakyoku, 2-5-6 Izumicho Kokubunji, Tokyo, Japan.

PROBLEMY PRAWA PRZEWOZOWEGO. see LAW

380.5 CN ISSN 0702-0996
QUEBEC (PROVINCE). COMMISSION DES TRANSPORTS DU QUEBEC. RAPPORT ANNUEL.* a. (Commission des Transports du Quebec) Editeur Officiel du Quebec, 1283 Bd. Charest Ouest, Quebec, P.Q. G1N 2C9, Canada. TEL 413-643-3895.
 Formerly: Quebec (Province). Commission des Transports. Rapports des Activites de la Commission des Transports du Quebec (ISSN 0318-5303)

380.5 330 CN
QUEBEC (PROVINCE). MINISTERE DE L'INDUSTRIE ET DU COMMERCE. DIRECTION DE L'ANALYSE ET DE LA PREVISION ECONOMIQUES. irreg.? Ministere de l'Industrie et du Commerce, 2700 Einstein, Quebec G1P 3W8, Canada. TEL 418-643-1344.

796.5 US
R V BUYERS GUIDE. (Recreational Vehicle) 1982. a. $3.95. T L Enterprises, Inc., 29901 Agoura Rd., Agoura, CA 91301. TEL 818-991-4980. Ed. Bill Estes. adv. circ. 100,000.

387 623.8 UK ISSN 0080-0422
REED'S NAUTICAL ALMANAC. (In three editions: European, American East Coast & Mediteranean) 1931. a. $20. Thomas Reed Publications Ltd., 80 Coombe Rd., New Malden, Surrey KT3 4QS, England. Ed. Jean Fowler. index.

380.5 US ISSN 0516-9445
REFERENCE BOOK OF HIGHWAY PERSONNEL. a. $5. American Association of State Highway and Transportation Officials, 444 N. Capitol St. N.W., Ste. 225, Washington, DC 20001. TEL 202-624-5800.

380.5 US
RESEARCH IN TRANSPORTATION ECONOMICS. 1983. a. $24.75 to individuals; institutions $49.50. J A I Press Inc., 36 Sherwood Pl., Greenwich, CT 06830. TEL 203-661-7602. Ed. Theodore E. Keller.

380.5 FR ISSN 0304-3320
RESEARCH ON TRANSPORT ECONOMICS/ RECHERCHE EN MATIERE D'ECONOMIE DES TRANSPORTS. 1968. a. 280 F.($56) (European Conference of Ministers of Transport) Organization for Economic Cooperation and Development, 19 rue de Franqueville, 75775 Paris Cedex 16, France (U.S. orders to: O.E.C.D. Publications and Information Center, 1750 Pennsylvania Ave., N.W., Washington, D.C. 20006) circ. 800. (also avail. in microfiche) Indexed: BMT. ●Also available online. Vendors: European Space Agency.
 Formerly: Recherche en Matiere d'Ecomomie des Transports (ISSN 0048-6922)

380.5 388.31 UK
ROAD DOCUMENTATION FOR DEVELOPING COUNTRIES. a. free. Transport and Research Laboratory, Overseas Unit, Old Wokingham Rd., Crowthorne, Berkshire, England. Ed. S.G. Jobbins. circ. 500.

380.5 US ISSN 0362-2800
SAN FRANCISCO BAY AREA RAPID TRANSIT DISTRICT. ANNUAL REPORT. 1958. a. San Francisco Bay Area Rapid Transit District, 800 Madison St., Oakland, CA 94607. TEL 415-465-4100. Ed. Michael Healy. illus. circ. 5,000. Key Title: Annual Report - San Francisco Bay Area Rapid Transit District.

388 UK ISSN 0048-9808
SCOTTISH TRANSPORT. 1963. a. £6.50 for 3 nos. Scottish Tramway and Transport Society, P.O. Box 78, Glasgow G3 6ER, Scotland. Ed. Brian T. Deans. adv. bk. rev. circ. 1,500. (reprint service avail. from UMI)
 Formerly: Scottish Tramlines.

380.1 CN ISSN 0707-9184
SNOWMOBILE ACCIDENTS, MANITOBA. 1972. a. contr. free circ. Department of Highways and Transportation, Safety Branch, 1075 Portage Ave., Winnipeg, Man. R3G 0S1, Canada. TEL 204-945-5751. circ. 350.

380.52 382 SA
SOUTH AFRICAN FREIGHT MANUAL. 1981. biennial. R.45. Thomson Publications S.A. (Pty) Ltd., Box 56182, Pinegowrie 2123, South Africa. Ed. Pete Bower. adv.

380.5 US ISSN 0362-2843
SOUTHERN CALIFORNIA RAPID TRANSIT DISTRICT. ANNUAL REPORT. 1964. a. free. Southern California Rapid Transit District, Marketing Department, 425 S. Main, Los Angeles, CA 90013. TEL 213-972-6000. illus. circ. 5,000. Key Title: Annual Report - Southern California Rapid Transit District.

380.5 US
SPECIALIZED TRANSPORTATION SERVICES, SERVICES GUIDE. 1983. irreg., no.5, 1986. $75. J.J. Keller and Associates, Inc., 145 W. Wisconsin Ave., Neenah, WI 54956. TEL 800-558-5011. Ed. George B. McDowell.

380.5 EI ISSN 0081-4962
STATISTICAL OFFICE OF THE EUROPEAN COMMUNITIES. STATISTIQUES DES TRANSPORTS. ANNUAIRE. (Text in Dutch, French, German, Italian) a. Rue Alcide de Gasperi, B.P. 1907, Luxembourg, Luxembourg (Dist. in the U.S. by: European Community Information Service, 2100 M St., N.W., Ste. 707, Washington, DC 20037)

STATISTICAL REPORTS OF CHANGWAT. see GEOGRAPHY

380.5 UK
STEAM HERITAGE YEARBOOK, PRESERVED TRANSPORT & INDUSTRIAL ARCHAEOLOGY GUIDE. 1968. a. £1.50. T E E Publishing, Edwards Centre, Regent St., Hinckley, Leics. LE10 0EB, England. Ed. C.L. Deith. adv. circ. 25,000.
 Former titles: Steam Year Book, Preserved Transport and Industrial Archaeology Guide; Steam and Organ Year Book and Preserved Transport Guide.

380.5 CN
SURFACE TRANSPORTATION R & D IN CANADA. 1963. a. Can.$23 to members; non-members Can.$34.50. Roads and Transportation Association of Canada, 1765 St. Laurent Blvd., Ottawa, Ont. K1G 3V4, Canada. TEL 613-521-4052. Ed. C D. James. index. circ. 800.
 Former titles: Transportation R & D in Canada (ISSN 0381-8284); Transportation Research in Canada; Road Research in Canada.

380.5 BE
TARIFICATION - FARE COLLECTION. 1983. irreg. International Union of Public Transport, Av. de l'Uruguay 19, B-1050 Brussels, Belgium.

380.5 SW
TRANSPORFORSKNINGKOMMISSION. RAPPORTER. 1976. irreg. (12-15/yr.) price varies. (Ingenioersvetenskapsakademien, Transportforskningskommissionen - Royal Swedish Academy of Engineering Sciences) Swedish Transport Research Commission, Grev Turegatan 12 A, 114 46 Stockholm, Sweden. Ed. Karl-Lennart Baang. circ. 2,000.

380.5 DK ISSN 0108-8157
TRANSPORT (AARLIG) Cover Title: Produktnoeglen for Transportemballageindkoebere. 1983. a. Kr.103.70. Teknisk Forlag A-S, Skelbaekgade 4, DK-1717 Copenhagen V, Denmark. illus.

380 UN ISSN 0252-4392
TRANSPORT & COMMUNICATIONS BULLETIN FOR ASIA & THE PACIFIC. 1950. a., latest no.57, 1985. price varies. United Nations Economic and Social Commission for Asia and the Pacific, United Nations Bldg., Rajadamnern Ave., Bangkok 2, Thailand (Dist. by: United Nations Publications, Room DC2-0853, New York, NY 10017; or Distribution and Sales Section, Palais des Nations, CH-1211 Geneva 10, Switzerland) bk. rev. charts. illus. stat. Indexed: P.A.I.S.
 Formerly: Transport and Communications Bulletin for Asia and the Far East (ISSN 0041-1396)

380.5 UK
TRANSPORT ENGINEER'S HANDBOOK. irreg. £13. Kogan Page Ltd., 120 Pentonville Rd., London N1 9JN, England.

380.5 900 UK ISSN 0041-1469
TRANSPORT HISTORY. 1968. a. £19.50($38.50) Graphmitre Ltd., 1 West St., Tavistock, Devon PL19 8DS, England. Ed. M. Lindsay-Browne. adv. bk. rev. illus. index. cum.index. circ. 2,000. (back issues avail.) Indexed: Br.Hum.Ind.

380.5 II
TRANSPORT INDUSTRY AND TRADE ANNUAL. 1963. a. $10. Praveen Corp., Sayajigani, Baroda 390005, India. Ed. C.M. Pandit. circ. 2,500.
 Formerly: Transport Industry and Trade Journal (ISSN 0041-1477)

388 UK ISSN 0306-9435
TRANSPORT MANAGER'S HANDBOOK. 1970. a. £16.95. ‡ Kogan Page Ltd., 120 Pentonville Rd., London N1 9JN, England. Ed. David Lowe. adv. charts. illus.

380.5 PL ISSN 0137-4435
TRANSPORT MUSEUMS. (Yearbook of the International Association of Transport Museums) (Text in English) irreg., vol.9, 1985. (Centralne Muzeum Morskie, Gdansk) Ossolineum, Publishing House of the Polish Academy of Sciences, Rynek 9, Wroclaw, Poland (Subscr. to: International Association of Transport Museums, Zeughaus Str. 1-5, Cologne, W. Germany (B.R.D.)) (Co-sponsor: International Association of Transport Museums)

380 AT
TRANSPORT SERVICES DIRECTORY. 1968. a. Trade Directories, Box 779, Toowong, Qld. 4066, Australia.

380.5 UK
TRANSPORT STUDIES GROUP. ANNUAL SEMINAR ON RURAL PUBLIC TRANSPORT. PAPERS AND PROCEEDINGS. 1972. biennial. £6. Polytechnic of Central London, Transport Studies Group, 35 Marylebone Rd., London NW1 5LS, England. Ed. Peter R. White. bk. rev. circ. 150.

331.88 MY
TRANSPORT WORKERS UNION. TRIENNIAL REPORT. (Text in English) triennial. Transport Workers Union, Transport Workers House, 21 Jalan Barat, Petaling Jaya, Malaysia.

380.5 US ISSN 0889-0889
TRANSPORTATION IN AMERICA; a statistical analysis of transportation in the United States. 1983. a. $30 to individuals; institutions $20. Transportation Policy Associates, 810 18th St., N.W., Washington, DC 20006 TEL 202-638-5244. (Subscr. to: Box 33633, Washington, DC 20033) Ed. Frank A. Smith. circ. 600. (back issues avail.)

380 918 US
TRANSPORTATION: LATIN AMERICAN INDUSTRIAL REPORT. 1985. a. $235 per country report. Aurora International, Box 9099, Bridgeport, CT 06601-2099. Ed. Andres C. Aquino.

380.5 US ISSN 0097-8515
TRANSPORTATION RESEARCH CIRCULAR.
irreg., no.295, 1985. price varies. National Research Council, Transportation Research Board, 2101 Constitution Ave., N.W., Washington, DC 20418. TEL 202-334-2934.

380.5 US ISSN 0091-2468
TRANSPORTATION RESEARCH FORUM. PROCEEDINGS: ANNUAL MEETING. 1962. a. $25. (Transportation Research Forum) Richard B. Cross Co., 103 S. Howard St., Box 405, Oxford, IN 47971 TEL 317-385-2255. (Dist. by Grant C. Vietsch, 181 E. Lake Shore Dr., Chicago, IL 60611) illus. stat. Key Title: Proceedings. Annual Meeting - Transportation Research Forum.

TRANSPORTATION STATISTICS IN THE UNITED STATES. see BUSINESS AND ECONOMICS — Domestic Commerce

380.5 US ISSN 0278-3819
TRANSPORTATION STUDIES. 1982. irreg., latest no.3. Gordon and Breach Science Publishers, Inc., 50 W. 23rd St., New York, NY 10010. Eds. Norman Ashford, William G. Bell.

TRANSPORTATION TELEPHONE TICKLER. see BUSINESS AND ECONOMICS — Trade And Industrial Directories

380.5 SW ISSN 0280-1183
TRANSPORTRAADET RAPPORT. 1980. irreg. price varies. Transportraadet, Box 1329, 171 26 Solna, Sweden. TEL 730-5880.

380.5 US ISSN 0082-9404
U.S. BUREAU OF THE CENSUS. CENSUS OF TRANSPORTATION. (Consists of 2 surveys: Truck Inventory and Use Survey and Commodity Transportation Survey) 1963. quinquennial. price varies. U.S. Bureau of the Census, Customer Services Dept., Washington, DC 20233 TEL 301-763-4100. (Orders to: Supt. of Documents, Washington, DC 20402) (also avail. in microfiche)

353.85 US ISSN 0092-3117
U.S. DEPARTMENT OF TRANSPORTATION. FISCAL YEAR BUDGET IN BRIEF.* a. U.S. Department of Transportation, Office of Budget, 400 Seventh St., S.W., Washington, DC 20590. Key Title: Budget in Brief - Department of Transportation (Washington)

380.5 US ISSN 0099-2267
U.S. DEPARTMENT OF TRANSPORTATION. OFFICE OF UNIVERSITY RESEARCH. AWARDS TO ACADEMIC INSTITUTIONS BY THE DEPARTMENT OF TRANSPORTATION. a. U.S. Department of Transportation, Office of University Research, 400 7th St., S.W., Washington, DC 20590. TEL 202-655-4000. Key Title: Awards to Academic Institutions by the Department of Transportation.

388.3 US
U.S. FEDERAL HIGHWAY ADMINISTRATION. HIGHWAY AND URBAN MASS TRANSPORTATION. 1970. irreg. (2-3/yr.) price varies. U.S. Federal Highway Administration, 400 Seventh St. S.W., Washington, DC 20590. TEL 202-426-0632. charts. illus. Indexed: Ind.U.S.Gov.Per. Tr.& Indus.Ind.

625.7 016 US ISSN 0068-6115
UNIVERSITY OF CALIFORNIA, BERKELEY. INSTITUTE OF TRANSPORTATION STUDIES. LIBRARY REFERENCES. 1955. irreg., no.78, 1978. price varies. University of California, Berkeley, Institute of Transportation Studies Library, 412 McLaughlin Hall, Berkeley, CA 94720. TEL 415-642-6000. Ed. Michael Kleiber.

385.1 CN
UNIVERSITY OF MANITOBA. CENTER FOR TRANSPORTATION STUDIES. ANNUAL REPORT. 1969. a. free. University of Manitoba, Center for Transportation Studies, Rm. 515, University Centre, Winnipeg, Man. R3T 2N2, Canada. TEL 204-474-9116.

385.1 CN ISSN 0076-3977
UNIVERSITY OF MANITOBA. CENTER FOR TRANSPORTATION STUDIES. OCCASIONAL PAPER. 1968. irreg. University of Manitoba, Center for Transportation Studies, Rm. 515, University Centre, Winnipeg, Man. R3T 2N2, Canada. TEL 204-474-9116.

385 CN ISSN 0316-7984
UNIVERSITY OF MANITOBA. CENTER FOR TRANSPORTATION STUDIES. RESEARCH REPORT. 1967. irreg. price varies. University of Manitoba, Center for Transportation Studies, Rm. 515, University Centre, Winnipeg, Man. R3T 2N2, Canada. TEL 204-474-9116.

380.5 CN ISSN 0076-3993
UNIVERSITY OF MANITOBA. CENTER FOR TRANSPORTATION STUDIES. SEMINAR SERIES ON TRANSPORTATION. PROCEEDINGS. 1967. a. Can.$3. University of Manitoba, Center for Transportation Studies, Rm. 515, University Centre, Winnipeg, Man. R3T 2N2, Canada. TEL 204-474-9116.
Incorporating: Colloquim Series on Transportation. Proceedings (ISSN 0069-584X)

380.5 CN ISSN 0318-1251
UNIVERSITY OF TORONTO-YORK UNIVERSITY. JOINT PROGRAM IN TRANSPORTATION. ANNUAL REPORT. a. University of Toronto-York University Joint Program in Transportation, 42 St. George St., Toronto, Ont. M5S 2E4, Canada. TEL 416-978-7282.

380.5 PL ISSN 0208-4821
UNIWERSYTET GDANSKI. WYDZIAL EKONOMIKI TRANSPORTU. ZESZYTY NAUKOWE. EKONOMIKA TRANSPORTU LADOWEGO. (Text in Polish; summaries in English and Russian) 1971. irreg. price varies. Uniwersytet Gdanski, Ul. Czerwonej Armii 110, 81-824 Sopot, Poland. circ. 300.

354.931 NZ
URBAN TRANSPORT COUNCIL. REPORT. 1982. a. NZ.$1.30. Urban Transport Council, Box 10-144, Wellington, New Zealand. stat. circ. 100.
Formerly: New Zealand. Urban Public Passenger Transport Council. Report.

380.5 DK
VIRKSOMHEDS NYTS. 1984. a. Thomson Communications (Scandinavia) A-S, Struenseegade 7-9, DK-2200 Copenhagen N, Denmark. circ. 19, 654.

380.5 UR
VSESOYUZNYI NAUCHNO-ISSLEDOVATEL'SKII INSTITUT TRANSPORTNOGO STROITEL'STVA. TRUDY. vol.106, 1977. irreg. 0.83 Rub. per no. Izdatel'stvo Transport, Basmannyi Tupik, 6a, Moscow B-175, Russian S.F.S.R., U.S.S.R. Ed.Bd. circ. 1,000. Indexed: Chem.Abstr.

WASHINGTON. UTILITIES AND TRANSPORTATION COMMISSION. RAILROAD-HIGHWAY GRADE CROSSING ACCIDENTS. SUMMARY AND ANALYSIS. see TRANSPORTATION — Railroads

354 AT
WESTERN AUSTRALIA. TRANSPORT COMMISSION. ANNUAL REPORT OF THE COMMISSIONER OF TRANSPORT. 1934. a. free contr.circ. Department of Transport, 136-138 Stirling Highway, Nedlands, W.A. 6009, Australia. circ. 200.

380.5 US ISSN 0271-4396
WESTERN TRANSPORTATION LAW SEMINAR. PAPERS AND PROCEEDINGS. 1978. a. Association of Transportation Practitioners, 1211 Connecticut Ave., N.W., Ste. 310, Washington, DC 20036. TEL 202-466-2080.
Supersedes in part: Transportation Law Seminar. Papers and Proceedings (ISSN 0164-1689)

TRANSPORTATION — Abstracting, Bibliographies, Statistics

338 AO
ANGOLA. DIRECCAO DOS SERVICOS DE ESTATISTICA. ESTATISTICA DOS VEICULOS MOTORISADOS. 1967. a. Direccao dos Servicos de Estatistica, Ministerio do Planeamento e Coordenacao Economica, C.P. 1215, Luanda, Angola. circ. 750.

315.2 JA
ANNUAL STATISTICS OF ACTUAL PRODUCTION OF RAILWAY CARS/TETSUDO SHARYOTO SEISAN DOTAI TOKEI NENPO. (Text in Japanese) 1954. a. Ministry of Transport, Data Processing Division - Un'Yu-sho Daijin Kanbo. Joho Kanri-bu, Minister's Secretariat, 2-1-3 Kasumigaseki, Chiyoda-ku, Tokyo 100, Japan.

387.7 AT ISSN 0729-6096
AUSTRALIA. AIR TRANSPORT STATISTICS. AIRPORT TRAFFIC DATA. 1980. a. free. Department of Aviation, Central Statistical Section, Box 367, Canberra City 2601, Australia. charts. circ. 450.

387.7 AT ISSN 0727-6672
AUSTRALIA. AIR TRANSPORT STATISTICS. AUSTRALIAN AIR DISTANCES. 1982. biennial. free. Department of Aviation, Central Statistical Section, Box 367, Canberra City 2601, Australia. charts. circ. 550.

387.7 AT ISSN 0727-2774
AUSTRALIA. AIR TRANSPORT STATISTICS. FLIGHT CREW LICENCES. 1978. a. free. Department of Aviation, Central Statistical Section, Box 367, Canberra City, 2601, Australia. circ. 350. (back issues avail.)

385.264 310 AT
AUSTRALIA. NON-GOVERNMENT RAILWAYS STATISTICS. 1979. a. free. Federal Bureau of Transport Economics, P.O. Box 501, Canberra, A.C.T. 2601, Australia. Ed. F.S. Poole. charts. circ. 100.
Formerly: Australia. Land Transport Statistics. Non-Government Railways (ISSN 0727-2804)

388 016 620 AT ISSN 0312-2115
AUSTRALIAN ROAD INDEX. 1975. a. Aus.$60. Australian Road Research Board, Box 156 (Bag 4), Nunawading, Vic. 3131, Australia.
●Available only online. Vendors: AUSINET.

AUSTRALIAN ROAD RESEARCH IN PROGRESS. see ENGINEERING — Abstracting, Bibliographies, Statistics

388.3 IT
AUTOMOBILE IN CIFRE. a. L.25000($25) Associazione Nazionale fra le Industrie Automobilistiche, Corso G. Ferraris 61, 10128 Turin, Italy. (Co-sponsor: Unione Italiana Costruttori Autoveicoli) stat.

388 US
AUTOMOTIVE LITERATURE INDEX. 1981. quinquennial. $29.95. Wallace Publishing, 2307 Shoreland Ave., Toledo, OH 43611. TEL 419-729-9065. Ed. A. Wallace. bk. rev. film rev. play rev. charts. illus. cum.index. circ. 1,000. (back issues avail.)

380.5 IT
AUTOVEICOLI CIRCOLANTI IN ITALIA. a. L.24000($25) Associazione Nazionale fra le Industrie Automobilistiche, Corso G. Ferraris 61, 10128 Turin, Italy. (Co-sponsor: Unione Italiana Costruttori Autoveicoli) stat.

388 II ISSN 0067-6462
BASIC ROAD STATISTICS OF INDIA. Hindi edition: Mool Sarak Ankrey. 1948. a. Rs.79.40 for Hindi edt.; $3.78 for English edt. Ministry of Shipping and Transport, Transport Research Division, I D A Bldg., Jamnagar House, Shahjahan Rd, New Delhi 110011, India (Orders to: Controller of Publications, Civil Lines, New Delhi 110006, India)

386 BE ISSN 0067-5539
BELGIUM. INSTITUT NATIONAL DE STATISTIQUE. STATISTIQUE DE LA NAVIGATION INTERIEURE. (Text in Dutch and French) 1971. a. 230 Fr. Institut National de Statistique, 44 rue de Louvain, 1000 Brussels, Belgium.
Incorporating: Belgium. Institut National de Statistique. Statistique de la Navigation du Rhin (ISSN 0067-5520)

TRANSPORTATION — ABSTRACTING, BIBLIOGRAPHIES, STATISTICS

338.4   BE   ISSN 0067-5555
BELGIUM. INSTITUT NATIONAL DE STATISTIQUE. STATISTIQUE DES VEHICULES A MOTEUR NEUFS MIS EN CIRCULATION. (Text in Dutch and French) 1955. a. 290 Fr. Institut National de Statistique, 44 rue de Louvain, B-1000 Brussels, Belgium.

016 947 387   US
BIBLIOGRAPHY OF MARITIME AND NAVAL HISTORY PERIODICAL ARTICLES. 1972. irreg. Texas A & M University, Sea Grant College Program, College Station, TX 77843-4115. index. cum.index: 1970-1979.

623.82 016   UK
BRITISH SHIP RESEARCH ASSOCIATION. B.S.R.A. BIBLIOGRAPHIES. 1963. irreg. £10($12) per no. British Maritime Technology Ltd., Wallsend Research Station, Wallsend, Tyne and Wear NE28 6UY, England. bibl.

387.7   CN   ISSN 0705-4343
CANADA. STATISTICS CANADA. AIR PASSENGER ORIGIN AND DESTINATION. CANADA-UNITED STATES REPORT/ ORIGINE ET DESTINATION DES PASSAGERS AERIENS. RAPPORT SUR LE TRAFIC CANADA-ETAT UNIS. (Catalogue 51-205) (Text in English and French) 1968. a. Can.$74($87) Statistics Canada, Communications Division, 3rd Floor, R.H. Coats Bldg., Ottawa, Ont. K1A 0T6, Canada TEL 613-993-7276. (Subscr. to: Publications Sales and Services, Ottawa, Ont. K1A 0T6, Canada) (also avail. in microform from MML)

387.7   CN   ISSN 0068-7057
CANADA. STATISTICS CANADA. AVIATION STATISTICS CENTRE. SERVICE BULLETIN/ BULLETIN DE SERVICE DU CENTRE DES STATISTIQUES DE L'AVIATION. (Catalog 51-004) (Text in English and French) 1968. irreg (service bulletin) Can.$85($95) Statistics Canada, Communications Division, 3rd Floor, R.H. Coats Bldg., Ottawa, Ont. K1A 0T6, Canada TEL 613-993-7276. (Subscr. to: Publications Sales and Services, Ottawa, Ont. K1A 0T6, Canada) (also avail. in microform from MML)

387   CN   ISSN 0225-1507
CANADA. STATISTICS CANADA. COASTWISE SHIPPING STATISTICS. (Catalogue 54-210) (Text in English and French) 1978. a. Can.$42($43) Statistics Canada, Communications Division, 3rd Floor, R.H. Coats Bldg., Ottawa, Ont. K1A 0T6, Canada TEL 613-993-7276. (Subscr. to: Publications Sales and Services, Ottawa, Ont. K1A 0T6, Canada)

388   CN   ISSN 0383-5766
CANADA. STATISTICS CANADA. PASSENGER BUS AND URBAN TRANSIT STATISTICS/ STATISTIQUE DU TRANSPORT DES VOYAGEURS PAR AUTOBUS ET DU TRANSPORT URBAIN. (Catalogue 53-215) (Text in English and French) 1956. a. Can.$32($33) Statistics Canada, Communications Division, 3rd Floor, R.H. Coats Bldg., Ottawa, Ont. K1A 0T6, Canada TEL 613-993-7276. (Subscr. to: Publications Sales and Services, Ottawa, Ont. K1A 0T6, Canada) (also avail. in microform from MML)

388.3   CN   ISSN 0703-654X
CANADA. STATISTICS CANADA. ROAD MOTOR VEHICLES-FUEL SALES/VEHICULES AUTOMOBILES-VENTES DE CARBURANTS. (Catalogue 53-218) (Text in English, French) 1960. a. Can.$10($11) Statistics Canada, Communications Division, 3rd Floor, R.H. Coats Bldg., Ottawa, Ont. K1A 0T6, Canada TEL 613-993-7276. (Subscr. to: Publications Sales and Services, Ottawa, Ont. K1A 0T6, Canada) (also avail. in microform from MML)
     Formerly: Canada. Statistics Canada. Motor Vehicle. Part 2. Motive Fuel Sales/Vehicules a Moteur. Partie 2. Ventes des Carburants (ISSN 0527-5830)

388.3   CN   ISSN 0706-067X
CANADA. STATISTICS CANADA. ROAD MOTOR VEHICLES-REGISTRATIONS/ VEHICULES AUTOMOBILES-IMMATRICULATIONS. (Catalogue 53-219) (Text in English, French) 1960. a. Can.$10($11) Statistics Canada, Communications Division, 3rd Floor, R.H. Coats Bldg., Ottawa, Ont. K1A 0T6, Canada TEL 613-993-7276. (Subscr. to: Publications Sales and Services, Ottawa, Ont. K1A 0T6, Canada) (also avail. in microform from MML)

385   CN   ISSN 0828-2897
CANADA. STATISTICS CANADA. SURFACE AND MARINE TRANSPORT. SERVICE BULLETIN/BULLETIN DE SERVICE TRANSPORTS TERRESTRES ET MARITIMES. (Catalogue 50-002) (Text in English, French) 1971. irreg., (approx. 10/yr.) Can.$75($85) Statistics Canada, Communications Division, 3rd Floor, R.H. Coats Bldg., Ottawa, Ont. K1A 0T6, Canada TEL 613-993-7276. (Subscr. to: Publications Sales and Services, Ottawa, Ont. K1A 0T6, Canada)
     Formerly (until 1984): Canada. Statistics Canada. Railway Transport. Service Bulletin (ISSN 0700-2211)

387   CN   ISSN 0380-0342
CANADA. STATISTICS CANADA. WATER TRANSPORTATION/TRANSPORT PAR EAU. (Catalogue 54-205) (Text in English and French) 1946. a. Can.$32($33) Statistics Canada, Communications Division, 3rd Floor, R.H. Coats Bldg., Ottawa, Ont. K1A 0T6, Canada TEL 613-993-7276. (Subscr. to: Publications Sales and Services, Ottawa, Ont. K1A 0T6, Canada) (also avail. in microform from MML)

380.5   UK   ISSN 0260-9886
CHARTERED INSTITUTE OF PUBLIC FINANCE AND ACCOUNTANCY. HIGHWAYS AND TRANSPORTATION. ACTUALS. 1980. a. £10. Chartered Institute of Public Finance and Accountancy, 3 Robert St., London WC2N 6BH, England.

380.5   UK   ISSN 0260-9894
CHARTERED INSTITUTE OF PUBLIC FINANCE AND ACCOUNTANCY. HIGHWAYS AND TRANSPORTATION STATISTICS. ESTIMATES. 1981. a. £14. Chartered Institute of Public Finance and Accountancy, 3 Robert St., London WC2N 6BH, England.

387.7 310   UK
CHARTERED INSTITUTE OF PUBLIC FINANCE AND ACCOUNTANCY. LOCAL AUTHORITY AIRPORTS. ACCOUNTS AND STATISTICS. ACTUALS STATISTICS. 1979. a. £10. Chartered Institute of Public Finance and Accountancy, 3 Robert St., London WC2N 6BH, England. (back issues avail.)
     Formerly: Chartered Institute of Public Finance and Accountancy. Local Authority Airports. Accounts and Statistics (ISSN 0260-9967)

318   CK
COLUMBIA. DEPARTAMENTO ADMINISTRATIVO NACIONAL DE ESTADISTICA. ANUARIO GENERAL DE ESTADISTICA - TRANSPORTES Y COMUNICACIONES. irreg.? Departamento Administrativo Nacional de Estadistica, Banco Nacional de Datos, Centro Administrativo Nacional, Avda. Eldorado, Bogota, Colombia.

380.5   FR
COMMENT EVALUER LA PART DU TRAFIC MARITIME DE NOTRE COMMERCE EXTERIEUR QUI ECHAPPE AUX PORTS FRANCAIS. 1975. a. Departement des Statistiques des Transports, Direction des Affaires Economiques, Financieres et Administratives, 55 rue Brillat-Savarin, 75658 Paris Cedex 13, France.

385.1 016   US   ISSN 0069-9314
CONTAINERIZATION: A BIBLIOGRAPHY. 1967. a. $3. Northwestern University, Transportation Center, 1936 Sheridan Rd., Evanston, IL 60201. TEL 312-492-7287. Ed. Dorothy V. Ramm.
     Formerly: Bibliography on Economics of Containerization.

387 314   DK   ISSN 0070-3486
DANMARKS SKIBE OG SKIBSFART/DANISH SHIPS AND SHIPPING. (Text in Danish; notes in English) 1921. a. Kr.43.44. Danmarks Statistik, Sejroegade 11, 2100 Copenhagen OE, Denmark.

380.5 016   US   ISSN 0070-6809
DOCTORAL DISSERTATIONS ON TRANSPORTATION. 1969. irreg. $3 for latest supplement. Northwestern University, Transportation Center, 1936 Sheridan Rd., Evanston, IL 60201. TEL 312-492-7287.

380.5   FJ
FIJI. BUREAU OF STATISTICS. SHIPPING STATISTICS. 1971. a. $1. Bureau of Statistics, Box 2221, Suva, Fiji.

385.1   FI   ISSN 0430-5272
FINLAND. TILASTOKESKUS. LIIKENNETILASTOLLINEN VUOSIKIRJA/ FINLAND. STATISTIKCENTRALEN. SAMFAERDSELSTATISTISKAARSBOK/ FINLAND. CENTRAL STATISTICAL OFFICE. YEARBOOK OF TRANSPORT STATISTICS. (Section XXXVI of Official Statistics of Finland) (Text in English, Finnish and Swedish) 1958. a. Fmk.43. Tilastokeskus, Annankatu 44, SF-00100 Helsinki 10, Finland (Subscr. to: Government Printing Centre, Box 516, SF-00100 Helsinki 10, Finland)

388.31   FI   ISSN 0355-2284
FINLAND. TILASTOKESKUS. TIELIIKENNEONNETTOMUUDET/FINLAND. STATISTISKCENTRALEN. VAEGTRAFIKOLYCKOR/FINLAND. CENTRAL STATISTICAL OFFICE. ROAD TRAFFIC ACCIDENTS. (Text in English, Finnish and Swedish) 1967. a. Fmk.60. Tilastokeskus, P.O. Box 504, SF-00101 Helsinki, Finland. (back issues avail.)

380.5   FR
FRANCE. DEPARTEMENT DES STATISTIQUES DE TRANSPORT. ANNUAIRE STATISTIQUE DES TRANSPORTS. a. Departement des Statistiques de Transport, Ministere des Transports, 55-57 rue Brillat-Savarin, 75658 Paris Cedex 13, France. circ. 1,000.

380.5   FR
FRANCE. DEPARTEMENT DES STATISTIQUES DE TRANSPORT. MEMENTO DE STATISTIQUES DES TRANSPORTS. a. Departement des Statistiques de Transport, Ministere des Transports, 55-57 rue-Brillat-Savarin, 75658 Paris Cedex 13, France.

388 314   GW   ISSN 0072-405X
GERMANY (FEDERAL REPUBLIC, 1949-). STATISTISCHES BUNDESAMT. FACHSERIE 8, VERKEHR, REIHE 3: STRASSENVERKEHR. irreg. price varies. W. Kohlhammer-Verlag GmbH, Abt. Veroeffentlichungen des Statistischen Bundesamtes, Philipp-Reis-Str. 3, Postfach 421120, 6500 Mainz 42, W. Germany (B.R.D.)

614 312   GW   ISSN 0072-4068
GERMANY (FEDERAL REPUBLIC, 1949-). STATISTISCHES BUNDESAMT. FACHSERIE 8, VERKEHR, REIHE 3.3: HAUSHAELTE UND FAMILIEN. m. (and a.) DM.57.60. W. Kohlhammer-Verlag GmbH, Abt. Veroeffentlichungen des Statistischen Bundesamtes, Philipp-Reis-Str. 3, Postfach 421120, 6500 Mainz 42, W. Germany (B.R.D.)

380.5 314   GW   ISSN 0072-3924
GERMANY (FEDERAL REPUBLIC, 1949-). STATISTISCHES BUNDESAMT. FACHSERIE 17, PREISE, REIHE 9: PREISE FUER VERKEHRSLEISTUNGEN. a. DM.7.40. W. Kohlhammer-Verlag GmbH, Abt. Veroeffentlichungen des Statistischen Bundesamtes, Philipp-Reis-Str. 3, Postfach 421120, 6500 Mainz 42, W. Germany (B.R.D.)

387   GR   ISSN 0072-7423
GREECE. NATIONAL STATISTICAL SERVICE. SHIPPING STATISTICS. 1967. a. $7. National Statistical Service, Publications and Information Division, 14-16 Lycourgou St., 10166 Athens, Greece. (Text in English and Greek)

301.6 380.5   GR
GREECE. NATIONAL STATISTICAL SERVICE. TRANSPORT AND COMMUNICATION STATISTICS. (Text in Greek) 1967. a. $10. National Statistical Service, Publications and Information Division, 14-16 Lycourgou St., 10166 Athens, Greece.

625 388.1 016   US   ISSN 0017-6222
H R I S ABSTRACTS. (Highway Research Information Service) 1968. q. $70. National Research Council, Transportation Research Board, Highway Research Information Service, 2101 Constitution Ave. N.W., Washington, DC 20418. TEL 202-334-3218. Ed.Bd. abstr. circ. 2,500. (also avail. in microfiche; reprint service avail. from UMI)

385　　　　　　II　　ISSN 0376-9909
INDIAN RAILWAYS YEARBOOK. (Text in
English) 1973/74. a. Railway Board, Directorate of
Statistics and Economics, Joint Director, Public
Relations, New Delhi 110001, India.

623.8　016　　　　UK　　ISSN 0309-3948
INSTITUTE OF MARINE ENGINEERS
TECHNICAL REPORTS. 1889. irreg. price varies.
Marine Management Holdings Ltd., Memorial
Bldg., 76 Mark Lane, London EC3R 7JN, England.
Ed. Roderick Smith. adv. abstr. charts. illus. index.
circ. 5,000. (also avail. in microform from MIM)
Indexed: Br.Tech.Ind. Chem.Abstr. Eng.Ind.
Met.Abstr. Ocean.Abstr. Pollut.Abstr. BMT.
Fluidex. ISMEC. World Alum.Abstr.
  Formerly: Institute of Marine Engineers.
Transactions (ISSN 0020-2924)

387　629.1　016　　UN　ISSN 0074-249X
INTERNATIONAL CIVIL AVIATION
ORGANIZATION. INDEXES TO I C A O
PUBLICATIONS. ANNUAL CUMULATION.
(Text in English) a. price varies. International Civil
Aviation Organization, 1000 Sherbrooke St. W.,
Montreal, Que. H3A 2R2, Canada.

INTERNATIONAL MEDIA GUIDE. CONSUMER
MAGAZINES WORLDWIDE. see
*ADVERTISING AND PUBLIC RELATIONS —
Abstracting, Bibliographies, Statistics*

385　　　　　　FR
INTERNATIONAL UNION OF RAILWAYS.
TABLEAUX ET GRAPHIQUES. (Text in French;
tables of contents in English, French and German)
1962. irreg. 50 F. International Union of Railways,
14 rue Jean Rey, 75015 Paris, France. charts.

330　　　　　　IE
IRELAND. CENTRAL STATISTICS OFFICE.
PARTICULARS OF VEHICLES REGISTERED
AND LICENSED FOR THE FIRST TIME. a.
Central Statistics Office, Earlsfort Terrace, Dublin
2, Ireland. (processed)

330　　　　　　IE
IRELAND. CENTRAL STATISTICS OFFICE.
STATISTICS OF PORT TRAFFIC. a. Central
Statistics Office, Earlsfort Terrace, Dublin 2,
Ireland. (processed)

380.3　310　　　　IS
ISRAEL. CENTRAL BUREAU OF STATISTICS.
ROAD ACCIDENTS WITH CASUALTIES. (Text
in English and Hebrew) 1950. a., latest issue,
no.761, 1984. price varies. Central Bureau of
Statistics, P.O.B. 13015, Jerusalem, Israel.

387　314　　　　IT　　ISSN 0075-1898
ITALY. ISTITUTO CENTRALE DI STATISTICA.
ANNUARIO STATISTICO DELLA
NAVIGAZIONE MARITTIMA. a. L.10000.
Istituto Centrale di Statistica, Via Cesare Balbo 16,
00100 Rome, Italy.

380.5　　　　　　MW
MALAWAI. NAITONAL STATISTICAL OFFICE.
TRANSPORT STATISTICS. 1980. a. K.9.00.
National Statistical Office, Box 333, Zomba,
Malawi.

380.5　016　　　　BE　　ISSN 0378-195X
METRO: A BIBLIOGRAPHY. 1964. biennial. 1800
Fr.($45) International Union of Public Transport,
Av. de l'Uruguay 19, B-1050 Brussels, Belgium.
(back issues avail.)

MOTOR SPECIFICATIONS & PRICES. see
TRANSPORTATION — Automobiles

388.34　310　　　　JA　　ISSN 0463-6635
MOTOR VEHICLE STATISTICS OF JAPAN. (Text
in English) 1958. a. free. Japan Automobile
Manufacturers Association - Nihon Jidosha
Kogyokai, Ote-machi Bldg., 1-6-1 Ote-machi,
Chiyoda-ku, Tokyo 100, Japan. illus. stat. circ. 7,
500.

387　　　　　　JA　　ISSN 0469-4783
NAGOYA PORT STATISTICS ANNUAL/
 NAGOYAKO TOKEI NENPO. (Text in Japanese)
1958. a. Nagoya Port Authority - Nagoyako Kanri
Kumiai, 1-8-21 Irifune, Minato-ku, Nagoya 455,
Japan. stat.

388.314　　　　SA
NATIONAL INSTITUTE FOR TRANSPORT AND
ROAD RESEARCH. TRANSPORT STATISTICS/
NASIONALE INSTITUUT VIR VERVOER- EN
PADNAVORSING. VERVOERSTATISTIEK.
(Text in Afrikaans and English) 1969. a. free.
National Institute for Transport and Road Research,
Box 395, Pretoria 0001, South Africa. Ed. C.C.
Hamilton. charts. illus. circ. 1,000.
  Formerly: National Institute for Transport and
Road Research. Road Statistics.

387　314.9　　　NE　ISSN 0168-4825
NETHERLANDS. CENTRAAL BUREAU VOOR
DE STATISTIEK. STATISTIEK VAN AAN-, AF-
EN DOORVOER. GOEDERENVERVOER PER
GOEDERENSOORT VAN EN NAAR DE
ZEEHAVENS VAN ROTTERDAM EN
AMSTERDAM. 1950. a. fl.24.50. Centraal Bureau
voor de Statistiek, Prinses Beatrixlaan 428,
Voorburg, Netherlands (Orders to: Staatsuitgeverij,
Christoffel Plantijnstraat, The Hague, Netherlands)
circ. 300.
  Formerly: Netherlands. Centraal Bureau voor de
Statistiek. Statistiek van het Internationaal
Zeehavenvervoer.

388.1　　　　　NE　ISSN 0168-5023
NETHERLANDS. CENTRAAL BUREAU VOOR
DE STATISTIEK. STATISTIEK VAN DE
VERKEERSONGEVALLEN OP DE OPENBARE
WEG. STATISTICS OF ROAD-TRAFFIC
ACCIDENTS. (Text in Dutch and English) 1947/
48. a. fl.23.95. Centraal Bureau voor de Statistiek,
Prinses Beatrixlaan 428, Voorburg, Netherlands
(Orders to: Staatsuitgeverij, Christoffel
Plantijnstraat, The Hague, Netherlands)

380.5　　　　　NZ　ISSN 0112-3629
NEW ZEALAND CENSUS OF TRANSPORT,
STORAGE & COMMUNICATION. 1979. irreg.
R.5.50. Department of Statistics, Private Bag,
Wellington, New Zealand (Subscr. to: Government
Printing Office, Publications, Private Bag,
Wellington, New Zealand)

380.5　　　　　NO　ISSN 0468-8147
NORWAY. STATISTISK SENTRALBYRAA.
SAMFERDSELSSTATISTIKK/TRANSPORT
AND COMMUNICATION STATISTICS.
(Subseries of its Norges Offisielle Statistikk) (Text
in English and Norwegian) 1958. a. Kr.55. Statistisk
Sentralbyraa - Central Bureau of Statistics, Box
8131-Dep., 0033 Oslo 1, Norway. circ. 1,350.

380.5　　　　　IT
ONERI FISCALI SULLA MOTORIZZAZIONE.
biennial (updates every six months) L.25000($50)
Associazione Nazionale fra le Industrie
Automobilistiche, Corso G. Ferraris 61, 10128
Turin, Italy. (Co-sponsor: Unione Italiana
Costruttori Autoveicoli) stat.

388　310　　　　PP
PAPUA NEW GUINEA. NATIONAL
STATISTICAL OFFICE. STATISTICAL
BULLETIN: REGISTERED MOTOR VEHICLES.
(Text in English) 1962. a. National Statistical
Office, P.O. Wards Strips, Papua New Guinea. circ.
484.

314　387　　　　PL　ISSN 0079-2667
POLAND. GLOWNY URZAD STATYSTYCZNY.
ROCZNIK STATYSTYCZNY GOSPODARKI
MORSKIEJ. YEARBOOK OF SEA ECONOMY
STATISTICS. (Subseries of its: Statystyka Polski)
1969. irreg., latest 1983. 65 Zl. Glowny Urzad
Statystyczny, Al. Niepodleglosci 208, 00-925
Warsaw, Poland. stat. illus. charts. circ. 1,040.

380.5　314　　　PL　ISSN 0079-2802
POLAND. GLOWNY URZAD STATYSTYCZNY.
ROCZNIK STATYSTYCZNY TRANSPORTU.
YEARBOOK OF TRANSPORT STATISTICS.
(Subseries of its: Statystyka Polski) 1967. irreg.,
latest 1986. 77 Zl. Glowny Urzad Statystyczny, Al.
Niepodleglosci 208, 00-925 Warsaw, Poland.

315.2　　　　　JA
PORT OF YOKOHAMA. ANNUAL STATISTICS.
(Text in Japanese) no.212, Nov. 1969. a. free. Port
and Harbor Bureau, Industry and Trade Center
Bldg., 2 Yamashita-cho Nakaku, Yokohama, Japan.
(processed)
  Formerly: Port of Yokohama. Monthly Statistics.
(ISSN 0032-4876)

380.5　301.16　314　　PO　ISSN 0377-2292
PORTUGAL. INSTITUTO NACIONAL DE
ESTATISTICA. SERVICOS CENTRAIS.
ESTATISTICAS DOS TRANSPORTES E
COMMUNICACOES: CONTINENTE, ACORES
E MADEIRA (Text in French, Portuguese) 1970.
a. Esc.600. Instituto Nacional de Estatistica, Avda.
Antonio Jose de Almeida 1, 1078 Lisbon Codex,
Portugal.

338.476　　　　　IT
QUADERNO INDUSTRIA AUTOMOBILISTICA
MONDIALE. a. L.15000($25) Associazione
Nazionale fra le Industrie Automobilistiche, Corso
G. Ferraris 61, 10128 Turin, Italy. (Co-sponsor:
Unione Italiana Costruttori Autoveicoli) stat.

388.1　　　　　ZA
REPORT ON PASSENGER ROAD TRANSPORT
IN ZAMBIA. 1968. a. K.3. Central Statistical
Office, P.O. Box 31908, Lusaka, Zambia.

016　629.2　620　　US　ISSN 0741-2029
S A E TECHNICAL LITERATURE ABSTRACTS.
1975. q. $76. Society of Automotive Engineers, 400
Commonwealth Dr., Warrendale, PA 15096. TEL
412-776-4841. cum.index: 1965-1985. (also avail. in
magnetic tape; back issues avail.) Indexed: Fluidex.
●Also available online. Vendors: Orbit Information
Technologies.
  Supersedes (1970-1975): S A E Quarterly
Abstracts.

380.5　　　　　FR
S.I.T.R.A.M. RESULTATS GENERAUX: TRAFIC
INTERIEUR - TRAFIC INTERNATIONAL.
(Systeme d'Information sur les Transports de
Machandises) 1971. a. free. Ministere des
Transports, de l'Urbanisme et du Logement,
Department des Statistiques des Transports, 55 rue
Brillat-Savarin, 75658 Paris Cedex 13, France.
  Formerly (until 1983): France. Departement des
Statistiques Transports. Resultats Generaux - Trafic
Interieur et International.

623.82　　　　NO　ISSN 0346-1025
SHIP ABSTRACTS; information service on ship
technology, ship operation and ocean engineering.
(Was available in hard copy until 1984) (Text and
summaries in English) 1973. 10/yr. Norges
Skipsforskningsinstitutt - Ship Research Institute of
Norway, Box 6099-Etterstad, Oslo 6, Norway. (Co-
sponsors: Stiching Coordinatie Maritiem Onderzoek;
Association of Finnish Shipbuilders; British Ship
Research Association; the Associations of Swedish
Shipbuilders and Shipowners) Ed. Svein Lunde.
abstr. circ. 1,100.
●Available only online.
  Incorporates (from Jan. 1977): Maritime
Information Review; Former titles: Scandinavian
Ship Abstract Journal & Artikkel-Indeks for Skip.

312.44　　　　SA
SOUTH AFRICA. CENTRAL STATISTICAL
SERVICE. ROAD TRAFFIC ACCIDENTS.
(Report No. 12-01) a., latest 1985. Central
Statistical Service, Private Bag X44, Pretoria 0001,
South Africa (Orders to: Government Printer,
Bosman St., Private Bag X85, Pretoria 0001,South
Africa)
  Formerly: South Africa. Department of Statistics.
Road Traffic Accidents (ISSN 0584-195X)

388.3　310　　　　SA
SOUTH AFRICA. CENTRAL STATISTICAL
SERVICE. STATISTICS OF MOTOR AND
OTHER VEHICLES. (Report No. 12-03) 1972. a.
Central Statistical Service, Private Bag X44, Pretoria
0001, South Africa (Orders to: Government Printer,
Bosman St., Private Bag X85, Pretoria 0001,South
Africa)
  Formerly: South Africa. Department of Statistics.
Statistics of Motor and Other Vehicles.

388　　　　　SA
SOUTH AFRICA. CENTRAL STATISTICAL
SERVICE. STATISTICS OF NEW VEHICLES
REGISTERED. (Report No. 12-02) a., latest 1983-
84. Central Statistical Service, Private Bag X44,
Pretoria 0001, South Africa (Orders to: Government
Printer, Bosman St., Private Bag X85, Pretoria 0001,
South Africa)
  Former titles: South Africa. Department of
Statistics. Statistics of New Vehicles Registered;
South Africa. Department of Statistics. Statistics of
New Vehicles Licensed.

614.86   SP   ISSN 0085-655X
SPAIN. DIRECCION GENERAL DE TRAFICO. ANUARIO ESTADISTICO DE ACCIDENTES. BOLETIN INFORMATIVO. 1962. a. Direccion General de Trafico, Gabinete de Estudios, Calle J. Valcarcel 28, 28071 Madrid, Spain. circ. 2,000.

614.86   SP   ISSN 0304-9191
SPAIN. DIRECCION GENERAL DE TRAFICO. ANUARIO ESTADISTICO GENERAL. 1960. a. Direccion General de Trafico, Gabinete de Estudios, Calle J. Valcarcel 28, 28071 Madrid, Spain. circ. 2,500.

STATISTICA DEGLI INCIDENTI STRADALI. see PUBLIC HEALTH AND SAFETY — Abstracting, Bibliographies, Statistics

STATISTICAL SUMMARY OF THAILAND. see AGRICULTURE — Abstracting, Bibliographies, Statistics

388.1   UN   ISSN 0081-5160
STATISTICS OF ROAD TRAFFIC ACCIDENTS IN EUROPE. 1956. a., latest vol.30, 1983. price varies. Economic Commission for Europe (ECE), Palais des Nations, 1211 Geneva 10, Switzerland (Or United Nations Publications, Rm. DC2-853, New York, NY 10017)

388.31 310   JA
STATISTICS OF ROAD TRAFFIC ACCIDENTS IN JAPAN. a. $7. International Association of Traffic and Safety Sciences, 6-20, 2-chome, Yaesu, Chuoku, Tokyo 104, Japan.

387.7   SW   ISSN 0348-2251
SWEDEN. LUFTFARTSVERKET. AARSBOK. 1976. a. Kr.35. Luftfartsverket - Board of Civil Aviation, S-601 79 Norrkoeping, Sweden. stat.

380   SW   ISSN 0082-0334
SWEDEN. STATISTISKA CENTRALBYRAAN. STATISTISKA MEDDELANDEN. SUBGROUP T (TRANSPORT AND OTHER FORMS OF COMMUNICATION) (Text in Swedish; table heads and summaries in English) N.S. 1963. irreg. Kr.800. Distribution, S-701 89 Oerebro, Sweden. circ. 1,000.

314.94 338.4   SZ
SWITZERLAND. BUNDESAMT FUER STATISTIK. EINGEFUEHRTE MOTORFAHRZEUGE/ VEHICULES A MOTEUR IMPORTES. (Text in French and German) a. Bundesamt fuer Statistik, Hallwylstr. 15, Ch-3003 Berne, Switzerland.
Continues in part: Switzerland. Statistisches Amt. Eingefuehrte Motorfahrzeuge; in Verkehr Gesetzte Neue Motorfahrzeuge.

388   SZ
SWITZERLAND. BUNDESAMT FUER STATISTIK. IN VERKEHR GESETZTE NEUE MOTORFAHRZEUGE/VEHICULES A MOTEUR NEUFS MIS EN CIRCULATION. (Text in French and German) a. Bundesamt fuer Statistik, Hallwaylstr. 15, CH-3003 Berne, Switzerland.
Continues in part: Switzerland. Statistisches Amt. Eingefuehrte Motorfahrzeuge: In Verkehr Gesetzte Neue Motorfahrzeuge.

387.7   AU
TAETIGEITSBERICHT DES VERKEHRS ARBEITSINSPEKTORATES FUER DAS JAHR (YEAR) 1952. biennial. free. Bundesministerium fuer oeffentliche Wirtschaft und Verkehr Verkehrsarbeitsinspektorat, Radetzskystr. 2, 1030 Vienna, Austria. circ. 850.

380.5 315   CH
TAIWAN ANNUAL STATISTICAL REPORT OF TRANSPORTATION/TAI-WAN SHENG CHIAO TUNG TUNG CHI NIEN PAO. (Text in Chinese and English) 1946. a. Taiwan Sheng Cheng Fu Chiao Tung Chu, Nan-Tou Hsien, Taiwan, Republic of China. stat.

380.5   FR
TRANSPORTS ROUTIERS DE MARCHANDISES EFFECTIVES PAR DES TRANSPORTEURS ETRANGERS SUR LE TERRITOIRE FRANCAIS. 1973. quadrennial. Departement des Statistiques des Transports, Direction des Affaires Economiques, Financieres et Administratives, 55 rue Brillat-Savarin, 75658 Paris Cedex 13, France.

380.5 016   US   ISSN 0083-0380
U.S. DEPARTMENT OF TRANSPORTATION. BIBLIOGRAPHIC LISTS. 1969. irreg. U.S. Department of Transportation, Library Services Division, 400 Seventh St. N.W., Washington, DC 20590 TEL 202-655-4000. (Order from: National Technical Information Service, 5285 Port Royal Rd., Springfield, VA 22151)

623.89 310   UY
URUGUAY. CENTRO DE NAVEGACION TRANSATLANTICA. ESTADISTICA. irreg. free. Centro de Navegacion Transatlantica, Montevideo, Uruguay. circ. X.

387   NN
VANUATU. NATIONAL PLANNING AND STATISTICS OFFICE. OVERSEAS SHIPPING AND AIRCRAFT STATISTICS/STATISTIQUES DE NAVIGATION MARITIME ET AERIENNE INTERNATIONALES. (Text and summaries in English and French) 1971. a. free. Informations Department, Statistics Division, NP 50, Port-vila, Vanuatu. stat. circ. 250. (processed)
Formerly: Vanuatu. Bureau of Statistics. Overseas Shipping and Aircraft Statistics/Statistiques de Navigation Maritime et Aerienne Internationales.

387   II
WATER TRANSPORT STATISTICS OF INDIA. 1969. a. $11.70. Ministry of Shipping and Transport, Transport Research Division, I D A Bldg., Jamnagar House, Shahjahan Rd., New Delhi 11001, India (Orders to: Controller of Publications, Civil Lines, Delhi 110006, India)
Formerly: India (Republic) Ministry of Shipping and Transport. Statistics of Water Transport Industries (ISSN 0081-5144)

387 016   UK   ISSN 0264-0775
WORLD PORTS AND HARBOURS ABSTRACTS. 1976. q. £93($142) B H R A Fluid Engineering, Cranfield, Bedford MK43 0AJ, England (Dist. in U.S. by: Learned Information Inc., 143 Old Marlton Pike, Medford, NJ 08055) Ed.Bd. bk. rev. abstr. index. cum.index.
●Also available online. Vendors: European Space Agency.
Incorporating (with vol. 7, Dec. 1982): International Dredging Abstracts (ISSN 0308-1400)

380.5   SZ   ISSN 0302-7902
WORLD TRANSPORT DATA/STATISTIQUES MONDIALES DE TRANSPORT. (Text in English and French) 1973. triennial. 80 Fr. International Road Transport Union, 3 rue de Varembe, B.P. 44, CH-1211 Geneva 20, Switzerland. circ. 4,000. (back issues avail.)

384 314   YU   ISSN 0513-0794
YUGOSLAVIA. SAVEZNI ZAVOD ZA STATISTIKU. SAOBRACAJ I VEZE. (Subseries of its Statisticki Bilten) (Edition also in English) 100 din.($5.56) Savezni Zavod za Statistiku, Kneza Milosa 20, Belgrade, Yugoslavia. illus. circ. 1,100.

TRANSPORTATION — Air Transport

387.7   US   ISSN 0271-065X
A O P A'S AIRPORTS U.S.A. 1962. a. $24.95. Aircraft Owners and Pilots Association, 421 Aviation Way, Frederick, MD 21701. TEL 301-695-2000. circ. 100,000.
Formerly: Aircraft Owners and Pilots Association. A O P A Airport Directory (ISSN 0065-4906)

387.7   UK   ISSN 0306-3550
ACCIDENTS TO AIRCRAFT ON THE BRITISH REGISTER. 1949. irreg. price varies. Civil Aviation Authority, C A A House, 45-59 Kingsway, London WC2B 6TE, England.

387.7   FR   ISSN 0065-3721
AEROPORTS DE PARIS. RAPPORT DU CONSEIL D'ADMINISTRATION. (Editions in English and French) a. free. Aeroports de Paris - Paris Airport Authority, Service Relations Publiques et Editions, 291 Bd. Raspail, 75675 Paris, France.

387.7   FR   ISSN 0078-947X
AEROPORTS DE PARIS. SERVICE STATISTIQUE. STATISTIQUE DE TRAFIC. 1951. irreg.? 123 F. Aeroports de Paris - Paris Airport Authority, Service Documentation et Statistiques, Orly Sud 103, 94396 Orly Aerogare Cedex, France.

387.736   FR
AEROPORTS DE PARIS. TRAFIC DES PRINCIPAUX AEROPORTS MONDIAUX. (Text in English and French) a. 90 F. Aeroports de Paris, Service Documentation et Statistiques, Orly Sud 103, 94396 Aerogare, France.

387.7   NZ   ISSN 0065-4817
AIR NEW ZEALAND. ANNUAL REPORT. 1965. a. free. Air New Zealand Ltd, 1 Queen St., Auckland, New Zealand (U.S. address: Ste. 1000, Equitable Airport Center, 9841 Airport Blvd., Los Angeles, CA 90045) circ. 14,000.

387.7   US
AIR TRANSPORT. 1937. a. free. Air Transport Association of America, 1709 New York Ave., N.W., Washington, DC 20006. TEL 202-626-4000.

387.7   CN   ISSN 0065-485X
AIR TRANSPORT ASSOCIATION OF CANADA. ANNUAL REPORT. 1960. a. Air Transport Association of Canada, 747 Metropolitan Life Bldg., 99 Bank St., Ottawa, Ont. K1P 6B9, Canada. TEL 613-233-7727. Ed. Donald H. Watson. circ. 1,000.

387.7   II
AIR TRANSPORTATION ANNUAL (BOMBAY) (Text in English) 1980. a. Rs.20($5) Amalgamated Press, Narang House, 41 Ambalal Doshi Marg, Bombay 400023, India. Ed. Jeanette da Silva. circ. 2,000.

387.7   RH
AIR ZIMBABWE ANNUAL REPORT. 1968. a. free. Air Zimbabwe Corporation, P.O. Box AP. 1, Harare Airport, Harare, Zimbabwe. circ. 2,000.
Formerly: Air Rhodesia Annual Report.

AIRLINE GUIDE TO FLIGHT ATTENDANT CAREER. see OCCUPATIONS AND CAREERS

387.7   US   ISSN 0095-4683
AIRLINE HANDBOOK. 1972. a. $16. AeroTravel Research Publications, Box 3694, Cranston, RI 02910. TEL 401-941-6140. Ed. Paul K. Martin. illus.

AIRMAN'S INFORMATION MANUAL. see AERONAUTICS AND SPACE FLIGHT

341.46   US
AVIATION CASES IN THE COURTS. irreg. (approx. 2/yr.) $80. Hawkins Publishing Co., Inc., Box 480, Mayo, MD 21106-0480. TEL 301-798-1677. Ed. Carl R. Eyler.

387.7   II   ISSN 0067-2645
AVIATION DIRECTORY OF ASIA.* 1956. a. Aeronautical Publications of India Private Limited, Santa Cruz Airport, Bombay 19, India.

BOSTON SEA AND AIR PORT HANDBOOK. see BUSINESS AND ECONOMICS — Trade And Industrial Directories

387.7   UK
BRITISH HELICOPTER ADVISORY BOARD HANDBOOK. 1972. a. free. (British Helicopter Advisory Board) Shephard Press Ltd., 111 High St., Burnham, Bucks. SL1 7JZ, England. Ed. Capt. E.H. Brown. adv. circ. 2,000.

387.7   CN
CALGARY AIRPORT BUSINESS DIRECTORY. 1977. a. Can.$5.00. Corvus Publishing Group Ltd., 1224-53 Ave. N.E., Ste. 158, Calgary, Alta. T2E 7E2, Canada. TEL 403-275-9457. Ed. Paul J. Skinner. adv. circ. 7,000. (back issues avail.)

387.7   US   ISSN 0069-1437
CENSUS OF U.S. CIVIL AIRCRAFT. 1965. a. $8.50. U.S. Federal Aviation Administration., Office of Management Systems, Department of Transportation, Washington, DC 20591 TEL 202-655-4000. (Orders to: NTIS, Springfield, VA 22161)

TRANSPORTATION — AIR TRANSPORT

387.7   UK
CONCORD INFLIGHT ENTERTAINMENT GUIDE. a. Headway Publications Ltd., Clareville House, 47 Whitcomb St., London WC2H 7DK, England. Ed. William Davis. circ. 180,000.

387.7   910.22   US
DETROIT NEWS TRAVEL DIRECTORY. biennial. free. Detroit News, Travel Advertising, 615 W. Lafayette, Detroit, MI 48231. TEL 313-222-2326. circ. 6,000.

387   SP   ISSN 0421-4986
ESTADISTICAS DE LA AVIACION CIVIL EN ESPANA. a. Ministerio del Aire, Subsecretaria de Aviacion Civil, Princessa 88, Madrid, Spain.

387.7   UN   ISSN 0071-2558
EUROPEAN CIVIL AVIATION CONFERENCE (REPORT OF SESSION) (Issued as a subseries of Air Transport. Series D: Reports) (Editions in English, French and Spanish) 1955. triennial since 1961 with intermediate sessions; 8th triennial, Strasbourg, 1973; 6th intermediate, Paris, 1974. price varies. International Civil Aviation Organization, 1000 Sherbrooke St. W., Montreal, Que. H3A 2R2, Canada.

387.74   614.86   US
FACTS AND ADVICE FOR AIRLINE PASSENGERS. 1979. biennial. $2. Aviation Consumer Action Project, Box 19029, Washington, DC 20036. TEL 202-785-3704. Ed.Bd.

387.73   US
FEDERAL AVIATION ADMINISTRATION: HIGH ALTITUDE POLLUTION PROGRAM. biennial. Federal Aviation Administration, Office of Environment and Energy, Washington, DC 20591.

387.82   UK
FLIGHT DIRECTORY OF BRITISH AVIATION. 1973. biennial. £25. Business Press International Ltd., Quadrant House, Sutton, Surrey SM2 5AS, England. Ed. Malcolm Guinsberg.

FLYING DOCTOR YEARBOOK. see *HOSPITALS*

387.7   US
GENERAL AVIATION STATISTICAL DATABOOK. 1980. a. $3. General Aviation Manufacturers Association, 1400 K St. N.W., Ste. 801, Washington, DC 20005. TEL 202-393-1500. stat.

387.7   UK
GREAT BRITAIN. AIR TRANSPORT USERS COMMITTEE ANNUAL REPORT. 1975. a. price varies. Air Transport Users Committee, 129 Kingsway, London WC2B 6NN, England. Ed. Richard Botwood. circ. 1,000.
    Formerly: Great Britain. Civil Aviation Authority. Air Transport Users Committee Annual Report.

387.7   UK   ISSN 0068-1229
GREAT BRITAIN. BRITISH AIRPORTS AUTHORITY. ANNUAL REPORT AND ACCOUNTS. 1966. a. £2. (British Airports Authority) B A A Plc., Corporate Office, 130 Wilton Rd., London SW1V 1LQ, England, England. Ed. F. Gibson Smith. illus. circ. 10,000.

387.71   UK   ISSN 0306-3569
GREAT BRITAIN. CIVIL AVIATION AUTHORITY. ANNUAL REPORT AND ACCOUNTS. 1949. a. price varies. Civil Aviation Authority, C A A House, 45-59 Kingsway, London WC2B 6TE, England.
    Formerly: Great Britain. Air Transport Licensing Board. Report (ISSN 0072-5617)

387.7   UK   ISSN 0072-5641
GREAT BRITAIN. CIVIL AVIATION AUTHORITY. CIVIL AVIATION PUBLICATIONS. 1946. irreg. price varies. Civil Aviation Authority, C A A House, 45-59 Kingsway, London WC2B 6TE, England.

387.7   UK
GREAT BRITAIN. CIVIL AVIATION AUTHORITY. GENERAL AVIATION AIRMISS BULLETIN; a review of selected incidents. irreg. £5. Civil Aviation Authority, C A A House, 45-59 Kingsway, London WC2B 6TE, England.
    Formerly: Great Britain. Civil Aviation Authority. General Aviation Airmisses (ISSN 0144-2481)

387.7   UK
GREAT BRITAIN. CIVIL AVIATION AUTHORITY. INTERNATIONAL REGISTER OF CIVIL AIRCRAFT. (Supplements avail.) a. £70. Civil Aviation Authority, CAA House, 45-59 Kingsway, London WCB 6TE, England. (also avail. in microfiche)

387.7   UK
GREAT BRITAIN. CIVIL AVIATION AUTHORITY. U.K. AIRLINES ANNUAL OPERATING, TRAFFIC & FINANCIAL STATISTICS. 1973. a. price varies. Civil Aviation Authority, CAA House, 45-59 Kingsway, London WC2B 6TE, England.
    Supersedes in part (as from 1983): Great Britain. Civil Aviation Authority. Annual Statistics.

387.7   UK
GREAT BRITAIN. CIVIL AVIATION AUTHORITY. U.K. AIRPORTS ANNUAL STATEMENTS OF MOVEMENTS, PASSENGERS AND CARGO. 1973. a. price varies. Civil Aviation Authority, CAA House, 45-59 Kingsway, London WC2B 6TE, England.
    Supersedes in part (as from 1983): Great Britain. Civil Aviation Authority. Annual Statistics.

386.736   FR
GUIDE PRATIQUE DES AEROPORTS ET DE L'AVIATION COMMERCIALE. 1975. a. 40 F. 30 rue de Trevise, 75009 Paris, France.

387.7   CN
HANDBOOK OF AIR TRANSPORT LEGISLATION. (Text in English and French) 1979. irreg. Can.$50. Canadian Transport Commission, Ottawa, Ont. K1A 0N9, Canada TEL 819-997-2560. (Avail. from: Canadian Government Publishing Centre, Supply and Services Canada, Ottawa, Ont. K1A 0S9, Canada) (looseleaf format)

387.7   US   ISSN 0739-5728
HELICOPTER ANNUAL. 1983. a. $35 to non-members. Helicopter Association International, 1619 Duke St., Alexandria, VA 22314-3406. TEL 703-683-4646. Ed. Daniel P. Warsley. adv. circ. 20,000.

387.742   UK
HICKMAN'S INTERNATIONAL AIR TRAVELLER. 1979. a. £6.95. Mitchell Beazley, 14 Manette St., London W1, England. Eds. R.H. Hickman, M.E. Hickman. circ. 20,000.

387.7   CN
I A T A ANNUAL REPORT. (Director General's report to the Annual General Meeting of the International Air Transport Association) (Text in English, French and Spanish) 1945. a. free; limited distribution. ‡ International Air Transport Association, 2000 Peel St., Montreal, Que. H3A 2R4, Canada. TEL 514-844-6311. circ. controlled.
    Formerly: State of the Air Transport Industry (ISSN 0081-4571)

387.7   CN
I A T A DANGEROUS GOODS REGULATIONS. (Editions in English, French, German, Spanish) 1957. a. $42. International Air Transport Association, 2000 Peel St., Montreal, Que. H3A 2R4, Canada. TEL 514-844-6311. circ. 55,000.

341.46   CN
I A T A LIVE ANIMALS REGULATIONS. (Editions in English, French and Spanish) 12th edt., 1985. a. $35. International Air Transport Association, 2000 Peel St., Montreal, Que. H3A 2R4, Canada.

387   UN   ISSN 0074-2481
I C A O CIRCULARS. (Editions in English, French, Spanish; some also issued in Russian) no.18, 1951. irreg. price varies. International Civil Aviation Organization, 1000 Sherbrooke St. W., Montreal, Que. H3A 2R2, Canada.

387.7   NE
INTERNATIONAL AIR SHOW GUIDE. (Text in English) 1981. a. fl.10. Flash Aviation, Postbus 855, 5600 AW Eindhoven, Netherlands. Ed. C. van den Heuvel. adv. bk. rev. circ. 10,000.
    Formerly: Aviation Focus.

387.7   CN
INTERNATIONAL AIR TRANSPORT ASSOCIATION. ANNUAL GENERAL MEETING. REPORTS AND PROCEEDINGS. (Text in English, French and Spanish) 1945. a. free. International Air Transport Association, 2000 Peel St., Montreal, Que. H3A 2R4, Canada. TEL 514-844-6311.
    Formerly: International Air Transport Association. Annual Report; Continues: Air Transport Association. Annual General Meeting Reports and Proceedings; Which was formerly: International Air Transport Association. Bulletin (ISSN 0074-1329)

387.7   SZ
INTERNATIONAL AIR TRANSPORT ASSOCIATION. INDUSTRY AUTOMATION AND FINANCE SERVICES DEPARTMENT. PUBLICATIONS. (Text in English) 1979. a. free. International Air Transport Association, Industry Automation and Finance Services, 26 Chemin de Joinville, Box 160, 1216 Cointrin-Geneva, Switzerland.
    Former titles: International Air Transport Association. Economics and Industry Finance Department. Bulletin; International Air Transport Association. Industry Research Division. Bulletin; International Air Transport Association. Industry Research Division. Service Information Bulletin.

387.7   FR
INTERNATIONAL CIVIL AIRPORTS ASSOCIATION. STATISTIQUES DE TRAFFIC. RESULTATS GENERAUX. (Text in English and French) 1962. a. 169 F. Aeroports de Paris, Service Documentation et Statistique, Orly Sud 103, 94396 Orly Aerogare, France. Ed. Rene Andre. bk. rev. circ. 600.
    Formerly: Western European Association. Statistiques de Traffic.

387   UN   ISSN 0074-221X
INTERNATIONAL CIVIL AVIATION ASSOCIATION. AERONAUTICAL AGREEMENTS AND ARRANGEMENTS. ANNUAL SUPPLEMENT. (Text in English) 1965. a. price varies. International Civil Aviation Organization, 1000 Sherbrooke St. W., Montreal, Que. H3A 2R2, Canada.

387.7   UN   ISSN 0074-2287
INTERNATIONAL CIVIL AVIATION ORGANIZATION. AIR NAVIGATION PLAN. AFRICA-INDIAN OCEAN REGION. (Editions in English, French and Spanish) 1954. irreg., 24th, 1983. price varies. International Civil Aviation Organization, 1000 Sherbrooke St. W., Montreal, Que. H3A 2R2, Canada.

387.7   UN
INTERNATIONAL CIVIL AVIATION ORGANIZATION. AIR NAVIGATION PLAN. CARIBBEAN REGION. (Editions in English, French and Spanish) 1956. irreg., 13th, 1985. price varies. International Civil Aviation Organization, 1000 Sherbrooke St. W., Montreal, Que. H3A 2R2, Canada.
    Third meeting: International Civil Aviation Organization. Air Navigation Plan. Caribbean and South American Regions (ISSN 0074-2295)

387.7   UN
INTERNATIONAL CIVIL AVIATION ORGANIZATION. AIR NAVIGATION PLAN. MIDDLE EAST AND ASIA REGIONS. (Supersedes its Middle East Region and its South East Asia Region) (Editions in English, French, Spanish) irreg., 13th, 1985. price varies. International Civil Aviation Organization, 1000 Sherbrooke St. W., Montreal, Que. H3A 2R2, Canada.
    Formerly: International Civil Aviation Organization. Air Navigation Plan. Middle East and South East Asia Regions (ISSN 0074-2317)

387.7   UN   ISSN 0074-2325
INTERNATIONAL CIVIL AVIATION ORGANIZATION. AIR NAVIGATION PLAN. NORTH ATLANTIC, NORTH AMERICAN AND PACIFIC REGIONS. (Supersedes its North Atlantic Region and its Pacific Region) (Editions in English, French, Spanish) irreg., 12th, 1984. price varies. International Civil Aviation Organization, 1000 Sherbrooke St. W., Montreal, Que. H3A 2R2, Canada.

TRANSPORTATION — AIR TRANSPORT

387.7   UN   ISSN 0074-2368
INTERNATIONAL CIVIL AVIATION ORGANIZATION. ASSEMBLY. REPORT AND MINUTES OF THE LEGAL COMMISSION. (Editions in Arabic, English, French, Russian, Spanish) irreg., 24th, Montreal, 1983. price varies. International Civil Aviation Organization, 1000 Sherbrooke St. W., Montreal, Que. H3A 2R2, Canada.

387.7   UN   ISSN 0074-2376
INTERNATIONAL CIVIL AVIATION ORGANIZATION. ASSEMBLY. REPORT OF THE ECONOMIC COMMISSION. irreg., 18th, 1971. price varies. International Civil Aviation Organization - Organisation de l'Aviation Civile Internationale, P.O. Box 400, Succursale: Place de l'Aviation Internationale, 1000 Sherbrooke Street West, Montreal, Quebec H3A 2R2, Canada.

387.7   UN   ISSN 0074-235X
INTERNATIONAL CIVIL AVIATION ORGANIZATION. ASSEMBLY. RESOLUTIONS. (Editions in Arabic, English, French, Russian, Spanish) 1965, 15th. irreg., 21st, Montreal, 1974. price varies. International Civil Aviation Organization, 1000 Sherbrooke St. W., Montreal, Que. H3A 2R2, Canada.

387   UN
INTERNATIONAL CIVIL AVIATION ORGANIZATION. COUNCIL. ANNUAL REPORT. (Editions in English, French, Russian, Spanish) a. price varies. International Civil Aviation Organization, 1000 Sherbrooke St. W., Que. H3A 2R2, Canada.

387   UN   ISSN 0074-2422
INTERNATIONAL CIVIL AVIATION ORGANIZATION. DIGESTS OF STATISTICS. SERIES AT. AIRPORT TRAFFIC. (Editions in English, French, Russian, Spanish) a., no.25, 1984. price varies. International Civil Aviation Organization, 1000 Sherbrooke St. W., Montreal, Que. H3A 2R2, Canada.
Monthly and yearly statistics for airports open to international traffic

387   UN   ISSN 0074-2430
INTERNATIONAL CIVIL AVIATION ORGANIZATION. DIGESTS OF STATISTICS. SERIES F. FINANCIAL DATA. (Editions in English, French, Russian, Spanish) a. price varies. International Civil Aviation Organization, 1000 Sherbrooke St. W., Montreal, Que. H3A 2R2, Canada.

387   UN   ISSN 0074-2449
INTERNATIONAL CIVIL AVIATION ORGANIZATION. DIGESTS OF STATISTICS. SERIES FP. FLEET, PERSONNEL. (Classification of its Digest of Statistics, issued from 1947. Digest and Series numbering maintained separately) (Editions in English, French, Russian and Spanish) a. price varies. International Civil Aviation Organization, 1000 Sherbrooke St. W., Montreal, Que. H3A 2R2, Canada.

387   UN   ISSN 0074-2457
INTERNATIONAL CIVIL AVIATION ORGANIZATION. DIGESTS OF STATISTICS. SERIES R. CIVIL AIRCRAFT ON REGISTER. (Editions in English, French, Russian, Spanish) 1961. a. price varies. International Civil Aviation Organization, 1000 Sherbrooke St. W., Montreal, Que. H3A 2R2, Canada.

387   UN   ISSN 0074-2465
INTERNATIONAL CIVIL AVIATION ORGANIZATION. DIGESTS OF STATISTICS. SERIES T. TRAFFIC. (Editions in English, French, Russian, Spanish) a. price varies. International Civil Aviation Organization, 1000 Sherbrooke St. W., Montreal, Que. H3A 2R2, Canada.
Monthly and yearly traffic statistics for scheduled airlines, information also provided by country

387   UN   ISSN 0074-2473
INTERNATIONAL CIVIL AVIATION ORGANIZATION. DIGESTS OF STATISTICS. SERIES TF. TRAFFIC FLOW. (Text in English, French, Spanish, Russian) a. price varies. International Civil Aviation Organization, 1000 Sherbrooke St. W., Montreal, Que. H3A 2R2, Canada.

387.7   UN   ISSN 0074-2503
INTERNATIONAL CIVIL AVIATION ORGANIZATION. LEGAL COMMITTEE. MINUTES AND DOCUMENTS (OF SESSIONS) (Editions in English, French and Spanish) triennial, 25th, Montreal, 1983. price varies. International Civil Aviation Organization, 1000 Sherbrooke St. W., Montreal, Que. H3A 2R2, Canada.

658   US   ISSN 0538-7442
INTERNATIONAL FEDERATION OF OPERATIONAL RESEARCH SOCIETIES. AIRLINE GROUP (A G I F O R S) PROCEEDINGS. 1961. a. $45. International Federation of Operational Research Societies, Airline Group, c/o Joe D. Hinson, 2725-21 Mendelken, Memphis, TN 38115. Ed. L.G. Klingen. circ. 300. (processed; back issues avail.)

387.7   UR   ISSN 0202-7887
ITOGI NAUKI I TEKHNIKI: VOZDUSHNYI TRANSPORT. irreg., latest vol.15, 1987. price varies. Vsesoyuznyi Institut Nauchno-Tekhnicheskoi Informatsii (VINITI), Baltiiskaya ul. 14, Moscow A-219, Russian S.F.S.R., U.S.S.R. (Subscr. to: Mezhdunarodnaya Kniga, Dimitrova ul. 39, 113095 Moscow, Russian S.F.S.R., U.S.S.R.)

387.7   UK
JANE'S AIRPORT EQUIPMENT. 1982. a. £58($137.50) Jane's Publishing Co., 238 City Rd., London E.C.1, England (Subscr.to: Jane's Publishing Inc., 20 Park plaza, Boston, MA 02116) Ed. David Rider. adv. index.

341.46   AG
JORNADAS NACIONALES DE DERECHO AERONAUTICO Y ESPACIAL. TRABAJOS. irreg. Universidad Nacional de Cordoba, Instituto de Derecho Aeronautico y Espacial, Ciudad Universitaria, Cordoba, Argentina.

387.7   NE   ISSN 0022-7374
K L M NEWS. (Text in Dutch, English, French, Spanish) 1946. irreg. free. ‡ K.L.M. Royal Dutch Airlines, Pb 7700, 1117 ZL Schiphol, Netherlands. Ed.Bd.

387.7   MW   ISSN 0076-3055
MALAWI. DEPARTMENT OF CIVIL AVIATION. ANNUAL REPORT. a. K.0.30. Government Printer, P.O. Box 37, Zomba, Malawi.

MASSACHUSETTS INSTITUTE OF TECHNOLOGY. FLIGHT TRANSPORTATION LABORATORY. F T L REPORTS AND MEMORANDA. see *AERONAUTICS AND SPACE FLIGHT*

387.742   AT
MORGAN INDEX ON AIRLINE TRAVEL (AUSTRALIA) 1973. a. Aus.$17.80. Roy Morgan Research Centre Pty. Ltd., Box 2282U, Melbourne, Vic. 3001, Australia.

387.7   KE   ISSN 0077-2666
NAIROBI AIRPORT. ANNUAL REPORT.* 1958. a. Director of Aerodromes, P.O. Box 19001, Nairobi, Kenya.

387.7   US
NATIONAL AIRSPACE SYSTEM PLAN: FACILITIES, EQUIPMENT AND ASSOCIATED DEVELOPMENT. a. U.S. Department of Transportation, Federal Aviation Administration, 800 Independence Ave., S.W., Washington, DC 20591.

387.7   US
NATIONAL TRANSPORTATION SAFETY BOARD SERVICE. 1972. irreg. (approx. 8-10/yr.) $210. Hawkins Publishing Co., Inc., Box 480, Mayo, MD 21106-0480. TEL 301-798-1677. Ed. Carl R. Eyler. circ. 80. (looseleaf format)

387.7   NE   ISSN 0168-552X
NETHERLANDS. CENTRAAL BUREAU VOOR DE STATISTIEK. STATISTIEK VAN DE LUCHTVAART. CIVIL AVIATION STATISTICS. (Text in Dutch and English) 1949. a. fl.16.50. Centraal Bureau voor de Statistiek, Prinses Beatrixlaan 428, Voorburg, Netherlands (Orders to: Staatsuitgeverij, Christoffel Plantijnstraat, The Hague, Netherlands)

387.7   US   ISSN 0091-6978
NEW JERSEY AIRPORT DIRECTORY. 1968. irreg., latest 1981. ‡ Department of Transportation, 1035 Parkway Ave., Trenton, NJ 08625. illus.

PACIFIC AVIATION YEARBOOK. see *AERONAUTICS AND SPACE FLIGHT*

387.736   US
PORT AUTHORITY OF NEW YORK AND NEW JERSEY. AVIATION ANNUAL REPORT. a. Port Authority of New York and New Jersey, Aviation Department, One World Trade Center, New York, NY 10048.

307.71   US
PORT AUTHORITY OF NEW YORK AND NEW JERSEY. AVIATION DEPARTMENT. AIRPORT STATISTICS. a. Port Authority of New York, and New Jersey, Aviation Department, Aviation Economics Division, 65 N One World Trade Center, New York, NY 10048. TEL 212-466-7000. stat.

387.7   AT
QANTAS AIRWAYS. REPORT. (Subseries of: Australia. Parliament. Parliamentary Papers) a. price varies. Australian Government Publishing Service, G.P.O. Box 84, Canberra, A.C.T. 2601, Australia. illus.

387.744   388.324   US
QUICK CALLER: BOSTON AREA AIR CARGO DIRECTORY. 1976. biennial. $7. Fourth Seacoast Publishing Co., Inc., 25300 Little Mack, St. Clair Shores, MI 48081 TEL 313-779-5570. (Subscr. to: Box 145, St. Clair Shores, MI 48080) Ed. Roger J. Buysse. circ. 10,000.

387.744   388.324   US
QUICK CALLER: DETROIT AREA AIR CARGO DIRECTORY. 1973. a. $7. Fourth Seacoast Publishing Co., Inc., 25300 Little Mack, St. Clair Shores, MI 48081 TEL 313-779-5570. (Subscr. to: Box 145, St. Clair Shores, MI 48080) Ed. Roger J. Buysse. circ. 10,000.

387.744   388.324   US
QUICK CALLER: MIAMI AREA AIR CARGO DIRECTORY. 1975. a. $7. Fourth Seacoast Publishing Co., Inc., 25300 Little Mack, St. Clair Shores, MI 48081 TEL 313-779-5570. (Subscr. to: Box 145, St. Clair Shores, MI 48080) Ed. Roger J. Buysse. circ. 10,000.

387.744   388.324   US
QUICK CALLER: SAN FRANCISCO BAY AREA AIR CARGO DIRECTORY. 1982. a. $7. Fourth Seacoast Publishing Co., Inc., 25300 Little Mack, St. Clair Shores, MI 48081 TEL 313-779-5570. (Subscr. to: Box 145, St. Clair Shores, MI 48080) Ed. Roger J. Buysse. circ. 10,000.

387.7   FR   ISSN 0080-066X
REGISTRE AERONAUTIQUE INTERNATIONAL. 1966. a. (with m. suppl.) 1070 F. Bureau Veritas, Registre International de Classification de Navires et d'Aeronefs, 92077 Paris la Defense Cedex 44, France. circ. 1,000. (also avail. in microfilm)

387.7   UN   ISSN 0085-5596
REVIEW OF ECONOMIC SITUATION OF AIR TRANSPORT. (Issued in ICAO Circular Series) (Editions in English, French, Russian, Spanish) triennial. price varies. International Civil Aviation Organization, 1000 Sherbrooke St. W., Montreal, Que. H3A 2R2, Canada.

387.7   SZ
DIE SCHWEIZERISCHE ZIVILLUFTFAHRT; l'aviation civile suisse. (Text in French, German) 1925. a. 12 Fr. Bundesamt fuer Zivilluftfahrt - Federal Office for Civil Aviation (Office Federal de l'Aviation Civile), Inselgasse, CH-3003 Berne, Switzerland. Ed. Daniel Ruhier. circ. 1,400.
Supersedes (from 1975): Schweizerische Luftverkehrsstatistik/Statistique du Trafic Aerien Suisse.

387.7   IS
TEUFAH. (Text in English) 1985. a. $10. Israel Shipping and Aviation Research Institute, P.O. Box 1860, Haifa 31 086, Israel.

TRANSPORTATION — AUTOMOBILES

387.7   CN
TORONTO AIRPORT BUSINESS DIRECTORY. 1979. a. Can.$5.00. Corvus Publishing Group Ltd., 1224-53 Ave. N.E., Ste. 158, Calgary, Alta. T2E 7E2, Canada. TEL 403-275-9457. Ed. Paul J. Skinner. adv. circ. 7,000. (back issues avail.)

387.7   US   ISSN 0886-4217
U S AVIATION REPORTS. 1968; cum. digest began 1982. a. $45 ($100 per vol. for cum. digest) Oceana Publications, Inc., 75 Main St., Dobbs Ferry, NY 10522. TEL 914-693-1320. Ed. Christopher Knauth.

387.7   US
U.S. FEDERAL AVIATION ADMINISTRATION. NATIONAL AVIATION SYSTEM: DEVELOPMENT AND CAPITAL NEEDS. 1969. irreg., latest issue 1980. free. U.S. Federal Aviation Administration, Department of Transportation, c/o Freda Johnson, 800 Independence Ave., Washington, DC 20591 TEL 202-655-4000. (Orders to: Supt. of Documents, Washington, DC 20402) illus. circ. 3,000.
    Former titles: U.S. Federal Aviation Administration. National Aviation System: Challenges of the Decade Ahead & U.S. Federal Aviation Administration. National Aviation System Policy Summary (ISSN 0092-4555)

387.74   US
U.S. NATIONAL TRANSPORTATION SAFETY BOARD. AIRCRAFT ACCIDENT REPORTS. (Formerly issued by Department of Transportation) irreg. $35 (brief format $40) U.S. National Transportation Safety Board, Department of Transportation, Washington, DC 20590 TEL 202-426-8787. (Orders to: National Technical Information Service, 5825 Port Royal Rd., Springfield, VA 22151)

387.7   CN
VANCOUVER AIRPORT BUSINESS DIRECTORY. 1978. a. Can.$3.50. Corvus Publishing Group Ltd., 1224-53 Ave. N.E., Ste. 158, Calgary, Alta. T2E 7E2, Canada. Ed. Paul J. Skinner. adv. circ. 7,000. (back issues avail.)

387.7   SZ   ISSN 0084-1366
WORLD AIR TRANSPORT STATISTICS. 1956. a. $55. International Air Transport Association, Economics and Industry Finance Department, 26 Chemin de Joinville, Box 160, 1216 Cointrin-Geneva, Switzerland. (back issues avail.)

387.7   US   ISSN 0084-1374
WORLD AIRLINE RECORD. 1948. irreg., 7th edt., 1972 (with q. supplements) $43.50. Roadcap Aviation Publications, 1030 S. Green Bay Rd., Lake Forest, IL 60045. TEL 312-234-4730. Ed. Roy R. Roadcap.

387.736   UK
WORLD AIRPORTS CONFERENCE. PROCEEDINGS. irreg., 7th, 1983. £24.50($35.50) (Institution of Civil Engineers) Thomas Telford Ltd., 1-7 Great George St., Westminster, London SW1P 3AA, England (Dist. in U.S. by: American Society of Civil Engineers, 345 E. 47th St., New York, NY 10017)

387.7   ZA
ZAMBIA. DEPARTMENT OF CIVIL AVIATION. ANNUAL REPORT. (Text in English) a. Government Printer, Box 30136, Lusaka, Zambia.

TRANSPORTATION — Automobiles

388.3 910.09   GW
A V D AUTO BORDBUCH. a. DM.4.80. A V D Verlag GmbH, Lyoner Str. 16, D-6000 Frankfurt/Main 71, W. Germany (B.R.D.) (back issues avail.)

629.2   US   ISSN 0065-2555
ADVANCES IN ENGINEERING. irreg. price varies. Society of Automotive Engineers, 400 Commonwealth Dr., Warrendale, PA 15096. TEL 412-776-4970.

AFTERMARKET BUSINESS BUYER'S GUIDE. see BUSINESS AND ECONOMICS — Marketing And Purchasing

AMERICAN ASSOCIATION FOR AUTOMOTIVE MEDICINE. PROCEEDINGS. see MEDICAL SCIENCES

343   US   ISSN 0093-4062
AMERICAN AUTOMOBILE ASSOCIATION. DIGEST OF MOTOR LAWS. (Vols. for 1965-79 compiled by its Legal Dept.; vols. for 1980-present compiled by its Traffic Safety Dept.) a. $6. American Automobile Association, 8111 Gatehouse Road, Falls Church, VA 22047. TEL 703-222-6000. Ed. Tom Luce. circ. 80,000. Key Title: Digest of Motor Laws.

388   629.286   UK   ISSN 0260-664X
AUSTIN HEALEY YEAR BOOK. 1978. a. Magpie Publishing Co., Holmerise, Seven Hills Rd., Cobham, Surrey, England. illus.

AUSTRALIAN ROAD RESEARCH BOARD. RESEARCH REPORT. see TRANSPORTATION

AUSTRALIAN ROAD RESEARCH BOARD. SPECIAL REPORT. see TRANSPORTATION

AUSTRALIAN ROAD RESEARCH BOARD. TECHNICAL MANUAL. see TRANSPORTATION

629.2   SA
AUTO DATA DIGEST. 1974. a. R.37. Mead & McGrouther (Pty) Ltd., 327 Surrey Ave., Box 1240, Ferndale, Randburg 2125, South Africa. Eds. O. Peruch, W. Calcutt. circ. 4,500.

629.2   GW   ISSN 0175-9531
DAS AUTO-INTERNATIONAL IN ZAHLEN/INTERNATIONAL AUTO STATISTICS. (Text in English, German) 1981. a. price varies. Verband der Automobilindustrie, Westendstr. 61, Postfach 17 05 63, 6000 Frankfurt 17, W. Germany (B.R.D.) (back issues avail.)

629.2   GW
AUTO-KATALOG. 1957. a. DM.12. Vereinigte Motor-Verlage GmbH und Co. KG, Leuschnerstr. 1, Postfach 1042, 7000 Stuttgart 1, W. Germany (B.R.D.) Ed. Rudolf Heitz. adv. abstr. index. circ. 295,000.
    Formerly: Auto-Modelle.

388.3 631.3   DK   ISSN 0106-0473
AUTO NYTS LEVERANDOERREGISTER. a. Thomson Communications (Scandinavia) A-S, Struenseegade 7-9, DK-2200 Copenhagen N, Denmark. adv. circ. 14,803.

629.2   FR   ISSN 0067-2424
AUTOCATALOGUE; guide technique de mecanique automobile. 1913. a. 173 F. Editions S.O.S.P., 59-61 Avenue de la Grande Annee, 75782 Paris Cedex 16, France. Ed. C.L. Lavaud. index.

388   RH
AUTOMOBILE ASSOCIATION OF ZIMBABWE. MEMBERS' HANDBOOK. 1923. biennial. membership. Automobile Association of Zimbabwe, Fanum House, 57 Samora Machel Ave., Harare, P.O. Box 585, Zimbabwe. adv. circ. 50,000.

338.476   JA
AUTOMOBILE INDUSTRY - JAPAN AND TOYOTA. (Text in English) 1972. a. free. Toyota Motor Corporation, Public Affairs Department, 1-4-18, Koraku, Bunkyo-ku, Tokyo 112, Japan. charts. illus. stat. circ. 7,000. Indexed: JCT.
    Formerly: Motor Industry of Japan; Incorporating: Toyota in Brief.

629.2   II   ISSN 0067-2548
AUTOMOBILE NEWS ANNUAL. (Text in English) 1947. a. Rs.15. Gidwaney's Publishing Co., 401 Arun Chambers, Tardeo Rd., Bombay 400034, India. Ed. Kishu Gidwaney.

629.2   SZ   ISSN 0084-7674
AUTOMOBILE YEAR/ANNEE AUTOMOBILE/AUTO-JAHR. (Editions in English, French, German) 1953. a. 69 Fr. Edipresse Publishing Group, Ave. de la Gare, 39, 1003 Lausanne, Switzerland (Dist. in UK by: Motor Racing Publications Ltd., Unit 6, The Pilton Estate, 46 Pitlake, Croydon CR0 3RY, England) Ed. J.-R. Piccard. adv. circ. 39,000.

318   US
AUTOMOBILES: LATIN AMERICAN INDUSTRIAL REPORT. (Avail. for each of 22 Latin American countries) 1985. a. $435 per country report per industry covered. Aurora International, Box 9099, Bridgeport, CT 06601-2099. TEL 203-368-0579. Ed. Andres C. Aquino.

629.286   US
AUTOMOTIVE AGE BUYER'S GUIDE. 1966. a. $5. Freed Crown Lee Publishing Inc., Box 2006, 6931 Van Nuys Blvd., CA 91405. TEL 213-997-0644. adv. circ. 35,374.

629.286   US
AUTOMOTIVE BODY REPAIR NEWS (YEAR) BUYERS GUIDE AND FACT BOOK. 1977. a. Stanley Publishing Co., 65 E. South Water St., Chicago, IL 60601. TEL 312-332-0210. Ed. Charles E. Rauhauser, Jr. adv. tr.lit. circ. 60,571.

338.3   US
AUTOMOTIVE CONTACT AUTOMOTIVE DIRECTORY. INDIANA. INDIANA. a. $27.95. Automotive Contact, Box 517, Terre Haute, IN 47808. TEL 812-232-2441. Ed. T.L. Spelman. adv. circ. 3,250.
    Formerly: Indiana Automotive Directory.

629   US
AUTOMOTIVE ENCYCLOPEDIA. Variant title: Goodhear-Willcox Automotive Encyclopedia. 1956. biennial. $23. Goodheart-Willcox Co., Inc., 123 West Taft Dr., South Holland, IL 60473. TEL 312-333-7200. Eds. William K. Toboldt, Larry Johnson. index.

338.476   JA
AUTOMOTIVE HERALD. FACTS & INFO; annual guide to Japan's auto industry. (Text in English) 1981. a. $54. Automotive Herald Co., Ltd., 3rd Shinto Bldg., 21-1 Shinbashi 5-chome, Minato-ku, Tokyo 105, Japan (U.S. address: Japan America Automotive Systems, Inc., 2424 W. Morse Ave., Chicago, IL 60645) Ed. Akira Shikakura. circ. 8,000.

692.2   SA
AUTOMOTIVE INDUSTRY DIRECTORY. 1981. a. R.35. Ramsay, Son & Parker (Pty) Ltd., Box 180, Howard Place 7450, Cape Town, South Africa. TEL 021-531 391. Ed. Jean Beechey. circ. 1,100.
    Formerly: Automotive Products Directory.

380.5   II
AUTOMOTIVE INDUSTRY OF INDIA - FACTS & FIGURES. (Text in English) 1966. a. Rs.50. All-India Automobile and Ancillary Industries Association, 80 Dr. Annie Besant Rd., Worli, Bombay 400018, India. Ed. S. Panikar. circ. 1,000.
    Formerly: Automotive and Ancillary Industry.

629.2   US
AUTOMOTIVE NEWS MARKET DATA BOOK. 1933. a. $22.50. (Automotive News) Crain Communications Inc. (Detroit), Automotive News, 1400 Woodbridge Ave., Detroit, MI 48207. TEL 313-446-6000. Ed. Andrew R. McGill. adv. circ. 65,638. (also avail. in microform from UMI; reprint service avail. from UMI)
    Formerly: Automotive News Almanac (ISSN 0067-2580)

629.286   CN   ISSN 0068-9629
AUTOMOTIVE SERVICE DATA BOOK. 1935. a. Can.$18($22) Maclean-Hunter Ltd., Business Publication Division, Maclean-Hunter Bldg., 777 Bay St., Toronto, Ont. M5W 1A7, Canada. TEL 416-596-5784. adv.

629.286   MX
AUTOMOTRIZ. 1968. a. Mex.$4250($25) Litoimpresores, S.A., Espana 396, 09880 Mexico, D.F., Mexico. Ed. Cesar Macazaga. adv.

796.77   IT
AUTOSPRINT ANNO. 1970. a. L.7000. Conti Editore Spa., Via del Lavoro 7, 40068 S. Lazzaro di Savena (Bologna), Italy. Ed. Carlo Cavicchi. adv. circ. 30,000.
    Racing Cars

388.3   DK
BIL-REVYEN. a. Bonniers Specialmagasiner, Noerre Farimagsgade 49, 1375 Copenhagen K, Denmark. adv. circ. 60,000.

338.476   DK   ISSN 0108-5018
BILENS AARSREVY. a. Bonnier Specialmagasiner, Noerre Farimagsgade 49, 1375 Copenhagen K, Denmark. circ. 31,000.

388.3   DK   ISSN 0901-6120
BILISMEN I DANMARK. 1967. a. free. Automobil-Importoerernes Sammenslutning, Ryvangs Alle 68, 2900 Hellerup, Denmark. Ed. Erik Ebsen Petersen.

TRANSPORTATION — AUTOMOBILES

796 380.1   FR
BOTTIN AUTO-CYCLE-MOTO. 1894. a. $70. Societe Didot Bottin, 28 rue du Docteur Finlay, 75738 Paris Cedex 15, France.
 Formerly: Bottin de l'Auto et du Cycle.

388.3   CN ISSN 0707-5014
BRITISH COLUMBIA MOTOR TRANSPORT DIRECTORY. 1978. a. Can.$34.95. British Columbia Motor Transport Association, 4090 Graveley St., Burnaby, B.C. V5C 3T6, Canada. TEL 604-299-7407. adv. circ. 850.

629.222   UK
BUYERS' GUIDE TO THE AUTOMOTIVE INDUSTRY OF GREAT BRITAIN FOR INTERNATIONAL BUYERS. a. £10 to non-members; members £6. Society of Motor Manufacturers and Traders Ltd., Forbes House, Halkin St., London SW1X 7DS, England.
 Formerly: Buyers' Guide to the Motor Industry of Great Britain.

388   CN
CANADIAN AUTOMOBILE ASSOCIATION. PUBLIC POLICY BOOKLET. 1975. a. Canadian Automobile Association, 1775 Courtwood Cresc., Ottawa, Ont. K2C 3J2, Canada. TEL 613-226-7631. Ed. Michael S. McNeil. circ. 4,000.

CANADIAN AUTOMOTIVE AFTERMARKET DIRECTORY/MARKETING GUIDE. see *BUSINESS AND ECONOMICS — Trade And Industrial Directories*

629.2   US
CAR AND DRIVER BUYERS GUIDE. 1957. a. $3.95. C B S Magazines, Car and Driver Department, 1515 Broadway, New York, NY 10036. TEL 212-719-6000. Don Coulter. adv. circ. 155,000.
 Formerly: Car and Driver Yearbook (ISSN 0069-0260)

388 658.8   US
CAR PRICES. 1965. a. $2.50 per no. People's Publishing Co., Inc., 901 W. Victoria St., Ste. B-2, Compton, CA 90220. TEL 707-822-8442. Ed. Rosemary Anderson. adv. stat. circ. 100,000.
 Formerly: American Car Prices.

CARAVAN FACTFINDER. see *TRAVEL AND TOURISM*

796.77   AT
CARS IN AUSTRALIA. ANNUAL. 1984. a. Hay Street Publications Pty Ltd, 405-411 Sussex St, Sydney, NSW 2000, Australia. Ed. Barry Cooke. circ. 40,000.

629.286   IT
CATALOGO MOTORISTICO. (Text in English, French, German, Italian) 1962. a. L.10000. Azienda Cataloghi Italiani, Piazzale Lugano 9, 20158 Milan, Italy. Ed. Lucio Torella. adv. circ. 35,000 (controlled)

629.2   FR ISSN 0069-1097
CATALOGUE DES CATALOGUES AUTOMOBILE. 1905. a. 300 F. Editions Professionnelles Glass France S.A.R.L., 14 av. Pierre Grenier, Boulogne-Billancourt, 92100 Paris, France. Ed. B. Louvigne. adv. circ. 11,000.

388.3   BE
CATALOGUE GENERAL DE L'INDUSTRIE ET DU COMMERCE AUTOMOBILE DE BELGIQUE. (Text in Dutch, English, French and German) 1950. a. Chambre Syndicale du Commerce Automobile de Belgique, Bd. de la Woluwe 46, 1200 Brussels, Belgium. adv.

388.3 918.904   UY
CENTUR. 1977. a. free. Centro Automovilista del Uruguay, Artigas 1773, Montevideo, Uruguay. Ed. Ever Cabrera Tornielli. adv. circ. 10,000.

CHAMBRE SYNDICALE NATIONALE DES ELECTRICIENS ET SPECIALISTES DE L'AUTOMOBILE. ANNUAIRE. see *ELECTRICITY AND ELECTRICAL ENGINEERING*

629.28   US ISSN 0069-3634
CHILTON'S AUTO REPAIR MANUAL; American cars from 1979 to 1986. 1968. a. price varies. Chilton Book Co., Automotive Editorial Department, Chilton Way, Radnor, PA 19089.

629.2   US
CHILTON'S IMPORT CAR REPAIR MANUAL; from 1979-1986. 1971. a. price varies. Chilton Book Co., Automotive Editorial Department, Chilton Way, Radnor, PA 19089. Ed.Bd.
 Former titles: Chilton's Import Automotive Repair Manual; Chilton's Import Car Repair Manual (ISSN 0084-8743); Chilton's Foreign Car Repair Manual.

338.4   US ISSN 0749-5579
CHILTON'S LABOR GUIDE AND PARTS MANUAL. MOTOR AGE PROFESSIONAL MECHANICS EDITION. 1927. a. Chilton Co., Chilton Way, Radnor, PA 19089. TEL 215-964-4723. illus.
 Former titles: Chilton's Motor-Age Professional Labor Guide and Parts Manual (ISSN 0361-9397) & Chilton's Motor Age Labor Guide and Parts Manual.

629.28   US ISSN 0363-2393
CHILTON'S MOTOR-AGE PROFESSIONAL AUTOMOTIVE SERVICE MANUAL. 1976. a. Chilton Book Co., Chilton Way, Radnor, PA 19089. TEL 215-964-4496. illus.
 Former titles: Chilton's Motor-Age Service Handbook (ISSN 0097-4773); Chilton's Automotive Service Manual.

629.224   US
CHILTON'S TRUCK AND VAN REPAIR MANUAL; gasoline and diesel engines, from 1977 to 1984. 1971. biennial. price varies. Chilton Book Co., Automotive Editorial Department, Chilton Way, Radnor, PA 19089.
 Formerly: Chilton's Truck Repair Manual (ISSN 0045-6721)

629.22   US ISSN 0097-8337
CONSUMER GUIDE MAGAZINE. (Each issue is on a specific subject) irreg. (32-44) $99. Consumer Guide Magazine, 3841 W. Oakton, Skokie, IL 60076. TEL 312-676-3470. illus.

796.77   IT
CONTATTO; la voce dell'automobilista. 1978. irreg. free. Automobil Club Brescia, Via Malta 4, Brescia, Italy.

CONTINENTAL MOTORING HOLIDAYS. see *TRAVEL AND TOURISM*

629.2 621.38   US
CONVERGENCE: INTERNATIONAL COLLOQUIUM ON AUTOMOTIVE ELECTRONIC TECHNOLOGY. PROCEEDINGS. biennial. Society of Automotive Engineers, 400 Commonwealth Dr., Warrendale, PA 15096. TEL 412-776-4970. (Co-sponsor: Institute of Electrical and Electronics Engineers)

659.1   US ISSN 0070-2277
CYCLE BUYERS GUIDE. 1968. a. $2.98 (free to subscribers of Cycle) C B S Magazines, Cycle (Subsidiary of: C B S, Inc.) 1515 Broadway, New York, NY 10036. Ed. Phil Schilling. adv. circ. 160,000.

796.5   GW
D C C - CARAVAN MODELLFUEHRER. a. (Deutscher Camping Club e.V.) D C C - Wirtschaftsdienst und Verlag GmbH, Postfach 400428, 8000 Munich 40, W. Germany (B.R.D.) adv. circ. 15,000.
 Camping

629.2   UK
DAILY EXPRESS GUIDE TO WORLD CARS. 1954. a. Express Newspapers PLC, 121-128 Fleet St., London EC4P 4JT, England. Ed. David Benson. adv. circ. 200,000.

796.77   UK
DAILY MAIL MOTOR REVIEW. 1954. a. £.80. Associated Newspapers Group Ltd., Carmelite House, London EC4Y JA, England.

629.28   US
DOMESTIC CARS, IMPORTED CARS AND TRUCKS, DOMESTIC LIGHT TRUCKS. MECHANICAL, AIR CONDITIONING AND TRANSMISSION SERVICE AND REPAIR.* 1915. a. Mitchell Manuals, 9889 Willow Creek Rd., San Diego, CA 92131. TEL 619-578-8770. Ed. Ken Young.
 Formerly: Domestic Cars. Tune-up, Mechanical Transmission Service & Repair.

629.2   US
EDMUND'S CAR PRICES. 1970. a. $3.50 per no. Edmund Publications Corp., 515 Hempstead Tpke., West Hempstead, NY 11552. TEL 516-292-0044. charts. illus. circ. 200,000.

629.2   US
EDMUND'S CAR SAVVY. 1973. a. $3.50. Edmund Publications Corp., 515 Hempstead Tpke., West Hempstead, NY 11552 TEL 516-292-0044. (Dist. by: Dell Distributing, Inc., One Dag Hammarskjold Plaza, 245 E. 47 St., New York, NY 10017) charts. illus. circ. 200,000.
 Formerly: Edmund's Auto-Pedia (ISSN 0270-5354)

388.3   US
EDMUND'S ECONOMY CAR BUYING GUIDE. 1980. a. $3.50. Edmund Publications Corp., 515 Hempstead Tpke., West Hempstead, NY 11552. TEL 516-292-0044. Ed. William Badnow. (back issues avail.)

EMERGENCY RESPONSE GUIDEBOOK. see *PUBLIC HEALTH AND SAFETY*

629.2   US ISSN 0489-5606
ENGINEERING KNOW-HOW IN ENGINE DESIGN. 1953. a. Society of Automotive Engineers, 400 Commonwealth Dr., Warrendale, PA 15096. TEL 412-776-4970. illus.

338.3   FR
ETUDES ET DOCUMENTATION DE LA R.T.A. (Revue Technique Automobile) 1946. irreg. 84 F. Editions pour l'Automobile et l'Industrie, 20-22 rue de la Saussiere, 92100 Boulogne-Billancourt, France. Ed. Pascal Cromback. adv. charts. illus. circ. 2,500.

796.77   FR
F I A YEAR BOOK OF AUTOMOBILE SPORT. a. Editions V.M., 116 bd. Malesherbes, 75017 Paris, France. circ. 7,000.

338.3   FR
FICHES TECHNIQUES R.T.A. (Revue Technique Automobile) 1978. irreg. 910 F. Editions Techniques pour l'Automobile et l'Industrie, 20-22 rue de la Saussiere, 92100 Boulogne-Billancourt, France. charts. illus. (looseleaf format)

338.3   FR
FICHES TECHNIQUES R.T.C. (Revue Technique Carrosserie) irreg. 410 F. Editions Techniques pour l'Automobile et l'Industrie, 20-22 rue de la Saussiere, 92100 Boulogne-Billancourt, France. charts. illus. (looseleaf format)

338.3   FR
FICHES TECHNIQUES R.T.D. (Revue Technique Diesel) irreg. 405 F. Editions Techniques pour l'Automobile et l'Industrie, 20-22 rue de la Saussiere, 92100 Boulogne-Billancourt, France.

GENERAL MOTORS PUBLIC INTEREST REPORT. see *BUSINESS AND ECONOMICS — Production Of Goods And Services*

388 629.2   US
GENERAL MOTORS SYMPOSIA SERIES. 1971. irreg. price varies. Plenum Publishing Corp., 233 Spring St., New York, NY 10013. TEL 212-620-8047.

629.2   GW ISSN 0072-145X
GERMAN MOTOR TRIBUNE. 1951. a. DM.30. (Export-Service Dupke) Broenner Verlag Breidenstein GmbH, Stuttgarter Str. 18-24, 6000 Frankfurt, W. Germany (B.R.D.) Ed. Werner Siebeneicher. adv. circ. 10,000.
 Export directory

388   UK
GLASS'S CAR CHECK BOOK. a. £10. Glass's Guide Service Ltd., Elgin House, St. George's Ave., Weybridge, Surrey KT13 0BX, England. adv.

388   UK
GLASS'S INDEX OF REGISTRATION MARKS. a. £10. Glass's Guide Service Ltd., Elgin House, St. George's Ave., Weybridge, Surrey KT13 0BX, England.

388.3   UK
GOODS VEHICLE COSTING AND PRICING HANDBOOK. irreg. £13.50. Kogan Page Ltd., 120 Pentonville Rd., London N1 9JN, England. Ed. David Lowe.

GUESTHOUSES, FARMHOUSES AND INNS IN BRITAIN. see *TRAVEL AND TOURISM*

629.286   VE
GUIA AUTOMOTRIZ DE VENEZUELA/ VENEZUELAN AUTOMOTIVE GUIDE. 1970. a. $15. Promotrix, S.R.L., Av. Libertador, cruce con calle Negrin, Apdo. 50045, Caracas 1050-A, Venezuela. Ed. Armando Ortiz P. adv. circ. 8,000.

629   MX
GUIA DE LA INDUSTRIA: AUTOMOTRIZ/ GUIDE TO INDUSTRY: AUTOMOTIVE. 1968. a. 2000($25) Editorial Cosmos, Espana No. 396, Col. Granjas Estrella, Mexico 09880 DF, Mexico. Ed. Cesar Macazaga O. adv. circ. 5,000.

916.9   MG
GUIDE ROUTIER ET TOURISTIQUE: MADAGASCAR, REUNION, MAURICE, COMORES ET SEYCHELLES. a. Automobile Club de Madagascar, Service du Guide Routier, B.P. 571, Antananarivo, Malagasy Republic. illus.

388.3   US
HILDY'S FORD BLUE BOOK. 1926. a. Cummins Publishing Company, 31600 Telegraph Rd., Ste. 200, Birmingham, MI 48010-3439. TEL 313-645-0300.

629.2   US   ISSN 0098-3551
I E E E VEHICULAR TECHNOLOGY CONFERENCE. RECORD. a. Institute of Electrical and Electronics Engineers, Inc., 345 E. 47th St, New York, NY 10017 TEL 212-705-7900. (Subscr. address: 445 Hoes Ln., Piscataway, NJ 08854) illus. Key Title: Record - Vehicular Technology Conference.

629.2   IT   ISSN 0073-7291
INDUSTRIA ITALIANA DEL CICLO E DEL MOTOCICLO. ANNUARIO. (Text in English, French, German, Italian and Spanish) 1960. a. free. Associazione Nazionale Ciclo, Motociclo e Accessori, Via M. Macchi 32, Milan, Italy. adv. index. circ. 12,000.

629.2   FR   ISSN 0073-7747
INDUSTRIE FRANCAISE DES MOTEURS A COMBUSTION INTERNE; repertoire alphabetique des constructeurs. 1953. irreg. free. Syndicat des Constructeurs de Moteurs a Combustion Interne, 10 av. Hoche, 75382 Paris Cedex 08, France.

614.86   US
INTERNATIONAL ASSEMBLY ON EMERGENCY MEDICAL SERVICES. PROCEEDINGS. 1982. a. U.S. Department of Transportation, National Highway Traffic Safety Administration, Washington, DC 20591.

629.286   US
INTERNATIONAL CONFERENCE ON VEHICLE STRUCTURAL MECHANICS. PROCEEDINGS. 1975. biennial. Society of Automotive Engineers, 400 Commonwealth Dr., Warrendale, PA 15096. TEL 412-776-4970.

629.2   UR
KONSTRUKTORSKO-TEKHNOLOGICHESKII INSTITUT AVTOMATIZATSII AVTOMOBILESTROENIYA. SBORNIK TRUDOV. irreg. price varies. Konstruktorsko-Tekhnologicheskii Institut Avtomatizatsii Avtomobilestroeniya, Chelyabinsk, Russian S.F.S.R., U.S.S.R. illus.

338.476   US   ISSN 0146-9932
M V M A MOTOR VEHICLE FACTS AND FIGURES. 1976. a. $7.50. ‡ Motor Vehicle Manufacturers Association of the U.S. Inc., 300 New Center Bldg., Detroit, MI 48202. TEL 313-872-4311. Key Title: Motor Vehicle Facts & Figures.
    Formed by the merger of: Automobile Facts and Figures (ISSN 0067-253X) & Motor Truck Facts (ISSN 0077-1643)

629.286   VE
MECANICA NACIONAL/NATIONAL MECHANICS. 1975. a. Bs.148. Gaisma Editores S.A., Calle Caurimare al lado, Edificio Parque Alto, Apdo. 68.431, Caracas 106, Venezuela. Ed. Janis Kleinbergs. adv. circ. 10,000.

MEMBERSHIP DIRECTORY & BUYER'S GUIDE. see *BUSINESS AND ECONOMICS — Trade And Industrial Directories*

338.3   FR
MOTEURS DIESEL. irreg. Editions Techniques pour l'Automobile et l'Industrie, 20-22 rue de la Saussiere, 92100 Boulogne-Billancourt, France. charts. illus.

629.2   UK
MOTOR AGENTS ASSOCIATION YEAR BOOK AND DIARY. 1983. a. Webecson Ltd., Strawberry St., Hull HU9 1EX, England.

629.2   US
MOTOR AUTO REPAIR MANUAL. 1938. a. $45. Hearst Magazines, Motor Manuals Department, 555 W. 57th St., New York, NY 10019. TEL 800-228-2028. index.
    Formerly: Motor's Auto Repair Manual (ISSN 0098-1745)
    Mechanical repair procedures for American-made cars

629.28   US   ISSN 0094-1514
MOTOR HANDBOOK. a. included in subscr. to Motor magazine. Hearst Magazines, Motor Manuals Department, 555 W. 57th St., 17th Fl., New York, NY 10019. TEL 212-903-5000. adv. illus.
    Continues: Motor's Handbook.

629.222   UK
MOTOR INDUSTRY OF GREAT BRITAIN (YEAR) WORLD AUTOMOTIVE STATISTICS. 1926. a. £38 to non-members; members £22. Society of Motor Manufacturers and Traders Ltd., Forbes House, Halkin St., London, SW1X 7DS, England. circ. 1,000.
    Formerly: Motor Industry of Great Britain (ISSN 0077-1597)

629.28   US
MOTOR LIGHT TRUCK TUNEUP & VAN REPAIR MANUAL. a. $42. Hearst Magazines, Motor Manuals Department, 555 W. 57th St., New York, NY 10019. TEL 800-228-2028. Ed. Louis C. Forier.
    Former titles: Motor Light Truck and Van Repair Manual; Motor Truck Repair Manual (ISSN 0098-3624); Motor Truck and Diesel Repair Manual (ISSN 0077-1724)

MOTOR MANUAL. see *TRANSPORTATION — Trucks And Trucking*

629.2   US   ISSN 0077-1716
MOTOR PARTS & TIME GUIDE. 1910. a. $50. Hearst Magazines, Motor Manuals Department, 555 W. 57th St., New York, NY 10019. TEL 800-228-2028. Ed. Philip Cunningham.
    Formerly: Motor's Flat Rate and Parts Manual.

614.86   UK
MOTOR ROAD TEST ANNUAL. 1949. a. £5. Specialist & Professional Press, Surrey House, 1 Throwley Way, Sutton, Surrey SM1 4QQ, England.

629.286   338.476   UK
MOTOR SPECIFICATIONS & PRICES. 1930. a. £16.50. Stone & Cox (Publications) Ltd., 44 Fleet St., London EC4Y 1BS, England. Ed. Ernest Holland. (back issues avail.)

388.3   SW   ISSN 0077-1619
MOTOR TRAFFIC IN SWEDEN. Swedish edition: Bilismen i Sverige. 1948. a. $35. (Bilindustri Foereningen - Association of Swedish Automobile Maufacturers and Wholesalers) AB Bilstatistik, Box 5514, S-114 85 Stockholm, Sweden. circ. 1,500.

629.286   JA
MOTOR VEHICLE ENGINEERING SPECIFICATIONS - JAPAN. (Text in Japanese) a. 10.900 Yen. Society of Automotive Engineers of Japan, Inc., 10-2, Goban-cho, Chiyoda-ku, Tokyo 102, Japan.

388.5   US   ISSN 0091-5793
MOTORCYCLE FACTS. a. free. National Safety Council, Statistics Division, 444 N. Michigan Ave., Chicago, IL 60611. TEL 312-527-4800. illus. stat.

388.3   US
N A F A ANNUAL REFERENCE BOOK. 1960. a. $15. National Association of Fleet Administrators, Inc., 120 Wood Ave. South, Iselin, NJ 08830. TEL 201-694-8100. Ed. Lori McDonough. adv. stat. circ. 3,300.
    Formerly: N A F A Conference Brochurand and Reference Book (ISSN 0550-8843)

629.222   UK
NATIONAL MOTOR MUSEUM PICTORIAL GUIDE. 1959. a. £1.20. (National Motor Museum Trust) Montagu Ventures Ltd., Beaulieu, Hampshire, England. Ed. M.E. Ware. adv. illus. stat. circ. 120,000.

629.28   US
NATIONAL SERVICE DATA: DOMESTIC. 1971. a. $35. Mitchell Manuals, Inc., Box 26260, San Diego, CA 92126. TEL 619-578-8770. Ed. Ken Young. illus. circ. 25,000.

NEW ZEALAND. MINISTRY OF TRANSPORT. TRAFFIC RESEARCH CIRCULAR. see *TRANSPORTATION*

NEW ZEALAND. MINISTRY OF TRANSPORT. TRAFFIC RESEARCH REPORT. see *TRANSPORTATION*

629   US
OFFICIAL N A S C A R YEARBOOK AND PRESS GUIDE. 1986. a. $6. U M I Publications, Inc., Box 30036, Charlotte, NC 28230. TEL 703-374-0420. Ed. Ivan Mothershead. adv. circ. 100,000. (back issues avail.)

629.2   US   ISSN 0475-1876
OLD CAR VALUE GUIDE. Variant title: Old Car Value Guide Annual. 1967. a. $10.95. (Craft Appraisal Service) Quentin Craft, Ed. & Pub., 1462 Vanderbilt, El Paso, TX 79935. TEL 915-592-5713. illus.

796.77   GW
OLDTIMER ADRESSEN LEXIKON; alle Adressen rund um den Oldtimer. 1984. a. F.Ch. Heel Verlag, Koenigwinterer Str. 528, 5300 Bonn 3, W. Germany (B.R.D.) Ed. Klaus Fey. circ. 15,000.

796.77   GW
OLDTIMER KATALOG; Marktuebersicht fuer klassischer Automobile. a. F.Ch. Heel Verlag, Koenigwinter Strasse 528-536, 5300 Bonn 3 (Oberkassel), W. Germany (B.R.D.) Ed. Halwart Schrader. circ. 10,000.

338.3   CN
ONTARIO. MINISTRY OF TRANSPORTATION AND COMMUNICATIONS. ONTARIO ROAD SAFETY ANNUAL REPORT. 1957. a. free. Ministry of Transportation and Communications, 1201 Wilson Ave., Downsview, Ont. M3M 1J8, Canada. TEL 416-248-3708. illus. stat.
    Formerly(until 1985): Ontario. Ministry of Transportation and Communications. Motor Vehicle Accident Facts; Continues: Ontario. Ministry of Transportation and Communications. Highway Traffic Collisions.

388.3   629.2   CN
OPPORTUNITIES UNLIMITED. biennial. free. Automotive Industries Association of Canada, 1272 Wellington St., Ottawa, Ont. K1Y 3A7, Canada. TEL 613-728-5821. Ed. Doug Jordan. circ. 40,000.

388.3   388   UR   ISSN 0320-3433
POLUTEHNILINE INSTITUUT TALLINN. TEORETICHESKOE I EKSPERIMENTAL'NOE ISSLEDOVANIE AVTOMOBIL'NYKH DOROG I AVTOMOBIL'NOGO TRANSPORTA ESTONSKOI S.S.R. V USLOVIYAKH INTENSIVNOI AVTOMOBILIZATSII. (Subseries of Its Toimetised) (Text in Russian; summaries in English or German) irreg. price varies. Polutehniline Instituut Tallinn, Ehitajate tee 5, Tallinn, Estonian S.S.R., U.S.S.R.

629.286   JA
PRODUCT GUIDE. 1982. irreg. $30.40. Automotive Herald Co., Ltd., 3rd Shinto Bldg., 21-1 Shinbashi 5-chome, Minato-ku, Tokyo 105, Japan (U.S. Address: Japan America Automotive Systems, Inc., 2424 W. Morse Ave., Chicago, IL 60645) Ed. Akira Shikakura. circ. 9,000.

R A C CONTINENTAL HANDBOOK AND HOTEL GUIDE. (Royal Automobile Club) see *TRAVEL AND TOURISM*

R A C HANDBOOK AND HOTEL GUIDE. (Royal Automobile Club) see *TRAVEL AND TOURISM*

R A C MOTOR SPORT YEAR BOOK. see *TRAVEL AND TOURISM*

796.77 US
ROAD & TRACK SPORTS & G T CARS. a. C B S Magazines, Road & Track, 1499 Monrovia Ave., Newport Beach, CA 92663. TEL 714-720-5300. adv.

629.28 US ISSN 0362-8205
S A E HANDBOOK. 1905. a. $140 4-vol. set. Society of Automotive Engineers, 400 Commonwealth Dr., Warrendale, PA 15096. TEL 412-776-4970.
●Also available online. Vendors: Orbit Information Technologies.

388 US ISSN 0148-7191
S A E TECHNICAL PAPERS. irreg. $4.50 to non-members; members $2.75. Society of Automotive Engineers, 400 Commonwealth Dr., Warrendale, PA 15096. TEL 412-776-4970. index. cum.index: 1965-1985. (back issues avail.) Indexed: Pollut.Abstr.

629.28 US ISSN 0096-736X
S A E TRANSACTIONS. a. $650. Society of Automotive Engineers, 400 Commonwealth Dr., Warrendale, PA 15096. TEL 412-776-4970. index. Indexed: Geotech.Abstr. Noise Pollut.Publ.Abstr.

388 US
ST. PAUL, MINNESOTA. TWIN CITIES AREA METROPOLITAN TRANSIT COMMISSION. ANNUAL REPORT. 1969. a. free. Twin Cities Area Metropolitan Transit Commission, 560 N. 6th St., Minneapolis, MN 55411-4398. TEL 612-349-7400. Ed. Sue Rohland. circ. 7,000.
Formerly: St. Paul, Minnesota. Metropolitan Transit Commission. Annual Report (ISSN 0082-710X)

388 SI
SINGAPORE MOTORING GUIDE. 1980. a. S.$4. Times Directories Private Ltd., 422 Thomson Rd., Singapore 1129, Singapore. circ. 12,000.

SOCIEDAD ESPANOLA DE AUTOMOVILES DE TURISMO. MEMORIA Y BALANCE. see *TRAVEL AND TOURISM*

629.28 US ISSN 0585-086X
STAPP CAR CRASH CONFERENCE PROCEEDINGS. 10th, 1967. a. Society of Automotive Engineers, 400 Commonwealth Dr., Warrendale, PA 15096. TEL 412-776-4970. Indexed: Biol.Abstr.

388.3 629.2 IT ISSN 0039-4254
STYLE AUTO; architettura della carrozzeria. (Text in English or Italian) 1964. a. L.5000($10) softbound; L.8000 ($13) hardbound. Style Auto Editrice, Corso Adriatico 26, 10129 Turin, Italy. Ed. Mario Dinarich. adv. illus.

388 SZ
SWITZERLAND. BUNDESAMT FUER STATISTIK. STRASSENVERKEHRSUNFAELLE/ ACCIDENTS DE LA CIRCULATION ROUTIERE EN SUISSE. (Text in French and German) 1963. a. 24 Fr. Bundesamt fuer Statistik, Hallwylstrasse 15, CH-3003 Berne, Switzerland. stat.

629.2 GW
TASCHENBUCH KAROSSERIE & FAHRZEUGTECHNIK. a. DM.14.90. Gentner Verlag, Forststr. 131, 7000 Stuttgart 1, W. Germany (B.R.D.)

629.2 GW
TASCHENFACHBUCH DER KRAFTFAHRZEUGBETRIEBE. 1953. a. DM.13.50. Krafthand-Verlag Walter Schulz, St.-Anna-Str. 26, 8939 Bad Woerishofen, W. Germany (B.R.D.) Ed. Walter Schulz.

338 629.2 GW ISSN 0083-548X
TATSACHEN UND ZAHLEN AUS DER KRAFTVERKEHRSWIRTSCHAFT. 1927. a. price varies. Verband der Automobilindustrie, Westendstr. 61, Postfach 17 05 63, 6000 Frankfurt 17, W. Germany (B.R.D.) (back issues avail.)

388.3 UK
TAXI DRIVERS COMPENDIUM. 1947. a. free to qualified personnel. Britannic Publicity & Publications Ltd., 8 Harewood Row, London NW1, England. Ed. J.V. Tame. adv. circ. 14,500.

600 UK ISSN 0082-2329
TECHNICAL SERVICE DATA (AUTOMOTIVE) 1935. a. £9.50. Palgrave Publishing Co. Ltd., 25 Windsor Street, Chertsey, Surrey KT16 8AX, England. Ed. C.T. Arden-White. circ. 16,000.

629.283 UK
TRUCK DRIVER'S HANDBOOK. a. £9.95. Kogan Page Ltd., 120 Pentonville Rd., London N1 9JN, England. Ed. David P. Soye.
Formerly: H G V Driver's Handbook.

TYRE AND RIM ASSOCIATION OF AUSTRALIA STANDARDS MANUAL. see *RUBBER*

629.2 US ISSN 0270-756X
U.S. DEPARTMENT OF ENERGY. ANNUAL REPORT TO CONGRESS ON THE AUTOMOTIVE TECHNOLOGY PROGRAM. 1979. a. U.S. Department of Energy, Office of Transportation Systems, Washington, DC 20585. TEL 202-252-8012. Ed. Saunders B. Kramer. Key Title: Annual Report to Congress on the Automotive Technology Development Program.

629.286 UK ISSN 0263-1083
V B R A DIRECTORY OF MEMBERS. 1960. a. £16. (Vehicle Builders and Repairers Association) V B R A Publications Ltd., Belmont House, 102 Finkle Ln., Gildersome, Leeds LS27 7TW, England. Ed. Robert Hadfield.
Formerly: V B R A Directory of the Vehicle Bodybuilding and Accident Repair Industries.

629.2 796.77 GW ISSN 0171-5046
V K G JAHRBUCH; Mitgliederverzeichnis. 1969. a. DM.20. Verband der Kraftfahrzeugteile- und Zweiradgrosshaendler e.V., Postfach 1861, Oberstr. 36-42, 4030 Ratingen, W. Germany (B.R.D.) Ed. Hans H. Eichler. adv. stat. circ. 1,000. (back issues avail.)

629 NN
VANUATU. NATIONAL PLANNING AND STATISTICS OFFICE. NEW MOTOR VEHICLE REGISTRATIONS AND MOTOR VEHICLES ON THE REGISTER/NOUVELLES IMMATRICULATIONS ET VEHICULES AUTOMOBILES IMMATRICULES. (Text in English and French) 1972. a. free. Informations Department, Statistics Division, NP 50, Port-Vila, Vanuatu. stat. circ. 300.
Formerly: Vanuatu. Bureau of Statistics. New Motor Vehicle Registrations and Motor Vehicles on the Register/Nouvelles Immatriculation et Vehicles Automobiles Immatricules.

388.1 DK ISSN 0083-5358
VEJTRANSPORTEN I TAL OG TEKST. (Text in Danish; notes in English) 1959. a. Kr.118. Automobil-Importoerernes Sammenslutning, Ryvangs Alle 68, 2900 Hellerup, Denmark. Ed. Erik Ebsen Petersen. index. cum.index every 7 years.

629.2 338 GW
VERBAND DER AUTOMOBILINDUSTRIE. JAHRESBERICHT. (Editions in English, German) a. free. Verband der Automobilindustrie, Westendstr. 61, Postfach 17 05 63, 6000 Frankfurt 17, W. Germany (B.R.D.)
Formerly: Verband der Automobilindustrie. Taetigkeitsbericht (ISSN 0083-5471)

629.386 SZ
VEREINIGUNG SCHWEIZERISCHER STRASSENFACHLEUTE. FORSCHUNGSBERICHTE. vol.5, 1974. irreg. price varies. Vereinigung Schweiz Strassenfachleute, Seefeldstr. 9, CH-8008 Zurich, Switzerland. charts. stat. circ. 130.
Former titles: Vereinigung Schweizerischer Strassenfachleute. Versuchsberichte; Vereinigung Schweizerischer Strassenfachmaenner. Versuchsbericht.

629.2 US ISSN 0083-7229
WARD'S AUTOMOTIVE YEARBOOK. 1938. a. $140. Ward's Communications, Inc., 28 W. Adams St., Detroit, MI 48226. TEL 313-962-4433. Ed. Harry R. Stark. adv. bk. rev. charts. illus. stat. index. circ. 5,087.

388.3 GW
WAS KOSTET DER GESCHAEFTSWAGEN? vol.11, 1977. a. DM.19.80. ADAC Verlag GmbH, Am Westpark 8, 8 Munich 70, Postfach 70 01 26, W. Germany (B.R.D.) circ. 7,000.
Formerly (until vol.15, 1979/80): Was Kostet Mein Auto?

388.4 US
WORLD AUTOMOTIVE MARKET. 1931. a. $22. (Automobile International) Johnston International Publishing Co., 386 Park Ave. South, New York, NY 10016. TEL 212-689-0120. Ed. Bernard Zinober. circ. 3,500.

338.476 US ISSN 0084-1463
WORLD CARS. 1962. a. $45.95. (Automobile Club of Italy, IT) Herald Books, Box 17, Pelham, NY 10803. TEL 914-576-1121. Ed. Anna Maria Losch.

629.2 US ISSN 0085-8307
WORLD MOTOR VEHICLE DATA. a. $35. Motor Vehicle Manufacturers Association of the U.S., Inc., 300 New Center Bldg., Detroit, MI 48202. TEL 313-872-4311. Dir. V.J. Adduci.

TRANSPORTATION — Computer Applications

625.7 651.8 US ISSN 0091-5122
AMERICAN ASSOCIATION OF STATE HIGHWAY AND TRANSPORTATION OFFICIALS. SUB-COMMITTEE ON COMPUTER TECHNOLOGY. NATIONAL CONFERENCE. PROCEEDINGS. 1983. a. $15. American Association of State Highway and Transportation Officials, U.S. Department of Transportation, 444 N. Capitol St. N.W., Ste. 225, Washington, DC 20001. TEL 202-624-5800. Ed. Keith F. Kohler. circ. controlled. Key Title: Proceedings - Committee on Computer Technology.

625 US
ASSOCIATION OF AMERICAN RAILROADS. DATA SYSTEMS DIVISION. PAPERS. a. price varies. Association of American Railroads, American Railroads Bldg., No. 3 Capitol Pl., 50 F St., N.W., Washington, DC 20001. TEL 202-639-5540.

387 623.82 NE
COMPUTER APPLICATIONS IN SHIPPING AND SHIPBUILDING. 1974. irreg., vol.10, 1983. price varies. Elsevier Science Publishers B.V., Box 211, 1000 AE Amsterdam, Netherlands. Eds. V. Fujita, T.J. Williams. index. Indexed: Sci.Abstr.

380.5 US
I E E E WORKSHOP ON AUTOMOTIVE APPLICATIONS OF ELECTRONICS (PUBLICATION) 1982. biennial. price varies. (I E E E, Industrial Electronics Society) Institute of Electrical and Electronics Engineers, Inc., 345 E. 47th St., New York, NY 10017 TEL 212-705-7900. (Subscr. addr.: 445 Hoes Ln., Piscataway, NJ 08854)
Formerly (until 1986): Automotive Applications on Microprocessors.

625 001.642 SA
NATIONAL INSTITUTE FOR TRANSPORT AND ROAD RESEARCH. USER MANUALS FOR COMPUTER PROGRAMS/NASIONALE INSTITUUT VIR VERVOER- EN PADNAVORSING. GEBRUIKERSHANDBOEKE VIR REKENAARPROGRAMME. 1976. irreg., no.16, 1984. price varies. National Institute for Transport and Road Research, Computer Information Centre for Transportation, Box 395, Pretoria 0001, South Africa.

352.7 624 UK
PLANNING AND TRANSPORT RESEARCH AND COMPUTATION. SUMMER ANNUAL MEETING. PROCEEDINGS. 1968. a. (approx. 20 vols./yr.) £125. Planning and Transport Research and Computation (International) Co., 110 Strand, London, WC2, England. circ. 350. Indexed: HRIS.

TRANSPORTATION — Railroads

625.1 US
AMERICAN RAILWAY ENGINEERING ASSOCIATION. PROCEEDINGS. a. $54. American Railway Engineering Association, 50 F St., N.W., Washington, DC 20001. Ed. Louis Cerny. Indexed: Geotech.Abstr.
Formerly: American Railway Engineering Association. Proceedings, Technical Conference (ISSN 0271-4450) & American Railway Engineering Association. Proceedings of the Annual Convention.

385 US ISSN 0097-7039
AMTRAK ANNUAL REPORT. 1971. a. National Railroad Passenger Corporation, 400 North Capitol St., N.W., Washington, DC 20001. TEL 202-383-3000. circ. 35,000.

385 BL
ANUARIO ESTATISTICO DAS FERROVIAS DO BRASIL. 1977. a. free. Rede Ferroviaria Federal, S.A., Departamento Geral de Estatistica, Rio de Janeiro, Brazil. adv. circ. 1,200.

625.1 GW ISSN 0341-0463
ARCHIV FUER EISENBAHNTECHNIK. 1952. a. price varies. Hestra-Verlag, Holzhofallee 33, Postfach 4244, 6100 Darmstadt 1, W. Germany (B.R.D.) adv. Indexed: Sci.Abstr. Fuel & Energy Abstr.

385 GW
B D E F - JAHRBUCH. 1982. a. DM.15. (Bund Deutscher Eisenbahn-Freunde) Uhle & Kleimann, Pettenpohlstr. 17, D-4990 Luebbecke 1, W. Germany (B.R.D.) circ. 3,500. (back issues avail.)

385 SW
BENELUX RAIL. (Text in Dutch and French) 1981. a. Kr.85($13) Frank Stenvalls Foerlag, Foereningsgatan 67, S-211 52 Malmoe, Sweden. Ed. Marcel Vleugels. illus. (back issues avail.)

385 UK ISSN 0263-0125
BLASTPIPE. 1981. irreg. £0.10 per no. Fakenham and Dereham Railway Society, c/o I Jowett, Market Place, East Harling, Norfolk NOR 12X, England. illus.

385.1 UK ISSN 0068-242X
BRITISH RAILWAYS BOARD. REPORT AND STATEMENT OF ACCOUNTS. 1963. a. price varies. British Railways Board, Euston Square, Box 100, London NW1 2DZ, England (Also avail from: H.M.S.O., c/o Liaison Officer, Atlantic House, London EC1P 1BW, England)

385.1 CM
CAMEROUN. REGIE NATIONALE DES CHEMINS DE FER. COMPTE RENDU DE GESTION. a. Regie Nationale des Chemins de Fer, Douala, Cameroon.

385 CM
CAMEROUN. REGIE NATIONALE DES CHEMINS DE FER. STATISTIQUES. irreg. Regie Nationale des Chemins de Fer, Douala, Cameroon. illus.

625.2 US
CAR AND LOCOMOTIVE CYCLOPEDIA. 1879. quadrennial. $60. Simmons-Boardman Publishing Corporation, 1809 Capitol Ave., Omaha, NE 10014. TEL 402-346-4300. Ed. K. Ellsworth. adv. bibl. charts. illus. circ. 6,500.

625 US ISSN 0069-1623
CENTRAL ELECTRIC RAILFANS' ASSOCIATION. BULLETIN. 1938. irreg., no.125, 1986. membership. Central Electric Railfans' Association, Box 503, Chicago, IL 60690. TEL 312-346-3723. Ed.Bd. circ. 2,000.

625 385 PL
CENTRALNY OSRODEK BADAN I ROZWOJU TECHNIKI KOLEJNICTWA. PRACE COBIRTK. (Text in Polish; summaries in English, French, German, Russian) 1959. irreg. (approx 4-5/yr.) price varies. Wydawnictwa Komunikacji i Lacznosci, Kazimierzowska 52, Warsaw, Poland. Ed.Bd. circ. 1, 400 (controlled)

385.1 US ISSN 0069-6048
COLORADO RAIL ANNUAL. 1963. a. (none published 1975) price varies. ‡ (Colorado Railroad Historical Foundation, Inc.) Colorado Railroad Museum, Box 10, Golden, CO 80401. TEL 303-279-4591. Ed. Cornelius W. Hauck. adv. bk. rev. index. circ. 4,500.

625.1 GW ISSN 0072-1549
D B REPORT. 1965. a. price varies. (Deutsche Bundesbahn) Hestra-Verlag, Holzhofallee 33, Postfach 4244, 6100 Darmstadt 1, W. Germany (B.R.D.) adv.

385 UK ISSN 0309-1465
DEVELOPING RAILWAYS. 1966. a. £2. Business Press International Ltd., Quadrant House, The Quadrant, Sutton, Surrey SM2 5AS, England. circ. 8,944. (reprint service avail. from UMI)
Former titles: International Railway Progress (ISSN 0074-7572); Overseas Railways.

621.2 US ISSN 0070-4830
DIESEL LOCOMOTIVE QUESTION & ANSWER MANUAL. 1950. irreg. $8. Railway Fuel and Operating Officers Association, Box 1189, Champaign, IL 61820-1189.
Formerly: Diesel Electric Locomotive Examination Book.

385 SZ
EISENBAHNGESCHICHTE DER VEREINIGTEN STAATEN VON AMERIKA. 1977. irreg. Birkhaeuser Verlag, P.O. Box 133, CH-4010 Basel, Switzerland.

625.1 GW ISSN 0071-0075
ELSNERS TASCHENBUCH DER EISENBAHNTECHNIK. a. DM.42.00. Tetzlaff Verlag GmbH, Havelstr. 9, 6100 Darmstadt 1, W. Germany (B.R.D.) Ed.Bd. adv. circ. 6,000.

EURAIL GUIDE; how to travel Europe and all the world by train. see TRAVEL AND TOURISM

385.1 SZ ISSN 0071-2264
EUROPEAN COMPANY FOR THE FINANCING OF RAILWAY ROLLING STOCK. ANNUAL REPORT. Short title: EUROFIMA Annual Report. (Text in English, French and German) 1957. a. free. European Company for the Financing of Railway Rolling Stock (EUROFIMA), Rittergasse 20, CH-4001 Basel 1, Switzerland. circ. 4,000.

385 UK
FELIXSTOWE DOCK & RAILWAY COMPANY DIARY. a. Welbecson Ltd., Strawberry St., Hull, Humberside, HU9 1EX, England.

385 UK ISSN 0262-3943
GUIDE TO STEAM TRAINS IN THE BRITISH ISLES. 1973. a. free. (Association of Railway Preservation Societies Ltd.) B.P. Oil Ltd., c/o J.C. Jeffery, Ed., 42 North St., Oundle, Peterborough PE8 4AL, England. circ. 175,000.

625.1 385 UK ISSN 0073-9839
INSTITUTION OF RAILWAY SIGNAL ENGINEERS. PROCEEDINGS. 1912. a. £4. Institution of Railway Signal Engineers, 21 Avalon Rd, Earley Reading Berks, England. Ed. L.G. Mackean. adv. circ. 2,000.

385 FR ISSN 0074-7580
INTERNATIONAL RAILWAY STATISTICS. STATISTICS OF INDIVIDUAL RAILWAYS. (Text in English, French, German) a. 200 F. International Union of Railways, 14 rue Jean Rey, 75015 Paris, France.

385 JA ISSN 0047-1925
J N R BULLETIN. (Text in English) 1973. a. free. Japanese National Railways, International Dept., 1-6-5 Marunouchi, Chiyoda-ku, Tokyo 100, Japan. Ed.Bd. charts. stat.

625.1 GW ISSN 0075-2479
JAHRBUCH DES EISENBAHNWESENS. 1950. a. price varies. (Deutsche Bundesbahn) Hestra-Verlag, Holzhofallee 33, Postfach 4244, 6100 Darmstadt 1, W. Germany (B.R.D.) adv.

385 GW ISSN 0075-2576
JAHRBUCH FUER BUNDESBAHNBEAMTE. 1968. a. DM.75. Walhalla-und Praetoria-Verlag, Dolomitenstr. 1, Postfach 301, 8400 Regensburg 1, W. Germany (B.R.D.) Eds. Hermann Borndorfer, Hartmut Adolf, Hugo Dessau.

385 GW
JAHRBUCH FUER EISENBAHNLITERATUR; ein kritischer Wegweiser zu lieferbaren, angezeigten und empfehlenswerten Buechern "rund um die Eisenbahn". 1984. a. DM.5. Horst-Werner Dumjahn Verlag, Immenhof 12, Postfach 1746, D-6500 Mainz 1, W. Germany (B.R.D.) (Subscr. to: V V A-Vereinigte Verlagsauslieferung, Postfach 7777, D-4830 Guetersloh 1, W. Germany (B.R.D.)) Ed. Horst-Werner Dumjahn. (back issues avail.)

385.1 UK ISSN 0075-3033
JANE'S FREIGHT CONTAINERS. 1968. a. £60($125) Jane's Publishing Co., 238 City Rd., London E.C.1, England (Subscr.to: Jane's Publishing Inc., 20 park Plaza, Boston MA 02116) Ed. Patrick Finlay. adv. index.

385.1 625.1 UK ISSN 0075-3084
JANE'S WORLD RAILWAYS. 1950. a. £57.50($125) Jane's Publishing Co., 238 City Rd., London E.C.1, England (Subscr.to: Jane's Publishing Inc., 20 Park Plaza, Boston, MA 02116) Ed. Geoffrey Freeman Allen. adv. index.

385 JA ISSN 0546-093X
JAPANESE NATIONAL RAILWAYS. FACTS AND FIGURES. a. free. Japanese National Railways - Nihon Kokuyu Tetsudo, International Dept., 1-6-5 Marunouchi, Chiyoda-ku, Tokyo 100, Japan. illus. stat.

625.1 US
JOINT A S M E/I E E E RAILROAD CONFERENCE. I E E E TECHNICAL PAPERS. Title varies (1983): Joint I E E E/A S M E Railroad Conference. a. price varies. Institute of Electrical and Electronics Engineers, Inc, 345 E. 47th St., New York, NY 10017 TEL 212-705-7900. (Subscr. address: 445 Hoes Ln., Piscataway, NJ 08854)
Former titles (1977-1980): Joint A S M E/I E E E/A A R Railroad Conference. I E E E Technical Papers; (1976): Joint A S M E/I E E E Railroad Technical Conference. I E E E Papers; (1975): Joint Railroad Conference. I E E E Papers; Joint Railroad Conference. Conference Record; Which superseded: Joint Railroad Technical Conference. Preprint (ISSN 0075-3998)

385 GW
KURSBUCH DER DEUTSCHEN MUSEUMS-EISENBAHNEN. 1978. a. DM.4. Verlag Uhle & Kleimann, Pettenponhlstr. 17, D-4990 Luebbecke 1, W. Germany (B.R.D.) Ed. Bernhard Uhle. circ. 14, 000. (back issues avail.)

385 GW ISSN 0170-4621
L O K REPORT REISEFUEHRER; Europa-Reisefuehrer fuer Eisenbahnfreunde. 1978. a. Arbeitsgruppe L O K Report e.V., Postfach 1280, D-4400 Muenster, W. Germany (B.R.D.) adv. illus. stats. index. (back issues avail.)

625.26 US ISSN 0076-0285
LOCOMOTIVE MAINTENANCE OFFICERS ASSOCIATION. ANNUAL PROCEEDINGS.* 1940. a. $6., or $10. for both preconvention report and the annual proceedings. Locomotive Maintenance Officers Association, 3144 Brereton Ct., Huntington, WV 25705. index.

625.26 US ISSN 0076-0293
LOCOMOTIVE MAINTENANCE OFFICERS ASSOCIATION. PRECONVENTION REPORT;* full text of all seven technical committee reports on diesel locomotive and M.U. train maintenance. a. $10 for both preconvention report and the annual proceedings. Locomotive Maintenance Officers Association, 3144 Brereton Ct., Huntington, WV 25705. Ed. C.M. Lipcomb. index.

385 MW ISSN 0076-3330
MALAWI RAILWAYS. ANNUAL REPORTS AND ACCOUNTS. Title varies: Malawi Railways. Directors' Reports and Accounts. 1932. a. free. Malawi Railways, Ltd., P.O. Box 5144, Limbe, Malawi. circ. 500.

621.2 US
MODERN LOCOMOTIVE HANDBOOK. 1950. irreg. $8. Railway Fuel and Operating Officers Association, Box 1189, Champaign, IL 61820-1189.

385 US ISSN 0077-3387
NATIONAL ASSOCIATION OF REGULATORY UTILITY COMMISSIONERS. PROCEEDINGS. a. $35. National Association of Regulatory Utility Commissioners, 1102 Interstate Commerce Commission Bldg., Box 684, Washington, DC 20044. TEL 202-898-2200.
 Formerly: National Association of Railroad and Utilities Commissioners. Proceedings.

385 NZ
NEW ZEALAND. RAILWAYS CORPORATION. ANNUAL REPORT. 1880? a. Railways Corporation, Wellington, New Zealand. illus. stat. circ. 750.
 Formerly: New Zealand. Railways Department. Annual Report.

385 SW
NORDENS JAERNVAEGAR. (Text in English and Swedish) 1966. a. Kr.85($13) Frank Stenvalls Foerlag, Foereningsgatan 67, S-211 52 Malmoe, Sweden. Ed. Frank Stenvall. illus. circ. 250. (back issues avail.)

385.1 PK
PAKISTAN RAILWAYS. YEARBOOK OF INFORMATION. (Text in English) a. Pakistan Railways, Moghalpura, Pakistan.
 Continues: Pakistan Western Railway. Yearbook of Information (ISSN 0078-8511)

385 BL ISSN 0102-4930
R F F S A. ANUARIO ESTATISTICO. 1960. a. free. Rede Ferroviaria Federal, S.A., Departamento Geral de Estatistica, Rio de Janeiro, Brazil.

385.26 US
RAILROAD STATION HISTORICAL SOCIETY. RAILROAD STATION MONOGRAPH. 1970. a. free to members. J-B Publishing Co., 430 Ivy Ave., Crete, NE 68333. Ed.Bd. bibl. illus. circ. 500.

657 385 US
RAILWAY ACCOUNTING RULES. a. price varies. Association of American Railroads, American Railroads Bldg., No. 3 Capitol Pl., 50 F St., N.W., Washington, DC 20001. TEL 202-639-2316.

385 UK ISSN 0079-9513
RAILWAY DIRECTORY AND YEARBOOK. a. $55. Business Press International Ltd., Quadrant House, The Quadrant, Sutton, Surrey Sm2 5AS, England. (reprint service avail. from UMI)

385 US ISSN 0079-9521
RAILWAY FUEL AND OPERATING OFFICERS ASSOCIATION. PROCEEDINGS. a. $15. Railway Fuel and Operating Officers Association, Box 1189, Champaign, IL 61820-1189.

385 US
RAILWAY LINE CLEARANCES.* 1897. a. $25. International Thomson Transport Press, 424 W. 33rd St., New York, NY 10001. TEL 212-714-3100. Ed. Paul Kelly. adv. circ. 2,000.

385 US ISSN 0094-2278
RAILWAY PASSENGER CAR ANNUAL. 1974. a. $10.50. R P C Publications, Box 296, Godfrey, IL 62035. Ed. W. David Randall. circ. 1,500.

625.1 GW ISSN 0079-9548
RAILWAY TECHNICAL REVIEW. (Text in English) 1952. a. price varies. Hestra-Verlag, Holzhofallee 33, Postfach 4244, 6100 Darmstadt 1, W. Germany (B.R.D.) adv. Indexed: Br.Rail.Bd.

385 UK ISSN 0082-5891
RAILWAY WORLD ANNUAL. 1947. a. price varies. Ian Allan Ltd., Coombelands House, Addlestone, Weybridge, Surrey KT15 0HY, England. circ. 8,500. (reprint service avail. from UMI)
 Former titles: Trains Annual; Trains Illustrated Annual.

385 II ISSN 0080-1933
REVIEW OF ACCIDENTS ON INDIAN GOVERNMENT RAILWAYS. (Text in English) 1957/58. a. Railway Board, Directorate of Safety, Joint Director, Public Relations, New Delhi 110001, India.

385 GW
REVISTA TECNICA DE LOS FERROCARRILES. 1952. a. DM.22.80. Hestra Verlag GmbH, Holzhofallee 33, 6100 Darmstadt, W. Germany (B.R.D.) Ed. Michael B. Brauckmann. adv. bk. rev. circ. 4,900.

625.1 US ISSN 0080-3316
ROADMASTERS AND MAINTENANCE OF WAY ASSOCIATION OF AMERICA. PROCEEDINGS. 1883. a. free to members and advertisers. Richard B. Cross Co., 103 S. Howard St., Box 405, Oxford, IN 47971. TEL 317-385-2255. Ed. Richard B. Cross. circ. 2,000.

385.1 SZ ISSN 0080-6048
SANKT GALLER BEITRAEGE ZUM FREMDENVERKEHR UND ZUR VERKEHRSWIRTSCHAFT: REIHE VERKEHRSWIRTSCHAFT. 1970. irreg., no.12, 1986. price varies. (Hochschule St. Gallen fuer Wirtschafts- und Sozialwissenschaften, Institut fuer Fremdenverkehr und Verkehrswirtschaft) Paul Haupt AG, Falkenplatz 14, 3001 Berne, Switzerland.

385 BL ISSN 0102-5694
SINTESE FERROVIARIA BRASILEIRA. 1981. irreg. free. Rede Ferroviaria Federal, S.A., Departamento Geral de Estatistica, Rio de Janeiro, Brazil.

385.314 BL
SISTEMA FERROVIARIO R F F S A. 1962. irreg. free. Rede Ferroviaria Federal, S.A., Departamento Geral de Estatistica, Rio de Janeiro, Brazil. adv. illus. circ. 1,200. (also avail. in microfiche)

385 BE ISSN 0081-119X
SOCIETE NATIONALE DES CHEMINS DE FER BELGES. RAPPORT ANNUEL. 1926/27. a. ‡ Nationale Maatschappij der Belgische Spoorwegen, 85 rue de France, B-1070 Brussels, Belgium. circ. controlled.

385 069.9 DK ISSN 0106-6927
SPORVEJSMUSEET SKJOLDENAESHOLM. AARSBERETNING. 1979. a. Kr.15. Sporvejshistorisk Selskab, Valloevej 24, 2700 Broenshoej, Denmark. Eds. Per Soegaard, Hans Andersen. illus. circ. 1,500.

385.1 US ISSN 0081-542X
STEAM PASSENGER SERVICE DIRECTORY. 1966. a. $6. ‡ Empire State Railway Museum, P.O. Box 666, Middletown, NY 10940. TEL 914-343-4219. Ed. Marvin H. Cohen. adv. circ. 15,000.

385 SW ISSN 0081-9964
SVERIGES JAERNVAEGAR/RAILWAYS OF SWEDEN. (Subseries of Sveriges Officiella Statistik: Transport- och Kommunikationsvaesen) 1953. a. Kr.25. Statens Jaernvaegars Huvudkontor - State Railways Head Office, S-105 50 Stockholm, Sweden. circ. 1,000.
 Supersedes: Allmaen Jaernvaegsstatistik; Statens Jaernvaegar.

385 CH
TAIWAN RAILWAY. (Text in Chinese and English) 1963. irreg. Taiwan Railway Administration, Taipei, Taiwan, Republic of China. Ed. J. Fan. illus. circ. 2,000.

625.1 AU
TECHNISCHE UNIVERSITAET WIEN. INSTITUT FUER EISENBAHNWESEN, SPEZIALBAHNEN UND VERKEHRSWIRTSCHAFT. ARBEITEN. 1971. biennial. ‡ Technische Universitaet Wien, Institut fuer Eisenbahnwesen, Spezialbahnen und Verkehrswirtschaft, Karlsplatz 13, A-1040 Vienna, Austria. Edwin Engel.

385.1 FR ISSN 0579-8256
THROUGH EUROPE BY TRAIN. 1951. irreg., latest 1985. free. International Union of Railways, 14 rue Jean Rey, 75015 Paris, France.

625.1 US
TRACK YEARBOOK. 1982. a. $15. Murphy-Richter Publishing Co., 2 N. Riverside Plaza, Rm. 2115, Chicago, IL 60606. TEL 312-454-1823. Ed. Michael J. Wujcik. adv. circ. 6,000.

385.1 NO
TRANSPORTOEKONOMISK INSTITUTT. AARSBERETNING. 1965. a. free. Transportoekonomisk Institutt - Institute of Transport Economics, Box 24 Roea, Oslo 7, Norway. Ed. Tore Thjoemoee.
 Formerly: Norges Teknisk-Naturvitenskapelige Forskningsraad. Transportoekonomisk Institutt. Aarsberetning (ISSN 0078-124X)

385 US ISSN 0163-4674
U.S. FEDERAL RAILROAD ADMINISTRATION. OFFICE OF SAFETY. ACCIDENT/INCIDENT BULLETIN. no.144, 1975. a. U.S. Federal Railroad Administration, Office of Safety, Washington, DC 20590. TEL 202-426-4000. Key Title: Accident/Incident Bulletin.
 Formerly: U.S. Federal Railroad Administration. Office of Safety. Accident Bulletin (ISSN 0092-1645)

625.1 UR
VSESOYUZNYI NAUCHNO-ISSLEDOVATEL'SKII INSTITUT VAGONOSTROENIYA. TRUDY. irreg. 1.10 Rub. Vsesoyuznyi Nauchno-Issledovatel'skii Institut Vagonostroeniya, Moscow, Russian S.F.S.R., U.S.S.R. illus.

380.3 CS
VYZKUMNY USTAV SPOJU. SBORNIK PRACI. (Text in Czech; summaries in English, French, German, Russian) 1974. irreg., (2-3/yr.) 10 Kcs. per no. Nakladatelstvi Dopravy a Spoju, Hybernska 5, 115 78 Prague 1, Czechoslovakia (Subscr. to: Artia, Ve Smeckach 30, 111 27 Prague 1) Ed. Milos Matura. charts illus.

385 614.85 US
WASHINGTON. UTILITIES AND TRANSPORTATION COMMISSION. RAILROAD-HIGHWAY GRADE CROSSING ACCIDENTS. SUMMARY AND ANALYSIS. a. Utilities and Transportation Commission, Highways-Licenses Bldg., Olympia, WA 98504. TEL 206-753-6420.

385 CN ISSN 0085-8188
WESTERN CANADIAN STEAM LOCOMOTIVE DIRECTORY. 1969. biennial. $1. Richard L. Coulton, Ed. & Pub., Bentley, Alberta, T0C 0J0, Canada. circ. 100.

TRANSPORTATION — Roads And Traffic

see also Engineering—Civil Engineering

624 690 US ISSN 0360-6996
A R T B A OFFICIALS AND ENGINEERS DIRECTORY, TRANSPORTATION AGENCY PERSONNEL. a. $17.50. American Road and Transportation Builders Association, A R T B A Bldg., 525 School St., S.W., Washington, DC 20024.

388.312 US
AMERICAN ASSOCIATION OF STATE HIGHWAY AND TRANSPORTATION OFFICIALS. PROCEEDINGS. a. $10. American Association of State Highway and Transportation Officials, 444 N. Capitol St. N.W., Ste. 225, Washington, DC 20001. TEL 202-624-5800. Indexed: HRIS.

388 625.7 AT ISSN 0572-1431
AUSTRALIAN ROAD RESEARCH BOARD. PROCEEDINGS. 1962. biennial. Australian Road Research Board, Box 156 (Bag 4) Nunawading, Vic. 3131, Australia. Indexed: Geotech.Abstr. HRIS. Noise Pollut.Publ.Abstr.

388 BL
BRASILIA. DEPARTAMENTO DE ESTRADAS DE RODAGEM DO DISTRITO FEDERAL. DIRETORIA GERAL. RELATORIO DE ATIVIDADES. 1978. a. free. Departamento de Estradas de Rodagem do Distrito Federal, Divisao de Programacao, 70000 Brasilia, DF, Brazil. circ. 300.
 Formerly: Brasilia. Departamento de Estradas de Rodagem do Distrito Federal. Diretoria Geral. Relatorio Anual.

TRANSPORTATION — ROADS AND TRAFFIC

388.1 FR
CAISSE NATIONALE DES AUTOROUTES. RAPPORT ANNUEL. a. Caisse Nationale des Autoroutes, 56 rue de Lille, 75356 Paris, France. Ed. J.F. Dupuis. illus.

388 UN
CENSUS OF MOTOR TRAFFIC ON MAIN INTERNATIONAL TRAFFIC ARTERIES. (Text in English and French) quinquennial; latest 1980. Economic Commission for Europe (ECE), Palais des Nations, 1211 Geneva 10, Switzerland (Or United Nations Publications, Room LX-2300, New York, NY 10017)
  Formerly: Census of Traffic on Main International Traffic Arteries (ISSN 0566-7631)

388.312 US
COLORADO STATE HIGHWAY CONDITION AND VOLUME REPORT. 1952. biennial. $7. Department of Highways, 4201 East Arkansas, Denver, CO 80222. TEL 303-757-9011. circ. 300.
  Formerly (until 1982): Colorado. Department of Highways. Traffic Volume Study (ISSN 0069-6013)

388.1 II
COMMERCE YEARBOOK OF ROAD TRANSPORT. (Text in English) a. Rs.35. Commerce Publications Limited, NKM International House, 178 Backbay Reclamation, Bombay 400020, India.

CONSTRUCTION INDUSTRIES OF MASSACHUSETTS DIRECTORY; a directory and catalog of highway and heavy construction in New England. see BUSINESS AND ECONOMICS — Trade And Industrial Directories

388.1 CR
COSTA RICA. MINISTERIO DE OBRAS PUBLICAS Y TRANSPORTES. MEMORIAS. irreg. Ministerio de Obras Publicas y Transportes, San Jose, Costa Rica.
  Continues: Costa Rica. Ministerio de Transportes. Memoria (ISSN 0589-8617)

388.1 352.7 DK ISSN 0107-0134
DANMARKS TEKNISKE HOEJSKOLE. INSTITUTET FOR VEJE, TRAFIK OG BYPLAN. NOTAT/TECHNICAL UNIVERSITY OF DENMARK. INSTITUTE OF ROADS, TRANSPORT AND TOWN PLANNING. PAPER. 1976. irreg. price varies. Danmarks Tekniske Hoejskole, Institutet for Veje, Trafik og Byplan, Bygning 115, 2800 Lyngby, Denmark. illus. circ. 100.

388 US ISSN 0070-329X
DELAWARE. DEPARTMENT OF HIGHWAYS AND TRANSPORTATION. TRAFFIC SUMMARY. 1957. a. $5. Department of Transportation, Bureau of Traffic, P.O. Box 778, Dover, DE 19901. TEL 302-735-4303. Ed. John J. Kirwan. circ. 400.

388.1 DK ISSN 0106-312X
DENMARK. STATENS VEJLABORATORIUM. LABORATORIERAPPORT. No.52, 1981. irreg. Statens Vejlaboratorium, Roskilde, Denmark.

388.1 DK
DENMARK. STATENS VEJLABORATORIUM. NOTAT. irreg. free. Statens Vejlaboratorium, Roskilde, Denmark.

388.1 DK ISSN 0109-2405
DENMARK. VEJDIREKTORATET. AARSBERETNING. 1983. a. free. Vejdirektoratet, Copenhagen, Denmark. illus.
  Formerly: Denmark. Vejdirektoratet. Aarsrapport.

388.31 DK
DENMARK. VEJDIREKTORATET. OEKONOMISK-STATISTISK AFDELING. TRAFIKRAPPORT. 1975. a. Vejdirektoratet, Oekonomisk Statistisk Afdeling, Copenhagen, Denmark. illus.
  Formerly: Denmark. Vejdirektoratet. Trafikrapport (ISSN 0106-7389)

388.1 DK ISSN 0108-1306
DETАILFORSKRIFTER FOR KOERETOEJER. 1977. a. Kr.35. Justitsministeriet, Faerdselssikkerhedsafdelingen, Postboks 2131, DK-1015 Copenhagen K, Denmark (Subscr. to: I.H. Schultz Boghandel A-S, Moentergade 19, DK-1116 Copenhagen K, Denmark)

388.1 US ISSN 0732-9792
FATAL ACCIDENT REPORTING SYSTEM. 1975. a. U.S. Department of Transportation, National Highway and Traffic Safety Administration, National Center for Statistics and Analysis, Washington, DC 20590 TEL 202-426-1828. (Subscr. to: Utilization and Storage Section, M-443.2, 400 7th St., S.W., Washington, DC 20590) circ. 4,000. (also avail. in microfiche)
  Formerly (until 1979): Fatal Accident Reporting System. Annual Report (ISSN 0147-6939)

388 GW
FORSCHUNGSGESELLSCHAFT FUER STRASSEN- UND VERKEHRSWESEN. ARBEITSGRUPPE MINERALSTOFFE IM STRASSENBAU. 1977. irreg. price varies. (Forschungsgesellschaft fuer Strassen- und Verkehrswesen) Kirschbaum Verlag, Siegfriedstr. 28, Postfach 210209, D-5300 Bonn 2, W. Germany (B.R.D.)

FRANCE. LABORATOIRE CENTRAL DES PONTS ET CHAUSSEES. RAPPORT DE RECHERCHE. see ENGINEERING — Civil Engineering

388 GW
GERMANY (FEDERAL REPUBLIC). BUNDESMINISTERIUM FUER VERKEHR. STRASSENBAUBERICHT. 1971. a. DM.15. (Bundesministerium fuer Verkehr) Verlag Dr. Hans Heger, Herderstr. 56, Postfach 200821, 5300 Bonn 2, W. Germany (B.R.D.) illus. circ. 1,500.

388.1 UK
GREAT BRITAIN. DEPARTMENT OF TRANSPORT. POLICY FOR ROADS: ENGLAND. (Issued in the series of Reports and Papers of the House of Commons. Report Year Ends Mar. 31) a. price varies. H.M.S.O., Box 569, London SE1 9NH, England. illus.
  Formerly: Great Britain. Department of Transport. Roads in England.

264 UK
HIGHWAY CODE. irreg. Department of Transport, 2 Marsham St., London SW1P 3EB, England.

HIGHWAY RESEARCH RECORD; general report on road research work done in India during (year) see ENGINEERING — Civil Engineering

388.1 II
I R C SPECIAL PUBLICATION. no.13, 1973. irreg. Rs.28. Indian Roads Congress, Jamnagar House, Shahjahan Rd., New Delhi 110011, India. bibl. charts.

624 II ISSN 0046-905X
INDIAN ROADS CONGRESS. JOURNAL. (Text in English) 1934. irreg., (approx. 4/yr.) $8.00. Indian Roads Congress, Jamnagar House, Shahjahan Rd., New Delhi 110011, India. Ed. Ninan Koshi. circ. 6, 500. Indexed: Eng.Ind. Geotech.Abstr. HRIS.

388.1 BL
INSTITUTO DE PESQUISAS RODOVIARIAS. RELATORIO DAS ATIVIDADES.* (Subseries of its Publicacao) irreg. Instituto de Pesquisas Rodoviarias, Rua Dom Gerardo 84, 12 Andar, 20000 Rio de Janeiro, Brazil.

388.31 US
INTERNATIONAL BRIDGE, TUNNEL AND TURNPIKE ASSOCIATION. REPORT OF THE ANNUAL MEETING. 1962. a. price varies. International Bridge, Tunnel and Turnpike Association, 2120 L St., N.W., Ste. 305, Washington, DC 20037. Dir. John J. Hassett. circ. 2,000.

625.7 US ISSN 0074-3348
INTERNATIONAL CONFERENCE ON THE STRUCTURAL DESIGN OF ASPHALT PAVEMENTS. PROCEEDINGS.* 1963. irreg., 1967, 2nd, Ann Arbor, Mich. c o Prof. Egon Tons, University of Michigan, Box 619, Ann Arbor, Michigan.

388.1 625.7 FR ISSN 0074-7815
INTERNATIONAL ROAD CONGRESSES. PROCEEDINGS. (Editions avail. in English and French) quadrennial since 1964; 1983 17th, Sydney. Permanent International Association of Road Congresses, 27 rue Guenegaud, 75006 Paris, France.

388.413 US
IOWA COUNTY ENGINEERS ANNUAL HIGHWAY REPORTS. SUMMARY. 1959. a. free. Department of Transportation, Office of Local Systems, 800 Lincoln Way, Ames, IA 50010. TEL 515-239-1101. circ. 250.

ITOGI NAUKI I TEKHNIKI: AVTOMOBIL'NYI I GORODSKOI TRANSPORT. see ENGINEERING — Civil Engineering

388.1 AU ISSN 0075-7306
KURATORIUM FUER VERKEHRSSICHERHEIT. KLEINE FACHBUCHREIHE. (Text in German; summaries in English, French) 1959. irreg., no.20, 1984. price varies. ‡ (Kuratorium fuer Verkehrssicherheit) Literas Universitaetsverlag, Berggasse 4, A-1030 Vienna, Austria. Ed.Bd. cum.index: 1959-1971. circ. 1,300. Indexed: Psychol.Abstr. Hwy.Res.Abstr. Psychopharmacol.Abstr.

388.1 DK ISSN 0109-6044
LAENGDEN AF OFFENTLIGE VEJE. 1983. a. free. Vejdirektoratet - Ministry of Public Works, Transport Dept., Frederiksholm Kanal 27, 1220 Copenhagen K, Denmark.

LINKS UND RECHTS DER AUTOBAHN; der Reisefuehrer und Reiseatlas speziell fuer die Autobahn. see HOTELS AND RESTAURANTS

388.3 US ISSN 0094-6265
MARYLAND. STATE HIGHWAY ADMINISTRATION. TRAFFIC TRENDS. 1963. irreg. free. State Highway Administration, Department of Transportation, Box 717, 300 W. Preston St., Baltimore, MD 21203. TEL 301-659-1122. stat. circ. 200. Key Title: Traffic Trends.

388 US
MISSOURI. DIVISION OF HIGHWAY SAFETY. HIGHWAY SAFETY PLAN. 1971. a. ‡ Division of Highway Safety, 301 W. High St., Jefferson City, MO 65102. TEL 314-751-4161. Ed. Vicky S. Williams. circ. controlled.
  Former titles: Missouri's Annual Highway Safety Program; Missouri Annual Highway Safety Work Program (ISSN 0091-1097)

625.7 388.31 US ISSN 0077-5614
NATIONAL COOPERATIVE HIGHWAY RESEARCH PROGRAM REPORTS. 1964. irreg., no.281, 1985. price varies. National Research Council, Transportation Research Board, 2101 Constitution Ave., N.W., Washington, DC 20418. TEL 202-334-2934. circ. 3,250.

625.7 US ISSN 0547-5570
NATIONAL COOPERATIVE HIGHWAY RESEARCH PROGRAM SYNTHESIS OF HIGHWAY PRACTICE. 1969. irreg., no.119, 1985. price varies. National Research Council, Transportation Research Board, 2101 Constitution Ave., N.W., Washington, DC 20418. TEL 202-334-2934.

388.31 625 SA ISSN 0379-6124
NATIONAL INSTITUTE FOR TRANSPORT AND ROAD RESEARCH. ANNUAL REPORT/ NASIONALE INSTITUUT VIR VERVOER- EN PADNAVORSING. JAARVERSLAG. (Text in Afrikaans and English) 1961. a. free. National Institute for Transport and Road Research, P.O. Box 395, Pretoria 0001, South Africa. Ed. G.J. Van N. Fourie. bibl. charts. illus. circ. 1,000.
  Formerly: National Institute for Road Research. Annual Report.

388.1 SA
NATIONAL INSTITUTE FOR TRANSPORT AND ROAD RESEARCH. BULLETINS. Alternative title: C S I R Research Reports. (Text in Afrikaans or English) 1956. irreg., no.17, 1980. free. National Institute for Transport and Road Research, Box 395, Pretoria 0001, South Africa. Indexed: Chem.Abstr.

388.1 SA
NATIONAL INSTITUTE FOR TRANSPORT AND ROAD RESEARCH. P A D SERIES. Alternate title: C S I R Special Reports. (Text in Afrikaans or English) irreg., no.54, 1984. National Institute for Transport and Road Research, Box 395, Pretoria 0001, South Africa.

TRANSPORTATION — ROADS AND TRAFFIC

625　　　　　　　　SA
NATIONAL INSTITUTE FOR TRANSPORT AND ROAD RESEARCH. TECHNICAL METHODS FOR HIGHWAYS/NASIONALE INSTITUUT VIR VERVOER- EN PADNAVORSING. TEGNIESE METODES VIR HOOFWEE. (Text in Afrikaans or English) 1978. irreg., no.7, 1981. price varies. National Institute for Transport and Road Research, Box 395, Pretoria 0001, South Africa.

388.312　　　　　　　SA
NATIONAL INSTITUTE FOR TRANSPORT AND ROAD RESEARCH. TECHNICAL RECOMMENDATIONS FOR HIGHWAYS/NASIONALE INSTITUUT VIR VERVOER- EN PADNAVORSING. TEGNIESE RIGLYNE VIR HOOFWEE. (Text in Afrikaans or English) 1970. irreg., no.17, 1984. free. National Institute for Transport and Road Research, Box 395, Pretoria 0001, South Africa.

388.1　　　　　　　US
NEBRASKA. DEPARTMENT OF ROADS. NEBRASKA SELECTED STATISTICS. a. Department of Roads, Highway Statistical Unit, Lincoln, NE 68509. illus.
    Former titles: Nebraska. Department of Roads. Highway Statistics: State and Local Road and Street Data for (Year); Nebraska Highway Statistics: State and Local Construction Mileage (ISSN 0099-0442)

388　　　　　US　ISSN 0091-844X
NEBRASKA. DEPARTMENT OF ROADS. TRAFFIC ANALYSIS UNIT. CONTINUOUS TRAFFIC COUNT DATA AND TRAFFIC CHARACTERISTICS ON NEBRASKA STREETS AND HIGHWAYS. 1968. a. Department of Roads, Transportation Planning Division, Box 94759-4759, Lincoln, NE 68509. TEL 402-464-0641. circ. controlled.

388.1　　　　　NE　ISSN 0168-4388
NETHERLANDS. CENTRAAL BUREAU VOOR DE STATISTIEK. TOEPASSING DER WEGENVERKEERSWET. STATISTICS OF THE APPLICATION OF THE ROAD TRAFFIC ACT. (Text in Dutch and English) 1951/52. irreg. fl.10.85. Centraal Bureau voor de Statistiek, Prinses Beatrixlaan 428, Voorburg, Netherlands (Orders to: Staatsuitgeverij, Christoffel Plantijnstraat, The Hague, Netherlands)

NEW ZEALAND. MINISTRY OF TRANSPORT. TRAFFIC RESEARCH REPORT. see *TRANSPORTATION*

388.1　　　　　NZ　ISSN 0549-0030
NEW ZEALAND. ROAD RESEARCH UNIT. BULLETIN. 1965. irreg. NZ.$5. Road Research Unit, P.O. Box 12041, Wellington, New Zealand. bk. rev. charts. illus. circ. 800.

388.1　　　　　NZ　ISSN 0111-0756
NEW ZEALAND. ROAD RESEARCH UNIT. OCCASIONAL PAPER. 1978. irreg. NZ.$5 per no. Road Research Unit, P.O. Box 12041, Wellington, New Zealand. bk. rev. charts. illus. circ. 200.

388.31　　　　　　　US
NOISE MANUAL. 1980. irreg. $20. Department of Transportation, Publications Section, 6002 Folsom Blvd., Sacramento, CA 95819. TEL 916-445-4616. Ed. M.M. Hatano. charts. illus. (also avail. in looseleaf format)

338.3　　　　　　　US
NORTH CAROLINA. DEPARTMENT OF TRANSPORTATION. OFFICE OF HIGHWAY SAFETY. SUMMARY OF ACTIVITIES. a. free. Department of Transportation, Office of Highway Safety, Raleigh, NC 27600. TEL 919-733-5007. illus. stat.
    Formerly: North Carolina Governor's Highway Safety Program. Summary of Activities (ISSN 0361-2295)

388　614　　　　　US
NORTH DAKOTA'S HIGHWAY SAFETY PLAN. 1967. a. free to qualified personnel. ‡ State Highway Department, Driver's License and Traffic Safety, Traffic Safety Programs Section, 600 E. Blvd. Ave., Bismarck, ND 58505-0178. TEL 701-224-2600. circ. controlled. (looseleaf format)
    Formerly: North Dakota's Highway Safety Work Programs.

388.1　　　　　　　US
OKLAHOMA. DEPARTMENT OF TRANSPORTATION. SUFFICIENCY RATING REPORT AND NEEDS STUDY: OKLAHOMA STATE TRANSPORTATION. 1966. biennial. free. Department of Transportation, Planning Division, 200 N.E. 21st., Oklahoma City, OK 73105. TEL 405-521-2579. illus. circ. 200.
    Formerly: Oklahoma. Department of Highways. Sufficiency Rating Report and Needs Study: Oklahoma State Highways (ISSN 0094-6230)

388.31　　　　　　　US
OKLAHOMA TURNPIKE AUTHORITY. ANNUAL REPORT TO THE GOVERNOR. 1954. a. free. Turnpike Authority, 3500 North Eastern, Box 11357, Oklahoma City, OK 73136. TEL 405-527-8331. charts. stat. circ. 1,000 (approx.)

388.31　　　　　　　US
OKLAHOMA TURNPIKE AUTHORITY. REPORT TO BONDHOLDERS. a. Turnpike Authority, 3500 N. Eastern, Box 11357, Oklahoma City, OK 73136. TEL 405-427-8331.

388.1　　　　　　　II
ORISSA STATE ROAD TRANSPORTATION CORPORATION. ANNUAL ADMINISTRATION REPORT. (Text in English) 1974/75. a. State Road Transportation Corporation, Cuttack 753001, India. stat.

625.7　　　　　US　ISSN 0079-8142
PURDUE UNIVERSITY. ROAD SCHOOL. PROCEEDINGS OF ANNUAL ROAD SCHOOL. (Subseries of: Engineering Bulletin. Engineering Extension Series) 1924. a. single copy free. Purdue University, School of Civil Engineering, West Lafayette, IN 47907. TEL 317-494-5600. Ed. D.G. Shurig. circ. 2,500.

388.1　　　　　DK　ISSN 0105-6956
RAPPORT FRA S T I K K; trafikuheld i Storkoebenhavn. 1977. a. free. Samarbejdsgruppen for Trafiksikkerhed i Kommuneerne i Koebenhavns-Omraadet, Gentofte Kommunes Tekniske Forvaltning, Sekretariat, Raadhuset, 2920 Charlottenlund, Denmark. illus. circ. 3,000.

385.1　388　　　UK　ISSN 0307-6822
ROAD ACCIDENTS IN GREAT BRITAIN. (Joint publication with Scottish Development Department and the Welsh Office) 1969. a. price varies. H.M.S.O., Box 569, London SE1 9NH, England.

ROAD DOCUMENTATION FOR DEVELOPING COUNTRIES. see *TRANSPORTATION*

388.1　　　　　　　DK
S V LEVERINGSBETINGELSER OG PROEVNINGSMETODER. vol.12, 1981. irreg. free. Statens Vejlaboratorium, Roskilde, Denmark.

388.3　　　　　　　CN
SASKATCHEWAN. GOVERNMENT INSURANCE OFFICE. PROVINCE OF SASKATCHEWAN MOTOR VEHICLE TRAFFIC ACCIDENTS. ANNUAL REPORT. a. Government Insurance Office, Regina, Saskatchewan, Canada. TEL 306-565-1200.

388.413　　　　　DK　ISSN 0107-5179
SIKKERHEDSMAESSIG VURDERING OG PRIORITERING AF MINDRE ANLAEGSARBEJDER PAA HOVEDLANDEVEJE. 1975. a. free. Vejdirektoratet - Ministry of Public Works, Transport Dept., Frederiksholm Kanal 27, 1220 Copenhagen K, Denmark. illus.
    Formerly: Denmark. Vejdirektoratet. Black-Spotundersoegelse paa Hovedlandeveje.

614.8　　　　　US　ISSN 0731-1966
STATE OF MICHIGAN'S ANNUAL HIGHWAY SAFETY PLAN. 1968. a. free. Department of State Police, Office of Highway Safety Planning, 111 S. Capital Ave., Lansing, MI 48913. Ed. B. Powell. illus. stat. circ. 50.
    Formerly (until 1978): Michigan. Office of Highway Safety Planning. Annual Highway Safety Work Plan (ISSN 0094-1069)

388.1　　　　　DK　ISSN 0106-7540
STOPINTERVIEWANALYSE. irreg. Vejdirektoratet - Ministry of Public Works, Transport Dept., Frederikssholm Kanal 27, 1220 Copenhagen K, Denmark. illus.
    Formerly: Trafikanalyse.

354.485　　　　SW　ISSN 0347-6057
SWEDEN. STATENS VAEG- OCH TRAFIKINSTITUT. VERKSAMHETSBERAETTELSE. English edition: Swedish National Road and Traffic Research Institute. Annual Report. a. Statens Vaeg- och Trafikinstitut, S-581 01 Linkoeping, Sweden.

338.1　　　　　SW　ISSN 0347-6030
SWEDEN. V T I RAPPORT. (Text in English and Swedish; summaries in English) 1971. irreg. (15-20/yr.) free. Swedish Road and Traffic Research Institute, S-581 01 Linkoeping, Sweden. circ. 800.

388.413　　　　　SW　ISSN 0281-4447
SWEDISH ROAD SAFETY OFFICE. ANALYSIS SECTION REPORT. (Text in Swedish, summaries in English) 1968. irreg. Swedish Road Safety Office, S-78186 Borlaenge, Sweden.

388.411　　　　　DK　ISSN 0105-5119
TECHNICAL UNIVERSITY OF DENMARK. INSTITUTE OF ROADS, TRANSPORT AND TOWN PLANNING. PAPERS AND REPORTS. (Text in Danish and English; summaries in English) 1937. irreg. Technical University of Denmark, Institute of Roads, Transport and Town Planning, Building 115, DK-2800 Lyngby, Denmark. circ. 50. (back issues avail.)

388.314　333.77　　　DK
TECHNICAL UNIVERSITY OF DENMARK. INSTITUTE OF ROADS, TRANSPORT AND TOWN PLANNING. REPORT. 1976. irreg., no. 19, 1978. Polytekniske Laereanstalt, Danmarks Tekniske Hoejskole, Instituttet for Vejbygning, Trafikteknik og Byplanlaegning, Bygning 115, DK-2800 Lyngby, Denmark. circ. 250.

353.9　　　　　US　ISSN 0095-1994
TENNESSEE. DEPARTMENT OF SAFETY. ANNUAL REPORT. 1971. a. free to qualified personnel. Department of Safety, 1150 Foster Ave., Nashville, TN 37210. TEL 615-251-5229. circ. 500. Key Title: Annual Report - Department of Safety.

388　　　　　US　ISSN 0082-5859
TRAFFIC LAWS COMMENTARY.* 1963. irreg., latest 1982. price varies. National Committee on Uniform Traffic Laws and Ordinances, 405 Church St., Box 1409, Evanston, IL 60204.

388.1　　　　　　　US
TRAFFIC SAFETY; a report on activities under the Highway Safety Act of 1966. 1966. a. U.S. National Highway Traffic Safety Administration, 400 Seventh St. N.W., Washington, DC 20590. (Co-sponsor: U.S. Federal Highway Administration) Indexed: CJPI.

388.1　330　　　DK　ISSN 0106-1852
TRAFIKOEKONOMISKE ENHEDSPRISER. 1977. a. free. Vejdirektoratet, Oekonomisk-Statistik Afdelning, Copenhagen, Denmark.

388.1　　　　　SA　ISSN 0379-4792
TRANSPORT AND ROAD DIGEST/VERVOER- EN PADOORSIG. 1977. irreg., no.50, 1985. National Institute for Transport and Road Research - Nasionale Instituut vir Vervoer- en Padnavorsing, Box 395, Pretoria 0001, South Africa. Ed. C.A. Kruger. circ. 3,000. Indexed: HRIS.

388　625.7　　　　　UK
TRANSPORT AND ROAD RESEARCH LABORATORY. RESEARCH REPORTS. irreg. £200. Transport and Road Research Laboratory, Old Wokingham Rd., Crowthorne, Berks. RG7 6AU, England.
    Supersedes (as of 1985): Road Notes (ISSN 0080-3294) & Transport and Road Research; Which was formerly: Road Research (ISSN 0080-3308)

388.1　　　　　　　UK
TRANSPORT STATISTICS GREAT BRITAIN. (Joint publication with the Scottish Development Department and Welsh Office) 1976. a. price varies. ‡ H.M.S.O., Box 569, London SE1 9NH, England. circ. 2,000.
    Incorporating: Great Britain. Department of the Environment. Highway Statistics (ISSN 0072-6893) & Passenger Transport in Great Britain (ISSN 0079-0133)

625.7 388   US   ISSN 0360-859X
TRANSPORTATION RESEARCH BOARD
SPECIAL REPORT. 1952. irreg., no.209, 1985.
price varies. National Research Council,
Transportation Research Board, 2101 Constitution
Ave., N.W., Washington, DC 20418. TEL 202-334-
2934. circ. 3,250. Indexed: GeoRef. Geotech.Abstr.
HRIS.
   Formerly (until no.144, 1974): Highway Research
Board Special Publication (ISSN 0077-5622)

625.7 388   US   ISSN 0361-1981
TRANSPORTATION RESEARCH RECORD. 1963.
irreg., no.1016, 1985. price varies. National
Research Council, Transportation Research Board,
2101 Constitution Ave., N.W., Washington, DC
20418. TEL 202-334-2934. circ. 3,250. Indexed:
Chem.Abstr. GeoRef. Geotech.Abstr.
Ocean.Abstr. Pollut.Abstr. Noise Pollut.Publ.Abstr.
Sel.Water Res.Abstr.
   Formerly (until 1974): Highway Research Record
(ISSN 0073-2206)

388   CN   ISSN 0581-8079
TRAVEL ON SASKATCHEWAN HIGHWAYS.
1958. biennial. free. Department of Highways and
Transportation, Planning Support Branch, 1855
Victoria Ave., Regina, Sask. S4P 3V5, Canada. TEL
306-787-4800. Ed. Jon J. Wyatt. circ. 1,000.

388.3   US   ISSN 0277-2310
U.S. DEPARTMENT OF TRANSPORTATION.
HIGHWAY SAFETY STEWARDSHIP REPORT.
1974. a. U.S. Department of Transportation, 400
Seventh St. N.W., Washington, DC 20590 TEL
202-655-4000. (Order from: Supt. of Documents,
Washington DC 20402) stat.
   Former titles: Highway Safety Improvement
Programs & Annual Report on Highway Safety
Improvement Programs (ISSN 0098-3209)

625.7   US   ISSN 0361-4204
U.S. FEDERAL HIGHWAY ADMINISTRATION.
FEDERALLY COORDINATED PROGRAM OF
HIGHWAY RESEARCH AND DEVELOPMENT.
1975. a. U.S. Federal Highway Administration,
Dept. of Transportation, Washington, DC 20591
TEL 202-426-0600. (Orders to: Supt. of Documents,
Washington, D.C. 20402) illus. Key Title: Federally
Coordinated Program of Highway Research and
Development.
   Continues: U.S. Federal Highway Administration.
Research and Development Program.

388.3   US
U.S. FEDERAL HIGHWAY ADMINISTRATION.
HIGHWAY STATISTICS. 1945. a. price varies.
U.S. Federal Highway Administration, Highway
Statistics Division, 400 Seventh St. S.W., DC 20590
TEL 202-426-0632. (Orders to: Supt. of Documents,
U.S. Government Printing Office, Washington, DC
20402) Ed. A. French.

388.413   GW
UNIVERSITAET MUENSTER. INSTITUT FUER
VERKEHRSWISSENSCHAFT. BEITRAEGE.
1954. irreg. (Universitaet Muenster, Institut fuer
Verkehrswissenschaft) Vandenhoeck & Ruprecht,
Verlagsbuchhandlung, Robert-Bosch-Breite 6,
Postfach 3753, D-3400 Goettingen, W. Germany
(B.R.D.) Ed. Helmut Seidenfuess.

388.31   SW
V T I ANNUAL REPORT. a. Statens Vaeg- och
Trafikinstitut - Swedish Road and Traffic Research
Institute, S-581 01 Linkoeping, Sweden. charts.

338.1   SW   ISSN 0347-6049
V T I MEDDELANDE. (Text in Swedish; summaries
in English) 1976. irreg. (50-60/yr.) free. Swedish
Road and Traffic Research Institute, S-581 01
Linkoeping, Sweden. Indexed: HRIS.

388 310   GW   ISSN 0083-5021
V W Z. (Verkehrswirtschaftliche Zahlen) 1954. a. free.
Bundesverband des Deutschen Gueterfernverkehrs
e.V., Haus des Strassenverkehrs, Postfach 930 260,
D-6000 Frankfurt-93, W. Germany (B.R.D.) Ed. G.
Dierschke. circ. 5,000.

388.1   DK   ISSN 0107-0614
VEJDATALABORATORIET. RAPPORT. 1965.
irreg. free. Vejdatalaboratoriet, Stationsalleen 42,
2730 Herlev, Denmark. illus.

388.31   AU   ISSN 0042-4048
VERKEHRSPSYCHOLOGISCHER
INFORMATIONSDIENST. 1962. irreg. (2-3/yr.)
free. Kuratorium fuer Verkehrssicherheit,
Verkehrspsychologisches Institut, Oelzeltgasse 3, A-
1031 Vienna, Austria. Ed. K. Hoefner. circ. 2,500.

388.1 625.7   US
VIRGINIA HIGHWAY AND TRANSPORTATION
CONFERENCE. PROCEEDINGS. 1947. a.
Department of Highways and Transportation, 1401
E. Broad St., Richmond, VA 23219. TEL 804-786-
2716. (Co-sponsor: Virginia Military Institute)
cum.index: 1947-69 (except 1968) circ. 375.
   Formerly: Virginia Highway Conference.
Proceedings (ISSN 0083-6370)

388   US   ISSN 0084-0572
WISCONSIN. DEPARTMENT OF
TRANSPORTATION. DIVISION OF
PLANNING AND BUDGET. HIGHWAY
MILEAGE DATA. (Former name of issuing body:
Division of Planning) 1946. a. $12. Department of
Transportation, Division of Planning, Box 7913,
4802 Sheboygan Ave., Madison, WI 53702. TEL
608-266-3661. circ. 200.

388   US   ISSN 0084-0580
WISCONSIN. DEPARTMENT OF
TRANSPORTATION. DIVISION OF
PLANNING. HIGHWAY TRAFFIC. Short title:
Wisconsin Highway Traffic. 1968. a. $14.50.
Department of Transportation, Division of Planning,
Data Development Section, 4802 Sheboygan Ave.,
Box 7913, Madison, WI 53707. TEL 608-266-1466.
circ. 300.
   Formerly: Wisconsin. Division of Highways.
System Planning Section. Highway Traffic in
Wisconsin Cities (ISSN 0512-0624)

388   US   ISSN 0098-0323
WISCONSIN TRAFFIC DATA - AUTOMATIC
TRAFFIC RECORDER; monthly average daily
traffic. Short title: Wisconsin Traffic Data - A T R.
1970. a. $14.69. Department of Transportation,
Division of Planning, Data Development Section,
4802 Sheboygan Ave., Box 7913, Madison, WI
53707. TEL 608-266-1466. circ. 125.
   Former titles: Wisconsin. Department of
Transportation. Automatic Traffic Recorder Data;
Wisconsin. Department of Transportation. Traffic
Planning Section. Automatic Recorder Station
Traffic Data (ISSN 0091-6080)

WORLD SURVEY OF CURRENT RESEARCH
AND DEVELOPMENT ON ROADS AND
ROAD TRANSPORT (YEAR) see
ENGINEERING — Civil Engineering

TRANSPORTATION — Ships And Shipping

387   UK
A B O I CATALOGUE.* 1974. a. Association of
British Oceanic Industries, 32-38 Leman St.,
London WI8 EW, England.

ABERDEEN PORT HANDBOOK. see BUSINESS
AND ECONOMICS — Trade And Industrial
Directories

387   BE
ACADEMIE DE MARINE. COMMUNICATIONS/
MARINE ACADEMIE. MEDEDELINGEN. (Text
in Dutch and French; summaries in English and
French) 1936/37. irreg. (approx. a.) 630 Fr. price
varies. Uitgeverij de Sikkel N.V., Nijverheidsstraat
8, 2150 Malle, Belgium. Ed. Walter Debrock. bibl.
illus.

387   PO
ADMINISTRACAO-GERAL DO PORTO DE
LISBOA. RELATORIO. 1935. a. free.
Administracao-Geral do Porto de Lisboa, Servico de
Relacoes Publicas, Cais do Sodre, 1293 Lisbon
Codex, Portugal. circ. 1,000.

387   IT
AGENDA NAUTICA. 1955. a. L.13000. Istituto
Idrografico della Marina, Passo Osservatorio, 4,
16126 Genoa, Italy. Ed.Bd. circ. 15,000.

387   US   ISSN 0271-8987
ALASKA SHIPPERS GUIDE. 1980. a. $9.95. Alaska
Northwest Publishing Company, Box 4-EEE,
Anchorage, AK 99509. TEL 907-274-0521. Ed.
Rick Paul. adv. circ. 9,920.

387   US
AMERICAN BUREAU OF SHIPPING. RECORD.
1869. a. with m. supplements. $400. American
Bureau of Shipping, 45 Eisenhower Dr., Box 910,
Paramus, NJ 07653-0910. TEL 201-368-9100. Ed.
William R. Hartman. circ. 209. Indexed: BMT.

387.5   US
AMERICAN MERCHANT MARINE
CONFERENCE. PROCEEDINGS. 1935. a. $6.50.
Propeller Club of the United States, 1030 15th St.,
N.W., Washington, DC 20005. TEL 202-898-0680.
Ed. Jasper S. Baker. circ. 2,500 (controlled)

387   FR   ISSN 0066-2550
ANNUAIRE DE LA MARINE MARCHANDE.
1904. a. 115 F. Comite Central des Armateurs de
France, 73 Bld. Haussmann, 75008 Paris, France.
adv. circ. 650.

623.82   JA   ISSN 0448-3294
ANNUAL STATISTICS OF MARITIME SAFETY.
(Text in Japanese) 1950. a. Maritime Safety Agency
- Kaijo Hoancho, 2-1-3 Kasumigaseki, Chiyoda-ku,
Tokyo 100, Japan. stat.

623.89   AT
ANNUAL SUMMARY OF AUSTRALIAN
NOTICES TO MARINERS. 1933. a. free.
Department of the Navy, Hydrographic Service,
Sydney, Australia. illus. index. circ. 3,200.

387 620   UK   ISSN 0261-2720
ANNUAL SUMMARY OF MERCHANT SHIPS
COMPLETED IN THE WORLD. 1892. a. free.
Lloyd's Register of Shipping, 71 Fenchurch St.,
London EC3M 4BS, England.
   Formerly: Annual Summary of Merchant Ships
Launched/Completed in the World; Annual
Summary of Merchant Ships Launched in the World
(ISSN 0066-4391)

387 380   UK   ISSN 0264-1259
ANTWERP HANDBOOK 1984. 1983. a. £5. Charter
Publications, Bank Chambers, Downham Market,
Norfolk PE38 9BU, England. Ed. James Moriarty.
adv. circ. 6,000.

ANTWERP PORT ANNUAL. see BUSINESS AND
ECONOMICS — Trade And Industrial Directories

386   BL
ANUARIO DE PORTOS E NAVIOS. a. $30. Revista
Tecnica e Informativa Ltda., Rua Leandro Martins
10, Caixa Postal 2791, Rio de Janeiro, Brazil. Ed.
Brasilio Accioly. adv. charts. stat.

382   UK
ARAB SHIPPING. 1978. a. only including
subscription to "Seatrade". Seatrade Publications
Ltd., Fairfax House, Colchester, Essex CO1 IRJ,
England. Ed. Deborah Seyman. adv. circ. 5,910.
   Formerly: Seatrade Guide to Arab Shipping
(ISSN 0141-4151)

387.54   UK
ARROWSMITH'S BRISTOL CHANNEL TIDE
TABLE. 1835. a. £1.20. J.W. Arrowsmith Ltd.,
Winterstoke Rd., Bristol BS3 2NT, England. adv.
circ. 5,000.

387 380   UK   ISSN 0262-1630
ASSOCIATED BRITISH PORTS HANDBOOK.
1982. a. £10. Charter Publications, Bank Chambers,
Downham Market, Norfolk PE38 9BU, England.
Ed. James Moriarty. adv. circ. 6,000.

387   UK
ASSOCIATED BRITISH PORTS HOLDINGS PLC.
ANNUAL REPORT AND ACCOUNTS. 1963. a.
free. Associated British Ports Holdings PLC, 150
Holborn, London EC1N 2LR, England.
   Formerly: British Transport Docks Board. Annual
Report and Accounts (ISSN 0068-2659)

TRANSPORTATION — SHIPS AND SHIPPING

387   623.8   629.1   FR   ISSN 0066-9814
ASSOCIATION TECHNIQUE MARITIME ET AERONAUTIQUE, PARIS. BULLETIN. (Text in French; summaries in English and French) 1890. a. 450 F. to non-members. Association Technique Maritime et Aeronautique, 47 rue de Monceau, 75008 Paris, France. Ed.Bd. index. circ. 1,000. (back issues avail.) Indexed: Appl.Mech.Rev.

387   CN
ATLANTIC CANADA SHIPPING PROJECT. ANNUAL CONFERENCE. PROCEEDINGS. 1978. a. Memorial University of Newfoundland, Maritime History Group, St. John's, Nfld. A1C 5S7, Canada. TEL 709-737-8428.

623.8   387   AT
AUSTRALIAN SHIPPING AND SHIPBUILDING. 1947. a. price varies. Australian Government Publishing Service, G.P.O. Box 84, Canberra, A.C.T. 2601, Australia.

387   BF
BAHAMAS. PORT AND MARINE DEPARTMENT. MINISTRY OF TRANSPORT. ANNUAL REPORT. a. Port and Marine Department, Ministry of Transport, Nassau, Bahamas.

387   SP
BARCELONA PORT; guia de servicios del puerto de Barcelona. 1978. a. 650 ptas.($10) Publicaciones Men - Car, Paseo de Colon 24, Barcelona 2, Spain. Eds. Juan y Manuel Cardona. adv. circ. 15,000.
Formerly: Port (Year)

387   UK
BARROW DOCKS AND SILLOTH DOCK TIDAL PREDICTIONS. a. Associated British Ports Holdings PLC, 150 Holborn, London EC1N 2LR, England.

387   II
BASIC PORT STATISTICS OF INDIA. 1970. a., latest edition in print 1976/1977. $27.54. Ministry of Shipping and Transport, Transport Research Division, I D A Bldg., Jamnagar House, Shahjahan Rd., New Delhi 110011, India (Orders to: Controller of Publications, Civil Lines, Delhi 110006, India)
Former titles: Port Transport Statistics of India; India Ports and Shipping Statistics.

387   BE
BELGIUM. ADMINISTRATION DE LA MARINE ET DE LA NAVIGATION INTERIEURE. RAPPORT ANNUEL SUR L'EVOLUTION DE LA FLOTTE DE PECHE. a. Administration de la Marine et de la Navigation Interieure, 104 rue d'Arlon, 1040 Brussels, Belgium.
Continues: Belgium. Administration de la Marine. Rapport Annuel sur l'Evolution de la Flotte de Peche.

623.82   US
BOATBUILDER'S INTERNATIONAL DIRECTORY; the boatbuilder's source book of designers, kit makers and suppliers. 1980. a. $6.50. Saffron Publishing, 1001 Bridgeway, Dept. 621, Sausalito, CA 94965. Ed. Donald W. Purdy. adv. bk. rev. circ. 10,000.

BOATING INDUSTRY MARINE BUYERS GUIDE. see BUSINESS AND ECONOMICS — Trade And Industrial Directories

BOSTON SEA AND AIR PORT HANDBOOK. see BUSINESS AND ECONOMICS — Trade And Industrial Directories

387   380   UK   ISSN 0265-8178
BRITISH COLUMBIA PORTS HANDBOOK 1984. 1984. biennial. £10. Charter Publications, Bank Chambers, Downham Market, Norfolk PE38 9BU, England. Ed. James Moriarty. adv. circ. 6,000.

623.82   UK
BRITISH MARINE INDUSTRIES FEDERATION HANDBOOK. 1947. a. £4. British Marine Industries Federation, Boating Industry House, Vale Rd., Weybridge, Surrey KT13 9NS, England. adv. circ. 1,500.
Formerly: Ship and Boat Builders National Federation Handbook.

386   UK   ISSN 0068-2683
BRITISH WATERWAYS BOARD. ANNUAL REPORT AND ACCOUNTS. 1963. a. price varies. British Waterways Board, Melbury House, Melbury Terrace, London NW1 6JX, England (Avail. from: H.M.S.O., c/o Liaison Officer, Atlantic House, London EC1P 1BW, England)

BULK HANDLING & TRANSPORT. see TRANSPORTATION

387.5   FR
BULLETIN OFFICIEL DE LA MARINE MARCHANDE. irreg.? Imprimerie Nationale, Service des Ventes, 59128 Flers en Escrebieux, France.

BULLINGER'S POSTAL AND SHIPPERS GUIDE FOR THE UNITED STATES AND CANADA. see COMMUNICATIONS — Postal Affairs

387   SW
C M I YEAR BOOK. 1978. a. (International Maritime Committee - Comite Maritime International) Almvist & Wiksell, P.O. Box 638, S-101 28 Stockholm, Sweden. circ. 2,500.
Supersedes in part (since 1978): International Maritime Committee. Documentation (ISSN 0538-8643)

387   380   UK   ISSN 0263-7073
CANARY ISLANDS SHIPPING HANDBOOK 1983/4. 1980. a. £3.50. Charter Publications, Bank Chambers, Downham Market, Norfolk PE38 9BU, England. Ed. James Moriarty. adv. circ. 6,000.

387   380   CN   ISSN 0318-3742
CAPTAIN LILLIE'S COAST GUIDE AND RADIOTELEPHONE DIRECTORY. 1936. biennial. Can.$16. Progress Publishing Co. Ltd., C-310 Marine Building, 355 Burrard St., Vancouver, B.C. V6C 2G6, Canada. TEL 604-685-4385.

387   JM
CARIBBEAN PORTS HANDBOOK. a. (Caribbean Shipping Association) Creative Communications, Inc., Ltd., P.O. Box 105, Kingston 10, Jamaica. Ed. Anthony A. Gambrill.

387   UK   ISSN 0268-0815
CASUALTY RETURN. 1891. a. £45. Lloyd's Register of Shipping, 71 Fenchurch St., London EC3M 4BS, England.
Former titles: Casualty Return Statistical Summary of Merchant Ships Totally Lost, Broken Up, Etc (ISSN 0261-2712) & Casualty Return Statistical Summary (ISSN 0008-7572); Merchant Ships Totally Lost, Broken Up, Etc.

387   NE
CATALOGUS SCHEEPVAART. a. Nijgh Periodieken B.V., Postbox 122, 3100 AC Schiedam, Netherlands. circ. 2,500.

387   AG
CENTRO DE NAVEGACION TRANSATLANTICA. C.N.T. HANDBOOK. RIVER PLATE HANDBOOK FOR SHIPOWNERS AND AGENTS. Cover title: Centro de Navegacion Transatlantica. C.N.T. Year Book; Ship Owners' and Agents' Handbook, River Plate Ports. (Text in English) 1972. every 3 years. $42. ‡ Centro de Navegacion Transatlantica, Maipu 521, 1006 Buenos Aires, Argentina. Ed. Victor L.M. Fricker. adv. circ. 2,000.
Continues a similar publication issued 1933-1966 as: M A R Year Book.

387   CE
CEYLON SHIPPING CORPORATION. ANNUAL REPORT & STATEMENT OF ACCOUNTS. (Text in English) a. Ceylon Shipping Corporation, Box 1718, Colombo, Sri Lanka.

623.8   SW   ISSN 0009-112X
CHALMERS TEKNISKA HOEGSKOLA. INSTITUTIONEN FOER SKEPPSHYDROMEKANIK. RAPPORT/ CHALMERS UNIVERSITY OF TECHNOLOGY. DEPARTMENT OF SHIP HYDROMECHANICS. REPORT. (Text in English or Swedish) 1959. irreg., no.56, 1978. ‡ Chalmers Tekniska Hoegskola, Institutionen foer Skeppshydromekanik, Fack, S-412 96 Goeteborg, Sweden. Ed. Curt Falkemo. charts. illus. circ. 150.

387   US
CHARTERING ANNUAL. 1953. a. $75. Maritime Research, Inc., 499 Ernston Rd., Box 805, Parlin, NJ 08859. TEL 201-727-8040. adv.

CHERBOURG PORT HANDBOOK. see BUSINESS AND ECONOMICS — Trade And Industrial Directories

387   BG
CHITTAGONG PORT AUTHORITY. YEARBOOK. (Text in English) a. Chittagong Port Authority, Box 2013, Chittagong, Bangladesh.
Formerly: Chittagong Port Trust. Yearbook of Information (ISSN 0069-3723)

387   380   UK   ISSN 0260-9290
CITY HANDBOOK; guide to the shipping services of the City of London. 1979. a. £10. (Charter Publications) Charter Publications, Bank Chambers, Downham Market, Norfolk PE38 9BX, England. charts. illus.

387   US
COAST MARINE AND TRANSPORTATION DIRECTORY.* a. $12. Pacific Shipper, Inc., 1137 Howard St., San Francisco, CA 94103. TEL 415-981-7171.

387.5   FR   ISSN 0069-5815
COLLOQUES INTERNATIONAUX D'HISTOIRE MARITIME. TRAVAUX.* 1957. irreg., 1967, 9th. price varies. Ecole Pratique des Hautes Etudes, 45-47 rue des Ecoles, 75005 Paris, France.

387.5   UK
COMECON MERCHANT SHIPS. 1978. a. £9.95. Kenneth Mason Publications Ltd., The Old Harbourmaster's, 8 North St., Emsworth, Hants. PO10 7DD, England. Ed. Ambrose Greenway.

387   II
COMMERCE YEARBOOK OF PORTS, SHIPPING AND SHIPBUILDING. (Text in English) 1974. a. Rs.50. Commerce Publications Limited, NKM International House, 178 Backbay Reclamation, Bombay 40020, Indian. Ed. Vadilal Dagli. illus. stat.
Continues: Commerce Yearbook of Shipping and Shipbuilding.

354.44   623.8   FR
CONSTRUCTION NAVALE; rapport du conseil d'administration, assemblee generale ordinaire. 1919. a. free. Chambre Syndicale des Constructeurs de Navires, 47 rue de Monceau, 75008 Paris, France. Ed. P. Castanie. circ. 3,200.

387   BL
DADOS ESTATISTICOS DA MOVIMENTACAO DE CARGA E PASSAGEIROS. Cover title: Dados Estatisticos da Navegacao. a. Empresa de Navegacao de Amazonia, S.A., Setor de Processamento de Dados Estatisticos, Av. Presidente Vargas 41, Belem, Para, Brazil. stat.

387   DK   ISSN 0107-8011
DANSK ILLUSTRERET SKIBSLISTE. 1980. a. Kr.220. Seapress, Postboks 288, 8100 Aarhus C, Denmark. Eds. Per Rungholm, Bent Mikkelsen. adv. illus. circ. 3,500.

DARWIN PORT HANDBOOK. see BUSINESS AND ECONOMICS — Trade And Industrial Directories

DENMARK. MILJOESTYRELSEN. HAVFORURENINGSLABORATORIUM. REPORT OF THE MARINE POLLUTION LABORATORY. see ENVIRONMENTAL STUDIES

DETROIT NEWS TRAVEL DIRECTORY. see TRANSPORTATION — Air Transport

387   GW   ISSN 0070-4377
DEUTSCHER KUESTEN-ALMANACH; ein Nachschlagewerk fuer die Berufs- und Sportschiffahrt in Nord- und Ostsee und auf den deutschen Seeschiffahrts-strassen. a. DM.29.80. Kroegers Buch- und Verlagsdruckerei, Blankeneser Bahnhofstr. 17, Postf. 550270, 2000 Hamburg 55, W. Germany (B.R.D.)
Formerly: Deutscher Fischerei-Almanach.

TRANSPORTATION — SHIPS AND SHIPPING

623.82   GW
DEUTSCHER SCHIFFBAU. 1962. a. free. Verband der Deutschen Schiffbauindustrie e.V., An der Alster 1, 2000 Hamburg 1, W. Germany (B.R.D.) circ. 1,750.

387   UK   ISSN 0070-6310
DIRECTORY OF SHIPOWNERS, SHIPBUILDERS AND MARINE ENGINEERS. 1902. a. £45($84) Transport Press (Subsidiary of: Business Press International Ltd.) Quadrant House, The Quadrant, Sutton, Surrey SM2 5AS, England. Ed. Keith Wilson. index. circ. 2,750.

387.1   AT
DOG WATCH. 1943. a. Aus.$5. ‡ (Shiplovers' Society of Victoria) Research Publications Pty., G.P.O. Box 1169K, Melbourne, Victoria, 3001, Australia. Ed. T.E. Goldfinch. adv. bk. rev. circ. 2, 000.
    Formerly: Annual Dog Watch (ISSN 0066-3921)

387   US
DOMESTIC WATERBORNE TRADE OF THE UNITED STATES. a. U.S. Maritime Administration, Nassif Bldg., 400 7th St., S.W., Washington, DC 20590 TEL 202-426-5812. (Orders to: Supt. of Documents, Washington, DC 20402)
    Continues: Domestic Oceanborne and Great Lakes Commerce of the United States (ISSN 0070-7058)

387 380   UK   ISSN 0265-1165
DOVER PORT HANDBOOK. 1983/4. a. £10. Charter Publications, Bank Chambers, Downham Market, Norfolk PE38 9BU, England. Ed. James Moriarty. adv. circ. 6,000.

387   BL
EMPRESA DE NAVEGACAO DA AMAZONIA. ESTATISTICA DA NAVEGACAO. a. Empresa de Navegacao da Amazonia, Av. Presidente Vargas 41, Belem, Para, Brazil. Dir. Eugenio Marques Frazao. charts.

387   NO
EUROPEAN RIG- AND SUPPLY SHIP OWNERS. (Text in English) a. Kr.120. Selvig Publishing A-S, Box 9070 Vaterland, 0134 Oslo 1, Norway.

387   IT
FACOLTA DI SCIENZE NAUTICHE. ANNALI. (Text in English and Italian) 1932. a. free. Istituto Universito Navale, Via Ammiraglio Acton 38, 80133 Naples, Italy. circ. 400. (back issues avail.)

387 338   UK   ISSN 0267-0879
FAIRPLAY MARINE COMPUTING GUIDE. 1984. a. £22($30) Fairplay Publications Ltd., 52-54 Southwark St., London SE1 1UJ, England. Ed. W.B. Peach.

387   UK   ISSN 0261-2356
FAIRPLAY WORLD PORTS DIRECTORY. 1869. biennial. £48($76) Fairplay Publications Ltd., 52-54 Southwark St., London SE1 1UJ, England.

387   UK   ISSN 0140-5047
FAIRPLAY WORLD SHIPPING YEAR BOOK. a. £29($51) Fairplay Publications Ltd., 52-54 Southwark St., London S.E.1, England. Ed. W.B. Peach.

387 380   UK   ISSN 0260-9282
FALMOUTH PORT AND INDUSTRY HANDBOOK 1984. 1981. a. Charter Publications, Bank Chambers, Downham Market, Norfolk PE38 9BU, England. Ed. John Ison. adv. circ. 6,000.

387   UK   ISSN 0144-8781
FAR EAST SHIPPING. 1980. a. included in subscription to Seatrade. Seatrade Publications Ltd., Fairfax House, Colchester, Essex CO1 1RJ, England.

623.89   DK   ISSN 0109-5811
FARVANDVAESENETS TRAFIKANALYSE. 1981. a. free. Farvandsdirektoratet, Nautisk Afdelning, Esplanaden 19, 1263 Copenhagen K, Denmark. (Co-sponsor: Royal Danish Administration of Navigation and Hydrography) illus.

387   NO
FEARNLEYS REVIEW. a. free. Fearnleys, Box 1158-Sentrum, Oslo 1, Norway. charts. stat.
    Formerly: Fearnly and Egers Chartering Co. Review.

347.75 387   US
FEDERAL MARITIME COMMISSION SERVICE. 1970. irreg. (10-12/yr.) $215. Hawkins Publishing Co., Inc., Box 480, Mayo, MD 21106-0480. TEL 301-798-1677. Ed. Carl R. Eyler. (looseleaf format)

387   UK
FELIXSTOWE SHIPPING DIARY. a. Welbecson Ltd., 3 Thomas St., Hull, Humberside HU9 1EJ, England.

387   FR   ISSN 0223-5358
FEUX ET SIGNAUX DE BRUME. 1950. irreg. Service Hydrographique et Oceanographique de la Marine, 3 av. Octave Greard, 75200 Paris Naval, France (Subscr. to: EPSHOM, BP 426, 29275 Brest Cedex, France)

387   UK
FINANCIAL TIMES WORLD SHIPPING YEARBOOK. a. £14($42) Financial Times, Bracken House, 10 Cannon St., London EC4P 4BY, England.
●Also available online. Vendors: DIALOG.

FORD'S DECK PLAN GUIDE. see *TRAVEL AND TOURISM*

387 380   UK   ISSN 0262-8880
FORTH PORTS HANDBOOK 1984. 1982. a. £10. Charter Publications, Bank Chambers, Downham Market, Norfolk PE38 9BU, England. Ed. James Moriarty. adv. circ. 6,000.

387   FR
FRANCE. COMMISSION CENTRALE POUR LA NAVIGATION DU RHIN. RAPPORT ANNUEL. 1835. a. 50 F. ‡ Commision Centrale pour la Navigation du Rhin, Palais du Rhin, 67082 Strasbourg Cedex, France. Ed. J. Martineau. charts. stat.

387.54   UK
GARSTON DOCKS TIDE TABLE. a. free. Associated British Ports Holdings PLC, 150 Holborn, London EC1N 2LR, England.

GENOA PORT AND SHIPPING HANDBOOK. see *BUSINESS AND ECONOMICS — Trade And Industrial Directories*

387   GW   ISSN 0070-4148
GERMAN MERCHANT FLEET; die Deutsche Handelsflotte. 1954. a. DM.435. Sehafen-Verlag Erik Blumenfeld GmbH und Co., Postfach 105605, 2000 Hamburg 1, W. Germany (B.R.D.) adv.

387 380   UK   ISSN 0262-1622
GOOLE PORT HANDBOOK. 1982. biennial. £2. Charter Publications, Bank Chambers, Downham Market, Norfolk PE38 9BU, England. Ed. John Ison. adv. illus. circ. 6,000.

387.5   UK   ISSN 0072-6591
GREAT BRITAIN. MERCANTILE NAVY LIST. a. with m. supplements. H.M.S.O., P.O.B. 569, London SE1 9NH, England. (reprint service avail. from UMI)

386   US   ISSN 0072-7318
GREAT LAKES RED BOOK. 1903. a. $5. Fourth Seacoast Publishing Co. Inc., Box 145, St. Clair Shores, MI 48080. TEL 313-779-5570. Ed. Amelia G. Sasso. adv. index. circ. 6,000.

387 380   UK   ISSN 0260-9517
GREAT YARMOUTH PORT AND INDUSTRY HANDBOOK. 1980. a. £10. Charter Publications, Bank Chambers, Downham Market, Norfolk PE38 9BU, England. Ed. James Moriarty. adv. illus. circ. 6,000.

386   US   ISSN 0072-7490
GREENWOOD'S GUIDE TO GREAT LAKES SHIPPING. 1958. a. $43 (approx.) Freshwater Press, Inc., 1701 E. 12th St., Ste. 3K.W, Cleveland, OH 44114-3201. TEL 216-241-0373. Ed. Michael J. Dills. adv. circ. 3,700.

387   GW
GUETERTRANSPORT IN SEEVERKEHR. 1954. a. DM.59. K.O. Storck Verlag, Stahltwiete 7, 2000 Hamburg 50, W. Germany (B.R.D.) Ed. H. Meder.
    Formerly: Fracht-Schiffahrts-Konferenzen.

387   JA
GUIDE & DIRECTORY OF PORT OF YOKOHAMA. (Text in English) a. Port and Harbor Bureau, Industry and Trade Center Bldg., Yamashita-cho, Nakaku, Yokohama, Japan.

387   UK
GUIDE TO PORT ENTRY. 1971. biennial. £125. Shipping Guides Ltd., 75 Bell St., Reigate, Surrey RH2 7AN, England. TEL (0276) 42255. Ed. Robert Pedlow. circ. 8,000.

387   JA
GUIDE TO THE PORT OF YOKOHAMA. (Includes Map) (Text in English and Japanese) a. free. Port and Harbor Bureau, Industry and Trade Center Bldg., Yamashita-cho, Nakaku, Yokohama, Japan.

387   GW
HAMBURG THE QUICK PORT; also Bremen and Weserports. (Text in English) 1958. a. DM.24. K.O. Storck Verlag, Stahltwiete 7, 2000 Hamburg 50, W. Germany (B.R.D.) Ed. H. Meder.

948   DK   ISSN 0085-1418
HANDELS- OG SOEFARTSMUSEET PAA KRONBORG. AARBOG. (Text in Danish; summaries in English or German) 1942. a. membership. Handels- og Soefartsmuseet paa Kronborg, DK-3000 Helsingoer, Denmark. Ed. Hans Jeppesen. adv. illus. cum.index. circ. 2,500.

387   IS
HASAPANUT HAYISRAELIT. a. IS.15($10) Israel Shipping and Aviation Research Institute, P.O. Box 1860, Haifa 31 086, Israel.

387.164 380.1   GW
HAZARDOUS CARGO CONTACTS. 1976. a. DM.38. K.O. Storck Verlag, Stahltwiete 7, 2000 Hamburg 50, W. Germany (B.R.D.) Ed. H. Meder.
    Formerly: Gefahrgut Kontakte.

387   UK   ISSN 0260-7786
HONG KONG HANDBOOK. 1981. a. £3.50. Rystom and Storck Publications Ltd., Downham Market, Norfolk PE38 9BX, England. adv. illus. charts. circ. 6,000.

387.1   FR   ISSN 0073-7720
INDUSTRIE DE LA MANUTENTION DANS LES PORTS FRANCAIS. 1964. a. Union Nationale des Industries de la Manutention dans les Ports Francais, 76 Av. Marceau, 75008 Paris, France.

386   US
INLAND RIVER GUIDE. 1972. a. $35. ‡ Waterways Journal, Inc., 319 N. Fourth St., 666 Security Bldg., St. Louis, MO 63102. TEL 314-241-7354. Ed. Dan Owen. adv. circ. 4,500.

386   US
INLAND RIVER RECORD. 1945. a. $25. ‡ Waterways Journal, Inc., 319 N. Fourth St., 666 Security Bldg., St. Louis, MO 63102. TEL 314-241-7354. Ed. Dan Owen. adv. circ. 3,800.

386   UK
INLAND WATERWAYS GUIDE. 1972. a. £1.95. (Inland Waterways Association) Brittain Publications, 137 George Lane, South Woodford, London E18, England. Ed. Rachael McLeod.

INSTITUT MEDITERRANEEN DES TRANSPORTS MARITIMES. see *TRANSPORTATION*

387   UK   ISSN 0267-2006
INSTITUTE OF CHARTERED SHIPBROKERS. REFERENCE BOOK AND LIST OF MEMBERS (YEAR) 1983. a. £25. Millbank Publications, 25 Catherine St., London WC2B 5JW, England. TEL 01-379-3036. Ed. K.J. Allen. adv. circ. 4,000.

623.89   US
INSTITUTE OF NAVIGATION. PROCEEDINGS OF THE ANNUAL MEETING. a. $40. Institute of Navigation, 815 15th St., N.W., Ste. 832, Washington, DC 20005.

387   FR   ISSN 0223-534X
INSTRUCTIONS NAUTIQUES. 1902. irreg. Service Hydrographique et Oceanographique de la Marine, 3 av. Octave Greard, 75200 Paris Naval, France (Subscr. to: EPSHOM, BP 426, 29275 Brest Cedex, France)

387 UK ISSN 0266-3996
INTERNATIONAL CARGO HANDLING COORDINATION ASSOCIATION. BUYERS' GUIDE TO MANUFACTURERS. 1984. a. £25. Millbank Publications, 25 Catherine St., London WC2B 5JW, England. Ed. K.J. Allen. adv. illus. circ. 2,000.

385 FR
INTERNATIONAL COMMISSION OF MARITIME HISTORY. COLLOQUES. ACTES. 1957. irreg. Service d'Edition et de Vente des Publications de l'Education Nationale, 13 rue du Four, 75006 Paris, France.

623.89 FR ISSN 0538-6128
INTERNATIONAL CONFERENCE ON LIGHTHOUSES AND OTHER AIDS TO NAVIGATION. (REPORTS) (Includes: "Discussion Reports" which are in English; occasionally in French) 1929. quinquennial. 200 Fr. International Association of Lighthouse Authorities - Association Internationale de Signalisation Maritime, 13 rue Yvon Villarceau, 75116 Paris, France.

387 BE
INTERNATIONAL HARBOUR CONGRESS. PROCEEDINGS/INTERNATIONAAL HAVENKONGRES. VERSLAGBOEK/CONGRES PORTUAIRE INTERNATIONAL. COMPTE-RENDU/INTERNATIONALE HAFENTAGUNG. BERICHTE. 1949. irreg., 8th, 1983. Koninklijke Vlaamse Ingenieursvereniging, Jan van Rijswijcklaan 58, B-2018 Antwerp, Belgium. Ed. K. Viv.

387 UK
INTERNATIONAL MARINE SAFETY DIRECTORY. 1984. biennial. £13.50. Industrial & Marine Publications Ltd., Queensway House, 2 Queensway, Redhill, Surrey RH1 1QS, England. Ed. Richard Allen.

623.89 BE
INTERNATIONAL NAVIGATION CONGRESS. PAPERS. (Text in English or French; summaries in English or French) quadrennial, 26th, 1985, Edinburgh. Permanent International Association of Navigation Congresses, 155 rue de la Loi, 1040 Brussels, Belgium.

380.5 623.89 BE
INTERNATIONAL NAVIGATION CONGRESS. PROCEEDINGS. (Text in English or French) quadrennial, 25th, 1981, Edinburgh. Permanent International Association of Navigation Congresses, 155 rue de la Loi, 1040 Brussels, Belgium (Subscr. to: Pergamon Press, Headington Hill Hall, Oxford OX3 0BW, England) circ. 4,000.

387 UK
INTERNATIONAL OFFSHORE CRAFT CONFERENCE. PROCEEDINGS. irreg., 2nd 1977; 3rd 1979. $50. Thomas Reed Industrial Press, 80 Coombe Rd., New Malden, Surrey KT3 4QS, England. Ed. Kenneth D. Troup.

623.8 UK ISSN 0074-8358
INTERNATIONAL SHIPPING AND SHIPBUILDING DIRECTORY. 1966. a. £35 for 2 vols. Benn Publications Ltd., 25 New Street Square, London EC4A 3JA, England. Ed. Richard Daykin. adv. circ. 2,162.

387 UK
INTERNATIONAL TUG CONVENTION PROCEEDINGS. 1969. biennial. $60. Thomas Reed Publications Ltd., 80 Coombe Rd., New Malden, Surrey KT3 4QS, England. Ed. Ken Troup. adv. circ. 1,000.

387 380 UK
IPSWICH PORT HANDBOOK 1984. 1980. a. £10. Charter Publications, Bank Chambers, Downham Market, Norfolk PE38 9BU, England. Ed. John Ison. adv. circ. 6,000.

387 380 UK ISSN 0260-924X
IRELAND PORTS & SHIPPING HANDBOOK. 1981. a. £10. Charter Publications, Bank Chambers, Downham Market, Norfolk PE38 9BX, England. Ed. James Moriarty. adv. illus. circ. 6,000.

387 IS
ISRAEL PORTS AUTHORITY. ANNUAL REPORT. (Text in English) a. Israel Ports Authority, Box 20121, Tel Aviv, Israel. illus.

ITALY. ISTITUTO CENTRALE DI STATISTICA. ANNUARIO STATISTICO DELLA NAVIGAZIONE MARITTIMA. see TRANSPORTATION — Abstracting, Bibliographies, Statistics

386 UR ISSN 0202-7879
ITOGI NAUKI I TEKHNIKI: VODNYI TRANSPORT. irreg., latest vol.11, 1986. price varies. Vsesoyuznyi Institut Nauchno-Tekhnicheskoi Informatsii (VINITI), Baltiiskaya ul. 14, Moscow A-219, Russian S.F.S.R., U.S.S.R. (Subscr. to: Mezhdunarodnaya Kniga, Dimitrova ul. 39, 113095 Moscow, Russian S.F.S.R., U.S.S.R.)

JANE'S FIGHTING SHIPS. see MILITARY

387 UK
JANE'S HIGH-SPEED MARINE CRAFT AND AIR CUSHION VEHICLES; Hovercraft and Hydrofoils. 1967. a. £50($99.50) Jane's Publishing Co., 238 City Rd., London E.C.1., England (Subscr.to: Jane's Publishing Inc., 20 Park Plaza, Boston, MA 02116) Ed. Roy McLeavy. adv. index.
Formerly (until 1986): Jane's Surface Skimmers (ISSN 0075-305X)

387 UK
JANE'S NAVAL REVIEW. 1981. a. Jane's Publishing Co., 238 City Rd., London E.C.1., England. Ed. John Moore. charts. illus.
Formerly: Jane's Naval Annual.

387 JA
JAPAN PORT INFORMATION. (Text in English) 1969. biennial. 9000 Yen($45) (Ships Agency Committee of Japan - Japan Inbestazusha) Japan Press Ltd, 2-12-8 Kita Aoyama, Minato-ku, Tokyo 107, Japan. Ed. Yoshio Wada.

387 GW ISSN 0075-6474
KOEHLERS FLOTTENKALENDER. JAHRBUCH FUER SCHIFFAHRT UND HAEFEN. 1901. a. DM.19.80. Koehlers Verlagsgesellschaft mbH, Steintorwall 17, Postfach 2352, 4900 Herford, W. Germany (B.R.D.) Ed. Egbert Thomer. adv. bk. rev. abstr. charts. illus. stat. circ. 20,000.

386 US ISSN 0075-7748
LAKE CARRIERS' ASSOCIATION. ANNUAL REPORT. 1885. a. not for sale. Lake Carriers' Association, 915 Rockefeller Bldg., Cleveland, OH 44113. TEL 216-621-1107. Ed. Glen G. Nekvasil. index. circ. 1,500.

387 DK ISSN 0108-7231
LANDSHAVNEPLANBIDRAG; Aalborg Havn. 1982. a. free. Havnevaesen, Administrationsbygningen, Vesterbro 104, 9000 Aalborg, Denmark.

387 UK ISSN 0260-7387
LIST OF SHIPOWNERS. 1955. a. £50. Lloyd's Register of Shipping, 71 Fenchurch St., London EC3M 4BS, England.

387 FR
LISTE DES SIGNAUX DISTINCTIFS ET INDICATIFS INTERNATIONAUX DES STATIONS FRANCAISES (NAVIRES, STATIONS TERRESTRES). 1941. a. price varies. Service Hydrographique et Oceanographique de la Marine, 3 av. Octave Greard, 75200 Paris Naval, France (Subscr. to: E P S H O M, B.P. 426, 29275 Brest Cedex, France) Ed.Bd. circ. 1,500. (also avail. in magnetic tape)

387.2 BE
LISTE OFFICIELLE DES NAVIRES DE MER BELGES ET DE LA FLOTTE DE LA FORCE NAVALE. a. Administration de la Marine et de la Navigation Interieure, 104 rue d'Arlon, 1040 Brussels, Belgium. illus.

387 HK
LLOYDS HONG KONG PORT SERVICES INDEX (YEAR) (Text in English) a. HK.$220. Far East Trade Press Limited, 15/F, Lockhart Centre, 301 Lockhart Rd., Hong Kong, Hong Kong. Ed. Iris Stoner. circ. 7,000.

387 UK ISSN 0268-3253
LLOYD'S MARINE EQUIPMENT GUIDE. a. £33($85) Lloyd's of London Press Ltd., Sheepen Place, Colchester, Essex CO3 3LP, England. Ed. Peter Driver. adv.

387 UK ISSN 0076-020X
LLOYD'S MARITIME ATLAS. 1951. biennial, 15th edt., 1986. $65. Lloyd's of London Press Ltd., Sheepen Place, Colchester, Essex CO3 3LP, England (Subscr. address in U.S.: Lloyd's of London Press Inc., 817 Broadway, New York, NY 10003) circ. 14,000.

387 UK ISSN 0268-327X
LLOYD'S MARITIME DIRECTORY. international shipping & shipbuilding directory. 1982. a. $160. Lloyd's of London Press Ltd., Sheepen Place, Colchester, Essex CO3 3LP, England (Subscr. addr.: 817 Broadway, New York, NY 10003) Ed. Peter Driver. adv.

387 UK
LLOYD'S NAUTICAL YEAR BOOK. 1892. a. $35. Lloyd's of London Press Ltd., Sheepen Place, Colchester, Essex CO3 3LP, England (Subscr. address in U.S.: Lloyd's of London Press Inc., 817 Broadway, New York, NY 10003) Ed. H.W. Arnold. adv. circ. 10,000.
Former titles: Lloyd's Nautical Yearbook and Calendar; Lloyd's Calendar and Nautical Yearbook (ISSN 0076-0196)

387 UK ISSN 0266-6197
LLOYD'S PORTS OF THE WORLD. 1982. a. $170. Lloyd's of London Press Ltd., Sheepen Place, Colchester, Essex CO9 3LP, England (Subscr. address in U.S.: Lloyd's of London Press Inc., 817 Broadway, New York, NY 10003)

387 UK ISSN 0261-6688
LLOYD'S REGISTER OF CLASSED YACHTS. 1981. a. £10. Lloyd's Register of Shipping, 71 Fenchurch St., London EC3M 4BS, England.
Supersedes: Lloyd's Register of Yachts.

387 UK ISSN 0076-0234
LLOYD'S REGISTER OF SHIPPING. STATISTICAL TABLES. 1878. a. £45. Lloyd's Register of Shipping, 71 Fenchurch St., London EC3M 4BS, England.

387 UK ISSN 0141-4909
LLOYD'S REGISTER OF SHIPS. 1764. a. (with m. supplements) £250. Lloyd's Register of Shipping, 71 Fenchurch St., London EC3M 4BS, England.

387 UK ISSN 0260-8839
LONDON PORT HANDBOOK 1984. 1981. a. £10. Charter Publications, Bank Chambers, Downham Market, Norfolk PE38 9BU, England. Ed. John Ison. adv. circ. 6,000.

387 UK
LONDON SHIPPING CONTACTS. (Text in English) 1978. a. Rystom and Storck Publications Ltd., Downham Market, Norfolk PE38 9BX, Great Britain (Subscr. to: Storck Shipping Publications, 15 Half Moon St., London W.1, Great Britain) Ed. Stuart Pearce.

387 380 UK ISSN 0266-0644
LOS ANGELES PORT AND SHIPPING HANDBOOK. 1984. a. Charter Publications, Bank Chambers, Downham Market, Norfolk PE38 9BU, England. Ed. James Moriarty. adv. circ. 6,000.

387 SP
MADRID TRANS-PORT. 1983. a. 650 ptas. Publicaciones Men-Car, Paseo de Colon 24, Barcelona 2, Spain. Eds. Juan and Manuel Cardona. adv. circ. 15,000.

387 GW ISSN 0542-6758
MARE BALTICUM. (Text in German, Polish, Scandinavian languages) 1965. irreg. DM.20. Ostseegesellschaft e.V., Parkallee 86, 2000 Hamburg 13, W. Germany (B.R.D.) adv. bk. rev. bibl. charts. illus. index. (back issues avail.)

387 AT
MARINE BOARD OF HOBART. ANNUAL REPORT. 1858. a. Marine Board of Hobart, Franklin Wharf, Tas. 7000, Australia. Ed. D.G.F. Taylor. circ. 600.

387 US
MARINE CATALOG AND BUYERS GUIDE. 1943. a. $35. Simmons-Boardman Publishing Corporation, 345 Hudson St., New York, NY 10014. TEL 212-620-7200. Ed. Nicholas Blenkey. adv. circ. 21,000.
Formerly: Marine Catalog (ISSN 0076-4450)

TRANSPORTATION — SHIPS AND SHIPPING

623.87 387 US ISSN 0076-4469
MARINE ENGINEERING/LOG ANNUAL MARITIME REVIEW AND YEARBOOK ISSUE. 1942. a. $9. Simmons-Boardman Publishing Corporation, 345 Hudson St., New York, NY 10014. TEL 212-620-7200. Ed. Nicholas Blenkey. adv. circ. 25,000. (also avail. in microform from UMI,BLH) Indexed: BMT. ISMEC.

387 US
MARINE ENGINEERING/LOG MARINE DIRECTORY. 1878. a. $30. Simmons-Boardman Publishing Corp., 345 Hudson St., New York, NY 10014. TEL 212-620-7200. Ed. Nicholas Blenkey. adv. bk. rev. tr.lit. circ. 25,000. (also avail. in microform from UMI,BLH; reprint service avail.)

623.81 US
MARINE EQUIPMENT CATALOG. 1984. a. $65. Maritime Activity Reports, 118 E. 25th St., New York, NY 10010. TEL 212-477-6700. Ed. Laura Ann Sciame. adv. circ. 12,000.

387 FR ISSN 0294-8508
MARINE MARCHANDE. (Special series of: Journal de la Marine Marchande) 1948. a. 160 F. Journal de la Marine Marchande, S.A., 190 bd. Haussmann, 75008 Paris, France. index.

623.8 JA
MARINE STANDARDIZATION IN JAPAN. (Text in Japanese) a. 1,500 Yen. Japan Marine Standards Association, 11 Mori Bldg., 6-4, Toranomon 2-Chome, Minato-Ku, Tokyo 105, Japan.
Formerly: Marine Standardization.

387 UK ISSN 0264-6420
MARITIME GUIDE. 1984. a. £55. Lloyd's Register of Shipping, 71 Fenchurch St., London EC3M 4BS, England.
Formerly: Appendix (ISSN 0261-1821)

387 CN
MARITIME HISTORY GROUP NEWSLETTER. 1976. a. free contr. circ. Memorial University of Newfoundland, Maritime History Group, St. John's, Nfld. A1C 5S7, Canada. TEL 709-737-8428.
Supersedes (after 1984): Canadian Shipping Project Newsletter (ISSN 0708-0727)

MARITIME MONOGRAPHS AND REPORTS. see MUSEUMS AND ART GALLERIES

387 UK ISSN 0261-281X
MEDWAY PORTS SHIPPING HANDBOOK. 1981. irreg. £2.50. Charter Publications, Bank Chambers, Downham Market, Norfolk PE38 9BU, England. illus.

MELBOURNE PORT AND SHIPPING HANDBOOK. see BUSINESS AND ECONOMICS — Trade And Industrial Directories

387 UK ISSN 0265-1173
MERSEY PORTS HANDBOOK (YEAR) 1983/4. a. £10. Charter Publications, Bank Chambers, Downham Market, Norfolk PE38 9BU, England. Ed. John Ison. adv. circ. 6,000.

387 UK ISSN 0265-8186
MONTREAL PORT AND SHIPPING HANDBOOK (YEAR) 1984. a. £10. Charter Publications, Bank Chambers, Downham Market, Norfolk PE38 9BU, England. Ed. James Moriarty. adv. circ. 6,000.

387 MJ
MONTSERRAT. PORT AUTHORITY. ANNUAL REPORT. a. Port Authority, Plymouth, Montserrat, W. Indies.

387 UK ISSN 0077-5185
NATIONAL MARITIME BOARD. (GREAT BRITAIN) YEAR BOOK.* 1922. a. 50p. National Maritime Board, St. Mary Ave., Rms. 30-32, London EC3A 8ET, England.

NATIONAL MARITIME MUSEUM. OCCASIONAL LECTURES SERIES. see MUSEUMS AND ART GALLERIES

387.5 PK
NATIONAL SHIPPING CORPORATION. REPORT AND ACCOUNTS. (Text in English) a. National Shipping Corporation, N S C Bldg., Moulvi Tamizuddin Khan Rd., Karachi, Pakistan.

623.89 UK ISSN 0077-619X
NAUTICAL ALMANAC. 1960. a. price varies. Royal Greenwich Observatory, c/o J. Dudley, Librarian, Herstmonceux Castle, Hailsham, E. Essex BN27 1RD, England. (Co-sponsors: H.M. Nautical Almanac Office; U.S. Naval Observatory, Washington, D.C.)

387 GW
NAUTICUS. 1896. irreg. DM.49.80. Verlag E.S. Mittler und Sohn GmbH, Steintorwall 17, Postfach 2352, 4900 Herford, W. Germany (B.R.D.) Ed. Viceadmiral Kampe. adv. abstr. charts. illus. stat. circ. 3,000.

387 FR ISSN 0077-6270
NAVIS; annuaire de la marine marchande, de la construction navale et des ports. 1942. a. 385 F. Rene Moreux et Cie, 190 bd. Haussmann, 75008 Paris, France. index.

386 314 NE ISSN 0168-5376
NETHERLANDS. CENTRAAL BUREAU VOOR DE STATISTIEK. STATISTIEK VAN DE INTERNATIONALE BINNENVAART. STATISTICS OF THE INTERNATIONAL INLAND SHIPPING. (Text in Dutch and English) 1948. a. fl.23.25. Centraal Bureau voor de Statistiek, Prinses Beatrixlaan 428, Voorburg, Netherlands (Orders to: Staatsuitgeverij, Christoffel Plantijnstraat, The Hague, Netherlands)

387.5 NE
NETHERLANDS. CENTRAAL BUREAU VOOR DE STATISTIEK. STATISTIEK VAN DE KOOPVAARDIJVLOOT. STATISTICS OF THE MERCHANT MARINE. (Text in Dutch and English) 1949. a. fl.9.25. Centraal Bureau voor de Statistiek, Prinses Beatrixlaan 428, Voorburg, Netherlands (Orders to: Staatsuitgeverij, Christoffel Plantijnstraat, The Hague, Netherlands)

387 NE ISSN 0168-5422
NETHERLANDS. CENTRAAL BUREAU VOOR DE STATISTIEK. STATISTIEK VAN DE ZEEVAART. STATISTICS OF SEABORNE SHIPPING. (Text in Dutch and English) 1948. a. fl.26. Centraal Bureau voor de Statistiek, Prinses Beatrixlaan 428, Voorburg, Netherlands (Orders to: Staatsuitgeverij, Christoffel Plantijnstraat, The Hague, Netherlands)

386 NE ISSN 0168-5325
NETHERLANDS. CENTRAAL BUREAU VOOR DE STATISTIEK VAN HET BINNENLANDS GOEDERENVERVOER. STATISTICS OF INTERNAL GOODS TRANSPORT IN THE NETHERLANDS. (Text in Dutch and English) 1948/49. a. fl.32.50. Centraal Bureau voor de Statistiek, Prinses Beatrixlaan 428, Voorburg, Netherlands (Orders to: Staatsuitgeverij, Christoffel Plantijnstraat, The Hague, Netherlands)

387 NE
NETHERLANDS. PROVISIONAL NATIONAL PORTS COUNCIL. JAARVERSLAG. 1970. a. free. Provisional National Ports Council, Koningskade 4, The Hague, Netherlands.
Formerly: Netherlands. Commissie Zeehavenoverleg. Jaarverslag (ISSN 0077-7552)

NEW SOUTH WALES PORTS HANDBOOK. see BUSINESS AND ECONOMICS — Trade And Industrial Directories

387 NZ ISSN 0545-7866
NEW ZEALAND SHIPPING DIRECTORY. 1962. a. $9. Mercantile Gazette Marketing, Box 20-034, Christchurch 5, New Zealand. Ed. B.M. Stoop. adv. illus.

387.5 JA
NIHON SHOSEN SEMPUKU TOKEI. 1972. a. free. Japanese Shipowners' Association, Research Division - Nihon Senshu Kyokai, c/o Kaiun Bldg., 2-6-4 Hirakawacho, Chiyoda-ku, Tokyo 102, Japan. circ. 2,800.

NORTH AMERICAN SOCIETY FOR OCEANIC HISTORY. PROCEEDINGS. see HISTORY — History Of North And South America

OAKLAND PORT AND SHIPPING HANDBOOK. see BUSINESS AND ECONOMICS — Trade And Industrial Directories

OCCASIONAL PAPERS IN MARITIME AFFAIRS; Australia's offshore maritime interests. see ENVIRONMENTAL STUDIES

386.8 US ISSN 0093-1799
OFFICIAL PORT OF DETROIT WORLD HANDBOOK. 1973. a. $4.95. Fourth Seacoast Publishing Co. Inc., Box 145, St. Clair Shores, MI 48080. TEL 313-779-5570. Ed. Roger J. Buysse. adv. illus. circ. 10,000.

387.1 US ISSN 0094-8454
OFFICIAL SOUTHERN CALIFORNIA PORTS MARITIME DIRECTORY AND GUIDE. 1974. a. $10. Civic-Data Corp., 523 Superior Ave., Newport Beach, CA 92663. TEL 714-646-1623. illus.

387 665.5 US ISSN 0887-6827
OFFSHORE SERVICE VESSELS; guide to the American fleet. 1977. a. $150. Fleet Data Service, 1713 Springbrook, Box 2576, Nacogdoches, TX 75963-2576. TEL 409-569-0375. Ed. James O. Covington. circ. 200. (looseleaf format; back issues avail.; avail on computer disc)

387 665.5 US ISSN 0887-6835
OFFSHORE TUGS; guide to the American fleet. 1978. a. $125. Fleet Data Service, 1713 Sprongbrook, Box 2576, Nacogdoches, TX 75963-2576. TEL 409-569-0375. Ed. James O. Covington. circ. 200.

387 FR ISSN 0474-5884
ORGANIZATION FOR ECONOMIC COOPERATION AND DEVELOPMENT. MARITIME TRANSPORT COMMITTEE. MARITIME TRANSPORT. 1954. a. $15. Organization for Economic Cooperation and Development, 2 rue Andre Pascal, 75775 Paris 26, France (U.S. orders to: O.E.C.D. Publications and Information Center, 1750 Pennsylvania Ave., N.W., Washington, D.C. 20006) (also avail. in microfiche)

387 JA
OUR PORT - PORT OF YOKOHAMA. a. Port and Harbor Bureau, Industry and Trade Center Bldg., Yamashita-cho, Nakaku, Yokohama, Japan.

387 380 UK ISSN 0263-4260
PANAMA HANDBOOK 1983. 1982. a. £10. Charter Publications, Bank Chambers, Downham Market, Norfolk PE38 9BU, England. Ed. James Moriarty. adv. circ. 6,000.

PENANG PORT HANDBOOK. see BUSINESS AND ECONOMICS — Trade And Industrial Directories

387.5 NO
PLATOU REPORT. 1947. a. free. R. S. Platou A-S, Fjordveien 1, P.O. Box 10, N-1322 Hoevik, Norway. illus.

623.82 PL
POLITECHNIKA GDANSKA. INSTYTUT OKRETOWY. RAPORT. 1982. a. price varies. Politechnika Gdanska, Ul. Majakowskiego 11/12, 80-952 Gdansk 6, Poland.

623.8 PL ISSN 0373-868X
POLITECHNIKA GDANSKA. ZESZYTY NAUKOWE. BUDOWNICTWO OKRETOWE. (Text in Polish; summaries in English and Russian) 1957. irreg. price varies. Politechnika Gdanska, Majakowskiego 11/12, 81-952 Gdansk 6, Poland (Dist. by: Osrodek Rozpowszechniania Wydawnictw Naukowych Pan, Palac Kultury i Nauki, 00-901 Warsaw, Poland)

387 UK
POOLE HANDBOOK. 1979. a. £10. Charter Publications, Bank Chambers, Downham Market, Norfolk PE38 9BU, England. Ed. John Ison. adv. circ. 6,000.
Formerly: Poole - Commercial Users Handbook 1983/4 (ISSN 0260-2547)

387 II
POOMPUHAR SHIPPING CORPORATION. ANNUAL REPORT. (Text in English) 1975. a. Poompuhar Shipping Corporation Ltd., Kuralagam, Madras 600001, India.

TRANSPORTATION — SHIPS AND SHIPPING

627.2 JA
PORT AND HARBOUR RESEARCH INSTITUTE. GUIDE/KOWAN GIJUTSU KENKYUSHO. GUIDE. irreg. exchange basis. Port and Harbour Technical Research Institute - Un'Yu-sho Kowan Gijutsu Kenkyusho, 1-1, 3-chome, Nagase, Yokosuka, Kanagawa 239, Japan. illus. Indexed: Geotech.Abstr.
 Formerly: Port and Harbour Technical Research Institute. Guide.

387 JM
PORT BUSTAMANTE HANDBOOK. 1972. a. free. Shipping Association of Jamaica, Confederation Life Building, 5-7 King Street, P.O. Box 40, Kingston 15, Jamaica. (Co-sponsor: Port Authority of Jamaica) Ed. T.A. Gambrill. circ. 1,700.
 Formerly (until 1977): Port of Kingston Handbook.

387 380 UK ISSN 0266-3856
PORT KELANG SHIPPING HANDBOOK. 1984. a. Charter Publications, Bank Chambers, Downham Market, Norfolk PE38 9BU, England. Ed. Gerry Cansdale. adv. circ. 6,000.

387 US
PORT OF BALTIMORE MAGAZINE. 1946. biennial since 1957. free. ‡ Maryland Port Administration, World Trade Center Baltimore, Baltimore, MD 21202. TEL 301-333-4550. Ed. Mel Tansill. adv. circ. 14,765.
 Formerly: Port of Baltimore Handbook (ISSN 0079-3981)

387 UK
PORT OF BRISTOL AUTHORITY. 1886. a. free to qualified personnel. Port of Bristol Authority, St. Andrews Rd., Avonmouth, Bristol BS11 9DQ, England. TEL 0272-823681. Ed. P. White. adv. circ. 3,000.
 Formerly: Port of Bristol. Handbook.

387 JA
PORT OF OSAKA/OSAKAKO. (Text in English and Japanese) 1955. a. free. Port and Harbour Bureau - Osaka-shi Kowan-Kyoku, 2-8-24 Chikko, Minato-ku, Osaka 552, Japan. stat.

387 GR
PORT OF PIRAEUS AUTHORITY. ANNUAL REPORT. a. Port of Piraeus Authority, Akti Miaouli II, Merarchias Corner, Piraeus, Greece.

382 US
PORT OF SEATTLE. ANNUAL REPORT. a. Port of Seattle, Public Information Department, Box 1209, Seattle, WA 98111. TEL 206-728-3266.

387.1 JA
PORT OF TOKYO. 1951. a. free. Tokyo Metropolitan Government, Port and Harbor Bureau, 3-8 Marunouchi, Chiyoda-ku, Tokyo, Japan. illus. circ. 7,000.

315.2 JA
PORT OF YOKOHAMA. ANNUAL REPORT. (Text in Chinese, English and Japanese) a. free. Port and Harbor Bureau, Industry and Trade Center Bldg., 2 Yamashita-cho, Nakaku, Yokohama, Japan. stat.

387 JA
PORT OF YOKOHAMA. PLANS FOR FUTURE. (Text in English) irreg. Port and Harbor Bureau, Industry & Trade Center Bldg., Yamashita-cho, Nakaku, Yokohama, Japan.

387 380 UK ISSN 0266-3848
PORT RASHID: DUBAI SHIPPING HANDBOOK. (Text in Arabic and English) 1984. a. Charter Publications, Bank Chambers, Downham Market, Norfolk PE38 9BU, England. Ed. James Moriarty. adv. circ. 6,000.

387 SA
PORTS OF SOUTH AFRICA. 1948. a. R.25. Industrial Publishing Co. (Pty) Ltd., P.O. Box 825, Florida 1710, South Africa. adv. circ. 3,500.

623.89 UK
REED'S COMMERCIAL SALVAGE PRACTICE. 1986. every 4 yrs. $600 including 3 annual reviews. Thomas Reed Publications Ltd., 80 Coombe Rd., New Malden, Surrey KT3 4QS, England. Ed. David Hancox.

623.89 UK ISSN 0263-3620
REED'S MEDITERRANEAN NAVIGATOR. 1983. a. $16. Thomas Reed Publications Ltd., 80 Coombe Rd., New Malden, Surrey KT3 4QS, England. Ed. Jean Fowler. adv. circ. 5,000.

623.89 UK
REED'S OCEAN NAVIGATOR. 1969. irreg. Thomas Reed Publications Ltd., Saracen's Head Buildings, 80 Coombe Rd., New Malden, Surrey KT3 4QS, England. circ. 5,000.

387 UK ISSN 0141-4143
REGISTER OF OFFSHORE UNITS, SUBMERSIBLES AND DIVING SYSTEMS. 1976. a. £45. Lloyd's Register of Shipping, 71 Fenchurch St., London EC3M 4BS, England.

387 FR
REGISTRE MARITIME. 1829. a. (with q. suppl.) 900 F. Bureau Veritas, Service Maritime, 17 bis, Place des Reflets, La Defense 2, 92400 Courbevoie, France. Ed. Berger Levrault. (also avail. in microfilm)
 Supersedes in part: Registre International de Classification de Navires et d'Aeronefs (ISSN 0080-0678)

387.2 UN ISSN 0085-560X
REVIEW OF MARITIME TRANSPORT. (Editions in English, French and Spanish) 1968. a. price varies. (United Nations Conference on Trade and Development (UNCTAD)) United Nations Publications, Palais des Nations, 1211 Geneva, Switzerland (Or United Nations Publications, Rm. DC2-853, New York, NY 10017)

ROLL ON ROLL OFF IN EUROPE; international guide for roll-on/roll off shipping. see BUSINESS AND ECONOMICS — International Commerce

ROUEN PORT AND SHIPPING HANDBOOK. see BUSINESS AND ECONOMICS — Trade And Industrial Directories

623.81 UK ISSN 0373-529X
ROYAL INSTITUTION OF NAVAL ARCHITECTS. SUPPLEMENTARY PAPERS. a. £15($38) Royal Institution of Naval Architects, 10 Upper Belgrave St., London SW1X 8BQ, England. illus.

623.81 UK ISSN 0035-8967
ROYAL INSTITUTION OF NAVAL ARCHITECTS. TRANSACTIONS. 1860. a. £45 to non-members. Royal Institution of Naval Architects, 10 Upper Belgrave St., London SW1X 8BQ, England. Ed. P.W. Ayling. circ. 1,000. Indexed: Br.Tech.Ind. BMT.

359.97 US ISSN 0163-2833
S A R STATISTICS. (Search and Rescue) a. U.S. Coast Guard, 2100 Second St., S.W., Washington, DC 20593. TEL 202-426-1830.

387 MY ISSN 0080-522X
SABAH. MARINE DEPARTMENT. ANNUAL REPORT. (Text in English) 1961. a. M.$2. Marine Department, Labuan, Sabah, Malaysia.

387 UK
ST. JAMES PRESS CAR FERRY GUIDE. 1979. a. £15. St. James Press Ltd., 5-11 Worship St., London EC2A 2AY, England. Ed. Annabel Roney. adv. circ. 5,000(controlled)

387 CN ISSN 0581-3298
SAINT LAWRENCE SEAWAY AUTHORITY. ANNUAL REPORT. (Text in English and French) 1985. a. free. Saint Lawrence Seaway Authority, Constitution Square, 360 Albert St., Ottawa, Ont. K1R 7X7, Canada. TEL 613-598-4614. circ. 3,000.

387.2 GW
SCHIFF UND ZEIT. 1973. irreg., vol.25, 1987. DM.19.80. (Deutsche Gesellschaft fuer Schiffahrts- und Marinegeschichte e. V.) Koehlers Verlagsgesellschaft mbH, Steintorwall 17, Postfach 2352, 4900 Herford, W. Germany (B.R.D.) Ed. Jochen Brennecke. illus.

623.82 US ISSN 0080-6803
SCHIFFBAUTECHNISCHEN GESELLSCHAFT. JAHRBUCH. a. price varies. (GW) Springer-Verlag, 175 Fifth Ave, New York, NY 10010 TEL 212-460-1500. (Also Berlin, Heidelberg, Tokyo and Vienna) (reprint service avail. from ISI)

387 GW
SCHIFFSLISTE; Verzeichnis der deutschen Reedereien & ihre Schiffe ueber 100 BRT. 1902. a. DM.47. Eckardt & Messtorff GmbH, Roedingsmarkt 16, 2000 Hamburg 11, W. Germany (B.R.D.) Ed. G.U. Detlefsen. adv. circ. 3,000.

387 US ISSN 0732-6882
SEA LETTER.* 1961. q. $10. National Maritime Museum Association, Presidio of San Francisco Bldg. 275, Crissy Field, San Francisco, CA 94129. TEL 415-673-0700. bk. rev. illus. circ. 2,000. (looseleaf format)
 Formerly: San Francisco Maritime Museum. Sea Letter (ISSN 0037-0010)

387 382 CN ISSN 0080-8423
SEAPORTS AND THE SHIPPING WORLD. ANNUAL ISSUE. 1957. a. Gallery Publications Ltd., 4634 St. Catherine St. W., Montreal, Que H3Z 1S3, Canada. TEL 514-934-0373. Ed. Brian Gallery. adv. circ. 1,200.

387 UK ISSN 0142-5056
SEATRADE U.S. YEARBOOK. 1985 edition published as: Seatrade North America Yearbook. 1979. a. included with subscription to Seatrade. Seatrade Publications Ltd., Fairfax House, Colchester, Essex CO1 1RJ, England. adv.

SEFUNIM. see ARCHAEOLOGY

SHARJAH PORTS HANDBOOK. see BUSINESS AND ECONOMICS — Trade And Industrial Directories

387.7 MM ISSN 0080-9268
SHIPPING AND AVIATION STATISTICS OF THE MALTESE ISLANDS. a. Central Office of Statistics, Auberge d'Italie, Valletta, Malta (Subscr. to: Information Division, Auberge de Castille, Valletta, Malta)

SHIPPING & PORTS DIRECTORY OF INDONESIA. see BUSINESS AND ECONOMICS — Trade And Industrial Directories

387.5 GW ISSN 0721-3220
SHIPPING STATISTICS YEARBOOK. 1973. biennial. price varies. Institut fuer Seeverkehrswirtschaft und Logistik Bremen - Institute of Shipping Economics and Logistics, Am Dom 5a, D-2800 Bremen 1, W. Germany (B.R.D.) stat. (back issues avail.)

387 UK
SHIPPING SURVEY. 1973. irreg. (2-4/yr.) Drewry Shipping Consultants Ltd., 34 Brook St., Mayfair, London W1Y 2LL, England.

387 DK
SKANDINAVISK SKIBSFARTS TEKNISKE AARSHEFTE. a. Nautisk Forlag, Bentzonsvej 54, Box 1462, 2000 Copenhagen F, Denmark. adv. circ. 3,000.

387 NO ISSN 0800-1235
SKANDINAVISKE SKIPSREDERIER/YEARBOOK OF SCANDINAVIAN SHIPOWNERS. (Text in English) 1936. a. Kr.264. Selvig Publishing A-S, P.O. Box 9070 Vaterland, 0134 Oslo 1, Norway. adv.

387 NO
SKIPSFARTENS INNKJOEPSBOK. a. Kr.250. Instituttet for Merkantil Informasjon A-S, P.O. Box 102, Lilleaker, 0216 Oslo 2, Norway. Ed. Erling Riisnaes. adv. circ. 5,000.

387 US
SOCIETY OF MARITIME ARBITRATORS. AWARD SERVICE. 1965. a. $400. ‡ Society of Maritime Arbitrators, 26 Broadway, Ste. 1200, New York, NY 10004. TEL 212-483-0616. circ. 300. (also avail. in microfiche)

623.8 US ISSN 0081-1661
SOCIETY OF NAVAL ARCHITECTS AND MARINE ENGINEERS. TRANSACTIONS. 1893. a. $45. Society of Naval Architects and Marine Engineers, One World Trade Center, Ste. 1369, New York, NY 10048. TEL 212-432-0310. index. circ. 7,000. Indexed: Ocean.Abstr. Pollut.Abstr. BMT. Petrol.Abstr.

TRANSPORTATION — TRUCKS AND TRUCKING

387   AG
SOUTH AMERICAN PORTS HANDBOOK. (Text in English) 1974. biennial. $65. Agencia Maritima Internacional S.A., 25 de Mayo 555-piso 20, 1002 Buenos Aires, Argentina. Ed. Frank V. H. Wylie. illus. circ. 1,500.
 Formerly (until 1976): Owners, Masters, Brokers and Agents Handbook on South American Caribbean and Pacific Ports in Venezuela, Colombia, Panama, Ecuador, Peru, Bolivia and Chile.

SOUTHAMPTON PORT HANDBOOK. see BUSINESS AND ECONOMICS — Trade And Industrial Directories

387.5   UK
SOVIET MERCHANT SHIPS. 1969. a. £9.95. Kenneth Mason Publications Ltd., The Old Harbourmaster's, 8 North St., Emsworth, Hants. PO10 7DD, England. Ed. Ambrose Greenway.

386   NE
STATISTIEK VAN DE SCHEEPVAARTBEWEGING IN NEDERLAND/ CENSUS OF INLAND SHIPPING IN THE NETHERLANDS AT LOCKS AND BRIDGES. (Text in Dutch and English) 1946. a. Centraal Bureau voor de Statistiek, Prinses Beatrixlaan 428, Voorburg, Netherlands (Orders to: Staatsuitgeverij, Christoffel Plantijnstraat, The Hague, Netherlands)

387   GW   ISSN 0073-0203
STATISTIK DES HAMBURGISCHEN STAATES; Handel und Schiffahrt des Hafens Hamburg. 1845. biennial. DM.26. ‡ Statistisches Landesamt, Steckelhoern 12, 2000 Hamburg 11, W. Germany (B.R.D.)

387.164   GW
STOWAGE AND SEGREGATION TO I M D G CODE. 1973. a. DM.85. K. O. Storck Verlag, Stahltwiete 7, 2000 Hamburg 50, W. Germany (B.R.D.) Ed. H. Meder.

SVEUCILISTE U ZAGREBU. FAKULTET STROJARSTVA I BRODOGRADNJE. ZBORNIK RADOVA. see ENGINEERING — Mechanical Engineering

387 380   UK   ISSN 0264-567X
SYDNEY PORTS HANDBOOK (YEAR) 1983/4. biennial. £5. Charter Publications, Bank Chambers, Downham Market, Norfolk PE38 9BU, England. Ed. James Moriarty. adv. circ. 6,000.

387   GW
TAEGLICHER HAFENBERICHT. JAHRESAUSGABE. a. DM.27.80. Seshafen-Verlag Erik Blumenfeld GmbH und Co., Postfach 105605, 2000 Hamburg 1, W. Germany (B.R.D.) charts. stat.

387 380   UK   ISSN 0265-1181
TEES AND HARTLEPOOL PORTS. 1983/4. a. £5. Charter Publications, Bank Chambers, Downham Market, Norfolk PE38 9BU, England. Ed. John Ison. adv. circ. 6,000.

387.5   JA
TOYAMA MERCANTILE MARINE COLLEGE. JOURNAL/TOYAMA SHOSEN KOTO SENMON GAKKO KENKYU SHUROKU. (Text in Japanese; some articles in English) 1968. a. Toyama Mercantile Marine College - Toyama Shosen Koto Senmon Gakko, 1-2 Ebie Neriai, Shinminato, Toyama 933-02, Japan. Ed. Henshu Iinkai. illus. circ. 140.

387   US   ISSN 0082-5867
TRAFFIC REPORT OF THE ST. LAWRENCE SEAWAY. irreg. U.S. Saint Lawrence Seaway Development Corporation, 400 7th St., S.W., Rm. 5424, Washington, DC 20590. TEL 202-426-3574.

387.5   FR
TRANSPORT MARITIME: ETUDES ET STATISTIQUES. 1956. a. 30 F. Comite Central des Armateurs de France, 73 bld. Haussmann, 75008 Paris, France. circ. 4,500.
 Formerly: Marine Marchand: Etudes et Statistiques (ISSN 0069-6439)

387.1   TI
TUNISIA. OFFICE DES PORTS NATIONAUX. BULLETIN ANNUEL DES STATISTIQUES. Cover title: Tunisia. Office des Ports Nationaux. Trafic Maritime. a. Office des Ports Nationaux, Tunis, Tunisia.

387 380   UK   ISSN 0265-8194
TURKEY PORT AND SHIPPING HANDBOOK 1984. 1984. a. £10. Charter Publications, Bank Chambers, Downham Market, Norfolk PE38 9BU, England. Ed. John Ison. adv. circ. 6,000.

387   UK
TURKISH SHIPPING. 1979. a. including subscription to "Seatrade". Seatrade Publications Ltd., Fairfax House, Colchester, Essex CO1 1RJ, England.
 Former titles (until 1984): Latin American Shipping & Seatrade Guide to Latin American Shipping (ISSN 0142-5064)

387.1   US   ISSN 0083-0305
U.S. ARMY. CORPS OF ENGINEERS. PORT SERIES.* 1921. irreg. U.S. Army, Corps of Engineers, Publications Office, Washington, DC 20310 TEL 202-272-6001. (Orders to: Supt. of Documents, Washington, DC 20402)

287   US   ISSN 0083-0755
U.S. FEDERAL MARITIME COMMISSION. ANNUAL REPORT. 1962. a. free. U.S. Federal Maritime Commission, 1110 L St. N.W., Washington, DC 20573. TEL 202-523-5707.

387   US   ISSN 0083-1670
U.S. MARITIME ADMINISTRATION. ANNUAL REPORT. 1950. a. U.S. Maritime Administration, Nassif Bldg., 400 7th St., S.W., Washington, DC 20590 TEL 202-426-5812. (Orders to: Supt. of Documents, Washington, DC 20402)

387   US   ISSN 0083-3207
U.S. SAINT LAWRENCE SEAWAY DEVELOPMENT CORPORATION. ANNUAL REPORT. 1954/55. a. U.S. Saint Lawrence Seaway Development Corporation, 400 7th St., S.W., Rm. 5424, Washington, DC 20590. TEL 202-426-3574.

387   PL   ISSN 0208-483X
UNIWERSYTET GDANSKI. WYDZIAL EKONOMIKI TRANSPORTU. ZESZYTY NAUKOWE. EKONOMIKA TRANSPORTU MORSKIEGO. (Text in Polish; summaries in English and Russian) 1971. irreg. price varies. Uniwersytet Gdanski, Ul. Czerwonej Armii 110, 81-824 Sopot, Poland. circ. 300.

386 333.91   SP
VALENCIA PORT; guia del servicios del puerto de Valencia. 1978. a. 650 ptas. Publicaciones Men-Car, Paseo de Colon 24, Barcelona 2, Spain. Eds. Juan and Manuel Cardona. adv. circ. 15,000.

387   UK   ISSN 0264-5661
VANCOUVER PORT HANDBOOK. 1983. biennial. £10. Charter Publications, Bank Chambers, Downham Market, Norfolk PE38 9BU, England. Ed. James Moriarty. adv. circ. 6,000.

387 900   NE
VEREENIGING NEDERLANDSCH HISTORISCH SCHEEPVAART MUSEUM TE AMSTERDAM. JAARVERSLAG. 1917. a. membership. Lands Zeemagazijn, Kattenburgerplein 1, 1018 KK Amsterdam, Netherlands. cum.index: 1917-1980. circ. 1,500.

387 551.3   DK   ISSN 0109-2049
VIND - NYT. 1979. irreg. free. Danish Maritime Institute, Hjortekaersvej 99, 2800 Lyngby, Denmark. Eds. M. Gunzenhauser, S.O. Hansen. bk. rev. illus. circ. 600.

VIRGINIA PORTS AND SHIPPING HANDBOOK. see BUSINESS AND ECONOMICS — Trade And Industrial Directories

387   US   ISSN 0083-7725
WATERBORNE COMMERCE OF THE UNITED STATES. 1952. a. (in 5 separate parts) price varies. U.S. Army Corps of Engineers, Water Resources Support Center, Box 61280, New Orleans, LA 70161. TEL 504-865-1121. circ. 1,100.

387.5   AT
WESTERN AUSTRALIAN COASTAL SHIPPING COMMISSION. ANNUAL REPORT. a. contr.circ. Coastal Shipping Commission, P.O. Box 394, Fremantle, Australia. stat.

387   NO   ISSN 0800-1200
WHERE TO BUILD - WHERE TO REPAIR. (Text in English) 1952. a. Kr.210. Selvig Publishing A-S, P.O. Box 9070 Vaterland, 0134 Oslo 1, Norway. adv.

387 380.1   GW
WIE ERREICHE ICH WEN? 1958. a. DM.23. K.O. Storck Verlag, Stahltwiete 7, 2000 Hamburg 50, W. Germany (B.R.D.) Ed. H. Meder.

387   NO
WORLD BULK TRADES. a. free. Fearnleys, Box 1158-Sentrum, Oslo 1, Norway. charts. stat.

387.164   US   ISSN 0162-0088
WORLD WIDE SHIPPING GUIDE. 1976. a. $35. World Wide Shipping Guide, Inc., 77 Moehring Dr., Blauvelt, NY 10913. adv. circ. 12,500.

387.5   PL
WYZSZA SZKOLA MORSKA. ZESZYTY NAUKOWE. irreg. 103 Zl. Wyzsza Szkola Morska w Gdyni - Merchant Marine Academy, Czerwonych Kosynierow 83, 81-225 Gdynia, Poland (Dist. by Ars Polona-Ruch, Krakowskie Przedmiescie 7, Warsaw, Poland) Ed. Bozena Sobolewska.

387   JA
YOKOHAMA PORT ACTIVITIES. (Text in English) a. Port and Harbor Bureau, Industry & Trade Center Bldg., Yamashita-cho, Makaku, Yokohama, Japan.

TRANSPORTATION — Trucks And Trucking

388.324   UK   ISSN 0308-9304
A B C FREIGHT GUIDE. a. Kogan Page Ltd., 120 Pentonville Rd., London N1, England. adv. circ. 3, 500.
 Incorporates: A B C Guide to Recovery Services; Formerly: A B C Goods Transport Guide (ISSN 0001-0421)

ABSTRACTS OF SUPREME COURT DECISIONS INTERPRETING THE INTERSTATE COMMERCE ACT. see LAW

388   CN   ISSN 0084-6171
ALBERTA MOTOR TRANSPORT DIRECTORY. 1947. a. Can.$25. Alberta Trucking Association, P.O. Box 5520, Station A, 5112 3 St. S.E., Calgary, Alberta T2H 1X9, Canada. TEL 403-468-3195. Ed. Jim Bradbury. adv. bk. rev. circ. 1,500.
 Formerly: Alberta Shippers Guide.

388.3   US   ISSN 0065-7271
AMERICAN ASSOCIATION OF MOTOR VEHICLE ADMINISTRATORS. ANNUAL CONFERENCE. PROCEEDINGS. 1957. a. American Association of Motor Vehicle Administrators, 1201 Connecticut Ave., N.W., Ste. 910, Washington, DC 20036. Ed. Robert S. Brown, Jr. circ. 1,000.

388.4   US
AMERICAN TRUCKING TRENDS - (YEAR) a. $25. American Trucking Associations, Statistical Analysis Department, 2200 Mill Road, Alexandria, VA 22314. TEL 703-838-1792. Dir. Ronald D. Roth.
 Former titles: American Trucking Trends. Statistical Report; American Trucking Associations Report (ISSN 0066-0892)

388.322   UK   ISSN 0068-4376
BUSES ANNUAL. a. price varies. Ian Allan Ltd., Coombelands House, Addlestone, Weybridge, Surrey KT15 0HY, England. circ. 8,500. (reprint service avail. from UMI)

388.324   CN
CANADIAN TRUCKERS' GUIDE. 1981. a. Can.$3.50 (free with subscr. to Trucking Canada) Wadham Publications, 1450 Don Mills Rd., Don Mills, Ont M3B 2X7, Canada. TEL 416-442-2000. Ed. Rolf Lockwood. adv. charts. illus. stat. tr.lit. index. circ. 25,000. (back issues avail.)

388.324 US
CARGO TANK HAZARDOUS MATERIAL
REGULATIONS. a. $22 to non-members; members
$17. National Tank Truck Carriers, Inc., 2200 Mill
Rd., Alexandria, VA 22314. TEL 703-838-1960.

388.324 SA
COMMERCIAL VEHICLE DATA DIGEST. a. R.37.
Mead & McGrouther (Pty) Ltd., 327 Surrey Ave.,
Box 1240, Ferndale, Randburg 2125, South Africa.
adv. circ. 4,667.

EASTERN TRANSPORTATION LAW SEMINAR
PAPERS AND PROCEEDINGS. see *LAW*

388.3 US
F & O S EXECUTIVE AND OWNERSHIP
REPORT. (Financial and Operating Statistics) a.
$115 or with subscr. to 2 other F & O S
publications. American Trucking Associations, Inc.,
2200 Mill Rd., Alexandria, VA 22314. TEL 703-
838-1792.

388.3 US ISSN 0160-4570
F & O S MOTOR CARRIER ANNUAL REPORT.
(Financial and Operating Statistics); results of
operations class I & II motor carriers of property;
regulated by the Interstate Commerce Commission.
a. $200. American Trucking Associations, Inc., 2200
Mill Rd., Alexandria, VA 22314. illus.
  Supersedes in part: F & O S (ISSN 0098-2245)

388.3 US ISSN 0099-2445
FINANCIAL ANALYSIS OF THE MOTOR
CARRIER INDUSTRY. 1946. a. $25. American
Trucking Associations, Inc., 2200 Mill Rd.,
Alexandria, VA 22314. illus. stat.

388.324 UK
HAULAGE MANUAL. 1970. biennial. £15. Road
Haulage Association, 104 New Kings Rd., London
SW6 4LN, England. Ed. Derek Witcher. adv. stat.
index. circ. 12,000.

629.2 SZ
I N U F A KATALOG. 1958. a. 32 Fr. Vogt-Schild
AG, Dornacherstr. 39, 4501 Solothurn 1,
Switzerland. Eds. Theodor Eckert, H.U. Haueter.
adv. bk. rev. circ. 5,500.
  Formerly: I N U F A: Internationaler
Nutzfahrzeug-Katalog/International Catalogue for
Commercial Vehicles (ISSN 0073-4292)

388.324 UK ISSN 0262-6195
INTERNATIONAL ROAD HAULAGE BY
UNITED KINGDOM REGISTERED VEHICLES.
1979. a. £10. Department of Transport, 43
Marsham St., London SW1P 3PY, England. Ed.
A.K. Pepper.
  Formerly (until 1980): International Road
Haulage by British Registered Vehicles (ISSN 0262-
4508)

388.3 IS ISSN 0075-1057
ISRAEL. CENTRAL BUREAU OF STATISTICS.
MOTOR VEHICLES. (Subseries of its Special
Series) (Text in Hebrew; summaries in English)
irreg., latest issue no.746, 1983. price varies. Central
Bureau of Statistics, Box 13015, Jerusalem, Israel.

KITCHIN'S ROAD TRANSPORT LAW. see *LAW*

388.324 CN ISSN 0713-8776
MANITOBA SHIP BY TRUCK DIRECTORY. 1958.
a. Can.$15. Manitoba Trucking Association, 25
Bunting St., Winnipeg, Man. R2X 2P5, Canada. Ed.
Bob Wilks. adv. circ. 1,500.
  Formerly: M T A Ship by Truck Directory.

381 US
MOTOR HOME & TRUCK CAMPER TRADE-IN
GUIDE. a. $11.95. Intertec Publishing Corp.,
Technical Book Division, 9221 Quivira Rd.,
Overland Park, KS 66212. TEL 913-888-4664.
(reprint service avail. from UMI)
  Former titles: Motor Home Trade-in Guide;
Official Motor Home Trade-in Guide (ISSN 0093-
1195)

388.3 UK ISSN 0077-1600
MOTOR MANUAL.* irreg. L.1.25. Hamlyn Group,
42 The Centre, Feltham, Middlesex, England.
Indexed: Gdlns.

388.324 US ISSN 0077-586X
NATIONAL TANK TRUCK CARRIER
DIRECTORY. 1954. a. $23 to non-members;
members $60. National Tank Truck Carriers, Inc.,
2200 Mill Rd., Alexandria, VA 22314. TEL 703-
838-1960. Ed. Patricia Whiting. adv. circ. 3,000.

388.3 NE ISSN 0168-4973
NETHERLANDS. CENTRAAL BUREAU VOOR
DE STATISTIEK. STATISTIEK DER
MOTORVOERTUIGEN. STATISTICS OF
MOTOR VEHICLES. (Text in Dutch and English)
1966. a. fl.14.10. Centraal Bureau voor de Statistiek,
Prinses Beatrixlaan 428, Voorburg, Netherlands
(Orders to: Staatsuitgeverij, Christoffel
Plantijnstraat, The Hague, Netherlands)
  Formerly: Netherlands. Centraal Bureau voor de
Statistiek. Statistiek der Motorrijtuigen (ISSN 0077-
698X)

388.324 US
OHIO TRUCK TIMES. 1950. biennial. $5. ‡ Ohio
Trucking Association, 50 W. Broad St., Ste. 1111,
Columbus, OH 43215. TEL 614-221-5375. Ed.
David F. Bartosic. adv. bk. rev. illus. circ. 8,000.
  Formerly (1950-1974): Ohio Trucking News
(ISSN 0030-1191)

QUICK CALLER: BOSTON AREA AIR CARGO
DIRECTORY. see *TRANSPORTATION — Air
Transport*

QUICK CALLER: DETROIT AREA AIR CARGO
DIRECTORY. see *TRANSPORTATION — Air
Transport*

QUICK CALLER: MIAMI AREA AIR CARGO
DIRECTORY. see *TRANSPORTATION — Air
Transport*

QUICK CALLER: SAN FRANCISCO BAY AREA
AIR CARGO DIRECTORY. see
TRANSPORTATION — Air Transport

388.324 US
RAND MCNALLY MOTOR CARRIERS' ROAD
ATLAS. a. Rand McNally & Co., 8255 N. Central
Pk. Ave., Skokie, IL 60076. TEL 312-673-9100.
adv. circ. 75,000.

388.324 US
RECIPROCITY GUIDE FOR PRIVATE MOTOR
CARRIERS. 1960. a. $25. Private Carrier
Conference, Inc., 2200 Mill Rd., Alexandria, VA
22314. TEL 203-838-1995. (Affiliate: American
Trucking Associations, Inc.) circ. 10,000.

388.324 UK
ROAD HAULAGE ASSOCIATION DIARY. a.
Welbecson Ltd., 3 Thomas St., Hull, Humberside
HU9 1EJ, England.

388.324 CN
SASKATCHEWAN TRUCKING-SHIP BY TRUCK
DIRECTORY. 1973. a. Can.$11. Saskatchewan
Trucking Association, 1335 Wallace St., Regina,
Sask. S4N 3Z5, Canada. TEL 306-569-9696. adv.
circ. 2,000.
  Formerly: Saskatchewan Motor Transport Guide
(ISSN 0707-0365)

388.3 SA
TRANSPORT MANAGER'S HANDBOOK;
incorporating Commercial Transport Equipment
Index. 1978. a. R.112. (Federation of Road
Transport Associations) Thomson Publications S.A.
(Pty) Ltd., Thomson House, Cnr. Will Scarlet &
Hendrik Verwoerd Dr., Randburg, P.O. Box 56182,
Pinegowrie 2123, South Africa. Ed. Lauren Joffee.
adv. circ. 3,014.
  Supersedes (1964-1978): Commercial Transport
Handbook and Buyer's Guide for S.A. (ISSN 0069-
6676)

388.324 UK
TRANSPORT OF GOODS BY ROAD IN GREAT
BRITAIN. 1972. a. £8. Department of Transport,
Statistics Transport Division, Romney House, Rm.
B.639, 43 Marsham St., London SW1P 3PY,
England. Ed. F. Johnson. charts. stat. circ. 250.
(looseleaf format; back issues avail.)

388.3 US ISSN 0362-5737
TRUCK BROKER DIRECTORY. a. $25. J.J. Keller &
Associates, Inc., 145 W. Wisconsin Ave., Neenah,
WI 54956. TEL 414-722-2849. adv.

388.324 CN ISSN 0564-3392
TRUCK DATA BOOK. vol.34, 1981. a. Can.$23.
Sanford Evans Communications Ltd., 1077 St.
James St., Box 6900, Winnipeg, Man. R3Q 3B1,
Canada. TEL 204-775-0201. Ed. Gary Henry.

388.324 US
TRUCK PERMIT GUIDE. 1974. irreg., no.78, 1987.
$119. J.J. Keller and Associates, Inc., 145 W.
Wisconsin Ave., Neenah, WI 54956. TEL 800-558-
5011. Ed. George B. McDowell.

388.324 US
TRUCKING SAFETY GUIDE. (Updated 4/yr.) 1974.
irreg., no.54, 1986. $119. J.J. Keller and Associates,
Inc., 145 W. Wisconsin Ave., Neenah, WI 54956.
TEL 800-558-5011. Ed. George B. McDowell.

388.324 US
VEHICLE SIZES AND WEIGHTS MANUAL.
(Updated 2/yr.) 1974. irreg., no.26, 1987. $85. J.J.
Keller and Associates, Inc., 145 W. Wisconsin Ave.,
Neenah, WI 54956. TEL 800-558-5011. Ed. George
B. McDowell.

388.3 US
WAREHOUSING/DISTRIBUTION DIRECTORY.
Variant title: M C D Warehousing Distribution
Directory. 1963. a. $71. ‡ Guide Services, Box
720455, Atlanta, GA 30328. TEL 404-955-3000.
Ed. David Wise. adv. circ. 20,000.
  Former titles: National Distribution Directory of
Local Cartage-Short Haul Carriers Warehousing
(ISSN 0364-9539); National Distribution Directory
(ISSN 0077-4219)

TRAVEL AND TOURISM

A A A CAMPBOOKS. (American Automobile
Association) see *SPORTS AND GAMES —
Outdoor Life*

A D A C - CAMPINGFUEHRER. BAND 1:
SUEDEUROPA. see *SPORTS AND GAMES —
Outdoor Life*

A D A C - CAMPINGFUEHRER. BAND 2:
DEUTSCHLAND, MITTELEUROPA,
NORDEUROPA. see *SPORTS AND GAMES —
Outdoor Life*

917.3 US ISSN 0090-8614
A L A SIGHTS TO SEE BOOK. 1971. a.
membership. (Automobile Legal Association) A L A
Auto & Travel Club, 888 Worcester St., Wellesley,
MA 02181. TEL 617-237-5200. illus. circ. 25,000.
  Formerly: Automobile Legal Association. A L A
Green Book.

A V D AUTO BORDBUCH. see
TRANSPORTATION — Automobiles

910.1 647.94 US
A Y H HANDBOOK. 1939. a. $5 to non-members.
American Youth Hostels, Inc., Box 37613,
Washington, DC 20013-7613. TEL 202-783-6161.
adv. circ. 125,000.
  Formerly: American Youth Hostels Guide and
Handbook (ISSN 0066-1201)

914.2 UK ISSN 0261-5924
ACTIVITY HOLIDAYS IN BRITAIN. 1974. a. £1.
F.H.G. Publications Ltd., Abbey Mill Business
Centre, Seedhill, Paisley PA1 1JN, Scotland. circ.
15,000.

910.202 UK
ADVENTURE HOLIDAYS. 1978. a. $8.95. Vacation-
Work, 9 Park End St., Oxford OX1 1HJ, England
(Dist. in U.S. by: Writer's Digest Books, 9933
Alliance Rd., Cincinatti, OH 45242) Ed. Susan
Griffith. circ. 10,000.

910 US
ADVENTURE TRAVEL NORTH AMERICA. 1972.
biennial. $12.95. Adventure Guides, Inc., 36 E. 57
St., New York, NY 10022. TEL 212-355-6334. Ed.
Pat Dickerman. Indexed: Access.
  Former titles: Adventure Travel (New York)
(ISSN 0195-8445); (until 1976): Adventure Trip
Guide (ISSN 0084-5965)

AGENT'S HOTEL GAZETTEER: AMERICA. see
HOTELS AND RESTAURANTS

AGENT'S HOTEL GAZETTEER: RESORTS OF EUROPE. see *HOTELS AND RESTAURANTS*

796.5   UK
ALAN ROGERS' GOOD CAMPS GUIDE FOR FRANCE. 1985. a. £1.70. Deneway Guides and Travel Ltd., P.O. Box 286, Rottingdean, Brighton, BN2 8AY, England. circ. 20,000.

796.54   UK   ISSN 0065-5686
ALAN ROGERS' SELECTED SITES FOR CARAVANNING AND CAMPING IN EUROPE. 1968. a. £2.60. Deneway Guides and Travel Ltd., P.O. Box 286, Rottingdean, Brighton, BN2 8AY, England. adv. circ. 20,000.

917.98   US   ISSN 0270-5370
ALASKA ALMANAC: FACTS ABOUT ALASKA. 1976. a. $5.95. Alaska Northwest Publishing Co., Box 4-EEE, Anchorage, AK 99509. TEL 907-274-0521. illus.
    Formerly: Facts About Alaska (ISSN 0361-7823)

910.2 917   US   ISSN 0065-5848
ALASKA TRAVEL GUIDE. 1960. a. $9.95. Box 15889, Salt Lake City, UT 84115. Ed. Tim Bell. adv. bk. rev. circ. 60,000.

917.3   CN   ISSN 0707-3151
ALGOMA OUTDOORS. 1977. a. free contr. circ. Algoma Kinniwabi Travel Association, 553 Queen St. E., Sault Ste. Marie, Ont. P6A 2A3, Canada. TEL 705-254-4293. illus.

917.9   US
ALL ABOUT ARIZONA, THE HEALTHFUL STATE. biennial. $5.95. Harian Publications, One Vernon Ave., Floral Park, NY 11001. TEL 516-437-3440. Ed. Thomas B. Lesure.

910.09 917   US   ISSN 0533-0653
ALL OF MEXICO AT LOW COST. biennial. $3.45. Harian Publications, One Vernon Ave., Floral Park, NY 11001. TEL 516-437-3440. Ed. Norman D. Ford. charts.

919.4   AT
ALL STATES TOURIST PARK GUIDE. 1948. a. Aus.$2.95. Newspress Pty. Ltd., Box 628E, Melbourne, Vic. 3001, Australia.

917   US   ISSN 0569-1966
AMERICA BY CAR. 1958. biennial. $4.95. Harian Publications, One Vernon Ave., Floral Park, NY 11001. TEL 516-437-3440. Ed. Norman D. Ford.

AMERICA'S CUP CHALLENGE AND GUIDE TO AUSTRALIA. see *SPORTS AND GAMES*

910.202 917.04   US
AMERICA'S FAVORITE NATIONAL PARKS. a. $5.95. Rand McNally & Co., Box 7600, Chicago, IL 60680. TEL 312-673-9100. illus.

914.2   UK
ANGLING HOLIDAYS IN IRELAND. 1986. a. $4. Libra House Ltd., P.O. Box 1127, Dublin 8, Ireland. TEL (011) 753935. Ed. Cathal Tyrrell. illus. circ. 10,793.

914.4   DK
ANNUAIRE SOUVENIR NORMAND. (Text in English and French; summaries in Danish) 1979. biennial. Kr.50. Dansk-Normannisk Selskab, Kultorvet 2, Postbox 85, DK-1003 Copenhagen K, Denmark. Ed. Folmer Wisti. adv. bk. rev. illus. circ. 1,000.
    Formerly: Souvenir Normand (ISSN 0106-5017)

915.1   CH
ANNUAL REPORT ON TOURISM STATISTICS, REPUBLIC OF CHINA. (Text in Chinese and English) 1972. a. free. Taipei Tourism Bureau, Box 1490, Taipei, Taiwan, Republic of China. Ed. Ta-Rong Chu. illus. circ. 2,000.

914.504   IT
ANNUARIO GENERALE DELLE IMPRESE DI VIAGGIO E TURISMO. 1970. a. L.8000. Advertising Master Publisher (A.M.P.), Giacomo Spartaco Bertoletti & C. s.a.s., Via Natale Battaglia 27, 20127 Milan, Italy. adv. circ. 10,000.

914   UK
APARTMENT GAZETTEER (EUROPE) a. £17. C.H.G. Travel Publications, Waterside House, West Common, Gerrards Cross, Bucks, England.

910   UK
ARABIAN HOTEL & TRAVEL GUIDE. a. £20. Beacon Publications PLC., York House, Newton Close, Park Farm, Wellingborough, Northamptonshire NN8 3UW, England.

910   YU
ARENATURIST. 1972. a. free. Arenaturist, Pula, Yugoslavia. Ed. Marijan Fistrovic.

338.4   US
ARKANSAS TRAVEL AND TOURISM REPORT. 1972. a. free. Department of Parks and Tourism, Tourism Division, One Capitol Mall, Little Rock, AR 72201. TEL 501-371-7777. Ed. Charles McLemore. illus. circ. 900.
    Formerly: Tourism in Arkansas. Activity Report.

AUSTRALIAN-AMERICAN NEWS N.S.W. ANNUAL EDITION. see *POLITICAL SCIENCE — International Relations*

919.4   AT
AUSTRALIAN TOURIST COMMISSION. ANNUAL REPORT. 1968. a. free. Australian Tourist Commission, 324 St. Kilda Rd, P.O. Box 73B, Melbourne 3001, Australia. illus. stat. circ. 250. (back issues avail.)

649.94   AT   ISSN 0156-0107
AUSTRALIAN YOUTH HOSTELS HANDBOOK. 1957. a. Aus.$1. Kingsgrove Press Pty. ltd., 43 Kingsway, Kingsgrove NSW 2208, Australia. Ed. F. Fitzpatrick. adv. circ. 130,000.

910   FI   ISSN 0355-2896
AUTOLLA ULKOMAILLE. 1965. a. Fmk.30. Autoliitto - Automobile and Touring Club of Finland, Kansakoulukatu 10, 00100 Helsinki, Finland. Ed. Reijo Kaukinen. adv. circ. 7,000.
    Formerly: Kansainvalinen Automatkailu (ISSN 0075-4900)

910.09   GW
DIE BADEPLAETZE IN DAENEMARK. irreg. DM.19.80. ADAC Verlag GmbH, Am Westpark 8, 8 Munich 70, Postfach 70 01 86, W. Germany (B.R.D.)

910.09   GW
DIE BADEPLAETZE IN JUGOSLAWIEN. irreg. DM.19.80. ADAC Verlag GmbH, Am Westpark 8, 8 Munich 70, Postfach 70 01 86, W. Germany (B.R.D.)

917.2   BF
BAHAMAS FAMILY ISLANDS TRAVEL GUIDE. 1972. a. $1. (Bahamas Family Islands Promotion Board) Star Publishers Ltd., P.O. Box 4855, Nassau, Bahamas. TEL 809-322-4527. Ed. Paul Bower. adv. illus. circ. 200,000.
    Former titles (until 1977): Bahamas Out Islands Travel Guide; Bahama Out Islands Tourist News.

917.2   US   ISSN 0067-2955
BAJA CALIFORNIA TRAVELS SERIES. 1965. irreg. (approx. 2/yr.), latest 1986. $30 (approx.) per vol. Dawson's Book Shop, 535 N. Larchmont Blvd, Los Angeles, CA 90004. TEL 213-469-2186. Eds. Edwin Carpenter, Glen Dawson. index in some vols.; cum.index planned. circ. 350.

919.7   BB
BARBADOS. PARKS AND BEACHES COMMISSION. ANNUAL REPORT. a. Parks and Beaches Commission, P.O. Box 111, Trident House, Bridgetown, Barbados, W. Indies.

919.704   BB
BARBADOS TOURIST BOARD. ANNUAL REPORT. no.14, 1972. a. $3. Barbados Tourist Board, Bridgewater, Barbados, W. Indies. charts. illus.

914.6   IS
BAZAK GUIDE TO SPAIN.* (Text in English) irreg. $4.95. Bazak Israel Guidebook Publishers Ltd., P.O. Box 6340, Jerusalem, Israel (U.S. Distributor: Harper & Row, 60 E. 42nd St., Ste. 411, New York, NY 10017) illus.

910.3   UK   ISSN 0267-3436
BED AND BREAKFAST IN BRITAIN. 1955. a. £1.25. F.H.G. Publications Ltd., Abbey Mill Centre, Seedhill, Paisley PA1 1JN, Scotland. Ed. Peter Clark.
    Formed by the merger of: Bed and Breakfast in South and Southwest England (ISSN 0067-4761) & Bed and Breakfast in Wales, Northern England and Scotland (ISSN 0067-477X)

914.2   UK   ISSN 0267-3363
BED & BREAKFAST STOPS. 1975. a. £1.25. F.H.G. Publications Ltd., Abbey Mill Business Centre, Seedhill, Paisley PA1 1JN, Scotland.

910.202   US
BED AND BREAKFAST U S A; guide to tourist homes and guest houses. 1977. a. $9.95. E.P. Dutton, Inc., 2 Park Ave., New York, NY 10016. TEL 212-725-1818. Ed. Sandra Soule. circ. 40,000.
    Formerly: Guide to Tourist Homes and Guest Houses.

914.2   UK
BED, BREAKFAST & EVENING MEAL. 1963. a. £1.10. Pastime Publications Ltd., 15 Dublin Street Lane South, Edinburgh EH1 3PX, Scotland. adv.

910.2   UK   ISSN 0067-5342
BELFAST AND NORTHERN IRELAND DIRECTORY. 1852. a. £17.50. Century Services, Ltd., 51-59 Donegall St., Belfast BT1 2GB, N. Ireland. adv. circ. 3,000.

910 330   SZ   ISSN 0067-6152
BERNER STUDIEN ZUM FREMDENVERKEHR. 1966. irreg. price varies. (Universitaet Bern, Forschungsinstitut fuer Fremdenverkehr) Verlag Peter Lang AG, Jupiterstr. 15, CH-3015 Bern, Switzerland. Ed. J. Krippendorf.

796.95 914.2   UK
BLAKES BOATING HOLIDAYS. 1974. a. free. Blakes Holidays Ltd., Wroxham, Norwich NR12 8DH, England. Ed. T.E. Howes. circ. 350,000.
    Supersedes: Blakes Boating in Britain & Blakes Boating in Europe. Blakes Boating in Britain & Blakes Boating in Europe superseded in part: Blakes Holidays Afloat, which was formed by the merger of: Blakes International Holidays Afloat & Norfolk Broads Holidays Afloat (ISSN 0078-1142)

914.2   UK
BRITAIN: HOTELS & RESTAURANTS. 1955. a. free to qualified personnel. British Tourist Authority, Thames Tower, Blacks Rd., London W6, England. adv.

910.2   UK
BRITAIN WELCOMES COACHES. 1978. a. free to qualified personnel. Lewis Productions Ltd., 31 Castle St., Kingston upon Thames, Surrey KT1 1ST, England. Ed. Rosemary Bray. adv. circ. 30,000.

914.2   UK   ISSN 0267-1468
BRITAIN'S BEST HOLIDAYS - A QUICK REFERENCE GUIDE. 1968. a. £1.25. F.H.G. Publications Ltd., Abbey Mill Business Centre, Seedhill, Paisley PA1 1JN, Scotland.
    Formerly: Guide to Britain's Best Holidays.

910.202   UK
BURKE'S GUIDE TO COUNTRY HOUSES. 1977. irreg. £25. Burke's Peerage Ltd., 56 Walton St., London SW3 1RB, England.

910.202   UK
BURKE'S INTRODUCTION TO IRISH ANCESTRY. 1976. irreg. £2. Burke's Peerage Ltd., 56 Walton St., London SW3 1RB, England.

910.202 917.04 330   US
BUSINESS TRAVELER'S CITY GUIDE. 1986. a. $9.95. Rand McNally & Co., Box 7600, Chicago, IL 60680. TEL 312-673-9100. Ed. Jean Postlewaite. illus.

914   FR   ISSN 0068-5151
CAHIERS DU TOURISME. (Issued in 5 parts: A-France; B-Etranger; C-Recherche Fondamentale et Appliquee: Methodologie; D-Statistiques; E-Divers) 1963. irreg., no.155, 1986. price varies. Universite d'Aix-Marseille III (Universite de Droit, d'Economie et des Sciences), Centre des Hautes Etudes Touristiques, Fondation Vasarely, 1 Av. Marcel Pagnol, 13090 Aix-en-Provence, France. circ. 140.

918.104 BL
CALENDARIO CULTURAL DO BRASIL.* 1976. a. Conselho Federal de Cultura, Palacio da Cultura, Rua da Imprensa, 2000 Rio de Janeiro, Brazil. illus.

917 796.5 US
CALIFORNIA - NEVADA CAMPBOOK. Cover title: R V and Tent Sites in California, Nevada. a. membership. American Automobile Association, 8111 Gatehouse Rd., Falls Church, VA 22047. TEL 703-222-6000. circ. 534,000.
Formerly (until 1980): California-Nevada Camping.

910.2 914 FR ISSN 0076-7735
CAMPING, CARAVANING IN FRANCE. Also known as: Michelin Annual Camping Guide for France. (Text in Dutch, English, French and German) a. $7.95. Michelin, Services de Tourisme, 46 av. de Breteuil, 75341 Paris 7, France (U.S. subscr. address: Michelin Guides and Maps, P.O. Box 3305, Spartanburg, SC. 29304-3305)

CAMPITUR: CAMPING, CARAVANING, VILLAGGI TURISTICI. see SPORTS AND GAMES — Outdoor Life

917.104 US
CANADA (YEAR) a. $11.95. Houghton Mifflin Co., Birnbaum Travel Guides, 60 E. 42nd St., Ste. 1624, New York, NY 10165. TEL 212-682-9440. Ed. Stephen Birnbaum.

917 CN ISSN 0709-9762
CANADA: TRAVEL INFORMATION. a. Tourism Canada, Publications, 235 Queen St., Ottawa, Ont. K1A 0H6, Canada. TEL 613-954-3852.

910.4 US
CAPE COD AND ISLANDS ATLAS AND GUIDE BOOK. a. $10.95. Butterworth Company of Cape Cod, Inc., 350 Main St., West Yarmouth, MA 02673. TEL 617-775-4438. Ed. Rod Schou. adv. circ. 30,000.

974 US
CAPE COD RESORT DIRECTORY. 1921. a. Cape Cod Chamber of Commerce Inc., Routes 6 and 132, Hyannis, MA 02601. TEL 617-362-3225. adv. circ. 250,000.

910.2 UK ISSN 0069-0317
CARAVAN & CHALET SITES GUIDE. a. £3. Haymarket Publishing Ltd., 38-42 Hampton Rd., Teddington, Middx. TW11 0JE, England. circ. 35,000.

910.202 AT
CARAVAN BUYERS MANUAL. 1946. a. Aus.$2.95. Newspress Pty. Ltd. (Subsidiary of: Age Publications) 603-611 Little Lonsdale St., Melbourne, Vic. 3000, Australia.

914.2 388.3 UK
CARAVAN FACTFINDER. 1972. a. £2.20. Link House Magazines Ltd., Link House, Dingwall Ave., Croydon CR9 2TA, England. Ed. B. Williams.
Incorporating: Caravan Yearbook (ISSN 0069-0333)

914 UK
CARAVAN INDUSTRY DIRECTORY. a. £5.75 (includes Caravan Industry & Park Operator) A. E. Morgan Publications Ltd., Stanley House, 9 West St., Epsom, Surrey KT18 7RL, England.

910.2 914 UK
CARAVAN SITES. 1955. a. £1.95. Link House Magazines Ltd., Link House, Dingwall Ave., Croydon CR9 2TA, England. Ed. B. Williams.
Formerly: Caravan Sites and Mobile Home Parks (ISSN 0069-0309)

919.704 US
CARIBBEAN, BERMUDA, AND THE BAHAMAS (YEAR) a. $11.95. Houghton Mifflin Co., Birnbaum Travel Guides, 60 E. 42nd St., Ste. 1624, New York, NY 10165. TEL 212-682-9440. Ed. Stephen Birnbaum.

919.704 BB
CARIBBEAN TOURISM STATISTICAL REPORT. 1978. a. $20. Caribbean Tourism Research Center, Mervue, Marine Gardens, Christ Church, Barbados, W. Indies. circ. 1,000.
Formerly: Caribbean Tourism Statistics.

796 917.1 CN
CATALOGUE OF CANADIAN RECREATION AND LEISURE RESEARCH. 1973. every 2-3 years. price varies. Ontario Research Council on Leisure, 77 Bloor St. W., 8th Floor, Toronto, Ont. M7A 2R9, Canada. circ. 5,000.

918 CJ
CAYMAN ISLANDS HOLIDAY GUIDE. 1972. a. $2. (Department of Tourism) Northwester Company Ltd., P.O. Box 243, George Town, Grand Cayman, British West Indies. Ed. Desmond Seales. circ. 200,000.

910.202 UY
CENTAUR. 1977. a. Centro Automovilista del Uruguay, Artigas 1773, Montevideo, Uruguay. Ed. Ever Cabrera Tornielli. adv.

CENTUR. see TRANSPORTATION — Automobiles

914.2 UK
CHERWELL GUIDE TO OXFORD. 1948. a. £1.80. Oxford Student Publications Ltd., Frewin Court, Cornmarket, Oxford OX1 2ED, England. Eds. James Lofthouse, Emily Bell. circ. 9,000.

910.2 914 UK ISSN 0069-3456
CHILDREN WELCOME; happy family holiday guide. 1956. a. £1. ‡ F.H.G. Publications Ltd., Abbey Mill Business Centre, Seedhill, Paisley PA1 1JN, Scotland. Ed. Peter Clark. index.

910.4 US ISSN 0277-0342
CITYGUIDE - THE SAN FRANCISCO BAY AREA AND NORTHERN CALIFORNIA. 1978. a. $5.95. Danella Publications, Box C, Sausalito, CA 94966. TEL 415-332-9601. Ed. Bella Levin. adv. circ. 40,000. (back issues avail.)

910.2 UK
COACHES & PARTIES WELCOME. 1977. a. free to qualified personnel. Lewis Productions Ltd., 31 Castle St., Kingston upon Thames, Surrey KT1 1ST, England. Ed. Rosemary Bray. adv. circ. 40,000.

CONFERENCES MEETINGS & EXHIBITIONS WELCOME. see MEETINGS AND CONGRESSES

974 US
CONNECTICUT VACATION GUIDE. 1968. a. free. Department of Economic Development, 210 Washington St., Hartford, CT 06106. Ed. Barbara J. Beeching. circ. 250,000.

917 US
CONNECTICUT WEST. 1970. a. $2. Foothills Trader, Inc., Central Ave., New Hartford, CT 06057. TEL 203-379-7517. Ed. Lillian J. Ludlam. adv. bibl. circ. 20,000.

CONNEXIONS; address book of alternative projects. see LITERARY AND POLITICAL REVIEWS

914.7 388 UK
CONTINENTAL MOTORING HOLIDAYS. 1972. a. 50. Contemporary Press Ltd., 21A Alma Square, London NW8 9QA, England. Ed. Brian Hedges.

910.202 UK
CONVENTION LONDON. a. Where Publications, 55-57 Great Marlborough St., London W1V 1DD, England. Ed. Y. French. circ. 30,000.

914.2 UK
CORNWALL BLUE BOOK GUIDE AND COUNTY HANDBOOK. 1927. a. E.J. Hubber, Ed. & Pub., 17 Mellanurawe Lane, Newquay, Cornwall, England. adv. circ. 20,000.

910.4 382 CY
CYPRUS. TOURISM ORGANISATION. ANNUAL REPORT. a. Tourism Organisation, Nicosia, Cyprus. charts. stat.

910.2 GW ISSN 0078-3943
D C C - CAMPING FUEHRER EUROPA. 1950. a. DM.19.80. (Deutscher Camping Club e.V.) D C C-Wirtschaftsdienst und Verlag GmbH, Postfach 400428, 8000 Munich 40, W. Germany (B.R.D.) adv. circ. 50,000.

796.5 GW
D C C - TOURISTIK SERVICE. a. (Deutscher Camping Club e.V.) D C C - Wirtschaftsdienst und Verlag GmbH, Postfach 400428, 8000 Munich 40, W. Germany (B.R.D.) adv.

TRAVEL AND TOURISM 1107

914.8 DK ISSN 0109-6125
DANMARKS TURIST VEJVISER. (Text in Danish, English and German) 1984. a. Kr.40.10. Glumsoe Bogtrykkeri, Noeddevej 10, 4171 Glumsoe, Denmark. illus.

DETROIT NEWS TRAVEL DIRECTORY. see TRANSPORTATION — Air Transport

914.8 DK ISSN 0107-8720
DEUTSCHER VOLKSKALENDER NORDSCHLESWIG. 1924. a. Kr.25. Deutscher Schul- und Sprachverein fuer Nordschleswig, Joergensgaard 5, 6200 Aabenraa, Denmark. illus. circ. 2,500.

910.4 UK
DEVON TOURISM REVIEW. 1981. a. £0.50 per no. Devon County Council, Property Department, Amentities and Countryside Division, County Hall, Topsham Rd., Exeter EX2 4QQ, England. Ed. Lesley Garlick. illus. charts. circ. 500.
Former titles (until 1985): Devon. Property Department. Tourism and Recreation. Annual Report & Devon County Planning Department. Tourism and Recreation. Annual Report (ISSN 0261-2445)

910.202 US
DIRECTORY OF COUNTRY CLUBS. 1987. a. $249. Chain Store Guide, 425 Park Ave, New York, NY 10022. TEL 212-371-9400.

910.09 US
DIRECTORY OF FREE VACATION & TRAVEL INFORMATION. 1977. irreg. $3.95. Pilot Books, 103 Cooper St., Babylon, NY 11702. TEL 516-422-2225. Ed. Raymond Carlson.
Formerly (until 1985): National Directory of Free Vacation and Travel Information.

910.09 US ISSN 0732-6572
DIRECTORY OF INCENTIVE TRAVEL INTERNATIONAL. 1977. a. $25. Harcourt Brace Jovanovich, Inc., 7500 Old Oak Blvd., Cleveland, OH 44130 TEL 216-243-8100. (Subscr. address: 1 E. First Ave., Duluth, MN 55802) Ed. Connie Goldstein. adv. bk. rev. circ. 40,061.
Former titles: Incentive Travel International; Directory of Incentive Travel International.

910 US
DIRECTORY OF LOW COST VACATIONS WITH A DIFFERENCE. 1986. irreg. $4.95. Pilot Books, 103 Cooper St., Babylon, NY 11702. TEL 516-422-2225. Ed. J. Crawford.

917 UK
DISCOVER NORTH AMERICA. 1980. a. free to qualified personnel. Discovery Press, 33-35 Crouch End Hill, London N8 8DH, England. Ed. Carol Chester. circ. 25,000.
Former titles (until 1986): Holiday U.S.A. and Canada Magazine; Holiday U.S.A.

915.204 UK
DISCOVER THE FAR EAST. 1986. a. Discovery Press, 33-35 Crouch End Hill, London N8 8DH, England. Ed. John Samson.

910.202 US ISSN 0277-8416
DISCOVERICARD DIRECTORY OF CITIES AND HOTELS.* 1980. a. $35. International Travel Resources, Inc., c/o Timothy J. Gaffney, Ed., Box 2675, Iowa City, IA 52244-2675. circ. 5,000.
Formerly: Discoveramericard Directory of Cities and Hotels.

917.904 US
DISNEYLAND (YEAR) a. $5.95. Houghton Mifflin Co., Birnbaum Travel Guides, 60 E. 42nd St, Ste. 1624, New York, NY 10165. TEL 212-682-9440. Ed. Stephen Birnbaum.

917.2 UK
DISNEYLAND ANNUAL. 1983. a. £3.25. World International Publishing Co., P.O. Box 111, Gt. Ducie St., Manchester, M60 3BL, England. Ed. Mae Broadley. adv.

DOMOVA POKLADNICA. see LITERATURE

910.202 US
DUDE RANCH MAGAZINE/DIRECTORY. 1935. a. $1. Dude Ranchers Association, Box 471, La Porte, CO 80535. TEL 303-493-7623. Ed. Amey E. Grubbs. circ. 10,000. (back issues avail.)

TRAVEL AND TOURISM

910.4 US
DUDE RANCHER. 1930. a. $1. Dude Ranchers Association, Box 471, LaPorte, CO 80535. TEL 303-493-7623. Ed. Amey Grubbs. adv. bk. rev. circ. 10,000. (back issues avail.)

DUTY & TAX-FREE SHOP WORLD GUIDE SERIES. VOL. 4: BEST "N" MOST IN D F S. see *BUSINESS AND ECONOMICS — International Commerce*

914.2 UK
EAST ANGLIA GUIDE. 1973. a. £1.75. East Anglia Tourist Board, Toppesfield Hall, Hadleigh, Suffolk, England. Ed. Mrs. E. Woolnough. adv. circ. 45,000.

917 796.5 US ISSN 0363-2091
EASTERN CANADA CAMPBOOK. Cover title: R V and Tent Sites in New Brunswick, Newfoundland, Nova Scotia, Ontario, Prince Edward Island, Quebec. a. membership. American Automobile Association, 8111 Gatehouse Rd., Falls Church, VA 22047. TEL 703-222-6000. circ. 234,000.
   Formerly (until 1980): Eastern Canada Camping.

910.202 910.03 US
ECONOMIC IMPACT OF THE NEGRO TRAVELER. 1963. biennial. $102.50. Travelers' Research Publishing Co., Inc., 11717 S. Vincennes Ave., Chicago, IL 60643. TEL 312-881-3712. Ed. Clarence M. Markham, Jr. stat. circ. 10,000. (tabloid format; back issues avail.)
   Formerly: Impact of the Negro Traveler.

910.09 US ISSN 0733-642X
ECONOMIC REVIEW OF TRAVEL IN AMERICA. a. $55. U S Travel Data Center, 1899 L St., N.W., Washington, DC 20036. TEL 202-293-1040. (reprint service avail. from CIS)
   Formerly: Travel in America.

910.2 338.4 SP ISSN 0070-864X
ECONOMIC REVIEW OF WORLD TOURISM. (Editions in English, French and Spanish) biennial. $24. World Tourism Organization, Capitan Haya 42, 28020 Madrid, Spain.

EGON RONAY'S GUIDE TO 500 GOOD RESTAURANTS IN MAJOR CITIES OF EUROPE. see *HOTELS AND RESTAURANTS*

918.1 BL
EMPRESA BRASILEIRA DE TURISMO. ANUARIO ESTATISTICO. 1970. a. (with supplement) price varies. Empresa Brasileira de Turismo, Rua Mariz e Barros 13, Rio de Janeiro 20270, Brazil. stat.

918.104 BL
EMPRESA BRASILEIRA DE TURISMO. CALENDARIO TURISTICO. English edition: Empresa Brasileira de Turismo. Tourist Calendar. a. free. Empresa Brasileira de Turismo, Rua Mariz e Barros 13, Rio de Janeiro 20270, Brazil.

914.2 US
ENGLAND AND SCOTLAND ON TWENTY-FIVE DOLLARS A DAY. 1980. a. $9.95. Frommer-Pasmantier Publishing Corp., 1230 Ave. of the Americas, New York, NY 10020. TEL 212-245-6400. Eds. S. Haggart, D. Porter.
   Former titles: England and Scotland on Twenty Dollars a Day (ISSN 0271-3977); Supersedes: England on Fifteen Dollars a Day.

914.2 UK ISSN 0267-3398
ENGLAND'S BEST HOLIDAYS. 1974. a. £1. F.H.G. Publications Ltd., Abbey Mill Business Centre, Seedhill, Paisley PA1 1JN, Scotland.

914 385 US ISSN 0085-0330
EURAIL GUIDE; how to travel Europe and all the world by train. 1971. a. $12.95. Eurail Guide Annual, 27540 Pacific Coast Highway, Malibu, CA 90265. TEL 213-457-7286. Eds. Kathryn S. Turpin, Marvin L. Saltzman.

EUROPA CAMPING UND CARAVANING. INTERNATIONALER FUEHRER. see *SPORTS AND GAMES — Outdoor Life*

910.202 IT
EUROPA FACILE; notizie pratiche per il turista. 1971. biennial, latest edt. 1986-87. L.7000 to non-members. Touring Club Italiano, Corso Italia 10, 20122 Milan, Italy. adv. illus. circ. 50,000.
   Continues: Touring Club Italiano. Servizio Informazioni Turistiche. Fascicoli di Documentazione per i Viaggi in Europa.

914 US
EUROPE (YEAR) a. $13.95. Houghton Mifflin Co., Birnbaum Travel Guides, 60 E. 42nd St., Ste. 1624, New York, NY 10165. TEL 212-682-9440. Ed. Stephen Birnbaum. Indexed: P.A.I.S.

914 US
EUROPE FOR BUSINESS TRAVELERS. a. $7.95. Houghton Mifflin Co., Birnbaum Travel Guides, 60 E. 42nd St., Ste. 1624, New York, NY 10165. TEL 212-682-9440. Ed. Stephen Birnbaum.

910.202 US
EUROPE ON TWENTY-FIVE DOLLARS A DAY. a. $10.95. Frommer-Pasmantier Publishing Corp., 1230 Ave. of the Americas, New York, NY 10020.
   Formerly: Europe on Fifteen Dollars a Day.

EXPLORATION; journal on the literature of exploration and travel. see *LITERATURE*

977 US
EXPLORE MINNESOTA ARTS AND ATTRACTIONS. biennial. free. Office of Tourism, 375 Jackson St., Ste. 250, St. Paul, MN 55101. circ. 100,000.
   Formerly: Minnesota Arts and Attractions Guide.

917.704 US
EXPLORE MINNESOTA BED AND BREAKFAST/ HISTORIC INNS. a. free. Office of Tourism, 375 Jackson St., Ste. 205, St. Paul, MN 55101. circ. 50,000.

EXPLORE MINNESOTA BIKING. see *SPORTS AND GAMES — Bicycles And Motorcycles*

917 796.5 US
EXPLORE MINNESOTA CAMPGROUNDS. 1984. a. free. Minnesota Office of Tourism, 375 Jackson St., 250 Skyway Level, St. Paul, MN 55101. TEL 612-296-5029. Ed. Bonnie Richter. circ. 100,000.
   Formerly: Camping Guide.

917.704 796 US
EXPLORE MINNESOTA CANOEING, BACKPACKING & HIKING. triennial. free. Office of Tourism, 375 Jackson St., Ste. 205, St. Paul, MN 55101. circ. 50,000.

910 917.047 US
EXPLORE MINNESOTA MINNETOURS. triennial. free. Office of Tourism, 375 Jackson St., Ste. 205, St. Paul, MN 55101. circ. 100,000.

917 796.93 US
EXPLORE MINNESOTA ON SKIS. a. free. Office of Tourism, 375 Jackson St., Ste. 205, St. Paul, MN 55101. circ. 53,000.
   Formerly: Guide to Skiing in Minnesota; Incorporating: Guide to Downhill Skiing in Minnesota; Guide to Cross Country Skiing in Minnesota.

914.4 UK
EXPLORING FRANCE. 1981. irreg. £4.95. Jarrold Colour Publications, Barrack Street, Norwich, NR3 1TR, England. Ed. Peter Titchmarsh.

910.09 US ISSN 0429-9639
FABULOUS MEXICO; where everything costs less. biennial. $2.50 per issue. Harian Publications, One Vernon Ave., Floral Park, NY 11001. TEL 516-437-3440.

FACTS AND ADVICE FOR AIRLINE PASSENGERS. see *TRANSPORTATION — Air Transport*

919 FK ISSN 0256-1824
FALKLAND ISLANDS JOURNAL. (Text in English) 1967. a. 60p. price varies. ‡ Lois Cottage, Stanley, Falkland Islands, South Atlantic. Ed.Bd. illus. circ. 400.

910.202 UK
FAMILY GUIDE ON WHERE TO GO. 1976. a. £2.25. Jarrold Colour Publications, Barrack St., Norwich NR3 1TR, England. Ed. Peter Titchmarsh. circ. 10,000.

910.2 UK ISSN 0071-3740
FAMILY HOLIDAY GUIDE. 1953. a. £1.25. ‡ Lewis Productions Ltd., 31 Castle St., Kingston Upon Thames, Surrey KT1 1ST, England. Ed. Jonathan Lewis. adv. circ. 75,000.

914.2 UK
FARM & COUNTRY HOLIDAYS. 1969. a. £1.10. Pastime Publications Ltd., 15 Dublin Street Lane South, Edinburgh EH1 3PX, Scotland. adv.

914.2 UK
FARM HOLIDAY GUIDE (ENGLAND, WALES & IRELAND) 1946. a. £1.50. F.H.G. Publications Ltd., Abbey Mill Business Centre, Seedhill, Paisley PA1 1JN, Scotland.
   Formed by the merger of: Farm Holiday Guide (England Edition) (ISSN 0267-2871) & Farm Holiday Guide (Wales Edition) (ISSN 0267-2898)

914.1 UK ISSN 0267-288X
FARM HOLIDAY GUIDE (SCOTLAND EDITION) a. £1.25. F.H.G. Publications Ltd., Abbey Mill Business Centre, Seedhill, Paisley PA1 1JN, Scotland.

914.2 IE
FARM HOLIDAYS IN IRELAND. 1970. a. $4. Libra House Ltd., Box 1127, Dublin 8, Ireland. TEL (01) 753935. Ed. Cathal Tyrrell. adv. illus. circ. 53,370.

796 US ISSN 0195-8437
FARM, RANCH AND COUNTRY VACATIONS. 1949. biennial. $9.95. Farm and Ranch Vacations, Inc., 36 E. 57 St., New York, NY 10022. TEL 212-355-6334. Ed. Pat Dickerman.
   Former titles: Country Vacations U.S.A. (ISSN 0147-3867); Farm, Ranch and Country Vacations; Farm, Ranch and Countryside Guide; Farm and Ranch Vacation Guide (ISSN 0085-0438)

912.16 US ISSN 0192-1347
FASTFACTS EUROPEAN HOTEL LOCATOR. 1978. a. $75. Denhamwood, Inc., 4069 Hayvenhurst Ave., Encino, CA 91436. TEL 818-783-2758. illus.

647.94 US ISSN 0197-9477
FASTFACTS U S A HOTEL MOTEL LOCATOR. 1979. a. $85. Denhamwood, Inc., 4069 Hayvenhurst Ave., Encino, CA 91436. TEL 818-783-2758.

917 US
FESTIVALS SOURCEBOOK; a reference guide to fairs, festivals and celebrations in agriculture, antiques, the arts, theatre and drama, arts and crafts, community, dance, ethnic events, film, folk, food and drink, history, Indians, marine, music, seasons and wildlife. 1977. irreg., 2nd edt., 1984. $135. Gale Research Company, Book Tower, Detroit, MI 48226. TEL 313-961-2242. Eds. Paul Wasserman, Edmond L. Applebaum.

970 US ISSN 0739-0769
FIELDING'S BERMUDA AND THE BAHAMAS. 1983. a. $7.95. Fielding Travel Books (Subsidiary of: William Morrow and Company, Inc.) 105 Madison Ave., New York, NY 10016. TEL 212-889-3050. Ed. Randy Ladenheim. index.

910.2 US
FIELDING'S CARIBBEAN. 1968. a. $12.95. Fielding Travel Books (Subsidiary of: William Morrow and Company, Inc.) 105 Madison Ave., New York, NY 10016. TEL 212-889-3050. index.

970 US ISSN 0739-0750
FIELDING'S ECONOMY CARIBBEAN. 1983. a. $8.95. Fielding Travel Books (Subsidiary of: William Morrow and Company, Inc.) 105 Madison Ave., New York, NY 10016. TEL 212-889-3050.

910.2 US ISSN 0739-0785
FIELDING'S ECONOMY EUROPE. 1967. a. $9.95. Fielding Travel Books (Subsidiary of: William Morrow and Company, Inc.) 105 Madison Ave., New York, NY 10016.
   Formerly: Fielding's Low-Cost Europe (ISSN 0095-6406)

910.2 US ISSN 0192-5326
FIELDING'S EUROPE. 1948. a. $12.95. Fielding Travel Books (Subsidiary of: William Morrow and Company, Inc.) 105 Madison Ave., New York, NY 10016. TEL 212-889-3050. index.
   Formerly: Fielding's Travel Guide to Europe (ISSN 0071-4801)

972 US ISSN 0739-0793
FIELDING'S MEXICO. 1983. a. $12.95. Fielding Travel Books (Subsidiary of: William Morrow and Company, Inc.) 105 Madison Ave., New York, NY 10016. TEL 212-889-3050. index.

910.2 US ISSN 0071-478X
FIELDING'S SELECTIVE SHOPPING GUIDE TO EUROPE. 1957. a. $5.95. Fielding Travel Books (Subsidiary of: William Morrow and Company, Inc.) 105 Madison Ave., New York, NY 10016. TEL 212-889-3050. index.

FINANCIAL TIMES INTERNATIONAL YEAR BOOKS: WORLD HOTEL DIRECTORY. see HOTELS AND RESTAURANTS

338.4 US
FLORIDA'S VISITORS. 1973? a. Department of Commerce, Division of Tourism, 107 W. Gaines St., Tallahassee, FL 32304. TEL 904-488-7300.
   Florida Tourist Study (ISSN 0430-6953)

917.304 US ISSN 0271-2776
FODOR'S ALASKA. 1979. a. $8.95. Fodor's Travel Guides, 2 Park Ave., New York, NY 10016.

917.304 US
FODOR'S AMERICAN CITIES ON A BUDGET. 1971. a. $12.95. Fodor's Travel Guides, 2 Park Ave., New York, NY 10016. Ed. E. Fodor.
   Formerly: Fodor's Budget Travel in America (ISSN 0192-8287)

919.04 US ISSN 0191-2321
FODOR'S AUSTRALIA, NEW ZEALAND AND THE SOUTH PACIFIC. a. $14.95. Fodor's Travel Guides, 2 Park Ave., New York, NY 10016. illus.

910.2 US ISSN 0071-6340
FODOR'S AUSTRIA. 1951. a. $13.95. Fodor's Travel Guides, 2 Park Ave., New York, NY 10016. Ed. Eugene Fodor.

910.2 US
FODOR'S BAHAMAS. a. $6.95. Fodor's Travel Guides, 2 Park Ave., New York, NY 10016. Ed. Eugene Fodor.
   Supersedes in part: Fodor's Caribbean and Bahamas (ISSN 0271-4760)

951 US
FODOR'S BEIJING, GUANGZHOU AND SHANGHAI. a. $6.95. Fodor's Travel Guides, 2 Park Ave., New York, NY 10016.

910.2 US ISSN 0071-6359
FODOR'S BELGIUM AND LUXEMBOURG. 1951. biennial. $13.95. Fodor's Travel Guides, 2 Park Ave., New York, NY 10016. Ed. Eugene Fodor.

919.704 US
FODOR'S BERMUDA. 1979. a. $8.95. Fodor's Travel Guides, 2 Park Ave., New York, NY 10016.

917.4 US
FODOR'S BOSTON. 1984. a? $7.95. Fodor's Travel Guides, 2 Park Ave., New York, NY 10016.

918.104 US ISSN 0163-0628
FODOR'S BRAZIL. 1978. a. $6.95. Fodor's Travel Guides, 2 Park Ave., New York, NY 10016.

914.04 US ISSN 0197-4998
FODOR'S BUDGET EUROPE. 1980. a. $11.95. Fodor's Travel Guides, 2 Park Ave., New York, NY 10016.
   Formerly (1972-1979): Fodor's Europe on a Budget (ISSN 0276-0738)

914.204 US
FODOR'S BUDGET TRAVEL BRITAIN. 1979. a. $5.95. Fodor's Travel Guides, 2 Park Ave., New York, NY 10016.
   Formerly: Fodor's Budget Britain (ISSN 0193-2381)

917.104 US
FODOR'S BUDGET TRAVEL CANADA. 1982. a. $6.95. Fodor's Travel Guides, 2 Park Ave., New York, NY 10016.
   Formerly: Fodor's Budget Canada.

919.604 US
FODOR'S BUDGET TRAVEL CARIBBEAN. 1979. a. $6.95. Fodor's Travel Guides, 2 Park Ave., New York, NY 10016. Ed. E. Fodor.
   Formerly: Fodor's Budget Caribbean (ISSN 0193-9122)

914.4 US
FODOR'S BUDGET TRAVEL FRANCE. 1980. a? $5.95. Fodor's Travel Guides, 2 Park Ave., New York, NY 10016.
   Formerly: Fodor's Budget France (ISSN 0194-4150)

914.304 US
FODOR'S BUDGET TRAVEL GERMANY. 1979. a. $5.95. Fodor's Travel Guides, 2 Park Ave., New York, NY 10016.
   Formerly: Fodor's Budget Germany (ISSN 0193-9033)

910 US
FODOR'S BUDGET TRAVEL ITALY. irreg. $5.95. Fodor's Travel Guides, 2 Park Ave., New York, NY 10016. Ed. Richard Moore.
   Formerly: Fodor's Budget Italy (ISSN 0270-787X)

915.204 US
FODOR'S BUDGET TRAVEL JAPAN. 1980. a. $6.95. Fodor's Travel Guides, 2 Park Ave., New York, NY 10016.
   Formerly: Fodor's Budget Japan (ISSN 0276-2552)

917.204 US
FODOR'S BUDGET TRAVEL MEXICO. 1979. a. $5.95. Fodor's Travel Guides, 2 Park Ave., New York, NY 10016.
   Formerly: Fodor's Budget Mexico (ISSN 0196-1829)

914.604 US
FODOR'S BUDGET TRAVEL SPAIN. 1979. a. $5.95. Fodor's Travel Guides, 2 Park Ave., New York, NY 10016.
   Formerly: Fodor's Budget Spain (ISSN 0270-7888)

917.9 US ISSN 0192-9925
FODOR'S CALIFORNIA. irreg., latest 1985. $11.95. Fodor's Travel Guides, 2 Park Ave., New York, NY 10016. Ed. E. Fodor.

917.104 US ISSN 0160-3906
FODOR'S CANADA. 1978. a. $12.95. Fodor's Travel Guides, 2 Park Ave., New York, NY 10016.

917.404 US
FODOR'S CAPE COD. 1982. a. $8.95. Fodor's Travel Guides, 2 Park Ave., New York, NY 10016.

910.2 US
FODOR'S CARIBBEAN. 1962. a. $12.95. Fodor's Travel Guides, 2 Park Ave., New York, NY 10016. Ed. Eugene Fodor.
   Supersedes in part: Fodor's Caribbean and Bahamas (ISSN 0271-4760); Former titles: Fodor's Caribbean, Bahamas and Bermuda (ISSN 0098-2547); Fodor's Guide to the Caribbean, Bahamas and Bermuda (ISSN 0071-6561)

910 US ISSN 0270-8183
FODOR'S CENTRAL AMERICA; Belize, Costa Rica, El Salvador, Guatemala, Honduras, Nicaragua, Panama. irreg., latest 1980. $12.95. Fodor's Travel Guides, 2 Park Ave., New York, NY 10016. Ed. R.C. Fisher.

917.704 US
FODOR'S CHICAGO. 1982. a. $6.95. Fodor's Travel Guides, 2 Park Ave., New York, NY 10016.
   Formerly: Fodor's Chicago and the Great Lakes.

917.804 US ISSN 0276-9018
FODOR'S COLORADO. 1981. a. $7.95. Fodor's Travel Guides, 2 Park Ave., New York, NY 10016.

914.704 US
FODOR'S EASTERN EUROPE. 1980. a. $15.95. Fodor's Travel Guides, 2 Park Ave., New York, NY 10016.

916 US ISSN 0147-8176
FODOR'S EGYPT. 1977. a. $12.95. Fodor's Travel Guides, 2 Park Ave., New York, NY 10016. Ed. Eugene Fodor. illus.

917 US ISSN 0192-3730
FODOR'S FAR WEST. 1975. biennial. $11.95. Fodor's Travel Guides, 2 Park Ave., New York, NY 10016. Ed. Eugene Fodor. illus.

917.5 US ISSN 0193-9556
FODOR'S FLORIDA. irreg., 2nd edt. 1980. $9.95. Fodor's Travel Guides, 2 Park Ave., New York, NY 10017.

910.2 US ISSN 0071-6383
FODOR'S FRANCE. 1951. a. $13.95. Fodor's Travel Guides, 2 Park Ave., New York, NY 10016. Ed. Eugene Fodor.

910.2 US
FODOR'S GERMANY. 1951. a. $13.95. Fodor's Travel Guides, 2 Park Ave., New York, NY 10016. Ed. Eugene Fodor.
   Former titles: Fodor's Germany: West and East (ISSN 0192-0952); Fodor's Germany (ISSN 0071-6391)

910.2 US ISSN 0071-6405
FODOR'S GREAT BRITAIN. 1951. a. $13.95. Fodor's Travel Guides, 2 Park Ave., New York, NY 10016. Ed. Eugene Fodor.

910.2 US ISSN 0071-6413
FODOR'S GREECE. 1951. a. $13.95. Fodor's Travel Guides, 2 Park Ave., New York, NY 10016. Ed. Eugene Fodor.

910.2 US ISSN 0071-6421
FODOR'S HAWAII. 1961. a. $11.95. Fodor's Travel Guides, 2 Park Ave., New York, NY 10016. Ed. Eugene Fodor.

910.2 US ISSN 0071-643X
FODOR'S HOLLAND. 1951. biennial. $12.95. Fodor's Travel Guides, 2 Park Ave., New York, NY 10016.

915 US
FODOR'S HONG KONG AND MACAU. 1984. a. $9.95. Fodor's Travel Guides, 2 Park Ave., New York, NY 10016.

910.2 US ISSN 0276-5500
FODOR'S INDIA & NEPAL. 1963. biennial. $16.95. Fodor's Travel Guides, 2 Park Ave., New York, NY 10016.
   Formerly: Fodor's India (ISSN 0362-0212); Which superseded: Fodor's Guide to India (ISSN 0071-6456)

910.2 US ISSN 0071-6464
FODOR'S IRELAND. 1968. a. $12.95. Fodor's Travel Guides, 2 Park Ave., New York, NY 10016.

910.2 US ISSN 0071-6588
FODOR'S ISRAEL. 1967. a. $13.95. Fodor's Travel Guides, 2 Park Ave., New York, NY 10016.

910.2 US ISSN 0071-6472
FODOR'S ITALY. 1951. a. $13.95. Fodor's Travel Guides, 2 Park Ave., New York, NY 10016.

910.2 US
FODOR'S JAPAN. 1962. a. $14.95. Fodor's Travel Guides, 2 Park Ave., New York, NY 10016.
   Supersedes in part: Fodor's Japan and Korea (ISSN 0098-1613); Which superseded in part: Fodor's Japan and East Asia (ISSN 0071-6480)

910.2 US
FODOR'S KOREA. a? Fodor's Travel Guides, 2 Park Ave., New York, NY 10016.
   Supersedes in part: Fodor's Japan and Korea (ISSN 0098-1613); Which superseded in part: Fodor's Japan and East Asia (ISSN 0071-6480)

914.69 US
FODOR'S LISBON. 1984. a. $5.95. Fodor's Travel Guides, 2 Park Ave., New York, NY 10016.

910.2 US ISSN 0071-6596
FODOR'S LONDON. 1971. a. $8.95. Fodor's Travel Guides, New York, NY 10016.

914.6 US
FODOR'S MADRID. a? $5.95. Fodor's Travel Guides, 2 Park Ave., New York, NY 10016.

910.2 US ISSN 0071-6499
FODOR'S MEXICO. 1972. a. $13.95. Fodor's Travel Guides, 2 Park Ave., New York, NY 10016.

914.3 US
FODOR'S MUNICH. 1984. a? $5.95. Fodor's Travel Guides, 2 Park Ave., New York, NY 10016.

917 US ISSN 0192-3412
FODOR'S NEW ENGLAND. 1975. biennial. $10.95. Fodor's Travel Guides, 2 Park Ave., New York, NY 10016. Ed. E. Fodor. illus.

917 US
FODOR'S NEW YORK CITY. 1975. irreg. $8.95. Fodor's Travel Guides, 2 Park Ave., New York, NY 10016. illus.
Former titles: Fodor's New York; Fodor's New York & New Jersey.

916.104 US
FODOR'S NORTH AFRICA. 1980. a. $15.95. Fodor's Travel Guides, 2 Park Ave., New York, NY 10016.

917.9 US
FODOR'S PACIFIC NORTH COAST. 1984. a? $9.95. Fodor's Travel Guides, 2 Park Ave., New York, NY 10016.

914.4 US ISSN 0149-1288
FODOR'S PARIS. 1973. a. $8.95. Fodor's Travel Guides, 2 Park Ave., New York, NY 10016.

915.104 US ISSN 0192-2378
FODOR'S PEOPLE'S REPUBLIC OF CHINA. 1979. a. $15.95. Fodor's Travel Guides, 2 Park Ave., New York, NY 10016.

910.2 US ISSN 0071-6510
FODOR'S PORTUGAL. 1951. a. $12.95. Fodor's Travel Guides, 2 Park Ave., New York, NY 10016.

914.504 US ISSN 0276-2560
FODOR'S ROME. 1979. a. $8.95. Fodor's Travel Guides, 2 Park Ave., New York, NY 10016.

917.9 US
FODOR'S SAN DIEGO. a. $7.95. Fodor's Travel Guides, 2 Park Ave., New York, NY 10016.

917.904 US
FODOR'S SAN FRANCISCO. 1982. a. $7.95. Fodor's Travel Guides, 2 Park Ave., New York, NY 10016.

910.2 US ISSN 0071-6529
FODOR'S SCANDINAVIA. 1951. a. $14.95. Fodor's Travel Guides, 2 Park Ave., New York, NY 10016.

914.1 US
FODOR'S SCOTLAND. a. $10.95. Fodor's Travel Guides, 2 Park Ave., New York, NY 10016.

917 US ISSN 0147-8680
FODOR'S SOUTH. 1975. a. $12.95. Fodor's Travel Guides, 2 Park Ave., New York, NY 10016. Ed.Bd. illus.

910.2 US ISSN 0071-6537
FODOR'S SOUTH AMERICA. 1966. a. $14.95. Fodor's Travel Guides, 2 Park Ave., New York, NY 10016.

910.2 US ISSN 0160-8991
FODOR'S SOUTHEAST ASIA. 1975. a. $14.95. Fodor's Travel Guides, 2 Park Ave., New York, NY 10016.
Supersedes in part: Fodor's Japan and East Asia (ISSN 0071-6480)

914.7 US ISSN 0095-1358
FODOR'S SOVIET UNION. 1975. a. $15.95. Fodor's Travel Guides, 2 Park Ave., New York, NY 10016. Eds. E. Fodor, R.C. Fisher. illus.

910.2 US ISSN 0071-6545
FODOR'S SPAIN. 1955. a. $13.95. Fodor's Travel Guides, 2 Park Ave., New York, NY 10016. Ed. Eugene Fodor.

914.8 US
FODOR'S STOCKHOLM, COPENHAGEN, OSLO, HELSINKI & REYKJAVIK. a. $6.95. Fodor's Travel Guides, 2 Park Ave., New York, NY 10016.

910.2 US ISSN 0071-6553
FODOR'S SWITZERLAND. 1951. a. $13.95. Fodor's Travel Guides, 2 Park Ave., New York, NY 10016.

910.2 US ISSN 0071-6618
FODOR'S TURKEY. 1969. a. $14.95. Fodor's Travel Guides, 2 Park Ave., New York, NY 10016.

917 US ISSN 0147-8745
FODOR'S U S A. 1976. a. $14.95. Fodor's Travel Guides, 2 Park Ave., New York, NY 10016. Ed. E. Fodor. illus.

914.3 US
FODOR'S VIENNA. 1984. a. $5.95. Fodor's Travel Guides, 2 Park Ave., New York, NY 10016.

910.2 US ISSN 0071-657X
FODOR'S YUGOSLAVIA. 1951. a. $13.95. Fodor's Travel Guides, 2 Park Ave., New York, NY 10016.

387.2 US ISSN 0096-1353
FORD'S DECK PLAN GUIDE. Short title: Deck Plan Guide. 1974. irreg., (approx. a.) $50 per issue. Ford's Travel Guides, 19448 Londelius St., Northridge, CA 91324. TEL 818-701-7414. Ed. Judith A. Howard. illus. circ. 5,000.

914.404 US
FRANCE (YEAR) a. $11.95. Houghton Mifflin Co., Birnbaum Travel Guides, 60 E. 42nd St., Ste. 1624, New York, NY 10165. TEL 212-682-9440. Ed. Stephen Birnbaum.

910.2 FR ISSN 0071-8734
FRANCE EN POCHE. TOTAL GUIDE.* 1970. a. Editions Vrille-Copalic, 32 Boulevard Flandrin, Paris 16e, France.

910 AU ISSN 0071-948X
FREMDENVERKEHR IN OESTERREICH. (Subseries of: Beitraege zur Oesterreichischen Statistik) 1956/57. a. S.570. ‡ (Oesterreichisches Statistisches Zentralamt) Oesterreichische Staatsdruckerei, Rennweg 12a, 1037 Vienna, Austria. circ. 600.

914 UK
FRENCH FARM AND VILLAGE HOLIDAY GUIDE. 1976. a. £4.75($12.95) F.H.G. Publications Ltd., Abbey Mill Business Centre, Seedhill, Paisley PA1 1JN, Scotland. adv. illus. circ. 20,000.

916.204 US
FROMMER'S DOLLARWISE GUIDE TO EGYPT. 1980. biennial. $9.95. Frommer-Pasmantier Publishing Corp., 1230 Ave. of the Americas, New York, NY 10020. TEL 212-245-6400. Ed. Marilyn Wood.

914.3 US ISSN 0731-4442
FROMMER'S DOLLARWISE GUIDE TO GERMANY. biennial. Frommer-Pasmantier Publishing Corp., 1230 Ave. of the Americas, New York, NY 10020. TEL 212-245-6400. Ed. D. Porter.
Formerly: Arthur Frommer's Dollarwise Guide to Germany (ISSN 0272-0035)

914.509 US
FROMMER'S DOLLARWISE GUIDE TO ITALY. 1969. biennial. $10.95. Frommer-Pasmantier Publishing Corp., 1230 Ave. of the Americas, New York, NY 10020. TEL 212-245-6400. Ed. Marilyn Wood.

917.404 US
FROMMER'S DOLLARWISE GUIDE TO NEW ENGLAND. 1978. biennial. $9.95. Frommer-Pasmantier Publishing Corp., 1230 Ave. of the Americas, New York, NY 10020. TEL 212-245-6400. Ed. Marilyn Wood.

790 US
FUNPARKS DIRECTORY. Variant title: Amusement Business's Funparks Directory. 1961. a. $18. Billboard Publications, Inc., Amusement Business Division, Box 24970, Nashville, TN 37202. TEL 615-748-8100. Ed. Steve Rogers. adv. circ. 5,200. (also avail. in microfilm)
Formerly: Funspots Directory (ISSN 0071-9951)
Annual market report and directory of amusement parks, tourist attractions and zoos in North America

910.4 301.4157 UK
GAIA'S GUIDE. 1973. a. $9.50. 11 Northington St., London WC1, England. Ed. Sandy Horn. adv. bk. rev. circ. 8,000.

918.304 CL ISSN 0431-1930
GEOCHILE. 1951. irreg. (Sociedad Geografica de Chile) Lord Cochrane S.A., Providencia 711, Santiago, Chile. illus. Indexed: GeoRef.

914.104 UK
GLIMPSE OF LONDON WITH AMERICAN EXPRESS. 1965. a. free. (American Express International, US) Clarke & Hunter (London) Ltd., 11 Old Bond St., London W1X 3DB, England. Ed. Michael Cope. adv. circ. 85,000.

796.5 UK ISSN 0142-5978
GOOD CAMPS GUIDE. 1976. a. £1.60. Deneway Guides and Travel Ltd., Box 286, Rottingdean, Brighton, Sussex BN2 8AY, England. Ed. Alan Rogers. adv. circ. 25,000.

910.202 UK
GOOD VALUE GUIDE. 1979. a. £5.95. Macdonald Orbis, Greater London House, Third Fl., Hampstead Rd., London NW1 7QX, X. (Co-publisher: Routiers Ltd.) Ed. Joanna Gray. circ. 17,500.
Formerly: British Relais Routiers Guide.

GOURMETOUR; gastronomy & travel guide. see *HOTELS AND RESTAURANTS*

914.204 US
GREAT BRITAIN AND IRELAND (YEAR) a. $11.95. Houghton Mifflin Co., Birnbaum Travel Guides, 60 E. 42nd St., Ste. 1624, New York, NY 10165. TEL 212-682-9440. Ed. Stephen Birnbaum.

914.95 GR ISSN 0432-6105
GREECE. (Text in English) 1950. a. National Tourist Organisation of Greece, General Direction of Promotion, Odos Amerikis 2, Athens, Greece. illus.

914.2 388 UK
GUESTHOUSES, FARMHOUSES AND INNS IN BRITAIN. a. £5.95 to non-members. Automobile Association, Fanum House, Basingstoke, Hants RG21 2EA, England. adv.
Formerly: Automobile Association. Budget Guide.

647 SP
GUIA DE HOTELES: ESPANA.* (Includes some material in English, French, German, Italian, Portuguese and Swedish) a. 350 ptas. Empresa Nacional de Turismo, Velazquez 47, 28001 Madrid, Spain. illus.
Continues: Hoteles de Spana; Guia Oficial Abreviada.

910.202 SP
GUIA DE VALENCIA: TURISTICA, URBANA, COMERCIAL. 1960. a. 225 ptas. Ediciones Gaisa, Gran via Marques de Turia 64, Valencia 5, Spain. Ed. S. L. Gaisa. illus. circ. 3,000.

917.204 HO
GUIA OFICIAL DE CENTRO-AMERICA. 1922. irreg. Apartado 494, Tegucigalpa, Honduras.

910.202 BL
GUIA QUATRO RODAS. BRAZIL. 1965. a. Editora Abril S A., Av. Otaviano Alves de Lima 4,400, Sao Paulo, Brazil. Ed. Victor Civita. adv. charts. illus. stat. circ. 280,000.

910.202 796.5 BL
GUIA QUATRO RODAS. CAMPING. 1980. a. $3.03 per. no. Editora Abril S A., Av. Otavian Alves de Lima 4,400, Sao Paulo, Brazil. Ed. Victor Civita. adv. charts. illus. stat. circ. 37,000.

910.202 BL
GUIA QUATRO RODAS. RIO DE JANEIRO. 1973. a. Editora Abril Ltda., Av. Otaviano Alves de Lima 4,400, Sao Paulo, Brazil. Ed. Victor Civita. adv. charts. illus. stat. circ. 42,000.

910.202 BL
GUIA QUATRO RODAS. RODOVIARIO. 1976. a. Editora Abril Ltda., Av. Otaviano Alves de Lima 4, 400, Sao Paulo, Brazil. Ed. Victor Civita. adv. charts. illus. stat. circ. 106,000.

910.202　　　BL
GUIA QUATRO RODAS. SAO PAULO. 1973. a. Editora Abril S A., Av. Otaviano Alves de Lima 4400, Sao Paulo, Brazil. Ed. Victor Civita. adv. charts. illus. stat. circ. 206,000.

910.202　　　BL
GUIA QUATRO RODAS. SUL. 1976. a. Editora Abril S A, Av. Otaviano Alves de Lima 4,400, Sao Paulo, Brazil. Ed. Victor Civita. adv. charts. illus. stat. circ. 39,000.

918.704　　　VE
GUIA TURISTICA DE CARACAS, LITORAL Y VENEZUELA.* a. (Camara Nacional de Turismo) Corporacion de Turismo Venezuela, Centro Capriles, 7o, Plaza Venezuela, Apdo. 50200, Caracas, Venezuela.

918.104　　　AG
GUIA TURISTICA DE ROSARIO Y SANTE FE. vol. 13, 1975. irreg. Talleres Graficos Amalevi, Calle Mendoza 1851, Rosario, Santa Fe, Argentina. Ed. Rafael Vinas Paris. adv. illus.

796　　　IT
GUIDA DELLO SCIATORE. no. 12, 1969/70. a. (Federazione Italiana Sport Invernali) Milano Sole Editore, Via Denti 2, 20133 Milan, Italy. adv.

914.504　　　IT　ISSN 0487-3750
GUIDA SARDEGNA D'OGGI. Title varies: Sardegna d'oggi; Guida Practica. 1955. irreg., 7th, 1976. L.4800. Poliedrica Editrice, Plaza Bologna 1 bis, Rome, Italy. charts. illus.

910.202　　　DK　ISSN 0106-3022
GUIDE I JYLLAND. 1979. a. Kr.28.50. Bureau Vildmosen, Solvej 5, 9293 Kongerslev, Denmark. illus.

916.2　　　UK
GUIDE TO CAIRO. 1985. irreg. £5.95. Michael Haag Ltd., P.O. Box 369, London NW3 4ER, England.

910　　　US
GUIDE TO CANADA. 1972. a. Rand McNally & Co., 8225 N. Central Pk., Skokie, IL 60076 (Orders to: Box 7600, Chicago, IL 60680) Ed. Len Hilts.
Formerly: Explore Canada (ISSN 0085-0373)

796.5　　　UK　ISSN 0267-3355
GUIDE TO CARAVAN AND CAMPING HOLIDAYS. 1975. a. £1.25. F.H.G. Publications Ltd., Abbey Mill Business Centre, Seedhill, Paisley PA1 1JN, Scotland.

910.202　　　US
GUIDE TO CRUISING THE CHESAPEAKE BAY. 1974. a. $19.95. Chesapeake Bay Communications, Inc., 1819 Bay Ridge Ave., Annapolis, MD 21403. TEL 301-263-2662. Ed. Ann Hayes.

916.7　　　UK
GUIDE TO EAST AFRICA. 1984. irreg. £5.95. Michael Haag Ltd., P.O. Box 369, London NW3 4ER, England.

916.2　　　UK
GUIDE TO EGYPT. 1981. irreg. £8.95. Michael Haag Ltd., Box 369, London NW3 4ER, England.
Formerly: Travelaid Guide to Egypt.

914.9　　　UK
GUIDE TO GREECE. 1978. irreg. £7.95. Michael Haag Ltd., Box 369, London NW3 4ER, England.
Formerly: Travelaid Guide to Greece.

910.09　　　UK
GUIDE TO PARTY BOOKING. a. British Leisure Publications, Windsor Court, East Grinstead, West Sussex RH19 1XA, England. circ. 12,000.
Formerly: A B C Guide to Party Booking.

910.202　　　UK
GULF GUIDE & DIARY. 1972. a. $15. World of Information, 21 Gold St., Saffron Walden, Essex CB10 1EJ, England. Ed. Richard Green. adv. illus. circ. 10,000.

GUT ESSEN/EATS & TREATS; hospitality in Frankfurt and Rhine Main Area. see *HOTELS AND RESTAURANTS*

915.1　　　KO
HANDBOOK OF KOREA. 1978. a. Korean Overseas Information Service, Ministry of Culture and Information, Sejongno 1, Seoul, S. Korea.

919.604　　　US
HAWAII (YEAR) a. $11.95. Houghton Mifflin Co., Birnbaum Travel Guides, 60 E. 42nd St., Ste 1624, New York, NY 10165. Ed. Stephen Birnbaum.

919
HAWAII ON 35 DOLLARS A DAY. a. $9.95. Frommer-Pasmantier Publishing Corp., 1230 Ave. of the Americas, New York, NY 10020. TEL 212-245-6400.
Former titles: Hawaii on 25 Dollars a Day (ISSN 0197-8527); Hawaii on 20 Dollars a Day.

919.69　　　US　ISSN 0066-412X
HAWAII VISITORS BUREAU. ANNUAL RESEARCH REPORT. 1953. a. $100 to non-members. Hawaii Visitors Bureau, 2270 Kalakaua Ave., Honolulu, HI 96815. TEL 808-923-1811. Ed. Evelyn K. Richardson. circ. 4,000.

854　　　II
HELLO DELHI. a. Newspread International, E-2 Greater Kailash II, New Delhi 0048, India.

HERALD CARAVANNING GUIDE. see *SPORTS AND GAMES — Outdoor Life*

914.2　　　UK　ISSN 0267-3371
HERITAGE BRITAIN. WHERE TO VISIT: WHERE TO STAY. 1984. a. £1.50. F.H.G. Publications Ltd., Abbey Mill Business Centre, Seedhill, Paisley PA1 1JN, Scotland.

914.204　　　UK
HOLIDAY HAUNTS IN GREAT BRITAIN. a. £1.95. Brittain Publications, 137 George Lane, South Woodfurd, London E18, England. Ed. Rachael McLeod.

910.2　　　UK
HOLIDAY HINTS HANDBOOK. 1960. a. 75p. Hoseasons Holidays, Sunway House, Oulton Broad, Lowestoft, Suffolk NR32 3LT, England.
Former titles: Norfolk Holiday Handbook (ISSN 0078-1150); Norfolk Holiday Hints Handbook.

914.2　　　UK
HOLIDAY HOMES, COTTAGES & APARTMENTS IN BRITAIN. a. £5.95 to non-members. Automobile Association, Fanum House, Basingstoke, Hants. RG21 2EA, England.
Former titles: Self-Catering in Britain; Guide to Holiday Houses, Cottages and Chalets.

914.204　　　UK
HOLIDAY ISLANDER. 1976. a. free. South News Publications, Box 1, Hayling Island PO11 9RL, England. Ed. Robert Godfrey. adv. bk. rev. circ. 10,000.
Former titles: Hayling Islander; (until 1984): Hayling Island Magazine.

914.204　　　UK
HOLIDAY NEWS SERIES. 1973. a. £0.10. Shoreham Publishing Co. Ltd., 87 Gloucester Rd., Brighton, East Sussex, England. Ed. Spencer Eade.

914.2　　　UK　ISSN 0266-4429
HOLIDAY PARKS. 1983. a. £1.50. Stone Industrial Publications Ltd., Andrew Hse., 2a Granville Road, Sidcup, Kent DA14 4BN, England. Ed. Robert Griffits. circ. 60,000.

914　　　UK　ISSN 0073-3024
HOLIDAYS IN BRITAIN. 1924. a. £1.95. Brittain Publications, 137 George Lane, South Woodfurd, London E18, England. Ed. Rachael McLeod. index.

HOLY PLACES OF PALESTINE. see *RELIGIONS AND THEOLOGY*

910.09　　　HO
HONDURAS. CONSEJO SUPERIOR DE PLANIFICACION ECONOMICA. PLAN OPERATIVO ANUAL. SECTOR TURISMO. a. Consejo Superior de Planificacion Economica, Secretaria Tecnica, Tegucigalpa, Honduras.

915　　　HK
HONG KONG STREETS AND PLACES. (Text in Chinese and English) no. 2, 1978. irreg. HK.$47. Government Land Surveyor, Buildings and Lands Department, Survey Mapping Office, Murray Bldg., Garden Rd., Hong Kong, Hong Kong. circ. 2,000.

910.2　　　UK
HOSEASONS BOATING HOLIDAYS. 1946. a. free. Hoseasons Holidays, Sunway House, Oulton Broad, Lowestoft, Suffolk NR32 3LT, England.
Formerly: Hoseasons Holiday Boats and Bungalows Hire (ISSN 0073-3431)

910.202　　　UK
HOSEASONS HOLIDAY-HOMES IN U.K. 1946. a. free. (Hoseasons Holidays) Sunway House, Lowestoft NR32 3LT, England. Ed. James Hoseason. circ. 1,000,000.
Formerly: Hoseasons Holiday-Homes.

647.94　　　US
HOSTELING HOLIDAYS. 1956. a. free. American Youth Hostels, Inc., Metropolitan New York Council, 75 Spring St., New York, NY 10012. TEL 212-431-7100. Ed. Chuck Reif. adv. circ. 65,000.

647　　　US
HOTELS & TOURISM: LATIN AMERICAN INDUSTRIAL REPORT. (Avail. for each of 22 Latin American countries) 1985. a. $435 per country report per industry covered. Aurora International, Box 9099, Bridgeport, CT 06601-2099. TEL 203-368-0579. Ed. Andres C. Aquino.

919　　　BF
HOTELS, MOTELS AND GUEST HOUSES IN NEW PROVIDENCE AND PARADISE ISLAND. 1980. a. B.$2. Ministry of Finance, Department of Statistics, Box N 3904, Nassau, Bahamas.

338.4　　　US
I C T A DIRECTORY. 1969. a. membership. Institute of Certified Travel Agents, 148 Linden St., Box 56, Wellesley, MA 02181. TEL 617-237-0280. Ed. Patricia Kane. circ. 13,000.
Formerly: I C T A Roster (ISSN 0094-3517)

917.04　　　US
I LOVE NEW YORK: THE FINGER LAKES TRAVEL GUIDE. 1951. a. $1.25. Finger Lakes Association, Inc., 309 Lake Street, Penn Yan, NY 14527. TEL 315-536-7488. Ed. Thelma Oswald. adv. circ. 65,000.
Formerly: Finger Lakes Travel Guide.

910.2　　　UK
I T M YEARBOOK. 1975. a. £7($9.30) (Institute of Travel Managers) J. Offord (Publications) Ltd., 12 The Avenue, Eastbourne, E. Sussex BN21 3YA, England. adv. circ. 1,500.

917　　　US
ILLINOIS TRAVEL AND RECREATION GUIDE. a. Rockford Map Publishers, Inc., 4525 Forest View Ave., Box 6126, Rockford, IL 61125.

910.09　　　US　ISSN 0730-9813
IMPACT OF TRAVEL ON STATE ECONOMIES. 1976. a. $60. U S Travel Data Center, 1899 L St., N.W., Washington, DC 20036. TEL 202-293-1040. (reprint service avail. from CIS)

914　382　　　US
INFORMATION MOSCOW, WESTERN EDITION. 1978. a. $15. U S Information Moscow, 3220 Sacramento St., San Francisco, CA 94115. TEL 415-922-2422. Eds. Anya Kucharev, Jocelyn Stoller. adv. bk. rev. bibl. charts. illus. tr.lit. circ. 7,000. (back issues avail.)
Former titles: U S Information Moscow & Information Moscow (ISSN 0163-5093)

917.204　　　CR
INSTITUTO COSTARRICENSE DE TURISMO. MEMORIA ANUAL. a. Instituto Costarricense de Turismo, San Jose, Costa Rica. illus.

917 642.5　　　CN
INTERNATIONAL GUIDE. 1977. a. Can.$6.95. Wake Holdings Ltd., Suite 111, 999 8th St., N.W., Calgary, Alta T2R 1J5, Canada. Ed. Bryan W. Johnstone. adv. circ. 25,000.

910.202　　　UK　ISSN 0268-5671
INTERNATIONAL MEETING PLACE; a guide to international conference & exhibition locations. 1986. a. £25. Millbank Publications, 25 Catherine St., London WC2B 5JW, England. TEL 01-379-3036. Ed. K.J. Allen. adv. charts. illus. circ. 3,000.

TRAVEL AND TOURISM

910.2   SZ   ISSN 0074-9133
INTERNATIONAL TOURING ALLIANCE. MINUTES OF THE GENERAL ASSEMBLY. (Text in English and French) 1898. a. free. International Touring Alliance, 2 Quai Gustave Ador, Geneva, Switzerland. circ. 150.

INTERNATIONAL VEGETARIAN HANDBOOK. see *NUTRITION AND DIETETICS*

910.2   GW   ISSN 0075-2150
JAEGER'S INTERTRAVEL; world guide to travel agencies, tour operators, countries, towns and hotels. (Text in English) 1959. a. DM.108. Jaeger-Verlag GmbH, Holzhofallee 38, Postfach 110320, 6100 Darmstadt, W. Germany (B.R.D.) adv.

382   GW   ISSN 0075-2649
JAHRBUCH FUER FREMDENVERKEHR. 1950. a. DM.50. Deutsches Wirtschaftswissenschaftliches Institut fuer Fremdenverkehr, Hermann-Sack-Str. 2, Postfach 264, 8000 Munich 33, W. Germany (B.R.D.) Ed. Manfred Zeiner. bk. rev. circ. 500 (approx.)

910.2   UK   ISSN 0075-3750
JEWISH TRAVEL GUIDE. 1950. a. $9.95. Jewish Chronicle Publications, 25 Furnival St., London EC4A 1JT, England (Dist. in N. America by: Sepher Hermon Press, Inc., 53 Park Place, New York, NY 10007) Ed. S. Lightman. adv. index. circ. 10,000.

915.6   JO
JORDAN. MINISTRY OF TOURISM AND ANTIQUITIES. TOURIST ARRIVALS IN NUMBERS. Variant title: Jordan. Ministry of Tourism and Antiquities. Travel Statistics. (Editions in Arabic and English) a. Ministry of Tourism & Antiquities, Jordan tourism authority, Box 224, Amman, Jordan. circ. 1,000.

KAKTUSBLUETE. see *CHILDREN AND YOUTH — About*

KARNATAKA. DEPARTMENT OF TOURISM. ANNUAL REPORT. see *PUBLIC ADMINISTRATION*

914.304   GW
KAUPERTS DEUTSCHLAND STAEDTE-, HOTEL- UND REISEFUEHRER. 1950. a. DM.19.50. Adressbuch-Gesellschaft Berlin mbH, Friedrichstr. 210, 1000 Berlin 61, W. Germany (B.R.D.) Ed. Heinz Spitzing. adv. circ. 8,500.

338.4   KE
KENYA. CENTRAL BUREAU OF STATISTICS. MIGRATION AND TOURISM STATISTICS. 1971. irreg., latest 1975/78. Central Bureau of Statistics, Ministry of Finance & Planning, Box 30266, Nairobi, Kenya (Orders to: Government Printing and Stationery Office, Box 30128, Nairobi, Kenya)

916.04   KE
KENYA TOURIST DEVELOPMENT CORPORATION. REPORT AND ACCOUNTS. (Text in English) a. Kenya Tourist Development Corporation, Box 42013, Nairobi, Kenya.

KULTURNOPOLITICKY KALENDAR. see *MEETINGS AND CONGRESSES*

914.2   UK
LAKESCENE - GUIDE TO CARLISLE THE BORDER. 1975. a. £1. Border Press Agency Ltd., 12 Lonsdale St., Carlisle, Cumbria CA1 1DD, England. Ed. John Barker. adv.

914.2   UK
LAKESCENE - LEISURE TIME IN LAKELAND. 1975. a. £0.60. Border Press Agency Ltd., 12 Lonsdale St., Carlisle, Cumbria CA1 1DD, England. Ed. John Barker. adv.

910.4   US
LEISUREGUIDE - ATLANTA. 1982. a. L I N Broadcasting Corp., 1370 Ave. of the Americas, New York, NY 10019. circ. 2,730,000.

917.4   US
LEISUREGUIDE - BOSTON. 1978. a. L I N Broadcasting Corp., 1370 Ave. of the Americas, New York, NY 10019. Ed. Peter C. Johnson. adv. circ. 2,979,000.

917   US
LEISUREGUIDE - CHICAGO. 1971. a. L I N Broadcasting Corp., 1370 Ave. of the Americas, New York, NY 10019. Ed. Peter C. Johnson. adv. circ. 3,800,000.

917   US
LEISUREGUIDE - HOUSTON. 1978. a. L I N Broadcasting Corp., 1370 Ave. of the Americas, New York, NY 10019. Ed. Peter C. Johnson. adv. circ. 3,186,000.

910.4   US
LEISUREGUIDE - KANSAS CITY. 1982. a. L I N Broadcasting Corp., 1370 Ave. of the Americas, New York, NY 10091. circ. 1,740,000.

917   US
LEISUREGUIDE - LOUISVILLE. 1979. a. L I N Broadcasting Corp., 1370 Ave. of the Americas, New York, NY 10019. Ed. Peter C. Johnson. adv. circ. 2,234,000.

910.4   US
LEISUREGUIDE - MILWAUKEE. 1982. a. L I N Broadcasting Corp., 1370 Ave. of the Americas, New York, NY 10019. circ. 950,000.

910.202   US
LEISUREGUIDE - MYRTLE BEACH.* 1971. a. Leisureguides, 2050 Coral Way, Miami, FL 33145. adv.

917.5   US
LEISUREGUIDE - ORLANDO. 1980. a. L I N Broadcasting Corp., 1370 Ave. of the Americas, New York, NY 10019. Ed. Peter C. Johnson. adv. circ. 3,100,000.

917.2   US
LEISUREGUIDE - PUERTO RICO. 1980. a. L I N Broadcasting Corp., 1370 Ave. of the Americas, New York, NY 10019. Ed. Peter C. Johnson. adv. circ. 3,045,000.

917   US
LEISUREGUIDE - THE FLORIDA GOLD COAST. 1974. a. L I N Broadcasting Corp., 1370 Ave. of the Americas, New York, NY 10019. Ed. Peter C. Johnson. adv. circ. 5,590,000.

910.4   US
LEISUREGUIDE - TWIN CITIES. 1982. a. L I N Broadcasting Corp., 1370 Ave. of the Americas, New York, NY 10019. circ. 1,800,000.

910.2 914   US   ISSN 0163-4585
LET'S GO: THE BUDGET GUIDE TO EUROPE. 1960. a. $9.95 per no. St. Martin's Press, 175 Fifth Ave., New York, NY 10010. TEL 212-674-5151. adv. circ. 60,000.
Formerly: Let's Go: The Student Guide to Europe (ISSN 0075-8868)

938 956   US
LET'S GO: THE BUDGET GUIDE TO GREECE, ISRAEL AND EGYPT - INCLUDING CYPRUS & TURKISH COAST. a. $8.95. (Harvard Student Agencies) St. Martin's Press, 175 Fifth Ave., New York, NY 10010. Ed. Scott W. Pink.
Formerly: Let's Go: The Budget Guide to Greece, Israel and Egypt (ISSN 0276-6779)

917.04   US   ISSN 0192-2920
LET'S GO: THE BUDGET GUIDE TO ITALY. 1981. a. $8.95 per no. (Harvard Student Agencies) St. Martin's Press, 175 Fifth Ave., New York, NY 10010. TEL 212-674-5151. Ed. Jeremy Metz.

917.04   US
LET'S GO: U S A. 1973. a. $9.95 per no. St. Martin's Press, 175 Fifth Ave., New York, NY 10010. TEL 212-674-5151. illus.
Formerly: Let's Go: The Student Guide to the United States and Canada (ISSN 0090-788X)

354   LB
LIBERIA. MINISTRY OF INFORMATION, CULTURAL AFFAIRS & TOURISM. ANNUAL REPORT TO THE SESSION OF THE LEGISLATURE. (Text in English) a. Ministry of Information, Cultural Affairs and Tourism, Monrovia, Liberia.

910.2 960   UK
LIBYA PAST AND PRESENT SERIES. 1970. irreg., (approx. 2 per year) 1970, vol.3. price varies. Oleander Press, 17 Stangsate Ave., Cambridge CB2 2QZ, England (U.S. address: 210 Fifth Ave., New York, N.Y. 10010) Ed. Philip Ward.
Formerly: Libyan Travel Series (ISSN 0075-9309)

LINKS UND RECHTS DER AUTOBAHN; der Reisefuehrer und Reiseatlas speziell fuer die Autobahn. see *HOTELS AND RESTAURANTS*

LIVABILITY DIGEST. see *HOUSING AND URBAN PLANNING*

910.09   VE
LIVING IN VENEZUELA. (Text in English) 1980. a. Bs.200($25) Venezuelan-American Chamber of Commerce and Industry - Camara Venezolano Americana de Comercio e Industria, Apdo. 5181, Caracas 1010A, Venezuela. adv. index. circ. 5,000. (back issues avail.)
Formerly: VenAmCham's Executive Newcomers Guide.

910.2 914   UK
LUXURY COACH TOURS IN BRITAIN & EUROPE. 1924. a. free. Galleon World Travel Ltd., Galleon House, 52 High St., Sevenoaks, Kent TN13 1JG, England (Dist. in U.S. by: Fourways Travel Ltd., 950 Third Ave., New York, NY 10022) index.
Formerly: Coach Tours in Britain and Ireland (ISSN 0069-4886)

910.202   UK
M E E D PRACTIAL GUIDE. KUWAIT. 1985. irreg. £9.00($20) per issue. Middle East Economic Digest Ltd., 21 John St., London WC1N 2BP, England (Distr. in U.S. by: Lynne Rienner Publishers Inc., 948 North St., no.8, Boulder, CO 80302) Ed. John Whelan. adv. bibl. illus. stat. index.

910.202   UK
M E E D PRACTICAL GUIDE. BAHRAIN. 1983. irreg. £9.99($20) per issue. Middle East Economic Digest Ltd., 21 John St., London WC1N 2BP, England (Distr. in U.S. by: Lynne Rienner Publishers Inc., 948 North St., no.8, Boulder, CO 80302) Ed. John Whelan. adv. bibl. illus. stat. index.

910.202   UK
M E E D PRACTICAL GUIDE. EGYPT. 1986. irreg. £9.99($20) per issue. Middle East Economic Digest Ltd., 21 John St., London WC1N 2BP, England (Distr. in U.S. by: Lynne Rienner Publishers Inc., 948 North St., no.8, Boulder, CO 80302) Ed. John Whelan. adv. bibl. illus. stat. index.

910.202   UK
M E E D PRACTICAL GUIDE. JORDAN. 1983. irreg. £9.99($20) per issue. Middle East Economic Digest Ltd., 21 John St., London WC1N 2BP, England (Distr. in U.S. by: Lynne Rienner Publishers Inc., 948 North St., no.8, Boulder, CO 80302) Ed. Jonn Whelan. adv. bibl. illus. stat. index.

910.04 956   UK
M E E D PRACTICAL GUIDE. OMAN. 1981. irreg. £9.99($20) per issue. Middle East Economic Digest Ltd., 21 John St., London WC1N 2BP, England. Ed. Trevor Mostyn. bibl. illus. stat. index.

910.202   UK
M E E D PRACTICAL GUIDE. QATAR. 1983. irreg. £9.99($20) per issue. Middle East Economic Digest Ltd., 21 John St., London WC1N 2BP, England (Distr. in U.S. by: Lynne Rienner Publishers Inc., 948 North St., no.8, Boulder, CO 80302) Ed. John Whelan. adv. bibl. illus. stat. index.

910.04 956   UK
M E E D PRACTICAL GUIDE. SAUDI ARABIA. 1981. irreg. £9.99($20) per issue. Middle East Economic Digest Ltd., 21 John St., London WC1N 2BP, England. Ed. Trevor Mostyn. bibl. illus. stat. index.

910.04 956   UK
M E E D PRACTICAL GUIDE. U A E. (United Arab Emirates) 1981. irreg. £9.99($20) per issue. Middle East Economic Digest Ltd., 21 John St., London WC1N 2BP, England. Ed. Trevor Mostyn.

910.202   CN
M F V A BROCHURE. 1972. a. free. Manitoba Farm Vacations Association, 525 Kylemore Ave., Winnipeg, MB R3L 1B5, Canada. TEL 204-475-6624. Ed. Irv Kroeker. circ. 5,000.

917.404   US
MAINE INVITES YOU. 1930. a. free. Maine Publicity Bureau, Inc., 97 Winthrop St., Hallowell, ME 04347. TEL 207-289-2423. Ed. India Howell. circ. 110,000.

916   MW
MALAWI: A GUIDE FOR THE VISITOR. (Text in English) a. free. Department of Tourism, Box 402, Blantyre, Malawi.

MALTA YEARBOOK. see *POLITICAL SCIENCE*

917.104   CN
MANITOBA VACATION GUIDE, CANADA. 1972. a. Department of Business Development and Tourism, 155 Carlton St., 7th floor, Winnipeg, MB. R3C 3H8, Canada. TEL 800-665-0040. Ed. Victor Pasta. adv. illus.
Formerly: Manitoba Vacation Handbook.

916.1   NO
MED BIL I EUROPA. 1951. a. membership. Norges Automobil-Forbund, Storgaten 2, Postboks 494, Oslo 1, Norway.

917.204   US
MEXICO (YEAR) a. $11.95. Houghton Mifflin Co., Birnbaum Travel Guides, 60 E. 42nd St., Ste. 1624, New York, NY 10165. TEL 212-682-9440. Ed. Stephen Birnbaum.

914.404   FR
MICHELIN GREEN GUIDE SERIES: ALPES. 1978. irreg. $8.95. Michelin, Services de Tourisme, 46 av. de Breteuil, 75341 Paris Cedex 7, France (U.S. subscr. addr.: Michelin Guides and Maps, P.O. Box 3305, Spartanburg, SC. 29304-3305)

914.36   FR
MICHELIN GREEN GUIDE SERIES: AUSTRIA. (Editions in English and French) irreg. $9.95 per no. Michelin, Services de Tourisme, 46 av. de Breteuil, 75341 Paris Cedex 7, France (U.S. subscr. address: Michelin Guides and Maps, P.O. Box 3305, Spartanburg, SC. 29304-3305)

914.404   FR
MICHELIN GREEN GUIDE SERIES: AUVERGNE. 1977. irreg. latest 1984. $8.95. Michelin, Services de Tourisme, 46 av. de Breteuil, 75341 Paris Cedex 7, France (U.S. subscr. addr.: Michelin Guides and Maps, P.O. Box 3305, Spartanburg, SC. 29304-3305)

914.404   FR
MICHELIN GREEN GUIDE SERIES: BELGIQUE - LUXEMBOURG. (Text in French) irreg.; latest 1986. $9.95 per no. Michelin, Service de Tourism, 46 av. de Breteuil, 75341 Paris Cedex France (U.S. subscr. address: Michelin Guides and Maps, P.O. Box 3305, Spartanburg, SC. 29304-3305)

914.404   FR
MICHELIN GREEN GUIDE SERIES: BELGIUM - LUXEMBOURG. (Text in Dutch) irreg. $9.95. Michelin, Service de Tourisme, 46 av. de Breteuil, 75346 Paris Cedex 7, France (U.S. subscr. address: Michelin Guides and Maps, P.O. Box 3305, Spartanburg, SC. 29304-3305)

914.404   FR
MICHELIN GREEN GUIDE SERIES: BOURGOGNE. irreg.; latest 1985. $8.95. Michelin, Service de Tourisme, 46 av. de Breteuil, 75341 Paris Cedex 7, France (U.S. subscr. addr.: Michelin Guides and Maps, P.O. Box 3305, Spartanburg, SC. 29034-3305)

914.4   FR
MICHELIN GREEN GUIDE SERIES: BRITTANY. (Editions in English, French and German) irreg.; latest 1983. $8.95 per no. Michelin, Services de Tourisme, 46 av. de Breteuil, 75341 Paris Cedex 7, France (U.S. subscr. address: Michelin Guides and Maps, P.O. Box 3305, Spartanburg, SC. 29304-3305)

914.4   FR
MICHELIN GREEN GUIDE SERIES: CHATEAUX OF THE LOIRE. (Editions in English and French) irreg.; latest 1985. $8.95 per no. Michelin, Services de Tourisme, 46 av. de Breteuil, 75341 Paris Cedex 7, France (U.S. subscr. address: Michelin Guides and Maps, P.O. Box 3305, Spartanburg, SC 29304-3305)

914.404   FR
MICHELIN GREEN GUIDE SERIES: CORSE. irreg.; latest 1985. $8.95. Michelin, Services de Tourisme, 46 av. de Breteuil, 75341 Paris Cedex 7, France (U.S. subscr. address: Michelin Guides and Maps, P.O. Box 3305, Spartanburg, SC 29304-3305)

914.404   FR
MICHELIN GREEN GUIDE SERIES: COTE ATLANTIQUE. irreg.; latest 1984. 8.95 F. Michelin, Service de Tourisme, 46 av. de Breteuil, 75341 Paris Cedex 7, France (U.S. subscr. address: Michelin Guides and Maps, P.O. Box 3305, Spartanburg, SC 29304-3305)

914.4   FR
MICHELIN GREEN GUIDE SERIES: DORDOGNE. English edition: Michelin Green Guide Series: Perigord. (Text in English & French) irreg.; latest 1985. $8.95. Michelin, Services de Tourism, 46 av. de Breteuil, 75341 Paris Cedex 7, France (U.S. subscr. address: Michelin Guides and Maps, P.O. Box 3305, Spartanburg, SC 29304-3305)

914.404   FR
MICHELIN GREEN GUIDE SERIES: ENVIRONS DE PARIS. irreg.; latest 1984. $8.95. Michelin, Service de Tourisme, 46 av. de Breteuil, 75341 Paris Cedex 7, France (U.S. subscr. address: Michelin Guides and Maps, P.O. Box 3305, Soartanburg, SC 29304-3305)

914.404   FR
MICHELIN GREEN GUIDE SERIES: FLANDRES, ARTOIS, PICARDIE. (Text in French) irreg.; latest 1985. $8.95. Michelin, Service de Tourisme, 46 av. de Breteuil, 75341 Paris Cedex 7, France (U.S. subscr. address: Michelin Guides and Maps, P.O. Box 3305, Spartanburg, SC 29304-3305)
Formerly: Michelin Green Guide Series: Nord de la France.

914.4   FR
MICHELIN GREEN GUIDE SERIES: FRENCH RIVIERA. (Editions in English, French and German) irreg.; latest 1985. $8.95 per no. Michelin, Services de Tourisme, 46 av.de Breteuil, 75341 Paris Cedex 7, France (U.S. subscr. address: Michelin Guides and Maps, P.O. Box 3305, Spartanburg, SC 29304-3305)

914.3   FR
MICHELIN GREEN GUIDE SERIES: GERMANY. (Editions in English and French) irreg.; latest 1983. $9.95 per no. Michelin, Services de Tourisme, 46 av. de Breteuil, 75341 Paris Cedex 7, France (U.S. subscr. address: Michelin Guides and Maps, P.O. Box 3305, Spartanburg, SC 29304-3305)

914.904   FR
MICHELIN GREEN GUIDE SERIES: HOLLANDE. (Editions in Dutch and French) irreg.; latest 1986. $9.95 per no. Michelin, Service de Tourisme, 46 av. de Breteuil, 75341 Paris Cedex 7, France (U.S. subscr. address: Michelin Guides and Maps, P.O. Box 3305, Spartanburg, SC 290304-3305)

914.5   FR
MICHELIN GREEN GUIDE SERIES: ITALY. (Editions in English, French, German and Italian) irreg.; latest 1983. $8.95 per no. Michelin, Services de Tourisme, 46 av. de Breteuil, 75341 Paris Cedex 7, France (U.S. subscr. address: Michelin Guides and Maps, P.O. Box 3305, Spartanburg, SC 29304-3305)

914.404   FR   ISSN 0293-9436
MICHELIN GREEN GUIDE SERIES: JURA. irreg.; latest 1985. $8.95. Michelin, 46 av. de Breteuil, 75341 Paris Cedex 7, France (U.S. subscr. address: Michelin Guides and Maps, P.O. Box 3305, Spartanburg, SC 29304-3305)

914.2   FR
MICHELIN GREEN GUIDE SERIES: LONDRES. (Text in French) irreg. $9.95 per no. Michelin, Services de Tourisme, 46 av. de Breteuil, 75341 Paris Cedex 7, France (U.S. subscr. addr.: Michelin Guides and Maps, P.O. Box 3305, Spartanburg, SC 29304-3305)

916.4   FR
MICHELIN GREEN GUIDE SERIES: MAROC. (Text in French) irreg.; latest 1985. $9.95 per no. Michelin, Services de Tourisme, 46 av. de Breteuil, 75341 Paris Cedex 7, France (U.S. subscr. addr.: Michelin Guides and Maps, P.O. Box 3305, Spartanburg, SC 29304-3305)

917.4   FR
MICHELIN GREEN GUIDE SERIES: NEW YORK (CITY) (Text in English and French) irreg. $9.95 per no. Michelin, Services de Tourisme, 46 av. de Breteuil, 75341 Paris Cedex 7, France (U.S. subscr. addr.: Michelin Guides and Maps, P.O. Box 3305, Spartanburg, SC 29304-3305)

914.4   FR
MICHELIN GREEN GUIDE SERIES: NORMANDY. (Editions in English & French) irreg.; latest 1986. $8.95 per no. Michelin, Services de Tourisme, 46 av. de Breteuil, 75341 Paris Cedex 7, France (U.S. subscr. addr.: Michelin Guides and Maps, P.O. Box 3305, Spartanburg, SC 29304-3305)

914.4   FR
MICHELIN GREEN GUIDE SERIES: PARIS. (Editions in English, French and German) irreg.; latest 1985. $9.95 per no. Michelin, Services de Tourisme, 46 av. de Breteuil, 75341 Paris Cedex 7, France (U.S. subscr. address: Michelin Guides and Maps, P.O. Box 3305, Spartanburg, SC 29304-3305)

914.69   FR
MICHELIN GREEN GUIDE SERIES: PORTUGAL. (Editions in English and French) irreg.; latest 1985. $9.95 per no. Michelin, Services de Tourisme, 46 av. de Breteuil, 75341 Paris Cedex 7, France (U.S. subscr. address: Michelin Guides and Maps, P.O. Box 3305, Spartanburg, SC 29304-3305)

914.404   FR
MICHELIN GREEN GUIDE SERIES: PROVENCE. (Editions in English, French and German) 1980. irreg.; latest 1985. $8.95. Michelin, Service de Tourisme, 46 av. de Breteuil, 75341 Paris Cedex 7, France (U.S. subscr. address: Michelin Guides and Maps, P.O. Box 3305, Spartanburg, SC 29304-3305)

914.404   FR
MICHELIN GREEN GUIDE SERIES: PYRENEES. irreg. $8.95. Michelin, Service de Tourisme, 46 av. de Breteuil, 75341 Paris Cedex 7, France (U.S.subscr.address: Michelin Guides and Maps, P.O Box 3305, Spartanburg, SC 29304-3305)

914.404   FR
MICHELIN GREEN GUIDE SERIES: ROME. (Text in English and French) irreg.; latest 1985. $9.95. Michelin, Service de Tourisme, 46 av. de Breteuil, 75341 Paris Cedex 7, France (U.S. subscr. address: Michelin Guides and Maps, P.O. Box 3305, Spartanburg, SC 29304-3305)

914.6   FR
MICHELIN GREEN GUIDE SERIES: SPAIN. (Editions in English, French, German and Spanish) irreg.; latest 1985. $9.95 per no. Michelin, Services de Tourisme, 46 av. de Breteuil, 75341 Paris Cedex 7, France (U.S. subscr. address: Michelin Guides and Maps, P.O. Box 3305, Spartanburg, SC 29304-3305)

914.94   FR
MICHELIN GREEN GUIDE SERIES: SWITZERLAND. (Editions in English and French) irreg.; latest 1985. $9.95 per no. Michelin, Services de Tourisme, 46 av. de Breteuil, 75341 Paris Cedex 7, France (U.S. subscr. address: Michelin Guides and Maps, P.O. Box 3305, Spartanburg, SC 29304-3305)

914.404   FR
MICHELIN GREEN GUIDE SERIES: VALLEE DU RHONE. irreg.; latest 1985. $8.95. Michelin, Service de Tourisme, 46 av. de Breteuil, 75341 Paris Cedex 7, France (U.S. subscr. address: Michelin Guides and Maps, P.O. Box 3305, Spartanburg, SC 29304-3305)

TRAVEL AND TOURISM

914.404   FR
MICHELIN GREEN GUIDE SERIES: VOSGES. (Editions in French and German) irreg.; latest 1986. $8.95. Michelin, Service de Tourisme, 46 av. de Breteuil, 75341 Paris Cedex 7, France (U.S. subscr. address: Michelin Guides and Maps, P.O. Box 3305, Spartanburg, SC 29304-3305)

910.2   914   FR   ISSN 0076-7743
MICHELIN RED GUIDE SERIES: BENELUX. (Text in Dutch, English, French and German) a. $14.95. Michelin, Services de Tourisme, 46 av. de Breteuil, 75341 Paris Cedex 7, France (U.S.subscr.address: Michelin Guides and Maps, P.O. Box 3305, Spartanburg, SC 29304-3305)

910.2   914   FR   ISSN 0076-7778
MICHELIN RED GUIDE SERIES: FRANCE. (Text in English, French, German and Italian) a. $15.95. Michelin, Services de Tourisme, 46 av. de Breteuil, 75342 Paris Cedex 7, France (U.S.subscr.address: Michelin Guides and Maps, P.O. Box 3305, Spartanburg, SC 29304-3305)

910.2   914   FR   ISSN 0076-7751
MICHELIN RED GUIDE SERIES: GERMANY. (Text in English, French, German and Italian) a. $15.95. Michelin, Services de Tourisme, 46 av. de Breteuil, 75341 Paris Cedex 7, France (U.S. subscr. addr.: Michelin Guides and Maps, P.O. Box 3305, Spartanburg, SC 29304-3305)

914.204   FR
MICHELIN RED GUIDE SERIES: GREAT BRITAIN AND IRELAND. (Text in English, French, German and Italian) a. $14.95. Michelin, Services de Tourisme, 46 av. de Breteuil, 75341 Paris Cedex 7, France (U.S.subscr.address: Michelin Guides and Maps, P.O. Box 3305, Spartanburg, SC 29304-3305) illus.

914.21   FR
MICHELIN RED GUIDE SERIES: GREATER LONDON. (Text in English, French, German & Italian) a. $3.95. Michelin, Services de Tourisme, 46 av. de Breteuil, 75341 Paris Cedex 7, France (U.S.subscr.address: Michelin Guides and Maps, P.O. Box 3305, Spartanburg, SC 29304-3305) illus.

914   FR   ISSN 0076-7786
MICHELIN RED GUIDE SERIES: ITALY. (Text in English, French, German and Italian) a. $15.95. Michelin, Services de Tourisme, 46 av. de Breteuil, 75341 Paris Cedex 7, France (U.S. subscr. address: Michelin Guide and Maps, P.O. Box 3305, Spartanburg, SC 29304-3305)

910.2   914   FR   ISSN 0076-7794
MICHELIN RED GUIDE SERIES: PARIS. (Notes: in two editions: (1) Multilingual (Dutch, French, German & Italian) and (2) English) a. $3.95. Michelin, Services de Tourisme, 46 av. de Breteuil, 75341 Paris Cedex 7, France (U.S. subscr. address: Michelin Guides and Maps, P.O. Box 3305, Spartanburg, SC 29304-3305)

910.2   914   FR   ISSN 0076-776X
MICHELIN RED GUIDE SERIES: SPAIN & PORTUGAL. (Text in English, French, German, Italian, Portuguese and Spanish) a. $14.95. Michelin, Services de Tourisme, 46 av. de Breteuil, 75341 Paris Cedex 7, France (U.S. subscr. addr.: Michelin Guide and Maps, P.O. Box 3305, Spartanburg, SC 29304-3305)

917   US
MICHIGAN TRAVEL AND RECREATION GUIDE. a. Rockford Map Publishers, Inc., 4525 Forest View Ave., Box 6126, Rockford, IL 61125.

917   796.5   US   ISSN 0734-2705
MIDEASTERN CAMPBOOK. Cover title: R V and Tent Sites in Delaware, District of Columbia, Maryland, New Jersey, Pennsylvania, Virginia, West Virginia. a. membership. American Automobile Association, 8111 Gatehouse Rd., Falls Church, VA 22047. TEL 703-222-6000. circ. 339,000.
Formerly (until 1980): Mideastern Camping (ISSN 0147-7285)

910   US   ISSN 0361-1361
MILEPOST; all-the-north-travel-guide. 1948. a. $12.95. Alaska Northwest Publishing Co., Box 4-EEE, Anchorage, AK 99509 TEL 907-274-0521. (Circ. Office: 130 Second Ave. S., Edmonds, WA 98020) Ed. Robert A. Henning. adv. charts. illus. stat. circ. 60,000.

910.202   US
MINNESOTA TRAVEL AND RECREATION GUIDE. a. Rockford Map Publishers, Inc., 4525 Forest View Ave., Box 6126, Rockford, IL 61125.

910.202   US
MOBIL TRAVEL GUIDE - MAJOR CITIES. (In 7 regional edts.: California & the West; Northeast; Great Lakes; Southeast; Southwest & South Central; Northwest & Great Plains States; Middle Atlantic States) 1960. a. $7.95. (Mobil Products) Rand McNally & Co., Box 7600, Chicago, IL 60680. TEL 312-673-9100. Ed. Helen Clark. illus. circ. 28,000. (also avail. in magnetic tape)

997   MJ
MONTSERRAT. STATISTICS OFFICE. TOURISM REPORT. irreg. Statistics Office, Government Headquarters, Plymouth, Montserrat.

659.2   US   ISSN 0890-9512
MORGAN REPORT ON DIRECTORY PUBLISHING. 1986. m. $48. Morgan-Rand Publications, Inc., 2200 Sansom St., Philadelphia, PA 19103. TEL 215-557-8200. Ed. Russell Perkins. adv. bk. rev. stats. tr.lit. circ. 900. (looseleaf format; back issues avail.)

910.202   GR
MOTION/KINESI. (Text in English, French, German and Greek) 1969. a. free. Olympic Airways S.A., Purchasing Department, West Airport Helliniko, 16604 Athens, Greece. Ed. C. Kontadakis. adv. circ. 500,000.
Formerly: Your Air Companion.

MOVING TO & AROUND ALBERTA. see *REAL ESTATE*

MOVING TO & AROUND MARITIMES & NEWFOUNDLAND. see *REAL ESTATE*

MOVING TO & AROUND SOUTHWESTERN ONTARIO. see *REAL ESTATE*

MOVING TO & AROUND WINNIPEG & MANITOBA. see *REAL ESTATE*

MOVING TO DALLAS/FORT WORTH. see *REAL ESTATE*

MOVING TO DENVER. see *REAL ESTATE*

MOVING TO OTTAWA/HULL. see *REAL ESTATE*

MOVING TO SASKATCHEWAN. see *REAL ESTATE*

MOVING TO THE SAN FRANCISCO BAY AND GREATER SACRAMENTO. see *REAL ESTATE*

MOVING TO VANCOUVER & B.C. see *REAL ESTATE*

MULTINATIONAL EXECUTIVE TRAVEL COMPANION. see *BUSINESS AND ECONOMICS — International Commerce*

910.09   SA
NANA NO PASUPORTO/SOUTHERN AFRICA PASSPORT. (Text in Japanese; occasionally in English) 1982. a. R.1($1.92) Media Link (Pty) Ltd, 55 Minors St., Yeoville, Johannesburg, South Africa. Ed. Godfrey Sheldon Busscham. adv. circ. 8,000. (back issues avail.)

910.202   US
NATIONAL DIRECTORY OF FREE TOURIST ATTRACTIONS. 1976. irreg., latest 1987. $3.95. Pilot Books, 103 Cooper St., Babylon, NY 11702. TEL 516-422-2225. Ed. Raymond Carlson, Maria Maiorino.

910.202   US
NATIONAL DIRECTORY OF LOW-COST TOURIST ATTRACTIONS. 1979. irreg. $3.50. Pilot Books, 103 Cooper St., Babylon, NY 11702. TEL 516-422-2225. Ed. Raymond Carlson.

910.202   US
NATIONAL DIRECTORY OF THEME PARKS AND AMUSEMENT AREAS. 1978. irreg. $2.95. Pilot Books, 103 Cooper St., Babylon, NY 11702. TEL 516-422-2225. Ed. Raymond Carlson.

910.09   US
NATIONAL TRAVEL EXPENDITURE STUDY: SUMMARY REPORT. 1975. a. $27. U S Travel Data Center, 1899 L. St., N.W., Washington, DC 20036. TEL 202-293-1040. (reprint service avail. from CIS)

917.1   CN   ISSN 0703-6566
NEW BRUNSWICK. DEPARTMENT OF TOURISM. ANNUAL REPORT. (Text in English and French) 1972. a. Department of Tourism, Marketing Branch, Advertising and Communications, P.O. Box 12345, Fredericton, N.B. E3B 5C3, Canada. TEL 506-453-2377. Ed.Bd. illus. circ. 600.

910.2   915.2   JA   ISSN 0077-8591
NEW OFFICIAL GUIDE: JAPAN. (Text in English) 1952. irreg. 5000 Yen($15.) (Japan National Tourist Organization - Nihon Boeki Shuppansha) Japan Travel Bureau Inc., 1-6-4 Marunouchi, Chiyoda-ku, Tokyo, Japan. index.
Formerly: Japan: the Official Guide.

917.53   US   ISSN 0097-8213
NEW SETTLER'S GUIDE FOR WASHINGTON, D.C. AND COMMUNITIES IN NEARBY MARYLAND AND VIRGINIA. 1972. a. $5.50. Robco, Inc., 8824 Tuckerman Lane, Potomac, MD 20854. TEL 301-299-7507. Ed. Robert B. Minogue. adv. illus. circ. 15,000.

974   US
NEW YORK STATE FAIR MAGAZINE. 1955. a. $2. New York State Fair, State Fairgrounds, Syracuse, NY 13209. Ed. Joseph J. LaGuardia. adv. circ. 30,000.
Formerly: New York State FairGround.

919.3   NZ
NEW ZEALAND VISITOR STATISTICS. 1973. a. free. Department of Tourist and Publicity, Private Bag, Wellington, New Zealand. adv.

916.69   NR
NIGERIA TOURIST GUIDE/GUIDE DU TOURISME NIGERIEN. Variant title: National Tourist Guide of Nigeria. 1969. irreg. Nigerian Tourist Association, 47 Marina, P.O. Box 2944, Lagos, Nigeria. adv. illus.

917.5   US   ISSN 0546-3432
NORMAN FORD'S FLORIDA. biennial. $4.95 per no. Harian Publications, One Vernon Ave., Floral Park, NY 11001. TEL 516-437-3440. Ed. Norman D. Ford. charts. illus.

917   796.5   US   ISSN 0147-8613
NORTH CENTRAL CAMPBOOK. Cover title: R V and Tent Sites in Iowa, Minnesota, Nebraska, North Dakota, South Dakota. a. membership. American Automobile Association, 8111 Gatehouse Rd., Falls Church, VA 22047. TEL 703-222-6000. circ. 265, 000.
Formerly (until 1980): North Central Camping.

914.1   UK   ISSN 0260-2415
NORTH OF SCOTLAND VISITOR; tourist guide to north of Scotland. 1980. a. £0.20. Scotsman Publications, 20 North Bridge, Edinburgh EH1 1YT, Scotland. illus.

910   917.7   US
NORTH SHORE DINING GUIDE. 1981. a. $1.50 per no. P B Communications, Inc., 874 Green Bay Rd., Winnetka, IL 60093. TEL 312-441-7892. Ed. Asher J. Birnbaum. adv. illus. circ. 50,000.

647.94   US   ISSN 0732-7315
NORTHEASTERN CAMPBOOK; including location maps. Cover title: R V and Tent Sites in Connecticut, Maine, Massachusetts, New Hampshire, New York, Rhode Island, Vermont. a. American Automobile Association, 8111 Gatehouse Rd., Falls Church, VA 22047. TEL 703-222-6000. illus. circ. 299,000.
Former titles (until 1980): Northeastern Camping (ISSN 0196-6456); Northeastern Camping and Trailering.

TRAVEL AND TOURISM

917.8 US
NORTHWESTERN CAMPBOOK; including location maps. Cover title: R V and Tent Sites in Idaho, Montana, Oregon, Washington, Wyoming. a. membership. American Automobile Association, 8111 Gatehouse Rd., Falls Church, VA 22047. TEL 703-222-6000. illus. circ. 367,000.
Former titles (until 1980): Northwestern Camping (ISSN 0095-4411); Northwestern Camping and Trailering.

917.04 US
NUDIST PARK GUIDE. 1966. a. $15. American Sunbathing Association, 1703 N. Main St., Kissimmee, FL 32743. TEL 305-933-2064. Ed. Arne Eriksen. adv. circ. 10,000.

OFFICIAL HOTEL & RESORT GUIDE. see HOTELS AND RESTAURANTS

910.4 700 UK
OFFICIAL SOUVENIR GUIDE TO THE EDINBURGH FESTIVAL. 1985. a. £1.90. Pastime Publications Ltd., 15 Dublin Street Lane South, Edinburgh EH1 3PX, Scotland. adv. circ. 50,000.

910 UK
OLEANDER TRAVEL BOOKS SERIES. a. Oleander Press, 17 Stansgate Ave., Cambridge CB2 2QZ, England (U.S. address: 210 Fifth Ave., New York, NY 10010)

950.04 US ISSN 0162-5950
ON-YOUR-OWN GUIDE TO ASIA; the budget handbook to East & Southeast Asia. 1976. biennial. $6.95. Volunteers in Asia, Inc., Box 4543, Stanford, CA 94305 TEL 415-326-7672. (Co-sponsor: Charles E. Tuttle Company) Ed. Terry George.

382 FR
ORGANIZATION FOR ECONOMIC COOPERATION AND DEVELOPMENT. TOURISM COMMITTEE. TOURISM POLICY AND INTERNATIONAL TOURISM IN O E C D MEMBER COUNTRIES. a. price varies. Organization for Economic Cooperation and Development, 2 rue Andre-Pascal, 75775 Paris Cedex 16, France (U.S. orders to: O.E.C.D. Publications and Information Center, 1750 Pennsylvania Ave. N.W., Washington, D.C. 20006) (also avail. in microfiche; back issues available)
Continues: International Tourism Policy in OECD Member Countries.

917.404 US ISSN 0734-4066
ORIGINAL NEW ENGLAND GUIDE. 1957. a. $3.50 per no. Historical Times, Inc., 2245 Kohn Rd., Box 8200, Harrisburg, PA 17105. TEL 717-657-9555. Ed. Kathie Kull. adv. circ. 200,000.
Supersedes: New England Guide (ISSN 0077-8222)

OTTAWA GUIDEBOOK. see PUBLIC ADMINISTRATION — Municipal Government

910.09 US
OUTLOOK FOR TRAVEL AND TOURISM. a. $80. U S Travel Data Center, 1899 L St., N.W., Washington, DC 20036. TEL 202-293-1040. charts. (reprint service avail. from CIS)
Formerly: Travel Outlook Forum Proceedings (ISSN 0160-4651)

OWEN'S BUSINESS DIRECTORY AND TRAVEL GUIDE. see BUSINESS AND ECONOMICS — International Commerce

PACIFIC BOATING ALMANAC. NORTHERN CALIFORNIA & NEVADA. see SPORTS AND GAMES — Boats And Boating

PACIFIC BOATING ALMANAC. OREGON, WASHINGTON, BRITISH COLUMBIA & SOUTHEASTERN ALASKA. see SPORTS AND GAMES — Boats And Boating

PACIFIC BOATING ALMANAC. SOUTHERN CALIFORNIA, ARIZONA, BAJA. see SPORTS AND GAMES — Boats And Boating

915 AT ISSN 0311-0826
PACIFIC TRAVEL DIRECTORY. 1973. a. Aus.$7.50. c/o Pacific Airlines News, Box 1, Surfers Paradise, Qld. 4217, Australia. Ed. A. H. McRobbie.

910.2 UK
PAINTING, HOLIDAYS AND ACTIVITY. 1924. a. free. Galleon World Travel Ltd., Galleon House, 2 High St., Sevenoaks, Kent TN13 1JG, England (Dist. in U.S. by: Fourways Travel Ltd., 950 Third Ave., New York, NY 10022)
Formerly: Painting Holidays (ISSN 0078-7833)

910.202 PK
PAKISTAN HOTELS & TOURISM. 1975. a. Rs.5. Bhatti Publications, 103/B Gulberg, Lahore, Pakistan. Ed. Mukhtar Bhatti. adv.

PANAMA NOW. see BUSINESS AND ECONOMICS — Domestic Commerce

910.2 AT
PAPUA NEW GUINEA HANDBOOK. 1954. irreg., 10th edt., 1980. Aus.$13.95. Pacific Publications (Australia) Pty. Ltd., P.O. Box 3408, G.P.O., Sydney, N.S.W. 2001, Australia. Ed. Russell Hunter. adv. index.
Formerly: Handbook of Papua and New Guinea (ISSN 0072-9868)

914.504 IT
PASSEGGIATE NEL LAZIO. 1977. irreg. price varies per vol. (Regione Lazio, Assessorato al Turismo) Bulzoni Editore, Via dei Liburni, 00185 Rome, Italy.

PETER STUYVESENT TRAVEL WATERSKI GUIDE. see SPORTS AND GAMES — Outdoor Life

PETER STUYVESENT TRAVEL WINDSURF GUIDE. see SPORTS AND GAMES — Outdoor Life

910.2 914 UK ISSN 0079-130X
PETS WELCOME; animal lovers' holiday guide. 1961. a. £1.50. ‡ F.H.G. Publications Ltd., Abbey Mill Business Centre, Seedhill, Paisley PA1 1JN, Scotland. Ed. Peter Clark.

299 910 US
PILGRIM'S GUIDE TO PLANET EARTH. 1974. irreg. $8.95. Arcline Publications, Box 1550, Pomona, CA 91769. TEL 714-623-1738. Ed. Parmatma Singh Khalsa. circ. 17,500.

910.09 CU
POLIMITAS. a. Instituto Nacional del Turismo, Malecon y G, Vedado, Havana, Cuba.

917.04 US
PORTLAND AND THE PACIFIC NORTHWEST. 1975. a. $6.50. Fox Publishing Co., 320 S.W. Stark, Suite 519, Portland, OR 97204. TEL 503-223-0051. Ed. Susan Monti. adv. circ. 13,500.

914.2 UK
PORTLAND SOUVENIR MAGAZINE. 1971. a. £0.25. Royal Naval Association, Portland Branch, 2 Clarence Rd., Portland, Dorset, England. Ed. John Barnes.

QUADERNI DE "LA TERRA SANTA". see RELIGIONS AND THEOLOGY

353.9 CN ISSN 0229-3811
QUEBEC (PROVINCE) DEPARTMENT OF RECREATION, FISH AND GAME. ANNUAL REPORT/MINISTERE DU LOISIR DE LA CHASSE ET DE LA PECHE. (Editions in English, French) 1980. a. free. Quebec (Province) Department of Recreation, Fish and Game, Quebec, P.Q., Canada. TEL 418-643-3895.
Formerly: Quebec (Province) Department of Tourism, Fish and Game. Annual Report (ISSN 0481-2786)

QUEEN'S PARK GUIDEBOOK. see PUBLIC ADMINISTRATION — Municipal Government

910.2 AT
QUEENSLAND TOURIST AND TRAVEL CORPORATION. ANNUAL REPORT. 1980. a. free. Queensland Tourist and Travel Corporation, 307 Queen St., G.P.O. Box 328, Brisbane, Qld. 4001, Australia. illus. circ. 400.

910.202 UK
R A C CONTINENTAL HANDBOOK AND HOTEL GUIDE. 1932. a. £4.50. (Royal Automobile Club) R A C Motoring Services Ltd., Box 100, R A C House, Lansdowne Rd., Croydon CR9 2JA, England. adv.
Former titles: R A C Continental Motoring Guide; (until 1982): R A C Continental Handbook.

796.77 UK
R A C HANDBOOK AND HOTEL GUIDE. 1904. a. £5.95. (Royal Automobile Club) R A C Motoring Services Ltd., Box 100, R A C House, Lansdowne Rd., Croydon CR9 2JA, England.
Formerly (until 1985): R A C Guide and Handbook.

796.77 UK
R A C MOTOR SPORT YEAR BOOK. 1956. a. R A C Motor Sport Association Ltd., 31 Belgrave Square, London SW1X 8QH, England. adv. circ. 38,000.

910.202 330 US
RAND McNALLY BUSINESS TRAVELER'S ROAD ATLAS; and guide to major cities. a. $10.95. Rand McNally & Co., Box 7600, Chicago, IL 60680. TEL 312-673-9100. Ed. Virginia Ure.

910.2 US ISSN 0079-9637
RAND McNALLY DISCOVER HISTORIC AMERICA. 1971. a. Rand McNally & Co., 8255 N. Central Park, Box 728, Skokie, IL 60076.
Formerly: Rand McNally Vacation Guide.

910.202 917.04 US
RAND McNALLY FAMILY ADVENTURE ROAD ATLAS. a. $7.95. Rand McNally & Co., Box 7600, Chicago, IL 60680. TEL 312-673-9100. Ed. Virginia Ure.

910.202 US
RAND McNALLY INTERSTATE ROAD ATLAS; United States, Canada, Mexico. a. $3.50. Rand McNally & Co., Box 7600, Chicago, IL 60680. TEL 312-673-9100. Ed. Virginia Ure. illus.

910.202 US
RAND McNALLY ROAD ATLAS. 1924. a. $5.95. Rand McNally & Co., 8255 N. Central Park Ave., Skokie, IL 60076. TEL 312-673-9100. Ed. John Manning. adv. circ. 2,200,000.

910.202 914.04 US
RAND McNALLY ROAD ATLAS & CITY GUIDE TO EUROPE. a. $12.95. Rand McNally & Company, Box 7600, Chicago, IL 60680. TEL 312-673-9100. Ed. Virginia Ure. illus.

910.202 US
RAND McNALLY ROAD ATLAS & VACATION GUIDE; United States, Canada, Mexico. a. $12.95. Rand McNally & Co., Box 7600, Chicago, IL 60202. TEL 312-673-9100. Ed. Virginia Ure.

910.202 914.204 US
RAND McNALLY ROAD ATLAS OF BRITAIN; the ultimate road atlas for travel in England, Scotland, and Wales. a. $12.95. Rand McNally & Company, Box 7600, Chicago, IL 60680. TEL 312-673-9100. Ed. Virginia Ure. illus.

910.202 914.04 US
RAND McNALLY ROAD ATLAS OF EUROPE. a. $6.95. Rand McNally & Co., Box 7600, Chicago, IL 60680. TEL 312-673-9100. Ed. Virginia Ure. illus.

910.202 917.04 US
RAND McNALLY VACATION PLACES RATED. 1986. irreg. $12.95. Rand McNally & Co., Box 7600, Chicago, IL 60680. TEL 312-673-9100.

910.2 914 UK ISSN 0267-3428
RECOMMENDED COUNTRY HOTELS OF BRITAIN. 1973. a. £1.95. F.H.G. Publications Ltd., Abbey Mill Business Centre, Seedhill, Paisley PA1 1JN, Scotland. Ed. Peter Clark.

914 UK
RECOMMENDED SHORT BREAK HOLIDAYS. a. £1. F.H.G. Publications Ltd., Abbey Mill Business Centre, Seedhill, Paisley PA1 1JN, Scotland. Ed. Peter Clark.
Formerly: Mini-Break Holidays in Britain (ISSN 0267-341X)

TRAVEL AND TOURISM

910.2 914   UK   ISSN 0080-0252
RECOMMENDED WAYSIDE INNS OF BRITAIN. 1962. a. £1.99. ‡ F.H.G. Publications Ltd., 18 High St., Paisley PA1 2BX, Scotland. Ed. Peter Clark.

917   CN
REGINA. 1976. a. Regina Tourist and Convention Bureau, 2145 Albert St., Regina, Sask. S4P 2W1, Canada. TEL 306-527-6631. circ. 20,000.

910.2   GW
REISEN IN DEUTSCHLAND; DEUTSCHES HANDBUCH FUER FREMDENVERKEHR. Volume 1 (ISSN 0177-2953); Volume 2 (ISSN 0177-2961) 1925. a. (2 volumes) DM.28 per vol. Jaeger-Verlag GmbH, Holzhofallee 38, Postfach 110320, 6100 Darmstadt, W. Germany (B.R.D.) adv.

910.09   DK   ISSN 0108-6812
REJSEBOGEN (YEAR); muligheder for ophold i udlandet af kortere eller laengere varighed. 1983. a. Kr.87. Forlaget Nuna, Fasanvej 3, 9670 Loegstoer, Denmark. Ed. Georg Harmsen. bk. rev. circ. 8,000.

910.09   US
RETIREMENT PARADISES OF THE WORLD. biennial. $4.95. Harian Publications, One Vernon Ave, Floral Park, NY 11001. TEL 516-437-3440. Ed. Norman D. Ford. illus.
    Supersedes: Bargain Paradises of the World (ISSN 0408-568X)

642.5 901.202   UK
ROUTIERS GUIDE TO FRANCE. (Editions in Dutch and English) 1934. a. £5.95. (Societe d'Exploitation de Journaux Techniques, FR) Macdonald Orbis, Greater London House, Third Fl., Hampstead Rd., London NW1 7QX, England. (Co-publisher: Routiers Ltd.) Ed. Joanna Gray. adv. charts. circ. 17,500.
    Formerly (until 1974): Guide des Relais Routiers.

910.09   US
S T A R SERVICE. 1960. base vol. plus bi-m. supplements. $155. (Sloane Travel Agency Reports) Star Service, Box 15610, Ft. Lauderdale, FL 33318-9985. TEL 305-472-8794. Ed. Robert D. Sloane. (looseleaf format)

910.2   UK
SCHOOLS AND COLLEGES WELCOME. 1978. a. free to qualified personnel. Lewis Productions Ltd., 31 Castle St., Kingston upon Thames, Surrey KT1 1ST, England. Ed. Rosemary Bray. adv. circ. 30,000.

914.1   UK
SCOTLAND: CAMPING AND CARAVAN SITES. 1960. a. £2. Scottish Tourist Board, 23 Ravelston Terrace, Edinburgh EH4 3EU, Scotland. adv. circ. 50,000.
    Former titles: Scotland for Touring Caravans; Scotland for Caravan Holidays.

914.2   UK
SCOTLAND FOR HILLWALKING. 1971. irreg. £1.75. Scottish Tourist Board, 23 Ravelston Terrace, Edinburgh EH4 3EU, Scotland. Ed. Donald J. Bennet. illus.

914.1   UK
SCOTLAND FOR THE MOTORIST. 1970. a. 1.10. Pastime Publications Ltd., 15 Dublin Street Lane South, Edinburgh EH1 3PX, Scotland. adv.

914.2   UK
SCOTLAND: SELF-CATERING ACCOMMODATION. 1971. a. £3.50. Scottish Tourist Board, 23 Ravelston Terrace, Edinburgh EH4 3EU, Scotland. charts. circ. 44,000.

914.1   UK
SCOTLAND: WHERE TO STAY, BED AND BREAKFAST. a. £2.20. Scottish Tourist Board, 23 Ravelston Terrace, Edinburgh EH4 3EU, Scotland. circ. 50,000.
    Formerly: Where to Stay in Scotland. Bed and Breakfast; Supersedes in part: Where to Stay in Scotland (ISSN 0083-9221)

914.1   UK
SCOTLAND: WHERE TO STAY, HOTELS AND GUEST HOUSES. 1947. a. £3.50. Scottish Tourist Board, 23 Ravelston Terrace, Edinburgh EH4 3EU, Scotland. circ. 60,000.
    Formerly: Where to Stay in Scotland. Hotels and Guest Houses; Supersedes in part: Where to Stay in Scotland (ISSN 0083-9221)

910.2   UK
SCOTLAND: 1001 THINGS TO SEE. 1970. irreg. £2.50. Scottish Tourist Board, 23 Ravelston Terrace, Edinburgh EH4 3EU, Scotland.
    Former titles: Scotland: 600 Things to See; Scottish Castles and Historic Houses (ISSN 0080-7931); Scotlands Castles.

914.2   UK   ISSN 0267-338X
SCOTLAND'S BEST HOLIDAYS. 1974. a. £1. F.H.G. Publications Ltd., Abbey Mill Business Centre, Seedhill, Paisley PA1 1JN, Scotland.

914.2   UK
SCOTLAND'S FOR ME. 1972. a. free. Scottish Tourist Board, 23 Ravelston Terrace, Edinburgh EH4 3EU, Scotland. charts. illus. circ. 900,000.
    Former titles: Enjoy Scotland; Scotland: A World of Difference.

914.2   UK   ISSN 0267-4599
SELF-CATERING AND FURNISHED HOLIDAYS. 1968. a. £1.25. F.H.G. Publications Ltd., Abbey Mill Business Centre, Seedhill, Paisley PA1 1JN, Scotland.
    Formerly: Furnished Holidays in Britain.

910.2   UK
SELF-CATERING HOLIDAY HOMES, CARAVANS & BOATS. 1958. a. £1. ‡ F.H.G. Publications Ltd., Abbey Mill Business Centre, Seedhill, Paisley PA1 1JN, Scotland. Ed. Peter Clark. index.
    Formerly: Furnished Holiday Homes and Caravans (ISSN 0071-996X)

910.4   UK
SELF CATERING HOLIDAYS. 1959. a. £1.10. Pastime Publications Ltd., 15 Dublin Street Lane South, Edinburgh EH1 3PX, Scotland. adv.

910   US
SENIOR CITIZEN'S GUIDE TO BUDGET TRAVEL IN THE UNITED STATES AND CANADA. 1983. irreg. $3.95. Pilot Books, Inc., 103 Cooper St., Babylon, NY 11702. TEL 516-422-2225.

916.8   SA
SHELL TOURIST GUIDE TO SOUTH AFRICA. a. R.4.40. Chris van Rensburg Publications (Pty) Ltd., Box 25272, Marshalltown 2107, South Africa. adv.

SKI HOLIDAYS SCOTLAND. see *SPORTS AND GAMES — Outdoor Life*

910.202   US
SOBEK'S ADVENTURE VACATION. 1983. a., 4th edt., 1986. membership. Sobek's International Explorers Society, Angels Camp, CA 95222. TEL 209-736-4524. Ed. Christian Kallen. adv. illus. index. circ. 60,000. (back issues avail.)
    Formerly: Adventure Book.

914.6 388.3   SP
SOCIEDAD ESPANOLA DE AUTOMOVILES DE TURISMO. MEMORIA Y BALANCE. 1953. a. free. Sociedad Espanola de Automoviles de Turismo, S.A., Paseo Castellana, 278, Madrid 16, Spain. charts. stat. circ. 1,000.

910.202 236   US
SOPHISTICATED LEISURE TRAVEL DIRECTORY. 1985. a. $8.95. Schueler Communications, 208 N. Townsend St., Syracuse, NY 13203. TEL 315-472-6948. Ed. Bruce Coville. adv. index. circ. 400,000.
    Formerly (until 1986): Seniority Travel Directory.

918   US   ISSN 0193-7944
SOUTH AMERICA (NEW YORK) 1980. a. $11.95. Houghton Mifflin Co., Birnbaum's Travel Guides, 60 E. 42nd St., Ste. 1624, New York, NY 10165. TEL 212-682-9440. Ed. Stephen Birnbaum. circ. 10,000.

910.2   US   ISSN 0081-2579
SOUTH AMERICAN HANDBOOK. a. Rand McNally & Co., 8255 N. Central Park, Box 728, Skokie, IL 60076.

917 796.5   US
SOUTH CENTRAL CAMPBOOK. Cover title: R V and Tent Sites in Arkansas, Kansas, Missouri, Oklahoma, Texas. a. membership. American Automobile Association, 8111 Gatehouse Rd., Falls Church, VA 22047. TEL 703-222-6000. circ. 274,000.
    Formerly (until 1980): South Central Camping (ISSN 0364-7161)

917 796.5   US   ISSN 0731-5112
SOUTHEASTERN CAMPBOOK. Cover title: R V and Tent Sites in Alabama, Florida, Georgia, Kentucky, Louisiana, Mississippi, North Carolina, South Carolina, Tennessee. a. membership. American Automobile Association, 8111 Gatehouse Rd., Falls Church, VA 22047. TEL 703-222-6000. circ. 389,000.
    Formerly (until 1980): Southeastern Camping (ISSN 0162-9166)

916.8 916.9   SA
SOUTHERN AFRICA AND THE INDIAN OCEAN ISLANDS TRAVEL TRADE DIRECTORY. 1974. a. $15. Da Gama Publishers (Pty) Ltd., 5th Fl., Harland House, 17 Loveday St., Box 61464, Marshalltown 2107, South Africa. Ed. Daphne de Freitas. adv. circ. 10,000.

917 796.5   US   ISSN 0731-8103
SOUTHWESTERN CAMPBOOK. Cover title: R V and Tent Sites in Arizona, Colorado, New Mexico, Utah. a. membership. American Automobile Association, 8111 Gatehouse Rd., Falls Church, VA 22047. TEL 703-222-6000. circ. 369,000.
    Formerly (until 1980): Southwestern Camping (ISSN 0094-2855)

910   SP
SPAIN. MINISTERIO DE COMERCIO Y TURISMO. ESTADISTICAS DE TURISMO. a. free. Ministerio de Comercio y Turismo, Alcala 44, Madrid 14, Spain.
    Formerly: Spain. Ministerio de Informacion y Turismo. Estadisticas de Turismo (ISSN 0081-346X)

914.6   SP
SPAIN. SECRETARIA GENERAL DE TURISMO. ANUARIO DE ESTADISTICAS DE TURISMO. a. (Ministerio de Transportes, Turismo y Comunicaciones, Secretaria General de Turismo) Ruan, S.A., Avda. de la Industria, 19 Alcobendas (Madrid), Spain.

910.202 301.415   NE
SPARTACUS INTERNATIONAL GAY GUIDE. (Text in English, French, German and Spanish) 1971. a. fl.35($20) Spartacus, Box 3496, 1001 AG Amsterdam, Netherlands. Ed. John D. Stamford. adv. illus.

914   DK
STADTFUHER KOPENHAGEN. (Text in German) a. Forlaget Folia ApS, St. Kongensgade 40, 1264 Copenhagen K, Denmark. adv. circ. 200,000.

974.9   US
STATE AND NATIONAL REGISTERS OF HISTORIC PLACES. 1977. a. free. Department of Environmental Protection, Office of New Jersey Heritage, John Fitch Plaza, Trenton, NJ 08625. TEL 609-292-2028. Ed. Susan Pringle. circ. 2,000.

914.2   UK
STATELY HOMES, MUSEUMS, CASTLES AND GARDENS IN BRITAIN. a. £5.95 to non-members. Automobile Association, Fanum House, Basingstoke, Hants. RG21 2EA, England. adv.
    Former titles: Stately Homes, Museums, Castles and Gardens & Britain's Heritage.

919   SI
SURVEY OF OVERSEAS VISITORS TO SINGAPORE. (Text in English) 1975. a. S.$10. Singapore Tourist Promotion Board, Research Department, Raffles City Tower 36-04, 250 North Bridge Road, Singapore 0617, Singapore. charts.

910.09   US
SURVEY OF STATE TRAVEL OFFICES. 1973. a. $60. U S Travel Data Center, 899 L. St., N.W., Washington, DC 20036. TEL 202-293-1040. (reprint service avail. from CIS)

338.7　　　　　II
TAMIL NADU TOURISM DEVELOPMENT CORPORATION. ANNUAL REPORT. (Text in English) a. Tamil Nadu Tourism Development Corporation, Shivalaya Bldg., 16 Commander-in-Chief Rd., Madras 600008, India.

914.2　　　　　UK
TASTE OF SCOTLAND. 1972. a. free. Scottish Tourist Board, 23 Ravelston Terrace, Edinburgh EH4 3EU, Scotland. illus.

TEACHERS' GUIDE TO OVERSEAS TEACHING; a complete and comprehensive guide of English-language schools and colleges overseas. see *EDUCATION*

910.202　　　　　US
TEMPORARY MILITARY LODGING AROUND THE WORLD. 1971. irreg., 6th edt. 1984. $8.95. Military Marketing Services, Inc., Box 4010, Arlington, VA 22204.

914　　　　　IT　　ISSN 0040-3652
TERAMO; le notizie del turismo. (Text in English, French, German and Italian) 1959. irreg. free. Ente Provinciale per Il Turismo di Teramo, Teramo, Italy. Dir. Giammario Sgattoni. bk. rev. charts. illus. tr.lit. circ. 10,000.

910.2 914　　　　　UK　　ISSN 0082-3805
THAMES BOOK. 1966. a. £2.95. Link House Magazines Ltd., Link House, Dingwall Ave., Croydon CR9 2TA, England.

910.2 919　　　　　US
THRUM'S ALL ABOUT HAWAII. 1970, 91st edt. a. $3.50. S B Printers, Inc., P.O. Box 100, Honolulu, HI 96810. TEL 808-537-5353. Ed. Arlene King Duncan. adv. circ. 25,000.
　Former titles: Almanac of the Pacific (ISSN 0065-6461) & All About Hawaii.

THUNDER BAY CAMPING GUIDE. see *SPORTS AND GAMES — Outdoor Life*

917.6　　　　　US　　ISSN 0361-4948
TOURBOOK: ALABAMA, LOUISIANA, MISSISSIPPI. Cover title: Alabama, Louisiana, Mississippi TourBook. a. membership. American Automobile Association, 8111 Gatehouse Rd., Falls Church, VA 22047. TEL 703-222-6000. illus. circ. 801,000.

917.89　　　　　US　　ISSN 0362-3599
TOURBOOK: ARIZONA, NEW MEXICO. Variant title: Arizona, New Mexico TourBook. a. membership. American Automobile Association, 8111 Gatehouse Rd., Falls Church, VA 22047. TEL 703-222-6000. illus. circ. 1,125,000.

917.6　　　　　US
TOURBOOK: ARKANSAS, KANSAS, MISSOURI, OKLAHOMA. Cover title: Arkansas, Kansas, Missouri, Oklahoma TourBook. a. membership. American Automobile Association, 8111 Gatehouse Rd., Falls Church, VA 22047. TEL 703-222-6000. circ. 1,042,000.

917.15　　　　　US　　ISSN 0363-1788
TOURBOOK: ATLANTIC PROVINCES AND QUEBEC. Cover title: Atlantic Provinces and Quebec; New Brunswick Newfoundland, Nova Scotia, Prince Edward Island, Quebec TourBook. a. membership. American Automobile Association, 8111 Gatehouse Rd., Falls Church, VA 22047. TEL 703-222-6000. (Co-sponsor: Canadian Automobile Association) illus. circ. 520,000.
　Formerly: Eastern Canada Tour Book (ISSN 0569-2857)

917.9　　　　　US
TOURBOOK: CALIFORNIA, NEVADA. Cover title: California, Nevada TourBook. a. membership. American Automobile Association, 8111 Gatehouse Rd., Falls Church, VA 22047. TEL 703-222-6000. circ. 2,675,000.

917.8　　　　　US　　ISSN 0362-9821
TOURBOOK: COLORADO, UTAH. Cover title: Colorado, Utah TourBook. a. membership. American Automobile Association, 8111 Gatehouse Rd., Falls Church, VA 22047. TEL 703-222-6000. circ. 943,000.

917.4　　　　　US
TOURBOOK: CONNECTICUT, MASSACHUSETTS, RHODE ISLAND. Cover title: Connecticut, Massachusetts, Rhode Island TourBook. a. membership. American Automobile Association, 8111 Gatehouse Rd., Falls Church, VA 22047. TEL 703-222-6000. illus. circ. 1,099,000.
　Supersedes in part: Northeastern Tour Book (ISSN 0468-6853)

917.59　　　　　US　　ISSN 0516-9674
TOURBOOK: FLORIDA. 1965. a. membership. American Automobile Association, 8111 Gatehouse Rd., Falls Church, VA 22047. TEL 703-222-6000. illus. circ. 2,097,000. Key Title: Florida Tour Book.

917.5　　　　　US　　ISSN 0361-4956
TOURBOOK: GEORGIA, NORTH CAROLINA, SOUTH CAROLINA. Cover title: Georgia, North Carolina, South Carolina TourBook. a. membership. American Automobile Association, 8111 Gatehouse Rd., Falls Church, VA 22047. TEL 703-222-6000. illus. circ. 1,979,000.

917　　　　　US
TOURBOOK: HAWAII. Cover title: Hawaii TourBook. a. membership. American Automobile Association, 8111 Gatehouse Rd., Falls Church, VA 22047. circ. 376,000.

917.9　　　　　US　　ISSN 0363-2695
TOURBOOK: IDAHO, MONTANA, WYOMING. Cover title: Idaho, Montana, Wyoming TourBook. a. membership. American Automobile Association, 8111 Gatehouse Rd., Falls Church, VA 22047. TEL 703-222-6000. illus. circ. 728,000.
　Supersedes in part: Northwestern Tour Book (ISSN 0094-078X); Continues: Northwestern States.

917　　　　　US
TOURBOOK: ILLINOIS, INDIANA, OHIO. Cover title: Illinois, Indiana, Ohio, TourBook. a. membership. American Automobile Association, 8111 Gatehouse Rd., Falls Church, VA 22047. TEL 703-222-6000. circ. 1,658,000.

917.68　　　　　US　　ISSN 0361-4964
TOURBOOK: KENTUCKY, TENNESSEE. Cover title: Kentucky, Tennessee TourBook. a. membership. American Automobile Association, 8111 Gatehouse Rd., Falls Church, VA 22047. TEL 703-222-6000. illus. circ. 1,440,000.

917.4　　　　　US
TOURBOOK: MAINE, NEW HAMPSHIRE, VERMONT. Cover title: Maine, New Hampshire, Vermont TourBook. a. membership. American Automobile Association, 8111 Gatehouse Rd., Falls Church, VA 22047. TEL 703-222-6000. circ. 878,000.
　Supersedes in part: Northeastern Tour Book (ISSN 0468-6853)

917　　　　　US
TOURBOOK: MICHIGAN, WISCONSIN. Cover title: Michigan, Wisconsin TourBook. a. membership. American Automobile Association, 8111 Gatehouse Rd., Falls Church, VA 22047. TEL 703-222-6000. circ. 850,000.

917　　　　　US　　ISSN 0364-0086
TOURBOOK: MID-ATLANTIC. Cover title: Mid-Atlantic-Delaware, District of Columbia, Maryland, Virginia, West Virginia TourBook. a. membership. American Automobile Association, 8111 Gatehouse Rd., Falls Church, VA 22047. TEL 703-222-6000. circ. 1,935,000.

917　　　　　US
TOURBOOK: NEW JERSEY, PENNSYLVANIA. Cover title: New Jersey, Pennsylvania TourBook. a. membership. American Automobile Association, 8111 Gatehouse Rd., Falls Church, VA 22047. TEL 703-222-6000. circ. 1,689,000.

917　　　　　US　　ISSN 0363-1540
TOURBOOK: NEW YORK. Cover title: New York TourBook. a. membership. American Automobile Association, 8111 Gatehouse Rd., Falls Church, VA 22047. TEL 703-222-6000. circ. 1,342,000.

917　　　　　US
TOURBOOK: NORTH CENTRAL. Cover title: North Central-Iowa, Minnesota, Nebraska, North Dakota, South Dakota TourBook. a. membership. American Automobile Association, 8111 Gatehouse Rd., Falls Church, VA 22047. TEL 703-222-6000. circ. 825,000.
　Formerly: North Central Tour Book (ISSN 0733-835X)

917　　　　　US
TOURBOOK: ONTARIO. Cover title: Ontario TourBook. a. membership. American Automobile Association, 8111 Gatehouse Rd., Falls Church, VA 22047. TEL 703-222-6000. circ. 750,000.

918　　　　　US
TOURBOOK: OREGON/WASHINGTON. Cover title: Oregon/Washington. a. membership. American Automobile Association, 8111 Gatehouse Rd., Falls Church, VA 22047. TEL 703-222-6000. circ. 911,000.

917　　　　　US
TOURBOOK: TEXAS. Cover title: Texas TourBook. a. membership. American Automobile Association, 8111 Gatehouse Rd., Falls Church, VA 22047. TEL 703-222-6000. circ. 933,000.

917.12　　　　　US　　ISSN 0362-3602
TOURBOOK: WESTERN CANADA AND ALASKA. Cover title: Western Canada and Alaska; Alberta, British Columbia, Manitoba, Saskatchewan, Northwest Territories, Yukon Territory and Alaska TourBook. a. American Automobile Association, 8111 Gatehouse Rd., Falls Church, VA 22047. TEL 703-222-6000. illus. circ. 669,000.

914.1　　　　　UK
TOURING GUIDE TO SCOTLAND. 1975. a. £10.95 to non-members. Automobile Association, Fanum House, Basingstoke, Hants RG21 2EA, England.

914.2　　　　　UK
TOURING IN FROM SALISBURY. (Text in English, French, German) 1983. a. £1.25. Salisbury District Council, Publicity Office, Bourne Hill, Salisbury SP1 3UZ, England (Subscr. to: Tourist Information Centre, Fish Row, Salisbury SP1 3UZ, England) Ed. John S. Guthrie. adv. circ. 30,000.
　Formerly (until 1987): Touring in Historic Wessex.

971.04　　　　　CN
TOURIST GUIDE BOOK OF ONTARIO. 1921. a. free. C A A Auto Club & Travel Agency, 1215 Ouellette Ave., P.O. Box 580, Windsor, Ont. N9A 9Z9, Canada. TEL 519-255-1212. Ed. Marlene S. Lancaster. adv. circ. 150,000.

917.104　　　　　CN
TOURIST GUIDE/TOURISTIQUE. (Text in French & English) a. Can.$2.50. Editeur Limite-Ltd., 300 Arran Ave., St. Lambert, Que. J4R 1K5, Canada. Ed. Lucien Fontaine. adv. circ. 50,000.

910.202　　　　　AT
TOURIST PARK GUIDE. 1946. a. Aus.$2.50. Newspress Pty Ltd. (Subsidiary of: Age Publications) 603-611 Little Lonsdale St., Melbourne, Vic. 3000, Australia. Ed. Gwen Haslar. adv. circ. 30,000.

910.202　　　　　US　　ISSN 0278-467X
TOURS AND VISITS DIRECTORY. irreg., 2nd edt., 1981. $98. Gale Research Company, Book Tower, Detroit, MI 48226. TEL 313-961-2242.
　Formerly: Behind the Scenes (ISSN 0270-3416)

380.058　　　　　ET　　ISSN 0564-0490
TRADE DIRECTORY AND GUIDE BOOK TO ETHIOPIA. 1954. a. Eth.$10($4.80) Ethiopian Chamber of Commerce, Box 517, Addis Ababa, Ethiopia. (reprint service avail. from ISI)

TRADESHOW & EXHIBIT MANAGER BUYERS GUIDE. see *BUSINESS AND ECONOMICS — Trade And Industrial Directories*

TRAILER LIFE'S RECREATIONAL VEHICLE CAMPGROUND AND SERVICES DIRECTORY. see *SPORTS AND GAMES — Outdoor Life*

910　　　　　SP　　ISSN 0082-6103
TRAVEL ABROAD: FRONTIER FORMALITIES. (Editions in English and French) 1955. a. $54. World Tourism Organization, Capitan Hata 42, 28020 Madrid, Spain.

910.09   US   ISSN 0276-8968
TRAVEL AND TOURISM RESEARCH ASSOCIATION. PROCEEDINGS OF THE ANNUAL CONFERENCE. 1970. a. $45. Bureau of Economic and Business Research, University of Utah, Graduate School of Business, K D G Bldg., Rm. 401, Salt Lake City, UT 84108. TEL 801-581-6333. Ed. Mari Lou Wood. charts. illus. circ. 900.

910.22   330.9   HK   ISSN 0255-8866
TRAVEL BUSINESS ANALYST. 1981. irreg. $200. Interasia Publications, 200 Lockhart Rd., 13th Floor, Hong Kong, Hong Kong. Ed. Murray Bailey.

910.09   US
TRAVEL DATA LOCATOR INDEX; a reference guide to current data on travel and recreation. irreg. $12. U S Travel Data Center, 1899 L St., N.W., Washington, DC 20036. TEL 202-293-1040. (reprint service avail. from CIS)

910.202   HK   ISSN 0256-4203
TRAVEL DIRECTORY. 1977. a. $25. Interasia Publications, 200 Lockhart Rd., 13th Floor, Hong Kong, Hong Kong. Ed. Murray Bailey. adv. bk. rev. illus. circ. 6,000.
Formerly: Asia Travel Trade Directory.

910   SA
TRAVEL GUIDE, S.A. a. R.7.60. Promco (Pty) Ltd., 1202 Radio City, Tulbagh Square, Cape Town 8001, South Africa. Ed. L.D. Solomon. adv.

914.1   US
TRAVEL GUIDE TO EUROPE. a. $8.95. American Automobile Association, 8111 Gatchouse Rd., Falls Church, VA 22047. TEL 703-222-6000. illus. circ. 133,000.
Formed by the merger of: British Isles and Ireland Travel Guide (ISSN 0095-1579) & Central Europe and Scandinavia Travel Guide (ISSN 0094-3657) & Eastern Europe Travel Guide (ISSN 0094-8632) & Southern Europe Travel Guide (ISSN 0094-3614)

919   US
TRAVEL GUIDE TO THE CARIBBEAN. a. $5.95. American Automobile Association, 8111 Gatehouse Rd., Falls Church, VA 22047. circ. 189,000.

914.95   GR
TRAVEL IN GREECE. (Text in Greek) 1970. a. Dr.450($3.30) Hellenews Ltd., 39 Amaroussiou-Halandriou Rd., Amaroussion, Athens, Greece. Ed. D. G. Kalofolias.

910.2   US   ISSN 0082-6146
TRAVEL INDUSTRY PERSONNEL DIRECTORY. 1951. a. $15. American Traveler, Capital Cities Media, Inc., 2 W. 46th St., New York, NY 10036. TEL 212-575-9000. Ed. Bette Sweeney. adv. index. circ. 7,000.

910.09   US   ISSN 0738-9515
TRAVEL INDUSTRY WORLD YEARBOOK. 1956. a. $56. Child & Waters, Inc., 516 Fifth Ave., New York, NY 10036. TEL 212-840-1935. Ed. Somerset Waters.

910.202   UK   ISSN 0264-7664
TRAVEL MANAGEMENT INTERNATIONAL; the comprehensive guide to world business travel. 1984. a. £25. Millbank Publications, 25 Catherine St., London WC2B 5JW, England. TEL 01-379-3036. Ed. K.J. Allen. adv. illus. circ. 4,000.

910.2   UK   ISSN 0041-2074
TRAVEL TRADE DIRECTORY. 1958. a. £23. Morgan-Grampian Book Publishing Co. Ltd., 30 Calderwood St., Woolwich, London SE18 6QH, England. Ed. Ian Laurie. adv. bk. rev. charts. illus. mkt. tr.lit. circ. 5,500.

914.2   UK   ISSN 0082-7932
TRAVEL TRADE DIRECTORY, U K AND IRELAND. 1958. a. Morgan-Grampian (Publishers) Ltd., Morgan-Grampian House, Calderwood St., London SE18 6QH, England. adv.

910.202   UK
TRAVEL TRADE LONDON. 1984. a. Where Publications, 55-57 Great Marlborough St., London W1V 1DD, England. Ed. Ylva French. circ. 25,000.

910   US
TRAVEL TRENDS IN THE UNITED STATES AND CANADA. 1960. irreg., latest edt., 1984. $45. University of Colorado, Graduate School of Business Administration, Boulder, CO 80309. TEL 303-492-8227. Ed. Charles R. Goelder. circ. 1,100.
Formerly: Travel Trends in the United States and Canadian Provinces (ISSN 0082-6200)

910.202   US
TRAVEL WEEKLY'S WORLD TRAVEL DIRECTORY; official guide to the worldwide travel industry. 1970. a. $95. Murdoch Magazines (Secaucus), 500 Harmon Meadow Blvd., Secaucus, NJ 07094. TEL 201-902-2000. adv. tr. lit. circ. 8,000.
Formerly: World Travel Directory.

917.204   MX
TRAVELERS GUIDE TO MEXICO. (Text in English) 1969. a. $10.95 per no. Prometur, S.A. de C.V., Apdo. 6-1007, 06600 Mexico, D.F., Mexico. adv. circ. 3,600,000.

916.7   UK   ISSN 0144-7661
TRAVELLER'S GUIDE TO CENTRAL AND SOUTHERN AFRICA. 1978. a. £9.95($19.95) I.C. Publications Ltd., Box 261, Carlton House, 69 Gt. Queen St., London WC2B 5BN, England. Ed. Alan Rake. (back issues avail.)

916.7   UK   ISSN 0144-7653
TRAVELLER'S GUIDE TO EAST AFRICA AND THE INDIAN OCEAN. 1978. a. £9.95($19.95) I.C. Publications Ltd., Box 261, Carlton House, 69 Gt. Queen St., London WC2B 5BN, England. Ed. Alan Rake. (back issues avail.)

916.1   UK   ISSN 0144-7637
TRAVELLER'S GUIDE TO NORTH AFRICA. 1978. a. £9.95($19.95) I.C. Publications Ltd., Box 261, Carlton House, 69 Gt. Queen St., London WC2B 5BN, England. Ed. Alan Rake.

915.6   UK
TRAVELLER'S GUIDE TO THE MIDDLE EAST. 1978. a. £9.95($19.95) I.C. Publications Ltd., Box 261, Carlton House, 69 Gt. Queen St., London WC2B 5BN, England. Ed. Terence Mirabelli. charts. illus.

916.6   UK   ISSN 0144-7645
TRAVELLER'S GUIDE TO WEST AFRICA. 1978. a. £9.95($19.95) I.C. Publications Ltd., Box 261, Carlton House, 69 Gt. Queen St., London WC2B 5BN, England. Ed. Alan Rake. bk. rev. illus. stat. (back issues avail.)

910.202   AT
TRAVELWEEK BLUE BOOK. 1983. a. Aus.$30. Peter Isaacson Publications, 45-50 Porter St., Prahran, Vic. 3181, Australia. Ed. Peter Finlayson.

910.09   UK
TRIP OUT. 1977. biennial. £2.95. G.P. Hamer, Ed. & Pub., 77 St. Mary's Grove, London W4 3LW, England. (back issues avail.)

910.09   DK   ISSN 0108-8734
TURISTFOERER. Variant title: Turistfoererforeningen. Medlemliste. 1975. a. free. (Turistfoerrerforeningen) Point Publishing ApS, Gersonsvej 33, 2900 Hellerup, Denmark. adv. circ. 3,600.

917   US
U S A FOR BUSINESS TRAVELERS. a. $7.95. Houghton Mifflin Co., Birnbaum Travel Guides, 60 E. 42nd St., Ste. 1624, New York, NY 10165. TEL 212-682-9440. Ed. Stephen Birnbaum.

719.32   US   ISSN 0083-2316
U.S. NATIONAL PARK SERVICE. HISTORICAL HANDBOOK SERIES. 1950. irreg. U.S. National Park Service, Interior Bldg., Washington, DC 20240 TEL 202-343-1100. (Orders to: Supt. Doc., Washington, DC 20402)

917   US
UNITED STATES (YEAR) a. $11.95. Houghton Mifflin Co., Birnbaum Travel Guides, 60 E. 42nd St., Ste. 1624, New York, NY 10165. TEL 212-682-9440. Ed. Stephen Birnbaum.

914   FR   ISSN 0395-8086
UNIVERSITE D'AIX-MARSEILLE 3. CENTRE DES HAUTES ETUDES TOURISTIQUES. COLLECTION "ESSAIS". 1976. irreg., no.243, 1986. 50 Fr. Universite d'Aix-Marseille III(Universite de Droit, d'Economie et des Sciences), Centre des Hautes Etudes Touristiques, Fondation Vasarely, 1 Av. Marcel Pagnol, 13090 Aix-en-Provence, France. Indexed: Rural Recreat.Tour.Abstr. World Agri.Econ.& Rural Social.Abstr.

914   FR   ISSN 0065-4965
UNIVERSITE D'AIX-MARSEILLE 3. CENTRE DES HAUTES ETUDES TOURISTIQUES. ETUDES ET MEMOIRES. 1963. irreg., no.100, 1986. price varies. Universite d'Aix-Marseille III (Universite de Droit, d'Economie et des Sciences), Centre des Hautes Etudes Touristiques, Fondation Vasarely, 1 Av. Marcel Pagnol, 13090 Aix-en-Provence, France.

919.604   NN
VANUATU IN FIGURES/VANUATU EN CHIFFRES. (Text in English and French) 1975. a. free. Informations Department, Statistics Division, NP 50, Port-vila, Vanuatu. stat. circ. 500.
Formerly: New Hebrides. Bureau of Statistics. Some Facts and Figures about the New Hebrides/ Quelques Fait et Chiffres Concernants les Nouvelles-Hebrides.

914.3   GW   ISSN 0083-5250
VARTA FUEHRER DURCH DEUTSCHLAND, WESTLICHER TEIL UND BERLIN; ausgewaehlte Hotels und Restaurants in der Bundesrepublik Deutschland. 1957. a. 39.80 dM. Redaktion VARTA-Fuehrer, Seedammweg 55, Postfach 1563, 6380 Bad Homburg, W. Germany (B.R.D.) Ed.Bd. adv. circ. 110,000.

910.2   UK   ISSN 0260-910X
VISIT CALIFORNIA WITH FYFE ROBERTSON. 1981. a. £1.95. Lewis Productions Ltd., 31 Castle St., Kingston-upon-Thames, Surrey KT1 1ST, England. Ed. David Jacobson. adv. circ. 60,000.

914.2   UK
WALES BEST HOLIDAYS. 1974. a. £1. F.H.G. Publications Ltd., Abbey Mill Business Centre, Seedhill, Paisley PA1 1JN, Scotland.
Formerly: Holidays in Wales (ISSN 0267-3401)

914.1   UK
WALKS AND TRAILS IN SCOTLAND. 1977. irreg. £1.50. Scottish Tourist Board, 23 Ravelston Terrace, Edinburgh EH4 3EU, Scotland.

917.504   US
WALT DISNEY WORLD (YEAR) a. $6.95. Houghton Mifflin Co., Birnbaum Travel Guides, 60 E. 42nd St., Ste. 1624, New York, NY 10165. TEL 212-682-9440. Ed. Stephen Birnbaum.

910.2   UK   ISSN 0260-9061
WEEKENDER. 1981. a. £1.25. Lewis Publications Ltd., 31 Castle St., Kingston-upon-Thames, Surrey KT1 1ST, England. Ed. David Jacobson. adv. circ. 60,000.

919.31   NZ
WEEKLY NEWS ANNUAL. 1901. a. NZ.$7.95. Wilson & Horton Ltd., 46 Albert St., Auckland, New Zealand. Ed. D.Faulls. adv. illus. circ. 16,000.
Formerly: New Zealand Annual (ISSN 0110-0831)

914   DK   ISSN 0085-8048
WELCOME TO FINLAND. (Text in English, French and German) 1962. a. Kr.45($10) Welscan AG, International Publishers, Hasenbuehlweg 3, CH-6300 Zug, Schweiz, Denmark. Ed. Irmeli Porkka. circ. 50,000.

914.1   UK   ISSN 0260-4426
WEST OF SCOTLAND VISITOR; a complete tourist guide to the West of Scotland. 1979. a. £0.20. Scotsman Publications, 20 North Bridge, Edinburgh EH1 1YT, Scotland. illus.

917.12 US
WESTERN CANADA ALASKA CAMPBOOK.
Cover title: R V and Tent Sites in Alberta, British Columbia, Manitoba, Northwest Territories, Saskatchewan, Yukon Territory and Alaska. a. membership. American Automobile Association, 8111 Gatehouse Rd., Falls Church, VA 22047. TEL 703-222-6000. circ. 283,000. Key Title: CampBook. Western Canada and Alaska.
 Formerly: Western Canada. Alaska Camping.

914.2 UK
WHAT TO DO IN THE NORFOLK BROADS. 1927. a. £2. Jarrold Colour Publications, Barrack St., Norwich NR3 1TR, England.

914.204 UK
WHAT'S ON NORTH WEST. a. free. Intercity Publications (N.W.) Ltd., 21 Roebuck Lane, Sale, Cheshire M33 1SY, England. adv. illus. circ. 100,000.

796 US
WHEELERS R V RESORT AND CAMPGROUND GUIDE: NORTH AMERICAN EDITION. 1972. a. $10.95. Print Media Services, Ltd., 1310 Jarvis Ave., Elk Grove Village, IL 60007. TEL 312-981-0100. adv. circ. 180,000.
 Supersedes regional editions of: Wheelers Recreational Vehicle Resort and Campground Guide; Which was formerly titled: Wheelers Trailer Resort and Campground Guide (ISSN 0090-600X)

WHERE TO EAT & ENTERTAIN - SINGAPORE. see HOTELS AND RESTAURANTS

WHERE TO EAT IN BERKSHIRE. see HOTELS AND RESTAURANTS

WHERE TO EAT IN BOURNEMOUTH, POOLE AND DORSET. see HOTELS AND RESTAURANTS

WHERE TO EAT IN BRISTOL, BATH & AVON. see HOTELS AND RESTAURANTS

WHERE TO EAT IN CANADA. see HOTELS AND RESTAURANTS

WHERE TO EAT IN CARDIFF, SWANSEA & SOUTH WALES. see HOTELS AND RESTAURANTS

WHERE TO EAT IN DEVON. see HOTELS AND RESTAURANTS

WHERE TO EAT IN EDINBURGH, FIFE AND THE LOTHIANS. see HOTELS AND RESTAURANTS

WHERE TO EAT IN GLOUCESTERSHIRE AND THE COTSWOLDS. see HOTELS AND RESTAURANTS

WHERE TO EAT IN GREATER MANCHESTER. see HOTELS AND RESTAURANTS

WHERE TO EAT IN HAMPSHIRE AND THE NEW FOREST. see HOTELS AND RESTAURANTS

WHERE TO EAT IN KENT. see HOTELS AND RESTAURANTS

WHERE TO EAT IN OXFORD AND OXFORDSHIRE. see HOTELS AND RESTAURANTS

WHERE TO EAT IN SOMERSET. see HOTELS AND RESTAURANTS

WHERE TO EAT IN SURREY. see HOTELS AND RESTAURANTS

WHERE TO EAT IN SUSSEX. see HOTELS AND RESTAURANTS

WHERE TO EAT IN THE CHANNEL ISLANDS. see HOTELS AND RESTAURANTS

WHERE TO EAT IN WILTSHIRE. see HOTELS AND RESTAURANTS

914.2 UK
WHERE TO GO IN THE THAMES AND CHILTERNS. 1980. a. £1. Thames & Chilterns Tourist Board, 8 Market Place, Abingdon, Oxon, England. adv. circ. 25,000.

914.2 UK
WHERE TO GO, WHAT TO DO IN THE SOUTH. a. £1. Heritage Publications, 6 Brook Court, Middlebridge St., Romsey, Hants. SO51 8HR, England. Ed. J. Dunning. circ. 17,000.

910.202 657 UK
WHERE TO STAY IN LONDON. 1980. a. Where Publications, 55-57 Great Marlborough St., London W1V 1DD, England. Ed. Mary Barham. circ. 40,000.

910.202 US
WISCONSIN TRAVEL AND RECREATION GUIDE. a. Rockford Map Publishers, Inc., 4525 Forest View Ave., Box 6126, Rockford, IL 61125.

WORKING ABROAD (LONDON) see BUSINESS AND ECONOMICS — Labor And Industrial Relations

910 709 US
WORLD CULTURAL GUIDES. irreg. Holt Rinehart and Winston, Inc., General Book Division, 383 Madison Ave., New York, NY 10017. TEL 212-688-9100.

910.2 FR ISSN 0070-6515
WORLD DIRECTORY OF TRAVEL AGENCIES. 1950. a. 360 F. ‡ International Hotel Association, 80 rue de la Roquette, 75011 Paris, France. circ. 5,500.

910.202 US
WORLD HOLIDAY AND TIME GUIDE. 1982. a. Morgan Guaranty Trust Company, 23 Wall St., New York, NY 10015.

910 SP
WORLD TOURISM ORGANIZATION. TOURIST BIBLIOGRAPHY. (Includes annual Legislation Supplement) (Text in English, French, Spanish) 3/yr. (with a. suppl.) $15. World Tourism Organization, Capitan Haya 42, 28020 Madrid, Spain. abstr.

YACHTSMAN'S GUIDE TO THE BAHAMAS. see SPORTS AND GAMES — Boats And Boating

647.94 UK
YOUTH HOSTELS ASSOCIATION (ENGLAND AND WALES) GUIDE. 1931. a. £1.75. Youth Hostels Association, Trevelyan House, St. Albans AL1 2DY, England. TEL (0727) 55215. Ed. Helen Gavine. adv. circ. 250,000.
 Formerly: Youth Hostels Association (England and Wales) Handbook.

TRAVEL AND TOURISM —
Abstracting, Bibliographies, Statistics

319 BB
BARBADOS. STATISTICAL SERVICE. DIGEST OF TOURISM STATISTICS. a. Statistical Service, National Insurance Building, 3rd FL., Fairchild St., Bridgetown, Barbados, W. Indies.

910.2 BE ISSN 0067-5547
BELGIUM. INSTITUT NATIONAL DE STATISTIQUE. STATISTIQUE DU TOURISME ET DE L'HOTELLERIE. (Text in Dutch and French) a. 48 Fr. Institut National de Statistique, 44 rue de Louvain, 1000 Brussels, Belgium.

959 016 SI ISSN 0068-0176
BOOKS ABOUT SINGAPORE. 1963. biennial. free. National Library, Stamford Road, Singapore 0617, Singapore. circ. 5,000.
 Formerly: Books About Malaysia.

916.8 316 BS
BOTSWANA. CENTRAL STATISTICS OFFICE. TOURIST STATISTICS. 1974. a. R.1. Central Statistics Office, Ministry of Finance and Development Planning, Private Bag 0024, Gaborone, Botswana (Orders to: Government Printer, Box 87, Gaborone, Botswana). charts. stat.

338.4 CN ISSN 0317-6738
CANADA. STATISTICS CANADA. TRAVEL BETWEEN CANADA AND OTHER COUNTRIES/VOYAGES ENTRE LE CANADA ET LES AUTRES PAYS. (Catalogue 66-201) (Text in English and French) 1920. a. Can.$25($26) Statistics Canada, Communications Division, 3rd Floor, R.H. Coats Bldg., Ottawa, Ont. K1A 0T6, Canada TEL 613-993-7276. (Subscr. to: Publications Sales and Services, Ottawa, Ont. K1A 0T6, Canada) (also avail. in microform from MML)

910.09 CE
CEYLON TOURIST BOARD. ANNUAL STATISTICAL REPORT. 1968. a. $10. Ceylon Tourist Board, Research Department, P.O. Box 1504, Colombo, Sri Lanka. circ. 1,000.

910.202 CK
COLOMBIA. CORPORACION NACIONAL DE TURISMO. BOLETIN DE ESTADISTICA TURISTICA. (YEAR) 1970. irreg., latest issue 1984. free. Corporacion Nacional de Turismo, Oficina de Planeacion, Calle 28 No. 13A-15, primer piso, Apdo. Aereo 8400, Bogota, Colombia. bk. rev. charts. stat. circ. 2,500.
 Formerly: Colombia. Corporacion Nacional de Turismo. Boletin de Investigaciones e Informacion Turistica.

301.32 312 CY ISSN 0253-8709
CYPRUS. DEPARTMENT OF STATISTICS AND RESEARCH. TOURISM, MIGRATION AND TRAVEL STATISTICS. (Text in English and Greek) 1973. a. cyprus pounds 3. Department of Statistics and Research, Ministry of Finance, Nicosia, Cyprus.

016 940 US ISSN 0070-8097
EAST EUROPE IN GERMAN BOOKS; a bulletin listing new books on East Europe published in the German language. 1971. irreg., vol.5, 1977. Park College, Governmental Research Bureau, Kansas City, MO 64152. TEL 816-741-2000. Ed. Jerzy Hauptmann.

312.8 910 GM
GAMBIA. CENTRAL STATISTICS DEPARTMENT. TOURIST STATISTICS. (Formerly issued by Central Statistics Division) a., latest 1982/1983. d.20. Central Statistics Department, Wellington St., Banjul, Gambia.

GEO KATALOG (YEAR). VOLUME 1. TOURISTISCHE VEROEFFENTLICHUNGEN. see GEOGRAPHY

910 314 GW ISSN 0072-1999
GERMANY (FEDERAL REPUBLIC, 1949-). STATISTISCHES BUNDESAMT. FACHSERIE 6, HANDEL, GASTGEWERBE, REISEVERKEHR; REIHE 7: REISEVERKEHR. irreg. price varies. W. Kohlhammer-Verlag GmbH, Abt. Veroeffentlichungen des Statistischen Bundesamtes, Philipp-Reis-Str. 3, Postfach 421120, 6500 Mainz 42, W. Germany (B. R. D.)

914.704 314 HU ISSN 0230-4414
HUNGARY. KOZPONTI STATISZTIKAI HIVATAL. IDEGENFORGALMI EVKONYV. a. 165 Ft. Statisztikai Kiado Vallalat, Kaszasdulo u. 2, P.O.B. 99, 1300 Budapest 3, Hungary (Subscr. to: Kultura, Box 149, H-1389 Budapest, Hungary)
 Supersedes: Idegenforgalmi Statisztika (ISSN 0209-4819)

338.4 IO
INDONESIA TOURIST STATISTICS. 1975. a. Directorate General of Tourism - Direktorat Jenderal Pariwisata, Jalan Kramat Raya, Box 409, Jakarta, Indonesia.

915.69 IS ISSN 0075-1405
ISRAEL TOURIST STATISTICS/TAYARUT BE-YISRAEL. (Subseries of the Bureau's Special Series) (Text in English and Hebrew) irreg., latest no. 732, 1982. $8 price varies. Central Bureau of Statistics, Box 13015, Jerusalem, Israel.

910 016　　　　　　UK　ISSN 0261-1392
LEISURE, RECREATION AND TOURISM
ABSTRACTS. 1977. q. £62($106) to non-members.
C.A.B. International, Farnham House, Farnham
Royal, Slough SL2 3BN, England (U.S. subscr. to:
Unipub, Box 433, Murray Hill Sta., New York, NY
10016) circ. 350. (also avail. in microfiche; back
issues avail.)
●Also available online. Vendors: BRS, CISTI,
DIMDI, DIALOG, European Space Agency.
　　Formerly: Rural Recreation and Tourism
Abstracts (ISSN 0308-0137)

916　　　　　　　　MW
MALAWI TOURISM REPORT. 1970. a.
K.2.50($2.50) ‡ National Statistical Office, Box 333,
Zomba, Malawi. stat. (processed)
　　Formerly: Malawi. National Statistical Office.
Tourist Report (ISSN 0085-302X)

338.4　　　　　　　MF
MAURITIUS. CENTRAL STATISTICAL OFFICE.
INTERNATIONAL TRAVEL AND TOURISM.
1974. a. Rs.40. Central Statistical Office, Rose Hill,
Mauritius (Orders to: G.P.O., Elizabeth II, Port
Louis, Mauritius)

910 310　　　　　　NE　ISSN 0168-5538
NETHERLANDS. CENTRAAL BUREAU VOOR
DE STATISTIEK. STATISTIEK
VREEMDELINGENVERKEER. TOURISM
STATISTICS. (Text in Dutch and English) 1952. a.
fl.20.75. Centraal Bureau voor de Statistiek, Prinses
Beatrixlaan 428, Voorburg, Netherlands (Orders to:
Staatsuitgeverij, Christoffel Plantijnstraat, The
Hague, Netherlands)

910.2　　　　　　　NE　ISSN 0168-3411
NETHERLANDS. CENTRAAL BUREAU VOOR
DE STATISTIEK. VAKANTIEONDERZOEK.
(Text in Dutch and English) 1954. a. Centraal
Bureau voor de Statistiek, Prinses Beatrixlaan 428,
Voorburg, Netherlands (Orders to: Staatsuitgeverij,
Christoffel Plantijnstraat, The Hague, Netherlands)
　　Formerly: Vakantiebesteding van de Nederlandse
Bevolking (ISSN 0077-7501)

332.1 314　　　　　NO　ISSN 0333-208X
NORWAY. STATISTISK SENTRALBYRAA.
REISELIVSTATISKK/STATISTICS ON TRAVEL.
(Subseries of its Norges Offisielle Statistikk) (Text
in Norwegian and English) 1977. a. Kr.45. Statistisk
Sentralbyraa, Box 8131 Dep., 0033 Oslo 1, Norway.
stat. circ. 1,000.

914.69　　　　　　 PO　ISSN 0377-2306
PORTUGAL. INSTITUTO NACIONAL DE
ESTATISTICA. ESTATISTICAS DO TURISMO.
CONTINENTE, ACORES E MADEIRA. (Text in
French and Portuguese) 1969. a. Esc.1275. Instituto
Nacional de Estatistica, Av. Antonio Jose de
Almeida, 1078 Lisbon Codex, Portugal (Orders to:
Imprensa Nacional, Casa da Moeda, Direccao
Comercial, rua D. Francisco Manuel de Melo 5,
1000 Lisbon, Portugal)
　　Formerly: Portugal. Instituto Nacional de
Estatistica. Estatisticas do Turismo.

910.09　　　　　　TZ　ISSN 0564-836X
REPORT ON TOURISM STATISTICS IN
TANZANIA. (Formerly issued by its Central
Statistical Bureau) 1968. irreg. Bureau of Statistics,
Box 796, Dar es Salaam, Tanzania (Orders to:
Government Publications Agency, Box 1801, Dar es
Salaam, Tanzania)

310　　　　　　　　SE
SEYCHELLES. DEPARTMENT OF FINANCE.
VISITOR SURVEY. a. R.5. Department of Finance,
Statistics Division, P.O.Box 206, Independence
House, Victoria, Republic of Seychelles.

960 316　　　　　　SE
SEYCHELLES. PRESIDENT'S OFFICE.
STATISTICS DIVISION. MIGRATION AND
TOURISM STATISTICS. a. Rs.15. President's
Office, Department of Finance, Statistics Division,
Box 206, Mahe, Seychelles.
　　Formerly: Seychelles. President's Office. Statistics
Division. Tourism and Migration Report.

915.95　　　　　　 SI
SINGAPORE TOURIST PROMOTION BOARD.
ANNUAL STATISTICAL REPORT ON VISITOR
ARRIVALS. 1969. a. S.$16.50. ‡ Singapore Tourist
Promotion Board, Research Department, Raffles
City Tower 36-04, 250 North Bridge Road,
Singapore 0617, Singapore. charts. stat. circ. 1,500.
(tabloid format)

SOUTH AFRICA. CENTRAL STATISTICAL
SERVICE. TOURISM AND MIGRATION. see
*POPULATION STUDIES — Abstracting,
Bibliographies, Statistics*

915.1　　　　　　　HK
STATISTICAL REVIEW OF TOURISM IN HONG
KONG. (Text in English) 1974. a. HK.$50($10)
Hong Kong Tourist Association, Research
Department, Box 2597, Hong Kong, Hong Kong.
circ. 5,000.
　　Supersedes: Hong Kong Tourist Association.
Digest of Annual Statistics.

319　　　　　　　　FJ
TOURISM AND MIGRATION STATISTICS. 1973.
a. $1.25. Bureau of Statistics, Box 2221, Suva, Fiji.
　　Supersedes: Statistical Report on Tourism in Fiji.

910 016　　　　　　SP
TOURISM COMPENDIUM. (Editions in English,
French and Spanish) 1959. a. $9. World Tourism
Organization, Capitan Haya 42, 28020 Madrid,
Spain.
　　Formerly: Tourist Bibliography (ISSN 0082-5468)

338.4　　　　　　　VB
TOURISM IN THE BRITISH VIRGIN ISLANDS.
1973. a. $3. Statistics Office, Finance Department,
Road Town, Tortola, British Virgin Islands. stat.

917.29　　　　　　 PR
TOURISM INDUSTRY OF PUERTO RICO.
SELECTED STATISTICS. 1970. a., latest issue
1984-85. free. ‡ Tourism Company of Puerto Rico,
Office of Statistics and Economic Studies, 301 San
Justo St., P.O. Box 4435, Old San Juan Sta., San
Juan, PR 00905. Ed. Maria I. Aponte. stat. circ. 1,
250. (processed)

910 310　　　　　　TR　ISSN 0082-6537
TRINIDAD AND TOBAGO. CENTRAL
STATISTICAL OFFICE. INTERNATIONAL
TRAVEL REPORT. 1955. a., latest 1981. T.T.$3.
Central Statistical Office, P.O. Box 98, 23 Park St.,
Port-of-Spain, Trinidad, W.I. (Orders to:
Government Printing Office, 48 St. Vincent St., Port
of Spain, Trinidad, W.I.)

910 314　　　　　　BU
TURIZUM/TOURISM. (Text in Bulgarian and
English) 1967. irreg. 0.74 lv. per issue. Ministerstvo
na Informatsiiata i Suobshteniiata, 18, Ul. Graf
Ignatiev, Sofia, Bulgaria. (Co-sponsor: Tsentralno
Statistichesko Upravlenie) stat. circ. 690.

910.2　　　　　　　SP
YEARBOOK OF TOURISM STATISTICS. (Text in
English, French and Spanish) 1953. a. $21. World
Tourism Organization, Capitan Haya 42, 28020
Madrid, Spain. (looseleaf format)
　　Former titles: World Tourism Statistics/
Statistiques du Tourisme Mondial/Estadisticas del
Turismo Mundial; International Travel Statistics
(ISSN 0074-9184)

910.09　　　　　　YU
YUGOSLAVIA. SAVEZNI ZAVOD ZA
STATISTIKU. TURIZAM. (Subseries of its
Statisticki Bilten) a. 30 din.($1.67) Savezni Zavod za
Statistiku, Kneza Milosa 20, Belgrade, Yugoslavia.
stat.

UROLOGY AND NEPHROLOGY

see *Medical Sciences — Urology and
Nephrology*

VETERINARY SCIENCE

636.089　　　　　　PL　ISSN 0860-2840
ACTA ACADEMIAE AGRICULTURAE AC
TECHNICAE OLSTENENSIS. VETERYNARIA/
VETERINARY MEDICINE. (Subseries of Its:
Zeszyty Naukowe) (Text in Polish; summaries in
English and Russian) 1972. irreg. price varies.
Akademia Rolniczo-Techniczna, Blok 21, 10-718
Olsztyn-Kortowo, Poland (Dist. by: Ars Polona-
Ruch, Krakowskie Przedmiescie 7, 00-901 Warsaw,
Poland) illus. Indexed: Curr.Cont.
　　Formerly: Weterynaria (ISSN 0324-9220)

636.089　　　　　　DK　ISSN 0065-1699
ACTA VETERINARIA SCANDINAVICA.
SUPPLEMENTUM. (Text in English, German or
French; summaries in English and German) 1961.
irreg. Kr.410 incl. main vols. (Societatum
Veteranariarum Scandanivacarum) Danske
Dyrlaegeforening, Alhambravej 15, DK-1826
Copenhagen V, Denmark. Indexed: Biol.Abstr.
Ind.Med. Nutr.Abstr. Dairy Sci.Abstr. Food Sci.&
Tech.Abstr.

ACTA ZOOLOGICA ET PATHOLOGICA
ANTVERPIENSIA. see *BIOLOGY — Zoology*

ADELAIDE. INSTITUTE OF MEDICAL AND
VETERINARY SCIENCE. ANNUAL REPORT
OF THE COUNCIL. see *MEDICAL SCIENCES*

636.089　　　　　　GW　ISSN 0301-2794
ADVANCES IN VERTERINARY MEDICINE/
FORTSCHRITTE DER VETERINAERMEDIZIN.
(Supplement to: Advances in Veterinary Medicine,
Series A, Series B, and Series C which is under the
title: Anatomia, Histologia, Embryologia) 1958.
irreg. price varies. Verlag Paul Parey (Berlin),
Lindenstr. 44-47, 1000 Berlin 61, W. Germany
(B.R.D.) bibl. illus. index. Indexed: Biol.Abstr.
Chem.Abstr. Excerp.Med. Sci.Cit.Ind. Food Sci.&
Tech.Abstr. Ind.Vet. Ind.Sci.Rev. Vet.Bull.

636.089　　　　　　US　ISSN 0065-3519
ADVANCES IN VETERINARY SCIENCE AND
COMPARATIVE MEDICINE. 1953. irreg., vol.30,
1985. Academic Press Inc., Orlando, FL 32887.
TEL 305-345-2000. Eds. C.A. Brandly, E.L.
Jungherr. index. Indexed: Biol.Abstr. Excerp.Med.
Ind.Med. Nutr.Abstr. Sci.Cit.Ind.
Anim.Breed.Abstr. Biotech.Abstr. Dairy Sci.Abstr.
Dent.Ind. Helminthol.Abstr. Ind.Sci.Rev. Ind.Vet.
Vet.Bull.
　　Continues: Advances in Veterinary Science.

636.089　　　　　　US
AMERICAN ANIMAL HOSPITAL ASSOCIATION.
ANNUAL MEETING SCIENTIFIC
PROCEEDINGS. a. $42 to non-members.
American Animal Hospital Association, Box 15899,
Denver, CO 80215-0899. TEL 303-279-2500.

636.089　　　　　　US　ISSN 0065-7182
AMERICAN ASSOCIATION OF EQUINE
PRACTITIONERS. PROCEEDINGS OF THE
ANNUAL CONVENTION. 1956, 2nd convention.
a. $20. American Association of Equine
Practitioners, 410 W. Vine St., Lexington, KY
40507. Ed. Frank Milne. circ. 2,500. (also avail. in
microfilm from UMI; back issues avail.) Indexed:
Helminthol.Abstr. Ind.Vet. Vet.Bull.

636.089　　　　　　US　ISSN 0098-3543
AMERICAN ASSOCIATION OF VETERINARY
LABORATORY DIAGNOSTICIANS.
PROCEEDINGS OF ANNUAL MEETING. 17th,
1974. a. $25. American Association of Veterinary
Laboratory Diagnosticians, c/o Charlotte L. Fox,
Ex. Dir., 3900 E. Timrod, Tucson, AZ 85712. Ed.
M.W. Vorhies. bibl. illus. circ. 700. Indexed:
Chem.Abstr. Ind.Vet. Vet.Bull. Key Title:
Proceedings of Annual Meeting - American
Association of Veterinary Laboratory
Diagnosticians.

636　　　　　　　　US　ISSN 0569-7832
AMERICAN SOCIETY OF ANIMAL SCIENCE.
WESTERN SECTION PROCEEDINGS. 1950? a.
$6. American Society of Animal Science, Western
Section, 309 W. Clark St., Champaign, IL 61820.
TEL 217-356-3182. circ. 600.

VETERINARY SCIENCE

636.089 US ISSN 0066-1147
AMERICAN VETERINARY MEDICAL
ASSOCIATION. DIRECTORY. 1920. a. $30.
American Veterinary Medical Association, 930 N.
Meacham Rd., Schaumburg, IL 60196. TEL 312-
885-8070. Ed. Mrs. J. La Frana. adv. circ. 35,000.
(reprint service avail. from UMI)

636.089 SP
ANALES DE LA UNIVERSIDAD HISPALENSE.
SERIE: VETERINARIA. irreg. price varies.
Universidad de Sevilla, San Fernando 4, Seville,
Spain. charts, illus.

636.089 UK
ANIMAL HEALTH INTERNATIONAL
DIRECTORY. 1984. a. $500. IMSWORLD
Publications Ltd., 11-13 Melton St., London NW1
2EH, England.
●Also available online.

636.089 UG
ANIMAL HEALTH RESEARCH CENTRE.
ANNUAL REPORT. (Text in English) a. Animal
Health Research Centre, Box 24, Entebbe, Uganda.
Indexed: Rev.Appl.Entomol.

636.089 UK ISSN 0142-6591
ANIMAL HEALTH TRUST. ANNUAL REPORT.
1963. a. £2.50. Animal Health Trust, Lanwades
Hall, Kennett, Newmarket, Suffolk CB8 7PN,
England (and 122 E. 55th St., New York, N.Y.
10022) Ed.Bd. adv. bk. rev. charts. illus. index.
circ. 3,500. Indexed: Biol.Abstr.
Formerly: Animal Health (ISSN 0003-3502)

636 AT
ANIMAL QUARANTINE. 1972. irreg. free.
Department of Primary Industry, P.O. Box 46,
Brisbane, Qld. 4001, Australia. circ. 4,000. Indexed:
Ind.Vet. Vet.Bull.

639.089 PL ISSN 0301-7737
ANNALES UNIVERSITATIS MARIAE CURIE-
SKLODOWSKA. SECTIO DD. MEDICINA
VETERINARIA. (Text in Polish or English;
summaries in English, Russian) 1949. a. price varies.
Uniwersytet Marii Curie-Sklodowskiej, Plac Marii
Curie-Sklodowskiej 5, 20-031 Lublin, Poland. Ed.
G. Staskiewicz. circ. 500. Indexed: Biol.Abstr.
Chem.Abstr. Landwirt.Zentralbl. Vet.Bull.

636.089 PL ISSN 0239-4243
ANNALES UNIVERSITATIS MARIAE CURIE-
SKLODOWSKA. SECTIO EE. ZOOTECHNIKA.
(Text in English or Polish; summaries in English,
and Russian) 1983. a. price varies. Uniwersytet
Marii Curie-Sklodowskiej, Plac Marii Curie-
Sklodowskiej 5, 20-031 Lublin, Poland. Ed. Ewald
Sasimowski. circ. 650.

ARANETA RESEARCH JOURNAL. see
AGRICULTURE

636.089 AT ISSN 0728-8425
AUSTRALIAN ADVANCES IN VETERINARY
SCIENCE. 1976. a. Aus.$25. Australian Veterinary
Association Ltd, 134-136 Hampden Rd., Artarmon,
N.S.W. 2064, Australia. Ed. P.M. Outteridge. adv.
circ. 4,000. (back issues avail.)

636.089 AT ISSN 0706-3504
AUSTRALIAN VETERINARY ASSOCIATION.
YEAR BOOK. 1981. a. Aus.$25. Australian
Veterinary Association, 134-136 Hampden Rd.,
Artarmon, NSW 2064, Australia.

636.089 UK
BLACK'S VETERINARY DICTIONARY. 1928.
irreg., (every 2-3 yrs.) A & C Black (Publishers)
Ltd., 35 Bedford Row, London WC1R 4JH,
England. Ed. Geoffrey P. West.

636.089 615 UK
BRITISH PHARMACOPOEIA (VETERINARY)
1977. irreg. £35. Department of Health & Social
Security, P.O. Box 276, London SW8 5DT,
England.

CENTRO DE EDAFOLOGIA Y BIOLOGIA
APLICADA. ANUARIO. see *AGRICULTURE —
Agricultural Economics*

636.089 AT ISSN 0812-7336
COMMONWEALTH SCIENTIFIC AND
INDUSTRIAL RESEARCH ORGANIZATION.
DIVISION OF ANIMAL HEALTH. RESEARCH
REPORT. 1966. biennial. Aus.$2. C.S.I.R.O.,
Division of Animal Health, Private Bag No. 1,
Glebe, N.S.W. 2037, Australia. circ. 1,000. Indexed:
Biol.Abstr. Ind.Vet. Rev.Appl.Entomol. Vet.Bull.
Formerly (until 1982): Commonwealth Scientific
and Industrial Research Organization. Division of
Animal Health. Annual Report (ISSN 0069-7273)

COMPARATIVE ANIMAL NUTRITION. see
BIOLOGY — Zoology

636.089 CU ISSN 0138-8134
CUBA. CENTRO DE INFORMACION Y
DOCUMENTACION AGROPECUARIO.
BOLETIN DE RESENAS. SERIE:
VETERINARIA. (Abstracts in English) 1974. irreg.
exchange basis. Centro de Informacion y
Documentacion Agropecuario, Gaveta Postal 4149,
Havana 4, Cuba (Dist. by: Ediciones Cubana,
Obispo No. 461, Aptdo. 605, Havana, Cuba)
Indexed: Agrindex.
Formerly: Cuba. Centro de Informacion y
Divulgacion Agropecuario. Boletin de Resenas.
Serie: Veterinaria.

636.089 CY
CYPRUS. CHIEF VETERINARY OFFICER.
ANNUAL REPORT. (Text in English) 1967. a.
Department of Veterinary Services, Nicosia, Cyprus.
circ. 275.

636.089 DK ISSN 0105-2543
DENMARK. KUNGL VETERINAER OG
LANDBOHOEJSKOLE. MEDDELELSER. irreg.
Kungl Veterinaer og Landbohoejskole, Afdelningen
for Planternes Ernaering, Thorvaldsens vej 40, DK-
1871 Frederiksberg, Denmark.

636.089 NE
DEVELOPMENTS IN ANIMAL AND
VETERINARY SCIENCES. 1976. irreg., vol.18,
1985. price varies. Elsevier Science Publishers B.V.,
Box 211, 1000 AE Amsterdam, Netherlands.

636.089 GR
EPISTIMONIKI EPITERIS KTENIATRIKIS
SCHOLIS. (Summaries in English) 1952. irreg.
Aristotelian University of Thessaloniki, Faculty of
Veterinary Medicine, Thessaloniki, Greece. Ed. A.
G. Spais. circ. 500. Indexed: Biol.Abstr.

636.089 GE ISSN 0138-5003
ERKRANKUNGEN DER ZOOTIERE. (Text in
English, French, German) 1967. a. (Akademie der
Wissenschaften der DDR) Akademie-Verlag Berlin,
Leipziger Str. 3-4, 1086 Berlin, E. Germany
(D.D.R.)

636.089 634.9 CS
FOLIA VENATORIA; pol'ovnicky zbornik. (Text in
Czech, Slovak; summaries in English, German,
Russian) 1971. a. price varies. (Forest Research
Institute, Federal Committee of Hunting
Associations in the CSSR) Priroda, Krizkova 9, 815
34 Bratislava, Czechoslovakia. Ed. Pavel Hell. bk.
rev. charts. illus. cum.index. Indexed: Biol.Abstr.

636.089 FR ISSN 0249-5740
FRANCE. CENTRE DE RECHERCHE
ZOOTECHNIQUE. DEPARTEMENT DE
GENETIQUE ANIMALE. BULLETIN
TECHNIQUE. 1968. irreg. price varies. Centre de
Recherche Zootechnique, Departement de
Genetique Animale, 78350 Jouy en Josas, France.
Ed. L. Ollivier. circ. 500. Indexed: Biol.Abstr.
Anim.Breed.Abstr.
Formerly: France. Centre de Recherche
Zoologique. Departement de Genetique Animale.
Bulletin Technique.

636.089 IT
GUIDA DI VETERINARIA E ZOOTECNIA; Italian
directory of veterinary drugs, feed additives and
manufacturers. (Text in Italian) 1966. irreg., 5th
edt., 1985. L.63000. Organizzazione Editoriale
Medico-Farmaceutica, Via Edolo 42, Box 10434,
20125 Milan, Italy (U.S. dist.: Drug Intelligence &
Clinical Pharmacy, Box 42435, Cincinnati, OH
45242) Ed. Silvia Marini.

636.089 UK
HANDBOOK OF MEDICINAL FEED
ADDITIVES. 1982. a. price varies. H G M
Publications, Abney House, Baslow, Bakewell,
Derbys, DE4 1RW, England. Ed. Howard G.
Mounsey. adv. circ. 3,000.

INDIAN POULTRY INDUSTRY YEARBOOK. see
AGRICULTURE — Poultry And Livestock

636.089 II ISSN 0304-7067
INDIAN VETERINARY RESEARCH INSTITUTE.
ANNUAL REPORT. (Text in English) 1947/48. a.
exchange basis. Indian Veterinary Research
Institute, Mukteswar-Kumaon, Izatnagar 243122,
Uttar Pradesh, India. circ. 1,500. Indexed:
Anim.Breed.Abstr.
Continues: Muktesar, India. Imperial Veterinary
Research Institute. Report.

636 CN ISSN 0581-3263
INFORMATION VETERINAIRE. vol.19, 1977.
irreg. free. Universite de Montreal, Faculte de
Medecine Veterinaire, C.P. 5000, St. Hyacinthe,
Que. J2S 7C6, Canada. TEL 514-343-6111. Ed. Dr.
Louis Phillippe Phaneuf. Indexed: Ind.Vet.

636.089 FR ISSN 0246-2303
INSTITUT D'ELEVAGE ET DE MEDECINE
VETERINAIRE DES PAYS TROPICAUX.
RAPPORT D'ACTIVITE. 1954. a. Institut
d'Elevage et de Medecine Veterinaire des Pays
Tropicaux, 10 rue Pierre Curie, 94704 Maison
Alfort Cedex, France. Ed.Bd. bibl. circ. 400. (back
issues avail.) Indexed: Biol.Abstr.

636.089 BL
INSTITUTO DE PESQUISAS VETERINARIAS
DESIDERIO FINAMOR. BOLETIM. (Text in
Portuguese; summaries in English) 1972. a. Instituto
de Pesquisas Veterinarias Desiderio Finamor, Caixa
Postal 2076, 90000 Porto Alegre, RS, Brazil. adv.
circ. 1,000. Indexed: Biol.Abstr. Vet.Bull.

INSTITUTUL AGRONOMIC CLUJ-NAPOCA.
BULETINUL. SERIA ZOOTEHNIE SI
MEDICINA VETERINARA. see
AGRICULTURE — Poultry And Livestock

INSTITUTUL AGRONOMIC ION IONESCU DE
LA BRAD. LUCRARI STIINTIFICE, SERIA
ZOOTECHNIE - MEDICINA VETERINARIA.
see *AGRICULTURE — Poultry And Livestock*

636.089 SW ISSN 0074-4026
INTERNATIONAL CONGRESS ON ANIMAL
REPRODUCTION AND ARTIFICIAL
INSEMINATION. PROCEEDINGS. 1948.
quadrennial., 7th, 1972, Munich; 8th, 1976, Krakow;
10th, 1984, Urbana. $60. International Standing
Committee on Physiology and Pathology of Animal
Reproduction, c/o Prof. Stig Einarsson, Dept. of
Obstetrics and Gynaecology, Swedish University of
Agricultural Sciences, 75007 Uppsala, Sweden. circ.
2,000. Indexed: Biol.Abstr.

636.089 GW ISSN 0074-6975
INTERNATIONAL MEETING ON CATTLE
DISEASES. REPORTS. (Each report published in
the host country) (Text in English, French and
German) 1960. biennial, 10th, Mexico, 1978. World
Association for Buiatrics, Bischofsholer Damm 15
(Rinderklinik), 3000 Hannover, W. Germany
(B.R.D.)

636.089 KE
INTERNATIONAL SCIENTIFIC COUNCIL FOR
TRYPANOSOMIASIS RESEARCH AND
CONTROL. (Text in English or French) 1951.
biennial. price varies. (Interafrican Bureau for
Animal Resources) Eleza Services Ltd., P.O. Box
30786, Nairobi, Kenya. Ed. K.M. Katondo. circ. 1,
000. (back issues avail.) Indexed: Biol.Abstr.

636.7 US
INTERNATIONAL SYMPOSIUM ON CANINE
HEARTWORM DISEASE. PROCEEDINGS.
1969. irreg., 2d, Jacksonville, 1971. $12. ‡
University of Florida, Institute of Food and
Agricultural Sciences, Department of Veterinary
Science, Gainesville, FL 32611. TEL 904-392-1733.
Ed. Richard E. Bradley. bibl. illus.

ISRAEL INSTITUTE OF ANIMAL SCIENCE.
SCIENTIFIC ACTIVITIES. see *MEDICAL
SCIENCES — Experimental Medicine, Laboratory
Technique*

VETERINARY SCIENCE

636.089   AU   ISSN 0075-2606
JAHRBUCH FUER DEN OESTERREICHISCHEN TIERARZT. 1950. a. S.208. Alois Goeschl und Co., Trummelhofgasse 12, A-1190 Vienna, Austria. Ed. Hiltraud Lechner.

636.089   JA   ISSN 0388-7421
JAPAN. NATIONAL VETERINARY ASSAY LABORATORY. ANNUAL REPORT. (Text and summaries in English and Japanese) 1963. a. Ministry of Agriculture, Forestry and Fisheries, National Veterinary Assay Laboratory, 1-15-1, Tokura, Kokubunji, Tokyo 185, Japan. Ed.Bd. (back issues avail.)

636   US   ISSN 0075-4129
JOURNAL OF ANIMAL SCIENCE. SUPPLEMENT. irreg., vol.61, 1985. $8. American Society of Animal Science, 309 W. Clark St., Champaign, IL 61820. TEL 217-356-3192. Ed. R.A. Merkel. Indexed: Ind.Med.

636.089   KE
KENYA AGRICULTURAL RESEARCH INSTITUTE. VETERINARY RESEARCH DEPARTMENT. ANNUAL REPORT. (Text in English) 1977. a. Kenya Agricultural Research Institute, Box 30148, Nairobi, Kenya. Indexed: Field Crop Abstr. Herb.Abstr. Rev.Appl.Entomol. Weed Abstr.

KONGELIGE VETERINAER OG LANDBOHOEJSKOLE. HAANDBOG. see *AGRICULTURE*

636.089   630   DK   ISSN 0106-8261
KONGELIGE VETERINAER OG LANDBOHOEJSKOLE. SKOVBRUGINSTITUTET. MEDDELELSER. 1975. irreg., no.17, 1984. Kongelige Veterinaer og Landbohoejskole, Skovbruginstitutet - Royal Veterinary and Agricultural University, Dept.of Forestry, Thorvaldsensvej 57, 1871 Frederiksberg C, Denmark. illus.

636.089   MW   ISSN 0076-3365
MALAWI. DEPARTMENT OF VETERINARY SERVICES AND ANIMAL INDUSTRY. ANNUAL REPORT. a. K.1.50. Government Printer, P.O. Box 37, Zomba, Malawi. Indexed: Anim.Breed.Abstr. Field Crop Abstr. Herb.Abstr.

636.089   MY   ISSN 0126-5652
MALAYSIAN VETERINARY JOURNAL.* (Text in English) 1955. a. M.$5. Malaysian Veterinary Association, University of Malaya, Lembah Pantai, Kuala Lumpur 22-11, Malaysia. Ed. A. Retnasabapathy. adv. bk. rev. charts. illus. circ. 350. Indexed: Biol.Abstr. Nutr.Abstr. Anim.Breed.Abstr. Dairy Sci.Abstr. Ind.Vet. Vet.Bull.

636.089   US   ISSN 0076-6542
MERCK VETERINARY MANUAL: A HANDBOOK OF DIAGNOSIS AND THERAPY FOR THE VETERINARIAN. 1955. irreg., 6th edt., 1986. $20. Merck and Co., Inc, Box 2000, Rahway, NJ 07065. TEL 201-574-4003. Ed. Clarence Fraser.

636.089   574.524   PL   ISSN 0540-6722
MONOGRAFIE PARAZYTOLOGICZNE. 1959. irreg., vol.10, 1985. price varies. Polskie Towarzystwo Parazytologiczne, Miodowa 10, 00-251 Warsaw, Poland (Dist. by: Ars Polona, Krakowskie Przedmiescie 7, 00-068 Warsaw, Poland) Ed. Leszek Grzywinski. bibl. illus. circ. 400. (back issues avail.) Indexed: Biol.Abstr.

636.089   AT   ISSN 0085-4026
NEW SOUTH WALES VETERINARY PROCEEDINGS.* 1965. a. price varies. Australian Veterinary Association, N.S.W. Division, 134-136 Hampden Rd., Artarmon, N.S.W. 2064, Australia. adv. circ. 1,000. Indexed: Ind.Vet. Vet.Bull.

636.089   NO
NORGES VETERINAERHOEGSKOLE. AARSMELDING/NORWEGIAN COLLEGE OF VETERINARY MEDICINE. ANNUAL REPORT. 1985. a. free. Norges Veterinaerhoegskole, P.O. Box 8146, 0033-Oslo 1, Norway.

636.089   NO   ISSN 0078-6721
NORGES VETERINAERHOEGSKOLE. PUBLIKASJONER/NORWEGIAN COLLEGE OF VETERINARY MEDICINE. PUBLICATIONS. 1981. a. free or on exchange basis. Norges Veterinaerhoegskole, P.O. Box 8146 Dep., 0033 Oslo 1, Norway. circ. 1,500. Indexed: Nutr.Abstr.

636.089   IE
PEGASUS. 1961. a. £10. Veterinary Students Union of Ireland, Veterinary College of Ireland, Ballsbridge, Dublin, 4, Ireland. Eds. James T.P. Walsh, James F.U. McInerney. adv. bk. rev. circ. 1, 500.
Formerly: A.V.S. Journal (ISSN 0066-9768)

591   US
PERSPECTIVES IN ETHOLOGY. 1973. irreg. Plenum Publishing Corp., 233 Spring St., New York, NY 10013. TEL 212-620-8047. Ed.Bd.

636.089   PL   ISSN 0079-3647
POLSKIE ARCHIWUM WETERYNARYJNE/ ARCHIWUM VETERINARIUM POLONICUM. (Text in Polish and English; summaries in English, Polish and Russian) 1951. irreg., vol.23, 1983. price varies. (Polska Akademia Nauk, Komitet Nauk Weterynaryjnych) Panstwowe Wydawnictwo Naukowe, Miodowa 10, 00-251 Warsaw, Poland (Dist. by: Ars Polona, Krakowskie Przedmiescie 7, 00-068 Warsaw, Poland) Ed. Edmund Prost. bibl. charts. illus. Indexed: Biol.Abstr. Chem.Abstr. Excerp.Med. Ind.Med. Nutr.Abstr. Anim.Breed.Abstr. Dairy Sci.Abstr. Field Crop Abstr. Herb.Abstr. Ind.Vet. Rev.Plant Path. Vet.Bull.

636.089   SZ
PROGRESS IN VETERINARY MICROBIOLOGY AND IMMUNOLOGY. (Text in English) 1985. irreg. (approx. 1/yr.) price varies. S. Karger AG, Allschwilerstr. 10, P.O. Box, CH-4009 Basel, Switzerland. Ed. R. Pandey. (reprint service avail.) Indexed: Biol.Abstr. Chem.Abstr. Curr.Cont. Ind.Med.

636.089   UK
REGISTERS & DIRECTORY OF VETERINARY SURGEONS. 1870. biennial. £8. Royal College of Veterinary Surgeons, 32 Belgrave Square, London SW1X 8QP, England. Ed. R. Marshall. adv. circ. 13,000.

636.089   IT   ISSN 0016-5700
RILANCIO; agricoltural veterinary zootechnical magazine. 1969. irreg. (9-12/yr.) free. Carlo Erba S.p.A., Via Carlo Imbonati 24, 20159 Milan, Italy. Ed. Prof. Bruno Mainardi. adv. abstr. index. circ. 35,000.

SPAIN. INSTITUTO NACIONAL DE INVESTIGACIONES AGRARIAS. COMUNICACIONES. SERIE: HIGIENE Y SANIDAD. see *AGRICULTURE — Poultry And Livestock*

636.089   US
U.S. DEPARTMENT OF AGRICULTURE. ANIMAL AND PLANT HEALTH INSPECTION SERVICE. REPORTED ARTHROPOD-BORNE ENCEPHALITIDES IN HORSES AND OTHER EQUIDAE. 1966. a. free. ‡ U.S. Animal and Plant Health Inspection Service, Federal Building, Hyattsville, MD 20782. TEL 301-436-8645. illus. stat. Indexed: Bibl.Agri.

636.089   US   ISSN 0082-8750
UNITED STATES ANIMAL HEALTH ASSOCIATION. PROCEEDINGS OF THE ANNUAL MEETING. no.73, 1969. a. $20. United States Animal Health Association, 6924 Lakeside Ave., Ste. 205, Richmond, VA 23228. circ. 1,200. (back issues avail.) Indexed: Ind.Med. Ind.Vet. Vet.Bull.
Supersedes: United States Livestock Sanitary Association. Proceedings.

636.089   SP   ISSN 0213-5434
UNIVERSIDAD DE MURCIA. ANALES DE VETERINARIA. 1985. a. ($1500) Universidad de Murcia, Secretariado de Publicaciones e Intercambio Cientifico, Santo Cristo, 1, 30001 Murcia, Spain. TEL 968 24 92 00.

636.089   GT
UNIVERSIDAD DE SAN CARLOS DE GUATEMALA. FACULTAD DE MEDICINA VETERINARIA Y ZOOTECNIA REVISTA. (Text in Spanish; summaries in English and Spanish) 1962. irreg. exchange basis. Universidad de San Carlos de Guatemala, Facultad de Medicina Veterinaria y Zootecnia, Ciudad Universitaria, Zona 12, Guatemala. Indexed: Biol.Abstr.

636   CN   ISSN 0383-8455
UNIVERSITE DE MONTREAL. FACULTE DE MEDECINE VETERINAIRE. ANNUAIRE. 1968. a. free. Universite de Montreal, Ecole de Medecine Veterinaire, C.P. 6128, Montreal, Que., Canada. TEL 514-343-6111.
Formerly: Ecole de Medecine Veterinaire, Saint-Hyacinthe, Quebec. Annuaire (ISSN 0383-8447)

UNIVERSITY OF DAR ES SALAAM. FACULTY OF AGRICULTURE, FORESTRY AND VETERINARY SCIENCE. ANNUAL RECORD OF RESEARCH. see *AGRICULTURE*

636.089   VE
VETERINARIA TROPICAL. (Text in Spanish; summaries in English and Spanish) 1976. a. $10 available on exchange. Centro Nacional de Investigaciones Agropecuarias, Apdo. 4653, Maracay 2101, Venezuela. Ed.Bd. bibl. charts. illus. Indexed: Helminthol.Abstr. Ind.Vet. Vet.Bull.
Formerly (until 1976): Instituto de Investigaciones Veterinarias. Boletin.

636.089   UK   ISSN 0083-5870
VETERINARY ANNUAL. 1959. a. £17.50. John Wright, Techno House, Redcliffe Way, Bristol BS1 6NX, England. index. circ. 2,500. Indexed: Biol.Abstr. Nutr.Abstr. Anim.Breed.Abstr. Vet.Bull.

636.089   PL   ISSN 0042-4870
VETERINARY INSTITUTE, PULAWY. BULLETIN. (Text and summaries in English) 1957. a. exchange basis. Instytut Weterynarii, c/o Dr. Tadeusz Zieba, Sec, Al. Partyzantow 55, 24-100 Pulawy, Poland. Ed. Stanislaw Cakala. circ. 500. Indexed: Biol.Abstr. Chem.Abstr. Nutr.Abstr. Ref.Zh. Anim.Breed.Abstr. Dairy Sci.Abstr. Landwirt.Zentralbl. Food Sci.& Tech.Abstr. Helminthol.Abstr. Ind.Vet. Vet.Bull.

636.089   AT   ISSN 0157-3136
VETERINARY PRESCRIBERS INDEX. 1979. a. Aus.$36. P V P Publications Pty Ltd., Box 278, Balgowlah, NSW 2093, Australia. circ. 3,000.

636   NZ
VETERINARY SURGEONS IN NEW ZEALAND; registered under the Veterinary Surgeons Act 1956 & persons entitled to use the title or description of veterinary practitioner. 1957. a. price varies. Government Printing Office, Private Bag, Wellington, New Zealand. circ. 1,000.

636.089   PL   ISSN 0208-5763
WARSAW AGRICULTURAL UNIVERSITY. S G G W-A R. ANNALS. VETERINARY MEDICINE. (Szkola Glowna Gospodarstwa Wiejskiego - Akademia Rolnicza) (Until 1980, part of Zeszyty Naukowe series of Akademia Rolnicza, Warsaw) (Text mainly in English; occasionally in French, German or Russian; summaries in Polish) 1957. irreg. $6. Warsaw Agricultural University Press, Ul. Nowoursynowska 166, 02-766 Warsaw, Poland (Dist. by: Ars Polona-Ruch, Krakowskie Przedmiescie 7, 00-068 Warsaw, Poland) Ed. T. Roskosz. Indexed: Chem.Abstr. Vet.Bull.

636.089   SP   ISSN 0084-2443
WORLD VETERINARY CONGRESS. PROCEEDINGS. 1863. quadrennial, 21st, 1979, Moscow; 22nd, 1983, Perth, 23rd, 1987, Montreal. price varies. World Veterinary Association, Secretariat, Isabel la Catolica 12, Madrid 13, Spain (Published by the organizing committee of each congress; for 21st Congress, inquire: USSR National Organizing Committee, Bld. B1, Room 404, Orlikov Per. 1/11, Moscow, USSR; for 23rd, inquire: Dr. Guy Lafreniere, President, Organizing Committee, Box 1117-Sucursale Desjardins, Complex Guy Favreau Tour Est 1002, Montreal H5B 1C2, Quebec, Canada) Ed. C. Main. bibl. circ. 5,000. Indexed: Anim.Breed.Abstr.

636.089 ZA
ZAMBIA. DEPARTMENT OF VETERINARY AND TSETSE CONTROL SERVICES. ANNUAL REPORT. (Text in English) a. Government Printer, Box 30136, Lusaka, Zambia.

ZENTRALINSTITUT FUER VERSUCHSTIERZUCHT. JAHRESBERICHT. see *BIOLOGY*

VETERINARY SCIENCE —
Abstracting, Bibliographies, Statistics

636 016 UK ISSN 0019-4123
INDEX VETERINARIUS; a classified subject and author index produced by computer processes of current literature on veterinary science with approximately 23,000 titles. 1931. m. (with annual cumulation) £283($499) to non-members. C.A.B. International, Bureau of Animal Health, Farnham House, Farnham Royal, Slough SL2 3BN, England. bibl. circ. 750. (also avail. in microfiche; back issues avail.) Indexed: Nutr.Abstr. Dairy Sci.Abstr. Helminthol.Abstr. Rev.Appl.Entomol. Rev.Plant Path.
●Also available online. Vendors: BRS, CISTI, DIMDI, DIALOG, European Space Agency.

595.7 016 UK ISSN 0305-0084
REVIEW OF APPLIED ENTOMOLOGY. SERIES B: MEDICAL AND VETERINARY. 1913. m. £100($181) to non-members. C.A.B. International, Institute of Entomology, Farnham House, Farnham Royal, Slough SL2 3BN, England. Ed.Bd. adv. bk. rev. abstr. index. circ. 1,250. (also avail. in microfilm; back issues avail.) Indexed: Chem.Abstr. Abstr.Hyg. Helminthol.Abstr. Rev.Appl.Entomol. Trop.Dis.Bull. Vet.Bull.
●Also available online. Vendors: BRS, CISTI, DIMDI, DIALOG, European Space Agency.

636.089 UK ISSN 0042-4854
VETERINARY BULLETIN; a monthly abstract journal on veterinary science. 1931. m. £227($392) to non-members. C.A.B. International, Bureau of Animal Health, Farnham House, Farnham Royal, Slough SL2 3BN, England. Ed. R. Mack. adv. bk. rev. abstr. circ. 1,900. (also avail. in microfiche; back issues avail.) Indexed: Chem.Abstr. Nutr.Abstr. Abstr.Hyg. Anim.Breed.Abstr. Biotech.Abstr. Dairy Sci.Abstr. Field Crop Abstr. Helminthol.Abstr. Herb.Abstr. Rev.Appl.Entomol. Trop.Dis.Bull.
●Also available online. Vendors: BRS, CISTI, DIMDI, DIALOG, European Space Agency.

WATER RESOURCES
see also *Environmental Studies*

333.19 639.2 PL ISSN 0860-2611
ACTA ACADEMIAE AGRICULTURAE AC TECHNICAE OLSTENENSIS. PROTECTIO AQUARUM ET PISCATORIA/WATER CONSERVATION AND INLAND FISHERIES. (Subseries of Its: Zeszyty Naukowe) (Text in Polish; summaries in English and Russian) 1956. irreg. price varies. Akademia Rolniczo-Techniczna, Blok 21, 10-718 Olsztyn-Kortowo, Poland (Dist. by: Ars Polona-Ruch, Krakowskie Przedmiescie 7, 00-901 Warsaw, Poland)
Formerly: Ochrona Wod i Rybactwo Srodladowe (ISSN 0324-9190)

333.7 628 US
ADVANCED WATER CONFERENCE. PROCEEDINGS. irreg., 3rd, 1971. price varies. Oklahoma State University, College of Engineering, Engineering Extension, 512 Engineering North, Stillwater, OK 74078. TEL 405-624-5276.

333.91 US
AMERICAN WATER RESOURCES SYMPOSIA. ANNUAL PROCEEDINGS. 1965. a., latest 1985, Tucson, Arizona. $35.95 to non-members; members $29.95. American Water Resources Association, 5410 Grosvenor Ln., Ste. 220, Bethesda, MD 20814. Indexed: GeoRef.
Formerly: American Water Resources Conferences. Annual Proceedings (ISSN 0066-1171)

628 US ISSN 0360-814X
AMERICAN WATER WORKS ASSOCIATION. PROCEEDINGS, A W W A ANNUAL CONFERENCE. a. American Water Works Association, 6666 W. Quincy Ave., Denver, CO 80235. TEL 303-794-7711. illus. Indexed: GeoRef. Key Title: Proceedings, A W W A Annual Conference.

627 BL
ANAIS HIDROGRAFICOS. 1933. a. free. Ministerio da Marinha, Diretoria de Hidrografia e Navegacao, Rio de Janeiro, Brazil. charts. illus. stat. circ. controlled.

333.91 US ISSN 0161-4924
ANNUAL NEW MEXICO WATER CONFERENCE. PROCEEDINGS. 1956. a. $5. New Mexico Water Resources Research Institute, Box 3167, New Mexico State University, Las Cruces, NM 88003. TEL 505-646-4337. Ed. Linda G. Harris. circ. 500.

333.91 AT ISSN 0003-7206
AQUA. 1949. a. free. Rural Water Commission of Victoria, 590 Orrong Rd., Armadale 3143, Victoria, Australia. Ed. L.J. Greenhill. charts. illus. mkt. pat. stat. cum.index: 1949-67 (in several vols.) circ. 5,000. Indexed: Aus.P.A.I.S. Fluidex.

AQUARICULTURE AND AQUATIC SCIENCES. JOURNAL. see *BIOLOGY*

333.91 US
ARIZONA. DEPARTMENT OF WATER RESOURCES. REPORT. irreg. Department of Water Resources, 99 E. Virginia, Ste. 800, Phoenix, AZ 85004. TEL 602-255-1554. Indexed: GeoRef.
Former titles: Arizona. Department of Water Resources. Bulletin; Arizona. Water Commission. Bulletin (ISSN 0360-7461); Arizona. State. State Land Department. Water Resources Report (ISSN 0403-0699)

333.91 US ISSN 0571-0278
ARKANSAS. GEOLOGICAL COMMISSION. WATER RESOURCES CIRCULARS. 1955. irreg., no. 12, 1975. price varies. Geological Commission, Vardelle Parham Geology Center, 3815 West Roosevelt Rd., Little Rock, AR 72204. TEL 501-663-9714. (back issues avail.) Indexed: GeoRef.

333.9 US ISSN 0067-043X
AUBURN UNIVERSITY. WATER RESOURCES RESEARCH INSTITUTE. ANNUAL REPORT. 1965. a. free. Auburn University, Water Resources Research Institute, 202 Hargis Hall, Auburn, AL 36849. TEL 205-826-5075. Ed. James C. Warman. circ. 600.

333.91 AT ISSN 0812-7735
AUSTRALIA. DEPARTMENT OF RESOURCES AND ENERGY. STREAMLINE UPDATE. irreg., (approx. 8/yr.) free. Department of Resources and Energy, G.P.O. Box 858, Canberra, A.C.T. 2601, Australia (Distr. addr.: Jolimont Centre, Northbourne Ave., Canberra City 2601, Australia)
●Also available online.

333.91 AT
AUSTRALIAN WATER RESOURCES COUNCIL. WATER RESOURCES SERIES. irreg. Department of Resources and Energy, Australian Water Resources Council, Box 858, Canberra, A.C.T. 2601, Australia.

628 MW ISSN 0084-7925
BLANTYRE WATER BOARD. ANNUAL REPORT AND STATEMENT OF ACCOUNTS. 1967. a. Blantyre Water Board, Box 30369, Chichiri, Blantyre 3, Malawi. stat. circ. 500.

627 BL
BRAZIL. SUPERINTENDENCIA DO DESENVOLVIMENTO DO NORDESTE. RELATORIO SINTETICO, ANDAMENTO DO PROGRAMA DE IRRIGACAO DO NORDESTE. 1971. irreg. Superintendencia do Desenvolvimento do Nordeste, Servico Publico Federal, Recife, Pernambuco, Brazil. illus. circ. 250.

BRITISH COLUMBIA. MINISTRY OF ENVIRONMENT AND PARKS. ANNUAL REPORT. see *CONSERVATION*

333.91 CN
BRITISH COLUMBIA WATER AND WASTE ASSOCIATION. PROCEEDINGS OF THE ANNUAL CONFERENCE.* a. free. Department of Fisheries & Oceans, 200 Kent St., Ottawa, Ont. K1A 0E6, Canada. TEL 613-995-2041. charts. illus.

354.66 631.7 UV
BURKINA FASO. DIRECTION DE L'HYDRAULIQUE ET DE L'EQUIPEMENT RURAL. SERVICE I.R.H. RAPPORT D'ACTIVITES. irreg. Direction de l'Hydraulique et de l'Equipement Rural, Service I.R.H., Ministere du Plan, du Developpement Rural, de l'Environnement et du Tourisme, Ouagadougou, Burkina Faso.
Formerly: Upper Volta. Direction de l'Hydraulique et de l'Equipement Rural. Service I.R.H. Rapport d'Activites.

333.9 US ISSN 0084-8263
CALIFORNIA. DEPARTMENT OF WATER RESOURCES. BULLETIN. a. price varies. Department of Water Resources, P.O. Box 388, Sacramento, CA 95802. TEL 916-445-9248. circ. controlled. Indexed: GeoRef.

333.9 US ISSN 0092-9158
CALIFORNIA. DEPARTMENT OF WATER RESOURCES. INVENTORY OF WASTE WATER PRODUCTION AND WASTE WATER RECLAMATION PRACTICES IN CALIFORNIA. (Subseries of its Bulletin) a. price varies. Department of Water Resources, P.O. Box 388, Sacramento, CA 95802. TEL 916-445-9248.

333.91 US
CALIFORNIA DIRECTORY OF WATER RESOURCES EXPERTISE. 1975. biennial. free. University of California, Davis, Water Resources Center, 2102 Wickson Hall, Davis, CA 95616. TEL 916-752-1544. Ed. Rex J. Woods. circ. 1,750.

333.91 US ISSN 0090-5968
CALIFORNIA STATE WATER PROJECT. (Subseries of California. Dept. of Water Resources. Bulletin) 1963. a. price varies. Department of Water Resources, Box 388, Sacramento, CA 95802. TEL 916-445-9248. illus. stat. circ. controlled. (back issues avail.)

333.91 US ISSN 0575-4941
CALIFORNIA WATER RESOURCES CENTER. CONTRIBUTION. irreg., no.193, Mar. 1985. California Water Resources Center, University of California, Davis, 2102 Wickson Hall, Davis, CA 95616. TEL 916-752-1544. bibl. charts. circ. 265. Indexed: GeoRef.

CANADA. AGRICULTURE CANADA. ANNUAL REPORT OF PRAIRIE FARM REHABILITATION ADMINISTRATION/ RAPPORT ANNUAL: RETABLISSEMENT AGRICOLE DES PRAIRIES. see *AGRICULTURE — Crop Production And Soil*

354 CN ISSN 0701-6786
CANADA. HYDROGRAPHIC SERVICE. ACTIVITY REPORT/CANADA. SERVICE HYDROGRAPHIQUE. RAPPORT DES ACTIVITES.* (Text in English and French) a. free. Department of Fisheries & Oceans, 200 Kent St., Ottawa, Ont. K1A 0E6, Canada. TEL 613-995-4031. illus.
Formed by the merger of: Canada. Hydrographic Service. Annual Report (ISSN 0704-3139) & Canada. Service Hydrographique. Rapport Annuel (ISSN 0704-3147)

333.91 016 NE ISSN 0920-9786
CATALOGUS VAN NEDERLANDSE ZEEKAARTEN EN ANDERE HYDROGRAFISCHE PUBLIKATIES/CATALOG OF CHARTS AND OTHER HYDROGRAPHIC PUBLICATIONS. (Text in Dutch, English) 1874. a. free. Ministerie van Defensie, c/o Hydrographer of the Royal Netherlands Navy, Box 90704, 2509 LS The Hague, Netherlands. Ed.Bd. circ. 800.
Formerly: Netherlands. Departement van Marine. Catalogus van Nederlandse Zeekaarten en Boekwerken.

WATER RESOURCES

628　　　　　　　　SW　ISSN 0280-4026
CHALMERS UNIVERSITY OF TECHNOLOGY. DEPARTMENT OF SANITARY ENGINEERING; Current reports on research in water supply and sewage disposal. (Text in Swedish; summaries in English) 1962. irreg. Kr.90. Chalmers University of Technology, Department of Sanitary Engineering - Chalmers Tekniska Hoegskolan, S-412 96 Goeteborg 5, Sweden. Ed. P. Balmer. charts. illus. circ. 100.

333.91　　　　　　　US　ISSN 0069-4657
CLEMSON UNIVERSITY. WATER RESOURCES RESEARCH INSTITUTE. REPORT. 1967. irreg., no.67, 1977. free; limited distribution. Clemson University, Water Resources Research Institute, Clemson, SC 29634-2900. circ. 200. Indexed: Pollut.Abstr. Water Resour.Abstr.

333.9　　　　　　　US　ISSN 0360-6864
COLUMBIA RIVER WATER MANAGEMENT REPORT. 1971. a. free. U.S. Army Corps of Engineers, Columbia River Water Management Group, Box 2870, Portland, OR 97208. TEL 503-221-6021. illus.

COMISION DE INTEGRACION ELECTRICA REGIONAL. RECURSOS ENERGETICOS DE LOS PAISES DE LA C I E R. see *PETROLEUM AND GAS*

627　　　　　　　　BL　ISSN 0589-3305
CONGRESSO LATINOAMERICANO DE HIDRAULICA (PAPERS)* irreg. Associacao Internacional de Pesquisas Hidraulicas, Av. Bento Goncalves 10600, Porto Allegre, Brazil.

333.9　　　　　　　US
COORDINATION DIRECTORY OF STATE AND FEDERAL WATER RESOURCE OFFICIALS IN THE MISSOURI RIVER BASIN. biennial. $4. Missouri Basin States Association, Ste. 1, 10834 Old Mill Rd., Omaha, NE 68154. TEL 402-330-5714.
　　Formerly: Directory of Federal and State Officials Engaged in Water Resource Development.

627　628.167　　　II
CURRENT PRACTICES IN DRYLAND RESOURCES AND TECHNOLOGY. a. $50. Geo-Environ Academia, A-42 Shastri Nagar, Jodhpur 342 003, India. (Co-sponsor: Scientific Publisher (Jodhpur)) Eds. Alam Singh, G.R. Chowdhary.
　　Former titles: Dryland Resources and Technology (ISSN 0254-8305); Until 1984: Desert Resources and Technology.

CURRENT PRACTICES IN ENVIRONMENTAL SCIENCE AND ENGINEERING. see *ENVIRONMENTAL STUDIES*

DANSKE HEDESELSKAB. FORSOEGSVIRKSOMHEDEN. BERETNING. see *FORESTS AND FORESTRY*

333.91　　　　　　US
DELAWARE RIVER BASIN BIENNIAL WATER RESOURCES CONFERENCE. PROCEEDINGS. 1962. biennial. membership. Water Resources Association of the Delaware River Basin, Box 867, Davis Rd., Valley Forge, PA 19481. TEL 215-783-0634.
　　Formerly: Delaware River Basin Water Resources Conference. Proceedings.

551.4　627　　　GW　ISSN 0340-5176
DEUTSCHES GEWAESSERKUNDLICHES JAHRBUCH. DONAUGEBIET. 1898. a. also avail. on exchange. Bayerisches Landesamt fuer Wasserwirtschaft, Lazarettstr. 67, 8000 Munich 19, W. Germany (B.R.D.) charts. stat. circ. 500. Indexed: GeoRef.

551.4　627　　　GW　ISSN 0340-5184
DEUTSCHES GEWAESSERKUNDLICHES JAHRBUCH. KUESTENGEBIET DER NORD- UND OSTSEE. 1941. a. DM.40. Landesamt fuer Wasserhaushalt und Kuesten, Saarbrueckenstr. 38, 2300 Kiel 1, W. Germany (B.R.D.) Ed. Mr. Benn. stat. index, cum.index. circ. controlled.

551　627　　　　GW　ISSN 0173-7260
DEUTSCHES GEWAESSERKUNDLICHES JAHRBUCH. RHEINGEBIET TEIL 2: MAIN. 1898. a. also avail. on exchange. Bayerisches Landesamt fuer Wasserwirtschaft, Lazarettstr. 67, 8000 Munich 19, W. Germany (B.R.D.) charts. stat. circ. 500.

333.91　　　　　　UK
DEVELOPING WORLD WATER. 1985. a. Grosvenor Press International, West Garden Place, Kendal St., London W2 2AQ, England. Ed. John Pickford. adv. circ. 15,000.

628　　　　　　　　GW　ISSN 0012-0030
DOKUMENTATIONSZENTRALE WASSER SCHRIFTENREIHE. 1963. irreg. price varies. (Fraunhofer-Gesellschaft) Erich Schmidt Verlag GmbH (Bielefeld), Viktoriastr. 44A, 4800 Bielefeld 1, W. Germany B.R.D. adv. bk. rev. bibl. circ. 750.
　　Formerly: Deutscher Arbeitskreis Wasser. Schriftenreihe.

627　620　　　　US
DREDGING SEMINAR. PROCEEDINGS. 1968. irreg. price varies. Texas A & M University, Center for Dredging Studies, College Station, TX 77843. TEL 409-845-3211. Ed. Dr. John B. Herbich. charts. circ. 800.

627　　　　　　　　US
ENGINEERING COMMITTEE ON OCEANIC RESOURCES. PROCEEDINGS OF THE GENERAL ASSEMBLY. irreg., 2nd, 1975, Tokyo. Engineering Committee on Oceanic Resources, 2101 Constitution Ave. N.W., Washington, DC 20418. TEL 202-334-2000.

627　　　　　　　　UN
F A O IRRIGATION AND DRAINAGE PAPERS. (Editions in English, French, Spanish) irreg., no.41, 1986. price varies. Food and Agriculture Organization of the United Nations, Distribution and Sales Section, Via delle Terme di Caracalla, I-00100 Rome, Italy (Dist. in U.S. by: Bernan Associates-Unipub, 4611-F Assembly Drive, Lanham, MD 20706-4391) Indexed: Excerp.Med.

627　　　　　　　　FI　ISSN 0355-0982
FINLAND. VESTIENTUTKIMUSLAITOS. JULKAISUJA/FINLAND. WATER RESEARCH INSTITUTE. PUBLICATIONS. (Text in Finnish; summaries in English) 1972. irreg. price varies. Valtion Painatuskeskus - Government Printing Centre, Annankatu 44, 00100 Helsinki 10, Finland. illus.

333.91　　　　　　US
GEORGIA. GEOLOGIC SURVEY. CIRCULAR 4. WATER USE IN GEORGIA. 1981. irreg. free. Department of Natural Resources, Georgia Geologic Survey, 19 Martin Luther King Jr. Dr., S.W., Rm. 400, Atlanta, GA 30334. TEL 404-656-3214.

333.7　333.7　　　GW
GERMANY (FEDERAL REPUBLIC, 1949-). BUNDESANSTALT FUER GEWAESSERKUNDE. JAHRESBERICHT. 1949-1962 suspended; resumed 1974. a. Bundesanstalt fuer Gewaesserkunde, Kaiserin-Augusta-Anlagen 15-17, D-5400 Koblkenz, W. Germany (B.R.D.) illus.

333.9　　　　　　UK　ISSN 0072-7245
GREAT BRITAIN. WATER RESOURCES BOARD. PUBLICATION. 1966. irreg. free. Water Resources Board, Reading Bridge House, Reading, Berks., England (Avail. from H.M.S.O., Atlantic House, Holborn Viaduct, London EC1P 1BN, England)

333.9　　　　　　UK　ISSN 0072-7253
GREAT BRITAIN. WATER RESOURCES BOARD. REPORT. 1963/64. a. price varies. Water Resources Board, Reading Bridge House, Reading, Berks., England (Avail. from H.M.S.O., c/o Liaison Officer, Atlantic House, Holborn Viaduct, London EC1P 1BN, England)

363.6　　　　　　CN　ISSN 0710-8702
GREAT LAKES SCIENCE ADVISORY BOARD. ANNUAL REPORT. 1975. a. free. International Joint Commission, 100 Ouellette Ave., Windsor, Ont. N9A 6T3, Canada. TEL 519-256-7821. Ed.Bd. circ. 8,000. Indexed: Environ.Abstr. Sel.Water Res.Abstr.
　　Formerly: Great Lakes Research Advisory Board. Annual Report.

HUNTER VALLEY RESEARCH FOUNDATION. WORKING PAPERS. see *STATISTICS*

333.91　　　　　　IS　ISSN 0333-5194
I O L R COLLECTED REPORTS. (Text in English) 1971. a. free. Israel Oceanographic and Limnological Research Ltd., P.O. Box 8030, Haifa 31 080, Israel.

551.4　　　　　　CN
INDEX DE REFERENCES: INVENTAIRE DES STATIONS HYDROMETRIQUES. 1968. irreg. Can.$2. Ministere des Richesses Naturelles, 1620 Blvd. de l'Entente, Quebec G1S 4N6, Canada. TEL 418-643-1344. illus. circ. 400.

333.91　551.4　　　GW
INSTITUT FUER WASSERWIRTSCHAFT, HYDROLOGIE UND LANDWIRTSCHAFTLICHEN WASSERBAU. 1958. irreg. DM.45 per no. Institut fuer Wasserwirtschaft, Hydrologie und landwirtschaftlichen Wasserbau, Callinstr. 32, 3000 Hannover 1, W. Germany (B.R.D.) (back issues avail.)

333.91　　　　　　RM
INSTITUTUL DE STUDII CERCETARI SI PROIECTARI PENTRU GOSPODARIREA APELOR. STUDII DE ECONOMIA APELOR. (Text in Rumanian; summaries in English, French and Russian.) 1972. irreg. Institutul de Studii Cercetari si Proiectari Pentru Gospodarirea Apelor, Splaiul Indepentei 294, Sector 6, Bucharest 17, Rumania. illus.

INSTITUUT VOOR CULTUURTECHNIEK EN WATERHUISHOUDING. JAARVERSLAG. see *AGRICULTURE — Crop Production And Soil*

INSTITUUT VOOR CULTUURTECHNIEK EN WATERHUISHOUDING. MEDEDELING. NIEUWE SERIE. see *AGRICULTURE — Crop Production And Soil*

INSTITUUT VOOR CULTUURTECHNIEK EN WATERHUISHOUDING. RAPPORTEN. NIEUWE SERIE. see *AGRICULTURE — Crop Production And Soil*

INSTITUUT VOOR CULTUURTECHNIEK EN WATERHUISHOUDING. REPORTS. see *AGRICULTURE — Crop Production And Soil*

INSTITUUT VOOR CULTUURTECHNIEK EN WATERHUISHOUDING. TECHNICAL BULLETINS. NEW SERIES. see *AGRICULTURE — Crop Production And Soil*

333.9　　　　　　PL　ISSN 0074-0586
INSTYTUT GOSPODARKI WODNEJ. PRACE.* (Text in Polish; summaries in English and Russian) 1961. irreg., 1971, no. 4, vol. 6. $8 per volume. Wydawnictwa Komunikacji i Lacznosci, Ul. Kazimierzowska 52, Warsaw, Poland (Dist. by Ars Polona-Ruch, Krakowskie Przedmiescie 7, Warsaw, Poland)

631.6　　　　　　II　ISSN 0538-5768
INTERNATIONAL COMMISSION ON IRRIGATION AND DRAINAGE. REPORT. (Text in English) 1951. a. International Commission on Irrigation and Drainage - Commission Internationale des Irrigations et du Drainage, 48 Nyaya Marg, Chanakyapuri, New Delhi 110021, India. circ. 2,000(controlled)

627　　　　　　　　UK
INTERNATIONAL SYMPOSIUM ON WAVE AND TIDAL ENERGY. PROCEEDINGS. 1978. irreg., 3rd, 1986. price varies. B H R A Fluid Engineering, Cranfield, Bedford MK43 0AJ, England (Dist. in U.S. by: Learned Information Inc., 143 Old Marlton Pike, Medford, NJ 08055)

333.91　　　　　　US　ISSN 0074-9575
INTERNATIONAL WATER CONFERENCE. PROCEEDINGS. 1941. a. $45. Engineers' Society of Western Pennsylvania, International Water Conference, Wm. Penn Hotel, 530 William Penn Pl., Pittsburgh, PA 15219. TEL 412-261-0710. Ed. Mary Jean Edgar. adv. cum.index: 1940-1974. circ. 1,700. Indexed: Chem.Abstr.

333.91　　　　　　US　ISSN 0535-4676
INTERSTATE COMMISSION ON THE POTOMAC RIVER BASIN. PROCEEDINGS. a. Interstate Commission on the Potomac River Basin, 6110 Executive Blvd., Ste. 300, Rockville, MD 20852. TEL 301-984-1908.

627　　　　　　　　PK
IRRIGATION RESEARCH INSTITUTE, LAHORE. REPORT. 1973. irreg. Irrigation Research Institute, The Mall, Lahore, Pakistan.

ISRAEL. METEOROLOGICAL SERVICE. RAINFALL SEASON. see *METEOROLOGY*

JOURNAL OF SOIL AND WATER CONSERVATION IN INDIA. see *CONSERVATION*

333.91 US ISSN 0160-2659
KANSAS WATER RESOURCES RESEARCH INSTITUTE. ANNUAL REPORT. 1964. a. free. Kansas Water Resources Research Institute, 44 Waters Hall, Manhattan, KS 66506. Ed. Floyd W. Smith. circ. 65. Indexed: GeoRef.

628 551.4 US
LOUISIANA WATER RESOURCES RESEARCH INSTITUTE. ANNUAL REPORT. 1965/66. a. Louisiana Water Resources Research Institute, 2514 Ceba Bldg., Louisiana State University, Baton Rouge, LA 70803. (Co-sponsor: U.S. Department of Interior) circ. controlled. Indexed: GeoRef.

MAJI REVIEW. see *ENERGY*

354 CN ISSN 0318-3912
MANITOBA. WATER SERVICES BOARD. ANNUAL REPORT. 1973. a. free. Water Services Board, 2022 Currie Blvd., Brandon, Man. R7A 6A3, Canada. circ. 300.

333.91 US ISSN 0076-4817
MARYLAND. GEOLOGICAL SURVEY. WATER RESOURCES BASIC DATA REPORT. 1966. irreg., no.15, 1985. price varies. Maryland Geological Survey, 2300 St. Paul St., Baltimore, MD 21218. TEL 301-554-5500. Indexed: GeoRef.

628 US
MICHIGAN STATE UNIVERSITY. INSTITUTE OF WATER RESEARCH. ANNUAL REPORT. 1966. a. free. ‡ Michigan State University, Institute of Water Research, 334 Natural Resources Bldg., East Lansing, MI 48824. TEL 517-353-3744. Ed. Frank M. D'Itri. illus. circ. 150. (processed; reprint service avail. from UMI) Indexed: GeoRef.

628 US ISSN 0580-9746
MICHIGAN STATE UNIVERSITY. INSTITUTE OF WATER RESEARCH. TECHNICAL REPORT. 1968. irreg., latest no. 47. price varies. Michigan State University, Institute of Water Research, 334 Natural Resources Bldg., East Lansing, MI 48824 TEL 517-353-3744. (Order from: National Technical Information Service, 5285 Port Royal Rd., Springfield, VA 22151) (back issues avail.; reprint service avail. from UMI) Indexed: GeoRef.

333.91 LE
MIDDLE EAST AND WORLD WATER DIRECTORY. (Text in English) 1980. biennial. $110 for two volumes; $65 for single volume. Middle East Publishing & Dist. Est., P.O. Box 135121, Beirut, Lebanon. Ed. Fathi Chatila. adv. circ. 5,100.

333.91 551.4 US ISSN 0076-9614
MISSOURI. DIVISION OF GEOLOGICAL SURVEY AND WATER RESOURCES. WATER RESOURCES REPORT. 1956. irreg., no.36, 1985. price varies. Department of Natural Resources, Division of Geology and Land Survey, Box 250, Rolla, MO 65401. TEL 314-364-1752.

333.9 US
MISSOURI BASIN STATES ASSOCIATION. ANNUAL REPORT. 1972/73. a. Missouri Basin States Association, Ste. 1, 10834 Old Mill Rd., Omaha, NE 68154. TEL 402-330-5714. illus.
Formerly: Missouri River Basin Commission. Annual Report (ISSN 0092-7945)

628 US
MONTANA WATER RESOURCES RESEARCH CENTER. ANNUAL REPORT. 1982. a. Montana University Joint Water Resources Research Center, Montana State University, 309 Montana Hall, Bozeman, MT 59717. TEL 406-994-6690. abstr.

333.91 SA
N I W R INFORMATION SHEET. 1974. irreg. R.3. National Institute for Water Research, Box 395, Pretoria 0001, South Africa. circ. 200.

627 JA
NAGOYA UNIVERSITY. WATER RESEARCH INSTITUTE. ANNUAL REPORT/SUIKEN KAGAKU KENKYUJO NENPO. (Text in Japanese) 1974. a. Nagoya University, Water Research Institute - Nagoya Daigaku Suishitsu Kagaku Kenkyu Shisetsu, Furo-cho, Chikusa-ku, Nagoya 464, Japan. illus.

333.91 US
NEBRASKA. NATURAL RESOURCES COMMISSION. STATE WATER PLANNING AND REVIEW PROCESS. irreg. Natural Resources Commission, 301 Centennial Mall South, Box 94876, Lincoln, NE 68509. TEL 402-471-2081. illus.
Formerly: Nebraska. Natural Resources Commission. State Water Plan Publication (Lincoln) (ISSN 0092-6442)

333.9 US ISSN 0077-6394
NEBRASKA WATER RESOURCES RESEARCH INSTITUTE, UNIVERSITY OF NEBRASKA. ANNUAL REPORT OF ACTIVITIES. a. free. Nebraska Water Resources Research Institute, University of Nebraska, Lincoln, NE 68503.

NEW ZEALAND AGRICULTURAL ENGINEERING INSTITUTE. ANNUAL REPORT. see *AGRICULTURE — Crop Production And Soil*

333.9 US ISSN 0078-1525
NORTH CAROLINA STATE UNIVERSITY. WATER RESOURCES RESEARCH INSTITUTE. REPORT. 1966. irreg., no.222, 1985. $8. ‡ North Carolina State University, Water Resources Research Institute, 225 Page Hall, Box 7912, Raleigh, NC 27695-7912. TEL 919-737-2815. Ed. David H. Moreau. bk. rev. circ. 150. Indexed: Pollut.Abstr. Sel.Water Res.Abstr.

OCEAN SCIENCE, RESOURCES AND TECHNOLOGY. see *EARTH SCIENCES — Oceanography*

333.9 US ISSN 0092-2528
OKLAHOMA WATER RESOURCES RESEARCH INSTITUTE. ANNUAL REPORT. 1966. a. Oklahoma Water Resources Research Institute, 203 Whitehurst Hall, Stillwater, OK 74078. TEL 405-624-7002. Ed. S.K. Dunn. illus. circ. 200. Key Title: Annual Report of the Oklahoma Water Resources Research Institute.

333.9 CN ISSN 0078-5156
ONTARIO. MINISTRY OF THE ENVIRONMENT. GROUND WATER BULLETIN. 1961. irreg. free. Ministry of the Environment, Water Resources Branch, 135 St. Clair Ave. W., Toronto, Ont. M4V 1P5, Canada. TEL 416-965-6141.

333.91 JA
OSAKA MUNICIPAL WATER WORKS BUREAU. ANNUAL REPORT. (Text in Japanese) 1949. a. free. Osaka Municipal Water Works Bureau, Water Examinination Laboratory, 1, Hama-Cho, Higasiyodogawa-Ku, Osaka-Shi 533, Japan. circ. 500.

627 DK ISSN 0107-4997
OVERSIGT OVER RAPPORTER M.M. VEDROERENDE VANDKRAFTUNDERSOEGELSER I GROENLAND. 1981. a. free. Ministeriet for Groenland, Raastofforvaltningen, Hausergade 3, 1128 Copenhagen K, Denmark.

POLIMERY V MELIORATSII I VODNOM KHOZYAISTVE. see *ENGINEERING — Hydraulic Engineering*

333.91 PL ISSN 0137-1363
POLITECHNIKA KRAKOWSKA. ZESZYTY NAUKOWE. BUDOWNICTWO WODNE I INZYNIERIA SANITARNA. (Text in Polish; summaries in English, French, German and Russian) 1957. irreg. price varies. Politechnika Krakowska, Ul. Warszawska 24, 31-155 Krakow, Poland (Dist. by: Ars Polona-Ruch, Krakowskie Przedmiescie 7, 00-068 Warsaw, Poland) bibl. charts. illus. circ. 200.

333.91 US
POTOMAC ISSUES. irreg. price varies. Interstate Commission on the Potomac River Basin, 6110 Executive Blvd., Ste. 300, Rockville, MD 20852. TEL 301-984-1908.

333.91 US
POTOMAC RIVER BASIN WATER QUALITY REPORTS. biennial. Interstate Commission on the Potomac River Basin, 6110 Executive Blvd., Ste. 300, Rockville, MD 20852. TEL 301-984-1908.
Formerly: Potomac River Water Quality Network (ISSN 0539-2047)

354.712 CN
PRAIRIE PROVINCES WATER BOARD ANNUAL REPORT. (First report covers period Oct. 30, 1969-Mar. 31, 1972) 1972. a. free. ‡ Prairie Provinces Water Board, Rm. 306, Motherwell Bldg., 1901 Victoria Ave., Regina, Sask. S4P 3R4, Canada. TEL 306-522-6671. circ. 400.

333.7 UR
PROBLEMY POLES'YA. 1972. irreg. 2.61 Rub. Akademiya Navuk Belarusskai S.S.R., Leninskii Prospekt 68, Minsk, Byelorussian S.S.R., U.S.S.R. bibl. illus.

333.9 US ISSN 0079-6956
PROJECT SKYWATER. ANNUAL REPORT. 1967. a. U.S. Bureau of Reclamation, Engineering and Research Center, Box 25007, Denver Federal Center, Denver, CO 80225. TEL 303-236-6741.

333.91 US
PURDUE UNIVERSITY. WATER RESOURCES RESEARCH CENTER. ANNUAL REPORT. 1966. a. free. Purdue University, Water Resources Research Center, Lilly Hall of Life Sciences, W. Lafayette, IN 47907. Ed. John H. Cushman. circ. 230.

333.91 II
RIVER BEHAVIOUR AND CONTROL. (Text in English) vol. 9, 1976. a. River Research Institute, 11-a Free School St., Calcutta 700016, India.

620 PL ISSN 0035-9394
ROZPRAWY HYDROTECHNICZNE/ HYDROTECHNICAL TRANSACTIONS. (Text in English, French; summaries in English, Polish, Russian) 1956. irreg., vol.46, 1984. price varies. (Polska Akademia Nauk, Instytut Budownictwa Wodnego) Panstwowe Wydawnictwo Naukowe, Miodowa 10, 00-251 Warsaw, Poland (Dist. by: Ars Polona, Krakowskie Przedmiescie 7, 00-068 Warsaw, Poland) Ed. R. Molisz. circ. 280. Indexed: Chem.Abstr. Fluidex. Geotech.Abstr.

551 GW ISSN 0172-665X
SCHRIFTENREIHE DES BAYER. LANDESAMTES FUER WASSERWIRTSCHAFT. 1975. irreg. (approx. 3/yr.) also avail. on exchange. Bayerisches Landesamt fuer Wasserwirtschaft, Lazarettstrasse 67, 8000 Munich 19, W. Germany (B.R.D.) circ. 500.

628.167 US ISSN 0720-0773
SEAWATER AND DESALTING. 1980. irreg. price varies. Springer-Verlag, 175 Fifth Ave., New York, NY 10010 TEL 212-460-1500. (Also Berlin, Heidelberg, Vienna) (reprint service avail. from ISI) *Desalination*

333.91 SA
SOUTH AFRICA. WATER RESEARCH COMMISSION. ANNUAL REPORT. 1971. a. free. Water Research Commission, Box 824, Pretoria 0001, South Africa. illus. circ. 2,300.

333.9 SA
SOUTH AFRICA. WATER RESEARCH COMMISSION. RESEARCH PROJECTS. a. Water Research Commission, Box 824, Pretoria 0001, South Africa.

551.4 US ISSN 0038-5425
SOVIET HYDROLOGY: SELECTED PAPERS. (English translation from the Russian) 1962. irreg. (4 nos./vol.) $165 for vol.19 to non-members; members $132. American Geophysical Union, 2000 Florida Ave. N.W., Washington, DC 20009. TEL 202-462-6903. Ed. B.S. Browzin. abstr. charts. illus. index. circ. 300. (also avail. in microfilm; reprint service avail. from ISI) Indexed: Excerp.Med. Geo.Abstr. GeoRef.

627 DK ISSN 0108-0466
SPILDEVANDSTEKNISK TIDSSKRIFT. 1973. irreg. (approx. 3-4/yr.) membership. Spildevandsteknisk Forening, c/o Bent Christensen, Egevangen 19, Sig, 6800 Varde, Denmark. Ed. Ole Poulsen. illus. circ. 600.

WATER RESOURCES

627   RM
STUDII DE IRIGATII SI DESECARI. (Text in Rumanian; summaries in English and French) a. Academia de Stiinte Agricole si Silvice, Institutul de Cercetari Pentru Imbunatatiri Funciare, B-dul Marasti, 61, Bucharest, Rumania (Subscr. to: ILEXIM, Str. 13 Decembrie Nr. 3, P.O. Box 136-137, Bucharest, Rumania)

333.9   UK   ISSN 0081-959X
SURFACE WATER YEAR BOOK OF GREAT BRITAIN. 1961. a. price varies. Water Resources Board, Reading Bridge House, Reading, Berks., England (Avail. from H.M.S.O., c/o Liaison Officer, Atlantic House, Holborn Viaduct, London EC1P 1BN, England)

333.9   US   ISSN 0094-6427
SUSQUEHANNA RIVER BASIN COMMISSION. ANNUAL REPORT. 1972. a. free. Susquehanna River Basin Commission, 1721 N. Front St., Harrisburg, PA 17102. TEL 717-238-0422. illus. Key Title: Annual Report - Susquehanna River Basin Commission.

627   333.91   US
TEXAS. WATER DEVELOPMENT BOARD. REPORT. 1950. irreg. free. Water Development Board, Box 13231, Capitol Station, Austin, TX 78711. TEL 512-463-7834. (also avail. in microfiche) Indexed: Chem.Abstr. Pollut.Abstr. Sel.Water Res.Abstr. GeoRef.
Former titles (1977-1985): Texas. Department of Water Resources. Report; (1965-1977): Texas. Water Development Board. Report (ISSN 0082-3562); (until 1965): Texas. Water Commission. Bulletin.

333.9   US
TEXAS WATER RESOURCES INSTITUTE. TECHNICAL REPORT. irreg. Texas A & M University, College Station, TX 77843. TEL 409-845-3211. illus.

THALASSIA SALENTINA. see *BIOLOGY — Botany*

333.91   DK   ISSN 0106-8334
TIDEVANDSTABELLER FOR DANMARK. (Text in Danish and English) 1977. a. Kr.30.50. Farvandsdirektoratet, Nautisk Afdeling, Esplanaden 19, DK-1263 Copenhagen K, Denmark.

333.91   UN
UNITED NATIONS. ECONOMIC AND SOCIAL COMMISSION FOR ASIA AND THE PACIFIC. NATURAL RESOURCES - WATER SERIES. 1964. irreg., no.60, 1985. price varies. United Nations Publications, Room DC2-0853, New York, NY 10017 (Or Distribution and Sales Sections, Palais des Nations, 1211 Geneva 10, Switzerland)
Formerly: United Nations. Department of International Economic adn Social Affairs. Natural Resources - Water Series.

333.91   UN   ISSN 0082-8130
UNITED NATIONS. ECONOMIC AND SOCIAL COMMISSION FOR ASIA AND THE PACIFIC. WATER RESOURCES DEVELOPMENT SERIES. 1964. irreg., latest no.59, 1985. price varies. United Nations Economic and Social Commission for Asia and the Pacific, United Nations Bldg., Rajamnern Ave., Bangkok 10200, Thailand (Dist. by: United Nations Publications, Room DC2-0853, New York, NY 10017; or Distribution and Sales Section, Palais des Nations, CH-1211 Geneva 10, Switzerland) (back issues avail.)

U.S. BUREAU OF RECLAMATION. ANNUAL REPORT. see *CONSERVATION*

333.91   US
U.S. BUREAU OF RECLAMATION. ENGINEERING AND RESEARCH CENTER. RESEARCH REPORTS. 1963. irreg., no.28, 1977. price varies. U.S. Bureau of Reclamation, Engineering and Research Center, Box 25007, Denver Federal Center, Denver, CO 80225. TEL 303-236-6741. (back issues avail.)
Former titles: U.S. Water and Power Resources Service. Engineering and Research Center. Research Reports; U.S. Bureau of Reclamation. Engineering and Research Center. Research Reports (ISSN 0501-7467)

U.S. DEPARTMENT OF THE ARMY. PROJECTS RECOMMENDED FOR DEAUTHORIZATION, ANNUAL REPORT. see *MILITARY*

U.S. WATER AND POWER RESOURCES SERVICE. ENGINEERING MONOGRAPH. see *ENGINEERING — Hydraulic Engineering*

333.91   GW
UNIVERSITAET HANNOVER. INSTITUT FUER SIEDLUNGSWASSERWIRTSCHAFT. VEROEFFENTLICHUNGEN. 1957. irreg., no.50, 1980. price varies. Universitaet Hannover, Institut fuer Siedlungswasserwirtschaft, Welfengarten 1, 3000 Hannover, W. Germany (B.R.D.)
Formerly: Technische Universitaet Hannover. Institut fuer Siedlungswasserwirtschaft. Veroeffentlichungen (ISSN 0073-0319)

333.91   US
UNIVERSITY OF ALASKA. INSTITUTE OF NORTHERN ENGINEERING. 1975. a. free. University of Alaska, Institute of Northern Engineering, Water Research Center, Fairbanks, AK 99775-1760. TEL 907-474-7775. Ed. Alan C. Paulson. circ. 1,800.
Former titles: University of Alaska. Institute of Water Resources-Engineering Experiment Station. Annual Report; University of Alaska. Institute of Water Resources. Annual Report (ISSN 0065-5953)

333.91   US   ISSN 0068-6301
UNIVERSITY OF CALIFORNIA, DAVIS. WATER RESOURCES CENTER. CONTRIBUTIONS. 1957. irreg., (5-7 nos. per yr.) free. ‡ University of California, Davis, Water Resources Center, Davis, CA 95616. TEL 916-752-1544. circ. 600. Indexed: Sel.Water Res.Abstr.

333.9   US   ISSN 0069-9063
UNIVERSITY OF CONNECTICUT. INSTITUTE OF WATER RESOURCES. REPORT SERIES. 1966. irreg., no.31, 1981. ‡ University of Connecticut, Institute of Water Resources, Storrs, CT 06268. TEL 203-486-4523. Indexed: GeoRef.

333.7   US
UNIVERSITY OF CONNECTICUT. INSTITUTE OF WATER RESOURCES. WETLANDS CONFERENCE. PROCEEDINGS. (Subseries of its Report) 1973. irreg., 3rd, 1976. University of Connecticut, Institute of Water Resources, Box U-37, Storrs, CT 06268. TEL 203-486-2000. charts. illus. (also avail. in microfiche from NTI) Indexed: Sel.Water Res.Abstr.

333.91   US
UNIVERSITY OF HAWAII. WATER RESOURCES RESEARCH CENTER. ANNUAL REPORT. 1966. a. free. University of Hawaii, Water Resources Research Center, 2540 Dole St., Holmes Hall 283, Honolulu, HI 96822. TEL 808-948-7847. Ed. Faith N. Fujimura. circ. 500. (back issues avail.)

333.9   628   US   ISSN 0073-1293
UNIVERSITY OF HAWAII. WATER RESOURCES RESEARCH CENTER. COLLECTED REPRINTS. 1969. biennial. price varies. ‡ University of Hawaii, Water Resources Research Center, 2540 Dole St., Honolulu, HI 96822. TEL 808-948-7847. Ed. Faith N. Fujimura. circ. 500. (also avail. in microfiche from NTI)

333.91   US
UNIVERSITY OF HAWAII. WATER RESOURCES RESEARCH CENTER. PROJECT BULLETIN. 1972. irreg. free. University of Hawaii, Water Resources Research Center, 2540 Dole St., Honolulu, HI 96822. TEL 808-948-7847.

333.91   US
UNIVERSITY OF HAWAII. WATER RESOURCES RESEARCH CENTER. RAIN WATER CISTERN SYSTEMS. 1982. irreg. $38. University of Hawaii, Water Resources Research Center, 2540 Dole St., Honolulu, HI 96822. TEL 808-948-7847. Ed. Faith N. Fujimura. charts.

333.9   628   US   ISSN 0073-1307
UNIVERSITY OF HAWAII. WATER RESOURCES RESEARCH CENTER. TECHNICAL REPORT. 1967. irreg. price varies. ‡ University of Hawaii, Water Resources Research Center, 2540 Dole St., Honolulu, HI 96822. TEL 808-948-7847. Ed. Faith N. Fujimura. circ. 300. (also avail. in microfiche from NTI) Indexed: Pollut.Abstr.

333.91   US
UNIVERSITY OF HAWAII. WATER RESOURCES RESEARCH CENTER. WORKSHOP SERIES. 1976. irreg. University of Hawaii, Water Resources Research Center, 2540 Dole St., Honolulu, HI 96822. TEL 808-948-7847.

333.9   627   US   ISSN 0073-4616
UNIVERSITY OF IDAHO. WATER RESOURCES RESEARCH INSTITUTE. ANNUAL REPORT. 1965. a. free. University of Idaho, Water Resources Research Institute, Moscow, ID 83843. TEL 208-885-6429. Ed. George L. Bloomsburg. circ. 400.

333.91   US   ISSN 0073-5434
UNIVERSITY OF ILLINOIS AT URBANA-CHAMPAIGN. WATER RESOURCES CENTER. ANNUAL REPORT. 1965. a. $5. ‡ University of Illinois at Urbana-Champaign, Water Resources Center, 208 N. Romine, Urbana, IL 61801. TEL 217-333-0536. Ed. Glenn E. Stout. (also avail. in microform from NTI)

333.91   US   ISSN 0073-5442
UNIVERSITY OF ILLINOIS AT URBANA-CHAMPAIGN. WATER RESOURCES CENTER. RESEARCH REPORT. 1966. irreg., no.205, 1984. price varies. ‡ University of Illinois at Urbana-Champaign, Water Resources Center, 208 N. Romine, Urbana, IL 61801. TEL 217-333-0536. Ed. Glenn E. Stout. (also avail. in microform from NTI) Indexed: Biol.Abstr. Pollut.Abstr.

333.91   US
UNIVERSITY OF ILLINOIS AT URBANA-CHAMPAIGN. WATER RESOURCES CENTER. SPECIAL REPORTS. 1968. irreg., no.15, 1984. price varies. University of Illinois at Urbana-Champaign, Water Resources Center, 208 N. Romine, Urbana, IL 60801. TEL 217-333-0536. Indexed: Biol.Abstr. Pollut.Abstr. GeoRef.

333.91   634.9   US
UNIVERSITY OF MINNESOTA. CENTER FOR NATURAL RESOURCE POLICY AND MANAGEMENT. WORKING PAPERS. 1984. irreg., latest issue no.2. University of Minnesota, Center for Natural Resource Policy & Management, 110 Green Hall, Dept. of Forest Resources, St. Paul, MN 55108. TEL 612-373-0846. Ed. James Perry. circ. 150. (back issues avail.)

627   333.9   AT   ISSN 0077-8818
UNIVERSITY OF NEW SOUTH WALES. WATER RESEARCH LABORATORY, MANLY VALE. LABORATORY RESEARCH REPORTS. 1959. irreg., no. 157, 1980. price varies. University of New South Wales, Water Research Laboratory, King St., Manly Vale, N.S.W. 2093, Australia. Indexed: Sel.Water Res.Abstr. GeoRef.

333.9   628   US
UNIVERSITY OF RHODE ISLAND. WATER RESOURCES CENTER. ANNUAL REPORT. 1965. a. 5. ‡ Rhode Island Water Resources Center, University of Rhode Island, Kingston, RI 02881. TEL 401-792-1000. Ed. Calvin Poon. circ. 800.

333.91   US
UNIVERSITY OF TEXAS AT AUSTIN. CENTER FOR RESEARCH IN WATER RESOURCES. TECHNICAL REPORT SERIES. 1964. irreg., latest, no.219. price varies. University of Texas at Austin, Center for Research in Water Resources, Austin, TX 78758-4497. TEL 512-471-3131. Indexed: Chem.Abstr.

333.91   US
UNIVERSITY OF TEXAS AT AUSTIN. CENTER FOR RESEARCH IN WATER RESOURCES. WATER RESOURCES SYMPOSIUM SERIES. 1968. irreg. price varies. University of Texas at Austin, Center for Research in Water Resources, 10100 Burnet Rd., Austin, TX 78758-4497. TEL 512-471-3131.
Former titles: University of Texas at Austin. Center for Research in Water Resources. Symposium Series; University of Texas at Austin. Center for Research in Water Resources. Resource Symposium Series.

333.91   US
UNIVERSITY OF WYOMING. WYOMING WATER RESEARCH CENTER. WATER CENTER SERIES. 1985. irreg. free. University of Wyoming, Wyoming Water Research Center, Box 3067, University Sta., Laramie, WY 82071. TEL 307-766-2143. Ed. Pamelia A. Murdock.

VALENCIA PORT; guia del servicios del puerto de Valencia. see *TRANSPORTATION — Ships And Shipping*

VANDERBILT UNIVERSITY. DEPARTMENT OF ENVIRONMENTAL AND WATER RESOURCES ENGINEERING. TECHNICAL REPORTS. see *ENVIRONMENTAL STUDIES*

353.9 US ISSN 0095-1978
VIRGINIA. STATE WATER CONTROL BOARD. ANNUAL REPORT. 1973. a. free. State Water Control Board, 2111 N. Hamilton St., P.O. Box 11143, Richmond, VA 23230. TEL 804-257-0056. illus. Key Title: Annual Report of the Virginia State Water Control Board.

353.9 US
VIRGINIA. STATE WATER CONTROL BOARD. BASIC DATA BULLETIN. 1930. irreg., no. 44, 1975. State Water Control Board, 2111 N. Hamilton St., Box 11143, Richmond, VA 23230. TEL 804-257-0056.

353.9 US
VIRGINIA. STATE WATER CONTROL BOARD. INFORMATION BULLETIN. no. 527, 1977. irreg. State Water Control Board, 2111 N. Hamilton St., Box 11143, Richmond, VA 23230. TEL 804-257-0056.

353.9 US
VIRGINIA. STATE WATER CONTROL BOARD. PLANNING BULLETIN. no. 304, 1976. irreg. State Water Control Board, 2111 N. Hamilton St., Box 11143, Richmond, VA 23230. TEL 804-257-0056. Indexed: GeoRef.

333.91 US
VIRGINIA. WATER RESOURCES RESEARCH CENTER. BULLETIN. 1965. irreg., latest no.142. free within Virginia; out-of-state $8 per no. Water Resources Research Center, Virginia Polytechnic Institute and State University, 617 N. Main St., Blacksburg, VA 24060. TEL 703-961-5624. abstr. bibl. illus. circ. 250. (also avail. in microfilm from UMI; back issues avail.) Indexed: Geo.Abstr. GeoRef.

614 333.7 HU ISSN 0133-3305
VIZGAZDALKODAS ES KORNYEZETVEDELEM. irreg. price varies. Orszagos Vizugyi Foigazgatosag, Kazinczy u. 37B, Budapest 7, Hungary. illus.

627 BU ISSN 0204-8248
VODNI PROBLEMI. 1975. irreg. 1.40 lv. per no. (Bulgarska Akademiia na Naukite, Institut po Vodni Problemi) Publishing House of the Bulgarian Academy of Sciences, Acad. G. Bonchev St., Bldg. 6, 1113 Sofia, Bulgaria. circ. 480.
Supersedes: Bulgarska Akademiia na Naukite. Institut po Vodni Problemi. Izvestiia.

608 540 GW ISSN 0083-6915
VOM WASSER; ein Fachbuch fuer Wasserchemie und Wasserreinigungstechnik. irreg., vol.67, 1986. price varies. (Gesellschaft Deutscher Chemiker, Fachgruppe Wasserchemie) V C H Verlagsgesellschaft mbH, Postfach 1260/1280, 6940 Weinheim, W. Germany (B.R.D.) (U.S. addr.: 220 East 23rd St., NY, NY, 10010-4606) adv. (reprint service avail. from ISI) Indexed: Biol.Abstr. Chem.Abstr. Excerp.Med.

628.1 333.7 GW ISSN 0511-3520
WASSER-KALENDER; Jahrbuch fuer das gesamte Wasserfach. 1966. a. price varies. Erich Schmidt Verlag GmbH (Berlin), Genthiner Str. 30g, 1000 Berlin 30, W. Germany (B.R.D.) Ed. R. Wagner. charts. stat. circ. 3,000.

333.7 628.1 GW ISSN 0512-5030
WASSER UND ABWASSER IN FORSCHUNG UND PRAXIS. (Text in German; summaries in English and French) 1969. irreg., vol.19, 1984. price varies. Erich Schmidt Verlag GmbH (Bielefeld), Viktoriastr. 44A, 4800 Bielefeld, W. Germany (B.R.D.)

333.7 340 628.1 GW ISSN 0508-1254
WASSERRECHT UND WASSERWIRTSCHAFT. 1960. irreg., vol.22, 1983. price varies. Erich Schmidt Verlag GmbH (Berlin), Genthiner Str. 30g, 1000 Berlin 30, W. Germany (B.R.D.) bibl. charts. illus. stat.

333.91 GW
WASSERVERSORGUNGS- UND ABWASSERTECHNIK. JAHRBUCH. a. Vulkan-Verlag Dr. W. Classen, Hollestr. 1G, Postfach 103962, D-4300 Essen, W. Germany (B.R.D.)

627 US ISSN 0083-7636
WATER. (Subseries of A I Ch E Symposium Series) irreg., latest 1980. price varies. American Institute of Chemical Engineers, 345 E. 47 St., New York, NY 10017. TEL 212-705-7657. (back issues avail.)

628.1 CN
WATER & POLLUTION CONTROL. DIRECTORY AND BUYERS' GUIDE. (Title varies slightly) 1962. a. Can.$15. Southam Communications Ltd., 1450 Don Mills Road, Don Mills, Ont. M3B 2X7, Canada. TEL 416-445-6641. Ed. Tom Davey. adv. bk. rev. illus. circ. 8,238.
Former titles: Water and Pollution Control. Directory and Handbook (ISSN 0318-0468); Water & Pollution Control Directory (ISSN 0511-3555)

338.7 II
WATER AND POWER DEVELOPMENT CONSULTANCY SERVICES. ANNUAL REPORT AND STATEMENT OF ACCOUNTS. (Report year ends Mar. 31) (Text in English) a. Water and Power Development Consultancy Services (India) Ltd., Kailash, 26 K. G. Marg, New Delhi 110001, India.

333.91 CN ISSN 0383-5472
WATER QUALITY DATA FOR ONTARIO STREAMS & LAKES. a. free. Ministry of the Environment, Water Resources Branch, 135 St. Clair Ave. W., Toronto, Ont. M4Y 1P5, Canada. TEL 416-965-6141.

628.1 AT ISSN 0085-8021
WATER RESEARCH FOUNDATION OF AUSTRALIA. REPORTS. 1959. irreg. Aus.$100. Water Research Foundation of Australia Ltd., Box 47, Kingsford, N.S.W. 2032, Australia. circ. 1,000. Indexed: Biol.Abstr. Aus.Sci.Ind. GeoRef.
Incorporating: Water Research Foundation of Australia. Bulletin (ISSN 0085-8013)

333.91 AT
WATER RESEARCH IN AUSTRALIA: CURRENT PROJECTS. 1982. a. free. Department of Resources and Energy, G.P.O. Box 858, Canberra, A.C.T. 2601, Australia. Ed. Sally Anderson. circ. 1,200.
●Also available online.
Former titles: Water Research in Australia (ISSN 0810-736X); Inventory of Water Resources Research.

333.91 US
WATER RESOURCES ASSOCIATION OF THE DELAWARE RIVER BASIN. ALERTING BULLETIN. irreg., no. 200, 1984. membership. Water Resources Association of the Delaware River Basin, Box 867, Davis Rd., Valley Forge, PA 19481. TEL 215-783-0634.

333.91 620 US
WATER RESOURCES MONOGRAPHS. 1971. irreg. American Geophysical Union, 2000 Florida Ave. N.W., Washington, DC 20009. TEL 202-462-6903. (reprint service avail. from ISI) Indexed: GeoRef.

333.9 US
WATER RESOURCES REPORT SERIES. irreg. $3. Texas Tech University, Water Resources Center, Box 4630, Lubbock, TX 79409. circ. 600.
Civil Engineering Report Series (ISSN 0095-1692)

551.4 333.9 US ISSN 0518-6374
WATER RESOURCES SUMMARY. 1962. irreg., latest issue 1973. price varies. ‡ Geological Commission, Vardelle Parham Geology Center, 3815 W. Roosevelt Rd, Little Rock, AR 72204. TEL 501-663-9714. illus.

333.91 US
WATERMARKS. 1965. irreg. free. University of Texas at Austin, Center for Research in Water Resources, Balcones Research Center, 10100 Burnet Rd., Austin, TX 78758. TEL 512-471-3131. Ed. Maria de la Luz Martinez. bk. rev. circ. 2,400.
Former titles: Center for Research in Water Resources Newsletter; C R W R News (ISSN 0049-3538)

333.91 US
WESTERN WASHINGTON UNIVERSITY. INSTITUTE FOR WATERSHED STUDIES. TECHNICAL REPORT SERIES. 1964. irreg., no. 26, 1978. free. Western Washington University, Institute for Watershed Studies, Bellingham, WA 98225. TEL 206-676-3510. Ed. David F. Brakke. charts. illus. stat.
Former titles: Western Washington State College. Aquatic Studies Program. Technical Report Series & Western Washington State College. Institute for Freshwater Studies. Technical Report Series.

333.91 UK
WHO'S WHO IN THE WATER INDUSTRY. 1975. a. £8. (National Water Council) Wheatland Journals Ltd., Penn House, Penn Place, Rickmansworth, Herts. WD3 1SN, England. Ed. R. Clarke. adv. circ. 4,500.

627 333.91 AU
WIENER MITTEILUNGEN: WASSER, ABWASSER, GEWAESSER. 1968. irreg. price varies. Technische Universitaet Wien, Institut fuer Wasserguete und Landschaftswasserbau, A-1040 Vienna, Austria. circ. 350. Indexed: Chem.Abstr.

627 UK ISSN 0260-504X
WIND AND WATER MILLS. 1980. a. £0.75 to non-members. Midland Wind and Water Mill Group, c/o John Bedington, 188 Merivale Rd., Smethwick, West Midlands B66 4EA, England. illus.

333.91 627 ZA ISSN 0084-4705
ZAMBIA. DEPARTMENT OF WATER AFFAIRS. REPORT. 1964. a. 30 n. Government Printer, P.O. Box 136, Lusaka, Zambia.

WATER RESOURCES — Abstracting, Bibliographies, Statistics

551.46 639.3 016
333.7 US ISSN 0140-5373
AQUATIC SCIENCES & FISHERIES ABSTRACTS. PART 1: BIOLOGICAL SCIENCES & LIVING RESOURCES. 1969. m. $522. (Food and Agriculture Organization of the U.N.) Cambridge Scientific Abstracts, 5161 River Rd., Bethesda, MD 20816. TEL 301-951-1400. Ed. Jon Sears. adv. abstr. bibl. index. (also avail. in magnetic tape; back issues avail.) Indexed: Cal.Tiss.Abstr. Chemorec.Abstr. Oncol.Abstr. Weed Abstr.
●Also available online. Vendors: Bureau National des Donnees Oceaniques, CISTI, DIMDI, DIALOG.
Supersedes in part: Aquatic Sciences and Fisheries Abstracts (ISSN 0044-8516); Which was formed by the merger of: Aquatic Biology Abstracts (ISSN 0003-7311); Current Bibliography for Aquatic Sciences and Fisheries (ISSN 0011-3239)

551.46 639.3 016 US ISSN 0140-5381
AQUATIC SCIENCES & FISHERIES ABSTRACTS. PART 2: OCEAN TECHNOLOGY, POLICY AND NON-LIVING RESOURCES. 1969. m. $377. Cambridge Scientific Abstracts, 5161 River Rd., Bethesda, MD 20816. TEL 301-951-1400. Ed. B. Engel. adv. abstr. bibl. index. (also avail. in magnetic tape) Indexed: Cal.Tiss.Abstr. Chemorec.Abstr. Oncol.Abstr. Weed Abstr.
●Also available online. Vendors: Bureau National des Donnees Oceaniques, CISTI, DIMDI, DIALOG.
Supersedes in part: Aquatic Sciences and Fisheries Abstracts (ISSN 0044-8516); Which was formed by the merger of: Aquatic Biology Abstracts (ISSN 0003-7311) & Current Bibliography for Aquatic Sciences and Fisheries (ISSN 0011-3239)

627 016 II ISSN 0523-302X
BIBLIOGRAPHY ON IRRIGATION, DRAINAGE, RIVER TRAINING AND FLOOD CONTROL/ BIBLIOGRAPHIE RELATIVE AUX IRRIGATIONS, AU DRAINAGE, A LA REGULARISATION DES COURS D'EAU ET LA MATRISE DES CRUES. (Text in English and French) 1954/56. a. $5.00 per copy. International Commission on Irrigation and Drainage - Commission Internationale des Irrigations et du Drainage, 48 Nyaya Marg, Chanakyapuri, New Delhi 110021, India. bk. rev. circ. 1,200. (back issues avail.)

1128 WELDING

333.91 310 UK ISSN 0141-7835
CHARTERED INSTITUTE OF PUBLIC FINANCE
AND ACCOUNTANCY. WATER SERVICES
CHARGES STATISTICS. 1978. a. £8. Chartered
Institute of Public Finance and Accountancy, 3
Robert St., London WC2N 6BH, England. (back
issues avail.)

CURRENT TITLES IN OCEAN, COASTAL, LAKE
& WATERWAY SCIENCES; reader's information
bulletin and service. see EARTH SCIENCES —
Abstracting, Bibliographies, Statistics

016 333.91 614.7 US ISSN 0143-3296
ECOLOGY ABSTRACTS. 1975. m. $468. Cambridge
Scientific Abstracts, 5161 River Rd., Bethesda, MD
20816. TEL 301-951-1400. Ed. Pam Clare. adv. bk.
rev. index. (also avail. in magnetic tape; back issues
avail.) Indexed: Cal.Tiss.Abstr. Chemorec.Abstr.
Oncol.Abstr.
●Also available online. Vendors: DIALOG.
Formerly: Applied Ecology Abstracts (ISSN
0305-3040)

GERMANY (FEDERAL REPUBLIC, 1949-).
STATISTISCHES BUNDESAMT. FACHSERIE
19, UMWELTSCHUTZ, REIHE 2:
WASSERVERSORGUNG UND
ABWASSERBESEITIGUNG. see ENERGY —
Abstracting, Bibliographies, Statistics

333.91 314 HU ISSN 0209-7915
HUNGARY. KOZPONTI STATISZTIKAI
HIVATAL. VIZGAZDALKODASI
STATISZTIKAI ZSEBKONYV. irreg. 40 Ft.
Statisztikai Kiado Vallalat, Kaszasdulo u. 2, P.O.B.
99, 1300 Budapest 3, Hungary (Subscr. to: Kultura,
Box 149, H-1389 Budapest, Hungary)

333.91 016 US ISSN 0731-6445
HYDRO-ABSTRACTS. 1968. m. $10 for 1st category;
$5 ea. for others; $120 for all categories.
Environmental Hydrology Corp., Box 14701,
University Sta., Minneapolis, MN 55414. TEL 612-
379-0901. (looseleaf format; also avail. in microform
from UMI) Indexed: GeoRef.
●Also available online.
Formerly (until 1980): Water Resources Abstracts
(ISSN 0043-1362)

630 016 II ISSN 0021-1672
IRRIGATION AND POWER ABSTRACTS. (Text in
English) 1943. bi-m. Rs.500($50) Central Board of
Irrigation and Power, Malcha Marg, Chanakyapuri,
New Delhi 110021. Ed. Shri C.V.J. Varma. adv. bk.
rev. abstr. bibl. index. cum.index. circ. 2,150.
(back issues avail.; reprint service avail. from UMI)
Indexed: Field Crop Abstr. Fluidex. Herb.Abstr.
Formerly: Abstracts of Current Technical
Literature.

NEW ZEALAND AGRICULTURAL
ENGINEERING INSTITUTE. CURRENT
PUBLICATIONS. see AGRICULTURE —
Abstracting, Bibliographies, Statistics

PIPELINES ABSTRACTS. see PETROLEUM AND
GAS — Abstracting, Bibliographies, Statistics

333.91 016 SA
SELECTED JOURNALS ON WATER. (Text in
English) 1975. m. free. South African Water Information
Centre, Council for Scientific and Industrial
Research, Box 395, Pretoria 0001, South Africa. Ed.
M. Laubscher. circ. 150.

333.91 628 016 US ISSN 0037-136X
SELECTED WATER RESOURCES ABSTRACTS.
1968. m. $115 (with index $145) U.S. Geological
Survey, Water Resources Scientific Information
Center, 425 National Center, Reston, VA 22092
TEL 703-860-7455. (Available from: NTIS,
Springfield, VA 22161) Ed. R.A. Jensen. index. circ.
2,000. (also avail. in microform from UMI; reprint
service avail. from UMI) Indexed: Petrol.Abstr.
●Also available online. Vendors: DIALOG,
Pergamon Infoline.

338.4 US ISSN 0094-4335
STATISTICS FOR WATER UTILITIES
INCLUDING WATER AUTHORITIES IN
PENNSYLVANIA. a. free. Department of
Commerce, Bureau of Policy, Planning, & Systems
Development, 474 Forum Bldg., Harrisburg, PA
17120. TEL 717-787-7532.

333.91 JA
SUIDO JIGYO NENPO/ANNUAL STATISTICS OF
WATER WORKS. (Text in Japanese) 1971. a. free.
Toyama City Water Works Bureau, 7-38
Shinsakura-Machi, Toyama city 930, Japan. index.
circ. 350. (back issues avail.)

WELDING

see Metallurgy — Welding

WOMEN'S INTERESTS

301.412 DK ISSN 0900-1565
AARBOG FOR KVINDEFORSKNING. 1984. a.
Kr.118. (Koebenhavns Universitet, Center for
Kvindeforskning og Undervisning) Tiderne Skrifter
Forlag, Sank Peders Straede 28B, DK-1453
Copenhagen, Denmark. Ed.Bd. illus.

396 PK
ALL PAKISTAN WOMEN'S ASSOCIATION.
TRIENNIAL CONFERENCE REPORT. (Text in
English) triennial. All Pakistan Women's
Association, Information and Research Bureau, 67-B
Garden Rd., Karachi 3, Pakistan.

ANGELSTONE. see LITERATURE — Poetry

301.412 CN
ANNUAIRE DES FEMMES DE MONTREAL.
English edition: Montreal Women's Directory.
(Editions in English and French) 1974. a.
Can.$8.95. Editions Communiqu'Elles, 3585 St-
Urbain, Montreal, Que. H2X 2N6, Canada. TEL
514-844-1761. Ed. Jacquie Manthorne. adv. circ. 8,
000.

AURORA (MADISON); S F science fiction/
speculative feminism. see ADVENTURE AND
ROMANCE

301.412 AT
AUSTRALIA. NATIONAL WOMEN'S ADVISORY
COUNCIL. ANNUAL REPORT. 1979. a.
Australian Government Publishing Service, G.P.O.
Box 84, Canberra, A.C.T. 2601, Australia. illus.

B W P A MAGAZINE. (British Women Pilots
Association) see AERONAUTICS AND SPACE
FLIGHT

301.42 US
BATTERED WOMEN'S DIRECTORY. 1976. irreg.,
latest 1985. $12. c/o Terry Mehlman, Box E-94,
Earlham College, Richmond, IN 47374. adv. bk.
rev. bibl. stat. circ. 2,000. (also avail. in microform)
Formerly: Working on Wife Abuse.

BETTER HOMES & DYKES. see
HOMOSEXUALITY

301.412 US
BIG APPLE DYKE NEWS. 1981. irreg. $10. B.A.D.
News, 192 Spring St., No.15, New York, NY
10012. TEL 212-226-2821. Ed.Bd. adv. bk. rev. circ.
5,000.

BLACK MARIA. see LITERATURE

301.412 PO
CADERNOS CONDICAO FEMININA. 1975. irreg.
price varies. Comissao da Condicao Feminina, Av.
da Republica, 32, 2 Esq, 1093 Lisbon Codex,
Portugal. circ. 2,000.

CALIFORNIA YOUTH AUTHORITY'S STATUS
OF FEMALE EMPLOYEES. REPORT. see
BUSINESS AND ECONOMICS — Labor And
Industrial Relations

301.412 CN ISSN 0705-6028
CANADA. ADVISORY COUNCIL ON THE
STATUS OF WOMEN. ANNUAL REPORT.
1973. a. free. Advisory Council on the Status of
Women - Conseil Consultatif Canadien de la
Situation de la femme, 110 O'Connor St., 9th Floor,
P.O. Box 1541, Station "B", Ottawa, Ont. K1P 5R5,
Canada. TEL 613-992-4975. circ. 10,000.

CANADA. WOMEN'S BUREAU. WOMEN IN THE
LABOUR FORCE. see BUSINESS AND
ECONOMICS — Labor And Industrial Relations

301.412 US ISSN 0735-4398
CELIBATE WOMAN; a journal for women who are
celibate or considering this liberating way of relating
to others. 1982. irreg. $8. Martha Allen, Ed. & Pub.,
3306 Ross Place, N.W., Washington, DC 20008.
TEL 202-966-7783. bk. rev.

391 US
CHICAGOLAND WEDDING GUIDE. 1983. a.
$2.50 per no. P B Communications, Inc., 874 Green
Bay Rd., Winnetka, IL 60093. TEL 312-441-7892.
Ed. Asher J. Birnbaum. adv. circ. 50,000.

CLIO; eine periodische Zeitschrift zur Selbsthilfe. see
MEDICAL SCIENCES

301.412 US ISSN 0147-8311
CONDITIONS; a feminist magazine of writing by
women, with an emphasis on writing by lesbians.
1977. a. $18 for 3 nos. to individuals; institutions
$28. Conditions, Inc., Box 56, Van Brunt Sta.,
Brooklyn, NY 11215. Ed.Bd. adv. bk. rev. circ. 3,
000. (back issues avail.) Indexed: A.I.P.P. Alt.Press
Ind.

301.42 US ISSN 0147-104X
CONTRIBUTIONS IN WOMEN'S STUDIES. 1978.
irreg., no.40, 1983. price varies. Greenwood Press,
88 Post Rd. W., Box 5007, Westport, CT 06881.
TEL 203-226-3571.

COVERED WAGON WOMEN. see HISTORY —
History Of North And South America

DE TEXTOS. see SOCIOLOGY

331.4 US ISSN 0273-2157
DIRECTORY OF SPECIAL OPPORTUNITIES FOR
WOMEN. 1981. irreg. $19. Garrett Park Press, Box
190F, Garrett Park, MD 20896. TEL 301-946-2553.
Ed. Martha Merrill Doss.

DYKE DIANNIC WICCA SEPARATIST AMAZON
MAGICK. see HOMOSEXUALITY

EARTH CIRCLES. see AGRICULTURE

301.412 BO
ESTUDIOS DE PROMOCION FEMENINA. 1978.
irreg., no.6, 1985. Centro de Investigaciones
Sociales, Casilla 6931 - Correo Central, La Paz,
Bolivia.

301.412 UK
EXPLORATIONS IN FEMINISM. no.7, 1981. irreg.
Women's Research and Resources Centre,
Explorations in Feminism Collective, 1a Gladys
Rd., London NW6 2PU, England.

305.412 054 FR ISSN 0014-5327
EXPRESSION; revue culturelle feminine
internationale. (Text in English, French and
German) 1964. a. membership. Editions Expression
et Communication, 1 ave de Chatou, 92561 Reuil-
Malmaison Cedex, France. Ed. Perigot De LaTour.
adv. illus. circ. 3,000. (tabloid format)

FACTS ON WOMEN AT WORK IN AUSTRALIA.
see BUSINESS AND ECONOMICS — Labor And
Industrial Relations

FEMMES EN LITTERATURE. see LITERATURE

FORD FOUNDATION ANNUAL REPORT. see
SOCIAL SCIENCES: COMPREHENSIVE
WORKS

GAIA'S GUIDE. see TRAVEL AND TOURISM

354 GH
GHANA. NATIONAL COUNCIL ON WOMEN
AND DEVELOPMENT. ANNUAL REPORT.
1976. a. National Council on Women and
Development, Box M.53, Accra, Ghana. circ. 3,000.

376 SW ISSN 0283-2399
GOETEBORG WOMEN'S STUDIES. a. Kr.125.
University of Gothenburg, P.O. Box 5096, S-402 22
Goeteborg, Sweden (Distr.in U.S. by: Humanities
Press Inc., 171 First Ave., Atlantic Highlands, NJ
07716-1289) Ed. Gunhild Kyle.

HARVARD WOMEN'S LAW JOURNAL. see LAW

346.969   US   ISSN 0092-9190
HAWAII. STATE COMMISSION ON THE STATUS
OF WOMEN. ANNUAL REPORT. 1972. irreg.,
latest Jul., 1985. State Commission on the Status
of Women, Attn.: Marion H. Shim, Exec. Sec., 335
Merchant St., No. 253, Honolulu, HI 96813-2907.
Ed. Marion Heen Shim. illus. circ. 400. Key Title:
Annual Report - State of Hawaii. State Commission
on the Status of Women.

052   SI   ISSN 0217-1058
HER WORLD ANNUAL. 1976. a. S.$8 per no.
Times Periodicals Private Ltd., I New Industrial
Rd., Singapore 1953, Singapore. circ. 34,000.

HIGHER EDUCATION OPPORTUNITIES FOR
MINORITIES AND WOMEN: ANNOTATED
SELECTIONS. see EDUCATION — Higher
Education

HUE POINTS. see ART

301   US
I C R W OCCASIONAL PAPER SERIES. 1984.
irreg. International Center for Research on Women,
1717 Massachusetts Ave., N.W., Ste. 501.,
Washington, DC 20036. (back issues avail.)

I W F A YEARBOOK. (International Women's
Fishing Association) see SPORTS AND
GAMES — Outdoor Life

301.412   US
IMAGE OF WOMAN. irreg. price varies. Abner
Schram Ltd., 36 Park St., Montclair, NJ 07042.
TEL 201-744-7755.

IN THE LIFE. see HOMOSEXUALITY

301.412   US   ISSN 0197-3401
INDEX/DIRECTORY OF WOMEN'S MEDIA.
1975. a. $12. Women's Institute for Freedom of the
Press, 3306 Ross Place, N.W., Washington, DC
20008. TEL 202-966-7783. Ed. Martha Leslie Allen.
adv. circ. 2,000. Indexed: HR Rep.

301.412   IO
INDONESIAN WOMEN'S CONGRESS.
BULLETIN/KONGRES WANITA INDONESIA.
BERITA. (Text in Indonesian) irreg. Indonesian
Women's Congress, Jl. H.O.S. Cokroaminoto 67,
Jakarta, Indonesia.

396   US   ISSN 0538-2912
INTER-AMERICAN COMMISSION OF WOMEN.
NEWS BULLETIN. Spanish edition: Inter-
American Commission of Women. Noticiero (ISSN
0538-2920) 1953. irreg., latest no.33. (Inter-
American Commission of Women (C I M))
Organization of American States, General
Secretariat of the Organization of American States,
Department of Publications, Washington, DC
20006. TEL 703-941-1617.

396   US   ISSN 0538-2920
INTER-AMERICAN COMMISSION OF WOMEN.
NOTICIERO. English edition: Inter-American
Commission of Women. News Bulletin (ISSN 0538-
2912) 1951. irreg., latest no. 33. (Inter-American
Commission of Women (C I M)) Organization of
American States, General Secretariat of the
Organization of American States, Washington, DC
20006. TEL 703-941-1617.

301.42   US
INTERNATIONAL WOMEN'S WRITING GUILD.
SYMPOSIUM MONOGRAPH. 1982. a. price
varies. International Women's Writing Guild, Box
810, Gracie Sta., New York, NY 10028. Ed. Greta
Hofmann Nemiroff.

KVINDER, KVINDER. see HOMOSEXUALITY

301.412   DK   ISSN 0108-3961
KVINDESTUDIER VED A U C. AARBOG.
(Aalborg Universitetscenter) (Forms also part of:
Serie om Kvindeforskning) 1982. a. Kr.132. (Institut
for Samfundsudvikling og Planaegning) Aalborg
Universitetsforlag, Aalborg, Denmark. illus.

L A R C NEWSLETTER. (Radcliffe College, Lesbian
Alumni) see HOMOSEXUALITY

301.412   AT   ISSN 0313-4288
L I P; feminist arts journal. 1976. a. Aus.$8.95. L I P
Magazine Co-operative, Box 139, Parkville, Vic.
3052, Australia. Ed.Bd. adv. bk. rev. circ. 1,500.

LAW & WOMEN SERIES. see LAW

920 301.412   FR
MEMOIRE DES FEMMES. 1978. irreg. price varies.
Editions Syros, 1 rue de Varenne, 75006 Paris,
France.

301.412   BO
MONOGRAFIAS DE PROMOCION FEMENINA.
1985. irreg. price varies. Centro de Investigaciones
Sociales, Casilla 6931 - Correo Central, La Paz,
Bolivia.

301.412 618   US
MONTHLY EXTRACT.* 1972. irreg. $5.50 for 6 nos.
New Moon Communications, 2 Hemlock Rd.,
Stamford, CT 06902. Ed.Bd. circ. 1,500. (also avail.
in microform from BLH)

301.412   US   ISSN 0047-830X
MOVING OUT; a feminist literary & arts journal.
1971. a. $6 to individuals; libraries $9. Box 21249,
Detroit, MI 48221. TEL 313-577-2424. Ed.Bd. adv.
bk. rev. illus. circ. 1,000. (also avail. in microform
from BLH; back issues avail) Indexed:
Wom.Stud.Abstr. A.I.P.P.

MUSICAL WOMAN. see MUSIC

301.41   CN
ONTARIO ADVISORY COUNCIL ON WOMEN'S
ISSUES. ANNUAL REPORT. 1974. a. free.
Ontario Advisory Council on Women's Issues, 880
Bay St., 5th floor, Toronto, Ont. M7A 1N3,
Canada. TEL 416-965-5824. illus. circ. 9,000.
    Former titles: Ontario. Advisory Council on
Women's Issues. Annual Report on the Status of
Women's Issues; Ontario. Status of Women Council.
Annual Report.

OPEN DOOR INTERNATIONAL FOR THE
EMANCIPATION OF THE WOMAN WORKER.
REPORT OF CONGRESS. see BUSINESS AND
ECONOMICS — Labor And Industrial Relations

353.9   US
P C S W ANNUAL REPORT. 1973. a. free.
Permanent Commission on the Status of Women, 90
Washington St., Hartford, CT 06106. TEL 203-566-
5702. Ed. Fredrica K. Gray.

PERFORMING WOMAN; a national directory of
professional women musicians. see MUSIC

POETESSA; the new woman's poetry journal. see
LITERATURE — Poetry

301.412   PO
PORTUGAL. COMISSAO DA CONDICAO
FEMININA. COLECCAO INFORMAR AS
MULHERES. 1979. irreg. Comissao da Condicao
Feminina, Avda. da Republica 32, 2 Esq., 1093
Lisbon Codex, Portugal.

301   PO
PORTUGAL. COMISSAO DA CONDICAO
FEMININA. NOTICIAS. 1985. irreg. free.
Comissao da Condicao Feminina, Avda. da
Republica 32, 2 Esq., 1093 Lisbon Codex, Portugal.

301.412 800   US   ISSN 0364-7609
PRIMAVERA (CHICAGO) 1975. a. $5. 1212 E. 59th
St., Chicago, IL 60637. Ed.Bd. adv. circ. 1,000.
(also avail. in microfilm from UMI; reprint service
avail. from UMI) Indexed: Amer.Hum.Ind.
Ind.Amer.Per.Verse.

PROFESSIONAL WOMEN AND MINORITIES; a
manpower data resource service. see
OCCUPATIONS AND CAREERS

ROOM; a woman's literary journal. see
LITERATURE — Poetry

301.412   US
SAGE YEARBOOKS IN WOMEN'S POLICY
STUDIES. 1976. a. $29.95 for hardcover; softcover
$14.95. Sage Publications, Inc., 2111 W. Hillcrest
Dr., Newbury Park, CA 91320 TEL 805-499-0721.
(And Sage Publications Ltd., 28 Banner St., London
C1Y 8QE, England) Ed.Bd. (back issues avail.)
    Formerly: Yearbook in Women's Policy Studies.

301.4157 808   US   ISSN 0275-6757
SAPPHIC TOUCH; a journal of lesbian erotica. 1981.
irreg. $7 per no. Pamir Productions, Box 40218, San
Francisco, CA 94140. Eds. Jeannie Karen, Sue
Skope.

WOMEN'S INTERESTS   1129

323 700   US   ISSN 0161-715X
SIBYL-CHILD. 1974. 3/yr. (in 1 vol.) $9. Sibyl-Child
Press, Inc., Box 1773, Hyattsville, MD 20788. TEL
202-723-5468. Eds. Saundra Maley, Nancy Prothro.
adv. bk. rev. bibl. illus. circ. 1,000. Indexed:
Wom.Stud.Abstr.

331.4   UK
SOCIETY FOR PROMOTING TRAINING OF
WOMEN. ANNUAL REPORT. 1859. a. free.
Society for Promoting Training of Women, Dean
Cottage, Village Lane, Hedgerley, Slough SL2 3UY,
England. circ. 500.

SOCIETY OF WOMEN ARTISTS. PUBLICATION.
see ART

821 820 305.412   NZ   ISSN 0110-1145
SPIRAL. 1976. irreg. NZ.$10 per no. Spiral
Collectives, Box 9600, Courtenay Place, Wellington,
New Zealand. Ed.Bd. adv. bk. rev. circ. 500. (back
issues avail.)

STUDIES IN WOMEN AND RELIGION. see
RELIGIONS AND THEOLOGY

UNCOVERINGS; research papers. see HISTORY —
History Of North And South America

376 301.412   US
UNIVERSITY OF MICHIGAN. CENTER FOR
CONTINUING EDUCATION OF WOMEN
NEWSLETTER. 1965. irreg. (1-2/yr.) free.
University of Michigan, Center for Continuing
Education of Women, 350 S. Thayer St., Ann
Arbor, MI 48104-1608. Ed. Nelvia Vant Hal. circ.
13,000.

301.412   SP   ISSN 0212-324X
VINDICACION FEMINISTA. 1976. irreg. 2250
ptas.($15) Partido Feminista de Espana, Bailen 38,
Barcelona 13, Spain. Ed. Lidia Falcon. illus.

W I D FORUM. (Office of Women in International
Development) see SOCIOLOGY

301   CN
WAGES FOR HOUSEWORK. CAMPAIGN
BULLETIN. 1976. irreg. (2-3/yr.) Can.$3. Toronto
Wages for Housework Committee, Box 38, Ste E,
Toronto, Ont. M6H 4E1, Canada. TEL 416-465-
6822. bk. rev. circ. 10,000. (tabloid format)

WISCONSIN WOMEN'S LAW JOURNAL. see
LAW

301.412   US   ISSN 0195-9743
WOMAN IN HISTORY. 1980. irreg., vol.7, 1983.
price varies. Monument Press, Box 160361, Las
Colinas, TX 75016-9998. (Co-publishers: Texas
Independent Press; Liberal Press; Tanglewuld Press)
Ed. Samantha Gonzales. circ. 300.

WOMAN POET. see LITERATURE — Poetry

052   UK
WOMAN'S OWN HOLIDAY READING. a. £0.90. I
P C Magazines Ltd., King's Reach Tower, Stamford
St., London SE1 9LS, England. circ. 250,000.

800 301.412   US   ISSN 0147-1759
WOMEN & LITERATURE; a journal of women
writers and the literary treatment of women. 1974;
N.S. 1981. a. price varies. Holmes & Meier
Publishers, Inc., 30 Irving Pl., New York, NY
10003. Ed. Janet M. Todd. adv. bk. rev. bibl. (also
avail. in microform from MIM,UMI; back issues
avail.) Indexed: Curr.Cont. Hum.Ind. M.L.A.
Amer.Hum.Ind. Arts & Hum.Cit.Ind.
Abstr.Engl.Stud.
    Formerly: Mary Wollstonecraft Journal (ISSN
0193-7103)

WOMEN AND MINORITIES IN SCIENCE AND
ENGINEERING. see ENGINEERING

331.4   II
WOMEN IN A DEVELOPING ECONOMY. 1975.
irreg. Allied Publishers Private Ltd., 15 Graham
Rd., Ballard Estate, Bombay 400038, India.

WOMEN IN CONTEXT. see MEDICAL SCIENCES

301.412 BB
WOMEN IN THE CARIBBEAN PROJECT. 1981. irreg., vol.7, 1986. University of the West Indies, Institute of Social and Economic Research, P.O. Box 64, Bridgetown, Barbados, W.I. Ed. Joycelin Massiah. circ. 500.

WOMEN - POEMS. see *LITERATURE — Poetry*

WOMEN TALKING, WOMEN LISTENING. see *LITERATURE — Poetry*

301.412 US ISSN 0276-7988
WOMEN'S ANNUAL. 1980. a. $35. G. K. Hall & Co., 70 Lincoln St., Boston, MA 02111. TEL 617-423-3990. Ed. Barbara Haber. circ. 800.

301.412 US
WOMEN'S COLLECTION NEWSLETTER. 1974. irreg. free. Northwestern University Library, Women's Collection Library, 1935 Sheridan Rd., Evanston, IL 60201. TEL 312-491-3635. Ed.Bd. abstr. bibl. circ. 1,500.

WOMEN'S NETWORK/RESEAU FEMMES. (Federation Nationale des Enseignants et des Enseignantes du Quebec) see *EDUCATION*

301.412 US
WOMEN'S ORGANIZATIONS: A NATIONAL DIRECTORY. 1986. irreg. (approx. 2-3/yr) $25. Garrett Park Press, Box 190B, Garrett Park, MD 20896. TEL 301-946-2553. Ed. Martha Merrill Doss.

301.412 US
WOMEN'S ORGANIZATIONS: A NEW YORK CITY DIRECTORY. 1982. irreg. New York City Commission on the Status of Women, 52 Chambers St., Ste. 207, New York, NY 10007. Ed. Lisa Kassel. circ. 5,000.

301.41 US ISSN 0092-6639
WOMEN'S ORGANIZATIONS & LEADERS DIRECTORY. 1973. biennial. $65. Today Publications and News Service, Inc., National Press Building, Washington, DC 20045. TEL 202-638-0348. Ed. Lester A. Barrer.

WORKING PAPERS ON WOMEN IN INTERNATIONAL DEVELOPMENT. see *BUSINESS AND ECONOMICS — International Development And Assistance*

920.72 UK
WORLD WHO'S WHO OF WOMEN. 1973. every 18 mos. price varies. Melrose Press Ltd., 3 Regal Lane, Soham, Ely, Cambridgeshire CB7 5BA, England. Ed. Dr. Ernest Kay. illus.

13TH MOON; a feminist literary magazine. see *LITERATURE*

WOMEN'S INTERESTS — Abstracting, Bibliographies, Statistics

301.412 US ISSN 0742-6941
BIBLIOGRAPHIES AND INDEXES IN WOMEN'S STUDIES. 1984. irreg. price varies. Greenwood Press, 88 Post Rd. W., Box 5007, Westport, CT 06881. TEL 203-226-3571.

301.412 016 GW ISSN 0344-1415
DIE FRAUENFRAGE IN DEUTSCHLAND. BIBLIOGRAPHIE. 1951. irreg(vol.2, 1985) price varies. (Deutscher Akademikerinnenbund) K. G. Saur Verlag KG, Peossenbacherstr. 2, 8000 Munich 71, W. Germany (B.R.D.) (U.S. and Canadian subscr. to: K.G. Saur Inc., 175 Fifth Ave., New York, N.Y. 10010) (reprint service avail. from UMI, ISI)

INDEX/DIRECTORY OF WOMEN'S MEDIA. see *WOMEN'S INTERESTS*

LESBIAN HERSTORY ARCHIVES NEWSLETTER. see *HOMOSEXUALITY*

301.412 016 UK ISSN 0262-5644
STUDIES ON WOMEN ABSTRACTS. 1983. bi-m. $140. Carfax Publishing Co., P.O. Box 25, Abingdon, Oxfordshire OX14 3UE, England (U.S. distr.: 85 Ash St., Hopkinton, MA 01748) Ed. June Purvis. adv. bk. rev. cum.index. (also avail. in microfiche; back issues avail.)

305.412 016 US ISSN 0049-7835
WOMEN STUDIES ABSTRACTS. 1972. q. $43 to individuals; institutions $84. Rush Publishing Co., Inc., Box 1, Rush, NY 14543. TEL 716-624-4418. Ed. Sara Stauffer Whaley. adv. bk. rev. index. circ. 1,000. (also avail. in microfilm from UMI; reprint service avail. from UMI)

WORD PROCESSING

see *Computers — Word Processing*

ZOOLOGY

see *Biology — Zoology*

Serials Available Online

A P I ABSTRACTS/LITERATURE.
American Petroleum Institute, Central Abstracting and Indexing Service, 156 William St., New York, NY 10038. TEL 212-587-9660.
Also available online. Vendors: Orbit Information Technologies. (867)

ABSTRACTS ON TROPICAL AGRICULTURE.
Royal Tropical Institute, Information and Documentation, Mauritskade 63, 1092 AD Amsterdam, Netherlands.
Also available online. Vendors: Orbit Information Technologies. (38)

ACCESS: THE SUPPLEMENTARY INDEX TO PERIODICALS.
John Gordon Burke Publishers, Inc., Box 1492, Evanston, IL 60204-1492.
Also available online. (2)

ACCOUNTANTS' INDEX.
American Institute of Certified Public Accountants, 1211 Ave. of the Americas, New York, NY 10036-8775. TEL 212-575-5515.
Also available online. Vendors: Orbit Information Technologies. (202)

ADVANCES IN PHARMACEUTICAL SCIENCES.
Academic Press Inc., Orlando, FL 32887. TEL 305-345-6000.
Also available online. (869)

AEROSPACE DEFENSE MARKETS AND TECHNOLOGY.
Predicasts, Inc., 200 University Circle Research Center, 11001 Cedar Ave., Cleveland, OH 44106. TEL 216-795-3000.
Also available online. Vendors: DIALOG. (813)

AGRICULTURAL ENGINEERING ABSTRACTS.
C.A.B. International, Farnham House, Farnham Royal, Slough SL2 3BN, England
Also available online. Vendors: BRS, CISTI, DIMDI, DIALOG, European Space Agency. (38)

AGRICULTURAL FINANCE OUTLOOK AND SITUATION.
U.S. Department of Agriculture, Economics Management Staff, Information Division, 1301 New York Ave., N.W., Washington, DC 20005 TEL 202-783-3238.
Also available online. Vendors: DIALOG. (44)

ALBERTA REPORTS.
Maritime Law Book Ltd., Box 302, Fredericton, N.B. E3B 4Y9, Canada. TEL 506-454-9921.
Also available online. Vendors: QL Systems Ltd. (650)

ALLOYS INDEX.
A M S International, Materials Information, Metals Park, OH 44073. TEL 216-338-5151.
Also available online. Vendors: CEDOCAR, CISTI, DIALOG, European Space Agency, Orbit Information Technologies. (801)

AMERICA: HISTORY AND LIFE. PART A: ARTICLE ABSTRACTS AND CITATION.
A B C-Clio, 2040 Alameda Padre Serra, Box 4397, Santa Barbara, CA 93140-4397. TEL 805-963-4221.
Also available online. Vendors: DIALOG. (562)

AMERICA: HISTORY AND LIFE. PART B: INDEX TO BOOK REVIEWS.
A B C-Clio, 2040 Alameda Padre Serra, Box 4397, Santa Barbara, CA 93110-4397. TEL 805-963-4221.
Also available online. Vendors: DIALOG. (562)

AMERICA: HISTORY AND LIFE. PART C: AMERICAN HISTORY BIBLIOGRAPHY.
A B C-Clio, 2040 Alameda Padre Serra, Box 4397, Santa Barbara, CA 93140-4397. TEL 805-963-4221.
Also available online. Vendors: DIALOG. (562)

AMERICAN CHEMICAL SOCIETY. DIRECTORY OF GRADUATE RESEARCH.
American Chemical Society, 1155 16th St., N.W., Washington, DC 20036. TEL 202-872-8065.
Also available online. (428)

AMERICAN HOSPITAL FORMULARY SERVICE DRUG INFORMATION.
American Society of Hospital Pharmacists, c/o Jean Rogers, Dir., Mkt. Svcs., 4630 Montgomery Ave., Bethesda, MD 20814. TEL 301-657-3000.
Also available online. Vendors: BRS, DIALOG, Mead Data Central. (869)

AMERICAN LIBRARY DIRECTORY.
R. R. Bowker Company, Database Publishing Group, 245 W. 17th St., New York, NY 10011. TEL 800-521-8110.
Also available online. Vendors: DIALOG. (673)

AMERICAN MEN AND WOMEN OF SCIENCE. PHYSICAL AND BIOLOGICAL SCIENCES.
R.R. Bowker Company, Database Publishing Group, 245 W. 17th St., New York, NY 10011. TEL 800-521-8110.
Also available online. Vendors: BRS, DIALOG. (133)

AMERICAN STATISTICS INDEX; a comprehensive guide and index to the statistical publications of the U.S. Government.
Congressional Information Service, Inc., 4520 East-West Hwy., Bethesda, MD 20814. TEL 301-654-1550.
Also available online. Vendors: DIALOG, Orbit Information Technologies. (1048)

ANALYTICAL CHEMISTRY.
American Chemical Society, 1155 16th St., N.W., Washington, DC 20036. TEL 202-872-8065.
Also available online. (326)

ANIMAL BREEDING ABSTRACTS; a monthly abstract of world literature.
C.A.B. International, Farnham House, Farnham Royal, Slough SL2 3BN, England
Also available online. Vendors: BRS, CISTI, DIMDI, DIALOG, European Space Agency. (149)

ANIMAL HEALTH INTERNATIONAL DIRECTORY.
IMSWORLD Publications Ltd., 11-13 Melton St., London NW1 2EH, England.
Also available online. (1121)

ANTARCTIC BIBLIOGRAPHY.
U.S. National Science Foundation, Office of Polar Programs, 1800 G St., N.W., Washington, DC 20550. TEL 202-655-4000.
Also available online. Vendors: Orbit Information Technologies. (541)

APICULTURAL ABSTRACTS.
International Bee Research Association, Hill House, Gerrards Cross, Bucks SL9 ONR, England.
Also available online. Vendors: DIALOG, European Space Agency. (38)

APPLIED SCIENCE AND TECHNOLOGY INDEX; a cumulative subject index to English language periodicals in the fields of aeronautics and space science, automation, chemistry, construction, earth sciences, electricity and electronics, etc.
H.W. Wilson Co., 950 University Ave., Bronx, NY 10452. TEL 212-588-8400.
Also available online. Vendors: Wilsonline. (476)

AQUATIC SCIENCES & FISHERIES ABSTRACTS. PART 1: BIOLOGICAL SCIENCES & LIVING RESOURCES.
Cambridge Scientific Abstracts, 5161 River Rd., Bethesda, MD 20816. TEL 301-951-1400.
Also available online. Vendors: Bureau National des Donnees Oceaniques, CISTI, DIMDI, DIALOG. (1127)

AQUATIC SCIENCES & FISHERIES ABSTRACTS.
PART 2: OCEAN TECHNOLOGY, POLICY
AND NON-LIVING RESOURCES.
 Cambridge Scientific Abstracts, 5161 River Rd.,
 Bethesda, MD 20816. TEL 301-951-1400.
 Also available online. Vendors: Bureau National des
 Donnees Oceaniques, CISTI, DIMDI, DIALOG.
 (1127)

ARTBIBLIOGRAPHIES MODERN.
 Clio Press Ltd., 55 St. Thomas' St., Oxford OX1
 1JG, England
 Also available online. Vendors: DIALOG. (113)

AUDIOCASSETTE FINDER.
 Access Innovations, Inc., Box 40130, Albuquerque,
 NM 87196. TEL 505-265-3591.
 Also available online. (422)

AUSTRALIA. DEPARTMENT OF RESOURCES
AND ENERGY. STREAMLINE UPDATE.
 Department of Resources and Energy, G.P.O. Box
 858, Canberra, A.C.T. 2601, Australia
 Also available online. (1123)

AUSTRALIAN ROAD INDEX.
 Australian Road Research Board, Box 156 (Bag 4),
 Nunawading, Vic. 3131, Australia.
 Available only online. Vendors: AUSINET. (1084)

AUSTRALIAN ROAD RESEARCH IN PROGRESS.
 Australian Road Research Board, Box 156 (Bag 4),
 Nunawading, Vic. 3131, Australia.
 Also available online. Vendors: AUSINET. (476)

AUSTRALIAN TRANSPORT INFORMATION
DIRECTORY.
 Australian Government Publishing Service (Griffith),
 109 Canberra Ave, Griffith, ACT 2603, Australia
 Also available online. Vendors: Bureau of Transport
 Economics. (1080)

AVERY INDEX TO ARCHITECTURAL
PERIODICALS.
 G. K. Hall & Co., 70 Lincoln St., Boston, MA
 02111. TEL 617-423-3990.
 Available only online. Vendors: Research Libraries
 Information Network. (100)

BIBLIOGRAPHY AND INDEX OF GEOLOGY.
 American Geological Institute, 4220 King St.,
 Alexandria, VA 22302-1507. TEL 703-379-2480.
 Also available online. Vendors: CISTI, DIALOG,
 Orbit Information Technologies. (381)

BIBLIOGRAPHY OF AGRICULTURE.
 Oryx Press, 2214 N. Central Ave., Phoenix, AZ
 85004-1483. TEL 602-254-6156.
 Also available online. Vendors: CISTI. (39)

BIBLIOGRAPHY OF BIOETHICS.
 Kennedy Institute of Ethics, National Reference
 Center for Bioethics Literature, Georgetown
 University, Washington, DC 20057.
 Also available online. Vendors: National Library of
 Medicine. (768)

BIBLIOGRAPHY OF EDUCATION THESES IN
AUSTRALIA.
 Australian Council for Educational Research,
 Radford House, Box 210, Hawthorn, Vic. 3122,
 Australia.
 Also available online. Vendors: AUSINET. (422)

BIBLIOGRAPHY ON COLD REGIONS SCIENCE
& TECHNOLOGY.
 U.S. Army, Cold Regions Research and Engineering
 Laboratory, 72 Lyme Rd., Hanover, NH 03755.
 TEL 603-646-4221.
 Also available online. Vendors: Orbit Information
 Technologies. (476)

BIOGRAPHY AND GENEALOGY MASTER
INDEX.
 Gale Research Company, Book Tower, Detroit, MI
 48226. TEL 313-961-2242.
 Also available online. Vendors: DIALOG. (136)

BIOGRAPHY INDEX; a quarterly index to
biographical material in books and magazines.
 H. W. Wilson Co., 950 University Ave., Bronx, NY
 10452. TEL 212-588-8400.
 Also available online. Vendors: Wilsonline. (136)

BIOLOGICAL AND AGRICULTURAL INDEX; a
subject index to periodicals in the fields of biology
and agriculture and related sciences.
 H.W. Wilson Co., 950 University Ave., Bronx, NY
 10452. TEL 212-588-8400.
 Also available online. Vendors: Wilsonline. (149)

BIOTECHNOLOGY RESEARCH ABSTRACTS.
 Cambridge Scientific Abstracts, 5161 River Rd.,
 Bethesda, MD 20816.
 Also available online. Vendors: DIALOG, Orbit
 Information Technologies. (149)

BOOK REVIEW DIGEST; an index to reviews of
current books.
 H.W. Wilson Co., 950 University Ave., Bronx, NY
 10452. TEL 212-588-8400.
 Also available online. Vendors: Wilsonline. (963)

BOOKS IN PRINT.
 R.R. Bowker Company, Database Publishing Group,
 245 W. 17th St., New York, NY 10011. TEL 800-
 521-8110.
 Also available online. Vendors: BRS, DIALOG.
 (124)

BOOKS IN PRINT SUPPLEMENT; a mid-year
updating service listing new and forthcoming books,
price changes, and out-of-print titles.
 R.R. Bowker Company, Database Publishing Group,
 245 W. 17th St., New York, NY 10011. TEL 800-
 521-8110.
 Also available online. Vendors: BRS, DIALOG.
 (124)

BOOKS OUT OF PRINT.
 R.R. Bowker Company, Database Publishing Group,
 245 W. 17th St., New York, NY 10011. TEL 800-
 521-8110.
 Also available online. Vendors: BRS, DIALOG.
 (124)

BRITISH BOOKS IN PRINT.
 J. Whitaker & Sons Ltd., 12 Dyott St., London
 WC1A 1DF, England
 Also available online. (124)

BRITISH CATALOGUE OF AUDIO-VISUAL
MATERIALS.
 British Library, Bibliographic Services, 2 Sheraton
 St., London W1V 4BH, England.
 Also available online. (1032)

BRITISH EXPORTS.
 Kompass Publishers Ltd., Windsor Court, East
 Grinstead House, East Grinstead, West Sussex
 RH19 1XD, England.
 Also available online. (253)

BRITISH LIBRARY. DOCUMENT SUPPLY
CENTRE. INDEX OF CONFERENCE
PROCEEDINGS RECEIVED.
 British Library, Document Supply Centre, Boston
 Spa, Wetherby, West Yorkshire LS23 7BQ,
 England.
 Also available online. (796)

BULLETIN SIGNALETIQUE. PART 521:
SOCIOLOGIE - ETHNOLOGIE.
 Centre National de la Recherche Scientifique,
 Centre de Documentation Sciences Humaines, 54
 bd. Raspail, 75260 Paris Cedex, France.
 Also available online. Vendors: European Space
 Agency. (1031)

BULLETIN SIGNALETIQUE. PART 524:
SCIENCES DU LANGAGE.
 Centre National de la Recherche Scientifique,
 Centre de Documentation Sciences Humaines, 54
 bd. Raspail, 75260 Paris Cedex, France.
 Also available online. Vendors: European Space
 Agency. (709)

BULLETIN SIGNALETIQUE D'INFORMATION
ADMINISTRATIVE.
 Documentation Francaise, 29-31 quai Voltaire,
 75340 Paris Cedex 07, France
 Also available online. Vendors: European Space
 Agency. (948)

BUSINESS PERIODICALS INDEX; a cumulative
subject index to English language periodicals in the
fields of accounting, advertising and public relations,
automation, banking, communications, economics,
finance and investments, insurance, labor,
management, etc.
 H. W. Wilson Co., 950 University Ave., Bronx, NY
 10452. TEL 212-588-8400.
 Also available online. Vendors: Wilsonline. (204)

BUSINESS WHO'S WHO OF AUSTRALIA.
 R.G. Riddell Pty. Ltd., 100 Alexander St., Crowns
 Nest, N.S.W. 2065, Australia.
 Also available online. Vendors: AUSINET. (303)

C.A.B. INTERNATIONAL BUREAU OF
AGRICULTURAL ECONOMICS. ANNOTATED
BIBLIOGRAPHIES SERIES A.
 C.A.B. International, Farnham House, Farnham
 Royal, Slough SL2 3BN, England.
 Also available online. Vendors: BRS, CISTI,
 DIMDI, DIALOG, European Space Agency. (39)

C.A.B. INTERNATIONAL BUREAU OF
AGRICULTURAL ECONOMICS. ANNOTATED
BIBLIOGRAPHIES. SERIES B:
AGRICULTURAL POLICY AND RURAL
DEVELOPMENT IN AFRICA.
 C.A.B. International, Farnham House, Farnham
 Royal, Slough SL2 3BN, England.
 Also available online. Vendors: BRS, CISTI,
 DIMDI, DIALOG, European Space Agency. (39)

C.A.B. INTERNATIONAL BUREAU OF
NUTRITION. ANNOTATED BIBLIOGRAPHIES.
 C.A.B. International, Farnham House, Farnham
 Royal, Slough SL2 3BN, England.
 Also available online. Vendors: BRS, CISTI,
 DIMDI, DIALOG, European Space Agency. (847)

C.A.B. INTERNATIONAL BUREAU OF SOILS.
ANNOTATED BIBLIOGRAPHIES.
 C.A.B. International, Farnham House, Farnham
 Royal, Slough SL2 3BN, England.
 Also available online. Vendors: BRS, CISTI,
 DIMDI, DIALOG, European Space Agency. (39)

C I S ABSTRACTS.
 International Labour Office, International
 Occupational Safety and Health Information Centre,
 CH-1211 Geneva 22, Switzerland.
 Also available online. Vendors: European Space
 Agency. (636)

C I S INDEX.
 Congressional Information Service, Inc., 4520 East-
 West Hwy., Ste. 800, Bethesda, MD 20814. TEL
 301-654-1550.
 Also available online. Vendors: Orbit Information
 Technologies. (948)

CADSCAN.
 Cadmium Association, 34 Berkeley Sq., London
 W1X 6AJ, England.
 Also available online. Vendors: Pergamon Infoline.
 (801)

CALCIFIED TISSUE ABSTRACTS.
 Cambridge Scientific Abstracts, 5161 River Rd.,
 Bethesda, MD 20816. TEL 301-951-1400.
 Also available online. Vendors: DIALOG. (149)

CANADIAN BUSINESS INDEX.
 Micromedia Ltd., 158 Pearl St., Toronto, Ont. M5H
 1L3, Canada. TEL 416-593-5211.
 Also available online. Vendors: CISTI, DIALOG,
 IST-INFORMATHEQUE, QL Systems Ltd. (205)

CANADIAN NEWS INDEX.
 Micromedia Ltd., 158 Pearl St., Toronto, Ont. M5H
 1L3, Canada. TEL 416-593-5211.
 Also available online. Vendors: CISTI, DIALOG,
 QL Systems Ltd. (647)

CERAMIC ABSTRACTS.
 American Ceramic Society, Inc., 65 Ceramic Dr.,
 Columbus, OH 43214. TEL 614-268-8645.
 Also available online. Vendors: Orbit Information
 Technologies, Pergamon Infoline. (320)

CHEM SOURCES - U.S.A.
 Directories Publishing Company, Inc., Box 1372,
 Ormond Beach, FL 32075 TEL 904-673-1241.
 Also available online. (304)

CHEMICAL ABSTRACTS SERVICE SOURCE INDEX.
Chemical Abstracts Service, Box 3012, Columbus, OH 43210 TEL 614-421-3600.
Also available online. Vendors: Orbit Information Technologies, STN International. (325)

CHEMICAL ENGINEERING ABSTRACTS.
Royal Society of Chemistry, University of Nottingham, Nottingham NG7 2RD, England
Also available online. Vendors: Data-Star, European Space Agency, Orbit Information Technologies, Pergamon Infoline. (476)

CHEMICAL REGULATION REPORTER; a weekly review of activity affecting chemical users and manufacturers.
The Bureau of National Affairs, Inc., 1231 25th St., N.W., Washington, DC 20037. TEL 202-452-4200.
Also available online. Vendors: Mead Data Central, WESTLAW. (494)

CHEMORECEPTION ABSTRACTS; chemical senses & applied techniques.
Cambridge Scientific Abstracts, 5161 River Rd., Bethesda, MD 20816. TEL 301-951-1400.
Also available online. Vendors: DIALOG. (325)

CHILDREN'S BOOKS IN PRINT.
R.R. Bowker Company, Database Publishing Group, 245 W. 17th St., New York, NY 10011. TEL 800-521-8110.
Also available online. (739)

CIVIL ENGINEERING HYDRAULICS ABSTRACTS.
B H R A Fluid Engineering, Cranfield, Bedford MK43 0AJ, England
Also available online. Vendors: European Space Agency. (476)

COAL ABSTRACTS.
I.E.A. Coal Research, 14/15 Lower Grosvenor Place, London SW1W 0EX, England.
Also available online. Vendors: BELINDIS, CISTI, INKA. (815)

CODE OF MARYLAND REGULATIONS.
Division of State Documents, Box 802, Annapolis, MD 21404. TEL 301-974-2486.
Also available online. (940)

COMMUNICATION THEORY IN THE CAUSE OF HUMANITY; notes on the application of theory to the strengthening of democratic institutions.
2346 Lansford Ave., Box 5095, San Jose, CA 95150.
Also available online. (634)

COMPUMATH CITATION INDEX.
Institute for Scientific Information, 3501 Market St., Philadelphia, PA 19104 TEL 215-386-0100.
Also available online. Vendors: BRS. (755)

COMPUTER & CONTROL ABSTRACTS.
INSPEC, I.E.E., Station House, Nightingale Rd., Hitchin, Herts. SG5 1RJ, England
Also available online. Vendors: BRS, CEDOCAR, CISTI, Data-Star, DIALOG, European Space Agency, JICST, Orbit Information Technologies, STN International, University of Tsukuba. (354)

COMPUTER AND INFORMATION SYSTEMS ABSTRACT JOURNAL; an abstract journal pertaining to the theory, design, fabrication and application of computer and information systems.
Cambridge Scientific Abstracts, 5161 River Rd., Bethesda, MD 20816. TEL 301-951-1400.
Also available online. Vendors: DIALOG. (354)

COMPUTER CONTENTS; semi-monthly compilation of tables of contents from more than 250 of the latest computer periodicals.
Find - S V P, 500 Fifth Ave., New York, NY 10110. TEL 212-354-2424.
Also available online. Vendors: DIALOG. (354)

COMPUTER READABLE DATABASES; a directory and data sourcebook.
American Library Association, 50 E. Huron, Chicago, IL 60611.
Also available online. Vendors: DIALOG. (354)

CONFERENCE PAPERS ANNUAL INDEX.
Cambridge Scientific Abstracts, 5161 River Rd., Bethesda, MD 20816. TEL 301-951-1400.
Also available online. Vendors: DIALOG. (4)

COTTON AND TROPICAL FIBRES ABSTRACTS.
C.A.B. International, Farnham House, Farnham Royal, Slough SL2 3BN, England
Also available online. Vendors: BRS, CISTI, DIMDI, DIALOG, European Space Agency. (40)

CRIMINAL JUSTICE PERIODICAL INDEX.
University Microfilms International, 300 N. Zeeb Road, Ann Arbor, MI 48106. TEL 313-761-4700.
Also available online. Vendors: DIALOG. (373)

CROP PHYSIOLOGY ABSTRACTS.
C.A.B. International, Farnham House, Farnham Royal, Slough SL2 3BN, England
Also available online. Vendors: BRS, CISTI, DIMDI, DIALOG, European Space Agency. (40)

CUMULATIVE BOOK INDEX; a world list of books in the English Language.
H. W. Wilson Co., 950 University Ave, Bronx, NY 10452. TEL 212-588-8400.
Also available online. Vendors: Wilsonline. (125)

CUMULATIVE INDEX TO NURSING & ALLIED HEALTH LITERATURE (C I N A H L)
Glendale Adventist Medical Center, Box 871, Glendale, CA 91209. TEL 818-577-7233.
Also available online. Vendors: BRS, BRS/Saunders Colleague, Data-Star, DIALOG. (769)

CURRENT AWARENESS IN BIOLOGICAL SCIENCES.
Pergamon Press, Inc., Journals Division, Maxwell House, Fairview Park, Elmsford, NY 10523 TEL 914-592-7700.
Also available online. Vendors: Pergamon Infoline. (150)

CURRENT BIOTECHNOLOGY ABSTRACTS.
Royal Society of Chemistry, University of Nottingham, Nottingham NG7 2RD, England.
Also available online. Vendors: Data-Star, European Space Agency, Orbit Information Technologies, Pergamon Infoline. (150)

CURRENT CONTENTS/CLINICAL MEDICINE.
Institute for Scientific Information, 3501 Market St., Philadelphia, PA 19104 TEL 215-386-0100.
Also available online. Vendors: BRS. (769)

CURRENT DIGEST OF THE SOVIET PRESS.
Current Digest of the Soviet Press, 1480 West Lane Ave., Columbus, OH 43221. TEL 614-292-4234.
Also available online. Vendors: DIALOG, Mead Data Central. (911)

CURRENT INDEX TO JOURNALS IN EDUCATION.
Oryx Press, 2214 N. Central Ave., Phoenix, AZ 85004-1483. TEL 602-254-6156.
Also available online. Vendors: BRS, CISTI, DIALOG, Orbit Information Technologies. (423)

CURRENT INDEX TO STATISTICS; applications-methods-theory.
American Statistical Association, 806 15th St., N.W., Washington, DC 20005. TEL 202-393-3253.
Also available online. Vendors: BRS, DIALOG, European Space Agency. (4)

CURRENT MATHEMATICAL PUBLICATIONS.
American Mathematical Society, Box 6248, Providence, RI 02940. TEL 401-272-9500.
Also available online. Vendors: BRS, DIALOG, European Space Agency. (755)

D L A BULLETIN.
University of California, Division of Library Automation, 186 University Hall, Berkeley, CA 94720. TEL 415-642-9485.
Also available online. (688)

DENMARK. RIGSBIBLIOTEKAREMBEDET. ACCESSIONSKATALOG; faelleskatalog over danske videnskabelige og faglige bibliotekers erhvervelser af udenlandsk litteratur.
Rigsbibliotekarembedet, Nyhavn 31E, DK-1051 Copenhagen K, Denmark.
Also available online. (125)

DICTIONARY OF CONTEMPORARY QUOTATIONS.
John Gordon Burke Publishers, Inc., Box 1492, Evanston, IL 60204-1492.
Also available online. (720)

DIRECTORY OF AMERICAN RESEARCH AND TECHNOLOGY.
R. R. Bowker Company, Database Publishing Group, 245 W. 17th St., New York, NY 10011. TEL 800-521-8110.
Also available online. Vendors: Pergamon Infoline. (1068)

DIRECTORY OF ASSOCIATIONS IN CANADA.
Micromedia Limited, 158 Pearl St., Toronto, Ont. M5H 1L3, Canada. TEL 416-593-5211.
Also available online. Vendors: CISTI. (462)

DIRECTORY OF CORPORATE AFFILIATIONS; who owns whom.
National Register Publishing Co. 3004 Glenview Rd., Wilmette, IL 60091. TEL 312-256-6067.
Also available online. (15)

DIRECTORY OF FEDERAL LABORATORIES.
High Tech Publishing Company, 10 Ridge Rd., Box 360, Ridge, NY 11961. TEL 516-924-6168.
Also available online. (306)

DIRECTORY OF FEDERALLY SUPPORTED RESEARCH IN UNIVERSITIES.
C.I.S.T.I. Publications, Ottawa, Ont. K1A 0S2, Canada. TEL 613-993-3736.
Also available online. Vendors: CISTI. (990)

DIRECTORY OF PUBLIC HIGH TECHNOLOGY CORPORATIONS.
American Investor Information Services, 311 Bainbridge St., Philadelphia, PA 19147-1543. TEL 215-925-2761.
Also available online. (307)

DOKUMENTATION RHEOLOGIE.
Bundesanstalt fuer Materialpruefung, Unter den Eichen 87, 1000 Berlin 45, W. Germany (B.R.D.)
Also available online. Vendors: INKA. (892)

DOKUMENTATION TRIBOLOGIE.
Bundesanstalt fuer Materialpruefung, Unter den Eichen 87, D-1000 Berlin 45, W. Germany (B.R.D.)
Also available online. Vendors: INKA. (476)

E I S CUMULATIVE.
Cambridge Scientific Abstracts, 5160 River Rd., Bethesda, MD 20816.
Also available online. Vendors: DIALOG. (501)

ECOLOGY ABSTRACTS.
Cambridge Scientific Abstracts, 5161 River Rd., Bethesda, MD 20816. TEL 301-951-1400.
Also available online. Vendors: DIALOG. (1128)

ECONOMIC TITLES/ABSTRACTS; semi-monthly providing concise information of interest to business, trade, industry, economic libraries and research institutes.
Martinus Nijhoff Publishers, Postbus 163, 3300 AD Dordrecht, Netherlands
Also available online. Vendors: BELINDIS, Data-Star, DIALOG. (207)

EDUCATION INDEX; an author-subject index to educational publications in the English language.
H.W. Wilson Co., 950 University Ave, Bronx, NY 10452. TEL 212-588-8400.
Also available online. Vendors: Wilsonline. (423)

EDUCATIONAL SOFTWARE SELECTOR.
Educational Products Information Exchange (EPIE) Institute, Box 839, Water Mill, NY 11976. TEL 516-283-4922.
Also available online. Vendors: CompuServe Consumer Information Service. (363)

ELECTRIC POWER INDUSTRY ABSTRACTS.
Edison Electric Institute, c/o Utility Data Institute, 2011 I St., N.W., Ste. 700, Washington, DC 20006.
Also available online. Vendors: Orbit Information Technologies. (461)

ELECTRICAL & ELECTRONICS ABSTRACTS.
INSPEC, I.E.E., Station House, Nightingale Rd., Hitchin, Herts. SG5 1RJ, England
Also available online. Vendors: BRS, CEDOCAR, CISTI, Data-Star, DIALOG, European Space Agency, JICST, Orbit Information Technologies, STN International, University of Tsukuba. (461)

ELECTRONIC PUBLISHING ABSTRACTS.
Pergamon Press, Inc., Journals Division, Maxwell House, Fairview Park, Elmsford, NY 10523 TEL 914-592-7700.
Also available online. Vendors: Orbit Information Technologies, Pergamon Infoline. (354)

ELECTRONICS AND COMMUNICATIONS ABSTRACTS JOURNAL; an abstract journal involving the theory, design and application of electronic devices and systems.
Cambridge Scientific Abstracts, 5161 River Rd., Bethesda, MD 20816. TEL 301-951-1400.
Also available online. Vendors: DIALOG. (345)

ENCYCLOPEDIA OF ASSOCIATIONS.
Gale Research Company, Book Tower, Detroit, MI 48226. TEL 313-961-2242.
Also available online. Vendors: DIALOG. (462)

ENERGY INFORMATION ABSTRACTS.
E I C Intelligence, Inc., 48 W. 38 St., New York, NY 10018. TEL 212-944-8500.
Also available online. Vendors: DIALOG, European Space Agency, Orbit Information Technologies. (468)

ENGINEERING INDEX MONTHLY AND AUTHOR INDEX; abstracting and indexing services covering sources of the world's engineering literature.
Engineering Information, Inc., 345 E. 47th St., New York, NY 10017 TEL 212-705-7600.
Also available online. Vendors: BRS, CEDOCAR, CISTI, Data-Star, DIALOG, European Space Agency, INKA, NERAC, Inc., Orbit Information Technologies, Pergamon Infoline, STN International. (476)

ENTOMOLOGY ABSTRACTS.
Cambridge Scientific Abstracts, 5161 River Rd., Bethesda, MD 20816. TEL 301-951-1400.
Also available online. Vendors: DIALOG. (150)

ESSOR; French industrial companies database.
Union Francaise d'Annuaires Profesionnels (U.F.A.P.), 13 Avenue Komarov, 78190 Trappes, France.
Also available online. (255)

EXCERPTA MEDICA. SECTION 1: ANATOMY, ANTHROPOLOGY, EMBRYOLOGY & HISTOLOGY.
Elsevier Science Publishers B.V., Box 211, 1000 AE Amsterdam, Netherlands.
Also available online. Vendors: BRS, DIALOG. (769)

EXCERPTA MEDICA. SECTION 2: PHYSIOLOGY.
Elsevier Science Publishers B.V., Box 211, 1000 AE Amsterdam, Netherlands.
Also available online. Vendors: BRS, DIALOG. (769)

EXCERPTA MEDICA. SECTION 3: ENDOCRINOLOGY.
Elsevier Science Publishers B.V., Box 211, 1000 AE Amsterdam, Netherlands.
Also available online. Vendors: BRS, DIALOG. (769)

EXCERPTA MEDICA. SECTION 4: MICROBIOLOGY: BACTERIOLOGY, MYCOLOGY AND PARASITOLOGY.
Elsevier Science Publishers B.V., Box 211, 1000 AE Amsterdam, Netherlands.
Also available online. Vendors: BRS, DIALOG. (769)

EXCERPTA MEDICA. SECTION 5: GENERAL PATHOLOGY AND PATHOLOGICAL ANATOMY.
Elsevier Science Publishers B.V., Box 211, 1000 AE Amsterdam, Netherlands.
Also available online. Vendors: BRS, DIALOG. (769)

EXCERPTA MEDICA. SECTION 6: INTERNAL MEDICINE.
Elsevier Science Publishers B.V., Box 211, 1000 AE Amsterdam, Netherlands.
Also available online. Vendors: BRS, DIALOG. (769)

EXCERPTA MEDICA. SECTION 7: PEDIATRICS AND PEDIATRIC SURGERY.
Elsevier Science Publishers B.V., Box 211, 1000 AE Amsterdam, Netherlands.
Also available online. Vendors: BRS, DIALOG. (769)

EXCERPTA MEDICA. SECTION 8: NEUROLOGY AND NEUROSURGERY.
Elsevier Science Publishers B.V., Box 211, 1000 AE Amsterdam, Netherlands.
Also available online. Vendors: BRS, DIALOG. (769)

EXCERPTA MEDICA. SECTION 9: SURGERY.
Elsevier Science Publishers B.V., Box 211, 1000 AE Amsterdam, Netherlands.
Also available online. Vendors: BRS, DIALOG. (769)

EXCERPTA MEDICA. SECTION 10: OBSTETRICS AND GYNECOLOGY.
Elsevier Science Publishers B.V., Box 211, 1000 AE Amsterdam, Netherlands.
Also available online. Vendors: BRS, DIALOG. (769)

EXCERPTA MEDICA. SECTION 11: OTORHINOLARYNGOLOGY.
Elsevier Science Publishers B.V., Box 211, 1000 AE Amsterdam, Netherlands.
Also available online. Vendors: BRS, DIALOG. (769)

EXCERPTA MEDICA. SECTION 12: OPHTHALMOLOGY.
Elsevier Science Publishers B.V., Box 211, 1000 AE Amsterdam, Netherlands.
Also available online. Vendors: BRS, DIALOG. (770)

EXCERPTA MEDICA. SECTION 13: DERMATOLOGY AND VENEREOLOGY.
Elsevier Science Publishers B.V., Box 211, 1000 AE Amsterdam, Netherlands.
Also available online. Vendors: BRS, DIALOG. (770)

EXCERPTA MEDICA. SECTION 14: RADIOLOGY.
Elsevier Science Publishers B.V., Box 211, 1000 AE Amsterdam, Netherlands.
Also available online. Vendors: BRS, DIALOG. (770)

EXCERPTA MEDICA. SECTION 15: CHEST DISEASES, THORACIC SURGERY AND TUBERCULOSIS.
Elsevier Science Publishers B.V., Box 211, 1000 AE Amsterdam, Netherlands.
Also available online. Vendors: BRS, DIALOG. (770)

EXCERPTA MEDICA. SECTION 16: CANCER.
Elsevier Science Publishers B.V., Box 211, 1000 AE Amsterdam, Netherlands.
Also available online. Vendors: BRS, DIALOG. (770)

EXCERPTA MEDICA. SECTION 17: PUBLIC HEALTH, SOCIAL MEDICINE & HYGIENE.
Elsevier Science Publishers B.V., Box 211, 1000 AE Amsterdam, Netherlands.
Also available online. Vendors: BRS, DIALOG. (958)

EXCERPTA MEDICA. SECTION 19: REHABILITATION AND PHYSICAL MEDICINE.
Elsevier Science Publishers B.V., Box 211, 1000 AE Amsterdam, Netherlands.
Also available online. Vendors: BRS, DIALOG. (770)

EXCERPTA MEDICA. SECTION 20: GERONTOLOGY AND GERIATRICS.
Elsevier Science Publishers B.V., Box 211, 1000 AE Amsterdam, Netherlands.
Also available online. Vendors: BRS, DIALOG. (552)

EXCERPTA MEDICA. SECTION 23: NUCLEAR MEDICINE.
Elsevier Science Publishers B.V., Box 211, 1000 AE Amsterdam, Netherlands.
Also available online. Vendors: BRS, DIALOG. (770)

EXCERPTA MEDICA. SECTION 24: ANESTHESIOLOGY.
Elsevier Science Publishers B.V., Box 211, 1000 AE Amsterdam, Netherlands.
Also available online. Vendors: BRS, DIALOG. (770)

EXCERPTA MEDICA. SECTION 25: HEMATOLOGY.
Elsevier Science Publishers B.V., Box 211, 1000 AE Amsterdam, Netherlands.
Also available online. Vendors: BRS, DIALOG. (770)

EXCERPTA MEDICA. SECTION 26: IMMUNOLOGY, SEROLOGY AND TRANSPLANTATION.
Elsevier Science Publishers B.V., Box 211, 1000 AE Amsterdam, Netherlands.
Also available online. Vendors: BRS, DIALOG. (770)

EXCERPTA MEDICA. SECTION 27: BIOPHYSICS, BIO-ENGINEERING AND MEDICAL INSTRUMENTATION.
Elsevier Science Publishers B.V., Box 211, 1000 AE Amsterdam, Netherlands.
Also available online. Vendors: BRS, DIALOG. (770)

EXCERPTA MEDICA. SECTION 28: UROLOGY AND NEPHROLOGY.
Elsevier Science Publishers B.V., Box 211, 1000 AE Amsterdam, Netherlands.
Also available online. Vendors: BRS, DIALOG. (770)

EXCERPTA MEDICA. SECTION 29: CLINICAL BIOCHEMISTRY.
Elsevier Science Publishers B.V., Box 211, 1000 AE Amsterdam, Netherlands.
Also available online. Vendors: BRS, DIALOG. (770)

EXCERPTA MEDICA. SECTION 31: ARTHRITIS AND RHEUMATISM.
Elsevier Science Publishers B.V., Box 211, 1000 AE Amsterdam, Netherlands.
Also available online. Vendors: BRS, DIALOG. (770)

EXCERPTA MEDICA. SECTION 32: PSYCHIATRY.
Elsevier Science Publishers B.V., Box 211, 1000 AE Amsterdam, Netherlands.
Also available online. Vendors: BRS, DIALOG. (770)

EXCERPTA MEDICA. SECTION 33: ORTHOPEDIC SURGERY.
Elsevier Science Publishers B.V., Box 211, 1000 AE Amsterdam, Netherlands.
Also available online. Vendors: BRS, DIALOG. (770)

EXCERPTA MEDICA. SECTION 34: PLASTIC SURGERY.
Elsevier Science Publishers B.V., Box 211, 1000 AE Amsterdam, Netherlands.
Also available online. Vendors: BRS, DIALOG. (770)

EXCERPTA MEDICA. SECTION 35: OCCUPATIONAL HEALTH AND INDUSTRIAL MEDICINE.
Elsevier Science Publishers B.V., Box 211, 1000 AE Amsterdam, Netherlands.
Also available online. Vendors: BRS, DIALOG. (770)

EXCERPTA MEDICA. SECTION 36: HEALTH ECONOMICS AND HOSPITAL MANAGEMENT.
Elsevier Science Publishers B.V., Box 211, 1000 AE Amsterdam, Netherlands.
Also available online. Vendors: BRS, DIALOG. (619)

EXCERPTA MEDICA. SECTION 38: ADVERSE REACTIONS TITLES.
Elsevier Science Publishers B.V., Box 211, 1000 AE Amsterdam, Netherlands.
Also available online. Vendors: BRS, DIALOG. (770)

EXCERPTA MEDICA. SECTION 46:
ENVIRONMENTAL HEALTH AND
POLLUTION CONTROL.
Elsevier Science Publishers B.V., Box 211, 1000 AE
Amsterdam, Netherlands.
Also available online. Vendors: BRS, DIALOG.
(501)

EXCERPTA MEDICA. SECTION 47: VIROLOGY.
Elsevier Science Publishers B.V., Box 211, 1000 AE
Amsterdam, Netherlands.
Also available online. Vendors: BRS, DIALOG.
(770)

EXCERPTA MEDICA. SECTION 48:
GASTROENTEROLOGY.
Elsevier Science Publishers B.V., Box 211, 1000 AE
Amsterdam, Netherlands.
Also available online. Vendors: BRS, DIALOG.
(770)

EXCERPTA MEDICA. SECTION 49: FORENSIC
SCIENCE.
Elsevier Science Publishers B.V., Box 211, 1000 AE
Amsterdam, Netherlands.
Also available online. Vendors: BRS, DIALOG.
(770)

EXCERPTA MEDICA. SECTION 50: EPILEPSY.
Elsevier Science Publishers B.V., Box 211, 1000 AE
Amsterdam, Netherlands.
Also available online. Vendors: BRS, DIALOG.
(770)

EXCERPTA MEDICA. SECTION 51: LEPROSY
AND RELATED SUBJECTS.
Elsevier Science Publishers B.V., Box 211, 1000 AE
Amsterdam, Netherlands.
Also available online. Vendors: BRS, DIALOG.
(770)

F D A DRUG BULLETIN.
U.S. Food and Drug Administration, 5600 Fisher's
Lane, Rockville, MD 20857. TEL 301-443-3220.
Also available online. (376)

FABA BEAN ABSTRACTS.
C.A.B. International, Farnham House, Farnham
Royal, Slough SL2 3BN, England
Also available online. Vendors: BRS, CISTI,
DIMDI, DIALOG, European Space Agency. (40)

FIELD CROP ABSTRACTS; monthly abstract journal
on world annual cereal, legume, root, oilseed and
fibre crops.
C.A.B. International, Farnham Royal, Slough SL2
3BN, England
Also available online. Vendors: BRS, CISTI,
DIMDI, DIALOG, European Space Agency. (40)

FILM & VIDEO FINDER.
Access Innovations, Inc., Box 40130, Albuquerque,
NM 87196. TEL 505-265-3591.
Also available online. (424)

FINANCE FOR NEW PROJECTS IN UK; guide to
private and public sector initiatives and grants.
Peat Marwick Mitchell & Co., 1 Puddle Dock,
Blackfriars, London EC4V 3PD, England.
Also available online. (244)

FINANCIAL TIMES WORLD SHIPPING
YEARBOOK.
Financial Times, Bracken House, 10 Cannon St.,
London EC4P 4BY, England.
Also available online. Vendors: DIALOG. (1100)

FINDEX; directory of market research reports, studies
and surveys.
National Standards Association, Inc., 1561 River
Rd., Bethesda, MD 20816. TEL 301-951-1389.
Also available online. Vendors: DIALOG. (284)

FINE CHEMICALS DIRECTORY.
Pergamon Journals, Inc., Maxwell House, Fairview
Park, Elmsford, NY 10523 TEL 914-592-7700.
Also available online. Vendors: Pergamon Infoline.
(328)

FLUID FLOW MEASUREMENT ABSTRACTS.
B H R A Fluid Engineering, Cranfield, Bedford
MK43 0AJ, England
Also available online. Vendors: European Space
Agency. (476)

FLUID SEALING ABSTRACTS.
B H R A Fluid Engineering, Cranfield, Bedford
MK43 0AJ, England
Also available online. Vendors: European Space
Agency. (476)

FOOD SCIENCE AND TECHNOLOGY
ABSTRACTS.
C.A.B. International, Farnham House, Farnham
Royal, Slough SL2 3BN, England
Also available online. Vendors: BRS, CISTI,
DIMDI, Data-Star, DIALOG, European Space
Agency, JICST, Orbit Information Technologies.
(521)

FOREST PRODUCTS ABSTRACTS.
C.A.B. International, Farnham House, Farnham
Royal, Slough SL2 3BN, England
Also available online. Vendors: BRS, CISTI,
DIMDI, DIALOG, European Space Agency. (529)

FORESTRY ABSTRACTS; compiled from world
literature.
C.A.B. International, Farnham House, Farnham
Royal, Slough SL2 3BN, England.
Also available online. Vendors: BRS, CISTI,
DIMDI, DIALOG, European Space Agency. (529)

FORESTRY ABSTRACTS. LEADING ARTICLE
REPRINT SERIES.
C.A.B. International, Farnham House, Farnham
Royal, Slough SL2 3BN, England.
Also available online. Vendors: BRS, CISTI,
DIMDI, DIALOG, European Space Agency. (529)

FORTSCHRITTE DER
ARZNEIMITTELFORSCHUNG.
Birkhaeuser Verlag, P.O. Box 133, CH 4010 Basel,
Switzerland.
Also available online. (871)

FOUNDATION CENTER NATIONAL DATA
BOOK.
Foundation Center, 79 Fifth Ave., New York, NY
10003. TEL 212-620-4230.
Also available online. Vendors: DIALOG. (1022)

FOUNDATION DIRECTORY.
Foundation Center, 79 Fifth Ave., New York, NY
10003. TEL 212-620-4230.
Also available online. Vendors: DIALOG. (1022)

FOUNDATION GRANTS INDEX.
Foundation Center, 79 Fifth Ave., New York, NY
10003. TEL 212-620-4230.
Also available online. Vendors: DIALOG. (1022)

GENERAL SCIENCE INDEX.
H.W. Wilson Co., 950 University Ave., Bronx, NY
10452. TEL 212-588-8400.
Also available online. Vendors: Wilsonline. (1004)

GENETICS ABSTRACTS.
Cambridge Scientific Abstracts, 5161 River Rd.,
Bethesda, MD 20816. TEL 301-951-1400.
Also available online. Vendors: DIALOG. (150)

GEOSCIENCE DOCUMENTATION; a bi-monthly
journal for the study of geoscience literature.
Geosystems, Box 40, Didcot, Oxon OX11 9BX,
England.
Also available online. Vendors: DIALOG. (382)

GEOSOURCES.
Geosystems, P.O. Box 40, Didcot, Oxon OX11
9BX, England.
Also available online. Vendors: DIALOG. (379)

GLACIOLOGICAL DATA.
World Data Center A for Glaciology (Snow and
Ice), CIRES, Campus Box 449, University of
Colorado, Boulder, CO 80309. TEL 303-497-5311.
Also available online. Vendors: Orbit Information
Technologies. (388)

GOVERNMENT SUPPORT FOR BRITISH
BUSINESS.
University of Strathclyde, Center for the Study of
Public Policy, Livingstone Tower, 26 Richmond
Street, Glasgow G1 1XH, Scotland.
Also available online. (245)

HARVARD WOMEN'S LAW JOURNAL.
Harvard University Law School, Women's Law
Journal, Langdell Hall, Cambridge, MA 02138. TEL
617-495-3100.
Also available online. Vendors: WESTLAW. (656)

HELMINTHOLOGICAL ABSTRACTS. SERIES A:
ANIMAL AND HUMAN HELMINTHOLOGY.
C.A.B. International, Farnham House, Farnham
Royal, Slough SL2 3BN, England.
Also available online. Vendors: BRS, CISTI,
DIMDI, DIALOG, European Space Agency. (41)

HELMINTHOLOGICAL ABSTRACTS. SERIES B:
PLANT NEMATOLOGY.
C.A.B. International, Farnham House, Farnham
Royal, Slough SL2 3BN, England.
Also available online. Vendors: BRS, CISTI,
DIMDI, DIALOG, European Space Agency. (41)

HERBAGE ABSTRACTS; monthly abstract journal
on grassland husbandry and fodder crop production.
C.A.B. International, Farnham House, Farnham
Royal, Slough SL2 3BN, England
Also available online. Vendors: BRS, CISTI,
DIMDI, DIALOG, European Space Agency. (41)

HISTORICAL ABSTRACTS. PART A: MODERN
HISTORY ABSTRACTS, 1450-1914.
A B C-Clio, 2040 Alameda Padre Serra, Box 4397,
Santa Barbara, CA 93140-4397. TEL 805-963-4221.
Also available online. Vendors: DIALOG. (563)

HISTORICAL ABSTRACTS. PART B: TWENTIETH
CENTURY ABSTRACTS, 1914 TO THE
PRESENT.
A B C-Clio, 2040 Alameda Padre Serra, Box 4397,
Santa Barbara, CA 93140-4397. TEL 805-963-4221.
Also available online. Vendors: DIALOG. (563)

HORTICULTURAL ABSTRACTS; compiled from
world literature and temperate and tropical fruits,
vegetables, ornaments, plantation crops.
C.A.B. International, Farnham House, Farnham
Royal, Slough SL2 3BN, England.
Also available online. Vendors: BRS, CISTI,
DIMDI, DIALOG, European Space Agency. (534)

HOSPITAL LITERATURE INDEX.
American Hospital Association, 840 N. Lake Shore
Dr., Chicago, IL 60611. TEL 312-280-6263.
Also available online. Vendors: DIMDI. (619)

HUMANITIES INDEX; an author and subject index
to periodicals in the fields of archaeology and
classical studies, area studies, folklore, history,
language and literature, literary and political
criticism, performing arts, philosophy, religion and
theology, and related subjects.
H.W. Wilson Co., 950 University Ave., Bronx, NY
10452. TEL 212-588-8400.
Also available online. Vendors: Wilsonline. (634)

HYDRO-ABSTRACTS.
Environmental Hydrology Corp., Box 14701,
University Sta., Minneapolis, MN 55414. TEL 612-
379-0901.
Also available online. (1128)

I M M ABSTRACTS; a survey of world literature on
the economic geology and mining of all minerals
(except coal), mineral processing and non-ferrous
extraction metallurgy.
Institution of Mining and Metallurgy, 44 Portland
Place, London W1N 4BR, England.
Also available online. (822)

I N I S ATOMINDEX.
International Atomic Energy Agency, Wagramer
Str. 5, Box 100, A-1400 Vienna, Austria
Also available online. Vendors: CISTI, European
Space Agency. (893)

IMMUNOLOGY ABSTRACTS.
Cambridge Scientific Abstracts, 5161 River Rd.,
Bethesda, MD 20816. TEL 301-951-1400.
Also available online. Vendors: DIALOG. (770)

INDEX CHEMICUS.
Institute for Scientific Information, 3501 Market St.,
Philadelphia, PA 19104 TEL 215-386-0100.
Also available online. Vendors: Telesystemes -
Questel. (325)

INDEX MEDICUS.
U.S. National Library of Medicine, 8600 Rockville
Pike, Bethesda, MD 20894 TEL 202-783-3238.
Also available online. Vendors: DIALOG. (771)

INDEX OF CURRENT RESEARCH ON PIGS.
C.A.B. International, Farnham House, Farnham
Royal, Slough SL2 3BN, England.
Also available online. Vendors: BRS, CISTI,
DIMDI, DIALOG, European Space Agency. (41)

INDEX OF ECONOMIC ARTICLES IN JOURNALS AND COLLECTIVE VOLUMES.
American Economic Association, 1313 21st. Ave. So., Nashville, TN 37212 TEL 615-322-2595.
Also available online. Vendors: DIALOG. (210)

INDEX TO DENTAL LITERATURE; an alphabetical author and subject index to dental literature.
American Dental Association, 211 E. Chicago Ave., Chicago, IL 60611. TEL 312-440-2500.
Also available online. Vendors: DIALOG. (771)

INDEX TO LEGAL PERIODICALS.
H.W. Wilson Co., 950 University Ave., Bronx, NY 10452. TEL 212-588-8400.
Also available online. Vendors: Mead Data Central, Wilsonline. (668)

INDEX TO THE CHRISTIAN SCIENCE MONITOR.
Bell & Howell Co., Newspaper Indexing Center, Microphoto Division, Old Mansfield Rd., Wooster, OH 44691. TEL 216-264-6666.
Also available online. (647)

INDEX TO THE LOS ANGELES TIMES.
Bell & Howell Co., Newspaper Indexing Center, Microphoto Division, Old Mansfield Rd., Wooster, OH 44691. TEL 216-264-6666.
Also available online. (647)

INDEX VETERINARIUS; a classified subject and author index produced by computer processes of current literature on veterinary science with approximately 23,000 titles.
C.A.B. International, Farnham House, Farnham Royal, Slough SL2 3BN, England.
Also available online. Vendors: BRS, CISTI, DIMDI, DIALOG, European Space Agency. (1123)

INDUSTRIAL AERODYNAMICS ABSTRACTS.
B H R A Fluid Engineering, Cranfield, Bedford MK43 0AJ, England
Also available online. Vendors: European Space Agency. (477)

INFORMATION SCIENCE ABSTRACTS.
Plenum Press, Electronic Publishing Division, 233 Spring St., New York, NY 10013. TEL 212-620-8468.
Also available online. Vendors: DIALOG. (688)

INSTITUTE OF PAPER CHEMISTRY. ABSTRACT BULLETIN.
Institute of Paper Chemistry, 1043 E. South River St., Box 1039, Appleton, WI 54912. TEL 414-734-9251.
Also available online. Vendors: DIALOG. (859)

INSURANCE PERIODICALS INDEX.
N I L S Publishing Company, Box 2507, Chatsworth, CA 91311 TEL 818-998-8830.
Also available online. Vendors: Mead Data Central. (642)

INTERNATIONAL AEROSPACE ABSTRACTS.
American Institute of Aeronautics and Astronautics, Technical Information Service, 555 W. 57th St., Ste. 1200, New York, NY 10019. TEL 212-247-6500.
Also available online. Vendors: DIALOG, European Space Agency, Mead Data Central. (22)

INTERNATIONAL BUILDING SERVICES ABSTRACTS.
Building Services Research and Information Association, Old Bracknell Lane West, Bracknell, Berks RG12 4AH, England.
Also available online. Vendors: European Space Agency, Pergamon Infoline. (554)

INTERNATIONAL JOURNAL OF ROCK MECHANICS AND MINING SCIENCES & GEOMECHANICS ABSTRACTS.
Pergamon Press, Inc., Journals Division, Maxwell House, Fairview Park, Elmsford, NY 10523 TEL 914-592-7700.
Also available online. Vendors: Pergamon Infoline. (822)

INTERNATIONAL NURSING INDEX INCLUDING NURSING CITATION INDEX.
American Journal of Nursing Co., 555 W. 57th St., New York, NY 10019. TEL 212-582-8820.
Also available online. Vendors: BRS, DIALOG. (771)

INTERNATIONAL OMBUDSMAN INSTITUTE BIBLIOGRAPHY.
International Ombudsman Institute, Faculty of Law, University of Alberta, Edmonton, Alta. T6G 2H5, Canada. TEL 403-432-3196.
Available only online. (668)

INTERNATIONAL PACKAGING ABSTRACTS.
Pergamon Press, Inc., Journals Division, Maxwell House, Fairview Park, Elmsford, NY 10523 TEL 914-592-7700.
Also available online. Vendors: Orbit Information Technologies, Pergamon Infoline. (855)

INTERNATIONAL PETROLEUM ABSTRACTS.
John Wiley & Sons Ltd., Baffins Lane, Chichester, Sussex PO19 1UD, England.
Also available online. Vendors: Pergamon Infoline. (868)

INTERNATIONAL PHARMACEUTICAL ABSTRACTS; key to the world's literature of pharmacy.
American Society of Hospital Pharmacists, c/o Jean Rogers, Dir., Mkt. Svcs., 4630 Montgomery Ave., Bethesda, MD 20814. TEL 301-657-3000.
Also available online. Vendors: BRS, DIALOG, European Space Agency. (873)

IRREGULAR SERIALS AND ANNUALS; an international directory.
R.R. Bowker Company, Database Publishing Group, 245 W. 17th St., New York, NY 10011. TEL 800-521-8110.
Also available online. Vendors: BRS, DIALOG, European Space Agency. (128)

JOHN MARSHALL LAW REVIEW.
John Marshall Law School, 315 S. Plymouth Ct., Chicago, IL 60604. TEL 312-987-1415.
Also available online. Vendors: WESTLAW. (658)

JOURNAL OF DRUG RESEARCH OF EGYPT.
National Organisation for Drug Control and Research, Drug Research and Control Center, 6, Abou-Hazem St., Pyramids Ave., Box 29, Cairo, Egypt.
Also available online. (871)

KELLY'S BUSINESS DIRECTORY; list of manufacturers and merchants (alphabetical and classified)
Kelly's Directories, Windsor Court, East Grinstead House, East Grinstead, West Sussex RH19 1XB, England.
Also available online. (310)

KELLY'S U.K. EXPORTS TO EUROPE.
Kelly's Directories, Windsor Court, East Grinstead House, East Grinstead, West Sussex RH19 1XB, England.
Also available online. (310)

KEY BRITISH ENTERPRISES.
Dun & Bradstreet Ltd., 26-32 Clifton St., London EC2P 2LY, England.
Also available online. Vendors: Pergamon Infoline. (196)

KEY TO ECONOMIC SCIENCE; semi-monthly review of abstracts on economics, finance, trade, industry, foreign aid, management, marketing, labour.
Martinus Nijhoff Publishers, Spuiboulevard 50, 3311 GR Dordrecht, Netherlands
Also available online. Vendors: BELINDIS, Data-Star, DIALOG. (212)

KOMPASS BELGIUM/LUXEMBOURG; repertoire de l'economie de la Belgique et du Luxembourg.
Kompass Belgium S.A., Av. Moliere 256, 1060 Brussels, Belgium
Also available online. (311)

KOMPASS UNITED KINGDOM; register of British industry and commerce.
Kompass Publishers Ltd., Windsor Court, East Grinstead House, East Grinstead, West Sussex RH19 1XD, England
Also available online. (311)

LABORATORY AND RESEARCH METHODS IN BIOLOGY AND MEDICINE.
Alan R. Liss, Inc., 41 E. 11th St., New York, NY 10003. TEL 212-475-7700.
Also available online. (782)

LEADSCAN; a review of recent technical literature on the uses of lead and its products.
Lead Development Association, 34 Berkeley Square, London W1X 6AJ, England.
Also available online. Vendors: Pergamon Infoline. (801)

LEGAL CONTENTS; semi-monthly compilation of tables of contents from more than 320 business magazines and journals.
Find-S V P, 500 Fifth Ave., New York, NY 10110. TEL 212-354-2424.
Also available online. Vendors: DIALOG. (668)

LEGAL RESOURCE INDEX.
Information Access Company, 11 Davis Dr., Belmont, CA 94002. TEL 800-227-8431.
Also available online. Vendors: BRS, DIALOG, Mead Data Central. (668)

LEISURE, RECREATION AND TOURISM ABSTRACTS.
C.A.B. International, Farnham House, Farnham Royal, Slough SL2 3BN, England
Also available online. Vendors: BRS, CISTI, DIMDI, DIALOG, European Space Agency. (1120)

LENTIL ABSTRACTS.
C.A.B. International, Farnham House, Farnham Royal, Slough SL2 3BN, England.
Also available online. Vendors: BRS, CISTI, DIMDI, DIALOG, European Space Agency. (42)

LIBRARY & INFORMATION SCIENCE ABSTRACTS.
Library Association Publishing Ltd., 7 Ridgmount St., London WC1E 7AE, England.
Also available online. Vendors: DIALOG, Orbit Information Technologies. (688)

LIBRARY LITERATURE; an index to library and information science.
H.W. Wilson Co., 950 University Ave., Bronx, NY 10452. TEL 212-588-8400.
Also available online. Vendors: Wilsonline. (688)

LINGUISTICS AND LANGUAGE BEHAVIOR ABSTRACTS.
Sociological Abstracts, Inc., Box 22206, San Diego, CA 92122. TEL 619-565-6603.
Also available online. Vendors: BRS, DIALOG. (709)

M L A INTERNATIONAL BIBLIOGRAPHY OF BOOKS AND ARTICLES ON THE MODERN LANGUAGES AND LITERATURES.
Modern Language Association of America, 10 Astor Place, New York, NY 10003. TEL 212-614-6314.
Also available online. Vendors: DIALOG. (128)

MAGAZINE INDEX.
Information Access Company, 11 Davis Dr., Belmont, CA 94002. TEL 800-227-8431.
Also available online. Vendors: BRS, DIALOG, Mead Data Central. (9)

MAIZE ABSTRACTS.
C.A.B. International, Farnham House, Farnham Royal, Slough SL2 3BN, England
Also available online. Vendors: BRS, CISTI, DIMDI, DIALOG, European Space Agency. (42)

MANAGEMENT AND MARKETING ABSTRACTS.
Pergamon Press, Inc., Journals Division, Maxwell House, Fairview Park, Elmsford, NY 10523 TEL 914-592-7700.
Also available online. Vendors: Pergamon Infoline. (213)

MANAGEMENT CONTENTS; semi-monthly compilation of tables of contents from more than 320 business magazines and journals.
Find-S V P, 500 Fifth Ave., New York, NY 10110. TEL 212-354-2424.
Also available online. Vendors: BRS, DIALOG, Mead Data Central, Orbit Information Technologies. (213)

MANITOBA REPORTS.
Maritime Law Book Ltd., Box 302, Fredericton, N.B. E3B 4Y9, Canada. TEL 506-454-9921.
Also available online. Vendors: QL Systems Ltd. (659)

MARTINDALE: THE EXTRA PHARMACOPOEIA.
Pharmaceutical Society of Great Britain, 1 Lambeth High St., London SE1 7JN, England
Also available online. Vendors: Data-Star, DIALOG. (871)

MARX KAROLY KOZGAZDASAGTUDOMANYI EGYETEM: DOKTORI ERTEKEZESEK.
Marx Karoly Kozgazdasagtudomanyi Egyetem, Dimitrov Ter 8, Budapest 9, Hungary.
Also available online. Vendors: DIALOG. (213)

MASS SPECTROMETRY BULLETIN.
Royal Society of Chemistry, University of Nottingham, Nottingham NG7 2RD, England
Also available online. Vendors: European Space Agency, Pergamon Infoline. (326)

MATHEMATICAL REVIEWS; a reviewing journal covering the world literature of mathematical research.
American Mathematical Society, Box 6248, Providence, RI 02940. TEL 401-272-9500.
Also available online. Vendors: BRS, DIALOG, European Space Agency. (755)

MEDICAL AND HEALTH CARE BOOKS AND SERIALS IN PRINT; an index to literature in health sciences.
R.R. Bowker Company, Database Publishing Group, 245 W. 17th St., New York, NY 10011. TEL 800-521-8110.
Also available online. Vendors: BRS, DIALOG. (771)

MEDIO AMBIENTE.
Universidad Austral de Chile, Instituto de Ecologia y Evolucion, Facultad de Ciencias, Casilla 567, Valdivia, Chile.
Also available online. (497)

MENTAL MEASUREMENTS YEARBOOK.
Buros Institute of Mental Measurements, 135 Bancroft, University of Nebraska-Lincoln, Lincoln, NE 68588-0348
Also available online. (935)

MERCK INDEX: AN ENCYCLOPEDIA OF CHEMICALS AND DRUGS.
Merck and Co., Inc, Box 2000, Rahway, NJ 07065. TEL 201-574-5403.
Also available online. Vendors: Telesystemes - Questel. (872)

METALS ABSTRACTS.
A S M International, Materials Information, Metals Park, OH 44073. TEL 216-338-5151.
Also available online. Vendors: CEDOCAR, CISTI, DIALOG, European Space Agency, INKA, Orbit Information Technologies. (801)

METEOROLOGICAL AND GEOASTROPHYSICAL ABSTRACTS.
American Meteorological Society, 45 Beacon St., Boston, MA 02108. TEL 617-227-2425.
Also available online. Vendors: DIALOG. (808)

MICROBIOLOGY ABSTRACTS. SECTION B. BACTERIOLOGY.
Cambridge Scientific Abstracts, 5161 River Rd., Bethesda, MD 20816. TEL 301-951-1400.
Also available online. Vendors: DIALOG. (168)

MICROCOMPUTER INDEX.
Database Services Inc., 2685 Marine Way, Ste. 1305, Mountain View, CA 94043-1125.
Also available online. Vendors: CISTI, DIALOG, Mead Data Central, VU/TEXT Information Services, Inc. (354)

MICROLOG INDEX.
Micromedia Ltd., 158 Pearl St., Toronto, Ont. M5H 1L3, Canada. TEL 416-593-5211.
Also available online. Vendors: CISTI. (9)

MIDDLE EAST: ABSTRACTS AND INDEX.
Northumberland Press, 1717 Boulevard of the Allies, Pittsburgh, PA 15219. TEL 412-281-6179.
Also available online. Vendors: DIALOG. (9)

MILLION DOLLAR DIRECTORY.
Dun's Marketing Services 49 Old Bloomfield Rd., Mtn. Lakes, NJ 07046. TEL 201-455-0900.
Also available online. (285)

MODERN AGING RESEARCH.
Alan R. Liss, Inc., 41 E. 11th St., New York, NY 10003. TEL 212-475-7700.
Also available online. (552)

N A S A SOFTWARE DIRECTORY.
High Tech Publishing Company, 10 Ridge Rd., Box 360, Ridge, NY 11961. TEL 516-924-6168.
Also available online. (363)

N C J R S DOCUMENT RETRIEVAL INDEX.
U.S. National Institute of Justice, National Criminal Justice Reference Service, Box 6000, Department F, MD 20850. TEL 301-251-5500.
Also available online. (371)

N I C E M INDEX TO 35MM EDUCATIONAL FILMSTRIPS.
Access Innovations, Inc., Box 40130, Albuquerque, NM 87196. TEL 505-265-3591.
Also available online. (424)

NATIONAL ASSOCIATION OF BOARDS OF PHARMACY. PROCEEDINGS.
National Association of Boards of Pharmacy, 1300 Higgins Rd., No. 103, Park Ridge, IL 60068-5743. TEL 312-698-6227.
Also available online. (872)

NATIONAL REPORTER.
Maritime Law Book Ltd., Box 302, Fredericton, N.B. E3B 4Y9, Canada. TEL 506-454-9921.
Also available online. Vendors: QL Systems Ltd. (660)

NEUROSCIENCES ABSTRACTS.
Cambridge Scientific Abstracts, 5161 River Rd., Bethesda, MD 20816.
Also available online. Vendors: DIALOG. (771)

NEW BRUNSWICK REPORTS.
Maritime Law Book Ltd., Box 302, Fredericton, N.B. E3B 4Y9, Canada. TEL 506-454-9921.
Also available online. Vendors: QL Systems Ltd. (661)

NEW TRADE NAMES IN THE RUBBER AND PLASTICS INDUSTRIES.
R A P R A Technology Ltd., Shawbury, Shrewsbury, Shropshire, England.
Also available online. Vendors: Pergamon Infoline. (985)

NEW YORK TIMES INDEX.
University Microfilms International, 300 N. Zeeb Rd., Ann Arbor, MI 48106.
Also available online. (646)

NEWFOUNDLAND & PRINCE EDWARD ISLAND REPORTS.
Maritime Law Book Ltd., Box 302, Fredericton, N.B. E3B 4Y9, Canada. TEL 506-454-9921.
Also available online. Vendors: QL Systems Ltd. (661)

NOVA SCOTIA REPORTS.
Maritime Law Book Ltd., Box 302, Fredericton, N.B. E3B 4Y9, Canada. TEL 902-667-3889.
Also available online. Vendors: QL Systems Ltd. (661)

NUTRITION ABSTRACTS AND REVIEWS. SERIES A: HUMAN AND EXPERIMENTAL.
C.A.B. International, Farnham House, Farnham Royal, Slough SL2 3BN, England
Also available online. Vendors: BRS, CISTI, DIMDI, DIALOG, European Space Agency. (847)

NUTRITION ABSTRACTS AND REVIEWS. SERIES B: LIVESTOCK FEEDS AND FEEDING.
C.A.B. International, Farnham House, Farnham Royal, Slough SL2 3BN, England
Also available online. Vendors: BRS, CISTI, DIMDI, DIALOG, European Space Agency. (42)

OCEANIC ABSTRACTS.
Cambridge Scientific Abstracts, 5161 River Rd., Bethesda, MD 20816. TEL 301-951-1400.
Also available online. Vendors: DIALOG, European Space Agency. (382)

ONTARIO APPEAL CASES.
Maritime Law Book Ltd., Box 302, Fredericton, N.B. E3B 4Y9, Canada. TEL 506-454-9921.
Also available online. Vendors: QL Systems Ltd. (661)

OUTLOOK (YEAR) PROCEEDINGS.
U.S. Department of Agriculture, World Agricultural Outlook Board, Rm. 5143 S. Bldg., Washington, DC 20250-3800. TEL 202-447-5447.
Also available online. Vendors: BRS, DIALOG. (48)

P A I S BULLETIN.
Public Affairs Information Service, Inc., 11 W. 40th St., New York, NY 10018-2693. TEL 212-869-6186.
Also available online. Vendors: BRS, Data-Star, DIALOG. (215)

P A I S FOREIGN LANGUAGE INDEX.
Public Affairs Information Service, Inc., 11 W. 40th St., New York, NY 10018. TEL 212-869-6186.
Also available online. Vendors: BRS, Data-Star, DIALOG. (215)

PAPER AND BOARD ABSTRACTS.
Pergamon Press Ltd., Headington Hill Hall, Oxford OX3 0BW, England.
Also available online. Vendors: Orbit Information Technologies, Pergamon Infoline. (859)

PERIODICALS IN PRINT IN JAPAN.
Media Research Center Inc., 5-10-1 Shinjuku, Shinjuku-ku, Tokyo 160, Japan.
Also available online. (130)

PETROLEUM ABSTRACTS.
University of Tulsa, Information Services Division, 600 South College, Tulsa, OK 74104. TEL 918-592-6000.
Also available online. Vendors: Orbit Information Technologies. (868)

PHARMACEUTICAL NEWS INDEX.
Data Courier, 620 S. Fifth St., Louisville, KY 40202. TEL 800-626-2823.
Available only online. Vendors: DIALOG. (873)

PHOTOGRAPHIC ABSTRACTS.
Pergamon Journals Ltd., Headington Hill Hall, Oxford, OX3 0BW, England.
Also available online. Vendors: Pergamon Infoline. (885)

PHYSICS ABSTRACTS.
INSPEC, I.E.E., Station House, Nightingale Rd., Hitchin, Herts. SG5 1RJ, England
Also available online. Vendors: BRS, CEDOCAR, CISTI, Data-Star, DIALOG, European Space Agency, JICST, Orbit Information Technologies, STN International, University of Tsukuba. (893)

PLANT BREEDING ABSTRACTS.
C.A.B. International, Farnham House, Farnham Royal, Slough SL2 3BN, England
Also available online. Vendors: BRS, CISTI, DIMDI, DIALOG, European Space Agency. (534)

PLANT GROWTH REGULATOR ABSTRACTS.
C.A.B. International, Farnham House, Farnham Royal, Slough SL2 3BN, England
Also available online. Vendors: BRS, CISTI, DIMDI, DIALOG, European Space Agency. (42)

POPULAR MAGAZINE REVIEW.
Data Base Communications Corp., Box 325, Topsfield, MA 01983. TEL 617-887-6667.
Also available online. Vendors: BRS. (11)

POTATO ABSTRACTS.
C.A.B. International, Farnham House, Farnham Royal, Slough SL2 3BN, England
Also available online. Vendors: BRS, CISTI, DIMDI, DIALOG, European Space Agency. (42)

POULTRY ABSTRACTS.
C.A.B. International, Farnham House, Farnham Royal, Slough SL2 3BN, England
Also available online. Vendors: BRS, CISTI, DIMDI, DIALOG, European Space Agency. (43)

PREDICASTS F & S INDEX EUROPE.
Predicasts, Inc., 200 University Circle Research Center, 11001 Cedar Ave., Cleveland, OH 44106. TEL 216-795-3000.
Also available online. Vendors: BRS, DIALOG. (216)

1138 SERIALS AVAILABLE ONLINE

PREDICASTS F & S INDEX INTERNATIONAL.
Predicasts, Inc., 200 University Circle Research Center, 11001 Cedar Ave., Cleveland, OH 44106. TEL 216-795-3000.
Also available online. Vendors: BRS, DIALOG. (216)

PREDICASTS F & S INDEX OF CORPORATE CHANGE.
Predicasts Inc., 200 University Circle Research Center, 11001 Cedar Ave., Cleveland, OH 44106. TEL 216-795-3000.
Also available online. Vendors: BRS, DIALOG. (216)

PREDICASTS F & S INDEX UNITED STATES.
Predicasts, Inc., 200 University Circle Research Center, 11001 Cedar Ave., Cleveland, OH 44106. TEL 216-795-3000.
Also available online. Vendors: BRS, DIALOG. (216)

PREDICASTS FORECASTS.
Predicasts, Inc., 200 University Circle Research Center, 11001 Cedar Ave., Cleveland, OH 44106. TEL 216-795-3000.
Also available online. Vendors: DIALOG. (216)

PSYCHOLOGICAL ABSTRACTS.
American Psychological Association, 1200 17th St., N.W., Washington, DC 20036. TEL 202-955-7600.
Also available online. Vendors: BRS, DIMDI, Data-Star, DIALOG, Orbit Information Technologies. (938)

PUBLISHERS, DISTRIBUTORS AND WHOLESALERS OF THE UNITED STATES.
R.R. Bowker Company, Database Publishing Group, 245 W. 17th St., New York, NY 10011. TEL 800-521-8110.
Also available online. Vendors: DIALOG. (316)

PUMPS AND OTHER FLUIDS MACHINERY ABSTRACTS.
B H R A Fluid Engineering, Cranfield, Bedford MK43 0AJ, England
Also available online. Vendors: European Space Agency. (746)

R A P R A ABSTRACTS.
R A P R A Technology Ltd., Shawbury, Shrewsbury SY4 4NR, England.
Also available online. Vendors: Orbit Information Technologies, Pergamon Infoline. (986)

R I L M ABSTRACTS OF MUSIC LITERATURE.
International Repertory of Music Literature, 33 W. 42 St., New York, NY 10036 TEL 212-790-4214.
Also available online. Vendors: DIALOG. (844)

RELIGION INDEX ONE: PERIODICALS.
American Theological Library Association, Religion Indexes, 5600 S. Woodlawn Ave., Chicago, IL 60637. TEL 312-947-9417.
Also available online. Vendors: BRS, DIALOG. (975)

RELIGION INDEX TWO: MULTI-AUTHOR WORKS.
American Theological Library Association, Religion Indexes, 5600 S. Woodlawn Ave., Chicago, IL 60637. TEL 312-947-9417.
Also available online. Vendors: BRS, DIALOG. (975)

RELIGIOUS AND INSPIRATIONAL BOOKS AND SERIALS IN PRINT.
R.R. Bowker Company, Database Publishing Group, 245 W. 17th St., New York, NY 10011. TEL 800-521-8110.
Also available online. Vendors: BRS, DIALOG. (130)

RESEARCH INDEX.
Business Surveys Ltd., P.O. Box 21, Dorking, RH5 4EE, Surrey, England.
Also available online. Vendors: Pergamon Infoline. (217)

RESEARCH ON TRANSPORT ECONOMICS/RECHERCHE EN MATIERE D'ECONOMIE DES TRANSPORTS.
Organization for Economic Cooperation and Development, 19 rue de Franqueville, 75775 Paris Cedex 16, France
Also available online. Vendors: European Space Agency. (1083)

RESOURCES IN EDUCATION.
Educational Resources Information Center, E R I C Processing and Reference Facility, 4833 Rugby Ave., Ste. 301, Bethesda, MD 20814 TEL 301-656-9723.
Also available online. Vendors: BRS, CISTI, DIALOG, Orbit Information Technologies. (425)

REVIEW OF APPLIED ENTOMOLOGY. SERIES A: AGRICULTURAL; consisting of abstracts of reviews of current literature on applied entomology throughout the world.
C.A.B. International, Farnham House, Farnham Royal, Slough SL2 3BN, England.
Also available online. Vendors: BRS, CISTI, DIMDI, DIALOG, European Space Agency. (43)

REVIEW OF APPLIED ENTOMOLOGY. SERIES B: MEDICAL AND VETERINARY.
C.A.B. International, Farnham House, Farnham Royal, Slough SL2 3BN, England.
Also available online. Vendors: BRS, CISTI, DIMDI, DIALOG, European Space Agency. (1123)

REVIEW OF PLANT PATHOLOGY; consisting of abstracts and reviews of current literature on plant pathology.
C.A.B. International, Farnham House, Farnham Royal, Slough SL2 3BN, England.
Also available online. Vendors: BRS, CISTI, DIMDI, DIALOG, European Space Agency. (150)

REVISTA DE CIENCIAS FARMACEUTICAS.
Universidade Estadual Paulista, Av. Vicente Ferreira 1278, Caixa Postal 630, 17.500 Marilia SP, Brazil.
Also available online. (872)

RICE ABSTRACTS.
C.A.B. International, Farnham House, Farnham Royal, Slough SL2 3BN, England
Also available online. Vendors: BRS, CISTI, DIMDI, DIALOG, European Space Agency. (43)

ROBOMATIX REPORTER.
E I C Intelligence, Inc., 48 W. 38th St., New York, NY 10018. TEL 800-223-6275.
Also available online. Vendors: DIALOG, European Space Agency. (354)

RURAL DEVELOPMENT ABSTRACTS.
C.A.B. International, Farnham House, Farnham Royal, Slough SL2 3BN, England
Also available online. Vendors: BRS, CISTI, DIMDI, DIALOG, European Space Agency. (949)

RURAL EXTENSION, EDUCATION AND TRAINING ABSTRACTS.
C.A.B. International, Farnham House, Farnham Royal, Slough SL2 3BN, England
Also available online. Vendors: BRS, CISTI, DIMDI, DIALOG, European Space Agency. (419)

S A E HANDBOOK.
Society of Automotive Engineers, 400 Commonwealth Dr., Warrendale, PA 15096. TEL 412-776-4970.
Also available online. Vendors: Orbit Information Technologies. (1093)

S A E TECHNICAL LITERATURE ABSTRACTS.
Society of Automotive Engineers, 400 Commonwealth Dr., Warrendale, PA 15096. TEL 412-776-4841.
Also available online. Vendors: Orbit Information Technologies. (1086)

S C I M P; European index of management periodicals.
European Business School Librarians Group, Manchester Business School Library, Booth St. West, Manchester M15 6PB, England.
Also available online. (217)

SAFETY SCIENCE ABSTRACTS JOURNAL.
Cambridge Scientific Abstracts, 5161 River Rd., Bethesda, MD 20816. TEL 301-951-1400.
Also available online. Vendors: DIALOG, Pergamon Infoline. (12)

SASKATCHEWAN REPORTS.
Maritime Law Book Ltd., Box 302, Fredericton, N.B. E3B 4Y9, Canada. TEL 506-454-9921.
Also available online. Vendors: QL Systems Ltd. (663)

SCIENCE CITATION INDEX.
Institute for Scientific Information, 3501 Market St., Philadelphia, PA 19104 TEL 215-386-0100.
Also available online. Vendors: BRS, CISTI, Data-Star, DIALOG. (1004)

SEED ABSTRACTS.
C.A.B. International, Farnham House, Farnham Royal, Slough SL2 3BN, England
Also available online. Vendors: BRS, CISTI, DIMDI, DIALOG, European Space Agency. (43)

SELECTED WATER RESOURCES ABSTRACTS.
U.S. Geological Survey, Water Resources Scientific Information Center, 425 National Center, Reston, VA 22092 TEL 703-860-7455.
Also available online. Vendors: DIALOG, Pergamon Infoline. (1128)

SHIP ABSTRACTS; information service on ship technology, ship operation and ocean engineering.
Norges Skipsforskningsinstitutt, Box 6099-Etterstad, Oslo 6, Norway.
Available only online. (1086)

SMALL ANIMAL ABSTRACTS.
C.A.B. International, Farnham House, Farnham Royal, Slough SL2 3BN, England
Also available online. Vendors: BRS, CISTI, DIMDI, DIALOG, European Space Agency. (43)

SOCIAL PLANNING, POLICY & DEVELOPMENT ABSTRACTS.
Sociological Abstracts Inc., Box 22206, San Diego, CA 92122.
Also available online. Vendors: BRS, DIALOG. (264)

SOCIAL SCIENCES CITATION INDEX.
Institute for Scientific Information, 3501 Market St., Philadelphia, PA 19104 TEL 215-386-0100.
Also available online. Vendors: BRS, CISTI, DIALOG. (1014)

SOCIAL SCIENCES INDEX; an author and subject index to periodicals in the fields of anthropology, area studies, economics, environmental science, geography, law and criminology, medical sciences, political science, psychology, public administration, sociology and related subjects.
H. W. Wilson Co., 950 University Ave., Bronx, NY 10452. TEL 212-588-8400.
Also available online. Vendors: Wilsonline. (1014)

SOCIOLOGICAL ABSTRACTS.
Sociological Abstracts, Inc., Box 22206, San Diego, CA 92122. TEL 619-565-6603.
Also available online. Vendors: BRS, Data-Star, DIALOG. (1031)

SOFTWARE ENCYCLOPEDIA.
R.R. Bowker Company, Database Publishing Group, 245 W. 17th St., New York, NY 10011. TEL 800-521-8110.
Also available online. Vendors: DIALOG. (363)

SOILS AND FERTILIZERS; abstracts of world literature.
C.A.B. International, Farnham House, Farnham Royal, Slough SL2 3BN, England
Also available online. Vendors: BRS, CISTI, DIMDI, DIALOG, European Space Agency. (43)

SOLID STATE ABSTRACTS JOURNAL; an abstract journal involving the physics, metallurgy, crystallography, chemistry and device technology of solids.
Cambridge Scientific Abstracts, 5161 River Rd., Bethesda, MD 20816. TEL 301-951-1400.
Also available online. Vendors: DIALOG. (893)

SORGHUM AND MILLETS ABSTRACTS.
C.A.B. International, Farnham House, Farnham Royal, Slough SL2 3BN, England
Also available online. Vendors: BRS, CISTI, DIMDI, DIALOG, European Space Agency. (43)

SOYABEAN ABSTRACTS.
C.A.B. International, Farnham House, Farnham Royal, Slough SL2 3BN, England
Also available online. Vendors: BRS, CISTI, DIMDI, DIALOG, European Space Agency. (43)

STANFORD JOURNAL OF INTERNATIONAL LAW.
Stanford University, Stanford Law School, Stanford, CA 94305. TEL 415-497-2465.
Also available online. Vendors: WESTLAW. (671)

SERIALS AVAILABLE ONLINE 1139

SUBJECT GUIDE TO BOOKS IN PRINT.
R.R. Bowker Company, Database Publishing Group, 245 W. 17th St., New York, NY 10011. TEL 800-521-8110.
Also available online. Vendors: DIALOG. (131)

SUBJECT GUIDE TO CHILDREN'S BOOKS IN PRINT.
R.R. Bowker Company, Database Publishing Group, 245 W. 17th St., New York, NY 10011. TEL 800-521-8110.
Also available online. (131)

TELEGEN REPORTER.
E I C Intelligence, 48 W. 38th St., New York, NY 10018. TEL 212-944-8500.
Also available online. Vendors: DIALOG, European Space Agency. (147)

TEXTILE TECHNOLOGY DIGEST.
Institute of Textile Technology, Charlottesville, VA 22902. TEL 804-296-5511.
Also available online. Vendors: DIALOG. (1076)

THOMAS REGISTER OF AMERICAN MANUFACTURERS AND THOMAS REGISTER CATALOG FILE.
Thomas Publishing Co., One Penn Plaza, 250 W. 34th St., New York, NY 10119. TEL 212-695-0500.
Also available online. Vendors: DIALOG. (285)

TOXICOLOGY ABSTRACTS.
Cambridge Scientific Abstracts, 5161 River Rd., Bethesda, MD 20816. TEL 301-951-1400.
Also available online. Vendors: DIALOG. (873)

TRIBOS - TRIBOLOGY ABSTRACTS.
B H R A Fluid Engineering, Cranfield, Bedford MK43 0AJ, England
Also available online. Vendors: European Space Agency. (477)

U K TRADE NAMES; including imported items.
Kompass Publishers Ltd., Windsor Court, East Grinstead House, East Grinstead, West Sussex RH19 1XD, England.
Also available online. (318)

ULRICH'S INTERNATIONAL PERIODICALS DIRECTORY.
R.R. Bowker Company, Database Publishing Group, 245 W. 17th St., New York, NY 10011. TEL 800-521-8110.
Also available online. Vendors: BRS, DIALOG, European Space Agency. (132)

UNION LIST OF SCIENTIFIC SERIALS IN CANADIAN LIBRARIES.
C.I.S.T.I. Publications, Ottawa, Ont. K1A 0S2, Canada. TEL 613-993-3736.
Also available online. Vendors: CISTI. (1005)

U.S. CROP REPORTING BOARD. CROP PRODUCTION.
U.S. Crop Reporting Board, Washington, DC 20250 TEL 202-655-4000.
Also available online. Vendors: DIALOG. (60)

UNITED STATES POLITICAL SCIENCE DOCUMENTS.
University of Pittsburgh, NASA Industrial Applications Center, 823 William Pitt Union, Pittsburgh, PA 15260. TEL 412-648-7000.
Also available online. Vendors: DIALOG. (910)

UNIVERSIDADE DE SAO PAULO. REVISTA DE FARMACIA E BIOQUIMICA.
Universidade de Sao Paulo, Faculdade de Farmacia e Bioquimica, Conj. das Quimicas-Cid. Universitaria, Caixa Postal 30786, Sao Paulo, Brazil.
Also available online. (873)

URBAN ABSTRACTS.
Research Library, London Residuary Body, County Hall, Rm. 514, London SE1 7PB, England
Also available online. Vendors: European Space Agency, Pergamon Infoline, Scicon Ltd. (950)

VERTICAL FILE INDEX; a subject and title index to selected pamphlet material.
H. W. Wilson Co., 950 University Ave., Bronx, NY 10452. TEL 212-588-8400.
Also available online. Vendors: Wilsonline. (13)

VETERINARY BULLETIN; a monthly abstract journal on veterinary science.
C.A.B. International, Farnham House, Farnham Royal, Slough SL2 3BN, England.
Also available online. Vendors: BRS, CISTI, DIMDI, DIALOG, European Space Agency. (1123)

VIROLOGY ABSTRACTS.
Cambridge Scientific Abstracts, 5161 River Rd., Bethesda, MD 20816. TEL 301-951-1400.
Also available online. Vendors: DIALOG. (773)

WALL STREET JOURNAL INDEX.
Dow Jones & Co., Inc., 200 Liberty St., New York, NY 10281 TEL 413-592-7761.
Also available online. (268)

WATER RESEARCH IN AUSTRALIA: CURRENT PROJECTS.
Department of Resources and Energy, G.P.O. Box 858, Canberra, A.C.T. 2601, Australia.
Also available online. (1127)

WEED ABSTRACTS; compiled from world literature.
C.A.B. International, Farnham House, Farnham Royal, Slough SL2 3BN, England
Also available online. Vendors: BRS, CISTI, DIMDI, DIALOG, European Space Agency. (44)

WER LIEFERT WAS?
Bezugsquellennachweis fuer den Einkauf "Wer Liefert Was?" GmbH, Novmannenweg 18-20, 2000 Hamburg 26, W. Germany (B.R.D.)
Also available online. (319)

WHO OWNS WHOM. UNITED KINGDOM AND REPUBLIC OF IRELAND.
Dun & Bradstreet Ltd., 26-32 Clifton St., London EC2P 1LY, England.
Also available online. Vendors: Pergamon Infoline. (319)

WHO OWNS WHOM, NORTH AMERICA.
Dun & Bradstreet Ltd., 26-32 Clifton St., London EC2P 1LY, England.
Also available online. Vendors: Pergamon Infoline. (286)

WHO'S WHO IN AMERICA.
Marquis Who's Who, Macmillan Directory Division, 3002 Glenview Rd., Wilmette, IL 60091. TEL 312-441-2387.
Also available online. Vendors: DIALOG. (135)

WORDS ON TAPE.
Meckler Publishing Corporation, 11 Ferry Lane West, Westport, CT 06880-5808. TEL 203-220-6967.
Also available online. Vendors: BRS. (133)

WORLD AGRICULTURAL ECONOMICS AND RURAL SOCIOLOGY ABSTRACTS; abstracts of world literature.
C.A.B. International, Farnham House, Farnham Royal, Slough SL2 3BN, England
Also available online. Vendors: BRS, CISTI, DIMDI, DIALOG, European Space Agency. (44)

WORLD ALUMINUM ABSTRACTS; a monthly review of the world's technical literature on aluminum.
Aluminum Association, Inc., 818 Connecticut Ave., N.W., Washington, DC 20006. TEL 202-862-5156.
Also available online. Vendors: DIALOG, European Space Agency. (802)

WORLD AROMATICS AND DERIVATIVES.
S R I International, World Petrochemicals Program, Menlo Park, CA 94025. TEL 415-326-6200.
Also available online. (325)

WORLD C4 HYDROCARBONS AND DERIVATIVES.
S R I International, World Petrochemicals Program, Menlo Park, CA 94025. TEL 415-326-6200.
Also available online. (325)

WORLD DIRECTORY OF PHARMACEUTICAL MANUFACTURERS.
IMSWORLD Publications Ltd., 11-13 Melton St., London NW1 2EH, England.
Also available online. (873)

WORLD DRUG MARKET MANUAL.
IMSWORLD Publications Ltd., 11-13 Melton St., London NW1 2EH, England.
Also available online. (873)

WORLD ETHYLENE AND DERIVATIVES.
S R I International, World Petrochemicals Program, Menlo Park, CA 94025. TEL 415-326-6200.
Also available online. (325)

WORLD LICENSE REVIEW.
IMSWORLD Publications Ltd., 11-13 Melton St., London NW1 3EH, England.
Also available online. (873)

WORLD METHANOL AND DERIVATIVES.
S R I International, World Petrochemicals Program, Menlo Park, CA 94025. TEL 415-326-6200.
Also available online. (325)

WORLD PATENTS ABSTRACTS JOURNALS.
Derwent Publications Ltd., Rochdale House, 128 Theobalds Rd., London WC1X 8RP, England
Also available online. Vendors: DIALOG, Orbit Information Technologies, Telesystemes - Questel. (861)

WORLD PORTS AND HARBOURS ABSTRACTS.
B H R A Fluid Engineering, Cranfield, Bedford MK43 0AJ, England
Also available online. Vendors: European Space Agency. (1087)

WORLD SURFACE COATING ABSTRACTS.
Pergamon Press Ltd., Headington Hill Hall, Oxford OX3 0BW, England.
Also available online. Vendors: Orbit Information Technologies, Pergamon Infoline. (856)

WORLD TEXTILE ABSTRACTS.
Shirley Institute, Manchester M20 8RX, England.
Also available online. Vendors: DIALOG, Pergamon Infoline. (1076)

ZAHRANICNE PERIODIKA V C S S R.
Univerzitna Kniznica, Michalska 1, 885 17 Bratislava, Czechoslovakia.
Available only online. (133)

ZENTRALBLATT FUER MATHEMATIK UND IHRE GRENZGEBIETE/MATHEMATICS ABSTRACTS.
Springer-Verlag, 175 Fifth Ave., New York, NY 10010 TEL 212-460-1500.
Also available online. Vendors: STN International. (755)

ZINCSCAN; a review of recent technical literature on the uses of zinc and its products.
Zinc Development Association, 34 Berkeley Square, London W1X 6AJ, England.
Also available online. Vendors: Pergamon Infoline. (802)

ZOOLOGICAL RECORD.
BioSciences Information Service (BIOSIS) U.K. Ltd., Garforth House, 54 Micklegate, Boston Spa, York YO1 1LF, England.
Also available online. Vendors: BRS, DIALOG. (150)

Vendor Listing/Serials Online

A U S I N E T
Information Management Group, 310 Ferntree Gully Rd., Clayton, Vic. 3168, Australia Tel: 554 8433
- Australian Road Index
- Australian Road Research in Progress
- Bibliography of Education Theses in Australia
- Business Who's Who of Australia

B E L I N D I S (Subsidiary of: Belgian Ministry of Economic Affairs)
Data Processing Centre, 30 rue de Mot, 1040 Brussels, Belgium Tel: (02) 233 6737, (02) 233 6111 Telex: 23509 energi B
- Coal Abstracts
- Economic Titles/Abstracts
- Key to Economic Science

B R S
1200 Route 7, Latham, NY 12110. Tel: 518-783-1161, 800-345-4BRS Telex: 710 444 4965
- Agricultural Engineering Abstracts
- American Hospital Formulary Service Drug Information
- American Men and Women of Science. Physical and Biological Sciences
- Animal Breeding Abstracts
- Books in Print
- Books in Print Supplement
- Books Out of Print
- C.A.B. International Bureau of Agricultural Economics. Annotated Bibliographies Series A
- C.A.B. International Bureau of Agricultural Economics. Annotated Bibliographies. Series B: Agricultural Policy and Rural Development in Africa
- C.A.B. International Bureau of Nutrition. Annotated Bibliographies
- C.A.B. International Bureau of Soils. Annotated Bibliographies
- Compumath Citation Index
- Computer & Control Abstracts
- Cotton and Tropical Fibres Abstracts
- Crop Physiology Abstracts
- Cumulative Index to Nursing & Allied Health Literature (C I N A H L)
- Current Contents/Clinical Medicine
- Current Index to Journals in Education
- Current Index to Statistics
- Current Mathematical Publications
- Electrical & Electronics Abstracts
- Engineering Index Monthly and Author Index
- Excerpta Medica. Section 1: Anatomy, Anthropology, Embryology & Histology
- Excerpta Medica. Section 2: Physiology
- Excerpta Medica. Section 3: Endocrinology
- Excerpta Medica. Section 4: Microbiology: Bacteriology, Mycology and Parasitology
- Excerpta Medica. Section 5: General Pathology and Pathological Anatomy
- Excerpta Medica. Section 6: Internal Medicine
- Excerpta Medica. Section 7: Pediatrics and Pediatric Surgery
- Excerpta Medica. Section 8: Neurology and Neurosurgery
- Excerpta Medica. Section 9: Surgery
- Excerpta Medica. Section 10: Obstetrics and Gynecology
- Excerpta Medica. Section 11: Otorhinolaryngology
- Excerpta Medica. Section 12: Ophthalmology
- Excerpta Medica. Section 13: Dermatology and Venereology
- Excerpta Medica. Section 14: Radiology
- Excerpta Medica. Section 15: Chest Diseases, Thoracic Surgery and Tuberculosis
- Excerpta Medica. Section 16: Cancer
- Excerpta Medica. Section 17: Public Health, Social Medicine & Hygiene
- Excerpta Medica. Section 19: Rehabilitation and Physical Medicine
- Excerpta Medica. Section 20: Gerontology and Geriatrics
- Excerpta Medica. Section 23: Nuclear Medicine
- Excerpta Medica. Section 24: Anesthesiology
- Excerpta Medica. Section 25: Hematology
- Excerpta Medica. Section 26: Immunology, Serology and Transplantation
- Excerpta Medica. Section 27: Biophysics, Bio-Engineering and Medical Instrumentation
- Excerpta Medica. Section 28: Urology and Nephrology
- Excerpta Medica. Section 29: Clinical Biochemistry
- Excerpta Medica. Section 31: Arthritis and Rheumatism
- Excerpta Medica. Section 32: Psychiatry
- Excerpta Medica. Section 33: Orthopedic Surgery
- Excerpta Medica. Section 34: Plastic Surgery
- Excerpta Medica. Section 35: Occupational Health and Industrial Medicine
- Excerpta Medica. Section 36: Health Economics and Hospital Management
- Excerpta Medica. Section 38: Adverse Reactions Titles
- Excerpta Medica. Section 46: Environmental Health and Pollution Control
- Excerpta Medica. Section 47: Virology
- Excerpta Medica. Section 48: Gastroenterology
- Excerpta Medica. Section 49: Forensic Science
- Excerpta Medica. Section 50: Epilepsy
- Excerpta Medica. Section 51: Leprosy and Related Subjects
- Faba Bean Abstracts
- Field Crop Abstracts
- Food Science and Technology Abstracts
- Forest Products Abstracts
- Forestry Abstracts
- Forestry Abstracts. Leading Article Reprint Series
- Helminthological Abstracts. Series A: Animal and Human Helminthology
- Helminthological Abstracts. Series B: Plant Nematology
- Herbage Abstracts
- Horticultural Abstracts
- Index of Current Research on Pigs
- Index Veterinarius
- International Nursing Index Including Nursing Citation Index
- International Pharmaceutical Abstracts
- Irregular Serials and Annuals
- Legal Resource Index
- Leisure, Recreation and Tourism Abstracts
- Lentil Abstracts
- Linguistics and Language Behavior Abstracts
- Magazine Index
- Maize Abstracts
- Management Contents
- Mathematical Reviews
- Medical and Health Care Books and Serials in Print
- Nutrition Abstracts and Reviews. Series A: Human and Experimental
- Nutrition Abstracts and Reviews. Series B: Livestock Feeds and Feeding
- Outlook (Year) Proceedings
- P A I S Bulletin
- P A I S Foreign Language Index
- Physics Abstracts
- Plant Breeding Abstracts
- Plant Growth Regulator Abstracts
- Popular Magazine Review
- Potato Abstracts
- Poultry Abstracts
- Predicasts F & S Index Europe
- Predicasts F & S Index International
- Predicasts F & S Index of Corporate Change
- Predicasts F & S Index United States
- Psychological Abstracts
- Religion Index One: Periodicals
- Religion Index Two: Multi-Author Works
- Religious and Inspirational Books and Serials in Print
- Resources in Education
- Review of Applied Entomology. Series A: Agricultural
- Review of Applied Entomology. Series B: Medical and Veterinary
- Review of Plant Pathology
- Rice Abstracts
- Rural Development Abstracts
- Rural Extension, Education and Training Abstracts

1142 VENDOR LISTING/SERIALS ONLINE

Science Citation Index
Seed Abstracts
Small Animal Abstracts
Social Planning, Policy & Development Abstracts
Social Sciences Citation Index
Sociological Abstracts
Soils and Fertilizers
Sorghum and Millets Abstracts
Soyabean Abstracts
Ulrich's International Periodicals Directory
Veterinary Bulletin
Weed Abstracts
Words on Tape
World Agricultural Economics and Rural Sociology Abstracts
Zoological Record

B R S SAUNDERS COLLEAGUE (Subsidiary of: C B S Inc.)
1290 Ave. of the Americas, New York, NY 10104. Tel: 212-765-4840, 212-333-7660
Cumulative Index to Nursing & Allied Health Literature (C I N A H L)

BUREAU NATIONAL DES DONNEES OCEANIQUES (Subsidiary of: Institut francais de Recherche pour l'Exploitation de la Mer)
Centre de Brest, BP 337, 29273 Brest Cedex, France Tel: (98) 45 8055 Telex: Oceanex 940627 F
Aquatic Sciences & Fisheries Abstracts. Part 1: Biological Sciences & Living Resources
Aquatic Sciences & Fisheries Abstracts. Part 2: Ocean Technology, Policy and Non-Living Resources

BUREAU OF TRANSPORT ECONOMICS
G.P.O. Box 501, Canberra, ACT 2601, Australia Tel: (062) 67 9811, (062) 67 9890 Telex: 61733
Cnr. Cooyong St. & Northbourne Ave., Braddon, ACT 2601, Australia
Australian Transport Information Directory

C E D O C A R
26 Bd. Victor, 75996 Paris Armees, France Tel: 33 1 4552 4321 Telex: 202778 F
Alloys Index
Computer & Control Abstracts
Electrical & Electronics Abstracts
Engineering Index Monthly and Author Index
Metals Abstracts
Physics Abstracts

C I S T I (Subsidiary of: National Research Council of Canada)
Ottawa, Ont. K1A 0S2, Canada Tel: 613-993-1210 Telex: 0533115
Agricultural Engineering Abstracts
Alloys Index
Animal Breeding Abstracts
Aquatic Sciences & Fisheries Abstracts. Part 1: Biological Sciences & Living Resources
Aquatic Sciences & Fisheries Abstracts. Part 2: Ocean Technology, Policy and Non-Living Resources
Bibliography and Index of Geology
Bibliography of Agriculture
C.A.B. International Bureau of Agricultural Economics. Annotated Bibliographies Series A
C.A.B. International Bureau of Agricultural Economics. Annotated Bibliographies. Series B: Agricultural Policy and Rural Development in Africa
C.A.B. International Bureau of Nutrition. Annotated Bibliographies
C.A.B. International Bureau of Soils. Annotated Bibliographies
Canadian Business Index
Canadian News Index
Coal Abstracts
Computer & Control Abstracts
Cotton and Tropical Fibres Abstracts
Crop Physiology Abstracts
Current Index to Journals in Education
Directory of Associations in Canada
Directory of Federally Supported Research in Universities
Electrical & Electronics Abstracts
Engineering Index Monthly and Author Index
Faba Bean Abstracts
Field Crop Abstracts
Food Science and Technology Abstracts
Forest Products Abstracts
Forestry Abstracts
Forestry Abstracts. Leading Article Reprint Series
Helminthological Abstracts. Series A: Animal and Human Helminthology
Helminthological Abstracts. Series B: Plant Nematology
Herbage Abstracts
Horticultural Abstracts
I N I S Atomindex
Index of Current Research on Pigs
Index Veterinarius
Leisure, Recreation and Tourism Abstracts
Lentil Abstracts
Maize Abstracts
Metals Abstracts
Microcomputer Index
Microlog Index
Nutrition Abstracts and Reviews. Series A: Human and Experimental
Nutrition Abstracts and Reviews. Series B: Livestock Feeds and Feeding
Physics Abstracts
Plant Breeding Abstracts
Plant Growth Regulator Abstracts
Potato Abstracts
Poultry Abstracts
Resources in Education
Review of Applied Entomology. Series A: Agricultural
Review of Applied Entomology. Series B: Medical and Veterinary
Review of Plant Pathology
Rice Abstracts
Rural Development Abstracts
Rural Extension, Education and Training Abstracts
Science Citation Index
Seed Abstracts
Small Animal Abstracts
Social Sciences Citation Index
Soils and Fertilizers
Sorghum and Millets Abstracts
Soyabean Abstracts
Union List of Scientific Serials in Canadian Libraries
Veterinary Bulletin
Weed Abstracts
World Agricultural Economics and Rural Sociology Abstracts

COMPUSERVE CONSUMER INFORMATION SERVICE
5000 Arlington Blvd., Columbus, OH 43220. Tel: 800-848-8990
Educational Software Selector

D I M D I (Subsidiary of: Deutsches Institut fuer Medizinische Dokumentation und Information)
Box 42 05 60, Weisshausstrasse 27, D-5000 Cologne, Federal Republic Of Germany Tel: (49) 221-4721-1, (42) 221-4724-270 Telex: 88 81 364 dim D
Agricultural Engineering Abstracts
Animal Breeding Abstracts
Aquatic Sciences & Fisheries Abstracts. Part 1: Biological Sciences & Living Resources
Aquatic Sciences & Fisheries Abstracts. Part 2: Ocean Technology, Policy and Non-Living Resources
C.A.B. International Bureau of Agricultural Economics. Annotated Bibliographies Series A
C.A.B. International Bureau of Agricultural Economics. Annotated Bibliographies. Series B: Agricultural Policy and Rural Development in Africa
C.A.B. International Bureau of Nutrition. Annotated Bibliographies
C.A.B. International Bureau of Soils. Annotated Bibliographies
Cotton and Tropical Fibres Abstracts
Crop Physiology Abstracts
Faba Bean Abstracts
Field Crop Abstracts
Food Science and Technology Abstracts
Forest Products Abstracts
Forestry Abstracts
Forestry Abstracts. Leading Article Reprint Series
Helminthological Abstracts. Series A: Animal and Human Helminthology
Helminthological Abstracts. Series B: Plant Nematology
Herbage Abstracts
Horticultural Abstracts
Hospital Literature Index
Index of Current Research on Pigs
Index Veterinarius
Leisure, Recreation and Tourism Abstracts
Lentil Abstracts
Maize Abstracts
Nutrition Abstracts and Reviews. Series A: Human and Experimental
Nutrition Abstracts and Reviews. Series B: Livestock Feeds and Feeding
Plant Breeding Abstracts
Plant Growth Regulator Abstracts
Potato Abstracts
Poultry Abstracts
Psychological Abstracts
Review of Applied Entomology. Series A: Agricultural
Review of Applied Entomology. Series B: Medical and Veterinary
Review of Plant Pathology
Rice Abstracts
Rural Development Abstracts
Rural Extension, Education and Training Abstracts
Seed Abstracts
Small Animal Abstracts
Soils and Fertilizers
Sorghum and Millets Abstracts
Soyabean Abstracts
Veterinary Bulletin
Weed Abstracts
World Agricultural Economics and Rural Sociology Abstracts

DATA-STAR
114 Jermyn St., Plaza Suite, London SW1Y 6HJ, United Kingdom Tel: (01) 930-5503, 44 1930-5503
Radio Suisee Ltd., Schwarztorstrasse 61, PO Box 3000, Berne 14, Switzerland Tel: 031 659500
Chemical Engineering Abstracts
Computer & Control Abstracts
Cumulative Index to Nursing & Allied Health Literature (C I N A H L)
Current Biotechnology Abstracts
Economic Titles/Abstracts
Electrical & Electronics Abstracts
Engineering Index Monthly and Author Index
Food Science and Technology Abstracts
Key to Economic Science
Martindale: the Extra Pharmacopoeia
P A I S Bulletin
P A I S Foreign Language Index
Physics Abstracts
Psychological Abstracts
Science Citation Index
Sociological Abstracts

DIALOG (Subsidiary of: Lockheed Corporation)
3460 Hillview Ave, Palo Alto, CA 94304. Tel: 415-858-3700, 800-3-DIALOG Telex: 334499 DIALOG
Learned Information, PO Box 8, Abingdon, Oxford OX13 6E6, United Kingdom Tel: (0865) 730969 Telex: 837704 Inform G
Aerospace Defense Markets and Technology
Agricultural Engineering Abstracts
Agricultural Finance Outlook and Situation
Alloys Index
America: History and Life. Part A: Article Abstracts and Citation
America: History and Life. Part B: Index to Book Reviews
America: History and Life. Part C: American History Bibliography
American Hospital Formulary Service Drug Information
American Library Directory
American Men and Women of Science. Physical and Biological Sciences
American Statistics Index
Animal Breeding Abstracts
Apicultural Abstracts
Aquatic Sciences & Fisheries Abstracts. Part 1: Biological Sciences & Living Resources
Aquatic Sciences & Fisheries Abstracts. Part 2: Ocean Technology, Policy and Non-Living Resources
Artbibliographies Modern
Bibliography and Index of Geology
Biography and Genealogy Master Index
Biotechnology Research Abstracts
Books in Print
Books in Print Supplement
Books Out of Print
C.A.B. International Bureau of Agricultural Economics. Annotated Bibliographies Series A

C.A.B. International Bureau of Agricultural Economics. Annotated Bibliographies. Series B: Agricultural Policy and Rural Development in Africa
C.A.B. International Bureau of Nutrition. Annotated Bibliographies
C.A.B. International Bureau of Soils. Annotated Bibliographies
Calcified Tissue Abstracts
Canadian Business Index
Canadian News Index
Chemoreception Abstracts
Computer & Control Abstracts
Computer and Information Systems Abstract Journal
Computer Contents
Computer Readable Databases
Conference Papers Annual Index
Cotton and Tropical Fibres Abstracts
Criminal Justice Periodical Index
Crop Physiology Abstracts
Cumulative Index to Nursing & Allied Health Literature (C I N A H L)
Current Digest of the Soviet Press
Current Index to Journals in Education
Current Index to Statistics
Current Mathematical Publications
E I S Cumulative
Ecology Abstracts
Economic Titles/Abstracts
Electrical & Electronics Abstracts
Electronics and Communications Abstracts Journal
Encyclopedia of Associations
Energy Information Abstracts
Engineering Index Monthly and Author Index
Entomology Abstracts
Excerpta Medica. Section 1: Anatomy, Anthropology, Embryology & Histology
Excerpta Medica. Section 2: Physiology
Excerpta Medica. Section 3: Endocrinology
Excerpta Medica. Section 4: Microbiology: Bacteriology, Mycology and Parasitology
Excerpta Medica. Section 5: General Pathology and Pathological Anatomy
Excerpta Medica. Section 6: Internal Medicine
Excerpta Medica. Section 7: Pediatrics and Pediatric Surgery
Excerpta Medica. Section 8: Neurology and Neurosurgery
Excerpta Medica. Section 9: Surgery
Excerpta Medica. Section 10: Obstetrics and Gynecology
Excerpta Medica. Section 11: Otorhinolaryngology
Excerpta Medica. Section 12: Ophthalmology
Excerpta Medica. Section 13: Dermatology and Venereology
Excerpta Medica. Section 14: Radiology
Excerpta Medica. Section 15: Chest Diseases, Thoracic Surgery and Tuberculosis
Excerpta Medica. Section 16: Cancer
Excerpta Medica. Section 17: Public Health, Social Medicine & Hygiene
Excerpta Medica. Section 19: Rehabilitation and Physical Medicine
Excerpta Medica. Section 20: Gerontology and Geriatrics
Excerpta Medica. Section 23: Nuclear Medicine
Excerpta Medica. Section 24: Anesthesiology
Excerpta Medica. Section 25: Hematology
Excerpta Medica. Section 26: Immunology, Serology and Transplantation
Excerpta Medica. Section 27: Biophysics, Bio-Engineering and Medical Instrumentation
Excerpta Medica. Section 28: Urology and Nephrology
Excerpta Medica. Section 29: Clinical Biochemistry
Excerpta Medica. Section 31: Arthritis and Rheumatism
Excerpta Medica. Section 32: Psychiatry
Excerpta Medica. Section 33: Orthopedic Surgery
Excerpta Medica. Section 34: Plastic Surgery
Excerpta Medica. Section 35: Occupational Health and Industrial Medicine
Excerpta Medica. Section 36: Health Economics and Hospital Management
Excerpta Medica. Section 38: Adverse Reactions Titles
Excerpta Medica. Section 46: Environmental Health and Pollution Control
Excerpta Medica. Section 47: Virology
Excerpta Medica. Section 48: Gastroenterology
Excerpta Medica. Section 49: Forensic Science
Excerpta Medica. Section 50: Epilepsy
Excerpta Medica. Section 51: Leprosy and Related Subjects

Faba Bean Abstracts
Field Crop Abstracts
Financial Times World Shipping Yearbook Findex
Food Science and Technology Abstracts
Forest Products Abstracts
Forestry Abstracts
Forestry Abstracts. Leading Article Reprint Series
Foundation Center National Data Book
Foundation Directory
Foundation Grants Index
Genetics Abstracts
Geoscience Documentation
Geosources
Helminthological Abstracts. Series A: Animal and Human Helminthology
Helminthological Abstracts. Series B: Plant Nematology
Herbage Abstracts
Historical Abstracts. Part A: Modern History Abstracts, 1450-1914
Historical Abstracts. Part B: Twentieth Century Abstracts, 1914 to the Present
Horticultural Abstracts
Immunology Abstracts
Index Medicus
Index of Current Research on Pigs
Index of Economic Articles in Journals and Collective Volumes
Index to Dental Literature
Index Veterinarius
Information Science Abstracts
Institute of Paper Chemistry. Abstract Bulletin
International Aerospace Abstracts
International Nursing Index Including Nursing Citation Index
International Pharmaceutical Abstracts
Irregular Serials and Annuals
Key to Economic Science
Legal Contents
Legal Resource Index
Leisure, Recreation and Tourism Abstracts
Lentil Abstracts
Library & Information Science Abstracts
Linguistics and Language Behavior Abstracts
M L A International Bibliography of Books and Articles on the Modern Languages and Literatures
Magazine Index
Maize Abstracts
Management Contents
Martindale: the Extra Pharmacopoeia
Marx Karoly Kozgazdasagtudomanyi Egyetem: Doktori Ertekezesek
Mathematical Reviews
Medical and Health Care Books and Serials in Print
Metals Abstracts
Meteorological and Geoastrophysical Abstracts
Microbiology Abstracts. Section B. Bacteriology
Microcomputer Index
Middle East: Abstracts and Index
Neurosciences Abstracts
Nutrition Abstracts and Reviews. Series A: Human and Experimental
Nutrition Abstracts and Reviews. Series B: Livestock Feeds and Feeding
Oceanic Abstracts
Outlook (Year) Proceedings
P A I S Bulletin
P A I S Foreign Language Index
Pharmaceutical News Index
Physics Abstracts
Plant Breeding Abstracts
Plant Growth Regulator Abstracts
Potato Abstracts
Poultry Abstracts
Predicasts F & S Index Europe
Predicasts F & S Index International
Predicasts F & S Index of Corporate Change
Predicasts F & S Index United States
Predicasts Forecasts
Psychological Abstracts
Publishers, Distributors and Wholesalers of the United States
R I L M Abstracts of Music Literature
Religion Index One: Periodicals
Religion Index Two: Multi-Author Works
Religious and Inspirational Books and Serials in Print
Resources in Education
Review of Applied Entomology. Series A: Agricultural
Review of Applied Entomology. Series B: Medical and Veterinary
Review of Plant Pathology
Rice Abstracts

Robomatix Reporter
Rural Development Abstracts
Rural Extension, Education and Training Abstracts
Safety Science Abstracts Journal
Science Citation Index
Seed Abstracts
Selected Water Resources Abstracts
Small Animal Abstracts
Social Planning, Policy & Development Abstracts
Social Sciences Citation Index
Sociological Abstracts
Software Encyclopedia
Soils and Fertilizers
Solid State Abstracts Journal
Sorghum and Millets Abstracts
Soyabean Abstracts
Subject Guide to Books in Print
Telegen Reporter
Textile Technology Digest
Thomas Register of American Manufacturers and Thomas Register Catalog File
Toxicology Abstracts
Ulrich's International Periodicals Directory
U.S. Crop Reporting Board. Crop Production
United States Political Science Documents
Veterinary Bulletin
Virology Abstracts
Weed Abstracts
Who's Who in America
World Agricultural Economics and Rural Sociology Abstracts
World Aluminum Abstracts
World Patents Abstracts Journals
World Textile Abstracts
Zoological Record

EUROPEAN SPACE AGENCY
Via Galileo Galilei, I-00044 Frascati (Rome), Italy Tel: (06) 396 94011 Telex: 610637 ESRIN1
Department of Trade & Industry, Ashdown House, Rm. 123, Victoria St., London SW1E 6RB, United Kingdom Tel: (01) 212-5638, (01) 212-8225
Agricultural Engineering Abstracts
Alloys Index
Animal Breeding Abstracts
Apicultural Abstracts
Bulletin Signaletique. Part 521: Sociologie - Ethnologie
Bulletin Signaletique. Part 524: Sciences du Langage
Bulletin Signaletique d'Information Administrative
C.A.B. International Bureau of Agricultural Economics. Annotated Bibliographies Series A
C.A.B. International Bureau of Agricultural Economics. Annotated Bibliographies. Series B: Agricultural Policy and Rural Development in Africa
C.A.B. International Bureau of Nutrition. Annotated Bibliographies
C.A.B. International Bureau of Soils. Annotated Bibliographies
C I S Abstracts
Chemical Engineering Abstracts
Civil Engineering Hydraulics Abstracts
Computer & Control Abstracts
Cotton and Tropical Fibres Abstracts
Crop Physiology Abstracts
Current Biotechnology Abstracts
Current Index to Statistics
Current Mathematical Publications
Electrical & Electronics Abstracts
Energy Information Abstracts
Engineering Index Monthly and Author Index
Faba Bean Abstracts
Field Crop Abstracts
Fluid Flow Measurement Abstracts
Fluid Sealing Abstracts
Food Science and Technology Abstracts
Forest Products Abstracts
Forestry Abstracts
Forestry Abstracts. Leading Article Reprint Series
Helminthological Abstracts. Series A: Animal and Human Helminthology
Helminthological Abstracts. Series B: Plant Nematology
Herbage Abstracts
Horticultural Abstracts
I N I S Atomindex
Index of Current Research on Pigs
Index Veterinarius
Industrial Aerodynamics Abstracts
International Aerospace Abstracts
International Building Services Abstracts
International Pharmaceutical Abstracts

Irregular Serials and Annuals
Leisure, Recreation and Tourism Abstracts
Lentil Abstracts
Maize Abstracts
Mass Spectrometry Bulletin
Mathematical Reviews
Metals Abstracts
Nutrition Abstracts and Reviews. Series A: Human and Experimental
Nutrition Abstracts and Reviews. Series B: Livestock Feeds and Feeding
Oceanic Abstracts
Physics Abstracts
Plant Breeding Abstracts
Plant Growth Regulator Abstracts
Potato Abstracts
Poultry Abstracts
Pumps and Other Fluids Machinery Abstracts
Research on Transport Economics/Recherche en Matiere d'Economie des Transports
Review of Applied Entomology. Series A: Agricultural
Review of Applied Entomology. Series B: Medical and Veterinary
Review of Plant Pathology
Rice Abstracts
Robomatix Reporter
Rural Development Abstracts
Rural Extension, Education and Training Abstracts
Seed Abstracts
Small Animal Abstracts
Soils and Fertilizers
Sorghum and Millets Abstracts
Soyabean Abstracts
Telegen Reporter
Tribos - Tribology Abstracts
Ulrich's International Periodicals Directory
Urban Abstracts
Veterinary Bulletin
Weed Abstracts
World Agricultural Economics and Rural Sociology Abstracts
World Aluminum Abstracts
World Ports and Harbours Abstracts

I N K A (Subsidiary of: Fachinformationszentrum Energie, Physik, Mathematik GMBH)
Leopoldshafen 2, D-7514 Eggentein, Federal Republic Of Germany Tel: 7247 82 4568, 49 7247 824553 Telex: 7826487 FIZED
Coal Abstracts
Dokumentation Rheologie
Dokumentation Tribologie
Engineering Index Monthly and Author Index
Metals Abstracts

I S T INFORMATHEQUE
2 Complexe Desjardins, Ste. 1317, Montreal, Que. H5B 1B3, Canada Tel: 514-284-1111, 800-361-7469
Canadian Business Index

J I C S T
c/o U S A C O Corp., Tsutsumi Bldg., 13-12 Shimbashi 1-chome, Minato-ku, Tokyo 105, Japan
Shirobu-Shushuka, 5-2 Nagatacho 2-chome, Chiyoda-ku, Tokyo 100, Japan Tel: 813-581-6411 Telex: 02223604 J
Computer & Control Abstracts
Electrical & Electronics Abstracts
Food Science and Technology Abstracts
Physics Abstracts

MEAD DATA CENTRAL (Subsidiary of: Mead Corporation)
Box 1830, Dayton, OH 45401. Tel: 800-227-4908
American Hospital Formulary Service Drug Information
Chemical Regulation Reporter
Current Digest of the Soviet Press
Index to Legal Periodicals
Insurance Periodicals Index
International Aerospace Abstracts
Legal Resource Index
Magazine Index
Management Contents
Microcomputer Index

N E R A C, INC.
Mansfield Professional Park, Storrs, CT 06268. Tel: 203-429-3000
Engineering Index Monthly and Author Index

NATIONAL LIBRARY OF MEDICINE (Subsidiary of: National Institutes of Health)
8600 Rockville Pike, Bethesda, MD 20209. Tel: 301-496-6193, 800-638-8480
Bibliography of Bioethics

ORBIT INFORMATION TECHNOLOGIES
(Subsidiary of: Pergamon Press, Inc.)
1340 Old Chain Bridge Rd., McLean, VA 22101. Tel: 703-442-0900, 800-336-7575
A P I Abstracts/Literature
Abstracts on Tropical Agriculture
Accountants' Index
Alloys Index
American Statistics Index
Antarctic Bibliography
Bibliography and Index of Geology
Bibliography on Cold Regions Science & Technology
Biotechnology Research Abstracts
C I S Index
Ceramic Abstracts
Chemical Abstracts Service Source Index
Chemical Engineering Abstracts
Computer & Control Abstracts
Current Biotechnology Abstracts
Current Index to Journals in Education
Electric Power Industry Abstracts
Electrical & Electronics Abstracts
Electronic Publishing Abstracts
Energy Information Abstracts
Engineering Index Monthly and Author Index
Food Science and Technology Abstracts
Glaciological Data
International Packaging Abstracts
Library & Information Science Abstracts
Management Contents
Metals Abstracts
Paper and Board Abstracts
Petroleum Abstracts
Physics Abstracts
Psychological Abstracts
R A P R A Abstracts
Resources in Education
S A E Handbook
S A E Technical Literature Abstracts
World Patents Abstracts Journals
World Surface Coating Abstracts

PERGAMON INFOLINE (Subsidiary of: Pergamon Press, Ltd.)
12 Vandy St., London EC2A 2DE, United Kingdom Tel: 01-377-4650 Telex: 8814614
1340 Old Chain Rd., McLean, VA 22101. Tel: 703-442-0900
Cadscan
Ceramic Abstracts
Chemical Engineering Abstracts
Current Awareness in Biological Sciences
Current Biotechnology Abstracts
Directory of American Research and Technology
Electronic Publishing Abstracts
Engineering Index Monthly and Author Index
Fine Chemicals Directory
International Building Services Abstracts
International Journal of Rock Mechanics and Mining Sciences & Geomechanics Abstracts
International Packaging Abstracts
International Petroleum Abstracts
Key British Enterprises
Leadscan
Management and Marketing Abstracts
Mass Spectrometry Bulletin
New Trade Names in the Rubber and Plastics Industries
Paper and Board Abstracts
Photographic Abstracts
R A P R A Abstracts
Research Index
Safety Science Abstracts Journal
Selected Water Resources Abstracts
Urban Abstracts
Who Owns Whom. United Kingdom and Republic of Ireland
Who Owns Whom, North America
World Surface Coating Abstracts
World Textile Abstracts
Zincscan

Q L SYSTEMS LTD.
112 Kent St., Tower B, Ste. 205, Ottawa, Ont. K1P 5P2, Canada Tel: 613-238-3499
Alberta Reports
Canadian Business Index
Canadian News Index
Manitoba Reports
National Reporter
New Brunswick Reports
Newfoundland & Prince Edward Island Reports
Nova Scotia Reports
Ontario Appeal Cases
Saskatchewan Reports

RESEARCH LIBRARIES INFORMATION NETWORK
Jordan Quadrangle, Stanford, CA 94305. Tel: 415-328-0920
Avery Index to Architectural Periodicals

S T N INTERNATIONAL
c/o Chemical Abstracts Service, 2540 Olentengy River Rd., Box 3012, Columbus, OH 43210. Tel: 614-421-3600, 800-848-6533 Telex: 6842086 CHMAB
Chemical Abstracts Service Source Index
Computer & Control Abstracts
Electrical & Electronics Abstracts
Engineering Index Monthly and Author Index
Physics Abstracts
Zentralblatt fuer Mathematik und ihre Grenzgebiete/Mathematics Abstracts

SCICON LTD
Kiln Farm, Brick Ln., Milton Keyes, Buckinghamshire MK11 3EJ, United Kingdom Tel: 44 908-5656 56 Telex: 826 693 SCICON G
Urban Abstracts

TELESYSTEMES - QUESTEL
83-85 bd. Vincent Auriol, 75013 Paris, France Tel: 33 (1) 582 6464 Telex: 204594 TELQUES F
Index Chemicus
Merck Index: An Encyclopedia of Chemicals and Drugs
World Patents Abstracts Journals

UNIVERSITY OF TSUKUBA
Gakujutsu Joho Shori Center, Tennodai, Sakura-mura, Niihari-gun, Ibaraki, Japan Tel: 81 298 53 2450
Computer & Control Abstracts
Electrical & Electronics Abstracts
Physics Abstracts

VU/TEXT INFORMATION SERVICES, INC. (Subsidiary of: Knight-Ridder Company)
2852 Bluebill Dr., Virginia Beach, VA 23456. Tel: 804-427-1555
1211 Chestnut St., Philadelphia, PA 19107. Tel: 215-665-3300, 800-258-8080
Microcomputer Index

WESTLAW (Subsidiary of: West Publishing Company)
50 W. Kellogg Blvd., Box 43526, St. Paul, MN 55164. Tel: 612-228-2433, 800-328-9352
Chemical Regulation Reporter
Harvard Women's Law Journal
John Marshall Law Review
Stanford Journal of International Law

WILSONLINE (Subsidiary of: H.W. Wilson Company)
950 University Ave, Bronx, NY 10452. Tel: 212-588-8400, 800-367-6700
Applied Science and Technology Index
Biography Index
Biological and Agricultural Index
Book Review Digest
Business Periodicals Index
Cumulative Book Index
Education Index
General Science Index
Humanities Index
Index to Legal Periodicals
Library Literature
Social Sciences Index
Vertical File Index

Cessations

020 FR ISSN 0066-9210
A D B S ANNUAIRE. 1966-1986. a. Association Francaise des Documentalistes et des Bibliothecaires Specialises, 5 ave. Franco-Russe, 75007 Paris, France.

616.863 016 AT
A F A D D LIBRARY PERIODICALS HOLDINGS LIST. 1980-1986. irreg. Australian Foundation on Alcoholism and Drug Dependence, G.P.O. Box 477, Canberra, ACT 2601, Australia.

664 574 UK
A F R C FOOD RESEARCH INSTITUTE. BIENNIAL REPORT. 1969-1985. biennial. (also avail. in microfiche) Agricultural & Food Research Council, Food Research Institute, Colney Lane, Norwich NR4 7UA, England.

660 US ISSN 0270-6229
A I CH E M I MODULAR INSTRUCTION. SERIES A: PROCESS CONTROL. 1980-1987. irreg. (back issues avail.) American Institute of Chemical Engineers, 345 E. 47th St., New York, NY 10017.

660 US ISSN 0270-7624
A I CH E M I MODULAR INSTRUCTION. SERIES B: STAGEWISE AND MASS TRANSFER OPERATIONS. 1980-1987. irreg. (back issues avail.) American Institute of Chemical Engineers, 345 E. 47th St., New York, NY 10017.

660 US ISSN 0270-7640
A I CH E M I MODULAR INSTRUCTION. SERIES D: THERMODYNAMICS. 1980-1987. irreg. (back issues avail.) American Institute of Chemical Engineers, 345 E. 47th St., New York, NY 10017.

660 US ISSN 0270-7659
A I CH E M I MODULAR INSTRUCTION. SERIES E: KINETICS. 1980-1986. irreg. (back issues avail.) American Institute of Chemical Engineers, 345 E. 47th St., New York, NY 10017.

660 US ISSN 0270-7667
A I CH E M I MODULAR INSTRUCTION. SERIES F: MATERIAL AND ENERGY BALANCES. 1980-1986. irreg. (back issues avail.) American Institute of Chemical Engineers, 345 E. 47th St., New York, NY 10017.

574 610 US
A L Z A CONFERENCE SERIES. 1972-1973. irreg. Plenum Publishing Corp., 233 Spring St., New York, NY 10013.

621.381 US
A-PLUS BUYER'S GUIDE. suspended. a. Ziff-Davis Publishing Co., Computer Publications Division, One Park Ave., New York, NY 10016.

200 GW ISSN 0173-0851
A Q. 1964-1980. irreg. A Q-Verlag, Erwin Stegentritt, Beim Weisenstein 6, 6602 Dudweiler, W. Germany (B.R.D.)
Formerly: Anti-Quarium.

950 KO ISSN 0066-8311
A S P A C SEMINAR ON AUDIO-VISUAL EDUCATION. PROCEEDINGS. 1969-1978. irreg. Asian and Pacific Council, Cultural and Social Centre, I.P.O. Box 3129, Seoul, S. Korea.

362.7 UK
ABERLOUR CHILD CARE TRUST. NEWSLETTER. 1885-1979. a. Aberlour Child Care Trust, 36 Park Terrace, Stirling FK8 2JR, England.
Formerly: Advance.

333.7 016 US
ABSTRACT NEWSLETTER: N A S A EARTH RESOURCES SURVEY PROGRAM. discontinued. w. (back issues avail.) (U.S. National Aeronautics and Space Administration) U.S. National Technical Information Service, 5285 Port Royal Rd., Springfield, VA 22151.
Former titles: Weekly Abstract Newsletter: N A S A Earth Resources Survey Program; Weekly Government Abstracts. N A S A Earth Resources Survey Program (ISSN 0364-6440)

551.7 016 BE ISSN 0304-5935
ABSTRACTS OF GEOCHRONOLOGY AND ISOTOPE GEOLOGY. 1972-1982, no.40. 4/yr. Belgian Centre for Geochronology, c/o Museum, Steenweg Op Leuven 11, B-1980 Tervuren, Belgium.

157 CU
ACADEMIA DE CIENCIAS DE CUBA. CENTRO PARA EL ESTUDIO DE LAS NEUROSIS. BOLETIN. 1977-1982 (no.6) irreg. Academia de Ciencias de Cuba, Centro para el Estudio de las Neurosis, Biblioteca Central de Ciencia y Tecnica, Apartado 2291, Zona 2, Havana, Cuba.

551.46 CU ISSN 0567-5782
ACADEMIA DE CIENCIAS DE CUBA. INSTITUTO DE OCEANOLOGIA. SERIE OCEANOLOGICA. 1968-19?? (no.36) irreg. Academia de Ciencias de Cuba, Instituto de Oceanologia, Avda. 1ra. no. 18406, Havana, Cuba.

370 US
ACCESS (WASHINGTON) ceased. irreg. Association for Educational Communications and Technology, 1126 16th St., Washington, DC 20036.

796.41 UK
ACROBATICS MAGAZINE. 1976-1981 (no.23) irreg. 6 Elizabeth Way, Hanworth, Feltham, Middlesex TW13 7PH, England.

001.3 FI ISSN 0355-578X
ACTA ACADEMIAE ABOENSIS. SERIES A: HUMANIORA. 1920-1986. irreg. Aabo Akademi, Domkyrkotorget 3, 20500 Aabo, Finland.

016 610 FR
ACTUALITES BIBLIOGRAPHIQUES EN MEDECINE, PHARMACIE ET SCIENCES BIOMEDICALES. 1973-1978. a. Sandoz Editions, B.P. 120, 92505 Rueil Malmaison Cedex, France.

545.822 US ISSN 0065-2091
ADVANCES IN ACTIVATION ANALYSIS. 1969-1972. irreg. Academic Press, Inc., Orlando, FL 32887.

615 US ISSN 0146-3810
ADVANCES IN GENERAL AND CELLULAR PHARMACOLOGY. 1976-19?? irreg. Plenum Publishing Corp., 233 Spring St., New York, NY 10013.

029.7 651.8 US ISSN 0065-2784
ADVANCES IN INFORMATION SYSTEMS SCIENCE. 1969-19?? irreg. Plenum Publishing Corp., 233 Spring St., New York, NY 10013.

133 US
ADVANCES IN PARAPSYCHOLOGICAL RESEARCH. 1977-1982. irreg. Plenum Publishing Corp., 233 Spring St., New York, NY 10013.

150 US ISSN 0065-325X
ADVANCES IN PSYCHOLOGICAL ASSESSMENT. 1968-1984. irreg. (also avail. in microform from UMI) Jossey-Bass, Inc., Publishers, 433 California St., San Francisco, CA 94104.

301.1 150 US
ADVANCES IN SOCIAL PSYCHOLOGY. 1985; ceased same year. irreg. Ablex Publishing Corp., 355 Chestnut St., Norwood, NJ 07648.

CESSATIONS

820   US   ISSN 0065-4000
AFRICAN LITERATURE TODAY. 1968-1976. a. (back issues avail.) (University of Sierra Leone, Fourah Bay College, SL) Africana Publishing Co. (Subsidiary of: Holmes & Meier Publishers, Inc.) 30 Irving Pl., New York, NY 10003.
    Supersedes: Association for African Literature in English. Bulletin.

338   UK
AIDS FOR INDUSTRY - NORTH WEST ENGLAND. 1981-1985. a. North West Industrial Development Association, Brazennose House (West Door), Brazennose St., Manchester M2 5AZ, England.

398   UR
AKADEMIYA NAUK BELORUSSKOI S.S.R. BELORUSSKII ETNOGRAFICHESKII SBORNIK. SERIYA FOL'KLORA I ETNOGRAFII. published only once, 1958. a. Akademiya Nauk Belorusskoi S.S.R., Institut Mastatstvaznaustva, Minsk, Byelorussian S.S.R., U.S.S.R.

541.37   UR   ISSN 0568-6776
AKADEMIYA NAUK S.S.S.R. SIBIRSKOE OTDELENIE. URAL'SKII NAUCHNYI TSENTR. INSTITUT ELEKTROKHIMII. TRUDY. 1960-1978. irreg. (also avail. in microfilm) Akademiya Nauk S.S.S.R., Ural'skii Nauchnyi Tsentr, Ul. Pervomaiskaya, 91, Sverdlovsk, Russian S.F.S.R., U.S.S.R.

380.1   US
ALABAMA INTERNATIONAL TRADE DIRECTORY. ceased. a. Department of Economic and Community Affairs, State Capitol, Montgomery, AL 36130.
    Formerly: Alabama World Trade Directory (ISSN 0095-1269)

368.4   US   ISSN 0095-4667
ALASKA MEDICAID STATUS REPORT. 1973-19?? a. Department of Health and Social Services, Division of Public Assistance, Pouch H-01, Juneau, AK 99811.
    Formerly: Alaska. Division of Medical Assistance. Medicaid Annual Status Report (ISSN 0095-4675)

331.12   US
ALASKA PLANNING INFORMATION. ceased. a. Department of Labor, Research and Analysis Section, Box 25501, Juneau, AK 99802.
    Formerly: Alaska Statewide Annual Planning Information.

531.64   665.5   CN   ISSN 0700-2645
ALBERTA. DEPARTMENT OF ENERGY AND NATURAL RESOURCES. ANNUAL REPORT. 1976-1985. a. Department of Energy and Natural Resources, Bramalea Bldg., 9920 108th St., Edmonton, Alta. T5K 2M4, Canada.

635   CN   ISSN 0706-3369
ALBERTA. HORTICULTURAL RESEARCH CENTER. ANNUAL REPORT. (Previously included in: Alberta. Department of Agriculture. Annual Report) 1970-19?? a. Department of Agriculture, Horticultural Research Center, Communications Branch, 7000 113 St., Edmonton, Alta. T6H 5T6, Canada

943   GW   ISSN 0516-5644
ALEMANNISCHES JAHRBUCH. 1953-1985. irreg. Verlag Konkordia, Eisenbahnstr. 31-33, Postfach 1240, 7580 Buehl Baden, W. Germany (B.R.D.)

574   US   ISSN 0065-6364
ALLAN HANCOCK MONOGRAPHS IN MARINE BIOLOGY. 1966-1983. irreg. Allan Hancock Foundation, University of Southern California, Los Angeles, CA 90089-0371.

500   AU
ALMANACH DER OESTERREICHISCHEN FORSCHUNG. 1978-1983. irreg. Verband der Wissenschaftlichen Gesellschaften Oesterreichs, Lindengasse 37, A-1070 Vienna, Austria.

340 016   US   ISSN 0065-7549
AMERICAN BAR FOUNDATION. RESEARCH CONTRIBUTIONS. 1967-1984. irreg. (1-10/yr.), no.2. (reprint service avail. from UMI) American Bar Foundation, 750 N. Lake Shore Dr., Chicago, IL 60611.

340   US
AMERICAN BAR FOUNDATION RESEARCH REPORTER. 1971-1985. irreg. (processed; reprint service avail. from UMI) American Bar Foundation, 1155 East 60th St., Chicago, IL 60637.
    Formerly: A B F Research Reporter (ISSN 0084-6317)

677   US   ISSN 0065-8588
AMERICAN HOME ECONOMICS ASSOCIATION. TEXTILES AND CLOTHING SECTION. TEXTILE HANDBOOK. 1960-19?? irreg. American Home Economics Association, 2010 Massachusetts Ave. N.W., Washington, DC 20036.

340   US
AMERICAN LAWYER GUIDE TO LEADING LAW FIRMS. 1981-1986. biennial. Am-Law Publishing Corporation, 600 Third Ave., New York, NY 10016.
    Formerly: American Lawyer Guide to Law Firms.

301   US   ISSN 0271-9487
AMERICAN MAN. 1980-1984 (vol.2) irreg. Haddad Communications, Box 693, Columbia, MD 21045.

157.72 616.855   US   ISSN 0065-9886
AMERICAN PSYCHOPATHOLOGICAL ASSOCIATION. PUBLICATIONS. ceased. irreg. (reprint service avail. from UMI) Johns Hopkins University Press, 701 W. 40th St., Ste. 275, Baltimore, MD 21211.

371.42   US
AMERICAN VOCATIONAL ASSOCIATION. YEARBOOK. (Each vol. has distinctive title) 1971-1985. a. American Vocational Association, 1410 King St., Alexandria, VA 22314-2715.

780   IS   ISSN 0066-1260
AMLI STUDIES IN MUSIC BIBLIOGRAPHY. 1970-1982. irreg. Haifa Music Museum and Amli Library, P.O. Box 45134, Haifa, Israel.

500   GW   ISSN 0080-5165
ANNALES UNIVERSITATIS SARAVIENSIS. REIHE: MATHEMATISCH-NATURWISSENSCHAFTLICHE FAKULTAET. 1963-198? a. (Universitaet des Saarlandes) Gebrueder Borntraeger Verlagsbuchhandlung, Johannesstr. 3A, 7000 Stuttgart 1, W. Germany (B.R.D.)

720   FR   ISSN 0066-2747
ANNUAIRE DES ARCHITECTES. (Extract from Annuaire du Batiment et des Travaux Publics) 1935-1984. a. (Societe des Architectes Diplomes de l'Ecole Speciale d'Architecture) Saint Lambert Editeur, Boite Postale 72, 13673 Aubagne Cedex, France.

327 382   MG
ANNUAIRE DU MADAGASCAR. (In 3 vols.) 1973-1987; suspended. a. Editions Madagascar Print and Press Company, B.P. 953, Antananarivo, Malagasy Republic.

616.742 016   US   ISSN 0097-921X
ANNUAL INDEX OF RHEUMATOLOGY. 1965-19?? a. Arthritis Foundation, American Rheumatism Association Section, 17 Executive Park Dr., N.E., Ste. 480, Atlanta, GA 30329.
    Formerly (until 1974): Index of Rheumatology (ISSN 0019-3933)

663 338.47   US   ISSN 0066-4367
ANNUAL STATISTICAL REVIEW: THE DISTILLED SPIRITS INDUSTRY. 1942-1984/85. a. Distilled Spirits Council of the United States, Inc., 1250 Eye St., N.W., Washington, DC 20008.

382   MX
ANUARIO DE COMERCIO EXTERIOR DE MEXICO. 1939-19?? irreg. Banco Nacional de Comercio Exterior, S.A., Gerencia de Publicaciones, Malintzin 28, Col. del Carmen, Coyoacan, Mexico D.F. 04100.
    Formerly: Comercio Exterior de Mexico.

861   AG
ANUARIO DE POETAS CONTEMPORANEOS. 1976-19?? a. Club de Poetas, Casilla de Correo 189, 1401 Buenos Aires, Argentina.

700   US
APPELLES: THE GEORGIA ARTS JOURNAL. 1979-1984; suspended. irreg. University of Georgia, Department of Art, Athens, GA 30602.

536.56   US
APPLICATIONS OF CRYOGENIC TECHNOLOGY. 1969-1979 (vol.9) irreg. (Cyrogenic Society of America) Scholium International, Inc., 265 Great Neck Rd., Great Neck, NY 11021.

289.9   US
AQUARIAN LIGHTS. 1979-1984. a. International Church of Ageless Wisdom, Inc., Box 101, Wyalusing, PA 18853.

331   DK   ISSN 0107-9743
ARBEJDSMARKEDETS REGELSAMLING. 1981-1986. a. Dansk Arbejdsgiverforening, Vester Volgade 113, Denmark.

913 016   UK   ISSN 0066-5967
ARCHAEOLOGICAL BIBLIOGRAPHY FOR GREAT BRITAIN AND IRELAND. 1950-1986. a. (back issues avail.) Council for British Archaeology, 112 Kennington Rd., London SE11 6RE, England.

720   UK   ISSN 0066-619X
ARCHITECTS' YEAR BOOK. 1944-19?? irreg. Granada Publishing Ltd., 8 Grafton St., London W1X 3LA, England.

720   US
ARCHITECTURAL HANDBOOK. 1976-19?? a. American Institute of Architects, California Council, 1303 J St., No. 200, Sacramento, CA 95814-2916.

630   AG   ISSN 0066-7242
ARGENTINA. ESTACION EXPERIMENTAL AGROPECUARIA MANFREDI. SERIE INFORMACION TECNICA. ceased with no.92. irreg. Instituto Nacional de Tecnologia Agropecuria, Estacion Experimental Agropecuaria Manfredi, 5988 Manfredi (Cordoba), Argentina.

338 318   AG
ARGENTINA. INSTITUTO NACIONAL DE ESTADISTICA Y CENSOS. INDICADORES INDUSTRIALES. SERIE I. 1974-1982. a. Instituto Nacional de Estadistica y Censos, Hipolito Yrigoyen 250, Buenos Aires, Argentina.

310   AG   ISSN 0066-7196
ARGENTINA. INSTITUTO NACIONAL DE ESTADISTICA Y CENSOS. INFORME SERIE E: EDIFICACIONE. ceased. irreg. Instituto Nacional de Estadistica y Censos, Hipolito Yrigoyen 250, Buenos Aires, Argentina.

312   AG
ARGENTINA. INSTITUTO NACIONAL DE ESTADISTICA Y CENSOS. SERIE INFORMACION DEMOGRAFICA. ceased 1970 (no.7) a. Instituto Nacional de Estadistica y Censos, Hippolito Yrigoyen 250, Buenos Aires, Argentina.

631   AG
ARGENTINA. INSTITUTO NACIONAL DE TECNOLOGIA AGROPECUARIA. SUELOS. ceased. irreg. Instituto Nacional de Tecnologia Agropecuaria, Centro de Investigaciones de Recursos Naturales, Casilla de Correo 25, 1712 Buenos Aires, Argentina.

355   US   ISSN 0004-2536
ARMY MUSEUM NEWSLETTER. 1969-19?? irreg. (2-4/yr.) (processed) U.S. Army, Center of Military History, Washington, DC 20314.

950   KO   ISSN 0066-8303
ASIAN AND PACIFIC COUNCIL. CULTURAL AND SOCIAL CENTRE. ANNUAL REPORT. 1969-1976. irreg. Asian and Pacific Council, Cultural and Social Centre, I.P.O. Box 3129, Seoul, S. Korea.

069.950   KO
ASIAN AND PACIFIC COUNCIL. MUSEUM CONFERENCE. PROCEEDINGS. ceased 1976. irreg. Asian and Pacific Council, Cultural and Social Centre, C.P.O. Box 3129, Seoul, S. Korea.

950   BG
ASIAN STUDIES. 1979-1985. a. Jahangirnagar University, Department of Government and Politics, Dacca, Bangladesh.

410 SP
ASOCIACION DE ACADEMIAS DE LA LENGUA ESPAÑOLA. COMISION PERMANENTE. BOLETIN. 1975-1976 (no.24) irreg. Asociacion de Academias de la Lengua Espanola, Comision Permanente, Calle de Felipe IV 4, Madrid 14, Spain.

382 UY
ASOCIACION LATINOAMERICANA DE LIBRE COMERCIO. ESTADISTICAS DE COMERCIO EXTERIOR - SERIE A: EXPORTACIONES. (Separate volume for each member country) 1972-19?? a. Asociacion Latinoamericana de Integracion, Cebollati 1461, Casilla de Correo 577, Montevideo, Uruguay.
  Formerly: Asociacion Latinoamericana de Libre Comercio. Comercio Exterior. Argentina. Exportacion (ISSN 0571-3870)

382 UY
ASOCIACION LATINOAMERICANA DE LIBRE COMERCIO. ESTADISTICAS DE COMERCIO EXTERIOR-SERIE B-IMPORTACIONES. (Separate volume for each member country) 1973-19?? a. Asociacion Latinoamericana de Integracion, Cebollati 1461, Casilla de Correo 577, Montevideo, Uruguay.
  Formerly: Asociacion Latinoamericana de Libre Comercio. Comercio Exterior Argentina. Importacion (ISSN 0571-3889)

382 UY
ASOCIACION LATINOAMERICANA DE LIBRE COMERCIO. ESTADISTICAS DE COMERCIO EXTERIOR-SERIE C-IMPORTACIONES ZONALES. (Separate volume for each member country) 1974-19?? a. Asociacion Latinoamericana de Integracion, Cebollati 1461, Casilla de Correo 577, Montevideo, Uruguay.
  Formerly: Asociacion Latinoamericana de Libre Comercio. Comercio Exterior Brasil. Importacion.

615 BL
ASSOCIACAO BRASILEIRA DA INDUSTRIA FARMACEUTICA. PESQUISA. 1976-19?? irreg. Associacao Brasileira da Industria Farmaceutica, Av. Beira Mar 262, CEP 20000 Rio de Janeiro, R J, Brazil.

636.089 US
ASSOCIATION OF ANIMAL ALLERGIC VETERINARY ASSOCIATION. NEWSLETTER. 1981-19??; suspended. irreg. Iowa State University, College of Veterinary Medicine, Ames, IA 50011.

535 US
ATMOSPHERIC OPTICS. 1970-19?? irreg. Consultants Bureau, Special Research Report, 233 Spring St., New York, NY 10013.

681 IT ISSN 0004-7309
ATTUALITA DI LABORATORIO. 1955-19?? irreg. Dott. G. Terzano & Co. S.p.A., Via Darwin 19-21, Milan, Italy.

500 AU
AUS OESTERREICHS WISSENSCHAFT. 1973-1980. irreg. Verband der Wissenschaftlichen Gesellschaften Oesterreichs, Lindgengasse 37, A-1070 Vienna, Austria.

629.13 GW ISSN 0067-0685
AUSRUESTUNG IN LUFT- UND RAUMFAHRT. 1966-1972 (no.6) irreg. R. Oldenbourg Verlag GmbH, Rosenheimer Str. 145, Postfach 801360, 8000 Munich 80, W. Germany (B.R.D.).

338.1 633 AT ISSN 0311-0788
AUSTRALIA. BUREAU OF AGRICULTURAL ECONOMICS. COARSE GRAINS: SITUATION AND OUTLOOK. 1954-1985, discontinued. a. Bureau of Agricultural Economics, Department of Primary Industry, G.P.O. Box 1563, Canberra, A.C.T. 2601, Australia
  Supersedes in part: Australia. Bureau of Agricultural Economics. Coarse Grains and Oilseeds Situation (ISSN 0084-702X); Australia. Bureau of Agricultural Economics. Coarse Grain Situation.

338.1 637 AT ISSN 0311-8843
AUSTRALIA. BUREAU OF AGRICULTURAL ECONOMICS. DAIRY PRODUCTS: SITUATION AND OUTLOOK. 1954-1985; discontinued. a. Bureau of Agricultural Economics, Department of Primary Industry, G.P.O. Box 1563, Canberra, A.C.T. 2601, Australia
  Supersedes: Australia. Bureau of Agricultural Economics. Dairy Situation (ISSN 0084-7038)

338.1 637.5 AT
AUSTRALIA. BUREAU OF AGRICULTURAL ECONOMICS. EGGS: SITUATION AND OUTLOOK. 1955-1985; discontinued. a. Bureau of Agricultural Economics, Department of Primary Industry, G.P.O. Box 1563, Canberra, A.C.T. 2601, Australia
  Supersedes: Australia. Bureau of Agricultural Economics. Egg Situation (ISSN 0084-7046)

338.1 AT ISSN 0311-2950
AUSTRALIA. BUREAU OF AGRICULTURAL ECONOMICS. FIBRE REVIEW. 1974-1976. a. Bureau of Agricultural Economics, Department of Primary Industry, G.P.O. Box 1563, Canberra, A.C.T. 2601, Australia
  Supersedes: Australia. Bureau of Agricultural Economics. Fibres Other Than Wool (ISSN 0045-0200)

338.1 636.2 AT ISSN 0311-0885
AUSTRALIA. BUREAU OF AGRICULTURAL ECONOMICS. MEAT: SITUATION AND OUTLOOK. 1953-1985; discontinued. a. Bureau of Agricultural Economics, Department of Primary Industry, G.P.O. Box 1563, Canberra, A.C.T. 2601, Australia
  Supersedes: Australia. Bureau of Agricultural Economics. Meat Situation (ISSN 0310-0685); Australia. Bureau of Agricultural Economics. Beef Situation (ISSN 0084-7011); Australia. Bureau of Agricultural Economics. Mutton and Lamb Situation (ISSN 0084-7054)

338.1 633 AT ISSN 0311-8789
AUSTRALIA. BUREAU OF AGRICULTURAL ECONOMICS. OILSEEDS: SITUATION AND OUTLOOK. 1955-1985; discontinued. a. Bureau of Agricultural Economics, Department of Primary Industry, G.P.O. Box 1563, Canberra, A.C.T. 2601, Australia
  Supersedes in part: Australia. Bureau of Agricultural Economics. Coarse Grains and Oilseeds Situation (ISSN 0084-702X)

350 631 AT ISSN 0311-8835
AUSTRALIA. BUREAU OF AGRICULTURAL ECONOMICS. SITUATION AND OUTLOOK (YEAR). COTTON. 1974-1985; discontinued. a. Bureau of Agricultural Economics, Department of Primary Industry, G.P.O. Box 1563, Canberra, A.C.T. 2601, Australia

350 338.1 AT ISSN 0810-6797
AUSTRALIA. BUREAU OF AGRICULTURAL ECONOMICS. SITUATION AND OUTLOOK (YEAR). FARM INPUTS. 1974-1985; discontinued. a. Bureau of Agricultural Economics, Department of Primary Industry, G.P.O. Box 1563, Canberra, A.C.T. 2601, Australia

350 639.2 AT ISSN 0810-6800
AUSTRALIA. BUREAU OF AGRICULTURAL ECONOMICS. SITUATION AND OUTLOOK (YEAR). FISH PRODUCTS. 1974-1985; discontinued. a. Bureau of Agricultural Economics, Department of Primary Industry, G.P.O. Box 1563, Canberra, A.C.T. 2601, Australia

633.11 338.1 AT ISSN 0310-9917
AUSTRALIA. BUREAU OF AGRICULTURAL ECONOMICS. WHEAT: SITUATION AND OUTLOOK. 1951-1985; discontinued. a. Bureau of Agricultural Economics, Department of Primary Industry, G.P.O. Box 1563, Canberra, A.C.T. 2601, Australia
  Formerly: Wheat Situation (ISSN 0043-4736)

382 319 AT ISSN 0705-0542
AUSTRALIA. BUREAU OF STATISTICS. AUSTRALIAN IMPORTS, COUNTRY BY COMMODITY. 1966-1986. a. Australian Bureau of Statistics, Box 10, Belconnen, A.C.T. 2616, Australia.
  Formerly: Australia. Bureau of Statistics. Australian Imports Bulletin (ISSN 0067-1916)

350 319.4 AT
AUSTRALIA. BUREAU OF STATISTICS. AUSTRALIAN MUNICIPAL INFORMATION SYSTEM. 1966-1986; suspended. a. (also avail. in microfiche) Australian Bureau of Statistics, Ground Floor, Wing 5, Cameron Offices, Belconnen, A.C.T. 2617, Australia.

350 319.4 AT
AUSTRALIA. BUREAU OF STATISTICS. CHILD CARE ARRANGEMENTS. 1969-1986; suspended. a. Australian Bureau of Statistics, Ground Floor, Wing 5, Cameron Offices, Belconnen, A.C.T. 2617, Australia.

350 319.4 AT
AUSTRALIA. BUREAU OF STATISTICS. CHILD CARE ARRANGEMENTS. PRELIMINARY. 1969-1986; suspended. irreg. Australian Bureau of Statistics, Ground Floor, Wing 5, Cameron Offices, Belconnen, A.C.T. 2617, Australia.

350 319.4 AT
AUSTRALIA. BUREAU OF STATISTICS. DIRECTORY OF A B S ENERGY STATISTICS. 1981-1986; suspended. irreg. Australian Bureau of Statistics, Ground Floor, Wing 5, Cameron Offices, Belconnen, A.C.T. 2617, Australia.

350 319.4 AT
AUSTRALIA. BUREAU OF STATISTICS. EX-SERVICE PERSONNEL. 1966-1986; suspended. irreg. Australian Bureau of Statistics, Ground Floor, Wing 5, Cameron Offices, Belconnen, A.C.T. 2617, Australia.

338.4 AT
AUSTRALIA. BUREAU OF STATISTICS. MANUFACTURING COMMODITIES: PRINCIPAL ARTICLES PRODUCED, AUSTRALIA. 1968-1986; suspended. a. Australian Bureau of Statistics, Box 10, Belconnen, A.C.T. 2616, Australia.

338.4 AT
AUSTRALIA. BUREAU OF STATISTICS. MANUFACTURING ESTABLISHMENTS: SUMMARY OF OPERATIONS BY INDUSTRY CLASS, AUSTRALIA. suspended 1986. a. Australian Bureau of Statistics, Box 10, Belconnen, A.C.T. 2616, Australia.

312 AT
AUSTRALIA. BUREAU OF STATISTICS. VICTORIAN OFFICE. DEMOGRAPHY SUMMARY STATEMENT, VICTORIA. 1961-1983; discontinued. a. Australian Bureau of Statistics, Victorian Office, Box 2796Y, G.P.O. Melbourne, Victoria 3001, Australia.
  Formerly: Australia. Bureau of Statistics. Victorian Office. Demography, Victoria (ISSN 0067-1096)

350 338.1 AT
AUSTRALIA. DEPARTMENT OF PRIMARY INDUSTRY. INDUSTRY PRICE INDEXES. 1972-1985, discontinued. a. Department of Primary Industry, Bureau of Agricultural Economics, G.P.O. Box 1563, Canberra, A.C.T. 2601, Australia.

387 639.2 AT
AUSTRALIAN CENTRE FOR MARITIME STUDIES. OCCASIONAL PAPERS IN MARITIME AFFAIRS; Australian maritime horizons in the 1980s. 1982-1986; suspended. a. (back issues avail.) Australian Centre for Maritime Studies, P.O. Box E20, Queen Victoria Terrace, Canberra 2600, Australia.

616.863 AT ISSN 0311-9629
AUSTRALIAN DIRECTORY OF SERVICES FOR ALCOHOLISM AND DRUG DEPENDENCE. 1975-1986. irreg. Australian Foundation on Alcoholism and Drug Dependence, G.P.O. Box 477, Canberra, ACT 2601, Australia.

350 338.1 AT
AUSTRALIAN IMPORTS OF DAIRY PRODUCE. 1972-1986. a. Department of Primary Industry, Dairy and Intensive Livestock Division, Edmund Barton Bldg., Broughton St., Barton, A.C.T. 2600, Australia.

CESSATIONS

622   AT
AUSTRALIAN MINERAL INDUSTRIES RESEARCH ASSOCIATION. BULLETIN. ceased 1979 (no.7) irreg. Australian Mineral Industries Research Association Ltd., 57-63 Exhibition St., 11th Fl., Melbourne, Vic. 3000, Australia.

549   AT
AUSTRALIAN MINERAL INDUSTRIES RESEARCH ASSOCIATION. NON-CONFIDENTIAL RESEARCH INFORMATION. 1967-1983. a. Australian Mineral Industries Research Association Ltd., 57-63 Exhibition St., 11th Fl., Melbourne, Vic. 3000, Australia, Vic. 3052.

797.1   DK
BAAD JUL. ceased. a. Bonniers Specialmagasiner, Noerre Farimagsgade 49, 1375 Copenhagen K, Denmark.

943 800 410   US   ISSN 0360-2206
BALKANISTICA; a journal of southeast European studies. 1975-1971/82 (vol.7) irreg. (American Association for Southeast European Studies) Slavica Publishers, Inc., Box 14388, Columbus, OH 43214.

808.8   US
BANANA RAG. 1971-197?; discontinued. a. Banana Productions, P.O. Box 3655, Vancouver V6B 3Y8, Canada.

658.3   BL
BANCO DA AMAZONIA. CENTRO DE DOCUMENTACAO E BIBLIOTECA. CONTEXTO BOLETIM. 1974; ceased after 2 issues. irreg. Banco da Amazonia, Centro de Documentacao e Biblioteca, Av. Presidente Vargas, 800 - 16. Andar, Belem, Brazil.

332   SP
BANCO DE FINANCIACION INDUSTRIAL. BANCA PRIVADA. 1966-1976. irreg. Banco de Financiacion Industrial, Servicio de Estudios, P. de la Castellano 112, Madrid 6, Spain.

382   CK   ISSN 0302-9611
BANCO DE LA REPUBLICA. REGISTROS DE EXPORTACION E IMPORTACION. ceased 1980. a. Banco de la Republica, Departamento de Investigaciones Economicas, Casilla de Correo 402, Bogata 1, Colombia.
    Formerly: Banco de la Republica. Bogota. Registros de Importaciones.

621.381   US
BANK MICROCOMPUTER DIRECTORY. 1983-1985. a. (reprint service avail.) Bank Administration Institute, 60 Gould Center, Rolling Meadows, IL 60008.

629.2   US   ISSN 0067-4338
BASIC AUTO REPAIR MANUAL. 1968-1984. irreg. Caroline House, Inc., 5 S. 250 Frontenac Rd., Naperville, IL 60540.

629.2   US   ISSN 0067-4362
BASIC BODYWORK AND PAINTING. 1969-1984. irreg. Caroline House, Inc., 5 S. 250 Frontenac Rd., Naperville, IL 60540.

629.2   US   ISSN 0067-4370
BASIC CAMS, VALVES AND EXHAUST SYSTEMS. 1968-1984. irreg. Caroline House, Inc., 5 S. 250 Frontenac Rd., Naperville, IL 60540.

629.2   US   ISSN 0067-4397
BASIC CHASSIS, SUSPENSION AND BRAKES. 1969-1984. irreg. Caroline House, Inc., 5 S. 250 Frontenac Rd., Naperville, IL 60540.

629.2   US   ISSN 0067-4400
BASIC CLUTCHES AND TRANSMISSIONS. 1968-1984. irreg. Caroline House, Inc., 5 S. 250 Frontenac Rd., Naperville, IL 60540.

629.2   US   ISSN 0067-4427
BASIC IGNITION AND ELECTRICAL SYSTEMS. 1969-1984. irreg. Caroline House, Inc., 5 S. 250 Frontenac Rd., Naperville, IL 60540.

620.106   US
BATTELLE INSTITUTE MATERIALS SCIENCE COLLOQUIA. 1972-1977. irreg. Plenum Publishing Corp., 233 Spring St., New York, NY 10013.

678   GW   ISSN 0005-6987
BAYER-MITTEILUNGEN FUER DIE GUMMI-INDUSTRIE. 1955-1981 (no.53) irreg. (1-2/yr.) Bayer AG, 5090 Leverkusen-Bayerwerk, W. Germany (B.R.D.)

355   GW   ISSN 0067-5253
BEITRAEGE ZUR WEHRFORSCHUNG. 1963-1976. irreg. (Arbeitskreis fuer Wehrforschung) Wehr und Wissen Verlagsgesellschaft GmbH, Heilsbachstr., Postfach 87, 5300 Bonn-Duisdorf, W. Germany (B.R.D.)

500 016   BE
BELGIUM. NATIONAAL FONDS VOOR WETENSCHAPPELIJK ONDERZOEK. BIBLIOGRAFIE/BELGIUM. FONDS NATIONAL DE LA RECHERCHE SCIENTIFIQUE. BIBLIOGRAPHIE. ceased in 1979. triennial. (back issues avail.) Nationaal Fonds voor Wetenschappelijk Onderzoek - Fonds National de la Recherche Scientifique, Egmontstraat 5, 1050 Brussels, Belgium.
    Formerly: Belgium. Nationaal Fonds voor Wetenschappelijk Onderzoek. Bibliografische Lijst van de Werken/Liste Bibliographique des Travaux.

943.8   UK   ISSN 0005-8645
BELLONA; kwartalnik. 1940-1967. a. Polish Institute and Sikorski Museum, 20 Princes Gate, London SW7 1WA, England.

051   US
BENNINGTON REVIEW. 1978-19?? a. (also avail. in microfilm from UMI; reprint service avail. from UMI) Bennington College, Bennington, VT 05201.

808.81   US
BERKELEY WORKS. 1981-1986 (no.4) a. 25 Yarmouth Rd., East Rockaway, NY 11518.

001   US   ISSN 0271-8189
BEST OF MICRO. 1978-19?? a. Micro Ink, Inc., Box 6502, Chelmsford, MA 01824.

581 016   BL   ISSN 0067-6586
BIBLIOGRAFIA BRASILEIRA DE BOTANICA. 1950-1981 (vol.13) irreg. Instituto Brasileiro de Informacao em Ciencia e Tecnologia, SCRN 708/709 Bloco B Loja 18E 30, 70740 Brasilia DF, Brazil.

016 791.43   RM   ISSN 0084-7828
BIBLIOGRAFIA INTERNATIONALA CINEMA/BIBLIOGRAPHIE INTERNATIONALE CINEMA. 1967-1974. a. Arhiva Nationala de Filme, Bd. Gh. Gheorghiu-Dej, Nr. 65, Bucharest C.P. 1-126, Rumania.

388.3   DK
BIL JUL. ceased. a. Palle Fogtdals A-S, Noerre Farmmimagsgade 49, 1364 Copenhagen K, Denmark.

598.2   US   ISSN 0067-8945
BIRD CONTROL SEMINAR. PROCEEDINGS. 1962-1983 (vol.9) triennal. Bowling Green State University, Department of Biological Sciences, Bowling Green, OH 43403.

830   DK   ISSN 0105-2071
BLIXENIANA. 1976-1985 (no.10) a. Karen Blixen Selskabet, Eksp. Dr. Holsts Vej 1, 8230 Aabyhoej, Denmark.

796.95   US
BOATING ALMANAC - FLORIDA. 1977-1985. a. Boating Almanac Co., Inc., 203 McKinsey Rd., Severna Park, MD 21146.

796.95   US
BOATING ALMANAC, VOL. 5-NORTH CAROLINA, SOUTH CAROLINA, GEORGIA. 1978-1985. a. Boating Almanac Co., Inc., 603 McKinsey Rd., Severna Park, MD 21146.

551   PO
BOLETIM MICROSSISMICO. suspended 1973. irreg. Universidade do Porto, Instituto Geofisico, Sierra do Pilar, Villa Nova de Gaia, Portugal.

551.22   PO   ISSN 0006-6109
BOLETIM SISMICO. 1958-1972. a. Universidade do Porto, Instituto Geofisico, Sierra do Pilar, Vila Nova de Gaia, Portugal.

382   UY
BOLETIN DE INFORMACION COMERCIAL. 1972-19?? m. Asociacion Latinoamericana de Integracion, Oficina de Informacion Comercial, Casilla 577, Montevideo, Uruguay.

070.5   UK   ISSN 0142-9523
BOOK DEALERS' AND COLLECTORS' YEAR-BOOK AND DIARY. 1978-1986. a. (back issues avail.) Europa Publications Ltd., 18 Bedford Sq., London WC1V 3JN, England.
    Incorporating: Miniature Book World (ISSN 0143-8743)

070.5   US
BOOK PUBLISHING ANNUAL; highlights, analysis and trends. 1983-1985. a. Bowker Magazine Group, Cahners Magazine Division, 249 W. 17th St., New York, NY 10011.
    Formerly (until 1984): Publishers Weekly Yearbook (ISSN 0000-0469)

070.5   IS   ISSN 0333-6166
BOOKS FROM ISRAEL. discontinued. a. Israel Export Institute, Book and Printing Center, Industry House, 29 Hamered St., P.O. Box 50084, Tel Aviv, Israel.

382   FR   ISSN 0068-0494
BOTTIN INTERNATIONAL. (In 2 vols.) 1895-1986. a. Societe Didot Bottin, 28, rue Docteur Finlay, 75738 Paris Cedex 15, France.

621.381   US   ISSN 0882-0082
BOWKER'S COMPLETE SOURCEBOOK OF PERSONAL COMPUTING. 1983-1986. a. R.R. Bowker Company, Database Publishing Group, 245 W. 17th St., New York, NY 10011.
    Formerly: Bowker/Bantam Complete Sourcebook of Personal Computing.

630   BL
BRAZIL. CONSELHO NACIONAL DE DESENVOLVIMENTO DE PECUARIA. MERCADO ATACADISTA DE GADO E CARNE: ANALISE DA VARIACAO DOS PRECOS. ceased. irreg. Ministerio da Agricultura, Conselho Nacional de Desenvolvimento de Pecuaria, Rio de Janeiro, Brazil.

630 334.683   BL
BRAZIL. INSTITUTO NACIONAL DE COLONIZACAO E REFORMA AGRARIA. ACAO ASSOCIATIVISTA. 1975-1976. irreg. Instituto Nacional de Colonizacao e Reforma Agraria, Palacio do Desenvolvimento 14, SBN 70057 Brasilia, Brazil.

370   BL   ISSN 0068-080X
BRAZIL. INSTITUTO NACIONAL DE ESTUDOS E PESQUISAS EDUCACIONAIS. CONFERENCIA NACIONAL DE EDUCACAO. ANAIS. 1965-19?? irreg. Instituto Nacional de Estudos e Pesquisas Educacionais, Esplanada dos Ministerios, Bloco L, Anexo 1 do MEC, 1 andar, 70047 Brasilia, D.F., Brazil, Brazil.

630 334.683   BL
BRAZIL. MINISTERIO DA AGRICULTURA. DEPARTAMENTO DE ASSISTENCIA AO COOPERATIVISMO. SERIE CONTABILIDADE. ceased. irreg. Ministerio da Agricultura, Departamento de Assistencia ao Cooperativismo, Rua do Carmo 88, Sao Paulo, Brazil.

630 334.683   BL
BRAZIL. MINISTERIO DA AGRICULTURA DEPARTAMENTO DE ASSISTENICA AO COOPERATIVISMO. SERIE INTEGRACAO. ceased. irreg. Ministerio da Agricultura, Departamento de Assistencia ao Cooperativismo, Rua do Carmo 88, Sao Paulo, Brazil.

942   US   ISSN 0068-1105
BRITAIN IN THE WORLD TODAY. 1962-19?? irreg. (reprint service avail. from UMI) Johns Hopkins University Press, 701 W. 40th St., Ste. 275, Baltimore, MD 21211

509   UK   ISSN 0068-1261
BRITISH ANTARCTIC SURVEY. SCIENTIFIC REPORTS. ceased. irreg. British Antarctic Survey, Madingley Rd., Cambridge CB3 OET, England.

631.5 CN
BRITISH COLUMBIA. MINISTRY OF AGRICULTURE AND FOOD. BERRY PRODUCTION GUIDE. ceased 1986. a. Ministry of Agriculture, Publications Office, Parliament Bldg., Victoria, B.C. V8W 2Z7, Canada.
    Formerly: Ministry of Agriculture. Berry Production Guide (ISSN 0706-4306)

380.1 663 UK ISSN 0263-3698
BRITISH DISTILLING INDUSTRY. 1980-198? biennial. Jordan & Sons Ltd., Jordan House, 47 Brunswick Pl., London N1 6EE, England.

380.1 070 UK ISSN 0263-2462
BRITISH NEWSPAPER INDUSTRY. 1978-19??; suspended. biennial. Jordan & Sons Ltd., Jordan House, 47 Brunswick Pl., London N1 6EE, England.

655 011 UK ISSN 0262-9763
BRITISH PAPERBACKS IN PRINT. 1960-19?? a. J. Whitaker & Sons Ltd., 12 Dyott St., London WC1A 1DF, England.
    Formerly (until 1982): Paperbacks in Print (ISSN 0031-1219)

327 UK
BRITISH POLICY IN ASIA: INDIA OFFICE MEMORANDA. ceased 1980 (vol.2) irreg. (microfiche) Mansell Publishing Ltd., 6 All Saints St., London N1 9RL, England

341 UK ISSN 0007-1676
BRITISH PRACTICE IN INTERNATIONAL LAW. 1962-1967. irreg. British Institute of International and Comparative Law, 17 Russell Square, London WC1B 5DR, England.
    Formerly: Contemporary Practice of the United Kingdom in the Field of International Law.

810 US
BROADSIDE CRITICS SERIES. 1971-19?? irreg. Broadside Press, Box 04257, Northwestern Station, Detroit, MI 48204-0257.

350 TI
LE BUDGET TUNISIEN. 1978-1980. a. Dar el Amal d'Edition, de Diffusion, et de Presse, Rue 2 Mars 1934, Tunis, Tunisia.

690 SA
BUILDING INDEX. 1982-1986. a. Avonwold Publishing Co., P.O. Box 52068, Saxonwold, South Africa.
    Formerly: I S A A Architect Directory.

560 IO
BULLETIN OF PREHISTORY/BERITA PRASEJARAH. 1974; ceased after one issue. irreg. National Archaeological Institute of Indonesia, Department of Prehistory - Lembaga Purbakala dan Peninggalan Nasional, Bidang Prasejarah, Jalan Kimia 12, P.O. Box 2533, Jakarta, Indonesia.

574.92 UK ISSN 0068-4198
BULLETINS OF MARINE ECOLOGY. 1939-1980 (vol.8, no.4) irreg. (Natural Environmental Research Council) Institute for Marine Environmental Research, Prospect Place, the Hoe, Plymouth, UK.

572 913 HT
BUREAU NATIONAL D'ETHNOLOGIE. PUBLICATION. 1943-1980. irreg. Bureau National d'Ethnologie, Angle Rue St. Honore et Ave. Magloire Ambroise, B P 915, Port-Au-Prince, Haiti.

301.16 910.03 US
BURRELLE'S BLACK MEDIA DIRECTORY. 1980-1984. biennial. Burrelle's Media Directories, 75 E. Northfield Ave., Livingston, NJ 07039.

301.16 946.406 US
BURRELLE'S HISPANIC MEDIA DIRECTORY. 1980-1984. biennial. Burrelle's Media Directories, 75 E. Northfield Ave., Livingston, NJ 07039.

659.1 US
BURRELLE'S SPECIAL GROUPS MEDIA DIRECTORY. ceased. a. Burrelle's Media Directories, 75 E. Northfield Ave., Livingston, NJ 07039.

301.16 301.412 US
BURRELLE'S WOMEN'S MEDIA DIRECTORY. 1980-1984. biennial. Burrelle's Media Directories, 75 E. Northfield Ave., Livingston, NJ 07039.

691 SW
C B I AARSBERAETTELSE/REPORT OF ACTIVITIES. 1972/73-1983. a. Cement- och Betonginstitutet - Swedish Cement and Concrete Research Institute, S-100 44 Stockholm, Sweden.

133.5 US
C C R S NEWSLETTER. 1977-19?? irreg. Los Angeles Community Church of Religious Science, 838 Fifth Ave., Los Angeles, CA 90005.

631.3 FR ISSN 0249-4779
C E M A G R E F BULLETIN D'INFORMATION. 1957-1986. irreg. (10-12/yr.) Centre National du Machinisme Agricole du Genie Rural, des Eaux et des Forets, Parc de Tourvoie, 92160 Antony, France.
    Formerly: C N E E M A Bulletin d'Information (ISSN 0007-8727)

631.3 FR ISSN 0249-4787
C E M A G R E F ETUDES. 1948-1986. irreg. (10-12/yr.) Centre National du Machinisme Agricole du Genie Rural, des Eaux et des Forets, Parc de Tourvoie, 92160 Antony, France.
    Formerly: C N E E M A Etudes (ISSN 0007-8735)

500 600 UK
C L A I M REPORT TO THE BRITISH LIBRARY AND DEVELOPMENT DEPARTMENT. 1969-1983. irreg. Centre for Library and Information Management, Loughborough University, Loughborough, Leics. LE11 3TU, England.
    Formerly: Cambridge University. Library Management Research Unit. Report to the Office for Scientific and Technical Information.

020 US ISSN 0034-1169
C L R RECENT DEVELOPMENTS. 1957-1986 (vol.14) irreg. Council on Library Resources, Inc., 1785 Massachusetts Ave., N.W., Washington, DC 20036.

615 BL ISSN 0068-4775
CADASTRO BRASILEIRO DE MATERIAS-PRIMAS FARMACEUTICAS, POR PRODUTO, POR FABRICANTE. 1966-19?? a. Associacao Brasileira da Industria Farmaceutica, Av. Beira Mar 262, CEP 20000 Rio de Janeiro, R J, Brazil.

800 CN ISSN 0068-4961
CAHIERS CANADIENS CLAUDEL. 1963-1978; discontinued. irreg. University of Ottawa Press, 603 Cumberland, Ottawa, Ont. K1N 6N5, Canada.

200 133 CN ISSN 0704-7924
CAHIERS DE RECHERCHES EN SCIENCES DE LA RELIGION. 1977-1984. a. (back issues avail.) Editions Bellarmin, 8100 bd. Saint-Laurent, Montreal, Que. H2P 2L9, Canada.
    Formerly: Cahiers du C R S R.

300 CN ISSN 0068-5097
CAHIERS DE SCIENCES SOCIALES. 1963-1981; discontinued. a. University of Ottawa Press, 603 Cumberland, Ottawa, Ont. K1N 6N5, Canada.

200 UK
CALENDARS AND INDEXES TO THE LETTERS AND PAPERS OF THE ARCHBISHOPS OF CANTERBURY IN LAMBETH PALACE LIBRARY. 1975-1980 (vol.3) irreg. Mansell Publishing Ltd., 6 All Saints St., London N1 9RL, England

330.9 US
CALIFORNIA DATA BRIEF. 1977-1986. irreg. (processed) University of California, Berkeley, Institute of Governmental Studies, Berkeley, CA 94720.

630 US
CALIFORNIA FARMLANDS PROJECT. WORKING PAPERS. 1982-1983. irreg. California Institute of Public Affairs, Box 10, Claremont, CA 91711.

622 CN ISSN 0229-8325
CANADA. MINERAL POLICY SECTOR. MINERAL SURVEY. ceased. a. Department of Energy, Mines and Resources, Mineral Policy Sector, Ottawa, Ontario K1A OE4, Canada
    Former titles: Canada. Mineral Development Center. Mineral Survey; Canada. Mineral Resources Branch. Mineral Survey (ISSN 0068-7839)

388 CN ISSN 0382-0939
CANADA. STATISTICS CANADA. FOR-HIRE TRUCKING SURVEY/ENQUETE SUR LE TRANSPORT ROUTIER DE MARCHANDISES POUR COMPTE D'AUTRUI. (Catalogue 53-224) 1970-1983. a. (also avail. in microform from MML) Statistics Canada, Communications Division, 3rd Floor, R.H. Coats Bldg., Ottawa, Ont. K1A 0T6, Canada

338 317 CN ISSN 0712-8762
CANADA. STATISTICS CANADA. SYSTEM OF NATIONAL ACCOUNTS, PROVINCIAL GROSS DOMESTIC PRODUCT BY INDUSTRY. (Catalogue 61-202) 1920-1984. a. (also avail. in microform from MML) Statistics Canada, Communications Division, 3rd Floor, R.H. Coats Bldg., Ottawa, Ont. K1A 0T6, Canada
    Formerly: Canada. Statistics Canada. System of National Accounts, Domestic Product by Industry/ Systeme de Comptabilite Nationale. Produit Interieur par Industrie: Releve de la Production (ISSN 0068-7227)

614 618 CN ISSN 0700-138X
CANADA. STATISTICS CANADA. THERAPEUTIC ABORTIONS/AVORTEMENTS THERAPEUTIQUES. (Catalog 82-211) 1972-1985. a. (also avail. in microform from MML) Statistics Canada, Communications Division, 3rd Floor, R.H. Coats Bldg., Ottawa, Ont. K1A 0T6, Canada

378.1 CN ISSN 0383-2406
CANADIAN CAMPUS CAREER DIRECTORY. 1968-1984. a. Whitsed Publishing Ltd., 47 Lake Shore Rd., E., Box 190, Missisauga, ON L6S 4L7, Canada.
    Former titles: Canadian Campus; Campus (Toronto) (ISSN 0045-4133)

282 CN
CANADIAN CATHOLIC HISTORICAL ASSOCIATION. ANNUAL REPORT. ceased 1975. a. Canadian Catholic Historical Association, c/o Rev. Edward Jackman, 355 Church Street, Toronto, Ont. L5B 1Z8, Canada.

633.1 CN
CANADIAN CORN. published only once. irreg. Grains Council, 760-360 Main St., Winnipeg, Man. R3C 3Z3, Canada.

651 CN
CANADIAN OFFICE REDBOOK. ceased 1986. a. Whitsed Publishing Ltd., 47 Lake Shore Rd., E., Box 190, Missisauga, ON LYS 4L7, Canada.

614 CN ISSN 0319-2644
CANADIAN PUBLIC HEALTH ASSOCIATION. PROCEEDINGS OF THE ANNUAL MEETING. 1974, published only once. irreg. Canadian Public Health Association, 1335 Carling Ave., Suite 210, Ottawa, Ont. K1Z 1E5, Canada.

624 CN ISSN 0375-605X
CANADIAN ROCK MECHANICS SYMPOSIUM. PROCEEDINGS. 1962-19?? irreg. Canadian Institute of Mining and Metallurgy, 400-1130 Sherbrooke St. W., Montreal, Quebec H3A 2M8, Canada.

792 CN ISSN 0226-5125
CANADIAN THEATRE CHECKLIST. ceased. a. York University, Faculty of Administrative Studies, c/o Prof. Joseph Green, 4700 Keele St., Downsview, Ont. M3J 1P3, Canada.
    Formerly: Checklist of Canadian Theatres (ISSN 0705-5064)

929 AT ISSN 0314-7894
CANDY FAMILY HISTORY NEWSLETTER. 1977-19??; suspended. irreg. (also avail. in microfiche) Candy Family Group, 147 Seventh Ave., Royston Park, S.A. 5070, Australia.

620 NZ ISSN 0069-0201
CANTERBURY ENGINEERING JOURNAL. 1970-19??, discontinued. irreg. no.5, 1975. University of Canterbury, School of Engineering, Private Bag, Christchurch, New Zealand.

371.42 US
CAREER RESOURCE DIRECTORY. ceased. irreg. Association for School, College and University Staffing, 301 S. Swift Rd., Addison, IL 60101-1499.

CESSATIONS

267   IT   ISSN 0069-0554
CARITAS INTERNATIONALIS.
INTERNATIONAL YEARBOOKS. 1965-19?? a.
Caritas Internationalis, Piazza San Calisto 16, 00153 Rome, Italy.

557   CN   ISSN 0069-0619
CARLETON UNIVERSITY, OTTAWA.
DEPARTMENT OF GEOLOGY. GEOLOGICAL PAPERS. 1958-1979. irreg. Carleton University, Department of Geology, Ottawa, Ont. K1S 5B6, Canada.

070 011   EC
CATALOGO COLECTIVO DE PUBLICACIONES PERIODICAS. ceased 1978. irreg. Superintendencia de Bancos, Biblioteca, 10 de Agosto 251, Casilla 424, Quito, Ecuador.

547.2   US   ISSN 0197-534X
CATALYSIS IN ORGANIC SYNTHESES; proceedings of conference. 1980, published only once. a. Academic Press, Inc., Orlando, FL 32887.

338.9   CJ
CAYMAN ISLANDS. DEPARTMENT OF FINANCE AND DEVELOPMENT. ESTIMATES OF GROSS DOMESTIC PRODUCT AND RELATED AGGREGATES. 1972, published only once. irreg. Department of Finance and Development, Grand Cayman Island, Cayman Islands, B.W.I.

320   US
CENTER FOR NATIONAL POLICY REVIEW. ANNUAL REPORT. ceased. a. Center for National Policy Review, 733 15th St, N.W., Ste. 1026, Washington, DC 20005.
    Formerly: Catholic University of America. School of Law. Center for National Policy Review. Annual Report.

382   FR   ISSN 0071-836X
CENTRE NATIONAL DU COMMERCE EXTERIEUR. ANNUAIRE. 1966-1985. a. Centre National du Commerce Exterieur, 10 Av. d'Iena, 75016 Paris, France.

374.013   UY
CENTRO INTERAMERICANO DE INVESTIGACION Y DOCUMENTACION SOBRE FORMACION PROFESIONAL. CUADRO COMPARATIVO Y FICHAS DESCRIPTIVAS. 1970-1978. a. Centro Interamericano de Investigacion y Documentacion Sobre Formacion Profesional, Avda. Uruguay 1238, Casilla de Correo 1761, Montevideo, Uruguay.

616.96   AG
CENTRO PANAMERICANO DE ZOONOSIS. BOLETIN INFORMATIVO. ENFERMEDADES TRANSMITIDAS POR ALIMENTOS EN LAS AMERICAS. 1974-19?? a. Centro Panamericano de Zoonosis, Casilla 3092 C.C., 1000 Buenos Aires, Argentina.
    Supersedes in part (since 1978): Centro Panamericano de Zoonosis. Boletin Informativo.

616.998   AG
CENTRO PANAMERICANO DE ZOONOSIS. BOLETIN INFORMATIVO. HIDATIDOSIS EN LAS AMERICAS. 1974-19?? a. Centro Panamericano de Zoonosis, Casilla 3092 Correo Central, 1000 Buenos Aires, Argentina.
    Supersedes in part (since 1978): Centro Panamericano de Zoonosis. Boletin Informativo.

616.998   AG
CENTRO PANAMERICANO DE ZOONOSIS. BOLETIN INFORMATIVO. LEPTOSPIROSIS EN LAS AMERICAS. 1974-19?? a. Centro Panamericano de Zoonosis, Casilla 3092 Correo Central, 1000 Buenos Aires, Argentina.
    Supersedes in part (since 1978): Centro Panamericano de Zoonosis. Boletin Informativo.

616.96   AG
CENTRO PANAMERICANO DE ZOONOSIS. BOLETIN INFORMATIVO. TUBERCULOSIS EN LAS AMERICAS. 1974-19?? a. Centro Panamericano de Zoonosis, Casilla 3092 Correo Central, 1000 Buenos Aires, Argentina.
    Supersedes in part (since 1978): Centro Panamericano de Zoonosis. Boletin Informativo.

666   US
CERAMICS AND GLASS: SCIENCE AND TECHNOLOGY SERIES. 1970-1974. irreg. Marcel Dekker, Inc., 270 Madison Ave., New York, NY 10016.
    Formerly: Ceramics and Glass Series (ISSN 0069-2239)

658.182   US   ISSN 0069-2395
CHAIN STORE AGE SUPERMARKET SALES MANUAL. (Part of July issue of Chain Store Age: Supermarket Edition) 1934-19?? a. Lebhar-Friedman, Inc., 425 Park Ave., New York, NY 10022.

100   US
CHARLES S. PEIRCE NEWSLETTER. 1973-1984. a. Texas Tech University, Institute for Studies in Pragmaticism, Library, Rm. 304-K, Lubbock, TX 79409.

015   US
CHECKLIST OF KENTUCKY STATE PUBLICATIONS. 1962-19?? a. (also avail. in microfilm) Department of Library and Archives, Division of Archives and Records, Box 537, Frankfort, KY 40602.

540   UK
CHEMFACTS: SCANDINAVIA. 1977-19??; suspended. a. Chemical Intelligence Services, 39A Bowling Green Lane, London EC1R 0BJ, England.

660   UK
CHEMICAL INDUSTRY YEAR BOOK. 1981-198?; suspended. a. Chemical Intelligence Services, 39A Bowling Green Lane, London EC1R 0BJ, England.

660   US
CHEMICAL PROCESSING & ENGINEERING: AN INTERNATIONAL SERIES. 1975-1977. irreg. Marcel Dekker, Inc., 270 Madison Ave., New York, NY 10016.

660   US
CHEMSPHERE AMERICAS. 1968-1986. irreg. Exxon Chemical Americas, Box 3272, Houston, TX 77001.
    Former titles: Exxon Chemicals Magazine; Enjay Magazine (ISSN 0013-8541)

811   US   ISSN 0737-5182
CHIAROSCURO. 1976-1986 (vol.586) a. Ithaca House, Box 6484, Ithaca, NY 14851.

330.9   CL
CHILE. OFICINA DE PLANIFICACION NACIONAL. INFORME ECONOMICO ANUAL. 1974-1982. a. Oficina de Planificacion Nacional, Biblioteca, Seccion Publicaciones, Ahumada 48, Casilla 9140, Santiago, Chile.

368   CN   ISSN 0711-3048
CHOOSING LIFE. 1980-1985. a. Stone & Cox Ltd., 323-366 Adelaide St. E., Toronto, Ont. M5A 3X9, Canada.

378.0025   US   ISSN 0276-0363
CHRONICLE GUIDE FOR TRANSFERS. ceased. biennial. Chronicle Guidance Publications, Inc., Box 1190, Moravia, NY 13118.
    Formerly (until 1981): Chronicle College Counseling for Transfers (ISSN 0160-9300)

367   US
CIRCLES OF FRIENDS; 200 new ways to make friends in Washington, D.C. and Baltimore. 1976-19?? a. Mail Order USA, Box 19083, Washington, DC 20036.

378   US   ISSN 0077-894X
CITY COLLEGE PAPERS; contributions to knowledge in all fields originating in lectures, research and scholarship at the City College of New York. 1965-1970; suspended. irreg. City College of New York, Library, Convent Ave. & 138th St., New York, NY 10031.

700 821   UK
CODEX BANDITO. 1981-1984 (no.6) irreg. Outcrowd, 3 Pleasant Villas, 189 Kent St., Mereworth, Maidstone, Kent ME18 5QN, England.

616.8 574.4   US   ISSN 0276-4695
COLD SPRING HARBOR REPORTS IN THE NEUROSCIENCES. 1980-198? irreg. (back issues avail.) Cold Spring Harbor Laboratory, Box 100, Cold Spring Harbor, NY 11724.

380   SP
COLECCION TEMAS DE AHORRO Y CREDITO. ceased. irreg. Confederacion Espanola de Cajas de Ahorros, Fondo para la Investigacion Economica y Social, Juan Hurtado de Mendoza 14, Madrid 16, Spain.

331   CN   ISSN 0229-4958
COLLECTIVE AGREEMENT EXPIRATION IN NOVA SCOTIA. discontinued 1985. a. Department of Labour and Manpower, Box 697, Halifax, N.S. B3J 2T8, Canada.

639.2   US   ISSN 0588-4462
COLORADO FISHERIES RESEARCH REVIEW. 1964-1981 (no.10) triennial. (back issues avail.) Division of Wildlife, 317 W. Prospect, Ft. Collins, CO 80526.
    Formerly: Fisheries Research Review (ISSN 0277-7436)

382   BL
COMERCIO EXTERIOR DO BRASIL; importacao. 1972-1980. a. Secretaria da Receita Federal, Coordenacao do Sistema de Informacoes Economico-Fiscais, Esplanada dos Ministerios, Bloco 5, 70079 Brasilia D.F., Brazil.

616.99   US   ISSN 0194-1666
COMMENTARIES ON RESEARCH IN BREAST DISEASE. 1980-1983 (vol.3) irreg. Alan R. Liss, Inc., 41 E. 11th St., New York, NY 10003.

380   EI
COMMISSION OF THE EUROPEAN COMMUNITIES. ENERGY SITUATION IN THE COMMUNITY. 1961-1984, discontinued. a. Office for Official Publications of the European Communities, P.O. Box 1003, L-2985 Luxembourg, Luxembourg
    Former titles: Commission of the European Communities. Conjoncture Energetique dans la Communaute (ISSN 0531-304X); Until 1962: European Coal and Steel Community. High Authority. Rapport sur la Situation Energetique de la Communaute et Perspective d'Approvisionnement dans la Communaute en 1962.

630 338.1   EI   ISSN 0069-6765
COMMISSION OF THE EUROPEAN COMMUNITIES. STUDIES: AGRICULTURAL SERIES. 1960-19??, discontinued. irreg. Office for Official Publications of the European Communities, P.O. Box 1003, L-2985 Luxembourg, Luxembourg

338.5   EI
COMMISSION OF THE EUROPEAN COMMUNITIES. STUDIES: COMPETITION-APPROXIMATION OF LEGISLATION. 1966-1983, discontinued. irreg. Office for Official Publications of the European Communities, P.O. Box 1003, L-2985 Luxembourg, Luxembourg
    Formerly: Commission of the European Communities. Etudes: Serie Concurrence-Rapprochement des Legislations (ISSN 0069-6706)

330   EI
COMMISSION OF THE EUROPEAN COMMUNITIES. STUDIES: DEVELOPMENT SERIES. 1967-1981, discontinued. irreg. Office for Official Publications of the European Communities, P.O. Box 1003, L-2985 Luxembourg, Luxembourg
    Formerly: Commission of the European Communities. Etudes: Serie Aide au Developpement (ISSN 0069-6692)

330   EI   ISSN 0069-6773
COMMISSION OF THE EUROPEAN COMMUNITIES. STUDIES: ECONOMIC AND FINANCIAL SERIES. 1962-1980, discontinued. irreg. Office for Official Publications of the European Communities, P.O. Box 1003, L-2985 Luxembourg, Luxembourg

330   EI
COMMISSION OF THE EUROPEAN COMMUNITIES. STUDIES: ENERGY SERIES. 1968-1981, discontinued. irreg. Office for Official Publications of the European Communities, P.O. Box 1003, L-2985 Luxembourg, Luxembourg
    Formerly: Commission of the European Communities. Etudes: Serie Energie (ISSN 0069-6714)

338 EI
COMMISSION OF THE EUROPEAN
COMMUNITIES. STUDIES: INDUSTRY SERIES.
discontinued. irreg. Office for Official Publications
of the European Communities, P.O. Box 1003, L-
2985 Luxembourg, Luxembourg
 Formerly: Commission of the European
Communities. Etudes: Serie Industrie (ISSN 0591-
1737)

385 EI ISSN 0069-679X
COMMISSION OF THE EUROPEAN
COMMUNITIES. STUDIES: TRANSPORT
SERIES. 1966-1982, discontinued. irreg. Office for
Official Publications of the European Communities,
P.O. Box 1003, L-2985 Luxembourg, Luxembourg

329 US ISSN 0163-3023
COMMONSENSE; a Republican journal of thought
and opinion. 1978-19??; discontinued. irreg.
Republican National Committee, Political/Research
Division, 310 First St., S.E., Washington, DC
20003.

769.56 UK ISSN 0142-7830
COMMONWEALTH CATALOGUE OF QUEEN
ELIZABETH STAMPS. 1952-19??, discontinued.
irreg. Urch, Harris & Co. Ltd., Clifton Heights,
Triangle West, Bristol BS8 1BQ, England.

910 UK
COMMONWEALTH FACT SHEETS. ceased. irreg.
Commonwealth Institute, Kensington High St.,
London W8 6NQ, England.

320.531 US ISSN 0193-3469
COMMUNIST. 1976-1979 (no.5); discontinued. irreg.
(Revolutionary Communist Party) R C P
Publications, Inc., Box 3486, Merchandise Mart,
Chicago, IL 60654.

330 370 US
COMMUNITY COMPUTER CENTERS.
NEWSLETTER. 1983-1986. irreg. (4-6/yr.)
Community Computer Centers, N.W. 258 Sunrise
Dr., Pullman, WA 99163.

900 300 US
COMPARATIVE FRONTIER STUDIES. 1975-1984
(no.19); suspended. irreg. University of Oklahoma,
Department of History, 455 W. Lindsey, Rm. 406,
Norman, OK 73019.

001.6 621.381 US ISSN 0000-0779
COMPUTER BOOKS AND SERIALS IN PRINT.
1984-1986. a. R.R. Bowker Company, Database
Publishing Group, 245 W. 17th St., New York, NY
10011.

355 US
CONFEDERATE REGIMENTAL HISTORIES.
1982-1987 (no.12, Jan.) irreg. (back issues avail.)
Confederate Publishing Co., Box 1712, University,
AL 35486.

636 US
CONFERENCE ON ARTIFICIAL
INSEMINATION AND EMBRYO TRANSFER
OF BEEF CATTLE. PROCEEDINGS. 1967-1986.
a. National Association of Animal Breeders, 401
Bernadette St., Box 1033, Columbia, MO 65205.
 Formerly: Conference on Artifical Insemination
of Beef Cattle. Proceedings (ISSN 0084-9146)

378 UK ISSN 0260-3853
CONSPECTUS FOR...OF FURTHER EDUCATION
IN THE INNER AND OUTER LONDON
REGION. 1978-19?? a. Civil Service Council for
Further Education, 28 Northumberland Ave.,
London WC2N, England.

640.73 US
CONSUMER PROTECTION DIRECTORY. 1973-
1975 (2nd edt.) irreg. Marquis Who's Who, Inc.,
200 E. Ohio St., Chicago, IL 60611.
 Supersedes in part: Directory of Consumer
Protection and Environmental Agencies.

676 US
CONTAINER NEWS WORLDWIDE
INTERMODAL DIRECTORY. 1971; never
published. a. Communication Channels, Inc., 6255
Barfield Rd., Atlanta, GA 30328.

338.4 IT ISSN 0069-9764
CONVEGNO NAZIONALE DEI
COMMERCIANTI DE MOBILI. ATTI E
RELAZIONI. suspended. a. Camera di Commercio,
Industria, Artigianato e Agricoltura di Pesaro, Corso
XI Settembre 116, 61100 Pesaro, Italy.

334 US
COOPERATIVES & THE LAW; annual proceedings.
1974-19?? a. University of Wisconsin-Extension,
University Center for Cooperatives, Lowell Hall,
610 Langdon St., Madison, WI 53706.

628 614.7 US ISSN 0065-4604
CORNELL AGRICULTURAL WASTE
MANAGEMENT CONFERENCE.
PROCEEDINGS. discontinued. New York State
College of Agriculture and Life Sciences, Cornell
University, Ithaca, NY 14853.
 Formerly: Cornell University Conference on
Agricultural Waste Management.

950 US ISSN 0070-0215
CORNELL UNIVERSITY. SOUTHEAST ASIA
PROGRAM. DATA PAPERS. 1951-1982. irreg.
(also avail. in microform from UMI) Cornell
University, Southeast Asia Program, 120 Uris Hall,
Ithaca, NY 14853.

312 CR
COSTA RICA. REVISTA DE ESTUDIOS Y
ESTADISTICAS. SERIE DEMOGRAFICA. 1961-
19??; discontinued. irreg. Direccion General de
Estadistica y Censos, Apdo. 10163, San Jose, Costa
Rica.

913 016 US ISSN 0070-0770
COUNCIL FOR OLD WORLD ARCHAEOLOGY:
C O W A SURVEYS AND BIBLIOGRAPHIES.
AREA 5: CENTRAL EUROPE. 1959-19?? irreg.
Council for Old World Archaeology, Boston
University, 232 Bay State Rd., Boston, MA 02215.

350 US ISSN 0099-006X
COUNCIL OF STATE GOVERNMENTS.
SOUTHERN LEGISLATIVE CONFERENCE.
SUMMARY, ANNUAL MEETING. 1977-19?? a.
Council of State Governments, Southern Legislative
Conference, 3384 Peachtree Rd. N.E., Room 830,
Atlanta, GA 30326.

352 US
COUNCIL ON MUNICIPAL PERFORMANCE.
ANNUAL REPORT. 1973-19?? a. Council on
Municipal Performance, 55 W. 44th St., 6th Fl.,
New York, NY 10036-6699.

365 US ISSN 0735-3928
CRIME AND JUSTICE. 1972-1974. irreg. (back
issues avail.) A M S Press, Inc., 56 E. 13th St., New
York, NY 10003.

300 SP
CUADERNOS CANARIOS DE CIENCIAS
SOCIALES. ceased. irreg. Confederacion Espanola
de Cajas de Ahorros, Alfredo Calderon 61, Las
Palmas de Gran Canaria, Spain.

155 US
CURRENT AUDIOVISUALS FOR MENTAL
HEALTH EDUCATION. ceased with 2nd edt.,
1979. irreg. Marquis Who's Who, Inc., 200 E. Ohio
St., Chicago, IL 60611.

331.11 CN ISSN 0382-1102
CURRENT LABOUR FORCE STATISTICS FOR
NOVA SCOTIA. 1966-1985. a. Department of
Labour and Manpower, Research Division, Box 697,
Halifax, N.S. B3J 2T8, Canada.

500 600 IS ISSN 0301-4657
CURRENT RESEARCH AND DEVELOPMENT
PROJECTS IN ISRAEL: NATURAL SCIENCES
AND TECHNOLOGY. ceased. irreg. (National
Council for Research and Development) National
Center of Scientific and Technological Information,
Box 20125, Tel-Aviv, Israel.
 Formerly: Directory of Current Research in
Israel: Physical and Life Sciences (ISSN 0070-539Y)

616.15 US ISSN 0190-1486
CURRENT TOPICS IN HEMATOLOGY. 1978-198?
(vol.5) a. Alan R. Liss, Inc., 41 E. 11th St., New
York, NY 10003.

616.4 US ISSN 0094-6761
CURRENT TOPICS IN MOLECULAR
ENDOCRINOLOGY. 1974-19?? irreg. Plenum
Publishing Corp., 233 Spring St., New York, NY
10013.

914.2 UK
CYCLISTS TOURING CLUB HANDBOOK. 1962-
19?? a. Ramblers Association, 1-5 Wandsworth Rd.,
London SW8 2LJ, England
 Former titles: Ramblers and Cyclists Bed and
Breakfast Guide & Ramblers Association Bed and
Breakfast Guide.

338 CY
CYPRUS. DEPARTMENT OF STATISTICS AND
RESEARCH. INDUSTRIAL PRODUCTION
SURVEY. discontinued. a. Department of Statistics
and Research, Ministry of Finance, Nicosia, Cyprus.
 Formerly: Cyprus. Department of Statistics and
Research. Annual Industrial Production Survey
(ISSN 0590-4854)

388.1 312.4 CY ISSN 0574-8399
CYPRUS. DEPARTMENT OF STATISTICS AND
RESEARCH. MOTOR VEHICLES AND ROAD
ACCIDENTS. 1960-19??; discontinued. a.
Department of Statistics and Research, Ministry of
Finance, Nicosia, Cyprus.

387.5 CY ISSN 0070-2439
CYPRUS. DEPARTMENT OF STATISTICS AND
RESEARCH. SHIPPING STATISTICS. 1954-19??;
discontinued. a. Department of Statistics and
Research, Ministry of Finance, Nicosia, Cyprus.
 Supersedes in part: Cyprus. Department of
Statistics and Research. Shipping and Aviation
Statistics; Which was formerly: Cyprus. Department
of Statistics and Research. Statistics of Imports,
Exports and Shipping.

331.2 312 CY ISSN 0253-8660
CYPRUS. DEPARTMENT OF STATISTICS AND
RESEARCH. WAGES, SALARIES AND HOURS
OF WORK. discontinued. a. Department of
Statistics and Research, Ministry of Finance,
Nicosia, Cyprus.

614 US ISSN 0160-1504
D I S C U S FACTS BOOK. ceased 1982. a. Distilled
Spirits Council of the United States, Inc., 1250 Eye
St., N.W., Washington, DC 20005.

637 UK ISSN 0144-5251
DAIRYMAN'S YEARBOOK. 1978-19??; suspended.
a. National Dairymen's Association, 19 Cornwall
Terrace, London NW1 4QP, England.

793 792 US ISSN 0886-3954
DANCE RESEARCH ANNUAL. 1968-1987. a. (back
issues avail.) Congress on Research in Dance,
Dance and Dance Education Department, New
York University, 35 W. 4th St., New York, NY
10003.
 Formerly: C O R D Research Annual.

028.5 UK
DANGERMOUSE ANNUAL. ceased 1986. a.
Independent Television Books Ltd., 247 Tottenham
Court Rd., London W1P 0AU, England.

531.64 DK
DANMARKS TEKNISKE BIBLIOTEK. UDDRAG.
1982-1985. a. (Danmarks Tekniske Bibliotek -
National Technological Library of Denmark)
Bibliotekscentralen, Telegrafvej 5, DK-2750
Ballerup, Denmark.
 Former titles: Uddrag af Energilitteratur paa
Danmarks Tekniske bibliotek, Soenderborg Tekniske
Bibliotek, Aarhus Tekniske Bibliotek (ISSN 0108-
402X) & Uddrag af Energilitteratur paa Danmarks
Tekniske Bibliotek (ISSN 0108-528X)

700 DK ISSN 0109-4165
DANSK KUNST. 1984-1986. a. (Kunstbogklubben)
Fogtdals Blade A-S, Noerre Farimagsgade 49, 1364
Copenhagen K, Denmark.

614.7 GW ISSN 0170-608X
DATEN UND DOKUMENTE ZUM
UMWELTSCHUTZ/DATA AND DOCUMENTS
ABOUT ENVIRONMENT PROTECTION. 1972-
1985. irreg. Universitaet Hohenheim,
Dokumentationsstelle, Paracelsusstr. 2, Postfach 70
05 62, 7000 Stuttgart 70, W. Germany (B.R.D.)

CESSATIONS

677 US ISSN 0070-2943
DAVISON'S KNIT GOODS TRADE. 1891-19?? a. Davison Publishing Co., Inc., Box 477, Ridgewood, NJ 07451.

808.8 US
DELIRIUM. 1975-1979 (no.415) a. Libra Press, Box 341, Wataga, IL 61488.

910 DK ISSN 0108-0504
DENMARK. GEOGRAFISK MAGASIN. ceased. irreg. Aarhus Universitet, Geografisk Institut, Vennelyst Blvd. 8, 8000 Aarhus C, Denmark.

628 016 IS ISSN 0011-9172
DESALINATION ABSTRACTS. 1966-1985. q. (tabloid format) (National Council for Research and Development) National Center of Scientific and Technological Information, Box 20125, Tel Aviv, Israel.

309 MX ISSN 0011-9199
DESARROLLO; estudios sobre estructuracion social. 1965-19?? irreg. Instituto Mexicano de Estudios Sociales, Av. Cuahtemoc 1486, Mexico, D.F., Mexico.

622 BL ISSN 0101-658X
DESTAQUES. 1974-19?? irreg. Ministerio das Minas e Energia, Centro de Documentacao, Esplanada dos Ministerios, Bloco J, 7 Andar, 70056 Brasilia DF, Brazil.

791.53 GW ISSN 0070-4490
DEUTSCHES INSTITUT FUER PUPPENSPIEL. FORSCHUNG UND LEHRE. 1964-1984. irreg. Deutsches Institut fuer Puppenspiel, Hattinerstr. 467, 4630 Bochum, W. Germany (B.R.D.)

330 CN ISSN 0708-2533
DEVINDEX; index to literature on third world economic and social development. 1976-1984. a. (also avail. in microfiche) International Development Research Centre, Box 8500, Ottawa, Ont. K1G 3H9, Canada.
   Formerly: Devindex Canada.

813.01 CN ISSN 0702-8520
DIME BAG: FICTION ISSUE. 1977-19?? irreg. Glendon College, 2275 Bayview Ave., Toronto, Ont. M4N 3M6, Canada.

378.1 US ISSN 0092-8526
DIRECTORY LISTING CURRICULUMS OFFERED IN THE COMMUNITY COLLEGES OF PENNSYLVANIA. 1967-19?? irreg. Department of Education, Box 911, Harrisburg, PA 17126.

362.1 CN ISSN 0707-0047
DIRECTORY OF LIFESTYLE CHANGE SERVICES. 1978-1983. irreg. University of British Columbia, School of Physical Education and Recreation, Lifestyle Referral Project, Vancouver, B.C. V6T 1W5, Canada.

674 CN
DIRECTORY OF MANUFACTURERS OF LUMBER, PLYWOOD, AND BUILDING MATERIALS MADE IN B.C. ceased 1981. irreg. Ministry of Economic Development, Parliament Bldgs., Victoria, B.C. V8V 1X4, Canada.

371.42 US
DIRECTORY OF PUBLIC SERVICE INTERNSHIPS; opportunities for the graduate, post graduate and mid-career professional. 1974-19?? biennial. National Society for Internships and Experiential Education, 122 St. Mary's St., Raleigh, NC 27605.

070.5 US ISSN 0275-3820
DIRECTORY OF PUBLISHING OPPORTUNITIES IN JOURNALS AND PERIODICALS. 1971-1981 (5th edt.) irreg. Marquis Who's Who, Inc., 200 E. Ohio St., Chicago, IL 60611.
   Former titles: Directory of Publishing Opportunities; Directory of Scholarly and Research Publishing Opportunities (ISSN 0070-623X)

328.38 US ISSN 0146-0323
DIRECTORY OF REGISTERED LOBBYISTS AND LOBBYIST LEGISLATION. 1973-1981 (5th edt.) irreg. Marquis Who's Who, Inc., 200 E. Ohio St., Chicago, IL 60611.
   Formerly: Directory of Registered Federal and State Lobbyists (ISSN 0092-1874)

500 IS ISSN 0334-3197
DIRECTORY OF RESEARCH INSTITUTES AND INDUSTRIAL LABORATORIES IN ISRAEL. 1962-1979. irreg. National Center of Scientific and Technological Information, Box 20125, Tel-Aviv, Israel.
   Formerly: Directory of Research Institutes and Industrial Research Units in Israel (ISSN 0334-2875)

340 396 US
DIRECTORY OF WOMEN LAW GRADUATES AND ATTORNEYS IN THE U.S.A. (In 5 vols.) 1972-19?? irreg. Ford Associates, 824 E. Seventh St., Auburn, IN 46706.
   Formerly (until 1977): Directory of Women Attorneys in the United States (ISSN 0092-1416)

053.1 GW ISSN 0173-007X
DISKURS; Bremer Beitraege zu Wissenschaft und Gesellschaft. 1979-1985. irreg. (back issues avail.) Universitaet Bremen, Bibliothekstr., Postfach 330440, D-2800 Bremen 33, W. Germany (B.R.D.)

384.5 SG
DISOO. 1969-1973. irreg. Office de Radiodiffusion-Television du Senegal (ORTS), 58 Bd. de la Republique, Dakar, Senegal.

634.9 IS
DIVISION OF FORESTRY RESEARCH. LEAFLET. 1956-1985. irreg. (back issues avail.) Division of Forestry, Agricultural Research Division, 42805 Ilanot, Lev Hasharon, Israel.

700 US
DOCUMENTS OF MODERN ART. ceased. irreg. Wittenborn and Co., 1018 Madison Ave., New York, NY 10021.

946.04 SP
DOMESTIC TOURISM STATISTICS. ceased. a. World Tourism Organization, OMT-Capitan Haya 42, 28020 Madrid, Spain.

919.04 AT ISSN 0729-5936
DOMESTIC TRAVEL IN QUEENSLAND. 1979-1986. a. Queensland Tourist and Travel Corporation, Research and Development Division, 307 Queen St., G.P.O. Box 328, Brisbane, Qld. 4001, Australia.

133 US
DOORWAYS TO THE MIND. 1973-19?? irreg. (Mind Development Association) Aries Productions, Inc., Box 29396, Sappington, MO 63126.
   Formerly: Pathways (Creve Coeur)

301 CN
DOSSIERS BEAUX-JEUX. 1976-1983. irreg. Editions Bellarmin, 8100 Bd. Saint-Laurent, Montreal, Que. H2P 2L9, Canada.

011 UK
DUMBARTON OAKS BIBLIOGRAPHIES; based on "Byzantinische Zeitschrift". 1973-1982. irreg. (Dumbarton Oaks Center for Byzantine Studies, US) Mansell Publishing Ltd., 6 All Saints St., London N1 9RL, England

372.6 BE
E B I C BANKS. ANNUAL REVIEW. ceased 1985. a. (European Banks International) Ebic S.A., 100 bd. du Souverain, 1170 Brussels, Belgium.

382 US
E C UPDATE. (European Community) 1982-198?; discontinued. irreg. (back issues avail.) United States Council for International Business, 1212 Ave. of the Americas, New York, NY 10036.

370 US
E R I C CLEARINGHOUSE ON TEACHER EDUCATION. BULLETIN. 1977-1985. irreg. (reprint service avail. from UMI,EDR) American Association of Colleges for Teachers Education, E R I C Clearinghouse on Teacher Education, One Dupont Circle, Ste. 610, Washington, DC 20036.
   Formerly: E R I C Clearinghouse on Teacher Education. Quarterly Information Bulletin.

382 BE
EAST-WEST TRADE YEARBOOK. 1978-1986, suspended. a. East-West S.P.R.L., 10 bd. Saint Lazare, 1210 Brussels, Belgium.

330 AT ISSN 0814-5504
ECONOMIC GROWTH OF THE AUSTRALIAN STATES. 1982-1985. a. Coopers & Lybrand W, Box 1815, North Sydney NSW 2060, Australia.

338.1 US ISSN 0070-8615
ECONOMIC QUESTIONS FOR ILLINOIS AGRICULTURE. 1969-1971 (Jan.) irreg. University of Illinois at Urbana-Champaign, Cooperative Extension Service, Urbana, IL 61801.

338.1 NZ ISSN 0111-1108
ECONOMIC REVIEW OF NEW ZEALAND AGRICULTURE. (Supplement to: Agricultural Economist) 1974-19??, discontinued. a. Ministry of Agriculture and Fisheries, Economic Division, Private Bag, Wellington, New Zealand.

370 FR
EDUCATION AND CULTURE. SECTION 3: OUT-OF-SCHOOL EDUCATION. 1963-198? irreg. Council of Europe, Council for Cultural Co-Operation, Publications in Section, Strasbourg, France
   Formerly (until 1979): Education in Europe. Section 3: Out-of-School Education (ISSN 0070-9204)

011 AT ISSN 0816-6773
EDUCATION DEPARTMENT OF VICTORIA. TEXTBOOKS. ceased. biennial. Education Department of Victoria, Materials Production, Curriculum Branch, 525 Collins St., Melbourne, Vic. 3000, Australia.

155 US
EDUCATION FOR HEALTH: THE SELECTIVE GUIDE. 1973; published only once. biennial. National Center for Health Education, 30 E. 29th St., New York, NY 10016.
   Formerly: Selective Guide to Audiovisuals for Mental Health and Family Life Education; Supersedes in part: Selective Guide to Materials on Mental Health and Family Life Education; Which was formerly titled: Information Resources Center for Mental Health and Family Hygiene. I R C Recommends.

370 016 US
EDUCATION INFORMATION GUIDE SERIES. 1978-19?? irreg. Gale Research Company, Book Tower, Detroit, MI 48226.

370.196 UK
EDUCATIONAL INTERNATIONAL. 1969-19?? a. Central Bureau for Educational Visits and Exchanges, Seymour Mens House, Seymour News, London W1H 9PE, England.
   Formed by the merger of: Education Exchange (ISSN 0046-1490) & Higher Education Exchange (ISSN 0305-3253)

621.31 US
ELECTRICAL CONTACTS. 1953-19?? a. (I E E E, Components, Hybrids, and Manufacturing Technology Society) Institute of Electrical and Electronics Engineers, Inc., 345 E. 47th St., New York, NY 10017

910.202 US
EMERALD SEAS. 1981-198? a. (In Cruise Network) T L Enterprises, Inc., 29901 Agoura Rd., Agoura, CA 91301.

331 CY
EMPLOYMENT, OUTPUT AND CAPITAL FORMATION IN THE INDUSTRIAL SECTOR. 1976-1984; discontinued. a. Ministry of Finance, Department of Statistics and Research, Nicosia, Cyprus.

621 US
ENERGY DIRECTORY. 1973-1983. irreg. E I C Intelligence, Inc., 48 W. 38 St., New York, NY 10018.

011 531.64 US
ENERGY FROM THE WIND - ANNOTATED BIBLIOGRAPHY. 1975-19?? irreg. (looseleaf format; back issues avail.) Colorado State University, College of Engineering, Solar Energy Applications Laboratory, Foothills Campus, Fort Collins, CO 80523.

720 309   US
ENVIRONMENTAL DESIGN PERSPECTIVES;
  viewpoints on the profession, education and
  research. (Subseries of: Man-Environment Systems -
  Focus Series) 1972-19?? irreg? Association for the
  Study of Man-Environment Relations, Box 57,
  Orangeburg, NY 10962.

574.192   US
ENZYMOLOGY SERIES. ceased 1975. irreg. Marcel
  Dekker, Inc., 270 Madison Ave., New York, NY
  10016.

330   DK
ERHVERVSSITUATIONEN. 1983-1986. a.
  Helsingoer Kommune, Erhvervsgruppen, c/o
  Teknisk Forvaltning, Moerdrupvej 15 A, 3060
  Espergaerde, Denmark.

341.7   SP   ISSN 0464-3755
ESCUELA DIPLOMATICA. CUADERNOS. 1960-
  1972. irreg. (back issues avail.) Escuela Diplomatica,
  Paseo de Juan 23, No. 5, Madrid 3, Spain.

318   GT
ESTADISTICAS DE VEHICULOS EN
  CIRCULACION EN GUATEMALA. (Former
  name of issuing body: Direccion General de
  Estadistica) 1972-19??; suspended. irreg. Instituto
  Nacional de Estadistica, Ministerio de Economia,
  8A Calle no. 9-55, Zona 1, Guatemala, Guatemala.

100   PO
ESTUDOS FILOSOFICOS. 1982-19?? irreg.
  Universidade Nova de Lisboa, Faculdade de
  Ciencias Sociais e Humanas, Departamento de
  Filosofia, Avenida de Berna, 24, 1000 Lisbon,
  Portugal.

320   US
ETHICS AND PUBLIC POLICY ESSAYS. ceased
  1986. irreg. Ethics and Public Policy Center, 1030
  15th St., N.W., Washington, DC 20005.
  Formerly: Ethics and Public Policy Reprints.

973   US
ETHNIC STUDIES INFORMATION GUIDE
  SERIES. ceased. irreg. Gale Research Company,
  Book Tower, Detroit, MI 48226.

944   FR   ISSN 0071-2140
ETUDES PICARDES. 1957-1985. irreg. (Societe
  d'Emulation Historique et Litteraire d'Abbeville)
  Editions A. et J. Picard, 82 Rue Bonaparte, 75006
  Paris, France.

540   UK
EUROPEAN CHEMICAL BUYER'S GUIDE. 1975-
  19?? a. Business Press International Ltd., Quadrant
  House, the Quadrant, Sutton, Surrey SM2 5AS,
  England.

668.4   UK   ISSN 0306-5502
EUROPEAN PLASTICS BUYERS GUIDE. 1931-
  19?? a. Business Press International Ltd., Quadrant
  House, the Quadrant, Sutton, Surrey SM2 5AS,
  England.
  Former titles: Europlastics Year Book (ISSN
  0068-2381); British Plastics Year Book.

798.4   IT
EUROPEAN RACING MANUAL. 1973-1976. a.
  Derby Societa Editrice, Corso di Porta Nuova 46,
  20121 Milan, Italy.

332.6 332   UK   ISSN 0262-7663
EXCHANGE RATE MOVEMENTS YEAR BOOK.
  1981-1984. a. Henley Centre for Forecasting, 2
  Tudor St, Blackfriars, London EC4Y 0AA, England.

622.15   US   ISSN 0071-3473
EXPLORATION GEOPHYSICS. ceased. irreg.
  Consultants Bureau, Special Research Report, 233
  Spring St., New York, NY 10013.

382   US   ISSN 0276-556X
EXPORT DOCUMENTATION HANDBOOK. 1977-
  198? a. plus q. updates. Dun's Marketing Services
  (Subsidiary of: Dun & Bradstreet Corporation) 49
  Old Bloomfield Ave., Mtn. Lakes, NJ 07046.

940   UK   ISSN 0261-9911
FACTS ABOUT LEWISHAM. published only once.
  irreg. Lewisham Local History Society, c/o J.
  Birchenough, 116 Manor Lane, Lee SE12 8LR,
  England.

301   BL
FACULDADE DE FILOSOFIA, CIENCIAS E
  LETRAS DE ARARAQUARA. CADEIRA DE
  SOCIOLOGIA E FUNDAMENTOS
  SOCIOLOGICOS DA EDUCAO. BOLETIM.
  1965-1969 (vol.4, no.1) irreg. Faculdade de
  Filosofia, Ciencias e Letras de Araraquara, Cadeira
  de Sociologia e Fundamentos Sociologicos da
  Educao, Praca Santos Dumont, C.P. 174,
  Araraquara, S.P., Brazil.

700 350   US
FEDERAL ART PATRONAGE NOTES. 1974-1983.
  irreg. (back issues avail.) Francis V. O'Connor, Ed.
  & Pub., 250 E. 73rd St., Apt. 11C, New York, NY
  10021.

631.8   UN   ISSN 0071-4615
FERTILIZER INDUSTRY SERIES. 1968-19??;
  discontinued. irreg. United Nations Industrial
  Development Organization, Box 300, A-1400
  Vienna, Austria

382   FR   ISSN 0071-4704
FICHES ANALYTIQUES DE LA PRESSE
  TECHNIQUE FRANCAISE. 1965-1985. irreg.
  Centre National du Commerce Exterieur, 10 Av.
  d'Iena, 75016 Paris, France.

310   FJ   ISSN 0071-4828
FIJI. BUREAU OF STATISTICS. ANNUAL
  STATISTICAL ABSTRACT. 1969/1971-19?? a.
  Bureau of Statistics, Box 2221, Suva, Fiji.

630   FJ
FIJI. MINISTRY OF AGRICULTURE &
  FISHERIES. BULLETIN. ceased. irreg. Ministry of
  Agriculture & Fisheries, Box 358, Suva, Fiji.
  Formerly: Fiji. Department of Agriculture.
  Bulletin.

778.5   DK   ISSN 0109-1174
FILM PREMIERER. 1983-1984. a. Danske
  Filminstitut, Store Soendervoldstraede, DK-1419
  Copenhagen, Denmark.

614.84   US   ISSN 0071-5425
FIRE PROTECTION HANDBOOK STUDY
  GUIDE. 1962-19?? irreg. Davis Publishing Co.,
  2015 McFarland Blvd., E., Tuscaloosa, AL 35405.

353.9   US   ISSN 0095-2060
FLORIDA. DEPARTMENT OF
  TRANSPORTATION. ANNUAL REPORT. 1915-
  19?? irreg. Department of Transportation, Office of
  Communication Services, Burns Bldg., Tallahassee,
  FL 32301.

629.132   US   ISSN 0190-6526
FLYING YEARBOOK. 1979-19?? a. C B S
  Magazines, Flying, 1515 Broadway, New York, NY
  10036.

382   US
FOCUS ON ISSUES. 1981-198?; discontinued. irreg.
  (looseleaf format; back issues avail.) United States
  Council for International Business, 1212 Ave. of the
  Americas, New York, NY 10036.

659.1 658.8   US
FOLIO: THE ADGUIDE. 1984-198? a. Folio
  Publishing Corp., Six River Bend, Box 4949,
  Stamford, CT 06907-0949.

070.5   US
FOLIO: 400. 1980-198? a. Folio Publishing Corp., Six
  River Bend, Box 4949, Stamford, CT 06907.

637   UK
FOODNEWS DAIRY PRODUCTS REVIEW.
  (Supplement to: Foodnews) 1976-19??. a. 22a Sidcup
  High St., Sidcup, Kent DA14 6EH, England.

069   GE
FORSCHUNGEN ZUR AELTESTEN
  ENTWICKLUNG DRESDENS. 1953-1981. irreg.
  (Landesmuseum fuer Vorgeschichte Dresden) V E B
  Deutscher Verlag der Wissenschaften, Postfach
  1216, 1080 Berlin, E. Germany (D.D.R.)

551.46   FR
FRANCE. I.F.RE.MER. CENTRE DE BREST.
  RECUEIL DES TRAVAUX. 1972-1978, no.10.
  irreg. Institut Francais de Recherche pour
  l'Exploitation de la Mer (IFREMER)-Centre de
  Brest, Service de la documentation et des
  Publications (SDP), B.P. 337, 29273 Brest Cedex,
  France.
  Former titles: France. Centre National pour
  l'Exploitation des Oceans. Centre Oceanologique de
  Bretagne. Recueil des Travaux (ISSN 0336-3112)

371.2   FR
FRANCE. INSTITUT NATIONAL DE
  RECHERCHE ET DE DOCUMENTATION
  PEDAGOGIQUES. CAHIERS DE
  DOCUMENTATION. 1960-198?, ceased. irreg.
  Centre National de Documentation Pedagogique, 29
  rue d'Ulm, 75230 Paris Cedex 05, France

370.025   FR   ISSN 0071-8963
FRANCE. INSTITUT NATIONAL DE
  RECHERCHE ET DE DOCUMENTATION
  PEDAGOGIQUES. REPERTOIRE
  D'ETABLISSEMENTS PUBLICS
  D'ENSEIGNEMENT ET DE SERVICES. 1967-
  19??, ceased. a. (Ministere de l'Education) France.
  Centre National de Documentation Pedagogique, 13
  rue du Four, 75006 Paris, France.

616.8   AG   ISSN 0016-271X
FUNDACION ROUX-OCEFA. ARCHIVOS. 1960-
  1977. irreg. (Sociedad Argentina de Neuropatologia)
  Fundacion Roux-Ocefa, Montevideo 81, Buenos
  Aires, Argentina.

370   UN   ISSN 0071-9870
FUNDAMENTALS OF EDUCATIONAL
  PLANNING. LECTURE-DISCUSSION SERIES.
  1966-1986; discontinued. irreg. International
  Institute for Educational Planning, 7-9 rue Eugene
  Delacroix, 75116 Paris, France.

621.38   UK   ISSN 0046-5593
G E C TELECOMMUNICATIONS JOURNAL.
  1930-1985. irreg. (General Electric Co. p.l.c. of
  England) G E C Telecommunications Ltd., Box 53,
  Coventry CV3 1HJ, England.
  Formerly: G E C-A E I Telecommunications.

301.2   II
GAUHATI UNIVERSITY. DEPARTMENT OF
  ANTHROPOLOGY. BULLETIN. 1972-1976. a.
  Gauhati University, Department of Anthropology,
  Gauhati 14, Assam, India.

574.87   US
GENETICS AND CELLULAR TECHNOLOGY
  SERIES. published only once, 1982. irreg. Marcel
  Dekker, Inc., 270 Madison Ave., New York, NY
  10016.

338 630   GW
GERMANY (FEDERAL REPUBLIC, 1949-).
  BUNDESMINISTERIUM FUER
  ERNAEHRUNG, LANDWIRTSCHAFT UND
  FORSTEN. AGRARBERICHT DER
  BUNDESREGIERUNG. 1956-1987. a.
  Bundesministerium fuer Ernaehrung, Landwirtschaft
  und Forsten, 5300 Bonn 1, W. Germany (B.R.D.)

530   IT   ISSN 0391-5905
GIORNALE DI FISICA. QUADERNI. 1976-19??;
  suspended. irreg. (Societa Italiana di Fisica) Editrice
  Compositori s.r.l., Viale 12 Giugno 1, Bologna
  40124, Italy.

268   US   ISSN 0160-2373
GLEANINGS (CAMBRIDGE) 1973-1981 (no.12)
  irreg. Monks of New Skete, c/o Brother Marc, Ed.,
  Cambridge, NY 12816.

909   US   ISSN 0072-4742
GLOBAL FOCUS SERIES. 1961-1977 (vol.17) irreg.
  (Institute of World Affairs) University of Wisconsin-
  Milwaukee, Box 413, Milwaukee, WI 53201.

910   UK
GOFFS TRAVELLERS GUIDE. ceased. a. Adprint,
  69 Thorpe Rd., Norwich, Norfolk NR1 1UA,
  England.

551.44   SP
GOURS. 1973-1984 (no.10) a. Fomento Martinense,
  Grupo Espeleologico, Calle Provenza 593-595,
  Barcelona 26, Spain.

1154   CESSATIONS

352   US
GOVERNANCE OF METROPOLITAN REGIONS. SERIES. 1972-19?? irreg. (reprint service avail. from UMI) (Resources for the Future Inc.) Johns Hopkins University Press, 701 W. 40th St., Ste. 275, Baltimore, MD 21211.

070   BL
GRANDES TEMAS DO JORNALISMO. 1982-19?? irreg. Editora Soma, Ltda., Rua Braulio Gomes, 141, 8 Andar, Sao Paulo, Brazil.

550   UK
GREAT BRITAIN. BRITISH GEOLOGICAL SURVEY. METRIC WELL INVENTORY. 1973-1983. irreg. British Geological Survey, Keyworth, Nottingham NG12 5GG, England.
 Formerly (until Jan.1984): Great Britain. Institute of Geological Sciences. Metric Well Inventory.

796   US
GREAT OUTDOORS ALMANAC. ceased 1985. a. Mariah Publications Corporation, 1165 N. Clark St., Chicago, IL 60610.

070 384   US
GREATER BOSTON MEDIA DIRECTORY. 1981-19?? biennial. New England Newsclip Agency, Inc., 5 Auburn St., Framingham, MA 01701.

378   US   ISSN 0046-6409
GREEN SHEET; University of Hawaii newsletter. 1968-1986 (Oct.) irreg. University of Hawaii at Manoa, Office of University Relations and Development, 2500 Campus Rd., Hawaii 2, Honolulu, HI 96822.

780.42   US
GREENSBORO SUBSTITUTE. 1982-1983. irreg. (back issues avail.) Parnassus Publishing Group, Box 5003, Greensboro, NC 27403.
 Formerly: Southern Fried Turnip Greens.

630   GT
GUATEMALA. INSTITUTO NACIONAL DE ESTADISTICA. ENCUESTA PECUARIA. (Former name of issuing body: Direccion General de Estadistica) 1974-1978. a. Instituto Nacional de Estadistica, Ministerio de Economia, 8A Calle No. 9-55, Zona 1, Guatemala, Guatemala.

620   US
GUIDE TO COMPUTER SOFTWARE FOR ARCHITECTS AND ENGINEERS. 1983-19?? a. (Architectural Record) McGraw-Hill Information Systems Co., 1221 Ave. of the Americas, New York, NY 10020.
 Formerly: Computer for Architects and Engineers.

690   US   ISSN 0160-7340
GUIDE TO MANUFACTURED HOMES. 1978-19?? irreg. National Association of Home Manufacturers, Home Manufacturers Council, 15th & M Sts., N.W., Washington, DC 20005.

551.46   US   ISSN 0072-9027
GULF RESEARCH REPORTS. 1961-1985. a. (reprint service avail. from UMI) Gulf Coast Research Laboratory, Ocean Springs, MS 39564-0951.

799.3   US   ISSN 0072-906X
GUNS AND AMMO ANNUAL. ceased 1984. a. Caroline House, Inc., 5 S. 250 Frontenac Rd., Naperville, IL 60540.

942   UK   ISSN 0306-3151
GWYNEDD ARCHIVES SERVICE. BULLETIN. ceased 1976. irreg. Gwynedd Archives Service, Gwynedd County Council, Caernarfon, Gwynedd LL55 1SH, Wales.

647.94   US
H.S.M.A. HOTEL FACILITIES DIGEST. ceased. a. Hotel Sales & Marketing Association International, 333 N. Gladstone Ave., Margate, NJ 08402.
 Formerly: H.S.M.A. Hotel-Motel Directory and Facilities Guide (ISSN 0072-9167)

320   DK   ISSN 0106-0392
HAANDBOG I DANSK POLITIK. 1978-1986. a. Mjoelner Edition S-A, DK-4720 Praestoe, Denmark.

574.5   PH   ISSN 0115-4990
HABITAT PHILIPPINES. 1980-1984. a. Forest Research Institute, College, Laguna 3720, Philippines.

769.569   US   ISSN 0273-0200
HARRIS POSTAGE STAMP PRICE INDEX; stamps of the United States and Canada since 1845. 1947-19?? a. H. E. Harris and Company, Box 7084, Portsmouth, NH 03801-7084.

570   US   ISSN 0073-0467
HARVARD BOOKS IN BIOLOGY. 1959-1971 (no.7) irreg. Harvard University Press, 79 Garden St., Cambridge, MA 02138.

956   US   ISSN 0073-0572
HARVARD MIDDLE EASTERN MONOGRAPHS. 1959-1978 (vol.23/24) irreg. Harvard University, Center for Middle Eastern Studies, Cambridge, MA 02138

509   US
HARVARD MONOGRAPHS IN THE HISTORY OF SCIENCE. ceased 1974. irreg. Harvard University Press, 79 Garden St., Cambridge, MA 02138.

950   US   ISSN 0073-0599
HARVARD ORIENTAL SERIES. 1883-1978 (no.48) irreg. Harvard University Press, 79 Garden St., Cambridge, MA 02138.

320   US
HARVARD POLITICAL STUDIES. ceased 1978. irreg. Harvard University Press, 79 Garden St., Cambridge, MA 02138.

947 491.8 891.8   US
HARVARD SLAVIC MONOGRAPHS. 1975-1979 (vol.7) irreg. Harvard University Press, 79 Garden St., Cambridge, MA 02138.

610   CY   ISSN 0253-8601
HEALTH STATISTICS. 1980-1984; discontinued. a. Ministry of Finance, Department of Statistics and Research, Nicosia, Cyprus.

635   US
HERB COLLECTOR'S MANUAL & MARKETING GUIDE; gingseng growers and collectors' handbook. 1946-1977. irreg. J. Kelly, Ed. & Pub., Box 7, Looneyville, WV 25259.

378   UK   ISSN 0309-9113
HIGHER EDUCATION CURRENT AWARENESS BULLETIN. 1967-1986 (no.513) fortn. University of Aston-in-Birmingham, Library, Gosta Green, Birmingham B4 7ET, England.
 Formerly (until 1973): Higher Education.

977   US
HISTORIC MICHIGAN TRAVEL GUIDE. 1975-198?; suspended. a. Historical Society of Michigan, 2117 Washtenaw Ave., Ann Arbor, MI 48104.
 Formerly: Historical Museums in Michigan.

500 610   US
HISTORICAL STUDIES IN THE LIFE SCIENCES. 1977-19?? a. (reprint service avail. from UMI) Johns Hopkins University Press, 701 W. 40th St., Ste. 275, Baltimore, MD 21211.

300   GW   ISSN 0173-2153
HISTORISCH SOZIALWISSENSCHAFTLICHE FORSCHUNGEN. 1977-1985. irreg. Klett-Cotta, P.O. Box 809, D-7000 Stuttgart 1, W. Germany (B.R.D.)

800 900   US   ISSN 0195-802X
HOFSTRA UNIVERSITY CULTURAL AND INTERCULTURAL STUDIES. 1980-1983(no.4) irreg. (back issues avil.) (Hofstra University) A M S Press, Inc., 56 E. 13th St., New York, NY 10003.

362   JA
HOKKAIDO REHABILITATION/HOKKAIDO RIHABIRTESHON GAKKAI ZASSHI. 1964-1970/71; suspended. irreg. Hokkaido Rehabilitation Association - Hokkaido Rihabiriteshon Gakkai, c/o Sapporo Ika Daigaku Seik Geka, Minami Ichijo Nishi-16-chome, Sapporo 060, Japan.

070.5   JA   ISSN 0046-7839
HON: A BOOK-BIN FOR SCHOLARS. 1970-19?? irreg. Yushodo Booksellers Ltd., 29 Sanei-cho, Shinjuku-ku, Tokyo 160, Japan.

800 920 011   GW   ISSN 0724-2603
HORVATH BLAETTER. 1983-1987. a. (back issues avail.) Edition Herodot im Rader Verlag, Kongress Str.5, D-5100 Aachen, W. Germany (B.R.D.)

657   US
HOSPITAL RATE DIRECTORY OF SOUTHERN NEW YORK. discontinued 1985. a. United Hospital Fund of New York, 55 Fifth Ave., New York, NY 10003.

310   CY   ISSN 0253-8628
HOSPITAL STATISTICS. 1980-1984; discontinued. a. Ministry of Finance, Department of Statistics and Research, Nicosia, Cyprus.

796.6   US
HOSTELING U.S.A; the official American youth hostels handbook. 1979-1983. irreg. East Woods Press Book, 429 E. Blvd., Charlotte, NC 28203.

690   US
HOUSTON BUILDING AND CONSTRUCTION DIRECTORY. 1982-198? a. Greystone Communications, 13027 Skymeadow, Houston, TX 77082.

001.3   DK   ISSN 0105-5216
HUMANIORA. 1975-1984 (no.6) biennial. Statens Humanitiske Forskningsraad, Holmens Kanal 7, 1060 Copenhagen K, Denmark.

301.16   US
HUMANISTIC STUDIES IN THE COMMUNICATIONS ARTS. ceased. irreg. Hastings House Publishers, Inc., c/o Richard Gallen & Co., 260 Fifth Ave., New York, NY 10001-6408.

374   CN   ISSN 0018-8891
I.C.E.A. CAHIERS. 1966-19?? (vol.9, no.1/2) irreg. Institut Canadien d'Education des Adultes, 506 Est rue Catherine, Suite 800, Montreal, Que., Canada.
 Formerly: Education des Adultes (ISSN 0424-5393)

677   US
I F I BULLETIN: TEXTILE NOTES. ceased. irreg. (looseleaf format) International Fabricare Institute, 12251 Tech Rd., Silver Spring, MD 20904.

664   US   ISSN 0073-9286
I F T WORLD DIRECTORY AND BUYERS' GUIDE. 1967-19?? a. Institute of Food Technologists, 221 N. La Salle St., Chicago, IL 60601.

341.1   GW   ISSN 0074-7289
I P R A STUDIES IN PEACE RESEARCH. 1966-1980? irreg. (International Peace Research Association, JA) Campus Verlag, Myliusstr. 15, 6000 Frankfurt 1, W. Germany (B.R.D.)

500   US
I S I ATLAS OF SCIENCE: VOL. 1: BIOCHEMISTRY AND MOLECULAR BIOLOGY. published only once, 1981. irreg. Institute for Scientific Information, 3501 Market St., Philadelphia, PA 19104
 Supersedes in part: I S I Atlas of Science (ISSN 0278-2898)

575.1   US
I S I ATLAS OF SCIENCE: VOL. 2: BIOTECHNOLOGY AND MOLECULAR GENETICS. (Includes Contents of Books Index, Author/Editor Index, Corporate Index and Permuterm Subject Index) published only once, 1981. irreg. Institute for Scientific Information, 3501 Market St., Pniladelphia, PA 19104
 Supersedes in part: I S I Atlas of Science.

639.2   FR   ISSN 0750-8743
I S T P M RAPPORTS TECHNIQUES. 1983-1985. irreg. Institut Scientifique et Technique des Peches Maritimes, Rue de l'Ile-d'Yeu, B.P. 1049, Nantes Cedex, France.

574.5   NE
I T C-U N E S C O INTERNATIONAL SEMINAR. PROCEEDINGS. 1966-19??; discontinued. a. International Institute for Aerospace Survey and Earth Sciences, P.O. Box 6, Enschede, Netherlands.
 Former titles: International Seminar on Integrated Surveys. Proceedings & Seminar on Integrated Surveys of Environment. Proceedings (ISSN 0080-8830)

700   GW   ISSN 0341-8448
ICONOGRAPHIA ECCLESIAE ORIENTALIS. ceased. irreg. Verlag Aurel Bongers, Dortmunder str. 67, Postfach 100 264, 4350 Recklinghausen, W. Germany (B.R.D.)

331.7　　　　　　　US
IDAHO. DEPARTMENT OF EMPLOYMENT.
ANNUAL RURAL EMPLOYMENT REPORT.
ceased. a. Department of Employment, Bureau of
Research and Analysis, Box 35, Boise, ID 83735.
　　Former titles: Idaho. Department of Employment.
Annual Rural Manpower Report; Idaho. Department
of Employment. Annual Farm Labor Report (ISSN
0091-0732)

026　610　016　　US　ISSN 0148-0650
ILLINOIS HEALTH SCIENCES LIBRARIES
SERIALS HOLDINGS LIST. 1973-1986 (vol.12) a.
(also avail. on microfiche) University of Illinois at
Chicago, Library of the Health Sciences, Box 7509,
Chicago, IL 60680.

741.640　　　　US　ISSN 0073-5477
ILLUSTRATORS: THE ANNUAL OF AMERICAN
ILLUSTRATION. 1959-19?? a. (back issues avail.)
(Society of Illustrators) Hastings House Publishers,
Inc., c/o Richard Gallen & Co., 260 Fifth Ave.,
New York, NY 10001-6408.

378　　　　　　　　CL
IMAGEN U.C.V. 1977-19?? a. (Universidad Catolica
de Valparaiso, Oficina de Planificacion y Estudios)
Ediciones Universitarias de Valparaiso, Casilla 1415,
Valparaiso, Chile.

539　　　　　　　　GW
IMPULSTECHNIKEN. ceased 1976. irreg. R.
Oldenbourg Verlag GmbH, Rosenheimer Str. 145,
Postfach 801360, 8000 Munich 80, W. Germany
(B.R.D.)

610　015　　　　US　ISSN 0162-6639
INDEX OF N L M SERIAL TITLES. 1972-19?? a.
National Library of Medicine, 8600 Rockville Pike,
Bethesda, MD 20209

011　　　　　　　CN　ISSN 0316-5019
INDEX OF 16 MM & 35 MM FEATURE LENGTH
FILMS AVAILABLE IN CANADA. 1947-1984.
irreg. Canadian Federation of Film Societies, Index
Committee, Box 6536, Stn.D, Calgary, Alberta T2P
2E1, Canada.
　　Formerly: Index of Feature Length Films (ISSN
0316-5000)

340　016　　　　　　UK
INDEX TO LEGAL ESSAYS. ceased 1983. irreg.
(British and Irish Association of Law Librarians)
Mansell Publishing Ltd., 6 All Saints St., London
N1 9RL, England
　　Formerly: Index to Legal Studies.

029　　　　　　　NZ　ISSN 0073-5957
INDEX TO NEW ZEALAND PERIODICALS.
1940-1986. 3/yr. (annual cumulations) (also avail. in
microfiche; back issues avail.) National Library of
New Zealand, Private Bag, Wellington, New
Zealand.

070　016　　　　　　TH
INDEX TO THAI NEWSPAPERS. 1964-19??;
suspended. irreg. National Institute of Development
Administration, Library and Information Center,
Klongjan, Bangkapi, Bangkok 10240, Thailand.

398　　　　　　　US　ISSN 0073-6996
INDIANA UNIVERSITY. FOLKLORE INSTITUTE.
MONOGRAPH SERIES. 1933-19?? irreg. Indiana
University, Folklore Institute, 504 N. Fess,
Bloomington, IN 47405.

333　350　　　　　　US
INDIANA UNIVERSITY. SCHOOL OF PUBLIC
AND ENVIRONMENTAL AFFAIRS.
OCCASIONAL PAPERS. 1972-19?? irreg. (back
issues avail.) Indiana University, School of Public
and Environmental Affairs, 400 E. Seventh,
Bloomington, IN 47401.

574.5　　　　　　　MX
INDICE DE PROYECTOS EN DESARROLLO EN
ECOLOGIA DE ZONAS ARIDAS/INDEX OF
CURRENT RESEARCH IN ARID ZONES
ECOLOGY/INDEX DES PROJECTS EN
DEVELOPPMENT SUR L'ECOLOGIE DES
ZONES ARIDES. 1978-1979. irreg. Instituto
Nacional de Investigaciones sobre Recursos
Bioticos, Apdo. Postal 63, 91000 Xalapa, Veracruz,
Mexico.

574.5　016　　　　MX
INDICE DE PROYECTOS EN DESARROLLO EN
ECOLOGIA TROPICAL/INDEX OF CURRENT
TROPICAL ECOLOGY RESEARCH. 1975-1980.
a. Instituto Nacional de Investigaciones sobre
Recursos Bioticos, Apdo. Postal 63, 91000 Xalapa,
Veracruz, Mexico.

070.5　　　　　　　CL
INDICE GENERAL DE LA REVISTA HOY. 1981-
1985. biennial. (back issues avail.) Servicio de
Extension de Cultura Chile, Portugal 12, Depto.46,
Santiago, Chile.

800　　　　　　　GW　ISSN 0073-7208
INDICES ZUR DEUTSCHEN LITERATUR. ceased.
irreg. Athenaeum-Verlag GmbH, Adelheidstr. 2,
Postfach 1220, 6240 Koenigstein im Taunus, W.
Germany (B.R.D.)

678　028　　　　　　GW
INFORMACIONES BAYER PARA LA
INDUSTRIA DEL CAUCHO. 1955-1981 (no.53)
irreg. (1-2/yr.) Bayer AG, 5090 Leverkusen-
Bayerwerk, W. Germany (B.R.D.)

678　　　　　　　　GW
INFORMATIONS BAYER POUR L'INDUSTRIE
DU CAOUTCHOUC. 1955-1981 (no. 53) irreg. (1-
2/yr.) Bayer AG, 5090 Leverkusen-Bayerwerk, W.
Germany (B.R.D.)

378　　　　　　　　US
INSIDE OUTSIDE BANKSTREET. ceased. irreg. (1-
2/yr.) Bank Street College of Education, 610 W.
112 St., New York, NY 10025.

371.002　　　　　US　ISSN 0271-535X
INSIDER'S GUIDE TO PREP SCHOOLS. ceased.
biennial. E. P. Dutton & Co., 2 Park Ave., New
York, NY 10016.

320　　　　　　　FR　ISSN 0078-995X
INSTITUT D'ETUDES POLITIQUES DE PARIS.
LIVRET. 1954-19??, ceased. biennial. Librarie
Vuibert, 63 Bld. Saint- Germain, 75005 Paris,
France.

338.1　　　　　　BE　ISSN 0303-8971
INSTITUT ECONOMIQUE AGRICOLE.
CAHIERS/L.E.I. SCHRIFTEN. 1962-1986 (Mar.)
irreg. Ministry of Agriculture, Institute Economique
Agricole, Manhattan Centre, 21 av. de Boulevard,
1210 Brussels, Belgium.

338.1　　　　　　　BE
INSTITUT ECONOMIQUE AGRICOLE.
COURRIER. 1971-1986 (Jun.) irreg. Ministry of
Agriculture, Institute Economique Agricole,
Manhattan Centre, 21 av. de Boulevard, 1210
Brussels, Belgium.

551.46　574.92　　　GW　ISSN 0068-0915
INSTITUT FUER MEERESFORSCHUNG,
BREMERHAVEN. VEROEFFENTLICHUNGEN.
1952-1986. irreg. Institut fuer Meeresforschung, Am
Handelshafen 12, Bremerhaven, W. Germany
(B.R.D.)

332　　　　　　　US　ISSN 0073-8778
INSTITUTE FOR MONETARY RESEARCH.
MONOGRAPHS. 1962-1983. irreg. Institute for
Monetary Research, 4813 Woodway Lane, N.W.,
Washington, DC 20016.

956　　　　　　　　LE
INSTITUTE FOR PALESTINE STUDIES. UNITED
NATIONS RESOLUTIONS ON PALESTINE
AND THE ARAB-ISRAELI CONFLICT SERIES.
1967-1981. a. Institute for Palestine Studies, Box
11-7164, Beirut, Lebanon
　　Formerly: Institute for Palestine Studies. Basic
Documents Series (ISSN 0073-8794)

368.01　　　　　UK　ISSN 0073-8980
INSTITUTE OF ACTUARIES. YEAR BOOK. 1929-
1986. a. Institute of Actuaries, Staple Inn Hall, High
Holborn, London, WC1V 7QJ, England.

510　　　　　　　　JA
INSTITUTE OF STATISTICAL MATHEMATICS.
ANNUAL REPORT/TOKEI SURI KENKYUSHO
NENPO. 1967-19??, ceased. a. Institute of
Statistical Mathematics - Tokei Suri Kenkyusho, 6-
7, 4-Chome, Minami Azabu, Minato-ku, Tokyo 106,
Japan.

333.71　　　　　　　UK
INSTITUTE OF WATER POLLUTION CONTROL
HANDBOOK. ceased. a. Adprint, 69 Thorpe Rd.,
Norwich, Norfolk NR1 3AU, England.

333.71　　　　　　　UK
INSTITUTION OF WATER ENGINEERS &
SCIENTISTS HANDBOOK. ceased. a. Adprint, 69
Thorpe Rd., Norwich, Norfolk NR1 3AU, England.

572　987　　　　　　VE
INSTITUTO DE ANTROPOLOGIA E HISTORIA.
ANUARIO. 1964-19?? a. Universidad Central de
Venezuela, Instituto de Antropologia e Historia,
Caracas, Venezuela.

320　016　　　　　　PO
INSTITUTO DE INVESTIGACAO CIENTIFICA
TROPICAL. BIBLIOGRAFIA CIENTIFICA.
1960-1981. a. Instituto de Investigacao Cientifica
Tropical, Centro de Documentacao e Informacao,
Rua Jau 47, 1300 Lisbon, Portugal.
　　Formerly: Junta de Investigacoes Cientificas do
Ultramar. Bibliografia Cientifica.

711　　　　　　　AG　ISSN 0074-0330
INSTITUTO TORCUATO DI TELLA. CENTRO DE
ESTUDIOS URBANOS REGIONALES.
DOCUMENTOS DE TRABAJO. 1969-19?? irreg.
Instituto Torcuato di Tella, Centro de Estudios
Urbanos y Regionales, Corrientes 2835, Cuerpo "A",
Piso 7, Buenos Aires 1193, Argentina.

330　　　　　　　AG　ISSN 0074-0349
INSTITUTO TORCUATO DI TELLA. CENTRO DE
INVESTIGACIONES ECONOMICAS.
DOCUMENTOS DE TRABAJO. 1966-19?? irreg.
Instituto Torcuato di Tella, 11 de Septiembre 2139,
Buenos Aires, C.P. 1428, Argentina.

301　　　　　　　AG　ISSN 0074-0357
INSTITUTO TORCUATO DI TELLA. CENTRO DE
INVESTIGACIONES SOCIALES.
DOCUMENTOS DE TRABAJO. 1965-19?? irreg.
Instituto Torcuato di Tella, 11 de Septiembre 2139,
Buenos Aires, C.P. 1428, Argentina.

338　370　　　　　　US
INSTRUCTOR COMPUTER DIRECTORY FOR
SCHOOLS. 1982-19?? a. Harcourt Brace
Jovanovich, Inc., 7500 Old Oak Blvd., Cleveland,
OH 44130

943　　　　　　　PL　ISSN 0074-0616
INSTYTUT SLASKI. KOMMUNIKATY. SERIA
NIEMCOZNAWCZA. 1961-19??, ceased. irreg.
Instytut Slaski, Instytut Naukowo-Badawczy, Ul.
Luboszycka 3, 45-036 Opole, Poland

943.8　　　　　　PL　ISSN 0074-0632
INSTYTUT SLASKI. WYDAWNICTWA. 1958-19??
irreg. Instytut Slaski, Instytut Naukowo-Badawczy,
Ul. Luboszycka 3, 45-036 Opole, Poland

368　　　　　　　　KO
INSURANCE STATISTICS YEARBOOK. 1972-
1983. a. Korea Non-Life Insurance Association, 80
Soosong-dong, 6th floor, Chongno-ku, Seoul, S.
Korea.

616.99　　　　　　US　ISSN 0190-1575
INTERNATIONAL ADVANCES IN SURGICAL
ONCOLOGY. 1978-19?? (vol.7) irreg. ●Also
available online. Alan R. Liss, Inc., 41 E. 11th St.,
New York, NY 10003.

960　015　　　　　　UK
INTERNATIONAL AFRICAN BIBLIOGRAPHY
CUMULATION; books, articles and papers in
African studies. ceased 1982. quinquennial.
(University of London, School of Oriental and
African Studies) Mansell Publishing Ltd., 6 All
Saints St., London N1 9RL, England

011　363.6　　　　　　US
INTERNATIONAL ASSOCIATION OF
CORONERS AND MEDICAL EXAMINERS.
PROCEEDINGS. 1970-1982. a. International
Association of Coroners and Medical Examiners,
6913 W. Plank Rd., Peoria, IL 61604.

622.33　　　　　　　US
INTERNATIONAL COAL EXPLORATION
SYMPOSIUM. PROCEEDINGS. 1976-1984. irreg.
(reprint service avail. from UMI) (World Coal
Magazine) Miller Freeman Publications, Inc., 500
Howard St., San Francisco, CA 94105.

CESSATIONS

619 SZ ISSN 0251-6810
INTERNATIONAL COLLOQUIUM ON
PROSPECTIVE BIOLOGY (PROCEEDINGS)
1973-1980. irreg. S. Karger AG, Allschwilerstrasse
10, P.O. Box, CH-4009 Basel, Switzerland.

616.6 SZ ISSN 0074-378X
INTERNATIONAL CONGRESS OF
NEPHROLOGY. PROCEEDINGS. 1960-1981.
irreg. (reprint service avail. from ISI) S. Karger AG,
Allschwilerstrasse 10, P.O. Box, CH-4009 Basel,
Switzerland.

574.1 US
INTERNATIONAL CONGRESS ON
PHOTOBIOLOGY. PROCEEDINGS. ceased.
irreg. Plenum Publishing Corp., 233 Spring St., New
York, NY 10013.

690 FR ISSN 0074-428X
INTERNATIONAL COUNCIL FOR BUILDING
RESEARCH, STUDIES AND
DOCUMENTATION. CONGRESS REPORTS.
1959-19??. ceased. triennial. International Council
for Building Research, Studies and Documentation,
4 Av. du Recteur Poincare, 75782 Paris Cedex 16,
France.

796.6 UK
INTERNATIONAL CYCLING GUIDE. 1980-198?
a. Tantivy Press, 136-148 Tooley St., London SE1
2TT, England

651.8 001.64 US
INTERNATIONAL DATA PROCESSING
CONFERENCE. PROCEEDINGS. (Published as
Sept. issue of Data Management) 1970-19??. a.
(reprint service avail. from UMI) Data Processing
Management Association, 505 Busse Highway, Park
Ridge, IL 60068.

650 378 US ISSN 0074-4611
INTERNATIONAL DIRECTORY OF PROGRAMS
IN BUSINESS AND COMMERCE. 1966-196?
irreg. American Assembly of Collegiate Schools of
Business, 605 Old Ballas Rd., St. Louis, MO 63141-
7011.

551 AT
INTERNATIONAL GONDWANA SYMPOSIUM.
PAPERS. ceased. irreg. Australian National
University Press, Pergamon Press Australia Pty.
Ltd., P.O. Box 544, Potts Point, Sydney, N.S.W.
2011, Australia.

616.9 UN ISSN 0538-7736
INTERNATIONAL HISTOLOGICAL
CLASSIFICATION OF TUMOURS. 1967-1980
(no.25) irreg. (slides in box accompany each text)
World Health Organization - Organisation Mondiale
de la Sante, Distribution and Sales Service, 20
Avenue Appia, CH-1211 Geneva 27, Switzerland.

001.53 382 US
INTERNATIONAL INFORMATION FLOWS. 1982-
198?; discontinued. irreg. United States Council for
International Business, 1212 Ave. of the Americas,
New York, NY 10036.

616.8 US ISSN 0091-0600
INTERNATIONAL JOURNAL OF
PSYCHOANALYTIC PSYCHOTHERAPY. 1972-
1985/86. irreg. (also avail. in microfilm from UMI;
reprint service avail. from UMI) Jason Aronson,
Inc., 230 Livingston St., No.941, Northvale, NJ
07647-1726.
 Incorporating (as of 1974): International Journal
of Psychiatry.

331 US ISSN 0074-6657
INTERNATIONAL LABOR STUDIES. 1959-19??;
discontinued. irreg. U.S. Bureau of International
Labor Affairs, Department of Labor, Washington,
DC 30210

639 CN ISSN 0074-7165
INTERNATIONAL NORTH PACIFIC FISHERIES
COMMISSION. ANNUAL REPORT. 1954-1985.
a. International North Pacific Fisheries Commission,
6640 N.W. Marine Dr., Vancouver, B.C. V6T 1X2,
Canada.

639 CN ISSN 0074-7157
INTERNATIONAL NORTH PACIFIC FISHERIES
COMMISSION. BULLETIN. 1955-1985. irreg.
International North Pacific Fisheries Commission,
6640 N.W. Marine Dr., Vancouver, B.C. V6T 1X2,
Canada.

639 CN ISSN 0535-1588
INTERNATIONAL NORTH PACIFIC FISHERIES
COMMISSION. STATISTICAL YEARBOOK.
1970-1985. a. International North Pacific Fisheries
Commission, 6640 N.W. Marine Drive, Vancouver,
B.C. V6T 1X2, Canada.

639 CN ISSN 0074-7254
INTERNATIONAL PACIFIC SALMON
FISHERIES COMMISSION. ANNUAL REPORT.
1937-1985. a. International Pacific Salmon Fisheries
Commission, Box 30, New Westminster, B.C. V3L
4X9, Canada.

639 CN ISSN 0074-7262
INTERNATIONAL PACIFIC SALMON
FISHERIES COMMISSION. BULLETIN. 1945-
1985. irreg. International Pacific Salmon Fisheries
Commission, Box 30, New Westminster, B.C. V3L
4X9, Canada.

639 CN ISSN 0074-7270
INTERNATIONAL PACIFIC SALMON
FISHERIES COMMISSION. PROGRESS
REPORT. 1956-1985. irreg. International Pacific
Salmon Fisheries Commission, Box 30, New
Westminster, B.C. V3L 4X9, Canada.

341.7 GW ISSN 0074-7297
INTERNATIONAL PEACE RESEARCH
ASSOCIATION. PROCEEDINGS OF THE
CONFERENCE. (Incl. in I P R A Studies in Peace
Research) 1965-1980? biennial. (International Peace
Research Association) Campus Verlag, Myliusstr.
15, Frankfurt 1, W. Germany (B.R.D.)

301 NO ISSN 0522-4497
INTERNATIONAL PEACE RESEARCH
INSTITUTE. BASIC SOCIAL SCIENCE
MONOGRAPHS. 1967-1982. irreg. International
Peace Research Institute, Raadhusgt. 4, Oslo 1,
Norway.

574.192 US ISSN 0074-7351
INTERNATIONAL PHOTOBIOLOGICAL
CONGRESS. PROCEEDINGS. 1954-19??
quadrennial. (International Committee of
Photobiology) Plenum Publishing Corp., 233 Spring
St., New York, NY 10013.

371.928 US
INTERNATIONAL RESEARCH SEMINAR ON
VOCATIONAL REHABILITATION OF THE
MENTALLY RETARDED. SPECIAL
PUBLICATIONS SERIES. ceased 1978. irreg.
American Association on Mental Deficiency, 1719
Kalorama Rd., N.W., Washington, DC 20009-2684.

370 US
INTERNATIONAL SCHOLARS DIRECTORY.
1972-1975. irreg. Marquis Who's Who, Inc., 200 E.
Ohio St., Chicago, IL 60611.

574.8 US
INTERNATIONAL SYMPOSIUM ON
MOLECULAR BIOLOGY. PROCEEDINGS.
1972-19?? irreg. (reprint service avail. from UMI)
Johns Hopkins University Press, 701 W. 40th St.,
Ste. 275, Baltimore, MD 21211.

551.4 627 US ISSN 0732-2607
INTERNATIONAL SYMPOSIUM ON URBAN
HYDROLOGY, HYDRAULIC
INFRASTRUCTURES AND WATER QUALITY
CONTROL. PROCEEDINGS. 1974-19?? a. (back
issues avail.) (University of Kentucky, College of
Engineering, Office of Continuing Education and
Extension) O E S Publications, College of
Engineering, Univ. of Kentucky, Lexington, KY
40506-0046.
 Former titles: International Symposium on Urban
Hydrology, Hydraulics and Sediment Control.
Proceedings; Urban Storm Runoff. Proceedings;
Until 1978: International Symposium on Urban
Storm Water Management. Proceedings.

919.04 AT ISSN 0729-5944
INTERNATIONAL TRAVEL IN QUEENSLAND.
1981-1986. a. Queensland Tourist and Travel
Corporation, Research and Development Division,
307 Queen St., G.P.O. Box 328, Brisbane, Qld.
4001, Australia.

331.88 SZ ISSN 0579-8302
INTERNATIONAL UNION OF FOOD AND
ALLIED WORKERS' ASSOCIATIONS.
TOBACCO WORKERS' TRADE GROUP
BOARD. MEETING. discontinued. irreg.
International Union of Food and Allied Workers'
Associations - Union Internationale des Travailleurs
de l'Alimentation et des Branches Connexes,
Secretariat, Rampe du Pont-Rouge 8, CH-1213
Petit-Lancy/Geneva, Switzerland.

520 UK ISSN 0539-1342
INTERNATIONAL WHO'S WHO IN POETRY.
1958-19?? irreg. Melrose Press Ltd., 3 Regal Lane,
Soham, Ely, Cambridgeshire CB7 5BA, England.

301 MY
INTISARI; research journal of wider Malaysia. 1971-
19?? irreg. Malaysian Sociological Research
Institute, Box 2112, Kuala Lumpur, Malaysia.

551 US
IOWA. GEOLOGICAL SURVEY. ANNUAL
REPORT OF THE STATE GEOLOGIST TO THE
GOVERNOR. 1893-19?? a. Geological Survey, 123
N. Capitol St., Iowa City, IA 52242.
 Formerly: Iowa. Geological Survey. Annual
Report of the State Geologist to the Geological
Board (ISSN 0361-7629)

016 500 600 US
IOWA STATE UNIVERSITY. LIBRARY. SERIES
IN BIBLIOGRAPHY. 1971-1987 (suspended) irreg.
Iowa State University Library, Ames., IA 50011.

052 UK ISSN 0260-8480
IRISH STUDIES. 1980-1987; suspended. a. Cambridge
University Press, Edinburgh Bldg., Shaftesbury Rd.,
Cambridge CB2 2RU, England

016 669.1 UK
IRON & STEEL INDUSTRY PROFILES. 1969-1984.
fortn. Institute of Metals, Metals Information, 1
Carlton House Terrace, London SW1Y 5DB,
England.

011 UK
ISIS CUMULATIVE BIBLIOGRAPHY. 1971-1985.
irreg. (Smithsonian Institution, History of Science
Society, US) Mansell Publishing Ltd., 6 All Saints
St., London N1 9RL, England

070.5 IS
ISRAELI PUBLISHERS AND AUTHORS AND
THEIR BOOKS ON THE WORLD PUBLISHING
SCENE. discontinued. irreg. Israel Export Institute,
Book and Printing Center, Industry House, 29
Hamered St., P.O. Box 50084, Tel Aviv, Israel.

300 IT ISSN 0391-321X
ISTITUZIONI CULTURALI. 1977-1985. irreg.
Liguori Editore s.r.l., Via Mezzocannone 19, 80134
Naples, Italy.

830 016 GE ISSN 0300-8436
JAHRESVERZEICHNIS DER
VERLAGSSCHRIFTEN UND EINER AUSWAHL
DER AUSSERHALB DES BUCHHANDELS
ERSCHIENENEN VEROEFFENTLICHUNGEN
DER D.D.R., DER B.R.D. UND WESTBERLINS
SOWIE DER DEUTSCHSPRACHIGEN WERKE
ANDERER LAENDER. 1796-1976. irreg. VEB
Verlag fuer Buch- und Bibliothekswesen,
Gerichtsweg 26, 7010 Leipzig, E. Germany
(D.D.R.)
 Formerly: Jahresverzeichnis des Deutschen
Schrifttums (ISSN 0075-2967)

510 US
JAMES K. WHITTEMORE LECTURES IN
MATHEMATICS GIVEN AT YALE
UNIVERSITY. ceased. irreg. Yale University Press,
92A Yale Sta., New Haven, CT 06520.

623.8 JA
JAPAN. SHIP RESEARCH INSTITUTE. PAPERS/
SENPAKU GIJUTSU KENKYUSHO OBUN
HOKOKU. 1951-1984. irreg. Ship Research
Institute - Un'Yu-sho Senpaku Gijutsu Kenkyusho,
Ministry of Transport, 6-38-1 Shinkawa, Mitaka-shi,
Tokyo 181, Japan.
 Formerly: Papers of Ship Research Institute.

340 320 JA ISSN 0075-3157
JAPAN ANNUAL OF LAW AND POLITICS. 1952-
1986. a. Science Council of Japan - Nihon
Gakujutsu Kaigi, 7-22-34 Roppongi, Minato-ku,
Tokyo 106, Japan.

330 016 JA ISSN 0911-8004
JAPANESE ANNUAL BIBLIOGRAPHY OF
ECONOMICS. ceased 1986. a. Science Council of
Japan - Nihon Gakujutsu Kaigi, 7-22-34 Roppongi,
Minato-ku, Tokyo 106, Japan.

330.9 IS ISSN 0447-6719
JERUSALEM CHAMBER OF COMMERCE.
BULLETIN. suspended 1985. (back issues avail.)
Jerusalem Chamber of Commerce, 10 Hillel St.,
Jerusalem 94581, Israel.

361 US ISSN 0075-3742
JEWISH SOCIAL SERVICE YEARBOOK. ceased. a.
Council of Jewish Federations, Inc., 730 Broadway,
2nd Fl., New York, NY 10003.

380 US
JIDDAH CHAMBER OF COMMERCE &
INDUSTRY ANNUAL TRADE DIRECTORY.
ceased 1983. a. Inter-Crescent Publishing Co., Inc.,
2021 Nieta Dr., Garden Grove, CA 92640.

301 US ISSN 0075-3866
JOHNS HOPKINS SERIES IN INTEGRATION
AND COMMUNITY BUILDING IN EASTERN
EUROPE. 1968-19?? irreg. (reprint service avail.
from UMI) Johns Hopkins University Press, 701 W.
40th St., Ste. 275, Baltimore, MD 21211.

915 JO
JORDAN. MINISTRY OF TOURISM AND
ANTIQUITIES. TOURISM ANNUAL REPORT.
ceased. a. Ministry of Tourism & Antiquities, Jordan
Tourism Authority, Box 224, Amman, Jordan.

800 US ISSN 0075-4099
JOURNAL FOR THE PROTECTION OF ALL
BEINGS. 1960-19?? irreg. City Lights Books, 261
Columbus Ave., San Francisco, CA 94133.

336 US
JULIAN BLOCK'S GUIDE TO YEAR-ROUND
TAX SAVINGS. ceased. a. Dow Jones-Irwin,
Homewood, IL 60430.

620 US ISSN 0145-0093
KANSAS STATE UNIVERSITY. CENTER FOR
ENERGY STUDIES. REPORT. (Subseries of:
Institute for Systems Design and Optimization.
Report) 1973-19?? irreg. Kansas State University,
Center for Energy Studies, Ward Hall, Manhattan,
KS 66502.

670 380 UK ISSN 0260-633X
KELLY'S DIRECTORY OF BRITISH INDUSTRY &
SERVICES IN SCOTLAND AND NORTHERN
IRELAND. 1980-198?, ceased. a. Kelly's
Directories Ltd., Windsor Court, East Grinstead
House, East Grinstead, West Sussex RH19 1XB,
England.

133.5 US ISSN 0748-8513
KEY (LANSDALE) 1979-19?? irreg. (10-13/yr.)
Association for Studying Chiron, 158 Poplar,
Ambler, PA 19002.

338 DK
KEY FIGURES ON DANISH INDUSTRY. 1964-
1984. biennial. Industriraadet, H.C. Andersens Blvd.
18, 1596 Copenhagen, Denmark.
 Formerly: Industriens Hovedtal.

700 GW ISSN 0445-2577
KLEINE IKONENBUECHEREI. ceased. irreg. Verlag
Aurel Bongers, Dortmunder str. 67, Postfach 100
264, 4350 Recklinghausen, W. Germany (B.R.D.)

574 591 BE
KONINKLIJK BELGISCH INSTITUUT VOOR
NATUURWETENSCHAPPEN.
VERHANDELINGEN/INSTITUT ROYAL DES
SCIENCES NATURELLES DE BELGIQUE.
MEMOIRES. 1900-1984. irreg. (back issues avail.)
Koninklijk Belgisch Instituut voor
Natuurwetenschappen - Institut Royal des Sciences
Naturelles de Belgique, Vautierstraat 29, 1040
Brussels, Belgium.

610 US ISSN 0361-0489
KROC FOUNDATION SERIES. 1973-19??, vol.19.
irreg. Alan R. Liss, Inc., 41 E. 11th St., New York,
NY 10003.

020 US
L A C U N Y OCCASIONAL PAPERS. 1972-1979
(no. 6) irreg. Library Association of the City
University of New York, c/o Kathleen Meier,
Hunter College Library, 695 Park Ave., New York,
NY 10021.

020 US ISSN 0362-448X
L J SPECIAL REPORTS. 1976-1985 (no. 25) irreg. R.
R. Bowker Company, Magazine Division, 205 E. 42
St., New York, NY 10017.

331.1 US ISSN 0075-7489
LABOR RELATIONS YEARBOOK. 1966-1984. a.
The Bureau of National Affairs, Inc., 1231 25th St.,
N.W., Washington, DC 20037.

320 US
LAISSEZ FAIRE ANARCHIST CATALOG. 1973-
19?? a. Laissez Faire Books, Inc., 532 Broadway,
New York, NY 10012.

333 US ISSN 0084-0785
LAND TENURE CENTER. NEWSLETTER. 1962-
1981 (no.70) irreg. University of Wisconsin-
Madison, Land Tenure Center, 1300 University
Ave., Madison, WI 53706.

327 980 US
LATIN AMERICAN INTERNATIONAL AFFAIRS.
1975-19?? irreg. (Center for Inter-American
Relations) Sage Publications, Inc., 2111 W. Hillcrest
Dr., Newbury Park, CA 91320

771.3 US ISSN 0093-9374
LEICA MANUAL. discontinued. irreg. Morgan &
Morgan, Inc., 145 Palisade St., Dobbs Ferry, NY
10522.

100 NE ISSN 0459-0007
LEIDSE WIJSGERIGE REEKS. 1966-1971. irreg.
Leiden University Press, c/o E.J. Brill Publishers,
Postbus 9000, 2300 PA Leiden, Netherlands.

971 CN ISSN 0383-9133
LILLOOET DISTRICT HISTORICAL SOCIETY.
BULLETIN. 1974-1981. irreg. Lillooet District
Historical Society, Box 441, Lillooet, B.C. V0K
1V0, Canada.

371.912 DK ISSN 0900-1174
LOGOS. 1976-1983. irreg. Koebenhavns Universitet,
Center for Audiologopaedi, Njalsgade 86, 2300
Copenhagen S, Denmark.

551 US
LONG ISLAND WATER RESOURCES BULLETIN.
1971-19?? (no.16) irreg. U.S. Geological Survey,
Water Resources Division (New York), 5 Aerial
Way, Syosset, NY 11791.

942 UK ISSN 0144-5898
LOOKBACK. 1980-1984. irreg. Andover Local
History Society, Andover Public Library, Chantry
Way, Andover, Hants. SP10 1LT, England.
 Formerly: Test Valley and Border Anthology.

027.7 US
LOUISIANA STATE UNIVERSITY. LIBRARY.
REPORT OF THE DIRECTOR. 1943-19?? a.
Louisiana State University Library, Baton Rouge,
LA 70803.

284 CN ISSN 0460-024X
LUTHERAN CHURCH IN AMERICA. WESTERN
CANADA SYNOD. MINUTES OF THE
ANNUAL CONVENTION. 1962-1984. a.
Lutheran Church in America, Western Canada
Synod, 9901 107th Street, Edmonton, Alberta T5K
1G4, Canada.

651.8 621.381 US ISSN 0361-5421
M P, THE MICROPROCESSOR; annual study of the
market and applications for the microprocessor and
microcomputers by E D N Magazine. (Special
annual issues of E D N) discontinued. a. Cahners
Publishing Co., Inc., Division of Reed Holdings,
Inc., 275 Washington St., Newton, MA 02158-1630.

976 016 US ISSN 0076-9525
M V C BULLETIN. (Mississippi Valley Collection)
1968-19?? irreg., approx. a. (back issues avail.)
(Memphis State University, John Willard Brister
Library) Memphis State University Press, Memphis,
TN 38152.

550 574 CN
MCGILL UNIVERSITY. INSTITUTE OF
OCEANOGRAPHY. BIENNIAL REPORT. 1965-
1987. biennial. McGill University, Institute of
Oceanography, 3620 University St., Montreal, P.Q.
H3A 2B2, Canada.
 Formerly: McGill University. Marine Sciences
Centre. Annual Report (ISSN 0541-6299)

551.5 CN ISSN 0076-1842
MCGILL UNIVERSITY, MONTREAL.
DEPARTMENT OF METEOROLOGY.
PUBLICATION IN METEOROLOGY. 1955-1985.
irreg. McGill University, Department of
Meteorology, 805 Sherbrooke St. W., Montreal,
Que., Canada.

978 US ISSN 0541-6507
MACKINAC HISTORY; an informal series of
illustrated vignettes. 1963-19?? irreg. (looseleaf
format) Mackinac Island State Park Commission,
Box 30028, Lansing, MI 48909.

380 US ISSN 0733-4931
MACRAE'S SOUTH CAROLINA STATE
INDUSTRIAL DIRECTORY. ceased 1985. irreg.
MacRae's Blue Book, Inc., 817 Broadway, New
York, NY 10003.
 Formerly: South Carolina State Industrial
Directory (ISSN 0162-0878)

398 HU ISSN 0200-5352
MAGYAR NEPMUVESZET EVSZAZADAI. ceased
1972 (vol.3) irreg. Istvan Kiraly Muzeum,
Szekesfehervar, Hungary.

614.7 016 US
MAN AND THE ENVIRONMENT
INFORMATION GUIDE SERIES. 1975-198?
irreg. Gale Research Company, Book Tower,
Detroit, MI 48226.

610 BL
MANUAL DO INTERNO E RESIDENTE. ceased.
a. Moreira Jr. Editora Ltda, Rua Pinheiros 504, Sao
Paulo, Brazil.

387 NE
MANUAL OF MARITIME STATISTICS. 1972-1980.
irreg. Netherlands Ministry of Transport, Maritime
Research Institute Netherlands, Box 1555, 3000 BN
Rotterdam, Netherlands.
 Formerly: Manual of Maritime Statistics of
Seaborne Trade and Shipping.

320 301.412 301.4157 NE
MANUSCRIPT; tijdschrift van mannen tegen het
patriarchaat. 1979-1986 (no.12) irreg. Stiftung
"Aktiv gegen Sexismus", Postbus 28, Eindhoven,
Netherlands.

551.46 US
MARINE SCIENCE. ceased 1974. irreg. Marcel
Dekker, Inc., 270 Madison Ave., New York, NY
10016.

338.1 NZ ISSN 0112-0603
MASSEY UNIVERSITY. CENTRE FOR
AGRICULTURAL POLICY STUDIES.
DISCUSSION PAPER. 1979-1980, ceased. irreg.
Massey University, Centre for Agricultural Policy
Studies, Palmerston North, New Zealand.
 Formerly: Massey University. Department of
Agricultural Economics and Farm Management.
Technical Discussion Paper.

690 US
MECHANIX ILLUSTRATED PLANS & PROJECTS.
1977-1985. a. C B S Publications, Home Mechanix,
1515 Broadway, New York, NY 10036.

616.98 AT ISSN 0025-7494
MEDICAL RESEARCH BULLETIN. 1965-1980
(no.7) irreg. Department of Veterans' Affairs, M. L.
C. Tower, Woden, A.C.T. 2606, Australia.

610 IE ISSN 0076-5996
MEDICAL RESEARCH COUNCIL (IRELAND).
REPORT. 1937-1986. a. Medical Research Council
of Ireland, 9 Clyde Rd., Dublin 4, Ireland.

610 US
MEDICINAL RESEARCH SERIES. 1967-19?? irreg.
Marcel Dekker, Inc., 270 Madison Ave., New York,
NY 10016.
 Formerly: Medicinal Research: A Series of
Monographs (ISSN 0076-6062)

CESSATIONS

574 US
MEMBRANE PROTEINS SERIES. 1977-1979. irreg. (also avail. in microfilm) Marcel Dekker, Inc., 270 Madison Ave., New York, NY 10016.

920 UK
MEN AND WOMEN OF DISTINCTION. 1980-198? irreg. Melrose Press Ltd., 3 Regal Lane, Soham, Ely, Cambridgeshire CB7 5BA, England.

800 811 US ISSN 0278-1190
MENDOCINO REVIEW. 1972-1986. a. Box 888, Mendocino, CA 95460.

800 US ISSN 0887-9273
MENSES. ceased 1985 (vol.4, no.2) irreg. (4-6/yr.) (tabloid format; back issues avail.) Menses, Inc., Box 192, Croton-on-Hudson, NY 10520.

808 US
MENU; a journal of arts and letters. published only once, 1985. a. Lunchroom Press, Box 36027, Grosse Pointe Farms, MI 48236.

550 GW ISSN 0721-8761
"METEOR" FORSCHUNGSERGEBNISSE. REIHE A/B: ALLGEMEINES, PHYSIK UND CHEMIE DES MEERES MARITIME METEOROLOGIE. 1966-198? irreg. (Deutsche Forschungsgemeinschaft) Gebrueder Borntraeger Verlagsbuchhandlung, Johannesstr. 3A, 7000 Stuttgart 1, W. Germany (B.R.D.)
  Incorporating: Meteor Forschungsergebnisse. Reihe A. Allgemeines, Physik und Chemie des Meeres (ISSN 0543-5900) & Meteor Forschungsergebnisse. Reihe B. Meteorologie und Aeronomie.

551 540 GW ISSN 0543-5935
"METEOR" FORSCHUNGSERGEBNISSE. REIHE D. BIOLOGIE. 1967-198? irreg. (Deutsche Forschungsgemeinschaft) Gebrueder Borntraeger Verlagsbuchhandlung, Johannesstr. 3A, 7000 Stuttgart 1, W. Germany (B.R.D.)

530 US ISSN 0076-6860
METHODS IN COMPUTATIONAL PHYSICS: ADVANCES IN RESEARCH AND APPLICATIONS. 1963-1977 (vol.17) irreg. (also avail. in microfiche) Academic Press, Inc., Orlando, FL 32887.

914.404 FR
MICHELIN GREEN GUIDE SERIES: CAUSSES CEVENNES. ceased. irreg. Michelin, Service de Tourisme, 46 av. de Breteuil, 75341 Paris Cedex, France

371.42 US ISSN 0076-7913
MICHIGAN. DIVISION OF VOCATIONAL EDUCATION. REPORT. 1918-19?? a. Department of Education, Division of Vocational Education, Box 30009, Lansing, MI 48909.
  Continues: Michigan. State Board of Control for Vocational Education. Annual Descriptive Report.

622 US ISSN 0085-3372
MICHIGAN MINERAL PRODUCERS ANNUAL DIRECTORY: 1970-1978. a. Department of Natural Resources, Geological Survey Division, Information Services Center, Box 30028, Lansing, MI 48909.
  Supersedes: Directory of Michigan Mineral Operators.

658 US ISSN 0736-2870
MICHIGAN PURCHASING DIRECTORY. 1983-1985. a. Pick Publications, Inc., 28715 Greenfield Rd., Southfield, MI 38076.

621.381 025 US ISSN 8755-5786
MICRO SOFTWARE REPORT (LIBRARY EDITION) 1983-198? a. Meckler Publishing, 11 Ferry Lane W., Westport, CT 06880.

576 SP ISSN 0026-2595
MICROBIOLOGIA ESPANOLA. 1947-1986 (vol.39) a. (Consejo Superior de Investigaciones Cientificas) Instituto Jaime Ferran de Microbiologia, Joaquin Costa 32, Madrid 6, Spain.

338 US
MIDEAST BUSINESS GUIDE. 1977-19?? irreg. News Circle Publishing Co., 6730 San Fernando, Box 3684, Glendale, CA 91201.

338.2 US ISSN 0085-3445
MINERAL INDUSTRY OF MICHIGAN ANNUAL STATISTICAL SUMMARY. 1963-1978. a. Department of Natural Resources, Geological Survey Division, Information Services Center, Box 30028, Lansing, MI 48909.
  Supersedes: Michigan's Mineral Industries.

338.1 US ISSN 0544-3512
MINNESOTA ECONOMIC DATA: COUNTRIES AND REGIONS. 1966-19?? irreg. (looseleaf format) University of Minnesota, Agricultural Extension Service, Department of Agricultural Economics, 277 Coffey Hall, St. Paul, MN 55105.

011 US
MINNESOTA PERIODICALS ON MICROFILM. 1972-19?? a. (microfilm; back issues avail.) Minnesota Scholarly Press, Box 224, Mankato, MN 56001.

977 US
MISSOURI HISTORICAL SOCIETY. ANNUAL REPORT. suspended. a. Missouri Historical Society, Jefferson Memorial Bldg., Forest Park, St. Louis, MO 63112.

625.19 385 UK
MODEL RAILWAY CONSTRUCTOR ANNUAL. 1978-1986; discontinued. a. (reprint service avail. from UMI) Ian Allan Ltd., Coombelands House, Addlestone, Weybridge, Surrey KT15 0HY, England.

510.78 US ISSN 0076-9908
MODERN ANALYTIC AND COMPUTATIONAL METHODS IN SCIENCE AND MATHEMATICS. 1963-1983 (vol.40) irreg. Elsevier Science Publishing Co., Inc. (New York), 52 Vanderbilt Ave., New York, NY 10017.

362.1 US
MODERN NURSING HOME DIRECTORY OF NURSING HOMES IN THE UNITED STATES, U.S. POSSESSIONS AND CANADA. ceased. irreg. McGraw-Hill Book Co., 1221 Ave. of the Americas, New York, NY 10020

541.3 UK
MODERN PHYSICS IN CHEMISTRY. 1976-1986, discontinued. irreg. Academic Press Inc. (London) Ltd., 24 Oval Rd., London NW1 7DX, England

917 UK
MONEYWISE GUIDE TO CALIFORNIA. 1982-198? irreg. Michael Haag Ltd., Box 369, London NW3 4ER, England.

340 CN ISSN 0077-0728
MONOGRAPHIES JURIDIQUES. 1967-1981; discontinued. irreg. (University of Ottawa, Faculty of Law) University of Ottawa Press, 603 Cumberland, Ottawa, Ont. K1N 6N5, Canada.

550 US
MONOGRAPHS IN GEOSCIENCE. 1967-19?? irreg. Plenum Publishing Corp., 233 Spring St., New York, NY 10013.

546 US
MONOGRAPHS IN INORGANIC CHEMISTRY. 1966-19?? irreg. Plenum Publishing Corp., 233 Spring St., New York, NY 10013.

537.6 530.4 US ISSN 0544-8417
MONOGRAPHS IN SEMICONDUCTOR PHYSICS. (Translated from Russian) 1963-19?? irreg. Plenum Publishing Corp., 233 Spring St., New York, NY 10013.

400 GW ISSN 0077-1031
MONOGRAPHS ON LINGUISTIC ANALYSIS. 1965-19?? (vol.5) irreg. (Ohio State University, Project on Linguistic Analysis, US) Walter de Gruyter & Co., Mouton Publishers, Postfach 110240, D-1000 Berlin 11, W. Germany (B.R.D.)

913 HU ISSN 0077-1392
MONUMENTA ANTIQUITATIS EXTRA FINES HUNGARIAE REPERTA QUAE IN MUSEO ARTIUM HUNGARICO ALIISQUE MUSEIS ET COLLECTIONIBUS HUNGARICIS CONSERVANTUR. 1968, published only once. irreg. (Magyar Tudomanyos Akademia) Akademiai Kiado, Publishing House of the Hungarian Academy of Sciences, P.O. Box 24, H-1363 Budapest, Hungary.

610 US
MOUSE IN BIOMEDICAL RESEARCH. 1981-1984. irreg. Academic Press, Inc., Orlando, FL 32887.

551.5 MZ
MOZAMBIQUE. SERVICO METEOROLOGICO. ANUARIO DE OBSERVACOES. PARTE I: OBSERVACOES DE SUPERFICIE. 1909-1978. a. Servico Meteorologico, C.P. 256, Maputo, Mozambique.

551.5 MZ
MOZAMBIQUE. SERVICO METEOROLOGICO. ANUARIO DE OBSERVACOES. PARTE II: OBSERVACOES DE ALTITUDE. 1909-1977. a. Servico Meteorologico, C.P. 256, Maputo, Mozambique.

026 960 US ISSN 0047-8350
MUNGER AFRICANA LIBRARY NOTES. 1970-19??; suspended until 1989. irreg. (5-6/yr.) (back issues avail.) California Institute of Technology, Munger Africana Library, Pasadena, CA 91125.

913 SP
MUSEO ARQUEOLOGICO NACIONAL. GUIAS. ceased. irreg. Museo Arqueologico Nacional, Serrano 13, Madrid 1, Spain.

913 SP
MUSEO ARQUEOLOGICO NACIONAL. PUBLICACIONES DIDACTICAS. ceased. irreg. Museo Arqueologico Nacional, Serrano 13, Madrid 1, Spain.

708.1 US ISSN 0739-5736
MUSEUM OF FINE ARTS, BOSTON. BULLETIN. 1903-19??; suspended. a. Museum of Fine Arts, 465 Huntington Ave., Boston, MA 02115.
  Former titles: M F A Bulletin (ISSN 0732-2895); until 1978: Boston Museum Bulletin (ISSN 0006-7997); Museum of Fine Arts. Bulletin.

780 016 US ISSN 0077-2429
MUSIC INDEXES AND BIBLIOGRAPHIES. 1970-19?? irreg. European American Music Corporation, Box 850, Valley Forge, PA 19482-0650.

780.65 US
MUSIC INDUSTRY DIRECTORY. ceased 1983 (7th edt.) a. Marquis Who's Who, Inc., 200 E. Ohio St., Chicago, IL 60611.
  Formerly (until 1980): Musician's Guide.

534.4 614.7 CN
MUSIC OF THE ENVIRONMENT SERIES. published only once, 1977. irreg. World Soundscape Project, Sonic Research Studio, Dept. of Communication, Simon Fraser University, Burnaby, B.C. V5A 1S6, Canada.

338.4 US ISSN 0092-8410
N.A.C.D.S. LILLY DIGEST. 1971-1986. a. (National Association of Chain Drug Stores) Eli Lilly & Co., General Offices and Principal Laboratories, Indianapolis, IN 46285.

639 CN ISSN 0704-4771
N A F O MEETING PROCEEDINGS. 1979, published only once. a. Northwest Atlantic Fisheries Organization, P.O. Box 638, Dartmouth, N.S. B2Y 3Y9, Canada.
  Formerly (until 1979): International Commission for the Northwest Atlantic Fisheries. Meetings Proceedings.

796.32 US ISSN 0362-3254
N A G W S GUIDE. BASKETBALL; official rules and interpretations. 1901-19?? a. American Alliance for Health, Physical Education, Recreation and Dance, National Association for Girls and Women in Sport, 1900 Association Dr., Reston, VA 22091.
  Formerly: Basketball Guide, with Official Rules and Standards (ISSN 0065-7018)

794.6 796.86 US
N A G W S GUIDE. BOWLING - GOLF. 1954/56-19?? biennial. American Alliance for Health, Physical Education, Recreation, and Dance, National Association for Girls and Women in Sport, 1900 Association Dr., Reston, VA 22091.
  Formerly: Bowling-Fencing Guide (ISSN 0099-0051)

797.21 US ISSN 0271-2199
N A G W S GUIDE. COMPETITIVE SWIMMING AND DIVING. 1949-19?? a. American Alliance for Health, Physical Education, Recreation and Dance, National Association for Girls and Women in Sport, 1900 Association Dr., Reston, VA 22091.
Supersedes in part: N A G W S Guide. Aquatics (ISSN 0361-719X)

796 US
N A G W S GUIDE. LACROSSE. 1939-19?? biennial. American Alliance for Health, Physical Education, Recreation and Dance, National Association for Girls and Women in Sport, 1900 Association Dr., Reston, VA 22091.
Supersedes in part: Field Hockey-Lacrosse Guide (ISSN 0065-7026)

796.42 US ISSN 0362-9481
N A G W S GUIDE. TRACK AND FIELD. 1937-19?? a. American Alliance for Health, Physical Education, Recreation, and Dance, National Association for Girls and Women in Sport, 1900 Association Dr., Reston, VA 22091.

639.9 015 UK ISSN 0143-1722
N C C INFORMATION AND LIBRARY SERVICES. BIBLIOGRAPHY SERIES. 1979-19?? irreg. Nature Conservancy Council, Information and Library Services, Northminster House, Peterborough PE1 1UA, England.

380.5 US
N F T A PORT OF BUFFALO HANDBOOK. 1967-19??; suspended. biennial. Niagara Frontier Transportation Authority, 181 Ellicott St., Buffalo, NY 14205.

370 016 US
N I C E M INDEX TO EDUCATIONAL SLIDES. 1973-1980. irreg. (also avail. in microfiche) •Also available online; back issues avail.) (National Information Center for Educational Media) Access Innovation, Inc., Box 40130, Albuquerque, NM 87196.

614 US
N I H FACTBOOK. 1976; published only once. irreg. (U.S. National Institutes of Health) Marquis Who's Who, Inc., 200 E. Ohio St., Chicago, IL 60611.

150 UK ISSN 0077-5010
N I I P BULLETIN. 1966-1977. irreg. National Institute of Industrial Psychology, c/o North East London Polytechnic Livingstone House, Livingstone Rd., London, E15 2LJ, England.

330.9 ET ISSN 0077-3506
NATIONAL BANK OF ETHIOPIA. LOCAL PRICES. 1963-1986. irreg. National Bank of Ethiopia, Economic Research and Planning Division, c/o Research Library, Box 5550, Addis Ababa, Ethiopia.

362.7 US ISSN 0190-7476
NATIONAL DIRECTORY OF CHILDREN & YOUTH SERVICES. 1979-1987 (5th ed.) biennial. (back issues avail.) (American Association for Protecting Children) Bookmakers Guild, Inc., 1430 Florida Ave., Ste. 202, Longmont, CO 80501.

796.332 US ISSN 0077-4588
NATIONAL FOOTBALL LEAGUE. RECORD MANUAL. 1947-1983. a. National Football League, 410 Park Ave., New York, NY 10022.

610.73 US
NATIONAL LEAGUE FOR NURSING. BACCALAUREATE PROGRAMS ACCREDITED FOR PUBLIC HEALTH NURSING. ceased. irreg. National League for Nursing, Council of Baccalaureate and Higher Degree Programs, 10 Columbus Circle, New York, NY 10019.
Formerly: National League for Nursing. Baccalaureate Programs Accredited for Public Health Nursing Preparation.

363.2 US
NEBRASKA LAW ENFORCEMENT TRAINING CENTER. ANNUAL REPORT. ceased. a. Nebraska Law Enforcement Training Center, Rt. 3, Box 50, Grand Island, NE 68801.

373 US
NEVADA. ADVISORY COUNCIL FOR VOCATIONAL-TECHNICAL EDUCATION. ANNUAL EVALUATION REPORT. ceased. a. Advisory Council for Vocational-Technical Education, Nye Bldg., Capitol Complex, Carson City, NV 89701.
Formerly: Nevada. Advisory Council for Manpower Training and Career Education. Annual Evaluation Report (ISSN 0093-9595)

614 CN
NEW BRUNSWICK. HEALTH SERVICES ADVISORY COUNCIL. ANNUAL REPORT/ RAPPORT ANNUEL. 1971-1985. a. Health Services Advisory Council, Box 6000, Fredericton, N.B. E3B 5HI, Canada.

378 370.73 US ISSN 0077-8168
NEW CAMPUS. (This Organization merged with A C H E (Association for Continuing Higher Education) in Oct. 1985) 1922-1985. a. Association for Continuing Professional Education, c/o John J. Dlabal, Jr., Northern Illinois University, DeKalb, IL 60115.

378 US
NEW ENGLAND BOARD OF HIGHER EDUCATION ISSUES. discontinued. irreg. New England Board of Higher Education, Wenham, MA 01984.

553 US ISSN 0092-1602
NEW JERSEY. DIVISION OF WATER RESOURCES. SPECIAL REPORT. ceased 1983 (no.39) irreg. Department of Environmental Protection, Division of Water Resources, Trenton, NJ 08625

553 US ISSN 0545-2252
NEW JERSEY. DIVISION OF WATER RESOURCES. WATER RESOURCES CIRCULARS. ceased 1970 (no.24) irreg. Department of Environmental Protection, Division of Water Resources, Trenton, NJ 08625.

368.4 US
NEW JERSEY. STATE AGENCY FOR SOCIAL SECURITY. ANNUAL REPORT. ceased 1982. a. State Agency for Social Security, 20 W. Front St., Trenton, NJ 08625.

974.9 US
NEW JERSEY INSTRUCTIONAL SERIES. 1963-19?? a. New Jersey Historical Society, 230 Broadway, Newark, NJ 07104.
Formerly: Cockpit (ISSN 0010-0102)

622 AT ISSN 0727-9264
NEW SOUTH WALES. DEPARTMENT OF MINERAL RESOURCES. ANNUAL REPORT. STATISTICAL SUPPLEMENT. 1972-1984, discontinued. a. Department of Mineral Resources and Development, G.P.O. Box 5288, Sydney, N.S.W. 2001, Australia.
Former titles: New South Wales. Department of Mines. Annual Report. Statistical Supplement; New South Wales. Department of Mineral Resources Development. Annual Report. Statistical Supplement.

622 660 AT ISSN 0077-8672
NEW SOUTH WALES. DEPARTMENT OF MINES. CHEMICAL LABORATORY. REPORT. 1961-1966, discontinued. irreg. Department of Mineral Resources & Development, Box 5288, Sydney, N.S.W. 2001, Australia.

622 559 AT ISSN 0077-8680
NEW SOUTH WALES. DEPARTMENT OF MINES. COALFIELDS BRANCH. REPORTS. 1962-1965, discontinued. irreg. Department of Mineral Resources & Development, Box 5288, Sydney, N.S.W. 2001, Australia.

790 NZ
NEW ZEALAND. COUNCIL FOR RECREATION AND SPORT. REPORT. 1974-1987. a. (Council for Recreation and Sport) Government Printer, P.O. Box 5122, Wellington, New Zealand.

607 NZ ISSN 0078-0154
NEW ZEALAND. NATIONAL RESEARCH ADVISORY COUNCIL. SENIOR AND POST DOCTORAL RESEARCH FELLOWSHIP AWARDS FOR RESEARCH IN NEW ZEALAND GOVERNMENT DEPARTMENTS. 1968-1986. a. National Research Advisory Council, P.O. Box 12240, Wellington, New Zealand.

769.56 AT ISSN 0729-2368
NEW ZEALAND AND DEPENDENCIES STAMP CATALOGUE. 1983-1986. irreg. Seven Seas Stamps Pty. Ltd., 62 Wingewarra St., Dubbo, NSW 2830, Australia.

613 AU ISSN 0028-9620
NEYDHARTINGER MOORPOST. 1950-19??; suspended. irreg. (looseleaf format) Moorbad Neydharting, Pfarrplatz 3-4, A-4010 Linz, Austria.

539.7 DK ISSN 0109-0054
NIELS BOHR INTERNATIONAL GOLD MEDAL. 1955-1981. triennial. Dansk Ingenioerforening, Ingenioerhuset, Vester Farimagsgade 20-31, 1606 Copenhagen V, Denmark.

364 340 UK ISSN 0262-4737
NIGERIAN CRIMINAL REPORTS. 1980-1983; suspended. a. African Law Reports, c/o Dr. A. Milner, Trinity College, Oxford, England.

770 US ISSN 0029-0513
NIKON WORLD. 1967-19??; discontinued. a. Nikon Inc., 623 Stewart Ave., Garden City, NY 11530.

614.7 US ISSN 0733-172X
NOISE POLLUTION PUBLICATIONS ABSTRACTS. (Includes document delivery service) 1981-1986 (vol.4, no.2) irreg. 12614 E. Park St., Cerritos, CA 90701.

636.089 NO ISSN 0078-6713
NORGES VETERINAERHOEGSKOLE. AARSBERETNING/NORWEGIAN COLLEGE OF VETERINARY MEDICINE. 1937-1986. a. Norges Veterinaerhoegskole, Postboks 8146, Oslo-Dep, 0033 Oslo 1, Norway.

658.8 DK ISSN 0108-7274
NORMTAL FOR KOEBMAEND. 1950-1984. irreg. Samvirkende Koebmandsforeninger i Danmark, Svanemoellevej 41, 2900 Hellerup, Denmark.

361.6 US ISSN 0095-1633
NORTH DAKOTA. SOCIAL SERVICE BOARD. STATISTICS. ceased 1977. a. Department of Human Services, State Capitol, Bismark, ND 58505.

630 UK
NORTH OF SCOTLAND COLLEGE OF AGRICULTURE, ABERDEEN. BULLETIN. 1970-19?? irreg. North of Scotland College of Agriculture, 581 King St., Aberdeen AB9 1UD, Scotland.

599.639 US ISSN 0078-1622
NORTH PACIFIC FUR SEAL COMMISSION. PROCEEDINGS OF THE ANNUAL MEETING. 1958-19?? a. North Pacific Fur Seal Commission, c/o National Marine Fisheries Service, Washington, DC 20235.

338 UK
NORTH WEST INDUSTRIAL DEVELOPMENT ASSOCIATION. ANNUAL REPORT. ceased 1985. a. North West Industrial Development Association, Brazennose House (West Door), Brazennose St., Manchester M2 5AZ, England.

614 310 NO ISSN 0332-7965
NORWAY. STATISTISK SENTRALBYRAA. ALKOHOL OG ANDRE RUSMIDLER/ ALCOHOL AND DRUGS. (Subseries of its Norges Offisielle Statistikk) ceased. a. Statistisk Sentralbyraa, Box 8131 Dep., 0033 Oslo 1, Norway.

301.4 NO ISSN 0332-7957
NORWAY. STATISTISK SENTRALBYRAA. FAMILIE STATISTIKK/FAMILY STATISTICS. (Subseries of its Norges Offisielle Statistikk) 1974-19??, ceased. irreg. Statistisk Sentralbyraa, Box 8131 Dep., 0033 Oslo 1, Norway.

623.82 FR ISSN 0078-2157
NOUVEAUTES TECHNIQUES MARITIMES. (Special series of: Journal de la Marine Marchande) ceased 1986. a. Journal de la Marine Marchande, S.A., 190 bd. Haussmann, 75008 Paris, France.

551.48 627   FR   ISSN 0071-8998
O.R.S.T.O.M. ANNALES HYDROLOGIQUES.
(Office de la Recherche Scientifique et Technique
Outre-Mer. Annales Hydrologiques) (Formerly its
Annuaire Hydrologique) 1949-59; N.S. 1959-1973.
irreg. O R S T O M, Institut Francais de Recherche
Scientifique pour le Developpement en Cooperation,
70-74 Route d'Aulnay, 93140 Bondy, France.

551   BL
OBSERVATORIO NACIONAL RIO DE JANEIRO.
CONTRIBUICOES CIENTIFICAS. 1977-1978
(no.9) irreg. Observatorio Nacional, Rua General
Bruce 586, Sao Cristovao, Rio de Janeiro, Brazil.

331.11   US
OCCUPATIONAL EMPLOYMENT IN
HOSPITALS IN NEW JERSEY. discontinued.
triennial. Department of Labor and Industry,
Division of Planning and Research, Office of
Demographic and Economic Analysis, Trenton, NJ
08625-0383.

336   GW
DER OEFFENTLICHE HAUSHALT; Archiv fuer
das oeffentliche Haushaltswesen. 1960-1979. irreg.
Verlag Otto Schwartz und Co., Annastr. 7, 3400
Goettingen, W. Germany (B.R.D.)

550   AU   ISSN 0078-351X
OESTERREICHISCHE MOORFORSCHUNG. 1954-
19??; suspended. irreg. Neydharting Verlag,
Pfarrplatz 3-4, A-4020 Linz, Austria.

790.1
OFFICIAL RULES OF SPORTS AND GAMES.
1949-19?? biennial. Sportshelf Ltd., Box 2294,
Gaithersburg, MD 20879-0294.

700   US
ON S I T E. (Sculpture in the Environment) 1973-
19?? irreg. Site, 65 Bleecker St., New York, NY
10012.

051   US
ON YOUR OWN. ceased 1984. a. 13-30 Corporation,
505 Market St., Knoxville, TN 37902.

620   CN
ONTARIO DIGEST (TORONTO) ceased 1980
(Apr.) irreg. Association of Professional Engineers
of Ontario, 1027 Yonge St., Toronto, Ont. M4W
3E5, Canada.

782.1   NE
OPERA JAARBOEK. 1980-1985. a. Nederlandse
Operastichting, Korte Leidseonarsstraat 12,
Marnixstraat 427, Amsterdam, Netherlands.

333.7   AT
OPERCULUM. 1971-1985. irreg. Australian Littoral
Society, Box 49, Moorooka, Qld. 4105, Australia.
  Supersedes: Queensland Littoral Society.
Newsletter (ISSN 0048-6353)

617   US   ISSN 0743-751X
OPHTHALMOLOGY ANNUAL. 1985-1986. a.
Appleton-Century-Crofts, 25 Van Zant St., East
Norwalk, CT 06855.

338.39   FR   ISSN 0474-5876
ORGANIZATION FOR ECONOMIC
COOPERATION AND DEVELOPMENT.
MACHINERY COMMITTEE. ENGINEERING
INDUSTRIES IN NORTH-AMERICA-EUROPE-
JAPAN. 1953/55-1980/83. irreg. (also avail. in
microfiche) Organization for Economic Cooperation
and Development, Machinery Committee, 2 rue
Andre Pascal, 75775 Paris 16, France

974 614.7 917.306
929   US
OUR HAMPTON HERITAGE. 1983-1984. a. (back
issues avail.) Dan' Papers Ltd., Main St.,
Bridgehampton, NY 11932.

338.91   US
OVERSEAS DEVELOPMENT COUNCIL.
COMMUNIQUE. 1971-19?? irreg. Overseas
Development Council, 1717 Massachusetts Ave.
N.W., Ste. 501, Washington, DC 20036.

338.9   US
OVERSEAS DEVELOPMENT COUNCIL.
DEVELOPMENT PAPERS. 1970-1984. irreg.
Overseas Development Council, 1717 Massachusetts
Ave. N.W., Ste. 501, Washington, DC 20036.

338.9   US   ISSN 0078-7108
OVERSEAS DEVELOPMENT COUNCIL.
MONOGRAPH SERIES. 1970-1982. irreg.
Overseas Development Council, 1717 Massachusetts
Ave. N.W., Ste. 501, Washington, DC 20036.

338.91   US
OVERSEAS DEVELOPMENT COUNCIL.
OCCASIONAL PAPERS. 1971-1978. irreg.
Overseas Development Council, 1717 Massachusetts
Ave. N.W., Ste. 501, Washington, DC 20036.

608.7 602.7   CN   ISSN 0380-6367
P T I C BULLETIN. 1962-1983. irreg., approx. 4/yr.
(back issues avail.) Patent and Trademark Institute
of Canada, Box 1298, Sta. B, Ottawa, Ont. K1P
5R3, Canada.

595.7   US   ISSN 0078-7515
PACIFIC INSECTS MONOGRAPHS. 1961-1986
(no.8) irreg. (Bishop Museum, Department of
Entomology) Bishop Museum Press, Box 19000-A,
Honolulu, HI 96817.

378   US   ISSN 0078-7620
PACIFIC NORTHWEST CONFERENCE ON
HIGHER EDUCATION. PROCEEDINGS. 1935-
1943; N.S. 1946-19?? a. (back issues avail. since
1950; reprint service avail. from UMI) Oregon State
University Press, 101 Waldo Hall, Corvallis, OR
97331.

500 607   PK   ISSN 0078-804X
PAKISTAN COUNCIL OF SCIENTIFIC AND
INDUSTRIAL RESEARCH. REPORT. 1953-1958.
a. Pakistan Council of Scientific and Industrial
Research, 39 Garden Rd., Karachi 0310, Pakistan.

389   PK   ISSN 0078-8457
PAKISTAN STANDARDS INSTITUTION.
REPORT. 1959/60-1967. a. Pakistan Standards
Institution, 39 Garden Road, Karachi 3, Pakistan.

056.9   BL
PARANA EM TRES DIMENSOES. 1973-19?? irreg.
Editora Mayo, Curitiba, Parana, Brazil.

539.7   US
PARTICLES AND NUCLEI SERIES. 1972-19??
irreg. Consultants Bureau, Special Research Report
(Subsidiary of: Plenum Publishing Corp.) 233 Spring
St., New York, NY 10013.

020   PO
PATRIMONIO CULTURAL. 1983-19??; suspended.
irreg. Instituto Portugues do Patrimonio Cultural,
Palacio Nacional de Ajude, 1300 Lisbon Codex,
Portugal.
  Supersedes (1969-19??): Bibliotecas e Arquivos de
Portugal.

371.9   US   ISSN 0099-0302
PENNSYLVANIA. DEPARTMENT OF
EDUCATION. SPECIAL EDUCATION
PROGRAMS-SERVICES. ceased. irreg.
Department of Education, Box 911, Harrisburg, PA
17126.

659.152   AT
PEOPLE IN WOOL. 1981-1985. a. Australian Wool
Corporation, 369 Royal Parade, Parkville, Vic. 3052,
Australia.

658.3   UK
PERSONNEL AND TRAINING DATABOOK.
1970-19?? a. Kogan Page Ltd., 120 Pentonville Rd.,
London N1 9JN, England.
  Formerly: Personnel and Training Management
Yearbook (ISSN 0306-6673)

576.64   US   ISSN 0072-9086
PERSPECTIVES IN VIROLOGY. 1958-1981 (vol.11)
irreg. Alan R. Liss, Inc., 41 E. 11th St., New York,
NY 10003.

770   US   ISSN 0079-1849
PHOTOGRAPHY ANNUAL. 1950-1986. a. C B S
Magazines, One Park Ave., New York, NY 10016.

770   US
PHOTOGRAPHY BUYERS GUIDE. 1957-1986. a. C
B S Magazines, One Park Ave., New York, NY
10016.
  Formerly: Photography Directory and Buying
Guide (ISSN 0079-1857)

537.622   UK
PHYSICS OF SEMICONDUCTORS. (Proceedings
published by host countries) ceased 1978. biennial.
Institute of Physics, Techno House, Redcliffe Way,
Bristol BS1 6NX, England
  Formerly: International Conference on Physics of
Semiconductors. Proceedings (ISSN 0074-3240)

352   NE
PLANNING AND MANAGEMENT. 1979-198?;
suspended. irreg. Dick Coutinho B.V., Badlaan 2,
Muiderberg, Netherlands.

309.1   NZ   ISSN 0111-4123
PLANNING RESEARCH INDEX. 1969-1985. a.
Ministry of Works and Development, Town and
Country Planning Directorate, Box 12041,
Wellington North, New Zealand.

800   UK
PLAYS OF THE YEAR. 1949-1979. irreg. Granada
Publishing Ltd., 8 Grafton St., London W1X 3LA,
England.

821   NZ
POETRY NEW ZEALAND. 1971-1986; discontinued.
biennial. John McIndoe Ltd., Box 694, Dunedin,
New Zealand.

811   US
POETRY PROJECT. 1978-1985. biennial. Cambric
Press, 901 Rye Beach Rd., Huron, OH 44839.
  Formerly: Cambric Poetry Project.

380.1 621.32   IT
POLILUCE - AZIENDE ITALIANE. 1980-198? a.
Tecniche Nuove s.r.l., Via Moscova 46/1, 20121
Milan, Italy.

410   PL   ISSN 0324-8038
POLITECHNIKA SLASKA. ZESZYTY NAUKOWE.
JEZYKI OBCE. 1970-1978 (No. 4) irreg.
Politechnika Slaska, W. Pstrowskiego 7, 44-100
Gliwice, Poland

660   DK
POLYMERTEKNISK ORIENTERING. 1980-198?
irreg. (Polymerteknisk Selskab) Dansk
Ingenioerforening, Vester Farimagsgade 29-31, 1606
Copenhagen V, Denmark.

540   US
POWDER COATINGS BUYER'S GUIDE. 1982-
1985. a. Technology Marketing Corp., 17 Park St.,
Norwalk, CT 06851.

891.85   PL   ISSN 0079-4767
PRACE LITERACKIE. 1959-1977 (vol.19) irreg. (also
avail. in microfilm) (Uniwersytet Wroclawski)
Ossolineum, Publishing House of the Polish
Academy of Sciences, Rynek 9, Wroclaw, Poland

051   US
PRELUDE TO FANTASY. 1978-1985 (no.4) irreg.
Hans-Peter Werner, Ed. & Pub., 2351 N.W., 3rd St.,
No. 203, St. Paul, MN 55112-7285.

338   CY
PRICE INDEX FOR THE MANUFACTURING
SECTOR. 1978-1984; discontinued. a. Ministry of
Finance, Department of Statistics and Research,
Nicosia, Cyprus.

840   CN
PRIX DE LA REVUE ETUDES FRANCAISES.
ceased 1980. irreg. Presses de l'Universite de
Montreal, C.P. 6128, Succ. A, Montreal, Que. H3C
3J7, Canada.

510   US   ISSN 0079-5739
PROBLEMS IN MATHEMATICAL ANALYSIS
REPORT. 1968-19?? irreg. Consultants Bureau,
Special Research Report (Subsidiary of: Plenum
Publishing Corp.) 233 Spring St., New York, NY
10013.

320   SW   ISSN 0552-2005
PROBLEMS OF THE BALTIC. 1962-1980. irreg.
Estonian Information Centre, Box 450, S104 30
Stockholm 45, Sweden.

382   PL
PROBLEMY HANDLU ZAGRANICZNEGO. 1971-
1983. irreg. (Instytut Koniunktur i Cen Handlu
Zagranicznego) Panstwowe Wydawnictwo
Ekonomiczne, Ul. Niecala 4A, Warsaw, Poland.

CESSATIONS

658   US
PROFILES AND TRENDS; hospital inpatient and ambulatory care in southern New York. discontinued 1985. a. (back issues avail.) United Hospital Fund of New York, 55 Fifth Ave., New York, NY 10003.
    Formerly: Ambulatory Care Statistics.

330.1   FR   ISSN 0079-5984
PROFITS. 1970-19??, ceased. irreg. Tchou Editeur, 6 rue du Mail, Paris 2e, France.

338   US   ISSN 0739-9405
PROGRAMMER'S MARKET. 1984-198? a. F & W Publications, Inc., 9993 Alliance Rd., Cincinnati, OH 45242.

543   US   ISSN 0079-6042
PROGRESS IN ANALYTICAL CHEMISTRY. (Represents: Proceedings of the Eastern Analytical Symposia.) 1968-19?? irreg. Plenum Publishing Corp., 233 Spring St., New York, NY 10013.

860   SP
PROSA GALEGA. 1976-1980 (no.3) irreg. Editorial Galaxia, Reconquista 1, Vigo, Spain.

610   US   ISSN 0275-3618
PROSTAGLANDIN AND RELATED LIPIDS. 1980-1982 (vol.2) irreg. Alan R. Liss, Inc., 41 E. 11th St., New York, NY 10003.

614.85   UK
PROTECTION DIRECTORY OF INDUSTRIAL & ENVIRONMENTAL PERSONNEL. vol.3, 1978/79-19??, ceased. a. (reprint service avail. from UMI) (Institution of Industrial Safety Offices) Alan Osborne & Associates, Unit 5, Seager Bldgs., Brookmill Road, London SE8, England.

330 016   PL   ISSN 0033-2445
PRZEGLAD ZACHODNICH CZASOPISM EKONOMICZNYCH. 1955-1972. irreg. (2-3/yr.) Polska Akademia Nauk, Zaklad Nauk Ekonomicznych, Palac Kultury i Nauki, Warsaw, Poland.

614.7 333.77   US
PSYCHE AND DESIGN. ceased. irreg. Association for the Study of Man-Environment Relations, Box 57, Orangeburg, NY 10962.
    Formerly: Man - Environment Systems/Focus Series.

910.202   UK
PUBBING, EATING AND SLEEPING IN THE SOUTH-WEST. Ceased. a. Heritage Publications, Merchants House, Barley Market St., Tavistock, Devon, England.

350   US   ISSN 0276-0843
PUBLIC AFFAIRS REVIEW. 1980-19?? a. Public Affairs Council, 1255 23rd St., N.W., Ste. 750, Washington, DC 20037.

350   UK
PUBLIC AUTHORITIES HANDBOOK. ceased. a. Adprint, 69 Thorpe Rd., Norwich, Norfolk NR1 3AU, England.

336.2   US   ISSN 0148-0863
PUBLIC REVENUES FROM ALCOHOL BEVERAGES. ceased 1984/85. a. Distilled Spirits Council of the United States, Inc., 1250 Eye St., N.W., Washington, DC 20005.

362   US   ISSN 0362-742X
PUBLIC WELFARE IN CALIFORNIA. 1958-1981. a. Health and Welfare Agency, Department of Social Services, Statistical Services Section, 744 P St., Mail Sta. 12-81, Sacramento, CA 95814.

860   AG
PUENTE: LECTURA PARA TODOS. ceased. irreg. Editorial Guadalupe, Mansilla 3865, Buenos Aires, Argentina.

330 621.381   US
PURCELL LETTER ON GRAPHICS FOR MANAGEMENT. ceased. irreg. W.R. Purcell Jr., Ed. & Pub., 29529 Buchanan Dr., Evergreen, CO 80439-8521.

001.3   AT
QUADERNI. 1965-1975. irreg. Istituto Italiano di Cultura - Italian Institute of Culture, 233 Domain Rd., South Yarra, Vic. 3141, Australia.

240   CN   ISSN 0079-9343
R.M. BUCKE MEMORIAL SOCIETY FOR THE STUDY OF RELIGIOUS EXPERIENCE. NEWSLETTER-REVIEW. 1966-19??; discontinued. irreg. R.M. Bucke Memorial Society, 1033 Pine Ave. W., Montreal, Que. H3A 1A1, Canada.

385   SW   ISSN 0347-030X
RAILWAY SCENE. 1968-1985; discontinued. irreg. Frank Stenvalls Foerlag, Foereningsgatan 67, S-211 52 Malmoe, Sweden.

340 332.1   US
RAND MCNALLY LIST OF BANK-RECOMMENDED ATTORNEYS. 1876-1985; discontinued. a. Rand McNally & Co., Financial Publishing Division, 8255 N. Central Park Ave., Skokie, IL 60076

610   US   ISSN 0079-9939
RECENT ADVANCES IN PLASMA DIAGNOSTICS. 1971-19?? irreg. Consultants Bureau, Special Research Report (Subsidiary of: Plenum Publishing Corp.) 233 Spring St., New York, NY 10013.

500   JA   ISSN 0286-715X
RECENT PROGRESS OF NATURAL SCIENCES IN JAPAN. ceased 1986 (vol.11) a. Science Council of Japan - Nihon Gakujutsu Kaigi, 7-22-34 Roppongi, Minato-ku, Tokyo 106, Japan.

780.65   UK
RECORD & TAPE DIRECTORY. ceased. a. Adprint, 69 Thorpe Rd., Norwich, Norfolk NR1 3AU, England.

790.1   US
RECREATION, SPORTS & LEISURE RESOURCE. 1984-198? a. Lakewood Publications, Inc., 50 S. 9th St., Minneapolis, MN 55402.

314 910.202   SP
REGIONAL BREAKDOWN OF WORLD TRAVEL STATISTICS. ceased. a. World Tourism Organization, Capitan Haya 42, 28020 Madrid, Spain.

500 016   US   ISSN 0080-0619
REGIONAL SCIENCE RESEARCH INSTITUTE. BIBLIOGRAPHY SERIES. 1961-1975 (no.5); suspended. irreg. Regional Science Research Institute, Box 3735, Peace Dale, RI 02883.

330   US   ISSN 0080-0627
REGIONAL SCIENCE RESEARCH INSTITUTE. MONOGRAPH SERIES. 1965-1978 (no.7); suspended. irreg. Regional Science Research Institute, Box 3735, Peace Dale, RI 02883.

670   FR
REPERTOIRE DES ENTREPRISES ARTISANALES. ceased. a. (Chambre de Metiers Departementale) Union Francaise d'Annuaires Professionnels, 13 av. Vladimir Komarov, B.P. 36, 78192 Trappes Cedex, France.
    Formerly: Guide-Annuaire Officiel de l'Artisanat et de Metiers.

371.8 332.7   CK
REVISTA A P I C E/A P I C E JOURNAL. 1975-19?? irreg. (back issues avail.) Asociacion Panamericana de Instituciones de Credito Educativo, Calle 38 no. 8-56, Apdo. Aereo 17388, Bogota, Colombia.

340   PN   ISSN 0302-6655
REVISTA JURIDICA PANAMENA. discontinued 1976 (vol.6) irreg. Universidad de Panama, Centro de Investigacion Juridica, Estafeta Universitaria, Panama, Panama.

368.4   MX   ISSN 0482-6876
REVISTA MEXICANA DE SEGURIDAD SOCIAL. 1971-1985 (Dec.) irreg. Instituto Mexicano del Seguro Social, San Jeronimo Lidice, Mexico 20, D.F., Mexico.

330   US
RICE UNIVERSITY. PROGRAM OF DEVELOPMENT STUDIES. DISCUSSION PAPERS. 1970-19?? irreg. (12-16/yr.) Rice University, Program of Development Studies, 121 Sewall Hall, Houston, TX 77001.

860   AG
RIO NEGRO, ARGENTINA. DIRECCION PROVINCIAL DE CULTURA. MONOGRAFIAS. 1972-19?? irreg. Direccion Provincial de Cultura, Roca 250, Viedma, Rio Negro, Argentina.

001.535   US
ROBOTICS AND C A D/C A M MARKET PLACE. published only once, 1984. a. R.R. Bowker Company, Database Publishing Group, 245 W. 17th St., New York, NY 10011.

913   GW   ISSN 0076-2733
ROEMISCH-GERMANISCHES ZENTRALMUSEUM, MAINZ. AUSSTELLUNGSKATALOGE. 1966-198? irreg. Dr. Rudolf Habelt GmbH, Am Buchenhang 1, 5300 Bonn 1, W. Germany (B.R.D.).

300   DK   ISSN 0106-8911
ROSKILDE UNIVERSITETSCENTER. INSTITUT FOR SOCIALVIDENSKAB. INSTITUTTETS SKRIFTSERIE. 1982-1986 (no.20) irreg. Roskilde Universitetscenter, Institut for Socialvidenskab, Postbox 260, 4000 Roskilde, Denmark.

677.3   AT
ROUSEABOUT. 1980-1985. irreg. Australian Wool Corporation, 369 Royal Parade, Parkville, Vic. 3052, Australia.

500   CN   ISSN 0080-4304
ROYAL CANADIAN INSTITUTE. PROCEEDINGS. 1879-19?? a. Royal Canadian Institute, 191 College St., Toronto 2b, Ontario, Canada.

500   CN   ISSN 0080-4312
ROYAL CANADIAN INSTITUTE. TRANSACTIONS. 1889-19?? irreg. Royal Canadian Institute, 191 College St., Toronto 2b, Ontario, Canada.

333.33   UK   ISSN 0308-1451
ROYAL INSTITUTION OF CHARTERED SURVEYORS YEAR BOOK. 1975-1985. a. Kelly's Directories, Ltd., Windsor Court, East Grinstead House, East Grinstead, West Sussex RH19 1XB, England.

510   UK
ROYAL IRISH ACADEMY. CONFERENCE ON NUMERICAL ANALYSIS. PROCEEDINGS. 1977-19??, discontinued. biennial. Academic Press Inc. (London) Ltd., 24-28 Oval Rd., London NW1 7DX, England

913 700   UK   ISSN 0309-393X
ROYAL SCOTTISH MUSEUM INFORMATION SERIES: ART & ARCHAEOLOGY. (Former name of issuing body: Royal Scottish Museum) 1979-1984; suspended. irreg. (back issues avail.) National Museums of Scotland, Chambers St., Edinburgh EH1 1JF, Scotland.

551   UK   ISSN 0307-5052
ROYAL SCOTTISH MUSEUM INFORMATION SERIES: GEOLOGY. (Former name of issuing body: Royal Scottish Museum) 1970-1984 (no.9); suspended. irreg. (back issues avail.) National Museums of Scotland, Chambers St., Edinburgh EH1 1JF, Scotland.

500.9   UK   ISSN 0307-5036
ROYAL SCOTTISH MUSEUM INFORMATION SERIES: NATURAL HISTORY. (Former name of issuing body: Royal Scottish Museum) 1973-1983 (no.10); suspended. irreg. (back issues avail.) National Museums of Scotland, Chambers St., Edinburgh EH1 1JF, Scotland.

600   UK   ISSN 0307-5044
ROYAL SCOTTISH MUSEUM INFORMATION SERIES: TECHNOLOGY. (Former name of issuing body: Royal Scottish Museum) 1972-1985 (no.3); suspended. irreg. (back issues avail.) National Museums of Scotland, Chambers St., Edinburgh EH1 1JF, Scotland.

634.9   RW
RWANDA. PROJET PILOTE FORESTIER. BULLETIN D'INFORMATION. suspended. a. Projet Pilote Forestier, B.P. 1, Kibuye, Rwanda.

350　　　　　　　　　　　US
S C A N. (Superior California Administration Newsletter) 1974-19?? a. (back issues avail.) California State University at Chico, School of Behavioral and Social Sciences, Chico, CA 95929.

539　621.48　　　　　　　BE
S C K ANNUAL REPORT. 1962-1984. a. Studiecentrum voor Kernenergie - Centre d'Edude de l'Energie Nucleaire, Boeretang 200, B-2400 MOL, Belgium.
　　Formerly: Studiecentrum voor Kernenergie. Annual Scientific Report (ISSN 0081-7155)

020.9　　　　　　US　ISSN 0273-2343
S H A R E; a directory of feminist library workers. (Sisters Have Resources Everywhere) 1975-19?? irreg. Women Library Workers, 2027 Parker, Berkeley, CA 94704.

020　　　　　　SW　ISSN 0348-243X
S K R-MEDDELANDEN. Ceased (No.6, 1983) irreg. Kungliga Biblioteket, Box 5039, S-102 41 Stockholm, Sweden.

382　　　　　　SP　ISSN 0080-9985
S L A M: TRADE YEAR BOOK OF AFRICA/S L A M: ANNUAIRE COMMERCIAL DE L'AFRIQUE. 1962-1980. irreg. Editorial Office, German Perez Carasco 63, Madrid 27, Spain.
　　Formerly: Spanish, Lusitanian, American Trade Directory.

364　　　　　　　　　　　US
SAGE RESEARCH PROGRESS SERIES IN CRIMINOLOGY. 1977-198? irreg. (back issues avail.) (American Society for Criminology) Sage Publications, Inc., 2111 W. Hillcrest Dr., Newbury Park, CA 91320.

570　　　　　　US　ISSN 0080-5467
SAINT BONAVENTURE UNIVERSITY. SCIENCE STUDIES. 1932-1976 (vol.32) a. St. Bonaventure University, c/o Stephen Eaton, Ed., Ten Mile Rd., Allegany, NY 14706.

338.1　　　　　CY　ISSN 0253-8636
SALES OF VINE PRODUCTS MANUFACTURED IN CYPRUS. discontinued. a. Department of Statistics and Research, Ministry of Finance, Nicosia, Cyprus.

340　　　　　　　　　　　US
SAN FERNANDO VALLEY LAW REVIEW. 1967-19?? a. 8353 Sepulveda Blvd., Sepulveda, CA 91343.
　　Formerly: University of San Fernando Valley Law Review (ISSN 0042-000X)

301.2　016　　　　　　　SW
SCANDINAVIAN AFRICANA. 1981-198?, discontinued. irreg. Nordiska Afrikainstitutet - Scandinavian Institute of African Studies, Box 1703, S-751 47 Uppsala, Sweden.

642.58　371　　　　　　　US
SCHOOL BREAKFAST NEWSLETTER. ceased. irreg. Department of Education, 333 Market St., Harrisburg, PA 17108.
　　Supersedes in part: School Food Services Bulletin (ISSN 0036-6552)

333.7　　　　　　　　　　GW
SCHRIFTENREIHE AUS DEN NATURSCHUTZGEBIETEN BAYERNS. published only once, 1978. irreg. (Landesamt fuer Umweltschutz) R. Oldenbourg Verlag GmbH, Rosenheimer Str. 145, 8000 Munich 80, W. Germany (B.R.D.).

614.7　　　　　　　　　　GW
SCHRIFTENREIHE CHEMISCHE ANALYTIK UND UMWELTTECHNOLOGIE. ceased 1979. irreg. (Landesamt fuer Umweltschutz) R. Oldenbourg Verlag GmbH, Rosenheimer Str. 145, 8000 Munich 80, W. Germany (B.R.D.).

531.64　　　　　　　　　GW
SCHRIFTENREIHE KERNENERGIE. 1978 (ceased with one issue) irreg. (Landesamt fuer Umweltschutz) R. Oldenbourg Verlag GmbH, Rosenheimer Str. 145, 8000 Munich 80, W. Germany (B.R.D.).

333.7　　　　　　　　　　GW
SCHRIFTENREIHE NATURSCHUTZ UND LANDSCHAFTSPFLEGE. ceased 1981. irreg. (Landesamt fuer Umweltschutz) R. Oldenbourg Verlag GmbH, Rosenheimer Str. 145, 8000 Munich 80, W. Germany (B.R.D.)

011　310　　　　　　　　SZ
SCHWEIZERISCHE BIBLIOGRAPHIE FUER STATISTIK UND VOLKSWIRTSCHAFT/ BIBLIOGRAPHIE SUISSE DE STATISTIQUE ET D'ECONOMIE POLITIQUE. 1937-1984. biennial. Schweizerische Gesellschaft fuer Statistik und Volkswirtschaft u. Bundesamt fuer Statistik - Societe Suisse de Statistique et d'Economie, Hallwylstr. 15, 3003 Berne, Switzerland.

500　　　　　　SZ　ISSN 0252-2969
SCHWEIZERISCHEN NATURFORSCHENDEN GESELLSCHAFT. JAHRBUCH. ceased 1986. a. (back issues avail.) (Schweizerische Naturforschende Gesellschaft) Birkhaeuser Verlag AG, P.O. Box 133, CH-4010 Basel, Switzerland.
　　Formerly: Verhandlungen der Schweizerischen Naturforschenden Gesellschaft.

338.1　630　　　JA　ISSN 0911-8012
SCIENCE COUNCIL OF JAPAN. ANNUAL REPORT ON THE PROGRESS OF AGRICULTURE. 1951-1986 (no.33) a. Science Council of Japan - Nihon Gakujutsu Kaigi, 7-22-34 Roppongi, Minato-ku, Tokyo 106, Japan.
　　Formerly: Science Council of Japan. Annual Report of the Development of Agriculture in Japan (ISSN 0546-109X)

894.2　951.7　　　US　ISSN 0080-8377
SCRIPTA MONGOLICA. 1952-1969. irreg.? (Harvard-Yenching Institute) Harvard University Press, 79 Garden St., Cambridge, MA 02138.

551.4　　　　　US　ISSN 0037-0118
SEAHORSE. 1964-1982. irreg. Hydro Products, A Tetra Tech Co., 11777 Sorrento Valley Rd., San Diego, CA 92121.

510　　　　　　SP　ISSN 0085-6029
SEMINARIO MATEMATICO GARCIA DE GALDEANO. PUBLICACIONES. 1959-1985(vol.33) irreg. Seminario Matematico Garcia de Galdeano, Facultad de Ciencias, Zaragoza, Spain.

001.3　　　　　　　　　　US
SEMIOTIC SCENE. 1976-19?? irreg. Semiotic Society of America, Box 10, Bloomington, IN 47402.
　　Incorporating: B L S-Bulletin of Literary Semiotics.

370　　　　　　　　　　　DK
SERIE OM UDDANNELSESFORSKNING. 1979-1987. irreg. Aalborg Universitetscenter, Institut for Uddannelse og Socialisering, Fibigerstraede 3, 9220 Aalborg OE, Denmark.

628.96　　　　　　　　　AT
SERVING AUSTRALIAN AGRICULTURE. 1969-1986; discontinued. a. Agricultural and Veterinary Chemicals Association of Australia Ltd., P.O. Box 3968, Sydney NSW 2001, Australia.
　　Formerly (until 1984): A V C A Directory.

340　　　　　　　　　　　UK
SHAW'S LEGAL DIARY. 1983-198? a. Shaw & Sons Ltd., Shaway House, Lower Sydenham, London SE26 5AE, England.

614.7　　　　　　　　　　US
SIERRA CLUB. INTERNATIONAL REPORT. 1972-19??; discontinued. irreg. (looseleaf format) Sierra Club, 730 Polk St., San Francisco, CA 94109.

810　　　　　　US　ISSN 0037-5306
SILO. 1962-19?? a. Bennington College, Bennington, VT 05201.

616.8　　　　　SZ　ISSN 0302-5128
SLEEP. ceased. biennial. (reprint service avail. from ISI) S. Karger AG, Allschwilerstrasse 10, P.O. Box, CH-4009 Basel, Switzerland.

800　　　　　　　　　　　US
SLOW LORIS READER. 1971-1974? a. Slow Loris Press, 923 Highview St., Pittsburgh, PA 15206.
　　Supersedes (after vol.4, no.1,): Rapport (Pittsburgh)

572　911　　　　NE　ISSN 0081-0398
SOCIAAL-GEOGRAFISCHE STUDIEN. 1955-19?? irreg. Van Gorcum, Box 43, 9400 AA Assen, Netherlands.

300　　　　　　CN　ISSN 0081-0460
SOCIAL SCIENCE STUDIES. 1966-1981; discontinued. irreg. (University of Ottawa) University of Ottawa Press, 603 Cumberland, Ottawa, Ont. K1N 6N5, Canada.

574　　　　　　AG　ISSN 0037-8380
SOCIEDAD ARGENTINA DE BIOLOGIA. REVISTA. 1924-1980. irreg. (Sociedad Argentina de Biologia) Instituto de Biologia y Medicina Experimental, Obligado 2490, 1428 Buenos Aires, Argentina.

860　　　　　　　　　　　SP
SOCIEDAD ESPANOLA DE LITERATURA GENERAL Y COMPARADA. ANUARIO. 1978-1981. a. Ediciones Catedra, Don Ramon de la Cruz 67, Madrid, Spain.

633.1　338.1　　　　　　BL
SORGO - UMA ALTERNATIVA ECONOMICA. ceased 1974. a. Fundacao de Economia e Estatistica, Sao Manoel 466, 90000 Porto Alegre, RS, Brazil.

336　　　　　　US　ISSN 0494-8203
SOURCE REFERENCES FOR FACTS AND FIGURES ON GOVERNMENT FINANCE. ceased 1984 (Apr.) biennial. Tax Foundation, Inc., One Thomas Circle, N.W., Ste. 500, Washington, DC 20005.

362.6　　　　　　　　　　US
SOURCEBOOK ON AGING. 1977-1979 (2nd edt.) irreg. Marquis Who's Who, Inc., 200 E. Ohio St., Chicago, IL 60611.

155.937　301　　　　　　US
SOURCEBOOK ON DEATH AND DYING. 1982; published only once. irreg. Marquis Who's Who, Inc., 200 E. Ohio St., Chicago, IL 60611.

613.2　　　　　　　　　　US
SOURCEBOOK ON FOOD AND NUTRITION. 1978-1982 (3rd edt.) irreg. Marquis Who's Who, Inc., 200 E. Ohio St., Chicago, IL 60611.

338.1　　　　　SA　ISSN 0300-5747
SOUTH AFRICA. MAIZE BOARD. REPORT ON GRAIN SORGHUM AND BUCKWHEAT FOR THE FINANCIAL YEAR. (Report year ends April 30) ceased. a. Maize Board - Mielieraad, P.O. Box 669, Pretoria 0001, South Africa.

296　920　　　　　　　　SA
SOUTH AFRICAN JEWRY AND WHO'S WHO. suspended. irreg. (University of the Witwatersrand Medical School) Alex White & Company, 22 Yaron Ave. Lea Glen Roodeport, P.O. Box 825, Florida 1710, South Africa.

700　721　　　　　　　　SA
SOUTH AFRICAN NATIONAL GALLERY. BULLETIN. 1980-1986, suspended. irreg. South African National Gallery, Box 2420, Cape Town 8000, South Africa.

664.1　　　　　　　　　　SA
SOUTH AFRICAN SUGAR YEAR BOOK. 1917-1985. a. South African Sugar Association, Box 1209, Durban 4000, South Africa.

614.7　　　　　AT　ISSN 0311-4805
SOUTH AUSTRALIA. DEPARTMENT OF ENVIRONMENT AND PLANNING. COASTLINE. 1973-1985. irreg. Department of Environment and Planning, G.P.O. Box 667, Adelaide, S.A. 5001, Australia.

614.7　　　　　AT　ISSN 0159-3641
SOUTH AUSTRALIA. DEPARTMENT OF ENVIRONMENT AND PLANNING. DIRECTORY OF NON-GOVERNMENT ENVIRONMENTAL GROUPS IN SOUTH AUSTRALIA. 1979-1985. irreg. Department of Environment and Planning, G.P.O. Box 667, Adelaide, S.A. 5001, Australia.

910.09　　　　　　　　　AT
SOUTH PACIFIC HOLIDAYS. ceased. a. Hay Street Publications Pty Ltd, 405-411 Sussex St, Sydney, NSW 2000, Australia.

CESSATIONS

520 US ISSN 0147-2003
SOUTHWEST REGIONAL CONFERENCE FOR ASTRONOMY AND ASTROPHYSICS. PROCEEDINGS. 1975-1984; suspended. a. (also avail. in microfiche) Southwest Regional Conference for Astronomy and Astrophysics, Department of Physics, Texas Tech University, Lubbock, TX 79409.

632 SP ISSN 0211-4682
SPAIN. INSTITUTO NACIONAL DE INVESTIGACIONES AGRARIAS. ANALES. SERIE: AGRICOLA. 1971-1985 (vol.28) irreg. (1-2/yr.) Instituto Nacional de Investigaciones Agrarias, Jose Abascal 56, 28003 Madrid, Spain.
  Supersedes in part: Spain. Instituto Nacional de Investigaciones Agronomicas. Anales; (1927-1969): Boletin de Patologia Vegetal y Entomologia Agricola (ISSN 0366-2381); Formed by the merger of: Spain. Instituto Nacional de Investigaciones Agrarias. Anales. Serie: Produccion Vegetal (ISSN 0376-1851); Spain. Instituto Nacional de Investigaciones Agrarias. Anales. Serie: Proteccion Vegetal; Which superseded in part: Spain. Instituto Nacional de Investagaciones Agronomicas. Anales (ISSN 0210-2501)

634.9 500 SP ISSN 0211-9102
SPAIN. INSTITUTO NACIONAL DE INVESTIGACIONES AGRARIAS. ANALES. SERIE: FORESTAL. (Subseries of Instituto Nacional de Investigaciones Agrarias. Anales) ceased 1985 (vol.9) irreg. (back issues avail.) Instituto Nacional de Investigaciones Agrarias, Jose Abascal 56, Madrid 3, Spain.
  Formerly: Spain. Instituto Nacional de Investigaciones Agrarias. Anales. Serie: Recursos Naturales (ISSN 0210-2471)

636 SP ISSN 0211-4674
SPAIN. INSTITUTO NACIONAL DE INVESTIGACIONES AGRARIAS. ANALES. SERIE: GANADERA. 1971-1985 (vol.22) irreg. Instituto Nacional de Investigaciones Agrarias, Jose Abascal 56, Madrid 3, Spain.
  Formed by the merger of: Spain. Instituto Nacional de Investigaciones Agrarias. Anales. Serie: Higiene y Sanidad Animal (ISSN 0210-2498); Spain. Instituo Nacional de Investigaciones Agrarias. Anales. Serie: Produccion Animal (ISSN 0376-1843); Which superseded in part: Spain. Instituto Nacional de Investigaciones Agronomicas. Anales (ISSN 0020-4129)

630 SP
SPAIN. INSTITUTO NACIONAL DE INVESTIGACIONES AGRARIAS. ANALES. SERIE: TECHNOLOGIA. ceased 1979 (no.5) irreg. Instituto Nacional de Investigaciones Agrarias, Jose Abascal 56, Madrid 3, Spain.

370 SP ISSN 0561-4619
SPAIN. MINISTERIO DE EDUCACION Y CIENCIA. JUNTA NACIONAL CONTRA EL ANALFABETISMO. BOLETIN. 1951-1962. a. Ministerio de Educacion y Ciencia, Junta Nacional Contra el Analfabetismo, Los Madrazo 17, Madrid, Spain.

620 UK
SPANNER (LONDON) ceased. a. (City and Guilds College Union) Dominion Press Ltd., Dominion House, 101 Southwark St., London, SE1 oJH, England.
  Incorporates: Guild's Engineer.

616.4 US ISSN 0193-0982
SPECIAL TOPICS IN ENDOCRINOLOGY AND METABOLISM. 1979-1985 (vol.7) irreg. Alan R. Liss, Inc., 41 E. 11th St., New York, NY 10003.

589 UK ISSN 0306-2074
SPORE RESEARCH. discontinued. irreg. Academic Press Inc. (London) Ltd., 24-28 Oval Rd., London NW1 7DX, England

370 US ISSN 0081-4237
STANDARD EDUCATION ALMANAC. 1968-1984 (17th edt.) a. Marquis Who's Who, Inc., 200 E. Ohio St., Chicago, IL 60611.

610 US
STANDARD MEDICAL ALMANAC. 1977-1979 (2nd edt.) irreg. Marquis Who's Who, Inc., 200 E. Ohio St., Chicago, IL 60611.

617.102 US ISSN 0081-427X
STANDARD NOMENCLATURE OF ATHLETIC INJURIES. 1966-19?? irreg. American Medical Association, Committee on Sports Injuries, 535 N. Dearborn St., Chicago, IL 60610.

350 II ISSN 0081-4504
STATE GOVERNMENT UNDERTAKINGS IN GUJARAT. 1960/61-1976/77. a. Bureau of Economics and Statistics, Sector No. 18, Gandhinagar, India.

382 314 EI ISSN 0081-4857
STATISTICAL OFFICE OF THE EUROPEAN COMMUNITIES. ASSOCIES STATISTIQUE DU COMMERCE EXTERIEUR. ANNUAIRE. 1968-1983; discontinued. a. B.P. 1907, Luxembourg, Luxembourg

338 EI
STATISTICAL OFFICE OF THE EUROPEAN COMMUNITIES. INDUSTRIAL STATISTICS. SHORT TERM TRENDS. ceased. irreg. Statistical Office of the European Communities, B.P. 1907, Luxembourg, Luxembourg

330 316 EI ISSN 0081-492X
STATISTICAL OFFICE OF THE EUROPEAN COMMUNITIES. OVERSEAS ASSOCIATES. ANNUAIRE STATISTIQUES DES ETATS AFRICAINS ET MALGACHE. ceased. a. Rue Alcide de Gasperi, B.P. 1907, Luxembourg, Luxembourg

336 314 EI ISSN 0081-4938
STATISTICAL OFFICE OF THE EUROPEAN COMMUNITIES. RECETTES FISCALES. ANNUAIRE. ceased. a. Rue Alcide de Gasperi, B.P. 1907, Luxembourg, Luxembourg

301 EI ISSN 0081-4989
STATISTICAL OFFICE OF THE EUROPEAN COMMUNITIES. STATISTIQUES SOCIALES. ANNUAIRE. ceased. a. Rue Alcide de Gasperi, B.P. 1907, Luxembourg, Luxembourg

621.389 AT ISSN 0312-0104
STEREO BUYER'S GUIDE. CASSETTES. 1971-1986. a. Australian Hi-Fi Publications Pty. Ltd., Box 341, Mona Vale, N.S.W. 2103, Australia.

621.389 AT ISSN 0312-004X
STEREO BUYER'S GUIDE. DIRECTORY. 1971-1985. a. Australian Hi-Fi Publications Pty. Ltd., Box 341, Mona Vale, N.S.W. 2103, Australia.

621.389 AT ISSN 0312-0074
STEREO BUYER'S GUIDE. SPEAKERS. 1971-1986. a. Australian Hi-Fi Publications Pty. Ltd., Box 341, Mona Vale, N.S.W. 2103, Australia.

943.7 CS ISSN 0585-4172
STREDOCESKY SBORNIK HISTORICKY. 1957-1981 (vol.16) irreg. Statni Oblastni Archiv Praha, Horska 7, 128 00 Praha 2, Czechoslovakia

380 UK
STUBBS DIRECTORY; professional and commercial products and services. 1879-19?? a. (also avail. in magnetic tape) Dun & Bradstreet Ltd., 6-8 Bonhill St., London EC2A 4BU, England.
  Formerly (until 1979): Stubbs Buyers Guide (ISSN 0081-6043)

554 914 PL ISSN 0081-6418
STUDIA GEOGRAFICZNO-FIZYCZNE Z OBSZARU OPOLSZCZYZNY. 1968-19??, ceased. irreg. Instytut Slaski, Instytut Naukowo-Badawczy, Luboszycka 3, Opole, Poland.

943.8 PL ISSN 0081-7058
STUDIA Z DZIEJOW OSADNICTWA. (Subseries of Polska Akademia Nauk. Instytut Historii Kultury Materialnej. Studia i Materialy) 1963-1970 (vol. 8) irreg. (Polska Akademia Nauk, Instytut Historii Kultury Materialnej) Ossolineum, Publishing House of the Polish Academy of Sciences, Rynek 9, 50-106 Wroclaw, Poland

970 GW ISSN 0081-7503
STUDIES IN AMERICAN HISTORY. 1963-19?? irreg. Walter de Gruyter & Co., Mouton Publishers, Postfach 110240, D-1000 Berlin 11, W. Germany (B.R.D.)

810 GW ISSN 0081-752X
STUDIES IN AMERICAN LITERATURE. 1964-19?? irreg. Walter de Gruyter & Co., Mouton Publishers, Postfach 110240, D-1000 Berlin 11, W. Germany (B.R.D.)

370 US
STUDIES IN EDUCATION. 1959-19?? a. West Texas State University, College of Education, Box 208, WT Station, Canyon, TX 79016.

820 GW ISSN 0081-7899
STUDIES IN ENGLISH LITERATURE. 1965-19?? irreg. Walter de Gruyter & Co., Mouton Publishers, Postfach 110240, D-1000 Berlin 11, W. Germany (B.R.D.)

860 GW ISSN 0081-8534
STUDIES IN SPANISH LITERATURE. 1971-19?? irreg. Walter de Gruyter & Co., Mouton Publishers, Postfach 110240, D-1000 Berlin 11, W. Germany (B.R.D.)

500 SW ISSN 0081-8704
STUDIES IN THE THEORY OF SCIENCE. 1969-1976. irreg. Goeteborgs Universitet, Department of Theory of Science and Research, Vaestra Hamngatan 3, S-411 17 Gothenburg, Sweden.

340 SW ISSN 0348-1964
STUDIES OF LAW IN SOCIAL CHANGE AND DEVELOPMENT. 1977-1981. irreg. Nordiska Afrikainstitutet - Scandinavian Institute of African Studies, Box 1703, S-751 47 Uppsala, Sweden.

614.77 EI
STUDIES ON THE RADIOACTIVE CONTAMINATION OF THE SEA. ANNUAL REPORT. discontinued. a. (European Atomic Energy Community) Office for Official Publications of the European Communities, P.O. Box 1003, L-2985 Luxembourg, Luxembourg

157.63 616.86 CN ISSN 0228-8648
SUBSTANCE ABUSE BOOK REVIEW INDEX. 1980-1984. a. Addiction Research Foundation of Ontario, 33 Russell St., Toronto, Ont. M5S 2S1, Canada.

631.8 661.63 US ISSN 0081-9255
SULPHUR INSTITUTE. TECHNICAL BULLETIN. 1963-19?? irreg. Sulphur Institute, 1725 K St. N.W., Washington, DC 20006.

661.63 US ISSN 0163-0644
SULPHUR RESEARCH & DEVELOPMENT. 1977-19?? a. (back issues avail.) Sulphur Institute, 1725 K St., N.W., Washington, DC 20006.

991.4 PH
SULU STUDIES. 1972-1974. a. Notre Dame of Jolo College, Jolo, Sulu 7601, Philippines

314 SW
SWEDEN. STATISTISKA CENTRALBYRAAN BIBLIOTEK. STATISTIK FRAAN INTERNATIONELLA ORGAN. 1974-1986. a. Statistics Distribution, S-701 89 Oerebro, Sweden.
  Former titles: Sweden. Statistiska Centralbyraan Bibliotek. Internationella Organ. Statistik (ISSN 0280-7629) & Aktuell Internationell Statistik i SCBs Bibliotek.

314 331 SW ISSN 0082-0180
SWEDEN. STATISTISKA CENTRALBYRAAN. INFORMATION I PROGNOSFRAGOR/ FORECASTING INFORMATION. 1965-1985. irreg. Statistics Distribution, S-701 89 Oerebro, Sweden.

331.1 351.4 SW ISSN 0348-811X
SWEDEN. STATISTISKA CENTRALBYRAAN. STATSANSTAELLDA/GOVERNMENT EMPLOYEES. 1954-1986. irreg. Statistiska Centralbyraan, Distribution, S-701 89 Oerebro, Sweden.

770 UK
SYMPOSIUM ON PHOTOGRAPHIC GELATIN. PROCEEDINGS. 1974-19??, discontinued. irreg. (Royal Photographic Society of Great Britain, Scientific and Technical Group) Academic Press Inc. (London) Ltd., 24-28 Oval Rd., London NW1 7DX, England.

338.9　　　　　US
T A I C H CATEGORY REPORTS: DEVELOPMENT ASSISTANCE PROGRAMS OF U.S. NON-PROFIT ORGANIZATIONS ABROAD. 1973-19?? irreg. (American Council of Voluntary Agencies for Foreign Service, Inc) Technical Assistance Information Clearing House, 200 Park Ave. S., New York, NY 10003.

338　　　　　US　　ISSN 0738-4912
T A I C H DIRECTORY; U.S. nonprofit organizations in development assistance abroad. ceased. a. (American Council of Voluntary Agencies for Foreign Service, Inc.) Technical Assistance Information Clearing House, 200 Park Ave. South, New York, NY 10003

792　　　　　US
T C G NATIONAL WORKING CONFERENCE. PROCEEDINGS. 1976-1982. biennial. Theatre Communications Group, 355 Lexington Ave., New York, NY 10017.

800　　　　　II　　ISSN 0082-1454
TAGORE STUDIES. 1969-1980. a. Tagore Research Institute, c/o Ms. Pronoti Mukerji, Rabindra Charcha Bhavan, Kalighat Park, Calcutta 700 026, India.

630 581　　　　CH
TAIWAN AGRICULTURAL RESEARCH INSTITUTE. BULLETIN. 1950-1979. irreg. Taiwan Agricultural Research Institute, Taichung, Taiwan, Republic of China.

350　　　　　II　　ISSN 0082-1594
TAMIL NADU. LEGISLATIVE COUNCIL. QUINQUENNIAL REVIEW. 1952/57-1980/84. quinquennial. Legislative Council Secretariat, Fort St. George, Madras 600009, India.

387　　　　　US
TAMPA PORT HANDBOOK. 1978-1985/86. a. Howard Publications, Inc., 33 S. Hogan St., Ste. 230, Box 4728, Jacksonville, FL 32201.

384 355　　　　GW　　ISSN 0082-1861
TASCHENBUCH FUER DEN FERNMELDEDIENST. 1960-1979 (vol.7) a. Wehr und Wissen Verlagsgesellschaft GmbH, Heilsbachstr., Postfach 87, 5300 Bonn-Duisdorf, W. Germany (B.R.D.)

355　　　　　GW　　ISSN 0082-1942
TASCHENBUCH FUER LOGISTIK. 1961-1977 (vol.7) a. Wehr und Wissen Verlagsgesellschaft GmbH, Heilsbachstr., Postfach 87, 5300 Bonn-Duisdorf, W. Germany (B.R.D.)

336　　　　　US
TAX FOUNDATION. PROCEEDINGS OF CONFERENCES. 1953-1985. a. Tax Foundation, Inc., Public Information Department, One Thomas Circle, N.W., Ste. 500, Washington, DC 20005.

378　　　　　US
TEACHER CERTIFICATION RECIPROCITY POLICIES IN THE U.S. 1969-198? biennial. (back issues avail.) Association for School, College & University Staffing, 301 S. Swift Rd., Addison, IL 16101-1499.
  Formerly: Certification Reciprocity Policies in the U.S.

382　　　　　GW　　ISSN 0033-0876
TECHNIC INTERNATIONAL. 1967-1981. irreg. Droste-Verlag GmbH, Pressehaus am Martin-Luther-Platz, 4000 Duesseldorf 1, W. Germany (B.R.D.)
  Formerly: German Exporter (ISSN 0016-8742)

676.3　　　　US
TECHNICAL ASSOCIATION OF THE PULP AND PAPER INDUSTRY. PAPER SYNTHETICS CONFERENCE. PROCEEDINGS. discontinued. a. Technical Association of the Pulp and Paper Industry, Inc., Technology Park/Atlanta, Box 105113, Atlanta, GA 30348.

678　　　　　GW
TECHNICAL NOTES FOR THE RUBBER INDUSTRY. 1955-1981 (no.53) irreg. (1-2/yr.) Bayer AG, 5090 Leverkusen-Bayerwerk, W. Germany (B.R.D.)

682.11　　　　US
TEENS & BOYS DIRECTORY. ceased 1986 (Sep.) a. Larkin-Pluznick-Larkin, Inc., 210 Boylston St., Chestnut Hill, MA 02167

330.9　　　　US
TEXAS: TRENDS AND FORECASTS. 1983-1985. irreg. University of Texas at Austin, Bureau of Business Research, Box 7459, Austin, TX 78713.

332.6　　　　TH　　ISSN 0082-3783
THAI INVESTMENT REVIEW. 1968-198? a. Business (Thailand) Co., Ltd., 185 Soi Putta-O Soth, New Road, Bangkok 10500, Thailand.

930　　　　　IT　　ISSN 0082-4097
THESAURISMATA. 1962-1982; suspended. a. Istituto Ellenico di Studi Bizantini e Post-Bizantini, Castello 3412, 3412 Venezia, Italy.

810　　　　　US
THOREAU SOCIETY BOOKLETS. 1942-19??; discontinued. irreg. (reprint service avail. from UMI) Thoreau Society, Inc., State University College, Geneseo, NY 14454.

282　　　　　DK
TIDENS TEGN; et aar med kirken. 1981-1985. a. Katolsk Forlag, Bredgade 69, A st., 1260 Copenhagen K, Denmark.

910.202　　　　US
TIME ZONES. ceased. a. (Transamerica Airlines) Halsey Publishing Co., 12955 Biscayne Blvd., No. 202, North Miami, FL 33181.

612 016　　　　JA　　ISSN 0082-4518
TISSUE CULTURE STUDIES IN JAPAN: THE ANNUAL BIBLIOGRAPHY/NIHON SOSHIKI BAIYO KENKYU NENPO. 1957-1980. a. Japanese Tissue Culture Association - Nihon Soshiki Baiyo Gakkai, c/o Tokyo Daigaku Igakubu Kaibogaku Kyoshito, 7-3-1 Hongo, Bunkyo-ku, Tokyo 113, Japan.

379　　　　　US　　ISSN 0737-1888
TODAY'S EDUCATION: EDUCATIONAL SUPPORT EDITION. ceased. a. National Education Association of the United States, 1201 16th St., N.W., Washington, DC 20036.

623 551.46　　　US　　ISSN 0085-7297
TOPICS IN OCEAN ENGINEERING. 1969-1976. irreg. (reprint service avail. from UMI) (University of Hawaii) Gulf Publishing Co., Box 2608, Houston, TX 77001.

810　　　　　US　　ISSN 0041-2171
TREE. 1970-1978; suspended. a. Tree Books, Box 9005, Berkeley, CA 94709.

676　　　　　CN　　ISSN 0041-2295
TREND. 1963-1983. irreg. Pulp and Paper Research Institute of Canada, 570 St. Johns Blvd., Pointe Claire, Que. H9R 3J9, Canada.

331.2　　　　CN　　ISSN 0227-1362
TRENDS IN COLLECTIVE AGREEMENT SETTLEMENT WAGE RATE CHANGES IN NOVA SCOTIA. 1975-1985. a. (back issues avail.) Department of Labour and Manpower Research Division, Box 697, Halifax, N.S. B3J 2T8, Canada.
  Formerly (until 1978): Trends in Collective Agreement Base Rate Changes in Nova Scotia (ISSN 0382-1773)

331.2　　　　CN　　ISSN 0381-3258
TRENDS IN COLLECTIVE BARGAINING SETTLEMENTS IN NOVA SCOTIA. 1975-1985. a. Department of Labour, Economics and Research Division, Box 697, Halifax, N.S., Canada.

388.324　　　　AT　　ISSN 0816-2905
TRUCK & BUS ROAD TESTS. 1979-1985. a. (reprint service avail. from UMI) Shennen Publishing & Publicity Co., 64 Kippax St., Surry Hills, N.S.W. 2010, Australia.
  Formerly: Truck and Bus Tests and Specs.

362　　　　　US　　ISSN 0085-7408
TRUE TO LIFE. 1970-19?? irreg. Reproductive Health Resources, Inc., 1507 21st St., Suite 100, Sacramento, CA 95814

338　　　　　AT
U B D REGISTER OF INDUSTRY & COMMERCE: SOUTH AUSTRALIA. 1974-1985. discontinued. a. Universal Business Directories Pty. Ltd., 64 Talavera Rd., Macquarie Park, N.S.W. 2113, Australia.
  Formerly: U B D Australia Wide Business Guide: South Australia.

796.332　　　　US　　ISSN 0742-4299
U S F L GUIDE AND REGISTER. (United States Football League) 1984-198?; discontinued. a. Sporting News Publishing Co., 1212 N. Lindbergh Blvd., St. Louis, MO 63132

615.11　　　　US　　ISSN 0091-3839
U S P GUIDE TO SELECT DRUGS. 1973-1981; discontinued. irreg. United States Pharmacopeial Convention, Inc., 12601 Twinbrook Parkway, Rockville, MD 20852.

535　　　　　UK　　ISSN 0144-2317
U.V. SPECTROMETRY GROUP. BULLETIN. (Ultra Violet) 1949-1984 (vol.11) a. (back issues avail.) U.V. Spectrometry Group, c/o Dr. M. Barnard, Perkin-Elmer Ltd., Beaconsfield, England.
  Formerly (until 1973): Photoelectric Spectrometry Group Bulletin (ISSN 0079-1814)

630.8　　　　US　　ISSN 0092-1939
U.S. AGRICULTURAL RESEARCH SERVICE. A R S-S. ceased. irreg. U.S. Science and Education Administration, Southern Region, P. O. Box 53326, New Orleans, LA 70153.

340 658.8 663.1　　US
U.S. BUREAU OF ALCOHOL, TOBACCO AND FIREARMS. ANNUAL REPORT. ceased. a. U.S. Department of the Treasury, Bureau of Alcohol, Tobacco and Firearms, Washington, DC 20226.

630.2　　　　US
U.S. DEPARTMENT OF AGRICULTURE. EASTERN REGIONAL RESEARCH CENTER. PUBLICATIONS AND PATENTS. 1948-1983. a. U.S. Department of Agriculture, Eastern Regional Research Center, 600 E. Mermaid Lane, Philadelphia, PA 19118.
  Formerly: Eastern Utilization Research and Development Division. Publications and Patents (ISSN 0012-8945)

309.2　　　　US　　ISSN 0091-6234
U.S. GENERAL ACCOUNTING OFFICE. SOCIAL DEVELOPMENT ACTIVITIES IN LATIN AMERICA PROMOTED BY THE INTER-AMERICAN FOUNDATION: REPORT TO THE CONGRESS BY THE COMPTROLLER GENERAL OF THE UNITED STATES. (Report year ends June 30.) no longer available. a. U.S. General Accounting Office, 441 G St. N.W., Room 6417, Washington, DC 20548.

719.32　　　　US　　ISSN 0083-2324
U.S. NATIONAL PARK SERVICE. SOURCE BOOKS SERIES. 1942-19?? irreg. U.S. National Park Service, Interior Bldg., Washington, DC 20240.

500　　　　　US　　ISSN 0083-2375
U.S. NATIONAL SCIENCE FOUNDATION. N S F FACTBOOK. 1971-1975 (2nd edt.) irreg. Marquis Who's Who, Inc., 200 E. Ohio St., Chicago, IL 60611.

382　　　　　US
UNITED STATES COUNCIL FOR INTERNATIONAL BUSINESS. ANNUAL REPORT. ceased. a. United States Council for International Business, 1212 Ave. of the Americas, New York, NY 10036.

500　　　　　IS　　ISSN 0333-5526
UNITED STATES-ISRAEL BINATIONAL SCIENCE FOUNDATION. PROJECT-REPORT ABSTRACTS. 1980, published only once. United States-Israel Binational Science Foundation, P.O. Box 7677, Jerusalem 91076, Israel.

572 913.031　　　CU
UNIVERSIDAD DE LA HABANA. CENTRO DE INFORMACION CIENTIFICAS Y TECNICA. CIENCIAS. SERIE 9. ANTROPOLOGIA Y PREHISTORIA. 1972-1976 (no.17) irreg. Universidad de la Habana, Centro de Informacion Cientifica y Tecnica, Havana, Cuba.

630   UY   ISSN 0077-1279
UNIVERSIDAD DE LA REPUBLICA. FACULTAD DE AGRONOMIA. PUBLICACION MISCELANEA. 1956-19?? irreg. Universidad de Uruguay, Facultad de Agronomia, Avda. Garzon 780, Montevideo, Uruguay.

510   UY   ISSN 0077-1295
UNIVERSIDAD DE URUGUAY. INSTITUTO DE MATHEMATICA Y ESTADISTICA. PUBLICACIONES DIDACTICAS. 1956-1984. irreg. Universidad de Uruguay, Instituto de Matematica y Estadistica, J. Herrera y Reissig 565, Montevideo, Uruguay.

020 011   SP
UNIVERSIDAD DE VALLADOLID. FACULTAD DE MEDICINA. BIBLIOTECA. BOLETIN DE OBRAS INGRESADAS. 1967-1982. a. Universidad de Valladolid, Facultad de Medicina, Biblioteca, Avda. Ramon y Cajal no. 7, Valladolid, Spain.

330   PE
UNIVERSIDAD DEL PACIFICO. CENTRO DE INVESTIGACION. SERIE: COYUNTURA ECONOMICA. ceased. a. Universidad del Pacifico, Centro de Investigacion, Av. Salaverry 2020, Lima 11, Peru.

300   PE
UNIVERSIDAD DEL PACIFICO. CENTRO DE INVESTIGACION. SERIE: ENSAYOS. 1973-19?? irreg. Universidad del Pacifico, Centro de Investigacion, Av. Salaverry 2020, Lima 11, Peru.

378   PE
UNIVERSIDAD DEL PACIFICO. CENTRO DE INVESTIGACION. SERIE: MONOGRAFIAS. ceased. irreg. Universidad del Pacifico, Centro de Investigacion, Lima, Peru.

378   PE
UNIVERSIDAD DEL PACIFICO. CENTRO DE INVESTIGACION. SERIE: TRABAJOS DE INVESTIGACION. ceased. irreg. Universidad del Pacifico, Centro de Investigacion, Lima, Peru.

300   PE
UNIVERSIDAD DEL PACIFICO. DEPARTAMENTO DE CIENCIAS SOCIALES Y POLITICAS. SERIE: DEPARTAMENTOS ACADEMICOS. ceased. irreg. Universidad del Pacifico, Departamento de Ciencias Sociales y Politicas, Lima, Peru.

551   MX   ISSN 0076-7182
UNIVERSIDAD NACIONAL AUTONOMA DE MEXICO. INSTITUTO DE GEOFISICA. ANALES. 1955-1982 (vol.28) a. (back issues avail.) Universidad Nacional Autonoma de Mexico, Instituto de Geofisica, Circuito Exterior, Ciudad Universitaria, Mexico 20, D.F., Mexico.

300   BL   ISSN 0302-217X
UNIVERSIDADE FEDERAL DO RIO GRANDE DO SUL. INSTITUTO DE FILOSOFIA E CIENCIAS HUMANAS. REVISTA. 1973-1985. a. Universidade Federal do Rio Grande do Sul, Instituto de Filosofia e Ciencias Humanas, Porto Alegre, Rio Grande do Sul, Brazil.

720.16 026 016   IT   ISSN 0391-500X
UNIVERSITA DEGLI STUDI DI FIRENZE. FACOLTA DI ARCHITETTURA. BIBLIOTECA. BOLLETTINO DI SEGNALAZIONI E NOTIZIE BIBLIOGRAFICHE. 1975-1982 (no.7) irreg. Universita degli Studi di Firenze, Facolta di Architettura. Biblioteca, Via Micheli 2, 50122 Florence, Italy.

310   CN
UNIVERSITE DU QUEBEC. STATISTIQUES. 1973/74-1984/85. a. Universite du Quebec, 2875 Bd. Laurier, St. Foy, Que. G1V 2M3, Canada.

634.9   CN   ISSN 0041-9214
UNIVERSITE LAVAL. FONDS DE RECHERCHES FORESTIERES. BULLETIN. 1956-19?? irreg. Forest Research and Development Foundation, Fonds de Recherches Forestieres, 237 Principale St., St. Romuald, PQ G6W 5M6, Canada.

634.9   CN   ISSN 0079-838X
UNIVERSITE LAVAL. FONDS DE RECHERCHES FORESTIERES. CONTRIBUTION. 1956-19?? irreg. Forest Research and Development Foundation, 237 Principale Street, St. Romuald, PQ G6W 5M6, Canada.

301   BE   ISSN 0771-5323
UNIVERSITE LIBRE DE BRUXELLES. INSTITUT DE SOCIOLOGIE. ANNALES. ceased. a. (Universite Libre de Bruxelles, Institut de Sociologie) Editions de l'Universite de Bruxelles, Av. P. Heger 26, C.P. 163, B-1050 Brussels, Belgium.

301   BE   ISSN 0068-2985
UNIVERSITE LIBRE DE BRUXELLES. INSTITUT DE SOCIOLOGIE. CAHIERS. 1951-1984. irreg. Editions de l'Universite de Bruxelles, Av. P Heger 26, C.P. 163, B-1050 Brussels, Belgium.

338.91   UK   ISSN 0144-9486
UNIVERSITY COLLEGE OF SWANSEA. CENTRE FOR DEVELOPMENT STUDIES. MONOGRAPH SERIES. 1977-1985. irreg. (3-4/yr.) Geo Books, Regency House, 34 Duke St., Norwich NR3 3AP, England.

338.91   UK   ISSN 0144-9494
UNIVERSITY COLLEGE OF SWANSEA. CENTRE FOR DEVELOPMENT STUDIES. OCCASIONAL PAPERS SERIES. 1977-1985. irreg. (3-4/yr.) Geo Books, Regency House, 34 Duke St., Norwich NR3 3AP, England.

020   SA
UNIVERSITY OF CAPE TOWN. LIBRARIES. VARIA SERIES. 1959-1986; discontinued. irreg. University of Cape Town, Libraries, Rondebosch 7700, South Africa.

011   SA
UNIVERSITY OF CAPE TOWN. SCHOOL OF LIBRARIANSHIP BIBLIOGRAPHICAL SERIES. 1944-1986; discontinued. irreg. University of Cape Town, School of Librarianship, Rondebosch 7700, South Africa.

519   DK
UNIVERSITY OF COPENHAGEN. INSTITUTE OF MATHEMATICAL STATISTICS. LECTURE NOTES. 1972-1986, suspended. irreg. Koebenhavns Universitet, Institut for Matematisk Statistik, 5 Universitetsparken, 2100 Copenhagen OE, Denmark.

333.9 628   US
UNIVERSITY OF DELAWARE. WATER RESOURCES CENTER. ANNUAL REPORT. 1965-1982. a. University of Delaware, Delaware Water Resources Center, 101 Hullihen Hall, Newark, DE 19716.

333.91   US
UNIVERSITY OF HAWAII. WATER RESOURCES RESEARCH CENTER. GROUNDWATER IN HAWAII; a century of progress. published only once, 1981. irreg. University Press of Hawaii, 2840 Kolowalu St., Honolulu, HI 96822.

338.1   US
UNIVERSITY OF ILLINOIS. AGRICULTURAL EXPERIMENT STATION. BULLETIN. ceased. irreg. University of Illinois at Urbana-Champaign, College of Agriculture, Agricultural Experiment Station, 47 Mumford Hall, 1301 W. Gregory Dr., Urbana, IL 61801.

630   US   ISSN 0073-5299
UNIVERSITY OF ILLINOIS AT URBANA-CHAMPAIGN. COLLEGE OF AGRICULTURE. AGRICULTURAL COMMUNICATIONS RESEARCH REPORT. 1960-19?? irreg. University of Illinois at Urbana-Champaign, College of Agriculture, Office of Agricultural Communications, 67 Mumford Hall, 1301 W. Gregory Dr., Urbana, IL 61801.

378.1   US   ISSN 0011-3174
UNIVERSITY OF ILLINOIS AT URBANA-CHAMPAIGN. COLLEGE OF AGRICULTURE. CURRENT AFFAIRS. ceased. irreg. University of Illinois at Urbana-Champaign, College of Agriculture, 101 Mumford Hall, 1301 W. Gregory Dr., IL 61801.

630   US   ISSN 0073-5205
UNIVERSITY OF ILLINOIS AT URBANA-CHAMPAIGN. COLLEGE OF AGRICULTURE. SPECIAL PUBLICATION. 1960-19?? irreg. University of Illinois at Urbana-Champaign, College of Agriculture, 47 Mumford Hall, 1301 W. Gregory Dr., Urbana, IL 61801.

331   US   ISSN 0578-6371
UNIVERSITY OF IOWA. CENTER FOR LABOR AND MANAGEMENT. RESEARCH SERIES. ceased. irreg. University of Iowa, College of Business Administration, Center for Labor and Management, Phillips Hall, Iowa City, IA 52240.
Supersedes: University of Iowa. Center for Labor and Management. Monograph Series (ISSN 0075-045X)

708 700   US
UNIVERSITY OF KANSAS. SPENCER MUSEUM OF ART. MISCELLANEOUS PUBLICATIONS. 1952-19?? irreg. University of Kansas, Spencer Museum of Art, Lawrence, KS 66045.
Formerly: University of Kansas. Museum of Art. Miscellaneous Publications (ISSN 0075-501X)

330.9   US
UNIVERSITY OF KENTUCKY. CENTER FOR APPLIED ECONOMIC RESEARCH. ECONOMIC STUDIES SERIES. ceased. irreg. University of Kentucky, Center for Applied Economic Research, 451 Commerce Bldg., Lexington, KY 40506.

370   US
UNIVERSITY OF MONTANA. DIVISION OF EDUCATIONAL RESEARCH AND SERVICES. EDUCATION MONOGRAPH. ceased. irreg. University of Montana, School of Education, Missoula, MT 59812.

331.1   US
UNIVERSITY OF NOTRE DAME. SAINT MARY'S COLLEGE. LAW SCHOOL. DEPARTMENT OF ECONOMICS. CONFERENCE ON CHANGING FACTORS IN COLLECTIVE BARGAINING. PROCEEDINGS. 1953-1983 (Jun.) a. (back issues from 1958 avail.) University of Notre Dame, Department of Economics, Box 476, Notre Dame, IN 46556.

500.9   US   ISSN 0078-6047
UNIVERSITY OF OREGON. MUSEUM OF NATURAL HISTORY. BULLETIN. 1965-1983 (no.24) irreg. University of Oregon, Museum of Natural History, Eugene, OR 97403.

910   CN
UNIVERSITY OF OTTAWA. DEPARTMENT OF GEOGRAPHY. OCCASIONAL PAPERS. 1971-1981; discontinued. irreg. (tabloid format) University of Ottawa Press, 603 Cumberland, Ottawa, Ont. K1N 6N5, Canada.

338.1   AT   ISSN 0082-0563
UNIVERSITY OF SYDNEY. DEPARTMENT OF AGRICULTURAL ECONOMICS. RESEARCH BULLETIN. 1957-1986, discontinued. irreg. University of Sydney, Department of Agricultural Economics, Sydney, N.S.W. 2006, Australia.

657   US   ISSN 0081-7465
UNIVERSITY OF TEXAS, AUSTIN. BUREAU OF BUSINESS RESEARCH. STUDIES IN ACCOUNTING. 1966-1977. irreg. (reprint service avail. from UMI) University of Texas at Austin, Bureau of Business Research, Box 7459, Austin, TX 78712.

332   US   ISSN 0081-7570
UNIVERSITY OF TEXAS, AUSTIN. BUREAU OF BUSINESS RESEARCH. STUDIES IN BANKING AND FINANCE. 1958-1978. irreg. (reprint service avail. from UMI) University of Texas at Austin, Bureau of Business Research, Box 7459, Austin, TX 78712.

560   SA
UNIVERSITY OF THE WITWATERSRAND, JOHANNESBURG. BERNARD PRICE INSTITUTE FOR PALAEONTOLOGICAL RESEARCH. MEMOIR. discontinued 1986. irreg. University of the Witwatersrand, Johannesburg, Bernard Price Institute for Palaeontological Research, 1 Jan Smuts Ave., Johannesburg 2001, South Africa.

621.381 001.64   JA   ISSN 0564-8742
UNIVERSITY OF TOKYO. COMPUTER CENTER. REPORT. 1962-1976. a. University of Tokyo, Computer Center - Tokyo Daigaku Ogata Keisanki Senta, 2-11-6 Yayoi, Bunkyo-ku, Tokyo 113, Japan.

CESSATIONS

330   US
UNIVERSITY OF TOLEDO. BUSINESS RESEARCH CENTER. HODGE MEMORIAL GRADUATE LECTURES. 1968-19?? irreg. University of Toledo, College of Business Administration, 2801 W. Bancroft St., Toledo, OH 43606.

650   US
UNIVERSITY OF TOLEDO. BUSINESS RESEARCH CENTER. REGIONAL RESEARCH REPORTS. (Subseries of Toledo Business Report) 1962-19?? irreg. University of Toledo, College of Business Administration, 2801 W. Bancroft. St, Toledo, OH 43606.

333   US   ISSN 0084-0807
UNIVERSITY OF WISCONSIN, MADISON. LAND TENURE CENTER. REPRINT. 1965-1979 (no.138) irreg. University of Wisconsin-Madison, Land Tenure Center, 1300 University Ave., Madison, WI 53706.

333   US   ISSN 0084-0823
UNIVERSITY OF WISCONSIN, MADISON. LAND TENURE CENTER. TRAINING AND METHODS SERIES. 1964-1982 (no.29) irreg. University of Wisconsin-Madison, Land Tenure Center, 1300 University Ave., Madison, WI 53706.

622   US
URANIUM SEMINAR. PROCEEDINGS. ceased 1984. a. American Institute of Mining, Metallurgical, and Petroleum Engineers, Inc., Society of Mining Engineers, 345 E. 47th St., New York, NY 10017.

371.3   370   AT   ISSN 0813-1759
V I S E. OCCASIONAL PAPERS. 1981-1986, discontinued. irreg. Victorian Institute of Secondary Education, 582 St. Kilda Rd., Melbourne, Vic. 3004, Australia.

370   AT   ISSN 0314-724X
V I S E NEWS. 1977-1985, discontinued. irreg. Victorian Institute of Secondary Education, 582 St. Kilda Rd., Melbourne, Vic. 3004, Australia.

284   GW   ISSN 0083-5633
VEREINIGTE EVANGELISCH-LUTHERISCHE KIRCHE DEUTSCHLANDS. AMTSBLATT. 1948-1983. irreg. Lutherisches Kirchenamt, Richard-Wagner-Str. 26, D-3000 Hannover 1, W. Germany (B.R.D.)

070   384   US
VERMONT MEDIA DIRECTORY. 1979-19?? biennial. New England Newsclip Agency, Inc., 5 Auburn St., Framingham, MA 01701.

634.9   AT
VICTORIA. FOREST COMMISSION. ANNUAL REPORT. 1919-1984. a. Forest Commission, 601 Bourke St., Melbourne, Vic. 3001, Australia.

634.9   AT   ISSN 0083-5978
VICTORIA, AUSTRALIA. FORESTS COMMISSION. FORESTRY TECHNICAL PAPERS. 1959-1987 (no.29) irreg. State Forests and Lands Service, 601 Bourke St., Melbourne, Vic. 3001, Australia.

371.3   AT   ISSN 0813-5150
VIEWPRINTS. 1984-1986, discontinued. irreg. Victorian Institute of Secondary Education, 582 St. Kilda Rd., Melbourne, Vic. 3004, Australia.

975   US   ISSN 0734-5089
VIRGINIA HISTORICAL ABSTRACTS. published only once, 1983. 2/yr. •Also available online. Virginia History Services, Inc., Box 3751, Arlington, VA 22203-0751.

382   387   US   ISSN 0083-6532
VIRGINIA PORT AUTHORITY. BOARD OF COMMISSIONERS. ANNUAL REPORT. 1953-1986. a. Port Authority, 600 World Trade Center, Norfolk, VA 23510.

382   387   US   ISSN 0083-6516
VIRGINIA PORT AUTHORITY. FOREIGN TRADE ANNUAL REPORT: THE PORTS OF VIRGINIA. 1970-1986. a. Port Authority, 600 World Trade Center, Norfolk, VA 23510.
    Formerly: Foreign Trade Annual Report. Virginia Ports (ISSN 0095-3903)

574   US   ISSN 0083-7652
WATER IN BIOLOGICAL SYSTEMS. 1969-19?? irreg. Consultants Bureau, Special Research Report (Subsidiary of: Plenum Publishing Corp.) 233 Spring St., New York, NY 10013.

914.2   UK
WEEKENDER AND DAYTRIPPER. 1981-198?, ceased. a. Adprint, 69 Thorpe Rd., Norwich, Norfolk NR1 3AU, England.

380.5   AT
WEST AUSTRALIAN TRANSPORTER YEAR BOOK. 1965-19??, ceased. a. Wescolour Press, 340 High St., East Fremantle, WA 6158, Australia.

387   UK
WEST COUNTRY'S MARITIME STORY. 1983-198? irreg. Heritage Publications, Merchants House, Barley Market St., Tavistock, Devon, England.

622   AT   ISSN 0510-2014
WESTERN AUSTRALIA. GEOLOGICAL SURVEY. MINERAL RESOURCES BULLETIN. 1945-1984; suspended. irreg. (back issues avail.) Geological Survey of Western Australia, 66 Adelaide Terrace, Perth, WA 6000, Australia.

388   AT   ISSN 0310-6330
WESTERN AUSTRALIA. MAIN ROADS DEPARTMENT. TECHNICAL REPORT. 1973-19??, ceased. irreg. Main Roads Department, Waterloo Crescent, East Perth, W.A. 6000, Australia.

333.7   581   591   AT   ISSN 0726-2469
WESTERN AUSTRALIAN NATURE RESERVE MANAGEMENT PLAN. 1981-1986. irreg. (back issues avail.) Department of Conservation and Land Management, 108 Adelaide Terrace, Perth 6000, W.A., Australia.

633.1   CN
WHEATS OF THE WORLD. 1978-19?? irreg. Grains Council, 760-360 Main St., Winnipeg, Man. R3C 3Z3, Canada.

796.5   914.4   UK
WHERE TO CAMP IN FRANCE. ceased. a. Club of Great Britain & Ireland Ltd., 11 Lower Grosvenor Place, London SW1W 0EY, England.

796.5   914.3   UK
WHERE TO CAMP IN GERMANY. ceased. a. Club of Great Britain & Ireland Ltd., 11 Lower Grosvenor Place, London SW1W, England.

796.5   914.5   UK
WHERE TO CAMP IN ITALY. ceased. a. Club of Great Britain & Ireland Ltd., 11 Lower Grosvenor Place, London SW1W, England.

796.5   914.6   UK
WHERE TO CAMP IN SPAIN. ceased. a. Club of Great Britain & Ireland Ltd., 11 Lower Grosvenor Place, London SW1W, England.

914.2   UK
WHERE TO GO, WHAT TO DO IN THE S.W. ceased. a. Heritage Publications, Merchant's House, Barley Market St., Tavistock, Devon, England.

328.54   II
WHO IS WHO. 1961-1985. biennial. Legislative Council Secretariat, Fort St. George, Madras 600009, India.

792   US   ISSN 0508-6795
WHO'S WHERE; who's where in show business. ceased. biennial. Leo Shull Publications, 134 W. 44th St., New York, NY 10036.
    Title varies: Show Business Who's Where (ISSN 0488-7115)

700   US
WILLIAMSBURG DECORATIVE ART SERIES. 1974-1986. irreg. Colonial Williamsburg Foundation, Box C, Williamsburg, VA 23187.

970   US
WILLIAMSBURG EYEWITNESS TO HISTORY SERIES. 1959-1971. irreg. Colonial Williamsburg Foundation, Box C, Williamsburg, VA 23187.

028.5   UK
WIND IN THE WILLOWS ANNUAL. ceased. a. Independent Television Books Ltd., 247 Tottenham Court Rd., London W1P 0AU, England.

796   NE
WINTER EN SPORT. ceased. a. Kluwer Technische Tijdschriften B.V., Postbus 23, 7400 GA Deventer, Netherlands.

323.4   US
WOMEN'S REFERRAL SERVICE ANNUAL DIRECTORY. 1981-198? a. Women's Referral Service, Inc., 13630 Ventura Blvd., No. 374, Sherman Oaks, CA 91423-0374.

677   AT
WOOL NEWS. 1954-1985. irreg. Australian Wool Corporation, Public Relations Officer, Box 4867, Melbourne, Vic. 3000, Australia.
    Formerly: Wool News Digest.

636.089   GR   ISSN 0084-1404
WORLD ASSOCIATION FOR THE ADVANCEMENT OF VETERINARY PARASITOLOGY. PROCEEDINGS OF CONFERENCE. (Publisher varies) 1963-19??; now issued with journal, Veterinary Parasitology. biennial. World Association for the Advancement of Veterinary Parasitology, c/o C.A. Himonas, Sec.-Treas., Department of Applied Helminthology & Entomology, School of Veterinary Medicine, Aristotelian University, Thessalonika, Greece.

338.9   UN
WORLD BANK. ECONOMIC DEVELOPMENT INSTITUTE. E D I SEMINAR PAPERS. 1972-19?? irreg. World Bank, Economic Development Institute, 1818 H. St., N.W., Washington, DC 20433.

338.91   UN
WORLD BANK. STAFF WORKING PAPERS. 1967-19??; discontinued. irreg., approx. 60/yr. World Bank, 1818 H St., N.W., Washington, DC 20433.

382   UK
WORLD DIRECTORY OF MULTINATIONAL ENTERPRISES: RANKINGS AND INTERPRETATIONS. ceased 1982/83. biennial. Globe Book Services Ltd., Brunel Rd., Houndmills, Basingstoke, Hants. RG21 2XS, England.

783   UK
WORLD OF CHURCH MUSIC. 1963-1986, discontinued. a. (also avail. in microform from UMI; reprint service avail. from UMI) Royal School of Church Music, Addington Palace, Croydon CR9 5AD, England.
    Formerly (until 1980): English Church Music (ISSN 0071-0555)

780   UK
WORLD RECORD MARKETS. ceased 1976 (3rd edt.) a. Henry Melland Ltd., 23 Ridgmount St., London WC1E 7AH, England.

550   333.7   US   ISSN 0883-8100
WORLD RESOURCES INSTITUTE. JOURNAL. 1984-198?; discontinued. a. World Resources Institute, 1735 New York Ave., N.W., Washington, DC 20006.

910.202   SP
WORLD TOURISM ORGANIZATION. TOURIST DEPARTURES AND MAIN DESTINATIONS. ceased. a. World Tourism Organization, OMT-Capitan Haya 42, 28020 Madrid, Spain.

651.8   338   US
WORLDWIDE DIRECTORY OF COMPUTER COMPANIES. ceased 1973 (2nd edt.) irreg. Marquis Who's Who, Inc., 200 East Ohio Street, Chicago, IL 60611.
    Formerly: Directory of North American Computer Companies.

026   US
WORLDWIDE DIRECTORY OF FEDERAL LIBRARIES. 1973; published only once. irreg. Marquis Who's Who, Inc., 200 E. Ohio St., Chicago, IL 60611.

581   US   ISSN 0084-2648
WRIGHTIA; a botanical journal. 1945-1951. irreg. University of Texas at Dallas, Box 688, Richardson, TX 75080.

400 PL ISSN 0075-5281
WYZSZA SZKOLA PEDAGOGICZNA, KATOWICE. ZESZYTY NAUKOWE. SEKCJA JEZYKOZNAWSTWA. 1959-1968. a. Uniwersytet Slaski w Katowicach, Wyzsza Szkola Pedagogiczna, Ul. Bankowa 14, 40-007 Katowice, Poland.

800 US
YANDRO. 1953-19??; suspended. irreg. (back issues avail.) Coulson Publications, 2677W-500N, Hartford City, IN 47348.

336 US
YEAR END TAX PLANNING MANUAL. 1982-198? a. Warren, Gorham & Lamont, Inc., 210 South St., Boston, MA 02111.

370 US ISSN 0084-3784
YEARBOOK OF HIGHER EDUCATION. 1969-1984 (16th edt.) a. Marquis Who's Who, Inc., 200 E. Ohio St., Chicago, IL 60611.

712 US
YEARBOOK OF LANDSCAPE ARCHITECTURE. 1983-198?; discontinued. a. Van Nostrand Reinhold Company, Inc., 115 Fifth Ave., New York, NY 10003.

341.058 UK ISSN 0084-408X
YEARBOOK OF WORLD AFFAIRS. 1947-1984. a. (back issues avail.) (London Institute of World Affairs) Sweet & Maxwell Stevens Journals, 11 New Fetter Lane, London EC4P 4EE, England

301.4 US
YOUNG WOMAN. ceased 1984. a. 13-30 Corporation, 505 Market St., Knoxville, TN 37902.

330 PL ISSN 0044-1503
Z PRAC ZAKLADU NAUK EKONOMICZNYCH PAN. 1954-1972. irreg. Polska Akademia Nauk, Zaklad Nauk Ekonomicznych, Palac Kultury i Nauki, Warsaw, Poland.

943 PL ISSN 0084-5493
ZIEMA KOZIELSKA. STUDIA I MATERIALY. 1971-19??, ceased. irreg. Instytut Slaski, Instytut Naukowo-Badawczy, Luboszycka 3, Opole, Poland.

591 SA
ZOOLOGICAL SOCIETY OF SOUTHERN AFRICA. OCCASIONAL BULLETIN. 1959-1986. irreg. Zoological Society of Southern Africa, c/o J.P. Furstenberg, Department of Zoology, University of Port Elizabeth, P.O. Box 1600, Port Elizabeth 6000, South Africa.
Formerly: Zoological Society of Southern Africa. News Bulletin (ISSN 0044-5126)

370 PL ISSN 0084-5698
ZRODLA DO DZIEJOW MYSLI PEDAGOGICZNEJ. 1957-1979. irreg. (Polska Akademia Nauk, Komitet Nauk Pedagogicznych) Ossolineum, Publishing House of the Polish Academy of Sciences, Rynek 9, Wroclaw, Poland

500 PL ISSN 0084-5701
ZRODLA DO DZIEJOW NAUKI I TECHNIKI. 1957-1974 (vol. 16) irreg. (Polska Akademia Nauk, Zaklad Historii Nauki i Techniki) Ossolineum, Publishing House of the Polish Academy of Sciences, Rynek 9, 50-106 Wroclaw, Poland

400 GW ISSN 0084-5817
ZWEISPRACHIGE REIHE. 1964-19?? irreg. Max Hueber Verlag, Max-Hueber-Str.4, 8045 Ismaning, W. Germany (B.R.D.)

Index to Publications of International Organizations

Titles listed with page numbers refer to entries included in the Classified List of this Directory. Titles listed without page numbers refer to entries in the 26th edition of *Ulrich's International Periodicals Directory*. The index is divided into four sections; publications of international organizations, of international congresses, of the European Communities, and of the United Nations.

INTERNATIONAL ORGANIZATIONS

A D B Quarterly Review (Asian Development Bank)

A I C A R C Bulletin

A I L A Bulletin (Association Internationale de Linguistique Appliquee)

A L A M A R Informativo (Asociacion Latinoamericana de Armadores)

A P O Annual Report (Asian Productivity Organization) 287

A P O News (Asian Productivity Organization)

A R N A B Newsletter (African Research Network for Agricultural Byproducts)

A S A I H L. Seminar Reports (Association of Southeast Asian Institutions of Higher Learning) 431

Academie Internationale d'Histoire des Sciences. Collection des Travaux 986

Acta Colloquii Didactici Classici 689

Acta Geneticae Medicae et Gemellologiae: Twin Research

Acta Haematologica

Acta Musicologica

Acta Radiologica. Series 1: Diagnosis

Acta Radiologica. Series 2: Oncology, Radiation Therapy, Physics and Biology

Acute Care

Adelphi Papers

Aerospace U F O News

African Bulletin/Bulletin Africain

African Development Bank. Report by the Board of Directors/Banque Africaine de Developpement. Rapport du Conseil d'Administration 261

African Journal of Plant Protection/Revue Africaine de la Protection des Vegetaux

African News Sheet 637

African Tax Systems

Afro Asian Economic Review

Afro-Asian Publications 565

ALGOL Bulletin 357

Aluminum Smelters 814

America Cooperativa

Amnesty International Report 914

Anales Galdosianos 714

Anciens Pays et Assemblees d'Etats 902

Andrologia

Animals International

Annales de l'Economie Publique, Sociale et Cooperative/Annals of Public and Cooperative Economy

Annals of Glaciology 383

Annotated Bibliography of Literature on Cooperative Movements in South-East Asia

Annuaire des Arachnologistes Mondiaux 163

Annuaire des Centres de Recherche Demographique/Directory of Demographic Research Centers 920

Annuaire des Chercheurs Francais du Fonds de Bourses de Recherche Scientifique et Technique de l'Organisation du Traite de l'Atlantique Nord 432

Annuaire Economique des Pays Membres de l'Organisation de l'Unite Africaine/Economic Yearbook of Member States of the Organization of African Unity 241

Annual Report on Results of Treatment in Gynecological Cancer 774

Anthos

Anuario Estadistico Centroamericano de Comercio Exterior 202

Anuario Interamericano de Derechos Humanos/Inter-American Yearbook on Human Rights 669

Apiacta

Applied Neurophysiology

Arab Struggle

Archiv fuer Rechts- und Sozialphilosophie/Archives de Philosophie du Droit et de Philosophie Sociale/Archives for Philosophy of Law and Social Philosophy

Archiv fuer Rechts- und Sozialphilosophie. Beihefte 876

Archiv fuer Religionspsychologie 967

Asia-Pacific Scouting

Asian and Pacific Council. Food and Fertilizer Technology Center. Extension /Technical Bulletin

Asian and Pacific Labour

Asian and Pacific Quarterly

Asian Bulletin/Bulletin d'Asie

Asian Institute of Technology. Research Summary 1067

Asian News Sheet

Asian Peoples' Anti-Communist League. Charts About Chinese Communists on the Mainland 568

Asian Peoples' Anti-Communist League. China. Pamphlet

Asociacion

Asociacion Interamericana de Bibliotecarios y Documentalistas Agricolas. Boletin Especial 24

Asociacion Interamericana de Bibliotecarios y Documentalistas Agricolas. Boletin Informativo.

Association Euratom-Ital. Annual Report 24

Association Internationale d'Etudes du Sud-Est Europeen. Bulletin

Association Internationale d'Etudes Patristiques. Bulletin d'Information et de Liaison 967

Association Internationale pour l'Histoire du Verre. Bulletin 319

Association of Commonwealth Universities. Annual Report of the Council Together with the Accounts of the Association 432

Association of Institutes for European Studies. Annuaire 576

Association of Institutes for European Studies. Year-Book 576

Association of Southeast Asian Institutions of Higher Learning. Newsletter

Atlantic Mail 669

Atlantic Salmon Newsletter

Atomic Physics 896

Audiology

Automatic Data Processing Information Bulletin 360

Automatica

B E N E L U X Economic Union. Conseil Central de l'Economie. Rapport du Secretaire sur l'Activite du Conseil 287

B I C-Code (Bureau International des Containers-Code) 854

Babel

Bank for International Settlements. Annual Report 224

Batiment International/Building Research and Practice

Benelux Publikatieblad/Bulletin Benelux 939

Benelux Tijdschrift/Revue Benelux

Biblia Revuo

Bibliographia I U L A

Bibliographie de la Philosophie/Bibliography of Philosophy

Bibliographie Internationale de l'Humanisme et de la Renaissance 634

Bibliography on Irrigation, Drainage, River Training and Flood Control/Bibliographie Relative aux Irrigations, au Drainage, a la Regularisation des Cours d'Eau et la Matrise des Crues 1127

Biochemical Education

Biological Substances 138

Biology International: I U B S Newsmagazine (International Union of Biological Sciences)

Boreas

Brahmavidya 850

Building and Wood

Bulletin A I O S P/I A E V G/I V S B B (International Association for Educational and Vocational Guidance)

Bulletin d'Archeologie Sud-Est Europeenne. 83

Bulletin de Philosophie Medievale 877

Bulletin for International Fiscal Documentation

Bulletin G C I D (International Commission on Irrigation and Drainage, Greek National Committee)

Bulletin Geodesique

Bulletin of Peace Proposals

Bulletin of Volcanology

Bulletin on Applied Research for the Protection of Man at Work

Bureau International de l'Heure. Rapport Annuel 115

Bureau International des Societes Gerant les Droits d'Enregistrement et de Reproduction Mecanique. Bulletin 930

C.A.B. International Bureau of Agricultural Economics. Annotated Bibliographies. Series B: Agricultural Policy and Rural Development in Africa 39

C.A.B. International Bureau of Nutrition. Annotated Bibliographies 847

C.A.B. International. Forestry Bureau. Annotated Bibliographies 529

C.A.B. International. Mycological Institute. Phytopathological Papers 155

C A T C Electronic News (Commonwealth Air Transport Council)

C C I A Background Information (World Council of Churches, Commission on International Affairs) 968

C E R N Annual Report 887

C E R N Courier

C E R N-H E R A Reports 887

C E R N Reports 887

C E R N School of Computing. Proceedings 1005

C E R N School of Physics. Proceedings 887

C.I.A. Revue (Confederation Internationale des Accordeonistes) 834

C I A T Report (Centro Internacional de Agricultura Tropical) 25

C.I.C.A.E. Bulletin d'Information (Confederation Internationale des Cinemas d'Art et d'Essai) 823

C I N D A 892

C I N T E R F O R - Documentacion (Centro Interamericano de Investigacion y Documentacion Sobre Formacion Profesional)

C I N T E R F O R Estudios y Monografias (Centro Interamericano de Investigacion y Documentacion Sobre Formacion Profesional) 411

C I R A Bulletin (Centre International de Recherches sur l'Anarchisme)

C.I.R.P. Annals

C M A S Bulletin d'Information/C M A S Newsletter (Confederation Mondiale des Activites)

C M I News Letter (International Maritime Committee)

C M I Year Book 1099

Cahiers de Droit Fiscal International 669

Cahiers Ligures de Prehistoire et de Protohistoire 84

Catalogo de Publicaciones Latinoamericanas Sobre Formacion Profesional 849

Catalogus Musicus 834

Catalogus Translationem et Commentatorium 739

Centre International de Documentation Arachnologiques. Liste des Travaux Arachnologiques 149

Centre International de Liaison des Ecoles de Cinema et de Television. Bulletin d'Informations 347

Centro de Estudios Monetarios Latinoamericanos. Ensayos 226

Centro Interamericano de Investigacion y Documentacion Sobre Formacion Profesional. Boletin

Centro Interamericano de Investigacion y Documentacion Sobre Formacion Profesional. Informes 426

Centro Interamericano de Investigacion y Documentacion Sobre Formacion Profesional. Serie Bibliografica 411

Centro Latinoamericano de Economia Humana. Publicaciones

Chemistry International

Chemoreception Abstracts 325

Children in the Tropics

Child's Nervous System

Ch'indaba

Christian Democratic International. Information Bulletin

Christian Democratic Study and Documentation Center. Cahiers d'Etudes 903

Christian Jewish Relations

Christian Peace Conference

Chronicle of Parliamentary Elections and Developments 903

Chronobiologia

Ciencia Interamericana

Cites Unies

CODATA Bulletin (Committee on Data for Science and Technology)

Colecciones Basicas C I N T E R F O R (Centro Interamericano de Investigacion y Documentacion Sobre Formacion Profesional) 426

Collection of Documents for the Study of International Non-Governmental Relations 670

Colombo Plan Bureau. The Colombo Plan Council Report 261

Colombo Plan for Co-operative Economic and Social Development in Asia and the Pacific. Consultative Committee. Proceedings and Conclusions 261

Colombo Plan for Co-operative Economic and Social Development in Asia and the Pacific. Development Perspectives. Country Issues Papers by Member Governments to the Consultative Committee 261

Colombo Plan Newsletter

Comision Nacional Espanola de Cooperacion con la UNESCO. Revista de Informacion

Comite Consultatif pour la Masse et les Grandeurs Apparentees 808

Comite International de Cooperation dans les Recherches Nationales en Demographie. Actes des Seminaires 921

Comite International des Poids et Mesures. Comite Consultatif d'Electricite. (Rapport et Annexes) 808

Comite International des Poids et Mesures. Comite Consultatif de Photometrie et Radiometrie.(Rapport et Annexes) 808

Comite International des Poids et Mesures. Comite Consultatif de Thermometrie. Rapports et Annexes 808

Comite International des Poids et Mesures. Comite Consultatif des Unites (Rapport et Annexes) 808

Comite International des Poids et Mesures. Comite Consultatif pour la Definition de la Seconde. (Rapport et Annexes) 808

Comite International des Poids et Mesures. Comite Consultatif pour la Definition du Metre (Rapport et Annexes) 808

Comite International des Poids et Mesures. Comite Consultatif pour les Etalons des Mesure des Rayonnements Ionisants (Rapport et Annexes) 808

Comite International des Poids et Mesures. Proces-Verbaux des Seances 808

Comite International des Poids et Mesures. Systeme International d'Unites 808

Comites Francais de Geodesie et Geophysique. Annales 405

Commission for the Geological Map of the World. Bulletin 379

Commonwealth Geological Liaison Office. Special Publication

Commonwealth Universities Yearbook 433

Communication Arts International

Communication World (International Association of Business Communicators)

Communist Program 904

Compendio Estadistico Centroamericano 206

Compendium of University Entrance Requirements for First Degree Courses in the United Kingdom 433

Competition Policy in O E C D Countries 288

Composers of the Americas/Compositores de America 834

Confederacion Latinoamericana de Asociaciones Cristianas de Jovenes. Carta 969

Conference Generale des Poids et Mesures. Comptes Rendus des Seances 808

Conscience et Liberte

Consumers Directory 368

Controller

Convenios Centroamericanos de Integration Economica. 261

Convergence

Convergence: International Colloquium on Automotive Electronic Technology. Proceedings 1091

Cooperative Press in South-East Asia 645

Cooperative Trade Directory for Southeast Asia 238

Corporate Taxation in Latin America

Cotton. Part 1: Bi-monthly Review of the World Situation

Cotton. Part 2: World Statistics

Council of Europe. Directorate of Legal Affairs. Information Bulletin on Legislative Activities

Council of Europe. Documentation Centre for Education in Europe. Newsletter/Faits Nouveaux

Council of Europe. Documentation Section and Library. Bibliographical Bulletin. Series: Legal Affairs.

Council of Europe. Documentation Section and Library. Bibliographical Bulletin. Series: Political and Economic Affairs.

Council of Europe. Documentation Section and Library. Bibliographical Bulletin. Series: Social Affairs

Council of Europe. European Treaty Series 670

Council of Europe. Parliamentary Assembly. Documents; Working Papers/Documents de Seance 670

Council of Europe. Parliamentary Assembly. Orders of the Day, Minutes of Proceedings/Ordres du Jour, Proces Verbaux

Council of Europe. Parliamentary Assembly. Texts Adopted by the Assembly/Textes Adoptes Par l'Assemblee 670

Council of Europe. Standing Committee on the European Convention on Establishment (Individuals). Periodical Report. 913

Council of Europe Forum

Cross-Cultural Psychology Bulletin

Cultural Policy

Current Dialogue

Cytologia/Kitorogia

D E

Date Palm Journal

Democratic Journalist

Desert Locust Control Organization for Eastern Africa. Annual Report 54

Development

Dialogues et Cultures 693

Diamond World Review

Documentation Bulletin for South-East Asia

Drug and Alcohol Dependence

E A A S Newsletter (European Association for American Studies) 915

E B U Monographs, Legal and Administrative Series (European Broadcasting Union) 348

E B U Review. Geneva Edition (Programmes, Adminstration, Law) (European Broadcasting Union)

E B U Seminars for Producers and Directors of Educational Television for Schools and Adults (European Broadcasting Union) 348

E B U Workshops for Producers and Directors of Television Programmes for Children and Young People (European Broadcasting Union) 348

E C A R B I C A Journal (International Council on Archives, Eastern and Southern Africa Regional Branch)

E C Index 207

E F I L Documentation (European Federation for Intercultural Learning) 441

E F I L Newsletter (European Federation for Intercultural Learning)

E F T A Bulletin (European Free Trade Association)

E F T A Trade (European Free Trade Association) 255

E P P O Bulletin

E S A Bulletin (European Space Agency)

Earth Sciences Programme Newsletter

Earthquake Engineering and Structural Dynamics

Echo

Economic Review of World Tourism 1108

Economie Familiale/Home Economics

Ecumenical Review

Education and Culture. Section 1: Cultural Development 413

Education and Culture. Section 2: Higher Education and Research 413

Education in Europe. Cultural Development 413

Education in Europe. Section 1: Higher Education and Research 434

Educational Statistics in O E C D Countries (Organisation for Economic Cooperation and Development) 413

Electrochimica Acta

Electroencephalography and Clinical Neurophysiology

Enfant en Milieu Tropical

Engineering Industries in O E C D Member Countries: New Basic Statistics 288

Entomologische Zeitschrift

Environmental Policy and Law

Enzyme

Epilepsia

Episodes

Ergebnisse der Limnologie/Advances in Limnology 402

Estadistica

Estimated World Requirements of Narcotic Drugs 870

Estimated World Requirements of Narcotic Drugs. Supplement

EUDISED R & D Bulletin

Europastimme

European and Mediterranean Plant Protection Organization. Publications. Series B: Plant Health Newsletter 55

European Aspects, Law Series 655

European Aspects, Social Studies Series 1026

European Association for Animal Production. Publications 65

European Association for Animal Production. Symposia on Energy Metabolism 65

European Association of Exploration Geophysicists. Constitution and By-Laws, Membership List. 399

European Bibliography of Soviet, East European and Slavonic Studies/Bibliographie Europeenne des Travaux sur l'URSS et l'Europe de l'Est/ Europaische Bibliographie der Sowjet- und Oesteuropastudien 563

European Co-Operation 670

European Convention on Human Rights. Yearbook 913

European Coordination Centre for Research and Documentation in Social Sciences. Publications 1008

European Council of Jewish Community Services. Exchange

European Court of Human Rights. Publications. Series A: Judgments and Decisions/Cour Europeenne des Droits de l'Homme. Publications. Serie A: Arrets et Decisions 913

European Economic Review

European Federation of Finance House Associations. Annual Report 227

European Federation of Finance House Associations. Newsletter

European Free Trade Association. Annual Report 255

European Information Centre for Nature Conservation. Newsletter. Nature

European Journal of Biochemistry

European Journal of Political Research

European League for Economic Cooperation. Publications 262

European League for Economic Cooperation. Report of the Secretary General on the Activities of E.L.E.C. 262

European Organisation for Civil Aviation Electronics. General Assembly. Annual Report 18

European Organization for Nuclear Research. Liste des Publications Scientifiques/List of Scientific Publications 892

European Research

European Southern Observatory. Annual Report 115

1172 INDEX TO PUBLICATIONS OF INTERNATIONAL ORGANIZATIONS

European Taxation

European Yearbook 126

Exchange of Information on Research in European Law/Echange d'Informations sur les Recherches en Droit Europeen 668

Expression 1128

Extensions and Corrections to the U D C 677

Eye to Eye

F A M L I (Family Medicine Literature Index) 770

F.I.D./C.R. Report Series (International Federation for Documentation) 689

F I D Directory (International Federation for Documentation) 677

F I D News Bulletin (International Federation for Documentation)

F I D/R I Meetings Reports (International Federation for Documentation, Committee on Research on the Theoretical Basis of Information) 677

F I D/R I Series on Problems of Information Science (International Federation for Documentation, Committee on Research on the Theoretical Basis of Information) 677

F I F A News (International Federation of Association Football)

F I O D S Revue (Federation Internationale des Organisations de Donneurs de Sang Benevoles)

F I S Bulletin (International Ski Federation)

F I T Newsletter/F I T Nouvelles (Federation Internationale des Traducteurs)

Faith and Order Papers 969

Family Planning in Five Continents

Federacion Panamericana de Associaciones de Facultades de Medicina. Boletin

Federation Internationale de Gymnastique. Bulletin

Federation Internationale de Rugby Amateur. Annuaire 1038

Federation Internationale Motocycliste. Annuaire 1041

Fernschach

Fertilizers and Agriculture

Flashes from the Trade Unions

Fluoride

Folia Phoniatrica

Fontes Artis Musicae

Food Consumption Statistics in the O.E.C.D. Countries 521

Forage Network in Ethiopia Newsletter

Forum

Free Labour World

Futuribles

Futurology

General Treaty for Central American Economic Integration. Permanent Secretariat. Carta Informativa

General Treaty for Central American Economic Integration. Permanent Secretariat. Newsletter 262

Geodex Retrieval System for Geotechnical Abstracts

Geographical Distribution of Financial Flows to Developing Countries. (Disbursement) 262

Geothermics

Germplasm Newsletter

Giornale Storico della Lunigiana e del Territorio Lucense 584

Guide-Annuaire de l'Equipement Agricole 51

Guide to European Taxation. Taxation of Companies in Europe

Guides to European Taxation: Taxation of Patent Royalties, Dividends, Interest in Europe

Hague Conference on Private International Law. Actes et Documents 670

Handbook on the U.S. - German Tax Convention 296

Hebrew Christian

Hegel-Studien Beihefte 878

Histopathology

Human Rights Bulletin (New York)

Human Rights Teaching/Enseignement des Droits de l'Homme

Hydrological Sciences Journal/Journal des Sciences Hydrologiques

Hygie

I A B S E Report (International Association for Bridge and Structural Engineering) 481

I A G A News (International Association of Geomagnetism and Aeronomy) 399

I.A.J.R.C. Journal (International Association of Jazz Record Collectors)

I A L A Bulletin/Association Internationale de Signalisation Maritime. Bulletin de l' A I S M (International Association of Lighthouse Authorities)

I A L News (International Association of Laryngectomees)

I A S L Newsletter (International Association of School Librarianship)

I A T A Review (International Air Transport Association.)

I B A Review (International Bauxite Association)

I B I Newsletter (Intergovernmental Bureau for Informatics)

I C A Regional Bulletin (International Cooperative Alliance)

I C A S A L S Newsletter (International Center for Arid and Semi-Arid Land Studies)

I C C Annual Review (International Chamber of Commerce) 236

I C C Business World (International Chamber of Commerce)

I C E L References (International Council on Environmental Law) 501

I C E M Review (International Council for Educational Media)

I C E S Oceanographic Data Lists and Inventories 406

I C F T U Economic & Social Bulletin (International Confederation of Free Trade Unions)

I C H E International Commission on Human Ecology 72

I C I D Bulletin (International Commission on Irrigation and Drainage)

I C L A S Bulletin (International Council for Laboratory Animal Science)

I C M A Newsletter (International City Management Association)

I C M C Newsletter (International Catholic Migration Commission)

I C O M News/Nouvelles de l'I C O M (International Council of Museums)

I C P A Quarterly (International Commission for the Prevention of Alcoholism and Drug Dependency)

I C S U Newsletter (International Council of Scientific Unions)

I C V A News (International Council of Voluntary Agencies)

I E C Bulletin (International Electrotechnical Commission)

I E C Catalogue of Publications (International Electrotechnical Commission) 461

I E E E International Conference on Acoustics, Speech and Signal Processing. Proceedings 454

I E E E International Symposium on Electrical Insulation. I E E E Conference Record 454

I E S A Information (International Society for Electrosleep and Electroanaesthesia) 790

I F A P News/F I P A Nouvelles (International Federation of Agricultural Producers)

I F H P News Sheet (International Federation for Housing and Planning)

I F I P Information Bulletin (International Federation for Information Processing) 678

I F L A Directory (International Federation of Library Associations and Institutions) 678

I F L A Journal

I F L A Publications (International Federation of Library Associations and Institutions) 679

I F L Nieuws (International Friendship League)

I G F - Journal (International Graphical Federation)

I I A S A Annual Report (International Institute for Applied Systems Analysis) 358

I L C A Annual Report (International Livestock Centre for Africa) 66

I L C A Bulletin (International Livestock Centre for Africa)

I L C A Newsletter (International Livestock Centre for Africa)

I L C A Proceedings (International Livestock Centre for Africa) 66

I L C A Programme and Budget (International Livestock Centre for Africa) 66

I L C A Research Report (International Livestock Centre for Africa) 66

I M A C S News (International Association for Mathematics and Computers in Simulation)

I M F News (International Metalworkers Federation)

I M U Canberra Circular (International Mathematical Union)

I M Z Bulletin (International Music Centre)

I O J Newsletter (International Organization of Journalists)

I P D. Cahier/P A I D. Reports (Institut Panafricain pour le Developpement)

I P I Report (International Press Institute)

I P P F Co-operative Information Service (International Planned Parenthood Federation)

I P S F News Bulletin (International Pharmaceutical Students Federation)

I P T C News (International Press Telecommunications Council)

INDEX TO PUBLICATIONS OF INTERNATIONAL ORGANIZATIONS 1173

I R R I Annual
    Report (International Rice Research Institute) 63

I S O Bulletin (International Organization for Standardization)

I S O International Standards (International Organization for Standardization) 809

I S O Memento (International Organization for Standardization) 809

I S T A News Bulletin (International Seed Testing Association)

I S U Constitution (International Skating Union) 1033

I S U Regulations (International Skating Union) 1034

I T C Journal

I T M F Directory (International Textile Manufacturers Federation) 1074

I T U Review (International Typographical Union)

I U C N Annual Report (International Union for Conservation of Nature and Natural Resources) 365

I U C N Bulletin (International Union for Conservation of Nature and Natural Resources)

I.U.G.G. Chronicle (International Union of Geodesy and Geophysics)

I U P I W Views (International Union of Petroleum & Industrial Workers)

I U S S P Papers/U I E S P Documents de l'Union (International Union for the Scientific Study of Population) 922

I W G I A Documents (International Work Group for Indigenous Affairs) 72

I W G I A Newsletter (International Work Group for Indigenous Affairs) 72

Ibero-American Bureau of Education. Information and Publications Department Series V: Technical Seminars and Meetings 414

Ice

Index to Plant Chromosome Numbers 158

Inform Quarterly Newsletter

Information Bulletin for Catholic Rural Organizations

Infoterm Series (International Information Centre for Terminology, Vienna) 696

Ingenieria Sanitaria

Inspel

Institut International du Froid. Bulletin/International Institute of Refrigeration. Bulletin

Institut Panafricain pour le Developpement. Annuaire des Anciens Etudiants

Institut Panafricain pour le Developpement. Travaux Manuscrits 48

Instituto Indigenista Interamericano Serie de Ediciones Especiales 72

Instituto Interamericano de Cooperacion para la Agricultura - O E A. Documentos Oficiales 28

Instituto Interamericano del Nino. Boletin

Instituto Interamericano del Nino. Servicio Social. Informes Tecnicos 1018

Instituto Panamericano de Geografia e Historia. Boletin Aereo

Inter American Press Association. Committee on Freedom on the Press. Report

Inter American Press Association. Minutes of the Annual Meeting 646

Inter-American Bar Association. Letter to Members

Inter-American Center of Tax Administrators. Informativo/Newsletter

Inter-American Centre for Agricultural Documentation and Information. Documentacion e Informacion Agricola 41

Interamerican Children's Institute. Report of the General Director 1018

Inter-American Commission of Women. News Bulletin 1129

Inter-American Commission of Women. Noticiero 1129

Inter-American Council for Education, Science, and Culture. Final Report 415

Inter-American Council of Commerce and Production. Uruguayan Section. Publicaciones 263

Inter-American Development Bank. Annual Report 229

Inter-American Development Bank. Institute for Latin American Integration. Annual Report 263

Inter-American Economic and Social Council. Final Report of the Annual Meeting at the Ministerial Level 606

Inter-American Institute for Cooperation on Agriculture. Executive Committee. Yearly Meeting Report 29

Inter-American Institute for Cooperation on Agriculture. Informe Anual 29

Inter-American Review of Bibliography/Revista Interamericana de Bibliografia

Inter-American Tropical Tuna Commission. Annual Report/Comision Inter-Americana del Atun Tropical 510

Inter-American Tropical Tuna Commission. Bulletin/Comision Interamericana del Atun Tropical. Boletin 510

Inter-American Tropical Tuna Commission. Data Report 510

Interdependence

Intergovernmental Committee for Migration. Review of Achievements 922

InterMedia

International Abstracts in Operations Research 354

International Advertising Association. United Kingdom Chapter. Concise Guide to International Markets 15

International Aeronautic Federation. Annual Information Bulletin 19

International Air Transport Association. Annual General Meeting. Reports and Proceedings 1088

International Angiology

International Animated Film Association. Bulletin 824

International Archery Federation. Bulletin Officiel 1034

International Arthurian Society. Bibliographical Bulletin/Societe Internationale Arthurienne. Bulletin Bibliographique 739

International Association for Byzantine Studies. Bulletin d'Information et de Coordination 586

International Association for Mass Communications Research. Letter from the President 343

International Association for Plant Tissue Culture. Newsletter

International Association for Shell and Spatial Structures. Bulletin

International Association for the Exchange of Students for Technical Experience. Annual Report 441

International Association of Agricultural Librarians and Documentalists. Quarterly Bulletin

International Association of Dentistry for Children. Journal

International Association of Engineering Geology. Bulletin

International Association of French Studies. Cahiers 724

International Association of Geodesy. Central Bureau for Satellite Geodesy. Bibliography 551

International Association of Geodesy. Central Bureau for Satellite Geodesy. Information Bulletin 545

International Association of Geodesy. Commission Permanente des Marees Terrestres. Marees Terrestres Bulletin d'Information 399

International Association of Hydrogeologists. Memoires 403

International Association of Labour History Institutions. Bibliographische Information

International Association of Law Libraries. Directory 679

International Association of Liberal Religious Women. Newsletter 970

International Association of Theoretical and Applied Limnology. Communications 403

International Astronomical Union. Transactions 116

International Baccalaureate Office. Annual Bulletin 415

International Badminton Federation. Annual Statute Book 1034

International Bibliography of Selected Police Literature 374

International Bibliography of the Forensic Sciences 771

International Brain Research Organization Monograph Series 790

International Bureau of Fiscal Documentation. Annual Report 296

International Bureau of Fiscal Documentation. Publication 296

International Cancer News (International Union Against Cancer)

International Cataloguing

International Centre for Settlement of Investment Disputes. Annual Report 266

International Centre of Insect Physiology and Ecology. Annual Report 167

International Chamber of Commerce. Handbook 236

International Child Welfare Review

International Children's Center. Courrier

International Children's Centre. Paris. Report of the Director-General to the Executive Board 1027

International Children's Centre. Paris. Travaux et Documents 1027

International Civil Defence

International Classification

International College of Dentists. European Section. Newsletter 779

International Commission for Uniform Methods of Sugar Analysis. Report of the Proceedings of the Session 519

International Commission of Jurists. Review

International Commission on Irrigation and Drainage. Congress Reports 490

1174 INDEX TO PUBLICATIONS OF INTERNATIONAL ORGANIZATIONS

International Commission on Irrigation and Drainage. Report 1124

International Commission on Large Dams. Bulletin 482

International Commission on Radiological Protection. Report 792

International Committee for Historical Science. Bulletin d'Information 558

International Committee of the Red Cross. Annual Report/Rapport d'Activite/Informe de Actividad/Taetigkeitsbericht 1018

International Committee on Urgent Anthropological and Ethnological Research. Bulletin 72

International Confederation of Free Trade Unions. World Congress Reports 648

International Confederation of Societies of Authors and Composers 861

International Congress Science Series 796

International Cooperative Alliance. Cooperative Series 238

International Copper Information Bulletin 801

International Cotton Advisory Committee. Country Statements Presented in Connection with the Plenary Meetings 57

International Cotton Industry Statistics 1075

International Cotton-System Fibre Consumption Statistics 1076

International Council for Bird Preservation. British Section. Report 170

International Council for the Exploration of the Sea. Annales Biologiques 142

International Council for the Exploration of the Sea. Bulletin Statistique 406

International Council for the Exploration of the Sea. Cooperative Research Reports 406

International Council for the Exploration of the Sea. Journal du Conseil 406

International Council of Scientific Unions. Year Book 993

International Council on Archives. Committee on Conservation and Restauration. Committee on Archival Reprography (Bulletin) 679

International Court of Justice. Yearbook/Annuaire 670

International Customs Journal/Bulletin International des Douanes 296

International Dairy Federation. Annual Bulletin/Federation Internationale de Laiterie. Bulletin Annuel 62

International Dairy Federation. Annual Memento/Federation Internationale de Laiterie. Memento Annuel 62

International Dairy Federation. Catalogue of I D F Publications. Catalogue des Publications de la F I L 41

International Dairy Federation. International Standard/Federation Internationale de Laiterie. Norme Internationale 62

International Dental Journal

International Directory of Antiquarian Booksellers/Repertoire International de la Librairie Ancienne 962

International Directory of Building Research, Information and Development Organizations 185

International Directory of Prisoners' Aid Agencies 370

International Egg Commission. Market Review Situation & Outlook Report

International Egg Commission. Monthly Chick Placement Bulletin

International Egg Commission. Monthly News Bulletin

International Egg Commission. Monthly News Sheet

International Egg Commission. Six-Monthly Statistical Bulletin

International Electrotechnical Commission. Repertoire/International Electrotechnical Commission. Directory 456

International Electrotechnical Commission. Yearbook/Annuaire 456

International Federation for Documentation. P-Notes 679

International Federation for Housing and Planning. Directory 623

International Federation of Commercial Clerical and Technical Employees. Newsletter

International Federation of Journalists and Travel Writers. Official List/Repertoire Officiel

International Federation of Secondary Teachers. International Bulletin/Federation Internationale des Professeurs de l'Enseignement Secondaire Officiel. Bulletin International/Internationale Vereinigung der Lehrer an Offentlichen Hoheren Schulen. Internationale Zeitschrift

International Fiscal Association. Yearbook 670

International Fiscal Harmonization Series 296

International Forum of Light Music in Radio 348

International Graphical Federation. Report of Activities 648

International Gravimetric Bureau. Bulletin d'Information

International Handbook of Universities and Other Institutions of Higher Education 436

International Hotel Guide 620

International Humanist

International Hydrographic Bulletin

International Hydrographic Organization. Yearbook 406

International Hydrographic Review

International Institute for Land Reclamation and Improvement. Annual Report 57

International Institute for Land Reclamation and Improvement. Bibliography 41

International Institute for Land Reclamation and Improvement. Publication 57

International Institute of Administrative Sciences. Reports of the International Congress 943

International Institute of Refrigeration. Proceedings of Commission Meetings 554

International Institute of Seismology and Earthquake Engineering. Bulletin 399

International Institute of Seismology and Earthquake Engineering. Individual Studies by Participants at I I S E E 400

International Institute of Seismology and Earthquake Engineering. Year Book 400

International Institute on the Prevention and Treatment of Alcoholism. Selected Papers 377

International Journal of Biometeorology

International Journal of Cancer

International Journal of Dermatology

International Journal of Early Childhood

International Journal of Government Auditing/Revue Internationale de la Verification des Comptes Publics/Revista Internacional de Entidades Fiscalizadoras Superiores

International Journal of Group Tensions 935

International Journal of Gynaecology and Obstetrics

International Journal of Legal Information

International Journal of Leprosy and Other Mycobacterial Diseases

International Journal of Oral and Maxillofacial Surgery

International Journal of Physical Education/Internationale Zeitschrift fuer Sportpaedagogik

International Journal of Psycho-Analysis

International Journal of Sport Psychology

International Journal of Systematic Bacteriology

International Journal of University Adult Education

International League for Human Rights. Annual Report 913

International Linguistic Association. Monograph 696

International Linguistic Association. Special Publications 696

International Music Council. German Committee. Referate Informationen

International Narcotic Enforcement Officers Association. Annual Conference Report 370

International Narcotics Control Board. Comparative Statement of Estimates and Statistics on Narcotic Drugs for (Year) 871

International Narcotics Control Board. Report for (Year) 871

International Narcotics Control Board. Statistics on Narcotic Drugs for (Year) 871

International Narcotics Control Board. Statistics on Psychotropic Substances for (Year) 871

International Naturist Guide/Internationaler FKK-Reisefuehrer/Guide Naturiste Internationale 1045

International Navigation Congress. Papers 1101

International Navigation Congress. Proceedings 1101

International Newsletter

International Nursing Review

International Office of Cocoa and Chocolate and the International Sugar Confectionary Manufacturers' Association. Annual Statistical Bulletin 522

International Oil Scouts Association. Official Publication

International Organization

International Organization of Consumers Unions. Proceedings 369

International Orthopaedics

International Pacific Halibut Commission (U.S. and Canada). Annual Report 510

International Pacific Halibut Commission (U.S. and Canada). Scientific Reports 510

International Peace Research Newsletter

International Pediatric Association. Bulletin

International Polar Motion Service. Annual Report/Kokusai Kyoku-Undo Kansoku Jigyo Nenpo 116

International Polar Motion Service. Monthly Notes/Kokusai Kyoku-Undo Kansoku Jigyo Geppo

International Police Association. Meeting of the International Executive Council 370

International
 Police Association. Travel Scholarships 371

International Political Science Abstracts/
 Documentation Politique Internationale 912

International Population Conference. Proceedings 922

International Press Institute. Survey

International Prisoners Aid Association. Newsletter

International Psychologist

International Railway Statistics. Statistics of Individual
 Railways 1094

International Rayon and Synthetic Fibres Committee.
 Statistical Yearbook 1076

International Rehabilitation Review 762

International Rescue Committee Annual Report 1018

International Review for Business Education/Revue
 Internationale pour l'Enseignement Commercial/
 Internationale Zeitschrift fuer Kaufmaennisches
 Bildungswesen/Rivista Internazionale per la Cultura
 Commerciale/Revista Internacional la Ensenanza
 Comercial

International Review of Administrative Sciences

International Review of Contemporary Law

International Review of Mission

International Review of the Red Cross

International Rubber Digest

International Seismological Centre. Bulletin

International Silk Association. Monthly Newsletter

International Skating Union. Ice Dancing Regulations 1034

International Social Science Council. Publications 1009

International Social Security Association. Etudes et
 Recherches/Studies and Research 640

International Social Security Review

International Social Work

International Society of Criminology. Bulletin 371

International Society of Plant Morphologists. Yearbook 158

International Society of Soil Science. Bulletin

International Statistical Handbook of Urban Public
 Transport/Recueil International de Statistiques des
 Transports Publics Urbains/Internationales Statistik-
 Handbuch fuer den Oeffentlichen Stadtverkehr 1081

International Statistical Review

International Studies Notes

International Sugar Organization. Annual Report 57

International Sugar Organization Statistical Bulletin

International Symposium on Canine Heartworm
 Disease. Proceedings 1121

International Textile Machinery Shipment Statistics 1076

International Textile Manufacturing 1074

International Tin Research Institute. Annual Report 798

International Union against Cancer. Manual/Union
 Internationale Contre le Cancer. Manuel 775

International Union for Inland Navigation. Annual
 Report 1082

International Union for Vacuum Science, Technique
 and Applications. News Bulletin

International Union of Alpine Associations. Bulletin/
 Union Internationale des Associations d'Alpinisme.
 Bulletin

International Union of Food and Allied Workers'
 Associations. News Bulletin

International Union of Geodesy and Geophysics.
 Monograph 545

International Union of Geodesy and Geophysics.
 Proceedings of the General Assembly 545

International Union of Physiological Sciences.
 Newsletter 172

International Union of Public Transport. Proceedings
 of the International Congress 1082

International Union of Public Transport. Technical
 Reports of the Congresses 1082

International Union of Students. Sport Bulletin

International Union of Tenants. International
 Information

International Whaling Commission. Report 510

International Wheat Council. Annual Report 29

International Wheat Council. Market Report

International Wheat Council. Record of Operations of
 Member Countries 29

International Wheat Council. Secretariat Papers 29

International Women's News

International Yearbook of the Underwater World/
 Annuaire International du Monde Sous-Marin

Internationale Berg- und Seilbahn-Rundschau/
 International Aerial Tramway Review

Internationale Gesellschaft fuer Geschichte der
 Pharmazie. Veroeffentlichungen. Neue Folge 871

Internationale Gesellschaft fuer Urheberrecht.
 Yearbook 861

Internationale Stiftung Mozarteum. Mitteilungen

Internationales Jahrbuch fuer Kartographie 545

Inter-Parliamentary Bulletin

Inter-Parliamentary Union. Series: "Reports and
 Documents" 906

Interpressgraphic

Intervirology

Inventaria Archaeologica Belgique 88

Inventaria Archaeologica Ceskoslovensko 88

Inventaria Archaeologica Denmark 88

Inventaria Archaeologica Deutschland 88

Inventaria Archaeologica Espana 88

Inventaria Archaeologica France 88

Inventaria Archaeologica Italia 88

Inventaria Archaeologica Jugoslavija 88

Inventaria Archaeologica Norway 88

Inventaria Archaeologica Oesterreich 88

Inventaria Archaeologica Pologne 88

Inventaria Archaeologica Ungarn 88

Jahrbuch fuer Liturgik und Hymnologie 970

Jazzforschung/Jazz Research 837

Jazzmen's Reference Book 837

Journal de Genetique Humaine

Journal of Cardiovascular Surgery

Journal of Glaciology

Journal of Hydraulic Research

Journal of Maxillofacial Surgery

Journal of Medical & Veterinary Mycology

Journal of Police Science and Administration

Journal of Reading

Journal of Rural Cooperation

Journal of Sports Medicine and Physical Fitness

Journal of Structural Learning

Journal of Terramechanics

Journal of Traffic Medicine

Jugend und Buch

Kidma

Kidney International

Klassische Homoeopathie

Labor

Labor Press and Information

Latin American Bulletin/Boletin de America Latina

Lead and Zinc Statistics

Leben und Umwelt

Lethaia

Ligue Internationale Contre la Concurrence Deloyale.
 Annuaire 258

Ligue Internationale Contre la Concurrence Deloyale.
 Communication

Local Government Newsletter (International Union of
 Local Authorities)

Log of the Star Class 1042

Lotus

M.I.I. Series (Muslim Intellectuals' International) 975

Market Frontier News

Materiaux & Constructions/Materials & Structures

Ma'yanot 504

Medailles

Media Development

Medical & Biological Engineering & Computing

Memento de l'O.I.V. (Office International de la Vigne
 et du Vin) 120

Metallography

Metro: A Bibliography 1086

Metrologia

Microtables Imports-Exports of O.E.C.D. Countries 258

Microwave Power Symposium. Proceedings 457

Migration News

Migration Today 923

Military Balance 812

Ministerial Formation

Monthly Letter on Evangelism

Muslim World

N A T O. Annual Economic Colloquia. Proceedings
 (North Atlantic Treaty Organization) 258

1176 INDEX TO PUBLICATIONS OF INTERNATIONAL ORGANIZATIONS

N A T O and the Warsaw Pact - Force Comparisons/ O T A N et le Pacte de Varsovie - Comparison des Forces en Presence (North Atlantic Treaty Organization) 917

N A T O Basic Documents/O T A N Documents Fondamentaux (North Atlantic Treaty Organization) 917

N A T O Final Communiques/O T A N Communiques Finals (North Atlantic Treaty Organization) 917

N A T O Handbook (North Atlantic Treaty Organization) 917

N A T O Review (North Atlantic Treaty Organization)

N A T O Scientific Publications. Newsletter (North Atlantic Treaty Organization)

Nature and Environment Series 366

Naturopa

Neuroendocrinology

New Perspectives

News from I C S I D (International Centre for Settlement of Investment Disputes)

News from O E C D

Newsletter on Radionuclides Migration in the Geosphere/Bulletin sur la Migration des Radionucleides dans la Geosphere

Nonviolence et Societe

Nordisk Statistisk Aarsbok/Yearbook of Nordic Statistics 1060

Nordisk Statistisk Skriftserie/Statistical Reports of the Nordic Countries 1060

Nordisk Statutsamling 661

North Atlantic Treaty Organization. Facts and Figures/Alliance Atlantique. Structure, Faits et Chiffres 917

Noticias de Galapagos

Nuclear Law Bulletin

Numen

O A S. General Secretariat. Annual Report (Organization of American States) 608

O E C D Economic Outlook (Organisation for Economic Cooperation and Development)

O E C D Economic Studies (Organisation for Economic Cooperation and Development)

O E C D Financial Statistics/Statistiques Financieres de l'O C D E (Organization for Economic Cooperation and Development) 215

O E C D Main Economic Indicators/Principaux Indicateurs Economiques (Organisation for Economic Cooperation and Development)

O E C D Observer (Organisation for Economic Cooperation and Development)

O I E C Bulletin (Catholic International Education Office)

O I V Bulletin (Office International de la Vigne et du Vin)

Odonto-Stomatologie Tropicale/Tropical Dental Journal

Olympic Review (Year)

One World

Onoma

Orbis

Orbis Geographicus 547

Organ Building Periodical/Zeitschrift fuer Orgelbau (International Society of Organbuilders) 840

Organization for Economic Cooperation and Development. Activities of O.E.C.D.: Report by the Secretary General 263

Organization for Economic Cooperation and Development. Annual Oil and Gas Statistics/ Statistiques Annuelles du Petrole et du Gaz Naturel 868

Organization for Economic Cooperation and Development. Catalogue of Publications 129

Organization for Economic Cooperation and Development. Council. Code de la Liberation des Mouvements de Capitaux. Code of Liberalisation of Capital Movements 231

Organization for Economic Cooperation and Development. Development Cooperation 263

Organization for Economic Cooperation and Development. Economic Surveys: Austria 247

Organization for Economic Cooperation and Development. Economic Surveys: Australia 247

Organization for Economic Cooperation and Development. Economic Surveys: Belgium-Luxembourg Economic Union 247

Organization for Economic Cooperation and Development. Economic Surveys: Canada 247

Organization for Economic Cooperation and Development. Economic Surveys: Denmark 247

Organization for Economic Cooperation and Development. Economic Surveys: France 247

Organization for Economic Cooperation and Development. Economic Surveys: Germany 247

Organization for Economic Cooperation and Development. Economic Surveys: Greece 247

Organization for Economic Cooperation and Development. Economic Surveys: Iceland 247

Organization for Economic Cooperation and Development. Economic Surveys: Ireland 247

Organization for Economic Cooperation and Development. Economic Surveys: Italy 247

Organization for Economic Cooperation and Development. Economic Surveys: Japan 247

Organization for Economic Cooperation and Development. Economic Surveys: Netherlands. 247

Organization for Economic Cooperation and Development. Economic Surveys: Norway 248

Organization for Economic Cooperation and Development. Economic Surveys: Portugal 248

Organization for Economic Cooperation and Development. Economic Surveys: Socialist Federal Republic of Yugoslavia 248

Organization for Economic Cooperation and Development. Economic Surveys: Spain 248

Organization for Economic Cooperation and Development. Economic Surveys: Sweden 248

Organization for Economic Cooperation and Development. Economic Surveys. Switzerland 248

Organization for Economic Cooperation and Development. Economic Surveys: Turkey 248

Organization for Economic Cooperation and Development. Economic Surveys: United Kingdom 248

Organization for Economic Cooperation and Development. Economic Surveys: United States 248

Organization for Economic Cooperation and Development. Energy Statistics 468

Organization for Economic Cooperation and Development. Foreign Trade by Commodities 215

Organization for Economic Cooperation and Development. Guide to Legislation on Restrictive Business Practices. Supplements

Organization for Economic Cooperation and Development. Labour Force Statistics (Yearbook) / Statistiques de la Population Active 215

Organization for Economic Cooperation and Development. Liaison Bulletin Between Research and Training Institutes 291

Organization for Economic Cooperation and Development. Library. Catalogue of Periodicals/ Catalogue des Periodiques 129

Organization for Economic Cooperation and Development. Library. Ouvrages et Periodiques Nouveaux Catalogues a la Bibliotheque/New Books and Periodicals Catalogued at the Library

Organization for Economic Cooperation and Development. Library. Special Annotated Bibliography: Automation. Bibliographie Speciale Analytique 354

Organization for Economic Cooperation and Development. Main Economic Indicators. Historical Statistics. Statistiques Retrospectives 215

Organization for Economic Cooperation and Development. Maritime Transport Committee. Maritime Transport 1102

Organization for Economic Cooperation and Development. Monthly Foreign Trade Statistics/ Statistiques Mensuel du Commerce Exterieur.

Organization for Economic Cooperation and Development. Nuclear Energy Agency. Activity Report 898

Organization for Economic Cooperation and Development. Quarterly Labour Statistics/ Statistiques Trimestrielles de la Population Active

Organization for Economic Cooperation and Development. Revenue Statistics of O.E.C.D. Member Countries 215

Organization for Economic Cooperation and Development. Reviews of Manpower and Social Policies 275

Organization for Economic Cooperation and Development. Special Committee for Iron and Steel. Iron and Steel Industry 799

Organization for Economic Cooperation and Development. Special Committee for Oil. Oil Statistics. Supply and Disposal 866

Organization for Economic Cooperation and Development. Tourism Committee. Tourism Policy and International Tourism in O E C D Member Countries 1115

Organization of African Unity. Inter-African Bureau for Soils. Bibliographie 42

Organization of African Unity. Scientific Technical and Research Commission. Publication 997

Organization of American States. Department of Cultural Affairs. Manuales del Bibliotecario 682

Organization of American States. Department of Scientific Affairs. Report of Activities 997

Organization of American States. Department of Scientific Affairs. Serie de Biologia: Monografias 145

Organization of American States. Department of Scientific Affairs. Serie de Fisica: Monografias 890

Organization of American States. Department of Scientific Affairs. Serie de Matematica: Monografias 751

Organization of American States. Department of Scientific Affairs. Serie de Quimica: Monografias 324

Organization of American States. General Assembly. Actas y Documentos 917

Organization of American States. Official Records. Indice y Lista General 608

INDEX TO PUBLICATIONS OF INTERNATIONAL ORGANIZATIONS 1177

Organization of the Petroleum Exporting Countries. Annual Report. 866

Organization of the Petroleum Exporting Countries. Annual Statistical Bulletin 866

P C R Information (World Council of Churches, Programme to Combat Racism)

P T T I Studies (Postal Telegraph and Telephone International)

Pan American Federation of Engineering Societies. Bulletin 473

Pan American Institute of Geography and History. Commission on Geophysics. Boletin 400

Pan American Institute of Geography and History. Commission on History. Bibliografias 608

Pan American Institute of Geography and History. Commission on History. Historiografias Americanas 608

Pan American Institute of Geography and History. Commission on History. Historiadores de America 608

Pan American Institute of Geography and History. Commission on History. Monumentos Historicos y Arqueologicos 608

Pan American Medical Women's Alliance. Newsletter 765

Panorama Democrate Chretien 907

Panorama Democrate Chretien/Panorama Democrata Cristiano/Christlich Demokratisches Panorama

Paraplegia

Parlements et Francophonie

Participation

Pax et Libertas

Peace and the Sciences

Peace Courier

Pedofauna 58

People

Permanent International Altaistic Conference (PIAC). Newsletter 853

Permanent International Association of Navigation Congresses. Bulletin

Phonetica

Photogrammetria

Phycologia

Phytomorphology

Planning and Administration 945

Planning & Administration

Polar Bears 177

Police Chief

Police Labor Review

Potash Review

Prison Information Bulletin

Psychotherapy and Psychosomatics

Quality

Quarterly Bulletin on Solar Activity

R & D Projects in Documentation and Librarianship

Radio - Television

Rail International/Schienen der Welt

Reading Research Quarterly

Reading Teacher

Reformation Review

Reformed World

Regnum Vegetabile 160

Rejuvenation

Repertorium Plantarum Succulentarum 160

Research in Reproduction

Research into Disease 765

Research on Transport Economics/Recherche en Matiere d'Economie des Transports 1083

Resumenes Analiticos C I N T E R F O R (Centro Interamericano de Investigacion y Documentacion sobre Formacion Profesional)

Review of Fisheries in O.E.C.D. Member Countries 512

Review of Income and Wealth

Review of International Cooperation

Review of Population Reviews

Review of the World Wheat Situation 33

Revista FeLaBan (Federacion Latinoamericana de Bancos)

Revista Geofisica

Revista Geografica

Revista Internacional de Vivienda Rural/International Rural Housing Journal 625

Revista Latinoamericana de Quimica

Revista Rotaria

Revue Africaine et Malgache de Psychologie

Revue de Bio-Mathematique/Biomathematics

Revue Internationale de Police Criminelle

Rivista di Studi Liguri/Revue d'Etudes Ligures

Rotarian

Rubber Statistical Bulletin

Scandinavian Journal of History

Scientia Horticulturae

Scientific World

Sedimentology

Seed Science and Technology

Selected Documents of the International Petroleum Industry 867

Selected Monographs on Taxation 298

Selection of International Railway Documentation/Abrege de Documentation Ferroviaire Internationale/Auszuege aus der Internationalen Eisenbahn-Dokumentation/Resumen de Documentacion Ferroviaria Internacional

Sennacieca Revuo 918

Situation de la Viticulture dans le Monde 120

Social Europe

Societe Francaise de Psycho-Prophylaxie Obstetricale. Bulletin Officiel

Socio-Economic Differential Mortality in Industrialized Societies 924

Solnechnaya Radiatsiya i Radiatsionnyi Balans. Mirovaya Set/Solar Radiation and Radiation Balance Data. The World Network

Sols Africains/African Soils

Sources of Contemporary Jewish Thought/Mekevot 712

South Pacific Commission. Annual Report 918

South Pacific Commission. Handbook 513

South Pacific Commission. Information Circular 513

South Pacific Commission. Information Document 513

South Pacific Commission. Technical Paper 1071

Southeast Asian Archives 571

Speleological Abstracts/Bulletin Bibliographique Speleologique 382

Sport International

Statistical Theory and Method Abstracts 12

Strategic Survey 918

Studi Genuensi 93

Studies in Conservation

Studies in Social History 1012

Studies on Taxation and Economic Development 299

Supplementary Service to European Taxation

Survey

T U I A F P W Information (Trade Union International of Agricultural, Forestry and Plantation Workers)

Taraxacum

Tax News Service

Taxon

Teachers of the World

Terra et Aqua

Textile Industry in O.E.C.D. Countries 1075

Theatre en Pologne/Theatre in Poland

Theosophist

Thrombosis and Haemostasis

Through Europe by Train 1095

Tidal Gravity Corrections 401

Torah Education

Tourism Compendium 1120

Trade Unions International of Workers in Commerce. Bulletin

Trade Unions International of Workers in Commerce. News

Transnational Associations/Associations Transnationales

Transport Museums 1083

Transport Workers of the World

Travel Abroad: Frontier Formalities 1117

Tropical Ecology

Typographical Journal

U I A-International Architect (International Union of Architects)

U.I.A.M.S. Bulletin Trimestriel (International Union for Moral and Social Action)

U.I.A.M.S. Informations (International Union for Moral and Social Action)

U I A Newsletter (Union Internationale des Architectes)

1178 INDEX TO PUBLICATIONS OF INTERNATIONAL ORGANIZATIONS

U I S Bulletin (Union Internationale de Speleologie)

U I T B B Bulletin (Trade Unions International of Workers of the Building, Wood and Building Materials Industries)

U I T Journal (Union International de Tir)

U I T P Biblio-Index (International Union of Public Transport)

U I T P Revue (International Union of Public Transport)

U R S I Information Bulletin (International Union of Radio Science)

Uganda Freshwater Fisheries Research Organization. Annual Report 513

Union Douaniere et Economique de l'Afrique Centrale. Bulletin des Statistiques Generales

Union Internationale de Protection de l'Enfance. Bibliotheque. Liste

Union Mondiale des Organisations Syndicales sur Bases Economique et Sociale Liberales. Conferences: Rapport 649

Union of European Football Associations. Handbook of U E F A 1040

United States Board on Books for Young People. Newsletter

Uranium: Resources, Production and Demand/Uranium: Ressources, Production et Demande

La Vie Oecumenique

Vigilancia Epidemiologica de las Encefalitis en las Americas

Visual Merchandising & Store Design

Voice of Silence Newsletter

Volunteer

Vox Sanguinis

Vsemirnoe Profsoyuznoe Dvizhenie

W A Y Forum (World Assembly of Youth)

W C O T P Report (World Confederation of Organizations of the Teaching Profession) 444

W F D Y News (World Federation of Democratic Youth)

W I Z O Review (Women's International Zionist Organization)

W R I Newsletter

Water Research

Water Science and Technology

Welding in the World/Soudage dans le Monde

Wereldverbond van Bouwvakarbeiders- en Houtbewerkersorganisaties. Bulletin

White Paper on Human Ecology 78

White Ribbon Bulletin

Widening Horizons

Word and Deed 977

Work Accomplished by the Inter-American Juridical Committee during its Meeting 667

World Advertising Expenditures 16

World Aeronautical Records 22

World Agriculture /I F A P News/Agriculture dans le Monde (International Federation of Agricultural Producers)

World Air Transport Statistics 1090

World Alliance of Y M C A's Directory 341

World Aluminum Abstracts 802

World Bibliography of Social Security/Bibliographie Universelle de Securite Sociale 220

World Communique

World Council of Churches. Office of Education. Education Newsletter

World Development Report 265

World Directory of Mathematicians 755

World Directory of Travel Agencies 1119

World Federation of Teachers' Unions. Information Letter 422

World Fertility Survey. Basic Documentation 930

World Highways

World Hockey

World Journal of Surgery

World List of Family Planning Agencies 179

World List of Universities, Other Institutions of Higher Education and University Organizations 431

World Methodist Historical Society. Historical Bulletin

World Mining Congress. Report 821

World of Music

World Scout Bureau Report 334

World Scouting/Scoutisme Mondial

World Scouting Newsletter/Bulletin du Scoutisme Mondial

World Student News

World Trade Union Movement

World Translation Index

World Transport Data/Statistiques Mondiales de Transport 1087

World Union for the Safeguard of Youth. Bulletin

World Wheat Statistics 44

World Youth/Jeunesse du Monde/Juventud del Mundo

World Zionist Press Service 539

Y M C A's of the World 341

Yearbook for Traditional Music 843

Yearbook of International Congress Proceedings 920

Yearbook of International Organizations 920

Yearbook of Tourism Statistics 1120

Yearbook of World Problems and Human Potential 920

Young Cinema and Theatre/Jeune Cinema et Theatre

Youth of the 21

Zahlentafeln der Physikalisch-Chemischen Untersuchungen des Rheinwassers/Tableaux Numeriques des Analyses Physico-Chimiques des Eaux du Rhin 500

Zeitschrift fuer Fremdenverkehr/Revue de Tourisme/Tourist Review

Zhenshchiny Mira

Zionist Literature 964

Zshurnalist 647

INTERNATIONAL CONGRESS PROCEEDINGS

A I E S E C Link (International Association of Students in Economics and Management)

Acoustical Imaging: Recent Advances in Visualization and Characterization 899

Acta Concilium Ophthalmologicum 785

Acta Endocrinologica Congress. Advance Abstracts 768

Acta Endocrinologica Panamericana 780

Acta I M E K O

Acta Medica et Sociologica 1023

Actualites Protozoologiques 162

African Regional Trade Union Conference. Report 648

Afro-Asian Peoples' Conference. Proceedings 565

Afro-Asian Peoples' Solidarity Organization. Council. Documents of the Session 565

Allergologicum; Transactions of the Collegium Internationale 773

Annuaire International des Jus de Fruits 119

Annual International Congress Calendar 795

Archivum 673

Asian Pacific Congress of Cardiology. Symposia 776

Assembly of Western European Union. Proceedings

Baptist World Alliance. Congress Reports 978

Biometeorology; Proceedings 803

Brown Boveri Symposia. Proceedings 451

Caribbean Congress of Labour. Report 648

Carnegie-Rochester Conference Series on Public Policy

Carotenoids Other Than Vitamin A 151

Center for High Energy Forming. International Conference. Proceedings 470

Chemistry of Natural Products 329

Clinical Neurosurgery; Proceedings 789

Colloques Internationaux d'Histoire Maritime. Travaux 1099

Colloquium on the Law of Outer Space. Proceedings 18

Colombo Plan for Co-operative Economic and Social Development in Asia and the Pacific. Consultative Committee. Proceedings and Conclusions 261

Committee of the Professional Photographers of Europe. General Assembly. Report of Proceedings 884

Comparative Education Society in Europe. Proceedings of the General Meeting 412

Confederation Europeenne pour la Therapie Physique. Congress Reports 759

Conference Internationale sur les Phenomenes d'Ionisation dans les Gaz. Comptes Rendus 331

Conferencia de Facultades Latinoamericanas de Derecho. (Documentos Oficiales) 654

Congres International d'Histoire des Sciences. Actes 990

Congreso Latinoamericano de Siderurgia. Memoria Tecnica 797

INDEX TO PUBLICATIONS OF INTERNATIONAL ORGANIZATIONS 1179

Congresos Indigenistas Interamericanos. Actas 71

Congress in Park and Recreation Administration. Programme 795

Congress in Park and Recreation Administration. Reports 1044

Congress International Medical de Pays de Langue Francaise de l'Hemisphere Americain. Rapports et Communications 759

Congress of International Congress Organizers and Technicians. Proceeding 795

Congresso Europeo di Storia Ospitaliera. Atti 616

Congresso Latinoamericano de Hidraulica (Papers) 1124

Coordination Chemistry 322

Council for the Social Sciences in East Africa. Social Science Conference. Proceedings 1007

Council of American Building Officials. One and Two Family Dwelling Code 183

Developments in Biological Standardization

E A P R Abstracts of Conference Papers (European Association for Potato Research) 55

Electra

Etudes Historiques 557

Eucarpia 156

European Academy of Allergy. Proceedings 773

European Association for Animal Production. Symposia on Energy Metabolism 65

European Association for Personnel Management. Congress Reports 286

European Brewery Convention. Proceedings of the International Congress 119

European Civil Aviation Conference (Report of Session) 1088

European Conference of Local and Regional Authorities. Official Reports of Debates 941

European Conference of Local and Regional Authorities. Texts Adopted 941

European Congress of Anaesthesiology. Proceedings 774

European Congress of Cardiology. Abstracts of Papers 776

European Congress of Cardiology. (Proceedings) 776

European Congress on Electron Microscopy 169

European Federation of Finance House Associations. Conference Proceedings 227

European Grassland Federation. Proceedings of the General Meeting 55

European League for Economic Cooperation. Reports of the International Congress 262

European Organization for Quality Control. Conference Proceedings 809

European Passenger Train Timetable Conference Minutes 1081

European Symposium on Concrete Pavements. Reports 481

Federation of European Biochemical Societies. (Proceedings of Meeting) 151

Food and Agriculture Organization of the United Nations Conference. Report 27

Guetertransport in Seeverkehr 1100

Hybrid Microelectronics Symposium. (Papers) 454

I A B S E Congress Report (International Association for Bridge and Structural Engineering) 481

I A T A Annual Report (International Air Transport Association) 1088

I C E V H Educator (International Council for Education of the Visually Handicapped) 444

I C H P E R Congress Proceedings (International Council on Health, Physical Education and Recreation) 762

I E E E International Conference on Communications. Conference Record 343

I E E E International Conference on Systems, Man, and Cybernetics. Proceedings 359

I E E E International Symposium on Circuits and Systems. Proceedings 454

I F A C Symposium on Multivariable Technical Control Systems. Proceedings (International Federation of Automatic Control) 491

I F L A Annual (International Federation of Library Associations and Institutions) 678

I F O S A. Minutes of the General Meeting (International Federation of Stationers' Associations) 286

I P A Conference Report 333

Instrumentation in the Pulp and Paper Industry 858

Inter-African Conference on Co-Operative Societies Meeting. Reunion 238

Inter-African Conference on Food and Nutrition. Programa e Informacoes 846

Inter-African Conference on Food and Nutrition. Report 846

Inter-African Conference on Industrial Commercial and Agricultural Education Meeting 441

Inter-African Conference on Medical Co-Operation. Meeting 762

Inter-African Conference on Social Science Meeting 1009

Inter-African Conference on the Treatment of Offenders. Meetings. Reunion 370

Inter-African Forestry Conference. Conference Forestiere Interafricaine (Communications) 525

Inter-African Labour Conference Reports, Recommendations and Conclusions 272

Inter-American Commission of Women. Special Assembly. Final Act/Comision Interamericana de Mujeres. Asamblea Extrarodinaria. Acta Final 913

Inter-American Development Bank. Board of Governors. Proceedings of the Meeting 229

International Academy of Legal Medicine and of Social Medicine. (Congress Reports) 782

International Actuarial Congress. Transactions 640

International Air Safety and Corporate Aviation Safety Seminar Proceedings 19

International Anatomical Congress. Proceedings 762

International Association for Cereal Chemistry. Working and Discussion Meetings Reports 519

International Association for Classical Archaeology. Proceedings of Congress 87

International Association for Cross-Cultural Psychology. International Conference. Selected Papers 934

International Association for Dental Research. Abstracts of the General Meeting 779

International Association for Hydraulic Research. Congress Proceedings 490

International Association for Scientific Study of Mental Deficiency. Proceedings of International Congress 790

International Association of Applied Psychology. Proceedings of Congress 935

International Association of Chain Stores. Report of Plenary Session 284

International Association of Democratic Lawyers. Congress Report 657

International Association of Gerontology. European Clinical Section Proceedings 552

International Association of Logopedics and Phoniatrics. Reports of Congress 790

International Association of Meteorology and Atmospheric Physics. Report of Proceedings of General Assembly 805

International Association of Milk Control Agencies. Proceedings of Annual Meetings 62

International Association of Museums of Arms and Military History. Congress Reports 828

International Association of Performing Arts Libraries and Museums. Congress Proceedings 106

International Association of Physical Education and Sports for Girls and Women. Proceedings of the International Congress 1034

International Association of Seed Crushers. Proceedings of the Annual Congress 29

International Association of State Lotteries. (Reports of Congress) 296

International Association of Students in Economics and Management. International Compendium. Annual Report 196

International Association of Thalassotherapy. Congress Reports 762

International Association of Workers for Maladjusted Children. Congress Reports 444

International Astronomical Union. General Assembly. Highlights 116

International Astronomical Union. Proceedings of Symposia 116

International Basketball Federation. Official Report of the World Congress 1039

International Beekeeping Congress. Reports 29

International Biodeterioration Symposium. Proceedings. Biodeterioration of Materials 168

International Biometeorological Congress. Summaries and Reports Presented to the Congress 142

International Biophysics Congress. Abstracts 150

International Botanical Congress. Abstracts of Papers 158

International Botanical Congress. Proceedings 158

International Cellular Plastics Conference. Proceedings 900

International Ceramic Congress. Proceedings 320

International Clean Air Congress. Proceedings 497

International College of Psychosomatic Medicine. Proceedings of the Congress 790

International Commission of Agricultural Engineering. Reports of Congress 57

International Commission of Sugar Technology. Proceedings of the General Assembly 519

International Commission on Illumination. Proceedings 455

International Commission on Irrigation and Drainage. Congress Reports 490

International Commission on Large Dams. Transactions 482

International Commission on Trichinellosis. Proceedings 777

International Committee for Standardization in Hematology. Symposia 783

International Committee of Onomastic Sciences. Congress Proceedings 696

International Comparative Literature Association. Proceedings of the Congress 724

International Confederation for Agricultural Credit. Assembly and Congress Reports 48

International Confederation of Free Trade Unions. World Congress Reports 648

International Conference for the Sociology of Religion 970

International Conference of Agricultural Economists. Proceedings 48

International Conference of Building Officals. Accumulative Supplement to the Uniform Codes 185

International Conference of Building Officials. Analysis of Revisions to the Uniform Building Code 185

International Conference of Building Officials. Building Department Administration 185

International Conference of Building Officials. Code Changes Committee. Annual Report 185

International Conference of Building Officials. Dwelling Construction Under the Uniform Building Code 185

International Conference of Building Officials. Plan Review Manual

International Conference of Building Officials. Uniform Code for the Abatement of Dangerous Buildings 185

International Conference of Building Officials. Uniform Fire Code 185

International Conference of Building Officials. Uniform Housing Code 185

International Conference of Building Officials. Uniform Mechanical Code 185

International Conference of Ethiopian Studies. Proceedings 566

International Conference of Social Work. Conference Proceedings 1018

International Conference on Acoustics. Reports 900

International Conference on Aerospace Computers in Rockets and Spacecraft. Proceedings 22

International Conference on Cloud Physics. Proceedings 805

International Conference on Computer Communications. (Proceedings) 360

International Conference on Computing Fixed Points with Applications. Proceedings 749

International Conference on Cosmic Rays. (Proceedings) 897

International Conference on Education. Final Report/ Conference International de l'Education. Rapport Final 415

International Conference on Electron and Ion Beam Science and Technology. Abstracts 888

International Conference on Fluid Sealing. Proceedings 491

International Conference on Global Impacts of Applied Microbiology. Proceedings 168

International Conference on Large High Voltage Electric Systems. Proceedings 455

International Conference on Lead. Proceedings 798

International Conference on Lighthouses and Other Aids to Navigation. (Reports) 1101

International Conference on Liquefied Natural Gas. Papers 865

International Conference on Low Temperature Physics. Reports 894

International Conference on Oral Biology. Proceedings 779

International Conference on Piagetian Theory and the Helping Professions. Proceedings 415

International Conference on Science and World Affairs. Proceedings 993

International Conference on Structural Mechanics in Reactor Technology. Proceedings 888

International Conference on the Environmental Impact of Aerospace Operations in the High Atmosphere. (Proceedings) 497

International Conference on the Physics of Electronic and Atomic Collisions. Abstracts of Contributed Papers and Invited Papers 897

International Conference on the Structural Design of Asphalt Pavements. Proceedings 1096

International Conference on Thermoelectric Energy Conversion. Proceedings 455

International Conference on Vehicle Structural Mechanics. Proceedings 1092

International Conference on World Politics. Conference Papers 916

International Congress for Byzantine Studies. Acts/ Congres International des Etudes Byzantines. Actes 586

International Congress for Cybernetics. Proceedings. Actes 359

International Congress for Logic, Methodology and Philosophy of Science. Proceedings 993

International Congress for Papyrology. Proceedings 87

International Congress for Stereology. Proceedings 489

International Congress for the Study of Pre-Columbian Cultures of the Lesser Antilles. Proceedings 73

International Congress of Angiology. Proceedings 776

International Congress of Anthropological and Ethnological Sciences. Proceedings 73

International Congress of Automatic Control. Proceedings 355

International Congress of Biochemistry. Proceedings 151

International Congress of Entomology 165

International Congress of Food Science and Technology. Proceedings 519

International Congress of Graphoanalysts. Proceedings 935

International Congress of Hematology. Proceedings 783

International Congress of Histochemistry and Cytochemistry. Proceedings 151

International Congress of History of Medicine. Proceedings 762

International Congress of Home Economics. Report 615

International Congress of Life Assurance Medicine. Proceedings 640

International Congress of Linguists. Proceedings 696

International Congress of Nephrology. Abstracts of Reports and Communications 795

International Congress of Occupational Therapy. Proceedings 762

International Congress of Orthoptists. Transactions 786

International Congress of Parasitology. Proceedings 175

International Congress of Pharmaceutical Sciences. Proceedings

International Congress of Primatology. Proceedings 73

International Congress of Psychology. Proceedings 935

International Congress of Psychopathological Art. Program. Programme 860

International Congress of Pure and Applied Chemistry. (Lectures) 323

International Congress of Radiology. (Reports) 792

International Congress of Sugarcane Technologists. Proceedings 519

International Congress of Verdi Studies. Proceedings. 836

International Congress on Alcoholism and Drug Dependence. Proceedings 377

International Congress on Animal Reproduction and Artificial Insemination. Proceedings 1121

International Congress on Clinical Chemistry. Abstracts 152

International Congress on Clinical Chemistry. Papers 152

International Congress on Combustion Engines. Proceedings 491

International Congress on Experimental Mechanics. Proceedings 489

International Congress on Hygiene and Preventive Medicine. Proceedings 886

International Congress on Metallic Corrosion. (Proceedings) 798

International Congress on the History of Art. Proceedings 106

International Congresses on Tropical Medicine and Malaria. (Proceedings) 777

International Convocation on Immunology. Papers 773

International Cooperative Alliance. Congress Report 238

International Cotton Advisory Committee. Country Statements Presented in Connection with the Plenary Meetings 57

International Council for Automatic Data Processing in Government Administration. Proceedings of Conference 360

International Council for Bird Preservation. Proceedings of Conferences 170

International Council for Laboratory Animal Science. Proceedings of the Symposium 762

International Council for Scientific Management. Proceedings of World Congress 280

International Council for the Exploration of the Sea. Rapports et Proces-Verbaux des Reunions 406

International Council on Archives. East and Central Africa Regional Branch. General Conference Proceedings 679

International Design Conference in Aspen. Report 643

INDEX TO PUBLICATIONS OF INTERNATIONAL ORGANIZATIONS 1181

International
Economic Association. Proceedings of the Conferences and Congresses 196

International Egg Marketing Conference. Proceedings 66

International Electron Devices Meeting. I E D M Technical Digest 456

International Eucharist Congress. Proceedings 982

International Falcon Movement. Conference Reports 335

International Federation for Documentation. Proceedings of Congress 679

International Federation for Medical Psychotherapy. Congress Reports 790

International Federation of Agricultural Producers. General Conference Proceedings 29

International Federation of Asian and Western Pacific Contractors' Associations. Proceedings of the Annual Convention 796

International Federation of Associations of Textile Chemists and Colorists. Reports of Congress 1074

International Federation of Catholic Universities. General Assembly. (Report) 436

International Federation of Fruit Juice Producers. Proceedings of Congress. Compte-Rendu du Congres 120

International Federation of Fruit Juice Producers. Rapport Annuel d'Activite 519

International Federation of Medical Students' Associations. Minutes and Reports of the General Assembly 762

International Federation of Operational Research Societies. Airline Group (A G I F O R S) Proceedings 1089

International Federation of Plantation, Agricultural and Allied Workers. Report of the Secretariat to the I F P A A W World Congress 48

International Federation of Prestressing. Congress Proceedings 482

International Foundry Congress. Papers and Communications 798

International Gas Union. Proceedings of World Gas Conferences 865

International Geographical Union. Papers 545

International Grassland Congress. Proceedings 57

International Harbour Congress. Proceedings/Internationaal Havenkongres. Verslagboek/Congres Portuaire International. Compte-Rendu/Internationale Hafentagung. Berichte 1101

International Hop Growers Convention. Report of Congress 63

International Horticultural Congress. Proceedings 533

International Humanist and Ethical Union. Proceedings of the Congress 878

International Hydrographic Conference. Reports of Proceedings 406

International Institute for Sugar Beet Research. Reports of the Winter Congress 57

International Institute of Administrative Sciences. Reports of the International Congress 943

International Institute of Ibero-American Literature. Congress Proceedings. Memoria 724

International Institute of Philosophy. Actes 878

International Institute of Public Finance. Papers and Proceedings 296

International Institute of Space Law. Colloquium. Proceedings 657

International Institute of Synthetic Rubber Producers. Annual Meeting Proceedings 985

International Institute on the Prevention and Treatment of Drug Dependence. Selected Papers 377

International Iron and Steel Institute. Report of Conference Proceedings 798

International Joint Conference on Artificial Intelligence. Advance Papers of the Conference

International Journal of Psycho-Analysis

International Law Association. Reports of Conferences 671

International League of Societies for Persons With Mental Handicap. World Congress Proceedings. 935

International Literary and Artistic Association. Proceedings and Reports of Congress 630

International Machine Tool Design and Research Conference. Proceedings 745

International Meeting of Animal Nutrition Experts. Proceedings 66

International Meeting on Cattle Diseases. Reports 1121

International Metalworkers' Congress. Reports 798

International Mineralogical Association. Proceedings of Meetings 817

International Navigation Congress. Proceedings 1101

International Office of Cocoa and Chocolate and the International Sugar Confectionary Manufacturers' Association. Report of the General Assembly 522

International Offshore Exploration Conference 406

International Olympic Academy. Report of the Sessions 1034

International Organization for Cooperation in Health Care. General Assembly. Report 762

International P.E.N. Congress. Report 724

International Pediatric Association. Proceedings of Congress 787

International Philatelic Federation. General Assembly. Proces-Verbal 875

International Political Science Association. World Congress 906

International Population Conference. Proceedings 922

International Potash Institute. Colloquium. Proceedings 57

International Potash Institute. Congress Proceedings 57

International Powder Metallurgy Conference. Proceedings-Modern Developments in Powder Metallurgy 798

International Publishers Association. Proceedings of Congress 962

International Quantum Electronics Conference. Digest of Technical Papers 456

International Road Congresses. Proceedings 1096

International Rubber Study Group. Summary of Proceedings of the Group Meetings and Assemblies 985

International School of Physics "Enrico Fermi". Italian Physical Society. Proceedings 889

International Seaweed Symposium. Proceedings 158

International Sedimentological Congress. Guidebook 389

International Skating Union. Minutes of Congress 1034

International Social Security Association. Reports of the General Assemblies of the ISSA 640

International Society for Rock Mechanics. Congress. Proceedings 482

International Society for Soil Mechanics and Foundation Engineering. Proceedings 482

International Society for Terrain-Vehicle Systems. Proceedings of International Conference 482

International Society of Blood Transfusion. Proceedings of the Congress 783

International Society of Internal Medicine. Congress Proceedings 762

International Society of Urology. Reports of Congress 795

International Statistical Institute. Bulletin. Proceedings of the Biennial Sessions 1057

International Superphosphate and Compound Manufacturers Association Limited. Technical Meeting. Proceedings 57

International Symposium on Atherosclerosis. Proceedings 777

International Symposium on Canine Heartworm Disease. Proceedings 1121

International Symposium on Chemical Reaction Engineering. Proceedings 478

International Symposium on Crop Protection. Proceedings 57

International Symposium on Fault-Tolerant Computing. Digest of Papers 352

International Symposium on Regional Development. Papers and Proceedings 623

International Symposium on Subscriber Loop and Services. Proceedings 456

International Symposium on Surface Physics. Solid-Vacuum Interface. Proceedings 889

International Symposium on Surgical Heart Disease. Proceedings 794

International Symposium on the Chemistry of Cement. Proceedings 323

International Television Symposium and Technical Exhibition, Montreux. (Papers) 348

International Thermal Spraying Conference. Preprint of Papers 802

International Touring Alliance. Minutes of the General Assembly 1112

International Trade Conference of Workers of the Building, Wood and Building Materials Industries. (Brochure) 185

International Trade Union Conference for Action Against Apartheid. Resolution 913

International Union for Conservation of Nature and Natural Resources. Proceedings and Papers of the Technical Meeting 365

International Union for Conservation of Nature and Natural Resources. Proceedings of the General Assembly 365

International Union for Quaternary Research. Congress Proceedings 389

International Union of Biological Sciences. General Assemblies. Proceedings 142

International Union of Building Societies and Savings Associations. Congress Proceedings 230

International Union of Crystallography. Abstracts of the Triennial Congress 327

International Union of Food and Allied Workers' Associations. Meeting of the Executive Committee. I. Documents of the Secretariat. II. Summary Report 648

1182 INDEX TO PUBLICATIONS OF INTERNATIONAL ORGANIZATIONS

International Union of Forestry Research Organizations. Congress Proceedings/Rapports du Congres/Kongressberichte 525

International Union of Latin Notaries. Proceedings of Congress 943

International Union of Physiological Sciences. Proceedings of Congress 172

International Union of Producers and Distributors of Electrical Energy. (Congress Proceedings) 456

International Union of Public Transport. Proceedings of the International Congress 1082

International Union of Radio Science. Proceedings of General Assemblies 348

International Union of School and University Health and Medicine. Congress Reports 415

International Union of Students. Congress and Executive Committee Meetings Resolutions 436

International Water Conference. Proceedings 1124

Internationaler Weltkongress der U F O-Forscher. Dokumentarbericht 20

Inter-Parliamentary Union. Conference Proceedings/ Union Interparlementaire. Comptes Rendus des Conferences 916

Istituto Internazionale di Studi Liguri. Collezione di Monografie Preistoriche Ed Archeologiche 88

Journees Biochimiques Latines. Rapports 152

Kongresa Libro 697

Lutheran World Federation. Proceedings of the Assembly 979

Macromolecular Chemistry (Oxford) 330

Mathematics and Computers in Simulation

Miles International Symposium 163

Mushroom Science 159

National/International Sculpture Conference. Proceedings 108

Nobel Symposium Series 631

North Atlantic Treaty Organization. Advisory Group for Aerospace Research and Development. A G A R D Annual Meeting 20

North Atlantic Treaty Organization. Advisory Group for Aerospace Research and Development. A G A R D Conference Proceedings 21

North Atlantic Treaty Organization. Expert Panel on Air Pollution Modeling. Proceedings 498

Open Door International for the Emancipation of the Woman Worker. Report of Congress 274

Organization of American States. Permanent Council. Decisions Taken at Meetings (Cumulated Edition) 608

Pacific Science Association. Congress and Inter-Congress Proceedings 997

Parapsychology Foundation. Proceedings of International Conferences 860

Pax Romana 983

Perugia Quadrennial International Conferences on Cancer. Proceedings 776

Photochemistry (Oxford) 332

Power Systems Computation Conference. P S C C Proceedings 474

Reinforced Plastics Congress 901

Rubber Research Institute of Malaysia. Planters Conference Proceedings 985

S D C E International Die Casting Congress. Transactions (Society of Die Casting Engineers, Inc.) 746

Scandinavian Corrosion Congress. Proceedings 800

Social Welfare Services in Japan 1020

South Pacific Commission. Report of S P C Fisheries Technical Meetings 513

Study of Time 117

Symposium (International) on Combustion 332

Trade Unions International of Chemical, Oil and Allied Workers. International Trade Conference. Documents 649

Transplantation Today 794

TropMed Seminars on Tropical Medicine. Proceedings 778

U I C C Technical Report Series (International Union Against Cancer) 776

U N I T A R Conference Reports (United Nations Institute for Training and Research) 671

Unesco. Records of the General Conference. Proceedings 919

Unesco. Records of the General Conference. Resolutions 919

Union Academique Internationale. Compte Rendu de la Session Annuelle du Comite 633

Union Mondiale des Organisations Syndicales sur Bases Economique et Sociale Liberales. Conferences: Rapport 649

Union of European Pedopsychiatrists. Proceedings 791

United Nations Issues Conference. Report 919

United Nations of the Next Decade Conference. Report 919

United Schools International. Documents of the Biennial Conference 665

Water Supply

Wenner Gren Center International Symposium Series 1003

Western Hemisphere Nutrition Congress. Proceedings 847

World Airports Conference. Proceedings 1090

World Association for Educational Research. Congress Reports 422

World Association of Girl Guides and Girl Scouts. Report of Conference 334

World Conference on Animal Production. Proceedings 68

World Congress of Psychiatry. Proceedings 791

World Congress of the Deaf. Proceedings. 376

World Congress of the W F D. Proceedings (World Federation of the Deaf) 376

World Congress on Fertility and Sterility. Proceedings 149

World Congress on the Prevention of Occupational Accidents and Diseases. Proceedings 636

World Congresses on Information Processing. Proceedings 686

World Council of Churches. General Assembly. Assembly-Reports 974

World Council of Churches. Minutes and Reports of the Central Committee Meeting 974

World Council of Young Men's Service Clubs. Minutes of the General Meeting 1021

World Crafts Council. General Assembly. Proceedings of the Biennial Meeting 112

World Energy Conference. Plenary Conferences. Transactions 467

World Food Production Conference Summary Report 521

World Forestry Congress. Proceedings 528

World Movement of Mothers. Reports of Meetings 1022

World Muslim Conference. Proceedings 976

World Union for the Safeguard of Youth. Conference Proceedings 1022

World Veterinary Congress. Proceedings 1122

World Zionist Organization. General Council. Addresses, Debates, Resolutions 977

World Zionist Organization. Zionist Congress. Kongres Ha-Tsiyoni. Hahlatot 911

World's Poultry Science Association. Report of the Proceedings of International Congress 68

World's Woman's Christian Temperance Union. Triennial Report 377

EUROPEAN COMMUNITIES

Bulletin of the European Communities

Bulletin of the European Communities. Supplement 242

Bureau Eurisotop. Cahiers d'Information 896

Bureau Eurisotop. Informations Technico-Economiques. 896

C E D E F O P News (European Centre for the Development of Vocational Training (CEDEFOP))

C E E International. Droit et Affaires (Communaute Economique Europeenne) 669

Commission of the European Communities. Annual Reports on the Progress of Research Work Promoted by the ECSC 953

Commission of the European Communities. Collection of Agreements 254

Commission of the European Communities. Community Law 670

Commission of the European Communities. Directorate of Taxation. Inventory of Taxes 294

Commission of the European Communities. Directory 670

Commission of the European Communities. Documentation Bulletin.

Commission of the European Communities. European Regional Development Fund. Annual Report 261

Commission of the European Communities. Financial Report 294

Commission of the European Communities. Investments in the Community Coal Mining and Iron and Steel Industries. Report on the Survey 815

Commission of the European Communities. Joint Research Centre, Ispra. Annual Report: Program Biology-Health Protection 139

Commission of the European Communities. Marches Agricoles: Serie "Prix". Notes Explicatif 45

Commission of the European Communities. Marches Agricoles: Serie "Prix". Produits Animaux 45

INDEX TO PUBLICATIONS OF INTERNATIONAL ORGANIZATIONS 1183

Commission of the European Communities. Marches Agricoles: Serie "Prix". Produits Vegetaux 46

Commission of the European Communities. Monthly Catalogue. Part A: Publications

Commission of the European Communities. Operation of Nuclear Power Stations 896

Commission of the European Communities. Report on Competition Policy/Rapport sur la Politique de Concurrence 288

Commission of the European Communities. Report on the Social Situation 1007

Commission of the European Communities. Specialized Department Terminology and Computer Applications. Bulletin de Terminologie et de Traduction 693

Commission of the European Communities. Studies: Social Policy Series 904

Commission of the European Communities. Trade Union Information Bulletin

Community Report

Comunita Europee

Council of the European Communities. Review of the Council's Work 243

Court of Justice of the European Communities. Report of Cases of the Court 670

Debates of the European Parliament 670

Delta

Developments in the European Communities. Report 243

Documentation Europeenne - Serie Agricole 26

Documentation Europeenne - Serie Syndicale et Ouvriere 271

E C Index 207

E E/Epargne Europe

E G Magazine (Europaeischen Gemeinschaften)

E I B - Information (European Investment Bank)

E P News 670

E U R O N O R M 809

Economic and Social Committee of the European Communities. Bulletin.

Energy Saving and Alternative Energy Sources Newsletter

Etudes Universitaires sur l'Integration Europeenne/ University Studies on European Integration 915

Euro Abstracts Section I. Euratom and EEC Research 892

Euro Abstracts Section II. Coal and Steel 822

Europe (Luxembourg)

European Atomic Energy Community. Contamination Radioactive des Denrees Alimentaires dans les Pays de la Communaute 953

European Atomic Energy Community. Resultats des Mesures de la Radioactivite Ambiante dans les Pays de la Communaute: Air-Retombee-Eaux 953

European Coal and Steel Community. Consultative Committee. Handbook 262

European Coal and Steel Community. Consultative Committee. Yearbook 262

European Court of Human Rights. Publications. Series B: Pleadings, Oral Arguments and Documents/Cour Europeenne des Droits de l'Homme. Publications. Serie B: Memoires, Plaidoiries et Documents 913

European Economic Community Savings Bank Group. Report 227

European Economy

European File

European Investment Bank. Annual Report 227

European Parliament. Bulletin

European Parliament. Committee Report 796

European Parliament. Working Documents 670

European Social Fund. Annual Report on the Activities of the New European Social Fund 444

European University News

Eurostat News

General Commission on Safety and Health in the Iron and Steel Industry. Report 635

General Report on the Activities of the European Communities 245

Green Europe

Information Market

Information Service of the European Communities. Newsletter on the Common Agricultural Policy 48

Information Service of the European Communities. Trade Union News 648

Institut de la Communaute Europeenne pour les Etudes Universitaires. Recherche. Research 436

Intertax

Joint Nuclear Research Center, Ispra, Italy. Annual Report 897

Mines Safety and Health Commission. Report/Organe Permanent pour la Securite dans les Mines de Houille. Rapport 818

New Technologies. Innovation Policy (Commission of the European Communities)

Official Journal of the European Communities. C Series: Information and Notices

Official Journal of the European Communities. L Series: Legislation

Results of the Business Survey Carried out Among Heads of Enterprises in the Community

Statistical Office of the European Communities. Animal Production

Statistical Office of the European Communities. Aussenhandel: Analitische Ubersichten. Foreign Trade: Analytical Tables 218

Statistical Office of the European Communities. Balances of Payments. Quarterly Data

Statistical Office of the European Communities. Basic Statistics 218

Statistical Office of the European Communities. Commerce Exterieur: Nomenclature des Pays 259

Statistical Office of the European Communities. Commerce Exterieur: Products C E C A 218

Statistical Office of the European Communities. Crop Production

Statistical Office of the European Communities. Energy Statistics. Yearbook 469

Statistical Office of the European Communities. Foreign Trade: Monthly Statistics

Statistical Office of the European Communities. Foreign Trade: Standard Country Classification 218

Statistical Office of the European Communities. Iron & Steel

Statistical Office of the European Communities. National Accounts. Yearbook 218

Statistical Office of the European Communities. Quarterly Bulletin of Energy Statistics

Statistical Office of the European Communities. Siderurgie Annuaire 802

Statistical Office of the European Communities. Social Statistics

Statistical Office of the European Communities. Statistical Studies and Surveys

Statistical Office of the European Communities. Statistique Agricole 43

Statistical Office of the European Communities. Statistiques des Transports. Annuaire 1083

Statistical Office of the European Communities. Statistiques Industrielles Annuaire 218

Statistical Office of the European Communities. Yearbook of Regional Statistics 218

Terminological Information

Trade Union News from the European Community

UNITED NATIONS

A C E I D Newsletter (Asian Centre of Educational Innovation for Development)

A D I Quarterly News Letter

A D O P T (Asian-Pacific and Worldwide Documents on Population Topics)

A F R O Technical Papers (Regional Office for Africa) 952

A F R O Technical Report Series. Reports of Meetings of Expert Committees (Regional Office for Africa) 952

Adult Education Information Notes

African Population Newsletter

African Trade/Commerce Africain 253

Agricultural Review for Europe 44

Agricultural Trade in Europe 45

Agrindex

Aircraft Accident Digest 17

Animal Production and Health Newsletter 792

Annotated Accessions List of Studies and Reports in the Field of Science Statistics 121

Annual Bulletin of Coal Statistics for Europe 814

Annual Bulletin of Electric Energy Statistics for Europe 461

Annual Bulletin of Gas Statistics for Europe/Bulletin Annuel de Statistiques de Gaz pour l'Europe 862

Annual Bulletin of General Energy Statistics for Europe 468

Annual Bulletin of Housing and Building Statistics for Europe 181

Annual Bulletin of Steel Statistics for Europe 801

Annual Bulletin of Trade in Chemical Products 287

Annual Bulletin of Transport Statistics for Europe 1080

Annual Report on Development Assistance to Mauritius 261

Annual Report on Development Assistance to the Seychelles 261

Annual Review of Engineering Industries and Automation 488

1184 INDEX TO PUBLICATIONS OF INTERNATIONAL ORGANIZATIONS

Annual Review of the Chemical Industry 287

Anuario Hidrologico del Istmo Centroamericano 402

Art 101

Asia Pacific Book News

Asian Bibliography

Asian Book Development

Asian Cultural Centre for Unesco. Organization and Activities 850

Asian Population Studies Series 920

B I B E Annual Summary (International Bulletin of Bibliography on Education) 422

B I B E Bulletin (International Bulletin of Bibliography on Education)

Basic Facts about the United Nations 914

Bibliographical Services Throughout the World 122

Boletin de Arte

Bulletin of Labour Statistics

Bulletin on Aging

Bulletin on Narcotics

C I F A Technical Papers (Food and Agriculture Organization of the United Nations, Committee for Inland Fisheries of Africa) 508

C I N D A 892

C I S Abstracts (International Labour Office) 636

C T C Reporter (Centre on Transnational Corporations)

Carnets de l'Enfance/Assignment Children

Catalog of World Bank Publications 261

Catalogue of Reproductions of Paintings Prior to 1860 103

Catalogue of Reproductions of Paintings, 1860-1973 103

Census of Motor Traffic on Main International Traffic Arteries 1096

Centro Latinoamericano de Demografia. Boletin Demografico

Centro Latinoamericano de Demografia. Notas de Poblacion

Centro Latinoamericano de Demografia. Serie OI: Publicaciones Conjuntas con Instituciones Nacionales de Paises de America Latina 921

Centro Pan-Americano de Febre Aftosa. Boletin

Ceres

Commodity Trade Statistics

Compendium on Development Assistance to Kenya 261

Composition of the W M O

Connaissance de l'Orient. Collection Unesco d'Oeuvres Representatives 719

Connect

Copyright

Copyright Bulletin

Copyright Laws and Treaties of the World. Supplements 860

Corriere Unesco

Cost of Social Security 1016

Cuadernos de la C E P A L (Comision Economica para America Latina (CEPAL)) 238

D O C P A L Resumenes Sobre Poblacion en America Latina/D O C P A L Latin American Population Abstracts

Date Palm Journal

Demographic Handbook for Africa/Guide Demographie de l'Afrique 921

Demographic Yearbook 921

Development Assistance to Malawi; Annual Report 262

Development Business

Development Forum

Development Information Abstracts 207

Diogenes/Revue Diogene

Direction of Trade Statistics

Directory of the National Productivity Organizations in A P O Member Countries 288

Directory: Organizations of the United Nations System in the United Republic of Tanzania 262

Disarmament 811

Documentation, Libraries and Archives: Bibliographies and Reference Works 687

Documentation, Libraries and Archives: Studies and Research 677

Droit d'Auteur

Earth Sciences Series 379

Earthscan Bulletin

Economic and Social Survey of Asia and the Pacific 243

Economic Bulletin for Asia and the Pacific

Economic Bulletin for Europe

Economic Survey of Europe 243

Economic Survey of Latin America and the Caribbean 243

Educacion Medica y Salud

Education in Asia and the Pacific: Reviews, Reports and Notes 413

Educational Building Digest 184

Educational Innovation and Information

Educational Studies and Documents 413

Electric Power in Asia and the Pacific 452

Energy Statistics Yearbook 465

Enfants du Monde

Estimated World Requirements of Narcotic Drugs 870

Estimated World Requirements of Narcotic Drugs. Supplement

Estudios e Informes de la C E P A L/C E P A L Studies and Reports (Comision Economica para America Latina (CEPAL)) 262

European Civil Aviation Conference (Report of Session) 1088

European Economy. Supplement A: Recent Economic Trends

European Economy. Supplement B: Economic Prospects - Business Survey Results

Everyone's United Nations 916

F A O Agricultural Development Paper 27

F A O Agricultural Services Bulletin (Food and Agriculture Organization of the United Nations (FAO)) 46

F A O Animal Production and Health Series (Food and Agriculture Organization of the United Nations) 65

F A O Commodity Review and Outlook 46

F A O Documentation-Current Bibliography (Food and Agriculture Organization of the United Nations)

F A O Economic and Social Development Paper (Food and Agriculture Organization of the United Nations) 194

F A O Fertilizer and Plant Nutrition Bulletin (Food and Agriculture Organization of the United Nations) 46

F A O Fertilizer Yearbook (Food and Agriculture Organization of the United Nations) 55

F A O Fisheries Circulars 508

F A O Fisheries Reports 508

F A O Fisheries Series 509

F A O Fisheries Technical Paper 509

F A O Food and Nutrition Series 846

F A O Forestry Studies (Food and Agriculture Organization of the United Nations) 524

F A O Irrigation and Drainage Papers (Food and Agriculture Organization of the United Nations) 1124

F A O Legislative Series 27

F A O Manuals in Fisheries Science 509

F A O Plant Protection Bulletin

F A O Regional Conference for Africa 27

F A O Regional Conference for Asia and the Pacific. Report 27

F A O Regional Conference for Europe. Report of the Conference 27

F A O Regional Conference for Latin America and the Caribbean. Report 27

F A O Regional Conference for the Near East. Report 27

F A O Terminology Bulletin 27

Farm Management Notes for Asia and the Far East 46

Finance and Development

Food and Agricultural Legislation

Food and Agriculture Organization of the United Nations. Agricultural Planning Studies 47

Food and Agriculture Organization of the United Nations. Asia and Pacific Plant Protection Commission. Information Letter 55

Food and Agriculture Organization of the United Nations. Asia and Pacific Plant Protection Commission. Quarterly Newsletter

Food and Agriculture Organization of the United Nations. Asia and Pacific Plant Protection Commission. Technical Document 55

Food and Agriculture Organization of the United Nations. Asia and the Pacific Commission on Agricultural Statistics. Periodic Report 40

Food and Agriculture Organization of the United Nations. Basic Texts 27

Food and Agriculture Organization of the United Nations. European Inland Fisheries Advisory Commission. Occasional Papers 509

Food and Agriculture Organization of the United Nations. European Inland Fisheries Advisory Commission. Technical Papers 509

Food and Agriculture Organization of the United Nations. Production Yearbook 47

INDEX TO PUBLICATIONS OF INTERNATIONAL ORGANIZATIONS 1185

Food and
  Agriculture Organization of the United Nations.
  Soils Bulletins 55

Food and Agriculture Organization of the United
  Nations. Trade Yearbook 47

Food and Agriculture Organization of the United
  Nations. World Soil Resources Reports 55

Food and Agriculture Organization of the United
  Nations Conference. Report 27

Food and Nutrition

Food and Nutrition Bulletin

Food Irradiation Newsletter 519

Foreign Trade Statistics of Africa. Series A: Direction
  of Trade 208

Foreign Trade Statistics of Africa. Series B: Trade by
  Commodity 208

Foreign Trade Statistics of Africa. Series C: Summary
  Tables/Statistiques Africaines du Commerce
  Exterieur. Serie C: Tableaux Recapitulatifs 208

Foreign Trade Statistics of Asia and the Pacific. Series
  A 208

Foreign Trade Statistics of Asia and the Pacific. Series
  B 208

Forestry Newsletter of the Asia-Pacific Region 525

Forum du Developpement

Freshwater and Aquaculture Contents Tables

Fundamentals of Educational Planning 441

G A T T Focus (General Agreement on Tariffs and
  Trade)

G A T T Studies in International Trade (General
  Agreement on Tariffs and Trade) 256

General Agreement on Tariffs and Trade. Basic
  Instruments and Selected Documents Series.
  Supplement 256

General Agreement on Tariffs and Trade. G A T T
  Activities in (Year) 256

General Agreement on Tariffs and Trade. International
  Trade 256

General Catalogue of Unesco and Unesco-Sponsored
  Publications 912

General Fisheries Council for the Mediterranean.
  Proceedings and Technical Papers. Debats et
  Documents Techniques 509

General Fisheries Council for the Mediterranean.
  Reports of the Sessions 509

General Fisheries Council for the Mediterranean.
  Studies and Reviews 509

Geological Correlation 386

Gilberto Amado Memorial Lecture 670

Guide to National Bibliographical Information Centres
  678

Guide to Sources of International Population
  Assistance 922

Health Physics Research Abstracts 958

Human Rights Bulletin

Human Rights Teaching/Enseignement des Droits de
  l'Homme

I A E A Library Film Catalog (International Atomic
  Energy Agency) 893

I A E A Technical Documents Series (International
  Atomic Energy Agency) 896

I A R C Monographs on the Evaluation of the
  Carcinogenic Risk of Chemicals to Humans
  (International Agency for Research on Cancer) 775

I A R C Scientific Publications (International Agency
  for Research on Cancer) 775

I B E D O C. International Network for Educational
  Information. Liason Bulletin (International Bureau
  of Education)

I C A O Bulletin (International Civil Aviation
  Organization)

I C A O Circulars (International Civil Aviation
  Organization) 1088

I C P A Quarterly (International Commission for the
  Prevention of Alcoholism and Drug Dependency)

I I E P Occasional Papers (International Institute for
  Educational Planning) 441

I I E P Research Reports (International Institute for
  Educational Planning) 441

I I E P Seminar Papers (International Institute for
  Educational Planning) 441

I L C A Proceedings (International Livestock Centre
  for Africa) 66

I L O Information (International Labour Office)

I L O Judgements of the Administrative Tribunal
  (International Labour Office)

I L O Publications (International Labour Office)

I L P E S Cuadernos (Instituto Latinamericano de
  Planificacion Economica y Social) 277

I M F Survey (International Monetary Fund)

I M O News

I M S Newsletter (International Marine Science)

I N I S Atomindex 893

I N I S Newsletter

I N I S Reference Series 679

I P F C Proceedings (Indo-Pacific Fishery
  Commission) 510

Ideas and Action Bulletin

Impact of Science on Society

Index to Proceedings of the General Assembly of the
  United Nations 912

Index Translationum 679

Indicators for the Telegram Retransmission System
  (TRS) - Telex Identification Codes 350

Indo-Pacific Fisheries Council. Regional Studies 510

Industrial Development Abstracts (United Nations
  Industrial Development Organization) 211

Industrial Property

Industrial Property, Statistics B/Propriete Industrielle,
  Statistiques B 862

Industry and Development

Industy and Technology Development News - Asia
  and the Pacific 262

Information Circular on Radiation Techniques and
  Their Applications to Insect Pests 792

Instituto de Nutricion de Centro America y Panama.
  Informe Anual 846

Intergovernmental Oceanographic Commission.
  Technical Series 406

International Atomic Energy Agency. Annual Report
  897

International Atomic Energy Agency. Bulletin

International Atomic Energy Agency. Legal Series
  657

International Atomic Energy Agency. Nuclear Power
  Reactors in the World 897

International Atomic Energy Agency. Panel
  Proceedings Series 897

International Atomic Energy Agency. Proceedings
  Series 897

International Atomic Energy Agency. Safety Series
  954

International Atomic Energy Agency. Technical
  Directories 897

International Atomic Energy Agency. Technical
  Report Series 897

International Bulletin on Atomic and Molecular Data
  for Fusion.

International Bureau of Education. Bulletin

International Catalogue of Occupational Safety and
  Health Films 636

International Centre for Theoretical Physics. Annual
  Report 888

International Civil Aviation Association. Aeronautical
  Agreements and Arrangements. Annual Supplement
  1088

International Civil Aviation Organization. Air
  Navigation Plan. Africa-Indian Ocean Region 1088

International Civil Aviation Organization. Air
  Navigation Plan. Caribbean Region 1088

International Civil Aviation Organization. Air
  Navigation Plan. Middle East and Asia Regions
  1088

International Civil Aviation Organization. Air
  Navigation Plan. North Atlantic, North American
  and Pacific Regions 1088

International Civil Aviation Organization.
  Airworthiness Committee. Report of Meeting 19

International Civil Aviation Organization. All-Weather
  Operations Panel. Report of Meeting 19

International Civil Aviation Organization. Assembly.
  Report and Minutes of the Legal Commission 1089

International Civil Aviation Organization. Assembly.
  Report of the Economic Commission 1089

International Civil Aviation Organization. Assembly.
  Report of the Technical Commission 19

International Civil Aviation Organization. Assembly.
  Resolutions 1089

International Civil Aviation Organization. Automated
  Data Interchange Systems Panel. Report of Meeting
  19

International Civil Aviation Organization. Council.
  Annual Report 1089

International Civil Aviation Organization. Digests of
  Statistics. Series AT. Airport Traffic 1089

International Civil Aviation Organization. Digests of
  Statistics. Series F. Financial Data 1089

International Civil Aviation Organization. Digests of
  Statistics. Series FP. Fleet, Personnel 1089

International Civil Aviation Organization. Digests of
  Statistics. Series R. Civil Aircraft on Register 1089

International Civil Aviation Organization. Digests of
  Statistics. Series T. Traffic 1089

International Civil Aviation Organization. Digests of
  Statistics. Series TF. Traffic Flow 1089

International Civil Aviation Organization. Indexes to I
  C A O Publications. Annual Cumulation 1086

International Civil Aviation Organization. Legal
  Committee. Minutes and Documents (of Sessions)
  1089

International Civil Aviation Organization. Library Information: Recent Accessions and Selected Articles

International Civil Aviation Organization. Obstacle Clearance Panel. Report of Meeting 19

International Civil Aviation Organization. (Panel On) Application of Space Techniques Relating to Aviation. Report of Meeting 19

International Civil Aviation Organization. Sonic Boom Panel. Report of the Meeting 19

International Civil Aviation Organization. Technical Panel on Supersonic Transport. Report of Meeting 20

International Civil Aviation Organization. Visual Aids Panel. Report of Meeting 20

International Conference on Education. Final Report/Conference International de l'Education. Rapport Final 415

International Council for Philosophy and Humanistic Studies. Bulletin 630

International Court of Justice. Yearbook/Annuaire 670

International Designs Bulletin

International Digest of Health Legislation

International Directory of Marine Scientists 142

International Directory of New and Renewable Energy 465

International Directory of Occupational Safety and Health Services and Institutions 635

International Finance Corporation. Report 229

International Financial Statistics 211

International Financial Statistics Yearbook 245

International Institute for Labour Studies. Public Lecture Series 272

International Institute for Labour Studies. Publications 272

International Institute for Labour Studies. Research Series 272

International Labour Conference. Reports to the Conference and Record of Proceedings 272

International Labour Documentation

International Labour Office. Legislative Series

International Labour Office. Official Bulletin. Series A 273

International Labour Office. Official Bulletin. Series B 273

International Labour Office. P R E A L C. Investigaciones sobre Empleo (Programa Regional del Empleo para America Latina y el Caribe) 245

International Labour Office. Special Report of the Director-General on the Application of the Declaration Concerning the Policy of Apartheid of the Republic of South Africa 913

International Labour Review

International Law Commission Yearbook 671

International Monetary Fund. Annual Report of the Executive Board 229

International Monetary Fund. Annual Report on Exchange Arrangements and Exchange Restrictions 229

International Monetary Fund. Balance of Payments Statistics 277

International Monetary Fund. Government Finance Statistics Yearbook 211

International Monetary Fund. Occasional Papers 229

International Monetary Fund. Pamphlet Series 230

International Monetary Fund. Selected Decisions of the International Monetary Fund and Selected Documents 230

International Monetary Fund. Staff Papers

International Monetary Fund. Summary Proceedings of the Annual Meeting of the Board of Governors 230

International Narcotics Control Board. Comparative Statement of Estimates and Statistics on Narcotic Drugs for (Year) 871

International Narcotics Control Board. Report for (Year) 871

International Narcotics Control Board. Statistics on Narcotic Drugs for (Year) 871

International Narcotics Control Board. Statistics on Psychotropic Substances for (Year) 871

International Oceanographic Tables 406

International Review of Criminal Policy 371

International Rice Commission. Newsletter

International Social Science Journal

International Studies in Education 415

International Telecommunication Union. Central Library. List of Recent Acquisitions/Union Internationale des Telecommunications. Bibliotheque Centrale. Liste des Acquisitions Recentes/Union Internacional de Telecommunicaciones. Biblioteca Central. Lista de Adquisiciones Recientes

International Telecommunication Union. Central Library. Liste des Periodiques. List of Periodicals. Lista de Revistas 345

International Telecommunication Union. Central Library. Listes des Publications Annuelles. List of Annuals. Lista de Publicaciones Anuales 345

International Telecommunication Union. List of Telegraph Offices Open for International Service 350

International Telecommunication Union. Operational Bulletin

International Telecommunication Union. Report on the Activities 350

International Trade Forum

International Trade Statistics Yearbook 211

International Understanding at School 415

Investment Africa 263

Joint F A O/W H O Codex Alimentarius Commission. Report of the Session 954

Journal of Development Planning 263

Labour and Society

Labour Education

Labour-Management Relations Series 273

Land Reform, Land Settlement and Cooperatives/Reforme Agraire, Colonisation et Cooperatives Agricoles/Reforma Agraria, Colonizacion y Cooperativas

Lifelong Education Network 416

List of Cables Forming the World Submarine Network 350

List of E C A Documents Issued/Liste des Documents Publies par la C E A 263

List of International Telephone Routes 350

Locust Newsletter 57

Management Development Series 280

Marine Science Contents Tables 150

Marques Internationales

Meetings on Atomic Energy

Mekong Bulletin 263

Monographs on Education 416

Monographs on Oceanographic Methodology 407

Monthly Bulletin of Statistics (FAO)/Bulletin Mensuel de Statistiques (FAO)/Boletin Mensual de Estadisticas (FAO)

Museum

Museums and Monuments Series 829

Mutation Breeding Newsletter 57

N A T I S - News 681

Namibia Studies Series 1010

Natural Resources Research 380

Nature and Resources

New Aquisitions in the U N E C A Library

New Trends in Biology Teaching 144

New Trends in Chemistry Teaching 324

New Trends in Integrated Science Teaching 448

New Trends in Mathematics Teaching 751

New Trends in Physics Teaching 889

News from C C I V S (Coordinating Committee for International Voluntary Service)

Notas Sobre la Economia y el Desarrollo

Nuclear Data Newsletter 897

Nuclear Fusion/Fusion Nucleaire

Objective: Justice

Occupational Safety and Health Series 636

Oficina Sanitaria Panamericana. Boletin

Operational Hydrology Reports 403

Ozone Layer Bulletin

P C T Gazette

Palestine Refugees Today

Pan American Health Organization. Bulletin

Periodicals of Asia and the Pacific

Personnel des Nations Unies et des Agences Specialisees en Republique de Rwanda 263

Perspectivas

Perspectives

Pesticide Residues in Food 955

Plant Genetic Resources Newsletter

Population Bulletin of the United Nations 924

Population Education in Asia and the Pacific Newsletter and Forum

Population Headliners

Population Newsletter

Population Studies 924

Practical Guide to the Use of the European Communities' Scheme of Generalized Tariff Preferences 259

Prices of Agricultural Products and Selected Inputs in Europe and North America 49

Propriete Industrielle

INDEX TO PUBLICATIONS OF INTERNATIONAL ORGANIZATIONS 1187

Prospects

Public Health in Europe 765

Public Health Papers 955

Quarterly Bulletin of Statistics for Asia and the Pacific

Quarterly Bulletin of Steel Statistics for Europe/ Statistiques de l'Acier pour l'Europe/Evropeiskaya Statistika Chernoi Metallurgii. Kvartal'nyi Byulleten'

Radiation Dosimetry Data; Catalogue 792

Rapport Annuel sur l'Assistance au Developpement: Rwanda 263

Rapport Annuel sur la Cooperation au Developpement - Burundi 264

Refugees

Refugees Magazine

Regional Development Dialogue

Regional Planning 1020

Report on Development Assistance to Ethiopia 264

Report on Development Cooperation to the Democratic Republic of the Sudan 264

Report on the World Health Situation 955

Reports and Papers in the Social Sciences 1011

Reports and Papers on Mass Communications 344

Review of Economic Situation of Air Transport 1089

Review of Maritime Transport 1103

Revista de la C E P A L (Comision Economica para America Latina (CEPAL))

Revue de Coree

Revue Internationale des Sciences Sociales

Rural Progress

Sample Surveys in the ESCAP Region 217

Science Policy Studies and Documents 999

Siren

Small Industry Bulletin for Asia and the Pacific 281

Social and Labour Bulletin

Social Development Newsletter

Social Science Journal 1011

Soils Newsletter 60

State of Food and Agriculture 34

Statistical Indicators for Asia and the Pacific

Statistical Information Bulletin for Africa/Bulletin d'Information Statistique pour l'Afrique 218

Statistical Office of the European Communities. Agricultural Prices

Statistical Yearbook for Asia and the Pacific/Annuaire Statistique pour l'Asie et le Pacifique 1064

Statistical Yearbook for Latin America/Anuario Estadistico de America Latina 1064

Statistics of Road Traffic Accidents in Europe 1087

Statistics of World Trade in Steel 802

Statistics on World Trade in Engineering Products. Bulletin 802

Steel Market 800

Studies and Documents on Cultural Policies 632

Studies and Reports in Hydrology Series 404

Studies in Mathematics Education/Etudes sur l'Enseignement des Mathematiques/Estudios en Educacion Matematica 442

Studies in the Processing, Marketing and Distribution of Commodities 285

Studies on Selected Development Problems in Various Countries in the Middle East 264

Study Abroad/Etudes a l'Etranger/Estudios en el Extranjero 442

Survey of Economic and Social Conditions in Africa 264

Table of International Telex Relations and Traffic 350

Technical Papers in Hydrology Series 404

Telecommunication Journal

Trade and Development: an U N C T A D Review (United Nations Conference on Trade and Development (UNCTAD)) 260

Trade and Development Report 260

Training for Agriculture and Rural Development 427

Transport & Communications Bulletin for Asia & the Pacific 1083

Tungsten Statistics

U I E Case Studies (Unesco Institute for Education) 420

U I E Monographs (Unesco Institute for Education) 420

U I E Studies on Post-Literacy and Continuing Education (Unesco Institute for Education) 427

U N C H S. Habitat News (United Nations, Centre for Human Settlements (Habitat))

U N C R D Bulletin (United Nations, Centre for Regional Development) 264

U N C R D Newsletter (United Nations, Centre for Regional Development)

U N C T A D. Monthly Bulletin (United Nations Conference on Trade and Development (UNCTAD))

U N C T A D Guide to Publications (United Nations Conference on Trade and Development (UNCTAD)) 219

U N Chronicle

U N D O C: Current Index (United Nations Documents)

U N E P Information (United Nations Environment Programme) 499

U N E P News

U N I D O Newsletter (United Nations Industrial Development Organization)

U N I S I S T Boletin de Informacion

U N I S I S T Newsletter (Unesco Programme of International Cooperation in Scientific and Technological Information) 685

U N I T A R Conference Reports (United Nations Institute for Training and Research) 671

U N I T A R Peaceful Settlement Series (United Nations Institute for Training and Research) 918

U N I T A R Regional Studies (United Nations Institute for Training and Research) 919

Unasylva

Unesco. Centro de Documentacion Cultural, Havana. Informaciones Trimestrales

Unesco. Records of the General Conference. Proceedings 919

Unesco. Records of the General Conference. Resolutions 919

Unesco. Regional Office for Education in Asia and the Pacific. Abstract Bibliography Series on Population Education 426

Unesco. Regional Office for Education in Asia and the Pacific. Bulletin 420

Unesco. Regional Office for Science and Technology for Africa. Bulletin

Unesco. Regional Office for Science and Technology for Latin American and the Caribbean. Boletin

Unesco. Report of the Director-General on the Activities of the Organization 919

Unesco. Scientific Maps and Atlases and Other Related Publications 132

Unesco. Statistics on Science and Technology/ Statistiques Relatives aux Science et a la Technologie/Estadisticas Relativas a la Ciencia y a la Tecnologia 1004

Unesco. Studies on Books and Reading 963

Unesco Asian Fiction Series 736

Unesco Courier

Unesco Earthquake Study Missions 401

Unesco Features

Unesco List of Documents and Publications

Unesco News

Unesco Review

Unesco Source Books on Curricula and Methods 449

Unesco Statistical Reports and Studies 1066

Unesco Statistical Yearbook 1066

Unesco Technical Papers in Marine Science 408

Unicef Information Bulletin

Unicef News

Union Postale

Union Postale Universelle. Actes 347

Union Postale Universelle. Statistique des Services Postaux 347

United Nations. Conference on Trade and Development. Trade and Development Board. Official Records 264

United Nations. Current Bibliographical Information

United Nations. Development Programme. Compendium of Approved Projects 264

United Nations. Division of Narcotic Drugs. Information Letter

United Nations. Economic and Social Commission for Asia and the Pacific. Development Papers 367

United Nations. Economic and Social Commission for Asia and the Pacific. Mineral Resources Development Series 820

United Nations. Economic and Social Commission for Asia and the Pacific. Natural Resources - Water Series 1126

United Nations. Economic and Social Commission for Asia and the Pacific. Water Resources Development Series 1126

United Nations. Economic and Social Council. Index to Proceedings 919

United Nations. Economic and Social Council. Official Records 919

United Nations. Economic Commission for Asia and the Pacific. Energy Resources Development Series 467

INDEX TO PUBLICATIONS OF INTERNATIONAL ORGANIZATIONS

United Nations. Multilateral Treaties Deposited with the Secretary-General 671

United Nations. National Accounts Statistics 219

United Nations. Population and Vital Statistics Report

United Nations. Regional Centre for Demographic Training and Research in Latin America. Serie A/Centro Latinoamericano de Demografia. Serie A: Informes sobre Investigaciones Realizadas 924

United Nations. Regional Centre for Demographic Training and Research in Latin America. Serie C/Centro Latinoamericano de Demografia. Serie C: Informes sobre Investigaciones Realizadas Por los Alumnos del Centro 924

United Nations. Regional Centre for Demographic Training and Research in Latin America. Serie D/Centro Latinoamericano de Demografia. Serie D: Traducciones, Estudios, Conferencias y Otros Trabajos Preparados por Profesores y Expertos Visitantes 924

United Nations. Security Council. Index to Proceedings 919

United Nations. Security Council. Official Records 919

United Nations. Statistical Yearbook 1066

United Nations. Trade and Development Board. Official Records. Supplements 919

United Nations. Trusteeship Council. Index to Proceedings 919

United Nations. Trusteeship Council. Official Records 919

United Nations. Trusteeship Council. Official Records. Supplements 919

United Nations. Yearbook 919

United Nations Commission on International Trade Law. Report on the Work of Its Session 671

United Nations Commission on International Trade Law. Yearbook 672

United Nations Conference on the Standardization of Geographical Names. Report of the Conference 549

United Nations Conference on the Standardization of Geographical Names. Technical Papers 549

United Nations Conference on Trade and Development: Proceedings 260

United Nations Congress on the Prevention of Crime and the Treatment of Offenders. Report 373

United Nations Disarmament Yearbook 813

United Nations Economic and Social Commission for Asia and the Pacific. Social Development Division. Social Work Education and Development 1021

United Nations Economic and Social Commission for Asia and the Pacific. Statistical Newsletter

United Nations Economic and Social Council. Disarmament Study Series 813

United Nations Economic Commission for Africa. Annual Report 264

United Nations Economic Commission for Africa. Statistical Newsletter 1066

United Nations Economic Commission for Western Asia. Population Bulletin

United Nations Environment Programme. Feature 499

United Nations Environment Programme. Governing Council. Report on the Work of its Session 499

United Nations Environment Programme. The State of the Environment; Report of the Executive Director 499

United Nations Industrial Development Organization. Development and Transfer of Technology Series 264

United Nations Institute for Namibia. Occasional Papers 1012

United Nations Institute for Namibia. Prospectus 420

United Nations Institute for Training and Research. Report of the Executive Director 919

United Nations Juridical Yearbook 672

United Nations Legislative Series 672

United Nations Library. Monthly Bibliography: Part 1

United Nations Library. Monthly Bibliography: Part 2

United Nations Regional Cartographic Conference for Asia and the Pacific. Report of the Conference 549

United Nations Regional Cartographic Conference for Asia and the Pacific. Technical Papers 549

United Nations Regional Cartographic Conference for the Americas. Report of the Conference 549

United Nations Regional Cartographic Conference for the Americas. Technical Papers 549

United Nations Research Institute for Social Development, Report 1012

United Nations Social Defence Research Institute. Publication 373

United Nations Statistical Office. Monthly Bulletin of Statistics

Vaccination Certificate Requirements and Health Advice for International Travel/Certificats de Vaccination Exiges et Conseils d'Hygiene pour les Voyages Internationaux 957

Vigilancia Epidemiologica de las Encefalitis en las Americas

W H O Offset Publications (World Health Organization) 959

W H O Technical Report Series (World Health Organization) 768

W M O Bulletin (World Meteorological Organization)

Waste Management Research Abstracts 959

Water Resources Journal

Weekly Epidemiological Record

Women at Work

World Animal Review

World Bank. Annual Report 265

World Bank. Commodity Trade and Price Trends 265

World Bank. Monthly Operational Summary

World Bank Atlas 265

World Bank Research News

World Bank Research Program: Abstracts of Current Studies 220

World Cartography 551

World Debt Tables 265

World Directory of Social Science Institutions 1015

World Economic Survey 250

World Food Problems 521

World Food Programme News

World Health

World Health Forum

World Health Organization. Bulletin

World Health Organization. Handbook of Resolutions and Decisions of the World Health Assembly and the Executive Board. 957

World Health Organization. Monograph Series 957

World Health Organization. Regional Office for Africa. Report of the Regional Committee. 957

World Health Organization. Regional Office for Africa. Report of the Regional Director 957

World Health Organization. Regional Office for the Eastern Mediterranean. Biennial Report of the Regional Director 957

World Health Organization. Regional Office for the Western Pacific. Annual Report of the Regional Director to the Regional Committee for the Western Pacific 958

World Health Organization. Regional Office for the Western Pacific. Report on the Regional Seminar on the Role of the Hospital in the Public Health Programme 618

World Health Organization. Work of W H O 958

World Health Statistics Annual 959

World Health Statistics Quarterly 959

World List of Social Science Periodicals 1015

World Meteorological Congress. Abridged Report with Resolutions 807

World Meteorological Congress. Proceedings 807

World Meteorological Organization. Annual Reports 807

World Meteorological Organization. Basic Documents 807

World Meteorological Organization. Executive Council Session. Abridged Final Reports with Resolutions 807

World Meteorological Organization. Reports of Sessions of Regional Associations 807

World Meteorological Organization. Reports of Sessions of Technical Commissions 807

World Meteorological Organization. Reports on Marine Science Affairs 409

World Meteorological Organization. Special Environmental Reports 500

World Meteorological Organization. Technical Notes 807

World Meteorological Organization. Weather Reporting. Volume A: Observing Stations 807

World Meteorological Organization. Weather Reporting. Volume B: Data Processing 807

World Meteorological Organization. Weather Reporting. Volume C: Transmissions 807

World Meteorological Organization. Weather Reporting. Volume D: Information for Shipping 807

World Trade Annual 260

World Trade Annual Supplement 260

World Weather Watch Planning Reports 807

Yearbook of Common Carrier Telecommunication Statistics/Annuaire Statistique des Telecommunications du Secteur Public 345

Yearbook of Fishery Statistics 514

Yearbook of Forest Products 531

Yearbook of International Commodity Statistics 220

Year Book of Labour Statistics. 220

Yearbook on Human Rights 914

Your United Nations 562

ISSN Index

Titles in the Bowker International Serials Database with ISSN are listed in this index. For title change, a reference is given to the ISSN of the new title. If a title has changed and a new ISSN has not been assigned (or has not been entered in the Bowker database serial record), a reference to the new title will be given. Duplicate listing of ISSN, with references to new titles and/or new ISSN, indicates that the serial has split. Ceased titles are identified by the symbol†.

ISSN	Title
0000-0019	Publishers Weekly
0000-0043	Irregular Serials and Annuals
0000-0051	Previews†
0000-0078	L J/S L J Hot Line (Library Journal/School Library Journal) see 0000-0493
0000-0094	Bowker Serials Bibliography Supplement see 0000-0892
0000-0140	Subject Collections
0000-0159	Subject Guide to Books in Print
0000-0167	Subject Guide to Children's Books in Print
0000-0175	Ulrich's International Periodicals Directory
0000-0191	Who's Who in American Art
0000-0205	Who's Who in American Politics
0000-0213	Willing's Press Guide
0000-0221	Internationales Bibliotheks-Handbuch
0000-0248	Scientific and Technical Books in Print see 0000-054X
0000-0256	Who's Who in der Politik†
0000-0264	Subject Guide to Forthcoming Books see 0015-8119
0000-0280	Book/Guide: Mystery, Detective and Suspense Stories†
0000-0299	Biometeorological Research Centre. Reports
0000-0302	Mystery & Detection Annual.
0000-0310	Books in Print Supplement
0000-0329	I B I D (International Bibliography, Information, Documentation) see 0256-1042
0000-0345	Canadian Serials Directory/Repertoire des Publications Seriees Canadiennes
0000-037X	Educational Media Yearbook see 8755-2094
0000-0388	International Index to Film Periodicals
0000-0434	Magazine Industry Market Place
0000-0450	Information Industry Market Place changed to North American Online Directory
0000-0469	Publishers Weekly Yearbook changed to Book Publishing Annual
0000-0485	Small Press
0000-0493	Library Hotline
0000-0507	Ulrich's Quarterly see 0000-0892
0000-0515	Books in Series in the United States see 0000-0906
0000-054X	Scientific and Technical Books and Serials in Print
0000-0574	Medical Books and Serials in Print see 0000-085X
0000-0590	Educational Film Locator changed to Educational Film/Video Locator
0000-0612	Religious Books and Serials in Print see 0000-0868
0000-0620	Publishers and Distributors of the United States see 0000-0671
0000-0663	Associations' Publications in Print†
0000-0671	Publishers, Distributors and Wholesalers of the United States
0000-0701	Law Information see 0000-0752
0000-0728	Law Information Update see 0000-0760
0000-0736	Books Out of Print
0000-0752	Bowker's Law Books and Serials in Print
0000-0760	Bowker's Law Books and Serials in Print Update
0000-0779	Computer Books and Serials in Print†
0000-0795	I B M Software Directory†
0000-0809	Business Mini/Micro Software Directory†
0000-0817	C P-M Software Directory†
0000-0825	El Hi Textbooks and Serials in Print
0000-0833	Retailers Microcomputer Market Place†
0000-085X	Medical and Health Care Books and Serials in Print
0000-0868	Religious and Inspirational Books and Serials in Print
0000-0892	Bowker International Serials Database Update
0000-0906	Books in Series
0000-0981	Ulrich's and Irregular Serials & Annuals on Microfiche
0001-0006	Mississippi News and Views†
0001-0022	A A A M Quarterly changed to A A A M Quarterly Journal
0001-0049	A A C E Bulletin see 0274-9696
0001-0057	A A C S B Bulletin†
0001-0065	A A C T E Publications Service†
0001-0073	A.A.E.A. Byline
0001-009X	A A L C Reporter
0001-0111	A A M A Apparel Management Letter†
0001-012X	A A M A Newsletter†
0001-0146	A A M News
0001-0154	A A M V A Bulletin
0001-0162	A.A.P.M. Quarterly Bulletin see 0094-2405
0001-0170	A A P S News Letter
0001-0189	A A Quarterly see 0261-6823
0001-0197	A.A.R.N. Newsletter
0001-0200	A A R P News Bulletin
0001-0227	A A S Newsletter changed to Space Times
0001-0235	Advertising Techniques see 0747-3168
0001-0243	A A T G Newsletter
0001-0251	A A T S E E L Newsletter
0001-026X	A A U P Bulletin see 0190-2946
0001-0278	A A U W Journal see 0161-5661
0001-0286	A A U W New York Division. Newsletter changed to A A U W New Yorker
0001-0308	A A Z P A Newsletter
0001-0316	A et U†
0001-0340	A B Bookman's Weekly
0001-0367	A B C - Nieuwsmagazine†
0001-0375	Die A B C-Zeitung
0001-0383	A B C A Bulletin (American Business Communication Association) see 8756-1972
0001-0391	A B C Air Cargo Guide and Directory see 0141-6529
0001-0413	A B C Film Review changed to Film Review
0001-0421	A B C Goods Transport Guide see 0308-9304
0001-043X	B and C News see 0163-447X
0001-0456	A B C Pol Sci
0001-0464	A B C Radio Guide†
0001-0472	A B C Rail Guide
0001-0480	A B C Shipping Guide changed to A B C Passenger Shipping Guide
0001-0502	A.B.D.
0001-0510	A B L C Journal changed to Textile Services
0001-0529	A B M A C Bulletin changed to Taiwan Review
0001-0545	A B N Correspondence
0001-0553	A B P - Association Belge des Paralyses. Bulletin
0001-0588	A C A News†
0001-0596	A C B Management
0001-060X	A.C.C.A. Canberra Comment changed to Australian Commerce Review
0001-0618	A. C. C. E. Reporter†
0001-0626	A C C E S S changed to A C C E L
0001-0634	Chemical Abstracts Service Source Index
0001-0642	A. C. E.
0001-0650	A C E†
0001-0669	A C E C Review
0001-0677	A C E N News†
0001-0693	A C E Research†
0001-0707	A C H A News (American College of Hospital Administrators) changed to Executive News
0001-0715	A.C.I. Informazioni
0001-0723	A C I L Bulletin†
0001-0731	A C changed to Fibrecement Review
0001-0766	A C M C Bulletin†
0001-0774	A C M C Newsletter see 0317-5006
0001-0782	Association for Computing Machinery. Communications
0001-0790	A C O S News
0001-0812	A C P A Newsletter changed to P I R I Newsletter
0001-0847	A.D.A. Forecast see 0095-8301
0001-0855	A D A News
0001-0863	A D A Newsletter changed to A D A Leadership Bulletin
0001-0871	A D A World changed to A D A Today
0001-088X	A D C Newsletter†
0001-0898	A D E Bulletin
0001-091X	Adib
0001-0928	A D K Nuusbrief changed to S A D K Nuusbrief

ISSN INDEX

0001-0936 A D L Bulletin
0001-0944 A D M
0001-0960 A D T Transmitter
0001-0979 A D T V - Nachrichten
0001-0987 A D V-Informationsdienst
0001-0995 A D W - Umschau†
0001-1002 A E A-M Newsletter/Journal
0001-1010 A E B U
0001-1029 A E C L Review see 0707-5588
0001-1037 A E D S Journal
0001-1045 A E D S Monitor
0001-1053 A E G - Schakels
0001-1061 A E G - Telefunken al Dia†
0001-107X A E G - Telefunken Progress†
0001-1088 A E Rho Monitor changed to Playback
0001-1096 A E Ue
0001-110X A U E W E S Journal
0001-1118 A E U Reports
0001-1126 A F A Informationen
0001-1134 A F E R
0001-1150 A F L - C I O Library Acquisition List
0001-1169 American Federationist see 0149-2489
0001-1177 A F L-C I O Free Trade Union News†
0001-1185 A F L-C I O News
0001-1193 A F R A Boletin Informativo
0001-1207 A F R E
0001-1223 A F S Cast Metals Research Journal see 0008-7467
0001-1231 A.F. Universite changed to Aspects de la France
0001-124X A F V-G2
0001-1258 A F Z changed to A F Z-Fischmagazin
0001-1274 A G A
0001-1282 A G A News†
0001-1290 Agasvets†
0001-1304 A. G. Bush Library Abstracts†
0001-1320 A G E C O - Documentation Siderurgique
0001-1339 A G I E S
0001-1347 A G P-Mitteilungen changed to Das Neue Unternehmen
0001-1355 A G R A News
0001-1371 A G V A News changed to A G V A Newsletter
0001-138X A.H.A. Newsletter changed to Perspectives (Washington)
0001-1398 A H A Review†
0001-1401 Aussenhandelsdienst der Industrie- und Handelskammern und Wirtschaftsverbaende
0001-1428 A H I L Quarterly see 0270-6717
0001-1436 A H R C Chronicle
0001-1452 A I A A Journal
0001-1460 A I A A Student Journal
0001-1479 A I A Journal see 0746-0554
0001-1487 A I A Memo see 0732-4073
0001-1495 Asociacion Interamericana de Bibliotecarios y Documentalistas Agricolas. Boletin Informativo
0001-1509 All India Congress Committee. Political and Economic Review†
0001-1517 A I C C News
0001-1541 A I Ch E Journal
0001-155X American Industrial Development Council. A I D C Journal see 0279-6430
0001-1568 A.I. Digest changed to Advanced Animal Breeder
0001-1576 A I F L D Report
0001-1584 A.I.L.A.
0001-1606 A I L Newsletter†
0001-1614 Modern Times
0001-1622 A I M S Newsletter
0001-1630 A I O E Labour News
0001-1649 A I P Educational Newsletter†
0001-1657 A. I. P. Information & Publication Newsletter†
0001-1665 A I P Newsletter see 0164-5420
0001-1673 A I Z
0001-1681 A J R Information
0001-169X A K†
0001-1703 A L A F O. Revista
0001-1746 A L A Washington Newsletter
0001-1754 A L B A Bowls
0001-1762 A L E C Report see 0115-6373
0001-1789 A Lampada
0001-1800 Atualidades Medicas†
0001-1819 A.M.A. changed to Assistant Masters & Mistresses Association. Report
0001-1827 A M A Audio News Journal†
0001-1835 A M A International Health Bulletin†
0001-1843 American Medical News
0001-1851 A M A X Journal†
0001-186X A M B A C. Noticiero
0001-1878 A M C H A M Newsletter
0001-1886 A. M. C. K. Mededelingsblad
0001-1908 A M D I Bollettino
0001-1916 A.M.I. Newsletter
0001-1932 A M News - Southern Africa
0001-1940 Ampujainlehti
0001-1967 A M S Management Bulletin changed to Management Success
0001-1975 A M T D A Journal see 0308-9274
0001-1983 A M Z
0001-1991 A.N.A. Club Bulletin see 0029-6090
0001-2025 A.N.F.I.A. Notiziario di Informazioni†
0001-2033 A.N.F.I.A. Notiziario Statistico
0001-2041 A N N Y see 0199-2864
0001-205X American Newspaper Publishers Association, Research Institute. R.I. Bulletins. see 0194-3243
0001-2068 A N U Historical Journal
0001-2076 A N Z Bank Quarterly Survey†
0001-2084 A O P A Pilot
0001-2092 A O R N Journal
0001-2114 A P A Monitor
0001-2122 A.P.A.V.E. Revue Technique
0001-2130 A P C A Abstracts†
0001-2157 A P C D Report see 0092-8593
0001-2181 A P E C
0001-2203 A P L A Bulletin
0001-2211 A P L Technical Digest see 0270-5214
0001-2246 A P R A Journal†
0001-2262 A P W A Newsletter
0001-2270 A P W A Reporter
0001-2289 A R A Log
0001-2297 A R E R S
0001-2300 A R G R Journal
0001-2319 A R M P News†
0001-2327 A R S H A Bulletin
0001-2335 A R S Hai Sird
0001-2343 Archiv fuer Rechts- und Sozialphilosophie
0001-2351 A S A E Transactions
0001-2378 A S A Newsletter†
0001-2386 A S B Bulletin
0001-2394 A.S.B.E. Letter
0001-2408 A S B S D Bulletin
0001-2416 A S C A Newsletter
0001-2424 A S C A P changed to A S C A P in Action
0001-2432 A S C E Publications Abstracts see 0734-1962
0001-2440 A S E A Bulletin†
0001-2459 A S E A Journal
0001-2467 A S E E International Engineering Education Newsletter†
0001-2475 A S H A
0001-2483 A S H P Newsletter
0001-2491 A S H R A E Journal
0001-2505 A S H R A E Transactions
0001-2513 A S I S Newsletter see 0095-4403
0001-2521 Aslib Book List
0001-253X Aslib Proceedings
0001-2548 A S L P Bulletin
0001-2556 A S M Bibliography Series
0001-2564 A S M T News†
0001-2580 A S P A C Newsletter of Cultural and Social Affairs†
0001-2599 A S P A Quarterly of Cultural and Social Affairs changed to Asian and Pacific Quarterly
0001-2602 A S P B A E Journal†
0001-2610 Planning
0001-2629 A S R C T Newsletter†
0001-2637 A S T A Travel News
0001-2645 A S T E Bulletin see 0888-7233
0001-2653 A S T M S Journal
0001-2661 A T A Associazione Tecnica dell'Automobile
0001-267X A T A News
0001-2688 Auto Touring
0001-2696 Acta Technica Belgica. Revue A T B: Metallurgie
0001-2718 A T E Newsletter
0001-2726 A T F Monthly Report changed to A T F Annual Report
0001-2734 A T G Bulletin
0001-2742 A T M N E Journal
0001-2750 A T O - A C E Newsletter†
0001-2769 A T P A S Bulletin see 0308-6895
0001-2777 A T R
0001-2785 A T Z
0001-2807 A U P E L F Revue see 0820-005X
0001-2815 Tissue Antigens
0001-2823 A U T Bulletin
0001-2831 The A V Magazine
0001-2858 A V A Magazine
0001-2866 A V A Member-Gram†
0001-2874 A V C Bulletin
0001-2890 A V Communication Review see 0148-5806
0001-2904 A V S News changed to A V S C News
0001-2912 A Votre Sante†
0001-2920 A W A Technical Review†
0001-2947 A W R Bulletin
0001-2955 Hostelert†
0001-2971 A A H E College and University Bulletin see 0162-7910
0001-298X Aakerifoeretagaren-Transportoeren see 0348-0356
0001-2998 Seminars in Nuclear Medicine
0001-3013 Aannemer changed to Bouwbedrijf
0001-303X Aaraaichi
0001-3048 Aaron Burr Association. Chronicle
0001-3056 Arrow (Kenosha)
0001-3064 Aavesh
0001-3072 Abacus
0001-3099 Abacus
0001-3102 Abbia
0001-3110 Abbigliamento Italiano changed to Abbigliamento
0001-3129 Abeille & Erable†
0001-3137 Abeille de France changed to Abeille de France et l'Apiculteur
0001-3153 Abel changed to Abel Value News
0001-3161 Aberdeen-Angus Journal see 0194-9543
0001-317X Aberdeen - Angus Review
0001-3188 Aberdeen Chamber of Commerce Journal†
0001-3196 University of Aberdeen. African Studies Group. Bulletin
0001-320X University of Aberdeen Review
0001-3218 Abitare
0001-3234 Abolition News changed to National Committee Against Repressive Legislation. Memo
0001-3242 About the House
0001-3269 Abracadabra
0001-3285 Abrasive Methods changed to Abrasive Engineering Society. Magazine
0001-3307 Abraxas†
0001-3331 Abridged Index Medicus
0001-334X Abridged Readers' Guide to Periodical Literature
0001-3358 Abril†
0001-3374 Absatzwirtschaft
0001-3382 Abside
0001-3404 Abstracts and Book Title Index Card Service (ABTICS)†
0001-3412 Abstracts for Social Workers see 0148-0847
0001-3420 Abstracts for the Advancement of Industrial Utilization of Cereal Grains†
0001-3439 Abstracts from Current Scientific and Technical Literature
0001-3447 B I C E R I Abstracts from Technical and Patent Publications.
0001-3455 Abstracts in Anthropology
0001-3463 Abstracts of Bulgarian Scientific Literature. Agriculture and Forestry. Veterinary Medicine
0001-3498 Abstracts of Bulgarian Scientific Literature. Geology and Geography see 0204-9406
0001-351X Abstracts of Bulgarian Scientific Literature. Mathematics, Physics, Astronomy, Geophysics, Geodesy see 0204-9449
0001-3528 Abstracts of Bulgarian Scientific Literature. Philosophy, Psychology and Pedagogics changed to Abstracts of Bulgarian Scientific Literature. Philosophy, Sociology, Science of Sciences, Psychology and Pedagogics
0001-3536 Abstracts of Bulgarian Scientific Medical Literature
0001-3544 Current Literature on Venereal Disease see 0195-7708
0001-3552 Abstracts of Efficiency Studies in the Hospital Service changed to Great Britain. Department of Health and Social Security. Notes on Good Practices
0001-3560 Abstracts of English Studies
0001-3579 Abstracts of Entomology
0001-3587 Abstracts of Folklore Studies†
0001-3595 Abstracts of Hospital Management Studies see 0194-4908
0001-3609 Abstracts of Instructional Materials in Vocational and Technical Education see 0160-2004
0001-3617 Abstracts of Mycology
0001-3625 Abstracts of North American Geology†
0001-3633 Abstracts of Photographic Science & Engineering Literature†
0001-3641 Abstracts of Research and Related Materials in Vocational and Technical Education see 0160-2004
0001-365X Abstracts of Romanian Scientific and Technical Literature
0001-3668 Abstracts of the Current Literature on TB and Other Respiratory Diseases see 0389-7389
0001-3676 Abstracts of Uppsala Dissertations in Science
0001-3684 Excerpta Criminologica see 0166-6231
0001-3692 Abstracts on Hygiene see 0260-5511
0001-3714 Revista de Microbiologia
0001-3730 Acacia Clarion
0001-3749 Academe see 0190-2946
0001-3757 Academia Argentina de Letras. Boletin
0001-3765 Academia Brasileira de Ciencias. Anais
0001-3773 Academia Colombiana. Boletin
0001-3781 Academia das Ciencias de Lisboa. Boletim
0001-379X Academia de Artes y Ciencias de Puerto Rico. Boletin
0001-3803 Academia Medico Quirurgica Espanola. Anales†
0001-3811 Academia Militar de Chorrillos. Revista
0001-382X Academia Nacional de la Historia. Boletin
0001-3838 Academia Nacional de Medicina. Boletim
0001-3846 Academia Paulista de Letras. Revista
0001-3854 Academia Peruana de Cirugia Revista
0001-3862 Academia Portena del Lunfardo. Boletin
0001-3889 Academia Republicii Socialiste Romania. Buletin de Informare Stiintifica, Geologia, Geografie†
0001-3897 Lingvistica-Filologie†
0001-3900 Academia Republicii Socialiste Romania. Buletin de Informare Stiintifica. Seria Matematica Astronomie†
0001-3919 Teoria si Istoria Literaturii si Artei; Buletin de Informare Stiintifica†
0001-3927 Academia Sinica. Institute of Chemistry. Bulletin
0001-3935 Academia Sinica. Institute of Ethnology. Bulletin
0001-3943 Academia Sinica. Institute of Zoology. Bulletin
0001-3951 Academic Achievement†
0001-396X Academic Therapy
0001-3994 Academie d'Architecture
0001-4001 Chirurgie

ISSN INDEX 1191

0001-401X Academie de Droit International de la Haye. Recueil des Cours
0001-4044 Academie des Sciences d'Outre-Mer, Paris. Comptes Rendus des Seances
0001-4060 Academie Internationale du Tourisme. Revue
0001-4079 Academie Nationale de Medecine. Bulletin
0001-4087 Academie Polonaise des Sciences. Bulletin. Serie des Sciences Biologiques *see* 0239-751X
0001-4095 Academie Polonaise des Sciences. Bulletin. Serie des Sciences Chimiques *changed to* Polish Academy of Sciences. Bulletin. Chemical Sciences
0001-4109 Academie Polonaise des Sciences. Bulletin. Serie des Sciences de la Terre *see* 0239-7277
0001-4117 Academie Polonaise des Sciences. Bulletin. Serie des Sciences Mathematiques, Astronomiques et Physiques *changed to* Polish Academy of Sciences. Bulletin. Mathematical Sciences
0001-4125 Academie Polonaise des Sciences. Bulletin. Serie des Sciences Techniques *see* 0239-7528
0001-415X Commission Royale d'Histoire. Bulletin
0001-4168 Academie Royale de Medecine de Belgique. Bulletin *see* 0377-8231
0001-4176 Academie Royale des Sciences d'Outre-Mer. Bulletin des Seances
0001-4184 Academie Serbe des Sciences et des Arts. Classe des Sciences Mathematiques et Naturelles. Bulletin. Nouvelle Serie *changed to* Academie Serbe des Sciences et des Arts. Classe des Sciences Mathematiques et Naturelles. Bulletin. Sciences Mathematiques
0001-4184 Academie Serbe des Sciences et des Arts. Classe des Sciences Mathematiques et Naturelles. Bulletin. Nouvelle Serie *see* 0352-5740
0001-4192 Academie Veterinaire de France. Bulletin
0001-4214 Revue Roumaine de Biochimie
0001-4249 Academy Bookman
0001-4265 Academy of General Dentistry. Journal *see* 0363-6771
0001-4273 Academy of Management. Journal
0001-4281 Academy of Medicine of Cleveland. Bulletin *changed to* Cleveland Physician
0001-4303 Academy of Toledo and Lucas County. Bulletin *changed to* Toledo Medicine
0001-4311 Academy of Medicine, Toronto. Bulletin
0001-432X Academy of Sciences of the U S S R. Bulletin. Physical Series
0001-4338 Academy of Sciences of the U S S R. Izvestiya. Atmospheric and Oceanic Physics
0001-4346 Academy of Science of the U S S R. Mathematical Notes
0001-4354 Academy of Sciences of the U S S R. Izvestiya. Physics of the Solid Earth
0001-4362 Population Biocharacterist *see* 0098-8618
0001-4370 Academy of Sciences of the U S S R. Oceanology
0001-4389 Pharmacology and Therapeutics in Dentistry†
0001-4397 Acadiana Profile
0001-4400 Acao†
0001-4419 Accademia delle Scienze di Torino. Atti. Part 1. Classe di Scienze Fisiche, Matematiche e Naturali
0001-4427 Accademia Medica Lombarda. Atti
0001-4435 Accademia Nazionale dei Lincei. Classe di Scienze Fisiche Matematiche e Naturali. Rendiconti
0001-4443 Accademia Nazionale di Agricoltura. Annali†
0001-4451 Accademie e Biblioteche d'Italia
0001-446X Accelerator (Saskatoon)
0001-4478 Accelerator *changed to* Accelerator Newsletter
0001-4486 Accent†
0001-4508 Accent on Living
0001-4516 Accent on Youth
0001-4559 Acciaio
0001-4567 L'Acciaio Inossidabile
0001-4575 Accident Analysis & Prevention
0001-4583 Accidents Claims Journal
0001-4591 Accidents, How They Are Caused and How to Prevent Them†
0001-4605 Accion
0001-4648 Accordion Horizons†
0001-4664 Accountancy
0001-4672 Accountancy Age
0001-4680 Accountancy, Business & Insurance Review
0001-4699 Accountancy Ireland
0001-4702 Accountant Journal *changed to* Institute of Chartered Accountants of Sri Lanka. Journal
0001-4710 Accountant
0001-4729 Accountant
0001-4737 Accountants Digest
0001-4745 Accountants' Journal
0001-4753 Accountants' Journal
0001-4761 Accountant's Magazine
0001-4788 Accounting and Business Research
0001-4796 Accounting & Data Processing Abstracts
0001-4818 Accounting Forum†
0001-4826 Accounting Review
0001-4834 Accounting Trends†
0001-4842 Accounts of Chemical Research
0001-4850 Acero y Energia
0001-4869 Achaab
0001-4877 Achats et Entretien du Materiel Industriel *see* 0396-6666
0001-4893 Acheteurs
0001-4907 Achievement
0001-4923 Acier†
0001-4931 Acier dans le Monde
0001-494X Acme
0001-4958 Aconcagua Iberoamerica-Europa†
0001-4966 Acoustical Society of America. Journal
0001-4974 Acoustics Abstracts
0001-4982 Inquinamento
0001-5008 Acquisitions Nouvelles en Pathologie Cardio-Vasculaire
0001-5040 Acropole†
0001-5059 Across from City Hall *changed to* Citizens Union Reports
0001-5067 Acrow Review
0001-5075 Act
0001-5083 Act
0001-5105 Acta Academiae Aboensis, Series B: Mathematica et Physica
0001-5113 Acta Adriatica
0001-5121 Acta Agriculturae Scandinavica
0001-513X Academia Scientiarum Hungarica. Acta Agronomica
0001-5148 Acta Allergologica *see* 0105-4538
0001-5156 Acta Anaesthesiologica *see* 0374-4965
0001-5164 Acta Anaesthesiologica Belgica
0001-5172 Acta Anaesthesiologica Scandinavica
0001-5180 Acta Anatomica
0001-5199 Acta Apostolicae Sedis. Commentarium Officiale
0001-5202 Acta Arachnologica
0001-5210 Academia Scientiarum Hungarica. Acta Archaeologica
0001-5229 Acta Archaeologica Carpathica
0001-5237 Acta Astronomica
0001-5253 Academia Scientiarum Hungarica. Acta Biochimica et Biophysica
0001-5261 Acta Biochimica Iranica†
0001-527X Acta Biochimica Polonica†
0001-5288 Acta Biologica†
0001-5296 Acta Biologica Cracoviensia. Botanica
0001-530X Acta Biologica Cracoviensia. Zoologia
0001-5318 Acta Biologica et Medica Germanica *see* 0232-766X
0001-5326 Acta Biologica Venezuelica
0001-5334 Acta Biologicae Experimentalis Sinica†
0001-5342 Acta Biotheoretica
0001-5350 Academiae Scientiarum Hungaricae. Acta Botanica *see* 0236-6495
0001-5369 Acta Botanica Fennica
0001-5377 Acta Cancerologica
0001-5385 Acta Cardiologica
0001-5393 Acta Chemica Scandinavica *see* 0302-4377
0001-5393 Acta Chemica Scandinavica *see* 0302-4369
0001-5407 Academia Scientiarum Hungarica. Acta Chimica *see* 0231-3146
0001-5415 Acta Chirurgiae Orthopaedicae et Traumatologiae Cechoslovaca
0001-5423 Acta Chirurgiae Plasticae
0001-5431 Academia Scientiarum Hungarica. Acta Chirurgica *see* 0231-4614
0001-544X Acta Chirurgica Austriaca
0001-5458 Acta Chirurgica Belgica
0001-5466 Acta Chirurgica Italica
0001-5474 Acta Chirurgica Iugoslavica
0001-5482 Acta Chirurgica Scandinavica
0001-5490 Acta Cientifica†
0001-5504 Acta Cientifica Venezolana
0001-5520 Acta Crystallographica *see* 0108-7673
0001-5520 Acta Crystallographica *see* 0108-7681
0001-5520 Acta Crystallographica *see* 0108-2701
0001-5547 Acta Cytologica
0001-5555 Acta Dermato-Venereologica
0001-5563 Acta Diabetologica Latina
0001-5571 Acta Diurna†
0001-558X Acta Electronica
0001-5598 Acta Endocrinologica
0001-5601 Acta Entomologica Bohemoslovaca
0001-561X Acta Entomologica Fennica
0001-5628 Academia Scientiarum Hungarica. Acta Ethnographica
0001-5636 Acta Forestalia Fennica
0001-5644 Acta Gastro-Enterologica Belgica
0001-5652 Human Heredity
0001-5660 Acta Geneticae Medicae et Gemellologiae: Twin Research
0001-5679 Academia Scientiarum Hungarica. Acta Geodaetica, Geophysica et Montanistica *see* 0374-1842
0001-5687 Acta Geographica
0001-5695 Academiae Scientiarum Hungarica. Acta Geologica *see* 0236-5278
0001-5709 Acta Geologica Polonica
0001-5717 Acta Geologica Sinica
0001-5725 Acta Geophysica Polonica
0001-5733 Acta Geophysica Sinica
0001-5741 Acta Gerontologica
0001-575X Acta Gerontologica et Geriatrica Belgica *changed to* Rejuvenation
0001-5768 Acta Gerontologica Japonica *changed to* Yokufukai Geriatric Journal
0001-5776 Acta Ginecologica
0001-5792 Acta Haematologica
0001-5806 Acta Haematologica Japonica
0001-5814 Acta Haematologica Polonica
0001-5822 Acta Hepato- Splenologica *see* 0172-6390
0001-5830 Academia Scientiarum Hungarica. Acta Historiae Artium
0001-5849 Academia Scientiarum Hungarica. Acta Historica
0001-5857 Acta Historica Leopoldina
0001-5865 Acta Historica Medicinae, Stomatologiae, Pharmaciae, Veterinae
0001-5881 Acta Homeopathica *see* 0301-1402
0001-589X Acta Iberica Radiologica-Cancerologica
0001-5903 Acta Informatica
0001-592X Academia Scientiarum Hungarica. Acta Juridica
0001-5938 Acta Leprologica
0001-5946 Academia Scientiarum Hungarica. Acta Linguistica
0001-5954 Academia Scientiarum Hungarica. Acta Mathematica *see* 0236-5294
0001-5962 Acta Mathematica
0001-5970 Acta Mechanica
0001-5989 Academia Scientiarum Hungarica. Acta Medica *see* 0236-5286
0001-5997 Acta Medica
0001-6004 Acta Medica Auxologica
0001-6012 Acta Medica Costarricense
0001-6039 Acta Medica Italica di Medicina Tropicale e Subtropicale e di Gastroenterologia
0001-6055 Acta Medica Nagasakiensia
0001-6071 Acta Medica Philippina
0001-608X Acta Medica Polona
0001-6098 Acta Medica Romana
0001-6101 Acta Medica Scandinavica
0001-611X Acta Medica Universitatis Kagoshimaensis
0001-6136 Acta Medica Veterinaria
0001-6152 Acta Medicinae Okayama. *see* 0386-300X
0001-6160 Acta Metallurgica
0001-6179 Acta Meteorologica Sinica
0001-6187 Academia Scientiarum Hungarica. Acta Microbiologica *see* 0231-4622
0001-6195 Acta Microbiologica Polonica
0001-6209 Acta Microbiologica Sinica
0001-6217 Academia Scientiarum Hungarica. Acta Morphologica *see* 0236-5391
0001-6225 Acta Morphologica Neerlando-Scandinavica
0001-6233 Acta Mozartiana
0001-6241 Acta Musicologica
0001-625X Acta Mycologica
0001-6268 Acta Neurochirurgica. Supplementa
0001-6268 Acta Neurochirurgica
0001-6276 Acta Neurologica
0001-6284 Acta Neurologica et Psychiatrica Belgica *see* 0300-9009
0001-6284 Acta Neurologica et Psychiatrica Belgica *see* 0300-8967
0001-6306 Acta Neurologica Latinoamericana
0001-6314 Acta Neurologica Scandinavica
0001-6322 Acta Neuropathologica
0001-6330 Acta Obsterica et Gynaecologica Japonica†
0001-6349 Acta Obstetrica et Gynecologica Scandinavica
0001-6357 Acta Odontologica Scandinavica
0001-6365 Acta Odontologica Venezolana
0001-6373 Academia Scientiarum Hungarica. Acta Oeconomica
0001-6381 Acta Oncologica†
0001-639X Acta Ophthalmologica
0001-6403 Acta Ophthalmologica Iugoslavica
0001-6411 Acta Ordinis Fratrum Minorum
0001-642X Acta Ordinis Sancti Augustini
0001-6438 Acta Orientalia
0001-6446 Academia Scientiarum Hungarica. Acta Orientalia
0001-6454 Acta Ornithologica
0001-6462 Acta Orthopaedica Belgica
0001-6470 Acta Orthopaedica Scandinavica
0001-6489 Acta Oto-Laryngologica
0001-6497 Acta Oto-Rhino-Laryngologica Belgica
0001-6500 Acta Oto-Rino-Laringologica Ibero-Americana *see* 0303-8874
0001-6519 Acta Otorrinolaringologica Espanola
0001-6527 Academia Scientiarum Hungarica. Acta Paediatrica *see* 0231-441X
0001-6535 Acta Paediatrica Belgica
0001-6543 Acta Paediatrica Japonica
0001-6551 Acta Paediatrica Latina
0001-656X Acta Paediatrica Scandinavica
0001-6578 Acta Paediatrica Sinica
0001-6586 Acta Paedopsychiatrica†
0001-6594 Acta Palaeobotanica
0001-6616 Acta Palaeontologica Sinica
0001-6624 Acta Pathologica et Microbiologica Scandinavica *see* 0108-0164
0001-6632 Acta Pathologica Japonica
0001-6640 Acta Pediatrica Espanola
0001-6659 Acta Pharmaceutica Hungarica
0001-6667 Acta Pharmaceutica Jugoslavica
0001-6675 Acta Pharmaceutica Suecica
0001-6683 Acta Pharmacologica et Toxicologica *see* 0901-9928
0001-6691 Acta Philologica Scandinavica
0001-6705 Academia Scientiarum Hungarica. Acta Physica *see* 0231-4428
0001-6713 Acta Physica Austriaca *see* 0177-7963
0001-6721 Acta Universitatis Szegediensis de Attila Jozsef Nominatae. Acta Physica et Chemica
0001-673X Acta Physica Polonica *see* 0587-4246

1192 ISSN INDEX

0001-673X Acta Physica Polonica *see* 0587-4254
0001-6748 Acta Physioligica et Pharmacologia Neerlandica†
0001-6756 Academia Scientiarum Hungarica. Acta Physiologica *see* 0231-424X
0001-6764 Acta Physiologica et Pharmacologica Latinoamericana *changed to* Acta Physiologica Latino Americana
0001-6772 Acta Physiologica Scandinavica
0001-6780 Academia Scientiarum Hungarica. Acta Phytopathologica
0001-6799 Acta Phytotaxonomica et Geobotanica
0001-6810 Acta Politica
0001-6829 Acta Poloniae Historica
0001-6837 Acta Poloniae Pharmaceutica†
0001-6845 Acta Polytechnica Scandinavica. Electrical Engineering Series
0001-6853 Acta Polytechnica Scandinavica. Chemical Technology and Metallurgy
0001-6861 Acta Polytechnica Scandinavica. Mathematics and Computing Machinery Series *see* 0355-2713
0001-687X Acta Polytechnica Scandinavica. Mechanical Engineering Series
0001-6888 Acta Polytechnica Scandinavica. Physics Including Nucleonics Series *see* 0355-2721
0001-6896 Acta Psiquiatrica y Psicologica de America Latina
0001-690X Acta Psychiatrica Scandinavica
0001-6918 Acta Psychologica
0001-6934 Acta Rheumatologica Scandinavica *see* 0300-9742
0001-6942 Acta Sagittariana
0001-6950 Acta Scholae Medicinalis Universitatis in Kioto†
0001-6969 Acta Universitatis Szegediensis de Attila Jozsef Nominatae. Acta Scientiarum Mathematicarum
0001-6977 Acta Societatis Botanicorum Poloniae
0001-6985 Acta Societatis Medicorum Upsaliensis *see* 0300-9734
0001-6993 Acta Sociologica
0001-7000 Acta Stomatologica Belgica
0001-7019 Acta Stomatologica Croatica
0001-7035 Academia Scientiarum Hungarica. Acta Technica
0001-7043 Ceskoslovenska Akademie Ved. Acta Technica
0001-7051 Acta Theriologica
0001-706X Acta Tropica
0001-7078 Acta Tuberculosea et Pneumologica Belgica *see* 0106-4339
0001-7094 Drug Therapy
0001-7108 Current Literature of Blood†
0001-7124 Acta Universitatis Carolinae: Biologica
0001-7132 Acta Universitatis Carolinae: Geologica
0001-7140 Acta Universitatis Carolinae: Mathematica et Physica
0001-7159 Acta Universitatis Lundensis Sectio: Medica, Mathematica, Scientiae Rerum Naturalium†
0001-7167 Acta Universitatis Palackianae, Facultatis Medicae *see* 0301-2514
0001-7175 Acta Universitatis Szegediensis de Attila Jozsef Nominatae. Acta Bibliothecaria
0001-7183 Acta Urologica Belgica
0001-7191 Acta Urologica Japonica
0001-7205 Academia Scientiarum Hungarica. Acta Veterinaria *see* 0236-6290
0001-7213 Acta Veterinaria
0001-7221 Acta Veterinaria Japonica
0001-723X Acta Virologica
0001-7248 Acta Vitaminologica *see* 0300-8924
0001-7264 Academia Scientiarum Hungarica. Acta Zoologica *see* 0236-7130
0001-7272 Acta Zoologica
0001-7280 Acta Zoologica et Pathologica Antverpiensia
0001-7299 Acta Zoologica Fennica
0001-7302 Acta Zoologica Sinica
0001-7310 Actas Dermo-Sifiliograficas
0001-7329 Actas Luso Espanolas de Neurologia y Psiquiatria *see* 0300-5062
0001-7345 Actes Pontificaux†
0001-7353 Actinides and Lanthanides Reviews†
0001-737X Action (Louisville) *changed to* Update (Louisville)
0001-7388 Action (New York)†
0001-7396 Action (Albany)
0001-740X Action†
0001-7418 Action Automobile et Touristique
0001-7426 Action et Fensee†
0001-7442 Action Line (Baltimore)
0001-7450 Action Municipale
0001-7469 Action Nationale
0001-7477 Action Poetique
0001-7485 Action-Reaction *see* 0360-1897
0001-7507 Action Sociale
0001-7523 Action Veterinaire
0001-754X Active Handicapped†
0001-7558 Active Service
0001-7566 Actividade Economica de Angola
0001-7574 C E E D. Actividades†
0001-7582 Actividades Petroleras
0001-7590 Activist†
0001-7604 Activitas Nervosa Superior
0001-7612 Activities of the Communist World Organizations†
0001-7620 A C Tivity
0001-7639 Actual
0001-7647 Actual Specifying Engineer *changed to* Consulting/Specifying Engineer
0001-7655 Actualidad Economica
0001-7671 Actualidad Pediatrica†
0001-768X Actualidades de Japon
0001-7701 General Relativity and Gravitation
0001-771X Actualite Economique
0001-7728 Actualite Juridique: Edition Droit Administratif
0001-7736 Actualite Juridique: Edition Propriete Immobiliere *see* 0001-7728
0001-7744 Actualite Missionnaire†
0001-7752 Actualite Pedagogique a l'Etranger†
0001-7760 Actualite Publicitaire
0001-7779 Actualite Terminologique
0001-7787 Actualites Cereales *changed to* Actualites Agricoles
0001-7795 Actualites et Culture Veterinaires†
0001-7809 Actualites Marines†
0001-7817 Actualites Odonto-Stomatologiques
0001-7825 Actuary
0001-7833 Actuel†
0001-7841 Actuele Onderwerpen-Reeks *changed to* A O (Year)
0001-785X Aktuelle Chirurgie
0001-7868 Aktuelle Urologie
0001-7884 Acustica
0001-7892 Ad
0001-7906 AD-Cards†
0001-7914 Ad Change
0001-7930 Ad Fontes
0001-7957 Ad Libs†
0001-7965 Ad Marginem
0001-7973 Ad Rem†
0001-7981 Behavioral Science in Progress†
0001-799X Adalbert-Stifter-Institut des Landes Oberoesterreich. Vierteljahresschrift
0001-8007 Adam
0001-8015 Adam International Review
0001-8023 Adam Magazine†
0001-804X Adansonia *see* 0240-8937
0001-8066 Adcrafter
0001-8074 Addiction and Drug Abuse Report *changed to* Substance Abuse Report
0001-8082 Addictions†
0001-8090 Adding Life to Years†
0001-8112 A D E G - Kaufmann
0001-8120 A D E G - Kurier
0001-8139 Adelaar
0001-8147 Adelaide Church Guardian
0001-8163 University of Adelaide. Graduates Union. Monthly Newsletter and Gazette *changed to* Lumen
0001-8171 Adem
0001-8198 Adhaesion
0001-8201 Adhesion Society of Japan. Journal
0001-821X Adhesives Age
0001-8228 Adhuna Sahitya
0001-8236 Adirondac
0001-8244 Behavior Genetics
0001-8252 Adirondack Life
0001-8260 Adler
0001-8279 Der Adler
0001-8295 Admap
0001-8317 Administratieve Arbeid†
0001-8325 Administration
0001-8333 Quarterly Journal of Administration
0001-835X Administrative Digest *changed to* Office Product News
0001-8368 Administrative Law Review
0001-8376 Administrative Management *see* 0884-5905
0001-8384 Administrative Officer *changed to* Alert! Top Executive & The Administrative Officer
0001-8392 Administrative Science Quarterly
0001-8406 Administrative Science Review
0001-8414 Administrator Quarterly
0001-8422 Administrator's Digest *see* 0746-6129
0001-8430 Administrators Notebook
0001-8449 Adolescence
0001-8473 Adult & Continuing Education Today
0001-8481 Adult Education *changed to* Adult Education Quarterly
0001-849X Adult Education
0001-8503 Adult Education in Finland
0001-8511 Adult Education in Nova Scotia†
0001-852X Adult Education in the Public Schools†
0001-8546 Adult Jewish Education†
0001-8562 Advance (Chicago)
0001-8570 Advance (St. Louis) *see* 0360-7119
0001-8589 Advance (Springfield)
0001-8597 Advance (New York) *see* 0271-5848
0001-8600 Advance Abstracts of Contributions on Fisheries and Aquatic Sciences in India†
0001-8619 Advance Australia
0001-8627 Advanced Battery Technology
0001-8635 Advanced Documentation List†
0001-8651 Advanced Publications†
0001-8678 Advances in Applied Probability
0001-8686 Advances in Colloid and Interface Science
0001-8694 Advances in Education
0001-8708 Advances in Mathematics
0001-8716 Advances in Molecular Relaxation Processes *see* 0167-7322
0001-8724 Advances in Neurological Sciences
0001-8732 Advances in Physics
0001-8740 Adveniat
0001-8759 Advent Christian Missions†
0001-8767 Adventbode *changed to* Advent
0001-8775 Adventure†
0001-8783 Adventure (Nashville)
0001-8791 Journal of Vocational Behavior
0001-8805 Adventure Road
0001-8813 Adventure Time†
0001-8821 Adventurer *see* 0263-8894
0001-883X Adventures in Western New York History
0001-8848 Excerpta Medica. Section 38: Adverse Reactions Titles
0001-8856 Advertentieblad
0001-8864 Advertisement Parade
0001-8880 Adweek†
0001-8899 Advertising Age
0001-8902 Advertising & Marketing for Manufactures†
0001-8910 Advertising and Marketing News *changed to* National Business Review
0001-8929 Advertising and Newspaper News *see* 0814-6942
0001-8961 Advertising Quarterly *see* 0265-0487
0001-897X Advertising Statistical Review *changed to* T V Advertising Statistical Review
0001-8988 Advertlink
0001-8996 Advocate (Malibu)
0001-9003 Advocate (New York)
0001-9011 Adyar
0001-902X Brahmavidya
0001-9038 Aegir
0001-9046 Aegyptus
0001-9054 Aequationes Mathematicae
0001-9062 Aerial†
0001-9070 Aerial Applicator
0001-9089 Sardegna-Agricoltura (Varese)
0001-9097 Aero
0001-9100 Aero
0001-9127 Aeroespacio
0001-9135 Aero Field†
0001-916X Aero Mundial
0001-9178 Aero Philatelist Annals†
0001-9186 Aero-Revue
0001-9194 Aerograph Research Notes†
0001-9216 Aerological Data of Japan
0001-9224 Aerologische Berichte
0001-9232 Aero Modeller
0001-9240 Aeronautical Journal
0001-9259 Aeronautical Quarterly *see* 0001-9240
0001-9267 Aeronautical Society of India. Journal
0001-9275 Aeronautique et l'Astronautique
0001-9283 Aeroporika Nea Kai Pathetike *changed to* Aeroporika Nea
0001-9291 Aerosol Age
0001-9313 Aerosol Report
0001-9321 Aerospace (Washington)
0001-933X Aerospace
0001-9364 Aerospace Historian
0001-9372 Aerospace International†
0001-9380 Aerospace Maintenance Safety *see* 0364-7145
0001-9402 Aerospace Medicine *see* 0095-6562
0001-9410 Aerospace Medicine and Biology; a Continuing Bibliography
0001-9429 Aerospace Safety *see* 0279-9308
0001-9445 Flieger-Revue
0001-9453 Aerotecnica *changed to* Aerotecnica, Missili e Spazio
0001-9461 Aerovoz
0001-9488 Aerzteblatt Rheinland-Pfalz
0001-9496 Aerztliche Forschung†
0001-950X Aerztliche Fortbildung†
0001-9518 Aerztliche Jugendkunde
0001-9526 Das Aerztliche Laboratorium
0001-9534 Aerztliche Praxis
0001-9542 Aerztliche Tonbandzeitung†
0001-9550 Aersceala
0001-9569 Aesculape†
0001-9585 AetnaIzer
0001-9593 Aevum
0001-9607 Affaersekonomi *changed to* Affaersekonomi Management
0001-9615 Affaires
0001-9623 Affairs of State†
0001-9658 Affaersvaerlden-Finanstidningen *see* 0345-3766
0001-9666 Affiches d'Alsace et de Lorraine-Moniteur des Soumissions et des Ventes de Bois de l'Est
0001-9674 Affirmation†
0001-9682 Afghanistan
0001-9690 Aficion Espanola
0001-9704 Afinidad
0001-9712 Afrasian Markets *changed to* Export Gazette
0001-9739 Africa†
0001-9747 Africa
0001-9755 Africa
0001-9763 Africa†
0001-978X Africa Diary
0001-9798 Africa Digest *see* 0306-8412
0001-981X Africa Institute. Bulletin *changed to* Africa Institute Bulletin
0001-9828 Africa Quarterly
0001-9836 Africa Report
0001-9844 Africa Research Bulletin. Series A: Political, Social and Cultural *changed to* Africa Research Bulletin. Series A: Political
0001-9852 Africa Research Bulletin. Series B: Economic, Financial and Technical *changed to* Africa Research Bulletin. Series B: Economic
0001-9860 Africa Samachar
0001-9879 Africa-Tervuren
0001-9887 Africa Today
0001-9909 African Affairs
0001-9925 African Aquarist†
0001-9933 African Arts
0001-9941 African Books Newsletter

ISSN INDEX 1193

ISSN	Title
0001-995X	African Bookshelf *changed to* Diplomatic Bookshelf & Review
0001-9968	African Challenge *changed to* Today's Challenge
0001-9976	African Communist
0001-9984	African Development *see* 0140-833X
0001-9992	African Historical Studies *see* 0361-7882
0002-001X	African Insurance Record
0002-0028	African Journal of Medical Sciences *see* 0309-3913
0002-0036	African Journal of Tropical Hydrobiology and Fisheries
0002-0044	African Labour News
0002-0052	African Law Digest
0002-0060	African Law Studies *see* 0732-9113
0002-0079	African M I M S *see* 0140-4415
0002-0087	African Notes
0002-0117	African Political Review *see* 0856-0056
0002-0133	African Recorder
0002-015X	African Scientist *changed to* African Scientist and Technologist
0002-0168	African Social Research
0002-0184	African Studies
0002-0192	African Studies Association of the United Kingdom. Bulletin *see* 0305-862X
0002-0206	African Studies Review
0002-0214	African Studies Newsletter *see* 0278-2219
0002-0222	African Succulent Plant Society. Bulletin†
0002-0230	African Target†
0002-0249	African Trader
0002-0265	African Violet Magazine
0002-0273	African Wildlife
0002-0281	Africana†
0002-029X	Africana Bulletin
0002-0303	Africana Library Journal *see* 0095-1080
0002-0311	Africana Marburgensia
0002-032X	Africana Notes and News
0002-0338	Africasia *changed to* Afrique-Asie
0002-0346	Afrika†
0002-0397	Afrika Spectrum
0002-0400	Afrika-Spiegel
0002-0419	Afrika Studiecentrum. Documentatieblad *see* 0166-2694
0002-0427	Afrika und Uebersee
0002-0443	Journal of Nursing Administration
0002-046X	Afrique & Culture†
0002-0478	Afrique Contemporaine
0002-0486	Afrique et l'Asie *see* 0399-0370
0002-0508	Afrique Litteraire et Artistique *changed to* Afrique Litteraire
0002-0516	Afrique Medicale
0002-0524	Afrique Mon Pays
0002-0532	Afrique Nouvelle†
0002-0540	Afrique Service
0002-0559	Afrique Urbaine†
0002-0575	Afro-American Studies *see* 0308-6860
0002-0591	Afro-Asia
0002-0613	Afro Asian Economic Review
0002-063X	Afro-Asian Labour Bulletin *changed to* Singaporean
0002-0648	Afro-Asia Peoples *changed to* Solidarity
0002-0664	Lotus
0002-0672	Afrox News
0002-0699	After Beat†
0002-0710	Agrarische Rundschau
0002-0729	Age and Ageing
0002-0737	Age de la Science†
0002-0745	Age of Achievement†
0002-0753	Age of Tomorrow
0002-0761	Agence d'Informations Europeennes. Bulletin
0002-077X	Revue Parlementaire
0002-0788	Agency Items *changed to* Agency News
0002-0796	Agenda
0002-080X	Agenor
0002-0826	Agent Commercial
0002-0834	Agente
0002-0869	Agenzia di Viaggi
0002-0877	Agenzia Economica Finanziaria
0002-0893	Agenzia Nazionale Informazioni Turistiche
0002-0907	Aggiornamenti Clinicoterapeutici *changed to* Gazzetta Medica Italiana Archivio per le Scienze Mediche
0002-0915	Aggiornamenti di Terapia Oftalmologica
0002-0923	Aggiornamenti in Ematologia†
0002-0931	Aggiornamenti di Ostetricia e Ginecologia *see* 0026-4784
0002-094X	Aggiornamenti Sociali
0002-0958	Aggiornamento Pediatrico
0002-0966	Aging (Washington)
0002-0974	Aging and Human Development *see* 0091-4150
0002-0982	Aging in the News†
0002-0990	Agmazine
0002-1008	Krankenpflege
0002-1024	Agra Europe
0002-1032	Agra University Journal of Research (Science)
0002-1040	Agradoot
0002-1059	Agraringenieur *see* 0341-2520
0002-1067	Agrarirodalmi Szemle
0002-1075	Landbouw-Economisch Instituut. Agrarisch Weekoverzicht
0002-1105	Agrartorteneti Szemle
0002-1113	Magyar Tudomanyos Akademia. Agrartudomanyok Osztalya. Kozlemenyek *changed to* Agrartudomanyi Kozlemenyek
0002-1121	Agrarwirtschaft
0002-113X	Agrekon
0002-1148	Agressologie
0002-1164	Agri Finance
0002-1172	Agri Hortique Genetica
0002-1180	Agri Marketing
0002-1199	Agri-Pick-Up
0002-1202	Agricoltore (Perugia)
0002-1210	Agricoltore Ferrarese
0002-1229	Agricoltore Trevisano
0002-1237	Agricoltura (Rome, 1952)
0002-1245	Agricoltura Aretina
0002-1253	Agricoltura Bergamasca†
0002-1261	Agricoltura delle Venezie
0002-127X	Agricoltura d'Italia
0002-1288	Agricoltura Nostra
0002-1296	Agricoltura Romagnola
0002-130X	Agriculteur du Sud-Est Magazine
0002-1318	Agricultor
0002-1326	Agricultor Venezolano
0002-1334	Agricultura
0002-1342	Agricultura al Dia†
0002-1369	Agricultural and Biological Chemistry Journal
0002-1377	Agricultural & Veterinary Chemicals and Agricultural Engineering
0002-1393	South Africa. Department of Agricultural Technical Services. Agricultural Bulletins *changed to* South Africa. Department of Agriculture. Agricultural Bulletins
0002-1407	Agricultural Chemical Society of Japan. Journal
0002-1415	Agricultural Co-Operative Bulletin†
0002-1423	Agricultural Economics Research
0002-144X	Agricultural Education
0002-1458	Agricultural Engineering
0002-1466	Agricultural Finance Review
0002-1474	Agricultural Gazette of New South Wales†
0002-1482	Agricultural History
0002-1490	Agricultural History Review
0002-1504	A I C Review *see* 0044-684X
0002-1512	Agricultural Letter
0002-1520	Agricultural Literature of Czechoslovakia
0002-1539	Agricultural Machinery Journal
0002-1547	Agricultural Marketing†
0002-1555	Agricultural Marketing
0002-1571	Agricultural Meteorology *see* 0168-1923
0002-158X	Agricultural News
0002-1598	Fertilizer Progress
0002-1601	U.S. Crop Reporting Board. Agricultural Prices
0002-161X	Agricultural Research
0002-1628	Agricultural Research Journal of Kerala
0002-1660	Agricultural Situation *see* 0270-5672
0002-1679	Agricultural Situation in India
0002-1687	Agriculture
0002-1695	Agriculture†
0002-1709	Agriculture
0002-1717	Agriculture Abroad
0002-1725	Agriculture and Agro-Industries Journal
0002-1733	Agriculture Checklist
0002-1741	Agriculture Decisions
0002-175X	Agriculture in Northern Ireland
0002-1776	Agriculture Pakistan *see* 0251-0480
0002-1784	Agrisul
0002-1792	Agro-Industrialist†
0002-1806	Israel. Meteorological Service. Agro-Meteorological Bulletin *see* 0333-7936
0002-1814	Agro-Service
0002-1822	Agroborealis
0002-1830	Agrochemia
0002-1849	Agrochemia
0002-1857	Agrochimica
0002-1865	Agrohemija
0002-1873	Agrokemia es Talajtan
0002-1881	Agrokhimiya
0002-189X	Agrometeorolosko Porocilo
0002-1903	Agronomia†
0002-1911	Agronomia Lusitana
0002-192X	Agronomia Tropical
0002-1938	Agronomics†
0002-1946	Agronomie Tropicale
0002-1954	Agronomski Glasnik
0002-1962	Agronomy Journal
0002-1970	Agros
0002-1989	Agrotehnicar
0002-1997	Agrotis
0002-2004	Agua†
0002-2012	Agway Cooperator
0002-2039	Ahijuna
0002-2047	Ahora
0002-2055	Ahorro†
0002-2063	Aid Newsletter *changed to* A M S A A Newsletter
0002-208X	Aidai-Echoes
0002-2098	Aika *see* 0355-0303
0002-2101	Aikakan Himiakan Amsagir
0002-211X	Aikya†
0002-2136	Ain Agricole
0002-2144	Ain Shams Medical Journal
0002-2152	Air Actualites
0002-2160	Air Almanac
0002-2179	Air and Space Age†
0002-2187	Air and Water News†
0002-2195	Air B P†
0002-2209	Air Cadet News *changed to* Air Cadet
0002-2225	Air Carrier Financial Statistics
0002-2241	Air Classics
0002-225X	Air Comprime
0002-2268	Air Conditioning & Refrigeration in India
0002-2276	Air Conditioning, Heating and Refrigeration News
0002-2284	Building Systems Design *see* 0199-8595
0002-2292	Air Currents *changed to* Citizens for Clean Air
0002-2306	Air-Cushion Vehicles†
0002-2330	Air Force Accounting and Finance Technical Digest *changed to* Accounting and Finance Tech Digest
0002-2349	Air Force and Space Digest *see* 0730-6784
0002-2357	Air Force Civil Engineer *see* 0362-188X
0002-2365	Air Force Comptroller
0002-2373	Air Force Driver *changed to* Driver
0002-2403	Air Force Times
0002-2411	Air Line Employee
0002-242X	Air Line Pilot
0002-2454	Air Navigation Radio Aids†
0002-2462	Air Pictorial
0002-2470	Air Pollution Control Association. Journal
0002-2489	Air Pollution Notes *changed to* Solid Waste Management
0002-2497	Air Pollution Titles
0002-2500	Air Progress
0002-2527	U D S Air Quality Control Digest *changed to* Air Quality Control Digest
0002-2535	Air Reservist Magazine
0002-2543	Air Transport World
0002-2551	Air Transportation *see* 0745-5100
0002-256X	Air Transport Magazine *see* 0005-2132
0002-2578	Air Travel *changed to* TravelScene
0002-2586	Air University Library Index to Military Periodicals
0002-2594	Air University Review
0002-2608	Air/Water Pollution Report
0002-2616	Air Weather Service Observer
0002-2624	Airadio News
0002-2640	Airconditioning and Refrigeration Business *see* 0279-4071
0002-2659	Aircraft
0002-2667	Aircraft Engineering *changed to* Aircraft Engineering and Aerospace Technology
0002-2675	Aircraft Illustrated
0002-2683	Aircraft Industry Record
0002-2691	A.O.P.A. Magazine
0002-2705	Airfix
0002-2713	Airframe *changed to* British Aerospace News
0002-2721	Airline Fleet Record
0002-273X	Airline Management and Marketing†
0002-2748	Airline Newsletter
0002-2756	Airman
0002-2764	Airman's Information Manual. Part 1. Basic Flight Manual and ATC Procedures *changed to* Airman's Information Manual. Official Guide to Basic Flight Information and A T C Procedures
0002-2772	Airman's Information Manual. Part 2: Airport Directory†
0002-2802	Airport Forum
0002-2829	Airport Services Management
0002-2853	Airports International *see* 0261-6513
0002-287X	Airways *see* 0032-0617
0002-2888	Airways International†
0002-2926	Aiton Review†
0002-2942	Asian Economies
0002-2950	Ajour *changed to* Ajour-Industri-Teknikk
0002-2969	Biologicheskii Zhurnal Armenii
0002-2977	Akademie der Wissenschaften und der Literatur. Geistes- und Sozialwissenschaftliche Klasse. Abhandlungen
0002-2985	Akademie der Wissenschaften und der Literatur, Mainz. Klasse der Literatur. Abhandlungen
0002-2993	Akademie der Wissenschaften und der Literatur, Mainz. Mathematisch-Naturwissenschaftliche Klasse. Abhandlungen
0002-3000	Akademische Monatsblaetter
0002-3019	Akademischer Dienst
0002-3027	Akademiya Meditsinskikh Nauk S.S.S.R. Vestnik
0002-3035	Akademiya Nauk Armyanskoi S.S.R. Izvestiya. Seriya Fizika
0002-3043	Akademiya Nauk Armyanskoi S.S.R. Izvestiya. Seriya Matematika
0002-3051	Akademiya Nauk Armyanskoi S.S.R. Izvestiya. Seriya Mekhanika
0002-306X	Akademiya Nauk Armyanskoi S.S.R. Izvestiya. Seriya Tekhnicheskikh Nauk
0002-3078	Akademiya Nauk Azerbaidzhanskoi S.S.R. Doklady
0002-3086	Akademiya Nauk Azerbaidzhanskoi S.S.R. Izvestiya. Seriya Biologicheskikh Nauk
0002-3094	Akademiya Nauk Azerbaidzhanskoi S.S.R. Izvestiya. Seriya Ekonomicheskikh Nauk

ISSN INDEX

ISSN	Title
0002-3108	Akademiya Nauk Azerbaidzhanskoi S.S.R. Izvestiya. Seriya Fiziko-Tekhnicheskikh i Matematicheskikh Nauk
0002-3116	Akademiya Nauk Azerbaidzhanskoi S.S.R. Izvestiya. Seriya Istoriya, Filosofiya i Pravo
0002-3124	Akademiya Nauk Azerbaidzhanskoi S.S.R. Izvestiya. Seriya Nauki o Zemle
0002-3132	Akademiya Nauk Azerbaidzhanskoi S.S.R. Izvestiya. Seriya Yazykoznanie, Literatura i Iskusstvo
0002-3140	Akademiya Nauk Estonskoi S.S.R. Izvestiya. Fizika. Matematika
0002-3159	Akademiya Nauk Estonskoi S.S.R. Izvestiya. Obshchestvennye Nauki
0002-3167	Akademiya Nauk Gruzinskoi S.S.R. Soobshcheniya
0002-3175	Akademiya Nauk Kazakhskoi S.S.R. Izvestiya. Seriya Geologicheskaya
0002-3183	Akademiya Nauk Kazakhskoi S.S.R. Izvestiya. Seriya Biologicheskaya
0002-3191	Akademiya Nauk Kazakhskoi S.S.R. Izvestiya. Seriya Fiziko - Matematicheskaya
0002-3205	Akademiya Nauk Kazakhskoi S.S.R. Izvestiya. Seriya Khimicheskaya
0002-3213	Akademiya Nauk Kazakhskoi S.S.R. Vestnik
0002-3221	Akademiya Nauk Kirgizskoi S.S.R. Izvestiya
0002-3248	Akademiya Nauk Latviiskoi S.S.R. Izvestiya. Seriya Khimicheskaya
0002-3264	Akademiya Nauk S.S.S.R. Doklady
0002-3299	Akademiya Nauk S.S.S.R. Institut Geologii Rudnykh Mestorozhdenii, Petrografii, Mineralogii i Geokhimii. Trudy†
0002-3302	Institut Teoreticheskoi Astronomii. Byulleten'
0002-3310	Akademiya Nauk S.S.S.R. Izvestiya. Energetika i Transport
0002-3329	Akademiya Nauk S.S.S.R. Izvestiya. Seriya Biologicheskaya
0002-3337	Akademiya Nauk S.S.S.R. Izvestiya. Seriya Fizika Zemli
0002-3345	Akademiya Nauk S.S.S.R. Izvestiya. Seriya Geologicheskaya
0002-3353	Akademiya Nauk S.S.S.R. Izvestiya. Seriya Khimicheskaya
0002-3361	Akademiya Nauk S.S.S.R. Izvestiya. Seriya Matematicheskaya
0002-337X	Akademiya Nauk S.S.S.R. Izvestiya. Seriya Neorganicheskie Materialy
0002-3388	Akademiya Nauk S.S.S.R. Izvestiya. Tekhnicheskaya Kibernetika
0002-3418	Akademiya Nauk S.S.S.R. Sibirskoe Otdelenie. Izvestiya. Seriya Biologicheskikh i Meditsinskikh Nauk
0002-3426	Akademiya Nauk S.S.S.R. Sibirskoe Otdelenie. Izvestiya. Seriya Khimicheskikh Nauk
0002-3434	Akademiya Nauk S.S.S.R. Sibirskoe Otdelenie. Izvestiya. Seriya Tekhnicheskikh Nauk
0002-3442	Akademiya Nauk S.S.S.R. Vestnik
0002-3450	Akademiya Nauk S.S.S.R. Institut Okeanologii. Trudy
0002-3469	Akademiya Nauk Tadzhikskoi S.S.R. Doklady
0002-3477	Akademiya Nauk Tadzhikskoi S.S.R. Izvestiya. Otdelenie Biologicheskikh Nauk
0002-3485	Akademiya Nauk Tadzhikskoi S.S.R. Izvestiya. Otdelenie Fiziko-Matematicheskikh i Geologo-Khimicheskikh Nauk
0002-3493	Akademiya Nauk Turkmenskoi S.S.R. Izvestiya. Seriya Biologicheskikh Nauk
0002-3507	Akademiya Nauk Turkmenskoi S.S.R. Izvestiya. Seriya Fiziko-Tekhnicheskikh, Khimicheskikh i Geologicheskikh Nauk
0002-3515	Akademiya Nauk S.S.S.R. Izvestiya. Seriya Fizika Atmosfery i Okeana
0002-354X	Akademiya Nauk Belarusskoi S.S.R. Doklady
0002-3558	Akademiya Navuk Belarusskai S.S.R. Vesti. Seryya Biyalagichnykh Navuk
0002-3566	Akademiya Navuk Belarusskai S.S.R. Vestsi. Seryya Fizika-Tekhnichnykh Navuk
0002-3574	Akademiya Navuk Belarusskai S.S.R. Vestsi. Seryya Fizika-Matematychnykh Navuk
0002-3590	Akademiya Navuk Belarusskai S.S.R. Vestsi. Seryya Khimichnykh Navuk
0002-3612	Akaroa Mail
0002-3620	Akashi
0002-3639	Akhand Anand
0002-3655	Akher Saa
0002-368X	Akita Journal of Rural Medicine
0002-3698	Akrides
0002-3701	Akron Dental Society. Bulletin
0002-371X	Akron Law Review
0002-3728	Akros†
0002-3744	Aktie
0002-3752	Die Aktiengesellschaft
0002-3760	Aktion†
0002-3787	Aktualne Problemy Informacji i Dokumentacji
0002-3809	Aktuelle Freie Praxis†
0002-3825	Aktuelle Kulturpolitik†
0002-3833	Aktuelle Probleme der Buergerlichen Philosophie see 0138-2721
0002-3841	Aktuelle Sammlung†
0002-385X	Aktuelle Steuer-Informationen changed to Steuer-Telex
0002-3884	Aktuellt Politik och Samhaelle see 0345-0635
0002-3892	Akuntansi & Administrasi
0002-3914	Akusticheskii Zhurnal
0002-3922	Akvariet
0002-3930	Akvarium a Terarium
0002-3949	Akwesasne Notes
0002-3957	Akzente
0002-3965	Ousbou' al-Arabi
0002-3973	Al-Abhath
0002-3981	Ahad
0002-399X	Dirasat al-Islamiyah
0002-4015	Ma'arif
0002-4023	Al-Machriq†
0002-4031	Arab Academy of Damascus. Journal
0002-4058	Al-Maskukat
0002-4066	Ai Nostri Amici
0002-4074	Ta'awun
0002-4082	Turath al-Sha'bi
0002-4090	A L A
0002-4112	Alabama Academy of Science. Journal
0002-4120	Alabama Architect†
0002-4139	Alabama Association of Secondary School Principals. Bulletin
0002-4147	Alabama Baptist Historian
0002-4155	Alabama Builder
0002-4163	Alabama Business†
0002-4171	Alabama Conservation
0002-418X	Alabama Contractor
0002-4198	Alabama Dental Association. Journal
0002-421X	Alabama Food Merchants Journal
0002-4228	Alabama Forest Products see 0275-6625
0002-4236	Alabama Historical Quarterly†
0002-4252	Alabama Journal of Medical Sciences
0002-4260	Alabama Junior College Librarian changed to Alabama Junior College Library Association Newsletter
0002-4279	Alabama Law Review
0002-4287	Alabama Lawyer
0002-4295	Alabama Librarian
0002-4309	Alabama Municipal Journal
0002-4325	Alabama Purchasor
0002-4333	Alabama Retail Trade see 0002-4163
0002-4341	Alabama Review
0002-435X	Alabama School Journal
0002-4368	Alabama Social Welfare†
0002-4384	Alabama Trucker
0002-4392	Alam Attijarat
0002-4406	Alambre
0002-4414	Alameda-Contra Costa Medical Association. Bulletin
0002-4422	Alamo
0002-4430	Alan Watts Journal†
0002-4465	Alaska Conservation Review†
0002-4473	Alaska Construction and Oil Report changed to Alaska Construction & Oil
0002-449X	Alaska Industry changed to Alaska Business and Industry
0002-4503	Alaska Journal†
0002-4511	Alaska Land Lines changed to Alaska's Resources
0002-452X	Alaska Law Journal changed to Alaska Bar Rag
0002-4546	Alaska Nurse
0002-4554	A M U Press Alaskana Series (Alaska Methodist University) changed to A P U Press Alaskana Book Series
0002-4562	Alaska Sourdough
0002-4570	Alaska Sourdough
0002-4589	Alaska Teacher changed to Alaska Teacher Newsletter
0002-4597	Alaska's Health and Welfare changed to Alaska. Department of Health and Social Services. Quarterly
0002-4600	Alata Internazionale
0002-4619	Alauda
0002-4627	Alba
0002-4643	Albania Oggi
0002-4651	Albania Report
0002-466X	Albany County Agriculture News changed to Extension News-Albany/Rensselaer/Saratoga/Washington Counties
0002-4678	Albany Law Review
0002-4686	Albany Regional Medical Program. Report†
0002-4708	Albert Einstein Medical Center. Journal†
0002-4716	Alberta Amateur see 0049-5778
0002-4724	Alberta Business Trends see 0317-3925
0002-4740	Alberta Calls
0002-4759	Alberta Conservative†
0002-4767	Alberta Farm Economist†
0002-4775	Alberta Gazette
0002-4783	Alberta Historical Review see 0316-1552
0002-4805	Alberta Journal of Educational Research
0002-4821	Alberta Law Review
0002-483X	Library Association of Alberta. Bulletin†
0002-4848	Alberta Medical Bulletin†
0002-4856	Alberta Magazine see 0228-1082
0002-4872	Alberta Oil and Gas Industry. Monthly Statistics see 0710-6874
0002-4880	Alberta School Trustee changed to Trustee
0002-4902	Alberta Transport Reporter
0002-4910	Albertina Studien†
0002-4929	Albrecht-Thaer-Archiv see 0365-0340
0002-4937	Album
0002-4953	Albuquerque Archaeological Society Newsletter
0002-4961	Albus
0002-497X	Alcalde
0002-4988	Alcan Magazine†
0002-4996	Alcan News†
0002-5003	Alcan Review changed to Aluminum Review
0002-5011	Alchimist†
0002-502X	Alcoholism
0002-5038	Alcoholism Review†
0002-5054	Alcool ou Sante
0002-5062	Alcor
0002-5089	Aldebaran Review
0002-5097	Alderley and Wilmslow and Knutsford Advertiser
0002-5100	Aldrichimica Acta
0002-5119	Aldus†
0002-5127	Aleh
0002-5135	Alemanha Internacional†
0002-5143	Alemas
0002-5151	Alergia
0002-5178	Alerta†
0002-5186	Alerte Atomique
0002-5208	Alexanor
0002-5216	Alfa
0002-5224	Alfred Hitchcock's Mystery Magazine
0002-5232	Algebra and Logic
0002-5240	Algebra Universalis
0002-5267	Algemeen Maconniek Tijdschrift
0002-5275	Algemeen Nederlands Tijdschrift voor Wijsbegeerte
0002-5283	Algemeen Politieblad van het Koninkrijk der Nederlanden
0002-5291	Algeria. Institut Pedagogique National. Bureau de Documentation et d'Information Scolaires Universitaires et Professionnelles. Informations et Documents†
0002-5305	Algeria. Sous-Direction des Statistiques. Bulletin de Statistiques Generales changed to Algeria. Direction des Statistiques et de la Comptabilite Nationale. Bulletin Trimestriel de Statistiques
0002-5313	Algerien en Europe
0002-5321	Universite d'Alger. Publications Scientifiques. Serie A: Mathematiques
0002-533X	Universite d'Alger. Publications Scientifiques. Serie B: Sciences Physiques
0002-5348	Algo
0002-5364	Algol see 0195-5365
0002-5380	Ali Nuove
0002-5399	Alieia
0002-5410	Alimentation au Quebec
0002-5429	Alimentazione Animale see 0390-0487
0002-5445	Aliupseeri see 0355-726X
0002-5453	Alive†
0002-5461	Alive (St. Louis)
0002-547X	Alive(Harrisonburg)†
0002-5488	Alkahest†
0002-5496	Alkohol-Industrie
0002-550X	Alkoholdebatt
0002-5518	Alkoholfraagen see 0345-0732
0002-5526	Alkoholikysymys changed to Mutta
0002-5534	All-Africa Church Music Association. Journal†
0002-5542	All-Church Press Newspapers
0002-5550	All Clear†
0002-5569	All England Law Reports
0002-5577	All Hands†
0002-5585	All-India Anglo-Indian Association. Review
0002-5593	All India Reporter
0002-5607	All Outdoors
0002-5623	All the World
0002-5631	Alla Bottega
0002-564X	Allam- es Jogtudomany
0002-5658	Allattani Kozlemenyek
0002-5666	Alle den Volcke
0002-5674	Alle Hens
0002-5682	Alle Kvinner†
0002-5690	Allegheny County Pharmacist
0002-5704	Allegro
0002-5712	Allemagne d'Aujourd'hui
0002-5720	Allemagne Internationale†
0002-5739	Allen Memorial Art Museum. Bulletin
0002-5747	Allergia
0002-5755	Allergie und Immunologie
0002-5771	Allers
0002-578X	Allers
0002-5798	Allgemeine Bau-Zeitung
0002-5801	Allgemeine Bauzeitung
0002-581X	Allgemeine Deutsche Gesellen-Zeitung†
0002-5828	Allgemeine Deutsche Imkerzeitung
0002-5836	Allgemeine Deutsche Lehrerzeitung see 0342-0671
0002-5852	Allgemeine Forst- und Jagdzeitung
0002-5860	Allgemeine Forstzeitschrift
0002-5879	Allgemeine Forstzeitung changed to Oesterreichische Forstzeitung
0002-5887	Allgemeine Homoeopathische Zeitung
0002-5895	Allgemeine Hotel- und Gaststaetten-Zeitung
0002-5909	Allgemeine Missionsnachrichten changed to Die Weltmission
0002-5917	A P R
0002-5925	Allgemeine Schweizerische Militaerzeitschrift
0002-5933	Allgemeine Sparkasse Linz. Kurz Notiert changed to Allgemeine Sparkasse. Kurz Notiert.
0002-5968	Allgemeine Vermessungs-Nachrichten

ISSN INDEX 1195

0002-5976 Allgemeine Waermetechnik
0002-5984 Nachrichten der Fachorganisationen *see* 0342-3573
0002-5992 Allgemeiner Muehlen-Markt
0002-600X Allgemeiner Samen- und Pflanzen Anzeiger
0002-6018 Allgemeines Statistisches Archiv
0002-6050 Alliance Israelite Universelle en France. Cahiers
0002-6069 Alliance Journal†
0002-6093 Alliance Review
0002-6107 Allied Industrial Worker
0002-6123 Allis-Chalmers Engineering Review†
0002-614X Alloy Digest
0002-6158 Allpress
0002-6166 Allround-Collector Address-List
0002-6174 Allsvensk Samling *changed to* Sverigekontakt
0002-6182 Allt i Hemmet
0002-6190 Allt om Hobby
0002-6204 Allt Om Mat
0002-6212 Alluminio e Nuova Metallurgia *see* 0365-3927
0002-6239 Alma *changed to* Paz e Alegria
0002-6247 Alma Mater†
0002-6255 Almanac of Current World Leaders *see* 0192-6802
0002-6263 Current World Leaders - Biography and News *see* 0192-6802
0002-6271 Almanaque Aeronautico†
0002-628X Almas
0002-6298 Der Almbauer
0002-6301 Aloe
0002-631X Aloft†
0002-6328 Along the Boardwalk†
0002-6336 Alpen
0002-6344 Alpengarten†
0002-6352 Alpenlaendische Bienenzeitung
0002-6379 Alpha *changed to* Prisma
0002-6395 Alpha-Mathematische Schuelerzeitschrift
0002-6409 Alpha News Digest *changed to* Alpha News
0002-6425 Alphabet†
0002-6433 Alphabet†
0002-6441 Alphabetic Subject Index to Petroleum Abstracts
0002-645X Alphian *changed to* Transportation Worldwide
0002-6468 Alpi Venete
0002-6476 Alpine Garden Society. Quarterly Bulletin
0002-6484 Alpinismus *see* 0177-3542
0002-6492 Alpino
0002-6506 Alt for Damerne
0002-6514 Alt-Katholische Kirchenzeitung
0002-6522 Alt-Katholische Kirchenzeitung *changed to* Christien Heute
0002-6530 Microform Review
0002-6549 Alta Direccion
0002-6557 Alta Frequenza
0002-6565 Alte und Moderne Kunst†
0002-6573 Das Altenheim
0002-6611 Alternative
0002-662X Alternative Press Index
0002-6638 Alternatives
0002-6646 Das Altertum
0002-6662 Altra Italia
0002-6670 Der Altsprachliche Unterricht
0002-6689 Aluminum
0002-6697 World Aluminum Abstracts
0002-6700 Johns Hopkins Hospital School of Nursing. Alumni Magazine
0002-6778 Amaru†
0002-6786 Amaterska Scena
0002-6794 Amatersky Film
0002-6816 Amateur Baseball News
0002-6832 Amateur Gardening
0002-6840 Amateur Photographer
0002-6859 Amateur Radio
0002-6867 Amateur Stage
0002-6875 Amateurtuinder
0002-6883 Amateur Winemaker
0002-6905 Ambassade van de U.S.S.R. in Nederland. Informatie-Bulletin†
0002-6913 Ambassador†
0002-6921 Ambassador of Peace *changed to* Young Companion
0002-693X Amber-Hi-Lites
0002-6948 Ambiance de Paris†
0002-6956 Ambience†
0002-6964 Ambienti†
0002-6972 Ambit
0002-6980 Ambix
0002-6999 Ambt en Plicht
0002-7006 Ambulatory Pediatric Association Newsletter
0002-7014 Ameghiniana
0002-7022 Amentia
0002-7049 America
0002-7057 Cooperative America *changed to* America Cooperativa
0002-7065 America: History and Life. Part A: Article Abstracts and Citation
0002-7081 America Indigena
0002-709X America Latina
0002-7103 Woman Physician *see* 0098-8421
0002-712X American Academy of Arts and Sciences. Bulletin
0002-7138 American Academy of Child Psychiatry. Journal
0002-7146 American Academy of Gold Foil Operators. Journal *see* 0361-7734
0002-7154 American Academy of Ophthalmology and Otolaryngology. Transactions *see* 0161-6420
0002-7162 American Academy of Political and Social Science. Annals
0002-7170 Council on the Study of Religion. Bulletin†
0002-7189 American Academy of Religion. Journal
0002-7197 Independent Agent
0002-7200 American Agent and Broker
0002-7219 American Agriculturist and Rural New Yorker *see* 0161-8237
0002-7227 American Aircraft Modeler†
0002-7235 Alumni Register *changed to* Illinois State University Alumni Today
0002-7243 American Analgesia Society. Journal
0002-7251 American Animal Hospital Association Bulletin *see* 0587-2871
0002-726X American Annals of the Deaf
0002-7286 American Anthropological Association. Newsletter *see* 0098-1605
0002-7294 American Anthropologist
0002-7316 American Antiquity
0002-7324 American Archives of Rehabilitation Therapy
0002-7359 American Art Journal
0002-7367 American Artisan†
0002-7375 American Artist
0002-7413 American Association of Colleges for Teacher Education. Bulletin *see* 0731-602X
0002-7421 American Association of Dental Examiners. Board Bulletin
0002-743X American Association of Fund-Raising Counsel. Bulletin *changed to* Fund-Raising Review
0002-7448 American Association of Nurse Anesthetists. Journal *see* 0094-6354
0002-7464 American Association of Petroleum Geologists. Bulletin *see* 0149-1423
0002-7472 American Association of State Libraries. President's Newsletter *see* 0044-9660
0002-7480 American Association of Teacher Educators in Agriculture. Journal
0002-7499 American Association of Teachers of Esperanto Quarterly Bulletin
0002-7502 American Association of Workers for the Blind. Dictionary Catalogue†
0002-7510 American Association of Workers for the Blind. News and Views *changed to* A E R Report
0002-7529 American Astrology
0002-7537 American Astronomical Society. Bulletin
0002-7545 American Automatic Merchandiser
0002-7561 American Banker
0002-757X American Baptist
0002-7596 American Bar Association Journal *see* 0747-0088
0002-760X American Bar News†
0002-7618 American Bard†
0002-7626 American Bee Journal
0002-7634 American Beef Producer†
0002-7642 American Behavioral Scientist
0002-7650 American Benedictine Review
0002-7669 American Bibliography of Agricultural Economics†
0002-7677 American Bicyclist & Motorcyclist
0002-7685 American Biology Teacher
0002-7707 American Book Publishing Record
0002-7715 American Breeds Magazine†
0002-7723 American Brewer†
0002-7731 American Building Supplies†
0002-7766 American Business Law Journal
0002-7774 Report on Alcohol *see* 0161-1267
0002-7782 American Cage-Bird Magazine
0002-7790 American Catholic Historical Society of Philadelphia. Records
0002-7804 American Cemetery
0002-7812 American Ceramic Society Bulletin
0002-7820 American Ceramic Society. Journal *changed to* American Ceramic Society Journal/Communications
0002-7839 American Chamber of Commerce Executives. Journal†
0002-7847 American Chamber of Commerce in Japan. Journal
0002-7863 American Chemical Society. Journal
0002-788X American Choral Foundation. Research Memorandum Series
0002-7898 American Choral Review
0002-7901 American Christmas Tree Growers' Journal *see* 0569-3845
0002-791X American Church News *see* 0149-4244
0002-7928 American Cinematographer
0002-7936 American City *see* 0149-337X
0002-7944 American College Health Association. Journal *see* 0744-8481
0002-7952 A C H A Action
0002-7960 American College of Chest Physicians Bulletin *see* 0149-6719
0002-7979 American College of Dentists. Journal
0002-7987 American College of Foot Orthopedists Newsletter
0002-7995 American College of Neuropsychiatrists. Bulletin
0002-8002 American College of Nurse-Midwives. Bulletin *see* 0091-2182
0002-8010 American College of Physicians. Bulletin *see* 0161-7478
0002-8029 American College of Preventive Medicine Newsletter
0002-8037 American College of Radiology. Bulletin *see* 0098-6070
0002-8045 American College of Surgeons. Bulletin
0002-8053 American Comparative Literature Association Newsletter *changed to* American Comparative Literature Association Newsletter
0002-8061 American Concrete Institute. Journal *see* 0889-3241
0002-8061 American Concrete Institute. Journal *see* 0889-325X
0002-807X American Cooner
0002-8088 American Corrective Therapy Journal
0002-810X American Craftmen's Council Outlook *changed to* A C C Outlook
0002-8118 American Criminal Law Quarterly *see* 0164-0364
0002-8126 American Criminologist†
0002-8134 American Crosby Clipper *changed to* American Clipper
0002-8142 American Dachshund†
0002-8150 American Dahlia Society. Bulletin
0002-8177 American Dental Association. Journal
0002-8185 American Dental Hygienists Association. Journal *see* 0091-3979
0002-8193 American Dialect Society Newsletter
0002-8207 American Dialect Society. Publications
0002-8215 American Dialog†
0002-8223 American Dietetic Association. Journal
0002-8231 American Society for Information Science. Journal
0002-8258 American Drycleaner
0002-8266 American Dyestuff Reporter
0002-8274 American Ecclesiastical Review†
0002-8282 American Economic Review
0002-8290 American Economist
0002-8304 American Education
0002-8312 American Educational Research Journal
0002-8320 American Entomological Society. Transactions
0002-8339 American Esperanto Magazine†
0002-8347 American Stock Exchange Stock Reports
0002-838X American Family Physician
0002-8398 American Farm Bureau Federations Official News Letter *see* 0197-5617
0002-8401 American Farm Youth†
0002-8436 American Fencing
0002-8444 American Fern Journal
0002-8452 American Field
0002-8460 American Film Institute. Education Membership Newsletter†
0002-8487 American Fisheries Society. Transactions
0002-8525 American Flint
0002-8533 American Forensic Association. Journal
0002-8541 American Forests
0002-855X American Foundation for the Blind Newsletter *changed to* A F B News
0002-8568 American Fruit Grower
0002-8576 American Funeral Director
0002-8584 American Gas Association Monthly
0002-8592 American Genealogist
0002-8606 American Geophysical Union. Transactions *see* 0096-3941
0002-8614 American Geriatrics Society. Journal
0002-8622 American-German Review†
0002-8630 American Girl (Inkprint Edition)†
0002-8649 American Glass Review
0002-8657 American Gold News
0002-8665 American Grocer
0002-8681 American Hampshire Herdsman
0002-869X American Harp Journal
0002-8703 American Heart Journal
0002-8711 American Helicopter Society. Journal
0002-872X American Hereford Journal
0002-8738 American Heritage
0002-8746 American Highways *see* 0147-4820
0002-8754 American Histadrut Cultural Exchange Institute. Bulletin†
0002-8762 American Historical Review
0002-8770 American History Illustrated
0002-8789 American Home†
0002-8797 American Horologist and Jeweler *see* 0279-6198
0002-8800 American Horticultural Magazine *see* 0096-4417
0002-8819 American Horticultural Society News and Views *see* 0096-4417
0002-8835 American Hungarian Review†
0002-8843 American Idea†
0002-886X American Import/Export Bulletin *changed to* Global Trade Executive
0002-8886 American Indian Law Newsletter
0002-8894 American Industrial Hygiene Association Journal
0002-8908 American Industry
0002-8916 American Inkmaker
0002-8940 Report on Food Markets *see* 0745-4503
0002-8959 American Institute of Food Distribution. Weekly Digest *see* 0745-4503
0002-8967 American Institute of Homeopathy. Journal
0002-8975 American Institute of Hypnosis. Journal
0002-8983 American Institute of Landscape Architects. Journal†
0002-8991 American Institute of Planners. Journal *see* 0194-4363
0002-9033 American-Israel Economic Horizons
0002-9041 American Jewelry Manufacturer
0002-905X American Jewish Archives
0002-9068 American Jewish Historical Quarterly *see* 0164-0178
0002-9084 American Jewish World
0002-9092 American Journal of Agricultural Economics
0002-9106 American Journal of Anatomy

1196 ISSN INDEX

0002-9114 American Journal of Archaeology
0002-9122 American Journal of Botany
0002-9149 American Journal of Cardiology
0002-9157 American Journal of Clinical Hypnosis
0002-9165 American Journal of Clinical Nutrition
0002-9173 American Journal of Clinical Pathology
0002-919X American Journal of Comparative Law
0002-9203 American Journal of Correction *see* 0190-2563
0002-9211 American Journal of Digestive Diseases *see* 0163-2116
0002-922X American Journal of Diseases of Children
0002-9238 American Journal of E E G Technology
0002-9246 American Journal of Economics and Sociology
0002-9254 American Journal of Enology and Viticulture
0002-9262 American Journal of Epidemiology
0002-9270 American Journal of Gastroenterology
0002-9289 American Journal of Hospital Pharmacy
0002-9297 American Journal of Human Genetics
0002-9300 American Journal of International Law
0002-9319 American Journal of Legal History
0002-9327 American Journal of Mathematics
0002-9335 American Journal of Medical Technology *see* 0741-5397
0002-9343 American Journal of Medicine
0002-9351 American Journal of Mental Deficiency
0002-936X American Journal of Nursing
0002-9378 American Journal of Obstetrics and Gynecology
0002-9386 American Journal of Occupational Therapy *see* 0272-9490
0002-9394 American Journal of Ophthalmology
0002-9416 American Journal of Orthodontics and Oral Surgery *changed to* American Journal of Orthodontics and Pentofacial Orthodontics
0002-9432 American Journal of Orthopsychiatry
0002-9440 American Journal of Pathology
0002-9459 American Journal of Pharmaceutical Education
0002-9467 American Journal of Pharmacy and the Sciences Supporting Health *see* 0730-7780
0002-9475 American Journal of Philology
0002-9483 American Journal of Physical Anthropology
0002-9491 American Journal of Physical Medicine
0002-9505 American Journal of Physics
0002-9513 American Journal of Physiology
0002-9521 American Journal of Proctology *see* 0162-6566
0002-953X American Journal of Psychiatry
0002-9548 American Journal of Psychoanalysis
0002-9556 American Journal of Psychology
0002-9564 American Journal of Psychotherapy
0002-9572 American Journal of Public Health and the Nation's Health *see* 0090-0036
0002-9580 American Journal of Roentgenology, Radium Therapy and Nuclear Medicine *see* 0361-803X
0002-9599 American Journal of Science
0002-9602 American Journal of Sociology
0002-9610 American Journal of Surgery
0002-9629 American Journal of the Medical Sciences
0002-9637 American Journal of Tropical Medicine and Hygiene
0002-9645 American Journal of Veterinary Research
0002-9653 Dimensions in American Judaism†
0002-9688 American Labor†
0002-970X American Landrace *changed to* American Landrace
0002-9718 American Laundry Digest
0002-9726 American Leather Chemists Association. Journal
0002-9734 American Legion Magazine
0002-9742 American Legion Press Association News-Letter
0002-9750 American Legislator†
0002-9769 American Libraries
0002-9777 American Library Association. Adult Services Division Newsletter†
0002-9785 American Library Association. Library Education Division. Newsletter†
0002-9793 American Library Directory Updating Service
0002-9815 American Literary Accents†
0002-9823 American Literary Realism: 1870-1910
0002-9831 American Literature
0002-9858 American Machinist (1963) *changed to* American Machinist & Automated Manufacturing
0002-9866 American Marine Engineer
0002-9874 American Maritime Cases
0002-9882 American Maritime Officer
0002-9890 American Mathematical Monthly
0002-9904 America Mathematical Society. Bulletin. *see* 0273-0979
0002-9912 American Mathematical Society. New Publications *see* 0361-4794
0002-9920 American Mathematical Society. Notices
0002-9939 American Mathematical Society. Proceedings
0002-9947 American Mathematical Society. Transactions
0002-9955 American Medical Association. Journal *see* 0098-7484
0002-9963 American Medical Technologists. Journal *see* 0741-5397
0002-9971 American Medical Writers Association. Bulletin *changed to* A M W A Journal
0002-9998 American Metal Market
0003-0007 American Meteorological Society. Bulletin
0003-0015 American-Mexican Medical Association. Journal
0003-0023 American Microscopical Society. Transactions
0003-0031 American Midland Naturalist
0003-004X American Mineralogist
0003-0066 American Motor Carrier
0003-0074 A M A News *changed to* American Motorcyclist
0003-0082 American Museum Novitates
0003-0090 American Museum of Natural History. Bulletin
0003-0104 American Music Center. Newsletter
0003-0112 American Music Teacher
0003-0139 American Musicological Society. Journal
0003-0147 American Naturalist
0003-0155 American Neptune
0003-0163 American Newspaper Boy *changed to* American Newspaper Carrier
0003-0171 American Notes & Queries
0003-018X American Nuclear Society Transactions
0003-0198 American Nurseryman
0003-0201 American Observer *changed to* Scholastic Update
0003-021X American Oil Chemists' Society. Journal
0003-0228 American Old Time Fiddlers News *changed to* American Fiddlers News
0003-0236 American Opinion *changed to* New American
0003-0244 American Optometric Association. Journal
0003-0252 American Orchid Society Bulletin
0003-0279 American Oriental Society. Journal
0003-0287 American Osteopathic Association. Journal *see* 0098-6151
0003-0295 American Oxonian
0003-0309 American Paint and Wallpaper Dealer *see* 0199-4328
0003-0317 American Paint Journal *see* 0098-5430
0003-0325 American Painting Contractor
0003-0333 American Paper Industry *see* 0161-1364
0003-0341 American Paper Institute. Monthly Statistical Summary *changed to* Paper, Paperboard, & Wood Pulp. Monthly Statistical Summary
0003-0376 American Pen†
0003-0392 American Perfumer and Cosmetics *see* 0361-4387
0003-0406 Abstracts of Air and Water Conservation Literature†
0003-0422 Abstracts of Refining Literature *changed to* A P I Abstracts/Literature
0003-0430 American Petroleum Institute. Abstracts of Refining Patents *changed to* A P I Abstracts/Patents
0003-0457 American Petroleum Institute. Division of Statistics & Economics. Weekly Statistical Bulletin *changed to* American Petroleum Institute. Division of Statistics. Weekly Statistical Bulletin
0003-0465 American Pharmaceutical Association. Journal *see* 0160-3450
0003-0473 American Philatelist
0003-0481 American Philosophical Quarterly
0003-049X American Philosophical Society. Proceedings
0003-0503 American Physical Society. Bulletin
0003-0511 American Pigeon Journal
0003-052X American Place Theatre. News†
0003-0538 American Podiatry Association. Journal *changed to* American Podiatric Medical Association. Journal
0003-0546 American Poet
0003-0554 American Political Science Review
0003-0562 American Polygraph Association. Journal *see* 0197-7024
0003-0570 American Portuguese Cultural Society. Journal *see* 0098-4981
0003-0589 American Potato Journal
0003-0619 American Primrose, Primula and Auricula Society, Quarterly *see* 0162-6671
0003-0627 Pharmacy Times
0003-0635 American Protestant Hospital Association. Bulletin *changed to* American Protestant Health Association. Bulletin
0003-0651 American Psychoanalytic Association. Journal
0003-066X American Psychologist
0003-0678 American Quarterly
0003-0686 American Racing Pigeon News
0003-0694 American Railway Engineering Association. Bulletin
0003-0708 American Rationalist
0003-0716 American Record Guide
0003-0724 American Recorder
0003-0732 American Red Cross Youth Journal†
0003-0740 American Red Cross Youth News *changed to* Young Horizons
0003-0775 American Report†
0003-0791 American Review of Eastern Orthodoxy
0003-0805 American Review of Respiratory Disease
0003-0813 American Review of World Health†
0003-0821 American Rhododendron Society. Quarterly Bulletin *see* 0745-7839
0003-083X American Rifleman
0003-0848 American Risk and Insurance Association. Commission on Insurance Terminology. Bulletin†
0003-0856 American Road Builder *see* 0149-4511
0003-0864 American Rock Garden Society Bulletin
0003-0872 American Rodding†
0003-0899 American Rose Magazine
0003-0902 American Salesman
0003-0910 American Scandinavian Review *see* 0098-857X
0003-0929 American Scene *see* 0730-5036
0003-0937 American Scholar
0003-0945 American School & University
0003-0953 American School Board Journal
0003-0961 American School News†
0003-097X American Schools of Oriental Research. Bulletin
0003-0988 American Scientific Affiliation. Journal: Evangelical Perspectives on Science and Christian Faith *changed to* Perspectives on Science and Christian Faith
0003-0996 American Scientist
0003-1003 American Secondary Education
0003-1011 American Security Council Washington Report†
0003-102X American Sephardi
0003-1038 American Shoemaking
0003-1046 American Small Stock Farmer†
0003-1054 American Society for Geriatric Dentistry. Journal
0003-1062 American Society for Horticultural Science. Journal
0003-1070 American Society for Psychical Research. Journal
0003-1089 American Society for the Study of Orthodontics. Journal†
0003-1097 American Society Legion of Honor Magazine *see* 0270-3793
0003-1100 American Society of Civil Engineers. Engineering Mechanics Division. Newsletter†
0003-1119 American Society of Civil Engineers. Proceedings
0003-1135 American Society of Civil Engineers. Structural Division. Newsletter†
0003-1143 American Society of Civil Engineers. Surveying & Mapping Division. Newsletter†
0003-1151 American Society of Civil Engineers. Waterways & Harbors Division. Newsletter†
0003-116X American Society of Farm Managers and Rural Appraisers. Journal
0003-1178 American Society of Newspaper Editors. Bulletin
0003-1186 American Society of Papyrologists. Bulletin
0003-1194 American Society of Psychosomatic Dentistry and Medicine. Journal *see* 0884-8297
0003-1208 American Society of Safety Engineers. Journal *see* 0099-0027
0003-1216 American Society of Sugar Beet Technologists. Journal
0003-1224 American Sociological Review
0003-1232 American Sociologist†
0003-1240 American Soft Drink Journal†
0003-1259 American Sokol
0003-1275 Soybean Profits†
0003-1283 American Speech
0003-1291 American Statistical Association. Journal *see* 0162-1459
0003-1305 American Statistician
0003-1313 American String Teacher
0003-1321 American Studies International
0003-1348 American Surgeon
0003-1356 American Surgical Dealer†
0003-1372 American Symphony Orchestra League. Newsletter *see* 0271-2687
0003-1380 American Teacher
0003-1399 American Theological Library Association. Newsletter
0003-1402 American Theosophist
0003-1410 American Transcendental Quarterly *see* 0149-9017
0003-1429 American Translator†
0003-1437 American Trial Lawyers Association Newsletter *see* 0364-8125
0003-1445 American Turf Monthly
0003-1453 American University Law Review
0003-1461 American Vegetable Grower
0003-147X American Vegetarian-Hygienist†
0003-1488 American Veterinary Medical Association. Journal
0003-1496 American Vocational Journal *changed to* Vocational Education Journal
0003-150X American Water Works Association. Journal
0003-1518 American Way
0003-1534 American West
0003-1550 American Zionist
0003-1569 American Zoologist
0003-1585 America's First Zoo *see* 0003-3537
0003-1593 America's Future
0003-1607 America's Textile Reporter†
0003-1615 The Americas
0003-1631 Amerikas Latvietis†
0003-1666 Amersfoortse Stemmen†
0003-1674 A M E X *changed to* A M E X Canada
0003-1682 Amgueddfa†
0003-1690 Amherst Alumni News *changed to* Amherst

ISSN INDEX 1197

0003-1704 Ami du Peuple
0003-1712 Amica *changed to* A M I C A Bulletin
0003-1720 Amicizia
0003-1739 Amicizia Ebraico-Cristiana di Firenze. Bollettino
0003-1747 Amico dell'Arte Cristiana
0003-1755 Amiga
0003-1763 Aminco Laboratory News†
0003-1771 Amis-Coop
0003-178X Amis de Han Ryner. Cahiers
0003-1798 Amis de la Radiesthesie
0003-1801 Amis de l'I.B.A.N.A. (Publication) *changed to* Ecole Nationale Superieure de Biologie Appliquee a la Nutrition et a l'Alimentation. Cahiers
0003-181X Amis de Milosz
0003-1828 Amis de Napoleon 3rd. Bulletin Interne *changed to* Nouveaux Cahiers du Second Empire
0003-1844 Amis des Roses
0003-1852 Amis du Chateau de Pau. Bulletin
0003-1860 Amis du Film et de la Television *changed to* Visions
0003-1879 Amistad†
0003-1887 S O S Amitie France. Bulletin National
0003-1895 Amities Catholiques Francaises
0003-1909 Amities Spirituelles. Bulletin
0003-1917 Amministrazione Socialista†
0003-1933 Amnesty Action
0003-1941 Amnesty International Monthly *see* 0308-6887
0003-195X Among Friends
0003-1968 Among Ourselves
0003-1984 Amor Artis Bulletin†
0003-1992 Amperland
0003-200X Amphora
0003-2018 Ampleforth Journal
0003-2026 Ampo
0003-2034 Amposta
0003-2042 Ampul
0003-2069 Amsterdam in de Markt†
0003-2077 Amsterdam-Rotterdam Bank. Economic Quarterly Review†
0003-2093 Kursblatt der Amtlich Nicht Notierten Wertpapiere - Geregelter Freiverkehr an der Wiener Boerse
0003-2107 Amtliche Veterinaernachrichten
0003-2115 Amtlicher Anzeiger
0003-2131 Amtliches Kreisblatt fuer den Kreis Herzogtum Lauenburg
0003-214X Berliner Wertpapierboerse. Amtliches Kursblatt
0003-2158 Wertpapierboerse in Stuttgart. Amtliches Kursblatt *changed to* Baden - Wuerttembergische Wertpapierboerse zu Stuttgart. Amtliches Kursblatt
0003-2166 Wiener Warenboerse. Amtliches Kursblatt. Holz
0003-2174 Wiener Warenboerse. Amtliches Kursblatt. Rohhaeute und Felle, Leder Treibriemen und Technische Lederartikel
0003-2190 Amtliches Schulblatt fuer den Regierungsbezirk Duesseldorf
0003-2204 Amtliches Schulblatt fuer die Volks-, Real- und Berufsschulen fuer den Bezirksregierung Trier
0003-2220 Amtsblatt der Oesterreichischen Justizverwaltung
0003-2239 Amtsblatt der Stadt Kapfenberg
0003-2247 Wels, Stadt. Amtsblatt
0003-2255 Wiener Neustadt. Amtsblatt der Stadt *changed to* Wiener Neustadt. Amtsblatt der Statutarstadt
0003-2263 Germany (Federal Republic, 1949-) Bundesminister fuer das Post- und Fernmeldewesen. Amtsblatt
0003-2271 Amtsblatt fuer das Land Vorarlberg
0003-228X Amtsblatt fuer den Regierungsbezirk Aurich†
0003-2328 Amtsblatt fuer die Erzdioezese Bamberg
0003-2336 Der Amtsvormund
0003-2344 Amusement Business
0003-2360 An Lef Kernewek†
0003-2379 An-Nahar Arab Report *changed to* An-Nahar Arab Report and Memo
0003-2387 Al-Nashra *see* 0889-8731
0003-2409 Anaesthesia
0003-2417 Der Anaesthesist
0003-2425 Anais Azevedos†
0003-2441 Anais de Farmacia e Quimica de Sao Paulo
0003-245X Anais Paulistas de Medicina e Cirurgia
0003-2468 Analecta Bollandiana
0003-2476 Analecta Cisterciensia
0003-2484 Anales Cientificos
0003-2492 Anales de Bromatologia
0003-2506 Anales de Mecanica y Electricidad
0003-2514 Anales de Medicina *changed to* Anales de Medicina
0003-2530 Anales del Instituto Corachan
0003-2549 Anales del Servicio de Psiquiatria
0003-2557 Anales Espanoles de Odontoestomatologia†
0003-2565 Beogradski Univerzitet. Pravni Fakultet. Anali
0003-2573 Analise Social
0003-2581 Analisis-Confirmado
0003-259X Analisis de Actualidades Societicas†
0003-2603 Analog Science Fact-Science Fiction *see* 0161-2328
0003-262X Analyse et Prevision *see* 0337-307X
0003-2638 Analysis
0003-2646 Analysis of Current Developments in the Soviet Union†
0003-2654 Analyst
0003-2662 Analyst
0003-2670 Analytica Chimica Acta
0003-2689 Analytical Abstracts
0003-2697 Analytical Biochemistry
0003-2700 Analytical Chemistry
0003-2700 Laboratory Guide to Instruments, Equipment and Chemicals. Lab Guide
0003-2719 Analytical Letters *changed to* Analytical Letters: Chemical Analysis/ Clinical and Biomedical Analysis
0003-2727 Anaqueles†
0003-2751 Anarchy†
0003-276X Anatomical Record
0003-2778 Anatomical Society of India. Journal
0003-2786 Anatomischer Anzeiger
0003-2794 Anbar Management Services Abstracts *see* 0001-4796
0003-2794 Anbar Management Services Abstracts *see* 0049-4100
0003-2794 Anbar Management Services Abstracts *see* 0305-067X
0003-2794 Anbar Management Services Abstracts *see* 0305-0653
0003-2808 Anbar Management Services Bibliography *see* 0261-0108
0003-2816 Anbar Management Services Joint Index *see* 0261-0094
0003-2824 Anblick
0003-2832 Anchor *changed to* Golden Gate Aquarist
0003-2840 Anchor
0003-2867 Ancilla *changed to* Mirjam
0003-2883 Ancora†
0003-2891 Andar per Ceramiche
0003-2905 Andean Air Mail and Peruvian Times†
0003-2913 Andelsbladet
0003-2921 Esotera
0003-293X Anderson College News *changed to* Signatures
0003-2948 Andes
0003-2956 Andhra Agricultural Journal
0003-2964 Andhra Pradesh Productivity Council. Target
0003-2972 Andover Newton Quarterly†
0003-2980 Andrews University Seminary Studies
0003-2999 Anesthesia and Analgesia
0003-3006 Anesthesia Progress
0003-3014 Anesthesie, Analgesie, Reanimation *see* 0750-7658
0003-3022 Anesthesiology
0003-3030 Ange Gardien
0003-3049 Angeiologie
0003-3057 Angel Hair†
0003-3073 Angheliaforos *changed to* Anichti Orizontes-Angheliaforos
0003-3081 Angelicum
0003-3103 Angels†
0003-3138 Angewandte Kosmetik *see* 0342-2968
0003-3146 Angewandte Makromolekulare Chemie
0003-3154 Angewandte Ornithologie
0003-3162 Angewandte Parasitologie
0003-3170 Angiologia
0003-3189 Angiologica *see* 0303-6847
0003-3197 Angiology
0003-3200 Angiopatias
0003-3219 Angle Orthodontist
0003-3227 Angler Tierzucht *see* 0171-7383
0003-3235 Anglers' Digest
0003-3243 Angler's Mail
0003-3251 Anglia
0003-326X Anglica
0003-3278 Anglican Digest
0003-3286 Anglican Theological Review
0003-3308 Angling Times
0003-3316 Anglo American Trade News *changed to* Atlantic
0003-3324 Anglo-Continental Dental Society. Journal *changed to* Journal of Restorative Dentistry
0003-3332 Anglo-German Medical Review†
0003-3340 Anglo-German Review
0003-3359 Anglo-Israel Trade Journal *see* 0260-3985
0003-3367 Anglo-Jewish Art and History†
0003-3375 Anglo-Norwegian Trade Journal
0003-3383 Anglo-Spanish Quarterly Review
0003-3391 Anglo Swiss Times†
0003-3405 Anglo-Welsh Review
0003-3413 Angola. Direccao dos Servicos de Estatistica. Boletim Mensal
0003-343X Instituto de Investigacao Cientifica de Angola. Relatorios e Communicacoes
0003-3448 Laboratorio de Engenharia de Angola. Boletim Informativo†
0003-3456 Angola. Direccao Provincial dos Servicos de Geologia e Minas. Boletim
0003-3464 Angora Goat & Mohair Journal
0003-3472 Animal Behaviour
0003-3480 Animal Blood Groups and Biochemical Genetics *see* 0268-9146
0003-3499 Animal Breeding Abstracts
0003-3502 Animal Health *see* 0142-6591
0003-3510 Animal Health Age†
0003-3537 Animal Kingdom
0003-3545 Animal Life†
0003-3553 Animal Nutrition and Health *changed to* Animal Health & Nutrition
0003-3561 Animal Production
0003-357X Animal Protection *changed to* A S P C A Report
0003-3588 Animal Science Journal of Pakistan *changed to* Bangladesh Journal of Animal Science
0003-3596 Animal Welfare Institute. Information Report *see* 0743-0841
0003-360X Animaldom
0003-3618 Wildlife *see* 0265-3656
0003-3634 Animals: Defender and Anti-Vivisection News *changed to* Campaigner & Animal's Defender
0003-3642 Animals Magazine *changed to* Animal Forum
0003-3650 Animaux de Laboratoire. Revue Bibliographique†
0003-3669 Animo
0003-3685 Ankara Universitesi. Veteriner Fakultesi. Dergisi
0003-3707 Ankh†
0003-3715 Anleggsmaskinen
0003-3723 Ann Arbor Argus†
0003-3731 Ann Arbor Review†
0003-3758 Annabel
0003-3766 Annabella
0003-3774 Annabelle *changed to* Annabelle
0003-3790 Annals of Science
0003-3804 Annalen der Physik
0003-3839 Annales Agronomiques†
0003-3847 Annales Botanici Fennici
0003-3855 Annales Chirurgiae et Gynaecologiae Fenniae *see* 0355-9521
0003-3863 Annales Collegii Medici Antverpiensis
0003-3871 Annales d'Anatomie Pathologique *see* 0242-6498
0003-388X Annales de Biologie Animale, Biochimie, Biophysique *see* 0181-1916
0003-3898 Annales de Biologie Clinique
0003-3901 Annales de Bourgogne
0003-391X Annales de Bretagne et des Pays de l'Ouest (Anjou, Maine, Touraine)
0003-3928 Annales de Cardiologie et d'Angeiologie
0003-3936 Annales de Chimie *see* 0151-9107
0003-3944 Annales de Chirurgie
0003-3952 Annales de Chirurgie Infantile *see* 0180-5738
0003-3960 Annales de Chirurgie Plastique
0003-3979 Societe Francaise de Dermatologie et de Syphiligraphie. Bulletin *see* 0151-9638
0003-3987 Anales de Edafologia y Agrobiologia
0003-3995 Annales de Genetique
0003-4002 Annales de Genetique et de Selection Animale *see* 0754-0264
0003-4010 Annales de Geographie
0003-4029 Annales de Geophysique *changed to* Annales de Geophysicae
0003-4037 Annales de la Nutrition et de l'Alimentation†
0003-4045 Annales de la Propagation de la Foi *see* 0336-335X
0003-4053 Annales de l'Amelioration des Plantes†
0003-4061 Annales de l'Anesthesiologie Francaise†
0003-407X Annales de l'Economie Collective *changed to* Annales de l'Economie Publique, Sociale et Cooperative
0003-4088 Annales de Limnologie
0003-4096 Annales de Medecine et de Pharmacie de Reims *see* 0301-4444
0003-410X Annales de Medecine Interne
0003-4118 Annales de Medecine Veterinaire
0003-4126 Annales de Medecine des Accidents et du Trafic Traumatologie
0003-4134 Annales de Normandie
0003-4142 Annales de Paleontologie *see* 0753-3969
0003-4150 Annales de Parasitologie Humaine et Comparee
0003-4169 Annales de Physique
0003-4177 Annales de Phytopathologie†
0003-4185 Annales de Radiologie
0003-4193 Annales de Recherches Veterinaires
0003-4207 Annales de Sciences Economiques Appliquees
0003-4215 Annales de Speleologie†
0003-4223 Annales de Technologie Agricole *changed to* Sciences des Aliments
0003-4231 Annales de Zoologie- Ecologie Animale†
0003-424X Annales de Zootechnie
0003-4266 Annales d'Endocrinologie
0003-4274 Annales des Falsifications de l'Expertise Chimique et Toxicologique
0003-4282 Annales des Mines
0003-4290 Annales des Mines de Belgique
0003-4312 Annales des Sciences Forestieres
0003-4320 Annales des Sciences Naturelles. Botanique et Biologie Vegetale
0003-4339 Annales des Sciences Naturelles. Zoologie et Biologie Animale
0003-4347 Annales des Telecommunications
0003-4355 Annales d'Histochimie *see* 0145-5680
0003-4363 Annales d'Hygiene de Langue Francaise *changed to* Medecine et Nutrition
0003-4371 Annales d'Oculistique *see* 0181-5512
0003-438X Annales d'Oto-Laryngologie et de Chirurgie Cervico Faciale
0003-4398 Annales du Midi
0003-4401 Annales d'Urologie
0003-441X Annales - Economies, Societes, Civilisations
0003-4428 Annales Entomologici Fennici
0003-4436 Annales Historiques de la Revolution Francaise
0003-4444 Annales Homeopathiques Francaises *changed to* Homeopathie
0003-4452 Annales Internationales de Criminologie

1198 ISSN INDEX

0003-4460 Annales Medicales de Nancy
0003-4479 Annales Medicinae Experimentalis et Biologiae Fenniae *see* 0302-2137
0003-4487 Annales Medico-Psychologiques
0003-4495 Annales Paediatrici Japonici
0003-4509 Annales Pharmaceutiques Francaises
0003-4517 Annales Scientifiques Textiles Belges†
0003-4525 Annales Textiles†
0003-4533 Annales Universitatis Saraviensis. Reihe: Medizin *changed to* Annales Universitatis Saraviensis. Medicinae
0003-4541 Annales Zoologici
0003-455X Annales Zoologici Fennici
0003-4568 Annali della Carita
0003-4576 Annali della Facolta di Agraria
0003-4584 Italy. Ministero della Pubblica Istruzione. Annali della Pubblica Istruzione
0003-4592 Annali di Chimica
0003-4614 Annali di Idrologia†
0003-4622 Annali di Matematica
0003-4630 Annali di Medicina Navale
0003-4649 Annali di Microbiologia ed Enzimologia
0003-4657 Annali di Ostetricia e Ginecologia (1879-1971) *see* 0300-0087
0003-4665 Annali di Ottamologia e Clinica Oculistica
0003-4673 Annali di Radiologia Diagnostica†
0003-469X Annali Italiani di Chirurgia
0003-4703 Annali Italiani di Dermatologia Clinica e Sperimentale
0003-4711 Annali Italiani di Pediatria†
0003-472X Annali Sclavo *changed to* Annali Sclavo Monograph
0003-4738 Annals of Allergy
0003-4746 Annals of Applied Biology
0003-4762 Annals of Clinical Research
0003-4770 Annals of Dentistry
0003-4789 Annals of General Practice *see* 0300-8495
0003-4800 Annals of Human Genetics
0003-4819 Annals of Internal Medicine
0003-4827 Annals of Iowa
0003-4835 Annals of Library Science and Documentation
0003-4843 Annals of Mathematical Logic *see* 0168-0072
0003-4851 Annals of Mathematical Statistics *see* 0090-5364
0003-486X Annals of Mathematics
0003-4878 Annals of Occupational Hygiene
0003-4886 Annals of Ophthalmology
0003-4894 Annals of Otology, Rhinology and Laryngology
0003-4908 Rheumatology and Physical Medicine *see* 0263-7103
0003-4916 Annals of Physics
0003-4932 Annals of Surgery
0003-4940 Annals of the Holy Childhood *changed to* It's Our World
0003-4967 Annals of the Rheumatic Diseases
0003-4975 Annals of Thoracic Surgery
0003-4983 Annals of Tropical Medicine and Parasitology
0003-4991 Annals of Wyoming
0003-5009 Annals of Zoology
0003-5017 L'Annee Biologique
0003-5033 Annee Psychologique
0003-505X Annonces de l'Industrie
0003-5076 Annotated Bibliography of Economic Geology†
0003-5084 Annotated Bibliography of Literature Produced by the Cooperative Movements in South-East Asia *changed to* Annotated Bibliography of Literature on Cooperative Movements in South-East Asia
0003-5092 Annotationes Zoologica Japonenses *see* 0289-0003
0003-5106 Announced Reprints†
0003-5114 Conference Board. Announcements of Mergers and Acquisitions†
0003-5130 Annual of Animal Psychology
0003-5149 Annuario di Diritto Comparato e di Studi Legislativi
0003-5165 Annunciatore Poligrafico
0003-519X Die Anregung
0003-5203 Annrinya
0003-5211 Anritsu Technical Bulletin
0003-522X Ans Werk
0003-5238 Der Anschnitt†
0003-5246 Ansearchin' News *changed to* Tennessee Genealogical Magazine, "Ansearchin'" News
0003-5254 Ansgarsjunioren *see* 0003-5262
0003-5262 Ansgarsposten
0003-5270 Anstoesse
0003-5289 Anstoss
0003-5300 Answer†
0003-5319 Antaeus
0003-5327 Antarctic
0003-5335 Antarctic Journal of the United States
0003-5351 Antarktiese Bulletin
0003-536X Antena
0003-5378 Antenna *see* 0101-9112
0003-5386 Antenna
0003-5394 Antenne Medicale
0003-5408 Antenni†
0003-5416 Anthologies of the Year *changed to* Poetry of the Year
0003-5424 Anthos
0003-5440 Anthropologiai Kozlemenyek
0003-5459 Anthropologica
0003-5467 Royal Anthropological Institute of Great Britain and Ireland. Library. Anthropological Index *changed to* Anthropological Index to Current Periodicals in the Library of the Museum of Mankind
0003-5475 Anthropological Journal of Canada†
0003-5483 Anthropological Linguistics
0003-5491 Anthropological Quarterly
0003-5505 Anthropological Society of Nippon. Journal
0003-5513 Anthropological Survey of India. Bulletin *changed to* Human Science
0003-5521 L'Anthropologie
0003-5548 Anthropologischer Anzeiger
0003-5556 Anthropologist
0003-5564 Anthropology U C L A
0003-5572 Anthropos
0003-5580 Anti-Apartheid News
0003-5599 Anti-Corrosion Methods and Materials
0003-5602 A R Staatkunde†
0003-5610 Anti-Vivisectionist *changed to* Liberator
0003-5629 Antibiotica
0003-5637 Antibiotiki
0003-5645 Antichita Viva
0003-5653 Antiek
0003-5661 Antigonish Review
0003-567X Antik Tanulmanyok
0003-5688 Antike Kunst
0003-5696 Antike und Abendland
0003-5718 Antilliaanse Nieuwsbrief
0003-5734 Antincendio e Protezione Industriale *changed to* Antincendio
0003-5742 Antioch College Reports *changed to* Antioch Report
0003-5769 Antioch Review
0003-5785 Antiquarian Horology and the Proceedings of the Antiquarian Horological Society
0003-5793 Antiquariat†
0003-5815 Antiquaries Journal
0003-5823 Antique Airplane Association News
0003-5831 Antique Automobile
0003-584X Antique Collecting
0003-5858 Antique Collector
0003-5866 Antique Dealer and Collectors' Guide
0003-5874 Antique Finder *see* 0003-584X
0003-5882 Antique Monthly
0003-5890 Antique Motor News and Atlantic Auto Advertiser *changed to* Collectors Car News
0003-5904 Antique Outboarder
0003-5912 Antique Trader *see* 0161-8342
0003-5939 Antiques *see* 0161-9284
0003-5947 Antiques Dealer
0003-5955 Antiques in Britain *changed to* Antiques Folio
0003-5963 Antiques Journal†
0003-598X Antiquity
0003-5998 Antiseptic
0003-6021 Antitrust & Trade Regulation Report
0003-603X Antitrust Bulletin
0003-6048 Antitrust Law and Economics Review
0003-6056 Antitrust Law Journal
0003-6064 Antonianum
0003-6072 Antonie van Leeuwenhoek Journal of Microbiology and Serology *changed to* Antonie van Leeuwenhoek Journal of Microbiology
0003-6099 Antriebstechnik
0003-6102 Antropologia e Historia de Guatemala (IDAEH)
0003-6110 Antropologica
0003-6129 Antropolognytt *changed to* Antropologiska Studier
0003-6137 Antropos
0003-6145 Antroposofia
0003-6161 Antur
0003-617X Antwerp Bee-Argus
0003-6188 Antwerps Havennieuws†
0003-620X Anukta
0003-6218 Anuvad
0003-6226 Anvil
0003-6234 Das Anwaltbuero†
0003-6242 Anyagmozgatas-Csomagolas
0003-6277 Anzeiger des Oesterreichischen Buchhandels
0003-6285 Anzeiger des Reiches der Gerechtigkeit
0003-6293 Anzeiger fuer die Altertumswissenschaft
0003-6307 Anzeiger fuer Schaedlingskunde und Pflanzenschutz *see* 0340-7330
0003-6315 Anzeiger Solothurn-Lebern
0003-6323 Aomori-ken Nogyo Kisho Junpo
0003-6331 Agriculture in Aomori
0003-634X Apalachee Diary†
0003-6358 Apartment Construction News *see* 0146-0919
0003-6366 Apartment Ideas *see* 0273-2858
0003-6390 Apeiron
0003-6412 Apercu Technique - Technisch Overzicht (A T O)
0003-6420 Aperture
0003-6439 Apex
0003-6455 Apiacta
0003-6471 Apicultor†
0003-648X Apicultural Abstracts
0003-6498 Apka Swasthya
0003-6501 Aplikace Matematiky
0003-651X Aplomb Zero
0003-6528 Apollo *changed to* Oeko.L.
0003-6536 Apollo
0003-6552 Aposento Alto
0003-6560 Apothecary
0003-6579 Apothekersblad
0003-6595 Appalachia
0003-6609 Appalachia Medicine†
0003-6617 Appalachian Lookout†
0003-6625 Appalachian Outlook
0003-6641 Appalachian Trailway News
0003-665X Appaloosa News *changed to* Appaloosa Journal
0003-6668 Apparecchi Elettrodomestici Nella Casa Moderna
0003-6676 Apparecchiature Idrauliche e Pneumatiche *see* 0374-3225
0003-6684 Apparel Executive†
0003-6749 Appel de Saint Vincent de Paul†
0003-6757 Appita
0003-6765 Apple†
0003-6773 Appliance Engineer *see* 0003-6781
0003-6781 Appliance
0003-679X Appliance Manufacturer
0003-6803 Appliance Service News
0003-6811 Applicable Analysis
0003-682X Applied Acoustics
0003-6838 Applied Biochemistry and Microbiology
0003-6846 Applied Economics
0003-6854 Applied Electrical Phenomena†
0003-6862 Applied Entomology and Zoology
0003-6870 Applied Ergonomics
0003-6889 Applied Graphics†
0003-6900 Applied Mechanics Reviews
0003-6919 Applied Microbiology *see* 0099-2240
0003-6935 Applied Optics
0003-6943 Applied Photography†
0003-6951 Applied Physics Letters
0003-696X Applied Plastics†
0003-6978 Journal of Applied Pneumatics
0003-6986 Applied Science and Technology Index
0003-6994 Applied Scientific Research
0003-701X Applied Solar Energy
0003-7028 Applied Spectroscopy
0003-7052 Appraisal
0003-7060 Appraisal Digest
0003-7079 Appraisal Institute Digest
0003-7087 Appraisal Journal
0003-7095 Appraiser
0003-7109 Apprenticeship News
0003-7117 Approach
0003-7125 Approach Magazine†
0003-7133 Approaches; a Periodical of Poems by Kentuckians *changed to* Kentucky Poetry Review
0003-7176 Apres - Demain
0003-7206 Aqua
0003-7222 Aqua Vite
0003-7230 New Aquarian Agent *changed to* Astrology - the New Aquarian Agent
0003-7257 Aquarien Magazin
0003-7265 Die Aquarien- und Terrarien-Zeitschrift
0003-7273 Aquarist and Pondkeeper
0003-729X Aquarium
0003-7303 Aquarius
0003-7311 Aquatic Biology Abstracts *see* 0140-5373
0003-7311 Aquatic Biology Abstracts *see* 0140-5381
0003-7338 Aqueduct News *see* 0092-0622
0003-7362 Aquinas
0003-7370 Ara
0003-7389 Arab
0003-7397 Arab Film and Television Center News
0003-7400 Arab Journal†
0003-7419 Arab News and Views†
0003-7435 Arab Oil Review
0003-7443 Arab Petroleum
0003-7451 A R R
0003-746X Arab Veterinary Medical Association. Journal
0003-7478 Arab World†
0003-7486 Arabian Horse News†
0003-7494 Arabian Horse World
0003-7524 Arable Farmer *see* 0300-2829
0003-7540 Araksha
0003-7559 Araldo di S. Antonio
0003-7567 Aramco World Magazine
0003-7583 Ararat
0003-7591 Arbeidskundig Tijdschrift *changed to* Bedrijfsvoering
0003-7605 Die Arbeit
0003-7613 Die Arbeit†
0003-7621 Arbeit, Beruf, und Arbeitslosenhilfe *changed to* Arbeit und Beruf
0003-763X Arbeit und Leistung *see* 0340-2444
0003-7648 Arbeit und Recht
0003-7656 Arbeit und Wirtschaft
0003-7664 Arbeits- und Sozialrecht
0003-7710 Arbeitsgemeinschaft fuer Jugendpflege und Jugendfuersorge. Mitteilungen *changed to* Forum Jugendhilfe
0003-7729 Arbeitsgemeinschaft Oesterreichischer Entomologen. Zeitschrift
0003-7737 Saarlaendischer Arbeitnehmer *changed to* Arbeitnehmer
0003-7745 Arbeitskreis Holz *see* 0341-0331
0003-7753 Arbeitsmedizin, Sozialmedizin, Arbeitshygiene *see* 0300-581X
0003-7761 Arbeitsrecht in Stichworten
0003-777X Arbeitsrecht und Arbeitslosenversicherung
0003-7796 Arbeitstechnische Merkhefte der Waldarbeit
0003-780X Arbeitsvorbereitung
0003-7818 Arbejdsgiveren
0003-7826 Arbejdslederen
0003-7834 Arbetsmiljoe
0003-7842 Arbetsledaren

ISSN INDEX 1199

0003-7850 Arbetsmarknaden†
0003-7869 Arbiter
0003-7877 Arbitration
0003-7885 Arbitration in the Schools
0003-7893 Arbitration Journal
0003-7907 Arbitro
0003-7915 Arbol de Fuego: Poesia
0003-7931 Arboricultural Association Journal *see* 0307-1375
0003-794X Arboriculture Fruitiere
0003-7958 Arborist's News *changed to* Journal of Arboriculture
0003-7966 Arbos†
0003-7974 L'Arc
0003-7982 Arcadia
0003-7990 Arcadie
0003-8008 Archaeologia Austriaca
0003-8032 Archaeologiai Ertesito
0003-8059 Archaeological Society of Central New York. Bulletin†
0003-8067 Archaeological Society of Delaware. Bulletin
0003-8075 Archaeological Society of Japan. Journal
0003-8091 A S A Newsletter *changed to* A S A Journal
0003-8105 Archaeologischer Anzeiger
0003-8113 Archaeology
0003-8121 Archaeology and Physical Anthropology in Oceania *changed to* Archaeology in Oceania
0003-813X Archaeometry
0003-8148 Archeia tes Pharmakeutikes (Athens)
0003-8156 Archeocivilisation†
0003-8164 Archeologia†
0003-8172 Archeologia Classica
0003-8180 Archeologia Polski
0003-8199 Archeological Newsletter†
0003-8202 Archeological Society of Virginia. Quarterly Bulletin
0003-8210 Archeologie
0003-8229 Archeologie Vivante
0003-8237 Archer†
0003-827X Archery World
0003-8288 Archibald Newsletter†
0003-8296 Archidiocesi di Monreale. Bollettino Ecclesiastico
0003-8326 Archief voor de Geschiedenis van de Katholieke Kerk in Nederland
0003-8369 Archimede
0003-8377 Archimedes†
0003-8385 Archimedes
0003-8393 Architect *changed to* Architect (W.A.)
0003-8407 Architect & Builder
0003-8415 Architect†
0003-8423 Architect & Contractor
0003-8431 Architect and Surveyor *changed to* Architect & Surveyor
0003-844X Architect Consulting Engineer-Product Bulletin Directory *changed to* Product Bulletin Directory.
0003-8458 Architekonike Kai Dikosmese†
0003-8466 Architects' Journal
0003-8490 Architecture Culture
0003-8504 Architectural Design
0003-8512 Architectural Design, Cost and Data *see* 0739-3946
0003-8520 Architectural Digest
0003-8547 Architectural Glass & Aluminium†
0003-8555 Architectural Institute of Japan. Transactions
0003-858X Architectural Record
0003-8598 Architectural Record Newsletter†
0003-8601 Architectural Research and Teaching *changed to* Journal of Architectural Research
0003-861X Architectural Review
0003-8628 Architectural Science Review
0003-8644 Arkhitektura
0003-8652 Architecture and Building Industry
0003-8679 Architecture Canada†
0003-8695 Architecture d'Aujourd'hui (Paris, 1929)
0003-8709 Architecture East Midlands†
0003-8717 Architecture Francaise *changed to* Architecture d'Aujourd'hui (Paris, 1930)
0003-8725 Architecture in Australia *changed to* Architecture Australia
0003-8733 Architecture New Jersey
0003-8741 Architecture Today
0003-875X Der Architekt
0003-8768 Der Architekt und der Bauingenieur
0003-8784 Architektur und Kultiviertes Wohnen *changed to* Architektur und Wohnen
0003-8792 Architektur und Wohnform *see* 0173-8046
0003-8806 Architektur Wettbewerbe *changed to* Architecture & Competitions
0003-8814 Architektura
0003-8830 Architettura
0003-8849 Archiv
0003-8857 Archiv†
0003-8865 Archiv der Gegenwart
0003-8873 Archiv der Internationalen Stefan Zweig-Gesellschaft
0003-8881 Julius Klaus- Stiftung. Archiv *see* 0300-984X
0003-889X Archiv der Mathematik
0003-8911 Archiv des Oeffentlichen Rechts
0003-892X Archiv des Voelkerrechts
0003-8938 Archiv for Pharmaci og Chemi
0003-8946 Archiv fuer Begriffsgeschichte
0003-8962 Archiv fuer das Eisenhuettenwesen *changed to* Steel Research - Archiv fuer das Eisenhuettenwesen
0003-8970 Archiv fuer das Studium der Neueren Sprachen und Literaturen
0003-8989 Archiv fuer Deutsche Postgeschichte
0003-8997 Archiv fuer die Civilistische Praxis
0003-9012 Archiv fuer die Gesamte Virusforschung *see* 0304-8608
0003-9020 Archiv fuer Druck und Papier†
0003-9039 Archiv fuer Elektrotechnik
0003-9047 Archiv fuer Energiewirtschaft
0003-9055 Archiv fuer Experimentelle Veterinaermedizin
0003-9063 Archiv fuer Fischereiwissenschaft
0003-908X Archiv fuer Gartenbau
0003-9098 Archiv fuer Gefluegelkunde
0003-9101 Archiv fuer Geschichte der Philosophie
0003-911X Archiv fuer Geschwulstforschung
0003-9128 Archiv fuer Gynaekologie *see* 0170-9925
0003-9136 Archiv fuer Hydrobiologie
0003-9152 Archiv fuer Japanische Chirurgie
0003-9160 Archiv fuer Katholisches Kirchenrecht
0003-9179 Archiv fuer Kinderheilkunde *see* 0300-8630
0003-9187 Archiv fuer Dermatologische Forschung *see* 0340-3696
0003-9195 Archiv fuer Klinische und Experimentelle Ohren-, Nasen- und Kehlkopfheilkunde *see* 0302-9530
0003-9209 Archiv fuer Kommunalwissenschaften
0003-9225 Archiv fuer Kriminologie
0003-9233 Archiv fuer Kulturgeschichte
0003-925X Archiv fuer Lebensmittelhygiene, Insbesondere fuer Fleisch-, Fisch- und Milchhygiene *changed to* Archiv fuer Lebensmittel Hygiene, Fleisch-, Fisch- und Milchhygiene
0003-9268 Archiv fuer Mathematische Logik und Grundlagenforschung
0003-9276 Archiv fuer Mikrobiologie *see* 0302-8933
0003-9284 Archiv fuer Molluskenkunde
0003-9292 Archiv fuer Musikwissenschaft
0003-9306 Archiv fuer Naturschutz und Landschaftsforschung
0003-9314 Archiv fuer Oeffentliche und Freigemeinnuetzige Unternehmen
0003-9330 Archiv fuer Orthopaedische und Unfallchirurgie *see* 0344-8444
0003-9357 Zeitschrift fuer Physiotherapie
0003-9365 Archiv fuer Protistenkunde
0003-9373 Archiv fuer Psychiatrie und Nervenkrankheiten *see* 0175-758X
0003-9381 Archiv fuer Reformationsgeschichte
0003-9403 Archiv fuer Sippenforschung
0003-9411 Archiv fuer Technisches Messen - A T M *see* 0171-8096
0003-942X Archives of Animal Nutrition
0003-9438 Archiv fuer Tierzucht
0003-9446 Archiv fuer Toxikologie *see* 0340-5761
0003-9462 Archiv fuer Vaterlaendische Geschichte und Topographie
0003-9470 Archiv Ostdeutscher Familienforscher
0003-9489 Archiva Veterinaria†
0003-9497 Archivalische Zeitschrift
0003-9500 Der Archivar
0003-9519 Archive for History of Exact Sciences
0003-9527 Archive for Rational Mechanics and Analysis
0003-9535 Archives
0003-9543 Archives Advocate†
0003-9551 Archives and Manuscripts
0003-956X Archives Belges de Dermatologie et de Syphiligraphie *see* 0301-8636
0003-9578 Archives Belges de Medecine Sociale, Hygiene, Medecine du Travail et Medecine Legale *changed to* Archives Belges de Medecine Sociale et d'Hygiene
0003-9586 Archives d'Anatomie, d'Histologie et d'Embryologie
0003-9594 Archives d'Anatomie Microscopique et de Morphologie Experimentale
0003-9608 Archives d'Anatomie Pathologique *changed to* Archives d'Anatomie et de Cytologie Pathologiques
0003-9616 Archives de Biochimie et Cosmetologie†
0003-9624 Archives de Biologie
0003-9632 Archives de Philosophie
0003-9640 Archives de Psychologie
0003-9659 Archives de Sociologie des Religions *see* 0335-5985
0003-9667 Archives de Zoologie Experimentale et Generale†
0003-9675 Archives des Lettres Modernes
0003-9683 Archives des Maladies du Coeur et des Vaisseaux
0003-9691 Archives des Maladies Professionnelles de Medecine du Travail et de Securite Sociale
0003-9705 Archives des Sciences
0003-9721 Revue Diplomatique *changed to* Archives Diplomatiques et Consulaires
0003-973X Archives d'Ophtalmologie *see* 0181-5512
0003-9748 Archives et Bibliotheques de Belgique
0003-9756 European Journal of Sociology
0003-9764 Archives Francaises de Pediatrie
0003-9772 Archives Francaises des Maladies de l'Appareil Digestif *see* 0399-8320
0003-9780 Archives Internationales de Pharmacodynamie et de Therapie
0003-9799 Archives Internationales de Physiologie et de Biochimie
0003-9802 Archives Internationales de Sociologie de la Cooperation et du Developpement
0003-9810 Archives Internationales d'Histoire des Sciences
0003-9829 Archives Italiennes de Biologie
0003-9837 Archives Juives
0003-9845 Archives Mediterraneennes de Medecine
0003-9853 Archives of American Art. Journal
0003-9861 Archives of Biochemistry and Biophysics
0003-987X Archives of Dermatology
0003-9888 Archives of Diseases in Childhood
0003-9896 Archives of Environmental Health
0003-990X Archives of General Psychiatry
0003-9918 Archives of Hygiene†
0003-9926 Archives of Internal Medicine
0003-9934 Archives of Medical Hydrology
0003-9942 Archives of Neurology
0003-9950 Archives of Ophthalmology
0003-9969 Archives of Oral Biology
0003-9977 Archives of Otolaryngology
0003-9985 Archives of Pathology *see* 0363-0153
0003-9993 Archives of Physical Medicine and Rehabilitation
0004-0002 Archives of Sexual Behavior
0004-0010 Archives of Surgery
0004-0029 Archives of Traditional Music. Trimester Report†
0004-0037 Archives Roumaines de Pathologie Experimentale et de Microbiologie
0004-0053 Archivio Botanico e Biogeografico Italiano
0004-0061 Archivio de Vecchi
0004-007X Archivio di Chirurgia Toracica e Cardiovascolare†
0004-0088 Archivio di Filosofia
0004-0096 Archivio di Fisiologia
0004-010X Archivio di Medicina Interna
0004-0118 Archivio di Ortopedia *changed to* Archivio di Ortopedia e Reumatologia
0004-0126 Archivio di Ostetricia e Ginecologia
0004-0134 Archivio di Ottalmologia *see* 0300-0109
0004-0142 Archivio di Patologia e Clinica Medica†
0004-0150 Archivio di Psicologia, Neurologia e Psichiatria
0004-0169 Archivio di Scienze Biologiche†
0004-0185 Archivio Monaldi per la Tisiologia e le Malattie dell'Apparato Respiratorio
0004-0193 Archivio E. Maragliano di Patologia e Clinica
0004-0207 Archivio Glottologico Italiano
0004-0215 Archivio Italiano delle Malattie dell'Apparato Digerente†
0004-0231 Archivio Italiano di Anatomia e Istologia Patologica†
0004-024X Archivio Italiano di Chirurgia†
0004-0258 Archivo Italiano di Otologia, Rinologia e Laringologia *changed to* Otorinolaringologica
0004-0266 Archivio Italiano di Patologia e Clinica dei Tumori
0004-0274 Archivio Italiano di Pediatria e Puericoltura†
0004-0312 Archivio per le Scienze Mediche *changed to* Gazzetta Medica Italiana Archivio per le Scienze Mediche
0004-0320 Archivio Stomatologico
0004-0339 Archivio Storico Italiano
0004-0347 Archivio Storico Lodigiano
0004-0355 Archivio Storico per la Calabria e la Lucania
0004-0363 Archivio Storico per la Sicilia Orientale
0004-0371 Archivio Storico Ticinese
0004-038X Archivmitteilungen
0004-0398 Archivni Casopis
0004-0401 Archivo de Ciencias Biologicas y Naturales, Teoricas y Aplicadas
0004-041X Archivio di Medicina Mutualistica†
0004-0428 Archivo Espanol de Arte
0004-0444 Archivo Historico de Miraflores. Boletin
0004-0452 Archivo Ibero-Americano
0004-0460 Archivio Italiano di Dermatologia, Venereologia e Sessuologia *changed to* Archivo Italiano di Urologia e Nefrologia
0004-0479 Archivio Veterinario Italiano
0004-0495 Archivos Argentinos de Reumatologia†
0004-0509 Archivos Argentinos de Tisiologia y Neumonologia
0004-0517 Archivos Argentinos Enfermedades del Aparato Digestivo
0004-0525 Archivos Bolivianos de Medicina
0004-0533 Archivos de Biologia y Medicina Experimentales
0004-0541 Archivos de Criminologia, Neuro-Psiquiatria y Disciplinas Conexas
0004-055X Archivos de Historia Potosina
0004-0568 Archivos de Medicina Experimental†
0004-0576 Archivos de Neurobiologia
0004-0584 Archivos de Pediatria del Uruguay
0004-0592 Archivos de Zootecnia
0004-0606 Archivos Dominicanos de Pediatria
0004-0614 Archivos Espanoles de Urologia
0004-0622 Archivos Latinoamericanos de Nutricion
0004-0630 Archivos Leoneses
0004-0649 Archivos Venezolanos de Puericultura y Pediatria
0004-0665 Archivum Franciscanum Historicum
0004-0673 Archivum Heraldicum
0004-0681 Archivum Histologicum Japonicum
0004-069X Archivum Immunologiae et Therapiae Experimentalis
0004-0711 Archiwista

ISSN INDEX

ISSN	Title
0004-072X	Archiwum Automatyki i Telemechaniki
0004-0738	Archiwum Budowy Maszyn†
0004-0754	Archiwum Gornictwa
0004-0762	Archiwum Historii Medycyny
0004-0770	Archiwum Hutnictwa
0004-0789	Archiwum Hydrotechniki
0004-0797	Archiwum Inzynierii Ladowej
0004-0800	Archiwum Mechaniki Stosowanej see 0373-2029
0004-0819	Arcispedale S. Anna di Ferrara†
0004-0835	Arcoscenico
0004-0843	Arctic
0004-0851	Arctic and Alpine Research
0004-086X	Arctic Circular†
0004-0878	Resource Development see 0824-4952
0004-0894	Area
0004-0908	Area Development Magazine
0004-0916	U.S. Department of Labor. Employment and Training Administration. Area Trends in Employment and Unemployment
0004-0932	Arena
0004-0959	Arena
0004-0967	Arepo†
0004-0975	Arethusa
0004-0983	Argentina
0004-0991	Argentina Automotriz
0004-1009	Argentina. Biblioteca del Congreso. Boletin changed to Argentina. Biblioteca del Congreso de la Nacion. Boletin
0004-1017	Argentina. Direccion Nacional de Estadistica y Censos. Boletin de Estadistica see 0325-1969
0004-1025	Argentina. Direccion Nacional de Asistencia Nacional. DAS
0004-1033	Pergamino, Argentine Republic. Estacion Experimental Agropecuario. Boletin de Divulgacion†
0004-1041	Argentina Futuro
0004-105X	Argentina Grafica
0004-1068	Argentina. Ministerio de Trabajo y Prevision. Boletin de Biblioteca see 0403-0133
0004-1076	Argentina. Servicio de Hidrografia Naval. Boletin
0004-1084	Argentine Science Fiction Review
0004-1106	Argentinos Lietuviu Balsas
0004-1114	Argosy†
0004-1130	Argot†
0004-1149	Argument for Frihet och Raett
0004-1157	Das Argument
0004-1165	Argus (Thunder Bay)
0004-1173	Argus
0004-1181	Argus (Bloomington)
0004-119X	Argus des Collectivites
0004-1203	Argus des Pharmaciens
0004-1211	Argus-Journal
0004-122X	Argus Menager see 0019-9354
0004-1238	Arhitektura-Urbanizam see 0350-3666
0004-1246	Arhiv Bioloskih Nauka†
0004-1254	Arhiv za Higijenu Rada i Toksikologiju
0004-1262	Arhiv za Poljoprivredne Nauke
0004-1270	Arhiv za Pravne i Drustvene Nauke
0004-1289	Arhiv za Zastitu Majke i Djeteta
0004-1297	Arhivski Pregled
0004-1300	Aria Compressa
0004-1319	Arid Lands Research Newsletter†
0004-1327	Ariel
0004-1335	Ariel
0004-1351	Arion†
0004-136X	Arithmetic Teacher
0004-1378	Arizona Academy of Science Journal changed to Arizona-Nevada Academy of Science. Journal
0004-1386	Arizona Advocate
0004-1394	Arizona Alumnus
0004-1408	Arizona and the West
0004-1424	Arizona Bar Journal
0004-1432	Arizona Beverage Journal changed to Arizona Beverage Analyst
0004-1440	Arizona Business Bulletin see 0093-0717
0004-1459	Arizona Dental Journal†
0004-1467	Arizona Economic Indicators†
0004-1475	Arizona Education News changed to Alert (Phoenix)
0004-1483	Arizona English Bulletin
0004-1491	Arizona Farmer-Ranchman changed to Arizona Farmer-Stockman
0004-1505	Arizona Grocer
0004-1521	Arizona Highways
0004-153X	Arizona Law Review
0004-1548	Arizona Librarian†
0004-1556	Arizona Medicine see 0093-0415
0004-1564	Arizona Mobile Citizen
0004-1572	Arizona Modern Business and Industry see 0193-7480
0004-1580	Arizona-New Mexico Contractor and Engineer changed to Builder Architect
0004-1599	Arizona Nurse
0004-1602	Arizona Pharmacist changed to Arizona Pharmacist
0004-1610	Arizona Quarterly
0004-1629	Arizona Review
0004-1637	Arizona Roadrunner†
0004-1653	Arizona Teacher see 0194-8849
0004-167X	Ark
0004-1688	Ark changed to Ark (1978)
0004-1696	Ark-Light Newsletter see 0094-0488
0004-170X	Ark/Ozark
0004-1718	Arkansas Archeologist
0004-1726	Arkansas Banker
0004-1742	Arkansas Business and Economic Review
0004-1750	Arkansas Cattle Business
0004-1769	Arkansas Dental Journal
0004-1777	Arkansas Department of Education Newsmagazine changed to Education Update (Little Rock)
0004-1785	Arkansas Farm Research
0004-1807	Arkansas Game & Fish Magazine
0004-1815	Arkansas Grocer
0004-1823	Arkansas Historical Quarterly
0004-1831	Arkansas Law Review
0004-184X	Arkansas Libraries
0004-1858	Arkansas Medical Society. Journal
0004-1866	Arkansas Municipalities see 0193-8371
0004-1874	Arkansas Oil and Gas Statistical Bulletin
0004-1882	Arka-Tech
0004-1890	Arkansas Valley Journal
0004-1904	Arkham Collector†
0004-1920	Arkhimedes
0004-1939	Arkhitektura S.S.S.R.
0004-1947	Arkhiv Anatomii, Gistologii i Embriologii
0004-1955	Arkhiv Patologii
0004-1963	Arhiv za Farmaciju
0004-1971	Arkitekt
0004-198X	Arkitekten
0004-1998	Arkitektnytt
0004-1998	Arkitektnytt issued with 0332-6578
0004-2005	A T
0004-2013	Arkitektur changed to Arkitektur DK
0004-2021	Arkitektur
0004-203X	Arkiv
0004-2048	Arkiv for Astronomi†
0004-2056	Chemica Scripta
0004-2064	Arkiv for Geofysik†
0004-2080	Arkiv foer Matematik
0004-2099	Arkiv for Mineralogi och Geologi†
0004-2102	Arkiv for Sjoerett
0004-2110	Arkiv for Zoologi see 0300-3256
0004-2129	Arkkitehti
0004-2145	Arma
0004-2153	Armament Data Sheets
0004-217X	Armchair Detective
0004-2188	Armed Forces Comptroller
0004-220X	Armed Forces Journal see 0196-3597
0004-2218	Armed Forces Medical Journal, India changed to Medical Journal Armed Forces, India
0004-2226	Armed Forces Writer & Journalist changed to National Association of Government Communicators. News
0004-2234	Armee changed to Armees d'Aujourd'hui
0004-2242	Armee et Defense
0004-2269	Armee-Motor
0004-2277	Armee-Rundschau
0004-2285	Armeiski Pregled
0004-2293	Armenia Today
0004-2307	Armenian-American Outlook changed to A M A A News
0004-2315	Armenian Church see 0199-8765
0004-2323	Armenian Digest
0004-2331	Armenian Guardian†
0004-234X	Armenian Mirror - Spectator
0004-2358	Armenian Reporter
0004-2366	Armenian Review
0004-2374	Armenian Weekly
0004-2382	Armenian Welfare Association of New York News
0004-2404	Armenytt
0004-2412	Armieri
0004-2420	Armor
0004-2447	Arms Control and National Security†
0004-2455	Army see 0191-975X
0004-2463	Army, Air Force & Naval Air Statistical Record
0004-2471	United States Army Aviation Digest
0004-248X	Army Aviation
0004-2498	Army Digest see 0093-8440
0004-251X	Army Journal see 0314-1039
0004-2528	Army Logistician changed to A Log Magazine
0004-2536	Army Museum Newsletter†
0004-2544	Army Orders†
0004-2552	Army Quarterly and Defence Journal
0004-2560	Army Research and Development see 0162-7082
0004-2579	Army Reserve Magazine
0004-2595	Army Times
0004-2617	Arnold Air Letter
0004-2625	Arnold Arboretum. Journal
0004-2633	Arnoldia
0004-265X	Ars Sutoria
0004-2668	Arquipelago changed to Voz di Povo
0004-2676	Arquitecto Peruano
0004-2706	Arquitectura
0004-2714	Arquivo de Patologia
0004-2722	Arquivo do Distrito de Aveiro†
0004-2730	Arquivos Brasileiros de Endocrinologia e Metabologia
0004-2749	Arquivos Brasileiros de Oftalmologia
0004-2757	Arquivos Brasileiros de Psicologia Aplicada changed to Arquivos Brasileiros de Psicologia
0004-2765	Arquivos Brasileiros de Tuberculose e Doencas do Torax
0004-2773	Arquivos Catarinenses de Medicina
0004-2781	Arquivos de Angola
0004-279X	Arquivos de Biologia†
0004-2803	Arquivos de Gastroenterologia
0004-2811	Arquivos de Higiene e Saude Publica†
0004-282X	Arquivos de Neuro-Psiquiatria
0004-2838	Universidade Federal de Minas Gerais. Curso de Odontologia. Arquivos do Centro de Estudos
0004-2846	Arredare la Casa†
0004-2854	Arredorama
0004-2870	Ars Aequi
0004-2889	Ars Buddhica
0004-2897	Ars Medici
0004-2900	Ars Medici et Nouveautes Medicales
0004-2919	Ars Organi
0004-2927	Ars Pharmaceutica
0004-296X	Art Alliance Bulletin
0004-2986	Art and Archaeology Newsletter
0004-2994	Art and Archaeology Technical Abstracts
0004-3001	Art & Artists
0004-301X	Art and Australia
0004-3028	Art and Craft in Education changed to Art & Craft
0004-3044	Art and Life
0004-3052	Art and Man
0004-3060	Indianapolis Museum of Art. Bulletin changed to Indianapolis Museum of Art. Quarterly Magazine
0004-3079	Art Bulletin
0004-3087	Art Chretien
0004-3095	Art d'Eglise†
0004-3109	Art Direction
0004-3125	Art Education
0004-3133	Art Enfantin changed to Creations
0004-315X	Art et Curiosite
0004-3168	Art et Decoration
0004-3184	Art Gallery
0004-3206	Art Gallery of South Australia. Bulletin†
0004-3214	Art in America
0004-3222	Art Index
0004-3230	Art International
0004-3249	Art Journal changed to Art Journal (Year)
0004-3265	Art Material Trade News
0004-3273	Artnews
0004-329X	Art of the Americas. Bulletin†
0004-3303	Art Quarterly
0004-3354	Arta
0004-3389	De Arte
0004-3397	Qui Arte Contemporanea†
0004-3400	Arte Cristiana
0004-3419	Arte e Poesia
0004-3443	Arte Lombarda
0004-3451	Arterama
0004-346X	El Arte Tipografico
0004-3478	Arteregalo
0004-3486	Artes
0004-3494	Artes Graficas see 0164-1905
0004-3508	Artes Graficas en Mexico
0004-3516	Artes Hispanicas†
0004-3524	Artes/Letras
0004-3532	Artforum
0004-3540	Artha
0004-3559	Artha Vijnana
0004-3567	Artha-Vikas
0004-3575	Arthaniti
0004-3583	Arthritis and Rheumatic Diseases Abstracts†
0004-3591	Arthritis and Rheumatism
0004-3605	Arthur D. Little. Industrial Bulletin changed to Arthur D. Little Inc. Bulletin
0004-3613	Arthur Young Journal†
0004-363X	Arti e Mercature
0004-3648	Artibus Asiae
0004-3664	Articles on Neoplasia changed to Current Articles on Neoplasia
0004-3672	Articoli Casalinghi
0004-3680	Artifact
0004-3702	Artificial Intelligence
0004-3710	Artificial Kidney Bibliography see 0363-2369
0004-3729	Artificial Limbs†
0004-3737	Artigiano Modenese
0004-3745	Artigliere
0004-3753	Artigos Selecionados
0004-377X	Artikkelindeks Foer Bygg†
0004-3788	Artilleri-Tidskrift
0004-3796	Artillerie, Armee & Technik
0004-380X	Artillerie Rundschau†
0004-3818	Artilleriiskii Zhurnal
0004-3826	Artillery Journal
0004-3834	Artis changed to Dieren
0004-3842	Artis
0004-3869	Artisan Staff Association Magazine changed to A S A Magazine
0004-3877	Artist
0004-3885	Artist
0004-3893	Artist Junior see 0004-3052
0004-3907	Artistes et Varietes
0004-3915	Artlook
0004-3931	Arts and Activities
0004-394X	Arts and Sciences (Brooklyn)
0004-3958	Arts Asiatiques
0004-3966	Arts en Auto
0004-3982	Arts et Industries
0004-3990	Arts et Manufactures
0004-4008	Arts et Metiers
0004-4024	Arts in Society†
0004-4032	Arts in Virginia
0004-4059	Arts Magazine (New York)
0004-4067	Arts Management
0004-4083	Arts of Asia
0004-4091	Arts Review
0004-4113	Artscanada
0004-4121	Artweek
0004-413X	Arunodayam
0004-4148	Arx†

ISSN INDEX 1201

ISSN	Title
0004-4156	Aryan Path†
0004-4164	Aryana
0004-4172	Arzneimittel-Forschung
0004-4180	Arzt in Niederoesterreich
0004-4202	As We Are†
0004-4210	Asahi Glass Company. Research Laboratory. Reports
0004-4229	Asbarez
0004-4237	Asbestos†
0004-4245	Asbestos Worker
0004-4253	Asbury Seminarian *changed to* Asbury Theological Journal
0004-427X	Ascent†
0004-4288	Aschehougs Leksikonservice†
0004-4296	Asecolda†
0004-430X	Aseguradores
0004-4318	Asfalt
0004-4326	Ashanti Times†
0004-4334	Ashford Advertiser *changed to* Ashford Extra
0004-4342	Achkhar
0004-4350	Ashland Dealer†
0004-4377	Ashtree Echo
0004-4385	Asi†
0004-4407	Asia Bulletin *see* 0161-4355
0004-4423	Asia Bulletin†
0004-4431	Asia Calling†
0004-444X	Asia Christian Colleges Association. Bulletin†
0004-4458	Asia Foundation Program Quarterly†
0004-4466	Asia Letter
0004-4474	Asia Magazine
0004-4482	Asia Major†
0004-4490	Asia Notebook *see* 0387-3927
0004-4504	Asia Scene *see* 0300-4341
0004-4520	Asian Almanac
0004-4539	Asian and Indian Skyways *changed to* Skyways
0004-4547	Asian Books Newsletter
0004-4555	Asian Economic Review
0004-458X	Asian Industry *changed to* Asian Business
0004-4598	Asian Institute of Technology. Newsletter *changed to* A I T Review
0004-4601	Asian Labour *changed to* Asian and Pacific Labour
0004-461X	Asian Medical Journal
0004-4628	Asian Outlook
0004-4636	Asian Printer†
0004-4644	Asian Recorder
0004-4652	Asian Review and Arts and Letters *see* 0038-2841
0004-4660	Asian Student†
0004-4679	Asian Studies
0004-4687	Asian Survey
0004-4695	Asiatic Research Bulletin†
0004-4709	Asiatic Society, Bombay. Journal
0004-4717	Asiatische Studien
0004-4725	Asie Nouvelle
0004-4733	Asien-Bibliographie†
0004-4741	Asociacion Argentina Criadores de Cerdos. Revista
0004-4768	Asociacion Bioquimica Argentina. Revista
0004-4776	Asociacion Colombiana de Facultades de Medicina. Cronica†
0004-4784	Asociacion Costarricense de Bibliotecarios. Boletin
0004-4792	Asociacion Cultural Humboldt. Boletin
0004-4806	Asociacion de Ex-Alumnos de la Escuela Nacional de Bibliotecarios. Boletin
0004-4814	Asociacion Franco-Mexicana de Ingenieros y Tecnicos. Boletin
0004-4822	Asociacion Geologica Argentina. Revista
0004-4830	Asociacion Medica Argentina. Revista†
0004-4849	Asociacion Medica de Puerto Rico. Boletin
0004-4857	Asociacion Mexicana de Facultades y Escuelas de Medicina. Boletin
0004-4865	Asociacion Nacional de Industriales. Revista Trimestral *changed to* Asociacion Nacional de Industriales. Revista Bimestral
0004-4873	Asociacion Numismatica Argentina. Revista
0004-4881	Asociacion Odontologica Argentina. Revista
0004-489X	Asociacion para Evitar la Ceguera en Mexico. Archivos
0004-4911	Aspect†
0004-4954	Asphalt†
0004-4962	Aspire†
0004-4970	Asprenas
0004-4989	Assam Information
0004-4997	Assam Review and Tea News
0004-5004	Assay *see* 0147-6629
0004-5012	Assayad
0004-5020	Assegai†
0004-5063	Assembly Engineering
0004-5071	Assessors Journal *see* 0731-0285
0004-508X	Assessors News Letter/A N L *see* 0731-0277
0004-5098	Assicurazione
0004-511X	Assicurazioni
0004-5128	Carnets de l'Enfance
0004-5136	Assignments in Management *see* 0740-0411
0004-5144	Education Sanitaire et Nutritionnelle d'Afrique Centrale
0004-5152	Assistant Librarian
0004-5187	Associacao Bahiana de Bibliotecarios. Informa
0004-5195	Associacao Brasileira de Pesquisas sobre Plantas Aromaticas e Oleos Essenciais. Boletim
0004-5209	Associacao Comercial de Lourenco Marques. Boletim†
0004-5217	Associacao Comercial do Amazonas. Boletim
0004-5225	Associacao Medica Brasileira. Boletim†
0004-5233	Associacao Medica Brasileira. Jornal
0004-5241	Associacao Medica Brasileira. Revista
0004-525X	Associacao Medica de Minas Gerais. Revista
0004-5268	Associacao Medica do Rio Grande do Sul. Revista *changed to* Revista A M R I G S
0004-5276	Associacao Paulista de Cirurgioes Dentistas. Revista
0004-5292	Association and Society Manager
0004-5306	Association Canadienne d'Education. Bulletin
0004-5314	Association Canadienne des Bibliothecaires de Langue Francaise. Bulletin *see* 0315-2340
0004-5322	Association de Geographes Francais. Bulletin
0004-5349	Association des Anciens Eleves des Ecoles Techniques Superieures de Geneve. Bulletin Technique *changed to* Association des Anciens Eleves de l'Ecole d'Ingenieurs de Geneve. Bulletin Technique
0004-5365	Association des Bibliothecaires Francais. Bulletin d'Informations
0004-5373	Association des Diplomes de Microbiologie de la Faculte de Pharmacie de Nancy. Bulletin *changed to* Microbia (Nancy)
0004-539X	Association des Medecins de Langue Francaise du Canada. Bulletin
0004-5403	Association for Asian Studies. Newsletter *changed to* Asian Studies Newsletter
0004-5411	Association for Computing Machinery. Journal
0004-542X	Association for Psychoanalytic Medicine. Bulletin
0004-5438	A R S C Journal
0004-5446	Association for the Advancement of Medical Instrumentation. Journal (JAAMI) *see* 0090-6689
0004-5454	Association for the Study of Perception. Journal
0004-5462	Revue Technique des Industries du Cuir
0004-5470	Association Francaise des Techniciens du Petrole. Revue *see* 0152-5425
0004-5497	Association Francaise pour l'Etude du Cancer. Bulletin *see* 0007-4551
0004-5500	Association Francaise pour l'Etude du Quaternaire. Bulletin
0004-5519	Association Generale des Medecins de France. Bulletin
0004-5527	Association Guillaume Bude. Bulletin
0004-5535	Art
0004-5543	Association Internationale des Numismates Professionels. Bulletin-Circular
0004-5551	Association Internationale d'Etudes du Sud-Est Europeen. Bulletin
0004-556X	Association Internationale Permanente des Congres de la Route. Bulletin
0004-5578	Association Management
0004-5586	Feuillets de l'A N A S *changed to* Revue Francaise de Service Social
0004-5608	Association of American Geographers. Annals
0004-5616	Association of American Medical Colleges. Bulletin†
0004-5632	Annals of Clinical Biochemistry
0004-5640	Association of College and University Concert Managers. Bulletin *changed to* A C U C A A Bulletin
0004-5659	Association of College Unions International. Bulletin
0004-5667	Association of College Unions International. Union Wire
0004-5675	Association of Collegiate Schools of Planning. Bulletin†
0004-5683	Association of Economic Geographers. Annals
0004-5691	Association of Engineering Geologists. Bulletin
0004-5713	Association of Engineers, Kerala State. Journal
0004-5721	Association of Food and Drug Officials of the United States. Quarterly Bulletin *see* 0195-4865
0004-573X	Association of Marshall Scholars and Alumni. Newsletter *changed to* Marshall News
0004-5748	Association of Nova Scotia Land Surveyors *see* 0380-9242
0004-5756	Association of Official Analytical Chemists. Journal
0004-5764	Association of Official Seed Analysts. News Letter
0004-5772	Association of Physicians of India. Journal
0004-5780	Association of Public Analysts. Journal
0004-5799	Association of Public Passenger Transport Operators. Journal†
0004-5810	Association of Teachers of Japanese. Journal-Newsletter *changed to* Association of Teachers of Japanese. Journal
0004-5837	Association of the Bar of the City of New York. Record
0004-5845	Association of University Evening Colleges. Newsletter *changed to* Five Minutes with A C H E
0004-5853	Association of Urban Universities Newsletter
0004-5861	Association pour le Developpement International de l'Observatoire de Nice. Bulletin d'Information *see* 0249-7522
0004-587X	Association Suisse des Electriciens. Bulletin
0004-5888	Association Technique de l'Industrie Papetiere. Feuillets Bibliographiques. *changed to* Centre Technique du Papier. Feuillets Bibliographiques
0004-5896	Association Technique de l'Industrie Papetiere. Revue
0004-590X	Associazione degli Africanisti Italiani. Bollettino
0004-5918	Notiziario (Arezzo)
0004-5934	Associazione Italiana Biblioteche. Bollettino d'Informazioni
0004-5950	Associazione Italiana Industriali Tintori Stampatori e Finitori Tessili. Notiziario
0004-5969	Associazione Italiana per l'Assistenza Agli Spastici. Notiziaro *changed to* Associazione Italiana Assistenza Spastici. Notiziario
0004-5977	Associazione Italiana Veterinari per Piccoli Animali. Bollettino
0004-5985	Associazione Nazionale Ex Internati. Bollettino Ufficiale
0004-5993	Associazione Nazionale Mutilati e Invalidi di Guerra. Sezione di Roma. Notiziario
0004-6000	Associazione Romana di Entomologia. Bollettino
0004-6019	Assurance Francaise
0004-6027	Assurances
0004-6035	Assurances Banques Transports†
0004-6043	Assureur Conseil *changed to* Revue l'Assureur Conseil
0004-6051	Assyrian Star
0004-606X	Aste Giudiziarie
0004-6078	Asti Informazioni Economiche
0004-6086	Astma- og Allergi-Nytt *see* 0801-3799
0004-6094	Astra
0004-6108	Astra
0004-6116	Astrado
0004-6124	Astral Projection†
0004-6132	Astrolabio
0004-6140	Astrological Magazine
0004-6175	Astrologischer Auskunftsbogen
0004-6183	Astrology
0004-6191	Astrology Guide
0004-6205	Astronautica Acta *see* 0094-5765
0004-6213	Astronautics and Aeronautics *see* 0740-722X
0004-6221	Astronautik
0004-623X	Astronautyka
0004-6248	Bulletin of the Astronomical Institutes of Czechoslovakia
0004-6256	Astronomical Journal
0004-6264	Astronomical Society of Japan. Publications
0004-6272	Astronomical Society of the Pacific. Leaflet†
0004-6280	Astronomical Society of the Pacific. Publications
0004-6299	Astronomicheskii Zhurnal
0004-6302	Astronomie
0004-6310	Astronomie in der Schule
0004-6337	Astronomische Nachrichten
0004-6345	Astronomisk Tidsskrift
0004-6353	Astronomy
0004-6361	Astronomy and Astrophysics
0004-637X	Astrophysical Journal
0004-6388	Astrophysical Letters
0004-6396	Astrophysics
0004-640X	Astrophysics and Space Science
0004-6434	At Cooper Union
0004-6450	At Home with the South African Permanent†
0004-6469	New Packaging
0004-6477	Atem *see* 0341-3403
0004-6485	Atemschutz-Informationen†
0004-6493	Atene e Roma
0004-6507	Atenea *see* 0716-1840
0004-6531	Ateneo Parmense. Acta Bio-Medica
0004-654X	Ateneo Parmense. Acta Naturalia
0004-6558	Ateneo Veneto†
0004-6574	Athenaeum
0004-6582	Athene†
0004-6590	Athenee
0004-6604	Athens Annals of Archaeology
0004-6612	Athens Chamber of Commerce and Industry. Monthly Bulletin
0004-6620	Institut Pasteur Hellenique. Archives
0004-6647	Athletic Director
0004-6655	Athletic Journal
0004-6663	Athletics Arena *changed to* Athletics Arena International
0004-6671	Athletics Weekly
0004-668X	Atletiekwereld
0004-6698	Athletik
0004-6701	Atlanta Magazine
0004-671X	Atlanta Economic Review *see* 0163-531X
0004-6736	Atlante
0004-6744	Atlantic Advocate
0004-6752	Atlantic Baptist
0004-6760	Atlantic Community Quarterly

1202 ISSN INDEX

0004-6787 Atlantic Mirror†
0004-6795 Atlantic Monthly
0004-6809 Atlantic Naturalist†
0004-6817 Atlantic Observer-Knickbocker International†
0004-6825 Atlantic Provinces Inter-University Committee on the Sciences. Newsletter
0004-6833 Atlantic Psychologist†
0004-6841 Atlantic Report
0004-685X Atlantic Sun
0004-6868 Atlantic Truck Transport Review *changed to* Atlantic Trucking
0004-6914 Marine/Atlantische Welt†
0004-6922 Atlas (Paris, 1960) *changed to* Atlas - Air France
0004-6930 Atlas *see* 0195-8895
0004-6965 Atmanirvrithi
0004-6973 Atmosphere *see* 0705-5900
0004-6981 Atmospheric Environment
0004-699X Air Pollution Abstracts†
0004-7007 Atoka
0004-7015 Atom
0004-7023 Atom†
0004-7031 Atom-Informationen
0004-7058 Atom News
0004-7066 Atom und Strom
0004-7074 Atomic Absorption and Flame Emission Spectroscopy Abstracts *see* 0309-1813
0004-7082 Atomic Data *see* 0092-640X
0004-7090 Atomic Energy in Australia†
0004-7104 Atomic Energy Law Journal
0004-7112 Atomic Energy Review†
0004-7120 Atomic Energy Society of Japan. Journal
0004-7139 I N I S Atomindex
0004-7147 Atomkernenergie *see* 0171-5747
0004-7155 A T O M K I Kozlemenyek
0004-7163 Atomnaya Energiya
0004-7171 Atomo e Industria
0004-718X Atomo Petrolio Elettricita
0004-7198 Kerntechnik *see* 0171-5747
0004-7201 Izotoptechnika
0004-721X Atomwirtschaft *see* 0365-8414
0004-7228 Atoomenergie en Haar Toepassingen *changed to* Energie-Spectrum
0004-7244 Att Bo†
0004-7252 Attentie Met Oog en Oor *changed to* Attentie
0004-7279 Atterraggio Forzato
0004-7287 Societa degli Ingegneri e degli Architetti in Torino. Atti e Rassegna Tecnica
0004-7309 Attualita di Laboratorio†
0004-7317 Attualita di Ostetricia e Ginecologia
0004-7325 Attualita Mediche
0004-7333 Attualita Mondiali *changed to* Informazioni e Attualita Mondiali
0004-7341 Atuagagdliutit
0004-7376 Au Fil du Rail
0004-7384 Au Grand Air
0004-7392 Auberge de la Jeunesse
0004-7414 Auburn Pharmacist†
0004-7422 Auckland City Art Gallery Quarterly†
0004-7449 Auckland Star
0004-7465 Auctioneer
0004-7473 Audecibel
0004-7481 Audenshaw Papers
0004-749X Audience†
0004-7503 Audience†
0004-7546 Audio Amateur
0004-7554 Audio Engineering Society. Journal
0004-7562 Audio-Visual Communications
0004-7570 Audio Visual Journal
0004-7589 Audio-Visual Language Journal *see* 0144-0888
0004-7597 Educational Media International
0004-7600 Audio-Vizualis Technikai es Modszertani Kozlemenyek *see* 0231-2379
0004-7619 Audiotecnica
0004-7627 Audiovisivi
0004-7635 Audiovisual Instruction *see* 8756-3894
0004-7643 Audit-Poetry
0004-7651 Auditor
0004-7686 American Birds
0004-7694 Audubon Magazine
0004-7708 Auerbach Computer Characteristics Digest *see* 0361-2783
0004-7716 Auerbach Computer Notebook International†
0004-7724 Auerbach Data Communications Reports *changed to* Data Communications Reports
0004-7732 Auerbach Data Handling Reports†
0004-7740 Auerbach Graphic Processing Reports†
0004-7775 Auerbach Software Reports *changed to* Applications Software Reports
0004-7775 Auerbach Software Reports *changed to* Systems Software Reports
0004-7783 Auerbach Standard E D P Reports
0004-7791 Auerbach Time Sharing Reports†
0004-7813 Aufbau
0004-7821 Aufbau
0004-783X Aufbereitungs-Technik/Mineral Processing
0004-7848 Aufbruch
0004-7864 Der Aufstieg†
0004-7872 Der Auftrag
0004-7880 Auftrag
0004-7899 Ran
0004-7902 Der Augenarzt
0004-7910 Augenoptik
0004-7929 Der Augenoptiker
0004-7945 Augsburg Echo
0004-7953 Augsburg in Zahlen
0004-7961 Augsburger Kulturnachrichten
0004-797X Augusta Magazine
0004-7988 Augustan
0004-7996 Augustana College Bulletin
0004-8003 Augustiniana
0004-8011 Augustinianum
0004-802X Augustinus
0004-8038 Auk
0004-8046 Aum *changed to* Aum: the Message of Sri Chinmoy
0004-8054 Aural News
0004-8062 Aurea Parma
0004-8070 Auricle
0004-8089 Aurora
0004-8097 Ausbau *changed to* Technik Heute
0004-8100 Der Ausbilder
0004-8119 Ausblick (Duesseldorf)
0004-8127 Ausgrabungen und Funde
0004-8143 Ausonia
0004-816X Statistik des Aussenhandels Oesterreichs *changed to* Austria. Statistisches Zentralamt. Aussenhandel Oesterreichs
0004-8178 Aussenhandelsdienst *changed to* B F G Aussenhandelsdienst
0004-8186 Der Aussenhandelskaufmann†
0004-8194 Aussenpolitik
0004-8208 Aussenpolitische Korrespondenz
0004-8216 Aussenwirtschaft
0004-8232 Aussenwirtschaftsdienst des Betriebs-Berater *see* 0340-7926
0004-8240 Aussprache†
0004-8259 Aussteuer Bett und Couch *changed to* Haustex
0004-8267 Austin Dental News *changed to* Tenth Times
0004-8275 Austral News *changed to* Australian Trading News
0004-8283 Australian Citrus News
0004-8291 Australian and New Zealand Journal of Medicine
0004-8305 Australasian Baker and Miller's Journal *changed to* Australasian Baking
0004-8313 Australasian Beekeeper
0004-8321 Australasian Catholic Record
0004-833X Australasian Corrosion Engineering
0004-8356 Australasian Grocer *see* 0156-0352
0004-8364 A I M M Proceedings *see* 0817-2668
0004-8372 Australasian Insurance and Banking Record *see* 0725-4644
0004-8380 Australasian Journal of Dermatology
0004-8399 Australasian Journal of Pharmacy
0004-8402 Australasian Journal of Philosophy
0004-8410 Australasian Manufacturer
0004-8437 Australasian Post
0004-8453 Australasian Printer
0004-8461 Australasian Radiology
0004-847X Australasian Soft Drink Journal *changed to* Australian Beverage Review
0004-8488 Australasian Sportsgoods and Toy Retailer
0004-8496 Australasian Stamp Collector
0004-850X A N Z Bank Business Indicators
0004-8542 Australia. Bureau of Statistics. Western Australian Office. Monthly Statistical Summary *see* 0727-2367
0004-8577 Australia. Bureau of Statistics. Quarterly Estimates of National Income and Expenditure, Australia
0004-8585 Australia. Bureau of Statistics. Western Australian Office. Quarterly Statistical Abstract†
0004-8607 Australia International†
0004-8615 Australia Newsletter†
0004-8623 Australian Academic and Research Libraries
0004-8631 Australian Accountant
0004-8658 Australian and New Zealand Journal of Criminology
0004-8666 Australian and New Zealand Journal of Obstetrics and Gynecology
0004-8674 Australian & New Zealand Journal of Psychiatry
0004-8682 Australian and New Zealand Journal of Surgery
0004-8690 Australian & New Zealand Journal of Sociology
0004-8704 Australian Antique Collector
0004-8712 V A C C Journal *changed to* Motor Industry Journal
0004-8720 Australian Automotive Engineering and Equipment *changed to* Automotive Engineer
0004-8739 Australian Baptist
0004-8747 Australian Bird Bander *see* 0155-0438
0004-8763 Australian Bookseller and Publisher
0004-8771 Australian Bride Magazine *changed to* Mode for Brides
0004-878X Australian Builder
0004-8798 Australian Building Science and Technology
0004-8801 Australian Business Communications†
0004-881X Australian Ceramic Society. Journal
0004-8828 Australian Chemical Engineering
0004-8836 Australian Chemical Processing and Engineering *see* 0728-3636
0004-8844 Australian Children Limited *changed to* Interaction (Canberra)
0004-8852 Australian Christian
0004-8887 Australian Coin Review
0004-8895 Australian College of Dental Surgeons. Annals. *see* 0158-1570
0004-8909 Australian College of Speech Therapists. Journal *changed to* Australian Journal of Human Communication Disorders
0004-8917 Australian Computer Journal
0004-8933 Australian Country Magazine *changed to* Farm Equipment
0004-8941 Australian Credit Manager *changed to* Credit Review
0004-895X Australian Cricket *changed to* Australian Cricket Newspaper
0004-8992 Australian Economic History Review
0004-900X Australian Economic Papers
0004-9018 Australian Economic Review
0004-9026 Australian Education Index
0004-9034 Australian Electrical World *see* 0726-7827
0004-9042 Australian Electronics Engineering
0004-9050 Australian Entomological Society. Journal
0004-9069 Australian External Territories†
0004-9077 Australian Family Safety
0004-9085 Australian Fashion News *see* 0312-0325
0004-9093 Australian Economic News†
0004-9107 Australian Fish Trades Review
0004-9115 Australian Fisheries
0004-9123 Australian Flying
0004-9131 Australian Food Manufacturer and Distributor†
0004-914X Australian Forest Research
0004-9158 Australian Forestry
0004-9166 Australian Gas Journal
0004-9174 Australian Gemmologist
0004-9182 Australian Geographer
0004-9190 Australian Geographical Studies
0004-9204 Australian Gliding
0004-9212 Australian Golf *changed to* Australian Golf (1978)
0004-9239 Australian Grapegrower *see* 0727-3606
0004-9255 Australian Hardware Journal
0004-9263 Australian Harness Sport
0004-928X Australian Home Beautiful
0004-9298 Australian Home Journal†
0004-9301 Australian Hot Rodding Review†
0004-931X Australian House and Garden
0004-9328 Australian Humanist†
0004-9344 A.I.A.S. Newsletter *see* 0729-4352
0004-9352 Australian Institute of Metals. Journal *see* 0160-7952
0004-9360 Australian Jewish Historical Society. Journal of Proceedings
0004-9379 Australian Jewish News
0004-9387 Australian Journal of Adult Education
0004-9395 Australian Journal of Agricultural Economics
0004-9409 Australian Journal of Agricultural Research
0004-9417 Australian Journal of Biological Sciences
0004-9425 Australian Journal of Chemistry
0004-9433 Australian Journal of Dairy Technology
0004-9441 Australian Journal of Education
0004-945X Australian Journal of Experimental Biology and Medical Science *changed to* Immunology and Cell Biology
0004-9468 Australian Journal of French Studies
0004-9476 Australian Journal of Marketing Research
0004-9484 Australian Journal of Music Education *changed to* International Journal of Music Education
0004-9492 Australian Journal of Physical Education *see* 0813-2283
0004-9506 Australian Journal of Physics
0004-9522 Australian Journal of Politics and History
0004-9530 Australian Journal of Psychology
0004-9549 Search
0004-9557 Australian Journal of Social Issues
0004-9565 Australian Journal of Social Work *see* 0312-407X
0004-9573 Australian Journal of Soil Research
0004-9581 Australian Journal of Statistics
0004-959X Australian Journal of Zoology
0004-9603 Australian Lapidary Magazine
0004-9611 Australian Law Journal
0004-962X Australian Leather Journal, Boot and Shoe Recorder *changed to* Australian Leather Journal
0004-9638 Australian Left Review
0004-9646 Australian Legal Monthly Digest
0004-9654 Australian Liberal
0004-9662 Communion
0004-9670 Australian Library Journal
0004-9689 Australian Library News†
0004-9697 Australian Literary Studies
0004-9700 Australian Lithographer *see* 0159-2319
0004-9719 Australian Machinery and Production Engineering
0004-9727 Australian Mathematical Society. Bulletin
0004-9743 Australian Meteorological Magazine
0004-9751 Australian Mineral Industry. Quarterly Review. *see* 0155-9419
0004-976X Australian Mining
0004-9808 Australian Municipal Journal
0004-9816 Australian National Bibliography
0004-9832 Australian National University News†
0004-9840 Australian Natural History
0004-9867 Australian Newsagent and Stationer
0004-9875 Australian Numismatic Journal
0004-9883 Australian Numismatic Society. Report
0004-9891 Australian Official Journal of Patents, Trade Marks, and Designs
0004-9905 Australian Outdoors
0004-9913 Australian Outlook
0004-9921 Australian Packaging
0004-993X Australian Paediatric Journal

ISSN INDEX

ISSN	Title
0004-9956	Australian Parks see 0311-8223
0004-9964	Australian Photography
0004-9972	Australian Physicist
0004-9980	Australian Pistol Shooters' Bulletin
0004-9999	Royal Australian Planning Institute Journal changed to Australian Planner
0005-0008	Australian Plants
0005-0016	Australian Plastics and Rubber Journal†
0005-0024	Australian Police Journal
0005-0059	Australian Presbyterian Life
0005-0067	Australian Psychologist
0005-0075	Australian Public Affairs Information Service see 0727-8926
0005-0083	Australian Purchasing
0005-0091	Australian Quarterly
0005-0105	Australian Railway Historical Society. Bulletin
0005-0148	Australian Refrigeration, Air Conditioning and Heating
0005-0164	Australian Road Research
0005-0180	Australian Safety News
0005-0199	Australian School Librarian
0005-0229	Australian Science Index†
0005-0237	Australian Seacraft
0005-0253	Australian Skindivers changed to N.S.W. Skindiver
0005-0261	Australian Society of Accountants. Bulletin†
0005-027X	Australian Special Library News
0005-0296	Australian Stamp Monthly
0005-030X	Australian Student†
0005-0318	Australian Sugar Journal†
0005-0326	Australian Surveyor
0005-0334	Australian Teacher of the Deaf
0005-0342	Australian Temperance Advocate changed to Temperance Advocate
0005-0350	Australian Thoroughbreds
0005-0369	Australian Timber Journal and Building Products Merchandiser changed to Australian Forest Industries Journal
0005-0377	Australian Tradition†
0005-0385	Australian Transport
0005-0393	Australian Traveller†
0005-0407	Australian Trotting Register
0005-0415	Australian University†
0005-0423	Australian Veterinary Journal
0005-044X	Australian Wine, Brewing & Spirit Review†
0005-0458	Australian Women's Weekly
0005-0474	Australia's Neighbors changed to Asian Pacific Review
0005-0482	Australijas Latvietis
0005-0490	Austria Export
0005-0504	I F E F, Austria Sekcio. Bulteno
0005-0512	Austria-Philatelist
0005-0520	Austrian Information
0005-0539	Austro-Motor†
0005-0555	Austroflug
0005-0563	Austropack
0005-0571	Auszuege aus den Gebrauchsmustern
0005-058X	Auszuege aus den Patentanmeldungen changed to Auszuege aus den Patentschriften
0005-0598	Auszuege aus Presseartikeln
0005-0601	Aut Aut
0005-0628	Author
0005-0652	Authority in Crisis†
0005-0660	Authorship
0005-0695	Autospark
0005-0709	Auto Age
0005-0717	Auto and Flat Glass Journal
0005-0725	Auto Club News Pictorial changed to Auto Club News
0005-0733	Auto Dealers' Digest
0005-0768	Auto-Journal
0005-0776	Auto Laundry News
0005-0792	Auto-Motor
0005-0806	Auto Motor und Sport
0005-0814	Auto Noticias
0005-0822	Auto Racing†
0005-0830	Autorevue
0005-0857	Auto-Technik
0005-0865	Auto Trim News
0005-0873	Autovisie
0005-0881	Auto-Volt
0005-089X	Auto-Writing changed to I I S T Bulletins
0005-0903	Autoaccessorio
0005-0911	Autobody and the Reconditioned Car
0005-092X	Autocar
0005-0938	Autocar et Cargo Routier†
0005-0946	Autoclub
0005-0954	Autoclub changed to Touring
0005-0962	Autoclub and Via changed to Via!
0005-0989	Autohaus
0005-0997	Autokampioen
0005-1004	Autolinea†
0005-1012	Automat
0005-1020	Automated Education Letter†
0005-1039	Automaten-Markt
0005-1047	Automatic Control see 0146-4116
0005-1055	Automatic Documentation and Mathematical Linguistics
0005-1063	Automatic Electric Technical Journal see 0273-141X
0005-1071	Automatic Machining
0005-108X	Automatic Welding†
0005-1098	Automatica
0005-1128	Automatie
0005-1136	Automatik changed to Messen Pruefen Automatisieren
0005-1152	Automation
0005-1160	Automation see 0146-1737
0005-1179	Automation and Remote Control
0005-1187	Automation Council News
0005-1217	Automation in Housing see 0740-3534
0005-1225	Automation Journal of Japan see 0388-1423
0005-1233	Automatisch-Verkaufen†
0005-125X	Automatizace
0005-1268	Automatizacija Poslovanja
0005-1284	Automazione e Strumentazione
0005-1292	Automatic Monitoring & Measuring
0005-1306	Automobil-Industrie
0005-1314	Revue Automobile
0005-1330	Automobile
0005-1349	Automobile
0005-1357	Automobile Abstracts see 0309-0817
0005-1373	Automobile Club di Milano. Notiziario Economico
0005-139X	Automobile in Southern Africa see 0304-8721
0005-1403	Automobile India
0005-1411	Automobile Law Reports Insurance Decisions changed to Automobile Law Reports - Insurance Cases
0005-142X	Automobile News
0005-1438	Automobile Quarterly
0005-1454	Automobilismo e Automobilismo Industriale changed to Automobilism
0005-1462	Automobilist changed to Away
0005-1470	Automotive Age changed to Auto Age
0005-1497	Automotive Cooling Journal
0005-1500	Automotive Design Engineering see 0307-6490
0005-1519	Automotive Fleet
0005-1527	Automotive Industries changed to Automotive Industries
0005-1543	Automotive Market Report and Auto Week
0005-1551	Automotive News
0005-156X	Automotive News of the Pacific Northwest
0005-1578	Automotive Retailer
0005-1586	Automotive Service changed to Service Station
0005-1594	Automobile International
0005-1608	Automotor
0005-1616	Automovil de Venezuela
0005-1659	Autoparade†
0005-1675	Autoproducts see 0164-4904
0005-1683	Autorama
0005-1691	Auto Revista
0005-1713	Autorevue†
0005-173X	Autosport
0005-1748	Autosprint
0005-1756	Autostrade
0005-1772	Autotoerist†
0005-1780	Autotransportes "Tres Estrellas de Oro"
0005-1799	Autoveteranen
0005-1802	Autoweek
0005-1810	Autowelt†
0005-1829	Autoworld
0005-1845	Auvergne Litteraire†
0005-1853	Auxiliaire des Fabricants de Cartonnages, Transformateurs de Papier, Industries et Arts Graphiques changed to Cartonnages et Complexes
0005-1861	Volunteer Leader
0005-1888	Avalanche†
0005-1896	Avances en Alimentacion y Mejora Animal
0005-190X	Avant-Garde†
0005-1918	Avant Garde
0005-1926	Avant Gardener
0005-1934	A M
0005-1942	A. D. Correspondence†
0005-1950	Avedik
0005-1969	Avenirs
0005-1977	Aventure Sous-Marine see 0425-5054
0005-1985	Avenue
0005-1993	Aves
0005-2000	Aves & Ovos
0005-2027	Avia
0005-2035	Avia
0005-2043	Avia Aeroespacial
0005-206X	Aviacao e Astronautica changed to Aviacao em Revista
0005-2078	Aviacion
0005-2086	Avian Diseases
0005-2094	Aviasport
0005-2108	Aviation et Astronautique changed to La Conquete de l'Air-Aviastro
0005-2116	National Aeronautics†
0005-2132	Aviation Magazine International
0005-2140	Aviation Mechanics Bulletin
0005-2159	Aviation Reports
0005-2167	Aviation Studies International. Official Price List
0005-2175	Aviation Week & Space Technology
0005-2183	Aviatsiia i Kosmonavtika
0005-2205	Aviazione di Linea Difesa e Spazio changed to Aviazione
0005-2213	Rivista di Avicoltura
0005-2221	Aviculteur Quebecois
0005-2248	Avicultura Brasileira
0005-2256	Avicultural Magazine
0005-2264	Avio-Nieuws see 0017-6818
0005-2272	Avion
0005-2280	Avis-Kronik-Index see 0106-147X
0005-2299	Labour and National Insurance
0005-2302	Avtomaticheskaya Svarka
0005-2310	Avtomatika i Telemekhanika
0005-2329	Avtomatika, Telemekhanika i Svyaz'
0005-2337	Avtomobil'naya Promyshlennost'
0005-2345	Avtomobil'nyi Transport
0005-2353	Avtomobil'nye Dorogi
0005-2361	Avvenire Agricolo (Parma)
0005-237X	Awake
0005-2388	Awakener
0005-2426	Axial
0005-2442	Ayrshire Cattle Society's Journal
0005-2450	Ayrshire Digest
0005-2469	Ayu
0005-2485	Ayurveda-Bharati
0005-2493	Ayurveda Doot
0005-2515	Azad Mazdur
0005-2523	Azerbaidzhan Tibb Zhurnaly
0005-2531	Azerbaidzhanskii Khimicheskii Zhurnal
0005-254X	Azimut
0005-2558	Azione
0005-2566	Azione Cooperativa
0005-2574	Aziya i Afrika Segodnya
0005-2590	Aztec Engineer†
0005-2604	Aztlan changed to Aztlan-International Journal of Chicano Studies Research
0005-2612	B A C I E Journal changed to Transition
0005-2639	B A G - Nachrichten
0005-2647	B A R C News
0005-2655	B A S F Review†
0005-2671	British Amateur Scientific Research Association see 0141-6413
0005-268X	B & T
0005-2698	B-U Nachrichten
0005-2701	B & Z†
0005-2728	B B A - Bioenergetics
0005-2736	B B A - Biomembranes
0005-2744	B B A-Enzymology†
0005-2760	B B A Lipids & Lipid Metabolism
0005-2779	B. B. A. Nieuws†
0005-2787	B B A-Nucleic Acids and Protein Synthesis†
0005-2795	B B A-Protein Structure†
0005-2809	B B B Tribune changed to Better Business Bureau
0005-2817	British Broadcasting Corporation. B B C Engineering†
0005-2833	Bokrevy
0005-2841	B C A News
0005-2868	B C I R A Abstracts of Foundry Literature see 0268-3393
0005-2876	B C L A Reporter
0005-2884	B.C. Motorist changed to Westworld Magazine
0005-2892	B C Power Engineer
0005-2906	B.C. Professional Engineer
0005-2930	B. C. Sports & Recreation Magazine†
0005-2949	B C Studies
0005-2957	B.C. Teacher
0005-2965	British Columbia Teachers' Federation. Newsletter
0005-2981	B D K-Mitteilungen†
0005-299X	B D V-Dienst Niedersachsen†
0005-3015	B. E. A. Bulletin†
0005-3023	B E A Magazine changed to Topline
0005-304X	B E M A Bulletin
0005-3058	B E N E L U X International
0005-3066	B H P Review
0005-3074	B H P Technical Bulletin
0005-3082	B I B - Liner
0005-3090	B I C C Bulletin†
0005-3112	B I I L†
0005-3120	Bibliotheque de Travail Junior
0005-3147	B I N O P Bulletin see 0249-6739
0005-3155	Bios
0005-3163	B.I.R.E.
0005-318X	B I T S
0005-3198	B L M
0005-3201	B M/E
0005-321X	B M G
0005-3228	B N A Policy & Practice Series
0005-3244	B N F Abstracts changed to B N F Nonferrous Metals Abstracts
0005-3252	B.O.A.C. Review changed to British Airways News
0005-3279	B R A Review see 0144-6339
0005-3287	Betriebssicherheit - B S
0005-3295	B S C S Newsletter see 0162-3613
0005-3309	B S I News
0005-3317	B.S.I. Quarterly changed to Chartered Building Societies Institute. Journal
0005-3325	B S P Magazine
0005-3333	B S R
0005-3341	B S S R Quarterly Newsletter changed to B S S R Newsletter
0005-335X	Bibliotheque de Travail
0005-3368	B T A /Buerotechnik und Automation see 0343-2319
0005-3376	B T E - Werbedienst see 0171-838X
0005-3392	B T O News
0005-3414	Bibliotheque de Travail 2d Degre
0005-3430	B V A Bulletin
0005-3449	B V E A Reporter
0005-3457	B V N. Boletin Informativo
0005-3465	B Z
0005-3473	B Z B
0005-3503	Babel
0005-3538	Babson Alumni Bulletin changed to Babson Bulletin
0005-3546	Babson's Washington Service†
0005-3554	Baby & Junior
0005-3562	Baby & Tiener†
0005-3570	Baby Care†
0005-3589	Baby Talk changed to Baby Talk Magazine
0005-3600	Bach
0005-3643	Back to Godhead
0005-366X	Backstretch
0005-3678	Bacteriological Reviews see 0146-0749
0005-3686	Bad und Kueche†

1204 ISSN INDEX

ISSN	Title
0005-3708	Bad Homburger Veranstaltungsspiegel Kurzeitung†
0005-3724	Baden - Wuerttembergisches Verwaltungsblat *see* 0340-3505
0005-3740	Badger Farm Bureau News†
0005-3759	Badger History†
0005-3767	Badger Legionnaire
0005-3775	Badger Sportsman
0005-3783	Badia Greca di Grottaferrata. Bollettino
0005-3791	Badminton
0005-3821	Archaeographie *changed to* Baecker - Zeitung
0005-383X	Baecker und Konditor
0005-3848	Baender, Bleche, Rohre
0005-3856	Baessler Archiv
0005-3864	Det Baesta ur Reader's Digest (Swedish Edition)
0005-3872	Baeuerlicher Ratgeber†
0005-3880	Bagdala
0005-3899	Baghdad Chamber of Commerce. Weekly Bulletin
0005-3902	Baghdad Observer
0005-3910	Bagin
0005-3929	Bagolah *changed to* Batnua
0005-3937	Bagvertising Weekly
0005-3945	Baha'i-Briefe†
0005-3953	Bahamas
0005-3961	Bahamas Weekly and Nassau Tourist News *changed to* Nassau and Paradise Island. Tourist News
0005-397X	Bahamian Review
0005-3988	Bahana
0005-3996	Hadshot Hahistadrut†
0005-4003	Baileya
0005-4011	Bajan and South Caribbean *changed to* Bajan
0005-402X	Bakelite Review†
0005-4054	Baker, Confectioner, Caterer *see* 0005-4100
0005-4062	Baker - Konditor
0005-4070	Baker Street Journal
0005-4097	Bakers Journal
0005-4100	Bakers Review
0005-4119	Bakers Weekly *see* 0005-4127
0005-4127	Bakery Production and Marketing
0005-4135	New Student Baker *changed to* Student Baker
0005-4143	Baking Research Association. Abstracts *see* 0430-7941
0005-4151	Baking Industries Journal *see* 0144-8374
0005-416X	Baking Industry
0005-4178	Bakkersvakblad *changed to* Bakker
0005-4186	Baksteen
0005-4194	Bal Bharati
0005-4208	Bal Sandesh
0005-4216	Balance
0005-4224	Balance of Payments Reports†
0005-4232	Balance Sheet
0005-4240	Banque Populaire Suisse. Balance Sheet Prospectus
0005-4259	Balans
0005-4267	Balcony Square *changed to* Underground
0005-4275	Balde Branco
0005-4283	Bulgarski Ezik
0005-4291	Baljivan
0005-4313	Balkan Studies
0005-433X	Ball State Teachers College Forum *see* 0888-188X
0005-4348	Ballet - Who *see* 0705-8063
0005-4356	E M U Faculty-Staff News. Library Supplement *changed to* Eastern Michigan University Faculty-Staff News. Center of Educational Resources Supplement
0005-4364	Ballon Kurier
0005-4380	Ballroom Dancing Times
0005-4399	Ballsout
0005-4402	Balneologia Polska
0005-4410	Balon
0005-4429	Balthazar
0005-4437	Baltic Exchange
0005-4453	Baltimore
0005-4447X	Baltimore Bulletin of Education†
0005-4488	Baltimore City Public Schools Staff Newsletter and Community Newsletter *changed to* Baltimore City Public Schools Staff Newsletter
0005-4496	Baltimore Engineer
0005-450X	Baltimore Jewish Times
0005-4518	Baltimore Museum of Art Record†
0005-4526	Baltische Briefe
0005-4534	Baltische Hefte
0005-4542	Bama'arakha
0005-4550	Chambre de Commerce et d'Industrie du Mali. Circulaire Mensuelle d'Information *changed to* Chambre de Commerce et d'Industrie du Mali. Bulletin Trimestriel
0005-4569	Bamat Hatzarkhan†
0005-4577	Israel. Ministry of Agriculture. Department of Fisheries. Bamidgeh
0005-4585	Banas
0005-4593	Banca d'Italia. Bollettino *see* 0392-467X
0005-4607	Banca Nazionale del Lavoro Quarterly Review
0005-4615	Banca y Comercio
0005-4623	Bancaria
0005-4631	Bancni Vestnik
0005-464X	Banco Central de Chile. Boletin Mensual
0005-4658	Banco Central de Costa Rica. Revista†
0005-4666	Banco Central de Honduras. Revista Trimestral†
0005-4674	Banco Central de la Republica Argentina. Boletin Estadistico
0005-4682	Banco Central de la Republica Dominicana. Boletin Mensual
0005-4690	Banco Central de Nicaragua. Boletin Trimestral *changed to* Banco Central de Nicaragua. Boletin Anual
0005-4704	Banco Central de Reserva de El Salvador. Revista Mensual
0005-4712	Banco Central de Reserva del Peru. Boletin
0005-4720	Banco Central de Venezuela. Revista†
0005-4739	Banco Central del Ecuador. Boletin
0005-4747	Banco Central del Uruguay. Boletin Estadistico Mensual *changed to* Banco Central del Uruguay. Departamento de Estadisticas Economicas. Boletin Estadistico
0005-4755	Banco Central del Uruguay. Seleccion de Temas Economicos *changed to* Banco Central del Uruguay. Seleccion de Temas
0005-4763	Banco Central do Brazil. Boletim
0005-478X	Banco de Angola. Boletim Trimestral†
0005-4798	Banco de Espana. Boletin Estadistico
0005-4801	Banco de Fomento Nacional. Boletim de Informacao†
0005-481X	Banco de Guatemala. Boletin Estadistico
0005-4828	Banco de la Republica. Revista Economia y Finanzas
0005-4844	Banco de Vizcaya. Noticiario Economico†
0005-4852	Banco di Sicilia. Informazioni Sulla Congiuntura
0005-4860	Banco do Brasil. Boletim
0005-4879	Banco Nacional Ultramarino. Boletim Trimestral†
0005-4887	Band *changed to* K B M - Kantoormarkt
0005-4909	Band†
0005-4917	Band- und Flechtindustrie
0005-4925	Band Journal
0005-4933	Bandwagon
0005-4968	Baner Ac Amserau Cymru *changed to* Y Faner
0005-4976	Bangkok Bank. Monthly Review
0005-4984	Banif's Investment Bulletin
0005-4992	Banijya Barta
0005-500X	Bank- en Effectenbedrijf
0005-5018	Bank-Betrieb *changed to* Die Bank
0005-5034	Bank Board Letter
0005-5042	Bank Equipment News *see* 0146-0900
0005-5050	Bank Installment Lending Newsletter *changed to* Consumer Lending Report
0005-5069	Bank Karamchari
0005-5077	Bankkaufmann
0005-5085	Bank Markazi Iran Bulletin
0005-5093	Bank Negara Malaysia. Quarterly Economic Bulletin *changed to* Bank Negara Malaysia. Bulletin Ekonomi Suku Tahunan/Quarterly Economic Bulletin
0005-5115	Bank News
0005-5123	Bank Notes
0005-5131	Bank of Canada Statistical Summary *see* 0045-1460
0005-514X	Bank of Canada Weekly Financial Statistics
0005-5158	Bank of England Quarterly Bulletin
0005-5166	Bank of Finland. Monthly Bulletin
0005-5174	Bank of Ghana. Quarterly Economic Bulletin
0005-5182	Bank of Greece. Monthly Statistical Bulletin
0005-5190	Bank of Hawaii Monthly Review *changed to* Bank of Hawaii Business Trends
0005-5204	Bank of India. Bulletin
0005-5212	Bank of Israel. Bulletin *changed to* Bank of Israel. Economic Review
0005-5220	Bank of Jamaica. Bulletin
0005-5239	Bank of Japan. Economic Statistics Monthly
0005-5247	Bank of Japan. Monthly Economic Review
0005-5255	Bank of Korea. Monthly Statistical Review *changed to* Bank of Korea. Monthly Statistical Bulletin
0005-5263	Bank of Libya. Economic Research Division. Economic Bulletin
0005-5271	Bank of London & South America. Revista Mensual†
0005-528X	Bank of London and South America Review†
0005-5298	Bank of Mauritius. Quarterly Review
0005-5301	Bank of Montreal Business Review
0005-531X	Bank of Nova Scotia. Monthly Review†
0005-5328	Bank of Sudan. Economic and Financial Bulletin *changed to* Bank of Sudan. Economic and Financial Statistics Review
0005-5336	Bank of Taiwan Quarterly
0005-5344	Bank of Thailand. Monthly Bulletin *see* 0125-605X
0005-5352	Bank of Tokyo Semiannual Report *changed to* Bank of Tokyo Annual Report
0005-5360	Bank of Tokyo Weekly Review *changed to* Tokyo Financial Review
0005-5379	Bank One
0005-5387	Banker
0005-5395	Banker & Tradesman
0005-5409	Bankers Digest *changed to* Special Office Brief
0005-5417	Bankers Digest
0005-5425	Banker's Letter of the Law
0005-5433	Bankers' Magazine (London) *see* 0737-6413
0005-5441	Bankers Magazine
0005-545X	Bankers' Magazine of Australasia *changed to* Australian Banker
0005-5468	Banking *changed to* A B A Banking Journal
0005-5492	Banking Law Journal
0005-5506	Banking News *changed to* Maryland Banking Quarterly
0005-5514	Bankinsurance News
0005-5522	Bankruptcy Law Reports
0005-5530	Bankvaerlden
0005-5549	Banner (Grand Rapids)
0005-5557	Banneret
0005-5565	Bano
0005-5573	Banque
0005-5581	Banque Centrale des Etats de l'Afrique de l'Ouest. Notes d'Information et Statistiques
0005-559X	Banque de Port-Said. Revue Economique Trimestrielle
0005-5603	Banque Nationale de Belgique. Bulletin
0005-5611	Banque Nationale de Paris. Revue†
0005-562X	Bantu Education Journal/Bantoe Onderwysblad *see* 0250-152X
0005-5662	Banyaszati es Kohaszati Lapok - Kohaszat
0005-5670	Baptist Bulletin
0005-5689	Baptist Challenge
0005-5697	Baptist Herald
0005-5700	Baptist History and Heritage
0005-5719	Baptist Leader
0005-5727	Baptist Program
0005-5743	Baptist Progress
0005-5751	Baptist Quarterly
0005-576X	Baptist Record
0005-5778	Baptist Times
0005-5786	Baptist Witness *see* 0726-4097
0005-5794	Baptist World
0005-5808	N A B E News†
0005-5816	Bar Examiner
0005-5824	Bar-Server†
0005-5840	Barat Review†
0005-5859	Baratz'ba
0005-5867	Baraza *changed to* Chemsa Bongo
0005-5875	Barba
0005-5883	Barbados Museum and Historical Society. Journal
0005-5891	Barclays Trade Review *see* 0250-2402
0005-5913	Barco Pesquero†
0005-5921	Bardic Echoes†
0005-5948	Barid Hollanda
0005-5956	Barkai
0005-5964	Barke†
0005-5972	Barmer Ersatzkasse *changed to* Die Barmer
0005-5980	Barmherzigkeit
0005-5999	Barn i Hem-Skola-Samhaelle
0005-6006	Barnard Bulletin
0005-6014	Baromfiipar *see* 0133-011X
0005-6049	Barron's National Business and Financial Weekly
0005-6073	Baseball Digest
0005-609X	Basic Journal Abstracts†
0005-6103	Basilicata
0005-6111	Basis
0005-6138	Basis
0005-6146	Basketbal *changed to* Play Off / Basketbal
0005-6154	Basketball *changed to* Basketball Monthly
0005-6162	Basketball Weekly
0005-6170	Basler Predigten
0005-6189	Basse Normandie Automobile
0005-6197	Basteria
0005-6219	Bat Research News
0005-6227	Bateaux
0005-6235	Baths Service *changed to* Baths Service and Recreation Management
0005-626X	Batiment
0005-6278	Baatnytt
0005-6308	Baton Rouge *changed to* Baton Rouge's Commerce
0005-6324	Battaglia Letteraria
0005-6332	Battaglie Postelegrafoniche
0005-6340	Battery Man
0005-6359	Batting the Breeze
0005-6367	Battleacts†
0005-6375	Bau†
0005-6383	Bau; Fachzeitschrift fuer Bautechnik, Baupraxis und Baumaschinen *changed to* Bau; Fachzeitschrift fuer Baupraxis, Bautechnik, Baumaschinen, Betriebsfuehrung und Kalkulation
0005-6391	Bau *see* 0172-2514
0005-6413	Bau & Bauindustrie†
0005-6421	Bau und Baustoff
0005-643X	Der Baustoffmarkt
0005-6448	Bauamt und Gemeindebau *see* 0005-6847
0005-6472	Baubeschlag Magazin mit Praktikus *changed to* Baubeschlag Magazin
0005-6480	Bingo
0005-6499	Bauen und Fertighaus
0005-6510	Bauen mit Holz
0005-6545	Bauen und Siedeln
0005-6553	Der Bauer
0005-6561	Bauern und Gaertner†
0005-657X	Bauforum
0005-6596	

ISSN INDEX 1205

ISSN	Title
0005-6618	Das Baugeruest
0005-6626	Baugeschaeft und Bauunternehmer
0005-6634	Baugewerbe
0005-6642	Bauinformation see 0323-8490
0005-6650	Bauingenieur
0005-6677	Baum Bugle
0005-6685	Baumaschine Baugeraet Baustoff changed to Baumaschine - Baugeraet - Baustelle
0005-6693	Baumaschine und Bautechnik
0005-6707	Baumaschinen und Baugeraette Revue†
0005-6715	Baumaschinen- und Baugeraete-Handel
0005-6723	B D Baumaschinendienst
0005-674X	Baumeister
0005-6758	Bauplanung - Bautechnik
0005-6766	Baupraxis†
0005-6782	Bausparkasse der Rheinprovinz†
0005-6790	Baustein
0005-6804	Baustoff- und Baubedarfs-Grosshandel
0005-6839	Bauunternehmer changed to Bau; Fachzeitschrift fuer Baupraxis, Bautechnik, Baumaschinen, Betriebsfuehrung und Kalkulation
0005-6847	Die Bauverwaltung
0005-6855	Bauwelt
0005-6863	Bauwirtschaft. Ausgabe B
0005-6871	Bauzeitung
0005-688X	Das Bauzentrum
0005-6928	New England Architect changed to Architecture: New England
0005-6936	Bay State F L Bulletin changed to Massachusetts Foreign Language Bulletin
0005-6944	Bay State Librarian
0005-6952	Bayavaya Uskalos
0005-6987	Bayer-Mitteilungen fuer die Gummi-Industrie†
0005-6995	Bayerische Akademie der Wissenschaften. Mathematisch-Naturwissenschaftliche Klasse. Abhandlungen
0005-7002	Bayerische Beamtenzeitung†
0005-7010	Bayerische Blaetter fuer Stenographie
0005-7029	Bayerische Boerse in Muenchen. Amtliches Kursblatt
0005-7045	Bayerische Gemeindezeitung
0005-7053	Bayerische Kleingaertner†
0005-7061	Das Bayerische Kraftfahrzeughandwerk
0005-7088	Der Metzgermeister
0005-7096	Bayerische Standesamt changed to Das Standesamt
0005-710X	Bayerische Akademie der Wissenschaften. Philosophisch-Historische Klasse. Abhandlungen
0005-7118	Bayerischer Landesverein fuer Familienkunde. Blaetter
0005-7126	Bayerisches Aerzteblatt
0005-7142	Bayerisches Justizministerialblatt
0005-7150	Bayerisches Landwirtschaftliches Jahrbuch
0005-7169	Bayerisches Landwirtschaftliches Wochenblatt
0005-7177	Bayerisches Sonntagsblatt fuer die Katholische Familie
0005-7185	Bayerisches Staatsministerium des Innern. Ministerialamtsblatt der Bayerischen Inneren Verwaltung
0005-7193	Bayerisches Staatsministerium fuer Arbeit und Soziale Fuersorge Amtsblatt. see 0340-1790
0005-7207	Bayerisches Staatsministerium fuer Unterricht und Kultus. Amtsblatt
0005-7215	Bayern in Zahlen changed to Bayerisches Landesamt fuer Statistik und Datenverarbeitung. Zeitschrift. Bayern in Zahlen.
0005-7223	Bayern Nachrichten†
0005-7231	Bayernturner
0005-724X	Baylor Business Studies†
0005-7258	Baylor Dental Journal
0005-7266	Baylor Geological Studies Bulletin
0005-7274	Baylor Law Review
0005-7282	Bayreuther Gemeindeblatt
0005-7312	Bazuin
0005-7320	Beacon
0005-7339	Beacon (New York)
0005-7347	Beacon
0005-7363	Beaconette
0005-7371	Be'ad Ve- Neged†
0005-738X	Beaken
0005-7398	Beam
0005-7401	Beamte im Lande Bremen see 0721-8206
0005-741X	Der Beamte in Rheinland-Pfalz
0005-7428	Bearing Engineer†
0005-7436	Beato Angelo
0005-7460	Beautiful British Columbia
0005-7495	Beauty Tips†
0005-7509	Beaux-Arts changed to Journal des Beaux-Arts
0005-7517	Beaver
0005-7525	Beaver
0005-7533	Bebidas
0005-755X	Beckman Report
0005-7568	Bedding
0005-7576	Bedford Stuyvesant Youth in Action Monthly Newsletter
0005-7584	Bedford Transport†
0005-7592	Bedfordshire Magazine
0005-7606	Bedriftsoekonomen see 0800-8159
0005-7630	Bedrijfsjournalist†
0005-7649	Bedrijfspluimveehouder changed to Pluimveehouderij
0005-7657	Bedrijfsvervoer changed to Vervoer en Transporttechniek
0005-7665	Bedside Nurse changed to Licensed Practical Nurse
0005-7673	Bedsitter
0005-7681	Det Bedste fra Reader's Digest (Danish Edition)
0005-769X	Beduin
0005-7703	Bee Craft
0005-7711	Bee-Hive changed to United Technologies Bee-Hive
0005-772X	Bee World
0005-7738	Beef
0005-7746	Beef and Sheep Farming see 0262-4559
0005-7754	Beekeeping
0005-7770	Beer Wholesaler
0005-7789	Beet†
0005-7797	F B U-Befael
0005-7800	Begegnung
0005-7819	Begegnung mit Polen
0005-7843	Behavioural Sciences and Community Development changed to Journal of Rural Development
0005-786X	Behavioral Research in Highway Safety†
0005-7878	Behavior Research Methods and Instrumentation see 0743-3808
0005-7886	Behavior Science Notes see 0094-3673
0005-7894	Behavior Therapy
0005-7916	Journal of Behavior Therapy and Experimental Psychiatry
0005-7924	Behavior Today
0005-7932	Behavioral Neuropsychiatry
0005-7940	Behavioral Science
0005-7959	Behaviour
0005-7967	Behaviour Research and Therapy
0005-7983	Behind the Headlines
0005-7991	Behinderte Kind see 0175-5854
0005-8009	Bei Uns
0005-8017	Beihefte zum Geologischen Jahrbuch see 0341-6429
0005-8017	Beihefte zum Geologischen Jahrbuch see 0341-6410
0005-8017	Beihefte zum Geologischen Jahrbuch see 0341-6399
0005-8017	Beihefte zum Geologischen Jahrbuch see 0341-6402
0005-8025	Contributions to Plasma Physics
0005-8041	Beitraege zur Biologie der Pflanzen
0005-805X	Beitraege zur Entomologie
0005-8068	Beitraege zur Geschichte der Arbeiterbewegung
0005-8076	Beitraege zur Geschichte der Deutschen Sprache und Literatur
0005-8084	Beitraege zur Linguistik und Informationsverarbeitung†
0005-8092	Literaturkunde. Beitraege
0005-8106	Musikwissenschaft. Beitraege
0005-8114	Beitraege zur Namenforschung
0005-8122	Beitraege zur Naturkundlichen Forschung in Suedwestdeutschland see 0176-3997
0005-8149	Beitraege zur Orthopaedie und Traumatologie
0005-8157	Beitraege zur Paedagogischen Arbeit
0005-8165	Beitraege zur Pathologie see 0344-0338
0005-8173	Beitraege zur Physik der Atmosphaere
0005-8181	Romanische Philologie. Beitraege
0005-819X	Beitraege zur Tabakforschung see 0173-783X
0005-8203	Beitraege zur Tropischen und Subtropischen Landwirtschaft und Tropen Veterinaermedizin see 0301-567X
0005-8211	Beitraege zur Vogelkunde
0005-822X	Bejaarden changed to Senior
0005-8238	B E K - Bruecke changed to Barmer Bruecke
0005-8246	Germany (Democratic Republic). Amt fuer Erfindungs- und Patentwesen. Bekanntmachungen
0005-8254	Bekhan Wa Bedan
0005-8262	Beklaednadsfolket
0005-8270	Bekleidung und Maschenware
0005-8289	Bekleidung und Waesche
0005-8297	Beku Nyusu
0005-8300	Bela Abela
0005-8319	Belarus'
0005-8327	Belaruskaja Carkva
0005-8335	Maandblad Belasting Beschouwingen
0005-8351	Belfagor
0005-8378	Belgian Chamber of Commerce in Great Britain Journal changed to Business Contact
0005-8386	Het Beste uit Reader's Digest (Belgian-Flemish Edition)
0005-8394	Belgian Trade Review changed to Belgian American Trade Review
0005-8408	Belgicatom
0005-8416	Belgique Hoteliere
0005-8424	Belgique Laitiere/Belgisch Zuivelbedrijf see 0770-2515
0005-8440	Tijdschrift voor Geneeskunde
0005-8459	Belgische Duivensport
0005-8467	Belgische Fruitrevue
0005-8475	Belgische Textielreiniging
0005-8483	Belgische Tuinbouw
0005-8491	Belgium: Economic and Technical Information
0005-8521	Belgium. Ministere des Affaires Economiques. Bibliotheque Centrale (Fonds Quetelet). Accroissements
0005-853X	Belgium. Ministere des Finances. Administration des Contributions. Bulletin des Contributions/Bulletin der Belastingen
0005-8556	Bell Journal of Economics and Management Science see 0741-6261
0005-8564	Bell Laboratories Record changed to A T & T Bell Laboratories Record
0005-8572	Bell Ringer
0005-8580	Bell System Technical Journal changed to A T & T Bell Laboratories Technical Journal
0005-8602	Bella (Milan, 1947)
0005-8610	Bellamy - Nieuws
0005-8629	Belleza y Moda
0005-8637	Bellezza
0005-8645	Bellona†
0005-8653	Belmont Teachers Association. Newsletter changed to Beacon
0005-8661	Beloit Poetry Journal
0005-867X	Belora†
0005-8696	Benavides
0005-8726	Benedictines
0005-8734	Benedictijns Tijdschrift
0005-8742	Benediktusbote
0005-8750	U.S. Unemployment Insurance Service. Benefit Series Service, Unemployment Insurance†
0005-8769	Benelux Economica en Statistisch Kwartaalbericht/Bulletin Trimestriel Benelux Economique et Statistique changed to Benelux Tijdschrift
0005-8777	Benelux Publikatieblad
0005-8785	Benfica
0005-8793	Bengal Medical Journal
0005-8807	Bengal: Past and Present
0005-8815	Bengali Literature
0005-884X	Bent of Tau Beta Pi
0005-8858	Benzin & Olie Bladet
0005-8866	Beratende Ingenieure
0005-8874	Berea Alumnus
0005-8890	Berean Searchlight
0005-8904	Denmark. Forsoegslaboratoriet. Beretning see 0105-6883
0005-8912	B H M. Berg- und Huettenmaennische Monatshefte.
0005-8920	Bergbauwissenschaften und Verfahrenstechnik†
0005-8939	Winter-Bergkamerad see 0340-1294
0005-8947	Das Bergmann-Echo
0005-8955	Bergomun
0005-8963	Der Bergsteiger
0005-8971	Bergverks-Nytt
0005-898X	Bergvriend
0005-9013	Berichte Biochemie und Biologie†
0005-9021	Bunsengesellschaft fuer Physikalische Chemie. Berichte
0005-9048	Berichte Physiologie, Physiologische Chemie und Pharmakologie†
0005-9056	Berichte ueber die Allgemeine und Spezielle Pathologie changed to Berichte Pathologie
0005-9072	Berichte ueber Die Gesamte Biologie Abt. A: Berichte ueber Die Wissenschaftliche Biologie see 0005-9013
0005-9080	Berichte ueber Landwirtschaft
0005-9099	Berichte zur deutschen Landeskunde†
0005-9102	Berichte zur Raumforschung und Raumplanung
0005-9110	Berichten van de Afdeling Volkskredietwezen
0005-9129	Berita Bibliografi see 0216-1273
0005-9145	Berita Selulosa
0005-9153	Berita Shell
0005-9161	Berkeley Barb†
0005-917X	Berkeley Monitor changed to Grassroots (Berkeley)
0005-9188	Berkeley Tribe†
0005-9196	Berkshire News changed to American Landrace
0005-920X	Berkshire Review
0005-9218	Magazine R V I - Info R V I changed to Info Renault Vehicules Industriels
0005-9226	Berlin
0005-9242	Berlin-Flugplan
0005-9250	Berlin Programm
0005-9269	Berliner Baer
0005-9277	Berliner Bank. Wirtschaftsbericht
0005-9285	Betten-Magazin
0005-9293	Berliner Leben†
0005-9307	Berliner Liberale Zeitung
0005-9323	Berliner Sozialversicherungs beamte und angestellte†
0005-9331	Berliner Statistik
0005-934X	Berliner Studentenzeitung
0005-9358	Berliner Turnzeitung
0005-9366	Berliner und Muenchener Tieraerztliche Wochenschrift
0005-9374	Sozialistische Politik†
0005-9382	Bermudian Magazine
0005-9390	Sint Bernardus
0005-9404	Berner Briefmarken-Zeitung
0005-9412	Berner Wochen Bulletin
0005-9420	Berner Zeitschrift fuer Geschichte und Heimatkunde
0005-9439	Bernice P. Bishop Museum Bulletin
0005-9455	Bertelsmann Briefe
0005-9471	Beruf und Gesinnung
0005-948X	Berufliche Bildung changed to Gewerkschaftliche Bildungspolitik
0005-9498	Berufs-Dermatosen see 0343-2432
0005-9501	Berufsberatung und Berufsbildung
0005-951X	Die Berufsbildende Schule

ISSN INDEX

0005-9528 Berufsbildende Schule Oesterreichs†
0005-9536 Berufsbildung
0005-9544 Berufsgenossenschaft see 0723-7561
0005-9560 Berufstaetige Frau Oesterreichs†
0005-9579 Besco News†
0005-9587 Besier's Hauswirtschaftliche†
0005-9595 Besser Verpacken changed to O V Z-Mitteilungen
0005-9609 Besseres Obst
0005-9617 Best in Documents†
0005-9625 Best Sellers
0005-9641 Best Songs†
0005-965X Best Wishes
0005-9668 Das Beste aus Reader's Digest (German Edition)
0005-9676 Das Beste aus Reader's Digest (Swiss-German Edition)
0005-9684 Det Beste fra Reader's Digest (Norwegian Edition)
0005-9692 Het Beste uit Reader's Digest (Dutch Edition)
0005-9706 Best's Review. Life/Health Insurance Edition
0005-9714 Best's Review. Property-Liability Insurance Edition see 0161-7745
0005-9722 Best's Weekly Digest changed to Best's Insurance Management Reports: Life-Health Edition
0005-9730 Bestsellers see 0744-3102
0005-9749 Bet ha-Talmud†
0005-9757 Beta Phi Mu Newsletter
0005-9765 Betail
0005-9773 Betar Jagat
0005-9781 Betelgeuse†
0005-979X Bet Mikra
0005-9803 Bethany Guide†
0005-9811 Bethany Nazarene College Today†
0005-982X Bethel College Bulletin
0005-9838 Bethlehem Express
0005-9846 Beton
0005-9854 Beton Arme
0005-9889 Beton i Zhelezobeton
0005-9897 Beton-Landbau see 0171-7952
0005-9900 Beton- und Stahlbetonbau
0005-9919 Betonituote
0005-9927 Betonstein-Zeitung see 0373-4331
0005-9935 Der Betrieb
0005-9943 Betrieb und Absatz†
0005-9951 Betriebliche Altersversorgung
0005-996X Betriebsausruestung changed to Betriebs und Ausruestung
0005-9986 Betriebswirtschafts-Magazin
0006-0003 Buerotechnik changed to Sysdata
0006-0011 Betriebswirtschaftliche Blaetter fuer die Praxis der Sparkassen und Girozentralen changed to Betriebswirtschaftliche Blaetter fuer die Praxis der Sparkassen und Landesbanken/Girozentralen
0006-0046 Better Breeding
0006-0054 Better Broadcasts News changed to Telemedium
0006-0062 Better Business†
0006-0070 Better Camping†
0006-0089 Better Crops with Plant Food
0006-0100 Better Driving†
0006-0119 Better Editing†
0006-0127 Better Education
0006-0151 Better Homes and Gardens
0006-016X Better Investing
0006-0186 Better Management
0006-0194 Better Radio and Television
0006-0208 Better Roads
0006-0216 Better Supervision†
0006-0224 Better Times
0006-0232 Better Tomorrows†
0006-0240 Better Transit Bulletin see 0029-4039
0006-0291 Between Ourselves changed to Horizons
0006-0305 Between the Lines see 0887-428X
0006-0313 Beursbengel
0006-033X Bevar†
0006-0356 Beverage Bulletin. Southern California
0006-0364 Beverage Industry News see 0274-9041
0006-0372 Beverage Media
0006-0399 Beverages
0006-0410 Beverly Review
0006-0429 Bewusster Leben
0006-0453 Bezpecnost a Hygiena Prace
0006-0461 Bhagirath
0006-047X Bharat Medical Journal†
0006-0488 Bharat Sevak
0006-0496 Bharatha Darshan
0006-050X Bharati Te Videshi Sahita
0006-0518 Bhavan's Journal
0006-0526 Bhopal Regional College of Education. Journal†
0006-0534 Bhubaneswar Review
0006-0542 Bhushan's World Trade Enquiries
0006-0569 Biafra Time
0006-0577 Bianco e Nero
0006-0585 Bibbia e Oriente
0006-0593 Bibel Heute
0006-0607 Bibel-Journalen
0006-0615 Bibel und Gemeinde
0006-0623 Bibel und Kirche
0006-064X Bibel und Liturgie
0006-0658 Bibeltrogna Vaenners Missionstidning
0006-0674 Bible Advocate and Herald of the Coming Kingdom see 0009-630X
0006-0690 Bible Collector†
0006-0704 Bible et Son Message see 0761-7267
0006-0712 Bible et Terre Sainte changed to Monde de la Bible
0006-0720 Bible et Vie Chretienne†
0006-0739 Bible Friend
0006-0747 Bible in New York changed to BibleWorld
0006-0755 Bible Society News changed to Word in Action: the Bible in the World
0006-0763 Bible Lands
0006-0771 Bible Readers' Union Bulletin see 0334-2166
0006-078X Bible Searchers
0006-0798 Bible Searchers: Teacher
0006-0801 American Bible Society Record
0006-081X Bible Standard and Herald of Christ's Kingdom
0006-0828 Bible-Time
0006-0836 Bible Today
0006-0844 Bible Translator see 0260-0943
0006-0844 Bible Translator see 0260-0935
0006-0860 Biblia
0006-0879 Biblia Revuo
0006-0887 Biblica
0006-0895 Biblical Archaeologist
0006-0909 Biblical Missions
0006-0917 Biblical Theology
0006-0925 Biblical Viewpoint
0006-0941 Bibliofilia
0006-0968 Bibliografia Argentina de Artes y Letras†
0006-0976 Bibliografia Brasileira Mensal†
0006-0992 Bibliografia Classificada
0006-100X Bibliografia Economica de Mexico changed to Bibliografia Economica de Mexico. Libros
0006-1018 Bibliografia Elettrotecnica
0006-1026 Bibliografia Historica de Espana e Hispanoamerica see 0537-3522
0006-1034 Bibliografia Internazionale di Scienze ed Arti
0006-1042 Bibliografia Italiana di Idraulica
0006-1050 Bibliografia Medica Internacional†
0006-1069 Bibliografia Mexicana
0006-1077 Bibliografia Nazionale Italiana
0006-1085 Bibliografia Venezolana
0006-1093 Bibliografia Zawartosci Czasopism
0006-1107 Statni Knihovna C S R. Bibliograficky Casopis†
0006-1115 Bibliograficky Katalog C S S R: Clanky v Ceskych Casopisech
0006-1123 Spolecenske Vedy. Rada 2: Bibliografie Ekonomicke Literatury see 0139-5203
0006-1158 Bibliografia Jugoslovenske Periodike see 0350-0349
0006-1166 Bibliografija Prispelih Knjiga Clanaka Iz Strucnih Casopisa i Drugih Dokumenata
0006-1182 Bibliographia I U L A-I F H P changed to Bibliographia I U L A
0006-1190 Bibliographia Africana
0006-1204 Bibliographia Anastatica see 0303-4550
0006-1212 Bibliographia Asiatica
0006-1220 Bibliographia Asiatica see 0004-4733
0006-1239 Bibliographia Geodaetica
0006-1247 Bibliographia Neuroendocrinologica†
0006-1255 Bibliographic Index
0006-1271 Bibliographical Bulletin for Welding and Allied Processes†
0006-128X Bibliographical Society of America. Papers
0006-1298 Bibliographie Africaine
0006-1301 Bibliographie Agricole Courante Roumaine†
0006-131X Bibliographie Americaniste†
0006-1328 Centre Technique du Cuir. Bibliographie Analytique et Signaletique†
0006-1336 Bibliographie de Belgique
0006-1344 Bibliographie de la France†
0006-1352 Bibliographie de la Philosophie
0006-1360 Bibliographie der Deutschen Bibliographien see 0301-4614
0006-1379 Bibliographie der Kunstblaetter†
0006-1387 Bibliographie der Pflanzenschutzliteratur
0006-1409 Bibliographie der Uebersetzungen Deutschsprachiger Werke
0006-1417 Bibliographie der Wirtschaftspresse
0006-1433 Bibliographie, Documentation, Terminologie†
0006-1441 Bibliographie du Quebec
0006-1468 Bibliographie Staat und Recht der Deutschen Demokratischen Republik (Vierteljahresbibliographie)†
0006-1476 World Bibliography of Social Security
0006-1484 Bibliographies of Atomic Energy Literature†
0006-1506 Bibliographische Berichte
0006-1514 Bibliographische Zeitschrift fuer Aesthetik†
0006-1522 Bibliography and Index of Geology Exclusive of North America see 0098-2784
0006-1530 Bibliography of Agriculture
0006-1557 Bibliography of Indian Fisheries changed to Indian Fisheries Abstracts
0006-1565 Bibliography of Reproduction
0006-1573 Bibliography of Systematic Mycology
0006-1581 Shu Mo Chi Kan. Bibliography Quarterly
0006-159X Biblion†
0006-1603 Bibliophilie see 0399-9742
0006-1611 Biblioteca
0006-162X Biblioteca Americana de Autores. Boletin†
0006-1646 Biblioteca de Menendez Pelayo. Boletin
0006-1654 Biblioteca della Liberta
0006-1662 Biblioteca do Sejur. Boletim
0006-1670 Tribunal Justica Estado da Guanabara. Biblioteca. Boletim changed to Rio de Janeiro, Brazil (State). Tribunal de Justicia. Biblioteca. Boletim
0006-1697 Biblioteca "Jose Artigas". Boletin
0006-1700 Biblioteca Labronica Notiziario
0006-1719 Universidad Nacional Autonoma de Mexico. Instituto de Investigaciones Bibliograficas. Boletin
0006-1727 Biblioteca Nacional Jose Marti. Revista
0006-1751 Biblioteca y Hemeroteca de Servicios Electricos del Gran Buenos Aires. Boletin Bibliografico changed to Servicios Electricos del Gran Buenos Aires S.A. Boletin Bibliografico
0006-176X Bibliotecas
0006-1778 Biblioteconomia†
0006-1786 Bibliotek for Laeger
0006-1808 Bibliotekar'
0006-1816 Bibliotekar
0006-1824 Bibliotek 70
0006-1832 Bibliotekarstvo
0006-1840 Biblioteket Presenterar Nya Boecker†
0006-1859 Biblioteki Z.N.E.P.A.N. Biuletyn Informacyjny†
0006-1867 Biblioteksbladet
0006-1913 Bibliotheca Orientalis
0006-1921 Bibliotheca Sacra
0006-193X Bibliotheck
0006-1948 Technische Hogeschool te Delft. Bibliotheek. Aanwinsten
0006-1956 Bibliotheekgids changed to Bibliotheek-en Archiefgids
0006-1964 Der Bibliothekar
0006-1972 Bibliotheksdienst
0006-1980 Bibliotheque de l'Ecole des Chartes
0006-1999 Bibliotheque d'Humanisme et Renaissance
0006-2006 Bulletin des Bibliotheques de France
0006-2014 Biblische Zeitschrift
0006-2022 Biblos
0006-2030 Biblos
0006-2057 Bichitra†
0006-2065 Bicycle Journal changed to Bicycle Business Journal
0006-2073 Bicycling
0006-209X Bielarus
0006-2111 Bien-Etre Social Canadien changed to Digeste Social
0006-212X Die Biene
0006-2146 Bienenvater
0006-2154 Bienenwelt
0006-2189 Big Farmer see 0274-6050
0006-2219 Bihar Industries
0006-2227 Bij de Haard
0006-2235 Bijbellessen voor de Kinderen
0006-2243 Bijbellessen voor de Sabbatschool
0006-2251 Bijblad bij de Industriele Eigendom
0006-226X Bijblijven
0006-2278 Bijdragen
0006-2286 Bijdragen tot de Geschiedenis
0006-2294 Bijdragen tot de Taal-, Land- en Volkenkunde
0006-2308 Bijeen
0006-2316 Bijou Magazine
0006-2324 Biken Journal
0006-2340 Bilanz
0006-2359 Bilanz- und Buchhaltungspraxis
0006-2367 Bilbransjen/Bilteknisk Fagblad
0006-2375 Bild der Wissenschaft
0006-2383 Bild und Ton
0006-2391 Bildende Kunst
0006-2405 Bildermaerchen†
0006-2413 Bildlexikon der Nutzhoelzer
0006-2421 Bildmessung und Luftbildwesen
0006-243X Bildnerische Erziehung†
0006-2448 Bildor changed to Building Business and Apartment Management Bildor
0006-2456 Bildung und Erziehung
0006-2464 Bilen og Baden changed to Bilen, Motor og Sport
0006-2472 Biliardo
0006-2502 Bill of Rights Newsletter see 0160-7731
0006-2510 Billboard
0006-2529 Bille-Anzeigen-Rundschau
0006-2537 Billed Bladet
0006-2545 Billiards & Snooker†
0006-2553 Billiken
0006-2561 Savez Sindikata Jugoslavije. Centralni Vec. Bilten changed to Savez Sindikata Jugoslavije. Veca S S J. Bilten
0006-257X Bilten Dokumentacije. Biljna Proizvodnja see 0351-2312
0006-2588 Bilten Dokumentacije. Elektrotehnika see 0351-238X
0006-2588 Bilten Dokumentacije. Elektrotehnika changed to Bilten Dokumentacije. Elektrotehnika i Elektronika. Proizvodnja Elektricnih Masina i Aparata. Ptt Usluge
0006-2596 Bilten Dokumentacije. Goriva i Maziva†
0006-260X Bilten Dokumentacije. Gradjevinarstvo i Arhitektura see 0352-1028
0006-260X Bilten Dokumentacije. Gradjevinarstvo i Arhitektura see 0351-2576
0006-260X Bilten Dokumentacije. Gradjevinarstvo i Arhitektura see 0351-2592
0006-2618 Bilten Dokumentacije. Hemija i Hemijska Industrija

ISSN	Title
0006-2626	Bilten Dokumentacije. Industrija Tekstila i Papira†
0006-2634	Bilten Dokumentacije. Masinska Tehnologija i Radne Masine see 0351-8906
0006-2642	Bilten Dokumentacije. Metalurgija
0006-2650	Bilten Dokumentacije. Pogonske Masine i Masinski Delovi see 0351-8906
0006-2669	Bilten Dokumentacije. Prehrambena Industrija see 0351-2479
0006-2677	Bilten Dokumentacije. Rudarstvo i Geologija
0006-2685	Bilten Dokumentacije. Saobracaj
0006-2693	Bilten Dokumentacije. Silikatna Industrija see 0351-2509
0006-2707	Bilten Dokumentacije. Stocna Proizvodnja i Veterinarstvo see 0351-2320
0006-2715	Bilten Dokumentacije. Sumarstvo i Drvna Industrija†
0006-2731	Bilten Pravne Sluzbe J N A
0006-2758	Bilten Zavoda za Osnovno Obrazovanje i Obrazovanje Nastavnika Sr Srbije
0006-2766	Bim
0006-2774	Iranian Journal of Plant Pathology
0006-2790	Bimestre†
0006-2804	Binario
0006-2812	Binden en Bouwen
0006-2863	BioDynamics
0006-2871	Bio-Graphic Quarterly†
0006-2898	Biomedical Engineering see 0309-1902
0006-2901	Bioastronautics Report†
0006-291X	Biochemical and Biophysical Research Communications
0006-2928	Biochemical Genetics
0006-2944	Biochemical Medicine see 0885-4505
0006-2952	Biochemical Pharmacology
0006-2960	Biochemistry
0006-2979	Biochemistry
0006-2995	Biochemistry and Experimental Biology†
0006-3002	Biochimica et Biophysica Acta
0006-3029	Biofizika
0006-3037	Biogenic Amines and Transmitters in the Nervous System see 0193-5186
0006-3053	Biography Index
0006-3061	Bioinorganic Chemistry see 0162-0134
0006-307X	Biokhimiya
0006-3088	Biologia changed to Biologia. A: Botany
0006-3088	Biologia changed to Biologia. B: Zoology
0006-3088	Biologia changed to Biologia. C: General Biology
0006-3088	Biologia changed to Biologia. D: Biochemistry and Molecular Biology
0006-3096	Biologia
0006-310X	Biologia Culturale†
0006-3118	Biologia Gabonica
0006-3126	Biology of the Neonate
0006-3134	Biologia Plantarum
0006-3142	Biologiai Kozlemenyek/Biological Publications see 0133-3844
0006-3150	Biologica Latina†
0006-3169	Biological Abstracts
0006-3177	Biological and Agricultural Index
0006-3185	Biological Bulletin
0006-3193	Biological Bulletin†
0006-3207	Biological Conservation
0006-3215	Biological Photographic Association. Journal see 0274-497X
0006-3223	Biological Psychiatry
0006-3231	Cambridge Philosophical Society. Biological Reviews
0006-324X	Biological Society of Washington. Proceedings
0006-3258	Biologie et Gastro-Enterologie see 0399-8320
0006-3266	Biologie Medicale
0006-3274	Der Biologieunterricht
0006-3282	Biologische Abhandlungen
0006-3290	Biologische Rundschau
0006-3304	Biologisches Zentralblatt
0006-3339	Biologist
0006-3347	Biologist
0006-3355	Biology and Human Affairs see 0143-5051
0006-3363	Biology of Reproduction
0006-338X	Biomedical Electronics†
0006-3398	Biomedical Engineering
0006-341X	Biometrics
0006-3428	Biometrie Humaines see 0758-2714
0006-3436	Biometrie-Praximetrie
0006-3444	Biometrika
0006-3479	Bionomic Briefs†
0006-3487	Bionomica
0006-3495	Biophysical Journal
0006-3509	Biophysics
0006-3517	Biophysik see 0301-634X
0006-3517	Biophysik see 0175-7571
0006-3525	Biopolymers
0006-3533	Bioquimica Clinica changed to Acta Bioquimica Clinica Latinoamericana
0006-3541	BioResearch Index see 0192-6985
0006-355X	Biorheology
0006-3568	BioScience
0006-3576	Biosophia
0006-3584	Biota†
0006-3592	Biotechnology and Bioengineering
0006-3606	Biotropica
0006-3614	Birbal
0006-3630	Bird-Banding see 0273-8570
0006-3649	Bird Life
0006-3657	Bird Study
0006-3665	Birds
0006-3673	Birds and Country
0006-3681	Birlik
0006-369X	Birmingham
0006-3703	Birmingham ABC & Midland Counties Railway Time Tables†
0006-3711	Birmingham Bar Association. Bulletin
0006-3746	University of Birmingham Chemical Engineer†
0006-3754	Birmingham World
0006-3762	Birney Arrow†
0006-3770	Birra e Malto
0006-3797	Biscuits, Biscottes, Panification Industrielle, Produits Dietetiques, Chocolat, Confiserie changed to Magazine des Industries Gourmandes
0006-3800	In the Field of Building†
0006-3827	Bismoi
0006-3835	Bit
0006-3843	Bit
0006-3878	Bitaon Heyl Ha-avir
0006-3886	Bitidningen
0006-3908	Bitterroot
0006-3916	Bitumen
0006-3924	Bitumen, Teere, Asphalte, Peche changed to Strassen- und Tiefbau Vereinigt mit Strasse-Bruecke-Tunnel, Bitumen-Teere-Asphalts-Peche
0006-3932	Bitzaron: the Hebrew Monthly of America changed to Bitzaron: a Quarterly of Hebrew Letters
0006-3940	Biuletyn Biblioteki Jagiellonskiej
0006-3967	Biuletyn Historii Sztuki
0006-3975	Biuletyn Informacyjny†
0006-3983	Biblioteka Narodowa. Biuletyn Informacyjny
0006-4017	Biuletyn Numizmatyczny
0006-4025	Poland. Glowny Urzad Statystyczny. Biuletyn Statystyczny
0006-4033	Zydowski Instytut Historyczny w Polsce. Biuletyn
0006-4068	Bjelovarski List
0006-4076	Blaa Stjaernan
0006-4084	Black Academy Review†
0006-4106	Black Belt Magazine
0006-4114	Black Business Digest†
0006-4122	Black Careers
0006-4149	Black Diamond
0006-4165	Black Enterprise
0006-4173	Black Hills Anemone changed to Black Hills State Today
0006-4246	Black Scholar
0006-4254	Black Student†
0006-4262	Black Swamp Review†
0006-4289	Black Times: Voices of the National Community†
0006-4297	Black Vanguard
0006-4319	Black World†
0006-4327	Blackboard Bulletin
0006-4335	Blackcountryman
0006-4351	Blackpool Hotel & Guest House Association. Journal
0006-4378	Blaetter der Freien Volksbuehne Berlin
0006-4386	Blaetter fuer Agrarrecht†
0006-4394	Blaetter fuer den Deutschlehrer
0006-4408	Blaetter fuer deutsche Landesgeschichte
0006-4416	Blaetter fuer Deutsche und Internationale Politik
0006-4424	Blaetter fuer Fraenkische Familienkunde
0006-4440	Blaetter fuer Grundstuecks-, Bau- und Wohnungsrecht
0006-4459	Blaetter fuer Heimatkunde
0006-4475	Blaetter fuer Steuerrecht, Sozial Versicherung und Arbeitsrecht
0006-4483	Blaetter fuer Volksliteratur
0006-4491	Blaetter fuer Zuercherische Rechtsprechung
0006-4505	Blagovest†
0006-4513	Blagues
0006-453X	Blake Newsletter see 0160-628X
0006-4548	Blake Studies
0006-4556	Blaaklint see 0345-1593
0006-4564	B T N†
0006-4580	B L A S A Newsletter changed to African Library Association of S.A. Newsletter
0006-4610	Blaue, Alpwirtschaftliche Monatsblaetter
0006-4629	Blaue Kreuz
0006-4637	Der Blaue Peter
0006-4645	A en D
0006-4653	Blauwe Kruis
0006-4661	Blauwe Wimpel
0006-467X	Bleb changed to Ark (Tiburon)
0006-4688	Blech-Rohre-Profile
0006-4688	Blech Rohre Profile changed to Sheet Metal Tubes Sections
0006-4696	Blessings of Liberty
0006-4718	Blick und Bild
0006-4734	Blick ins Fleischer-Fachgeschaeft
0006-4742	Blick Ins Land
0006-4750	Blick vom Hochhaus
0006-4769	Blickpunkt
0006-4777	Blijde Boodschap
0006-4785	Blijdorp Geluiden†
0006-4793	Blikkenslager- Roer- og Sanitets Mesteren see 0106-8881
0006-4807	Blind Advocate changed to Advocate
0006-4815	Blind Citizen
0006-4823	Blind Welfare
0006-4831	Blindas Tidskrift†
0006-4858	Zeitschrift fuer das Blinden- und Sehbehindertenbildungswesen see 0176-7836
0006-4866	Blindenwelt changed to Die Blindenselbsthilfe
0006-4874	Blindmaker see 0305-733X
0006-4882	Blitz
0006-4890	Bloc
0006-4904	Der Block
0006-4912	Blodau'r Ffair
0006-4920	Bloemenvriend
0006-4939	Bloemfontein Nuusbrief
0006-4947	Bloemheuwel-Nuus
0006-4955	Blomster
0006-4963	Blomster-Branschen
0006-4971	Blood
0006-498X	Blood Group News†
0006-4998	Blood-Horse
0006-5005	Blood Therapy Journal changed to Blood Therapy Journal International
0006-5013	Bloodlines Journal changed to Bloodlines
0006-5021	Blue Anchor
0006-503X	Blue and Gold Triangle of Lambda Kappa Sigma
0006-5048	Blue and White†
0006-5056	Bluebook†
0006-5064	Blue Cloud Quarterly
0006-5072	Blue Cross Reports. Research Series see 0095-6740
0006-5099	Blue Jay
0006-5102	Blue Triangle†
0006-5129	Bluegrass Music News
0006-5137	Bluegrass Unlimited
0006-5153	Blues Unlimited
0006-5161	Blues World
0006-517X	Bluestocking†
0006-5188	Bluestone†
0006-5196	Blumea
0006-5218	Blumenau em Cadernos
0006-5226	Blumenfreundin Blumenpost
0006-5242	Blut
0006-5250	Blutalkohol
0006-5269	Blyttia
0006-5277	B'nai B'rith Messenger
0006-5307	Scripts†
0006-5323	Trade and Industry see 0143-9111
0006-5331	Board of Trade Newsletter see 0164-7059
0006-534X	Board Manufacture Practice see 0306-4123
0006-5358	Boardman changed to Boardmember
0006-5366	Boat & Motor Dealer
0006-5374	Boating
0006-5404	Boating Industry
0006-5412	Bobbin
0006-5420	Scientific Pest Control†
0006-5439	Bode van het Heil in Christus
0006-5455	Boden und Gesundheit
0006-5463	Boden, Wand, Decke
0006-5471	Die Bodenkultur
0006-548X	Bodensee Hefte
0006-5498	Bodine Motorgram
0006-5501	Body
0006-5528	National Defense Medical Journal
0006-5544	Boek der Boeken changed to Schrift
0006-5560	Boekenband
0006-5579	Boekengids
0006-5587	Boekverkoper
0006-5595	Boer see 0772-7054
0006-5609	Boer en Tuinder
0006-5617	Boerderij
0006-5625	Boerenleenbank changed to Rabobank
0006-5633	Boern & Unge
0006-5641	Boersenblatt fuer den Deutschen Buchhandel
0006-565X	Boersenblatt fuer den Deutschen Buchhandel. Frankfurter Ausgabe
0006-5692	Bogens Verden
0006-5706	Bogormen
0006-5714	Bogoslovlje
0006-5722	Bogoslovni Vestnik
0006-5730	Bogtrykkerbladet
0006-5749	Bogvennen
0006-5765	B B R
0006-5773	Boi
0006-5781	Bois
0006-579X	Bois et Forets des Tropiques
0006-5803	Boissons de France "Saines et Legeres" see 0760-1999
0006-5811	Bok og Bibliotek
0006-582X	Bokbladet†
0006-5838	Bokmakierie
0006-5846	Bokvennen
0006-5854	Boletim Cultural da Guine Portuguesa
0006-5862	B I G (Boletim da Industria Grafica) changed to A B I G R A F em Revista
0006-5870	Boletim da Pesca changed to Revista do Pescador
0006-5897	Boletim de Bibliografia Portuguesa see 0253-3413
0006-5897	Boletim de Bibliografia Portuguesa see 0253-3421
0006-5897	Boletim de Bibliografia Portuguesa see 0253-343X
0006-5900	Boletim de Custos
0006-5919	Boletim de Desenvolvimento de Pessoal†
0006-5927	Boletim de Estudos de Pesca
0006-5935	Boletim de Minas
0006-5943	Boletim de Psicologia
0006-5951	Boletim do Leite e Seus Derivados
0006-596X	Boletim do Porto de Lisboa
0006-5978	Portos e Caminhos de Ferro de Mozambique changed to Mozambique. Direccao Nacional dos Portos e Caminhos de Ferro. Revista Trimestral.
0006-5994	Boletim Geoelectrico see 0870-4716

1208 ISSN INDEX

0006-6001 Mozambique. Servico Meteorologico. Boletim Geomagnetico Preliminar
0006-601X Boletim-Geral do Ultramar†
0006-6028 Boletim Geografico†
0006-6044 Mozambique. Servico Meteorologico. Boletim Meteorologico para a Agricultura
0006-6052 Boletim Meteorologico para a Agricultura†
0006-6060 Boletim Mineiro de Geografia
0006-6079 Boletim Paulista de Geografia
0006-6087 B R
0006-6095 Mozambique. Servico Meteorologico. Boletim Seismique
0006-6109 Boletim Sismico†
0006-6117 Boletim Tecnico da Petrobras
0006-6125 Boletin Agropecuario del Alto Valle†
0006-6133 Boletin Bibliografice de Revista "Signos"†
0006-6141 Boletin Bibliografico Boliviano
0006-6168 Boletin Bibliografico Mexicano
0006-6176 Boletin Chileno de Parasitologia
0006-6184 Banco de la Republica. Biblioteca Luis Angel Arango. Boletin Cultural y Bibliografico
0006-6192 Escuela Interamericana de Bibliotecologia. Boletin de Adquisiciones†
0006-6206 Boletin de Arte
0006-6249 Boletin de Estudios Economicos
0006-6257 Boletin de Estudios Oaxaquenos†
0006-6265 Boletin de Filologia Espanola†
0006-6273 Boletin de Formacion Cooperativa
0006-6281 Ministerio de Energia y Minas. Boletin de Geologia
0006-629X Boletin de Higiene y Epidemiologia *changed to* Revista Cubana de Higiene y Epidemiologia
0006-6303 Boletin de Historia y Antiguedades
0006-6311 Boletin de Informacion Dental *changed to* Revista Actualidad Estomatologica
0006-632X Boletin de Informacion Educativa†
0006-6338 Boletin de la Propiedad Industrial
0006-6346 Argentina. Ministerio de Trabajo y Seguridad Social. Boletin de Legislacion†
0006-6354 Boletin de Noticias†
0006-6362 Boletin del Deposito Legal de Obras Impresas *see* 0525-3675
0006-6389 Boletin Informativo†
0006-6397 Boletin Informativo sobre Estudios Latinoamericanos en Europa *see* 0304-2634
0006-6419 Boletin Juridico Militar
0006-6435 Boletin Mensual Climatologico†
0006-6451 Boletin Meteorologico de El Salvador†
0006-646X Boletin Naval
0006-6486 Boletin Produccion Animal†
0006-6494 Boletin Radiofonico T.V.
0006-6508 Boletin Uruguayo de Sociologia
0006-6524 Bolignyt *changed to* Vi Lejere
0006-6532 Bolivarian Review†
0006-6540 Bolivia
0006-6559 Bolivia - Land of Promise†
0006-6567 Bollettino delle Malattie dell'Orecchio, della Gola, del Naso *changed to* Otorinolaringologica
0006-6575 Bollettino di Pesca *changed to* Bollettino di Pesca, Piscicoltura e Idrobiologia
0006-6583 Bollettino di Studi Latini
0006-6591 Bollettino Storico Piacentino
0006-6605 I S L Bollettino Bibliografico†
0006-6613 Bollettino Bibliografico Internazionale per l'Apostolato delle Edizioni
0006-6621 Bollettino Bibliografico per le Scienze Morali e Sociale
0006-663X Bollettino Ceciliano
0006-6648 Bollettino Chimico Farmaceutico
0006-6656 D O X A Bollettino
0006-6664 Bollettino dei Brevetti per Invenzioni, Modelli e Marchi
0006-6680 Bollettino delle Accessioni di Periodici e Libri
0006-6699 Studio di Restauro Strini. Bollettino
0006-6702 Italy. Azienda Autonoma delle Ferrovie dello Stato. Informazioni Doc *changed to* Italy. Azienda Autonoma delle Ferrovie dello Stato. Informaioni Doc
0006-6710 Bollettino di Geodesia e Scienze Affini
0006-6729 Bollettino di Geofisica, Teorica ed Applicata
0006-6745 Bollettino di Libri Antichi e Moderni di Varia Cultura Esauriti e Rari
0006-6753 Italy. Laboratorio di Idrobiologia. Bollettino di Pesca Piscicoltura e Idrobiologia
0006-6761 Bollettino di Psicologia Applicata
0006-677X Bollettino d'Oculistica
0006-6788 Bollettino Ecclesiastico *changed to* Arcidiocesi di Reggio Calabria. Rivista Pastorale
0006-6796 Bollettino Economico
0006-680X Bollettino Emerografico di Economia Internazionale
0006-6826 Bollettino-Metallografico e di Odonto-Stoma-Tologia
0006-6834 Dati Meteorologico della Puglia e Luciania *changed to* Osservazioni di Meteorologia Agraria della Puglia e Basilicata
0006-6842 Italy. Consiglio dell'Ordine dei Medici di Torino. Bollettino Ordine dei Medici†
0006-6850 Bollettino Quindicinale dell'Emigrazione†
0006-6869 Bollettino Storico della Svizzera Italiana
0006-6877 Bollettino Tecnico Geloso
0006-6885 Bollettino Termomeccanica
0006-6893 Bollettino Tributario d'Informazioni
0006-6907 Bollettino Vincenziano
0006-6915 Bolsa de Valores de Mexico. Weekly Bulletin
0006-6923 Bolsa de Comercio de Buenos Aires. Boletin *changed to* Bolsa
0006-6931 Bolsa de Comercio de Rosario. Revista
0006-694X Bolsa de Valores do Rio de Janeiro. Boletim de Documentacao†
0006-6958 Bolwerk
0006-6966 Yelmo
0006-6974 Bombay Market
0006-6982 Bombay Natural History Society. Journal
0006-6990 Bon Appetit
0006-7016 Bona
0006-7024 Bona Espero
0006-7040 Bond and Money Market Review†
0006-7059 Bondline
0006-7067 Standard & Poor's Bond Outlook *see* 0731-1974
0006-7075 Bondholder's Register
0006-7091 Bondsspaarbanken *see* 0169-5401
0006-7113 Bonifatiusblatt
0006-7121 Bonjour
0006-713X Bonne Cuisine†
0006-7156 Bonner Meteorologische Abhandlungen
0006-7164 Bonner Zahlen†
0006-7172 Bonner Zoologische Beitraege
0006-7180 Bonsai Bulletin
0006-7199 Bonytt *see* 0800-1936
0006-7202 Book Club of California. Quarterly News-Letter
0006-7229 Book Collecting World
0006-7237 Book Collector
0006-7245 Book Exchange
0006-7253 Book-Keepers Journal *changed to* Administrative Accountant
0006-7261 Book Market†
0006-727X Book News†
0006-7288 Book News *changed to* Tartan Book Sales Catalog
0006-7296 Book News Letter
0006-730X Book-Of-The-Month Club News
0006-7318 Book Production Industry *see* 0273-8724
0006-7326 Book Review Digest
0006-7334 Rucksack *changed to* Rambler
0006-7342 Book Reviews of the Month†
0006-7350 Book Shopper Newsletter†
0006-7369 Book World
0006-7377 Bookbird
0006-7385 Booklist
0006-7393 Bookmark (Chapel Hill)
0006-7407 Bookmark (Albany)
0006-7415 Bookmark†
0006-7423 Books†
0006-7431 Books Abroad *changed to* World Literature Today
0006-7458 Books and Libraries at the University of Kansas
0006-7474 Books at Iowa
0006-7482 Books for Your Children
0006-7490 Books from Finland
0006-7504 Books from Hungary *see* 0324-3451
0006-7512 Books in Polish or Relating to Poland
0006-7520 Books of the Southwest
0006-7539 Bookseller
0006-7547 Bookseller
0006-7555 Bookseller Pustak Vikreta Baroda
0006-7563 Bookstore Journal
0006-7571 Boom-Pers Combinatie
0006-758X Boor
0006-7598 Boosey and Hawkes. Newsletter
0006-7601 Boost
0006-761X Boot- und Schiffbau†
0006-7636 Boote
0006-7644 Bootswirtschaft
0006-7652 Bor- es Cipotechnika
0006-7660 Bordeaux Chirurgical†
0006-7679 Borden Review of Nutrition Research†
0006-7695 Borderline Magazine†
0006-7709 Bore Da
0006-7717 Boreal *changed to* Boreal International
0006-7725 Borec
0006-7741 Borgazdasag
0006-775X Borghese
0006-7768 Borgyogyaszati es Venerologiai Szemle
0006-7784 Boris Kidric Institute of Nuclear Sciences. Bulletin†
0006-7792 Boern og Boeger
0006-7806 Borneo Research Bulletin
0006-7822 Boron in Glass
0006-7849 Borsa dei Noli
0006-7857 Borsa Marmi
0006-7865 Borussen-Echo
0006-7873 Disaster Prevention
0006-789X Bosch Technische Berichte
0006-7903 Bose Institute. Transactions
0006-792X Boss
0006-7946 Boston City Record
0006-7954 Boston College Industrial and Commercial Law Review *see* 0161-6587
0006-7997 Boston Museum Bulletin *see* 0739-5736
0006-8004 Boston Public Schools Review *changed to* B P S News
0006-8020 Boston Symphony Orchestra Program Book-Notes *changed to* Boston Symphony Orchestra Program
0006-8039 Boston University Journal†
0006-8047 Boston University Law Review
0006-8055 Botanica Marina
0006-8063 Academia Sinica. Botanical Bulletin
0006-8071 Botanical Gazette
0006-808X Botanical Magazine *changed to* Botanical Magazine, Tokyo
0006-8098 Botanical Museum Leaflets
0006-8101 Botanical Review
0006-811X Botanical Society of Bengal. Bulletin
0006-8128 Botanical Survey of India. Bulletin
0006-8136 Botanicheskii Zhurnal
0006-8144 Botanikai Kozlemenyek
0006-8152 Botanische Jahrbuecher fuer Systematik, Pflanzengeschichte und Pflanzengeographie
0006-8160 Botanische Tuinen en Het Belmonte Arboretum der Landbouwhogeschool Te Wageningen Mededelingen†
0006-8179 Botanische Staatssammlung Muenchen. Mitteilungen
0006-8187 Botanisk Tidsskrift *see* 0107-055X
0006-8195 Botaniska Notiser *see* 0107-055X
0006-8209 Bote
0006-8217 Bote aus der Apotheke†
0006-8225 Bote fuer Tirol
0006-8233 Both Sides Now
0006-8241 Bothalia
0006-8276 Botschafter des Kommenden Koenigs
0006-8284 Boucherie Francaise
0006-8292 Boulanger-Patissier *see* 0224-5027
0006-8306 Boumi Temple News
0006-8314 Boundary-Layer Meteorology
0006-8330 Bouwbelangen
0006-8349 Bouwen aan de Nieuwe Aarde
0006-8365 Bouwliteratuur Documentatie†
0006-8373 Bouwmachines
0006-8381 Bouwondernemer
0006-839X Bovagblad
0006-8403 Bow and Arrow
0006-8411 Bowlers Journal and Billiard Revue *see* 0164-9183
0006-842X Bowling Magazine
0006-8438 Bowling Notizie
0006-8446 Bowling Proprietor
0006-8454 Bowls in N.S.W
0006-8470 Box y Lucha
0006-8489 Boxboard Containers
0006-8497 Boxe Ring
0006-8519 Boxing News
0006-8527 Boxoffice
0006-8535 Boxwood Bulletin
0006-8543 Boyce Thompson Institute for Plant Research, Inc. Contributions†
0006-8551 Boys and Girls†
0006-856X Boys Baseball Bulletin *changed to* Pony Baseball Express Newsletter
0006-8578 Boys Brigade Gazette
0006-8586 Boys Club Bulletin
0006-8594 Boys Clubs of America. Journal *see* 0272-6513
0006-8608 Boys' Life (Inkprint Edition)
0006-8616 Brabant Tourisme
0006-8624 Brabantia
0006-8632 De Brabantse Leeuw
0006-8640 Bracara Augusta
0006-8667 Brackety - Ack
0006-8675 Bradfield College Chronicle
0006-8683 Bradford & Halifax Chambers of Commerce. Chamber of Commerce Journal
0006-8705 Bragantia
0006-8721 Brahmavadin
0006-873X Braille Book Review (Large Print Edition)
0006-8756 Braille Chess Magazine
0006-8764 Braille Digest
0006-8772 Braille Forum
0006-8780 Braille Journal of Physiotherapy
0006-8799 Braille Mainichi *changed to* Braille Mainichi Weekly
0006-8810 Braille Mirror
0006-8829 Braille Monitor (Inkprint Edition)
0006-8837 Braille Music Magazine
0006-8845 New Braille Musician *see* 0364-7501
0006-8853 Braille News Summary
0006-887X Braille Radio Times
0006-8888 Braille Rainbow
0006-8896 Braille Science Journal
0006-890X Braille Sporting Record
0006-8918 Braille Star Theosophist
0006-8926 Braille Sunday School Quarterly†
0006-8942 Braille Variety News†
0006-8950 Brain
0006-8969 Brain and Nerve
0006-8977 Brain, Behavior and Evolution
0006-8985 Brain News
0006-8993 Brain Research
0006-8993 Brain Research *issued with* 0165-3806
0006-8993 Brain Research *issued with* 0165-0173
0006-8993 Brain Research *issued with* 0169-328X
0006-9000 Brainstorms†
0006-9019 Brake and Front End Service *see* 0193-726X
0006-9027 Brand *changed to* Brand en Brandweer
0006-9035 Brand Aus
0006-9043 Brandeis University Bulletin†
0006-9051 Brandfoersvar *see* 0283-1155
0006-906X Die Brandhilfe
0006-9078 Branding Iron
0006-9086 Brandon's Shipper & Forwarder

0006-9108 Brandverhuetung und Brandbekaempfung *see* 0343-3560
0006-9116 Brandwacht
0006-9124 Brandweer†
0006-9132 Brangus Journal
0006-9140 Branicevo
0006-9159 Die Branntweinwirtschaft
0006-9167 Brazil Acucareiro
0006-9191 Brasil Jovem†
0006-9205 Brasil-Medico
0006-9248 Bratislavske Lekarske Listy
0006-9256 Bratrsky Vestnik
0006-9264 Bratstvo
0006-9272 Bratstvo
0006-9280 Brauereibesitzer und Braumeister *see* 0172-0589
0006-9299 Braunkohle Waerme und Energie *see* 0341-1060
0006-9310 Brautechnik Aktuell
0006-9361 Brazil. Biblioteca da Camara dos Deputados. Boletim *changed to* Brazil. Camara dos Deputados. Documentacao e Informacao
0006-9388 Brazil. Departamento de Agricultura. Boletim†
0006-9434 Brazil. Ministerio da Fazenda. Nucleo Regional de Administracao. Boletim Informativo *changed to* Brazil. Ministerio da Fazenda. Boletim Informativo da Secao de Documentacao
0006-9442 Brazil. Ministerio da Saude. Departamento Nacional de Endemias Rurais. Divisao de Cooperacao e Divulgacao. Boletim Bibliografico†
0006-9469 Pernambuco. Secretaria do Saneamento, Habitacao e Obras. Boletin Tecnico
0006-9477 Brazila Esperantisto
0006-9485 Brazilian Bulletin†
0006-9493 Brazilian Business†
0006-9507 Brazilian News Briefs *changed to* AmCham News Update
0006-9515 Bread of Life
0006-9523 Break-In
0006-9531 Breakthru
0006-954X Brecon and Radnor Farmer
0006-9566 Bref Rhone Alpes
0006-9574 Bremer Missionsschiff
0006-9582 Bremer Schulblatt
0006-9604 Brennpunkt†
0006-9612 B W K
0006-9620 Brennstoffchemie *see* 0014-0058
0006-9639 Bres-Planete *changed to* Bres'
0006-9647 Bretagne Reelle
0006-9663 Brethren Life and Thought
0006-9671 Breton News *changed to* Carn
0006-968X Breve, il Gruppo, la Cultura, l'Idee
0006-9698 Breviora
0006-9701 Brewers Bulletin
0006-971X Brewers Digest
0006-971X Brewers Digest Annual Buyers Guide and Brewery Directory
0006-9728 Brewers' Guardian†
0006-9736 Brewer
0006-9752 Brewing Trade Review *changed to* Brewing Review
0006-9760 Brick and Clay Record
0006-9779 Brickbats & Bouquets
0006-9787 Brides & Setting Up Home
0006-9795 Bride's Magazine *see* 0161-1992
0006-9809 Bridge of Eta Kappa Nu
0006-9817 Bridge†
0006-9825 Bridge
0006-9833 Most
0006-9841 Bridge Bulletin *changed to* South African Bridge Bulletin
0006-985X Bridge d'Italia
0006-9868 Bridge Magazine
0006-9876 Bridge World
0006-9884 Bridgeport Hospital News *changed to* Resource Magazine (Bridgeport)
0006-9892 Bridgeport News
0006-9906 Bridge Tidningen
0006-9914 Bridgeur
0006-9922 Brief *see* 0741-465X
0006-9930 Brief an Unsere Freunde *changed to* Enka Glanzstoff. Trend und Information
0006-9949 Brief aus Wahlwies
0006-9965 Southern Methodist University School of Law. Brief
0006-9973 Briefe an den Chef†
0006-9981 Briefe an den Mitarbeiter†
0006-999X Briefe an den Mitmenschen
0007-0009 Briefe fuer junge Steuerfachleute
0007-0017 Briefed†
0007-0025 Briefing Papers
0007-0033 Briefmarke
0007-0041 Briefmarken-Spiegel
0007-0068 Briefs†
0007-0076 Brieven Aan de Chef†
0007-0106 Brigham Young University Studies *see* 0278-1980
0007-0122 Brighton Head and Freak Magazine
0007-0130 Brighton Historical Society. Newsletter *changed to* Brighton Newsletter
0007-0149 Brighton Park Life
0007-0157 Brightonian
0007-0173 Brio
0007-0181 Bristol Building and Design Centre. Newsletter *changed to* Bristol Newsletter
0007-019X Bristol Medico-Chirurgical Journal†
0007-0203 Britannia†
0007-0211 Brith *changed to* Covenant Voice
0007-022X British Agents Review *changed to* British Commercial Agents Review
0007-0238 British Amateur Journalist
0007-0262 British Antarctic Survey. Bulletin
0007-0270 British Archaeological Abstracts
0007-0289 British Archer
0007-0297 British Astronomical Association. Journal
0007-0300 British Baker
0007-0319 British Bandsman
0007-0327 British Bee Journal
0007-0335 British Birds
0007-0343 British Book News
0007-0351 British Boot and Shoe Institution. Journal *see* 0263-1008
0007-036X British Bulletin of Publications on Latin America, the West Indies, Portugal and Spain *see* 0268-2400
0007-0378 British Bulletin of Spectroscopy *see* 0307-0026
0007-0394 British Ceramic Society. Publications
0007-0408 British Chamber of Commerce in Brazil. Information Circular *changed to* British Chamber of Commerce in Brazil. News & Views
0007-0416 British Chamber of Commerce of Turkey. Trade Journal
0007-0432 British Chemist†
0007-0440 British Chess Magazine
0007-0459 British Citizen†
0007-0467 British Clothing Manufacturer
0007-0475 B C U R A Monthly Bulletin†
0007-0483 British Columbia Catholic
0007-0513 British Columbia Government News
0007-0521 British Columbia Hospital News *changed to* B C H A News
0007-053X British Columbia Library Quarterly†
0007-0548 British Columbia Lumberman
0007-0556 British Columbia Medical Journal
0007-0564 British Columbia Music Educator
0007-0572 British Columbia Orchardist†
0007-0580 British Columbia School Trustee†
0007-0599 British Corrosion Journal
0007-0602 British Deaf News
0007-0610 British Dental Journal
0007-0629 British Dental Surgery Assistant
0007-0637 British Education Index
0007-0653 British Endodontic Society Journal *see* 0143-2885
0007-0661 British Engineer†
0007-067X British Esperantist
0007-0688 British Farmer and Stockbreeder†
0007-0696 British Federation of Master Printers. Members Circular *see* 0307-7195
0007-070X British Food Journal
0007-0718 British Foundryman
0007-0726 British Friesian Journal
0007-0734 British Goat Society. Monthly Journal
0007-0742 British Golf Greenkeeper *changed to* Golf Greenkeeping & Course Maintenance
0007-0750 British Grassland Society. Journal *see* 0142-5242
0007-0769 British Heart Journal
0007-0777 British Homing World
0007-0785 British Homoeopathic Journal
0007-0807 British Hotelier and Restaurateur
0007-0815 British Humanities Index
0007-0823 British Industry and Engineering
0007-0831 British Ink Maker *see* 0263-497X
0007-084X British Interplanetary Society Journal
0007-0858 British Italian Trade Review
0007-0866 British Jeweller
0007-0874 British Journal for the History of Science
0007-0882 British Journal for the Philosophy of Science
0007-0890 British Journal of Addiction
0007-0904 British Journal of Aesthetics
0007-0912 British Journal of Anaesthesia
0007-0920 British Journal of Cancer
0007-0939 British Journal of Chiropody
0007-0947 British Journal of Clinical Practice
0007-0955 British Journal of Criminology
0007-0963 British Journal of Dermatology
0007-0971 British Journal of Diseases of the Chest
0007-098X British Journal of Disorders of Communication
0007-0998 British Journal of Educational Psychology
0007-1005 British Journal of Educational Studies
0007-1013 British Journal of Educational Technology
0007-1021 British Journal of Experimental Pathology
0007-1048 British Journal of Haematology
0007-1056 British Journal of Herpetology *changed to* Herpetological Journal
0007-1064 British Journal of Hospital Medicine
0007-1072 British Journal of Industrial Medicine
0007-1080 British Journal of Industrial Relations
0007-1099 British Journal of Marketing *see* 0309-0566
0007-1102 British Journal of Mathematical and Statistical Psychology
0007-1110 British Journal of Medical Education *see* 0308-0110
0007-1129 British Journal of Medical Psychology
0007-1137 British Journal of Non-Destructive Testing
0007-1145 British Journal of Nutrition
0007-1161 British Journal of Ophthalmology
0007-117X British Journal of Oral Surgery *see* 0266-4356
0007-1188 British Journal of Pharmacology
0007-1196 British Journal of Photography
0007-120X British Journal of Physical Education
0007-1218 British Journal of Physiological Optics *see* 0275-5408
0007-1226 British Journal of Plastic Surgery
0007-1234 British Journal of Political Science
0007-1242 British Journal of Preventive and Social Medicine *see* 0141-7681
0007-1250 British Journal of Psychiatry
0007-1269 British Journal of Psychology
0007-1285 British Journal of Radiology
0007-1293 British Journal of Social and Clinical Psychology *see* 0144-6665
0007-1293 British Journal of Social and Clinical Psychology *see* 0144-6657
0007-1307 British Journal of Social Psychiatry†
0007-1315 British Journal of Sociology
0007-1323 British Journal of Surgery
0007-1331 British Journal of Urology
0007-134X British Journal of Venereal Diseases *changed to* Genitourinary Medicine
0007-1358 British Kinematography, Sound and Television *see* 0950-2114
0007-1366 British Lawn Tennis *changed to* Tennis
0007-1374 British Legion Journal *see* 0308-4949
0007-1390 British Master Patternmaker *changed to* British Pattern & Mould Maker
0007-1404 British Medical Abstracts†
0007-1412 British Medical Book List *see* 0140-2722
0007-1420 British Medical Bulletin
0007-1439 British Medical Index *see* 0140-2722
0007-1447 British Medical Journal
0007-1455 British Medical Register of Holiday Accommodation†
0007-1463 British Mouthpiece
0007-1471 British Museum (Natural History) Bulletin. Geology
0007-148X British Museum (Natural History) Bulletin. Mineralogy *see* 0007-1471
0007-1498 British Museum (Natural History) Bulletin. Zoology
0007-151X British Museum Quarterly†
0007-1528 British Mycological Society. Bulletin *changed to* Mycologist
0007-1536 British Mycological Society. Transactions
0007-1544 British National Bibliography
0007-1552 British National Film Catalogue
0007-1560 British Naturism
0007-1587 British Nuclear Energy Society. Journal *see* 0140-4067
0007-1595 British Ornithologists' Club. Bulletin
0007-1609 British Patents Abstracts
0007-1617 British Phycological Journal
0007-1625 British Plastics *see* 0306-3534
0007-1633 British Polio Fellowship. Bulletin
0007-1641 British Polymer Journal
0007-165X British-Portuguese Chamber of Commerce. Monthly Bulletin *changed to* Camara de Comercio Luso-Britanica. Monthly Magazine
0007-1668 British Poultry Science
0007-1676 British Practice in International Law†
0007-1684 British Printer
0007-1692 British Psychological Society. Bulletin
0007-1706 British Racehorse *see* 0260-7468
0007-1714 British Railways Board. Monthly Review of Technical Literature
0007-1722 British Record†
0007-1749 N L L Announcement Bulletin *see* 0144-7556
0007-1757 British Road Federation. Bulletin†
0007-1765 British Ship Research Association. Journal *see* 0268-9650
0007-1773 British Society for Phenomenology. Journal
0007-1781 British Society of Commerce. Review
0007-179X British Society of Dowsers. Journal
0007-1803 British-Soviet Friendship
0007-1811 British Stationer *changed to* C T N
0007-1838 British Steelmaker *see* 0265-0983
0007-1846 British Studies Monitor†
0007-1854 British Sugar Beet Review
0007-1862 British Tax Guide
0007-1870 British Tax Review
0007-1889 British Technology Index *see* 0260-6593
0007-1897 British Toys *changed to* British Toys & Hobbies Briefing
0007-1900 British Travel News†
0007-1927 British Vegetarian *see* 0260-3233
0007-1935 British Veterinary Journal
0007-1951 British Weekly and Christian World *changed to* British Weekly and Christian Record
0007-196X Brittonia
0007-1986 Public Health†
0007-1994 Broadcast Engineering
0007-2001 Broadcast Journal†
0007-201X Broadcasters Bulletin
0007-2028 Broadcasting
0007-2036 Broadsheet
0007-2044 Broadsheet
0007-2052 China Policy Study Group. Broadsheet†
0007-2109 Broadside and the Free Press†
0007-2133 Broadway
0007-215X Brodogradnja
0007-2168 Broed *see* 0345-181X
0007-2176 Broiler Industry

1210 ISSN INDEX

0007-2184 Bromeliad Society Bulletin *see* 0090-8738
0007-2192 Bromides in Agriculture
0007-2214 Bron†
0007-2222 Bronches *changed to* Bronches-Broncho-Pneumologie
0007-2230 Bronchi *changed to* Bronco-Pneumologia
0007-2249 Bronx County Historical Society. Journal
0007-2257 Bronx County Medical Society. Bulletin *changed to* Bronx Medicine
0007-2265 Bronx Real Estate and Building News *changed to* Bronx Realtor News
0007-2273 Bronxboro†
0007-2281 Bronze
0007-229X Brookings Bulletin *see* 0745-1253
0007-2303 Brookings Papers on Economic Activity
0007-232X Brooklyn Barrister
0007-2346 Brooklyn Heights Press and Cobble Hill News
0007-2354 Brooklyn Insurance Brokers Association. Bulletin *changed to* Messenger Reporter
0007-2362 Brooklyn Law Review
0007-2370 Brooklyn Longshoreman *changed to* 1814 Union News
0007-2397 Brooklyn Public Library Bulletin
0007-2400 Broom and Broom Corn News *changed to* Broom, Brush & Mop
0007-2419 Brot und Gebaeck *changed to* Getreide, Mehl und Brot
0007-2427 Broteria: Ciencias Naturais *changed to* Broteria Genetica
0007-2435 Brotherhood
0007-2443 Brotherhood of Maintenance of Way Employes. Journal *see* 0146-0625
0007-2451 Brothers Newsletter
0007-2478 Brown Alumni Monthly
0007-2486 Brown Boveri Review
0007-2494 Brown Gold
0007-2516 Brown Swiss Bulletin
0007-2524 Brownie
0007-2532 Browning Newsletter *see* 0095-4489
0007-2559 Browser†
0007-2567 Brud ar Yez hag ar Vro *see* 0399-7014
0007-2583 Bruecke
0007-2605 Bruecke†
0007-2621 Bruel & Kjaer Technical Review
0007-2648 Brug
0007-2656 Brug†
0007-2664 Bruehl
0007-2672 Brulot
0007-2680 Burns Beitraege fuer Klinische Chirurgie *see* 0023-8236
0007-2699 Brunswickan
0007-2702 Brushes *changed to* Brushmaking International
0007-2710 Brushware
0007-2729 B. B. B. Agenda†
0007-2745 Bryologist
0007-2753 B't
0007-2761 Buch der Zeit
0007-277X Buch und Bildung
0007-2788 Druck und Verarbeitung†
0007-2796 Buchhaendler Heute
0007-280X Landesmuseum fuer Kaernten. Buchreihe.
0007-2818 Buck Investment Letter†
0007-2826 Buckeye Beverage Journal *changed to* Ohio Beverage Journal
0007-2834 Buckeye Farm News
0007-2842 A D A C Motorwelt
0007-2869 Bucknell Review
0007-2885 Budapest
0007-2893 Budapester Rundschau
0007-2907 Budavox Telecommunication Review
0007-294X Budget
0007-2958 Budget Decorating *see* 0360-4993
0007-2974 Budivel'ni Materialy i Konstruktsii
0007-2982 Budo-Sport
0007-2990 Budownictwo Okretowe
0007-3016 Buecherkommentare *changed to* Lektuere
0007-3032 Buechergilde
0007-3040 Buecherschau
0007-3059 Buecherschiff
0007-3067 Der Buechsenmacher
0007-3075 Die Buehne
0007-3083 Die Buehnengenossenschaft
0007-3091 Buehnentechnische Rundschau
0007-3113 Buenos Aires Musical
0007-3121 Der Buerger im Staat
0007-313X Buero Modern *changed to* Carriere
0007-3148 Bueromarkt
0007-3156 Bueromaschinen-Mechaniker *see* 0340-2185
0007-3164 Buerotechnische Praxis†
0007-3172 Buerotechnische Sammlung
0007-3199 Buffalo Magazine *see* 0149-5070
0007-3210 Bugantics
0007-3229 Build
0007-3245 Builder†
0007-3261 Builder (Columbus)
0007-327X Builder/Architect *changed to* Builder Architect
0007-3288 Builders' Merchants' Journal *see* 0262-6063
0007-3296 Builders Report Pacific *see* 0194-6587
0007-330X Builders' Weekly Guide†
0007-3318 Building
0007-3326 Building Abstracts Service C I B
0007-3334 Building Alaska†
0007-3342 Building & Construction
0007-3350 Building & Contract Journal
0007-3369 S.A. Building Products News
0007-3377 Building & Heating Product Guide
0007-3385 Building and Management *changed to* Building Operating Manager
0007-3393 Building & Realty Record†
0007-3407 Building Design & Construction
0007-3415 Building Construction in Texas†
0007-3423 Building Design
0007-3431 Building Economist
0007-344X Building Equipment and Materials for South Africa *changed to* Building Equipment & Materials
0007-3458 Building Equipment News *changed to* Building Equipment and Materials
0007-3466 Building Forum
0007-3490 Building Operating Management
0007-3504 Building Materials†
0007-3512 Building Materials & Equipment
0007-3520 Building Materials Merchandiser *see* 0194-1321
0007-3539 Building Materials News
0007-3547 Building Official and Code Administrator
0007-3555 Building Permit Activity in Florida
0007-3563 Building Permit Values
0007-3571 Building Practice†
0007-358X Building Products News
0007-3598 Building Progress†
0007-3601 Building Research†
0007-361X Building Research News
0007-3628 Building Science *see* 0360-1323
0007-3636 Building Science Abstracts†
0007-3644 Building Services Contractor
0007-3652 Building Societies' Gazette
0007-3679 Building Stone News *changed to* Building Stone Magazine
0007-3687 Building Supply Dealer *changed to* Hardware Merchandising's Canadian Hardware Handbook
0007-3695 Building Supply News *changed to* Building Supply & Home Centers
0007-3709 Building Technology and Management
0007-3717 Building Tradesman
0007-3725 Buildings
0007-3733 Asian Regional Institute for School Building Research. Newsletter
0007-375X Nieuwsbrief†
0007-3768 Buitenspoor
0007-3776 Bukhgalterskii Uchet
0007-3784 Buletin de Informare in Bibliologie
0007-3792 Buletin de Informare Pedagogica *changed to* Probleme de Pedagogie Contemporana
0007-3806 Buletin de Informare Stiintifica Biologie†
0007-3822 Buletin de Informare Stiintifica. Fizica†
0007-3830 Istorie-Arheologie†
0007-3849 Buletin de Informare Stiintifica. Matematica, Mecanica, Astronomie†
0007-3857 Psihologie; Buletin de Informare Stiintifica†
0007-3865 Sociologie; Buletin de Informare Stiintifica†
0007-3873 Stiinte Economice; Buletin de Informare Stiintifica†
0007-3881 Stiinte Juridice; Buletin de Informare Stiintifica†
0007-389X Vyzkumny Ustav Rybarsky a Hydrobiologicky. Bulletin
0007-3903 Bulgaria Today
0007-3911 Bulgarian Films
0007-3938 Bulgarsko Geologichesko Druzhestvo. Spisanie
0007-3946 Bulgarian Review
0007-3954 Bulgarian Trade Unions
0007-3970 Bulgarska Akademiia na Naukite. Institut po Fiziologiia na Rasteniiata "Metodii Popov." Izvestiia *see* 0324-0290
0007-3989 Bulgarska Akademiia na Naukite. Spisanie
0007-3997 Bulgarski Knigopis. Seriia 1: Knigi, Notni, Graficheski i Kartografski
0007-4004 Bulgarski Voin
0007-4012 Bulgarsko Foto
0007-4020 Otkrytiya, Izobreteniya, Promyshlennye Obraztsy, Tovarnye Znaki
0007-4039 Bulletin
0007-4047 Bulletin; Belgium's Newsweekly in English
0007-4063 Centre de Documentation Siderurgique. Bulletin Analytique
0007-4071 Bulletin Analytique de Documentation Politique, Economique et Sociale Contemporaine
0007-408X Bulletin Analytique de Linguistique Francaise
0007-4098 Bulletin Analytique d'Entomologie Medicale et Veterinaire†
0007-4101 Bulletin Analytique Petrolier
0007-411X Bulletin Annote des Lois et Decrets
0007-4128 Bulletin Baudelairien
0007-4136 Bulletin Belge de Metrologie†
0007-4144 Bulletin Bi-Mensuel des Tirages
0007-4152 Bulletin Bibliographique de Documentation Technique des Charbonnages de France *changed to* Bulletin Bibliographique de Documentation Technique du Groupement des Industries Extractives
0007-4160 Bulletin Bibliographique International du Machinisme Agricole
0007-4187 Bulletin Biologique de la France et de la Belgique†
0007-4209 Bulletin Critique du Livre Francais
0007-4217 Bulletin de Correspondance Hellenique
0007-4225 Belgium. Ministere des Communications. Bulletin de Documentation†
0007-4233 Laboratoire de Recherches et de Controle du Caoutchouc. Bulletin de Documentation Bibliographique *changed to* L R C C Bulletin Bibliographique
0007-4241 Bulletin de Documentation Ceramique *changed to* CERINDEX: Bulletin de Documentation Ceramique
0007-4268 Bulletin de Documentation Pratiques des Impots Directs et des Taxes sur le Chiffre d'Affaires *changed to* Bulletin Fiscal
0007-4276 Bulletin de Documentation Pratique des Taxes sur le Chiffre d'Affaires *changed to* Bulletin Fiscal
0007-4284 Bulletin de Geophysique†
0007-4292 Bulletin de la Librairie Ancienne et Moderne†
0007-4306 Belgium. Administration Penitentiaire. Bulletin
0007-4314 A I M Bulletin *changed to* A I M Monastic Bulletin
0007-4322 Bulletin de Litterature Ecclesiastique
0007-4330 Bulletin de l'Oeuvre Apostolique
0007-4349 Bulletin de l'Oeuvre d'Orient
0007-4357 Bulletin de Madagascar†
0007-4365 Bulletin de Medecine Legale et de Toxicologie Medicale *see* 0249-6208
0007-4373 A U P E L F Bulletin de Nouvelles Breves *see* 0226-7454
0007-439X Bulletin de Physiopathologie Respiratoire *see* 0271-9983
0007-4411 Bulletin de Psychologie Scolaire et d'Orientation
0007-442X Bulletin de Theologie Ancienne et Medievale
0007-4438 Institut de Science Financiere et d'Assurances. Bulletin des Actuaires Diplomes
0007-4446 Bulletin des Agriculteurs
0007-4462 Data from the Greek Economic Life *see* 0041-0543
0007-4489 Bulletin des Lettres†
0007-4497 Bulletin des Sciences Mathematiques
0007-4500 Bulletin des Soies et Soieries *changed to* Textilyon: Bulletin des Soies et Soieries
0007-4519 Bulletin des Transports
0007-4535 Bulletin d'Information des Centrales Electriques†
0007-4543 France. Commissariat a l'Energie Atomique. Bulletin d'Informations Scientifiques et Techniques.†
0007-4551 Bulletin du Cancer
0007-456X Connaissance et Formation Par le Livre et l'Audiovisuel *changed to* Livres de France
0007-4578 Bulletin Economique du Cambresis
0007-4586 Bulletin Economique et Social du Maroc
0007-4594 E G U Bulletin
0007-4616 Bulletin Folklorique de l'Ile de France *changed to* Traditions de l'Ile de France
0007-4624 Bulletin for International Fiscal Documentation
0007-4632 Bulletin Geodesique
0007-4640 Bulletin Hispanique
0007-4659 Bulletin Historique et Scientifique de l'Auvergne
0007-4667 Bulletin Hygiene du Travail†
0007-4675 Bulletin Immobilier
0007-4683 Japanese Communist Party. Central Committee. Bulletin: Information for Abroad
0007-4691 Bulletin Mathematique
0007-4705 Bulletin Medical Franco-Japonais
0007-4713 France. Institut National de la Statistique et des Etudes Economiques. Bulletin Mensuel de Statistique
0007-473X Bulletin Monumental
0007-4748 Service Central d'Organisation et Methodes. O et M Bulletin *changed to* Service Central d'Organisation et Methodes. Revue
0007-4756 Bulletin of Applied Linguistics†
0007-4764 American Journal of Art Therapy
0007-4780 Bulletin of Bibliography and Magazine Notes *see* 0190-745X
0007-4799 Bulletin of Business Research†
0007-4802 Bulletin of Canadian Petroleum Geology
0007-4810 Bulletin of Concerned Asian Scholars
0007-4837 Bulletin of Dental Education
0007-4845 Bulletin of Endemic Diseases
0007-4853 Bulletin of Entomological Research
0007-4861 Bulletin of Environmental Contamination and Toxicology
0007-4888 Bulletin of Experimental Biology and Medicine
0007-4896 Bulletin of Grain Technology
0007-490X Bulletin of Hispanic Studies
0007-4918 Bulletin of Indonesian Economic Studies
0007-4926 Bulletin of Information on Current Research on Human Sciences Concerning Africa
0007-4942 Volunteer Service Bulletin *changed to* News from C C I V S
0007-4950 Bulletin of Labour Statistics
0007-4969 Bulletin of Legal Developments
0007-4977 Bulletin of Marine Science

ISSN INDEX 1211

0007-4985 Bulletin of Mathematical Biophysics *see* 0092-8240
0007-4993 Bulletin of Mathematical Statistics *see* 0286-522X
0007-5000 Bulletin of Mechanical Engineering Education†
0007-5027 Laboratory Medicine
0007-5035 Bulletin of Peace Proposals
0007-5043 Bulletin of Physical Education
0007-5051 Bulletin of Polish Medical Science and History†
0007-506X Bulletin of Prosthetics Research *changed to* Journal of Rehabilitation Research and Development
0007-5078 Bulletin of Rural Economics and Sociology *changed to* Journal of Rural Economics & Development
0007-5094 Science and Public Affairs Bulletin of the Atomic Scientists *see* 0096-3402
0007-5108 Bulletin of the Comediantes
0007-5116 Bulletin of the European Communities
0007-5124 Experimental Animals
0007-5132 Bulletin of the History of Dentistry
0007-5140 Bulletin of the History of Medicine
0007-5159 Bulletin of Tibetology
0007-5175 Bulletin Officiel Annote de Tous les Ministeres *changed to* Documentation Communale
0007-5183 Bulletin Officiel de la Propriete Industrielle *see* 0223-4092
0007-5191 Sport en Roumanie
0007-523X Bulletin on Narcotics
0007-5248 Bulletin on the Rheumatic Diseases
0007-5256 Bulletin Ornithologique
0007-5264 Bulletin Quotidien d'Afrique
0007-5272 Bulletin Quotidien d'Informations Textiles†
0007-5280 Belgium. Institut Royal Meteorologique. Bulletin Quotidien du Temps
0007-5302 Bulletin Signaletique des Telecommunications
0007-5310 Information Scientifique et Technique *changed to* P A S C A L Thema. Part 205: Sciences de l'Information. Documentation
0007-5329 Mathematiques Appliques-Informatique-Automatique *changed to* P A S C A L Explore. Part 34: Robotique. Automatique et Automatisation des Processus Industrieis
0007-5345 Bulletin Signaletique. Part 130: Physique *changed to* P A S C A L Folio. Part 10: Mecanique et Acoustique
0007-5353 Bulletin Signaletique. Part 140: Electricite-Electronique *changed to* P A S C A L Folio. Part 21: Electrotechnique
0007-5353 Bulletin Signaletique. Part 140: Electricite-Electronique *changed to* P A S C A L Explore. Part 20: Electronique et Telecommunications
0007-537X Bulletin Signaletique. Part 160: Structure de la Matiere I *changed to* P A S C A L Explore. Part 12: Etat Condense
0007-537X Bulletin Signaletique. Part 160: Structure de la Matiere 1 *changed to* P A S C A L Explore. Part 11: Physique Atomique et Moleculaire. Plasmas
0007-5388 Bulletin Signaletique. Part 161. Structure de la Matiere II *changed to* P A S C A L Explore. Part 13: Structure des Liquides et des Solides. Cristallographie
0007-5442 Bulletin Signaletique. Part 330: Sciences Pharmacologiques - Toxicologie *changed to* P A S C A L Explore. Part 63: Toxicologie
0007-5442 Bulletin Signaletique. Part 330: Sciences Pharmacologiques - Toxicologie *changed to* P A S C A L Folio. Part 70: Pharmacologie. Traitements Medicamenteux
0007-5450 Bulletin Signaletique. Part 340: Microbiologie-Virologie-Immunologie *changed to* P A S C A L Explore. Part 61: Microbiologie: Bacteriologie, Virologie, Mycologie, Protozoaires Pathogenes
0007-5450 Bulletin Signaletique. Part 340: Microbiologie-Virologie-Immunologie *changed to* P A S C A L Explore. Part 62: Immunologie
0007-5469 Bulletin Signaletique. Part 350. Pathologie Generale et Experimentale *changed to* P A S C A L Explore. Part 83: Anesthesie et Reanimation
0007-5477 Bulletin Signaletique. Part 351: Revue Bibliographique Cancer *changed to* P A S C A L Thema. Part 251: Cancerologie (Cancernet)
0007-5485 Bulletin Signaletique. Part 360. Biologie et Physiologie Animale *changed to* P A S C A L Thema. Part 260: Zoologie Fondamentale et Appliquee des Invertebres (Milieu Terrestre, Eaux Douces)
0007-5493 Bulletin Signaletique. Part 361. Endocrinologie et Reproduction *changed to* P A S C A L Folio. Part 54: Reproduction des Vertebres. Embryologie des Vertebres et des Invertebres
0007-5507 Bulletin Signaletique. 362: Diabete. Obesite. Maladies. *changed to* P A S C A L Explore. Part 81: Maladies Metaboliques
0007-5515 Bulletin Signaletique. Part 370. Biologie et Physiologie Vegetales *changed to* P A S C A L Folio. Part 55: Biologie Vegetale
0007-5523 Bulletin Signaletique. Part 380: Agronomie-Zootechnie-Phytopathologie-Industries Alimentaires *see* 0181-0030
0007-5531 Bulletin Signaletique. Part 390: Psychologie. Psychopathologie. Psychiatrie *changed to* P A S C A L Explore. Part 65: Psychologie. Psychopathologie. Psychiatrie
0007-554X Bulletin Signaletique. Part 519: Philosophie
0007-5566 Bulletin Signaletique. Part 521: Sociologie - Ethnologie
0007-5574 Bulletin Signaletique. Part 522: Histoire des Sciences et des Techniques
0007-5582 Bulletin Signaletique. Part 523: Histoire et Sciences de la Litterature
0007-5590 Bulletin Signaletique. Part 524: Sciences du Langage
0007-5612 Bulletin Signaletique. Part 526: Art et Archeologie
0007-5620 Bulletin Signaletique. Part 527: Sciences Religieuse *see* 0180-9296
0007-5639 Bulletin Signaletique. Part 528: Science Administrative *see* 0150-8695
0007-5647 Bulletin Signaletique. Part 730: Combustibles. Energie *changed to* P A S C A L Thema. Part 230: Energie
0007-5655 Bulletin Signaletique. Part 740: Metaux. Metallurgie *changed to* P A S C A L Thema. Part 240: Metaux. Metallurgie
0007-5663 Bulletin Signaletique. Part 761: Microscopie Electronique. Diffraction Electronique *changed to* P A S C A L Explore. Part 30: Microscopie Electronique et Diffraction Electronique
0007-5671 Bulletin Signaletique. Part 780: Polymeres *changed to* P A S C A L Folio. Part 24: Polymeres. Peintures. Bois
0007-568X Bulletin Signaletique. Part 880: Genie Chimique. Industries Chimique et Parachimique *changed to* P A S C A L Folio. Part 23: Genie Chimique. Industries Chimique et Parachimique
0007-5698 Bulletin Signaletique. Part 885: Eau et Assainissement. Pollution Atmospherique *changed to* P A S C A L Explore. Part 36: Pollution de l'Eau, de l'Air et du Sol
0007-5701 Bulletin Signaletique. Part 890: Industries Mecaniques-Genie Civil-Transports-Techniques Aerospatiales *changed to* P A S C A L Folio. Part 10: Mecanique et Acoustique
0007-571X Bulletin Signaletique. Part 900. Bulletin des Traductions *see* 0259-8264
0007-5728 Bulletin Synoptique de Documentation Thermique *see* 0337-4092
0007-5736 Bulletin Technique
0007-5744 Bulletin Technique de la Suisse Romande *changed to* Ingenieurs et Architectes Suisses
0007-5752 Bureau Veritas. Bulletin Technique
0007-5779 Bulletins of American Paleontology
0007-5787 Bollettino delle Scienze Mediche
0007-5795 Bullettino Storico Empolese
0007-5809 Bollettino Storico Pistoiese
0007-5817 Bumazhnaya Promyshlennost'
0007-5833 Bund der Deutschen Katholischen Jugend. Informationsdienst
0007-5841 Bund der Oeffentlich Bestellten Vermessungsingenieure. Mitteilungsblatt *changed to* B D V I - Forum
0007-585X Germany (Federal Republic, 1949-) Bundesanstalt fuer Arbeit. Amtliche Nachrichten
0007-5868 Bundesversorgungsblatt *changed to* Bundesarbeitsblatt
0007-5876 Die Bundesbahn
0007-5884 Bundesbaublatt
0007-5892 Bundesforschungsanstalt fuer Forst- und Holzwirtschaft, Hamburg. Mitteilungen
0007-5914 Bundesgesundheitsblatt
0007-5922 Austria. Hoehere Bundeslehr-und Versuchsanstalt fuer Wein-und Obstbau. Mitteilungen Klosterneuburg
0007-5930 Die Bundesverwaltung
0007-5949 Die Bundeswehr
0007-5965 Das Bunte Blatt
0007-5973 Bunte Blumenwelt
0007-5981 Bunte Oesterreich *changed to* Bunte
0007-6007 Bur
0007-6015 Burbujas
0007-6023 Burda Bunte Bild Rezepte†
0007-6031 Burda Moden
0007-604X Le Bureau
0007-6066 Bureau Briefs†
0007-6074 Bureaux de France
0007-6090 France. Bureau de Recherches Geologiques et Minieres. Bulletin. Section 2. Geologie Appliquee *changed to* France. Bureau de Recherches Geologiques et Minieres. Agence Francaise pour la Maitrise de l'Energie. Geothermie/Actualities
0007-6104 France. Bureau de Recherches Geologiques et Minieres. Bulletin. Section 1: Geologie de la France *changed to* France. Bureau de Recherches Geologiques et Minieres. Geologie de la France
0007-6112 France. Bureau de Recherches Geologiques et Minieres. Bulletin Section 4: Geologie Generale *see* 0153-8446
0007-6120 Hydrogeologie *changed to* France. Bureau de Recherches Geologiques et Minieres. Hydrogeologie
0007-6155 Philippines. Bureau of Agricultural Economics. Bureau of Agricultural Economics Reporter†
0007-6163 Bureau of Government Research Bulletin†
0007-6171 University of Rhode Island. Bureau of Government Research. Newsletter *see* 0273-7884
0007-618X U.S. Bureau of the Census. Bureau of the Census Catalog *changed to* U.S. Bureau of the Census. Census Catalog and Guide
0007-6201 Burgen und Schloesser
0007-621X Burgenlaendische Forschungen
0007-6228 Burgenlaendische Gemeinschaft
0007-6236 Burgenlaendische Heimatblaetter
0007-6244 Burgenlaendische Landwirtschaftskammer. Mitteilungsblatt
0007-6252 Burgenlaendisches Leben
0007-6260 Buried History
0007-6279 Burlington County Times Advertiser†
0007-6287 Burlington Magazine
0007-6295 Burma Medical Journal
0007-6309 Burning Bush
0007-6325 B T O /Buerotechnik und Organization *see* 0343-2319
0007-6333 Burroughs Bulletin
0007-6341 Burroughs Clearing House†
0007-635X Bus and Truck Transport *changed to* Truck Fleet
0007-6376 Busara
0007-6392 Buses
0007-6406 Business Abroad†
0007-6414 Business Administration *see* 0140-8453
0007-6422 Business Advertising†
0007-6430 Business Analyst
0007-6449 Business and Administration *changed to* Institute of Administration and Commerce of South Africa. Journal
0007-6457 Business and Economic Dimensions†
0007-6465 Business & Economic Review
0007-6473 Business and Finance
0007-6481 Business and Financial Indicators†
0007-6503 Business and Society
0007-6511 Business and Society†
0007-652X Business and Technology Sources†
0007-6538 Business Archives
0007-6562 Business Comments†
0007-6570 Business and Commercial Aviation
0007-6589 Business Conditions *see* 0164-0682
0007-6597 Business Conditions Digest
0007-6600 Business Conditions in Argentina†
0007-6627 Business Credit and Hire Purchase Journal
0007-6635 Business Day
0007-6643 Zrak'or
0007-666X Business Economics
0007-6678 Business Education Forum
0007-6686 Business Education Journal
0007-6694 Business Education World
0007-6708 Business Equipment Digest
0007-6716 Business Equipment Guide
0007-6732 Business Systems & Equipment†
0007-6740 U B S Business Facts and Figures
0007-6767 Business Forms Reporter *changed to* Business Forms and Systems
0007-6775 Business Graphics†
0007-6783 Business Herald
0007-6791 Business History
0007-6805 Business History Review
0007-6813 Business Horizons
0007-6821 Business in Brief†
0007-683X Business in Nebraska
0007-6856 Business Inquiry†
0007-6864 Business Insurance
0007-6872 Business International
0007-6880 Business Latin America
0007-6899 Business Lawyer
0007-6902 Business Literature *changed to* Business Information
0007-6929 Industrial Management & Data Systems
0007-6937 Business Management†
0007-6945 Business Memo from Belgium
0007-6961 Business Periodicals Index
0007-6988 Business Products *changed to* Special Report to the Office Products Industry
0007-6996 Business Quarterly
0007-7011 Federal Reserve Bank of Philadelphia Business Review
0007-702X Federal Reserve Bank of Dallas. Business Review *see* 0149-5364
0007-7038 Business Review and Economic News from Israel

0007-7046 Business Screen *changed to* Backstage
0007-7062 Business Service Checklist†
0007-7070 Business South Africa *changed to* Business S A
0007-7097 Business Systems & Equipment
0007-7100 Business Today
0007-7119 Business Travel *changed to* Business Travel World
0007-7127 Business Trends in New York State
0007-7135 Business Week
0007-7151 Businessman
0007-716X Businessman and the Law & Your Product and the Law *changed to* Your Business and the Law
0007-7178 Businessmen's Expectations
0007-7194 Buskap og Avdraatt
0007-7208 Bussi-Baer
0007-7216 Bustan†
0007-7224 Bustleton-Somerton News Gleaner *changed to* NewsGleaner - Bustleton - Somerton Edition
0007-7232 Busy Bees' News
0007-7240 Butane Propane
0007-7259 Butane - Propane News
0007-7267 Butcher Workman†
0007-7275 Butter-Fat
0007-7291 Butterfly
0007-7305 Butterick Home Catalog *changed to* Butterick Sewing World
0007-7313 Butterley Foundry News†
0007-7321 Butterworths Consolidated Legislation Service of South Africa. Monthly Bulletin
0007-733X Buttons†
0007-7356 Buvar
0007-7364 Buxom Belle Courier
0007-7372 Buyer
0007-7380 Buyers' Guide
0007-7402 Buyers Purchasing Digest
0007-7429 Byarozka
0007-7437 Byelorussian-American Union. Bulletin†
0007-7445 Bygd
0007-7453 Bokvaennen *see* 0345-7982
0007-7461 Bygg *changed to* Byggaktuelt
0007-7488 Bygge Nyt
0007-7496 Byggehaandvaerket
0007-750X Byggeindustrien
0007-7518 Byggekunst
0007-7542 Bygglitteratur†
0007-7550 Byggmaestaren†
0007-7569 Byggnadsarbetaren
0007-7577 Byggnadsindustrin *see* 0349-3733
0007-7585 Byggnadsingenjoren- Team
0007-7593 Byggnadskonst *see* 0281-658X
0007-7607 Byggnadstidningen
0007-7623 Bygmesteren
0007-7631 Byminner
0007-764X Hospital Equipment *changed to* Hospital Engineering Association of Japan. Journal
0007-7658 Byplan
0007-7666 Gosudarstvennyi Komitet Soveta Ministrov S.S.S.R. po Voprosam Truda i Zarabotnoi Platy. Byulleten'
0007-7674 Byulleten' Inostrannoi Kommercheskoi Informatsii
0007-7682 Moskovskoe Obshchestvo Ispytatelei Prirody. Geologicheskii Otdel. Byulleten'
0007-7690 Byulleten' Stroitel'noi Tekhniki
0007-7704 Byzantinische Zeitschrift
0007-7712 Byzantinoslavica
0007-7720 Canadian Review of American Studies
0007-7739 C A E News
0007-7763 C A H P E R Journal *see* 0273-6896
0007-7771 C.A.H.S. Journal
0007-778X Cal
0007-7798 C A L F News
0007-7801 C A M†
0007-7836 C A R D A N. Fiches Analytiques†
0007-7844 Council for the Advancement of Small Colleges. Newsletter†
0007-7852 C. A. S. I. Transactions†
0007-7860 C A T C A Journal†
0007-7879 C A T V Magazine *changed to* V U E Magazine
0007-7887 C A U T Bulletin
0007-7895 C A U T Newsletter *see* 0007-7887
0007-7925 Select†
0007-7933 C B E Bulletin *see* 0196-4984
0007-7941 C B M News
0007-795X C B Magazine
0007-7968 C.B.R.I. Abstracts
0007-7976 C C A R Journal *see* 0149-712X
0007-7984 C C B Outlook (Inkprint Edition)
0007-7992 Accounting Articles
0007-800X C C I T U Labour Bulletin†
0007-8018 C D A Newsletter *see* 0703-5764
0007-8026 C D I U P A. Bulletin Bibliographique *see* 0223-9159
0007-8034 C E A Forum
0007-8050 C E A Advisor
0007-8069 C E A Critic
0007-8077 O E C D. Isotope Generator Information Centre *changed to* O E C D. Newsletter on Isotopic Generators and Batteries
0007-8093 C E A P Bulletin†
0007-8107 C E A Voice
0007-8123 C E C Newsletter *changed to* Last Word
0007-8131 C E C Update†
0007-814X C E D A G Informativo†
0007-8158 C E D A M Notiziario Bibliografico
0007-8166 C. E. D. Contact†
0007-8174 C. E. D. Dokumentoj†
0007-8204 English Education
0007-8212 C E F News *changed to* C-E-F Trailblazer
0007-8220 C E F P Journal
0007-8247 C E N
0007-8255 C E N
0007-8271 C E N S I S Quindicinale di Note e Commenti
0007-828X C E N T O Newsletter†
0007-8301 C E R I L H Bulletin Analytique
0007-8328 C E R N Reports
0007-8336 C E S I N News
0007-8344 C F Letter *see* 0091-536X
0007-8352 C G D Betriebstraete-Mitteilungen
0007-8360 C G Information *changed to* C G Kurier
0007-8387 C I A S Centro de Investigacion y Accion *see* 0325-1306
0007-8395 Ciba Journal *changed to* CIBA-Geigy Journal
0007-8409 Ciba Technical Notes *see* 0142-4904
0007-8417 C I C I A M S News/Nouvelles/ Nachrichten
0007-8425 C.I.E. Newsletter
0007-8433 C I L Oval†
0007-8441 C I M M Y T Annual Report on Maize and Wheat Improvement *see* 0304-5439
0007-8441 C I M M Y T Annual Report on Maize and Wheat Improvement *see* 0304-548X
0007-845X C I M Notes *changed to* Cleveland Institute of Music (Newsletter)
0007-8468 C. I. M. Notiziario
0007-8484 C I R F Abstracts *changed to* T & D Abstracts
0007-8506 C.I.R.P. Annals
0007-8514 C I S Index
0007-8530 C. K. of A. Journal
0007-8549 C L A Journal
0007-8557 C L A Newsletter
0007-8565 Cumann Leabharlannaithe Scoile. C L S Bulletin†
0007-8573 C L U Journal *see* 0742-9517
0007-8581 C. M. A. A. Newsletter†
0007-8603 C M A S Bulletin d'Information
0007-8611 C.M.B. Newsletter
0007-862X C M D†
0007-8646 C.M.J. Quarterly *changed to* Shalom
0007-8654 C M M
0007-8662 C/M News *changed to* C/M News
0007-8670 C M R†
0007-8689 C M S News *see* 0311-0737
0007-8697 C M T Health Sciences TV Bulletin *changed to* H E S C A Feedback
0007-8700 C. N. A. P. T. Bulletin†
0007-8727 C N E E M A Bulletin d'Information *see* 0249-4779
0007-8735 C N E E M A Etudes *see* 0249-4787
0007-8743 C N E E M A Nouvelles *see* 0249-5686
0007-8751 C N E N Notiziario *changed to* E N E A Notiziario/Energia e Innovazione
0007-8808 C O P H Bulletin
0007-8816 C O P N I P List†
0007-8824 C O P P E Boletim Informativo *changed to* C O P P E Noticiario
0007-8832 C O S M E P Newsletter *changed to* C O S M E P Newsletter (1981)
0007-8859 C O T A L
0007-8867 C P A†
0007-8875 C. P. C. Monthly Report†
0007-8883 C P C U News
0007-8891 C P E C Taxpayers News†
0007-8905 C P H Commentator *see* 0162-7929
0007-8921 C P S Reporter
0007-893X C Q
0007-8956 C Q Guide to Current American Government *see* 0196-612X
0007-8964 C Q Ham Radio
0007-8972 Foodservice & Hospitality
0007-8980 C R C Critical Reviews in Analytical Chemistry
0007-8999 C R C Critical Reviews in Environmental Control
0007-9006 C R C Critical Reviews in Food Technology *see* 0099-0248
0007-9014 C R C Critical Reviews in Radiological Sciences and Nuclear Medicine *see* 0147-6750
0007-9030 Illinois Drug Process *see* 0195-2099
0007-9049 C R E Information
0007-9057 C R V Newsletter†
0007-9065 C S A Quarterly Review†
0007-9073 C S C Newsletter
0007-9081 C.S.E.R. Selezione *see* 0391-3457
0007-9103 C.S.I.R.O. Wildlife Research *see* 0310-7833
0007-9111 C S I R Library Information & Accessions†
0007-912X C S I R O Abstracts *see* 0311-5836
0007-9138 C S I R O Food Preservation Quarterly *see* 0310-9070
0007-9154 C S I R Recorder†
0007-9162 C S I R Research Review *see* 0301-6145
0007-9197 C S U Collegian *changed to* Fort Collins Journal
0007-9200 C T A Action *changed to* C T A Action
0007-9219 C T V D: Cinema - TV - Digest
0007-9227 C W A News
0007-9235 Ca-A Cancer Journal for Clinicians
0007-9243 Ca Va
0007-926X Cabellian†
0007-9278 Cabinet Maker & Retail Furnisher
0007-9286 Cable *changed to* Lost & Found
0007-9294 Cablecasting-Cable TV Engineering†
0007-9308 Cables and Transmission *see* 0242-1283
0007-9316 Cabore
0007-9332 Cacaos, Cafes, Sucres
0007-9340 Cacau Atualidades†
0007-9367 Cactus and Succulent Journal
0007-9375 Cactus and Succulent Journal of Great Britain *see* 0264-3405
0007-9391 Cad†
0007-9405 Cadenza
0007-9421 Cadernos de Biblioteconomia, Arquivistica e Documentacao
0007-943X Cadernos de Jornalismo e Comunicacao†
0007-9456 Cadet Journal and Gazette
0007-9464 Les Dossiers CADRECO
0007-9472 Cadres and Profession *see* 0398-3145
0007-9480 Caducee
0007-9502 Caesaraugusta
0007-9510 Cafe et Cacao
0007-9537 Cafe Solo
0007-9545 Cafeteria Motel Bladet *changed to* Cafeteria Bladet
0007-9553 Caffe†
0007-9561 Cage & Aviary Birds
0007-957X Civilisation Libertaire
0007-9596 Cahiers Astrologiques
0007-960X Cahiers Bibliques Trimestriels *see* 0222-9714
0007-9618 Cahiers Bourbonnais et du Centre
0007-9626 Cahiers Bruxellois
0007-9634 Canada Music Book *see* 0700-4745
0007-9650 Cahiers d'Action Litteraire
0007-9669 Cahiers de l'Actualite Religieuse et Sociale
0007-9677 Cahiers d'Agriculture Pratique des Pays Chauds *see* 0395-9481
0007-9685 Cahiers d'Anesthesiologie
0007-9693 Cahiers d'Archeologie et d'Histoire du Berry
0007-9715 Cahiers de Bibliographie Therapeutique Francaise. Edition Medicale
0007-9723 Cahiers de Biologie Marine
0007-9731 Cahiers de Civilisation Medievale
0007-974X Cahiers de Droit
0007-9758 Cahiers de Droit Europeen
0007-9766 Cahiers de Geographie du Quebec
0007-9774 Cahiers de Josephologie
0007-9782 Cahiers de Kinesitherapie
0007-9790 Cahiers de la Ceramique, du Verre et des Arts du Feu
0007-9804 Association Belge de Documentation. Cahiers de la Documentation/Bladen voor de Documentatie
0007-9812 Cahiers de la Methode Naturelle *changed to* Cahiers de la Methode Naturelle en Medecine
0007-9820 Cahiers de la Puericultrice
0007-9839 Cahiers de la Reconciliation
0007-9847 Cahiers de la Renaissance Vaudoise
0007-9855 Cahiers de l'Afrique Occidentale et de l'Afrique Equatoriale
0007-9863 Cahiers de l'Enfance Inadaptee†
0007-9871 Cahiers de Lexicologie
0007-9898 Cahiers de l'Iroise
0007-991X Cahiers de l'Oronte
0007-9936 Cahiers de Medecine Interprofessionnelle
0007-9952 France. Institut National de Recherche et de Securite pour la Prevention des Accidents du Travail et des Maladies Professionnelles. Cahiers de Notes Documentaires
0007-9960 Cahiers de Nutrition et de Dietetique
0007-9979 Cahiers de Reeducation & de Readaptation Fonctionnelles†
0007-9987 Cahiers de Sociologie Economique
0007-9995 Cahiers de Sociologie et de Demographie Medicales
0008-0004 Cahiers de Topologie et Geometrie Differentielle†
0008-0012 Cahiers de Tunisie
0008-0020 Cahiers des Ameriques Latines. Serie - Sciences de l'Homme *changed to* Cahiers des Ameriques Latines
0008-0039 Cahiers des Naturalistes
0008-0047 Cahiers des Religions Africaines
0008-0055 Cahiers d'Etudes Africaines
0008-0063 Cahiers d'Etudes Cathares
0008-008X Cahiers d'Histoire (Lyon)
0008-0101 Cahiers du Chemin†
0008-011X Cahiers du Cinema
0008-0128 Club de la Grammaire. Cahiers
0008-0136 Cahiers du Communisme
0008-0152 Cahiers du Monde Hispanique et Luso-Bresilien (Caravelle)
0008-0160 Cahiers du Monde Russe et Sovietique
0008-0179 Cahiers du Nursing *changed to* Infirmiere Auxiliaire
0008-0195 Cahiers Economiques de Bruxelles
0008-0209 Cahiers Economiques et Sociaux
0008-0217 Cahiers Francais
0008-0233 Cahiers Galilee *changed to* Galilee
0008-0241 Cahiers Geologiques
0008-025X Cahiers Haut-Marnais
0008-0268 Cahiers Integres de Medecine†
0008-0276 Cahiers Internationaux de Sociologie
0008-0284 Cahiers Internationaux de Symbolisme
0008-0292 Cahiers J E B *changed to* J E B

ISSN INDEX 1213

0008-0292 Cahiers J E B *changed to* J E B Special
0008-0292 Cahiers J E B *changed to* J E B-Points
0008-0306 Cahiers Jean Tousseul†
0008-0314 Cahiers Laennec†
0008-0330 Cahiers Lyonnais d'Histoire de la Medecine†
0008-0365 Cahiers Naturalistes
0008-0373 Cahiers Numismatiques
0008-0381 Cahiers O.R.S.T.O.M. Serie Hydrologie *see* 0246-1528
0008-0403 Cahiers O.R.S.T.O.M. Serie Sciences Humaines *see* 0768-9829
0008-0411 Cahiers Oceanographiques†
0008-042X Cahiers Pedagogiques
0008-0438 Cahiers Pierre Loti†
0008-0446 Cahiers pour l'Analyse†
0008-0454 Cahiers Raciniens
0008-0462 Cahiers Rationalistes
0008-0497 Cahiers Vilfredo Pareto
0008-0519 Caiet de Documentare Cinematografica
0008-0527 Caiet Pentru Literatura si Istoriografie
0008-0535 Cake and Cockhorse
0008-0543 Cal-Tax News
0008-056X Calabria Nobilissima
0008-0578 Calavo Newsletter *changed to* Calavo Newsletter
0008-0586 Calcified Tissue Abstracts
0008-0594 Calcified Tissue Research *see* 0171-967X
0008-0616 Calcoin News
0008-0624 Calcolo
0008-0632 Calculi†
0008-0659 Calcutta Mathematical Society. Bulletin
0008-0667 Calcutta Medical Journal
0008-0675 Calcutta Municipal Gazette
0008-0683 Calcutta Statistical Association. Bulletin
0008-0691 University of Calcutta. Department of English. Bulletin *changed to* University of Calcutta. Department of English. Journal
0008-0705 University of Calcutta. University College of Medicine. Bulletin
0008-0721 Calendar *changed to* C B C Features
0008-073X Calendar of Coming Meetings of Interest to Historians†
0008-0756 Calendar of Events in the New Pennsylvania *changed to* Pennsylvania Quarterly Calendar of Events
0008-0764 Calendar of Forthcoming Scientific and Technological Meetings to Be Held in Israel *see* 0333-6131
0008-0772 Calendar of Sports Events†
0008-0802 California A F L - C I O News
0008-0829 California Academy of Sciences. Academy Newsletter
0008-0837 California Agency Bulletin *changed to* California Insurance
0008-0845 California Agriculture
0008-0853 California Agriculture Department Biennial Report†
0008-0861 California Air Environment†
0008-0896 California Apparel News
0008-090X California-Arizona Cotton
0008-0918 California Bowling News
0008-0926 California Business
0008-0934 California C P A Quarterly *see* 0273-835X
0008-0942 California Cattleman
0008-0950 California Courier
0008-0969 California Covenanter *changed to* Pacific Southwest Covenanter
0008-0977 California Dental Association. Journal
0008-0985 California Dental Association. Newsletter†
0008-1000 California. Division of Mines and Geology. Bulletin
0008-1019 California Elementary Administrator†
0008-1027 California Engineer
0008-1051 California Farmer
0008-106X Western Financial Journal†
0008-1078 California Fish and Game
0008-1094 California Forestry and Forest Products
0008-1108 California Future Farmer†
0008-1116 California Garden
0008-1124 California Grange News
0008-1140 California Highway Patrolman
0008-1167 California Historical Society. Notes *see* 0095-6465
0008-1175 California Historical Society Quarterly *see* 0162-2897
0008-1191 California Industrial Relations Reports
0008-1205 California Journal
0008-1213 California Journal of Educational Research *changed to* Educational Research Quarterly
0008-1221 California Law Review
0008-123X California Librarian†
0008-1248 California Livestock News *changed to* California Sheepman's Quarterly
0008-1256 California Management Review
0008-1264 California Medicine *see* 0093-0415
0008-1272 California Men's and Women's Stylist *changed to* Mens Apparel News
0008-1280 California Mental Health Research Digest†
0008-1299 California Mining Journal
0008-1302 California Monthly
0008-1310 California Nurse
0008-1329 Pacific Oil World
0008-1337 California Optometrist Association. Journal *see* 0273-804X
0008-1345 Nord Nytt
0008-1353 California Palace of the Legion of Honor. Bulletin†
0008-1361 California Pelican
0008-1388 California Pharmacy *changed to* California Pharmacist
0008-140X California Probation, Parole and Correctional Association. Journal *changed to* Crime and Corrections
0008-1418 California Professor *changed to* C C A Advocate
0008-1426 California Public Survey†
0008-1434 California Publisher
0008-1442 California Rancher *changed to* California Grower & Rancher
0008-1450 California Real Estate Magazine
0008-1477 California Safety News†
0008-1485 California Savings and Loan Journal *changed to* California Hotline
0008-1493 California School Administrator†
0008-1507 California School Boards
0008-1515 California School Employee
0008-1523 California School Libraries *see* 0196-3309
0008-1558 California Southern Baptist
0008-1566 California State Employee
0008-1574 California State Publications
0008-1582 California Tech
0008-1604 California Vector Views†
0008-1612 California Veterinarian
0008-1620 California Water Pollution Control Association. Bulletin
0008-1639 California Western Law Review
0008-1647 Western Tide *changed to* U S I U News
0008-1655 California Wineletter
0008-1663 California Woman
0008-1671 California Youth Authority Quarterly†
0008-1698 Call (New York)
0008-1701 Call Board
0008-1728 Call
0008-1736 Call Number†
0008-1744 Call Number
0008-1760 Calore
0008-1779 Calvary Review
0008-1787 Calvijn
0008-1795 Calvin Theological Journal
0008-1809 Calzado en Mexico *see* 0008-1817
0008-1817 Calzado y Teneria
0008-1833 Camag Bibliography Service
0008-1841 Camara Argentina de Productos Quimicos. Boletin Informativo
0008-185X Camara de Comercio de Bogota. Boletin
0008-1868 Comerciante
0008-1876 Camara de Comercio de la Guaira. Boletin Estadistico.
0008-1884 Camara de Comercio de Lima. Boletin Semanal
0008-1892 Comercio y Produccion
0008-1906 Camara de Comercio Luso-Americana. Boletim *changed to* Camara de Comercio Americana. Boletim
0008-1914 Camara de Comercio Uruguayo-Britanica. Revista
0008-1922 Camara Nacional de Comercio de Managua. Boletin *changed to* Camara de Comercio de Nicaragua. Boletin Comercial
0008-1930 Camara Oficial de Comercio, Industria y Navegacion de Barcelona. Boletin
0008-1949 Camera Textil de Mexico. Revista Tecnica *changed to* Revista Tecnica Textil-Vestido
0008-1973 Cambridge Law Journal
0008-1981 Cambridge Philosophical Society. Proceedings. Mathematical and Physical Sciences *see* 0305-0041
0008-199X Cambridge Quarterly
0008-2007 Cambridge Review
0008-2023 Cambridgeshire, Huntingdon & Peterborough Life
0008-2031 Camden County Record
0008-204X Camellia Journal
0008-2058 Cameo Newsletter *changed to* New York (State) Office for the Aging. Newsletter
0008-2066 Camera
0008-2074 Camera†
0008-2082 CamerArt
0008-2090 Camera Canada
0008-2104 Camera Club Journal
0008-2112 Camara de Industria y Comercio Argentino-Alemana. Boletin
0008-2120 Camera di Commercio di Milano *changed to* Realta Economica
0008-2139 Camera di Commercio Industria Artigianato e Agricoltura. Dati e Notizie†
0008-2147 Camera di Commercio, Industria, Artigianato e Agricoltura di Belluno. Rassegna Economica
0008-2155 Camera Mainichi†
0008-2163 Camera Nu *changed to* Camera Palet
0008-2171 Camera Thirty-Five†
0008-218X Cameral†
0008-2198 Chambre de Commerce, d'Industrie et des Mines du Cameroun. Bulletin d'Information
0008-221X Camillusbode
0008-2236 Caminos
0008-2244 Caminos del Aire†
0008-2252 Camion
0008-2260 Cammino
0008-2279 Cammino Economico
0008-2287 Camp Fire Girl *see* 0092-1289
0008-2295 Camp Management†
0008-2309 Campaign
0008-2317 Campaign Insight
0008-2325 Campeggio Italiano
0008-2341 Campesino
0008-235X Campesino
0008-2376 Camping Magazine
0008-2384 Camping & Caravaning
0008-2406 C S E News
0008-2414 Camping-Caravanning-Revue
0008-2430 Camping Industry†
0008-2449 Camping Journal *changed to* Caravan Camping-Journal
0008-2465 Campo
0008-2473 El Campo
0008-2481 Campus (Lennoxville)
0008-249X Campus Call†
0008-2503 Campus Crier *changed to* Observer (Ellensburg)
0008-2511 Campus Estrien *changed to* Collectif
0008-252X Campus Leader
0008-2538 Campus Life
0008-2554 Canada Agriculture†
0008-2562 Canada Armenian Press *changed to* Canada Armenian Press. Newsletter
0008-2570 Canada. Statistics Canada. Air Carrier Operations in Canada/Operations des Transporteurs Aeriens au Canada
0008-2589 Canada. Bureau of Statistics. Credit Statistics. *see* 0380-0741
0008-2597 Canada. Bureau of Statistics. Industry Division. Air Conditioning and Equipment *changed to* Canada. Statistics Canada. Air Conditioning & Refrigeration Equipment
0008-2600 Canada. Statistics Canada. Biscuits and Confectionery/Biscuits et Confiserie†
0008-2619 Canada. Statistics Canada. Production of Canada's Leading Minerals/Production es Principaux Mineraux du Canada†
0008-2627 Canada. Statistics Canada. Restaurant Statistics *see* 0226-2320
0008-2635 Canada Courier†
0008-2643 Canada. Department of Fisheries and Forestry. Bi-Monthly Research Notes *see* 0228-9989
0008-2651 Canada. Statistics Canada. Consumption, Production and Inventories of Rubber/ Consommation, Production et Stocks de Caoutchouc†
0008-266X Canada. Statistics Canada. Service Bulletin. Energy Statistics†
0008-2686 Canada. Fisheries Research Board. Journal *see* 0706-652X
0008-2694 Canada Income Tax Guide
0008-2708 Canada Labour Service
0008-2716 Canada Lutheran *see* 0831-4446
0008-2732 Canada Poultryman
0008-2740 Canada Tax Cases
0008-2759 Canada Tax Service
0008-2775 Canadan Uutiset
0008-2791 Canada's Mental Health
0008-2805 Canadian
0008-2813 Canadian Administrator
0008-2821 Canadian Aeronautics and Space Journal
0008-283X Canadian Affairs†
0008-2848 Canadian Aircraft Operator
0008-2856 Canadian Anaesthetists' Society. Journal
0008-2864 Canadian Arabian News
0008-2872 Canadian Architect
0008-2880 Canadian Armed Forces Review *changed to* Government and Military Business
0008-2899 C A H P E R Journal
0008-2902 Canadian Association of Radiologists. Journal
0008-2937 Canadian Author & Bookman
0008-2945 Canadian Automotive Trade
0008-2953 Canadian Aviation
0008-2961 Canadian Ayrshire Review
0008-297X Canadian Banker *see* 0822-6830
0008-2988 Canadian Baptist
0008-3003 Canadian Bar Review
0008-3011 Canadian Beverage Review
0008-3038 Broadcaster
0008-3046 Canadian Botanical Association. Bulletin
0008-3054 Canadian Boy†
0008-3070 Canadian Building
0008-3089 Canadian Building Abstracts
0008-3097 Canadian Building Digest
0008-3100 Canadian Business
0008-3127 Canadian Cartographer *see* 0317-7173
0008-3143 Cattlemen
0008-3151 Canadian Certified Accountant *see* 0318-742X
0008-316X Canadian Chartered Accountant *see* 0317-6878
0008-3178 Canadian Chemical Education†
0008-3194 Canadian Chiropractic Association. Journal
0008-3208 Canadian Church Historical Society Journal
0008-3216 Canadian Churchman
0008-3232 Canadian Clothing Journal
0008-3240 Canadian Co-Operative Digest†
0008-3259 Canadian Composer
0008-3275 Canadian Consumer
0008-3283 Canadian Controls & Instrumentation *changed to* Canadian Controls & Instrumentation (1983)
0008-3291 Canadian Copper
0008-3305 Canadian Council for International Co-Operation. Bulletin†

1214 ISSN INDEX

0008-3313 Canadian Council of Professional Engineers. News Brief/Communique†
0008-3321 Canadian Council of Resource Ministers. References†
0008-3348 Canadian Criminal Cases
0008-3356 Canadian Current Law
0008-3364 Canadian Datasystems
0008-3372 Canadian Dental Association. Journal
0008-3380 Canadian Dental Hygienist
0008-3399 Canadian Dietetic Association. Journal
0008-3402 Canadian Dimension
0008-3429 Canadian Doctor
0008-3437 Canadian Documentation Centre, Fitness and Sport. Bulletin†
0008-3445 Canadian Education Association. Newsletter
0008-3453 Canadian Education Index
0008-3461 Canadian Electronics Engineering
0008-347X Canadian Entomologist
0008-3488 Canadian Estate and Gift Tax Reports *changed to* Canadian Estate Planning and Administration Reports
0008-3496 Canadian Ethnic Studies
0008-350X Canadian Family Physician
0008-3518 Canadian Farm Economics
0008-3526 Canadian Farm Equipment Dealer†
0008-3534 Canadian Federation of Music Teachers' Associations. News Bulletin *see* 0319-6356
0008-3542 Canadian Feed & Grain Journal†
0008-3550 Canadian Field-Naturalist
0008-3577 Canadian Flight
0008-3585 Canadian Florist, Greenhouse and Nursery
0008-3631 Canadian Forum
0008-364X Canadian Funeral Service *see* 0319-3225
0008-3658 Canadian Geographer
0008-3674 Canadian Geotechnical Journal
0008-3682 Canadian Golf Review†
0008-3690 Canadian Government Publications Monthly Catalogue *see* 0709-0412
0008-3704 Canadian Grocer
0008-3720 Canadian Hairdresser
0008-3739 Canadian Hereford Digest
0008-3747 Canadian High News *changed to* Teen Generation
0008-3755 Canadian Historical Review
0008-3763 Canadian Home Economics Journal
0008-3771 Canadian Home Leaguer *changed to* Home Leaguer
0008-378X Canadian Horse *see* 0830-0593
0008-3798 Canadian Hospital *see* 0317-7645
0008-3801 Canadian Hotel & Restaurant
0008-381X Canadian Imperial Bank of Commerce. Commercial Letter *changed to* Canadian Imperial Bank of Commerce. Spectrum
0008-3828 Canadian Independent Adjuster
0008-3836 Canadian Industrial Equipment News
0008-3844 Canadian Information Processing Society. Quarterly Bulletin *see* 0315-5986
0008-3860 Canadian Institute of Food Technology Journal/Institut Canadien de Technologie Alimentaire *see* 0315-5463
0008-3879 Canadian Insurance
0008-3887 Canadian Interiors
0008-3895 Canadian Jaycee
0008-3909 Canadian Jersey Breeder
0008-3917 Canadian Jeweller
0008-3925 Canadian Jewish Chronicle Review *see* 0008-3941
0008-3941 Canadian Jewish News
0008-395X Canadian Jewish Weekly†
0008-3968 Canadian Journal of African Studies
0008-3976 Canadian Journal of Agricultural Economics
0008-3984 Canadian Journal of Animal Science
0008-3992 Canadian Journal of Arms Collecting *changed to* Arms Collecting
0008-4018 Canadian Journal of Biochemistry *see* 0829-8211
0008-4026 Canadian Journal of Botany
0008-4034 Canadian Journal of Chemical Engineering
0008-4042 Canadian Journal of Chemistry
0008-4050 Canadian Journal of Comparative Medicine *see* 0830-9000
0008-4069 Canadian Journal of Corrections *see* 0704-9722
0008-4077 Canadian Journal of Earth Sciences
0008-4085 Canadian Journal of Economics
0008-4093 Canadian Journal of Genetics and Cytology/Journal Canadien de Genetique et de Cytologie *see* 0831-2796
0008-4107 Canadian Journal of History
0008-4115 Canadian Journal of History of Sport and Physical Education *changed to* Canadian Journal of History of Sport
0008-4123 Canadian Journal of Hospital Pharmacy
0008-4131 Canadian Journal of Linguistics
0008-414X Canadian Journal of Mathematics
0008-4158 Canadian Journal of Medical Technology
0008-4166 Canadian Journal of Microbiology
0008-4182 Canadian Journal of Ophthalmology
0008-4190 Canadian Journal of Pharmaceutical Sciences†
0008-4204 Canadian Journal of Physics
0008-4212 Canadian Journal of Physiology and Pharmacology
0008-4220 Canadian Journal of Plant Science
0008-4239 Canadian Journal of Political Science
0008-4247 Canadian Journal of Psychiatric Nursing
0008-4255 Canadian Journal of Psychology
0008-4263 Canadian Journal of Public Health
0008-4271 Canadian Journal of Soil Science
0008-428X Canadian Journal of Surgery
0008-4301 Canadian Journal of Zoology
0008-4328 Canadian Labor Law Reports
0008-4336 Canadian Labour
0008-4344 Canadian Lacombe Breeders Association. Newsletter
0008-4352 Canadian Library Journal
0008-4360 Canadian Literature
0008-4387 Canadian Marketer†
0008-4395 Canadian Mathematical Bulletin
0008-4409 Canadian Medical Association Journal
0008-4417 Canadian Mennonite†
0008-4425 Canadian Messenger of the Sacred Heart
0008-4433 Canadian Metallurgical Quarterly
0008-4441 Canadian Metalworking/Machine Production†
0008-445X Canadian Military Engineer†
0008-4468 Canadian Military Journal
0008-4476 Canadian Mineralogist
0008-4506 Canadian Modern Language Review
0008-4522 Canadian Motorcycling *changed to* Cycle C M A
0008-4549 Canadian Music Educator
0008-4557 Canadian Commission for UNESCO. Bulletin
0008-4565 Canadian News Facts
0008-4573 Canadian Numismatic Journal
0008-4581 Canadian Nurse *changed to* Canadian Nurse/L'Infirmiere Canadienne
0008-459X Canadian Nurseryman *see* 0315-4874
0008-4611 Canadian Occupational Safety
0008-462X Canadian Office Products and Stationery
0008-4638 Canadian Journal of Operational Research and Information Processing *see* 0315-5986
0008-4654 Canadian Packaging
0008-4662 Canadian Paint and Finishing†
0008-4670 Patent Office Record (Canada)
0008-4689 Canadian Patent Reporter
0008-4697 Peace Research
0008-4719 Canadian Periodical Index
0008-4727 Canadian Personnel & Industrial Relations Journal
0008-4743 Canadian Pharmaceutical Journal
0008-4751 Canadian Physiotherapy Association Journal/Association Canadienne de Physiotherapie Revue *see* 0300-0508
0008-476X Canadian Plant Disease Survey
0008-4778 Canadian Plastics
0008-4786 Canadian Podiatrist
0008-4794 Canadian Postmaster
0008-4808 Canadian Poultry Review†
0008-4816 Canadian Printer and Publisher
0008-4816 Printing Product Guide
0008-4824 Canadian Psychiatric Association Journal *see* 0706-7437
0008-4840 Canadian Public Administration
0008-4859 Canadian Publishers Directory
0008-4867 Canadian Pulp and Paper Industry *see* 0713-5807
0008-4867 Canadian Pulp and Paper Industry *see* 0225-7572
0008-4875 Canadian Rail
0008-4883 Canadian Railway Club. Official Proceedings *see* 0226-157X
0008-4891 Canadian Reader†
0008-4905 Canadian Realtor *changed to* Canadian Real Estate
0008-4913 Canadian Register *see* 0383-1620
0008-493X Canadian Research and Development *see* 0319-1974
0008-4948 Canadian Review of Sociology and Anthropology
0008-4956 Canadian Rockhound†
0008-4972 Canadian Sailor
0008-4980 Canadian Shipping and Marine Engineering
0008-4999 Canadian Slavic Studies/Revue Canadienne d'Etudes Slaves *see* 0090-8290
0008-5006 Canadian Slavonic Papers
0008-5022 Canadian Society of Exploration Geophysicists. Journal
0008-5030 Canadian Society of Forensic Science Journal
0008-5049 Canadian Sociology and Anthropology Association. Bulletin†
0008-5057 Canadian Spectroscopy *see* 0045-5105
0008-509X Canada. Statistics Canada. Canadian Statistical Review/Revue Statistique du Canada
0008-5103 Canadian Surveyor
0008-5111 Canadian Tax Journal
0008-512X Canadian Tax Papers
0008-5138 Canadian Tax Reports
0008-5154 Canadian Technical Information News *changed to* Canadian Technical and Scientific Information News Journal
0008-5162 Canadian Telephone and Cable Television Journal *see* 0318-0069
0008-5189 Canadian Tobacco Grower
0008-5197 Canadian Tourism†
0008-5200 Canadian Transportation and Distribution Management
0008-5219 Canadian Travel Courier
0008-5235 Canadian Tuberculosis and Respiratory Disease Association. Bulletin *changed to* Canadian Lung Association. Bulletin
0008-5243 Canadian U F O Report†
0008-5251 Canadian Underwriter
0008-5278 Canadian Vending
0008-5286 Canadian Veterinary Journal
0008-5294 Canadian Weather Review†
0008-5308 Canadian Weekly Law Sheet
0008-5316 Canadian Weekly Publisher *see* 0380-8025
0008-5324 Canadian Welder & Fabricator
0008-5332 Canadian Welfare *see* 0704-5263
0008-5340 Western Canadian Journal of Anthropology *see* 0706-4845
0008-5367 Canadian Wings *changed to* Wings Newsmagazine of Canada
0008-5383 Canadian Zionist
0008-5391 Canadiana
0008-5405 Canard Enchaine
0008-5413 Canberra Consumer
0008-5421 Canberra Post
0008-543X Cancer
0008-5448 Cancer Bulletin *see* 0740-820X
0008-5456 Cancer Chemotherapy Abstracts *see* 0095-7895
0008-5464 Cancer News
0008-5472 Cancer Research
0008-5480 Cancro
0008-5502 Candle *see* 0262-5474
0008-5510 Candle (Macomb)
0008-5537 Baked Snack Industry *see* 0745-1032
0008-5553 Cane Growers Quarterly Bulletin†
0008-5588 Canning and Packing *see* 0040-795X
0008-560X Canning Trade *see* 0191-6181
0008-5618 Cannocchiale
0008-5626 Canoe-Camper
0008-5642 Canoeing in Britain *see* 0308-7565
0008-5650 Canon Law Abstracts
0008-5677 Canteras y Explotaciones
0008-5685 Canterbury Chamber of Commerce. Economic Bulletin
0008-5693 Canterbury Diocesan Notes *see* 0260-9924
0008-5715 Cantiere *see* 0029-6325
0008-5723 Canto dell'Assemblea†
0008-5731 Canto Gregoriano†
0008-5758 Canyon Cinemanews *changed to* Cinemanews
0008-5774 Capaha Arrow
0008-5782 Cape Cod Illustrated†
0008-5790 Cape Librarian
0008-5804 Cape of Good Hope. Department of Nature Conservation. Newsletter *changed to* Cape of Good Hope. Department of Nature Conservation and Museum Services. Annual Report
0008-5812 Cape Rock Journal *see* 0146-2199
0008-5820 Cape Town Photographic Society Syllabus
0008-5839 Capital
0008-5847 Capital
0008-5855 Capital Changes Reports
0008-5871 Capital en Accion *changed to* San Juan en Accion
0008-588X Capital Goods Review
0008-5898 Capital Voice
0008-591X Capitolium†
0008-5936 Capper's Weekly
0008-5944 Capricho
0008-5952 C C C O News Notes
0008-5960 Capsule News†
0008-5979 Captions†
0008-5987 Car
0008-5995 Car
0008-6002 Car and Driver
0008-6010 Car Craft
0008-6029 Car-del Scribe
0008-6037 Car Mechanics
0008-6053 Car Rental & Leasing Insider Newsletter
0008-607X Car Wash Review *changed to* American Carwash Review
0008-6088 Cara
0008-6096 Carabinier de Lausanne
0008-610X Carabiniere
0008-6118 Caracola
0008-6126 Caractere
0008-6134 Caracteres
0008-6142 Caravan *changed to* Caravan Magazine
0008-6150 Caravan
0008-6169 Caravan Bladet
0008-6177 Caravaning
0008-6185 Caravaning
0008-6193 Caravanner
0008-6207 Caravel†
0008-6215 Carbohydrate Research
0008-6223 Carbon
0008-6231 Carbon Black Abstracts†
0008-624X Carcanet *see* 0308-2636
0008-6258 Carcinogenesis Abstracts
0008-6266 Commonwealth Forestry Bureau. Card Title Service†
0008-6274 Cardamom News *changed to* Cardamom
0008-6290 Cardinal Poetry Quarterly†
0008-6312 Cardiology
0008-6320 Cardiologia nel Mondo
0008-6347 Cardiology Digest *changed to* Cardiology Digest (1979)
0008-6355 Cardiovascular Nursing
0008-6363 Cardiovascular Research
0008-6371 Cardiovascular Research Center Bulletin†

ISSN INDEX 1215

0008-638X Care†
0008-641X Cargill Crop Bulletin *changed to* Cargill Bulletin
0008-6436 Caribbean Challenge
0008-6444 Caribbean Conservation Association. Newsletter *changed to* Caribbean Conservation News.
0008-6452 Caribbean Journal of Science
0008-6460 Caribbean Journal of Science and Mathematics†
0008-6495 Caribbean Quarterly
0008-6509 Caribbean Report†
0008-6517 Caribbean Research Institute. Quarterly Report†
0008-6525 Caribbean Review
0008-6533 Caribbean Studies
0008-655X Caridade
0008-6568 Caries Research
0008-6576 Carillon
0008-6592 Carinski Pregled
0008-6606 Carinthia 1
0008-6614 Caritas
0008-6622 Caritas-Korrespondenz
0008-6630 Carleton *see* 0315-1859
0008-6649 Carleton Miscellany†
0008-6657 Laboratoire Carlsberg. Comptes Rendus des Travaux *see* 0105-1938
0008-6665 Carmel
0008-6673 Carmelus
0008-6681 Carnegie Magazine
0008-669X Carnets de Zoologie
0008-6703 Carnival
0008-6711 Carnivore Genetics Newsletter
0008-672X Carolina Christian
0008-6738 Carolina Cooperator *see* 0195-3346
0008-6746 Carolina Country
0008-6762 Carolina Genealogist†
0008-6770 Carolina Golfer
0008-6789 Carolina Highways
0008-6797 Carolina Quarterly
0008-6800 Carolina Sportsman
0008-6819 Carolinian†
0008-6835 Carovana†
0008-6843 Carpenter
0008-6851 Carpet Review *see* 0263-4236
0008-6886 Carrefour
0008-6894 Carrell
0008-6908 Carreteras
0008-6916 Carriage Journal
0008-6924 Carrier Reports
0008-6932 Carroll Business Bulletin
0008-6940 Carrosserie
0008-6959 Carrozziere Italiano
0008-6967 Cars & Car Conversions
0008-6975 Cars & Parts
0008-6983 Carta Cultural de Venezuela
0008-6991 Cartabianca
0008-7009 Cartactual
0008-7017 Carte Blanche†
0008-7025 Carte Segrete
0008-7033 Carthusian
0008-7041 Cartographic Journal
0008-705X Cartonnagebedrijf *changed to* Kartonnagemarkt
0008-7068 Cartoonist Profiles
0008-7076 Cartophilic Notes & News
0008-7114 Caryologia
0008-7122 Casa
0008-7149 Casa de la Cultura Ecuatoriana. Revista†
0008-7157 Casa de las Americas
0008-7165 Casa do Douro Boletim†
0008-7173 Casa Vogue
0008-7181 Casabella
0008-719X Casana
0008-7203 Casas y Jardines
0008-7211 Cascade Caver
0008-722X Cascades†
0008-7238 Case and Comment (Rochester)
0008-7246 Case & Counsel
0008-7254 Case Western Reserve Journal of International Law
0008-7262 Case Western Reserve Law Review
0008-7270 Cash and Carry News *changed to* Convenience Store
0008-7289 Cash Box
0008-7297 Cash Crop Farming†
0008-7300 Cashew Bulletin
0008-7319 Cashier
0008-7327 C & S
0008-7335 Casopis Lekaru Ceskych
0008-7343 Narodni Muzeum v Praze. Casopis: Rada Historicka
0008-7351 Narodni Muzeum. Casopis: Oddil Prirodovedny *changed to* Narodni Muzeum v Praze. Casopis: Rada Prirodovedna
0008-736X Casopis pro Mezinarodni Pravo†
0008-7378 Casopis pro Mineralogii a Geologii
0008-7394 Casopis pro Pestovani Matematiky
0008-7408 Cassa di Risparmio delle Provincie Lombarde Quarterly
0008-7416 Cassa di Soccorso e Malattia per i Dipendenti dell'Azienda Trasporti Municipali di Milano. Bollettino d'Informazione
0008-7424 Cassazione Penale
0008-7440 Cassella-Riedel Archiv
0008-7467 International Cast Metals Journal†
0008-7475 Castanea
0008-7483 Casteel†
0008-7491 Il Castello
0008-7505 Castillos de Espana
0008-7513 Casting Engineering *see* 0273-9607
0008-7521 Castings
0008-753X Castoro†
0008-7548 Burmah International†
0008-7556 Castrum Peregrini
0008-7564 Casual Living and Summer and Casual Furniture *changed to* Casual Living
0008-7572 Casualty Return Statistical Summary *see* 0268-0815
0008-7580 Casualty Simulation
0008-7599 Cat
0008-7610 Catalogo Nacional del Envase, Embalaje y Artes Graficas Aplicadas *changed to* Catalogo Espanol del Envase, Embalaje y Artes Graficas Aplicadas
0008-7629 Catalogue & Index
0008-7645 Catalysis Reviews *see* 0161-4940
0008-7661 Catalyst (Peterborough)
0008-767X Catalyst (Philadelphia)
0008-7688 Catalyst for Environmental Quality *see* 0194-1445
0008-7696 Catch
0008-770X Catch Society of America. Journal†
0008-7726 Catechist
0008-7734 Catechistes *changed to* Temps et Paroles
0008-7742 Catechistes d'Aujourd'hui *changed to* Points de Repere
0008-7750 Universidad de Granada. Catedra Francisco Suarez. Anales
0008-7777 Caterer & Hotelkeeper
0008-7807 Catering Executive†
0008-7815 Catering Industry Employee
0008-7823 Catering Quarterly†
0008-784X Caterpillar *see* 0730-305X
0008-7866 Cathcart Chronicle
0008-7874 Cathedral Age
0008-7882 Cathode Press†
0008-7890 New Earth
0008-7904 Catholic Advance
0008-7912 Catholic Biblical Quarterly
0008-7920 Catholic Book Review *changed to* Canadian Book, Film and Record Review
0008-7939 Religious Book Guide *see* 0279-9588
0008-7947 Catholic Business Education Review†
0008-7971 Catholic Chronicle
0008-7998 Catholic Digest
0008-8005 Catholic Documentation†
0008-8013 Catholic Education Today†
0008-8021 Catholic Film Newsletter *see* 0362-0875
0008-803X Catholic Fireside
0008-8048 Catholic Forester
0008-8056 Catholic Free Press
0008-8064 Catholic Gazette
0008-8072 Catholic Herald
0008-8080 Catholic Historical Review
0008-8099 Catholic Hospital *see* 0226-5923
0008-8102 Medical Service
0008-8110 Catholic Institutional Management†
0008-8129 Catholic Journalist
0008-8137 Catholic Lawyer
0008-8145 Catholic Leader
0008-8161 Catholic Library Association. Northern Illinois Chapter. Newsletter
0008-8188 Parish and Lending Library News *changed to* Parish and Community Libraries News
0008-820X Catholic Library World
0008-8218 Catholic Life
0008-8226 Catholic Medical Quarterly
0008-8234 Catholic Messenger
0008-8242 Catholic Mind†
0008-8250 Catholic News†
0008-8269 Catholic Nurse†
0008-8277 Catholic Peace Fellowship Bulletin
0008-8285 Catholic Periodical and Literature Index
0008-8293 Catholic Pictorial
0008-8307 Catholic Press Directory
0008-8315 Catholic Review (Baltimore)
0008-8323 Catholic Review (New York)
0008-8331 Catholic Rural Life
0008-834X Catholic School Editor†
0008-8366 Catholic Standard
0008-8390 Catholic University Law Review
0008-8404 Catholic Virginian
0008-8412 Catholic Voice
0008-8420 Catholic Weekly
0008-8439 Catholic Weekly
0008-8447 Catholic Witness
0008-8455 Catholic Woman's Journal†
0008-8463 Catholic Worker
0008-8471 Catholic Workman
0008-848X Catholic World *changed to* New Catholic World
0008-8498 Catholica†
0008-8501 Catholica
0008-851X Catholica Unio
0008-8528 Catolicismo†
0008-8536 Catonsville Roadrunner†
0008-8544 Cats Magazine
0008-8552 Cattleman
0008-8579 Caustic
0008-8609 Cavalier Daily
0008-8625 Caves and Karst†
0008-8641 Caxtonian†
0008-865X Cayuga County Farm and Home News *see* 0002-158X
0008-8668 Cebu y Derivados
0008-8676 Cecidologia Internationale
0008-8684 Cedars-Sinai Medical Center Compass
0008-8692 Ceiba
0008-8706 Selebriamo
0008-8714 Celestial Mechanics
0008-8722 Celik
0008-8730 Cell & Tissue Kinetics
0008-8749 Cellular Immunology
0008-8757 Cellule
0008-8765 Cellulosa e Carta
0008-8773 Celtic News *changed to* Carn
0008-8781 Celuloide
0008-8803 Cement
0008-8811 Cement
0008-882X Cement
0008-8838 Cement & Concrete†
0008-8846 Cement and Concrete Research
0008-8854 Cement Technology *see* 0263-6050
0008-8862 Cement, Lime and Gravel *changed to* Quarry Management
0008-8870 Cement og Beton *see* 0029-1307
0008-8889 Cement Special
0008-8897 Cement, Wapno, Gips
0008-8919 Cemento-Hormigon
0008-8927 Cemento Portland
0008-8935 Cenacolo
0008-8943 Cenhadwr†
0008-8951 Cenicafe
0008-896X Cenobio
0008-8978 Centaur†
0008-8986 Centauros
0008-8994 Centaurus
0008-9001 Centenary College Conglomerate
0008-901X Centennial Review *see* 0162-0177
0008-9036 Center for Children's Books. Bulletin
0008-9044 Center for Chinese Research Materials. Newsletter
0008-9052 University of Michigan. Center for Coordination of Ancient and Modern Studies. Newsletter†
0008-9079 Center for Law Enforcement Research Information†
0008-9087 Center for Research Libraries. Newsletter *see* 0275-4924
0008-9095 Center for Soviet and East-European Studies in the Performing Arts. Bulletin
0008-9117 Center Forum†
0008-9125 Center for the Study of Democratic Institutions. Center Magazine
0008-9133 Center for Teaching About Peace and War. Newsletter *changed to* Center for Peace and Conflict Studies/Detroit Council for World Affairs. Newsletter
0008-9141 Cento
0008-9168 Centraal Orgaan voor de Handel in Aardappelen, Groenten en Fruit†
0008-9176 Central African Journal of Medicine
0008-9184 Central African Zionist Digest
0008-9192 Central Asiatic Journal
0008-9206 Central Bank News†
0008-9214 Central Bank News Digest *see* 0115-1401
0008-9222 Central Bank of Ceylon. Bulletin
0008-9230 Central Bank of Cyprus. Bulletin
0008-9249 Central Bank of Egypt. Economic Review
0008-9257 Central Bank of Iraq. Quarterly Bulletin
0008-9265 Central Bank of Jordan. Quarterly Bulletin *changed to* Central Bank of Jordan. Monthly Statistical Bulletin
0008-9273 Central Bank of Malta. Quarterly Review
0008-9281 Central Bank of Nigeria. Economic and Financial Review
0008-929X Central Bank of Nigeria. Monthly Report
0008-9303 Philippine Financial Statistics
0008-9311 Central Bible Quarterly†
0008-9346 Central Constructor†
0008-9362 Central Europe Journal†
0008-9389 Central European History
0008-9397 Central Glass and Ceramic Research Institute. Bulletin
0008-9400 Central Ideas†
0008-9419 Central Illinois Historical Messenger *changed to* Historical Messenger
0008-9427 Central Inland Fisheries Research Institute. Bulletin
0008-9443 Central Japan Journal of Orthopaedic & Traumatic Surgery
0008-9451 Central Michigan Life
0008-946X Central New York Academy of Medicine. Bulletin
0008-9478 Central New York Regional Medical Program. Bulletin†
0008-9494 Central News†
0008-9508 Central Opera Service Bulletin
0008-9524 Central Pennsylvania Labor News
0008-9559 Central States Archaeological Journal
0008-9575 Central States Speech Journal
0008-9583 Centralblatt fuer das Gesamte Forstwesen
0008-9591 Centralny Osrodek Informacji Budownictwa. Biuletyn-Informacja *changed to* Biuletyn Informacyjny o Budownictwie
0008-9605 Centre Catholique des Intellectuels Francais. Recherches et Debats
0008-9621 Centre de Conjoncture Africaine et Malgache. Bulletin d'Information *changed to* C C A M Information
0008-963X Centre de Documentation Siderurgique. Circulaire d'Informations *changed to* Revue de Metallurgie. Cahiers d'Information Techniques
0008-9648 Centre de Formation des Journalistes. Feuillets
0008-9664 Centre de Recherche et d'Information Socio-Politiques. Etudes Africaines†

0008-9672 Societe Nationale des Petroles d'Aquitaine. Centre de Recherches de Pau. Bulletin *see* 0396-2687
0008-9680 Centre de Recherches et d'Etudes Oceanographiques. Travaux
0008-9699 Universite Libre de Bruxelles. Centre d'Etude des Pays de l'Est. Revue du Centre d'Etude des Pays de l'Est et du Centre National pour l'Etude des Etats de l'Est *changed to* Universite Libre de Bruxelles. Centre d'Etude des Pays de l'Est. Revue des Pays de l'Est
0008-9702 Centre d'Etude des Matieres Plastiques. Bulletin de Documentation
0008-9710 Shikshak
0008-9737 Universite Libre de Bruxelles. Centre d'Etudes de Recherche Operationnelle. Cahiers
0008-9761 Centre d'Etudes Socialistes. Cahiers†
0008-9788 Centre d'Information Civique, Paris. Etudes
0008-980X Centre International d'Etude des Textiles Anciens. Bulletin de Liaison
0008-9818 Centre International d'Etudes Romanes. Bulletin *changed to* Centre International d'Etudes Romanes. Revue Trimestrielle
0008-9826 Centre Medical†
0008-9842 Federation Protestante de France. Centre d'Etudes et de Documentation. Bulletin *see* 0181-7671
0008-9850 Centre Scientifique et Technique du Batiment. Cahiers
0008-9869 Centre Technique du Bois et de l'Ameublement. Bulletin Bibliographique *see* 0295-5717
0008-9877 Centre Technique du Bois et de l'Ameublement. Bulletin d'Informations Techniques *changed to* C T B Info
0008-9885 Centre Technique du Bois et de l'Ameublement. Cahiers
0008-9907 Centro America Odontologica
0008-9915 Instituto de Investigacao Cientifica de Mocambique. Centro de Documentacao Cientifica. Boletim†
0008-9931 Portugal. Ministerio do Ultramar. Centro de Documentacao Tecnico-Economica. Boletim Bibliografico
0008-994X Centro de Documentacion. Boletin
0008-9958 Centro de Estudios Monetarios Latinoamericanos. Boletin Mensual *changed to* Centro de Estudios Monetarios Latinoamericanos. Boletin Bimensual
0008-9966 Centro de Estudios Sociales del Valle de los Caidos. Boletin *see* 0303-9889
0008-9990 Centro de Historia del Estado Falcon. Boletin
0009-000X Regno - Documenti
0009-0026 Centro di Documentazione Sul Movimento dei Disciplinati. Quaderni *changed to* Centro di Ricerca e di Studio Sul Movimento dei Disciplinati. Quaderni
0009-0034 Centro Interamericano de Vivienda y Planeamiento. Lista de Nuevas Adquisiciones†
0009-0042 Centro Interamericano de Vivienda y Planeaminento. Suplemento Informativo *changed to* S I N D U. Noticiero
0009-0050 Centro Latino Americano de Fisica Noticia†
0009-0069 Centro Latino Americano de Pesquisas em Ciencias Sociais. Boletim Bibliografia
0009-0085 Centro Nacional de Informacion de Ciencias Medicas. Revista de Resumenes. Cuaderno 2. Cirugia†
0009-0093 Centro Nacional de Informacion de Ciencias Medicas. Revista de Resumenes. Cuaderno 4. Higiene, Epidemiologia, Medios de Diagnostico y Otros†
0009-0107 Centro Nacional de Informacion de Ciencias Medicas. Revista de Resumenes. Cuaderno 1. Medicina†
0009-0115 Centro Nacional de Informacion de Ciencias Medicas. Revista de Resumenes. Cuaderno 3. Pediatria†
0009-0123 Centro Naval. Boletin
0009-0131 Centro Pan-Americano de Febre Aftosa. Boletin
0009-014X Centro Regional de Pesquisas Educacionais Jaoa Pinheiro. Boletim Informativo†
0009-0158 Century
0009-0166 Century†
0009-0174 Ceol
0009-0190 Ceramic Arts & Crafts
0009-0204 Ceramic Awareness Bulletin†
0009-0212 Ceramic Forum†
0009-0220 Ceramic Industry
0009-0247 Ceramic Scope
0009-0255 Ceramic Society of Japan. Journal
0009-0263 Ceramic Trade News & Catalog File *changed to* Ceramic Projects
0009-028X Ceramic Italian nell'Edilizia *see* 0392-4890
0009-0301 Ceramics *see* 0305-7623
0009-031X Ceramics Japan
0009-0328 Ceramics Monthly
0009-0336 Ceramique Moderne
0009-0344 Cercle d'Etudes Numismatiques. Bulletin
0009-0352 Cereal Chemistry
0009-0360 Cereal Science Today *see* 0146-6283
0009-0379 Ceres
0009-0387 Cerkev v Sedanjem Svetu
0009-0395 Cernakov Odkaz *changed to* Slobodne Slovensko
0009-0409 Certificated Engineer
0009-0417 Certified Accountants Journal *see* 0306-2406
0009-0425 Certified General Accountant *see* 0318-742X
0009-0433 Certified Milk†
0009-0441 Cerveny Kvet
0009-045X Cervi's Rocky Mountain Journal *changed to* Rocky Mountain Business Journal
0009-0468 Ceska Literatura
0009-0476 Ceska Mykologie
0009-0484 Ceske Listy†
0009-0492 Ceskoslovenska Akademie Ved. Vestnik
0009-0506 Ceskoslovenska Armada
0009-0514 Ceskoslovenska Dermatologie
0009-0522 Ceskoslovenska Epidemiologie, Mikrobiologie, Imunologie
0009-0530 Ceskoslovenska Farmacie
0009-0549 Ceskoslovenska Fotografie
0009-0557 Ceskoslovenska Fysiologie
0009-0565 Ceskoslovenska Gastroenterologie a Vyziva
0009-0573 Ceskoslovenska Hygiena
0009-0581 Ceskoslovenska Neurologie *see* 0301-0597
0009-059X Ceskoslovenska Oftalmologie
0009-0603 Ceskoslovenska Otolaryngologie
0009-0611 Ceskoslovenska Patologie
0009-062X Ceskoslovenska Psychologie
0009-0638 Ceskoslovenska Rusistika
0009-0646 Ceskoslovenska Spolecnost Mikrobiologicka. Bulletin
0009-0654 Ceskoslovenska Stomatologie
0009-0670 Rybarstvi
0009-0689 Ceskoslovenske Zdravotnictvi
0009-0697 Ceskoslovensky Architekt
0009-0700 Ceskoslovensky Casopis pro Fysiku
0009-0719 Ceskoslovensky Hornik a Energetik
0009-0727 Ceskoslovensky Kolorista
0009-0735 Ceskoslovensky Rozhlas a Televize
0009-0743 Ceskoslovensky Sach
0009-0751 Ceskoslovensky Vojak
0009-0778 Cesky Bratr
0009-0786 Cesky Jazyk a Literatura
0009-0794 Cesky Lid
0009-0808 Ceux des F F A
0009-0816 Ceylon Coconut Planters' Review *changed to* Coconut Bulletin
0009-0824 Ceylon Coconut Quarterly *changed to* Cocos
0009-0832 Sri Lanka Journal of Historical and Social Studies
0009-0840 Ceylon Journal of the Humanities *changed to* Sri Lanka Journal of the Humanities
0009-0859 Ceylon Labour Gazette *changed to* Sri Lanka Labour Gazette
0009-0867 Sri Lanka Library Review
0009-0875 Ceylon Medical Journal
0009-0883 Ceylon National Bibliography *changed to* Sri Lanka National Bibliography
0009-0891 Ceylon Veterinary Journal *changed to* Sri Lanka Veterinary Journal
0009-0905 Avicultura Industrial
0009-0913 Chacra *changed to* Campo Moderno y Chacra
0009-0921 Chain Merchandiser
0009-093X Chain Saw Age
0009-0948 Chain Saw Industry & Power Equipment Dealer
0009-0972 Chalkmarks†
0009-0980 Challenge *see* 0045-849X
0009-0999 Challenge (London, 1961)
0009-1006 Challenge (London)
0009-1014 Challenge (Sandbach)
0009-1049 Challenge (New York)
0009-1057 Challenge†
0009-1065 New Stationer†
0009-1073 Challenge (Richmond)†
0009-1103 Chalmers†
0009-112X Chalmers Tekniska Hoegskola. Institutionen foer Skeppshydromekanik. Rapport
0009-1138 Dublin Chamber of Commerce Journal *changed to* Trade-Links Journal
0009-1146 Chamber of Commerce of the U.S. Newsletter *changed to* Organization Dateline
0009-1154 Chamber of Commerce of the U.S. Association Letter
0009-1162 Chamber of Mines Journal *changed to* Mining and Engineering
0009-1189 Chambre de Commerce et d'Industrie de Meurthe et Moselle. Bulletin Mensuel *see* 0240-7426
0009-1197 Chambre de Commerce de Bruxelles. Bulletin Officiel *changed to* Entreprendre
0009-1200 Chambre de Commerce et d'Industrie de Marseille. Cahiers de Documentation†
0009-1219 Chambre de Commerce et d'Industrie de Paris. Bulletin Mensuel
0009-1227 Chambre de Commerce et d'Industrie de Rouen. Bulletin Economique
0009-1235 Chambre de Commerce Francaise du Japon. Bulletin†
0009-126X Chambre Syndicale des Mines de Fer de France. Bulletin Technique
0009-1286 Chaminade College Newsletter *changed to* Chaminade University Newsletter
0009-1294 Champagne News
0009-1308 Champignon
0009-1316 Champignoncultuur
0009-1324 Champion†
0009-1332 Champak
0009-1359 Chandrabhaga (West Bengal)
0009-1367 Change *see* 0335-1971
0009-1383 Change (New Rochelle)
0009-1413 Changing Education†
0009-1421 Changing Schools†
0009-143X Changing Times
0009-1456 Channel *see* 0025-4142
0009-1464 Channel (New Paltz)†
0009-1480 Gambit†
0009-1499 Channel Viewer *changed to* Channel TV Times
0009-1502 Channels (Omaha)†
0009-1510 Channels (New York)
0009-1529 Channels of Blessing
0009-1537 Chanoyu *changed to* Chanoyu Quarterly
0009-1553 Chantecoq†
0009-1561 Chanticleer
0009-1588 Chantiers†
0009-1596 Chantiers Cooperatifs
0009-160X Les Chantiers du Cardinal
0009-1618 Chantiers Pedagogiques
0009-1626 Children's Book Review†
0009-1634 Chapeaux et Coiffures de France *see* 0047-8512
0009-1642 Chaplain *see* 0149-4236
0009-1650 Chappaqua Speculator†
0009-1669 Character Potential†
0009-1685 Charbonnages de France. Publications Techniques
0009-1707 Charing Cross Hospital Gazette *changed to* Charing Cross Medical Gazette
0009-1715 Charisma *changed to* Touch
0009-1723 Charity and Children
0009-1731 Charivari†
0009-174X Charlatan: Interdisciplinary Journal†
0009-1758 Charles Buchan's Football Monthly *changed to* Football Monthly
0009-1766 Charles C. Adams Center for Ecological Studies. Occasional Papers
0009-1774 Charles S. Peirce Society. Transactions
0009-1790 Charlotte-Mecklenburg School Report†
0009-1804 Charm *changed to* Kapperskrant
0009-1812 Charm†
0009-1820 Charmant†
0009-1839 Charme†
0009-1847 Charolais Banner
0009-188X Chartered Accountant
0009-1898 Chartered Accountant in Australia
0009-1901 Chartered Engineer†
0009-1928 Chartered Secretary
0009-1936 Chartered Surveyor *changed to* Chartered Surveyor Weekly
0009-1944 Chartotheca Translationum Alphabetica
0009-1952 Chase
0009-1960 Chasovoi
0009-1979 Chasse et Peche *changed to* Chasse-Peche-Tir
0009-1987 Chat
0009-1995 Chatelaine
0009-2002 Chaucer Review
0009-2010 Chaud - Froid - Plomberie
0009-2029 Chauffage - Ventilation - Conditionnement
0009-2037 Chauffage-Plomberie†
0009-2061 Chavhata Weekly
0009-2096 Checklist of Congressional Hearings *changed to* Congress in Print
0009-2126 Cheering Words
0009-2142 Cheese Reporter
0009-2150 Chef Magazine *see* 0192-7116
0009-2177 Chefs
0009-2185 Chelsea
0009-2207 Chemexcil Export Bulletin
0009-2223 Chemia Analityczna
0009-2231 Chemia Stosowana. Seria A: Zagadnienia Technologii Chemicznej *see* 0376-0898
0009-224X Chemia Stosowana. Seria B. Zagadnienia Inzynierii i Apartury Chemicznej *changed to* Inzynieria Chemiczna i Procesowa
0009-2258 Chemical Abstracts
0009-2266 Chemical Abstracts - Applied Chemistry Sections *see* 0090-8363
0009-2274 Chemical Abstracts - Macromolecular Sections
0009-2282 Chemical Abstracts - Organic Chemistry Sections
0009-2290 Chemical Abstracts - Physical and Analytical Chemistry Sections *changed to* Chemical Abstracts - Physical, Inorganic and Analytical Chemistry Sections
0009-2304 Chemical Abstracts - Biochemistry Sections
0009-2312 Chemical Age *see* 0262-4230
0009-2320 Chemical Age of India
0009-2347 Chemical and Engineering News
0009-2355 Chemical and Petroleum Engineering
0009-2363 Chemical & Pharmaceutical Bulletin
0009-2371 Chemical and Process Engineering *see* 0370-1859
0009-238X Chemical-Biological Activities(CBAC)†

0009-2398 Chemical Bond
0009-2401 Chemical Bulletin
0009-241X Chemical Communications *see* 0022-4936
0009-2436 Chemical Economy and Engineering Review
0009-2452 Chemical Engineer and Transactions of the Institution of Chemical Engineers *see* 0302-0797
0009-2460 Chemical Engineering
0009-2479 Chemical Engineering Education
0009-2509 Chemical Engineering Science
0009-2517 Chemical Engineering World
0009-2525 Chemical Equipment
0009-2533 Chemical Era
0009-2541 Chemical Geology
0009-255X Chemical Highlights
0009-2576 Chemical Industry News
0009-2584 Chemical Industry Report†
0009-2592 Chemical Instrumentation *see* 0743-5797
0009-2606 Chemical Market Abstracts *see* 0161-8032
0009-2614 Chemical Physics Letters
0009-2622 Chemical Processing *see* 0305-439X
0009-2630 Chemical Processing
0009-2649 Chemical Processing & Engineering *see* 0302-7678
0009-2665 Chemical Reviews
0009-2673 Chemical Society of Japan. Bulletin
0009-2681 Chemical Society, London. Quarterly Reviews *see* 0306-0012
0009-269X Chemical Substructure Index
0009-2703 Chemical Technology *changed to* Chemtech
0009-2711 Chemical Titles
0009-272X Chemical Week
0009-2738 Chemicals & Allied Products Export News
0009-2746 Chemicals-International
0009-2754 Chemicals, Quarterly Industry Report†
0009-2770 Chemicke Listy
0009-2789 Chemicky Prumysl
0009-2797 Chemico-Biological Interactions
0009-2800 Chemie-Anlagen und Verfahren
0009-2819 Chemie der Erde
0009-2827 Chemie en Techniek†
0009-2835 Chemie fuer Labor und Betrieb
0009-2843 Chemie in der Schule
0009-2851 Chemie in Unserer Zeit
0009-286X Chemie-Ingenieur-Technik
0009-2886 Chemik
0009-2894 Chemiker-Zeitung
0009-2908 Chemin
0009-2916 Cheminot
0009-2924 Chemins de Fer
0009-2932 Chemisch Weekblad *see* 0167-2746
0009-2940 Chemische Berichte
0009-2959 Chemische Industrie
0009-2967 Chemische Industrie International
0009-2975 Chemischer Informationsdienst
0009-2983 Chemische Rundschau
0009-3017 Chemisier l'Elegance Masculine *changed to* Elegance Masculine-Mylord
0009-3025 Chemist
0009-3033 Chemist & Druggist
0009-3041 Chemist & Drugstore News
0009-305X Chemistry *see* 0190-597X
0009-3068 Chemistry and Industry
0009-3076 Chemistry and Industry in New Zealand *changed to* Chemistry and Industry and Laboratory Management
0009-3084 Chemistry and Physics of Lipids
0009-3092 Chemistry and Technology of Fuels and Oils
0009-3106 Chemistry in Britain
0009-3114 Chemistry in Canada *see* 0823-5228
0009-3122 Chemistry of Heterocyclic Compounds
0009-3130 Chemistry of Natural Compounds
0009-3149 Chemists Review
0009-3157 Chemotherapy
0009-3165 Chemotherapy
0009-3173 Chempress
0009-3203 Cherie Moda
0009-322X Cherokee Nation News *changed to* Cherokee Advocate
0009-3238 Cherry Circle *changed to* C A A Magazine
0009-3262 Chesapeake Science *see* 0160-8347
0009-3289 Cheshire Life
0009-3297 Cheshire Smile
0009-3300 Chesopiean
0009-3319 Chess
0009-3335 Chess Digest†
0009-3343 Chess in Australia
0009-3351 Chess Life and Review *see* 0197-260X
0009-336X Chess 'n Checkers' *changed to* Pool Checker Masters
0009-3378 Kyoto University. Chest Disease Research Institute. Bulletin
0009-3386 Chester White Journal
0009-3394 Chestnut Hill Local
0009-3408 Chetwynd Reporter *changed to* Chetwynd Echo
0009-3424 Chez Nous
0009-3432 Chhandita
0009-3459 Chiba Medical Society. Journal *see* 0303-5476
0009-3467 Monthly Report of Meteorology, Chiba Prefecture
0009-3483 Chic†
0009-3491 Chicago Academy of Sciences. Bulletin
0009-3505 Chicago Bar Record
0009-3513 Chicago Bowler
0009-3521 Chicago Daily Hide and Tallow Bulletin
0009-353X Chicago Dental Society Fortnightly Review *see* 0091-1666
0009-3548 Chicago Fire Fighter†
0009-3556 Chicago Genealogist
0009-3564 Chicago Herpetological Society. Bulletin
0009-3572 Chicago Illini
0009-3580 Chicago Journalism Review†
0009-3599 Chicago-Kent Law Review *changed to* Chicago-Kent Law Review
0009-3602 Chicago Magazine†
0009-3610 Chicago Maroon
0009-3629 Chicago Medical School Quarterly†
0009-3637 Chicago Medicine
0009-3653 Chicago Police Star†
0009-3661 Chicago Psychoanalytic Literature Index
0009-367X Chicago Purchasor
0009-3696 Chicago Review
0009-3718 Chicago Studies
0009-3734 University of Chicago. Pritzker School of Medicine. Alumni Association. Bulletin *changed to* University of Chicago. Pritzker School of Medicine. Alumni Association. Magazine
0009-3742 Chicagoland Food News
0009-3769 Chicagoland's Real Estate Advertiser *changed to* Real Estate Magazine
0009-3777 Chicano Community Newspaper *changed to* El Chicano
0009-3785 Chichester News
0009-3793 Chicory
0009-3807 Chief *see* 0746-7761
0009-3831 Education of Earth Science
0009-384X Chiiki Fukushi
0009-3858 Chikitsak Samaj
0009-3866 Storage Battery
0009-3874 Animal Husbandry
0009-3882 Child and Family
0009-3890 Child and Man
0009-3904 Child Care†
0009-3920 Child Development
0009-3939 Child Development Abstracts and Bibliography
0009-3947 Child Education
0009-3963 Child Health Investigation†
0009-3971 Child Life
0009-398X Child Psychiatry and Human Development
0009-3998 Child Psychiatry Quarterly
0009-4005 Child Study Journal
0009-4013 Child Wear†
0009-4021 Child Welfare
0009-403X Childbirth Education†
0009-4048 Childbirth Without Pain Education Association. Newsletter *changed to* Childbirth Without Pain Education Association. Memo
0009-4056 Childhood Education
0009-4064 Children *see* 0361-4336
0009-4072 Mental Retardation News *see* 0199-9435
0009-4080 Children's Digest
0009-4099 Children's Digest *see* 0272-7145
0009-4102 Friend
0009-4110 Children's Hospital Notes
0009-4129 Children's Hospital of the District of Columbia. Clinical Proceedings *see* 0092-7813
0009-4137 Children's House Magazine *changed to* Children's House/Children's World
0009-4153 Children's Own
0009-4161 Children's Playmate
0009-417X Children's Styles
0009-4196 Children's Theatre Review
0009-420X Children's World
0009-4218 Child's Guardian
0009-4226 Chile - Economic Notes†
0009-4234 Chile-Economic Background Information†
0009-4242 Chile. Ejercito. Anexo Historico. Memorial
0009-4277 Chiltern Life†
0009-4285 Chimes
0009-4315 Chimica e l'Industria
0009-4323 Chimie Actualites
0009-4331 Chimie Analytique *see* 0365-4877
0009-4366 Chimie et Technique
0009-4374 European Journal of Medicinal Chemistry
0009-4382 China Glass & Tableware
0009-4404 China News Analysis
0009-4412 China Notes
0009-4420 China Pictorial
0009-4439 China Quarterly
0009-4447 China Reconstructs
0009-4455 China Report
0009-4471 China Today†
0009-448X China Trade Report
0009-4501 Chinatown News
0009-451X Chinchilla-Zucht†
0009-4528 Chinese Bulletin *changed to* Chinese-Canadian Bulletin
0009-4536 Chinese Chemical Society. Journal
0009-4544 Chinese Culture
0009-4552 Chinese Economic Studies
0009-4560 Chinese Education
0009-4579 Chinese Journal of Administration
0009-4587 Chinese Journal of Microbiology *changed to* Chinese Journal of Microbiology and Immunology
0009-4595 Chinese Language Teachers Association. Journal
0009-4609 Chinese Law and Government
0009-4617 Chinese Literature
0009-4625 Chinese Sociology and Anthropology
0009-4633 Chinese Studies in History
0009-4641 Chinese Voice
0009-465X Ch'ing Documents
0009-4668 Ching Feng
0009-4684 Chirimo
0009-4692 Chirogram†
0009-4706 Chiropodist
0009-4714 Chiropody Review
0009-4722 Der Chirurg
0009-4749 Chirurgia degli Organi di Movimento
0009-4757 Chirurgia e Patologia Sperimentale
0009-4765 Chirurgia Gastroenterologica (Italian Edition)
0009-4773 Chirurgia Italiana
0009-4781 Chirurgia Maxillofacialis and Plastica
0009-479X Chirurgia Narzadow Ruchu i Ortopedia Polska
0009-4811 Chirurgia Triveneta
0009-482X Chirurgia Veterinaria†
0009-4838 Chirurgien-Dentiste de France
0009-4846 Chirurgische Praxis
0009-4862 Chitalishte
0009-4870 Chitrali
0009-4897 Map
0009-4900 Map's Companion *changed to* Map and Landscape
0009-4919 Chlodnictwo
0009-4935 Choc-Talk†
0009-4943 Chocolaterie, Confiserie de France *changed to* Magazine des Industries Gourmandes
0009-4951 Chogin Research *see* 0287-2404
0009-496X Choice
0009-4978 Choice (Middletown)
0009-4986 Choice†
0009-4994 Choisir
0009-5001 Choix Artistique et Litteraire
0009-501X Choppers Magazine *see* 0194-9888
0009-5028 Choral Journal
0009-5036 Der Chordirigent
0009-5044 Chorleiter†
0009-5052 Christ et France-sur le Roc *changed to* Sur le Roc
0009-5060 Der Christ im Zwanzigsten Jahrhundert
0009-5087 Christ und Buch
0009-5109 Christ und Welt *changed to* Deutsche Zeitung Christ und Welt
0009-5117 Christadelphian
0009-5133 Christelijk-Historisch Tijdschrift†
0009-5141 Christelijk Oosten
0009-515X Onze Vacatures†
0009-5176 Christelijke Muziekbode *changed to* Muziekbode
0009-5184 Die Christengemeinschaft
0009-5192 Christenlehre
0009-5206 Christian *see* 0092-8372
0009-5214 Christian Adventurer
0009-5222 Christian Advocate *changed to* Today's Ministry
0009-5249 Christian Attitudes on Jews and Judaism *see* 0144-2902
0009-5265 Christian Beacon
0009-5273 Christian Bookseller *see* 0749-2510
0009-5281 Christian Century
0009-5303 Christian Communications
0009-5311 Christian Cynosure†
0009-532X Christian Economics *changed to* Answers to Economic Problems
0009-5338 Christian Endeavor World
0009-5346 Christian Family†
0009-5354 Christian Herald (Chappaqua)
0009-5362 Christian Heritage†
0009-5370 Christian Home†
0009-5389 Christian Home & School
0009-5397 Christian Institutes of Islamic Studies Bulletin *changed to* Christian Institutes of Islamic Studies Bulletin
0009-5400 Christian Labor Herald†
0009-5419 Christian Leader
0009-5427 Christian Life
0009-5435 Christian Living
0009-5443 Christian Medical Association of India. Journal
0009-5451 Christian Medical College Alumni Journal
0009-546X Christian Medical Society Journal
0009-5478 Christian Messenger
0009-5486 Christian Minister
0009-5494 Christian Monthly
0009-5508 Today's Christian Mother *changed to* Today's Christian Parent
0009-5516 Christian News
0009-5524 Christian News Bulletin†
0009-5532 Christian News from Israel
0009-5540 Christian Nurse
0009-5559 Christian Order
0009-5567 Christian Peace Conference
0009-5575 Christian Record
0009-5583 Christian Record Talking Magazine
0009-5591 Christian Recorder†
0009-5605 Christian Rural Fellowship. Bulletin†
0009-5613 Christian Science Journal
0009-563X Christian Science Sentinel
0009-5648 Christian Socialist
0009-5656 Christian Standard
0009-5664 Christian Statesman
0009-5672 Christian Teacher†
0009-5680 Vanguard (Toronto)
0009-5699 Christian Voice
0009-5702 Christian Woman
0009-5710 Christiane†
0009-5729 Christianisme au Vingtieme Siecle

1218 ISSN INDEX

0009-5745 Christianity and Crisis
0009-5753 Christianity Today
0009-5761 Christlich-Paedagogische Blaetter
0009-5788 Die Christliche Frau
0009-5796 Christliche Innerlichkeit
0009-580X Christoffel-Blindenmission. Bericht
0009-5818 Christophorus
0009-5826 Youth Alive *see* 0190-6569
0009-5834 Christus
0009-5850 Christus en Israel†
0009-5869 Die Christus-Post
0009-5877 Christus Rex *changed to* Social Studies
0009-5885 Christusruf†
0009-5893 Chromatographia
0009-5907 Chromatographic Reviews *see* 0021-9673
0009-5915 Chromosoma
0009-5931 Chronica
0009-594X S U N Y Research (Year)
0009-5958 Chronicle†
0009-5974 Chronicle†
0009-5982 Chronicle of Higher Education
0009-5990 Chronicle of the Horse
0009-6008 Chronicle of U S Classic Postal Issues
0009-6024 Chronicles of Oklahoma
0009-6040 Chronique de l'I R S A C
0009-6059 Chronique de Politique Etrangere *changed to* Studia Diplomatica
0009-6067 Chronique d'Egypte
0009-6075 Chronique des Mines et de la Recherche Miniere *changed to* France. Bureau de Recherches Geologiques et Minieres. Agence Francaise pour la Maitrise de l'Energie. Geothermie/Actualities
0009-6083 Transport Echo
0009-6121 Chronique Sociale de France†
0009-6148 Chroniques de l'Art Vivant†
0009-6172 Chronmy Przyrode Ojczysta
0009-6180 Chronos
0009-6199 Chrysalis†
0009-6202 Chubu Institute of Technology. Memoirs
0009-6210 Chuck Wagon *changed to* Food & Service
0009-6229 Chugoku Agricultural Research *changed to* Kinki Chugoku Agricultural Research
0009-6237 Chugoku Electric Power Co. Technical Laboratory Report
0009-6245 Chulpan Moonwha
0009-6253 Chung-Ang Herald
0009-6261 Chung Chi Bulletin
0009-6296 Chuo Law Review
0009-630X Church Advocate
0009-6318 Church and Community†
0009-6334 Church & State
0009-6342 Church and Synagogue Libraries
0009-6350 Church Army Review *changed to* Church Army. Frontline News
0009-6385 Church Growth Bulletin *see* 0731-1125
0009-6393 Church Herald
0009-6407 Church History
0009-6415 Church Labor Letter†
0009-6423 Media: Library Services Journal *changed to* Church Media Library Magazine
0009-6431 Clergy Journal
0009-644X Church Music *see* 0305-4438
0009-6466 Church Musician
0009-6474 Church News
0009-6482 Church Observer
0009-6490 Church of England Historical Society (Diocese of Sydney). Journal
0009-6504 Church of God Missions
0009-6512 Church of Ireland Gazette
0009-6520 Church of Light Quarterly
0009-6539 Church Panorama†
0009-6547 Church Quarterly†
0009-6555 Church Renewal†
0009-6563 Church Scene
0009-6571 Church Teacher *see* 0307-5982
0009-658X Church Times
0009-6598 Church Woman
0009-6601 Church World
0009-661X Churchman
0009-6628 Churchman's Human Quest
0009-6636 Churchman's Magazine
0009-6652 Casting and Forging *changed to* Casting, Forging & Heat Treatments
0009-6679 Cibles
0009-6687 Ciceroniana
0009-6709 Ciel et Terre
0009-6717 Ciencia Aeronautica
0009-6725 Ciencia e Cultura
0009-6733 Ciencia e Investigacion
0009-675X Ciencia Interamericana
0009-6768 Ciencia y Naturaleza
0009-6776 Ciencias
0009-6784 Ciencias Administrativas†
0009-6792 Ciencias Neurologicas†
0009-6814 Cigar Makers' Official Journal†
0009-6822 Cigarette Card News and Trade Card Chronicle
0009-6830 Cimaise
0009-6849 Cimarron Review
0009-6873 Cincinnati Journal of Medicine *see* 0163-0075
0009-6881 Cincinnati Law Review
0009-6903 Cincinnati Purchasor
0009-6911 Cinderella Philatelist
0009-692X Cine al Dia *changed to* Cine-Oja
0009-6946 Cine Cubano
0009-6954 Cine News
0009-6970 Cine Technicians' Association of South India. Journal *changed to* C.T.A. Journal
0009-7004 Cineaste
0009-7012 Cineclube do Porto. Boletim Circular *see* 0704-061X
0009-7020 Cinecronache
0009-7039 Cineforum
0009-7047 Cinema†
0009-7063 Cinema†
0009-7071 Cinema/Canada (Montreal)
0009-708X Cinema de Amadores
0009-7101 Cinema Journal
0009-711X Cinema Nuovo
0009-7128 Cinema Pratique
0009-7144 Cinema Rangam†
0009-7152 Cinema e Societa
0009-7160 Cinemasud
0009-7179 Cinematografia in Presa†
0009-7187 Cinematografia Ita
0009-7195 Cines d'Orient†
0009-7209 Cinesiologie
0009-7225 Cinque Foil
0009-7241 Circolo Letterario†
0009-725X Circolo Matematico di Palermo. Rendiconti
0009-7268 Circolo Speleologico Romano. Notiziario
0009-7284 Circuit Magazine†
0009-7292 Circuit News
0009-7306 Circuits Manufacturing
0009-7314 Colegio Oficial de Farmaceutico. Circular Farmaceutica
0009-7322 Circulation
0009-7330 Circulation Research
0009-7349 Circulo
0009-7357 Circulo Odontologico de Rosario. Revista
0009-7365 Circus *changed to* Circus (1979)
0009-7373 Cirque dans l'Univers
0009-7381 Cirugia del Uruguay
0009-739X Cirugia Espanola
0009-7403 Cirugia Plastica Uruguaya
0009-7411 Cirugia y Cirujanos
0009-7438 Citatel
0009-7446 Citation
0009-7489 Cahiers de Cite Libre
0009-7497 Citeaux
0009-7500 Cites et Villes†
0009-7527 Cithara
0009-7535 Cities and Villages
0009-7543 Citizen (Denver)
0009-7551 Citizen and Week End Review
0009-756X Citizens' Business
0009-7578 Citrograph
0009-7586 Citrus and Vegetable Magazine
0009-7594 Citrus Industry Magazine
0009-7608 Citrus World†
0009-7616 Citta di Milano†
0009-7624 Patavium†
0009-7632 Citta di Vita
0009-7640 Citta e Societa
0009-7667 Cittadino Canadese
0009-7675 City†
0009-7683 City Almanac
0009-7691 City Art Museum of Saint Louis. Bulletin *changed to* St. Louis Art Museum. Bulletin
0009-7705 City Beautiful
0009-7713 City Business Courier
0009-7721 City Club Comments *changed to* City Club Gadfly
0009-7748 City Press†
0009-7756 Ciudad de Dios
0009-7764 Civic Administration *see* 0315-1972
0009-7772 Civic Affairs
0009-7780 Civic Forum
0009-7799 Civic Leader†
0009-7810 Civil Air Patrol News
0009-7845 Civil Engineer in South Africa
0009-7853 Civil Engineering (New York) *see* 0360-0556
0009-7861 Civil Engineering and Public Works Review *see* 0305-6473
0009-787X Civil Engineering, Construction & Public Works Journal†
0009-7888 Civil Engineering Contractor
0009-790X Civil Liberties (New York)
0009-7918 Civil Liberties Bulletin†
0009-7926 Civil Liberties in New York *changed to* N.Y. Civil Liberties
0009-7934 Civil Liberties Reporter
0009-7942 Rights, Opportunities, Action Reporter†
0009-7969 Civil Rights Digest *changed to* New Perspectives
0009-7985 Civil Service Journal *see* 0198-8557
0009-8000 Civil Service Leader
0009-8019 Civil Service News Releases *changed to* Civil Service News
0009-8027 Civil Service Opinion *changed to* Opinion
0009-8035 Civil Service Review/Revue du Service Civil *changed to* Public Service Alliance of Canada. Review/Revue
0009-8051 Civil Service Sports Quarterly†
0009-806X Civil Transport Data Sheets
0009-8078 Civil War History
0009-8086 Civil War Round Table Digest
0009-8094 Civil War Times Illustrated
0009-8108 Civil War Token Society. Journal
0009-8132 Civilingenjoersfoerbundets Tidskrift *see* 0348-6087
0009-8140 Civilisations†
0009-8140 Civilisations
0009-8159 Civilt Foersvar
0009-8167 Civilta Cattolica
0009-8175 Civilta' della Strada†
0009-8191 Civitas
0009-8205 Cizi Jazyky ve Skole
0009-8213 Clan McLaren Society, U S A. Quarterly
0009-8221 Clare Market Review†
0009-823X Claridad
0009-8256 Clarin Economico
0009-8264 Clark County School Letter *changed to* Educator
0009-8272 Clark Now
0009-8280 C L A S S: Reading†
0009-8299 Classe e Stato†
0009-8310 Classic Car
0009-8329 Classic Film Collector *see* 0275-8423
0009-8337 Classical Bulletin
0009-8345 Classical Folia†
0009-8353 Classical Journal
0009-8361 Classical Outlook
0009-837X Classical Philology
0009-8388 Classical Quarterly
0009-840X Classical Review
0009-8418 Classical World
0009-8426 Classici del Giallo
0009-8434 Classification Management
0009-8450 Classified Abstract Archive of the Alcohol Literature†
0009-8477 Classified Documentation List of Current Scientific Literature. Monthly Bulletin *changed to* C S M C R I Documentation List Monthly Bulletin
0009-8485 Classroom Interaction Newsletter *see* 0749-4025
0009-8493 Claudia
0009-8507 Claudia
0009-8515 Claudia
0009-8523 Clausthaler Geologische Abhandlungen
0009-854X Clavier
0009-8558 Clay Minerals
0009-8566 Canadian Clay and Ceramics *changed to* Canadian Ceramics Quarterly
0009-8574 Clay Science
0009-8582 Claycraft *see* 0306-1841
0009-8590 Claymore
0009-8604 Clays and Clay Minerals
0009-8620 Clean Water Report
0009-8639 Manual of Maintenance *changed to* Maintenance Buyers Guide
0009-8647 Clean Air
0009-8655 Clearing House
0009-8663 Clearinghouse Announcements in Science & Technology†
0009-8671 Clearinghouse on Self-Instructional Materials for Health Care Facilities. Bulletin†
0009-868X Clearinghouse Review
0009-8698 Clearway
0009-8701 Cleft Palate Journal
0009-871X Clemson University. College of Architecture. Semester Review
0009-8728 Cleo en la Moda
0009-8736 Clergy Review
0009-8744 Clerk *changed to* A P E X
0009-8752 Clessidra
0009-8787 Cleveland Clinic Quarterly *see* 0891-1150
0009-8809 Cleveland Engineering
0009-8817 Cleveland Food Dealer
0009-8825 Cleveland Jewish News
0009-8833 Cleveland Medical Library. Bulletin†
0009-8841 Cleveland Museum of Art. Bulletin
0009-885X Cleveland Public Library Staff Association. News and Views
0009-8876 Cleveland State Law Review
0009-8884 Business Bulletin†
0009-8892 Clevelander
0009-8906 Clic Fotografiamo
0009-8914 Clima Commerce International
0009-8930 Climate Control
0009-8957 Climatological Data for Jakarta Observatory
0009-8965 Climb†
0009-8973 Climber and Rambler *changed to* Climber
0009-8981 Clinica Chimica Acta
0009-899X Clinica de Endocrinologia y Metabolismo. Boletin†
0009-9007 Clinica Europea
0009-9015 Clinica Geral†
0009-9023 Clinica Ortopedica†
0009-9031 Clinica Ostetrica e Ginecologica *see* 0304-0313
0009-904X Clinica Otorinolaringoiatrica *changed to* Nuova, Clinica Otorinolaringoiatrica
0009-9058 Clinica Pediatrica
0009-9066 Clinica Psichiatrica
0009-9074 Clinica Terapeutica
0009-9082 Clinica Veterinaria
0009-9090 Clinical Allergy
0009-9104 Clinical and Experimental Immunology
0009-9112 Clinical Anesthesia†
0009-9120 Clinical Biochemistry
0009-9139 Quarterly Literature Reports. Clinical Biochemistry†
0009-9147 Clinical Chemistry
0009-9155 Clinical Electroencephalography
0009-9163 Clinical Genetics
0009-918X Clinical Neurology
0009-9201 Clinical Obstetrics and Gynecology
0009-921X Clinical Orthopaedics and Related Research
0009-9228 Clinical Pediatrics
0009-9236 Clinical Pharmacology and Therapeutics

ISSN INDEX 1219

0009-9244 Clinical Psychologist
0009-9252 Clinical Radiology *changed to* Japanese Journal of Clinical Radiology
0009-9279 Clinical Research
0009-9295 Clinical Symposia
0009-9309 Clinical Toxicology *see* 0731-3810
0009-9317 Clinical Trends in Rheumatology†
0009-9325 Clinical Trials Journal
0009-9333 Clinicas Obstetricas y Ginecologicas
0009-9341 Clinician
0009-935X Clinique
0009-9368 La Clinque, Ophtalmologique
0009-9376 Clio
0009-9384 Clio: Devoted to Commercials
0009-9414 Clipsheet†
0009-9422 Clique
0009-9430 Clock Tower *changed to* Clocktower
0009-9449 C M A Close-Up
0009-9465 Clothes *see* 0161-973X
0009-9473 Clothesline *changed to* National Clothesline
0009-9503 Club
0009-9511 Club Alpino Italiano. Rivista Mensile *changed to* Club Alpino Italiano. Rivista
0009-952X Club and Institute Journal
0009-9538 Club Committee & Northern Free Trade News
0009-9546 Club du Griffon d'Arret a Poil Dur Korthal. Bulletin
0009-9554 Club Executive *see* 0192-2718
0009-9562 Club Folk†
0009-9570 Club Francais de la Medaille
0009-9589 Club Management
0009-9597 Club Managers Journal *changed to* Secretaries and Managers Journal of Australia
0009-9600 Fussball Club Pforzheim. Club-Nachrichten
0009-9619 Club News *see* 0886-8832
0009-9627 Club Operations†
0009-9635 Club Secretary
0009-9651 Clube Filatelico de Portugal. Boletim
0009-966X Clube Militar Naval. Anais
0009-9678 Salcofoon†
0009-9716 C M I Descriptions of Pathogenic Fungi and Bacteria
0009-9724 Co-Ed *changed to* Choices (New York)
0009-9740 Co-Op Highlights
0009-9759 Co-Op Maandblad†
0009-9767 Co-Op Report†
0009-9783 Cooperatie
0009-9805 Cooperative Information Bulletin *changed to* Cooperative Perspective
0009-9813 Co-Operative Management & Marketing *see* 0307-8604
0009-9821 Co-Operative News
0009-9848 Co-operative Review
0009-9856 Co-Operatives Quarterly
0009-9864 Co-Partnership *changed to* Industrial Participation
0009-9872 Coach and Athlete *changed to* Coach and Athlete Magazine
0009-9880 Coaching Clinic†
0009-9899 Coaching Journal and Bus Review
0009-9902 Coagulation *see* 0301-0147
0009-9910 Coal Age
0009-9929 Coal and Steel†
0009-9945 Coal Miner†
0009-9961 Coal Mining and Processing *see* 0749-1948
0009-997X Coal News
0009-9988 Coal Research†
0009-9996 Canada. Statistics Canada. Coarse Grains Review/Revue des Cereales Secondaire†
0010-0005 Coast
0010-003X Coat of Arms
0010-0056 Cobbers†
0010-0064 Cobouw
0010-0072 Sonntagsblatt - Coburger Heimatglocken
0010-0080 Cock
0010-0099 Cockpit *changed to* Vliegtuigparade
0010-0102 Cockpit *changed to* New Jersey Instructional Series
0010-0110 Cockpit
0010-0137 Cocoa Statistics†
0010-0145 Coconut Bulletin *changed to* Indian Coconut Journal
0010-0161 Cocuk Sagligi ve Hastaliklari Dergisi
0010-017X Coda
0010-0188 Codes Larcier
0010-0196 Codex†
0010-020X Codicillus
0010-0226 Coeur
0010-0234 Coeur et Medecine Interne *see* 0248-8663
0010-0250 Coffee Mazdoor Sahakari
0010-0277 Cognition
0010-0285 Cognitive Psychology
0010-0293 Cogwheel†
0010-0307 Cohesion†
0010-034X Coiffure de Paris
0010-0358 Coiffure et Beaute†
0010-0366 Coimbra Medica†
0010-0374 Coin Dealer†
0010-0390 Coin Monthly *changed to* Coin Monthly (1980)
0010-0404 Coin-Op *see* 0092-2811
0010-0412 Coin Prices
0010-0420 Coin Slot *see* 0043-9304
0010-0439 Coin, Stamp, Antique News *see* 0702-3162
0010-0447 Coin World
0010-0455 Coinage
0010-0463 Coinamatic Age
0010-0471 Coins
0010-0501 Coke and Chemistry U.S.S.R.
0010-0528 Coke Research Report *see* 0305-9545
0010-0536 Coke Review *see* 0305-8131
0010-0544 Colada
0010-0552 Colby Library Quarterly
0010-0560 Colegio de Abogados de la Ciudad de Buenos Aires. Boletin Informativo
0010-0579 Colegio de Abogados de Puerto Rico. Revista
0010-0587 Colegio de Abogados. Revista
0010-0595 Colegio de Bibliotecarios Colombianos.(Revista)†
0010-0609 Colegio de Ingenieros Arquitectos y Agrimensores de Puerto Rico. Revista
0010-0617 Colegio de Ingenieros de Caminos, Canales y Puertos. Boletin de Informacion
0010-0625 Colegio de Ingenieros de Venezuela. Boletin Informativo
0010-0633 Colegio de Profesores de Venezuela. Seccional No. 1. Boletin. Informativo
0010-0641 Colegio Medico de El Salvador. Archivas
0010-065X Coleopterists Bulletin
0010-0676 Colfeian
0010-0684 Colgate *changed to* Colgate Scene
0010-0692 Collage†
0010-0706 Collage
0010-0722 Collana di Monografie Turistiche†
0010-0730 Collectanea Botanica
0010-0749 Collectanea Franciscana
0010-0757 Collectanea Mathematica
0010-0765 Collection of Czechoslovak Chemical Communications
0010-0773 Femme Chic
0010-0781 Collections Baur. Bulletin
0010-079X Collective Bargaining Negotiations & Contracts
0010-0803 Collective Bargaining Review
0010-0811 Collectivites-Express
0010-082X Collector
0010-0838 Collectors Club Philatelist
0010-0854 Collector's World†
0010-0862 College *see* 0277-4720
0010-0870 College & Research Libraries
0010-0889 College and University
0010-0900 College and University Business *see* 0194-2263
0010-0919 College and University Business Officer *see* 0147-877X
0010-0935 College and University Personnel Association. Journal
0010-0943 College and University Safety Newsletter *changed to* Campus Safety Newsletter
0010-0951 College Board Review
0010-096X College Composition and Communication
0010-0986 College Echoes†
0010-0994 College English
0010-1001 Education et Societe†
0010-101X College Law Bulletin†
0010-1028 College Library Notes†
0010-1044 College of Dental Surgeons of the Province of Quebec. Information *changed to* Order of Dentists of Quebec. Information
0010-1052 University of North Dakota. College of Education. Record *see* 0887-9486
0010-1060 College of Emporia Compass†
0010-1087 College of Physicians of Philadelphia. Transactions & Studies
0010-1095 College of Physicians, Surgeons and Gynecologists of South Africa. Transactions *see* 0375-3220
0010-1117 College Press Review *see* 0739-1056
0010-1125 College Press Service
0010-1133 Journal of College Radio
0010-1141 College Store Executive
0010-115X College Store Journal
0010-1168 College Student Personnel Abstracts *see* 0748-4364
0010-1176 College Student Personnel Institute. Newsletter†
0010-1184 College Student Survey *see* 0146-3934
0010-1192 College Voice (Trenton)
0010-1206 Collegian
0010-1214 Collegiate Journalist†
0010-1222 Collegiate News and Views†
0010-1230 Collegiate Scene†
0010-1249 Collegio
0010-1265 Collezionista-Italia Filatelica
0010-1281 Colliery Guardian
0010-129X Collins Signal Magazine†
0010-1303 Colloid Journal of the U S S R
0010-1311 Colloquium†
0010-132X Colloqui Cremonese
0010-1338 Colloquia Germanica
0010-1346 Colloquium†
0010-1354 Colloquium Mathematicum
0010-1370 Colombia. Departamento Administrativo Nacional de Estadistica. Boletin de Estadistica
0010-1389 Colombia. Ministerio de Defensa. Boletin
0010-1397 Colombia Today
0010-1419 Colombo Plan Newsletter
0010-1427 Colombophilie Belge
0010-1435 Colonial Courier
0010-1443 C N L
0010-146X Color Engineering†
0010-1478 Color Engineering†
0010-1494 Colorado and Rocky Mountain Motor Carrier *changed to* Highland Highways
0010-1516 Colorado Beverage Analyst
0010-1524 Colorado Business Review†
0010-1532 Colorado C P A Report†
0010-1540 Colorado Councillor *changed to* Colorado Kairos
0010-1559 Colorado Dental Association. Journal
0010-1567 Colorado Editor
0010-1583 Colorado Engineer
0010-1605 Colorado F.P.†
0010-163X Colorado Journal of Pharmacy
0010-1648 Colorado Magazine *see* 0272-9377
0010-1656 Colorado Manpower Review *changed to* Colorado Labor Force Review
0010-1664 Colorado Municipalities
0010-1672 Colorado Music Educator
0010-1680 Colorado Nurse
0010-1699 Colorado Outdoors
0010-1702 Colorado Prospector
0010-1710 Colorado Quarterly†
0010-1729 Colorado Rancher and Farmer
0010-1745 Colorado School of Mines. Mineral Industries Bulletin *see* 0192-6179
0010-1761 Colorado State Library Newsletter *changed to* Centennial State Libraries
0010-1788 Colores y Pinturas
0010-1796 Colorado-Rocky Mountain West†
0010-1818 Colour Review†
0010-1826 Colourage
0010-1834 Cols-Bleus
0010-1842 Colstonian
0010-1850 Coltivatore e Giornale Vinicolo Italiano†
0010-1869 Columbia (New Haven)
0010-1877 Columbia Basin Farmer
0010-1885 Columbia College Pre-Med†
0010-1893 Columbia Daily Spectator
0010-1907 Columbia Forum†
0010-1915 Columbia Jester
0010-1923 Columbia Journal of Law and Social Problems
0010-1931 Columbia Journal of Transnational Law
0010-194X Columbia Journalism Review
0010-1958 Columbia Law Review
0010-1966 Columbia Library Columns
0010-1982 Columbia Review
0010-1990 C.S.P.A.A. Bulletin†
0010-2016 Columbia University. Ancient Near Eastern Society. Journal *changed to* Ancient Near Eastern Society. Journal
0010-2024 Columbian (Chicago)
0010-2032 Squires *changed to* Squires Newsletter
0010-2059 Columbus Business Forum†
0010-2075 Column *changed to* Scan
0010-2091 Columns (Fairmont)
0010-2105 Comarca de Suzano
0010-2113 Combat†
0010-2121 Combat
0010-213X Combat Crew
0010-2156 Toesj/Combo
0010-2164 International Laboratory
0010-2172 Combustion†
0010-2180 Combustion and Flame
0010-2199 Combustion Institute. Western States Section. Papers
0010-2202 Combustion Science & Technology
0010-2237 Comentarios Bibliograficos Americanos
0010-2245 Comercio
0010-2253 Comercio
0010-227X Comercio & Mercados
0010-2288 Comercio Colombo Americano
0010-2296 Comercio Ecuatoriano
0010-2326 Comercio Hispano Britanico
0010-2334 Comercio Portugues *changed to* Comercio, Industria, Servicos
0010-2342 Comercio y Produccion
0010-2350 Comercio y Produccion
0010-2369 Comhar
0010-2377 Coming up *changed to* Perspective (Berkeley)
0010-2385 Comino
0010-2407 Comissao de Desenvolvimento Economico do Estado do Amazonas. Boletim Informativo
0010-2415 Comite Belge d'Histoire des Sciences. Notes Bibliographiques/Belgisch Komitee voor de Geschiedeis der Wetenschappen. Bibliograpische Notas *see* 0771-6826
0010-2423 Economic and Social Committee of the European Communities. Bulletin.
0010-2431 Olympic Review (Year)
0010-244X Comites de Prevention du Batiment et des Travaux Publics. Cahiers
0010-2458 Officiel des Comites d'Entreprise et Services Sociaux
0010-2482 Commanders Digest *see* 0270-9015
0010-2504 Commando *changed to* Paratus
0010-2512 Commandos *changed to* Junior Life
0010-2520 Comme les Autres
0010-2539 Comment†
0010-2547 Comment (London) *changed to* Focus
0010-2555 Comment
0010-2571 Commentarii Mathematici Helvetici
0010-2598 Commentarium pro Religiosis et Missionariis
0010-2601 Commentary
0010-2628 Commentationes Mathematicae Universitatis Carolinae
0010-2644 Commentator†
0010-2652 Commentator

1220 ISSN INDEX

ISSN	Title
0010-2660	Comments on Argentine Trade
0010-2679	Comments on Astrophysics and Space Physics *see* 0146-2970
0010-2687	Comments on Atomic and Molecular Physics
0010-2695	Comments on Earth Sciences: Geophysics *see* 0276-8577
0010-2709	Comments on Nuclear & Particle Physics
0010-2725	Commerce
0010-2733	Commerce International
0010-2741	Commerce
0010-275X	Commerce
0010-2768	Commerce
0010-2776	Commerce†
0010-2784	Commerce & Industry†
0010-2792	Commerce & Industry Monthly Journal
0010-2806	Commerce des Combustibles†
0010-2814	Commerce du Levant
0010-2822	Commerce Education *changed to* Journal of Commerce Education
0010-2830	Commerce Franco-Suisse
0010-2849	Commerce in France
0010-2865	Commerce Industrial and Mining Review
0010-2873	Commerce Moderne Urbanisme et Commerce *see* 0396-714X
0010-2881	Australia. Perth Chamber of Commerce. Commerce News†
0010-2911	Commercial Bulletin
0010-292X	Commercial Car Journal *see* 0734-1423
0010-2938	Commercial Courier
0010-2946	Decor and Contract Furnishing *see* 0020-5494
0010-2954	Commercial Expansion Reporter *see* 0036-3456
0010-2989	Commercial Fisheries Review *see* 0090-1830
0010-2997	Australian Commercial Fishing & Marketing
0010-3004	Commercial Grower *see* 0262-3765
0010-3012	Commercial Herald
0010-3039	Commercial Journal
0010-3047	Commercial Kitchen and Dining Room *see* 0190-8553
0010-3055	Commercial Law Journal
0010-3063	Commercial Motor
0010-3071	Allied Trades Association. Commercial News
0010-308X	Commercial Opinion *changed to* AssoCom Review
0010-3098	Commercial Record
0010-3101	Oregon Feed, Seed and Suppliers Association. Commericial Review *changed to* Oregon Feed, Seed Grain and Suppliers Association. Commercial Review
0010-311X	Commercial Teacher *changed to* Focus on Business Education
0010-3136	Commercial Vehicles†
0010-3144	Commercial West
0010-3160	Commercium
0010-3179	Commission
0010-3209	Commission on Accreditation of Service Experiences. Newsletter *changed to* American Council on Education. Office on Educational Credit and Credentials. News
0010-3217	Commitment†
0010-3225	Commodity Chart Service *changed to* C R B Futures Chart Service
0010-3233	Commodity Trade Statistics
0010-3241	Commodity Yearbook Statistical Abstract Service
0010-325X	Common Ground
0010-3276	Common Life
0010-3314	Commonplace Book
0010-3322	Commons, Open Spaces and Footpaths Preservation Society. Journal
0010-3330	Commonweal
0010-3357	Commonwealth
0010-3365	Commonwealth Magazine
0010-3373	Commonwealth Education Liaison Committee Newsletter†
0010-3381	Commonwealth Forestry Review
0010-3403	Commonwealth Jeweller and Watchmaker *changed to* Jeweller, Watchmaker and Giftware
0010-3411	Commonwealth
0010-342X	Commonwealth Producer
0010-3438	Commonwealth Secretariat Rice Bulletin†
0010-3446	Communaute Autogestion†
0010-3454	Communaute Chretienne
0010-3497	Communicatio Socialis
0010-3500	Communication Arts International
0010-3519	Communication Arts
0010-3527	Communication Disorders†
0010-3535	Communication: Journalism Education Today
0010-3543	Communication Reports†
0010-3551	Orvostorteneti Kozlemenyek
0010-356X	Communications
0010-3586	Communications Business *changed to* Communications and Cable T V Business
0010-3608	Communications in Behavioral Biology *see* 0163-1047
0010-3616	Communications in Mathematical Physics
0010-3624	Communications in Soil Science and Plant Analysis
0010-3632	Communications News
0010-3640	Communications on Pure and Applied Mathematics
0010-3683	Communicator†
0010-3691	Communidades†
0010-3705	Communio
0010-3713	Communio Viatorum
0010-3721	Communique *changed to* This Week in Wood County Schools
0010-3756	Communist Viewpoint
0010-3772	Community
0010-3780	Community Comments *see* 0277-6189
0010-3802	Community Development Journal
0010-3829	Community Development Society. Journal
0010-3837	Community Health†
0010-3845	Community Health *changed to* Post Rock
0010-3853	Community Mental Health Journal
0010-3861	Community Mental Health Services. Newsletter *changed to* Access (Tallahassee)
0010-3888	Community School and Its Administration†
0010-3896	Community Schools Gazette *changed to* Community Homes Gazette
0010-3918	Community Teamwork†
0010-3926	Commutation et Electronique *see* 0242-1283
0010-3934	Compact *see* 0736-7511
0010-3942	Compact†
0010-3959	Companheiros
0010-3985	Companion of St. Francis and St. Anthony
0010-3993	Companion†
0010-4019	Company Law Journal†
0010-4027	Company News and Notes
0010-4035	Comparative and General Pharmacology *see* 0306-3623
0010-4043	Comparative and International Education Society. Newsletter
0010-4051	Comparative and International Law Journal of Southern Africa
0010-4078	Comparative Drama
0010-4086	Comparative Education Review
0010-4108	Comparative Group Studies *see* 0090-5526
0010-4116	Comparative Law Review
0010-4124	Comparative Literature
0010-4132	Comparative Literature Studies
0010-4140	Comparative Political Studies
0010-4159	Comparative Politics†
0010-4167	Comparative Romance Linguistics Newsletter
0010-4175	Comparative Studies in Society and History
0010-4191	Compass (Asbury Park) *changed to* Compass Quarterly
0010-4205	A I C S Compass
0010-4213	Compass (Norman)
0010-4248	Compensation Review *changed to* Compensation and Benefit Review
0010-4299	Comple
0010-4310	Component Technology†
0010-4329	Comportamiento Humano
0010-4337	Composer
0010-4353	Composers, Authors and Artists of America
0010-4361	Composites
0010-437X	Compositio Mathematica
0010-4388	Compost Science *see* 0276-5055
0010-4396	Compostelle *changed to* Compostelle, Cahiers du Centre d'Etudes Compostellanes
0010-440X	Comprehensive Psychiatry
0010-4418	Comprendre
0010-4426	Compressed Air
0010-4450	Computable
0010-4469	Computer Abstracts
0010-4477	Computer Age
0010-4485	Computer-Aided Design
0010-4507	Computer and Information Systems *see* 0191-9776
0010-4523	Computer Applications Service†
0010-4531	Computer Bulletin
0010-454X	Computer Characteristics Review *see* 0093-416X
0010-4558	Computer Decisions
0010-4566	Computer Design
0010-4574	Computer Digest *see* 0093-7290
0010-4582	Computer Display Review
0010-4590	Computer Education
0010-4620	Computer Journal
0010-4639	Computer Management
0010-4647	Computer News *issued with* 0010-4469
0010-4655	Computer Physics Communications
0010-4663	Computer Praxis *changed to* Informationstechnik - I T
0010-468X	Computer Programs in Biomedicine *see* 0169-2607
0010-4728	Computer Science Newsletter *see* 0315-4661
0010-4736	Computer Services†
0010-4760	Computer Survey
0010-4787	Computer Weekly
0010-4795	Computers and Automation *see* 0361-1442
0010-4809	Computers and Biomedical Research
0010-4817	Computers and the Humanities
0010-4825	Computers in Biology and Medicine
0010-4833	Computers in Medicine Abstracts†
0010-4841	Computerworld
0010-485X	Computing
0010-4868	Computing Newsletter for Schools of Business†
0010-4884	Computing Reviews
0010-4892	Computing Surveys *see* 0360-0300
0010-4906	Computopia
0010-4914	Comte de Jette Bulletin
0010-4922	Comune (Rome)
0010-4930	Comune Democratico
0010-4949	Comune di Bologna. Notiziario Settimanale *changed to* Bologna
0010-4957	Comune di Roma. Ufficio di Statistica e Censimento. Bollettino Statistico
0010-4965	Comune di Rome. Ufficio de Statistica e Censimento. Notiziario Statistico Mensile
0010-4973	Comuni d'Europa
0010-5007	Instituto de Ciencias da Informacao Comunicacoes & Problemas
0010-5015	Comunicacoes Bioquimicas
0010-5023	Comunidad†
0010-504X	Comunita
0010-5058	Comunita Europee
0010-5066	Comunita Internazionale
0010-5074	Comunita Israelitica di Milano. Bollettino
0010-5082	Combustion, Explosion and Shock Waves
0010-5090	Con Edison Library Bulletin
0010-5104	Con Safos
0010-5112	Concept
0010-5120	Concept of Pakistan
0010-5147	Conceptos de Matematica
0010-5155	Conceptus
0010-5163	Concern (New York)
0010-5171	Concern†
0010-5198	Concerning Food & Nutrition†
0010-5201	Concerning Poetry
0010-5228	Conciliatore
0010-5236	Concilium
0010-5244	Concord†
0010-5252	Concordia
0010-5260	Concordia Historical Institute Quarterly
0010-5287	Concordia Torch
0010-5309	Concours Medical
0010-5317	Concrete
0010-5333	Concrete Construction
0010-5341	Concrete Construction and Architecture
0010-535X	Concrete Industry Bulletin
0010-5368	Concrete Products
0010-5376	Concrete Quarterly
0010-5392	Conditional Reflex *see* 0093-2213
0010-5414	Condor†
0010-5422	Condor (Los Angeles)
0010-5457	Confectioner
0010-5465	Confectionery and Tobacco News *changed to* C T N
0010-5473	Confectionery Production
0010-549X	Confederacion de Camaras Nacionales de Comercio. Carta Semanal†
0010-5503	Confederacion Sudamericana de Asociaciones Cristianas de Jovenes. Noticias *changed to* Asociacion
0010-5511	Confederate Historical Society. Journal†
0010-5546	Conference Board Record *changed to* Across the Board
0010-5554	Conference Board Statistical Bulletin
0010-5570	Conference on Latin American History Newsletter
0010-5589	Conferences du Cenacle
0010-5597	Conferences, Exhibitions and Executive Travel *see* 0260-8316
0010-5600	Conferencias
0010-5627	Confi†
0010-5635	Confidencias†
0010-5651	Confidential Confessions†
0010-566X	Confidential Detective Cases†
0010-5678	Confinia Neurologia *see* 0302-2773
0010-5686	Confinia Psychiatrica†
0010-5694	Confins
0010-5708	Confort
0010-5716	Confrontation
0010-5732	Confronto†
0010-5740	Congiuntura Estera
0010-5759	Congiuntura Italiana
0010-5767	Congo-Afrique *see* 0049-8513
0010-5775	Congo Disque
0010-5783	Congo Magazine *changed to* Zaire Ya Sika
0010-5805	Congo. Centre National de la Statistique et des Etudes Economiques. Bulletin Mensuel de la Statistique
0010-5813	Congregation Cistercienne de Senaque et de la Pieuse Ligue Universelle pour les Ames de l'Abbaye de Lerins. (Publication) *changed to* Lerins
0010-5821	Congregational Library. Bulletin
0010-583X	Congregational Monthly *see* 0306-7262
0010-5848	Christian Leader†
0010-5856	Congregationalist
0010-5872	American Jewish Congress. Congress Bi-Weekly *see* 0163-1365
0010-5880	Congress Bulletin†
0010-5899	Congressional Digest
0010-5902	Congressional Monitor
0010-5910	Congressional Quarterly Service. Weekly Report
0010-5929	Rivista di Coniglicoltura
0010-5937	Conjunto
0010-5945	Conjuntura Economica
0010-5953	Connaissance de la Campagne†
0010-5961	Connaissance de la Mer†
0010-597X	Connaissance de la Vigne et du Vin
0010-5988	Connaissance des Arts *see* 0293-9274
0010-6003	Connaissance des Plastiques†
0010-602X	Connaitre la Wallonie
0010-6038	Connchord

0010-6046 Connecticut Action†
0010-6054 Connecticut Antiquarian
0010-6070 Connecticut Bar Journal
0010-6089 Connecticut C P A
0010-6097 Connecticut Conference Missioner†
0010-6100 Connecticut Conservation Reporter†
0010-6119 Connecticut Government
0010-6127 Connecticut Health Bulletin
0010-6135 Connecticut Industry *see* 0199-686X
0010-6143 Connecticut. Labor Department. Bulletin
0010-6151 Connecticut Law Review
0010-616X Connecticut Libraries
0010-6178 Connecticut Medicine
0010-6208 Connecticut Purchaser *changed to* New England Purchaser/Connecticut Purchaser
0010-6216 Connecticut Review†
0010-6232 Connecticut State Dental Association. Journal
0010-6240 Connecticut Teacher†
0010-6259 Connecticut Woodlands
0010-6267 Connection†
0010-6275 Connoisseur
0010-6283 Connoisseur's Guide†
0010-6291 Conocimiento de la Nueva Era
0010-6305 Conoscenza
0010-6313 Conparlist
0010-6348 Conquiste del Lavoro
0010-6356 Conradiana
0010-6364 Argentina. Consejo Nacional de Investigaciones Cientificas y Tecnicas. Informaciones
0010-6410 Conselho Estadual de Educacao de Sao Paulo. Acta
0010-6429 Consensus (Toronto) *changed to* Momentum
0010-6445 Conservacionista†
0010-6461 Conservation Education Association Newsletter
0010-647X Conservation News†
0010-6488 Conservation Report *see* 0736-9522
0010-6496 Conservation Volunteer *changed to* Minnesota Volunteer
0010-650X Conservationist
0010-6518 Conservative and Unionist Central Office. Monthly News *changed to* Conservative and Unionist Central Office. Conservative News Line
0010-6542 Conservative Judaism
0010-6550 Conservatoire de Musique de Geneve. Bulletin
0010-6569 Consiglio di Stato
0010-6577 Consol News
0010-6593 Consommation
0010-6607 Constabulary Gazette
0010-6623 Constitutional and Parliamentary Information
0010-6631 Construcao Sao Paulo
0010-6658 Constructeur
0010-6674 Construction *changed to* Builder N.S.W.
0010-6690 Construction in Southern Africa†
0010-6704 Construction
0010-6712 Construction Advisor†
0010-6739 Construction Digest
0010-6747 Construction Electrique *changed to* Industries Electriques et Electroniques
0010-6755 Construction Equipment Distribution
0010-6763 Construction Equipment Magazine *see* 0192-3978
0010-6771 Construction Equipment Operation and Maintenance
0010-678X Construction Foreman's and Supervisor's Letter *see* 0744-7167
0010-6798 Construction Francaise *see* 0335-2021
0010-6828 Construction Industries and Trade Journal *changed to* Construction Industries and Trade Annual
0010-6836 Construction Labor Report
0010-6844 Construction Methods and Equipment *see* 0270-1588
0010-6852 Construction Moderne
0010-6860 Construction News
0010-6879 Construction Plant Hire *changed to* Plant Hire
0010-6887 Construction Products *changed to* Spectrum (Middletown)
0010-6895 Construction Products & Technology†
0010-6917 Construction Review
0010-6925 Construction Specifier
0010-6941 Construction West†
0010-695X Constructional Review
0010-6968 Constructioneer
0010-6976 Constructions Equipements pour les Loisirs
0010-6992 Constructive Action for Good Mental Health *changed to* Constructive Action Newsletter
0010-700X Constructive Triangle *changed to* A M S Constructive Triangle
0010-7018 Constructor
0010-7034 Construire
0010-7042 Consudel
0010-7050 Consulente Immobiliare
0010-7069 Consultant (Greenwich)
0010-7077 Consultant (Midland)†
0010-7085 Consultant (Wake)
0010-7093 Consulting Engineer
0010-7107 Consulting Engineer *changed to* Consulting/Specifying Engineer
0010-7115 Consumers Affairs Bulletin *changed to* Co-Op Consumers
0010-7123 Consumer Bulletin *changed to* Consumers' Research Magazine
0010-7131 Consumer Buying Prospects *changed to* Economic Prospects
0010-7158 Consumer Education Forum†
0010-7174 Consumer Reports
0010-7182 Consumers Digest
0010-7190 Consumers Voice
0010-7212 Contabilidad Administracion *changed to* Contaduria. Administracion
0010-7220 Austria Contact
0010-7239 Contact
0010-7247 Contact (London, 1955) *see* 0309-4928
0010-7255 Contact (Bromley)
0010-7263 Contact†
0010-7271 Contact Lens *see* 0306-9575
0010-728X Contact Lens Medical Bulletin *see* 0733-8902
0010-7301 Contact Point
0010-731X Contactblad
0010-7328 O A A G. Bulletin†
0010-7352 Container in Italia e nel Mondo *changed to* Eurotransports Illustrato-Container in Italia e nel Mondo
0010-7360 Container News
0010-7379 Containerisation International
0010-7387 Containers and Packaging†
0010-7395 Contamination Control *see* 0090-2519
0010-7409 Contamination Newsletter†
0010-7417 Contante y Sonante
0010-7468 Contemporary Authors
0010-7476 Contemporary Education
0010-7484 Contemporary Literature
0010-7492 Contemporary Literature in Translation†
0010-7514 Contemporary Physics
0010-7522 Contemporary Poland
0010-7530 Contemporary Psychoanalysis
0010-7549 Contemporary Psychology
0010-7557 Contemporary Religions in Japan *see* 0304-1042
0010-7565 Contemporary Review
0010-7573 Contemporary Writers in Christian Perspective†
0010-7581 Contenido
0010-759X Contents of Contemporary Mathematical Journals *see* 0361-4794
0010-7603 Contents Pages: Electronics and Electricity†
0010-7611 Contents Pages of Iranian Science and Social Science Journals†
0010-762X Contenuti
0010-7646 Jaybee
0010-7662 Contigo *changed to* T V Contigo
0010-7689 Continental *changed to* Hamilton History and Political Science Review
0010-7697 Continental Bulletin
0010-7719 Continental Iron and Steel Trade Reports
0010-7727 Continental Magazine (Dearborn)†
0010-7735 Continental Paint and Resin News *see* 0266-7800
0010-7743 Continentaler Stahlmarkt
0010-776X Continuing Education Report†
0010-7778 Continuous Learning†
0010-7794 Conto Dertien *changed to* Tussen Ons in
0010-7816 Contra Costa County School Bulletin *changed to* Contra Costa County Office of Education Newsletter
0010-7824 Contraception
0010-7832 Contract
0010-7840 Contract Bridge Bulletin
0010-7859 Contract Journal *changed to* Contract Journal (1979)
0010-7867 Contracting and Construction Engineer *changed to* Resources Industry - Quarry Mine & Construction Equipment
0010-7875 Contracting in the Carolinas
0010-7883 Contractor and Plant Manager†
0010-7913 Contractors' Electrical Equipment *see* 0192-1274
0010-793X Contrary Investor
0010-7948 Contrast
0010-7956 Contratista
0010-7964 Contrepoint
0010-7972 Instituto Ecuatoriano de Ciencias Naturales. Contribuciones
0010-7980 University of Wyoming. Contributions to Geology
0010-7999 Contributions to Mineralogy and Petrology
0010-8014 Controcorrente
0010-8022 Control and Instrumentation
0010-8030 Control and Science Record†
0010-8049 Control Engineering
0010-8073 Controller
0010-8081 Controlli Numerici e Macchine *see* 0393-3911
0010-809X Controspazio†
0010-8103 Controvento
0010-8111 Convegno Musicale
0010-812X Convegno
0010-8138 Convenience Store Journal†
0010-8146 Convergence
0010-8154 Convergence
0010-8170 Conversation et Traduction
0010-8189 Converter
0010-8197 Converting Industry *see* 0032-8707
0010-8200 Conveyancer and Property Lawyer
0010-8227 Convivium†
0010-8235 Convivium, Filosofia, Psicologia, Humanidades
0010-8243 Convorbiri Literare
0010-8251 Cook County Highway News†
0010-826X Cookbook Digest
0010-8286 Cooks Continental Timetable *see* 0144-7467
0010-8294 Cooks Staff Magazine *changed to* Internationally Speaking
0010-8308 Coop-Habitat
0010-8316 Cooperacion Libre
0010-8332 Cooperation
0010-8340 Cooperation *see* 0294-8303
0010-8359 Cooperation Agricole
0010-8367 Cooperation and Conflict
0010-8375 Cooperation et Developpement *see* 0395-9481
0010-8383 Cooperation Technique *see* 0395-9481
0010-8391 Cooperative Accountant
0010-8413 Cooperative Builder
0010-843X Cooperative Education Association Newsletter
0010-8448 Cooperative Farmer
0010-8456 Cooperativismo & Nordeste†
0010-8464 Cooperator
0010-8472 Cooperator†
0010-8480 Cooperazione di Credito
0010-8499 Cooperazione e Societa
0010-8502 Cooperazione Educativa
0010-8510 Cooperazione Italiana
0010-8529 Coopercotia
0010-8537 Cooper's Hero-Hobby†
0010-8545 Coordination Chemistry Reviews
0010-857X Copper†
0010-8596 Copper Abstracts *see* 0309-2216
0010-8626 Copyright
0010-8634 Copyright Bulletin
0010-8642 Copyright Society of the U.S.A. Bulletin *changed to* Copyright Society of the U.S.A. Journal
0010-8650 Cor et Vasa
0010-8669 Coranto
0010-8677 Corcoran Gallery of Art Bulletin†
0010-8685 Cord
0010-8707 Corduroy†
0010-8723 C O R E S T A
0010-8731 Cork Historical and Archaeological Society. Journal
0010-874X Cork Weekly Examiner & Weekly Herald *changed to* Irish Weekly Examiner
0010-8758 Cormoran†
0010-8766 Cormoran y Delfin
0010-8782 Cornell Countryman
0010-8790 Cornell Engineer
0010-8804 Cornell Hotel & Restaurant Administration Quarterly
0010-8812 Cornell International Law Journal
0010-8820 Cornell Journal of Social Relations
0010-8839 Cornell Law Forum
0010-8847 Cornell Law Review
0010-8855 Cornell Newsletter, Chemicals-Pesticides Program†
0010-8863 Cornell Plantations
0010-8871 Cornell Program in Oral History. Bulletin *changed to* Documentation Newsletter
0010-888X Cornell International Agricultural Development Bulletin *changed to* Cornell International Agricultural Bulletin
0010-8898 Cornell University Medical College Alumni Quarterly
0010-8901 Cornell Veterinarian
0010-8936 Coronet†
0010-8944 Corpoandes *changed to* Corporacion de los Andes. Revista
0010-8952 Corporate Communications Report
0010-8987 Corporate Planning: Formation, Operation and Management†
0010-8995 Corporate Practice Commentator
0010-9029 Correction Sidelights†
0010-9045 Corrections Digest
0010-9053 Corrective Psychiatry and Journal of Social Therapy *see* 0093-1551
0010-9061 Correio Agro-Pecuario
0010-9088 Correio Serrano
0010-910X Correo del Sur
0010-9118 Correo Economico
0010-9142 Corridor *changed to* Wordworks
0010-9150 Corriere Nucleare†
0010-9169 Corriere dei Ciechi
0010-9177 Corriere dei Congressi†
0010-9185 Corriere dei Piccoli
0010-9193 Corriere dei Trasporti
0010-9207 Corriere del Farmacista
0010-9215 Corriere del Teatro
0010-9231 Corriere di Caracas
0010-924X Corriere d'Italia
0010-9258 Corriere Fitopatologico
0010-9266 Corriere Internazionale del Teatro
0010-9274 Corriere Italiano
0010-9282 Corriere Sindacale†
0010-9290 Corriere Stenografico
0010-9304 Corrispondenza Socialista
0010-9312 Corrosion
0010-9320 Corrosion Abstracts†
0010-9339 Corrosion Abstracts
0010-9347 Corrosion Control Abstracts
0010-9355 Corrosion Engineering
0010-9371 Corrosion Prevention and Control
0010-938X Corrosion Science
0010-941X Body Fashions *see* 0360-3520
0010-9428 Corset, Bra & Lingerie Magazine *changed to* Intimate Fashion News
0010-9436 Corset de France
0010-9444 Corsetry and Underwear *see* 0308-9886
0010-9452 Cortex

1222 ISSN INDEX

0010-9525 Cosmic Research
0010-9533 Cosmoglotta
0010-9541 Cosmopolitan
0010-955X Cosmopolitan Contact
0010-9568 Cosmorama Pictorial
0010-9576 Cosmos
0010-9592 Cost and Management *see* 0831-3881
0010-9606 Cost Engineer
0010-9614 Cost Engineering†
0010-9622 Value Engineering Digest/Defense Contract Guide *changed to* Value Engineering and Management Digest/Defense Contract Guide
0010-9630 Camara de Comercio. Boletin Informativo *changed to* Comercio
0010-9649 Costruire Laterizi†
0010-9657 Costruttori Romani
0010-9665 Costruzioni
0010-9673 Costruzioni Metalliche
0010-9681 Cote d'Azur Agricole et Horticole
0010-969X Cote des Coupons
0010-9711 Coton et Fibres Tropicales
0010-972X Coton et Fibres Tropicales. Bulletin Bibliographique
0010-9746 Cotswold Life
0010-9789 Cotton and General Economic Review *changed to* Cotton Outlook
0010-9797 Cotton Digest *changed to* Cotton Digest International
0010-9800 Cotton Gin and Oil Mill Press
0010-9819 Cotton Growing Review
0010-9835 Cotton's Progress†
0010-9843 Cottonwood *changed to* Cottonwood
0010-9851 Couleurs
0010-986X Coulisse Diplomatique *see* 0015-3516
0010-9886 Council Fire†
0010-9894 Council for Research in Music Education. Bulletin
0010-9916 Council for the Protection of Rural England. Quarterly Bulletin *see* 0268-5795
0010-9924 Church Council of Greater Seattle. Occasional News *changed to* Source (Seattle)
0010-9932 Tanners' Council of America, Inc. Council News
0010-9940 Council of Associations of University Student Personnel Services. Journal†
0010-9967 Council on America's Military Past. Periodical.
0010-9975 American Council on Consumer Interests. Newsletter
0010-9983 Council of Library Technology. Newsletter *changed to* Council on Library/Media Technical Assistants. Newsletter
0010-9991 Councilor
0011-0000 Counseling Psychologist
0011-0019 Counselor (Wheaton)
0011-0027 Counselor (Langhorne)
0011-0035 Counselor Education and Supervision
0011-0043 Counselor's Information Service†
0011-0051 Count Dracula Society Quarterly *changed to* Castle Dracula
0011-0086 Country & Western Express
0011-0094 Country and Western Roundabout
0011-0108 Country & Western Spotlight
0011-0124 Country Churchman
0011-0132 Country
0011-0159 Country Landowner
0011-0167 Country Life *changed to* National Country Life
0011-0175 Country Life†
0011-0183 Country Life in British Columbia
0011-0191 Country Living (Owego)
0011-0205 Country Living (Covington)
0011-0213 Country Quest
0011-023X Country-Side
0011-0248 Country Song Roundup
0011-0256 Country Standard
0011-0264 Countryman
0011-0272 Countryman
0011-0280 Countryside *see* 8750-7595
0011-0299 Countrywide Sports†
0011-0302 Countrywoman
0011-0310 County Councils Gazette
0011-0353 County Progress
0011-037X Courage†
0011-0396 Courier
0011-040X Courier (New York)†
0011-0418 Courier *changed to* Syracuse University Library Associates Courier
0011-0426 Courier
0011-0434 Voedingsblad
0011-0442 Courrier Australien
0011-0450 Courrier Avicole†
0011-0469 Courrier: Cahiers d'Etudes et d'Informations *changed to* Association des Eleves et Anciens Eleves de l'Ecole Nationale Superieure des Postes et Telecomunications. Cahiers d'Etudes et d'Information
0011-0477 Courrier de la Nature, l'Homme et l'Oiseau
0011-0485 Courrier de la Normalisation *see* 0223-4866
0011-0493 Courrier de la Republique
0011-0507 Courrier des Echecs
0011-0515 Courrier des Messageries Maritimes *changed to* Compagnie Generale Maritime. Courrier
0011-0523 Courrier d'Information-Rearmement Moral *changed to* Changer/Tribune de Caux
0011-0531 Centre International d'Etudes Poetiques. Courrier
0011-0558 Courrier du Secretariat International de l'Enseignement Universitaire des Sciences Pedagogiques†
0011-0566 Courrier du Verre *changed to* Architecture de Lumiere Courrier du Verre
0011-0574 Courrier Europeen
0011-0604 Courrier Industriel et Scientifique
0011-0620 Courrier Musical de France†
0011-0639 Courrier Vauclusien
0011-0647 Court Review
0011-0655 Couture†
0011-0671 Covenant Companion
0011-0701 Cover Note†
0011-071X Covered Bridge Topics
0011-0728 Covjek i Prostor
0011-0736 Coyote's Journal
0011-0744 Craft Horizons *see* 0194-8008
0011-0752 Craft, Model & Hobby Industry *changed to* Craft and Needlework Age
0011-0779 Craftsman *changed to* Leather Craftsman
0011-0787 Cranberries
0011-0795 Cranbrook Magazine†
0011-0809 Crane News†
0011-0825 Cranial Academy Newsletter
0011-0833 Crawdaddy; Magazine of Rock *see* 0163-9404
0011-0841 Crazyhorse
0011-085X C R C Critical Reviews in Solid State Sciences *see* 0161-1593
0011-0868 Creationist†
0011-0876 Creative Camera
0011-0884 Creative Crafts *see* 0146-6607
0011-0892 Creative Drama†
0011-0906 Creative Plastics†
0011-0930 Creative Writing
0011-0973 Credit and Financial Management
0011-0981 Credit and Financial Newsletter†
0011-099X Credit Communal de Belgique. Bulletin Trimestriel
0011-1007 Credit Executive
0011-1023 Credit Suisse. Bulletin
0011-1031 Credit Retailer
0011-1058 Credit Union Executive
0011-1066 Credit Union Magazine
0011-1074 Credit World
0011-1090 Credito Popolare
0011-1104 Creditreform
0011-1139 Creel†
0011-1147 Creem
0011-1155 Creighton Law Review
0011-1163 Crematienieuws *changed to* Ooit
0011-1171 Crescendo
0011-118X Crescendo International
0011-1198 Cresset
0011-1201 Creuset, la Voix des Cadres *changed to* Cadres et Maitrise
0011-121X Cri du Monde†
0011-1228 Crianca e Escola *changed to* Escola Fundamental
0011-1236 Cricket
0011-1252 Cricket Quarterly†
0011-1260 Cricketer *see* 0266-7398
0011-1287 Crime & Delinquency
0011-1295 Crime Control Digest
0011-1309 Crime Detective†
0011-1317 Criminal Law Bulletin
0011-1325 Criminal Law Journal
0011-1333 Criminal Law Quarterly
0011-1341 Criminal Law Reporter
0011-135X Criminal Law Review
0011-1368 Criminalia†
0011-1376 Criminologist
0011-1384 Criminology
0011-1406 Crisi e Letteratura
0011-1422 Crisis (New York, 1910)
0011-1430 Crisis & Change
0011-1449 Cristallo
0011-1457 Cristianismo y Sociedad
0011-1465 Christ to the World
0011-1473 Criterio
0011-1481 Criterion†
0011-149X Critic (Chicago)†
0011-1503 Critica
0011-1511 Critica d'Arte
0011-152X Critica Marxista
0011-1538 Critica Sociale†
0011-1546 Critica Sociologica
0011-1554 Critica Storica
0011-1562 Critical Quarterly
0011-1589 Criticism
0011-1597 Criticon
0011-1600 Critique
0011-1619 Critique: Studies in Modern Fiction
0011-1627 Croatia Press
0011-1643 Croatica Chemica Acta
0011-1651 Croce
0011-166X Crochet†
0011-1686 Croissance des Jeunes Nations
0011-1694 Crol
0011-1708 Cromos
0011-1716 T T P I Trade Gazette
0011-1724 Cronaca Politica†
0011-1732 Cronache Calabresi
0011-1740 Cronache d'Altri Tempi†
0011-1759 Chronica Dermatologica
0011-1767 Cronache di Archeologia e di Storia dell'Arte *changed to* Cronache di Archeologia
0011-1775 Cronache Economiche
0011-1783 Cronache Farmaceutiche
0011-1791 Cronica de Holanda
0011-1805 Cronica Medica†
0011-1813 Cronica Universitaria†
0011-183X Crop Science
0011-1848 Crop Science Society of Japan. Proceedings *changed to* Japanese Journal of Crop Science
0011-1864 Crops & Soils *see* 0162-5098
0011-1872 Crops in India
0011-1880 Croquet Gazette
0011-1899 Cross†
0011-1902 Cross & Cockade Journal
0011-1910 Cross and Crown *see* 0162-6760
0011-1945 Cross Country News
0011-1953 Cross Currents
0011-1961 Cross of Languedoc
0011-197X Cross Tie Bulletin *see* 0097-4536
0011-1988 Crossbow
0011-2011 Crossed Flags†
0011-202X Crossroads†
0011-2046 Crossroads (Newark) *changed to* Crossroads U.S.A. (Newark)
0011-2054 Crossroads (New York)
0011-2070 Crow's Forest Products Digest†
0011-2089 Croydon Advertiser
0011-2100 Crucible
0011-2119 Crucible
0011-2127 Crusade *changed to* Leadership Today
0011-2143 Crusade Messenger *changed to* Crusader
0011-2151 Crusader (Memphis)
0011-216X Crustaceana
0011-2186 Crux
0011-2194 Cruzada Eucaristica
0011-2208 Cruzado
0011-2216 Cruzeiro
0011-2224 Cry California *see* 0744-8686
0011-2232 Ceylon Journal of Medical Science
0011-2240 Cryobiology
0011-2259 Cryogenic Information Report
0011-2275 Cryogenics
0011-2283 Cryogenics and Industrial Gases†
0011-2291 Immortality Magazine†
0011-2305 Crystal Lattice Defects *see* 0732-8699
0011-2313 C S A and the Consumer
0011-2321 Ctenar
0011-2348 Cuaderno Cultural
0011-2356 Cuadernos Americanos
0011-2364 Cuadernos de Arquitectura *changed to* Quaderns d'Arquitectura i Urbanisme
0011-2372 Cuadernos de Botanica Canaria†
0011-2380 Cuadernos de Critica
0011-2429 Cuadernos de la Boca del Riachuelo
0011-2445 Cuadernos de Literatura†
0011-2453 Cuadernos de Orientacion Familiar
0011-2488 Cuadernos de Ruedo Iberico
0011-250X Cuadernos Hispanoamericanos
0011-2526 Cuadernos Latinoamericanos de Economia Humana *changed to* Centro Latinoamericano de Economia Humana. Publicaciones
0011-2534 Cuadernos para el Dialogo†
0011-2550 Cuadernos Trimestrales de Poesia
0011-2569 Cuadernos Universitarios
0011-2577 Cuadernos Valencianos de Historia de la Medicina y de la Ciencia
0011-2585 Cuba - Foreign Trade†
0011-2593 Cuba Internacional
0011-2607 Cuba Noticias Economicas
0011-2615 Cuba. Oficina Nacional de Invenciones, Informacion Tecnica y Marcas. Boletin Oficial
0011-2623 Cuba Socialista†
0011-2631 Cuban Studies Newsletter/Boletin de Estudios Cubanos *see* 0361-4441
0011-264X Cucciolo
0011-2658 Cue *see* 0028-7369
0011-2666 Cue of Theta Alpha Phi
0011-2674 Cuento
0011-2690 Cuir
0011-2704 Cuisine et Vins de France
0011-2720 Cukoripar
0011-2739 Culinary Times
0011-2747 Cultivador Moderno
0011-2755 Cultura
0011-2763 Cultura Boliviana
0011-2771 Cultura e Scuola
0011-278X Cultura Hispanica
0011-2798 Cultura nel Mondo
0011-2801 Cultura Popolare†
0011-281X Cultura Turcica
0011-2828 Cultural Affairs†
0011-2836 Cultural Comercial
0011-2844 Cultural Events in Africa
0011-2852 Cultural Forum†
0011-2860 Cultural Hermeneutics *see* 0191-4537
0011-2879 Cultural News from Germany *changed to* Kulturbrief - A German Review
0011-2887 Cultural News from India†
0011-2895 Cultural Research Institute. Bulletin
0011-2925 Culture Francaise
0011-2941 Groningen
0011-2976 Cumberland Presbyterian
0011-2984 Cumbria
0011-300X Cumulative Book Index
0011-3018 Cumulative Index to Nursing Literature *see* 0146-5554
0011-3026 Cumulative Stock Profits
0011-3034 Cuoio Pelli Materie Concianti
0011-3050 Cupula†
0011-3069 Curator
0011-3107 Curling *changed to* Svensk Curling
0011-3115 Curling Review
0011-3123 Current

ISSN INDEX 1223

0011-3131 Current (Washington, 1960)
0011-3158 Current Abstracts of Chemistry and Index Chemicus *see* 0891-6055
0011-3166 Current Abstracts of the Soviet Press *see* 0011-3425
0011-3174 University of Illinois at Urbana-Champaign. College of Agriculture. Current Affairs†
0011-3182 Current Affairs Bulletin
0011-3190 Indo-Pacific Fisheries Council. Current Affairs Bulletin†
0011-3204 Current Anthropology
0011-3212 Current Archaeology
0011-3220 Cryogenic Data Center. Current Awareness Service *see* 0364-0868
0011-3239 Current Bibliography for Aquatic Sciences and Fisheries *see* 0140-5373
0011-3239 Current Bibliography for Aquatic Sciences and Fisheries *see* 0140-5381
0011-3247 Current Bibliography of Epidemiology†
0011-3255 Current Bibliography on African Affairs
0011-3263 Current Bibliography on Science and Technology: Nuclear Engineering
0011-3271 Current Bibliography on Science and Technology: Chemistry and Chemical Engineering (Foreign)
0011-3298 Current Bibliography on Science and Technology: Electronics and Electrical Engineering
0011-3301 Current Bibliography on Science and Technology: Earth Science, Mining and Metallurgy
0011-331X Current Bibliography on Science and Technology: Mechanical Engineering
0011-3328 Current Bibliography on Science and Technology: Management Science and Systems Engineering
0011-3336 Current Bibliography on Science and Technology: Pure and Applied Physics.
0011-3344 Current Biography
0011-3352 Current Books for Academic Libraries *see* 0360-473X
0011-3360 Current Compensation References
0011-3379 C C-A F V/Current Contents, Agricultural, Food and Veterinary Sciences *see* 0090-0508
0011-3387 C C-B S E/Current Contents, Behavioral, Social and Educational Sciences *see* 0092-6361
0011-3395 Current Contents/Engineering and Technology *see* 0095-7917
0011-3409 Current Contents/Life Sciences
0011-3417 Current Contents, Physical and Chemical Sciences *see* 0163-2574
0011-3425 Current Digest of the Soviet Press
0011-3433 Current Documents from the German Democratic Republic
0011-3468 Current Events (Fredericton) *changed to* N.B. Power News
0011-3484 Current Events
0011-3492 Current Events
0011-3506 Current Food Additives Legislation†
0011-3514 Current Geographical Publications
0011-3522 Current Hawaiiana
0011-3530 Current History
0011-3557 Current Index to Conference Papers†
0011-3565 Current Index to Journals in Education
0011-3573 Current Indian Statutes
0011-359X Current Journals in Baker Library. Part One - Author and Title†
0011-3603 Current Journals in Baker Library. Part Two - Subject†
0011-3611 Current Laboratory Practice†
0011-362X Current Law
0011-3638 Current Leather Literature
0011-3646 Current Legal Bibliography†
0011-3654 Current Literature in Traffic and Transportation
0011-3662 Current Literature on Aging
0011-3689 Current Medical Abstracts for Practitioners†
0011-3700 Current Medical Practice
0011-3719 Current Medicine for Attorneys†
0011-3727 Current Municipal Problems
0011-3735 Current Musicology
0011-3751 Current Notes on International Affairs *see* 0311-7995
0011-3778 Current Papers in Electrical & Electronics Engineering
0011-3786 Current Papers in Physics
0011-3794 Current Papers on Computers & Control
0011-3824 Current Podiatry *changed to* Journal of Current Podiatric Medicine
0011-3832 Current Practices†
0011-3840 Current Problems in Surgery
0011-3859 Current Publications in Legal and Related Fields
0011-3867 Current Publications in Family Planning *see* 0039-3665
0011-3883 Current Scene†
0011-3891 Current Science
0011-3905 Current Science
0011-3913 Current Slang†
0011-3921 Current Sociology
0011-393X Current Therapeutic Research
0011-3948 Current Tissue Culture Literature *see* 0090-0753
0011-3964 Current Topics in Radiation Research†
0011-3972 U.S. Bureau of Labor Statistics. Current Wage Developments
0011-3999 Current Work in the History of Medicine
0011-4006 Currents *see* 0738-7776
0011-4014 Currents in Modern Biology *see* 0303-2647
0011-4022 Curriculum†
0011-4049 Curriculum Theory Network *see* 0362-6784
0011-4057 Cursillo
0011-4065 Curtain and Drapery Department Magazine *changed to* Interior Textiles
0011-4081 Curved Horn Newspaper *changed to* Fordham University. Review
0011-409X Cushman Foundation for Foraminiferal Research. Contributions *see* 0096-1191
0011-4103 Custodian's Letter†
0011-4111 Custom Applicator
0011-412X Custom Tailor
0011-4146 Customs Bulletin
0011-4154 Customs Imports and Exports Journal
0011-4162 Cutis
0011-4170 Cutler-Hammer Record
0011-4189 Cutting Tool Engineering
0011-4197 Cutting Tools
0011-4200 Cuvar Jadrana
0011-4219 Cybernetic Medicine
0011-4227 Cybernetica
0011-4235 Cybernetics
0011-4243 Cybernetics Abstracts
0011-426X Cycle†
0011-4278 Cycle Guide
0011-4286 Cycle World
0011-4294 Cycles
0011-4316 Cycling
0011-4324 Cycling and Motorcycling *changed to* Cycling & Motorcycling with the Scooter
0011-4359 Cyclo-Flame†
0011-4375 Cygnet
0011-4383 Cykel- och Sporthandlaren *changed to* Cykel- och Sport Fritidshandlaren
0011-4391 Cykel- och Mopednytt *see* 0280-3038
0011-4413 Cyklistika
0011-4421 Cylchgrawn Llyfrgell Genedlaethol Cymru
0011-443X Cylinder Theory Reports
0011-4448 Cymru'r Plant
0011-4456 Cyprus Bulletin
0011-4464 Cyprus. Department of Statistics & Research. Quarterly Statistical Digest†
0011-4480 Cyprus. Ministry of Labour and Social Insurance. Quarterly Review *see* 0256-8314
0011-4499 Cyrano de Paris
0011-4510 Cystic Fibrosis. Quarterly Annotated References†
0011-4529 Cytobios
0011-4537 Cytogenetics *see* 0301-0171
0011-4545 Cytologia
0011-4553 Czasopismo Stomatologiczne
0011-4561 Czasopismo Techniczne *see* 0137-5911
0011-4561 Czasopismo Techniczne *see* 0137-592X
0011-457X Czechoslovak Engineering Sciences Abstracts†
0011-4588 Czechoslovak Film
0011-4596 Czechoslovak Film Press News *changed to* Film & Video News
0011-460X Czechoslovak Foreign Trade
0011-4618 Czechoslovak Heavy Industry
0011-4626 Czechoslovak Journal of Physics. Section B *changed to* Czechoslovak Journal of Physics
0011-4634 Czechoslovak Life
0011-4642 Czechoslovak Mathematical Journal
0011-4650 Czechoslovak Motor Review
0011-4677 Czechoslovak Woman†
0011-4685 Quattroruote Mare†
0011-4693 D/A *see* 0161-5785
0011-4707 D A C News
0011-4723 D A Review†
0011-4731 D A S U P
0011-474X D A V Magazine
0011-4758 D B - Kundenbrief
0011-4766 D B - Deutsche Bauzeitung - Die Bauzeitung *see* 0721-1902
0011-4782 D B Z
0011-4790 D B Z
0011-4804 D D F - das Drogisten Fachblatt
0011-4812 D D R - Sport†
0011-4820 D D R - Verkehr
0011-4839 D D Z†
0011-4847 D E C A Distributor *see* 0279-473X
0011-4871 D E S A L Reportaje†
0011-4898 D E W Technische Berichte *see* 0724-7265
0011-4901 D F V L R - Nachrichten
0011-491X D F Z†
0011-4928 D G Z
0011-4936 D.H. Lawrence Review
0011-4952 D I N Mitteilungen & Elektronorm
0011-4987 D K - Mitteilungen
0011-4995 D L - Q T C *see* 0178-269X
0011-5002 D L W Informationen zur Bau- und Einrichtungspraxis *see* 0172-2867
0011-5010 D L Z
0011-5029 D M
0011-5037 D M A A Washington Newsletter *changed to* Washington Report (Washington, 1982)
0011-5045 D M G Newsletter†
0011-5053 D M I - Nachrichten *see* 0342-0957
0011-5061 Deadline Data on World Affairs
0011-507X D N Z International
0011-5088 D.O.
0011-510X D P W V - Nachrichten
0011-5118 D R C Newsletter *changed to* D R C News
0011-5126 D R P A Log *changed to* Delaware Valley Business Magazine
0011-5142 D S F-Journal
0011-5150 D S H Abstracts†
0011-5169 D S T Z - Deutsche Stenografenzeitung
0011-5177 D.V.B.A. Publicaciones Tecnicas
0011-5185 D W I - Berichte†
0011-5193 D W V - Mitteilungen
0011-5207 Da-a /U dela
0011-5223 Dacca University Studies. Part A: Humanities
0011-5231 Dachshund
0011-524X Dade County Teacher *changed to* U T D Today
0011-5258 Dados
0011-5266 Daedalus (Cambridge)
0011-5282 D A F Trucks Magazine
0011-5290 Daffodil Journal
0011-5304 Dagspressen
0011-5320 Daheim bei der W A G
0011-5339 Dahl, Dunn & Hargitt's Moving Average Commodity Service†
0011-5347 Large Dams
0011-5355 Daiichi Kogyo Seiyaku Review
0011-5371 Daily Athenaeum
0011-538X Daily Blessing
0011-5398 Daily Cardinal
0011-5401 Daily Construction Service
0011-541X Daily Gleaner-Farmers Weekly
0011-5428 Daily Gleaner-Food Supplement
0011-5444 Daily Kent Stater
0011-5452 Daily Law Journal Record *changed to* Journal Record
0011-5460 Daily News Record
0011-5495 Daily Telegraph Magazine *changed to* Telegraph Sunday Magazine
0011-5509 Daily Variety
0011-5517 South Africa. Weather Bureau. Daily Weather Bulletin/Daaglikse Weerbulletin
0011-5525 Daily Word
0011-5533 Daily World *changed to* People's Daily World
0011-5541 Dainichi-Nippon Cables Review *changed to* Mitsubishi Cable Industries Review
0011-5568 Dairy Council Digest
0011-5576 Dairy Farmer
0011-5592 Dairy Goat Journal
0011-5606 Dairy Guide
0011-5614 Dairy Herd Management
0011-5622 Dairy Industries *see* 0308-8197
0011-5657 Dairy Industry Newsletter†
0011-5673 Dairy Record *changed to* Dairy Foods
0011-5681 Dairy Science Abstracts
0011-569X Dairy Shorthorn Journal *changed to* Shorthorn Journal
0011-5703 Dairy Situation *changed to* U.S. Department of Agriculture. Dairy Outlook and Situation
0011-572X Dairyman
0011-5738 Dairynews
0011-5746 Milk Reporter *changed to* Milk Marketer
0011-5754 Dais *changed to* Monopoly
0011-5762 Dak Tar
0011-5789 Dakota Farmer *changed to* Farmer/Dakota Farmer
0011-5800 Dalesman
0011-5819 Dalhousie Gazette
0011-5827 Dalhousie Review
0011-5835 Dallas
0011-5843 Dallas Bible College News *changed to* Dallas Bible College Herald
0011-586X Dallas Medical Journal
0011-5878 Dallas Notes *changed to* Iconoclast
0011-5894 Daltons Weekly
0011-5908 Damals
0011-5916 Damernas Vaerld
0011-5959 Damspel
0011-5975 Dan Smoot Report†
0011-5983 Dance & Dancers
0011-5991 Dance Films Association and Dance Society Newsletter *changed to* Dance on Camera News
0011-6009 Dance Magazine
0011-6017 Dance News†
0011-6033 Dance Perspectives†
0011-6041 Dance Scope†
0011-605X Dancing Times
0011-6068 Dandy
0011-6076 Danfoss Journal
0011-6084 Danish Journal
0011-6092 Danish Medical Bulletin
0011-6106 Danmarks Amtsraad
0011-6114 Danmarks Geologiske Undersoegelse
0011-6130 Danmarks Havfaskeri *see* 0011-6270
0011-6149 Danmarks Nationalbank. Monetary Review
0011-6157 Danmarksposten
0011-6165 Dansbalans *changed to* Volksdans
0011-6173 Danses
0011-6181 Dansk Arbejde
0011-6203 Dansk Artilleri-Tidsskrift
0011-6211 Dansk Botanisk Arkiv *see* 0078-5237
0011-622X Dansk Brandvaern *see* 0106-6072
0011-6238 Dansk Bridge
0011-6270 Dansk Fiskeritidende
0011-6297 Dansk Geologisk Forening. Bulletin
0011-6300 Dansk Grossist Tidende
0011-6319 Dansk Institutions Tidsskrift
0011-6327 Dansk Jagt

1224 ISSN INDEX

0011-6335 Dansk-Kemi
0011-6351 Nye Dansk Landbrug†
0011-636X Dansk Mejeritidende†
0011-6378 Dansk Missionsblad
0011-6386 Dansk Musiktidsskrift†
0011-6394 Dansk Ornithologisk Forenings Tidsskrift
0011-6408 Dansk Paedagogisk Tidsskrift
0011-6424 Dansk Pelsdyravl
0011-6432 Dansk Psykolognyt
0011-6440 Dansk Radio Industri *see* 0108-6626
0011-6459 Dansk Reklame *changed to* Markedsfoering
0011-6475 Dansk Skovforenings Tidsskrift
0011-6483 Dansk Smede-Tidende
0011-6491 Dansk Svejsetidende *changed to* Svejsetidende
0011-6505 Dansk Teknisk Tidsskrift
0011-6513 Dansk Tidsskrift for Farmaci *see* 0302-248X
0011-6548 Dansk Vejtidsskrift
0011-6556 Danske Bogmarked
0011-6564 Danske Dyrlaegeforening. Medlemsblad *changed to* Dansk Veterinaertidsskrift
0011-6572 Danske Kommuner
0011-6629 Danske Vognmaend
0011-6637 Darbininkas
0011-6645 Daring Confessions
0011-6653 Daring Romance *changed to* My Personal Love Secrets
0011-667X Dark Horse†
0011-6688 Dark Shadows†
0011-6696 Umma
0011-6718 Darpon
0011-6726 D'Ars
0011-6734 Darshana International
0011-6750 Dartmouth College Library Bulletin
0011-6769 Dartnell Office Adminstration Service†
0011-6777 Dartnell Sales and Marketing Service†
0011-6793 Darwiniana
0011-6807 Dasein
0011-6823 Data Journal *changed to* Tass News and Journal
0011-6831 Data Management†
0011-684X Data Processing *see* 0950-5849
0011-6858 Data Processing Digest
0011-6866 Data Processing in Education *see* 0093-7290
0011-6874 Data Processing Magazine†
0011-6882 Data Processing Practitioner†
0011-6890 Data Processor†
0011-6939 Data Systems *see* 0046-6212
0011-6947 Data Trend *changed to* Modern Office
0011-6963 Datamation
0011-6971 Dataweek†
0011-698X Dateline Delhi
0011-7005 Datenjournal
0011-7013 Daughters of the American Revolution Magazine
0011-703X Davar
0011-7048 Davka
0011-7064 Dawn†
0011-7080 Day by Day
0011-7102 Daybreak
0011-7110 Israel. Ministry of Agriculture. Department of Fisheries. Dayig u-Midgeh be-Yisrael
0011-7129 Daytime T V
0011-7145 Db, the Sound Engineering Magazine
0011-7153 D.C. Gazette *changed to* Progressive Review
0011-7161 Echo (De Aar)
0011-7188 De Paul Law Review
0011-7196 Deadwood†
0011-720X Deaf American
0011-7218 Dealerscope *changed to* Dealerscope Merchandising
0011-7234 Dean Sherman's Forest Industry Affairs Letter *changed to* Forest Industry Affairs
0011-7250 Decalogue Journal
0011-7269 Deccan Geographer
0011-7285 Deciduous Fruit Grower
0011-7293 Decimal Currency and Metrication News†
0011-7307 Decision (Minneapolis)
0011-7315 Decision Sciences
0011-7323 Decisions of the Comptroller General of the United States
0011-7331 U.S. Department of the Interior. Decisions of the Department of the Interior
0011-734X Deco Trefoil†
0011-7358 Decor
0011-7374 Decorating Contractor *see* 0263-7936
0011-7382 Decorating Craft Ideas Made Easy *changed to* Creative Ideas for Living
0011-7404 Decorating Retailer
0011-7412 Decorating Your First Home†
0011-7420 Decoration - Ameublement
0011-7447 D E C U Scope
0011-7455 Dedalo†
0011-7471 Deep-Sea Research and Oceanographic Abstracts *see* 0198-0149
0011-748X Defence Science Journal
0011-7498 Defender (Wilmington)
0011-7501 Defender
0011-7528 Defenders of Wildlife News *see* 0162-6337
0011-7552 Defense de l'Occident†
0011-7579 Defense des Vegetaux
0011-7587 Defense Law Journal
0011-7595 Defense Management Journal
0011-7609 Defense Manager *see* 0092-1491
0011-7625 Defense Transportation Journal
0011-7633 Defensor-Chieftain
0011-7641 Defesa Nacional
0011-765X Defesa Nacional
0011-7668 Deficience Mentale/Mental Retardation *changed to* Entourage
0011-7676 Definition†
0011-7684 Dein Freund†
0011-7692 Dein Reich Komme
0011-7706 Deirdre
0011-7714 Dekalb Literary Arts Journal
0011-7722 Delavska Enotnost
0011-7730 Delaware Archaeology†
0011-7749 Delaware Geological Survey Reports of Investigations
0011-7765 Delaware History
0011-7773 Delaware Library Association Bulletin
0011-7781 Delaware Medical Journal
0011-779X Delaware Today
0011-7803 D V I Magazine *changed to* Delaware Valley Business Magazine
0011-782X Delfts Bouwkundig Studenten Gezelschap Styles. Mededelingen
0011-7846 Delhi Law Times
0011-7854 Delhi Medical Journal
0011-7862 Deli News
0011-7870 Delinquency and Society†
0011-7889 Delirante
0011-7897 Deliverer
0011-7927 Delmarva Report†
0011-7935 Delo
0011-7943 Delo in Varnost
0011-796X Delphin
0011-7978 Delta (Tigre)
0011-7986 Delta (Plymouth)
0011-7994 Delta (Budapest)
0011-801X Delta (Washington) *see* 0025-570X
0011-8028 Delta Epsilon Sigma Bulletin *changed to* Delta Epsilon Sigma Journal
0011-8036 Delta Farm Press
0011-8044 Delta Kappa Gamma Bulletin
0011-8052 Delta Pi Epsilon Journal
0011-8060 Paper Book
0011-8079 Deltawerken
0011-8087 Deltion Diikiseos Epichiriseon
0011-8095 Deltion Dimotikis Vivliothikis Hermoupoleos†
0011-8109 International Committee on Irrigation and Drainage. Greek National Committee. Bulletin *changed to* Bulletin G C I D
0011-8117 Greek Speleological Society. Deltion
0011-8133 National Foundation "King Paul." Deltion *changed to* Protovoulia
0011-8141 DeLuxe General Rewind†
0011-815X Demag Kurier
0011-8168 Demain
0011-8176 Demama
0011-8184 D E Mly
0011-8192 Democrat†
0011-8206 Democratic German Report†
0011-8214 Democratic Journalist
0011-8222 Democratie Moderne
0011-8249 Demografia
0011-8265 Demografie
0011-8281 Demography and Development Digest
0011-829X Demokraat
0011-8303 Demokratische Gemeinde
0011-8311 Die Demokratische Schule
0011-832X Demos
0011-8338 Demosta
0011-8346 Radio Waves and Examination
0011-8362 Den'gi i Kredit
0011-8370 Denken en Doen
0011-8389 Electric Furnace Steel
0011-8397 Denkisha No Kagaku
0011-8419 Denmark. Civilforsvarsstyrelsen. Orientation†
0011-8427 Denmark Quarterly Review
0011-8435 Radio, TV, HiFi & Electronics†
0011-8451 Densei Technical Journal
0011-8478 Electrophotography
0011-8486 Dental Abstracts
0011-8508 Dental Assistant
0011-8516 Dental Association of South Africa. Journal
0011-8524 Dental Cadmos
0011-8532 Dental Clinics of North America
0011-8540 Dental Concepts†
0011-8559 Dental-Dienst
0011-8567 Dental Digest *see* 0033-6572
0011-8575 Dental Echo
0011-8583 Dental Economics
0011-8591 Dental Guidance Council for Cerebral Palsy. Bulletin *changed to* Dental Guidance Council on the Handicapped. Journal
0011-8605 Dental Health†
0011-863X Dental Industry Newsletter†
0011-8656 Das Dental-Labor
0011-8664 Dental Laboratory News
0011-8672 Dental Laboratory Review
0011-8680 Dental Management
0011-8699 Dental Mirror
0011-8702 Dental Outlook
0011-8710 Dental Practice
0011-8729 Dental Practitioner and Dental Record *see* 0300-5712
0011-8737 Dental Products Report
0011-8745 National University of Iran. Dental School. Journal
0011-877X Dental Student *changed to* Dental Student
0011-8788 Dental Survey†
0011-8796 Dental Technician
0011-8826 Denver Art Museum. Quarterly†
0011-8834 Denver Law Journal *changed to* Denver University Law Review
0011-8850 Denver Public Library News *see* 0020-1405
0011-8869 Denver Quarterly
0011-8877 Osmania Medical College. Department of History of Medicine. Bulletin *see* 0304-9558
0011-8885 Department Store Employees Union. Local Twenty One Guide†
0011-8893 Department Store Management *changed to* Department Store Economist
0011-8907 Department Store Suppliers *changed to* I.R.D.S.
0011-8915 Department Store Workers' Union. Local 1-S News
0011-8931 Depeche Commerciale et Agricole
0011-8958 Depeche Mode
0011-8966 Depositaire de France
0011-8974 Derby *changed to* Esquire & Derby
0011-8982 Derby Enterprise *see* 0144-6118
0011-8990 Derbyshire Life and Countryside
0011-9008 Derevoobrabatyvayushchaya Promyshlennost'
0011-9016 Dergi†
0011-9024 Dermato-Venerologie *see* 0028-386X
0011-9032 Dermatologia†
0011-9040 Dermatologia Ibero Latino-Americano *see* 0210-5187
0011-9059 International Journal of Dermatology
0011-9075 Dermatologica
0011-9083 Dermatologische Monatsschrift
0011-9091 Dermatology and Urology/Hifu to Hitsunyo *changed to* Nishi Nihon Journal of Dermatology
0011-9105 Dermatology Digest *see* 0198-6643
0011-9113 Derriere le Miroir *changed to* Reperes
0011-9121 Belgian Patents Report *changed to* Belgian Patents Abstracts
0011-913X Japanese Patents Report *changed to* Japanese Patents Report. Examined
0011-9148 Deryn
0011-9156 Des Moines. Public Library. Monthly Memo
0011-9164 Desalination *changed to* Membrane Science and Desalination
0011-9172 Desalination Abstracts†
0011-9199 Desarrollo†
0011-9202 Desarrollo Administrativo†
0011-9210 Descant
0011-9229 Desert Call
0011-9245 Design
0011-9253 Design *see* 0732-0973
0011-9261 Design
0011-927X Design†
0011-9288 Design & Components in Engineering†
0011-9296 Design & Development†
0011-930X Design and Environment *changed to* Urban Design Newsletter
0011-9318 Design Australia†
0011-9342 Design Engineering
0011-9350 Design Engineering
0011-9393 Design International *changed to* Design International. Issue B
0011-9393 Design International *changed to* Design International. Issue A
0011-9407 Design News
0011-9415 Design Quarterly
0011-9423 Designer
0011-9431 Designer
0011-944X Designscape†
0011-9474 Desmos
0011-9490 Dessa Mina Minsta
0011-9512 Dessinateurs et Techniciens *changed to* Dessin et Technique
0011-9520 Dessins et Modeles Internationaux *see* 0250-7730
0011-9539 Dessous Elegants *see* 0010-9436
0011-9547 Destellos Evangelicos†
0011-9555 Destin *changed to* Destin International
0011-9563 Destino†
0011-9571 Detail
0011-958X Detergents and Specialties *changed to* H A P P I: Household & Personal Products Industry
0011-9598 Detonator *changed to* Envoy (New York)
0011-9601 Detroit Dental Bulletin
0011-9636 Detroit Institute of Arts. Bulletin
0011-9644 Detroit Jewish News *changed to* Detroit Jewish News Ltd. Partnership
0011-9652 Detroit Lawyer
0011-9660 Detroit and Suburban Lutheran *changed to* Tri-County Lutheran
0011-9679 Detroit Schools *changed to* Call to Action
0011-9687 Detroit Society for Genealogical Research. Magazine
0011-9695 Detroit Teacher
0011-9709 Detroiter
0011-9725 Dettaglio Tessile e dell'Abbigliamento†
0011-9741 Deutsch als Fremdsprache
0011-9741 Deutsch als Fremdsprache *issued with* 0323-3766
0011-975X Die Deutsche Buehne
0011-9784 Deutsche Agrartechnik *see* 0323-3308
0011-9822 Deutsche Akademie fuer Staedtebau und Landesplanung. Mitteilungen
0011-9830 Deutscher Altphilologen-Verband. Mitteilungsblatt
0011-9849 Der Deutsche Apotheker

0011-9857 Deutsche Apotheker Zeitung
0011-9865 Deutsche Architektur *see* 0323-3413
0011-9873 Der Deutsche Arzt
0011-9881 Deutsche Aussenpolitik†
0011-989X Deutsche Automobil Revue†
0011-9911 Deutsche Baumeister†
0011-992X Deutsche Baumschule
0011-9938 Der Deutsche Beamte
0011-9946 Deutsche Berufs- und Fachschule *see* 0172-2875
0011-9954 Deutsche Bibliographie. Das Deutsche Buch†
0011-9989 Deutsche Buecherschau†
0012-0006 Deutsche Bundesbank. Monatsberichte
0012-0022 Deutsche Circus-Zeitung *changed to* Die Circuszeitung
0012-0030 Dokumentationszentrale Wasser Schriftenreihe
0012-0057 Deutsche Eisenbahntechnik *see* 0323-3553
0012-0073 Deutsche Entomologische Zeitschrift
0012-0081 Der Deutsche Fall Schirmjaeger†
0012-009X Defazet
0012-0103 Sozialistische Finanzwirtschaft
0012-0111 Deutsche Fischerei-Zeitung *changed to* Zeitschrift fuer die Binnenfischerei der DDR
0012-012X Der Deutsche Forstmann
0012-0138 Deutsche Gaertnerboerse *changed to* G B und G W - Gaertnerboerse und Gartenwelt
0012-0162 Deutsche Gefluegelwirtschaft *see* 0340-3858
0012-0189 Deutsche Geologische Gesellschaft. Zeitschrift
0012-0197 Deutsche Gesellschaft fuer Geologische Wissenschaften. Berichte. Reihe A: Geologie und Palaeontologie, Reihe B: Mineralogie und Lagerstaettenforschung†
0012-0200 Deutsche Gesellschaft fuer Versicherungsmathematik. Blaetter
0012-0219 Deutsche Gesundheitswesen *see* 0233-1608
0012-0227 Deutsche Getraenke-Industrie *see* 0724-4266
0012-0235 Deutsche Gewaesserkundliche Mitteilungen
0012-0251 Deutsche Handelskammer in Oesterreich (Bulletin)
0012-026X Deutsche Hebammen-Zeitschrift
0012-0278 Deutsche Hebe- und Foerdertechnik
0012-0286 Deutsche Hotel Zeitung *changed to* D G Deutsche Gaststaette/Deutsche Hotel-Zeitung Gastwirt und Hotelier
0012-0294 Der Deutsche Hugenott
0012-0308 Deutsche Hydrographische Zeitschrift
0012-0316 Deutsche Ingenieurschule *see* 0340-448X
0012-0324 Deutsche Jaeger-Zeitung *see* 0720-4523
0012-0332 Deutsche Jugend
0012-0340 Deutsche Kameramann *see* 0343-5571
0012-0375 Deutsche Kunst und Denkmalpflege
0012-0391 Deutsche Landwirtschaft *see* 0023-3811
0012-0413 Deutsche Lebensmittel-Rundschau
0012-0421 Deutsche Lehrerzeitung
0012-043X Deutsche Literaturzeitung
0012-0448 Das Deutsche Malerblatt
0012-0456 Deutsche Mathematiker Vereinigung. Jahresbericht
0012-0464 Deutsche Mechaniker Zeitung†
0012-0472 Deutsche Medizinische Wochenschrift
0012-0480 Deutsche Milchwirtschaft
0012-0502 Deutsche Musikbibliographie
0012-0510 Deutsche National-Zeitung
0012-0545 Deutsche Nationalbibliographie. Reihe C: Dissertationen und Habilitationsschriften
0012-0553 Der Deutsche Pelztierzuechter
0012-057X Deutsche Polizei
0012-0588 Deutsche Post
0012-0596 Deutsche Post
0012-060X Deutsche Rechtsprechung
0012-0618 Deutsche Rentenversicherung
0012-0626 Deutsche Rheologische Gesellschaft. Berichte *see* 0340-8388
0012-0634 Der Deutsche Rundfunk- Einzelhandel
0012-0650 Deutsche Schachblaetter
0012-0677 Deutsche Schaefereizeitung
0012-0685 Deutscher Schreiner *changed to* D D S - Der Deutscher Schreiner und Tischler
0012-0693 Die Deutsche Schrift
0012-0707 Deutsche Schuetzenzeitung
0012-0723 Das Deutsche Schuhmacherhandwerk
0012-0731 Die Deutsche Schule
0012-074X Deutsche Krankenpflege-Zeitschrift
0012-0758 Deutsche Seiler-Zeitung
0012-0766 Deutsche Sparkassenzeitung
0012-0774 Deutsche Steuer-Zeitung: Ausgabe A *see* 0724-5637
0012-0782 Deutsche Steuer-Zeitung. Ausgabe B *see* 0724-553X
0012-0790 Deutsche Stomatologie der D D R *see* 0302-4725
0012-0804 Der Deutsche Strassenverkehr
0012-0812 Deutsche Studien
0012-0820 Der Deutsche Tabakbau
0012-0839 Deutsche Textiltechnik *see* 0323-3804
0012-0847 Deutsche Tieraerztliche Wochenschrift *see* 0341-6593
0012-0855 Der Deutsche Tischlermeister
0012-0863 Deutsche Uhrmacher-Zeitschrift *see* 0017-1689
0012-0871 Deutsche Umschau
0012-0901 D V Z
0012-091X Deutsche Versicherungszeitschrift†
0012-0936 Deutsche Vierteljahrsschrift fuer Literaturwissenschaft und Geistesgeschichte
0012-0944 Neue Volkskunst†
0012-0960 Allgemeine Deutsche Weinfachzeitung *see* 0723-1350
0012-0979 Der Deutsche Weinbau
0012-0987 Deutsche Wissenschaftliche Kommission fuer Meeresforschung. Berichte *see* 0341-6836
0012-0995 Deutsche Wohnungswirtschaft
0012-1010 Zahn- Mund- und Kieferheilkunde
0012-1029 Deutsche Zahnaerztliche Zeitschrift
0012-1037 Zeitschrift fuer Neurologie *see* 0340-5354
0012-1045 Deutsche Zeitschrift fuer Philosophie
0012-1053 Deutsche Zeitschrift fuer Verdauungs- und Stoffwechselkrankheiten
0012-1061 Deutscher Germanisten-Verband. Mitteilungen
0012-1088 Deutscher Alpenverein
0012-1096 Deutscher Drucker
0012-110X Der Fass- und Weinkuefer†
0012-1118 Deutscher Jaeger *see* 0340-7829
0012-1126 Deutscher Kantinen Anzeiger *changed to* Kantinen Anzeiger
0012-1134 Deutscher Lebensmittelgrosshandel
0012-1142 Deutscher Lebensmittelhandel
0012-1169 Deutscher Palaestina-Verein. Zeitschrift
0012-1177 Deutscher Studenten-Anzeiger
0012-1185 Deutscher Verein fuer Oeffentliche und Private Fuersorge. Nachrichtendienst
0012-1193 Deutsches Adelsblatt
0012-1207 Deutsches Aerzteblatt
0012-1215 Deutsches Architektenblatt
0012-1223 Deutsches Archiv fuer Erforschung des Mittelalters
0012-1231 D A R
0012-124X Deutsches Dachdecker-Handwerk *changed to* Das Dachdecker-Handwerk
0012-1258 Deutsches Elektrohandwerk *changed to* D E - der Elektromeister und Deutsches Elektrohandwerk
0012-1274 Deutsches Handwerksblatt
0012-1282 Deutsches Industrieinstitut Beitraege†
0012-1304 Deutsches Institut fuer Wirtschaftsforschung. Wochenbericht
0012-1312 Jahrbuch fuer Volkskunde und Kulturgeschichte *see* 0138-4503
0012-1320 Deutsches Medizinisches Journal†
0012-1339 Deutsches Museum. Abhandlungen und Berichte
0012-1347 Deutsches Steuerrecht
0012-1363 Deutsches Verwaltungsblatt
0012-1371 Deutsches Volksheimstaettenwerk. Informationsdienst
0012-138X Deutsches Waffen-Journal
0012-1398 Deutschkurse
0012-1401 Deutschland - Frankreich†
0012-141X Deutschland-Magazin
0012-1428 Deutschland Archiv
0012-1436 Deutschland-Berichte
0012-1444 Deutschland-Informationen†
0012-1452 Der Deutschland- Sammler†
0012-1460 Deutschunterricht
0012-1479 Zielsprache Deutsch
0012-1487 Deutschunterricht in Suedafrika
0012-1509 Deux Mille†
0012-1533 Developing Economies
0012-155X Development and Change
0012-1576 Development Digest†
0012-1592 Development, Growth and Differentiation
0012-1606 Developmental Biology
0012-1622 Developmental Medicine and Child Neurology
0012-1630 Developmental Psychobiology
0012-1649 Developmental Psychology
0012-1657 Developpement et Civilisations†
0012-1665 Devenir Historico
0012-1673 Devil's Advocate†
0012-1681 Devon and Cornwall Notes and Queries
0012-1703 Devon Life
0012-1711 Devotion au Saint-Esprit *see* 0396-969X
0012-172X Dewey Newsletter†
0012-1746 Dharma
0012-1754 Di Cyan and Brown Bulletin *changed to* Di Cyan Bulletin
0012-1762 Dia Medico
0012-1770 Diabete *see* 0338-1684
0012-1789 Diabete et Nutrition
0012-1797 Diabetes
0012-1800 Diabetes in the News *see* 8750-1244
0012-1819 Diabetes Literature Index†
0012-1827 Diabetes Newsletter *changed to* Diabetes Update
0012-1851 Diabetiker *see* 0341-8812
0012-186X Diabetologia
0012-1878 Diafora
0012-1886 Diaghonios†
0012-1894 Diagnosi - Laboratorio e Clinica†
0012-1908 Internal Medicine and Diagnosis News *see* 0274-5542
0012-1916 Diagnostica†
0012-1924 Diagnostica
0012-1932 Diagnostyka Laboratoryjna
0012-1959 Diakonia†
0012-1967 Diakonia
0012-1975 Diakonie im Rheinland
0012-1983 Diakonische Werk *see* 0342-1643
0012-1991 Dial†
0012-2009 D A I R S and Systems for Instruction Newsletter†
0012-2017 Dialectica
0012-2025 Dialetti d'Italia
0012-2033 Dialog
0012-2041 Dialog
0012-2068 Dialogi
0012-2084 Dialogo
0012-2092 Dialogo
0012-2106 Dialogos
0012-2122 Dialogos
0012-2130 Dialogue†
0012-2157 Dialogue: A Journal of Mormon Thought
0012-2165 Dialogue†
0012-2181 Dialogue
0012-219X Dialogue
0012-2203 Dialogue†
0012-2211 Dialogue (New York, 1962) Braille edition of 0012-222X
0012-222X Dialogue (New York, 1962)†
0012-2238 Dialogue (New York, 1966)†
0012-2246 Dialogue (Milwaukee)
0012-2262 Dialogue (Washington)
0012-2270 Dialogue Calcutta *changed to* Dialogue India
0012-2289 Dialogue on Campus
0012-2297 Dialoguer
0012-2300 Diamond News and South African Jeweller
0012-2319 Diamond Walnut News *changed to* Sun-Diamond Grower
0012-2327 Diana
0012-2335 Diana
0012-2343 Diana
0012-2351 Diana Armi
0012-236X Diane
0012-2378 Diapason
0012-2386 Diario Italiano†
0012-2416 Dibevo *changed to* Dibevo Vakblad
0012-2432 Dickens Studies Newsletter *see* 0742-5473
0012-2440 Dickensian
0012-2459 Dickinson Law Review
0012-2467 Dictionnaire Permanent de la Construction
0012-2475 Dictionnaire Permanent Droit des Affaires
0012-2483 Dictionnaire Permanent Entreprise Agricole
0012-2491 Dictionnaire Permanent Fiscal
0012-2505 Dictionnaire Permanent Rural *changed to* Dictionnaire Permanent Rural (Droit, Social, Agricole)
0012-2513 Dictionnaire Permanent Social
0012-253X Die Casting Engineer
0012-2548 Diecasting & Metal Moulding†
0012-2556 Diemaking, Diecutting and Converting *see* 0163-9234
0012-2564 Dienen und Fuehren *changed to* Unterwegs
0012-2572 Dienender Glaube
0012-2580 Sonntagschulmitarbeiter
0012-2602 Diesel and Gas Turbine Progress *see* 0744-0073
0012-2610 Diesel Equipment Superintendent
0012-2629 Diesel-Lehti
0012-2637 Dietetique d'Aujourd'hui
0012-2645 Dietsche Warande en Belfort
0012-2653 Difesa Sociale
0012-2661 Differential Equations
0012-267X Diffusion Data *see* 0377-6883
0012-2688 Difofu *changed to* Sedibeng
0012-2696 Difusion Economica
0012-2718 Digest des Revues Techniques *changed to* Bulletin Bibliographique des Laboratoires Professionnels Francais et Belge
0012-2734 U.S. National Labor Relations Board. Digest of Decisions of the National Labor Relations Board *changed to* Classified Index of N.L.R.B. and Related Court Decisions
0012-2742 Digest of Investment Advices
0012-2750 Digest of Labour Cases
0012-2769 Digest of Neurology & Psychiatry
0012-2777 Digest of Opinions of the Attorney General
0012-2785 U.S. Library of Congress. Congressional Research Service. Digest of Public Bills and Resolutions *changed to* U.S. Library of Congress. Congressional Research Service. Digest of Public General Bills and Resolutions
0012-2807 Journal for Special Educators of the Mentally Retarded *see* 0741-9325
0012-2815 Digest of the Soviet Ukrainian Press†
0012-2823 Digestion
0012-2831 Digital Integrated Circuit D.A.T.A. Book†
0012-284X Dikobraz
0012-2858 Diliman Review
0012-2866 Dimanche
0012-2874 Dime Novel Round-Up
0012-2882 Dimension
0012-2890 Dimension: Journal of Pastoral Concern†
0012-2904 Dimensioni
0012-2920 Dimossiotis *changed to* Nea Dimossiotis
0012-2939 Dinamica Economica

ISSN INDEX

ISSN	Title
0012-2971	Dines Letter
0012-3005	Dinaman
0012-3013	Dinteria
0012-3021	Diocesan Digest†
0012-303X	Diogene†
0012-3048	Diogenes
0012-3072	Diplomania see 0016-4364
0012-3080	Diplomatic Bookshelf changed to Diplomatic Bookshelf & Review
0012-3099	U.S. Department of State. Diplomatic List
0012-3102	Diplomatic List of Arrivals & Departures
0012-3110	Diplomatist
0012-3129	Diplomlandwirt see 0340-7810
0012-3137	Dippy Post†
0012-3145	Spain. Direccion General de Archivos y Bibliotecas. Boletin†
0012-3161	Power Electronics†
0012-320X	Direction et Gestion des Entreprises
0012-3218	Direction for Youth Leaders†
0012-3226	Direction of Trade see 0252-306X
0012-3234	Directions†
0012-3242	Director
0012-3250	Director
0012-3277	Directory of Chemical Producers-U.S.A.
0012-3293	Directory of Published Proceedings. Series S E M T - Science, Engineering, Medicine and Technology
0012-3307	Directory of Published Proceedings. Series S S H - Social Sciences/Humanities
0012-3323	Direttore Commerciale
0012-3331	Direzione Aziendale
0012-3358	Dirigente Construtor
0012-3366	Dirigente Industrial
0012-3374	Dirigente Rural
0012-3390	Diritto Aereo
0012-3404	Diritto del Lavoro
0012-3412	Diritto delle Radiodiffusioni e delle Telecomunicazioni
0012-3420	Diritto di Autore
0012-3439	Diritto e Giurisprudenza
0012-3447	Diritto e Pratica Tributaria
0012-3455	Diritto Ecclesiastico changed to Diritto Ecclesiastico e Rassegna di Diritto Matrimoniale
0012-3471	Diritto Internazionale†
0012-348X	Diritto Marittimo
0012-351X	Discipline and Grievances
0012-351X	Discipline and Grievances see 0271-3462
0012-3528	Discobolo
0012-3544	Discographical Forum
0012-3560	Discoteca Alta Fedelta changed to Discoteca Hi Fi
0012-3579	Discount Merchandiser
0012-3587	Discount Store News
0012-3595	Discours Social
0012-3625	Discovery (New Haven)
0012-3641	Discovery (Northbrook)
0012-365X	Discrete Mathematics
0012-3668	Discretio
0012-3676	Discus
0012-3684	Discussion sur l'Alphabetisation see 0024-4503
0012-3692	Chest
0012-3706	Diseases of the Colon and Rectum
0012-3714	Diseases of the Nervous System see 0160-6689
0012-3730	Diskus
0012-3765	Dispatcher (San Francisco, 1942)
0012-3773	Dispensing Optician changed to Dispensing Optics
0012-3781	Display International†
0012-3803	Display World see 0745-4295
0012-3811	Disposables and Nonwovens
0012-382X	Disque-Ton†
0012-3846	Dissent (New York)
0012-3862	Dissertationes Mathematicae
0012-3870	Dissertationes Pharmaceuticae et Pharmacologicae see 0301-0244
0012-3889	Distaff†
0012-3900	Distributie en Zelfbediening,D6†
0012-3927	Distribution/Warehouse Cost Digest changed to Warehouse and Physical Distribution Productivity
0012-3935	Distribution d'Aujourd'Hui
0012-3951	Distribution Worldwide see 0273-6721
0012-396X	C M I Distribution Maps of Plant Diseases
0012-3986	Distributive Worker
0012-401X	District Heating
0012-4028	District Mail
0012-4036	District Management†
0012-4044	District Nursing see 0301-0821
0012-4060	District of Columbia Dental Society. Journal†
0012-4079	District of Columbia Nurses Association. Quarterly Review†
0012-4087	Distrofia Muscolare
0012-4109	D I T
0012-4125	Dithmarschen
0012-4133	Detail
0012-4141	Divadelni Noviny
0012-4206	Divine Life
0012-4214	Divine Word Messenger†
0012-4222	Divinitas
0012-4230	Divorce Chats
0012-4249	Israel. Knesset. Divrei ha-Knesset
0012-4257	Divus Thomas
0012-4265	Divya Vani
0012-4273	Dix-Septieme Siecle
0012-4281	Dixie Contractor
0012-4303	Dixon Line†
0012-4311	Djezair
0012-432X	Djur-Expressen changed to Djurens Vaarld
0012-4338	Djur och Natur†
0012-4346	Djurskyddet
0012-4354	Dnipro
0012-4370	Do It Yourself
0012-4389	Do It yourself-Markt changed to Muster und Farbe
0012-4397	Do It Yourself Retailing†
0012-4400	Doberman News†
0012-4419	Dock and Harbour Authority
0012-4427	Docket
0012-4435	Doctor
0012-4443	Doctor Communist†
0012-446X	Doctrine and Life
0012-4478	Document Reproductie
0012-4486	Documenta Ophthalmologica
0012-4494	Documentacion Administrativa
0012-4508	Documentaliste
0012-4516	Documentatie†
0012-4524	Documentatie Verkeerseconomie en Aanverwante Onderwerpen†
0012-4532	Documentatieblad see 0167-5850
0012-4540	Netherlands. Ministerie van Onderwijs en Wetenschappen. Documentatieblad see 0167-6644
0012-4559	Documentatio Geographica see 0341-2431
0012-4567	Societe Nationale des Chemins de Fer Belges. Documentaire see 0771-517X
0012-4583	Documentation - Technique, Scientifique et Commerciale
0012-4591	International Cooperative Alliance. Regional Office and Education Centre for South-East Asia. Documentation Bulletin changed to Documentation Bulletin for South-East Asia
0012-4613	Documentation Catholique
0012-4621	Documentation Commerciale et Comptable
0012-463X	Documentation East-European Agricultural Literature†
0012-4648	Documentation Economique†
0012-4656	Documentation Francaise Illustree†
0012-4680	Documentation Rapide du Chef d'Enterprise see 0395-451X
0012-4699	Documentation Sociale†
0012-4702	Electricite de France. Documentation Technique
0012-4710	Documentazione sui Paesi dell'Est
0012-4729	Documenti di Architettura†
0012-4737	Documenti di Vita Comunale
0012-4753	Documentos
0012-477X	Documents et Debats
0012-4788	Documents et Statistiques†
0012-480X	Dodge Construction News. Chicago Edition
0012-4826	Doelmatig Bedrijfsbeheer changed to D B - Tijdschrift voor Doelmatig Bedrijfsbeheer
0012-4850	Dog News see 0309-1031
0012-4877	Dog Review of Southern Africa†
0012-4885	Dog World
0012-4893	Dog World
0012-4907	Dogar's General Knowledge Digest
0012-4931	Dohanyipar
0012-494X	Doklady - Earth Science Sections
0012-4958	Doklady Biochemistry
0012-4966	Doklady Biological Sciences
0012-4974	Doklady Biophysics
0012-4982	Doklady Botanical Sciences
0012-4990	Doklady Chemical Technology
0012-5008	Doklady Chemistry
0012-5016	Doklady Physical Chemistry
0012-5024	Dokumentacija za Gradevinarstvo i Arhitekturu
0012-5032	Dokumentacja Geograficzna
0012-5067	Dokumentation der Deutschen Binnenschiffahrt†
0012-5075	Dokumentation der Gesetze und Verordnungen Osteuropas
0012-5091	Dokumentation der Zeit†
0012-5105	Dokumentation fuer Bodenmechanik - Grundbau - Felsmechanik - Ingenieurgeologie
0012-5113	Dokumentation - Jugendfoschung, Jugendhilfe, Jugendpolitik see 0342-3964
0012-513X	Dokumentation Sozialmedizin, Oeffentlicher Gesundheitsdienst, Arbeitsmedizin changed to Dokumentation Sozialmedizin, Oeffentlicher Gesundheitsdienst, Gesundheitserziehung
0012-5148	Dokumentation Strasse
0012-5156	Dokumentation Wasser
0012-5172	Dokumente
0012-5180	Documentation Study changed to Information Science and Technology Association. Journal
0012-5229	Doll Talk
0012-5237	Dollar-Bonds & Euro-Bonds
0012-5245	Dollars and Sense
0012-5253	Dolphin changed to Dewan Perintis
0012-5261	Dolphin Book Club News
0012-527X	Domei News†
0012-5288	Domenica
0012-5296	Domenica del Corriere
0012-530X	Domestic Equipment Trader
0012-5318	Domestic Heating see 0308-9614
0012-5326	Domestic Heating News changed to Domestic Heating Plus Plumbing: Bathrooms
0012-5342	Dominion Engineer
0012-5350	Dominion Law Reports
0012-5369	Domov
0012-5377	Domus
0012-5393	Don
0012-5407	Don Universel du Sang see 0253-1321
0012-5415	Donauraum†
0012-5423	Der Donauschwabe
0012-544X	Dono
0012-5458	Dookola Swiata
0012-5474	Doorbraak
0012-5482	Doorkijk
0012-5490	Doors to Latin America†
0012-5504	Doortocht
0012-5512	Dopester†
0012-5520	Doprava
0012-5547	Dorf Aktuell see 0340-7837
0012-5555	Dorfschule†
0012-5563	Dornier-Post
0012-5571	Road
0012-5598	Dorset Farmer
0012-561X	Doshkol'noe Vospitanie
0012-5636	Dostignuca
0012-5652	Dotacion
0012-5660	Dotaito Nyusus Reta†
0012-5679	Dots and Taps
0012-5687	Dottore in Scienze Agrarie
0012-5695	Douai Magazine
0012-5709	Double Liaison
0012-5717	Douglas Library Notes†
0012-5725	Dow Diamond changed to Elements
0012-575X	Dow Theory Comment
0012-5768	Down Beat
0012-5776	Down East Magazine
0012-5784	Down Library Lane†
0012-5806	Downside Review
0012-5814	Downstate Reporter†
0012-5822	Downtown Idea Exchange
0012-5849	Dr. Shelton's Hygienic Review†
0012-5857	Draegerheft
0012-5865	Draft Horse Journal
0012-5873	Drag Racing†
0012-5881	Dragoco Report
0012-589X	Dragon
0012-5911	Draht
0012-592X	DrahtWelt
0012-5938	Drake Law Review
0012-5946	Drama
0012-5954	Drama and Theatre†
0012-5962	Drama Review
0012-5989	Dramatics
0012-5997	Dramatika
0012-6004	Dramatists Guild Quarterly
0012-6012	Dramma
0012-6020	Drapers Record
0012-6055	Drehpunkt
0012-6063	Die Drei
0012-6071	Dreihammer
0012-608X	Dreikoenigsbote
0012-6098	Dreiser Newsletter
0012-6101	Dresdner Monats-Blaetter
0012-611X	Dressmaking
0012-6128	Dressvertising Weekly
0012-6136	Drevarsky Vyskum
0012-6144	Drevo
0012-6152	Drew Gateway
0012-6160	Drexel Library Quarterly†
0012-6179	Drexel Technical Journal†
0012-6187	Drie Talen
0012-6209	Rijksuniversiteit te Groningen. Nedersaksisch Instituut. Driemaandelijkse Bladen
0012-6225	Drill Bit changed to Southwestern Oil World
0012-625X	Drinks International
0012-6268	Der Dritte Weg
0012-6306	Droga changed to Droga Helvetica
0012-6322	Drogerie-Journal†
0012-6330	Drogist
0012-6349	Drogistenblad Vergulde Gaper changed to D W
0012-6357	Drogownictwo
0012-6365	Droit d'Auteur
0012-6373	Droit de Vivre
0012-639X	Droit et Economie
0012-6411	Droit et Liberte
0012-642X	Droit Maritime Francais
0012-6438	Droit Social
0012-6454	Drovers Journal
0012-6462	Druck-Print
0012-6470	Druck und Papier
0012-6489	Druckformenherstellung†
0012-6500	Der Druckspiegel
0012-6519	Druckwelt
0012-6527	Drug and Cosmetic Industry
0012-6535	1199 News
0012-6543	Drug and Therapeutics Bulletin
0012-6551	Drug Digest†
0012-656X	Drug Information Bulletin see 0092-8615
0012-6578	Drug Intelligence & Clinical Pharmacy
0012-6586	Drug Merchandising
0012-6608	Drug Research Reports: The Blue Sheet see 0162-3605
0012-6616	Drug Topics
0012-6624	Drug Trade News see 0278-1530
0012-6632	Drugarce
0012-6640	Druggist†
0012-6667	Drugs
0012-6683	Drugs Made in Germany
0012-6691	Drugs of Today changed to Medicamentos de Actualidad/Drugs of Today

ISSN INDEX

ISSN	Title
0012-6713	Drukkerswereld *changed to* Repro en Druk
0012-6721	Drum
0012-6748	Drum Corps News
0012-6756	Druzhba Narodov
0012-6764	Druzina in Dom
0012-6772	Drvna Industrija
0012-6799	Dryade
0012-6802	Drycleaners News
0012-6829	Drycleaning World *changed to* Laundry Cleaning World
0012-6837	Du
0012-6853	Dual Dictionary Coordinate Index to Petroleum Abstracts *see* 0162-329X
0012-6861	Dublin Historical Record
0012-687Y	Dublin Magazine
0012-6896	Dublin University Law Review†
0012-690X	Dubrovacki Vjesnik
0012-6918	Dubuque Leader
0012-6934	Duca-Post
0012-6942	Duckett's Register†
0012-6950	Ducks Unlimited
0012-6977	Duepiu
0012-7019	Duesseldorfer Amtsblatt
0012-7027	Duesseldorfer Hefte
0012-7043	Duiker Krant
0012-7051	Duitse Kroniek
0012-706X	Duivengazet†
0012-7078	Duke Divinity School Review†
0012-7086	Duke Law Journal
0012-7094	Duke Mathematical Journal
0012-7108	Duke University Library Newsletter
0012-7116	Duluthian
0012-7124	Dundee Chamber of Commerce Journal *see* 0306-0241
0012-7132	Dune Buggies & Hot VWs
0012-7159	Dunlop Industrial Rubber News†
0012-7167	Dunn & Hargitt's Commodity Service
0012-7175	Dun's Review *changed to* Business Month
0012-7183	Duodecim
0012-7191	Duquesne Hispanic Review†
0012-7205	Duquesne Review†
0012-7213	Duquesne University Law Review *see* 0093-3058
0012-7221	Durban High School Old Boys' Club. Bulletin
0012-723X	Durban Museum Novitates
0012-7264	Durez Molder
0012-7272	Durham County Local History Society. Bulletin
0012-7280	Durham University Journal
0012-7299	Duroc News
0012-7302	Dust†
0012-7310	Dutch-Australian Weekly
0012-7337	D V M Newsmagazine
0012-7353	Dyna
0012-7361	Dyna
0012-737X	Dynamic
0012-7388	Dynamic Maturity *see* 0148-799X
0012-7396	Dynamic Supervision
0012-740X	Dynamische Psychiatrie
0012-7418	Dynamite/International
0012-7434	Dysk Olimpijski†
0012-7450	E A R O P H News and Notes
0012-7469	E A S A *changed to* Engineers' News
0012-7477	E A Z
0012-7485	E B B A News *changed to* North American Bird Bander
0012-7493	E B U Review. Geneva Edition (Programmes, Adminstration, Law)
0012-7507	E D C†
0012-7515	E E E-Magazine of Circuit Design Engineering *changed to* E D N Magazine
0012-7523	E D P Analyzer
0012-7531	E D P Daily†
0012-754X	E D P Industry Report and Market Review *see* 0742-647X
0012-7558	E D P Weekly *changed to* Computer Age. E D P Weekly
0012-7590	E E G-E M G
0012-7604	E E I Bulletin *see* 0364-474X
0012-7612	E E I Statistical Releases. Electric Output
0012-7639	E E O†
0012-7647	E F D S S News *see* 0013-8231
0012-7655	E F T A Bulletin
0012-7671	E G
0012-768X	E I M Mededelingen
0012-7701	E L F
0012-771X	E L N A Bulteno *see* 0030-5065
0012-7744	E.M.G. Handmade Gramophones. Monthly Letter
0012-7760	E M N I D-Informationen
0012-7779	E M O Bulletin†
0012-7787	E M O National Digest *see* 0317-3518
0012-7795	E-M Synchronizer†
0012-7809	E N A P I†
0012-7825	Eos
0012-7841	E P I C Bulletin†
0012-7876	E. R. A. Journal†
0012-7884	E.R.B. Newsletter
0012-7892	E R D A†
0012-7922	E R I C News Plus†
0012-7957	E R T (Electronics-Radio-TV) *changed to* Elektroniika & Automaatio
0012-7965	E S/Espana Semanal *changed to* Espana Hoy
0012-7981	E S G - Nachrichten
0012-799X	E S R O/E L D O Bulletin *see* 0376-4265
0012-8007	E S S A World *see* 0014-0821
0012-8015	Essor Economique et Commercial
0012-8023	E T V Newsletter
0012-8031	Elektrontechnische Zeitschrift. Ausgabe B *changed to* E T Z Zeitschrift fuer Elektrische Energietechnik
0012-804X	E U R I S I†
0012-8058	E und M
0012-8066	E V
0012-8074	Elektronik-Zeitung *changed to* Elektronik-Technologie
0012-8082	Eagle (Washington)
0012-8104	Eagle and Boys' World
0012-8112	Eagle
0012-8139	Early American
0012-8147	Early American Industries Association. Chronicle
0012-8155	Early American Life
0012-8163	Early American Literature
0012-8171	Early Childhood Education
0012-8198	Earnshaw's Infants' & Children's Review *see* 0161-2786
0012-821X	Earth and Planetary Science Letters
0012-8228	Earth Science
0012-8236	Earth Science Bulletin
0012-8244	Earth Science Journal†
0012-8252	Earth Science Reviews
0012-8287	Earthquake Notes
0012-8295	East
0012-8309	East Africa Journal†
0012-8317	Journal of the East Africa Natural History Society and National Museum
0012-8325	East African Agricultural and Forestry Journal
0012-8333	East Africa Journal of Rural Development *changed to* Eastern Africa Journal of Rural Development
0012-8341	East African Management Journal
0012-835X	East African Medical Journal
0012-8368	East African Trade and Industry *changed to* Review of Trade and Industry
0012-8376	East and West
0012-8384	East and West Series
0012-8392	East Anglian Magazine†
0012-8406	East Asia Millions
0012-8414	East Asian Cultural Studies
0012-8430	East Europe†
0012-8449	East European Quarterly
0012-8457	East European Trade
0012-8465	East London Papers†
0012-8473	Perspective
0012-8481	East Midland Geographer
0012-849X	Bangladesh. Bureau of Statistics. Monthly Bulletin of Statistics *changed to* Monthly Statistical Bulletin of Bangladesh
0012-8503	East Pakistan Bureau of Statistics. Weekly Information Service†
0012-852X	East Riding Archaeologist
0012-8538	East Side Chamber of Commerce Newsletter
0012-8546	East Sussex Farmer
0012-8570	East-West
0012-8589	East/West
0012-8597	East-West Center Magazine†
0012-8600	East-West Commerce
0012-8627	East-West Digest
0012-8635	East-West Review†
0012-8643	Eastbournian
0012-8651	Easter Seal Bulletin *changed to* National Easter Seal Communicator
0012-866X	Eastern Africa Economic Review
0012-8678	Eastern Africa Law Review
0012-8686	Eastern Anthropologist
0012-8708	Eastern Buddhist
0012-8724	Eastern Cape Naturalist *changed to* Naturalist
0012-8732	Eastern Churches News Letter
0012-8740	Eastern Churches Review *see* 0144-8722
0012-8759	Eastern Dental Society Bulletin
0012-8767	Eastern Economist
0012-8775	Eastern European Economics
0012-8783	International Journal of Politics *see* 0891-1916
0012-8791	Eastern Evening News
0012-8805	Eastern Fruit Grower†
0012-8813	Eastern Horizon†
0012-8821	Eastern Journal of International Law
0012-883X	Eastern Kansas Register
0012-8848	Eastern Librarian
0012-8856	Eastern Metals Review *changed to* Engineering & Metals Review
0012-8864	Eastern News
0012-8872	Eastern Pharmacist
0012-8880	Eastern Railway Magazine
0012-8899	Eastern Massachusetts Regional Library System. Eastern Region News
0012-8902	Eastern Review Magazine *see* 0094-3649
0012-8910	Eastern School Law Review†
0012-8937	Eastern Trade Gazette *changed to* Eastern Trade
0012-8945	Eastern Utilization Research and Development Division. Publications and Patents *changed to* U.S. Department of Agriculture. Eastern Regional Research Center. Publications and Patents
0012-8953	Eastern Worker
0012-8961	Eastern World
0012-897X	Organic Chemical Bulletin *see* 0270-4265
0012-8996	Eaton Livia†
0012-9003	Information Eaux
0012-9011	Ebony
0012-902X	Ecclesia†
0012-9038	Ecclesia
0012-9046	Ecclesia *changed to* Kiongozi
0012-9054	Ecclesiastica Xaveriana *changed to* Theologica Xaveriana
0012-9089	Echo†
0012-9097	Echo†
0012-9119	Echo
0012-9127	Echo (Bethal)
0012-9135	Echo
0012-9143	Echo
0012-916X	Economic Echo from Yugoslavia *changed to* Yugoslavia Echo
0012-9178	Echo Africain
0012-9208	Echo de la Finance
0012-9224	Echo de la Liberte de l'Ouest
0012-9232	Echo de la Presse et de la Publicite
0012-9240	Echo de la Timbrologie
0012-9259	Echo de l'Imprimerie et des Arts Graphiques *see* 0012-9232
0012-9267	Echo des Depositaires des Libraires et des Marchands de Journaux
0012-9275	Echo des Eglises Wallonnes
0012-9283	Echo des Recherches
0012-9305	Echo uit Afrika *changed to* Echo uit Afrika en Andere Werelddelen
0012-9321	Echoes
0012-933X	Echoes
0012-9356	Echos du Monde Classique
0012-9372	Echo's voor de Textielkleinhandel†
0012-9380	Eclair†
0012-9402	Ecologae Geologicae Helvetiae
0012-9410	Eco
0012-9429	Eco Contemporaneo†
0012-9437	Eco-Cuoio delle Industrie e del Commercio del Cuoio e delle Calzature
0012-9445	Eco de Nayarit
0012-9453	Eco degli Oratori e dei Circoli Giovanili
0012-947X	Eco del Seguro
0012-9488	Eco della Riviera
0012-9496	Eco della Scuola Nuova
0012-9518	Eco dell'Educazione Ebraica
0012-9526	Eco dell'Industria Tessile
0012-9534	Eco d'Italia
0012-9542	Eco-Tessili
0012-9550	Ecole de Specialisation de l'Artillerie Anti-Aerienne. Bulletin d'Information
0012-9569	Ecole en Afrique†
0012-9577	Ecole et la Vie†
0012-9585	Ecole Maternelle Francaise
0012-9593	Ecole Normale Superieure. Annales Scientifiques
0012-9607	Ecologia Agraria
0012-9615	Ecological Monographs
0012-9623	Ecological Society of America. Bulletin
0012-9631	Ecologist†
0012-9658	Ecology
0012-9666	Ecology Today†
0012-9682	Econometrica
0012-9690	Economia†
0012-9704	Economia
0012-9712	Economia
0012-9720	Economia
0012-9747	Economia Aretina
0012-9763	Economia Dominicana
0012-9771	Economia e Credito
0012-978X	Economia e Lavoro
0012-9798	Economia e Storia†
0012-9801	Economia Internacional
0012-981X	Economia Internazionale
0012-9828	Economia Internazionale delle Fonti di Energia†
0012-9836	Economia Montana
0012-9844	Economia Mundial
0012-9852	Economia Nuova per Un Mondo Nuovo
0012-9860	Economia Salvadorena
0012-9879	Economia Trentina
0012-9887	Economia y Administracion
0012-9895	Economia y Ciencias Sociales
0012-9917	Economic Abstracts *see* 0165-4748
0012-9925	Economic Activity *changed to* Western Australia. Economic and Business Review
0012-9933	Economic and Business Bulletin *see* 0148-6195
0012-995X	Economic & Business Review
0012-9968	Economic and Financial Review†
0012-9976	Economic and Political Weekly
0012-9984	Economic and Social Review
0012-9992	East African Community. Economic and Statistical Review
0013-0001	Economic Botany
0013-001X	Economic Brief†
0013-0028	Commercial Bank of Greece. Economic Bulletin
0013-0044	Economic Bulletin of Ghana
0013-0079	Economic Development and Cultural Change
0013-0095	Economic Geography
0013-0109	Economic Geology *see* 0361-0128
0013-0117	Economic History Review
0013-0125	Economic Indicators
0013-0133	Economic Journal
0013-0141	Economic Leaflets
0013-015X	Economic News about Turkey†
0013-0168	Economic News
0013-0176	Economic News of Bulgaria
0013-0184	Economic Notes
0013-0192	Economic Observer†
0013-0206	Economic Opportunity Report
0013-0222	Economic Planning
0013-0249	Economic Record

0013-0257 Economic Report from Germany†
0013-0265 Economic Reporter
0013-0273 Economic Review
0013-0281 Economic Review
0013-029X Economic Review
0013-0303 Economic Review
0013-0311 Economic Review and Report *changed to* International Understanding
0013-032X Economic Review of the Arab World
0013-0346 Economic Situation in the Community *changed to* European Economy
0013-0354 Economic Society of Australia and New Zealand. New South Wales and Victorian Branches. Economic Papers
0013-0362 Economic Studies
0013-0370 Goetabanken
0013-0389 Economic Times
0013-0397 Economic Topics Series†
0013-0400 Economic Trends
0013-0419 Revista Economica
0013-0427 Economica
0013-0435 Economia de Cordoba
0013-0443 Economicos Tachydromos
0013-0451 Economics of Planning
0013-0478 Economie
0013-0494 Economie Appliquee
0013-0508 Economie Electrique†
0013-0524 Economie et Medecine Animales†
0013-0532 Economie in Limburg *changed to* G O M - Economie in Limburg
0013-0540 Economie Libanaise et Arabe
0013-0559 Economie Rurale
0013-0567 Economies et Societes. Serie EM. Economie Mathematique et Econometrie
0013-0575 Economisch en Sociaal Tijdschrift
0013-0583 Economisch-Statistische Berichten
0013-0613 Economist
0013-0621 Economist
0013-063X Economist
0013-0648 Economista
0013-0656 Economista
0013-0672 Economiste Egyptien
0013-0680 Ecos
0013-0699 Ecos de Portugal
0013-0702 Ecotass
0013-0710 Ecrits de Paris
0013-0761 Ecumenical Courier
0013-077X Czech Ecumenical News *changed to* Czechoslovak Ecumenical News
0013-0788 National†
0013-0796 Ecumenical Review
0013-080X Ecumentist
0013-0818 Edda
0013-0826 Die Edelkatze
0013-0842 Edesipar
0013-0877 Edilizia alle Fiere *see* 0393-8050
0013-0885 Edilizia Moderna†
0013-0893 Edinburgh Academy Chronicle
0013-0907 Edinburgh Dental Hospital Gazette†
0013-0915 Edinburgh Mathematical Society. Proceedings
0013-0923 Edition†
0013-0931 Editor†
0013-094X Editor & Publisher-the Fourth Estate
0013-0958 Editorial Research Reports
0013-0966 Editorials on File
0013-0974 Editor's Notebook†
0013-0982 Edizioni Nostre *changed to* Pagine Aperte
0013-0990 Edjer Grakanutian Yev Arvesdi
0013-1008 Edmonton Public Library. News Notes. *see* 0319-2156
0013-1016 Edmundite
0013-1024 EdPress Newsletter *changed to* EDPRESS News
0013-1032 Edubusiness†
0013-1067 Educacion
0013-1075 Educacion
0013-1083 Educacion Dental†
0013-1091 Educacion Medica y Salud
0013-1105 Educador Social†
0013-1113 Educadores
0013-1121 Educate†
0013-113X Educateur
0013-1148 Educateur et Bulletin Corporatif
0013-1156 Education (Sydney)
0013-1164 Education
0013-1172 Education
0013-1180 Education
0013-1199 Education†
0013-1202 Education *changed to* Education News
0013-1202 Education *see* 0259-207X
0013-1210 Education Abstracts†
0013-1229 Education and Culture *see* 0252-0958
0013-1237 Education and Training of the Mentally Retarded *changed to* Education and Training in Mental Retardation
0013-1245 Education and Urban Society
0013-1253 Education Canada
0013-1261 Education Daily
0013-127X Education Digest
0013-1288 Education Enfantine
0013-1296 Education Equipment
0013-130X Education Equipment and Services Review†
0013-1318 Education et Developpement
0013-1326 Education for Teaching *see* 0309-877X
0013-1334 Education Gazette
0013-1342 Victoria, Australia. Department of Education. Education Gazette and Teachers' Aid
0013-1350 Education in Chemistry
0013-1369 French News *changed to* France Education
0013-1377 Education in Science
0013-1385 Education Index
0013-1407 Education Libraries Bulletin
0013-1415 Education Musicale
0013-1423 Education
0013-1431 Education News
0013-144X Education Newsletter *changed to* Education San Diego County
0013-1458 Education of the Visually Handicapped
0013-1474 Education Physique et Sport
0013-1482 Education Quarterly
0013-1490 Education Quebecoise†
0013-1504 Education Recaps†
0013-1512 Education Reporter
0013-1520 Education Summary†
0013-1547 Education Today
0013-1563 Education Trends *changed to* Outlook in Education
0013-1571 Education U.S.A.
0013-158X Education Weekly†
0013-1598 Education Welfare Officer *see* 0263-0664
0013-1601 Educational Administration Abstracts
0013-161X Educational Administration Quarterly
0013-1628 Educational Administration Reporter†
0013-1644 Educational and Psychological Measurement
0013-1652 Educational Books and Equipment†
0013-1660 Educational Broadcasting Review *see* 0093-8149
0013-1679 Educational Bulletin *changed to* D P I Dispatch
0013-1687 Educational Courier†
0013-1695 Educational Development
0013-1725 Educational Forum
0013-1741 Educational Freedom
0013-175X Educational Horizons
0013-1768 Educational India
0013-1784 Educational Leadership
0013-1792 Educational Magazine†
0013-1806 Educational Marketer
0013-1814 Educational Media†
0013-1830 Transvaal. Education Department. Educational News Flashes
0013-1849 Educational Perspectives
0013-1857 Educational Philosophy and Theory
0013-1865 Educational Product Report *changed to* E P I E Publication Membership
0013-1873 Educational Record
0013-1881 Educational Research
0013-189X Educational Researcher
0013-1911 Educational Review
0013-192X Educational Review
0013-1938 Educational Screen and Audio Visual Guide *changed to* A V Guide: the Learning Media Magazine
0013-1946 Educational Studies
0013-1954 Educational Studies in Mathematics
0013-1962 Educational Technology
0013-1970 Educational Broadcasting International *see* 0262-0251
0013-1989 Educational Theatre Journal *see* 0192-2882
0013-1997 Educational Theatre News
0013-2004 Educational Theory
0013-2012 Educator *changed to* Guru Malaysia
0013-2020 Educator
0013-2055 Educator's Dispatch†
0013-2071 Educazione alla Sicurezza
0013-208X Educazione Musicale†
0013-2098 Educazione Sanitaria *see* 0391-6200
0013-2101 Eendracht *changed to* W I K
0013-211X Eendrachtbode†
0013-2128 Eerste Hulp†
0013-2136 Eesti Loodus
0013-2144 Akademiya Nauk Estonskoi S.S.R. Izvestiya. Biologiya
0013-2152 Eesti Post†
0013-2160 Efemerides Costarricenses†
0013-2179 Effektivt Forsvar†
0013-2187 Effektivt Landbrug
0013-2195 Effeta
0013-2209 Efficacy†
0013-2217 Effluent and Water Treatment Journal
0013-2225 Effort *changed to* Jeu de Dames
0013-2233 Efluvios†
0013-2241 Egerer Zeitung
0013-225X Egeszseg†
0013-2268 Egeszsegtudomany
0013-2276 Egeszsegugyi Gazdasagi Szemle
0013-2306 Egg Industry†
0013-2322 L'Eglise Canadienne
0013-2330 Eglise en Alsace
0013-2349 Eglise et Theologie
0013-2357 Eglise Qui Chante
0013-2365 Eglise Vivante†
0013-2373 Egretta
0013-2381 Egypt Travel Magazine
0013-239X Egypte Contemporaine
0013-2403 Egyptian Cotton Gazette
0013-2411 Egyptian Medical Association. Journal
0013-242X Egyptian Orthopaedic Journal
0013-2438 Egyptian Pharmaceutical Journal†
0013-2446 Egyptian Public Health Association Journal
0013-2454 Egyptian Surgical Society Quarterly Review
0013-2462 Ehe *changed to* Partner Beratung
0013-2470 Ehe und Familie
0013-2489 Rundbrief Ehemaliger Schueler und Freunde der Schulbrueder
0013-2497 Eichholzbrief
0013-2500 Eier-Wild-Gefluegel-Markt
0013-2519 Eigen Huis *changed to* Eigen Huis en Interieur
0013-2527 Eigene Garten - Eigene Haus *changed to* Das Eigene Haus
0013-2543 Film Making
0013-2551 Eight O'Clock *changed to* Sunday Star
0013-256X 1820 *changed to* Settler
0013-2578 1860 Settler
0013-2586 Eighteenth-Century Studies
0013-2594 Eighteen Month Forecast of Japan's Economy *see* 0910-075X
0013-2608 Eigse
0013-2624 Eimreidin
0013-2632 Ein- und Verkaufsfuehrer der Oesterreichischen Uhren- und Schmuckwirtschaft
0013-2640 Eine Welt der Vereinten Nationen
0013-2659 Einheit
0013-2667 Einheit und Fortschritt†
0013-2683 Eire-Ireland
0013-2705 Eisbericht
0013-2713 Eisdiele & Milchbar†
0013-273X Journal of Hygienic Chemistry
0013-2756 Eisenbahn
0013-2764 Eisenbahn-Amateur
0013-2772 Eisenbahn-Landwirt
0013-2780 Eisenbahnpraxis
0013-2799 Eisenbahner
0013-2802 Eisenbahner. Ausgabe A & B *changed to* D B
0013-2810 Der Eisenbahningenieur
0013-2829 Eisenbahntechnik
0013-2837 Eisenbahn-technische Praxis
0013-2845 Eisenbahntechnische Rundschau
0013-2853 Eisenwaren-Boerse
0013-2861 Eisenwaren-Zeitung
0013-287X Eisma's Schildersblad
0013-2888 Either/Or†
0013-2896 Ejendomsmaegleren
0013-2918 Ejercito
0013-2926 Ekalabya
0013-2934 Ekistic Index
0013-2942 Ekistics
0013-2969 Wiadomosci Ekologiczne
0013-2977 Ekonomen
0013-2985 Ekonomia†
0013-2993 Ikonomiceska Misal
0013-3000 Ekonomicheskii Byulleten Niderlandov
0013-3019 Ekonomicheskie Nauki
0013-3027 Ekonomicko-Matematicky Obzor
0013-3035 Ekonomicky Casopis
0013-3051 Ekonomika i Zhizn'
0013-306X Ekonomika Poljoprivreda
0013-3078 Ekonomika Preduzeca *changed to* Ekonomika Udruzenog Rada
0013-3086 Ekonomika Radyanskoi Ukrainy
0013-3094 Ekonomika Sel'skogo Khozyaistva
0013-3108 Ekonomika Stavebnictva
0013-3116 Ekonomika Stroitel'stva
0013-3124 Ekonomika Zemedelstvi *changed to* Ekonomika Polnohospodarstva
0013-3132 Ekonomicheskaya Gazeta
0013-3167 Ekonomisk Revy†
0013-3175 Ekonomiska Laeget†
0013-3183 Ekonomiska Samfundets Tidskrift
0013-3191 Ekonomist
0013-3205 Ekonomista
0013-3213 Ekonomska Analiza/Economic Analysis *see* 0351-286X
0013-3221 Radna Jedinica *changed to* Organizacija Samoupravljanja OUR
0013-323X Ekonomska Misao
0013-3256 Ekonomska Revija
0013-3264 Ekonomski Anali
0013-3272 Ekonomski Glasnik
0013-3299 Ekran
0013-3302 Ekran
0013-3310 Zhurnal Eksperimental'noi i Klinicheskoi Meditsiny
0013-3329 Eksperimental'naya Khirurgiya i Anesteziologiya *see* 0201-7563
0013-3353 Ekspress-Informatsiya. Automobilestroenie†
0013-3361 Ekspress-Informatsiya. Avtomobil'nyi Transport†
0013-3396 Ekspress-Informatsiya. Elektricheskie Mashiny i Apparaty†
0013-340X Ekspress-Informatsiya. Elektricheskie Stantsii, Seti i Sistemy†
0013-3426 Ekspress-Informatsiya. Fotokinoapparatura. Nauchnaya i Prikladnaya Fotografiya†
0013-3434 Ekspress-Informatsiya. Garazhi i Garazhnoe Oborudovanie†
0013-3442 Ekspress-Informatsiya. Gidroenergetika†
0013-3450 Ekspress-Informatsiya. Gornorudnaya Promyshlennost'†
0013-3477 Ekspress-Informatsiya. Iskusstvennye Sooruzheniya na Avtomobil'nykh Dorogakh†
0013-3493 Ekspress-Informatsiya. Khimicheskaya Tekhnologiya Pererabotki Vysokopolimernykh Materialov†
0013-3507 Ekspress-Informatsiya. Khimiya i Pererabotka Nefti i Gaza†
0013-3515 Ekspress-Informatsiya. Khimia i Tekhnologiya Neorganicheskikh Veshchestv†
0013-354X Ekspress-Informatsiya. Kozhevenno-Obuvnaya Promyshlennost' *changed to* Ekspress-Informatsiya. Kozhevennaya Promyshlennost'

ISSN INDEX 1229

0013-354X Ekspress-Informatsiya. Kozhevenno-Obuvnaya Promyshlennost' *changed to* Ekspress-Informatsiya. Obuvnaya Promyshlennost'
0013-3558 Ekspress-Informatsiya. Lokomotivostroenie Vagonostroenie†
0013-3574 Ekspress-Informatsiya. Myasnaya i Molochnaya Promyshlennost'†
0013-3582 Ekspress-Informatsiya. Nefte- i Gazodobyvayushchaya Promyshlennost'†
0013-3590 Ekspress-Informatsiya. Obogashchenie Poleznykh Iskopaemykh†
0013-3612 Ekspress-Informatsiya. Pishchevaya Promyshlennost'†
0013-3620 Ekspress-Informatsiya. Pod'emno-Transportnoe Mashinostroenie†
0013-368X Ekspress-Informatsiya. Protsessy i Apparaty Khimicheskikh Proizvodstv *see* 0207-5024
0013-3698 Ekspress-Informatsiya. Put' i Stroitel'stvo Zheleznykh Dorog *see* 0134-7683
0013-3701 Ekspress-Informatsiya. Radiolokatsiya, Televidenie, Radiosvyaz'†
0013-371X Ekspress-Informatziya. Radiotekhnika Sverkhvysokikh Chastot i Kvantovaya Radiotekhnika *see* 0131-0437
0013-371X Ekspress-Informatsiya. Radiotekhnika Sverkhvysokikh Chastot i Kvantovaya Radiotekhnika *see* 0131-0208
0013-3736 Ekspress-Informatsiya. Rybnaya Promyshlennost'†
0013-3744 Ekspress-Informatsiya. Sel'skokhozyaistvennye Mashiny i Orudiya. Mekhanizatsiya Sel'skokhozyaistvennykh Rabot†
0013-3752 Ekspress-Informatsiya. Silikatnye Stroitel'nye Materialy†
0013-3787 Ekspress-Informatsiya. Steklo, Keramika i Ogneupory†
0013-3795 Ekspress-Informatsiya. Stroitel'stvo i Ekspluatatsiya Avtomobilnykh Dorog†
0013-3809 Ekspress-Informatsiya. Sudostroenie†
0013-3825 Ekspress-Informatsiya. Tara i Upakovka *see* 0131-0526
0013-3833 Ekspress-Informatsiya. Tekhnicheskaya Ekspluatatsiya Podvizhnogo Sostava i Tyaga Poezdov†
0013-3884 Ekspress-Informatsiya. Tekstil'naya Promyschlennost'†
0013-3892 Ekspress-Informatsiya. Teoriya i Praktika Nauchnoi Informatsii†
0013-3906 Ekspress-Informatsiya. Teploenergetika†
0013-3914 Ekspress-Informatsiya. Traktorostroenie†
0013-3922 Ekspress-Informatsiya. Transport i Khranenie Nefti i Gaza†
0013-3930 Ekspress-Informatsiya. Tsellyulozno-Bumazhnaya Promyshlennost'†
0013-3957 Ekspress-Informatsiya. Ugol'naya Promyshlennost'†
0013-3965 Ekspress-Informatsiya. Vodnyi Transport†
0013-3973 Ekspress-Informatsiya. Vozdushnyi Transport†
0013-3981 Ekspress-Informatsiya. Vychislitel'naya Tekhnika†
0013-399X El
0013-4007 El Branschen
0013-4023 El Paso Archaeology
0013-4031 El Paso Economic Review *see* 8750-6033
0013-404X El Salvador. Direccion General de Estadistica y Censos. Boletin Estadistico
0013-4058 Elam
0013-4066 Elan
0013-4074 Elder Statesman
0013-4082 Elders
0013-4090 E L D O - E S R O Scientific and Technical Review *see* 0379-2285
0013-4104 Electra
0013-4112 Electric Heat and Air Conditioning *see* 0190-1370
0013-4139 Electric Power Statistics (Washington)†
0013-4147 Electric Railway Society. Journal
0013-4155 Electric Technology U.S.S.R.
0013-4163 Electric Traction *see* 0818-5204
0013-4171 Electric Vehicles for Industry *changed to* Electric Vehicles
0013-418X Electrical & Electronic Trader
0013-421X Electrical and Electronics Incorporated Engineers *see* 0306-8552
0013-4228 Electrical and Radio Trading
0013-4236 Electrical Apparatus Service-Volt/Age *see* 0190-1370
0013-4244 Electrical Business
0013-4252 Electrical Communication
0013-4260 Electrical Construction and Maintenance
0013-4279 Electrical Contractor (Sydney)
0013-4287 Electrical Contractor and Maintenance Supervisor *changed to* Electricity Canada
0013-4295 Electrical Contractor and Retailer *see* 0308-7174
0013-4309 Electrical Engineer
0013-4317 Electrical Equipment
0013-4325 Electrical Equipment *changed to* E E-Electronic/Electrical Product News
0013-4333 Electrical Equipment News
0013-435X Electrical India
0013-4376 Electrical Power Engineer
0013-4384 Electrical Review
0013-4414 Electrical Times
0013-4422 Electrical Wholesaler
0013-4430 Electrical Wholesaling
0013-4449 Electrical Workers' Journal *changed to* I B E W Journal
0013-4457 Electrical World
0013-4465 Electricidade *see* 0870-5364
0013-4481 Electricite
0013-449X Electricite de France. Direction des Etudes et Recherches. Bulletin. Serie A: Nucleaire, Hydraulique, Thermique
0013-4503 Electricite de France. Direction des Etudes et Recherches. Bulletin. Serie B: Reseaux Electriques, Materiels Electriques
0013-4511 Electricite de France. Direction des Etudes et Recherches. Bulletin. Serie C: Mathematiques-Informatique
0013-452X Electricite pour Vous *changed to* Pour Vous
0013-4538 Electricity and Electronics
0013-4546 Electricity in Building *see* 0362-1324
0013-4562 Electrified Industry *see* 0194-4746
0013-4589 Electro Optics
0013-4597 Electrophysiological Technologists' Association. Proceedings and Journal *see* 0307-5095
0013-4600 Electro-Procurement *see* 0163-6197
0013-4619 Electro Radio Mercuur *changed to* E R M
0013-4627 Elektrotechniek
0013-4635 Electro-Technology†
0013-4643 Electro-Technology
0013-4651 Electrochemical Society. Journal
0013-466X Electrochemical Society of India. Journal
0013-4678 Electrochemical Society of Japan. Journal (Denki Kagaku) *changed to* Electrochemistry and Industrial Physical Chemistry
0013-4686 Electrochimica Acta
0013-4694 Electroencephalography and Clinical Neurophysiology
0013-4708 Electrolysis Digest†
0013-4716 Electromechanical Design†
0013-4732 Electromyography *see* 0301-150X
0013-4740 Electron†
0013-4759 Electron *changed to* Sound & Vision
0013-4767 Electron
0013-4775 Electroanalytical Abstracts†
0013-4783 Electronic Age†
0013-4791 Electronic & Appliance Specialist†
0013-4805 S.E.R.T. Journal *see* 0141-061X
0013-4813 Electronic Application News
0013-4821 Electronic Applications Bulletin *changed to* Electronic Components and Applications
0013-483X Electronics Today *see* 0047-9624
0013-4848 Electronic Capabilities†
0013-4864 Electronic Components *see* 0307-2401
0013-4872 Electronic Design
0013-4880 Electronic Distributing and Marketing *changed to* Electronic Purchaser
0013-4899 Electronic Engineer *changed to* E E Systems Engineering Today
0013-4902 Electronic Engineering
0013-4910 Electronic Equipment News
0013-4929 Electronic Instrument Digest†
0013-4937 Electronic News
0013-4945 Electronic Packaging and Production
0013-4953 Electronic Products Magazine
0013-4961 Electronic Progress
0013-497X Electronic Servicing *see* 0278-9922
0013-4988 Electronic Technician *see* 0278-9922
0013-4996 Electronics Trends (Washington) *changed to* Electronic Market Trends
0013-5011 Electronic Trends: International†
0013-502X Electronica†
0013-5046 Elternblatt†
0013-5054 Electronica y Fisica Aplicada†
0013-5062 Electronicien
0013-5070 Electronics *see* 0883-4989
0013-5097 Electronics Abstracts Journal *see* 0361-3313
0013-5100 Electronics and Communications†
0013-5119 Electronics and Communications Abstracts
0013-5127 Electronics and Power
0013-5135 Electronics Australia
0013-5143 Electronics Digest†
0013-516X Electronics for You
0013-5178 Electronics Illustrated *see* 8755-0423
0013-5186 Electronics and Instrumentation *changed to* Current
0013-5194 Electronics Letters
0013-5208 Electronics Record†
0013-5216 Electronics Today *see* 0142-7229
0013-5224 Electronics Weekly
0013-5232 Electronics World†
0013-5259 Electronique Industrielle *see* 0398-1851
0013-5267 Electronique Medicale†
0013-5283 Electronique Professionnelle Belge
0013-5305 Electroplating and Metal Finishing *see* 0264-2506
0013-5313 Electrotecnia Popular
0013-5321 Electrotehnica *changed to* Electrotehnica, Electronica si Automatica. Electrotehnica
0013-5348 Eleftherotypia
0013-5372 Elektricheskie Stantsii
0013-5380 Elektrichestvo
0013-5399 Elektrie
0013-5402 Elektrik Muhendisligi
0013-5410 Elektrikeren
0013-5437 Elektrische Bahnen
0013-5445 E M A - Elektrische Maschinen
0013-5461 Die Elektrizitaet
0013-547X Elektrizitaet *see* 0340-7519
0013-5488 Elektrizitaetsverwertung†
0013-5496 Elektrizitaetswirtschaft
0013-550X Elektro
0013-5518 Elektro-Anzeiger
0013-5542 E H - Elektro Handel
0013-5550 Elektro Nachrichten†
0013-5569 Der Elektro-Praktiker
0013-5577 Elektromarkt
0013-5585 Biomedizinische Technik
0013-5607 Elektron *see* 0374-3098
0013-5615 Electronaut
0013-5623 Elektronica en Telecommunicatie *changed to* Nederlands Elektronica- en Radiogenootschap. Tijdschrift.
0013-5631 Elektronik *see* 0109-2359
0013-564X Elektronik-Teknik & Marknad *changed to* Elektroniknyheterna
0013-5658 Elektronik
0013-5666 Elektronik-Anzeiger *see* 0720-101X
0013-5674 Elektronik Journal
0013-5690 Elektronikk
0013-5704 Angewandte Informatik
0013-5712 Journal of Information Processing and Cybernetics
0013-5720 Elektronische Rechenanlagen mit Computer-Praxis *changed to* Informationstechnik - I T
0013-5739 Elektronnaya Obrabotka Materialov
0013-5747 Elektronorm *see* 0011-4952
0013-5755 Elektroprivreda *changed to* Elektroprivreda Jugoslavije
0013-5763 Elektropromishlenost i Priborostroene
0013-5771 Elektrosvyaz'
0013-578X Elektrotechnicky Casopis
0013-5798 Elektrotechnicky Obzor
0013-581X Elektrotechnik
0013-5828 Elektrotehnicar
0013-5844 Elektrotehnika
0013-5852 Elektrotehniski Vestnik
0013-5860 Elektrotekhnika
0013-5887 Elektrowirtschaft
0013-5895 Elektuur
0013-5909 Elelmezesi Ipar
0013-5917 Elelmiszertudomany *see* 0139-3006
0013-5933 Elementa
0013-5941 Elementary Counselor *see* 0036-6536
0013-595X Elementary Electronics *see* 0279-070X
0013-5968 Elementary English *see* 0360-9170
0013-5976 Elementary School Guidance & Counseling
0013-5984 Elementary School Journal
0013-5992 Elementary Teacher's Ideas and Materials Workshop
0013-600X Elemente
0013-6018 Elemente der Mathematik
0013-6026 Elements, Produits, Services
0013-6042 Elenco dei Quotidiani e Periodici Italiani†
0013-6050 Elenco Ufficiale dei Protesti Cambiari Levati Nella Provincia di Torino
0013-6069 Elepaio
0013-6077 Elet es Tudomany
0013-6085 Eletronica Popular *see* 0101-9112
0013-6093 Elettrificazione
0013-6115 Elettrodomus†
0013-6123 Elettronica e Telecomunicazioni
0013-6131 Elettrotecnica
0013-6158 Elevator World
0013-6166 Eleventh District Dental Society. Bulletin
0013-6182 Elim Evangel
0013-6190 Elinstallatoeren
0013-6204 Eliot Sharp's Tax Exempt Newsletter *changed to* Eliot Sharp's Municipal Newsletter
0013-6212 Elisabethbode
0013-6220 Elisha Mitchell Scientific Society. Journal
0013-6247 Elizabeth†
0013-6255 Elizabethan†
0013-6263 Elks Magazine
0013-6298 Elle
0013-6301 Ellery Queen's Anthology
0013-631X Ellery Queen's Mystery Magazine. Braille Edition†
0013-6328 Ellery Queen's Mystery Magazine
0013-6336 Ellinika
0013-6352 Eloquenza
0013-6379 Elovilag *see* 0007-7356
0013-6395 Elseviers Magazine
0013-6409 Elsevier Select
0013-6417 Elta
0013-6425 Elteknik *see* 0346-6310
0013-6433 Schweizer Zeitschrift fuer die Junge Familie *changed to* Wir Eltern
0013-6441 Elternblatt
0013-645X Der Elternbrief
0013-6468 Eltheto†
0013-6484 Elvis Monthly
0013-6506 Emajl-Keramika-Staklo
0013-6522 Emantalehti
0013-6530 Embalagem
0013-6557 Emballage Digest
0013-6565 Emballage Moderne *see* 0247-8390
0013-6573 Emballages
0013-6581 Emballering
0013-6603 Embotellador *changed to* Beverage World (Spanish Edition)
0013-6611 Embroidery
0013-662X Ementario da Legislacao do Petroleo

ISSN	Title
0013-6638	Ementario Forense
0013-6646	Emergency Health Services Newsletter†
0013-6654	Emergency Medicine
0013-6662	Emerita
0013-6697	Emigrato Italiano
0013-6700	Emigrazione
0013-6719	Emmanuel
0013-6727	Emory Magazine
0013-6743	Forum (Syracuse)
0013-676X	Empire State Geogram
0013-6786	Empire State Iris Society Newsletter
0013-6794	Empire State Mason
0013-6808	Employee Benefit Plan Review
0013-6816	Employee Relations Bulletin see 0744-7779
0013-6824	Employee Relations in Action
0013-6832	Employers' Review
0013-6840	U.S. Bureau of Labor Statistics. Employment and Earnings
0013-6859	Great Britain. Department of Employment. Employment Gazette
0013-6875	Employment Relations Abstracts see 0273-3234
0013-6883	Employment Review
0013-6891	Empoli
0013-6905	Empress Chinchilla Breeder
0013-6913	Emuna†
0013-6921	En Avant
0013-693X	En Concreto
0013-6956	En Haa†
0013-6964	En Marche
0013-6972	En Viaje†
0013-6980	Enact
0013-6999	Enamelling Newsletter†
0013-7006	Encephale
0013-7057	Encore: a Quarterly of Verse & Poetic Arts
0013-7065	Encounter†
0013-7073	Encounter
0013-7081	Encounter (Indianapolis)
0013-709X	Encounter Today†
0013-7103	Encres Vives
0013-7111	Encuentro†
0013-712X	Encyclopaedia Africana. Information Report
0013-7138	Encyclopaedia Moderna†
0013-7146	Encyclopedie Politique Arabe. Documents et Notes
0013-7154	End-Use Markets for Plastics
0013-7170	Endeavour
0013-7200	Endocrinologia Experimentalis
0013-7219	Endocrinologia Japonica
0013-7227	Endocrinology
0013-7235	Endocrinology Index†
0013-7243	Endocrinologya y Terapeutica†
0013-7251	Endokrinologie changed to Experimental and Clinical Endocrinology
0013-726X	Endoscopy
0013-7278	Energetik
0013-7286	Energetika
0013-7294	Energetyka
0013-7308	Energia Elettrica
0013-7316	Energia es Atomtechnika
0013-7324	Energia Nuclear
0013-7332	Energia Nucleare†
0013-7340	Energie†
0013-7359	Energie changed to Energie Spektrum
0013-7405	Energieanwendung
0013-7421	Energietechnik
0013-743X	Energiewirtschaftliche Tagesfragen
0013-7448	Energija
0013-7456	Energomashinostroenie
0013-7464	Energy changed to Energy Dialogue
0013-7472	Energy and Character
0013-7480	Energy Conversion see 0196-8904
0013-7502	Energy Developments†
0013-7510	Energy Info†
0013-7529	Energy International see 0260-7840
0013-7537	Energy Management Report issued with 0031-6466
0013-7545	Enfance
0013-7553	Enfant
0013-7561	Enfant en Milieu Tropical
0013-757X	Enfants du Monde
0013-7596	Enfys
0013-7618	Engage see 0164-5528
0013-7626	Japanese Society for Horticultural Science. Journal
0013-7634	New Information on Horticulture changed to New Information on Horticulture: Flowers
0013-7634	New Information on Horticulture changed to New Information on Horticulture: Vegetables
0013-7642	Engelhard Industries Technical Bulletin†
0013-7669	Engenharia†
0013-7707	Engenharia changed to Engenharia Civil
0013-7723	Engenheiro Moderno†
0013-774X	Engine Data Sheets
0013-7758	Engineer
0013-7766	Engineer of Southern California see 0277-3183
0013-7774	Engineering changed to Engineering Times
0013-7782	Engineering
0013-7790	Engineering Construction World see 0020-6415
0013-7804	Engineering and Contract Record changed to Canadian Construction Record
0013-7812	Engineering and Science
0013-7839	Engineering Bulletin†
0013-7855	Engineering Capacity Register see 0306-0179
0013-7871	Engineering: Cornell Quarterly
0013-788X	Engineering Cybernetics changed to Soviet Journal of Computer & Systems Sciences
0013-7898	Engineering Designer†
0013-7901	Engineering Digest
0013-791X	Engineering Economist
0013-7928	Facts from Gatorland†
0013-7936	Engineering Forum
0013-7944	Engineering Fracture Mechanics
0013-7952	Engineering Geology
0013-7960	Engineering Index see 0162-3036
0013-7979	Engineering Index Card-A-Lert†
0013-7987	Engineering Industries & Trade Journal
0013-7995	Engineering Industries Journal changed to Engineering Industries Gazette
0013-8010	Engineering Journal see 0013-7901
0013-8029	Engineering Journal
0013-8037	Engineering Manpower Bulletin
0013-8053	Engineering Production†
0013-8061	Engineering News
0013-807X	Engineering News-Record changed to E N R
0013-8088	Engineering Outlook at the University of Illinois at Urbana-Champaign changed to Engineering Outlook
0013-810X	Engineering Research News
0013-8118	Engineering Societies of New England. Journal changed to New England Engineering Journal
0013-8126	Engineering Technician in the News changed to Certified Engineering Technician
0013-8134	Engineering Times
0013-8142	Engineers and Engines Magazine
0013-8150	Engineers' Club of St. Louis. Journal changed to Gateway Engineer
0013-8169	Engineers' Digest
0013-8177	Coast Guard Engineer's Digest
0013-8185	English
0013-8193	Englisch an Volkshochschulen see 0342-6173
0013-8215	English
0013-8223	English Churchman changed to English Churchman & St. James's Chronicle
0013-8231	English Dance and Song
0013-824X	English for Immigrants†
0013-8266	English Historical Review
0013-8274	English Journal
0013-8282	English Language Notes
0013-8290	English Language Teaching see 0307-8337
0013-8304	E L H
0013-8312	English Literary Renaissance
0013-8312	English Literary Renaissance Supplements
0013-8339	English Fiction in Transition see 0364-3549
0013-8355	English Quarterly
0013-8363	English Record
0013-8371	English-Speaking Union News changed to E-S U News
0013-838X	English Studies
0013-8398	English Studies in Africa
0013-8401	English Westerners' Brand Book
0013-841X	English Westerners' Tally Sheet
0013-8436	Enigma
0013-8444	Engineers
0013-8460	Vinyls and Polymers
0013-8479	Enlightenment Essays
0013-8487	Enlite†
0013-8495	Enoch Pratt Free Library. Staff Reporter
0013-8509	Enquiry
0013-8517	Enquiry
0013-8533	Ensanian Physicochemical Institute. Journal
0013-8541	Enjay Magazine changed to Chemsphere Americas
0013-855X	Ensayo
0013-8576	Techniques Industrielles see 0768-9454
0013-8584	Enseignement Mathematique
0013-8592	Ensemble†
0013-8606	Ensign
0013-8614	Ensino Secundario
0013-8622	Ente Provinciale per Il Turismo di Nuoro. Notiziario
0013-8630	Entente Africaine
0013-8657	Enterprise
0013-8665	Enterprise†
0013-8673	Enterprise
0013-8681	Enterprise
0013-8703	Entomologia Experimentalis et Applicata
0013-8711	Entomologica Scandinavica
0013-872X	Entomological News
0013-8738	Entomological Review
0013-8746	Entomological Society of America. Annals
0013-8754	Entomological Society of America. Bulletin
0013-8762	Entomological Society of India. Bulletin of Entomology
0013-8770	Entomology changed to Insect
0013-8789	Entomological Society of Southern Africa. Journal
0013-8797	Entomological Society of Washington. Proceedings
0013-8800	Entomologie et Phytopathologie Appliquees
0013-8819	Entomologische Arbeiten aus dem Museum G. Frey, Tutzing-Bei Muenchen†
0013-8827	Entomologische Berichten
0013-8835	Entomologische Blaetter fuer Biologie und Systematik der Kaefer
0013-8843	Entomologische Zeitschrift
0013-8851	Entomologiske Meddelelser
0013-886X	Entomologisk Tidskrift
0013-8886	Entomologiste
0013-8894	Entomologist's Gazette
0013-8908	Entomologist's Monthly Magazine
0013-8916	Entomologist's Record
0013-8924	Entomology Abstracts
0013-8932	Florida. Department of Agriculture and Consumer Services. Entomology Circular
0013-8940	South Africa. Department of Agricultural Technical Services. Entomology Memoirs changed to South Africa. Department of Agriculture. Entomology Memoirs
0013-8959	Entomophaga
0013-8975	Entr'Acte
0013-8991	Entre/Nous changed to Hydro-Presse
0013-9033	Entrepreneur en Plomberie-Chauffage see 0032-1591
0013-9041	Entrepreneur Menuisier
0013-905X	Entreprise
0013-9084	Entropie
0013-9092	Entscheidung
0013-9149	Environment†
0013-9157	Environment
0013-9165	Environment and Behavior
0013-9173	Environment and Planning see 0308-518X
0013-9181	Environment Information Access see 0093-3287
0013-919X	Environment Monthly†
0013-9203	Environment Report
0013-9211	Environment Reporter
0013-922X	Environmental Action
0013-9238	Environmental Control News for Southern Industry
0013-9254	Environmental Education see 0095-8964
0013-9262	Environmental Engineering see 0374-356X
0013-9270	Environmental Health
0013-9289	Environmental Health changed to Indian Journal of Environmental Health
0013-9319	Environmental Mutagen Society Newsletter changed to Mutation Research
0013-9327	Environmental Pollution see 0143-1471
0013-9327	Environmental Pollution see 0143-148X
0013-9343	Environmental Quarterly†
0013-9351	Environmental Research
0013-936X	Environmental Science & Technology
0013-9386	Environmental Spectrum
0013-9394	Envoi
0013-9408	Envoy (Pittsburg)
0013-9416	Enzymes in Medicine†
0013-9424	Enzymologia see 0300-8177
0013-9432	Enzyme
0013-9475	Epatologia
0013-9491	Ephemerides Iuris Canonici
0013-9505	Ephemerides Liturgicae
0013-9513	Ephemerides Theologicae Lovanienses
0013-9521	L'Epicier
0013-953X	Epicure†
0013-9548	Epicurean
0013-9556	Epidemiological Review†
0013-9564	Epigraphia Indica
0013-9572	Epigraphica
0013-9580	Epilepsia
0013-9610	Episcopal Recorder
0013-9629	Episcopalian
0013-9645	Epistemologie Sociologique†
0013-9653	Epistolodidaktika
0013-9661	Epites- Epiteszettudomany
0013-967X	Epitesugyi Szemle
0013-9688	Genike Stratiotike Epitheoresis†
0013-9696	Greek Review of Social Research
0013-970X	Epitoanyag
0013-9718	Epoca
0013-9726	Epoca
0013-9734	Epos, a Quarterly of Poetry†
0013-9742	Epuletgepeszet
0013-9750	Equal Justice†
0013-9777	Equal Opportunity in Federal Government changed to Spotlight on Affirmative Employment Programs
0013-9815	Equals One
0013-9831	Equestrian Trails
0013-984X	Equinews
0013-9874	Equipment Industriel†
0013-9882	Equipment Mechanique des Chantiers changed to Equipement Mecanique, Carrieres et Materiaux
0013-9890	Equity News
0013-9912	Er Ruft
0013-9920	Era changed to Philomel
0013-9939	E R A
0013-9947	Eranos
0013-9963	Erbe und Auftrag
0013-9971	Ercilla
0013-998X	Erdbau†
0013-9998	Die Erde
0014-0007	Erdkreis
0014-0015	Erdkunde
0014-0031	Az Erdo
0014-004X	Erdoel-Erdgas Zeitschrift see 0179-3187
0014-0058	Erdoel und Kohle, Erdgas, Petrochemie

ISSN INDEX 1231

ISSN	Title
0014-0066	Erdogazdasag es Faipar
0014-0074	Erevna
0014-0082	Erfahrungsheilkunde
0014-0090	Erfahrungswissenschaftliche Blaetter
0014-0104	Erfolgs- und Erwerbspost
0014-0112	Ergokratische Schule fuer Dauernden. Frieden (Publication) *changed to* Die Ergokratische Schule
0014-0120	Ergonomia
0014-0139	Ergonomics
0014-0147	Erhversoekonomisk Tidsskrift
0014-0155	Erhvervs-Bladet
0014-0163	Eric/Crier Newsletter†
0014-0171	Ericsson Review
0014-018X	Ericsson Technics†
0014-0201	Ermlandbriefe
0014-021X	Ernaehrungs-Umschau
0014-0228	Ernaehrungsdienst
0014-0236	Die Ernaehrungsindustrie
0014-0252	Eroeffnungen
0014-0260	Erre U
0014-0279	Die Ersatzkasse
0014-0309	Erwerbsobstbau
0014-0317	Dynamic†
0014-0325	Erziehung und Unterricht
0014-0333	Erziehungskunst
0014-0341	Escalpelo
0014-0368	Escort†
0014-0376	Escribano *changed to* Escribano
0014-0384	Escrow Newsletter†
0014-0392	Escudo†
0014-0422	Universidad de Panama. Escuela de Bibliotecologia. Boletin *changed to* Universidad de Panama. Departamento de Bibliotecologia. Boletin
0014-0430	Argentina. Escuela Superior de Guerra. Revista *changed to* Argentina. Escuela de Defensa Nacional. Revista
0014-0449	Escursionismo
0014-0457	Escutcheon†
0014-0481	Espaces et Societes
0014-049X	Espana Agraria *changed to* Espana Agricola
0014-0546	Espanol en Australia
0014-0554	Espansione
0014-0562	Esparavel
0014-0570	Espectaculos†
0014-0589	Espectador
0014-0597	Espejo†
0014-0600	Esperanta Ligilo
0014-0619	Der Esperantist
0014-0635	Esperanto
0014-0643	Esperanto en Skotlando
0014-0651	Esperanto-Gazeto†
0014-066X	Esperanto-Lingvo Internacia
0014-0678	Esperienza
0014-0686	Esperienze Amministrative
0014-0694	Espero
0014-0708	Espiral†
0014-0716	Espiritu
0014-0724	Espoir
0014-0732	Espoir du Monde
0014-0740	Esportazione
0014-0759	Esprit
0014-0767	Esprit Createur
0014-0775	Esprit et Vie
0014-0783	Esprit Libre
0014-0791	Esquire *see* 0194-9535
0014-0805	Esquire's Good Grooming Guide†
0014-0813	Esquiu
0014-0821	N O A A†
0014-083X	Essay and General Literature Index
0014-0848	Essay Proof Journal
0014-0856	Essays in Criticism
0014-0864	Essays in Economics†
0014-0880	Essence
0014-0902	Essenze-Derivati Agrumari
0014-0910	Essex Countryside
0014-0937	Essex County Medical Society. Bulletin
0014-0945	Essex Farmers Journal *changed to* Essex Farmer
0014-0953	Essex Institute. Historical Collections
0014-0961	Essex Journal
0014-097X	Esso Agricola
0014-0988	Esso Air World *changed to* Exxon Air World
0014-0996	Esso Aviation News Digest *changed to* Exxon Aviation News Digest
0014-1003	Esso Dealer
0014-102X	Esso News *changed to* Esso in Malaysia
0014-1038	Esso Rivista
0014-1046	Essobron
0014-1062	Essor du Comminges
0014-1089	Est
0014-1100	Est Sesia
0014-1127	Estacion Experimental. Dr. Mario Cassinoni. Facultad de Agronomia. Boletin Tecnico†
0014-1135	Estadistica
0014-1151	Spain. Instituto Nacional de Estadistica. Estadistica Espanola
0014-1178	Folha Mensal do Estado das Culturas e Previsao de Colheitas *see* 0870-2594
0014-1186	Estafeta Literaria *see* 0210-0835
0014-1194	Estano
0014-1208	Estanzuela - Investigacion Agricola†
0014-1216	Estate Planning (Englewood Cliffs)
0014-1224	Estate Planning Checklists and Forms
0014-1240	Estates Gazette
0014-1259	Estates Times
0014-1267	Est et Ouest
0014-1275	Estetica Ambrosiana
0014-1283	Esteticka Vychova
0014-1291	Estetika
0014-1313	Estetyka†
0014-1321	Estheticienne
0014-133X	Estilo *see* 0325-0229
0014-1356	Estomatologia†
0014-1372	Estonian Events *changed to* Baltic Events
0014-1380	Extra Twenty-Two Hundred South
0014-1399	Estrella†
0014-1410	Estudios Americanos†
0014-1429	Estudios Andinos
0014-1437	Estudios Biblicos
0014-1445	Estudios Centro Americanos
0014-1453	Estudios Clasicos
0014-1461	Estudios de Derecho
0014-147X	Estudios de Historia Moderna y Contemporanea de Mexico
0014-1496	Estudios Geograficos
0014-150X	Estudios Historicos sobre San Sebastian. Boletin
0014-1518	Estudios Internacionales†
0014-1542	Estudios Sindicales y Cooperativos†
0014-1550	Estudios sobre el Communismo
0014-1569	Estudios Sobre Hospitales
0014-1577	Estudios Sobre la Union Sovietica†
0014-1585	Estudos Agronomicos†
0014-1607	Estudos Leopoldenses
0014-1623	Estudos Politicos e Sociais
0014-1631	L'Etain et ses Usages
0014-164X	ETC
0014-1658	Eter-Aktuellt
0014-1666	Eterna Sabiduria - Spanish Braille for Theosophists†
0014-1682	Eternity
0014-1690	Ethical Record
0014-1704	Ethics: An International Journal of Social, Political and Legal Philosophy
0014-1712	Ethiopia in the World Press†
0014-1720	Ethiopia Observer†
0014-1739	Ethiopian Geographical Journal†
0014-1747	Ethiopian Library Association. Bulletin
0014-1755	Ethiopian Medical Journal
0014-178X	Ethnie Francaise
0014-1798	Ethnographia
0014-1801	Ethnohistory
0014-181X	Ethnologische Zeitschrift†
0014-1828	Ethnology
0014-1836	Ethnomusicology *changed to* Journal for Ethnomusicology
0014-1844	Ethnos
0014-1909	Etruscan†
0014-1917	Etude Comparative Benelux sur les Salaires†
0014-1941	Etudes
0014-195X	Etudes Anglaises
0014-1968	Etudes Ardennaises *see* 0035-3272
0014-1976	Etudes Balkaniques
0014-1992	Etudes Cinematographiques
0014-200X	Etudes Classiques
0014-2018	Etudes Dahomeennes
0014-2026	Etudes de Lettres
0014-2034	Etudes Economiques†
0014-2042	Banque Francaise et Italienne. Etudes Economiques
0014-2069	Banque des Etats de l'Afrique Centrale. Etudes et Statistiques
0014-2077	Etudes Evangeliques†
0014-2085	Etudes Francaises
0014-2093	Etudes Franciscaines†
0014-2107	Etudes Freudiennes
0014-2115	Etudes Germaniques
0014-2123	Etudes Internationales
0014-2131	Etudes Internationales de Psycho-Sociologie Criminelle†
0014-214X	Etudes Litteraires
0014-2158	Etudes Normandes
0014-2166	Etudes Philosophiques
0014-2182	Etudes Rurales
0014-2204	Etudes Sociales
0014-2212	Etudes Sociales et Syndicales
0014-2239	Etudes Theologiques et Religieuses
0014-2247	Etudes Tsiganes
0014-2255	World Student News
0014-2263	Etyka
0014-2271	Eucharist†
0014-2298	Euhemer
0014-2301	E U M I G - Lupe
0014-2328	Euphorion
0014-2336	Euphytica
0014-2352	Euro Abstracts *changed to* Euro Abstracts Section I. Euratom and EEC Research
0014-2387	Euro Piano
0014-2409	EUROCOM Press Information†
0014-2417	Eurographie
0014-2425	Euromed†
0014-2433	Euromoney
0014-2441	Euromonitor Review *see* 0308-3446
0014-2468	Europa
0014-2476	Europa-Archiv
0014-2484	Europa Chemie
0014-2492	Europa Ethnica
0014-2514	Europa Industrie Revue. Maschinenmarkt und Elektrotechnik *see* 0341-5783
0014-2522	Europa-Korrespondenz
0014-2530	Europa Libera
0014-2549	Europa Medica†
0014-2557	Europa Medica *changed to* Panminerva Medica-Europa Medica
0014-2565	Revista Clinica Espanola
0014-2573	Europa Medicophysica
0014-259X	Eurosport *changed to* Sportshop
0014-2603	Europa Star
0014-2611	Europa-Union *changed to* Europaeische Zeitung
0014-262X	Europa-Verkehr†
0014-2638	Europaeer Diskutieren†
0014-2646	Europaeische Begegnung *see* 0014-2468
0014-2670	Europaeische Mode nach Mass†
0014-2697	Europaeische Technische Informationen *changed to* Lagern und Fordern
0014-2700	Europaeisches Immobilien Journal†
0014-2727	Europastimme
0014-2751	Europe
0014-276X	Europe & Oil†
0014-2794	Europe-Echecs
0014-2808	Europe en Formation
0014-2816	Europe France Outremer *changed to* Europe Outremer
0014-2824	Europe Oil-Telegram
0014-2832	Europe Orientale†
0014-2840	Witchcraft *see* 0085-8250
0014-2859	European Board Markets†
0014-2867	European Business Review†
0014-2875	European Chemical News
0014-2891	European Community *see* 0191-4545
0014-2905	European Documentation - a Survey†
0014-2921	European Economic Review
0014-293X	European Federation for the Protection of Waters. Information Bulletin†
0014-2948	European Grocery Letter
0014-2956	European Journal of Biochemistry
0014-2964	European Journal of Cancer *see* 0277-5379
0014-2972	European Journal of Clinical Investigation
0014-2980	European Journal of Immunology
0014-2999	European Journal of Pharmacology
0014-3006	European Judaism
0014-3014	European Marketing Research Review *see* 0304-4297
0014-3022	European Neurology
0014-3030	European Numismatics
0014-3057	European Polymer Journal
0014-3065	Potato Research
0014-3073	European Railways†
0014-3081	European Review†
0014-309X	European Shipbuilding†
0014-3103	European Studies *changed to* Exploring Europe
0014-3111	European Studies Review *changed to* European History Quarterly
0014-312X	European Surgical Research
0014-3138	European Taxation
0014-3146	European Teacher†
0014-3154	European Transport Law
0014-3162	European Trends
0014-3170	European University News
0014-3189	Europeo
0014-3197	Europese Documentatie†
0014-3235	Eurosud
0014-3243	Eurotec
0014-3251	Eurotransports Illustrato *changed to* Eurotransports Illustrato-Container in Italia e nel Mondo
0014-326X	Evangelische-Lutherische Kirche in Thueringen. Amtsblatt
0014-3278	Eva
0014-3286	Eva
0014-3294	Eva†
0014-3308	Eva Express
0014-3316	Evaluation Engineering *see* 0149-0370
0014-3324	Evangelical Baptist
0014-3332	Evangelical Beacon
0014-3340	Evangelical Friend
0014-3359	Evangelical Missions Quarterly
0014-3367	Evangelical Quarterly
0014-3375	Evangelical Truth
0014-3383	Evangelie en Maatschappij
0014-3391	Sonntagsblatt fuer die Evangelisch-Lutherische Kirche in Bayern. Ausgabe Oberfranken
0014-3405	Evangelisch-Soziale Warte *changed to* S V A-Zeitung
0014-3413	Der Evangelische Erzieher
0014-3421	Evangelische Kinderpflege fuer Kindergarten, Hort, Heim und Familie *see* 0342-7145
0014-343X	Evangelische Kirche in Deutschland. Amtsblatt
0014-3472	Evangelische Missionszeitschrift *see* 0342-9423
0014-3480	Der Evangelische Religionslehrer an Beruflichen Schulen†
0014-3502	Evangelische Theologie
0014-3529	Evangelische Landeskirche in Wuerttemberg. Amtsblatt
0014-3553	Evangelischer Nachrichtendienst in der DDR
0014-3561	Evangelisches Gemeindeblatt Berlin
0014-3588	Evangelisches Gemeindeblatt fuer Muenchen *changed to* Muenchner Gemeindeblatt
0014-360X	Evangelisches Gemeindeblatt fuer Wuerttemberg
0014-3618	Evangelisches Schulblatt†
0014-3626	Evangelist
0014-3642	Evanjelicky Hlasnik
0014-3650	Evans-Novak Political Report
0014-3669	Evansville Public Library and Vanderburgh County Public Library. Staff News Bulletin *changed to* Evansville-Vanderburgh County Public Library. Staff News Bulletin
0014-3677	Evansville-Vanderburgh School Corporation. Public Schools Bulletin†

ISSN INDEX

0014-3685 Eve†
0014-3693 Evelyn Waugh Newsletter
0014-3731 Event *changed to* Metropinion
0014-374X Event
0014-3804 Everywoman's Daily Horoscope *changed to* Popular Astrology
0014-3812 Eve's Weekly
0014-3820 Evolution
0014-3839 Panelectronics
0014-3855 Evolution Psychiatrique
0014-3863 Evoluzione Agricola
0014-3871 E W G-Warenhandel
0014-388X Ex-C B I Roundup
0014-3901 Ex Libris†
0014-391X Ex Libris
0014-3928 Ex Ore Infantium
0014-3936 Ex-Serviceman
0014-3944 Ex-Umbra
0014-3952 Exakte Aesthetk†
0014-3960 Examen de la Situacion Economica de Mexico
0014-3979 Examiner
0014-3987 Excalibur
0014-3995 Excavating Contractor
0014-4002 Excavator
0014-4010 Exceptional Child Education Abstracts *see* 0160-4309
0014-4029 Exceptional Children
0014-4037 Excerpta Botanica. Sectio A: Taxonomica et Chorologica
0014-4045 Excerpta Botanica. Sectio B: Sociologica
0014-4053 Excerpta Medica. Section 1: Anatomy, Anthropology, Embryology & Histology
0014-4061 Excerpta Medica. Section 2: Physiology
0014-407X Excerpta Medica. Section 3: Endocrinology
0014-4088 Excerpta Medica. Section 4: Microbiology-Bacteriology, Virology, Mycology and Parasitology *changed to* Excerpta Medica. Section 4: Microbiology: Bacteriology, Mycology and Parasitology
0014-4096 Excerpta Medica. Section 5: General Pathology and Pathological Anatomy
0014-410X Excerpta Medica. Section 6: Internal Medicine
0014-4118 Excerpta Medica. Section 7: Pediatrics *changed to* Excerpta Medica. Section 7: Pediatrics and Pediatric Surgery
0014-4126 Excerpta Medica. Section 8: Neurology and Neurosurgery
0014-4134 Excerpta Medica. Section 9: Surgery
0014-4142 Excerpta Medica. Section 10: Obstetrics and Gynecology
0014-4150 Excerpta Medica. Section 11: Otorhinolaryngology
0014-4169 Excerpta Medica. Section 12: Ophthalmology
0014-4177 Excerpta Medica. Section 13: Dermatology and Venereology
0014-4185 Excerpta Medica. Section 14: Radiology
0014-4193 Excerpta Medica. Section 15: Chest Diseases, Thoracic Surgery and Tuberculosis
0014-4207 Excerpta Medica. Section 16: Cancer
0014-4215 Excerpta Medica. Section 17: Public Health, Social Medicine & Hygiene
0014-4223 Excerpta Medica. Section 18: Cardiovascular Diseases and Cardiovascular Surgery
0014-4231 Excerpta Medica. Section 19: Rehabilitation and Physical Medicine
0014-424X Excerpta Medica. Section 20: Gerontology and Geriatrics
0014-4258 Excerpta Medica. Section 21: Developmental Biology and Teratology
0014-4266 Excerpta Medica. Section 22: Human Genetics
0014-4274 Excerpta Medica. Section 23: Nuclear Medicine
0014-4282 Excerpta Medica. Section 24: Anesthesiology
0014-4290 Excerpta Medica. Section 25: Hematology
0014-4304 Excerpta Medica. Section 26: Immunology, Serology and Transplantation
0014-4312 Excerpta Medica. Section 27: Biophysics, Bio-Engineering and Medical Instrumentation
0014-4320 Excerpta Medica. Section 28: Urology and Nephrology
0014-4339 Excerpta Medica. Section 29: Biochemistry *see* 0300-5372
0014-4355 Excerpta Medica. Section 31: Arthritis and Rheumatism
0014-4363 Excerpta Medica. Section 32: Psychiatry
0014-4371 Excerpta Medica. Section 33: Orthopedic Surgery
0014-438X Excerpta Medica. Section 34: Plastic Surgery
0014-4398 Excerpta Medica. Section 35: Occupational Health and Industrial Medicine
0014-4436 Exchange†
0014-4444 Exchange†
0014-4452 Exchange & Commissary News
0014-4460 Exchange and Mart
0014-4479 Echangiste Universel
0014-4487 Exchangite
0014-4509 Executive *see* 0145-3963
0014-4525 Executive Fitness Newsletter
0014-4533 Executive Grocer†
0014-455X Executive Housekeeper†
0014-4568 Executive Life†
0014-4576 Executive Men's Arts Series *changed to* Executive Men's Advertising Service
0014-4584 Executive Reading
0014-4592 Executives Wealth Report†
0014-4622 Exeter University Gazette
0014-4649 Exhibition Bulletin
0014-4665 Exil et Liberte†
0014-4673 Existential Psychiatry†
0014-4681 Exlibris-Nyt
0014-469X Expanded Shale Concrete Facts *changed to* Expanded Shale Lightweight Concrete Facts
0014-4703 Expansion
0014-4711 Cahiers de l'Expansion Regionale *see* 0240-9925
0014-472X Expecting
0014-4738 Expedition
0014-4754 Experientia
0014-4762 Experientiae
0014-4770 Experiment
0014-4797 Experimental Agriculture
0014-4800 Experimental and Molecular Pathology
0014-4819 Experimental Brain Research
0014-4827 Experimental Cell Research
0014-4835 Experimental Eye Research
0014-4851 Experimental Mechanics
0014-486X Experimental Medicine and Microbiology†
0014-4878 Experimental Medicine and Surgery†
0014-4886 Experimental Neurology
0014-4894 Experimental Parasitology
0014-4908 Experimentelle Pathologie *see* 0232-1513
0014-4916 Experimentation Animale†
0014-4924 Experimentelle Technik der Physik
0014-4932 Experiodica
0014-4940 Explicator
0014-4959 Exploration†
0014-4967 Explorations *see* 0360-6511
0014-4975 Explorations
0014-4983 Explorations in Economic History
0014-4991 Explorer
0014-5009 Explorer (Cleveland)
0014-5017 Explorer (Indiana)
0014-5025 Explorers Journal
0014-5033 Exploring *changed to* Exploring Journal
0014-505X Explosives & Pyrotechnics
0014-5068 Explosivstoffe
0014-5076 Exponent
0014-5084 Export
0014-5092 Export†
0014-5106 Export Anzeiger†
0014-5122 Export Courier
0014-5130 Export Direction†
0014-5149 Export-Import News
0014-5165 Export Management†
0014-5173 Export Polygraph International (E I P)
0014-5181 Export Shipping Manual
0014-519X Export
0014-5203 Revista Mensal de Exportacao
0014-5211 Exportmarkten†
0014-522X Expositor Bautista
0014-5238 Expositor Biblico (Teacher Edition)
0014-5246 Expository Times
0014-5254 Expovisie
0014-5262 Express†
0014-5270 Express
0014-5289 Express Documents
0014-5327 Expression
0014-5343 Expression†
0014-5351 Expression†
0014-536X Expression One
0014-5378 Extebank Monthly Economic Report
0014-5386 Extemporale
0014-5394 Extensao em Minas Gerais
0014-5408 Extension Service Review *see* 0162-9875
0014-5416 Extensions†
0014-5424 Extensions and Corrections to the U D C
0014-5432 External Affairs *see* 0381-4890
0014-5440 New Zealand Foreign Affairs Review
0014-5459 External Studies Gazette
0014-5467 Stamp Digest
0014-5475 American Digest of Foreign Orthopaedic Literature†
0014-5483 Extrapolation
0014-5491 Eye, Ear, Nose & Throat Monthly *see* 0145-5613
0014-5513 Eyeopener
0014-5521 Eyewitness
0014-553X F A A Aviation News *see* 0362-7942
0014-5548 F A B I Revue d'Information
0014-5556 F A C T A Newsletter
0014-5564 F.A.I. Abstract Service
0014-5580 F A O Documentation-Current Index *see* 0304-582X
0014-5599 F A O Aquaculture Bulletin†
0014-5610 F A O Forestry and Forest Industries Bulletin for Latin America†
0014-5629 F A O Information *changed to* World Agriculture, Forestry and Fisheries
0014-5637 F A O Plant Protection Bulletin
0014-5645 F A P I G
0014-5661 F and S International *see* 0270-4528
0014-567X F and S Index of Corporations and Industries *see* 0270-4544
0014-5688 F B I Law Enforcement Bulletin
0014-570X F C H News Briefs
0014-5718 F C I B Bulletin *changed to* F C I B International Bulletin
0014-5734 F C N L Washington Newsletter
0014-5742 F C X Patron†
0014-5750 F D A Papers *see* 0362-1332
0014-5769 Freien Deutschen Gewerschaftsbundes. Rundschau *see* 0323-5750
0014-5777 F.D.I. Newsletter
0014-5785 F E & Z N
0014-5793 F E B S Letters
0014-5807 F E N; Australian Factory Equipment News *see* 0728-9413
0014-5815 F F Communications
0014-584X M F D-Zeitung *changed to* Schweizer Soldat
0014-5874 F I D News Bulletin
0014-5890 F I G A News *changed to* F I G A
0014-5904 F I R A Bulletin
0014-5912 F.I.R.O. Quaderni
0014-5920 F L A C S
0014-5939 F L C Newsletter *see* 0882-908X
0014-5955 F M G - Fachblatt
0014-5963 F M *changed to* Vox: Hebdomadaire Militaire
0014-5971 F M Guide
0014-5998 F.N. Orienterung
0014-6013 F O A Orienterar Om
0014-603X F O I Center Report†
0014-6048 F.O. Licht's Europaeisches Zuckerjournal *changed to* F.O. Licht's International Sugar Report
0014-6056 F.O. Lichts's International Molasses Report
0014-6072 F.P.A. Journal *see* 0309-6866
0014-6080 F P C News (U.S. Federal Power Commission) *changed to* F E R C News
0014-6102 F R C C *changed to* B C S Newsletter
0014-6110 F R E N *changed to* Florida Rural Electric News
0014-6137 F R I Monthly Portfolio
0014-6145 Der Sportjournalist
0014-6153 F u Pressedienst Wissenschaft†
0014-6161 F V I†
0014-6196 Fabian News
0014-6226 Fabrieksorganisatie†
0014-6234 Fabriksarbetaren
0014-6242 Fabula
0014-6269 Face au Risque
0014-6277 Face-To-Face†
0014-6285 Facettes
0014-6293 Fachberater
0014-6307 Der Fachberater†
0014-6315 Fachberater fuer das Deutsche Kleingartenwesen
0014-6323 Fachberichte fuer Metallbearbeitung
0014-634X Fachblatt der Bundesinnung der Metallgiesser, Guertler, Graveure, Metalldrucker†
0014-6366 F F S B *changed to* Handels-Magazin F S B und Fachblatt fuer Selbstbedienung
0014-6374 Fachhefte fuer Chemigraphie, Lithographie und Tiefdruck
0014-6382 Fachpresse *changed to* Schweizer Fachpresse
0014-6390 Die Fachschule
0014-6412 Fachzeitschrift fuer den Buerofachhandel *changed to* Fachzeitung fuer den Buerofachhandel
0014-6420 Facilities for Atmospheric Research *see* 0091-2026
0014-6447 Die Fackel
0014-6455 Fackfoereningsroerelsen *see* 0346-895X
0014-6463 Facklaeraren
0014-6471 Fackliga Vaerldsrorelsen
0014-648X Universita degli Studi di Perugia. Facolta di Medicina e Chirurgia. Annali
0014-6501 F B; A Fact Book on Higher Education *changed to* Fact Book for Higher Education
0014-651X Fact Finder
0014-6536 De Facto *changed to* Uni-Press
0014-6544 Purchasing
0014-6552 Factory Equipment & Materials for Southern Africa
0014-6579 Factory Equipment News
0014-6595 Factory Mutual Record
0014-6617 Facts and Comparisons *changed to* Facts and Comparisons
0014-6633 Facts on Dental Health & Smoking†
0014-6641 Facts on File
0014-665X Lisbon. Universidade. Faculdade de Ciencias. Revista. Serie 2. Seccao A. Ciencias Matematicas†
0014-6676 Universidade de Sao Paulo. Faculdade de Farmacia e Bioquimica. Revista *see* 0370-4726
0014-6684 Faculdade de Farmacia e Odontologia de Araraquara. Revista *see* 0101-3793
0014-6684 Faculdade de Farmacia e Odontologia de Araraquara. Revista *see* 0101-1774
0014-6714 Universidad de la Republica. Facultad de Arquitectura. Revista†
0014-6722 Universidad Nacional de Cordoba. Facultad de Ciencias Medicas. Revista
0014-6730 Universidad de Zaragoza. Facultad de Medicina. Archivos†
0014-6749 Universite de Toulouse II (le Mirail). Annales†
0014-679X Faenza
0014-6803 Fahr mit Uns
0014-6811 Fahr Betriebsleben
0014-682X Fahrlehrer†
0014-6838 Fahrschule
0014-6846 Fahrt Frei

ISSN	Title
0014-6854	Der Fahrzeug- und Metall-Lackierer
0014-6862	Fahrzeug und Karosserie
0014-6870	Der Fahrzeughandel
0014-6889	Faims et Soifs des Hommes
0014-6897	Faipar
0014-6919	Fair Employment Report
0014-6927	Fair Lady
0014-6943	Fairchild Tropical Garden Bulletin
0014-6951	Faire Face
0014-696X	Fairfield County Economy†
0014-6978	Fairfield County Press†
0014-6986	Fairplay Shipping Journal see 0307-0220
0014-6994	Fait Public†
0014-7001	Faith and Form
0014-701X	Faith and Freedom
0014-7028	Faith and Thought
0014-7036	Faith and Unity†
0014-7044	Faith for Daily Living
0014-7052	Facts and Tendencies
0014-7079	Falcon†
0014-7087	Faller-Magazin see 0170-0510
0014-7095	Famiglia Cristiana
0014-7109	Familia†
0014-7117	Familia
0014-7125	Familia Crista
0014-7133	Familie Journalen
0014-7141	Familien
0014-715X	Familienblatt
0014-7168	Familienfreund†
0014-7176	Familienverband Avenarius. Familienzeitschrift
0014-7184	Famille Nouvelle
0014-7206	Family Circle
0014-7214	Family Coordinator see 0197-6664
0014-7230	Family Handyman
0014-7249	Family Health see 0279-3547
0014-7257	Family Health Bulletin†
0014-7265	Family History
0014-7273	Family Housebeating see 0006-5374
0014-7281	Family Law
0014-729X	Family Law Quarterly
0014-7303	Family Life
0014-7311	Family Perspective
0014-732X	Family Physician
0014-7338	Family Planning see 0309-1112
0014-7346	Family Planning News changed to Pathways in Population Planning
0014-7354	Family Planning Perspectives
0014-7362	Family Planning Quarterly†
0014-7370	Family Process
0014-7389	Family Puzzlers
0014-7397	Family Safety changed to Family Safety & Health
0014-7435	Famous Artists Magazine†
0014-7443	Famous Monsters of Filmland changed to Famous Monsters
0014-7451	Famous Photographers†
0014-746X	Famous Writers Magazine†
0014-7478	Fanfare†
0014-7486	Fangst og Fiske changed to Maritime News
0014-7494	Fant†
0014-7524	Fante di Quadri
0014-7532	Far East see 0048-251X
0014-7540	Far East Architect and Builder see 0264-8164
0014-7559	Far East Engineer†
0014-7567	Far East Medical Journal see 0301-0376
0014-7583	Far East Trade and Development†
0014-7591	Far Eastern Economic Review
0014-7605	Far Eastern University Journal†
0014-7613	F A R Horizons Newletter†
0014-763X	Far West Magazine
0014-7648	Far West News see 0746-4541
0014-7656	Faraday†
0014-7664	Faraday Society. Discussions see 0301-7249
0014-7672	Faraday Society. Transactions see 0300-9599
0014-7672	Faraday Society. Transactions see 0300-9238
0014-7680	Die Farbe
0014-7699	Farbe und Lack
0014-7702	Farbe und Raum
0014-7710	Farben-Chemiker changed to Fett
0014-7737	Farbenkreis, Oesterreichische Malerzeitung
0014-7745	Fare Box
0014-777X	Jern og Farge changed to Jernvare Bygg Hobby
0014-7788	Farhang-e Iran Zamin
0014-7796	Farm
0014-7818	Big Farm Management changed to Farm Business
0014-7826	Farm and Dairy
0014-7834	Farm & Power Equipment
0014-7842	Farm and Ranch Bulletin†
0014-7850	Farm Building Express†
0014-7869	Farm Building News changed to Rural Builder
0014-7877	Farm Buildings Digest see 0265-5373
0014-7885	Farm Chemicals and Croplife see 0092-0053
0014-7893	Farm City Week Newsletter
0014-7907	Farm Credit Banks of Baltimore. News & Views†
0014-7931	Farm Economist changed to Oxford Agrarian Studies
0014-7958	Farm Equipment
0014-7974	U.S. Department of Agriculture. Economic Research Service. Farm Income Situation see 0099-1066
0014-7982	Farm Index see 0270-5672
0014-7990	Farm Industry News see 0199-6924
0014-8008	Farm Journal
0014-8016	Farm Labor†
0014-8024	Farm Letter
0014-8032	Farm Light & Power
0014-8040	Farm Machine Design Engineering†
0014-8059	Farm Management
0014-8075	Farm Policy†
0014-8083	Farm Pond Harvest
0014-8091	Farm Quarterly†
0014-8105	Farm Safety Review†
0014-8113	Farm Service News changed to N J D A Report
0014-8121	Farm Store Merchandising
0014-813X	Farm Supplier
0014-8148	Farm Technology changed to Ag Consultant
0014-8164	Farmaceuten†
0014-8172	Farmaceuticky Obzor
0014-8199	Farmaceutisk Tidende
0014-8202	Farmaceutski Glasnik
0014-8210	Farmacevtisk Revy
0014-8229	Farmacevtski Vestnik
0014-8237	Farmacia
0014-8245	Farmacia Nuova
0014-8253	Farmacista Sociale
0014-8261	Farmacja Polska
0014-827X	Farmaco
0014-8288	Farmacognosia†
0014-8296	Terapeutica Razonada†
0014-8318	Farmakologiya i Toksikologiya
0014-8326	Farmakoterapi
0014-8334	Farmand
0014-8350	Farmer
0014-8369	Farmer & Parliament
0014-8377	Farmer-Labor Press
0014-8393	Farmers Club. Journal
0014-8415	Farmers' Friend
0014-8423	Farmers Guardian
0014-844X	Farmers Newsletter
0014-8458	Farmers Union Herald changed to Co-Op Country News
0014-8466	Farmers Weekly
0014-8474	Farmers Weekly
0014-8482	Farmers Weekly
0014-8504	Farming in Zambia
0014-8512	Foreign Acquisitions Newsletter†
0014-8520	Farmis - Reptilen
0014-8547	Farmweek
0014-8555	Il Faro
0014-8563	Faro Dominical changed to Marchemos
0014-8571	Farogh-I-Urdu
0014-858X	Farol†
0014-8598	Faarskoetsel
0014-8601	Pharmacy
0014-8644	Fashion Accessories
0014-8660	Fashion Calendar
0014-8679	Fashion Forecast
0014-8695	Fashion Week†
0014-8709	Fashionweek see 0312-0325
0014-8725	Fast Food see 0097-8043
0014-8733	Fast Grunn
0014-8741	Fasteners†
0014-875X	Fastline Monthly†
0014-8776	Fate
0014-8784	Res Medicae
0014-8792	Fateh
0014-8814	Fathers of the Church
0014-8822	Fathom (Norfolk)
0014-8830	Fatima Findings
0014-8849	Fatos and Fotos changed to Fatos
0014-8865	U.S. Department of Agriculture. Fats and Oils Situation changed to U.S. Department of Agriculture. Oil Crops Outlook and Situation
0014-8873	Fatti E Notizie
0014-8881	Fauna
0014-8903	Fauna och Flora
0014-892X	Faversham Papers
0014-8938	Fax Forecast
0014-8946	Feasta
0014-8962	Feddes Repertorium
0014-8970	Die Feder
0014-9004	Federal Accountant see 0883-1483
0014-9039	Federal Bar Journal see 0279-4691
0014-9047	Federal Bar News see 0279-4691
0014-9063	Federal Contracts Report
0014-9071	Federal Employee
0014-908X	Federal Fire Council News Letter†
0014-911X	Federal Notes†
0014-9128	Federal Probation
0014-9136	Washington Environmental Protection Report
0014-9144	Federal Reserve Bank of Atlanta. Monthly Review see 0732-1813
0014-9152	Federal Reserve Bank of Kansas City. Monthly Review see 0161-2387
0014-9160	Federal Reserve Bank of New York. Monthly Review see 0147-6580
0014-9179	Federal Reserve Bank of Richmond. Monthly Review see 0094-6893
0014-9187	Federal Reserve Bank of St. Louis. Review
0014-9195	Federal Reserve Bank of San Francisco. Monthly Review see 0363-0021
0014-9209	Federal Reserve Bulletin
0014-9225	Federal Statistics Users' Conference. Newsletter
0014-9233	Federal Times
0014-9241	Federalist changed to World Citizen/Federalist Letter
0014-9268	Federaliste Europeen
0014-9276	Federated Ironworkers' Association of Australia. Labor News
0014-9284	Federatie Contact changed to Contour
0014-9306	Federation of State Medical Boards of the United States. Federation Bulletin
0014-9314	Federation of Synagogues of South Africa. Federation Chronicle changed to Jewish Tradition
0014-9330	Federation des Entreprises de l'Industrie des Fabrications Metalliques, Mecaniques, Electriques et de la Transformation des Matieres Plastiques. Bulletin d'Information Mensuel changed to Federation des Entreprises de l'Industrie des Fabrications Metalliques, Mecaniques, Electriques et de la Transformation des Matieres Plastiques. Revue Mensuelle
0014-9349	Federation des Industries Belges. Bulletin see 0771-2987
0014-9357	Federation des Societes d'Histoire Naturelle de Franche-Comte. Bulletin see 0753-4655
0014-9365	Federation Francaise des Societes de Sciences Naturelles. Revue see 0336-8300
0014-9373	Entreprise Europeenne
0014-939X	Federation Nationale de l'Industrie Laitiere. Bulletin d'Information
0014-9411	Federation News
0014-942X	Federation News
0014-9438	American Beekeeping Federation. News Letter
0014-9446	Federation of American Societies for Experimental Biology. Federation Proceedings see 0892-6638
0014-9454	Federation of Canadian Archers. Official Bulletin changed to F C A Official Newsletter
0014-9470	Federation of Indian Chambers of Commerce and Industry. Fortnightly Review changed to Economic Trends
0014-9489	F. W. I. News
0014-9497	Federazione Italiana Medici Igienisti. Bolletino d'Informazioni Agli Iscritti
0014-9500	Federazione Medica
0014-9519	Federazione Nazionale Stampa Italiana. Bollettino†
0014-9527	Quaerendo
0014-9535	Feed Industry see 0191-9334
0014-9543	Feed Bulletin
0014-9551	Feed/Grain Equipment Times see 0163-4119
0014-956X	Feed Management
0014-9578	U.S. Department of Agriculture. Feed Situation see 0278-0127
0014-9586	Feed Trade
0014-9594	Feedback changed to Feedback for Improving Vocational-Technical and Career Education
0014-9608	Feedback†
0014-9616	Feedlot changed to Feedlot Management
0014-9624	Feedstuffs
0014-9632	Feet†
0014-9659	Fegato
0014-9667	Chung Kung Yen Chiu
0014-9675	Fei-Ching Yueh-Pao/Chinese Communist Affairs Monthly changed to Chung-Kuo Ta-Lu Yen-Chiu
0014-9683	Feingeraetetechnik
0014-9691	Feinkost-Revue
0014-9713	Feinwerktechnik see 0340-1952
0014-9721	Feiten, Cijfers, Meningen changed to Mensen op Straat
0014-973X	Feju
0014-9748	Feld und Wald changed to Agrar-Praxis
0014-9756	Feld Wald Wasser
0014-9764	Feldgrau†
0014-9772	Fel'dsher i Akusherka
0014-9780	Feldweibel
0014-9799	Feldwirtschaft
0014-9802	Feliciter
0014-9810	Fellowship
0014-9829	Fellowship for Freedom in Medicine. Bulletin see 0305-9324
0014-9837	Fellowship in Prayer
0014-9853	Femina
0014-9861	Femina changed to Femina Maanadens Magasin
0014-987X	Femina and Woman's Life†
0014-9888	Feminidades†
0014-9896	Femme Chic†
0014-990X	Femme d'Aujourd'hui et Patrie Suisse-Actualites changed to La Femme D'Aujourd'Hui
0014-9918	Femme-Lines
0014-9926	Femme Pratique
0014-9934	Femmes au Village
0014-9942	Femmes Chefs d'Entreprise
0014-9950	Femmes d'Aujourd'hui
0014-9977	Fence Industry see 0885-8411
0014-9985	Fendt-Nachrichten†
0015-0002	Fenix
0015-0010	Fennia
0015-0029	Das Fenster
0015-0037	Ferguson-Florissant Schools
0015-0053	Fermentatio see 0770-1713
0015-007X	Fermettes et Residences Secondaires changed to Combat Nature
0015-0088	Fernkurs Textiltechnik
0015-0096	Fernmelde Impulse†
0015-010X	Der Fernmelde-Ingenieur

ISSN	Title
0015-0118	Fernmelde Praxis
0015-0126	Fernmeldetechnik†
0015-0134	Fernseh-Informationen
0015-0142	Fernseh- und Kino-Technik
0015-0150	Fernsehen und Bildung†
0015-0177	Ferrocarriles *changed to* Ferrocarriles Mexicanos
0015-0185	Ferrocarriles y Tranvias
0015-0193	Ferroelectrics
0015-0207	Ferronales
0015-0215	Ferroviere
0015-0223	Ferskvandsfiskeribladet
0015-0231	Fertigteilbau und Industrialisiertes Bauen *see* 0340-2967
0015-024X	Fertigungstechnik und Betrieb
0015-0258	Feed and Farm Supplies *changed to* Milling Feed and Farm Supplies
0015-0266	Fertiliser News
0015-0282	Fertility and Sterility
0015-0290	Fertilizer Abstracts†
0015-0304	Fertilizer International
0015-0312	Fertilizer Solutions *see* 0199-9869
0015-0320	Der feste Grund
0015-0339	Feste Prophetische Wort†
0015-0347	Festina Lente
0015-0355	Festiniog Railway Magazine
0015-0363	Festival
0015-0371	Fetes et Saisons
0015-038X	Fette-Seifen-Anstrichmittel *changed to* Fett
0015-0401	Feuerungstechnik - Gebaeudetechnik *changed to* Feuerungstechnk, Energie & Umwelt
0015-041X	Feuille Anarchiste
0015-0428	Feuille Officielle de la Protection Civile
0015-0452	Feuillets du Praticien
0015-0479	Fiamma†
0015-0495	Fiat Lux
0015-0509	Fib-Aktuellt *changed to* Veckans Stopp
0015-0509	Fib-Aktuellt *changed to* Fib-Aktuellt
0015-0517	Fibonacci Quarterly
0015-0525	Fibra†
0015-0533	Fibre and Fabric†
0015-0541	Fibre Chemistry
0015-055X	Fibre e Colori *see* 0033-9067
0015-0568	Fibre Science and Technology *see* 0266-3538
0015-0576	Fibula†
0015-0592	Fichero Bibliografico Hispanoamericano
0015-0606	Fichero Medico Terapeutico Purissimus
0015-0614	Fiches Medicales
0015-0630	Fiddlehead
0015-0649	Field
0015-0657	Field
0015-0673	Field & Stream
0015-069X	Field Crop Abstracts
0015-0703	Field Museum of Natural History Bulletin
0015-0711	Arkansas Archeological Society. Field Notes
0015-072X	Field Notes†
0015-0746	Fieldiana: Botany
0015-0754	Fieldiana: Zoology
0015-0762	Fields *see* 0744-4052
0015-0770	Fields Within Fields...Within Fields†
0015-0797	Fiere e Mostre
0015-0800	Fifth Estate
0015-0819	Fifth Wheel
0015-0827	Fifty Millesimal
0015-0835	Figaro
0015-0843	Figaro Litteraire†
0015-0851	Figurino Moderno
0015-086X	Figyelo
0015-0878	Fiinta Romaneasca†
0015-0886	Fiji Agricultural Journal
0015-0894	Fiji. Bureau of Statistics. Current Economic Statistics
0015-0908	Fiji Farmer†
0015-0916	Fiji. Government Printing Department. Publications Bulletin
0015-0924	Fiji. Geological Survey. Bulletin *see* 0379-1580
0015-0932	Fikrun Wa Fann
0015-0940	Filatelia Italiana
0015-0959	Filatelie
0015-0967	Filatelija
0015-0975	Filatelista
0015-0983	Filateliya S.S.S.R.
0015-0991	Filipino-American Herald
0015-1009	Filipino Teacher
0015-1017	Film *see* 0108-5697
0015-1025	Film
0015-1033	Film
0015-1041	Film
0015-105X	Film *see* 0046-368X
0015-1068	Film a Doba
0015-1076	Schweizer Schmalfilm *changed to* Film & Foto mit Video
0015-1106	Film and Television Technician
0015-1114	Film und Ton-Magazin†
0015-1122	Film Artiste†
0015-1130	Film Bild Ton *changed to* A V-Praxis
0015-1149	Film-Echo/Filmwoche
0015-1157	Film Bulletin†
0015-1165	Film Bulletin
0015-1173	Film Canadiana: The Canadian Film Institute Yearbook of Canadian Cinema†
0015-1181	Film Collectors Registry†
0015-119X	Film Comment
0015-1203	Critic
0015-1211	Film Culture
0015-1238	Film Fan Monthly†
0015-1262	Film Francais-Cinematographie Francais *see* 0397-8702
0015-1270	Film Heritage†
0015-1289	Film Index
0015-1297	Film Information†
0015-1300	Film Italiano†
0015-1319	Film Journal Advertiser†
0015-1327	Film Library Quarterly†
0015-1335	Film-Lyd-Bilde†
0015-1343	Film News *changed to* Film & Video News (1979)
0015-1351	Film og Kino
0015-136X	Polish Film
0015-1378	Film/Pop-Telescoop *changed to* Pop-Telescoop
0015-1386	Film Quarterly
0015-1416	Film, Szinhaz, Muzsika
0015-1424	Fernseh und Film Technikum†
0015-1440	Film und Recht
0015-1459	Film User *see* 0305-2249
0015-1467	Film Weekly†
0015-1475	Film World†
0015-1505	Filmclub Action-Mitteilungen
0015-1513	Filmcritica
0015-1521	Filme e Cultura *changed to* Filme Cultura
0015-153X	Filmfacts†
0015-1548	Filmfare
0015-1556	Filmjournalen
0015-1564	Filmkompas *changed to* Groepsmedia
0015-1572	Filmkritik
0015-1580	Filmkultura
0015-1599	Filmkunst
0015-1602	Filmlist *see* 0037-4830
0015-1610	Filmmakers' Newsletter *see* 0194-4339
0015-1629	Filmograph†
0015-1645	Filmovy Prehled
0015-1653	Filmowy Osrodek Badawczo - Rozwojowy "Techfilm". Przeglad Dokumentacyjny†
0015-1661	Filmrutan
0015-167X	Films & Filming
0015-1688	Films in Review
0015-1696	Filmschau
0015-170X	Filmska Kultura
0015-1734	Filmspiegel
0015-1742	Filmtheater-Praxis *changed to* Filmtheater-Praxis - Werbung Heute
0015-1777	Filologia e Letteratura *changed to* Critica Letteraria
0015-1785	Filologiai Kozlony
0015-1815	Filomata
0015-1823	Filosofia
0015-1831	Filosoficky Casopis
0015-1858	Filosofskie Nauki
0015-1866	Filozofija
0015-1874	Filson Club History Quarterly
0015-1882	Filtration & Separation
0015-1890	Filtration Engineering†
0015-1904	Findiver†
0015-1912	Finance†
0015-1920	Finance a Uver
0015-1939	Finance & Commerce *changed to* Finance & Society
0015-1947	Finance and Development
0015-1955	Finance and Trade Review
0015-1963	Finance Facts
0015-1971	Finance Taxation & Company Law
0015-198X	Financial Analysts Journal
0015-1998	Financial Executive *changed to* Financial Executives
0015-2005	Financial Express
0015-2013	Financial Mail
0015-2021	Financial Post
0015-203X	Great Britain. Central Statistical Office. Financial Statistics
0015-2056	Financial Times of Canada
0015-2064	Financial World
0015-2072	Financieel Overheidsbeheer
0015-2080	Financiele Flitsen†
0015-2099	Financiele Koerier
0015-2102	Financiero
0015-2110	Financing Agriculture
0015-2129	Financing Foreign Operations
0015-2137	Finansi i Kredit
0015-2145	Finansije
0015-2153	Finanstidende
0015-2161	Finansy S.S.S.R.
0015-217X	Finante si Credit†
0015-2188	Finanz-Revue
0015-2196	Finanz-Rundschau
0015-220X	Finanz und Wirtschaft
0015-2218	Finanzarchiv
0015-2226	Finanzas al Dia
0015-2242	Finanziere
0015-2250	Finanzjournal mit Gebuehren-und Verkehrsteuerbeitragen
0015-2269	Finanznachrichten
0015-2277	Finanzrechtliche Erkenntnisse des Verwaltungsgerichtshofes
0015-2285	Findings†
0015-2307	Fine Arts†
0015-2331	Finis Terrae†
0015-234X	Finish†
0015-2358	Finishers' Management
0015-2366	Finite String *changed to* Computational Linguistics
0015-2374	Sueder-Elbe Wochenblatt fuer Sued Hamburg *changed to* Elbe Wochenblatt
0015-2390	Finland. Tilastokeskus. Tilastokatsauksia
0015-2412	Finnfacts
0015-2420	Finnische Handelsrundschau *changed to* Technik aus Finnland
0015-2439	Finnish American Chamber of Commerce Newsletter *changed to* Finnish American Chamber of Commerce Newsletter
0015-2447	Finnish Game Research
0015-2455	Finnish Paper and Timber†
0015-2463	Finnish Trade Review
0015-248X	Finsk Tidskrift
0015-2498	Finska Kemistsamfundet. Meddelanden *see* 0355-1628
0015-2501	Finska Laekaresaellskapet. Handlingar
0015-251X	Finskij Torgovyj Zhurnal
0015-2528	Fiori di S. Antonio
0015-2536	Fiorisce Un Cenacolo
0015-2544	Fire
0015-2552	Fire Chief
0015-2560	Fire Command *see* 0746-9586
0015-2587	Fire Engineering
0015-2595	Fire Fighting in Canada
0015-2609	Fire International
0015-2617	Fire Journal
0015-2625	Fire News
0015-2641	Fire Protection Review *changed to* Fire & Security Protection
0015-2668	Fire Service Information
0015-2684	Fire Technology
0015-2714	Fireside Chats
0015-2722	Firing Line
0015-2730	Firmenkraftfahrer†
0015-2749	First *see* 0199-2066
0015-2757	First Hawaiian Bank. Economic Indicators
0015-2773	First National Bank of Chicago. Business and Economic Review†
0015-2781	First National Bank of Chicago. International Economic Review†
0015-279X	Citibank. Monthly Economic Letter†
0015-2803	First to Final
0015-2811	Fiscaal Tijdschrift voor de Euromarkt *changed to* Intertax (Dutch Edition)
0015-282X	Fiscalite du Marche Commun *see* 0165-2826
0015-2838	Fisch und Fang
0015-2846	Fischer Edition News†
0015-2854	Das Fischerblatt
0015-2862	Fischers Tarif Nachrichten fuer Eisenbahn und Kraftwagen
0015-2897	Fish and Game Sportsman *see* 0709-1532
0015-2900	Fish Boat/Sea Food Merchandising
0015-2919	Fish Culturist
0015-2927	Fish Friers Review
0015-2943	Fish Trades Gazette *changed to* Fish Trader
0015-2951	Fisheries of Canada†
0015-2978	Fisherman†
0015-2986	Fisherman
0015-2994	Fishermen's News
0015-3001	Fishery Technology
0015-301X	Fishing and Hunting News
0015-3028	Fishing Gazette†
0015-3036	Fishing News
0015-3044	Fishing News International
0015-3052	Tackle & Guns
0015-3060	Fishing Tackle Trade News
0015-3079	Fishing World
0015-3087	Fishpaste†
0015-3095	Fiskaren
0015-3109	Fiskehandleren†
0015-3117	Norway. Fiskeridirektoratet. Skrifter. Serie Havundersoekelser
0015-3125	Fiskeritidskrift foer Finland
0015-3133	Fiskets Gang
0015-3141	Fitness and Health†
0015-3176	Five Associated University Libraries. Newsletter†
0015-3184	Five/Six *see* 0149-7820
0015-3206	Fizika
0015-3214	Fizika i Khimiya Obrabotki Materialov
0015-3222	Fizika i Tekhnika Poluprovodnikov
0015-3230	Fizika Metallov i Metallovedenie
0015-3249	Fizika Tverdogo Tela
0015-3257	Fizikai Szemle
0015-3265	Fiziko-Matematichesko Spisanie
0015-3273	Fiziko-Tekhnicheskie Problemy Razrabotki Poleznykh Iskopaemykh
0015-329X	Fiziologicheskii Zhurnal
0015-3303	Fiziologiya Rastenii
0015-3311	Fiziologichnyi Zhurnal
0015-332X	Fizkul'tura i Sport
0015-3338	Fjaederfae
0015-3346	Fjarmalatidindi
0015-3354	Fjoerfe
0015-3362	Flacara
0015-3370	Flag Bulletin
0015-3389	Flair†
0015-3400	Flakten†
0015-3419	Flama†
0015-3427	Flambeau
0015-3435	Flambeau
0015-346X	Flame Notes†
0015-3478	Flamingo†
0015-3486	Flammes Vives
0015-3494	Flash
0015-3508	Flash
0015-3516	Flash Actualite
0015-3524	Flash Art *changed to* Flash Art Italia
0015-3532	Flavour Industry *see* 0143-8441
0015-3540	De Fleanende Krie
0015-3575	Fleisch
0015-3583	Fleisch und Feinkost†
0015-3605	Fleischer Offerten-Dienst *see* 0170-0499
0015-3613	Die Fleischerei

ISSN INDEX 1235

0015-363X Die Fleischwirtschaft
0015-3648 Fleur de Lys
0015-3680 Der Flieger
0015-3699 Luftwaffe
0015-3702 Flight Comment
0015-3710 Flight International
0015-3729 Flight Magazine *see* 0361-5030
0015-3737 Flight Safety Bulletin
0015-3753 Floor & Wall Covering News†
0015-3761 Floor Covering Weekly
0015-377X Flooring & Carpet Specifier†
0015-3796 Biochemie und Physiologie der Pflanzen(B P P)
0015-380X Flora
0015-3818 Flora og Fauna
0015-3826 Floresta
0015-3834 Floricoltura Pesciatina
0015-3842 Florida A A A Motorist *changed to* A A A World (Miami)
0015-3850 Florida Academy of Sciences. Quarterly Journal *see* 0098-4590
0015-3869 Florida Agriculture *changed to* FloridAgriculture
0015-3877 Florida Alligator *see* 0889-2423
0015-3885 Florida Sportsman
0015-3893 Florida Anthropologist
0015-3907 Florida Architect†
0015-3915 Florida Bar Journal
0015-3923 Florida Builder
0015-3931 Florida Cancer News
0015-394X Florida Catholic Newspaper
0015-3958 Florida Cattleman and Livestock Journal
0015-3974 Florida Conservation News†
0015-3982 Florida Contractor and Builder *changed to* Florida Construction Industry
0015-3990 Florida State Dental Society. Journal *see* 0360-1676
0015-4008 Florida. Department of Agriculture. Division of Plant Industry. News Bulletin *changed to* Florida. Department of Agriculture and Consumer Services. Plant Industry News
0015-4016 Florida Education *see* 0744-6063
0015-4024 Florida Educational Research and Development Council. Research Bulletin
0015-4032 Florida Engineering Society. Journal
0015-4040 Florida Entomologist
0015-4059 Florida Explorer†
0015-4067 Florida Family Physician
0015-4075 Florida Field Report *see* 0015-4091
0015-4083 Florida Food & Grocery News
0015-4091 Florida Grower and Rancher
0015-4105 Florida Health Notes†
0015-4113 Florida Historical Quarterly
0015-4121 Florida Industrial Arts Quarterly Bulletin
0015-413X Florida Journal of Commerce/Seafarer *see* 0160-225X
0015-4148 Florida Medical Association. Journal
0015-4164 Florida Municipal Record
0015-4172 Florida Naturalist
0015-4180 Communique (Hollywood)†
0015-4199 Florida Nurse
0015-4202 Florida Pharmaceutical Journal *see* 0161-746X
0015-4210 Florida Planning and Development *see* 0145-5885
0015-4229 Florida Police Journal
0015-4237 Florida Prisoner Statistics†
0015-4245 Florida Purchaser
0015-4253 Florida Quarterly†
0015-4261 Florida Reading Quarterly
0015-4288 Florida School Herald
0015-4296 Florida Schools†
0015-430X Florida State University. Institute for Social Research. Governmental Research Bulletin†
0015-4318 Florida Supplement
0015-4326 Florida Trend
0015-4334 Florida Truck News
0015-4369 Florida Wildlife
0015-4385 Florist
0015-4393 Florist
0015-4407 Florist and Nursery Exchange *see* 0037-0797
0015-4415 Florist Trade Magazine
0015-4423 Florists' Review
0015-4431 Flottans Maen
0015-444X Flourish†
0015-4458 Flow Line†
0015-4466 Flower and Feather†
0015-4482 Home Garden *see* 0014-7230
0015-4490 Flower News
0015-4504 Flowering Plants of Africa
0015-4512 Flue Cured Tobacco Farmer
0015-4520 Mitteldeutscher Kurier
0015-4547 Flug Revue
0015-4563 Der Flugleiter
0015-458X Flug und Modell-Technik
0015-4598 Flugsport-Informationen *changed to* Flug-Informationen
0015-461X Fluid *changed to* Fluidtechnik
0015-4628 Fluid Dynamics
0015-4636 Fluid Milk and Cream Report†
0015-4644 Fluid Power Abstracts
0015-4660 Fluid Sealing Abstracts
0015-4687 Fluidics Quarterly *see* 8755-8564
0015-4709 Fluorescence News†
0015-4717 Fluoridation Reporter†
0015-4725 Fluoride
0015-4733 Flur und Furche
0015-4741 Fly Fisherman
0015-475X Flyghorisont
0015-4776 Flygposten
0015-4784 Flygrevyn
0015-4792 FlygvapenNytt
0015-4806 Flying
0015-4822 Flying Angel
0015-4830 Flying Lady
0015-4849 Flying Models
0015-4857 Flying Physician
0015-4865 Aerospace Review†
0015-4873 Flying Saucer News
0015-4881 Flying Saucer Review
0015-489X Flying Saucers *changed to* Search - Flying Saucers
0015-4911 Flyleaf†
0015-492X Flyv
0015-4938 Canadian Journal of Radiography, Radiotherapy, Nucleography *changed to* Canadian Journal of Radiography, Radiation Therapy, Nuclear Medicine
0015-4954 Focus†
0015-4962 National Association of State Boards of Education. Focus *changed to* National Association of State Boards of Education. State Board Connection
0015-4970 Focus (Chicago)†
0015-5004 Focus (New York, 1950)
0015-5012 Bausch and Lomb Focus *changed to* Educational Focus
0015-5020 National Committee on the Education of Migrant Children. Focus†
0015-5039 Focus (New York, 1964)†
0015-5047 Focus (Columbus, 1967)
0015-5055 South Africa International
0015-5063 Focus on Public Affairs *changed to* Focus on Governmental Affairs
0015-508X Focus/Midwest *see* 0036-2972
0015-5098 Focus on Industry and Commerce
0015-511X Focus on Exceptional Children
0015-5128 Focus on Film†
0015-5136 Focus on Guidance *see* 0193-7375
0015-5152 Focus on Indiana Libraries
0015-5160 Focus on Jamaica†
0015-5179 Focus on Saskatchewan Libraries *changed to* Focus (Regina)
0015-5195 Focus: Social and Preventive Medicine
0015-5209 Foden News†
0015-5217 Foer Biblisk Tro *see* 0345-1453
0015-5225 Foerbundet Svenska Finlandsfrivilliga. Tidning
0015-5233 Foerdermittel-Journal
0015-5241 Foerdern und Heben
0015-525X Foerderungsdienst
0015-5268 F I V Meddelanden
0015-5276 Foeretagaren
0015-5284 Foersamlings- och Pastoratsfoervaltning *changed to* Svenska Kyrkans
0015-5292 Foerskolan
0015-5306 Foersvarstjaenstemannen
0015-5314 Fogorvosi Szemle
0015-5322 Fogra-Literaturdienst
0015-5330 Fogra-Mitteilungen
0015-5349 F O I Digest†
0015-5357 Foi et Vie
0015-5365 Foi et Vie de l'Eglise au Diocese de Toulouse
0015-5373 Foil
0015-539X Fold es Eg
0015-5403 Foldrajzi Ertesito
0015-5411 Foldrajzi Kozlemenyek
0015-542X Foldtani Kozlony
0015-5438 Folger Library Newsletter
0015-5446 Folha Bancaria
0015-5454 Folha Medica
0015-5470 Folia Allergologica *see* 0303-8432
0015-5489 Folia Biochimica et Biologica Graeca
0015-5497 Folia Biologica
0015-5500 Folia Biologica
0015-5519 Folia Clinica et Biologica†
0015-5527 Folia Clinica Internacional†
0015-5543 Folia Forestalia
0015-5551 Folia Geobotanica et Phytotaxonomica
0015-5578 Folia Hereditaria et Pathologica
0015-5586 Folia Histochemica et Cytochemica *changed to* Folia Histochemica et Cytobiologica
0015-5594 Folia Humanistica
0015-5608 Folia Medica†
0015-5616 Folia Medica Cracoviensia
0015-5624 Netherlands Journal of Medicine
0015-5632 Folia Microbiologica
0015-5640 Folia Morphologica
0015-5659 Folia Morphologica†
0015-5667 Folia Ophtalmologica Japonica
0015-5675 Folia Orientalia
0015-5683 Folia Parasitologica
0015-5691 Folia Pharmacologica Japonica
0015-5705 Folia Phoniatrica
0015-5713 Folia Primatologica
0015-5721 Folia Psychiatrica et Neurologica Japonica
0015-573X Folia Quaternaria
0015-5748 Folia Veterinaria
0015-5756 Folio (Birmingham)
0015-5764 Folio†
0015-5772 Folio
0015-5780 Folio (Waltham)†
0015-5799 Folio Pharmaceutica
0015-5802 Folium Diocesanum Bauzanense-Brixinense
0015-5810 Folk og Fritid
0015-5829 Folk Style
0015-5837 Folkeskolen
0015-5845 Folkevirke
0015-5853 Folkforsvaret†
0015-5861 Folkets Vael *changed to* Folkets-Vael/DKSN-RIA Informerar
0015-587X Folklore
0015-5888 Folklore
0015-5896 Folklore
0015-590X Folklore Brabancon
0015-5918 Folklore de France
0015-5926 Folklore Forum
0015-5950 Folklore Society of Greater Washington Newsletter
0015-5969 Folklore Suisse
0015-6000 Follia di New York
0015-6019 Contrary Investor Follow-up Service
0015-6027 Fomento†
0015-6035 Fomento de la Produccion
0015-6043 Revista de Fomento Social
0015-6051 Fondation Eugene Ysaye. Bulletin d'Information
0015-606X Fondazione Giorgio Ronchi. Atti
0015-6078 Fonderia
0015-6086 Fonderia Italiana
0015-6108 Fonderie Belge†
0015-6116 Fondeur d'Aujourd'hui *see* 0249-3136
0015-6124 Fondo Nacional de las Artes. Informativo†
0015-6132 Confederacion Espanola de Cajas de Ahorros. Fondo para la Investigacion Economica y Social. Boletin de Documentacion†
0015-6140 Fono Forum
0015-6159 Platenwereld†
0015-6167 Foenstret
0015-6175 Fontane-Blaetter
0015-6183 Fontes Archaeologici Pragenses
0015-6191 Fontes Artis Musicae
0015-6213 Food Agriculture and Plantation Journal
0015-6221 Food and Agricultural Legislation
0015-6256 Food and Cookery Review
0015-6264 Food and Cosmetics Toxicology *see* 0278-6915
0015-6272 Food and Drug Packaging
0015-6280 Food & Equipment Product News *see* 0199-7696
0015-6302 Hospitality-Food and Lodging *see* 0148-0766
0015-6310 Food & Nutrition News
0015-6329 Food and Nutrition Notes and Reviews *see* 0728-4713
0015-6337 Food Chemical News
0015-6353 Food Distributors News *changed to* Food Distributors Magazine
0015-6361 Food Drug Cosmetic Law Journal
0015-637X Food Engineering *see* 0193-323X
0015-6388 Food Executive
0015-6396 Food Farming and Agriculture
0015-640X Food Fish Situation Outlook *see* 0091-8105
0015-6418 Food from Poland†
0015-6426 Food Hygienic Society of Japan. Journal
0015-6442 Food in Canada
0015-6450 Food Industries of South Africa
0015-6469 Food Ingredients & Equipment *see* 0149-5895
0015-6477 Food Manufacture
0015-6493 Food Merchants Advocate
0015-6507 Food Outlook *changed to* Retail Food Price Report
0015-6515 Food Plant Equipment *see* 0747-2536
0015-6523 Food Processing
0015-6531 Food Processing Industry
0015-654X Food Product Development *see* 0279-0726
0015-6558 Food Promotions
0015-6566 Food Research Institute Studies in Agricultural Economics, Trade, and Development *see* 0193-9025
0015-6574 Food Science and Technology Abstracts
0015-6582 Food-Scope†
0015-6604 Food Service Magazine *see* 0746-1887
0015-6639 Food Technology
0015-6647 Food Technology in Australia
0015-6655 Food Technology in New Zealand
0015-6663 Food Trade News
0015-6671 Food Trade Review
0015-668X Food World *changed to* World Food Review
0015-6698 Foodpack
0015-6701 Foodpress†
0015-6728 Foodsman
0015-6752 Football Clinic†
0015-6760 Football Digest
0015-6787 Football Pictorial *changed to* Football Monthly
0015-6795 Football Record
0015-6809 Footplate
0015-6817 Footwear Fashions
0015-6825 Footwear Manufacturers Journal†
0015-6833 Footwear News
0015-6841 Footwear Weekly *see* 0306-3437
0015-685X For Reference
0015-6868 For Teens Only†
0015-6884 For the Defense
0015-6892 For You from Czechoslovakia
0015-6906 Forage and Grassland Progress†
0015-6914 Forbes
0015-6922 Forbes Magazine's Restaurant Guide†
0015-6930 Forbrukeren†
0015-6949 Foerbundskontakt *changed to* Soedra
0015-6981 Ford Estate
0015-699X Ford Foundation Letter
0015-7007 Ford-Nachrichten
0015-7015 Ford Times
0015-7031 Ford Wereld†

0015-704X Fordham Law Review
0015-7058 Ford's Freighter Travel Guide *changed to* Ford's Freighter Travel Guide and Waterways of the World
0015-7066 Ford's International Cruise Guide
0015-7074 Forecast *changed to* Y Seren
0015-7082 Forecast Data Bank Cumulative Sheets
0015-7090 Forecast for Home Economics *changed to* Forecast for the Home Economist
0015-7104 Advance Weather Forecasts†
0015-7112 Forefront *changed to* Howard University Journal of Science
0015-7120 Foreign Affairs
0015-7139 Foreign Affairs Bulletin
0015-7155 Foreign Affairs Reports
0015-7163 Foreign Agriculture
0015-718X Foreign Language Annals
0015-7198 Foreign Language Beacon *changed to* Beacon (Georgia)
0015-721X Foreign Chemical Patent News
0015-7228 Foreign Policy
0015-7244 Foreign Projects Newsletter
0015-7260 Foreign Radio Amateur Callbook Magazine *changed to* Foreign Callbook
0015-7279 Foreign Service Journal
0015-7287 U.S. Department of State. Foreign Service List†
0015-7317 Foreign Trade Bulletin
0015-7325 Foreign Trade Review
0015-7333 Foreman's Letter
0015-735X Forensic
0015-7368 Forensic Science Society. Journal
0015-7384 Forest and Bird
0015-7392 Forest and Timber
0015-7406 Forest Farmer
0015-7422 Forest History *see* 0094-5080
0015-7430 Forest Industries
0015-7449 Forest Log
0015-7457 Forest Notes
0015-7473 Forest Products Journal
0015-7481 Forest Research Institute and Colleges, Dehra Dun. Quarterly News Letter
0015-749X Forest Science
0015-7503 Foresta
0015-7511 Foresters Miscellany
0015-752X Forestry
0015-7538 Forestry Abstracts
0015-7546 Forestry Chronicle
0015-7546 Forestry Chronicle *issued with* 0068-8991
0015-7570 Forestry Marketing Bulletin *changed to* Sawlog
0015-7589 Forests & People
0015-7597 Foret
0015-7619 Foeretagsekonomi Bokfoeraren-Revisorn
0015-7627 Forex Service *changed to* International Business Regulations Report
0015-7635 Forge†
0015-766X Form
0015-7678 Form
0015-7686 Form & Function
0015-7694 Form und Geist
0015-7708 Form und Technik *see* 0012-6470
0015-7716 Forma et Functio†
0015-7724 Formage des Materiaux *changed to* Travail des Metaux Par Deformation
0015-7732 Formage et Traitements des Metaux *changed to* Machine Moderne
0015-7740 Format
0015-7759 Format
0015-7767 Formazione e Lavoro
0015-7775 Graveur Flexograf
0015-7791 Formosan Science
0015-7805 Forms of Business Agreements
0015-7813 Fornvaennen
0015-783X Foro Italiano
0015-7848 Foro Napoletano
0015-7864 Foro Penale
0015-7880 Foersaakringstidningen
0015-7899 Forschung im Ingenieurwesen
0015-7902 Forschungen zur Volks- und Landeskunde
0015-7910 Vierteljahresberichte - Probleme der Entwicklungslaender
0015-7929 Forsikringstidende
0015-7937 Forskning och Framsteg
0015-7945 Norges Almenvitenskapelige Forskiningsraad. Forskningsnytt†
0015-7953 Institutet foer Metallforskning. Forskningsverksamheten
0015-7961 Der Forst- und Holzwirt
0015-797X Forstliche Mitteilungen
0015-7988 Forstliche Umschau
0015-7996 Forstpflanzen-Forstsamen
0015-8003 Forstwissenschaftliches Centralblatt
0015-8011 Foersvarsmedicin†
0015-802X Fort Beaufort Advocate
0015-8038 Fort Dodge Biochemic Review†
0015-8054 Fort Hare Papers
0015-8070 Fort Ticonderoga Museum. Bulletin
0015-8089 Fort Worth
0015-8097 Fort Worth Commercial Recorder
0015-8100 Forth Valley Chamber of Commerce Quarterly Bulletin *changed to* Central Scotland Chamber of Commerce Quarterly Bulletin
0015-8119 Forthcoming Books
0015-8127 Fortnightly Journal of Industry & Commerce
0015-8135 Fortpflanzung, Besamung und Aufzucht der Haustiere. Biologie, Pathologie und Hygiene†
0015-8151 Fortschritte auf dem Gebiete der Roentgenstrahlen und der Nuklearmedizin *see* 0340-1618
0015-816X Fortschritte der Kieferorthopaedie
0015-8178 Fortschritte der Medizin
0015-8186 Fortschritte der Mineralogie
0015-8194 Fortschritte der Neurologie, Psychiatrie und Ihrer Grenzgebiete *changed to* Fortschritte der Neurologie, Psychiatrie
0015-8208 Fortschritte der Physik†
0015-8216 Fortschrittliche Betriebs-fuehrung *changed to* Fortschrittliche Betriebsfuehrung und Industrial Engineering
0015-8224 Der Fortschrittliche Landwirt
0015-8232 Fortuna Italiana
0015-8240 Fortune
0015-8259 Fortune *changed to* Fortune Magazine
0015-8275 Fortune News
0015-8283 Forty Acres and a Mule†
0015-8291 Education Forum†
0015-8305 Forum (Washington, 1963)
0015-8313 Forum
0015-8321 Forum†
0015-833X Forum
0015-8356 Forum (Chicago, 1965) *see* 0885-856X
0015-8364 Forum†
0015-8372 Forum†
0015-8380 Forum†
0015-8399 Forum (Scranton)
0015-8402 Forum
0015-8410 Forum (Houston)†
0015-8445 Forum
0015-8453 Forum - Revista Invatamintului Superior
0015-847X Forum Botanicum
0015-8488 Forum de la Force Terrestre
0015-8496 Forum der Letteren
0015-850X Forum des Praktischen Arztes
0015-8518 Forum for Modern Language Studies
0015-8526 Forum for the Advancement of Toxicology in Colleges of Pharmacy. Newsletter *changed to* Forum for the Advancement of Toxicology
0015-8534 Forum Haus Ortlohn. Freundsbrief *changed to* Forum. Berichte aus der Arbeit
0015-8542 Forum of Education
0015-8550 Forum on Public Affairs†
0015-8577 Forumeer
0015-8585 Foervaltningsraettslig Tidskrift
0015-8593 Forward *see* 0731-3675
0015-8615 Forward *changed to* Civil Aviation in Pakistan: Half-Yearly Newsletter
0015-8623 Forward in Erie *changed to* Forward
0015-8631 Forward in Europe *see* 0252-0958
0015-864X Forward Markets Bulletin
0015-8658 Special Education - Forward Trends *changed to* British Journal of Special Education
0015-8674 Foss†
0015-8690 Foto-Film-Video-Tip
0015-8704 Foto-Kino Revija
0015-8712 Foto-Magazin
0015-8720 Foto-Notiziario
0015-8755 Foto & Film Prisma†
0015-8771 Fotocamara con Popular Photography
0015-8798 Fotograferne†
0015-8801 Fotografia *see* 0324-8453
0015-881X Fotografia Universal
0015-8828 Fotografie
0015-8836 Fotografie
0015-8844 Fotohaendler *changed to* Fotowirtschaft
0015-8879 Fotokino-Magazin
0015-8895 Foton
0015-8909 Fotonyheterna
0015-8933 Foundation Facts
0015-8941 Foundation for Reformation Research. Bulletin of the Library *changed to* Sixteenth Century Bibliography
0015-895X Foundation for Reformation Research. Newsletter *changed to* Center for Reformation Research. Newsletter
0015-8968 Foundation Law Review
0015-8976 Foundation News
0015-8984 Foundation Time
0015-8992 Foundations *changed to* American Baptist Quarterly
0015-900X Foundations of Language *see* 0378-4177
0015-9018 Foundations of Physics
0015-9026 F.W.P. Journal *changed to* Founding, Welding, Production Engineering Journal
0015-9034 Foundry *see* 0360-8999
0015-9042 Foundry Trade Journal
0015-9069 Fountainhead†
0015-9077 Four and Five
0015-9093 Peace and Freedom
0015-9107 Four Quarters
0015-9115 Four States Genealogist†
0015-9123 Four Wheeler Magazine
0015-914X Fourier
0015-9158 La Fournee
0015-9174 Fourrure et Peau en Poil†
0015-9182 Foursquare World Advance
0015-9190 Fourth Estate
0015-9204 Fourth International†
0015-9212 Fox-Report†
0015-9220 Foxfire
0015-9239 Foyers Mixtes
0015-9247 Fra Fysikkens Verden
0015-9255 Fra Haug og Heidni
0015-9271 Fracastoro
0015-928X Fragen der Freiheit
0015-9298 Fragmenta Balcanica Musei Macedonici Scientiarum Naturalium
0015-9301 Fragmenta Faunistica
0015-931X Fragmenta Floristica et Geobotanica
0015-9336 Fragments *changed to* Banque Populaire Suisse. Journal
0015-9344 Fragments
0015-9352 Fraktemann
0015-9360 Saadd och Skoerd *see* 0021-7433
0015-9379 Franc-Rire
0015-9387 Francais au Nigeria
0015-9395 Francais dans le Monde
0015-9409 Francais Moderne
0015-9417 France/Loisirs†
0015-9425 France-Cuir†
0015-9433 France-Theatre
0015-9441 France a Table†
0015-9476 France-Algerie†
0015-9484 France Alimentaire
0015-9506 France Catholique *changed to* France Catholique-Ecclesia
0015-9530 France. Commissariat General au Tourisme. Bulletin Mensual de Statistique du Tourisme *see* 0753-311X
0015-9549 France Dimanche
0015-9557 Societe d'Edition de Periodiques Sportifs
0015-9565 France Graphique
0015-9573 France Horlogere
0015-959X France Informations
0015-9603 France. Institut National de la Sante et de la Recherche Medicale. Bulletin *changed to* France. Institut National de la Sante et de la Recherche Medicale. Bulletin d'Information
0015-962X France Medicale†
0015-9646 France. Ministere de l'Agriculture. Bulletin Technique d'Information (1945) *changed to* France. Ministere de l'Agriculture. Bulletin Technique d'Information
0015-9654 France. Ministere de l'Economie et des Finances. Statistiques et Etudes Financieres *changed to* France. Ministere de l'Economie et des Finances. Statistiques et Etudes Financieres. Finance Publique. Serie Bleue
0015-9670 France Mutualite
0015-9689 France Peche *see* 0296-3353
0015-9697 France Pharmacie
0015-9700 France-Pologne, Peuples Amis
0015-9719 France. Ministere de la Defense Nationale. Bulletin d'Information Technique et Scientifique
0015-9727 France. Ministere de la Defense Nationale. Bulletin Officiel
0015-9735 France. Secretariat d'Etat a la Marine. Bulletin d'Information de la Marine Nationale†
0015-9743 Problemes Politiques et Sociaux
0015-9751 France-U.S.A
0015-9778 Franchising Around the World *changed to* Franchising Investments Around the World
0015-9786 Francis Bolen's Newsletter
0015-9794 Franciskaans Leven
0015-9808 Franciscan *changed to* Inside San Francisco State University
0015-9816 Franciscan Herald†
0015-9840 Franciscana
0015-9867 Franco-British Trade Review *changed to* Info
0015-9875 Franco Vida†
0015-9905 Frankenland
0015-9921 Frankford News Gleaner *changed to* NewsGleaner - Frankford - Oxford Circle Edition
0015-993X Frankfurter Blaetter fuer Heimatvertriebene
0015-9964 Frankfurter Gastronomie
0015-9972 Frankfurter Handwerk†
0015-9980 Frankfurter Hausfrauen Zeitung†
0015-9999 Frankfurter Hefte
0016-0008 Frankfurter Lehrerblatt†
0016-0024 Frankfurter Wochenschau *changed to* Frankfurter Woche
0016-0032 Franklin Institute. Journal
0016-0040 Franklin Township Sentinel
0016-0059 Franse Boek *changed to* Rapports Franse Boek
0016-0067 Franziskanische Studien
0016-0075 Investment Survey of Warrants *changed to* F R A Warrant Service
0016-0083 Fraser's Circular
0016-0091 Frate Francesco
0016-0105 Fraternal Monitor
0016-0113 Fraternity Month†
0016-0121 Frau
0016-013X Frau im Beruf
0016-0148 Frau im Leben
0016-0172 Frau und Frieden
0016-0199 Neue Mode - Frau und Mutter
0016-0202 Frau und Politik
0016-0210 Die Frau von Heute
0016-0229 Frauen der Ganzen Welt
0016-0237 Der Frauenarzt
0016-0245 Frauenkulter *changed to* Frau und Kultur
0016-0288 Fred och Frihet
0016-0296 Freddo
0016-030X Free China Review
0016-0318 Free China Weekly *see* 0255-9870

ISSN INDEX 1237

0016-0326	Free Church Chronicle	0016-1500	Fritidsgaarden†	0016-2663	Functional Analysis and Its Applications
0016-0334	Free Church of Scotland. Monthly Record	0016-1519	Fritt Kjoepmannskap	0016-2671	Fund Guide Internationak *changed to* Portfolio and Fund Guide International
0016-0342	Free Enterprise *changed to* American Patriot	0016-1527	Fritzsche-D & O Library Bulletin†	0016-268X	Fund Raising Management
		0016-1535	Il Friuli Medico	0016-2698	Fundacion Jimenez Diaz. Boletin
0016-0350	Free Labour World	0016-1543	Foersvarsforskningsreferat	0016-2701	Fundacion John Boulton. Boletin Historico†
0016-0369	Free Lance	0016-156X	Der Froehliche Kreis		
0016-0377	Free-Lance Report	0016-1586	From Italy†	0016-271X	Fundacion Roux-Ocefa. Archivos†
0016-0385	Free-Lance Writing & Photography *changed to* Free-Lance Writing	0016-1594	From Italy Clothing *see* 0016-1586	0016-2728	Fundament
		0016-1608	From New York†	0016-2736	Fundamenta Mathematicae
0016-0423	Boston Free Press†	0016-1616	From Nine to Five	0016-2744	Fundamentalist
0016-0431	Free Press Weekly Report on Farming *see* 0317-8552	0016-1624	From the California State Librarian†	0016-2760	FundScope†
		0016-1632	From the State Capitals. Agricultural and Food Products *changed to* From the State Capitals. Agriculture	0016-2779	Die Fundstelle
0016-044X	Free Ranger Inter-Tribal News Service *see* 0730-1766			0016-2787	Funeral Forum
				0016-2809	Funeral Service Journal
0016-0458	Free State Libraries	0016-1691	From the State Capitals. General Bulletin *see* 0741-3475	0016-2817	Funk Fachhaendler†
0016-0474	Free Trader†			0016-2825	Funk-Technik†
0016-0482	Free World Horizons	0016-1705	From the State Capitals. Highway Financing and Construction†	0016-2841	Funkschau
0016-0504	Freedom			0016-285X	Funktsional'nyi Analiz i Ego Prilozheniya
0016-0512	Freedom & Union†	0016-1713	From the State Capitals. Housing and Redevelopment *see* 0741-3483		
0016-0520	Freedom at Issue			0016-2876	Fuoco
0016-0547	Freedom First	0016-1748	From the State Capitals. Insurance Regulation	0016-2884	Fur Age Weekly
0016-0555	Freedom Magazine			0016-2892	Fur and Feather, Rabbits and Rabbit Keeping *changed to* Fur & Feather
0016-0571	Freedom of Vision	0016-1764	From the State Capitals. Juvenile Delinquency and Family Relations *see* 0741-3505		
0016-061X	Freedomways			0016-2906	Fur & Feathers
0016-0644	Freeland†			0016-2914	Fur Bulletin
0016-0652	Freeman	0016-1780	From the State Capitals. Liquor Control *see* 0734-0842	0016-2922	Fur-Fish-Game. Harding's Magazine
0016-0660	Freemason			0016-2930	Fur Market Review *see* 0260-2393
0016-0679	Freeport Memorial Library. News Bulletin†	0016-1799	From the State Capitals. Merchandising *see* 0741-3467	0016-2957	Fur and Leather Review *see* 0260-2393
				0016-2965	Fur Taker
0016-0687	Freethinker	0016-1810	From the State Capitals. Motor Vehicle Regulation	0016-2973	Fur Trade Journal of Canada *see* 0381-8535
0016-0695	Freezer Provisioning and Portion Control *see* 0192-2807				
		0016-1829	From the State Capitals. Off-Street Parking *see* 0749-2774	0016-2981	Fur Weekly News
0016-0709	Freiburger Studentenzeitung			0016-299X	Die Furche
0016-0725	Freiburger Zeitschrift fuer Philosophie und Theologie	0016-1845	From the State Capitals. Personnel Management *see* 0741-3521	0016-3007	Home Furnishing†
				0016-3015	Furnishing World *see* 0007-9278
0016-075X	Freie Lehrerstimme	0016-1888	From the State Capitals. Public Utilities	0016-304X	Furniture Design and Manufacturing *see* 0192-8058
0016-0768	Freie Presse-Korrespondenz	0016-1896	From the State Capitals. Racial Relations *see* 0741-353X		
0016-0776	Freie Religion			0016-3058	Furniture History
0016-0784	Die Freie Wohnungswirtschaft	0016-1926	From the State Capitals. Sewage and Waste Disposal *changed to* Waste Disposal and Pollution	0016-3066	Furniture News *see* 0194-360X
0016-0792	F D P Informationsdienst†			0016-3074	Furniture South *changed to* Furniture World
0016-0806	Freies Bayern				
0016-0814	Freies Leben†	0016-1934	From the State Capitals. Small Loans, Sales Finance, Banking *see* 0749-2812	0016-3082	Furniture Warehouseman *see* 0092-7449
0016-0830	Freigeistige Aktion *changed to* Der Humanist				
		0016-1942	Local Non-Property *see* 0741-3556	0016-3090	Furniture Workers Press
0016-0849	Freight	0016-2019	Front	0016-3104	Furniture World and Furniture Buyer and Decorator
0016-0857	Freight *changed to* Commercial Transport	0016-2027	Front		
		0016-2043	Front Page Detective	0016-3112	Furrow
0016-0857	Freight *changed to* Freight World	0016-2078	Frontier†	0016-3120	Furrow
0016-0865	Freight & Container Transportation†	0016-2086	Frontier†	0016-3139	Fuersorger *changed to* Suchtprobleme und Sozialarbeit
0016-0881	Freight News *changed to* Freight News Weekly	0016-2094	Frontier		
		0016-2108	Frontier News	0016-3147	Fusilier
0016-089X	Freighter Travel News	0016-2116	Frontier Nursing Service Quarterly Bulletin	0016-3155	Fusion
0016-0903	Freiheitlicher Oberoesterreichischer Landeslehrer Verein. Zeitschrift *changed to* Freiheitlicher Oberoesterreichischer Lehrerverein. Zeitschrift			0016-3171	Fusion Facts†
		0016-2132	Frontiera	0016-318X	Fusion Facts†
		0016-2159	Frontiers†	0016-321X	Fussball-Jugend†
		0016-2167	Frontiers of Plant Science	0016-3228	Der Fussballtrainer
		0016-2175	Frontlijn	0016-3244	Futur†
0016-0911	Die Freiheitsglocke	0016-2183	Frontpage	0016-3252	Futura
0016-092X	Der Freiwillige	0016-2191	Frozen Food Age	0016-3260	Future *changed to* Jaycees Magazine
0016-0938	Freizeit-Mode *changed to* Sportshop	0016-2205	Frozen Foods *changed to* Frozen and Chilled Foods	0016-3287	Futures
0016-0946	Der Freizeitgaertner			0016-3295	Futures Market Service
0016-0954	Fremdenverkehr-Reiseland-Oesterreich *see* 0254-5292	0016-2221	Fruechte und Gemuese	0016-3317	Futurist
		0016-2248	Fruit Belge	0016-3325	Futuro
0016-0962	Fremdenverkehr *changed to* Der Fremdenverkehr-Tourismus & Kongress	0016-2256	Fruit Trades Journal	0016-3341	Futurum†
		0016-2264	Fruit of the Vine	0016-335X	4H-Journalen *see* 0281-1278
0016-0970	Fremdsprachen	0016-2272	Fruit Varieties and Horticultural Digest *see* 0091-3642	0016-3376	Fyzika ve Skole *changed to* Matematika a Fyzika ve Skole
0016-0997	Fremonitor				
0016-1004	Fremont Schools	0016-2280	Fruit World and Market Grower†	0016-3384	Fysioterapeuten
0016-1012	Fremsyn	0016-2299	Fruits	0016-3392	Fysisk Tidsskrift
0016-1020	Fremtiden	0016-2302	Fruitteelt	0016-3406	G A
0016-1039	French-American Commerce	0016-2310	Frutticoltura	0016-3414	G A O Review
0016-1047	French Canadian and Acadian Genealogical Review	0016-2329	Ftiziologia *changed to* Revista de Igiena, Bacteriologie, Virusologie, Parazitologie, Pneumoftiziologie. Pneumoftiziologie	0016-3422	G A T F Newsletter†
				0016-3449	G C A Newsletter *changed to* Voice for Girls
0016-1071	French Historical Studies				
0016-108X	French Notes & Queries†			0016-3457	G D I Information†
0016-1098	French Patents Abstracts	0016-2353	Fuehrungskraefte Foerdern†	0016-3465	G D I Test Universal *see* 0016-3457
0016-1101	French Railway Techniques†	0016-2361	Fuel	0016-3473	G D I Topics *changed to* Brennpunkte
0016-111X	French Review	0016-237X	Ful-, Orr-, Gegegyogyaszat	0016-3481	G.D.R. Peace Council. Information
0016-1128	French Studies	0016-2388	Fuel Abstracts and Current Titles *see* 0140-6701	0016-349X	G D R Review
0016-1136	Frequenz			0016-3503	G E N
0016-1144	Freres d'Armes	0016-2396	Fuel Oil News	0016-3511	G F M-Mitteilungen zur Markt- und Absatzforschung *see* 0170-723X
0016-1152	Fresenius' Zeitschrift fuer Analytische Chemie	0016-240X	Fules		
		0016-2418	Fueloil and Oil Heat *see* 0148-9801	0016-3538	G I T
0016-1160	Fresno County Medical Society. Bulletin *changed to* Vital Signs (Fresno)	0016-2426	Fuer Alle†	0016-3554	G L C A Newsletter†
		0016-2434	Fuer Arbeit und Besinnung	0016-3562	G L V Mitteilungen
0016-1187	Freundin	0016-2442	Fuer Heute	0016-3570	GmbH-Rundschau
0016-1209	Freyr	0016-2450	Fuer Sie	0016-3597	G O†
0016-1217	Fri Koepenskap	0016-2469	Fuerstenfelder Grenzlandecho	0016-3600	G P *see* 0002-838X
0016-1225	Friar Magazine†	0016-2477	Fuerza Nueva	0016-3619	G R A Reporter
0016-1233	Friday Flash	0016-2493	Fuji Bank Bulletin	0016-3627	G S N. Gesneriad Saintpaulia News
0016-1268	Friend	0016-2507	Keio University. Fujihara Memorial Faculty of Engineering. Proceedings. *see* 0286-4215	0016-3635	Grossmont Educator *changed to* G E A Educator
0016-1276	Friend of Animals				
0016-1284	Friend O'Wildlife				
0016-1292	Friendly Companion	0016-2515	Fujitsu	0016-3651	G W F Gas- und Wasserfach *changed to* Wasser/Abwasser - G W F
0016-1314	Friendly World†	0016-2523	Fujitsu Scientific & Technical Journal		
0016-1322	Friends Journal	0016-2531	Red Double-Barred Cross	0016-366X	G W: George Washington University Magazine *see* 0279-2435
0016-1330	Friends of the San Bernardino County Library. News Letter†	0016-254X	Fukuoka Acta Medica		
		0016-2558	Fukuoka District Meteorological Observatory. Unusual Meteorological Report	0016-3678	Gaangsport
0016-1349	Friends of Youth Newsletter *changed to* Target (Renton)			0016-3686	Catholic Broadcasters Association. Newsletter *changed to* Unda - U S A Newsletter
0016-1357	Friends' Quarterly	0016-2566	Fukuoka District Meteorological Observatory. Technical Times	0016-3694	Gabriel
0016-1365	Friends World News			0016-3708	Gabriele *changed to* Sekretariat
0016-1373	Fries Landbouwblad	0016-2574	Fukuoka Prefecture. Monthly Report of Meteorology	0016-3716	Gaceta
0016-1381	Friesch Rundvee-Stamboek. Mededelingen *see* 0168-7565			0016-3724	La Gaceta
		0016-2582	Fukushima Medical Journal	0016-3759	Gaceta de la Universidad
0016-1403	Friesia *see* 0107-055X	0016-2590	Fukushima Journal of Medical Science	0016-3767	Gaceta Economica
0016-1411	Frigotechnica *changed to* Frigotherma	0016-2604	Fulcrum	0016-3775	Gaceta Hipica
0016-142X	Frihet	0016-2612	Fuldaer Geschichtsblaetter	0016-3783	Gaceta Ilustrada
0016-1438	Frimaerkesamleren	0016-2620	Full Cry	0016-3791	Honduras. Corte Suprema de Justicia. Gaceta Judicial
0016-1446	Fripound	0016-2639	Filmmuseum-Cinematheek *changed to* Filmmuseum Cinematheek Journaal		
0016-1454	Friseurhandwerk Friseurspiegel			0016-3805	Gaceta Matematica
0016-1470	Friseurwelt	0016-2655	Fun for Middlers *changed to* Rainbow (Valley Forge)	0016-3813	Gaceta Medica de Mexico
0016-1489	Frisur *see* 0323-410X			0016-3821	Gaceta Medica Espanola

ISSN	Title
0016-383X	Gaceta Militar y Naval†
0016-3848	Gaceta Politecnica
0016-3856	Gaceta Pre Militar†
0016-3864	Gaceta Rural
0016-3880	Gacetilla Agricola de Holanda†
0016-3902	Garten- und Freizeitmarkt
0016-3910	Gaiato
0016-3929	Gairm
0016-3945	Musical Instruments News *changed to* Music Trade in Japan
0016-3953	Gakushuin Economic Papers
0016-397X	Gala *changed to* Gala International
0016-3988	Galamukani!
0016-3996	Galaxia
0016-4003	Galaxy
0016-4011	Galencia Acta†
0016-402X	Galeon
0016-4038	Galerie *changed to* Arts-Magazine
0016-4046	Galerie Raymond Creuze. Bulletin†
0016-4054	Galesburg Labor News
0016-4070	Gallagher Report
0016-4089	Gallaudet Today
0016-4097	Galleria
0016-4100	Galley Sail Review
0016-4119	Gallia
0016-4127	Gallia Prehistoire
0016-4143	Gallneukirchner Bote *changed to* Diakonie
0016-4151	El Gallo News
0016-416X	Gallo *changed to* Quaderni del Gallo
0016-4178	Galloway News
0016-4186	Galloway Times†
0016-4194	Gallup Opinion Index *see* 0731-6143
0016-4216	Galpakabita
0016-4224	Galvano *changed to* Galvano-Organo-Traitements de Surface
0016-4240	Galvanotecnica *changed to* Galvanotecnica e Processi al Plasma
0016-4259	Gam on Yachting
0016-4275	Gambit†
0016-4283	Gambit
0016-4313	Gamecock
0016-4321	Gameskeeeper and Countryside *see* 0261-2208
0016-433X	Gamekeepers' Gazette *changed to* Shooting & Conservation
0016-4348	Games and Toys *changed to* Toys and Games Trader
0016-4356	Gamesletter *see* 0016-4364
0016-4364	Gamesman†
0016-4380	Gamma
0016-4402	Gan v'Nof
0016-4429	Gandalf's Garden
0016-4437	Gandhi Marg
0016-4445	Gandhian Thought
0016-4453	Gangan
0016-4461	Ganganatha Jha Research Institute. Journal *changed to* Ganganatha Jha Kendriya Sanskrit Vidyapeetha. Journal
0016-4488	Ophthalmology
0016-4496	Ganmitram
0016-450X	Gann *see* 0910-5050
0016-4518	Ganterie-Vetements de Peau†
0016-4526	Garage
0016-4542	Garage & Officina
0016-4550	Garage, Tankstelle und Servicestation *changed to* Tankstelle und Garage
0016-4569	Garcia de Orta†
0016-4585	Garden Journal *see* 0191-3999
0016-4593	Garden News
0016-4607	Garden Path
0016-4615	Garden Stater†
0016-4623	Garden Supplies Retailer†
0016-4631	Garden Writers Bulletin
0016-464X	Gardener
0016-4682	Gardeners Chronicle/Horticultural Trade Journal *changed to* Horticulture Week
0016-4712	Garment Worker
0016-4720	Garten und Landschaft
0016-4739	Das Gartenamt
0016-4747	Gartenbau
0016-4755	Gartenbau†
0016-4763	Der Gartenbauingenieur
0016-4771	Gartenbauwirtschaft mit Gartenbau Nachrichten *changed to* Gartenbauwirtschaft
0016-478X	Gartenbauwissenschaft
0016-4798	Gartenwelt *changed to* G B und G W - Gaertnerboerse und Gartenwelt
0016-4801	Gary Library Bulletin *changed to* Gary Graphique
0016-4828	Gas
0016-4836	Gas Magazine *see* 0161-4851
0016-4844	Gas Abstracts
0016-4852	Gas and Oil Power *see* 0308-4795
0016-4860	Gas & Sanitair Mercuur†
0016-4887	Gas Chromatography Abstracts *see* 0538-7590
0016-4895	Gas Chromatography Literature-Abstracts & Index
0016-4909	Gas - Erdgas/G W F
0016-4925	Gas in Industry and Commerce *changed to* Natural Gas
0016-4933	Gas in Industry *see* 0194-2468
0016-495X	Gas Liquefatti - le Apparecchiature
0016-4968	Gas Processing/Canada *see* 0319-5759
0016-4976	Gas Scope
0016-4984	Gas Marketing *see* 0308-7026
0016-4992	Gas Showroom *see* 0308-7026
0016-500X	Gas Turbine Magazine *see* 0149-4147
0016-5018	Gas, Wasser, Waerme
0016-5034	Gas-Beispiele†
0016-5042	Gasoline News
0016-5069	Monthly Gasoline Stand
0016-5077	Gastro-Enterologie Quotidienne
0016-5085	Gastroenterology
0016-5093	Gastroenterology Abstracts and Citations†
0016-5107	Gastrointestinal Endoscopy
0016-5115	Gastronomie *changed to* Plaisirs
0016-5123	Gastronomie-Rundschau
0016-514X	Gastronomo
0016-5158	Gastwirt
0016-5166	Gastwirt und Hotelier *changed to* D G Deutsche Gaststaette/Deutsche Hotel-Zeitung Gastwirt und Hotelier
0016-5182	Gasverwendung†
0016-5190	Gateway
0016-5204	Gateway
0016-5239	Gaudeamus
0016-5247	Gaudeamus
0016-5255	Gauge "O" Guild Gazette
0016-5263	Gaveshana†
0016-5271	Gawein *changed to* Gedrag & Gezondheid
0016-5298	Gay Scene
0016-5301	Gayana: Botanica
0016-531X	Gayana: Zoologica
0016-5328	Gaz d'Aujourd'Hui
0016-5352	Gaz, Woda i Technika Sanitarna
0016-5360	Gazdasag
0016-5379	Gazer
0016-5395	Gazeta Cukrownicza
0016-5409	Gazeta da Farmacia†
0016-5514	Gazeta Matematica. Serie A *changed to* Gazeta Matematica
0016-5441	Gazetta Matematica. Serie B *changed to* Gazeta Matematica
0016-545X	Gazeta Medica da Bahia†
0016-5468	Gazeta Mobil†
0016-5484	Gazette†
0016-5492	Gazette
0016-5506	Gazette Apicole
0016-5514	Gazette de la Region du Nord
0016-5522	Gazette des Archives
0016-5530	Gazette des Beaux Arts
0016-5557	Gazette Medicale de France
0016-5565	Gazette Numismatique Suisse
0016-5573	Gazette Officielle du Tourisme
0016-5581	Gazovaya Promyshlennost'
0016-559X	Gazzetta Antiquaria
0016-5603	Gazzetta Chimica Italiana
0016-5611	Gazzetta Commerciale†
0016-562X	Gazzetta della Domenica
0016-5638	Gazzetta delle Arti
0016-5646	Gazzetta Farmaceutica†
0016-5654	Gazzetta Filatelica
0016-5662	Gazzetta Internazionale di Medicina e Chirurgia
0016-5670	Gazzetta Medica Italiana *changed to* Gazzetta Medica Italiana Archivio per le Scienze Mediche
0016-5697	Gazzetta Sanitaria
0016-5700	Rilancio
0016-5719	Gazzettino della Scuola
0016-5727	Gebaeudigereiniger-Handwerk *changed to* Rationell Reinigen
0016-5735	Gebetsapostolat und Seelsorge
0016-5743	Gebrauchsgraphik *see* 0302-9794
0016-5751	Geburtshilfe und Frauenheilkunde
0016-5778	Gedeeld Domein†
0016-5786	Gedistilleerd, Wijn, Bier en Frisdranken†
0016-5794	Gefaehrdetenhilfe
0016-5808	Gefaehrliche Ladung
0016-5824	Gefluegel-Boerse
0016-5832	Geflugel und Kleinvieh *changed to* Schweizerische Gefluegelzeitung
0016-5840	Gegenbaurs Morphologisches Jahrbuch
0016-5859	Gegenwart
0016-5867	Gegenwart
0016-5875	Gegenwartskunde
0016-5883	Gehoert Gelesen (Munich, 1954)
0016-5913	Geisinger Medical Center. Bulletin†
0016-5921	Geist und Leben
0016-593X	Surgery
0016-5956	Gekkan Kibbutz *changed to* Cooperative Life
0016-5964	Monthly Journal of Gasoline Service Stations
0016-5972	Petroleum Monthly
0016-5980	Pharmaceuticals Monthly
0016-5999	Gelatiere Italiano
0016-6006	Die Gelben Hefte
0016-6014	Gelders Oudheidkundig Contactbericht
0016-6022	Geloteknhika
0016-6030	Gem†
0016-6049	Gemeenteblad van Amsterdam
0016-6057	Gemeentefinancien *changed to* B & G
0016-6065	Gemeenteleven
0016-6073	Die Gemeinde
0016-609X	Gemeindebote
0016-6103	Gemeindebote *changed to* Kirche in Marburg
0016-6111	Gemeindebrief
0016-612X	Die Gemeindekasse
0016-6146	Gemeindekurier
0016-6154	Evangelische Pfarrgemeinde A.B. Wien-Favoriten-Christuskirche. Gemeindebrief
0016-6170	Gemeindeverwaltung in Rheinland - Pfalz
0016-6200	Gemeinsames Amtsblatt des Landes Baden-Wuerttemberg
0016-6219	Gemeinschaft der Wohnungseigentuemer-Informationen *changed to* G D W Informationen
0016-6227	Gemeinwirtschaft
0016-6235	Gemengde Branche(1948) *changed to* Gemengde Branche (1978)
0016-6243	Gemischtwarenhandel
0016-6251	Gems†
0016-626X	Gems & Gemology
0016-6278	Gems and Minerals *see* 0274-8193
0016-6286	Gemuese
0016-6308	Gemueseproduktion *see* 0138-3280
0016-6316	Prosit
0016-6324	Genadeklanken
0016-6332	Contemporary Library Trends *changed to* Libraries Today
0016-6359	Genealogical Helper
0016-6367	Genealogical Magazine of New Jersey
0016-6375	Genealogical Quarterly†
0016-6383	Genealogie
0016-6391	Genealogists' Magazine
0016-6405	Geneologist's Post *changed to* Pennsylvania Traveler-Post
0016-6421	Genealogy Club of America Magazine *see* 0098-7689
0016-643X	Geneeskunde
0016-6448	Geneeskunde en Sport
0016-6464	Geneeskundige Gids†
0016-6472	Genen en Phaenen†
0016-6480	General and Comparative Endocrinology
0016-6499	General and Municipal Workers' Union *changed to* G M B Journal
0016-6502	General Aviation
0016-6510	General Aviation *see* 0191-927X
0016-6537	General Federation Clubwoman *see* 0745-2209
0016-6545	General Insurance Guide
0016-6553	General Linguistics
0016-657X	Strobotactics†
0016-660X	General Topology and Its Applications *see* 0166-8641
0016-6634	Genesee Valley Buyer *see* 0192-9607
0016-6642	Genesee Valley Chemunications
0016-6669	Genesis 2
0016-6677	Genetic Psychology Monographs *see* 8756-7547
0016-6685	Genetica Agraria
0016-6693	Genetica Iberica
0016-6707	Genetica
0016-6715	Genetica Polonica
0016-6723	Genetical Research
0016-6731	Genetics
0016-674X	Genetics Abstracts
0016-6758	Genetika
0016-6766	Genetika i Selektsiia
0016-6774	Geneve-Afrique†
0016-6812	Genie Civil
0016-6820	Genie Construction
0016-6839	Genie Medical
0016-6847	Genie Rurale
0016-6863	Genio Rurale
0016-6871	Genitori†
0016-6898	Genos
0016-6901	Genova
0016-691X	Genova Statistica *changed to* Notiziario Statistico Mensile
0016-6928	Genre
0016-6936	Gens Nostra, "Ons Geslacht"
0016-6944	Gente
0016-6952	Gente
0016-6960	Gentes
0016-6979	Gentlemen's Quarterly
0016-6987	Genus
0016-6995	Geobios
0016-7002	Geochemical Journal
0016-7029	Geochemistry International
0016-7037	Geochimica et Cosmochimica Acta
0016-7053	Geocom Bulletin *changed to* Bibliography of Economic Geology
0016-7061	Geoderma
0016-707X	Geodesia
0016-7088	Geodesy and Aerophotography *changed to* Mapping Sciences & Remote Sensing
0016-7096	Geodeticky a Karaficky Obzor
0016-710X	Geodetski List
0016-7118	Geodezia es Kartografia
0016-7126	Geodeziya i Kartografiya
0016-7134	Geodezja i Kartografia
0016-7142	Geoexploration
0016-7169	Geofisica Internacional
0016-7177	Geophysical Transactions
0016-7185	Geoforum
0016-7193	Geograficky Casopis
0016-7207	Geografiya v Shkole
0016-7215	Geografisch Tijdschrift
0016-7223	Geografisk Tidsskrift
0016-7231	Geografiska Annaler *see* 0435-3676
0016-7231	Geografiska Annaler *see* 0435-3684
0016-724X	Geografiska Notiser
0016-7266	Geografski Horizont
0016-7274	Geografski Obzornik
0016-7282	Geographia Polonica
0016-7290	Geographica
0016-7312	Geographica Helvetica
0016-7339	Geographical Abstracts B (Biogeography, Climatology and Cartography) *see* 0268-7887
0016-7363	Geographical Analysis
0016-7371	Geographical Association of Nigeria. Journal *see* 0029-0084
0016-738X	Geographical Association of Tanzania Journal
0016-7398	Geographical Journal
0016-7401	Geographical Knowledge†
0016-741X	Geographical Magazine†
0016-7428	Geographical Review
0016-7436	Geographical Review of Afghanistan

ISSN INDEX 1239

0016-7444 Geographical Review of Japan. Series A
0016-7452 Geographische Berichte
0016-7460 Geographische Rundschau
0016-7479 Geographische Zeitschrift
0016-7487 Geography
0016-7509 Geography Teacher†
0016-7517 Geography Teacher
0016-7525 Geokhimiya
0016-7533 Geologia y Metalurgia
0016-7541 Geologic Notes *see* 0272-9873
0016-755X Geologica Bavarica
0016-7568 Geological Magazine
0016-7576 Geological, Mining and Metallurgical Society of India. Bulletin
0016-7584 Geological, Mining and Metallurgical Society of India. Quarterly Journal
0016-7592 Geological Society of America. Abstracts with Programs
0016-7606 Geological Society of America. Bulletin
0016-7614 Geological Society of Australia. Journal *see* 0812-0099
0016-7622 Geological Society of India. Journal
0016-7630 Geological Society of Japan. Journal
0016-7649 Geological Society. Journal
0016-7657 Geological Society of South Africa. Quarterly News Bulletin/Geologiese Vereniging van Suid-Afrika. Kwarataalikse Nuusbulletin *changed to* Geological Society of South Africa. Geobulletin
0016-7681 Geological Survey of South Australia. Report of Investigations
0016-769X Geologicheskii Zhurnal Armenii
0016-7703 Geologichnii Zhurnal (Ukrainian) *see* 0201-8489
0016-772X Geologicky Pruzkum
0016-7738 Geologicky Zbornik
0016-7746 Geologie en Mijnbouw
0016-7762 Izvestiya Vysshikh Uchebnykh Zavedenii. Seriya Geologiya i Razvedka
0016-7789 Geologija
0016-7797 Geologische Blaetter fuer Nordost-Bayern und Angrenzende Gebiete
0016-7800 Geologische Bundesanstalt, Vienna. Jahrbuch
0016-7835 Geologische Rundschau
0016-7843 Geologische Gesellschaft, Vienna. Mitteilungen *see* 0251-7493
0016-7851 Geologisches Jahrbuch *see* 0341-6429
0016-7851 Geologisches Jahrbuch *see* 0341-6410
0016-7851 Geologisches Jahrbuch *see* 0341-6399
0016-7851 Geologisches Jahrbuch *see* 0341-6402
0016-786X Geologiska Foereningens i Stockholm. Foerhandlinger
0016-7878 Geologists' Association. Proceedings
0016-7886 Geologiya i Geofizika†
0016-7894 Geologiya Nefti i Gaza
0016-7908 Geologiya Rudnykh Mestorozhdenii
0016-7924 Geoloski Vjesnik
0016-7932 Geomagnetism and Aeronomy
0016-7940 Geomagnetizm i Aeronomiya
0016-7959 Geometra
0016-7967 Geometre
0016-7975 Geominas
0016-7983 Geophysical Abstracts†
0016-8009 Royal Astronomical Society Geophysical Journal
0016-8017 Japan. Meteorological Agency. Geophysical Magazine
0016-8025 Geophysical Prospecting
0016-8033 Geophysics
0016-8041 Leipzig. Universitaet. Geophysikalisches Institut. Veroeffentlichungen. Zweite Serie *see* 0138-2357
0016-8076 George Washington Law Review
0016-8084 Georgetown Dental Journal *see* 0730-0808
0016-8092 Georgetown Law Journal
0016-8106 Georgetown Medical Bulletin
0016-8114 Georgia Journal of Science
0016-8122 Georgia Agricultural Research†
0016-8130 Georgia Alumni Record
0016-8149 Georgia AnchorAge
0016-8157 Georgia Augusta
0016-8173 Georgia Business *see* 0279-3857
0016-8181 Georgia C. P. A†
0016-819X Georgia Dental Association. Journal
0016-822X Georgia Engineer
0016-8254 Georgia Farmer†
0016-8262 Georgia Future Farmer
0016-8270 Georgia Game and Fish *see* 0147-720X
0016-8289 Georgia Government Review *see* 0160-323X
0016-8297 Georgia Historical Quarterly
0016-8300 Georgia Law Review
0016-8319 Georgia Librarian
0016-8335 Georgia Nursing
0016-8351 Georgia Professional Engineer
0016-836X Georgia Progress *changed to* Georgia
0016-8378 Georgia Rehabilitation News†
0016-8386 Georgia Review
0016-8394 Georgia School Boards Bulletin
0016-8416 Georgia State Bar Journal
0016-8424 Georgia State University Signal
0016-8432 Georgia Straight
0016-8440 Georgia Tech Alumnus *changed to* Tech Topics
0016-8459 Georgia Tech Engineer *changed to* Exponent
0016-8467 Georgian
0016-8483 Geoscience Documentation
0016-8491 Geotechnical Abstracts
0016-8505 Geotechnique
0016-8521 Geotectonics
0016-853X Geotektonika
0016-8548 Geotektonische Forschungen
0016-8556 Geotimes
0016-8564 Geotitles Weekly *changed to* Geotitles
0016-8572 Gep
0016-8580 Gepgyartastechnologia
0016-8599 Geraniums around the World
0016-8602 Gereedschap
0016-8610 Gereformeerd Theologisch Tijdschrift
0016-8629 Gereformeerde Kerken in Noord-Brabant en Limburg. Kerkblad
0016-867X Geriatrics
0016-8688 Geriatrics Digest†
0016-8696 Gerlands Beitraege zur Geophysik
0016-870X Gerling-Informationen fuer Geschaeftsfreunde†
0016-8718 German American Trade News *changed to* German American Trade
0016-8726 German Constructions†
0016-8742 German Exporter *see* 0033-0876
0016-8777 German Life and Letters
0016-8785 German Medical Monthly†
0016-8793 German News
0016-8807 German Patents Abstracts
0016-8823 German Postal Specialist
0016-8831 German Quarterly
0016-884X Philosophy and History
0016-8858 German Tribune
0016-8866 Germana Esperanta Fervojista Asocio. Bulteno
0016-8874 Germania
0016-8882 Germanic Notes
0016-8890 Germanic Review
0016-8904 Germanisch-Romanische Monatsschrift
0016-8912 Germanistik
0016-8920 Germantown Courier
0016-8963 Germany Stamp News
0016-898X Gerontologia *see* 0304-324X
0016-8998 Gerontologia Clinica *see* 0304-324X
0016-9005 Gerontologie (Year)
0016-9013 Gerontologist
0016-9021 Geschaeftsmann und Christ
0016-903X Geschaeftsmappe fuer Gemeinden und Standesaemter†
0016-9048 Geschaeftsreisen *changed to* Verband
0016-9056 Geschichte in Wissenschaft und Unterricht
0016-9064 Geschichten aus dem Wienerwald *changed to* W Wintern
0016-9072 Geschichtsunterricht und Staatsburgerkunde
0016-9080 Gesellschaft fuer Natur- und Voelkerkunde Ostasiens. Nachrichten
0016-9099 Gesellschaft und Politik
0016-9102 Gesellschaftspolitische Kommentare
0016-9129 Gesetz- und Verordnungsblatt fuer Schleswig-Holstein
0016-9145 Gesher
0016-9153 Gesichertes Leben
0016-9161 Gesnerus
0016-920X Gesta
0016-9218 Gestions Hospitalieres
0016-9226 Gesund durch Sauna†
0016-9234 Gesund Leben
0016-9242 Gesunde Mensch†
0016-9269 Gesundheit in Betrieb und Familie
0016-9285 Gesundheitsnachrichten
0016-9293 Gesundheitspolitik†
0016-9307 Gesundheitspolitische Umschau
0016-9315 Gesundheitswesen und Desinfektion *see* 0340-997X
0016-9323 Getraenke-Industrie
0016-9331 Getraenkehandel
0016-934X Getroster Tag
0016-9374 Geuzen Penning†
0016-9390 Gewaltfreie Aktion
0016-9412 Gewerbliche Rundschau *changed to* Chef-Magazin fuer Klein- und Mittelbetriebe
0016-9420 Gewerblicher Rechtsschutz und Urheberrecht
0016-9439 Gesellen-Mitteilungen *see* 0343-4052
0016-9447 Gewerkschaftliche Monatshefte
0016-9455 Gewerkschaftliche Rundschau
0016-9463 Gewerkschafts Presse
0016-948X Geyer's Dealer Topics *changed to* Geyer's Office Dealer
0016-9498 Gezinsblad
0016-9501 Gezond Limburg
0016-951X Gezondheid en Ziekenfonds†
0016-9528 Gezondheidszorg†
0016-9536 Ghana Geographical Association. Bulletin
0016-9544 Ghana Journal of Science†
0016-9552 Ghana Library Journal
0016-9560 Ghana Medical Journal
0016-9579 Ghana News
0016-9587 Ghana Review
0016-9595 Ghana Teacher's Journal *changed to* Ghana Journal of Education
0016-9609 Ghana Today *changed to* New Ghana
0016-9617 Ghana Workers' Bulletin *changed to* T U C News
0016-9625 Gheoponica
0016-9633 Ghost Dance
0016-965X Giardino Fiorito
0016-9668 Gib Acht
0016-9676 Stamp Monthly
0016-9684 Gibson Report
0016-9706 Gidroliznaya i Lesokhimicheskaya Promyshlennost'
0016-9714 Gidrotekhnicheskoe Stroitel'stvo
0016-9722 Gidrotekhnika i Melioratsiya
0016-9730 Gids
0016-9757 Giervalk-Gerfaut
0016-9765 Giesserei
0016-9773 Giesserei-Erfahrungsaustausch
0016-9781 Giesserei-Praxis
0016-979X Giesserei Rundschau
0016-9803 Giessereitechnik
0016-9854 Gift Buyer International
0016-9889 Gifts & Decorative Accessories
0016-9900 Gigiena i Sanitariya
0016-9919 Gigiena Truda i Professional'nye Zabolevaniya
0016-9935 Technology and Industries†
0016-9943 Gil Vicente†
0016-9951 Gilbert and Sullivan Journal
0016-9978 Gildenfreund†
0016-9986 Gildenweg
0016-9994 Giligia†
0017-0003 Gimlaoth†
0017-0011 Ginekologia Polska
0017-002X Jugoslavenska Ginekologija i Opstetricija *changed to* Yugoslav Gynecology and Perinatology
0017-0046 Ginnasta
0017-0054 Giocattoli
0017-0062 Gioia
0017-0070 Giornale Botanico Italiano
0017-0089 Giornale Critico della Filosofia Italiana
0017-0097 Giornale degli Economisti e Annali di Economia
0017-0100 Giornale degli Uccelli
0017-0119 Giornale dei Distillatori
0017-0127 Giornale dei Genitori
0017-0135 Giornale degli Allevatori
0017-0143 Giornale del Bieticoltore
0017-0151 Commercio Turismo
0017-016X Giornale del Genio Civile
0017-0186 Giornale del Mezzogiorno
0017-0208 Giornale della Cogne
0017-0216 Giornale della Libreria
0017-0224 Giornale dell'Arteriosclerosi
0017-0232 Giornale dello Spettacolo
0017-0240 Giornale dell'Officina
0017-0259 Giornale di Barga
0017-0267 Giornale di Batteriologia, Virologia ed Immunologia ed Annali dell'Ospedale Maria Vittoria di Torino *see* 0390-5462
0017-0267 Giornale di Batteriologia, Virologia ed Immunologia ed Annali dell'Ospedale Maria Vittoria di Torino *see* 0390-5454
0017-0275 Giornale di Clinica Medica
0017-0283 Giornale di Fisica
0017-0291 Giornale di Geologia
0017-0305 Giornale di Gerontologia
0017-0313 Giornale di Igiene e Medicina Preventiva
0017-0321 Giornale di Malattie Infettive e Parassitarie
0017-033X Giornale di Mathematiche di Battaglini
0017-0364 Giornale di Medicina Militare
0017-0380 Giornale di Microbiologia
0017-0399 Giornale di Psichiatria e di Neuropatologia†
0017-0429 Giornale Economico
0017-0437 Giornale Italiano delle Malattie del Torace
0017-0445 Giornale Italiano di Chemioterapia
0017-0453 Giornale Italiano di Chirurgia
0017-047X Giornale Italiano di Patologia e Scienze Affini
0017-0496 Giornale Storico della Letteratura Italiana
0017-050X Giornale Storico della Lunigiana e del Territorio Lucense
0017-0518 Giornalismo Europeo
0017-0526 Giovane Critica
0017-0534 Giovane Montagna
0017-0542 Gioventu Evangelica
0017-0550 Girard Home News
0017-0569 Girl Crusader
0017-0577 Girl Scout Leader
0017-0593 Girls' Brigade Gazette
0017-0615 Gissing Newsletter
0017-0623 Giurisprudenza Italiana
0017-0631 Giustizia Civile
0017-064X Giustizia Nuova
0017-0658 Giustizia Penale
0017-0682 Gjuteriet
0017-0690 Glaces et Verres†
0017-0704 Glacier Francais
0017-0712 Glaciological Notes *see* 0149-1776
0017-0720 Glad Tidings
0017-0739 Glad Tidings of Good Things
0017-0747 Glamour
0017-0755 Glarmestertidende
0017-0763 Glas-Email-Keramo-Technik†
0017-0771 Glas Istre
0017-078X Glas och Porslin
0017-0798 Glas Omladine
0017-0801 Glas Podravine
0017-081X Glas Podrinja
0017-0828 Glas Trebinja
0017-0836 Glasblaeser
0017-0852 Glasforum
0017-0860 Glasgow Chamber of Commerce. Journal
0017-0879 Glasgow Herald Trade Review†
0017-0887 Glasgow Illustrated
0017-0895 Glasgow Mathematical Journal
0017-0917 Glasgow University Guardian
0017-0925 Glasnik

ISSN INDEX

ISSN	Title
0017-0933	Glasnik Advokatske Komore Vojvodine
0017-0941	Glasnik Hemijskog Drustva/Societe Chimique, Belgrade. Bulletin *changed to* Serbian Chemical Society. Journal
0017-095X	Glasnik Matematicki
0017-0976	Glasnik Poljoprivredne Proizvodnje, Prerade i Plasmana
0017-0984	Glass
0017-0992	Glass Age
0017-100X	Glass and Ceramics
0017-1018	Glass Digest
0017-1026	Glass Industry
0017-1042	Glass, Potteries and Ceramic Journal *changed to* Glass, Potteries and Ceramic Annual
0017-1050	Glass Technology
0017-1069	Glass Workers News†
0017-1077	Glass Workshop
0017-1085	Glastechnische Berichte
0017-1093	Glasteknisk Tidskrift
0017-1107	Glaswelt/Deutsche Glaserzeitung
0017-1123	Glaube und Tat
0017-1131	Gleaner *changed to* Rutgers Gleaner
0017-114X	Gleanings in Bee Culture
0017-1166	Gledista
0017-1174	Glenbow†
0017-1204	Globe and Laurel
0017-1212	Globe and Mail Report on Business
0017-1220	Globen†
0017-1239	Glocke†
0017-1247	Glocke
0017-1263	Glos Nauczycielski
0017-1271	Glossa†
0017-1298	Glotta
0017-1301	Gloucester Diocesan Gazette
0017-131X	Gloucestershire Farmer *changed to* Gloucestershire and North Avon Farmer
0017-1328	Gloucestershire Life and Countryside *changed to* Somerset and Avon Life
0017-1336	Giovani in Dialogo
0017-1344	Glowna Biblioteka Lekarska. Biuletyn
0017-1352	Gloxinian
0017-1360	Glucose Informatie†
0017-1387	Glueckauf-Forschungshefte
0017-1395	Gluecklisches Leben-der Stille Weg *changed to* Lebensschutz
0017-1409	Gnade und Herrlichkeit
0017-1417	Gnomon
0017-1425	Gnosis†
0017-1433	Go (Burlingame)
0017-1441	Go (Charlotte)
0017-145X	Go Boating
0017-1476	Go Greyhound
0017-1484	Goa Today
0017-1506	Gobbles
0017-1522	Goetheana Periodico Literario
0017-1549	Goettingische Gelehrte Anzeigen
0017-1557	Gold Bulletin
0017-1573	Gold und Silber
0017-1581	Golden Eye
0017-159X	Golden Magazine *see* 0009-3971
0017-162X	Golden West Purchasor
0017-1638	Di Goldene Keyt
0017-1646	Der Goldene Pfennig
0017-1654	Die Sphinx
0017-1670	Goldmanns Mitteilungen fuer den Buchhandel
0017-1689	Goldschmiede Zeitung - European Jeweler und Uhrmacherzeitschrift
0017-1697	Goldsmith-Nagan Bond and Money Market Letter *changed to* Reporting on Governments/Bond and Money Market Letter
0017-1700	Goleuad
0017-1727	Golf
0017-1735	Golf
0017-176X	Golf Digest
0017-1794	Golf Journal
0017-1808	Golf
0017-1816	Golf Monthly
0017-1824	Golf Shop Operations
0017-1832	Golf Singapore Review
0017-1840	Golf Superintendent *see* 0192-3048
0017-1867	Golf/U.S.A†
0017-1883	Golf World
0017-1891	Golf World
0017-1905	Golfdom *see* 0148-3706
0017-1913	Golfer
0017-1948	Golos Radzimy
0017-1956	Goltdammer's Archiv fuer Strafrecht
0017-1964	Gomitolo
0017-1980	Gong
0017-1999	Gong
0017-2014	Gonubie Gazette *changed to* Times of Gonubie
0017-2022	Good Counsel†
0017-2030	Good Earth *see* 0816-6668
0017-2049	Good Farming†
0017-2073	Good Health *see* 0306-462X
0017-2081	Good Housekeeping
0017-209X	Good Housekeeping
0017-2111	Good Motoring
0017-212X	Good News†
0017-2138	Good News *changed to* New York Good News
0017-2146	Good News
0017-2154	Confident Living
0017-2162	Good News Crusades *see* 0164-7253
0017-2170	Good Packaging Magazine
0017-2189	Good Reading *changed to* Good Reading for Everyone
0017-2197	Good Times†
0017-2219	Goodyear Revue†
0017-2227	Gopher Historian *see* 0148-6659
0017-2235	Gopher Music Notes
0017-2243	Gordian
0017-2251	Christian Scholar's Review
0017-226X	Gornik
0017-2278	Gornyi Zhurnal
0017-2286	Gorskostopanska Nauka
0017-2294	Gorteria
0017-2308	Goshen College Bulletin
0017-2332	Gospel Carrier
0017-2340	Gospel Herald
0017-2359	Gospel Messenger
0017-2367	Gospel Standard
0017-2383	Gospel Truth
0017-2391	Gospel Witness *changed to* Indian Lutheran
0017-2405	Gospodarka Materialowa
0017-2413	Gospodarka Paliwami i Energia
0017-2421	Gospodarka Planowa
0017-243X	Gospodarka Rybna
0017-2448	Gospodarka Wodna
0017-2456	Gospodarstvo
0017-2472	Gothique
0017-2480	Gottes Wort
0017-2499	Gottesdienst und Kirchenmusik
0017-2510	Gotteskinder *changed to* Regenbogen
0017-2529	Gouden Sleutels
0017-2537	Gouden Uren
0017-2553	Gourmet
0017-257X	Government and Opposition
0017-2588	Government Business Worldwide *changed to* Defense & Economy World Report
0017-2588	Government Business Worldwide Reports
0017-2596	Government Contractor
0017-260X	Government Employee Relations Report
0017-2618	Government Equipment Reports *changed to* Defense & Economy World Report
0017-2626	Government Executive
0017-2642	Government Product News
0017-2650	Government Purchasing Digest *see* 0017-2642
0017-2669	Government Standard *changed to* Government Standard/Agenda
0017-2677	Governmental Research Newsletter *see* 0196-7355
0017-2693	Gown
0017-2707	Gownsman†
0017-2715	Goya
0017-2723	Gozdarski Vestnik
0017-2731	Kirjapainotaito-Graafikko
0017-2758	Gracas do Servo de Deus: Padre Cruz
0017-2774	Gradbeni Vestnik
0017-2782	Grade Teacher *changed to* Instructor
0017-2790	Roots
0017-2804	Graduate Careers
0017-2812	Graduate Careers in Science and Technology†
0017-2839	Graduate Research in Education and Related Disciplines *changed to* Graduate Research in Urban Education and Related Disciplines
0017-2863	Graffitti†
0017-2871	Druk en Papier *changed to* Drukwerk
0017-288X	Grafia
0017-2898	Grafica†
0017-291X	Grafico
0017-2928	Grafico
0017-2936	Graficus
0017-2944	Grafiek
0017-2952	Grafische Literatuur Centrale†
0017-2979	Grafisk Faktorstidning
0017-2987	Grafisk Revy *see* 0017-288X
0017-2995	Grafiske Fag
0017-3002	Grafiskt Forum
0017-3029	Grain Age
0017-3053	Grain Bulletin†
0017-3061	Grain Market News and Feed Market News *changed to* Grain and Feed Market News
0017-3061	Grain Market News and Feed Market News *changed to* Livestock, Meat and Wool Market News
0017-307X	Revue Technique Automobile
0017-3088	Gralswelt
0017-310X	Gramophone
0017-3118	Gran Pavese†
0017-3126	Gran Tiramolla
0017-3134	Grana
0017-3142	Grande Hotel
0017-3185	Grani
0017-3207	Granite Cutters Journal†
0017-3223	Granma
0017-3231	Granta
0017-324X	Granthagar
0017-3258	Grapevine
0017-3274	Graphic Antiquarian†
0017-3282	Graphic Arts Abstracts
0017-3290	Graphic Arts Bulletin†
0017-3304	Graphic Arts Buyer†
0017-3312	Graphic Arts Monthly and the Printing Industry *changed to* Graphic Arts Monthly
0017-3320	Graphic Arts Patent Abstracts†
0017-3339	Graphic Arts Product News†
0017-3347	Graphic Arts Progress *see* 0090-8207
0017-3355	Graphic Arts Supplier News *changed to* In-Plant Reproductions & Electronic Publishing
0017-3363	Graphic Arts Unionist *changed to* GraphiCommunicator
0017-341X	Graphic Trends†
0017-3428	Graphics: U.S.A *changed to* Graphic Design: U.S.A
0017-3436	Graphicus
0017-3452	Graphis
0017-3479	Graphische Revue Oesterreichs
0017-3487	Graphs and Notes on the Economic Situation in the Community *changed to* European Economy
0017-3495	Grasas y Aceites
0017-3517	Grass Roots Forum
0017-3525	Grasso Mededelingen *changed to* Grassortiment
0017-3541	Grassroots Editor
0017-3568	Gravure *see* 0163-9234
0017-3576	Gravure Technical Association Bulletin *changed to* Gravure Bulletin
0017-3584	Gray and Ductile Iron News *changed to* Metalcaster
0017-3592	Graybar Outlook
0017-3606	Grazhdanskaya Aviatsiya
0017-3614	Great Basin Naturalist
0017-3630	Great Britain. Central Statistical Office. Statistical News
0017-3657	Great Britain Journal *changed to* G B Journal
0017-3665	Great Lakes News Letter
0017-3673	Great Plains Journal
0017-3681	Great Plains National Instructional Television Library Newsletter *see* 0738-7555
0017-369X	Great Speckled Bird†
0017-3703	Greater Amusements and International Projectionist
0017-3711	Greater Indianapolis *see* 0279-3180
0017-3754	Greater Milwaukee Dental Bulletin
0017-3762	Delaware Valley Business Fortnight†
0017-3770	Greater Pittsburgh†
0017-3789	Portland Commerce *changed to* Portland Magazine
0017-3797	Greater Rochester Commerce†
0017-3819	Grecia de Ayer, de Hoy y de Siempre†
0017-3835	Greece and Rome
0017-3851	Greek Bibliography†
0017-386X	Greek Gazette
0017-3886	Greek Observer
0017-3894	Greek Orthodox Theological Review
0017-3908	Greek Report
0017-3916	Greek, Roman and Byzantine Studies
0017-3924	Green and White
0017-3932	Green Book
0017-3940	Green Cross†
0017-3967	Green Island
0017-3975	Green Pyne Leaf†
0017-3983	Green Revolution
0017-3991	Green River Current
0017-4009	Green River Review
0017-4017	Green Tree†
0017-4041	Greenfield Review
0017-4068	Greenleaf†
0017-4076	Green's Commodity Market Comments†
0017-4084	Greensboro Review
0017-4092	Greensward
0017-4106	Greeting Card Magazine *changed to* Greetings
0017-4114	Gregorianum
0017-4122	Gregoriusblad†
0017-4149	Grenoble Universite. Faculte des Lettres et Sciences Humaines. Centre de Documentation et de Recherches Bibliographiques. Bulletin d'Information†
0017-4157	Greyhound
0017-4165	Greyhound Owner & Breeder
0017-4181	Grial
0017-419X	Gridley Wave
0017-4203	Griekenland Bulletin *changed to* Internationale Korrespondentie
0017-422X	Griffin Report of New England *see* 0192-4400
0017-4254	Grille
0017-4289	Grit
0017-4297	Grit and Steel
0017-4300	Grito†
0017-4319	Grits and Grinds†
0017-4327	Grits and Grinds (Swedish edition)†
0017-4335	Grive
0017-4343	Grlica
0017-4351	Grocer
0017-436X	Grocer Management/Western†
0017-4378	Grocers' and Storekeepers' Journal of Western Australia
0017-4386	Grocers Gazette
0017-4394	Grocery Marketing
0017-4416	Grocery Communications
0017-4440	Grocery Review
0017-4459	Groei†
0017-4467	Groei *see* 0169-281X
0017-4483	De Groene Amsterdammer
0017-4491	Groenten en Fruit
0017-4505	Grondboor en Hamer
0017-4521	Groninger Landbouwblad *changed to* Landbode (Groningen)
0017-453X	Gronk
0017-4548	Gronkopings Veckoblad
0017-4556	Groenland
0017-4564	Groote Schrijver-Genesiusblad *see* 0165-8867
0017-4572	Groothandel in Levensmiddelen *changed to* Missets Distrifood
0017-4599	Gross Wartenberger Heimatblatt
0017-4602	Entschluss
0017-4610	Grosse Pointe Public Library. Newsletter†

ISSN INDEX 1241

ISSN	Title
0017-4637	Grosseteste Review
0017-4645	Grosswetterlagen Europas
0017-4653	Ground Engineering
0017-467X	Ground Water
0017-4688	Grounds Maintenance
0017-4696	Groundsman
0017-470X	Group Health and Welfare News *see* 0887-9087
0017-4718	Group Leader's Workshop
0017-4726	Group Practice *see* 0199-5103
0017-4734	Group Psychotherapy *see* 0731-1373
0017-4742	Group Research Report
0017-4750	Group Travel†
0017-4769	Oregon Quality Newsletter *changed to* Oregon Development
0017-4777	Grower
0017-4785	Grower
0017-4793	Growth
0017-4807	Growth and Acquisition Guide†
0017-4815	Growth and Change
0017-4831	Strongest Funds
0017-484X	Growth Stock Digest†
0017-4858	Grubensicherheit *see* 0344-239X
0017-4866	Grudnaya Khirurgiya
0017-4874	Die Waage
0017-4904	Grundfoerbaettring†
0017-4912	Grundig Technische Informationen†
0017-4920	Grundlagen der Landtechnik
0017-4939	Grundlagenstudien aus Kybernetik und Geisteswissenschaft
0017-4947	Gruppenpsychotherapie und Gruppendynamik
0017-4955	Gruzlica i Choroby Pluc *see* 0376-4761
0017-4971	Guaira†
0017-498X	Guajana†
0017-4998	Guanabara Industrial†
0017-5005	Guardia Nacional
0017-5013	Guardian†
0017-5021	Guardian
0017-503X	Guards Magazine
0017-5048	Guatemala. Instituto Nacional de Estadistica. Boletin Estadistico
0017-5056	Guatemala Indigena
0017-5064	Guatemala Pediatrica
0017-5080	Guepes
0017-5110	Guernsey Breeders' Journal
0017-5137	Der Gueterverkehr
0017-5145	Guia Aeronautico
0017-5153	Guia Guarani
0017-5161	Guia para Maestros de Ninos†
0017-5188	Guida Allo Spettacolo
0017-5218	Guidance Report†
0017-5226	Guide (Hagerstown)
0017-5234	Today's Guide
0017-5242	Guide *see* 0273-3145
0017-5269	Guide Post
0017-5285	Guide to Indian Periodical Literature
0017-5293	Guide to Microforms in Print *see* 0164-0747
0017-5307	Guide to Social Science and Religion in Periodical Literature
0017-5315	Guide to the American Left *see* 8756-0208
0017-5323	Guidepost
0017-5331	Guideposts
0017-534X	Guider *changed to* Guiding
0017-5366	Guild Gardener. Newsletter†
0017-5374	Guild Gazette *changed to* Guild and City Gazette
0017-5382	Guild Guide *see* 0194-2174
0017-5390	Guild Practitioner *see* 0730-532X
0017-5404	Guild Reporter
0017-5412	Guilde du Livre
0017-5439	Guilds of Weavers, Spinners and Dyers. Quarterly Journal *changed to* Journal for Spinners, Weavers & Dyers
0017-5455	Guion
0017-5463	Guitar Player
0017-5471	Guitar Review
0017-548X	Guitare et Musique Chansons Poesie
0017-5501	Gujarat Labour Gazette
0017-551X	Gujarat Law Reporter
0017-5528	Gujarat Law Times
0017-5536	Gujarat Revenue Tribunal Law Reporter
0017-5544	Guldsmedebladet
0017-5560	Gulf Coast Lumberman and Building Distributor *see* 0192-4389
0017-5587	Gulf Review†
0017-5609	Gummibereifung
0017-5617	Gun Report
0017-5625	Gun Talk
0017-5633	Gun Week *see* 0195-1599
0017-5641	Gun World
0017-565X	Gumma Journal of Medical Science *changed to* Gumma Reports on Medical Sciences
0017-5668	Gunma University. Faculty of Education. Science Reports
0017-5676	Guns
0017-5684	Guns & Ammo
0017-5692	Guns Review
0017-5706	Gurukul Kangri Vishwavidyalaya
0017-5714	Gurukula Prakashana†
0017-5730	Gustav-Adolf-Blatt
0017-5749	Gut
0017-5765	Gute Fahrt
0017-5781	Gute Nachrichten
0017-579X	Gute Reise
0017-5803	Die Gute Tat
0017-5811	Le Gutenberg
0017-582X	Guter Rat
0017-5838	Guthrie Clinic Bulletin *see* 0882-696X
0017-5846	Guy†
0017-5854	Guyana Business
0017-5862	Guyana Information Bulletin *changed to* Guyana Information Bulletin
0017-5870	Guy's Hospital Gazette
0017-5897	Gwyddonydd(y)
0017-5900	Gyermekgyogyaszat
0017-5919	Gymnasieingenjoeren *changed to* T L I - Ingenjoren
0017-5927	Gymnasieskolen
0017-5935	Das Gymnasion†
0017-5943	Gymnasium
0017-5951	Gymnasium Helveticum
0017-596X	Gymnastikk og Turn
0017-5978	Gymnastikledaren *changed to* Svensk Gymnastik
0017-5986	Gynecologic Investigation *see* 0378-7346
0017-5994	Der Gynaekologe
0017-6001	Gynaekologische Rundschau
0017-601X	Gynecologie et Obstetrique et Federation des Societes de Gynecologie et d'Obstetrique. Bulletin *see* 0368-2315
0017-6028	Gynecologie Pratique *see* 0301-2204
0017-6036	Gyogyszereszet
0017-6044	Gyogyszereszeti es Gyogyszerterapias Dokumentacios Szemle *see* 0138-9289
0017-6052	Gyorstajekoztato a Magyar Konyvtartudomanyi Irodalomrol *see* 0133-736X
0017-6087	Gypsy Lore Society. Journal†
0017-6095	Gypsies for Christ
0017-6109	H A Bulletin†
0017-6117	H & S Reports
0017-6125	H & W†
0017-6141	H C I Journal *see* 0144-3704
0017-615X	H C R Bulletin *changed to* Refugees
0017-6176	H E A News Flash†
0017-6192	H N O
0017-6206	H. P†
0017-6214	H R D News *see* 0098-1435
0017-6222	H R I S Abstracts
0017-6230	H S M A Bulletin and Idea Exchange *changed to* H S M A World
0017-6249	H S U Brand
0017-6257	H S V - Post
0017-6265	H T A Contact *changed to* H T A Advocate
0017-6273	H T A Horizon†
0017-629X	HTS'er†
0017-6303	H U D Challenge Magazine *see* 0196-1969
0017-6311	H U D Newsletter
0017-632X	Haagse Jazz Club
0017-6346	Habinjan
0017-6354	Habinyan
0017-6362	Habit
0017-6370	Habitat†
0017-6397	Habitat†
0017-6400	Habitation†
0017-6419	Habitation
0017-6443	Haboneh†
0017-6451	Hacettepe Bulletin of Medicine-Surgery/ Hacettepe Tip Cerrahi Bulteni *changed to* Hacettepe Medical Journal
0017-646X	Hinukh†
0017-6478	Hacia la Luz
0017-6486	Hacienda
0017-6508	Hadashot Me ha-Chaim ha-Datiyim Be Israel
0017-6516	Hadassah Magazine
0017-6524	Hadoar
0017-6532	Hadorom
0017-6540	Hadtortenelmi Kozlemenyek
0017-6559	Haematologia
0017-6575	Haematologica Latina†
0017-6605	Encouragement
0017-6613	Kir-Ou-Kirk
0017-6621	Hahnemannian
0017-6656	Haiku *see* 0703-1831
0017-6664	Haiku Highlights *see* 0364-359X
0017-6680	Addis Ababa University. College of Technology. Library Bulletin
0017-6699	Hailer†
0017-6702	Hair & Beauty
0017-6710	Hair and Makeup Trends†
0017-6729	Hair Beauty Magazine†
0017-6737	Hair Magic†
0017-6753	Hairdressers' Guide
0017-6761	Hairdressers' Journal *changed to* Hairdressers' Journal International
0017-677X	Hairenik
0017-6788	Haiti. Institut Haitien de Statistique. Bulletin Trimestriel de Statistique
0017-6796	Hakku
0017-680X	Halle aux Cuirs†
0017-6818	I D†
0017-6834	Halve Maen
0017-6842	Ham Radio *see* 0148-5989
0017-6850	Hamaapil
0017-6877	Hamburg in Zahlen
0017-6885	Hamburg Journal†
0017-6915	Hamburger Aerzteblatt†
0017-6931	Hamburger Export-Woche
0017-694X	Hamburger Hafen-Nachrichten und Schiffsabfahrten *see* 0341-0862
0017-6966	Hamburger Lehrerzeitung
0017-6982	Hamburger Sport-Mitteilungen
0017-6990	Hamburger Vorschau
0017-7024	Hamdard Medical Digest *see* 0250-7188
0017-7032	Hamdden†
0017-7040	Hamevaser
0017-7059	Ha-Mifal
0017-7067	Hamilton Alumni Review
0017-7075	Hamilton County Pharmacist
0017-7083	Mizrah he-Hadash
0017-7091	Mlonai
0017-7113	Hampshire
0017-7121	Hampshire Farmer
0017-7148	Hand Vol Pluis
0017-7156	Handarbeit
0017-7164	Handasah ve-Adrikhalut
0017-7172	Handbags and Accessories *changed to* Accessories
0017-7180	Handbal
0017-7199	Handbook of Basic Economic Statistics
0017-7202	Handbuch des Bauherrn
0017-7210	Handbuch des Hausbesitzers†
0017-7229	Der Handel
0017-7237	Handel en Nywerheid†
0017-7245	Handel Zagraniczny
0017-7253	Handelingen der Staten-Generaal
0017-7261	Agentur *changed to* Agentur
0017-7288	Handelsbelangen†
0017-7296	Handelsblatt
0017-730X	Handelskammer Hamburg. Mitteilungen *changed to* Hamburger Wirtschaft
0017-7318	Handelslaget *see* 0781-7347
0017-7326	Handelsnytt
0017-7334	Chambre de Commerce Neerlandaise pour la Belgique et le Luxembourg. Revue Commerciale
0017-7342	Denmark. Danmarks Statistik. Handelsstatistiske Meddelelser. Maanedsstatistik over Udenrigshandelen-Monthly Bulletin of External Trade *see* 0108-5506
0017-7350	Handelswoche *see* 0323-7168
0017-7369	Handenarbeid *changed to* Beeldpraat
0017-7377	Handes Amsorya
0017-7385	Handling & Shipping *see* 0194-603X
0017-7393	Handloader
0017-7407	Handweaver and Craftsman†
0017-7415	Handwerken Ariadne *changed to* Ariadne
0017-7423	Handy Shipping Guide
0017-7431	Hanford Project News *changed to* Hanford News
0017-744X	Korea Development Bank. Monthly Economic Review
0017-7458	Hannibal Labor Press†
0017-7474	Hannoversches Pferd
0017-7482	Hanover News
0017-7504	Hansa
0017-7520	Animal Reproduction Techniques
0017-7539	Hanson's Latin America Letter
0017-7547	Japanese Journal of Criminal Psychology
0017-7555	Olam ha-Zeh
0017-7563	Happening in New York†
0017-7571	Praklit
0017-758X	Harangue
0017-761X	Harbinger (Crystal City)
0017-7636	Harbour and Shipping
0017-7644	Hard Fibres†
0017-7652	Hardlines Wholesaling†
0017-7660	Hardware Age *see* 8755-254X
0017-7679	Hardware & Farm Equipment
0017-7687	Hardware Consultant *see* 0361-5294
0017-7695	Hardware Merchandiser *see* 0017-7741
0017-7709	Hardware Merchandiser
0017-7717	Hardware Merchandising
0017-7725	Hardware Retailer *changed to* Do-it-Yourself Retailing
0017-7733	Hardware Review
0017-7741	Hardware Trade Journal
0017-7768	Ha-Refuah
0017-7776	Harian Press *see* 0278-4947
0017-7806	Harmonica Accordeon et Musique
0017-7822	Harmonie *see* 0757-0139
0017-7830	Die Harmonika†
0017-7849	Harmonizer
0017-7857	Harness Horse
0017-7865	Israel Pharmaceutical Journal
0017-7873	Harper's Bazaar
0017-789X	Harper's Magazine
0017-7903	Harpers Wine and Spirit Gazette
0017-7938	Harris-Report†
0017-7946	Harrison Tape Catalog *changed to* Harrison Tape Guide
0017-7954	Harry S. Truman Library Institute Research Newsletter *see* 0363-1028
0017-7962	Hartford Agent
0017-7970	Hartford Hospital Bulletin†
0017-7989	Hartford Studies in Literature *see* 0196-2280
0017-8004	Harvard Advocate
0017-8012	Harvard Business Review
0017-8020	Harvard Business School Bulletin
0017-8039	Harvard Civil Rights - Civil Liberties Law Review
0017-8047	Harvard Divinity Bulletin
0017-8055	Harvard Educational Review
0017-8063	Harvard International Law Journal
0017-808X	Harvard Journal on Legislation
0017-8098	Harvard Lampoon
0017-8101	Harvard Law Record
0017-811X	Harvard Law Review
0017-8128	Harvard Law School Bulletin
0017-8136	Harvard Library Bulletin
0017-8144	Harvard Project Physics. Newsletter†
0017-8160	Harvard Theological Review
0017-8179	Harvard Today†
0017-8195	Harvest Farm Magazine
0017-8209	Harvest Years *see* 0163-2027
0017-8217	Harvester
0017-8225	Harvester
0017-8233	Haryana Cooperation

ISSN INDEX

0017-8241	Haryana Health Journal
0017-825X	Haryana Journal of Education
0017-8268	Haryou-Act News†
0017-8276	Harzburger Hefte see 0302-6671
0017-8284	Sifrut
0017-8306	Hasler-Mitteilungen
0017-8314	Hassadeh
0017-8322	Hastings Law Journal
0017-8330	Hat Worker†
0017-8349	Hataassiya changed to M'lakha V'ta'asiya
0017-8357	Hatchet changed to G W Hatchet
0017-8381	Hatvertising Weekly
0017-839X	Hauenstein Verlag. Mitteilungsblatt changed to Ring-Post
0017-8403	Haus und Grund
0017-842X	Hausfrau
0017-8438	Haustechnische Rundschau
0017-8454	Hauswirtschaft und Wissenschaft
0017-8462	Hauswirtschaftsmeisterin changed to Rationelle Hauswirtschaft
0017-8470	Der Hautarzt
0017-8497	Havebladet
0017-8500	Haven
0017-8519	Havenloods
0017-8527	Hawadess
0017-8535	Hawaii AFL-CIO News changed to Hawaii AFL-CIO Nupepa
0017-8543	Hawaii Beverage Guide
0017-8551	Hawaii Business and Industry changed to Hawaii Business
0017-856X	Business Historical Society. Bulletin see 0007-6805
0017-8578	Hawaii Guardsman changed to Pupukahi
0017-8586	Hawaii Library Association Journal changed to H L A Journal
0017-8594	Hawaii Medical Journal
0017-8616	Hawaii State Dental Association. Journal changed to Hawaii Dental Journal
0017-8624	Hawaiian Shell News
0017-8632	Hawkeye United Methodist changed to Hawkeye
0017-8640	Hay Guetron
0017-8667	Hayastanyaitz Yegeghetzy see 0199-8765
0017-8675	Yahad Digest changed to Yahad
0017-8683	Aiastani Kensabanakan Andes
0017-8691	Yatsiv
0017-8705	Areiniki Dzain changed to Hayreniky Dzayn
0017-8713	Head, Heart, Hands & Health in Virginia
0017-8721	Head Start Newsletter†
0017-873X	Head Teachers Review
0017-8748	Headache
0017-8756	Headland changed to New Headland
0017-8764	Headlight
0017-8780	Foreign Policy Association. Headline Series
0017-8799	Heads Up†
0017-8829	Healing Hand
0017-8837	Health changed to Health News Digest
0017-8845	Health see 0308-602X
0017-8853	Health†
0017-8861	Health
0017-887X	Health
0017-8888	Health and Efficiency
0017-8896	Health and Physical Education Bulletin see 0707-3186
0017-890X	Health and Strength
0017-8926	Ofakim
0017-8950	Health Education changed to Health Promotion
0017-8969	Health Education Journal
0017-8977	Health Foods Retailing
0017-8985	Health for All see 0018-0696
0017-8993	Health Information Digest†
0017-9019	Health Insurance Underwriter
0017-9027	Health Insurance Viewpoints changed to Health Care Viewpoint
0017-9035	Health Laboratory Science†
0017-9043	Health News†
0017-9051	Health-Pac changed to Health - P A C Bulletin
0017-906X	Health, Physical Education, and Recreation Microcard Bulletin see 0090-5119
0017-9078	Health Physics
0017-9086	Weekly Government Abstracts. Health Planning changed to Abstract Newsletter: Health Planning & Health Services Research
0017-9116	Health Services Journal
0017-9124	Health Services Research
0017-9132	Health Trends
0017-9140	Health Visitor
0017-9159	Healthways Magazine†
0017-9167	Healthy Living
0017-9175	Hear This
0017-9183	Hearing†
0017-9191	Hearing and Speech News see 0162-5667
0017-9205	Hearing Dealer see 0092-4466
0017-9248	Heart Bulletin†
0017-9256	Heart of America Purchaser
0017-9272	Heartbeat of St. Joseph's Hospital changed to Heartbeat of St. Joseph's Medical Center
0017-9280	Hearth and Home†
0017-9299	Hearthstone†
0017-9302	Hearts of Oak Journal†
0017-9310	International Journal of Heat and Mass Transfer
0017-9329	Heat Engineering
0017-9345	Heat Treating
0017-9353	Heating, Air Conditioning & Refrigeration†
0017-937X	Heating and Ventilating Engineer and Journal of Air Conditioning changed to Heating and Ventilating Engineer
0017-9388	Heating and Ventilating News changed to H & V News
0017-9396	Heating and Ventilating Review
0017-940X	Heating/Piping/Air Conditioning
0017-9418	Heating, Plumbing, Air Conditioning
0017-9426	Heavy Construction News
0017-9434	Heavy Duty Trucking
0017-9442	Hebezeuge und Foerdermittel
0017-9477	Hebrew Christian
0017-9485	Hechos y Dichos†
0017-9493	Hed ha-Hinukh
0017-9507	Hedeselskabets Tidsskrift
0017-9515	Heemschut
0017-9523	Heer en Mode†
0017-9531	Heerbaan see 0165-988X
0017-9566	Heghapoghagan Albom
0017-9590	Heights (Chestnut Hill)
0017-9604	Die Heilberufe
0017-9612	Das Heilige Band
0017-9620	Heiliger Dienst
0017-9647	Heilpaedagogische Forschung
0017-9655	Vierteljahresschrift fuer Heilpaedagogik und ihre Nachbargebiete
0017-9671	Heim und Anstalt
0017-968X	Heim und Herd see 0174-3058
0017-9698	Heima Er Bezt
0017-9701	Die Heimat
0017-9728	Heimat und Kirche†
0017-9736	Heimat und Staat†
0017-9752	Heimat-Zeitung Roemerstaedter Laendchen
0017-9779	Heimatland
0017-9787	Heimatland Lippe
0017-9809	Das Heimatmuseum Alsergrund
0017-9817	Heimatschutz
0017-9833	Heimatwerk
0017-9841	Heimen
0017-985X	Heimevernsbladet
0017-9868	Die Heimstatt
0017-9876	Heimtex
0017-9884	Heirs†
0017-9906	H L H, Zeitschrift fuer Heizung, Lueftung, Klimatechnik, Haustechnik changed to H L H, Heizung, Lueftung, Klima, Haustechnik
0017-9914	Hejnal Mariacki
0017-9922	Helan Medical Magazine
0017-9930	Helferbrief see 0173-7872
0017-9949	Die Helferin des Arztes
0017-9957	Helgolaender Wissenschaftliche Meeresuntersuchungen see 0174-3597
0017-9965	Helicopter World†
0017-9973	Helictite
0017-9981	Helikon
0017-999X	Helikon
0018-0009	Helinium
0018-0025	Hellenic-American Chamber of Commerce. Newsletter
0018-0033	Hellenic Herald
0018-005X	Hellenic Shipping International
0018-0068	Elliniki Ktiniatriki
0018-0076	Hellenicos Erythros Stavros Neotitos
0018-0084	Hellenika
0018-0092	Hellenike Cheirougike
0018-0114	Helmantica
0018-0130	Helminthological Society of Washington. Proceedings
0018-0149	Helse
0018-0157	Helsenytt
0018-0173	Helvetia Archaeologica changed to Archaeologie der Schweiz
0018-0181	Helvetica Chirurgica Acta
0018-019X	Helvetica Chimica Acta
0018-0211	Helvetica Odontologica Acta changed to Schweizerische Monatsschrift fuer Zahnmedizin
0018-022X	Helvetica Paediatrica Acta
0018-0238	Helvetica Physica Acta
0018-0246	Hem och Fritid
0018-0262	Hembygden
0018-0270	Hemecht
0018-0289	Hemel en Dampkring see 0165-0211
0018-0297	Hemerocallis Journal see 0744-0219
0018-0300	Hemisphere†
0018-0319	Hemispherica†
0018-0327	Hemmets Journal
0018-0335	Hemmets Vaen
0018-0343	Hemtraedgaarden
0018-0351	Hemvaernet
0018-036X	Hendrik Pierson Vereniging (Publication) changed to Hendrik Pierson Stichting (Publication)
0018-0386	Hennepin Reporter
0018-0394	Hennes†
0018-0408	Henry E. Huntington Library and Art Gallery. Calendar of Exhibitions changed to Huntington Library, Art Gallery and Botanical Gardens. Calendar
0018-0416	Henry Ford Hospital Medical Journal
0018-0424	Henry George News see 0734-4031
0018-0432	Hep changed to Hip
0018-0467	Herald
0018-0475	Herald of Christian Science
0018-0483	Herald of Freedom†
0018-0491	Herald of Health
0018-0505	Herald of Health†
0018-0521	Herald of Library Science
0018-053X	Heraldo del Espiritismo see 0034-4478
0018-0548	Heraldo Mercantil Internacional
0018-0556	Heraldos del Rey changed to Conquistadores (Student Edition)
0018-0572	Herb Grower Magazine†
0018-0580	Herba Hungarica
0018-0599	Herba Polonica
0018-0602	Herbage Abstracts
0018-0629	Hercules Chemist†
0018-0637	Hercynia
0018-0645	Herder-Korrespondenz
0018-0661	Hereditas
0018-067X	Heredity
0018-0688	Herefordshire Farmer
0018-0696	Here's Health
0018-070X	Black Music Review†
0018-0718	Heritage of Vermilion County
0018-0726	Heritage - Southwest Jewish Press
0018-0734	Herkenning
0018-0742	Hermanus News†
0018-0750	Hermathena
0018-0777	Hermes
0018-0785	Hermes Exchange†
0018-0793	Herold
0018-0807	Herold (Munich)
0018-0815	Herold des Kostbaren Blutes
0018-0823	Heroldo de Esperanto
0018-0831	Herpetologica
0018-084X	Herpetological Review
0018-0858	Der Herr†
0018-0866	Husholdningslaereren (Vaeloese)
0018-0874	Herrenjournal
0018-0890	Herst†
0018-0904	Hertfordshire Countryside Illustrated see 0306-672X
0018-0912	Hertha
0018-0920	Hervormd Arnhem
0018-0939	Hervormd Nederland
0018-0947	Hervormd Wageningen
0018-0955	Hervormde Gemeente Musselkanaal. Kerkblad
0018-0971	Herzogia
0018-098X	Hesperia
0018-0998	Hesperide†
0018-1005	Hesperis - Tamuda
0018-1013	Hesperus†
0018-103X	Hessische Blaetter fuer Volksbildung
0018-1056	Hessische Erzieher†
0018-1064	Hessische Familienkunde
0018-1072	Hessischer Gaertner
0018-1080	Hessische Gross- und Aussenhandel changed to Grosshandel-Aussenhandel
0018-1099	Hessische Jugend
0018-1102	Hessische Standesbeamte†
0018-1110	Hestesport
0018-1129	Het Torentje
0018-1137	Heterofonia
0018-1145	Heuristics†
0018-1153	Hewlett-Packard Journal
0018-1188	Hey Lady
0018-1196	Heythrop Journal
0018-120X	HiCall
0018-1218	Hi-Fi/Stereo Buyers' Guide†
0018-1226	Audio Record Review see 0142-6230
0018-1242	Hi-Tension News
0018-1269	Hiballer Miner changed to Hiballer Contractor Miner
0018-1277	Hibernia changed to Hibernia Weekly
0018-1285	Hidalguia
0018-1293	Hide and Leather Bulletin
0018-1307	Hides and Skins Quarterly†
0018-1315	Hidro Mecanica en la Construccion Mexicana
0018-1323	Hidrologiai Kozlony
0018-1331	Hydrology and Meteorology
0018-134X	Hidrotehnica, Gospodarirea Apelor, Meteorologia changed to Hidrotehnica
0018-1358	Hidrotehnicka Bibliografija
0018-1382	HiFi Stereophonie changed to Stereoplay
0018-1390	Skin Research
0018-1404	Clinical Dermatology
0018-1412	High Change & Unitholder†
0018-1420	High Country
0018-1439	High Energy Chemistry
0018-1447	High Energy Physics Index
0018-1455	High Fidelity
0018-1463	High Fidelity/Musical America changed to Musical America
0018-1471	High Plains Journal
0018-148X	High Points
0018-1498	High School Journal
0018-1501	High Speed Ground Transportation Journal see 0197-6729
0018-151X	High Temperature Physics changed to High Temperature
0018-1536	High Temperature Science
0018-1544	High Temperatures - High Pressures
0018-1552	High Voltage Engineering Corporation Newsletter†
0018-1560	Higher Education
0018-1579	Higher Education and National Affairs
0018-1587	Higher Education and Research in the Netherlands changed to Counterpart - the International Dimension of Higher Education in the Netherlands
0018-1595	Secondary Education see 0143-1749
0018-1609	Higher Education Review
0018-1617	Highland Hotelkeeper & Touristmaker
0018-1625	Highlights
0018-1641	Highlights at B P L changed to Bloomfield Public Library Highlights
0018-165X	Highlights for Children

ISSN	Title
0018-1668	Highlights of Agricultural Research
0018-1676	Highway
0018-1684	Highway
0018-1692	Highway Builder
0018-1706	Highway Common Carrier Newsletter
0018-1722	Highway Mail
0018-1730	Highway Research Abstracts see 0095-2648
0018-1749	Highway Research News changed to T R News
0018-1757	Highway Transport†
0018-1765	Highway User see 0094-7393
0018-1773	Highways changed to Highways
0018-1781	Highways. Current Literature see 0091-1410
0018-179X	Hika
0018-1803	Leather Technology
0018-1811	Leather Chemistry
0018-182X	Hikone Ronso†
0018-1854	Hillbilly†
0018-1862	Hillel Gate
0018-1889	Himachal Agricultural Newsletter
0018-1897	Himavanta
0018-1900	Himmat
0018-1927	Hinduism
0018-1935	Hindustan Antibiotics Bulletin
0018-1943	Hindustan Chamber Review
0018-1951	Statistical Quality Control
0018-1978	Hinterland
0018-1986	Hints to Potato Growers
0018-2001	Hippokrates†
0018-201X	Hippologisk Tidsskrift
0018-2028	Hiradastechnika
0018-2036	Hiram Poetry Review
0018-2044	Hiroshima Medical Association. Journal
0018-2052	Hiroshima Journal of Medical Sciences
0018-2060	Hiroshima University. Faculty of Engineering. Bulletin
0018-2079	Hiroshima Mathematical Journal
0018-2087	Hiroshima Daigaku Igaku Zasshi
0018-2095	His changed to U Magazine
0018-2117	Hisairdec News†
0018-2125	Hispalis Medica
0018-2133	Hispania
0018-2141	Hispania
0018-215X	Hispania Sacra
0018-2168	Hispanic American Historical Review
0018-2176	Hispanic Review
0018-2184	El Hispano
0018-2192	Hispano Americano
0018-2206	Hispanofila
0018-2214	Histochemical Journal
0018-2222	Histochemie/Histochemistry/Histochimie see 0301-5564
0018-2230	Histoire de la Medecine†
0018-2257	Histoire Sociale
0018-2273	Historama
0018-229X	Historia
0018-2311	Historia
0018-2346	Historia Natural y pro Natura
0018-2354	Historia y Vida
0018-2362	Historiallinen Aikakauskirja
0018-2370	Historian
0018-2389	Historic Aviation†
0018-2397	Historic Kern
0018-2419	Historic Preservation
0018-2427	Historica
0018-2435	Historical Abstracts see 0363-2717
0018-2435	Historical Abstracts see 0363-2725
0018-2443	Historical Aviation Album
0018-2451	Historical Firearms Society of South Africa. Journal
0018-246X	Historical Journal
0018-2478	Historical Journal of Japan
0018-2486	Historical Magazine of the Protestant Episcopal Church
0018-2494	Historical Methods Newsletter see 0161-5440
0018-2508	Historical New Hampshire
0018-2516	Historical Review
0018-2524	Historical Review of Berks County
0018-2532	Historical Society of Haddonfield. Bulletin
0018-2540	Historical Society of Nigeria. Journal
0018-2559	Historical Studies
0018-2567	Historical Wyoming†
0018-2575	Historicky Casopis
0018-2583	Historie a Vojenstvi
0018-2591	Historiographer
0018-2605	Das Historisch-Politische Buch
0018-2613	Historische Zeitschrift
0018-2621	Historisches Jahrbuch
0018-263X	Historisk Tidskrift
0018-2648	History
0018-2656	History and Theory
0018-2664	History Book Club Review
0018-2680	History of Education Quarterly
0018-2699	History of Education Society Bulletin
0018-2702	History of Political Economy
0018-2710	History of Religions
0018-2737	History of the Twentieth Century†
0018-2745	History Teacher
0018-2753	History Today
0018-2761	Hit†
0018-277X	Hitachi Review
0018-2788	Hitachi Zosen Technical Review
0018-2796	Hitotsubashi Journal of Commerce and Management
0018-280X	Hitotsubashi Journal of Economics
0018-2842	Hjemmet
0018-2869	Hlas l'Udu
0018-2885	Hoard's Dairyman
0018-2893	Hobart Weldworld†
0018-2907	Hobbies, the Magazine for Collectors changed to Antiques & Collecting Hobbies
0018-2923	Hobby (Stuttgart)
0018-2931	Hobby Bulletin see 0165-5949
0018-2958	Hochfrequenztechnik und Elektroakustik†
0018-2974	Das Hochschulwesen
0018-2982	Hockey Circle
0018-2990	Hockey e Pattinaggio†
0018-3008	Hockey Field
0018-3016	Hockey News
0018-3032	Hockey Sport†
0018-3040	Hodowla Roslin, Aklimatyzacja i Nasiennictwo
0018-3059	Hoechstrichterliche Finanzrechtsprechung
0018-3067	Hoeden & Boetiek†
0018-3075	Tidsskriftet den Hoegre Skolen see 0332-7167
0018-3083	Die Hoehere Schule†
0018-3091	Hoehle
0018-3105	Hoehlenpost
0018-3113	Hoer Zu
0018-3121	Hoergeschaedigte Kinder
0018-3156	Hoesch changed to Estel
0018-3164	Hoffheimer Nachrichten†
0018-3172	Hofstra Chronicle changed to Chronicle (Hempstead)
0018-3180	Hog Farm Management
0018-3199	Hog Guide
0018-3210	Hogar
0018-3229	Hogar Cristiano
0018-3245	Hohe Bruecke
0018-3253	Hohenzollerische Heimat
0018-327X	Hoiku No Tomo
0018-3288	Hoja de Informacion Economica
0018-3296	Hoja del Lunes de Lugo
0018-330X	Hoja del Lunes de Orense
0018-3334	Hoejskolebladet
0018-3342	Health Care
0018-3350	Health and Physical Education
0018-3369	Review of Tuberculosis for Public Health Nurse
0018-3377	Hokkaido Journal of Orthopedic & Traumatic Surgery
0018-3385	Hokkaido Veterinary Medical Association. Journal
0018-3393	Hokkaido University of Education. Journal. Section 2 B. Biology, Geology and Agriculture
0018-3415	Hokkaido National Agricultural Experiment Station. Research Bulletin
0018-3431	Hokkaido Librarians Study Circle. Bulletin
0018-344X	Hokkaido University. Faculty of Agriculture. Journal
0018-3458	Hokkaido University. Faculty of Fisheries. Bulletin
0018-3466	Hokkaido University. Faculty of Fisheries. Memoirs
0018-3474	Hokkaido University. Faculty of Science. Journal. Series 4: Geology and Mineralogy
0018-3482	Hokkaido University. Faculty of Science. Journal. Series 1: Mathematics see 0385-4035
0018-3490	Agriculture in Hokkaido
0018-3504	Hokkaido Fisheries Experimental Station. Journal
0018-3512	Holectechniek†
0018-3520	Holiday changed to Travel-Holiday
0018-3539	Holiday Inn changed to Holiday Inn Companion
0018-3555	Holidays in Romania
0018-3563	Holland Herald
0018-3571	Holland Shipbuilding, Marine Engineering and Shipping Herald changed to Holland Shipbuilding
0018-358X	Holland Shipping and Trading changed to Holland's Export Magazine
0018-3598	Hollandia Varia†
0018-3601	Hollands Maandblad
0018-361X	Hollandse Huis†
0018-3628	Hollar†
0018-3636	Hollingsworth Register
0018-3644	Hollins Critic
0018-3652	Hollins Symposium†
0018-3660	Hollywood Reporter
0018-3687	Holstein-Friesian Journal changed to Holstein Journal
0018-3695	Holstein-Friesian World see 0199-4239
0018-3709	Holsteiner Pferd changed to Pferde
0018-3717	Holt Investment Advisory
0018-3725	Holy Cross
0018-3741	Holy Name Monthly†
0018-375X	Holz-Kunststoff see 0341-0331
0018-3768	Holz als Roh- und Werkstoff
0018-3776	Holz im Handwerk
0018-3784	Holz-Kurier
0018-3792	Holz-Zentralblatt
0018-3806	Holzarbeiter-Zeitung
0018-3814	Holzbau
0018-3822	H O B - Die Holzbearbeitung
0018-3830	Holzforschung
0018-3849	Holzforschung und Holzverwertung
0018-3857	Holzindustrie†
0018-3865	Die Holzschwelle
0018-3881	Holztechnologie
0018-3911	Home and Auto Retailer changed to Aftermarket Business
0018-392X	Home and Building
0018-3938	Home & Country
0018-3946	Home and Family
0018-3954	Home and Garden Supply Merchandiser see 0195-1386
0018-3962	Home and Health changed to Vitalite
0018-3970	Home Builder News
0018-3997	Home Business Digest changed to Mail Order Selling & Small Business World
0018-4004	Home Ec News
0018-4012	Home Echoes see 0705-7830
0018-4039	Home Finders Directory
0018-4047	Home Furnishings Daily see 0162-9158
0018-4055	Home Goods Retailing
0018-4063	Home Improvements see 0746-2344
0018-4071	Home Life
0018-408X	Home Missions see 0279-5345
0018-411X	Home Office Report†
0018-4128	Home Rule†
0018-4152	Homecare
0018-4160	Homefinder
0018-4179	Homefront I A D†
0018-4195	Perspectives-In Long Term Care†
0018-4209	Homemakers's Magazine
0018-4217	Homemakers Guide†
0018-4225	Homeopathie Francaise
0018-4233	Homes and Gardens
0018-4241	Homes Overseas
0018-425X	Homesewing Trade News
0018-4268	Homiletic and Pastoral Review
0018-4276	Homiletische Monatshefte
0018-4284	Homin Ukrainy
0018-4292	Homine
0018-4314	Revue l'Homme Libre
0018-4322	Homme Nouveau
0018-4349	Hommes et Commerce - Horizons et Conjoncture see 0223-5846
0018-4357	Hommes et Fonderie
0018-4381	Hommes et Techniques†
0018-439X	Hommes et Terres du Nord
0018-4403	Hommes Libres
0018-4411	Hommes Volants
0018-442X	Homo
0018-4446	Homeopathic Sandesh†
0018-4454	Homoeopathic Science Quarterly†
0018-4489	Homoeopathisch Maandblad changed to Homoeopathisch Tijdschrift
0018-4500	Hon & Han
0018-4519	Art & Architecture
0018-4527	Hondenwereld
0018-4535	Honduras Pediatrica
0018-4551	Honey
0018-456X	Honeyguide
0018-4578	Hong Kong Economic Papers
0018-4586	Hong Kong Enterprise
0018-4594	Hong Kong Manager
0018-4616	Hong Kong Travel Bulletin
0018-4632	Honnold Library Record†
0018-4640	Honolulu Magazine see 0441-2044
0018-4659	Honolulu Weekly Snooper
0018-4675	Honourable Company of Master Mariners. Journal
0018-4683	Hoof Beats
0018-4691	Dimensie†
0018-4705	Hoofdlijnen
0018-4721	Hoosharar
0018-473X	Hoosier Banker
0018-4748	Hoosier Farmer
0018-4756	Hoosier Genealogist
0018-4764	Hoosier Independent
0018-4772	Hoosier Legionnaire
0018-4780	Hoosier Outdoors
0018-4799	Hoosier Purchasor
0018-4810	Hoosier Schoolmaster
0018-4829	Hooyce†
0018-4837	Hopeapeili†
0018-4845	Hopfen-Rundschau
0018-4853	Hopital d'Aujourd'hui see 0317-3739
0018-4861	Hopital a Paris
0018-487X	Hopitaux Civils et Militaires. Gazette
0018-4888	Hoppe-Seyler's Zeitschrift fuer Physiologische Chemie changed to Biological Chemistry Hoppe-Seyler
0018-4896	Hoppenstedt-Monatskurstabellen see 0170-5822
0018-4918	Horatio Alger Newsboy see 0028-9396
0018-4934	Hoerelsen
0018-4942	Die Horen
0018-4977	Horizon (Tuscaloosa)
0018-4985	Horizons changed to A C A News
0018-5000	Horizons in Leisure†
0018-5019	Horizons Unlimited
0018-5027	Horizontes
0018-5043	Hormone and Metabolic Research
0018-5051	Hormones see 0301-0163
0018-506X	Hormones and Behavior
0018-5078	Horn Book Magazine
0018-5086	Hornet
0018-5108	Horological Journal
0018-5116	Horoscope
0018-5124	Horoscope Quotidien Eclair
0018-5132	Hors Cote
0018-5140	Horse and Hound
0018-5159	Horse & Rider
0018-5167	Horse and Show Inc†
0018-5175	Horse Lover's Magazine changed to Horse Lover's National Magazine
0018-5191	Horse World
0018-5205	Horsefeathers
0018-5213	Horseless Carriage Gazette
0018-5221	Horseman
0018-523X	Horseman and Fair World
0018-5256	Horsemen's Journal
0018-5264	Horsetrader
0018-5272	Horticultura see 0106-0546
0018-5280	Horticultural Abstracts

ISSN INDEX

ISSN	Title
0018-5299	Horticultural Research *changed to* Crop Research
0018-5302	Horticultural Society of New York. Bulletin†
0018-5329	Horticulture
0018-5337	Hortikultura
0018-5345	HortScience
0018-5361	Hose & Nozzle†
0018-537X	Hosiery Abstracts *see* 0260-8553
0018-5388	Hosiery and Textile Journal
0018-5396	Hosiery and Underwear
0018-540X	Hosiery Newsletter *changed to* Hosiery News
0018-5418	Hosiery *changed to* Hosiery Report Weekly
0018-5426	British Knitting Industry *see* 0307-2517
0018-5442	Arquivos dos Hospitais e da Faculdade de Ciencias Medicas da Santa Casa de Sao Paulo
0018-5477	Hospital *see* 0308-0234
0018-5485	Hospital (Los Angeles)
0018-5493	Hospital Abstract Service†
0018-5507	Hospital Abstracts *changed to* Health Service Abstracts
0018-5515	Hospital and Health Care *changed to* Australian Hospital
0018-5523	Hospital Administration *changed to* Hospital & Health Services Administration
0018-5531	Hospital Administration
0018-5558	Hospital Affairs in New York State†
0018-5566	Health Care Product News
0018-5574	Hospital Association of New York State. News
0018-5582	Hospital Building and Engineering *see* 0300-5720
0018-5590	Hospital Bureau Market News†
0018-5612	Hospital de Mataro. Anales†
0018-5620	Hospital Equipment & Supplies
0018-5639	Hospital Accounting *see* 0735-0732
0018-5647	Hospital for Joint Diseases Orthopaedic Institute. Bulletin
0018-5655	Hospital Formulary Management *see* 0098-6909
0018-5663	Hospital Forum *changed to* Healthcare Forum
0018-568X	Hospital General†
0018-5701	Hospital Highlights *changed to* Hospital Highlights (Year)
0018-571X	Hospital International†
0018-5728	Hospital Law Manual and Quarterly Service *changed to* Hospital Law Manual. Attorneys
0018-5736	Hospital Literature Index
0018-5760	Hospital Oftalmologico de Nuestra Senora de la Luz. Boletin
0018-5779	Hospital Pharmacy *changed to* White Sheet
0018-5787	Hospital Pharmacy
0018-5795	Hospital Physician
0018-5817	Hospital Progress *see* 0882-1577
0018-5825	Hospital Purchasing *see* 0300-5461
0018-5833	Hospital R.S.A.
0018-5841	Hospital Supervision *see* 0363-020X
0018-585X	Hospital Supervisor's Bulletin
0018-5868	Hospital Topics
0018-5876	Hospital Tribune†
0018-5884	Hospital Vargas. Archivos
0018-5906	Hospitales y Clinicas
0018-5914	Hospitalia
0018-5922	Hospitalier
0018-5930	Hospitalis
0018-5949	Hospitality *changed to* Hospitality & Convention News
0018-5973	Hospitals
0018-5981	Hospitals' Association Journal†
0018-599X	Hospodar
0018-6007	Hot Car *see* 0265-6183
0018-6023	Hot Rod Industry News†
0018-6031	Hot Rod
0018-6066	Hotel *changed to* Hotel Voice
0018-6074	Hotel and Club Voice *changed to* Hotel Voice
0018-6082	Hotel and Motel Management
0018-6104	Catering and Hotel Management†
0018-6120	Hotel-Gasthof-Pension/H G P *changed to* Hotel 2000
0018-6139	Hotel Gazette of South Australia
0018-6147	Hotel Herald†
0018-6171	Hotel Motel and Restaurant†
0018-618X	Hotel/Motel Buyer's Directory†
0018-6201	Hotel & Restaurant
0018-6221	Hotel Restaurant
0018-6228	Hotel Review *changed to* Hotel Review of Western Australia
0018-6279	Hoteles de Colombia
0018-6287	Hotelier
0018-6295	Hotelier & Caterer
0018-6309	Hotellerie Magazine
0018-6317	Hotelli- ja Ravintolalehti *see* 0357-749X
0018-6333	Hotelnews
0018-6341	Practice in Prosthodontics
0018-6368	Houille Blanche
0018-6384	Hounds and Hunting
0018-6392	House & Bungalow
0018-6406	House & Garden
0018-6414	House and Home *see* 0161-0619
0018-6422	House Beautiful
0018-6430	House Beautiful's Building Manual
0018-6457	House Beautiful's Home Decorating
0018-6465	House Beautiful's Home Remodeling
0018-6473	House Buyer
0018-6481	House of Tang Family News†
0018-649X	House Physician Reporter†
0018-6503	Housecraft *changed to* Modus
0018-652X	Housewares Promotions
0018-6554	Housing Affairs Letter
0018-6562	Housing and People†
0018-6570	Housing and Planning References
0018-6589	Housing and Planning Review *changed to* Housing and Planning Review
0018-6597	Housing and Renewal Index *see* 0094-2324
0018-6600	Housing and Urban Affairs†
0018-6619	Housing and Urban Development Trends†
0018-6627	Housing Authority Journal
0018-6635	Housing Finance
0018-6643	Housing Quarterly *changed to* Building Review
0018-6651	Housing Review
0018-666X	H D A World†
0018-6678	Houston *see* 0745-9807
0018-6686	Houston Geological Society. Bulletin
0018-6694	Houston Law Review
0018-6708	Houston, Texas. Museum of Fine Arts Bulletin
0018-6732	Houtwereld
0018-6740	Houtz†
0018-6767	Hoverfoil News
0018-6805	Howard Collector†
0018-6813	Howard Law Journal
0018-6856	Hoy Dia
0018-6899	Hromkla†
0018-6902	Hrvatska Revija
0018-6910	Hrvatski Katolicki Glasnik
0018-6929	Hsien Tai Hsueh Yuan *changed to* Chieh-Hsueh Yu Wen-Hua
0018-6937	Hsin Ju Chia
0018-6945	Hsinhua Selected News Items *changed to* Hsinhua Weekly
0018-6953	Huaral
0018-6961	Hubbard School System Office of Curriculum and Instruction. Digest Newsletter *changed to* Insight (Hubbard)
0018-6988	Hudba a Zvuk†
0018-6996	Hudebni Rozhledy
0018-7003	Hudebni Veda
0018-702X	Hudson Review
0018-7054	Ovum
0018-7070	Huisarts en Wetenschap
0018-7089	Huisgenoot
0018-7097	Huismuziek
0018-7119	Huizer Kerkblad
0018-7127	Hule Mexicano y Plasticos
0018-7135	Human Side *changed to* Human Side of Supervision
0018-7143	Human Biology
0018-7151	Human Context†
0018-716X	Human Development
0018-7178	Human Ecology Forum
0018-7194	Human Events
0018-7208	Human Factors
0018-7216	Human Geography
0018-7224	Human Industrial Design
0018-7232	Human Issue *changed to* New Kent Quarterly
0018-7240	Human Mosaic
0018-7259	Human Organization
0018-7267	Human Relations
0018-7275	Human Relations Tips and Trends *see* 0097-8345
0018-7283	Human Relations News of Chicago
0018-7291	Human Relations Training News *changed to* Social Change
0018-7305	Human Voice *see* 0145-983X
0018-7321	Humana†
0018-733X	Humane Society of the United States. News *changed to* Humane Society of the United States News (1977)
0018-7348	Humangenetik *see* 0340-6717
0018-7356	Humanidades
0018-7364	Humanisme
0018-7372	Humanisme et Entreprise
0018-7380	Humanist *see* 0306-512X
0018-7399	Humanist
0018-7402	Humanist in Canada
0018-7410	Humanist News *changed to* Humanist Newsletter
0018-7429	Humanist Outlook
0018-7437	Quest†
0018-7445	Humanitas
0018-7453	Humanitas†
0018-7488	Humanitas†
0018-7496	Humanitas *see* 0193-2748
0018-750X	Humanite Rouge *see* 0754-281X
0018-7518	Humanities Scientifique *changed to* Documents et Recherches-Sciences
0018-7526	Humanities
0018-7534	Humanities. Classes de Lettres. Sections Modernes *changed to* Documents et Recherches
0018-7542	Humanities Association Review†
0018-7550	Humanities. Classes de Lettres. Section Classiques *changed to* Documents et Recherches
0018-7569	Humanities. Cycle d'Observation. Classes de 4 et 3 *changed to* Documents et Recherches
0018-7577	Humanities in the South
0018-7585	Humberside
0018-7615	Humboldt
0018-7623	Humboldt (Portuguese Edition)
0018-7631	Humboldtglocke
0018-7666	Humpty Dumpty's Magazine for Little Children *see* 0273-7590
0018-7690	Hundsport
0018-7704	Hungara Vivo
0018-7712	Hungarian Agricultural Review
0018-7720	Hungarian Building Bulletin
0018-7739	Hungarian Exporter *see* 0324-7473
0018-7747	Hungarian Foreign Trade
0018-7755	Hungarian Heavy Industries *see* 0139-035X
0018-7763	Hungarian Review *see* 0209-5386
0018-7771	Hungarian Technical Abstracts *see* 0237-0808
0018-778X	Hungarian Trade Union News
0018-7798	Hungarofilm Bulletin
0018-7801	Hungary. Kozponti Statisztikai Hivatal. Ipari es Epitoipari Statisztikai Ertesito
0018-781X	Hungary. Kozponti Statisztikai Hivatal. Statisztikai Havi Kozlemenyek
0018-7828	Hungary. Kozponti Statisztikai Hivatal. Teruleti Statisztika
0018-7852	Hunterdon Historical Newsletter
0018-7860	Hunter's Horn
0018-7879	Hunting Dog†
0018-7887	Hunting Group Review
0018-7895	Huntington Library Quarterly
0018-7909	Huon News
0018-7917	Huron Church News
0018-7925	Huron Road Hospital. Scientific Bulletin *changed to* Huron Road Hospital. Scientific Bulletin
0018-7933	Hurra Juventus
0018-795X	Hus og Hjem *changed to* Ugebladet Hus og Hjem
0018-7968	Husbyggaren
0018-7976	Huset Vaart
0018-7984	Husfreyjan
0018-7992	Hushaallslaeraren
0018-800X	Husipar
0018-8018	Husmandshjemmet *changed to* Landbrugsmagasinet Husmandshjemmet
0018-8026	Husmodern
0018-8034	Husmorbladet
0018-8050	Hutmacher-, Modisten- und Schirrmmacher-Zeitung
0018-8069	Hutnicke Listy
0018-8077	Hutnik
0018-8085	Hutoipar
0018-8093	Hvedekorn
0018-8107	Hvidvare-Nyt
0018-8115	Hydata†
0018-8131	Hydraulic Pneumatic Power *see* 0306-4069
0018-814X	Hydraulics and Pneumatics
0018-8158	Hydrobiologia
0018-8166	Hydrobiological Journal
0018-8182	Hydrocarbon News *see* 0031-6466
0018-8190	Hydrocarbon Processing
0018-8212	Hydrospace *changed to* Offshore Services & Technology
0018-8220	Hydrotechnical Construction
0018-8239	Hygien Forum†
0018-8247	Higiena i Zdraveopazvane
0018-8263	Hygienist
0018-8271	Hymn
0018-8298	Hymylehti
0018-831X	Hyperbaric Medicine Newsletter *changed to* Pressure (Bethesda)
0018-8328	Hyperion (Austin)
0018-8336	Hyphen
0018-8344	Hypnosis Quarterly *see* 0882-6072
0018-8352	Hypothese†
0018-8360	Hyresgaesten
0018-8387	I A G Journal *see* 0579-5486
0018-8395	T A M
0018-8409	I A P A News
0018-8425	Institute of Administrative Research. Research Bulletin *changed to* H M L I Research Bulletin
0018-8441	I A S L I C Bulletin
0018-845X	I A S L I C Newsletter
0018-8468	I A S L News for You (Illinois Association of School Librarians) *changed to* I A M E News for You
0018-8476	I A T U L Proceedings *changed to* I A T U L Quarterly
0018-8484	I A U News *changed to* Interamericana
0018-8492	International Association of University Professors & Lecturers. Communication†
0018-8506	Bulletin d'Information de la Region Parisienne *see* 0396-9975
0018-8514	I and N Reporter
0018-8522	I B A Municipal Statistical Bulletin†
0018-8530	I. B. A. News†
0018-8549	I B A Statistical Bulletin†
0018-8557	I B B - Information†
0018-8565	I B B Bulletin *changed to* I B E Bulletin
0018-8581	I B E A S
0018-859X	I B E W - A F L - C I O. Local 1470 Journal
0018-8603	I. B. Flash-Edition Batiment†
0018-8611	I B I S
0018-862X	I B L A
0018-8638	I B M Iran News Bulletin†
0018-8646	I B M Journal of Research and Development
0018-8654	I B M Kwartaalschrift *changed to* I B M Nieuws
0018-8662	I B M Nachrichten
0018-8670	I B M Systems Journal

ISSN INDEX 1245

ISSN	Title
0018-8697	I B Nachrichten
0018-8700	I B P Boletim *changed to* Petroleo e Petroquimica
0018-8735	I C A Information†
0018-8743	I C A Information Bulletin *changed to* I C A Regional Bulletin
0018-8751	I C A News†
0018-876X	I C A Newsletter
0018-8778	I C A O Bulletin
0018-8786	Icare
0018-8794	Instituto Colombiano Agropecuario. Revista I C A
0018-8808	I C A S A L S Newsletter
0018-8816	I C A T U Review
0018-8824	I C B
0018-8832	I C C News *changed to* I C C Information
0018-8840	I C C Newsletter *changed to* I B I Newsletter
0018-8859	I C C Practitioners' Journal *changed to* Transportation Practitioners Journal
0018-8867	I C C W News Bulletin
0018-8875	I C D Letterette
0018-8883	Institut Canadien d'Education des Adultes. Bulletin *changed to* I C E A Bulletin de Liaison
0018-8891	I.C.E.A. Cahiers†
0018-8913	I C F Quarterly
0018-8921	I C F T U Economic & Social Bulletin
0018-8948	I C I A Information Bulletin†
0018-8972	I C N Calling†
0018-8980	I C O F T News Review
0018-8999	I C O M News
0018-9006	I C P A Quarterly Bulletin *changed to* I C P A Quarterly
0018-9014	I C P Quarterly *see* 0272-1171
0018-9030	I C S I D Information Bulletin *see* 0145-2118
0018-9049	I C S S R Newsletter
0018-9065	I C V A News
0018-9073	I D B Newsletter†
0018-9081	I D I A†
0018-909X	I D O C International Documentation on the Contemporary Church *see* 0160-7553
0018-9103	I D O R T†
0018-9111	Probleme de Informare si Documentare
0018-912X	Discover the Bible
0018-9138	I E C Bulletin
0018-9146	I.E.E. - I.E.R.E. Proceedings - India
0018-9154	I E E E Almanack
0018-9162	Computer
0018-9197	I E E E Journal of Quantum Electronics
0018-9200	I E E E Journal of Solid State Circuits
0018-9219	Institute of Electrical and Electronics Engineers. Proceedings
0018-9235	I E E E Spectrum
0018-9243	I E E E Student Journal†
0018-9251	I E E E Transactions on Aerospace and Electronic Systems
0018-926X	I E E E Transactions on Antennas and Propagation
0018-9278	I E E E Transactions on Audio and Electroacoustics *see* 0096-3518
0018-9286	I E E E Transactions on Automatic Control
0018-9294	I E E E Transactions on Biomedical Engineering
0018-9308	I E E E Transactions on Broadcast and Television Receivers *see* 0098-3063
0018-9316	I E E E Transactions on Broadcasting
0018-9324	I E E E Transactions on Circuit Theory *see* 0098-4094
0018-9332	I E E E Transactions on Communication Technology *see* 0090-6778
0018-9340	I E E E Transactions on Computers
0018-9359	I E E E Transactions on Education
0018-9367	I E E E Transactions on Electrical Insulation
0018-9375	I E E E Transactions on Electromagnetic Compatibility
0018-9383	I E E E Transactions on Electron Devices
0018-9391	I E E E Transactions on Engineering Management
0018-9405	I E E E Transactions on Engineering Writing and Speech *see* 0361-1434
0018-9413	I E E E Transactions on Geoscience Electronics *see* 0196-2892
0018-9421	I E E E Transactions on Industrial Electronics and Control Instrumentation *see* 0278-0046
0018-943X	I E E E Transactions on Industry and General Applications *see* 0093-9994
0018-9448	I E E E Transactions on Information Theory
0018-9456	I E E E Transactions on Instrumentation and Measurement
0018-9464	I E E E Transactions on Magnetics
0018-9472	I E E E Transactions on Systems, Man and Cybernetics
0018-9480	I E E E Transactions on Microwave Theory and Techniques
0018-9499	I E E E Transactions on Nuclear Science
0018-9502	I E E E Transactions on Parts, Materials and Packaging *see* 0148-6411
0018-9510	I E E E Transactions on Power Apparatus and Systems†
0018-9510	I E E E Transactions on Power Apparatus and Systems *see* 0885-8977
0018-9510	I E E E Transactions on Power Apparatus and Systems *see* 0885-8969
0018-9510	I E E E Transactions on Power Apparatus and Systems *see* 0885-8950
0018-9529	I E E E Transactions on Reliability
0018-9537	I E E E Transactions on Sonics and Ultrasonics *see* 0885-3010
0018-9545	I E E E Transactions on Vehicular Technology
0018-9553	I E E News *see* 0013-5127
0018-9561	I E E T E Bulletin *changed to* Electrical and Electronics Incorporated Engineer
0018-957X	I E N Pubblicazioni
0018-9596	I E Review
0018-9618	I. E. S. Lighting Review†
0018-9626	I E S P E. Boletim†
0018-9634	I F A N Bulletin. Serie A: Sciences Naturelles
0018-9642	I F A N Bulletin. Serie B: Sciences Humaines
0018-9650	I F A P News
0018-9685	I F L A News *see* 0340-0352
0018-9693	I F L - Mitteilungen
0018-9707	I F L Nieuws
0018-9715	I F M - S E I Bulletin
0018-9723	I F M A News
0018-9731	I F O Studien
0018-974X	I F O Schnelldienst
0018-9758	I. F. Stone's Weekly†
0018-9766	I G A Grocergram
0018-9774	I G C Monthly†
0018-9782	I G F - Journal
0018-9790	I G T - Nieuws†
0018-9804	I G U Bulletin
0018-9820	I H I Engineering Review
0018-9839	I H K Wuppertal. Wirtschaftliche Mitteilungen
0018-9847	I.H.V.E. Journal *changed to* Building Services
0018-9855	I I C
0018-9863	I I C A. Documentacao
0018-9871	I I E Report†
0018-988X	Status Report (Washington)
0018-9898	I. I. R. B.†
0018-991X	I J A Report
0018-9936	I K Z *changed to* I K Z - Haustechnik
0018-9944	I L A Catalyst *see* 0730-711X
0018-9952	I L A Intercambio Latinoamericano†
0018-9960	I L A R News
0018-9979	I L A Reporter
0018-9995	I L P A Reporter *changed to* I L C A Reporter
0019-0012	I M C Journal†
0019-0020	I M M Abstracts
0019-0063	I M S Bulletin
0019-0071	I M Z Bulletin
0019-008X	Imboniselo
0019-0136	I N F O
0019-0144	I N F O Journal
0019-0152	I N P A Advertising Newsletter *changed to* Idea Newsletter
0019-0160	International Newspaper Promotion Association Advertising Copy Service Newsletter†
0019-0179	Inpho
0019-0187	I N P S Boletim Informativo *changed to* Informe I N P S
0019-0195	I N P S Mensario Estatistico *changed to* I N A M P S em Dados
0019-0209	France. Institut National de la Statistique et des Etudes Economiques. Annales
0019-0217	Inspel
0019-0225	Argentina. Instituto Nacional de Tecnologia Industrial. Boletin I N T I *see* 0325-934X
0019-0233	I N T Informativo
0019-0241	Inqabayokulinda
0019-025X	I P A Forum†
0019-0268	I P A Review
0019-0276	I P A S E Biblioteca Informa
0019-0292	I P E G. Boletim Informativo†
0019-0314	I P I Report
0019-0330	I P M Digest
0019-0349	Instituut voor Plantenziektenkundig Onderzoek. Mededeling
0019-0357	I P P F Medical Bulletin
0019-0365	International Philosophical Quarterly
0019-039X	I P S F News Bulletin
0019-0403	I P S S Bulletin
0019-0411	I. P. V. D. F. Boletim Mensal†
0019-042X	I R A L
0019-0446	I R B Revista
0019-0454	I. R. Concepts†
0019-0462	I. R. I. Journal†
0019-0497	I R M P Impact†
0019-0500	I R R A Newsletter
0019-0535	Workers' Power†
0019-0543	I S A C S Bulletin†
0019-0551	Instrumentation Index†
0019-056X	I S A L Abstracts†
0019-0578	I S A Transactions
0019-0586	I S B A Journal
0019-0594	Iscor News
0019-0608	I S C P A Bulletin *changed to* Tickmark
0019-0624	I S E A Communique
0019-0632	I S I Bulletin
0019-0640	Standard and Poor's I S L Daily Stock Price Index. American Stock Exchange. *changed to* Standard & Poor's Daily Stock Price Record. American Exchange
0019-0659	Standard and Poor's I S L Daily Stock Price Index. New York Stock Exchange *changed to* Standard & Poor's Daily Stock Price Record. New York Stock Exchange
0019-0691	I S S Letter *changed to* T A I S S A Letter
0019-0713	I S T A News Bulletin
0019-073X	I T
0019-0748	I T A Bulletin *changed to* Institut du Transport Aerien. Monthly Bulletin
0019-0756	I T A Bulletin†
0019-0772	I T A-Engenharia†
0019-0780	I T A Studies
0019-0799	I T F Newsletter
0019-0810	I T L†
0019-0829	I T L Review of Applied Linguistics
0019-0837	I T Novine
0019-0845	I T R
0019-0853	I T U Review
0019-0861	I U E News
0019-087X	I U L A Newsletter *changed to* Local Government Newsletter
0019-0888	I U S Y Survey *changed to* I U S Y Bulletin
0019-0896	I V L Nytt
0019-090X	I.V.-Nieuws *changed to* Vorm
0019-0918	I V S
0019-0926	I Y F European Bulletin†
0019-0934	Iade
0019-0942	Iatrika Pepragmena
0019-0950	Iatriki
0019-0977	Ibarske Novosti
0019-0993	Ibero-Romania†
0019-1000	Ibid
0019-1019	Ibis
0019-1027	Icarus
0019-1035	Icarus
0019-1043	Ice
0019-1051	Ice Cap News
0019-106X	Ice Cream & Frozen Confectionery
0019-1078	Hagtidindi
0019-1108	Ichthyologica
0019-1159	Idaho Agricultural Science†
0019-1167	Idaho Business and Economic Review†
0019-1175	Idaho Transportation Department. Highway Information
0019-1183	Idaho Education News *changed to* I E A Reporter (1976)
0019-1205	Idaho Law Review
0019-1213	Idaho Librarian
0019-1221	Idaho Pharmacist
0019-1248	Idaho Wildlife Review *changed to* Idaho Wildlife
0019-1256	Idaho Woodland Farmer†
0019-1264	Idaho Yesterdays
0019-1272	Idea†
0019-1280	Idea
0019-1299	Idea
0019-1310	Idea Source Guide
0019-1329	Idea Zoofila†
0019-1345	Ideal Companion
0019-1353	Ideal Education
0019-1361	Ideal Home
0019-137X	Ideals
0019-1388	Ideas†
0019-140X	Ideas y Valores
0019-1426	Ideen des Exakten Wissens *see* 0340-0220
0019-1434	Idees pour Tous *changed to* Idees pour Tous - Speciale Hebdo
0019-1442	Ideggyogyaszati Szemle
0019-1450	Identification News
0019-1485	Idiom†
0019-1507	Idisze Szriftn
0019-1523	Idrijski Razgledi
0019-1531	Iets
0019-154X	If†
0019-1566	Wirtschaftsbilderheft BRD und Ausland *see* 0170-3617
0019-1574	Japana Medicina Revuo
0019-1582	Medicine and Gospel
0019-1590	Medical Science and Medical Care
0019-1604	Medicine and Biology
0019-1612	Studies on History of Medicine
0019-1620	Revista de Igiena, Bacteriologie, Virusologie, Parazitologie, Pneumoftiziologie. Igiena
0019-1639	Igiene e Sanita Pubblica
0019-1647	Igiene Mentale
0019-1655	Igiene Moderna
0019-1663	Igitur Revista Literaria
0019-1671	Iglesia Evangelica del Rio de la Plata. Revista Parroquial
0019-168X	Igloos
0019-1698	Ignis *see* 0282-0595
0019-1701	Ihre Brigitte†
0019-171X	Ija Webonere
0019-1728	Ikai Jiho
0019-1736	Journal of Medical Instruments
0019-1744	Ikon
0019-1752	Ikon†
0019-1779	Ilanga
0019-1795	Iliff Review
0019-1809	Illiana Genealogist
0019-1817	Illiana Research Report†
0019-1825	Illinet Output *changed to* Off-Line
0019-1833	Illinois Agricultural Economics†
0019-1841	Illinois Alumni News

0019-185X Illinois Banker
0019-1868 Illinois Baptist
0019-1876 Illinois Bar Journal
0019-1892 Illinois Beverage Journal
0019-1906 Illinois Braille Messenger (Inkprint Edition)
0019-1914 Illinois Building News
0019-1922 Illinois Business Review
0019-1930 Illinois Central Gulf News *changed to* Main Line News
0019-1949 Illinois County and Township Official
0019-1957 Illinois Courts Bulletin
0019-1973 Illinois Dental Journal
0019-1981 Illinois Business and Economic Development *see* 0161-7885
0019-199X Illinois. Department of Public Health. Division of Disease Control. Weekly Report *changed to* Illinois. Department of Public Health. Division of Disease Control. Monthly Report
0019-2015 Illinois Engineer
0019-2023 Illinois English Bulletin
0019-2031 Illinois Geographical Society. Bulletin
0019-204X Illinois Health Messenger†
0019-2058 Illinois History
0019-2082 Illinois Journal of Mathematics
0019-2090 Illinois Labor Bulletin†
0019-2104 Illinois Libraries
0019-2112 Illinois Master Plumber Magazine
0019-2120 Illinois Medical Journal
0019-2139 Illinois Municipal Review
0019-2147 Illinois Music Educator
0019-2155 Illinois Parks & Recreation
0019-2163 Illinois Pharmacist *see* 0195-2099
0019-2171 Illinois Police Association. Official Journal
0019-2201 Illinois Research
0019-221X Illinois School Board Journal
0019-2228 Illinois School Research *see* 0163-822X
0019-2236 Illinois Schools Journal
0019-2252 Illinois State Academy of Science. Transactions
0019-2260 Illinois State Chamber of Commerce. Current Report *changed to* Voice of Illinois Business
0019-2287 Illinois State Historical Society. Journal *see* 0748-8149
0019-2295 Illinois Quarterly†
0019-2309 Illinois Truck News
0019-2317 Illinois Wildlife
0019-2325 Illovo Digest†
0019-2333 Illuminating Engineering *see* 0360-6325
0019-2333 Illuminating Engineering *see* 0099-4480
0019-2341 Illuminating Engineering Institute of Japan. Journal
0019-235X Illumination Annual *changed to* Divine Path
0019-2368 Illuminations *see* 0046-5410
0019-2384 Illumino-Tecnica
0019-2392 Illustrated Bristol News
0019-2406 Illustrated Carpenter and Builder *see* 0306-3216
0019-2414 Illustrated Life Rhodesia *changed to* Illustrated Life & Talk
0019-2422 Illustrated London News
0019-2430 Illustrated Weekly of India
0019-2457 Illustration 63
0019-2465 Illustrator
0019-2473 Illustrazione Pubblicitaria
0019-2481 Illustre Protestant†
0019-249X Illustrerad Motor Sport
0019-2511 Illustrierte Rundschau der Gendarmerie *changed to* Illustrierte Rundschau der Oesterreichischen Gendarmerie
0019-252X Ilmailu
0019-2538 Ilocos Review
0019-2546 I L T A M Newsletter
0019-2554 Ilusao *changed to* Almanaque Ilusao
0019-2562 Ilusion y Aventura†
0019-2570 Ilustrovana Politika
0019-2597 Im Lande der Bibel
0019-2635 Revue du Cinema
0019-2651 Image Technology†
0019-2694 Imago†
0019-2708 Imballaggio
0019-2716 Imbongi
0019-2724 Imfama (Inkprint Edition)
0019-2732 Der Imkerfreund
0019-2740 Immagini/Forma *changed to* Immagini/Technika
0019-2759 Immanuel's Witness *see* 0308-5252
0019-2767 Immex†
0019-2775 Immigration Bar Bulletin *see* 0884-3244
0019-2783 Immortality Newsletter *see* 0362-0085
0019-2791 Immunochemistry *see* 0161-5890
0019-2805 Immunology
0019-2813 Casting Digest
0019-2821 Impact (Wheaton)
0019-2848 Impact (Valley Forge)†
0019-2856 Impact (Columbia)
0019-2864 Impact - Africa†
0019-2872 Impact of Science on Society
0019-2880 Impacto
0019-2899 Impacts
0019-2902 Imparcial
0019-2910 Imperial Oil Review *see* 0700-5156
0019-2929 Impermeabile Europeo†
0019-2945 Impianti Industriali†
0019-2961 Import†
0019-297X Import Bulletin *changed to* Journal of Commerce Import Bulletin
0019-2988 Importer *changed to* Importer/Electronics
0019-3003 Impresa Pubblica
0019-3011 Impressions
0019-302X Imprimerie Nouvelle
0019-3038 Imprint (Bristol)
0019-3046 Imprint
0019-3054 Imprint
0019-3062 Imprint
0019-3089 Improving College and University Teaching *see* 8756-7555
0019-3097 Impuls†
0019-3100 In†
0019-3127 Animaland
0019-3135 In Brief†
0019-3143 In Britain
0019-3151 In de Rechte Straat
0019-316X In de Waagschaal
0019-3186 In Famiglia
0019-3194 In Jewish Bookland *changed to* Jewish Books in Review
0019-3216 In Particular†
0019-3224 Printing Industry†
0019-3232 In-Plant Printer *changed to* In-Plant Printer & Electronic Publisher
0019-3240 In-Plant Reprographics†
0019-3259 In Review†
0019-3267 In Step *changed to* Lutherans in Step
0019-3283 In Touch (Pinner)
0019-3291 In Transit
0019-3321 In Your Hands
0019-333X Monthly Newspaper Techniques *changed to* Newspaper Techniques
0019-3356 Incentive Marketing *see* 0266-7991
0019-3364 Incentive Marketing (New York)
0019-3399 Inchieste di Urbanistica e Architettura
0019-3402 Co-Incidences *see* 0705-4165
0019-3410 Incidenza
0019-3429 Income Opportunities
0019-3437 Income-Tax Journal
0019-3453 Income Tax Reports
0019-3461 Incomes Data Report
0019-347X Incontri Culturali†
0019-3488 Incontri Meridionali *changed to* Corrispondenza Meridionale
0019-3496 L'Incontro
0019-3518 Weekly Law Reports
0019-3526 Incorporated Law Society of Northern Ireland. Gazette†
0019-3534 Incorporated Linguist *changed to* Linguist
0019-3542 Incredible Idaho†
0019-3550 Incunable†
0019-3569 I N D A C
0019-3577 Indagationes Mathematicae *issued with* 0023-3358
0019-3585 Indeks
0019-3593 Indonesian Biological and Agricultural Index/Indeks Biologi Dan Pertanian di Indonesia *changed to* Index of Biology, Agriculture and Agro Economy
0019-3631 Independent *changed to* Western Sunday Independent
0019-3658 Independent Adjuster
0019-3666 Independent American
0019-3674 Independent Banker
0019-3682 Independent Coal Operator *changed to* Coal Operator
0019-3690 Independent College Funds of America Bulletin†
0019-3712 Independent Film Journal *changed to* Film Journal
0019-3720 Independent Formosa†
0019-3747 Independent School†
0019-3755 Independent School Bulletin *see* 0145-9635
0019-3763 Independent Shavian
0019-378X Index Analytique†
0019-3798 Index Bibliographique de Botanique Tropicale†
0019-3801 Index Bibliographique du Vide - Vacuum Index†
0019-3836 Index de la Litterature Nucleaire Francaise†
0019-3844 Index India
0019-3852 Index Indo-Asiaticus
0019-3860 Index: Industrial Extension for the Forest Products Industry†
0019-3879 Index Medicus
0019-3887 Index Medicus Danicus†
0019-3895 Index of Fungi
0019-3909 Index of Dermatology and Dermapathology *see* 0090-1245
0019-3917 Index of Mathematical Papers
0019-3925 Index of New Products†
0019-3933 Index of Rheumatology *see* 0097-921X
0019-3941 Index of Veterinary Specialities
0019-3968 Index to Australian Book Reviews†
0019-3976 Index to Current E E G Literature *see* 0013-4694
0019-3984 Index to Current Malaysian, Singapore, and Brunei Periodicals†
0019-3992 Index to Dental Literature
0019-400X Index to Foreign Legal Periodicals
0019-4018 Index to Forthcoming Russian Books†
0019-4026 Index to Indian Economic Journals
0019-4034 Index to Indian Legal Periodicals
0019-4042 Index to Indian Medical Periodicals
0019-4069 Index to Latin American Periodicals†
0019-4077 Index to Legal Periodicals
0019-4085 Index to Office Equipment and Supplies *see* 0305-635X
0019-4093 Index to Periodical Articles Related to Law
0019-4107 Index to Religious Periodical Literature *see* 0149-8428
0019-4115 Index to the Literature of Magnetism†
0019-4123 Index Veterinarius
0019-4131 Indexer
0019-414X India Book House News†
0019-4158 India Calling
0019-4166 India Cultures Quarterly *changed to* India Cultures
0019-4174 India. Central Statistical Organization. Monthly Abstract of Statistics
0019-4182 India in Industries†
0019-4204 India. Ministry of Finance. Finance Library. Weekly Bulletin
0019-4212 India News
0019-4220 India Quarterly
0019-4239 India Today and Tomorrow
0019-4247 Indian Academy of Applied Psychology. Journal
0019-4255 Indian Academy of Dentistry. Journal†
0019-4263 Indian Academy of Medical Sciences. Annals *see* 0379-038X
0019-4271 Indian Academy of Philosophy. Journal
0019-428X Indian Academy of Sciences. Proceedings *see* 0370-0097
0019-4298 Indian Administrative and Management Review *changed to* Indian Review of Management and Future
0019-4301 Indian Advocate
0019-4328 Indian Agricultural News Digest†
0019-4336 Indian Agriculturist
0019-4344 Journal of Indian and Buddhist Studies
0019-4352 Indian and Eastern Engineer
0019-4360 Indian & Eastern Pharmacy
0019-4379 Indian and Foreign Review
0019-4387 Indian Anthropological Society. Journal
0019-4395 Indian Antiquary†
0019-4409 Indian Architect
0019-4417 Indian Aviation
0019-4425 Indian Bee Journal
0019-4433 Indian Book Industry
0019-4441 Indian Book Review Supplement
0019-445X Indian Books
0019-4476 Indian Business Review†
0019-4484 Indian Cashew Journal
0019-4492 Indian Ceramics
0019-4506 Indian Chemical Engineer
0019-4514 Indian Chemical Journal†
0019-4522 Indian Chemical Society. Journal
0019-4530 Indian Church History Review
0019-4549 Indian Coffee
0019-4557 Indian Communist†
0019-4565 Indian Concrete Journal
0019-4573 Indian Construction News
0019-4581 Indian Cooperative Review
0019-459X Indian Cotton Mills Federation Journal
0019-4603 Indian Dairyman
0019-4611 Indian Dental Association. Journal
0019-462X Indian Drugs
0019-4638 Indian Drugs and Pharmaceuticals Industry
0019-4646 Indian Economic and Social History Review
0019-4654 Indian Economic Diary
0019-4662 Indian Economic Journal
0019-4670 Indian Economic Review
0019-4689 Indian Education
0019-4697 Indian Education Abstracts
0019-4700 Indian Educational Review
0019-4719 Indian Engineering Exporter
0019-4727 Indian-Eskimo Association of Canada Bulletin *see* 0073-6341
0019-4735 Indian Export Trade Journal
0019-4751 Indian Exporter Quarterly†
0019-476X Indian Factories Journal
0019-4778 Indian Farm Mechanization
0019-4786 Indian Farming
0019-4808 Indian Food Packer
0019-4816 Indian Forester
0019-4824 Indian Geographical Journal
0019-4832 Indian Heart Journal
0019-4840 Indian Historian *see* 0199-9052
0019-4867 Indian Homoeopathic Gazette
0019-4875 Indian Horticulture
0019-4883 Indian Hotelier and Caterer
0019-4905 Indian Institute of Advanced Study, Simla. Bulletin *changed to* I I A S Newsletter
0019-4913 Indian Institute of Architects. Journal†
0019-4921 Indian Institute of Bankers. Journal
0019-493X Indian Institute of Metals. Transactions
0019-4948 Indian Institute of Public Opinion. Quarterly Economic Report
0019-4956 Indian Institute of Road Transport. Monthly Bulletin
0019-4964 Indian Institute of Science. Journal
0019-4972 Indian Institute of World Culture. Transactions
0019-4980 I I T C Bulletin
0019-4999 Indian Investment Centre. Monthly Newsletter
0019-5006 Indian Journal of Adult Education
0019-5014 Indian Journal of Agricultural Economics
0019-5022 Indian Journal of Agricultural Sciences
0019-5030 Indian Journal of American Studies
0019-5049 Indian Journal of Anaesthesia
0019-5057 Indian Journal of Animal Health
0019-5065 Indian Journal of Applied Chemistry *see* 0019-4522

ISSN INDEX 1247

0019-5073 Indian Journal of Applied Psychology
0019-5081 Indian Journal of Biochemistry *see* 0301-1208
0019-509X Indian Journal of Cancer
0019-5103 Indian Journal of Chemistry *see* 0376-4710
0019-5103 Indian Journal of Chemistry *see* 0376-4699
0019-5111 Indian Journal of Chest Diseases and Allied Sciences
0019-512X Indian Journal of Commerce
0019-5138 Journal of Communicable Diseases
0019-5146 Indian Journal of Dairy Science
0019-5154 Indian Journal of Dermatology
0019-5162 Indian Journal of Dermatology and Venereology *changed to* Indian Journal of Dermatology, Venereology and Leprology
0019-5170 Indian Journal of Economics
0019-5189 Indian Journal of Experimental Biology
0019-5197 Indian Journal of Experimental Psychology†
0019-5200 Indian Journal of Genetics and Plant Breeding
0019-5219 Indian Journal of Gerontology
0019-5227 Indian Journal of Helminthology
0019-5235 Indian Journal of History of Science
0019-5243 Indian Journal of Homoeopathic Medicine
0019-5251 Indian Journal of Horticulture
0019-526X Indian Journal of Hospital Pharmacy
0019-5278 Indian Journal of Industrial Medicine
0019-5286 Indian Journal of Industrial Relations
0019-5294 Indian Journal of International Law
0019-5308 Indian Journal of Labour Economics
0019-5316 Indian Journal of Marketing
0019-5324 Indian Journal of Mathematics
0019-5340 Indian Journal of Medical Research
0019-5359 Indian Journal of Medical Sciences
0019-5367 Indian Journal of Medicine & Surgery
0019-5375 Indian Journal of Mental Retardation
0019-5383 Indian Journal of Meteorology and Geophysics *see* 0252-9416
0019-5391 Indian Journal of Occupational Health
0019-5413 Indian Journal of Orthopaedics
0019-5421 Indian Journal of Otolaryngology
0019-5448 Indian Journal of Pathology & Bacteriology *changed to* Indian Journal of Pathology & Microbiology
0019-5456 Indian Journal of Pediatrics
0019-5464 Indian Journal of Pharmaceutical Education
0019-5472 Indian Journal of Pharmacy *see* 0250-474X
0019-5480 Indian Journal of Physics and Proceedings of the Indian Association for the Cultivation of Science
0019-5499 Indian Journal of Physiology and Pharmacology
0019-5502 Indian Journal of Plant Physiology
0019-5510 Indian Journal of Political Science
0019-5529 Indian Journal of Poultry Science
0019-5537 Indian Journal of Power and River Valley Development
0019-5545 Indian Journal of Psychiatry
0019-5553 Indian Journal of Psychology *changed to* Indian Journal of Psychological Medicine
0019-5561 Indian Journal of Public Administration
0019-557X Indian Journal of Public Health
0019-5588 Indian Journal of Pure and Applied Mathematics
0019-5596 Indian Journal of Pure & Applied Physics
0019-560X Indian Journal of Radiology
0019-5618 Indian Journal of Science and Industry *see* 0367-8245
0019-5618 Indian Journal of Science and Industry *see* 0367-6722
0019-5626 Indian Journal of Social Research
0019-5634 Indian Journal of Social Work
0019-5642 Indian Journal of Sociology
0019-5650 Indian Journal of Surgery
0019-5669 Indian Journal of Technology
0019-5677 Indian Journal of the History of Medicine *changed to* Indian Institute of History of Medicine. Bulletin (Madras)
0019-5685 Indian Journal of Theology
0019-5693 Indian Journal of Theoretical Physics
0019-5707 Indian Journal of Tuberculosis
0019-5715 Indian Journal of Veterinary Science and Animal Husbandry *changed to* Indian Journal of Animal Sciences
0019-5723 Indian Labour Journal
0019-5731 Indian Law Institute. Journal
0019-574X Indian Leather
0019-5758 Indian Leather Technologists' Association. Journal
0019-5766 Indian Libertarian†
0019-5774 Indian Librarian
0019-5782 Indian Library Association. Bulletin
0019-5790 Indian Library Science Abstracts
0019-5804 Indian Literature
0019-5812 Indian Management
0019-5820 Indian Management Abstracts
0019-5839 Indian Mathematical Society. Journal
0019-5847 Indian Medical Association. Journal
0019-5855 Indian Medical Forum
0019-5863 Indian Medical Gazette
0019-5898 Indian Medical Record
0019-5901 Indian Merchants' Chamber. Journal
0019-591X Indian Military Academy Journal
0019-5928 Indian Mineralogist
0019-5936 Indian Minerals
0019-5944 Indian Mining & Engineering Journal
0019-5979 Indian Movie News *changed to* Indian Movie News
0019-5987 Indian Museum Bulletin
0019-5995 Indian Music Journal
0019-6002 Indian National Bibliography
0019-6029 Indian News†
0019-6037 Indian News Index†
0019-6045 Indian Oil and Soap Journal†
0019-6053 Indian P.E.N.
0019-6061 Indian Pediatrics
0019-607X Indian Perfumer
0019-6088 Indian Periodicals Record *changed to* Journal of Indexing & Reference Work
0019-6096 Indian Philosophy & Culture†
0019-610X Indian Plastics Review†
0019-6126 Indian Political Science Review†
0019-6142 Indian Poultry Gazette *changed to* Avian Research
0019-6150 Indian Poultry Review
0019-6169 Indian Practitioner
0019-6177 Indian Press Index
0019-6185 Indian Print & Paper
0019-6193 Indian Progress
0019-6207 Indian Promenade
0019-6223 Indian Publisher and Bookseller
0019-6231 Indian Pulp and Paper
0019-624X Indian Radio Amateur
0019-6258 Indian Railway Gazette
0019-6266 Indian Railway Technical Bulletin
0019-6274 Indian Railways
0019-6282 Indian Record
0019-6290 Indian Recorder & Digest†
0019-6304 Indian Review
0019-6312 Indian Rubber & Plastics Age
0019-6320 Indian Rubber Bulletin†
0019-6339 Indian Science Abstracts
0019-6347 Indian Seafoods
0019-6355 Indian Silk
0019-6363 Indian Society of Agricultural Statistics. Journal
0019-6371 Indian Society of Earthquake Technology. Bulletin
0019-638X Indian Society of Soil Science. Journal
0019-6398 International Journal of Contemporary Sociology
0019-6401 Indian Spices
0019-641X Indian Steel Age
0019-6428 Indian Sugar
0019-6436 Indian Textile Journal
0019-6444 Indian Trade Journal
0019-6452 Indian Truth
0019-6460 Indian Vegetarian Congress Quarterly
0019-6479 Indian Veterinary Journal
0019-6487 Indian Witness
0019-6495 Indian Writing Today†
0019-6509 Indiana
0019-6517 Indiana Alumni Magazine
0019-6525 Indiana Audubon Quarterly
0019-6533 Indiana Business and Industry *see* 0273-7930
0019-6541 Indiana Business Review
0019-655X Indiana Covered Bridge Society. Newsletter
0019-6568 Indiana Dental Association. Journal
0019-6576 Indiana. Department of Public Welfare. Semi-Annual Statistical Series
0019-6584 Indiana English Journal *changed to* Indiana English
0019-6606 Indiana Family Planner *see* 0146-1117
0019-6614 Indiana Folklore *changed to* Indiana Folklore and Oral History
0019-6622 Indiana Freemason
0019-6630 Indiana Herald
0019-6649 Indiana History Bulletin
0019-6665 Indiana Law Journal
0019-6673 Indiana Magazine of History
0019-6681 Indiana Nurse†
0019-6703 Indiana Plumbing-Heating-Cooling Contractor
0019-6711 Indiana Publisher
0019-672X Indiana Reading Quarterly
0019-6738 Indiana Slant
0019-6746 Indiana Social Studies Quarterly *see* 0889-0293
0019-6754 Indiana State Board of Health Bulletin
0019-6762 Indiana State Library. Extension Division Bulletin†
0019-6770 Indiana State Medical Association. Journal *see* 0746-8288
0019-6789 Indiana Statesman
0019-6797 Indiana Teacher *changed to* I S T A Advocate
0019-6800 Indiana University Bookman
0019-6819 Indiana University. Folklore Institute Journal *see* 0737-7037
0019-6827 Indiana University. Graduate Library School Alumni Newsletter *changed to* Indiana University. School of Library and Information Science. Alumni Newsletter
0019-6835 Viewpoints *see* 0160-8398
0019-6851 India's Stamp Journal
0019-686X Indica
0019-6908 Indicateur Universel des P.T.T.
0019-6916 Luxembourg. Service Central de la Statistique et des Etudes Economiques. Indicateurs Rapides
0019-6924 Indicator
0019-6932 Indicator
0019-6940 Indicator Digest
0019-6959 Indicatore Cartotecnico
0019-6967 Indicatore Grafico
0019-6975 Indice
0019-7009 Indice de Precios al Consumidor para San Salvador, Mejicanos y Villa Delgado *changed to* Indice de Precios al Consumidor
0019-7017 Indice de Precios al Consumidor para Familias Obreras en Puerto Rico
0019-7025 Indice de Precios al Consumidor
0019-7033 Indice Economico Colombiano†
0019-705X Indice Medico Colombiano†
0019-7068 Indice Medico Espanol
0019-7084 Indice Penale
0019-7114 Indiscret de Paris
0019-7149 Individual Psychologist†
0019-7157 Individual Psychology News Letter†
0019-7165 Individualist
0019-7181 Indo-African Trade Journal†
0019-719X Indo-Asia
0019-7211 Indo-British Review
0019-722X Indo-Canadian
0019-7238 Indo-German Review†
0019-7246 Indo-Iranian Journal
0019-7262 Indogermanische Forschungen
0019-7270 Indonesia *changed to* Indochina
0019-7289 Indonesia (Ithaca)
0019-7297 Indonesia Letter
0019-7319 Indonesian Abstracts *see* 0216-4167
0019-7351 Indonesian Planned Parenthood Association News†
0019-7378 Indus Digest†
0019-7386 Industria
0019-7394 Industria
0019-7408 Industria
0019-7416 Industria *changed to* Industria: Rivista di Economia Politica Industriale
0019-7424 Industria *changed to* Industrie Revu
0019-7459 Industria Alimenticia
0019-7467 Industria Avicola
0019-7475 Industria Britanica†
0019-7483 Industria Conserve
0019-7491 Industria Cotoniera
0019-7521 Industria del Legno e del Mobile *changed to* L M l'Industria del Legno e del Mobile
0019-753X Industria del Mobile
0019-7548 Industria della Carta
0019-7556 Industria della Gomma
0019-7564 Industria della Vernice†
0019-7602 Industria e Desenvolvimento
0019-7610 Industria Italiana dei Laterizi
0019-7629 Industria Italiana dei Plastici *changed to* Europlast
0019-7637 Industria Italiana del Cemento
0019-7645 Industria Italiana Elettrotechnica ed Elettronica *changed to* Tecnologie Elettriche
0019-7661 Industria Lombarda
0019-767X Industria Meridionale†
0019-7688 Industria Militar
0019-7696 Industria Mineraria
0019-770X Industria Portuguesa†
0019-7718 Industria & Produtividade
0019-7734 Industria Saccarifera Italiana
0019-7742 Industria Textil Sud Americana
0019-7750 Industria Textila *changed to* Industria Usoara-Textile, Tricotaje, Confectii Textile
0019-7769 Industria Toscana
0019-7777 Industria Turistica
0019-7785 Industria Usoara *changed to* Industria Usoara-Pielarie, Confectii de Piele, Prelucrarea Cauciucului si Maselor Plastice, Sticla, Ceramica Fina, Articole Casnice, Utilaje Pentru Industria Usoara
0019-7793 Industrial Accountant
0019-7815 Industrial Advertising & Marketing *changed to* Advertising & Marketing
0019-7823 Industrial Aerodynamics Abstracts
0019-784X Industrial and Commercial Photographer *changed to* Professional Photographer
0019-7858 Industrial and Commercial Training
0019-7866 Industrial and Engineering Chemistry†
0019-7912 Industrial and Labor Relations Forum†
0019-7920 Industrial and Labor Relations Report *see* 0736-6396
0019-7939 Industrial and Labor Relations Review
0019-7963 Industrial and Welfare Catering *see* 0306-2538
0019-7971 Industrial Archaeology
0019-8005 Industrial Arts and Vocational Education *see* 0091-8601
0019-8013 Industrial Banker *see* 0097-8345
0019-8021 Industrial Bulletin *changed to* Industrial Product Bulletin
0019-8056 Industrial Canada†
0019-8064 Industrial Ceylon†
0019-8099 Industrial Courier
0019-8102 Industrial Court Reporter
0019-8110 Industrial Design *see* 0192-3021
0019-8145 Industrial Diamond Review
0019-8153 Industrial Distribution
0019-8161 Industrial Distributor News *changed to* I M P O Distributor News
0019-817X Industrial Ecology†
0019-8196 Industrial Editor†
0019-820X Industrial Egypt
0019-8226 Engineering Management†
0019-8234 Industrial Engineering
0019-8242 Industrial Engineering and Management
0019-8269 Industrial Enterprise
0019-8277 Industrial Equipment News
0019-8285 Industrial Equipment News (New York)
0019-8307 Industrial Fabric Products Review

0019-8307 Industrial Fabric Products Review Buyer's Guide
0019-8315 Industrial Finishing *see* 0264-2506
0019-8323 Industrial Finishing
0019-834X Industrial Gas†
0019-8358 Industrial Gerontology *see* 0161-2514
0019-8366 Industrial Health
0019-8374 Industrial Heating
0019-8382 Industrial Hygiene Digest
0019-8390 Industrial Hygiene Review†
0019-8412 Industrial India
0019-8439 Industrial Japan *see* 0386-6076
0019-8447 Industrial Laboratory
0019-8455 Industrial Machinery News
0019-8471 Industrial Management
0019-848X Sloan Management Review
0019-8498 Industrial Marketing *see* 0745-5933
0019-8501 Industrial Marketing Management
0019-8528 Industrial Mathematics
0019-8536 Industrial Medicine and Surgery *see* 0362-4064
0019-8544 Industrial Minerals
0019-8552 Industrial Models & Patterns
0019-8579 Industrial Nottingham
0019-8587 Industrial Philippines
0019-8595 Industrial Photography
0019-8609 Industrial Photography and Commercial Camera *see* 0313-4393
0019-8617 Industrial Progress
0019-8625 Industrial Property
0019-8633 Industrial Puerto Rico
0019-8641 Industrial Purchasing Agent
0019-8668 Industrial Recovery
0019-8676 Industrial Relations
0019-8684 Industrial Relations *changed to* Personnel Today
0019-8692 Industrial Relations Journal
0019-8706 Industrial Relations Law Digest†
0019-8714 Industrial Relations News *changed to* Human Resource Management News
0019-8722 Industrial Research *see* 0746-9179
0019-8757 Industrial Safety *see* 0262-3226
0019-8765 Industrial Safety & Health Bulletin
0019-8773 Industrial Security *see* 0145-9406
0019-8781 Industrial Society
0019-879X Industrial Supervisor *see* 0734-3302
0019-8803 Industrial Times
0019-8838 Industrial Tribunal Reports†
0019-8846 Industrial Tyneside *changed to* Industrial Tyne & Wear
0019-8854 Progress Wales
0019-8862 Industrial Water Engineering†
0019-8870 Industrial Worker
0019-8889 Industrial World
0019-8897 Industrialisierung des Bauens†
0019-8927 Industrialization Forum†
0019-8935 Industrials: Four Hundred & Twenty Five Canadian Weekly Stock Charts *see* 0383-2945
0019-8943 Industrias de la Alimentacion†
0019-8951 Industrias Lacteas *see* 0744-625X
0019-896X Die Industrie
0019-8978 Industrie†
0019-8986 Industrie- und Handelskammer Frankfurt am Main. Mitteilungen
0019-8994 Ostschwaebische Wirtschaft *changed to* Wirtschaft in Ostwuerttemberg
0019-901X Industrie Alimentari
0019-9028 Industrie & Nachwuchs†
0019-9036 Industrie-Anzeiger
0019-9044 Societe Francaise de Ceramique. Traductions Brevets. *changed to* Industrie Ceramique
0019-9060 Industrie du Petrole en Europe-Gaz-Chimie *see* 0220-3294
0019-9087 Industrie Francaise du Coton et des Fibres Alliees
0019-9095 Industrie Hoteliere de France et d'Outre Mer *changed to* Industrie Hoteliere
0019-9109 Industrie Lackierbetrieb
0019-9125 Producteur de Lait
0019-9141 Industrie-Post†
0019-9168 Messe Industriespiegel
0019-9176 Industrie Textile
0019-9192 Industrie und Handel
0019-9206 Profit *see* 0721-0477
0019-9214 Der Industrie- und Handelsvertreter
0019-9230 Industriel de Cote d'Ivoire
0019-9249 Industrieel Eigendom
0019-9257 Industriell Teknik†
0019-9265 Industrielle Einkauf *see* 0341-4507
0019-9281 Management-Zeitschrift *changed to* I O Management-Zeitschrift
0019-929X Industriemagazin
0019-9303 Industriemeister Nachrichten
0019-932X Industries Atomiques *changed to* Industries Atomiques et Spatiales
0019-9354 Industries et Techniques
0019-9362 Industrie et Travaux d'Outre-Mer *changed to* Industries et Developpement International
0019-9370 Industries Mecaniques
0019-9389 Industries Nautiques
0019-9397 Proclim *changed to* Promoclim A: Applications Thermiques et Aerauliques
0019-9397 Proclim *changed to* Promoclim B: Bulletin du Genie Climatique
0019-9419 Industrijska Istrazivanja
0019-9427 Industritjaenstemannen *changed to* S I F Tidningen
0019-9435 Industry
0019-9443 Industry & Finance
0019-9451 Industry & Trade Review
0019-946X Industry of Free China
0019-9494 Industry Today†
0019-9508 Infancia e Juventude
0019-9516 Infant and Nursery School Equipment
0019-9524 Infanteria
0019-9532 Infantry
0019-9540 Infantry Journal
0019-9559 Infants to Teens Wear Buyers
0019-9567 Infection and Immunity
0019-9591 Infirmiere *see* 0301-0813
0019-9605 Infirmiere Canadienne *changed to* Canadian Nurse/L'Infirmiere Canadienne
0019-9613 Infirmiere Francaise
0019-9656 Info
0019-9680 Infor-Austria†
0019-9702 Inform - Letter *changed to* Inform Quarterly Newsletter
0019-9710 Informa†
0019-9729 Informacao Agricola
0019-9737 Informacao Semanal C A C E X
0019-9753 Informacio-Elektronika
0019-9761 Informacion Comercial Espanola. Boletin Semanal *changed to* Informacion Comercial Espanola. Boletin Economico
0019-977X Informacion Comercial Espanola. Revista Mensual *changed to* Informacion Comercial Espanola
0019-9788 Informacion Educativa *changed to* Argentina. Centro Nacional de Documentacion e Informacion Educativa. Informaciones y Documentos
0019-9796 Informacion Farmaceutica
0019-9818 Informaciones del Brasil†
0019-9826 Informatsiya o Bibliotechnom Dele i Bibliografii za Rubezhom†
0019-9834 Informacja Ekspresowa *changed to* Instytut Obrobki Skrawaniem. Przeglad Dokumentacyjny
0019-9869 Informador
0019-9885 Informateur *changed to* Etudes Rwandaises; l'Informateur
0019-9893 Informateur de la Quinzaine
0019-9907 Informatie
0019-9915 Informatik
0019-9923 Informatika
0019-9931 Information about the Oil Industry/for the Oil Industry
0019-994X Information Agricole
0019-9958 Information and Control *see* 0890-5401
0019-9966 Information and Records Management *see* 0739-9049
0019-9974 Information Bulletin for the Southern Hemisphere†
0019-9982 Information Bulletin on Isotopic Generators†
0019-9990 Information *see* 0345-5300
0020-000X Information de Sages-Femmes†
0020-0018 Information Dentaire
0020-0026 Information d'Histoire de l'Art†
0020-0034 Information Dietetique
0020-0042 Information Display
0020-0050 Information Economique Africaine
0020-0077 Information fuer auslaendische Studienbewerber an oesterreichischen Hochschulen
0020-0085 Information from the Peace Movement of the German Democratic Republic
0020-0093 Information Geographique
0020-0107 Information Juive
0020-0123 Information Litteraire
0020-0131 Information Los Angeles *changed to* Key, This Week in Los Angeles and Southern California
0020-0166 Tajekoztato a Kulfoldi Kozgazdasagi Irodalomrol. Series A, Referatumok/ Information on the Foreign Economic Literature, Series A *changed to* Kulfoldi Kozgazdasagi Irodalmi Szemle. Series A
0020-0174 Information om Rehabilitering
0020-0190 Information Processing Letters
0020-0220 Information Retrieval and Library Automation Newsletter *changed to* Information Retrieval & Library Automation
0020-0239 Information Science Abstracts
0020-0247 Information Science in Canada†
0020-0255 Information Sciences
0020-0263 Information Scientist *see* 0165-5515
0020-0271 Information Storage and Retrieval *see* 0306-4573
0020-028X Hopital, Information Therapeutique†
0020-0298 Information Transports
0020-0301 Information ueber Aktuelle Probleme der Marxistisch-Leninistischen Philosophie in der U.d.S.S.R. *see* 0138-2055
0020-031X Informationsdienst fuer die Private Krankenversicherung *see* 0343-9321
0020-0328 Informationen aus dem Philosophischen Leben in der D.D.R. *see* 0138-242X
0020-0336 Informationen aus Orthodontie und Kieferorthopaedie
0020-0344 Informationen fuer die Fischwirtschaft
0020-0352 Informationen fuer die Frau
0020-0379 Informationen ueber die Fischwirtschaft des Auslandes
0020-0387 Informationen zur Kernforschung und Kerntechnik *changed to* Fachinformationszentrum Energie, Physik, Mathematik. Kernforschungszentrum. Konferenzberichte. Kernforschung, Kerntechnik
0020-0395 Soziologische Forschung in der D.D.R. Informationen
0020-0409 Informations Aeronautiques *changed to* Informations Aeronautiques et Spatiales
0020-0417 Informations & Documents
0020-0425 Informations Bancaires et Financieres
0020-0433 Informations Canadiennes
0020-0441 Informations Catholiques Internationales *changed to* Actualite Religieuse dan le Monde
0020-045X Informations - Chimie
0020-0468 Informations du Caoutchouc *see* 0247-3518
0020-0476 Informations Etudes Outre-Mer†
0020-0484 Federation des Comites d'Alliance Ouvriere. Informations Ouvrieres
0020-0492 Informations Rapides de l'Administration Francaise
0020-0506 Statistiques des Enseignements†
0020-0522 Informations Techniques des Directions des Services Veterinaires
0020-0530 Informations Universitaires et Professionnelles Internationales†
0020-0549 Informationsdienst des Deutschen Rates der Europaeischen Bewegung *changed to* Europaeisches Forum
0020-0581 Informationsdienstkartei (I D K) *changed to* Fachdokumentation Agrargeschichte
0020-0611 Informatique *changed to* Informatique Professionnelle
0020-0638 Informativni Bilten Radnickog Sveucilista "Mosa Pijade"†
0020-0654 Informativo Bamerindus
0020-0662 Informatology†
0020-0670 P. I. M. R. Informator Patentowy†
0020-0689 Informatore Agrario
0020-0697 Informatore Botanico Italiano
0020-0700 Informatore del Marmista
0020-0719 Informatore di Ortoflorofrutticoltura†
0020-0727 Informatore Filatelico
0020-0735 Informatore Fitopatologico
0020-0743 Informatore Medico-Sociale
0020-076X Informatore Turistico
0020-0778 Informatore Zootecnico
0020-0786 Informazione Industriale
0020-0794 Informazione Mediterranea
0020-0816 Informazioni Sociali
0020-0832 Estacion Experimental Agropecuaria Pergamino. Informe Tecnico *see* 0325-1799
0020-0840 Informer
0020-0883 Informes de la Construccion
0020-0891 Infrared Physics
0020-0905 Ingegnere
0020-0913 Ingegnere Italiano†
0020-0921 Ingegnere Libero Professionista†
0020-093X Ingegneria Chimica†
0020-0948 Ingegneria Civile
0020-0956 Ingegneria Ferroviaria
0020-0964 Ingegneria Meccanica†
0020-0980 Ingegneria Sanitaria
0020-0999 Ingenieria
0020-1014 Ingenieria Arquitectura Construccion
0020-1022 Ingenieria Civil
0020-1030 Ingenieria e Industria
0020-1049 Ingenieria Electrica y Mecanica†
0020-1057 Ingenieria Hidraulica en Mexico *changed to* Recursos Hidraulicos
0020-1065 Ingeneria Internacional Construccion *see* 0020-6415
0020-1073 Ingenieria Naval
0020-1081 Ingenieria Quimica†
0020-109X Ingenieria y Arquitectura†
0020-1111 Ingeniero Andino†
0020-112X Ingeniero Westinghouse†
0020-1138 L'Ingenieur
0020-1154 Ingenieur-Archiv
0020-1162 Ingenieur Chimiste†
0020-1170 Der Ingenieur der Deutschen Bundespost
0020-1197 Ingenieurs *changed to* Equipement Industriel/Industriele Uitrusting
0020-1200 Ingenieurs de l'Automobile
0020-1219 Ingenieurs et Cadres de France
0020-1227 Ingenieur et Technicien *changed to* Revue de l'Entreprise
0020-1235 Ingenieursblad
0020-1243 Ingenioer- og Bygningsvaesen *changed to* Ingenioeren
0020-126X Ingenioerens Ugeblad *changed to* Ingenioeren
0020-1278 Ingenjoersvetenskapsakademiens Meddelanden†
0020-1308 Inglewood Public Library Quarterly Report
0020-1324 Respiratory Care *see* 0730-8418
0020-1340 Iniziativa Europea *changed to* Sinistra Europea
0020-1359 Iniziativa Isontina
0020-1383 Injury
0020-1391 Injury Valuation Reports and Special Research Reports
0020-1405 Inkling (Denver)†
0020-1413 Inkoop *changed to* Bedrijfsvoering
0020-1421 Inkop†

ISSN INDEX 1249

0020-1448 Inlaendsk Tidningstaxa
0020-1456 Inland
0020-1464 Inland Africa *changed to* A I M International
0020-1472 Inland Architect
0020-1502 Inland Printer/American Lithographer *see* 0744-6616
0020-1510 Inland Register
0020-1537 Inland Seas
0020-1553 Inner Space†
0020-1561 Innere Kolonisation *see* 0341-1869
0020-157X Innes Review
0020-1588 Innisfail Canegrower
0020-1596 Inniu
0020-160X Innkjoep
0020-1618 Innominate
0020-1626 Du Pont Innovation†
0020-1642 Innsbrucker Theater- und Konzertspiegel
0020-1650 Inorganic and Nuclear Chemistry Letters *see* 0277-5387
0020-1669 Inorganic Chemistry
0020-1685 Inorganic Materials
0020-1693 Inorganica Chimica Acta
0020-1707 Inpho Oesterreich
0020-1715 Input - Kentucky Quarterly†
0020-1723 Inquirer
0020-1731 Inquiry (Coral Gables)†
0020-174X Inquiry
0020-1758 Japan Printer
0020-1766 Printing World
0020-1774 Inscape (Phoenix)†
0020-1790 Insect Biochemistry
0020-1804 Insecta Matsumurana
0020-1812 Insectes Sociaux /Social Insects
0020-1820 Insectocutor News†
0020-1839 Insektenboerse *see* 0013-8843
0020-1847 Inside Detective
0020-1855 Inside Education†
0020-1863 Inside Kenya Today
0020-1871 Insieme (Milan)
0020-1901 Insight†
0020-191X Insight: Notre Dame†
0020-1936 Insight
0020-1944 Insight (Hagerstown)
0020-1960 Insight & Opinion *changed to* Insight Publication
0020-2002 Insinoorilehti†
0020-2010 Insinooriuutiset
0020-2029 Insite
0020-2045 Netherlands. Inspectie voor het Brandweerwezen. Maandelijkse Mededelingen *changed to* Maandelijkse Mededelingen van de Inspectie voor het Brandweerwezen
0020-2053 Inspection News *changed to* Equifax Journal
0020-2061 Inspiration
0020-207X Installateur
0020-2088 Installateur Rhone-Alpes†
0020-2096 Installatie
0020-2118 Installatore Italiano
0020-2126 Installment Retailing *changed to* N A I C Reporter
0020-2134 Instantanes Criminologiques
0020-2142 Instantanes Medicaux
0020-2150 Instantanes Techniques†
0020-2177 Institut Archeologique du Luxembourg. Bulletins
0020-2185 Institut Belge du Petrole. Annales
0020-2207 Institut d'Amenagement et d'Urbanisme de la Region Parisienne. Cahiers *see* 0153-6184
0020-2223 Institut des Actuaires Francais. Bulletin Trimestriel
0020-2231 I F R E M E R. Revue des Travaux
0020-2266 Institut Economique et Social des Classes Moyennes. Bulletin d'Information
0020-2274 Institut Francais du Petrole. Revue et Annales des Liquides Combustibles *changed to* Institut Francais du Petrole. Revue
0020-2304 Institut fuer Orientforschung. Mitteilungen†
0020-2312 Institut fuer Raumordnung. Informationen *see* 0303-2493
0020-2320 Institut fuer Wissenschaft und Kunst. Mitteilungen
0020-2339 Institut Henri Poincare. Annales. Section A: Physique Theorique
0020-2347 Institut Henri Poincare. Annales. Section B: Calcul des Probabilites et Statistiques
0020-2355 Institut International d'Administration Publique. Bulletin *changed to* Revue Francais d'Administration Publique
0020-2363 Institut Maurice Thorez. Cahiers d'Histoire *changed to* Cahiers d'Histoire (Paris)
0020-2371 Institut Napoleon. Revue
0020-238X Institut National de la Recherche Agronomique de Tunisie. Documents Techniques
0020-2398 France. Institut National de la Statistique et des Etudes Economiques. Departements et Territoires d'Outre Mer. Bulletin Bibliographique
0020-2401 Institut National des Appellations d'Origine des Vins et Eaux-de-Vie. Bulletin
0020-241X Institut National des Industries Extractives. Bulletin Technique "Mines et Carrieres"†
0020-2428 Institut National des Industries Extractives. Fiches de Documentation†
0020-2436 Belgium. Institut National du Logement. Bulletin d'Information/Informatie Bulletin†
0020-2444 Institut Pasteur. Annales *see* 0769-2625
0020-2444 Institut Pasteur. Annales *see* 0769-2609
0020-2452 Institut Pasteur. Bulletin
0020-2460 Institut Pasteur d'Algerie. Archives
0020-2479 Institut Pasteur de la Guyane Francaise. Archives†
0020-2487 Institut Pasteur de Lyon. Revue
0020-2495 Institut Pasteur de Madagascar. Archives
0020-2509 Institut Pasteur de Tunis. Archives
0020-2517 Institut Royal Meteorologique de Belgique Contributions†
0020-2525 Belgium. Institut Royal Meteorologique. Observations Geophysiques
0020-2533 Belgium. Institut Royal Meteorologique. Observations Ionospheriques et du Rayonnement Cosmique
0020-2541 Belgium. Institut Royal Meteorologique. Observations Synoptiques
0020-255X Belgium. Institut Royal Meteorologique. Publications
0020-2568 Institut Technique du Batiment et des Travaux Publics. Annales
0020-2606 Institute for Defence Studies and Analyses. Journal
0020-2614 Pennsylvania State University. Institute for Research on Land and Water Resources. Newsletter *changed to* Pennsylvania State University. Environmental Resources Research Institute. Newsletter
0020-2622 Institute for Social Research. Newsletter
0020-2630 Institute for the Study of Nonviolence Journal†
0020-2649 Institute for the Study of the U S S R. Bulletin†
0020-2665 Institute for Workers' Control. Bulletin *see* 0306-1892
0020-2673 Young Men's Institute. Institute Journal
0020-2681 Institute of Actuaries. Journal
0020-269X Institute of Actuaries Students' Society. Journal
0020-2703 University of Ghana. Institute of African Studies. Research Review
0020-2711 Institute of Animal Technicians. Journal *see* 0264-4754
0020-272X Institute of Bankers in Ireland. Journal
0020-2738 Institute of Bankers. Journal†
0020-2746 Motor Management *changed to* Motor Industry Management
0020-2754 Institute of British Geographers. Transactions
0020-2762 Institute of Burial and Cremation Administration. Journal
0020-2770 Institute of Civil Defence. Journal
0020-2800 Institute of Consulting Engineers. Journal
0020-2827 Institute of Developing Economies. Library Bulletin
0020-2835 Institute of Developement Studies Bulletin *see* 0308-5872
0020-2843 Institute of Early American History and Culture. News Letter
0020-2851 Institute of Economic Research. Journal
0020-286X Institute of Electrical Communication Engineers of Japan. Journal *see* 0373-6121
0020-2878 Railway Electric Rolling Stocks
0020-2886 Institute of Fuel. Journal *see* 0144-2600
0020-2894 University of London. Institute of Historical Research. Bulletin *see* 0950-3471
0020-2908 Landscape Design
0020-2916 Institute of Management Sciences Bulletin *see* 0092-2102
0020-2924 Institute of Marine Engineers. Transactions *see* 0309-3948
0020-2932 Institute of Mathematics and Its Applications. Journal *see* 0272-4960
0020-2932 Institute of Mathematics and Its Applications. Journal *see* 0272-4979
0020-2940 Measurement and Control
0020-2959 Institute of Medical Laboratory Technology. Gazette *changed to* I M L S. Gazette
0020-2967 Institute of Metal Finishing. Transactions
0020-2983 Institute of Mine Surveyors of South Africa. Journal
0020-3009 Institute of Navigation. Journal *see* 0373-4633
0020-3017 Institute of Outdoor Drama Newsletter
0020-3025 Institute of Pacific Research. Journal†
0020-3033 Institute of Paper Chemistry. Abstract Bulletin
0020-3041 Institute of Paper Chemistry. Keyword Supplement *changed to* Institute of Paper Chemistry. Keyword Index to Abstract Bulletin
0020-3076 Petroleum Review
0020-3084 Institute of Physical and Chemical Research. Reports
0020-3092 Institute of Physical and Chemical Research. Scientific Papers
0020-3106 Institute of Public Health. Bulletin
0020-3114 Institute of Rail Transport. Journal
0020-3122 Transport Engineer
0020-3130 Institute of Science Technology. Bulletin
0020-3157 Institute of Statistical Mathematics. Annals
0020-3165 University of Dacca. Institute of Statistical Research and Training. Bulletin *changed to* Journal of Statistical Research
0020-3173 Institute of the Motor Industry. Journal *changed to* Motor Industry Management
0020-3181 Chartered Institute of Transport. Journal *see* 0144-3453
0020-319X Institute of Weights and Measures Administration Monthly Review *see* 0302-3249
0020-322X Institutet Foer Maltdrycksforskning. Meddelande†
0020-3238 Institution of Agricultural Engineers. Journal and Proceedings *see* 0308-5732
0020-3246 Institution of Chemical Engineers. Diary
0020-3254 Institution of Chemists (India). Journal
0020-3270 Institution of Electrical Engineers. Proceedings *see* 0143-702X
0020-3270 Institution of Electrical Engineers. Proceedings *changed to* I E E Proceedings Part H: Microwaves, Antennas & Propagation
0020-3270 Institution of Electrical Engineers. Proceedings *see* 0143-7100
0020-3270 Institution of Electrical Engineers. Proceedings *see* 0143-7038
0020-3270 Institution of Electrical Engineers. Proceedings *see* 0143-7046
0020-3270 Institution of Electrical Engineers. Proceedings *see* 0143-7054
0020-3270 Institution of Electrical Engineers. Proceedings *see* 0143-7062
0020-3270 Institution of Electrical Engineers. Proceedings *see* 0143-7089
0020-3270 Institution of Electrical Engineers. Proceedings *see* 0143-7070
0020-3297 Institutions of Engineers, Australia. Civil Engineering Transactions *see* 0159-2068
0020-3300 Institution of Engineers, Australia. Transactions. Electrical Engineering
0020-3319 Institution of Engineers, Australia. Journal *changed to* Engineers Australia
0020-3327 Institution of Engineers, Australia. Mechanical and Chemical Engineering Transactions *see* 0313-5519
0020-3327 Institution of Engineers, Australia. Mechanical and Chemical Engineering Transactions *see* 0157-9762
0020-3335 Institution of Engineers-In-Charge. Transactions
0020-3343 Institution of Engineers (India). Bulletin
0020-3351 Institution of Engineers (India). Chemical Engineering Division. Journal
0020-336X Institution of Engineers (India). Civil Engineering Division. Journal
0020-3378 Institution of Engineers (India). Electronics and Telecommunication Engineering Division. Journal
0020-3386 Institution of Engineers (India). Electrical Engineering Division. Journal
0020-3394 Institution of Engineers (India). Mining and Metallurgy Division. Journal *see* 0257-442X
0020-3408 Institution of Engineers (India). Mechanical Engineering Division. Journal
0020-3416 Institution of Engineers (India). Public Health Engineering Division. Journal *changed to* Institution of Engineers (India). Environmental Engineering Division. Journal
0020-3424 Institution of Fire Engineers Quarterly *changed to* Fire Engineers Journal
0020-3432 Institution of Gas Engineers. Journal *see* 0306-6444
0020-3475 Institution of Marine Technologists. Journal
0020-3483 Institution of Mechanical Engineers. Proceedings *see* 0263-7138
0020-3483 Institution of Mechanical Engineers. Proceedings *see* 0263-7146
0020-3483 Institution of Mechanical Engineers. Proceedings *see* 0265-1904
0020-3505 Institution of Municipal Engineers. Journal *changed to* Municipal Engineer
0020-3513 Institution of Public Health Engineers. Journal *see* 0300-5925
0020-3521 Institution of Radio and Electronics Engineers Australia. Proceedings *see* 0725-2986
0020-3556 Institution of Water Engineers. Journal *see* 0309-1600
0020-3572 Institutional Distribution
0020-3580 Institutional Investor
0020-3599 Institutional Laundry *changed to* Laundry Cleaning World
0020-3602 Institutional Management *see* 0144-3704
0020-3610 Institutions/Volume Feeding Management *see* 0273-5520
0020-3629 Instituto Agronomico do Sul. Escola de Agronomia Eliseu Maciel. Arquivos de Entomologia. Serie A & Serie B

1250 ISSN INDEX

0020-3637 Instituto Americano de Estudios Vascos. Boletin
0020-3645 Instituto Barraquer. Anales
0020-3653 Instituto Biologico. Arquivos
0020-3661 Instituto Biologico da Bahia. Boletim
0020-367X Instituto Brasil-Estados Unidos. Boletim
0020-3688 Instituto Brasileiro de Bibliografia e Documentacao. Noticias†
0020-370X Instituto Caro y Cuervo. Noticias Culturales
0020-3718 Instituto Cultural Peruano Norteamericano. Boletin *changed to* Instituto Cultural Peruano Norteamericano. Newsletter
0020-3726 Instituto de Angola. Boletim *changed to* Uniao dos Escritores Angolanos. Boletim
0020-3734 Instituto de Angola. Boletim Analitico *changed to* Uniao dos Escritores Angolanos. Boletim Analitico
0020-3742 Instituto de Angola. Boletim Bibliografico *changed to* Uniao dos Escritores Angolanos. Boletim Bibliografico
0020-3750 Universidad Nacional Mayor de San Marcos. Instituto de Biologia Andina. Archivos *changed to* Archivos de Biologia Andina
0020-3769 Instituto de Biologia Aplicada. Publicaciones†
0020-3777 Lisbon. Instituto de Biologia Maritima. Notas e Estudos *see* 0870-1245
0020-3785 Instituto de Cardiologia de Mexico. Archivos
0020-3807 Instituto de Ciencias Sociales. Revista
0020-3815 Instituto de Cultura Puertorriquena. Revista
0020-3823 Instituto de Derecho Privado. Boletin
0020-3831 Academia de Ciencias de Cuba. Instituto de Documentacion e Informacion Cientifica y Tecnica. Boletin *see* 0138-6107
0020-384X Instituto de Estudios Asturianos. Boletin
0020-3858 Estudios Medicos y Biologicos. Boletin
0020-3874 Universidade de Sao Paulo. Instituto de Estudos Brasileiros. Revista
0020-3882 Instituto de Fomento Pesquero. Boletin Cientifico *changed to* Serie Investigacion Pesquera
0020-3890 Instituto de Geografia e Historia Militar do Brasil. Revista
0020-3912 Instituto de Investigacao Cientifica de Angola. Boletim
0020-3939 Chile. Servicio Nacional de Geologia y Mineria. Boletin
0020-3947 Anales de Antropologia
0020-3955 Instituto de Investigaciones Medica. Bulletin†
0020-3963 Instituto de Zoonosis e Investigacion Pecuaria Revista
0020-3971 I M M E Boletin
0020-398X Instituto de Pesquisas e Experimentacao Agropecuarias do Sul. Biblioteca. Boletim Bibliografico. *changed to* Rio Grande do Sul. Unidade Executiva de Pesquisa Agropecuaria Estadual. Boletim Bibliografico
0020-4005 Instituto de Prevision Social. Boletin
0020-4013 Instituto de Salubridad y Enfermedades Tropicales, Revista *see* 0034-8384
0020-4021 Instituto de Zoologia "Dr. Augusto Nobre". Publicacoes
0020-403X Istituto di Patologia del Libro "Alfonso Gallo." Bollettino *see* 0391-5972
0020-4048 Instituto Ingenieros Civiles de Espana. Boletim Informativo *changed to* Instituto de la Ingenieria de Espana. Hoja Informativa
0020-4056 Instituto Interamericano del Nino. Boletin
0020-4064 Instituto Italiano di Cultura. Bulletin†
0020-4099 Instituto Latinoamericano de Relaciones Internacionales. Trabajos
0020-4102 Instituto Nacional de Antropologia e Historia. Boletin†
0020-4129 Spain. Instituto Nacional de Investigaciones Agronomicas. Anales†
0020-4129 Spain. Instituto Nacional de Investigaciones Agronomicas. Anales *see* 0211-4674
0020-4129 Spain. Instituto Nacional de Investigaciones Agronomicas. Anales *see* 0210-2463
0020-4137 Instituto Nacional de Investigaciones Agronomicas. Boletin†
0020-4145 Instituto Nacional de la Vivienda. Boletin Interior de Informacion†
0020-4153 Instituto Nacional de Pesca del Ecuador. Boletin Cientifico y Tecnico†
0020-4161 Argentina. Instituto Nacional de Tecnologia Agropecuaria. Departamento de Especializacion. Publicacion Didactica†
0020-417X Universidad de Oriente. Instituto Oceanografico. Boletin
0020-4188 Instituto Panamericano de Geografia e Historia. Boletin Aereo
0020-4196 Instituts fuer Landeskunde. Neueingaenge der Bibliothek und Kartensammlung†
0020-4218 Instituto Historico e Geografico de Juiz de Fora
0020-4226 Institutul de Cercetari Piscicole. Buletinul *changed to* Institutul de Cercetari si Proiectari Alimentare. Sectia Cercetare Piscicola. Buletinul de Cercetari Piscicole
0020-4234 Institutul Geologie si Geofizica. Memoire
0020-4242 Institutul Politehnic "Gherghe Gheorghiu-Dej." Buletin *changed to* Institutul Politehnic Bucuresti. Buletin
0020-4269 Instructional Materials Intercom†
0020-4277 Instructional Science
0020-4285 Instructor *changed to* Instructor
0020-4293 Instrument and Apparatus News *changed to* Chilton's I A N (Instrumentation & Control News)
0020-4307 Instrument and Control Engineering†
0020-4323 Instrument Practice for Process Control and Automation†
0020-4331 Instrumentalist
0020-434X Instrumentatie†
0020-4358 Honeywell Instrumentatie Nieuws
0020-4366 Instrumentation†
0020-4382 Instrumentation Technology *see* 0192-303X
0020-4390 Instrumentenbau-Zeitschrift *changed to* Musik International
0020-4404 Instruments and Control Systems *see* 0746-2395
0020-4412 Instruments and Experimental Techniques
0020-4420 Instruments & Laboratoires†
0020-4447 Instytut Ciezkiej Syntezy Organicznej. Zeszyty Naukowe
0020-4455 Instytut Gospodarstwa Spolecznego. Biuletyn *changed to* Biuletyn I G S
0020-4463 Instytut Medycyny Morskiej w Gdansku. Biuletyn/Institute of Marine Medicine in Gdansk. Bulletin *changed to* Instytut Medycyny Morskiej i Tropikalnej w Gdyni. Bulletin
0020-4471 Instytut Metali Niezelaznych. Przeglad Dokumentacyjny†
0020-448X Instytutu Ochrony Roslin. Biuletyn
0020-4498 Instytut Urbanistyki i Architektury. Biuletyn†
0020-4501 Instytut Urbanistyki i Architektury. Przeglad Informacyjny†
0020-451X Instytut Lacznosci. Prace
0020-4528 Instytut Obrobki Skrawaniem. Zeszyty Naukowe
0020-4536 Insula
0020-4544 Insulation/Circuits *see* 0745-4309
0020-4560 Insurance†
0020-4579 Insurance Adjuster
0020-4587 Insurance Advocate
0020-4595 Insurance Agent and Broker in Canada *see* 0008-3879
0020-4609 Insurance and Actuarial Society of Glasgow. Newsletter†
0020-4617 Insurance Broker *see* 0384-5958
0020-4625 Insurance Broker-Age†
0020-4633 Insurance Brokers' Monthly *see* 0260-2385
0020-465X Insurance Counsel Journal *changed to* Defense Counsel Journal
0020-4668 Insurance Economics Surveys
0020-4676 Insurance Exchange Magazine *changed to* Illinois Underwriter
0020-4684 Insurance Field
0020-4706 Insurance Index†
0020-4714 Insurance Journal
0020-4722 Insurance Law Journal†
0020-4730 Insurance Law Reports: Fire & Casualty
0020-4757 Insurance Lines
0020-4765 Insurance Literature *changed to* Insurance and Employee Benefits Literature
0020-4773 Insurance Mail
0020-479X Insurance Record†
0020-4803 Insurance Record
0020-4811 Insurance Review
0020-482X Insurance Salesman *see* 0199-4581
0020-4846 Insuranceweek
0020-4854 Intanda News
0020-4862 Integrateducation
0020-4870 Integrated Management†
0020-4889 Integrated Personnel Services Index†
0020-4900 Intelligence Digest *changed to* Intelligence Digest (Cheltenham)
0020-4919 Intensive Agriculture
0020-4927 Inter
0020-4943 Inter-American Economic Affairs
0020-4978 Inter-American Music Bulletin†
0020-4986 Inter-American News†
0020-5001 Inter Auto Ecoles de France/Inter Auto Route
0020-501X Inter-Continental Press Guide
0020-5028 Inter/Ed†
0020-5036 Inter Electronique†
0020-5044 Integre C.H.U†
0020-5052 Nordens Kristne Laeger Meddelelser *changed to* Inter Medicos
0020-5079 Inter-Parliamentary Bulletin
0020-5087 Inter-School & Inter-Varsity Christian Fellowship
0020-5095 Inter-State Milk Producers Review *see* 0195-5314
0020-5109 Andy Warhol's Interview *see* 0149-8932
0020-5117 Interaction (St. Louis)
0020-5125 Interafrique Presse
0020-5133 Interamerican
0020-515X Interauteurs†
0020-5168 Interavia: World Review of Aviation-Astronautics-Avionics *changed to* Interavia: Aerospace Review
0020-5176 Interavia Air Letter
0020-5184 Intercambio
0020-5192 Inter Cambio
0020-5206 Interceptor†
0020-5214 Interceram
0020-5222 Interchange†
0020-5249 Intercollegiate Review
0020-5265 Intercon
0020-5273 Intercom (New York)
0020-529X Interconair Aviazione e Marina Internazionale
0020-5303 Intercontinental Press *changed to* Intercontinental Press
0020-532X Intercultural Education†
0020-5338 Interdiscipline
0020-5346 Intereconomics
0020-5362 Interesse
0020-5389 Interest and Dividends†
0020-5397 Interet Europeen: Europe et Regions†
0020-5419 Interface (Bethesda)
0020-5451 Interfaith Observer†
0020-5478 Interim†
0020-5494 Interior Design
0020-5508 Interior Design
0020-5516 Interiors *see* 0164-8470
0020-5532 Interline Reporter
0020-5567 Interlinks†
0020-5575 Interlit
0020-5583 Intermedia News and Feature Service
0020-5605 Intermediair
0020-5613 Intermediaire des Chercheurs et Curieux
0020-5621 Intermediaire des Genealogistes
0020-563X Intermediate Teacher†
0020-5656 Intermountain Contractor
0020-5664 Intermountain Economic Review *see* 0195-8550
0020-5672 Intermountain Farmer *changed to* I F A Cooperator
0020-5680 Intermountain Food Retailer
0020-5699 Intermountain Industry
0020-5702 Transport Management *changed to* Distributie en Transport Management
0020-5710 Internacia Esperanto-Muzeo en Wien. Informilo
0020-5737 Internal *changed to* New York University Report
0020-5745 Internal Auditor
0020-5761 Internal Revenue Bulletin
0020-577X Internasjonal Politikk
0020-5796 International Abstract†
0020-580X International Abstracts in Operations Research
0020-5818 International Abstracts of Biological Sciences *see* 0733-4443
0020-5826 International Accountant†
0020-5834 International Advertiser†
0020-5842 International Aerospace Abstracts
0020-5850 International Affairs
0020-5869 International Affairs
0020-5877 International African Bibliography
0020-5885 International Alliance of Theatrical Stage Employees and Moving Picture Machine Operators of the United States and Canada. Official Bulletin
0020-5893 International and Comparative Law Quarterly
0020-5907 International Anesthesiology Clinics
0020-5915 International Archives of Allergy and Applied Immunology
0020-5923 International Archives of Occupational Health *see* 0340-0131
0020-5931 International Art Market†
0020-594X International Association for Analog Computation. Proceedings *see* 0378-4754
0020-5958 International Association for Mathematical Geology. Journal
0020-5966 International Association of Agricultural Librarians and Documentalists. Quarterly Bulletin
0020-5974 I A E I News
0020-6008 International Association of Personnel in Employment Security. News
0020-6016 International Association of Pupil Personnel Workers. Journal
0020-6024 International Association of Scientific Hydrology. Bulletin *see* 0262-6667
0020-6032 International Association of Universities. Bulletin
0020-6059 International Associations *see* 0250-4928
0020-6067 International Atomic Energy Agency. Bulletin
0020-6075 List of Bibliographies on Nuclear Energy†
0020-6091 Audiology
0020-6105 International Aviation Review†
0020-6121 International Bank Note Society Magazine
0020-613X International Behavioural Scientist
0020-6148 International Beverage News
0020-6156 International Bibliography of Automatic Control†
0020-6172 International Boat Industry
0020-6180 International Bookbinder†
0020-6199 International Bottler and Packer
0020-6202 International Brahman Review†
0020-6229 International Broadcast Engineer
0020-6245 International Bulletin for the Printing and Allied Trades†
0020-627X International Business Contacts†

ISSN INDEX 1251

0020-6288 International Business Equipment
0020-6296 International Centre for Local Credit. Bulletin *changed to* Local Finance
0020-630X International Centre for Theoretical Physics. Monthly Bulletin†
0020-6318 International Chemical Engineering
0020-6326 International Chemical Register *changed to* Chemical Trade Magazine
0020-6334 International Chemical Worker *see* 0162-637X
0020-6342 International Child Welfare Review
0020-6350 International Christian Broadcasters Bulletin†
0020-6369 International Civil Defence
0020-6377 International Civil Engineering Monthly†
0020-6385 Commerce Today *see* 0190-6275
0020-6393 International Commission of Jurists. Review
0020-6407 International Conciliation†
0020-6415 International Construction
0020-6423 International Construction Reporter
0020-6431 International Consumer†
0020-644X International Cooperative Training Journal *see* 0090-9580
0020-6466 International Council for the Exploration of the Sea. Journal du Conseil
0020-6482 International Credit Bank. Quarterly Review†
0020-6490 International Currency Review
0020-6504 International Cycle Sport
0020-6512 International Defense Review
0020-6520 International DeMolay Cordon†
0020-6539 International Dental Journal
0020-6555 International Development Review/ Revista del Desarrollo Internacional/ Revue du Developpement International *changed to* Development
0020-6563 International Digest of Health Legislation
0020-6571 International Drug Therapy Newsletter
0020-658X International Dyer, Textile Printer, Bleacher and Finisher
0020-6598 International Economic Review
0020-6601 International Educational and Cultural Exchange†
0020-661X International Egg Commission. Market Review Situation & Outlook Report
0020-6628 International Egg Commission. Six-Monthly Statistical Bulletin
0020-6644 International Electronics†
0020-6652 International Executive
0020-6660 International Federation for Housing and Planning Bulletin *changed to* I F H P News Sheet
0020-6687 International Federation of European Contractors of Building and Public Works Review *see* 0014-9373
0020-6695 International Federation of Gynaecology and Obstetrics. Journal *see* 0020-7292
0020-6709 International Federation of Pedestrians. International Bulletin *changed to* Voice of the Pedestrian
0020-6717 International Financial News Survey *see* 0047-083X
0020-6725 International Financial Statistics
0020-675X International Flying Farmer
0020-6768 International Folk Music Council. Bulletin *see* 0739-1390
0020-6784 International Forum
0020-6792 International Franchise Association. Legal Bulletin *changed to* Franchising World
0020-6806 International Friendship League. Newsletter
0020-6814 International Geology Review
0020-6830 International Grafik
0020-6849 International Guide to Classical Studies†
0020-6857 International Guide to Indic Studies†
0020-6865 International Guide to Medieval Studies
0020-6911 International Hotel Review *see* 0744-3897
0020-692X International Humanism *changed to* International Humanist
0020-6938 International Hydrographic Bulletin
0020-6946 International Hydrographic Review
0020-6970 Institut International du Froid. Bulletin
0020-6997 International Insurance Monitor
0020-7004 International Intertrade Index
0020-7020 International Journal
0020-7039 International Journal
0020-7047 International Journal for Philosophy of Religion
0020-7063 International Journal of Accounting Education and Research
0020-7071 International Journal of American Linguistics
0020-708X International Journal of Applied Radiation and Isotopes *changed to* International Journal of Radiation Applications and Instrumentation. Part A: Applied Radiation and Isotopes
0020-7098 International Journal of Arbitration
0020-7101 International Journal of Bio-Medical Computing
0020-711X International Journal of Biochemistry
0020-7128 International Journal of Biometeorology
0020-7136 International Journal of Cancer
0020-7144 International Journal of Clinical and Experimental Hypnosis
0020-7152 International Journal of Comparative Sociology
0020-7160 International Journal of Computer Mathematics
0020-7179 International Journal of Control
0020-7187 International Journal of Early Childhood
0020-7209 International Journal of Electrical Engineering Education
0020-7217 International Journal of Electronics
0020-7225 International Journal of Engineering Science
0020-7233 International Journal of Environmental Studies
0020-7276 International Journal of Game Theory
0020-7284 International Journal of Group Psychotherapy
0020-7292 International Journal of Gynaecology and Obstetrics
0020-7306 International Journal of Health Education *changed to* Hygie
0020-7314 International Journal of Health Services
0020-7322 International Journal of Insect Morphology and Embryology
0020-7330 International Journal of Legal Research†
0020-7349 International Journal of Leprosy *see* 0148-916X
0020-7357 International Journal of Machine Tool Design and Research *changed to* International Journal of Machine Tools Design and Manufacture
0020-7365 International Journal of Magnetism†
0020-7373 International Journal of Man-Machine Studies
0020-7381 International Journal of Mass Spectrometry and Ion Physics *changed to* International Journal of Mass Spectrometry and Ion Processes
0020-739X International Journal of Mathematical Education in Science and Technology
0020-7403 International Journal of Mechanical Sciences
0020-7411 International Journal of Mental Health
0020-7438 International Journal of Middle East Studies
0020-7446 International Journal of Neurology
0020-7454 International Journal of Neuroscience
0020-7462 International Journal of Non-Linear Mechanics
0020-7470 International Journal of Nondestructive Testing *see* 0140-072X
0020-7489 International Journal of Nursing Studies
0020-7497 International Journal of Offender Therapy *see* 0306-624X
0020-7500 International Journal of Orthodontics *changed to* American Journal of Orthodontics and Pentofacial Orthodontics
0020-7519 International Journal for Parasitology
0020-7527 International Journal of Physical Distribution *changed to* International Journal of Physical Distribution & Materials Management
0020-7535 International Journal of Powder Metallurgy *see* 0361-3488
0020-7543 International Journal of Production Research
0020-7578 International Journal of Psycho-Analysis
0020-7594 Journal International de Psychologie
0020-7608 International Journal of Quantum Chemistry
0020-7616 International Journal of Radiation Biology
0020-7624 International Journal of Rock Mechanics and Mining Sciences *see* 0148-9062
0020-7632 International Journal of Slavic Linguistics and Poetics
0020-7640 International Journal of Social Psychiatry
0020-7659 International Journal of Sociology
0020-7675 International Journal of Sociometry and Sociatry *changed to* Handbook of International Sociometry.
0020-7683 International Journal of Solids and Structures
0020-7691 International Journal of Speleology†
0020-7705 International Journal of Symbology†
0020-7713 International Journal of Systematic Bacteriology
0020-7721 International Journal of Systems Science
0020-773X International Journal of the Addictions
0020-7748 International Journal of Theoretical Physics
0020-7756 International Labour Documentation
0020-7764 International Labour Office. Legislative Series
0020-7772 International Labour Office. Official Bulletin *see* 0378-5882
0020-7772 International Labour Office. Official Bulletin *see* 0378-5890
0020-7780 International Labour Review
0020-7799 International Language Reporter *changed to* Eco-Logos
0020-7810 International Lawyer
0020-7829 International Legal Materials
0020-7837 International Library Review
0020-7845 International Licensing
0020-7853 International Lighting Review
0020-7888 International Management
0020-7896 International Management Information Business Digest†
0020-7918 International Marine Science *changed to* I M S Newsletter
0020-7926 International Mathematical News
0020-7950 International Medieval Bibliography. Annual Subject Guide *changed to* International Medieval Bibliography
0020-7969 International Mental Health Research Newsletter *changed to* Transnational Mental Health Research Newsletter
0020-7977 International Microform Journal of Legal Medicine *changed to* International Microform Journal of Legal Medicine and Forensic Sciences
0020-7985 International Migration
0020-8000 International Mining Equipment *see* 0010-1281
0020-8019 International Molders' and Allied Workers' Journal
0020-8027 International Monetary Fund. Staff Papers
0020-8035 International Monetary Issues *changed to* Gold, Money, Commodities
0020-8051 International Musician
0020-806X International Narcotic Report *see* 0148-4648
0020-8086 International News Items†
0020-8094 International News Letter *changed to* International Report
0020-8124 International Nursing Index *changed to* International Nursing Index Including Nursing Citation Index
0020-8132 International Nursing Review
0020-8140 International Odd Fellow†
0020-8159 International Operating Engineer
0020-8167 International Ophthalmology Clinics
0020-8175 International Organization of Good Templars Journal *changed to* Globe
0020-8183 International Organization
0020-8191 International Paper Board Industry
0020-8213 International Peace Research Newsletter
0020-823X International P.E.N. Bulletin of Selected Books *changed to* P E N International
0020-8248 International Perfumer *see* 0305-0319
0020-8256 International Pest Control
0020-8264 International Pharmaceutical Abstracts
0020-8272 International Pharmacopsychiatry *see* 0302-282X
0020-8280 International Photo Technik
0020-8299 International Photographer
0020-8302 International Piano Library Bulletin†
0020-8337 International Polar Motion Service. Monthly Notes
0020-8345 International Political Science Abstracts
0020-8353 Potters Herald†
0020-837X International Press Journal
0020-8396 International Prisoners Aid Association. Newsletter
0020-840X International Problems
0020-8418 International Prospect
0020-8426 International Psychiatry Clinics†
0020-8434 International Public Relations Review *see* 0033-3700
0020-8442 Rail International
0020-8450 International Railway Journal *see* 0744-5326
0020-8477 International Rehabilitation Review
0020-8485 International Relations†
0020-8493 International Reporter
0020-8507 International Reports
0020-8523 International Review of Administrative Sciences
0020-8566 International Review of Education
0020-8574 International Review of History and Political Science†
0020-8582 International Review of Mission
0020-8604 International Review of the Red Cross
0020-8639 Trade and Economic Development†
0020-8647 International Ropeway Review†
0020-8655 International Rubber Digest
0020-8663 International Seed Testing Association. Proceedings *see* 0251-0952
0020-8671 International Seismological Centre. Bulletin
0020-8698 International Silk Association. Bulletin *see* 0290-8271
0020-8701 International Social Science Journal
0020-871X International Social Security Review
0020-8728 International Social Work
0020-8760 International Society of Soil Science. Bulletin
0020-8779 International Statistical Institute Review *see* 0306-7734
0020-8787 Stewardess and Flight Service *see* 0915-2210
0020-8795 International Stock Report *see* 0364-5711
0020-8809 International Student Newsletter *changed to* F.S.S.C. Newsletter
0020-8817 International Studies
0020-8825 International Studies of Management and Organization
0020-8833 International Studies Quarterly
0020-8841 International Sugar Journal
0020-885X International Sugar Organization Statistical Bulletin
0020-8868 International Surgery†
0020-8876 International Swimmer
0020-8884 World Federation of Teachers' Unions. Information Letter
0020-8892 International Teamster
0020-8930 International Theatre†
0020-8957 International Trade Forum
0020-8981 International Trade Review
0020-899X International Trade Union News†
0020-9007 International Transport Workers' Journal†
0020-9015 International Travel *changed to* Travelweek

1252 ISSN INDEX

0020-9023 International Trotter and Pacer *changed to* Harness Horsemen International
0020-9058 I U C N Bulletin
0020-9066 International Union for Vacuum Science, Technique and Applications. News Bulletin
0020-9074 International Union of Food and Allied Workers' Associations. News Bulletin
0020-9090 International Whaling Statistics
0020-9104 Wheelspin News
0020-9112 International Wildlife
0020-9120 International Women's News
0020-9139 International Woodworker
0020-9147 Elektrowaerme International *see* 0340-3521
0020-9147 Elektrowaerme International *see* 0340-3513
0020-9155 International Zoo-News
0020-9163 Internationale - A. M. R.
0020-918X I B R
0020-9198 Internationale Bibliographie der Versicherungsliteratur†
0020-9201 I B Z
0020-921X I B N
0020-9236 Internationale Elektronische Rundschau *changed to* Nachrichten-Elektronik & Telematik
0020-9252 Internationale Kirchliche Zeitschrift
0020-9260 Internationale Luftwaffen Revue *changed to* Luftwaffen Revue
0020-9309 Internationale Revue der gesamten Hydrobiologie
0020-9317 Internationale Spectator
0020-9325 Internationale Stiftung Mozarteum. Mitteilungen
0020-9341 Internationale Transport-Zeitschrift
0020-935X Internationale Wirtschaft
0020-9368 Internationale Wirtschafts-Briefe
0020-9376 Internationale Zeitschrift fuer Angewandte Physiologie Einschliesslich Arbeitsphysiologie *see* 0301-5548
0020-9384 Gas Waerme International
0020-9392 Internationale Zeitschrift fuer Klinische Pharmakologie, Therapie und Toxikologie *see* 0174-4879
0020-9406 Internationale Zeitschrift fuer Vitamin-Forschung *see* 0300-9831
0020-9422 Internationaler Holzmarkt
0020-9430 Internationales Afrikaforum
0020-9449 Internationales Asienforum
0020-9457 Internationales Biographisches Archiv *changed to* Internationales Biographisches Archiv - Personen Aktuell
0020-9465 Internationales Europaforum *see* 0049-7134
0020-9473 Internationales Freies Wort
0020-9481 Internationales Gewerbearchiv
0020-949X Internationales Handbuch *changed to* Internationales Handbuch - Laender Aktuell
0020-9503 Internationales Recht und Diplomatie
0020-9511 Internationales Verkehrswesen
0020-952X Internationella Studier
0020-9538 Interni†
0020-9546 Internist *changed to* Internist: Health Policy in Practice
0020-9554 Der Internist
0020-9562 Internist Observer†
0020-9570 Internistische Praxis
0020-9597 Interplanetary News
0020-9619 Interpressgrafik *changed to* Interpressgraphic
0020-9635 Interpretation
0020-9643 Interpretation (Richmond)
0020-966X Buffalo and Erie County Public Library Bulletin
0020-9678 Interpreter (Dayton)
0020-9686 Interpreter Releases
0020-9694 Quarterly Report on Public Welfare in Arkansas†
0020-9708 Interracial Books for Children *see* 0146-5562
0020-9716 Interstages†
0020-9724 Interstampa della Capitale†
0020-9732 Interstate Oil Compact Commission. Committee Bulletin
0020-9740 Interstellar Communication *changed to* Interstellar Bulletins
0020-9759 Intervalo†
0020-9783 Interwing Weekly Review
0020-9791 Intimate Apparel *see* 0360-3520
0020-9805 Intimate Confessions
0020-9813 Intimate Story
0020-983X Into Europe *changed to* New Europe
0020-9848 Intra-Science Chemistry Reports *see* 0276-8585
0020-9864 Intrepid
0020-9872 Inuktitut
0020-9880 Invalidensport *changed to* Behindertensport
0020-9902 Invention Intelligence
0020-9910 Inventiones Mathematicae
0020-9929 Inverness Courier
0020-9937 Investicni Vystavba
0020-9953 Investigacion Pesquera
0020-9961 Investigaciones en Sociologia
0020-9988 Investigative Ophthalmology *see* 0146-0404
0020-9996 Investigative Radiology
0021-0005 Investigative Urology *see* 0022-5347
0021-0013 Investigator
0021-003X Investing, Licensing & Trading Conditions Abroad
0021-0048 Investment Analyst
0021-0064 Investment & Marketing
0021-0072 Investment Bulletin *changed to* A I C Investment Bulletin
0021-0080 Investment Dealers' Digest
0021-0080 Directory of Corporate Financing
0021-0110 Investment Quality Trends
0021-0153 Investor
0021-0161 Investors Chronicle and Stock Exchange Gazette *changed to* Investors Chronicle
0021-0218 Investors League Bulletin†
0021-0250 Inward Light
0021-0269 Inyala News
0021-0277 Inzinierske Stavby
0021-0293 Inzhenernyi Zhurnal *changed to* Inzhenerno-Fizicheskii Zhurnal
0021-0307 Inzicht
0021-0315 Inzynieria i Budownictwo
0021-0331 Io
0021-034X Ion
0021-0358 Ionian
0021-0374 Ionospheric Data *see* 0111-7122
0021-0382 Ionospheric Data in Japan
0021-0390 Ionospheric Predictions†
0021-0404 Ios
0021-0420 Iowa Adult Education Association. Newsletter *changed to* I A L L Eye-Opener
0021-0439 Iowa Architect
0021-0447 Iowa Association of School Librarians. Library Lines *changed to* Iowa Media Message
0021-0455 Iowa Bird Life
0021-0463 Business and Industry
0021-0471 Iowa Conservationist†
0021-0498 Iowa Dental Journal
0021-0501 Iowa Engineer
0021-051X Iowa Farm Bureau Spokesman
0021-0528 Iowa Food Dealer†
0021-0536 Iowa Journal of Social Work *changed to* Social Development Issues
0021-0552 Iowa Law Review
0021-0560 Iowa Legionnaire
0021-0579 Iowa Library Quarterly†
0021-0587 Iowa Medical Society. Journal *changed to* Iowa Medicine
0021-0595 Iowa Municipalities
0021-0609 Iowa Music Educator
0021-0617 Iowa P T A Bulletin
0021-0625 Iowa Plumbing, Heating, Cooling Contractor
0021-0633 Iowa Police Journal
0021-0641 Iowa A E C News *see* 0162-2412
0021-065X Iowa Review
0021-0668 Iowa School Board Dialogue
0021-0676 Iowa Science Teachers Journal
0021-0684 Iowa State Journal of Science *see* 0092-6345
0021-0706 Iowa Transit *changed to* Hawkeye Engineer
0021-0714 Iowa Veterinarian†
0021-0722 Iowan
0021-0730 Iowa's People†
0021-0749 Ipargazdasag
0021-0757 Ipari Energiagazdalkodas *changed to* Energiagazdalkodas
0021-0765 Epirotiki Estia
0021-0773 Iqbal Review
0021-0781 Iran News
0021-079X Iran Oil Journal
0021-0803 Iran Trade and Industry
0021-082X Iranian Journal of Dermatology
0021-0846 Iranian Library Association Bulletin†
0021-0854 Iranian Petroleum Institute. Bulletin
0021-0862 Iranian Studies
0021-0870 Iranica Antiqua
0021-0889 Iraq
0021-0897 Iraq Natural History Museum. Bulletin *changed to* Iraq Natural History Museum. Bulletin
0021-0900 Iraq. Central Statistical Organization. Summary of Foreign Trade Statistics
0021-0919 Iraq. Statistics Bureau. Quarterly Bulletin of Foreign Trade Statistics†
0021-0927 Iraqi Medical Professions' Association. Journal
0021-0935 Ireland *changed to* Ireland Today
0021-0943 Ireland of the Welcomes
0021-0951 Ireland's Own
0021-096X Ireland's Press and Print†
0021-0978 Irenikon
0021-0986 I R G-M I R Bulletin *changed to* Nonviolence et Societe
0021-1001 Iris
0021-101X Iris an Gharda *changed to* Garda Review
0021-1028 Irish Accountant and Secretary†
0021-1036 Irish Agricultural and Creamery Review *see* 0790-732X
0021-1052 Irish Astronomical Journal
0021-1060 Irish Banking Review
0021-1079 Irish Bee-Keeper
0021-1087 Irish Builder and Engineer
0021-1095 Irish Catering Review *changed to* Hotel and Catering Review
0021-1109 Irish Chemist and Druggist *changed to* Irish Pharmacy Journal
0021-1117 Irish Contracts Weekly
0021-1133 Irish Dental Association. Journal
0021-1141 Irish Electrical Industries Review
0021-115X Irish Engineers *see* 0332-1711
0021-1168 Irish Farmers' Journal
0021-1176 Irish Farming News†
0021-1184 Irish Field
0021-1192 Irish Forestry
0021-1206 Irish Georgian Society. Bulletin
0021-1214 Irish Historical Studies
0021-1222 Irish Independent
0021-1249 Irish Journal of Agricultural Economics and Rural Sociology
0021-1257 Irish Journal of Education
0021-1265 Irish Journal of Medical Sciences
0021-1273 Irish Jurist
0021-1281 Irish Law Times and Solicitors' Journal *changed to* Irish Law Times and Solicitors' Journal. New Series
0021-129X Irish Medical Association. Journal *changed to* Irish Medical Journal
0021-1303 Irish Messenger of the Sacred Heart *changed to* Sacred Heart Messenger
0021-1311 Irish Naturalists' Journal
0021-132X Irish Numismatics†
0021-1338 Irish Nurses' Journal *changed to* World of Irish Nursing
0021-1354 Irish Nursing News *changed to* Irish Nursing Newsletter
0021-1362 Irish Plumbing and Heating Engineer *changed to* Irish Heating and Ventilating News
0021-1370 Irish Statistical Bulletin
0021-1389 Irish Sword
0021-1397 Irish Tatler and Sketch *changed to* I T Magazine
0021-1400 Irish Theological Quarterly
0021-1419 Irish Travel Trade News†
0021-1427 Irish University Review
0021-1443 Irish World and Gaelic American
0021-1451 Irish Yachting and Motorboating *changed to* Ireland Afloat
0021-1478 Irodalomtortenet
0021-1486 Irodalomtorteneti Kozlemenyek
0021-1494 Irohin Yoruba
0021-1508 Iron Age *changed to* Chilton's Iron Age: Manufacturing Management
0021-1516 Iron Age Metalworking International *see* 0163-030X
0021-1524 Iron and Steel *see* 0143-7798
0021-1532 Statistical Office of the European Communities. Iron & Steel
0021-1559 Iron and Steel Engineer
0021-1575 Iron and Steel Institute of Japan. Journal
0021-1583 Iron and Steel Institute of Japan. Transactions
0021-1591 Iron and Steel Monthly Statistics *see* 0308-9770
0021-1605 Iron and Steel Translations *changed to* Ferrous and Non-Ferrous Science and Technology Lists-British Industrial and Scientific International Translations
0021-1613 Iron & Steel Journal of India
0021-1621 Iron Worker†
0021-163X Ironworker
0021-1648 Food Irradiation /Irradiation des Aliments (ISSN 0021-1648) *see* 0301-049X
0021-1656 Irrigation Age
0021-1664 Irrigation and Power
0021-1672 Irrigation and Power Abstracts
0021-1680 Irrigazione e Drenaggio
0021-1699 Medical Treatment
0021-1710 Iscani†
0021-1737 Isenkraemmerbladet *changed to* Isenkram-Goer-det-Selv/ Byggemarkedet
0021-1753 Isis
0021-1761 Iskra
0021-177X Iskusstvo
0021-1788 Iskusstvo Kino
0021-1796 Isla Literaria†
0021-180X Al-Islam
0021-1818 Der Islam
0021-1826 Islam and the Modern Age
0021-1834 Islamic Culture
0021-1842 Islamic Quarterly
0021-1850 Islamic Review†
0021-1885 Isolation et Revetements *see* 0244-2019
0021-1893 Isotope†
0021-1907 Isotope and Radiation Research
0021-1915 Isotopenpraxis
0021-1923 Isotopes and Radiation Technology†
0021-1931 Isotopics†
0021-194X Israel
0021-1958 Israel Annals of Psychiatry and Related Disciplines†
0021-1974 Israel Book World *see* 0333-953X
0021-1982 Israel. Central Bureau of Statistics. Monthly Bulletin of Statistics
0021-1990 Israel. Central Bureau of Statistics. Foreign Trade Statistics Quarterly *changed to* Israel. Central Bureau of Statistics. Annual Foreign Trade Statistics
0021-2008 Israel. Central Bureau of Statistics. Monthly Price Statistics
0021-2016 Israel Diamonds
0021-2032 Israel Digest of Press and Events in Israel and the Middle East *changed to* Israel Digest
0021-2040 Israel Economist
0021-2059 Israel Exploration Journal
0021-2067 Israel Export and Trade Journal *changed to* Israel Aussenhandel
0021-2075 Israel Financial Review
0021-2083 Israel Horizons
0021-2091 Israel Illustrated *see* 0007-7038
0021-2113 Israel Investors' Report *see* 0334-3898

ISSN INDEX 1253

0021-213X Israel Journal of Botany
0021-2148 Israel Journal of Chemistry
0021-2164 Israel Journal of Earth Sciences
0021-2172 Israel Journal of Mathematics
0021-2180 Israel Journal of Medical Sciences
0021-2199 Israel Journal of Physiotherapy
0021-2202 Israel Journal of Technology
0021-2210 Israel Journal of Zoology
0021-2229 Israel Labour Party Bulletin†
0021-2237 Israel Law Review
0021-2245 Israel†
0021-2253 Israel Medical Association. Quarterly Review
0021-2261 Israel. Meteorological Service. Series B: Observational Data. Monthly Weather Report
0021-227X Israel Museum News *see* 0333-7499
0021-2288 Israel Numismatic Journal
0021-230X Israel Seaman
0021-2318 I S L I C Bulletin
0021-2326 Israel. Ministry of Justice. Patent Office. Patents and Designs Journal
0021-2334 Die Gemeinde
0021-2342 Israelitisches Wochenblatt fuer die Schweiz
0021-2350 Israel's Oriental Problems *changed to* Sephardi Heritage
0021-2369 Issue†
0021-2377 Issues & Studies
0021-2385 Issues in Criminology *see* 0094-7571
0021-2415 Istarski Mozaik
0021-2423 Istina
0021-2431 Istituto Carlo Forlanini. Annali†
0021-244X Istituto Centrale del Restauro. Bollettino†
0021-2458 Istituto di Architettura e Urbanistica. Rassegna
0021-2474 Istituto di Studi Romani. Rassegna d'Informazioni *changed to* Istituto Nazionale di Studi Romani. Rassegna d'Informazioni
0021-2482 Istituto Italiano degli Attuari. Giornale
0021-2490 Istituto Italiano di Cultura. Newsletter†
0021-2504 Istituto Lombardo Accademia di Scienze e Lettere. Rendiconti. A
0021-2512 Istituto Mobiliare Italiano. Quarterly Economic Review†
0021-2520 Istituto Nazionale della Previdenza Sociale. Atti Ufficiali
0021-2539 I N A I L Notiziario Statistico
0021-2547 Istituto Sieroterapico Milanese. Bollettino
0021-2555 Istituto Storico e di Cultura dell'Arma del Genio. Bollettino
0021-2571 Istituto Superiore di Sanita. Annali
0021-258X Istituto Tecnico
0021-2598 Istituto Vaccinogeno e dei Consorzi Provinciali Antitubercolari. Rivista†
0021-261X Istmo
0021-2644 Istorijski Glasnik
0021-2652 Istorijski Zapisi
0021-2660 Istoriya S.S.S.R.
0021-2679 Istruzione Tecnica *see* 0535-899X
0021-2717 It Starts in the Classroom
0021-2725 It-Torca
0021-2733 Italdoc
0021-2741 Italia
0021-275X Italia Agricola
0021-2768 Italia che Scrive
0021-2776 Italia Forestale e Montana
0021-2792 Italia Medica *changed to* Italia Medica - Vitalita
0021-2806 Italia Missionaria
0021-2822 Italia Nostra
0021-2830 Italia Numismatica
0021-2849 Italia Scacchistica
0021-2857 Italia sul Mare
0021-2873 Italian American Business
0021-289X Italian Business†
0021-2903 Italian Chamber of Commerce in Chicago. Bulletin
0021-2911 Italian Economic Survey
0021-292X Italian General Review of Dermatology
0021-2938 Italian Journal of Biochemistry
0021-2954 Italian Quarterly†
0021-2970 Italiana Stil Maglia
0021-2989 Italian Stock Market
0021-2997 Italian Trade Topics
0021-3004 Italian Trends
0021-3020 Italica (New York)
0021-3063 Italy - Documents and Notes
0021-3071 Annali della Sanita Pubblica
0021-308X Italy and Nigeria†
0021-3098 Italy Canada Trade
0021-3101 Italy. Centro per la Statistica Aziendale. Index
0021-3136 Italy. Istituto Centrale di Statistica. Bollettino Mensile di Statistica
0021-3144 Italy. Ministero dei Trasporti e dell'Aviazione Civile. Azienda Autonoma delle Ferrovie dello Stato. Bollettino Statistico Mensile
0021-3187 Itineraires
0021-3209 Itinerarium
0021-3225 Acta Biologica Iugoslavica. Serija C: Iugoslavica Physiologica et Pharmacologica Acta
0021-3233 Yunost'
0021-3241 Iura
0021-325X Ius Canonicum
0021-3268 Iustitia
0021-3276 Ivy Leaf
0021-3284 Iwate Medical Association. Journal
0021-3306 Iyyun
0021-3314 Outdoor America
0021-3349 Izmeritel'naya Tekhnika
0021-3357 Izmir Chamber of Commerce Review
0021-3381 Izraz
0021-339X Fountain
0021-3411 Izvestiya Vysshikh Uchebnykh Zavedenii. Seriya Fizika
0021-342X Timiryazevskaya Sel'skokhozyaistvennaya Akademiya. Izvestiya
0021-3438 Izvestiya Vysshikh Uchebnykh Zavedenii. Seriya Chernaya Metallurgiya
0021-3446 Izvestiya Vysshikh Uchebnykh Zavedenii. Seriya Matematika
0021-3454 Izvestiya Vysshikh Uchebnykh Zavedenii. Seriya Priborostroenie
0021-3462 Izvestiya Vysshikh Uchebnykh Zavedenii. Seriya Radiofizika
0021-3470 Izvestiya Vysshikh Uchebnykh Zavedenii. Seriya Radioelektronika
0021-3489 Izvestiya Vysshikh Uchebnykh Zavedenii. Seriya Tekhnologiya Legkoi Promyshlennosti
0021-3497 Izvestiya Vysshikh Uchebnykh Zavedenii. Seriya Tekhnologiya Tekstil'noi Promyshlennosti
0021-3500 J A F News Letter†
0021-3519 J A G Journal *changed to* Naval Law Review
0021-3527 J A G Bulletin *see* 0094-8381
0021-3551 Japan Agricultural Research Quarterly
0021-356X J. B. Speed Art Museum Bulletin
0021-3578 J C I World *changed to* Leader (Coral Gables)
0021-3594 B J E Bulletin *changed to* Up-to-Date with B J E
0021-3608 J E E: Japan Electronic Engineering *see* 0385-4507
0021-3616 J E I: Japan Electronic Industry *see* 0385-4515
0021-3624 J E I
0021-3632 J E M F Newsletter *changed to* J E M F Quarterly
0021-3640 J E T P Letters
0021-3659 J E T S Journal†
0021-3667 Journal of General Education
0021-3675 Japanese Journal of Medical Electronics and Biological Engineering
0021-3691 J M Action *changed to* J-M Future
0021-3705 J N F Illustrated
0021-3713 J N K V V News
0021-3721 J N K V V Research Journal
0021-3748 J O L A Technical Communications†
0021-3756 J O T (Journal fuer Oberflaechentechnik) *see* 0170-4044
0021-3764 J S M E Bulletin
0021-3772 J T A Daily News Bulletin
0021-3780 J W B Circle
0021-3799 J.W.V.A. Bulletin
0021-3802 Formule 1†
0021-3810 Jacetania
0021-3829 Jack and Jill (Inkprint Edition)
0021-3837 Jack London Newsletter
0021-3845 Jack-Pine Warbler
0021-3861 Jacksonville Magazine
0021-387X Jacobsen's Fats & Oils Bulletin
0021-3888 Jadeed Science
0021-3896 Jaegerblatt
0021-390X Jag
0021-3918 Jagawani
0021-3926 Jagd und Jaeger in Rheinland-Pfalz
0021-3942 Der Jagdgebrauchshund
0021-3950 Der Jagdspaniel
0021-3969 Jagriti
0021-3977 Jagt og Fiskeri
0021-3985 Jahrbuch der Absatz - und Verbrauchsforschung
0021-3993 Jahrbuch fuer Internationales Recht *see* 0344-3094
0021-4000 Jahrbuch fuer Psychologie, Psychotherapie, und Medizinische Anthropologie *see* 0300-869X
0021-4019 Jahrbuecher fuer Geschichte Osteuropas
0021-4027 Jahrbuecher fuer Nationaloekonomie und Statistik
0021-4035 Jain Jagran
0021-4043 Jain Journal
0021-4051 Jakt-Fiske-Friluftsliv *changed to* Jakt-Fiske
0021-406X Jaktmaker och Fiskevatten
0021-4078 Jalkine
0021-4094 Jamaica Chamber of Commerce Journal
0021-4108 Jamaica. Department of Statistics. Rural Retail Price Index *changed to* Statistical Institute of Jamaica. Consumer Price Indices
0021-4116 News Review
0021-4124 Jamaica Journal
0021-4132 Jamaica Public Health
0021-4140 Jamaican Nurse
0021-4159 Jamaican Weekly Gleaner
0021-4167 Missionland
0021-4183 James Joyce Quarterly
0021-4191 Jamia Educational Quarterly†
0021-4205 Jana Sangh Patrika
0021-4213 Janaman
0021-4221 Janata
0021-423X Jantantra
0021-4248 Janus†
0021-4256 Janus†
0021-4264 Janus
0021-4272 Janus & S C T H
0021-4280 Japan Academy. Proceedings *changed to* Japan Academy. Proceedings. Series A: Mathematical Sciences
0021-4280 Japan Academy. Proceedings *changed to* Japan Academy. Proceedings. Series B: Physical and Biological Sciences
0021-4299 Japan-America Society of Washington. Bulletin
0021-4302 Japan Architect
0021-4310 Seigyo Kogaku *changed to* Systems and Controls
0021-4329 Japan Automotive News
0021-4337 Japan Book News†
0021-4345 Japan Camera Trade News
0021-4353 Japan Christian Activity News
0021-4361 Japan Christian Quarterly
0021-437X Japan Diabetic Society. Journal *changed to* Japan Diabetes Society. Journal
0021-4388 Japan Economic Journal
0021-4396 Japan Foundrymen's Society. Journal
0021-440X Japan Harvest
0021-4418 Japan Illustrated†
0021-4426 Japan Institute of Metals. Bulletin
0021-4434 Japan Institute of Metals. Transactions
0021-4442 Japan Interior Design
0021-4469 Japan Labor Bulletin
0021-4477 Japan Lumber Journal
0021-4485 Japan. Maritime Safety Agency. Hydrographic Department. Hydrographic Bulletin
0021-4493 Japan Medical Association. Journal
0021-4507 Japan Medical Gazette†
0021-4515 Japan Medical News
0021-4523 Japan Metal Bulletin
0021-4531 Japan Missionary Bulletin
0021-454X Japan Orthodontic Society. Journal
0021-4558 Japan Patent News *changed to* Japan Patent Report
0021-4574 Japan Plastics†
0021-4582 Japan Plastics Age
0021-4590 Japan Quarterly
0021-4604 Japan Report (New York)
0021-4620 Japan Sea Regional Fisheries Research Laboratory. Bulletin
0021-4639 Japan Sewage Works Association. Journal
0021-4647 Japan Shipbuilding & Marine Engineering
0021-4655 Japan Socialist Review
0021-4663 Japan Society for Aeronautical and Space Sciences. Journal
0021-4671 Japan Society for Cancer Therapy. Journal
0021-468X Japan Society of Civil Engineers. Journal
0021-4701 Japan Society of London. Bulletin
0021-471X Japan Society of Mathematical Education. Journal
0021-4728 Japan Society of Mechanical Engineers. Journal
0021-4736 Japan Stock Journal
0021-4744 Japan Telecommunications Review
0021-4760 Japan Trade Bulletin *see* 0388-0311
0021-4779 Japan Welding News†
0021-4787 Japan Welding Society. Journal
0021-4795 Japan Wood Research Society. Journal
0021-4809 Japanese Archives of Internal Medicine
0021-4817 Japanese Association for Infectious Diseases. Journal
0021-4825 Japanese Association of Mineralogists, Petrologists and Economic Geologists. Journal
0021-4833 Economic Survey of Japan
0021-4841 Japanese Economic Studies
0021-485X Japanese Forestry Society. Journal
0021-4868 Japanese Heart Journal
0021-4876 Japan Institute of Metals. Journal
0021-4884 Japanese Journal of Allergology
0021-4914 Japanese Journal of Applied Entomology and Zoology
0021-4922 Japanese Journal of Applied Physics
0021-4930 Japanese Journal of Bacteriology
0021-4949 Japanese Journal of Cancer Clinics
0021-4957 Japanese Journal of Child Psychiatry *see* 0289-0968
0021-4965 Japanese Journal of Clinical and Experimental Medicine
0021-4973 Japanese Journal of Clinical Dermatology
0021-4981 Japanese Journal of Clinical Electron Microscopy *changed to* Journal of Clinical Electron Microscopy
0021-499X Japanese Journal of Dermatology: Series A & B
0021-5007 Japanese Journal of Ecology
0021-5015 Japanese Journal of Educational Psychology
0021-5023 Japanese Journal of Ethnology
0021-5031 Japanese Journal of Experimental Medicine
0021-504X Japanese Journal of Genetics
0021-5066 Japanese Journal of Geophysics†
0021-5074 Japanese Journal of Human Genetics
0021-5082 Japanese Journal of Hygiene
0021-5090 Japanese Journal of Ichthyology
0021-5104 Japanese Journal of Limnology
0021-5112 Japanese Journal of Medical Science and Biology
0021-5120 Japanese Journal of Medicine
0021-5139 Japanese Journal of Microbiology *see* 0385-5600
0021-5147 Japanese Journal of Nutrition
0021-5155 Japanese Journal of Ophthalmology
0021-5163 Japanese Journal of Oral Surgery

1254 ISSN INDEX

0021-5171 Japanese Journal of Parasitology
0021-518X Japanese Journal of Pediatrics
0021-5198 Japanese Journal of Pharmacology
0021-5201 Japanese Weekly on Pharmacy and Chemistry
0021-521X Japanese Journal of Physiology
0021-5228 Japanese Journal of Plastic & Reconstructive Surgery
0021-5236 Japanese Journal of Psychology
0021-5244 Japanese Journal of Studies on Alcohol *changed to* Japanese Journal of Alcohol Studies and Drug Dependence
0021-5252 Japanese Journal of Thoracic Surgery
0021-5260 Japanese Journal of Tropical Agriculture
0021-5279 Japanese Journal of Tuberculosis and Chest Diseases†
0021-5287 Japanese Journal of Urology
0021-5295 Japanese Journal of Veterinary Science
0021-5309 Japanese Journal of Zootechnical Science
0021-5325 Japanese Orthopaedic Association. Journal
0021-5333 Japanese Patents Abstracts *changed to* Japanese Patents Report. Examined
0021-5341 Japanese Periodicals Index. Humanities and Social Science Section
0021-535X Japanese Poetry in English†
0021-5368 Japanese Psychological Research
0021-5376 Food and Nutrition/Eiyo to Shokuryo *changed to* Japanese Society of Nutrition and Food Science. Journal
0021-5384 Japanese Society of Internal Medicine. Journal
0021-5392 Japanese Society of Scientific Fisheries. Bulletin
0021-5406 Japanese Society of Starch Science. Journal
0021-5414 Japanese Sociological Review
0021-5449 Jardin des Arts *changed to* Arts-Magazine
0021-5465 Jardin Ouvier de France *see* 0240-5024
0021-5481 Jardins de France
0021-5503 Jardin et Logis *see* 0772-1099
0021-5511 Jarmuvek, Mezogazdasagi Gepek
0021-552X Jaernhandlaren
0021-5546 Jaernvaegteknik†
0021-5554 Jaune et la Rouge
0021-5562 Javeriana
0021-5570 Jax
0021-5597 Jazykovedny Casopis
0021-5600 Jazz
0021-5619 Jazz - Rhythm & Blues *changed to* Jazz
0021-5627 Jazz & Pop†
0021-5635 Jazz Forum
0021-5643 Jazz Hot
0021-5651 Jazz Journal *see* 0140-2285
0021-566X Jazz Magazine
0021-5678 Jazz Monthly†
0021-5686 Jazz Podium
0021-5694 Jazz Report†
0021-5708 Musikrevue†
0021-5716 Jazz Times
0021-5724 Der Jazzfreund
0021-5740 Je Crois
0021-5759 Jeune Garde *changed to* Combat Socialiste
0021-5767 Jean's Journal of Poems *changed to* Jean's Journal
0021-5775 Jedinstvo
0021-5783 Jedlesee†
0021-5791 Jednota
0021-5805 Jednotna Skola
0021-5813 Jeevan Jauban
0021-5821 Jefferson Medical College Alumni Bulletin
0021-583X J. E. M.†
0021-5848 J E N-Bulteno (Junularo Esperantista de Nord-Ameriko *see* 0030-5065
0021-5856 Jenaer Jahrbuch†
0021-5872 Jenga
0021-5880 Jeopardy
0021-5899 Jernindustri
0021-5902 Jernkontorets Annaler *see* 0280-4239
0021-5910 Jerry Kluttz's Federal Employe Newsletter *changed to* Mike Causey's Federal Employe Newsletter
0021-5929 Jersey
0021-5945 Jersey Concrete†
0021-5953 Jersey Journal
0021-5961 Jersey Publisher
0021-5988 Jesuit†
0021-5996 Jet
0021-6003 Jet Cargo News
0021-602X Jetline Schedules
0021-6038 Jeugd
0021-6054 Jeugdboekengids
0021-6062 Jeugdnatuurwachter
0021-6070 J N†
0021-6089 Jeune Afrique
0021-6100 Jeune Revolutionnaire *changed to* Information Ouvrieres
0021-6119 Jeune (S)†
0021-6127 Quebec Science
0021-6135 Jeunes
0021-6143 Jeunes Annees
0021-6151 Jeunes Avocats
0021-616X Jeunes des Auberges
0021-6208 Jeunesse et Orgue
0021-6224 Jeunesses Numismatiques *changed to* Vie Numismatique
0021-6232 Revue Internationale des Jeux et Jouets
0021-6240 Jevrejski Pregled
0021-6259 Jewel of Africa
0021-6267 Jewelers' Circular-Keystone *see* 0194-2905
0021-6275 Jeweller and Metalworker *see* 0307-580X
0021-6283 Jewelry Clip Review *changed to* Costume Jewelry Review
0021-6291 Jewelry Workers' Bulletin
0021-6305 Jewish Affairs
0021-6313 Jewish Affairs
0021-6321 Jewish Braille Review
0021-633X Jewish Chronicle
0021-6348 Jewish Civic Press
0021-6356 Jewish Collegiate Observer *changed to* Kol Yavneh
0021-6364 Jewish Community Bulletin *changed to* Northern California Jewish Bulletin
0021-6372 Jewish Community Center Program Aids
0021-6380 Jewish Current Events
0021-6399 Jewish Currents
0021-6402 Jewish Defense League Newsletter *changed to* Jewish Defense League Iton
0021-6410 Jewish Digest†
0021-6429 Jewish Education
0021-6437 Jewish Exponent
0021-6453 Jewish Frontier
0021-6461 Jewish Gazette
0021-647X Jewish Herald
0021-6488 Jewish Herald-Voice
0021-6534 Jewish Journal of Sociology
0021-6542 Jewish Labor Movement. Bund Archives. Bulletin†
0021-6550 Jewish Ledger
0021-6569 Jewish Liberation Journal†
0021-6577 Jewish Life†
0021-6585 Jewish Memorial Hospital Bulletin†
0021-6615 Jewish Observer
0021-6623 Jewish Observer and Middle East Review†
0021-6631 Jewish Parent†
0021-6658 Jewish Post and Opinion
0021-6666 Jewish Press (Omaha)
0021-6674 Jewish Press (Brooklyn)
0021-6682 Jewish Quarterly Review
0021-6690 Jewish Review *changed to* Jewish Review (1983)
0021-6704 Jewish Social Studies
0021-6712 Jewish Social Work Forum
0021-6739 Jewish Standard
0021-6747 Jewish Standard
0021-6755 Jewish Telegraph
0021-6763 J T A Weekly News Digest
0021-6771 Jewish Times *changed to* Boston Jewish Times
0021-678X Jewish Transcript
0021-6801 Jewish Vanguard
0021-681X Jewish Vegetarian
0021-6828 Jewish Voice
0021-6852 Jewish Week and American Examiner *changed to* Jewish Week
0021-6860 Jewish Weekly News
0021-6879 Jewish Western Bulletin
0021-6887 Jewish Youth Monthly *changed to* Jewish Youth
0021-6895 Jews and the Jewish People
0021-6909 Jews in Eastern Europe†
0021-6917 Jez
0021-6925 Jezik
0021-6933 Jezik in Slovstvo
0021-6941 Jezyk Polski
0021-695X Jicarilla Chieftain
0021-6968 Jikeikai Medical Journal
0021-6976 Jiwan Dhara
0021-6984 Free World
0021-700X Jnanadhara
0021-7042 Jobber and Warehouse Executive
0021-7050 Jobber News
0021-7069 Jobber Topics
0021-7077 Joblinglass†
0021-7093 Jobson's Investment Digest of Australia and New Zealand *see* 0075-3785
0021-7115 Jockey Club
0021-7131 Joedisk Orientering
0021-714X Joel†
0021-7158 Joeygram *changed to* Calliope (Baltimore)
0021-7166 Jogtudomanyi Kozlony
0021-7174 Johann Wilhelm Klein
0021-7182 Johannesburg Stock Exchange Monthly Bulletin
0021-7190 John Herling's Labor Letter
0021-7204 John Liner Letter
0021-7212 John Marshall Journal of Practice and Procedure *see* 0270-854X
0021-7220 John Milton Talking Book
0021-7239 John Rylands Library. Bulletin *see* 0301-102X
0021-7255 Johns Hopkins Magazine
0021-7263 Johns Hopkins Medical Journal†
0021-7271 Johnson Drillers Journal†
0021-728X Johnsonian News Letter
0021-7298 Information and Documentation *changed to* Journal of Information Processing and Managements
0021-7301 Desfile
0021-731X Joint Acquisitions List of Africana
0021-7336 National Defence College Gazette
0021-7344 Jok†
0021-7379 Jonge Handen *changed to* Splinter
0021-7387 Jonge Kampvechter *changed to* Wyzer
0021-7395 Jonge Kerk
0021-7409 Jonge Muziek
0021-7417 Stakkato
0021-7433 Traktor Journalen
0021-7441 Jordbruksekonomiska Meddelanden
0021-745X Jordbrukskasseroerelsen *see* 0346-9670
0021-7468 Jordemodern
0021-7476 Jorden Runt
0021-7484 Jordens Folk - Etnografisk Revy†
0021-7514 Jornal Brasileiro de Neurologia *see* 0101-8469
0021-7522 Jornal de Estomatologia
0021-7530 Jornal de Letras e Artes
0021-7557 Jornal de Pediatria
0021-7565 Jornal de Poesia
0021-7573 Jornal do Medico
0021-759X Josephinum Newsletter
0021-7603 Josephite Harvest
0021-7611 Joslin Diabetes Foundation. Newsletter *changed to* Joslin Magazine
0021-762X Journal Asiatique
0021-7638 Journal Bandeirante†
0021-7654 Journal Belge de Rhumatologie et de Medecine Physique *changed to* Clinical Rheumatology
0021-7662 Journal d'Agriculture Tropical et de Botanique Appliquee *see* 0183-5173
0021-7670 Journal d'Analyse Mathematique
0021-7689 Journal de Chimie Physique et de Physicochimie Biologique
0021-7697 Journal de Chirurgie
0021-7719 Journal de Conchyliologie
0021-7735 Journal de France des Appellations d'Origine†
0021-7743 Journal de Genetique Humaine
0021-7751 Journal de Kinesitherapie *see* 0302-427X
0021-776X Journal de la Construction de la Suisse Romande
0021-7778 Journal de la Corse Agricole
0021-7786 Journal de la Marine Marchande
0021-7808 Journal de l'Amateur d'Art
0021-7824 Journal de Mathematiques Pures et Appliquees
0021-7832 Journal de Mecanique
0021-7859 Journal de Medecine de Besancon†
0021-7867 Bordeaux Medical
0021-7875 Journal de Medecine de Caen†
0021-7883 Journal de Medecine de Lyon
0021-7891 Journal de Medecine de Montpellier†
0021-7905 Journal de Medecine de Strasbourg†
0021-7913 Journal de Medecine et de Chirurgie Pratiques
0021-7921 Journal de Microscopie *see* 0395-9279
0021-793X Journal de Pharmacologie†
0021-7948 Journal de Physiologie
0021-7956 Journal de Psychologie Normale et Pathologique†
0021-7964 Journal de Radiologie d'Electrologie et de Medecine Nucleaire *see* 0227-9363
0021-7972 Journal de Recherches Atmospheriques *changed to* Atmospheric Research
0021-7980 Journal de Semiologie Medicale†
0021-7999 Journal Dentaire du Quebec
0021-8006 Journal Historique des Bernier
0021-8014 Journal des Combattants
0021-8022 Journal des Communautes *see* 0020-0107
0021-8030 Journal des Communes
0021-8049 Journal des Finances
0021-8057 Journal des Horticulteurs et Maraichers. *changed to* Horticulteurs et Maraichers Romands
0021-8065 Journal des Ingenieurs
0021-8073 Journal des Instituteurs et des Institutrices
0021-8081 Journal des Medecins du Nord & de l'Est
0021-8111 Journal des Sciences Medicales de Lille
0021-812X Journal des Tribunaux
0021-8138 Journal d'Hotel
0021-8170 Journal du Droit International
0021-8189 Journal du Four Electrique et des Industries Electrochimiques *changed to* Journal Francais de l'Electrothermie
0021-8197 Journal du Textile
0021-8200 Journal d'Urologie et de Nephrologie *see* 0248-0018
0021-8219 Journal Europeen de Toxicologie *changed to* European Journal of Toxicology and Environmental Hygiene
0021-8227 Journal Export
0021-8235 Journal for Anthroposophy
0021-8243 Journal for Geography/Tydskrif vir Aardrykskunde *see* 0378-5327
0021-8251 Journal for Research in Mathematics Education
0021-8278 Journal for Technical and Vocational Education in South Africa
0021-8286 Journal for the History of Astronomy
0021-8294 Journal for the Scientific Study of Religion
0021-8308 Journal for the Theory of Social Behaviour
0021-8324 Journal Francais de Medecine et Chirurgie Thoraciques†
0021-8332 Journal Francais d'Oto-Rhino-Laryngologie et Chirurgie Maxillo-Faciale *see* 0398-9771
0021-8340 Journal Francais Langenscheidt†
0021-8359 Journal fuer Hirnforschung
0021-8367 Journal fuer Marktforschung†
0021-8375 Journal fuer Ornithologie
0021-8383 Journal fuer praktische Chemie

ISSN INDEX

0021-8405 Journal Mondial de Pharmacie†
0021-8413 Journal Musical Francais-Musica Disques†
0021-8421 Journal of Abdominal Surgery
0021-843X Journal of Abnormal Psychology
0021-8448 Journal of Accountancy
0021-8456 Journal of Accounting Research
0021-8464 Journal of Adhesion
0021-8472 Journal of Administration Overseas *see* 0271-2075
0021-8480 Journal of Adventist Education
0021-8499 Journal of Advertising Research
0021-8502 Journal of Aerosol Science
0021-8510 Journal of Aesthetic Education
0021-8529 Journal of Aesthetics and Art Criticism
0021-8537 Journal of African History
0021-8553 Journal of African Law
0021-8561 Journal of Agricultural and Food Chemistry
0021-857X Journal of Agricultural Economics
0021-8588 Journal of Agricultural Meteorology
0021-8596 Journal of Agricultural Science
0021-860X Journal of Agriculture†
0021-8618 Journal of Agriculture of Western Australia
0021-8626 Journal of Agriculture-South Australia†
0021-8634 Journal of Agricultural Engineering Research
0021-8642 Journal of Air Law and Commerce
0021-8650 Journal of Air Traffic Control
0021-8669 Journal of Aircraft
0021-8677 Journal of Alcohol Education *see* 0090-1482
0021-8685 Journal of Alcoholism; Bulletin of Alcoholism *see* 0735-0414
0021-8693 Journal of Algebra
0021-8707 Journal of Allergy *see* 0091-6749
0021-8715 Journal of American Folklore
0021-8723 Journal of American History
0021-8731 Journal of American Indian Education
0021-874X Journal of American Insurance
0021-8758 British Association for American Studies. Newsletter *changed to* Journal of American Studies
0021-8766 Journal of Analytical Chemistry of the U S S R
0021-8774 Journal of Analytical Psychology
0021-8782 Journal of Anatomy
0021-8790 Journal of Animal Ecology
0021-8804 Journal of Animal Morphology and Physiology
0021-8812 Journal of Animal Science
0021-8820 Journal of Antibiotics
0021-8839 Journal of Apicultural Research
0021-8847 Journal of Applied Bacteriology
0021-8855 Journal of Applied Behavior Analysis
0021-8863 Journal of Applied Behavioral Science
0021-8871 Journal of Applied Chemistry *see* 0268-2575
0021-888X Journal of Applied Chemistry of the U S S R
0021-8898 Journal of Applied Crystallography
0021-8901 Journal of Applied Ecology
0021-891X Journal of Applied Electrochemistry
0021-8928 Journal of Applied Mathematics and Mechanics
0021-8936 Journal of Applied Mechanics
0021-8944 Journal of Applied Mechanics and Technical Physics
0021-8952 Journal of Applied Meteorology *see* 0733-3021
0021-8960 Journal of Applied Nutrition
0021-8979 Journal of Applied Physics
0021-8987 Journal of Applied Physiology *changed to* Journal of Applied Physiology
0021-8995 Journal of Applied Polymer Science
0021-9002 Journal of Applied Probability
0021-9010 Journal of Applied Psychology
0021-9029 Journal of Applied Social Psychology
0021-9037 Journal of Applied Spectroscopy
0021-9045 Journal of Approximation Theory
0021-9053 Journal of Arizona History
0021-9061 Journal of Arkansas Education *see* 0161-7753
0021-907X Journal of Art History
0021-9088 Journal of Art Studies
0021-9096 Journal of Asian and African Studies
0021-910X Journal of Asian History
0021-9118 Journal of Asian Studies
0021-9126 Journal of Asiatic Studies
0021-9134 Journal of Asthma Research *see* 0277-0903
0021-9142 Journal of Astronautical Sciences
0021-9150 Atherosclerosis
0021-9169 Journal of Atmospheric and Terrestrial Physics
0021-9177 Journal of Auditory Research
0021-9185 Journal of Autism and Childhood Schizophrenia *see* 0162-3257
0021-9193 Journal of Bacteriology
0021-9207 Journal of Band Research
0021-9215 Journal of Bank Research†
0021-9223 Journal of Basic Engineering *see* 0098-2202
0021-9223 Journal of Basic Engineering *see* 0094-4289
0021-9231 Journal of Biblical Literature
0021-924X Journal of Biochemistry
0021-9258 Journal of Biological Chemistry
0021-9266 Journal of Biological Education
0021-9274 Journal of Biological Psychology-Worm Runner's Digest†
0021-9282 Journal of Biological Sciences
0021-9290 Journal of Biomechanics
0021-9304 Journal of Biomedical Materials Research
0021-9320 Journal of Biosocial Science
0021-9339 Journal of Black Poetry *changed to* Kitabu Cha Jua
0021-9347 Journal of Black Studies
0021-9355 Journal of Bone and Joint Surgery: American Volume
0021-9363 Journal of Botany of the United Arab Republic *changed to* Egyptian Journal of Botany
0021-9371 Journal of British Studies
0021-938X Journal of Broadcasting *see* 0883-8151
0021-9398 Journal of Business (Chicago)
0021-9401 Journal of Business (South Orange) *changed to* Mid-Atlantic Journal of Business
0021-941X Journal of Business Administration
0021-9436 Journal of Business Communication
0021-9444 Journal of Business Education *see* 0883-2323
0021-9460 Journal of Business Law
0021-9487 Journal of Canadian Petroleum Technology
0021-9495 Journal of Canadian Studies
0021-9509 Journal of Cardiovascular Surgery
0021-9517 Journal of Catalysis
0021-9525 Journal of Cell Biology
0021-9533 Journal of Cell Science
0021-9541 Journal of Cellular Physiology
0021-955X Journal of Cellular Plastics
0021-9568 Journal of Chemical and Engineering Data
0021-9576 Journal of Chemical Documentation *see* 0095-2338
0021-9584 Journal of Chemical Education
0021-9592 Journal of Chemical Engineering of Japan
0021-9606 Journal of Chemical Physics
0021-9614 Journal of Chemical Thermodynamics
0021-9622 Journal of Chemicals and Allied Industries
0021-9630 Journal of Child Psychology and Psychiatry and Allied Disciplines *changed to* Journal of Child Psychology and Psychiatry
0021-9649 Journal of Christian Camping
0021-9657 Journal of Christian Education
0021-9665 Journal of Chromatographic Science
0021-9673 Journal of Chromatography
0021-9681 Journal of Chronic Diseases
0021-969X Journal of Church and State
0021-9703 Journal of Church Music
0021-9711 Journal of Clinical Chiropractic *see* 0097-4706
0021-972X Journal of Clinical Endocrinology and Metabolism
0021-9738 Journal of Clinical Investigation
0021-9746 Journal of Clinical Pathology
0021-9754 Journal of Clinical Pharmacology and New Drugs *see* 0091-2700
0021-9762 Journal of Clinical Psychology
0021-9770 Journal of College Placement *changed to* Journal of Career Planning and Employment
0021-9789 Journal of College Student Personnel
0021-9797 Journal of Colloid and Interface Science
0021-9800 Journal of Combinatorial Theory *see* 0097-3165
0021-9800 Journal of Combinatorial Theory *see* 0095-8956
0021-9819 Journal of Commerce
0021-9827 Journal of Commerce *see* 0361-5561
0021-9835 Journal of Commerce & Independent Review *changed to* Daily Commerce
0021-9843 Journal of Commerce & Industry *changed to* Journal of Commerce, Industry & Transportation
0021-9851 Journal of Commerce
0021-986X Journal of Commercial Bank Lending
0021-9886 Journal of Common Market Studies
0021-9894 Journal of Commonwealth Literature
0021-9908 Journal of Commonwealth Political Studies *see* 0306-3631
0021-9916 Journal of Communication
0021-9924 Journal of Communication Disorders
0021-9932 Journal of Comparative Administration *see* 0095-3997
0021-9940 Journal of Comparative and Physiological Psychology *see* 0735-7044
0021-9940 Journal of Comparative and Physiological Psychology *see* 0735-7036
0021-9967 Journal of Comparative Neurology
0021-9975 Journal of Comparative Pathology
0021-9983 Journal of Composite Materials
0021-9991 Journal of Computational Physics
0022-0000 Journal of Computer and System Sciences
0022-0019 Journal of Conchology
0022-0027 Journal of Conflict Resolution
0022-0035 Journal of Connoisseurship and Art Technology†
0022-0043 Journal of Constitutional & Parliamentary Studies
0022-0051 Journal of Constitutional Law *see* 0377-0907
0022-006X Journal of Consulting and Clinical Psychology
0022-0078 Journal of Consumer Affairs
0022-0086 Journal of Consumer Credit Management†
0022-0094 Journal of Contemporary History
0022-0116 Journal of Contemporary Psycho
0022-0124 Journal of Continuing Education Nursing
0022-0132 Journal of Cooperative Education
0022-0140 Journal of Extension
0022-0159 Journal of Correctional Education
0022-0167 Journal of Counseling Psychology
0022-0175 Journal of Creative Behavior
0022-0183 Journal of Criminal Law
0022-0191 Journal of Criminal Law
0022-0205 Journal of Criminal Law, Criminology and Police Science *see* 0091-4169
0022-0213 Journal of Critical Analysis
0022-0221 Journal of Cross Cultural Psychology
0022-023X Ophthalmic Surgery
0022-0248 Journal of Crystal Growth
0022-0256 Journal of Cuneiform Studies
0022-0264 Journal of Current Laser Abstracts
0022-0272 Journal of Curriculum Studies
0022-0280 Journal of Cybernetics *see* 0196-9722
0022-0299 Journal of Dairy Research
0022-0302 Journal of Dairy Science
0022-0310 Journal of Data Education *changed to* Journal of Computer Information Systems
0022-0329 Data Management *changed to* Data Management
0022-0337 Journal of Dental Education
0022-0345 Journal of Dental Research
0022-0353 Journal of Dentistry for Children
0022-0361 Journal of Detergents and Collective Chemistry and Physics *changed to* Journal of Collective Chemistry and Physics
0022-037X Journal of Developing Areas
0022-0388 Journal of Development Studies
0022-0396 Journal of Differential Equations
0022-040X Journal of Differential Geometry
0022-0418 Journal of Documentation
0022-0426 Journal of Drug Issues
0022-0434 Journal of Dynamic Systems, Measurement and Control
0022-0442 Journal of Earth Sciences
0022-0450 Journal of East Asiatic Studies
0022-0469 Journal of Ecclesiastical History
0022-0477 Journal of Ecology
0022-0485 Journal of Economic Education
0022-0493 Journal of Economic Entomology
0022-0507 Journal of Economic History
0022-0515 Journal of Economic Literature
0022-0531 Journal of Economic Theory
0022-0558 Journal of Ecumenical Studies
0022-0574 Journal of Education (Boston)
0022-0582 Sierra Leone Journal of Education
0022-0590 Journal of Education and Psychology
0022-0604 Journal of Education for Librarianship *see* 0748-5786
0022-0612 Journal of Education for Social Work *changed to* Journal of Social Work Education
0022-0620 Journal of Educational Administration and History
0022-0639 Journal of Educational Administration
0022-0647 Journal of Educational Data Processing†
0022-0655 Journal of Educational Measurement
0022-0663 Journal of Educational Psychology
0022-0671 Journal of Educational Research
0022-068X Journal of Educational Research and Extension
0022-0698 Journal of Educational Technology *see* 0007-1013
0022-0701 J E T: Journal of Educational Thought
0022-071X Journal of Elastoplastics. *see* 0095-2443
0022-0728 Journal of Electroanalytical Chemistry and Interfacial Electrochemistry
0022-0736 Journal of Electrocardiology
0022-0744 Journal of Electron Microscopy
0022-0752 Journal of Embryology and Experimental Morphology *see* 0950-1991
0022-0787 Journal of Employment Counseling
0022-0795 Journal of Endocrinology
0022-0809 Engineering Education
0022-0817 Journal of Engineering for Industry
0022-0825 Journal of Engineering for Power *changed to* Journal of Turbomachinery
0022-0833 Journal of Engineering Mathematics
0022-0841 Journal of Engineering Physics
0022-0868 Journal of English and Germanic Philology *see* 0363-6941
0022-0884 Journal of English Teaching Techniques†
0022-0892 Journal of Environmental Health
0022-0906 Journal of Environmental Sciences
0022-0914 Journal of Ethiopian Law†
0022-0922 Journal of Ethiopian Studies
0022-0930 Journal of Evolutionary Biochemistry and Physiology
0022-0949 Journal of Experimental Biology
0022-0957 Journal of Experimental Botany
0022-0965 Journal of Experimental Child Psychology
0022-0973 Journal of Experimental Education
0022-0981 Journal of Experimental Marine Biology and Ecology
0022-099X Journal of Experimental Medical Sciences†
0022-1007 Journal of Experimental Medicine
0022-1015 Journal of Experimental Psychology *see* 0278-7393
0022-1015 Journal of Experimental Psychology *see* 0097-7403
0022-1015 Journal of Experimental Psychology *see* 0096-3445

1255 herapy

…hology *see*

…in

…ology

…are

… and Quantitative

… & Flammability†
… Biology
…uid Mechanics
… Fluorine Chemistry
… of Food Science
… of Food Science and Technology
…al of Food Technology
…rnal of Forensic Medicine *see* 0379-0738
… Journal of Forensic Sciences
… Journal of Forestry
…X Journal of Fuel and Heat Technology *see* 0367-1119
…1228 Journal of Fukien History
…-1236 Journal of Functional Analysis
…22-1244 Journal of Gem Industry
…022-1252 Journal of Gemmology and Proceedings of the Gemmological Assocation of Great Britain *changed to* Journal of Gemmology
0022-1260 Journal of General and Applied Microbiology
0022-1279 Journal of General Chemistry of the U S S R
0022-1287 Journal of General Microbiology
0022-1295 Journal of General Physiology
0022-1309 Journal of General Psychology
0022-1317 Journal of General Virology
0022-1325 Journal of Genetic Psychology
0022-1333 Journal of Genetics
0022-1341 Journal of Geography
0022-135X Journal of Geography
0022-1368 Journal of Geological Education
0022-1376 Journal of Geology
0022-1384 Journal of Geology of the United Arab Republic *changed to* United Arab Republic Journal of Geology
0022-1392 Journal of Geomagnetism and Geoelectricity
0022-1406 Journal of Geophysical Research *changed to* J G R: Journal of Geophysical Research: Oceans and Atmospheres
0022-1414 Journal of Geriatric Psychiatry
0022-1422 Journal of Gerontology
0022-1430 Journal of Glaciology
0022-1449 Journal of Graphoanalysis
0022-1457 Journal of Health and Physical Education *changed to* Journal of Health, Physical Education and Recreation
0022-1465 Journal of Health and Social Behavior
0022-1481 Journal of Heat Transfer
0022-149X Journal of Helminthology
0022-1503 Journal of Heredity
0022-1511 Journal of Herpetology
0022-152X Journal of Heterocyclic Chemistry
0022-1538 Journal of High Temperature Science *see* 0018-1536
0022-1546 Journal of Higher Education
0022-1554 Journal of Histochemistry and Cytochemistry
0022-1562 Journal of Historical Research
0022-1570 Journal of Home Economics
0022-1589 Journal of Horticultural Science
0022-1597 Hospital and Community Psychiatry
0022-1619 Journal of Hospital Pharmacy *see* 0025-7621
0022-1651 Journal of Human Relations†
0022-166X Journal of Human Resources
0022-1678 Journal of Humanistic Psychology
0022-1686 Journal of Hydraulic Research
0022-1694 Journal of Hydrology
0022-1708 Journal of Hydrology (N.Z.)
0022-1716 Journal of Hydronautics†
0022-1724 Journal of Hygiene
0022-1732 Journal of Hygiene, Epidemiology, Microbiology and Immunology
0022-1759 Journal of Immunological Methods
0022-1767 Journal of Immunology
0022-1775 Journal of Indian History
0022-1783 Journal of Indian Pharmaceutical Manufacturers
0022-1791 Journal of Indian Philosophy
0022-1805 Journal of Individual Psychology *see* 0277-7010
0022-1813 Man/Society/Technology *changed to* Technology Teacher
0022-1821 Journal of Industrial Economics
0022-183X Journal of Industrial Engineering
0022-183X Journal of Industrial Engineering *see* 0019-8234
0022-1856 Journal of Industrial Relations
0022-1864 Journal of Industrial Teacher Education
0022-1872 Journal of Industry *see* 0818-4674
0022-1880 Journal of Industry and Trade†
0022-1899 Journal of Infectious Diseases
0022-1902 Journal of Inorganic and Nuclear Chemistry *see* 0277-5387
0022-1910 Journal of Insect Physiology
0022-1929 Journal of Insurance *see* 0749-8667
0022-1937 Journal of Interamerican Studies and World Affairs
0022-1945 Journal of Interdisciplinary Cycle Research
0022-1953 Journal of Interdisciplinary History
0022-1961 Journal of Internal Medicine *changed to* Internal Medicine
0022-197X Journal of International Affairs
0022-1988 Journal of International and Comparative Studies *see* 0091-2573
0022-1996 Journal of International Economics
0022-2003 Journal of International Law and Economics *changed to* George Washington Journal of International Law and Economics
0022-2011 Journal of Invertebrate Pathology
0022-202X Journal of Investigative Dermatology
0022-2038 Journal of Irreproducible Results
0022-2046 Journal of Islamic Studies
0022-2054 Journal of J.J. Group of Hospitals and Grant Medical College
0022-2062 Journal of Japanese Botany
0022-2070 Journal of Japanese Chemistry†
0022-2089 Journal of Jewish Communal Service
0022-2097 Journal of Jewish Studies
0022-2100 Journal of Jinsen Medical Sciences†
0022-2119 Journal of Karyopathology
0022-2135 Journal of Labelled Compounds *see* 0362-4803
0022-2143 Journal of Laboratory and Clinical Medicine
0022-2151 Journal of Laryngology and Otology
0022-216X Journal of Latin American Studies
0022-2186 Journal of Law and Economics
0022-2194 Journal of Learning Disabilities
0022-2208 Journal of Legal Education
0022-2216 Journal of Leisure Research
0022-2224 Visible Language
0022-2232 Journal of Librarianship
0022-2240 Journal of Library Automation *see* 0730-9295
0022-2267 Journal of Linguistics
0022-2275 Journal of Lipid Research
0022-2283 Journal of Livestock and Agriculture *changed to* St. Joseph Journal of Livestock and Agriculture
0022-2291 Journal of Low Temperature Physics
0022-2305 Journal of Lubrication Technology *see* 0742-4787
0022-2313 Journal of Luminescence
0022-233X Journal of Macromolecular Science. Part A. Chemistry
0022-2348 Journal of Macromolecular Science. Part B. Physics
0022-2356 Journal of Macromolecular Science. Part C. Reviews in Macromolecular Chemistry *see* 0736-6574
0022-2364 Journal of Magnetic Resonance
0022-2372 Journal of Mammalogy
0022-2380 Journal of Management Studies
0022-2399 Journal of Management Studies
0022-2402 Journal of Marine Research
0022-2410 Journal of Maritime Law and Commerce
0022-2429 Journal of Marketing
0022-2437 Journal of Marketing Research
0022-2445 Journal of Marriage and the Family
0022-2453 Journal of Materials. (J M L S A) *see* 0090-3973
0022-2461 Journal of Materials Science
0022-247X Journal of Mathematical Analysis and Applications
0022-2488 Journal of Mathematical Physics
0022-2496 Journal of Mathematical Psychology
0022-250X Journal of Mathematical Sociology
0022-2518 Indiana University Mathematics Journal
0022-2526 Studies in Applied Mathematics
0022-2542 Journal of Mechanical Engineering Science *see* 0263-7154
0022-2550 Government Mechanical Laboratory of Japan. Journal†
0022-2569 Journal of Mechanisms *see* 0094-114X
0022-2577 Journal of Medical Education
0022-2585 Journal of Medical Entomology
0022-2593 Journal of Medical Genetics
0022-2607 Medical Laboratory Technology *see* 0308-3616
0022-2615 Journal of Medical Microbiology
0022-2623 Journal of Medicinal Chemistry
0022-2631 Journal of Membrane Biology
0022-264X Journal of Mental Deficiency Research
0022-2658 Journal of Mental Health
0022-2666 Journal of Mental Subnormality *see* 0374-633X
0022-2674 Journal of Metals *see* 0148-6608
0022-2704 Journal of Microbiology of the United Arab Republic *changed to* Egyptian Journal of Microbiology
0022-2712 Journal of Micrographics *changed to* Inform (Silver Spring)
0022-2720 Journal of Microscopy
0022-2739 Journal of Microwave Power
0022-2747 Journal of Milk and Food Technology *see* 0362-028X
0022-2755 Journal of Mines, Metals and Fuels
0022-2771 Journal of Mississippi History
0022-278X Journal of Modern African Studies
0022-2798 Journal of Modern Education†
0022-2801 Journal of Modern History
0022-281X Journal of Modern Literature
0022-2828 Journal of Molecular and Cellular Cardiology
0022-2836 Journal of Molecular Biology
0022-2844 Journal of Molecular Evolution
0022-2852 Journal of Molecular Spectroscopy
0022-2860 Journal of Molecular Structure
0022-2879 Journal of Money, Credit & Banking
0022-2887 Journal of Morphology *see* 0362-2525
0022-2895 Journal of Motor Behavior
0022-2909 Journal of Music Theory
0022-2917 Journal of Music Therapy
0022-2925 Journal of Narrative Technique
0022-2933 Journal of Natural History
0022-2941 Journal of Natural Sciences and Mathematics
0022-295X Journal of Navy Civilian Manpower Management *see* 0364-0426
0022-2968 Journal of Near Eastern Studies
0022-2976 Journal of Necromantic Numismatics†
0022-2984 Journal of Negro Education
0022-2992 Journal of Negro History *see* 0028-2529
0022-300X Journal of Nematology
0022-3018 Journal of Nervous and Mental Disease
0022-3026 Journal of Neuro-Visceral Relations *see* 0300-9564
0022-3034 Journal of Neurobiology
0022-3042 Journal of Neurochemistry
0022-3050 Journal of Neurology, Neurosurgery and Psychiatry
0022-3069 Journal of Neuropathology and Experimental Neurology
0022-3077 Journal of Neurophysiology
0022-3085 Journal of Neurosurgery
0022-3093 Journal of Non-Crystalline Solids
0022-3107 Journal of Nuclear Energy *see* 0306-4549
0022-3115 Journal of Nuclear Materials
0022-3123 Journal of Nuclear Medicine *see* 0161-5505
0022-3131 Journal of Nuclear Science and Technology
0022-314X Journal of Number Theory
0022-3158 Journal of Nursing Education
0022-3166 Journal of Nutrition
0022-3174 Indian Journal of Nutrition and Dietetics
0022-3182 Journal of Nutrition Education
0022-3190 Journal of Obstetrics and Gynaecology of India
0022-3204 Journal of Obstetrics and Gynaecology of the British Commonwealth *see* 0306-5456
0022-3212 Journal of Occupational Medicine
0022-3239 Journal of Optimization Theory and Applications
0022-3247 Journal of Oral Medicine
0022-3255 Journal of Oral Surgery *see* 0278-2391
0022-3263 Journal of Organic Chemistry
0022-3271 Journal of Organic Chemistry of the U S S R
0022-328X Journal of Organometallic Chemistry
0022-3298 Journal of Orgonomy
0022-3301 Journal of Oriental Research
0022-331X Journal of Oriental Studies
0022-3336 Journal of Outdoor Education
0022-3344 Journal of Pacific History
0022-3352 J.P.T. Journal of Paint Technology *see* 0361-8773
0022-3360 Journal of Paleontology
0022-3379 Journal of Palynology
0022-3387 Journal of Parapsychology
0022-3395 Journal of Parasitology
0022-3409 Journal of Pastoral Care
0022-3417 Journal of Pathology
0022-3425 Journal of Peace *see* 0022-3433
0022-3433 Journal of Peace Research
0022-345X Journal of Pediatric Ophthalmology *see* 0191-3913
0022-3468 Journal of Pediatric Surgery
0022-3476 Journal of Pediatrics
0022-3484 Journal of Periodontal Research
0022-3492 Journal of Periodontology
0022-3506 Journal of Personality
0022-3514 Journal of Personality and Social Psychology
0022-3522 Journal of Petroleum Technology *see* 0149-2136
0022-3530 Journal of Petrology
0022-3549 Journal of Pharmaceutical Sciences
0022-3557 Journal of Pharmaceutical Sciences of the United Arab Republic *see* 0301-5068
0022-3565 Journal of Pharmacology and Experimental Therapeutics
0022-3573 Journal of Pharmacy and Pharmacology
0022-3581 Journal of Phi Rho Sigma
0022-359X Journal of Philippine Librarianship
0022-3603 Journal of Philippine Statistics
0022-3611 Journal of Philosophical Logic
0022-362X Journal of Philosophy
0022-3638 Journal of Photographic Science
0022-3646 Journal of Phycology
0022-3654 Journal of Physical Chemistry
0022-3662 Journal of Physical Education *changed to* Journal of Physical Education and Program
0022-3670 Journal of Physical Oceanography
0022-3689 Journal of Physics A-General *see* 0305-4470
0022-3697 Journal of Physics and Chemistry of Solids
0022-3700 Journal of Physics B: Atomic and Molecular Physics
0022-3719 Journal of Physics C: Solid State Physics
0022-3727 Journal of Physics D: Applied Physics
0022-3735 Journal of Physics E: Scientific Instruments
0022-3743 Journal of Physics of the Earth

ISSN INDEX 1257

0022-3751	Journal of Physiology
0022-376X	Journal of Planning and Property Law *see* 0307-4870
0022-3778	Journal of Plasma Physics
0022-3786	D E Journal *see* 0147-6998
0022-3794	Journal of Podiatric Medicine†
0022-3808	Journal of Political Economy
0022-3816	Journal of Politics
0022-3824	Journal of Polygraph Studies *changed to* Journal of Polygraph Science
0022-3840	Journal of Popular Culture
0022-3859	Journal of Postgraduate Medicine
0022-3867	Journal of Practical Nursing
0022-3883	Journal of Presbyterian History *see* 0886-5159
0022-3891	Journal of Personality Assessment
0022-3905	Journal of Property Management
0022-3913	Journal of Prosthetic Dentistry
0022-3921	Journal of Protozoology
0022-393X	Journal of Psychedelic Drugs *see* 0279-1072
0022-3948	Journal of Psychiatric Nursing *see* 0279-3695
0022-3956	Journal of Psychiatric Research
0022-3964	Journal of Psychoanalysis in Groups *see* 0093-4763
0022-3972	Journal of Psychological Researches
0022-3980	Journal of Psychology
0022-3999	Journal of Psychosomatic Research
0022-4006	Journal of Public Health Dentistry
0022-4014	Journal of Public Law *see* 0094-4076
0022-4030	Journal of Purchasing *see* 0094-8594
0022-4049	Journal of Pure and Applied Algebra
0022-4057	Journal of Pure and Applied Sciences
0022-4065	Journal of Quality Technology
0022-4073	Journal of Quantitative Spectroscopy and Radiative Transfer
0022-409X	Journal of Range Management
0022-4103	Journal of Reading
0022-4111	Journal of Reading Behavior
0022-412X	Journal of Recreational Mathematics
0022-4138	Journal of Refrigeration†
0022-4146	Journal of Regional Science
0022-4154	Journal of Rehabilitation
0022-4162	Journal of Rehabilitation in Asia
0022-4170	Journal of Rehabilitation of the Deaf
0022-4189	Journal of Religion
0022-4197	Journal of Religion and Health
0022-4200	Journal of Religion in Africa
0022-4219	Journal of Religious Education *changed to* Journal of Christian Education of the African Methodist Episcopal Church
0022-4227	Journal of Religious History
0022-4235	Journal of Religious Thought
0022-4243	Journal of Reprints for Antitrust Law & Economics
0022-4251	Journal of Reproduction and Fertility
0022-426X	Journal of Research and Development in Education
0022-4278	Journal of Research in Crime and Delinquency
0022-4286	Journal of Research in Indian Medicine
0022-4294	Journal of Research in Music Education
0022-4308	Journal of Research in Science Teaching
0022-4316	U. S. National Bureau of Standards. Journal of Research. Section C: Engineering and Instrumentation†
0022-4324	Journal of Research on the Lepidoptera
0022-4332	U.S. National Bureau of Standards. Journal of Research. Section A. Physics and Chemistry *see* 0160-1741
0022-4340	U.S. National Bureau of Standards. Journal of Research. Section B. Mathematical Sciences *see* 0160-1741
0022-4359	Journal of Retailing
0022-4367	Journal of Risk and Insurance
0022-4375	Journal of Safety Research
0022-4383	Journal of San Diego History
0022-4391	Journal of School Health
0022-4405	Journal of School Psychology
0022-4413	Journal of Science and Engineering Research
0022-4421	Journal of Science and Technology *see* 0264-9187
0022-443X	Journal of Science of Labour
0022-4456	Journal of Scientific and Industrial Research
0022-4464	Journal of Secondary Education *see* 0145-2061
0022-4472	Journal of Sedimentary Petrology
0022-4480	Journal of Semitic Studies
0022-4499	Journal of Sex Research
0022-4502	Journal of Ship Research
0022-4510	Journal of Small Animal Practice
0022-4529	Journal of Social History
0022-4537	Journal of Social Issues
0022-4545	Journal of Social Psychology
0022-4553	Journal of Societal Issues†
0022-4561	Journal of Soil and Water Conservation
0022-457X	Journal of Soil and Water Conservation in India
0022-4588	Journal of Soil Science
0022-4596	Journal of Solid State Chemistry
0022-460X	Journal of Sound and Vibration
0022-4618	Journal of South African Botany *see* 0254-6299
0022-4634	Journal of Southeast Asian Studies
0022-4642	Journal of Southern History
0022-4650	Journal of Spacecraft and Rockets
0022-4669	Journal of Special Education†
0022-4677	Journal of Speech and Hearing Disorders
0022-4685	Journal of Speech and Hearing Research
0022-4693	Journal of Spelean History
0022-4707	Journal of Sports Medicine and Physical Fitness
0022-4715	Journal of Statistical Physics
0022-4723	Journal of Steel Castings Research†
0022-4731	Journal of Steroid Biochemistry
0022-474X	Journal of Stored Products Research
0022-4758	Journal of Strain Analysis *see* 0309-3247
0022-4766	Journal of Structural Chemistry
0022-4774	Journal of Structural Learning
0022-4790	Journal of Surgical Oncology
0022-4804	Journal of Surgical Research
0022-4812	Journal of Symbolic Logic
0022-4820	Journal of Systems Engineering *see* 0308-9541
0022-4839	Journal of Systems Management†
0022-4847	Journal of Taiwan Agricultural Research *changed to* Journal of Agricultural Research of China
0022-4855	Journal of Tamil Studies
0022-4863	Journal of Taxation
0022-4871	Journal of Teacher Education
0022-4898	Journal of Terramechanics
0022-4901	Journal of Texture Studies
0022-4928	Journal of the Atmospheric Sciences
0022-4936	Journal of the Chemical Society. Chemical Communications
0022-4944	Chemical Society, London. Journal. Section A: Inorganic, Physical and Theoretical Chemistry *see* 0300-9246
0022-4952	Chemical Society, London. Journal. Section C: Organic Chemistry *see* 0300-922X
0022-4979	Karnatak University. College of Education. Journal
0022-4987	Journal of the Dianetic Sciences *changed to* Dianetic Journal Notes
0022-4995	Journal of the Economic and Social History of the Orient
0022-5002	Journal of the Experimental Analysis of Behavior
0022-5010	Journal of the History of Biology
0022-5029	Journal of the History of Buddhism†
0022-5037	Journal of the History of Ideas
0022-5045	Journal of the History of Medicine and Allied Sciences
0022-5053	Journal of the History of Philosophy
0022-5061	Journal of the History of the Behavioral Sciences
0022-507X	Journal of the Indian Medical Profession
0022-5088	Journal of the Less-Common Metals
0022-5096	Journal of the Mechanics and Physics of Solids
0022-510X	Journal of the Neurological Sciences
0022-5118	Journal of the New African Literature and the Arts†
0022-5126	Journal of the Reading Specialist *changed to* Reading Research and Instruction
0022-5134	Journal of the Royal Artillery
0022-5142	Journal of the Science of Food and Agriculture
0022-5150	Denison University. Journal of the Scientific Laboratories†
0022-5169	Journal of the West
0022-5177	Journal of the West Australian Nurses†
0022-5185	Journal of Theological Studies
0022-5193	Journal of Theoretical Biology
0022-5207	Journal of Therapy
0022-5215	Journal of Thermal Analysis
0022-5223	Journal of Thoracic and Cardiovascular Surgery
0022-5231	Journal of Thought
0022-524X	Journal of Transpersonal Psychology
0022-5258	Journal of Transport Economics and Policy
0022-5266	Journal of Transport History
0022-5274	Journal of Transportation Medicine
0022-5282	Journal of Trauma
0022-5290	Journal of Tropical Geography *see* 0129-7619
0022-5304	Journal of Tropical Medicine and Hygiene
0022-5320	Journal of Ultrastructure Research *see* 0889-1605
0022-5339	Journal of Undergraduate Mathematics
0022-5347	Journal of Urology
0022-5355	Journal of Vacuum Science and Technology *see* 0734-2101
0022-5355	Journal of Vacuum Science and Technology *see* 0734-211X
0022-5363	Journal of Value Inquiry
0022-5371	Journal of Verbal Learning and Verbal Behavior *see* 0749-596X
0022-538X	Journal of Virology
0022-5398	Journal of Vitaminology *see* 0301-4800
0022-5401	Journal of West African Languages
0022-541X	Journal of Wildlife Management
0022-5428	Columbia Journal of World Business
0022-5436	Journal of World History†
0022-5444	Journal of World Trade Law
0022-5452	Journal of Yugoslav Foreign Trade
0022-5460	Journal of Zoology
0022-5495	Journal Pratique de Droit Fiscal et Financier *changed to* Journal de Droit Fiscal
0022-5509	Journalism†
0022-5517	Journalism Educator
0022-5525	Journalism Monographs
0022-5533	Journalism Quarterly *see* 0196-3031
0022-5541	Journalist
0022-555X	Journalist
0022-5568	Zhurnalist
0022-5576	Der Journalist
0022-5584	Journalist
0022-5592	Journalisten
0022-5622	Journee des Fruits & Legumes
0022-5630	Journee du Batiment†
0022-5649	Journee Vinicole
0022-5665	Journeyman Barber *see* 0148-2114
0022-5681	Jours de France
0022-569X	Joy†
0022-5703	Joy & Light
0022-5711	Jucunda Laudatio
0022-572X	Judaica
0022-5738	Judaica Bohemiae
0022-5746	Judaica Book Guide†
0022-5754	Judaica Book News
0022-5762	Judaism
0022-5770	Judean
0022-5800	Judicature
0022-5819	Judo
0022-5827	Judo Echo *changed to* Judo Echo
0022-5843	Judo Kokokan†
0022-5851	Judy *changed to* Judy and Tracy
0022-5878	Jugend & Technik
0022-5886	Jugend Film Fernsehen *see* 0341-6860
0022-5894	Jugend in Arbeit *changed to* Jugend in Schule und Beruf
0022-5908	Jugend Kurier†
0022-5916	Jugend und Buch
0022-5924	Jugenddorf-Zeitung *changed to* Klinge
0022-5932	Jugendherberge
0022-5940	Jugendhilfe
0022-5959	Jugendpost
0022-5967	Jugendwacht *changed to* Dafuer
0022-5975	Jugendwohl
0022-6009	Jugi/Ajiste *changed to* Ticket
0022-6017	Jugoslavenska Advokatura†
0022-6025	Jugoslavia Pervojisto
0022-6033	Jugoslavija
0022-6041	Yugoslavskie Profsoyuzy
0022-605X	Jugoslawische Touristenzeitung
0022-6068	Jugoslovenska i Inostrana Dokumentacija Zastite na Radu
0022-6076	Jugoslovenska Revija za Kriminologiju i Krivicno Pravo
0022-6084	Jugoslovenska Revija za Medjunarodno Pravo
0022-6114	Jugoslovenski Pregled
0022-6130	Jugoslovensko Vinogradarstvo i Vinarstvo
0022-6149	Jugovinil
0022-6157	Juguetes y Juegos de Espana
0022-6165	Juillard†
0022-6173	Juilliard News Bulletin
0022-6203	Juncture - Where Ideas Meet†
0022-622X	Junge Christliche Arbeitnehmer. Befreing *changed to* Aktion
0022-6246	Das Junge Elektrohandwerk
0022-6262	Der Junge Florist
0022-6270	Junge Gaertner†
0022-6289	Junge Gemeinde
0022-6297	Junge Generation
0022-6300	Der Junge Kaufmann
0022-6319	Junge Kirche
0022-6335	Der Junge Metallhandwerwer
0022-6343	Junge Sammler
0022-636X	Junge Stimme†
0022-6378	Der Junge Textilverkaeufer
0022-6394	Junger Tischler†
0022-6416	Junge Wirtschaft *changed to* Unternehmer
0022-6424	Jungfreiheitliche†
0022-6432	Junghandwerker im Kraftfahrzeug-Betrieb *changed to* Autofachmann
0022-6440	Eisenhardt-Post
0022-6467	Jungscharhelfer
0022-6475	Junior
0022-6483	Junior Age†
0022-6505	Junior Bookshelf
0022-6521	Junior Church Paper†
0022-653X	Junior College Journal *changed to* Community, Technical, and Junior College Journal
0022-6548	Junior College Research Review *changed to* Junior College Resource Review
0022-6556	Junior Dental *see* 0393-0505
0022-6564	Junior Education Equipment *see* 0262-5717
0022-6572	Junior Farmer and 4-H Enthusiast
0022-6602	Texas Historian
0022-6610	Institution of General Technician Engineers Journal *see* 0308-650X
0022-6629	Junior Keynotes
0022-6637	Junior League *changed to* Junior League Review
0022-6645	Jet Cadet *see* 0162-5217
0022-6661	Junior Members Round Table. News Notes *see* 0736-8879
0022-667X	Junior News†
0022-6688	Junior Scholastic
0022-6696	Junior Statesman *changed to* Junior Statement
0022-670X	Junior Student†
0022-6718	Junior Trails
0022-6726	Quest (St. Louis)†
0022-6734	Junta Nacional da Cortica Boletim *changed to* Instituto dos Produtos Florestais - Cortica. Boletim
0022-6742	Junta Nacional da Marinha Mercante. Boletim *changed to* Portugal. Direccao Geral de Marinha do Comercio. Boletim
0022-6769	Juntendo Medical Journal
0022-6777	Juridica†

ISSN INDEX

ISSN	Title
0022-6785	Juridical Review
0022-6793	Jurimetrics Journal
0022-6807	Juris
0022-6815	Jurisprudence Association. Journal
0022-6823	Jurisprudence Automobile
0022-6831	Jurisprudence du Port d'Anvers
0022-684X	Jurisprudencia e Doutrina
0022-6858	Jurist
0022-6874	Juristen changed to Juristen og Oekonomen
0022-6882	Juristenzeitung
0022-6890	Juristische Analysen†
0022-6912	Juristische Blaetter
0022-6920	Juristische Rundschau
0022-6939	Juristische Schulung
0022-6947	J U S changed to J U S E K
0022-6955	Jus
0022-6963	Jus Gentium
0022-6971	Jussens Venner
0022-698X	Just Between Office Girls changed to Office Guide
0022-6998	P L A Newsletter see 0163-5506
0022-7013	Justice
0022-703X	Justice of the Peace
0022-7048	Justice Weekly
0022-7056	Justicia
0022-7064	Justiz-Ministerial-Blatt fuer Hessen
0022-7099	Jute and Jute Fabrics- Pakistan changed to Jute and Jute Fabrics-Bangladesh
0022-7102	Jute and Synthetics Review†
0022-7129	Jute Markets and Prices
0022-7137	Jutro Polski
0022-7145	Juvenile Braille Monthly†
0022-7153	Juvenile Court Judges Journal see 0161-7109
0022-7161	Juvenile Merchandising
0022-717X	Juvenile Rechabite†
0022-7196	Juventud
0022-720X	Juventud en Accion†
0022-7218	Juventud Panadera
0022-7226	Juzen Medical Society. Journal
0022-7234	Jyotish Kalp†
0022-7242	K A C B Royal Auto
0022-7250	K A G P Journal see 0090-5089
0022-7269	K A H P E R Journal changed to K A H P E R D Journal
0022-7277	K & C
0022-7285	K B S Anvisningar/K B S Directions changed to K B S Tekniska Foereskrifter
0022-7293	K B S-Rapporter
0022-7307	K E A Publications changed to K E A Research Publications
0022-7323	K F Z Werkstaette
0022-734X	K L A Bulletin see 0732-5452
0022-7358	K L A Bulletin
0022-7366	K L M Literatuuroverzicht
0022-7374	K L M News
0022-7390	K M U Monthly Newsletter changed to K M U News Report
0022-7404	K-Rautaviesti see 0355-3086
0022-7439	K V P News
0022-7447	K.W.F. - Nieuws changed to Tijdschrift Kanker
0022-7463	Kaarsvlam
0022-7471	Kachiku to Eiyo†
0022-748X	Kadima
0022-7498	Kadmos
0022-7501	Kaelte see 0343-2246
0022-751X	Kaelte- und Klima Rundschau changed to Temperatur Technik
0022-7528	Kaelte Klima-Praktiker changed to K I Klima, Kaelte, Heizung
0022-7552	Kaerntner Gemeindeblatt
0022-7560	Kaerntner Heimatleben
0022-7579	Kaerntner Landes-Zeitung
0022-7587	Kaerntner Museumsschriften
0022-7595	Kaerntner Naturschutzblaetter
0022-7609	Kaffee und Tee Markt
0022-7625	Science
0022-7633	Science and Technology Information Service
0022-7641	Current Bibliography on Science and Technology: Civil Engineering and Architecture
0022-765X	Toyama Science and Technical Documents
0022-7668	Japan Association for Philosophy of Science. Journal
0022-7676	Chemical Engineering
0022-7684	Chemistry and Chemical Industry
0022-7692	Journal of History of Science
0022-7706	Monthly Report of Agricultural Meteorology, Kagoshima Prefecture
0022-7714	Kahertaja
0022-7722	Acta Anatomica Nipponica
0022-7730	Technical Highlights from Overseas changed to Technology Highlight
0022-7757	Kairos
0022-7765	Kairos†
0022-779X	Kaiserswerther Mitteilungen
0022-7803	Shipping
0022-782X	Kajian Ekonomi Malaysia
0022-7838	Kakao und Zucker
0022-7846	Kakteen und Andere Sukkulenten
0022-7854	Japanese Journal of Nuclear Medicine
0022-7862	Kakyevole
0022-7870	Kalaikathir
0022-7889	Kalakeli
0022-7900	Kalbos Kultura
0022-7919	Kaleidoscope (Springfield)
0022-7927	Kaleidoscope†
0022-7935	Kalendarium†
0022-7943	Kali†
0022-796X	Kalibreur
0022-7978	Kalimat Al-Mar'ah†
0022-7994	Kalki
0022-8028	Kalyan
0022-8036	Kalyan Kalpataru†
0022-8052	Kamakoti Vani
0022-8060	Kameradengruss†
0022-8109	Kamera und Schule
0022-8133	Kameralehti
0022-8141	University of Leiden. Kamerlingh Onnes Laboratory. Communications
0022-815X	Japan T A P P I
0022-8168	Paper & Pulp Statistical Monthly
0022-8176	Kamm und Schere
0022-8184	Kammer-Nachrichten
0022-8192	Kammerspiele Muenchen changed to Muenchner Kammerspiele
0022-8206	Campana
0022-8214	Kampanje!
0022-8230	Kampf dem Krieg
0022-8249	Kampf dem Laerm see 0174-1098
0022-8257	Kampftruppen changed to Europaeische Wehrkunde. Ausgabe "A"
0022-8265	Kampioen
0022-8273	Kamratposten
0022-8281	Kanadai Magyarsag
0022-829X	Kanaski Srbobran
0022-8311	Journal of Radiology and Physical Therapy†
0022-832X	Kanazawa University. Faculty of Technology. Memoirs
0022-8338	Kanazawa University. Science Reports
0022-8346	Kandang Kerbau Hospital Bulletin changed to Singapore Journal of Obstetrics & Gynaecology
0022-8354	Kandelaar
0022-8362	Nursing
0022-8370	Japanese Journal of Nursing Research
0022-8397	Kanot-Nytt
0022-8400	Kansai Medical School. Journal changed to Kansai Medical University. Journal
0022-8419	Kansallis-Osake-Pankki. Economic Review
0022-8427	Kansantaloudellinen Aikakauskirja
0022-8435	Kansas!
0022-8443	Kansas Academy of Science. Transactions
0022-8451	Kansas Anthropological Association. Newsletter changed to Kansas Anthropological Association. Journal
0022-8478	Kansas Banker
0022-8486	Kansas Bar Association. Journal
0022-8494	Kansas Beverage News
0022-8516	Kansas City Grocer
0022-8524	Kansas City Jewish Chronicle
0022-8532	Kansas Economic Development Report†
0022-8540	Kansas Electric Farmer see 0091-9586
0022-8559	Kansas Engineer
0022-8567	Kansas Entomological Society. Journal
0022-8575	Kansas Farm Bureau News
0022-8583	Kansas Farmer changed to Kansas Farmer
0022-8591	Kansas Fish and Game see 0279-9030
0022-8605	Kansas Food Dealers Bulletin
0022-8613	Kansas Government Journal
0022-8621	Kansas Historical Quarterly see 0149-9114
0022-863X	Kansas Job Opportunities†
0022-8648	Kansas Journal of Sociology see 0732-913X
0022-8656	Kansas Judicial Council Bulletin
0022-8672	Kansas Law Enforcement Journal changed to Kansas Peace Officer
0022-8699	Kansas Medical Society. Journal see 8755-0059
0022-8702	Kansas Music Review
0022-8710	Kansas Nurse
0022-8729	Kansas Ornithological Society. Bulletin
0022-8737	Kansas Publisher
0022-8745	Kansas Quarterly
0022-8753	Kansas Restaurant
0022-8761	Kansas School Board Journal†
0022-877X	Kansas School Naturalist
0022-8788	Kansas Speech and Hearing Association Journal changed to Kansas Speech-Language-Hearing Association Journal
0022-8796	Kansas State Dental Association. Journal changed to Kansas Dental Association. Journal
0022-880X	Kansas. State Department of Education. Special Education Section. Typical Report†
0022-8818	Kansas State Teachers College Alumni Association. Alumni News changed to Spotlight (Emporia)
0022-8826	Kansas Stockman
0022-8834	Kansas Teacher
0022-8842	Kansas Transporter changed to Mid-America Transporter
0022-8850	University of Kansas Science Bulletin
0022-8869	Kansas Water News†
0022-8877	Kant-Studien
0022-8885	Kantinen
0022-8893	Kantoor en Efficiency
0022-8907	Kantoor-School-Huis
0022-8923	Kanu-Sport
0022-894X	Kappa Delta Epsilon Current
0022-8958	Kappa Delta Pi Record
0022-8966	Karachi Commerce Weekly
0022-8974	Karachi University Gazette
0022-8982	Karakter changed to Interaktie
0022-8990	Karamu
0022-9008	Karate and Oriental Arts
0022-9016	Karate Illustrated
0022-9024	Karayollari Teknik Bulteni
0022-9032	Kardiologia Polska
0022-9040	Kardiologiya
0022-9059	Karlovacki Tjednik
0022-9075	Karma Album Review†
0022-9083	Karnatak Granthalaya
0022-9105	Die Karpatenpost
0022-9113	Kartei der Praktischen Medizin
0022-913X	Karting
0022-9148	Kartofel' i Ovoshchi
0022-9156	Der Kartoffelbau
0022-9164	Kartographische Nachrichten
0022-9172	Karty Dokumentacyjne
0022-9199	Karys
0022-9202	Fossils
0022-9210	Kashmir Affairs
0022-9229	Kasityo ja Teollisuus
0022-9237	Kasr-el-Aini Journal of Surgery
0022-9245	Kasseler Sonntagsblatt
0022-9253	Kastner & Oehler Firmen-Zeitung
0022-9261	Kasturi
0022-927X	Kasvatus
0022-9288	Katallagete
0022-9296	Katedra
0022-930X	Katera i Yakhty
0022-9318	Katha-Sahitya
0022-9326	Kathakali†
0022-9342	Archief van de Kerken
0022-9350	Metamedica
0022-9377	Katholische Frauenbewegung Oesterreichs. Fuehrungsblatt
0022-9385	Katholische Gedanke see 0340-8280
0022-9393	Katholische Hochschuljugend Oesterreichs-Blaetter changed to Wiener Blaetter
0022-9407	Katholischen Missionen changed to K M - Die Katholischen Missionen
0022-9415	Katilolehti
0022-9423	Katipo
0022-9431	Katolikus Szemle
0022-9458	Katsaus
0022-9466	Kauchuk i Rezina
0022-9474	Kaufhaus und Warenhaus
0022-9482	Kaunis Koti see 0355-2950
0022-9490	Kauppa ja Koti
0022-9504	Kaupparekisteri
0022-9520	Kautschuk und Gummi. Kunststoffe
0022-9539	Kaviamuthu
0022-9547	Kavita
0022-9555	Kayak†
0022-9563	Kayhan-e-Bacheha
0022-9571	Kaytannon Maamies
0022-9598	Kazak
0022-9601	Keel ja Kirjandus
0022-961X	Keen Teen
0022-9636	Keeping Posted
0022-9644	Keeping Posted with N C S Y
0022-9652	Keeping the Record Straight†
0022-9660	Keeping up with Elementary Education changed to Educating Children: Early and Middle Years
0022-9679	Keesing's Contemporary Archives
0022-9687	Kehilwenyane
0022-9695	Keidanren Review
0022-9709	Keio Economic Studies
0022-9717	Keio Journal of Medicine
0022-9725	Economic Science
0022-9733	Economic Review
0022-9741	Economic Review
0022-975X	Journal of Political Economy
0022-9768	Journal of Economics
0022-9776	Tuberculosis
0022-9784	Kelderblom
0022-9792	Keltia
0022-9806	Keltner Commodity Letter†
0022-9822	Kemian Teollisuus see 0355-1628
0022-9830	Kemija u Industriji
0022-9857	Kemio Internacia†
0022-9865	Kemisti
0022-9873	Kemixon Reporter
0022-9881	Kemphaan
0022-989X	Kempo Nyusu changed to Kempo News
0022-9903	Kempton Park Parade†
0022-992X	Kenko Hoken Shimbun changed to Sukoyaka Kempo
0022-9938	Public Health Education
0022-9946	Longer and Healthier Life
0022-9954	Kenkyuseika Yoshisyu see 0385-6437
0022-9962	Kennel Gazette
0022-9970	K en O changed to K & O voor Jeugdwelzijnswerk
0022-9997	Monthly Report of Price and Wage in Construction Engineering
0023-0014	Kent Archaeological Review
0023-0022	Kent Farmer
0023-0030	Kent Life
0023-0049	Kent Messenger
0023-0065	Kentering†
0023-0073	Kentuckiana Purchasor
0023-0081	Kentucky Academy of Science. Transactions
0023-009X	Kentucky Accountant changed to Bottom Line (Louisville)
0023-0103	Kentucky Ancestors
0023-0111	Kentucky Banker
0023-012X	Kentucky Beverage Journal
0023-0146	Kentucky Civil War Round Table. Bulletin
0023-0170	Kentucky Education News see 0164-3959
0023-0197	Kentucky English Bulletin
0023-0200	Kentucky Farm Bureau News

ISSN INDEX 1259

ISSN	Title
0023-0219	Kentucky Farmer
0023-0227	Kentucky Folklore Record
0023-0235	Kentucky Happy Hunting Ground
0023-0243	Kentucky Historical Society. Register
0023-0251	Kentucky Labor News
0023-026X	Kentucky Law Journal
0023-0294	Kentucky Medical Association. Journal
0023-0316	Kentucky Nurse Association Newsletter *changed to* Kentucky Nurse
0023-0324	Kentucky Press
0023-0332	Kentucky Foreign Language Quarterly *changed to* Romance Quarterly
0023-0359	Kentucky School Journal†
0023-0367	Kentucky State Bar Journal *see* 0164-9345
0023-0421	Kenya Farmer
0023-043X	Kenya Mirror *changed to* Mambo
0023-0448	Kenya Police Review
0023-0464	Kenya Teacher Journal
0023-0472	Kenya Weekly News
0023-0480	Kep- es Hangtechnika
0023-0499	Kerala Commerce and Industry *changed to* Vyavasaya Keralam
0023-0502	Kerala Labour & Industries Review
0023-0510	Kerala Law Journal
0023-0529	Kerala Law Times
0023-0537	Kerala Sree
0023-0553	Keramik-Freunde der Schweiz. Mitteilungsblatt
0023-0561	Keramische Zeitschrift
0023-057X	Kereskedelmi Szervezes†
0023-0588	Kerk en Wereld†
0023-0596	Kerkblad
0023-0618	Kerkbode van Gereformeerde Kerken in Noord en Zuid-Holland *changed to* Kerkbode van Nederlands Gereformeerde Kerken
0023-0626	Kerknieuws van de Hervormde Gemeente Schoonebeek†
0023-0634	Kern County Dental Society Newsletter
0023-0642	Kernenergie
0023-0650	Kerngetallen van Europese Effecten†
0023-0669	Kerngetallen van Nederlandse Effecten
0023-0677	Kerteszet es Szoleszet *see* 0133-381X
0023-0685	Kerugma
0023-0693	Kerygma
0023-0707	Kerygma und Dogma
0023-0715	Keshet†
0023-0723	Kesho *changed to* Afrika Ya Kesho
0023-0731	Keuken
0023-074X	Kexue Tongbao
0023-0758	Key (Grand Rapids)†
0023-0766	Key (Philadelphia)
0023-0774	Key Figures to European Securities†
0023-0782	Key Houston
0023-0790	U.S. Department of State. Key Officers in Foreign Service Posts
0023-0804	Key Reporter
0023-0839	Key to Christian Education
0023-0855	Key to the Dayton Scene *changed to* Key Dayton Scene
0023-0863	Key to Toronto
0023-0952	Keya-the Journal for You†
0023-0987	Keystone Folklore Quarterly *see* 0149-8444
0023-0995	Keystone Motorist
0023-1010	Khad Patrika
0023-1029	Khadi Gramodyog
0023-1037	Khadya Vigyan
0023-1045	Khao Kan-Faifa
0023-1053	Khao Setthakit Kan-Kaset
0023-1061	Khartoum†
0023-107X	Khatoon Mashriq
0023-1088	Kheti
0023-1096	Khilauna
0023-110X	Khimicheskaya Promyshlennost'
0023-1118	Khimicheskie Volokna
0023-1126	Khimicheskoe i Neftyanoe Mashinostroenie
0023-1134	Khimiko-farmatsevticheskii Zhurnal
0023-1142	Khimiya i Zhizn'
0023-1150	Khimiya Prirodnykh Soedinenii
0023-1169	Khimiya i Tekhnologiya Topliv i Masel
0023-1177	Khimiya Tverdogo Topliva
0023-1185	Khimiya v Sel'skom Khozyaistve
0023-1193	Khimiya Vysokikh Energii†
0023-1207	Khirurgiya
0023-1215	Khlebopekarnaya i Konditerskaya Promyshlennost'
0023-1223	Khliborob Ukrainy
0023-1231	Khlopkovodstvo
0023-124X	Kholodil'naya Tekhnika
0023-1258	Khudozhnik
0023-1274	Kibernetika
0023-1282	Kick to Corruption
0023-1290	Kicker-Sportmagazin
0023-1304	Kidney
0023-1312	Kids†
0023-1347	Kieler Milchwirtschaftliche Forschungsberichte
0023-1355	Kigyoho Kenkyu†
0023-1363	Kijk op het Noorden
0023-1371	Farming Mechanization
0023-138X	Quarterly Information of Sugar Industry
0023-1398	Komuna (Kikinda)
0023-1401	Kilpailunvapauslehti *see* 0356-5092
0023-141X	Kim/Trefle *changed to* Tefle/Kim
0023-1428	Kimya Muhendisligi
0023-1436	Kin
0023-1444	Kind en Zondag
0023-1452	Kindai Chugoku Kenkya Senta Iho†
0023-1460	Kindai Eiga
0023-1479	Contemporary Architecture
0023-1495	Kinderaerztliche Praxis
0023-1509	Kinderdorfbote
0023-1517	Kindergartner *see* 0276-3435
0023-1541	Kine Weekly†
0023-1576	Kinesitherapie Scientifique
0023-1584	Kinetics and Catalysis
0023-1606	Kingbird
0023-1614	Kingdom Digest
0023-1630	Libya. Census and Statistical Department. Monthly Cost of Living Index for Tripoli Town
0023-1649	Kingsman
0023-1657	Kinki University. Bulletin of Pharmacy
0023-1673	Kino
0023-1681	Kinomekhanik
0023-169X	Kinotechnik
0023-1703	Kinship
0023-1711	Kinyu Keizai
0023-172X	Kioskejer-Bladet
0023-1738	Kipling Journal
0023-1746	Kiplinger Agricultural Letter
0023-1754	Kiplinger Florida Letter
0023-1762	Kiplinger Tax Letter
0023-1770	Kiplinger Washington Letter
0023-1789	Kirche
0023-1797	Kirchenblatt fuer die Reformierte Schweiz:
0023-1800	Der Kirchenchor
0023-1819	Der Kirchenmusiker
0023-1827	Kirchliches Amtsblatt fuer das Bistum Essen
0023-1843	Kirjastolehti
0023-1851	Kiryat Sefer
0023-186X	Kirke og Kultur
0023-1878	Kiserletes Orvostudomany
0023-1886	Kiswahili
0023-1894	Kitab†
0023-1908	Kitikanto Medical Journal
0023-1916	Kitano Hospital Journal of Medicine
0023-1924	Kitazato Archives of Experimental Medicine
0023-1932	Kitchen Business *see* 0730-2487
0023-1940	Kiva
0023-1959	Kivung
0023-1967	Kiwanis Magazine
0023-1975	Kizito
0023-1983	Kjemi
0023-1991	Kjoleteknikk og Fryseriniaering *see* 0048-9301
0023-2017	Klagenfurt
0023-2025	Klassekampen
0023-2033	Akroterion
0023-2041	Klei en Keramiek *changed to* Klei/Glas/Keramiek
0023-2068	Kleine Chorzeitung
0023-2076	Kleintier-Praxis
0023-2084	Kleio
0023-2106	Kleuterwerld *see* 0165-4772
0023-2114	Kliatt Paperback Book Guide *see* 0199-2376
0023-2149	Klinicheskaya Meditsina
0023-2157	Klinika Oczna
0023-2165	Klinische Monatsblaetter fuer Augenheilkunde und Augenarztliche Fortbildung
0023-2173	Klinische Wochenschrift
0023-2181	Klok en Klepel
0023-219X	Klub *changed to* Klubi Khudozhestvennaya Samodeyatel'nost'
0023-2203	Klub Slowenischer Studenten in Wien. Information
0023-2211	Klueter Blaetter
0023-222X	Die Kluge Hausfrau
0023-2238	Kmecki Glas
0023-2246	Kneipp
0023-2254	Kneipp Blaetter
0023-2262	Knight†
0023-2270	Knight's Industrial Reports *see* 0309-0558
0023-2289	Knip
0023-2297	Knit Directions *changed to* Textile Directions
0023-2300	Knitting Times
0023-2335	Knitting Industry†
0023-2351	Knitwear and Stockings *see* 0308-9886
0023-2378	Knizhnoe Obozrenie
0023-2386	Knjigovoda
0023-2394	Knjigovodstvo
0023-2408	Knjizevnost
0023-2416	Knjizevne Novine
0023-2424	Knjiznica
0023-2432	Konditor-Zeitung
0023-2440	Know Britain
0023-2467	A P S S Know How (Associated Public School Systems) *changed to* H M L I Research Bulletin
0023-2483	Know Your World *see* 0163-4844
0023-2491	Knowledge Industry Report†
0023-2505	Kobber- og Blikkenslagermesteren
0023-2513	Kobe Journal of Medical Sciences
0023-2521	Kobe Plant Protection and Plant Quarantine Information
0023-2548	Kobieta i Zycie
0023-2556	Kobunshi Kagaku *see* 0386-2186
0023-2564	Polymer Application
0023-2572	Kochniano Anees
0023-2599	Kodai Mathematical Seminar Reports *see* 0386-5991
0023-2602	Kodak Dealer News†
0023-2610	Kodin Kuvalehti
0023-2629	Koebenhavns Havneblad
0023-2637	Koeling†
0023-2645	Koelner Monatszahlen *see* 0177-6355
0023-2653	Koelner Zeitschrift fuer Soziologie und Sozialpsychologie
0023-267X	Koepelt
0023-2688	Koepmannen
0023-2696	Koerpererziehung†
0023-270X	Koers
0023-2718	Kyushu University. Faculty of Engineering. Technology Reports
0023-2726	N A L News
0023-2734	Kogyo Kagaku Zasshi *see* 0369-4577
0023-2742	Kohle und Heizoel
0023-2750	Koinonia†
0023-2777	Factory Management
0023-2785	Essences of Japan
0023-2807	Mind and Society
0023-2815	Koks i Khimiya
0023-2823	Koks, Smola, Gaz
0023-2831	Journal of Dental Health
0023-284X	Aircraft Engineering
0023-2858	Japan Air Self Defense Force. Aeromedical Laboratory. Reports
0023-2866	Journal of International Law and Diplomacy
0023-2912	Kolloidnyi Zhurnal
0023-2939	Kolorisztikai Ertesito
0023-2947	Kolpingblatt
0023-2963	Komal Patra
0023-298X	Komfort in Haus und Garten†
0023-3005	Die Kommenden
0023-3013	Kommentar
0023-3048	Oesterreichische Akademie der Wissenschaften. Kommission fuer Musikforschung. Mitteilungen
0023-3056	Kommunal Litteraturtjaenst *see* 0349-5426
0023-3064	Kommunal Skoltidning *see* 0347-5484
0023-3072	Kommunal Tidskrift *see* 0347-5484
0023-3080	Kommunikation†
0023-3099	Kommunist
0023-3102	Kommunist Belorussii
0023-3110	Kommunist Ukrainy
0023-3129	Kommunisti Tochikiston
0023-3137	Kommunitaet
0023-3161	Komuna (Belgrade)
0023-317X	Komuna Esperanto-Gazeto
0023-3188	Komunikasi
0023-3196	Komunikaty Mazursko-Warminskie
0023-320X	Komunist
0023-3234	Konditorei und Cafe
0023-3250	Der Konditormeister†
0023-3277	Konepajamies
0023-3285	Konevodstvo i Konnyi Sport
0023-3293	Konfeksjon†
0023-3307	Kongelige Danske Videnskabernes Selskab. Historisk-Filosofiske Skrifter
0023-3323	Kongelige Danske Videnskabernes Selskab. Matematisk-Fysiske Meddelelser
0023-3331	Kongelige Danske Videnskabernes Selskab. Matematisk-Fysiske Skrifter†
0023-334X	Agricultural Chemicals Monthly
0023-3358	Koninklijke Nederlandse Akademie van Wetenschappen. Series A: Mathematical Sciences. Proceedings
0023-3366	Koninklijke Nederlandse Akademie van Wetenschappen. Series B: Physical Sciences. Proceedings *changed to* Koninklijke Nederlandse Akademie van Wetenschappen. Series B: Palaeontology, Geology, Physics and Chemistry. Proceedings
0023-3374	Biological and Medical Sciences. Proceedings *changed to* Koninklijke Nederlandse Akademie van Wetenschappen Series C: Biological and Medical Sciences. Proceedings
0023-3390	Koninklijke Shell-Post *changed to* Shell-Post
0023-3404	Koninklijke Academie voor Nederlandse Taal- en Letterkunde. Verslagen en Mededelingen
0023-3412	Tractatenblad van het Koninkrijk der Nederlanden
0023-3420	Konjunktur und Krise†
0023-3439	Konjunktur von Morgen
0023-3447	Konjunkturberichte
0023-3455	Konjunkturdienst *changed to* Konjunktur
0023-3463	Konjunkturlaget
0023-3471	Konjunkturni Barometar
0023-3498	Konjunkturpolitik
0023-3501	Konkreet
0023-3544	Konkuriito Jaanaru *see* 0387-1061
0023-3552	Konkurs, Treuhand- und Schiedsgerichtswesen
0023-3560	Konsertnytt
0023-3579	Konservatorium Nuus
0023-3587	Konservnaya i Ovoshchesushil'naya Promyshlennost'
0023-3595	Konsonanz
0023-3609	Konsthistorisk Tidskrift
0023-3625	Konstruktion im Maschinen-, Apparate- und Geraetebau *see* 0720-5953
0023-3633	Konstruktiver Ingenieurbau Berichte
0023-365X	Kontakt
0023-3668	Kontakt†
0023-3676	Kontakt Drei und Zwanzig
0023-3692	Kontakto
0023-3706	Kontinent†
0023-3722	Kontorsvaerlden
0023-3730	Kontorteknikk *see* 0332-8201
0023-3749	Kontraste Impuls
0023-3757	Kontur
0023-3765	Kontynenty
0023-3773	Konyvtari Figyelo
0023-3811	Kooperation

ISSN INDEX

ISSN	Title
0023-382X	Kooperationen
0023-3838	K L F Tidskrift *see* 0024-015X
0023-3846	Kooperatoeren
0023-3862	Koepmannen
0023-3870	Koppeling
0023-3889	Korea Exchange Bank. Monthly Review
0023-3897	Korea Herald
0023-3900	Korea Journal
0023-3919	Korea Observer
0023-3927	Korea Research Society for Dental Materials. Journal
0023-3935	Korea Times
0023-3943	Korea Trade
0023-396X	Korean Business Journal
0023-3978	Korean Economic Journal
0023-3994	Korean Journal of International Law
0023-4001	Korean Journal of Parasitology
0023-401X	Korean Journal of Public Health
0023-4028	Korean Medical Association. Journal
0023-4036	Korean Nature
0023-4044	Journal of Social Sciences and Humanities
0023-4052	Korean Scientific Abstracts
0023-4079	Koreansk Journal
0023-4087	Korneuburger Kulturnachrichten
0023-4095	Koroze a Ochrana Materialu
0023-4109	Koroth
0023-4117	Korpsblad Rijkspolitie *changed to* Rijkspolitie Magazine
0023-4125	Korrespondens /Utbildningskontakt†
0023-4141	Korrosion och Ytskydd *changed to* Modern Ytbehandling
0023-415X	Kortars
0023-4168	Kosmetik-Parfum-Drogen-Rundschau mit Aerosol-Aspect†
0023-4176	Kosmetikerinnen-Fachzeitung - Parfuemerie Journal *see* 0342-2976
0023-4184	Kosmetische Monatschrift†
0023-4192	Kosmicheskaya Biologiya i Meditsina *see* 0321-5040
0023-4206	Kosmicheskie Issledovaniya
0023-4214	Kosmobiologie *changed to* Meridian
0023-4222	Kosmorama
0023-4230	Kosmos
0023-4249	Kosmos. Series A. Biologia *changed to* Kosmos
0023-4257	Kosmos Tis Psychis
0023-4265	Kostenrechnungspraxis
0023-4281	Kotiliesi
0023-429X	Kountry Korral†
0023-4303	Kovave†
0023-4311	Kovoexport *changed to* Kovoexport-Investa
0023-432X	Kovove Materialy
0023-4338	Kozarstvi
0023-4346	Kozgazdasagi Szemle
0023-4354	Kozhevenno-Obuvnaya Promyshlennost'
0023-4362	Kozlekedestudomanyi Szemle
0023-4370	Kraaiennest†
0023-4389	Kracht van Omhoog
0023-4397	Kraftfahrzeug und Motorrad-Kurier *changed to* Kraftfahrzeug-Gewerbe Suedbaden
0023-4400	Kraftfahrzeugvermieter *changed to* Der Autovermieter
0023-4419	K F T
0023-4427	Kraftfutter
0023-4435	Krafthand
0023-4443	Kraftverkehr
0023-446X	Krajina
0023-4478	Krakowskie Studia Prawnicze
0023-4486	Krankendienst
0023-4494	Krankengymnastik
0023-4508	Krankenhaus-Umschau
0023-4516	Krankenhausarzt
0023-4524	Krankenversicherung
0023-4532	Kranti
0023-4567	Kratylos
0023-4583	Kredietbank. Weekly Bulletin
0023-4591	Kredit und Kapital
0023-4605	Kresge Art Center Bulletin†
0023-4613	Krestanska Revue
0023-4621	Kridangan
0023-463X	Der Kriegsblinde
0023-4648	Kriegsgraeberfuersorge
0023-4656	Krikos
0023-4664	Krikos Ton Vathmoforon
0023-4672	Krila Armije
0023-4680	Kriminal Journalen
0023-4699	Kriminalistik
0023-4702	Kriminalistik und Forensische Wissenschaften
0023-4710	Krishak Samachar
0023-4729	Krishan
0023-4737	Krishanu
0023-4745	Krishnachura
0023-4753	Kristall und Technik *see* 0232-1300
0023-4761	Kristallografiya
0023-477X	Kristaus Karaliaus Laivas
0023-4788	Kristet Samhaellsliv†
0023-4796	Kristliga Esperantofoerbundets Medlemsblad
0023-4818	Kritika
0023-4826	Kritika†
0023-4834	Kritische Justiz
0023-4842	Kritischer Katholizismus†
0023-4850	Krmiva
0023-4869	Kroeber Anthropological Society. Papers
0023-4877	Krokodil
0023-4885	Krolikovodstvo i Zverovodstvo
0023-4893	Kroniek van Afrika *changed to* African Perspectives
0023-4907	Kroniek van het Ambacht/Klein- en Middenbedrijf
0023-4923	Kronika
0023-494X	Kruidenier *changed to* Food-Magazine
0023-4958	Krul's Maandblad voor Stoom- en Chemische Wasserijen, Ververijen en Wassalons
0023-4974	Kryl'ya Rodiny
0023-4982	Ktaadn†
0023-4990	Kudzu†
0023-5008	Kuehn Archiv†
0023-5016	Kuerbiskern
0023-5032	Air Cleaning
0023-5040	Kukuruza
0023-5059	Kulde *see* 0048-9301
0023-5067	Kulfold Mezogazdasaga†
0023-5075	Kulfoldi Folyoiratok Tartalomjegyzeke†
0023-5083	Kulisy
0023-5113	Kultur
0023-5121	Kulturberichte aus Niederoesterreich
0023-513X	Kultur un Lebn
0023-5148	Kultura
0023-5156	Kultura
0023-5164	Kultura
0023-5172	Kultura i Spoleczenstwo
0023-5180	Kul'tura i Zhyttya
0023-5199	Kul'tura i Zhizn'
0023-5202	Kultura Slova
0023-5210	Kulturberichte aus Tirol
0023-5229	Kulturgemeinschaft "der Kreis." Mitteilungen
0023-5237	Kulturgeografi†
0023-5245	Kulturgeografiske Skrifter
0023-5253	Kulturni Radnik
0023-5261	Kulturni Zivot
0023-5296	Kumamoto University. Faculty of Engineering. Technical Reports
0023-530X	Kumamoto University. Institute of Constitutional Medicine. Bulletin
0023-5318	Kumamoto Journal of Science. Series A: Mathematics, Physics and Chemistry *see* 0385-6763
0023-5326	Kumamoto Medical Journal
0023-5334	Kumamoto University. Faculty of Engineering. Memoirs
0023-5342	Kumar
0023-5350	Kungliga Skogs- och Lantbruksakademiens. Tidskrift
0023-5369	Kungliga Krigsvetenskapsakademien. Handlingar och Tidskrift
0023-5377	Kungliga Svenska Vetenskapsademiens. Handlingar†
0023-5385	Kunnallistekniikka
0023-5393	Kunst des Orients
0023-5415	Kunst og Kultur
0023-5423	Kunst und das Schoene Heim *changed to* Die Kunst
0023-5431	Kunst und Kirche
0023-544X	Kunst und Literatur
0023-5458	Kunst und Stein
0023-5474	Kunstchronik
0023-5490	Kunstgeschichtliche Anzeigen†
0023-5504	Der Kunsthandel
0023-5512	Kunstnachrichten
0023-5539	Kunststoff Dokumentum
0023-5555	Kunststoff-Rundschau *see* 0172-6374
0023-5563	Kunststoffe
0023-5571	K I B *see* 0343-3129
0023-558X	Kunststoffe - Plasticos *see* 0303-4011
0023-5598	Kunststoffe-Plastics
0023-5601	Kunststofftechnik *see* 0172-6374
0023-561X	Das Kunstwerk
0023-5628	Kupfer-Mitteilungen *see* 0309-2216
0023-5636	Kurdish Facts†
0023-5660	Kurukshetra
0023-5679	Kurume Medical Journal
0023-5687	Kurz und Buendig†
0023-5695	Kurzauszuege aus dem Schrifttum fuer das Eisenbahnwesen *changed to* Information Eisenbahn
0023-5717	Kuspi
0023-5725	Kusunoki Noho
0023-5733	Kutlwano
0023-5741	Kuuloviesti
0023-575X	Kuwait al-Youm
0023-5768	Kuwait. Central Statistical Office. Monthly Digest of Statistics *changed to* Kuwait. Central Statistical Office. Annual Statistical Abstract
0023-5776	Kuwait Medical Association. Journal
0023-5784	Kuwait†
0023-5792	Kuwaiti
0023-5806	Kuznechno-shtampovochnoe Proizvodstvo
0023-5814	Kvakera Esperantisto
0023-5822	Kvaellsstunden
0023-5830	Kvasny Prumysl
0023-5849	Kvety
0023-5857	Kvinner og Klaer
0023-5865	Kwartalnik Architektury i Urbanistyki
0023-5873	Kwartalnik Geologiczny
0023-5881	Kwartalnik Historii Kultury Materialnej
0023-589X	Kwartalnik Historii Nauki i Techniki
0023-5903	Kwartalnik Historyczny
0023-5911	Kwartalnik Neofilologiczny
0023-592X	Kwartalnik Opolski
0023-5938	Kwartalnik Pedagogiczny
0023-5946	Kybernetik *see* 0340-1200
0023-5954	Kybernetika
0023-5962	Kyklos
0023-5970	Kylteknisk Tidskrift *see* 0048-9301
0023-5989	Kymppi
0023-5997	Educational Review
0023-6004	Polar News
0023-6012	Kyoto Prefectural University of Medicine. Medical Society. Journal
0023-6020	Fire Prevention
0023-6039	Kyoto University. Bulletin of Stomatology
0023-6063	Kyoto University. Faculty of Engineering. Memoirs
0023-6071	Kyoto University. Institute for Chemical Research. Bulletin
0023-608X	Kyoto University. Journal of Mathematics
0023-6098	Kyoto University. Misaki Marine Biological Institute. Bulletin
0023-6101	Kyoto University of Education. Bulletin. Series B: Mathematics and Natural Science
0023-611X	Kypros
0023-6128	Kyrios†
0023-6136	Kyrkofoerfattningar
0023-6144	Kyushu Neuro-Psychiatry
0023-6152	Kyushu University. Faculty of Agriculture. Journal
0023-6160	Kyushu University. Faculty of Engineering. Memoirs
0023-6179	Kyushu University. Faculty of Science. Memoirs. Series D: Geology
0023-6195	Kyushu University. Research Institute for Applied Mechanics. Reports
0023-6217	L A M Y A Revista Mensual
0023-6225	L A R C Reports†
0023-6241	L & N *changed to* Seaboard System News
0023-625X	L B I News
0023-6268	L G A-Rundschau
0023-6276	L G M Mededelingen
0023-6292	L I D News Bulletin†
0023-6306	L K A B-Tidningen†
0023-6314	L K H H Accountant *see* 0147-2208
0023-6322	Laerarinnornas Missionsfoerening. Meddelande till L M F. *see* 0345-7842
0023-6330	L M S-Lingua
0023-6349	L O G A
0023-6365	L S A Bulletin
0023-6373	L S C R R C Newsletter†
0023-6381	Laurence Scott Engineering Bulletin
0023-639X	L S E Magazine
0023-6403	L S U Alumni News *changed to* L S U Magazine
0023-6411	L S U Engineering News
0023-642X	L V I Teknillingen Aikakaus-Lehti *changed to* L V I
0023-6438	Lebensmittel-Wissenschaft und Technologie
0023-6446	La-Ya'aran†
0023-6454	Lab World†
0023-6462	Labeo
0023-6470	Labo-Pharma *see* 0758-6922
0023-6489	Labor
0023-6497	Labor
0023-6500	Labor Arbitration Awards
0023-6519	Labor Chronicle
0023-6527	Labor Developments Abroad†
0023-6535	Labor Education News *changed to* Workers Education Local 189. Newsletter
0023-6543	Labor Education Viewpoints†
0023-656X	Labor History
0023-6578	Labor in Print†
0023-6586	Labor Law Journal
0023-6594	Labor Leader
0023-6616	Labor Record
0023-6632	Labor Safety Newsletter *changed to* Labor Newsletter
0023-6640	Labor Today
0023-6667	Labor World
0023-6675	Laboratoire Central des Industries Electriques. Bulletin d'Information *see* 0220-9535
0023-6683	Laboratoires Squibb. Recueil de Nouvelles†
0023-6691	Laboratorio
0023-6705	Laboratorio de Engenharia de Mocambique. Boletim Tecnico de Informacoes *changed to* Laboratorio de Engenharia de Mocambique. Boletin Tecnico
0023-6713	Soul Illustrated *changed to* Soul
0023-6721	Laboratoriums-Praxis†
0023-6748	Laboratornoe Delo
0023-6764	Laboratory Animal Science
0023-6772	Laboratory Animals
0023-6780	L A C News Letter *see* 0308-9568
0023-6799	Laboratory Digest†
0023-6810	Laboratory Equipment
0023-6829	Laboratory Equipment Digest
0023-6837	Laboratory Investigation
0023-6845	Laboratory Management
0023-6853	Laboratory Practice
0023-6888	Laborer
0023-6896	Labour and Employment Gazette
0023-690X	Labour Arbitration Cases
0023-6934	Labour Gazette
0023-6942	Labour History
0023-6950	Labour in Exile
0023-6969	Labour in Israel
0023-6977	Labour Law Journal
0023-6985	Labour Monthly†
0023-6993	Labour Organiser†
0023-7000	Labour Research
0023-7027	Labour Woman†
0023-7035	Labour World
0023-7043	Labris *changed to* Ko-Ko
0023-7051	Lacerta
0023-706X	Lach-Manoeuvre
0023-7078	Lackawanna Jurist

ISSN INDEX

ISSN	Title
0023-7086	Lacrosse
0023-7094	Lada'at
0023-7108	Ladder†
0023-7116	Laeder och Skor see 0040-4845
0023-7124	Ladies Home Journal (Inkprint Edition)
0023-7140	Ladue Public Schools Bulletin
0023-7159	Ladugaardsfoermannen
0023-7167	Lady
0023-7175	Lady see 0343-3366
0023-7183	Ladycom: The Military Lifestyle Magazine changed to Military Lifestyle Magazine
0023-7191	Lady's Circle
0023-7205	Laekartidningen
0023-7213	Laeknabladid
0023-7256	Lagena
0023-7272	Lagos Weekend
0023-7280	Lagrimal Trifurca
0023-7299	Lahey Clinic Foundation Bulletin†
0023-7310	Lajpat Bhawan Journal changed to Better Life
0023-7329	Lake Carriers' Association. Bulletin†
0023-7345	Lakeland Boating see 0744-9194
0023-7353	Lakimies
0023-7361	Lakimiesuutiset
0023-737X	Lakokrasochnye Materialy i ikh Primenenie
0023-7388	Lal-Baugh
0023-7396	Lalit Kala Contemporary
0023-740X	Lalita changed to Priya
0023-7418	Lamp (New York)
0023-7426	Lamp Journal see 0162-9077
0023-7442	Lampetten
0023-7450	Lana Moda
0023-7469	Lancashire Life
0023-7477	Lancaster County Historical Society. Journal
0023-7485	Lancaster Farming
0023-7493	Lance
0023-7515	Lanciana
0023-7523	Land
0023-7531	Land
0023-7531	Land-Consumerpart
0023-754X	Land
0023-7558	Der Land- und Forstwirtschaftliche Betrieb
0023-7574	Land and Liberty
0023-7582	Land en Water†
0023-7590	Land and Water Development see 0192-9453
0023-7612	Land and Water Law Review
0023-7639	Land Economics
0023-7655	Land Pollution Reporter
0023-768X	Land Use Digest
0023-7698	Land van Valkenburg
0023-7701	Land Worker
0023-7728	Landarzt see 0341-9835
0023-7736	Landbode (The Hague)
0023-7744	Landbote
0023-7752	Landbouw en Plantenziekten†
0023-7760	Landbouwdocumentatie
0023-7779	Landbouwweekblad
0023-7795	Landbouwmechanisatie
0023-7817	Bedrijfsontwikkeling. Editie Akkerbouw changed to Bedrijfsontwikkeling
0023-7833	Landbrukstidende
0023-7841	Koninklijk Instituut voor de Tropen. Afdeling Plattelandsontwikkeling. Landendocumentatie
0023-7868	Schleswig-Holstein Kultusminister. Nachrichtenblatt
0023-7876	Landesamtsblatt fuer das Burgenland
0023-7884	Landesgesetzblatt fuer das Land Salzburg
0023-7906	Landesmuseum fuer Naturkunde zu Muenster in Westfalen. Abhandlungen changed to Westfaelisches Museum fuer Naturkunde. Abhandlungen
0023-7922	Landesversicherungsanstalt Hessen. Nachrichten
0023-7930	Landfall
0023-7949	Landis und Gyr Mitteilungen
0023-7957	Landjugend
0023-7965	Landman changed to Mielies
0023-7973	Landmaschinen-Handwerk-Handel
0023-7981	Landmaschinen-Markt changed to Agrartechnik
0023-799X	Landowning in Scotland
0023-8007	Die Landpost
0023-8015	Landsbygdens Folk
0023-8023	Landscape
0023-8031	Landscape Architecture
0023-8058	Landschaft und Stadt
0023-8066	Landskab
0023-8074	Landstingens Tidskrift see 0282-4485
0023-8082	Fachzeitschrift fuer Alle Bereiche der Agrarkultur und laendliches Bauen changed to Landtechnik
0023-8104	Das Landvolk
0023-8112	Landwirt changed to Suedtiroler Landwirt
0023-8120	V W D - Landwirtschaft und Ernaehrung†
0023-8147	Landwirtschaftliche Forschung
0023-8163	Landwirtschaftliche Zeitschrift Rheinland
0023-8171	Landwirtschaftliches Jahrbuch der Schweiz†
0023-818X	Landwirtschaftliches Zentralblatt. Abteilung 1: Landtechnik see 0233-2655
0023-8198	Landwirtschaftliches Zentralblatt. Abteilung 2: Pflanzliche Produktion see 0233-2701
0023-8201	Landwirtschaftliches Zentralblatt. Abteilung 3: Tierzucht, Tierernaehrung, Fischerei see 0233-2752
0023-821X	Landwirtschaftliches Zentralblatt. Abteilung 4: Veterinaermedizin see 0233-2809
0023-8228	Langage Total
0023-8236	Langenbecks Archiv fuer Chirurgie
0023-8244	Langenscheidt's English Monthly†
0023-8252	Langenscheidt's Sprach-Illustrierte
0023-8279	Language-Teaching Abstracts see 0261-4448
0023-8287	Language and Automation†
0023-8295	Language and Language Behavior Abstracts see 0888-8027
0023-8309	Language and Speech
0023-8317	Language and Style
0023-8325	Language Association of Eastern Africa. Journal
0023-8333	Language Learning
0023-8341	Language Sciences†
0023-8368	Langue Francaise
0023-8376	Langues Modernes
0023-8384	Lansing Labor News
0023-8406	Lantern
0023-8414	Lantern
0023-8422	Lantern
0023-8430	Lantmaestaren
0023-8457	Lapidary Journal
0023-8473	Laputa Gazette and Faculty News†
0023-8481	Lara Lamont
0023-849X	Laerartidningen/Svensk Skoltidning
0023-8503	Lares
0023-8511	Larvae du Golden Gate
0023-852X	Laryngoscope
0023-8538	Las Polski
0023-8546	Las Vegas Voice
0023-8554	Laser changed to Laser und Optoelektronik
0023-8589	Laser Focus see 8755-1853
0023-8600	Laser Journal†
0023-8600	Laser Report
0023-8627	Chinese Studies in Philosophy
0023-8635	Last Day Messenger
0023-8651	Last Post
0023-866X	Lastauto Omnibus
0023-8678	Lastbilen
0023-8686	Lastebilen
0023-8694	Lastechniek
0023-8716	Lather†
0023-8740	Latin American Books Newsletter
0023-8759	Latin American Calendar†
0023-8767	Latin American Digest†
0023-8791	Latin American Research Review
0023-8805	Latin American Studies Association Newsletter changed to L A S A Forum
0023-8813	Latin American Theatre Review
0023-8821	Latin Teaching†
0023-883X	Latinitas
0023-8856	Latomus
0023-8872	Laettbetong
0023-8899	Latvija
0023-8902	Latvija Amerika
0023-8910	Latvijas P.S.R. Preses Hronika
0023-8937	Laufende Mitteilungen Zum Stand der Politischen Bildung in der Bundesrepublik Deutschland†
0023-8961	Laundry and Cleaning changed to Laundry and Cleaning News
0023-897X	Laundry and Cleaning International changed to Laundry & Cleaning News International
0023-8988	Laurel Messenger
0023-8996	Laurel of Phi Kappa Tau
0023-9003	Laurel Review (New Orleans) see 0145-8388
0023-9003	Laurel Review (Buckhannon)
0023-9011	Laurentian University Review
0023-902X	Laurentianum
0023-9038	Laval Administration
0023-9046	Laval Medical see 0315-5153
0023-9054	Laval Theologique et Philosophique
0023-9062	Lavender Band
0023-9070	Lavoro e Medicina†
0023-9089	Lavoro Italiano
0023-9097	Lavoro Neuropsichiatrico
0023-9119	Lavoro Sud†
0023-9135	Lavoura
0023-9143	Lavoura Arrozeira
0023-916X	Law changed to A D L Law Report
0023-9178	Law and Computer Technology see 0278-3916
0023-9186	Law and Contemporary Problems
0023-9194	Law and Order
0023-9208	Law and Policy in International Business
0023-9216	Law & Society Review
0023-9224	Law and the Social Order see 0164-4297
0023-9232	New South Wales Weekly Notes see 0312-1674
0023-9240	Law Books Published
0023-9259	Law Guardian see 0306-3348
0023-9267	Law Institute Journal
0023-9275	Law Librarian
0023-9283	Law Library Journal
0023-9291	Royal National Institute for the Blind. Law Notes. Extracts
0023-9305	Law Notes see 0094-5277
0023-9321	Law Officer†
0023-933X	Law Quarterly Review
0023-9356	Buffalo Law Review
0023-9364	Law Society Gazette
0023-9372	Law Society Journal
0023-9380	Law Society's Gazette
0023-9399	Law Thesaurus
0023-9402	Lawn Care
0023-9410	Lawn Equipment Journal changed to Outdoor Power Equipment
0023-9437	Lawyer
0023-9445	Lawyer of the Americas changed to Inter-American Law Review
0023-9453	Lawyer's Association. Journal
0023-947X	Lawyer's Medical Journal†
0023-9488	Lawyers' Recreation
0023-9518	Laymen's Movement Review changed to Catalogue of Conferences, Seminars, Workshop
0023-9526	Lazio
0023-9534	Havre changed to Escale
0023-9542	Leabharlann
0023-9550	Lead
0023-9569	Lead Abstracts see 0950-1584
0023-9577	Lead and Zinc Statistics
0023-9585	Leader†
0023-9593	Leader†
0023-9607	Leader
0023-964X	Leaflet
0023-9666	Leaguer
0023-9674	Lealtad
0023-9682	Learn†
0023-9690	Learning and Motivation
0023-9704	Learning for Living see 0141-6200
0023-9712	Learning Resources†
0023-9739	Leather
0023-9747	Leather and Shoes
0023-9755	L I R I Monthly Circular
0023-9763	Leather Manufacturer
0023-9771	Leather Science
0023-978X	Leather Titles Service†
0023-9798	Leathergoods see 0264-8555
0023-9801	Leathergoods Buyer†
0023-981X	Leatherneck
0023-9828	Leathers
0023-9836	Leaves of Twin Oaks
0023-9852	Lebanese Medical Journal
0023-9860	Lebanon. Direction Centrale de la Statistique. Bulletin Statistique Mensuel
0023-9887	Leben see 0303-4283
0023-9895	Leben und Gesundheit see 0179-7360
0023-9909	Lebende Sprachen
0023-9917	Lebendige Erde
0023-9925	Lebendige Familie changed to Praxis Bilden und Erziehen
0023-9933	Lebendige Schule†
0023-9941	Lebendiges Zeugnis
0023-995X	Lebenshilfe see 0173-9573
0023-9968	Thema Null changed to Blaue Feder
0023-9976	Lebensmittel-Grosshandel/Susswaren-Zeitung changed to Food and Nonfood
0023-9992	Lebensmittel Praxis
0024-001X	Lebensmittelhaendler see 0047-4282
0024-0028	Lebensmittelindustrie
0024-0036	Lebensmittelpost see 0047-4282
0024-0044	Lebensversicherungsmedizin
0024-0052	Lebensweiser†
0024-0060	Lebone la Kgalalelo Isibani Sobu Ngcwele changed to Lebone la Kgalalelo
0024-0079	Lecciones y Ensayos†
0024-0087	Lectura†
0024-0095	Lectura†
0024-0109	Lectura para Todos†
0024-0125	Lecture et Tradition
0024-0133	Lectures Francaises
0024-015X	Ledarforum
0024-0168	Ledarskap och Loensamhet
0024-0176	Das Leder
0024-0184	Leder Echo
0024-0192	L S L
0024-0214	Lederwaren-Report
0024-0222	Ledger†
0024-0230	Lediga Platser
0024-0249	Leeds African Studies Bulletin
0024-0257	Leeds Arts Calendar
0024-0273	Leeds Journal
0024-0281	Leeds Philosophical and Literary Society. Proceedings. Literary and Historical Section
0024-029X	Communist News
0024-0303	Left
0024-032X	Lega Navale
0024-0338	Legal Aid Briefcase changed to N L A D A Briefcase
0024-0354	Legal Eagles News changed to Lawyer-Pilots Bar Association Journal
0024-0362	Legal Executive
0024-0370	Legal Record†
0024-0389	Legerkoerier
0024-0400	Leggi
0024-0419	Leggi delle Comunita' Europee†
0024-0427	Legioen van Maria
0024-0435	Legion
0024-0451	Legionair
0024-046X	New Jersey School Boards Association. Legislative Bulletin changed to New Jersey School Boards Association. School Leader
0024-0478	Legislative Conference Reporter changed to P S C Clarion
0024-0486	Legislative Research Checklist see 0190-6623
0024-0494	Legislative Roundup†
0024-0508	Legislator
0024-0524	Legislazione Italiana
0024-0532	Legno changed to Mondolegno
0024-0540	Legon Observer†

ISSN INDEX

ISSN	Title
0024-0567	Lehigh Valley Safety News†
0024-0575	Ligstraal/Lehlasedi
0024-0591	Spark
0024-0605	Lehrer in Friseurklassen *see* 0723-7928
0024-0613	Leibesuebungen *changed to* T U S - Turnen und Sport
0024-0621	Leica-Fotografie
0024-063X	Leica Photography
0024-0648	Leicester & County Chamber of Commerce Journal
0024-0656	Leicestershire Farmer *see* 0306-0160
0024-0664	Leicestershire Historian
0024-0672	Rijksmuseum van Natuurlijke Historie. Zoologische Mededelingen
0024-0699	Leipuri
0024-0702	Leistung
0024-0710	Leisure Painter
0024-0729	Leisure Time†
0024-0737	Der Leitende Angestellte
0024-0745	Lekarz Wojskowy
0024-0761	Lemouzi
0024-0788	Lenau-Forum
0024-0796	Lenguaje y Ciencias
0024-0818	Leningradskii Universitet. Vestnik. Seriya Ekonomika, Filosofiya i Pravo
0024-0826	Leningradskii Universitet. Vestnik. Seriya Fizika i Khimiya
0024-0834	Leningradskii Universitet. Vestnik. Seriya Geologiya i Geografiya
0024-0842	Leningradskii Universitet. Vestnik. Seriya Istoriya, Yazyk i Literatura
0024-0850	Leningradskii Universitet. Vestnik. Seriya Matematika, Mekhanika i Astronomiya
0024-0869	Leninyan Ugiov
0024-0877	Lenkurt Demodulator *changed to* G T E Lenkurt Demodulator
0024-0885	Lentaja†
0024-0893	Lente (Inkprint Edition)†
0024-0907	Lenzinger Berichte
0024-0915	Leo Baeck Institut. Bulletin
0024-0923	Leodiensian
0024-094X	Leonardo: Art Science and Technology
0024-0958	Leone
0024-0966	Lepidopterist's Society. Journal
0024-0974	Lepidopterological Society of Japan. Transactions
0024-1008	Leppro *see* 0386-3980
0024-1016	Leprologia
0024-1024	Leprosy in India *changed to* Indian Journal of Leprosy
0024-1040	Lerindustrien†
0024-1059	Lernen und Leisten *see* 0340-6040
0024-1067	Les
0024-1075	Leserzeitschrift†
0024-1083	Lesestunde mit dem Grossen Freizeit-Programm
0024-1091	Leshonenu La'am
0024-1105	Lesnictvi
0024-1113	Lesnoe Khozyaistvo
0024-1121	Lesotho-Canada†
0024-1148	Lesovedenie
0024-1156	Letectvi a Kosmonautika
0024-1164	Lethaia
0024-1172	Letopis' Gazetnykh Statei
0024-1180	Letopis na Periodichna Pechat *see* 0324-0398
0024-1180	Letopis na Periodichna Pechat *see* 0324-0347
0024-1199	Letopis' Pechatnykh Proizvedenii Izobrazitel'nogo Iskusstva
0024-1202	Letopis' Zhurnal'nykh Statei
0024-1210	Letras
0024-1229	Letras de Ayer y de Hoy†
0024-1245	Letras Potosinas
0024-1261	Let's Find Out
0024-1288	Let's Live
0024-1296	Letter to Libraries *changed to* Letter to Libraries
0024-130X	Letterato
0024-1326	Lettere d'Affari
0024-1334	Lettere Italiane
0024-1350	Lettore di Provincia
0024-1369	Lettres
0024-1377	Lettres et Medecins†
0024-1385	Lettres et Poesie
0024-1393	Lettres Francaises†
0024-1407	Lettres Nouvelles†
0024-1415	Lettres Romanes
0024-1423	Lettrisme
0024-1431	Lettura Stenografica
0024-144X	Letture
0024-1458	Cineschedario - Letture Drammatiche
0024-1466	Leukemia Abstracts†
0024-1482	Leuvense Bijdragen
0024-1490	Levant Morgenland
0024-1504	Levante
0024-1512	Leveltari Kozlemenyek
0024-1520	Levende Natuur
0024-1539	Levende Talen†
0024-1555	Levend Woord
0024-1555	H L *changed to* Missets Distrifood
0024-1563	Leviathan *see* 0360-1765
0024-1571	Levnedsmiddelbladet *see* 0105-6654
0024-158X	Legislacao Federal e Marginalia
0024-1598	Lex
0024-161X	Lexington Philharmonic Society Newsletter
0024-1628	College of the Bible Quarterly *see* 0160-8770
0024-1636	Ley
0024-1652	Rijksmuseum van Natuurlijke Historie. Zoologische Verhandelingen
0024-1660	Leyland Journal†
0024-1679	Leyte-Samar Studies
0024-1687	Liaison†
0024-1709	Federation Nationale des Anciens Combattants et Coalets des Transmissions. Liaison des Transmissions
0024-1717	Liaisons
0024-1725	Liaisons Sociales
0024-1733	Al Liamm
0024-1741	Liaudies Balsas†
0024-175X	Libelle
0024-1792	Liberal Catholic
0024-1806	Liberal Context†
0024-1814	Liberal Debatt *see* 0345-3685
0024-1822	Liberal Education
0024-1830	Liberal Opinion†
0024-1849	Liberal Party Organisation. Liberal News
0024-1857	Liberal Ungdom
0024-1865	Liberated Guardian *changed to* City Star
0024-1873	Liberation
0024-1881	Liberation†
0024-189X	Liberation†
0024-1903	Liberation News Service
0024-1911	Liberation News Service
0024-1954	Liberia
0024-1962	Liberian Age
0024-1970	Liberian Law Journal
0024-1989	Liberian Studies Journal
0024-2004	Libertarian
0024-2012	Libertarian Connection *changed to* Connection (Fairfax)
0024-2020	Liberte
0024-2047	Libertijn†
0024-2055	Liberty (Washington, 1906)
0024-2063	Liberty *see* 0790-5068
0024-208X	Liberty *see* 0360-3342
0024-2098	Liberty Letter *changed to* Spotlight (Washington)
0024-2101	Libra†
0024-2128	Librairie Ancienne et Moderne. Bulletin *changed to* Bulletin du Bibliophile
0024-2144	Libraries in International Development. Newsletter†
0024-2152	Librarium
0024-2160	Library
0024-2179	Library & Information Science Abstracts
0024-2187	Library Associate†
0024-2195	Library Association Record
0024-2209	Library Binder *see* 0735-8571
0024-2217	Library Bookseller
0024-2225	State University of New York. Upstate Medical Center. Library Bulletin†
0024-2233	Library Chronicle (Philadelphia)†
0024-2241	Library Chronicle (Austin)
0024-225X	Library-College Journal *see* 0091-7281
0024-2276	Library Counselor†
0024-2284	Library for the Blind and Physically Handicapped. Newsletter†
0024-2292	Library Herald
0024-2306	Library History
0024-2330	Library Keynotes
0024-2349	Library Leaves†
0024-2357	Library Lines†
0024-2365	Contra Costa County Library Link†
0024-2373	Library Literature
0024-239X	Library Materials on Africa *see* 0305-862X
0024-2411	Library Notes†
0024-242X	Washington University. School of Medicine Library. Library Notes *changed to* Washington University. School of Medicine Library. Library Newsletter
0024-2438	Library Notes
0024-2446	North Dakota Library Notes†
0024-2454	Library Occurrent *see* 0275-777X
0024-2462	Library Opinion†
0024-2489	Library Periodicals Directory†
0024-2497	Library Progress†
0024-2500	Library Publicity Clippings†
0024-2519	Library Quarterly
0024-2527	Library Resources & Technical Services
0024-2535	Library Review
0024-2543	Library Science with a Slant to Documentation
0024-2551	Library Service News
0024-2578	Library System†
0024-2586	Library Technology Reports
0024-2594	Library Trends
0024-2608	Library World†
0024-2616	Library World *see* 0307-4803
0024-2632	L S A
0024-2640	Libreria†
0024-2659	Libreria
0024-2667	Libri
0024-2683	Libri e Riviste d'Italia
0024-273X	Libro Espanol
0024-2764	Libros†
0024-2772	Licensed Beverage Journal
0024-2780	Licensed Bookmaker & Betting Office Proprietor
0024-2802	Licensed Retailer
0024-2810	Licensee
0024-2829	Lichamelijke Opvoeding
0024-2845	Lichenologist
0024-2853	Lichtbogen
0024-287X	Lichthoeve-Kinderwerk *changed to* Lichthoeve
0024-2861	Lichttechnik *changed to* Licht
0024-2888	Licitationen
0024-2896	Licke Novine
0024-290X	Lide a Zeme
0024-2918	Lien
0024-2926	Lien Entre Meres et Peres de Pretres
0024-2942	Liens
0024-2950	Lietuviu Dienos
0024-2969	Lietuvos Fizikos Rinkinys
0024-3000	Akademiya Nauk Litovskoi S.S.R. Trudy. Seriya B *see* 0131-3851
0024-3019	Life (Chicago)
0024-3027	Life and Breath *changed to* Life & Lung
0024-3035	Life and Health *see* 0749-3509
0024-3043	Life and Health†
0024-306X	Life and Work
0024-3078	Life Association News
0024-3086	Life-Boat
0024-3094	Life Boy Link†
0024-3132	Life Insurance Planning
0024-3140	Life Insurance Selling
0024-3159	Life International†
0024-3167	Life Lines†
0024-3175	Life of Faith *changed to* Christian Family
0024-3183	Life Office Management Association. Bulletin *changed to* L.O.M.A. Resource
0024-3191	Systems and Procedures Review *changed to* L.O.M.A. Resource
0024-3205	Life Sciences (1973)
0024-3221	Life Underwriters Association of the City of New York. Bulletin
0024-3264	Ligament *changed to* Aktiviteitensektor. Maandblad
0024-3272	Die Ligdraer
0024-3299	Light and Life *see* 0162-1890
0024-3302	Light and Lighting†
0024-3310	Light Aviation
0024-3329	Light Horse *changed to* Horse & Rider
0024-3345	Light Metal Age
0024-3353	Light of New York†
0024-3361	Light of the Moon
0024-337X	Light Engineering†
0024-3388	Light Steam Power *changed to* Steam Power
0024-3396	Lightbearer
0024-340X	Lighter
0024-3418	Lighting Equipment News
0024-3426	Lighting Research and Technology
0024-3434	Ligne de Communication†
0024-3442	Ligstraal/Umsebe/Umtha
0024-3450	Liguorian
0024-3469	Liiketaloudellinen Aikakauskirja
0024-3477	Lijecnicki Vjesnik†
0024-3485	Lillabulero†
0024-3493	Lille Chirurgical
0024-3507	Lille Medical *changed to* Lille Medical
0024-3523	Limba Romana
0024-354X	Limen
0024-3558	Limi†
0024-3582	Limnological Society of Southern Africa. Newsletter *see* 0377-9688
0024-3590	Limnology and Oceanography
0024-3604	Limnos *see* 0037-0487
0024-3612	Limonadier de Paris
0024-3620	Limosa
0024-3639	Linacre Quarterly
0024-3647	Linage†
0024-3663	Lincoln Business†
0024-3671	Lincoln Herald
0024-368X	Lincoln Law Review†
0024-3698	Lincoln Library Bulletin
0024-3701	Lincolnian
0024-371X	Lincolnshire Life
0024-3728	Linde Berichte aus Technik und Wissenschaft
0024-3744	Lineagrafica
0024-3752	Linea Italiana
0024-3760	Linea Maschile e Femminile†
0024-3779	Linea Z
0024-3787	Lineamaglia
0024-3795	Linear Algebra and Its Applications
0024-3809	Linear Integrated Circuit D.A.T.A. Book *see* 0270-9988
0024-3817	Lineastruttura
0024-3825	Linen Supply News *see* 0195-0118
0024-3833	Linens/Domestics & Bath Products
0024-3841	Lingua
0024-385X	Lingua e Stile
0024-3868	Lingua Nostra
0024-3876	Lingue del Mondo
0024-3892	Linguistic Inquiry
0024-3906	Linguistic Reporter†
0024-3914	Linguistic Society of Japan. Journal
0024-3922	Linguistica
0024-3930	Linguistische Berichte
0024-3949	Linguistics
0024-3957	Linguistique
0024-3965	Lingvologia Revuo†
0024-3973	Linieofficeren
0024-399X	Link†
0024-4007	Link
0024-4015	Link-Up†
0024-4023	Linking Ring
0024-404X	Links
0024-4066	Linnean Society. Biological Journal
0024-4074	Linnean Society. Botanical Journal
0024-4082	Linnean Society. Zoological Journal
0024-4090	Linneana Belgica
0024-4104	Linn's Weekly Stamp News *see* 0161-6234
0024-4112	Linoticias†
0024-4139	Linzer Theaterzeitung
0024-4147	Linzer Woche
0024-4155	Legkaya Atletika
0024-4163	Lion (Oak Brook)

ISSN	Title
0024-4171	Lion en Espanol
0024-418X	Len i Konoplya
0024-4198	Lion
0024-4201	Lipids
0024-421X	Liquified Petroleum Gas Report *changed to* Inventories of Natural Gas Liquids & Liquified Refinery Gases
0024-4228	Liquified Natural Gas†
0024-4236	Liquor Store Magazine
0024-4244	Lira
0024-4260	Lisbon. Instituto Gulbenkian de Cienca. Arquivo. Section A. Estudos Matematicos e Fisico-Matematicos†
0024-4279	Instituto Maternal, Lisbon. Revista Clinica *see* 0302-4326
0024-4309	List-O-Tapes
0024-4317	List of Accessions to the Science Museum Library *changed to* Science Museum Library Bulletin
0024-4333	List of Selected Articles on I C A O and Civil Aviation *changed to* International Civil Aviation Organization. Library Information: Recent Accessions and Selected Articles
0024-4341	List of Technical Studies and Experimental Housing Projects†
0024-435X	Listen
0024-4384	Listen†
0024-4392	Listener
0024-4406	Listener in T V *changed to* Scene
0024-4430	Listino Ufficiale della Borsa Valori di Torino
0024-4449	Listy Cukrovarnicke
0024-4457	Listy Filologicke
0024-4465	Listy Sv. Frantiska
0024-4449X	Liteinoe Proizvodstvo
0024-4503	Literacy Discussion†
0024-4511	Literary Cavalcade
0024-452X	Literary Criterion
0024-4538	American Reference Books Annual
0024-4546	Literary Guild Newsletter†
0024-4554	Literary Half-Yearly
0024-4562	Literary Herald†
0024-4570	Literary Quarterly of the Yugoslav Pen-Centre†
0024-4589	Literary Review
0024-4597	Literary Sketches
0024-4600	Literary Studies
0024-4627	Der Literat
0024-4635	Literatur- Eildienst Roche *changed to* Hexagon Roche
0024-4643	Literatur in Wissenschaft und Unterricht
0024-4651	Literatur-Schnelldienst Kunststoffe und Kautschuk *changed to* Literatur-Schnelldienst Kunststoffe Kautschuk Fasern
0024-4678	Literatur Zum Bibliothekswesen†
0024-4686	Literatura i Mastatstva
0024-4694	Literatura Kajero
0024-4708	Literatura Ludowa
0024-4724	Literatura v Shkole
0024-4740	Literature and Ideology *see* 0702-7532
0024-4759	Literature and Psychology
0024-4767	Literature East & West
0024-4775	Literature, Music, Fine Arts
0024-4783	Literature on Economic Development and Planning - a Select Bibliography†
0024-4791	Literaturen Zbor
0024-4805	Rat fuer Formgebung. Literaturhinweise
0024-4821	Literaturna Ukrayina
0024-483X	Literaturnaya Armeniya
0024-4848	Literaturnaya Gazeta
0024-4856	Literaturnaya Rossiya
0024-4864	Literaturnyi Azerbaidzhan
0024-4872	Literaturrundschau
0024-4899	Literauur-Overzicht Personeelsaangelegenheden *changed to* Literatuurinformatie Personeelsbeleid en Orgeanisatie
0024-4902	Lithology and Mineral Resources
0024-4910	Lithopinion†
0024-4929	Lithoprinter Week *changed to* Litho Week
0024-4937	Lithos
0024-4953	Litmus
0024-4961	Litografia Oggi
0024-497X	Litologiya i Poleznye Iskopaemye
0024-4988	Litterair Paspoort†
0024-4996	Litterature de Jeunesse†
0024-5011	Little Bronzed Angel†
0024-502X	Little Flower†
0024-5054	Little Review
0024-5062	Little Ship
0024-5070	Little Square Review†
0024-5089	Lituanus
0024-5100	Liturgisches Jahrbuch
0024-5119	Life and Worship *see* 0305-4438
0024-5127	Liv og Helse†
0024-5135	Livarski Vestnik
0024-5143	Live Lines
0024-5151	Liverpool Bulletin†
0024-516X	U.S. Department of Agriculture. Livestock and Meat Situation *changed to* U.S. Department of Agriculture. Livestock and Poultry Outlook and Situation
0024-5178	Livestock Breeder Journal *changed to* Beefweek
0024-5208	Livestock Market Digest
0024-5224	Living
0024-5232	Living Blues
0024-5240	Living Church
0024-5259	Living Health Newsletter†
0024-5267	Living Judaism *changed to* Manna
0024-5275	Living Light
0024-5283	Living Museum
0024-5291	Living Tapes†
0024-5305	Living Wilderness *see* 0736-6477
0024-5313	Livingston County Agricultural News
0024-5321	Livornocronaca
0024-533X	Livre et l'Estampe
0024-5348	Livres
0024-5364	Livros de Portugal
0024-5372	Livrustkammaren
0024-5380	Livs
0024-5399	Livsmedelsteknik
0024-5402	Ljevarstvo
0024-5410	Ljusglimtar *changed to* Evangeliska Oestasienmissionen
0024-5437	Llais Llyfrau
0024-5445	Llan
0024-5453	Llangollen Broadsheet
0024-5461	Lloydia *see* 0163-3864
0024-547X	Lloyds Bank Review
0024-5488	Lloyd's Law Reports
0024-550X	Lloyd's Log
0024-5518	Local Government Administration
0024-5526	Local Government Bulletin
0024-5534	Local Government Chronicle
0024-5542	Local Government Finance *see* 0305-9014
0024-5569	Local Government Journal of Western Australia†
0024-5577	Munisipale en Openbare Dienste†
0024-5585	Local Historian
0024-5607	Local Preachers Magazine
0024-5615	Local Self-Government
0024-5623	All India Institute of Local Self Government. Quarterly Journal
0024-5631	Local Taxation†
0024-5658	Locating Gold *changed to* Locating Gold, Gems, & Minerals
0024-5666	Locations & Ventes
0024-5674	Locations Vacances
0024-5704	Lockheed Orion Service Digest
0024-5712	Lockheed Reports *changed to* Patrol Log
0024-5720	Locksmith Ledger and Security Register *changed to* Locksmith Ledger
0024-5739	Loco-Revue
0024-5747	Locomotive Engineer
0024-5755	Lodging and Food-Service News *see* 0885-6877
0024-5763	Lodigiano Sudmilano
0024-5771	Lodzki Numizmatyk
0024-578X	Loefgrenia
0024-5798	Log
0024-581X	Log Analyst
0024-5828	Log of Mystic Seaport
0024-5836	Logique et Analyse
0024-5844	Logistics Review *see* 0047-4991
0024-5852	Logistics Spectrum
0024-5887	Logos
0024-5895	Lohos
0024-5917	Lok Rajya
0024-5925	Lok Udyog†
0024-5941	Lokomotivtechnik†
0024-595X	Loktantra Samiksha
0024-5976	Lon og Virke *see* 0105-032X
0024-5984	London Archaeologist
0024-5992	London Spokesman *see* 0262-7922
0024-600X	London Calling
0024-6018	London Clinic Medical Journal†
0024-6026	London Corn Circular
0024-6034	London Diary of Social Events†
0024-6042	London Hilton Magazine
0024-6050	London Hospital Gazette†
0024-6069	London Information
0024-6077	London Letter†
0024-6085	London Magazine
0024-6093	London Mathematical Society. Bulletin
0024-6107	London Mathematical Society. Journal *see* 0024-6115
0024-6115	London Mathematical Society. Proceedings
0024-6123	London Mystery Magazine *see* 0307-9112
0024-6131	London Philatelist
0024-614X	London Review
0024-6158	London Society. Journal
0024-6166	London Times Index†
0024-6174	London Town
0024-6182	London Weekly Advertiser *changed to* London and Local Advertiser
0024-6190	London Weekly Diary of Social Events
0024-6204	Cymro Llundain
0024-6220	Long Cane News Letter
0024-6247	Long Island Builder *changed to* Builder
0024-6255	Long Island Catholic
0024-6263	Long Island Courant†
0024-628X	Long Island Forum
0024-6298	Long Island University Magazine†
0024-6301	Long Range Planning
0024-631X	Long Room
0024-6328	Longitude
0024-6336	Look†
0024-6344	Look and Learn†
0024-6352	Look & Listen
0024-6360	Look Around
0024-6379	Look at Finland
0024-6387	Look Fortnightly *changed to* Look Magazine
0024-6409	Looking Ahead *changed to* Looking Ahead
0024-6417	Looking Back
0024-6425	Lookout
0024-6433	Lookout
0024-6441	Looming
0024-645X	Loon
0024-6476	Looys
0024-6492	Lore
0024-6514	Loris
0024-6522	Los Angeles
0024-6530	Los Angeles Bar Bulletin *see* 0162-2900
0024-6549	Los Angeles Citizen
0024-6557	Los Angeles County Museum of Art. Bulletin†
0024-6565	Los Angeles County Regional Plannning Commission. Quarterly Bulletin *see* 0363-5775
0024-6573	Los Angeles Free Press
0024-6581	Image†
0024-6603	Eisenwaren Allgemeine
0024-6611	Loshen und Leben
0024-662X	Loteria
0024-6638	Lotta Contro la Tubercolosi *changed to* Lotta Contro la Tubercolosi e le Malattie Polmonari Sociali
0024-6654	Lottery Gazette
0024-6662	Lottoroscopo
0024-6670	Lotus Bleu
0024-6689	Intergroup Relations Newsletter†
0024-6719	Loughborough University of Technology Gazette
0024-6727	Louis Braille
0024-6735	Louisiana Agriculture
0024-6743	Louisiana Baptist Builder
0024-6751	Louisiana Business Review†
0024-6778	Louisiana Conservationist
0024-6786	Louisiana Dental Association. Journal
0024-6794	Louisiana Engineer
0024-6816	Louisiana History
0024-6832	Louisiana Insurer
0024-6840	Louisiana L P-Gas News
0024-6859	Louisiana Law Review
0024-6867	L L A Bulletin
0024-6875	Louisiana Methodist†
0024-6891	Louisiana-Revy
0024-6905	Louisiana Schools *see* 0162-2773
0024-6913	Louisiana Senior Citizen†
0024-6921	Louisiana State Medical Society. Journal
0024-693X	Louisiana Studies *changed to* Southern Studies: an Interdisciplinary Journal of the South
0024-6948	Louisville
0024-6956	Louvain Medical
0024-6964	Louvain Studies
0024-6980	Lov og Rett
0024-6999	Lovacki Vjesnik
0024-7014	Lovec
0024-7022	Lovejoy's Guidance Digest
0024-7030	Low Bidder
0024-7049	Low Cost Automation Review†
0024-7057	Lowell Observatory Bulletin
0024-7065	Lowry-Cocroft's Review of the Food Service Literature†
0024-7073	Loyola News *changed to* Loyola Students Association. Link
0024-7081	Loyola University of Chicago Law Journal
0024-709X	Liquefied Petroleum Gas
0024-7103	L P-Gas
0024-7111	Lraber Asarakakan Gitutyunneri
0024-7154	Lubrication Engineering
0024-7162	Lubrificazione Industriale e per Autoveicoli *see* 0391-8645
0024-7170	Lucas Engineering Review†
0024-7189	Luce
0024-7197	Luce e Immagini *changed to* Vision & Luci Sulla Via†
0024-7200	Luci Sulla Via†
0024-7219	Lucknow Librarian
0024-7235	Lucy Moda†
0024-7243	Lufkin Line†
0024-7251	Luft- und Kaeltetechnik
0024-7286	Luister
0024-7294	Lumber Co-Operator
0024-7316	Lumberman *changed to* Philippine Lumberman
0024-7332	Lumiere
0024-7340	Lumiere du Monde
0024-7359	Lumiere et Vie
0024-7367	Lumo
0024-7375	Luna Monthly *changed to* Luna
0024-7383	Luonnon Tutkija
0024-7391	Luscinia
0024-7413	Luso-Brazilian Review
0024-7421	Lustrum
0024-743X	Lutheran
0024-7448	Lutheran Education
0024-7456	Lutheran Forum
0024-7464	Lutheran Layman
0024-7472	Lutheran Libraries
0024-7480	Lutheran Messenger for the Blind
0024-7499	Lutheran Quarterly†
0024-7502	Lutheran Scholar *see* 0362-708X
0024-7510	Lutheran Sentinel
0024-7537	Lutheran Spokesman
0024-7545	Lutheran Standard
0024-7553	Lutheran Theological Journal
0024-7561	Lutheran Welfare in New Jersey *changed to* Lutheran Times in New Jersey
0024-757X	Lutheran Witness
0024-7588	Lutheran Witness-Reporter Edition†
0024-7596	Lutheran Women
0024-760X	Lutheran World†
0024-7618	Lutherische Monatshefte
0024-7626	Die Lutherkirche
0024-7634	Lutra

ISSN	Title
0024-7642	Lutte Contre le Cancer *changed to* Vivre
0024-7650	Lutte Ouvriere
0024-7669	Lux
0024-7685	Lux Vera
0024-7693	Luz
0024-7715	Luz Apostolica†
0024-7723	Luz del Cosmos†
0024-7731	Luz Y Verdad†
0024-774X	Lyd & Tone†
0024-7758	Journal of Reproductive Medicine
0024-7766	Lymphology†
0024-7774	Lynx
0024-7782	Lyon Chirurgical
0024-7812	Lyons Music News *see* 0093-0164
0024-7820	Lyric
0024-7839	Lyric Opera News
0024-7847	Lyrica Germanica†
0024-7863	Lys Mykyta
0024-7871	Lyudyna i Svit
0024-788X	M A C Flyer
0024-7898	M A C Gopher
0024-791X	M A S C A Newsletter *see* 0198-0106
0024-7944	M & B Laboratory Bulletin†
0024-7952	M B A†
0024-7960	M B A A Technical Quarterly
0024-7995	M C-Nytt
0024-8002	M D en Espanol
0024-8010	Medical Newsmagazine *changed to* M D Magazine
0024-8029	M D Moebel Interior Design *see* 0343-0642
0024-8045	M D S
0024-807X	M D'S Wife *see* 0163-0512
0024-810X	M E D *changed to* Medical Electronics
0024-8118	M E N Economic Weekly
0024-8134	M F C News
0024-8142	M F M-Moderne Fototechnik
0024-8150	M G A Bulletin *changed to* Mushroom Journal
0024-8169	M G Conquest†
0024-8185	M.H.S. Miscellany
0024-8207	M I Contact *changed to* Marconi Instruments Contact
0024-8215	M L A International Bibliography of Books and Articles on the Modern Languages and Literatures
0024-8231	M L B Log
0024-824X	M'-le Magazine de Madame†
0024-8258	M.M.E.A. Music News *see* 0147-2550
0024-8266	Astronomical Society of Southern Africa. Monthly Notes
0024-8282	M O N Y News
0024-8320	M R A Information Service *changed to* New World News
0024-8347	M R I Quarterly *changed to* Viewpoint
0024-8355	M Report
0024-8363	M S A Monthly Bulletin
0024-8398	M S H A†
0024-8428	M S O A Journal
0024-8444	M S S C Exchange
0024-8452	M S S P A Bugle†
0024-8460	M S U Business Topics†
0024-8479	M S U Mathematics Letter *changed to* M S U Mathematics Newsletter
0024-8487	M T A News†
0024-8495	Weekly Bulletin
0024-8509	M T M
0024-8517	M T T
0024-8525	M T Z
0024-8533	Meridiano Dodici†
0024-8541	Maailma ja Me
0024-855X	Maal og Minne
0024-8568	Maalarilehti
0024-8592	Drenthe
0024-8606	Maandblad Suiker Unie
0024-8614	Maandblad tegen de Kwakzalverij
0024-8630	Maandblad voor Bedrijfsadministratie en Organisatie
0024-8649	Maandblad voor de Varkensfokkerij *changed to* Maandblad Varkens
0024-8657	Maandblad voor het Land- en Tuinbouwonderwijs
0024-8665	Nederduitse Gereformeerde Kerk van Natal Gemeente Vryheid. Maandbrief
0024-8673	Maandschrift Economie
0024-869X	Maandschrift voor Kindergeneeskunde *changed to* Tijdschrift voor Kindergeneeskunde
0024-8703	Maandstatistiek Buitenlandse Handel†
0024-8711	Netherlands. Centraal Bureau voor de Statistiek. Maandstatistiek van de Bevolking
0024-872X	Netherlands. Centraal Bureau voor de Statistiek. Maandstatistiek van de Binnenlandse Handel *see* 0166-9281
0024-8738	Netherlands. Centraal Bureau voor de Statistiek. Maandstatistiek van de Buitenlandse Handel per Goederensoort
0024-8746	Netherlands. Centraal Bureau voor de Statistiek. Maandstatistiek van de Buitenlandse Handel per Land
0024-8754	Netherlands. Centraal Bureau voor de Statistiek. Maandstatistiek van de Landbouw
0024-8762	Maandstatistiek van Het Financiewezen†
0024-8770	Netherlands. Centraal Bureau voor de Statistiek. Maandstatistiek Verkeer en Vervoer
0024-8789	Maanedsskrift for Praktisk Laegegering *see* 0373-2746
0024-8797	Maanmittausinsinoori *see* 0356-7869
0024-8819	Maarakennus ja Kuljetus
0024-8827	Maatalous
0024-8835	Scientific Agricultural Society of Finland. Journal *see* 0782-4386
0024-8843	Maatschappijbelangen
0024-8886	Macabre†
0024-8894	Macaroni Journal†
0024-8908	McCall's
0024-8924	McCall's Needlework & Crafts
0024-8940	McCall's Fabrics Plus†
0024-8959	Macchine
0024-8967	Macchine e Motori Agricoli *changed to* Macchine e Motori Agricoli - I M A il Trattorista
0024-8975	McCormick Quarterly†
0024-9009	Macedonian Tribune
0024-9017	Macelleria Italiana
0024-9025	McGill Dental Review
0024-9033	McGill Journal of Education
0024-9041	McGill Law Journal
0024-905X	McGill Medical Journal
0024-9068	McGill News
0024-9076	McGill University, Montreal. Industrial Relations Centre. Review†
0024-9092	Machine and Machinery
0024-9106	Machine and Tool Blue Book
0024-9114	Machine Design
0024-9122	Machine Design & Control†
0024-9130	Machine Moderne *see* 0047-536X
0024-9149	Machine-Outil†
0024-9157	Machine Shop and Engineering Manufacture†
0024-9165	Machine Tool Engineering†
0024-9173	Machine-Tool Review†
0024-919X	Machinery and Production Engineering
0024-9203	Machinery Lloyd *changed to* International Industry
0024-9211	Machinery Market and the Machinery and Engineering Materials Gazette *changed to* Machinery Market
0024-922X	Machines and Tooling *see* 0144-6622
0024-9238	Machines Francaises†
0024-9246	Machinisme Agricole Tropical
0024-9254	Maclean's Guide *see* 0380-9552
0024-9262	Maclean's
0024-9270	McMaster University Library Research News
0024-9297	Macromolecules
0024-9300	Mad
0024-9319	Mad
0024-9327	Mad og Gaester†
0024-9335	Mada
0024-9343	Madam
0024-9351	Madam
0024-936X	Madame
0024-9378	Made in Europe *changed to* Made in Europe. General Merchandise
0024-9386	Made in Poland†
0024-9394	Mademoiselle
0024-9408	Mademoiselle Gymnast *see* 0276-1041
0024-9416	Madencilik
0024-9424	Madhumeh *changed to* Diabetic Association of India. Journal
0024-9432	Madhuri
0024-9459	Madhya Pradesh Law Journal
0024-9467	Madhya Pradesh Medical Journal†
0024-9483	Madison Avenue
0024-9513	Madison Select *changed to* Madison Magazine
0024-9521	Indonesian Journal of Geography
0024-953X	Madjalah Manager†
0024-9548	Madjalah Persatuan Dokter Gigi Indonesia
0024-9556	Madjalah Pertanian
0024-9564	Madjalah Kedokteran Surabaja *see* 0303-7932
0024-9572	Madonna *changed to* Sacred Heart Messenger
0024-9580	Madonna di Barbana
0024-9599	Madonna di Castelmonte
0024-9602	Madras Agricultural Journal
0024-9610	Madras Labour Gazette. *changed to* Tamil Nadu Labour Journal
0024-9629	Spain. Consejo Superior de Investigaciones Cientificas. Instituto de Farmacologia Experimental. Archivos *changed to* Archivos de Farmacologia y Toxicologia
0024-9637	Madrono
0024-9645	Danish Dairy Industry
0024-9653	Maelstrom†
0024-9661	Der Maerker
0024-967X	Maerkische Zeitung
0024-9688	Maerklin-Magazin
0024-9696	Maestro
0024-9718	Mafeking Mail and Botswana Guardian
0024-9726	Magadh University Journal
0024-9750	Magazin fuer Fortschrittliche Haustechnik und Wohnkultur†
0024-9769	Magazin fuer Haus und Wohnung
0024-9785	Magazin Vier und Zwanzig *changed to* Initiative
0024-9793	Media Industry Newsletter *changed to* M I N Media Industry Newsletter
0024-9807	Magazine Litteraire
0024-9815	Maclean *see* 0383-8714
0024-9823	Magazine of Bank Administration *changed to* Bank Administration
0024-9831	Magazine of Concrete Research
0024-984X	Magazine of Fantasy and Science Fiction
0024-9858	Magazine of Wall Street *changed to* Wall Street and U S Business News
0024-9866	Magazyn Polski
0024-9874	Magazzini e Trasporti *changed to* Magazzini e Trasporti - Logistica
0024-9890	Maghreb *see* 0336-6324
0024-9904	Magic Cauldron
0024-9912	"Magische" Welt
0024-9920	Magistrate
0024-9947	Maglie Calze Industria
0024-9955	Magna Graecia
0024-9963	Magneet-Revue†
0024-9971	Magistrate
0024-998X	Magnetohydrodynamics
0024-9998	Kongresszentralblatt fuer die Gesamte Innere Medizin *changed to* Zentralblatt Innere Medizin
0025-0007	Magnificat
0025-0015	Magnitnaya Gidrodinamika
0025-0023	Magnus *see* 0165-9677
0025-0031	Maguey†
0025-004X	Magyar Allatorvosok Lapja
0025-0058	Magyar Aluminium
0025-0066	Magyar Belorovosi Archivum *see* 0133-5464
0025-0074	Magyar Epitoipar
0025-0082	Magyar Epitomuveszet
0025-0090	Magyar Filozofiai Szemle
0025-0104	Magyar Fizikai Folyoirat
0025-0112	Magyar Folyoiratok Repertoriuma *see* 0133-6894
0025-0120	Magyar Geofizika
0025-0147	Magyar Jog
0025-0155	Magyar Kemiai Folyoirat
0025-0163	Magyar Kemikusok Lapja
0025-0171	Magyar Konyvszemle
0025-018X	Magyar Mezogazdasag
0025-0198	Magyar Mezogazdasagi Bibliografia
0025-021X	Magyar Noorvosok Lapja
0025-0228	Magyar Nyelv
0025-0236	Magyar Nyelvor
0025-0244	Magyar Onkologia
0025-0252	Magyar Orvosi Bibliografia
0025-0260	Magyar Pedagogia
0025-0279	Magyar Pszichologiai Szemle
0025-0287	Magyar Radiologia
0025-0295	Magyar Sebeszet
0025-0309	Magyar Textiltechnika
0025-0317	Magyar Traumatologia, Orthopedia es Helyreallito-Sebeszet
0025-0325	Magyar Tudomany
0025-0333	Magyar Tudomanyos Akademia. Biologiai Tudomanyok Osztalya. Kozlemenyek†
0025-035X	Magyar Tudomanyos Akademia. Matematikai es Fizikai Tudomanyok Osztalya. Kozlemenyek *see* 0133-3399
0025-0368	Magyar Tudomanyos Akademia. Nyelv- es Irodalomtudomanyi Osztaly. Kozlemenyek†
0025-0376	Magyar Tudomanyos Akademia. Filozofiai es Tortenettudomanyi Osztaly. Kozlemenyek†
0025-0384	Magyar Zene
0025-0392	Maharashtra
0025-0406	Maha Bodhi
0025-0414	Mahajanmer Lagna
0025-0422	Maharaja Sayajirao University of Baroda. Journal
0025-0430	Maharashtra Co-Operative Quarterly
0025-0449	Maharashtra, India. Directorate of Industries. Industrial Bulletin†
0025-0465	Maharashtra Law Journal
0025-0473	Maharashtra Parichaya†
0025-0481	Maharashtra Quarterly Bulletin of Economics and Statistics
0025-049X	Mahenjodaro
0025-0503	Mahfil: a Quarterly of South Asian Literature *see* 0091-5637
0025-0511	Die Mahnung
0025-052X	Maehrisch-Schlesische Heimat†
0025-0538	Maia
0025-0562	Mail Trade
0025-0570	Main Currents in Modern Thought†
0025-0597	Main Roads†
0025-0600	Main Sheet
0025-0619	Maine Business Indicators
0025-0643	Maine Fish and Game Magazine *see* 0360-005X
0025-0651	Maine Law Review
0025-0678	Maine Life Magazine
0025-0686	Maine Manpower *changed to* Maine Labor Market Digest
0025-0694	Maine Medical Association. Journal†
0025-0708	Maine Nature†
0025-0716	Maine, New Hampshire, Vermont Beverage Journal
0025-0732	Maine on the Grow *changed to* Mark Maine News
0025-0759	Maine State Labor News *changed to* Maine Labor News
0025-0775	Maine Teacher
0025-0783	Maine Times
0025-0791	Maine Townsman
0025-0805	Maine Water Utilities Association. Journal
0025-0813	Mainichi Graphic
0025-083X	Mainliner *changed to* United
0025-0848	Mainly
0025-0856	Mainostaja *changed to* Mark Markkinoinnin Ammattilenti
0025-0864	Mainosuutiset
0025-0872	Maintenance *changed to* Maintenance Management
0025-0880	Maintenance
0025-0899	Maintenance Engineering†

ISSN INDEX

ISSN	Title
0025-0910	Maintenance News†
0025-0929	Maintenance Supplies
0025-0937	Maison-Dieu
0025-0945	Maison et Jardin
0025-0953	Maison Francaise
0025-0988	Maitre Electricien
0025-0996	Maitre Imprimeur
0025-1003	International Phonetic Association. Journal
0025-102X	Majallah†
0025-1038	Diwan al-Tadween al-Qanouni Majallat *changed to* Adala
0025-1046	Majallat Shi'r
0025-1089	Makedonski Jazik
0025-1119	Makerere Medical Journal
0025-1127	Matekon
0025-1135	Makina Muehendisleri Odasi Haftalik Haberler Gazetesi
0025-1151	Making Music†
0025-116X	Makromolekulare Chemie
0025-1178	Mala Ukrstenica
0025-1186	Malabar Herald†
0025-1208	Maladosts'
0025-1216	Malahat Review
0025-1224	Malamalama†
0025-1232	Maaleri
0025-1240	Malawi Mwezi Uno/Malawi This Month *changed to* Boma Lathu
0025-1267	Malawi Patent Journal and Trade Marks Journal
0025-1275	Malayan Forester *see* 0302-2935
0025-1283	Malayan Law Journal
0025-1291	Malayan Nature Journal
0025-1305	Malaysia†
0025-1313	Quarterly Bulletin of Statistics Relating to the Mining Industry of Malaysia
0025-1321	Malaysian Agricultural Journal
0025-133X	Malaysian Journal of Education *changed to* South-East Asian Journal of Educational Studies
0025-1348	Malaysian Management Review
0025-1364	Malermesteren
0025-1372	Malerzeitung Drei Schilde
0025-1380	Mallasjuomat *see* 0356-3014
0025-1399	Mallige
0025-1402	Malm *changed to* Graengeskontakten
0025-1410	Malmoe Museum. Aktuellt†
0025-1429	Studia Historyczne
0025-1437	Malta. Central Office of Statistics. Quarterly Digest of Statistics
0025-1445	Maltechnik-Restauro
0025-1453	Malyatko
0025-1461	Mammalia
0025-147X	Mamme e Bimbi
0025-1496	Man
0025-150X	Man and His Music†
0025-1518	Man and Metal†
0025-1526	Man and Society†
0025-1534	Man and World
0025-1542	Man-Environment-Communication Center Report†
0025-1550	Man - Environment Systems
0025-1569	Man in India
0025-1577	Man in New Guinea *changed to* Research in Melanesia
0025-1615	Manab Mon
0025-1623	Manage
0025-1631	Management†
0025-164X	Management
0025-1658	Management
0025-1666	Management Abstracts *see* 0307-3580
0025-1674	Management Accountant
0025-1682	Management Accounting
0025-1690	Management Accounting
0025-1704	Management & Operations†
0025-1712	Management Australia†
0025-1720	Management Consultant†
0025-1739	Management Controls *changed to* Management Focus
0025-1747	Management Decision
0025-1771	Management Ideas
0025-178X	Management in Nigeria
0025-1798	Management Index†
0025-1801	Management Industrial *see* 0374-4795
0025-181X	Management International Review
0025-1828	Management Japan
0025-1836	Management Horizons
0025-1844	Management News *changed to* Managers' Forum
0025-1860	Management Quarterly
0025-1895	Management Review
0025-1909	Management Science
0025-1925	Management Today
0025-1933	Management's Bibliographic Data†
0025-1941	Managerial Planning *see* 0094-064X
0025-195X	Manager's Letter†
0025-1968	Manager's Magazine
0025-1976	Manas
0025-1984	Manas
0025-1992	Manchester Chamber of Commerce. Record
0025-200X	Manchester Guardian Weekly
0025-2018	Manchester Medical Gazette *see* 0261-7099
0025-2026	Manchester Review†
0025-2034	Manchester School of Economic and Social Studies
0025-2042	Manchete *changed to* Manchete Esportiva
0025-2077	Manequim
0025-2085	Manhattan Almanac *changed to* New York Almanac
0025-2093	Manhattan College Engineer
0025-2107	Manhattan East
0025-2123	Manhattan Review†
0025-2166	Manifold
0025-2174	Manion Forum†
0025-2182	Manitoba *changed to* Manitoba Business Review
0025-2190	Manitoba Archaeological Newsletter *see* 0705-2669
0025-2204	Manitoba Association of School Librarians Newsletter *see* 0315-9124
0025-2239	Manitoba Co-Operator
0025-2247	Manitoba Dental Association. Bulletin
0025-2255	Manitoba Medical Review†
0025-2271	Manitoba Professional Engineer
0025-2298	Manitoban
0025-231X	Mankato State Daily Reporter *changed to* Mankato State Reporter
0025-2328	Mankind
0025-2336	Mankind†
0025-2344	Mankind Quarterly
0025-2352	Mannskapsavisa *see* 0332-9062
0025-2360	Mannus *changed to* Volksleben
0025-2379	Manoir-Express *changed to* Manoir-Echo
0025-2387	Manovella
0025-2395	Manpower Magazine *changed to* Worklife Magazine
0025-2409	Manpower and Applied Psychology
0025-2433	Manpower Trends *changed to* Maryland Labor Market Dimensions
0025-2441	ManRoot†
0025-245X	Man's Conquest†
0025-2468	Man's Illustrated†
0025-2476	Man's Magazine
0025-2484	Manse Mail†
0025-2506	Mantova
0025-2514	Manuelle Medizin
0025-2522	Manufacturers Agent
0025-2530	Manufacturers' Monthly
0025-2549	Marketing in Action & Manufacturing and the Law *changed to* Your Business and the Law
0025-2557	Manufacturing Chemist and Aerosol News
0025-2565	Manufacturing Clothier
0025-2573	Manufacturing Confectioner
0025-2581	Manufacturing Optics International†
0025-259X	Manufaktur *see* 0332-5520
0025-2603	Manuscripta
0025-2611	Manuscripta Mathematica
0025-262X	Manuscripts
0025-2638	Manuskripte
0025-2646	Manutencion y Almacenaje
0025-2654	Manutention-Stockage *changed to* Logistiques Magazine
0025-2662	Manutention Mecanique et Automation
0025-2670	Many Smokes *changed to* Wildfire
0025-2689	Mapocho†
0025-2697	Die Mappe
0025-2700	Maquinas & Metais
0025-2719	Maquinas y Equipos
0025-2727	Mar *changed to* Clube Naval Revista
0025-2735	Mar y Pesca
0025-2743	Marathon World
0025-2751	Marathwada University Journal
0025-2778	Marburger Umschau†
0025-2808	March of Education†
0025-2824	Marcha
0025-2840	Marche Suisse des Machines
0025-2859	Marches Tropicaux et Mediterraneens
0025-2867	Marcolian
0025-2883	Marconi Review *see* 0264-9187
0025-2891	Marechal
0025-2905	Maree de France
0025-2913	Marg
0025-2921	Margin
0025-293X	Marginales
0025-2948	Marginalien
0025-2956	Margriet
0025-2972	Maria
0025-2980	Mariages
0025-2999	Mariahilfer Pfarrbote
0025-3006	Marian†
0025-3014	Marianist
0025-3022	Mariannhill
0025-3049	Marie-Claire
0025-3057	Marie-France
0025-3065	Regard de Foi
0025-3073	Marien Report†
0025-309X	Marina Italiana
0025-3103	Marina Mercantile
0025-312X	Marine & Recreation News
0025-3138	Marine and Air Catering†
0025-3146	Marine Biological Association of India. Journal
0025-3154	Marine Biological Association of the United Kingdom. Journal
0025-3162	Marine Biology
0025-3170	Marine Corps Gazette
0025-3197	Marine Digest
0025-3200	Marine Engineer and Naval Architect *changed to* Shipbuilding & Marine Engineering International
0025-3219	Marine Engineering/Log
0025-3227	Marine Geology
0025-3235	Marine Geophysical Researches
0025-3243	Marine News
0025-3251	Marine Observer
0025-326X	Marine Pollution Bulletin
0025-3278	Marine Products *changed to* Marine Retailer
0025-3286	Marine Resources Digest/Marine Biology Digest†
0025-3294	Marine-Rundschau
0025-3308	Marine Science Contents Tables
0025-3316	Marine Technology
0025-3324	Marine Technology Society Journal
0025-3332	Marine Equipment News
0025-3340	Marineblad
0025-3359	Mariner's Mirror
0025-3367	Mariners Weather Log
0025-3375	Marinnytt
0025-3383	Marion
0025-3391	Maritime *see* 0161-9373
0025-3405	Maritime Co-Operator *see* 0703-5357
0025-3413	Maritime Command Trident
0025-3421	Maritime Exchange Bulletin *changed to* Maritime Association of the Port of New York-New Jersey. Newsletter
0025-343X	Maritime Farmer and Co-Operative Dairyman
0025-3448	Maritime Reporter and Engineering News
0025-3464	Maritime Worker
0025-3472	Maritimes
0025-3480	Marjolaine
0025-3499	Mark Twain Journal
0025-3502	Markedsfoering
0025-3510	Markedskommunikasjon†
0025-3529	Marker *changed to* Arch
0025-3537	Market
0025-3545	West Virginia. Department of Agriculture. Market Bulletin
0025-3553	Market Frontier News
0025-3561	Market Industries News
0025-357X	Market Place†
0025-3588	Market Research *see* 0308-3047
0025-3596	Market Research Abstracts
0025-360X	Market Research Facts and Trends
0025-3618	Market Research Society. Journal
0025-3634	Marketing
0025-3642	Marketing
0025-3650	Marketing
0025-3677	U.S. Department of Agriculture. Economic Research Service. Marketing and Transport Situation *see* 0099-1066
0025-3685	Marketing/Communications†
0025-3707	Marketing Image
0025-3723	Marketing in Europe
0025-3731	Marketing in Hungary†
0025-374X	Marketing Information Guide†
0025-3774	Marketing Journal
0025-3790	Marketing News
0025-3812	Marketing World†
0025-3820	Markham Review
0025-3839	Marking Industry
0025-3847	Markkinointi-Myyntimiehet *changed to* Mark Markkinoinnin Ammattilenti
0025-3855	Marknaden
0025-3863	Markt
0025-3871	Marktwirtschaft *see* 0302-6671
0025-388X	Maroc-Medical†
0025-3901	Maroquinerie, Sellerie et Bagages de France
0025-391X	Marple's Business Roundup *see* 0279-960X
0025-3928	Marquee
0025-3936	Marques Internationales
0025-3944	Marquetarian
0025-3952	Marquette Business Review†
0025-3960	Marquette Engineer
0025-3979	Marquette Journal
0025-3987	Marquette Law Review
0025-3995	Marquette Tribune
0025-4002	Marquette University Magazine *changed to* Marquette
0025-4010	Marriage *changed to* Marriage and Family Living
0025-4029	Mars in Cathedra
0025-4037	Mars-Magazine
0025-4053	Marseille Medical
0025-4061	Mart
0025-4088	Chambre de Commerce et d'Industrie de la Martinique. Bulletin *see* 0396-2458
0025-4096	Maruee
0025-410X	Marx Memorial Library. Quarterly Bulletin
0025-4118	Marxism Today
0025-4126	Marxist Studies
0025-4134	Marxist Veekshanam
0025-4142	Maryknoll
0025-4150	Maryland and Delaware Genealogist
0025-4169	Baptist True Union
0025-4177	Maryland Bar Journal
0025-4185	Maryland C. P. A. Quarterly†
0025-4193	Maryland Conservationist†
0025-4207	Maryland Crime Report *changed to* Maryland Crime Control Directory
0025-4215	Maryland-Delaware-D. C. Press News
0025-4223	Maryland Fruit Grower
0025-4231	Maryland Herpetological Society. Bulletin
0025-424X	Maryland Historian
0025-4258	Maryland Historical Magazine
0025-4266	Maryland History Notes *changed to* Maryland Historical Society. News and Notes
0025-4274	Maryland Horse
0025-4282	Maryland Law Review
0025-4290	Maryland *changed to* Maryland Magazine
0025-4304	Maryland Municipal News *changed to* Municipal Maryland
0025-4312	Maryland Music Educator
0025-4339	Maryland P T A Bulletin
0025-4347	Maryland Pharmacist
0025-4355	Maryland State Dental Association. Journal

1266 ISSN INDEX

0025-4363 Maryland State Medical Journal *changed to* Maryland Medical Journal
0025-4371 Maryland Teacher†
0025-4398 Maryland Veterinarian†
0025-441X Mas Chistes†
0025-4428 Masada
0025-4436 Masalah Bangunan†
0025-4444 Die Maschine
0025-4460 Maschinen- und Stahlbauindustrie in Oesterreich *changed to* Maschinen und Stahlbau
0025-4479 Maschinenbau†
0025-4487 Maschinenbau und Fertigungstechnik der U d S S R
0025-4495 Maschinenbautechnik
0025-4517 Maschinenschaden
0025-4533 Maschinenwelt-Elektrotechnik
0025-4541 MascuLines
0025-455X Mashinostroene
0025-4568 Mashinostroitel'
0025-4576 Mashinovedenie
0025-4584 Mashriq
0025-4606 Maske und Kothurn
0025-4614 Maskin *changed to* Produksion
0025-4622 Maskinbefaelet
0025-4630 Maskinstationen *see* 0109-0291
0025-4649 Maslozhirovaya Promyshlennost'
0025-4657 Mason Clinic. Bulletin *changed to* Virginia Mason Clinic Bulletin
0025-4665 Masonic Record
0025-4681 Masonry
0025-469X Masque
0025-4703 Masque
0025-4711 Masque
0025-472X Mass Media Ministries. Bi-Weekly Newsletter *changed to* Mass Media Newsletter
0025-4738 Mass Spectrometry Bulletin
0025-4762 Massachusetts Bureau of Library Extension. Newsletter *changed to* Currents (Boston)
0025-4770 Massachusetts C P A Review
0025-4789 Massachusetts College of Pharmacy. Bulletin
0025-4797 Massachusetts Daily Collegian
0025-4800 Massachusetts Dental Society. Journal
0025-4819 Massachusetts Heritage†
0025-4827 Massachusetts Institute of Technology. Research Laboratory of Electronics. Quarterly Progress Report *see* 0163-9218
0025-4835 Massachusetts Law Quarterly *see* 0163-1411
0025-4843 Massachusetts Nurses Association. Bulletin *see* 0163-0784
0025-4851 Massachusetts Physician *see* 0192-2963
0025-486X Massachusetts Professional Engineer *changed to* New England Engineering Journal
0025-4878 Massachusetts Review
0025-4894 Massachusetts State Labor Council AFL-CIO Newsletter
0025-4908 Massachusetts Teacher†
0025-4916 Massachusetts Trends in Employment and Unemployment *changed to* Massachusetts Trends, Labor Force, Employment, Unemployment
0025-4924 Massachusetts Wildlife
0025-4932 Massimario de Il Foro Italiano
0025-4940 Massimario della Giurisprudenza Italiana
0025-4959 Massimario di Giurisprudenza del Lavoro
0025-4975 Massis
0025-4983 Master Baker, Confectioner & Caterer
0025-4991 Master Builders' Journal
0025-5009 Master Carriers Journal *changed to* Freight Carriers
0025-5017 Master Detective
0025-5025 Master Drawings
0025-5041 Master Plumber
0025-505X Master Plumber and Heating Contractor†
0025-5092 Masterpainter *changed to* British Decorator
0025-5106 Masters Abstracts
0025-5114 Master's Thesis Abstracts Bulletin†
0025-5122 Masthead
0025-5130 Mate *changed to* Climate
0025-5149 Matemaattisten Aineiden Aikakauskirja *changed to* Dimensio
0025-5157 Matematicheskii Sbornik
0025-5165 Matematicki Vesnik
0025-5173 Mathematica Slovaca
0025-5181 Matematika v Shkole
0025-519X Matematikai Lapok
0025-522X Mater Ecclesiae *changed to* Ecclesia Mater
0025-5238 Materia Medica Nordmark†
0025-5246 Materia Medica Polona
0025-5254 Materiaal, Metodiek, Mededelingen *changed to* M.3
0025-5262 Material Handling Engineering
0025-5270 Material und Organismen
0025-5289 Materiale Plastice
0025-5297 Materialehaandtering og Transport Nyt *see* 0106-1666
0025-5300 Materialpruefung
0025-5319 Materials Engineering
0025-5327 Materials Evaluation
0025-5335 Materials Handling and Management†
0025-5343 Materials Management & Distribution
0025-5351 Materials Handling News
0025-536X Materials on Asia and Africa-Accession list and Review *see* 0913-025X
0025-5378 Materials Protection *see* 0094-1492
0025-5386 Materials Reclamation Weekly
0025-5394 Materials Research and Standards/MIRS *see* 0090-1210
0025-5408 Materials Research Bulletin
0025-5416 Materials Science and Engineering
0025-5432 Materiaux & Constructions
0025-5440 Materidouska
0025-5459 Materie Plastiche ed Elastomeri
0025-5467 Materiel d'Enterprise *changed to* Construction
0025-5475 Maternal and Child Care†
0025-5491 Maternidade e Infancia
0025-5505 Mathematica
0025-5513 Mathematica Japonica
0025-5521 Mathematica Scandinavica
0025-553X Mathematicae Notae
0025-5548 Mathematical Algorithms†
0025-5556 Mathematical Association of India. Bulletin
0025-5564 Mathematical Biosciences
0025-5572 Mathematical Gazette
0025-5580 Mathematical Log
0025-5602 Mathematical Pie
0025-5610 Mathematical Programming
0025-5629 Mathematical Reviews
0025-5637 Mathematical Sciences Employment Register†
0025-5645 Mathematical Society of Japan. Journal
0025-5653 Mathematical Spectrum
0025-5661 Mathematical Systems Theory
0025-567X Matematicheskie Zametki
0025-570X Mathematics Magazine
0025-5718 Mathematics of Computation
0025-5726 Mathematics of the U S S R-Izvestiya
0025-5734 Mathematics of the U S S R-Sbornik
0025-5742 Mathematics Student
0025-5750 Mathematics Student Journal *see* 0095-7089
0025-5769 Mathematics Teacher
0025-5785 Mathematics Teaching
0025-5793 Mathematika
0025-5807 Der Mathematikunterricht
0025-5831 Mathematische Annalen
0025-584X Mathematische Nachrichten
0025-5858 Universitaet Hamburg. Mathematisches Seminar. Abhandlungen
0025-5866 Der Mathematische und Naturwissenschaftliche Unterricht
0025-5874 Mathematische Zeitschrift
0025-5904 Mathitiki Estia
0025-5912 Mati
0025-5920 Matica
0025-5939 Letopis Matice Srpske
0025-5955 Matilda Ziegler Magazine for the Blind
0025-5963 Matkailumaailma *see* 0359-0607
0025-598X Matrix *changed to* Professional Communicator
0025-5998 Matrix and Tensor Quarterly†
0025-6021 Mature Years
0025-603X Mature Years-New Directions†
0025-6048 Mauricien Medical
0025-6056 Mauritius. Central Statistical Office. Quarterly Digest of Statistics *changed to* Mauritius. Central Statistical Office. Bi-Annual Digest of Statistics
0025-6064 Mauritius Times
0025-6072 Mausolee
0025-6099 Mavoschool *changed to* Nieuw Zicht
0025-6102 Max-Planck-Gesellschaft zur Foerderung der Wissenschaften Mitteilungen *see* 0341-7778
0025-6129 May Day Pictorial News
0025-6137 May Trends
0025-6153 Maydica
0025-6161 Mayfair
0025-617X Mayfair News *changed to* NewsGleaner - Mayfair - Northeast Edition
0025-6188 Mayibuye
0025-6196 Mayo Clinic Proceedings
0025-620X Mazdaznan - Blatt
0025-6218 Mazputnins
0025-6234 Mbioni
0025-6242 Mvelaphanda *see* 0250-1910
0025-6269 Me
0025-6277 Me Naiset
0025-6285 Meander
0025-6293 Meanjin Quarterly *changed to* Meanjin
0025-6307 Measurement and Evaluation in Guidance *see* 0748-1756
0025-6315 National Council on Measurement in Education. Measurement News *see* 0731-1745
0025-6323 Measurements and Data *see* 0148-0057
0025-6331 Measuring for Medicine & the Life Sciences†
0025-634X Meat†
0025-6358 Meat Board Reports
0025-6366 Meat Industry *changed to* Meat Industry
0025-6374 Meat Industry
0025-6390 Meat Processing *changed to* Meat Processing
0025-6412 Meat Trades Journal
0025-6420 Mecanica Popular
0025-6447 M A G *see* 0531-755X
0025-6455 Meccanica†
0025-6463 Meccano Magazine†
0025-6471 Mech
0025-6501 Mechanical Engineering
0025-651X Mechanical Engineering News
0025-6528 Mechanical Handling *see* 0025-5351
0025-6536 Mechanical Sciences Abstracts *changed to* Mechanical Sciences
0025-6544 Mechanics of Solids
0025-6552 Mechanik
0025-6560 Mechanisch Transport en Opslag *changed to* Bedrijfstransport
0025-6579 South African Materials Handling News *changed to* Promat News
0025-6587 Mechanix Illustrated *see* 8755-0423
0025-6595 Mechanizacia
0025-6609 Mecman - Technique
0025-6625 Medailles
0025-6633 Medal Collector
0025-6641 MedBooks†
0025-665X Medborgaren
0025-6668 Norske Myrselskap. Meddelelser *see* 0332-5229
0025-6676 Meddelelser om Groenland *see* 0106-1046
0025-6676 Meddelelser om Groenland *see* 0106-1054
0025-6676 Meddelelser om Groenland *see* 0106-1062
0025-6692 Medecin du Quebec
0025-6714 Etudes Medicales
0025-6722 Medecine du Sport
0025-6730 Medecine et Gastronomie†
0025-6749 Medecine et Hygiene
0025-6757 Medecine et Travail
0025-6773 Medecine Infantile
0025-6781 Medecine Interne†
0025-6811 Medecine Practicienne†
0025-682X Medecine Tropicale
0025-6838 Medecins de Groupe
0025-6854 Bedrijfsontwikkeling. Editie Tuinbouw *changed to* Bedrijfsontwikkeling
0025-6870 Medhjalparen *see* 0349-2559
0025-6889 Media†
0025-6897 Media & Methods
0025-6900 Media Decisions *see* 0195-4296
0025-6919 Media-Informatiedienst
0025-6927 Medianite
0025-6943 Medical Abstract Service†
0025-6951 Medical Affairs *see* 0092-8577
0025-696X Medical & Biological Engineering *see* 0140-0118
0025-6978 Medical and Biological Illustration *see* 0140-511X
0025-6986 Medical Annals of the District of Columbia†
0025-7001 Medical Aspects of Human Sexuality
0025-701X Medical Association for Prevention of War. Proceedings *see* 0748-8009
0025-7028 Medical Association of Georgia. Journal
0025-7036 Medical Association of Thailand. Journal
0025-7044 Medical Association of the State of Alabama. Journal *see* 0738-4947
0025-7060 Medical Book News
0025-7079 Medical Care
0025-7087 Medical Care Review
0025-7095 Medical Centre Journal
0025-7109 Medical Checklist
0025-7117 Medical Chronicle
0025-7125 Medical Clinics of North America
0025-7133 Medical College and Hospital, Calcutta. Bulletin
0025-7141 Medical College of Virginia Quarterly†
0025-715X Medical Counterpoint†
0025-7168 Medical Digest†
0025-7176 Medical Digest *changed to* Medical Digest (1979) Education in Family Medicine
0025-7184 Medical Digest
0025-7192 Medical Ecology and Clinical Research†
0025-7206 Medical Economics
0025-7222 Medical Electronics & Communications Abstracts
0025-7230 Medical Electronics News *changed to* Medical Electronics and Equipment News
0025-7257 Medical Group Management
0025-7265 Medical Group News *changed to* Medical Group News & In-Office Testing Advances
0025-7273 Medical History
0025-729X Medical Journal of Australia
0025-7303 Medical Journal of Malaya *see* 0300-5283
0025-7311 Medical Lab *see* 0023-6845
0025-732X Medical Letter on Drugs and Therapeutics
0025-7338 Medical Library Association. Bulletin
0025-7346 National Library of Medicine. Current Catalog Proofsheets
0025-7354 Medical Marketing & Media
0025-7370 Medical Missionary News
0025-7389 Medical Missionary *changed to* Medical Mission Sisters News
0025-7397 Medical-Moral Newsletter
0025-7400 Medical Officer *see* 0300-8347
0025-7435 Medical Post
0025-7451 Medical Quarterly *see* 0046-9130
0025-746X Medical Radiography and Photography
0025-7478 Medical Record
0025-7486 Medical Record News *see* 0273-9976
0025-7494 Medical Research Bulletin†
0025-7508 Medical Research Engineering†
0025-7524 Medical Society of New Jersey. Journal *changed to* New Jersey Medicine
0025-7532 Medical Society of the County of Kings and Academy of Medicine of Brooklyn. Bulletin *changed to* K C M S Bulletin

ISSN INDEX   1267

ISSN	Title
0025-7540	Medical Socioeconomic Research Sources†
0025-7559	Medical Staff in Action†
0025-7567	Medical-Surgical Review†
0025-7583	Medical Times
0025-7605	Medical Tribune *see* 0279-9340
0025-7613	Medical University of South Carolina. Medical University News *changed to* Medical University of South Carolina. Medical University Review
0025-7621	Medical World
0025-763X	Medical World News
0025-7648	Medicamenta†
0025-7656	Medicamentos de Actualidad *changed to* Medicamentos de Actualidad/Drugs of Today
0025-7664	Medicamundi
0025-7672	Medicare Report
0025-7680	Medicina
0025-7699	Medicina
0025-7702	Medicina
0025-7729	Medicina
0025-7753	Medicina Clinica
0025-7761	Medicina Clinica e Sperimentale†
0025-777X	Medicina Contemporanea†
0025-7788	Medicina Cutanea *see* 0210-5187
0025-7796	Medicina Danas
0025-7818	Medicina del Lavoro
0025-7826	Medicina Dello Sport
0025-7834	Medicina e Morale†
0025-7842	Medicina Espanola
0025-7850	Journal of Medicine *changed to* Journal of Medicine (Clinical, Experimental and Theoretical)
0025-7869	Revista de Medicina Interna, Neurologie, Psihiatrie, Neuro-Chirurgie, Dermato-Venerologie. Medicina Interna
0025-7877	Medicina Nei Secoli
0025-7893	Medicina Psicosomatica
0025-7907	Medicina Rural†
0025-7915	Medicina Sociale
0025-7923	Medicina Tedesca†
0025-7931	Respiration
0025-794X	Medicina Tropical *changed to* Revista Cubana de Medicina Tropical
0025-7958	Medicina Tropical
0025-7966	Medicinar
0025-7974	Medicine
0025-7982	Medicine and Medicaments Courier
0025-7990	Medicine and Science in Sports *see* 0195-9131
0025-8008	Medicine & Surgery
0025-8016	Medecine Europeene
0025-8032	Medicine Today†
0025-8040	Medicinsk Forum
0025-8059	Medicinska Foereningarnas Tidskrift *see* 0347-0989
0025-8067	Medicinska Revija
0025-8075	Meditsinskaya Tekhnika
0025-8091	Medicinski Glasnik
0025-8105	Medicinski Pregled
0025-8113	Medicinski Radnik
0025-8121	Medicinski Razgledi
0025-813X	Medico†
0025-8148	Medico d'Italia
0025-8164	Medico-Legal Bulletin
0025-8172	Medico-Legal Journal
0025-8180	Medico Moderno†
0025-8202	Medicos†
0025-8210	Medicus†
0025-8229	Medjimurje
0025-8237	Medion†
0025-8245	Medisch Contact
0025-8261	Options Mediterraneennes†
0025-827X	Mediterranean Diplomatic Observer
0025-8296	Mediterranee
0025-830X	Meditsinskii Zhurnal Uzbekistana
0025-8318	Meditsinskaya Gazeta
0025-8326	Meditsinskaya Parazitologiya i Parazitarnye Bolezni
0025-8334	Meditsinskaya Radiologiya
0025-8342	Meditsinskaya Sestra
0025-8350	Medium
0025-8377	Saskatchewan Association of Media Specialists. Medium *changed to* Medium
0025-8385	Medium Aevum
0025-8393	Medizin in Bild und Ton†
0025-8407	Medizin und Ernaehrung†
0025-8415	Medizin und Sport
0025-8431	Medizinhistorisches Journal
0025-844X	Medizinische Bild†
0025-8466	Das Medizinische Laboratorium†
0025-8474	Medizinische Monatsschrift *see* 0342-9601
0025-8482	Medizinische Neuerscheinungen
0025-8490	Der Medizinische Sachverstaendige
0025-8504	Medizinische Technik *see* 0344-9416
0025-8512	Die Medizinische Welt
0025-8539	Nordisk Numismatisk Union. Medlemsblad
0025-8547	Foerfattaren
0025-8555	Medjunarodni Problemi
0025-8571	Medusa
0025-8601	Medycyna Doswiadczalna i Mikrobiologia
0025-861X	Medycyna Komunikacyjna
0025-8628	Medycyna Weterynaryjna
0025-8636	Medycyna Wiejska
0025-8652	Meetings and Conventions
0025-8679	Megamot
0025-8687	Megaphone (Canton)
0025-8695	Megaphone (Dallas)
0025-8709	Megaphone (Georgetown)
0025-8717	Meglio
0025-8725	Meharri-Dent
0025-8741	Meidensha Review *changed to* Meiden Review
0025-875X	Meie Post
0025-8768	Meie Tee
0025-8776	Meieriposten
0025-8784	Meiklejohn Civil Liberties Library. Acquisitions *changed to* What's Happening to the Law
0025-8792	Mein Eigenheim
0025-8814	Mein Standpunkt†
0025-8822	Fuer Sozialforschung. Journal
0025-8830	M E J
0025-8857	Mekeel's Stamp News
0025-8865	Mekhanika Polimerov *see* 0203-1272
0025-8873	Mekhanizatsiya i Avtomatizatsiya Proizvodstva
0025-8881	Mekhanizatsiya i Elektrifikatsiya Sotsialisticheskogo Sel'skogo Khozyaistva *see* 0206-572X
0025-8903	Mekhanizatsiya Stroitel'stva
0025-8911	Melanges de Science Religieuse
0025-892X	Revue Andre Malraux Review
0025-8938	Melbourne University Law Review
0025-8954	Mele
0025-8970	Melk en Zuivel *changed to* Zuivelkoerier
0025-8989	Melliand Textilberichte International *see* 0341-0781
0025-8997	Melodie
0025-9004	Melodie und Rhythmus
0025-9012	Melody Maker
0025-9020	Melos *see* 0170-8791
0025-9039	Melyepitestudomanyi Szemle
0025-9047	Memeler Dampfboot
0025-9055	Memento General Tequi Quincaillerie
0025-9063	Memisa Nieuws
0025-9071	Memo
0025-908X	Memo from Belgium
0025-9101	Memo Key *changed to* Business Education Today
0025-911X	Center for Research on Learning and Teaching. Memo to the Faculty†
0025-9128	Revue de Metallurgie. Memoires Scientifiques *changed to* Revue de Metallurgie. Memoires et Etudes Scientifiques
0025-9136	Defense Academy. Memoirs
0025-9144	Memon Alam
0025-9152	Mexico. Direccion de Estadistica y Estudios Economicos. Memorandum Tecnico
0025-9160	Memorial de l'Artillerie Francaise
0025-9179	Memorial des Percepteurs et Receveurs des Communes
0025-9195	Memoires C.E.R.E.S.
0025-9209	Memphis State Business Review *see* 0279-8174
0025-9217	Men Only
0025-9225	Menadzer u Privredi *changed to* Privreda i Rukovodjenje
0025-9233	Menckeniana
0025-9241	Mendel Newsletter†
0025-925X	Mendeleev Chemistry Journal
0025-9268	Mendocino County Historical Society. Newsletter
0025-9284	Menninger Clinic. Bulletin
0025-9292	Menninger Perspective
0025-9314	Mennonitische Rundschau
0025-9322	Mennonit†
0025-9330	Mennonite
0025-9349	Mennonite Brethren Herald
0025-9357	Mennonite Historical Bulletin
0025-9365	Mennonite Life
0025-9373	Mennonite Quarterly Review
0025-9381	Mennonite Research Journal *see* 0148-4036
0025-939X	Menorah
0025-9411	Men's and Boys' Wear Buyers
0025-942X	Men's Art Service
0025-9438	Men's Clip Review *changed to* Menswear Advertising
0025-9454	Mens en Maatschappij
0025-9462	Mens en Melodie
0025-9470	Mens en Onderneming *changed to* Mens en Organisatie
0025-9489	Humanist
0025-9497	Men's Fashions†
0025-9500	Men's Hairstylist and Barber's Journal *changed to* Salon Talk
0025-9519	Men's Wear
0025-9527	Men's Wear†
0025-9535	Men's Wear of Canada
0025-9543	Mensa Bulletin
0025-9586	Mensajero Forestal†
0025-9608	Mensch und Welt†
0025-9616	Das Menschenrecht
0025-9624	Mensucat Meslek Dergisi
0025-9632	Mental Health
0025-9667	Mental Health in Australia
0025-9683	M H†
0025-9691	Mental Retardation Abstracts *see* 0191-1600
0025-9748	Mercado da Borracha no Brasil. Boletim Mensual
0025-9764	Mercados de Grasas y Acietes†
0025-9772	Mercadotecnia
0025-9780	Corriere Mercantile Politico d'Informazioni
0025-9799	Mercante Gazette of New Zealand *changed to* New Zealand Mercantile Gazette
0025-9810	Mercantile Law Reporter†
0025-9829	Mercato Metalsiderurgico
0025-9837	Mercator *see* 0533-070X
0025-9845	Mercer Actuarial Bulletin *changed to* Mercer Bulletin
0025-9853	Mercer Cluster
0025-987X	Mercer Law Review
0025-9888	Merchandising Week *changed to* Dealerscope Merchandising
0025-990X	Mercian Geologist
0025-9918	Merck Sharp & Dohme Review†
0025-9926	Mercur
0025-9934	Mercure
0025-9950	Mercurius *changed to* F N V - Magazine
0025-9969	Mercury (Los Angeles)
0025-9985	Finland. Merentutkimuslaitoksen. Julkaisu *see* 0357-1076
0025-9993	Meres es Automatika
0026-0002	Meresugyi Kozlemenyek
0026-0010	Mergers & Acquisitions
0026-0029	Merian
0026-0037	Meridiano
0026-0045	Merino Breeders' Journal
0026-0061	Merk†
0026-007X	Merkenblad B E N E L U X
0026-0088	Merkonomi
0026-0096	Merkur
0026-010X	Merkur Magazin fuer Volksgesundheit
0026-0118	Merkuriusz Polski-Zycie Akademickie†
0026-0126	Merleg
0026-0142	Merova Technika *changed to* Ceskoslovenska Standardizace
0026-0150	Merrill-Palmer Quarterly
0026-0169	Merrimac *changed to* M T I Reporter
0026-0185	Mesias
0026-0193	Mesures Regulation Automatisme
0026-0215	Message de l'Immaculee†
0026-0223	Message de Verite†
0026-0231	Message (Hagerstown)
0026-024X	Messager
0026-0258	Messager de la Haute Savoie
0026-0266	Messager de l'Exarchat du Patriarche Russe en Europe Occidentale
0026-0274	Messager Evangelique
0026-0290	Messages du Secours Catholique
0026-0304	Messaggero dei Ragazzi
0026-0312	Messaggero di S. Antonio
0026-0339	Messen und Pruefen *changed to* Messen Pruefen Automatisieren
0026-0347	Messen - Steuern - Regeln
0026-0355	Messenger (Elgin)
0026-0363	Messenger
0026-0371	Messenger
0026-0398	Messer und Schere
0026-0401	Messidor
0026-0428	Messtechnische Briefe fuer Elektrisches Messen Mechanischer Groessen
0026-0436	Mester†
0026-0452	Meta
0026-0460	Metaal & Kunststof
0026-0479	Metaal en Techniek
0026-0487	Metaalbewerking *changed to* M B Produktiertechniek
0026-0495	Metabolism: Clinical and Experimental
0026-0509	Metabolismo
0026-0517	Metal
0026-0525	Metal Building Review
0026-0533	Metal Bulletin
0026-0541	Metal Construction and British Welding Journal *see* 0307-7896
0026-055X	Metal Fabricating News
0026-0568	Metal Fabricator†
0026-0576	Metal Finishing
0026-0584	Metal Finishing Abstracts *see* 0950-5199
0026-0606	Metal Finishing Plant and Processes *see* 0950-5202
0026-0614	Meidensha Review *changed to* Kinzoku Hyomen Gijutsu
0026-0622	Metal Forming *changed to* Metallurgia: the Journal of Metals Technology, Metal Forming and Thermal Processing
0026-0630	U D S Metal Joining Digest *changed to* Metal Joining Digest
0026-0649	Metal Polisher, Buffer and Plater†
0026-0657	Metal Powder Report
0026-0665	Metal Progress *see* 0882-7958
0026-069X	Metal Science and Heat Treatment
0026-069X	Metal Stamping
0026-0703	Metal Trades Department. Bulletin†
0026-072X	Metal Worker
0026-0738	Metalektro Visie *changed to* Metalektro Profiel
0026-0746	Metall
0026-0754	Metallarbetaren
0026-0762	Metalle
0026-0789	Metallhandwerk and Metalltechnik *changed to* Metallhandwerk und Technik
0026-0797	Metalloberflaeche
0026-0800	Metallography
0026-0819	Metallovedenie i Termicheskaya Obrabotka Metallov
0026-0827	Metallurg
0026-0835	Metallurgia *changed to* Metallurgia: the Journal of Metals Technology, Metal Forming and Thermal Processing
0026-0843	Metallurgia Italiana
0026-0851	C R M Metallurgical Reports†
0026-086X	Metallurgical Transactions *see* 0360-2133

0026-0878 Metallurgie *see* 0751-588X
0026-0894 Metallurgist
0026-0908 Metallverarbeitung
0026-0924 Metals Abstracts
0026-0932 Metals Abstracts Index
0026-0940 Metals and Materials
0026-0959 Metals and Minerals Review
0026-0975 Metals Week
0026-0983 Metalurgia A B M
0026-1009 Metalworking Digest
0026-1017 Metalworking Economics†
0026-1025 Chilton's Iron Age Management *see* 0891-4036
0026-1033 Metalworking Production
0026-105X Metanoia†
0026-1068 Metaphilosophy
0026-1076 Metapsichica
0026-1084 Metaux
0026-1092 Meteoor†
0026-1114 Meteoritics
0026-1122 Israel. Meteorologia Be-Israel. *changed to* Israel. Meteorological Society. Meteorologia Be-Israel
0026-1130 Meteorological and Geoastrophysical Abstracts
0026-1149 Meteorological Magazine
0026-1165 Meteorological Society of Japan. Journal
0026-1173 Meteorologicke Zpravy
0026-1181 Meteorologie
0026-119X Meteorologiya i Gidrologiya
0026-1203 Meteorologische Abhandlungen
0026-1211 Meteorologische Rundschau
0026-1238 Methodist History
0026-1246 Methodist Homes Quarterly *changed to* Horizon (Neptune)
0026-1254 Methodist Message *changed to* Pelita Methodist
0026-1262 Methodist Recorder
0026-1270 Methods of Information in Medicine
0026-1289 Metiers Graphiques†
0026-1297 Metlfax
0026-1300 Zemedelska Informatika
0026-1319 Metodiky pro Zavadeni Vysledku Vyzkumu do Praxe
0026-1327 Metra†
0026-1335 Metrika
0026-1343 Metro†
0026-136X Intelligence Report *changed to* Metro Denver
0026-1378 Metro Memo†
0026-1386 Metroecónomica
0026-1394 Metrologia
0026-1408 Metrology and Inspection *changed to* Quality Today
0026-1416 Metron†
0026-1424 Metron
0026-1467 Metropolitan *see* 0162-6221
0026-1475 Metropolitan†
0026-1483 Metropolitan Area Digest†
0026-1491 Metropolitan Computer News†
0026-1505 Metropolitan Council of the Twin Cities Area. Newsletter†
0026-1513 Statistical Bulletin - Metropolitan Life *see* 0741-9767
0026-1521 Metropolitan Museum of Art. Bulletin
0026-153X Metropolitan Nashville Board of Education. News and Views
0026-1556 Metropolitan Pensioner
0026-1564 Metropolitan Restaurant News *changed to* Metro Food Service News
0026-1580 Metropolitan Star *see* 0745-8509
0026-1599 Metropolitan Washington Board of Trade News *see* 0274-5496
0026-1602 Metsa Ja Puu
0026-1629 Metsastys ja Kalastus
0026-1637 Metterdaad†
0026-1645 Metzger und Wurster
0026-1653 Meubles et Decors *changed to* Decors
0026-1661 Meunerie Belge†
0026-1688 Mevo
0026-1696 Mexican-American Review *changed to* Business Mexico
0026-170X Mexican Life†
0026-1726 Mexico Agricola
0026-1734 Mexico. Archivo General de la Nacion. Boletin
0026-1750 Universidad Nacional Autonoma de Mexico. Revista
0026-1769 Mexico. Direccion General de Estadistica. Revista de Estadistica
0026-1777 Instituto Politecnico Nacional. Escuela National de Ciencias Biologicas. Anales
0026-1785 Mexico Farmaceutico
0026-1793 Mexico Heroico
0026-1807 Mexico Industrial
0026-1815 Mexico Mercantil
0026-1858 Mexletter
0026-1866 Meyers Modeblatt
0026-1882 Mezhdunarodnyi Sel'skokhozyaistvennyi Zhurnal
0026-1890 Mezogazdasagi Technika
0026-1904 Mezogazdasagi Vilagirodalom
0026-1912 Eurosud - Il Mezzogiorno e le Comunita' Europee†
0026-1939 Mi Mladi
0026-1947 Miami Business Review†
0026-1955 Miami Valley Dairyman *changed to* Milk Marketer
0026-1971 Mias†
0026-198X Michel-Rundschau
0026-1998 Michigan A F L - C I O News
0026-2005 Michigan Academician
0026-2021 Michigan Beverage News
0026-203X Michigan Botanist
0026-2056 Michigan Business Review *see* 0098-1923
0026-2072 Michigan Christian Advocate
0026-2102 Michigan Dental Association. Journal
0026-2110 Michigan Documents
0026-2129 Teacher's Voice *see* 0883-573X
0026-2137 Michigan Engineer†
0026-2145 Michigan Entomologist *see* 0090-0222
0026-2153 Michigan Farmer
0026-2161 Michigan Farm News
0026-217X Michigan Florist
0026-2188 Michigan Heritage *changed to* Family Trails
0026-2196 Michigan History
0026-2218 Michigan in Books†
0026-2226 Michigan Journal of Secondary Education *changed to* Secondary Education Today
0026-2234 Michigan Law Review
0026-2242 Michigan Librarian *changed to* Michigan Librarian
0026-2250 Michigan Magazine Index
0026-2277 Michigan Manufacturer and Financial Record†
0026-2285 Michigan Mathematical Journal
0026-2293 Michigan Medicine
0026-2315 Michigan Milk Messenger
0026-2323 Michigan Motor Carrier-Folks *changed to* Michigan Trucking Today
0026-2331 Michigan Municipal Review
0026-234X Michigan Music Educator
0026-2358 Michigan Natural Resources
0026-2366 Michigan Nurse
0026-2374 Michigan Osteopathic Journal
0026-2382 Michigan Out-Of-Doors
0026-2404 Michigan Pharmacist
0026-2412 Michigan Industry
0026-2420 Michigan Quarterly Review
0026-2439 Michigan School Board Journal
0026-2447 Michigan State Bar Journal *see* 0164-3576
0026-2455 Michigan State Economic Record†
0026-2463 Michigan State University Alumni Magazine
0026-2471 Michigan Technic
0026-248X Michigan Tradesman *see* 0193-0257
0026-251X Michigan's Occupational Health
0026-2528 Mic Mac News
0026-2536 Micro-Library Bulletin
0026-2544 Micro News Bulletin *changed to* Inform (Silver Spring)
0026-2560 Micro Tips *changed to* Componenten Visie
0026-2579 Microbial Genetics Bulletin†
0026-2595 Microbiologia Espanola†
0026-2609 Bacteriologia, Virusologia, Parazitologia, Epidemiologia *see* 0301-7338
0026-2617 Microbiology
0026-2633 Microbios
0026-265X Microchemical Journal
0026-2668 Microcosm†
0026-2676 Microcritica
0026-2692 Microelectronics Journal
0026-2706 Microelectronics Abstracts†
0026-2714 Microelectronics and Reliability
0026-2722 Microelectronics Digest†
0026-2730 Microfacts Advertising Reference File†
0026-2749 Microfilm Newsletter *see* 0883-9808
0026-2765 Micrographics News & Views†
0026-2781 Micronesian Reporter
0026-279X Micronesica
0026-2803 Micropaleontology
0026-2811 Journal of Microphotography *changed to* Journal of Micrographics
0026-282X Microscope
0026-2838 Microscopy
0026-2846 Microstructures†
0026-2854 Microtecnic
0026-2862 Microvascular Research
0026-2870 University of Utah. Microwave Device and Physical Electronics Laboratory Quarterly Report
0026-2889 Microwave Energy Applications Newsletter *see* 0276-7961
0026-2897 Microwave Journal
0026-2900 Microwave Tube D.A.T.A. Book *see* 0271-0773
0026-2919 Microwaves and R F
0026-2927 Mid-America
0026-2935 Mid-America Insurance
0026-2943 Mid-Atlantic Apothecary *see* 0003-6560
0026-2986 Mid-Continent Mortician†
0026-3001 Mid East†
0026-301X Mid-East Commerce
0026-3036 Mid-Towner†
0026-3044 Mid-West Contractor
0026-3052 Mid-West Truckman†
0026-3079 American Studies
0026-3095 Middle East Business Digest *changed to* Africa Middle East Business Digest
0026-3117 Middle East Express
0026-3133 Middle East Information Series *see* 0097-9791
0026-3141 Middle East Journal
0026-315X Middle East Monitor
0026-3176 Middle East Perspective†
0026-3184 Middle East Studies Association Bulletin
0026-3192 Middle East Trade
0026-3206 Middle Eastern Studies
0026-3214 Middle Way
0026-3222 Middlesex Hospital Journal
0026-3230 MidEast Report
0026-3249 Midland
0026-3257 Midland Bank Review
0026-3273 Midland Industrialist†
0026-3281 Midland Medical Review†
0026-3311 Midlands Industry and Commerce
0026-332X Midstream
0026-3338 Midwest Automotive News
0026-3346 Midwest Chaparral
0026-3354 Midwest Eighty-Eight Manufacturing
0026-3362 Midwest Electrical News†
0026-3370 Midwest Engineer
0026-3397 Midwest Journal of Political Science *see* 0092-5853
0026-3400 Midwest Landscaping *see* 0194-7257
0026-3419 Midwest Modern Language Association. Bulletin *see* 0742-5562
0026-3427 Midwest Motor Transport News
0026-3435 Midwest Motorist
0026-3443 Midwest Museums Conference. Quarterly
0026-3451 Midwest Quarterly
0026-346X Midwest Review of Public Administration *see* 0275-0740
0026-3478 Midwestern Dentist
0026-3486 Midwestern Druggist†
0026-3494 Midwestern Nigeria Gazette *changed to* Bendel State Gazette
0026-3516 Midwife and Health Visitor *see* 0306-9699
0026-3524 Midwives Chronicle
0026-3532 Mie Medical Journal
0026-3540 Miedzynarodowe Czasopismo Rolnicze
0026-3559 Maize News
0026-3567 Miesiecznik Literacki
0026-3575 Migrant
0026-3583 Migration News
0026-3591 Migrations
0026-3605 Mijn Stokpaardje
0026-3613 Mijnwerker†
0026-3621 Mike Shayne Mystery Magazine
0026-363X Mikhtav Lehaver
0026-3648 Mikologiya i Fitopatologiya
0026-3672 Mikrochimica Acta
0026-3680 Mikrokosmos
0026-3699 Mikroniek
0026-3702 Mikroskopie
0026-3710 Mil
0026-3729 Camera di Commercio Industria Artigianato e Agricoltura di Milano. Notiziario Commerciale
0026-3737 Milap Weekly
0026-3753 Milch-Praxis *see* 0343-0200
0026-3761 Milch - Fettwaren - Eier - Handel
0026-377X Milchsuppe
0026-3788 Milchwissenschaft
0026-380X Milestones
0026-3826 Militaergeschichtliche Mitteilungen
0026-3842 Militaerpsykologiske Meddelelser
0026-3850 Militaert Tidsskrift
0026-3869 Militaire Spectator
0026-3877 Militant
0026-3885 Militant
0026-3893 Militant Truth *changed to* Independent Voice
0026-3907 Militaer-Kuechenchef
0026-3915 Militaria†
0026-3923 Militaerwesen†
0026-3931 Military Affairs
0026-394X Military Aircraft & Missile Data Sheets
0026-3958 Military Chaplain
0026-3966 Military Collector & Historian
0026-3974 Military Digest†
0026-3982 Military Engineer
0026-3990 Military Government Journal and Newsletter *see* 0045-7035
0026-4008 Military Historical Society. Bulletin
0026-4016 Military History Journal
0026-4024 Military Intelligence
0026-4032 Military Journalist *see* 0095-635X
0026-4040 Military Law Review
0026-4067 Military Market
0026-4075 Military Medicine
0026-4083 Military Modelling
0026-4105 Military Police Journal†
0026-4121 Military Record of Atomic C B R Happenings *changed to* Military Record of Atomic C B R Happenings. Armament Data Sheets
0026-413X Military Research Letter
0026-4148 Military Review
0026-4156 Militia Christi *changed to* Kerk en Vrede
0026-4164 Miljoespegeln
0026-4172 Milk Industry
0026-4180 Milk Producer
0026-4199 Milk Producer
0026-4229 Milking Shorthorn Journal *see* 0145-8264
0026-4253 Mill News Letter
0026-427X Millinery and Boutique†
0026-4288 Millinery Research *changed to* Wigs, Hats and Accessories
0026-4296 Milling *changed to* Milling Feed and Farm Supplies
0026-430X Mills Stream
0026-4318 Milton College Blue and Gold†
0026-4326 Milton Quarterly
0026-4350 Milwaukee Courier
0026-4377 Milwaukee Reader
0026-4385 Mimos
0026-4407 North and South†
0026-4415 Minaret *changed to* Minaret Monthly International
0026-4423 Mind

ISSN INDEX 1269

0026-4431 Mynd
0026-4458 Mind over Matter†
0026-4474 Mindszenty Report
0026-4490 Mine Medical Officers' Association of South Africa. Proceedings
0026-4504 Mine Ventilation Society of South Africa. Journal
0026-4512 Mined-Land Conservation†
0026-4520 Mineracao Metalurgia
0026-4539 Earth and Mineral Sciences
0026-4547 Mineral Industries Newsletter†
0026-4555 California Geology
0026-4563 Mineral Research and Exploration Institute of Turkey. Bulletin
0026-4571 Mineral Wealth
0026-458X Minerales
0026-4598 Mineralium Deposita
0026-4601 Mineralogical Abstracts
0026-461X Mineralogical Magazine
0026-4628 Mineralogical Record
0026-4652 Minerals Research Laboratory Bulletin *changed to* Minerals Research Laboratory Newsletter
0026-4660 Minerals Science and Engineering†
0026-4679 Mineria
0026-4687 Miners' International News†
0026-4695 Minerva
0026-4709 Minerva Aerospaziale
0026-4717 Minerva Anestesiologica
0026-4725 Minerva Cardioangiologica
0026-4733 Minerva Chirurgica *changed to* Minerva Chirurgica-Chirurgia
0026-4741 Minerva Dermatologica *see* 0533-7712
0026-475X Minerva Dietologica *changed to* Minerva Dietologica e Gastroenterologica
0026-4776 Minerva Gastroenterologica *changed to* Minerva Dietologica e Gastroenterologica
0026-4784 Minerva Ginecologica
0026-4806 Minerva Medica
0026-4849 Minerva Medicolegale
0026-4857 Minerva Mediconucleare *see* 0392-0208
0026-4873 Minerva Nefrologica *changed to* Minerva Urologica e Nefrologica
0026-4881 Minerva Neurochirurgica *changed to* Journal of Neurosurgical Sciences
0026-489X Minerva Nipiologica *see* 0392-4416
0026-4903 Minerva Oftalmologica
0026-4911 Minerva Ortopedica
0026-4938 Minerva Otorinolaringologica *changed to* Otorinolaringologica
0026-4946 Minerva Pediatrica
0026-4954 Minerva Pneumologica
0026-4962 Minerva Radiologica *see* 0033-8362
0026-4970 Minerva Stomatologica
0026-4989 Minerva Urologica *changed to* Minerva Urologica e Nefrologica
0026-4997 Minervas Kvartalsskrift†
0026-5012 Mines and Factories Journal†
0026-5020 Mines and Minerals†
0026-5039 Mines and Oils; Four Hundred and Fifty Canadian Weekly Stock Charts *see* 0383-2953
0026-5047 Mines et Metallurgie†
0026-5055 Mines Golden *changed to* Mines Magazine
0026-5063 Mineur d'Auvergne *changed to* Centre Midi Magazine
0026-5071 Mineurs de France
0026-508X Mingay's Electrical Supplies Guide†
0026-5098 Mingay's News *see* 0728-9383
0026-5101 Mingay's Price Service *changed to* Mingay's Product Service
0026-5128 Miniature Book News†
0026-5152 Mining and Minerals Engineering *see* 0369-1632
0026-5160 Mining Congress Journal *see* 0277-8688
0026-5179 Mining Engineer
0026-5187 Mining Engineering
0026-5209 Mining Geology
0026-5217 Mining Industry and Trade Journal *changed to* Mining Industry & Trade Annual
0026-5225 Mining Journal
0026-5241 Mining Record
0026-525X Mineral Resources Review
0026-5268 Chamber of Mines of South Africa. Mining Survey
0026-5276 Mining Technology
0026-5284 Belgium. Ministere de l'Education Nationale et de la Culture Francaise. Bulletin d'Information *changed to* Belgium. Ministere de l'Education Nationale et de la Culture Francaise. Revue
0026-5292 Cuba. Ministerio del Commercio Exterior. Revista
0026-5306 Ministerium
0026-5314 Ministry
0026-5322 Trinidad and Tobago. Ministry of Petroleum and Mines. Monthly Bulletin *changed to* Trinidad and Tobago. Ministry of Energy and Natural Resources. Monthly Bulletin
0026-5330 Ministry Theological Review†
0026-5357 Minkus Stamp Journal *changed to* Minkus Stamp & Coin Journal
0026-5365 Minneapolis District Dental Journal†
0026-5381 Minnesota A. A. A. Motorist†
0026-539X Minnesota Academy of Science. Journal
0026-5403 Minnesota Archaeologist
0026-5411 Minnesota Chemist
0026-542X Minnesota. Department of Agriculture. Agronomy Services Newsletter†
0026-5438 Minnesota. Department of Education. Public Library Newsletter
0026-5446 Minnesota Education News *see* 0889-2474
0026-5454 Minnesota Education Report *changed to* Education Update (St. Paul)
0026-5462 Minnesota Engineer†
0026-5489 Minnesota Food Guide *changed to* Minnesota Grocer
0026-5497 Minnesota History
0026-5500 Minnesota Horticulturist
0026-5519 Minnesota I R C News *changed to* Insights (Minneapolis)
0026-5527 Minnesota Journal of Education†
0026-5535 Minnesota Law Review
0026-5543 Minnesota Legal Register: Opinions of the Minnesota Attorney General
0026-5551 Minnesota Libraries
0026-556X Minnesota Medicine
0026-5578 Minnesota Municipalities *changed to* Minnesota Cities
0026-5586 Minnesota Nursing Accent
0026-5594 Minnesota Optometrist
0026-5616 Minnesota Pharmacist
0026-5624 Minnesota Police Journal
0026-5632 Minnesota Press†
0026-5659 Minnesota Reading Quarterly†
0026-5667 Minnesota Review
0026-5675 Minnesota Science
0026-5691 Minnesota Technolog
0026-5705 Minnesota Welfare *changed to* People (St. Paul)
0026-5721 Minus One *changed to* The Egoist
0026-573X Minute
0026-5748 Minuzzolo *changed to* L.G. Argomenti
0026-5756 Mio Bebe
0026-5764 Mio Lavora†
0026-5780 Mira
0026-5802 Miraculous Medal
0026-5810 Miroir du Centre
0026-5829 Mirovaya Ekonomika i Mezhdunarodnye Otnosheniya
0026-5837 Sooke Mirror
0026-5845 Mirror
0026-5861 Miscellanea Barcinonensia†
0026-587X Miscellanea Francescana
0026-5888 Miscellanea Storica della Valdelsa
0026-5896 Miscellany
0026-590X Miscellany
0026-5918 Miss Chatelaine *see* 0708-4927
0026-5934 Bakkerswereld
0026-5942 Bouwwereld
0026-5950 Missets Horeca
0026-5977 Missi
0026-5993 Missile/Ordnance Letter
0026-6000 Espace†
0026-6019 Missili e Spazio *changed to* Aerotecnica, Missili e Spazio
0026-6027 Mission *see* 0199-4433
0026-6035 Mission de l'Eglise
0026-6043 Missionary Aviation *changed to* Mission Aviation Life Link
0026-6051 Missionary News Service
0026-606X Missionary Research Library. Occasional Bulletin *see* 0272-6122
0026-6078 Missionary Review†
0026-6086 Missionhurst
0026-6094 Mondo e Missione
0026-6108 Missioni Domenicane
0026-6116 Missions-Etrangeres
0026-6124 Mission. Messages
0026-6132 Missionsbaneret
0026-6159 Mississippi Banker
0026-6167 Mississippi Business Review†
0026-6175 Mississippi E P A News
0026-6183 Mississippi Educational Advance *see* 0164-8683
0026-6191 Mississippi Educational Journal *see* 0164-8683
0026-6205 Mississippi Farm Bureau News
0026-6213 Mississippi Farm Report†
0026-6221 Mississippi Farm. Research *see* 0091-4460
0026-6248 Mississippi Folklore Register
0026-6256 Mississippi Game and Fish *see* 0732-6602
0026-6264 Mississippi Grocers' Guide
0026-6272 Mississippi Language Crusader
0026-6280 Mississippi Law Journal
0026-6299 Mississippi Legion-Aire
0026-6302 Mississippi Library News *see* 0194-388X
0026-6310 Mississippi Magic†
0026-6329 Mississippi Methodist Advocate *changed to* Mississippi United Methodist Advocate
0026-6337 Mississippi Municipalities
0026-6353 Mississippi Notes *changed to* Mississippi Music Educator
0026-637X Mississippi Quarterly
0026-6388 Mississippi R N
0026-6396 Mississippi State Medical Association. Journal
0026-640X Mississippi State University. Forest Products Utilization Laboratory. Research Report
0026-6418 Mississippi Valley Journal of Business and Economics *changed to* Review of Business and Economic Research
0026-6426 Mississippi Valley Lumberman *changed to* Building Material Retailer
0026-6434 Mississippi Valley Stockman-Farmer *see* 0192-7140
0026-6442 Mississippi's Business
0026-6477 Missouri Architect
0026-6493 Missouri Botanical Garden. Annals
0026-6507 Missouri Botanical Garden Bulletin
0026-6515 Missouri Conservationist
0026-6523 Missouri Dental Association. Journal *changed to* Missouri Dental Journal
0026-6531 Missouri Disaster Planning and Operations Newsletter *see* 0197-6672
0026-6558 Missouri Engineer
0026-6574 Missouri Farm Bureau News
0026-6582 Missouri Historical Review
0026-6590 Missouri Historical Society. Bulletin *see* 0198-9375
0026-6604 Missouri Law Review
0026-6612 Missouri L P-Gas Talks *changed to* M L P G A News
0026-6620 Missouri Medicine
0026-6647 Missouri Municipal Review
0026-6655 Missouri Nurse
0026-6663 Missouri Pharmacist
0026-6671 Missouri Press News
0026-668X Missouri Ruralist
0026-6698 Missouri School Board
0026-6701 Missouri School Music
0026-671X Missouri Speleology
0026-6728 Missouri Teamster
0026-6760 Mita Journal of Economics
0026-6779 Die Mitarbeit†
0026-6787 Mithila Institute of Post Graduate Studies and Research in Sanskrit Learning. Bulletin
0026-6809 M E R I's Monthly Circular. Survey of Economic Conditions in Japan
0026-6817 Mitsubishi Heavy Industries Technical Review
0026-6825 Mitsui Zosen Technical Review
0026-6841 Mitteilungen aus der Gebiete der Lebensmitteluntersuchung und Hygiene
0026-6868 Mitteilungen aus der Rheinischen Rinderzucht
0026-6876 Mitteilungen aus Statistik und Verwaltung der Stadt Wien *changed to* Statistische Mitteilungen
0026-6884 Mitteilungen der Deutschen Patentanwaelte
0026-6892 Industrie- und Handelskammer Reutlingen. Mitteilungen†
0026-6906 Wiener Urania. Mitteilungen
0026-6922 Oberoesterreichisches Volksbildungswerk. Mitteilungen
0026-6930 Mitteilungen fuer den Aussenhandel†
0026-6949 Mitteilungen ueber Textilindustrie *changed to* Mittex: Mitteilungen ueber Textilindustrie
0026-6957 Dokumentation fuer Umweltschutz und Landespflege
0026-6965 Mitteilungsblatt der Genossenschaftlichen Frauenorganisation†
0026-6973 Mitteilungsblatt fuer Dolmetscher und Uebersetzer
0026-6981 Mizan: U S S R-China-Africa-Asia†
0026-699X Mizrachi Weg†
0026-7007 Mizrrachi Woman *changed to* Amit Woman
0026-7023 Mlad Borec
0026-7031 Mladost
0026-704X Mljekarstvo
0026-7058 Mlynsko-Pekarensky Prumysl a Technika Skladovani Obili
0026-7066 Mnemonic†
0026-7074 Mnemosyne
0026-7090 Moebelvaerlden *see* 0345-7737
0026-7104 Mobila
0026-7112 Mobile
0026-7120 Mobile and Recreational Housing Merchandiser *see* 0191-9768
0026-7139 Mobile Home *see* 0268-4594
0026-7147 Mobile Home Park Management *changed to* Mobile Home Park Management & Developer
0026-7163 Mobile Home Reporter and Recreation Vehicle News *changed to* Manufactured Housing Reporter
0026-7171 Mobile Homes & Recreational Vehicles in Canada *changed to* Canadian Recreational Vehicle Industry
0026-7198 Mobile Living
0026-7201 Mobile Living in Canada *changed to* Mobile Living in Canada-Manufactured Homes/Canada
0026-7228 Mobilia†
0026-7244 Moccasin
0026-7252 Moda dei Bimbi
0026-7279 Mode
0026-7295 Model Airplane News
0026-7309 Model Car Science†
0026-7317 Model *see* 0036-5432
0026-7325 Model Engineer
0026-7333 Model Maker and Model Boats *see* 0144-2910
0026-7341 Model Railroader
0026-735X Model Railway Constructor
0026-7368 Model Railways *changed to* Your Model Railway
0026-7384 Modelbouwer
0026-7392 Modele Magazine
0026-7406 Modele Reduit d'Avion
0026-7414 Modele Reduit de Bateau
0026-7422 Modelleisenbahner

1270 ISSN INDEX

0026-7430 Modena *changed to* Modena Economica
0026-7449 Moderat Debatt
0026-7457 Modern Age
0026-7465 Modern and Classical Language Bulletin *see* 0318-5176
0026-7473 Modern Applications News for Design and Manufacturing *see* 0277-9951
0026-7481 Modern Asia *changed to* Far East Business
0026-749X Modern Asian Studies
0026-7503 Modern Austrian Literature
0026-7511 Modern Beauty Shop *see* 0148-4001
0026-752X Modern Boating
0026-7538 Modern Brewery Age
0026-7546 Modern Bride
0026-7554 Modern Caravan *changed to* Caravan Magazine
0026-7562 Modern Casting
0026-7570 Modern Ceylon Studies†
0026-7597 Modern Churchman
0026-7600 Modern Concepts of Cardiovascular Disease
0026-7619 Modern Concrete *see* 0279-4705
0026-7635 Modern Converter†
0026-7651 Modern Dairy
0026-766X Modern Dance and Dancer†
0026-7678 Modern Data *changed to* Minimicro News
0026-7678 Modern Data *see* 0364-9342
0026-7686 Modern Datateknik†
0026-7694 Modern Drama
0026-7708 Modern English *see* 0306-9346
0026-7716 Modern Farming†
0026-7724 Modern Fiction Studies
0026-7732 Modern Fishing
0026-7759 Modern Franchising†
0026-7775 Modern Geology
0026-7791 Modern Government *see* 0360-7941
0026-7805 Modern Grocer
0026-7813 Modern Gymnast *see* 0276-1041
0026-7821 Modern Haiku
0026-783X Modern Hospital *see* 0160-7480
0026-7848 Modern Images
0026-7856 Modern International Drama
0026-7864 Modern Jeweler *see* 0193-208X
0026-7872 Modern Kantoor†
0026-7880 Modern Knitting
0026-7899 Modern Knitting Management†
0026-7902 Modern Language Journal
0026-7910 M L N
0026-7929 Modern Language Quarterly
0026-7937 Modern Language Review
0026-7945 Modern Languages
0026-7953 Modern Law and Society
0026-7961 Modern Law Review
0026-8003 Modern Machine Shop
0026-8011 Modern Man†
0026-802X Modern Manufacturing *changed to* Factory Management
0026-8038 Modern Materials Handling
0026-8046 Modern Maturity
0026-8054 Modern Media
0026-8070 Modern Medicine
0026-8089 Modern Medicine of Australia *see* 0312-875X
0026-8097 Modern Medicine of Canada
0026-8100 Modern Medicine of Great Britain
0026-8119 Modern Medicine of New Zealand†
0026-8127 Modern Metals
0026-8143 Modern Motor
0026-816X Modern Needlecraft
0026-8178 Modern Nursing Home *see* 0160-7480
0026-8194 Drug News
0026-8208 Modern Office Procedures *changed to* Modern Office Technology
0026-8216 Modern Ondernemerschap *changed to* Ondernemers-Visie
0026-8224 Modern Packaging *see* 0746-3820
0026-8232 Modern Philology
0026-8240 Modern Photography
0026-8259 Modern Plant Operation and Maintenance†
0026-8267 Modern Plastering *changed to* Specialist Building Finishes
0026-8275 Modern Plastics
0026-8283 Modern Plastics International
0026-8291 Modern Poetry in Translation *see* 0268-1390
0026-8305 Modern Poetry Studies
0026-8313 Modern Power & Engineering†
0026-833X Modern Purchasing
0026-8356 Modern Railways
0026-8364 Refrigeration and Air Conditioning *see* 0263-5739
0026-8380 Modern Review
0026-8399 Modern Romances
0026-8402 Modern Schoolman
0026-8410 Modern Schools†
0026-8429 Modern Screen†
0026-8437 Modern Society†
0026-8445 Modern Steel Construction
0026-8453 Modern Stores and Offices†
0026-8461 Modern Sunbathing Quarterly†
0026-847X Modern Design/Modern Textil†
0026-8488 Modern Textiles Magazine *see* 0279-5027
0026-8496 Modern Tire Dealer
0026-850X Modern Tramway and Light Railway Review *see* 0144-1655
0026-8518 Modern Trans†
0026-8526 Modern Treatment†
0026-8534 Modern Utopian *see* 0199-9346
0026-8542 Modern Veterinary Practice
0026-8550 Modern Vocational Trends†
0026-8577 Moderna Spraak
0026-8585 Moderna Transporter†
0026-8593 Moderne Frau *see* 0031-630X
0026-8607 Das Moderne Heim
0026-8623 Moderne Jordflytning *see* 0107-1866
0026-8631 Kontorbladet
0026-864X Die Moderne Kueche
0026-8666 Moderne Sprachen
0026-8674 Moderne Welt†
0026-8704 Modernes Hotel
0026-8712 Modernes Wohnen
0026-8720 Moderni Rizeni
0026-8739 Modes & Travaux
0026-8747 Modes de Paris
0026-8755 Modetelegramm†
0026-8763 Modine Gunch *changed to* Madison Review
0026-8771 Modische Linie (Ausgabe B)
0026-878X Modische Maschen
0026-8828 Modus Operandi†
0026-8836 Moebel und Raum†
0026-8844 Moebel und Wohnraum
0026-8852 Moellen
0026-8860 Mofussil
0026-8887 Moissons de l'Esprit†
0026-8895 Moj Pas
0026-8917 Wood Industry
0026-8925 Molecular and General Genetics
0026-8933 Molecular Biology
0026-8941 Molecular Crystals and Liquid Crystals *changed to* Molecular Crystals and Liquid Crystals
0026-895X Molecular Pharmacology
0026-8968 Molecular Photochemistry†
0026-8976 Molecular Physics
0026-8984 Molekulyarnaya Biologiya (Moscow)
0026-8992 Molennieuws/Windmill News *see* 0169-6459
0026-900X Molineria y Panaderia
0026-9018 Molini d'Italia
0026-9026 Molochnaya Promyshlennost'
0026-9034 Molochnoe i Myasnoe Skotovodstvo
0026-9042 Moloda Ukraina
0026-9050 Molodaya Gvardiya
0026-9077 Molodoi Kommunist
0026-9093 Molula-Qhooa
0026-9107 Molybdaen-Dienst†
0026-9115 Molykote†
0026-9131 Momento
0026-914X National Catholic Educational Association. Momentum *changed to* National Catholic Educational Association. Journal
0026-9166 Mon Jardin et Ma Maison
0026-9174 Mon Journal Confidences *changed to* Confidences Magazine
0026-9204 Monat†
0026-9212 Interkantonale Kontrollstelle fuer Heilmittel. Monatsbericht
0026-9220 Oesterreichische Landwirtschaft. Monatsberichte
0026-9247 Monatshefte fuer Chemie
0026-9255 Monatshefte fuer Mathematik
0026-9263 Monatshefte fuer Veterinaermedizin
0026-9271 Monatshefte fuer Deustschen Unterricht *changed to* Monatshefte
0026-9298 Monatsschrift fuer Kinderheilkunde
0026-9301 Monatsschrift fuer Kriminologie und Strafrechtsreform
0026-931X Monatsschrift fuer Lungenkrankheiten und Tuberkulosebekaempfung†
0026-9328 Monatschrift fuer Ohrenheilkunde und Laryngo-Rhinologie *changed to* Laryngologie, Rhinologie, Otologie
0026-9336 Monatsschrift fuer Unfallheilkunde, Versicherungs- , Versorgungs- und Verkehrsmedizin *see* 0341-5694
0026-9344 Mondo Lingvo Problemo *see* 0272-2690
0026-9352 Monday Morning†
0026-9360 Monde
0026-9379 Monde de l'Electricite
0026-9387 Monde des Philatelistes
0026-9395 Monde Diplomatique
0026-9417 Monde Gitan†
0026-9425 Monde Juif
0026-9433 Monde Libertaire
0026-9441 Travaux Souterrains†
0026-9468 Mondo†
0026-9476 Mondo Afro-Asiatico
0026-9484 Mondo Agricolo
0026-9492 Mondo Aperto
0026-9506 Mondo Bancario
0026-9522 Mondo Economico
0026-9530 Mondo Finanziario†
0026-9557 Mondo Occidentale *changed to* Americana
0026-9565 Mondo Odontostomatologico
0026-959X Moneda y Credito
0026-9611 Moneta e Credito
0026-9638 Jamaica. Department of Statistics. Monetary Statistics *changed to* Statistical Institute of Jamaica. Monetary Statistics Report
0026-9646 Moneysworth
0026-9654 Mongolian Society Bulletin *changed to* Mongolian Studies
0026-9662 Monist
0026-9689 Moniteur des Pharmacies et des Laboratoires
0026-9700 Moniteur des Travaux Publics et du Batiment
0026-9719 M O C I
0026-9727 Moniteur du Regne de la Justice
0026-9735 Moniteur Professionel de l'Electricite
0026-9743 Monitor *changed to* San Francisco Catholic
0026-9751 Monitor *see* 0198-7208
0026-976X Monitor Ecclesiasticus
0026-9786 Monitore Zoologico Italiano
0026-9794 Monkey
0026-9808 Monmouth Educator
0026-9816 Monmouthshire Farmer
0026-9832 Monographien zur Geschichte des Mittelalters
0026-9840 Monroe News Leader *changed to* Monroe Dispatch
0026-9859 Monsanto Magazine†
0026-9875 Montan-Berichte *see* 0005-8912
0026-9883 Montan-Rundschau *see* 0005-8912
0026-9891 Montana
0026-9905 Montana Agriculture *changed to* Montana Farm Bureau Spokesman
0026-9913 Montana Beverage News
0026-9921 Montana Business Quarterly
0026-993X Montana Education *changed to* M.E.A. Today
0026-9964 Montana Law Forum†
0026-9972 Montana Law Review
0026-9980 Montana League of Cities & Towns. Newsletter
0026-9999 Montana Legionnaire
0027-0008 Montana Masonic News
0027-0016 Montana Outdoors†
0027-0024 Montana Wool Grower
0027-0032 Montaneros de Aragon
0027-0040 Montazhnye i Spetsial'nye Raboty v Stroitel'stve
0027-0059 Montclair Art Museum. Bulletin *changed to* Montclair Art Museum. Bulletin/Newsletter
0027-0067 Montclair Public Schools†
0027-0075 Montclair Schools†
0027-0105 Montes
0027-0113 Museo Nacional de Historia Natural. Communicaciones Zoologicas
0027-0121 Museo Nacional de Historia Natural. Communicaciones Botanicas
0027-013X Universidad de la Republica. Facultad de Ingenieria y Agrimensura. Boletin *changed to* Universidad de la Republica. Facultad de Ingenieria. Boletin
0027-0148 Montfort
0027-0156 Montgomery-Bucks Dental Society. Bulletin
0027-0172 Month
0027-0180 New Zealand. Department of Statistics. Monthly Abstract of Statistics
0027-0199 Monthly Bank Clearings
0027-0202 Monthly Bibliography of Medical Reviews†
0027-0210 Monthly Bulletin of African Materials†
0027-0229 Monthly Bulletin of Agricultural Economics and Statistics (FAO) *see* 0379-0010
0027-0237 Egypt. Central Agency for Public Mobilisation and Statistics. Monthly Bulletin of Foreign Trade
0027-0245 Iraq. Central Statistical Organization. Monthly Bulletin of Foreign Trade Statistics *changed to* Iraq. Central Statistical Organization. Quarterly Bulletin of Foreign Trade Statistics
0027-0253 Monthly Bulletin of Ionospheric Characteristics Recorded at Johannesburg and Capetown *changed to* Monthly Bulletin of Ionospheric Characteristics Recorded at Johannesburg and Hermanus
0027-0261 Indian Bureau of Mines. Bulletin of Mineral Information
0027-027X Monthly Business Failures
0027-0288 U.S. Library of Congress. Monthly Checklist of State Publications
0027-0296 Monthly Climatic Data for the World
0027-030X Monthly Commentary on Indian Economic Conditions
0027-0318 Monthly Cotton Linters Review
0027-0326 Monthly Cotton Report
0027-0334 Pakistan Central Cotton Committee. Monthly Cotton Review
0027-0342 Ontario. Ministry of Agriculture and Food. Monthly Crop and Livestock Report
0027-0377 Zambia. Central Statistical Office. Monthly Digest of Statistics
0027-0385 Monthly Digest of Tax Articles
0027-0407 Monthly Film Bulletin
0027-0415 Monthly Frequency Tables of Visibility, Cloud & Wind
0027-0423 Monthly Guardian
0027-0431 M I M S
0027-044X U.S. Bureau of Labor Statistics. Monthly Review *see* 0098-1818
0027-0458 Monthly Listings of Neuro-Psychiatric Literature†
0027-0466 Monthly Mailer *changed to* I F I Fabricare News
0027-0482 Monthly Radiation Summary
0027-0490 Monthly Radiation Values for Bergen, Norway†
0027-0504 Monthly Railway Statistics
0027-0512 International Canada *see* 0381-4890
0027-0520 Monthly Review

ISSN INDEX 1271

ISSN	Title
0027-0539	Australia. Bureau of Statistics. Monthly Review of Business Statistics see 0727-1689
0027-0547	Monthly Statistics of Foreign Trade of India
0027-0563	Monthly Statistics of Korea
0027-058X	Monthly Summary of Business Conditions in Southern California
0027-0598	Monthly Summary of Jute and Gunny Statistics
0027-0601	Pakistan Jute Association. Monthly Summary of Jute Goods Statistics changed to Quarterly Summary of Jute Goods Statistics
0027-061X	Monthly Technical Review†
0027-0628	Jamaica. Department of Statistics. Monthly Trade Bulletin changed to Statistical Institute of Jamaica. External Trade Summary Tables
0027-0636	Great Britain. Meteorological Office. Monthly Weather Report
0027-0644	Monthly Weather Review
0027-0660	Monti e Boschi changed to Monti e Boschi
0027-0695	Ecole Publique changed to Trans-Parent
0027-0709	Montreal General Hospital News
0027-0717	Quebec Medical
0027-0725	Montreal. Museum of Fine Arts. Quarterly Review†
0027-0733	Monument in Cantos and Essays†
0027-0741	Monumenta Nipponica
0027-075X	Monumental News-Review see 0160-7243
0027-0768	Monuments Historiques de la France
0027-0776	Monumentum†
0027-0806	Moody Monthly
0027-0814	Moody's Bank & Finance Manual
0027-0822	Moody's Bond Survey
0027-0830	Moody's Handbook of Common Stocks
0027-0849	Moody's Industrials changed to Moody's Industrial News Reports
0027-0857	Moody's Municipals and Governments changed to Moody's Municipals and Government News Reports
0027-0865	Moody's O T C Industrials changed to Moody's O T C Industrial News Reports
0027-0881	Moody's Stock Survey†
0027-089X	Moody's Transportation changed to Moody's Transportation News Reports
0027-0903	Moon see 0167-9295
0027-0911	Moon Magazine
0027-0954	Moose
0027-0962	Moottoriviesti see 0041-4468
0027-0970	Moottori see 0359-7636
0027-0989	Mopac News†
0027-1004	Morality in Media Newsletter
0027-1012	North American Moravian
0027-1020	Moravian Music Foundation. News Bulletin see 0278-0763
0027-1047	Morehouse College Bulletin
0027-1055	Moreland News and Views
0027-1071	Morgagni
0027-1098	Morgan Horse
0027-1101	Morgonbris
0027-111X	Mormon Americana changed to New Mormon Americana Bibliography
0027-1136	Mornaricki Glasnik
0027-1144	Morning Rays†
0027-1160	Morocco Tourism
0027-1179	Morokami
0027-1187	Morris Arboretum Bulletin†
0027-1195	Morsingboen
0027-1209	Morsko Ribarstvo
0027-1217	Morskoi Flot
0027-1241	Mortgage Banker see 0730-0212
0027-125X	Morton Arboretum Quarterly
0027-1268	Mortuary Management
0027-1276	Mosaic
0027-1284	Mosaic (Washington)
0027-1306	Moscow News
0027-1314	Moscow University Chemistry Bulletin
0027-1322	Moscow University Mathematics Bulletin
0027-1330	Moscow University Mechanics Bulletin
0027-1349	Moscow University Physics Bulletin
0027-1357	Moskovskii Universitet. Vestnik. Seriya 12: Pravo
0027-1365	Moskovskii Universitet. Vestnik. Seriya Ekonomika, Filosofiya changed to Moskovskii Universitet. Vestnik. Seriya 7: Ekonomika
0027-1365	Moskovskii Universitet. Vestnik. Seriya Ekonomika, Filosofiya changed to Moskovskii Universitet. Vestnik. Seriya 8: Filosofiya
0027-1381	Moskovskii Universitet. Vestnik. Seriya 5: Geografiya
0027-139X	Moskovskii Universitet. Vestnik. Seriya Istoricheskie Nauki changed to Moskovskii Universitet. Vestnik. Seriya 9: Istoriya
0027-1403	Moskovskoe Obshchestvo Ispytatelei Prirody. Biologicheskii Otdel. Byulleten'
0027-1411	Moskva
0027-142X	Mosquito News changed to American Mosquito Control Association. Journal
0027-1446	Mosul University. College of Medicine. Annals
0027-1454	Mosupa - Tsela
0027-1470	Mot-Bau
0027-1500	Mother
0027-1527	Mother Cabrini Messenger
0027-1535	Mother Earth News
0027-1543	Mother India
0027-1551	Mothers' Manual changed to Mothers Today
0027-156X	Mothers-to-Be/American Baby see 0044-7544
0027-1594	Motion Picture Daily†
0027-1616	Motion Picture Herald see 0146-5023
0027-1624	Motion Picture Magazine†
0027-1632	Motion Pictures Technical Bulletin
0027-1667	Motive†
0027-1675	Moto†
0027-1683	Moto Revija
0027-1691	Motociclismo
0027-1713	Motor
0027-1721	Motor
0027-173X	Motor
0027-1748	Motor Magazine
0027-1756	Motor
0027-1764	Motor
0027-1772	Motor Age see 0193-7022
0027-1780	Motor Boat and Yachting
0027-1799	Motor Boating & Sailing
0027-1802	Motor Business
0027-1829	Motor Caravan and Camping changed to Motorcaravan & Motorhome Monthly
0027-1837	Motor Cycle†
0027-1845	Motor Cycle and Cycle Trader
0027-1853	Motor Cycle News
0027-1888	Motor-Dienst und Erdoel-Nachrichten changed to Motor und Erdoel
0027-190X	Motor in Canada
0027-1926	Motor Italia
0027-1934	Motor News changed to Michigan Living
0027-1942	Motor News Analysis
0027-1950	Motor Reise Revue
0027-1977	Motor Service
0027-1985	Motor Service changed to Garage & Transport
0027-1993	Motor-Service & Autoteknisk Tidsskridt
0027-2000	Motor Ship
0027-2019	Motor Sport
0027-2027	Motor Trade Executive
0027-2035	Motor Trade Journal
0027-2043	Motor Trader
0027-2051	Motor Trader and Fleet Operator
0027-206X	Motor Transport
0027-2078	Motor Transportation Hi-Lights
0027-2086	Motor Travel see 0890-7471
0027-2094	Motor Trend
0027-2108	Motor Truck
0027-2116	Motor Truck News changed to Iowa Trucking Lifeliner
0027-2124	Motor West†
0027-2140	Motorbranschen
0027-2159	Motorbranschens Registeringsstatistik see 0027-2140
0027-2167	Enthusiast
0027-2175	Revs Motorcycle News (Revs)
0027-2205	Motorcyclist
0027-2213	Motorfoereren
0027-2221	Motorhome Life see 0744-074X
0027-223X	Motorindia
0027-2248	Motoring
0027-2256	Motoring Life
0027-2264	Motoring News
0027-2299	Motorist
0027-2302	Motorists Guide to New & Used Car Prices
0027-2310	Motorland
0027-2337	Motorliv
0027-2345	Motorman
0027-2361	Motorpraxis†
0027-237X	Das Motorrad
0027-2388	Motortidningen Kart†
0027-2396	Motrix
0027-2485	Mount Allison Record
0027-2493	Mount Holyoke Alumnae Quarterly
0027-2507	Mount Sinai Journal of Medicine
0027-2523	Mount Washington Observatory News Bulletin
0027-254X	Mountain Geologist
0027-2558	Mountain Life and Work
0027-2566	Mountain†
0027-2574	Mountain Path
0027-2582	Mountain-Plains Library Quarterly see 0145-6180
0027-2590	Mountain States Banker see 0005-5123
0027-2612	Mountain Visitor
0027-2620	Mountaineer
0027-2639	Mousaion
0027-2647	Tele-Moustique
0027-2655	Mouthpiece
0027-2671	Mouvement Social
0027-268X	Movie
0027-2698	Movie Life†
0027-2701	Movie Maker see 0268-0750
0027-271X	Movie Mirror
0027-2736	Movie News
0027-2744	Movie Stars†
0027-2779	Movie World†
0027-2787	Movieland and TV Time see 0731-9991
0027-2809	Movimento di Liberazione in Italia see 0392-3568
0027-2817	Movimento Operaio e Socialista
0027-2833	Movoznavstvo
0027-2841	Moyen Age
0027-2868	Mozaiek Katholiek Verbond voor Kinderbescherming. Maandblad†
0027-2892	Moznayim
0027-2906	M.S. for Medical Secretaries†
0027-2914	Muanyag es Gumi
0027-2930	El Mueble
0027-2949	Die Muehle und Mischfuttertechnik
0027-2957	Muell und Abfall
0027-2965	Mueller Clipper
0027-2973	Muenchener Medizinische Wochenschrift
0027-2981	Muenchner Woche
0027-299X	Das Muenster
0027-3007	Muenzen und Medaillen
0027-3015	Muszaki Egyetemi Konyvtaros
0027-3023	Muszaki Lapszemle. Anyagmozatas, Csomagolas/Technical Abstracts. Materials Handling, Packaging see 0230-5348
0027-3031	Muhammad Speaks changed to A M Journal
0027-304X	Muhendis ve Makina
0027-3066	Mujer de America
0027-3104	Mukta
0027-3120	Mulino
0027-3139	Mullard Technical Communications changed to Electronic Components and Applications
0027-3147	Multi†
0027-3155	Multihull International
0027-3171	Multivariate Behavioral Research†
0027-318X	Munca Sanitara changed to Viata Medicala-Cadre Medii
0027-3198	Zahnaerztlicher Anzeiger
0027-321X	Office International de Bibliographie. Communications Mundaneum
0027-3228	Mundartfreunde Oesterreichs. Mitteilungen
0027-3244	Mundo Cristao†
0027-3252	Mundo Cristiano
0027-3287	Mundo Economico
0027-3295	Mundo Electrico
0027-3309	Mundo Hispanico†
0027-3317	Mundo Hospitalario†
0027-3325	Mundo Madereru
0027-3333	Mundo Nuevo
0027-335X	Mundo Social†
0027-3384	Mundus
0027-3392	Mundus
0027-3406	Mundus Artium
0027-3414	Munibe
0027-3422	Municipal Administration and Engineering changed to Local Government in Southern Africa
0027-3449	Municipal Attorney
0027-3457	Municipal Engineering see 0143-4187
0027-3465	Municipal Engineers Journal
0027-3473	Municipal Finance changed to Government Finance Review
0027-3481	Municipal Finance News Letter changed to M F O A Newsletter
0027-3503	Municipal Law Court Decisions
0027-352X	Municipal League of Seattle and King County. Municipal News
0027-3538	Municipal Ordinance Review
0027-3546	Municipal Recreation Pools, Rink & Parks changed to Pool Industry Canada
0027-3554	New York Municipal Reference & Research Center Notes†
0027-3562	Municipal Review see 0261-5118
0027-3570	Municipal South†
0027-3589	Municipal World
0027-3597	Municipality
0027-3600	Munka
0027-3619	Munkavedelem
0027-3627	Munson-Williams-Proctor Institute. Bulletin
0027-3635	Muotisorja see 0355-192X
0027-3643	Muoviviesti see 0355-7839
0027-366X	Murimi†
0027-3678	Murmesteren
0027-3686	Murray Hill News
0027-3716	Murrelet
0027-3724	Musart see 0363-6569
0027-3732	Muscular Dystrophy Journal
0027-3740	Muscular Dystrophy News see 8750-2321
0027-3767	Musee Carnavalet. Bulletin
0027-3775	Musee du Soir†
0027-3783	Musee Ingres. Bulletin
0027-3791	Musee National de Varsovie. Bulletin
0027-3805	Musee Neuchatelois
0027-3813	Museen in Koeln. Bulletin see 0178-4218
0027-3821	Musees de Geneve
0027-383X	Musees et Collections Publiques de France
0027-3848	Musees et Monuments Lyonnais. Bulletin
0027-3856	Musees Royaux des Beaux-Arts de Belgique. Bulletin
0027-3872	Musei e Gallerie d'Italia
0027-3880	Museo Argentino de Ciencias Naturales "Bernardino Rivadavia". Instituto Nacional de Investigacion de las Ciencias Naturales. Revista. Geologia
0027-3899	Museo de Ciencias Naturales. Boletin
0027-3902	Museo de Historia Natural de San Rafael. Revista Cientifica de Investigaciones changed to Museo Municipal de Historia Natural de San Rafael. Revista
0027-3910	Museo Nacional de Historia Natural. Boletin
0027-3945	Museo Nacional de Historia Natural. Noticiario Mensual

1272 ISSN INDEX

ISSN	Title
0027-3953	Museo Nazionale del Cinema. Notiziario†
0027-3961	Museo Trentino del Risorgimento e della Lotta per la Liberta. Bollettino
0027-397X	Museologist
0027-3988	Museu Bocage. Arquivos
0027-3996	Museum
0027-4003	Museum
0027-402X	Museum Alliance Quarterly *see* 0040-3733
0027-4038	Museum Boymans-van Beuningen. Bulletin†
0027-4046	Museum Graphic†
0027-4054	Museum Helveticum
0027-4062	New Brunswick Museum. Memo *see* 0703-0606
0027-4089	Museum News
0027-4100	Museum of Comparative Zoology. Bulletin
0027-4127	Museum of Modern Art. Members Newsletter†
0027-4135	Museum of the Fur Trade Quarterly
0027-4143	Museumjournaal
0027-4151	Museums Association Monthly Bulletin *see* 0307-2525
0027-416X	Museums Journal
0027-4178	Museumskunde
0027-4186	Museumsnytt
0027-4194	Courrier Roumain
0027-4208	Music *see* 0164-3150
0027-4216	Music & Artists†
0027-4224	Music and Letters
0027-4232	Music & Musicians
0027-4240	Music Article Guide
0027-4259	Music at Georgia†
0027-4283	Music Cataloging Bulletin
0027-4291	Music City News
0027-4313	Music Director *see* 0046-4155
0027-4321	Music Educators Journal
0027-433X	Music in Education†
0027-4348	Music Index
0027-4356	Music Industry
0027-4364	Music Journal
0027-4372	Music Leader
0027-4380	Music Library Association. Notes
0027-4399	Music Maker†
0027-4402	Music Ministry†
0027-4410	Music News from Prague
0027-4437	Music Now
0027-4445	Music Review
0027-4461	Music Teacher
0027-447X	Music Tempo
0027-4488	Music Trades
0027-4496	Music World†
0027-450X	Musica
0027-4518	Musica
0027-4526	Musica e Dischi
0027-4534	Musica Iberoamericana
0027-4542	Musica Jazz
0027-4550	Musica Universita
0027-4569	Musicae Sacrae Ministerium
0027-4577	Musical Box Society. Bulletin *changed to* Musical Box Society International Technical Journal
0027-4585	Musical Denmark
0027-4615	Musical Merchandise Review
0027-4623	Musical Opinion
0027-4631	Musical Quarterly
0027-464X	Musical Salvationist
0027-4658	Musical Show
0027-4666	Musical Times
0027-4674	Musicalbrande
0027-4682	Musicasia†
0027-4690	Impulse
0027-4704	Musik in der Schule
0027-4712	Musik-Informationen *changed to* Musik-Info
0027-4720	Musik och Ljudteknik
0027-4739	Musik og Handel†
0027-4747	Musik und Bildung
0027-4755	Musik und Gesellschaft
0027-4763	Musik und Gottesdienst
0027-4771	Musik und Kirche
0027-478X	Musikern
0027-4798	Musikerziehung
0027-4801	Die Musikforschung
0027-481X	Musikhandel
0027-4828	Das Musikinstrument
0027-4836	Musiklivet-Vaar Saang
0027-4844	Musikrevy
0027-4860	Muslim Africa
0027-4887	Muslim Digest
0027-4895	Muslim Review
0027-4909	Muslim World
0027-4917	Mustang Review†
0027-4925	Muster *changed to* Livestock & Grain Producers
0027-4933	Muszaki-Gazdasagi Tajekoztato
0027-4941	Muszaki Lapszemle. Uzemszervezes, Ipargazdasag/Technical Abstracts. Business Organization, Industrial Economics *see* 0231-0759
0027-495X	Muszaki Lapszemle. Banyaszat/Technical Abstracts. Mining *see* 0231-0651
0027-4968	Muszaki Lapszemle. Elektrotechnika, Hiradastechnika *see* 0231-0783
0027-4976	Muszaki Lapszemle. Elelmiszeripart†
0027-4984	Muszaki Lapszemle. Energia/Technical Abstracts. Energy *see* 0231-0678
0027-4992	Muszaki Lapszemle. Faipar, Papir-es Nyomdaipar/Technical Abstracts. Wood and Paper Industry, Printing *see* 0231-0740
0027-500X	Muszaki Lapszemle. Fizika, Meres- es Muszertechnika, Automatika/Technical Abstracts. Physics, Measurement and Instrument Technology, Automation *see* 0231-0643
0027-5018	Muszaki Lapszemle. Gepeszet *see* 0231-0694
0027-5018	Muszaki Lapszemle. Gepeszet *see* 0231-0686
0027-5026	Muszaki Lapszemle. Kemia Vegyipar/Technical Abstracts. Chemistry, Chemical Industry *see* 0231-0775
0027-5034	Muszaki Lapszemle. Kohaszat, Onteszet/Technical Abstracts. Metallurgy, Foundry *see* 0231-0708
0027-5042	Muszaki Lapszemle. Kozlekedes/Technica l Abstracts. Transport *see* 0231-1941
0027-5042	Muszaki Lapszemle. Kozleke des/Technical Abstracts. Transportation *see* 0231-0724
0027-5042	Muszaki Lapszemle. Kozlekedes/Technical Abstracts. Transportation *see* 0231-3928
0027-5042	Muszaki Lapszemle. Kozlekedes/Technological Abstracts. Transportation *see* 0231-0767
0027-5050	Muszaki Lapszemle. Melyepites, Vizepites/Technical Abstracts. Civil and Hydraulic Engineering *see* 0231-0732
0027-5069	Muszaki Lapszemle. Textilipar, Eob- es Eorfeldolgozoipar/Technical Abstracts. Textile Industry, Leather and Leatherprocessing Industry *see* 0209-9578
0027-5085	Muszaki Tudomany†
0027-5093	Mut
0027-5115	Mutech Chemical Engineering Journal†
0027-5123	Mutisia
0027-5131	Mutter
0027-514X	Muttersprache
0027-5158	Mutual Benefit Estate and Tax Letter†
0027-5182	Mutual Funds Guide
0027-5204	Mutual Review *see* 0148-8899
0027-5212	Mutualiste de Touraine
0027-5220	Mutualita' Democratica
0027-5239	Mutualite
0027-5247	Muveszettorteneti Ertesito
0027-5255	Muzejni a Vlastivedna Prace
0027-5263	Muzeum
0027-5271	Muzicka Omladina
0027-528X	Muziek Expres
0027-5298	Muziek Mercuur
0027-5301	Muziekhandel
0027-531X	Muzika
0027-5328	Muzilo†
0027-5336	Muzsika
0027-5344	Muzyka
0027-5352	Muzykal'naya Zhizn'
0027-5360	Muzzle Blasts
0027-5379	My Baby†
0027-5387	My Devotions
0027-5409	My Home and Family
0027-5417	My i Svit
0027-5425	My Career
0027-5433	My Magazine of India
0027-545X	My Story
0027-5468	My Volk†
0027-5484	My Weekly Reader (Summer Editions) *changed to* D.J.'s Summer Weekly Reader
0027-5484	My Weekly Reader (Summer Editions) *changed to* Zip's Summer Weekly Reader
0027-5484	My Weekly Reader (Summer Editions) *see* 0745-9130
0027-5492	Myasnaya Industriya S.S.S.R
0027-5506	Myastenia Gravis Foundation. Newsletter
0027-5514	Mycologia
0027-5522	Mycological Papers
0027-5530	Mycopathologia et Mycologia - Applicata *see* 0301-486X
0027-5549	Mycophile
0027-5557	Mykosen
0027-5565	Mylpaal†
0027-5573	Mysindia†
0027-5581	Mysl Polska
0027-559X	Mysore Commerce
0027-5603	Mysore Economic Review
0027-5611	Mysore Industrial Diary†
0027-562X	Mysore Labour Journal *changed to* Karnataka Labour Journal
0027-5638	Mysterium
0027-5662	N A A F I News
0027-5670	A. D. A. S. Quarterly Review†
0027-5689	N.A.B.A. Review
0027-5697	N A B E T News
0027-5700	N A B P Quarterly *changed to* N A B P Newsletter
0027-5719	N A C†
0027-5727	N A C C Attack *see* 0571-8597
0027-5735	N A C D L Journal *see* 0360-5361
0027-5743	N A C O News and Views *changed to* County News
0027-5751	N A C I F S Technical Bulletin *changed to* N A C U F S Journal
0027-576X	N A C W P I Journal
0027-5778	Cars and Trucks *see* 0195-1564
0027-5786	N A D A Auto Auction True Values Guide *changed to* Official Used Car Trade-In Guide
0027-5824	N A F S A Newsletter
0027-5832	N A H B Journal *see* 0744-1193
0027-5840	N A H B Washington Scope *see* 0744-1193
0027-5859	N A I I News Memo†
0027-5867	N A I I Press Samplings
0027-5875	N.A.I.L.M. News
0027-5883	N A I S Report†
0027-5891	Two Wheeler Dealer
0027-5905	N A L L D Journal 0891-2521
0027-5913	N A M M Music Retailer News
0027-5921	N A M Reports *see* 0191-5215
0027-593X	N A N T I S News†
0027-5948	N A O T Notes *changed to* Organ Teacher
0027-5956	Air Pollution Abstracts†
0027-5964	N A P I A Bulletin
0027-5972	N A R D Journal
0027-5980	N A R G U S Bulletin†
0027-5999	N A S C A R Newsletter
0027-6006	N A S C Quarterly
0027-6014	N A S P A Journal
0027-6022	N A S W News
0027-6030	N A T E S A Scope *changed to* Professional Electronics
0027-6049	N A T News
0027-6057	N A T O Letter *see* 0255-3813
0027-6073	N A T S Bulletin *see* 0884-8106
0027-609X	N A V A News *changed to* Communications Industries Report
0027-6103	N A W G A Management and Controller's Bulletin†
0027-6111	N & M†
0027-612X	N B C News *see* 0380-8599
0027-6138	N B O Abstracts
0027-6146	N.B.O.B. Orgaan *changed to* Unie van Beveiligings- en Bewakingspersoneel. Orgaan
0027-6154	N. B. O. Building Information Bulletin†
0027-6162	N B R I Information Sheet
0027-6170	N C A A News
0027-6189	N C A E News Bulletin
0027-6219	N C A Today†
0027-6227	N C A W E News
0027-6235	N C C D News†
0027-6243	N C C-Interface
0027-6251	N C C P A Newsletter *changed to* C M A Newsletter
0027-6278	N C D C Bulletin
0027-6308	N C E Today *see* 0194-3359
0027-6316	N C I Newsletter†
0027-6332	N C M A Newsletter *changed to* Contract Management
0027-6340	N C S A W Report *changed to* International Society for Animal Rights Report
0027-6367	N.C.W. News
0027-6383	Prosecutor
0027-6405	N E A Reporter *see* 0734-7219
0027-6413	N E A Research Bulletin†
0027-6421	N E C News
0027-643X	N E D A Journal/Electronic Merchandising
0027-6448	N E L A Newsletter
0027-6456	N E P P C O News†
0027-6464	N E R B A *changed to* C I M Construction Journal
0027-6480	N E S D E C News *changed to* N E S D E C Exchange
0027-6499	N F A Reports†
0027-6502	N F I Bulletin *changed to* Hardware Today
0027-6510	N F Legal Legislative Reporter News Bulletin (National Foundation of Health, Welfare and Pension Plans) *see* 0458-9599
0027-6529	N G Z *changed to* N G Z Service Manager
0027-6537	Conservation Commission News
0027-6545	N H D S Newsletter
0027-6553	N H K Technical Journal
0027-6561	N H K Technical Report
0027-657X	N H K Laboratories Note
0027-6596	N H S C News
0027-660X	Granite State School Leader *changed to* Granite State School Leader
0027-6618	N I A *see* 0165-1439
0027-6634	N I E Journal *changed to* Journal of Indian Education
0027-6642	N I F Weekly
0027-6669	N I M Abstracts†
0027-6685	N I N
0027-6731	N I T Newsletter *see* 0193-578X
0027-6758	N J E A Review
0027-6766	N K B
0027-6774	N K B Research Monthly *see* 0385-2350
0027-6782	N L G I Spokesman
0027-6790	N L L Review *see* 0264-1615
0027-6804	N L N News *see* 0276-5284
0027-6839	N M L Technical Journal
0027-6855	N M U Pilot
0027-6863	N O D A Bulletin *changed to* N O D A News
0027-6871	N O M D A Spokesman
0027-6898	N P L Technical Bulletin
0027-6901	N P N Bulletin†
0027-691X	N R A Newsletter *changed to* Renditions
0027-6928	N R C D Bulletin *see* 0266-6960
0027-6944	N H F A Reports *see* 0149-2276
0027-6952	N R I Journal†
0027-6979	N R T A Journal†
0027-6987	N R T A News Bulletin

0027-7002 National Society for Programmed Instruction. Journal *changed to* Performance & Instruction Journal
0027-7010 N S S News
0027-7029 New South Wales Contract Reporter†
0027-7037 N T A Journal
0027-7045 N T D R A Dealer News
0027-7053 N T L Institute News and Reports†
0027-707X N T Z Nachrichtentechnische Zeitschrift *changed to* N T Z Zeitschrift fuer Informationstechnik und Telekommunikation
0027-7088 N U B E News *changed to* B I F U Report
0027-7096 N U E A Spectator *changed to* Continuing Higher Education Review
0027-710X Centrale Suiker Maatschappij. Voorlichtingsblad *see* 0165-9375
0027-7126 Nya Argus
0027-7134 N Y L A Bulletin
0027-7142 N Y L I C Review
0027-7150 N Y P M A Bulletin
0027-7169 N Y S S A Bulletin *see* 0095-2273
0027-7177 New Zealand Baptist
0027-7185 Electrical Industry
0027-7193 N. Z. H. Maandblad†
0027-7207 New Zealand Institute of Architects Journal
0027-7215 N Z L A Newsletter *see* 0110-4373
0027-7223 N. Z. Licensee
0027-724X New Zealand Shipping Gazette
0027-7266 N Z T C A Journal
0027-7274 N.Z. Truth
0027-7282 New Zealand Valuer
0027-7304 Na Pua Okika o Hawaii Nei/Orchids of Hawaii *see* 0099-8745
0027-7312 Na Stroikakh Rossii
0027-7320 Na Vijven†
0027-7339 Naaimachine-Nieuws
0027-7347 Naamloos Nieuws *changed to* Milacroniek
0027-7355 Naar Morgen
0027-7363 Nach der Arbeit
0027-7371 Nachal'naya Shkola
0027-738X Nachrichten aus Chemie und Technik *see* 0341-5163
0027-7398 Nachrichten aus der Aerztlichen Mission
0027-7401 Oesterreichisches Chemiefaser-Institut. Nachrichten†
0027-7428 Nachrichten fuer Die Zivile Luftfahrt, Deutsche Demokratische Republik
0027-7436 Nachrichten fuer Dokumentation
0027-7444 Nachrichten fuer Seefahrer
0027-7452 Nachrichtenblatt der Bayerischen Entomologen
0027-7460 Deutsche Gesellschaft fuer Geschichte der Medizin, Naturwissenschaft und Technik. Nachrichtenblatt
0027-7479 Nachrichtenblatt des Deutschen Pflanzenschutzdienstes
0027-7487 Nachrichtenblatt fuer die Buersten- und Pinselindustrie *changed to* Brossapress-Nachrichtenblatt fuer die Buersten- und Pinselindustrie
0027-7495 Nachrichtentechnik *see* 0323-4657
0027-7509 Nacion
0027-7525 Nadel Faden Fingerhut†
0027-7533 Naeringsrevyen
0027-7541 Nafta
0027-755X Nafta
0027-7568 Nagaoka Technical College. Research Reports
0027-7576 Nagarjun
0027-7584 Nagarlok
0027-7592 Nagoya Port Statistics Monthly
0027-7606 Nagoya City University. Medical Association. Journal
0027-7614 Japan. Government Industrial Research Institute, Nagoya. Technical News
0027-7622 Nagoya Journal of Medical Science
0027-7630 Nagoya Mathematical Journal
0027-7649 Nagoya Medical Journal
0027-7657 Nagoya University. Faculty of Engineering. Memoirs
0027-7681 Naho†
0027-769X Die Naehrung
0027-7703 Nahrungsmittel
0027-7711 Nailaer Zeitung†
0027-772X Lead and Zinc
0027-7738 Names
0027-7746 Namib Times
0027-7754 Namibia
0027-7762 Namrugram†
0027-7770 Nanak Prakash Patrika
0027-7797 Nanyang University. Bulletin *changed to* Chronicle. Nanyang University. Newsletter
0027-7800 Napa-Solano Dental Society. District Six. Newsletter *changed to* Oracle
0027-7827 Napoleon
0027-7835 Napoli Nobilissima
0027-7843 Napred
0027-7851 Narciso
0027-786X Narcotics Control Digest
0027-7886 Narod†
0027-7894 Narod Polski
0027-7908 Narodna Armija
0027-7932 Narodne Novine
0027-7940 Narodne Noviny
0027-7959 Narodni Borac
0027-7975 Narodni List
0027-7983 Narodni Sumar
0027-8017 Narodno Stvaralastvo - Folklor
0027-8025 Narodno Zdravlje†
0027-8033 Narodnoe Obrazovanie
0027-8041 Narody Azii i Afriki *see* 0130-6995
0027-805X Narragansett Naturalist†
0027-8068 Nas Chov
0027-8076 Revija (Belgrade)
0027-8084 Nas Jezik
0027-8092 Nas Put/Our Way *see* 0702-3855
0027-8106 Nas Svijet
0027-8114 Nas Vesnik†
0027-8122 Nasa Rec
0027-8130 Nasa Rijec
0027-8149 Nasa Stampa
0027-8157 Nasa Strucna Skola
0027-8165 Nasa Zakonitost
0027-819X Nase Planine
0027-8203 Nase Rec
0027-8211 Nase Vojsko
0027-8238 Nash Sovremennik
0027-8246 Nash Swit
0027-8254 Nashe Slovo
0027-8262 Nasi Dani
0027-8270 Nasi Zbori
0027-8319 Nasza Droga†
0027-8327 Panorama Polska
0027-8335 Natal University News†
0027-8343 Natal Wildlife
0027-8351 Nataller *changed to* Tempo
0027-8378 Nation
0027-8408 Nation Europa
0027-8416 National Association of College Admissions Counselors. Newsletter *changed to* N A C A C Bulletin
0027-8424 National Academy of Sciences. Proceedings *see* 0273-1134
0027-8424 National Academy of Sciences. Proceedings *changed to* National Academy of Sciences of the United States of America. Proceedings. Physical Sciences
0027-8432 National Academy of Sciences. National Academy of Engineering. National Research Council. Institute of Medicine. News Report
0027-8459 National Adoptalk *changed to* Adoptalk
0027-8491 N A C News *changed to* R A S E - N A C News
0027-8505 National Agricultural Library Catalog†
0027-8513 National Alliance
0027-8521 National Amateur
0027-853X National AMVET
0027-8548 National and Grindlays Review *changed to* Grindlays Bank Review
0027-8556 National Antiques Review†
0027-8572 National Assembly Library Review
0027-8580 National Assembly Review
0027-8602 National Association of Colleges and Teachers of Agriculture. Journal *see* 0149-4910
0027-8610 National Association of Educational Broadcasters Newsletter *changed to* Current (Washington, 1982)
0027-8629 National Association of Private Psychiatric Hospitals. Journal *changed to* Psychiatric Hospital
0027-8637 National Association of Private Psychiatric Hospitals. News Letter *changed to* National Association of Private Psychiatric Hospitals. Newsline
0027-8645 National Association of Regulatory Utility Commissioners. Bulletin
0027-8653 National Association of Secondary School Principals. Bulletin *see* 0192-6365
0027-8661 National Association of Soil and Water Conservation Districts. Tuesday Letter *see* 0047-8733
0027-867X National Association of Summer Sessions. Newsletter *changed to* North American Association of Summer Sessions. Newsletter
0027-8688 National Association of Watch and Clock Collectors. Bulletin
0027-8718 National Athletic Trainers Association. Journal *see* 0160-8320
0027-8726 National Auricula & Primula Society (Northern) Year Book
0027-8742 National Bank of Egypt. Economic Bulletin
0027-8750 National Bank of Ethiopia. Quarterly Bulletin
0027-8769 National Beauty School Journal
0027-8777 National Bibliography of Botswana
0027-8793 National Bowlers Journal and Billiard Revue *see* 0164-9183
0027-8807 National Builder
0027-8815 National Buildings Organisation. Journal
0027-8823 U.S. National Bureau of Standards. Technical News Buletin *see* 0093-0458
0027-8831 National Business Woman
0027-884X National Button Bulletin
0027-8858 National Cactus and Succulent Journal *see* 0264-3405
0027-8866 Cancer Care and the National Cancer Foundation. Report About the Services Your Contributions Support†
0027-8874 National Cancer Institute. Journal
0027-8882 National Candy Wholesaler *see* 0162-5136
0027-8890 National Capital Pharmacist
0027-8912 National Catholic Guidance Conference Journal *see* 0160-7960
0027-8920 National Catholic Register
0027-8939 National Catholic Reporter
0027-8955 National Chamber of Trade Journal *changed to* Distributor
0027-8963 National Chinchilla Breeders of Canada. Bulletin
0027-898X National Chronicle
0027-9013 National Civic Review
0027-9021 National Coffee Association News Letter *changed to* National Coffee Association of U.S.A. Newsletter
0027-9048 American Bankruptcy Law Journal
0027-9064 National Contract Management Journal *changed to* National Contract Management Journal (1980)
0027-9072 National Council for Homemaker Service. News *changed to* National HomeCaring Council. News
0027-9080 National Cremation *changed to* Cremationist of North America
0027-9099 National Custodian *changed to* Cleaning Management
0027-9102 National Decency Reporter *changed to* C D L Reporter
0027-9110 National Defence Academy. Journal†
0027-9129 N.D.A. Quarterly *changed to* National Dental Association Journal
0027-9145 National Diary
0027-9153 Japan. National Diet Library. Monthly Bulletin
0027-9161 Japan. National Diet Library. Newsletter
0027-917X N.D.T.I. Review†
0027-9188 National Education
0027-9196 National Educational Secretary
0027-920X National Elementary Principal *see* 0271-6062
0027-9218 National Engineer
0027-9226 National Farmers Union Washington Newsletter
0027-9234 National Federation of Housing Societies. Quarterly Bulletin *changed to* Voluntary Housing
0027-9242 National Federation of Science Abstracting and Indexing Services. Federation Newsletter *see* 0090-0893
0027-9250 National Fisherman
0027-9269 National Fluoridation News
0027-9277 U.S. Department of Agriculture. Economic Research Service. National Food Situation *see* 0161-4274
0027-9293 National Franchise Reports†
0027-9315 National Future Farmer *changed to* National Future Farmer
0027-9323 National Gallery of Canada. Bulletin *see* 0711-2866
0027-9331 National Gardener
0027-934X National Genealogical Society Quarterly
0027-9358 National Geographic
0027-9374 National Geographical Journal of India
0027-9382 National Geophysical Research Institute. Bulletin *see* 0378-6307
0027-9390 National Glass Budget *see* 0890-3743
0027-9404 National Guardian *changed to* Scottish Licensed Trade Guardian
0027-9412 National Guardsman *see* 0163-3945
0027-9420 National Health Federation. Bulletin *changed to* Health Freedom News
0027-9439 National Hearing Aid Journal *changed to* Hearing Journal
0027-9447 National Hog Farmer
0027-9455 National Horseman
0027-9471 Animal Shelter Shoptalk *changed to* Advocate
0027-948X National Humane Review *changed to* Advocate
0027-9501 National Institute Economic Review
0027-951X Japan. National Institute of Animal Health Quarterly†
0027-9528 National Institute of Sciences of India. Bulletin *see* 0378-6242
0027-9544 National Jeweler
0027-9552 National Jewish Monthly *see* 0279-3415
0027-9560 National Journal *see* 0360-4217
0027-9587 National Lampoon
0027-9609 National Leaders Magazine†
0027-9617 National League Journal of Insured Savings Associations *see* 0740-5464
0027-9625 National Legal Magazine *see* 0041-2538
0027-9633 National Library News
0027-9641 National Library of Medicine. Current Catalog
0027-965X National Library of Medicine News
0027-9668 National Live Stock Producer†
0027-9676 National Medical and Dental Association. Bulletin
0027-9684 National Medical Association. Journal
0027-9706 National Merchandiser†
0027-9714 National Messenger *changed to* Upper Case
0027-9722 National Model Railroad Association. Bulletin
0027-9730 National Museums and Monuments of Rhodesia. Occasional Papers *see* 0250-300X
0027-9730 National Museums and Monuments of Rhodesia. Occasional Papers *changed to* National Museums and Monuments Administration. Occasional Papers. Series A: Human Sciences
0027-9749 National Music Council Bulletin†
0027-9765 National News†
0027-9773 British Association of Colliery Management. National News Letter

1274 ISSN INDEX

ISSN	Title
0027-9781	National News of the Blind†
0027-9803	National Observer†
0027-9811	National Oceanographic Data Center. Newsletter†
0027-9838	National P T A Bulletin†
0027-9846	National Palace Museum Bulletin
0027-9854	National Palace Museum Newsletter
0027-9862	Newsletter - National Parking Association changed to Parking World
0027-9870	National Parks and Conservation Magazine see 0276-8186
0027-9889	National Petroleum News
0027-9897	National Pharmaceutical Association. Journal
0027-9900	National Pilots Association News Bulletin changed to National Pilots Association News
0027-9927	National Press Club Record
0027-9935	National Press Photographer changed to News Photographer
0027-9943	National Program Letter
0027-9951	National Prospector's Gazette & Treasure Hunter's News†
0027-996X	National Provisioner
0027-9978	National Public Accountant
0027-9994	National Real Estate Investor
0028-0011	National Research Council of Thailand. Journal
0028-0038	National Review
0028-0046	National Review Bulletin†
0028-0054	National Review of Criminal Sciences
0028-0062	National Review of Social Sciences
0028-0089	National Rural Letter Carrier
0028-0097	National Safety
0028-0100	National Safety News changed to Safety & Health
0028-0119	National Science Museum. Bulletin see 0385-2431
0028-0119	National Science Museum. Bulletin see 0385-244X
0028-0119	National Science Museum. Bulletin see 0385-2423
0028-0127	National Sculpture Review changed to Sculpture Review
0028-0135	National Service to Regional Councils. Special Reports see 0196-4003
0028-0143	National Service to Regional Councils. Newsletter changed to National Association of Regional Councils. Regional Focus
0028-0151	National Service to Regional Councils. Regional Review†
0028-016X	National Sheriff
0028-0178	National Shorthand Reporter
0028-0186	National Society for Medical Research. Bulletin†
0028-0208	National Speed Sport News
0028-0216	National Speleological Society. Bulletin see 0146-9517
0028-0232	National Stamp News†
0028-0259	Greece. National Statistical Service. Monthly Statistical Bulletin of Public Finance see 0256-3592
0028-0267	National Stock Dog
0028-0275	National Taiwan University. College of Medicine. Memoirs
0028-0283	National Tax Journal
0028-0291	National Technical Report
0028-0305	National Timber Industry changed to Western Timber Industry
0028-0313	National Tuberculosis and Respiratory Disease Association Bulletin see 0092-5659
0028-0321	National U. Weekly†
0028-033X	National Underwriter. Life & Health Insurance Edition
0028-0348	National Union Catalog see 0734-7650
0028-0356	National Union of the Footwear, Leather and Allied Trades Monthly Journal and Report changed to National Union of the Footwear, Leather and Allied Trades Journal and Report
0028-0364	National Voice of Salesmen
0028-0372	National Voter
0028-0399	National Westminster Bank Review
0028-0402	National Wildlife
0028-0410	National Wool Grower
0028-0429	National Writers Club. Bulletin for Professional Members changed to Professional Freelance Writers Directory
0028-0437	Der Nationale Demokrat
0028-0453	Nationaloekonomisk Tidsskrift
0028-047X	Nation's Business
0028-0488	Nation's Cities see 0164-5935
0028-0496	Nation's Health
0028-050X	Nations Nouvelles
0028-0518	Nation's Restaurant News
0028-0526	Nation's Schools see 0194-2263
0028-0534	Native Nevadan
0028-0542	Native Voice
0028-0550	Natturufraedingurinn
0028-0577	Natur, Kultur und Jagd see 0340-4277
0028-0585	Natur og Museum
0028-0593	Natur und Heimat
0028-0607	Natur und Land
0028-0615	Natur und Landschaft
0028-0623	Natur-und Nationalparke†
0028-0631	Natura
0028-064X	Natura
0028-0666	Natura Mosana
0028-0674	Natura
0028-0682	Natural and Applied Science Bulletin
0028-0704	Natural Health World
0028-0712	Natural History
0028-0720	Natural History Society of Northumberland Durham and Newcastle Upon Tyne. Transactions see 0144-221X
0028-0739	Natural Resources Journal
0028-0747	Natural Resources Lawyer changed to Natural Resources & Environment
0028-0755	Natural Rubber News
0028-0763	Natural Science in Schools changed to Teaching Science
0028-0771	Naturalist
0028-0798	Naturaliste Canadien
0028-0801	Naturalistes Belges
0028-081X	Der Naturarzt
0028-0828	Naturbrunnen changed to Der Mineralbrunnen
0028-0836	Nature
0028-0844	Nature and Resources and Man and Biosphere Programme. Bulletin see 0547-9665
0028-0852	Nature Conservancy News
0028-0860	Nature Study
0028-0887	Naturen
0028-0895	Naturens Verden
0028-0909	Nature's Path†
0028-0917	Naturforschende Gesellschaft zu Freiburg. Berichte
0028-0925	Naturfreund
0028-0933	Naturgemaesser Land- und Gartenbau
0028-0941	Naturheilpraxis
0028-095X	Naturhistorisches Museum in Wien. Monatsprogramm
0028-0968	Naturisme
0028-0976	Naturist und Welt†
0028-0984	Naturkautschuk
0028-0992	Naturkunde in Westfalen changed to Natur- und Landschaftkunde
0028-100X	Naturopath
0028-1018	Naturschutz- und Naturparke
0028-1026	Naturstein
0028-1034	Die Naturstein-Industrie
0028-1042	Die Naturwissenschaften
0028-1050	Naturwissenschaftliche Rundschau
0028-1077	Natuur en Landschap changed to Natuur en Milieu
0028-1085	Natuur en Museum
0028-1093	Natuur en Techniek
0028-1107	Natuurhistorisch Maandblad
0028-1115	Natya
0028-1123	Nauchen Zhivot
0028-1131	Nauchno-Tekhnicheskaya Informatsiya changed to Nauchno-Tekhnicheskaya Informatsiya. Seriya 1. Organizatsiya i Metodika Informatsionnoi Raboty
0028-1212	Filologicheskie Nauki
0028-1220	Nauncni Skupovi u SFRJ i u Inostranstvu see 0350-011X
0028-1239	Nauka i Religiya
0028-1247	Nauka i Suspil'stvo
0028-1255	Nauka i Tekhnika
0028-1263	Nauka i Zhizn'
0028-1271	Nauka Polska
0028-128X	N A U N L U
0028-1298	Naunyn-Schmiedeberg's Archives of Pharmacology
0028-1301	Natur und Museum
0028-131X	Nautakarja
0028-1336	Nautical Magazine
0028-1344	Nautilus
0028-1352	Nautilus
0028-1379	Nautisk Tidskrift
0028-1409	Naval Affairs
0028-1417	Naval Aviation News
0028-1425	Naval Engineers Journal
0028-1441	Naval Research Logistics Quarterly
0028-145X	Naval Research Reviews†
0028-1468	Naval Stores Review and Terpene Chemicals changed to Naval Stores Review
0028-1484	Naval War College Review
0028-1492	Navalkatha
0028-1506	Navbharat Times
0028-1514	Navetex changed to Modis
0028-1522	Navigation (Washington)
0028-1530	Navigation
0028-1549	Revue de la Navigation Fluviale Europeenne, Ports et Industries
0028-1557	Navigator
0028-1565	Navigatoer see 0107-4806
0028-1581	Navioneer
0028-159X	Navires Ports & Chantiers
0028-1603	Navis
0028-1611	Navitecnia changed to Navitecnia y Comercio Maritimo
0028-162X	Navnirman
0028-1646	Navy see 0144-3194
0028-1654	Navy Chaplains Bulletin
0028-1662	Navy News
0028-1670	Navy News
0028-1689	Navy: the Magazine of Sea Power changed to Sea Power
0028-1697	Navy Times
0028-1700	Nazareth
0028-1727	Nea Agrotiki Epitheorisis
0028-1735	Nea Hestia
0028-1743	Middle East Council of Churches. News Bulletin†
0028-1751	Near East Foundation News†
0028-176X	Near East Report
0028-1778	Near North News
0028-1786	Nebelspalter
0028-1794	Nebraska Alumnus
0028-1808	Nebraska Beverage Analyst
0028-1816	Nebraska Bird Review
0028-1832	Nebraska Dental Association. Journal†
0028-1840	Nebraska Education News changed to Nebraska Ed News
0028-1859	Nebraska History
0028-1867	Nebraska Journal of Economics and Business see 0747-5535
0028-1875	Nebraska Legionnaire
0028-1883	Nebraska Library Association Quarterly
0028-1891	Nebraska Mortar and Pestle
0028-1905	Nebraska Municipal Review
0028-1913	Nebraska Newspaper
0028-1921	Nebraska Nurse
0028-193X	Nebraska on the March†
0028-1948	Nebraska Retailer
0028-1964	Nebraskaland
0028-1972	Nedele†
0028-1980	Nedeljne Novine
0028-1999	Nedeljne Novosti
0028-2006	Nederduitse Gereformeerde Teologiese Tydskrif
0028-2014	Nederland-Israel
0028-2022	Nederland-U S S R Instituut. Maandberichten
0028-2030	Nederlands Archief voor Kerkgeschiedenis
0028-2049	Nederlands Archievenblad
0028-2057	Nederlands Bosbouw Tijdschrift
0028-2073	Nederlands Korfbalblad
0028-2081	Nederlandsch Maandblad voor Philatelie changed to Philatelie
0028-209X	Netherlands Milk and Dairy Journal
0028-212X	Nederlands Theologisch Tijdschrift
0028-2138	Netherlands International Law Review
0028-2154	Nederlands Tijdschrift voor Criminology see 0165-182X
0028-2162	Nederlands Tijdschrift voor Geneeskunde
0028-2170	Nederlands Tijdschrift voor Medische Studenten†
0028-2189	Nederlands Tijdschrift voor Natuurkunde changed to Nederlands Tijdschrift voor Natuurkunde A en B
0028-2197	Nederlands Tijdschrift voor Psychiatrie see 0303-7339
0028-2200	Nederlands Tijdschrift voor Tandheelkunde
0028-2227	Nederlands Weekblad voor de Groothandel in Levensmiddelen†
0028-2243	European Journal of Obstetrics and Gynecology see 0301-2115
0028-2251	Nederlandsch-Turkse Vereeniging. Berichten†
0028-226X	Nederlandsche Leeuw
0028-2278	Nederlandse Gedachten
0028-2294	Nederlandse Onderneming changed to Onderneming
0028-2308	Nederlandse Sport Federatie. Technisch Bulletin changed to Nederlandse Sport Federatie. Technische Mededelingen
0028-2324	Nederlandse Vereniging van Huisvrouwen Afdeling Amsterdam. Maandbericht†
0028-2332	Nederlandse Vereniging van Vrouwen met Academische Opleiding. Mededelingen
0028-2340	Nederlandse Vereniging voor Zeegeschiedenis. Mededelingen changed to Tijdschrift voor Zeegeschiedenis
0028-2359	Needle's Eye
0028-2375	Neen†
0028-2383	Neerlandia
0028-2391	Neerlands Postduiven Orgaan
0028-2405	Neerlands Volksleven
0028-2421	Neftekhimiya
0028-243X	Neftyanik
0028-2448	Neftyanoe Khozyaistvo
0028-2456	Negocios y Bancos
0028-2464	Negotiation Research Digest†
0028-2472	Negotiations News changed to New Jersey School Boards Association. School Leader
0028-2480	Negro American Literature Forum see 0148-6179
0028-2502	Negro Braille Magazine changed to Merrick/Washington Magazine for the Blind
0028-2510	Negro Heritage changed to Black Heritage
0028-2529	Negro History Bulletin
0028-2537	Negro Traveler and Conventioneer changed to Traveler & Conventioneer
0028-2545	Niege et Glace changed to Ski-Flash Magazine
0028-2553	Neill Letter of Contrary Opinion changed to Fraser Opinion Letter
0028-2561	Neirofiziologiya
0028-2588	Neman
0028-2596	Nematologica
0028-260X	Nemuno Krastas
0028-2626	Nemzetor
0028-2642	Neo Aftokinito
0028-2677	Neophilologus
0028-2685	Neoplasma
0028-2693	Neos Kosmos
0028-2707	Nepal Gazette Translation Service changed to Nepal Recorder
0028-2715	Nepal Medical Association. Journal
0028-2723	Nepal Press Digest
0028-2731	Nepal Press Report

ISSN INDEX 1275

0028-274X Nepal Rastra Bank. Quarterly Economic Bulletin
0028-2758 Nepal Review Monthly†
0028-2766 Nephron
0028-2774 Neprajzi Kozlemenyek
0028-2782 Neptune Nautisme
0028-2790 Neptunus
0028-2804 Der Nervenarzt
0028-2812 Nestor
0028-2820 Net
0028-2847 Netherhall News†
0028-2855 Netherlands - American Trade *changed to* Holland - U S A & Netherlands News
0028-2871 Amsterdam. Bureau van Statistiek. Maandbericht
0028-2901 Netherlands Economic Bulletin for the Foreign Press *changed to* Netherlands News
0028-291X Statistisch Kwartaaloverzicht Hilversum *changed to* Statistisch Jaaroverzicht Hilversum
0028-2928 Netherlands Journal of Agricultural Science
0028-2944 Netherlands Journal of Plant Pathology
0028-2960 Netherlands Journal of Zoology
0028-2979 Netherlands. Ministerie van Cultuur, Recreatie en Maatschappelijk Werk. Centrale Afdeling Internationale Betrekkingen. Informatie Bulletin†
0028-2987 Netherlands. Ministerie van Onderwijs en Wetenschappen. Pedagogische Bibliografie
0028-2995 Netherlands Patents Report
0028-3002 Netherlands. Rijksmuseum. Bulletin *see* 0569-9665
0028-3029 Netsu Kanri *see* 0302-1289
0028-3045 Networks
0028-3053 Neue Technik und Wirtschaft†
0028-307X Angestellte *changed to* Die Angestellten
0028-3088 Neue Betriebswirtschaft†
0028-3096 Neue Blaetter des Theaters in der Josefstadt
0028-310X Neue Blaetter fuer Taubstummenbildung *see* 0342-4898
0028-3118 Das Neue Buch
0028-3126 Die Neue Buecherei
0028-3134 Der Neue Bund
0028-3142 Neue Deutsche Hefte
0028-3150 Neue Deutsche Literatur
0028-3169 Das Neue Erlangen
0028-3177 Neue Gesellschaft *see* 0177-6738
0028-3193 Das Neue Handwerk
0028-3207 Neue Huette
0028-3223 Neue Illustrierte Wochenschau
0028-3231 Neue Justiz
0028-324X Der Neue Kaufmann
0028-3258 Neue Kommentare
0028-3274 Der Neue Mahnruf
0028-3282 Neue Museumskunde
0028-3290 Neue Musikzeitung
0028-3304 Die Neue Ordnung in Kirche, Staat, Gesellschaft, Kultur
0028-3320 Neue Politische Literatur
0028-3339 Neue Produkte
0028-3347 Neue Rundschau
0028-3355 Neue Sammlung
0028-3371 Neue Stenographische Praxis
0028-338X Neue Steuerpraxis
0028-3398 Neue Technik
0028-3401 Neue Technik im Buero
0028-341X Neue Uhrmacher-Zeitung *changed to* Schmuck und Uhren
0028-3444 Neue Wege
0028-3452 Neue Werbung
0028-3460 Neue Wirtschafts-Briefe
0028-3479 Zeitschrift fuer Parapsychologie und Grenzgebiete der Psychologie
0028-3495 Neue Zeitschrift fuer Missionswissenschaft
0028-3509 Neue Zeitschrift fuer Musik *see* 0170-8791
0028-3517 Neue Zeitschrift fuer Systematische Theologie und Religionsphilosophie
0028-3525 Neue Zeitschrift fuer Wehrrecht
0028-3533 Neuen Buecher†
0028-3568 Zions Freund
0028-3576 Die Neueren Sprachen
0028-3584 Der Neuerer. Ausgabe A B C
0028-3592 Neues Beginnen *changed to* Theorie und Praxis der Sozialen Arbeit
0028-3606 Neues Bei Uns *changed to* STEWEAG-Rundschau
0028-3614 Neues Dorf
0028-3622 Neues Forvm *changed to* Forvm
0028-3630 Neues Jahrbuch fuer Geologie und Palaeontologie, Monatshefte
0028-3649 Neues Jahrbuch fuer Mineralogie. Monatshefte
0028-3657 Neues Leben
0028-3665 Neues Leben
0028-3673 Neues Optikerjournal
0028-3681 Neues Polizeiarchiv
0028-3711 Neuheiten und Erfinderdienst *changed to* Erfinder und Neuheitendienst
0028-3754 Neuphilologische Mitteilungen
0028-3770 Neuro-Chirurgie
0028-3797 Neuropaediatrie *see* 0174-304X
0028-3800 Neurobiologia
0028-3819 Neurochirurgia
0028-3827 Neuroendocrine Control Mechanism†
0028-3835 Neuroendocrinology
0028-3843 Neurologia i Neurochirurgia Polska
0028-386X Revista de Medicina Interna, Neurologie, Psihiatrie, Neuro-Chirurgie, Dermato-Venerologie
0028-3878 Neurology
0028-3886 Neurology India
0028-3894 Neuropatologia Polska
0028-3908 Neuropharmacology
0028-3916 Neuropsichiatria
0028-3924 Neuropsichiatria Infantile *see* 0393-361X
0028-3932 Neuropsychologia
0028-3940 Neuroradiology
0028-3959 Neuroscience Translations *see* 0097-0549
0028-3967 Neurosciences Research Program Bulletin†
0028-3975 Neurospora Newsletter *changed to* Fungal Genetics Newsletter
0028-3983 Neusprachliche Mitteilungen aus Wissenschaft und Praxis
0028-4009 Neva
0028-4017 Nevada Business Review *see* 0148-5881
0028-4033 Nevada Education Journal
0028-4041 Nevada Highway News†
0028-405X Nevada Highways and Parks *changed to* Nevada
0028-4068 Nevada Libraries *changed to* High Roller
0028-4084 Nevada Outdoors and Wildlife Review†
0028-4092 Nevada State Bar Journal *see* 0092-6086
0028-4106 Nevada State Library. Official Nevada Publications *changed to* Nevada Official Publications
0028-4114 Neve International
0028-4122 Nevesport Illustrato
0028-4130 New†
0028-4149 New Magazine†
0028-4165 New African†
0028-4173 Witches Newsletter *see* 0049-7754
0028-4181 New Amberola Graphic
0028-4203 New American & Canadian Poetry†
0028-4211 New American Review *changed to* American Review
0028-4238 New Associations and Projects
0028-4246 New Atlantis†
0028-4254 New Aurora
0028-4262 Green Mountain Post
0028-4270 New Beacon (Inkprint Edition)
0028-4289 New Blackfriars
0028-4297 New Book Review†
0028-4300 New Books†
0028-4319 New Books in Business and Economics *changed to* Harvard Business School. Baker Library. Recent Additions to Baker Library
0028-4327 New Books on Family Planning
0028-4335 New Books on World Affairs *changed to* Council Spotlight Book Notes
0028-4351 New Brunswick Economic Statistics†
0028-436X New Building *changed to* New Building Projects
0028-4378 New Business Incorporations
0028-4394 New Canadian
0028-4408 New Captain George's Whizzbang†
0028-4424 New Church Messenger *changed to* Messenger (San Francisco)
0028-4459 New Coin
0028-4467 New Collage Magazine
0028-4475 New Commonwealth *see* 0305-750X
0028-4491 New Construction
0028-4505 New Cornwall†
0028-4513 New Dawn†
0028-4521 New Dawn *changed to* Dawn
0028-453X New Day
0028-4548 New Day†
0028-4556 New Day *changed to* New Century
0028-4564 Ontario New Democrat
0028-4572 New Democrat†
0028-4599 New Dimensions†
0028-4602 New Dimensions in Education *see* 0317-0349
0028-4610 New Directions
0028-4629 New Directions *changed to* Valley Commerce
0028-4637 New Driver†
0028-4645 New Edinburgh Review *see* 0267-6672
0028-4653 New England Advertising Week
0028-4661 New England Apparel Retailer *changed to* Fashion Retailer
0028-470X New England Construction
0028-4726 New England Economic Review
0028-4734 New England Electrical News†
0028-4742 New England Furniture News†
0028-4750 New-England Galaxy†
0028-4785 New England Historical and Genealogical Register
0028-4793 New England Journal of Medicine
0028-4807 New England Journal of Optometry
0028-4823 New England Law Review
0028-4831 New England Letter *changed to* First National Bank of Boston. Economic Review
0028-484X New England Printer and Lithographer *see* 0162-8771
0028-4858 New England Purchaser *changed to* New England Purchaser/Connecticut Purchaser
0028-4866 New England Quarterly: A Historical Review of New England Life and Letters
0028-4874 New England Railroad Club. Official Proceedings
0028-4882 New England Reading Association. Journal
0028-4890 New England Real Estate Journal
0028-4912 New England Social Studies Bulletin
0028-4920 New England Square Dance Caller
0028-4939 New England Water Works Association. Journal
0028-4947 New Englander *see* 0164-3533
0028-4955 New Entomologist
0028-4963 New Equipment Digest
0028-4971 New Equipment News
0028-498X New Equipment News
0028-4998 New Era
0028-5013 New Era†
0028-5021 New Era (Ely)
0028-5048 New Era
0028-5056 New Era Laundry & Cleaning Lines
0028-5064 New Ethicals *see* 0311-905X
0028-5072 New Factory Report†
0028-5080 New Forerunner†
0028-5099 New Future *changed to* News and Views: for Young Workers
0028-5102 New Generation†
0028-5110 New Geographical Literature and Maps†
0028-5129 New Germany Reports†
0028-5137 New Guard
0028-5145 New Guinea and Australia, the Pacific and South-East Asia†
0028-5153 New Guinea Bulletin†
0028-5161 New Guinea Periodical Index†
0028-517X New Guinea Psychologist†
0028-5188 New Guinea Research Bulletin†
0028-5196 New Hampshire Alumnus
0028-520X New Hampshire Audubon News *see* 0162-5284
0028-5234 New Hampshire Educator
0028-5242 New Hampshire Highways
0028-5250 New Hampshire Horizons†
0028-5269 N H L A Newsletter
0028-5277 New Hampshire Motor Transport†
0028-5285 New Hampshire Natural Resources *changed to* Fish & Game Highlights of New Hampshire
0028-5293 New Hampshire Polyglot
0028-5307 New Hampshire Profiles
0028-5315 New Hampshire Quarter Notes
0028-5331 New Haven I N F O
0028-5374 New Horizons
0028-5382 New Horizons in Education
0028-5390 New Hungarian Quarterly
0028-5404 New Idea
0028-5412 New Illustrator *changed to* Light on the Word for Adult Teachers
0028-5420 New in Dentistry†
0028-5439 New Individualist Review†
0028-5455 New Jersey Academy of Science. Bulletin
0028-5463 New Jersey Academy of Science. Newsletter
0028-5498 New Jersey Air, Water and Waste Management Times *changed to* New Jersey Outdoors
0028-5528 N J A O P S Journal
0028-5536 New Jersey Banker
0028-5544 New Jersey Bell
0028-5552 New Jersey Beverage Journal
0028-5560 New Jersey Business
0028-5579 New Jersey Business Woman
0028-5587 New Jersey Club Woman and Even'tide†
0028-5595 New Jersey Correction News†
0028-5609 New Jersey Council News
0028-5617 New Jersey County Government†
0028-5633 New Jersey Days†
0028-5668 New Jersey Division of Veterans Services Information Bulletin. *changed to* New Jersey Bureau of Veterans Services Information Bulletin
0028-5676 New Jersey Economic Review†
0028-5684 New Jersey Education *see* 0199-4557
0028-5692 New Jersey Elementary School Principals Association. Bulletin *see* 0001-8414
0028-5706 New Jersey Equine Industry News
0028-5714 New Jersey Federation of Planning Officials. Federation Planner
0028-5722 New Jersey Federation of Planning Officials. Federation Planning Information Reports
0028-5757 New Jersey History
0028-5765 New Jersey Journal of Optometry
0028-5773 New Jersey Journal of Pharmacy
0028-5781 New Jersey Labor Herald
0028-579X New Jersey Landings†
0028-5803 New Jersey Law Journal
0028-5811 New Jersey Libraries
0028-582X New Jersey Messenger
0028-5838 New Jersey Motor Truck Association. Bulletin
0028-5846 New Jersey Municipalities
0028-5854 New Jersey Music and Arts†
0028-5862 New Jersey Nature News *changed to* New Jersey Audubon
0028-5870 N J S N A Newsletter *changed to* New Jersey Nurse
0028-5897 New Jersey Parent Teacher
0028-5900 New Jersey Professional Engineer
0028-5919 New Jersey Realtor
0028-5927 N J S D C Research Bulletin
0028-5935 New Jersey Speech and Hearing Association. Journal
0028-5951 New Jersey State Bar Journal *see* 0195-0983
0028-6001 New Journal

0028-601X New Journal of Statistics and Operational Research
0028-6044 New Leader
0028-6052 Money Management and Unitholder
0028-6060 New Left Review
0028-6079 New Life
0028-6087 New Literary History
0028-6095 New Literature on Automation
0028-6125 New Messenger (Braille Edition)†
0028-6141 New Mexico Beverage Journal *see* 0194-813X
0028-6168 New Mexico Business†
0028-6184 New Mexico Extension News†
0028-6192 New Mexico Farm & Ranch
0028-6206 New Mexico Historical Review
0028-6214 New Mexico Law Review
0028-6222 New Mexico Libraries†
0028-6230 New Mexico Lobo
0028-6249 New Mexico Magazine
0028-6257 New Mexico Municipal League. Municipal Reporter
0028-6265 New Mexico Musician
0028-6273 New Mexico Nurse
0028-6281 New Mexico Professional Engineer
0028-6303 New Mexico School Review†
0028-6338 New Mexico Wildlife
0028-6354 New Morality
0028-6362 New Musical Express
0028-6370 New Nation†
0028-6389 New Norfolk *changed to* Tidewater Virginian
0028-6397 New Orleans Port Record
0028-6400 New Orleans Review
0028-6419 New Outlook
0028-6427 New Outlook
0028-6435 New Outlook for the Blind *see* 0145-482X
0028-6443 New Philosophy
0028-6451 New Physician
0028-646X New Phytologist
0028-6478 New Poetry *changed to* Brouhaha
0028-6486 New Polish Publications
0028-6494 New Politics†
0028-6524 New Product Newsletter *changed to* International New Product Newsletter
0028-6532 New Race
0028-6540 New Rambler
0028-6559 New Records
0028-6567 New Reference Books at U C L A†
0028-6575 New Renaissance
0028-6583 New Republic
0028-6591 New Research Centers
0028-6605 New Review *changed to* New Review of East-European History (1981)
0028-6613 New Scholar
0028-6621 New Scholasticism
0028-663X New School Bulletin†
0028-6656 New Schools Exchange Newsletter†
0028-6664 New Scientist
0028-6672 New Scotian *see* 0704-0652
0028-6680 New Serial Titles
0028-6729 New Society
0028-6745 New South *see* 0093-9293
0028-6761 New South Wales Government Publications. Monthly List *changed to* New South Wales Government. Legislation Issued
0028-677X New South Wales Industrial Gazette
0028-6788 New South Wales Library Bulletin†
0028-6796 New South Wales Official Publications Received in the Library of New South Wales
0028-6818 New South Wales. Soil Conservation Service Journal
0028-6826 New South Wales Statistical Bulletin†
0028-6834 New Spotlight
0028-6842 New Statesman
0028-6869 New Technical Books
0028-6877 New Testament Abstracts
0028-6885 New Testament Studies
0028-6907 New Trail
0028-6966 New Window†
0028-6974 New Woman
0028-6990 New World
0028-7008 New World
0028-7016 New World *see* 0149-970X
0028-7032 New World
0028-7067 New World Review *changed to* Update U S S R
0028-7075 New Worlds
0028-7083 New Writing from Zambia
0028-7091 New York Academy of Medicine. Bulletin
0028-7105 New York Academy of Medicine. News Notes
0028-7113 New York Academy of Sciences. Transactions
0028-7121 New York Amsterdam News
0028-713X New York Auto Repairs
0028-7164 New York Construction News
0028-7180 New York Column†
0028-7199 New York Entomological Society. Journal
0028-7210 New York Fish and Game Journal
0028-7229 New York Folklore Quarterly *see* 0361-204X
0028-7237 New York Genealogical and Biographical Record
0028-7245 New York Generator
0028-7253 New York Historical Society Quarterly†
0028-727X New York Holstein Friesian News *see* 0279-8611
0028-7288 New York Convention & Visitors Bureau. Quarterly Calendar of Events
0028-7296 New York Journal of Dentistry
0028-730X New York L P N *changed to* New York L P N and Technician
0028-7318 New York Law Forum *see* 0145-448X
0028-7342 New York Letter Carriers' Outlook
0028-7369 New York Magazine
0028-7385 New York Motorist
0028-7431 New York Podiatrist†
0028-7466 New York Public Library. Bulletin *see* 0160-0168
0028-7474 New York Purchasing Review *see* 0192-7973
0028-7482 New York Quarterly
0028-7490 New York Retailer†
0028-7504 New York Review of Books
0028-7512 New York State Archeological Association. Bulletin *changed to* New York State Archaeological Association. Bulletin and Journal
0028-7547 New York State Bar Journal
0028-7555 New York State Bulletin *changed to* New York State Register
0028-7563 New York State Conference of Mayors and Other Municipal Officials. Legal Bulletin†
0028-7571 New York State Dental Journal
0028-7598 New York State Education†
0028-761X New York State Housing and Community Renewal Reporter†
0028-7628 New York State Journal of Medicine
0028-7644 New York State Nurses Association. Journal
0028-7652 New York State Nurses Association. Report
0028-7660 New York State Pharmacist *see* 0163-1586
0028-7679 New York State Planning News *changed to* New York Planning News
0028-7687 New York State Psychologist
0028-7709 New York State School Boards Association Journal
0028-7741 New York State Society of Dentistry for Children. Bulletin
0028-7768 New York State Statistical Reporter†
0028-7776 New York State Taxpayer *changed to* C P E S Taxpayer
0028-7784 New York Theatre Critics' Reviews
0028-7806 New York Times Book Review
0028-7814 New York Times Large Type Weekly
0028-7830 New York Times School Weekly†
0028-7849 New York Times Student Weekly†
0028-7857 New York University. Center for International Studies. Policy Papers†
0028-7865 New York University Journal of Dentistry†
0028-7873 New York University Journal of International Law and Politics
0028-7881 New York University Law Review
0028-789X New York University Medical Center News
0028-7903 New York University Medical Quarterly *changed to* N Y U Physician
0028-792X New Yorker
0028-7938 Farm Research *see* 0361-5367
0028-7946 New Yugoslav Law *see* 0350-2252
0028-7962 New Zealand Archaeological Association. Newsletter
0028-7989 New Zealand Camellia Bulletin
0028-7997 New Zealand Christian Pacifist *changed to* Peacemaker
0028-8004 New Zealand Coal†
0028-8012 New Zealand Commerce
0028-8020 New Zealand Company Director and Sharemarket Survey *changed to* Company Director & Professional Administrator
0028-8039 New Zealand Countrywoman
0028-8047 New Zealand Dental Journal
0028-8063 New Zealand Electrical Journal *see* 0111-5839
0028-8071 New Zealand Electrician
0028-808X New Zealand Engineering
0028-8098 New Zealand Farmer
0028-8101 New Zealand Financial Times *see* 0111-8021
0028-811X New Zealand. Forest Service. Forest Research Institute. Research Leaflet†
0028-8128 New Zealand Furnishing and Appliance World†
0028-8136 New Zealand Gardener
0028-8144 New Zealand Geographer
0028-8160 New Zealand Hardware Journal
0028-8179 New Zealand Holiday†
0028-8187 New Zealand Home Journal†
0028-8195 New Zealand Horological Journal
0028-8209 New Zealand Horse & Pony
0028-8217 New Zealand Hospital
0028-8225 New Zealand Institute of Chemistry. Journal *changed to* Chemistry in New Zealand
0028-8233 New Zealand Journal of Agricultural Research
0028-8241 New Zealand Journal of Agriculture
0028-825X New Zealand Journal of Botany
0028-8268 New Zealand Journal of Dairy Technology *see* 0300-1342
0028-8276 New Zealand Journal of Educational Studies
0028-8284 New Zealand Journal of Forestry *see* 0112-9597
0028-8292 New Zealand Journal of Geography
0028-8306 New Zealand Journal of Geology and Geophysics
0028-8314 New Zealand Journal of Health, Physical Education and Recreation
0028-8322 New Zealand Journal of History
0028-8330 New Zealand Journal of Marine and Freshwater Research
0028-8349 New Zealand Journal of Medical Laboratory Technology
0028-8357 New Zealand Journal of Public Administration *see* 0110-5191
0028-8365 New Zealand Journal of Science†
0028-8373 New Zealand Law Journal
0028-8381 New Zealand Libraries
0028-8403 New Zealand Local Government
0028-8411 New Zealand Manufacturer†
0028-842X New Zealand Marine Sciences Newsletter
0028-8438 New Zealand Meat Producer†
0028-8446 New Zealand Medical Journal
0028-8454 New Zealand Medical Record†
0028-8489 New Zealand Monthly Review
0028-8497 New Zealand National Bibliography
0028-8500 New Zealand News U.K.
0028-8519 New Zealand Newsletter *changed to* Letter from New Zealand
0028-8527 New Zealand Numismatic Journal
0028-8535 New Zealand Nursing Journal
0028-8543 New Zealand Outdoor
0028-8586 New Zealand Plastics *changed to* Plastics & Packaging
0028-8594 New Zealand Plumbing Review
0028-8608 New Zealand Potter
0028-8624 New Zealand Railway Observer
0028-8632 New Zealand Rationalist and Humanist
0028-8640 New Zealand Export Review†
0028-8667 New Zealand Science Review
0028-8675 Service Station News *changed to* Motor Trade News
0028-8683 New Zealand Slavonic Journal
0028-8705 New Zealand Society of Periodontology. Bulletin *see* 0111-1485
0028-8713 New Zealand Speech Therapists Journal *see* 0110-571X
0028-8721 New Zealand Stamp Monthly
0028-873X New Zealand Stock Market Review†
0028-8748 New Zealand Tablet
0028-8756 New Zealand Tenders Gazette
0028-8799 New Zealand Trotting Calendar
0028-8802 New Zealand Wildlife
0028-8829 New Zealand Woman's Weekly
0028-8837 Newark *changed to* Metro-Newark!
0028-8845 Newark Beth Israel Medical Center. Journal†
0028-8853 Newark Churchman *see* 0277-2272
0028-887X Newcastle Medical Journal†
0028-8888 Newfoundland Gazette
0028-8918 Newport History
0028-8926 Newport Newstory†
0028-8942 News About Z - 39 *see* 0163-626X
0028-8969 News & Letters
0028-9019 News Explorer *see* 0736-0592
0028-9035 News for Farmer Cooperatives *see* 0364-0736
0028-9043 Habitat
0028-9051 News for You
0028-9094 News from Pondy
0028-9116 News from Romania
0028-9132 News from South Africa†
0028-9140 News from the Center†
0028-9159 News from the Gutter
0028-9167 News from the Home Front *changed to* National Asthma Center News
0028-9175 News from the Library†
0028-9183 News from the Vineyards†
0028-9191 News Front *see* 0194-9225
0028-9205 News in Engineering
0028-9221 News 'n Views†
0028-923X News, Notes, and Quotes
0028-9256 Newark Museum. News Notes *changed to* Newark Museum. Exhibitions & Events
0028-9264 News of New York
0028-9272 News of Norway
0028-9280 News of the World
0028-9299 News of the World's Children
0028-9302 News of the Yivo
0028-9310 News on Russian Medicine and Biochemistry†
0028-9329 Scholastic News Pilot *see* 0744-916X
0028-9337 News Review†
0028-9353 News Trade Weekly
0028-9361 News Trails *see* 0736-0576
0028-937X News-View†
0028-9388 Newsagent†
0028-9396 Newsboy
0028-940X Bangkok Standard *changed to* Living in Thailand
0028-9418 Newsette
0028-9426 Newsletter for Birdwatchers
0028-9434 Newsletter for Research in Psychology *see* 0092-394X
0028-9442 Newsletter from behind the Iron Curtain†
0028-9450 Newsletter of Computer Archaeology†
0028-9469 Newsletter on Comparative Studies of Communism†
0028-9485 Newsletter on Intellectual Freedom
0028-9493 Newsletter on Isotopic Generators and Batteries†
0028-9507 Newsletter on Newsletters
0028-9523 Newsletter on the State of the Culture†
0028-9531 Newsman
0028-954X Newspaper Collector's Gazette†

ISSN INDEX 1277

0028-9558 Newspaper Controller *changed to* Newspaper Financial Executives Journal
0028-9566 Trabajador del Periodismo
0028-9574 Newsreel†
0028-9582 Newsseeker†
0028-9590 Newstime *see* 0736-0622
0028-9604 Newsweek
0028-9620 Neydhartinger Moorpost†
0028-9639 Nharireyomurindi
0028-9655 Nia Voceto *changed to* Kalejdoskopo
0028-9663 Niagara Frontier†
0028-9744 Niederoesterreichische Landes-Landwirtschaftskammer. Amtlicher Marktbericht
0028-9752 Niederrheinische Industrie- und Handelskammer Duisberg Wesel zu Duisberg. Wirtschaftliche Mitteilungen *changed to* NiederrheinKammer
0028-9779 Niedersaechsische Gemeinde
0028-9787 Niedersaechsischer Staatsanzeiger
0028-9795 Niedersaechsisches Aerzteblatt
0028-9809 Niekas†
0028-9817 Nieman Reports
0028-9825 Nieuw Archief voor Wiskunde
0028-9833 Nieuw Geluid
0028-9841 Nieuw Ruimzicht *changed to* Ruimzicht
0028-9868 Nieuw Vlaams Tijdschrift†
0028-9876 Nieuw Wereld Nieuws
0028-9892 Nieuwe Linie†
0028-9906 Nieuwe Literatuur over Oorlog en Vrede *changed to* Trans-Actie
0028-9922 Nieuwe Taalgids
0028-9930 Nieuwe West Indische Gids
0028-9949 Nieuws Uit Zuid-Afrika†
0028-9965 Nieuwsblad voor de Boekhandel *see* 0167-4765
0028-999X Verantwoord Levensverkeer
0029-0009 Nigeria English Studies Association Journal
0029-0017 Nigeria. Federal Office of Statistics. Digest of Statistics
0029-0025 Nigeria Lawyers' Quarterly
0029-0033 Nigeria Magazine
0029-0041 Nigeria Trade Journal
0029-005X Nigerian Christian
0029-0068 Nigerian Commercial Vehicle User
0029-0076 Nigerian Field
0029-0084 Nigerian Geographical Journal
0029-0092 Nigerian Journal of Economic & Social Studies
0029-0106 Nigerian Journal of Islam
0029-0114 Nigerian Journal of Science
0029-0122 Nigerian Libraries
0029-0130 Nigerian Opinion†
0029-0157 Nigerian Schoolmaster
0029-0173 Nigrizia
0029-0181 Nihon Butsuri Gakkaishi
0029-019X Science Council of Japan. Monthly Report
0029-0211 Japan Gas Association. Journal
0029-022X Society of Rubber Industry. Journal
0029-0238 Japanese Journal of Smooth Muscle Research
0029-0254 Japanese Poultry Science
0029-0262 Japanese Economic Indicators
0029-0270 Japan Society of Mechanical Engineers. Transactions
0029-0289 Mycological Society of Japan. Transactions
0029-0297 Japanese Stomatological Society. Journal
0029-0300 Folia Endocrinologica Japonica
0029-0319 Nihon no Jidosha†
0029-0327 Japan Science and Technology
0029-0335 Journal of Japanese Scientists
0029-0343 Japanese Association of Physical Medicine, Balneology and Climatology. Journal
0029-0351 Japan Plastics Journal
0029-036X Japan Refrigeration and Air Conditioning News
0029-0378 Japan Institute of Labour. Journal
0029-0386 Acta Neonatologica Japonica
0029-0394 Journal of Food Science and Technology
0029-0408 Japanese Television
0029-0416 Horological Institute of Japan. Journal
0029-0424 Nihon University Journal of Medicine
0029-0432 Nihon University. School of Dentistry. Journal
0029-0440 Niigata Medical Journal
0029-0459 Nijhoff Information
0029-0467 Nijhoff's Index Op Nederlandse en Vlaamse Periodieken†
0029-0483 Japan Chemical Industry Association Monthly
0029-0491 Nikkei Business
0029-0505 Nikkyoso Kyoiku Shimbun
0029-0513 Nikon World†
0029-0521 Nillmijmeringen†
0029-053X Nimrod
0029-0556 Nineteen†
0029-0564 Nineteenth-Century Fiction *changed to* Nineteenth-Century Literature (Berkeley)
0029-0572 Human Medicine
0029-0580 Ninth District Conditions *see* 0271-5287
0029-0602 Japanese Association of Groundwater Hydrology. Journal
0029-0610 Society of the Science of Soil and Manure of Japan. Journal *changed to* Japanese Journal of Soil Science & Plant Nutrition
0029-0629 Japanese Journal of Fertility and Sterility
0029-0645 Japan Broncho-Esophagological Society. Journal
0029-0653 Japan Precious Metals and Watch News
0029-067X Musashino Electrical Communication Laboratory. Review of the Electrical Communication Laboratory
0029-0688 Niranjan
0029-0696 Nirmok
0029-070X Nisarg Ane Arogya
0029-0718 Nishi Nihon Kisho Geppo†
0029-0726 Nishinihon Journal of Urology
0029-0734 Nissan Diesel Technical Review
0029-0742 Nissan Graphic
0029-0750 Nippon Institute for Biological Science. Journal
0029-0769 Niti†
0029-0777 Nitrogen
0029-0785 Poultry Researches
0029-0793 Annales de Physique Biologique & Medicale *changed to* Journal de Biophysique et Medecine Nucleaire
0029-0823 No More Hiroshimas†
0029-0831 Brain and Development/No to Hattatsu *changed to* No to Hattatsu
0029-084X No Walls Broadsheet†
0029-0858 Nobel Hefte
0029-0874 Nogaku Kenkyu
0029-0882 Agriculture and Better Farming
0029-0904 Nogyo No Kairyo†
0029-0912 Agriculture and Economy
0029-0920 Noi Donne
0029-0939 Noi Giovani
0029-0947 Noise & Vibration Bulletin
0029-0963 Nok Lapja
0029-0971 Agricultural Machinery News
0029-098X Nokigu Nyusu *changed to* Agricultural Machinery News
0029-1013 Canada. Statistics Canada. Non-Ferrous Scrap Metal†
0029-1021 Non-Destructive Testing *see* 0308-9126
0029-103X Non-Foods Merchandising
0029-1056 Non-Manual Worker in the Free Labour World *changed to* International Federation of Commercial Clerical and Technical Employees. Newsletter
0029-1080 Noncello
0029-1102 Nonferrous Report†
0029-1137 Noord-Amsterdammer
0029-1145 Noord-Brabant
0029-1161 Nor Or
0029-1188 Nord e Sud
0029-1196 Nordfriesland
0029-120X Nord Economique
0029-1226 Norden
0029-1234 Nordens Tidning†
0029-1242 Nordeste
0029-1269 Nordhaeuser Nachrichten
0029-1277 Nordic Hydrology
0029-1285 Nordisk Administrativt Tidsskrift
0029-1307 Nordisk Betong
0029-1315 Nordisk Domssamling
0029-1323 Nordisk Exlibris Tidsskrift
0029-1331 Nordisk Fagpresse *see* 0106-0120
0029-134X Nordisk Filateli
0029-1374 Nordisk Hygienisk Tidskrift *see* 0355-3140
0029-1382 Nordisk Jaernbane Tidskrift
0029-1390 Nordisk Kriminalteknisk Tidsskrift
0029-1404 Nordisk Kvaekartidskrift *see* 0345-6005
0029-1412 Nordisk Matematisk Tidskrift *changed to* Normat: Nordisk Matematisk Tidskrift
0029-1420 Nordisk Medicin
0029-1439 Nordisk Mejeri-Tidsskrift *see* 0109-3207
0029-1447 Nordisk Missions Tidsskrift *changed to* Mission
0029-1455 Nordisk Psykiatrisk Tidsskrift
0029-1463 Nordisk Psykologi
0029-1471 Nordisk Tidskrift foer Doevundervisningen *changed to* Nordisk Tidskrift foer Hoersel och Doevundervisning
0029-148X Nordisk Tidskrift Foer Bok- och Biblioteksvaesen
0029-1498 Nordisk Tidskrift for Fotografi
0029-1501 Nordisk Tidskrift for Vetenskap, Konst och Industri
0029-151X Nordisk Tidsskrift for International Ret
0029-1544 Nordisk Tidsskrift for Special-Optikere *changed to* Nordisk Tidsskrift for Optikere
0029-1552 Nordisk Tidsskrift for Tale og Stemme†
0029-1579 Nordisk Veterinaermedicin
0029-1587 Nordiska Institutet Foer Faergforskning. Litteraturoversigt†
0029-1595 Nordost-Archiv
0029-1609 Nordwestdeutsche Gesellschaft fuer Innere Medizin. Kongressbericht
0029-1617 Nordwestdeutsches Handwerk
0029-1625 Norelco Reporter *changed to* Electron Optics Reporter
0029-1633 Norfolk and Western *changed to* Norfolk Southern World
0029-1641 Norfolk Botanical Garden Society Bulletin
0029-165X Norfolk Fair
0029-1676 Norges Bank. Economic Bulletin
0029-1684 Norges Bondeblad *changed to* Bondebladet
0029-1692 Norges Forsvar
0029-1706 Norges Industri
0029-1722 Norges Utenrikshandel *changed to* Eksport Aktuelt
0029-1730 Norges Vel†
0029-1757 Monthly Statistics on Agriculture, Forestry and Fisheries
0029-1773 Norin Tosho Shiryo Geppo
0029-1781 Normalizace *changed to* Ceskoslovenska Standardizace
0029-179X Normalizacja
0029-1803 Normandie Industrielle
0029-1811 Normandie Protestante *changed to* Nord-Normandie
0029-182X Norois
0029-1838 Norrlaendsk Tidskrift
0029-1846 Norseman
0029-1854 Norsk Artilleri-Tidsskrift
0029-1862 Norsk Bibliografisk Bibliotek
0029-1870 Norsk Bokfortegnelse Aarskatalog
0029-1889 Norske Bokhandlertidende *changed to* Bok og Samfunn
0029-1897 Norwegian Journal of Entomology†
0029-1900 Norsk Fagfoto
0029-1919 Norsk Faktortidende
0029-1927 Norsk Farmaceutisk Selskap. Meddelelser *see* 0800-2606
0029-1935 Norsk Farmaceutisk Tidsskrift
0029-1943 Norsk Filosofisk Tidsskrift
0029-1951 Norsk Geografisk Tidsskrift
0029-196X Norsk Geologisk Tidsskrift
0029-1978 Norsk Grafisk Tidsskrift
0029-1986 Norsk Hagetidend
0029-1994 Norsk Idrett
0029-2001 Norske Laegeforening. Tidsskrift
0029-201X Norsk Luftmilitaert Tidsskrift
0029-2028 Norsk Militaert Tidsskrift
0029-2036 Norsk Motorblad
0029-2044 Norsk Musikerblad
0029-2052 Norsk Pedagogisk Tidskrift
0029-2060 Norsk Retstidende
0029-2079 Norsk Sjoemannsforbund. Medlemsblad
0029-2087 Norsk Skogbruk
0029-2095 Norsk Skogindustri *changed to* Skogindustri
0029-2109 Norsk Skole†
0029-2117 Norsk Skoleblad
0029-2117 Norsk Skoleblad *issued with* 0042-2029
0029-2125 Norsk Skomakertidende†
0029-2133 Norsk Skotoey *changed to* SKO
0029-2141 Norsk Slektshistorisk Tidsskrift
0029-215X Norsk Styrmansblad *see* 0801-1400
0029-2168 Norsk Tekstiltidende
0029-2176 Norsk Teologisk Tidsskrift
0029-2184 Norsk Tidende for det Industrielle Rettsvern. Del 3: Moenstre
0029-2192 Norsk Tidende for det Industrielle Rettsvern. Del 2: Varemerker
0029-2206 Norsk Tidende for det Industrielle Rettsvern. Del 1: Patenter
0029-2214 Norsk Tidsskrift for Misjon
0029-2222 Norsk Tidsskrift for Sjovesen
0029-2249 Norsk Tidsskrift om Alkoholspoersmaalet *see* 0332-5512
0029-2257 Norsk Ukeblad
0029-2265 Norsk V V S
0029-2273 Norsk Veterinaertidsskrift
0029-229X Norske Skogforsoksvesen. Meddelelser†
0029-2303 Norske Tannlegeforenings Tidende
0029-2311 Norske Videnskaps-Akademi. Historisk-Filosofisk Klasse. Avhandlinger Two
0029-2338 Norske Videnskaps-Akademi. Matematisk-Naturvidenkapelig Klasse. Skrifter *changed to* Norske Videnskaps-Akademi. Naturvidenskapelig Klasse. Skrifter
0029-2354 Norte†
0029-2362 North†
0029-2370 North American Gladiolus Council Bulletin
0029-2397 North American Review
0029-2419 North Carolina Anvil
0029-2427 North Carolina Architect
0029-2435 North Carolina Christian Advocate
0029-2451 North Carolina Education
0029-246X North Carolina Folklore *changed to* North Carolina Folklore Journal
0029-2478 North Carolina Foreign Language Teacher *changed to* North Carolina Foreign Language Review
0029-2494 North Carolina Historical Review
0029-2508 North Carolina Journal of Speech *changed to* North Carolina Journal of Speech Communication
0029-2516 North Carolina Law Enforcement Journal†
0029-2524 North Carolina Law Review
0029-2540 North Carolina Libraries
0029-2559 North Carolina Medical Journal
0029-2567 North Carolina Museum of Art. Bulletin†
0029-2575 North Carolina Museum of Art. Calendar of Art Events†
0029-2591 North Carolina Public Schools†
0029-2605 North Carolina Report†
0029-2613 North Carolina School Boards Association Bulletin *changed to* Voice of North Carolina School Boards Association
0029-2648 North Central Association Quarterly
0029-2672 North Country
0029-2680 North Country Libraries†

1278 ISSN INDEX

0029-2699 North Country Reference & Research Resources Council. Newsletter
0029-2702 North Dakota Employment Trends†
0029-2710 North Dakota History
0029-2729 North Dakota Industrial News *changed to* North Dakota Economic Development Commission News
0029-2737 North Dakota Journal of Education
0029-2745 North Dakota Law Review
0029-2753 North Dakota Music Educator
0029-2761 North Dakota Outdoors
0029-277X North Dakota Quarterly
0029-2788 North Dakota Rural Electric Magazine *changed to* North Dakota R E C Magazine
0029-280X North East Coast Institution of Engineers and Shipbuilders. Transactions
0029-2818 North East Group for the Study of Labour History Bulletin *changed to* North East Labour History Bulletin
0029-2842 North Jersey Business Review *changed to* Jersey Business Review
0029-2850 North Jersey Highlander
0029-2877 North Loop News
0029-2885 East Midlands Bibliography
0029-2907 North Texas Retailer *changed to* Retailer and Marketing News
0029-2923 North West Lancashire Chamber of Commerce Journal *changed to* Chacom
0029-294X North Wind-Skagway's Newspaper†
0029-2958 North Woods Call
0029-2982 Northeast Business†
0029-2990 Northeast Horseman *changed to* Show Horse
0029-3016 N E D C O Producers' Guide *changed to* N E D C O Today
0029-3032 Northeastern News
0029-3040 Northern Architect
0029-3067 Northern Circuit†
0029-3075 Northern District Dental Society. Dental Mirror
0029-3083 Northern Engineer
0029-3091 Northern Illinois University Business Report†
0029-3105 Northern Ireland Legal Quarterly
0029-3113 Northern Ireland Libraries *see* 0023-9542
0029-313X Northern Junket†
0029-3148 Northern Lights
0029-3156 Northern Logger and Timber Processer
0029-3164 Northern Miner
0029-3180 Northern Minnesota Review†
0029-3199 Northern Neighbors
0029-3210 Northern Railway Newsletter
0029-3253 Northian
0029-3261 Northland
0029-327X Northliner Magazine
0029-3296 Northwest Anthropological Research Notes
0029-330X Northwest Architect *see* 0149-9106
0029-3326 Northwest Association of Secondary and Higher Schools. Committee on Research and Service. Newsletter. *changed to* Northwest Association of Schools and Colleges, Committee on Research and Service. Newsletter
0029-3334 Northwest Community Hospital Medical Bulletin
0029-3350 Northwest Farm Equipment Journal
0029-3369 Northwest Folklore†
0029-3377 Northwest Insurance
0029-3393 Northwest Motor
0029-3407 Northwest Ohio Quarterly
0029-3415 Northwest Passage
0029-3423 Northwest Review
0029-3431 Salmon-Trout Steelheader
0029-344X Northwest Science
0029-3458 Northwest Skier *see* 0274-9149
0029-3466 Northwest Sportsman†
0029-3474 Northwest Technocrat
0029-3490 Northwestern Jeweler
0029-3504 Northwestern Lumber Dealer *changed to* Building Material Retailer
0029-3512 Northwestern Lutheran
0029-3520 Northwestern Management Reporter†
0029-3539 Northwestern Miller†
0029-3547 Unigard Mutuality†
0029-3555 Northwestern Ontario Timber Operators' Association. Log Book†
0029-3563 Northwestern Report†
0029-3571 Northwestern University Law Review
0029-358X Northwestern University Medical School Magazine *changed to* Northwestern University Medical Center Magazine
0029-3601 Norveg
0029-361X Norvega Esperantisto
0029-3628 Norway†
0029-3636 Norway. Statistisk Sentralbyraa. Statistisk Maanedshefte /Monthly Bulletin of Statistics
0029-3644 Norwegian American Commerce
0029-3652 Norwegian Archaeological Review
0029-3660 Norwegian Commercial Banks Financial Review *changed to* Financial Review
0029-3679 Norwegian Fishing and Maritime News *changed to* Maritime News
0029-3709 Norwegian Shipping News *changed to* Shipping News International
0029-3717 Nos Lettres. Informations
0029-3725 Nos Oiseaux
0029-3741 Theatre Amateur *see* 0398-0049
0029-3768 Nostra Voce
0029-3776 Nostre Scuole
0029-3784 Nostri Cani
0029-3792 Nostri Ragazzi
0029-3806 Nostro Mondo†
0029-3814 Nostro Tempo
0029-3822 Nota Bene†
0029-3857 Notaro
0029-3865 Centro Brasileiro de Pesquisas. Fisicas. Notas de Fisica†
0029-3881 Notas Sobre la Economia y el Desarrollo de America Latina *changed to* Notas Sobre la Economia y el Desarrollo
0029-389X Notatki Plockie
0029-3903 Note di Pastorale Giovanile
0029-392X Note Stiri de Cenaclu
0029-3946 Notes a Tempo
0029-3954 Notes Africaines
0029-3962 Notes and Abstracts in American and International Education
0029-3970 Notes and Queries
0029-3997 France. Commissariat a l'Energie Atomique. Notes d'Information
0029-4004 Notes et Etudes Documentaires
0029-4012 F E E Notes
0029-4020 Notes from the Tarlton Law Library
0029-4039 Notes from Underground
0029-4047 Notes on Contemporary Literature
0029-4055 Notes on Current Politics *see* 0307-7039
0029-4063 Commercial Bank of Greece. Notes on Foreign Trade *changed to* Commercial Bank of Greece. Notes on Foreign Trade and Main Economic Data
0029-4071 Notes on Mississippi Writers
0029-408X Notes on Selected Acquisitions†
0029-4098 Notes on Tin
0029-4101 Notes on Water Pollution *see* 0307-6652
0029-411X Nothing Doing in London†
0029-4128 Noticia Geomorfologica†
0029-4136 Noticiarie a Imprensa Falada e Escrita
0029-4144 Noticiario - Odontologia
0029-4152 Noticias (New York)
0029-4160 Fundacion Servicio para el Agricultor. Noticias Agricolas
0029-4187 Noticias de Suecia†
0029-4195 Noticias del Trabajo
0029-425X Noticiero de la Fe
0029-4276 Noticioso Perea
0029-4292 Sew Business
0029-4306 Notitiae
0029-4314 Notiziario Agricolo†
0029-4322 Notiziario d'Arte
0029-4330 Notiziario di Aviazione Civile *changed to* Aviazione Civile
0029-4349 Notiziario della Lega Italiana per la Lotta Contro i Tumori e dei Centri Oncologici†
0029-4357 Notiziario di Aviazione†
0029-4365 Notiziario di Caccia e Pesca-Tiro a Volo
0029-4373 Notiziario Famiglie Numerose
0029-4381 I S T A T. Notiziario
0029-439X Notiziario Medico Farmaceutico
0029-4403 Notiziario Orto Frutticolo dei Prodotti Agricolo-Alimentari *changed to* Export Alimentare e dei Prodotti Agricoli
0029-442X Notiziario Tecnico Worthington *changed to* Ingegneria e Fluidi
0029-4438 Notizie Olivetti
0029-4446 Notizie per gli Industriali della Provincia di Siena *changed to* Informatore Industriale
0029-4454 Notizie Rapide *see* 0391-6367
0029-4462 Notnaya Letopis'
0029-4470 Notornis
0029-4489 Notre Bourbonnais
0029-4497 Notre Dame Alumnus *see* 0161-987X
0029-4500 Notre Dame English Journal *changed to* Religion and Literature
0029-4519 Notre Dame Journal of Education†
0029-4527 Notre Dame Journal of Formal Logic
0029-4535 Notre Dame Lawyer *changed to* Notre Dame Law Review
0029-4543 Notre Dame Technical Review
0029-4551 Notre Formation *see* 0765-5762
0029-456X Notre Temps
0029-4578 Les Notres
0029-4586 Nottingham French Studies
0029-4594 Notulae Entomologicae
0029-4608 Notulae Naturae
0029-4616 Noturno†
0029-4624 Nous
0029-4632 Nous Deux Presente
0029-4659 Nouveau Cinemonde†
0029-4675 Nouveau Journal de Charpente-Menuiserie-Parquets
0029-4705 A I U Les Nouveaux Cahiers
0029-4713 Nouvel Observateur
0029-473X Nouvelle Etoile
0029-4748 Nouvelle Famille Educatrice
0029-4756 Nouvelle France
0029-4764 Nouvelle Frontiere
0029-4772 Nouvelle Hygiene
0029-4780 Nouvelle Revue d'Optique Appliquee *see* 0150-536X
0029-4799 Nouvelle Revue Franc-Comtoise
0029-4802 Nouvelle Revue Francaise
0029-4810 Nouvelle Revue Francaise d'Hematologie
0029-4837 Nouvelle Revue Pedagogique†
0029-4845 Nouvelle Revue Theologique
0029-4853 Nouvelles Archives Hospitalieres
0029-487X Nouvelles de Chretiente
0029-4888 Nouvelles de l'Estampe
0029-490X Nouvelles Esthetiques
0029-4918 Nouvelles Etudes Marxistes *changed to* Tribune Internationale
0029-4926 Nouvelles Graphiques
0029-4934 Nouvelles Industrielles et Commerciales et de Midi-Pyrenees
0029-4942 Nouvelles Litteraires, Arts, Sciences, Spectacles
0029-4969 Nova
0029-4977 Nova†
0029-4985 Nova
0029-4993 Nova
0029-5000 Nova Act Regiae Societatis Scientiarum Upsaliensis *changed to* Acta Universitatis Upsaliensis
0029-5019 Nova Ecclesia
0029-5027 Nova et Vetera
0029-5035 Nova Hedwiga
0029-5051 Nova Proizvodnja
0029-506X Nova Scotia *changed to* Nova Scotia Times
0029-5078 Nova Scotia Export Quarterly†
0029-5094 Nova Scotia Medical Bulletin
0029-5108 Nova Scotia Teachers Union Newsletter *see* 0382-408X
0029-5116 Novas de Alegria
0029-5124 Novaya i Noveishaya Istoriya
0029-5132 Novel: A Forum on Fiction
0029-5140 Novena *see* 0308-0617
0029-5159 Novidaded Fotoptica *changed to* Revista Fotoptica
0029-5167 Novinar
0029-5175 Novinarstvo
0029-5191 Novinky Literatury: Prehledy Informativni Literatury *changed to* Prehledy Informativni Literatury
0029-5205 Novinky Literatury: Zdravotnictvi
0029-5248 Noviny Vnitrniho Obchodu
0029-5264 Novitur†
0029-5272 Novosti *changed to* Novosti Iz Jugoslavije
0029-5280 Novoe Vremya
0029-5302 Novy Orient
0029-5310 Novy Shliakh
0029-5329 Novyi Mir
0029-5337 Novyj Zhurnal
0029-5345 Now
0029-5353 Now *changed to* Montana AgResearch
0029-537X Nowa Szkola
0029-5388 Nowe Drogi
0029-5396 Nowe Rolnictwo
0029-540X Nowotwory
0029-5426 Ag-Chem Age
0029-5434 Nozzle
0029-5442 Nsanja Ya Olonda
0029-5450 Nuclear Technology
0029-5469 Nuclear Canada
0029-5477 Nuclear Data *see* 0092-640X
0029-5477 Nuclear Data *see* 0090-3752
0029-5485 Nuclear Energy *see* 0262-5091
0029-5507 Nuclear Engineering International
0029-5515 Nuclear Fusion
0029-5523 Nuclear India
0029-5531 Nuclear Industry
0029-554X Nuclear Instruments and Methods *see* 0168-9002
0029-5558 Nuclear Magnetic Resonance Abstracts Service *see* 0733-2629
0029-5566 Nuklearmedezin
0029-5574 Nuclear News
0029-5574 Nuclear News Buyers Guide
0029-5582 Nuclear Physics *changed to* Nuclear Physics, Section A
0029-5582 Nuclear Physics *see* 0550-3213
0029-5604 Nuclear Safety
0029-5612 Nuclear Science Abstracts (United States Energy Research and Development Administration) *see* 0004-7139
0029-5620 Nuclear Science Information of Japan
0029-5639 Nuclear Science and Engineering
0029-5647 Nuclear Science Journal
0029-5655 Nuclear Standards News
0029-5663 Nuclelec†
0029-5671 Recherche
0029-568X Nucleus
0029-5698 Nucleus
0029-5701 Nuestra Arquitectura
0029-571X Nuestra Historia
0029-5728 Nuestra Industria. Revista Economica†
0029-5736 Nuestra Industria. Revista Tecnologia *changed to* Revista Tecnologica
0029-5752 Nuestro Amigo
0029-5760 Nuestro Anhelo
0029-5787 Nuestro Holando
0029-5795 Nuestro Tiempo
0029-5809 Nuestros Ninos (Student Edition)†
0029-585X Nueva Pompeya
0029-5868 Nueva Revista de Filologia Hispanica
0029-5884 Nuevo Ambiente *changed to* Habitat
0029-5914 Nuklearna Energija *see* 0351-689X
0029-5922 Nukleonika
0029-5949 Numaga
0029-5965 Number Three St. Jame's Street
0029-5973 Numen
0029-5981 International Journal for Numerical Methods in Engineering
0029-599X Numerische Mathematik
0029-6007 Numero Economique du Vendredi
0029-6015 Numisma
0029-6023 Numismatic Circular

ISSN INDEX 1279

0029-6031 Numismatic Literature
0029-604X Numismatic News
0029-6058 Numismatic Scrapbook *see* 0010-0447
0029-6066 Numismatic Society of India. Journal
0029-6074 Numismaticke Listy
0029-6082 Numismatisches Nachrichtenblatt
0029-6090 Numismatist†
0029-6112 Nuntempa Bulgario†
0029-6139 Nuorten Sarka
0029-6155 Nuova Corrente
0029-6163 Nuova Critica
0029-6171 Nuova Economia
0029-618X Nuova Era†
0029-6198 Nuova Gazzetta di Calabria
0029-6201 Nuova Rassegna
0029-621X Nuova Rivista Internazionale
0029-6228 Nuova Rivista Musicale Italiana
0029-6236 Nuova Rivista Storica
0029-6244 Nuova Rivista Tributaria
0029-6252 Nuova Tecnica Ospedaliera *see* 0392-4831
0029-6260 Nuova Venezia
0029-6279 Nuova Veterinaria†
0029-6287 Nuovi Annali di Igiene e Microbiologia
0029-6295 Nuovi Argomenti
0029-6309 Nuovo Agora Omaggio
0029-6317 Nuovo Bollettino Bibliografico Sardo
0029-6325 Il Nuovo Cantiere
0029-6333 Nuovo Chirone
0029-635X Nuovo Didaskaleion†
0029-6368 Nuovo Diritto
0029-6376 Nuovo Mezzogiorno
0029-6384 Nuovo Osservatore
0029-6392 Nuovo Pensiero Militare
0029-6406 Nursery Business
0029-6414 Nursery Days *see* 0275-9667
0029-6422 Nursery World
0029-6430 Nurseryman and Garden Centre
0029-6457 Nursing†
0029-6465 Nursing Clinics of North America
0029-6473 Nursing Forum
0029-649X Nursing Homes†
0029-6503 Nursing Journal of India
0029-6511 Nursing Mirror *changed to* Nursing Times, Nursing Mirror
0029-652X Nursing News *changed to* Connecticut Nursing News
0029-6538 New Hampshire Nursing News
0029-6546 Nursing News (Brooklyn)
0029-6554 Nursing Outlook
0029-6562 Nursing Research
0029-6570 Nursing Standard
0029-6589 Nursing Times *changed to* Nursing Times, Nursing Mirror
0029-6597 Nutida Musik
0029-6619 Nutrition Abstracts and Reviews *see* 0309-1295
0029-6619 Nutrition Abstracts and Reviews *see* 0309-135X
0029-6627 Nutrition Information Bulletin *see* 0309-0531
0029-6635 Nutrition Reports International
0029-6643 Nutrition Reviews
0029-6651 Nutrition Society. Proceedings
0029-666X Nutrition Today
0029-6678 Nutrition and Metabolism *see* 0250-6807
0029-6686 Nutzfahrzeug
0029-6694 Nuus Oor Afrika
0029-6708 Nuwe Protestant
0029-6716 Nux
0029-6724 Ny Boky No Loharanom-Pandrosoana†
0029-6732 Ny Fremtid
0029-6783 Nye Bonytt *see* 0800-1936
0029-6791 Nyelvtudomanyi Kozlemenyek
0029-6813 Nykytekstiili
0029-683X Nyt for Hospitalslaboranter
0029-6848 Nyt Fra Historien
0029-6864 Norwegian Journal of Zoology†
0029-6872 O A C Newsletter *changed to* Artspace (Columbus)
0029-6910 O A S Chronicle†
0029-6937 O & M
0029-6953 Biologico
0029-6961 O C L A E Revista
0029-702X O E C D Foreign Trade Statistics. Series A *changed to* Organization for Economic Cooperation and Development. Monthly Foreign Trade Statistics/Statistiques Mensuel du Commerce Exterieur.
0029-7038 Organization for Economic Cooperation and Development. Liaison Bulletin Between Research and Training Institutes
0029-7054 O E C D Observer
0029-7062 Organization for Economic Cooperation and Development. Provisional Oil Statistics/Statistiques Petrolieres Provisoires *changed to* Organization for Economic Cooperation and Development. Annual Oil and Gas Statistics/Statistiques Annuelles du Petrole et du Gaz Naturel
0029-7070 O E C T A Review *changed to* O E C T A Reporter
0029-7089 O G B-Bildungsfunktionaer†
0029-7097 O I R T Information†
0029-7127 O I V Bulletin
0029-7135 O L A Bulletin
0029-7143 O L O G O S
0029-7151 O L W
0029-716X O M I Farm News†
0029-7178 O. M. I. Missions†
0029-7194 O M V - Zeitschrift
0029-7208 O P Z - Dokumentation *changed to* Betriebswirtschaftliche O P W Z - Dokumentation
0029-7216 O R M P Newsletter†
0029-7224 Cahiers O.R.S.T.O.M. Serie Entomologie Medicale et Parasitologie
0029-7232 Cahiers O.R.S.T.O.M. Serie Geologie *see* 0766-5105
0029-7240 Cahiers O.R.S.T.O.M. Serie Hydrobiologie *see* 0240-8783
0029-7259 Cahiers O.R.S.T.O.M. Serie Pedologie
0029-7275 O S S T F Bulletin *see* 0319-2121
0029-7283 O S U Research Review†
0029-7291 O T C Chart Manual
0029-7305 O.T.C. Market Chronicle *see* 0360-1773
0029-7313 O T F Reporter *see* 0316-3903
0029-7321 O T Kaner
0029-733X O T O†
0029-7356 Oak Leaf
0029-7372 Oak Ridge Associated Universities. Newsletter†
0029-7380 Oakhamian
0029-7399 Aomori Prefecture. Monthly Report of Meteorology
0029-7402 Die Oase
0029-7429 Ob/Gyn Digest *see* 0198-9197
0029-7437 Ob. Gyn. News
0029-7445 Ob-Gyn Observer†
0029-7461 Savez Geodetskih Inzenjera i Geometara Hrvatske. Obavijesti *changed to* Savez Geodetskih Inzenjera i Geometara Hrvatske. Geodet
0029-747X Obcan
0029-7488 Oberflaeche *see* 0170-4044
0029-7496 Oberfraenkische Wirtschaft
0029-7518 Oberlin Alumni Magazine
0029-7526 Oberlin Review
0029-7534 Oberoesterreichische F P O - Nachrichten fuer Freiheit und Recht
0029-7542 Oberoesterreichische Gemeindezeitung
0029-7550 Oberoesterreichische Heimatblaetter
0029-7569 Oberoesterreichisches Reise Journal *changed to* Reise-Journal
0029-7585 Obiter Dicta
0029-7593 Objective: Justice
0029-7615 Objets et Mondes
0029-7623 Obogashchenie Rud
0029-764X Andragogija
0029-7658 Obrero Ferroviario
0029-7674 Observation, Opinion, Orientation *see* 0318-9236
0029-7682 Belgium. Institut Royal Meteorologique. Observations Climatologiques
0029-7690 Belgium. Institut Royal Meteorologique. Observations d'Ozone
0029-7704 Observatory
0029-7712 Observer
0029-7720 Observer†
0029-7739 Observer (Rockford)
0029-7763 Obshchestvennye Nauki v Uzbekistane
0029-7771 Obst- und Weinbau *changed to* Obst - Wein - Garten
0029-778X Obst-Gemuese
0029-7798 Obst und Garten
0029-781X Revista de Pediatrie, Obstetrica, Ginecologie. Obstetrica si Ginecologie
0029-7828 Obstetrical & Gynecological Survey
0029-7844 Obstetrics and Gynecology
0029-7852 Obzor
0029-7860 Obzornik
0029-7879 Occident†
0029-7887 Occult Gazette *changed to* Royal Cosmic Theology
0029-7909 Occupational Hazards
0029-7917 Occupational Health
0029-7925 Occupational Health Newsletter *changed to* Environmental Health and Safety News
0029-7933 Occupational Health Nursing *changed to* American Association of Occupational Health Nurses Journal
0029-7941 Occupational Health Review†
0029-7968 U.S. Bureau of Labor Statistics. Occupational Outlook Quarterly
0029-7976 Occupational Psychology *see* 0305-8107
0029-7984 Occupational Safety and Health Abstracts *see* 0302-7651
0029-8018 Ocean Engineering
0029-8026 Ocean Industry
0029-8042 Ocean Oil Weekly Report
0029-8069 Ocean Science News
0029-8077 Oceania
0029-8085 Oceanic Citation Index *see* 0093-6901
0029-8093 Oceanic Index *see* 0093-6901
0029-8115 Oceanic Linguistics
0029-8123 Oceanite
0029-8131 Oceanographical Society of Japan. Journal
0029-814X Oceanologia et Limnologia Sinica
0029-8158 Oceanology†
0029-8174 Oceans
0029-8182 Oceanus
0029-8190 Ochanomizu Women's University. Natural Science Report *changed to* Ochanomizu University. Natural Science Report
0029-8204 Ochrana Prirody *changed to* Pamatky a Priroda
0029-8220 Ochrona Pracy
0029-8239 Ochrona Roslin
0029-8247 Ochrona Zabytkow
0029-8263 Ocrotirea Naturii si a Mediului Inconjurator
0029-8271 Octagon
0029-828X Octobre
0029-8328 Oculus
0029-8336 Odbrana
0029-8344 Odbrana i Zastita
0029-8360 Der Odenwald
0029-8387 Odjek
0029-8395 Odontoiatria
0029-8409 Odontologia *see* 0120-2855
0029-8417 Odontologia Chilena
0029-8425 Odontologia Uruguaya
0029-8433 Odontological Bulletin
0029-8441 Odontologisk Revy *see* 0347-9994
0029-845X Scandinavian Journal of Dental Research
0029-8468 Odontologiska Foreningens Tidskrift
0029-8476 Odontologiste des Hopitaux†
0029-8484 Odontology
0029-8492 Odontoprotesti
0029-8506 Odontostomatological Progress
0029-8514 Odrodzenie i Reformacja w Polsce
0029-8522 Odu
0029-8530 Odvjetnik
0029-8549 Oecologia
0029-8557 Oecologica Plantarum *see* 0243-7651
0029-8573 Das Oeffentliche Gesundheitswesen
0029-8581 Das Oeffentliche Haushaltswesen in Oesterreich
0029-859X Die Oeffentliche Verwaltung
0029-8603 Oeffentliche Wirtschaft *changed to* Oeffentliche Wirtschaft und Gemeinwirtschaft
0029-862X L'Oeil
0029-8638 Oekonomik Gartenbau†
0029-8646 Oekonomisk Kronik
0029-8654 Oekumenische Rundschau
0029-8662 Oel- und Gasfeuerung *see* 0720-3438
0029-8689 Oel†
0029-8697 Oelhydraulik und Pneumatik
0029-8700 Oil World
0029-8719 Oertliche Raumheizung†
0029-8727 Oes†
0029-8735 Oeste†
0029-8751 Oesterreich-Nederland
0029-876X Oesterreichische Krankenhaus Zeitung
0029-8786 Oesterreichische Aerztezeitung
0029-8840 Oesterreichischer Alpenverein. Akademische Sektion Graz. Mitteilungen
0029-8859 Oesterreichische Apotheker-Zeitung
0029-8867 Oesterreichische Arbeitsgemeinschaft fuer Rehabilitation. Information
0029-8875 Der Oesterreichische Arzt
0029-8883 Oesterreichische Autorenzeitung
0029-8891 Oesterreichische Bauzeitung
0029-8905 Oesterreichische Bauernzeitung
0029-8921 Oesterreichische Blaetter fuer Gewerblichen Rechtsschutz und Urheberrecht
0029-8956 Brandverhuetung
0029-8972 Oesterreichische Camping & Caravaning Revue *changed to* Camping
0029-8980 Oesterreichische Caritas Zeitschrift *changed to* Caritas
0029-8999 Oesterreichische Dachdecker- und Pflasterer-Zeitung *changed to* Dach und Wand Abdichtung
0029-9006 Oesterreichische Dentisten - Zeitschrift
0029-9030 Die Oesterreichische Feuerwehr
0029-9057 Der Oesterreichische Filmamateur
0029-9065 Der Oesterreichische Friseur
0029-9073 Strassengueterverkehr
0029-9081 Oesterreichische Fussbodenzeitung
0029-909X Oesterreichische Galerie. Mitteilungen
0029-9103 Oesterreichische Gastgewerbe-Zeitung *changed to* Oesterreichische Gastgewerbe-Hotelzeitung
0029-9111 Oesterreichische Gefluegelwirtschaft
0029-912X Oesterreichische Gemeinde-Zeitung
0029-9138 Oesterreichische Geographische Gesellschaft. Mitteilungen
0029-9146 Oesterreichische Gesellschaft fuer Filmwissenschaft. Mitteilungen *changed to* Oesterreichische Gesellschaft fuer Filmwissenschaft, Kommunikations- und Medienforschung. Mitteilungen
0029-9154 Oesterreichische Gesellschaft fuer Holzforschung. Schrifttumskarteidienst
0029-9162 Oesterreichische Glaserzeitung
0029-9170 Das Oesterreichische Graphische Gewerbe
0029-9189 Oesterreichische Hausbesitz
0029-9200 Die Oesterreichische Hoehere Schule
0029-9219 Oesterreichische Ingenieur Zeitschrift *changed to* O I A Z. Oesterreichische Ingenieur und Architekten Zeitschrift
0029-9227 Der Oesterreichische Installateur
0029-9235 Oesterreichische Installateurzeitung
0029-9243 Der Oesterreichische Jungarbeiter
0029-9251 Oesterreichische Juristen - Zeitung
0029-926X Oesterreichische Kunststoff Zeitung *changed to* Oesterreichische Kunststoff - Zeitschrift
0029-9278 Laenderbank Boerseninformationen *changed to* Laenderbank Boerse
0029-9286 Oesterreichische Leder- und Haeutewirtschaft
0029-9294 Oesterreichische Mechaniker *changed to* Mechanik
0029-9308 Oesterreichische Monatshefte
0029-9316 Oesterreichische Musikzeitschrift

1280 ISSN INDEX

0029-9324 Oesterreichische Naehmaschinen- und Fahrrad-Zeitung *changed to* Oesterreichische Naehmaschinen- und Zweirad-Zeitung
0029-9332 Oesterreichische Nationalbank. Mitteilungen des Direktoriums
0029-9340 Oesterreichische Notariats-Zeitung
0029-9359 Oesterreichische Numismatische Gesellschaft. Mitteilungen
0029-9367 C W F
0029-9375 Oesterreichische Osthefte
0029-9383 Oesterreichische Paedagogische Warte *changed to* K L O E Impulse
0029-9391 Oesterreichische Papier-Zeitung
0029-9405 Oesterreichische Raumausstatterzeitung
0029-9421 Oesterreichische Schachzeitung†
0029-943X Oesterreichische Schlosser-und Maschinenbauerzeitung†
0029-9448 Oesterreichische Schmiede-Zeitung†
0029-9456 Oesterreichische Schuhhaendler *changed to* Schuh-Revue
0029-9464 Oesterreichische Schuhmacher - Zeitung *changed to* Der Oesterreichischer Schuhmarkt
0029-9499 Der Oesterreichische Spengler und Kupferschmied
0029-9502 Oesterreichische Foerster Zeitung
0029-9510 Oesterreichische Steuer und Wirtschaftskarei *changed to* Steuer und Wirtschaftskartei
0029-9529 Oesterreichische Steuer - Zeitung
0029-9537 Austria Tabakwerke A. G. Fachliche Mitteilungen†
0029-9545 Oesterreichische Textil-Mitteilungen
0029-9553 Oesterreichische Textil Zeitschrift *changed to* Mode und Material
0029-9561 Oesterreichische Trafikanten-Zeitung
0029-957X Der Oesterreichische Volkswirt
0029-9588 Oesterreichische Wasserwirtschaft
0029-9596 Oesterreichische Zahnaerzte - Zeitung
0029-9618 O Z E
0029-9626 Oesterreichische Zeitschrift fuer Kunst und Denkmalpflege
0029-9634 Oesterreichische Zeitschrift fuer Oeffentliches Recht. Neue Folge *see* 0378-3073
0029-9642 Oesterreichische Zeitschrift fuer Stomatologie *see* 0175-7784
0029-9650 Oesterreichische Zeitschrift fuer Vermessungswesen *changed to* Oesterreichische Zeitschrift fuer Vermessungswesen und Photogrammetrie
0029-9669 Oesterreichische Zeitschrift fuer Volkskunde
0029-9677 Der Oesterreichische Zimmermeister
0029-9685 Oesterreichische Zoll und Steuer Nachrichten
0029-9693 Der Oesterreichische Arbeitsgemeinschaft fuer Ur- und Fruhgeschichte. Mitteilungen
0029-9707 Oesterreichisches Institut fuer Raumplanung. Mitteilungen
0029-9715 Oesterreichischer Alpenverein. Mitteilungen
0029-9723 Oesterreichischer Blindenverband. Mitteilungen
0029-9731 Oesterreichischer Brieftaubensport
0029-974X Kameradschaft der Wiener Panzer-Division. Mitteilungsblatt
0029-9758 Der Oesterreichische Kleingaertner
0029-9766 Oesterreichischer Kleintierzuechter
0029-9774 Oesterreichischer Luftfahrt Pressedienst *changed to* Oesterreichische Luftfahrt Presse
0029-9782 Oesterreichischer Markenanzeiger
0029-9790 Oesterreichischer Personenverkehr
0029-9804 Oesterreichischer Wohnungs-Geschaefts- und Realitaeten-Anzeiger
0029-9820 Oesterreichisches Archiv fuer Kirchenrecht
0029-9839 Oesterreichisches Bank-Archiv
0029-9847 Oesterreichisches Cafe Journal
0029-9855 Elektro and Radio *changed to* Elektro Journal
0029-9863 Berichte und Informationen
0029-988X Oesterreichisches Hotel-und Gastronomie-Journal
0029-9898 Oesterreichisches Institut fuer Wirtschaftsforschung. Monatsberichte
0029-9901 Oesterreichisches Jugendrotkreuz. Arbeitsblaetter
0029-991X Oesterreichisches Klerus Blatt†
0029-9928 Oesterreichisches Kolpingblatt
0029-9936 Leben-Wirken *changed to* Mensch und Ziel
0029-9944 Oesterreichisches Patentblatt
0029-9952 Oesterreichisches Standesamt
0029-9987 Oesterreichs Fischerei
0029-9995 Oesterreichs Paddelsport *changed to* Oesterreichs Kanusport
0030-0004 Oesterreichs Presse, Werbung, Graphik *changed to* Pressehandbuch (Year)
0030-0012 Oesterreichs Weidwerk
0030-0047 Of Consuming Interest†
0030-0055 Of Sea and Shore†
0030-0071 Off Our Backs
0030-0098 Offene Kreis†
0030-0101 Offene Tore
0030-011X Offene Tueren
0030-0128 Office
0030-0136 Office Administration *changed to* Office Product News
0030-0144 Office Products *changed to* Office Products Dealer Buying Guide and Directory
0030-0179 Office Equipment & Methods
0030-0187 Office Equipment News
0030-0217 Management in Action *see* 0025-1747
0030-0233 Office Products Dealer†
0030-0241 Office Products News *see* 0744-2815
0030-025X Office Supervisor's Bulletin *changed to* Supervisor's Bulletin for Administration and Office Support Group
0030-0268 Officer
0030-0284 Official Board Markets
0030-0292 Official Container Directory
0030-0306 Official Detective Stories
0030-0314 Official Gazette of Guyana
0030-0322 Official Guide of the Railways and Steam Navigation Lines of the United States, Puerto Rico, Canada, Mexico and Cuba, Airline Schedules *see* 0190-6704
0030-0330 Official Journal (Patents)
0030-0349 Official Journal of Industrial and Commercial Property
0030-0357 Official Motor Freight Guide
0030-0365 Official Oil in North Dakota *see* 0363-2512
0030-0373 Official Railway Equipment Register
0030-0381 Official Steamship Guide
0030-039X Officiel de la Couleur†
0030-0403 Officiel de la Couture et de la Mode de Paris
0030-0411 Officiel de la Droguerie
0030-042X Officiel de la Librairie†
0030-0438 Officiel de la Photographie et du Cinema
0030-0446 Officiel de l'Ameublement: Ameublement Informations *changed to* Nouvel Officiel de l'Ameublement
0030-0454 Officiel de l'Automobile
0030-0462 Officiel des Plastiques et du Caoutchouc
0030-0500 Officiel des Spectacles
0030-0519 Officiel du Cycle, du Motocycle et de la Motoculture *changed to* Officiel du Cycle et du Motocycle
0030-0535 Officiel: Magazine des Menagers *see* 0335-9956
0030-0551 Officier de Reserve *changed to* Ares
0030-056X Officer de Police
0030-0586 Offizieller Salzburger Wochenspiegel
0030-0594 Offsetpraxis
0030-0608 Offshore (Tulsa)
0030-0624 Oficina Moderna
0030-0632 Oficina Sanitaria Panamericana. Boletin
0030-0667 Revista de Chirurgie, Oncologie, O.R.L., Radiologie, Stomatologie. Oftalmologie
0030-0675 Oftal'mologicheskii Zhurnal
0030-0683 Ofthalmologika Chronika *changed to* Greek Annals of Ophthalmology
0030-0691 Ogam
0030-0705 Oggi
0030-0713 Oglas za Pomorce
0030-0721 Ogonek
0030-073X Ogoniok
0030-0756 Ogrodnictwo
0030-0764 Ohio Academy of Science News
0030-0772 Ohio AFL-CIO News and Views
0030-0780 Society of Ohio Archivists Newsletter *changed to* Ohio Archivist
0030-0799 Ohio Association of School Librarians' Bulletin *see* 0192-6942
0030-0802 Ohio Banker
0030-0861 Ohio Contractor
0030-087X Ohio Dental Journal
0030-0888 Ohio Family Physician News
0030-0896 Ohio Farmer
0030-090X Ohio Florists Association. Bulletin
0030-0918 Ohio Forestry Association. Bulletin†
0030-0926 Ohio Grange *changed to* Ohio Granger
0030-0934 Ohio History
0030-0950 Ohio Journal of Science
0030-0977 Ohio Library Trustee
0030-0985 Ohio Motorist
0030-0993 Ohio Nurses Review
0030-1019 Ohio Parent Teacher *see* 0199-0918
0030-1027 Ohio Pharmacist
0030-1035 Ohio Reading Teacher
0030-1043 Ohio Report on Research and Development in Biology, Agriculture and Home Economics *changed to* Ohio Report
0030-1051 Ohio Researcher†
0030-1078 Ohio School Boards Journal
0030-1086 Ohio Schools
0030-1116 Ohio State Lantern
0030-1124 Ohio State Medical Journal
0030-1132 Ohio State University. College of Medicine. Journal
0030-1140 Ohio State University. Institute of Polar Studies. Newsletter†
0030-1159 Ohio State University Libraries Notes†
0030-1167 Ohio State University Monthly *see* 0744-8899
0030-1183 Ohio Tavern News
0030-1191 Ohio Trucking News *changed to* Ohio Truck Times
0030-1205 Ohio University Post *changed to* Post
0030-1213 Ohio Veterinarian *changed to* Ohio Veterinary Medical Association. Newsletter
0030-1221 Ohio Wesleyan Magazine
0030-123X Ohio Woodlands/Conservation in Action
0030-1248 Ohioana Quarterly
0030-1256 Ohio's Health†
0030-1264 Ohmio†
0030-1272 Ohnicek
0030-1280 Oiga
0030-1299 Oikos
0030-1302 Oikoumenikon†
0030-1310 Lifestream of Progress *changed to* Oil: Lifestream of Progress
0030-1329 Oil & Chemical Worker
0030-1337 Oil and Colour Chemists' Association. Journal
0030-1345 Oil & Gas Discoveries†
0030-1353 Oil, Gas & Petrochem Equipment
0030-1388 Oil & Gas Journal
0030-1396 Oil and Gas Tax Quarterly
0030-1418 Oil Caravan Weekly
0030-1426 Oil, Chemical and Atomic Workers International Union. Union News *see* 8756-1727
0030-1434 Oil Daily
0030-1442 Oil Mill Gazetter
0030-1450 Oil News
0030-1469 Oil, Paint and Drug Reporter *see* 0090-0907
0030-1485 Oil Technologists Association of India. Journal
0030-1493 Oilgas
0030-1507 Oils and Oilseeds Journal†
0030-1515 Oilweek
0030-1523 Oise Agricole
0030-1531 Oiseau et la Revue Francaise d'Ornithologie
0030-154X Okajima's Folia Anatomica Japonica
0030-1558 Medical Association of Okayama. Journal
0030-1566 Mathematical Journal of Okayama University
0030-1574 Okeanologiya
0030-1590 Okhrana Truda i Sotsial'noe Strakhovanie
0030-1612 Okki
0030-1620 Oklahoma Union Farmer
0030-1639 Oklahoma
0030-1647 Oklahoma Banker
0030-1655 Oklahoma Bar Association. Journal *changed to* Oklahoma Bar Journal
0030-1663 Oklahoma Beverage News
0030-1671 Oklahoma Business Bulletin
0030-168X Oklahoma C. P. A†
0030-1698 Oklahoma Cowman
0030-1701 Oklahoma Current Farm Economics
0030-171X Oklahoma Daily
0030-1728 Oklahoma Register (Oklahoma City)
0030-1736 Oklahoma Geology Notes
0030-1744 Oklahoma Labor Market
0030-1752 Oklahoma Law Review
0030-1760 Oklahoma Librarian
0030-1779 Oklahoma Mason
0030-1787 Oklahoma Nurse
0030-1795 Oklahoma Observer
0030-1809 Oklahoma Odd Fellow
0030-1817 Oklahoma Parent-Teacher
0030-1833 Oklahoma Reader
0030-1841 Oklahoma Retailer
0030-185X Oklahoma School Board Journal
0030-1868 Oklahoma State Dental Association. Journal *see* 0164-9442
0030-1876 Oklahoma State Medical Association. Journal
0030-1884 Oklahoma Teacher *changed to* O E A Focus
0030-1892 Oklahoma Today
0030-1906 Oekonomi og Politik
0030-1914 Oekonomisk Revy
0030-1922 Okonomisk Virksomhedsledelse *changed to* Lederskab og Loensomhed
0030-1949 Oktobar
0030-1957 Oktyabr'
0030-1965 Old Bottle Magazine *changed to* Old Bottle Magazine/Popular Archaeology
0030-1973 Old English Newsletter
0030-199X Old Lady of Threadneedle Street
0030-2007 Old Man
0030-2023 Old Motor (London)
0030-2031 Old-Time New England†
0030-204X Old Timers' Bulletin
0030-2058 Old West
0030-2066 Das Oldenburger Sportpferd
0030-2074 Oldenburgische Familienkunde
0030-2082 Oleagineux
0030-2090 Oleario
0030-2104 Oleodinamica - Pneumatica *see* 0391-8645
0030-2112 Olie *changed to* Shell-Venster
0030-2120 Oljebladet *see* 0006-2367
0030-2139 Olomeinu
0030-2147 Oltre il Cielo
0030-2155 Oltremare†
0030-2163 Olympian (San Francisco)
0030-2171 Olympic Training Film Profiles *see* 0740-1906
0030-218X Oma
0030-2201 Omaha District Dental Society. Chronicle
0030-221X Omaha Profile *see* 0162-5241
0030-2228 Omega (Farmingdale)
0030-2244 Omin Kasin *see* 0355-1873
0030-2260 Omnia Medica et Therapeutica
0030-2279 Omnibus-Revue
0030-2287 Omnipraticien Francais
0030-2317 Instytut Metali Niezelaznych. Biuletyn
0030-2325 On Course†
0030-2333 On Dit
0030-2341 On Target†

ISSN INDEX 1281

ISSN	Title
0030-2368	On the Road (Cape Town)
0030-2376	On the Sound†
0030-2384	On the Track†
0030-2392	On Watch
0030-2406	Oncologia si Radiologia *changed to* Revista de Chirurgie, Oncologie, O.R.L., Radiologie, Oftalmolgie, Stomatologie. Oncologie
0030-2406	Oncologia si Radiologia *see* 0481-6684
0030-2414	Oncology
0030-2430	Onde Electrique
0030-2449	Onder Chevron Vlag *changed to* Chevron Motor
0030-2457	Onder de Vlam
0030-2465	Onderstepoort Journal of Veterinary Research
0030-2473	Onderwijs en Media†
0030-2481	Onderwijs en Opvoeding
0030-2503	One Church
0030-2511	One-Design and Offshore Yachtsman *changed to* Sailing World
0030-252X	One in Christ
0030-2546	1001 Custom & Rod Ideas†
0030-2554	1001 Decorating Ideas *see* 0278-0844
0030-2562	One/Two†
0030-2597	Japanese Musicological Society. Journal
0030-2600	Art of Music
0030-2619	Onlooker
0030-2627	Onomastica†
0030-2635	Ons Beroepsonderwijis *changed to* Magazine Voortgezet Onderwijs
0030-2643	Ons Bou *changed to* Tagtig
0030-2651	Ons Erfdeel
0030-266X	Ons Fruitteeltblad *see* 0772-7054
0030-2678	Ons Geestelijk Leven
0030-2686	Ons Huis†
0030-2694	Ons Jeug
0030-2708	Ons Jonge Platteland(OJP)†
0030-2716	Ons Kompas†
0030-2724	Ons Leger
0030-2732	Ons Platteland
0030-2740	Ons Politeuma *changed to* Ons Burgerschap
0030-2759	Reisiesduif *changed to* Racing Pigeon
0030-2767	Ons Trekpaard†
0030-2775	Ons Vee
0030-2783	Ons Wapen
0030-2791	Ons Zeewezen *see* 0165-8182
0030-2805	Ons Ziekenhuis†
0030-2813	Japan Journal of Logopedics and Phoniatrics
0030-2821	Science of Hot Springs
0030-283X	Ontario Association of Children's Aid Societies. Journal
0030-2848	Ontario Churchman
0030-2856	Ontario College of Pharmacy. Bulletin†
0030-2864	Ontario Dental Association. Journal *see* 0300-5275
0030-2872	Ontario. Ministry of Agriculture and Food. Monthly Dairy Report.
0030-2902	Ontario Education
0030-2910	Ontario Film Association. Bulletin *see* 0315-6923
0030-2929	Ontario Fish and Wildlife Review†
0030-2937	Ontario Gazette
0030-2945	Families
0030-2953	Ontario History
0030-297X	Ontario Hydro News *changed to* Hydro News
0030-2988	Ontario Hydro Research Quarterly†
0030-2996	Ontario Library Review†
0030-3011	Ontario Mathematics Gazette
0030-302X	Ontario Medical Review
0030-3038	Ontario Milk Producer
0030-3054	Ontario Psychologist
0030-3062	O P A L
0030-3070	Ontario Register†
0030-3089	Ontario Reports
0030-3097	Ontario Securities Commission. Monthly Bulletin *changed to* O S C Bulletin
0030-3100	Ontario Securities Commission. Weekly Summary *changed to* O S C Bulletin
0030-3119	Ontario Showcase *see* 0713-6315
0030-3127	Ontario Statute Citator
0030-3135	Ontladingen
0030-3143	Ontode *see* 0375-9504
0030-3151	Ontological Thought *changed to* Emissary
0030-316X	Ontwaak!
0030-3186	Onward-Voorwaarts *changed to* Volkstem
C030-3208	Onze Luchtmacht
0030-3224	Onze Vogels
0030-3232	Onze Wereld
0030-3259	Oomoto
0030-3267	Oorspronkelijk Christendom
0030-3275	Oost en West
0030-3283	Civis Mundi
0030-3291	Oostenrijkse Handelsdelegatie in Nederland *changed to* Oostenrijkse Economische Berichten
0030-3305	Op Cit
0030-333X	Op Leeftijd *changed to* Leef Tijd
0030-3348	Opakowanie
0030-3356	Opbouw
0030-3372	Open
0030-3399	Open Deur
0030-3402	Open Deur
0030-3410	Open Door†
0030-3429	Open Forum
0030-3437	Open Road and the Professional Driver†
0030-3445	Open Shelf†
0030-3453	Open Venster
0030-3461	Openbaar Vervoer (Amsterdam, 1928)†
0030-3488	Openbare Uitgavent†
0030-3496	Public Work, Construction & Transport *changed to* Public Works
0030-350X	Openings†
0030-3518	Oper und Konzert
0030-3526	Opera
0030-3577	Opera/Canada
0030-3585	Opera Journal
0030-3593	European Intelligence†
0030-3607	Opera News
0030-3615	Operation L A P L†
0030-3623	Operational Research Quarterly *see* 0160-5682
0030-3631	Operations Forestieres et de Scierie
0030-364X	Operations Research
0030-3658	Operations Research/Management Science
0030-3666	Operations Research Society of America. Bulletin *see* 0161-0295
0030-3690	Opernwelt
0030-3720	Ophthalmic Literature
0030-3739	Ophthalmic Optician *see* 0268-5485
0030-3747	Ophthalmic Research
0030-3755	Ophthalmologica
0030-3763	Ophthalmologist†
0030-3771	Opinie *see* 0167-093X
0030-3798	Opinion†
0030-3836	Klank en Weerklank
0030-3844	Belgisch-Nederlands Tijdschrift voor Oppervlaktetechnieken van Metalen
0030-3852	Opportunities
0030-3879	Opsaal
0030-3887	Opsearch
0030-3895	Opstina
0030-3909	Optica Acta
0030-3917	Optica Pura y Aplicada
0030-3925	Optical Journal and Review of Optometry *see* 0147-7633
0030-3941	Optical Society of America. Journal *see* 0740-3232
0030-395X	Optical Spectra *see* 0731-1230
0030-3976	Opticien Belge
0030-3984	Opticien-Lunetier
0030-3992	Optics and Laser Technology
0030-400X	Optics and Spectroscopy
0030-4018	Optics Communications
0030-4026	Optik
0030-4034	Optika i Spektroskopiya
0030-4050	Optima
0030-4069	Optimist
0030-4077	Opto-Electronics *see* 0306-8919
0030-4085	Optometric Management
0030-4093	Optometric Weekly *changed to* International Eyecare
0030-4107	Optometric World
0030-4115	Optometrie
0030-4123	Optometrie
0030-4131	Opus†
0030-414X	Opuscula Medica
0030-4158	Opuscula Zoologica†
0030-4166	Or Hamizrach†
0030-4174	Ora et Labora
0030-4182	Orafo Orologiaio
0030-4190	Orafo Valenzano *changed to* Valenza Gioielli
0030-4204	Oral Health
0030-4212	Oral Research Abstracts†
0030-4220	Oral Surgery, Oral Medicine and Oral Pathology
0030-4239	Orang Peladang
0030-4247	Orange County Apartment House News *changed to* Orange County Apartment News
0030-4255	Orange County Business *changed to* Orange County Business Journal
0030-4263	Orange County Genealogical Society. Quarterly *changed to* Orange County California Genealogical Society Quarterly
0030-4271	Orange County Farm News
0030-428X	Orange County Illustrated
0030-4298	Orange County Jewish Heritage
0030-431X	Orangeburg Historical and Genealogical Record
0030-4328	Oranje-Nassau Post†
0030-4336	Orante
0030-4344	Oratoire
0030-4352	Oratoriana
0030-4360	Organismo†
0030-4379	Orbis
0030-4387	Orbis (Philadelphia)
0030-4395	Orbis Geographicus
0030-4425	Orbis
0030-4433	Orbit
0030-445X	Orbita†
0030-4468	Das Orchester
0030-4476	Orchid Review
0030-4484	Orchideeen
0030-4492	Ord och Bild
0030-4506	Ordem dos Medicos. Boletim
0030-4514	Order of Scottish Clans Lion Rampant†
0030-4530	Ordine Nuovo *changed to* Linea
0030-4549	Ordinismo†
0030-4557	Ordnance *see* 0092-1491
0030-4565	Ordre National des Medecins. Bulletin
0030-4581	Ordu Dergisi
0030-459X	Ore
0030-4603	Oregon Agri-Record
0030-4611	Oregon Agriculture†
0030-462X	Oregon Beverage Analyst
0030-4638	Oregon Business Review†
0030-4646	Oregon Churchman *changed to* Oregon Episcopal Churchman
0030-4654	Oregon Commercial Fisheries Newsletter *changed to* Oregon Commercial Fisheries
0030-4662	Oregon Daily Emerald
0030-4670	Oregon Dental Association. Journal
0030-4689	Oregon Education
0030-4697	Oregon Grange Bulletin
0030-4700	Oregon Health Bulletin†
0030-4727	Oregon Historical Quarterly
0030-4735	Oregon Library News
0030-4743	Oregon Music Educator
0030-4751	Oregon Nurse
0030-476X	Oregon Optometrist *see* 0274-6549
0030-4778	Oregon Ornamental and Nursery Digest *changed to* Ornamentals NorthWest Newsletter
0030-4786	Oregon Purchasor
0030-4794	Oregon Science Teacher
0030-4808	Oregon Sportsman and Conservationist *see* 0164-7881
0030-4816	Oregon State Bar Bulletin
0030-4832	Oregon State University. Forest Research Laboratory. Index†
0030-4840	Oregon Teamster
0030-4859	Oregon Voter Digest
0030-4867	Orella
0030-4875	Orfeo
0030-4883	Organ
0030-4905	Organi di Trasmissione
0030-4913	Organic Gardening and Farming *see* 0884-3252
0030-4921	O M R - Organic Magnetic Resonance *see* 0749-1581
0030-493X	O M S - Organic Mass Spectrometry
0030-4948	Organic Preparations and Procedures International
0030-4956	Organic Reactivity†
0030-4964	Organisation Gestion des Enterprises
0030-4972	Organisation Internationale pour l'Etude des Langues Anciennes Par Ordinateur. Revue
0030-5006	Organische Land -und Gartenkultur†
0030-5014	Organiser†
0030-5022	Organizacija Kadrovska Politika *see* 0350-1531
0030-5049	Organizacion Mercantil *changed to* Noticia Comercial del Oriente
0030-5057	Organizacja - Metody - Technika *changed to* Organizacja - Metody - Technika w Administracji Panstwowej
0030-5065	E L N A Newsletter
0030-5073	Organizational Behavior and Human Performance *see* 0749-5978
0030-5081	Organizer†
0030-509X	Organizzazione Ferroviaria
0030-5103	Organizzazione Industriale†
0030-5111	Organometallic Chemistry Reviews. Section A: Subject Reviews *see* 0022-328X
0030-512X	Annual Surveys *see* 0022-328X
0030-5138	Organometallic Compounds
0030-5146	Organometallics in Chemical Synthesis†
0030-5154	Organon†
0030-5162	Organorama
0030-5170	Orgue
0030-5189	Oriens Antiquus
0030-5197	Oriens Extremus
0030-5219	Orient
0030-5227	Orient
0030-5243	South Pacific Travel Trade News *changed to* Thomsons Travel
0030-5251	Orientacion Docente
0030-526X	Orientacion Economica†
0030-5278	Oriental Art
0030-5294	Oriental Economist *changed to* Tokyo Business Today
0030-5308	Oriental Geographer
0030-5316	Oriental Insects
0030-5324	Oriental Institute. Journal
0030-5332	Oriental Rug
0030-5340	Oriental Society of Australia. Journal
0030-5359	Oriental Tide
0030-5367	Orientalia
0030-5375	Orientalia Christiana Periodica
0030-5383	Orientalistische Literaturzeitung
0030-5391	Orientamenti Pedagogici
0030-5405	Orientamenti Sociali†
0030-5413	Orientation Professionnelle/Vocational Guidance *see* 0833-0530
0030-543X	Orientations
0030-5464	Oriente Europeo†
0030-5472	Oriente Moderno
0030-5480	Orientering *changed to* Ny Tid
0030-5499	Orientering
0030-5502	Orientierung
0030-5510	Origin
0030-5529	The Original Art Report
0030-5537	University of Victoria. Department of Hispanic and Italian Studies. Original Works†
0030-5545	Original Works; Art, Poetry, Fiction†
0030-5553	Oriole
0030-557X	Orion
0030-5588	Orissa Education
0030-5596	Orita
0030-560X	Orizont
0030-5618	Orizzonti Aperti
0030-5634	Orizzonti Professionali
0030-5642	Orkester Journalen
0030-5650	Orkestra
0030-5669	Orleans Parish Medical Society. Bulletin
0030-5677	Ormanci Gazetesi
0030-5685	Ornis Fennica
0030-5693	Ornis Scandinavica

ISSN INDEX

ISSN	Title
0030-5707	Ornithologische Beobachter
0030-5715	Ornithologische Gesellschaft in Bayern. Anzeiger
0030-5723	Ornithologische Mitteilungen
0030-5731	Ornithologische Arbeitsgruppe Mitteilungen *changed to* Lanioturdus Ornithologische Arbeitsgruppe Mitteilungen
0030-5758	Oro y Hora
0030-5774	Orphan's Messenger and Advocate of the Blind *changed to* St. Joseph's Messenger and Advocate of the Blind
0030-5790	Orpheus
0030-5804	Orphic Lute
0030-5812	Orta Dogu†
0030-5839	Orthodox Word
0030-5855	Orthopaedic Medicine Surgery *see* 0009-9325
0030-5863	Orthopaedics/Oxford†
0030-5871	Orthopaedieschuhmachermeister *changed to* Orthopaedieschuhtechnik
0030-588X	Orthopaedische Praxis
0030-5898	Orthopedic Clinics of North America
0030-5901	Orthopedic Surgery
0030-591X	Orthopod
0030-5928	Orthotics and Prosthetics
0030-5936	Ortodoncia
0030-5944	Ortodontia
0030-5952	Ortodox Kyrkotidning
0030-5979	Ortopedici e Sanitari
0030-5987	Ortopediya, Travmatologiya i Protezirovanie
0030-5995	Die Ortskrankenkasse
0030-6002	Orvosi Hetilap
0030-6010	Orvosi Konyvtaros
0030-6029	Orvosi Szemle†
0030-6037	Orvoskepzes
0030-6045	Orvostudomany†
0030-6053	Oryx
0030-6061	Orzecznictwo Sadow Polskich i Komisji Arbitrazowych
0030-607X	Orzel Bialy†
0030-6088	Osaka District Meteorological Observatory. Monthly Report
0030-610X	Osaka Economic Papers *changed to* Osaka Daigaku Keizaigaku - Osaka Economic Papers
0030-6118	Osaka Medical College. Journal
0030-6126	Osaka Journal of Mathematics
0030-6134	Osaka Institute of Technology. Memoirs. Series B: Liberal Arts
0030-6142	Osaka Medical College. Bulletin
0030-6150	Osaka Odontological Society. Journal
0030-6169	Osaka University. Medical Journal
0030-6177	Osaka University. Faculty of Engineering. Technology Reports
0030-6185	Osgoode Hall Law Journal
0030-6193	Osiguranje i Privreda
0030-6207	Journal of the Oslo City Hospitals
0030-6223	Osnovaniya, Fundamenty i Mekhanika Gruntov
0030-6231	Ospedale
0030-624X	Ospedale al Mare. Archivo.
0030-6258	Ospedali d'Italia
0030-6266	Ospedali d'Italia-Chirurgia
0030-6274	Ospedali Italiani-Pediatria
0030-6282	Polska Akademia Nauk. Osrodek Dokumentacji i Informacji Naukowej. Biuletyn *changed to* Zagadnienia Informacji Naukowej
0030-6290	Osservatore Legale
0030-6304	Osservatore Politico Letterario
0030-6320	Osservatore Tributario e Rassegna Tributaria†
0030-6339	Ostdeutscher Literatur-Anzeiger†
0030-6355	Ostchandleren
0030-6363	Osten
0030-6371	Osteopathic Physician†
0030-638X	Osteroder Zeitung
0030-6398	Oesterreich-Polen, Austria-Polska
0030-6428	Osteuropa
0030-6436	Osteuropa-Naturwissenschaft und Technik†
0030-6444	Osteuropa-Recht
0030-6452	Osteuropaeische Rundschau†
0030-6460	Osteuropa-Wirtschaft
0030-6479	Ostfriesland
0030-6487	Ostkirchliche Studien
0030-6495	Ostkusten *see* 0347-4275
0030-6509	Osto ja Materiaalijohto *see* 0356-7931
0030-6517	Ostomy Quarterly
0030-6525	Ostrich
0030-6533	Osuuskauppalehti *see* 0781-7347
0030-655X	Otazky Miru a Socialismu
0030-6576	Other Voices†
0030-6592	Oto†
0030-6614	Oto-Laryngological Society of Australia. Journal
0030-6622	Journal of Otolaryngology of Japan
0030-6630	Oto-Rino-Laringologia Italiana†
0030-6649	Oto-Rino Laringologie
0030-6657	Otolaryngologia Polska
0030-6665	Otolaryngologic Clinics of North America
0030-6673	Audio-Digest Otorhinolaryngology *see* 0271-1354
0030-6681	Otrok in Druzina
0030-669X	Otsuka Pharmaceutical Factory. Journal
0030-6703	Ottar
0030-6711	Otto Rank Association. Journal†
0030-672X	Oud-Holland
0030-6738	Oud Utrecht. Maandblad
0030-6746	Oude Paden
0030-6754	Ouest Industriel, Maritime, Agricole et Commercial
0030-6762	Our Age†
0030-6789	Our Animals
0030-6797	Our Boys
0030-6800	Our Children
0030-6819	Educating in Faith
0030-6835	Animals
0030-6843	Our Family
0030-6851	Our Fourfooted Friends
0030-686X	Our Generation
0030-6878	Our Lady of the Sacred Heart *changed to* Annals Magazine
0030-6886	Our Lady's Digest
0030-6894	Our Little Friend
0030-6916	Our Navy†
0030-6924	Our Northland Diocese
0030-6932	Our Paper
0030-6940	Our Public Lands *see* 0732-3581
0030-6959	Our Special
0030-6967	Our Sunday Visitor
0030-6975	Our World
0030-6983	Our World†
0030-6991	Ouranos-Giel-Insolite *see* 0472-2744
0030-7025	Outdoor California
0030-7033	Outdoor Education *changed to* Council on Outdoor Education. Newsletter
0030-705X	Outdoor Illinois *see* 0148-3390
0030-7068	Outdoor Indiana
0030-7076	Outdoor Life
0030-7092	Outdoor News Bulletin
0030-7106	Outdoor Oklahoma
0030-7122	Outdoor Power Products for Recreational and Garden Merchandising *see* 0381-5528
0030-7130	Outdoor Recreation Action†
0030-7157	Wonderful West Virginia
0030-7165	Outdoor World†
0030-7173	Outdoors Magazine *see* 0004-9905
0030-7181	Outdoors Unlimited
0030-719X	Outlook†
0030-7203	Outlook *see* 0306-7262
0030-7211	Outlook
0030-7238	Outlook (Wake Forest)
0030-7246	Standard & Poor's Outlook
0030-7254	Outlook
0030-7262	Outlook
0030-7270	Outlook on Agriculture
0030-7289	Outpost
0030-7297	Outposts *changed to* Outposts Poetry Quarterly
0030-7300	Outreach *changed to* Intercom
0030-7319	Outrider
0030-7327	Outward Bound
0030-7335	Over Alle Grenser
0030-7343	Over the Bridge†
0030-7351	Standard and Poor's Over-The-Counter *changed to* Standard & Poor's Daily Stock Price Record. Over the Counter Exchange
0030-736X	Over-the-Counter Securities Review *see* 0161-0694
0030-7378	Over the Hills†
0030-7386	Overbrook Adviser
0030-7394	Overdrive
0030-7408	Overflow†
0030-7416	Overland
0030-7424	Overseas
0030-7432	Overseas Building Notes
0030-7440	Overseas Development
0030-7475	Uebersee-Post - Europa-Post
0030-7491	Overseas Review *see* 0307-7039
0030-7505	Trinidad and Tobago. Central Statistical Office. Overseas Trade. Bi-Monthly Report
0030-7513	Overseas Trading
0030-7548	Overtones†
0030-7556	Overture
0030-7564	Overview (Chicago)
0030-7572	Ovtsevodstvo
0030-7580	Owl of Minerva
0030-7602	Owlet *changed to* Insight (Akron)
0030-7629	Ox Head
0030-7645	Oxford
0030-7653	Oxford Economic Papers
0030-7661	Oxford Medical School Gazette
0030-767X	Oxford University. Institute of Statistics. Bulletin *see* 0305-9049
0030-7688	Oxfordshire Farmer *changed to* Oxford and Berkshire Farmer
0030-7696	Oxidation and Combustion Reviews†
0030-770X	Oxidation of Metals
0030-7718	Afn Shvel
0030-7726	Hokkaido University. Research Institute of Applied Electricity. Bulletin
0030-7734	Kyushu University. Research Institute for Applied Mechanics. Bulletin
0030-7750	Ozarker
0030-7769	Ozarks Mountaineer
0030-7777	Ozone Data for the World
0030-7785	R A I Orgaan *see* 0166-1922
0030-7793	P A N S *see* 0143-6147
0030-7807	P.A.R. News Analysis *changed to* P A R Analysis
0030-7815	P A R D Bulletin
0030-7823	P and I†
0030-7831	P & S Quarterly *changed to* P & S Journal
0030-784X	P B S Aktuell
0030-7858	P Ch C Journal of Educational Research
0030-7866	P C M - P C E†
0030-7874	P C M R Message†
0030-7904	P E D
0030-7912	Pegg/Professional Engineering, Geologist, Geophysicist *see* 0823-1745
0030-7920	Panorama Economico Latinoamericano
0030-7947	P E P *changed to* P S I: Report Series
0030-7955	Mundo Policial
0030-7963	P F M
0030-798X	P H P *see* 0910-4607
0030-7998	P I B Monthly *changed to* Publishers Information Bureau Report
0030-8005	P I C I C News
0030-8013	P I E F Newsletter *see* 0276-6558
0030-8048	P J G B *see* 0260-6739
0030-8056	P K
0030-8064	Port of London
0030-8080	P M.†
0030-8099	P M A Newsletter
0030-8102	P M E A News
0030-8110	Photomethods for Industry *see* 0146-0153
0030-8129	P M L A
0030-8145	P M Newsletter (Blackburn) *see* 0141-1241
0030-8153	P.M.O. Notes
0030-817X	P N E U Journal *changed to* W E S Journal
0030-8188	P N L A Quarterly
0030-8196	P N P A Press
0030-820X	P P G Products
0030-8218	P P S T A Herald *changed to* P P S T A Report
0030-8226	P R Aids' Party Line
0030-8242	Profodcil Bulletin
0030-8250	P R S Journal
0030-8269	P S (Washington)
0030-8277	P S A Journal
0030-8285	P.S. for Private Secretaries *changed to* P.S. for Professional Secretaries
0030-8315	P.S.: Postscript to Education *changed to* Alumnews
0030-8323	P.S. Public Schools in Action†
0030-834X	P T B Mitteilungen *changed to* P T B Mitteilungen Forschen und Pruefen
0030-8358	P T M
0030-8366	P T T Bedrijf
0030-8374	P T T Informations
0030-8382	Telecommunicatie
0030-8390	P T T-Zbornik *changed to* P T T Novice
0030-8404	P U D O C Bulletin†
0030-8412	P. U.-Kaner†
0030-8420	P.U.R. Executive Information Service
0030-8439	P V
0030-8447	Paarl Post
0030-8455	Paarlse Padwyser *changed to* Strooidak Pace†
0030-8471	Pace†
0030-8528	Pacific Bakers News
0030-8536	Pacific Banker and Business *see* 8750-6718
0030-8544	Pacific Builder and Engineer
0030-8560	Pacific Business Magazine†
0030-8579	Pacific Citizen
0030-8587	Pacfic Coast Nurseryman and Garden Supply Dealer *see* 0192-7159
0030-8617	Pacific Coast Society of Orthodontists. Bulletin
0030-8625	Pacific Community†
0030-8633	Pacific Community *changed to* Asia Pacific Community
0030-8641	Pacific Discovery
0030-865X	Pacific Factory *changed to* Western Machining & Metalworking
0030-8668	Pacific Fruit News
0030-8676	Pacific Historian
0030-8684	Pacific Historical Review
0030-8692	Pacific Hosteller
0030-8706	Pacific Hotel-Motel News†
0030-8714	Pacific Insects *see* 0735-6250
0030-8722	Pacific Islands Monthly
0030-8730	Pacific Journal of Mathematics
0030-8757	Pacific Law Journal
0030-8765	P M L/Life *changed to* Soundings (Newport Beach)
0030-8781	Pacific Neighbors†
0030-879X	Pacific News *changed to* Pacific Rail News
0030-8803	Pacific Northwest Quarterly
0030-8811	Pacific Northwest Underwriter†
0030-882X	Pacific Northwesterner
0030-8838	Pacific Orchid Society of Hawaii. Bulletin *see* 0099-8745
0030-8846	Pacific Purchasor
0030-8854	Pacific Research and World Empire Telegrams *changed to* Pacific Research
0030-8862	Pacific Review
0030-8870	Pacific Science
0030-8889	Pacific Science Association. Information Bulletin
0030-8900	Pacific Shipper
0030-8919	Pacific Sociological Review *see* 0731-1214
0030-8943	Pacific Traffic
0030-8951	Pacific Travel News
0030-896X	Pacific Tribune
0030-8978	Pacific Viewpoint
0030-8986	Pacific Yachting
0030-9001	Pack *changed to* Pack-Distribution
0030-901X	Pack-o-Fun *see* 0146-6607
0030-9028	Package Development *see* 0274-4996
0030-9044	Package Engineering *see* 0746-3820
0030-9052	Packages & People†
0030-9060	Packaging
0030-9087	Packaging Abstracts *see* 0260-7409

ISSN	Title
0030-9095	Packaging Bulletin see 0091-0120
0030-9109	Packaging Design see 0032-8510
0030-9117	Packaging Digest
0030-9125	Packaging/India
0030-9133	Packaging News
0030-9141	Packaging Technology changed to Packaging Technology and Management
0030-9168	Packer
0030-9184	Packung und Transport im Chemiebetrieb. see 0343-7183
0030-9192	Padova e la sua Provincia
0030-9206	Padova Economica
0030-9214	Padre Santo
0030-9222	Padres' Trail
0030-9230	Paedagogica Historica
0030-9249	Paedagogik
0030-9257	Paedagogik Heute†
0030-9265	Paedagogik und Schule in Ost und West
0030-9273	Paedagogische Rundschau
0030-9281	Paedagogisches Institut der Stadt Wien. Mitteilungen
0030-929X	Paedagogisches Institute Salzburg. Mitteilungen changed to Paedagogische Mitteilungen
0030-9311	Paediatrica Indonesiana
0030-932X	Paediatrie und Grenzgebiete
0030-9338	Paediatrie und Paedologie
0030-9346	Paediatrische Praxis
0030-9362	Page
0030-9389	Pages
0030-9397	Pages†
0030-9400	Pagine di Storia della Medicina see 0025-7877
0030-9427	Pahlavi Medical Journal changed to Iranian Journal of Medical Sciences
0030-9435	Paideia
0030-9443	Paikallislehdisto
0030-946X	Paint and Resin Patents†
0030-9478	Paint and Varnish Production see 0098-7786
0030-9508	Paint Manufacture see 0261-5746
0030-9516	Paint Oil and Colour Journal see 0370-1158
0030-9524	Paint Technology see 0369-9420
0030-9532	Painter & Allied Trades Journal
0030-9540	Paintindia
0030-9567	Pais e Filhos
0030-9575	Pajara Pinta†
0030-9583	Pajtas
0030-9591	Pak Jamhuriat
0030-9605	Pak-Scout
0030-9613	Pakin
0030-9621	Pakistan Accountant
0030-963X	Pakistan Affairs
0030-9648	Pakistan Armed Forces Medical Journal
0030-9656	Pakistan Army Journal
0030-9664	Pakistan Book News†
0030-9680	Pakistan Chemist & Druggist†
0030-9699	Pakistan Cottons
0030-9702	Pakistan Council for National Integration. Review†
0030-9710	Pakistan Dental Review
0030-9745	Pakistan Economist see 0253-1941
0030-9753	Pakistan Engineer
0030-977X	Pakistan Exports
0030-9788	Pakistan Geographical Review†
0030-9796	Pakistan Historical Society. Journal
0030-980X	Pakistan Horizon
0030-9818	Pakistan Journal of Forestry
0030-9826	Pakistan Journal of Geriatrics†
0030-9834	Pakistan Journal of Health
0030-9842	Pakistan Journal of Medical Research
0030-9850	Pakistan Journal of Pharmacy
0030-9869	Pakistan Journal of Psychology†
0030-9877	Pakistan Journal of Science
0030-9885	Pakistan Journal of Scientific and Industrial Research
0030-9893	Pakistan Journal of Soil Science changed to Bangladesh Journal of Soil Science
0030-9907	Pakistan Journal of Surgery, Gynaecology, and Obstetrics
0030-9915	Pakistan Journal of Veterinary Science changed to Bangladesh Veterinary Journal
0030-9923	Pakistan Journal of Zoology
0030-994X	Pakistan Labour Cases
0030-9958	All Pakistan Legal Decisions
0030-9966	Pakistan Library Bulletin
0030-9982	Pakistan Medical Association. Journal
0030-9990	Pakistan Medical Forum†
0031-0018	Pakistan Medical Review
0031-0026	Pakistan. Ministry of Information & Broadcasting. Progress of the Month†
0031-0034	Pakistan Monitor
0031-0042	Pakistan News Digest changed to Weekly Commentary and Pakistan News Digest
0031-0050	Pakistan Press Index†
0031-0069	Pakistan Quarterly†
0031-0077	Pakistan Review†
0031-0085	Pakistan Science Abstracts
0031-0093	Pakistan Stamps
0031-0107	Pakistan Studies†
0031-0115	Pakistan Tax Decisions
0031-0123	Pakistan Weather Review - Monthly Weather Report
0031-0131	Pakkaus
0031-0158	El Palacio
0031-0166	Paladijn†
0031-0174	Palaeobotanist
0031-0182	Palaeogeography, Palaeoclimatology, Palaeoecology
0031-0204	Palaeontological Society of Japan. Transactions and Proceedings
0031-0220	Palaeontologische Zeitschrift
0031-0239	Palaeontology
0031-0247	Palaeovertebrata
0031-0255	Palaestra
0031-0263	Palaestra Latina†
0031-0298	PaleoBios
0031-0301	Paleontological Journal
0031-031X	Paleontologicheskii Zhurnal
0031-0328	Palestine Exploration Quarterly
0031-0336	Palestine Refugees Today
0031-0344	Palestra
0031-0360	Palimpsest
0031-0379	Palladio
0031-0387	Pallas
0031-0395	Pallottis Werk
0031-0417	Palm Beach Life
0031-0425	Palm Springs Life
0031-0433	Palmer Writer†
0031-0441	Palmos Tou Geneous†
0031-045X	Palomino Horses
0031-0468	Palontorjunta
0031-0476	Palontorjuntatekniika
0031-0492	Palynological Bulletin see 0022-3379
0031-0506	Pamatky Archeologicke
0031-0514	Pamietnik Literacki
0031-0522	Pamietnik Teatralny
0031-0530	Pamir Monthly changed to Pamir Magazine
0031-0549	Pammatone changed to San Martino
0031-0557	Pamphleteer Monthly†
0031-0565	Pan-African Journal
0031-059X	Pan American Review
0031-0603	Pan-Pacific Entomologist
0031-0611	Pan Pipes of Sigma Alpha Iota changed to Sigma Alpha Iota Quarterly: Pan Pipes
0031-0638	Panadero Latinoamericano/Latin American Baker see 0744-625X
0031-0646	Panama Canal Review†
0031-0662	Pancevac
0031-0697	Pandecte Neon Noman Kediataghmaton
0031-0719	Pandora changed to Pandora: a Washington Women's News Journal
0031-0735	Panel†
0031-0743	Excerpta Medica. Section 49: Forensic Science
0031-076X	Panhandle Magazine
0031-0778	Panidealistische Umschau†
0031-0786	Panjab Past and Present
0031-0794	Panjab University Economist changed to Pakistan Economic and Social Review
0031-0808	Panminerva Medica changed to Panminerva Medica-Europa Medica
0031-0824	Panorama (Fortitude Valley)
0031-0840	Panorama changed to Colorado Women's College. Bulletin
0031-0859	Panorama†
0031-0867	Panorama
0031-0875	Panorama†
0031-0883	Panorama
0031-0891	Panorama Ballesterense changed to Reportero
0031-0913	Panorama Democrate Chretien
0031-093X	Panorama Economico†
0031-0948	Panorama Medical†
0031-0964	Panorama Polnocy
0031-0972	Panpere
0031-0980	Panstwo i Prawo
0031-0999	Pantheon see 0720-0056
0031-1006	Panther changed to Advocate (Johnstown)
0031-1014	Pantograph
0031-1022	Pantuflas del Obispo
0031-1049	Papeis Avulsos de Zoologia
0031-1057	Papel
0031-1065	Papeles de Son Armadans†
0031-1081	Paper Age
0031-109X	Printing Abstracts
0031-1103	Paper and Twine Journal
0031-1111	Paper Bulletin see 0142-5307
0031-112X	Paper Facts and Figures
0031-1138	Paper, Film and Foil Converter
0031-1146	Paper Maker†
0031-1154	Paper-Maker see 0306-8234
0031-1162	Paper Money
0031-1170	Paper Sales
0031-1189	Paper Technology see 0306-252X
0031-1197	Paper Trade Journal
0031-1200	Paper Trends†
0031-1219	Paperbacks in Print see 0262-9763
0031-1227	Paperboard Packaging
0031-1235	Paperbound Books in Print
0031-1243	Paperi ja Puu
0031-1251	Papers in Linguistics: International Journal of Human Communication
0031-126X	Papers in Meteorology and Geophysics
0031-1278	Papers in Psychology†
0031-1286	Papers of Woodrow Wilson
0031-1294	Papers on Language and Literature
0031-1308	Papeterie
0031-1316	Papeterist
0031-1324	Papetier de France
0031-1332	Papetier Libraire
0031-1340	Das Papier
0031-1359	Papier- und Buchgewerbe-Rundschau
0031-1367	Papier Carton et Cellulose
0031-1375	Papier und Druck
0031-1383	Papiergeschichte†
0031-1391	Papierhandels-Fachblatt
0031-1405	Der Papiermacher
0031-1413	Papierwereld†
0031-1421	Papir a Celuloza
0031-143X	Papirhandleren
0031-1448	Papiripar
0031-1456	Pappershandlaren changed to Papper och Kontor
0031-1464	Papua New Guinea Agricultural Journal changed to Papua New Guinea Journal of Agriculture, Forestry and Fisheries
0031-1472	Papua New Guinea Journal of Education
0031-1480	Papua New Guinea Medical Journal
0031-1510	Papua New Guinea Overseas Migration changed to Papua New Guinea International Arrivals and Departures
0031-1529	Papua New Guinea. Quarterly Retail Price Index changed to Papua New Guinea. National Statistical Office. Consumer Price Index
0031-1537	Papua and New Guinea. Quarterly Summary of Statistics changed to Papua New Guinea. Abstract of Statistics
0031-1545	Para Elite
0031-1553	Parabas
0031-1561	Paraboles
0031-1588	Parachutist
0031-1596	Parade†
0031-160X	Parade
0031-1618	Parade and Foto-Action
0031-1642	Parag
0031-1650	Paragone
0031-1669	Paragraphs changed to Network (Arlington)
0031-1677	Paraguay. Direccion General de Estadistica y Censos. Boletin Estadistico
0031-1685	Paraguay Industrial y Comercial
0031-1715	Parallelo Trentotto
0031-1723	Parameters
0031-1731	Parametro
0031-174X	Parana em Paginas
0031-1758	Paraplegia
0031-1766	Paraplegia News
0031-1790	Parapsychology Bulletin†
0031-1804	Parapsychology Review
0031-1812	Parasitica
0031-1820	Parasitology
0031-1847	Parazitologiya
0031-1863	Parent Educator†
0031-188X	Parents' Bulletin
0031-1898	Parents et Instituteurs†
0031-1901	Parents et Maitres†
0031-191X	Parents' Magazine and Better Family Living see 0195-0967
0031-1928	Lexington School for the Deaf. Parents' Newsletter. changed to Sounds of Lexington
0031-1936	Parents Voice
0031-1952	Parfuemerie und Kosmetik
0031-1979	Parichiti
0031-1987	Paris
0031-2002	Paris District. Journal des Communes†
0031-2010	Paris Gaz Relations changed to Gaz Relations
0031-2029	Paris Match
0031-2037	Paris Review
0031-2045	Paris-Sud
0031-2053	Pariser Kurier
0031-2061	Parish Councils Review see 0308-3594
0031-207X	Parish News†
0031-2088	Parishioner
0031-2096	Pariyal Kalyan
0031-210X	Park
0031-2118	Park Administration
0031-2126	Park East
0031-2134	Park Maintenance see 0192-2505
0031-2142	Park News†
0031-2169	Park Slope Civic Council. Civic News
0031-2177	Parkdalian
0031-2193	Parking
0031-2207	Dierenpark Wassenaar Zoo. Parknieuws†
0031-2215	Parks and Recreation
0031-2223	Parks and Recreation changed to Leisure Manager
0031-2231	Recreation Canada
0031-224X	Parks and Sports Grounds
0031-2282	Parliamentarian
0031-2290	Parliamentary Affairs
0031-2312	Parmamedica
0031-2320	Parnasso
0031-2347	Paroisse et Liturgie changed to Communautes et Liturgies
0031-2355	Parola del Passato
0031-2363	Parola del Popolo†
0031-2371	Parola e Il Libro
0031-2398	Parole di Vita
0031-2401	Parole e le Idee
0031-2428	Parrocchia
0031-2436	Parson and Parish
0031-2444	U.S. Agency for International Development. Participant Journal†
0031-2460	Particle Accelerators
0031-2479	Particles and Nuclei†
0031-2487	Particulate Matter†
0031-2509	Partiinaya Zhizn'
0031-2517	Activist†
0031-2525	Partisan Review
0031-2533	Partisans†
0031-255X	Partizanov Vesnik
0031-2568	Partners
0031-2576	Parts Line
0031-2584	Pas a Past
0031-2592	Paseo del Rio Showboat
0031-2606	Pashupalan see 0023-1088

ISSN INDEX

ISSN	Title
0031-2614	Pasicrisie Belge
0031-2622	Pasidibala
0031-2630	Pasinomie
0031-2649	Pasque Petals
0031-2657	Pasquino
0031-2665	Passaic County Historical Society. Bulletin†
0031-2673	Passaic County Medical Society. Bulletin†
0031-2681	Passauer Bistumsblatt
0031-2703	Passenger Pigeon
0031-2711	Passerelle
0031-272X	Passport
0031-2738	Password
0031-2746	Past and Present: a Journal of Historical Studies
0031-2754	Pastor Evangelico *changed to* Obrero Cristiano
0031-2762	Pastoral Life
0031-2789	Pastoral Psychology
0031-2797	Pastoral Review
0031-2800	Pastoralblaetter
0031-2819	Pastoralist and Grazier Newsletter *changed to* Pastoralist and Grazier
0031-2827	Wissenschaft und Praxis in Kirche und Gesellschaft *see* 0720-6259
0031-2835	Patent and Trademark Review†
0031-286X	Patent Journal Including Trademarks and Models
0031-2878	Patent Licensing Gazette *changed to* World Technology
0031-2894	Patentblatt
0031-2908	Patentni Glasnik
0031-2916	Finland. Patentti- ja Rekisterihallitus. Patenttilehti/Patenttidning/Patent Gazette
0031-2932	Path of Truth
0031-2940	Pathfinder
0031-2959	Schweizerische Zeitschrift fuer Allgemeine Pathologie und Bakteriologie *see* 0304-3568
0031-2967	Pathologia Europaea†
0031-2975	Pathologia Veterinaria *see* 0300-9858
0031-2983	Pathologica
0031-2991	Patologicheskaya Fiziologiya i Eksperimental'naya Terapiya
0031-3009	Pathologie Biologie
0031-3017	Pathologist†
0031-3025	Pathology
0031-305X	Patient Care
0031-3068	Patisserie Francaise Illustree
0031-3076	Patissier de l'Ile-De-France†
0031-3084	Patna Journal of Medicine
0031-3092	Patna University Journal
0031-3106	Patologia
0031-3114	Patologia Polska
0031-3122	Patranu
0031-3130	Patria Indipendente
0031-3149	Patrimonium
0031-3165	Patronat Francais *see* 0399-8975
0031-3173	Patronato Genovese Pronatura "A. Anfossi." Notiziario†
0031-3181	Patrys
0031-319X	Pattern Makers' Journal
0031-3203	Pattern Recognition
0031-3211	Patterns *see* 0146-1397
0031-322X	Patterns of Prejudice
0031-3238	Patterson's California Beverage Gazetteer
0031-3246	Paukenslag
0031-3262	Paunch
0031-3270	Pauze
0031-3289	Pavliha
0031-3297	Pavo
0031-3300	Pax†
0031-3319	Pax Bulletin *see* 0306-7645
0031-3327	Pax et Libertas
0031-3335	Pax Regis
0031-3351	Pay Planning†
0031-336X	Pay Planning Checklist and Forms†
0031-3386	Pays Bas-Normand
0031-3394	Pays Lorrain
0031-3408	Paz e Terra†
0031-3416	Pcela
0031-3432	Peabody Journal of Education
0031-3440	Peabody Notes *changed to* Peabody News
0031-3459	Peabody Reflector
0031-3467	Peace
0031-3491	Peace and Freedom
0031-3513	Peace and the Sciences
0031-353X	Peace Monitor
0031-3548	Peace News
0031-3564	Peace Plans
0031-3572	Peace Press
0031-3580	Excerpta Medica. Section 48: Gastroenterology
0031-3599	Peace Research Abstracts Journal
0031-3602	Peacemaker
0031-3610	Peach-Times
0031-3629	Peak
0031-3637	Peak District Mines Historical Society. Bulletin
0031-3653	Peanut Farmer
0031-3661	Peanut Journal and Nut World
0031-367X	Peat Abstracts
0031-3696	Pebble
0031-370X	Peche au Canada†
0031-3718	Peche et les Poissons
0031-3726	Peche Maritime
0031-3734	Pecheur et Chasseur Suisses *changed to* Pecheur Romand
0031-3742	Pecheurs d'Hommes†
0031-3750	Pecsi Muszaki Szemle
0031-3777	Pedagogia e Vita
0031-3785	Pedagogiai Szemle
0031-3793	Pedagogic Reporter
0031-3807	Pedagogija
0031-3815	Pedagogika
0031-3823	Pedagogisch Forum *see* 0166-5855
0031-3831	Scandinavian Journal of Educational Research
0031-384X	Pedagoski Rad
0031-3858	Pedagoski Zivot
0031-3866	Pedale d'Oro
0031-3874	Arrive *see* 0144-2694
0031-3882	Pediatria
0031-3890	Pediatria
0031-3904	Revista de Pediatrie, Obstetrica, Ginecologie. Pediatrie
0031-3912	Pediatria e Puericultura
0031-3920	Pediatria Moderna
0031-3939	Pediatria Polska
0031-3947	Pediatria Pratica
0031-3955	Pediatric Clinics of North America
0031-3963	United Hospitals of Newark. Babies Hospital Unit. Pediatric Conferences *see* 0097-5982
0031-398X	Pediatric News
0031-3998	Pediatric Research
0031-4005	Pediatrics (Elk Grove Village)
0031-4013	Pediatrics Digest *see* 0198-6341
0031-4021	Pediatrie (Lyon)
0031-403X	Pediatriya
0031-4048	Pediatriya, Akusherstvo ta Ginekologiya
0031-4056	Pedobiologia
0031-4064	Pedologist
0031-4072	Pegasus *see* 0318-5753
0031-4080	Pegasus Journal
0031-4099	Peiling
0031-4110	Peking Informers
0031-4129	Beijing Review
0031-4137	Pelagos
0031-4145	Pelerin du Vingtieme Siecle
0031-4153	Pelican†
0031-4161	Pelican News
0031-417X	Pelita
0031-4188	Pellervo
0031-4226	Pembrokeshire Farmer
0031-4242	Pen Woman
0031-4250	Pendle Hill Pamphlets
0031-4293	Peninsula Living
0031-4307	Peninsula Poets
0031-4315	Penmen's News Letter
0031-4331	Penn Dental Journal
0031-434X	Pennsylvania Angler
0031-4366	Pennsylvania. Board of Probation and Parole. Monthly Statistical Report
0031-4374	Pennsylvania. Board of Probation and Parole. Quarterly Statistical Report *see* 0031-4366
0031-4382	Pennsylvania Business Survey
0031-4390	Pennsylvania C P A Spokesman *changed to* Pennsylvania C P A Journal
0031-4404	Pennsylvania Chiefs of Police Association Bulletin
0031-4412	Pennsylvania Contractor
0031-4420	Pennsylvania Dental Association. Newsletter†
0031-4439	Pennsylvania Dental Journal
0031-4455	Pennsylvania Education
0031-4471	Pennsylvania Farmer
0031-448X	Pennsylvania Flower Growers. Bulletin
0031-4498	Pennsylvania Folklife
0031-4501	Pennsylvania Forests
0031-451X	Pennsylvania Game News
0031-4528	Pennsylvania History
0031-4536	Pennsylvania Holstein News†
0031-4544	Pennsylvania Human Relations Report†
0031-4552	Pennsylvania Jewish Life†
0031-4587	Pennsylvania Magazine of History and Biography
0031-4595	Pennsylvania Medicine
0031-4609	Pennsylvania Message
0031-4617	Pennsylvania Nurse
0031-4625	Pennsylvania Optometrist†
0031-4633	Pennsylvania Pharmacist
0031-4641	Pennsylvania Professional Engineer *changed to* Engineer (Pittsburgh)
0031-465X	Pennsylvania Psychiatric Quarterly†
0031-4668	Pennsylvania School Boards Association. Bulletin *see* 0162-3559
0031-4676	Pennsylvania School Journal†
0031-4692	Pennsylvania Traveler *changed to* Pennsylvania Traveler-Post
0031-4706	Pennsylvania Veterinarian†
0031-4714	Pennsylvanian
0031-4730	Pensador†
0031-4749	Pensamiento
0031-4757	Pensamiento Politico†
0031-4765	Pensamiento y Accion
0031-4781	Pensee Catholique
0031-479X	La Pensee Francaise
0031-4803	Pensez Plastiques
0031-4811	Pensiero†
0031-482X	Pensiero Mazziniano
0031-4838	Pensiero Nazionale
0031-4846	Pensiero Politico
0031-4854	Pensioen Bulletin
0031-4862	Pension and Welfare News *see* 0098-1753
0031-4870	Pentagon
0031-4889	Pentagramma *changed to* Primi Piani
0031-4897	Pentecostal Evangel
0031-4900	International Pentecostal Holiness Advocate
0031-4919	Pentecostal Messenger
0031-4927	Pentecostal Testimony
0031-4935	Penthouse
0031-496X	Penzugyi Szemle
0031-4978	People *changed to* Pix - People
0031-4986	People†
0031-4994	People†
0031-5001	People†
0031-501X	People (Kansas City)
0031-5028	People's Action†
0031-5036	People's Korea
0031-5044	People's World
0031-5052	Peoria Labor News *changed to* Labor Paper
0031-5087	Pepinieristes Horticulteurs Maraichers *see* 0035-3302
0031-5117	Perception & Psychophysics
0031-5125	Perceptual and Motor Skills
0031-5133	Perceptual-Cognitive Development†
0031-5141	Perchtoldsdorfer Pfarrbote
0031-5168	Percussionist and Percussive Notes *changed to* Percussive Notes
0031-5176	Perets
0031-5184	Perfect Home†
0031-5192	Perfekt Kindermode
0031-5206	Perfekt Mode
0031-5214	Performance (Washington, 1977) *see* 0148-5407
0031-5222	Performing Arts
0031-5230	Performing Arts in Canada
0031-5249	Performing Arts Review *see* 0733-5113
0031-5257	Performing Right *see* 0309-0019
0031-529X	Periodica de Re Morali Canonica Liturgica
0031-5303	Periodica Mathematica Hungarica
0031-5311	Periodica Polytechnica. Chemical Engineering
0031-532X	Periodica Polytechnica. Electrical Engineering
0031-5338	Periodica Polytechnica. Engineering, Maschinen- und Bauwesen *see* 0324-6051
0031-5346	Periodica Polytechnica. Architecture
0031-5362	Periodicum Biologorum
0031-5397	Periodontology Today
0031-5400	Peripherals Weekly *changed to* Peripherals Digest
0031-5427	Periscope (Hartsville)†
0031-5435	Perito Industriale†
0031-5443	N.T.U.C. Perjuangan *changed to* Singaporean
0031-546X	Perlin et Pinpin *changed to* Perlin
0031-5478	Permanences
0031-5486	Permanencia
0031-5508	Permanent International Altaistic Conference (PIAC). Newsletter
0031-5516	Permanent Way†
0031-5524	Permanent Way Institution. Journal and Report of Proceedings
0031-5532	P S I†
0031-5540	Perpetual Motion Journal†
0031-5559	Perpustakaan†
0031-5567	Nederlandse Hervormde Kerk. Persbureau. Weekbulletin
0031-5575	Persklaar *changed to* Intercom
0031-5591	Personal Injury Valuation Handbooks
0031-5605	Personal
0031-5613	Personal Romances
0031-5621	Personalist *see* 0279-0750
0031-563X	Personality†
0031-5648	Personnality *changed to* Personnality
0031-5656	Personeelbeleid
0031-5699	Personhistorisk Tidskrift
0031-5702	Personnel
0031-5729	Personnel Administrator
0031-5737	Personnel and Guidance Journal *see* 0748-9633
0031-5745	Personnel Journal
0031-5753	Personnel Literature
0031-577X	Personnel Management Abstracts
0031-5788	International Personnel Management Association. Personnel News *changed to* I P M A News
0031-580X	Personnel Policies Forum *see* 0361-7467
0031-5818	Australia. Department of Labour and National Service. Personnel Practice Bulletin *see* 0312-455X
0031-5826	Personnel Psychology
0031-5834	Personnel Quarterly *changed to* L.O.M.A. Resource
0031-5842	Persoon en Gemeenschap†
0031-5850	Persoonia
0031-5869	Persoverzicht
0031-5885	Perspective (Augusta) *changed to* Maine. Arts Commission. Newsletter
0031-5893	Perpective (St. Louis)†
0031-5915	Perspective†
0031-5923	Perspective
0031-5931	Perspective (Olympia)†
0031-594X	Peace Courier
0031-5958	Perspectives: Journal of General and Liberal Studies *see* 0890-9792
0031-5974	Federation Nationale des Clubs Perspectives et Realities *changed to* Perspectives et Realities
0031-5982	Perspectives in Biology and Medicine
0031-5990	Perspectives in Psychiatric Care
0031-6016	Perspectives of New Music
0031-6032	Perspectives Psychiatriques
0031-6059	Perspektywy
0031-6067	Peru. Biblioteca Nacional. Boletin
0031-6075	Pesca Italiana
0031-6091	Pescare
0031-6105	Peshawar Times†

ISSN INDEX 1285

0031-6121 Pest Control
0031-613X Pesticide Science
0031-6148 Pesticides
0031-6156 Pesticides Monitoring Journal†
0031-6164 Pesum Padam
0031-6180 P S M *see* 0162-8666
0031-6229 Petermanns Geographische Mitteilungen
0031-6237 Petfish Monthly *changed to* Petfish Practical Fishkeeping Monthly
0031-6245 Petfood Industry
0031-6253 Petit Journal du Brasseur
0031-6261 Petit Meunier
0031-627X Petit Moniteur des Assurances
0031-6296 Petnaest Dana
0031-630X Petra
0031-6318 Petri-Heil
0031-6326 Petro/Chem Engineer *see* 0031-6466
0031-6334 Petrobras†
0031-6342 PetroChemical News
0031-6350 Petrol si Gaze *changed to* Mine, Petrol si Gaze
0031-6369 Arab Oil & Gas
0031-6407 Petroleo Interamericano *see* 0093-7851
0031-6415 Petroleo y Mineria de Venezuela
0031-6423 Petroleum Abstracts
0031-6431 Modern Bulk Transporter
0031-644X Petroleum and TBA Marketer *see* 0362-7799
0031-6458 Petroleum Chemistry U.S.S.R.
0031-6466 Petroleum Engineer International
0031-6490 Petroleum Outlook
0031-6504 Petroleum Press Service *see* 0306-395X
0031-6512 Petroleum Refining Developments†
0031-6539 Petroleum Taxation Report *changed to* Petroleum Taxation/Legislation Report
0031-6547 Petroleum Times *see* 0141-4437
0031-6555 Petroleum Today†
0031-6563 Petrolieri d'Italia
0031-6571 Petrolio
0031-658X Petronio
0031-6598 Petrotecnica
0031-661X Peuple
0031-6644 Pewter Collectors' Club of America. Bulletin
0031-6652 Pez y la Serpiente
0031-6660 Pfaelzer Bauer
0031-6679 Pfaelzer Heimat
0031-6687 Pfaelzer Saenger
0031-6695 Pfalz am Rhein
0031-6709 Pfarrbrief
0031-6725 Pfizer Spectrum†
0031-6733 Pflanzenarzt
0031-6741 Pflanzenernaehrung und Duengung†
0031-675X Pflanzenschutzberichte
0031-6768 Pfluegers Archiv
0031-6776 Pflugschar†
0031-6784 Die Pforte
0031-6792 Peradarstvo
0031-6806 Phaphama!
0031-6814 Phare
0031-6822 Pharetra
0031-6849 Pharma Times
0031-6857 Pharmaca
0031-6865 Pharmaceutica Acta Helvetiae
0031-6873 Pharmaceutical Journal
0031-689X Pharmaceutical Research Institute. Bulletin
0031-6903 Pharmaceutical Society of Japan. Journal
0031-692X Pharmacien
0031-6938 Pharmacien de France
0031-6946 Pharmacien de Reserve
0031-6954 Pharmacien Rural
0031-6970 European Journal of Clinical Pharmacology
0031-6989 Pharmacological Research Communications
0031-6997 Pharmacological Reviews
0031-7004 Pharmacologist
0031-7012 Pharmacology
0031-7020 Rational Drug Therapy
0031-7039 Pharmacotoxicologia et Therapia Clinica†
0031-7047 Pharmacy in History
0031-7063 Pharmacy News
0031-7071 Pharmacy Trade
0031-708X Pharmakeftikon Deltion
0031-7098 Pharmakopsychiatrie - Neuro-Psychopharmakologie *see* 0176-3679
0031-7101 Pharmanews†
0031-711X Die Pharmazeutische Industrie
0031-7128 Pharmazeutische Rundschau
0031-7136 Pharmazeutische Zeitung
0031-7144 Die Pharmazie
0031-7152 Pharmindex
0031-7160 Pharos
0031-7179 Pharos
0031-7187 Phare†
0031-7209 Phi Delta Epsilon News & Scientific Journal
0031-7217 Phi Delta Kappan
0031-7233 Philadelphia Magazine
0031-725X Philadelphia College of Pharmacy and Science Bulletin
0031-7268 Philadelphia County Dental Society. Bulletin
0031-7276 Philadelphia Dental Laboratory Association Journal†
0031-7306 Philadelphia Medicine
0031-7314 Philadelphia Museum of Art. Bulletin
0031-7322 Mid-Atlantic Purchasing
0031-7349 South Africa. Philatelic Services. Philatelic Bulletin/Filateliebulletin *changed to* South Africa. Philatelic Services and Intersapa. Philatelic Bulletin/Filateliebulletin
0031-7365 Philatelic Trader and Stationer *changed to* Philatelic Trader
0031-7373 Philatelist *see* 0260-6739
0031-7381 Philatelic Exporter
0031-739X Philately *see* 0265-8216
0031-7403 Philately from Australia
0031-7438 Philippine Abstracts *see* 0115-8724
0031-7446 Philippine Agricultural Situation
0031-7454 Philippine Agriculturist
0031-7462 Philippine Architecture & Building Journal
0031-7470 Philippine Architecture, Engineering & Construction Record
0031-7489 Philippine Business Index
0031-7497 Philippine Dental Association. Journal
0031-7500 Philippine Economic Journal
0031-7527 Philippine Educational Forum
0031-7535 Philippine Federation of Private Medical Practitioners. Journal
0031-7543 Philippine Fishing Journal
0031-7551 Philippine Geographical Journal
0031-7578 Philippine Health Journal *changed to* Philippine Health Education Journal
0031-7594 Philippine Journal of Business and Finance
0031-7608 Philippine Journal of Cancer
0031-7616 Philippine Journal of Child-Youth Development
0031-7624 Philippine Journal of Education
0031-7632 Philippine Journal of Leprosy *changed to* Philippine Journal of Dermatology and Leprosy
0031-7640 Philippine Journal of Nutrition
0031-7659 Philippine Journal of Ophthalmology
0031-7667 Philippine Journal of Pediatrics
0031-7675 Philippine Journal of Public Administration
0031-7683 Philippine Journal of Science
0031-7691 Philippine Journal of Surgical Specialties
0031-7705 Philippine Journal of Veterinary Medicine
0031-7713 Philippine Junior Red Cross Magazine
0031-7721 Philippine Law Journal
0031-773X Philippine Manager
0031-7748 Philippine Medical Association. Journal
0031-7764 Philippine Progress†
0031-7780 Philippine Review of Economics and Business
0031-7799 Philippine Scientific Journal
0031-7802 Philippine Social Sciences and Humanities Review
0031-7810 Philippine Sociological Review
0031-7829 Philippine Statistician
0031-7837 Philippine Studies
0031-7845 Philippine Tax Journal
0031-7853 Philippine Women's University Administrative News
0031-787X Philippines Labor Relations Journal
0031-7888 Philippines Transportation
0031-7896 Philips Cronache *changed to* Cronache
0031-790X Philips Music Herald†
0031-7926 Philips Technical Review
0031-7969 Philobiblon
0031-7977 Philological Quarterly
0031-7985 Philologus
0031-7993 Philosopher's Index
0031-8000 Philosophia
0031-8019 Philosophia Mathematica
0031-8027 Philosophia Naturalis
0031-8035 Philosophia Reformata
0031-8043 Philosophical Association. Journal†
0031-8051 Philosophical Books
0031-806X Philosophical Forum
0031-8078 Philosophical Journal†
0031-8086 Philosophical Magazine
0031-8094 Philosophical Quarterly
0031-8108 Philosophical Review
0031-8116 Philosophical Studies
0031-8140 Philosophische Probleme des Sozialistischen Aufbaus und der Technischen Revolution *see* 0232-8798
0031-8159 Philosophische Rundschau
0031-8167 Philosophische Zeitspiegel
0031-8175 Philosophischer Literaturanzeiger
0031-8183 Philosophisches Jahrbuch
0031-8191 Philosophy
0031-8205 Philosophy and Phenomenological Research
0031-8213 Philosophy and Rhetoric
0031-8221 Philosophy East and West
0031-823X Philosophy Forum *see* 0260-4027
0031-8248 Philosophy of Science
0031-8256 Philosophy Today
0031-8264 Philotelia
0031-8272 Philwomenian
0031-8280 Phlebologie *changed to* Societe Francaise de Phlebologie. Bulletin
0031-8299 Phoenix
0031-8310 Phoenix†
0031-8329 Phoenix
0031-8337 Phoenix†
0031-8353 Phoenix Jewish News *see* 0747-444X
0031-837X Phoenix Quarterly
0031-8388 Phonetica
0031-8396 Phoni Tou Evangeliou
0031-8426 Phosphorus and Potassium
0031-8434 Phosphorus in Agriculture *changed to* Fertilizers and Agriculture
0031-8442 Photo
0031-8450 Photo-Cine-Expert *changed to* Photo-Cine-Expert (1979)
0031-8469 Photo-Cine-Revue *changed to* Photo-Revue
0031-8477 Photo-Cinema, Film, Amateur-Son *changed to* Photomagazine
0031-8485 Photo Dealer†
0031-8515 Photographic Processor†
0031-8523 Photo Interpretation
0031-8531 Photo Marketing
0031-854X Photo News
0031-8566 Photo Screen
0031-8574 Photo-Technik und - Wirtschaft†
0031-8582 Canadian Photography *changed to* Photo/Video
0031-8590 Photo Trade News *see* 0816-1909
0031-8604 Photo Trade of Japan†
0031-8612 Photo Trader *changed to* Photo & Video Trader
0031-8639 Photo Typesetting
0031-8647 Photo Weekly
0031-8655 Photochemistry and Photobiology
0031-8663 Photogrammetria
0031-8671 Photogrammetric Engineering *see* 0099-1112
0031-868X Photogrammetric Record
0031-8698 Photographer
0031-8701 Photographic Abstracts
0031-871X Photographic Applications in Science and Technology *see* 0360-7216
0031-8728 Photographic Business and Product News *changed to* Studio Photography
0031-8736 Photographic Journal
0031-8744 Photographic Processing
0031-8760 Photographic Science and Engineering *changed to* Journal of Imaging Science
0031-8779 Photographic Trade News
0031-8809 Photography *changed to* 35MM Photography
0031-8817 Photography and Travel *changed to* Creative Photography
0031-8833 Photon
0031-8841 Photoplatemakers Bulletin *see* 8750-2224
0031-885X Photoplay (1946)†
0031-8868 Phronesis
0031-8876 Phytiatrie-Phythopharmacie
0031-8884 Phycologia
0031-8892 Phykos
0031-8906 Phylon
0031-8922 Physica Fennica *see* 0031-8949
0031-8930 Physica Norvegica *see* 0031-8949
0031-8949 Physica Scripta
0031-8965 Physica Status Solidi (A). Applied Research
0031-8973 Physical Education Newsletter
0031-8981 Physical Educator
0031-899X Physical Review *see* 0556-2791
0031-899X Physical Review *see* 0163-1829
0031-9007 Physical Review Letters
0031-9015 Physical Society of Japan. Journal
0031-9023 Physical Therapy
0031-9031 Physicians' Association of Madras. Journal
0031-904X Physicians' Basic Index†
0031-9058 Physicians' Drug Manual
0031-9066 Physician's Management
0031-9082 Physico-Chemical Biology
0031-9090 Physics and Chemistry of Glasses
0031-9104 Physics and Chemistry of Liquids
0031-9112 Physics Bulletin
0031-9120 Physics Education
0031-9147 Physics in Canada
0031-9155 Physics in Medicine and Biology
0031-9163 Physics Letters *changed to* Physics Letters. Section A: General, Atomic and Solid State Physics
0031-9163 Physics Letters *changed to* Physics Letters. Section B: Nuclear, Elementary Particle and High-Energy Physics
0031-9163 Physics Letters *see* 0370-1573
0031-9171 Physics of Fluids
0031-918X Physics of Metals and Metallography
0031-9198 Physics of Sintering *see* 0350-820X
0031-9201 Physics of the Earth and Planetary Interiors
0031-921X Physics Teacher (College Park)
0031-9228 Physics Today
0031-9236 Physik der Kondensierten Materie/Physique de la Matiere Condensee/Physics of Condensed Matter *see* 0722-3277
0031-9244 Physik in der Schule
0031-9252 Physik in Unserer Zeit
0031-9260 Physikalische Berichte *see* 0170-7434
0031-9279 Physikalische Blaetter
0031-9287 Physikalische Medizin und Rehabilitation *changed to* Aerztezeitschrift fuer Naturheilverfahren
0031-9295 Der Physikunterricht
0031-9309 Physiologia Bohemoslovaca
0031-9317 Physiologia Plantarum
0031-9325 Physiological Chemistry and Physics *changed to* Physiological Chemistry and Physics and Medical N M R
0031-9333 Physiological Reviews
0031-9341 Physiological Society of Japan. Journal
0031-935X Physiological Zoology
0031-9368 Physiologie Vegetale
0031-9376 Physiologist
0031-9384 Physiology and Behavior

ISSN INDEX

ISSN	Title
0031-9392	Physiotherapie
0031-9406	Physiotherapy
0031-9414	Physis
0031-9422	Phytochemistry
0031-9430	Phytologia
0031-9449	Phytomorphology
0031-9457	Phyton
0031-9465	Phytopathologia Mediterranea†
0031-9473	Phytopathological Society of Japan. Annals
0031-9481	Journal of Phytopathology
0031-949X	Phytopathology
0031-9503	Phytopathology News
0031-9511	Phytoprotection
0031-952X	Pi Mu Epsilon Journal
0031-9538	Pianeta
0031-9546	Piano Guild Notes
0031-9554	Piano Quarterly
0031-9562	Piano Technicians Journal
0031-9570	Pianura
0031-9589	Picchiarello†
0031-9600	Piccolo Missionario *changed to* Piemme
0031-9619	Picket Post *changed to* Valley Forge Journal
0031-9627	Pick'n' and Sing'n' Gather'n'. Newsletter
0031-9635	Pictorial†
0031-9643	Pictorial Life *changed to* Florida's Gold Coast
0031-9651	Pictorial News Review
0031-966X	Picturegoer†
0031-9678	Pictures & Prints†
0031-9686	Pictures on Exhibit†
0031-9694	Picturescope
0031-9708	Pie
0031-9716	Pierian Spring†
0031-9732	Pig Breeders Gazette†
0031-9740	Pig Farmer
0031-9759	Pig Farming
0031-9775	Pig Progress†
0031-9783	Pigeon News†
0031-9791	Piggin String
0031-9805	Pilgrim
0031-9813	Pilgrim Society Notes *see* 0885-4947
0031-983X	Pin High†
0031-9856	Pine Cone
0031-9864	Rap†
0031-9872	Pinellas Teacher *changed to* Action (Clearwater)
0031-9880	Pingrin
0031-9899	Pinheiros Farmaceutico†
0031-9902	Pinkster Protestant
0031-9910	Pinpointer
0031-9929	Pins and Needles†
0031-9937	Pinto Horse
0031-9945	Pintores
0031-9953	Pinturas y Acabados Industriales
0031-9961	Rivista degli Infermieri
0031-997X	Pioneer *changed to* Pioneer
0031-9988	Pioneer†
0032-0005	Pioneer America *changed to* Material Culture
0032-0021	Pioneer Woman *see* 0888-191X
0032-003X	Pioner
0032-0048	Pionerskaya Pravda
0032-0056	Pionier
0032-0099	Pionir-Kekec
0032-0102	Pioneriya
0032-0110	Pionyrske Noviny *changed to* Sedmicka Pionyru
0032-0129	Pioppicoltura *see* 0012-9836
0032-0137	Pipeline
0032-0145	Pipe Line Industry
0032-0153	Pipe Line News *see* 0148-4443
0032-0161	Pipe Smoker's Ephemeris
0032-0196	Pipeline & Underground Utilities Construction
0032-020X	Pipes and Pipelines International
0032-0226	P I R A Newspaper Information Service *changed to* P I R A Newsbrief
0032-0234	Piraiki-Patraiki
0032-0242	Pirkka
0032-0250	Pirquet Bulletin of Clinical Medicine *changed to* Virchow-Piquet Medical Society. Proceedings
0032-0269	Pirsch *see* 0340-7829
0032-0277	Piscator
0032-0285	Piscines
0032-0293	Pit & Quarry
0032-0307	Pitman Journal *changed to* Memo International
0032-0315	Pittsburgh Business Review†
0032-0323	Pittsburgh Catholic
0032-0331	Pittsburgh Legal Journal
0032-034X	Pittsburgh Musician
0032-0358	Pittsburgh Symphony Orchestra Program
0032-0374	Catholic Guild News *changed to* Word for Word
0032-0382	Pivot
0032-0390	Pix *changed to* Pix - People
0032-0404	Pjichk
0032-0420	Plain Truth (Pasadena)
0032-0439	Plain Truth†
0032-0447	Plains Anthropologist
0032-0471	Boum *changed to* Allons
0032-048X	Plaisir de France *see* 0293-9274
0032-0501	Plaisirs de la Peche
0032-051X	Plaisirs Equestre
0032-0528	Plamuk
0032-0536	Plan
0032-0544	Plan *changed to* Plan Canada
0032-0552	Plan
0032-0560	Plan
0032-0579	Plan
0032-0587	Plan Ahead
0032-0595	Plan and Print
0032-0609	Plan og Arbeid
0032-0617	Plane & Pilot
0032-0633	Planetary and Space Science
0032-065X	Planned Parenthood Report†
0032-0668	Planned Savings
0032-0676	Planner
0032-0684	Planning & Changing
0032-0692	Planning and Development in the Netherlands†
0032-0706	Planning Comment†
0032-0714	Planning Outlook
0032-0749	Planovane Hospodarstvi
0032-0757	Planovoe Khozyaistvo
0032-0765	Planseeberichte fuer Pulvermetallurgie†
0032-0773	Plant Administration and Engineering *see* 0315-9183
0032-0781	Plant and Cell Physiology
0032-079X	Plant and Soil
0032-0803	Plant Breeding Abstracts
0032-0811	Plant Disease Reporter *see* 0191-2917
0032-082X	Plant Engineering
0032-0838	Plant Engineers†
0032-0846	Plant Life *changed to* Herbertia
0032-0854	Plant Operating Management†
0032-0862	Plant Pathology
0032-0870	Florida. Department of Agriculture and Consumer Services. Plant Pathology Circular
0032-0889	Plant Physiology
0032-0897	Plant Protection Abstracts
0032-0919	Plant Science Bulletin
0032-0935	Planta
0032-0943	Planta Medica
0032-096X	Planters Bulletin
0032-0978	Planters' Chronicle
0032-0986	Planters Journal and Agriculturist
0032-0994	Plantes Medicinales et Phytotherapie
0032-101X	Plants & Gardens *see* 0362-5850
0032-1028	Plasma Physics *see* 0741-3335
0032-1052	Plastic and Reconstructive Surgery
0032-1060	Plastic Industry Notes†
0032-1079	Plastic Laminating†
0032-1087	Plastic-Revue Edition Schweiz†
0032-1095	Plastica *changed to* Kunststof en Rubber
0032-1109	Plasticke Hmoty a Kaucuk *changed to* Plasty a Kaucuk
0032-1117	Plasticonstruction *see* 0343-3129
0032-1125	Plasticos *changed to* Plasticos
0032-1133	Plasticos em Revista
0032-1141	Plasticos y Resinas†
0032-115X	Plastics Abstracts†
0032-1168	Plastics and Rubber Weekly
0032-1176	Plastics Design & Processing†
0032-1192	Plastics in Engineering†
0032-1206	Plastics Industry News, Japan
0032-1214	Plastics Industry Notes†
0032-1222	Plastics, Paint and Rubber *changed to* Plastics and Rubber News
0032-1249	Plastics, Rubber and Leather Industries Journal
0032-1257	Plastics Technology
0032-1265	Plastics Trends†
0032-1273	Plastics World
0032-129X	Plastiques Informations *see* 0032-1303
0032-1303	Plastiques Modernes et Elastomeres
0032-1311	Plastnytt *changed to* Plastindustrien
0032-132X	Plastvaerlden†
0032-1338	Plastverarbeiter
0032-1346	Plateau
0032-1354	Plateau†
0032-1370	Platform (Manchester)
0032-1389	Platform (Luddendenfoot)
0032-1397	Plating *see* 0360-3164
0032-1400	Platinum Metals Review
0032-1435	Plavi Vjesnik†
0032-1443	Play Schools Newsletter
0032-1451	Playback†
0032-146X	Playbill
0032-1478	Playboy
0032-1486	Players Magazine†
0032-1508	Playhour
0032-1516	Playing Fields†
0032-1532	Playmen
0032-1540	Plays
0032-1559	Plays & Players
0032-1567	Playthings
0032-1591	Plomberie-Chauffage et Climatisation
0032-1605	Plomjo
0032-1621	Plug
0032-163X	Plumb Line
0032-1656	Plumbing
0032-1672	Plumbing Equipment News and Heating Engineer *see* 0308-373X
0032-1680	Wholesaler
0032-1699	Plumbing and Heating Journal
0032-1702	Plus†
0032-1729	Plutonium-Dokumentation *changed to* Plutonium-Dokumentation/Transplutonium-Elemente
0032-1737	Plymouth Bulletin
0032-1753	Plymouth Traveler†
0032-1761	Plyn
0032-177X	Plywood and Panel *see* 0744-6853
0032-1788	Plywood World *changed to* Wood World
0032-1796	Pobeda
0032-180X	Pochvovedenie
0032-1826	Pocket List of Railroad Officials
0032-1869	Podnikova Organizace
0032-1877	Poe Newsletter *see* 0090-5224
0032-1885	Poem
0032-1893	Poesia de Venezuela
0032-1907	Poesia en la Calle
0032-1915	Poesia-Poesia
0032-194X	Poet
0032-1958	Poet and Critic
0032-1966	Poet Lore
0032-1974	Cahiers de Litterature et de Poesie: Poetes et Leurs Amis
0032-1982	Poeti della Nuova Italia
0032-1990	Poeti Italiani Contemporanei†
0032-2024	Poetique
0032-2032	Poetry (Chicago)
0032-2040	Poetry & Audience
0032-2059	Poetry Australia
0032-2075	Poetry India†
0032-2083	Poetry Market
0032-2105	Poetry Nippon
0032-2113	Poetry Northwest
0032-2148	Poetry Prevue *see* 0190-2253
0032-2156	Poetry Review
0032-2164	Poetry Singapore†
0032-2199	Poetry Venture†
0032-2202	Poetry Wales
0032-2229	Serie Poeyana *changed to* Poeyana
0032-2237	Poezja
0032-2245	Pogledi
0032-227X	Poids Lourd
0032-2288	Poilu Lorrain
0032-230X	Point of View
0032-2318	Point of View
0032-2326	Point Three
0032-2334	Point to Point Communication *see* 0305-3601
0032-2342	Pointer†
0032-2369	Points et Contrepoints
0032-2377	Poirieria
0032-2385	Poissonnier Belge
0032-2393	Pojistny Obzor
0032-2407	Pokret
0032-2415	Pokrof
0032-2423	Pokroky Matematiky, Fyziky a Astronomie
0032-2431	Pola Esperantisto
0032-244X	Poland
0032-2458	Poland and Germany (East & West)†
0032-2466	Poland China World *see* 8750-1880
0032-2474	Polar Record
0032-2482	Polar Times
0032-2490	Polarforschung
0032-2504	Pole et Tropiques
0032-2520	Polet
0032-2547	Poletarac
0032-2555	Police
0032-2563	Police†
0032-258X	Police Journal
0032-2598	Police Life
0032-2601	Police Times *changed to* Police Times
0032-261X	Police World
0032-2628	Policia Portuguesa Revista Ilustrada†
0032-2636	Policlinico. Sezione Chirurgica
0032-2644	Policlinico. Sezione Pratica
0032-2652	Policy *see* 0263-6700
0032-2660	Policy, Fact and Comment *changed to* P R P Comment
0032-2679	Policy Holder Insurance Journal *changed to* Policy Holder Insurance News
0032-2687	Policy Sciences
0032-2709	Poligrafico Italiano
0032-2717	Poligrafiya
0032-2725	Polimery
0032-2733	Polimlje
0032-2741	Polio-France
0032-2768	Poliplasti e Plastici Rinforzati *changed to* Poliplasti e Plastici Rinforzati (1978)
0032-2776	Polish Academy of Sciences. Review *changed to* Journal of Polish Science
0032-2784	Polish Affairs
0032-2792	Polish American Journal
0032-2806	Polish American Studies
0032-2814	Polish Building Abstracts†
0032-2822	Polish Co-Operative Review
0032-2849	Polish Economic Survey
0032-2857	Polish Facts and Figures†
0032-2881	Polish Foreign Trade
0032-289X	Polish Literature†
0032-2903	Polish Machinery News†
0032-2911	Polish Maritime News
0032-2938	Polish Medical Journal†
0032-2946	Polish Music
0032-2954	Polish News
0032-2962	Polish Perspectives
0032-2970	Polish Review
0032-2989	Polish Scientific Periodicals-Contents†
0032-2997	Polish Sociological Bulletin
0032-3004	Polish Technical and Economic Abstracts
0032-3012	Polish Technical Review
0032-3020	Polish Weekly†
0032-3039	Polish Western Affairs
0032-3047	Polish Western Association of America. Quarterly
0032-3055	Politecnica
0032-3063	Politica del Diritto
0032-3071	Politica e Mezzogiorno
0032-3101	Politica Internazionale (Florence)
0032-3128	Political Affairs
0032-3152	Political Companion†
0032-3160	Memo from C O P E
0032-3179	Political Quarterly
0032-3187	Political Science
0032-3195	Political Science Quarterly
0032-3209	Political Scientist

ISSN	Title
0032-3217	Political Studies
0032-3225	Politicheskoe Samoobrazovanie
0032-3233	Politicka Ekonomie
0032-3241	Politicka Misao
0032-325X	Politico
0032-3268	Politics
0032-3276	Politics
0032-3284	Politics and Money
0032-3292	Politics and Society
0032-3306	Politics†
0032-3322	Politie-Dierenbescherming *changed to* Politie, Dier en Milieu
0032-3349	Politiek en Cultuur
0032-3357	Politiidrett
0032-3365	Politiikka
0032-3381	Politika-Ekspres
0032-339X	Politikin Zabavnik
0032-3403	Politikon
0032-342X	Politique Etrangere *changed to* Politique Etrangere de la France
0032-3438	Politische Dokumentation
0032-3446	Die Politische Meinung
0032-3454	Politische Perspektiven
0032-3470	Politische Vierteljahresschrift
0032-3489	Politisk Tidskrift
0032-3497	Polity
0032-3500	Polityka
0032-3519	Die Polizei
0032-3527	Die Polizei im Lande Berlin
0032-3535	Polizei Technik Verkehr *changed to* Polizeiverkehr und Technik
0032-3543	Polizeimagazin
0032-3551	Polizeischau†
0032-356X	Polizia Moderna
0032-3578	Polja
0032-3594	Polka
0032-3608	Polled Hereford World
0032-3616	Pollen et Spores
0032-3624	Pollution Abstracts
0032-3632	Pollution Atmospherique
0032-3659	Pollution Equipment News
0032-3667	Polo
0032-3675	Pologne et les Affaires Occidentales
0032-3683	Polonia
0032-3713	Polska Bibliografia Analityczna Mechaniki
0032-3721	Polska Sztuka Ludowa
0032-373X	Polski Przeglad Chirurgiczny
0032-3756	Polski Tygodnik Lekarski
0032-3764	Polskie Archiwum Hydrobiologii
0032-3772	Polskie Archiwum Medycyny Wewnetrznej
0032-3780	Polskie Pismo Entomologiczne
0032-3799	Annales Societatis Mathematicae Polonae. Seria 1: Commentationes Mathematicae
0032-3802	Polskie Towarzystwo Jezykoznawcze. Biuletyn
0032-3829	Polyclinic Journal†
0032-3837	Polygraph *changed to* Interamericana
0032-3845	Der Polygraph
0032-3861	Polymer
0032-3888	Polymer Engineering and Science
0032-3896	Polymer Journal
0032-390X	Polymer Mechanics/Mekhanika Polimerov *see* 0191-5665
0032-3918	Polymer News
0032-3926	Polymer Report. Japan†
0032-3934	Polymer Preprints
0032-3942	Polymer Science & Technology Post†
0032-3950	Polymer Science, U.S.S.R.
0032-3969	Polymerics†
0032-3977	Quarterly Literature Reports. Polymers†
0032-3985	Polymya
0032-3993	Polymus†
0032-4000	Polynesian Society. Journal
0032-4019	Polyphonie *see* 0035-3736
0032-4027	Polysar Progress (1965) *changed to* Polysar Progress
0032-4035	Polyscope Automatik und Elektronik *changed to* Polyscope Plus
0032-4051	Polytechnic
0032-406X	Polytechnic Engineer
0032-4078	Bouwkunde Wegen- en Waterbouw *changed to* Architectuur/Bouwen
0032-4116	Polytechnische Bildung und Erziehung
0032-4124	Polyteknikeren
0032-4132	Pomhaj Boh
0032-4140	Pomiary - Automatyka - Kontrola
0032-4159	Pomme de Terre Francaise
0032-4167	Pommern
0032-4175	Pomologie Francaise†
0032-4183	Pomona Today
0032-4205	Pompebledden
0032-4213	Ponny *see* 0346-4687
0032-4221	Pont†
0032-423X	Ponte
0032-4256	Pony
0032-4272	Pool 'n Patio†
0032-4280	Pool News *see* 0194-5351
0032-4299	Poona Agricultural College Magazine
0032-4302	Poor Richard's Almanack†
0032-4310	Poor Richard's Report *see* 0516-9623
0032-4329	Poor's Investment Advisory Survey *changed to* Standard & Poor's Investment Advisory Survey
0032-4337	Pootaardappelhandel *changed to* Aardappelwereld
0032-4345	Pop-Foto/Tuney Tunes *changed to* Popfoto
0032-4353	Pope Speaks
0032-4361	El Popola Cinio
0032-437X	Popolo del Friuli-Venezia Giulia
0032-4388	Popayan
0032-440X	Populaer Elektronik og Viden *changed to* Populaer Elektronik og High Fidelity
0032-4418	Populaer Filateli
0032-4442	Populaer Radio og TV Teknik *see* 0105-4880
0032-4450	Popular Bridge
0032-4469	Camping *see* 0266-7878
0032-4477	Popular Ceramics
0032-4485	Popular Electronics *see* 0745-1458
0032-4493	Popular Flying
0032-4507	Popular Gardening†
0032-4515	Popular Government
0032-4523	Popular Hot Rodding
0032-4531	Popular Imported Cars *changed to* Small Cars /Magazine
0032-454X	Popular Mechanics†
0032-4558	Popular Mechanics
0032-4574	Popular Motoring
0032-4582	Popular Photography
0032-4590	Popular Photography's Woman†
0032-4604	Popular Plastics *changed to* Popular Plastics
0032-4620	Popular Rotorcraft Flying
0032-4639	Popular Science and Technology
0032-4647	Popular Science Monthly *see* 0161-7370
0032-4663	Population
0032-468X	Population Bulletin
0032-4698	Population Chronicle†
0032-4701	Population Index
0032-471X	Population Review
0032-4728	Population Studies
0032-4736	Population Statistics Hilversum *changed to* Statistisch Jaaroverzicht Hilversum
0032-4744	Por Alquimia
0032-4752	Poradnik Bibliotekarza
0032-4779	Polymer Friends for Rubber, Plastics and Fiber
0032-4787	Porodica i Dijete
0032-4795	Poroshkovaya Metallurgiya
0032-4809	Port
0032-4817	Port of Baltimore Bulletin
0032-4825	Port of Houston Magazine
0032-4833	Port of Karachi†
0032-4841	Port of Norfolk News Letter†
0032-485X	Port of Sydney *see* 0313-4075
0032-4868	Port of Toledo News
0032-4876	Port of Yokohama. Monthly Statistics. *changed to* Port of Yokohama. Annual Statistics.
0032-4884	Portals of Prayer
0032-4892	Portcullis
0032-4906	Porter Library Bulletin *changed to* Kansas State College of Pittsburg. Library Bulletin
0032-4914	Portico
0032-4922	Presence Orthodoxe
0032-4930	Portland Physician†
0032-4949	Porto di Livorno†
0032-4957	Il Porto di Savona
0032-4965	Porto di Venezia
0032-4973	Portos e Navios
0032-4981	Portrait *changed to* Maryland Today
0032-499X	Portraits of Prominent U.S.S.R. Personalities†
0032-5007	International Freighting Weekly
0032-5015	Ports O'Call
0032-5023	Portsmouth Chamber of Commerce. Newsletter *changed to* Portsmouth Chamber of Commerce. Report
0032-5031	Portugal-an Information Review†
0032-504X	Portugal. Direccao-Geral dos Servicos Florestais e Aquicolas. Gabinete de Estudos Economicos e Estatisticos. Cadernos†
0032-5066	Portugal Evangelico
0032-5082	Portugal. Instituto Nacional de Estatistica. Boletim Mensal *changed to* Portugal. Instituto Nacional de Estatistica. Boletim Mensal de Estatistica: Continente, Acores e Madeira
0032-5090	Laboratorio Nacional de Engenharia Civil. Boletim Mensal de Informacao *changed to* Laboratorio Nacional de Engeharia Civil. Boletim de Informacao Tecnica
0032-5112	Portugal Ministerio da Economia. Comissao Reguladora do Comercio de Arroz. Informacao Bibliografica do Arroz†
0032-5120	Portugal Ministerio da Saude e Assistencia, Direccao-Geral da Assistencia. Informacao Social†
0032-5139	Portugal. Ministerio dos Negocios Estrangeiros. Boletim de Informacao Economica†
0032-5147	Portugaliae Acta Biologica
0032-5155	Portugaliae Mathematica
0032-5163	Portuguese Journal
0032-5171	Poruka Borca
0032-5198	Poseidon
0032-5201	Possev
0032-521X	Posh†
0032-5228	Positions Lutheriennes
0032-5236	Post
0032-5244	Post†
0032-5252	Post Magazine and Insurance Monitor
0032-5260	Post Mark†
0032-5279	Post Mortem
0032-5287	Post Office Electrical Engineers' Journal *see* 0262-401X
0032-5295	Post Office Engineering Union Journal *changed to* National Communications Union Journal
0032-5309	Post Office Telecommunications Journal†
0032-5317	Postal and Telegraph Herald
0032-5325	Postal Bell
0032-5333	Postal Bulletin
0032-5341	Postal History Journal
0032-535X	Postal Journal
0032-5368	Postal Life
0032-5376	Postal Record
0032-5384	Postal Supervisor
0032-5392	Postal Worker *see* 0790-6277
0032-5406	Poste e Telecomunicazioni
0032-5414	Postepy Astronomii
0032-5422	Postepy Biochemii
0032-5430	Postepy Fizyki
0032-5449	Postepy Higieny i Medycyny Doswiadczalnej
0032-5457	Postepy Nauk Rolniczych
0032-5473	Postgraduate Medical Journal
0032-5481	Postgraduate Medicine
0032-549X	Posthalter-Kurier†
0032-5503	Postmaennens Tidning
0032-5511	Postmasters Advocate
0032-552X	Postmasters Gazette
0032-5538	Pot-Au-Feu
0032-5546	Potash Review
0032-5554	Potato and Onion World†
0032-5562	Potato Chipper *changed to* Chipper/Snacker
0032-5570	Potato Councillor
0032-5589	Potato Grower News
0032-5600	Potencia
0032-5619	Potentials in Marketing
0032-5635	Potomac Appalachian Trail Club. Bulletin *changed to* Potomac Appalachian
0032-5643	Potomac View *changed to* Nova Report on Lung Health and Wellness
0032-566X	Potravinar
0032-5678	Pottery Quarterly
0032-5686	Poty Cuntu
0032-5708	Poultry and Egg Situation *changed to* U.S. Department of Agriculture. Livestock and Poultry Outlook and Situation
0032-5716	Poultry and Eggs Marketing
0032-5724	Poultry Digest
0032-5732	Poultry Farmer
0032-5740	Poultry Guide
0032-5767	Poultry International
0032-5775	Poultry Market Review
0032-5783	Poultry Press
0032-5791	Poultry Science
0032-5805	Poultry Tribune
0032-5813	Poultry World
0032-5821	Poumon et le Coeur *see* 0761-8417
0032-583X	Pour la Vie
0032-5856	Poverty
0032-5864	Poverty and Human Resources Abstracts *see* 0099-2453
0032-5872	Poverty Law Reports†
0032-5880	Povratak u Zivot
0032-5899	Powder Metallurgy
0032-5910	Powder Technology
0032-5929	Power
0032-5937	Power and Plant in Southern Africa *changed to* Power & Plant Engineering in South Africa
0032-5953	Power Engineer†
0032-5961	Power Engineering (New York)
0032-5988	Power Farming
0032-5996	Power Farming and Better Farming Digest *see* 0311-1911
0032-6003	Power for Living
0032-6011	Power for Today
0032-6038	Power Laundry & Cleaning News†
0032-6046	Power Life *changed to* Freeway
0032-6054	Power Management†
0032-6062	Power Record†
0032-6070	Power Transmission Design
0032-6089	Powerboat
0032-6119	Polytechnic-Window of the Netherlands
0032-6127	Pozarni Ochrana
0032-6135	Pozarni Technika *see* 0032-6127
0032-6143	Poznaj Swiat
0032-6151	Poznaj Swoj Kraj
0032-616X	Pozoriste
0032-6178	Prabuddha Bharata
0032-6186	Praca i Zabezpieczenia Spoleczne
0032-6194	Praca Szkolna *changed to* Ogniwo
0032-6208	Prace a Mzda
0032-6216	Instytut Elektrotechniki. Prace
0032-6232	Instytut Naftowy. Prace
0032-6240	Instytut Technologii Drewna. Prace
0032-6259	Instytut Tele- i Radiotechniczny. Prace
0032-6267	Mineralogia Polonica
0032-6275	Muzeum Ziemi. Prace
0032-6283	Przemyslowy Instytut Telekomunikacji. Prace
0032-6291	Pracovni Lekarstvi
0032-6305	Practica Oto-Rhino-Laryngologica *see* 0301-1569
0032-6313	Practica Otologica Kyoto
0032-6321	Practical Accountant
0032-633X	Practical Anthropology *see* 0091-8296
0032-6348	Practical Boat Owner
0032-6356	Practical Camper *changed to* Camper
0032-6364	Practical Christianity *changed to* Contact (Aldershot)
0032-6372	Practical Electronics
0032-6380	Scholastic Voice

0032-6399 Practical Gardening
0032-6410 Practical Knowledge
0032-6429 Practical Lawyer
0032-6437 Practical Motorist *changed to* Motorist
0032-6445 Practical Photography
0032-6453 Practical Psychology
0032-647X Television (London, 1934)
0032-6488 Practical Woodworking
0032-6518 Practitioner
0032-6534 Praehistorische Forschungen†
0032-6542 Der Praeparator
0032-6550 Pragati
0032-6569 Prager Volkszeitung
0032-6577 Pragmatist in Art†
0032-6585 Prague Bulletin of Mathematical Linguistics
0032-6593 Praha - Moskva
0032-6607 Prairie Club Bulletin
0032-6615 Prairie Farmer
0032-6623 Prairie Gleaner
0032-664X Prairie Messenger
0032-6666 Prairie Rose
0032-6674 Prairie School Review†
0032-6682 Prairie Schooner
0032-6690 Prajnan
0032-6704 Praksa
0032-6720 Prakticke Zubni Lekarstvi
0032-6739 Prakticky Lekar
0032-6747 Prakticna Zena
0032-6755 Praktiker
0032-6763 Praktiko†
0032-6771 Praktische Forstwirt fuer die Schweiz *see* 0378-6919
0032-678X Praktische Mettallographie
0032-6798 Praktische Psychologie†
0032-6801 Der Praktische Schaedlingsbekaempfer
0032-681X Der Praktische Tierarzt
0032-6828 Praline
0032-6836 Pram Retailer†
0032-6844 Pram & Nursery Trader
0032-6852 Pramo
0032-6860 Prapor
0032-6879 Prasna
0032-6887 Pratfall†
0032-6895 Materiaux et Techniques
0032-6909 Pratique du Soudage *see* 0035-127X
0032-6917 Pratishruti
0032-6925 Prato - Storia ed Arte
0032-6933 Pratt Cannon *changed to* Pratt Reports
0032-695X Pravna Misla
0032-6968 Pravna Misal
0032-6976 Pravnik
0032-6984 Pravny Obzor
0032-6992 Pravoslavnaya Zhyzn'
0032-700X Pravoslavno Misao
0032-7018 Pravoslavnaya Rus'
0032-7034 Praxis der Kinderpsychologie und Kinderpsychiatrie
0032-7042 Praxis der Mathematik
0032-7069 Praxis der Pneumologie *see* 0342-7498
0032-7077 Praxis der Psychotherapie *see* 0171-791X
0032-7085 Praxis des Neusprachlichen Unterrichts
0032-7093 Pre-Investment News *changed to* Action U N D P
0032-7093 Pre-Investment News *changed to* Development Business
0032-7107 Worship and Preaching
0032-7123 Precision†
0032-7131 Precision
0032-714X Precision Metal
0032-7166 Predicasts *see* 0278-0135
0032-7174 Predicasts Electronic Trends *changed to* Electronics Trends(Cleveland)
0032-7182 Prediction
0032-7212 Der Prediger und Katechet
0032-7220 Predskolska Vychova
0032-7239 Preet Lari
0032-7247 Prefabbricare
0032-7255 Prefabbricazione
0032-7263 Preface
0032-7271 Pregled
0032-7298 Pregled Problema Mentalno Retardiranih Osoba
0032-731X Pregled Zakonodavstva u Stranim Drzavama
0032-7328 Prehlad Lesnickej, Drevarskej, Celulozovej a Papiernickej Literatury†
0032-7336 Prehled Lesnicke a Myslivecke Literatury
0032-7344 Novinky Literatury: Prehled Pedagogicke Literatury *changed to* Prehled Pedagogicke Literatury
0032-7352 Dokumentacni Listkova Sluzba
0032-7360 Prehledy Leteckotechnicke Literatury
0032-7379 Prehledy Potravinarske Literatury
0032-7387 Premier Plan†
0032-7409 Premio
0032-7433 Prensa Confidencial
0032-745X Prensa Medica Argentina
0032-7468 Prensa Medica Mexicana†
0032-7476 Prent 190
0032-7484 Preparative Biochemistry
0032-7506 Prepodavanie Istorii v Shkole
0032-7514 Prepravni a Tarifni Vestnik
0032-7522 Presbyterian Guardian
0032-7530 Presbyterian Herald
0032-7549 Presbyterian Journal†
0032-7557 Presbyterian Life *changed to* United Presbyterian A.D.
0032-7565 Presbyterian Outlook
0032-7573 Presbyterian Record
0032-7581 Rush-Presbyterian-St. Luke's Medical Bulletin†
0032-759X Presbyterian Survey
0032-7611 Prescribers' Journal
0032-762X Presence†
0032-7638 Presence Africaine
0032-7654 Presence des Lettres des Arts *changed to* Presence des Lettres et des Arts Emergences
0032-7662 Presence du Cinema
0032-7689 Presencia
0032-7697 Present
0032-7700 Present Truth and Herald of Christ's Epiphany
0032-7719 Presente†
0032-7727 Presenza Pastorale
0032-7735 Preservation News
0032-7751 President
0032-7778 Wisconsin Library Association. President's Newsletter *see* 0043-6518
0032-7786 Preslia
0032-7794 Germany (Federal Republic, 1949-) Presse- und Informationsamt. Bulletin
0032-7808 Press and Public Relations
0032-7816 Press Booklets
0032-7824 Press Woman
0032-7832 Presse Actualite *changed to* Medias Pouvoirs
0032-7840 Presse der Sowjetunion
0032-7859 Belgium. Commissariat General au Tourisme. Bulletin†
0032-7867 Presse Medicale *see* 0301-1518
0032-7875 Presse Thermale et Climatique
0032-7883 Pressens Tidning
0032-7891 Presseschau Ostwirtschaft
0032-7905 Pressespiegel Blicknach Drueben *changed to* Pressespiegel aus Zeitungen und Zeitschriften der DDR
0032-7913 Pressluft *changed to* Druckluftechnik
0032-7921 Prestige de l'Hotellerie, de la Restauration et de Tourism *changed to* Resto-Flash
0032-793X Prestressed Concrete Institute. Journal
0032-7948 South Africa. Weather Bureau. Newsletter/Nuusbrief
0032-7956 Pretres Diocesains
0032-7964 Pretzel Baker†
0032-7972 Preussenland
0032-7980 Preuves
0032-8006 Prevention
0032-8014 Prevention of Blindness News *changed to* Prevent Blindness News
0032-8022 Prevention Routiere
0032-8030 Prevention Routiere dans l'Entreprise
0032-8049 Previdencia Social†
0032-8057 Previdenza Agricola
0032-8065 Previdenza Sociale
0032-8081 Previdenza Sociale Nella Stampa Estera†
0032-809X Previdenza Sociale nell'Artigianato
0032-8103 Preview†
0032-8111 Preview†
0032-812X Previsoes Ionosfericas M U F
0032-8138 Przeglad Bibliograficzny Pismiennictwa Ekonomicznego
0032-8146 Priapus†
0032-8154 Pribory i Sistemy Upravleniya
0032-8162 Pribory i Tekhnika Eksperimenta
0032-8170 Price Waterhouse Review
0032-8200 Priest
0032-8219 Landbouw-Economisch Instituut. Prijsstatistiek
0032-8227 Prikazi in Studije
0032-8235 Prikladnaya Matematika i Mekhanika
0032-8243 Prikladnaya Mekhanika
0032-8251 Primalinea
0032-826X Primary Bookshelf†
0032-8278 Primary Days
0032-8286 Primary Friend
0032-8308 Primary Producer *changed to* Dairyman's Digest and Primary Producer
0032-8316 Primary Treasure
0032-8324 Primate News
0032-8332 Primates
0032-8340 Primavera
0032-8359 Prime Areas
0032-8367 Primer Acto†
0032-8375 Primera Plana
0032-8383 Primicia
0032-8405 Princeton Engineer
0032-843X Princeton University. Art Museum. Record
0032-8448 Princeton University Cutaneous Research Project Reports
0032-8456 Princeton University Library Chronicle
0032-8472 Principe de Viana
0032-8480 Principes
0032-8499 Prinsejagt
0032-8502 Prinses†
0032-8510 Print
0032-8529 Print
0032-8537 Print Collector's Newsletter
0032-8553 Print Project Amerika†
0032-8561 Print Room†
0032-8588 Printing and Publishing†
0032-8596 Printing Equipment and Materials *see* 0032-8715
0032-860X Printing Impressions
0032-8618 Printing†
0032-8626 Printing News
0032-8634 Printing Plates†
0032-8642 Printing Product Information Cards
0032-8650 Printing Management *see* 0032-860X
0032-8685 Printing Technology *see* 0308-4205
0032-8707 Printing Trades Journal†
0032-8715 Printing World
0032-8731 Priroda
0032-874X Priroda
0032-8758 Prirodovedne Prace Ustavu C S A V v Brne
0032-8766 Prirodni Vedy ve Skole
0032-8774 Prirucka Casopisu Zena a Moda *changed to* Prakticka Zena
0032-8790 Prism International
0032-8804 Prisma Lectuurvoorlichting/Book Reviews for Public Libraries
0032-8812 Prisma†
0032-8847 Prismet
0032-8855 Prison Journal
0032-8863 Prison Officers Magazine *changed to* Gatelodge
0032-8871 Private Carrier
0032-888X Private Eye
0032-8898 Private Library
0032-8901 Private Pilot
0032-891X Private Practice
0032-8928 Private Practice News†
0032-8936 Private Printer & Private Press†
0032-8944 Private Wirtschaft†
0032-8960 Privreda
0032-8995 Privredni Vjesnik
0032-9002 Privredno Pravni Prirucnik
0032-9010 Prizewinner *changed to* Enter-Prizes
0032-9037 Pro Magazin
0032-9045 Pro
0032-9053 Pro Football Weekly
0032-907X Pro Medico†
0032-9088 Pro Medico
0032-9096 Pro Metal†
0032-910X Pro Patria
0032-9118 Pro Senectute *changed to* Zeitlupe
0032-9134 Pro Tem
0032-9142 Pro Veritate
0032-9150 Proa
0032-9177 Probe (Santa Barbara)
0032-9185 Probe
0032-9193 Probe (Rockville Centre)
0032-9215 Probe (Memphis)
0032-9223 Problemas
0032-9231 Probleme Agricole†
0032-9258 Probleme des Friedens und des Sozialismus
0032-9266 Probleme Economice†
0032-9290 Problemes d'Outre-Mer†
0032-9304 Problemes Economiques
0032-9312 Problemes Sociaux Congolais *changed to* Problemes Sociaux Zairois
0032-9320 Problemes Sovietiques†
0032-9339 Problemi
0032-9347 Problemi della Pedagogia
0032-9355 Problemi della Sicurezza Sociale†
0032-9363 Problemi di Gestione
0032-9371 Problemi na Izkustvoto
0032-938X Problemi Spoljne Trgovine i Konjunkture
0032-9398 Problemist
0032-941X Problems of Communism
0032-9428 Problemy Osvoeniya Pustyn'
0032-9436 Problems of Economics
0032-9444 Problems of Forensic Medicine & Criminalistics†
0032-9452 Journal of Ichthyology
0032-9460 Problems of Information Transmission
0032-9479 Problems of the Peoples of the USSR†
0032-9487 Problemy
0032-9495 Problemy Alkoholizmu
0032-9509 Problemy Endokrinologii i Gormonoterapii *see* 0375-9660
0032-9517 Problemy Inwestowania i Rozwoju *changed to* Problemy Rozwoju Budownictwa
0032-9525 Problemy Transportu Samochodowego†
0032-9533 Problemy Tuberkuleza
0032-9541 Problemy Uczelni i Instytutow Medycznych *see* 0137-7183
0032-955X Procedes et Equipements Electroniques†
0032-9568 Proceedings in Print
0032-9576 Journal of Technical Physics
0032-9592 Process Biochemistry
0032-9606 Process Engineering, Plant and Control *see* 0370-1859
0032-9614 Process Journal *see* 0032-8529
0032-9622 Proche-Orient Chretien
0032-9630 Proche-Orient Etudes Economiques
0032-9649 Proche-Orient Etudes Juridiques
0032-9665 Prodotti di Marca
0032-9681 Produccion
0032-969X Produce News
0032-9703 Producers Guild of America. Journal†
0032-972X Producers Review†
0032-9738 Product Design and Development *changed to* Chilton's Product Design and Development
0032-9746 Product Design Engineering†
0032-9762 Product Finishing
0032-9770 Product Licensing Index *changed to* P L I Know How
0032-9789 American Hotel and Motel Association. Product News. *changed to* American Hotel and Motel Association. Buyers Guide for Hotels & Motels.
0032-9797 European Plant Equipment News†
0032-9819 Production
0032-9827 Weekly Production and Drilling Statistics *see* 0227-3357
0032-9843 Production and Inventory Management
0032-9851 Production Engineer
0032-9878 Production Journal
0032-9908 Productividad
0032-9924 Productivity
0032-9932 Productivity Letter†

0032-9940 Products Finishing
0032-9967 Produktion
0032-9975 Produktivnost
0033-0000 Produzione Animale
0033-0019 Proefstation voor de Groenten- en Fruitteelt onder Glas. Mededelingen *changed to* Proefstation voor Tuinbouw onder Glas
0033-0043 Professional Builder *changed to* Professional Builder
0033-0051 Professional Engineer (Washington)†
0033-006X Professional Engineer
0033-0078 Professional Engineer
0033-0086 Professional Engineer in Nova Scotia *see* 0225-851X
0033-0094 Professional Fisherman's Association of Tasmania Magazine *see* 0156-3548
0033-0108 Professional Flashes†
0033-0116 Professional Gardener *changed to* Grounds Management Forum
0033-0124 Professional Geographer
0033-0132 Professional Golfer *see* 0161-1259
0033-0140 Professional Medical Assistant
0033-0159 Professional Nutritionist†
0033-0167 Professional Photographer
0033-0175 Professional Psychology *see* 0735-7028
0033-0183 Professional Public Service *changed to* Professional Institute of the Public Service of Canada. Journal
0033-0191 Professional Sanitation Management
0033-0205 Professioni Infermieristiche†
0033-0213 Professions et Entreprises
0033-0221 Professor *changed to* Professor an A H S & B H S
0033-023X Profile†
0033-0248 Profile (Kansas City)†
0033-0256 Profile *changed to* Harbinger (Detroit)
0033-0280 Profit Sharing
0033-0299 Profitable Hobby Merchandising *changed to* Profitable Craft Merchandising
0033-0329 Profoto
0033-0337 Program
0033-0353 Norsk Rikskringkasting. Programbladet
0033-037X Programme Communiste
0033-0396 Programmed Learning & Educational Technology
0033-0434 Progres
0033-0442 Progres Islamique†
0033-0450 Progres Medical
0033-0469 Progres Scientifique†
0033-0477 Progresele Stintei†
0033-0485 Progreso
0033-0507 Progresos de Patologia y Clinica†
0033-0515 Progresos de Pediatria y Puericultura†
0033-0523 Progresos de Terapeutica Clinica†
0033-054X Progress
0033-0566 Progress
0033-0574 Progress
0033-0582 Deurbraak *changed to* Newsline
0033-0590 Progress†
0033-0604 Progress against Cancer
0033-0612 Progress & Care
0033-0620 Progress in Cardiovascular Diseases
0033-0639 Progress in Dermatology
0033-0655 Progress in Organic Coatings
0033-0663 Progress of Education
0033-068X Progress of Theoretical Physics
0033-0698 Progres Social†
0033-0701 Progressi in Patologia Cardiovascolare
0033-071X Progressi in Radiologia *changed to* Progressi in Radiologia
0033-0728 Progressio
0033-0736 Progressive (Madison)
0033-0744 Progressive Agriculture in Arizona *see* 0744-5474
0033-0752 Progressive Architecture
0033-0760 Progressive Farmer
0033-0779 Progressive Fish-Culturist
0033-0787 Progressive Grocer
0033-0809 Progressive Plastics†
0033-0817 Progressive Railroading
0033-0825 Progressive Teacher
0033-0833 Progressive Woman†
0033-0841 Progressive Worker
0033-085X Progressive World†
0033-0868 Progresso Fotografico
0033-0876 Technic International†
0033-0884 Projet
0033-0892 Project - Guidelines to Equal Opportunity *see* 0006-4122
0033-0906 Project Concern News *changed to* Concern News
0033-0914 Project†
0033-0922 Project on Linguistics Analysis Reports†
0033-0957 Projekt
0033-0981 Proletaire
0033-099X Prolipsis Ton Atychimaton
0033-1007 Prologue (Medford)
0033-1023 National Arts Centre. Calendar of Events
0033-1031 Prologue (Washington)
0033-1058 Promeny
0033-1066 Promesses†
0033-1082 Promethee
0033-1090 Promien
0033-1112 Promoting Church Music *see* 0307-6334
0033-1120 Promotion des Affaires
0033-1139 Promotor de Educacion Cristiana
0033-1147 Prompt
0033-1155 Promyshlennaya Energetika
0033-1163 Promyshlennost' Armenii
0033-1171 Promyshlennost' Belorussii
0033-118X Promyshlennoe Stroitel'stvo
0033-1201 Pronab
0033-121X Proof
0033-1228 Proof Sheet *changed to* S A L S in Brief
0033-1236 Proofs
0033-1244 Propaganda
0033-1260 Propane/Canada
0033-1279 Propel
0033-1287 Properties
0033-1295 Property and Compensation Reports *changed to* Property, Planning and Compensation Reports
0033-1309 Property Journal
0033-1317 Property Mail†
0033-1325 Property Survey†
0033-1333 Prophetic News and Israel's Watchman *see* 0033-135X
0033-1341 Prophetic Newsletter
0033-135X Prophetic Witness
0033-1368 Prophylaxe (Heidelberg) *see* 0340-7047
0033-1376 Propiedad Intelectual†
0033-1384 Propos en l'Air *changed to* A P a la Une
0033-1392 Propos Utiles aux Medecins
0033-1414 Propria Cures (PC)
0033-1422 Proprieta Edilizia Lombarda
0033-1430 Propriete Industrielle
0033-1449 Propriete Industrielle Nucleaire†
0033-1465 Proscopos
0033-1481 Prospect
0033-1503 Prospectives *see* 0337-307X
0033-1511 Prospectives
0033-1538 Prospects in Education *changed to* Prospects
0033-1546 University of Michigan Journal of Law Reform
0033-1554 Prosperite
0033-1562 Prospetti†
0033-1570 Nuove Prospettive
0033-1597 Prostor
0033-1600 Prostor in Cas†
0033-1619 Prosveta
0033-1635 Prosvetni Rabotnik
0033-1643 Prosvetni Delavec
0033-1651 Prosvetni Pregled
0033-166X Prosvjeta†
0033-1678 Prosvjetni List
0033-1686 Prosvjetni Rad
0033-1708 Protection
0033-1716 Protection†
0033-1724 Protection Civile et Securite Industrielle *changed to* Securite Civile et Industrielle
0033-1732 Protection of Metals
0033-1759 Protestant en de Weg *changed to* Tenminste
0033-1767 Protestantesimo
0033-1783 Protetyka Stomatologiczna
0033-1791 Proteus
0033-1805 Proteus
0033-1821 Protistologica
0033-183X Protoplasma
0033-1848 Prove di Letteratura
0033-1856 Provence Historique
0033-1864 Providence Hospital of Southfield. Medical Bulletin†
0033-1872 Province de Liege-Tourisme
0033-1880 Province du Maine
0033-1902 Provincia di Forli in Cifre
0033-1910 Provincia di Padova in Cifre
0033-1929 Provincia Social
0033-1937 Provoker†
0033-1945 Provost Parade
0033-1953 Proyecto Hidrometeorologico Centroamericano. Boletin Informativo†
0033-1988 Prumysl Potravin
0033-2003 Przeglad Antropologiczny
0033-2011 Przeglad Artystyczny *changed to* Sztuka
0033-202X Przeglad Biblioteczny
0033-2038 Przeglad Budowlany
0033-2046 Przeglad Dokumentacyjny Materialow Ogniotrwalych
0033-2054 Przeglad Dokumentacyjny Maszyn Rolniczych
0033-2062 Przeglad Dokumentacyjny Elektrotechniki
0033-2070 Przeglad Dokumentacyjny Polskiego i Zagranicznego Pismiennictwa Kolejowego
0033-2089 Elektronika
0033-2097 Przeglad Elektrotechniczny
0033-2100 Przeglad Epidemiologiczny
0033-2119 Przeglad Gastronomiczny
0033-2127 Przeglad Geodezyjny
0033-2135 Przeglad Geofizyczny
0033-2143 Przeglad Geograficzny
0033-2151 Przeglad Geologiczny
0033-216X Przeglad Gorniczy
0033-2178 Przeglad Historyczno-Oswiatowy†
0033-2186 Przeglad Historyczny
0033-2194 Przeglad Humanistyczny
0033-2208 Przeglad Kolejowy Drogowy *see* 0137-284X
0033-2216 Przeglad Kolejowy Elektrotechniczny *see* 0137-2858
0033-2224 Przeglad Kolejowy Mechaniczny *see* 0137-2963
0033-2232 Przeglad Komunikacyjny
0033-2240 Przeglad Lekarski
0033-2259 Przeglad Mechaniczny
0033-2275 Przeglad Odlewnictwa
0033-2283 Przeglad Orientalistyczny
0033-2291 Przeglad Papierniczy
0033-2313 Przeglad Piekarski i Cukierniczy
0033-2321 I.B. Informacja Biezaca
0033-233X Bibliografia Analityczna Bibliotekoznawstwa i Informacji Naukowej
0033-2348 Przeglad Pismiennictwa Zagadnien Informacji
0033-2356 Przeglad Socjologiczny
0033-2364 Przeglad Spawalnictwa
0033-2372 Przeglad Statystyczny
0033-2380 Przeglad Techniczny Tygodnik
0033-2399 Przeglad Telekomunikacyjny
0033-2402 Przeglad Ustawodawstwa i Czasopism Prawniczych Socjalistycznych Krajow Europy†
0033-2410 Przeglad Wlokienniczy
0033-2429 Przeglad Wybranych Czasopism Prawniczych Krajow Zachodnich†
0033-2437 Przeglad Zachodni
0033-2445 Przeglad Zachodnich Czasopism Ekonomicznych†
0033-2453 Przeglad Zagranicznej Literatury Naukowej z Zakresu Genetyki i Hodowli Roslin
0033-2461 Przeglad Zbozowo - Mlynarski
0033-247X Przeglad Zoologiczny
0033-2488 Przekroj
0033-2496 Przemysl Chemiczny
0033-250X Przemysl Spozywczy
0033-2518 Przewodnik Bibliograficzny
0033-2526 Przeglad Dermatologiczny
0033-2534 Przyjaciolka
0033-2542 Psallite
0033-2569 Psi Chi Newsletter
0033-2577 Psihijatrijska Njega/Psychiatric Care *changed to* Vjesnik Medicinskih Sestara i Medicinskih Tehnicara Hrvatske
0033-2585 Psionic Medicine
0033-2615 Psyche
0033-2623 Psyche
0033-264X Psychiatria Clinica *see* 0254-4962
0033-2658 Psychiatria et Neurologia Japonica (Tokyo, 1899)
0033-2666 Psychiatria, Neurologia, Neurochirurgia†
0033-2674 Psychiatria Polska
0033-2682 Psychiatric Communications†
0033-2690 Psychiatric Forum
0033-2704 Psychiatric News
0033-2712 O P. Psychiatric Opinion *see* 0163-2655
0033-2720 Psychiatric Quarterly
0033-2739 Psychiatrie, Neurologie und Medizinische Psychologie
0033-2747 Psychiatry
0033-2755 Psychiatry and Medical Practice Bulletin†
0033-2771 Psychiatry Digest *see* 0278-4602
0033-278X Psychiatry in Medicine *see* 0091-2174
0033-2798 Psychic *see* 0147-7625
0033-2801 Psychic News
0033-2828 Psychoanalytic Quarterly
0033-2836 Psychoanalytic Review
0033-2844 Physchogram†
0033-2852 Psychologia
0033-2860 Psychologia Wychowawcza
0033-2879 Psychologica Belgica
0033-2887 Psychological Abstracts
0033-2895 Psychological Association of Trinidad and Tobago. Journal
0033-2909 Psychological Bulletin
0033-2917 Psychological Medicine
0033-2925 Psychological Perspectives
0033-2933 Psychological Record
0033-2941 Psychological Reports
0033-295X Psychological Review
0033-2968 Psychological Studies
0033-2976 Psychologie *see* 0036-7869
0033-2984 Psychologie Francaise
0033-2992 Psychologie und Praxis *changed to* Psychologie und Praxis
0033-300X Psychologie v Ekonomicke Praxi
0033-3018 Psychologische Beitraege
0033-3034 Psychologische Menschenkenntnis
0033-3042 Psychologische Rundschau
0033-3050 Psychologist Magazine
0033-3077 Psychology
0033-3085 Psychology in the Schools
0033-3093 Psychology Quarterly
0033-3107 Psychology Today
0033-3115 Psycholoog
0033-3123 Psychometrika
0033-3131 Psychonomic Science†
0033-314X Psychopathologie Africaine
0033-3158 Psychopharmacology
0033-3166 Psychopharmacology Abstracts†
0033-3174 Psychosomatic Medicine
0033-3182 Psychosomatics
0033-3190 Psychotherapy and Psychosomatics
0033-3204 Psychotherapy: Theory, Research and Practice *changed to* Psychotherapy
0033-3212 Psykisk Haelsa
0033-3239 Ptitsevodstvo
0033-3263 Pubdisco News
0033-3271 Public Address Engineers Journal *changed to* Public Address
0033-328X Public Administration *see* 0313-6647
0033-3298 Public Administration
0033-3301 Public Administration†
0033-331X Public Administration Abstracts and Index of Articles *changed to* Documentation in Public Administration

1290 ISSN INDEX

0033-3328 Public Administration News and Views *see* 0149-8797
0033-3336 Public Administration Recruiter *see* 0149-8797
0033-3344 Public Administration Review
0033-3352 Public Administration Review
0033-3360 Public Administration Survey
0033-3387 Public Affairs Bulletin†
0033-3395 Public Affairs Comment
0033-3409 Public Affairs Information Service. Bulletin *changed to* P A I S Bulletin
0033-3417 Public Affairs Report
0033-3425 Public Aid in Illinois†
0033-3433 Public Cleansing *changed to* Wastes Management
0033-3441 Public Contract Law Journal
0033-345X Public Employee Press
0033-3468 Public Enterprise Recorder
0033-3476 Public Finance
0033-3484 Public Health†
0033-3492 Public Health†
0033-3506 Public Health
0033-3522 Public Health Laboratory†
0033-3530 Public Health News†
0033-3549 Public Health Reports *see* 0090-2918
0033-3557 Public Interest
0033-3565 Public Law
0033-3573 Public Library of Youngstown and Mahoning County. Staff Bulletin *changed to* Biblio-Files
0033-3581 Public Library Trustee†
0033-3603 Public Lighting *changed to* Lighting Journal
0033-3611 Public Management
0033-362X Public Opinion Quarterly
0033-3638 Public Personnel Review *see* 0091-0260
0033-3646 Public Policy (Cambridge) *see* 0276-8739
0033-3654 Public Power
0033-3662 Public Relations *see* 0307-9252
0033-3670 Public Relations Journal
0033-3689 Public Relations Journal of India
0033-3697 Public Relations News
0033-3700 Public Relations Quarterly
0033-3719 Public Relations Reporter†
0033-3727 P R Revue
0033-3735 Public Roads
0033-3743 Public Safety Systems†
0033-3751 Public Schools of New York City. Staff Bulletin *changed to* Learning in New York
0033-376X Public Servant
0033-3786 Public Service Review
0033-3794 Public Undertakings
0033-3808 Public Utilities Fortnightly
0033-3816 Public Welfare
0033-3840 Public Works
0033-3867 Publicaciones Cientificas Alter†
0033-3875 Publication Management†
0033-3883 Publicationes Mathematicae
0033-3913 Media News Keys
0033-3921 Publicity Review
0033-3948 Publieke Werken *see* 0046-5577
0033-3956 Publik†
0033-3972 Publisher†
0033-3999 Publitransport
0033-4006 Publizistik
0033-4014 Pueblo†
0033-4030 Puerto Rico Libre†
0033-4049 Puerto Rico Living
0033-4073 Pneumonologie/Pneumonology *see* 0341-2040
0033-4081 Pulp and Paper
0033-409X Pulp & Paper International
0033-4103 Pulp and Paper Magazine of Canada *see* 0316-4004
0033-4111 Pulp Era†
0033-4138 Christian Ministry
0033-4146 Pulpit Digest *see* 0160-838X
0033-4154 Pulpwood Production *see* 0160-6433
0033-4162 Pulse†
0033-4170 Pulse (Lafayette)†
0033-4197 Pulse (Tulsa)†
0033-4200 Pulse Beat
0033-4219 Pulse of Public School Adult Education *changed to* A A A C E Newsletter
0033-4227 Pulse of Youth
0033-4251 Pult
0033-426X Pumps - Pompes - Pumpen *changed to* World Pumps
0033-4278 Punch
0033-4286 Pungolo del Sud
0033-4294 Pungolo Verde
0033-4308 Punjab Educational Journal†
0033-4316 Punjab Fruit Journal
0033-4324 Punjab Horticultural Journal
0033-4332 Punjab Law Reporter
0033-4340 Punjab Medical Journal
0033-4359 Haryana Veterinarian
0033-4367 Punto de Partida
0033-4375 Punto de Vista†
0033-4391 Punto Omega
0033-4405 Puppenspiel und Puppenspieler
0033-4421 Puppet Post†
0033-443X Puppetry Journal
0033-4448 Purchasing (Newton)
0033-4456 Purchasing Bulletin *see* 0306-1922
0033-4472 Purchasing Journal *see* 0265-2072
0033-4480 Purchasing Week *see* 0093-1659
0033-4502 Purdue Alumnus
0033-4510 Purdue Engineer
0033-4529 Purdue Pharmacist
0033-4537 Purdue University. School of Electrical Engineering. Annual Research Summary
0033-4545 Pure and Applied Chemistry
0033-4553 Pure and Applied Geophysics
0033-4561 Pure-Bred Dogs, American Kennel Gazette
0033-4588 Pure Verite
0033-4596 Pure Water†
0033-4642 Purple Thumb†
0033-4669 Purpose†
0033-4677 Pursuit & Symposium†
0033-4685 Pursuit *changed to* Pursuit/S I T U
0033-4693 Pustakalaya
0033-4707 Pustakalaya Sandesh
0033-4715 Put' i Putevoe Khozyaistvo
0033-474X Pyrenees
0033-4758 Pythagoras†
0033-4766 Pythagoras†
0033-4774 Q B Beam
0033-4782 A F C I Q. Bulletin *changed to* Qualite, Industrie, Controle
0033-4790 Q I M P Quarterly
0033-4804 Q L†
0033-4812 Q S T
0033-4820 Q T C
0033-4839 Kadmoniot
0033-4863 Quaderni del Conoscitore di Stampe *changed to* Conoscitore di Stampe
0033-4898 Quaderni dello Sport†
0033-491X Quaderni di Clinica Ostetrica e Ginecologica
0033-4928 Quaderni di Criminologia Clinica *changed to* Rassegna Penitenziaria e Criminologica
0033-4952 Quaderni di Sociologia
0033-4960 Quaderni Ibero-Americani
0033-4979 Quaderni Sclavo di Diagnostica Clinica e di Laboratorio
0033-4987 Quaderni Urbinati di Cultura Classica
0033-4995 Quadrangle†
0033-5002 Quadrant
0033-5010 Quadrant
0033-5029 Quadrante Sardo†
0033-5037 Quaestiones Entomologicae
0033-5045 Quaker Campus
0033-5053 Quaker History
0033-5061 Quaker Life
0033-507X Quaker Monthly
0033-5088 Quaker Religious Thought
0033-5096 Quaker Service Bulletin
0033-5118 Electrical Contractor
0033-5134 Qualitas Plantarum et Materiae Vegetabiles *see* 0377-3205
0033-5142 Qualite *see* 0373-8809
0033-5169 Quality
0033-5177 Quality and Quantity
0033-5193 Quality Control
0033-5207 Quality Control and Applied Statistics
0033-5215 Quality Engineer *see* 0306-2856
0033-5231 Quality of Sheffield *changed to* Quality of Sheffield and South Yorkshire
0033-524X Quality Progress
0033-5266 Quarry
0033-5274 Quarry Managers' Journal *changed to* Quarry Management
0033-5290 Quarterly Analysis of Failures
0033-5304 Quarterly Bibliography of Economics
0033-5312 Quarterly Blue Book on Joint Stock Companies in India
0033-5320 Canada. Statistics Canada. Quarterly Bulletin of Agricultural Statistics†
0033-5339 Building *changed to* Papua New Guinea. National Statistical Office. Building Statistics
0033-5347 Quarterly Check -List of Ethnology & Sociology†
0033-5355 Quarterly Check-List of Biblical Studies *see* 0033-5428
0033-5363 Quarterly Check-List of Classical Studies
0033-5371 Quarterly Check-List of Economics & Political Science†
0033-538X Quarterly Check-List of Linguistics
0033-5398 Quarterly Check-List of Literary History: English, French, German†
0033-5401 Quarterly Check-List of Medievalia
0033-541X Quarterly Check-List of Musicology
0033-5428 Quarterly Check-List of Oriental Studies
0033-5436 Quarterly Check-List of Psychology
0033-5444 Quarterly Check-List of Renaissance Studies *see* 0033-5401
0033-5452 Quarterly Construction Statistics
0033-5479 Quarterly Dental Review *see* 0300-5712
0033-5487 Quarterly Digest of Urban and Regional Research†
0033-5495 Quarterly Economic Review *changed to* Country Reports
0033-5509 U.S. Federal Trade Commission. Quarterly Financial Report: United States Manufacturing Corporations *see* 0098-681X
0033-5517 Quarterly Inventory of Economic Research on New England†
0033-5525 Quarterly Journal of Crude Drug Research *changed to* International Journal of Crude Drug Research
0033-555X Quarterly Journal of Experimental Psychology *see* 0272-4987
0033-555X Quarterly Journal of Experimental Psychology *see* 0272-4995
0033-5568 Quarterly Journal of Forestry
0033-5576 Quarterly Journal of Indian Studies in Sciences†
0033-5584 Quarterly Journal of Indian Studies in Social Sciences *changed to* Asian Economic and Social Review
0033-5592 Quarterly Journal of Indian Studies in Technical Knowledge†
0033-5606 Quarterly Journal of Mathematics
0033-5614 Quarterly Journal of Mechanics and Applied Mathematics
0033-5622 Quarterly Journal of Medicine
0033-5630 Quarterly Journal of Speech
0033-5649 Quarterly Journal of Studies on Alcohol *see* 0096-882X
0033-5657 Quarterly Journal of Surgical Sciences
0033-5665 Quarterly Journal of Taiwan Land Credit
0033-5673 Psychiatria et Neurologia Japonica (Tokyo, 1949)
0033-569X Quarterly of Applied Mathematics
0033-5711 Quarterly Predictions of National Income and Expenditure
0033-572X Quarterly Report to Investors in Puerto Rican Securities†
0033-5754 Quarterly Review of Agricultural Economics *see* 0156-7446
0033-5762 Quarterly Review of Australian Education. *see* 0311-6875
0033-5770 Quarterly Review of Biology
0033-5789 Quarterly Review of Drilling Statistics *changed to* Quarterly Completion Report
0033-5797 Quarterly Review of Economics and Business
0033-5800 Quarterly Review of Historical Studies
0033-5819 Quarterly Review of Literature *changed to* Quarterly Review of Literature Poetry Series
0033-5835 Quarterly Reviews of Biophysics
0033-5843 Australia. Bureau of Statistics. Quarterly Summary of Australian Statistics.†
0033-5851 Quarterly Summary of Business Statistics, New York State
0033-586X Quartet *see* 0011-9210
0033-5878 Quatre Verites
0033-5894 Quaternary Research
0033-5908 Quatro Rodas
0033-5916 Quattroruote
0033-5924 Quattrosoldi†
0033-5940 Que Tal
0033-5967 Quebec Home & School News
0033-5975 Quebec Industriel
0033-5983 Quebec Official Gazette
0033-5991 Quebec/Travail†
0033-6009 Queen *see* 0141-0547
0033-6017 Queen
0033-6025 Queen's Highway†
0033-6033 Queens Medical Magazine
0033-6041 Queen's Quarterly
0033-6068 Queensborough
0033-6084 Queensland Country Life
0033-6092 Queensland Country Woman
0033-6106 Queensland Dairyfarmer
0033-6114 Queensland Electrical Contractor
0033-6122 Queensland Fruit and Vegetable News
0033-6149 Queensland Government Mining Journal
0033-6157 Queensland Heritage†
0033-6165 Q. Industry†
0033-6181 Queensland Justice of the Peace and Reports *see* 0312-1658
0033-6203 Queensland Motor Industry *changed to* Q A C C Motor Trader
0033-6211 Queensland Nurses Journal†
0033-622X Queensland Shopkeeper *see* 0034-6144
0033-6238 Queensland Teachers' Journal
0033-6246 Die Quelle
0033-6262 Querce
0033-6270 Query
0033-6289 Quest *changed to* New Quest
0033-6297 Quest (Champaign)
0033-6300 Little Magazine
0033-6319 Quest (Chardon)†
0033-6327 Quest (Pullman)
0033-6335 Questa Sicilia
0033-6343 Question†
0033-6351 Questions Actuelles du Socialisme
0033-636X Questions Internat *changed to* Nouvelles Questions
0033-6378 Questitalia
0033-6386 Quetta Times
0033-6432 Quid
0033-6440 Quiet Please *changed to* Noise News Digest
0033-6459 Quilates
0033-6467 Quill†
0033-6483 Quill (Summit)
0033-6491 Quill and Quire
0033-6505 Quill and Scroll
0033-6521 Quimica e Industria
0033-653X Quimica Iberoamericana†
0033-6548 Quincailliers de France *changed to* Quincailliers de France-l'Argus Menager
0033-6556 Quincy College Bulletin
0033-6572 Quintessence International
0033-6599 Quintessenz Journal
0033-6602 Quinto Lingo
0033-6610 Quis Custodiet *changed to* Law & Justice
0033-6629 Quixote
0033-6637 Quo Vadis
0033-6661 Quondam
0033-667X Quote Magazine
0033-6688 Quotes Ending†

ISSN INDEX

ISSN	Title
0033-6696	R. A. C. S. Newsletter†
0033-670X	R A E C Gazette *changed to* Torch
0033-6718	R A E News
0033-6734	R A News
0033-6742	R A P
0033-6750	R A P R A Abstracts
0033-6769	R A S
0033-6777	R A S Kennel Control Journal
0033-6785	R A U - Rapport
0033-6793	R & D Contracts Monthly
0033-6807	R & D Management
0033-6815	R & L News
0033-6823	R and R Magazine *changed to* Sales Builder Magazine
0033-6831	R C A Review
0033-684X	R C M Magazine
0033-6858	R C M P Quarterly
0033-6866	R-C Modeler
0033-6874	Refa Nachrichten
0033-6882	R E L C Journal
0033-6890	R E S. Reticuloendothelial Society. Journal *see* 0741-5400
0033-6904	R E S News Exchange
0033-6912	R I B A Library Bulletin *see* 0266-4380
0033-6939	R I C S Abstracts and Reviews *changed to* R I C S Library Information Service Abstracts and Reviews
0033-6947	R I C S Technical Information Service. Weekly Briefing *changed to* R I C S Library Information Service. Weekly Briefing
0033-6955	R I L M Abstracts of Music Literature
0033-6963	R I O Newsletter†
0033-6971	R J
0033-698X	R L A
0033-7021	R N
0033-703X	R O C
0033-7048	R O S C
0033-7056	R P A Bulletin
0033-7064	R P M Weekly
0033-7072	R Q
0033-7099	R S A World†
0033-7102	Railway Control Systems *see* 0033-8826
0033-7129	R S I
0033-7137	R.T.A. Journal *changed to* N.T.A. Journal
0033-7145	R T E Guide
0033-7153	R T N D A Communicator
0033-7161	R T T Y Journal
0033-7196	R W D S U Record
0033-720X	R X Sports and Travel†
0033-7218	R Z - Illustrierte Romanzeitung
0033-7226	Raadgevend-Ingenieur†
0033-7234	Raam†
0033-7242	Rabbits in Canada
0033-7250	Rabels Zeitschrift fuer auslaendisches und internationales Privatrecht
0033-7269	Raccolto *see* 0040-3776
0033-7277	Race *see* 0306-3968
0033-7285	Race News
0033-7293	Race Relations†
0033-7315	Race Relations and Industry
0033-7323	Race Relations Bulletin *see* 0142-971X
0033-7331	Race Relations Law Survey†
0033-734X	Race Relations News
0033-7358	Race Today
0033-7366	Racing & Football Outlook
0033-7374	Racing Car News
0033-7390	Racing Pigeon
0033-7404	Racing Pigeon Pictorial
0033-7412	Racing Report†
0033-7420	Racing Specialist
0033-7439	Racing Star Weekly
0033-7447	Racquette
0033-7455	Das Rad
0033-7463	Rad
0033-748X	Denmark. Statens Husholdningsraad. Raad og Resultater
0033-7498	Rad und Schiene *see* 0172-0554
0033-7501	Radar
0033-751X	Radar and Electronics *changed to* I. P. R. E. Review
0033-7528	Radcliffe Quarterly
0033-7536	Informacije Rade Koncar *see* 0350-5537
0033-7544	Radford Review†
0033-7552	Radiaesthesie - Geopathie - Strahlenbiologie *changed to* Radiaesthesie
0033-7560	Radiation Botany *see* 0098-8472
0033-7579	Radiation Effects
0033-7587	Radiation Research
0033-7617	Radical America
0033-7625	Radical Humanist
0033-7641	Radical Therapist†
0033-765X	Radio
0033-7668	Radio - Plans
0033-7676	Radio - Television
0033-7684	Radio Active *see* 0811-9929
0033-7692	Radio Aids to Marine Navigation
0033-7706	Radio Amateur Callbook Magazine: U S Listings *changed to* U S Callbook
0033-7722	Radio and Electronic Engineer *see* 0267-1689
0033-7730	Radio & Electronics
0033-7749	Radio & Television
0033-7757	Radio und Television *changed to* R T V
0033-7781	Radio Chassis Television
0033-779X	Radio Club of America. Proceedings
0033-7803	Radio Communication
0033-7811	Techniques Electroniques et Audiovisuelles *see* 0397-6424
0033-782X	Radio Constructor *see* 0374-4361
0033-7838	Radio Control Models & Electronics
0033-7846	Radio, Electrical & Furniture Merchandiser†
0033-7854	Radio Electronica *see* 0168-7840
0033-7862	Radio-Electronics
0033-7870	Radioelectronics and Communications Systems
0033-7889	Radio Engineering and Electronic Physics *see* 8756-6648
0033-7897	Radio Fernseh Phono Praxis†
0033-7900	Radio Fernsehen Elektronik
0033-7927	Radio Japan News
0033-7935	Radio Mentor Electronic†
0033-7943	Radio Mozambique†
0033-7951	Radio Nederland *changed to* Radio Nederland Programme Schedule
0033-796X	Radio Portugal Listeners Magazine†
0033-7986	Radio Propagation Predictions for Southern Africa
0033-7994	Radio R E F
0033-8001	Radio Research Laboratory. Journal
0033-801X	Radio Research Laboratory. Review
0033-8028	Radio Revue TV-Electronique Industrielle
0033-8036	Radio Rivista†
0033-8052	Radio Technica
0033-8060	Radio Times
0033-8079	Radio Times of India†
0033-8087	R T H†
0033-8095	Radio - TV - Electronic Service *changed to* R T E
0033-8109	Radio-TV Wereld *see* 0027-5298
0033-8133	Radio y Television†
0033-8141	Radio y Television Practica
0033-815X	Radio Z S
0033-8168	Radio-Amater
0033-8176	Radiobiologia, Radioterapia e Fisica Medica *see* 0003-4673
0033-8184	Radiobiologia - Radioterapia
0033-8192	Radiobiologiya
0033-8206	Radiobiology†
0033-8214	Radiobote
0033-8222	Radiocarbon
0033-8249	Radiochimie†
0033-8257	Radiocorriere-TV
0033-8273	Radiographer
0033-8281	Radiography
0033-829X	Radioisotope Report *changed to* Radiation Report
0033-8303	Radioisotopes
0033-8311	Radiokhimiya
0033-832X	Der Radiologe
0033-8338	Radiologia
0033-8346	Radiologia Clinica et Biologica *see* 0254-881X
0033-8354	Radiologia Diagnostica
0033-8362	Radiologia Medica
0033-8370	Radiologia y Medicina Nuclear
0033-8389	Radiologic Clinics of North America
0033-8397	Radiologic Technology†
0033-8400	Radiological Health Data and Reports. *see* 0091-6722
0033-8419	Radiology
0033-8427	Radiology/Today & Tomorrow†
0033-8443	Radiophysics and Quantum Electronics
0033-8451	Radioprotection
0033-846X	Radioschau *see* 0254-4318
0033-8478	Radiotechnika
0033-8486	Radiotekhnika
0033-8494	Radiotekhnika i Elektronika
0033-8516	Radiovy Konstrukter *changed to* Amaterske Radio B
0033-8532	Radius
0033-8540	Radmarkt
0033-8559	Imunoloski Zavod. Radovi
0033-8567	Centar za Proucananje i Suzbijanje Alkoholizma i Drugih Ovisnosti. Radovi
0033-8575	Radovi Medicinskog Fakulteta u Zagrebu
0033-8583	Radovi Poljoprivrednog Fakuteta Univerziteta u Sarajevu
0033-8591	Raduga
0033-8605	Radyans'ka Osvita
0033-8621	Rag
0033-8648	Ragguaglio Librario
0033-8656	Ragione
0033-8672	Ragtimer
0033-8680	Rehabilitacia
0033-8699	Rahnema-Ye Ketab†
0033-8702	Raiffeisenblatt fuer Niederoesterreich und Wien†
0033-8710	Raiffeisenbote
0033-8729	Spoor
0033-8737	R M F
0033-8745	Railnews
0033-8761	Railroad Magazine *see* 0163-7266
0033-877X	Railroad Model Craftsman
0033-8788	U.S. Railroad Retirement Board. Quarterly Review†
0033-8796	Railway Yardmaster†
0033-880X	Railroading *changed to* Railroading Series
0033-8818	Railway Advocate
0033-8826	Railway Age
0033-8834	Railway and Canal Historical Society Journal
0033-8842	Railway and Locomotive Historical Society. Bulletin *see* 0090-7847
0033-8850	Railway Carmen's Journal
0033-8869	Railway Clerk/Interchange *changed to* Interchange (Rockville)
0033-8893	Railway Forum†
0033-8907	Railway Gazette *see* 0373-5346
0033-8915	Railway Locomotives and Cars *see* 0033-8826
0033-8923	Railway Magazine
0033-8931	Railway Modeller
0033-894X	Railway Research & Engineering News. Section A
0033-8958	Railway Research & Engineering News. Section B
0033-8966	Railway Research & Engineering News. Sections D,E,F and G
0033-8974	Railway Review *changed to* Transport Review
0033-8990	Railway Steel Topics†
0033-9008	Railway Technical Research Institute (J N R). Quarterly Reports
0033-9016	Railway Track & Structures
0033-9032	Railway World
0033-9040	Railways Institute Magazine
0033-9067	Textilia
0033-9075	Raison Presente
0033-9083	Rajasthan Board Journal of Education
0033-9105	Rajasthan Srama Patrika†
0033-9113	Rakam
0033-9121	Rakennuslehti
0033-913X	Rakennustekniikka
0033-9148	Rallye Racing
0033-9156	Ramakrishna Mission Institute of Culture. Bulletin
0033-9164	Ramparts†
0033-9172	Ranch Romances†
0033-9180	Randolph-Macon Alumni Bulletin *changed to* Randolph-Macon College. Bulletin
0033-9199	Range†
0033-9202	Rangefinder
0033-9229	Ranger Rick's Nature Magazine *changed to* Ranger Rick
0033-9237	Ranger *changed to* Scout
0033-9245	Ransomer
0033-9261	Rapid Handler†
0033-9296	Rapport†
0033-930X	Racquet
0033-9318	Rasprostranenie Pechati
0033-9334	Rassegna Chimica
0033-9342	Rassegna Cinofila†
0033-9350	Camera di Commercio di la Spezia. Rassegna Commerciale *see* 0391-7983
0033-9369	Associazione Nazionale Commercianti, Gas Liquefatti. Bolletino Informativo
0033-9377	Rassegna dei Lavori Pubblici
0033-9385	Rassegna del Lavoro
0033-9407	Rassegna del Mercato
0033-9415	Rassegna dell'Arbitrato
0033-9423	Rassegna della Letteratura Italiana
0033-9431	Rassegna della Letteratura Odontoiatrica
0033-944X	Rassegna della Letteratura Sui Cicli Economici
0033-9458	Rassegna della Stampa
0033-9466	Rassegna dell'Istruzione Secondaria *changed to* Rassegna dell'Istruzione
0033-9482	Rassegna di Cultura e Vita Scolastica
0033-9504	Rassegna di Diritto Cinematografico, Teatrale e della Radiotelevisione
0033-9512	Rassegna di Diritto Pubblico
0033-9539	Rassegna di Ipnosi e Medicina Psicosomatica *changed to* Rassegni di Ipnosi
0033-9547	Rassegna di Legislazione Italiana Nei Rapporti Internazionali†
0033-9555	Rassegna di Medicina Sperimentale
0033-9563	Rassegna di Patologia dell' Apparato Respiratorio
0033-9571	Rassegna di Pedagogia
0033-958X	Rassegna di Politica e di Storia
0033-9601	Rassegna di Servizio Sociale
0033-9628	Rassegna di Studi Penitenziari *changed to* Rassegna Penitenziaria e Criminologica
0033-9636	Rassegna di Studi Psichiatrici
0033-9644	Rassegna di Teologia
0033-9652	Rassegna ed Archivio di Chirurgia†
0033-9679	Rassegna Giuridica Ed Economica sui Danni di Guerra
0033-9687	Rassegna Grafica
0033-9695	Rassegna Internazionale di Clinica e Terapia
0033-9725	Rassegna Italiana di Linguistica Applicata
0033-9733	Rassegna Italiana di Ricerca Psichica
0033-975X	Rassegna Lucchese
0033-9768	Rassegna Medica e Culturale†
0033-9776	Rassegna Medica Sarda
0033-9784	Rassegna Melodrammatica
0033-9792	Rassegna Mensile di Israel
0033-9806	Rassegna Musicale Curci
0033-9814	I S L E. Rassegna Parlamentare - Schedario Legislativo *changed to* I S L E. Rassegna Parlamentare
0033-9822	Rassegna Petrolifera
0033-9830	Rassegna Quindicinale dell'Agricoltura *changed to* Ecomese
0033-9849	Rassegna Sindacale
0033-9857	Rassegna Sovietica
0033-9865	Rassegna Speleologica Italiana†
0033-9873	Rassegna Storica del Risorgimento
0033-9881	Rassegna Storica Toscana
0033-9903	Rassegna Tecnica Enel *changed to* Rassegna Tecnica di Problemi dell'Energia Elettrica

0033-9911 Rassegna Trimestrale di Odontoiatria
0033-992X Rassegna di Urologia e Nefrologia†
0033-9938 Raster†
0033-9946 Rastitel'nye Resursy
0033-9962 Rateko
0033-9970 Rateksa *see* 0108-6626
0033-9989 Der Ratgeber
0033-9997 Ratgeber fuer Kranke und Gesunde *changed to* Ratgeber aus der Apotheke
0034-0006 Ratio
0034-0014 Ratio *see* 0035-6816
0034-0030 Individualist
0034-0049 Rational Living *see* 0748-1985
0034-0073 Rationelles Buero *see* 0340-3491
0034-009X Raumausstattung Report†
0034-0103 Raumfahrtforschung *see* 0342-068X
0034-0111 Raumforschung und Raumordnung
0034-012X Rautakaupan Uutiset *changed to* Kodinrakentaja
0034-0138 Rave†
0034-0146 Raven
0034-0162 Ray Palmer's Forum†
0034-0170 Rayito (Counselor's Edition)†
0034-0197 Rayons
0034-0200 Rays of Sunshine *see* 0039-5412
0034-0227 Razgledi
0034-0235 Razon y Fe
0034-0243 Razonoda Miliona
0034-0251 Razprave in Gradivo
0034-026X Razvedka i Okhrana Nedr
0034-0286 Re: Arts and Letters *changed to* Re: Artes Liberales
0034-0294 Re: Search†
0034-0308 Reach *see* 0745-1172
0034-0316 Reach Out†
0034-0324 Reaching Out *changed to* Feelings
0034-0332 Reactor Technology†
0034-0359 Read Magazine
0034-0367 Readaption *see* 0823-9436
0034-0375 Reader's Digest
0034-0383 Reader's Digest (Asian Edition)
0034-0391 Reader's Digest (Australian Edition)
0034-0405 Reader's Digest (British Edition)
0034-0413 Reader's Digest (Canadian-English Edition)
0034-0421 Reader's Digest (Indian Edition)
0034-043X Reader's Digest (Japanese Edition)
0034-0448 Reader's Digest (New Zealand Edition)
0034-0456 Reader's Digest (South African Edition)
0034-0464 Readers' Guide to Periodical Literature
0034-0472 Reading
0034-0502 Reading Horizons
0034-0510 Reading Improvement
0034-0537 Reading Newsreport†
0034-0545 Reading Quarterly†
0034-0553 Reading Research Quarterly
0034-0561 Reading Teacher
0034-057X Reaktorn
0034-0588 Real†
0034-0596 Real Academia de Ciencias Exactas, Fisicas y Naturales. Revista
0034-060X Real Academia de Cordoba de Ciencias, Bellas Letras y Nobles Artes. Boletin
0034-0618 Real Academia de Farmacia. Anales
0034-0626 Real Academia de la Historia. Boletin
0034-0634 Real Academia Nacional de Medicina. Anales
0034-0642 Real Confessions Magazine
0034-0669 Real Estate and Stock Journal *changed to* Victorian Real Estate Journal
0034-0677 Real Estate Appraiser *see* 0271-258X
0034-0693 Real Estate Investment Planning Checklist and Forms
0034-0707 Real Estate Forum
0034-0715 Real Estate Insider Newsletter
0034-0723 Real Estate Investment Ideas
0034-0731 Real Estate Investment Planning
0034-074X Real Estate Journal
0034-0758 Real Estate Law Brief Case†
0034-0766 Real Estate News (New York)†
0034-0774 Real Estate Record and Builder's Guide
0034-0790 Real Estate Review
0034-0804 Real Estate Today
0034-0839 Real Life Confessions
0034-0847 Real Living
0034-0855 Real Property, Probate and Trust Journal
0034-0863 Real Sociedad Arqueologica. Boletin Arqueologico
0034-0871 Real Sociedad Espanola de Fisica y Quimica. Anales. Serie A: Fisica *see* 0211-6243
0034-088X Real Sociedad Espanola de Fisica y Quimica. Anales. Serie B: Quimica *changed to* Real Sociedad Espanola de Fisica y Quimica. Anales de Quimica
0034-0898 Real West
0034-091X Realist†
0034-0960 Reality
0034-0979 Reality
0034-0987 Reality
0034-0995 Realta
0034-1029 Realta Sovietica†
0034-1037 Realtor Headlines†
0034-1045 Realty and Building
0034-1053 Realty and Chain Store Renting Leads *changed to* Realty
0034-1061 Realty Review†
0034-107X Reaper
0034-1096 Reassurance *see* 0153-3614
0034-1118 Rebe und Wein
0034-1142 Rec Naroda
0034-1150 Recall†
0034-1169 C L R Recent Developments†
0034-1185 Recent Publications on Governmental Problems
0034-1193 Recenti Progressi in Medicina
0034-1207 Recenzija
0034-1215 Rechabite
0034-1223 Recherche Aerospatiale
0034-1231 C A R D A N. Bulletin d'Information et de Liaison†
0034-124X Recherche Sociale
0034-1258 Recherches de Science Religieuse
0034-1266 Recherches de Theologie Ancienne et Medievale
0034-1274 Recherches Economiques de Louvain
0034-1282 Recherches Sociographiques
0034-1290 Rechnoi Transport
0034-1312 Recht der Jugend und des Bildungswesens
0034-1320 Recht der Schiffahrt
0034-1339 Recht im Amt
0034-1355 Rechtsarchiv der Wirtschaft *changed to* Recht der Wirtschaft
0034-1363 Rechtspflegerblatt
0034-1371 Rechtsprechung der Bau-Ausfuehrung *changed to* Rechtsprechung Zum Privaten Baurecht
0034-138X Rechtsprechung in Strafsachen
0034-1398 Rechtstheorie
0034-1401 Rechtswissenschaftliche Dokumentation *see* 0138-1385
0034-141X Reclamation Era *see* 0733-6446
0034-1436 Reclamation Safety News *see* 0270-4447
0034-1452 Recommend: Florida
0034-1479 Reconciliation Quarterly
0034-1487 Reconstruction
0034-1495 Reconstructionist
0034-1509 Rencontre Orient Occident†
0034-1517 Record†
0034-1525 Lancashire Authors' Association. Record
0034-1541 Record (New York, 1940)
0034-155X Record Collector (Heanor)
0034-1568 Record Collector (Ipswich)
0034-1592 Record Research
0034-1606 Record Retailer *see* 0265-1548
0034-1614 Record Stockman
0034-1622 Record World
0034-1630 Recorded Sound†
0034-1649 Recorder
0034-1657 Recorder†
0034-1665 Recorder and Music *see* 0306-4409
0034-1673 Recording Engineer-Producer
0034-1703 Records and Statistics†
0034-1711 Records Management Journal†
0034-172X Records Management Quarterly *see* 0191-1503
0034-1738 Records of Huntingdonshire
0034-1746 Records of the Month†
0034-1770 Recreation Management *see* 0744-3676
0034-1827 Recruiting Trends
0034-1835 Recueil Dalloz-Sirey
0034-1843 Recueil de Medecine Veterinaire d'Alfort
0034-1851 Recueil des Brevets d'Invention
0034-1878 Recueil Juridique de l'Est Securite Sociale
0034-1886 Recueil Officiel des Marques de Fabrique et de Commerce†
0034-1916 Recuperatie *changed to* Magazine Recycling
0034-1924 Recuperation
0034-1932 Recusant History
0034-1940 Red and Black (Washington)
0034-1959 Red and Green
0034-1967 Red Cedar Review
0034-1975 Red Clay Reader†
0034-1983 Red Cross Newsletter *changed to* Good Neighbor
0034-1991 Panorama†
0034-2009 Red Hill Press *see* 0147-4936
0034-2017 Red Mole *see* 0142-6575
0034-2025 Red Notes
0034-2033 Red Poll News
0034-2041 Red Shield *changed to* Red Shield News
0034-2068 Red Star Weekly
0034-2076 Red Tape
0034-2092 Redaktions-Archiv
0034-2106 Redbook
0034-2114 Reddingwezen
0034-2122 Redeemer's Voice
0034-2130 Redlands Bulldog
0034-2165 Redstart
0034-2181 Redwood Rancher *changed to* Redwood Rancher Country
0034-219X Reed's Aircraft & Equipment News†
0034-2203 Reed's Marine Equipment News *see* 0140-8046
0034-2211 Reeducation
0034-222X Reeducation Orthophonique
0034-2238 Reel
0034-2246 Referateblatt zur Raumordnung *see* 0341-2512
0034-2254 Referatekartei Korrosion-Korrosionsschutz†
0034-2262 Bibliographie Philosophie
0034-2297 Referativnyi Zhurnal. Avtomobil'nyi i Gorodskoi Transport
0034-2300 Referativnyi Zhurnal. Biologiya
0034-2327 Referativny Zhurnal. Elektrotekhnika i Energetika *changed to* Referativnyi Zhurnal. Elektrotekhnika
0034-2343 Referativnyi Zhurnal. Fizika
0034-2351 Referativnyi Zhurnal. Geodeziya *see* 0375-9717
0034-236X Referativnyi Zhurnal. Geofizika
0034-2378 Referativnyi Zhurnal. Geografiya
0034-2386 Referativnyi Zhurnal. Gornoe Delo
0034-2394 Gornye Mashiny *see* 0373-6415
0034-2408 Referativnyi Zhurnal. Issledovanie Kosmicheskogo Prostranstva
0034-2416 Referativnyi Zhurnal. Khimicheskoe i Kholodil'noe Mashinostroenie *see* 0370-8098
0034-2424 Referativnyi Zhurnal. Kotlostroenie
0034-2432 Referativnyi Zhurnal. Legkaya Promyshlennost'
0034-2440 Referativnyi Zhurnal. Lesovedenie i Lesovodstvo
0034-2459 Referativnyi Zhurnal. Mashinostroitel'nye Materialy, Konstruktsii i Raschet Detali Mashin. Gidroprivod
0034-2467 Referativnyi Zhurnal. Matematika
0034-2475 Referativnyi Zhurnal. Meditsinskaya Geografiya
0034-2483 Referativnyi Zhurnal. Mekhanika
0034-2491 Referativnyi Zhurnal. Metallurgiya
0034-2505 Referativnyi Zhurnal. Metrologiya i Izmeritel'naya Tekhnika
0034-2513 Referativnyi Zhurnal. Nasosostroenie i Kompressorstroenie *changed to* Referativnyi Zhurnal. Nasosostroenie i Kompressorostroenie. Kholodil'noe Mashinostroenie
0034-2521 Referativnyi Zhurnal. Oborudovanie Pishchevoi Promyshlennosti
0034-253X Referativnyi Zhurnal. Organizatsiya Upravleniya Promyshlennost'yu *see* 0132-5639
0034-2548 Referativnyi Zhurnal. Pochvovedenie i Agrokhimiya
0034-2556 Referativnyi Zhurnal. Promyshlennyi Transport
0034-2580 Referativnyi Zhurnal. Tekhnologiya i Oborudovanie Tsellyulozno-vumazhnogo i Poligraficheskogo Proizvodstva†
0034-2599 Referativnyi Zhurnal. Tekhnologiya Mashinostroeniya
0034-2602 Referativnyi Zhurnal. Traktory i Sel'skokhozyaistvennye Mashiny i Orudiya
0034-2610 Referativnyi Zhurnal. Truboprovodnyi Transport
0034-2629 Referativnyi Zhurnal. Turbostroenie
0034-2637 Referativnyi Zhurnal. Voprosy Tekhnicheskogo Progressa i Organizatsii Proizvodstva v Mashinostroenii
0034-2645 Referativnyi Zhurnal. Vzaimodeistvie Raznykh Vidov Transporta i Konteinernye Perevozki
0034-2653 Referativnyi Zhurnal. Yadernye Reaktory
0034-2661 Referativnyi Zhurnal. Zhivotnovodstvo i Veterinariya *see* 0206-5525
0034-267X Referativnyi Zhurnal. Radiotekhnika
0034-2688 Referatovy Vyber z Anestesiologie a Resuscitace
0034-2696 Referatovy Vyber z Chirurgie
0034-270X Referatovy Vyber z Chorob Infekcnich
0034-2718 Referatovy Vyber z Dermatovenerologie
0034-2726 Referatovy Vyber z Endokrinologie
0034-2734 Referatovy Vyber z Fysiologie
0034-2742 Referatovy Vyber z Gastroenterologie
0034-2750 Referatovy Vyber z Gerontologie a Geriatrie
0034-2769 Referatovy Vyber z Kardiologie, Fysiologie a Patologie Obehoveho Ustroji
0034-2777 Referatovy Vyber z Lekarenstvi
0034-2785 Referatovy Vyber z Lekarskeho Tisku o Vychove a Doskolovani Zdravotnickych Pracovniku†
0034-2793 Referatovy Vyber z Neurologie
0034-2807 Referatovy Vyber z Oftalmologie
0034-2815 Referatovy Vyber z Onkologie
0034-2823 Referatovy Vyber z Ortopedie, Traumatologie a Pribuznych Oboru
0034-2831 Referatovy Vyber z Otorhinolaryngologie a Foniatrie
0034-284X Referatovy Vyber z Patologicke Anatomie
0034-2858 Referatovy Vyber z Pediatrie
0034-2866 Referatovy Vyber z Porodnictvi a Gynekologie
0034-2874 Referatovy Vyber z Rentgenologie
0034-2882 Referatovy Vyber z Revmatologie
0034-2890 Referatovy Vyber z Pneumologie a Tuberkulosy
0034-2904 Referatovy Vyber ze Sportovni Mediciny/Abstracts of Sports Medicine *changed to* Referatovy Vyber ze Sportovni Mediciny a Lecebne Rehabilitace
0034-2912 Japan. National Diet Library. Reference
0034-2947 Reflector
0034-2963 Reflector
0034-2971 Reflets et Perspectives de la Vie Economique
0034-298X Reflets Guildiens†
0034-3005 Reflexion *see* 0384-8167
0034-3013 Kontakt und Reflexionen *changed to* Kontakt
0034-3021 Reformatio
0034-303X Reformation Review

0034-3048 Reformation Today
0034-3056 Reformed World
0034-3064 Reformed Review
0034-3072 Reformed Theological Review
0034-3080 Reformer
0034-3102 Refractories
0034-3110 Refractories Journal
0034-3129 Refrigerated Transporter
0034-3137 Refrigeration
0034-3145 Refrigeration Service and Contracting (Troy)
0034-3153 Refuah Veterinarith *changed to* Israel Journal of Veterinary Medicine
0034-3161 Refuat Hape Vehashinaim
0034-317X Regan Report on Hospital Law
0034-3188 Regan Report on Medical Law
0034-3196 Regan Report on Nursing Law
0034-320X Regards sur le Comite d'Etablissement d'Orly Sud
0034-3218 Regelrecht
0034-3250 Regensburger Bistumsblatt
0034-3269 Der Reggeboge
0034-3285 T V Panorama *changed to* Panorama/Ons Land
0034-3293 Regio Basiliensis
0034-3315 Region Six Sentinel
0034-3323 Regional Action†
0034-3331 Regional and Urban Economics-Operational Methods *see* 0166-0462
0034-334X International Seismological Centre. Regional Catalogue of Earthquakes
0034-3358 Regional Cultural Institute. Journal
0034-3366 Regional Development Newsletter *see* 0310-5946
0034-3374 Regional Plan News *changed to* Regional Plan News
0034-3382 Regional Review Quarterly *see* 0196-4003
0034-3390 Regional Spotlight
0034-3404 Regional Studies
0034-3412 Regione e Potere Locale
0034-3420 Region's Agenda
0034-3439 Regionwide†
0034-3471 Regmaker
0034-348X Regmi Research Series
0034-3498 Regno - Attualita
0034-3501 Rehabilitation in South Africa
0034-351X Japanese Journal of Rehabilitation Medicine
0034-3528 Rehabilitation†
0034-3536 Die Rehabilitation
0034-3552 Rehabilitation Counseling Bulletin
0034-3579 Rehabilitation Literature†
0034-3587 Rehabilitation Record *changed to* U.S. Health Care Financing Administration Forum
0034-3609 Rehovot
0034-3617 Reinforced Plastics
0034-3625 Reiniger und Waescher
0034-3633 Reino
0034-3641 Reinsurance Reporter
0034-365X Reinwardtia
0034-3668 Deutsche Reisebuero-Zeitung
0034-3676 Reiseliv i Norge *changed to* Reiseliv
0034-3684 Reiss-Davis Clinic Bulletin†
0034-3692 Reiter Revue International
0034-3714 Refrigeration
0034-3722 Refrigeration and Air Conditioning Technology *see* 0034-3714
0034-3749 Rekenschap
0034-3765 Relacoes Humanas†
0034-3773 Relais
0034-3781 Relations
0034-379X Relations Industrielles
0034-3803 Relations Latines
0034-3811 Relations Publiques Informations
0034-382X Relay Association Journal *changed to* Cablevision News
0034-3838 Relazioni†
0034-3846 Relazioni Internazionali
0034-3854 Etocomunicazione *changed to* Etocom (1980)
0034-3862 Relazioni Sociali†
0034-3897 Relics
0034-3900 Relics†
0034-3935 Religioese Graphik
0034-3943 Religion and Church in the Communist Orbit†
0034-3951 Religion and Society
0034-396X Religion and Society *see* 0093-2582
0034-3978 R C D A - Religion in Communist Dominated Areas
0034-3986 Religion in Life *see* 0270-9287
0034-401X Religion Teacher's Journal
0034-4036 Religiose nell'Apostolato Diretto
0034-4044 Religious & Theological Abstracts
0034-4052 Religious and Theological Resources†
0034-4060 Religious Book Review Index
0034-4079 Religious Broadcasting
0034-4087 Religious Education
0034-4095 Religious Humanism
0034-4109 R N A Newsletter
0034-4117 Religious Periodicals Index†
0034-4125 Religious Studies
0034-4141 Reluire *see* 0758-413X
0034-4168 Remag
0034-4176 Remainders' Book Italiano
0034-4184 Remanso
0034-4192 Remarques Africaines *changed to* Remarques Arabo-Africaines
0034-4206 Remedes des Corps et des Ames *see* 0048-7228
0034-4214 Remedial Education *see* 0268-2141
0034-4230 Reminder†
0034-4249 Remodeling Contractor (Arlington)
0034-4257 Remote Sensing of Environment
0034-4265 Removals and Storage
0034-4273 Rempart
0034-4281 Renaissance *changed to* New Reformation
0034-429X Renaissance and Reformation
0034-4311 Renaissance Deux-Mille *changed to* Tribune Gaulliste
0034-4338 Renaissance Quarterly
0034-4346 Renascence
0034-4362 Renderer *see* 0090-8932
0034-4370 Rendez-Vous
0034-4389 Rendez Vous
0034-4397 Rendez-Vous de la Mode
0034-4400 Rendezvous
0034-4419 Rendiconti
0034-4427 Rendiconti di Matematica
0034-4451 Renfro Valley Bugle
0034-446X Renovacion
0034-4478 Renovacion
0034-4486 Renovatio
0034-4494 Renovation *see* 0041-5103
0034-4508 Rensselaer Engineer
0034-4516 Rent-All Magazine†
0034-4524 Rental Equipment Register
0034-4532 Rental Laundry Management *changed to* Laundry Cleaning World
0034-4540 Rentner und Pensionist
0034-4567 Repertoire Bibliographique de la Philosophie
0034-4575 Repertoire des Voyages
0034-4583 Repertoire Permanent des Groupes Financiers et Industriels *changed to* Repertoire des Groupes d'Entreprises
0034-4591 Repertorio Analitico della Stampa Italiana. Quotidiani e Periodici†
0034-4613 Repertorio Centroamericano†
0034-463X Repertorium Verpakte Geneesmiddelen Periodiek Overzicht voor Artsen *changed to* Repertorium
0034-4648 Repertuar Khudozhestvennoi Samodeyatel'nosti
0034-4664 Report from Germany†
0034-4672 Report of Ionosphere and Space Research in Japan *see* 0386-5444
0034-4680 Report on Education of the Disadvantaged
0034-4699 Report on Education Research
0034-4702 Report on Preschool Education *changed to* Report on Preschool Programs
0034-4737 Report on World Affairs
0034-4745 Reportage
0034-4753 Reporter
0034-4788 Reporter
0034-4796 Reporter for Conscience' Sake
0034-480X Reporter of Construction Equipment *changed to* Equipment Today
0034-4818 Reportero Industrial
0034-4826 I A B C Notebook†
0034-4834 Reporting on Governments
0034-4842 Union of Japanese Scientists and Engineers. Reports of Statistical Application Research
0034-4869 Reports on Higher Education *see* 0511-7666
0034-4877 Reports on Mathematical Physics
0034-4885 Reports on Progress in Physics
0034-4893 Representation
0034-4907 Representative Research in Social Psychology
0034-4923 Reprint Expediting Service Bulletin *see* 0275-682X
0034-4931 Reprints from the Soviet Press
0034-4958 Reproduction
0034-4966 Reproduction Paper News Bulletin *changed to* Reproduction Bulletin
0034-4974 Reproductions Review *changed to* In-Plant Reproductions & Electronic Publishing
0034-4982 Reprographics
0034-5016 China, Republic. National Central Library. Newsletter
0034-5024 South Africa. Department of Statistics. Bulletin of Statistics *changed to* South Africa. Central Statistical Service. Bulletin of Statistics
0034-5032 Republic Weekly with Newsday
0034-5040 Republica Argentina. Transporte Aereo. Noticiero
0034-5059 Republican†
0034-5067 Republican Battle Line *see* 0145-1677
0034-5075 Republican Journal
0034-5091 Res Gestae†
0034-5105 Resale Weekly
0034-5113 Research†
0034-5121 Research and Farming *see* 0732-4766
0034-513X Research and Industry
0034-5148 Research and Sponsored Programs at Notre Dame *changed to* Notre Dame Report
0034-5156 Research Association of Powder Technology, Japan. Journal. *see* 0386-6157
0034-5164 Research Communications in Chemical Pathology and Pharmacology
0034-5172 Alberta Research Council. Bulletins
0034-5180 Alberta Research Council. Information Series
0034-5199 Research/Development *see* 0746-9179
0034-5202 Research Film†
0034-5210 Research in African Literatures
0034-5229 Research in Education *see* 0098-0897
0034-5237 Research in Education
0034-5245 Research in Librarianship
0034-5253 Research in Reproduction
0034-5261 Research in the Life Sciences†
0034-527X Research in the Teaching of English
0034-5288 Research in Veterinary Science
0034-5296 Research Index
0034-530X Hokkaido University. Research Institute for Catalysis. Journal†
0034-5318 Research Institute for Mathematical Sciences. Publications
0034-5326 Research into Higher Education Abstracts
0034-5334 Research Management
0034-5342 Research News†
0034-5350 Research Papers in Physical Education *changed to* Carnegie Research Papers
0034-5369 University of North Carolina. Institute for Research in Social Science. Research Reviews.†
0034-5377 American Alliance for Health, Physical Education and Recreation. Research Quarterly *see* 0270-1367
0034-5393 California University Center for Research and Development in Higher Education. Research Reporter†
0034-5407 American Institute for Economic Research. Research Reports
0034-5415 Research Reports in Social Science†
0034-5431 Research Society of Pakistan. Journal
0034-5458 Researcher†
0034-5466 Researches on Population Ecology
0034-5474 Resena de Hispanoamerica†
0034-5490 Reservbefal
0034-5504 Reserve Bank of Australia. Statistical Bulletin *see* 0725-0320
0034-5512 Reserve Bank of India. Bulletin
0034-5520 Reserve Bank of Malawi. Economic and Financial Review *see* 0376-5725
0034-5539 Reserve Bank of New Zealand. Bulletin
0034-5547 Reserve Marine
0034-5555 Resident and Staff Physician
0034-5571 Resin Review
0034-5598 Resistenza†
0034-5636 Resort Management *changed to* Resort & Hotel Management
0034-5652 Resource†
0034-5660 Resources for Youth Ministry
0034-5687 Respiration Physiology
0034-5695 Respond†
0034-5709 Response (Flushing)
0034-5725 Response (New York)
0034-575X Ressorgiment†
0034-5792 Restaurante
0034-5806 Restaurator
0034-5814 Restauratoeren
0034-5822 Restoration & Eighteenth Century Theatre Research
0034-5830 Restoration Herald
0034-5857 Results of the Business Survey Carried out Among Heads of Enterprises in the Community
0034-5865 Resumen†
0034-5873 Resumenes Analiticos Sobre Defensa y Seguridad Nacional/Abstracts of Military Bibliography *changed to* Abstracts of Military Bibliography
0034-5881 Resumenes de Articulos Cientificos y Tecnicos. Serie A: Quimica Industrial *changed to* Alerta Informativa. Serie A: Quimica Industrial
0034-589X Resumenes de Articulos Cientificos y Tecnicos. Serie B: Fisica Aplicada *see* 0210-6825
0034-5903 Resumenes de Articulos Cientificos y Tecnicos. Serie C: Ciencia y Tecnica de los Metales *changed to* Alerta Informativa. Serie C: Ciencia y Tecnica de los Metales
0034-5911 Resumenes de Articulos Cientificos y Tecnicos. Serie D: Ingenieria y Tecnologia Varias *see* 0210-7007
0034-592X Resumenes de Articulos Cientificos y Tecnicos. Serie E: Economia de la Empresa *see* 0210-7023
0034-5946 Mozambique. Servico Meteorologico. Resumos Meteorologicas para a Aeronautica†
0034-5970 Resurgence
0034-5989 Retail Ad News†
0034-5997 Retail Advertising Week
0034-6012 Retail Business
0034-6020 Retail Chemist *see* 0009-3033
0034-6039 Retail Clerks Advocate†
0034-6047 Retail Control
0034-6055 Retail Food Price Bulletin *see* 0028-6168
0034-6063 Retail Jeweller
0034-608X Retail Lumberman *changed to* Building Material Retailer
0034-6098 Retail Newsagent, Bookseller and Stationer *changed to* Retail Newsagent Tobacconist Confectioner
0034-6136 Retail World
0034-6144 Retailer of Queensland
0034-6152 Retarded
0034-6160 Retired Officer
0034-6179 Retirement Life (Washington)
0034-6187 Rettens Gang
0034-6195 Rjettur
0034-6209 Reuma
0034-6217 Reuma Bulletin
0034-6233 Reumatologia
0034-6241 Reus Avicola y Agricola
0034-625X Revealing Confession

0034-6268 Revealing Romances†
0034-6276 Reveil de Djibouti *changed to* Nation Djibouti
0034-6284 Reveil Missionnaire
0034-6292 Reveil Socialiste de Lannemezan
0034-6306 Reveille
0034-6314 Revetements Sols et Murs†
0034-6322 American Logistics Association Review *see* 0273-7485
0034-6330 Review†
0034-6349 Review: Worldwide Reinsurance
0034-6357 Review
0034-6373 Review and Expositor
0034-6381 Review and Herald *see* 0161-1119
0034-639X Review for Religious
0034-6403 Review of Agricultural Economics Malaysia†
0034-6438 Review of Plant Pathology
0034-6446 Review of Black Political Economy
0034-6454 Review of Business
0034-6462 Alaska Review of Business and Economic Conditions *see* 0162-5403
0034-6489 Review of Communist Scientific and Political Publications (Soviet Union)†
0034-6497 Review of Czechoslovak Medicine *changed to* Czechoslovak Medicine
0034-6500 Turkiye Is Bankasi. Review of Economic Conditions
0034-6519 Bank Leumi Economic Review *see* 0334-9160
0034-6527 Review of Economic Studies
0034-6535 Review of Economics and Statistics
0034-6543 Review of Educational Research
0034-6551 Review of English Studies
0034-656X Review of Existential Psychology and Psychiatry
0034-6578 Review of Ghana Law
0034-6586 Review of Income and Wealth
0034-6594 Review of Indonesian and Malayan Affairs *changed to* R I M A: Review of Indonesian and Malaysian Affairs
0034-6608 Review of International Cooperation
0034-6616 Review of Marketing and Agricultural Economics
0034-6624 Review of Medical and Veterinary Mycology
0034-6632 Review of Metaphysics
0034-6640 Review of National Literatures
0034-6659 Nutrition and Food Science
0034-6667 Review of Palaeobotany and Palynology
0034-6675 Review of Physical Chemistry of Japan†
0034-6683 Review of Physics in Technology *see* 0305-4624
0034-6691 Review of Polarography
0034-6705 Review of Politics
0034-6713 Review of Popular Astronomy†
0034-6721 Review of Religions
0034-673X Review of Religious Research
0034-6748 Review of Scientific Instruments
0034-6756 Standard and Poor's Review of Securities Regulation *changed to* Standard & Poor's Review of Securities Commodities Regulation
0034-6764 Review of Social Economy
0034-6772 Review of Soviet Medical Sciences†
0034-6780 Review of Surgery *see* 0149-7944
0034-6799 Review of Economic Conditions in Italy
0034-6802 Review of the News *changed to* New American
0034-6810 Review of the River Plate
0034-6829 Magyar Jog es Kulfoldi Jogi Szemle *see* 0025-0147
0034-6853 Reviews of Geophysics and Space Physics *see* 8755-1209
0034-6861 Reviews of Modern Physics
0034-687X Reviews of Pure and Applied Chemistry†
0034-6888 Revija (Osijek)
0034-6896 Revija Skolstva i Prosvetna Dokumentacija *see* 0351-0697
0034-690X Revija za Kriminalistiko in Kriminologijo
0034-6918 Revision og Regnskabsvaesen
0034-6926 Revista A P H
0034-6934 Revista Aerea Latinoamericana
0034-6942 Revista Aeronautica
0034-6950 Revista Aguas e Energia Eletrica de Sao Paulo†
0034-6969 Revista Alamar†
0034-6977 Revista Alentejana
0034-6985 Anales de Legislacion Argentina
0034-6993 Revista Argentina de Angiologia
0034-7019 Revista Argentina de Ciencia Politica
0034-7027 Revista Argentina de Psicologia
0034-7043 Revista Arhivelor
0034-706X Revista Bancaria Brasileira
0034-7078 Revista Biblica
0034-7086 Revista Bibliotecilor†
0034-7094 Revista Brasileira de Anestesiologia
0034-7108 Revista Brasileira de Biologia
0034-7116 Revista Brasileira de Cancerologia
0034-7124 Revista Brasileira de Cirurgia
0034-7140 Revista Brasileira de Economia
0034-7159 Revista Brasileira de Energia Eletrica†
0034-7167 Revista Brasileira de Enfermagem
0034-7175 Revista Brasileira de Estatistica
0034-7183 Revista Brasileira de Estudos Pedagogicos
0034-7191 Revista Brasileira de Estudos Politicos
0034-7205 Revista Brasileira de Filosofia†
0034-7213 Revista Brasileira de Folclore†
0034-723X Revista Brasileira de Geografia
0034-7256 Revista Brasileira de Malariologia e Doencas Tropicais
0034-7264 Revista Brasileira de Medicina
0034-7280 Revista Brasileira de Oftalmologia
0034-7299 Revista Brasileira de Oto-Rino-Laringologia
0034-7302 Revista Brasileira de Patologia Clinica
0034-7329 Revista Brasileira de Politica Internacional
0034-7337 Revista Brasileira de Saude Mental
0034-7353 Revista Campinense de Cultura
0034-7361 C E C Revista
0034-737X Ceres *changed to* Ceres. Revista
0034-7388 Revista Chilena de Neuropsiquiatria
0034-7396 Revista Chilena de Pediatria†
0034-740X Revista Chilena de Entomologia
0034-7418 Revista Colombiana de Ciencias Quimico Farmaceuticas
0034-7426 Revista Colombiana de Matematicas
0034-7434 Revista Colombiana de Obstetricia y Ginecologia
0034-7442 Revista Colombiana de Pediatria y Puericultura
0034-7450 Revista Colombiana de Psiquiatria
0034-7469 Revista Comercial de Nicaragua
0034-7477 Revista Conservadora del Pensamiento Centroamericano *see* 0378-3340
0034-7485 Revista Cubana de Ciencia Agricola
0034-7493 Revista Cubana de Cirugia
0034-7507 Revista Cubana de Estomatologia
0034-7515 Revista Cubana de Farmacia
0034-7523 Revista Cubana de Medicina
0034-7531 Revista Cubana de Pediatria
0034-754X Revista Cultului Mozaic
0034-7558 Bolsa de Valores de Sao Paulo. Revista†
0034-7566 Revista da Construcao Civil
0034-7582 Revista da Madeira
0034-7590 Revista de Administracao de Empresas
0034-7604 Revista de Administracao Municipal
0034-7612 Revista de Administracao Publica
0034-7620 Revista de Administracion Publica
0034-7647 Revista de Aeronautica y Astronautica
0034-7655 Revista de Agricultura
0034-7671 Revista de Agricultura *see* 0138-7251
0034-7698 Revista de Agroquimica y Tecnologia de Alimentos
0034-7701 Revista de Antropologia
0034-771X Revista de Archivos, Bibliotecas y Museos
0034-7728 Revista de Bellas Artes†
0034-7736 Revista de Biologia
0034-7744 Revista de Biologia Tropical
0034-7752 Revista de Chimie
0034-7779 Revista de Ciencias Economicas *see* 0325-0814
0034-7779 Revista de Ciencias Economicas *see* 0325-0830
0034-7787 Revista de Ciencias Juridicas†
0034-7817 Revista de Ciencias Sociales
0034-7825 Revista de Compendios de Articulos de Economia
0034-7833 Revista de Conservatorio†
0034-7841 Revista de Criminalistica do Rio Grande do Sul†
0034-785X Revista de Cultura Brasilena
0034-7868 Revista de Derecho
0034-7876 Revista de Derecho Comercial *changed to* Revista de Derecho Comercial y de la Empresa
0034-7884 Revista de Derecho Deportivo
0034-7892 Revista de Derecho Internacional y Ciencias Diplomaticas
0034-7906 Revista de Derecho, Jurisprudencia y Administracion
0034-7914 Revista de Derecho Penal y Criminologia†
0034-7922 Revista de Derecho Privado
0034-7930 Revista de Derecho Puertorriqueno
0034-7949 Revista de Derecho y Ciencias Politicas
0034-7957 Revista de Derecho y Ciencias Sociales *changed to* Revista de Derecho
0034-7965 Revista de Derecho y Legislacion†
0034-7973 Revista de Diagnostico Biologico†
0034-7981 Revista de Dialectologia y Tradiciones Populares
0034-8007 Revista de Direito Administrativo
0034-8015 Revista de Direito Publico
0034-8023 Revista de Ciencia Politica
0034-804X Revista de Economia Latinoamericana
0034-8066 Revista de Economia y Estadistica
0034-8074 Revista de Educacion
0034-8082 Revista de Educacion
0034-8090 Revista de Enfermagem†
0034-8104 Revista de Engenharia do Estado da Guanabara
0034-8112 Revista de Engenharia Mackenzie
0034-8139 Revista de Entomologia de Mocambique†
0034-8147 Revista de Espiritualidad
0034-8155 Revista de Estudios Agro-Sociales
0034-8163 Revista de Estudios de la Vida Local
0034-8171 Revista de Estudios de Teatro *changed to* Instituto Nacional de Estudios de Teatro. Boletin
0034-818X Revista de Estudios Hispanicos
0034-8198 Revista de Etnografie si Folclor
0034-8201 Revista de Farmacia e Odontologia *changed to* Especialidades Odontologicas
0034-8228 Revista de Filosofia†
0034-8236 Revista de Filosofia
0034-8244 Revista de Filosofia†
0034-8252 Revista de Filosofia
0034-8260 Revista de Filosofie
0034-8279 Revista de Geofisica
0034-8287 Revista de Ginecologia e d'Obstetricia†
0034-8295 Revista de Guimaraes
0034-8309 Revista de Historia
0034-8317 Revista de Historia†
0034-8325 Revista de Historia de America
0034-8333 Revista de Ideas Esteticas†
0034-8341 Revista de Indias
0034-835X Revista de Informacao Legislativa
0034-8368 Revista de Intendencia
0034-8376 Revista de Investigacion Clinica
0034-8384 Revista de Investigacion en Salud Publica†
0034-8392 Revista de Istorie si Teorie Literara
0034-8406 Revista de la Defensa Nacional†
0034-8422 Revista de la Integracion *see* 0325-1675
0034-8430 Revista de la Sanidad de Policia *changed to* Peru. Fuerzas Policiales. Revista de la Sanidad
0034-8457 Revista de las Fuerzas Armadas
0034-8473 Revista de las Fuerzas Armadas
0034-8481 Revista de Legislacion Argentina
0034-8511 Revista de Marina
0034-852X Revista de Marina
0034-8538 Revista de Marina del Peru
0034-8546 Revista de Marinha
0034-8554 Revista de Medicina
0034-8570 Revista de Metalurgia
0034-8589 Revista de Neumologia y Cirugia de Torax
0034-8597 Revista de Neuro-Psiquiatria
0034-8600 Revista de Nutricion y Aterosclerosis
0034-8619 Revista de Obras Publicas
0034-8627 Revista de Obras Sanitarias de la Nacion
0034-8635 Revista de Occidente
0034-8643 Revista de Otorrinolaringologia *changed to* Revista de Otorrinolaringologia y Cirugia de Cabeza y Cuello
0034-8651 Revista de Pedagogia†
0034-866X Revista de Tecnologia Educativa
0034-8678 Revista de Pedagogie
0034-8686 Revista de Planeacion y Desarrollo
0034-8694 Revista de Planificacion†
0034-8708 Revista de Plasticos Modernos
0034-8732 Revista de Prevencion
0034-8740 Revista de Psicoanalisis
0034-8759 Revista de Psihologie
0034-8767 Revista de Psiquiatria Dinamica
0034-8775 Revista de Publicaciones Navales
0034-8783 Revista de Referate in Bibliologie
0034-8791 Filosofie-Logica; Revista de Referate, Recenzii si Sinteze†
0034-8805 Istorie- Etnografie Revista de Referate, Recenzii si Sinteze†
0034-8813 Lingvistica-Filologie; Revista de Referate, Recenzii si Sinzeze†
0034-8821 Psihologie; Revista de Referate Recenzii si Sinteze†
0034-883X Sociologie; Revista de Referate Recenzii si Sinteze†
0034-8848 Stiinte Economice; Revista de Referate, Recenzii si Sinteze†
0034-8856 Stiinte Juridice; Revista de Referate, Recenzii si Sinteze†
0034-8864 Teoria si Istoria Literaturii si Artei; Revista de Referate, Recenzii si Sinteze†
0034-8872 Revista de Resumenes†
0034-8880 Revista de Revistas
0034-8899 Revista de Sanidad e Higiene Publica
0034-8902 Revista de Santander
0034-8910 Revista de Saude Publica
0034-8937 Revista de Servicio Social
0034-8961 Revista de Telecomunicacion
0034-897X Revista de Trabajo
0034-8988 Revista de Trabajo
0034-8996 Revista de Urologia†
0034-9003 Costa Rica. Archivo Nacional. Revista
0034-902X Circulo Odontologico del Sur. Revista†
0034-9046 Revista del Ejercito
0034-9054 Revista del Ejercito y Armada
0034-9070 Revista del Hogar
0034-9089 I D I E M Revista†
0034-9100 Revista del Pacifico†
0034-9119 Revista del Suboficial
0034-9127 Czechoslovak Glass Review *changed to* Glass Review
0034-9135 Rivista dell'Informazione
0034-9143 Revista Dental de Chile
0034-9178 Revista Diesel†
0034-9186 Diners
0034-9194 Revista Diplomatica e Internacional
0034-9208 Revista do Ar
0034-9216 Sao Paulo (City) Arquivo Municipal. Revista
0034-9224 Revista do Comercio de Cafe
0034-9240 Revista do Servico Publico
0034-9259 Revista dos Criadores
0034-9267 Revista dos Transportes†
0034-9275 Revista dos Tribunais
0034-9283 Revista Economica
0034-9291 Revista Economica†
0034-9305 Revista Ecuatoriana de Educacion†
0034-9313 Revista Ecuatoriana de Medicina y Ciencias Biologicas
0034-933X Sol
0034-9356 Revista Espanola de Anestesiologia y Reanimacion
0034-9372 Revista Espanola de Derecho Canonico
0034-9380 Revista Espanola de Derecho Internacional
0034-9399 Revista Espanola de Derecho Militar
0034-9402 Revista Espanola de Fisiologia
0034-9410 Revista Espanola de Gerontologia *changed to* Revista Espanola de Geriatria y Gerontologia

0034-9429 Revista Espanola de la Opinion Publica *see* 0210-5233
0034-9437 Revista Espanola de las Enfermedades del Aparato Digestivo
0034-9445 Revista Espanola de Obstetricia y Ginecologia
0034-9453 Revista Espanola de Oto-Neuro-Oftalmologia y Neurocirugia
0034-9461 Revista Espanola de Pedagogia
0034-947X Revista Espanola de Pediatria
0034-9496 Revista Farmaceutica
0034-950X Revista Ferroviaria
0034-9526 Revista Finlay†
0034-9534 Revista Fiscal e de Legislacao de Fazenda†
0034-9542 Revista Gaucha de Odontologia
0034-9550 Revista Genealogica Latina
0034-9569 Revista General de Marina
0034-9577 Revista Geografica de Valparaiso
0034-9585 Revista Goiana de Medicina
0034-9593 Revista Hispanica Moderna
0034-9607 Revista I M C Y C
0034-9615 Revista Iberica de Endocrinologia†
0034-9623 Revista Iberica de Parasitologia
0034-9631 Revista Iberoamericana
0034-964X Revista Iberoamericana de Seguridad Social†
0034-9658 Revista I B Y S†
0034-9666 Revista Imposto Fiscal
0034-9690 Revista Interamericana de Psicologia
0034-9704 Revista Interamericana de Radiologia
0034-9712 Revista Internacional de Sociologia
0034-9720 Revista Internacional y Diplomatica
0034-9739 Revista Juridica
0034-9747 Revista Juridica de Buenos Aires†
0034-9771 Revista Latinoamericana de Microbiologia
0034-9798 Revista Latinoamericana de Siderurgia *changed to* Siderurgia Latinoamericana
0034-9801 Revista Latinoamericana de Sociologia†
0034-981X Revista Literaria Azor
0034-9828 Cenit
0034-9844 Manana
0034-9852 Revista Manizales
0034-9860 Revista Maritima Brasileira
0034-9887 Revista Medica de Chile
0034-9909 Revista Medica de Costa Rica
0034-9917 Revista Medica de Valparaiso
0034-9925 Revista Medica del Hospital General de Mexico S.S.A.
0034-9933 Revista Medica del Paraguay
0034-9941 Revista Medica do Estado da Guanabara *see* 0100-0195
0034-995X Revista Medicala
0034-9976 Revista Mexicana de Ciencia Politica *see* 0185-1918
0034-9984 Revista Mexicana de Cirugia, Ginecologia y Cancer
0035-001X Revista Mexicana de Fisica
0035-0028 Revista Mexicana de Ingenieria y Arquitectura†
0035-0044 Revista Mexicana de la Propiedad Industrial y Artistica
0035-0079 Revista Mexicana de Psicologia†
0035-0087 Revista Mexicana de Sociologia
0035-0109 Revista Militar†
0035-0117 Revista Militar
0035-0125 Revista Militar Brasileira
0035-0133 Revista Militar
0035-0141 Revista Militar del Peru
0035-015X Revista Militar y Naval†
0035-0168 Revista Minelor *changed to* Mine, Petrol si Gaze
0035-0176 Revista Mineria, Geologia y Mineralogia
0035-0184 Revista Municipal†
0035-0192 Revista Musical Chilena
0035-0206 Revista Muzeelor *changed to* Revista Muzeelor si Monumentelor. Muzee
0035-0214 Revista Nacional da Pesca
0035-0222 Revista Nacional de Agricultura
0035-0257 Revista Odontologica *see* 0325-1071
0035-0265 Revista Odontologica de Concepcion†
0035-0273 Revista Odontologica de Merida *changed to* Universidad de Los Andes. Facultad de Odontologia. Revista
0035-0281 Revista Odontologica de Puerto Rico
0035-029X Revista Padurilor-Industria Lemnului-Celuloza si Hirtie *changed to* Industria Lemnului
0035-029X Revista Padurilor-Industria Lemnului-Celuloza si Hirtie *changed to* Revista Padurilor-Industria Lemnului, Celuloza si Hirtie. Celuloza si Hirtie
0035-029X Revista Padurilor-Industria Lemnului, Celuloza si Hirtie *changed to* Revista Padurilor
0035-0303 Revista para Parvulos y Principiantes†
0035-0311 Revista para Uniones de Adultos *changed to* Accion
0035-032X Revista para Uniones de Intermedios *changed to* Ahora
0035-0338 Revista para Jovenes *changed to* Adelante
0035-0346 Revista para Uniones de Primarios†
0035-0354 Revista Paraguaya de Sociologia
0035-0362 Revista Paulista de Medicina
0035-0370 Revista Peruana de Derecho Internacional
0035-0389 Revista Portuguesa de Ciencias Veterinarias
0035-0397 Revista Portuguesa de Estomatologia e Cirurgia Maxilo-Facial
0035-0419 Revista Portuguesa de Quimica
0035-0427 Revista Referativo de la Construccion *changed to* Servicio Referativo de la Construccion
0035-0435 Revista Romana de Drept
0035-0443 Revista Rotaria
0035-0451 Revista Signos de Valparaiso
0035-046X Revista Sindical de Estadistica
0035-0478 Sur
0035-0486 Revista Tamaulipas
0035-0516 Revista Telegrafica Electronica
0035-0524 Revista Textil
0035-0532 Revista Transporturilor *changed to* Revista Transporturi Auto, Navale si Aeriene
0035-0567 Rivista Veneta†
0035-0575 Revista Venezolana de Folklore†
0035-0583 Revista Venezolana de Sanidad y Asistencia Social
0035-0591 Revista Venezolana de Urologia
0035-0605 Revista do Livro†
0035-0621 Revolution Africaine
0035-0656 Revue "A" /Tijdschrift "A" *see* 0771-1107
0035-0672 Revue Administrative
0035-0699 Revue Algerienne des Sciences Juridiques, Politiques et Economiques *changed to* Revue Algerienne des Sciences Juridiques, Economiques et Politiques
0035-0702 Revue Algologique *see* 0181-1568
0035-0710 Revue Analytique d'Education Physique et de Sport†
0035-0729 Revue
0035-0737 Revue Archeologique
0035-0745 Revue Archeologique de l'Est et du Centre-Est
0035-0753 Revue Archeologique du Centre *see* 0220-6617
0035-077X Revue Belge d'Archeologie et d'Histoire de l'Art
0035-0788 Revue Belge de Droit International
0035-0818 Revue Belge de Philologie et d'Historie
0035-0826 Revue Belge de Psychologie et de Pedagogie
0035-0834 Revue Belge de Securite Sociale
0035-0850 Revue Belge des Vins & Spiritueux
0035-0869 Revue Belge d'Histoire Contemporaire
0035-0877 Revue Belge d'Histoire Militaire
0035-0885 Revue Belge d'Homoeopathie
0035-0893 Revue Benedictine
0035-0907 Revue Biblique
0035-0915 Revue Canadienne de Biologie *changed to* Experimental Biologie
0035-0931 Revue Congolaise des Sciences Humaines†
0035-0958 Revue Critique de Droit International Prive
0035-0966 Revue Critique de Jurisprudence Belge
0035-0974 Revue d'Allemagne *changed to* Revue d'Allemagne et des Pays de Langue Allemande
0035-0990 Revue d'Ascetique et de Mystique *changed to* Revue d'Histoire de la Spiritualite
0035-1008 Revue d'Auvergne
0035-1016 Revue de Belles-Lettres
0035-1024 Revue de Bio-Mathematique
0035-1032 Revue de Chimie Minerale
0035-1040 Revue de Chirurgie Orthopedique et Reparatrice de l'Appareil Moteur
0035-1059 Revue de Comminges
0035-1067 Revue de Cytologie et de Biologie Vegetales *see* 0181-7582
0035-1075 Defense Nationale
0035-1083 Revue de Droit Intellectuel l'Ingenieur-Conseil
0035-1091 Revue de Droit International de Sciences Diplomatiques et Politiques
0035-1105 Revue de Droit International et de Droit Compare
0035-1113 Revue de Droit Social
0035-1121 Revue de Geographie Alpine
0035-113X Revue de Geographie de Lyon
0035-1148 Revue de Geographie de Montreal *see* 0705-7199
0035-1156 Revue de Geographie du Maroc
0035-1164 Revue de Geographie Physique et de Geologie Dynamique *see* 0241-1407
0035-1172 Revue de Kinesitherapie *see* 0302-427X
0035-1199 Revue de la Cooperation Scolaire†
0035-1210 Revue de la France Libre
0035-1237 Revue de la Police Nationale
0035-1245 Revue de la Presse Arabe
0035-1253 Revue de la Protection†
0035-1261 Revue de la Securite
0035-127X Revue de la Soudure
0035-1288 Revue de l'Agenais
0035-1296 Revue de l'Agriculture
0035-130X Revue de l'Alcoolisme
0035-1318 Revue de l'Aluminium†
0035-1326 Revue de l'Art
0035-1334 Revue de Laryngologie - Otologie - Rhinologie
0035-1342 Revue de l'Avranchin et du Pays de Granville
0035-1350 Revue de l'Economie du Centre-Est
0035-1369 Revue de l'Economie Meridionale
0035-1377 Revue de l'Education Physique
0035-1385 Revue de l'Embouteillage et des Industries Connexes *changed to* Conditionnement des Liquides-Embouteillage
0035-1393 Revue de l'Enseignement Philosophique
0035-1407 Revue de l'Enseignement Superieur
0035-1415 Revue de l'Est *changed to* Revue d'Etudes Comparatives Est-Ouest.
0035-1423 Revue de l'Histoire des Religions
0035-1431 Revue de l'Industrie Minerale *see* 0302-2129
0035-144X Revue de l'Infirmiere et de l'Assistante Sociale *changed to* Revue de l'Infirmiere
0035-1458 Revue de Linguistique Romane
0035-1466 Revue de Litterature Comparee
0035-1474 Revue de l'Occident Musulman et de la Mediterranee
0035-1482 Revue de Madagascar†
0035-1490 Flair
0035-1504 Revue de Mathematiques Speciales
0035-1512 Revue de Medecine†
0035-1520 Revue de Medecine Aeronautique et Spatiale *changed to* Medecine Aeronautique et Spatiale - Medecine Subaquatique et Hyperbare
0035-1539 Revue de Medecine Moderne
0035-1547 Revue de Medecine Psychosomatique
0035-1555 Revue de Medecine Veterinaire
0035-1563 Revue de Metallurgie *changed to* Revue de Metallurgie. Cahiers d'Information Techniques
0035-1571 Revue de Metaphysique et de Morale
0035-158X Revue de Metrologie Pratique et Legale
0035-1598 Revue de Micropaleontologie
0035-1601 Revue de Musicologie
0035-161X Revue de Neuropsychiatrie de l'Ouest
0035-1628 Revue de Neuropsychiatrie Infantile et d'Hygiene Mentale de l'Enfance *changed to* Neuropsychiatrie de l'Enfance et de l'Adolescence
0035-1636 Revue de Pathologie Comparee†
0035-1644 Revue de Pediatrie
0035-1652 Revue de Philologie, de Litterature et d'Histoire Anciennes
0035-1660 Revue de Phonetique Appliquee
0035-1679 Revue de Physiologie Subaquatique et Medecine Hyperbare†
0035-1687 Revue de Physique Appliquee
0035-1709 Revue de Psychologie Appliquee
0035-1725 Revue de Qumran
0035-1733 Revue de Science Criminelle et de Droit Penal Compare
0035-1741 Revue de Science Financiere†
0035-175X Revue de Statistique Appliquee
0035-1768 Revue de Stomatologie et de Chirurgie Maxillo-Faciale
0035-1776 Revue de Synthese
0035-1784 Revue de Theologie et de Philosophie
0035-1792 Revue de Tuberculose et de Pneumologie *see* 0301-0279
0035-1806 Revue de Zoologie Agricole et de Pathologie Vegetale†
0035-1814 Revue de Zoologie et de Botanique Africaines *changed to* Revue de Zoologie Africaine
0035-1822 Revue d'Ecologie et de Biologie du Sol
0035-1849 Revue d'Egyptologie†
0035-1865 Revue d'Elevage et de Medecine Veterinaire des Pays Tropicaux
0035-1873 Lebanese Dental Journal†
0035-1881 Revue der Reclame *changed to* Kontekst
0035-1903 Revue des Agents de Police *changed to* Flute
0035-1911 Revue des Applications de l'Electricite *see* 0035-2926
0035-192X Revue des Assureurs-Vie *see* 0380-3147
0035-1938 Revue des Caisses d'Epargne
0035-1954 Revue des Corps de Sante des Armees *see* 0300-4937
0035-1962 Revue des Deux Mondes *changed to* Revue de Deux Mondes: Litterature, Histoire, Arts et Sciences
0035-1970 Revue des Disques et de la Haute Fidelite *changed to* Hifi Musique. Revue des Disques et de la Haute Fidelite
0035-1989 Revue des Droits de l'Homme†
0035-1997 Revue des Ecoles
0035-2004 Revue des Etudes Anciennes
0035-2012 Revue des Etudes Augustiniennes
0035-2020 Revue des Etudes Cooperatives *changed to* Revue des Etudes Cooperatives, Mutualistes et Associatives
0035-2039 Revue des Etudes Grecques
0035-2047 Revue des Etudes Italiennes
0035-2055 Revue des Etudes Juives
0035-2063 Revue des Etudes Sud-Est Europeennes
0035-2071 Revue des Fermentations et des Industries Alimentaires *changed to* Belgian Journal of Food Chemistry and Biotechnology
0035-208X Revue des Finances Communales
0035-2098 Revue des Hotesses†
0035-2101 Offrir *changed to* Offrir International
0035-211X Revue des Langues Vivantes†
0035-2128 Revue des Lettres
0035-2136 Revue des Lettres Modernes
0035-2144 Revue des Materiaux de Construction et de Travaux Publics *see* 0397-006X
0035-2152 Revue des P T T de France *changed to* Revue des Postes et Telecommunications de France
0035-2160 Revue des Questions Scientifiques
0035-2179 Cahiers des Ingenieurs Agronomes
0035-2187 Revue des Sciences Economiques†

0035-2195 Revue des Sciences Humaines
0035-2209 Revue des Sciences Philosophiques et Theologiques
0035-2217 Revue des Sciences Religieuses
0035-2241 Revue des Societes Savantes de Haute Normandie
0035-225X Revue des Tabacs
0035-2284 Revue Desjardins
0035-2292 Revue d'Esthetique
0035-2306 Revue d'Etudes Militaires, Aeriennes et Navales
0035-2314 Revue d'Histoire de la Deuxieme Guerre Mondiale
0035-2322 Revue d'Histoire de la Gaspesie *see* 0227-1370
0035-2330 Revue d'Histoire de la Medecine Hebraique
0035-2349 Revue d'Histoire de la Pharmacie
0035-2357 Revue d'Histoire de l'Amerique Francaise
0035-2365 Revue d'Histoire Diplomatique
0035-2373 Revue d'Histoire du Theatre
0035-2381 Revue d'Histoire Ecclesiastique
0035-239X Revue d'Histoire Economique et Sociale *see* 0752-5702
0035-2403 Revue d'Histoire et de Philosophie Religieuses
0035-2411 Revue d'Histoire Litteraire de la France
0035-242X Revue d'Hygiene du Travail†
0035-2438 Revue d'Epidemiologie, Medecine Sociale et Sante Publique *see* 0398-7620
0035-2446 Revue d'Hygiene et Medecine Scolaire et Universitaire†
0035-2462 Revue d'Informatique Medicale†
0035-2470 Revue d'Odonto-Stomatologie du Midi de la France
0035-2497 Revue d'Oto-Neuro-Ophtalmologie†
0035-2500 Revue du Bois Detail†
0035-2519 Revue du Bois et de ses Applications
0035-2527 Revue du Bouton†
0035-2535 Revue du Cethedec *see* 0765-0019
0035-2543 Revue du Cinema International & TV†
0035-2551 Revue du Clerge Africain†
0035-256X Revue du Droit du Travail†
0035-2578 Revue du Droit Public et de la Science Politique en France et a l'Etranger
0035-2586 Revue du Genie Militaire *changed to* Bulletin Technique du Genie (1960)
0035-2594 Revue du Jouet
0035-2608 Revue du Louvre et des Musees de France
0035-2616 Revue du Marche Commun
0035-2624 Revue du Nord
0035-2632 Revue du Notariat
0035-2640 Revue du Praticien
0035-2659 Revue du Rhumatisme et des Maladies Osteoarticulaires
0035-2667 Revue du Rouergue
0035-2675 Revue du Son *changed to* Nouvelle Revue du Son
0035-2683 Asia Quarterly†
0035-2705 Revue du Travail
0035-2713 Revue du Tresor
0035-273X Revue du Vin de France
0035-2748 Revue du Vivarais
0035-2756 Acta Technica Belgica. Revue E: Electricite Courants Forts. Electrotechnique Generale et ses Applications
0035-2764 Revue Economique
0035-2772 Revue Economique et Sociale
0035-2780 Revue Economique Francaise
0035-2799 Revue Economique Franco Suisse
0035-2802 Revue Europeenne des Papiers Cartons-Complexes†
0035-2810 Revue Fiscale *changed to* Journal de Droit Fiscal
0035-2829 Revue Forestiere Francaise
0035-2845 Revue Francaise d'Allergologie *changed to* Revue Francaise d'Allergologie et Immunologie Clinique
0035-2861 Revue Francaise de Bridge
0035-287X Revue Francaise de Droit Aerien
0035-2896 Revue Francaise de Gerontologie *changed to* Revue de Geriatrie
0035-290X Revue Francaise de Gynecologie et d'Obstetrique
0035-2918 Revue Francaise de l'Agriculture†
0035-2926 Revue Francaise de l'Electricite†
0035-2934 Revue Francaise de l'Energie *see* 0303-240X
0035-2942 Revue Francaise de Psychanalyse
0035-2950 Revue Francaise de Science Politique
0035-2969 Revue Francaise de Sociologie
0035-2977 Revue Francaise de Transfusion *see* 0338-4535
0035-2985 Revue Francaise des Affaires Sociales
0035-2993 Revue Francaise des Bijoutiers Horlogers *changed to* Bijoutier
0035-3000 Revue Francaise des Corps Gras
0035-3019 Revue Europeenne d'Etudes Cliniques et Biologiques *see* 0753-3322
0035-3027 Revue Francaise d'Etudes Politiques Africaines
0035-3035 Revue Francaise d'Informatique et de Recherche Operationnelle *see* 0399-0516
0035-3035 Revue Francaise d'Informatique et de Recherche Operationnelle *see* 0399-0559
0035-3035 Revue Francaise d'Informatique et de Recherche Operationnelle *see* 0399-0524
0035-3035 Revue Francaise d'Informatique et de Recherche Operationnelle *see* 0399-0532
0035-3035 Revue Francaise d'Informatique et de Recherche Operationnelle *see* 0399-0540
0035-3043 Revue Francaise d'Odonto-Stomatologie *see* 0300-9815
0035-3078 Revue Generale Belge *changed to* Revue Generale pour l'Humaniste des Temps Nouveaux
0035-3086 Revue Generale de Droit
0035-3094 Revue Generale de Droit International Public
0035-3108 Revue Generale de l'Air et de l'Espace†
0035-3116 Revue Generale de l'Electricite
0035-3124 Revue Generale de l'Enseignement des Deficients Auditifs
0035-3132 Revue Generale de l'Etancheite et de l'Isolation
0035-3140 Revue Generale de l'Hotellerie, de la Gastronomie et du Tourisme
0035-3159 Revue Generale de Thermique
0035-3167 Revue Generale des Assurances Terrestres
0035-3175 Revue Generale des Caoutchoucs et Plastiques
0035-3183 Revue Generale des Chemins de Fer
0035-3191 Revue Generale des Routes et des Aerodromes
0035-3205 Revue Generale du Froid
0035-3213 Revue Geographique de l'Est
0035-3221 Revue Geographique des Pyrenees et du Sud-Ouest
0035-323X Revue Graphique-Imprivaria
0035-3248 Acta Technica Belgica. Revue H F: Electricite Courants Faibles. Electronique Telecommunications
0035-3256 Revue Hellenique de Droit International
0035-3264 Revue Historique
0035-3272 Revue Historique Ardennaise
0035-3280 Revue Historique de Droit Francais et Etranger
0035-3299 Revue Historique des Armees
0035-3302 Revue Horticole
0035-3310 Revue Independante
0035-3329 Revue Internationale de Criminologie et de Police Technique†
0035-3337 Revue Internationale de Droit Compare
0035-337X Revue Internationale de la Propriete Industrielle et Artistique
0035-3396 Revue Internationale de Police Criminelle
0035-340X Revue Internationale de Psychologie Appliquee†
0035-3418 Comptabilite Economique Universelle-Scientifique
0035-3434 Revue Internationale des Hautes Temperatures et des Refractaires
0035-3442 Revue Internationale des Industries Agricoles. Bulletin Analytique†
0035-3450 Revue Internationale des Produits Tropicaux
0035-3469 Revue Internationale des Services de Sante des Armees de Terre, de Mer et de l'Air
0035-3477 Revue Internationale des Tabacs
0035-3485 Revue Internationale d'Ethnopsychologie Normale et Pathologique†
0035-3493 Revue Internationale d'Oceanographie Medicale
0035-3515 Revue Internationale du Droit d'Auteur
0035-3531 Revue Internationale du Trachome et des Maladies Oculaires des Pays Tropicaux et Sub Tropicaux *see* 0301-5017
0035-354X International Review for Business Education
0035-3566 Revue Juridique et Economique de Sud-Quest *changed to* Revue Economique du Sud-Ouest
0035-3582 Revue de l'Air Liquide†
0035-3590 Revue Laitiere Francaise
0035-3604 Revue Legale
0035-3620 Revue Mabillon
0035-3639 Revue Medicale de Bruxelles
0035-3655 Revue Medicale de la Suisse Romande
0035-3663 Revue Medicale de Liege
0035-368X Revue Militaire Suisse
0035-3698 Revue Moderne
0035-371X Revue-Moteur *changed to* Moteur et Equipement
0035-3728 Revue Municipale
0035-3736 Revue Musicale
0035-3744 Revue Musicale de Suisse Romande
0035-3752 Revue Nationale de le Chasse
0035-3779 Revue Neuchateloise *changed to* Nouvelle Revue Neuchateloise
0035-3787 Revue Neurologique
0035-3795 R N D
0035-3809 Revue Nouvelle
0035-3825 Revue Penitentiaire et de Droit Penal
0035-3833 Revue Philosophique de la France et de l'Etranger
0035-3841 Revue Philosophique de Louvain
0035-385X Revue Politique et Parlementaire
0035-3868 Revue Pratique du Froid *changed to* Journal R P F
0035-3876 Revue Pratique des Questions Commerciales et Economiques†
0035-3884 Societe Calviniste de France. Revue Reformee
0035-3892 Revue Roumaine des Sciences Sociales. Serie de Psychologie
0035-3906 Revue Romane
0035-3914 Revue Roumaine de Biologie. Serie Botanique *changed to* Revue Roumaine de Biologie. Serie Biologie Vegetale
0035-3922 Revue Roumaine de Biologie. Serie Zoologie *changed to* Revue Roumaine de Biologie. Serie Biologie Animale
0035-3930 Revue Roumaine de Chimie
0035-3957 Revue Roumaine de Linguistique
0035-3965 Revue Roumaine de Mathematiques Pures et Appliquees
0035-3973 Revue Roumaine de Medecine Interne *changed to* Revue Roumaine de Medecine. Serie Medecine Interne
0035-3981 Revue Roumaine de Neurologie et Psychiatrie *see* 0301-7303
0035-399X Revue Roumaine de Physiologie *changed to* Revue Roumaine de Morphologie, d'Embryologie et de Physiologie. Serie Physiologie
0035-4007 Revue Roumaine de Morphologie, d'Embryologie et de Physiologie. Serie Morphologie et Embryologie
0035-4015 Revue Roumaine d'Endocrinologie *changed to* Revue Roumaine de Medecine. Serie Endocrinologie
0035-4023 Revue Roumaine des Sciences Sociales. Serie de Sciences Juridiques
0035-4031 Revue Roumaine des Sciences Sociales. Serie de Philosophie et de Logique
0035-404X Revue Roumaine des Sciences Sociales. Serie de Sciences Economiques
0035-4066 Revue Roumaine des Sciences Techniques. Serie Electrotechnique et Energetique
0035-4074 Revue Roumaine des Sciences Techniques. Serie de Mecanique Appliquee
0035-4082 Revue Roumaine d'Inframicrobiologie *changed to* Revue Roumaine de Medecine. Serie Virologie
0035-4090 Revue Roumaine de Physique
0035-4104 Revue Scolaire†
0035-4112 Revue Senegalaise de Droit
0035-4120 Servir
0035-4139 Revue Socialiste
0035-4147 Revue Stomato-Odontologique du Nord de la France
0035-4163 Revue Suisse de Numismatique
0035-4171 Revue Suisse de Viticulture et Arboriculture *changed to* Revue Suisse de Viticulture, Arboriculture et Horticulture
0035-418X Revue Suisse de Zoologie
0035-4198 Revue Suisse des Marches Agricoles *changed to* Schweizerischer Bauernverband. Information
0035-4201 Revue Suisse du Trafic Routier†
0035-421X Revue Syndicale Suisse
0035-4228 Revue Technique des Hotels, Restaurants, Bars, Brasseries, Limonadiers, Tabacs, Habitats Collectifs
0035-4252 Revue de la Technique Europeenne *changed to* Indicateur Industriel
0035-4260 Revue Technique Luxembourgeoise
0035-4279 Revue Technique Thomson - C S F
0035-4287 Revue Textile Melliand†
0035-4295 Revue Thomiste
0035-4317 Revue Trimestrielle de Droit Europeen
0035-4325 Revue Trimestrielle de Droit Sanitaire et Social
0035-4333 Revue Tunisienne des Sciences Sociales
0035-4341 Revue Universelle des Mines, de la Metallurgie, de la Mecanique, des Travaux Publics, des Sciences et des Arts Appliques a l'Industrie†
0035-435X Revue Universitaire de Science Morale *changed to* Reseaux
0035-4376 Revues Medicales Normandes†
0035-4384 Revue de Droit Penal et de Criminologie
0035-4406 Revuo Orienta
0035-4422 Rexevents
0035-4449 Rheinhessische Wirtschaft
0035-4457 Rheinisch-Westfaelische Boerse zu Duesseldorf. Amtliches Kursblatt
0035-4465 Rheinisch-Westfaelisches Institut fuer Wirtschaftsforschung. Mitteilungen
0035-4473 Rheinische Vierteljahrsblaetter
0035-4481 Rheinisches Aerzteblatt
0035-449X Rheinisches Museum fuer Philologie
0035-4511 Rheologica Acta
0035-452X Rheology Abstracts
0035-4538 Rheology Bulletin
0035-4546 Rheumatism
0035-4554 Rheumatologia, Balneologia, Allergologia
0035-4562 Rhode Island Beverage Journal
0035-4570 Rhode Island Business Quarterly *see* 8755-5123
0035-4589 Rhode Island College Alumni Association. Review *changed to* Perspectives (Providence)
0035-4597 Rhode Island. Department of State Library Services. Newsletter
0035-4600 Rhode Island. Department of Labor and Employment Security. Employment Bulletin *changed to* Rhode Island. Department of Employment Security. Employment Bulletin
0035-4619 Rhode Island History
0035-4635 Rhode Island Resources†

ISSN INDEX 1297

0035-4643 Rhode Island State Dental Society. Journal *changed to* Rhode Island Dental Association. Journal
0035-466X Rhodeo
0035-4678 Rhodes Newsletter *changed to* Rhodes Review
0035-4686 Rhodesia Agricultural Journal *changed to* Zimbabwe Agricultural Journal
0035-4694 Rhodesia and World Report
0035-4708 Rhodesia Calls *changed to* Africa Calls From Zimbabwe
0035-4716 Zimbabwe. National Archives. Occasional Papers
0035-4724 Zimbabwe Railways Magazine *changed to* Railroader
0035-4732 Rhodesia Science News *changed to* Zimbabwe Science News
0035-4759 Rhodesian Commentary *see* 0304-7628
0035-4775 Rhodesian Farmer *changed to* Farmer
0035-4791 Rhodesian Industrialist
0035-4805 Rhodesian Insurance Review *changed to* Insurance Review
0035-4813 Rhodesia, Zambia and Malawi Journal of Agricultural Research *changed to* Zimbabwe Journal of Agricultural Research
0035-4821 Rhodesian Journal of Economics
0035-483X Rhodesia Law Journal *changed to* Zimbabwe Law Journal
0035-4848 Rhodesian Librarian *changed to* Zimbabwe Librarian
0035-4864 Rhodesian Property & Finance
0035-4872 Rhodesian Railway Review *changed to* Railway Review
0035-4880 Rhodesian Tobacco Journal *changed to* Zimbabwe Tobacco Today
0035-4899 Rhodesian Viewpoint†
0035-4902 Rhodora
0035-4929 Rhumatologie†
0035-4953 Ribarski List
0035-4961 Rice Journal
0035-497X Rice Review *changed to* Farmer
0035-4988 Rice University Review†
0035-4996 Rice University Studies†
0035-5011 Ricerca Scientifica
0035-502X Ricerche Bibliche e Religiose†
0035-5038 Ricerche di Matematica
0035-5046 Ricerche Didattiche
0035-5054 Ricerche Economiche
0035-5062 Ricerche Filosofiche†
0035-5070 Ricerche Storiche (Reggio Emilia)
0035-5089 Richard Cotten's Conservative Viewpoint
0035-5097 Richesses de France
0035-5100 Greater Richmond Chamber of Commerce. Research Bulletin†
0035-5119 Richmond County History
0035-5135 Richting
0035-5143 Ridge News†
0035-516X Riding
0035-5186 Ridotto
0035-5194 Riechstoffe, Aromen, Koerperpflegemittel *see* 0341-440X
0035-5216 Rifle Magazine *see* 0162-3583
0035-5224 Rifleman
0035-5240 Riforma della Scuola
0035-5259 Riforma Medica
0035-5267 Rig
0035-5283 Rights
0035-5291 Rights & Reviews†
0035-5305 Rehabilitation
0035-5313 Rijk der Vrouw
0035-533X Rijksuniversiteit te Gent. Faculteit Landbouwwetenschappen. Mededelingen
0035-5348 Rijksuniversiteit te Groningen. Mededelingenblad *changed to* Universiteitskrant Groningen
0035-5356 St. Paul's Economic Review
0035-5364 Sweden.Kungliga Biblioteket. Notiser Fraan Riksbibliotekarien†
0035-5372 Rimba Indonesia
0035-5380 Rinascita
0035-5402 Rinderproduktion *see* 0138-3337
0035-5410 Ring
0035-5429 Ring
0035-5437 Ring-Rund†
0035-5445 Ringdoc Profile Booklets
0035-5453 Ringing World
0035-5461 Ringling Museums Newsletter *see* 0731-7956
0035-5488 Folia Odontologica Practica
0035-550X Journal of Clinical Pediatrics
0035-5518 Ripley's Believe It or Not
0035-5526 Ripon Forum
0035-5534 Ripresa Nazionale
0035-5550 Rise Hvezd
0035-5569 Risiko *changed to* Voetnoot
0035-5585 Risk†
0035-5593 Risk Management
0035-5607 Risorgimento
0035-5615 Risparmio
0035-5623 Risveglio del Molise e del Mezzogiorno
0035-5631 Ritenour School District News *changed to* Ritenour News
0035-564X Intercom (Overland) *changed to* Ritenour Reporter
0035-5682 Riverlander *changed to* Riverlander Notes
0035-5690 Riverside County Farm and Agricultural Business News *changed to* Riverside County Agriculture
0035-5704 Riverside Quarterly†
0035-5720 Riviere
0035-5739 Rivista Abruzzese
0035-5747 Rivista Aeronautica - Missilistica *see* 0391-6162
0035-5755 Rivista Agricola dell'O C D E†
0035-5763 Rivista Amministrativa della Repubblica Italiana
0035-5771 Rivista Araldica
0035-5801 Rivista Chirurgia Pediatrica†
0035-581X Rivista Critica di Storia della Filosofia *changed to* Rivista di Storia della Filosofia
0035-5836 Rivista degli Infortuni e delle Malattie Professionali
0035-5852 La Rivista dei Combustibili
0035-5860 Rivista del Catasto e dei Servizi Tecnici Erariali
0035-5879 Rivista del Cinematografo†
0035-5887 Rivista del Diritto Commerciale e del Diritto Generale delle Obbligazioni
0035-5895 Rivista del Diritto della Navigazione†
0035-5917 Rivista del Nuovo Cimento
0035-5925 Rivista del Porto di Napoli
0035-595X Rivista della Guardia di Finanza
0035-5968 Rivista della Ortoflorofrutticoltura Italiana
0035-5976 Rivista della Proprieta' Industriale e della Concorrenza†
0035-5984 Rivista della Proprieta Intellettuale Ed Industriale†
0035-5992 Rivista della Strada *see* 0393-8077
0035-600X Consacrazione e Servizio
0035-6018 Rivista delle Societa
0035-6026 Rivista di Agricoltura Subtropicale e Tropicale
0035-6034 Rivista di Agronomia
0035-6042 Rivista di Archeologia Cristiana
0035-6050 Rivista di Biologia
0035-6069 Rivista di Chirurgia Pediatrica†
0035-6077 Rivista di Clinica Pediatrica *see* 0026-4946
0035-6085 Rivista di Cultura Classica e Medioevale
0035-6093 Rivista di Diritto Civile
0035-6107 Rivista di Diritto del Lavoro *changed to* Rivista Italiana di Diritto del Lavoro
0035-6115 Rivista di Diritto Economia e Tecnica della Pesca
0035-6123 Rivista di Diritto Europeo
0035-6131 Rivista di Diritto Finanziario e Scienza delle Finanze
0035-614X Rivista di Diritto Industriale
0035-6158 Rivista di Diritto Internazionale
0035-6166 Rivista di Diritto Internazionale e Comparato del Lavoro
0035-6174 Rivista di Diritto Internazionale Privato e Processuale
0035-6182 Rivista di Diritto Processuale
0035-6190 Rivista di Economia Agraria
0035-6204 Rivista di Emoterapia e Immunoematologia
0035-6212 Rivista di Estetica
0035-6220 Rivista di Filologia e di Istruzione Classica
0035-6239 Rivista di Filosofia
0035-6247 Rivista di Filosofia Neoscolastica
0035-6255 Rivista di Gastro-Enterologia
0035-6263 Ingegneria
0035-6271 Rivista di Legislazione Scolastica Comparata†
0035-628X Rivista di Lugano
0035-6298 Universita degli Studi di Parma. Rivista di Matematica
0035-6301 Rivista di Meccanica
0035-631X Rivista di Medicina Aeronautica e Spaziale
0035-6328 Rivista di Meteorologia Aeronautica
0035-6336 Rivista di Neurobiologia
0035-6344 Rivista di Neurologia
0035-6352 Rivista di Neuropsichiatria e Scienze Affini
0035-6360 Rivista di Organizzazione Aziendale†
0035-6379 Rivista di Ostetricia e Ginecologia†
0035-6387 Rivista di Parassitologia
0035-6395 Rivista di Pastorale Liturgica
0035-6409 Rivista di Patologia Clinica e Sperimentale *changed to* Rivista di Patologia e Sperimentazione Clinica
0035-6417 Rivista di Patologia e Clinica
0035-6425 Rivista di Patologia e Clinica della Tubercolosi *see* 0302-4717
0035-6433 Rivista di Patologia Nervosa e Mentale
0035-6441 Rivista di Patologia Vegetale
0035-645X Rivista di Politica Agraria
0035-6468 Rivista di Politica Economica
0035-6476 Rivista di Polizia
0035-6484 Rivista di Psichiatria
0035-6492 Rivista di Psicoanalisi†
0035-6506 Rivista di Psicologia
0035-6514 Rivista di Scienze Preistoriche
0035-6522 Rivista di Servizio Sociale
0035-6530 Rivista di Sociologia†
0035-6549 Rivista di Statistica Applicata
0035-6557 Rivista di Storia della Chiesa in Italia
0035-6565 Rivista di Storia della Medicina†
0035-6573 Rivista di Storia e Letteratura Religiosa
0035-6581 Rivista di Studi Classici
0035-659X Rivista di Studi Crociani
0035-6603 Rivista di Studi Liguri
0035-6611 Rivista di Studi Politici Internazionali
0035-662X Rivista di Suinicoltura
0035-6638 Rivista di Vita Spirituale
0035-6646 Rivista di Zootecnia *changed to* Rivista di Zootecnia e Veterinaria
0035-6654 Rivista Diocesana del Patriarcato di Venezia
0035-6662 Rivista Diocesana Riminì†
0035-6689 Rivista Generale Italiana di Chirurgia
0035-6697 Rivista Geografica Italiana
0035-6700 Rivista Giuridica della Circolazione e dei Trasporti
0035-6719 Rivista Internazionale di Dialogo†
0035-6727 Rivista Internazionale di Filosofia del Diritto
0035-6735 Rivista Internazionale di Filosofia Politica e Sociale e Diritto Comparato†
0035-6743 Rivista Internazionale di Psicologia e Ipnosi
0035-6751 Rivista Internazionale di Scienze Economiche e Commerciali
0035-676X Rivista Internazionale di Scienze Sociali
0035-6778 Rivista Italiana del Petrolio†
0035-6786 Rivista Italiana del Tracoma e di Patologia Oculare Virale Ed Esotica†
0035-6794 Rivista Italiana della Saldatura
0035-6808 Rivista Italiana delle Sostanze Grasse
0035-6816 Impresa
0035-6824 Rivista Italiana di Diritto Sociale
0035-6832 Rivista Italiana di Economia Demografia E Statistica
0035-6840 Rivista Italiana di Ginecologia†
0035-6867 Rivista Italiana di Musicologia
0035-6875 Rivista Italiana di Ornitologia
0035-6883 Rivista Italiana di Paleontologia e Stratigrafia
0035-6905 Rivista Italiana di Stomatologia
0035-6913 Rivista Italiana di Studi Napoleonici
0035-6921 Rivista Italiana d'Igiene
0035-6948 Rivista Italiana Essenze Profumi, Piante Officianali, Aromi, Saponi, Cosmetici, Aerosol†
0035-6956 Rivista Liturgica
0035-6964 Rivista Marittima
0035-6972 Rivista della Citta di Trieste
0035-6980 Rivista Militare
0035-6999 Rivista Militare della Svizzera Italiana
0035-7022 Rivista Penale
0035-7030 Rivista Rosminiana di Filosofia e di Cultura
0035-7049 Rivista Siciliana della Tubercolosi e delle Malattie Respiratorie
0035-7065 Rivista Storica del Mezzogiorno
0035-7073 Rivista Storica Italiana
0035-7081 Rivista Tecnica di Cinematografia
0035-709X Rivista Tributaria
0035-7103 Rivista Trimestrale†
0035-7138 Riv'on l'Inyanei Misim/Quarterly Tax Journal *see* 0334-3065
0035-7146 Rizeni Ekonomiky v Socialistickych Zemich *changed to* Rizeni Ekonomiky
0035-7154 R.L.C.'s Museum Gazette
0035-7162 Australia. Bureau of Statistics. Road Accident Fatalities *changed to* Australia. Bureau of Statistics. Road Traffic Accidents Involving Fatalities, Australia
0035-7170 Road Ahead
0035-7189 Road & Track
0035-7200 Road Apple Review
0035-7219 Road International†
0035-7227 Road Maps of Industry *changed to* Economic Road Maps
0035-7235 Raad och Roen
0035-7243 Road Rider
0035-7251 Road Tar†
0035-726X Road Test/Dune Buggy†
0035-7294 Road Transport and Contracting
0035-7308 Road Transporter *changed to* Road Transporter of Australia
0035-7316 Road Way
0035-7324 Roadrunner *changed to* Wow
0035-7332 Roads and Road Construction
0035-7340 Roads and Streets *see* 0362-0506
0035-7359 Roanoke Historical Society. Journal *changed to* Roanoke Valley Historical Society Journal
0035-7367 Roanoke Review
0035-7375 Roaring Twenties (Seabrook) *see* 0147-6165
0035-7383 Robert Dumm Piano Review†
0035-7391 Robot
0035-7405 Rochester Engineer
0035-7413 Rochester History
0035-743X Rock and Roll Songs *see* 8756-3487
0035-7448 Rock Mechanics *see* 0723-2632
0035-7456 Rock Mechanics Abstracts *see* 0148-9062
0035-7464 Rock Products
0035-7480 Rocket†
0035-7502 Rocketeer *changed to* Rocketeer
0035-7510 Rockhurst Hawk
0035-7529 Rocks and Minerals
0035-7537 Rocks & Minerals in Canada
0035-7553 Rockwell Water Journal
0035-757X Rocky Mountain Druggist *see* 0191-6394
0035-7588 Rocky Mountain Food Dealer
0035-7596 Rocky Mountain Journal of Mathematics
0035-760X Rocky Mountain Medical Journal *see* 0199-7343
0035-7618 Rocky Mountain Mineral Law Review *see* 0148-6489
0035-7626 Rocky Mountain Modern Language Association. Bulletin *see* 0361-1299
0035-7634 Rocky Mountain Social Science Journal *changed to* Social Science Journal

ISSN INDEX

ISSN	Title
0035-7642	Western Association of Africanists. Newsletter
0035-7650	Rocky Mountain Union Farmer
0035-7669	Rocznik Historii Czasopismiennictwa Polskiego *see* 0137-2998
0035-7677	Roczniki Chemii *see* 0137-5083
0035-7685	Roczniki Filozoficzne
0035-7715	Panstwowy Zaklad Higieny. Roczniki
0035-7723	Roczniki Teologiczno-Kanoniczne
0035-7758	Rodeo Sports News *see* 0161-5815
0035-7766	Rodina a Skola
0035-7774	Digest of Science of Labour
0035-7782	Roedovre Avis
0035-7790	Roeh Hacheshbon
0035-7812	Roemische Quartalschrift fuer Christliche Altertumskunde und Kirchengeschichte
0035-7820	Roentgenpraxis
0035-7839	Roester i Radio-TV
0035-7847	Rohm and Haas Reporter
0035-7855	Rohre-Rohrleitungsbau-Rohrleitungstransport *changed to* 3 R - International
0035-7863	Rohstoff-Rundschau
0035-7871	Rolandino†
0035-788X	Roll Call
0035-7898	Roll Sign
0035-7901	Der Roller
0035-791X	Rolling Stone
0035-7928	Rolling Stone of Tampa†
0035-7936	Rollins Sandspur
0035-7944	Rolls-Royce News†
0035-7952	Rolls Royce Owner
0035-7960	Roma e Provincia Attraverso la Statistica
0035-7979	Roman-Zeitung
0035-7995	Romance Notes
0035-8002	Romance Philology
0035-8029	Romania
0035-8037	Revista de Statistica
0035-8045	Romanian Books
0035-8053	Romanian Bulletin
0035-8061	Romanian Engineering
0035-807X	Romanian Foreign Trade
0035-8088	Romanian Review
0035-8096	Rumanian Scientific Abstracts
0035-810X	Romanian Scientific Abstracts. Social Sciences†
0035-8118	Romanic Review
0035-8126	Romanische Forschungen
0035-8142	Romantikk
0035-8150	Rome Report of Business Publication Advertising *changed to* Media Records Report of Business Publication Advertising
0035-8169	Rond de Tafel
0035-8177	Rondom het Boek
0035-8185	Ronzatore
0035-8193	Roofing Contractor
0035-8207	Rooi Rose
0035-8215	Roopa-Lekha
0035-8231	Ropa a Uhlie
0035-824X	Rope News *changed to* Rope Newsletter
0035-8258	Rorinstallatoren *changed to* V V S-Forum
0035-8266	Rosacruz
0035-8274	Rosario de Maria
0035-8282	Il Rosario e la Nuova Pompei
0035-8290	Rosebank Record†
0035-8304	Roseburg Woodsman
0035-8312	Rosenberg Library Bulletin†
0035-8320	Roses and Gold from Our Lady of the Ozarks†
0035-8339	Rosicrucian Digest
0035-8355	Ross Reports Television
0035-8363	Rossica Society of Russian Philately Journal
0035-8371	Rostlinna Vyroba
0035-838X	Rotarian
0035-8401	Rotary
0035-8428	Rote Revue *changed to* Profil
0035-8444	Rothwell Advertiser
0035-8452	Rotor & Wing *see* 0191-6408
0035-8487	Rotterdam - Europoort - Delta
0035-8495	Rotunda
0035-8525	Rough Notes
0035-8533	Round Table
0035-8541	Round-up - Children's Services†
0035-855X	Roundup (El Paso)
0035-8568	Route
0035-8584	Rowing
0035-8606	Royal Air Force College Journal
0035-8614	Royal Air Force News
0035-8630	Royal Air Forces Quarterly†
0035-8649	Royal Arch Mason
0035-8657	Royal Army Chaplains Department. Quarterly Journal *changed to* Great Britain. Royal Army Chaplains' Department. Journal
0035-8665	Royal Army Medical Corps. Journal
0035-8673	Royal Army Pay Corps Journal
0035-8681	Royal Army Veterinary Corps. Journal†
0035-869X	Royal Asiatic Society of Great Britain and Ireland. Journal
0035-8711	Royal Astronomical Society. Monthly Notices
0035-872X	Royal Astronomical Society of Canada. Journal
0035-8738	Royal Astronomical Society. Quarterly Journal
0035-8746	Royal Australian Chemical Institute. Proceedings *see* 0314-4240
0035-8762	Royal Australian Historical Society. Journal
0035-8770	Royal Bank of Canada. Monthly Letter *see* 0229-0243
0035-8789	Royal Central Asian Society. Journal *see* 0306-8374
0035-8797	Royal College of General Practitioners. Journal
0035-8800	Royal College of Physicians and Surgeons of Canada. Annals
0035-8819	Royal College of Physicians of London. Journal
0035-8827	Royal College of Surgeons in Ireland. Journal. *changed to* Irish Colleges of Physicians and Surgeons. Journal
0035-8835	Royal College of Surgeons of Edinburgh. Journal
0035-8843	Royal College of Surgeons of England. Annals
0035-8851	Royal Commonwealth Society Library Notes
0035-886X	Royal Commonwealth Society. Newsletter *changed to* Commonwealth Outlook
0035-8878	Royal Engineers Journal
0035-8894	Royal Entomological Society of London. Transactions *changed to* Ecological Entomology
0035-8908	Royal Gazette
0035-8916	Royal Historical Society of Queensland Bulletin
0035-8924	Royal Horticultural Society Journal *see* 0308-5457
0035-8932	R I B A Journal *changed to* Architect
0035-8940	Royal Institute of Chemistry Reviews *see* 0306-0012
0035-8967	Royal Institution of Naval Architects. Transactions
0035-8975	Royal Irish Academy. Proceedings. Section A: Mathematical, Astronomical and Physical Science *changed to* Royal Irish Academy. Proceedings. Section A: Mathematical and Physical Sciences
0035-8983	Royal Irish Academy. Proceedings. Section B: Biological, Geological and Chemical Sciences
0035-8991	Royal Irish Academy. Proceedings. Section C: Archaeology, Celtic Studies, History, Linguistics and Literature
0035-9009	Royal Meteorological Society. Quarterly Journal
0035-9017	Royal Microscopical Society. Proceedings
0035-9025	Royal Military Police Journal
0035-9033	Royal Naval Medical Service. Journal
0035-9041	Royal Naval Sailing Association Journal
0035-905X	Royal Neighbor
0035-9068	Royal Nepal Economist†
0035-9076	Royal Pioneer
0035-9084	Royal Service
0035-9092	Royal Society International Scientific Information Services. Bulletin†
0035-9106	Royal Society of Antiquaries of Ireland. Journal
0035-9114	Royal Society of Arts. Journal
0035-9122	Royal Society of Canada. Transactions
0035-9130	Royal Society of Health Journal
0035-9149	Royal Society of London. Notes and Records
0035-9157	Royal Society of Medicine. Proceedings *see* 0141-0768
0035-9165	Royal Society of Medicine. Section of Odontology Proceedings†
0035-9173	Royal Society of New South Wales. Journal and Proceedings
0035-9181	Royal Society of New Zealand. Transactions *see* 0303-6758
0035-919X	Royal Society of South Africa. Transactions
0035-9203	Royal Society of Tropical Medicine and Hygiene Transactions
0035-9211	Royal Society of Victoria. Proceedings
0035-922X	Royal Society of Western Australia. Journal
0035-9238	Royal Statistical Society. Journal. Series A: General
0035-9246	Royal Statistical Society. Journal. Series B: Methodological
0035-9254	Royal Statistical Society. Journal. Series C: Applied Statistics
0035-9262	Royal Tehran Hilton
0035-9270	Royal Television Society. Journal *see* 0308-454X
0035-9289	Royal United Service Institution. Journal *see* 0307-1847
0035-9297	University of Malta. Faculty of Arts. Journal†
0035-9300	Royalauto
0035-9319	Royale Federation Colombophile Belge. Bulletin Federal *changed to* Royale Federation Colombophile Belge. Bulletin National
0035-9327	Rozhl'ady†
0035-9335	Rozhlasova Prace
0035-9343	Rozhledy Matematicko-Fyzikalni
0035-9351	Rozhledy v Chirurgii
0035-9378	Narodni Technicke Muzeum. Rozpravy
0035-9386	Rozprawy Elektrotechniczne
0035-9394	Rozprawy Hydrotechniczne
0035-9408	Rozprawy Inzynierskie
0035-9416	Rozvoj Mistniho Hospodarstvi
0035-9424	Rtam
0035-9432	Rub-Off†
0035-9440	Rubber Age *see* 0146-0706
0035-9467	Rubber Chem Lines†
0035-9475	Rubber Chemistry and Technology
0035-9483	Rubber Developments
0035-9491	Rubber India
0035-9513	Rubber News
0035-9521	Rubber Research Institute of Sri Lanka. Quarterly Journal *changed to* Rubber Research Institute of Sri Lanka. Journal
0035-953X	Rubber Research Institute of Malaysia. Journal
0035-9548	Rubber Statistical Bulletin
0035-9556	Rubber Statistical News Sheet†
0035-9564	Rubber Trends
0035-9572	Rubber World
0035-9580	Ruby
0035-9599	Ruch Filozoficzny
0035-9602	Ruch Literacki
0035-9610	Ruch Muzyczny
0035-9629	Ruch Prawniczy, Ekonomiczny i Socjologiczny
0035-9637	Rudarski Glasnik
0035-9645	Rudarsko-Metalurski Zbornik
0035-9661	Ruedo
0035-9688	Rudy
0035-9696	Rudy i Metale Niezelazne
0035-970X	La rue
0035-9726	Rugby
0035-9742	Rugby League Week
0035-9750	Rugby News *changed to* Rugby (Year)
0035-9777	Rugby World *changed to* Rugby World and Post
0035-9793	Rukovet
0035-9815	Romania Today
0035-9823	Ruminskii Biulleten Naucinoi Informatii. Estestvennie Nauki *changed to* Ruminskii Biulleten Naucinoi Informatii. Estestvennie Nauki. Meditinskie Nauki
0035-9831	Ruminskii Biuleten Naucinoi Informatii. Obscestvennie Nauki†
0035-9866	Rundfunk- Fernseh- Grosshandel *changed to* Rundfunk - Fernseh - Wirtschaft
0035-9874	Rundfunk und Fernsehen
0035-9882	Rundfunkjournalistik in Theorie und Praxis
0035-9890	Rundfunktechnische Mitteilungen
0035-9904	Rundschau fuer den Deutschen Einzelhaendler
0035-9912	Rundschau fuer Internationale Damenmode
0035-9920	Hotel- Gastgewerbe
0035-9939	Runner's World
0035-9955	Ruota Diorama
0035-9963	Rupambara
0035-998X	Ruperto-Carola
0035-9998	Rural and Urban Roads *changed to* Roads
0036-0007	Rural Councillor
0036-0015	Rural District Review *see* 0306-3240
0036-0023	Rural Education News
0036-0058	Rural India
0036-0066	Rural Kentuckian
0036-0074	Rural Life†
0036-0082	Rural Missions *changed to* T N T
0036-0090	Rural Research. A C S I R O Quarterly
0036-0104	Rural Roundup
0036-0112	Rural Sociology
0036-0120	Rural Youth
0036-0139	Ruralista
0036-0147	Ruritan
0036-0155	Rusky Jazyk *changed to* Rusky Jazyk ve Skole
0036-0163	Russell: The Journal of the Bertrand Russell Archives
0036-0171	Russell's Official National Motor Coach Guide
0036-018X	Russia Cristiana *changed to* L'Altra Europa
0036-0201	Russian Castings Production†
0036-021X	Russian Chemical Reviews
0036-0228	Russian Engineering Journal *see* 0144-6622
0036-0236	Russian Journal of Inorganic Chemistry
0036-0244	Russian Journal of Physical Chemistry
0036-0252	Russian Language Journal
0036-0260	Russian Language Monthly†
0036-0279	Russian Mathematical Surveys
0036-0287	Russian Messenger/Russkij Vistnik *changed to* U R O B A Messenger
0036-0295	Russian Metallurgy
0036-0309	Russian Oil and Gas Bulletin
0036-0317	Russian Orthodox Journal
0036-0325	Russian Pharmacology and Toxicology
0036-0341	Russian Review
0036-035X	Russisch *changed to* Zielsprache Russisch
0036-0368	Russkaya Rech'
0036-0376	Russkii Yazyk v Shkole
0036-0384	Russkii Yazyk za Rubezhom
0036-0406	Russky Golos
0036-0414	Russland and Wir
0036-0422	Ruta Dominicana
0036-0430	Rutas de Pasion
0036-0449	Rutgers-Camden Law Journal *see* 0277-318X
0036-0457	Rutgers Alumni Magazine *changed to* Rutgers
0036-0465	Rutgers Law Review
0036-0473	Rutgers University. Libraries. Journal
0036-0481	Rwanda-Carrefour d'Afrique *changed to* Releve

ISSN INDEX 1299

0036-049X Rybnoe Khozyaistvo
0036-0511 Rydge's
0036-052X Rynki Zagraniczne
0036-0538 Rehabilitation
0036-0546 Rythmes du Monde†
0036-0570 South African Banking
0036-0597 S A C O Tidningen *see* 0347-0342
0036-0600 South African Cerebral Palsy Journal
0036-0627 South African Chemical Processing *changed to* Power & Plant Engineering in South Africa
0036-0643 South African Draughtsman
0036-0651 S A E - Australasia
0036-0678 S A E S T Transactions
0036-0708 S A F E - Nachrichten
0036-0716 S A F T O Exporter
0036-0724 South African Friesland Journal
0036-0740 S A H S Newsletter
0036-0759 S.A. Hairdressing and Beauty Culture
0036-0767 S A I P A
0036-0775 S A I S Review
0036-0783 S A L A Newsletter/S A B V Nuusbrief *see* 0256-6710
0036-0791 S A M A
0036-0805 Advanced Management Journal
0036-0813 S A M P E Journal†
0036-0821 S A M P E Quarterly
0036-083X S A M *changed to* Adweek/Midwest
0036-0848 South African Machine Tool Review
0036-0856 South Africa Motoring Mirror *changed to* South Africa Motor
0036-0864 S A N B
0036-0872 S A N T A News
0036-0880 S A N T A Bantu *changed to* S A N T A Health Magazine
0036-0899 S. A. News for the Deaf†
0036-0929 S.A.R. & H. Employees' Review *changed to* Emplo Review/Tydskrif
0036-0945 S.A. Road Transport *changed to* S.A. Road Transport Journal
0036-0953 SASSAR†
0036-097X S A T I S†
0036-0988 S A U K-S A B C Bulletin *changed to* Personnality
0036-0996 Sweden. Statens Avtalsverk. Information Fraan S A V *changed to* Sweden. Statens Arbetsgivarverk. Arbetsgivarverket Informerar
0036-1003 South African Wool and Textile Research Institute. Bulletin
0036-1011 S.A. Worker
0036-102X S B
0036-1038 S-B Gazette/Sutters Bourgeoisie Gazette *see* 0038-9900
0036-1046 S B I C/Venture Capital *changed to* Venture Capital Journal
0036-1062 Bibliotheque de Travail avec Supplement†
0036-1070 S B Z - Sanitaer-Technik, Heizungs-, und Lueftungsbau *see* 0342-8184
0036-1089 S C A A Viewpoint†
0036-1100 S C A T Bulletin *see* 0701-1024
0036-1119 S C A-Tidningen
0036-1127 S.C.E.T.A. Bulletin de Documentation *changed to* S C E T A Documentation
0036-1135 S C J
0036-1143 S C L A Data†
0036-116X Santa Casa di Loreto. Messaggio
0036-1178 S.D.C. Bulletin
0036-1186 S D L Newsletter†
0036-1194 S D R-Kontakt
0036-1224 S E A G Boletin del Algodon *changed to* E A G Publicaciones
0036-1232 S E A G Boletin del Maiz *changed to* E A G Publicaciones
0036-1240 S E A G Boletin del Trigo *changed to* E A G Publicaciones
0036-1267 S E D O C
0036-1275 S E H A Newsletter and Proceedings
0036-1291 S E M Newsletter *changed to* Ethnomusicology Newsletter
0036-1313 S E S A Proceedings (Society for Experimental Stress Analysis) *changed to* S E M Proceedings
0036-1321 S E V Bulletin *changed to* Bulletin S E V/V S E
0036-1364 S F W A Bulletin
0036-1372 Slovenska Akademia Vied. Geologicky Ustav D. Stura: Zbornik: Zapadne Karpaty
0036-1380 S H E N†
0036-1399 S I A M Journal on Applied Mathematics
0036-1402 S I A M Journal on Control *see* 0363-0129
0036-1410 S I A M Journal on Mathematical Analysis
0036-1429 S I A M Journal on Numerical Analysis
0036-1437 S I A M Newsletter *changed to* S I A M News
0036-1445 S I A M Review
0036-147X S I C A S H Newsletter *changed to* S I G L A S H Newsletter
0036-1488 Sida; Contributions to Botany
0036-1496 S.I.D. Proceedings
0036-150X S I E C U S Newsletter *see* 0091-3995
0036-1518 S I E T Studies *changed to* S E D M E
0036-1526 S I G S P A C†
0036-1534 S I I/Socialist International Information *see* 0049-0946
0036-1542 S I L B I Bollettino
0036-1550 S I L News *changed to* Individual Liberty
0036-1569 S J M Bulletin/Scandinavian Steel and Metal News *changed to* Skrot och Miljoteknik
0036-1585 S Z
0036-1607 Special Libraries Association. Geography and Map Division. Bulletin
0036-1615 S L F Tidningen†
0036-1631 S L R Camera *changed to* S L R Photography
0036-164X S M E A
0036-1666 S.M.M.B. Bulletin *see* 0309-0809
0036-1682 S M P T E Journal
0036-1704 S. M. U. H. Bulletin *see* 0399-0966
0036-1720 S N E C M A *see* 0750-7569
0036-1755 New York State School Nurse-Teachers Association. Journal *changed to* N Y S S N T A Journal
0036-1763 S Nine Two Way Radio *see* 0145-4560
0036-1771 S. O. L. A. I. A. T
0036-178X S O S Messenger
0036-1798 S. O. S. Soviet Jewry†
0036-181X S P A Journal†
0036-1836 Student Personnel Association for Teacher Education. Journal *see* 0735-6846
0036-1844 S P E Journal *see* 0091-9578
0036-1852 S P I C
0036-1860 S P I E Journal *see* 0091-3286
0036-1879 Sweden. Sjukvaardens och Socialvaardens Planerings- och Rationaliseringsinstitut. S P R I Litteraturtjaenst
0036-1887 S R F Resume *changed to* Resume
0036-1909 S S R C Newsletter *see* 0266-2639
0036-1925 S S S Newsletter (Simulation in the Service of Society) *see* 0037-5497
0036-1933 S & T A-Scienza e Tecnologia degli Alimenti†
0036-1941 S T A Educator†
0036-1976 S T E L C O - Scope†
0036-1984 S U C Bulletin
0036-1992 S U D A M Biblioteca. Informa
0036-200X S U D E NE. Boletim da Biblioteca†
0036-2018 S U H A F-Tidningen *changed to* Universitetslaeraren
0036-2034 Society of St. Vincent de Paul. Bulletin for Southern Africa
0036-2050 Czechoslovak Society of Arts and Sciences. Zpravy S V U
0036-2069 South West Africa Scientific Society. Newsletter
0036-2085 S.W.L.A. Newsletter†
0036-2093 S Y R-Information med Fruktodlaren *see* 0348-7032
0036-2107 Commercial Transport *changed to* Commercial Transport
0036-2107 Commercial Transport *changed to* Freight World
0036-2115 Saarbruecker Hefte
0036-2123 Saastopankki
0036-2131 Sabah Society. Journal
0036-214X Sabbath Recorder
0036-2158 Sabena Revue
0036-2174 Sabouraudia: Journal of Medical and Veterinary Mycology *see* 0268-1218
0036-2182 Saco-Lowell Bulletin *changed to* Platt Saco Lowell Bulletin
0036-2190 Sacra Doctrina
0036-2204 Sacramento Business
0036-2212 Sacramento Observer
0036-2239 Sacramento Teacher†
0036-2247 Sacramento Valley Union Labor Bulletin
0036-2255 Sacred Music
0036-2263 Sacred Organ Journal
0036-2271 Saddle and Bridle
0036-228X Sadelmager-og Tapetserer Tidende
0036-231X Holzindustrie†
0036-2328 Saenger- und Musikantenzeitung
0036-2336 Saenger-Zeitung
0036-2344 Saeugetierkundliche Mitteilungen
0036-2352 Safari†
0036-2360 Safe and Security News
0036-2379 Safe Deposit Bulletin
0036-2387 Safe Driver
0036-2395 Safe Engineering†
0036-2409 SAFECO Agent
0036-2417 Safer (Volkswagen) Motoring *changed to* V W Motoring
0036-2425 Safer Oregon *changed to* Update (Salem)
0036-2433 Safety†
0036-2441 Safety at Sea International
0036-245X Safety Briefs
0036-2468 Safety Digest *see* 0377-8592
0036-2476 Safety Energizer†
0036-2484 Safety in Industry *see* 0377-8592
0036-2492 Safety in Mines Abstracts *see* 0141-9803
0036-2514 Environmental Control & Safety Management†
0036-2549 Safety Review†
0036-2557 Safety Standards *see* 0090-4589
0036-2565 Saga†
0036-2573 Sagan-Sprottauer Heimatbriefe
0036-2581 Saguenay Medical
0036-259X Saagverken
0036-2603 Sahakar *changed to* Satyachar
0036-2611 Sahakari Jagat
0036-262X Sahamies
0036-2638 Sahara
0036-2646 Saharien
0036-2654 Sahifat Al-Tarbiya
0036-2670 Sahko-Elektriciten i Finland/Sahko-Electricity in Finland *changed to* Sahko-Electricity and Electronics
0036-2689 Journal of Accidental Medicine *see* 0387-4095
0036-2700 Sail
0036-2719 Sailing
0036-2727 Sailing Industry News†
0036-2735 Sailplane and Gliding
0036-2743 Sainik Samachar
0036-2751 St. Andrews Review
0036-276X St. Anthony Messenger
0036-2778 St. Bartholomew's Hospital Journal
0036-2794 Triomphe Saint-Cyr
0036-2808 St. Dunstan's Review
0036-2824 St. Francis Xavier University Contemporary and Alumni News *changed to* St. Francis Xavier University Alumni News
0036-2832 St. Gallen
0036-2840 Saint George's Hospital Gazette
0036-2859 St. Hallvard
0036-2867 Saint Hubert
0036-2875 St. Hubertus
0036-2883 St. John Review
0036-2891 St. John's Hospital Dermatological Society. Transactions *see* 0307-6938
0036-2905 St. John's Law Review
0036-2921 St. Jude's Magazine†
0036-293X St. Louis Commerce
0036-2948 St. Louis Countian
0036-2956 St. Louis Genealogical Society Quarterly
0036-2964 St. Louis Jewish Light
0036-2972 St. Louis Journalism Review
0036-2980 St. Louis Park Medical Center. Bulletin *changed to* Park-Nicollet Medical Foundation Bulletin
0036-2999 St. Louis Pharmacists' Association Magazine
0036-3006 St. Louis Purchaser
0036-3014 Saint Louis University Research Journal
0036-3022 St. Louis Review
0036-3030 Saint Louis University Law Journal
0036-3057 Saint-Luc Medical
0036-3065 St. Lucas Allgemeine Glaserzeitung *see* 0342-5142
0036-3081 St. Luke's Hospital Gazette†
0036-309X St. Luke's Journal *changed to* St. Luke's Journal of Theology
0036-3103 St. Mark's Review
0036-3111 St. Martin's Review
0036-312X St. Mary's Hospital Gazette
0036-3138 Saint Mary's University Journal
0036-3146 Saint Paul Area Chamber of Commerce Action†
0036-3154 St. Paul News
0036-3162 St. Poeltner Dioezesanblatt
0036-3170 St. Poeltner Kirchenzeitung *changed to* Kirche Bunt
0036-3189 St. Regis News, Southern Edition *changed to* St. Regis News
0036-3200 St. Thomas's Hospital Gazette *see* 0306-3860
0036-3219 Saint Vincent de Paul Record
0036-3227 St. Vladimir's Theological Quarterly
0036-3243 Sainte Therese de Lisieux. Annales
0036-3251 Saints' Herald
0036-326X Sairaala
0036-3278 Sairaanhoitaja-Sjukskoterskan
0036-3286 Collecting and Breeding
0036-3294 Saison
0036-3316 Saiva Siddhanta
0036-3324 Saivite Light *changed to* Gracious Light
0036-3340 Sakharnaya Promyshlennost'
0036-3359 Sakharnaya Svekla
0036-3367 Sal†
0036-3375 Salamandra
0036-3383 Salem County Historical Society Newsletter
0036-3391 Sales†
0036-3405 Sales Executive
0036-3413 Sales Management *changed to* Sales & Marketing Management
0036-3421 Sales Manager's Bulletin
0036-3448 Sales/Promotion *see* 0708-6024
0036-3456 Sales Prospector
0036-3464 Sales/Slants†
0036-3472 Sales Tax Advices
0036-3480 Salesian
0036-3502 Salesianum
0036-3510 Salesman's Opportunity Magazine *see* 0741-3750
0036-3529 Salmagundi
0036-3537 Salmanticensis
0036-3545 Salmon and Trout Magazine
0036-3553 Salon Owner *changed to* American Salon
0036-357X Salpisma
0036-360X Salt Lick
0036-3618 Salt Water Sportsman
0036-3634 Salud Publica de Mexico
0036-3642 Salus Militiae
0036-3650 Salut les Copains *changed to* Salut
0036-3669 Salvage Bids
0036-3677 Salzburger Wirtschaft
0036-3693 Samaj Kalyan
0036-3715 Samarbete
0036-3723 Samaritano
0036-3731 Samaru Agricultural Newsletter *see* 0331-6742
0036-3782 Samhaellsgemenskap
0036-3804 Sammelwerk Bauzentrumring†
0036-3820 Sammler Express

1300 ISSN INDEX

0036-3839 Samoa Times
0036-3847 Samostiina Ukrayina†
0036-3855 Samouprava Zavarovancev†
0036-3871 Sampada
0036-388X Samphire†
0036-3898 Sample Case
0036-391X Samson Technology Trends†
0036-3928 Samtiden
0036-3944 Samvirke
0036-3952 San Antonian *see* 0279-0785
0036-3960 San Antonio
0036-3979 San Antonio District Dental Society. Journal *changed to* San Antonio District Dental Society Newsletter
0036-3987 San Beda Review
0036-3995 San Bernardino County Library Newsletter†
0036-4002 San Diego Business†
0036-4010 San Diego County Dental Society. Bulletin *changed to* Facets (San Diego)
0036-4029 Door
0036-4037 San Diego Law Review
0036-4045 San Diego
0036-4053 San Diego Numismatic Society. Bulletin
0036-4061 San Diego Physician
0036-407X American Federation of Musicians Local 325
0036-4088 San Francisco
0036-4096 San Francisco Bay Guardian
0036-410X San Francisco Business
0036-4118 San Francisco Camera
0036-4126 San Francisco Earthquake†
0036-4134 San Francisco Labor *changed to* Northern California Labor
0036-4142 San Francisco Medical Society. Bulletin *changed to* San Francisco Medicine
0036-4169 San Francisco Unified School District Newsletter†
0036-4185 San Jose Post-Record
0036-4215 San Luis Valley Historian
0036-4223 San Marino (Repubblica) Bollettino Ufficiale
0036-424X San Salvatore da Horta
0036-4258 Sanatorio Sao Lucas. Boletim
0036-4266 Sand Castles†
0036-4282 Sandal Prints†
0036-4290 Sandlapper *see* 0195-282X
0036-4304 SANE World
0036-4312 Saneamento
0036-4320 Sangeet Kala Vihar *see* 0251-012X
0036-4339 Sangeet Natak
0036-4355 Sangre
0036-4363 Sangue della Redenzione†
0036-4371 Industrial and Technological Information of Yokkaichi City
0036-438X Industrial Training
0036-4398 Industrial Vehicles
0036-4401 Sanitaer- und Heizungstechnik
0036-4428 University of California. Sanitary Engineering and Environmental Health Research Laboratory. News Quarterly
0036-4436 Sanitary Maintenance
0036-4444 Sanity
0036-4460 Sannio Elegante
0036-4479 Sanomalehtimies
0036-4487 Sanop Kwa Kyongyong
0036-4495 Acta Sericologica
0036-4517 Santa Clara County Historical and Genealogical Quarterly *changed to* Santa Clara County Connection
0036-4525 Santa Clara County in Action†
0036-4541 Santa Fe Magazine†
0036-455X Santa Gertrudis Journal
0036-4568 Sante de l'Abeille
0036-4576 Sante et Sport
0036-4584 Sante, Liberte et Vaccination
0036-4606 Santo dei Voli
0036-4614 Santuario de Aparecida
0036-4622 Santuario della Madonna delle Rocche
0036-4630 Santuario di N.S.D. Grazie e di S. Maria Goretti
0036-4649 Sanyo Kasei News
0036-4657 Sao Paulo
0036-4665 Instituto de Medicina Tropical de Sao Paulo. Revista
0036-4681 Sapere
0036-469X Sapeur-Pompier
0036-4703 Sapientia
0036-4711 Sapienza
0036-472X Sapporo Medical Journal
0036-4738 Sarah Lawrence Journal†
0036-4746 S.L. Literary Review *changed to* Sarah Lawrence Review
0036-4754 Sarasvat
0036-4762 Sarawak Gazette
0036-4770 Sardegna Economica
0036-4789 Sardegna Informazioni
0036-4797 Sarika
0036-4819 S A R P *changed to* Servamus
0036-4827 Sarsia
0036-4835 Sarvodaya
0036-4843 Sash
0036-4851 SaskTel News
0036-4878 Saskatchewan Archaeology Newsletter *see* 0227-7514
0036-4886 Saskatchewan Bulletin
0036-4894 Saskatchewan Gazette
0036-4908 Saskatchewan History
0036-4916 Saskatchewan Law Review
0036-4924 Saskatchewan Library†
0036-4940 Saskatchewan Motorist
0036-4975 Saturday Night
0036-4983 Saturday Review *see* 0091-620X
0036-4991 Satya Prakash
0036-5009 Sau og Geit
0036-5025 Saucers, Space & Science†
0036-5033 Sauna Nachrichten mit Sauna Archiv
0036-5041 Sauvegarde de l'Enfance
0036-505X Sauvegarde des Chantiers
0036-5068 Savacou
0036-5084 Savant *see* 0822-7896
0036-5092 Savez Omladine
0036-5106 Saving Health
0036-5114 Savings and Loan News *see* 0746-1321
0036-5122 Savings Association News *changed to* New York League News
0036-5130 Savings Bank Journal *see* 0740-5464
0036-5149 Savita
0036-5157 Savoia
0036-5165 Savoir et Beaute *changed to* Cahiers du C A C E F
0036-5173 Savremena Praksa
0036-519X Savremenik
0036-5203 Savremeno Domacinstvo
0036-5211 Saxons Veckotidning
0036-522X Sbirka Soudnich Rozhodnuti a Stanovisek
0036-5238 Sbirka Zlepsovacich Navrhu a Pokrokovych Vyrobnich Zkusenosti *see* 0322-9564
0036-5246 Sbornik Archivnich Praci
0036-5254 Ceskoslovenska Spolecnost Zemepisna. Sbornik *changed to* Ceskoslovenske Geograficke Spolecnosti. Sbornik
0036-5270 Sbornik Geologickych Ved: Antropozoikum
0036-5289 Sbornik Geologickych Ved: Hydrogeologie, Inzenyrska Geologie
0036-5297 Sbornik Geologickych Ved: Paleontologie
0036-5300 Sbornik Geologickych Ved: Technologie, Geochemie
0036-5319 Sbornik Geologickych Ved: Uzita Geofyzika
0036-5327 Sbornik Lekarsky
0036-5335 Narodni Muzeum v Praze. Sbornik. Rada A: Historie
0036-5343 Narodni Muzeum v Praze. Sbornik. Rada B: Prirodni Vedy
0036-5351 Narodni Muzeum v Praze. Sbornik. Rada C: Literarni Historie
0036-536X V S D a V u D Sobornik Praci†
0036-5378 Sbornik U V T I Z - Genetika a Slechteni
0036-5386 Sbornik U V T I Z - Meliorace
0036-5394 Sbornik U V T I Z - Ochrana Rostlin
0036-5408 Scabbard and Blade Journal
0036-5416 Scala International
0036-5424 Scale Modeler
0036-5432 Scale Models
0036-5467 Scan (New York)
0036-5475 Scan *changed to* Newscan
0036-5483 Scandia
0036-5491 Scandinavian Economic History Review
0036-5505 Scandinavian Journal of Rehabilitation Medicine
0036-5513 Scandinavian Journal of Clinical & Laboratory Investigation
0036-5521 Scandinavian Journal of Gastroenterology
0036-553X Scandinavian Journal of Haematology
0036-5548 Scandinavian Journal of Infectious Diseases
0036-5556 Scandinavian Journal of Plastic and Reconstructive Surgery
0036-5564 Scandinavian Journal of Psychology
0036-5572 Scandinavian Journal of Respiratory Diseases *see* 0106-4339
0036-5580 Scandinavian Journal of Thoracic and Cardiovascular Surgery
0036-5599 Scandinavian Journal of Urology and Nephrology
0036-5602 Scandinavian Public Library Quarterly
0036-5610 Scandinavian Research Information Notes†
0036-5629 Scandinavian Shipping Gazette
0036-5637 Scandinavian Studies
0036-5653 Scandinavica
0036-5661 Scanlan's Monthly†
0036-567X Scarabee
0036-5696 Scautismo
0036-570X Scelte del Consumatore†
0036-5718 Scen och Salong
0036-5726 Scena
0036-5734 Scena
0036-5742 Scena Illustrata
0036-5777 Scene from Oceana†
0036-5793 Scenes et Pistes
0036-5831 Schach-Echo
0036-584X Schacklub Hietzing Nachrichtenblatt *changed to* Schachklub Hietzing Memphis Nachrichtenblatt
0036-5882 Schakels†
0036-5890 Schakend Nederland
0036-5904 Schakt-Bladet
0036-5920 Scharnhorst Auslese
0036-5939 Das Schaufenster (Passau)
0036-5947 Die Schaulade
0036-5955 Schedario
0036-5971 Scheepspraat *changed to* Fama
0036-5998 Scheppend Ambacht
0036-6005 Scherma
0036-6013 Schiedamse Gemeenschap†
0036-6021 Schienenfahrzeuge
0036-603X Schiff und Hafen *changed to* Schiff und Hafen /Kommandobruecke
0036-6048 Schiffbau-Normung *see* 0011-4952
0036-6056 Schiffbauforschung
0036-6064 Schiffstechnik
0036-6072 Schilder *changed to* Kleur
0036-6080 Norda Schimmel Briefs *see* 0090-1903
0036-6099 Schip en Werf
0036-6102 Schippersblad†
0036-6110 Schism, a Journal of Divergent American Opinion†
0036-6129 Schizophrenia *changed to* Journal of Orthomolecular Medicine
0036-6137 Schlager fuer Dich
0036-6145 Schlern
0036-6153 Schlesien
0036-6161 Schleswig-Holstein
0036-617X Der Schluessel
0036-6188 Der Schluessel†
0036-6196 Schmalenbachs Zeitschrift fuer Betriebswirtschaftliche Forschung
0036-6218 Schmiertechnik *see* 0724-3472
0036-6226 Schmierungstechnik
0036-6234 Schmollers Jahrbuch fuer Wirtschafts- und Sozialwissenschaften *see* 0342-1783
0036-6250 Schoeffe
0036-6269 Schoen - Visie
0036-6307 Schoenwereld
0036-6315 Schoevers Koerier
0036-6331 Scholarly Books in America†
0036-634X Scholarly Publishing
0036-6358 Scholars' Choice
0036-6366 Scholarships, Fellowships, Loans News Service *changed to* Scholarships, Fellowships and Loans News Service and Counselors Information Services
0036-6382 Scholastic Coach
0036-6390 Scholastic Editor Graphics/ Communications *see* 0745-2357
0036-6404 Scholastic News Ranger *see* 0736-055X
0036-6412 Scholastic Scope
0036-6439 School Administrator
0036-6447 School and Community
0036-6455 School and Society *see* 0161-7389
0036-6463 School Arts
0036-6471 School Board†
0036-648X School Boards Newsletter *changed to* School Board Notes
0036-6498 School Buildings Equipment and Supplies *changed to* School Buildings Equipment and Supplies and School Government Chronicle
0036-6501 School Bus Fleet
0036-651X School Business Affairs
0036-6528 School Community Observer *changed to* Daybreak
0036-6536 School Counselor
0036-6544 School en Godsdienst
0036-6552 School Food Services Bulletin *changed to* School Lunch Newsletter
0036-6552 School Food Services Bulletin *changed to* School Breakfast Newsletter
0036-6560 School Government Chronicle *changed to* School Buildings Equipment and Supplies and School Government Chronicle
0036-6579 School Health Review *see* 0097-0050
0036-6587 School Law Review†
0036-6595 School Librarian
0036-6609 School Libraries *see* 0278-4823
0036-6617 School Library *changed to* School Media Centre
0036-6641 School Lunch Journal *see* 0160-6271
0036-6668 School Music News
0036-6676 School Musician Director and Teacher
0036-6684 School News†
0036-6692 School News *changed to* EdNews
0036-6706 Michigan State University. School of Labor and Industrial Relations. Newsletter
0036-6730 School Press Review
0036-6749 School Product News *changed to* School and College Product News
0036-6765 School Research Information Service Quarterly *see* 0147-9741
0036-6773 School Review *see* 0195-6744
0036-6781 School Safety *changed to* School Safety World
0036-679X School Science
0036-6803 School Science and Mathematics
0036-6811 School Science Review
0036-682X School Shop
0036-6838 School Tie *changed to* Education News
0036-6846 School Times†
0036-6854 School Trustee
0036-6862 School Yarn Magazine
0036-6889 Schoolblad
0036-6897 Schoolgirl Story Magazine
0036-6900 Schools in Action†
0036-6919 Schott-Kurier *changed to* Schott Aktuell
0036-6927 Schouw
0036-6943 Evangelischer Bund in Oesterreich. Schriftenreihe
0036-696X Schriftenreihe fuer die Evangelische Frau
0036-6978 Geschichte der Naturwissenschaften, Technik und Medizin. Schriftenreihe *changed to* N T M Geschichte der Naturwissenschaften, Technik und Medizin. Schriftenreihe
0036-6986 Das Schrifttum der Agrarwirtschaft
0036-6994 Schrifttumkartei Bauwesen *see* 0722-060X

ISSN INDEX 1301

0036-7001 Schrifttumkartei Beton *see* 0722-060X
0036-701X Schrifttumsuebersicht Laermminderung *see* 0344-7758
0036-7044 Schuh-Kurier
0036-7060 Schuh-Zeitung
0036-7079 Schuhmarkt
0036-7087 Schuhwirtschaft†
0036-7095 Schul- und Sportstaettenbau
0036-7109 Schule und Europa†
0036-7117 Schule und Gesellschaft†
0036-7125 Schulfernsehen
0036-7133 Schutz und Wehr†
0036-715X Schwann Record and Tape Guide *see* 0160-1571
0036-7168 Schweineproduktion *see* 0138-3388
0036-7176 Schweinezucht und Schweinemast
0036-7184 Schweissen und Schneiden
0036-7192 Schweisstechnik
0036-7206 Schweisstechnik
0036-7214 Schweizerische Arbeitslehrerinnen-Zeitung
0036-7230 Schweiz, Suisse, Svizzera, Switzerland *changed to* Schweiz, Suisse, Svizzera, Svizra, Switzerland
0036-7257 Schweizer Aluminium Rundschau
0036-7273 Schweizer Archiv fuer Neurologie, Neurochirurgie und Psychiatrie
0036-7281 Schweizer Archiv fuer Tierheilkunde
0036-729X Schweizer Auto-Verkehr†
0036-7303 Schweizer Baublatt
0036-7311 Schweizer Brauerei-Rundschau *changed to* Brauerei und Getraenke-Rundschau
0036-732X Schweizer Buch
0036-7338 Schweizer Buchhandel
0036-7346 Schweizer Frauenblatt
0036-7354 Schweizer Hundesport
0036-7362 Schweizer Illustrierte
0036-7370 Schweizer Journal
0036-7389 Schweizer Kavallerist
0036-7397 Schweizer Maschinenmarkt
0036-7400 Schweizer Monatshefte
0036-7419 Schweizer Musiker-Revue
0036-7427 Schweizer Naturschutz
0036-7435 Schweizer Pedicure
0036-7443 Schweizer Schule
0036-746X Schweizer Treuhaender
0036-7478 Schweizer Uhr *changed to* Uhren Rundschau
0036-7486 Schweizerische Aerztezeitung
0036-7508 Schweizerische Apotheker-Zeitung
0036-7516 Schweizerische Arbeitgeber-Zeitung
0036-7524 Schweizerische Bauzeitung *changed to* Schweizer Ingenieur und Architekt
0036-7532 Schweizerische Beobachter
0036-7540 Schweizerische Bienen-Zeitung
0036-7559 Schweizerische Blatter fuer Heizung und Luftung
0036-7567 Schweizerische Drogistenzeitung
0036-7575 Schweizerische Entomologische Gesellschaft. Mitteilungen
0036-7583 Schweizerische Fachschrift fuer Buchbindereien *changed to* Bindetechnik
0036-7591 Schweizerische Gesellschaft der Offiziere des Munitionsdienstes. Bulletin
0036-7613 Schweizerische Juristen-Zeitung
0036-763X Schweizerische Landwirtschaftliche Forschung
0036-7648 Schweizerische Landwirtschaftliche Monatshefte†
0036-7656 Schweizerische Lehrerzeitung
0036-7672 Schweizerische Medizinische Wochenschrift
0036-7680 Schweizerische Metzger-Zeitung
0036-7699 Schweizerische Mineralogische und Petrographische Mitteilungen
0036-7702 Schweizerische Monatsschrift fuer Zahnheilkunde *changed to* Schweizerische Monatsschrift fuer Zahnmedizin
0036-7710 Schweizerische Musikzeitung†
0036-7729 Schweizerische Nationalbank. Monatsbericht
0036-7737 Schweizerische Photorundschau
0036-7745 Schweizerische Schachzeitung
0036-7753 Schweizerische Schreinerzeitung
0036-7761 Schweizerische Uhrmacher Zeitung *changed to* Schweizerische Uhrmacher- und Goldschmiede-Zeitung
0036-777X Schweizerische Vereinigung fuer Atomenergie. Bulletin
0036-7788 Schweizerische Vereinigung fuer Klinische Chemie. Bulletin *see* 0253-035X
0036-7796 Schweizerische Weinzeitung
0036-780X Schweizerische Wirte-Zeitung
0036-7818 Schweizerische Zeitschrift fuer Forstwesen
0036-7826 Schweizerische Zeitschrift fuer Gemeinnuetzigkeit
0036-7834 Schweizerische Zeitschrift fuer Geschichte
0036-7842 Swiss Journal of Hydrology
0036-7869 Schweizerische Zeitschrift fuer Psychologie und ihre Anwendungen
0036-7877 Schweizerische Zeitschrift fuer Sozialversicherung *changed to* Schweizerische Zeitschrift fuer Sozialversicherung und berufliche Vorsorge
0036-7885 Schweizerische Zeitschrift fuer Sportmedizin
0036-7893 Schweizerische Zeitschrift fuer Strafrecht
0036-7907 Schweizerische Zeitschrift fuer Vermessung, Photogrammetrie und Kulturtechnik *changed to* Mensuration, Photogrammetrie, Genie Rural
0036-7923 Schweizerischer Zeitungsverleger-Verband. Bulletin *changed to* Schweizerischer Verband der Zeitungs- und Zeitschriftenverleger. Bulletin
0036-7931 Schweizerisches Archiv fuer Verkehrswissenschaft und Verkehrs-Politik *changed to* Schweizerische Zeitschrift fuer Verkehrswirtschaft
0036-794X Schweizerisches Archiv fuer Volkskunde
0036-7958 Schweizerisches Gutenbergmuseum†
0036-7966 Schweizerisches Kaufmaennisches Zentralblatt *changed to* Schweizerische Kaufmaennische Zeitung
0036-7974 Schweizerisches Patent-, Muster- und Marken-Blatt
0036-7982 Schweizerisches Rotes Kreuz *changed to* Actio
0036-7990 Schweizerisches Zentralblatt fuer Staats- und Gemeindeverwaltung
0036-8008 G W A - Gas Wasser Abwasser
0036-8016 Schweizerjaeger
0036-8024 Schweizerische Zeitschrift fuer Militaermedizin *changed to* Schweizerische Zeitschrift fuer Militaer- und Katastrophenmedizin
0036-8032 Schwenkfeldian
0036-8040 Sci
0036-8059 Sci-Tech News
0036-8067 Sci/Tech Quarterly Index†
0036-8075 Science
0036-8083 Scienze
0036-8091 Physics Abstracts
0036-8105 Electrical & Electronics Abstracts
0036-8113 Computer & Control Abstracts
0036-8121 Science Activities
0036-813X Science Affairs†
0036-8148 Science and Children
0036-8156 Science and Culture
0036-8164 Science and Engineering
0036-8172 Doshisha University. Science and Engineering Review
0036-8180 Science and Industry†
0036-8237 Science and Society
0036-8245 Science and Technology
0036-8253 Science Books *see* 0098-342X
0036-8261 Science Bulletin
0036-827X Science Citation Index
0036-8288 Science Curriculum Improvement Study Newsletter†
0036-8296 Science Digest†
0036-830X Science Dimension *changed to* Science and Technology Dimensions
0036-8318 Science du Sol *see* 0335-1653
0036-8326 Science Education
0036-8334 Science Education News†
0036-8342 Science et Nature
0036-8350 Science et Peche
0036-8369 Science et Vie
0036-8377 Science Fiction Review†
0036-8385 Science for Schools
0036-8407 Science in Parliament
0036-8423 Science News
0036-8458 Science of Mind
0036-8466 Science of the Soul
0036-8474 Science on the March *see* 0160-0664
0036-8482 Science Policy Reviews†
0036-8504 Science Progress
0036-8520 Science Review†
0036-8539 Science Studies *changed to* Us
0036-8547 Science Teacher *see* 0261-5916
0036-8555 Science Teacher
0036-858X Science Today
0036-858X Sciences Today
0036-8598 Science Tools
0036-8601 Science World
0036-861X Sciences
0036-8628 Sciences & l'Enseignement des Sciences†
0036-8636 Sciences et Avenir
0036-8652 Sciences et Techniques
0036-8679 Scientia
0036-8687 Scientia
0036-8695 Scientia Electrica
0036-8709 Scientia Pharmaceutica
0036-8717 Scientiae
0036-8725 Scientiarum Historia†
0036-8733 Scientific American
0036-8741 S T A R
0036-875X Science and Australian Technology *see* 0310-9100
0036-8768 Scientific, Engineering, Technical Manpower Comments
0036-8776 Information-Part 1-News/Sources/Profiles *see* 0360-5817
0036-8784 Scientific Information Notes
0036-8792 Industrial Lubrication & Tribology
0036-8814 Scientific Progress/Wetenskaplike Vordering *see* 0038-2353
0036-8822 Scientific Research Council of Jamaica. Journal
0036-8830 Scientific Researches *changed to* Bangladesh Journal of Scientific and Industrial Research
0036-8857 Scientific World
0036-8865 Scienza dell'Alimentazione *see* 0391-4887
0036-8881 Scienza e Tecnica Agraria
0036-889X Scienza e Tecnica Lattiero-Casearia
0036-8903 Scienze ed il Loro Insegnamento *changed to* Scienze, la Matematica e Il Loro Insegnamento
0036-892X Scierie & Charpente†
0036-8962 Scopcraeft†
0036-8970 Scope†
0036-8989 Scope *changed to* Health Student
0036-8997 Scope (Minneapolis)
0036-9012 Scope
0036-9020 Scopus
0036-9039 Score†
0036-9055 Scotland *changed to* Business Scotland
0036-9063 Scotland's Magazine†
0036-9071 Scots Independent
0036-908X Scots Law Times
0036-911X Scottish Art Review
0036-9128 Scottish Bankers Magazine
0036-9136 Scottish Baptist Magazine
0036-9144 Scottish Birds
0036-9152 Scottish Clubman *changed to* Motorscot
0036-9160 Scottish Curler
0036-9195 Scottish Farmer
0036-9209 Scottish Field
0036-9217 Scottish Forestry
0036-9225 Scottish Geographical Magazine
0036-9233 Scottish Grocer
0036-9241 Scottish Historical Review
0036-925X Scottish Home and Country
0036-9276 Scottish Journal of Geology
0036-9284 Scottish Journal of Occupational Therapy†
0036-9292 Scottish Journal of Political Economy
0036-9306 Scottish Journal of Theology
0036-9314 Scottish Law Gazette
0036-9322 Scottish Licensed Trade News
0036-9330 Scottish Medical Journal
0036-9349 Scottish Miner
0036-9357 Scottish Pharmacist†
0036-9365 Scottish Plumbing and Heating Monthly *changed to* Plumbing and Heating
0036-9373 Scottish Primary Quarterly†
0036-939X Scottish Schoolmaster†
0036-9411 Scottish Studies
0036-942X Scottish Sunday School Teacher†
0036-9446 Scottish Women's Temperance News
0036-9454 Scott's Monthly Journal *changed to* Scott Stamp Monthly
0036-9470 Scout Pionnier *changed to* Pionnier
0036-9489 Scouting
0036-9500 Scouting Magazine
0036-9519 Scoutledaren
0036-9527 Scrap Age
0036-9535 Scraper†
0036-9543 Screen
0036-9551 Screen
0036-956X Screen Actor
0036-9586 Point of Sale & Screenprinting
0036-9594 Screen Printing
0036-9608 Screen Stories†
0036-9616 Screenland†
0036-9624 Screw
0036-9632 Scribblings†
0036-9640 Scriblerian *see* 0190-731X
0036-9721 Scripta Medica
0036-973X Scripta Mercaturae
0036-9748 Scripta Metallurgica
0036-9764 Scripta Theologica
0036-9772 Scriptorium
0036-9780 Scripture Bulletin
0036-9799 Scroll of Phi Delta Theta
0036-9802 Scugnizzo
0036-9810 Scuola Cattolica
0036-9837 Scuola di Base
0036-9845 Italy. Scuola di Guerra. Biblioteca. Bolletino
0036-9853 Scuola e Citta
0036-9861 Scuola e Didattica
0036-987X Scuola e l'Uomo
0036-9888 Scuola Italiana Moderna
0036-9896 Scuola Media†
0036-990X Scuola Normale Superiore di Pisa. Annali. Lettere, Storia e Filosofia *changed to* Scuola Normale Superiore di Pisa. Annali. Classe di Lettere e Filosofia
0036-9918 Scuola Normale Superiore di Pisa. Annali. Scienze, Fisiche e Matematiche *changed to* Scuola Normale Superiore di Pisa. Annali. Classe di Scienze
0036-9926 Scuola Viva
0036-9942 Sdelovaci Technika
0036-9950 Se Vuoi
0036-9977 Sea Breezes
0036-9985 Sea Cadet *changed to* Navy News. Sea Cadet Edition
0037-0010 San Francisco Maritime Museum. Sea Letter *see* 0732-6882
0037-0029 Sea Secrets *changed to* Sea Frontiers/Sea Secrets
0037-0037 Sea Spray
0037-0045 Maryland-Washington-Delaware Beverage Journal *changed to* Maryland-Washington Beverage Journal
0037-0053 Seaby's Coin and Medal Bulletin
0037-0061 Seacraft *see* 0005-0237
0037-007X Seafarer
0037-0096 Seafarer's Log *see* 0160-2047
0037-010X Seafood Export Journal
0037-0118 Seahorse†
0037-0126 Seal†
0037-0142 Seaman
0037-0150 Seaports and the Shipping World

0037-0169 Seara Medica Neurocirurgica
0037-0177 Seara Nova
0037-0185 Search *see* 0022-6726
0037-0193 Search and Seizure Bulletin
0037-0207 Search: Chemical Materials & Products Division†
0037-0215 Search: Coal, Coke & Mineral Tars Division†
0037-0223 Search: CPI Marketing & Statistics Division†
0037-0231 Search: Drugs Division†
0037-024X Search: Dyes, Pigments & Coatings Division†
0037-0258 Search: Essential Oils, Soaps & Toiletries Division†
0037-0266 Search: Fertilizers Division†
0037-0274 Search: Foodstuffs Division†
0037-0282 Search: Inorganic Chemicals Division†
0037-0290 Search (Amherst) *changed to* Search - Flying Saucers
0037-0304 Search: Metals Division†
0037-0312 Search: Non-Metallic Minerals Division†
0037-0320 Search: Oils, Fats & Waxes Division†
0037-0339 Search: Organic Chemicals Division†
0037-0347 Search: Pesticides Division†
0037-0355 Search: Petroleum Division†
0037-0363 Search: Plastics & Resins Division†
0037-0371 Search: Pulp & Paper Division†
0037-038X Search: Rubber Division†
0037-0398 Search: Textiles Division†
0037-0401 Searcher
0037-041X Searcher
0037-0428 Seatrade
0037-0436 Seattle Audubon Society Notes *changed to* Earthcare Northwest
0037-0444 Seattle Business
0037-0452 Seattle-King County Dental Society. Journal
0037-0460 Seattle Folklore Society Newsletter
0037-0479 Seattle University Spectator *changed to* Spectator (Seattle)
0037-0487 Seaway Review
0037-0495 Adhesion and Adhesives
0037-0509 Sechaba
0037-0517 Secolul 20
0037-0576 Second Line
0037-0584 Secondary Raw Materials *changed to* Recycling Today
0037-0592 Secret Confessions
0037-0606 Secret Place
0037-0622 Secretary
0037-0649 Secrets
0037-0657 Securitas
0037-0665 Securities Regulation & Law Report
0037-069X Security Systems Digest
0037-0703 Security World *changed to* Security
0037-0711 Sedia e Il Mobile†
0037-0738 Sedimentary Geology
0037-0746 Sedimentology
0037-0754 See
0037-0762 See India
0037-0770 Seed and Nursery Trader *changed to* Australian Horticulture
0037-0789 Seed Trade News
0037-0797 Seed World
0037-0800 Seedsmen's Digest
0037-0819 Seeing Eye Guide
0037-0827 Seek
0037-0843 Schiffahrt International /Seekiste *see* 0342-491X
0037-0851 Seer(Inkprint Edition)†
0037-086X Seeverkehr†
0037-0878 Der Seewart†
0037-0886 Seewirtschaft
0037-0894 Sefarad
0037-0916 Seglarbladet
0037-0924 Segnalatore Musicale delle Edizioni Carrara *changed to* Carrara
0037-0932 Segnalazioni Cinematografiche
0037-0940 Camera di Commercio Italiana per la Gran Bretagna e il Commonwealth. Segnalazioni
0037-0959 Segnalazioni Stradali *see* 0391-2019
0037-0967 Segretario del Comune e della Provincia†
0037-0975 Sehen und Hoeren
0037-0991 Seihin News†
0037-1009 Bookbinding Industry
0037-1017 Japanese Biochemical Society. Journal
0037-1025 Life and Environment
0037-1033 Orthopedics and Traumatology
0037-1041 Seine et Paris†
0037-105X Production Research
0037-1068 Modern Materials Handling
0037-1076 Tokyo Journal of Psychoanalysis†
0037-1084 Seishin Studies
0037-1092 Japanese Junior Red Cross
0037-1106 Seismological Society of America. Bulletin
0037-1114 Seismological Society of Japan. Journal
0037-1122 Seiva
0037-1130 Sejl og Motor
0037-1149 Sekretarska Praxe
0037-1157 Selbst Ist der Mann *changed to* Selbst mit 1000 Tips
0037-1165 Selbsthilfe
0037-1173 Sele Arte†
0037-1181 Selecciones de Libros *see* 0211-4143
0037-119X Selecciones de Teologia
0037-1203 Selecciones del Reader's Digest (Chilean Edition)
0037-1246 Selecciones del Reader's Digest (Iberian Edition)
0037-1262 Selecoes Zootecnicas†
0037-1297 Selected Abstracts of Non-U.S. Literature on Production and Industrial Uses of Radioisotopes†
0037-1300 University of California, Berkeley. Library School Library. Selected Additions to the Library School Library Collection
0037-1327 Crime and Delinquency Literature *see* 0146-9177
0037-1335 Selected Philippine Periodical Index†
0037-1343 Selected Rand Abstracts
0037-1351 Princeton University. Industrial Relations Sections Selected References
0037-136X Selected Water Resources Abstracts
0037-1378 Selection du Reader's Digest (Canadian-French Edition)
0037-1386 Selection du Reader's Digest (French Edition)
0037-1394 Selection du Reader's Digest (Swiss-French Edition)
0037-1408 Selection du Reader's Digest (Belgian-French Edition)
0037-1416 Belgium. Office Belge du Commerce Exterieur. Informations du Commerce Exterieur
0037-1424 Selection of International Railway Documentation
0037-1432 Selective Abstracting Service: Welding and Allied Processes *see* 0340-4749
0037-1459 Selektsiya i Semenovodstvo
0037-1467 Selenium and Tellurium Abstracts *changed to* C A Selects Topics
0037-1483 Selezione Dal Reader's Digest (Italian Edition)
0037-1491 Selezione di Picchiarello *changed to* Top Mix
0037-1505 Selezione per l'Avicoltore
0037-1513 Selezione Tessile
0037-1521 Selezione Veterinaria
0037-153X Self
0037-1556 Self-Knowledge
0037-1564 Self-Realization
0037-1572 Self Service and Supermarket *changed to* Super Marketing
0037-1599 Selling
0037-1602 Selling Christmas Decorations†
0037-1610 Selling Sporting Goods *see* 0279-6678
0037-1629 Selling Today
0037-1637 Selmer Bandwagon†
0037-1688 Sel'skokhozyaistvennaya Literatura S.S.S.R.
0037-1718 Selskostopanska Tekhnika
0037-1734 Semailles†
0037-1750 Semaine Commerciale
0037-1769 Annales de Pediatrie
0037-1793 Semana
0037-1807 Semana Medica†
0037-1815 Semana Medica de Centroamerica y Panama
0037-1823 Semana Medica de Mexico
0037-184X Semana Vitivinicola
0037-1858 Semanario Israelita
0037-1866 Sembrador
0037-1874 Semeador Baptista
0037-1882 Gemengo Textiel†
0037-1890 Sementi Elette
0037-1904 Semiconductor Diode & S C R D.A.T.A. Book *see* 0271-0803
0037-1912 Semigroup Forum
0037-1939 Seminar
0037-1947 Seminar†
0037-1963 Seminars in Hematology
0037-198X Seminars in Roentgenology
0037-1998 Semiotica
0037-2005 Seema†
0037-2013 Semper Floreat *changed to* Semper
0037-203X Sempre Pronto
0037-2064 Textile Review
0037-2072 Japan Research Association for Textile End-Uses. Journal
0037-2080 S E R Tidningen
0037-2099 Senales
0037-2102 Senckenbergiana Biologica
0037-2110 Senckenbergiana Lethaea
0037-2129 Sendbote des Herzens Jesu
0037-2145 Seneca Review
0037-2153 Senegal. Direction de la Statistique. Bulletin Statistique et Economique Mensuel *changed to* Senegal. Ministere de l'Economie et des Finances. Bulletin Statistiques et Economique
0037-2161 Senftenegger Monatsblatt fuer Genealogie und Heraldik†
0037-217X Dyeing & Finishing
0037-2188 Sen'i to Kogyo†
0037-2196 Senior Citizens News *changed to* S R S News
0037-2218 Senior Golfer
0037-2234 Senior News
0037-2242 Senior Scholastic *changed to* Scholastic Update
0037-2250 Seniorscope†
0037-2269 Sent *changed to* Share
0037-2277 Miscellanea Bryologica et Lichenologica†
0037-2285 Congenital Anomalies
0037-2315 Sentinel (Ottawa)
0037-234X Sentinella Agricola
0037-2366 Separation Science *see* 0149-6395
0037-2374 Sepia†
0037-2390 Sept Jours de l'Economie Britannique *changed to* Semaine Economique et Financiere en Grande Bretagne
0037-2404 Sept Jours de l'Economie Francaise†
0037-2412 Sequences
0037-2420 Sequoia
0037-2439 Serafico Vessillo
0037-2447 Serials Bulletin†
0037-2455 Journal of Sericultural Science of Japan
0037-2463 Series Haematologica†
0037-248X Sermon Builder
0037-2498 Serpe
0037-2501 Serra d'Or
0037-251X Serra-Post†
0037-2528 Serrurerie Constructions Metalliques *changed to* Structures Menuiserie Fermetures Actualities
0037-2536 Serviam
0037-2544 Service†
0037-2552 Service and Indemnity
0037-2560 Service de la Carte Geologique d'Alsace et de Lorraine. Bulletin *see* 0302-2692
0037-2579 Revue Technique Diesel
0037-2595 Service Economique & Financier "Secofi"
0037-2609 Service Employee
0037-2617 Service News
0037-2625 Service Protestant Francais de Presse et d'Information *changed to* Bulletin d'Information Protestant
0037-2633 Service Social
0037-2641 Service Social dans le Monde
0037-265X Service Station
0037-2668 Service Station & Garage Management
0037-2676 Service Station Management and Merchandising *see* 0037-2668
0037-2684 Service World Reports *changed to* I/V 400 Chain Report
0037-2692 Servicio Nacional Tecnico del Carton Ondulado. Revista†
0037-2706 Servicios Publicos *see* 0099-1694
0037-2714 Portugal. Servico de Administracao Militar. Revista Mensal *changed to* Portugal. Servico de Administracao Militar. Revista Bimestral
0037-2722 Servico de Odontologia Santaria. Boletim *changed to* Equipe de Odontologia Sanitaria. Boletim
0037-2730 Portugal. Servicos Geologicos. Comunicacoes
0037-2757 Servir Mieux
0037-2765 Servire
0037-2773 Servizio della Parola
0037-2781 Italy. Ministero dell'Interno. Rassegna degli Archivi di Stato
0037-279X Servizio Informazioni Avio
0037-2803 Servizio Migranti
0037-2811 Sesenta
0037-282X Session Cases
0037-2838 Sessuologia *changed to* Rivista di Sessuologia
0037-2846 Sestina Sveta v Obrazech†
0037-2862 Setimo Ceu
0037-2870 Seto Marine Biological Laboratory. Publications
0037-2889 Square Dancing†
0037-2897 Settanta Anni di Calcio†
0037-2900 Settegiorni
0037-2919 Settimana del Sordomuto *changed to* Settimana del Sordo
0037-2927 Settimana Medica
0037-2935 Settimanale di Diritto e Legislazione del Lavoro†
0037-2943 Seura *changed to* Seura (1979)
0037-2951 Seva-Bharati
0037-2986 Seven Arts†
0037-2994 Seven Arts Digest†
0037-3001 Seven Arts Guide†
0037-301X Seventeen
0037-3028 Seventeenth-Century News
0037-3036 73 Amateur Radio *see* 0883-234X
0037-3044 Sewanee News
0037-3052 Sewanee Review
0037-3060 Sexology *see* 0199-7149
0037-3087 Sekstant
0037-3095 Sexual Behavior†
0037-3117 S-Gravenhage *changed to* Den Haag
0037-3125 Shabistan Urdu Digest
0037-3133 Shade Tree
0037-3168 Shaftesbury Review
0037-3176 Shaheen
0037-3184 Shahpar†
0037-3214 Shakespeare Newsletter
0037-3222 Shakespeare Quarterly
0037-3230 Shakhmatnyi Byulleten'
0037-3249 Shakhmaty v S.S.S.R.
0037-3257 Shale Shaker
0037-3265 Shalom
0037-3273 Shama
0037-3281 Shankar's Weekly†
0037-329X Shantih
0037-3311 Shareholder
0037-3346 Shavian
0037-3354 Shaw Review *see* 0741-5842
0037-3362 Shawcover†
0037-3370 She
0037-3389 She†
0037-3400 Sheep Breeder and Sheepman
0037-3419 Sheera Udyog†
0037-3435 Sheet Metal Industries
0037-3494 Shelfmark
0037-3508 Shell Aviation News†
0037-3516 Shell Bitumen Review
0037-3524 Shell Chronicle
0037-3532 Shell Dealer News
0037-3540 Shell Hausnachrichten *changed to* Hausnachrichten

ISSN INDEX

ISSN	Title
0037-3559	Shell Revue†
0037-3567	Erdoel
0037-3575	Shellfish Situation and Outlook *see* 0098-8014
0037-3583	Shenandoah
0037-3605	Shepherd's Call
0037-3613	Shepherd's Magazine
0037-3621	Sherlock Holmes Journal
0037-3648	Shetkari
0037-3656	Sheviley Hahinuch
0037-3664	Audio-Visual Education
0037-3672	Shield
0037-3680	Shikoku Entomological Society. Transactions
0037-3699	Shikoku Acta Medica
0037-3702	Shikoku National Agricultural Experiment Station. Bulletin
0037-3710	Tokyo Dental College Society. Journal
0037-3729	Shilo Stag
0037-3737	New Flowers
0037-3745	New Nippon Electric Technical Review†
0037-3761	New Cities
0037-377X	Shingle
0037-3788	Shinkan News for Readers
0037-3796	Nerve Chemistry *changed to* Japanese Neurochemical Society. Bulletin
0037-3818	Shinshu University. Faculty of Engineering. Journal
0037-3826	Shinshu Medical Journal
0037-3834	Ship & Boat International
0037-3842	Ship-Shape†
0037-3850	Shipbuilding and Shipping Record *see* 0306-347X
0037-3885	Shipping and Port Review†
0037-3893	Shipping Digest
0037-3907	Shipping Executive
0037-3915	Shipping Gazette
0037-3923	Shipping Register and Shipbuilder
0037-3931	Shipping World & Shipbuilder
0037-394X	Ships Monthly
0037-3958	Shipyard Review
0037-3966	Shire & Municipal Record
0037-3974	Shirley Link *see* 0306-0748
0037-3982	Shiryo Gaido†
0037-3990	Japanese Journal of Education of the Handicapped
0037-4008	Shituf
0037-4024	Shkola i Proizvodstvo
0037-4032	Shoe and Leather Journal *see* 0705-1433
0037-4040	Shoe and Leather News
0037-4067	Shoe Service Wholesaler†
0037-4075	Shoe Workers' Journal†
0037-4083	Shoes on Parade
0037-4091	Plant Protection
0037-4105	Shokuhin To Kagaku
0037-4113	Journal of Child Health
0037-4121	Clinical Pediatrics
0037-413X	Shooroth
0037-4148	Shooting Industry
0037-4156	Shooting Sport/Tir Sportif/Tiro Deportivo/Shiess-Sport *changed to* U I T Journal
0037-4164	Shooting Times and Country Magazine
0037-4172	Shop Equipment & Shopfitting News
0037-4180	Shop Fitting and Equipment Monitor†
0037-4199	Shop Property
0037-4202	Shopfitting International†
0037-4210	Shopping Center Directory
0037-4229	Shopping Guide *changed to* Home Services
0037-4237	Shore and Beach
0037-4245	Short Story
0037-4253	Short-Term Economic Survey of Principal Enterprises in Japan *changed to* Short-Term Economic Survey of Enterprises in Japan
0037-4261	Short Wave Magazine
0037-427X	Shorthorn News
0037-4288	Shorthorn World†
0037-430X	Show-Business
0037-4318	Show Business
0037-4326	Show-Me Libraries
0037-4334	Show-Me Missouri Legionnaire
0037-4342	Showa Medical Association. Journal
0037-4350	Showcase
0037-4377	Japanese Journal of Pharmacognosy
0037-4385	Shreveport Magazine *see* 0744-3064
0037-4393	Shropshire Magazine
0037-4407	Shubyo to Engei
0037-4415	Mercury Magazine
0037-4423	Operation
0037-4431	Shveinaya Promyshlennost'
0037-444X	Si-De-Ka Magazine
0037-4466	Siberian Mathematical Journal
0037-4474	Sibirskii Matematicheskii Zhurnal
0037-4482	Sibylle
0037-4504	Sicher ist Sicher
0037-4512	Sichere Arbeit
0037-4520	Sicherheit Bergbau, Energiewirtschaft, Metallurgie *changed to* Sicherheit Bergbau, Energiewirtschaft, Geologie, Metallurgie
0037-4539	Sicherheit Zuerst
0037-4547	Sicherheitstechniker-Korrespondenz
0037-4563	Sicilia
0037-4571	Sicilia Archeologica
0037-458X	Siculorum Gymnasium
0037-4598	Sicurezza Sociale
0037-4601	Sidemount Reporter
0037-461X	7 Tage
0037-4628	Sicle a Mains
0037-4652	Siemens Data Report *changed to* Siemens-Magazin COM
0037-4660	Siemens Electromedica *see* 0340-5389
0037-4679	Siemens Electronic Components Bulletin *see* 0173-1726
0037-4687	Elektrodienst
0037-4695	Siemens Informationen Fernsprech-Vermittlungstechnik *see* 0344-4724
0037-4725	Sierra Club Bulletin *see* 0161-7362
0037-4733	Sierra Leone
0037-4741	Sierra Leone. Central Statistics Office. Quarterly Statistical Bulletin†
0037-475X	Sierra Leone Studies†
0037-4768	Sierra Leone Trade Journal
0037-4784	Siete Dias Ilustrados
0037-4792	Sifriya Laam
0037-4806	Sight and Sound
0037-4814	Sight & Sound Marketing
0037-4822	Sightsaving Review *see* 0735-5688
0037-4830	Sightlines
0037-4849	Sigma†
0037-4857	Sigma
0037-4865	Sigma-T
0037-4873	Sign (Union City)†
0037-4903	Signa†
0037-4911	Signal†
0037-492X	Signal
0037-4938	Signal (Fairfax)
0037-4946	Signal (Upminster)†
0037-4954	Signal
0037-4970	Signal International
0037-4997	Signal und Draht
0037-5004	Signal und Schiene
0037-5012	Signal 8-2
0037-5020	Signalman's Journal
0037-5039	Signature
0037-5055	Signs of the Times
0037-5063	Signs of the Times
0037-5071	Signs of the Times
0037-508X	Sigurnost
0037-5098	Siipikarja
0037-5101	Sika
0037-511X	Sikh Courier
0037-5128	Sikh Review
0037-5136	Sikio *changed to* Kenrail
0037-5136	Sikio *changed to* Tanzania Railways Corporation. Habari za Reli
0037-5144	Sikkim†
0037-5152	Sikorsky News
0037-5160	Siksha - O - Sahitya
0037-5179	Silarus
0037-5187	Silent Advocate
0037-5195	Silent Messenger
0037-5209	Silent Picture†
0037-5217	Silhouette
0037-5225	Silicates Industriels
0037-5233	Silikattechnik
0037-5241	Silikaty
0037-525X	Silk and Rayon Industries of India *changed to* Man-Made Textiles in India
0037-5268	Silk Screen
0037-5276	Silliman Christian Leader†
0037-5284	Silliman Journal
0037-5292	Silnicni Doprava *changed to* Silnicni Obzor
0037-5306	Silo†
0037-5314	Silpakon
0037-5322	Sil's'ke Budivnytstvo
0037-5330	Silva Fennica
0037-5349	Silvae Genetica
0037-5357	Silver-Rama *see* 0747-4482
0037-5365	Silver Screen†
0037-5373	Silvicultura†
0037-539X	Simian
0037-5403	Simiente
0037-5411	Simiolus
0037-542X	Simmenthal Club†
0037-5446	Simon Fraser University. Library. Information Bulletin†
0037-5454	Simon Stevin
0037-5462	Simon van der Stel Foundation. Bulletin *changed to* Restorica
0037-5470	Simon's Town Historical Society Bulletin
0037-5497	Simulation (San Diego)
0037-5500	Simulation & Games
0037-5519	Simulation Councils Proceedings *see* 0735-9276
0037-5527	Sin Nombre†
0037-5535	Sinai Hospital of Detroit. Bulletin
0037-5543	Sindacato Moderno
0037-556X	Sindicato Nacional de la Pesca Boletin de Informacion
0037-5578	Sindicato Nacional Textil. Boletin de Informacion
0037-5594	Sinfonian Newsletter *see* 8750-5347
0037-5608	Sinfonie Scacchistiche
0037-5616	Sinformation
0037-5624	Sing Out!
0037-5632	Singabout; Journal of Australian Folksong *see* 0157-3381
0037-5640	Singapore. Department of Statistics. Monthly Digest of Statistics.
0037-5659	Singapore International Chamber of Commerce. Economic Bulletin
0037-5675	Singapore Medical Journal†
0037-5683	Singapore Paediatric Society. Journal†
0037-5705	Singapore Trade and Industry *see* 0129-2951
0037-5713	Singapore Travel News *see* 0129-5020
0037-5721	Singende Kirche
0037-573X	Singer Showcase *see* 0026-816X
0037-5748	Single Parent
0037-5756	Sinn und Form
0037-5764	Sino Azul
0037-5772	Sintese Politica, Economica e Social *changed to* Sintese
0037-5780	Sintesi Economica
0037-5799	Sintesis Informativa Economica y Financiera
0037-5802	Sintesis *changed to* Sintesis - A L A D I
0037-5810	Sion
0037-5829	Sioux City Journal Farm Weekly
0037-5837	Sipapu
0037-5853	Siren†
0037-5861	Standard *changed to* Maanadens Standard
0037-5888	Sistematica
0037-5896	Sistemi e Automazione
0037-590X	Sisters Today
0037-5918	Situation Agricole en France *see* 0153-162X
0037-5926	Situation Economique *changed to* Banque de France. Enquete Mensuelle de Conjoncture
0037-5934	Situation in Argentina†
0037-5942	Gesellschaft Naturforschender Freunde zu Berlin. Sitzungsberichte. Neue Folge
0037-5950	Sivam
0037-5969	Seventies *changed to* Eighties
0037-5985	S J-Nytt
0037-5993	Sjaloom *changed to* Achtergrond
0037-6000	Sjoesport
0037-6019	Sjukgymnasten
0037-6027	Tidskrift foer Sveriges Sjukskoeterskor†
0037-6035	Skagerak
0037-6043	Skakbladet
0037-6051	Skakelblad *changed to* University of Pretoria. Annual Report
0037-606X	Skandinavisk Aktuarietidskrift *see* 0346-1238
0037-6086	Skandinavisk Motor Journal *changed to* Motor-Journalen Bilen
0037-6094	Faerg och Lack Scandinavia
0037-6108	Skandinaviska Banken. Quarterly Review *see* 0347-3139
0037-6124	Skate
0037-6132	Skating
0037-6140	Skeet Shooting Review
0037-6159	Ski
0037-6167	Ski
0037-6175	Ski Area Management
0037-6191	Ski Business†
0037-6205	Helice *see* 0762-7378
0037-6213	Ski Racing
0037-6221	Ski Runner
0037-623X	Ski-Schweizer Skisport
0037-6248	Skier (Brattleboro)†
0037-6256	Skiers Gazette *changed to* Mountain Gazette
0037-6264	Skiing
0037-6299	Skiing Trade News
0037-6310	Ringsport
0037-6329	Skillings' Mining Review
0037-6337	Skin & Allergy News
0037-6345	Skin Diver Magazine
0037-6361	Skipsteknikk *changed to* Skipsrevyen
0037-637X	Sklar a Keramik
0037-6388	Sko-Magasinet
0037-6396	Skogeieren
0037-640X	Skogen
0037-6418	S L A-Tidskriften†
0037-6426	Skogsaegaren†
0037-6442	Skol Vreizh- l'Ecole Bretonne
0037-6450	Skola Danas
0037-6469	Skolans Artikelservice
0037-6477	Barn och Kultur
0037-6485	Skolefilm†
0037-6493	Skolepsykologi
0037-6515	Skolledaren
0037-6523	Skolska Televizija
0037-6531	Skolske Novine
0037-654X	Skolski Vjesnik
0037-6558	Skolta Mondo†
0037-6566	Skolvaerlden
0037-6574	Skotoidetaljisten *changed to* SKO
0037-6582	Skov og So
0037-6590	Skraeddarmaestaren *see* 0346-1386
0037-6604	Sky and Telescope
0037-6620	Skylights†
0037-6647	Skyscraper Management *changed to* Skylines
0037-6663	Skytte-Bladet
0037-6671	Skyways
0037-668X	Slaboproudy Obzor
0037-6698	Slager
0037-6701	Slagerij *changed to* Vlees en Vleeswaren
0037-671X	Slagersambacht
0037-6736	Slavia
0037-6744	Slavia Orientalis
0037-6752	Slavic and East European Journal
0037-6779	Slavic Review
0037-6787	Slavica Slovaca
0037-6795	Slavonic and East European Review
0037-6809	Sleep Bulletin *changed to* Sleep Bulletin (1978)
0037-6817	Sleep-Learning Association. Journal
0037-6825	Slevarenstvi
0037-6833	Slezsky Sbornik
0037-6841	Slijtersvakblad
0037-685X	Slingervel
0037-6868	Sloboda
0037-6876	Sloboda
0037-6884	Slobodna Rec
0037-6892	Sloejd och Ton†
0037-6906	Slovenska Chemicka Spolocnost. Chemical Papers

0037-6914 Slovak Press Digest
0037-6922 Slovansky Prehled
0037-6930 Slovenska Akademia Vied. Biologicke Prace
0037-6949 Slovenska Archeologia
0037-6957 Slovenska Drzava
0037-6965 Slovenska Hudba†
0037-6973 Slovenska Literature
0037-6981 Slovenska Rec
0037-699X Slovenske Divadlo
0037-7007 Slovenske Pohlady na Literaturu a Umenie
0037-7015 Slovensky Hlas
0037-7023 Slovensky Narodopis
0037-7031 Slovo a Slovesnost
0037-704X Slow Learning Child *see* 0156-6555
0037-7058 Slowakei
0037-7074 Sluzba Bozja
0037-7082 Sluzba Lidu
0037-7090 Sluzben Glasnik na Sojuzot za Fizicka Kultura na Makedonija
0037-7104 Sluzbene Novine Opcine Karlovac
0037-7112 Opcina Podravska Slatina. Sluzbeni Glasnik
0037-7120 Sluzbeni Glasnik Opcine Rovinj
0037-7147 Sluzben Vesnik na Socijalisticka Republika Makedonija
0037-7155 Sluzbeni Vjesnik Opcine Buje, Novigrad i Umag
0037-7163 Sluzbeni Vjesnik Opcine Krizevci
0037-7171 Smaaskipfart *changed to* Skipsrevyen
0037-718X Small Boat *changed to* Yacht and Boat Owner
0037-7198 Voice of Small Business
0037-7201 Small Offset Printing *see* 0263-4384
0037-721X Small Pond
0037-7228 Small Press Review
0037-7244 Small Stock Magazine *see* 8750-7595
0037-7252 Small Trader and Wholesaler *changed to* Trader
0037-7260 Small World
0037-7279 Small World *changed to* Volkswagen's World
0037-7287 Smit-las *changed to* Smitweld Reportage
0037-7295 Holecpost
0037-7317 Smith College Studies in Social Work
0037-7325 Smith's Trade News *changed to* C T N
0037-7333 Smithsonian
0037-7341 Smithsonian Torch *changed to* Torch
0037-735X Smog
0037-7368 Smokeless Air *see* 0300-5143
0037-7376 Smuffeltje†
0037-7406 Snack Food
0037-7414 Snack Foods Merchandiser *see* 0026-7805
0037-7449 Sneha Sandesh†
0037-7457 Snips
0037-7473 Snowy Egret
0037-7481 Soap and Chemical Specialties *see* 0091-1372
0037-749X Soap, Perfumery and Cosmetics
0037-7503 Soaring
0037-7511 Slaski Kwartalnik Historyczny "Sobotka"
0037-752X Sobre Educacion Superior†
0037-7538 Soccer News†
0037-7546 Soccer Star†
0037-7554 Soccer World
0037-7562 Soccorso Perpetuo di Maria
0037-7589 Sociaal-Economische Raad. Informatie- en Documentatie Bulletin *see* 0920-4849
0037-7597 Sociaal-Economische Wetgeving *changed to* Tijdschrift voor Europees en Economisch Recht
0037-7600 Sociaal Maandblad Arbeid
0037-7619 Socialnytt
0037-7627 Social Action
0037-7635 Social Action *see* 0164-5528
0037-7643 Social and Economic Administration *see* 0144-5596
0037-7651 Social and Economic Studies
0037-766X Social Biology
0037-7678 Social Casework
0037-7686 Social Compass
0037-7694 Social Crediter
0037-7708 Social Debatt i Tidningar och Tidskrifter *see* 0349-9375
0037-7716 Social Defence
0037-7724 Social Education
0037-7732 Social Forces
0037-7740 Social Health News *changed to* V D News
0037-7759 Social Horizon
0037-7767 Social Justice Review
0037-7775 Washington Bulletin *see* 0149-2578
0037-7783 Social Policy
0037-7791 Social Problems
0037-7805 Church and Society
0037-7813 Social Psychiatry
0037-783X Social Research
0037-7848 Social Science *see* 0278-2308
0037-7864 Social Sciences Information
0037-7872 Social Science Record
0037-7880 Social Science Reporter and Public Relations Research Review†
0037-7899 Social Sciences and Humanities Index *see* 0094-4920
0037-7899 Social Sciences and Humanities Index *see* 0095-5981
0037-7902 Social Security Abstracts†
0037-7910 Social Security Bulletin
0037-7929 Social Security Rulings on Federal Old-Age, Survivors, Disability and Health Insurance, Supplemental Security Income, and Miners Benefits
0037-7937 Social Service†
0037-7945 Social Service Outlook†
0037-7953 Social Service Quarterly†
0037-7961 Social Service Review
0037-797X Social Services in Wisconsin†
0037-7996 Social Studies
0037-8003 Social Studies Teacher†
0037-8011 Social Survey
0037-802X Social Theory and Practice
0037-8038 Social Welfare
0037-8046 Social Work
0037-8054 Social Work
0037-8062 Social Work Education Reporter
0037-8070 Social Work Today
0037-8089 Social Worker
0037-8097 Sociale Wetenschappen
0037-8100 Socialfoerfattningar
0037-8127 Socialisme
0037-8143 Socialismo Democratico *changed to* Umanita
0037-8151 Socialismo Settanta†
0037-816X Socialist Action
0037-8178 Socialist Commentary†
0037-8186 Socialist Digest
0037-8194 Socialist Forum
0037-8208 Socialist India
0037-8216 Sotsialisticheskii Trud
0037-8224 Socialist Leader *see* 0305-0297
0037-8232 Socialist Monitor†
0037-8240 Socialist Revolution *see* 0161-1801
0037-8259 Socialist Standard
0037-8275 Socialista
0037-8283 Socialista†
0037-8291 Socialisticka Skola
0037-8305 Socialisticka Zakonnost
0037-8313 Socialisticke Zemedelstvi
0037-8321 Socialisticky Obchod
0037-833X Socialmedicinsk Tidskrift
0037-8364 Sociedad Americana de Oftalmologia y Optometria. Archivos
0037-8372 Sociedad Antioquena de Ingenieros. Boletin
0037-8380 Sociedad Argentina de Biologia. Revista†
0037-8402 Sociedad Bolivariana de Venezuela. Revista
0037-8410 Sociedad Canaria de Pediatria. Boletin†
0037-8429 Sociedad Castellano-Astur-Leonosa de Pediatria. Boletin
0037-8437 Sociedad Cientifica Argentina. Anales
0037-8453 Sociedad Colombiana de Ortodoncia. Revista
0037-8461 Sociedad Colombiana de Quimicos Farmaceuticos. Boletin
0037-847X Sociedad Cubana de Historia de la Medicina. Revista†
0037-8488 Sociedad Cubana de Ingenieros. Revista†
0037-8496 Sociedad de Bibliotecarios de Puerto Rico. Boletin†
0037-850X Sociedad de Biologia de Concepcion. Boletin
0037-8518 Sociedad de Ciencias Naturales la Salle. Memoria
0037-8526 Sociedad de Cirugia de Rosario. Boletines
0037-8534 Sociedad de Medicina Veterinaria de Chile. Revista
0037-8550 Sociedad Espanola de Ceramica. Boletin *changed to* Sociedad Espanola de Ceramica y Vidrio. Boletin
0037-8569 Sociedad Espanola de Socorros Mutuos y Beneficencia. Boletin
0037-8577 Sociedad Geografica de Colombia. Boletin
0037-8585 Sociedad Geografica de Lima, Peru. Boletin
0037-8607 Gazeta de Baixada
0037-8615 Sociedad Matematica Mexicana. Boletin
0037-8623 Sociedad Quimica del Peru. Boletin
0037-8631 Sociedad Rural Argentina. Anales
0037-864X Sociedad Rural Argentina. Boletin
0037-8658 Sociedad Vasco-Navarra de Pediatria. Boletin
0037-8666 Sociedade Brasileira de Estudos sobre Discos Voadores. Boletim
0037-8674 Sociedade Brasileira de Geografia. Boletim
0037-8682 Sociedade Brasileira de Medicina Tropical. Revista
0037-8712 Sociedade Paranaense de Matematica. Boletim
0037-8720 Societa Astronomica Italiana. Memorie
0037-8739 Societa di Studi Valdesi. Bollettino
0037-8747 Societa Entomologica Italiana. Bollettino e Memorie
0037-8755 Societa Geografica Italiana. Bollettino
0037-8763 Societa Geologica Italiana. Bolletino e Memorie *changed to* Societa Geologica Italiana. Bollettino, Memorie e Rendiconti.
0037-8771 Societa Italiana di Biologia Sperimentale. Bollettino
0037-878X Societa Italiana di Cardiologia. Bollettino *changed to* Cardiologia
0037-8798 Societa Italiana di Farmacia Ospedaliera. Bollettino
0037-8801 Societa Italiana di Fisica. Bollettino *changed to* Il Nuovo Saggiatore
0037-8828 Societa Italiana di Mineralogia e Petrologia. Rendiconti
0037-8844 Societa Italiana di Scienze Naturali e del Museo Civico di Storia Naturale. Atti
0037-8852 Societa Medica Chirurgica, Cremona. Bollettino
0037-8879 Societas†
0037-8887 Archivum Historicum Societatis Iesu
0037-8895 Societe Archeologique, Historique, Litteraire & Scientifique du Gers. Bulletin
0037-8909 Societe Belge de Geologie, de Paleontologie et d'Hydrologie. Bulletin *changed to* Societe Belge de Geologie. Bulletin
0037-8917 Societe Belge de Photogrammetrie. Bulletin Trimestriel *see* 0771-7873
0037-8925 Societe Belge d'Etudes Geographiques. Bulletin/Belgische Vereniging voor Aardrijkskundige Studies. Tijdschrift
0037-8933 Societe Belge d'Etudes Napoleoniennes. Bulletin†
0037-8941 Societe Botanique de France. Bulletin *see* 0181-1797
0037-895X Societe Centrale d'Education et d'Assistance pour les Sourds-Muets en France. Bulletin d'Information†
0037-8968 Societe Chimique de France. Bulletin
0037-8984 Societe d'Anthropologie de Paris. Bulletin & Memoires
0037-8992 Bulletin d'Archeologie et de Statistique de la Drome *changed to* Revue Dromoise
0037-900X Societe d'Astronomie Populaire de Toulouse. Bulletin Mensuel *see* 0154-4101
0037-9018 Societe de Biogeographie. Compte Rendu *changed to* Societe de Biogeographie. Compte Rendu des Seances
0037-9026 Societe de Biologie et de ses Filiales. Comptes Rendus des Seances
0037-9034 Societe de Botanique du Nord de la France. Bulletin
0037-9042 Societe de Chimie Biologique. Bulletin *see* 0300-9084
0037-9050 Societe de l'Histoire du Protestantisme Francais. Bulletin
0037-9069 Societe de Linguistique de Paris. Bulletin
0037-9077 Societe de Mythologie Francaise Bulletin
0037-9085 Societe de Pathologie Exotique et de ses Filiales. Bulletin
0037-9093 Societe de Pharmacie de Bordeaux. Bulletin
0037-9107 Societe de Pharmacie de Lyon. Bulletin des Travaux
0037-9115 Societe de Pharmacie de Montpellier. Travaux†
0037-9123 Societe de Pharmacie de Nancy. Bulletin *see* 0301-0635
0037-9131 Societe de Pharmacie de Strasbourg. Bulletin
0037-914X Societe de Statistique de Paris. Journal *changed to* Societe de Statistique de Paris. Journal
0037-9158 Societe d'Emulation du Bourbonnais. Bulletin
0037-9166 Societe des Africanistes. Journal *see* 0399-0346
0037-9174 Societe des Americanistes. Journal
0037-9182 Societe des Amis de Montaigne. Bulletin
0037-9190 Societe des Antiquaires de l'Ouest. Bulletin
0037-9204 Societe des Antiquaires de Picardie. Quarterly Bulletin
0037-9212 Revue Francaise d'Histoire du Livre
0037-9220 Societe des Chirurgiens de Paris. Bulletin et Memoires†
0037-9247 Societe des Sciences Medicales du Grand-Duche de Luxembourg. Bulletin
0037-9255 Societe des Sciences Naturelles et Physiques du Maroc. Bulletin
0037-9263 Etudes et Expansion *see* 0773-0543
0037-9271 Societe Entomologique de France. Annales
0037-928X Societe Entomologique de France. Bulletin
0037-9298 Societe Entomologique de Mulhouse. Bulletin
0037-9301 Societe Entomologique du Quebec. Annales *changed to* Revue d'Entomologie du Quebec
0037-931X Societe Francaise de Ceramique. Bulletin. *changed to* Industrie Ceramique
0037-9328 Societe Francaise de Mineralogie et de Cristallographie. Bulletin *see* 0180-9210
0037-9336 Societe Francaise de Mycologie Medicale. Bulletin
0037-9344 Societe Francaise de Numismatique. Bulletin
0037-9352 Societe Francaise de Philosophie. Bulletin
0037-9360 Societe Francaise de Physique. Bulletin
0037-9379 Societe Francaise d'Egyptologie. Bulletin
0037-9387 Societe Genealogique Canadienne-Francaise. Memoires
0037-9395 Societe Geologique de Belgique. Annales
0037-9409 Societe Geologique de France. Bulletin
0037-9417 Societe Geologique de France. Compte Rendu Sommaire des Seances *see* 0037-9409
0037-9425 Societe Historique et Archeologique du Perigord. Bulletin

0037-9441 Societe Industrielle de Mulhouse. Bulletin
0037-945X Societe Internationale de Chirurgie. Bulletin *see* 0364-2313
0037-9468 Societe Internationale de Psycho-Prophylaxie Obstetricale. Bulletin Officiel *changed to* Societe Francaise de Psycho-Prophylaxie Obstetricale. Bulletin Officiel
0037-9476 Societe Mathematique de Belgique. Bulletin
0037-9484 Societe de Mathematique de France. Bulletin *changed to* Societe Mathematique de France. Bulletin et Memoires
0037-9492 Societe Medico-Chirurgicale des Hopitaux et Formations Sanitaires des Armees. Bulletin
0037-9506 Societe Paul Claudel. Bulletin
0037-9514 Societe Prehistorique Francaise. Bulletin
0037-9522 Societe Royale Belge de Gynecologie et d'Obstetrique. Bulletin
0037-9530 Societe Royale Belge des Electriciens. Bulletin
0037-9549 Societe Royale Belge des Ingenieurs et des Industriels. Revue†
0037-9557 Societe Royale de Botanique de Belgique. Bulletin
0037-9565 Societe Royale des Sciences de Liege. Bulletin
0037-9573 Societe Royale Forestiere de Belgique. Bulletin
0037-9581 Societe Scientifique de Bretagne. Bulletin
0037-959X Societe Scientifique de Bruxelles. Annales. Sciences Mathematiques, Astronomiques et Physiques
0037-9603 Societe Vaudoise des Sciences Naturelles. Bulletin
0037-9611 Societe Vaudoise des Sciences Naturelles. Memoires
0037-962X Societe Zoologique de France. Bulletin
0037-9638 Societes Belges de Medecine Tropicale, de Parasitologie et de Mycologie. Annales *see* 0365-6527
0037-9646 Bulletin des Societes Chimiques Belges
0037-9662 Society and Culture
0037-9670 Society and Leisure†
0037-9689 Current Titles in Electrochemistry
0037-9697 Society for Analytical Chemistry. Proceedings *see* 0144-557X
0037-9700 Society for Army Historical Research. Journal
0037-9719 S C U P News and Journal *see* 0736-0983
0037-9727 Society for Experimental Biology and Medicine. Proceedings
0037-9735 Society for Historical Archaeology. Newsletter
0037-9743 Society for Italic Handwriting. Journal
0037-9751 Society for Psychical Research. Journal
0037-976X Society for Research in Child Development. Monographs
0037-9778 Society for the Bibliography of Natural History. Journal *see* 0260-9541
0037-9786 Society for the Study of State Governments. Journal
0037-9794 Society of Actuaries. Transactions (General)
0037-9808 Society of Architectural Historians. Journal
0037-9816 Society of Archivists. Journal
0037-9824 Society of Chartered Property and Casualty Underwriters. Annals *see* 0162-2706
0037-9832 Society of Cosmetic Chemists. Journal *see* 0142-5463
0037-9840 Society of Dairy Technology. Journal
0037-9859 Society of Dyers and Colourists. Journal
0037-9867 Society of Engineers. Journal and Transactions
0037-9875 Society of Fiber Science and Technology, Japan. Journal
0037-9883 Society of Film & Television Arts. Journal†
0037-9905 Society of Health of Nigeria. Journal
0037-9913 Society of Independent Professional Earth Scientists. Newsletter
0037-9921 Society of Leather Trades' Chemists. Journal *see* 0144-0322
0037-993X Society of Malawi Journal
0037-9948 Society of Medalists. News Bulletin†
0037-9956 Society of Medical Friends of Wine. Bulletin
0037-9964 Society of Mining Engineers of A I M E. Transactions†
0037-9972 Society of Occupational Medicine Transactions *see* 0301-0023
0038-0008 Society of Professional Investigators. Bulletin
0038-0016 Society of Public Teachers of Law Journal *see* 0261-3875
0038-0024 Society of Research Administrators. Journal
0038-0032 Society of Rheology. Transactions *see* 0148-6055
0038-0059 Society of Photographic Science and Technology of Japan. Bulletin
0038-0067 Society of Women Engineers. Newsletter *see* 0272-7838
0038-0075 Society Page
0038-0091 Socijalna Politika
0038-0105 Socijalni Rad
0038-0121 Socio-Economic Planning Sciences
0038-013X Sociocom Directory of Positions†
0038-0148 Sociologia†
0038-0156 Sociologia
0038-0164 Sociologia Internationalis
0038-0172 Sociologia Neerlandica *changed to* Netherlands' Journal of Sociology
0038-0180 Sociologia Religiosa†
0038-0199 Sociologia Ruralis
0038-0202 Sociological Abstracts
0038-0210 S A
0038-0229 Sociological Bulletin
0038-0237 Sociological Focus
0038-0245 Sociological Inquiry
0038-0253 Sociological Quarterly
0038-0261 Sociological Review
0038-027X Sociological Symposium *see* 0273-2173
0038-0288 Sociologicky Casopis
0038-0296 Sociologie du Travail
0038-030X Sociologie et Societes
0038-0318 Sociologija
0038-0326 Sociologija Sela
0038-0334 Sociologische Gids
0038-0342 Sociologisk Forskning
0038-0350 Sociologiske Meddelelser *see* 0901-0025
0038-0369 Sociologist
0038-0377 Sociologus
0038-0385 Sociology
0038-0393 Sociology and Social Research
0038-0407 Sociology of Education
0038-0415 Sociology of Education Abstracts
0038-0431 Sociometry *see* 0190-2725
0038-044X Socionomen *see* 0282-1001
0038-0458 Socioscoop *changed to* De Bijstaander
0038-0466 Socker Handlingar†
0038-0474 Sodobna Pedagogika
0038-0482 Sodobnost
0038-0490 Soedra Afrika. Informations Bulletin *see* 0346-9158
0038-0504 Soekaren
0038-0512 Soendags-B.T.
0038-0520 Soefart
0038-0547 Soft Drink Industry *see* 0148-6187
0038-0555 Soft Drink "Insider" Newsletter *see* 0148-6713
0038-0571 Soft Drinks *see* 0098-2318
0038-058X Soft Drinks Trade Journal *changed to* Soft Drinks
0038-0598 Soft Serve & Drive-in Field†
0038-061X Software Age†
0038-0628 Software Central†
0038-0636 Software Digest (Annandale) *changed to* Software Industry Report
0038-0644 Software: Practice & Experience
0038-0652 Software World
0038-0660 Sogo Kango
0038-0687 Soil & Health Journal
0038-0695 Soil and Water
0038-0709 Soil Association. Journal *see* 0307-2576
0038-0717 Soil Biology and Biochemistry
0038-0741 Soil Mechanics and Foundation Engineering
0038-075X Soil Science
0038-0768 Soil Science & Plant Nutrition
0038-0776 Soil Science Society of America. Proceedings *see* 0361-5995
0038-0784 Soil Sense†
0038-0792 Soils and Fertilizers
0038-0806 Soils & Foundations
0038-0814 Soins†
0038-0822 Sokol Polski
0038-0830 Geodetic Society of Japan. Journal
0038-0849 El Sol
0038-0857 Sol de Uruapan
0038-0865 Sol Institiae *changed to* Utrechts Universiteitsblad
0038-0881 Solaire Reflexen *changed to* Utrechts Universiteitsblad
0038-0903 Solanus
0038-092X Solar Energy
0038-0938 Solar Physics
0038-0946 Solar System Research
0038-0954 Soldado Argentino
0038-0962 Der Soldat
0038-0989 Soldat und Technik
0038-0997 Soldaten Kurier†
0038-1012 Soleil
0038-1039 Solia
0038-1047 Solicitors' Journal
0038-1055 Solid Fuel
0038-1063 Solid-Liquid Flow Abstracts
0038-108X Solid State Abstracts *changed to* Solid State Abstracts Journal
0038-1098 Solid State Communications
0038-1101 Solid-State Electronics
0038-111X Solid State Technology
0038-1128 Solid Waste Report
0038-1136 Solid Wastes Management/Refuse Removal Journal *see* 0745-6921
0038-1152 Solidarity
0038-1160 Solidarity
0038-1187 Solon
0038-1195 Solothurner-Zeitung
0038-1209 Sols Africains
0038-1217 Sols-Soils†
0038-1241 Solution *changed to* Amplifier
0038-125X Solvent Extraction Reviews†
0038-1268 Somali National Bank. Bulletin *changed to* Central Bank of Somalia. Bulletin
0038-1276 Somborske Novine
0038-1284 Some/Thing†
0038-1292 Someni
0038-1314 Somerset Farmer
0038-1322 Somerset Gazette†
0038-1349 Something Else Newsletter†
0038-1357 Sonderschule
0038-1365 Song Hits
0038-1373 Songwriter's Review†
0038-1381 Sonjog
0038-139X Sonntagspost
0038-1411 Sonntag
0038-142X Sonoma County Herald-Recorder *changed to* Sonoma County Daily Herald-Recorder
0038-1438 Sonorum Speculum *changed to* Key Notes
0038-1446 Sons of Italy News
0038-1454 Sons of Italy Times
0038-1462 Sons of Norway Viking
0038-1489 Gosudarstvennyi Astronomicheskii Institut im. P.K. Shternberga. Soobshcheniya
0038-1500 Sooner L P G Times
0038-1519 Sooner State Press†
0038-1527 Sophia
0038-1551 Sorby Natural History Society Newsletter
0038-156X Sorrisi e Canzoni T.V. (Milan)
0038-1578 Japanese Society of Phycology. Bulletin *changed to* Japanese Journal of Phycology
0038-1586 Japan Society for Technology of Plasticity. Journal
0038-1594 Sosiaalinen Aikakauskirja
0038-1608 Sosial Trygd
0038-1616 Sosialistinen Aikakauslehti
0038-1624 Sosialoekonomen
0038-1632 Sosialt Arbeid *changed to* Helse og Sosial Forum
0038-1659 Sot la Nape
0038-1667 Soteria
0038-1675 Sotilasaikakauslehti
0038-1691 Sotsialisticheskaya Zakonnost'
0038-1705 Sotsialistychna Kul'tura
0038-1713 Sotsial'noe Obespechenie
0038-173X Soudage et Techniques Connexes
0038-1748 Souder
0038-1756 Soul
0038-1764 Soul Force†
0038-1799 Sound *see* 0300-5364
0038-1802 Sound & Image†
0038-1810 Sound and Vibration
0038-1829 Sound and Vision *see* 0305-3601
0038-1837 Sound Ideas *see* 0888-0387
0038-1845 Sound & Communications
0038-1853 Soundings (Santa Barbara)
0038-1861 Soundings (Knoxville)
0038-187X Sounds of Truth and Tradition
0038-1896 Source
0038-190X SourceBook for Interior Planning and Design
0038-1934 South Africa. Department of Agricultural Technical Services. Science Bulletins *changed to* South Africa. Department of Agriculture. Science Bulletins
0038-1942 South Africa. Weather Bureau. Monthly Weather Report/Maandelikse Weerverslag
0038-1969 South African Archaeological Bulletin
0038-1977 South African Architectural Record *changed to* Architecture S.A. (Johannesburg)
0038-1985 South African Association for the Advancement of Science. Newsletter†
0038-1993 South African Bakery and Confectionery Review
0038-2000 South African Banker
0038-2019 South African Bee Journal
0038-2027 South African Builder
0038-2035 S.A. Building and Decorating Materials *see* 0007-3369
0038-2043 South African Cancer Bulletin
0038-206X South African Chartered Accountant
0038-2078 South African Chemical Institute. Journal *see* 0379-4350
0038-2094 South African Chessplayer
0038-2116 South African Citrus Journal *changed to* South African Citrus and Sub-Tropical Fruit Journal
0038-2132 South African Digest
0038-2140 South African Engineer *changed to* Current
0038-2159 South African Fire Services Institute. Quarterly
0038-2167 South African Forestry Journal
0038-2175 South African Garage and Motor Engineer *changed to* Motor World
0038-2183 South African Garden & Home
0038-2205 S.A. Medical Equipment News *changed to* S.A. Hospital Supplies
0038-2213 South African Institute of Assayers and Analysts. Journal
0038-2221 South African Institute of Electrical Engineers. Transactions
0038-223X South African Institute of Mining and Metallurgy. Journal
0038-2256 South African Insurance Magazine†
0038-2264 South African Jersey†
0038-2272 S. A. Jewellery & Gifts†
0038-2280 South African Journal of Economics
0038-2299 South African Journal of Laboratory and Clinical Medicine†
0038-2302 South African Journal of Medical Laboratory Technology
0038-2310 South African Journal of Medical Sciences†

1306 ISSN INDEX

0038-2329 South African Journal of Obstetrics and Gynecology *see* 0038-2469
0038-2337 South African Journal of Occupational Therapy
0038-2353 South African Journal of Science
0038-2361 South African Journal of Surgery
0038-237X South African Lapidary Magazine
0038-2388 South African Law Journal
0038-2396 South African Law Reports
0038-240X South African Libraries/Suid-Afrikaanse Biblioteke *see* 0256-8861
0038-2418 South African Library. Quarterly Bulletin
0038-2442 South African Mechanical Engineer
0038-2450 S.A. Mechanised Handling Equipment *changed to* Promat News
0038-2469 South African Medical Journal
0038-2477 South African Mining Equipment *changed to* South African Mining & Engineering Journal
0038-2485 South African Motor-Cyclist
0038-2493 South African Music Teacher
0038-2507 South African Nursing Journal *changed to* Nursing News
0038-2515 South African Observer
0038-2523 South African Outlook
0038-2531 S.A. Packaging *changed to* Pack & Print
0038-254X South African Panorama
0038-2558 South African Pharmaceutical Journal
0038-2566 South African Philatelist
0038-2574 South African Press Review *see* 0015-5055
0038-2582 S.A. Printer *changed to* Pack & Print
0038-2590 South African Racehorse *changed to* South African Racehorse
0038-2604 South African Red Cross News Digest *changed to* South African Red Cross Society (Cape Region). Newsletter
0038-2612 South African Refractionist
0038-2620 South African Reserve Bank. Quarterly Bulletin
0038-2647 South African Review†
0038-2655 South African Rider
0038-2671 South African Shipping News and Fishing Industry Review†
0038-2698 South Africa Bureau of Standards. Bulletin
0038-2701 South African Stationery Trades Journal *changed to* Stationery
0038-271X South African Statistical Journal
0038-2728 South African Sugar Journal
0038-2736 South African Survey Journal
0038-2744 South African Table Tennis News
0038-2752 South African Tax Cases Reports *changed to* Juta's Tax Service
0038-2760 South African Transport
0038-2779 South African Treasurer
0038-2787 South African Typographical Journal
0038-2795 South African Union Lantern
0038-2809 South African Veterinary Medical Association. Journal *see* 0301-0732
0038-2817 South African Yachting, Powerboats, Sailing, Waterski *see* 0256-7431
0038-2841 South Asian Review†
0038-285X South Asian Studies
0038-2876 South Atlantic Quarterly
0038-2892 South Australian Electrical Contractor
0038-2906 South Australian Government Gazette
0038-2922 South Australian Institute of Architects' Monthly Bulletin
0038-2949 Central Times *changed to* New Times
0038-2957 South Australian Motor
0038-2965 South Australian Naturalist
0038-2973 South Australian Ornithologist
0038-2981 South Australian Racing Calendar
0038-3015 South Australian Teachers Journal
0038-3023 South Australiana†
0038-3031 South Bay Economic Review *changed to* Daily Breeze Economic Review
0038-304X South Carolina Economic Indicators
0038-3058 South Carolina Education Journal†
0038-3066 South Carolina Education News Emphasis *changed to* S C E A Emphasis
0038-3074 South Carolina Farmer-Grower†
0038-3082 South Carolina Historical Magazine
0038-3090 South Carolina History Illustrated†
0038-3104 South Carolina Law Review
0038-3112 South Carolina Librarian
0038-3120 South Carolina Magazine†
0038-3139 South Carolina Medical Association. Journal
0038-3147 South Carolina Methodist Advocate *changed to* South Carolina United Methodist Advocate
0038-3155 South Carolina Nursing†
0038-3163 South Carolina Review
0038-3171 South Carolina Schools
0038-318X South Carolina. State Department of Education. Office of General Education Media Services Newsletter†
0038-3198 South Carolina Wildlife
0038-3201 South Carolina Young Farmer and Future Farmer
0038-321X South Central Bulletin *changed to* South Central Review
0038-3228 South Coast Herald
0038-3252 South Dakota Bird Notes
0038-3260 South Dakota Business Review
0038-3279 South Dakota Conservation Digest
0038-3287 South Dakota Dental Association. Newsletter
0038-3295 Farm & Home Research
0038-3309 South Dakota High Liner
0038-3317 South Dakota Journal of Medicine
0038-3325 South Dakota Law Review
0038-3341 South Dakota Musician
0038-3368 South Dakota Review
0038-3376 South Dakota State Library Commission Bulletin†
0038-3384 South Dakota Stockgrower
0038-3406 South East Asia Journal of Theology†
0038-3414 South-East Asia Treaty Organization. Economic Bulletin†
0038-3422 South East London & Kentish Mercury
0038-3430 South End
0038-3465 South India Churchman
0038-3473 South Indian Horticulture
0038-3481 South Indian Teacher
0038-349X South Pacific Bulletin†
0038-3503 South Penn Motorist *changed to* A A A Traveler (York, 1983)
0038-352X South Shore Record
0038-3538 South Street Reporter *changed to* Seaport: New York's History Magazine
0038-3546 South Texas Law Journal *changed to* South Texas Law Review
0038-3562 South Wales Institute of Architects. Journal†
0038-3570 South Wales Institute of Engineers. Proceedings
0038-3597 Southam Building Guide
0038-3600 Southeast Asia Quarterly *changed to* Southeast Asia Journal
0038-3619 Southeast Asian Journal of Tropical Medicine and Public Health
0038-3627 Southeast Furniture & Appliance News†
0038-3643 Southeastern Dairy Review
0038-3651 Southeastern Drug Journal *see* 0192-5792
0038-366X Southeastern Geographer
0038-3678 Southeastern Geology
0038-3686 Southeastern Librarian
0038-3694 Southeastern Peanut Farmer
0038-3708 Southeastern Poultry Times *see* 0048-4989
0038-3716 Southeasterner
0038-3724 Southend-on-Sea and District Chamber of Trade and Industry. Monthly Journal *changed to* Southend-on-Sea & District Chamber of Commerce, Trade & Industry. Monthly Journal
0038-3732 Southerly
0038-3775 Southern Africa†
0038-3791 Southern Africa Textiles†
0038-3805 Southern and Southwestern Railway Club. Proceedings
0038-3813 Southern Association of Colleges and Schools. Proceedings
0038-3821 Southern Automotive Journal†
0038-383X Southern Banker
0038-3848 Southern Baptist Educator
0038-3856 Southern Bell Views
0038-3864 Southern Building
0038-3872 Southern California Academy of Sciences. Bulletin
0038-3902 Southern California Guide
0038-3910 Southern California Law Review
0038-3929 Southern California Quarterly
0038-3937 Southern California Rancher†
0038-3945 Southern California Dental Laboratory Association. Bulletin
0038-3953 Southern California Teamster
0038-397X Southern Cemetery
0038-3988 Southern Connecticut Business Journal *see* 0300-7529
0038-4003 Southern Cooperator
0038-4011 Southern Cross
0038-402X Southern Dairy Products Journal
0038-4038 Southern Economic Journal
0038-4046 Southern Economist
0038-4054 Southern Engineer
0038-4070 Southern Exposure (Talladega)
0038-4089 Southern Exposure Library Staff Bulletin
0038-4097 Southern Farm Equipment *changed to* National Farm Equipment and Supply
0038-4119 Southern Florist and Nurseryman *changed to* Nursery Manager
0038-4127 Southern Folklore Quarterly
0038-4135 Southern Funeral Director
0038-4143 Southern Gardens
0038-4151 Southern Garment Manufacturer *changed to* Southern Garment
0038-416X Southern Hardware†
0038-4186 Southern Humanities Review
0038-4208 Southern Industrial Supplier
0038-4224 Southern Israelite *see* 0892-3345
0038-4232 Southern Jeweler
0038-4240 Southern Jewish Weekly
0038-4259 Southern Journal of Business *see* 0148-2963
0038-4267 Southern Journal of Education Research *see* 0279-0688
0038-4275 Southern Journal of Optometry
0038-4283 Southern Journal of Philosophy
0038-4291 Southern Literary Journal
0038-4305 Southern Living
0038-4313 Southern Lumberman
0038-433X Southern Medical Bulletin *see* 0097-5419
0038-4348 Southern Medical Journal
0038-4364 Southern Methodist University. Industrial Information Services. Newsletter†
0038-4372 Southern Motor Cargo
0038-4380 Southern News and Views
0038-4399 Southern Outdoors/Gulf Coast Fisherman *see* 0199-3372
0038-4402 Southern Patriot *see* 0199-8668
0038-4410 Southern Pharmaceutical Journal *see* 0192-5792
0038-4461 Southern Plumbing, Heating, Cooling
0038-447X Southern Poetry Review
0038-4488 Southern Pulp and Paper Manufacturer *see* 0270-5222
0038-4496 Southern Quarterly
0038-450X Southern Railways
0038-4518 Southern Research Institute Bulletin
0038-4526 Southern Review
0038-4534 Southern Review
0038-4542 Southern Sawdust†
0038-4577 Southern Sociologist
0038-4585 Southern Speech Journal *see* 0361-8269
0038-4593 Southern Stationer and Office Outfitter *changed to* Southern Office Dealer
0038-4607 Southern Textile News
0038-464X Southern Wings
0038-4658 Southwest Advertising and Marketing *changed to* Adweek/Southwest
0038-4666 Southwest Furniture News *changed to* Home Furnishings
0038-4674 Southwest Jewish Chronicle
0038-4690 Southwest Kansas Register
0038-4704 Southwest News-Herald
0038-4712 Southwest Review
0038-4720 Southwest Water Works Journal *see* 0196-0717
0038-4739 Southwestern Art *changed to* Art Insight/Southwest
0038-4747 Southwestern Association on Indian Affairs. Quarterly†
0038-4763 Southwestern Collegian†
0038-478X Southwestern Historical Quarterly
0038-4798 Independent Jeweler *changed to* Independent Jeweler (1978)
0038-4801 Southwestern Journal of Anthropology *see* 0091-7710
0038-481X Southwestern Journal of Philosophy *see* 0276-2080
0038-4828 Southwestern Journal of Theology
0038-4836 Southwestern Law Journal
0038-4844 Southwestern Lore
0038-4852 Southwestern
0038-4860 Southwestern Medicine†
0038-4879 Southwestern Miller *see* 0091-4843
0038-4887 Southwestern Minnesota Education Association Bulletin†
0038-4895 Southwestern Musician
0038-4909 Southwestern Naturalist
0038-4917 Southwestern News
0038-4925 Southwestern Philosophical Society. Newsletter
0038-4941 Social Science Quarterly
0038-495X Southwestern Veterinarian
0038-4968 Souvenirs and Novelties
0038-4976 Sou'wester (Edwardsville)
0038-4984 Sou'wester (South Bend)
0038-500X Sovetakan Arvest
0038-5018 Sovetakan Grakanutiun
0038-5026 Sovetakan Mankavarzh
0038-5034 Sovetskaya Arkheologiya
0038-5050 Sovetskaya Etnografiya
0038-5069 Sovetskaya Geologiya
0038-5077 Sovetskaya Meditsina
0038-5085 Sovetskaya Muzyka
0038-5093 Sovetskaya Pedagogika
0038-5107 Sovetskaya Torgovlya
0038-5123 Sovetskii Ekran
0038-514X Soviet Union
0038-5158 Sovetskii Shakhter
0038-5166 Sovetskie Arkhivy
0038-5174 Sovetskie Profsoyuzy
0038-5182 Sovetskoe Finnougrovedenie
0038-5190 Sovetskoe Foto
0038-5204 Sovetskoe Gosudarstvo i Pravo
0038-5220 Soviet Military Review
0038-5239 Sovetskoe Zdravookhranenie
0038-5247 Sovety Deputatov Trudyashchikhsya *changed to* Sovety Narodnykh Deputatov
0038-5263 Soviet and Eastern European Foreign Trade
0038-5271 Soviet Antarctic Expedition Information Bulletin†
0038-528X Soviet Anthropology and Archeology
0038-5298 Soviet Applied Mechanics
0038-5301 Soviet Astronomy A.J. *changed to* Soviet Astronomy
0038-531X Soviet Atomic Energy
0038-5328 Soviet Automatic Control/Avtomatyka *see* 0882-570X
0038-5336 Soviet-Bloc Research in Geophysics, Astronomy, and Space *changed to* U S S R Report: Space
0038-5344 Soviet Chemical Industry
0038-5360 Soviet Education
0038-5379 Soviet Electrical Engineering
0038-5387 Soviet Electrochemistry
0038-5395 Soviet Film
0038-5409 Soviet Genetics
0038-5417 Soviet Geography - Review and Translation *changed to* Soviet Geography
0038-5425 Soviet Hydrology: Selected Papers
0038-5441 Soviet Inventions Illustrated
0038-545X Soviet Jewish Affairs
0038-5468 Soviet Jewry Action Newsletter
0038-5484 Soviet Journal of Non-Ferrous Metals
0038-5492 Soviet Journal of Nondestructive Testing

ISSN	Title
0038-5506	Soviet Journal of Nuclear Physics
0038-5514	Soviet Journal of Optical Technology
0038-5522	Soviet Land
0038-5530	Soviet Law and Government
0038-5549	Soviet Life
0038-5557	Soviet Literature
0038-5565	Soviet Materials Science
0038-5581	Soviet Mining Science
0038-559X	Soviet Neurology and Psychiatry
0038-5603	Soviet News
0038-5611	Soviet Panorama see 0038-5549
0038-562X	Soviet Physics - Acoustics
0038-5638	Soviet Physics - Crystallography
0038-5646	Soviet Physics - J E T P
0038-5654	Soviet Physics - Solid State
0038-5662	Soviet Physics - Technical Physics
0038-5670	Soviet Physics - Achievements changed to Soviet Physics - Uspekhi
0038-5689	Soviet Physics - Doklady
0038-5697	Soviet Physics Journal
0038-5700	Soviet Physics - Semiconductors
0038-5719	Soviet Plant Physiology
0038-5727	Soviet Plastics†
0038-5735	Soviet Powder Metallurgy and Metal Ceramics
0038-5743	Soviet Progress in Chemistry
0038-5751	Soviet Psychology
0038-576X	Soviet Radiochemistry
0038-5786	Soviet Review
0038-5794	Soviet Review
0038-5816	Soviet Science Review†
0038-5824	Soviet Sociology
0038-5832	Soviet Soil Science
0038-5840	Soviet Statutes and Decisions
0038-5859	Soviet Studies
0038-5867	Soviet Studies in History
0038-5875	Soviet Studies in Literature
0038-5883	Soviet Studies in Philosophy
0038-5891	Soviet Technology Bulletin†
0038-5905	Soviet Weekly
0038-5913	Soviet Woman
0038-5921	Sovietica†
0038-5948	Sovremennik
0038-5956	Sovremennoe Polskoe Pravo
0038-5964	Sovremeno Pretprijatie
0038-5972	Sovremenost
0038-5980	Sower
0038-5999	Sowjetstudien†
0038-6006	Sowjetwissenschaft
0038-6014	Soybean Digest
0038-6030	Der Sozialdemokrat
0038-6049	Soziale Berufe
0038-6057	Soziale Selbstverwaltung
0038-6065	Soziale Sicherheit
0038-6073	Soziale Welt
0038-609X	Sozialer Fortschritt
0038-6103	Der Sozialistische Akademiker†
0038-6111	Sozialistische Arbeitswissenschaft
0038-6138	Sozialistische Demokratie†
0038-6146	Sozialistische Erziehung
0038-6154	Sozialistische Forstwirtschaft
0038-6170	Sozialkunde Heute†
0038-6189	Sozialpaedagogik
0038-6197	Sozialpolitik und Arbeitsrecht
0038-6200	Sozial Versicherung - Arbeitsschutz†
0038-6219	Space (London)
0038-6227	Space†
0038-6235	Space Age Market Research
0038-6243	Space Business Daily News Service see 0889-0404
0038-6251	Space Business Week†
0038-6278	Space Letter
0038-6286	Space Life Sciences changed to Origins of Life and Evolution of the Biosphere
0038-6294	Space Propulsion see 0363-8219
0038-6308	Space Science Reviews
0038-6324	Space-Wise
0038-6332	Space World
0038-6340	Spaceflight
0038-6367	Spafaswap
0038-6375	Spain. Departamento de Fomento y Difusion Internacional. Documentacion†
0038-6391	Spain. Instituto Nacional de Estadistica. Boletin Mensual de Estadistica
0038-6413	Spain. Ministerio de Industria. Registro de la Propreidad Industrial. Boletin Oficial
0038-6448	Span (Stowmarket)†
0038-6456	Spanish Cultural Index
0038-6464	Spanish Newsletter†
0038-6499	Spare Time
0038-6502	Sparebankbladet
0038-6510	Der Sparefroh
0038-6529	Sparekassetidende see 0107-9530
0038-6537	Sparer Magazin†
0038-6545	Sparfraemjaren see 0346-1602
0038-6553	Spark
0038-6561	Sparkasse†
0038-657X	Sparkling Gems†
0038-6588	Sparrow changed to Sparrow Poverty Pamphlets
0038-6596	Spartacist
0038-6618	Frosch†
0038-6626	Speaking of "Columbias"
0038-6634	Spear
0038-6650	Spearhead†
0038-6677	Spear's Special Situation Reports†
0038-6685	Specchio del Libro per Ragazzi†
0038-6693	Special
0038-6715	Special Events in Georgia†
0038-6723	Special Libraries
0038-6731	Special Libraries Association. Biological Sciences Division. Reminder†
0038-6782	Special Libraries Association. Publishing Division. Bulletin†
0038-6855	Specialities†
0038-6863	Specializzazione
0038-6871	Specialty Advertising Report changed to Ideasworth
0038-688X	Specialty Baker's Voice
0038-6898	Specialty Foods Magazine†
0038-6901	Specialty Salesman and Franchise Opportunities see 0738-4211
0038-6936	Specijalna Skola
0038-6944	Spectacle du Monde
0038-6952	Spectator
0038-6960	Spectator†
0038-6995	Spectroscopia Molecular†
0038-7002	Spectroscopical Society of Japan. Journal
0038-7010	Spectroscopy Letters
0038-7029	Spectrovision changed to Scan
0038-7061	Spectrum (Amherst)
0038-7088	Spectrum†
0038-7096	Spectrum der Herenmode
0038-710X	Spectrum International
0038-7126	Speculator†
0038-7134	Speculum
0038-7142	Speech and Drama
0038-7150	Speech and Hearing Association of Virginia. Journal
0038-7169	Speech Monographs see 0363-7751
0038-7177	Speech Teacher see 0363-4523
0038-7185	Speed Age†
0038-7193	Speed and Custom Dealer changed to Specialty & Custom Dealer
0038-7207	Speed and Custom Equipment News see 0018-6023
0038-7215	Speed and Supercar†
0038-7223	Speed Mechanics†
0038-7231	Speedway Post†
0038-724X	Speedway Star
0038-7258	D O E
0038-7266	Spejlet
0038-7274	Spektrum
0038-7282	S P E L D Information
0038-7290	Speleologia Emiliana
0038-7304	Speleologist
0038-7312	Spelewei†
0038-7320	Speling
0038-7339	Spelling Progress Bulletin†
0038-7347	Spenser Newsletter
0038-7355	Sperimentale
0038-738X	Spettacolo
0038-7398	Spettatore Internazionale†
0038-7401	Spettatore Musicale
0038-741X	Sphincter
0038-7428	Sphinx
0038-7436	Sphinx-Magazin
0038-7444	Spica
0038-7452	Der Spiegel
0038-7460	Spiegel der Historie†
0038-7479	Spiegel der Letteren
0038-7487	Spiegel Historiael
0038-7495	Spiegelreflex - Praxis Reflex changed to Reflex
0038-7509	Spiel und Theater
0038-7517	Der Spielplan
0038-7525	Das Spielzeug
0038-7533	Spin†
0038-755X	Spinning Wheel†
0038-7584	Spirit
0038-7592	Spirit & Life
0038-7606	Spiritual Book News
0038-7614	Spiritual Frontiers†
0038-7622	Spiritual Healer
0038-7630	Spiritual Life
0038-7649	Spiritualita
0038-7657	Spiritudsen- und Weinhandel
0038-7665	Spiritus
0038-7681	Spokane Affairs
0038-7711	Spokane, Washington. Official Gazette
0038-772X	Spoken English
0038-7738	Spokeswoman†
0038-7746	Spolem
0038-7754	Spoljnopoliticka Dokumentacija
0038-7770	Sport
0038-7789	International Union of Students. Sport Bulletin
0038-7797	Sport
0038-7800	Sport Age†
0038-7819	Sport and Recreation see 0144-7181
0038-7827	Sport-Auto
0038-7835	Sport Aviation
0038-7851	Sport en Spel
0038-786X	Sport Fishery Abstracts
0038-7878	Sport Flying†
0038-7908	Sport in the U.S.S.R.
0038-7916	Sport Italia
0038-7924	Sport- und Baederbauten see 0344-6492
0038-7932	Sport und Technik
0038-7959	Sportartikel-Sportmode changed to Speil-Sport-Freizeit-Mode
0038-7967	Sportdykaren
0038-7991	Sportimes
0038-8017	Sporting Goods Dealer
0038-805X	Sporting News
0038-8076	Sporting Shooter†
0038-8084	Shooting Times
0038-8092	Sportivnaya Zhizn' Rossii
0038-8106	Sportivnye Igry
0038-8114	Sportovni a Umelecka Gymnastika changed to Sportovni-Moderni Gymnastika
0038-8122	Sportowiec
0038-8130	Sportparade
0038-8149	Sports Afield
0038-8165	Sports Car Graphic see 0027-2094
0038-8173	Sports Car World
0038-8181	Sports and Recreation Equipment†
0038-8211	Sportsfiskeren
0038-822X	Sports Illustrated
0038-8238	Sports Loisirs, Education Physique†
0038-8254	Sports Trader
0038-8270	Sportshelf News†
0038-8289	Sportski Ribolov changed to Ribolov
0038-8297	Sportswear on Parade
0038-8300	Sportyvna Gazeta
0038-8319	Sposa
0038-8343	Spot News from Abroad†
0038-8351	Spotlight†
0038-8386	Spotlight
0038-8408	Spotlight on South Africa†
0038-8416	P D C A 74 see 0735-9713
0038-8424	Spots and Stripes see 0163-416X
0038-8432	Spotted News
0038-8440	Spraakvaard
0038-8459	Sprachdienst
0038-8467	Die Sprache
0038-8475	Sprache im Technischen Zeitalter
0038-8483	Sprachkunst
0038-8491	Sprachlabor†
0038-8505	Der Sprachmittler
0038-8513	Sprachspiegel
0038-8521	Spraak og Spraakundervisning†
0038-853X	Sprawy Miedzynarodowe
0038-8548	Sprechsaal fuer Keramik, Glas, Email, Silikate see 0341-0676
0038-8556	Sprig of Shillelagh†
0038-8564	Spring Arbor College Bulletin changed to Spring Arbor College Journal
0038-8572	Spring Thirty-One Hundred†
0038-8580	Springfield-Illinois-Review of Business & Economic Conditions†
0038-8599	Springfield. Massachusetts. City Library Bulletin
0038-8602	Springfield Public Schools. News and Views
0038-8610	Springfielder changed to Concordia Theological Quarterly
0038-8629	Springs & Brakpan Advertiser
0038-8637	Sprinkler Bulletin
0038-8645	Sprog og Kultur†
0038-867X	Spur changed to Young Country
0038-8688	Spur of Virginia see 0098-5422
0038-8696	Spurk
0038-870X	Der Spurkranz
0038-8718	Sputnik
0038-8726	Sputnik Junior
0038-8734	Square Dance see 0091-3383
0038-8750	Squilla
0038-8769	Squilla di S. Gerardo
0038-8777	Srecanja
0038-8785	Srednee Spetsial'noe Obrazovanie
0038-8793	Srpska Akademija Nauka i Umetnosti. Glasnik†
0038-8807	Sruth†
0038-8815	St. Paul's Printer
0038-8823	Staal†
0038-884X	Der Staat
0038-8858	Staat und Recht
0038-8866	Staatsbibliothek Preussischer Kulturbesitz. Mitteilungen
0038-8874	Staatsbuerger
0038-8882	Staatspensioenen
0038-8890	Stacks†
0038-8904	Stad Gods
0038-8912	Stadio Club†
0038-8920	Stadion
0038-8939	Stadlinger Post
0038-8947	Stads & Havneningenioeren
0038-8963	Stadsbyggnad
0038-8971	Stadt Linz
0038-898X	Stadt- und Gebaeudetechnik
0038-8998	Stadtbau-Informationen
0038-9013	Stadtverkehr
0038-9021	S I N Information†
0038-903X	Staedtebund see 0342-7706
0038-9048	Der Staedtetag
0038-9056	Starch
0038-9064	Staff and Line changed to Inforcadre
0038-9072	Staff Spectator†
0038-9080	Stage and Cinema changed to Cinema & T V
0038-9099	Stage and Television Today
0038-9102	Stage Centre changed to Manitoba Theatre Centre. House Programme
0038-9110	Stage in Canada†
0038-9129	Stagioni changed to Quattro Stagioni
0038-9145	Stahlbau
0038-9153	Stain Technology
0038-9161	Stained Glass
0038-917X	Stainless Steel
0038-9188	Stakker changed to Elvas-Krant
0038-9196	Stalt†
0038-920X	Stal'
0038-9218	Steel in the U S S R
0038-9226	Stalactite
0038-9234	Stamboeker changed to Veeverbetering
0038-9242	Stamford Collegian changed to Stamford Journal
0038-9269	Stamp Collecting see 0265-8216
0038-9277	Stamp Lover
0038-9293	Stamp News
0038-9307	Stamp Weekly†
0038-9315	Stamp Wholesaler
0038-9323	Stampa Medica
0038-934X	Stamping/Diemaking†
0038-9358	Stamps
0038-9366	Stand Magazine
0038-9374	Standard

0038-9382 Standard (Evanston)
0038-9390 Standard (Boston)
0038-9404 Standard *see* 0740-9680
0038-9412 Standard and Poor's Security Owner's Stock Guide *see* 0737-4135
0038-9420 Standard & Poor's Stock Summary
0038-9439 Standard Bank Review *see* 0305-9553
0038-9447 Standard Bearer (Sacramento)
0038-9455 Standard Rate and Data Service. Print Media Production Data
0038-9463 Standard Rate and Data Service. Direct Mail List Rates and Data
0038-948X Standard Rate and Data Service. Business Publication Rates and Data
0038-9498 Standard Rate and Data Service. Canadian Advertising Rates and Data
0038-9501 Dati e Tariffe Pubblicitarie
0038-951X Media Daten
0038-9528 Medios Publicitarios Mexicanos *changed to* Directorio M P M - Medios Impresos
0038-9536 Standard Rate and Data Service. Network Rates and Data†
0038-9544 Standard Rate and Data Service. Newspaper Rates and Data
0038-9552 Standard Rate and Data Service. Spot Television Rates and Data
0038-9560 Standard Rate and Data Service. Spot Radio Rates and Data
0038-9579 Tarif Media
0038-9587 Standard Rate and Data Service. Weekly Newspaper Rates and Data *see* 0162-8887
0038-9595 Standard Rate and Data Service. Consumer Magazine and Farm Publication Rates and Data *changed to* Standard Rate and Data Service. Consumer Magazine and Agri-Media Rates and Data
0038-9609 Standard Rate and Data Service. Transit Advertising Rates and Data†
0038-9617 Standard-Serie *changed to* Record-Serie
0038-9625 Standardisering
0038-9633 Standards Action
0038-9641 Standards and Specifications Information Bulletin
0038-965X Standards/Canada *changed to* Focus
0038-9668 Standards Engineering
0038-9676 A N S I Reporter
0038-9684 Standards: Monthly Additions
0038-9692 Standarty i Kachestvo
0038-9706 Stander
0038-9714 Standing Conferences of Women's Organisations. Newsletter *changed to* Newsletter of Women's Forum and the Standing Conferences of Women's Organisations
0038-9722 Der Standpunkt
0038-9730 Standpunte
0038-9749 Stanford Alumni Almanac†
0038-9757 Stanford Chaparral
0038-9765 Stanford Law Review
0038-9781 Stanford M.D.†
0038-979X Stanford Observer
0038-9803 Stanford University. Graduate School of Business. Bulletin *see* 0164-6605
0038-9811 Stanki i Instrumenty
0038-982X Stanovnistvo
0038-9838 Staple Cotton Review *changed to* StaplReview
0038-9846 Star and Garter Magazine
0038-9854 Star & Lamp of Pi Kappa Phi
0038-9862 Star & Style
0038-9870 Star of Zion
0038-9889 Star Serviceman
0038-9900 Star West
0038-9919 Stardock
0038-9927 Starlights
0038-9935 Start
0038-9943 Start & Speed
0038-9951 Start und Aufstieg
0038-996X Startling Detective
0038-9978 Stash Capsules†
0038-9986 Stat (Milwaukee)
0038-9994 The State..
0039-0003 State Bank of India. Monthly Review
0039-0011 State Bank of Pakistan. Bulletin
0039-002X State Bar of California. Journal *see* 0161-9241
0039-0046 State Education Journal Index
0039-0038 State Bar of New Mexico. Bulletin and Advance Opinions
0039-0054 State Engineer†
0039-0070 New Jersey School Boards Association. School Board Notes *changed to* New Jersey School Boards Association. School Leader
0039-0089 State Geologists Journal
0039-0097 State Government
0039-0119 State Government News
0039-0143 State Principals Association. Bulletin *changed to* Maine Secondary School Principals' Association. Newsletter
0039-0151 State Service *see* 0265-0975
0039-016X State Transport News *changed to* Journal of Transport Management
0039-0178 State Underwriter *see* 0198-683X
0039-0186 State University of New York. College at Buffalo. Record *changed to* Buffalo State Record
0039-0194 State University College of Arts and Science at Geneseo. School of Library Science. Newsletter *changed to* State University College of Arts & Science at Geneseo. School of Library and Information Science. Newsletter
0039-0208 State University of New York. Downstate Medical Center. Faculty Briefs *changed to* Focus
0039-0232 Staten Island Historian
0039-0240 Staten Island Institute of Arts & Sciences. Proceedings
0039-0259 Sweden. Statens Naturvaardsverk. Publikationer
0039-0267 Sweden. Statens Planverk. Statens Planverk Aktuellt *see* 0280-4131
0039-0275 Statens Vaextskyddsanstalt. Meddelanden†
0039-0291 States†
0039-0305 Statesman
0039-0313 Statesman
0039-0321 Statesman Weekly
0039-0348 Stati Uniti d'Europa
0039-0356 Station Seismographique de Lisboa. Bulletin Seismique
0039-0364 Stationer's
0039-0372 Stationery Trade Review
0039-0380 Statistica
0039-0399 Statistica del Turismo
0039-0402 Statistica Neerlandica
0039-0410 U.S. Securities and Exchange Commission. Statistical Bulletin *see* 0272-7846
0039-0437 Statistical Methods in Linguistics *changed to* Linguistic Calculation
0039-0445 Statistical News Summary†
0039-0453 Statistical Office of the European Communities. Foreign Trade: Monthly Statistics
0039-0461 Statistical Office of the European Communities. General Statistical Bulletin†
0039-047X Statistical Office of the European Communities. Industrial Statistics†
0039-0488 Statistical Office of the European Communities. Social Statistics
0039-050X Statistical Reporter†
0039-0518 Statistical Theory and Method Abstracts
0039-0526 Statistician
0039-0534 Yugoslavia. Savezni Zavod za Statistiku. Statisticka Revija
0039-0542 Statisticki Pregled Socijalisticke Republike Bosne i Hercegovine
0039-0550 Revue Statistique du Quebec *changed to* Quebec (Province) Bureau of Statistics. Statistiques
0039-0569 State Bank of Pakistan. Statistics on Co-Operative Banks†
0039-0577 State Bank of Pakistan. Statistics on Scheduled Banks
0039-0585 Austria. Bundeskammer der Gewerblichen Wirtschaft. Statistik und Dokumnentation. Information *changed to* Austria. Bundeskammer der Gewerblichen Wirtschaft. Fremdenverkehr in Zahlen
0039-0593 Statistika
0039-0607 Bank of Israel. Banking Statistics *changed to* Bank of Israel. Current Banking Statistics
0039-0615 Belgium. Institut National de Statistique. Statistique de la Navigation Maritime†
0039-0623 Bourse de Paris. Statistiques Mensuelles
0039-0631 Statistische Hefte
0039-064X Statistische Praxis†
0039-0682 Denmark. Danmarks Statistik. Statistiske Undersogelser
0039-0690 Hungary. Kozponti Statisztikai Hivatal. Statisztikai Szemle
0039-0704 Statni Statky
0039-0712 Statsanstaelld
0039-0720 Statsoekonomisk Tidsskrift
0039-0747 Statsvetenskaplig Tidskrift
0039-0755 Status of Your Vestal Schools *changed to* V C S Newsletter
0039-0763 Statutes and Notifications
0039-0771 Staub, Reinhaltung der Luft
0039-078X Stavebnicky Casopis
0039-0798 Stavebnik
0039-0801 Stavivo
0039-081X Stazione Zoologica di Napoli. Pubblicazioni *changed to* History and Philosophy of the Life Sciences
0039-081X Stazione Zoologica di Napoli. Pubblicazioni *see* 0173-9565
0039-0828 Steam & Fuel Users' Journal
0039-0836 Steam and Heating Engineer *see* 0307-7950
0039-0844 Steamboat Bill
0039-0852 Steaua
0039-0879 Stedebouw en Volkshuisvesting
0039-0887 Stedfast Magazine†
0039-0895 Industry Week
0039-0909 Steel Castings Abstracts†
0039-0917 Steel Facts *changed to* Steel (Year)
0039-0925 Steel Horizons *see* 0149-1997
0039-0941 Steel Labor *changed to* Steelabor
0039-095X Steel Times
0039-0968 Steel Trade
0039-0976 Steelwork in South Africa *see* 0010-6690
0039-0984 Steering Wheel *changed to* Cab Driver
0039-0992 Steiermark, das Land der Vielfalt
0039-100X Steinbeck Quarterly
0039-1018 Steinbruch und Sandgrube
0039-1026 Steine Sprechen
0039-1034 Steinmetz und Bildhauer
0039-1042 Steirische Berichte
0039-1050 Steirische Gemeinde-Nachrichten
0039-1077 Steirische Handelszeitung
0039-1085 Steirische Kriegsopfer Zeitung
0039-1093 Steirische Statistiken
0039-1107 Steirische Wirtschaft
0039-1115 Steklo i Keramika
0039-1131 Stelutis Alpinis
0039-1158 Stendhal Club. Quarterly
0039-1166 Stenografisk Tidsskrift
0039-1174 Der Stenopraktiker
0039-1182 Stephen Crane Newsletter†
0039-1190 Stephenson Locomotive Society Journal
0039-1204 Ster
0039-1212 Stereo Headphones
0039-1220 Stereo Review
0039-1239 Stern *changed to* Stern Magazin
0039-1247 Sterna
0039-1255 Sterne
0039-1263 Sterne und Weltraum
0039-1271 Der Sternenbote
0039-128X Steroids†
0039-1298 Steering Wheel
0039-1328 Stevens Indicator
0039-1344 Steward Anthropological Society. Journal
0039-1387 Paardesport in Ren en Draf
0039-1409 Wirtschaft und Wissenschaft†
0039-1417 Stiinta si Tehnica
0039-1425 Stijl *changed to* Women
0039-1433 Stil Novo
0039-1441 Stile Casa *changed to* Casa Stile
0039-1484 Stimme und Weg†
0039-1492 Stimmen der Zeit
0039-1514 Stimulus†
0039-1522 Stirpes
0039-1557 Stock and Crops *changed to* Zimbabwe Tobacco Today
0039-1565 Stock and Land
0039-1573 Stock Car-Hot Rod Journal†
0039-1581 Stock Exchange Journal†
0039-1611 Stock Exchange of New Zealand *changed to* Stock Exchange Journal of New Zealand
0039-162X Stock Journal
0039-1638 Stock Market Magazine
0039-1654 Stockholms Handelskammare. Meddelanden *see* 0345-4495
0039-1662 Stockton-San Joaquin County Public Library Newsletter†
0039-1670 Stokvis Expres *changed to* Inzicht
0039-1689 Stolica
0039-1697 Stoma *see* 0044-166X
0039-1700 Stomatologia
0039-1719 Revista de Chirurgie, Oncologie, O.R.L., Radiologie, Oftalmologie, Stomatologie. Stomatologie
0039-1727 Stomatologica *changed to* Parodontologia e Stomatologia Nuova
0039-1735 Stomatologiya
0039-1743 Stomatoloski Glasnik Srbije
0039-1778 Stone Industries
0039-1786 Stonehenge†
0039-1794 Stony Brook†
0039-1808 Stop
0039-1816 Stopanski Pregled
0039-1824 Stoperitidende
0039-1832 Storage Handling Distribution
0039-1859 Store Planning Service
0039-1867 Stores
0039-1875 Storia Contemporanea
0039-1891 Storia e Nobilta
0039-1905 Storia e Politica†
0039-1913 Storia Illustrata
0039-1921 Storie di Cucciolo†
0039-193X Storie di Tiramolla *changed to* Racolta Storie di Tiramolla
0039-1948 Storie e Fiabe†
0039-1956 Storkjoekken
0039-1964 Storkoek *changed to* Restauranger & Storkoek
0039-1972 Storm Data
0039-1980 Stormklockan
0039-1999 Story Art
0039-2006 Story Friends
0039-2014 Story of Life†
0039-2022 Discovery (Winona Lake) *see* 0273-3145
0039-2030 Storyville
0039-2049 Strad
0039-2057 Strade Aperte
0039-2065 Strade e Traffico†
0039-2073 Strahlentherapie; Zeitschrift fuer Radiologie und Onkologie *see* 0179-7158
0039-2081 Straight *changed to* Straight (1981)
0039-2103 Strain
0039-2111 Radio-Electronica
0039-212X Strandjaegeren
0039-2138 Strani Pravni Zivot. Serija D: Teorija, Zakonodavstvo, Praksa
0039-2146 Die Strasse
0039-2162 Strasse und Autobahn
0039-2170 Strasse und Nuechternheit *changed to* Freie Fahrt
0039-2189 Strasse und Verkehr
0039-2197 Strassen- und Tiefbau *changed to* Strassen- und Tiefbau Vereinigt mit Strasse-Bruecke-Tunnel, Bitumen-Teere-Asphalts-Peche
0039-2200 Strassenbau-Technik *see* 0005-6634

0039-2219 Strassenverkehrstechnik
0039-2235 Strategie†
0039-2243 Strathclyde Telegraph
0039-2251 Straub Clinic Proceedings *changed to* Straub Proceedings
0039-226X Street and Highway Lighting†
0039-2278 Streiflichter†
0039-2294 Stremez
0039-2308 Strength & Health Magazine
0039-2316 Strength of Materials
0039-2324 Streven†
0039-2340 Stride
0039-2359 Igaku No Ayumi
0039-2375 Stroitel'
0039-2383 Stroitel'naya Mekhanika i Raschet Sooruzhenii
0039-2391 Stroitel'nye i Dorozhnye Mashiny
0039-2405 Stroitel'stvo i Arkhitektura
0039-2413 Stroitel'stvo i Arkhitektura Leningrada *changed to* Leningradskaya Panorama
0039-2421 Stroitel'stvo i Arkhitektura Moskvy
0039-243X Stroitel'stvo i Arkhitektura Uzbekistana
0039-2448 Stroitel'stvo Truboprovodov
0039-2456 Strojirenska Vyroba
0039-2464 Strojirenstvi
0039-2472 Strojnicky Casopis
0039-2480 Strojniski Vestnik
0039-2499 Stroke
0039-2502 Association of Lunar and Planetary Observers. Journal
0039-2510 Strom & See
0039-2537 Strophes
0039-2545 Strout World
0039-2553 Structural Engineer *changed to* Structural Engineer. Part A
0039-2553 Structural Engineer *changed to* Structural Engineer. Part B
0039-2561 Structural Mechanics *see* 0890-5452
0039-257X Structure
0039-2588 Struggle
0039-260X Strumenti & Musica
0039-2618 Strumenti Critici
0039-2626 Stud and Stable *changed to* Pacemaker International
0039-2634 Stud. Med.
0039-2669 Student†
0039-2677 Student
0039-2685 Student (Nashville)
0039-2693 Student
0039-2715 Student Advocate†
0039-2723 Student Federalist *changed to* World Citizen/Federalist Letter
0039-2731 Student Impact *see* 0195-153X
0039-274X Student Lawyer (Chicago)
0039-2758 Student Life
0039-2766 Student Life Highlights *see* 0746-3545
0039-2790 Student Times International
0039-2804 Student Voice
0039-2839 Danske Studerendes Faellesraad. Studenterbladet
0039-2847 Studentische Politik†
0039-2855 Studentravel Magazine
0039-2863 Students' Digest†
0039-2871 Students Quarterly Journal *see* 0013-5127
0039-288X S L
0039-2898 Studi Biblici
0039-2901 Studi Cattolici
0039-291X Studi di Sociologia
0039-2936 Studi Emigrazione
0039-2944 Studi Francesi
0039-2952 Studi Germanici
0039-2960 Studi Grafici
0039-2979 Studi Internazonali di Filosofia *see* 0270-5664
0039-2987 Studi Italiani di Filologia Classica
0039-2995 Studi Romani
0039-3002 Studi Salentini
0039-3010 Studi Senesi
0039-3037 Studi Storici
0039-3045 Studi Storici dell'Ordine dei Servi di Maria
0039-3053 Studi Sul Lavoro†
0039-3061 Studi Teatrali†
0039-307X Studi Urbinati. Serie A: Diritto
0039-3088 Studi Urbinati. Serie B: Letteratura, Storia, Filosofia
0039-310X Studia Canonica
0039-3126 Studia Cywilistyczne
0039-3134 Studia Demograficzne
0039-3142 Studia Filozoficzne
0039-3150 Studia Forestalia Suecica
0039-3169 Studia Geophysica et Geodaetica
0039-3177 Instytut Przemyslu Drobnego i Rzemiosla Studia i Informacje *changed to* Instytut Ekonomiki Uslug i Drobnej Wytworczosci. Studia i Informacje
0039-3185 Studia Leibnitiana
0039-3193 Studia Linguistica
0039-3207 Studia Liturgica
0039-3215 Studia Logica
0039-3223 Studia Mathematica
0039-3231 Studia Mediewistyczne
0039-324X Studia Metodologiczne. Dissertationes Methodologicae
0039-3258 Studia Monastica
0039-3266 Studia Musicologica Academiae Scientiarum Hungaricae
0039-3274 Studia Neophilologica
0039-3282 Studia Orientalia
0039-3290 Studia Papyrologica†
0039-3304 Studia Patavina
0039-3312 Studia Prawnicze
0039-3320 Studia Psychologica
0039-3339 Studia Romanica et Anglica Zagrabiensia
0039-3347 Studia Rosenthaliana
0039-3355 Studia Slaskie
0039-3363 Studia Slavica Academiae Scientiarum Hungaricae
0039-3371 Studia Socjologiczne
0039-338X Studia Theologica
0039-3398 Studia Universitatis "Babes-Bolyai". Biologia
0039-3401 Studia Universitatis "Babes-Bolyai". Chemia
0039-341X Studia Universitatis "Babes-Bolyai". Geologia. Geographia
0039-3428 Studia Universitatis "Babes-Bolyai". Historia
0039-3436 Studia Universitatis "Babes-Bolyai". Series Mathematica-Physica *changed to* Studia Universitatis "Babes-Bolyai". Mathematica
0039-3444 Studia Universitatis "Babes-Bolyai". Philologia
0039-3452 Studiekamraten
0039-3460 Studiemappen†
0039-3495 Studies
0039-3525 Studies in Adult Education *changed to* Studies in the Education of Adults
0039-3533 Studies in African Linguistics
0039-3541 Studies in Art Education
0039-3568 Studies in Bibliography and Booklore
0039-3576 Studies in Black Literature†
0039-3584 Studies in Burke and His Time *see* 0193-5380
0039-3592 Studies in Comparative Communism
0039-3606 Studies in Comparative International Development
0039-3614 Studies in Comparative Local Government *changed to* Planning & Administration
0039-3622 Studies in Comparative Religion
0039-3630 Studies in Conservation
0039-3649 Studies in English Literature
0039-3657 Studies in English Literature 1500-1900
0039-3665 Studies in Family Planning
0039-3673 Studies in Germanics†
0039-3681 Studies in History and Philosophy of Science
0039-369X Studies in History and Society†
0039-3703 Studies in Iowa History†
0039-3711 Studies in Islam
0039-3738 Studies in Philology
0039-3754 Studies in Race and Nations†
0039-3762 Studies in Romanticism
0039-3770 Studies in Scottish Literature†
0039-3789 Studies in Short Fiction
0039-3797 Studies in Soviet Thought
0039-3800 Studies in the Humanities
0039-3819 Studies in the Literary Imagination
0039-3827 Studies in the Novel
0039-3835 Studies in the Twentieth Century†
0039-3851 Studies on Oriental Music
0039-386X Studies on the Soviet Union†
0039-3886 Studii si Cercetari de Antropologie
0039-3916 Studii si Cercetari de Documentare
0039-3940 Studii si Cercetari de Fizica
0039-3959 Studii si Cercetari de Fiziologie†
0039-3967 Studii si Cercetari de Geologie, Geofizica si Geografie. Geografie
0039-3983 Studii si Cercetari de Istoria Artei. Seria Arta Plastica
0039-3991 Studii si Cercetari de Istoria Artei. Seria Teatru-Muzica-Cinematografie
0039-4009 Studii si Cercetari de Istorie Veche *changed to* Studii si Cercetari de Istorie Veche si Arheologie
0039-4017 Studii si Cercetari de Mecanica Aplicata
0039-4041 Studii si Cercetari Juridice
0039-405X Studii si Cercetari Lingvistice
0039-4068 Studii si Cercetari Matematice
0039-4084 Studio
0039-4092 Studio†
0039-4106 Studio
0039-4114 Studio International
0039-4122 Studio Light
0039-4130 Studium
0039-4149 Studium Generale†
0039-4157 Study Encounter†
0039-4165 Stuekulturer
0039-4181 Stuff†
0039-419X Stukadoorspatroon *changed to* N A V A S
0039-4203 Stuurwiel
0039-4211 Stuwing *changed to* Toorts
0039-422X Stvaranje
0039-4238 Style (DeKalb)
0039-4246 Style
0039-4254 Style Auto
0039-4262 Style for Men†
0039-4289 Stylus (Brockport)
0039-4319 Styret *changed to* Cykelbranchen
0039-4335 Sub-Postmaster
0039-4351 Subject Index to Children's Magazines *see* 0743-9873
0039-436X Suboticke Novine
0039-4378 Subsidia Medica†
0039-4386 Subsidia Pataphysica *changed to* Organographes du Cymbalum Pataphysicum
0039-4394 Subterranean Sociology Newsletter
0039-4424 Success Unlimited *changed to* Success (New York)
0039-4432 Successful Farming: Farm Computer News
0039-4440 Successo†
0039-4459 Succhi di Frutta e Bevande Gassate†
0039-4467 Succulenta
0039-4491 Sucrerie Francaise
0039-4505 Sud Africa - Ieri, Oggi, Domani *changed to* Realta Sudafricana
0039-4521 Sudebnomeditsinskaya Ekspertiza
0039-453X Sudene Informa
0039-4556 Sudetenpost
0039-4564 Sudhoffs Archiv
0039-4572 Suedost-Gesellschaft. Mitteilungen *see* 0340-174X
0039-4580 Sudostroenie
0039-4599 Suecana Extranea†
0039-4610 Suedamerika
0039-4629 Suedtirol in Wort und Bild
0039-4637 Suedwestfaelische Wirtschaft
0039-4645 Suenos
0039-4653 Suesswaren
0039-4661 Suffolk Cooperative Library System. Newsletter†
0039-467X Suffolk County Agricultural News
0039-4688 Suffolk County Dental Society. Bulletin *changed to* Suffolk Dentistry
0039-4696 Suffolk University Law Review
0039-470X Mathematics
0039-4726 Sugar Bulletin
0039-4734 Sugar Journal
0039-4742 Sugar y Azucar
0039-4750 Sugarbeet Grower
0039-4777 Sugarland
0039-4793 Suggestion Systems Quarterly *changed to* Performance (Chicago)
0039-4807 Suid-Afrikaanse Akademie vir Wetenskap en Kuns. Nuusbrief
0039-4823 Suiker-Facetten *changed to* Kwartaalblad Suiker
0039-484X Water Temperature Research
0039-4858 Water Science
0039-4866 Fisheries World
0039-4874 Suisse Horlogere et Revue Internationale de l'Horlogerie *changed to* Suisse Horlogere et Revue Europeenne de l'Horlogerie-Bijouterie
0039-4882 Sukh Datta
0039-4890 Sulphur
0039-4904 Sulphur Institute Journal *see* 0160-0680
0039-4912 Sulzer Technical Review
0039-4947 Sumarios de Odontologia
0039-4955 Sumitomo Bank Review
0039-4963 Sumitomo Light Metal Technical Reports
0039-4971 Summa†
0039-498X Summa Brasiliensis Mathematicae†
0039-4998 Summary of Available Applicants and Summary of Academic, Industrial, and Government Openings†
0039-5005 Summary of Labor Arbitration Awards
0039-5021 Summer Texan *changed to* Daily Texan
0039-5056 Summit (Big Bear Lake)
0039-5072 Summons
0039-5080 Sun
0039-5099 Sun Dance *changed to* Detroit Sun
0039-5102 Sun
0039-5110 Sun & Health†
0039-5137 Sun Seeker†
0039-5145 Sunbelt Dairyman
0039-5153 Sunday†
0039-5161 Sunday
0039-517X Sunday Companion†
0039-5188 Sunday Digest
0039-5196 Sunday Express
0039-520X Sunday Gleaner
0039-5218 Sunday Independent
0039-5226 Sunday Mail
0039-5234 Sunday Mainichi
0039-5242 Sunday Mercury
0039-5250 Bible-in-Life Pix
0039-5277 Sunday Post
0039-5285 Sunday School Counselor
0039-5315 Sunday Sun
0039-5323 Sunday Times *see* 0111-5782
0039-5358 Sunday Truth *changed to* Sunday Sun
0039-5366 Sundhedsbladet
0039-5374 Sun (New York)
0039-5382 Sunflower
0039-5390 Sunlore
0039-5404 Sunset
0039-5412 Sunshine
0039-5420 Sunshine
0039-5439 Sunshine & Health
0039-5447 Sunshine State Agricultural Research Report *changed to* Florida Agricultural Research
0039-5455 Sunt Foernuft
0039-5471 Suo
0039-548X Suomalainen
0039-5498 Suomalaiset B-Referaatit *changed to* Rakennustieto
0039-5501 Suomen Elainlaakarilehti
0039-551X Suomen Hammaslaakariseura. Toimituksia
0039-5528 Suomen Kalastuslehti
0039-5544 Suomen Kunnallislehti
0039-5552 Suomen Kuvalehti
0039-5560 Suomen Laakarilehti
0039-5579 Laakintavoimistelija
0039-5587 Suomen Lehdisto
0039-5595 Suomen Maataloustieteellisen Seuran Julkaisuja†
0039-5609 Osuustoimintalehti
0039-5617 Suomen Puutalous *see* 0781-6758
0039-5625 Suomen Silta

ISSN	Title
0039-5633	Suomi Merella
0039-565X	Super Omnia Charitas†
0039-5676	Super Service Station
0039-5692	Super Stock & Drag Illustrated
0039-5706	Superba
0039-5714	Superconducting Devices and Materials†
0039-5765	Superlove†
0039-5773	Supermachos†
0039-5781	Supermarket
0039-579X	Supermarket Management†
0039-5803	Supermarket News
0039-5811	Supermarketing see 0196-5700
0039-582X	Supernovelas changed to Supernovelas Capricho
0039-5846	Supertiendas†
0039-5854	Supervision
0039-5862	Supervisor changed to Modern Management
0039-5870	Supervisor Nurse changed to Nursing Management
0039-5889	Supervisor's Bulletin
0039-5897	Supervisors Quarterly changed to Teacher Educator
0039-5919	Supervisory Management
0039-5927	Supplementary Service to European Taxation
0039-5935	Supply House Times
0039-5951	Supreme Court Cases
0039-596X	Supreme Court Notes
0039-5978	Supreme Court Practice
0039-5994	Sur l'Eau†
0039-6001	Industrial Finishing and Surface Coatings see 0264-2506
0039-6028	Surface Science
0039-6036	Surfer
0039-6052	Surfing East†
0039-6060	Surgery
0039-6087	Surgery, Gynecology & Obstetrics
0039-6095	Surgical Business see 0745-4678
0039-6109	Surgical Clinics of North America
0039-6117	Surgical Journal of Delhi
0039-6125	Surgo
0039-6133	Surinaamse Landbouw
0039-6141	Suriname Zending changed to Hernhutter Suriname Zending
0039-615X	Surplus Record
0039-6168	Surrealist Transformation
0039-6176	Surrey N.F.U. Journal changed to Central Southern Farmer
0039-6184	Sursum Corda
0039-6192	Survey
0039-6206	Survey of Anesthesiology
0039-6214	Survey of Current Affairs
0039-6222	Survey of Current Business
0039-6230	Survey of International Development†
0039-6249	Quarterly Survey of Japanese Finance and Industry changed to Japanese Finance and Industry: Quarterly Survey
0039-6257	Survey of Ophthalmology
0039-6265	Great Britain. Directorate of Overseas Surveys. Survey Review changed to Great Britain. Commonwealth Association of Surveying and Land Economy. Survey Review
0039-6273	Surveying and Mapping
0039-6303	Surveyor-Local Government Technology changed to Surveyor
0039-6311	Surveys of the Work of British Writers changed to Writers & Their Work
0039-632X	Survival changed to Alberta Public Safety Services News & Notes
0039-6338	Survival
0039-6354	Survive see 0740-5537
0039-6362	Sus Hijos†
0039-6370	Sushama
0039-6397	Sussex Life
0039-6427	Sveiseteknikk
0039-6435	Svensk Bergs- och Brukstidning
0039-6443	Svensk Bokfoerteckning
0039-6451	Svensk Bokhandel
0039-646X	Svensk Botanisk Tidskrift
0039-6478	Svensk Bridge
0039-6486	Svensk Dam Tidning
0039-6494	Nord-Emballage
0039-6508	Svensk Export
0039-6516	Svensk Faerghandel
0039-6524	Svensk Farmaceutisk Tidskrift
0039-6532	Svensk Filatelistisk Tidskrift
0039-6540	Svensk Fotografisk Tidskrift
0039-6559	Svensk Guldsmeds en Tidning changed to Guldsmedstidningen
0039-6575	Svensk Handelstidning Justita
0039-6583	Svensk Jakt
0039-6591	Svensk Juristtidning
0039-6605	Kemisk Tidskrift
0039-6613	Svensk Lantmaeteritidskrift
0039-6621	Svensk Leksaksrevy
0039-663X	Svensk Litteraturtidskrift†
0039-6648	Svensk Lokaltrafik
0039-6664	S M T see 0027-1764
0039-6672	Svensk Omnibustidning see 0282-7654
0039-6680	Svensk Papperstidning
0039-6699	Svensk Pastoral Tidskrift
0039-6702	Svensk Sjoefarts Tidning
0039-6729	Svensk Snickeritidskrift see 0346-2846
0039-6737	Svensk Sparbankstidskrift see 0346-1602
0039-6745	Svensk Tandlaekare-Tidskrift see 0347-9994
0039-6753	Svensk Tapetseraretidning
0039-6761	Svensk Teologisk Kvartalskrift
0039-677X	Svensk Tidskrift
0039-6788	Svensk Tidskrift for Industriellt Rattsskydd
0039-6796	Svensk Traevaru- och Papersmassetidning
0039-680X	Svensk Ur- Optik Tidning changed to Ur Optik
0039-6818	Svensk Valltidskrift†
0039-6826	Svensk Veckotidning
0039-6834	Gasnytt
0039-6842	Svenska Litteratursaellskapet i Finland. Skrifter
0039-6869	Svenska Mejiernas Riksfoerening. Meddelande†
0039-6877	Svenska Mejeritidningen see 0345-830X
0039-6885	Svenska Museer
0039-6893	Svenska. Riksarkivet. Meddelanden
0039-6907	Svenska Tidningsartiklar
0039-6915	Svenska Tidskriftsartiklar
0039-6923	Svenska Vaegfoereningens Tidskrift
0039-6931	Svenska Kraftverksfoereningens Publikationer†
0039-694X	Svenskt Fiske changed to Sportfiskaren
0039-6958	Sverige-Nytt
0039-6966	Sveriges Flotta changed to Under Svensk Flagg
0039-6982	Tandlaekartidningen†
0039-6990	Sveriges Utsadesfoerenings Tidskrift
0039-7008	Svet†
0039-7016	Svet Motoru
0039-7024	Svet Sovetu changed to Svet Socialismu
0039-7032	Svet v Obrazech
0039-7059	Svetlost
0039-7067	Svetotekhnika
0039-7075	Svetova Literatura
0039-7083	Svetsaren
0039-7091	Svetsen
0039-7105	Zvezda
0039-7113	Svijet (Zagreb)
0039-7121	Svijet (Sarajevo)
0039-713X	Svinovodstvo
0039-7148	Svisa Espero changed to Svisa Esperanto Revuo
0039-7156	Svit/Light
0039-7180	Swap Shop changed to Administrator's Swap Shop Newsletter
0039-7199	Swarajya
0039-7202	Swatantra in Parliament†
0039-7210	Swatantra Newsletter†
0039-7229	Swaziland Recorder†
0039-7245	Sweden Now
0039-7253	Sweden. Statistiska Centralbyraan. Allmaan Maanadsstitistik
0039-7261	Sweden. Statistiska Centralbyraan. Statistik Tidskrif changed to Journal of Official Statistics
0039-727X	Sweden. Statistiska Centralbyraan. Utrikeshandel. Kvartalsstatistik
0039-7288	Sweden. Statistiska Centralbyraan. Utrikeshandel. Maanadsstatistik
0039-7296	Swedish Economy
0039-730X	Swedish Forestry Association. Magazine
0039-7318	Swedish Journal of Economics see 0347-0520
0039-7326	Swedish Pioneer Historical Quarterly see 0730-028X
0039-7342	Sweet Briar College. Alumnae Magazine changed to Sweet Briar Alumnae Magazine
0039-7377	Swiat see 0031-6059
0039-7385	Swimming Pool Review changed to Swimming Pool
0039-7393	Swimming Pool Weekly and Swimming Pool Age see 0279-134X
0039-7415	Swimming Technique
0039-7423	Swimming Times
0039-7431	Swimming World
0039-744X	Swing Journal
0039-7458	Swing Through the Air changed to Sportparachutist
0039-7466	Swiss Bank Corporation. Bulletin see 0304-2162
0039-7474	Swiss Journal
0039-7482	Swiss Observer†
0039-7490	Swiss Review of World Affairs
0039-7504	Swiss Technics†
0039-7512	Swiss Watch†
0039-7520	Swiss Watch and Jewelry Journal
0039-7547	Sword of the Lord
0039-7563	Sybarite Review
0039-7571	Sydan
0039-758X	Sydney Jewish News changed to Australian Jewish Times
0039-7598	Sydney Stock Exchange Limited Gazette see 0045-0901
0039-7601	Sydney Tourist Guide
0039-761X	Sydney Water Board Journal
0039-7628	Sykepleien
0039-7636	S Y L F Nytt
0039-7652	Sylvaply News changed to MacMillan Bloedel Building Materials News
0039-7660	Sylwan
0039-7679	Symbolae Osloenses
0039-7695	Symposium
0039-7709	Symposium
0039-7717	Syn og Segn
0039-7725	Synagogue School changed to Impact! (New York)
0039-7733	Synagogue Service†
0039-7741	Syndicalisme Hebdo changed to Syndicalisme Hebdo
0039-775X	Syndicalisme C F T C
0039-7776	Syndicat des Critiques Litteraires. Bulletin
0039-7784	Syndicat National des Officers de la Marine Marchande C.F.D.T. Bulletin de Liaison
0039-7830	Synopsis Revue†
0039-7849	Synpunkt
0039-7857	Synthese
0039-7873	Who Put the Bomp changed to Bomp
0039-7881	Synthesis
0039-789X	Synthesis in Inorganic and Metalorganic Chemistry see 0094-5714
0039-7903	Synthesis Microbiologica†
0039-7911	Synthetic Communications
0039-792X	Syracuse Chemist
0039-7938	Syracuse Law Review
0039-7946	Syria
0039-7954	Syria. Central Bureau of Statistics. Summary of Foreign Trade Statistics changed to Syria. Central Bureau of Statistics. Summary of Foreign Trade
0039-7962	Syrie et Monde Arabe
0039-7989	Systematic Zoology
0039-8004	Systemation Service see 0563-0355
0039-8012	Systeme D
0039-8020	Systems & Communications
0039-8039	Systems Education Forum†
0039-8047	Systems Technology†
0039-8055	Systems, Technology and Science for Law Enforcement and Security Newsletter see 0271-7565
0039-8071	Szabadalmi Kozlony es Vedjegyertesito
0039-808X	Szamvitel es Ugyviteltechnika
0039-8098	Szazadok
0039-8101	Szemeszet
0039-811X	Szene
0039-8128	Szigma
0039-8136	Szinhaz
0039-8144	Szklo i Ceramika
0039-8152	Szpilki
0039-8160	T.I.T. Journal of Life Sciences
0039-8179	T A†
0039-8195	T A C Quarterly Circular
0039-8209	T A I C H News†
0039-8217	T.A. Informations
0039-8225	T A L B Talks†
0039-8233	T A M S Journal
0039-8241	T A P P I changed to T A P P I Journal
0039-8268	T A V R changed to Territorial Army Magazine
0039-8292	T E A News
0039-8306	T E A Newsletter
0039-8314	T E C Report
0039-8322	T.E.S.O.L. Quarterly
0039-8330	T F C Nieuws
0039-8349	T G A Cosmetic Journal see 0090-0591
0039-8357	Textile Institute and Industry see 0260-6518
0039-839X	T. I. P. Informatie†
0039-8403	T I P R O Reporter
0039-8411	T I S C O Technical Journal
0039-842X	T N A News
0039-8438	T N C - Aktuellt
0039-8446	T N O-Nieuws changed to T N O-Project
0039-8454	T.P.A. Travelers
0039-8462	T P Annales
0039-8470	T.P.L. News
0039-8497	T T A
0039-8500	T T G International changed to T T G Europa
0039-8519	T V Communications see 0745-2802
0039-8527	T V Comic†
0039-8535	I V A†
0039-8543	T V Guide
0039-8551	T V Hebdo
0039-8578	T V Radio Mirror changed to T V Mirror
0039-8608	T V Times†
0039-8624	T V Times
0039-8632	T W A Ambassador
0039-8640	T W A U News
0039-8659	T W U Express
0039-8667	T Z fuer Praktische Metallbearbeitung changed to T Z fuer Metallbearbeitung
0039-8675	Ta Kung Pao
0039-8683	Taag
0039-8691	Taal in Tongval
0039-8705	Taalgenoot
0039-8721	Tabak
0039-873X	Tabak
0039-8748	Tabak Journal International
0039-8756	Tabakpflanzer Oesterreichs
0039-8772	Tabakverschleisser Oesterreichs
0039-8780	Table et Cadeau
0039-8799	Table Tennis News
0039-8802	Tableau de Bord des Industries Francaises†
0039-8829	Tables of Redemption Values for U.S. Savings Bonds, Series A-E changed to Tables of Redemption Values for U.S. Savings Bonds, Series E and Tables of Redemption Values for U.S. Savings Bonds, Series EE
0039-8837	Tablet
0039-8845	Tablet
0039-8853	Tableware International and Pottery Gazette see 0143-7755
0039-8888	Tachydromos
0039-8896	Tactics†
0039-890X	Facultad de Medicina de Sevilla. Revista†

ISSN INDEX

ISSN	Title
0039-8926	Taeglicher Wetterbericht see 0341-2970
0039-8934	Wiener Tagebuch
0039-8942	Tageszeitung fuer Brauerei changed to Brauerei-Forum
0039-8950	Tagus
0039-8969	Tahqiqat e Eqtesadi
0039-8977	Taide
0039-8993	Refractories
0039-9000	Japan Society of Air Pollution. Journal
0039-9019	Air Pollution News†
0039-9027	Tail-Wagger and Family Magazine†
0039-9043	Tailor and Men's Wear changed to Menswear Magazine
0039-9051	Taipei Pictorial
0039-906X	Japanese Journal of Physical Fitness changed to Japanese Journal of Physical Fitness and Sports Medicine
0039-9078	Taiwan†
0039-9086	Taiwan
0039-9094	Taiwan Chengliang
0039-9108	Taiwan Industrial Panorama
0039-9116	Taiwan Museum. Quarterly Journal
0039-9124	Taiwan Trade Monthly†
0039-9140	Talanta
0039-9159	Talespinner†
0039-9175	Talim-O-Tarbiat
0039-9183	Talking Book Topics (Large Print Edition)
0039-9191	Talking Machine Review changed to Talking Machine Review International
0039-9213	Talks and Tales
0039-9221	Taller
0039-9248	Talon
0039-9256	Tamarack Review†
0039-9264	Tamarind Fact Sheets†
0039-9280	Tamil Arasu
0039-9299	Tamil Culture
0039-9310	Tamil Nadu Information
0039-9329	Tamil Nadu Police Journal
0039-9345	Tan see 0163-3007
0039-9353	Tandlaegebladet
0039-937X	Tanecni Listy
0039-9388	Tangent†
0039-940X	Tangerine
0039-9418	Tank
0039-9434	Report of Coal Mine Safety†
0039-9442	Tanner
0039-9450	Protein, Nucleic Acid, Enzyme
0039-9469	Tanzania. Bureau of Statistics. Quarterly Statistical Bulletin
0039-9477	Tanzania Education Journal
0039-9485	Tanzania Notes & Records
0039-9493	Tanzania Trade and Industry see 0856-0161
0039-9507	Tanzania Zamani
0039-9515	Tanzarchiv see 0720-3896
0039-9531	Tape Record
0039-954X	Studio Sound see 0133-5944
0039-9566	Tapetenzeitung Tapete und Bodenbelag see 0720-6593
0039-9574	Tapetsereren†
0039-9582	Tapissier Decorateur
0039-9590	Taproots†
0039-9604	Taptoe
0039-9612	Tar Heel Economist
0039-9620	Tar Heel Nurse
0039-9639	Tar River Poetry
0039-9655	Target
0039-9663	Tarheel Banker
0039-968X	Tarheel Wheels
0039-9698	Tarikh
0039-9711	Tarsadalmi Szemle
0039-9728	Tartarino
0039-9736	Speeluinvereniging Tarwewijk. Mededlingenblad
0039-9760	Tasmanian Education Gazette
0039-9787	Tasmanian Fruitgrower & Farmer
0039-9795	Tasmanian Government Gazette
0039-9809	Tasmanian Historical Research Association. Papers and Proceedings
0039-9817	Tasmanian Journal of Agriculture†
0039-9825	Tasmanian Journal of Education see 0314-2531
0039-9833	Australia. Bureau of Statistics. Tasmanian Office. Monthly Summary of Statistics see 0314-2094
0039-9841	Tasmanian Motor News
0039-985X	Tasmanian Motor Trader
0039-9892	Tatka
0039-9906	Tatler & Bystander
0039-9914	Tatrzanski Orzel
0039-9922	Finland. Patentti- ja Rekisterihallitus. Tavaramerkkilehti/Varumarkestidning/Trademark Gazette
0039-9930	Tawow†
0039-9949	Tax Administrators News
0039-9957	Tax Adviser
0039-9965	Tax Affairs
0039-9973	Tax Alert†
0039-999X	Tax Coordinator see 0163-996X
0040-0017	United States Tax Court Reports
0040-0025	Tax Executive
0040-0041	Tax Law Review
0040-005X	Tax Lawyer
0040-0068	Philippines. National Tax Research Center. Tax Monthly
0040-0076	Tax News Service
0040-0084	Tax Planning
0040-0092	Tax Planning Ideas
0040-0106	Tax Policy†
0040-0114	Tax Foundation's Tax Review see 0737-3481
0040-0122	Tax Times
0040-0130	Taxa Droske Tidende changed to Dansk Taxi Tidende
0040-0149	Taxation
0040-0157	Taxation
0040-0165	Taxation for Accountants
0040-0173	Taxation Record Journal
0040-0181	Taxes
0040-0203	Taxes Interpreted†
0040-0211	Taxi News Digest
0040-022X	Taxitrafiken
0040-0238	Taxia Fungorum changed to Mycological Flora
0040-0246	Taxicab Management†
0040-0254	Taxinews
0040-0262	Taxon
0040-0270	Taxpayer
0040-0289	Taxpayer
0040-0297	Tchahert
0040-0300	Te Ao Hou†
0040-0319	Te Maori changed to Te Awatea
0040-0327	Te-ve Guia
0040-0343	Tea and Coffee Trade Journal
0040-036X	Tea Quarterly changed to Sri Lanka Journal of Tea Science
0040-0378	Tea Research Foundation of Central Africa. Quarterly Newsletter
0040-0386	Tea Room, Restaurant and Catering Journal†
0040-0394	Teach†
0040-0408	Teacher
0040-0416	Teacher
0040-0424	Teacher Education in New Countries†
0040-0440	Teacher of the Blind see 0264-6196
0040-0459	Teacher of the Deaf changed to British Association of Teachers of the Deaf. Journal
0040-0467	Teacher Paper†
0040-0483	Teachers' Journal changed to V T U Journal
0040-0505	Message of the Teacher
0040-0521	Teacher's World
0040-053X	Teaching†
0040-0556	T A D see 0046-1482
0040-0564	Teaching All Nations changed to East Asian Pastoral Review
0040-0572	Teaching & Training
0040-0580	Teaching Beginners changed to Teaching Under 5's
0040-0599	Teaching Exceptional Children
0040-0602	Teaching History
0040-0610	Teaching History
0040-0629	Teaching Juniors changed to Teaching 7-10's
0040-0645	Teaching Pictures for Bible Searchers
0040-0653	Teaching Primaries changed to Teaching 5-7's
0040-0661	Milwaukee Public Schools Superintendent's Bulletin changed to Milwaukee Public Schools Staff Bulletin
0040-067X	Teaching Teenagers see 0308-356X
0040-0688	Teaching Tools for Consumer Ed changed to Teaching Tools for Consumer Reports
0040-0696	Team
0040-0718	Teamwork in Industry changed to Worklife
0040-0734	Crippled Children
0040-0750	Teatern
0040-0769	Teatr
0040-0777	Teatr
0040-0785	Teatral'naya Zhizn'
0040-0793	Teatro
0040-0807	Teatro e Cinema†
0040-0815	Teatrul
0040-0823	Tebiwa changed to Tebiwa
0040-0831	Tech Air
0040-0858	Tech Talk see 0002-242X
0040-0866	Technica
0040-0874	Technical Association of Graphic Arts of Japan. Bulletin changed to Japanese Society of Printing Science and Technology. Bulletin
0040-0882	Technical Association of Malaysia. Journal see 0127-6441
0040-0890	Technical Book Review Index
0040-0904	Technical Co-Operation
0040-0912	Education and Training
0040-0920	Technical Education Abstracts
0040-0939	Technical Education Newsletter changed to A T E A Journal
0040-0947	Technical Film International Bulletin see 0138-9157
0040-0955	T.I.
0040-0963	National Association of Teachers in Further and Higher Education. Technical Journal see 0308-1907
0040-0971	Technical Photography
0040-098X	Technical Progress in Israel†
0040-0998	Manila. Department of Public Works. Communications Technical Statistical Review changed to M P W Bulletin
0040-1005	Technical Survey†
0040-1013	Technicar see 0008-5995
0040-103X	Technicien du Film changed to Technicien du Film et de la Video
0040-1056	Technicka Praca
0040-1064	Technicky Tydenik
0040-1072	Technicuir
0040-1099	Die Technik†
0040-1102	Technik und Betrieb†
0040-1110	Technika
0040-1137	Technika i Gospodarka Morska
0040-1145	Technika Lotnicza i Astronautyczna
0040-1153	Technika Motoryzacyjna
0040-1161	Technika Poszukiwan Geologicznych
0040-117X	Technikgeschichte
0040-1188	Technion Magazine
0040-1196	Technique Chaussure
0040-1226	Technique et Pratique Agricoles changed to I T P A. Letters
0040-1250	Technique Moderne
0040-1269	Technique Pharmaceutique changed to Sciences et Technique Pharmaceutiques
0040-1277	Technique Routiere
0040-1285	Techniques†
0040-1293	Techniques C E M
0040-1307	Techniques de l'Air Comprime†
0040-1323	Techniques du Petrole changed to Techniques Petrole Petrochimie
0040-1331	Techniques Economiques
0040-1358	Techniques for Teachers of Adults see 0740-0578
0040-1374	Techniques Hospitalieres, Medico-Sociales et Sanitaires
0040-1382	Techniques Nouvelles†
0040-1390	Technisch Gemeenteblad†
0040-1420	Technische Information Armaturen
0040-1439	Technische Mitteilungen
0040-1447	A E G-Telefunken. Technische Mitteilungen†
0040-1455	R F Z. Technische Mitteilungen
0040-1471	P T T Technische Mitteilungen
0040-148X	Technische Rundschau
0040-1498	T U Technische Ueberwachung changed to T U - Technische Ueberwachung. Sicherheit Zuverlaessigkeit und Umweltschutz in Wirtschaft und Verkehr
0040-1501	Technische Universitaet Clausthal. Mitteilungsblatt
0040-151X	Schweizerische Technische Zeitschrift
0040-1536	Technischer Ansporn†
0040-1544	Technischer Fortschritt (Duesseldorf)
0040-1552	Technischer Handel
0040-1560	Technisches Journal†
0040-1587	Technocracy Digest
0040-1595	Technocrat†
0040-1609	Technocrat changed to Techno Japan
0040-1617	Technocratic Trendevents†
0040-1625	Technological Forecasting and Social Change
0040-1641	Technology changed to Fertilizer Technology
0040-165X	Technology and Culture
0040-1676	Technology Ireland
0040-1692	Technology Review
0040-1706	Technometrics
0040-1714	Tecnica
0040-1722	Tecnica de la Regulacion y Mando Automatico changed to Regulacion y Mando Automatico
0040-1730	Tecnica del Frio
0040-1757	Tecnica dell'Aria Compressa†
0040-1765	Tecnica dell'Arte
0040-1773	Tecnica e Circolazione Autostradale
0040-1781	Tecnica e Industria
0040-179X	Tecnica e Invencion
0040-1803	Tecnica e Ricostruzione
0040-1811	Tecnica e Uomo
0040-182X	Tecnica Hospitalaria
0040-1838	Tecnica Industrial†
0040-1846	Tecnica Italiana
0040-1854	Tecnica Mecanica†
0040-1862	Tecnica Molitoria
0040-1889	Tecnica Pecuaria en Mexico
0040-1897	Tecnica Sanitaria
0040-1900	Tecnica Textil Internacional
0040-1919	Tecnicas Financieras†
0040-1927	Tecniche dell'Automazione e Robotica
0040-1943	Tecnologia Alimentaria
0040-1951	Tectonophysics
0040-196X	Tedenska Tribuna changed to Teleks
0040-1978	Tednik
0040-1986	Teen Guide†
0040-1994	Teen Life†
0040-2001	Teen
0040-2044	Teen World†
0040-2060	Teens' and Boys' Outfitter see 0195-2137
0040-2087	Teenways†
0040-2095	Tees-Side Journal of Commerce
0040-2109	Teg och Teknik†
0040-2117	Tegel
0040-2125	Tegen de Tuberculose
0040-2133	Tegenwoordig
0040-2141	Tegl
0040-215X	Tegnikon†
0040-2168	Tekhniceska Misal
0040-2176	Tehnika
0040-2184	Teilhard Review changed to Teilhard Review and Journal of Creative Evolution
0040-2192	Teintex see 0019-9176
0040-2222	Tekenen des Tijds†
0040-2230	Tekhnicheskaya Estetika
0040-2249	Tekhnika Kino i Televideniya
0040-2257	Tekhnika Molodezhi
0040-2273	Journal of Labor Hygiene in Iron and Steel Industry
0040-2303	Tekniikka see 0020-2010
0040-2311	Teknisk Information†
0040-232X	Teknisk Nyt
0040-2338	Teknisk Skoletidende
0040-2346	Teknisk Tidskrift see 0550-8754
0040-2354	Teknisk Ukeblad-Teknikk changed to Teknisk Ukeblad
0040-2362	Tekniskt Forum see 0533-070X

1312 ISSN INDEX

0040-2370 Tekstiililehti
0040-2389 Tekstilna Industrija
0040-2397 Tekstil'naya Promyshlennost'
0040-2400 Tel Hashomer Hospital Proceeding†
0040-2419 Tel Quel
0040-2427 Tele (Swedish Edition)
0040-2443 Telemagazine
0040-2451 Tele-Scout†
0040-2486 Telecommunication Journal of Australia
0040-2494 Telecommunications (Norwood)
0040-2508 Telecommunications and Radio Engineering
0040-2524 Teledyne Ryan Aeronautical Reporter†
0040-2532 Teleflora Spirit *changed to* Flowers &
0040-2540 Telefood Magazine
0040-2575 Telegraph
0040-2583 Telegraph Worker Journal
0040-2591 Telekomunikace
0040-2605 Telekomunikacije
0040-2621 Telemetry Journal†
0040-263X Telephone Engineer and Management
0040-2648 Telephone Review Magazine†
0040-2656 Telephony
0040-2664 Telepro
0040-2672 Teleprograma
0040-2680 Telepulestudomanyi Kozlemenyek
0040-2699 Telerama
0040-2702 Telescope (Detroit)
0040-2710 Telesis
0040-2729 Telesna Vychova Mladeze
0040-2737 Telespazio
0040-2745 Telespiegel *changed to* Der Oesterreichische Schulfunk mit Telespiegel
0040-2753 Teleteknik.
0040-277X Television/Radio Age
0040-2788 Broadcast
0040-2818 Telhan Patrika
0040-2826 Tellus *see* 0280-6495
0040-2826 Tellus *see* 0280-6509
0040-2834 Telonde
0040-2850 Telovychovny Pracovnik
0040-2869 Temas
0040-2877 Temas Administrativos *changed to* Revista Universidad E A F I T
0040-2885 Temas Contemporaneos
0040-2915 Temas Sociales
0040-2923 Temoignage Chretien
0040-2958 Temple Apothecary
0040-2966 Temple David Bulletin
0040-2974 Temple Law Quarterly
0040-2982 Tempo (London, 1939)
0040-2990 Tempo†
0040-3008 Tempo (New York)
0040-3016 Tempo (New York, 1955)†
0040-3024 Tempo
0040-3040 Tempo Economico
0040-3067 Temps Libre Informations *changed to* Enjeu
0040-3075 Temps Modernes
0040-3083 Tenant
0040-3113 Tenders *see* 0812-2288
0040-3121 Tenneco
0040-313X Tennessee Academy of Science. Journal
0040-3148 Tennessee Agricultural Experiment Station. Bulletin
0040-3156 Tennessee Alumnus
0040-3180 Tennessee Archaeologist
0040-3199 Tennessee Banker
0040-3202 Tennessee Conservationist
0040-3229 Tennessee Farm and Home Science
0040-3245 Tennessee Farmer
0040-3253 Tennessee Folklore Society Bulletin
0040-3261 Tennessee Historical Quarterly
0040-327X Tennessee Law Enforcement Journal
0040-3288 Tennessee Law Review
0040-3296 Tennessee Librarian *see* 0162-1564
0040-330X Tennessee Life Insurance News *see* 0194-4312
0040-3318 Tennessee Medical Association. Journal
0040-3334 Tennessee Musician
0040-3342 Tennessee Nurses Association. Bulletin
0040-3350 Tennessee Planner†
0040-3369 Tennessee Poetry Journal†
0040-3377 Tennessee Public Welfare Record *see* 0360-4608
0040-3385 Tennessee Dental Association. Journal
0040-3393 Tennessee Survey of Business *see* 0099-0973
0040-3407 Tennessee Teacher
0040-3415 Tennessee Town and City
0040-3423 Tennis
0040-3431 Tennis Tidningen
0040-344X Tennis de France
0040-3458 Golf Europeen
0040-3466 Tennis U. S. A.
0040-3474 Tennis World
0040-3482 Tenrikyo
0040-3490 Tenside - Detergents *changed to* Tenside Surfactants Detergents
0040-3504 Tensor
0040-3520 Tentoonstellingsagenda *changed to* Tentoonstellingsboeke
0040-3539 Teollisuuslehti *see* 0358-7673
0040-3547 Teollisuustekniikka
0040-3555 Teologinen Aikakauskirja
0040-3563 Teoresi
0040-3571 Teoreticheskie Osnovy Khimicheskoi Tekhnologii
0040-358X Teorie a Praxe Telesne Vychovy
0040-3598 Teorija in Praksa
0040-3601 Teoriya i Praktika Fizicheskoi Kul'tury
0040-361X Teoriya Veroyatnostei i ee Primenenie
0040-3628 Teosofi i Norden
0040-3636 Teploenergetika
0040-3644 Teplofizika Vysokikh Temperatur
0040-3652 Teramo
0040-3660 Terapevticheskii Arkhiv
0040-3679 Terapia†
0040-3687 Terapia†
0040-3695 Terapia Moderna
0040-3709 Teratology
0040-3717 Termeszet Vilaga
0040-3725 Termotecnica
0040-3733 Terra
0040-3741 Terra
0040-375X Terra Ameriga
0040-3768 Terra e Sole
0040-3776 Terra e Vita
0040-3784 Terra Santa
0040-3792 Terra Umbra†
0040-3806 Terrazzo Topics
0040-3814 Terre
0040-3822 Terre Cuite†
0040-3830 Terre de Chez Nous
0040-3865 Terre et la Vie
0040-389X Terres Australes et Antarctiques Francaises†
0040-3903 Terveydenhoitolehti *see* 0355-1903
0040-3911 Terveys
0040-392X Terzo Mondo
0040-3938 Tesoro Eucaristico
0040-3946 Test
0040-3962 Testigo†
0040-3970 Textil & Beklaednings†
0040-3989 Testimonianze
0040-3997 Testing, Instruments, and Controls *changed to* Non-Destructive Testing - Australia
0040-4004 Tete†
0040-4012 Tethys
0040-4020 Tetrahedron
0040-4039 Tetrahedron Letters
0040-4047 Railway Pictorial
0040-4055 Monthly Statistics of Actual Production of Railway Cars
0040-4071 Tevyne
0040-4101 Texaco Tempo†
0040-4128 Texas A & M University. College of Liberal Arts. Review†
0040-4136 Texas A & M University Library Notes
0040-4144 Texas Academy of Science. Newsletter†
0040-4152 Texas Agriculture *changed to* Texas Agriculture
0040-4160 Texas and Southwest Hotel-Motel Review *see* 8750-4634
0040-4179 Texas Architect
0040-4187 Texas Bar Journal
0040-4195 Financial Trend
0040-4209 Texas Business Review
0040-4241 Texas Coach
0040-425X Texas Concho Register *changed to* West Texas Angelus
0040-4284 Texas Dental Journal
0040-4314 Texas Fashions†
0040-4322 Texas Food Merchant
0040-4330 Texas F F A Magazine
0040-4349 Texas Highways
0040-4357 Texas Hospitals
0040-4365 Texas Industrial Expansion
0040-4373 Texas Industry *changed to* T. A. B. Quarterly
0040-4381 Texas International Law Forum *see* 0163-7479
0040-439X Texas Jewish Post
0040-4403 Texas Journal of Science
0040-4411 Texas Law Review
0040-442X Texas Lawman
0040-4438 Texas Libraries
0040-4446 Texas Library Journal
0040-4454 Texas LP-Gas News
0040-4462 Texas Manpower Trends *changed to* Texas Labor Market Review
0040-4470 Texas Medicine
0040-4489 Texas Methodist *changed to* United Methodist Reporter
0040-4497 Texas Motorist *changed to* A A A World (Houston)
0040-4519 Texas Observer
0040-4527 Texas Oil Jobber *changed to* Texas Oil Marketer
0040-4535 Texas Oil Journal†
0040-4543 Texas Ornithological Society. Bulletin
0040-4551 Texas Outlook
0040-456X Texas Parade *see* 0164-7628
0040-4578 Texas Parent-Teacher *changed to* P T A Communicator
0040-4586 Texas Parks and Wildlife Magazine
0040-4608 Texas Poultry and Egg News *see* 0048-4989
0040-4616 Texas Presbyterian *changed to* Presbyterian (Denton)
0040-4624 Texas Press Messenger *changed to* T P A Messenger
0040-4632 Texas Professional Engineer
0040-4640 Texas Public Employee
0040-4659 Texas Quarterly†
0040-4675 Texas Reports on Biology and Medicine†
0040-4683 Texas Schools *changed to* T S T A Texas Schools
0040-4691 Texas Studies in Literature and Language
0040-4705 Texas Study of Secondary Education Research Bulletin
0040-4721 Texas Techsan
0040-473X Texas Town & City
0040-4748 Texas Transportation Researcher
0040-4756 Texas Veterinary Medical Journal
0040-4764 Technika Chronika
0040-4772 Texpress
0040-4780 Text†
0040-4799 France. Institut National de Recherche et de Documentation Pedagogiques. Textes et Documents pour la Classe *see* 0395-6601
0040-4810 Textiel-Visie/Weekly (Amsterdam) *changed to* TextielVisie
0040-4829 Textil
0040-4845 Textil och Konfektion
0040-4853 Textil Praxis International
0040-4861 Textil-Revue
0040-487X Textil-Wirtschaft
0040-4888 Textilbranschen
0040-4896 Textile Bulletin†
0040-490X Textile Chemist and Colorist
0040-490X American Association of Textile Chemists and Colorists. Buyer's Guide
0040-4926 Textile Dyer and Printer
0040-4934 Textile Engineer *changed to* Ramifications
0040-4969 Textile History†
0040-4977 Textile India
0040-4985 Textile Industries *changed to* America's Textiles
0040-4993 Textile Industry & Trade Journal
0040-5000 Textile Institute. Journal
0040-5019 Textile Journal of Australia *see* 0816-3588
0040-5027 Textile Labor *see* 0271-5848
0040-5035 Textile Machinery
0040-5043 Textile Machinery Society of Japan. Journal (English Edition).
0040-5051 Textile Machinery Society of Japan. Proceedings *see* 0371-0580
0040-506X Textile Machinery Society of Japan. Transactions *see* 0371-0580
0040-5078 Textile Magazine
0040-5086 Textile Magazine
0040-5094 Textile Maintenance Reporter
0040-5116 Textile Month
0040-5124 Textile News
0040-5132 Textile Organon
0040-5140 Textile Panamericanos
0040-5159 Textile Production *changed to* World Fibre News
0040-5167 Textile Progress
0040-5175 Textile Research Journal
0040-5191 Textile Technology Digest
0040-5205 Textile Trends
0040-5213 Textile World
0040-5221 Officiel du Pret a Porter
0040-523X Textiles of Ireland and Linen Trade Circular *changed to* Textile Times International
0040-5248 Textiles Suisses
0040-5264 Textilia
0040-5280 Textilis *changed to* Tex-Textilis
0040-5299 Textilmesteren†
0040-5302 Textilreinigung†
0040-5329 Text und Kritik
0040-5345 Thai Fisheries Gazette
0040-5353 Thai Journal of Development Administration
0040-5361 Thai Junior Red Cross Magazine
0040-537X Thailand Illustrated†
0040-5388 Thailand. National Statistical Office. Quarterly Bulletin of Statistics
0040-5396 Thames Valley Countryside *see* 0306-672X
0040-5418 Theater der Zeit
0040-5442 Theater-Rundschau
0040-5450 Theaternachrichten *changed to* Theater in Graz
0040-5469 Theatre Crafts
0040-5477 Theatre Design and Technology
0040-5485 Theatre Documentation†
0040-5493 Theatre en Pologne
0040-5507 Theater Heute
0040-5515 Theatre Information Bulletin
0040-5523 Theatre Notebook
0040-5531 Theatre Organ
0040-5558 Theatre Organ Review
0040-5566 Theatre Research *see* 0307-8833
0040-5574 Theatre Survey
0040-5604 Theatron
0040-5612 Theologia Reformata
0040-5620 Theological Education
0040-5639 Theological Studies
0040-5655 Theologie und Philosophie
0040-5663 Theologisch-Praktische Quartalschrift
0040-5671 Theologische Literaturzeitung
0040-568X Theologische Revue
0040-5698 Theologische Rundschau
0040-5701 Theologische Zeitschrift
0040-571X Theology
0040-5728 Theology Digest
0040-5736 Theology Today
0040-5744 Theoretica Chimica Acta
0040-5752 Theoretical and Applied Genetics
0040-5760 Theoretical and Experimental Chemistry
0040-5779 Theoretical and Mathematical Physics
0040-5787 Theoretical Chemical Engineering Abstracts
0040-5795 Theoretical Foundations of Chemical Engineering
0040-5809 Theoretical Population Biology
0040-5817 Theoria
0040-5825 Theoria
0040-5833 Theory and Decision
0040-5841 Theory Into Practice

ISSN INDEX 1313

ISSN	Title
0040-585X	Theory of Probability and Its Applications
0040-5868	Theosofia
0040-5876	Theosophical Journal
0040-5884	Theosophical Movement
0040-5892	Theosophist
0040-5906	Theosophy
0040-5914	Therapeutic Recreation Journal
0040-5922	Therapeutique†
0040-5930	Therapeutische Umschau
0040-5949	Therapia Hungarica
0040-5957	Therapie
0040-5965	Therapie der Gegenwart
0040-5973	Therapiewoche
0040-599X	Thermal Abstracts see 0140-4237
0040-6007	Thermal Analysis Review see 0306-0438
0040-6015	Thermal Engineering
0040-6023	Thermiek
0040-6031	Thermochimica Acta
0040-604X	Thesaurus
0040-6058	These Times†
0040-6066	Theta (Carrollton)
0040-6074	Theta
0040-6082	Thin Films see 0305-3091
0040-6090	Thin Solid Films
0040-6112	Think†
0040-6120	Third Branch
0040-6139	Third Degree
0040-6155	Magazine of Metals Producing see 0149-1210
0040-6171	This England
0040-6198	This is London
0040-6201	This Is West Texas
0040-6228	This Magazine Is About Schools see 0381-3746
0040-6244	This Month in London†
0040-6252	This Month in Your Library
0040-6260	This Paper Belongs to the People
0040-6279	Key-This Week in Chicago
0040-6309	This Week changed to This Week in Western North Carolina
0040-6317	This Week in the Nation's Capital
0040-6325	Thomist
0040-6341	Thomson C S F. Revue Technique
0040-6368	Thoracic Medicine and Surgery
0040-6376	Thorax
0040-6384	Thoraxchirurgie - Vaskulaere Chirurgie see 0171-6425
0040-6392	Thoreau Journal Quarterly see 0730-868X
0040-6406	Thoreau Society Bulletin
0040-6414	Thoroughbred Record and the Racing Calendar changed to Thoroughbred Record
0040-6430	Thoth†
0040-6449	Thought†
0040-6457	Thought
0040-6465	Thought†
0040-6449	Three Banks Review changed to Royal Bank of Scotland Review
0040-6511	Three Crafts Journal†
0040-6520	Three Crowns
0040-6538	Three/Four changed to Vine
0040-6546	Three Hundred Thirty-Eight News
0040-6554	3M Panorama
0040-6562	Threshold
0040-6589	Throb
0040-6597	Thrombosis et Diathesis Haemorrhagica see 0340-6245
0040-6600	Through to Victory†
0040-6619	Thru the Garden Gate
0040-6635	Thunder
0040-6643	Thunderbolt
0040-6651	Thursday†
0040-666X	Thyssenforschung see 0340-5060
0040-6686	Ti Saluto Fratello
0040-6694	Tibet im Exil†
0040-6708	Tibetan Review
0040-6716	Tic
0040-6732	Ticitl
0040-6740	Tiden
0040-6759	Tiden
0040-6767	Tidens Ekko†
0040-6775	Tidens Kvinder†
0040-6791	Tidings
0040-6805	Tidnings Nytt
0040-6821	Tidskrift foer Kriminalvaard
0040-683X	Tidskrift foer Kustartilleriet
0040-6848	Tidskrift foer Schack
0040-6856	Tidskrift foer Yrkesutbildning
0040-6872	Tidskrift foer Dokumentation
0040-6880	Tidsskrift for Groenlands Retsvaesen
0040-6899	Tidskrift foer Svenska Folkhoegskolan see 0348-4769
0040-6902	Sveriges Advokatsamfund. Tidskrift changed to Advokaten
0040-6937	Tidskrift i Fortifikation
0040-6945	Tidskrift i Sjovasendet
0040-6953	Juridiska Foereningen i Finland. Tidskrift
0040-6961	Tidskriften Bostadsnaemnden
0040-6988	Tidskriften Heimdal
0040-7003	Tidskriften Landstaten
0040-7011	Tidskriften Taxeringsnaemden
0040-702X	Tidsskrift for Danske Sygehuse
0040-7038	Tidsskrift for Faareavl
0040-7046	Tidsskrift for Fjerkraeavl see 0045-9607
0040-7062	Tidsskrift for Hermetikkindustri changed to Naeringsmiddelindustrien
0040-7070	Tidsskrift for Industri see 0045-9623
0040-7089	Tidsskrift for Jordmoedre
0040-7100	Tidsskrift for Kortbolge Radio changed to OZ
0040-7119	Tidsskrift for Landokonomi
0040-7135	Tidsskrift for Planteavl
0040-7143	Tidsskrift for Rettsvitenskap
0040-7151	Tidsskrift for Revisjon og Regnskapsvesen see 0332-7795
0040-716X	Tidsskrift for Samfunnsforskning
0040-7178	Tidsskrift for Skogbruk†
0040-7186	Tidsskrift for Soevaesen
0040-7194	Tidsskrift for Teologi og Kirke
0040-7208	Tidsskrift for Textilteknik see 0107-5373
0040-7216	Tidsskrift for Voksenopplaering changed to Nordisk Tidskrift for Folkbildning och Vuxenundervisning
0040-7224	Tidsskriftet Ny Tid og Vi
0040-7232	Tie
0040-7240	Tiefbau, Ingenieurbau, Strassenbau
0040-7259	Tiefkuehl Praxis International changed to G V - Praxis
0040-7267	Tielehti see 0355-7855
0040-7275	Tiempo
0040-7283	Tiempo de Cine
0040-7291	Tier
0040-7305	Das Tierreich
0040-7313	Tierfreund changed to Schweizer Tierschutz
0040-733X	Tierra
0040-7348	Tierra y dos Mares†
0040-7356	Tiers Monde
0040-7364	Der Tierzuechter
0040-7372	Tiesa
0040-7380	Tiger Beat
0040-7402	Tiili
0040-7410	Vereniging Koninklijke Nederlandsche Heide Maatschappij. Tijdschrift changed to Vereniging Koninklijke Nederlandsche Heide Maatschappij. Heidemijtijdschrift
0040-7429	Tijdschrift voor Architectuur en Beeldende Kunsten†
0040-7437	Tijdschrift voor Bestuurswetenschappen en Publiekrecht
0040-7445	Tijdschrift voor Chemie & Instrument changed to Chemie & Instrument
0040-7453	Tijdschrift voor Diergeneeskunde
0040-7461	Tijdschrift voor Economie changed to Tijdschrift voor Economie en Management
0040-747X	Tijdschrift voor Economische en Sociale Geografie
0040-7488	Tijdschrift voor Effectief Directiebeleid†
0040-7496	Tijdschrift voor Entomologie
0040-750X	Tijdschrift voor Filosofie
0040-7518	Tijdschrift voor Geschiedenis
0040-7526	Nederlands Geodetisch Tijdschrift
0040-7550	Tijdschrift voor Nederlandse Taal- en Letterkunde
0040-7569	Tijdschrift voor Oppervlaktetechnieken van Metalen see 0030-3844
0040-7577	Tijdschrift voor Opvoedkunde see 0166-5855
0040-7593	Tijdschrift voor Revalidatie changed to Revalidatie
0040-7607	Tijdschrift voor Sociale Geneeskunde changed to Tijdschrift voor Sociale Gezondheidszorg
0040-7615	Tijdschrift voor Sociale Wetenschappen
0040-7623	Tijdschrift voor Vervoerswetenschap
0040-764X	Tijdspiegel
0040-7658	Tilastollisia Kuukaustitietoja Helsingista see 0357-3362
0040-7666	Tile and Architectural Ceramics see 0192-9550
0040-7674	Tile and Till†
0040-7682	Till Rors (Med Segel och Motor) changed to Paa Kryss och till Rors
0040-7704	Tim changed to Maky
0040-7712	T I M
0040-7720	Timber changed to Timber and Timber Products
0040-7739	Timber and Plywood see 0262-6071
0040-7755	Timber Development Association of India. Journal
0040-7763	Timber Grower
0040-7771	Timber Journal†
0040-778X	Timber Supply Review
0040-7798	Timber Trades Journal and Woodworking Machinery see 0262-6071
0040-781X	Time
0040-7828	Time and Tide
0040-7836	Time & Tide
0040-7852	Time Machine
0040-7879	Times and Challenge
0040-7887	Times Educational Supplement
0040-7895	Times Literary Supplement
0040-7909	Times of Israel
0040-7917	Times of the Americas
0040-7925	Timken
0040-7933	Timmerfabrikant
0040-7941	Tin and Its Uses
0040-795X	Tin International
0040-7968	Tin News
0040-7976	Tin Printer and Box Maker see 0040-795X
0040-7984	Tintoria
0040-8018	Tip
0040-8026	Tip-O-Texan†
0040-8034	Tipperary Star
0040-8042	Tips and Topics in Home Economics
0040-8050	Welsh Farmer
0040-8069	Tir Sportif en France†
0040-8077	Tiramolla
0040-8085	Tire Review
0040-8093	Federacion Nacional del Tiro Olimpico Espanol. Revista Informativa changed to Federacion Nacional del Tiro Olimpico Espanol. Boletin Informativo
0040-8107	Tirol†
0040-8115	Tiroler Heimatblaetter
0040-8123	Tisch und Kueche changed to T U K Inform
0040-8131	Der Tischler
0040-814X	Tischtennis-Schau
0040-8158	Tish
0040-8166	Tissue & Cell
0040-8174	Tissue Culture Abstracts†
0040-8182	Titanic Commutator
0040-8190	Title News
0040-8204	Titogradska Tribina
0040-8212	Titular
0040-8239	Tlalocan
0040-8247	To Free Mankind changed to World Citizen/Federalist Letter
0040-8255	Nisaki Mas i Kea
0040-8263	Toastmaster
0040-8271	Tobacco
0040-828X	Tobacco†
0040-8298	Tobacco Abstracts
0040-8301	Tobacco Intelligence†
0040-8328	Tobacco Reporter changed to Tobacco Reporter
0040-8336	Tobacco Retailers Journal changed to Retail Tobacconist
0040-8344	U.S. Department of Agriculture. Economics Management Staff. Tobacco Situation changed to U.S. Department of Agriculture. Tobacco Outlook and Situation
0040-8352	Dialogue (Birmingham)†
0040-8360	Today
0040-8379	Today†
0040-8387	Today changed to Today in Africa
0040-8409	Today in Anaheim/Orange County†
0040-8417	Today in France
0040-8433	Today in San Diego
0040-8441	Today's Catholic Teacher
0040-845X	Today's Chef changed to Today's Chef-Food Service Executive
0040-8468	Today's Child Newsmagazine†
0040-8476	Today's Children†
0040-8484	Today's Education see 0737-1888
0040-8484	Today's Education see 0272-529X
0040-8484	Today's Education see 0272-3581
0040-8492	Todays Family†
0040-8514	Today's Health see 0279-3547
0040-8522	Today's Housing Briefs†
0040-8549	Today's Parish
0040-8565	Today's Secretary†
0040-8573	Today's Speech see 0146-3373
0040-8581	Today's Teens†
0040-859X	Today's Transport International
0040-8603	Todo
0040-8611	Todo es Historia†
0040-8638	Toerist see 0005-1772
0040-8646	Wudd
0040-8654	Toga Calabrese
0040-8697	Toho University Medical Society. Journal
0040-8700	Tohoku University. Institute for Agricultural Research. Bulletin
0040-8719	Tohoku Medical Journal
0040-8727	Tohoku Journal of Agricultural Research
0040-8735	Tohoku Journal of Experimental Medicine
0040-8743	Tohoku Mathematical Journal
0040-8751	Tohoku Psychologica Folia
0040-876X	Tohoku Archivo por Orthopedia Kej Akcidenta Hirurgio changed to Tohoku Archives of Orthopaedic Surgery and Traumatology
0040-8778	Tohoku University. Research Institute of Mineral Dressing and Metallurgy. Bulletin
0040-8786	Tohoku University. Science Reports. Series 1: Physics, Chemistry, Astronomy see 0388-5607
0040-8794	Tohoku University. Science Reports. Series 4: Biology†
0040-8808	Tohoku Geophysical Journal
0040-8816	Tohoku University. Science Reports of the Research Institutes. Series A: Physics, Chemistry, and Metallurgy
0040-8824	Tohoku University. Faculty of Engineering. Technology Reports
0040-8832	Toilers of the Deep
0040-8859	Toison d'Or
0040-8867	Tokai Regional Fisheries Research Laboratory
0040-8875	Toko-Ginecologia Practica
0040-8883	Tokushima Journal of Experimental Medicine
0040-8891	University of Tokushima. Faculty of Engineering. Bulletin
0040-8905	Tokyo Dental College. Bulletin
0040-8913	Tokyo Medical College. Journal
0040-8921	Tokyo Journal of Climatology
0040-893X	Tokyo Medical and Dental University. Bulletin
0040-8948	Tokyo Municipal News
0040-8956	Tokyo National Museum News
0040-8964	Tokyo Medical Association. Journal
0040-8972	University of Tokyo. College of General Education. Scientific Papers
0040-8972	University of Tokyo. Earthquake Research Institute. Bulletin

ISSN	Title
0040-8980	University of Tokyo. Faculty of Science. Journal. Section 1A: Mathematics
0040-8999	University of Tokyo. Faculty of Science. Journal. Section 2: Geology, Mineralogy, Geography, Geophysics
0040-9006	University of Tokyo. Institute of Industrial Science. Report
0040-9014	Tokyo University of Fisheries. Journal
0040-9022	Tokyo Women's Medical College. Journal
0040-9030	Tolar Creek Syndicate†
0040-9049	Toldbladet
0040-9057	Toledo Business News
0040-9065	Toledo City Journal
0040-9081	Toledo Jewish News
0040-909X	Tolkien Journal see 0146-9339
0040-9103	Tolpolski's Chronicle
0040-9111	Tolvmansbladet changed to Erhvervs-Jordbruget
0040-912X	Tom Thumb
0040-9146	Tomorrow Through Research changed to Technology Today
0040-9154	Tomorrow's Man†
0040-9170	Toneel Teatraal
0040-9189	Tong-Tong see 0165-6546
0040-9200	Tonindustrie-Zeitung und Keramische Rundschau changed to T I Z Fachberichte
0040-9219	Manufacturing Engineering and Management see 0361-0853
0040-9227	Tooling
0040-9243	Tooling & Production
0040-9251	Toonzaal†
0040-926X	Top Gear†
0040-9286	Top of the News
0040-9308	Topcu Dergisi†
0040-9316	Topic News Weekly
0040-9324	Topical Dates & Facts Newsletter†
0040-9332	Topical Time
0040-9340	Topicator
0040-9367	Topics
0040-9375	Topique - Revue Freudienne
0040-9383	Topology
0040-9391	Tora Ya Tebelo
0040-9405	Torah Umesorah Report†
0040-9413	Audio & Electronics
0040-9448	Torch (Chicago)
0040-9456	Torch of Knowledge†
0040-9472	Torfyanaya Promyshlennost'
0040-9499	Tornado†
0040-9502	Foro Universitario
0040-9510	Metropolitan Toronto Board of Trade. Journal changed to Metropolitan Toronto Business Journal
0040-9529	Toronto Boys and Girls House Subscription Reviews†
0040-9537	Toronto Calendar Magazine
0040-9553	Toronto Railway Club. Official Proceedings
0040-9561	University of Toronto News see 0042-0212
0040-957X	Torque†
0040-9588	Torre
0040-9596	Torre Civica†
0040-960X	Torre Davidica
0040-9618	Torrey Botanical Club. Bulletin
0040-9634	Tortenelmi Szemle
0040-9642	Toshiba Review
0040-9650	Japan Society of Library Science. Annals
0040-9669	Library World
0040-9677	Tot 'n Teen Fashions
0040-9693	Total Comfort Dealer
0040-9723	Totem
0040-9731	Tour de Feu see 0294-4030
0040-974X	Tourama changed to Hotel Tourama of Rhodesia
0040-9758	Touring
0040-9766	Touring Freizeit changed to Freizeit
0040-9782	Tourisme Informations†
0040-9804	Tourist Time†
0040-9820	Tout pour Vous
0040-9839	Tout-Rouen
0040-9855	Toute l'Electronique
0040-9863	Toutou - Journal
0040-9898	Toward Freedom
0040-9901	Tower†
0040-991X	Tower Smiling see 0190-3284
0040-9928	Towers
0040-9952	Town and Country
0040-9960	Town and Country Planning
0040-9979	Town & Village
0040-9995	Town Planning and Local Government Guide
0041-0012	New Zealand Planning Institute. Town Planning Quarterly see 0111-9435
0041-0020	Town Planning Review
0041-0039	Town Talk about Toronto†
0041-0047	Towns & Cities Magazines†
0041-0063	Towson State Journal of International Affairs
0041-0071	Toxicity Bibliography†
0041-008X	Toxicology and Applied Pharmacology
0041-0101	Toxicon
0041-011X	Toy & Hobby World
0041-0128	Toy Trader†
0041-0136	Toy Trader
0041-0144	Toyo Soda Manufacturing Company. Scientific Report
0041-0152	Toyoda Technical Review changed to Toyoda Machine Works Technical Review
0041-0160	Toys†
0041-0179	Toys see 0160-8010
0041-0195	Toys International changed to Toys International and the Retailer
0041-0209	Tozhil Udayam changed to Tozhil Uravu
0041-0233	Fomento del Trabajo Nacional. Economia Nacional, Internacional de la Empresa changed to Horizonte Empresarial
0041-0241	Trabajos de Estadistica e Investigacion Operativa
0041-025X	Trabajos de Hematologia y Hemoterapia†
0041-0276	Traces
0041-0284	Track & Field News
0041-0292	Track and Field Quarterly Review
0041-0306	Track Newsletter†
0041-0314	Track Technique see 0742-3918
0041-0330	Tracker
0041-0349	Tracks
0041-0357	Tract Messenger
0041-0365	Trade-A-Plane
0041-0373	Trade and Industry
0041-0381	Trade and Industry of Japan see 0388-0311
0041-039X	Trade and Tours†
0041-0403	Trade Channel
0041-0411	Trade Chronicle
0041-042X	Trade Digest changed to World Fairs Guide
0041-0438	Trade Marks Journal
0041-0446	Trade Marks Journal
0041-0454	Trade Marks Journal
0041-0462	Trade of the Maltese Islands changed to Malta Trade Statistics
0041-0470	Trade Review of the Week†
0041-0489	Trade Trends†
0041-0497	Trade Union Courier
0041-0500	Trade Union Information†
0041-0519	Trade Union News Bulletin from Norway†
0041-0527	Trade Union Press changed to Flashes from the Trade Unions
0041-0535	Trade Union Record
0041-0543	Trade with Greece
0041-0551	Trade with Italy
0041-056X	Trademark Reporter
0041-0586	Trading Post
0041-0594	Tradition
0041-0608	Tradition (New York)
0041-0624	Trae Nyt
0041-0632	Traeindustrien see 0105-8738
0041-0659	Traffic Bulletin†
0041-0675	Traffic Engineering see 0162-8178
0041-0683	Traffic Engineering & Control
0041-0691	Traffic Management
0041-0705	Traffic Manager
0041-0713	Traffic Quarterly see 0278-9434
0041-0721	Traffic Safety
0041-073X	Traffic World
0041-0748	Trail and Landscape
0041-0756	Trail and Timberline
0041-0764	Trailblazer†
0041-0772	Trailer-Body Builders
0041-0780	Trailer Life
0041-0799	Trailer Topics Magazine†
0041-0802	Trailer Travel Magazine see 0160-3000
0041-0829	Train Collectors Quarterly
0041-0837	Train Dispatcher
0041-0845	Trainsheet
0041-0853	Trained Men changed to Training Digest
0041-0861	Training and Development Journal changed to Training and Development Journal (1978)
0041-087X	Training Briefs†
0041-0888	Training Directors Newsletter†
0041-0896	Training in Business and Industry see 0095-5892
0041-090X	Training Officer
0041-0918	Training School Bulletin†
0041-0926	Trainmaster
0041-0934	Trains
0041-0950	Traitement Thermique
0041-0969	Traktoeren
0041-0977	Traktor- og Landbrugsbladet
0041-0985	Traktor Aktuell
0041-1000	Tramontane
0041-1027	Tranciatura Stampaggio
0041-1035	Trans-Action-Social Science and Modern Society see 0147-2011
0041-1043	Transair changed to Australian Way
0041-1051	Transactional Analysis Bulletin see 0362-1537
0041-106X	Transafrican Journal of History
0041-1078	Transatlantic Review†
0041-1086	Transatom Bulletin see 0259-8264
0041-1108	Transcultural Psychiatric Research Review
0041-1116	Transdex Index
0041-1124	Transformacion
0041-1132	Transfusion
0041-1140	Transistor
0041-1167	Transit of Chi Epsilon
0041-1175	Transit Postmark Collector
0041-1183	Transit Record
0041-1191	Transition see 0564-108X
0041-1205	Transition
0041-1213	Transitrends†
0041-1221	Translation changed to In Other Words
0041-123X	Translation Talk†
0041-1256	Translations Register-Index†
0041-1264	Translatoeren
0041-1272	Transmisiones
0041-1280	Transmission and Distribution
0041-1302	Transparent
0041-1310	Transpatent
0041-1337	Transplantation
0041-1345	Transplantation Proceedings
0041-1361	Transport
0041-137X	Transport
0041-1388	Transport and Communications
0041-1396	Transport and Communications Bulletin for Asia and the Far East see 0252-4392
0041-140X	Transport Commercial changed to Moteur et Equipement
0041-1418	Transport-Communications Monthly Review changed to Indian Highways
0041-1426	Transport-Dienst changed to Transport-Dienst & Wirtschaftscorrespondent
0041-1434	Transport Economics†
0041-1442	Transport et Tourisme
0041-1450	Transport Theory and Statistical Physics
0041-1469	Transport History
0041-1477	Transport Industry and Trade Journal changed to Transport Industry and Trade Annual
0041-1485	Transport Journal
0041-1493	Transport Journal of Australia
0041-1523	Transport-Nytt
0041-1531	Transport Salaried Staff Journal
0041-154X	Transport Teknik
0041-1558	Transport Topics
0041-1566	Transport und Lager
0041-1574	Transport und Lagertechnik changed to Transport, Foerder- und Lagertechnik
0041-1582	Transport und Schiffahrt†
0041-1590	Transportation Ad Views†
0041-1604	Transportation Engineer
0041-1612	Transportation Journal
0041-1639	Translog
0041-1647	Transportation Research see 0191-2607
0041-1647	Transportation Research see 0191-2615
0041-1655	Transportation Science
0041-1663	Standard and Poor's Transportation Securities Weekly Outlook changed to Standard & Poor's Transportation Securities
0041-1671	Transportation Technology see 0308-1060
0041-168X	Transporte
0041-1698	Transportes Moderno
0041-1701	Transportnoe Stroitel'stvo
0041-171X	Transvaal Education Bulletin†
0041-1728	Transvaal Educational News
0041-1736	Transvaal Farmer†
0041-1744	Transvaal Gardener
0041-1752	Transvaal Museum. Annals
0041-1760	Trap & Field
0041-1779	Trapani Nuova
0041-1787	Trasfusione del Sangue
0041-1795	Trasporti Aerei
0041-1809	Trasporti Industriali changed to Trasporti Industriali e Movimentazione
0041-1817	Trasporti Pubblici
0041-1825	Trattamenti dei Metalli†
0041-1833	Trattamenti e Finitura - Superfici
0041-1841	I M A Trattorista changed to Macchine e Motori Agricoli - I M A il Trattorista
0041-185X	Travail et Methodes
0041-1868	Travail Humain
0041-1876	Travailleur du Livre
0041-1892	Saagverken/Traevarunindustrin see 0036-259X
0041-1906	Travaux
0041-1914	Travaux de Peinture†
0041-1930	Travaux et Jours†
0041-1965	Travel changed to Travel-Holiday
0041-1973	TravelAge West
0041-1981	Travel Agency
0041-199X	Travel Agent
0041-2007	Travel & Leisure
0041-2015	Travel Management Daily
0041-2023	Travel Marketing Newsletter†
0041-2031	Travel Times†
0041-204X	Travel Times
0041-2058	Travel Trade Magazine see 0311-2179
0041-2066	Travel Trade
0041-2074	Travel Trade Directory
0041-2082	Travel Weekly
0041-2090	Travel World
0041-2104	TravelAge East
0041-2112	Traveler†
0041-2120	Travelling†
0041-2139	Treasure
0041-2155	U.S. Treasury Department. Treasury Bulletin
0041-2163	Treasury Information Bulletin†
0041-2171	Tree†
0041-2198	Tree-Ring Bulletin
0041-2201	Tree Talks
0041-221X	Trees
0041-2228	Trees†
0041-2236	Trees in South Africa
0041-2244	Trefoil
0041-2260	Trekker changed to Trekkerskrant
0041-2279	Tremplin
0041-2287	Trend†
0041-2295	Trend†
0041-2317	Trend in Engineering
0041-2325	Trenden
0041-2333	Standard & Poor's Trendline Current Market Perspectives
0041-2341	Trends see 0729-6509
0041-2368	Bauma-Trends

ISSN INDEX 1315

ISSN	Title
0041-2376	Trends (Arlington)†
0041-2384	Trends in Adjusting
0041-2406	Trends in Management-Stockholder Relations
0041-2449	Mercer Business Magazine
0041-2457	Trgovinski Glasnik
0041-2481	Florida. Department of Agriculture and Consumer Services. Tri-Ology Technical Report
0041-249X	Tri-State Food News
0041-2503	Tri-State Trader see 0888-5451
0041-2511	Triad
0041-252X	Triades
0041-2538	Trial
0041-2546	Trial Lawyer's Guide
0041-2554	Trial Lawyers Quarterly
0041-2562	Inklusief
0041-2570	Triangle (Lakeland)
0041-2597	Triangle
0041-2600	Triangle of Mu Phi Epsilon
0041-2619	Triangle Pointer
0041-2643	Tribal Spokesman†
0041-266X	Tribina
0041-2678	Tribology see 0301-679X
0041-2694	Tribos - Tribology Abstracts
0041-2708	Tribritta
0041-2716	Tribuene
0041-2724	Tribuna
0041-2767	Tribuna Musical
0041-2775	Tribuna Odontologica†
0041-2783	Tribuna Politica
0041-2791	Tribuna Postale changed to Tribuna Postale e delle Telecomunicazioni
0041-2805	Tribunal de Justica do Estado do Rio Grande do Sul. Revista de Jurisprudencia
0041-2813	Tribunal Federal de Recursos. Revista changed to Revista Trimestral de Jurisprudencia
0041-2821	Tribune
0041-2848	Tribune des Nations
0041-2864	Tribune Graphologique
0041-2872	Tribune Libre
0041-2899	Tributi Sugli Affari
0041-2902	Tricolor
0041-2910	Tricontinental - Edition Francais†
0041-2929	Trident†
0041-2945	Trierer Theologische Zeitschrift
0041-2953	Trierer Zeitschrift fuer Geschichte und Kunst des Trierer Landes und seiner Nachbargebiete
0041-2961	Trieste
0041-297X	Trilce de Poesia
0041-3003	Trim U Fit†
0041-3011	Trimestre Economico
0041-302X	Trinaesti Maj
0041-3046	Trinidad and Tobago. Central Statistical Office. Quarterly Economic Report
0041-3062	Trinity News
0041-3097	TriQuarterly
0041-3119	Triton changed to Diver
0041-3127	Triumph
0041-3135	Triveni
0041-3143	Trivsel†
0041-316X	Trompie changed to Student
0041-3178	Trons Segrar
0041-3186	Tropenlandwirt
0041-3208	Tropical Abstracts see 0304-5951
0041-3216	Tropical Agriculture
0041-3224	Tropical Agriculturist
0041-3232	Tropical and Geographical Medicine
0041-3240	Tropical Diseases Bulletin
0041-3259	Tropical Fish Hobbyist
0041-3267	Tropical Medicine
0041-3275	Tropical Medicine and Hygiene News
0041-3283	Tropical Products Quarterly†
0041-3291	Tropical Science
0041-3321	Tros-Kompas
0041-333X	Trottingbred†
0041-3348	Trotwaer
0041-3356	Trotzdem
0041-3364	Trout
0041-3372	Trout and Salmon
0041-3380	Truck and Bus Transportation
0041-3399	Truck Insider Newsletter
0041-3410	Trucking Business changed to Heavy Truck Business
0041-3429	Trucking News†
0041-3437	Trudbenik
0041-3445	Trudov Invalid
0041-3453	Gosudarstvennyi Astronomicheskii Institut im. P.K. Shternberga. Trudy
0041-3461	True†
0041-347X	True Confessions†
0041-3488	True Confessions
0041-3496	True Confidential Confessions
0041-350X	True Detective
0041-3518	True Experience†
0041-3534	True Life Secrets
0041-3542	True Love†
0041-3550	True Love
0041-3569	True Modern Romances
0041-3585	True Romance†
0041-3593	True Story†
0041-3607	Treasure World see 0195-2692
0041-3615	True West
0041-3658	Truppendienst
0041-3666	Truppenpraxis
0041-3674	Trustee
0041-3682	Trusts and Estates
0041-3690	Truth
0041-3704	Truth about Communism†
0041-3712	Truth Seeker
0041-3720	Trybuna Spoldzielcza
0041-3739	Tryckluft†
0041-3747	Trziste Povrca i Voca†
0041-3755	Trziste Stoke i Stochih Proizoda
0041-3763	T M P M
0041-3771	Tsitologiya
0041-378X	Tsopano News
0041-3798	Soil Mechanics and Foundation Engineering
0041-3801	Tsukumo Earth Science
0041-381X	Communication Industries
0041-3836	Tu Cher Wen Cher Reader's Digest (Chinese Edition)
0041-3844	Tu Sei Me
0041-3852	Tuatara†
0041-3860	Tuatara
0041-3879	Tubercle
0041-3887	Tuberkulozis es Tudobetegsegek changed to Pneumonologia Hungarica
0041-3895	Tuberkulozis es Tudogyogyaszat Referalo Szemle†
0041-3909	Tubular Structures
0041-3917	Tudomanyos es Muszaki Tajekoztatas
0041-3925	Turk Idare Dergisi
0041-3933	Tuesday
0041-3941	Tufts Dental Outlook†
0041-3968	Tuiles et Briques changed to Connaissance des Ceramiques
0041-3976	Tuinbouwberichten see 0772-7054
0041-3984	Tuinderij
0041-3992	Tulane Law Review
0041-400X	Tulane Medicine: Faculty and Alumni changed to Tulane Medicine
0041-4018	Tulane Studies in Geology and Paleontology
0041-4026	Tulanian
0041-4034	Tulimuld
0041-4042	Tulsa
0041-4050	Tulsa Law Journal
0041-4069	Tulsa Lawyer
0041-4085	Tummelplatz
0041-4093	Tumor Research: Experimental and Clinical
0041-4107	Tungsram Technische Mitteilungen
0041-4115	Tunisia. Institut National de la Statistique. Bulletin Mensuel de Statistique
0041-4123	Tunisie Economique
0041-4131	La Tunisie Medicale
0041-414X	Tunnels & Tunnelling
0041-4158	Turf and Sport Digest
0041-4182	Turist
0041-4190	Turist
0041-4204	Turisticke Novine
0041-4212	Turisticni Vestnik†
0041-4220	Turk Dili
0041-4239	Turk Kulturu
0041-4247	Turk Tarih Kurumu. Belgeler
0041-4255	Turk Tarih Kurumu. Belleten
0041-4263	Turkey. Devlet Istatistik Enstitusu. Aylik Istatistik Bulteni/Monthly Bulletin of Statistics
0041-4271	Turkey World
0041-4298	Turkish Digest†
0041-4301	Turkish Journal of Pediatrics
0041-431X	Turkish Medical Association. Journal/ Turk Tip Cemiyeti Mecmuasi changed to Turk Tip Dernegi Dergisi
0041-4328	Turkish National Bibliography
0041-4336	Turkiye Cumhuriyet Merkez Bankasi. Aylik Bulten
0041-4344	Bibliography of Articles in Turkish Periodicals
0041-4352	Tumori
0041-4360	Turrialba
0041-4379	Tussen de Rails
0041-4395	Tutti Fotografi
0041-4409	Tuttitalia†
0041-4417	Tutto Cucciolo
0041-4441	Tuttosport
0041-445X	Tuttoville
0041-4468	Tuulilasi
0041-4476	T.V. changed to Science et Culture
0041-4484	T V and Movie Play†
0041-4492	T V and Movie Screen
0041-4506	T V Digest changed to T V Times (St. Paul)
0041-4514	T V Publicity Outlets - Nationwide changed to All T V Publicity Outlets - Nationwide
0041-4522	T.V. Sorrisi e Canzoni (Rome)
0041-4530	T V Star Parade†
0041-4549	Tvai
0041-4565	Tvorchestvo
0041-4573	Twainian
0041-4581	Twee N
0041-459X	Twentieth Century†
0041-4611	Twentieth Century Fund. Newsletter
0041-462X	Twentieth Century Literature
0041-4638	Twentieth Century Studies†
0041-4646	Twigs see 0163-1209
0041-4654	Twin Circle changed to Catholic Twin Circle Weekly Magazine
0041-4662	Two Bridges News†
0041-4670	Two Rivers
0041-4689	Two Wheeler†
0041-4700	Two Wheels
0041-4719	Two Worlds
0041-4727	Tworczosc
0041-4751	Tydskrif vir Geesteswetenskappe
0041-476X	Tydskrif vir Letterkunde
0041-4778	Journal for Secondary Education†
0041-4786	Tydskrif vir Natuurwetenskappe†
0041-4794	Tydskrif vir Rasse-Aangeleenthede
0041-4808	Tygodnik Powszechny
0041-4816	Tyo - Terveys - Turvallisuus
0041-4824	Typetalks Magazine†
0041-4832	Typographical Journal
0041-4840	Typografische Monatsblaetter
0041-4859	Tyres and Accessories
0041-4867	Tsement
0041-4891	Tsvetnye Metally
0041-4905	Tsvetovodstvo
0041-4921	U. A. L. Economic and Financial Review†
0041-493X	U A M P T†
0041-4948	Egypt. Ministry of Tourism. Statistical Bulletin
0041-4972	U A W Fair Practices Fact Sheet†
0041-4980	U A W Washington Report
0041-4999	Alumni U B C Chronicle
0041-5006	U B N†
0041-5014	U C L A Graduate Journal†
0041-5030	U E C Journal†
0041-5049	U E News (Don Mills)
0041-5057	U E G Boletim changed to Boletim U E R J
0041-5065	U E News (New York)
0041-5073	U F O Investigator†
0041-5081	U F O - Nachrichten
0041-509X	U H S Bulletin changed to H I A S Reporter
0041-5103	U.I.A.M.S. Informations
0041-5111	U I C C Bulletin changed to International Cancer News
0041-512X	U I R Research Newsletter
0041-5146	U I T P Biblio-Index
0041-5154	U I T P Revue
0041-5162	U.I.U. Journal
0041-5170	U.K. Press Gazette
0041-5189	U L L I C O Bulletin
0041-5200	U M Profiles changed to Montanan
0041-5219	U N A F. Bulletin de Liaison see 0220-9926
0041-5227	U N C T A D Guide to Publications
0041-5243	Unesco Bulletin for Libraries see 0379-122X
0041-5251	Unesco. Oficina Regional de Educacion para America Latina y el Caribe. Boletin de Educacion†
0041-526X	Unesco Chronicle changed to Unesco News
0041-5278	Unesco Courier
0041-5286	Unesco Features
0041-5294	UNESCO Philippines
0041-5308	U N H C R Report changed to Refugees Magazine
0041-5324	U N I A P A C changed to U N I A P A C. International
0041-5340	Unicef News
0041-5359	U N I S A English Studies
0041-5367	U N Monthly Chronicle see 0251-7329
0041-5375	U N U C I
0041-5383	U.P.A. Journal†
0041-5405	U P E N
0041-5421	University Review†
0041-543X	U R S I Information Bulletin
0041-5456	U S A F Instructors Journal†
0041-5464	U S A Record
0041-5472	U S B W A Tip-Off
0041-5480	U S C O L D Newsletter
0041-5502	U S G A Green Section Record
0041-5537	U S News & World Report
0041-5545	U S S R and Third World
0041-5553	U S S R Computational Mathematics and Mathematical Physics
0041-5561	U S U Staff News
0041-557X	U T
0041-5588	U. T. C†
0041-5642	Ubulum†
0041-5650	U C L A Law Review
0041-5669	Ude og Hjemme
0041-5677	Udenrigs Handel og Industri Information
0041-5685	Udenrigsministeriet Tidsskrift changed to Eksport
0041-5693	Udenrigspolitiske Skrifter
0041-5707	Uebersee Rundschau
0041-5715	Ufahamu
0041-5731	Ufficio Moderno - Pubblicita
0041-574X	Uganda Journal
0041-5758	Uganda. Ministry of Planning and Economic Development. Statistics Division. Quarterly Economic and Statistical Bulletin
0041-5766	Uganda Teacher†
0041-5774	Ugeskrift for Agronomer see 0106-0546
0041-5782	Ugeskrift for Laeger
0041-5790	Ugol'
0041-5804	Ugol' Ukrainy
0041-5812	Uhli
0041-5820	Uhr changed to Uhren-Juwelen-Schmuck
0041-5839	Uhren Juwelen
0041-5847	Uhren und Schmuck
0041-5855	Uhrenjournal changed to Uhren-und Schmuck Journel
0041-5863	Uit de Pluimveepers see 0168-1168
0041-5871	Uit de Verf changed to Bouwvaria
0041-588X	Uit Europoortkringen
0041-5901	Uit Ons Werk†
0041-591X	Uitgelezen
0041-5936	Uitlotings-Archief
0041-5944	Uitzicht
0041-5952	Uj Iras
0041-5979	Ukiyo-e Art
0041-5987	Ukrainian Bulletin†
0041-5995	Ukrainian Mathematical Journal
0041-6002	Ukrainian News

0041-6010 Ukrainian Quarterly
0041-6029 Ukrainian Review
0041-6037 Ukrainian Voice
0041-6045 Ukrainskii Khimicheskii Zhurnal
0041-6053 Ukrainskii Matematicheskii Zhurnal
0041-6061 Ukrains'kyi Istoryk
0041-607X Ukrainian Medical Association of North America. Journal
0041-6088 Ukraina
0041-6096 Ukrains'ka Mova i Literatura v Shkoli
0041-6142 Ukrains'kyi Samostijnyk†
0041-6150 Ukulima Wa Kisasa
0041-6177 Finland. Tullihallituksen Tilastotoimisto. Ulkomaankauppa-Kuukausijulkaisu/ Foreign Trade Monthly Bulletin *changed to* Finland. Tullihallitus. Ulkomaankauppa/Utrikeshandel/ Foreign Trade
0041-6185 Ulster Commentary†
0041-6193 Ulster Medical Journal
0041-6207 Ulster Motorist
0041-6215 Ulster Young Farmer
0041-6223 Ultima Moda
0041-624X Ultrasonics
0041-6258 Ultreya
0041-6266 Ulysses S. Grant Association. Newsletter†
0041-6274 Umafrika
0041-6282 Umana†
0041-6290 Umanesimo†
0041-6320 Umetnost
0041-6339 Umpqua Trapper
0041-6347 Weltraumfahrt - Raketentechnik *changed to* Umschau, das Wissenschafts Magazin
0041-6355 Umwelt
0041-6371 Economic Bulletin for Asia and the Far East *see* 0378-455X
0041-638X Economic Bulletin for Europe
0041-6398 Economic Bulletin for Latin America *changed to* Revista de la C E P A L
0041-6401 Statistical Bulletin for Latin America *changed to* Statistical Yearbook for Latin America
0041-641X U N A Nursing Journal†
0041-6428 Una Sancta†
0041-6436 Unasylva
0041-6444 Unausforschlicher Reichtum
0041-6452 Unauthorized Practice News†
0041-6460 Under Glass†
0041-6479 Under the Sign of Pisces: Anais Nin and Her Circle†
0041-6487 Undergraduate Journal of Philosophy†
0041-6533 Undersea Technology *see* 0093-3651
0041-6541 Underseas Cable World†
0041-655X Understanding
0041-6576 Understanding Japan
0041-6584 Undervisning og Velferd
0041-6592 Underwater Letter
0041-6606 Underwater Naturalist
0041-6614 Underwater Journal and Information Bulletin *see* 0302-3478
0041-6622 Underwriters' Report
0041-6649 Unzer Weg†
0041-6657 Unga Oernar
0041-6665 Jornal dos Espectaculos *changed to* Jornal da A P E C
0041-6681 Unicorn Folio†
0041-6703 Unidad†
0041-6711 Unidad Cristiana-Oriente Cristiano†
0041-672X Uniform Commercial Code Law Journal
0041-6738 Uniforms and Accessories Review
0041-6754 Unijapan Film Quarterly†
0041-6762 Unilit
0041-6770 Union
0041-6800 Union Agricultural Cooperative of Syra. Bulletin†
0041-6819 Union Agriculture
0041-6827 Assembly of Western European Union. Monthly Information Bulletin
0041-6835 Union Democracy in Action *changed to* Union Democracy Review
0041-6843 Union des Aveugles de Guerre. Bulletin Mensuel
0041-6851 Union Douaniere et Economique de l'Afrique Centrale. Bulletin des Statistiques Generales
0041-686X Electrical Union World
0041-6878 Union Farmer
0041-6908 Union Industrial Uruguaya. Guia de Socios y de Productos *changed to* Products of Uruguay
0041-6916 U I A Information *changed to* U I A Newsletter
0041-6924 Union Labor News
0041-6932 Union Matematica Argentina. Revista
0041-6940 Union Medicale Balkanique. Archives
0041-6959 Union Medicale du Canada
0041-6975 Leeds Student
0041-6991 Union Postal Clerk and Postal Transport Journal *see* 0044-7811
0041-7009 Union Postale
0041-7017 Union Recorder
0041-7025 Union Seminary Quarterly Review
0041-7033 Union Signal
0041-7041 Union Sociale
0041-705X Union Technique de l'Automobile du Motorcycle et du Cycle. Bulletin Mensuel de Documentation *changed to* U T A C. Bulletin de Documentation
0041-7068 Union-Tribune Index of San Diego Business Activity
0041-7076 Unione degli Industriali della Provincia di Imperia. Notiziario†
0041-7084 Unione Matematica Italiana. Bolletino
0041-7092 Unionist
0041-7106 Unitholder *see* 0028-6052
0041-7122 Unitarian Universalist World
0041-7130 Unitas
0041-7149 Unitas
0041-7157 Unite Stenographique
0041-7165 United Arab Republic Journal of Veterinary Science *changed to* Egyptian Journal of Veterinary Science
0041-7173 United Asia†
0041-7181 United Association Journal
0041-719X United Bible Societies. Bulletin
0041-7203 United Business Service *changed to* United & Babson Investment Report
0041-7211 Journal of Current Social Issues†
0041-722X United Church Herald *changed to* United Church of Christ A.D.
0041-7238 United Church Observer
0041-7246 United Church Review†
0041-7262 United Evangelical
0041-7270 United Evangelical Action
0041-7289 United Kingdom Atomic Energy Authority. List of Publications Available to the Public
0041-7300 United Lutheran
0041-7319 United Methodist Periodical Index†
0041-7327 United Mine Workers Journal
0041-7335 Asian Development Institute. Newsletter *changed to* A D I Quarterly News Letter
0041-7343 United Nations. Current Bibliographical Information
0041-7351 U N D E X *see* 0250-5584
0041-736X Economic Bulletin for Africa†
0041-7378 Quarterly Bulletin of Steel Statistics for Europe
0041-7386 International Social Development Review†
0041-7394 United Nations Library. Monthly List of Books Catalogued in the Library of the United Nations. *see* 0251-6616
0041-7408 United Nations Library. Monthly List of Selected Articles *see* 0251-6624
0041-7416 United Nations. Population and Vital Statistics Report
0041-7424 U.N. Quarterly Housing Construction Summary for Europe *changed to* Annual Bulletin of Housing and Building Statistics for Europe
0041-7432 United Nations Statistical Office. Monthly Bulletin of Statistics
0041-7440 United Neighborhood Houses. News
0041-7459 United Paper *see* 0363-6437
0041-7475 United Rubber Worker
0041-7483 U S A (New York)†
0041-7491 United States Air Force Medical Service Digest
0041-7505 U.S. Army Natick Laboratories. Activities Report *see* 0099-6335
0041-7513 U.S. Army Recruiting and Career Counseling Journal *changed to* Recruiter Journal
0041-753X United States Book Exchange Newsletter *see* 0364-5215
0041-7548 U S Catholic
0041-7556 U. S. Chemical Patents†
0041-7564 U.S. Coast Guard. Merchant Marine Council. Proceedings *see* 0364-0981
0041-7572 U.S. Consumer *changed to* Consumer Newsweekly
0041-7580 United States: Cotton Quality Reports for Ginnings
0041-7610 U.S. Department of State. Bulletin
0041-7629 U.S. Department of State. Newsletter *see* 0278-1859
0041-7637 U S Farm News
0041-7645 U.S. Federal Home Loan Bank Board. Journal†
0041-7653 U S Fur Rancher *see* 0744-7701
0041-7661 U S Glass, Metal & Glazing
0041-7688 G R I (U.S. Government Reports Index) *see* 0097-9007
0041-770X U.S.I. Journal
0041-7718 United States Investor *see* 0148-8848
0041-7726 L C Card Number Index to the National Union Catalog
0041-7734 U.S. Library of Congress. Accessions List: India†
0041-7742 U.S. Library of Congress. Accessions List: Indonesia, Malaysia, Singapore and Brunei *see* 0096-2341
0041-7769 U.S. Library of Congress. Accessions List: Middle East
0041-7785 U.S. Library of Congress. Books: Subjects *see* 0096-8803
0041-7793 U.S. Library of Congress Catalog - Music and Phonorecords *see* 0092-2838
0041-7807 Library of Congress Catalog. Motion Pictures and Filmstrips *changed to* National Union Catalog. Audiovisual Materials
0041-7815 U.S. Copyright Office. Catalog of Copyright Entries. Third Series. Part 1. Books and Pamphlets *see* 0163-7290
0041-7815 U.S. Copyright Office. Catalog of Copyright Entries. Third Series. Part 1. Books and Pamphlets, Including Serials and Contributions to Periodicals *see* 0163-7304
0041-784X U.S. Copyright Office. Catalog of Copyright Entries. Third Series. Part 2. Periodicals *see* 0163-7304
0041-7858 U.S. Copyright Office. Catalog of Copyright Entries. Third Series. Parts 3-4. Drama and Works Prepared for Oral Delivery *see* 0163-7312
0041-7866 U.S. Copyright Office Catalog of Copyright Entries. Third Series. Part 5. Music *see* 0163-7312
0041-7874 U.S. Copyright Office. Catalog of Copyright Entries. Third Series. Part 6. Maps and Atlases *see* 0163-7347
0041-7882 U.S. Copyright Office. Catalog of Copyright Entries. Third Series. Parts 7-11A. Works of Art *see* 0163-7339
0041-7890 U.S. Library of Congress. Cataloging Service *see* 0160-8029
0041-7904 U.S. Library of Congress. Information Bulletin
0041-7912 U.S. Library of Congress. L.C. Classification - Additions and Changes
0041-7920 U.S. Library of Congress Pl-480 Newlsetter *see* 0095-0629
0041-7939 U.S. Library of Congress. Quarterly Journal†
0041-7947 U.S. Library of Congress. Subject Headings Used in the Dictionary Catalogs of the Library of Congress *changed to* U.S. Library of Congress Subject Headings Supplement
0041-7955 United States Municipal News *changed to* Mayor
0041-7971 United States National Student Association Newsletter *see* 0098-5570
0041-798X U.S. Naval Institute. Proceedings
0041-7998 U.S. Navy Medical News Letter *see* 0364-6807
0041-8013 U S P Boletim Informativo†
0041-8021 U.S. Patent Office. Official Gazette *see* 0098-1133
0041-8021 U.S. Patent Office. Official Gazette *see* 0360-5132
0041-803X United States Patents Quarterly
0041-8048 U S Piper
0041-8056 United States Review†
0041-8072 Gosudarstvennaya Biblioteka S.S.S.R. im. V.I. Lenina. Informatsionnyi Byulleten' Novykh Inostrannykh Knig, Postupivshikh v Biblioteku. Seriya 1: Fiziko-Matematicheskie i Khimicheskie Nauki; Nauki o Zemle; Tekhnika i Tekhnicheskie Nauk
0041-8080 Gosudarstvennaya Biblioteka S.S.S.R. im. V.I. Lenina. Informatsionnyi Byulleten' Novykh Inostrannykh Knig, Postupivshikh v Biblioteku. Seriya 3: Obshchestvennye Nauki; Khudozhestvennaya Literatura; Iskusstvo
0041-8099 United States Ski News†
0041-8129 U S Tax Week
0041-8137 United States Tobacco and Candy Journal
0041-8153 United Synagogue Review
0041-8161 United Teacher *changed to* New York Teacher
0041-817X Uniter
0041-8188 Daily Word
0041-8188 Unity Daily Word *see* 0041-8188
0041-820X Universal News *see* 0197-1506
0041-8218 Universalist
0041-8226 Universe
0041-8234 Universidad
0041-8250 Universidad Argentina de la Empresa. Revista†
0041-8277 Universidad Autonoma de Santo Domingo. Biblioteca Central. Boletin de Adquisiciones
0041-8285 Universidad Central de Venezuela. Facultad de Agronomia. Revista
0041-8293 Universidad Central de Venezuela. Facultad de Derecho. Revista *changed to* Universidad Central de Venezuela. Facultad de Ciencias Juridicas y Politicas. Revista
0041-8307 Universidad Central de Venezuela. Facultad de Farmacia. Revista
0041-8323 Universidad de Antioquia. Instituto de Antropologia. Boletin de Antropologia *changed to* Universidad de Antioquia. Departamento de Antropologia. Boletin de Antropologia
0041-8331 Universidad de Buenos Aires. Facultad de Filosofia y Letras. Gaceta†
0041-834X Universidad de Buenos Aires. Instituto Bibliotecologico. Boletin Informativo†
0041-8358 Universidad de Chile. Anales†
0041-8366 Universidad de Chile. Biblioteca. Instituto de Economia. Boletin *changed to* Universidad de Chile. Facultad de Ciencias Economicas y Adinistrativas. Biblioteca. Lista de Memorias y Libros Seleccionados
0041-8374 Universidad de Chile. Boletin
0041-8390 Universidad de Cuenca. Anales
0041-8404 Universidad de Guadalajara. Instituto de Astronomia y Meteorologia. Informacion
0041-8412 Universidad de Guayaquil. Facultad de Ciencias Medicas. Revista
0041-8420 Universidad de la Habana. Departmento de Actividades Culturales. Revista

ISSN INDEX 1317

0041-8439 Universidad de la Republica. Facultad de Ciencias Economicas y Administracion. Instituto de Estadistica. Indice de Precios al Consumidor
0041-8447 Universidad de la Republica. Facultad de Humanidades y Ciencias. Publicaciones†
0041-8455 Universidad de la Republica. Hospital de Clinicas. Informe Estatistico
0041-848X Universidad de Narino. Biblioteca Central. Boletin Informativo y Bibliograficas†
0041-8498 Universidad Autonoma de Nuevo Leon. Centro de Investigaciones Economicas. Boletin Bimestral
0041-851X Universidad de Puerto Rico. Escuela de Derecho. Revista Juridica
0041-8528 Universidad de Puerto Rico. Servicio de Extension Agricola. Boletin Ganadero†
0041-8536 Universidad de Yucatan. Revista *see* 0186-7180
0041-8544 Universidad Externado de Colombia. Revista
0041-8552 Universidad Hispalense. Anales. Series: Filosofia y Letras, Derecho, Medicina, Ciencias y Veterinaria *see* 0210-7678
0041-8579 Universidad Industrial de Santander. Boletin Informativo†
0041-8587 Universidad Industrial de Santander. Revista *see* 0120-0852
0041-8609 Universidad Mayor de San Andres. Gaceta Universitaria†
0041-8617 Universidad Boliviana Mayor de San Simon. Instituto de Estudios Sociales y Economicos. Revista
0041-8625 Universidad Nacional de la Plata. Revista
0041-8633 Boletin Mexicano de Derecho Comparado
0041-8641 Noticias de la Biblioteca
0041-865X Universidad Nacional de Cordoba. Instituto de Administracion. Revista *changed to* Revista de Ciencias Administrativas
0041-8668 Universidad Nacional de Cuyo. Facultad de Ciencias Economicas. Revista
0041-8676 Universidad Nacional de la Plata. Facultad de Agronomia. Revista
0041-8684 Universidad Nacional de Rosario. Facultad de Ciencias, Ingenieria y Arquitectura. Instituto de Fisiografia y Geologia. Publicaciones
0041-8714 Universidad Nacional Mayor de San Marcos. Boletin Universitario†
0041-8730 Universidad Pontificia Bolivariana†
0041-8749 Universidad Tecnica Federico Santa Maria. Boletin Informativo†
0041-8765 Universidade de Coimbra. Museum Zoologico. Memorias e Estudos *changed to* Ciencia Biologica: Biologia Molecular e Celular
0041-8781 Universidade de Sao Paulo. Hospital das Clinicas. Revista
0041-8803 Universidade de Sao Paulo. Museu de Arte Contemporanea. Boletim Informativo
0041-8811 Universidad del Zulia. Revistas
0041-8838 Universidade Federal de Minas Gerais. Escola de Engenharia. Revista
0041-8846 Universidade Federal de Santa Maria. Faculdade de Farmacia e Bioquimica. Revista
0041-8854 Arquivos de Ciencias do Mar
0041-8862 Revista de Ciencias Sociales
0041-8870 Universidade Federal do Ceara. Departamento de Ciencias Sociais e Filosofia. Documentos
0041-8889 Universidade Federal do Ceara. Faculdade de Medicina. Revista *changed to* Universidade Federal do Ceara. Centro de Ciencias da Saude. Revista de Medicina
0041-8900 Universidade do Parana. Departamento do Botanica e Farmacognosia. Boletim *see* 0301-2123
0041-8919 Universidade Federal do Rio de Janeiro. Faculdade de Odontologia. Anais
0041-8927 Universidade Federal do Rio Grande do Norte. Instituto de Biologia Marinha. Boletim *changed to* Universidade Federal do Rio Grande do Norte. Centro de Biociencias. Departamento de Oceanografia e Limnologia. Boletim
0041-8935 Universidades
0041-8943 Universita degli Studi Perugia. Istituto di Anatomia e Istologia. Lavori†
0041-8951 Universita degli Studi di Cagliari. Facolta di Scienza. Seminario. Rendiconti
0041-896X Universita degli Studi di Firenze. Istituto di Statistica. Documentazione
0041-8978 Universita degli Studi di Genova. Istituto di Geologia. Atti
0041-8986 Universita degli Studi di Modena. Seminario Matematico e Fisico. Atti
0041-8994 Universita di Padova. Seminario Matematico. Rendiconti
0041-9001 Universita Urbinate. Notiziario Mensile†
0041-9036 Etudes Scientifiques
0041-9044 Universitario
0041-9052 Universitas
0041-9060 Universitas
0041-9079 Universitas
0041-9087 Universitas Comeniana. Acta Pharmaceuticae
0041-9095 Universitas Medica
0041-9109 Universitatea "Al. I. Cuza" din Iasi. Analele Stiintifice. Sectiunea 1a: Matematica
0041-9117 Universitatea "Al. I. Cuza" din Iasi. Analele Stiintifice. Sectiunea 1c: Chimie†
0041-9125 Universitatea "Al. I. Cuza" din Iasi. Analele Stiintifice. Sectiunea 3a: Istorie
0041-9133 Universitatea "Al. I. Cuza" din Iasi. Analele Stiintifice. Sectiunea 2a: Biologie
0041-9141 Universitatea "Al. I. Cuza" din Iasi. Analele Stiintifice. Sectiunea 1b: Fizica
0041-915X Universite de Lausanne. Faculte des Lettres. Publications
0041-9168 Universite de Montreal. Institute Botanique. Contributions†
0041-9176 Universite de Paris. Annales†
0041-9184 Universite de Paris VI (Pierre et Marie Curie). Institut de Statistique. Publications
0041-9192 Universite de Tehran. Faculte des Lettres et des Sciences Humaines. Revue
0041-9206 Universite d'Ottawa. Revue
0041-9214 Universite Laval. Fonds de Recherches Forestieres. Bulletin†
0041-9230 Universities Quarterly *see* 0951-5224
0041-9249 University†
0041-9257 University Affairs
0041-9265 University Bookman
0041-9273 University College Hospital Magazine *changed to* Too Much - University College Hospital Magazine
0041-9281 University College Quarterly†
0041-929X University Engineer†
0041-9303 University Equipment†
0041-9311 University Film Association. Journal *see* 0742-4671
0041-932X University Jewish Voice†
0041-9346 University of Alabama in Birmingham. Medical Center Bulletin *changed to* University of Alabama, Birmingham. Medical Center
0041-9354 University of Alaska. Anthropological Papers
0041-9362 University of Alaska. Geophysical Institute. Report Series
0041-9370 University of Alberta. Department of Chemistry. Division of Theoretical Chemistry. Technical Report
0041-9389 University of Arizona. Agricultural Experiment Station. Technical Bulletin†
0041-9397 University of Auckland Gazette *changed to* University of Auckland News
0041-9400 University of Auckland. Fine Arts Library Bulletin
0041-9419 University of Baghdad. Faculty of Medicine. Journal
0041-9427 University of British Columbia Library. Asian Studies Division. List of Catalogued Books†
0041-9435 University of California U C News Clip Sheet *changed to* U C Clip Sheet
0041-9443 University of California. Institute of Governmental Studies Library. Accessions List
0041-946X University of California. Seismographic Stations. Bulletin
0041-9486 University of Chicago. Department & Graduate School of Education. Newsletter *changed to* Education on the Midway
0041-9494 University of Chicago Law Review
0041-9508 University of Chicago Magazine
0041-9516 University of Colorado Law Review
0041-9524 University of Dayton Review
0041-9532 University of Denver Alumni News *changed to* University of Denver News
0041-9559 Journal of Urban Law *changed to* University of Detroit Law Review
0041-9567 University of Edinburgh Journal
0041-9583 University of Florida Law Review
0041-9605 University of Ghana Law Journal
0041-9613 University of Ibadan. Department of Linguistics and Nigerian Languages. Research Notes
0041-963X University of Illinois Law Forum *see* 0276-9948
0041-9648 University of Iowa. School of Library Science. Newsletter *changed to* University of Iowa. School of Library and Information Science. Newsletter
0041-9656 University of Iowa Studies in Natural History†
0041-9672 University of Kansas. Museum of Art. Register *changed to* Spencer Museum of Art. Register
0041-9680 University of Kansas Newsletter†
0041-9702 University of Kansas School of Medicine and Medical Center. Bulletin *changed to* University of Kansas Medical Center. Bulletin
0041-9737 University of Leeds Review
0041-9745 University of Liberia Journal
0041-977X University of London. School of Oriental and African Studies. Bulletin
0041-9788 Library Review
0041-9796 University of Manila Law Gazette
0041-9818 University of Miami Law Review
0041-9826 University of Michigan Medical Center Journal†
0041-9834 University of Michigan. Museum of Paleontology. Contributions
0041-9842 University of Michigan. Division of Research Development and Administration. Research News
0041-9850 Michigan Today
0041-9869 University of Minnesota Alumni News *changed to* Minnesota (Minneapolis)
0041-9877 University of Montana Law School News†
0041-9885 University of Nebraska. Museum Notes
0041-9893 University of North Carolina School of Library Science. Alumni Association Bulletin. *changed to* News from Chapel Hill
0041-9907 University of Pennsylvania Law Review
0041-9915 University of Pittsburgh Law Review
0041-9923 University of Portland Review
0041-9931 University of Puerto Rico Dental School Newsletter†
0041-994X University of Puerto Rico. Journal of Agriculture
0041-9958 University of Queensland. Computer Centre. Computer Centre Bulletin†
0041-9974 University of Rochester Library Bulletin
0041-9990 University of San Carlos. University Bulletin
0042-000X University of San Fernando Valley Law Review *changed to* San Fernando Valley Law Review
0042-0018 University of San Francisco Law Review
0042-0026 University of Saskatchewan. University News†
0042-0034 University of Sheffield. Diary of Events *changed to* University of Sheffield. Diary of Events
0042-0050 University of South Carolina Governmental Review *changed to* Public Affairs Bulletin
0042-0077 University of South Florida Language Quarterly
0042-0085 Trojan Family *see* 8750-7927
0042-0093 University of Sydney. Australian Language Research Centre. Occasional Papers†
0042-0107 University of Sydney. Gazette
0042-0115 University of Sydney. Postgraduate Committee in Medicine. Bulletin
0042-0123 University of Teheran. Journal of Veterinary Faculty
0042-0131 University of Teheran. Faculty of Science. Quarterly Bulletin
0042-014X University Medical
0042-0158 U E Business Review
0042-0174 University of the State of New York Bulletin†
0042-0182 University of the Witwatersrand, Johannesburg. University Gazette†
0042-0190 University of Toledo Law Review
0042-0204 University of Toronto. Department of Computer Science. Technical Reports
0042-0212 University of Toronto Alumni Magazine
0042-0220 University of Toronto Law Journal
0042-0239 University of Toronto Medical Journal
0042-0247 University of Toronto Quarterly
0042-0255 University of Toronto Undergraduate Dental Journal
0042-0271 University of Virginia News Letter
0042-0298 University of Washington Business Review *see* 0194-0430
0042-0301 University of Washington. College of Education Record†
0042-031X University of Waterloo. Gazette
0042-0328 University of Western Australia Law Review
0042-0336 University of Western Ontario Medical Journal
0042-0344 University of Western Ontario. Alumni Gazette
0042-0352 University of Windsor Review
0042-0360 University (Philippines)
0042-0379 University Review *see* 0146-4930
0042-0387 University Seminar Directory†
0042-0395 University Vision†
0042-0409 L'Universo
0042-0417 Universum†
0042-0425 Univerzitet Danas
0042-0433 Uniwersytet Warszawski. Instytut Geograficzny. Katedra Klimatologii. Biuletyn†
0042-0441 Unlisted Drugs
0042-045X Unlisted Drugs on Cards
0042-0468 Unscheduled Events
0042-0476 Unsearchable Riches
0042-0484 Unser Neustadt
0042-0492 Unser Schaffen
0042-0506 Unser Usait
0042-0549 Unsere Wirtschaft
0042-0565 Unterhaltungskunst
0042-0573 Unternehmensforschung/Operations Research/Recherche Operationnelle *see* 0340-9422
0042-0581 Der Unternehmer
0042-059X Unternehmung†
0042-0603 Unterricht Heute†
0042-0611 Unterrichtsblaetter fuer die Bundeswehrverwaltung
0042-062X Unterrichtspraxis
0042-0638 Unterstufe
0042-0646 Uomini e Idee

ISSN	Title
0042-0654	Uomini e Libri
0042-0700	Upholstering Industry see 0744-138X
0042-0735	Upper Room
0042-0778	Uradni Vestnik Obcin Ormoz in Ptuj
0042-0786	Ural-Altaische Jahrbuecher
0042-0794	Urania
0042-0816	Urban Affairs Quarterly
0042-0824	Urban and Rural Planning Thought
0042-0832	Urban and Social Change Review
0042-0840	Urban Crisis Monitor†
0042-0859	Urban Education
0042-0867	Urban Employment†
0042-0875	Urban Georgia
0042-0883	Urban History Newsletter†
0042-0891	Urban Land
0042-0905	Urban Lawyer
0042-0913	Urban Memo†
0042-0921	Urban Renewal and Low-Income Housing see 0383-3003
0042-0948	Urban Reporter†
0042-0956	Urban Research Bulletin/Bulletin de Recherches Urbaines see 0318-8140
0042-0964	Urban Research News†
0042-0972	Urban Review
0042-0980	Urban Studies
0042-1006	Urban World†
0042-1014	Urbanisme
0042-1022	Urbanistica
0042-1030	Urbe
0042-1057	A D A B Sangbad
0042-1065	Urdu Namah
0042-1081	Urmager-Tidende changed to Ure & Optik
0042-1103	Urologe-Ausgabe A see 0340-2592
0042-1111	Urologe-Ausgabe B changed to Der Urologe. Section B
0042-112X	Urologia
0042-1138	Urologia Internationalis
0042-1146	Urological Survey see 0022-5347
0042-1154	Urologiya i Nefrologiya
0042-1162	Urology and Nephrology see 0301-1623
0042-1170	Urology Digest see 0197-7709
0042-1189	Uruguay Filatelico
0042-1197	Urval
0042-1200	Urzica
0042-1219	U.S. Federal Register. (Microfiche Edition)
0042-1227	U S Medicine
0042-1235	Us Wurk
0042-1243	Use of English
0042-1251	Usine Automation†
0042-126X	Usine Nouvelle
0042-1286	Usines et Industries
0042-1294	Uspekhi Fizicheskikh Nauk
0042-1308	Uspekhi Khimii
0042-1316	Uspekhi Matematicheskikh Nauk
0042-1324	Uspekhi Sovremennoi Biologii
0042-1340	Eko-Index
0042-1359	Ustredni Ustav Geologicky. Vestnik
0042-1367	Ut de Smidte fan de Fryske Akademy
0042-1375	Utah Cattleman
0042-1383	Utah Construction Report
0042-1391	Utah Eagle†
0042-1405	Utah Economic and Business Review
0042-1413	U E A Action
0042-1421	Utah Geological and Mineral Survey. Quarterly Review see 0362-6288
0042-143X	Utah Historical Quarterly
0042-1448	Utah Law Review
0042-1456	Utah Libraries†
0042-1464	Utah Medical Bulletin†
0042-1472	Utah P T A Bulletin changed to Sound-off
0042-1499	Utah Publisher and Printer†
0042-1502	Utah Science
0042-1529	Utah State Historical Society Newsletter
0042-1537	Utan Grans
0042-1553	Ute och Hemma
0042-157X	Uthon
0042-1588	Utility Purchasing & Stores
0042-160X	Utrikespolitiska Institut. Archives changed to World Press Archives
0042-1618	Uttar Bharat Bhoogol Patrika
0042-1626	Uttar Pradesh. State Planning Institute. Quarterly Bulletin of Statistics
0042-1642	Uusi Maailma see 0355-3043
0042-1650	Uw Koninkrijk Kome
0042-1669	Uw Rijk Kome†
0042-1685	Uzbekskii Biologicheskii Zhurnal
0042-1693	Uzbekskii Geologicheskii Zhurnal
0042-1707	Uzbekskii Khimicheskii Zhurnal
0042-1723	V A S L A
0042-174X	V D I - Forschungshefte
0042-1758	V D I-Nachrichten
0042-1766	V D I-Z
0042-1774	V D K-Mitteilungen changed to V D K-Mitteilungen Sozialpolitische Fachzeitschrift
0042-1782	V D M A-Wirtschaftsbild†
0042-1790	V E A News
0042-1804	V F D B: Zeitschrift fuer Forschung und Technik im Brandschutz
0042-1820	V.F.W. Magazine
0042-1839	V I C A
0042-1847	V I P: The Playboy Club Magazine
0042-1871	V-Illustriert
0042-188X	V Mire Knig
0042-1898	V. G. R. O-Mededelingen†
0042-1901	Vereinigung Schweizerischer Petroleum-Geologen und -Ingenieure. Bulletin
0042-191X	V S S D A Newsletter changed to V S B A Newsletter
0042-1928	V S T Revue
0042-1944	V V S
0042-1952	V W changed to Auto Toeruit
0042-1960	V W D-Kaffee-Spezialdienst†
0042-1979	V W D-Kaffee Uebersee Sonderdienst†
0042-1987	V W D-Kakao-Spezialdienst†
0042-1995	Va-Nytt
0042-2002	Vaar Bostad
0042-2010	Vaar Fana
0042-2029	Vaar Skole†
0042-2037	Vaart Vern
0042-2053	Vacature
0042-207X	Vacuum
0042-2118	Vaeddelobsbladet
0042-2126	Vaerksteds Nyt see 0106-0104
0042-2134	Vaerldshorisont
0042-2142	Vaerldsmarknad†
0042-2150	Vaestgoetalitteratur
0042-2169	Vaextskyddsnotiser
0042-2177	Vaeg- och Vattenbyggaren
0042-2185	Vaegnytt
0042-2193	Vagabond†
0042-2215	Vakblad voor Biologen
0042-2223	Vakblad voor de Bloemisterij
0042-2231	Vakblad voor de Meubelindustrie see 0165-4543
0042-224X	Vakblad voor Textielreiniging changed to Textielverzorging
0042-2266	Vakuum-Technik
0042-2274	Vale do Rio dos Sinos see 0100-039X
0042-2290	Valitut Palat
0042-2304	Valle Santa di Rieti
0042-2312	Vallecchi Informa
0042-2339	Valley Views†
0042-2347	Enforcement Journal
0042-2363	Valparaiso University Law Review
0042-2371	Valsalva
0042-238X	Valuation Magazine
0042-2398	Value Line Convertible Survey see 0146-7581
0042-2401	Value Line Investment Survey
0042-241X	Valuer
0042-2428	Valuer
0042-2436	Valve Information Report changed to Impact - Valves
0042-2444	Nav-Chitrapat
0042-2479	Vancouver Art Gallery. Bulletin see 0315-5226
0042-2495	Vancouver Public Aquarium Newsletter see 0700-9275
0042-2509	Vand†
0042-2517	Vanderbilt Hustler
0042-2525	Vanderbilt International see 0090-2594
0042-2533	Vanderbilt Law Review
0042-2541	Vanfoerebladet
0042-255X	Vanguard (San Francisco)
0042-2568	Vanguard (Milwaukee)
0042-2584	Vanity Fair see 0018-4551
0042-2614	Vantaggio
0042-2622	Vanyajati
0042-2630	Vapor Trail's Competition News and Manufacturing Report changed to Vapor Trail's Boating News & International Yachting & Cruiser and Manufacturers Report
0042-2649	Vaar Faagelvaerld
0042-2657	Vaar Foeda
0042-2665	Var Konst
0042-2673	Vaar Kyrka
0042-2681	Vaar Naering
0042-269X	Vaara Hundar
0042-2703	Vaara Paelsdjur
0042-2711	Varazdinske Vijesti
0042-272X	Variator
0042-2738	Variety
0042-2754	Vaerldspolitikens Dagsfragor
0042-2762	Varlik
0042-2770	Varme og Sanitets Nyt
0042-2789	Varsity
0042-2797	Varsity
0042-2800	Vaart Foersvar
0042-2819	Apropaa Roeda Korset changed to Vaart Roeda Kors
0042-2827	Vartavaha†
0042-2843	Vaskeri-Tidende changed to Vask-Rens-Rengoering
0042-2851	Vassar Quarterly
0042-286X	Vaste Goederen changed to Vastgoed
0042-2878	Vasudha Monthly
0042-2886	Vatten
0042-2908	Vauxhall Motorist†
0042-2924	Vcelarstvi
0042-2932	Ve Venezuela
0042-2940	Veckojournalen changed to Maanadsjournalen
0042-2959	Vector†
0042-2983	Vedanta Kesari
0042-2991	Vedecky Svet†
0042-3009	Vedetta†
0042-3017	Verkhovnyi Sovet S.S.S.R. Vedomosti
0042-3025	Vee-en Vleeshandel†
0042-3033	Bedrijfsontwikkeling. Editie Veehouderij changed to Bedrijfsontwikkeling
0042-305X	Vega
0042-3084	U.S. Department of Agriculture. Economics Management Staff. Vegetable Situation see 0277-9900
0042-3092	Vegetables Newsletter
0042-3106	Vegetatio
0042-3114	Vehicle System Dynamics
0042-3122	Veilig Vliegen
0042-3130	Veilig Werken changed to Doen & Laten
0042-3149	De Veiligheid/Safety changed to Arbeidsomslandigheden
0042-3157	Veilingberichten†
0042-3165	Veja
0042-3173	Vejen Frem
0042-3181	Vela e Motore
0042-3211	Veliger
0042-322X	Velikogoricki List
0042-3238	Velki
0042-3246	Vellez Music News
0042-3254	Veltro
0042-3262	Veluws Kerkblad
0042-3297	Vend see 0042-3327
0042-3319	Vending Engineer†
0042-3327	Vending Times
0042-3343	Vene
0042-3351	Veneficus
0042-336X	Turismo in Italia changed to Italia Turistica
0042-3378	Venezuela. Archivo General de la Nacion. Boletin
0042-3394	Venezuela. Ministerio de Minas e Hidrocarburos. Carta Semanal changed to Venezuela. Ministerio de Energia y Minas. Carta Semanal
0042-3408	Venezuela. Ministerio de Minas e Hidrocarburos. Informations changed to Venezuela. Ministerio de Energia y Minas. Informations
0042-3416	Venezuela. Ministerio de Minas e Hidrocarburos. Monthly Bulletin changed to Venezuela. Ministerio de Energia y Minas. Quarterly Bulletin
0042-3424	Venezuela Odontologia
0042-3432	Venezuela Up-to-Date†
0042-3440	Vent - Art
0042-3459	Ventana
0042-3483	Venture
0042-3491	Ventura County Historical Society Quarterly
0042-3548	Venture changed to Loughborough Student
0042-3556	Venture-the Traveler's World†
0042-3564	Ventures†
0042-3572	Venturi
0042-3580	Venus: Japanese Journal of Malacology
0042-3599	Vera Giustizia Sociale
0042-3610	Anzeiger des Verbandes der Antiquare Oesterreichs
0042-3629	Verband der Bibliotheken des Landes Nordrhein-Westfalen. Mitteilungsblatt
0042-3637	Verband Oesterreichischer Landsmannschaften Nachrichten-und Mitteilungsblatt
0042-3645	Verband Schweizerischer Verkehrsvereine und der Verband Schweizerischer Kur- und Verkehrsdirektoren. Bulletin†
0042-3653	Verbraucher-Politische Korrespondenz
0042-3661	Verbraucher Rundschau
0042-3688	Verbum†
0042-3696	Verbum
0042-370X	Communion†
0042-3718	Verdad y Vida
0042-3726	Vysoka Skola Banska. Sbornik Vedeckych Praci: Rada Hutnicka
0042-3734	Verdi
0042-3750	Verein der Freunde Carnuntums. Mitteilungen
0042-3769	S.W.A. Scientific Society. Verein fuer Hochlenforschung. Arbeitsberichte†
0042-3777	Verein fuer Krebsforschung. Mitteilungen
0042-3785	V G B Mitteilungen see 0372-5715
0042-3807	Nachrichten V S B/S V D changed to Arbido-B
0042-3815	Schweizerische Vereinigung der Versicherungsmathematiker. Mitteilungen
0042-3831	Verein Schweizerischer Lithographiebesitzer. Mitteilungen†
0042-384X	Vereinte Nationen
0042-3858	Vereniging van Vrienden van de Nederlandse Ceramiek. Mededelingenblad changed to Nederlandse Vereniging van Vrienden van de Ceramiek. Mededelingenblad
0042-3866	Vereniging voor Naamkunde. Mededelingen changed to Naamkunde
0042-3874	Vereniging voor Nederlandse Muziekgeschiedenis. Tijdschrift
0042-3882	Vereniging voor Oppervlaktetechnieken van Metalen. Documentatieservice changed to Vereniging voor Oppervlaktetechnieken van Materialen. Documentatieservice
0042-3890	Verfahrenstechnische Berichte
0042-3904	Verfkroniek
0042-3912	Verge†
0042-3920	Vergleichende Paedagogik
0042-3939	Verhuetet Unfaelle
0042-3947	Veritas
0042-3955	Veritas
0042-3963	Veritas
0042-3971	Verite changed to Magnificat - la Verite
0042-398X	Verkeersrecht
0042-3998	Verkeerstechniek changed to Verkeerskunde
0042-4013	Verkehrsblatt
0042-4021	Verkehrsmedizin und ihre Grenzgebiete
0042-403X	Verkehrspraktiker see 0023-4443
0042-4048	Verkehrspsychologischer Informationsdienst
0042-4056	Verkstaederna

ISSN INDEX 1319

ISSN	Title
0042-4064	Verladen†
0042-4099	Der Vermessungsingenieur
0042-4102	Vermessungstechnik
0042-4110	Vermessungstechnische Rundschau (VR) see 0340-5141
0042-4129	Vermissa Herald
0042-4137	Vermont Blackboard changed to Vermont - N E A Today
0042-4145	Vermont Catholic Tribune
0042-4161	Vermont History
0042-417X	Vermont Life
0042-420X	Vero Dialogo
0042-4234	Verona Fathers Missions changed to Comboni Missions
0042-4242	Verona Fedele
0042-4250	Wiener Boersekammer. Verordnungsblatt
0042-4269	Verpackung
0042-4277	Verpackung
0042-4293	Verpackungs Berater
0042-4307	Verpackungs-Rundschau
0042-4315	Verpakken
0042-4323	Verre Naasten Naderbij changed to Culturen
0042-4331	Verres et Refractaires
0042-434X	Vers Demain
0042-4358	Versicherungswirtschaft
0042-4366	Versiones†
0042-4374	Verso l'Azzurro
0042-4382	Versorgungswirtschaft
0042-4390	Versuchsstation fuer das Gaerungsgewerbe in Wien. Mitteilungen
0042-4412	Vertegenwoordiger
0042-4420	Vertex
0042-4439	Vertical File Index
0042-4447	Vertice
0042-4455	Vertiflite
0042-4463	Vertragssystem changed to Wirtschaftsrecht
0042-4471	Vertriko Visie†
0042-448X	Vervoer changed to Vervoer en Transporttechniek
0042-4498	Die Verwaltung
0042-4501	Verwaltungsarchiv
0042-451X	Verwarming en Ventilatie
0042-4528	Verzekerings-Archief
0042-4536	Veseli Svet
0042-4544	Vesmir
0042-4552	Udruzenje Pravoslavnog Svestenstva S.F.R. Jugoslavije. Glavni Savez. Vesnik
0042-4560	Vestes changed to Australian Universities' Review
0042-4579	Vestire changed to Vestire Uomo
0042-4587	Vestnik
0042-4595	Ceskoslovenska Spolecnost Zoologicka. Vestnik
0042-4609	Vestnik Dermatologii i Venerologii
0042-4617	Vestnik Drevnei Istorii
0042-4625	Vestnik Khirurgii im. I.I. Grekova
0042-4633	Vestnik Mashinostroeniya
0042-4641	Federalni Ministerstvo Financi. Vestnik see 0322-9653
0042-465X	Vestnik Oftal'mologii
0042-4668	Vestnik Otorinolaringologii
0042-4676	Vestnik Rentgenologii i Radiologii
0042-4684	Vestnik Sel'skokhozyaistvennoi Nauki Kazakhstana
0042-4692	Vestnik Statistiki
0042-4706	Vestnik Svyazi
0042-4714	Urad pro Normalizaci a Mereni. Vestnik
0042-4749	Vsesoyuznyi Nauchno-Issledovatel'skii Institut Zheleznodorozhnogo Transporta. Vestnik
0042-4757	Vestnik Vysshei Shkoly
0042-4765	Veteran
0042-4773	Veteran and Vintage changed to Collector's Car
0042-4781	Veteran Car
0042-4811	Veterantics
0042-482X	Veterinaria Mocambicana†
0042-4838	Veterinario y la Industria†
0042-4846	Veterinariya
0042-4854	Veterinary Bulletin
0042-4862	Veterinary Economics
0042-4870	Veterinary Institute, Pulawy. Bulletin
0042-4889	Veterinary Medicine/Small Animal Clinician changed to Veterinary Medicine
0042-4897	Veterinary Practice
0042-4900	Veterinary Record
0042-4919	Pionyr
0042-4935	Vetus Testamentum
0042-4943	Vi Bilaegare med Hem och Hobby changed to Vi Bilaegare
0042-4951	Vi Menn
0042-4978	Via
0042-4986	Via Libera
0042-4994	Via Migliore
0042-5001	Via Port of New York changed to Via Port of New York-New Jersey
0042-5028	Vialidad
0042-5036	Viata Medicala - Pentru Cadre Superioare changed to Viata Medicala - Pentru Medici
0042-5044	Viata Militara
0042-5052	Viata Romineasca
0042-5060	Vibrations†
0042-5079	Vichiana
0042-5087	Vickers Voice
0042-5095	Victoria Government Gazette
0042-5109	Victoria Reports†
0042-5117	Victoria University of Wellington Law Review
0042-5125	Victorian
0042-5141	Victorian Dry Cleaner†
0042-515X	Victoria Farmer changed to V F G A Newsletter
0042-5184	Victorian Naturalist
0042-5192	Victorian Newsletter
0042-5206	Victorian Poetry
0042-5214	Victorian Reports
0042-5222	Victorian Studies
0042-5230	Victoria's Resources see 0814-4680
0042-5265	Vida Pastoral see 0507-7184
0042-5281	Vide
0042-529X	Vidici
0042-5303	Vidura
0042-5311	Vidya changed to Oriente e Occidente
0042-532X	Vidyodaya
0042-5338	Vie Asistenziali changed to Promozione Sociale
0042-5346	Vie Canine†
0042-5362	Vie Catholique du Berry
0042-5370	Vie Collective
0042-5400	Vie Communale et Departementale
0042-5419	Vie de la Douane
0042-5427	Vie de la Recherche Scientifique
0042-5435	Vie des Arts
0042-5451	Vie des Transports
0042-546X	Qui Touring
0042-5478	Vie du Rail
0042-5486	Vie et Bonte see 0301-0260
0042-5516	Vie et Milieu
0042-5524	Vie et Sante
0042-5567	Vie Judiciaire
0042-5583	Vie Medicale
0042-5591	Vie Musicale†
0042-5605	Vie Sociale
0042-5613	Vie Spirituelle
0042-5621	Vie Theresienne
0042-563X	Vie Urbaine
0042-5656	Vient de Paraitre†
0042-5672	Naturforschende Gesellschaft in Zuerich. Vierteljahrsschrift
0042-5680	Vierteljahresschrift Wirtschaft und Verwaltung†
0042-5702	Vierteljahrshefte fuer Zeitgeschichte
0042-5710	Vietnam
0042-5745	Vietnam International Information Bulletin changed to Vietnam/South East Asia International
0042-5788	Vietnambulletinen
0042-5796	Vieux Jardinier see 0772-1099
0042-580X	View from the Bottom†
0042-5818	Viewpoints
0042-5834	Viewpoint (London, 1965)
0042-5842	Viewpoint (London, 1970)
0042-5850	Viewpoint†
0042-5869	Viewpoint (Indianapolis)†
0042-5877	Viewpoints changed to Humanist Viewpoints
0042-5893	Views†
0042-5907	Views and Ideas on Mankind†
0042-5915	Views & Reviews
0042-5931	Viga en el Ojo
0042-594X	Vigencia
0042-5958	Vigilance
0042-5966	Vigilance†
0042-5974	Vigilancia
0042-6024	Vigilia
0042-6032	Vigiliae Christianae
0042-6040	Vignes & Raisins
0042-6059	Vigo County Public Library Staff Bulletin†
0042-6075	Vigyan Pragati
0042-6083	Vijesti Muzealaca i Konzervatora Hrvatske
0042-6091	Vijnan Karmee
0042-6105	Vikan
0042-6113	Viikkosanomat†
0042-6121	Vikram
0042-613X	Vikrant
0042-6156	Villa & Hem i Sverige†
0042-6164	Villa de Madrid
0042-6172	Village see 0264-4002
0042-6180	Village Voice
0042-6199	Villager (Bronxville)
0042-6202	Villager
0042-6210	Villamossag
0042-6229	Villanova Law Review
0042-6237	Ville-Giardini
0042-6245	Viltis
0042-6288	Vinduet
0042-6296	Vingehjulet changed to D S B Bladet
0042-630X	Vini d'Italia
0042-6318	Vinodelie i Vinogradarstvo S.S.S.R.
0042-6326	Vinohrad
0042-6334	Vins d'Alsace
0042-6350	Vintage Ford
0042-6369	Vintage Jazz Mart
0042-6385	Vinyl Technology Newsletter†
0042-6393	Vinzenzbote changed to Dienen und Helfen
0042-6407	Viola-Traedgaardsvaerlden
0042-6415	Viomichaniki Epitheorissis
0042-6423	Patholgische Anatomie changed to Virchows Archiv. Section A: Pathological Anatomy and Histopathology
0042-6431	Virchows Archiv. Abt. B. Zellpathologie-Cell Pathology see 0340-6075
0042-644X	Virginia Accountant
0042-6458	Virginia Advocate changed to Virginia United Methodist Advocate
0042-6466	Virginia Agricultural Economics
0042-6474	Virginia Cavalcade
0042-6482	Virginia. Department of Agriculture. Bulletin
0042-6490	Virginia Economic Indicators
0042-6504	Virginia Forward†
0042-6512	Virginia Geographer
0042-6547	Virginia Highway Bulletin changed to Virginia Department of Highways and Transportation Bulletin
0042-6555	Virginia Historical Society. Occasional Bulletin
0042-6563	Virginia Journal of Education†
0042-6571	Virginia Journal of International Law
0042-658X	Virginia Journal of Science
0042-6598	Kirkus Reviews
0042-6601	Virginia Law Review
0042-661X	Virginia Law Weekly
0042-6636	Virginia Magazine of History and Biography
0042-6652	Virginia Minerals
0042-6660	Virginia Municipal Review changed to Virginia Review
0042-6687	Virginia Museum Bulletin see 0363-3519
0042-6695	Virginia Nurse Quarterly see 0270-7780
0042-6709	Virginia P T A Bulletin
0042-6717	Virginia Pharmacist
0042-6725	Virginia Polytechnic Institute and State University. Extension News
0042-6733	Virginia Poultryman
0042-6741	Virginia Publisher and Printer changed to Virginia's Press
0042-675X	Virginia Quarterly Review
0042-6768	Virginia Record
0042-6776	Virginia School Boards Association Newsletter
0042-6784	Virginia Town & City
0042-6792	Virginia Wildlife
0042-6806	Virittaajaa
0042-6822	Virology
0042-6830	Virology Abstracts
0042-6849	Viroviticki List
0042-6857	Virus
0042-6865	Visages de l'Ain†
0042-6873	Visao
0042-6881	Vishwakarma
0042-6911	Vision
0042-692X	Vision Magazine
0042-6938	Weyerhaeuser World changed to Weyerhaeuser Today
0042-6946	Vision and Voice†
0042-6954	Vision - Europe†
0042-6962	Vision Letter
0042-6970	Vision of India†
0042-6989	Vision Research
0042-7004	Visnyk
0042-7020	Visnyk Sil's'kogospodar'skoi Nauki
0042-7039	Vispera†
0042-7047	Visserij
0042-7098	Vista changed to In Touch (Marion)
0042-7101	Vista
0042-711X	Vista see 0094-5072
0042-7128	Vistazo
0042-7136	Visti Ukrayins'kykh Inzheneriv
0042-7152	Visual Education†
0042-7160	Visual Medicine†
0042-7179	Visva - Bharati Patrika
0042-7187	Visva-Bharati Journal of Philosophy
0042-7195	Visva - Bharati Quarterly
0042-7209	Viswa Rachana
0042-7217	Viswasilpi
0042-7233	Vita Cattolica
0042-7241	Vita dell'Infanzia
0042-725X	Vita e Pensiero
0042-7268	Vita e Salute
0042-7276	Vita Giuseppina
0042-7284	La Vita in Cristo e Nella Chiesa
0042-7292	Vita Italiana
0042-7306	Vita Latina
0042-7330	Vita Consacrata
0042-7349	Vita Scolastica
0042-7357	Vita Sindacale Bergamasca
0042-7365	Vita Sociale
0042-7381	Vital Christianity
0042-739X	Vital Issues†
0042-7411	Vital Notes on Medical Periodicals†
0042-742X	Vital Speeches of the Day
0042-7438	Vital Statistics Monthly Report†
0042-7446	Vitalita changed to Italia Medica - Vitalita
0042-7470	Vitchyzna
0042-7489	Vitesse - Speed
0042-7497	Vitezna Kridla
0042-7500	Vitis
0042-7519	Vitreous Enameller
0042-7527	Vivant Univers
0042-7543	Vivarium
0042-7551	Viviamo
0042-756X	Vivienda
0042-7578	Vivir
0042-7586	Rivista del Clero Italiano
0042-7594	Vivliothiki Ghoneon
0042-7608	Vivre en Harmonie
0042-7616	Vizugyi Kozlemenyek
0042-7624	Vjesnik Komune changed to Daruvarski List
0042-7632	Vjesnik Rada
0042-7640	Vjesnik U Srijedu†
0042-7659	Vjesnik Nadbiskupije Splitsko-Makarske
0042-7667	Vlaamse Chemische Vereniging. Mededelingen†
0042-7675	Vlaamse Gids
0042-7683	Vlaanderen
0042-7691	Vleesdistributie en Vleestechnologie

ISSN INDEX

ISSN	Title
0042-7705	Vliegende Hollander
0042-7713	Voz de Mocambique
0042-7721	Foreign Trade
0042-773X	Vnitrni Lekarstvi
0042-7756	Vocation†
0042-7764	Vocational Guidance Quarterly see 0889-4019
0042-7772	Vocations for Social Change changed to Workforce
0042-7780	Voce
0042-7802	Voce Bruzia
0042-7810	Voce degli Italiani
0042-7829	Voce del Tabaccaio
0042-7837	Voce della Fiera
0042-7845	Voce della Madonna delle Grazie
0042-7853	Voce di Ferrara
0042-7861	Voce di Siracusa
0042-787X	Voce Nuova changed to Voce della Regione
0042-7888	Voci Fraterne
0042-790X	Vodohospodarsky Casopis
0042-7918	Vodosnabzhenie i Sanitarnaya Tekhnika
0042-7926	Voeding
0042-7934	Voedingsmiddelentechnologie
0042-7942	Voeest-Alpine Betriebskurier
0042-7950	Voegel der Heimat
0042-7977	Voetbal International
0042-7985	Vogeljaar
0042-7993	Die Vogelwelt
0042-8000	Vogue
0042-8019	Vogue Australia
0042-8027	Vogue (Italy)
0042-8035	Vogue Living
0042-8043	Vogue Pattern Book International see 0095-2788
0042-8051	Queens Voice changed to New York Voice
0042-806X	National Institute of Rug Cleaning Voice see 0886-9901
0042-8078	Voice of A G S
0042-8086	Voice of Ahinsa
0042-8094	Voice of Buddhism
0042-8108	Voice of Business†
0042-8116	Voice of Freedom†
0042-8132	Voice of Islam
0042-8140	Voice of Jamaica
0042-8159	Voice of Liberty
0042-8167	Voice of Methodism
0042-8175	Voice of Missions
0042-8183	Voice of the Black Community
0042-8191	Voice of the Cement, Lime, Gypsum and Allied Workers
0042-8213	Voice of the Nazarene - A Universal Challenger
0042-8221	Voice of the People
0042-8248	Voice of the Unions†
0042-8256	Voice of Youth
0042-8264	Full Gospel Business Men's Voice
0042-8272	Voices
0042-8280	Voices International
0042-8299	Voicespondent
0042-8302	Phase Zero†
0042-8329	Voie de la Paix
0042-8337	Volk auf dem Weg
0042-8345	Voix de l'Edition de la Presse et de l'Audiovision
0042-837X	Voix des Enseignants
0042-8388	Voix du Silence changed to Voice of Silence Newsletter
0042-8396	Voix et Visages
0042-840X	Vojni Glasnik
0042-8418	Vojnik
0042-8426	Vojno Delo
0042-8442	Vojnoistorijski Glasnik
0042-8450	Vojnosanitetski Pregled
0042-8469	Vojnotehnicki Glasnik
0042-8485	Vokrug Sveta
0042-8493	Volksgesundheit
0042-8507	Volkshochschule Brigittenau. Mitteilungsblatt†
0042-8515	Volkshochschule im Westen
0042-8523	Volkskunde, Driemaandelijks Tijdschrift voor de Studie van het Volksleven
0042-8531	Volkskunde in Oesterreich
0042-854X	Volksmacht
0042-8558	Volksmusik see 0323-5106
0042-8574	Volkstuin
0042-8582	Wirtschaftswoche: Volkswirt changed to Wirtschaftswoche
0042-8590	Switzerland. Bundesamt fuer Industrie, Gewerbe und Arbeit. Volkswirtschaft
0042-8612	Volonte du Commerce et de l'Industrie changed to Volonte du Commerce, de l'Industrie et des Prestataires de Services
0042-8620	Volt
0042-8639	Volta Review
0042-8671	Volunteer
0042-868X	Volunteer Views changed to Volunteer in Education
0042-8698	Volunteer World changed to News from C C I V S
0042-8701	Volunteer's Digest†
0042-871X	Vom S I H fuer Sie changed to Auf Nummer Sicher
0042-8728	Die Voorligter
0042-8736	Voprosy Ekonomiki
0042-8744	Voprosy Filosofii
0042-8752	Voprosy Ikhtiologii
0042-8779	Voprosy Istorii
0042-8787	Voprosy Kurortologii, Fizioterapii i Lechebnoi Fizicheskoi Kul'tury
0042-8795	Voprosy Literatury
0042-8809	Voprosy Meditsinskoi Khimii
0042-8817	Voprosy Neirokhirurgii
0042-8825	Voprosy Okhrany Materinstva i Detstva
0042-8833	Voprosy Pitaniya
0042-8841	Voprosy Psikhologii
0042-885X	Voprosy Revmatizma changed to Revmatologiya
0042-8868	Voprosy Yazykoznaniya
0042-8884	Vorarlbergs Gewerbliche Wirtschaft changed to Vorarlbergs Wirtschaft Aktuell
0042-8892	Vorschau Europa see 0342-1716
0042-8914	Vorschau-Tabelle see 0723-5259
0042-8922	Vorschriften fuer die Veterinaerverwaltung†
0042-8930	Vorwaerts
0042-8949	Vorwaerts
0042-8957	Vospitanie Shkol'nikov
0042-8965	Votre Beaute
0042-8973	Votre Maison
0042-8981	Vou†
0042-899X	Vox Romanica
0042-9007	Vox Sanguinis
0042-9015	Vox Theologica†
0042-9031	Voyages†
0042-9058	Voenno-Istoricheskii Zhurnal
0042-9066	Voennyi Vestnik
0042-9074	Voennye Znaniya
0042-9082	Voz de la Biblioteca Universitaria†
0042-9090	Voz del Pueblo
0042-9104	Vozhatyi
0042-9112	Vredesactie†
0042-9120	Vredesopbouw changed to Vrede
0042-9139	Vriend
0042-9147	Vriend der Kinderen†
0042-9155	Vriend van Oud en Jong
0042-9171	Vriendenkring van Het Rembrandthuis. Kroniek†
0042-9198	Vrishchik
0042-921X	Vrouw in Middenstand en Burgerij changed to Vrouw
0042-9228	Free State Educational News
0042-9236	Vsemirnoe Profsoyuznoe Dvizhenie
0042-9244	Vsezoyuznaya Akademiya Sel'skokhozyaistvennykh Nauk im. V.I. Lenina. Doklady
0042-9279	Vsesvit
0042-9287	Vu Par les Belges†
0042-9309	Vukovarske Novine
0042-9317	Vuoriteollisus
0042-9325	Vyapar
0042-935X	Vynalezy changed to Vynalezy a Zlepsovaci Navrhy
0042-9368	Vysokomolekulyarnye Soedineniya
0042-9376	Vystavba a Architektura
0042-9384	Vytis
0042-9392	Vytvarnictvo, Fotografia, Film
0042-9406	Vyziva a Zdravie
0042-9414	Vyziva Lidu
0042-9422	Vyzvol'nyi Shlyakh
0042-9430	W A A C C S Motor Industry
0042-9449	W A C L Bulletin changed to Freedom Digest
0042-9465	W.A. Grower
0042-949X	W.A. Teachers' Journal changed to Western Teacher
0042-9503	W.A.V.A.E. News changed to W V A Lifeline
0042-9511	W A W Newsletter
0042-952X	W & L
0042-9538	W & V
0042-9562	W B F O
0042-9589	W D
0042-9635	W E M Newsletter
0042-9643	W F L N Philadelphia Guide changed to W F L N Philadelphia Guide to Events and Places
0042-9651	Chicago Guide see 0362-4595
0042-966X	W G A Geschaeftsbericht
0042-9678	W G O - Monatshefte fuer Osteuropaeisches Recht
0042-9686	World Health Organization. Bulletin
0042-9694	W H O Chronicle†
0042-9716	W I N†
0042-9732	W I Z O Review
0042-9740	Indo-Iran Journal
0042-9767	W M O Bulletin
0042-9775	W N Y F
0042-9783	W P M Newsletter (World Presbyterian Missions) changed to Network (Decatur)
0042-9791	W R L News
0042-9805	Washington Recreation and Park Society. News changed to Washington Recreation and Park Association. Syllabus-Bulletin
0042-983X	W S D A News
0042-9872	W W I Mitteilungen changed to W S I Mitteilungen
0042-9899	W Z E Wissenschaftliche Zeitschrift der Elektrotechnik†
0042-9902	Wacht te Kooi
0042-9929	Waerme- und Stoffuebertragung
0042-9937	Waescherei- und Reinigungs-Praxis
0042-9945	Waffen- und Kostumkunde
0042-9953	Wagenbouwnieuws†
0042-9961	Waggoner
0042-997X	Karosseriebauer und Wagner†
0042-9988	Wagtail
0042-9996	Die Wahrheit
0043-0005	Waiblinger Anzeigenblatt†
0043-0013	Wakayama Medicine
0043-0021	Wakayama Prefecture. Monthly Report of Meteorology
0043-003X	Wake Forest Law Review
0043-0048	Die Waldarbeit
0043-0056	Wales
0043-0064	Walkabout†
0043-0072	Walker Watchword†
0043-0099	Wall Street Reports
0043-0102	Wall Street Transcript
0043-0129	Wallaces Farmer
0043-0137	Wallerstein Laboratories Communications†
0043-0145	Wallpaper and Wallcoverings changed to Wallcoverings
0043-0153	Wallpaper, Paint and Wallcovering changed to W P W Decor
0043-0161	Walls & Ceilings
0043-017X	Walt Whitman Review see 0737-0679
0043-0188	Walters Art Gallery. Bulletin
0043-0196	Wanasan
0043-020X	War Communiques
0043-0218	War Cry
0043-0226	War Cry
0043-0234	War Cry
0043-0242	War Cry
0043-0250	War Cry
0043-0269	War on Hunger see 0735-1755
0043-0277	War/Peace Report see 0305-0629
0043-0307	Waratah†
0043-0315	Ward's Auto World
0043-0323	Ward's Bulletin
0043-0331	Warenzeichenblatt. Teil 1: Angemeldete Zeichen
0043-034X	Warenzeichenblatt. Teil 2: Eingetragene Zeichen
0043-0358	Warmte†
0043-0374	Warship International
0043-0382	Balai Penyelidikan Perusahaan Perkebunan Gula. Warta Bulanan
0043-0390	Warwickshire and Worcestershire Life
0043-0404	Was Tun
0043-0412	Wascana Review
0043-0420	Washburn Law Journal
0043-0439	Washington Academy of Sciences. Journal
0043-0447	Washington Afro-American
0043-0455	Washington and Jefferson Literary Journal†
0043-0463	Washington & Lee Law Review
0043-0471	Washington Atomic Energy Report and Guideletter changed to Washington Atomic Energy Report
0043-0501	Washington Coach
0043-051X	Washington County Education News
0043-0536	Washington Dental Service Newsletter
0043-0544	Washington Diocese
0043-0552	Washington Education†
0043-0560	Washington Food Dealer Magazine
0043-0587	Washington Grange News changed to Grange News
0043-0609	Washington International Arts Letter
0043-0617	Washington Law Review
0043-0633	Washington Monthly
0043-0641	Washington Motorist
0043-065X	Washington Music Educator see 0147-4367
0043-0684	Washington Newspaper
0043-0692	Washington Plumbing and Heating Contractor
0043-0706	Washington Purchaser†
0043-0714	Washington Report (Washington, 1979) changed to Business Counsel
0043-0730	Washington Report on Medicine and Health changed to Health Legislation Science Trends
0043-0749	Washington Sounds see 0162-5667
0043-0757	Washington State Entomological Society Proceedings
0043-0773	Washington State Journal of Nursing†
0043-0781	Washington State Research Council Monthly Report changed to Washington Research Council. Notebook
0043-0803	Washington State School Directors Association Newsletter changed to Signal (Olympia)
0043-0811	Washington State University. Mathematics Notes
0043-082X	Washington State University. Research Studies†
0043-0838	Washington State Voter
0043-0846	Washington University Law Quarterly
0043-0862	Washingtonian
0043-0897	Wasmann Journal of Biology
0043-0927	Wasser und Boden
0043-0951	Wasser und Energiewirtschaft changed to Wasser, Energie, Luft
0043-096X	Wasserwirtschaft
0043-0978	Wasserwirtschaft-Wassertechnik (W W T)
0043-0986	Wasserwirtschaftliche Mitteilungen
0043-0994	Waste Age
0043-1001	Wastewater Works News
0043-1028	Wat Kan Ons Opvoer'
0043-1036	Watchmaker, Jeweller & Silversmith
0043-1079	Watchtower
0043-1087	Water and Pollution Control
0043-1117	Water and Sewage Works see 0273-2238
0043-1125	Water and Waste Treatment
0043-1133	Water and Wastes Digest
0043-1141	Water and Wastes Engineering see 0273-2238
0043-115X	Water and Water Engineering see 0301-7028
0043-1168	Water Bodem Lucht†
0043-1176	

ISSN INDEX 1321

0043-1184 Water Conditioning *changed to* Water Conditioning and Purification
0043-1192 Water Conditions in Wisconsin†
0043-1206 Water Desalination Report
0043-1222 Water in the News†
0043-1249 Water Law Newsletter
0043-1257 Water Management Bulletin†
0043-1265 Water News
0043-1273 Water Newsletter
0043-1281 Water Pollution Abstracts *see* 0748-2531
0043-129X Water Pollution Control
0043-1303 Water Pollution Control Federation. Journal
0043-1311 Water Polo Scoreboard†
0043-1338 Water Power *see* 0306-400X
0043-1346 U D S Water Quality Control Digest *changed to* Water Quality Control Digest
0043-1354 Water Research
0043-1362 Water Resources Abstracts *see* 0731-6445
0043-1370 Water Resources Bulletin
0043-1397 Water Resources Research
0043-1400 Water Resources Review *changed to* National Water Conditions
0043-1435 Water Spectrum†
0043-1443 Water Well Journal
0043-1451 Waterkampioen
0043-146X Waterloo Campus *see* 0700-5105
0043-1486 Waterschapsbelangen
0043-1508 Watersheds†
0043-1516 Watersport†
0043-1524 Waterways Journal
0043-1532 Watsonia
0043-1559 Wave Hill News†
0043-1567 Wavriensia
0043-1575 Way (London, 1961)
0043-1583 Shlach *changed to* Way - Ukrainian Catholic Bi-Weekly
0043-1591 Way-Catholic Viewpoints *changed to* Way (San Francisco)
0043-1605 Way of Life
0043-1613 Wayne County Farm and Home News *changed to* Extension (Alton)
0043-1621 Wayne Law Review
0043-163X Wayne State University Alumni News
0043-1648 Wear
0043-1656 Weather
0043-1664 Weather Vane
0043-1672 Weatherwise
0043-1680 Webb Society Quarterly Journal
0043-1699 Webe Mit
0043-1710 Wee Wisdom (Inkprint Edition)
0043-1729 Weed Abstracts
0043-1737 Weed Research
0043-1745 Weed Science
0043-1753 Weeds, Trees and Turf
0043-1761 Week-End
0043-177X Weekblad Cinema
0043-1788 Weekblad voor Bloembollencultuur *changed to* Bloembollencultuur
0043-180X Weekend *changed to* Weekend News
0043-1818 Weekend
0043-1826 Weekend Magazine†
0043-1834 Weekly Letter Commentary†
0043-1842 Weekly Livestock Reporter
0043-1850 Weekly Market Bulletin
0043-1869 National Braille Press. Weekly News†
0043-1877 Weekly News *changed to* Sunday Herald
0043-1885 Weekly People *see* 0199-350X
0043-1893 Weekly Pharmacy Reports: The Green Sheet
0043-1907 National Promotion Audit†
0043-1915 Weekly Review *changed to* Intelligence Digest (Cheltenham)
0043-1923 Weekly Statistical Sugar Trade Journal
0043-194X Weekly Times
0043-1966 Weekly Underwriter†
0043-1974 Weekly Weather and Crop Bulletin, National Summary†
0043-1982 Weekly Weather Report of Pakistan & Kashmir
0043-2008 Weekly Wool Chart *changed to* Wool Record Weekly Market Report
0043-2016 Weg en Waterbouw†
0043-2024 Weg und Ziel
0043-2032 Weg zur Gesundheit
0043-2040 Wege zum Menschen
0043-2059 Wege zur Sozialversicherung
0043-2067 Wegen
0043-2075 Gornictwo Odkrywkowe
0043-2105 Wegwijzer
0043-2113 Wehr und Wirtschaft *changed to* Wehrtechnik, Vereinigt mit Wehr und Wirtschaft
0043-2121 Wehrausbildung in Wort und Bild *changed to* Wehrausbildung
0043-2156 Wehrmedizinische Monatsschrift
0043-2180 Weight Watchers
0043-2199 Weimarer Beitraege
0043-2202 Weiss-Blaue Rundschau
0043-2210 Welcome to Czechoslovakia
0043-2229 Welcome to Singapore†
0043-2237 Welder
0043-2245 Welding and Metal Fabrication
0043-2253 Welding Design and Fabrication
0043-227X Welding Engineer *see* 0043-2253
0043-2288 Welding in the World
0043-2296 Welding Journal
0043-230X Welding Production†
0043-2318 Welding Research Abroad
0043-2326 Welding Research Council Bulletin
0043-2342 Welfare in Review *changed to* Human Needs
0043-2369 Welfare Reporter†
0043-2385 Welfarer†
0043-2407 Welldoer
0043-2415 Wells Fargo Bank Business Review
0043-2431 Welsh History Review
0043-244X Welsh Music
0043-2458 Welsh Nation
0043-2466 Welsh Rugby
0043-2474 Welsh Secondary Schools Review
0043-2482 Welt der Arbeit
0043-2490 Die Welt der Buecher
0043-2512 Die Molkerei-Zeitung Welt der Milch
0043-2520 Die Welt der Slaven
0043-2539 Welt des Islams
0043-2555 Welt Agni *changed to* Welt Spirale und Agni Yoga
0043-2563 Welt und Sport†
0043-258X Weltblick†
0043-2598 Die Weltbuehne
0043-2601 Die Weltgewerkschaftsbewegung
0043-261X Weltkunst
0043-2636 Weltwirtschaftliches Archiv
0043-2644 Weltweite Hilfe
0043-2652 Die Weltwirtschaft
0043-2679 Die Wende
0043-2687 Wendepunkt†
0043-2695 Wending
0043-2709 Werbegeschenk-Berater *see* 0341-5600
0043-2725 Werbung in Oesterreich
0043-2741 Wereldmarkt†
0043-275X Wereldwijzer
0043-2776 Werkmeister und Techniche Arbeitsleiter/Contremaitre et Agent de Maistrise *changed to* Werkmeister
0043-2784 Werkpaedagogische Hefte†
0043-2792 Werkstatt und Betrieb
0043-2806 Werkstattstechnik *see* 0340-4544
0043-2814 Werkstoffe *see* 0176-6058
0043-2822 Werkstoffe und Korrosion
0043-2830 Werkzeitung des Schweizerischen Industrie *changed to* W Z : Wirtschaftszeitung fuer Alle
0043-2849 Die Weser
0043-2857 Weserlotse
0043-2865 Wesfarmers News *changed to* Western Farmer and Grazier
0043-2873 Wesley Historical Society. Proceedings
0043-289X Wesleyan Advocate
0043-2911 Wesleyan News†
0043-292X Wessex Life†
0043-2954 West-Ost-Journal
0043-2962 West Africa
0043-2970 West African Builder and Architect
0043-2989 West African Journal of Biological and Applied Chemistry
0043-2997 West African Journal of Education
0043-3004 West African Medical Journal
0043-3020 West African Science Association Journal *see* 0029-0114
0043-3039 West African Technical Review ABC *see* 0266-6677
0043-3047 West & East
0043-3055 West Australian Craftsman
0043-3071 West Bengal Labour Gazette
0043-3098 West Cameroon Monthly Digest of Statistics†
0043-3101 West Coast Druggist *see* 0191-6394
0043-311X West Coast Review
0043-3128 West Country Homefinder *see* 0018-4160
0043-3136 West Georgia College Review
0043-3144 West Indian Medical Journal
0043-3152 West Indies Chronicle *see* 0142-4742
0043-3179 West Pakistan Journal of Agricultural Research *see* 0251-0480
0043-3187 West Texas Register *changed to* West Texas Catholic
0043-3195 West Virginia Agriculture & Forestry†
0043-3209 West Virginia Archaeologist†
0043-3217 West Virginia C.P.A.
0043-3225 West Virginia Dental Journal
0043-3241 West Virginia Hillbilly *changed to* New West Virginia Hillbilly
0043-325X West Virginia History
0043-3268 West Virginia Law Review
0043-3276 West Virginia Libraries
0043-3284 West Virginia Medical Journal
0043-3292 West Virginia Pharmacist†
0043-3306 West Virginia Progress†
0043-3314 West Virginia School Boards Association. Bulletin. *changed to* Communicator (Charleston)
0043-3322 West Virginia School Journal *see* 0274-8606
0043-3330 West Virginia. State Department of Health. Weekly Morbidity Report *changed to* State of the State's Health
0043-3349 West Virginia University Magazine *changed to* West Virginia University Alumni Magazine
0043-3357 WestArt
0043-3365 Westchester Business Journal
0043-3373 Westchester County Press
0043-339X Westchester Realtor
0043-342X Westerly
0043-3438 Westermanns Monatshefte *changed to* Westermann's
0043-3454 Western†
0043-3462 Western American Literature
0043-3470 Western Apparel Industry *see* 0192-1878
0043-3489 Western Australia. Government Gazette
0043-3527 Western Buddhist†
0043-3535 Western Builder
0043-3551 Western Carolina University Journal of Education†
0043-3578 Western Collector *changed to* Avon Collectors Newsletter
0043-3594 Western Confectioner and Tobacconist *changed to* Candy World Illustrated
0043-3624 Western Construction and Industry *changed to* Western Commerce & Industry Magazine
0043-3640 Western Economic Journal *see* 0095-2583
0043-3659 Western Electric Engineer *changed to* Engineer
0043-3675 Western European Education
0043-3691 Western Farm Equipment
0043-3705 Western Fire Journal *changed to* American Fire Journal
0043-3721 Western Fisheries†
0043-373X Western Folklore
0043-3764 Western Fruit Grower
0043-3780 Western Grocer and Food Store Manager *see* 0705-906X
0043-3799 Western Grower & Shipper
0043-3802 Western Heart
0043-3810 Western Historical Quarterly
0043-3829 Western Horizons
0043-3837 Western Horseman
0043-3845 Western Humanities Review
0043-3853 Western Illinois University Bulletin†
0043-387X Western Livestock Journal *see* 0192-2815
0043-3888 Western Lumber and Building Materials Merchant *see* 0739-9723
0043-390X Western Manufacturing *changed to* Western Plant Operation
0043-3918 Western Meat Industry *changed to* Meat and Poultry Magazine
0043-3934 Western Miner
0043-3942 Western Mobile News
0043-3950 Western Motor Fleet
0043-3977 Western New York Motorist
0043-3985 Western Oil Reporter *changed to* Western Oil World
0043-3993 Western Ontario History Nuggets†
0043-4000 Western Outdoors
0043-4019 Western Pacific Orthopaedic Association. Journal
0043-4027 Western Paint Review *changed to* Paint & Decorating Magazine
0043-4035 Western Pennsylvania Historical Magazine
0043-4051 Western Plains Library System Newsletter
0043-4078 Western Political Quarterly
0043-4086 Western Printer & Lithographer†
0043-4094 Western Producer
0043-4108 Western Railroader *see* 0149-4996
0043-4124 Western Real Estate News
0043-4132 Western Recorder
0043-4140 Case Western Reserve University. School of Dentistry. Dental Alumni Bulletin *changed to* Case Western Reserve University School of Dentistry: Dental Alumni News
0043-4175 Western School Law Review†
0043-4191 Western Socialist†
0043-4205 Western Speech *changed to* Western Journal of Speech Communication
0043-4213 Western Stamp Collector *see* 0277-3899
0043-4221 Western States Jewish Historical Quarterly *changed to* Western States Jewish History
0043-423X Western Sun *changed to* Labor Voice
0043-4256 Western Underwriter†
0043-4280 Western Wear and Equipment *changed to* Western & English Fashions
0043-4299 Western World Review†
0043-4310 Westernews *see* 0191-5959
0043-4329 Western's World†
0043-4345 Westhoek†
0043-4361 Westinghouse Engineer†
0043-437X Westminster Review *changed to* Westminster
0043-4388 Westminster Theological Journal
0043-440X Westport Historical Quarterly†
0043-4418 Der Westpreusse
0043-4426 Westsider *see* 0148-0146
0043-4434 Westways
0043-4442 Wetenschap en Samenleving
0043-4450 Wetter und Leben
0043-4477 Whaley-Eaton Foreign Letter†
0043-4485 Wharton Quarterly†
0043-4493 What†
0043-4507 What Goes on in Medicine *changed to* What Goes on in Continuing Medical Education
0043-4523 What's Happening†
0043-454X What's New at Colgate *changed to* Colgate Scene
0043-4558 What's New in Advertising and Marketing
0043-4574 What's New in Co-Op Information†
0043-4582 What's New in Food and Drug Research†
0043-4590 What's New in Home Economics
0043-4612 What's News in Reinsurance†
0043-4620 What's on for Young People†
0043-4639 What's on in Aberdeen *changed to* What's on and Where to Shop in Aberdeen
0043-4647 What's on in Calcutta

0043-4655 What's on in Glasgow
0043-4663 What's on in Jersey
0043-4671 What's on in London
0043-468X What's on in Ottawa
0043-4698 Australia. Bureau of Statistics. Wheat Industry *changed to* Australia. Bureau of Statistics. Wheat, Australia
0043-4701 Wheat Life
0043-471X Wheat Review†
0043-4728 Wheat Scoop†
0043-4736 Wheat Situation *see* 0310-9917
0043-4744 Wheel Clicks
0043-4752 Wheel of Delta Omicron
0043-4760 Wheeled Sportsman†
0043-4779 Wheels
0043-4787 Wheels Afield *see* 0027-2094
0043-4795 Whenever Whatever *changed to* Rainbow (Valley Forge)
0043-4809 Where *see* 0266-6278
0043-4817 Where to Go in London and Around *see* 0264-3227
0043-4825 Whereas†
0043-4841 Which?
0043-485X Whip
0043-4868 Whitaker's Books of the Month and Books to Come
0043-4876 White Collar
0043-4884 White Collar Management
0043-4892 White Collar Report *see* 0891-4141
0043-4906 White County Heritage
0043-4922 White Fathers†
0043-4930 White Horse and Fleur de Lys *see* 0140-0991
0043-4965 White Ribbon Bulletin
0043-4973 White Ribbon Magazine
0043-499X White Tops
0043-5007 White Wing Messenger
0043-5015 Whiteshell Echo
0043-5023 Whitley Bulletin *see* 0261-3824
0043-5031 Whole Earth Catalog *see* 0749-5056
0043-504X Wholesale Commodity Prices
0043-5058 Wholesale Food Prices
0043-5066 Industrial Engineering Management Science *changed to* Technology Transfer
0043-5082 Wiadomosci Archeologiczne/Bulletin Archeologique Polonais
0043-5090 Wiadomosci Botaniczne
0043-5104 Wiadomosci Chemiczne
0043-5112 Wiadomosci Elektrotechniczne
0043-5120 Wiadomosci Gornicze
0043-5139 Wiadomosci Hutnicze
0043-5147 Wiadomosci Lekarskie
0043-5155 Wiadomosci Numizmatyczne
0043-5163 Wiadomosci Parazytologiczne
0043-5171 Wiadomosci Sluzby Hydrologicznej i Meteorologicznej *see* 0208-6263
0043-518X Poland. Glowny Urzad Statystyczny. Wiadomosci Statystyczne
0043-5198 Wiadomosci Telekomunikacyjne
0043-5201 Poland. Urzad Patentowy. Wiadomosci
0043-521X Wiadomosci Warsztatowe
0043-5228 Wichita *changed to* Wichita Business
0043-5236 Wichtigste fuer den Chef *changed to* Chef
0043-5244 Widnokregi
0043-5252 Wiederbelebung-Organersatz-Intensivmedizin *see* 0175-3851
0043-5260 Wielewaal
0043-5309 Wiener Entomologische Gesellschaft. Zeitschrift
0043-5317 Wiener Geschichtsblaetter
0043-5325 Wiener Klinische Wochenschrift
0043-5333 Wiener Library Bulletin†
0043-5341 Wiener Medizinische Wochenschrift
0043-535X Wiener Tieraerztliche Monatsschrift
0043-5376 Wiener Zeitschrift fuer Innere Medizin und ihre Grenzgebiete. *see* 0303-8173
0043-5406 Wigs & Hairpieces†
0043-5414 Wijsgerig Perspectief op Maatschappij en Wetenschap
0043-5422 Wild und Hund
0043-5430 Wilderness Camping *see* 0277-867X
0043-5449 Wilderness Travel Magazine†
0043-5457 Wildlife Crusader
0043-5473 Wildlife Disease Association. Journal *see* 0090-3558
0043-5481 Wildlife in Australia
0043-549X Wildlife in North Carolina
0043-5503 Wildlife News *changed to* International Wildlife (Canadian Edition)
0043-5511 Wildlife Review (Fort Collins)
0043-552X Wildlife Society News *see* 0091-7648
0043-5538 Wildlife Views†
0043-5546 Roux' Archiv fuer Entwicklungsmechanik der Organismen *see* 0340-0794
0043-5554 Willamette Bridge†
0043-5562 Willamette Law Journal *see* 0191-9822
0043-5589 William & Mary Law Review
0043-5597 William and Mary Quarterly
0043-5600 William and Mary Review
0043-5619 Comments on Current World Affairs *see* 0274-5852
0043-5627 Williams' Family Bulletin†
0043-5635 Wilmington Public Schools. Profile†
0043-5643 Wilson Bulletin
0043-5651 Wilson Library Bulletin
0043-566X Wiltshire Farmer
0043-5678 Wimpel
0043-5686 Win Magazine *changed to* Wind
0043-5694 W I N B A N News†
0043-5708 Wind Bell
0043-5716 Windless Orchard
0043-5724 Window†
0043-5759 House & Garden (London)
0043-5775 Off Licence News
0043-5783 Wine-Butler *see* 0141-6014
0043-5791 Wine Magazine†
0043-5805 Wine Review†
0043-5813 Wine, Spirit & Malt†
0043-5821 Wineletter†
0043-583X Wines and Vines
0043-5848 Winged Arrow†
0043-5856 Winged Foot
0043-5864 Winged Head
0043-5880 Wings
0043-5899 Wings
0043-5902 Wings at Home *see* 0704-6804
0043-5910 Wings Over Africa *see* 0261-2399
0043-5929 Wingspan *changed to* B C A L News
0043-5937 Winner (Washington)
0043-5953 Der Winzer
0043-5961 Wir Blenden Auf†
0043-597X Wir Herbergs Freunde *changed to* Jugendherbergswerk
0043-5988 Wir und Unsere Welt
0043-5996 Wire
0043-6011 Wire Industry
0043-602X Wire Journal *see* 0277-4275
0043-6046 Wire World International
0043-6062 Wireless World *changed to* Electronics & Wireless World
0043-6089 Wirkendes Wort
0043-6097 Wirkerei- und Strickerei-Technik
0043-6100 Die Wirtschaft
0043-6119 Wirtschaft: Ausgabe A *see* 0232-4768
0043-6135 Wirtschaft und Recht
0043-6143 Wirtschaft und Statistik
0043-6151 Wirtschaft und Wettbewerb
0043-616X Wirtschaft und Wissen *changed to* Angestellten Magazin
0043-6186 Wirtschaftliche Mitteilungen/Informations Economiques *changed to* Marches Etrangers
0043-6194 Wirtschaft und Investment
0043-6208 Wirtschaftsblaetter *changed to* B F G Wirtschaftsblaetter
0043-6240 Wirtschaftsbericht ueber die Lateinamerikanischen Laender sowie Spanien und Portugal *changed to* Wirtschaftsbericht Lateinamerika
0043-6259 Wirtschaftsberichte
0043-6275 Wirtschaftsdienst
0043-6283 Wirtschaftskonjunktur
0043-6291 Wirtschaftspolitische Blaetter
0043-6305 Wirtschaftspolitische Chronik *see* 0721-3808
0043-6321 Der Wirtschaftstreuhaender
0043-633X Wirtschaftswissenschaft
0043-6348 Wisconsin A A A Motor News *see* 0162-3591
0043-6356 Wisconsin Agriculturist
0043-6364 Wisconsin Archeologist
0043-6380 Wisconsin Bar Bulletin
0043-6399 Wisconsin Beverage Journal
0043-6402 Wisconsin C P A
0043-6410 Wisconsin Conservation Bulletin *see* 0736-2277
0043-6453 Wisconsin Engineer
0043-6488 Wisconsin Jewish Chronicle
0043-6496 Wisconsin Journal of Education†
0043-650X Wisconsin Law Review
0043-6518 W L A Newsletter
0043-6526 Wisconsin Library Bulletin†
0043-6534 Wisconsin Magazine of History
0043-6542 Wisconsin Medical Journal
0043-6550 Wisconsin Mental Hygiene Review†
0043-6569 Wisconsin Newsletter†
0043-6577 Wisconsin Parent Teacher Bulletin *changed to* Wisconsin Parent Teacher
0043-6585 Wisconsin Pharmacist
0043-6593 Wisconsin Pharmacy Extension Bulletin†
0043-6615 Wisconsin Professional Engineer
0043-6623 Wisconsin Rehabilitation†
0043-6631 Wisconsin Review
0043-664X Wisconsin School Board News *changed to* Wisconsin School News
0043-6658 Wisconsin School Musician
0043-6666 Wisconsin Sociologist
0043-6674 Wisconsin State Dental Society. Journal *see* 0091-4185
0043-6682 Wisconsin State Laboratory of Hygiene. Laboratory Newsletter†
0043-6690 Wisconsin State Universities Report†
0043-6704 Wisconsinsuror *changed to* Wisconsin Insuror
0043-6712 Wisconsin Tales and Trails *see* 0095-4314
0043-6739 Wisconsin Then and Now *see* 0196-1306
0043-6747 Wisconsin's Health *see* 0146-2768
0043-6755 Wise Owl News *changed to* Prevent Blindness News
0043-6763 Mitteilungen aus dem Wissenschaftlichen Bibliothekswesen der DDR
0043-678X Wissenschaft und Weisheit†
0043-6798 Wissenschaft und Weltbild
0043-6801 A E G-Telefunken. Wissenschaftliche Berichte†
0043-6828 Deutsche Gesellschaft fuer Ernaehrung. Wissenschaftliche Veroeffentlichungen†
0043-6836 Friedrich-Schiller-Universitaet Jena Mathematisch-Naturwissenschaftliche Reihe. Wissenschaftliche Zeitschrift
0043-6844 Hochschule fuer Verkehrswesen "Friedrich List". Wissenschaftliche Zeitschrift
0043-6879 Karl-Marx-Universitaet, Leipzig. Wissenschaftliche Zeitung *changed to* Karl-Marx-Universitaet, Leipzig. Wissenschaftliche Zeitschrift
0043-6895 Paedagogischen Hochschule, Potsdam. Gesellschafts und Sprachwissenschaftliche u. Math. Nat. Reihe. Wissenschaftliche Zeitschrift†
0043-6917 Technische Hochschule Ilmenau. Wissenschaftliche Zeitschrift
0043-6925 Technische Universitaet Dresden. Wissenschaftliche Zeitschrift
0043-6933 Rostock Universitaet. Wissenschaftliche Zeitschrift. Gesellschafts- und Sprachwissenschaftliche Reihe *changed to* Rostock Wilhelm-Pieck-Universitaet. Wissenschaftliche Zeitschrift. Gesellschafts-Wissenschaftliche Reihe
0043-6941 Wissenschaftlicher Dienst fuer Ostmitteleuropa *see* 0340-3297
0043-695X Wissenschaftlicher Dienst Suedosteuropa *see* 0722-480X
0043-6976 Wissenschaftsrecht, Wissenschaftsverwaltung, Wissenschaftsfoerderung
0043-6984 With
0043-6992 Within Our Gates *changed to* Open House
0043-700X Without Prejudice
0043-7018 Without the Camp *changed to* New Day
0043-7050 Witte Krant†
0043-7069 Witte Museum Quarterly†
0043-7077 Witterung in Oesterreich. Monatsuebersicht
0043-7085 Witterung in Uebersee
0043-7093 Wittgenstein
0043-7107 Wivenhoe Park Review
0043-7123 Woche in Australien
0043-7131 Wochenblatt fuer Papierfabrikation
0043-714X Wofford Bibliopolist†
0043-7158 Wohnen und Siedeln
0043-7166 Wohnungseigentum
0043-7174 Wojsko Ludowe
0043-7182 Wojskowy Przeglad Historyczny
0043-7190 Wojskowy Przeglad Lotniczy†
0043-7212 Wolkenridder
0043-7220 Woman
0043-7239 Woman Magazine
0043-7255 Woman Bowler
0043-7263 Woman, Bride and Home†
0043-7271 Woman C P A
0043-728X Woman Constitutionalist†
0043-7298 Woman Engineer
0043-7301 Woman Golfer†
0043-7328 Woman's Day
0043-7336 Woman's Day
0043-7344 Woman's Journal
0043-7352 Woman's National Magazine *changed to* Woman's National Farm & Garden Magazine
0043-7360 Woman's Own
0043-7379 Woman's Pulpit†
0043-7387 Woman's Realm
0043-7395 Knitting *changed to* Sewing & Knitting
0043-7409 Woman's Way Weekly
0043-7417 Woman's Weekly
0043-7425 Woman's World†
0043-7433 Women: A Journal of Liberation†
0043-7441 Women in Business
0043-745X Women in Council†
0043-7468 Women Lawyers Journal
0043-7476 Women of the Whole World
0043-7492 Women-To-By-Of-and About†
0043-7506 Women Today
0043-7514 Women's American O R T Reporter
0043-7522 Women's Dress Buyers *changed to* Women's, Misses & Jr. Dress Buyers
0043-7530 Women's Employment
0043-7549 Women's Intimate Apparel Buyers
0043-7557 Women's League Outlook
0043-7565 Women's Sportswear Buyers *changed to* Women's, Misses & Jr. Sportswear Buyers
0043-7573 Women's Track and Field World *see* 0193-8312
0043-7581 Women's Wear Daily *changed to* Women's Wear Daily
0043-759X Women's World
0043-7603 Women's Zionist Council of South Africa. News and Views *changed to* Women's Zionist Organization of South Africa. News and Views
0043-762X Wood *see* 0262-6071
0043-7646 Wood & Equipment News
0043-7654 Wood and Fiber *see* 0735-6161
0043-7662 Wood & Wood Products
0043-7670 Wood Construction and Building Materialist†
0043-7689 Wood Heat Quarterly†
0043-7697 Wood Preserving *see* 0099-1716
0043-7700 Wood Science†
0043-7719 Wood Science and Technology
0043-7727 Woodall's Trailer Travel *see* 0160-3000
0043-7743 Pulp and Paper Research Institute of Canada. Woodlands Papers†
0043-7751 Woodmen of the World Magazine
0043-776X Woodworker
0043-7778 Woodworking & Furniture Digest†
0043-7786 Woodworking Industry†

ISSN INDEX 1323

ISSN	Title
0043-7808	Wool and Woolens of India
0043-7816	Wool Intelligence (and Fibres Supplement)†
0043-7824	Wool News
0043-7832	Wool Record and Textile World *changed to* Wool Record
0043-7840	Wool Sack
0043-7867	U.S. Department of Agriculture. Economic Research Service. Wool Situation *see* 0744-2890
0043-7875	Wool Technology and Sheep Breeding
0043-7883	Woollens & Worsteds of India
0043-7891	Worcester Art Museum. News Bulletin and Calendar *see* 0193-9564
0043-7905	Worcester Medical News
0043-7913	Worcester Polytechnic Institute. Journal *see* 0148-6128
0043-7921	Worcester Punch†
0043-7948	Word
0043-7956	Word
0043-7980	Word Ways
0043-7999	On the Line (Scottdale)
0043-8014	Work Boat
0043-8022	Work Study
0043-8030	Work Study and Management Services *see* 0307-6768
0043-8057	Workbench
0043-8065	Queensland Worker *see* 0045-0979
0043-809X	Workers World
0043-8103	Working for Boys†
0043-8111	Workmen's Circle Call
0043-812X	Works†
0043-8146	Workshop *see* 0308-6283
0043-8154	World
0043-8162	World†
0043-8170	Canada & the World
0043-8189	World Affairs
0043-8200	World Affairs
0043-8219	World Agricultural Economics and Rural Sociology Abstracts
0043-8227	World Agriculture /Agriculture dans le Monde *changed to* World Agriculture /I F A P News
0043-8235	World and the School
0043-8243	World Archaeology
0043-826X	World Aviation Directory
0043-8278	World Bowls Magazine
0043-8286	World Buddhism†
0043-8294	World Calendar of Forthcoming Meetings: Metallurgical and Related Fields *changed to* World Calendar of Forthcoming Meetings: Metallurgy and Materials Science
0043-8308	World Call *see* 0092-8372
0043-8324	World Christian Digest†
0043-8332	World Christian Education†
0043-8340	World Coffee & Tea
0043-8359	World Coins†
0043-8375	World Construction *see* 0020-6415
0043-8383	World Convention Dates *changed to* Convention World
0043-8391	World Crops *changed to* Agriculture International
0043-8405	World Dredging & Marine Construction
0043-8413	World Encounter
0043-8421	World Farming *changed to* Agribusiness Worldwide
0043-843X	World Federalist *see* 0252-9505
0043-8448	World Federation
0043-8464	World Fellowship of Buddhists Review
0043-8472	World Fisheries Abstracts†
0043-8480	World Fishing
0043-8502	World Health
0043-8510	World Health Statistics Report *see* 0379-8070
0043-8529	World Highways
0043-8537	World Hunger *changed to* Action for Development
0043-8561	World Industrial Reporter
0043-857X	World Informo
0043-8588	World Irrigation†
0043-8596	World Jewry†
0043-860X	World Journal of Psychosynthesis
0043-8634	World Leprosy News†
0043-8642	World Marxist Review
0043-8669	World Medicine
0043-8677	World Meetings: Outside United States and Canada
0043-8685	World Meetings: Social and Behavioral Sciences, Education and Management *see* 0194-6161
0043-8693	World Meetings: United States and Canada
0043-8707	World Mining *changed to* World Mining Equipment
0043-874X	World News of the Week *changed to* World Newsmap of the Week
0043-8758	World Metal Statistics
0043-8774	World of Music
0043-8782	World of Pretzels†
0043-8790	World Oil
0043-8804	World Order
0043-8812	New World Outlook
0043-8820	World Over†
0043-8839	World Parish
0043-8847	World Petroleum†
0043-8855	International Oil News *changed to* International Oil News: Management Edition
0043-8871	World Politics
0043-888X	World Ports *changed to* W W S/World Wide Shipping
0043-8898	World-Product Casts *changed to* Worldcasts: Product Edition
0043-8901	World Progress
0043-891X	World Radio Bulletin†
0043-8928	World Refrigeration and Air Conditioning†
0043-8936	World-Regional Casts *changed to* Worldcasts: Regional Edition
0043-8944	World Report on Technical Advancement
0043-8952	Credit Union World Reporter
0043-8979	World Review of Animal Production
0043-8987	World Revolution†
0043-8995	World Scouting
0043-9002	World Scouting Newsletter
0043-9010	World Ships on Order
0043-9029	World Shopping *changed to* World Shopping Encyclopedia
0043-9037	World Soccer
0043-9045	World Space Directory Including Oceanology†
0043-9053	World Sports *changed to* Sportsworld
0043-9061	World Stamps
0043-907X	W S C F Newsletter†
0043-9088	World Surface Coating Abstracts
0043-9096	World Survey
0043-910X	World Tennis
0043-9118	World Textile Abstracts
0043-9126	World Tobacco
0043-9134	World Today
0043-9142	World Trade
0043-9150	World Trade Bulletin
0043-9169	World Travel†
0043-9177	World Traveler†
0043-9185	World Union
0043-9215	World Vision
0043-9223	World War II Historical Association. Newsletter *changed to* World War Enthusiast 1939-1945
0043-9231	World Week *changed to* Scholastic Update
0043-9258	World Wood
0043-9274	World Youth
0043-9282	Worldmission†
0043-9290	World's Children
0043-9304	World's Fair
0043-9312	Worlds of If†
0043-9320	World's Paper Trade Review *see* 0306-8234
0043-9339	World's Poultry Science Journal
0043-9355	Worldwide Art Book Bibliography†
0043-9363	Worldwide Art Catalogue Bulletin
0043-9371	Worldwide Marketing Horizons†
0043-9398	Worldwide Projects and Installation Planning *see* 0091-4800
0043-9401	Wormwood Review
0043-941X	Worship
0043-9428	Das Wort fuer Heute†
0043-9444	Wort und Weg
0043-9452	Wrangler's Roost
0043-9460	Wrecking & Salvage Journal
0043-9479	Wrestler†
0043-9495	Wretched Mess News†
0043-9509	Wright Advisory Report *changed to* Wright Bankers' Service
0043-9517	Writer (Boston)
0043-9525	Writer's Digest
0043-9533	Writers Guild of America, West. Newsletter
0043-9541	Writers Newsletter *changed to* J R G Newsletter
0043-9568	Writer's Review *see* 0260-2776
0043-9576	Writers' World
0043-9592	Wszechswiat
0043-9606	Wuerttembergisches Wochenblatt fuer Landwirtschaft
0043-9614	Wuerzburg-Heute
0043-9622	Das Wuestenrot-Heim
0043-9630	Wychowanie Fizyczne i Sport. Studia i Materialy
0043-9649	Wynalazczosc; Racjonalizacja *changed to* Temat - Wynalazczosc i Racjonalizacja
0043-9657	Wynboer
0043-9665	Wyoming Archaeologist
0043-9673	Wyoming Beverage Analyst
0043-9681	Wyoming Education News
0043-969X	Wyoming Educator
0043-9703	Wyoming Employment Outlook†
0043-9711	Wyoming Future Farmer†
0043-972X	Wyoming History News
0043-9738	Wyoming Library Roundup
0043-9754	Wyoming P T A News†
0043-9762	Big Wyoming Progress Reports *changed to* Wyoming Progress Report
0043-9770	Wyoming Rural Electric News
0043-9797	Pulse *changed to* Medical Wire
0043-9800	Wyoming Stockman Farmer
0043-9819	Wyoming Wildlife
0043-9827	Wyoming Wool Grower
0043-9851	X-Ray Fluorescence Spectrometry Abstracts
0043-986X	Xaloc
0043-9878	Xaverian†
0043-9886	Xaverian Weekly
0043-9916	Y.M.H.A. Bulletin *changed to* Y Bulletin
0043-9924	Y W C A Magazine†
0043-9932	Yacht
0043-9940	Yachting
0043-9959	Yachting
0043-9975	Yachting Italiano-Atomare *changed to* Yachting Italiano
0043-9983	Yachting Monthly
0043-9991	Yachting World
0044-0000	Yachts and Yachting
0044-0019	Yachtsman's Wife†
0044-0027	Yadernaya Fizika
0044-0035	Practical Pharmacy
0044-0043	Pharmacy Companion
0044-0051	Yale Alumni Magazine
0044-006X	Yale Economic Essays†
0044-0078	Yale French Studies
0044-0086	Yale Journal of Biology and Medicine
0044-0094	Yale Law Journal
0044-0108	Yale Literary Magazine *see* 0148-4605
0044-0124	Yale Review
0044-0132	Yale Review of Law and Social Action†
0044-0140	Yale Scientific Magazine *see* 0091-0287
0044-0167	Yale/Theatre *see* 0161-0775
0044-0175	Yale University Library Gazette
0044-0183	Yamashina Institute for Ornithology. Miscellaneous Reports *changed to* Yamashina Institute for Ornithology. Journal
0044-0191	Yankee
0044-0205	Yankee Oilman
0044-0213	Yaqeen International
0044-023X	Yarn (Your Auckland Railway News)
0044-0256	Yavneh Studies
0044-0280	Rashut ha-Nemalim be-Yisrael, Yedion *changed to* Nemalim be-Israel. Berashut
0044-0310	Yememhiran Dimts
0044-0329	Yememhiran Melkt
0044-0337	Yeni Sinema
0044-0345	Yeon-Gu Weolbo
0044-0353	Yes *see* 0315-467X
0044-0361	Yesodot†
0044-037X	Yesteryears
0044-0388	Yevanhelskyj Ranok
0044-0396	Yhteishyva
0044-040X	Yid
0044-0418	Yiddishe Heim
0044-0426	Yiddishe Kultur
0044-0434	Yiddisher Kemfer
0044-0442	Yidishe Shprakh
0044-0469	Yleiselektroniikka *changed to* Elektroniikkauutiset
0044-0485	Yoga
0044-0493	Yoga Institute. Journal *changed to* Yoga and Total Health
0044-0507	Yoga - Mimamsa
0044-0515	Yojana
0044-0523	Yokohama Mathematical Journal
0044-0531	Yokohama Medical Bulletin
0044-054X	Yontev Bleter
0044-0558	Yonago Medical Association. Journal
0044-0574	Yorker News *changed to* Heritage (Cooperstown)
0044-0582	Yorkshire Architect
0044-0590	Bulletin of Economic Research
0044-0612	Yorkshire Journal
0044-0620	Yorkshire Life
0044-0639	Yorkshire Ridings Magazine
0044-0647	Yorkshire Terrier Quarterly†
0044-0663	Monthly Statistics of Paper Distribution
0044-0671	Fish Culture
0044-068X	You and Your World†
0044-0698	Welcome to Cyprus
0044-0701	You†
0044-071X	T Q
0044-0728	Young Children
0044-0736	Young Citizen
0044-0744	Young Citizen *changed to* Scholastic News: News Citizen
0044-0752	Young Engineer & Scientist
0044-0760	Young Folk†
0044-0787	Young Ideas
0044-0795	Young India
0044-0809	Young Israel Viewpoint
0044-0817	Young Judaean
0044-0833	Young Miss *see* 0888-5842
0044-0841	Young Musicians
0044-0876	Young Scotland†
0044-0884	Young Socialist
0044-0892	Young Socialist - The Organizer *see* 0360-0157
0044-0906	Young Soldier
0044-0914	Young Sower *changed to* Search
0044-0922	Young Teen Power *changed to* Teen Power (1979)
0044-0957	Young Writer
0044-0973	Youngstown Jewish Times
0044-0981	Your Astrology†
0044-099X	Your Business†
0044-1007	Your Child
0044-1015	Your Edmundite Missions News Letter
0044-1031	Your Garden
0044-104X	Your Health
0044-1058	Your Library Presents†
0044-1074	Your New Baby†
0044-1082	Your Personal Astrology Magazine
0044-1090	International Rider and Driver *see* 0094-3355
0044-1104	Your Public Schools
0044-1112	Your Schools
0044-1139	You're the Critic†
0044-1155	Youth Aliyah Review
0044-1171	Youth and Nation
0044-118X	Youth & Society
0044-1201	Youth Chronicle
0044-121X	Youth Happiness *changed to* Young & Alive (Large Print Edition)
0044-1228	Youth Hosteller *changed to* Y H A Magazine
0044-1236	Youth in Action†
0044-1244	Youth Life *changed to* Union of Yugoslav Youth. Newsletter

1324 ISSN INDEX

0044-1252 Youth Program Service *changed to* Emmaus Letter
0044-1260 Youth Review
0044-1309 Yritystalous *see* 0358-4208
0044-1317 Yrkesopplaering *see* 0332-5814
0044-1325 Yudhagama
0044-1333 Yugoslav Life
0044-1341 Yugoslav Survey
0044-135X Yugoslav Trade Unions
0044-1368 Yugoslavia Export†
0044-1376 Yukon News
0044-1384 Yunak
0044-1392 Yunyi Naturalist
0044-1406 Yunyi Tekhnik
0044-1414 Yuvak
0044-1422 Z
0044-1449 Zeitschrift fuer Dialektologie und Linguistik
0044-1457 Informationsdienst Bibliothekswesen
0044-1465 Z I S Mitteilungen
0044-1473 Z Naszej Oficyny†
0044-1481 Z Otchlani Wiekow
0044-149X Z Pola Walki
0044-1503 Z Prac Zakladu Nauk Ekonomicznych PAN†
0044-1511 Z V und Z V
0044-152X Za Domovinu
0044-1538 Za i Przeciw
0044-1554 Za Rubezhom
0044-1562 Zaaier
0044-1570 Zacchia†
0044-1589 Zadarska Revija
0044-1597 Zagadnienia Drgan Nieliniowych
0044-1600 Zagadnienia Ekonomiki Rolnej
0044-1619 Zagadnienia Naukoznawstwa
0044-1627 Zagaglia
0044-1651 Zahnaerztliche Praxis
0044-166X Z W R
0044-1678 Der Zahnarzt
0044-1686 Zahntechnik
0044-1694 Zahradnicke Listy *changed to* Zahradnictvo
0044-1708 Zabrana Skod
0044-1716 Zajednica
0044-1724 Zambia Library Service Bulletin†
0044-1732 Zambia Mail *changed to* Zambia Daily Mail
0044-1783 Zapatos y Zapaterias
0044-1791 Zapiski Historyczne
0044-1805 Vsesoyuznoe Mineralogicheskoe Obshchestvo. Zapiski
0044-1813 Zapowiedzi Wydawnicze
0044-1821 Zaragoza
0044-183X Zaranie Slaskie
0044-1848 Zarja
0044-1856 Zashchita Metallov
0044-1864 Zashchita Rastenii
0044-1872 Zastita
0044-1880 Zastita Rada
0044-1899 Zastosowania Matematyki
0044-1902 Zavarivanje
0044-1910 Zavodskaya Laboratoriya
0044-1929 Zbior Dokumentow
0044-1937 Zbornik za Drustvene Nauke
0044-1945 Zdorov'e
0044-1953 Zdravie
0044-1961 Zdravookhranenie Belorussii
0044-197X Zdravookhranenie Rossiiskoi Federatsii
0044-1988 Zdravotni Technika a Vzduchotechnika
0044-1996 Zdravotnicke Noviny
0044-2011 Zdrowie Publiczne
0044-202X Zealandia
0044-2038 Zeichen der Zeit
0044-2046 Zeichnen in Technik, Architektur, Vermessung *changed to* Zeichnen Fachzeitschrift fuer Alle Bereiche Technischen Zeichnens
0044-2054 Zeiss Information
0044-2062 Zeiss-Mitteilungen ueber Fortschritte der Technischen Optik†
0044-2070 Die Zeit
0044-2089 Die Zeit im Buch
0044-2097 Zeit- und Kulturarchiv *changed to* Internationales Handbuch - Zeitarchiv
0044-2100 ZeitBild
0044-2119 Zeitgeist†
0044-2127 Zeitschrift des Bernischen Juristenvereins
0044-2135 Deutscher Verein fuer Kunstwissenschaft. Zeitschrift
0044-2151 Journal of Agronomy and Crop Science
0044-216X Zeitschrift fuer Aegyptische Sprache und Altertumskunde
0044-2178 Zeitschrift fuer Aerztliche Fortbildung
0044-2186 Zeitschrift fuer Aesthetik und allgemeine Kunstwissenschaft
0044-2194 Zeitschrift fuer Agrargeschichte und Agrarsoziologie
0044-2216 Zeitschrift fuer Allgemeine Wissenschaftstheorie
0044-2224 Zeitschrift fuer Alternsforschung
0044-2232 Zeitschrift fuer Anatomie und Entwicklungsgeschichte *see* 0340-2061
0044-2240 Journal of Applied Entomology
0044-2259 Zeitschrift fuer Angewandte Geologie
0044-2267 Zeitschrift fuer Angewandte Mathematik und Mechanik
0044-2275 Zeitschrift fuer Angewandte Mathematik und Physik
0044-2283 Zeitschrift fuer Angewandte Physik *see* 0721-7250
0044-2291 Zeitschrift fuer Angewandte Zoologie
0044-2305 Anglistik und Amerikanistik. Zeitschrift
0044-2313 Zeitschrift fuer Anorganische und Allgemeine Chemie
0044-2321 Zeitschrift fuer Arbeitsrecht und Sozialrecht
0044-233X Zeitschrift fuer Archaeologie
0044-2348 Zeitschrift fuer Auslaendisches Oeffentliches Recht und Voelkerrecht
0044-2356 Zeitschrift fuer Balkanologie
0044-2364 Zeitschrift fuer Bayerische Landesgeschichte
0044-2372 Zeitschrift fuer Betriebswirtschaft
0044-2380 Zeitschrift fuer Bibliothekswesen und Bibliographie
0044-2399 Zeitschrift fuer Bienenforschung *see* 0044-8435
0044-2402 Zeitschrift fuer Chemie
0044-2410 Zeitschrift fuer das Gesamte Familienrecht
0044-2429 Zeitschrift fuer das Gesamte Genossenschaftswesen
0044-2437 Zeitschrift fuer das Gesamte Handelsrecht und Wirtschaftsrecht
0044-2461 Zeitschrift fuer den Erdkundeunterricht
0044-247X Zeitschrift fuer den Lastenausgleich
0044-2496 Zeitschrift fuer Deutsche Philologie
0044-2518 Zeitschrift fuer Deutsches Altertum und Deutsche Literatur
0044-2526 Zeitschrift fuer die Alttestamentliche Wissenschaft
0044-2534 Zeitschrift fuer die Gesamte Experimentelle Medizin Einschliesslich Experimenteller Chirurgie *see* 0300-9130
0044-2542 Zeitschrift fuer die Gesamte Innere Medizin und ihre Grenzgebiete
0044-2550 Journal of Institutional and Theoretical Economics
0044-2585 Zeitschrift fuer die Gesamte Versicherungswissenschaft
0044-2593 Zeitschrift fuer die Geschichte der Juden†
0044-2615 Zeitschrift fuer die Neutestamentliche Wissenschaft und die Kunde der Aelteren Kirche
0044-2623 Zeitschrift fuer die Zuckerindustrie *see* 0344-8657
0044-2631 Zeitschrift fuer Erkrankungen der Atmungsorgane
0044-264X Zeitschrift fuer Ernaehrungswissenschaft
0044-2658 Erzmetall
0044-2666 Zeitschrift fuer Ethnologie
0044-2674 Zeitschrift fuer Evangelische Ethik
0044-2682 Zeitschrift fuer Evangelische Rundfunk- und Fernseharbeit Medium *see* 0025-8350
0044-2690 Zeitschrift fuer Evangelisches Kirchenrecht
0044-2704 Zeitschrift fuer Experimentelle Chirurgie
0044-2712 Zeitschrift fuer Experimentelle und Angewandte Psychologie
0044-2720 Zeitschrift fuer Fischerei und deren Hilfswissenschaften†
0044-2739 Zeitschrift fuer Flugwissenschaften
0044-2747 Zeitschrift fuer Franzoesische Sprache und Literatur
0044-2755 Zeitschrift fuer Fremdenverkehr
0044-2763 Zeitschrift fuer Ganzheitsforschung
0044-2771 Zeitschrift fuer Gastroenterologie
0044-278X Zeitschrift fuer Geburtshilfe und Gynaekologie *see* 0300-967X
0044-2801 Zeitschrift fuer Geophysik *see* 0340-062X
0044-281X Zeitschrift fuer Gerontologie
0044-2828 Zeitschrift fuer Geschichtswissenschaft
0044-2836 Zeitschrift fuer Gletscherkunde und Glazialgeologie
0044-2844 Zeitschrift fuer Haut- und Geschlechtskrankheiten *see* 0301-0481
0044-2852 Zeitschrift fuer Heereskunde
0044-2860 Zeitschrift fuer Hoergeraete Akustik *see* 0172-8261
0044-2887 Zeitschrift fuer Jagdwissenschaft
0044-2895 Zeitschrift fuer katholische Theologie
0044-2909 Zeitschrift fuer Kinderchirurgie und Grenzgebiete *see* 0174-3082
0044-2925 Zeitschrift fuer Kirchengeschichte
0044-2941 Zeitschrift fuer Krankenpflege/Revue Suisse des Infirmieres *changed to* Krankenpflege
0044-295X Zeitschrift fuer Kreislaufforschung *see* 0300-5860
0044-2968 Zeitschrift fuer Kristallographie
0044-2976 Zeitschrift fuer Kulturaustausch
0044-2984 Zeitschrift fuer Kulturtechnik und Flurbereinigung
0044-2992 Zeitschrift fuer Kunstgeschichte
0044-300X Zeitschrift fuer Landeskultur†
0044-3018 Zeitschrift fuer Laryngologie, Rhinologie, Otologie und ihre Grenzgebiete *changed to* Laryngologie, Rhinologie, Otologie
0044-3026 Zeitschrift fuer Lebensmittel Untersuchung und-Forschung
0044-3034 Zeitschrift fuer Luftrecht und Weltraumrechtsfragen *see* 0340-8329
0044-3042 Zeitschrift fuer Markt, Meinungs- und Zukunftsforschung
0044-3050 Zeitschrift fuer Mathematische Logik und Grundlagen der Mathematik. Zeitschrift
0044-3069 Zeitschrift fuer Medizinische Labortechnik *see* 0323-5637
0044-3077 Zeitschrift fuer Medizinische Mikrobiologie und Immunologie *see* 0300-8584
0044-3085 Zeitschrift fuer Menschenkunde und Zentralblatt fuer Graphologie, Ausdruckswissenschaft und Charakterkunde *changed to* Zeitschrift fuer Menschenkunde. Zentralblatt fuer Schriftpsychologie und Schriftvergleichung
0044-3093 Zeitschrift fuer Metallkunde
0044-3107 Zeitschrift fuer Mikroskopisch-Anatomische Forschung
0044-3115 Zeitschrift fuer Militaergeschichte *changed to* Militaergeschichte
0044-3123 Zeitschrift fuer Missionswissenschaft und Religionswissenschaft
0044-3131 Zeitschrift fuer Morphologie der Tiere *see* 0720-213X
0044-314X Zeitschrift fuer Morphologie und Anthropologie
0044-3158 Journal of Economics (New York)
0044-3166 Zeitschrift fuer Naturforschung. Ausgabe A. *see* 0340-4811
0044-3174 Zeitschrift fuer Naturforschung. Ausgabe B. *see* 0340-5087
0044-3182 Zeitschrift fuer Naturheilkunde
0044-3190 Zeitschrift fuer Niederdeutsche Familienkunde *changed to* Nordeutsche Familienkunde in Verbindung mit der Zeitschrift fuer Niederdeutsche Familienkunde
0044-3204 Zeitschrift fuer Oeffentliche Fuersorge
0044-3220 Zeitschrift fuer Orthopaedie und ihre Grenzgebiete
0044-3239 Zeitschrift fuer Ostforschung
0044-3247 Zeitschrift fuer Paedagogik
0044-3255 Zeitschrift fuer Parasitenkunde
0044-3263 Zeitschrift fuer Pflanzenernaehrung und Bodenkunde
0044-3271 Zeitschrift fuer Pflanzenkrankheiten und Pflanzenschutz
0044-328X Zeitschrift fuer Pflanzenphysiologie *changed to* Journal of Plant Physiology
0044-3301 Zeitschrift fuer Philosophische Forschung
0044-331X Zeitschrift fuer Phonetik, Sprachwissenschaft und Kommunikationsforschung
0044-3328 Zeitschrift fuer Physik. *see* 0340-2193
0044-3336 Zeitschrift fuer Physikalische Chemie
0044-3344 Zeitschrift fuer Physikalische Medizin†
0044-3360 Zeitschrift fuer Politik
0044-3379 Zeitschrift fuer Praeventivmedizin *changed to* Sozial- und Praeventivmedizin
0044-3387 Zeitschrift fuer Praktische Anaesthesie, Wiederbelebung und Intensivtherapie *see* 0174-1837
0044-3395 Zeitschrift fuer Psycho-Somatische Medizin *see* 0340-5613
0044-3409 Zeitschrift fuer Psychologie
0044-3417 Zeitschrift fuer Psychotherapie und Medizinische Psychologie *see* 0173-7937
0044-3425 Zeitschrift fuer Radiaesthesie
0044-3433 Zeitschrift fuer Rechtsmedizin
0044-3441 Zeitschrift fuer Religions- und Geistesgeschichte
0044-345X Zeitschrift fuer Rheumaforschung *see* 0340-1855
0044-3468 Zeitschrift fuer Saeugetierkunde
0044-3476 Zeitschrift fuer Schweizerische Archaeologie und Kunstgeschichte
0044-3484 Zeitschrift fuer Schweizerische Kirchengeschichte
0044-3492 Zeitschrift fuer Slavische Philologie
0044-3506 Zeitschrift fuer Slawistik
0044-3522 Zeitschrift fuer Sozialberatung†
0044-3557 Zeitschrift fuer Therapie†
0044-3565 Zeitschrift fuer Tierphysiologie, Tierernaehrung und Futtermittelkunde
0044-3573 Zeitschrift fuer Tierpsychologie *see* 0179-1613
0044-3581 Zeitschrift fuer Tierzuechtung und Zuechtungsbiologie
0044-359X Zeitschrift fuer Tropenmedizin und Parasitologie *see* 0177-2392
0044-3603 Zeitschrift fuer Unfallmedizin und Berufskrankheiten
0044-3611 Zeitschrift fuer Urologie und Nephrologie
0044-362X Zeitschrift fuer Vergleichende Physiologie *see* 0340-7594
0044-362X Zeitschrift fuer Vergleichende Physiologie *changed to* Journal of Comparative Physiology. B: Biochemical, Systematic, and Environmental Physiology
0044-3638 Zeitschrift fuer Vergleichende Rechtswissenschaft
0044-3646 Zeitschrift fuer Vergleichende Sprachforschung
0044-3654 Zeitschrift fuer Verkehrssicherheit
0044-3662 Zeitschrift fuer Verkehrsrecht
0044-3670 Zeitschrift fuer Verkehrswissenschaft
0044-3697 Zeitschrift fuer Versuchstierkunde
0044-3700 Zeitschrift fuer Volkskunde
0044-3719 Zeitschrift fuer Wahrscheinlichkeitstheorie und Verwandte Gebiete *see* 0178-8051
0044-3727 Zeitschrift fuer Wasser- und Abwasserforschung

ISSN INDEX

ISSN	Title
0044-3743	Z W F/C I M
0044-3751	Zeitschrift fuer Wirtschaftsgeographie
0044-376X	Microscopica Acta†
0044-3778	Zeitschrift fuer Wissenschaftliche Zoologie. Abteilung A†
0044-3786	Zeitschrift fuer Wuerttembergische Landesgeschichte
0044-3794	Zeitschrift fuer Zellforschung und Mikroskopische Anatomie see 0302-766X
0044-3808	Zeitschrift fuer Zoologische Systematik und Evolutionsforschung
0044-3816	Zeitschrift Interne Revision
0044-3824	Zeitschriftendienst Musik
0044-3832	Zeitungs- und Zeitschriftenhandel see 0341-8073
0044-3840	Zeitwende/Die Neue Furche changed to Zeitwende
0044-3867	Zellstoff und Papier
0044-3875	Zemedelska Skola
0044-3883	Zemedelska Technika
0044-3891	Zemedelska a Lesni Zamestnanec changed to Socialisticky Zemedelec
0044-3905	Zement-Kalk-Gips see 0722-4400
0044-3913	Zemledelie
0044-3921	Zemlja Sovjeta
0044-3948	Zemlya i Vselennaya
0044-3956	Zen Bow changed to Zen Bow Newsletter
0044-3972	Zending changed to Vandaar
0044-3980	Zenit
0044-3999	Zenit†
0044-4006	Zenken Journal
0044-4022	Zentralblatt fuer Aero- und Astronautik†
0044-4030	Zentralblatt fuer Allgemeine Pathologie und Pathologische Anatomie
0044-4049	Zentralblatt fuer Arbeitsmedizin und Arbeitsschutz see 0340-7047
0044-4081	Zentralblatt fuer Bibliothekswesen
0044-409X	Zentralblatt fuer Chirurgie
0044-4103	Zentralblatt fuer Didaktik der Mathematik
0044-4111	Zentralblatt fuer die Gesamte Kinderheilkunde see 0722-8953
0044-412X	Zentralblatt fuer die Gesamte Neurologie und Psychiatrie see 0722-3064
0044-4138	Zentralblatt fuer die Gesamte Ophthalmologie und ihre Grenzgebiete see 0722-9933
0044-4146	Zentralblatt fuer die Gesamte Radiologie see 0722-3072
0044-4154	Zentralblatt fuer die Gesamte Rechtsmedizin und ihre Grenzgebiete see 0722-3056
0044-4189	Zentralblatt fuer Geologie und Palaeontologie. Teil II: Palaeontologie
0044-4197	Zentralblatt fuer Gynaekologie
0044-4200	Zentralblatt fuer Hals-, Nasen- und Ohrenheilkunde Sowie Deren Grenzgebiete see 0340-5214
0044-4219	Zentralblatt fuer Haut- und Geschlechtskrankheiten Sowie Deren Grenzgebiete /Dermatology changed to Zentralblatt Haut- und Geschlechtskrankheiten/Dermatology
0044-4227	Zentralblatt fuer Industriebau
0044-4235	Zentralblatt fuer Mathematik und ihre Grenzgebiete/Mathematics Abstracts
0044-4251	Zentralblatt fuer Neurochirurgie
0044-426X	Zentralblatt fuer Phlebologie see 0301-1526
0044-4278	Zentralblatt fuer Sozialversicherung, Sozialhilfe und Versorgung
0044-4286	Zentralblatt fuer Verkehrs-Medizin, Verkehrs-Psychologie, Luft- und Raumfahrt-Medizin†
0044-4294	Zentralblatt fuer Veterinaermedizin. see 0721-0981
0044-4294	Zentralblatt fuer Veterinaermedizin see 0721-1856
0044-4308	Zentralorgan fuer die Gesamte Chirurgie und ihre Grenzgebiete see 0722-6985
0044-4316	Zentralsparkasse der Gemeinde Wien. Information
0044-4340	Zero One
0044-4383	Zeszyty Problemowe Gornictwa
0044-4391	Zeszyty Historyczne
0044-4405	Katolicki Uniwersytet Lubelski. Zeszyty Naukowe
0044-4413	Fasciculi Mathematici
0044-443X	Zeszyty Teoretyczno-Polityczne see 0137-3609
0044-4448	Zheleznodorozhnyi Transport
0044-4456	Zhenshchiny Mira
0044-4464	Zhilishchnoe i Kommunal'noe Khozyaistvo
0044-4472	Zhilishchnoe Stroitel'stvo
0044-4480	Zhivotnovodstvo
0044-4499	Zhovten'
0044-4502	Zhurnal Analiticheskoi Khimii
0044-4510	Zhurnal Eksperimental'noi i Teoreticheskoi Fiziki
0044-4529	Zhurnal Evolyutsionnoi Biokhimii i Fiziologii
0044-4537	Zhurnal Fizicheskoi Khimii
0044-4553	Russkaya Pravoslavnaya Tserkov'. Moskovskaya Patriarkhiya. Zhurnal
0044-4561	Zhurnal Nauchnoi i Prikladnoi Fotografii i Kinematografii
0044-457X	Zhurnal Neorganicheskoi Khimii
0044-4588	Zhurnal Nevropatologii i Psikhiatrii im. S.S. Korsakova
0044-4596	Zhurnal Obshchei Biologii
0044-460X	Zhurnal Obshchei Khimii
0044-4618	Zhurnal Prikladnoi Khimii
0044-4626	Zhurnal Prikladnoi Mekhaniki i Tekhnicheskoi Fiziki
0044-4634	Zhurnal Strukturnoi Khimii
0044-4642	Zhurnal Tekhnicheskoi Fiziki
0044-4650	Zhurnal Ushnykh, Nosovykh i Gorlovykh Boleznei
0044-4669	Zhurnal Vychislitel'noi Matematiki i Matematicheskoi Fiziki
0044-4677	Zhurnal Vysshei Nervnoi Deyatel'nosti
0044-4693	Ziegelindustrie see 0341-0552
0044-4707	Ziekenfondsgids†
0044-4715	Ziekenhuis
0044-4723	Zimbabwe Review changed to Revolution
0044-4731	Zinc Abstracts see 0950-1592
0044-474X	Alte und Neue Zinnfiguren
0044-4758	Zion
0044-4766	Zionist Collegiate†
0044-4774	Zionist Literature
0044-4782	Zionist Record and S.A. Jewish Chronicle
0044-4790	Zion's Herald see 0098-9282
0044-4812	Ziva
0044-4820	Ziviler Bevoelkerungsschutz. ZB†
0044-4839	Zivilverteidigung
0044-4847	Zivocisna Vyroba
0044-4855	Zivot i Skola
0044-4863	Zivotne Prostredie
0044-4871	Zlaty Maj
0044-488X	Znak
0044-4898	Znamya
0044-4928	Zobozdravstveni Vestnik
0044-4936	Zodiac†
0044-4944	Zodiac changed to Helix
0044-4952	Zodiaque
0044-4979	Zolnierz Polski
0044-4995	Zona: Revista de Comercio Latino-Americana
0044-5002	Zondagsmis
0044-5010	Zone
0044-5029	Zoo Anvers
0044-5037	Zoo†
0044-5045	Zoolog see 0315-5064
0044-5053	Zoologia see 0301-2123
0044-5061	Ricerche di Zoologia Applicata alla Caccia changed to Ricerche di Biologia della Selvaggina
0044-5088	Zoologica
0044-5096	Zoologica Africana see 0254-1858
0044-510X	Zoologica Poloniae
0044-5118	Zoological Magazine†
0044-5126	Zoological Society of Southern Africa. News Bulletin changed to Zoological Society of Southern Africa. Occasional Bulletin
0044-5134	Zoologicheskii Zhurnal
0044-5142	Folia Zoologica
0044-5150	Zoologische Beitraege
0044-5169	Der Zoologische Garten
0044-5177	Zoologische Jahrbuecher. Abteilung fuer Anatomie und Ontogenie der Tiere
0044-5185	Zoologische Jahrbuecher. Abteilung fuer Allgemeine Zoologie und Physiologie der Tiere
0044-5193	Zoologische Jahrbuecher. Abteilung fuer Systematik, Oekologie und Geographie der Tiere
0044-5223	Zoologisches Museum Hamburg. Entomologische Mitteilungen
0044-5231	Zoologischer Anzeiger
0044-5258	Zoologisk Revy
0044-5274	Zoon†
0044-5282	Zoonooz
0044-5290	Zooprofilassi†
0044-5304	Zoo's Letter changed to Zoosletter
0044-5312	Zootechnia
0044-5320	Brazil. Instituto de Zootecnia. Zootecnia
0044-5339	Zorgenkind see 0166-4298
0044-5347	Japan Shipping and Shipbuilding changed to Zosen
0044-5355	Zpravodaj V Z L U
0044-5371	Zuchthygiene
0044-538X	Zucker see 0344-8657
0044-5401	Zuechtungskunde
0044-5428	Zuid-Afrika
0044-5436	Zuivelnieuws
0044-5452	Zukunft
0044-5460	Zukunft
0044-5479	Zulqarnain
0044-5487	Zum Nachdenken
0044-5509	Zur Geschichte der Pharmazie see 0341-0099
0044-5517	Zurita
0044-5525	Zvaranie
0044-5533	Zvezdina Revija
0044-555X	Zvuk
0044-5576	Zwingli
0044-5584	Zycie i Mysl
0044-5592	A - Rivista Anarchica
0044-5614	A B C Decor
0044-5622	A B S E E S
0044-5649	A D P Newsletter†
0044-5657	A F - Architekturforum
0044-5681	A I M
0044-569X	A Is A Newsletter changed to A Is A
0044-5711	A R I S
0044-5746	Aboriginal Quarterly†
0044-5762	Revista del Frio
0044-5800	Abstracts of Hungarian Economic Literature
0044-5819	Abstracts on Health Effects of Environmental Pollutants
0044-5827	Abundance
0044-5835	Academy of Parish Clergy. Journal†
0044-5843	Acadia Bulletin
0044-5851	Acadiensis: Journal of the History of the Atlantic Region
0044-586X	Acarologia
0044-5878	Accident Prevention
0044-5894	Accion Empresarial
0044-5908	Accion Indigenista see 0185-058X
0044-5916	Accountants and Secretaries Educational Journal
0044-5924	Accountants" Washington Taxletter†
0044-5932	A C E
0044-5940	Acoma†
0044-5967	Acta Amazonica
0044-5975	Academia Scientiarum Hungarica. Acta Antiqua
0044-5983	Acta Botanica Neerlandica
0044-5991	Acta Histochemica et Cytochemica
0044-6009	Acta Hospitalia
0044-6017	Acta Medica del Valle changed to Colombia Medica
0044-6025	Acta Medica Iranica
0044-6033	Acta Physiologica Polonica†
0044-6041	Acta Socio-Medica Scandinavica see 0300-8037
0044-605X	Acta Veterinaria Scandinavica
0044-6068	Action
0044-6092	Action Era Vehicle
0044-6106	Action Populaire
0044-6130	Actualidade Universitaria†
0044-6149	Actualite de la Medecine Officielle et Medecine Naturelle
0044-6157	Actualite Fiduciaire
0044-6165	Actualites Industrielles Lorraines
0044-6173	Aktuelle Traumatologie
0044-6181	Adam and Eve
0044-6203	Alcoholism and Drug Addiction Research Foundation. Journal changed to Addiction Research Foundation. Journal
0044-6211	Adelaide. National Gallery of South Australia see 0004-3206
0044-622X	Adelaide. Stock Exchange. Official Record†
0044-6238	Adelante (Orlando)
0044-6254	Adhesifs changed to Assemblages Adhesifs
0044-6262	Administracion, Desarrollo, Integracion
0044-6289	A C O A
0044-6300	Administrative Scene
0044-6319	Administrator†
0044-6327	Administrator†
0044-6335	Adolescent Medicine
0044-6343	Adult & Child see 0092-4032
0044-636X	Advanced Technology Libraries
0044-6378	Advances in Urethane Science and Technology
0044-6386	Adventures in Experimental Physics changed to Adventures in Science
0044-6394	Adverse Drug Reaction Bulletin
0044-6408	Ad. Activities†
0044-6416	Advocate (West Vancouver)
0044-6432	Aero News†
0044-6459	Les Affaires
0044-6467	Affirm
0044-6475	Africa
0044-6483	Africa Confidential
0044-6491	Africa Letter
0044-6513	Africa Now see 0711-6683
0044-653X	African Crescent
0044-6556	African Jewish Newspaper
0044-6564	African Journal of Pharmacy and Pharmaceutical Sciences
0044-6580	African Missionary changed to S M A - the African Missionary
0044-6602	African Religious Research†
0044-6610	African Studies Association of the West Indies. Bulletin
0044-6629	African Urban Notes changed to African Urban Studies
0044-6645	Africana i Nordiska Vetenskapliga. Bibliotek see 0348-8691
0044-6661	Afrique et Parole†
0044-667X	Afriscope
0044-6696	After School
0044-670X	Afterthought
0044-6718	Agency Sales/With Agent and Representative see 0162-3656
0044-6726	Agora
0044-6734	Agra University. Bulletin
0044-6742	Agregation
0044-6750	Agri Sept changed to Le Nouvel Agriculteur
0044-6769	Agrichemical Age
0044-6785	Agricultura†
0044-6793	Agricultura em Sao Paulo
0044-6807	Agricultural Engineering Australia
0044-6823	Agriculture and Farming†
0044-6831	Agrifack
0044-684X	Agrologist
0044-6858	Agronomia Mocambicana
0044-6874	Agronomist
0044-6882	Agrosintesis
0044-6890	Agua
0044-6904	Ahead: Australian Health Advisory Digest†
0044-6912	Aichi-Gakuin Journal of Dental Science
0044-6920	Aikamerkki
0044-6963	Air Enthusiast see 0306-5634
0044-6971	Air et Cosmos
0044-698X	Air over Arizona†
0044-7005	Airfair Interline

ISSN INDEX

ISSN	Title
0044-7013	Airline Passengers Association News *changed to* A P A Holiday
0044-7021	Airport Report
0044-703X	Laisve†
0044-7048	Akron Business and Economic Review
0044-7064	Alaluz
0044-7072	Albania Today
0044-7080	Alberta Bowhunter and Archer
0044-7099	Alberta Builder†
0044-7129	Alberta Education Council. Newsletter†
0044-7137	A H E A Newsletter
0044-7145	Alberta Landrace Association. Newsletter
0044-7153	Alberta, Lands, Forests, Parks, Wildlife†
0044-7161	A M T A News Bulletin *see* 0709-4272
0044-7218	Alcheringa†
0044-7226	Alcoholism & Alcohol Education
0044-7234	Alert (Wahroonga)
0044-7242	Alert (Crows Nest) *changed to* Wormald Journal
0044-7250	Alexandria Journal of Agricultural Research
0044-7277	Alianza Federal de Pueblos Libres. Vox de la Alianza
0044-7293	All India Institute of Medical Sciences, New Delhi. Bulletin†
0044-7307	All India Ophthalmological Society. Journal *see* 0301-4738
0044-734X	Alliance
0044-7358	Allo Dix-Huit
0044-7374	Alm und Weide *changed to* Alm und Bergbauer
0044-7382	Alternative *see* 0148-8414
0044-7390	Alternatives Journal *changed to* Guide to Self-Directed Living Bulletin
0044-7412	Amanuensis†
0044-7439	Ambassador†
0044-7447	Ambio
0044-7455	Ambulance *changed to* Ambulance Service Journal
0044-7463	Amenagement et Nature
0044-7471	Amerasia Journal
0044-748X	Latinskaya Amerika
0044-7498	American Academic Association for Peace in the Middle East. Bulletin *see* 0097-9791
0044-7501	American Alumni Council Commentary†
0044-751X	American Antiquarian Society. Proceedings
0044-7528	American-Arab Association for Commerce & Industry. Bulletin
0044-7536	A A M Bulletin *changed to* Aviso
0044-7544	American Baby
0044-7552	A B A Bulletin *see* 0045-1312
0044-7560	A L I-A B A/C L E Review
0044-7579	AMCHAM Journal *changed to* Business Journal
0044-7587	A C S Single Article Announcement
0044-7595	S C A L A C S
0044-7609	A C A Journal of Chiropractic *see* 0744-9984
0044-7617	American Chronicle†
0044-7625	American Cinemeditor
0044-7633	American Classical Review
0044-7641	Nurses Association of the American College of Obstetricians and Gynecologists. Bulletin News *see* 0884-2175
0044-765X	American Cotton Grower *see* 0194-9772
0044-7676	American Federation of Television and Radio Artists. A F T R A *changed to* AFTRA
0044-7684	American Film Institute Report†
0044-7692	American Fisheries Society. Newsletter *see* 0363-2415
0044-7714	American Indian Crafts and Culture *see* 0099-0361
0044-7722	A S†
0044-7749	American Laboratory
0044-7757	A L A Zurnals†
0044-7765	A M A Update†
0044-7773	American Notary
0044-7781	Nursing Research Report†
0044-779X	American Philological Association. Directory of Members
0044-7803	American Politics Quarterly
0044-7811	American Postal Worker
0044-782X	A P W A Washington Report *see* 0160-001X
0044-7838	American Revolution†
0044-7854	A S E A Newsletter†
0044-7889	A S M News (Metals Park)
0044-7897	A S M News
0044-7900	American Society for Neo-Hellenic Studies. Newsletter
0044-7919	A S P R Newsletter
0044-7927	A S T R Newsletter
0044-7935	American Society of Architectural Hardware Consultants. News and Views *see* 0361-5294
0044-7943	American Society of Cartographers. Bulletin
0044-7951	American Society of Civil Engineers. Engineering Mechanics Division. Journal *see* 0733-9399
0044-796X	American Society of Civil Engineers. Hydraulics Division. Journal *see* 0733-9429
0044-7978	American Society of Civil Engineers. Irrigation and Drainage Division. Journal *see* 0733-9437
0044-7986	American Society of Civil Engineers. Sanitary Engineering Division. Journal *see* 0733-9372
0044-7994	American Society of Civil Engineers. Soil Mechanics and Foundation Division. Journal *see* 0733-9410
0044-8001	American Society of Civil Engineers. Structural Division. Journal *see* 0733-9445
0044-801X	American Society of Civil Engineers. Transportation Engineering Division. Journal *see* 0733-947X
0044-8028	American Society of Civil Engineers. Waterways, Harbors, and Coastal Engineering Division. Journal *see* 0733-950X
0044-8044	American Society of Planning Officials. A S P O Planning Advisory Service *see* 0460-8266
0044-8052	A S D A Newsletter *see* 0277-3627
0044-8060	American Studies in Scandinavia
0044-8079	American Zionist Federation. News and Views
0044-8087	Ami de la Boulangerie *changed to* Nouvelles de la Boulangerie
0044-8095	Ami des Jardins et de la Maison
0044-8117	Ami du Charcutier, du Boucher et du Salaisonnier *changed to* Ami du Professionnel en Alimentation
0044-8125	Amino Acids, Peptide and Protein Abstracts *see* 0143-3326
0044-8133	Amis d'Andre Gide. Bulletin
0044-815X	Ampute de Guerre
0044-8168	Amra
0044-8176	Analecta Linguistica
0044-8184	Anales de Ortopedia y Traumatologia
0044-8192	Analysen und Prognosen ueber die Welt von Morgen
0044-8206	Anapress
0044-8214	Anasthesiologische Praxis *see* 0303-6200
0044-8222	Ancestor
0044-8249	Angewandte Chemie
0044-8257	A.C.A. Review
0044-8265	Anglo-Soviet Journal
0044-8273	Anglo-Ukranian News†
0044-8281	Angola Bulletin *see* 0166-0373
0044-829X	Animal Defence League of Canada. News Bulletin
0044-832X	Annals of Economic and Social Measurement†
0044-8338	Annals of Immunology *see* 0324-8534
0044-8346	Irish Booklore *changed to* Irish Booklore - New Series
0044-8362	Antepasados
0044-8370	Anthropological Society of Oxford. Journal
0044-8389	Antioquia Medica
0044-8400	Apartment News *changed to* Apartment Owner-Builder
0044-8419	Apero†
0044-8427	Apiculture in Western Australia†
0044-8435	Apidologie
0044-8451	Applied Radiology *see* 0160-9963
0044-8486	Aquaculture
0044-8508	Aquarium Society of New South Wales, Monthly Journal
0044-8516	Aquatic Sciences and Fisheries Abstracts *see* 0140-5373
0044-8516	Aquatic Sciences and Fisheries Abstracts *see* 0140-5381
0044-8524	Aqui
0044-8540	Arab-Canada Newsletter *see* 0703-9018
0044-8559	Arab News†
0044-8567	Arbetsgivaren *see* 0349-6740
0044-8575	West Virginia University. Department of Biology. Arboretum Newsletter *changed to* West Virginia University. Department of Biology. Core Arboretum Bulletin
0044-8591	Archaeology in Montana
0044-8605	Archeologicke Rozhledy
0044-8613	Archipel
0044-8621	Architect
0044-863X	Architectura
0044-8648	A A Notes†
0044-8672	Architekt
0044-8680	Architektura a Urbanizmus
0044-8699	Archiv Orientalni
0044-8702	Archives Medicales de Normandie†
0044-8710	Archives of Child Health
0044-8729	Archives of Labor History and Urban Affairs Newsletter *changed to* Archives of Labor and Urban Affairs Newsletter
0044-8737	Archivio Storico Siracusano
0044-8745	Archivium Hibernicum
0044-8753	Archivum Mathematicum
0044-8761	Archiwum Procesow Spalania/Archives of Combustion Processes *see* 0208-4198
0044-877X	Arctic Frontiers†
0044-8788	Areas of Concern
0044-8796	Arecanut and Spices Bulletin *changed to* Indian Cocoa, Arecanut & Spices Journal
0044-8818	Argosy Weekly
0044-8826	Argus (College Park) *changed to* Argus Magazine
0044-8850	A S D M Newsletter *changed to* Sonorensis
0044-8869	Arizona Safety Sad-Istics *see* 0147-3743
0044-8877	University of Arizona Library. Bibliographic Bulletin
0044-8885	Ark River Review
0044-8893	Arkansas L P News
0044-8907	Arkansas Poultry Times
0044-8915	Arkkitehtiuutiset
0044-8931	Armed Citizen News
0044-894X	Armenian Observer
0044-8958	Armidale, New South Wales. Teachers' College. Bulletin *changed to* Armidale College of Advanced Education. Bulletin
0044-8966	Armor
0044-8974	Armstrong Logic
0044-8982	Arquivos Fluminenses de Odontologia†
0044-9008	Ars
0044-9016	Art Gallery of Greater Victoria. Bulletin *see* 0317-2031
0044-9024	Art Gallery of Ontario. Coming Events *see* 0829-4437
0044-9032	ARLIS Newsletter *see* 0307-4722
0044-9059	Art Teachers Association of Victoria. Journal *changed to* Interacta
0044-9067	Arte Nuova Oggi *changed to* Arte Nuova
0044-9075	Artefact
0044-9091	Arthur
0044-9105	Artificial Rainfall Newsletter†
0044-913X	Artistic Pakistan†
0044-9148	Asahi Camera
0044-9164	Asia Focus†
0044-9172	Asia Research Bulletin
0044-9180	Asian Beacon
0044-9199	Asian Development Bank. Newsletter *changed to* A D B Quarterly Review
0044-9202	Asian Music
0044-9210	Asian Periodicals *changed to* Periodicals of Asia and the Pacific
0044-9229	A P O News
0044-9245	Asian Studies Professional Review†
0044-9253	Revista Astronomica
0044-9261	A I T I M Boletin de Informacion Tecnica
0044-9288	A N A B A Boletin *see* 0210-4164
0044-930X	A N E C
0044-9318	Asociacion Peruana de Astronomia. Boletin
0044-9326	Asociacion Rural del Uruguay. Revista
0044-9369	Associacao Brasileira de Educacao Agricola Superior. A B E A S Informa
0044-9393	A C A Reports *changed to* Vantage Point: Issues in American Arts
0044-9407	Association Canadienne des Bibliothecaires de Langue Francaise. Nouvelles de l'A C B L F *see* 0316-0963
0044-9415	Association des Architects de la Province de Quebec. Bulletin *see* 0316-9200
0044-9423	Archives
0044-9458	A.F.E.A.S. Bulletin *see* 0705-3851
0044-9466	Association for Preservation Technology. Bulletin
0044-9482	Association for the Advancement of Agricultural Sciences in Africa. Journal *changed to* African Journal of Agricultural Sciences
0044-9490	A I L A Bulletin
0044-9504	A I O S P Bulletin *see* 0251-2513
0044-9539	Association of British Columbia Librarians. Newsletter†
0044-9547	Association of Canadian Distillers. A C D Bulletin†
0044-9555	Association of Canadian Faculties of Dentistry. Newsletter
0044-9563	A C U Bulletin of Current Documentation (ABCD)
0044-958X	A E N Bulletin *see* 0270-6881
0044-9598	Association of Engineers, India. Journal
0044-9601	A G B Notes
0044-961X	A G B Reports
0044-9628	Association of Law Teachers. Journal *see* 0306-9400
0044-9636	Association of New Jersey Conservation Commissions Newsletter *changed to* A N J E C Report
0044-9652	A R L Minutes
0044-9660	A S L A President's Newsletter†
0044-9687	A T S S Bulletin
0044-9695	A U A Newsletter
0044-9709	Association pour l'Histoire de Belle-Ile-En-Mer. Bulletin Trimestriel
0044-9725	Association Senegalaise pour l'Etude du Quaternaire de l'Ouest African. Bulletin de Liaison *changed to* Association Senegalaise pour l'Etude du Quaternaire Africain. Bulletin de Liaison
0044-9733	Associazione Italiana di Cartografia. A I C Bolletino
0044-9741	A P A C Inform
0044-975X	A I S C A T Informazioni
0044-9768	Astarte†
0044-9776	Asthma Welfarer
0044-9784	Astrological Review
0044-9792	Astrology and Athrishta
0044-9806	Astronomical Society of South Australia. Bulletin
0044-9814	Astronomical Society of Victoria. Journal†
0044-9822	Astronomy & Space†
0044-9830	At Home and Abroad *see* 0306-9028
0044-9849	Atenea
0044-9865	Athenes-Presse Libre†

ISSN INDEX 1327

0044-9873 Athletic Administration
0044-9881 Atlantic Control States Beverage Journal
0044-989X Atlantic Provinces Economic Council. Newsletter
0044-9903 Atlantic Provinces Numismatic Association. Newsletter
0044-9911 Atlantic Review (St. Johns)
0044-9954 Atomic Absorption Newsletter *see* 0195-5373
0044-9962 Attak *see* 0167-5303
0044-9970 W R R I News Report
0044-9989 Audience and Programme Research
0045-0006 Auditor's Computer Update Digest†
0045-0014 Audubon Leader
0045-0030 Auris
0045-0049 Ausbildung und Beratung in Land- und Hauswirtschaft
0045-0073 Australasian Insurance Journal
0045-0081 Australasian Kennel Review and Dog News†
0045-009X Australasian Model Railroad Magazine *changed to* Australian Model Railway Magazine
0045-0103 A S E Journal
0045-0111 Australia. Bureau of Statistics. Balance of Payments, Australia
0045-012X Industrial Information Bulletin†
0045-0138 Australia. Department of National Development. Nat/Dev†
0045-0146 Australia. Department of the Northern Territory. Northern Territory Affairs†
0045-0170 A N Z A News
0045-0189 Australia. Northern Territory Division. Northern Newsletter *see* 0728-4276
0045-0197 Australia Now
0045-0200 Australia. Bureau of Agricultural Economics. Fibres Other Than Wool *see* 0311-2950
0045-0219 Australian and New Zealand Association for Medieval and Renaissance Studies. Bulletin†
0045-0235 Australian Angler *see* 0158-572X
0045-0243 Australian Apprenticeship Advisory Committee. Apprenticeship News†
0045-026X Australian Author
0045-0286 Australian Bankruptcy Bulletin
0045-0294 Australian Bee Journal
0045-0308 Australian Biblical Review
0045-0316 Australian Birdwatcher
0045-0324 Australian Boating Industry
0045-0332 Australian Bridge
0045-0340 Australian Chemical Industry Directory†
0045-0359 Australian Chiropractors Association. Journal
0045-0383 Australian Computer Society. Canberra Branch. Bulletin *changed to* Canberra Computer Bulletin
0045-0391 A C O S S Quarterly *see* 0157-6321
0045-0391 A C O S S Quarterly *see* 0004-9557
0045-0405 Australian Current Law
0045-0413 Australian Current Law Review†
0045-0421 Australian Dental Journal
0045-043X Australian Environmental Report *see* 0311-0931
0045-0448 Australian Films
0045-0456 Australian Furnishing Trade Journal
0045-0472 Australian Goat World
0045-0480 Australian Government News†
0045-0499 Australian G P *changed to* Private Doctor
0045-0510 Australian Hand Weaver and Spinner
0045-0537 Australian Home Gardener†
0045-0545 Australian Institute of Agricultural Science. Journal
0045-0553 Australian Institute of Dairy Factory Managers and Secretaries. Butter Fats and Solids
0045-057X Management Diary *changed to* Management Review
0045-0588 Australian Jersey Journal
0045-0596 Australian Journal of Advanced Education *changed to* Journal of Advanced Education
0045-060X Australian Journal of Experimental Agriculture and Animal Husbandry *see* 0816-1089
0045-0618 Australian Journal of Forensic Sciences
0045-0626 Australian Journal of Instrumentation and Control†
0045-0634 Australian Journal of Mental Retardation *see* 0726-3864
0045-0642 Australian Journal of Optometry *changed to* Clinical and Experimental Optometry
0045-0650 Australian Journal of Sports Medicine *changed to* Australian Journal of Science and Medicine in Sport
0045-0669 Australian Labor Party. A.L.P.
0045-0677 Australian Maps
0045-0693 Australian Meat Board. Meat Producer and Exporter *changed to* Australian Meat and Livestock Corporation. Meat Producer and Exporter
0045-0707 A M D E L Bulletin
0045-0715 A.M.R.A. Journal
0045-0731 A N C O L D Bulletin
0045-074X Australian National Drycleaner
0045-0758 Australian Nurses' Journal
0045-0766 Australian Occupational Therapy Journal
0045-0774 Australian O.C.C.A. Proceedings and News *changed to* Surface Coatings Australia
0045-0782 Australian Orchid Review
0045-0820 Australian Retail Tobacconist
0045-0847 Australian Roads†
0045-0855 Australian Science Teachers' Journal
0045-0863 Australian Sea Spray Weekly *see* 0311-7839
0045-0898 Australia Stevedoring Industry Authority. Monthly Statistics
0045-0901 Australian Stock Exchange Journal
0045-091X Australian Teacher *changed to* Teachers Guild of New South Wales. Proceedings
0045-0928 Australian Technical Teacher
0045-0936 Australian Tobacco Journal†
0045-0944 Australian Trader
0045-0960 Australian Welding Research†
0045-0979 Australian Worker
0045-1002 Auto-Neige†
0045-1010 Auto und Reise
0045-1053 Automobile & Tractor
0045-1061 Automobile Connoisseur
0045-107X Automotive Marketing *see* 0193-3264
0045-1088 Automotive Messenger
0045-110X Automotive Transport Labour Relations Association. Monthly Labour Bulletin†
0045-1118 Autonomi
0045-1126 Autotouring *changed to* Touring Club Magazine
0045-1142 Auvergne Economique
0045-1150 Avant-Scene Cinema
0045-1169 Avant Scene Theatre
0045-1177 Aviacion y Astronautica
0045-1185 Aviation Historical Society of Australia. Journal
0045-1193 International Aviation Mechanics Journal
0045-1207 Aviation Safety Digest
0045-1223 Aware†
0045-1231 Awareness†
0045-124X Ayn Rand Letter†
0045-1258 Azor *see* 0572-2969
0045-1266 B E E
0045-1274 B P Shield International *changed to* B P Shield
0045-1282 Ba Shiru
0045-1290 Background to South African and World News†
0045-1304 Badger Herald
0045-1312 Badminton U.S.A.†
0045-1320 Baha'i World
0045-1347 Ballet-Hoo
0045-1355 Balloon *changed to* Atkinsonian
0045-1363 Baltimore Health News *changed to* Perspectives (Baltimore)
0045-138X Bamah
0045-1398 Banana Bulletin
0045-1401 Banco de Guatemala. Informe Economico
0045-1428 Bangladesh Journal of Biological and Agricultural Sciences *changed to* Bangladesh Journal of Biological Sciences
0045-1436 Bank Directory of Canada
0045-1444 Bank Melli Iran. Bulletin
0045-1460 Bank of Canada. Review
0045-1479 Bank of Tanzania. Economic Bulletin
0045-1487 Bank Operations Report
0045-1495 Bank Pembangunan Indonesia. Newsletter
0045-1509 Bank Street Reporting *changed to* Bank Street News-Reviews-Reporting
0045-1533 Banque Canadienne Nationale. Bulletin Mensuel†
0045-1541 Bar Executive Key Handbook†
0045-155X Barnet Marksman
0045-1576 Battle Line *see* 0145-1677
0045-1584 Beat Instrumental and International Recording Studio *changed to* Beat Instrumental Songwriting & Recording Magazine
0045-1592 Beaverbrook Art Gallery
0045-1606 Bedriftsoekonomisk Informasjon *changed to* Oekonomisk Rapport
0045-1614 Bedryfsleiding/Business Management *see* 0378-9098
0045-1622 Beef & You†
0045-1649 Beer in Canada†
0045-1657 Beermat *see* 0306-7912
0045-1673 B R S Monthly Index†
0045-169X Beitraege zur Konfliktforschung
0045-1703 Belgium. Institut National de Statistique. Bulletin de Statistique
0045-172X Benefits International *changed to* Benefits & Compensation International
0045-1738 Bensiini Uutiset
0045-1746 Bergens Privatbanks Kvartalsskrift *see* 0332-6756
0045-1762 Berliner Bauwirtschaft
0045-1770 Beseda Nasi Vesnice
0045-1789 Betrifft: Erziehung *changed to* Paedagogik Heute
0045-1797 Better Boating†
0045-1800 Better Business Bureau of Metropolitan New York. News Review†
0045-1819 Better Business Bureau of Metropolitan New York. Report to Business *changed to* Report to Business
0045-1827 Beverly Hills Bar Association. Journal
0045-1835 Bias
0045-186X Bibliografie van de Nederlandse Taal- en Literatuur Wetenschap
0045-1878 Bibliographic Society of Canada. Index Committee. Newsletter†
0045-1886 Bibliographie Nationale de la Tunisie†
0045-1894 Bibliographie Selective des Publications Officielles Francaise†
0045-1908 Bibliographies of Chemists†
0045-1916 Bibliographische Informationen aus der Technik und Ihren Grundlagenwissenschaften†
0045-1924 Bibliography of Articles on Physical and Health Education, Sport and Allied Subjects *changed to* Bibliographical Index on Physical and Health Education, Sport and Allied Subjects
0045-1932 Bibliography on High Pressure Research
0045-1940 Biblionews and Australian Notes and Queries
0045-1959 Biblioteca Teatrale
0045-1967 Bibliotheque Nationale. Bulletin *see* 0825-1746
0045-1975 Big Bike Magazine *see* 0194-9888
0045-1983 Big Book of Metalworking Machinery
0045-2009 Bil-Nyt *changed to* Motor-Journalen Bilen
0045-2025 Biochemical Systematics *see* 0305-1978
0045-2033 Biological Science
0045-205X Biologie in Unserer Zeit
0045-2068 Bioorganic Chemistry
0045-2076 Bird Keeping in Australia
0045-2084 Black Bag
0045-2114 Black Books Bulletin†
0045-2157 Black Flag
0045-2165 Black Graphics International
0045-2181 Black Law Journal
0045-219X Black Lechwe
0045-2203 Black Lines: a Journal of Black Studies†
0045-222X Black Maria
0045-2238 Black News Digest
0045-2246 Black Oracle *see* 0198-1064
0045-2270 Blackfish
0045-2289 Bleu et Rouge
0045-2297 Blues & Soul Music Review
0045-2300 Boardroom Reports
0045-2319 Bodyshop
0045-2351 Boian News Service
0045-236X BolaffiArte *changed to* Arte
0045-2378 Boletim de Materiais Dentarios
0045-2386 Boletim de Vulgarizacao Veterinaria†
0045-2394 Boletin de Ciencias Politicas y Sociales
0045-2424 Bollettino di Magistratura Democratica
0045-2432 Bollettino Bibliografico Sardo e Archivio Tradizioni Popolari
0045-2467 Bolsa de Cereales. Revista Institucional
0045-2483 Bonsai in Australia
0045-2505 Book Angles†
0045-2513 Book Trolley *see* 0305-9340
0045-2521 Bookplates in the News
0045-253X Books *see* 0266-4208
0045-2556 Books for Young People†
0045-2564 Books in Canada
0045-2572 Books in English
0045-2580 Border Business Digest *changed to* Cumbria Weekly Digest
0045-2599 Bosch Kurier†
0045-2602 Boston After Dark *see* 0163-3015
0045-2629 Botanica
0045-2637 Botaniste *see* 0181-7582
0045-2653 Bouliste et le Petanquier *see* 0336-8424
0045-2688 Boys Village Report *changed to* Dellcrest News
0045-2696 Brannmannen
0045-270X Brasil Florestal
0045-2718 Brauer und Maelzer *see* 0341-7115
0045-2726 M A M (Mensario de Arquivo Nacional) *see* 0102-700X
0045-2742 Brazil. Superintendencia do Desenvolvimento da Amazonia. S U D A M Documenta
0045-2750 Bread Manufacturer and Pastrycook of Western Australia
0045-2769 Break Through†
0045-2777 Breakthrough
0045-2785 Breves Nouvelles de France *see* 0398-9682
0045-2793 Brian Bex Report *changed to* American Record
0045-2823 Bridge (New York) *changed to* Bridge: Asian American Perspectives
0045-2831 Brigade
0045-2858 Bristol Diocesan Gazette *changed to* Bristol Diocesan News
0045-2866 Britain and Overseas
0045-2874 British Advent Messenger *see* 0309-3654
0045-2890 British Caribbean Philatelic Journal
0045-2904 British Columbia Art Teachers' Association. Newsletter *see* 0316-1544
0045-2912 B.C. Association of Teachers of Classics. Newsletter *see* 0316-2508
0045-2947 British Columbia Counsellors' Association. Newsletter *see* 0705-8802
0045-2955 British Columbia English Teacher *see* 0316-0173
0045-2963 British Columbia Historical News
0045-2971 British Columbia Hotelman†
0045-2998 British Columbia Mountaineer
0045-3005 British Columbia Museums Association. Museum Round Up
0045-3013 B C Outdoors
0045-303X British Columbia Snow Survey Bulletin
0045-3048 British Columbia Social Studies Teachers' Association. Newsletter *see* 0315-8527
0045-3056 British Columbia Tax Reports
0045-3064 British Columbia Thoroughbred
0045-3072 Phycological Newsletter

0045-3080 B.C. Voice
0045-3099 British Iron and Steel Research Association. Open Report List changed to British Steel Corporation. Corporate Development Laboratory. Open Report List
0045-3102 British Journal of Social Work
0045-3110 British Naturopathic Journal and Osteopathic Review†
0045-3129 B N A Topics
0045-3137 British Racing News
0045-3145 British Society of Rheology. Bulletin
0045-3153 British Speleological Association. Bulletin see 0142-1832
0045-317X B M I: the Many Worlds of Music
0045-3188 Broadcasting Bibliophile's Booknotes changed to Communication Booknotes: Recent Titles in Telecommunications, Information & Media
0045-3226 Broken Spoke
0045-3234 Bromeletter
0045-3242 B.A.C.A. Calendar of Cultural Events
0045-3250 Bruce County Historical Notes†
0045-3269 Brush
0045-3277 Belgium. Institut Royal Meteorologique. Bulletin Mensuel: Pollution Atmospherique. Fumee et So Deux†
0045-3285 Buckeye Review
0045-3293 Buck's Safety Management AID†
0045-3315 Buddhist Quarterly see 0265-2900
0045-3323 Budgerigar Bulletin
0045-3331 Museo Social Argentino. Boletin
0045-334X Buffalo
0045-3366 Milwaukee Bugle
0045-3374 Buhiti
0045-3382 Builder
0045-3412 Building Ideas†
0045-3420 Building News changed to Australian Building News
0045-3447 University of Stellenbosch. Bureau for Economic Research. Building Survey see 0586-4941
0045-348X Bullet
0045-3498 Bulletin Bibliographique de la Prevention see 0302-7651
0045-3501 Bulletin de l'Afrique Noire
0045-351X Bulletin Jugend und Literatur
0045-3536 Bulwark
0045-3544 Bureaucrat
0045-3552 Burning Spear†
0045-3587 Business and Professional Woman
0045-3595 Business and Professional Woman
0045-3617 Business Aviation changed to Business Aviation Weekly
0045-3625 Business Dynamics see 0361-3852
0045-3633 Business Ideas and Facts†
0045-3641 Business Venezuela
0045-3668 Businessman's Law
0045-3676 Bust†
0045-3684 Buyers' Market
0045-3692 Buzz
0045-3706 C I D X Messenger
0045-3714 Cable
0045-3730 Cahiers Bibliographiques des Lettres Quebecoise†
0045-3749 Cahiers de Litterature et de Linguistique Applique†
0045-3765 Cahiers d'Outre-Mer
0045-3773 Cahiers du Bilinguisme
0045-3781 Cahiers du Travailleur Intellectuel
0045-379X Cahiers Spartacus
0045-3803 University of Cairo. Faculty of Medicine. Medical Journal
0045-3811 Caisses et Emballages en Bois†
0045-3838 Calcutta Gazette
0045-3846 Calcutta Review
0045-3854 Calcutta Weekly Notes
0045-3862 Calcuttan
0045-3870 Caledonian
0045-3889 Calgary Livestock Market Journal†
0045-3900 California Builder and Engineer
0045-3919 C C A C Review
0045-3927 California Condor changed to Raptor Report
0045-3935 California Grocers Advocate†
0045-3943 California Institute of Technology. Division of Geological and Planetary Sciences. Report on Geological and Planetary Sciences for the Year
0045-3951 California News Index†
0045-396X California News Reporter†
0045-3978 California Quarterly
0045-3986 University of California, Los Angeles. Chicano Studies Center. Creative Series†
0045-3994 University of California, Los Angeles. Chicano Studies Center. Monographs changed to University of California, Los Angeles. Chicano Studies Research Center. Monographs
0045-4001 Caliper
0045-401X Call
0045-4036 Call and Post
0045-4044 Callboard
0045-4052 Calquarium
0045-4087 Cameroun Litteraire†
0045-4095 CAMmunique†
0045-4109 Campaigner
0045-4125 Camping
0045-4133 Campus (Toronto) see 0383-2406
0045-415X Statistics Canada Weekly see 0380-0547
0045-4168 Canada. Department of Agriculture. Forage Notes changed to Canada. Agriculture Canada. Forage Notes
0045-4176 Canada. Department of Energy, Mines, and Resources. Departmental Map Library. Acquisitions of Maps, Atlases and Gazeteers†
0045-4192 Canada Gazette: Part 1: Government, Divorce, Bankruptcy Notices, Etc
0045-4206 Canada Gazette: Part 2: Statutory Orders and Regulations
0045-4214 Canada Japan Trade Council. Newsletter
0045-4230 Canada Supreme Court Reports
0045-4249 Canada-Svensken
0045-4257 Canada Today/d'Aujourd'hui (Washington)
0045-4265 Canada Travel Digest†
0045-4273 Canada Trust Bulletin†
0045-4281 Canada - U.K. Trade News changed to Can - U.K. Link
0045-429X Canada. Western Forest Products Laboratory. Information Reports see 0708-6172
0045-4303 Canada's Business Climate
0045-4311 Canadian Aberdeen-Angus News
0045-432X Canadian Agricultural Engineering
0045-4338 Canadian Air Comments changed to Atlas Copco Comments
0045-4354 Canadian Association for Laboratory Animal Science Newsletter
0045-4389 Canadian Association of Medical Clinics. Bulletin changed to Group Practice in Canada
0045-4397 Canadian Association of Medical Record Librarians. Bulletin changed to C C H E A/C H R A. Bulletin.
0045-4419 Canadian Association of Social Workers. Newsletter†
0045-4427 Canadian Athletic Director and Coach
0045-4435 C. B. A. Bulletin†
0045-4451 Canadian Barber and Men's Hairstylists changed to Canadian Men's Hairstylist and Barber
0045-446X Canadian Bee Journal†
0045-4486 Canadian Biographical Studies†
0045-4494 Canadian Boating
0045-4508 Canadian Building News
0045-4524 Canadian Chamber of Commerce. Newsletter†
0045-4540 Canadian Chess Chat
0045-4559 Transit Canada†
0045-4567 Canadian Coach†
0045-4575 Canadian Coin Box
0045-4583 Canadian Community Publisher see 0380-8025
0045-4605 Canadian Council of Churches. Council Communicator
0045-4613 Canadian Council of Teachers of English. Newsletter
0045-4621 Canadian Courses and Seminars changed to Short Courses and Seminars
0045-463X Canadian Criminology and Corrections Association. Bulletin see 0823-9436
0045-4648 Canadian Curling News
0045-4656 Canadian Daily Stock Charts
0045-4702 C E M A Newsletter changed to Scanner
0045-4729 C.F.C.F. News for the Canadian Camper see 0316-280X
0045-4737 Canadian Far Eastern Newsletter
0045-4745 Canadian Farmer see 0041-6037
0045-477X Canadian Fiction
0045-4788 Canadian Field Hockey News
0045-480X Canadian Film Institute. Bulletin changed to Images
0045-4834 Canadian Football News
0045-4850 Canadian Forces Dental Services Quarterly†
0045-4869 C F A News†
0045-4877 Canadian Forwarder
0045-4885 Canadian Fruitgrower
0045-4893 Canadian Government Programs and Services
0045-4907 Canadian Guernsey Breeders' Journal changed to Canadian Guernsey Journal
0045-4915 Canadian Handgun
0045-4931 Canadian Imperial Bank of Commerce. Foreign Trade News†
0045-494X Canadian Importers Association. Importers' Bulletin
0045-4958 Canadian India Times
0045-4966 Canadian Industrial Relations and Personnel Developments
0045-4974 Canadian Industrial Traffic League. Traffic Notes changed to Canadian Industrial Transportation League. Transportation Info
0045-4982 C I C A Dialogue
0045-4990 Canadian Insurance Law Reports
0045-5008 Canadian Interline News†
0045-5024 Canadian Ionospheric Data
0045-5059 Canadian Jewish Outlook see 0834-0242
0045-5067 Canadian Journal of Forest Research
0045-5075 Canadian Journal of Optometry
0045-5083 Canadian Journal of Otolaryngology see 0381-6605
0045-5091 Canadian Journal of Philosophy
0045-5105 Canadian Journal of Spectroscopy
0045-5121 Canadian Leathercraft
0045-5156 Canadian Manager
0045-5164 Canadian Mathematical Congress. Notes, News and Comments changed to Canadian Mathematical Society. Notes, News and Comments
0045-5172 Canadian Music Educators Association. Newsletter
0045-5202 Canadian Numismatic Research Society. Transactions
0045-5229 Canadian Opera Guild. Guild News changed to Overtures (Toronto)
0045-5237 Canadian Paper Money Journal
0045-5245 Canadian Parachutist see 0319-3896
0045-5253 Canadian Philatelist
0045-527X Canadian Red Book
0045-530X Canadian Risk Management and Business Insurance see 0821-6916
0045-5318 Canadian Sales and Credit Law Guide changed to Canadian Commercial Law Guide
0045-5326 Canadian Sales Tax Reports
0045-5334 Canadian Scene
0045-5342 Canadian Securities Law Reports
0045-5369 Canadian Society for Education through Art. Newsletter
0045-5377 Canadian Society of Laboratory Technologists. Bulletin
0045-5385 Canadian Sports Digest
0045-5393 Canadian Steam
0045-5407 Canadian Stock Market Point and Figure Summary†
0045-5423 Canadian Swine
0045-5431 Canadian Teacher of the Deaf see 0382-7976
0045-544X Canadian Theosophist
0045-5458 Canadian Training Methods see 0225-6320
0045-5466 Canadian Transport
0045-5482 Canadian Travel News see 0319-7093
0045-5490 Canadian Travel Press
0045-5504 Canadian Trot Canadien see 0704-0733
0045-5512 Canadian Union of Public Employees. Journal changed to Canadian Union of Public Employees. The Public Employee
0045-5520 Canadian Vocational Journal
0045-5539 Canadian Warehousing Association. C W A Reporter†
0045-5571 Canadian Wildlife and Fisheries Newsletter Bulletin see 0318-5133
0045-5598 Canadian Wool Grower and Sheep Breeder see 0319-7387
0045-5601 Canberra and District Historical Society. Journal see 0313-5977
0045-561X Canberra Comment changed to Australian Commerce Review
0045-5628 Canberra Survey
0045-5636 Candido
0045-5660 Capella†
0045-5687 Capitol Studies see 0734-3469
0045-5695 Caps and Flints
0045-5709 Car Buyer†
0045-5717 Car Tips†
0045-5725 Caravan Industry and Park Operator changed to Caravan Business
0045-5733 Carbide Journal see 0192-8333
0045-5741 Cardiac Rehabilitation†
0045-575X Cardiovascular & Metabolic Diseases†
0045-5776 Career Development†
0045-5792 Caribbean Business News
0045-5830 Carleton Education Bulletin†
0045-5857 Carolina Centerscope†
0045-5865 Carolina Tips
0045-5873 Carolinian
0045-5881 Cartologica
0045-5903 Cash & Carry
0045-5911 Cashew News Teller changed to Cashew Causerie
0045-592X Castle Street Circular see 0266-8750
0045-5938 J S A S (Journal Supplement Abstract Service) changed to Psychological Documents
0045-5946 Catalogue of Replacement Books for Children's Library Collections†
0045-5954 Catalyst changed to Book Marks
0045-5962 Catalyst for the Scottish Viewpoint
0045-5970 Catholic Agitator
0045-5989 Catholic Citizen
0045-5997 Cavalletto e Tavolozza
0045-6004 Caveat Emptor changed to Caveat Emptor Consumers Bulletin
0045-6020 Celebrity Bulletin
0045-6039 Cell Differentiation
0045-6047 Cent Blagues
0045-6055 C R R I Road Abstracts
0045-6063 Centre Canadien International de Recherches et d'Information sur l'Economie Publique et Cooperative. Revue du Canadien see 0384-8744
0045-608X Centre de Recherche en Civilisation Canadienne-Francaise. Bulletin see 0825-2777
0045-6098 C H I S S Cahiers
0045-6101 Centre International pour le Credit Communal changed to Local Finance
0045-611X Ecuador. Centro de Desarrollo Industrial. Boletin Industrial
0045-6128 Centro de Estudios Educativos. Revista see 0185-1284
0045-6152 Ceramurgia
0045-6179 Cercles des Jeunes Naturalistes. Feuillets du Club changed to Feuillets du Naturaliste
0045-6187 Ceskoslovensky Casopis Historicky

ISSN INDEX 1329

0045-6195 Ceylon Forester *changed to* Sri Lanka Forester
0045-6209 Ceylon Trade Journal†
0045-6217 Congress News
0045-6225 Chakra†
0045-6233 Challenge (Washington) *changed to* New Challenge (Washington)
0045-625X Challenge
0045-6268 Challenger†
0045-6276 Chambre de Commerce, d'Agriculture, d'Industrie et des Mines du Gabon. Bulletin
0045-6292 Chambre de Commerce du Sud de la Tunisie. Bulletin Economique
0045-6306 Chambre de Commerce Francaise au Canada. Revue *see* 0318-7306
0045-6314 Champion†
0045-6330 Channel (Wellesley)†
0045-6349 Chaplin
0045-6365 Chat†
0045-6381 Chelsea Spelaeological Society Newsletter
0045-639X Chemical Industry Notes
0045-6403 Chemical Insight
0045-6411 C R C Critical Reviews in Biochemistry
0045-642X C R C Critical Reviews in Bioengineering *see* 0278-940X
0045-6446 C R C Critical Reviews in Toxicology
0045-6454 C R C Critical Reviews in Microbiology
0045-6470 Chemical Society, London. Journal. Section B: Physical Organic Chemistry *see* 0300-9580
0045-6497 Chemical Take-Off
0045-6500 Chemical Weekly
0045-6519 Chemische Technik
0045-6527 Chemists' Quarterly *see* 0115-2130
0045-6535 Chemosphere
0045-656X Chesapeake Bay Magazine
0045-6578 Chess Canada
0045-6594 Chess Player†
0045-6608 Chevre
0045-6616 C A G L A Newsletter *changed to* Chicago Area Group on Latin America. Occasional Papers
0045-6624 Chicagoland Development
0045-6632 Child Care Quarterly *changed to* Child and Youth Care Quarterly
0045-6640 Child Education Quarterly *changed to* Infant Projects
0045-6659 Child Welfare League Newsletter *changed to* Children's Voice
0045-6667 Children's Aid Society News *changed to* Children's Aid Society News
0045-6675 C.A.S. Record *see* 0319-7468
0045-6691 Children's Apparel Merchandising Aids
0045-6705 Children's Libraries Newsletter *changed to* Orana
0045-6713 Children's Literature in Education
0045-6721 Chilton's Truck Repair Manual *changed to* Chilton's Truck and Van Repair Manual
0045-6756 China Monthly†
0045-6764 China Now
0045-6780 Christian Brothers of the Australian and New Zealand Provinces. Our Studies *changed to* Catholic School Studies
0045-6799 Christian Communications Journal in Africa†
0045-6802 Christian Graduate *see* 0264-598X
0045-6810 Christian Institute for Ethnic Studies in Asia. Bulletin
0045-6829 Christian Patriot†
0045-6845 Christian Research Institute. Newsletter *changed to* Christian Research Journal
0045-6861 Church and Clergy Finance
0045-687X Church and School Equipment News
0045-6888 Ciencia Agronomica
0045-6896 Ciervo
0045-6918 Cine-Revue
0045-6926 Cinema
0045-6942 Circulo Odontologico de Cordoba. Revista
0045-6969 C L News†
0045-6977 Citta Futura
0045-6985 City and Suburban Travel
0045-6993 City College Alumnus
0045-7019 City of Ottawa Coin Club. Monthly Bulletin
0045-7027 Civic Affairs
0045-7035 Civil Affairs Journal & Newsletter
0045-7043 Civil & Military Law Journal
0045-7051 Civil Liberties
0045-706X Civil Rights Newsletter
0045-7116 Clave
0045-7159 Climbing
0045-7175 Clinical Trends in Anesthesiology†
0045-7183 Clio Medica
0045-7205 Club Management in Australia
0045-7213 Club Mirror
0045-723X Coastal Zone Management
0045-7248 Cocina y Hogar
0045-7256 Cocoa Growers Bulletin
0045-7272 Coin Launderer and Cleaner
0045-7280 Coin Wholesaler
0045-7310 C O D I A
0045-7329 Colegio Nacional de Enfermeras. Revista
0045-7337 Coleopterists Newsletter *see* 0010-065X
0045-7345 Collective Bargaining Settlements in New York State
0045-7361 College Canada
0045-737X College Law Digest
0045-7388 College of Physicians and Surgeons of Ontario. Interim Report
0045-740X Colony *changed to* Question Mark
0045-7426 Colorado Journal of Educational Research†
0045-7434 C T R C Newsletter†
0045-7469 Combat pour l'Homme *see* 0244-7878
0045-7477 Combat Syndicaliste *see* 0014-0724
0045-7523 Comfort Engineering *changed to* Environmental Design
0045-754X Commerce *changed to* Australian-American Dialog
0045-7558 Commerce et Distribution†
0045-7566 Commercial Bank of Australia. Economic Review†
0045-7574 Commercial Bank of Ethiopia Market Report
0045-7620 Commonwealth and Colonial History Newsletter
0045-7639 Commonwealth Professional
0045-7647 Commonwealth Scientific and Industrial Research Organization. Industrial Research News
0045-7663 Communication
0045-7671 Communicator (Ann Arbor) *changed to* Great Lakes Communicator
0045-768X Communicator of Technical Information *changed to* Communicator (Hatfield)
0045-7698 Communika
0045-7701 Communitarian *see* 0199-9346
0045-771X Community *changed to* Community (Alexandria)
0045-7728 Community College Social Science Quarterly *changed to* Community College Social Science Journal
0045-7736 Community Education Journal†
0045-7787 Company Law Institute of India. Reports of Company Cases Including Banking & Insurance
0045-7809 Compass
0045-7817 Compulsory Military Service and the Objector†
0045-7825 Computer Methods in Applied Mechanics and Engineering
0045-7833 Computer Operations†
0045-7841 Computer Price Guide
0045-785X Computer Program Abstracts†
0045-7868 Computer Programs in Science and Technology†
0045-7892 Computer Society of India. Journal
0045-7906 Computers & Electrical Engineering
0045-7930 Computers & Fluids
0045-7949 Computers & Structures
0045-7957 Computing Newsletter for Community Colleges *see* 0045-7965
0045-7965 Computing Newsletter for Instructors of Data Processing
0045-7981 Comunita Mediterranea
0045-799X Concerns
0045-8007 Concrete Abstracts
0045-8015 Concrete Pipe News
0045-8023 Confederation Nationale de la Construction. Annuaire
0045-804X Conference Board of the Mathematical Sciences. Newsletter†
0045-8058 Conference on Great Lakes Research. Proceedings *see* 0380-1330
0045-8066 Conflux†
0045-8082 Congiuntura Economica Lombarda
0045-8120 Connecticut Nutmegger
0045-8139 I P S Local Government Newsletter†
0045-8147 Conquest *changed to* Diabetes Conquest
0045-8155 Conservation Council of Ontario. Bulletin†
0045-8163 Consolidated Report of the Condition of Banks Operating in Puerto Rico
0045-8171 Consoliere†
0045-8198 Construction Metallique *changed to* C T I C M-Construction Metallique
0045-8201 Consultants News
0045-8236 Consumer Comment
0045-8252 Consumer Interest†
0045-8260 Consumer News†
0045-8279 Consumerism-New Developments for Business†
0045-8309 Contact in Urban and Regional Affairs *see* 0711-6780
0045-8317 Contacto *changed to* Contacto: Mini-Abstracts
0045-8325 Contacts
0045-8333 Contemporary Indian Literature†
0045-835X Content
0045-8368 Contents of Recent Economics Journals
0045-8376 Continental Franchise Review
0045-8384 Continuing Education Directory for Metropolitan Toronto
0045-8406 Contractspeler
0045-8414 Contrasts
0045-8422 Convenience Store News
0045-8430 C A I D Newsletter (Convention of American Instructors of the Deaf) *changed to* Advocate for Education of the Deaf
0045-8449 Conventions, Meetings, Incentive World†
0045-8457 Cooperateur de France
0045-8465 C E I R (Cooperative Economic Insect Report) *see* 0363-0889
0045-8473 Cooperative Educational Abstracting Service *changed to* International Bureau of Education. Bulletin
0045-849X Cooperator†
0045-8503 Cooperator's Bulletin
0045-8511 Copeia
0045-8538 Core Teacher
0045-8546 Cormorant *see* 0362-9368
0045-8554 Cormorant News Bulletin
0045-8562 Cornell University. Libraries. Bulletin†
0045-8570 Cornish Nation
0045-8635 Correctional Process *see* 0823-9436
0045-8643 Correio Portugues
0045-8651 Correo Hispano-Americano
0045-866X Corriere Canadese
0045-8678 Corrosion Y Proteccion
0045-8686 Corse Mediterranee Medicale *see* 0302-9263
0045-8716 Cosmorama
0045-8732 COSPAR Information Bulletin
0045-8740 Costa Rica. Instituto Geografico Nacional. Informe Semestral
0045-8759 Cotton Development
0045-8775 Council for Planning & Conservation. Newsletter†
0045-8791 C P L Newsletter
0045-8813 Countdown (Wichita)†
0045-8848 Country Bizarre
0045-8856 Country Life
0045-8864 Courier *changed to* B.C. Corrections Courier
0045-8872 C F B Cold Lake Courier
0045-8899 Courrier du Parlement
0045-8902 Courrier du Vietnam
0045-8910 Courrier Pedagogigue *changed to* Courrier du Francais-Cadre
0045-8929 Coursing News *changed to* Greyhound Review
0045-8937 Cowan Investment Survey. Weekly Market Digest *changed to* Cowan Investment Survey. Midas
0045-897X Creative Moment *changed to* Creative Moment World Poetry and Criticism
0045-8988 Creative Teacher†
0045-8996 Creative Urge†
0045-9003 Credit Union National Association. Research and Economics Department. R E Statistical Bulletin *changed to* Credit Union National Association. Research Division. Research Bulletin
0045-9011 Creditalk
0045-902X Crime and Delinquency Abstracts†
0045-9038 Criminal Justice Newsletter
0045-9046 Crisis Intervention
0045-9054 Cristiani nel Mondo
0045-9062 Critic†
0045-9070 Critical Digest
0045-9089 Critique Socialiste
0045-9097 Critiques de l'Economie Politique
0045-9100 Cross Reference *see* 0740-9982
0045-9119 Crossroads
0045-9127 Crown
0045-9135 Crucible
0045-9151 Cryptogram†
0045-9178 Cuadernos de Historia de la Salud Publica
0045-9186 Cuadernos de Historia Economica de Cataluna†
0045-9194 Cuadernos de Informacion Cientifica†
0045-9208 Cuisine Collective
0045-9216 Cultivar *changed to* Cultivar 2000
0045-9232 Cultura Antiqua
0045-9240 Culture and Education *changed to* Education for the Disadvantaged Child
0045-9259 Cultured Dairy Products Journal
0045-9267 Cultuurtechnisch Tijdschrift
0045-9275 Cumberland-Samford Law Review *see* 0360-8298
0045-9283 Current Citations on Communication Disorders *changed to* Current Citations on Communication Disorders: Hearing and Balance
0045-9283 Current Citations on Communication Disorders *changed to* Current Citations on Communications Disorders: Language, Speech, and Voice
0045-9291 Current Engineering Practice
0045-933X Current Physics Advance Abstracts: Solid State†
0045-9348 Current Physics Microform
0045-9380 Current Problems in Pediatrics
0045-9399 Current Problems in Radiology *see* 0363-0188
0045-9429 Cyprus To-day
0045-9445 Czas
0045-9453 Czasopismo Geograficzne
0045-9461 Czechoslovak Economic Digest
0045-947X Czechoslovak Science & Technology Digest†
0045-9488 Czechoslovak Scientific and Technical Periodicals Contents
0045-9496 Dafni†
0045-9534 Dalhousie University. University News *changed to* Dalhousie University. University News This Week
0045-9534 Dalhousie University. University News *changed to* Dalhousie University. University News This Month
0045-9542 Dalka
0045-9550 Dallas. Methodist Hospital. Bulletin of the Medical Staff†
0045-9569 Dallas News *changed to* Iconoclast
0045-9577 Dance/America
0045-9585 Danmarks Handels Tidende
0045-9593 Dansk Bygge Journal†
0045-9607 Dansk Erhvervsfjerkrae
0045-9615 Dansk Handelsblad
0045-9623 Dansk Industri
0045-9631 Dansk Ungdom og Idraet

ISSN INDEX

0045-964X Danske Realskole *changed to* Tidens Skole
0045-9658 Darshak
0045-9666 Data†
0045-9674 Data-Canada†
0045-9690 Data Processing Management Association. Magazine
0045-9704 Datapro Seventy
0045-9739 Davidsonia†
0045-9747 De Nos Mains
0045-9755 De Rebus
0045-9771 Deacon
0045-9801 Deccan College. Postgraduate & Research Institute. Bulletin
0045-981X Decennie 2†
0045-9836 Defending All Outdoors†
0045-9844 Delaware Basin Bulletin†
0045-9852 Delaware Conservationist
0045-9879 Delikt en Delinkwent
0045-9887 Delinquency Prevention Reporter *see* 0092-5438
0045-9895 Delta del Parana
0045-9909 Democratic Commitment
0045-9917 Dental Association of Thailand. Journal
0045-9933 Dental Hygienist *changed to* C D H A Journal
0045-9941 Dental Radiography and Photography†
0045-995X Dental Student News†
0045-9968 Dentoscope†
0045-9984 Departements et Communes
0045-9992 Derecho Penal Contemporaneo
0046-0001 Dermatology in Practice†
0046-001X Desarrollo Economico
0046-0028 Desarrollo Rural en las Americas
0046-0036 Descent
0046-0044 Desert Rancher
0046-0060 Designer & Builder in Asia†
0046-0079 Despatch
0046-0087 Despatch *see* 0227-034X
0046-0095 Detective†
0046-0117 Deutsche Baecker Zeitung
0046-0141 Deutsche Vereinigung von Winnipeg. Mitteilungen
0046-015X Deutsches Wirtschafts Institut, Berlin. D W I Forschungshefte *see* 0323-3901
0046-0168 Deux-Tiers†
0046-0184 Devonport News
0046-0192 Diabetes
0046-0206 Dialogo Social
0046-0222 Diana's Bimonthly
0046-0249 Digest of Executive Opportunities†
0046-0265 Dimension
0046-029X Dinny's Digest
0046-0303 Dio e Popolo
0046-032X Dire
0046-0338 Direct from Cuba
0046-0346 Discussion *changed to* American Film
0046-0362 Disposable Soft Goods *see* 0163-4429
0046-0370 Disposables International†
0046-0389 Dissonance†
0046-0435 Dixie Logger and Lumberman *see* 0192-7124
0046-0443 Djassin'foue
0046-0451 Doctor
0046-0478 Documentation par l'Image
0046-0486 Documentos de Educacion Cooperativa *see* 0210-7295
0046-0494 Doings†
0046-0508 Dokita
0046-0516 S I C C Dolphin *changed to* College Voice (Staten Island)
0046-0540 Domestic Heating Engineer *changed to* Comfort Engineering
0046-0559 Dominion Companies Law Reports *changed to* Canada Corporations Law Reports
0046-0567 Dominion Tax Cases
0046-0583 Domino *changed to* Schweizer Buch-Spiegel
0046-0591 Donna di Casa
0046-0605 Donnybrook Report: Photography†
0046-0621 Dorset
0046-063X Doshisha Literature
0046-0648 Down Under
0046-0656 Downtown Athletic Club Journal
0046-0664 Downtown Developments†
0046-0672 Dravo Review
0046-0680 Dressage *see* 0147-796X
0046-0702 Drilling Contractor
0046-0710 Drive *changed to* Drive
0046-0729 Driveway Reporter
0046-0737 Druckindustrie
0046-0745 Drug Education Report *see* 0091-2395
0046-0753 Drug Forum†
0046-0788 Duckological *changed to* From Duck Country
0046-0796 Duesseldorf
0046-080X Duitse Boek *see* 0167-2185
0046-0818 DukEngineer
0046-0826 Duodecimal Bulletin
0046-0834 Du Pont Magazine
0046-0842 Dutch Quarterly Review of Anglo American Letters
0046-0869 E E
0046-0877 E F B
0046-0885 E I
0046-0915 Eagle's Eye
0046-0931 Earthquake Information Bulletin
0046-0966 East St. Louis Monitor
0046-0974 Eastern Film†
0046-0990 Easyriders
0046-1016 Eau Vive *changed to* L'Eau Vive
0046-1024 Eburnea
0046-1032 Ecclaire

0046-1059 Echo (Huntsville)
0046-1067 Echo (Skokie)
0046-1083 Echo des Vieux de France *changed to* Echo de l'Union
0046-1091 Echoes of History†
0046-1105 Eclectic Theosophist
0046-1121 Ecology Law Quarterly
0046-113X Economia
0046-1148 Economia Cafetera
0046-1180 Economic Research Corporation. Research Review†
0046-1199 Economic Analysis and Policy
0046-1202 Economie de l'Energie
0046-1245 EdCentric†
0046-1253 Edge
0046-1261 Editing Technology *see* 0736-7260
0046-127X Editor's Newsletter†
0046-1288 Edmonton Livestock Market News *changed to* Western Beef Producers News
0046-1296 Edmonton Native News
0046-1318 Edmonton Stamp Club Bulletin
0046-1326 Edseletter
0046-1334 Educacao
0046-1369 Education†
0046-1377 Education and Culture†
0046-1385 Education and Psychology Review
0046-1407 Education Commission of the States Bulletin
0046-1415 Education Equipment Selector
0046-1423 Education in Eastern Africa
0046-1431 Education Mathematique†
0046-144X Education News from Metrologic
0046-1474 Educational Broadcasting *changed to* Instructional Broadcasting
0046-1482 Educational Digest
0046-1490 Education Exchange *changed to* Educational International
0046-1504 Educational Forum†
0046-1520 Educational Psychologist
0046-1539 Educational Reporter
0046-1547 E T S Developments
0046-1555 Educator *changed to* National Educator
0046-1571 Educators Negotiating Service *changed to* Employers Negotiating Service
0046-158X Educator's Purchasing Guide†
0046-1598 Effective Teaching with Programmed Instruction†
0046-1601 Eglise de Quebec *changed to* Pastorale-Quebec
0046-161X Egyptian Journal of Genetics and Cytology
0046-1628 Eirene
0046-1636 Eisenhower College Newsletter *changed to* Eisenhower
0046-1660 Electrical Contractor (Jolimont)
0046-1679 Electrical Equipment Selector *see* 0013-4317
0046-1695 Electrical Week *changed to* Electric Utility Week
0046-1709 Electromagnetic Metrology Current Awareness Service†
0046-1717 Electronic Equipment Monitor
0046-1725 Electronic Products *see* 0046-1717
0046-1733 Electronics Communicator
0046-1741 Electronics of America
0046-175X Electronique et Microelectronique Industrielles *see* 0398-1851
0046-1776 Elektro-Handel
0046-1784 Elektromonteur *changed to* Elektrotechnik
0046-1792 Elements
0046-1806 Elements of Technology
0046-1814 Eletronica em Foco
0046-1822 Eleveur Maine Anjou
0046-1830 Ellipse
0046-1849 Eltern
0046-1857 Embassy
0046-1865 Embassy of Switzerland Bulletin
0046-1881 Emily Dickinson Bulletin *see* 0164-1492
0046-1903 Employer
0046-1946 Enchantment
0046-1954 Encore (New York) *see* 0161-6536
0046-1962 Enfance et la Mode
0046-1970 Enfant Exceptionnel *see* 0827-1844
0046-1989 Engineer (Washington)
0046-1997 Engineer in Education Newsletter†
0046-2004 Engineering and Construction†
0046-2012 Engineering Design Graphics Journal
0046-2020 Engineering Horizons†
0046-2039 Engineering in Medicine
0046-2055 Engineering News of India *changed to* Engineering & Metals Review
0046-208X English in Australia
0046-2098 English Usage in Southern Africa
0046-2101 Enseignants
0046-211X Enseignement *see* 0823-5651
0046-2136 Enterpriser
0046-2144 Entre-Nous
0046-2152 Enterprises Agricoles
0046-2160 Entreprise et l'Homme
0046-2187 Envers et l'Endroit†
0046-2217 Environment Improvement Case History Report Service†
0046-2225 Environmental Affairs *see* 0190-7034
0046-2241 G A T F Environmental Control Report
0046-225X Environmental Entomology
0046-2268 Excerpta Medica. Section 46: Environmental Health *see* 0300-5194
0046-2276 Environmental Law (Portland)
0046-2284 Environmental Law Reporter

0046-2306 Indexed Article Titles *changed to* Environmental Periodicals Bibliography
0046-2314 Environmental Quality Report†
0046-2330 Environmental Technology and Economics
0046-2349 Envoy†
0046-2357 Kruidenier
0046-2365 Epidemiology Notes and Communicable Disease Morbidity Report *see* 0095-313X
0046-2373 Eprouvette *changed to* Defisicence
0046-2381 Saint John Viewpoint *changed to* Tucker Park Press
0046-239X Equipe
0046-2403 Era
0046-2411 Erasmus Review†
0046-242X Erdoel-Dienst
0046-2438 Ergo
0046-2446 Ergonomics Abstracts
0046-2454 Ergot
0046-2489 Escutcheon
0046-2497 Espace Geographique
0046-2500 Esperanto - Interlangue Universelle
0046-2519 Esperanto Contact†
0046-2527 Esperanto Teacher
0046-2535 Espoir de la Nation Togolaise†
0046-256X Est-Ovest
0046-2578 Estrategia
0046-2586 Et la Lumiere Fut
0046-2608 Ethnopsychologie *see* 0007-9987
0046-2616 Ethnologie Francaise
0046-2632 Etnia
0046-2640 Etudes Polemologiques†
0046-2659 Etudes Renaniennes Bulletin
0046-2667 Eureka
0046-2683 Europaeisches Bau-Forum†
0046-2705 Europe Left
0046-273X European Civil Engineering Abstracts *see* 0332-4095
0046-2756 European Demographic Information Bulletin†
0046-2772 European Journal of Social Psychology
0046-2802 European Studies Newsletter
0046-2837 Translation News†
0046-2853 Evangelical Magazine
0046-2861 Events
0046-287X Everybody's Money
0046-2896 Executive Review†
0046-2926 Experimental Study of Politics
0046-2977 Expression
0046-2985 Eye†
0046-3000 F T Abstracts in Science & Technology†
0046-3019 F Y I (Washington)†
0046-3027 Fabbrica e Stato
0046-3035 Fabricator
0046-306X Facets of Freshwater
0046-3086 Factory and Office Selector†
0046-3116 Komitee Zuidelijk Afrika. Angola Comite. Facts and Reports
0046-3124 Facts, Figures and Film *changed to* T V Facts, Figures and Film
0046-3140 Facts on Fish†
0046-3159 F A C C C Bulletin
0046-3167 Fag Rag
0046-323X Family Service Highlights†
0046-3248 Fanfare *see* 0217-765X
0046-3256 Fanfares
0046-3264 Far East Week by Week
0046-3272 Far Eastern Law Review
0046-3280 Farbenhaendler *changed to* Heim und Farbe
0046-3299 Farm and Country
0046-3302 Farm and Food Research
0046-3329 Farm Supply Store†
0046-3337 Farmer's Digest
0046-337X Fauna†
0046-3396 Features and News from Behind the Iron Curtain *changed to* Freedom Communications International News Agency
0046-3418 Federal Labor-Management Consultant *changed to* Federal Labor-Management and Employee Relations Consultant
0046-3426 Federal Librarian†
0046-3434 Federal Linguist†
0046-3442 Federal Program Monitor†
0046-3450 Federal Reserve Bank of Chicago. Banking Briefs†
0046-3469 Federal Reserve Bank of Chicago. International Letter
0046-3477 F E W's News and Views *changed to* F E W's News and Views
0046-3523 Federation des Travaux Publics et des Transports. Revue *changed to* Infos Federales
0046-3531 F I E J Bulletin†
0046-354X Federacion Odontologica Colombiana. Revista
0046-3558 F A H Review *changed to* Federation of American Health Systems Review
0046-3566 Federation of British Columbia Naturalists. Newsletter *changed to* B.C. Naturalist
0046-3582 Federation of Victorian Film Societies. Federation News *see* 0158-3778
0046-3604 Feed and Farm Supply Dealer
0046-3620 Feldpost
0046-3639 Feline Practice
0046-3647 Feltornithologen *see* 0107-3729
0046-3655 Femeia
0046-3663 Feminist Studies
0046-368X Fernsehen und Film†
0046-3698 Ferrocarriles Argentinos

ISSN INDEX 1331

ISSN	Title
0046-3701	Fettesian
0046-3728	Fibre Market News
0046-3736	Fiction
0046-3760	Fighting Back†
0046-3787	Film Journal†
0046-3809	Film Review Index see 0094-6818
0046-3817	Films - Learning Corporation of America†
0046-3825	Films a l'Ecran
0046-3841	Revista Filologia Moderna changed to Filologia Moderna
0046-385X	Filozofia
0046-3876	Financial Daily see 0279-0734
0046-3892	Financial Management
0046-3906	Financne Studie‡
0046-3922	Finishing Highlights†
0046-3957	First-Fleeters
0046-3965	Fish Trades Review
0046-3973	Fisheries Council of Canada. Bulletin
0046-399X	Fitofilo
0046-4031	Flame and Flavour
0046-404X	Flap Internacional
0046-4058	Flashpoint see 0308-1230
0046-4082	Florafacts
0046-4090	Florida Audiovisual Association. A V A News changed to Florida Media Quarterly
0046-4112	Florida Contractor
0046-4120	Florida. Department of Agriculture and Consumer Services. Market Bulletin changed to Florida Market Bulletin
0046-4139	Florida. Department of State. Division of Archives. Archives and History News†
0046-4147	Florida Libraries†
0046-4155	Florida Music Director
0046-4171	F P changed to Florida Psychologist
0046-4201	Flow†
0046-421X	Flower Arranger
0046-4228	Flyfishers Journal
0046-4236	Flyer International
0046-4244	Flying Fish Newsletter†
0046-4260	Focus
0046-4287	Focus changed to Tell
0046-4295	Focus on Asian Studies
0046-4317	Focus on Mental Health
0046-4325	Focus on Pakistan†
0046-4333	Folio (Stamford)
0046-435X	Fontes Linguae Vasconum
0046-4368	Food Aid Bulletin†
0046-4384	Food and Nutrition
0046-4414	Food Industry Futures: a Strategy Service
0046-4422	Foodcorp Quarterly
0046-4449	Football Association News see 0306-1132
0046-4457	Football News†
0046-4473	For Adults Only changed to More (Raleigh)
0046-4481	Forages
0046-449X	Forbruker-Rapporten
0046-4511	Force Ouvriere Hebdo†
0046-4538	Ford World
0046-4546	Foreign Agricultural Trade of the United States
0046-4554	Foreign Investment News†
0046-4570	Forensic Science Gazette
0046-4597	Forestdale News changed to Bano Biggyan Patrika
0046-4600	Foret Privee
0046-4619	Forets de France et Action Forestiere
0046-4627	Formation Premilitaire et Physique†
0046-4643	Foersvar i Nutid
0046-4651	Fort Concho Report
0046-466X	Fort Worth Como Monitor
0046-4678	Universidade do Ceara. Boletim†
0046-4686	Forthcoming International Scientific and Technical Conferences
0046-4708	Forum for the Discussion of New Trends in Education
0046-4716	Forum Internationale†
0046-4732	Lutheran Forum. Forum Letter
0046-4759	Forward Atlanta changed to Forward Metro Atlanta
0046-4767	Foster Parent Nourricier see 0705-1123
0046-4775	Foto-Avisen
0046-4783	Foto und Film Rundschau†
0046-4791	Fotoarte
0046-4805	Fotografi
0046-4813	Advances in Thanatology
0046-4848	Fourth Estate†
0046-4856	Fox†
0046-4864	Fra Ribe Amt
0046-4872	Francaise Frisonne Pied Noire see 0240-0154
0046-4899	France Agricole
0046-4910	France Forum
0046-4937	Annales d'Hydrobiologie†
0046-4945	France Pays-Bas Informations Rapides
0046-4961	Franklin County Historical Review
0046-497X	Frau im Spiegel
0046-4988	Fredonia Statement changed to Statement (Fredonia)
0046-5003	Free Market†
0046-5011	Free Press†
0046-502X	Freedom from Hunger Campaign/Ideas and Action Bulletin changed to Freedom from Hunger Campaign/Action for Development
0046-5038	Freedom to Read Foundation News
0046-5046	Freight Forwarding
0046-5054	Freighter Travel-Letter
0046-5062	Frendz
0046-5070	Freshwater Biology
0046-5097	Friday Report
0046-5100	Friend International
0046-5119	Friendly Way†
0046-5135	Friidrott
0046-5143	Frivakt
0046-5151	Froid et la Climatisation
0046-5178	Mibifnim
0046-5186	Front and Center
0046-5208	Front Rouge
0046-5216	Frontiersman
0046-5224	Frugt, Groent og Blomster
0046-5240	Fruit Intelligence†
0046-5259	Fulbright Newsletter
0046-5267	Full Tide
0046-5275	Fulton County (Illinois) Historical Society Newsletter changed to Fulton County (Illinois) Historical & Genealogical Society Newsletter
0046-5291	Fur, Feathers and Fins†
0046-5305	Furies†
0046-5313	Furniture and Furnishings†
0046-5321	Furniture Index†
0046-5364	Gaceta Textil
0046-5372	Galvano Teknisk Tidsskrift changed to Overglade Teknikk
0046-5380	Gambia News Bulletin
0046-5399	Ganagrinco
0046-5402	Ganita
0046-5410	Gar
0046-5429	Garage and Transport Equipment changed to Garage and Automotive Retailer
0046-5437	Gartneryrket
0046-5445	Garuda†
0046-5453	Garuda Indonesian Airways Magazine changed to Garuda Magazine
0046-5461	Gas Chromatography-Mass Spectrometry Abstracts
0046-547X	Gastgewerbe changed to D G Deutsche Gaststaette/Deutsche Hotel-Zeitung Gastwirt und Hotelier
0046-5496	Gay Liberator†
0046-550X	Gay Sunshine†
0046-5518	Gazdalkodas
0046-5526	Gazette des Hopitaux†
0046-5542	Gazette Officielle de la Peche
0046-5569	Gee Report†
0046-5577	Gemeentewerken
0046-5593	G E C Telecommunications Journal†
0046-5607	General Practitioner
0046-5615	Generazione Zero
0046-5623	Genhinen†
0046-5658	Geodex Retrieval System for Geotechnical Abstracts
0046-5666	Geographer
0046-5690	Geographical Review of India
0046-5704	Geographical Society of New South Wales. Geography Bulletin
0046-5712	Geographical View Point
0046-5720	Geologi
0046-5755	Geometriae Dedicata
0046-5763	Geophysical Surveys see 0169-3298
0046-578X	Georgia Journal of International and Comparative Law
0046-5798	Georgia Music News
0046-5801	Geoscience Information Society. Newsletter changed to G.I.S. Newsletter
0046-581X	Geoscope
0046-5828	Geotechnical Engineering
0046-5836	German-American Studies changed to Yearbook of German-American Studies
0046-5879	Getreide und Mehl changed to Getreide, Mehl und Brot
0046-5895	Ghala†
0046-5909	Ghana Bulletin of Theology†
0046-5917	Ghana Farmer
0046-5925	Ghana Social Science Journal
0046-5933	Giessereiforschung
0046-5941	Ginecologia Brasileira†
0046-5968	Giornale Italiano di Cardiologia
0046-5984	Giorni
0046-5992	Glas Kanadskin Srba
0046-600X	Glasgow Dental Journal†
0046-6018	Glassposten
0046-6034	Glos Polski-Gazeta Polska
0046-6042	Go
0046-6050	Goeteborgs - Koepmannen
0046-6069	Golden Gate North†
0046-6077	Golden Legacy
0046-6085	Golden Spike†
0046-6093	Das Goldene Blatt
0046-6107	Gondolier changed to Boat/America
0046-6115	Gonzaga Law Review
0046-6123	Good Gardening†
0046-6131	Good Healthkeeping†
0046-614X	Good News†
0046-6158	Good Old Days
0046-6174	Goodfruit Grower
0046-6182	Goodfruit Grower. Supplement changed to Goodgrape Grower
0046-6190	Goool†
0046-6212	Government Data Systems
0046-6220	Government Purchasing Guide
0046-6239	Grace
0046-6247	Graduado†
0046-6263	Grains changed to Negoce et Agriculture
0046-6271	Grande Sinal
0046-628X	Grands-Musees†
0046-6298	Granite see 0741-5028
0046-6301	Granite State Libraries
0046-631X	Graphoscope
0046-6328	Grassroots (Carbondale) see 0017-3541
0046-6344	Great Lakes Sportsman†
0046-6352	Greater World
0046-6379	Greek-American Trade
0046-6395	Green Egg†
0046-6409	Green Sheet†
0046-6417	Green 'un†
0046-6433	Gridweek changed to Gridweek (1979)
0046-6441	Grosshandelskaufmann changed to Handel
0046-645X	Ground Water Age
0046-6468	Group Process†
0046-6476	Grower
0046-6484	Growing Minds
0046-6492	Growing Older see 0726-4240
0046-6506	Growing Point
0046-6514	Gruppendynamik
0046-6522	Guam Recorder
0046-6549	Guatemala Filatelica
0046-6557	Guayacan
0046-6565	Guest and Host†
0046-659X	Gulf Coast Plumbing - Heating - Cooling News
0046-6603	Gullsmedkunst
0046-6638	Guppy Digest
0046-6646	Guyana Development Corporation. Industrial Review†
0046-6654	Guyana Journal
0046-6662	Guynews†
0046-6670	Gymnast see 0276-1041
0046-6689	Habit†
0046-6697	Hablemos de Cine
0046-6700	Hackney Journal
0046-6719	Haiku Byways changed to Byways
0046-6735	Halifax Board of Trade. Commercial News
0046-6743	Halifax Wildlife Association. The Four Seasons
0046-6751	Royal Botanical Gardens, Hamilton, Ont. Gardens' Bulletin
0046-676X	Hamore
0046-6778	Handball
0046-6786	Handbook of Environmental Management Series†
0046-6794	Handchirurgie
0046-6808	Der Handelsvertreter und Handelsmakler
0046-6816	Haandverk og Industri
0046-6832	Happiness Holding Tank
0046-6840	Hardsyssels Aarbog
0046-6859	Harian's the Traveler's Newsletter†
0046-6875	Harris Survey Column Subscription see 0273-1037
0046-6891	Harvard Dental Alumni Bulletin
0046-6905	Harvard University. Graduate School of Education Association. Bulletin
0046-6913	Haryana Electricity
0046-6921	Haryana Labour Journal
0046-693X	Haustechnischer Anzeiger see 0341-4817
0046-6948	Hawaii Farm Science†
0046-6980	Headmasters Association Review changed to Secondary Heads Association Review
0046-6999	Headpiece†
0046-7006	Health†
0046-7014	Health and Vision
0046-7022	Health Devices
0046-7049	Health Food Trader changed to Natural Food Trader
0046-7057	Health for Life
0046-7065	Health in New Brunswick changed to New Brunswick. Department of Health. Happenings in Health / Actualites Sante
0046-7073	Health in New South Wales†
0046-709X	Health Planning in Illinois†
0046-7103	Health Sciences TV Bulletin†
0046-7111	Heart Care
0046-7146	Heat Pipe Technology†
0046-7154	Hebdo de la Blanchisserie - Teinturerie
0046-7170	Hedmark Slektshistorielags Tidsskrift
0046-7197	Helderberg Review†
0046-7227	Hemelspleet
0046-7235	Hemicrania†
0046-7243	Hemingway Notes see 0276-3362
0046-7251	Hemophilia Today
0046-7278	Her World
0046-7286	Heraldo del Cine
0046-7294	Here Now†
0046-7316	Heron
0046-7324	Herz Kreislauf
0046-7332	Hi-Fidelity & Video Review†
0046-7340	Hi-Fi Newsletter†
0046-7359	Hibueras
0046-7367	High Fidelity Trade News see 0739-8123
0046-7375	Higher Education in the States†
0046-7383	Highway
0046-7391	Highway Engineering in Australia
0046-7405	Highway Users Federation. Federation Reporter†
0046-7413	Hikobia
0046-7421	Hill Monitor†
0046-7448	Him†
0046-7456	Himalayan Observer
0046-7472	Hiroshima University Dental Society. Journal
0046-7480	Hispania
0046-7499	Histoire au Pays de Matane
0046-7502	Histoire d'Aujourd'hui
0046-7510	Histoire en Savoie
0046-7537	Historian†

ISSN	Title
0046-7545	Historical Journal of Barmera and District†
0046-7553	Historical Musings†
0046-7561	Historie
0046-757X	Historiens et Geographes
0046-7596	Historisk Tidskrift foer Finland
0046-760X	History of Education
0046-7618	History of Medicine†
0046-7626	Hjemmet
0046-7634	Hjukrunarfelag Islands. Timarit see 0250-4731
0046-7642	Hobart and William Smith Colleges Official Publication changed to Hobart and William Smith Colleges Bulletin
0046-7650	Hobby
0046-7677	Hoch und Tiefbau
0046-7693	Hockey Digest
0046-7707	Hockey World changed to Hockey Pictorial World
0046-7715	Hoefslag
0046-7723	Hogar y la Moda
0046-774X	Holly Letter see 0738-2421
0046-7758	Home Beer and Winemaking
0046-7766	Home Economics and Domestic Subjects see 0265-6930
0046-7774	Home Economics Research Journal
0046-7812	Homoeopathic World
0046-7820	Homoeopathy
0046-7839	Hon: a Book-Bin for Scholars†
0046-7855	Honneur et Fidelite
0046-7863	Honourable Artillery Company Journal
0046-7901	Horizons du Fantastique
0046-791X	Horizont
0046-7928	Horn Call
0046-7936	Horses
0046-7995	Hospital Indicators†
0046-8010	Hospital Medical Practice
0046-8037	Hospitais Civis de Lisboa. Boletim Clinico
0046-8045	Hot Bike†
0046-8088	Houses for Sale changed to New Homes and Apartment Guide
0046-8096	Housing Australia changed to Housing Victoria
0046-8134	Human Behavior†
0046-8150	Human Design
0046-8169	Human Ecology (Park Ridge)
0046-8177	Human Pathology
0046-8185	Human Rights
0046-8193	Human Rights Bulletin
0046-8207	H R W Newsletter†
0046-8215	Human Rights in U.S.S.R†
0046-8223	Human Rights News and Views changed to Human Rights News
0046-8231	Human Settlements see 0255-271X
0046-824X	Humanistische Union. Mitteilungen
0046-8258	Humanitas†
0046-8266	Humanities Journal see 0882-5475
0046-8274	Humbard Christian Report
0046-8304	Hungarian Library and Information Science Abstracts
0046-8312	Hunter Natural History†
0046-8339	Husdjur
0046-8347	Husholdningslaereren (Copenhagen)
0046-8371	I E E E Publications Bulletin
0046-838X	I E E E Transactions on Manufacturing Technology see 0148-6411
0046-8398	I E T: Zeitschrift fuer Elektrische Informations- und Energietechnik†
0046-8401	I S L A
0046-841X	I S M†
0046-8428	I W K
0046-8436	University of Ibadan. Library. Library Record
0046-8444	Ibero-Americana
0046-8452	Icelandic Canadian
0046-8487	Idaho Economic Indicators†
0046-8495	I E A Reporter changed to I E A Reporter (1976)
0046-8517	Ide
0046-8541	Idealistic Studies
0046-855X	Identity changed to Aboriginal and Islander Identity
0046-8568	Idiom
0046-8576	Idoles†
0046-8592	Ikorok†
0046-8606	Illinois Education News changed to State of Education
0046-8622	Illinois State Genealogical Society Quarterly
0046-8630	Illinois University. Department of Urban & Regional Planning. Research Bureau. Newsletter changed to Planning and Public Policy
0046-8665	Images du Transport changed to Magazine du Transport Routier
0046-869X	Impact (Ottawa)†
0046-8703	Impact (London)
0046-8711	Impegno Settanta
0046-872X	Impianti Manutenzione Trasporti†
0046-8754	In Re changed to San Francisco Attorney Magazine
0046-8762	In-Short
0046-8770	In Step with the Visiting Nurse Association of Brooklyn changed to V N A Newsletter
0046-8797	Inbavan Tanah Air
0046-8819	Inchiesta
0046-8827	Incorporated Swimming Teacher see 0306-0403
0046-8843	Independent Republic Quarterly
0046-8851	Independent Weekly
0046-8886	Index to Chinese Periodicals-Humanities and Social Sciences see 0378-0112
0046-8894	Index to Chinese Periodicals-Science and Technology see 0378-0112
0046-8908	Index to Current Urban Documents
0046-8916	Index to the American Banker changed to Index to the American Banker
0046-8924	Index to the Times changed to Times Index
0046-8932	India Abroad
0046-8940	India. Directorate of Jute Development. Jute Bulletin changed to India. Directorate of Jute Development. Jute Development Journal
0046-8959	India Weekly
0046-8967	Indian Affairs
0046-8975	Indian Archives
0046-8983	Indian Geotechnical Journal
0046-8991	Indian Journal of Microbiology
0046-9009	Indian Journal of Psychometry and Education
0046-9017	Indian Journal of Regional Science
0046-9025	Indian Manager
0046-9033	I P I R I Journal
0046-905X	Indian Roads Congress. Journal
0046-9068	Indian Tourist
0046-9076	Indian Trader
0046-9092	Indian Welding Journal
0046-9106	Indiana Law Review
0046-9114	Indiana. University. Libraries. Library Newsletter†
0046-9122	M E R P Memo
0046-9130	Indiana University. School of Medicine. Review†
0046-9149	Indien
0046-9157	Exceptional Parent
0046-9165	Indonesian Current Affairs Translation Bulletin†
0046-9173	Indonesian Review of International Affairs
0046-9181	Industria Lechera
0046-919X	Industrial Bookshelf changed to Business/Management Book Review
0046-9203	Industrial Informika
0046-9211	Industrial Launderer
0046-9246	Industrial Relations Review and Report
0046-9254	Industrial Sewing Machine Times see 0305-7046
0046-9270	Industrialist
0046-9319	Brewers Association of Canada. Industry Notes†
0046-9327	Informateur des Chefs d'Entreprises Libres
0046-9343	Information G
0046-9351	Information Historique
0046-936X	Information Immobiliere
0046-9378	Information-Part 2-Reports/ Bibliographies see 0360-0971
0046-9386	Comite Belge de la Distribution. Information Specialisee
0046-9394	Informationen der Afrika-Studienstelle changed to I F O Mitteilungen der Abteilung Entwicklungslaender
0046-9408	Informationen zur Politischen Bildung
0046-9416	Informations Aerauliques et Thermiques†
0046-9432	Informations Laitieres
0046-9459	Informations Sociales
0046-9483	Informatologia Yugoslavica
0046-9491	Informazioni di Parapsicologia
0046-9505	Informer changed to Tourist Talks
0046-9513	Ingenieur-Constructeur†
0046-9521	Ingenieur et le Technicien de l'Enseignement Technique changed to Technologies et Formations
0046-9556	Innenriksske Blad og Tidsskrifter see 0333-0451
0046-9564	Innovation World
0046-9572	Innovator (Ann Arbor)
0046-9580	Inquiry (Chicago)
0046-9599	Inquisitor
0046-9629	Inside Canberra
0046-9653	Insight (St. Paul)†
0046-9661	Insita changed to Ars Populi
0046-967X	Instant Research on Peace and Violence see 0356-7893
0046-9688	I F E P P Informations
0046-9696	Institut fuer Gesellschaftspolitik. Mitteilungen
0046-970X	I P W Berichte
0046-9718	I I E E Bulletin†
0046-9726	Belgium. Institut National d'Assurance Maladie Invalidite. I.N.A.M.I. Bulletin d'Information
0046-9734	Institut Panafricain pour le Developpement. Annuaire des Anciens Etudiants
0046-9742	I.A.P. Professional Photography in Australia see 0159-8880
0046-9750	Institute of Brewing. Journal (London)
0046-9769	I C B Review (Institute of Canadian Bankers) see 0822-6830
0046-9777	C F A Digest
0046-9785	Institute of Club Managers and Secretaries. Club Guide
0046-9793	Institute of Commerce, London. Magazine
0046-9807	Institute of Electrical Inspectors. I.E.I. Journal
0046-984X	Institute of Southeast Asian Studies. Library. Accessions List
0046-9858	Institution of Chemical Engineers. Transactions see 0302-0797
0046-9858	Institution of Chemical Engineers. Transactions changed to Chemical Engineering Research & Design
0046-9866	Institution of Engineers, Australia. Brisbane Division. Technical Papers changed to Institution of Engineers, Australia. Queensland Division. Technical Papers
0046-9874	Institution of Engineers Australia. South Australian Division. Bulletin†
0046-9882	Institution of Engineers, Jamaica. Journal
0046-9890	Instituto Agricola Catalan de San Isidro. Revista†
0046-9912	Instituto Brasileiro de Mercado de Capitais. Boletim de Documentacao†
0046-9920	I C A Informa
0046-9939	Instituto de Pesca, Sao Paulo. Boletim
0046-9947	Instituto de Pesquisa Agropecuaria do l'Este. Pesquisa e Experimentos. Comunicado Technico†
0046-9955	Instituto de Soldadura. Boletim†
0046-9963	Instituto Estadual de Hematologia Arthur de Siqueira Cavalcanti. Boletim
0046-9971	Instituto Forestal Latinoamericano de Investigacion y Capacitacion. Boletin Bibliografico. changed to Bibliografia Forestal Latinoamericana
0046-998X	Instituto Historico e Geografico Brasileiro. Revista
0046-9998	Pan American Institute of Geography and History. Commission on Cartography. Cartografia†
0047-0007	Boletin de la Integracion see 0325-1675
0047-0015	Institutul Central de Documentare Tehnica. Revista de Titluri: Aspecte Ale Economiei Mondiale changed to Institutul National de Informare si Documentare Stiintifica si Tehnica Revista de Titluri: Economia Mondiala si Nationala
0047-0023	Institutul National de Informare si Documentare Stiintifica si Tehnica Revista de Titluri: Arhitectura. Sistematizare. Constructii†
0047-0031	Institutul Central de Documentare Tehnica. Revista de Titluri: Cibernetica. Automatizarea changed to Institutul National de Informare si Documentare Stiintifica si Tehnica Revista de Titluri: Automatica
0047-0031	Institutul Central de Documentare Tehnica. Revista de Titluri: Cibernetica. Automatizarea changed to Institutul National de Informare si Documentare Stiintifica si Tehnica Revista de Titluri: Cibernetica
0047-004X	Institutul Central de Documentare Tehnica. Revista de Titluri: Cresterea Animalel changed to Institutul National de Informare si Documentare Stiintifica si Tehnica Revista de Titluri: Agricultura. Cresterea Animalelor
0047-0058	Institutul National de Informare si Documentare Stiintifica si Tehnica Revista de Titluri: Constructii de Masini†
0047-0066	Institutul Central de Documentare Tehnica. Revista de Titluri: Cultura Plantelor changed to Institutul National de Informare si Documentare Stiintifica si Tehnica Revista de Titluri: Agricultura. Cultura Plantelor
0047-0074	Institutul National de Informare si Documentare Stiintifica si Tehnica. Revista de Titluri: Coroziune. Protectia Suprafetelor†
0047-0082	Institutul National de Informare si Documentare Stiintifica si Tehnica Revista de Titluri: Conducerea si Organizarea Intreprinderilor†
0047-0090	Institutul Central de Documentare Tehnica. Revista de Titluri: Energetica. Electrotehnica changed to Institutul National de Informare si Documentare Stiintifica si Tehnica. Revista de Titluri: Energetica
0047-0090	Institutul Central de Documentare Tehnica. Revista de Titluri: Energetica. Electrotehnica changed to Institutul National de Informare si Documentare Stiintifica si Tehnica. Revista de Titluri: Electrotehnica
0047-0104	Institutul National de Informare si Documentare Stiintifica si Tehnica Revista de Titluri: Eficienta Economica. Pret de Cost. Evidenta Contabila si Statistica†
0047-0112	Institutul Central de Documentare Tehnica. Revista de Titluri: Electronica. Telecomunicatii changed to Institutul National de Informare si Documentare Stiintifica si Tehnica. Revista de Titluri: Telecomunicatii
0047-0120	Institutul National de Informare si Documentare Stiintifica si Tehnica Revista de Titluri: Frecare. Uzura. Ungere. Intretinerea si Repararea Utilajelor†

ISSN INDEX

0047-0139 Institutul Central de Documentare Tehnica. Revista de Titluri: Gospodarirea Apelor *changed to* Institutul National de Informare si Documentare Stiintifica si Tehnica Revista de Titluri: Gospodarirea Apelor. Hidrotehnica
0047-0147 Institutul National de Informare si Documentare Stiintifica si Tehnica Revista de Titluri: Industria Alimentara†
0047-0155 Institutul Central Documentare Tehnica. Revista de Titluri: Industria Chimica *changed to* Institutul National de Informare si Documentare Stiintifica si Tehnica Revista de Titluri: Chimie
0047-0163 Institutul National de Informare si Documentare Stiintifica si Tehnica Revista de Titluri: Informare Documentare†
0047-0171 Institutul Central de Documentare Tehnica. Revista de Titluri: Industria Lemnului *changed to* Institutul National de Informare si Documentare Stiintifica si Tehnica Revista de Titluri: Lemn. Celuloza. Hirtie
0047-018X Institutul National de Informare si Documentare Stiintifica si Tehnica Revista de Titluri: Industria Miniera†
0047-0198 Institutul Central de Documentare Tehnica. Revista de Titluri: Industria Petrolului si a Gazelor Naturale *changed to* Institutul National de Informare si Documentare Stiintifica si Tehnica Revista de Titluri: Petrol si Gaze
0047-0201 Institutul National de Informare si Documentare Stiintifica si Tehnica Revista de Titluri: Industria Usoara†
0047-021X Institutul National de Informare si Documentare Stiintifica si Tehnica Revista de Titluri: Metalurgie†
0047-0228 Institutul Central de Documentare Tehnica. Revista de Titluri: Mecanizarea Agriculturii *changed to* Institutul National de Informare si Documentare Stiintifica si Tehnica Revista de Titluri: Agricultura. Mecanizarea Agriculturii
0047-0236 Institutul Central de Documentare Tehnica. Revista de Titluri: Marketing. Organizarea Desfacerii Produselor si a Activitatii de Servicii *changed to* Institutul National de Informare si Documentare Stiintifica si Tehnica Revista de Titluri: Marketing. Organizarea Desfacerii si a Prestarilor de Servicii
0047-0244 Institutul National de Informare si Documentare Stiintifica si Tehnica, Revista de Titluri: Mecanica. Rezistenta Materialelor. Mecanisme†
0047-0260 Institutul National de Informare si Documentare Stiintifica si Tehnica Revista de Titluri Organizarea Productiei si a Muncii†
0047-0279 Institutul Central de Documentare Tehnica. Revista de Titluri: Poluarea Aerului si Apei. Tratarea Deseurilor *changed to* Institutul National de Informare si Documentare Stiintifica si Tehnica Revista de Titluri: "Poluarea si Protectia Mediului Inconjurator"
0047-0287 Institutul National de Informare si Documentare Stiintifica si Technica. Revista de Titluri: Protectia Muncii†
0047-0295 Institutul Central de Documentare Tehnica. Revista de Titluri: Poligrafie. Reprografie *changed to* Institutul National de Informare si Documentare Stiintifica si Tehnica. Revista de Titluri: Poligrafie
0047-0295 Institutul Central de Documentare Tehnica. Revista de Titluri: Poligrafie. Reprografie *changed to* Institutul National de Informare si Documentare Stiintifica si Tehnica. Revista de Titluri: Reprografie
0047-0309 Institutul Central de Documentare Tehnica. Revista de Titluri: Silvicultura. Expoatare Forestiera *changed to* Institutul National de Informare si Documentare Stiintifica si Tehnica Revista de Titluri: Silvicultura
0047-0317 Institutul Central de Documentare Tehnica. Revista de Titluri: Sistemul Informational Economic. Masini si Echipamet de Birou *changed to* Institutul National de Informare si Documentare Stiintifica si Tehnica Revista de Titluri: Teoria Informatiei. Informatica
0047-0325 Institutul National de Informare si Documentare Stiintifica si Tehnica Revista de Titluri: Tehnica Fotografica si Cinematografica†
0047-0333 Institutul National de Informare si Documentare Stiintifica si Technica. Revista de Titluri: Transport Intern. Ambalare. Depozitare.†
0047-0341 Institutul National de Informare si Documentare Stiintifica si Tehnica Revista de Titluri: Tehnica Masurarii. Controlul Calitatii†
0047-035X Institutul National de Informare si Documentare Stiintifica si Tehnica Revista de Titluri: Transporturi Cai de Comuncatie†
0047-0368 Institutul National de Informare si Documentare Stiintifica si Tehnica. Revista de Titluri: Scientica. Cercetare. Proiectare. Estetica Indusriala†
0047-0376 Instruments India
0047-0384 Insurgent Sociologist
0047-0392 Integration
0047-0406 Intelligence Survey
0047-0414 Inter-Com; Washington Area Librarians
0047-0422 I M C O Bulletin *changed to* I M O News
0047-0430 Interchange
0047-0449 Interchange†
0047-0457 Interchange (Portland)
0047-0465 Interchange *changed to* Population Education Interchange
0047-0473 Intercom†
0047-049X Interior†
0047-0511 Intermountain Jewish News
0047-0538 International Afro-American Museum. Newsletter *changed to* Afro-American Museum of Detroit. Newsletter
0047-0554 I A C P Law Enforcement Legislation and Litigation Report†
0047-0562 I A C P Law Enforcement Legislative Research Digest†
0047-0570 International Bank for Reconstruction and Development. Statement of Loans†
0047-0589 International Bar Journal *see* 0143-7453
0047-0597 International Barbed Wire Gazette
0047-0619 International Book Year Newsletter *changed to* Book Promotion News
0047-0627 International Business Digest†
0047-0635 International Cataloguing
0047-0651 I C M A Newsletter
0047-0678 International Commission of Jurists. Journal *see* 0020-6393
0047-0686 International Dostoevsky Society Bulletin *changed to* Dostoevsky Studies
0047-0694 International Export Association. Export News
0047-0716 International Institute for Population Studies. Newsletter *changed to* Institute for Population Sciences. Newsletter
0047-0724 International Journal of Government Auditing
0047-0732 International Journal of Group Tensions
0047-0740 International Journal of Nuclear Medicine and Biology *changed to* International Journal of Radiation Applications and Instrumentation. Part B: Nuclear Medicine and Biology
0047-0759 International Journal of Radiation Engineering
0047-0767 International Journal of Sport Psychology
0047-0783 Co-operative Information†
0047-0791 International Labour Office. Minutes of the Governing Body†
0047-083X I M F Survey
0047-0856 I N I S Newsletter
0047-0864 International Oil Scouts Association. Official Newsletter *see* 0277-6812
0047-0880 International Planned Parenthood Federation. Library Bulletin *see* 0309-6904
0047-0899 International Press Cutting Service: Modern Plastics and Engineering
0047-0902 International Press Cutting Service: Ceramics - Porcelain - Refractory - Cement - Glass
0047-0910 International Press Cutting Service: Chemical Process Engineering. Drugs - Pharmaceuticals
0047-0929 International Press Cutting Service: Dyestuff Industry and Chemicals
0047-0937 International Press Cutting Service: Electronics and Electricals Industry
0047-0945 International Press Cutting Service: Fermented Wines, Liquers, Brandy, Gin, Rum, Whisky, Beer and Alcoholic Drinks
0047-0953 International Press Cutting Service: Import - Export - Licenses
0047-0961 International Press Cutting Service: Jute, Gunny, Hessian, Burlap, Coir
0047-097X International Press Cutting Service: Labour Welfare - Industrial Legislation and Personnel Management
0047-0988 International Press Cutting Service: Leather - Hides - Skin - Footwear
0047-0996 International Press Cutting Service: Machine Tool and Iron Steel Industry
0047-1003 International Press Cutting Service: Mines & Minerals (Coal/Ores)
0047-1011 International Press Cutting Service: Non-Ferrous Metals - Aluminium
0047-102X International Press Cutting Service: Oils (Vegetable) Fats - Soap - Animalfeed
0047-1038 International Press Cutting Service: Paper - Pulp - Board/Straw
0047-1046 International Press Cutting Service: Petroleum - Petrochemicals - Fertilisers - Agricultural Chemistry
0047-1054 International Press Cutting Service: Plywood - Timber - Particle Board
0047-1062 International Press Cutting Service: Rubber and Rubber Technology
0047-1070 International Press Cutting Service: Scientific Instruments, Laboratory Equipment & Chemicals
0047-1089 International Press Cutting Service: Sugar - Gur - Khandasari
0047-1097 International Press Cutting Service: Taxation - Finance - Company Law
0047-1100 International Press Cutting Service: Tea and Coffee News
0047-1119 International Press Cutting Service: Textile News
0047-1127 International Press Cutting Service: Tender Notifications (Indian & Global)
0047-1135 International Press Cutting Service: Tobacco News
0047-1143 International Press Cutting Service: Wheat & Wheat Products (Rice/Food Grains)
0047-1151 International Press Cutting Service: Processed Food Products/Spices
0047-116X International Psychologist
0047-1178 International Relations
0047-1208 International Review of Music Aesthetics and Sociology *changed to* International Review of the Aesthetics and Sociology of Music
0047-1216 I T C C Review
0047-1224 International Telecommunication Union. Operational Bulletin
0047-1240 International Understanding at School
0047-1259 I.U.G.G. Chronicle
0047-1267 International Union of Geological Sciences. Geological Newsletter *see* 0705-3797
0047-1275 International Wealth Success Newsletter
0047-1291 Interprete
0047-1305 I F C O News
0047-1321 Intervention
0047-1348 Investa *changed to* Kovoexport-Investa
0047-1356 Investor's Digest of Canada
0047-1372 Invitation to Snowmobiling†
0047-1380 Involvement *see* 0319-1443
0047-1399 Iowa Geographer *see* 0199-994X
0047-1402 University of Iowa. Libraries. Newsletter
0047-1410 Iran Family Planning Bulletin†
0047-1429 Iraq News Bulletin
0047-1437 Irish Ancestor
0047-1445 Irish Bacon News
0047-1453 Irish Equipment News
0047-1461 Irish Hardware and Allied Trader
0047-147X Irish Medical Times
0047-1488 Irish Pulse†
0047-1496 Iron Man†
0047-150X Ironwood
0047-1518 Irrigation Journal
0047-1542 Islas
0047-1550 Isotype Titles *changed to* Zidis
0047-1569 Israel. Department of Antiquities and Museums. Archaeological News *changed to* Israel. Department of Antiquities and Museums. Archaeological Newsletter
0047-1577 Israel Gerontological Society. Information Bulletin
0047-1585 Israel Oil News†
0047-1593 Israel Shipping Research Institute. Journal *see* 0334-2751
0047-1607 Issue
0047-1623 Istanbul Universitesi. Tip Fakultesi. Tip Fakultesi Mecmuasi *see* 0301-7362
0047-1631 I A I Informa†
0047-164X It Ain't Me Babe†
0047-1658 Italian-Australian Bulletin of Commerce
0047-1666 Italix†
0047-1674 Ivoire Dimanche
0047-1690 Jack O'Dwyer's Newsletter *changed to* Jack O'Dwyer's P R Newsletter
0047-1712 Jakemate
0047-1720 Jamaica Churchman
0047-1739 Janus†
0047-1755 Japan Chemical Week
0047-1763 Japan Dental Association. Journal
0047-1771 Japan Foreign Trade Journal†
0047-1798 Japan Society of Civil Engineers. Transactions†
0047-181X Japanese Business Journal†
0047-1828 Japanese Circulation Journal
0047-1836 Japanese Journal for the Midwife
0047-1852 Japanese Journal of Clinical Medicine
0047-1860 Japanese Journal of Clinical Pathology
0047-1879 Japanese Journal of Industrial Health
0047-1887 Japanese Journal of Legal Medicine
0047-1895 Japanese Journal of Nurses' Education
0047-1917 Japanese Journal of Veterinary Research
0047-1925 J N R Bulletin
0047-1933 Jasmin†
0047-1941 Javelin *changed to* Fleele
0047-1968 Jeremiad†
0047-1976 Jeugd en Samenleving
0047-1984 Jeunesse Ouvriere
0047-1992 Jeunesse Ouvriere Chretienne *changed to* Equipe Ouvriere
0047-200X Jewish Radical
0047-2018 Jewish Veteran
0047-2034 Jobs in Social Work†
0047-2042 Johnstown Motorist *changed to* Motorist (Johnstown)
0047-2050 Joka Poika *see* 0781-7177
0047-2077 Jornal Brasileiro de Medicina
0047-2085 Jornal Brasileiro de Psiquiatria
0047-2093 Jornal de Letras
0047-2123 Journal de la Navigation

0047-2131 Journal de la Police Nationale†
0047-214X Journal de la Publicite et des Techniques de la Promotion et Publi-Magazine
0047-2158 Journal de Mathematiques Elementaires†
0047-2166 Journal de Pharmacie de Belgique
0047-2174 Journal de Tanger
0047-2182 Journal des Caisses d'Epargne
0047-2212 Journal for the Study of Judaism *changed to* Journal for the Study of Judaism in the Persian, Hellenistic and Roman Period
0047-2220 Journal of Applied Rehabilitation Counseling
0047-2239 Journal of Architectural Education
0047-2255 Journal of Canadian Fiction
0047-2263 Journal of Caribbean History
0047-228X Journal of Clinical Child Psychology
0047-2298 Journal of Coated Fibrous Materials *see* 0093-4658
0047-2301 Journal of Collective Negotiations in the Public Sector
0047-231X Journal of College Science Teaching
0047-2328 Journal of Comparative Family Studies
0047-2336 Journal of Contemporary Asia
0047-2352 Journal of Criminal Justice
0047-2360 Journal of Development Administration
0047-2379 Journal of Drug Education
0047-2395 Journal of Educational Technology Systems
0047-2409 Journal of Entomology (A) *see* 0307-6962
0047-2417 Journal of Entomology (B) *see* 0307-6970
0047-2425 Journal of Environmental Quality
0047-2433 Journal of Environmental Systems
0047-2441 Journal of European Studies
0047-245X Journal of Food Distribution Research
0047-2468 Journal of Geometry
0047-2476 Journal of Geriatrics†
0047-2484 Journal of Human Evolution
0047-2492 Journal of Intergroup Relations
0047-2506 Journal of International Business Studies
0047-2514 Journal of Irish Literature
0047-2522 Journal of Korean Affairs†
0047-2530 Journal of Legal Studies
0047-2549 Journal of Marketing and Economic Research
0047-2557 Journal of Mathematical and Physical Sciences
0047-2573 Journal of Medieval and Renaissance Studies
0047-2581 Journal of Mexican American History
0047-259X Journal of Multivariate Analysis
0047-262X Journal of Nursing
0047-2638 Journal of Operational Psychiatry†
0047-2646 Journal of Organizational Communication†
0047-2662 Journal of Phenomenological Psychology
0047-2670 Journal of Photochemistry
0047-2689 Journal of Physical and Chemical Reference Data
0047-2697 Journal of Political and Military Sociology
0047-2700 Journal of Political Studies
0047-2719 Journal of Popular Film *see* 0195-6051
0047-2727 Journal of Public Economics
0047-2735 Journal of Religious Studies
0047-2743 Journal of Remote Sensing†
0047-2751 Journal of Rural Development and Administration
0047-276X Journal of Russian Studies
0047-2778 Journal of Small Business Management
0047-2786 Journal of Social Philosophy
0047-2794 Journal of Social Policy
0047-2816 Journal of Technical Writing and Communication
0047-2824 Journal of Technology
0047-2840 Journal of the New Harbinger *see* 0190-2741
0047-2867 Journal of Theology for Southern Africa
0047-2875 Journal of Travel Research
0047-2883 Journal of Value Engineering†
0047-2891 Journal of Youth and Adolescence
0047-2905 Journal on the Handicapped Child†
0047-2913 Journal Pakistan†
0047-293X Journalistes Francais
0047-2956 Juco Review
0047-2972 Judges' Journal
0047-2980 Judo-Koerier *changed to* Budo Koerier
0047-2999 Jungle
0047-3014 Juris Doctor†
0047-3030 K
0047-3049 K F Z-Betrieb und Automarkt *see* 0722-7841
0047-3057 K-Kauppa Ja Myyja *changed to* Kehittyvae Kauppa
0047-3065 K-3 Bulletin of Teaching Ideas and Materials†
0047-3073 Kaeltetechnik-Klimatisierung *changed to* K I Klima, Kaelte, Heizung
0047-3081 Kainai News
0047-309X Kajian Veterinar *see* 0126-9437
0047-3103 Kalakalpam
0047-3111 Kalakshetra *changed to* Kalakshetra Quarterly
0047-312X Kalori
0047-3138 Makerere University. Library. Library Bulletin and Accessions List
0047-3146 Kanadai Fuggetlen Hirlap *changed to* Magyar Naplo (Toronto, 1966)
0047-3154 Kanadsky Slovak
0047-3170 Kansas Professional Engineer
0047-3189 Kansas State Engineer
0047-3197 Karachi. Chamber of Commerce and Industry. Trade Journal†
0047-3200 Karaki†
0047-3219 Karavana†
0047-3227 Die Karawane
0047-3235 Karibu Tanzania†
0047-3243 Karjantuote *changed to* Meijeriteollisuus
0047-3251 Karjatalous
0047-326X Karnatak University, Dharwad, India. Bulletin†
0047-3278 Kart og Plan
0047-3286 Kasari†
0047-3294 Katholischer Digest
0047-3308 Kauneus ja Terveys
0047-3316 Kauppateknikko
0047-3340 Kenya Journal of Adult Education†
0047-3359 Kerala Industry
0047-3367 Kerala Sabha
0047-3375 Keretapi
0047-3383 Kesatuan Bulletin
0047-3391 Keste Damena
0047-3405 Kettenwirk-Praxis
0047-3413 Keynote *see* 0272-6513
0047-343X Kirjakauppalehti
0047-3456 Kirkens Verden†
0047-3472 Kneipp-Bademeister†
0047-3499 Knox Alumnus *changed to* Knox Alumnus
0047-3510 Koettbranschen
0047-3537 Kommunalt Tidsskrift†
0047-3545 Konditormestrenes Medlemsblad *changed to* Bager-Konditor
0047-3553 Konfekturehandleren
0047-3561 Koninklijke Officiers Schermbond. Kos-Gebeuren
0047-3588 Korea Focus†
0047-3596 Korea Today†
0047-360X Korean Medical Abstracts
0047-3618 Korean Nurse
0047-3626 Korps Komando *changed to* Mari Jo
0047-3634 Korrosjons-Nytt
0047-3650 Kosmos
0047-3677 Kotiseutu
0047-3685 Kotitalous
0047-3693 Krishnamurti Foundation. Bulletin
0047-3715 Kryds-Avisen†
0047-3731 Kulturen Zivot
0047-3766 Kunststoff-Journal
0047-3774 L A S I E
0047-3839 Labor Arbitration in Government
0047-3855 Laboratory Product News
0047-3863 Labores del Hogar
0047-3871 Labour *changed to* Labor Press and Information
0047-388X Labour Research Department. Fact Service
0047-3898 Lago
0047-3901 Lagos Librarian
0047-391X Lakaskultura
0047-3928 Lambda Alpha Journal of Man
0047-3936 Lamp
0047-3944 Lamp in the Spine†
0047-3952 Land Reform, Land Settlement and Cooperatives
0047-3960 Landbonyt
0047-3979 Landesverband der Tonkuenstler und Musiklehrer. Mitteilungsblatt
0047-3995 Landmaschinen-Rundschau
0047-4002 Landwirt im Ausland *see* 0343-6462
0047-4010 Die Landwirtschaft
0047-4029 Landwirtschaftsblatt Weser-Ems
0047-4037 Language and Literature†
0047-4045 Language in Society
0047-4053 Lantern's Core
0047-4061 Lanzadera†
0047-407X Lapsi Ja Nuoriso *see* 0355-3736
0047-4088 Lariat
0047-410X Laser Raman Spectroscopy Abstracts *see* 0309-5320
0047-4126 Lastebileieren
0047-4134 Latin American Literary Review
0047-4142 Literacy Advance
0047-4169 Law and Society Newsletter *changed to* Law and Society Quarterly
0047-4177 Law Council of Australia. Law Council Newsletter *see* 0159-7531
0047-4185 Law Report News†
0047-4193 Law Review Digest
0047-4207 Lawasia
0047-4215 LawLab Journal *changed to* Expert Witness Journal
0047-4231 Lazio Ieri e Oggi
0047-424X Leadership
0047-4258 League of Pity Paper *changed to* Wings
0047-4274 Leben und Erziehen
0047-4282 Der Lebensmittelkaufmann
0047-4290 Lebensmitteltechnik
0047-4304 Lecturas
0047-4312 Lederwaren-Zeitung *changed to* In Leder
0047-4320 Leeds and West Riding Topic *changed to* Leeds & Yorkshire Topic
0047-4339 Leeds Weekly Citizen
0047-4355 Leichtathletik
0047-4363 Leisure
0047-438X Leka Nuhou†
0047-4401 Ragioni Critiche
0047-441X Letras da Provincia
0047-4428 Letras de Hoje
0047-4436 Lettres Mensuelles; Revue Philosophique et Sociale
0047-4444 Levende Gedachten
0047-4452 Lex
0047-4460 Liberal
0047-4479 Liberalt Perspektiv *changed to* Populist
0047-4495 Liberation War
0047-4509 Libertarian Analysis†
0047-4517 Libertarian Forum
0047-4525 Library Action
0047-4533 Library Association of Australia. University and College Libraries Section. News Sheet†
0047-4541 Library Trustees Foundation of New York State. Newsletter
0047-4568 Libros Nuevos†
0047-4576 L E S Nouvelles
0047-4584 Licht und Leben
0047-4592 Life Threatening Behavior *see* 0363-0234
0047-4614 Life in America†
0047-4630 Lifeliner
0047-4649 Light (London, 1881)
0047-4657 Light (London, 1969)
0047-4665 Lillit
0047-4681 Lincolnshire Agricultural and Industrial Sales and Wants
0047-469X Linde Distributor Progress†
0047-4703 Lingua e Cultura
0047-4711 Lingua e Literatura
0047-472X Sprache und Literatur in Wissenschaft
0047-4746 Linnean Society of New South Wales. Proceedings
0047-4754 Liquified Petroleum Gas *changed to* L.P. Gas News
0047-4762 Listening Index *changed to* A M P S Broadcast Media
0047-4770 Literacy: a Newsletter *changed to* Adult Education Information Notes
0047-4789 Literacy Documentation†
0047-4797 Literary Repository†
0047-4800 Litterature
0047-4819 Little Flower Monthly†
0047-4827 Liverpool Newsletter
0047-4835 Living City
0047-4843 Living Earth†
0047-4851 Living Historical Farms Bulletin
0047-486X Living in South Carolina
0047-4878 Living Music
0047-4894 Llewellyn *see* 0145-885X
0047-4908 Lloyd's Weekly Casualty Reports
0047-4916 Lo Gai Saber *changed to* Gai Saber
0047-4924 Local Government in South Australia†
0047-4959 Locus
0047-4967 Logberg-Heimskringla
0047-4975 Logger†
0047-4983 Loggers World
0047-4991 Logistics and Transportation Review
0047-5009 Logistik Technik und Versorgung†
0047-5017 Loisirs Nautiques
0047-5025 London City Mission Magazine *changed to* Span (London)
0047-5033 London Collector
0047-505X Los†
0047-5068 W C N Commercial News
0047-5076 Los Angeles County Medical Association. Bulletin *see* 0162-7163
0047-5084 Los Angeles County Museum of Art. Graphic Arts Council. Newsletter†
0047-5106 Louisiana Researcher†
0047-5122 Louisiana Tech Engineer
0047-5149 Loyalist Gazette
0047-5157 Ludd's Mill
0047-5165 Lugha Yetu
0047-5173 Lumen†
0047-522X Luton Commerce and Trade Journal *changed to* Chiltern Enterprise
0047-5246 M D of Canada†
0047-5254 M H Builders News *changed to* M H/R V Builders News
0047-5262 M I S
0047-5270 M S News
0047-5289 M S T English Quarterly
0047-5297 M T A Journal
0047-5300 M U M
0047-5319 Maanmittaus
0047-5327 Maansiirto
0047-5335 Macdonald Journal
0047-5351 Machinery & Machine Tool Journal
0047-536X Machines Production
0047-5378 Machinist
0047-5386 McKee-Pedersen Instruments. M P I Applications Notes†
0047-5394 McKinsey Quarterly
0047-5416 Madagascar; Revue de Geographie
0047-5424 Made in Europe. Technical Equipment Catalog
0047-5432 Madrona
0047-5467 Magic and Spells Quarterly†
0047-5475 Magic Carpet
0047-5491 Magnesium Monthly Review
0047-5513 Magyar Elet
0047-5521 Magyar Hirlap†
0047-5548 Maine Trail
0047-5572 Mak†
0047-5599 Malayan Economic Review *changed to* Singapore Economic Review
0047-5610 Malaysia in History
0047-5629 Malaysian Digest
0047-5637 Mallee Horticulture Digest†
0047-5653 Management†
0047-567X Management Development Centre, Dacca. Quarterly Bulletin *see* 0378-7532
0047-5688 Management Education & Development
0047-570X Management in Government
0047-5718 Management-Scope

ISSN INDEX

ISSN	Title
0047-5726	Manager Magazin
0047-5734	University of Santo Tomas. Faculty of Civil Law. Law Review
0047-5742	University of Santo Tomas. Graduate School. Journal of Graduate Research
0047-5750	U.S.T. Library Bulletin†
0047-5769	Manitoba Journal of Education†
0047-5785	Manpower and Vocational Education Weekly *changed to* Vocational Training News
0047-5793	Manpower Documentation
0047-5807	Mantenimiento Ingenieria de Fabricas *see* 0276-7317
0047-5815	Manufacturing Engineer *changed to* Industrial Technology and Machine Tools
0047-5823	Manx Star
0047-5858	Maquettes-Plastiques *changed to* Maquettes Plastique Magazine
0047-5866	Mar
0047-5874	Marathon
0047-5904	Marelli *changed to* Ercole Marelli
0047-5912	Marga
0047-5920	Mariemou
0047-5939	Marine and Outdoor Trades *see* 0705-8993
0047-5947	Marine Aquarist
0047-5955	Marine Engineers Review
0047-5963	Maritime Express†
0047-5971	Maritimes Tax Reports
0047-598X	Market Research in Benelux *see* 0308-3446
0047-5998	Market Research in Germany *see* 0308-3446
0047-6005	Market Research in Italy *see* 0308-3446
0047-603X	Marmi Graniti Pietre
0047-6048	Marquette University Education Review†
0047-6056	Marriage Counseling Quarterly *changed to* Marriage and Family Counselors Quarterly
0047-6064	Marturion
0047-6072	Marxistiskt Forum
0047-6080	Maryland Nurse
0047-6099	Maryland Researcher
0047-6102	Maskinmesteren
0047-6110	Road of the Party
0047-6129	Massachusetts Correctional Association. Correctional Research Bulletin†
0047-6137	Massachusetts Journal of Mental Health†
0047-6153	Massachusetts Researcher†
0047-6161	Massachusetts Studies in English
0047-617X	Master Builder *changed to* Builder
0047-6188	Master Indicator of the Stock Market
0047-6196	Master Photographer
0047-6218	Material Management Journal and Review *changed to* Focus (Lansing)
0047-6234	Materials Handling and Storage *changed to* Materials Handling & Distribution
0047-6242	Mathematical Association of South Australia. S.A. Mathematics Teacher *changed to* Mobius
0047-6250	Mathematical Association of Tanzania. Bulletin *see* 0856-065X
0047-6269	Mathematics Education
0047-6277	Mathematische Operationsforschung und Statistik *see* 0323-3944
0047-6277	Mathematische Operationsforschung und Statistik *see* 0233-1934
0047-6285	Matthew Bender Tax Letter *changed to* Washington Tax and Business Report
0047-6293	Mawazo
0047-6315	Me Jane
0047-6323	Measurement in Education†
0047-6331	Meat and Allied Trades Federation of Australia. Western Australian Division. Meat Industry†
0047-634X	Meat and Livestock Commission, Bucks, England. International Market Survey
0047-6358	Meat Packers Council of Canada. Facts, Figures, Comment *changed to* Canadian Meat Council. Facts, Figures, Comment
0047-6366	Meat Trades Journal of Australia *see* 0156-2681
0047-6374	Mechanisms of Ageing and Development
0047-6390	Medaille Militaire
0047-6404	Medecine d'Afrique Noire
0047-6412	Medecine et Chirurgie Digestives
0047-6420	Medecine et Collectivite
0047-6439	Media and Consumer *see* 0010-194X
0047-6447	Media Mix Newsletter *changed to* Media Mix
0047-6455	Medical Assistance†
0047-6463	Medical Chronicle Monthly†
0047-6471	M C G Today
0047-648X	Medical Dimensions†
0047-6498	Medical Equipment *see* 0110-4578
0047-651X	Medical Journal of Zambia
0047-6528	Medical News Fortnightly
0047-6536	Medical News, Medicine and Law
0047-6552	Medical Progress through Technology
0047-6560	Medical Research Council Newsletter
0047-6587	Medico-Legal Society of New South Wales. Proceedings
0047-6595	Medico-Legal Society of Victoria. Proceedings
0047-6609	Mediterraneo
0047-6641	Meetings on Atomic Energy
0047-665X	Meie Elu
0047-6668	Mekong Monthly Bulletin *see* 0252-5348
0047-6676	Melbourne. Royal Melbourne Hospital. Quarterly†
0047-6692	American Association of State Colleges and Universities. Memo: to the President
0047-6706	Memorial-Sloan Kettering Cancer Center. Clinical Bulletin†
0047-6714	Memphis State University Law Review
0047-6730	Men's Week†
0047-6749	Mental Health News†
0047-6757	Mental Hygiene News†
0047-6765	Mental Retardation (Washington)
0047-6773	Mercury (San Francisco)
0047-6781	Merseyside Business News†
0047-679X	Message
0047-6803	Message of Life†
0047-6838	Metal and Engineering†
0047-6854	M T I A News Bulletin *changed to* M T I A Input
0047-6862	Metal Trades Journal *see* 0047-6838
0047-6870	Metaletter
0047-6889	Metallbericht
0047-6897	Metals Australasia
0047-6919	Methodist Church Music Society Bulletin
0047-6927	Metier d'Art du Quebec
0047-6935	Metro Guide. Halifax-Dartmouth Current Events
0047-6943	Metro Teen Scene†
0047-696X	Metropolitan Area Planning Council Regional Report
0047-6978	M A U D E P Newsletter
0047-6986	Metsastaja
0047-6994	Mexican Newsletter
0047-701X	C I A B Circular†
0047-7028	Mexico Forestal
0047-7036	Mexico Ganadero†
0047-7052	Michigan Academy of Science, Arts, and Letters. Academy Letter
0047-7060	Michigan Society for Respiratory Therapy. Journal
0047-7087	Michigan Civil Rights Commission Newsletter
0047-7095	Michigan Dental Hygienist Association. Bulletin
0047-7109	Michigan. Department of Commerce. Corporation and Securities Bureau. Securities Bulletin *changed to* Update (Lansing)
0047-7117	Michigan Food News
0047-7125	Michigan Reading Journal
0047-7133	Michigan Researcher
0047-7141	Michigan State University. Center for International Programs. International Report†
0047-715X	Michigan State University. Latin American Studies Center. Newsletter†
0047-7168	Summation†
0047-7184	Microfilm Techniques†
0047-7192	Microinfo
0047-7214	Microwave Systems News *changed to* Microwave Systems News & Technology
0047-7222	Midden
0047-7230	Middle East Economic Digest
0047-7249	Middle East International
0047-7257	Middle East Observer
0047-7265	M E R I P Report *see* 0888-0328
0047-7273	Midi-Minuit Fantastique
0047-7281	Midland Cooperator
0047-729X	Midland History
0047-7311	Midwest Purchasing
0047-732X	Midwest Racing News
0047-7338	Migrant Echo†
0047-7346	Militaertechnik
0047-7354	Militaer Teknisk Tidskrift
0047-7362	Militaerseelsorge
0047-7370	Military Collectors News
0047-7389	Military History of Texas and the Southwest
0047-7397	Voenno-Meditsinskii Zhurnal
0047-7400	Milk News
0047-7419	Milk Topics
0047-7427	Mill Trade Journal
0047-7443	Mineria y Metalurgia, Plasticos y Electricidad
0047-7478	Miniaturbahnen
0047-7508	M L N Bulletin *changed to* M L N New Directions
0047-7524	Mirror of the Month†
0047-7540	Mississippi Housing Newsletter†
0047-7559	Mississippi Review
0047-7567	Missouri Highways†
0047-7575	U M K C Law Review
0047-7583	Mlezi
0047-7591	Mobil & Motor
0047-7605	Mobile Home and Trailer News *changed to* Manufactured Home News
0047-7648	Modelisme
0047-7664	Modern Astronomy†
0047-7672	Modern Athlete and Coach
0047-7699	Modern Farmer *changed to* Modern Farming
0047-7702	Modern Greek Studies Association Bulletin
0047-7710	Modern Kemi†
0047-7729	Modern Language Studies
0047-7737	Modern Office *changed to* Modern Office
0047-7753	Modern Unionist
0047-7761	Modern Woman
0047-777X	Moderna Organizacija *see* 0350-1531
0047-7788	Modersmaalet
0047-7796	Moebel-Kultur
0047-780X	Der Moebelspediteur
0047-7826	Molecular Sieve Abstracts†
0047-7834	Monarchist
0047-7842	Monatsschrift Deutscher Zahnaerzte *see* 0340-1766
0047-7850	Monde Arabe†
0047-7869	Mondo Occulto *changed to* Nuovo Mondo Occulto
0047-7877	Monete e Medaglie
0047-7885	Monika
0047-7893	Moniteurs *changed to* M.A.
0047-7907	Monographs for Teachers of French *see* 0815-7138
0047-7915	Monster Times†
0047-7923	Montagne et Alpinisme
0047-7931	Montana Food Distributor
0047-794X	Montana Oil Journal
0047-7958	Montana Post
0047-7966	Montana Public Affairs Report†
0047-7974	Montana Rural Electric News *changed to* Rural Montana
0047-7982	Montana. State University. Library. Recent Acquisitions†
0047-7990	Montana Stockgrower
0047-8008	Montana's Treasure Acres†
0047-8016	Montevecchio†
0047-8032	Australia. Bureau of Statistics. South Australian Office. Monthly Summary of Statistics, South Australia.
0047-8040	Tax Features
0047-8059	Montreal Children's Hospital. Children's News
0047-8075	Montreal. Stock Exchange. Monthly Review *changed to* Montreal Exchange. Monthly Review
0047-8083	Moon Rainbow
0047-8091	MORE
0047-8105	Moreana
0047-813X	Mortgage and Real Estate Executives Report
0047-8148	Mosca Profana
0047-8164	Mosella
0047-8172	Mother & Baby
0047-8180	Moto Revue
0047-8199	Motor
0047-8210	Motor Manual *changed to* Australian Motor Manual
0047-8261	Mountain and Plain History Notes *see* 0272-8907
0047-8288	Movie/TV Marketing
0047-830X	Moving Out
0047-8318	Ms
0047-8326	Mufulira Mirror *changed to* Mining Mirror
0047-8342	Mundo Taquigrafico†
0047-8350	Munger Africana Library Notes†
0047-8369	Municipal Engineer
0047-8377	Munnpleien
0047-8385	Murmur
0047-8407	Muscle Training Illustrated
0047-8415	Muscular Development
0047-8423	Music & Arts†
0047-8431	Music and the Teacher
0047-844X	Music Educators National Conference. Contemporary Music Project. C M P Newsletter†
0047-8466	Musical Newsletter†
0047-8474	Der Musikmarkt
0047-8482	Mutter und Kind
0047-8490	Mutual Fund Performance Monthly†
0047-8504	Mutual Funds Forum†
0047-8512	Mylord†
0047-8539	Mysore Journal of Agricultural Sciences
0047-8555	Mythic Society. Quarterly Journal
0047-8563	N P†
0047-8598	Nachrichten zur Wirtschafts- und Sozialpolitik
0047-8601	Naering i Nord
0047-861X	Naftika Chronika
0047-8628	Nairang Da'ijist
0047-8636	Nairobi Handbook†
0047-8644	Nande
0047-8660	Nashotah Review†
0047-8679	Nashville, Tennessee. Children's Museum. Museum Notes†
0047-8687	N C P C Newsletter†
0047-8695	Nassau Lawyer
0047-8717	N A R D A News
0047-8733	National Association of Conservation Districts. Tuesday Letter
0047-8741	N A J E Educator *see* 0730-9791
0047-8768	National Braille Mail
0047-8784	National Congress of American Indians. Bulletin *changed to* Sentinel/Bulletin - N C A I News
0047-8792	National Council of Women of Australia. Bulletin
0047-8806	National Council on Alcoholism. Friday Letter†
0047-8822	National C F News Bulletin†
0047-8830	National Democrat†
0047-8857	National Electronics Council. Review *see* 0305-2257
0047-8865	National Folk†
0047-8881	N I C A Outlook *see* 0270-3963
0047-8903	National League of Cities. Congressional Report *changed to* N L C Washington Report to the Nations Cities
0047-8938	N L F A Feed-Lines *changed to* Beef Business Bulletin

1336 ISSN INDEX

0047-8946 National Maritime S A R Review *see* 0093-2124
0047-8962 British Israel World Federation. National Message *changed to* National Message
0047-8989 N O L P E School Law Journal†
0047-8997 N O L P E Notes
0047-9012 National Parks Journal
0047-9020 N.P.A. Journal
0047-9047 National Police Journal†
0047-9055 National Research Council, Canada. Division of Mechanical Engineering and National Aeronautical Establishment. Quarterly Bulletin†
0047-9063 National Saver *see* 0047-9071
0047-9071 National Savings Newsletter†
0047-908X N S S F N S News
0047-9101 N S A C Newsletter *changed to* Advocate (Albany)
0047-911X National Times
0047-9128 National Trust of Australia (New South Wales) National Trust Bulletin *see* 0811-0964
0047-9136 N T I Newsletter
0047-9144 Native People†
0047-9152 Natural Health Bulletin
0047-9160 Natural Life Styles†
0047-9195 Nebraska Art Association Quarterly *changed to* Nebraska Art Association Newsletter
0047-9209 Nebraska Law Review
0047-9217 Nebraska Resources
0047-9233 Nederlands Tijdschrift voor Vacuumtechniek
0047-9241 Nederlandse Krijgsman
0047-925X Needle Arts
0047-9276 Neerlandica Extra Muros†
0047-9284 Neerlands Voetbal *changed to* K N V Ber
0047-9292 Negotiations Management *changed to* Inside Negotiations
0047-9306 Negro Lawmaker Journal†
0047-9314 Neighbors - Interracial Living
0047-9322 Nelson Gallery and Atkins Museum. Gallery Events *changed to* Nelson-Atkins Museum of Art. Calendar of Events
0047-9330 Nepal Digest
0047-9349 Nepalese Perspective†
0047-9357 Nepriklausoma Lietuva
0047-9365 Netherlands Journal of Veterinary Science†
0047-9373 Network/Urban Coalition
0047-9381 Neue Apotheken Illustrierte
0047-939X Neue Barke *changed to* Lektuere
0047-9403 Neue Bergbautechnik
0047-9411 Neurocirugia†
0047-942X Neuroelectric News
0047-9438 Neuropsihijatrija *changed to* Neurologija
0047-9446 Neutron Activation Analysis Abstracts
0047-9454 Nevada Engineer†
0047-9462 Nevada Historical Society Quarterly
0047-9470 Nevada Livestock and Agriculture Journal†
0047-9489 Nevada Rancher
0047-9497 R C U Report†
0047-9500 New Age
0047-9519 New American Electronics Literature and Technical Data
0047-9527 New Banner†
0047-9543 New Brunswick Historical Society. Historical Review†
0047-9551 N.B. Naturalist
0047-956X New Chislehurst Announcer
0047-9578 New Church Herald†
0047-9594 New Critic *changed to* Saturday Review Book Club News
0047-9608 New Diffusionist†
0047-9616 New Directions (Washington)
0047-9624 New Electronics
0047-9632 New Engineer†
0047-9640 N E A P Q News†
0047-9659 New England Marine Resources Information *changed to* Marine Resources Information
0047-9683 New Focus *changed to* Emerging
0047-9691 New French Books†
0047-9705 New Frontiers in Education
0047-9721 New Hellas
0047-973X New Human Services Newsletter *see* 0094-5129
0047-9756 New Jersey Environmental Times *changed to* New Jersey Outdoors
0047-9772 New Jersey Historical Commission Newsletter
0047-9810 New Mexico Transporter†
0047-9829 New Patriot
0047-9837 New Priorities *see* 0305-0629
0047-9845 New Products Medical-Surgical *see* 0009-9325
0047-9853 New Promotions and Competitions
0047-987X New Shetlander
0047-9888 Bush Fire Bulletin†
0047-990X New South Wales. Fire Service. Fire News
0047-9918 New South Wales Journal of Optometry
0047-9926 New South Wales Pastoral Conditions *see* 0034-6616
0047-9934 New South Wales Police News
0047-9942 New Times (Phoenix) *see* 0273-9836
0047-9950 New Unity†
0047-9969 New Wave
0047-9977 New Ways†
0047-9985 New Writing†
0047-9993 New York (City) Economic Development Administration. Office of Public Affairs. Economic and Other Indicators†
0048-0002 New York Denik†
0048-0037 New York Liberty Dispatch†
0048-0045 New York State Migrant Center. Newsletter†
0048-0053 New York State Environment
0048-0061 New York (State) Office of Planning Coordination. O P C News Summary†
0048-0088 New York Times Biographical Edition *see* 0161-2433
0048-0118 New Zealand Camera *see* 0110-3989
0048-0134 New Zealand Journal of Forestry Science
0048-0142 New Zealand Sanitarian *see* 0112-0212
0048-0150 New Zealand Surveyor
0048-0169 New Zealand Veterinary Journal
0048-0177 Newfoundland Amateur†
0048-0185 Newfoundland. Department of Education. Newsletter *changed to* School World
0048-0193 Newfoundland Medical Association. Newsletter *see* 0705-6702
0048-0215 News and Farmer
0048-0223 News from Zambia†
0048-0231 News of the New World
0048-024X Newscope - Current Events Edition *changed to* Newscope - Middle/Intermediate/Junior High School Edition
0048-0258 Newscope-Science Edition
0048-0266 Newscope - Secondary Current Events Edition *changed to* Newscope - High School/College Edition
0048-0274 Newshunter *changed to* Hunter Magazine
0048-0282 Newsletter of Biomedical Safety & Standards
0048-0304 Newspeace *changed to* Peacelinks
0048-0320 Niagara Frontier Purchaser *changed to* Empire Niagara Purchaser
0048-0339 Niedersaechsischer Jaeger
0048-0355 Nieuwe Pockets en Paperbacks
0048-0363 Nigeria Confidential
0048-0371 Nigerian Accountant
0048-038X Nigerian Business Digest
0048-0398 Nigerian Insurance Monitor
0048-0401 Nigerian Journal of Contemporary Law
0048-041X Nile Gazette
0048-0428 Nippon Acta Radiologica
0048-0444 Nippon Medical School. Journal
0048-0452 Nippon Steel News
0048-0460 Niv Hamidrashia
0048-0479 Noir et Rouge†
0048-0495 Nordisk Jordbrugsforskning
0048-0509 Nordisk Tidsskrift for Specialpaedagogik
0048-0541 Norkontakt
0048-0568 Norrona†
0048-0576 Norsk Dampkjelforening. Meddelelser *see* 0800-7896
0048-0584 Norsk Drosjeeierblad *changed to* Taxi
0048-0592 Norsk Husflid
0048-0606 Norsk Skibsfoerertidende
0048-0614 Norsk Tidsskrift for Sjakk
0048-0630 N A C L A News *see* 0149-1598
0048-0657 North Carolina Bar *see* 0164-6850
0048-0665 North Carolina Researcher†
0048-0673 N C I Catalyst
0048-0681 North Dakota Education News
0048-069X North Dakota Society of Medical Technologists. Newsletter
0048-0711 Northampton and County Independent *changed to* Independent Image
0048-0746 Northeastern Regional Antipollution Conference. Proceedings†
0048-0754 Northern Air
0048-0762 Northern Industry
0048-0770 Northern Ireland. Ministry of Education. Education Statistics
0048-0789 Northern Libraries Bulletin
0048-0797 Northern Teacher
0048-0800 Special Schools Bulletin *see* 0310-5709
0048-0835 Nos Chasses
0048-0843 Nos Maisons Familiales de Vacances
0048-0886 Noticias da Africa do Sul *changed to* S.A. Panorama
0048-0908 Noticiero Quimico
0048-0916 Notizie dall'Albania
0048-0924 Notre Comte
0048-0932 Notre Dame Journal
0048-0940 Nottingham Topic
0048-0967 Nouvelle Ecole
0048-0975 Nouvelle Revue Internationale
0048-0983 Nova Scotia Reports
0048-1009 Novum Testamentum
0048-1017 Nowi Dni
0048-1025 Nuclear Active
0048-1033 Nuclear Magnetic Resonance Spectrometry Abstracts
0048-1041 Nucleic Acids Abstracts *see* 0143-3318
0048-105X Nucleonics Week
0048-1076 Nueva Cultura *see* 0011-2755
0048-1084 Nueva Narrativa Hispanoamericana†
0048-1106 Nuggets
0048-1114 Numismatic Messenger†
0048-1122 Nuova Tradotta
0048-1165 Nurse in Israel
0048-119X Nuwe Afrikaner
0048-1203 Ny Jord *see* 0332-5229
0048-1211 Nya Cyklisten
0048-122X Det Nye
0048-1238 Nye Boeger om Film *see* 0107-0894
0048-1246 O A G Travel Planner *see* 0193-3299
0048-1254 O.R.L. Digest *see* 0198-7038
0048-1262 Oak Ridge National Laboratory Review
0048-1270 Oberflaeche
0048-1289 Objectif Monde Uni†
0048-1297 Obra de Cooperacion Sacerdotal Hispanoamericana. Mensaje Iberoamericano *changed to* Comision Episcopal de Misiones y Cooperacion Entre las Iglesias. Mensaje Iberoamericano
0048-1319 Observateur Africain
0048-1335 Observations from the Treadmill
0048-1378 Occupational Health New Zealand *see* 0301-0384
0048-1386 Ocean Soundings *see* 0025-3324
0048-1394 Ochrana Fauny†
0048-1408 Odd Fellow
0048-1416 Oesterreichische Bau-Wirtschaft
0048-1424 Oesterreichische Buergermeister Zeitung
0048-1440 Oesterreichische Militaerische Zeitschrift
0048-1459 Oesterreichische Foto-Zeitung
0048-1467 Oesterreichische Schulfunk *changed to* Der Oesterreichische Schulfunk mit Telespiegel
0048-1475 Oesterreichische Tieraerztezeitung
0048-1483 Oesterreichische Touristenzeitung
0048-1505 Official Karate
0048-1513 Official Organ Blue Book
0048-1521 Pan-American Coffee Bureau. Boletin Mensual†
0048-153X Ohio Archaeologist
0048-1548 Ohio Insect Information†
0048-1556 Ohio Jersey News
0048-1564 Ohio Researcher†
0048-1572 Ohio State Law Journal
0048-1580 Oil Palm News *see* 0041-3216
0048-1599 Oklahoma Farm Bureau Farmer
0048-1602 Oklahoma Highwayman†
0048-1610 Oklahoma Rural News
0048-1629 Okyeame
0048-1637 Old Cars *changed to* Old Cars Weekly
0048-1645 Old Contemptible
0048-1653 Old Time Music
0048-1661 Omicron Nu *changed to* Omicron Nu Newsletter
0048-1696 Onderwatersport
0048-170X One-Ten *see* 0092-5667
0048-1734 Ontario Amateur
0048-1742 Ontario Archaeological Society. Arch Notes
0048-1750 Ontario Companies Law Guide *changed to* Ontario Corporations Law Guide
0048-1769 Ontario Education Review *changed to* O E A Review
0048-1785 Ontario Forests†
0048-1793 Ontario Geography Teachers Association Monograph *changed to* Ontario Association for Geographic & Environmental Education. Monograph
0048-1807 Ontario Journal and Tax Sale Register
0048-1815 Ontario Numismatist
0048-1823 Ontario Plumbing Inspectors Association. Bulletin
0048-1831 Ontario Research Foundation. Newsletter *see* 0712-9467
0048-1858 Ontario Shade Tree Council. Newsletter
0048-1866 Ontario Tax Reports
0048-1882 Onward†
0048-1890 Op Safari
0048-1904 Open Access
0048-1912 Open Court Newsletter *changed to* Educator: Open Court Newsletter
0048-1920 Open Home†
0048-1939 Open Letter
0048-1947 Open Road
0048-1955 Ophthalmology Digest (1979)†
0048-2013 Optics *see* 0308-7670
0048-2021 Optikko
0048-203X Optometry Today
0048-2064 Oral Implantology
0048-2080 Orben Comedy Letter†
0048-2099 Orben's Comedy Fillers†
0048-2110 Orbit Weekly†
0048-2129 Ordo
0048-2137 Oregon A S C D Curriculum Bulletin *changed to* Curriculum Bulletin
0048-2145 Oregon Environmental Council Newsletter *changed to* Earthwatch Oregon
0048-2153 Research and Development Perspectives *changed to* Center (Eugene)
0048-2161 Organists Review
0048-217X Organizacija i Kadrovi
0048-2196 Organized Farmer *see* 0383-2244
0048-220X Orient
0048-2242 Orissa Homoeopathic Bulletin
0048-2269 Orthodox Church
0048-2277 Volund
0048-2285 Ospedale Psichiatrico
0048-2293 Osteopathic Hospital *changed to* Osteopathic Hospital Leadership
0048-2331 Ottawa Law Review
0048-234X University of Ottawa. Aesculapian Society. Medical Review†
0048-2358 A P M Bulletin
0048-2366 Ouest Medical†
0048-2382 Our Children *changed to* Activnews
0048-2390 Our Local Sixty Six
0048-2404 Our Town
0048-2420 Outdoor Guide†
0048-2447 Outdoorman†

ISSN INDEX 1337

0048-2455 Outdoorsman†
0048-2463 Outlook†
0048-2471 Outlook†
0048-2498 Ouvrier Senegalais
0048-251X Overseas Advertising
0048-2528 Overseas Books
0048-2536 Overseas Hindustan Times
0048-2544 Overseas Press Bulletin *changed to* Overseas Press Club Bulletin
0048-2560 Oxford Consumer
0048-2579 Oxford Mission
0048-2587 P D & D International†
0048-2595 P G/Prisonniers de Guerre *changed to* P G - C A T M
0048-2609 P R Reporter
0048-2617 Pacific Alert *see* 0882-0929
0048-2625 P A T A Indonesia
0048-2633 Pacific Marketer
0048-2641 Pacific Sun
0048-265X Pacifist
0048-2668 Package
0048-2676 Packaging News
0048-2684 Packaging Review
0048-2692 Pakistan Educational Review†
0048-2706 Pakistan Heart Journal
0048-2714 P L A Newsletter
0048-2722 Pakistan Pediatric Journal
0048-2749 Pakistan Survey *changed to* Dakshinesia
0048-2757 Pakistan Textile Journal
0048-2765 Palabra†
0048-2773 Palette†
0048-2781 Palmetto Piper
0048-282X Panorama (Boston)
0048-2838 Panorama Aujourd'hui
0048-2846 Panorama des Entreprises†
0048-2854 Papel Impreso
0048-2862 Paperprintpack India
0048-2870 Papers on Far Eastern History
0048-2889 Papetier
0048-2897 Papier und Kunststoff Verarbeiter
0048-2919 Papua and New Guinea Education Gazette
0048-2935 Paragraphic
0048-2951 Parassitologia
0048-296X Paratracks *changed to* Son of Paratracks
0048-2978 Parent Cooperative Preschools International Journal *changed to* Co-operatively Speaking
0048-2986 Parenteral Drug Association. Bulletin *see* 0279-7976
0048-2994 Parliamentary Journal
0048-3001 Parliamentary Studies *see* 0301-9047
0048-301X Parnassos
0048-3028 Parnassus: Poetry in Review
0048-3036 Parsiana
0048-3044 Partisan
0048-3079 National Asphalt Pavement Association. Paving Forum *changed to* H M A T
0048-3087 Pax
0048-3095 Pazifische Rundschau
0048-3109 Pearl Gazette†
0048-3117 Pecan Quarterly *changed to* Pecan South Including Pecan Quarterly
0048-3133 Pediatric Clinics of India
0048-315X Pedra e Cal
0048-3176 Die Pelzwirtschaft
0048-3192 Pennant
0048-3206 Pennsylvania Academy of Ophthalmology and Otolaryngology. Transactions
0048-3214 Pennsylvania Geology
0048-3230 Pennsylvania News *changed to* P M H A News
0048-3249 Pennsylvania Researcher
0048-3257 Pennsylvania Road Builder
0048-3273 Penny Wise Motoring
0048-3281 Pensioners Voice
0048-329X People
0048-3303 People
0048-3311 People for Progress†
0048-332X People United to Save Humanity. P.U.S.H.-Operation Push
0048-3338 People Watching†
0048-3354 New Zealand People's Voice
0048-3362 People's Voice†
0048-3370 Periodista
0048-3389 Western Society of Periodontology. Journal
0048-3397 Periscoop†
0048-3400 Periscope
0048-3419 Faculdade de Odontologia de Pernambuco. Revista
0048-3435 Personal Injury Researcher
0048-3443 Personal Report for the Executive
0048-3451 Personnel Guide to Canada's Travel Industry
0048-346X Personnel Management *see* 0156-904X
0048-3478 Personnel News for School Systems *changed to* Wages and Benefits
0048-3486 Personnel Review
0048-3494 Perspective (Washington)
0048-3508 Perspectives (Washington, 1971)
0048-3516 Perspectives Euro Africaines
0048-3524 Perspectives in Defense Management†
0048-3532 Perspectives Syndicalistes *changed to* Pense et Lutte
0048-3540 Royal Perth Hospital. Journal†
0048-3559 Perth. Stock Exchange. Official Record†
0048-3567 Pesquisa Medica
0048-3575 Pesticide Biochemistry and Physiology
0048-3583 Petersen's PhotoGraphic Magazine *see* 0199-4913
0048-3591 Petroleum Gazette
0048-3605 Petts Wood Post
0048-3613 P.G. Football Newsletter
0048-3621 Pharmaceutical Salesman *see* 0161-8415
0048-363X Pharmacognosy Titles†
0048-3648 Pharmascope
0048-3656 Pharmazeutische Praxis
0048-3664 Pharmazie in Unserer Zeit
0048-3672 Pharos *changed to* Pharos International
0048-3699 Phi Sigma Iota Newsletter *changed to* Phi Sigma Iota Forum
0048-3702 Philadelphia Tribune
0048-3710 Philatelic Journalist
0048-3729 P T S Journal
0048-3737 Philatopic Magazine
0048-3745 Philippine Economy and Industrial Journal
0048-3753 Philippine Entomologist
0048-3761 Philippine Journal of Animal Industry
0048-377X Philippine Journal of Fisheries
0048-3796 Philippine Journal of Linguistics
0048-380X Philippine Journal of Mental Health
0048-3818 Philippine Journal of Nursing
0048-3826 Philippine Journal of Plant Industry
0048-3834 Philippine Journal of Soils
0048-3842 Philippine Mining & Engineering Journal
0048-3850 Philippine Planning Journal
0048-3869 Philippine Sugar Institute Quarterly *changed to* Philippine Sugar Commission. Quarterly
0048-3877 Philippines Quarterly
0048-3885 Philologica Pragensia
0048-3893 Philosophia
0048-3907 Philosophic Research and Analysis *see* 0732-4944
0048-3915 Philosophy and Public Affairs
0048-3923 Philosophy of Education Society of Great Britain. Proceedings *see* 0309-8249
0048-3931 Philosophy of the Social Sciences
0048-3966 Der Foto-Markt†
0048-3974 Photo-Memo
0048-3982 Photo Reporter†
0048-3990 Photographe Professionnel†
0048-4008 Photographic Journal of the Sun†
0048-4016 Photography North
0048-4024 Physical Review Abstracts
0048-4059 Physiological Plant Pathology *see* 0885-5765
0048-4083 Physiotherapists' Quarterly
0048-4105 Piano-Tuners Quarterly
0048-4113 Pick's World Currency Report†
0048-4121 Pictorial Education *see* 0309-3484
0048-413X Pictorial Education Quarterly *changed to* Junior Projects
0048-4148 Pielegniarka i Polozna
0048-4156 Pig Breeders Gazette
0048-4164 Pigeon Racing News & Gazette
0048-4172 Piltdown Newsletter†
0048-4180 Pink Sheet on the Left *see* 0278-0585
0048-4199 Pioneer
0048-4202 Pioneer
0048-4229 Pirogue
0048-4237 Pisciculture Francaise
0048-4245 Pitture e Vernici
0048-4253 Place†
0048-4261 Placedart†
0048-427X Plaisirs de la Chasse
0048-4288 Planet
0048-4296 Planner's Notebook *changed to* Practicing Planner
0048-4296 Planner's Notebook *see* 0001-2610
0048-430X Planning Advisory Service Reports *see* 0160-8266
0048-4318 Planning in Northeastern Illinois
0048-4326 P I B C News
0048-4334 Plant Genetic Resources Newsletter
0048-4342 Plant Varieties and Seeds Gazette
0048-4350 Plaste und Kautschuk
0048-4369 Plastforum *changed to* Plastforum Scandinavia
0048-4385 Plastics Southern Africa
0048-4415 Playboard
0048-4423 Playfair Cricket Monthly†
0048-444X Plebeian†
0048-4466 P L E R U S
0048-4474 Ploughshares
0048-4482 Plural Societies
0048-4490 Plymothian
0048-4504 Pneumatik Digest
0048-4512 Poder Politico
0048-4547 Poesia Hispanica†
0048-4563 Poesie Presente
0048-458X Poetry
0048-4598 Poetry Information *see* 0260-9339
0048-4601 Poetry Miscellany
0048-461X Poetry of Our Times†
0048-4636 Point and Figure Digest†
0048-4695 Police Nationale
0048-4709 Policia Espanola *changed to* Policia
0048-4717 Policlinico. Sezione Medica
0048-4725 Poliisimies
0048-4733 Polska Akademia Nauk. Wydzial Nauk Medycznych. Annals *see* 0001-608X
0048-4741 Polish Institute of Arts and Sciences in America. Information Bulletin†
0048-475X Politieke Dokumentatie
0048-4768 Polizeiblatt fuer das Land Baden-Wuerttemberg†
0048-4776 Polizei und Verkehrsjournal *changed to* Polizei Journal
0048-4784 Pollution
0048-4806 Polymer India†
0048-4822 Popular Culture Association Newsletter *changed to* Popular Culture Association. Newsletter and Popular Culture Methods
0048-4830 Popular Dogs†
0048-4849 Population Newsletter
0048-4857 Porfeydd†
0048-4865 Port of Melbourne Quarterly *changed to* Port Panorama
0048-4881 Portland Magazine
0048-489X Portside
0048-4903 Portugaliae Physica
0048-4911 Positif
0048-492X Posta si Telecomunicatii†
0048-4946 Postgraduate Medicine Quarterly Abstracts†
0048-4954 Pottery in Australia
0048-4962 Poultry Fancier
0048-4970 Poultry Meat *see* 0007-2176
0048-4989 Poultry Times
0048-5004 Pourquoi
0048-5012 Powder Metallurgy International
0048-5020 Powder Metallurgy Science & Technology†
0048-5039 Power
0048-5047 Power & Industry in Asia†
0048-5071 Practical Education and School Crafts *see* 0264-8156
0048-508X Practical Forms and Precedents (New South Wales)
0048-511X Prairies Tax Reports†
0048-5128 Der Praktische Arzt
0048-5136 Praxis der Beregnungswirtschaft†
0048-5144 Precision Shooting
0048-5160 Premisa
0048-5179 Prensa Chilena y Sus Comentarios
0048-5187 Presbyterian Leader *see* 0010-5848
0048-5195 Presence Francophone†
0048-5209 Press Forum *changed to* Depthnews
0048-5233 Prevention
0048-5241 Prevention *changed to* Prevoyance
0048-525X Preview Abstracts in Physics and Astronomy†
0048-5268 Preview of Bermuda
0048-5276 Prim-Aid†
0048-5284 Primary Education
0048-5306 Principality of Liechtenstein - A Documentary Handbook
0048-5314 Print-Equip News
0048-5322 Printers News
0048-5330 Printers News
0048-5349 Prism *changed to* Pratt Reports
0048-5357 Prisma
0048-5365 Prison Law Reporter†
0048-5373 Prisoners Rights Newsletter *see* 0048-5365
0048-5381 Pro Motion
0048-539X Probation *see* 0264-5505
0048-5411 Problemi di Ulisse†
0048-5438 Professional Engineer *see* 0158-3158
0048-5446 Professional Engineer in Industry Newsletter†
0048-5454 Professional Officer
0048-5489 Progreso
0048-5497 Progress in Fire Retardancy†
0048-5500 Progress in Materials Science†
0048-5519 Progress in Physical Therapy†
0048-5543 Promise M/R†
0048-5551 Propeller Club Quarterly
0048-5578 Prophetic Expositor
0048-5608 Prosperity
0048-5616 Protection†
0048-5624 Protection Management *changed to* Corporate Security
0048-5632 Proud
0048-5640 Proud Black Images†
0048-5659 Proust Research Association Newsletter
0048-5667 Proverbium†
0048-5675 Przeglad Psychologiczny
0048-5683 PSI *changed to* I Am
0048-5691 Psicologia e Lavoro
0048-5713 Psychiatric Annals
0048-5721 Psychiatric Outpatient Services in Los Angeles County†
0048-573X Psychic Observer†
0048-5748 Psychological Issues
0048-5756 Psychologie Medicale
0048-5764 Psychopharmacology Bulletin
0048-5772 Psychophysiology
0048-5799 Public Administration *changed to* Public Administration and Finance Newsletter
0048-5802 Public Affairs†
0048-5810 Public Affairs Information Service Foreign Language Index *changed to* P A I S Foreign Language Index
0048-5829 Public Choice
0048-5853 Public Finance Quarterly
0048-5888 Public Ledger
0048-5896 Public Relations Australia†
0048-5926 Public Service *changed to* Public Service-Staff Vacancies Weekly
0048-5942 Publishers' Auxiliary
0048-5950 Publius
0048-5977 Puhelin
0048-6000 Pulse
0048-6019 Punjab Agricultural University. Journal of Research
0048-6027 Punjab Punch
0048-6035 Purchasing Management Newsletter†
0048-6043 Pyrethrum Post
0048-6051 O and M Bulletin *changed to* Management in Government
0048-606X Q E D Renaissance *see* 0194-8431

1338 ISSN INDEX

0048-6078 Q I M A
0048-6108 Quantity Surveyor *see* 0007-3431
0048-6116 Quarry Mine and Pit *changed to* Resources Industry - Quarry Mine & Construction Equipment
0048-6124 Quarter Racing World *see* 0364-9237
0048-6132 Quarterly Bibliography of Computers and Data Processing *see* 0270-4846
0048-6159 Quarterly Bulletin of Statistics for Asia and the Far East *see* 0125-0019
0048-6167 Quarterly Bulletin on Solar Activity
0048-6175 Quarterly Journal of Management Development *changed to* Organization & Administrative Sciences
0048-6183 Quarterly Market Projection†
0048-6191 Quarterly Statistical Bulletin for Africa†
0048-6205 Quarto Mondo
0048-6213 Quasi
0048-6221 Que Pasa†
0048-623X Que Pasa in Puerto Rico *changed to* Que Pasa
0048-6248 Quebec Aujourd' Hui†
0048-6256 Quebec-Histoire†
0048-6299 Quebec Tax Reports
0048-6302 Queens Bar Bulletin
0048-6310 Queen's Intramural Law Journal *changed to* Queen's Law Journal
0048-6329 Queens Own Highlander
0048-6337 Queensland. Guidance and Special Education Branch. Special Schools Bulletin for Teachers of Exceptional Children *see* 0313-6728
0048-6345 Q H A Review
0048-6353 Queensland Littoral Society. Newsletter *changed to* Operculum
0048-6361 Queensland Master Builder
0048-637X Queensland Master Plumber
0048-6388 Queensland Roads
0048-6396 Monthly Summary of Statistics, Queensland
0048-6418 Administrators' Bulletin†
0048-6426 Quest for Higher Productivity *changed to* Productivity Australia
0048-6434 Quest in Education
0048-6442 Questo Nostro Ambiente†
0048-6450 Queyras
0048-6477 Journal de la Quincaillerie†
0048-6493 Quinzaine Litteraire
0048-6507 R E
0048-6523 Racehorse *changed to* Raceform Handicap Book
0048-654X Radharc
0048-6582 R C A Plain Talk and Technical Tips *changed to* Communicator (Indianapolis)
0048-6590 RadioFernseh-Haendler *see* 0343-4206
0048-6604 Radio Science
0048-6612 Rail Engineering International
0048-6639 Railroad Modeler
0048-6647 Railway Digest International
0048-6663 Rakennustaito
0048-668X Rally
0048-671X Ramus
0048-6744 Rassegna di Medicina del Traffico
0048-6760 Rassegna di Neuropsichiatria e Scienze Affini†
0048-6779 Rassegna Internazionale di Logica
0048-6787 Rassegna Odontotecnica
0048-6809 Ratcliffian
0048-6817 Rating and Valuation Reporter
0048-6825 Raum und Siedlung *changed to* Structur
0048-6833 Rautatieliikenne
0048-6841 Razon y Fabula†
0048-685X Real Estate Institute of Queensland. Real Estate Journal
0048-6868 Real Estate Law Journal
0048-6884 Realist†
0048-6892 Realites Malgaches *changed to* Zava Misy
0048-6906 Reason
0048-6922 Recherche en Matiere d'Ecomomie des Transports *see* 0304-3320
0048-6930 Recherche Spatiale†
0048-6949 Rechte Lijn
0048-6957 Record - Dossier *changed to* Phosphore
0048-6965 Records Management Report†
0048-6973 Recreation Property Ontario *changed to* Ontario Cottager
0048-6981 Recursos Hidricos
0048-7007 Red Comb Poultry Journal *changed to* Red Comb Journal
0048-7023 Red Cross Quarterly
0048-7031 Red Cross Senior *changed to* Link-up
0048-7066 Reeves Journal
0048-7090 Regione Toscana†
0048-7104 R N A B C News
0048-7112 R N A O News
0048-7120 Rehabilitacion
0048-7139 Rehabilitation Digest
0048-7155 Reign of the Sacred Heart
0048-7163 Universite de Reims. Institut de Geographie. Travaux
0048-7171 Reinsurance
0048-718X Relay Engineer *see* 0308-4213
0048-7198 Relazioni Clinico Scientifiche
0048-7201 Relevo†
0048-721X Religion
0048-7228 Remedes
0048-7236 Remedial Education *see* 0311-1954
0048-7260 Report on Indian Legislation†
0048-7279 Reports on Rheumatic Diseases
0048-7287 Die Republik
0048-7295 R E T S Digest
0048-7325 Research Journal of Philosophy
0048-7333 Research Policy
0048-7341 Researcher
0048-7368 Reserve Bank of Australia. Currency†
0048-7376 Resources (Washington, 1959)
0048-7392 Respiratory Therapy *changed to* Respiratory Management
0048-7406 Restaurant News
0048-7422 Retail Operations News Bulletin†
0048-7430 Rettung
0048-7449 Reumatismo
0048-7457 Reuse/Recycle
0048-7465 Review of Books and Religion *see* 0890-0841
0048-7473 International Review of Contemporary Law
0048-7481 Review of Law & Social Change
0048-749X Review of Regional Studies
0048-7511 Reviews in American History
0048-752X Reviews in Analytical Chemistry
0048-7538 Reviews on Coatings and Corrosion *changed to* Corrosion Reviews
0048-7546 Reviews on Drug Interactions *see* 0334-2190
0048-7554 Reviews on Environmental Health
0048-7562 Reviews on Reactive Species in Chemical Reactions *see* 0162-7546
0048-7570 Reviews on Silicon, Germanium, Tin and Lead Compounds
0048-7589 Reviews on Deformation Behavior of Materials
0048-7597 Revista Agropecuaria
0048-7600 Revista Argentina de Cirurgia
0048-7619 Revista Argentina de Radiologia
0048-7627 Revista Argentina de Urologia y Nefrologia
0048-7643 Revista Brasileira de Tecnologia
0048-7651 Revista Chilena de Literatura
0048-766X Revista Chilena de Obstetricia y Ginecologia
0048-7678 Revista Cubana de Ciencias Veterinarias
0048-7708 Revista de Geografia
0048-7716 Revista de la Sanidad Militar Argentina
0048-7724 Revista de Medicina Veterinaria y Parasitologia *changed to* Universidad Central de Venezuela. Facultad de Ciencias Veterinarias. Revista
0048-7732 Revista de Obstetricia y Ginecologia de Venezuela
0048-7740 Revista de Psicologia Normal e Patologica
0048-7759 Revista de Soldadura
0048-7767 Revista Dental
0048-7775 Revista Ecuatoriana de Higiene y Medicina Tropical
0048-7783 Revista Educativa†
0048-7791 Revista Espanola de Reumatismo y Enfermedades Osteoarticulares
0048-7848 Revista Medico-Chirurgicala
0048-7856 Revista Odonto-Estomatologica
0048-7880 Revista Portuguesa de Pediatria e Puericultura
0048-7902 Revue Avicole
0048-7910 Revue Belge du Feu
0048-7929 Revue de Droit et d'Economie Immobiliere *see* 0556-7297
0048-7937 Revue de Jurisprudence Commerciale
0048-7945 Revue de l'Atherosclerose†
0048-7953 Revue de l'Habitat Francais
0048-7988 Revue d'Histoire de l'Eglise de France
0048-7996 Revue d'Histoire des Sciences et de Leurs Applications
0048-8003 Revue d'Histoire Moderne et Contemporaine
0048-8038 Revue Economique Franco-Allemande
0048-8062 Revue Francaise d'Endocrinologie Clinique, Nutrition et Metabolisme
0048-8097 Revue Generale de Botanique
0048-8100 Revue Generale des Transmissions *changed to* Revue Generale des Transmissions Mecaniques, Hydrauliques, Pneumatiques, Commandes et Asservissements
0048-8143 Revue Internationale de Philosophie
0048-8151 Revue Internationale d'Onomastique
0048-816X Revue Ivoirienne de Droit
0048-8178 Revue Roumaine d'Etudes Internationales
0048-8186 Revue Technique du Batiment et des Constructions Industrielles
0048-8208 Revue Trimestrielle de Droit Commercial *see* 0244-9358
0048-8216 Rhode Island. University. U. R. I. Commercial Fisheries Newsletter†
0048-8224 Rhodes Report†
0048-8232 Rhodesian Caravaner and Outdoor Life *changed to* Caravaner and Outdoor Life
0048-8267 Ricardian
0048-8275 Ricemill News *changed to* R C L Magazine
0048-8291 Ricerche di Automatica
0048-8305 Right On
0048-8321 Risques du Metier
0048-8348 Rivista del Colore
0048-8364 Rivista di Anatomia Patologica e di Oncologia
0048-8372 Rivista di Diritto Sportivo
0048-8399 Rivista di Idrobiologia
0048-8402 Rivista Italiana di Scienza Politica
0048-8410 Rivista Oto-Neuro-Oftalmologica
0048-8429 Rivista Tributaria Ticinese
0048-8437 Roan Antelope *changed to* Mining Mirror
0048-8445 Rock & Folk
0048-8453 Rock & Gem
0048-8461 Rocket
0048-847X Rockhound†
0048-8496 Rod & Line†
0048-850X Rodale's Environment Action Bulletin *see* 0013-922X
0048-8518 Roeien
0048-8526 Roerfag
0048-8534 Rogue Digger
0048-8542 Rolling Along
0048-8550 Romania Literara
0048-8577 Romanian Journal of Chemistry
0048-8593 Romantisme
0048-8631 Rotary Down Under
0048-8658 Romania: Documents-Events
0048-8666 Roundabout
0048-8674 Rountree Report†
0048-8690 Royal Canadian Legion's Coaching Review†
0048-8704 The Royal Life Saving Society-U.K. Quarterly Journal
0048-8712 Royal National Institute for the Blind. School Magazine
0048-8720 R S P C A Today
0048-8739 Royal Town Planning Institute Journal *see* 0309-1384
0048-8747 Rubber, Plastic and Cable Industries Journal
0048-8755 Rund Um den Pelz International *changed to* Pelz International
0048-8771 Running Board
0048-878X Rural Arkansas
0048-8798 Rural Education Review†
0048-8801 Rural Electric Missourian *see* 0164-8578
0048-881X Russian Literature Triquarterly
0048-8828 Russian Ultrasonics
0048-8836 Rutebiltidende
0048-8844 Rutgers Journal of Computers and the Law *see* 0735-8938
0048-8852 Rutland Historical Society Newsletter *changed to* Rutland Historical Society Quarterly
0048-8860 Rx Bulletin†
0048-8879 Ryde Recorder
0048-8887 Rydge's Construction, Civil Engineering and Mining Review *changed to* Rydge's C C E M-Construction, Civil Engineering and Mining
0048-8895 S F Greats†
0048-8917 S M/Sales Meetings *see* 0148-4052
0048-8933 Sabretache
0048-8941 Sackbut†
0048-895X Saddle and Striker
0048-8968 Safety Canada
0048-8976 Sage Professional Papers in International Studies†
0048-8984 Sahkourakoitsija
0048-8992 Saint Louis Chronicle
0048-900X St. Paul Dispatch & Pioneer Press Newspaper Index *changed to* Index to the St. Paul Pioneer Press and Dispatch
0048-9018 Saisons d'Alsace
0048-9026 Salary and Merit *changed to* Wages and Benefits
0048-9034 Sales and Marketing in Australia†
0048-9050 Salvage Locator
0048-9069 S A E
0048-9077 San Bernardino County Museum Association. Newsletter†
0048-9107 Sante Publique
0048-9115 Santiago
0048-9123 Santo Tomas Nursing Journal
0048-914X Saskatchewan Administrator
0048-9166 Saskatchewan Care *changed to* S A S C H Newsletter
0048-9174 Saskatchewan Farm Science *see* 0707-7793
0048-9182 Saskatchewan Genealogical Society. Bulletin
0048-9190 Saskatchewan Guidance and Counseling Association. Guidelines
0048-9204 Saskatchewan Indian
0048-9212 Saskatchewan Journal of Educational Research and Development†
0048-9220 Saskatchewan Medical Quarterly†
0048-9239 Saturday Evening Post
0048-9247 Savings Banks Institute. Journal
0048-9255 Scalpel and Tongs
0048-9263 Scandinavian-American Bulletin
0048-9271 Scandinavian Audiology
0048-928X Scandinavian Canadian Businessman†
0048-9301 Scandinavian Refrigeration
0048-931X Scene
0048-9328 Schach
0048-9336 Scheidewege†
0048-9344 Schietsport
0048-9352 Schiltrom†
0048-9360 Schizophrenics Anonymous International. Bulletin *changed to* Health and Nutrition Update
0048-9387 School Bell
0048-9409 School Guidance Worker *changed to* Guidance & Counselling
0048-9417 School Health Bulletin
0048-9425 School Library Association of Queensland. Journal
0048-9433 School Library Newsletter†
0048-9441 S M S G Newsletter

0048-9476 School Services Curriculum Perspectives†
0048-9484 Schulverwaltungsblatt fuer Niedersachsen
0048-9492 Schuss
0048-9506 Die Schwalbe
0048-9514 Schweizer Hotel Journal
0048-9522 Schweizer Volkskunde
0048-9530 Schweizerische Zeitschrift fuer Nachwuchs und Ausbildung†
0048-9549 Schwestern Revue
0048-9581 Science and Government Report
0048-9603 Science Education News
0048-962X Science Fantasy†
0048-9646 Science Fiction Research Association Newsletter
0048-9654 Science Fiction Times
0048-9662 Science for the People
0048-9670 Science in Agriculture
0048-9689 Science of Man†
0048-9697 Science of the Total Environment
0048-9700 Science Policy *see* 0302-3427
0048-9719 S T A News *see* 0381-6036
0048-9727 Sciences Medicales
0048-9743 Scope: Recreational Vehicle and Camping News *changed to* Scope Camping News
0048-9751 Scots Magazine
0048-976X Scottish Cooperator *changed to* Co-Operative News (Scottish Edition)
0048-9778 Scottish Institute of Missionary Studies Bulletin
0048-9786 S L A News
0048-9794 Scottish Literary News *see* 0305-0785
0048-9808 Scottish Transport
0048-9816 Scout Leader
0048-9824 Scrap and Waste Reclamation and Disposal†
0048-9832 Screenings
0048-9859 S G M News Digest *changed to* S G M News
0048-9867 Sea Classics†
0048-9875 Sea Grant Seventies *see* 0197-3460
0048-9883 Sealandair
0048-9891 Seaposter
0048-9905 Sear
0048-9913 Search (Nashville)
0048-9921 Search (Washington, D.C.) *see* 0741-8485
0048-9948 Seattle Centerstage
0048-9956 Second Coming
0048-9964 Second Order
0048-9972 Second Souffle
0048-9980 Second Wave
0048-9999 Secondary Curriculum Letter *changed to* Curriculum Letter
0049-0008 Secularist
0049-0016 Security Distributing & Marketing
0049-0024 Security Gazette
0049-0032 Seed Producers Review *changed to* Australian Seed Producers Review
0049-0040 Seed Scoop
0049-0059 Seguranca
0049-0067 Selecciones Municipales
0049-0075 Selecoes Odontologicas
0049-0083 Select†
0049-0091 Select Bibliography on Higher Education†
0049-0105 Selected References on Environmental Quality as It Relates to Health†
0049-0113 Selective Service Law Reporter *see* 0193-3906
0049-0156 Semaine Juridique
0049-0164 Semina
0049-0172 Seminars in Arthritis & Rheumatism
0049-0199 Senior Citizens Today
0049-0202 Sentinel (Willowdale)
0049-0210 Srpski Arhiv za Celokupno Lekarstvo
0049-0229 Service to Business and Industry - B P L
0049-0237 Service World International *see* 0744-3897
0049-0253 Sesame Street
0049-027X Seventeen's Make It!†
0049-0296 Severn and Wye Review†
0049-030X Sewing Machine Times *changed to* Knitting and Sewing Machine Times
0049-0326 Sexologie†
0049-0334 Shareholder and New Investor†
0049-0342 Shawensis†
0049-0369 Ship Repair and Maintenance *changed to* Shipcare & Maritime Management
0049-0385 Sh'ma
0049-0393 Shopping Center World
0049-0393 Shopping Center World Product and Service Directory
0049-0415 Shotgun News
0049-0423 Shuttle, Spindle & Dyepot
0049-0431 Sic†
0049-044X Sierra Club. National News Report
0049-0466 Sign World
0049-0474 N B F A A Signal *see* 0199-6835
0049-0504 Sillon†
0049-0512 Simmons Review
0049-0520 S I A Journal
0049-0547 Singapore Undergrad
0049-0555 Singles-Mingles
0049-0563 Sinnets Helse
0049-0571 Sinopse de Cardiologia *changed to* Sinopse de Medicina Interna
0049-058X Sinopse de Gastroenterologia *changed to* Sinopse de Medicina Interna
0049-0598 Sintesis
0049-0601 Sinteza
0049-061X Sioniste
0049-0628 Sirjana
0049-0636 Sistema Nervoso†
0049-0652 Ski Scene†
0049-0660 Skolnytt *see* 0356-7842
0049-0679 Skotoey *changed to* SKO
0049-0687 Skylook *see* 0270-6822
0049-0709 Slavic Gospel News *changed to* Breakthrough (Wheaton)
0049-0725 Sleutelaar *changed to* N O W Nieuws
0049-0733 Slice of Pizza†
0049-075X Slimming and Nutrition *see* 0144-8129
0049-0776 Smoke Signals
0049-0806 Sno-Fari News Events *changed to* Colorado Outfitter
0049-0822 SnoTrack *changed to* Snowmobile
0049-0849 Sobre los Derivados de la Cana de Azucar
0049-0857 Social Change
0049-0865 Social Dimension Newsletter†
0049-0881 Social Reformer
0049-089X Social Science Research
0049-0911 Social Sciences
0049-092X Social Sciences in Canada
0049-0946 Socialist Affairs
0049-0954 Socialist Press Bulletin
0049-0962 Socialni Politika
0049-0970 Socialt Forum *see* 0347-5484
0049-0989 Boletin S A C M†
0049-0997 Sociedad Dominicana de Geografia Boletin†
0049-1004 Sociedad Mexicana de Geografia y Estadistica. Boletin
0049-1039 Sociedade de Lingua Portuguesa. Boletim
0049-1055 Societe des Ecrivains Canadiens. Bulletin
0049-1063 Societe d'Etudes et de Preparation aux Examens Publics et Prives. Revue d'Etudes
0049-108X Societe Francaise de Photogrammetrie. Bulletin *see* 0244-6014
0049-1098 Societe Historique Acadienne. Cahiers
0049-1101 Societe Medicale d'Afrique Noire de Langue Francaise. Bulletin *changed to* Dakar Medical
0049-111X Etudes Prehistoriques†
0049-1128 Societe Royale Belge d'Entomologie. Bulletin et Annales†
0049-1136 Societe Royale Zoologique de Belgique. Annales
0049-1144 S.A.M. News International *changed to* What's Happening
0049-1152 Society for Ancient Numismatics. S A N Journal
0049-1160 S A A D Digest
0049-1179 Society for the Study of Labour History. Bulletin
0049-1187 Society of Archer-Antiquaries. Newsletter *see* 0144-7424
0049-1195 Society of Architectural Historians Newsletter
0049-1209 Society of Manufacturing Engineers. Technical Digest
0049-1217 Sociolinguistics Newsletter
0049-1225 Sociologia
0049-1233 Sociological Analysis *see* 0306-2481
0049-1241 Sociological Methods & Research
0049-125X Soenderjysk Maanedsskrift
0049-1276 Sol
0049-1292 Solidarite Ouvriere
0049-1306 Somerset and Dorset Notes and Queries
0049-1330 Sosialistisk Perspektiv
0049-1349 Sotainvalidi
0049-1381 S A Athlete
0049-1403 South African Financial Gazette
0049-1411 South African Metrication News†
0049-142X South African Studies†
0049-1438 South Australia. Department of Education. Education Gazette
0049-1446 South Australian Dairymen's Journal *see* 0818-7169
0049-1454 South Australian Garden Guide†
0049-1470 South Australian State Reports
0049-1489 South Carolina Dental Journal†
0049-1497 Medical University of South Carolina. Bulletin *changed to* Auctus
0049-1519 South Coast Sun
0049-1527 South Eastern Latin Americanist
0049-1535 South Vietnam in Struggle
0049-1543 S.W.A. Boer†
0049-1551 Southeast Asia†
0049-156X Southern California Dental Association. Journal *see* 0008-0977
0049-1616 Southern MotoRacing
0049-1624 Southern Purchasor
0049-1640 Southern Stars
0049-1659 Southern Utah News
0049-1667 Southwest Skier *changed to* Skier
0049-1683 Southwestern Journal of Social Education
0049-1691 S P R P C Reports *changed to* Omnibus
0049-1705 Sou'wester
0049-1713 Soviet Analyst
0049-173X Soviet Journal of Developmental Biology
0049-1748 Soviet Journal of Quantum Electronics
0049-1756 Soviet Power Engineering†
0049-1764 Soviet Progress in Polyurethanes†
0049-1772 Sower *changed to* Sower (1979)
0049-1780 Space Adventures†
0049-1802 Spanish Today
0049-1810 Spastics News *changed to* Disability Now
0049-1829 Spear†
0049-1837 Special Education Newsletter
0049-1845 Special Interest Autos
0049-1861 Spektrum
0049-187X Spoke Wheels†
0049-1888 Spokesman
0049-190X Sport Heroes *changed to* Hockey Illustrated
0049-1926 Sport und Mode
0049-1934 Sporting Investor Method Magazine†
0049-1942 Sporting Press
0049-1950 Sporting Star†
0049-1985 Sports Merchandiser *changed to* Sports Trend
0049-1993 Sportshandleren *changed to* Sport
0049-2000 Spotlight (Bath)
0049-2019 Sprachpflege
0049-2027 Squadron†
0049-2035 Stagione delle Arti, del Libro, e del Turismo†
0049-2051 Stampa Sud
0049-206X Standard-Bearer (New York)
0049-2078 Standpunkte und Dokumente
0049-2086 Stanford Law School Journal
0049-2108 Stanford University Campus Report
0049-2116 Star (Carville)†
0049-2140 State of the Nation†
0049-2159 State Supplies
0049-2167 Statement of the Assets and Liabilities of the Chartered Banks of Canada
0049-2175 Statistical Indicators in E C A F E Countries *see* 0252-4457
0049-2183 Switzerland. Directorate General of Customs. Monthly Statistics
0049-2205 Steel Construction
0049-2213 Steel Pipe News†
0049-2221 Steroidologica *see* 0301-0163
0049-223X Der Steuerberater
0049-2248 Sti og Varde
0049-2272 Stock Car
0049-2280 Stockowners' Digest
0049-2329 Street Chopper *changed to* Custom Cycle
0049-2337 Street Level†
0049-2345 Strobe†
0049-2353 Stromata
0049-2361 Studi e Problemi di Critica Testuale
0049-237X Studies in Logic and the Foundations of Mathematics
0049-2388 University of Illinois. Department of Linguistics. Working Papers *changed to* Studies in the Linguistic Sciences
0049-2396 Studii si Cercetari de Biochimie
0049-2418 Sub-Normal Children's Welfare Association. Welfare News
0049-2426 Sub-Stance
0049-2434 S F M A Bulletin *changed to* F M A Bulletin
0049-2442 Success (Peterborough)
0049-2450 Sud
0049-2469 Sudan Engineering Society. Journal
0049-2477 Sugar News
0049-2531 Sundet Rundt
0049-254X Bulletin of Sung and Yuan Studies
0049-2558 Sunstone Review (Santa Fe)†
0049-2566 Suomen Invalidi *changed to* I T - Invalidityoe
0049-2574 Super-8 Filmaker *see* 0276-3494
0049-2590 Supermarket and Retailer
0049-2612 Supreme Court Researcher
0049-2620 Sur les Sentiers de l'Ecole Active†
0049-2639 Surface Wave Abstracts
0049-2647 Surgelation
0049-2655 Survie de l'Ame Humaine *see* 0151-4016
0049-2663 Svensk Idrott
0049-2671 Svensk Skidsport
0049-268X Svensk Socialvardstidning *see* 0346-5365
0049-2698 Svensk Ishockeymagasin *see* 0345-4347
0049-2701 Swedish Journal of Agricultural Research
0049-271X Swinton Journal
0049-2728 Swiss Canadian News
0049-2736 Syndicats de Roumanie
0049-2744 Syndicats Vietnamiens
0049-2752 Synergist†
0049-2760 B E C Synoptic
0049-2787 Terveystyo *see* 0356-3081
0049-2795 Systems/Stelsels *changed to* Computer Systems in S.A.
0049-2817 Taamuli
0049-2825 Die Tabak Zeitung
0049-2833 Tactile†
0049-2868 Take Over
0049-2876 Talent News and Views *changed to* Whitmark Magazine
0049-2884 Taliesin
0049-2906 Talk
0049-2914 Tallow Light†
0049-2922 Tambor
0049-2930 Tamkang Journal of Mathematics
0049-2949 Tamkang Review
0049-2957 Tangley Oaks Reading Guide†
0049-2973 Tanzania. Bureau of Statistics. Employment and Earnings *changed to* Tanzania. Bureau of Statistics. Survey of Employment
0049-2981 Tanzania Police Journal
0049-3007 Tasmanian Association for the Teaching of English. Journal *see* 0311-1784
0049-3015 Tasmanian Fisheries Research
0049-3023 Tasmanian Hotel Review†
0049-304X Taxi

ISSN INDEX

ISSN	Title
0049-3058	Taxi Drivers Voice†
0049-3066	Tchad et Culture
0049-3074	Teacher *changed to* M T A Association A E M
0049-3082	Teacher in Wales†
0049-3090	Teacher-Librarian
0049-3112	Teacher Today†
0049-3139	Teachers World *see* 0309-3484
0049-3147	Teaching of English
0049-3155	Technical Communication
0049-3171	Technicka Knihovna
0049-3198	Technology Mart†
0049-3201	I I T Tecnologia
0049-3228	Teen's Star†
0049-3252	Tele Presse
0049-3287	Telecine†
0049-3295	Teleguide
0049-3309	Teletronics *see* 0310-6411
0049-3317	Television Sponsors Directory
0049-3325	TeleVizier
0049-3333	Temas de Orientacion Agropecuaria
0049-335X	Tempo
0049-3368	Tempus†
0049-3376	Tenants Outlook†
0049-3392	Tennessee Parent-Teacher *changed to* Tennessee Parent - Teacher Bulletin
0049-3406	Tennessee School Board Bulletin
0049-3422	Tennessee Vo-Tech News†
0049-3430	Tenth†
0049-3449	Teologia y Vida
0049-3473	Terre Africaine
0049-3481	Teton
0049-349X	Texas Agricultural Progress†
0049-3503	Texas Dental Assistants Association. Bulletin *changed to* Texas Dental Assistants Association. Newsletter
0049-3511	Texas Farm & Ranch News
0049-352X	Texas Metro
0049-3538	C R W R News *changed to* Watermarks
0049-3546	Textil
0049-3554	Textile Asia
0049-3562	Textile Labour/Canadian Edition *see* 0271-5848
0049-3589	Thai Journal of Agricultural Science
0049-3597	Theatre Enfance et Jeunesse
0049-3600	Theatre Quarterly
0049-3619	Theatre-Quebec†
0049-3635	Theologia
0049-3643	Theologia Practica
0049-3651	Theological Times
0049-366X	Theologie und Glaube
0049-3678	Theoretical Physics Journal *changed to* Solid State Abstracts Journal
0049-3686	Theoria to Theory†
0049-3694	Theosophy in Australia
0049-3708	Theosophy in New Zealand
0049-3716	Therapeutica Nova *changed to* Probatum Est
0049-3724	Thin-Layer Chromatography Abstracts
0049-3740	Third World Reports
0049-3759	This Fortnight in Pakistan†
0049-3767	This Is Calgary *changed to* Calgary
0049-3783	This Week†
0049-3791	This Week in Israel
0049-3805	Thomas
0049-3813	T P S Bulletin *changed to* T P S Bulletin
0049-3821	Thoroughbred of California
0049-3848	Thrombosis Research
0049-3856	Sygeplejersken
0049-3864	Tieraerztliche Umschau
0049-3880	Tijdschrift voor Bejaarden-, Kraam- en Ziekenverzorging
0049-3899	Tijdschrift voor Gastro-Enterologie†
0049-3910	Time Out
0049-3929	Times Higher Education Supplement
0049-3945	Tobacco International
0049-3953	Tobacco Review†
0049-3961	Tobakk-Frukt-Sjokolade
0049-397X	Tocher
0049-3988	Today in Mining†
0049-4003	Today's Girl†
0049-402X	Tohoku Regional Fisheries Research Laboratory. Bulletin
0049-4038	Toike Oike
0049-4046	Tokyo Book Development Centre. Newsletter *see* 0388-5593
0049-4054	Freshwater Fisheries Research Laboratory, Tokyo. Bulletin *see* 0389-5858
0049-4062	Toledo Museum News†
0049-4070	Tomorrow's Newspaper†
0049-4089	Tonnage Club Farm News†
0049-4100	Top Management Abstracts
0049-4119	Top of the News with Fulton Lewis†
0049-4127	Topic
0049-4135	Topical Stamp Handbooks
0049-4143	Torax
0049-416X	Torch (Chicago) *changed to* Torchlight
0049-4178	Torch of Homoeopathy†
0049-4186	Toronto Jewish Press
0049-4194	Toronto Life
0049-4216	Toronto Stock Exchange Review
0049-4224	Toronto Symphony News *changed to* Toronto Symphony Magazine
0049-4232	Toronto Vegetarian Association. Newsletter
0049-4283	Touristik Aktuell
0049-4291	Town and Countryside†
0049-4313	T P I C News *see* 0708-5397
0049-4321	Trade and Commerce
0049-433X	Trade Unions International of Workers in Commerce. Bulletin
0049-4348	Trade Winds from Japan†
0049-4356	Traedgaardsnytt
0049-4372	Tramway Museum Society. Journal
0049-4380	Trans Tasman
0049-4402	Transit News†
0049-4410	Transit-Times
0049-4429	Transition
0049-4445	Transition *changed to* Perspective (Boston)
0049-4461	Transport
0049-447X	Transport Routier du Quebec
0049-4488	Transportation
0049-4496	Transportation and Distribution Management†
0049-450X	Transportation Law Journal
0049-4518	Transportation Safety Association of Ontario. Bulletin
0049-4526	Transportation Safety Association of Ontario. Drivers' News Letter
0049-4542	Travel and Camera *see* 0041-2007
0049-4577	Travelnews
0049-4585	TravLtips Freighter Bulletin *see* 0162-9816
0049-4593	Treasure (Twentynine Palms)
0049-4615	Trefoil Trail
0049-4623	Trend
0049-4631	Tribuna Farmaceutica
0049-464X	Tribuna Italiana
0049-4658	Tribune-Post
0049-4666	Tribune Psychique
0049-4674	Tribune Socialiste†
0049-4682	Tricontinental
0049-4690	Trident
0049-4704	Universita degli Studi di Trieste. Istituto di Matematica. Rendiconti
0049-4712	Trinitarian Bible Society Quarterly Record
0049-4720	Tripura Review†
0049-4739	Troisieme Civilisation
0049-4747	Tropical Animal Health and Production
0049-4755	Tropical Doctor
0049-4763	Tropical Grasslands
0049-478X	Truck Trends
0049-4801	Tundra Times
0049-481X	Tungsten News
0049-4828	Tungsten Statistics
0049-4836	Tupart Monthly Reports on the Underground Press†
0049-4844	Turkish Bulletin of Hygiene and Experimental Biology
0049-4852	Turkiye Muhendislik Haberleri
0049-4887	Tvaettnytt *changed to* Rent
0049-4917	Two Tone
0049-4925	Two-Year College Mathematics Journal *see* 0746-8342
0049-4933	Tydskrif vir Volkskunde en Volkstaal
0049-495X	Typog†
0049-4968	New York Typographical Union Number Six. Bulletin
0049-4976	U F O - Nyt
0049-4984	Unicef Information Bulletin
0049-500X	Ubique†
0049-5026	Uganda Schools Newsletter
0049-5034	Ugens Politik†
0049-5042	Uhrenfachgeschaeft
0049-5069	Uj Konyvek
0049-5077	Ukrainian Canadian
0049-5107	Ulster Tatler
0049-5123	Umeni
0049-5131	Umweltschutz
0049-514X	Unabashed Librarian
0049-5166	U E C A Publication *changed to* E C A Publication
0049-5174	Underground Lamp Post
0049-5190	Une Semaine de Paris-Pariscope
0049-5204	Unesco. Centro de Documentacion Cultural, Havana. Informaciones Trimestrales
0049-5212	Unesco. Regional Centre for Book Development in Asia, Karachi. Newsletter *changed to* Asia Pacific Book News
0049-5220	Unidad Latina†
0049-5239	Unifier†
0049-528X	Union Herald
0049-5298	Manhattan-Bronx Postal Union. Union Mail *changed to* New York Metro Area Postal Union. Union Mail
0049-5301	Union Research Service†
0049-531X	Unitarian
0049-5328	U C O News *changed to* Co-Op Cornerstone
0049-5344	United Florists News *changed to* United Flowers-by-Wire Canada Journal
0049-5379	U N I D O Documents Checklist†
0049-5387	U N I D O Newsletter
0049-5395	U N I T A R News†
0049-5433	United Reformed Church History Society. Journal
0049-5441	United Senior Citizens of Ontario. Bulletin *see* 0382-0068
0049-5468	B N D D Bulletin *see* 0098-3470
0049-5484	U.S. National Clearinghouse for Poison Control Centers. Bulletin†
0049-5506	Universe
0049-5514	Universita Karlova. Fakulta Vseobecneho Lekarstvi. Pobocka v Hradci Kralove. Sbornik Vedeckych Praci
0049-5522	Universita Karlova. Fakulta Vseobecneho Lekarstvi. Pobocka v Hradci Kralove. Sbornik Vedeckych Praci: Supplementum
0049-5530	Universitas
0049-5557	Unmuzzled Ox
0049-5581	Unser Kleeblatt *changed to* Fragezeider
0049-559X	Unspeakable Visions of the Individual
0049-562X	Urania
0049-5638	Urban Affairs Today†
0049-5654	Urban Data Service Report *changed to* Baseline Data Report
0049-5662	Urban Life and Culture *changed to* Journal of Contemporary Ethnography
0049-5689	Urban Rights†
0049-5697	Urbat *see* 0241-6794
0049-5700	Urethane Plastics and Products
0049-5719	Urogallo†
0049-5735	Utbildningstidningen
0049-576X	V E News *see* 0318-0867
0049-5778	V E 6
0049-5794	Valeurs Actuelles
0049-5808	Valiseesti
0049-5816	Vancouver Calendar Magazine
0049-5824	Vancouver Numismatic Society. News Bulletin
0049-5832	Vancouver Stock Exchange Review
0049-5867	Vaar Industri†
0049-5883	Vasama
0049-5891	Vasculum
0049-5905	Vegetarian Courier
0049-5913	Velocidad
0049-5921	Verbindungstechnik
0049-5948	Verfahrenstechnik *changed to* Chemical Engineering and Processing
0049-5956	Vermont Libraries†
0049-5964	Vern og Velferd *changed to* Arbeidsmiljoe
0049-5972	La Vernice
0049-5999	Versandhausberater
0049-6006	Versicherungskaufmann
0049-6014	Versicherungsvermittlung
0049-6022	Vertical
0049-6030	Vesey Street Letter *changed to* N.Y. County Lawyer
0049-6057	Die Veterinaermedizin
0049-6065	Veterinary Doctor and Veterinary Digest†
0049-6073	Vibration
0049-6081	Vibrations *see* 0739-4683
0049-609X	Vickers News
0049-6103	Victoria. Department of Agriculture. Dairyfarming Digest†
0049-6111	Victoria, Australia. Education Department. Curriculum and Research Bulletin†
0049-6138	Victorian Computer Bulletin
0049-6146	Victorian Horticulture Digest†
0049-6154	V I E R Bulletin
0049-6162	Australia. Bureau of Statistics. Victorian Office. Victorian Monthly Statistical Review *see* 0158-202X
0049-6170	Victorian Municipal Directory
0049-6189	Victorian Periodicals Newsletter *see* 0709-4698
0049-6197	Vic Rail News *see* 0814-7078
0049-6200	Victorian Tobacco Grower†
0049-6227	Vida Nostra *changed to* Vida Nostra Revolum
0049-6235	Video *see* 0310-6411
0049-6243	Videocassette Newsletter *see* 0145-9023
0049-6278	Vie du Rail Outremer *see* 0181-1878
0049-6286	Vie Mutualiste
0049-6294	Vie Publique
0049-6308	Viehhandel
0049-6316	Vieilles Maisons Francaises
0049-6340	Vietnam Digest
0049-6359	Vietnam Economic Report†
0049-6367	Vietnam: Yesterday and Today†
0049-6375	Vietnam Youth
0049-6383	View from Ottawa *see* 0702-8210
0049-6405	Viewpoint†
0049-6421	Vigilante *changed to* Hotel and Catering
0049-643X	Vigneron Champenois
0049-6448	Viking
0049-6464	V I N A Quarterly
0049-6472	Virginia Dental Journal
0049-6480	Virginia Gazette
0049-6499	Virginia Researcher
0049-6510	Vision Index†
0049-6529	Visite
0049-6537	Visor
0049-6545	Vista Femenina Centroamericana
0049-657X	Vivre†
0049-660X	Vivres-Voeding *changed to* Federation Belge des Enterprises de Distribution. Courrier Hebdomadaire
0049-6618	V F I Information Bulletin†
0049-6626	Voce dell'Africa†
0049-6634	Voce d'Italia in Canada
0049-6650	Vogelwarte
0049-6669	Voice (Westchester)
0049-6677	Voix de la Construction†
0049-6685	Voix de la Resistance
0049-6693	Voix des Parents
0049-6707	Voix du Retraite
0049-6715	Volare Necesse Est
0049-6723	Volkswagen Greats *see* 0273-6748
0049-6731	Volley Kroniek *changed to* Volleybal
0049-674X	Volume Retail Merchandising†
0049-6804	Vrachebnoe Delo
0049-6812	Vrije Pers†
0049-6820	Wirtschaft und Technik im Transport *changed to* Foerdertechnik
0049-6847	A Wake Newslitter†

0049-6871 Wallonie Art et Histoire†
0049-688X War Cry
0049-6898 War Cry
0049-6901 Warrior
0049-691X Washington International Business Report
0049-6928 Washington Researcher†
0049-6952 Washington Wildlife†
0049-6960 Watchmakers of Victoria *see* 0725-055X
0049-6979 Water, Air, and Soil Pollution
0049-6987 Water Pollution Control Federation. Highlights
0049-6995 Water Rights and Quality News and Views *changed to* California Waterscape
0049-7002 Water Skier
0049-7010 Water Talk
0049-7037 Wayne Engineer
0049-7045 Wealth of Nations
0049-7061 Weekly Nation
0049-707X Weekly Unity†
0049-7088 Weewish Tree†
0049-7096 Weights and Measures Review
0049-710X Weimaraner *see* 0162-315X
0049-7126 Weltbild
0049-7134 Weltgescheen
0049-7142 Werk und Leben *changed to* Magazin fuer Mitarbeiter - Werk und Leben
0049-7150 Werk und Zeit
0049-7169 Wertpapier
0049-7177 West†
0049-7185 West Australian Gardener
0049-7193 West Bengal
0049-7207 Mechanical Engineering Bulletin
0049-7215 West Coast Poetry Review†
0049-7223 West End
0049-7231 West Indian Sportsman
0049-724X West Texas Livestock Weekly *see* 0162-5047
0049-7258 West Virginia Economic Indicators†
0049-7266 Westchester Historian
0049-7274 Westchester Law Journal
0049-7282 Western Association of Map Libraries. Information Bulletin
0049-7312 Western Australia. Education Department. Education Circular
0049-7320 Western Australia. Forest Department. Forest Focus *changed to* Western Australia. Department of Conservation and Land Management. Landscope
0049-7347 Western Australian Institute of Technology Gazette†
0049-7371 Western Canadian Lumber Worker
0049-738X Western Cleaner and Launderer
0049-7398 Western Floors
0049-7436 W I D News
0049-7444 Western Living
0049-7460 Western Ontario Farmer *changed to* Ontario Farmer (Western Edition)
0049-7479 Western Outdoor News
0049-7487 Western Outfitter
0049-7495 Western Potter†
0049-7517 Western Temperance Herald
0049-7525 Western Weekly Reports
0049-7533 What's New†
0049-7541 Wheel
0049-755X Wheel Extended
0049-7568 Wheelchair Competitor *changed to* Achievement
0049-7584 White Pelican
0049-7592 Whooper *changed to* S W F News
0049-7614 Widening Horizons
0049-7622 Wiesbadener Leben
0049-7630 Wilcox Report *changed to* Wilcox Report Newsletter
0049-7649 Wilmington Journal
0049-7657 Wind Rose
0049-7673 Window†
0049-7681 Windsor Sportsmen's News
0049-7703 Wirtschaft Zwischen Nord- und Ostsee
0049-7711 Das Wirtschaftseigene Futter
0049-772X W A V A Dispatch†
0049-7746 Wisconsin Researcher†
0049-7754 Witches International Craft Associates. W I C A Newsletter
0049-7762 Wloptoonakun†
0049-7770 Woman Activist
0049-7797 Women and Film†
0049-7800 Women in Kenya†
0049-7819 Women in Struggle†
0049-7827 Women Speaking†
0049-7835 Women Studies Abstracts
0049-7843 Women's Army Corps Journal†
0049-786X Womens Press
0049-7878 Women's Studies
0049-7886 Wood Duck
0049-7908 Wood Products Industry Abstracts Bulletin *see* 0360-3083
0049-7916 Wood Research
0049-7924 Wood World†
0049-7940 Woodworkers and Painters Journal *see* 0042-5842
0049-7959 Word and Way
0049-7967 Word Processing Report *changed to* Office Automation Report
0049-7975 Workers Action
0049-8017 World Agricultural Report†
0049-8025 World Animal Review
0049-8033 W A Y Forum
0049-805X World Ecology Two Thousand†
0049-8068 W F P A News *changed to* Animals International
0049-8076 W F D Y News
0049-8084 World Food Programme News
0049-8092 World Future Society Bulletin *changed to* Futures Research Quarterly
0049-8106 World Gift Review Monthly Newsletter
0049-8114 Weekly Epidemiological Record
0049-8122 World Medical Journal
0049-8130 World Peace News
0049-8149 World Sugar News
0049-8157 World Tanker Fleet Review
0049-8165 World Tribune
0049-822X Wyoming Valley Motorist *changed to* Valley Motorist
0049-8238 X-Ray on Current Affairs in Southern Africa
0049-8246 X R S - X-Ray Spectrometry
0049-8254 Xenobiotica
0049-8262 Xi Psi Phi Quarterly
0049-8289 Yatri
0049-8319 Yoga Life International†
0049-8327 Yoga Quarterly Review
0049-8335 Yokohama Plant Protection News
0049-8343 You†
0049-8351 Young Age
0049-836X Young Alliance†
0049-8394 Your Church
0049-8424 Your Horoscope Guide
0049-8432 Your Region in Action *changed to* Your Region
0049-8440 Youth Action†
0049-8459 Youth Mirror
0049-8467 Youth Report *see* 0160-9696
0049-8475 Yrke
0049-8483 Yugoslavia
0049-8505 Zahir
0049-8513 Zaire-Afrique
0049-8521 Zambia Farmer†
0049-853X Zambia Library Association. Journal
0049-8572 Zdravotnicka Pracovnice
0049-8580 Zeitschrift fuer Analytische Psychologie und ihre Grenzgebiete *see* 0301-3006
0049-8599 Zeitschrift fuer Auslaendische Landwirtschaft
0049-8602 Zeitschrift fuer Bewaesserungswirtschaft
0049-8610 Zeitschrift fuer die Gesamte Hygiene und ihre Grenzgebiete
0049-8629 Zeitschrift fuer Eigenheimfreunde *changed to* Domus Magazin
0049-8637 Zeitschrift fuer Entwicklungspsychologie und Paedagogische Psychologie
0049-8645 Zeitschrift fuer Lateinamerika Wien
0049-8653 LiLi
0049-8661 Zeitschrift fuer Romanische Philologie
0049-867X Zeitschrift fuer Sozialpsychologie
0049-8688 Zeitschrift fuer Werkstofftechnik
0049-8696 Zentralblatt fuer Pharmazie, Pharmakotherapie und Laboratoriumsdiagnostik
0049-8718 Z P G National Reporter *see* 0199-0071
0049-8750 Zonneland
0049-8769 Zoological Society of India. Journal
0049-8777 Zootecnia e Veterinaria *see* 0020-0735
0049-8785 Zuidafrikaanse Koerier†
0052-2678 World Council of Young Men's Service Clubs. Minutes of the General Meeting
0065-0005 A B Bookman's Yearbook
0065-0013 A B C British Columbia Lumber Trade Directory and Year Book
0065-003X A B C Europe Production
0065-0048 A B C of Book Trade
0065-0072 Ag Engineers Notebook
0065-0080 A.I. Voeikov Main Geophysical Observatory, Leningrad. Data of Measurements of Electric Field Strength of the Atmosphere at Various Altitudes by the Results of Soundings
0065-0099 A.I. Voeikov Main Geophysical Observatory, Leningrad. Results of Ground Observations of Atmospheric Electricity. Additional Issue
0065-0102 A V E in Japan
0065-0129 A. W. Mellon Lectures in the Fine Arts
0065-0137 Aachener Geschichtsverein. Zeitschrift
0065-0145 Dansk Skolehistorie. Aarbog *changed to* Uddannelshistorie. Selskabet for Dansk Skolehistorie. Aarbog
0065-017X Aarhus Universitet. Matematisk Institut. Lecture Notes Series
0065-0188 Aarhus Universitet. Matematisk Institut. Various Publications Series
0065-0196 Aarsbok foer Skolan
0065-020X Aarsbok foer Sveriges Kummuner
0065-0218 Norges Landbrukshoegskole. Institutt for Bygningsteknikk. Byggekostnadsindeks for Driftsbygninger i Jordbruket. Prisutviklingen
0065-0226 Norges Landbrukshoegskole. Institutt for Bygningsteknikk. Aarsmelding/Annual Report
0065-0234 Norges Landbrukshoegskole. Institutt for Bygningsteknikk. Melding
0065-0242 Norges Landbrukshoejskole. Institutt for Jordskifte og Eiendomsutforming. Melding *see* 0801-2334
0065-0269 Hong Kong. Fisheries Research Station. Bulletin†
0065-0277 University of Aberdeen. Department of Forestry. Economic Survey of Private Forestry
0065-0285 Aberystwyth Memoranda in Agricultural, Applied and Biometeorology†
0065-0293 Wales. National Library. Handlist on Manuscripts in the National Library of Wales
0065-0307 Abhandlungen aus dem Gesamten Buergerlichen Recht, Handelsrecht und Wirtschaftsrecht
0065-0315 Abhandlungen Moderner Medizin†
0065-0323 Abhandlungen und Materialen zur Publizistik
0065-0358 Abhandlungen zur Handels- und Sozialgeschichte
0065-0366 Abhandlungen zur Philosophie, Psychologie und Paedagogik
0065-0374 About Zambia†
0065-0382 Abr-Nahrain
0065-0390 Abr-Nahrain. Supplements
0065-0412 Absorption Spectra in the Ultraviolet and Visible Region
0065-0420 Abstracts of Belgian Geology and Physical Geography†
0065-0439 Abstracts of Gothenburg Dissertations in Science†
0065-0447 Academia Campinense de Letras. Publicacoes
0065-0455 Academia Espanola, Madrid. Anejos del Boletin
0065-0463 Academia Guatemalteca de Estudios Genealogicos, Heraldicos e Historicos. Revista
0065-0471 Academia Hondurena de la Lengua. Boletin
0065-048X Institutul de Istorie si Arheologie - Cluj-Napoca. Anuarul
0065-0498 Institut de Speologie Emil Racovitza. Travaux
0065-0501 Academia Scientiarum Fennica. Proceedings/Sitzungsberichte *see* 0356-6927
0065-051X Academic Underachiever†
0065-0544 Academie des Inscriptions et Belles-Lettres. Etudes et Commentaires
0065-0552 Academie des Sciences. Annuaire
0065-0560 Academie des Sciences. Index Biographique des Membres et Correspondants
0065-0579 Academie des Sports, Paris. Annuaire
0065-0587 Academie Francaise. Annuaire
0065-0595 Academie Royale de Medecine de Belgique. Memoires. *see* 0377-8231
0065-0609 Academie Royale des Sciences, des Lettres et des Beaux Arts de Belgique. Index Biographique des Membres, Correspondants et Associes
0065-0625 Academy for Educational Development. Academy Papers†
0065-0633 Academy of American Franciscan History. Documentary Series
0065-0641 Academy of American Franciscan History. Monograph Series
0065-065X Academy of American Franciscan History. Propaganda Fide Series
0065-0668 Academy of Management. Proceedings
0065-0676 A N P H I Papers
0065-0684 Academy of Political Science. Proceedings
0065-0692 Academy of the Hebrew Language. Specialized Dictionaries
0065-0714 Accademia Musicale Chigiana. Quaderni *see* 0069-3391
0065-0722 Accademia dei Fisiocritici, Siena. Sezione Medico-Fisica *see* 0390-7783
0065-0730 Accademia Etrusca di Cortona. Annuario
0065-0757 Accademia Nazionale Italiana di Entomologia. Rendiconti
0065-0765 Accademia Patavina di Scienze Lettere ed Arti. Collana Accademica
0065-0781 Accademia Toscana di Scienze e Lettere La Colombaria. Studi
0065-079X Accepted Dental Therapeutics
0065-082X Accidents in North American Mountaineering
0065-0846 Accounting Research Studies†
0065-0862 Accredited Institutions of Higher Education *see* 0270-1715
0065-0870 Acoustical Holography *see* 0270-5117
0065-0889 Acronyms and Initialisms Dictionary *see* 0270-4404
0065-0897 Acta Academiae Regiae Gustavi Adolphi
0065-0900 Acta Ad Archaeologiam et Artium Historiam Pertinentia (Monograph)
0065-0919 Acta Agraria et Silvestria. Series Agraria
0065-0927 Acta Agraria et Silvestria. Series Silvestris
0065-0935 Acta Agraria et Silvestria. Series Zootechnica
0065-0943 Acta Agriculturae Scandinavica. Supplementum *issued with* 0001-5121
0065-0951 Acta Agrobotanica
0065-096X Acta Allergologica. Supplementum *changed to* Allergy. Supplementum
0065-0986 Acta Archaeologica Lodziensia
0065-0994 Acta Archaelogica Lundensia: Monographs of Lunds Universitets Historiska Museum. Series in 8
0065-1001 Acta Archaelogica Lundensia: Monographs of Lunds Universitets Historiska Museum. Series in 4
0065-101X Acta Archaeologica
0065-1028 Acta Arctica
0065-1036 Acta Arithmetica
0065-1044 Acta Baltico - Slavica

0065-1052 Acta Bernensia: Beitraege zur Praehistorischen, Klassischen und Juengeren Archaeologie
0065-1060 Acta Bibliothecae Regiae Stockholmiensis
0065-1079 Acta Bibliothecae Universitatis Gothoburgensis
0065-1095 Acta Biologica Hellenica *see* 0750-7321
0065-1109 Acta Borealia A. Scientia†
0065-1125 Taiwania
0065-1133 Acta Chemica Scandinavica. Supplementum†
0065-1141 Acta Classica
0065-115X Acta Concilium Ophthalmologicum
0065-1168 Acta Criminologica *see* 0316-0041
0065-1176 Acta Dermatologica
0065-1184 Acta Embryologiae Experimentalis *see* 0391-9706
0065-1192 Acta Endocrinologica Panamericana
0065-1206 Acta Facultatis Medicae Fluminensis
0065-1214 Medicinska Misla
0065-1222 Acta Geobotanica Barcinonensia *see* 0210-7597
0065-1230 Acta Geographica†
0065-1249 Acta Geographica Lodziensia
0065-1257 Acta Geographica Lovaniensia
0065-1265 Acta Geologica Taiwanica
0065-1281 Acta Histochemica
0065-1303 Acta Historica
0065-1311 Acta Historica Scientiarum Naturalium et Medicinalium
0065-132X Acta Hydrobiologica
0065-1338 Acta Hydrophysica
0065-1346 Acta Juridica
0065-1354 Acta Jutlandica
0065-1370 Acta Manilana
0065-1389 Acta Medicae Historiae Patavina
0065-1397 Acta Medicinae Legalis et Socialis
0065-1400 Acta Neurobiologiae Experimentalis
0065-1419 Acta Neurochirurgica. Supplement *see* 0001-6268
0065-1427 Acta Neurologica Scandinavica. Supplementum
0065-1435 Acta Neuropathologica. Supplement
0065-1443 Acta Nuntiaturae Gallicae
0065-1451 Acta Ophthalmologica. Supplementum
0065-146X Acta Pacis Westphalicae
0065-1478 Acta Parasitologica Polonica
0065-1508 Acta Pharmacologica et Toxicologica. Supplementum *see* 0901-9936
0065-1516 Acta Philologica
0065-1524 Acta Philologica
0065-1532 Acta Philologica Aenipontana
0065-1540 Acta Philosophica et Theologica
0065-1559 Acta Physica Austriaca. Supplement
0065-1567 Acta Phytomedica
0065-1575 Acta Phytotaxonomica Barcinonensia†
0065-1583 Acta Protozoologica
0065-1591 Acta Psychiatrica Scandinavica. Supplementum
0065-1605 Acta Psychologica - Gothoburgensia
0065-1613 Acta Psychologica Taiwanica *changed to* Chinese Journal of Psychology
0065-1621 Acta Radiobotanika et Genetika
0065-1656 Acta Scientiarum Socialium
0065-1672 Acta Theologica Danica
0065-1699 Acta Veterinaria Scandinavica. Supplementum
0065-1702 Acta Visbyensia
0065-1710 Acta Zoologica Cracoviensia
0065-1729 Acta Zoologica Lilloana
0065-1737 Acta Zoologica Mexicana†
0065-1753 Action in Pharmacy
0065-177X Action Universitaire
0065-1788 Activite Economique de la Haute-Normandie *changed to* Regards sur l'Economie de la Haute-Normandie
0065-1796 Actrascope *see* 0315-484X
0065-180X Actua. Special Enfants
0065-1818 Actualite Rhumatologique Presentee au Praticien
0065-1826 Actualites Endocrinologiques†
0065-1850 Adan E. Treganza Anthropology Museum. Papers
0065-1869 Adansonia. Memoires†
0065-1877 Adaptations Series
0065-1885 Addiction Research Foundation of Ontario. Bibliographic Series
0065-1907 Adelaide. Institute of Medical and Veterinary Science. Annual Report of the Council
0065-1915 Adelaide Law Review
0065-1923 Aden Magazine†
0065-1931 Adhesives Red Book *changed to* Adhesives Age Directory
0065-194X Adlai Stevenson Institute of International Affairs. Annual Report†
0065-1966 Kenya Institute of Administration. Journal
0065-1974 Administrator
0065-1982 Administrators in Action†
0065-1990 Admission Requirements of American Dental Schools *see* 0091-729X
0065-2008 Adolescent Psychiatry
0065-2024 Zuerl's Adressbuch der Deutschen Luft- und Raumfahrt
0065-2032 Adressbuch fuer den Deutschsprachigen Buchhandel
0065-2067 Advance of Christianity through the Centuries†
0065-2075 Advanced Accountancy Seminar. Proceedings†
0065-2091 Advances in Activation Analysis†
0065-2113 Advances in Agronomy
0065-2121 Advances in Alicyclic Chemistry
0065-213X Advances in Alicyclic Chemistry. Supplement†
0065-2148 Advances in Analytical Chemistry and Instrumentation†
0065-2156 Advances in Applied Mechanics
0065-2164 Advances in Applied Microbiology
0065-2180 Advances in Astronomy and Astrophysics†
0065-2199 Advances in Atomic and Molecular Physics
0065-2210 Advances in Biochemical Engineering
0065-2229 Advances in Biochemical Psychopharmacology
0065-2245 Advances in Biological and Medical Physics
0065-2253 Advances in Biology of Skin†
0065-2261 Advances in Biomedical Engineering and Medical Physics†
0065-227X Advances in Biophysics
0065-2288 Advances in Blood Grouping†
0065-2296 Advances in Botanical Research
0065-230X Advances in Cancer Research
0065-2318 Advances in Carbohydrate Chemistry and Biochemistry
0065-2326 Advances in Cardiology
0065-2334 Advances in Cardiopulmonary Diseases†
0065-2342 Advances in Catalysis and Related Subjects *see* 0360-0564
0065-2350 Advances in Cell and Molecular Biology†
0065-2377 Advances in Chemical Engineering
0065-2385 Advances in Chemical Physics
0065-2393 Advances in Chemistry Series
0065-2407 Advances in Child Development and Behavior
0065-2415 Advances in Chromatography
0065-2423 Advances in Clinical Chemistry
0065-2431 Advances in Communication Systems†
0065-244X Advances in Comparative Physiology and Biochemistry
0065-2458 Advances in Computers
0065-2466 Advances in Control Systems *see* 0090-5267
0065-2474 Advances in Corrosion Science and Technology
0065-2482 Advances in Cryogenic Engineering
0065-2490 Advances in Drug Research
0065-2504 Advances in Ecological Research
0065-2539 Advances in Electronics and Electron Physics
0065-2555 Advances in Engineering
0065-2563 Advances in Environmental Science and Technology
0065-2571 Advances in Enzyme Regulation
0065-258X Advances in Enzymology and Related Areas of Molecular Biology
0065-2598 Advances in Experimental Medicine and Biology
0065-2601 Advances in Experimental Social Psychology
0065-261X Advances in Fluorine Research and Dental Caries Prevention†
0065-2628 Advances in Food Research
0065-2644 Advances in Free Radical Chemistry†
0065-2652 Advances in Gas Chromatography†
0065-2660 Advances in Genetics
0065-2687 Advances in Geophysics
0065-2709 Advances in Gerontological Research
0065-2717 Advances in Heat Transfer
0065-2725 Advances in Heterocyclic Chemistry
0065-2733 Advances in High Pressure Research†
0065-2741 Advances in High Temperature Chemistry
0065-275X Advances in Human Genetics
0065-2768 Advances in Hydroscience
0065-2776 Advances in Immunology
0065-2784 Advances in Information Systems Science†
0065-2792 Advances in Inorganic Chemistry and Radiochemistry
0065-2806 Advances in Insect Physiology
0065-2814 Advances in Instrumentation
0065-2822 Advances in Internal Medicine
0065-2830 Advances in Librarianship
0065-2849 Advances in Lipid Research
0065-2857 Advances in Machine Tool Design and Research *changed to* International Journal of Machine Tools Design and Manufacture
0065-2865 Advances in Macromolecular Chemistry†
0065-2873 Advances in Magnetic Resonance
0065-2881 Advances in Marine Biology
0065-2903 Advances in Metabolic Disorders
0065-2911 Advances in Microbial Physiology
0065-292X Advances in Microbiology of the Sea *see* 0161-8954
0065-2938 Advances in Microcirculation
0065-2946 Advances in Microwaves
0065-2954 Advances in Molten Salt Chemistry
0065-2962 Advances in Morphogenesis†
0065-2970 Advances in Nuclear Physics
0065-2989 Advances in Nuclear Science and Technology
0065-2997 Advances in Obstetrics and Gynaecology *see* 0304-4246
0065-3004 Advances in Ophthalmology *see* 0250-3751
0065-3012 Advances in Optical and Electron Microscopy
0065-3020 Advances in Oral Biology
0065-3039 Advances in Oral Surgery *changed to* Update in Oral Surgery
0065-3047 Advances in Organic Chemistry†
0065-3055 Advances in Organometallic Chemistry
0065-3063 Advances in Orthodontics *changed to* Update in Orthodontics
0065-3071 Advances in Oto-Rhino-Laryngology
0065-308X Advances in Parasitology
0065-3098 Advances in Particle Physics†
0065-3101 Advances in Pediatrics
0065-311X Advances in Pedodontics†
0065-3128 Advances in Periodontics *changed to* Update in Periodontics
0065-3136 Advances in Pharmaceutical Sciences
0065-3144 Advances in Pharmacology and Chemotherapy
0065-3152 Advances in Photochemistry
0065-3160 Advances in Physical Organic Chemistry
0065-3187 Advances in Plasma Physics†
0065-3195 Advances in Polymer Science
0065-3217 Advances in Probability *changed to* Advances in Probability and Related Topics
0065-3225 Advances in Prosthodontics†
0065-3233 Advances in Protein Chemistry
0065-3241 Advances in Psychobiology†
0065-325X Advances in Psychological Assessment†
0065-3268 Advances in Psychosomatic Medicine
0065-3276 Advances in Quantum Chemistry
0065-3284 Advances in Quantum Electronics†
0065-3292 Advances in Radiation Biology
0065-3306 Advances in Radiation Chemistry†
0065-3322 Advances in Reproductive Physiology†
0065-3357 Advances in Solid State Physics†
0065-3365 Advances in Space Science and Technology†
0065-3373 Advances in Space Science and Technology
0065-3381 Advances in Stereoencephalotomy
0065-339X Advances in Steroid Biochemistry and Pharmacology *changed to* Advances in Steroid Biochemistry and Pharmacology (Year)
0065-3403 Advances in Structure Research by Diffraction Methods†
0065-3411 Advances in Surgery
0065-342X Advances in Teratology *see* 0306-2090
0065-3438 Advances in the Astronautical Sciences
0065-3446 Advances in the Biosciences
0065-3454 Advances in the Study of Behavior
0065-3500 Advances in Tuberculosis Research†
0065-3519 Advances in Veterinary Science and Comparative Medicine
0065-3527 Advances in Virus Research
0065-3535 Advances in Water Pollution Research†
0065-3543 Advancing Frontiers of Plant Sciences†
0065-3578 Advertiser's Annual
0065-3586 Ad Guide: an Advertiser's Guide to Scholarly Periodicals
0065-3594 Advertising and Press Annual of Africa *changed to* Promadata
0065-3640 Advertising Statistical Review†
0065-3659 Advertising Standards Authority, London. Annual Report
0065-3667 Aeldre Danske Tingboeger
0065-3683 Aeromedical Reviews *changed to* U.S. Air Force. School of Aerospace Medicine. Standard Technical Report Series
0065-3691 Aeromodeller Annual†
0065-3713 Aeronomica Acta
0065-3721 Aeroports de Paris. Rapport du Conseil d'Administration
0065-373X National Aerospace and Electronics Conference. Record *see* 0547-3578
0065-3756 Aerospace Materials Buyers Guide†
0065-3764 Aerospace Medical Association. Annual Scientific Meeting; Preprints†
0065-3772 Aerospace Safety Buyers Guide†
0065-3780 Revue Aerospatiale
0065-3799 Affaires et Gens d'Affaires
0065-3802 Africa Annual†
0065-3810 Africa Annual
0065-3829 Africa at a Glance: A Quick Reference of Facts and Figures on Africa†
0065-3845 Africa Contemporary Record. Annual Survey and Documents
0065-3853 Africa Institute. Annual Report *changed to* Africa Institute. Chairman's Report
0065-3861 Africa Institute. Communications†
0065-3888 Africa Institute. Special Publications *changed to* Africa Institute. Occasional Publications
0065-3896 Africa South of the Sahara
0065-3918 African Bibliographic Center, Washington, D.C. Biblioresearch Series†
0065-3926 African Bibliographic Center, Washington, D.C. Current Reading List Series†
0065-3934 African Bibliographic Center, Washington D.C. Special Bibliographic Series *see* 0749-2308
0065-3942 African Bibliographic Center, Washington, D.C. Special Bibliographic Series: Labor in Africa†
0065-3985 African Language Studies†
0065-4000 African Literature Today†
0065-4019 African Music
0065-4027 African Regional Trade Union Conference. Report
0065-4043 African Social Security Series *see* 0379-7074

ISSN INDEX 1343

0065-4051 Indiana University. Research Center for the Language Sciences. African Studies *see* 0073-7062
0065-406X African Studies Series
0065-4086 African Wildlife News *see* 0270-0360
0065-4116 Africana Collectanea Series†
0065-4140 Journal of African Studies
0065-4159 Afrika-Studiecentrum. Communications†
0065-4167 Afrique Industrie. Informations. *see* 0301-8520
0065-4191 Afro-Asian Peoples' Conference. Proceedings
0065-4248 Agence pour la Securite de la Navigation Aerienne en Afrique et a Madagascar. Direction de l'Exploitation Meteorologique. Publications. Serie 1
0065-4256 Agenda de la Quincaillerie
0065-4264 Agenda del Dirigente di Azienda
0065-4272 Agent's and Buyer's Guide
0065-4299 Agents and Actions
0065-4337 Agrarian Development Studies
0065-4345 Agrarmarkt-Studien
0065-4353 Agrarpolitik und Marktwesen†
0065-4361 A S G Eingliederung Heimatvertriebener Landwirte auf Vollbauernstellen†
0065-437X Agrarsoziale Gesellschaft. Geschaefts- und Arbeitsbericht
0065-4388 Agrarsoziale Gesellschaft. Rundbriefe *see* 0179-7603
0065-440X Agricultura Espanola *changed to* Agricultura Espanola en (Year)
0065-4418 North Carolina Agricultural Chemicals Manual
0065-4426 Agricultural Development Bank of Pakistan. Annual Report and Statement of Accounts
0065-4434 Agricultural Economics Bulletin for Africa†
0065-4442 Michigan State University. Agricultural Economics Report
0065-4469 Agricultural Economist
0065-4477 Agricultural Engineers Yearbook of Standards *changed to* A S A E Standards
0065-4485 Agricultural Pesticide Society. Annual Meeting. Proceedings *see* 0227-7980
0065-4493 Agricultural Progress
0065-4507 Great Britain. Institute of Animal Physiology. Report
0065-4515 Agricultural Research Council of Malawi. Annual Report *changed to* Malawi. Department of Agricultural Research. Annual Report
0065-4523 Agricultural Research Guyana
0065-4531 Agricultural Research Index *changed to* Agricultural Research Centres
0065-454X Agricultural Society of Nigeria. Proceedings
0065-4558 Agricultural Statistics, England and Wales *see* 0262-2394
0065-4566 Agricultural Statistics of Bangladesh *changed to* Yearbook of Agricultural Statistics of Bangladesh
0065-4574 Agricultural Statistics of Greece
0065-4582 Agricultural Statistics, Scotland *changed to* Economic Report on Scottish Agriculture
0065-4590 Agricultural Statistics, United Kingdom
0065-4604 Cornell Agricultural Waste Management Conference. Proceedings†
0065-4612 U.S. Department of Agriculture. Agriculture Handbook
0065-4639 U.S. Department of Agriculture. Agriculture Information Bulletin
0065-4647 Agro-Ecological Atlas of Cereal Growing in Europe†
0065-4655 Agro-Nouvelles
0065-4663 Agronomy: a Series of Monographs
0065-4671 Agronomy Abstracts
0065-468X Ahmadu Bello University. Centre of Islamic Legal Studies. Journal
0065-4698 Ahmadu Bello University. Department of Geography. Occasional Paper
0065-471X Ahmadu Bello University. Institute for Agricultural Research. Annual Report
0065-4728 Ahmadu Bello University. Institute for Agricultural Research. Soil Survey Bulletin
0065-4744 Ahmadu Bello University. Institute of Administration. Traditional Land Tenure Surveys†
0065-4752 Ahmadu Bello University. Institute of Education. Paper
0065-4760 Ahmadu Bello University. Northern History Research Scheme. Papers *changed to* Ahmadu Bello University. Northern History Research Scheme. Interim Report
0065-4779 Ahmedabad Textile Industry's Research Association. Proceedings of the Management Conference†
0065-4787 Ailleurs et Demain; Classiques
0065-4809 Air Conditioning, Ventilating and Heating Equipment *changed to* H V A C Red Book of Heating, Ventilating and Air Conditioning Equipment
0065-4817 Air New Zealand. Annual Report
0065-4841 Air Safety Forum†
0065-485X Air Transport Association of Canada. Annual Report
0065-4876 Aircraft Accident Digest
0065-4892 Aircraft Engines of the World†
0065-4906 Aircraft Owners and Pilots Association. A O P A Airport Directory *see* 0271-065X
0065-4914 Airline Guide to Stewardess & Stewards Career *changed to* Airline Guide to Flight Attendant Career
0065-4949 Universite d'Aix-Marseille I. Centre d'Etudes des Societes Mediterraneennes. Cahiers
0065-4965 Universite d'Aix-Marseille 3. Centre des Hautes Etudes Touristiques. Etudes et Memoires
0065-4973 Universite d'Aix-Marseille I. Faculte des Lettres et Sciences Humaines. Annales†
0065-4981 Universite d'Aix-Marseille I. Centre d'Etudes et de Recherches Helleniques. Publications
0065-499X Universite d'Aix-Marseille. Faculte des Lettres et Sciences Humaines. Travaux et Memoires†
0065-5007 Universite d'Aix-Marseille I. Institut d'Histoire des Pays d'Outre-Mer. Etudes et Documents
0065-5015 Akademie der Wissenschaften der DDR. Geodaetisches Institut. Veroeffentlichungen *changed to* Akademie der Wissenschaften der DDR. Zentralinstitut fuer Physik der Erde. Veroeffentlichungen
0065-5023 Zentralinstitut fuer Physik der Erde. Seismologischer Dienst Jena. Seismologische Bulletin†
0065-5066 Akademie der Wissenschaften. Berlin. Jahrbuch *see* 0304-2154
0065-5198 Akademie der Wissenschaften, Berlin. Sektion fuer Vor- und Fruehgeschichte. Schriften *see* 0138-3361
0065-5228 Akademie der Wissenschaften, Berlin. Volkskundliche Veroeffentlichungen *see* 0138-3167
0065-5260 Akademie der Wissenschaften, Berlin. Zentralinstitut fuer Sprachwissenschaft. Schriften *see* 0138-5852
0065-5287 Akademie der Wissenschaften, Goettingen. Nachrichten 1. Philologisch-Historische Klasse
0065-5295 Akademie der Wissenschaften, Goettingen. Nachrichten 2. Mathematisch-Physikalische Klasse
0065-5309 Deutsche Geodaetische Kommission. Veroeffentlichungen: Reihe A. Theoretische Geodaesie
0065-5317 Deutsche Geodaetische Kommission. Veroeffentlichungen: Reihe B. Angewandte Geodaesie
0065-5325 Deutsche Geodaetische Kommission. Veroeffentlichungen: Reihe C. Dissertationen
0065-5333 Deutsche Geodaetische Kommission. Veroeffentlichungen: Reihe D. Tafelwerke
0065-5341 Deutsche Geodaetische Kommission. Veroeffentlichungen: Reihe E. Geschichte und Entwicklung der Geodaesie
0065-535X Oesterreichische Akademie der Wissenschaften, Vienna. Mathematisch-Naturwissenschaftliche Klasse. Anzeiger *see* 0379-0207
0065-5376 Oesterreichische Akademie der Wissenschaften. Praehistorische Kommission. Mitteilungen
0065-5384 Akademie fuer Fuehrungskraefte der Wirtschaft. Taschenbuecher zur Betriebspraxis
0065-5392 Akademie fuer Staatsmedizin, Duesseldorf. Jahrbuch *see* 0172-2131
0065-5503 Koninklijke Nederlandse Akademie van Wetenschappen. Afdeling Natuurkunde, Verhandelingen. Eerste Reeks
0065-5511 Koninklijke Nederlandse Akademie van Wetenschappen. Afdeling Letterkunde. Verhandelingen. Nieuwe Reeks
0065-552X Koninklijke Nederlandse Akademie van Wetenschappen. Afdeling Natuurkunde. Verhandelingen. Tweede Reeks
0065-5538 Akademische Vortraege und Abhandlungen
0065-5554 Akiyoshi-dai Science Museum. Bulletin *changed to* Akiyoshi-dai Museum of Natural History. Bulletin
0065-5562 Aktion fuer Kultur und Politik *see* 0002-3760
0065-5589 Aktuelle Problcmc in der Chirurgie *changed to* Aktuelle Probleme in Chirurgie und Orthopadie
0065-5597 Aktuelle Probleme in der Klinischen Biochemie *see* 0300-1725
0065-5600 Aktuelle Probleme in der Psychiatrie, Neurologie, Neurochirurgie
0065-5619 Aktuellt och Historiskt *changed to* Militaerhistorisk Tidskrift
0065-5627 Al-Hikma†
0065-5635 Alabama Geological Society. Guidebook for the Annual Field Trip
0065-5643 A P A Newspaper Directory *changed to* Alabama Press Association. Rate and Data Guide
0065-5686 Alan Rogers' Selected Sites for Caravanning and Camping in Europe
0065-5694 Alaska Agricultural Statistics
0065-5708 Alaska. Department of Fish and Game. Annual Report
0065-5724 Alaska. Division of Geological and Geophysical Surveys. Annual Report†
0065-5732 Alaska. Division of Geological and Geophysical Surveys. Geochemical Report†
0065-5759 Alaska. Division of Geological and Geophysical Surveys. Information Circular
0065-5767 Alaska. Division of Geological and Geophysical Surveys. Laboratory Note *changed to* Alaska. Division of Geological and Geophysical Surveys. Report of Investigations
0065-5775 Alaska. Division of Geological and Geophysical Surveys. Laboratory Report *changed to* Alaska. Division of Geological and Geophysical Surveys. Geologic/Professional Report
0065-5783 Alaska. Division of Geological and Geophysical Surveys. Miscellaneous Paper†
0065-5805 Alaska. Employment Security Division. Workforce Estimates, by Industry and Area *see* 0362-4196
0065-5813 Alaska Petroleum and Industrial Directory
0065-5821 Annual Report of the Public Libraries of Alaska†
0065-583X Alaska State Plan for the Construction of Hospitals and Medical Facilities†
0065-5848 Alaska Travel Guide
0065-5864 University of Alaska. Geophysical Institute. Contributions. Series A†
0065-5872 University of Alaska. Geophysical Institute. Contributions. Series B†
0065-5929 University of Alaska. Institute of Marine Science. Technical Report
0065-5937 Institute of Social, Economic and Government Research. Reports *changed to* Institute of Social and Economic Research. Reports
0065-5945 I S E G R Research Notes *changed to* I S E R Research Notes
0065-5953 University of Alaska. Institute of Water Resources. Annual Report *changed to* University of Alaska. Institute of Northern Engineering
0065-5961 University of Alaska. Mineral Industry Research Laboratory. Report
0065-597X Alberta. Department of Agriculture. Annual Report *changed to* Alberta Agriculture. Annual Report
0065-5996 Alberta Poetry Yearbook†
0065-6003 Alberta Society of Petroleum Geologists. Geological Guide *changed to* Canadian Society of Petroleum Geologists. Bulletin
0065-6046 University of Alberta. Department of Agricultural Economics and Rural Sociology. Research Bulletin *changed to* University of Alberta. Department of Rural Economy. Bulletin
0065-6062 University of Alberta. Department of Computing Science. Publication *see* 0316-4683
0065-6070 University of Alberta. Faculty of Business Administration and Commerce. Research Studies in Business†
0065-6089 Alberta Writers Speak Overland to the Klondike
0065-6097 Albertan Geographer
0065-6100 Graefe's Archive for Clinical and Experimental Ophthamology
0065-6119 Alcoholism and Drug Addiction Research Foundation. Annual Report *changed to* Addiction Research Foundation of Ontario. Annual Report
0065-6127 Alcoy; Fiesta de Moros y Cristianos
0065-6143 Aldrich Entomology Club. Newsletter
0065-6151 Alessandria, Italy. Centro Documentazione e Richerche Economico-Sociali. Quaderni CeDRES
0065-616X Alexander Lectures
0065-6186 Alfred Benzon Symposium. Proceedings
0065-6216 Alfred P. Sloan Foundation. Report
0065-6232 Observatoire Astronomique d'Alger. Annales
0065-6240 Algorytmy†
0065-6259 Aligarh Muslim University, Aligarh, India. Department of History. Publication
0065-6267 Alimentation et la Vie *changed to* Alimentation et la Vie - Nouvelle Presentation
0065-6275 Aliso
0065-6283 All India Crime Prevention Society. Annual Report and Audited Statement of Accounts
0065-6291 All India Government Travellers Bungalows Annual Recorder
0065-6305 All India Leather Directory†
0065-6313 All-Pakistan Income-Tax Reports and Returns and Income-Tax Revenue Statistics†
0065-6321 All Pakistan Women's Association. Annual Report†
0065-633X All-Time Favorite Poetry†
0065-6348 Allam es Jogtudomany Uttoroi†
0065-6364 Allan Hancock Monographs in Marine Biology†

1344 ISSN INDEX

0065-6372 Allergologicum; Transactions of the Collegium Internationale
0065-6410 Allied Artists of America. Exhibition Catalog
0065-6429 Allionia
0065-6461 Almanac of the Pacific *changed to* Thrum's All About Hawaii
0065-647X Almanac of World Military Power†
0065-650X Almanach du Peuple
0065-6526 Almanach Sceny Polskiej
0065-6542 Alpha Annual†
0065-6569 Alpine Journal
0065-6585 Alt-Thueringen
0065-6593 Altbabylonische Briefe im Umschrift und Uebersetzung
0065-6607 Altdeutsche Textbibliothek. Ergaenzungsreihe
0065-6623 Altech
0065-6631 Naturkundliches Museum "Mauritianum" Altenburg. Abhandlungen und Berichte *see* 0233-173X
0065-6658 Aluminum Standards and Data
0065-6666 Aluminum Statistical Review
0065-6674 Amakusa Marine Biological Laboratory. Contributions
0065-6682 Amakusa Marine Biological Laboratory. Publications
0065-6690 Amateur Athletic Association. Handbook
0065-6704 Amateur Chamber Music Players. Directory
0065-6712 Percy Thrower's Guide to Modern Gardening *changed to* Amateur Gardening Guide
0065-6739 Amateur Softball Association of America. Official Guide and Rule Book
0065-6747 Amateur Trapshooting Association. Official Trapshooting Rules
0065-6755 Amazoniana; Limnologia et Oecologia Regionalis Systemae Fluminis Amazonas
0065-6763 America - Problema
0065-6771 America en Cifras†
0065-678X America Votes
0065-6798 American Academy for Jewish Research. Proceedings of the A A J R
0065-6801 American Academy in Rome. Memoirs
0065-681X American Academy in Rome. Papers and Monographs
0065-6836 American Academy of Arts and Letters. Proceedings *see* 0145-8493
0065-6852 American Academy of Child Psychiatry. Journal. Monograph†
0065-6860 American Academy of Environmental Engineers. Roster
0065-6879 A A M A Executive *changed to* Medical Administration Executive
0065-6887 American Academy of Optometry Series†
0065-6895 American Academy of Orthopaedic Surgeons. Committee on Instructional Courses. Instructional Course Lectures
0065-6909 American Academy of Pediatrics. Committee on Infectious Diseases. Report
0065-6917 American Academy of Political and Social Science. Monographs†
0065-6925 American Alpine Journal
0065-6933 American Anthropological Association. Annual Report and Directory†
0065-6941 American Anthropologist. Special Publication†
0065-6968 American Art Directory
0065-6976 American Assembly (Background Papers and Final Report) *see* 0569-2245
0065-6984 American Association for Conservation Information. Yearbook†
0065-700X A A H P E R Archery-Riding Guide *changed to* N A G W S Guide. Archery-Fencing
0065-7018 Basketball Guide, with Official Rules and Standards *see* 0362-3254
0065-7026 Field Hockey-Lacrosse Guide *changed to* N A G W S Guide. Field Hockey
0065-7026 Field Hockey-Lacrosse Guide *changed to* N A G W S Guide. Lacrosse
0065-7034 Soccer-Speedball Guide *see* 0190-9363
0065-7042 Tennis-Badminton-Squash Guide *see* 0272-863X
0065-7050 Volleyball Guide *changed to* N A G W S Guide. Volleyball
0065-7085 American Association for the Advancement of Science. Publications†
0065-7107 American Association of Cereal Chemists. Monograph Series
0065-7115 Standard Methods of Clinical Chemistry†
0065-7123 A A C T E Yearbook†
0065-7131 American Assembly of Collegiate Schools of Business. Accredited Schools, Officers, Committees *changed to* American Assembly of Collegiate Schools of Business. Membership Directory.
0065-7158 American Association of Cost Engineers. Transactions of the Annual Meeting
0065-7182 American Association of Equine Practitioners. Proceedings of the Annual Convention
0065-7190 American Association of Foot Specialists. Program Journal *changed to* American College of Foot Specialists. Annual Yearbook
0065-7204 American Association of Genito-Urinary Surgeons. Transactions
0065-7239 American Association of Community and Junior Colleges. Governmental Affairs Special†
0065-7255 A A L L Publications Series
0065-7263 American Association of Medical Milk Commissions. Methods and Standards for the Production of Certified Milk
0065-7271 American Association of Motor Vehicle Administrators. Annual Conference. Proceedings
0065-728X American Association of Obstetricians and Gynecologists. Transactions
0065-7298 American Association of Pathologists and Bacteriologists. Symposium. Monographs
0065-731X American Association of Petroleum Geologists. Memoir
0065-7328 A A S A Convention Reporter†
0065-7344 A A S C U Studies
0065-7352 American Association of Textile Chemists and Colorists. Products Buyer's Guide *see* 0040-490X
0065-7360 American Association of Theological Schools in the United States and Canada. Bulletin *see* 0362-1472
0065-7379 American Association of Theological Schools in the United States and Canada. Directory *changed to* Association of Theological Schools in the United States and Canada. Directory
0065-7395 American Association of Workers for the Blind. Proceedings *changed to* American Association of Workers for the Blind. Annual Report
0065-7417 A A S Microfiche Series
0065-7433 A A S Photo-Bulletin
0065-7441 American Bankers Association. National Automation Conference. Proceedings *see* 0095-5396
0065-745X American Bantam Association. Yearbook
0065-7468 American Baptist Education Association. Report†
0065-7476 Federal Government Legal Career Opportunities *changed to* Now Hiring
0065-7492 American Bar Association. Section of Labor-Relations Law. Report *see* 0270-4889
0065-7522 American Bar Association. Standing Committee on Legal Assistance for Servicemen. Occasional Newsletter *changed to* Legal Assistance Newsletter
0065-7549 American Bar Foundation. Research Contributions†
0065-7565 American Blue Book of Funeral Directors
0065-759X American Book Trade Directory
0065-7603 American Broncho-Esophagological Association. Transactions
0065-7611 American Bureau of Metal Statistics. Year Book *see* 0360-9553
0065-762X American Camellia Yearbook
0065-7638 American Catholic Philosophical Association. Proceedings
0065-7646 American Cement Directory
0065-7654 American Ceramic Society. Special Publications†
0065-7662 American Chamber of Commerce for Brazil. Annual Directory
0065-7670 American Chamber of Commerce in France. Directory
0065-7689 A M C H A M Morocco
0065-7697 American Chamber of Commerce of Venezuela. Yearbook and Membership Directory *changed to* Venezuelan - American Chamber of Commerce and Industry. Yearbook and Membership Directory
0065-7700 A C S Laboratory Guide *see* 0003-2700
0065-7719 A C S Monographs
0065-7727 American Chemical Society. Abstracts of Papers (at the National Meeting)
0065-7735 American Chemical Society. Abstracts of Papers (at the Regional Meetings)
0065-7743 Annual Reports in Medicinal Chemistry
0065-7778 American Clinical and Climatological Association. Transactions
0065-7786 American College of Apothecaries. Proceedings†
0065-7794 American College of Hospital Administrators. Directory *changed to* American College of Healthcare Executives. Directory
0065-7816 American College Public Relations Association. Directory *changed to* Council for Advancement and Support of Education. Membership Directory
0065-7832 A C T Monograph Series
0065-7840 A C T Research Service Report *see* 0569-3993
0065-7875 A C I Manual of Concrete Practice
0065-7883 A C I Monograph†
0065-7891 American Concrete Institute. Special Publication
0065-7905 American Conference of Academic Deans. Proceedings
0065-7913 American Congress on Surveying and Mapping. Papers from the Annual Meetings *see* 0277-2876
0065-793X American Cooperation Yearbook
0065-7948 American Correctional Association. Annual Congress of Correction. Proceedings
0065-7956 State and Federal Correctional Institutions *see* 0190-2555
0065-7964 American Council of Independent Laboratories. Directory
0065-7980 Accredited Colleges of Pharmacy *changed to* Accredited Professional Programs of Colleges and Schools of Pharmacy
0065-7999 American Country Life Association. Proceedings of the Annual Conference†
0065-8006 American Crystallographic Association. Transactions
0065-8014 American Culture†
0065-8022 American Dance Therapy Association. Proceedings of the Annual Conference†
0065-8030 Annual Report on Dental Education
0065-8049 Dental Students' Register *see* 0065-8030
0065-8057 American Dental Association. Council on Dental Education. Requirements and Registration Data: State Dental Examining Boards†
0065-8073 American Dental Directory
0065-8081 American Dexter Cattle Association. Herd Book
0065-809X American Doctoral Dissertations
0065-8103 American Drop-Shippers Directory
0065-8138 American Theatre Association. Annual Directory of Members
0065-8162 American Entomological Institute. Memoirs
0065-8170 American Entomological Society. Memoirs
0065-8189 American Ephemeris and Nautical Almanac *changed to* Astronomical Almanac
0065-8197 American Ethnological Society. Monographs
0065-8200 American Ethnological Society. Proceedings of Spring Meeting
0065-8219 American Exploration and Travel
0065-8308 American Film Review *changed to* American Film & Video Review
0065-8316 American Folk Music Occasional
0065-8324 American Folklore Society. Bibliographical and Special Series†
0065-8332 American Folklore Society. Memoirs†
0065-8359 American Foundation for the Blind. Annual Report
0065-8367 A F B Research Bulletin *see* 0145-482X
0065-8375 American Foundrymen's Society. Transactions
0065-8391 Gas Utility and Pipeline Industry Projections†
0065-8413 American Geographical Society of New York. Occasional Publication†
0065-8421 American Geographical Society of New York. Research Series†
0065-843X American Geographical Society of New York. Special Publication†
0065-8448 American Geophysical Union. Geophysical Monograph *changed to* American Geophysical Union. Geophysical Monograph Book Series
0065-8456 American Goat Society. Year Book
0065-8480 American Gynecological Society. Transactions of the A G S *changed to* American Gynecological and Obstetrical Society. Transactions of the A G O S
0065-8499 American Heart Association. Monographs
0065-8510 American Helicopter Society. National Forum. Proceedings *changed to* American Helicopter Society. Annual Forum. Proceedings
0065-8529 American-Hellenic Chamber of Commerce. Business Directory *see* 0065-8537
0065-8537 American-Hellenic Chamber of Commerce. Business Directory. Special Issue
0065-8545 American Histadrut Cultural Exchange Institute. Annual Arden House Conference. Proceedings†
0065-8553 American Histadrut Cultural Exchange Institute. Round Table Pamphlet Series†
0065-8561 American Historical Association. Annual Report
0065-8588 American Home Economics Association. Textiles and Clothing Section. Textile Handbook†
0065-8596 American Humane Association. National Humane Report *changed to* American Humane Association Annual Report
0065-860X American Imago
0065-8618 American Industrial Arts Association. Addresses and Proceedings of the Annual Convention†
0065-8634 American Industrial Arts Association. Yearbook *see* 0084-6333
0065-8642 American Industrial Real Estate Association. Journal†
0065-8650 American Institute for Marxist Studies. Bibliographic Series

ISSN INDEX 1345

ISSN	Title
0065-8669	American Institute for Marxist Studies. Historical Series†
0065-8677	American Institute for Marxist Studies. Monograph Series†
0065-8693	A I A A Roster
0065-8715	American Institute of Aeronautics and Astronautics. Selected Reprint Series†
0065-8723	A I A Building Construction Legal Citator. Supplement†
0065-874X	American Institute of Certified Public Accountants. Division of Federal Taxation. Statements on Responsibilities in Tax Practice
0065-8758	American Institute of Certified Public Accountants. Committee on Practice Review. Practice Review Bulletin†
0065-8766	American Institute of Certified Public Accountants. Management Advisory Services. Guideline Series†
0065-8774	American Institute of Certified Public Accountants. Practical Accounting and Auditing Problems†
0065-8782	American Institute of Certified Public Accountants. Statements on Auditing Procedure†
0065-8790	A I Ch E Continuing Education Series†
0065-8804	A I Ch E Monograph Series
0065-8812	A I Ch E Symposium Series
0065-8820	American Institute of Graphic Arts. Journal†
0065-8847	American Institute of Islamic Studies. Bibliographic Series
0065-8855	American Institute of Musicology. Miscellanea
0065-8871	American Institute of Ultrasound in Medicine. Annual Scientific Conference. Program *changed to* American Institute of Ultrasound in Medicine. Annual Scientific Conference. Proceedings
0065-891X	American Institutes for Research. Seminar Series†
0065-8928	American Jewish Committee. Institute of Human Relations. Pamphlet Series. *changed to* American Jewish Committee. Institute of Human Relations. Paperback Series
0065-8936	American Jewish Communal History
0065-8944	American Jewish Historical Society. News *see* 0732-0914
0065-8987	American Jewish Year Book
0065-8995	American Journal of Jurisprudence
0065-9010	A J S Information Report Series†
0065-9029	American Junior Colleges†
0065-9037	American Laryngological, Rhinological and Otological Society. Transactions
0065-9045	American Law Institute. Annual Meeting. Proceedings
0065-9053	Official Lawn Bowls Handbook *changed to* Official Lawn Bowls Almanac
0065-907X	A L A Studies in Librarianship
0065-9088	L T P Publications†
0065-9096	A L A Social Responsibilities Round Table Newsletter *see* 0749-1670
0065-910X	American Library Directory
0065-9118	American Life Collector's Annual†
0065-9142	American Literary Scholarship
0065-9150	American Littoral Society. Special Publications
0065-9185	American Management Association. Research Studies
0065-9193	American Management Association. Seminar Program
0065-9215	A M A Abstracts of Papers of the Conferences *changed to* American Marketing Association. Annual Marketing Educators' Conference. Proceedings
0065-9231	American Marketing Association. Proceedings *changed to* American Marketing Association. Annual Marketing Educators' Conference. Proceedings
0065-924X	American Marketing Association. Reprint Series†
0065-9258	American Mathematical Society. Colloquium Publications
0065-9266	American Mathematical Society. Memoirs
0065-9274	Selected Translations in Mathematical Statistics and Probability
0065-9282	Translations of Mathematical Monographs
0065-9290	American Mathematical Society. Translations. Series 2
0065-9304	A M A Drug Evaluations†
0065-9312	Current Procedural Terminology *see* 0276-8283
0065-9320	Medical and Surgical Motion Pictures†
0065-9339	American Medical Directory *changed to* American Medical Directory
0065-9347	American Men and Women of Science. Physical and Biological Sciences
0065-938X	American Merchant Marine Library Association. Report
0065-9401	American Meteorological Society. Meteorological Monographs
0065-9436	American Midland Naturalist Monograph Series
0065-9452	American Museum of Natural History. Anthropological Papers
0065-9479	American Neurological Association. Transactions†
0065-9487	A E C/A N S Monographs *changed to* Nuclear Science Technology Monograph Series
0065-9495	A N A Clinical Sessions†
0065-9517	American Nurses' Association. House of Delegates. Reports†
0065-9533	American Ophthalmological Society. Transactions
0065-9541	American Oriental Series
0065-955X	American Orthoptic Journal
0065-9576	American Osteopathic College of Radiology. Newsletter. *changed to* Viewbox
0065-9630	A P I Research Project 44. Selected Values of Properties of Hydrocarbons and Related Compounds. Category A: Tables of Selected Values of Physical and Thermodynamic Properties of Hydrocarbons *changed to* Thermodynamics Research Center. Hydrocarbon Project. Selected Values of Properties of Hydrocarbons and Related Compounds. Category A: Tables of Selected Values of Physical and Thermodynamic Properties of Hydrocarbons
0065-9649	A P I Research Project 44. Selected Values of Properties of Hydrocarbons and Related Compounds. Category B: Selected Infrared Spectral Data *changed to* Thermodynamics Research Center. Hydrocarbon Project. Selected Values of Properties of Hydrocarbons and Related Compounds. Category B: Selected Infrared Spectral Data
0065-9657	A P I Research Project 44. Selected Values of Properties of Hydrocarbons and Related Compounds. Category C: Selected Ultraviolet Spectral Data *changed to* Thermodynamics Research Center. Hydrocarbon Project. Selected Values of Properties of Hydrocarbons and Related Compounds. Category C: Selected Ultraviolet Spectral Data
0065-9665	A P I Research Project 44. Selected Values of Properties of Hydrocarbons and Related Compounds. Category D: Selected Raman Spectral Data *changed to* Thermodynamics Research Center. Hydrocarbon Project. Selected Values of Properties of Hydrocarbons and Related Compounds. Category D: Selected Raman Spectral Data
0065-9673	A P I Research Project 44. Selected Values of Properties of Hydrocarbons and Related Compounds. Category E: Selected Mass Spectral Data *changed to* Thermodynamics Research Center. Hydrocarbon Project. Selected Values of Properties of Hydrocarbons and Related Compounds. Category E: Selected Mass Spectral Data
0065-9681	A P I Research Project 44. Selected Values of Properties of Hydrocarbons and Related Compounds. Category F: Selected Nuclear Magnetic Resonance Data *changed to* Thermodynamics Research Center. Hydrocarbon Project. Selected Values of Properties of Hydrocarbons and Related Compounds. Category F: Selected Nuclear Magnetic Resonance Data
0065-9703	American Philological Association. Special Publications
0065-9711	American Philological Association. Transactions and Proceedings *see* 0362-9945
0065-9711	American Philological Association. Transactions and Proceedings *see* 0360-5949
0065-972X	American Philosophical Association. Proceedings and Addresses
0065-9738	American Philosophical Society. Memoirs
0065-9746	American Philosophical Society. Transactions
0065-9762	American Philosophical Society. Yearbook
0065-9770	American Podiatry Association. Desk Reference and Directory *changed to* American Podiatric Medical Association. Desk Reference and Directory
0065-9797	American Power Boat Association. A P B A Rule Book
0065-9800	American Printing House for the Blind, Louisville, Kentucky. Department of Educational Research. Annual Report *changed to* American Printing House for the Blind, Louisville, Kentucky. Department of Educational Research. Report of Research and Development Activities
0065-9819	A P I C S Annual Conference Proceedings *changed to* American Production and Inventory Control Society. Annual International Conference Proceedings
0065-9827	American Psychiatric Association. Biographical Directory†
0065-9843	American Psychoanalytic Association. Journal. Monograph
0065-9886	American Psychopathological Association. Publications†
0065-9894	American Public Gas Association. Memorandum Bulletins *changed to* American Public Gas Association. Newsletter
0065-9932	American Public Works Association. Research Foundation. Special Reports
0065-9940	American Railway Bridge and Building Association. Proceedings
0065-9959	American Reference Books Annual
0065-9967	American Register of Exporters and Importers *see* 0272-1163
0065-9975	American Register of Inter-Corporate Ownership *changed to* Directory of Inter-Corporate Ownership
0065-9991	American Research Center in Egypt. Journal
0066-0000	American Rose Annual
0066-0027	American School of Prehistoric Research. Bulletins
0066-0035	American Schools of Oriental Research. Annual
0066-0043	American Science Manpower†
0066-0051	American Series of Foreign Penal Codes
0066-006X	American Society for Abrasive Methods. Technical Conference. Proceedings *see* 0363-8065
0066-0086	American Society for Cybernetics. Proceedings of the Annual Symposium
0066-0116	American Society for Horticultural Science. Tropical Region. Proceedings of the Annual Meeting
0066-0124	A S I S Handbook and Directory *changed to* American Society for Information Science. Handbook and Directory
0066-0132	American Society for Neurochemistry. Transactions
0066-0159	American Society for Quality Control. Transactions of Annual Technical Conferences *see* 0360-6929
0066-0183	Annual Book of A S T M Standards. Volume 01.01. Steel-Piping, Tubing, Fittings
0066-0191	Annual Book of A S T M Standards. Part 2. Ferrous Castings, Ferro Alloys *changed to* Annual Book of A S T M Standards. Volume 01.02. Ferrous Castings, Ferro Alloys; Shipbuilding
0066-0205	Annual Book of A S T M Standards. Part 3. Steel Strip, Bar, Rod, Wire, Chain, and Spring; Wrought Iron; Metallic Coated Products; Ferrous Surgical Implants *changed to* Annual Book of A S T M Standards. Volume 01.03. Steel Plate, Sheet, Strip Wire
0066-0213	Annual Book of A S T M Standards. Part 4. Structural Steel; Concrete Reinforcing Steel; Pressure Vessel Plate; Steel Rails; Wheels, and Tires; Bearing Steel; Steel Forgings *changed to* Annual Book of A S T M Standards. Volume 01.04. Steel-Structural, Reinforcing, Pressure Vessel; Railway
0066-0221	Annual Book of A S T M Standards. Part 6. Copper and Copper Alloys (Including Electrical Conductors) *changed to* Annual Book of A S T M Standards. Volume 02.01. Copper and Copper Alloys
0066-023X	Annual Book of A S T M Standards. Part 7. Die-Cast Metals; Light Metals and Alloys (Including Electrical Conductors) *changed to* Annual Book of A S T M Standards. Volume 02.02. Die-Cast Metals; Aluminum and Magnesium Alloys
0066-0248	Annual Book of A S T M Standards. Part 7. Nonferrous Metals and Alloys (Including Corrosion Tests); Electrodeposited Metallic Coatings; Metal Powders; Surgical Implants. *changed to* Annual Book of A S T M Standards. Volume 02.04. Nonferrous Metals-Nickel, Lead, Tin Alloys, Precious, Primary, Reactive Metals
0066-0256	Annual Book of A S T M Standards. Part 9. Cement; Lime; Gypsum *changed to* Annual Book of A S T M Standards. Volume 04.01. Cement; Lime; Gypsum
0066-0264	Annual Book of A S T M Standards. Part 14. Concrete and Mineral Aggregates (Including Manual of Concrete Testing) *changed to* Annual Book of A S T M Standards. Volume 04.02. Concrete and Mineral Aggregates (Including Manual of Concrete and Aggregate Testing)
0066-0272	Soil and Rock; Skid Resistance *changed to* Annual Book of A S T M Standards. Volume 04.03. Road and Paving Materials; Traveled Surface Characteristics

ISSN INDEX

0066-0280 Annual Book of A S T M Standards. Part 12. Chemical-Resistant Nonmetallic Materials; Clay and Concrete Pipe and Tile; Masonry Mortars and Units; Asbestos-Cement Products; Natural Building Stones *changed to* Annual Book of A S T M Standards. Volume 04.05. Chemical-Resistant Materials; Vitrified Clay, Concrete; Masonry; Mortars; Fiber-Cement Products

0066-0299 Annual Book of A S T M Standards. Part 17. Refractories, Glass and Other Ceramic Materials; Manufactured Carbon and Graphite Products *changed to* Annual Book of A S T M Standards. Volume 15.01. Refractories, Manufactured Carbon and Graphite Products; Activated Carbon

0066-0299 Annual Book of A S T M Standards. Part 17. Refractories, Glass and Other Ceramic Materials; Manufactured Carbon and Graphite Products *changed to* Annual Book of A S T M Standards. Volume 15.02. Glass; Ceramic Whitewares

0066-0302 Annual Book of A S T M Standards. Part 18. Thermal and Cryogenic Insulating Materials; Building Seals and Sealants; Fire Tests; Building Constructions; Environmental Acoustics *changed to* Annual Book of A S T M Standards. Volume 04.06. Thermal Insulation; Environmental Acoustics

0066-0310 Annual Book of A S T M Standards. Part 15. Paper; Packaging; Cellulose; Casein; Flexible Barrier Materials; Carbon Paper; Leather *changed to* Annual Book of A S T M Standards. Volume 15.09. Paper; Packaging; Flexible Barrier Materials; Business Copy Products

0066-0329 Annual Book of A S T M Standards. Part 22. Wood; Adhesives *changed to* Annual Book of A S T M Standards. Volume 04.09. Wood

0066-0329 Annual Book of A S T M Standards. Part 22. Wood; Adhesives *changed to* Annual Book of A S T M Standards. Volume 15.06. Adhesives

0066-0337 Annual Book of A S T M Standards. Part 17. Petroleum Products - Fuels; Solvents; Burner Fuel Oils; Lubricating Greases; Hydraulic Fluids *changed to* Annual Book of A S T M Standards. Volume 05.01. Petroleum Products and Lubricants (1)

0066-0345 Annual Book of A S T M Standards. Part 18. Petroleum Products - Measurement and Sampling; Liquefied Petroleum Gases; Light Hydrocarbons; Plant Spray Oils; Aerospace Materials; Sulfonates; Crude Petroleum; Petroleum; Wax; Graphite *changed to* Annual Book of A S T M Standards. Volume 05.02. Petroleum Products and Lubricants (2)

0066-0353 Annual Book of A S T M Standards. Part 26. Gaseous Fuels; Coal and Coke *changed to* Annual Book of A S T M Standards. Volume 05.05. Gaseous Fuels; Coal and Coke

0066-0361 Annual Book of A S T M Standards. Part 20. Paint, Varnish, Lacquer, and Related Products - Materials Specifications and Tests; Naval Stores; Industrial Aromatic Hydrocarbons and Related Chemicals *changed to* Annual Book of A S T M Standards. Volume 06.03. Paint - Fatty Oils and Acids, Solvents, Miscellaneous; Aromatic Hydrocarbons

0066-037X Annual Book of A S T M Standards. Volume 06.01. Paint - Tests for Formulated Products and Applied Coatings

0066-0388 Annual Book of A S T M Standards. Part 30. Soap; Engine Coolants; Polishes; Halogenated Organic Solvents; Activated Carbon *changed to* Annual Book of A S T M Standards. Volume 15.05. Engine Coolants; Halogenated Organic Solvents; Industrial Chemicals

0066-0396 Annual Book of A S T M Standards. Part 23. Water; Atmospheric Analysis *changed to* Annual Book of A S T M Standards. Volume 11.01. Water (1)

0066-040X Annual Book of A S T M Standards. Volume 07.01. Textiles--Yarn, Fabrics, and General Test Methods

0066-0418 Annual Book of A S T M Standards. Part 33. Textiles--Fibers, Zippers; High Modulus Fibers *changed to* Annual Book of A S T M Standards. Volume 07.02. Textiles--Fibers, Zippers

0066-0426 Annual Book of A S T M Standards. Part 26. Plastics--Specifications; Methods of Testing Pipe, Film, Reinforced and Cellular Plastics *changed to* Annual Book of A S T M Standards. Volume 08.02. Plastics (2): D 1601 to D 3099

0066-0434 Annual Book of A S T M Standards. Part 35. Plastics--General Test Methods; Nomenclature *changed to* Annual Book of A S T M Standards. Volume 08.01. Plastics (1): C 177 to D 1600

0066-0442 Annual Book of A S T M Standards. Part 28. Rubber; Carbon Black; Gaskets *changed to* Annual Book of A S T M Standards. Volume 09.02. Rubber Products, Industrial--Specifications and Related Test Methods; Gaskets; Tires

0066-0450 Annual Book of A S T M Standards. Part 39. Electrical Insulating Materials--Test Methods *changed to* Annual Book of A S T M Standards. Volume 10.01. Electrical Insulation, Composites, and Coatings--Solids

0066-0469 Annual Book of A S T M Standards. Part 41. General Test Methods (Nonmetal); Statistical Methods; Space Simulation; Particle Size Measurement; Deterioration of Nonmetallic Materials *changed to* Annual Book of A S T M Standards. Volume 14.02. General Test Methods, Nonmetal; Laboratory Apparatus; Statistical Methods; Appearance of Materials; Durability of Nonmetallic Materials

0066-0477 Annual Book of A S T M Standards. Part 31. Metals--Physical, Mechanical, Nondestructive, and Corrosion Tests, Metallography, Fatigue, Effect of Temperature. *changed to* Annual Book of A S T M Standards. Volume 03.01. Metals-Mechanical Testing; Elevated and Low-Temperature Tests Metallography

0066-0485 Annual Book of A S T M Standards. Volume 03.05. Chemical Analysis of Metals; Metal Bearing Ores

0066-0493 Annual Book of A S T M Standards. Volume 00.01. Index

0066-0507 Annual Book of A S T M Standards. Part 8. Magnetic Properties; Metallic Materials for Thermostats and Contacts; Materials for Electron Devices and Microelectronics *changed to* Annual Book of A S T M Standards. Volume 03.04. Magnetic Properties; Metallic Materials for Thermostats, Electrical Resistance, Heating, Contacts

0066-0515 A S T M Proceedings

0066-0523 American Society for Testing and Materials. Compilation of A S T M Standards in Building Codes

0066-0531 American Society for Testing and Materials. Data Series Publications

0066-054X American Society for Testing and Materials. Five-Year Index to A S T M Technical Papers and Reports

0066-0558 American Society for Testing and Materials. Special Technical Publications

0066-0566 A S A Special Publication

0066-0582 American Society of Bakery Engineers. Proceedings of the Annual Meeting

0066-0590 C L U Forum Report†

0066-0604 American Society of Civil Engineers. Transactions

0066-0620 A S H R A E Handbook and Product Directory *changed to* A S H R A E Handbook

0066-0639 American Society of International Law. Newsletter

0066-0647 American Society of International Law. Proceedings *see* 0272-5045

0066-0655 American Society of Ophthalmologic and Otolaryngologic Allergy. Transactions†

0066-068X American Society of Sanitary Engineering. Year Book

0066-0698 American Society of Traffic and Transportation, Ohio Chapter. Proceedings of the Annual Seminar†

0066-0701 American Society of University Composers. Proceedings†

0066-071X A S H A Monographs†

0066-0736 American Statistical Association. Business and Economic Statistics Section. Proceedings

0066-0752 American Statistical Association. Social Statistics Section. Proceedings

0066-0760 American Stock Exchange. AMEX Databook *changed to* American Stock Exchange. AMEX Fact Book

0066-0779 American Stock Exchange. Annual Report

0066-0795 American Studies Research Centre. Newsletter

0066-0809 American Studies Series†

0066-0833 American Surgical Association. Transactions

0066-0868 American Theological Library Association. Conference. Summary of Proceedings

0066-0884 American Trail Series

0066-0892 American Trucking Associations Report *changed to* American Trucking Trends - (Year)

0066-0922 American Universities and Colleges

0066-0930 American Universities Field Staff. Reports. Central and Southern Africa Series *changed to* Fieldstaff Reports. Central and Southern Africa Series

0066-0949 American Universities Field Staff. Reports. East Africa Series *changed to* Fieldstaff Reports. East Africa Series

0066-0973 American Universities Field Staff. Reports. Mexico and Caribbean Area *changed to* Fieldstaff Reports. North America Series

0066-0981 American Universities Field Staff. Reports. North Africa Series *changed to* Fieldstaff Reports. North Africa Series

0066-104X American Universities Field Staff. Reports. Southeast Europe Series *changed to* Fieldstaff Reports. Southeast Europe Series

0066-1058 American Universities Field Staff. Reports. West Africa Series *changed to* Fieldstaff Reports. West Africa Series.

0066-1082 American Universities Field Staff. Annual Report of the Executive Director†

0066-1104 American Universities Field Staff. List of Publications†

0066-1112 American Universities Field Staff. Select Bibliography: Asia, Africa, Eastern Europe, Latin America. Supplement†

0066-1147 American Veterinary Medical Association. Directory

0066-1155 American Veterinary Radiology Society. Journal *see* 0196-3627

0066-1171 American Water Resources Conferences. Annual Proceedings *changed to* American Water Resources Symposia. Annual Proceedings

0066-118X American Waterways Series†

0066-1201 American Youth Hostels Guide and Handbook *changed to* A Y H Handbook

0066-121X Americans Before Columbus

0066-1228 A C A Index

0066-1236 Americans for Constitutional Action. Report

0066-1244 Amino Acides, Peptides, Proteines. Cahier†

0066-1252 Amities Philosophiques Internationales. Bulletin

0066-1260 Amli Studies in Music Bibliography†

0066-1287 Rijksinstituut voor Oorlogsdocumentatie. Documenten

0066-1295 Rijksinstituut voor Oorlogsdocumentatie. Monografieen

0066-1309 Amsterdam-Rotterdam Bank. Annual Report

0066-1317 Universiteit van Amsterdam. Fysisch Geografisch en Bodemkundig Laboratorium. Publikaties

0066-1325 Universiteit van Amsterdam. Zoologisch Museum. Bulletin

0066-1333 Anadolu Sanati Arastirmalari

0066-1341 Anaesthesiology and Resuscitation *see* 0171-1814

0066-135X Analecta Biblica

0066-1368 Analecta Boerhaaviana

0066-1376 Analecta Gregoriana

0066-1392 Analecta Romana Instituti Danici

0066-1406 Analecta Romana Instituti Danici. Supplementum

0066-1414 Analecta Vaticano-Belgica. Deuxieme Serie. Section A: Nonciature de Flandre

0066-1422 Analecta Vaticano-Belgica. Deuxieme Serie. Section B: Nonciature de Cologne

0066-1430 Analecta Vaticano-Belgica. Deuxieme Serie. Section C: Nonciature de Bruxelles

0066-1449 Analecta Vaticano-Belgica. Premiere Serie: Documents Relatifs aux Anciens Dioceses de Cambrai, Liege, Therouanne et Tournai

0066-1465 Anales de Cirugia

0066-1473 Anales de Moral Social y Economica

0066-1481 Analog: Stories Selected from Analog Science Fact and Science Fiction†

0066-149X Analyses of Natural Gases of the United States

0066-152X Analyst†

0066-1538 Analytical Calorimetry

0066-1546 Anatolian Studies

0066-1554 Anatolica

0066-1562 Anatomische Gesellschaft. Verhandlungen

0066-1589 Anciens Pays et Assemblees d'Etats

0066-1600 Ancient Pakistan†

0066-1619 Ancient Society

0066-1627 M.D. Anderson Hospital and Tumor Institute. General Report

0066-1635 M.D. Anderson Hospital and Tumor Institute. Research Report

0066-1651 Andhra Pradesh, India. Department of Archaeology. Epigraphy Series *changed to* Andhra Pradesh, India. Department of Archaeology and Museums. Epigraphy Series

0066-166X Andhra Pradesh, India. Department of Archaeology. Museum Series *changed to* Andhra Pradesh, India. Department of Archaeology and Museums. Museum Series

0066-1678 Andhra University Humanities and Sciences Series†
0066-1686 Andhra University Memoirs in Oceanography
0066-1694 Andrew W. Mellon Foundation. Report
0066-1708 Andrews University. Monographs
0066-1724 Anesthesiologie Europeenne et Mediterraneenne. Annuaire†
0066-1732 Anesthesiologie Francaise. Annuaire†
0066-1759 Angewandte Botanik
0066-1767 Angewandte Forschung in der Bundesrepublik Deutschland†
0066-1783 Anglers' Annual *changed to* Fishing Waters
0066-1791 Anglica Germanica. British Studies in Germanic Languages and Literatures†
0066-1805 Anglistica
0066-1848 Angola. Direccao dos Servicos de Estatistica. Estatisticas do Comercio Externo
0066-1899 Canada. Agriculture Canada. Animal Research Institute. Research Report *changed to* Canada. Agriculture Canada. Animal Research Centre. Research Report
0066-1910 Anleitung fuer die Chemische Laboratoriumspraxis *changed to* Anleitung fuer die Chemische Laboratoriumspraxis/Chemical Laboratory Practice
0066-1929 Annales Academiae Medicae Bialostocensis
0066-1937 Annales Academiae Medicae Cracoviensis. Index Dissertationum Editarum
0066-1945 Annales Academiae Medicae Stetinensis
0066-1953 Annales Academiae Scientiarum Fennicae. Series A, I: Mathematica
0066-1961 Annales Academiae Scientiarum Fennicae. Series A, II: Chemica
0066-197X Annales Academiae Scientiarum Fennicae. Series A, III: Geologica-Geographica
0066-1988 Annales Academiae Scientiarum Fennicae. Series A, 4: Biologica†
0066-1996 Annales Academiae Scientiarum Fennicae. Series A, V: Medica
0066-2003 Annales Academiae Scientiarum Fennicae. Series A, VI: Physica
0066-2011 Annales Academiae Scientiarum Fennicae. Series B
0066-2054 Annales de Chirurgie Thoracique et Cardio-Vasculaire
0066-2062 Annales de Demographie Historique
0066-2070 Annales de Gastroenterologie et d'Hepatologie
0066-2119 Annales d'Esthetique
0066-2127 Annales d'Ethiopie†
0066-2135 Annales d'Etudes Internationales
0066-2143 Annales Francaises de Chronometrie et de Micromecanique *see* 0294-1228
0066-216X Annales Malgaches. Series Lettres et Sciences Humaines *changed to* Universite de Madagascar. Annales. Serie Lettres et Sciences Humaines
0066-2186 Annales Moreau de Tours
0066-2194 Annales Odonto-Stomatologiques†
0066-2216 Annales Polonici Mathematici
0066-2224 Annales Silesiae
0066-2232 Annales Universitatis Mariae Curie-Sklodowska. Sectio C. Biologia
0066-2240 Annales Universitatis Mariae Curie-Sklodowska. Sectio D. Medicina
0066-2259 Annali del Mezzogiorno†
0066-2275 Annali di Sociologia
0066-2283 Quaderni Internazionali di Storia Economica e Sociale
0066-2291 Annals of Clinical Research. Supplementum
0066-2348 Annee Epigraphique; Revue des Publications Epigraphiques Relatives a l'Antiquite Romaine
0066-2356 Annee Politique
0066-2364 Annee Politique Africaine
0066-2372 Annee Politique Suisse
0066-2380 Universite Libre de Bruxelles. Institut de Sociologie. Annee Sociale
0066-2399 Annee Sociologique
0066-2402 Annee Therapeutique en Ophtalmologie *see* 0301-4495
0066-2410 Annotated Bibliography and Index of the Geology of Zambia
0066-2445 Annotated Guide to Taiwan Periodical Literature
0066-2453 Annuaire Administratif de la Republique du Mali
0066-2461 Annuaire Administratif et Judiciaire de Belgique
0066-247X Annuaire Biographique du Cinema et de la Television en France et en Belgique
0066-2488 Annuaire Catholique de France
0066-2518 Annuaire de la Chapellerie et de la Mode†
0066-2526 Annuaire de la Chaussure et des Cuirs
0066-2534 Annuaire de la France Rurale dans le Marche Commun
0066-2542 Annuaire de la Maree
0066-2550 Annuaire de la Marine Marchande
0066-2569 Annuaire de la Noblesse de France et d'Europe
0066-2577 Annuaire de la Papeterie Francaise *changed to* Annuaire de la Papeterie
0066-2585 Annuaire de la Presse et de la Publicite
0066-2593 Annuaire de l'Activite Nucleaire Francaise
0066-2607 Annuaire de l'Afrique du Nord
0066-2615 Annuaire de l'Ameublement et des Industries s'y Rattachant *changed to* Annuaire de l'Ameublement
0066-2623 Annuaire de l'Armement a la Peche
0066-264X Annuaire de l'Eclairage
0066-2658 Annuaire de Legislation Francaise et Etrangere
0066-2674 Annuaire de l'Industrie du Caoutchouc et de ses Derives
0066-2690 Annuaire de l'Industrie et du Commerce France-Afrique
0066-2704 Annuaire de l'U.R.S.S. *see* 0397-8249
0066-2712 Annuaire Dentaire
0066-2720 Annuaire des Annuaires *changed to* Repertoire des Annuaires
0066-2739 Annuaire des Arachnologistes Mondiaux
0066-2747 Annuaire des Architectes†
0066-2763 Annuaire des Boissons et des Liquides Alimentaires
0066-2771 Annuaire des Chercheurs Francais du Fonds de Bourses de Recherche Scientifique et Technique de l'Organisation du Traite de l'Atlantique Nord
0066-278X Annuaire des Caisses d'Epargne; France et Outre-Mer *changed to* Annuaire du Reseau Ecureuil
0066-2798 Annuaire des Chambres de Commerce et d'Industrie
0066-281X Annuaire des Docteurs (Lettres) de l'Universite de Paris et Autres Universites Francaises
0066-2828 Annuaire des Entreprises d'Afrique Noire, des Organismes Officiels et Professionels d'Outre-Mer, des Organismes de Cooperation Francais, Etrangers et Internationaux *changed to* Annuaire des Entreprises et Organismes d'Outre-Mer
0066-2844 Annuaire des Geographes de la France et de l'Afrique Francophone *changed to* Repertoire des Geographes Francais
0066-2860 Annuaire des Instituts de Religieuses en France
0066-2895 Annuaire des Mouvement de Jeunesse†
0066-2909 Annuaire des Negociants en Combustibles†
0066-2917 Annuaire des Organismes d'Habitat Rural *changed to* Guide de l'Habitat et de l'Amenagement Rural
0066-2933 Groupement des Societes Immobilieres d'Investissement. Annuaire
0066-2941 Annuaire des Stations Hydro-Minerales, Climatiques, et Balneaires de France et des Etablissements Medicaux *changed to* Annuaire des Stations Thermales et Climatiques et des Etablissements Medicaux Francais
0066-295X Annuaire Diplomatique et Consulaire de la Republique Francaise
0066-2968 Annuaire du Cinema et Television *changed to* Annuaire du Cinema et Television-Video
0066-2976 Annuaire du Corps Interministeriel des Ingenieurs des Telecommunications
0066-300X Annuaire du Marketing
0066-3018 Annuaire du Quebec
0066-3026 Annuaire du Spectacle
0066-3042 Annuaire Economique de la Tunisie
0066-3069 Guide Europeen de l'Amateur d'Art, de l'Antiquaire et du Bibliophile
0066-3077 Annuaire Europeen des Directeurs Commerciaux et de Marketing
0066-3085 Annuaire Francais de Droit International
0066-3107 Annuaire Franco-Asiatique†
0066-3115 Annuaire Franco-Italien
0066-3123 Annuaire Franco-Suisse†
0066-3131 Annuaire Fructidor
0066-3158 Annuaire General de la Pharmacie Francaise
0066-3174 Jaarboek der Schone Kunsten
0066-3182 Annuaire General des Cooperatives Francaises et de Leurs Fournisseurs; France, Afrique et Marche Commun
0066-3204 Guide de l'Organisation et de la Modernisation des Industries et Collectives *changed to* Guide de l'Organisation de l'Informatique et de la Formation
0066-3212 Annuaire-Guide International de l'Energie Atomique et des Autres Energies *changed to* Guide International de l'Energie Nucleare
0066-3255 Annuaire International des Jus de Fruits
0066-3263 Annuaire International des Ventes
0066-328X Annuaire Luxembourgeois; Annuaire LUX pour l'Industrie, le Commerce et l'Artisant†
0066-3298 Annuaire Medical de l'Hospitalisation Francaise.
0066-3301 Annuaire National de la Kinesitherapie†
0066-331X Annuaire National de la Musique†
0066-3328 Annuaire National de l'Aviculture
0066-3352 Annuaire National des Beaux-Arts
0066-3379 Annuaire National des Fournisseurs des Administrations Francaises
0066-3387 Annuaire National des Lettres
0066-3395 Annuaire National des Specialistes en Gynecologie-Obstetrique et des Competents Exlusifs en Gynecologie et Obstetrique
0066-3417 Annuaire National des Specialistes Qualifies en Chirurgie
0066-3425 Annuaire National des Specialistes Qualifies Exclusifs des Maladies de l'Appareil Digestif
0066-345X Annuaire National des Specialistes Qualifies Exclusifs en Dermatologie et Venereologie
0066-3468 Annuaire National des Specialistes Qualifies Exclusifs en Electroradiologie
0066-3476 Annuaire National des Specialistes Qualifies Exclusifs en Neuropsychiatrie
0066-3514 Annuaire National des Specialistes Qualifies Exclusifs en Pediatrie
0066-3522 Annuaire National des Specialistes Qualifies Exclusifs en Rhumatologie
0066-3549 Annuaire National des Transports
0066-3557 Annuaire National du Verre†
0066-3565 Annuaire O.G.M.
0066-3581 Annuaire Paris: Bijoux
0066-362X Annuaire Protestant; la France Protestante et les Eglises de Langue Francaise
0066-3638 Quatre Mille Imprimeries Francaises
0066-3646 Annuaire Statistique de la Belgique
0066-3654 Annuaire Statistique de la France
0066-3689 Annuaire Statistique de la Tunisie
0066-3697 Annuaire Statistique de l'Industrie Francaise du Jute†
0066-3719 Annuaire Statistique du Maroc
0066-3727 Annuaire Suisse de Science Politique
0066-3743 Annuaires Francais et Listes d'Adresses Susceptibles d'Interesser le Commerce et l'Industrie
0066-376X Annual Banff Regional Conference for School Administrators. Report†
0066-3778 Annual Basic Hobby Industry Trade Directory *changed to* Hobby Publications Annual Trade Directory
0066-3786 Annual Bibliography of English Language and Literature
0066-3808 Annual Bulletin of Coal Statistics for Europe
0066-3816 Annual Bulletin of Electric Energy Statistics for Europe
0066-3824 Annual Bulletin of Gas Statistics for Europe
0066-3832 Annual Bulletin of Historical Literature
0066-3859 Annual Bulletin of Transport Statistics for Europe
0066-3875 Annual Coffee Statistics *changed to* Mercadeo de Cafe nos Estados Unidos e no Canada
0066-3883 Annual Conference of Model Reporting Area for Blindness Statistics. Proceedings†
0066-3913 Annual Directory of Booksellers in the British Isles Specialising in Antiquarian and Out-Of-Print Books
0066-3921 Annual Dog Watch *changed to* Dog Watch
0066-3964 Annual Estimates of the Population of Scotland
0066-3972 N U T Guide to Careers Work
0066-3999 Annual Industry Survey of Computer and Software and Services Industry†
0066-4014 Annual of Advertising, Editorial and Television Art and Design *changed to* Art Directors Annual
0066-4030 Annual Progress in Child Psychiatry and Child Development
0066-4049 Annual Register of Grant Support: a Directory of Funding Soures
0066-4057 Annual Register World Events
0066-4065 Oklahoma. Department of Libraries. Annual Report and Directory of Libraries in Oklahoma *changed to* Annual Report of Oklahoma Libraries
0066-4065 Oklahoma. Department of Libraries. Annual Report and Directory of Libraries in Oklahoma *changed to* Annual Directory of Oklahoma Libraries
0066-409X Annual Reports in Organic Synthesis
0066-4103 Annual Reports on N M R Spectroscopy
0066-412X Hawaii Visitors Bureau. Annual Research Report
0066-4138 Annual Review in Automatic Programming
0066-4146 Annual Review of Astronomy and Astrophysics
0066-4154 Annual Review of Biochemistry
0066-4162 Annual Review of Ecology and Systematics
0066-4170 Annual Review of Entomology
0066-4189 Annual Review of Fluid Mechanics
0066-4197 Annual Review of Genetics
0066-4200 Annual Review of Information Science and Technology
0066-4219 Annual Review of Medicine *changed to* Annual Review of Medicine: Selected Topics in the Clinical Sciences
0066-4227 Annual Review of Microbiology
0066-4235 Annual Review of N M R Spectroscopy *see* 0066-4103
0066-4243 Annual Review of Nuclear Science *see* 0163-8998
0066-4251 Annual Review of Pharmacology *see* 0362-1642
0066-426X Annual Review of Physical Chemistry
0066-4278 Annual Review of Physiology
0066-4286 Annual Review of Phytopathology
0066-4294 Annual Review of Plant Physiology
0066-4308 Annual Review of Psychology

0066-4332 Silver Market
0066-4340 Annual Review of United Nations Affairs
0066-4359 Annual Safety Education Review†
0066-4367 Annual Statistical Review: The Distilled Spirits Industry†
0066-4375 Annual Summary of Business Statistics, New York State
0066-4383 Annual Summary of Information on Natural Disasters†
0066-4391 Annual Summary of Merchant Ships Launched in the World *see* 0261-2720
0066-4405 Annual Survey of African Law
0066-4413 Annual Survey of American Law
0066-443X Annual Survey of Psychoanalysis†
0066-4456 Annuale Mediaevale
0066-4464 Annuario Cattolico d'Italia
0066-4472 Annuario Ceramica
0066-4480 Annuario della Comunita Lombarda†
0066-4499 Annuario dell'Industria Italiana della Gomma
0066-4502 Annuario dell'Agricoltura Italiana
0066-4510 Annuario Politecnico Italiano†
0066-4545 Annuario Statistico Italiano
0066-4553 Anorganische und Allgemeine Chemie in Einzeldarstellungen *see* 0172-7966
0066-4596 Anschriften Deutscher Verlage und Auslaendischer Verlage mit Deutschen Auslieferungen
0066-460X Anschriften Deutschsprachiger Zeitschriften *see* 0419-005X
0066-4618 Anson G. Phelps Lectureship on Early American History
0066-4626 Antarctic Bibliography
0066-4634 Antarctic Research Series *changed to* Antarctic Research Book Series
0066-4642 Antemurale
0066-4677 Anthropological Forum
0066-4685 Anthropologie
0066-4693 Anthropologische Gesellschaft, Vienna. Mitteilungen
0066-4715 Anthropology of the North. Translations from Russian Sources†
0066-4723 Anthropos
0066-4758 Antibiotics and Chemotherapy
0066-4766 Antichita Classica e Cristiana
0066-4774 Antichthon
0066-4782 Antike Kunst. Beihefte
0066-4804 Antimicrobial Agents and Chemotherapy
0066-4812 Antipode
0066-4839 Antiquitas. Reihe 1. Abhandlungen zur Alten Geschichte
0066-4847 Antiquitas. Reihe 2. Abhandlungen aus dem Gebiete der Vor- und Fruehgeschichte
0066-4855 Antiquitas. Reihe 3. Abhandlungen zur Vor- und Fruehgeschichte, zur Klassischen und Provinzial-Roemischen Archaeologie und zur Geschichte des Altertums
0066-4863 Antiquitas. Reihe 4. Beitraege zur Historia-Augusta-Forschung
0066-4871 Antiquites Africaines
0066-488X Israel. Ministry of Education and Culture. Department of Antiquities and Museums. Atiqot (English Series)
0066-4898 Antiquites Nationales
0066-4928 Antologia del Folklore Musical Chileno†
0066-4936 Antologias del Pensamiento Politico†
0066-4979 Kunsthistorische Musea, Antwerp. Schone Kunsten†
0066-5010 Anuario Bibliografico Costarricense
0066-5045 Anuario Colombiano de Historia Social y de la Cultura
0066-5053 Anuario de Cinema†
0066-5061 Anuario de Estudios Medievales
0066-507X Anuario de Filologia
0066-5088 Anuario de Historia Economica y Social
0066-5096 Anuario de la Mineria de Chile
0066-510X Anuario de Relojeria y Arte en Metal para Espana e Hispanoamerica
0066-5118 Anuario del Comercio Exterior Latino-Americano
0066-5126 Anuario de Psicologia
0066-5169 Mexico. Direccion General de Estadistica. Anuario Estadistico Compendiado†
0066-5177 Anuario Estadistico de Espana
0066-5185 Anuario Estadistico de los Andes; Venezuela
0066-5193 Angola. Direccao dos Servicos de Estatistica. Anuario Estatistico
0066-5207 Anuario F.H.I. Argentina: Frutas y Hortalizas Industriarizadas y Frescas
0066-5215 Anuario Filosofico
0066-5223 Anuario Geografico del Peru
0066-5231 Anuario Industrial de Minas Gerais *changed to* Guia Economico e Industrial do Estado de Minas Gerais
0066-524X Anuario Martiano *changed to* Centro de Estudios Martianos. Anuario
0066-5274 Yearbook for Inter-American Musical Research†
0066-5282 Anzeiger fuer Slavische Philologie
0066-5304 Aphidologists' Newsletter†
0066-5320 Apocrypha Novi Testamenti†
0066-5339 Apollonia†
0066-5347 Apotheker - Jahrbuch
0066-5363 Financial Review
0066-5371 Appalachian Gas Measurement Short Course, West Virginia University. Proceedings†
0066-538X Appalachian Underground Corrosion Short Course, West Virginia University. Proceedings†
0066-5398 Appel Service; Repertoire d'Adresses Utiles pour le Commerce et l'Industrie
0066-5401 Appliance Technical Conference. Preprints†
0066-541X Applied Chemistry Series†
0066-5436 A F R I Miscellaneous Report†
0066-5444 Applied Forestry Research Institute. Research Report†
0066-5452 Applied Mathematical Sciences
0066-5460 North-Holland Series in Applied Mathematics and Mechanics
0066-5479 Applied Mathematics and Mechanics
0066-5487 Applied Mineralogy. Technische Minerologie
0066-5495 Applied Optics. Supplement
0066-5509 Applied Physics and Engineering
0066-5517 Applied Polymer Symposium. Papers
0066-5533 Applied Solid State Science
0066-5576 Approaches to Semiotics
0066-5592 Aquatica†
0066-5606 Aqui
0066-5614 Aquinas Lecture Series
0066-5622 Arab and Afro-Asian Monograph Series *changed to* Institute for Arab Studies. Publications and Studies
0066-5630 Arab Book Annual
0066-5657 Arabidopsis Information Service. Newsletter
0066-5665 Arbeiten aus dem Paul-Ehrlich-Institut, dem Georg-Speyer-Haus und dem Ferdinand-Blum-Institut
0066-5673 Arbeiten zur Angewandten Statistik
0066-5681 Arbeiten zur Geschichte des Antiken Judentums und des Urchristentums
0066-569X Arbeiten zur Paedagogik
0066-5703 Arbeiten zur Rechtsvergleichung
0066-5711 Arbeiten zur Theologie. Reihe 1
0066-572X Arbeiten zur Theologie. Reihe 2†
0066-5738 Arbeitsblaetter fuer Restauratoren
0066-5746 A R D - Jahrbuch
0066-5754 Rheinisch-Westfaelische Akademie der Wissenschaften. Veroeffentlichungen *changed to* Rheinisch-Westfaelische Akademie der Wissenschaften. Vortraege Natur- Ingenieur-und Wirtschaftswissenschaften
0066-5770 Arbeitsgemeinschaft zur Verbesserung der Agrarstruktur in Hessen. A V A-Beratungsunterlagen†
0066-5789 Arbeitsgemeinschaft zur Verbesserung der Agrarstruktur in Hessen. A V A-Hefte†
0066-5797 Arbeitsgemeinschaft zur Verbesserung der Agrarstruktur in Hessen. A V A-Materialsammlungen†
0066-5800 Arbeitsgemeinschaft zur Verbesserung der Agrarstruktur in Hessen. A V A-Sonderhefte†
0066-5819 Arbeitsgemeinschaft zur Verbesserung der Agrarstruktur in Hessen. A V A Bezugshefte†
0066-5843 Arbeitsmedizin†
0066-5851 Arbeitsmedizinische Fragen in der Ophthalmologie†
0066-586X Arbeitsrecht der Gegenwart
0066-5878 Arboretum Kornickie
0066-5886 Archaeo-Physika
0066-5894 Archaeologia Cantiana
0066-5908 Archaeologia Geographica
0066-5924 Archaeologia Polona
0066-5932 Archaeologica Slovaca. Catalogi
0066-5940 Archaeologica Slovaca. Fontes
0066-5967 Archaeological Bibliography for Great Britain and Ireland†
0066-5975 Archaeological Exploration of Sardis. Monographs
0066-5983 Archaeological Journal
0066-6009 Archaeologische Funde und Denkmaeler des Rheinlandes
0066-6017 Archaeologische Gesellschaft Koeln. Schriftenreihe†
0066-6025 Archeologische Kaarten van Belgie
0066-6033 Archaeologische Mitteilungen aus Iran. Neue Folge
0066-6041 Archeion
0066-605X Archeologia (Wroclaw)
0066-6068 Archeologie et Civilisation†
0066-6084 Archeologie Mediterraneenne
0066-6092 Archigram
0066-6114 Architect and Contractors Yearbook
0066-6122 Architectes *changed to* Architectes - Architecture
0066-6149 Architects, Builders and Contractors Pocket Book†
0066-6157 Architects, Contractors & Engineers Guide to Construction Costs
0066-6165 Architect's Detail Library†
0066-6173 Architect's Handbook of Professional Practice
0066-6181 Architects Standard Catalogues *changed to* A S C Mini-File
0066-619X Architects' Year Book†
0066-6203 Architectural and Archaeological Society of Durham and Northumberland. Transactions. New Series *changed to* Durham Archaeological Journal
0066-6211 A A Papers†
0066-622X Architectural History
0066-6238 Architecture at Rice University†
0066-6262 Architecture in Greece
0066-6270 Architectura
0066-6297 Archiv fuer Diplomatik, Schriftgeschichte, Siegel- und Wappenkunde
0066-6327 Archiv fuer Geschichte des Buchwesens
0066-6335 Archiv fuer Geschichte von Oberfranken
0066-636X Archiv fuer Hessische Geschichte und Altertumskunde
0066-6378 Archiv fuer Kinderheilkunde. Beihefte *see* 0373-3165
0066-6386 Archiv fuer Liturgiewissenschaft
0066-6416 Archives for Meteorology, Geophysics, and Bioclimatology. Series A: Meteorology and Geophysics/Archiv Fuer Meteorologie, Geophysik und Bioklimatologie. Series A. *see* 0177-7971
0066-6424 Archives for Meteorology, Geophysics, and Bioclimatology. Series B: Climatology, Environmental Meteorology, Radiation Research/Archiv fuer Meteorologie, Geophysik und Bioklimatologie. Series B *changed to* Theoretical and Applied Climatology
0066-6432 Archiv fuer Mittelrheinische Kirchengeschichte
0066-6440 Archiv fuer Orientforschung
0066-6459 Archiv fuer Papyrusforschung und Verwandte Gebiete
0066-6475 Archiv fuer Psychologie
0066-6491 Archiv fuer Schlesische Kirchengeschichte
0066-6505 Archiv fuer Sozialgeschichte
0066-6513 Archiv fuer Voelkerkunde
0066-6521 Archivalia Medica†
0066-653X Archives and the User
0066-6548 Archives Bakounine
0066-6556 Archives Claudeliennes
0066-6564 Archives de Philosophie du Droit
0066-6572 Archives des Lettres Canadiennes
0066-6580 Archives d'Ethnologie Francaise *see* 0046-2616
0066-6599 Archives in Trade Union History and Theory Series†
0066-6602 Archives Internationales de Finances Publiques†
0066-6610 Archives Internationales d'Histoire des Idees
0066-6629 Archives of Archaeology†
0066-6637 Archives of Asian Art
0066-6645 Archives of Maryland†
0066-6653 Archives Suisses d'Anthropologie Generale†
0066-6661 Archivio del Teatro Italiano
0066-667X Archivo di Oceanografia e Limnologia
0066-6688 Archivio Italiano per la Storia della Pieta
0066-6696 Archivio Linguistico Veneto. Quaderni.
0066-670X Archivio Putti di Chirurgia degli Organi di Movimento
0066-6718 Archivio Storico Italiano. Biblioteca
0066-6734 Archivo Epistolar Colombiano
0066-6742 Archivo Espanol de Arqueologia
0066-6750 Archivos Argentinos de Dermatologia
0066-6769 Archivos de Investigacion Medica
0066-6777 Archivos de Oftalmologia de Buenos Aires
0066-6785 Archivum Historiae Pontificae
0066-6793 Archivum
0066-6807 Archivum Romanicum. Biblioteca. Serie 1: Storia Letteratura-Paleografia
0066-6815 Archivum Romanicum. Biblioteca. Serie 2: Linguistica
0066-6823 Archiwum Akustyki
0066-6831 Archiwum Dziejow Oswiaty
0066-684X Archiwum Energetyki
0066-6858 Archiwum Etnograficzne†
0066-6866 Archiwum Filologiczne
0066-6874 Archiwum Historii Filozofii i Mysli Spolecznej
0066-6882 Archivum Iuridicum Cracoviense
0066-6890 Archiwum Kryminologii
0066-6904 Archiwum Literackie
0066-6912 Archiwum Mineralogiczne
0066-6939 Arctic Anthropology
0066-6947 Arctic Bibliography†
0066-6955 Arctic Institute of North America. Annual Report†
0066-6963 Arctic Institute of North America. Newsletter *see* 0315-2561
0066-6971 Arctic Institute of North America. Research Paper†
0066-698X Arctic Institute of North America. Technical Paper†
0066-6998 Arctos; Acta Philologica Fennica. Supplementum†
0066-7005 Argentina. Consejo Federal de Inversiones. Bibliografia Sobre el Desarrollo Economico Nacional†
0066-7021 Argentina. Departamento de Estadistica Educativa. Boletin Informativo.
0066-703X Argentina. Departamento de Estudios Historicos Navales. Serie A: Cultura Nautica
0066-7048 Argentina. Departamento de Estudios Historicos Navales. Serie B: Historia Naval Argentina
0066-7056 Argentina. Departamento de Estudios Historicos Navales. Serie C: Biografias Navales Argentinas
0066-7080 Argentina. Departamento de Estudios Historicos Navales. Serie J: Libros y Impresos Raros

ISSN INDEX 1349

0066-7099 Argentina. Direccion de Investigaciones Forestales. Misceleneas Forestales†
0066-7102 Argentina. Direccion de Investigaciones Forestales. Notas Silvicolas†
0066-7110 Argentina. Direccion de Investigaciones Forestales. Notas Tecnologicas Forestales *see* 0325-9781
0066-7129 Argentina. Direccion de Investigaciones Forestales. Planificacion del Desarrollo Forestal†
0066-7145 Argentina. Servicio Nacional Minero Geologico. Anales
0066-7153 Argentina. Servicio Nacional Minero Geologico. Boletin
0066-7161 Argentina. Servicio Nacional Minero Geologico. Estadistica Minera
0066-717X Argentina. Servicio Nacional Minero Geologico. Revista
0066-7188 Argentina. Instituto Nacional de Derecho Aeronautico y Espacial†
0066-7196 Argentina. Instituto Nacional de Estadistica y Censos. Informe Serie E: Edificacione†
0066-7242 Argentina. Estacion Experimental Agropecuaria Manfredi. Serie Informacion Tecnica†
0066-7269 Argentina. Junta Nacional de Carnes. Sintesis Estadistica
0066-7277 Combustible. *changed to* Argentina. Direccion General de Evaluacion Energetica. Anuario de Combustibles.
0066-7285 Argentina. Oficina Sectorial de Desarrollo de Energia. Anuarios Estadisticos. Energia Electrica *changed to* Argentina. Direccion General de Evaluacion Energetica. Anuario Energia Electrica.
0066-7293 Argentina. Secretaria de Guerra. Direccion de Estudios Historicos. Boletin Bibliografico
0066-7331 Argentina. Servicio de Inteligencia Naval. Bibliotecas de la Armada. Boletin Bibliografico.
0066-734X Argus de la Poesie Francaise
0066-7358 Arheologia Moldovei
0066-7366 Arid Zone Research†
0066-7382 Arizona. Department of Public Safety. Annual Report†
0066-7390 Arizona. Department of Public Safety. Statistical Reviews *see* 0066-7382
0066-7404 Arizona Forestry Notes
0066-7412 Arizona Geological Society Digest
0066-7447 Arizona Model United Nations†
0066-7455 Arizona State University. Bureau of Educational Research and Services. Educational Services Bulletin.†
0066-7463 Arizona State University. Bureau of Educational Research and Services. Research and Services Bulletin.†
0066-748X Arizona State University, Tempe. Institute of Public Administration. Monograph. *changed to* Arizona State University. Center for Public Affairs. Monograph.
0066-751X University of Arizona. College of Education. Monograph Series†
0066-7536 University of Arizona. Department of English. Graduate English Papers *see* 0275-5203
0066-7560 E E S Series Report†
0066-7587 University of Arizona. Laboratory of Tree-Ring Research. Papers†
0066-7609 University of Arizona. Optical Sciences Center. Newsletter†
0066-7617 University of Arizona. Optical Sciences Center. Technical Report†
0066-7641 Continuing Education in Business Administration†
0066-7668 Arkiv for Nordisk Filologi
0066-7684 Arlington Historical Magazine
0066-7706 University of New England. Department of Geography. Monograph Series in Geography
0066-7714 University of New England. Department of Geography. Research Series in Applied Geography†
0066-7730 University of New England. Exploration Society. Report†
0066-7749 Armorial†
0066-7765 Arnamagnaean Institute. Bulletin *see* 0107-1475
0066-7781 Arnoldia Rhodesia *see* 0250-6386
0066-7803 Arqueologicas
0066-7811 Arquivo de Anatomia e Antropologia
0066-782X Arquivos Brasileiros de Cardiologia
0066-7846 Arquivos de Cirurgia Clinica e Experimental
0066-7854 Arquivos de Patologia Geral e Anatomia Patologica
0066-7862 Arquivos de Tisiologia†
0066-7870 Arquivos de Zoologia
0066-7900 Ars Quatuor Coronatorum
0066-7919 Ars Suecica
0066-7927 Art and Artists of the Monterey Peninsula
0066-7935 Art Bulletin of Victoria
0066-7943 Art Directors Club Milano†
0066-7951 Art et les Grandes Civilisations
0066-796X Art Gallery of South Australia. Special Exhibitions†
0066-7978 Art in Its Context: Studies in Ethno-Aesthetics. Field Reports†
0066-7986 Art in Its Context: Studies in Ethno-Aesthetics. Museum Series†
0066-8036 Arthropods of Florida and Neighboring Land Areas
0066-8044 Arthur Holmes Society. Journal
0066-8079 Universidade de Lisboa. Faculdade de Ciencias. Instituto Botanico. Artigo de Divulgacao
0066-8087 Artists' Guide
0066-8095 Arts
0066-8133 Arts Council of Great Britain. Annual Report and Accounts
0066-815X Arts of Mankind†
0066-8168 Arts Patronage Series
0066-8176 Arv
0066-8184 Arvernia Biologica: Botanique
0066-8192 Arznei-Telegramm
0066-8214 Handbook of Asbestos Textiles†
0066-8222 Ascidian News
0066-8230 Asia - Africa World Trade Register
0066-8249 Centro de Estudios Orientales. Anuario
0066-8265 Asia Monograph Series
0066-8281 Asian and African Studies
0066-829X Asian and Pacific Archaeology Series
0066-8303 Asian and Pacific Council. Cultural and Social Centre. Annual Report†
0066-8311 A S P A C Seminar on Audio-Visual Education. Proceedings†
0066-8346 Asian and Pacific Marketing Conference. Proceedings†
0066-8354 Asian Annual
0066-8362 Asian Book Trade Directory
0066-8370 Asian Development Bank. Annual Report
0066-8389 Asian Development Bank. Board of Governors. Summary of Proceedings (of the) Annual Meeting
0066-8397 Asian Development Bank. Occasional Papers
0066-8419 Asian Journal of Pharmacy
0066-8435 Asian Perspectives
0066-8443 Asian Philosophical Studies†
0066-8451 Asian Population Studies Series
0066-846X A P O Annual Report
0066-8486 Asian Studies at Hawaii Monograph Series
0066-8508 Asien - Afrika - Lateinamerika *see* 0232-8410
0066-8532 Aslib Occasional Publications
0066-8540 Asociacion Espanola Contra el Cancer. Memoria de la Assemblea General *changed to* Asociacion Espanola Contra el Cancer. Memoria Tecnico-Administrativa
0066-8567 Asociacion Nacional del Cafe. Departamento de Asuntos Agricolas. Informe Anual
0066-8591 Asociacion Venezolana de Archiveros. Coleccion Doctrina
0066-8613 Asociacion Venezolana de Enfermeras Profesionales. Boletin
0066-8656 Aspects of Adhesion
0066-8672 Aspects of Education
0066-8699 Assembly Directory and Handbook *changed to* Assembly Technology Buyer's Guide
0066-8702 Assembly Engineering Master Catalog *changed to* Assembly Technology Buyer's Guide
0066-8710 Associated Church Press. Directory
0066-8729 Associated Colleges of Illinois. Report
0066-8753 Associated Public Schools Systems. Yearbook
0066-8761 Bibliography of Publications of University Bureaus of Business and Economic Research *changed to* University Research in Business and Economics: a Bibliography of (Year) Publications
0066-877X Associated Western Universities. Annual Report *changed to* Associated Western Universities. Program Report
0066-8796 Association Belge pour l'Etude, l'Essai et l'Emploi des Materiaux. Publication A.B.E.M
0066-880X Association Belge pour l'Etude, l'Essai et l'Emploi des Materiaux. Publication Groupement†
0066-8818 Association Belge pour l'Etude, l'Essai et l'Emploi des Materiaux. Proces Verbal de l'Assemblee Generale Ordinaire
0066-8826 Association Canadienne des Bibliothecaires de Langue Francaise. Rapport *see* 0316-0955
0066-8842 Association Canadienne-Francaise pour l'Avancement des Sciences. Annales
0066-8850 Association Canadienne-Francaise pour l'Avancement des Sciences. Bulletin *see* 0571-5288
0066-8877 Association de l'Ecole Nationale Superieure des Bibliothecaires. Annuaire
0066-8893 Association des Amis d'Alfred de Vigny. Bulletin
0066-8907 Association des Amis de Pierre Teilhard de Chardin. Bulletin
0066-8915 Association des Anatomistes. Bulletin
0066-8923 Association of Attenders and Alumni of the Hague Academy of International Law. Yearbook
0066-8931 Association des Bibliothecaires Francais. Annuaire
0066-894X Documents A B F†
0066-8958 Association des Bibliotheques Ecclesiastiques de France. Bulletin de Liaison
0066-8982 I C A M Annuaire
0066-8990 Association des Institutions d'Enseignement Secondaire. Annuaire
0066-9008 Association des Societes et Fonds Francais d'Investissement. Annuaire
0066-9016 Association des Traducteurs et Interpretes de l'Ontario. Repertoire
0066-9024 Association des Universites Partiellement Ou Entierement de Langue Francaise. Cahiers†
0066-9032 Association des Universites Partiellement Ou Entierement de Langue Francaise. Colloques et Congres. Comptes Rendus†
0066-9040 Association Euratom-Ital. Annual Report
0066-9075 Association for Childhood Education International. Yearbook†
0066-9083 Association for Commonwealth Literature and Language Studies. Bulletin
0066-9091 Association for Computing Machinery. Proceedings of National Conference
0066-9105 Association for Education of the Visually Handicapped. Selected Papers from A E V H Biennial Conferences†
0066-9156 A S C U S Annual - Teaching Opportunities for You *changed to* A S C U S Annual - A Job Search Handbook for Educators
0066-9164 A S C U S Directory of Membership and Subject Field Index
0066-9172 Association for Social Anthropology in Oceania. Monograph Series
0066-9210 A D B S Annuaire†
0066-9229 Association Francaise des Ingenieurs du Caoutchouc et des Plastiques. Annuaire
0066-9237 Association Francaise des Ingenieurs et Chefs d'Entretien. Annuaire
0066-9245 Association Francaise des Ingenieurs et Techniciens de l'Aeronautique et de l'Espace. Annuaire *changed to* Association Aeronautique et Astronautique de France. Annuaire
0066-9253 Union des Association Francaises de Relations Publiques. Annuaire
0066-927X Association Francaise des Techniciens et Ingenieurs de Securite et des Medecins du Travail. Annuaire
0066-9288 Association Francaise des Experts de la Cooperation Technique Internationale. Annuaire
0066-9296 Association Francaise d'Informatique et de Recherche Operationnelle. Annuaire *changed to* Association Francaise pour la Cybernetique Economique et Technique. Annuaire
0066-9318 Association Nationale de la Recherche Technique. Information et Documentation†
0066-9350 Association of American Geographers. Commission on College Geography. General Series Publications†
0066-9369 Association of American Geographers. Resource Papers *changed to* Resource Publications in Geography
0066-9393 Association of American Geographers. Monograph Series†
0066-9407 Association of American Law Schools. Proceedings
0066-9423 Medical School Admission Requirements, United States and Canada
0066-9431 Association of American Pesticide Control Officials. Official Publication
0066-944X Association of American Pesticide Control Officials. Pesticide Chemicals Official Compendium†
0066-9458 Association of American Physicians. Transactions
0066-9466 Association of Asphalt Paving Technologists. Proceedings
0066-9474 Association of Canadian Map Libraries. Annual Conference Proceedings *see* 0318-2851
0066-9482 Association of Canadian Map Libraries. Newsletter *see* 0318-2851
0066-9490 Association of Canadian Schools of Business. Proceedings of the Annual Conference *changed to* Administrative Sciences Association of Canada. Proceedings, Annual Conference
0066-9539 Association of Colleges for Further and Higher Education. Year Book *changed to* Association of Colleges for Further and Higher Education. Handbook
0066-9547 Association of European Paediatric Cardiologists. Proceedings *see* 0167-5273
0066-9555 Association of Faculties of Pharmacy of Canada. Proceedings
0066-9563 Association of Graduate Schools in Association of American Universities. Journal of Proceedings and Addresses†
0066-9571 Association of Island Marine Laboratories of the Caribbean. Proceedings
0066-958X Association of Japanese Geographers. Special Publication
0066-9598 Association of Life Insurance Medical Directors of America. Transactions

0066-9601 Association of Midwest Fish and Game Commissioners. Proceedings *changed to* Association of Midwest Fish and Wildlife Agencies. Proceedings
0066-961X Association of Official Analytical Chemists. Official Methods of Analysis
0066-9628 Association of Pacific Coast Geographers. Yearbook
0066-9652 A R L Newsletter
0066-9679 A S A Monographs *changed to* A S A Research Methods in Social Anthropology
0066-9687 Association of Southeast Asian Institutions of Higher Learning. Handbook: Southeast Asian Institutions of Higher Learning
0066-9695 A S A I H L. Seminar Reports
0066-9709 A T M Occasional Papers
0066-9725 Association of Universities and Colleges of Canada. Annual Meeting. Proceedings†
0066-9741 Association of University Evening Colleges. Proceedings *changed to* Association for Continuing Higher Education. Proceedings
0066-975X Association of University Summer Sessions. Summary Report
0066-9768 A.V.S. Journal *changed to* Pegasus
0066-9776 T.A. Documents
0066-9784 A.E.T.F.A.T. Index
0066-9792 Association Scientifique de la Precontrainte. Sessions d'Etudes
0066-9806 Association Technique de l'Industrie du Gaz en France. Compte Rendu du Congres†
0066-9814 Association Technique Maritime et Aeronautique, Paris. Bulletin
0066-9822 Associazione Elettrotecnica Ed Elettronica Italiana. Rendiconti della Riunione Annuale
0066-9830 Associazione Genetica Italiana. Atti
0066-9857 Associazione Internazionale della Stampa Medica. Bollettino Bibliografico†
0066-9865 Associazione Italiana Laringectomizzati. Atti (Del) Convegno Nazionale
0066-9873 Associazione Medica Chirurgica di Tivoli e della Val d'Aniene. Atti e Memorie
0066-989X Assurances Generales de France. Informations *see* 0761-7593
0066-9903 Assyriological Studies
0066-9911 Asterisks†
0066-992X Asticou
0066-9938 Astrology and Horse Racing†
0066-9946 Astronautics Year†
0066-9962 Astronomical Ephemeris *changed to* Astronomical Almanac
0066-9970 Astronomical Ephemeris of Geocentric Places of Planets
0066-9997 Astronomical Society of Australia. Proceedings
0067-0006 Astronomical Society of Victoria. Astronomical Yearbook
0067-0014 Astronomische Grundlagen fuer den Kalender
0067-0022 Astronomy and Astrophysics Abstracts
0067-0030 Astrophysica Norvegica†
0067-0049 Astrophysical Journal. Supplement Series
0067-0057 Astrophysics and Space Science Library
0067-0073 Athens Center of Ekistics. Research Report
0067-009X Mongrafie della Scuola Archeologica di Atene e delle Missioni Italiane in Oriente
0067-0103 Centre des Sciences Sociales d'Athenes. Publications†
0067-012X Athletisme Francais *changed to* Athlerama (Today)
0067-0138 Israel. Ministry of Education and Culture. Department of Antiquities and Museums. Atiqot (Hebrew Series)
0067-0162 Atlantic Provinces Economic Council. Annual Report
0067-0197 Atlantic Provinces Inter-University Committee on the Sciences. Annual Report
0067-0200 Atlantic Provinces Studies†
0067-0219 Atlantic Yearbook†
0067-0227 Atlantide Report. Scientific Results of the Danish Expedition to the Coasts of Tropical West Africa
0067-0235 Atlantische Tijdingen *changed to* Atlantisch Perspektief
0067-0243 Atlas Arqueologico de la Republica Mexicana†
0067-0251 Atlas de la Economia Colombiana†
0067-026X Atlas d'Attraction Urbaine.†
0067-0286 Atlas des Structures Agraires au Sud du Sahara†
0067-0294 Atlas Flory Polskiej i Ziem Osciennych
0067-0308 Atlas of External Diseases of the Eye†
0067-0316 Atlas Polskich Strojow Ludowych
0067-0324 Atlas Rozmieszczenia Drzew i Krzewow w Polsce
0067-0332 Atlas Rozmieszczenia Roslin Zarodnikowych w Polsce. Seria Iv. Watrobowce. Hepaticae†
0067-0340 Colorado State University. Atmospheric Science Paper
0067-0367 A E C L Report Series
0067-0383 Atomic Energy of Canada. Annual Report
0067-0405 Atomic Energy of Canada. List of Publications
0067-0421 Auburn Forestry Forum†
0067-043X Auburn University. Water Resources Research Institute. Annual Report
0067-0456 Auckland Institute and Museum. Bulletin
0067-0464 Auckland Institute and Museum. Records
0067-0480 University of Auckland Historical Society. Annual
0067-0499 University of Auckland. Library. Bibliographical Bulletin
0067-0510 Auckland University Law Review
0067-0537 Audarena Stadium Guide and International Directory
0067-0545 Audio Annual *changed to* Hi Fi News & Record Review Annual
0067-0553 Audiovisual Market Place *changed to* Audio Video Market Place
0067-057X Augustana Library Publications
0067-0588 Augustana Historical Society, Rock Island, Illinois. Publications
0067-0618 Aus dem Schweizerischen Landesmuseum
0067-0634 Buecher fuer Alle *changed to* Buecher (Year)
0067-0642 Aus Forschung und Kunst
0067-0669 Auslaendische Aktiengesetze
0067-0685 Ausruestung in Luft- und Raumfahrt†
0067-0707 University of Texas, Austin. Center for Neo-Hellenic Studies. Bulletin†
0067-0715 Australasian Corrosion Directory†
0067-0731 Australia. Bureau of Statistics. Banking and Currency Bulletin†
0067-074X Australia. Bureau of Statistics. Building and Construction Bulletin†
0067-0758 Australia. Bureau of Statistics. Commonwealth Finance†
0067-0766 Australia. Bureau of Statistics. Causes of Death, Australia
0067-0774 Australia. Bureau of Statistics. Commonwealth Taxation Assessment Bulletin†
0067-0782 Australia. Bureau of Statistics. Demography (Population and Vital) Bulletin†
0067-0790 Australia. Bureau of Statistics. Insurance and Other Private Finance Bulletin†
0067-0804 Australia. Bureau of Statistics. Imports Cleared for Home Consumption, Australia†
0067-0812 Australia. Bureau of Statistics. Labour Report *changed to* Australia. Bureau of Statistics. Labour Statistics, Australia
0067-0820 Australia. Bureau of Statistics. Manufacturing Commodities Bulletin†
0067-0839 Australia. Bureau of Statistics. Manufacturing Industry Bulletin†
0067-0847 Australia. Bureau of Statistics. Non-Rural Primary Industries†
0067-0855 Australia. Bureau of Statistics. Northern Territory Statistical Summary
0067-0871 Australia.Bureau of Statistics. Rural Industries Bulletin†
0067-088X Australia. Bureau of Statistics. South Australian Office. Births, South Australia
0067-0898 Australia. Bureau of Statistics. South Australian Office. Deaths, South Australia
0067-0901 Australia. Bureau of Statistics. South Australian Office. Divorces, South Australia
0067-0928 Australia. Bureau of Census and Statistics. South Australian Office. Factories *changed to* Australia. Bureau of Statistics. South Australian Office. Manufacturing Establishments, Details of Operations by Industry
0067-0936 Australia. Bureau of Statistics. South Australian Office. General Insurance†
0067-0979 Australia. Bureau of Statistics. South Australian Office. Projections of Population†
0067-0987 Australia. Bureau of Statistics. South Australian Office. Agriculture: General Summary-South Australia†
0067-1002 Australia. Bureau of Statistics. Transport and Communication Bulletin†
0067-1029 Australia. Bureau of Statistics. Tasmanian Office. Demography†
0067-1037 Australia. Bureau of Statistics. Tasmanian Office. Finance *see* 0312-7850
0067-1045 Australia. Bureau of Statistics. Tasmanian Office. Labour, Wages and Prices *see* 0814-9593
0067-1053 Australia. Bureau of Statistics. Tasmanian Office. Primary Industries (Excluding Mining) *changed to* Australia. Bureau of Statistics. Tasmanian Office. Agriculture, Tasmania
0067-1061 Australia. Bureau of Statistics. Tasmanian Office. Social *see* 0314-1705
0067-107X Australia. Bureau of Statistics. Tasmanian Office. Trade and Shipping *changed to* Australia. Bureau of Statistics. Tasmanian Office. Interstate Trade
0067-1096 Australia. Bureau of Statistics. Victorian Office. Demography, Victoria *changed to* Australia. Bureau of Statistics. Victorian Office. Demography Summary Statement, Victoria
0067-1126 Australia. Bureau of Statistics. Victorian Office. Hospital Morbidity†
0067-1134 Australia. Bureau of Statistics. Victorian Office Industrial Accidents and Workers Compensation. Statistics *changed to* Australia. Bureau of Statistics. Victorian Office. Industrial Accidents and Workers Compensation
0067-1142 Australia. Bureau of Statistics. Victorian Office. Government Finance *changed to* Australia. Bureau of Statistics. Victorian Office. Local Government Finance, Victoria
0067-1150 Australia. Bureau of Statistics. Victorian Office. Primary and Secondary Education, Victoria *changed to* Australia. Bureau of Statistics. Victorian Office. National Schools Statistics, Victoria
0067-1169 Australia. Bureau of Statistics. Value of Production Bulletin†
0067-1193 Australia. Bureau of Statistics. Victorian Office. Tertiary Education†
0067-1207 Australia. Bureau of Statistics. Victorian Office. Victorian Pocket Yearbook
0067-1223 Australia. Bureau of Statistics. Victorian Office. Victorian Yearbook
0067-124X Australia. Bureau of Statistics. Western Australian Office. Abstract of Statistics of Local Government Areas. *changed to* Australia. Bureau of Statistics. Western Australian Office. Local Government, Western Australia
0067-1282 Australia. Bureau of Statistics. Western Australian Office. Local Government Revenue and Expenditure: Budget Estimates†
0067-1290 Australia. Bureau of Statistics. Western Australian Office. Population, Dwellings and Vital Statistics†
0067-1312 Australia. Bureau of Meteorology. Bulletin
0067-1320 Australia. Bureau of Meteorology. Meteorological Study
0067-1339 Australia. Bureau of Mineral Resources, Geology and Geophysics. Pictorial Index of Activities†
0067-1347 Australia. Department of Industry and Commerce. Annual Report *see* 0728-6856
0067-1355 Australia. Department of Education. A.C.T. Education Directory†
0067-1436 Australia. Department of Primary Industry. Operation of the Fishing Industry, A.C.T. Annual Report
0067-1444 Australia. Department of the Treasury. Income Tax Statistics
0067-1452 Australia. Forestry and Timber Bureau. Bulletins *changed to* Commonwealth Scientific and Industrial Research Organization. Division of Forest Research. Bulletins
0067-1460 Australia. Forestry and Timber Bureau. Forest Resources Newsletter *see* 0314-1438
0067-1479 Australia. Forestry and Timber Bureau. Leaflets *changed to* Commonwealth Scientific and Industrial Research Organization. Division of Forest Research. Leaflets
0067-1495 Australia Handbook
0067-1509 Australia Mineral Industry Review *see* 0084-7488
0067-1517 Australia. National Capital Development Commission. Annual Report
0067-155X Australian Academy of Science. Records *changed to* Historical Records of Australian Science
0067-1568 Australian Academy of Science. Reports
0067-1576 Australian Academy of Science. Science and Industry Forum Reports
0067-1584 Australian Academy of Science. Year Book
0067-1592 Australian Academy of the Humanities. Proceedings
0067-1606 Australian Advertising Rate and Data Service
0067-1622 Australian and New Zealand Law List and Legal Compendium *changed to* Australian and New Zealand Law List
0067-1630 Australian Association of Adult Education. Monograph†
0067-1649 Australian Association of Adult Education. Proceedings of the National Conference†
0067-1657 Australia. Atomic Energy Commission. Research Establishment. A A E C/E
0067-1665 Australia. Atomic Energy Commission. Research Establishment. A A E C/M
0067-1703 Australian Biochemical Society. Proceedings
0067-172X Australian Books in Print
0067-1738 Australian Books
0067-1754 Australia. Bureau of Statistics. Australian Capital Territory. Statistical Summary
0067-1762 Australian Coal Industry Research Laboratories. Annual Report

ISSN INDEX 1351

0067-1789 Australian College of Ophthalmologists Transactions. *changed to* Australian and New Zealand Journal of Ophthalmology
0067-1819 Australian Computer Society. Council. Report†
0067-1835 Australian Council for Educational Research. Occasional Papers
0067-1843 Australian Digest
0067-186X Australia. Bureau of Statistics. Australian Exports Bulletin *see* 0705-0534
0067-1878 Australian Government Publications
0067-1894 Australian Honey Board. Annual Report
0067-1916 Australia. Bureau of Statistics. Australian Imports Bulletin *see* 0705-0542
0067-1924 Australian Journal of Botany
0067-1940 Australian Journal of Marine and Freshwater Research
0067-1959 Australian Market Guide
0067-1967 Australian Museum, Sydney. Memoirs *changed to* Australian Museum, Sydney. Records Supplements
0067-1975 Australian Museum, Sydney. Records
0067-1983 Australian National Accounts. National Income and Expenditure†
0067-2017 Australian National University, Canberra. Department of International Relations. Documents and Data Paper†
0067-2025 Australian National University, Canberra. Department of International Relations. Workpaper†
0067-2033 Australian National University, Canberra. Department of Political Science. Occasional Paper. *changed to* Australian National University, Canberra. Research School of Social Sciences. Department of Political Science. Occasional Papers
0067-2041 Australian National University, Canberra. Faculty of Asian Studies. Occasional Papers†
0067-2076 Australian Photography Directory *changed to* Australian Photography Photo-Directory
0067-2084 Australian Physiological and Pharmacological Society. Proceedings
0067-2106 Rural Industry Directory
0067-2130 Australian Society for Medical Research Proceedings *see* 0305-1870
0067-2149 Australian Society of Animal Production. Proceedings *see* 0728-5965
0067-2165 Australian Studies in Health Service Administration
0067-2173 Australian Sugar Year Book
0067-2181 Australian Telecommunication Monographs
0067-219X Australia. Australian Water Resources Council. Hydrological Series
0067-222X Australian Wool *see* 0311-9882
0067-2238 Australian Zoologist
0067-2246 Australiana Facsimile Editions†
0067-2262 Austria. Bundesministerium fuer Land- und Forstwirtschaft. Taetigkeitsbericht
0067-2270 Austria. Bundesministerium fuer Unterricht und Kunst. Erziehung, Wissenschaft, Forschung *changed to* Austria. Bundesministerium fuer Unterricht und Kunst. Schriftenreihe
0067-2289 Austria. Bundesministerium fuer Unterricht und Kunst. Jahresbericht†
0067-2297 Oesterreichisches Staatsarchiv. Mitteilungen
0067-2300 Austria. Statistisches Zentralamt. Die Wohnbautaetigkeit
0067-2319 Beitraege zur Oesterreichischen Statistik
0067-2327 Austria. Statistisches Zentralamt. Ergebnisse der Landwirtschaftlichen Statistik
0067-2335 Austria. Statistisches Zentralamt. Die Natuerliche Bevoelkerungsbewegung
0067-2343 Oesterreichische Hochschulstatistik
0067-2351 Austria. Zentralanstalt fuer Meteorologie und Geodynamik. Jahrbuch
0067-2378 Austrian History Yearbook
0067-2386 Author's and Writer's Who's Who *see* 0143-8263
0067-2408 Auto Racing Guide†
0067-2416 Auto-Universum
0067-2424 Autocatalogue
0067-2432 Autocourse†
0067-2491 Automatic Support Systems Symposium for Advanced Maintainability. Proceedings *changed to* Autotestcon
0067-2521 Automobile Buyers' Guide†
0067-253X Automobile Facts and Figures *see* 0146-9932
0067-2548 Automobile News Annual
0067-2572 Automotive Mass Marketer *see* 0702-8318
0067-2580 Automotive News Almanac *changed to* Automotive News Market Data Book
0067-2610 Avant-Siecle
0067-2629 Aventure des Civilisations†
0067-2637 Aves del Arca
0067-2645 Aviation Directory of Asia
0067-2653 Aviation et Astronautique†
0067-2661 Aviation Medical Education Series
0067-2696 Ayer Directory of Newspapers, Magazines, and Trade Publications *changed to* Gale Directory of Publications
0067-270X Azania
0067-2734 B B A Library†
0067-2742 B.G. Rudolph Lectures in Judaic Studies
0067-2777 Bacteriological Proceedings *see* 0094-8519
0067-2793 Badania z Dziejow Spolecznych i Gospodarczych
0067-2807 Badania Fizjograficzne nad Polska Zachodnia. Seria A. Geografia Fizyczna
0067-2815 Badania Fizjograficzne nad Polska Zachodnia. Seria B. Biologia *changed to* Badania Fizjograficzne nad Polska Zachodnia. Seria B. Botanika
0067-2823 Badania Nad Dziejami Przemyslu i Klasy Robotniczej W Polsce†
0067-2831 Kommission fuer Geschichtliche Landeskunde in Baden-Wuerttemberg. Veroeffentlichungen. Reihe A. Quellen
0067-284X Staatliche Kunstsammlungen in Baden-Wuerttemberg. Jahrbuch
0067-2858 Badischer Landesverein fuer Naturkunde und Naturschutz, Freiburg. Mitteilungen. Neue Folge
0067-2866 Badlands Natural History Association. Bulletin†
0067-2874 Badman†
0067-2882 Badminton Association of England. Official Handbook *see* 0262-1940
0067-2890 University of Baghdad. Biological Research Centre. Bulletin
0067-2904 University of Baghdad. College of Science. Bulletin *changed to* Iraqi Journal of Science
0067-2912 Bahamas Handbook and Businessman's Annual *changed to* Bahamas Handbook
0067-2947 Baily's Hunting Directory
0067-2955 Baja California Travels Series
0067-2963 Baker and Bakery Management Handbook and Buyers Guide†
0067-298X Balance of Payments of Japan†
0067-2998 Balance of Payments of Sierra Leone
0067-3005 Balance of Payments of Trinidad and Tobago
0067-3013 Balanza de Pagos de Chile†
0067-3021 Balanza de Pagos de Espana
0067-303X Baldwin Lectures in Teacher Education *changed to* Baldwin Lectures
0067-3048 Bale Catalogue of Israel Stamps *changed to* Bale Catalogue of Israel Postage Stamps
0067-3064 Baltica
0067-3072 Baltimore College of Dental Surgery, Journal†
0067-3080 Baltimore Museum of Art. Annual†
0067-3099 Baltische Studien
0067-3102 Baltisches Recht; das Recht Estlands, Lettlands und Litauens in Vergangenheit und Gegenwart†
0067-3110 Chambre de Commerce et d'Industrie du Mali. Precis Fiscal, Commercial, des Changes et des Echanges
0067-3129 Bampton Lectures in America
0067-3161 Banca d'Italia. Assemblea Generale Ordinaria dei Partecipanti.
0067-3188 Somali National Bank. Report and Balance Sheet *changed to* Central Bank of Somali. Annual Report and Statement of Accounts
0067-320X Banco Central de Costa Rica. Memoria Anual
0067-3218 Banco Central de Honduras. Memoria
0067-3226 Banco Central de Nicaragua. Informe Anual
0067-3234 El Salvador. Superintendencia de Bancos y Otras Instituciones Financieras. Estadisticas: Seguros, Finanzas, Capitalizacion *changed to* El Salvador. Superintendencia de Bancos y Otras Instituciones Financieras. Estadisticas: Seguros, Finanzas, Bancos
0067-3250 Banco Central de Venezuela. Informe Economico
0067-3269 Banco Central de Venezuela. Memoria
0067-3277 Banco Central del Ecuador. Memoria del Gerente General
0067-3285 Banco Central del Paraguay. Memoria
0067-3315 Banco de Espana. Informe Anual
0067-3323 Banco de la Republica Cuentas Nacionales†
0067-3331 Banco de la Republica Disposiciones†
0067-334X Guia para el Inversionista.†
0067-3366 Banco de la Republica Series Estadisticas y Graficos.†
0067-3374 Banco de Mexico. Informe Anual
0067-3390 Banco Nacional de Fomento, Tegucigalpa. Memoria Anual *changed to* Banco Nacional de Desarrollo Agricola. Memoria Anual
0067-3412 Bancroftiana
0067-3439 Indian Statistical Institute. Documentation Research and Training Centre. D R T C Annual Seminar
0067-3455 University of Agricultural Sciences, Bangalore. Annual Report
0067-3463 University of Agricultural Sciences, Bangalore. Research Series†
0067-3471 U A S Extension Series
0067-348X U A S Miscellaneous Series
0067-3498 Bangkok, Thailand. College of Education. Thesis Abstract Series
0067-3501 Bank Administration Institute. Accounting Bulletins†
0067-351X Bank Administration Institute. Annual Report†
0067-3528 Bank Officer Salary Survey *see* 0525-4620
0067-3536 Bank Administration Institute. Personnel Policies and Practices *changed to* Biennial Survey of Bank Personnel Policies and Practices
0067-3544 Bank Administration Institute. Security Bulletins†
0067-3560 Bank for International Settlements. Annual Report
0067-3587 Bank of Canada. Annual Report
0067-3595 Bank of Canada. Staff Research Studies *see* 0713-7931
0067-3617 Central Bank of Ceylon. Report and Accounts *changed to* Bank of Ceylon. Annual Report and Accounts
0067-3625 Bank of England. Report *see* 0308-5279
0067-3633 Hawaii Annual Economic Review
0067-3641 Bank of Israel. Main Points of the Annual Report
0067-365X Bank of Israel. Annual Report
0067-3668 Bank of Jamaica. Report and Statement of Accounts
0067-3676 Bank of Japan. Annual Report of the Policy Board *changed to* Bank of Japan. Annual Report
0067-3684 Bank of Japan. Business Report
0067-3692 Bank of Japan. Special Paper
0067-3706 Bank of Korea. Annual Report
0067-3714 Bank of Libya. Annual Report of the Board of Directors
0067-3722 Bank of Mauritius. Annual Report
0067-3730 Bank of Sierra Leone. Annual Report *changed to* Bank of Sierra Leone. Annual Report and Statement of Accounts
0067-3749 Bank of Sudan. Report
0067-3757 Bank of Tanzania. Economic and Operations Report
0067-3765 Bank of Tanzania. Economic Report *see* 0067-3757
0067-3773 Bank of Thailand. Annual Economic Report
0067-3781 Bankangestellte *changed to* Deutsches Banken-Handbuch (Year)
0067-379X Bankers Almanac and Year Book
0067-3803 Bankers' Who's Who
0067-3811 Banking Statistics of Pakistan
0067-382X Bankwirtschaftliche Forschungen
0067-3846 Banque Centrale de Syrie. Bulletin Periodique *changed to* Central Bank of Syria. Quarterly Bulletin
0067-3854 Banque Centrale de Tunisie. Bulletin
0067-3862 Banque Centrale de Tunisie. Rapport d'Activite
0067-3889 Banque Centrale des Etats de l'Afrique de l'Ouest. Rapport Annuel
0067-3897 Banque Centrale des Etats de l'Afrique de l'Ouest. Rapport d'Activite.
0067-3900 Banque des Etats de l'Afrique Centrale. Rapport d'Activite
0067-3919 Banque de Bruxelles. Rapport Annuel *changed to* Banque de Bruxelles Lambert. Rapports de l'Exercice
0067-3927 Banque de France. Compte-Rendu
0067-3935 Banque de la Republique du Burundi. Rapport Annuel
0067-3943 Banque de l'Union Europeenne. Informations Economiques et Financieres. *see* 0245-761X
0067-3951 Banque des Mots
0067-396X Banque du Maroc. Rapport Annuel
0067-3978 Banque Nationale de Belgique. Rapport sur les Operations
0067-4001 Banque Nationale du Congo. Rapport Annuel *see* 0300-1172
0067-401X Banque Nationale Malagasy de Developpement. Rapport d'Activite *changed to* Bankin'Ny Indostria. Rapport Annuel
0067-4028 Banque Populaire Suisse. Information
0067-4036 Banque Togolaise de Developpement. Rapport Annuel *changed to* Banque Togolaise de Developpement. Rapport d'Activites
0067-4044 Bantu Treasury
0067-4052 Baptist Handbook†
0067-4060 Baptist Missionary Society, London. Annual Report
0067-4079 Baptist Missionary Society, London. Official Report and Directory of Missionaries
0067-4087 Baptist Union of Western Canada. Yearbook
0067-4095 Baptist World Alliance. Congress Reports
0067-4109 Bar-Ilan: Annual of Bar-Ilan University
0067-4125 Barbados. Statistical Service. Overseas Trade Report
0067-4141 Universidad de Barcelona. Biblioteca Central. Catalogos de la Production Editorial Barcelona *see* 0210-6833
0067-4168 Patronato Municipal de la Vivienda de Barcelona. Memoria
0067-4176 Universidad de Barcelona. Facultad de Farmacia. Memoria
0067-4184 Universidad de Barcelona. Instituto de Arqueologia y Prehistoria. Publicaciones Eventuales
0067-4206 Die Barke
0067-4222 Baroque
0067-4230 Barque's Pakistan Trade Directory and Who's Who

0067-4249 Barsoomian
0067-4265 Baseball Dope Book *see* 0162-5411
0067-4273 Baseball Guide
0067-4281 Baseball Register *see* 0162-542X
0067-4303 Gewerbemuseum Basel. Schriften†
0067-4311 Oeffentliche Kunstsammlung. Jahresbericht
0067-4338 Basic Auto Repair Manual†
0067-4362 Basic Bodywork and Painting†
0067-4370 Basic Cams, Valves and Exhaust Systems†
0067-4389 Basic Carburetion and Fuel Systems†
0067-4397 Basic Chassis, Suspension and Brakes†
0067-4400 Basic Clutches and Transmissions†
0067-4419 Basic Facts about the United Nations
0067-4427 Basic Ignition and Electrical Systems†
0067-4443 Basic Science Symposium Series†
0067-446X Basis†
0067-4478 Basler Beitraege zur Ethnologie†
0067-4486 Basler Beitraege zur Geographie
0067-4494 Basler Drucke†
0067-4508 Basler Studien zur Deutschen Sprache und Literatur
0067-4524 Basler Veroeffentlichungen zur Geschichte der Medizin und der Biologie
0067-4532 Basler Wirtschaftswissenschaftliche Vortraege†
0067-4540 Basler Zeitschrift fuer Geschichte und Altertumskunde
0067-4575 Bau und Baustoff Handbuch†
0067-4583 Baubeschlag-Taschenbuch
0067-4591 Bauernhaeuser der Schweiz
0067-4605 Bauhinia
0067-463X Bausteine zur Geschichte des Neuhochdeutschen *changed to* Bausteine zur Sprachgeschichte des Neuhochdeutschen
0067-4648 Instituto Nacional de la Pesca de Cuba. Centro de Investigaciones Pesqueras. Boletin de Divulgacion Tecnica†
0067-4656 Centro de Investigaciones Pesqueras. Contribuciones *changed to* Revista Cubana de Investigaciones Pesqueras. Boletines Bibliograficos
0067-4664 Bauwelt Katalog
0067-4672 Bayer-Symposien
0067-4702 Bayerisches Beamten-Jahrbuch (Year)
0067-4710 Bayerisches Forstdienst-Taschenbuch
0067-4729 Bayerisches Jahrbuch fuer Volkskunde
0067-4745 Beaufortia
0067-4761 Bed and Breakfast in South and Southwest England *see* 0267-3436
0067-477X Bed and Breakfast in Wales, Northern England and Scotland *see* 0267-3436
0067-4788 Bedford Institute of Oceanography. A O L Data Series *changed to* Bedford Institute of Oceanography. Data Report
0067-4796 Atlantic Oceanographic Laboratory. A O L Report *changed to* Bedford Institute of Oceanography. Report
0067-480X Bedford Institute of Oceanography. Biennial Review *see* 0229-8910
0067-4826 Bedfordshire Historical Record Society. Publications
0067-4834 Bedrijfschap voor de Lederwarenindustrie. Jaarverslag
0067-4893 Beihefte der Bonner Jahrbuecher
0067-4907 Sonderbaende zur Theologischen Zeitschrift
0067-4915 Beilsteins Handbuch der Organischen Chemie. Fourth Supplement
0067-4931 Beiruter Texte und Studien
0067-4966 Beitraege zum Rundfunkrecht
0067-4974 Technische Beitraege zur Archaeologie
0067-5008 Beitraege zur Geologie von Thueringen†
0067-5016 Beitraege zur Gerichtlichen Medizin
0067-5024 Beitraege zur Geschichte der Philosophie und Theologie des Mittelalters Neue Folge
0067-5040 Geschichte des Buchwesens. Beitraege
0067-5059 Beitraege zur Geschichte des Religioesen und Wissenschaftlichen Denkens†
0067-5067 Beitraege zur Harmonikalen Grundlagenforschung
0067-5075 Beitraege zur Heilpaedagogik und Heilpaedagogischen Psychologie†
0067-5083 Beitraege zur Hygiene und Epidemiologie
0067-5091 Beitraege zur Inkunabelkunde. Dritte Folge
0067-5105 Beitraege zur Kinderpsychotherapie
0067-5113 Krebsforschung. Beitraege†
0067-5121 Beitraege zur Kunst des Christlichen Ostens
0067-5148 Beitraege zur Meereskunde
0067-5164 Beitraege zur Oberpfalzforschung
0067-5172 Beitraege zur Oekumenischen Theologie
0067-5180 Beitraege zur Praktischen Medizin†
0067-5199 Beitraege zur Rheumatologie
0067-5202 Beitraege zur Romanischen Philologie des Mittelalters
0067-5210 Beitraege zur Sexualforschung
0067-5237 Beitraege zur Strafvollzugswissenschaft
0067-5245 Beitraege zur Ur- und Fruehgeschichtlichen Archaeologie des Mittelmeerkulturraumes
0067-5253 Beitraege zur Wehrforschung†
0067-5261 Beitraege zur Westfaelischen Familienforschung
0067-527X Brazil. Instituto de Pesquisas Agropecuarias do Norte. Boletim Tecnico†
0067-5288 Instituto de Pesquisas Agropecuarias do Norte. Circular†
0067-5296 Instituto de Pesquisas Agropecurarias do Norte. Communicado Tecnico†
0067-5342 Belfast and Northern Ireland Directory
0067-5350 Belfast History and Philosophical Society. Proceedings and Reports
0067-5369 Belgium. Administration des Eaux et Forets. Station de Recherche des Eaux et Forets. Travaux. Serie D. Hydrobiologie *changed to* Belgium. Station de Recherches Forestieres et Hydrobiologiques. Travaux. Serie D. Hydrobiologie
0067-5385 Belgium. Conseil National du Travail. Rapport du Secretaire sur l'Activite du Conseil†
0067-5393 Belgium. Conseil Superieur des Classes Moyennes. Rapport Annuel du Secretaire General
0067-5407 Belgium. Nationaal Fonds voor Wetenschappelijk Onderzoek. Jaarverslag
0067-5415 Activities des Aerodromes Belges *changed to* Belgium. Institut National de Statistique. Statistiques des Transports
0067-5423 Belgium. Institut National de Statistique. Annuaire Statistique de l'Enseignement *changed to* Belgium. Ministere de l'Education Nationale et de la Culture Francaise. Annuaire Statistique de l'Enseignement
0067-5431 Belgium. Institut National de Statistique. Annuaire Statistique de Poche
0067-544X Belgium. Institut National de Statistique. Batiments et Logements *changed to* Belgium. Institut National de Statistique. Statistiques de la Construction et du Logement
0067-5458 Belgium. Institut National de Statistique. Mouvement de la Population des Communes†
0067-5466 Belgium. Institut National de Statistique. Statistiques Agricoles
0067-5482 Belgium. Institut National de Statistique. Statistique Annuelle du Trafic International des Ports *changed to* Belgium. Institut National de Statistique. Statistique du Trafic International des Ports
0067-5490 Belgium. Institut National de Statistique. Statistiques Demographiques
0067-5504 Belgium. Institut National de Statistique. Statistique des Accidents de la Circulation sur la Voie Publique
0067-5512 Belgium. Institut National de Statistique. Statistique des Accidents de Roulage *see* 0067-5504
0067-5520 Belgium. Institut National de Statistique. Statistique de la Navigation du Rhin *see* 0067-5539
0067-5539 Belgium. Institut National de Statistique. Statistique de la Navigation Interieure
0067-5547 Belgium. Institut National de Statistique. Statistique du Tourisme et de l'Hotellerie
0067-5555 Belgium. Institut National de Statistique. Statistique des Vehicules a Moteur Neufs Mis en Circulation
0067-5563 Belgium. Institut National de Statistique. Statistiques Sociales
0067-5571 Belgium. Ministere de la Prevoyance Sociale. Annuaire Statistique de la Securite Sociale/Statistisch Jaarboek van de Sociale Zeherheid†
0067-558X Belgium. Ministere de la Prevoyance Sociale. Rapport General sur la Securite Sociale/Algemeen Verslag over de Sociale Zekerheid
0067-5598 Belgium. Ministere de l'Education Nationale et de la Culture Francaise. Rapport Annuel
0067-5601 Bibliotheque Africaine. Catalogue des Acquisitions. Catologus van de Aanwinsten
0067-561X Belgium. Office Belge du Commerce Exterieur. Bijvoegsel B B H. Reeks B
0067-5628 I C E Supplement. Serie C
0067-5644 Belgium. Office National de l'Emploi. Rapport Annuel *changed to* Belgium. Office National de l'Emploi. Etudes Economiques et Sociales
0067-5652 Societe National du Logement. Rapport Annuel
0067-5660 Vojni Muzej, Belgrade. Vesnik
0067-5687 Universidade Federal de Minas Gerais. Instituto de Pesquisas Radioativas. Relatorios Anuais†
0067-5695 Beloit Poetry Journal. Chapbook
0067-5709 B E M A Engineering Directory
0067-5717 Benjamin F. Fairless Lectures
0067-5725 Benn's Hardware Directory *see* 0261-1465
0067-5733 Bent
0067-5768 Berg- und Huettenmaennische Monatshefte. Supplement†
0067-5792 Bergischer Geschichtsverein. Zeitschrift
0067-5806 Berichte des Vereins Natur und Heimat und des Naturhistorischen Museums zu Luebeck
0067-5814 Nursing Journal of Singapore
0067-5822 Berkeley Analyses of Molecular Spectra†
0067-5830 Berkeley Journal of Sociology
0067-5849 Biologische Bundesanstalt fuer Land- und Forstwirtschaft, Berlin-Dahlem. Mitteilungen
0067-5857 Historische Kommission zu Berlin. Einzelveroeffentlichungen
0067-5865 Berlin. Freie Universitaet. Institut fuer Statistik und Versicherungsmathematik. Berichte *see* 0066-5673
0067-5881 Freie Universitaet Berlin. Osteuropa-Institut. Bibliographische Mitteilungen
0067-589X Freie Universitaet Berlin. Osteuropa-Institut. Erziehungswissenschaftliche Veroeffentlichungen
0067-5903 Freie Universitaet Berlin. Osteuropa-Institut. Historische Veroeffentlichungen
0067-5911 Freie Universitaet Berlin. Osteuropa-Institut. Philosophische und Soziologische Veroeffentlichungen
0067-592X Freie Universitaet Berlin. Osteuropa-Institut. Slavistische Veroeffentlichungen
0067-5938 Freie Universitaet Berlin. Osteuropa-Institut. Wirtschaftswissenschaftliche Veroeffentlichungen
0067-5954 Hochschule fuer Oekonomie "Bruno Leuschner" Berlin. Wissenschaftliche Zeitschrift
0067-5962 Museum fuer Voelkerkunde, Berlin. Veroeffentlichungen. Neue Folge. Abteilung: Afrika
0067-5989 Museum fuer Voelkerkunde, Berlin. Veroeffentlichungen. Neue Folge. Abteilung: Suedsee
0067-5997 R I A S-Funkuniversitaet, Berlin. Forschung und Information *changed to* R I A S-Funkuniversitaet, Berlin. Schriftenreihe. Forschung und Information
0067-6004 Staatliche Museen zu Berlin. Jahrbuch. Forschungen und Berichte
0067-6039 Technische Universitaet Berlin. Institut fuer Sozialoekonomie der Agrarentwicklung. Taetigkeitsbericht *see* 0170-8376
0067-6047 Berlin, Theater und Drama†
0067-6055 Berliner Byzantinistische Arbeiten
0067-6063 Berliner Handelsregister Verzeichnis
0067-6098 Berliner Tierpark-Buch
0067-611X Berlinische Reminiszenzen
0067-6128 Berner Beitraege zur Nationaloekonomie
0067-6136 Berner Beitraege zur Soziologie
0067-6144 Berner Kriminologische Untersuchungen
0067-6152 Berner Studien zum Fremdenverkehr
0067-6160 Bernice Pauahi Bishop Museum, Honolulu. Occasional Papers
0067-6179 Bernice Pauahi Bishop Museum, Honolulu. Special Publications
0067-6195 Berytus Archeological Studies
0067-6233 Best American Short Stories
0067-6276 Borestone Mountain Poetry Awards†
0067-6284 Best Short Plays
0067-6292 Best Sports Stories
0067-6306 Bestands-Statistik der Kraftfahrzeuge in Oesterreich
0067-6314 Bestimmungsbuecher zur Bodenfauna Europas†
0067-6330 Bestsellers du Monde Entier†
0067-6349 Bestuurlike Informasie
0067-6357 Beta Phi Mu Chapbook
0067-6365 Beton- und Fertigteil-Jahrbuch
0067-6381 Schriftenreihe Betriebswirtschaftliche Beitraege zur Organisation und Automation†
0067-639X Betriebswirtschaftliche Mitteilungen *changed to* Management Praxis
0067-642X Better Building Bulletin†
0067-6454 Bharat Krishak Samaj. Year Book
0067-6462 Basic Road Statistics of India
0067-6470 Bialostockie Towarzystwo Naukowe. Prace
0067-6489 Akademia Medyczna im. J. Marchlewskiego w Bialymstoku. Roczniki
0067-6535 Biblical Research
0067-6543 Bibliografi over Danmarks Offentlige Publikationer
0067-6551 Bibliografia Analitica a Periodicelor Romanesti†
0067-656X Bibliografia Bibliotecologica Argentina
0067-6578 Bibliografia Boliviana *changed to* Bio-Bibliografia Boliviana
0067-6586 Bibliografia Brasileira de Botanica†
0067-6594 Bibliografia Brasileira de Ciencias Agricolas *changed to* Bibliografia Brasileira de Agricultura (year)
0067-6608 Bibliografia Brasileira de Ciencias Sociais
0067-6616 Bibliografia Brasileira de Direito
0067-6624 Bibliografia Brasileira de Documentacao
0067-6632 Bibliografia Brasileira de Educacao
0067-6640 Bibliografia Brasileira de Fisica
0067-6659 Bibliografia Brasileira de Livros Infantis†
0067-6667 Bibliografia Brasileira de Matematica
0067-6675 Bibliografia Brasileira de Medicina
0067-6683 Bibliografia Brasileira de Quimica *see* 0100-0756
0067-6691 Bibliografia Brasileira de Zoologia
0067-6705 Bibliografia Cubana
0067-6721 Bibliografia Historii Polskiej
0067-6748 Bibliografia Oficial Colombiana†
0067-6756 Bibliografia Portuguesa de Construcao Civil *changed to* Bibliografia Portuguesa de Engenharia Civil

ISSN INDEX 1353

0067-6764 Bibliografia Sobre a Economia Portuguesa†
0067-6772 Bibliografia Ticinese
0067-6780 Bibliograficky Zbornik
0067-6799 Bibliografija Medicinske Periodike Jugoslavije
0067-6802 Bibliographia Medica Cechoslovaca
0067-6829 Bibliographia Scientiae Naturalis Helvetica
0067-6837 Bibliographic Annual in Speech Communication†
0067-6853 Bibliographica Judaica
0067-6861 Bibliographical Selection of Museological Literature *changed to* Selected Bibliography of Museological Literature
0067-687X Bibliographical Society of Canada. Facsimile Series
0067-6888 Bibliographical Society of Canada. Monographs
0067-6896 Bibliographical Society of Canada. Papers
0067-6918 Bibliographie Annuelle de l'Histoire de France
0067-6926 Bibliographie Annuelle de Madagascar
0067-6934 Bibliographie Cartographique Internationale†
0067-6942 Bibliographie de la Litterature Francaise du Moyen Age a Nos Jours†
0067-6950 Bibliographie der Chemisch-Archaeologischen Literatur†
0067-6969 Bibliographie der Paedagogischen Veroeffentlichungen in der Deutschen Demokratischen Republik
0067-6977 Bibliographie der Sozialethik†
0067-6985 Bibliographie en la Langue Francaise d'Histoire du Droit de 987 a 1875 *changed to* Bibliographie en Langue Francaise d'Histoire du Droit de 987 a 1914
0067-6993 Bibliographie Geographique Internationale
0067-7000 Bibliographie Internationale de l'Humanisme et de la Renaissance
0067-7027 Bibliographie Programmierter Unterricht *see* 0523-2678
0067-7043 Bibliographie d'Histoire Luxembourgeoise
0067-706X Bibliographie zur Symbolik, Ikonographie und Mythologie
0067-7094 Bibliographies in Paint Technology†
0067-7116 Bibliographies on the Near East†
0067-7132 Bibliography and Reference Series†
0067-7159 Bibliography of Asian Studies
0067-7175 Bibliography of Canadian Bibliographies
0067-7183 Bibliography of Developmental Medicine and Child Neurology. Books and Articles Received
0067-7191 Bibliography of Historical Works Issued in the United Kingdom†
0067-7205 Bibliography of Interlingual Scientific and Technical Dictionaries†
0067-7213 Bibliography of Old Norse-Icelandic Studies
0067-7256 Bibliography of South African Government Publications
0067-7264 Bibliography of Surgery of the Hand
0067-7272 Bibliography of the Geology of Missouri
0067-7280 Bibliography of the History of Medicine
0067-7302 Bibliography of the Middle East
0067-7310 Bibliography of Works by Polish Scholars and Scientists Published outside Poland in Languages Other Than Polish
0067-7329 Bibliography on Foreign and Comparative Law: Books and Articles in English.
0067-7353 Bibliography on Satellite Geodesy and Related Subjects *changed to* International Association of Geodesy. Central Bureau for Satellite Geodesy. Bibliography
0067-7361 Bibliography on Smoking and Health
0067-737X Bibliohrafichnyi Pokazhchyk Ukrains'koi Presy Poza Mezhamy Ukrainy†
0067-7388 Biblioteca de Arheologie
0067-7396 Biblioteca de Cultura Vasca†
0067-740X Biblioteca de Teologia
0067-7418 Biblioteca di Bibliografia Italiana
0067-7434 Biblioteca di Labeo
0067-7442 Biblioteca di Storia Toscana Moderna e Contemporanea Studi e Documenti
0067-7450 Biblioteca di Studi Etruschi
0067-7469 Biblioteca do Educador Profissional
0067-7477 Bibliotheca Germanica. Handbuecher, Texte und Monographien aus dem Gebiete der Germanischen Philologie
0067-7493 Biblioteca Istorica
0067-7507 Biblioteca Praehistorica Hispana
0067-7515 Bibliotheca Romanica
0067-7523 Biblioteca Storica Toscana *changed to* Biblioteca Storica Toscana. Serie I
0067-7531 Biblioteconomia e Bibliografia. Saggi e Studi
0067-754X Biblioteczka Ateisty
0067-7558 Biblioteczka Kopernikanska†
0067-7582 Biblioteczka Wiedzy O Slasku. Seria Archeologiczna†
0067-7590 Biblioteczka Wiedzy O Slasku. Seria Etnograficzna†
0067-7604 Biblioteczka Wiedzy O Slasku. Seria Historyczna†
0067-7612 Biblioteczka Wiedzy O Slasku. Seria Literatura Ludowa†
0067-7620 Biblioteczka Wiedzy O Slasku. Seria Przyrodnicza†
0067-7639 Biblioteka Archeologiczna
0067-7655 Biblioteka Etnografii Polskiej
0067-7671 Biblioteka Klasykow Pedagogiki†
0067-7698 Biblioteka Krakowska
0067-7701 Biblioteka Mechaniki Stosowanej
0067-7728 Biblioteka Nawigatora†
0067-7736 Biblioteka Pisarzow Polskich *see* 0519-8631
0067-7760 Biblioteka Popularnonaukowa†
0067-7779 Biblioteka Sluchacza Koncertowego. Seria Wprowadzajaca
0067-7787 Towarzystwo Literackie im. A. Mickiewicza. Biblioteka
0067-7795 Biblioteka Wiadomosci Statystycznych
0067-7809 Biblioteka Zagadnien Gospodarczych Polski†
0067-7817 Bibliotheca Aegyptiaca
0067-7825 Bibliotheca Africana Droz†
0067-7833 Bibliotheca Anatomica
0067-7841 Bibliotheca Arnamagnaeana
0067-785X Bibliotheca Arnamagnaeana. Supplementum
0067-7868 Bibliotheca Athena
0067-7876 Bibliotheca Australiana
0067-7884 Bibliotheca Bibliographica Aureliana
0067-7892 Bibliotheca Botanica
0067-7906 Bibliotheca Cardiologica
0067-7914 Bibliotheca Celtica
0067-7922 Bibliotheca del Planeamiento Educativo
0067-7930 Bibliotheca Emblematica†
0067-7965 Bibliotheca Helvetica Romana
0067-7981 Bibliotheca Historica Romaniae. Studies
0067-799X Bibliotheca Historica Romaniae. Monographies
0067-8007 Bibliotheca Hungarica Antiqua
0067-8015 Bibliotheca Ibero-Americana
0067-8023 Bibliotheca Indonesica
0067-8031 Bibliotheca Latina Medii et Recentiori Aevi
0067-8058 Bibliotheca Microbiologia *see* 0301-3081
0067-8066 Bibliotheca Mycologica
0067-8082 Bibliotheca Oeconomica
0067-8090 Bibliotheca Ophthalmologica *see* 0250-3751
0067-8104 Bibliotheca Orientalis Hungarica
0067-8112 Bibliotheca Phycologica
0067-8120 Bibliotheca Phonetica†
0067-8139 Bibliotheca Primatologica *see* 0301-4231
0067-8147 Bibliotheca Psychiatrica
0067-8163 Bibliotheca Seraphico-Capuccina
0067-8198 Bibliotheca Nutritio et Dieta
0067-8201 Bibliothek der Klassischen Altertumswissenschaften. Neue Folge
0067-821X Bilder aus Deutscher Vergangenheit†
0067-8228 Bibliothek fuer das Gesamtgebiet der Lungenkrankheiten†
0067-8236 Bibliothek und Wissenschaft
0067-8244 Bibliotheque Arctique et Antarctique†
0067-8260 Bibliotheque de la Mer
0067-8279 Bibliotheque de la Revue d'Histoire Ecclesiastique
0067-8295 Bibliotheque de Sciences Religieuses†
0067-8309 Bibliotheque des Cahiers Archeologiques
0067-8325 Bibliotheque d'Etudes Balkaniques
0067-8333 Bibliotheque Europeenne†
0067-8341 Bibliotheque Francaise et Romane. Serie A: Manuels et Etudes Linguistiques
0067-835X Bibliotheque Francaise et Romane. Serie B: Editions Critiques de Textes
0067-8368 Bibliotheque Francaise et Romane. Serie C: Etudes Litteraires
0067-8376 Bibliotheque Francaise et Romane. Serie D: Initiation, Textes et Documents
0067-8384 Bibliotheque Francaise et Romane. Serie E: Langue et Litterature Francaises au Canada
0067-8406 Bibliotheque Historique Vaudoise
0067-8414 Bibliotheque Ideale†
0067-8422 Bibliotheque Introuvable
0067-8430 Bibliotheque Philosophique de Louvain
0067-8457 Bibliotheque Rencontre des Lettres Anciennes et Modernes†
0067-8473 Bidrag til H. C. Andersens Bibliografi
0067-8481 Bidrag till Kaennedom av Finlands Natur och Folk
0067-849X Biennale Internationale de la Tapisserie *changed to* Catalogue Biennale Internationale de Lausanne
0067-8538 Bijdragen tot de Bibliotheekwetenschap
0067-8546 Bijdragen tot de Dierkunde
0067-8554 Bijdragen tot de Geschiedenis van Arnhem
0067-8562 Bilateral Studies in Private International Law†
0067-8570 Bild des Menschen in der Wissenschaft†
0067-8589 Bildungsplanung in Oesterreich†
0067-8597 Campus Attractions *see* 0732-0124
0067-8600 Billboard's International Buyer's Guide of the Music-Record-Tape Industry
0067-8627 International Directory of Recording Studios *changed to* Billboard's International Recording Studio and Equipment Directory
0067-8643 Die Binnengewaesser
0067-8651 Binsted's Directory of Food Trade Marks and Brand Names
0067-8678 Biochemistry of Disease
0067-8686 Biochemical Preparations†
0067-8708 Biofeedback and Self-Control†
0067-8716 Biogeographical Society of Japan. Bulletin
0067-8724 Biograficke Studie
0067-8732 Biographical Encyclopedia of Pakistan
0067-8740 Biographies de Personnalites Francaises Vivantes†
0067-8775 Biological Macromolecules Series†
0067-8783 B S C S Bulletin Series†
0067-8791 B S C S Special Publication†
0067-8805 Biologie du Sol *see* 0378-181X
0067-8821 Biomathematics
0067-8848 Biomedical Engineering Series of Monographs *changed to* Biomedical Engineering and Health Systems: A Wiley-Interscience Series
0067-8856 Biomedical Sciences Instrumentation
0067-8864 Biomembranes
0067-8872 Biometeorological Research Centre. Monograph Series
0067-8880 Biometeorological Research Centre. Special Monograph Series
0067-8899 Verzeichnis Lieferbarer Buecher
0067-8902 Biometeorology; Proceedings
0067-8910 Biophysical Society. Abstracts
0067-8929 Biophysics Series†
0067-8937 Biosis: List of Serials *see* 0162-2048
0067-8945 Bird Control Seminar. Proceedings†
0067-8953 University of Birmingham. Centre for Urban and Regional Studies. Occasional Papers
0067-8961 University of Birmingham. Centre for Urban and Regional Studies. Urban and Regional Studies
0067-897X Bituminous Coal Data *see* 0145-417X
0067-8988 Bituminous Coal Facts *changed to* Coal Facts
0067-8996 Biuletyn Fonograficzny†
0067-9003 Biuletyn Geologiczny
0067-902X Biuletyn Polonistyczny
0067-9038 Biuletyn Peryglacjalny
0067-9070 Black Experience in Children's Books
0067-9100 Black Orpheus
0067-9119 Black Review†
0067-9127 Blaetter fuer Technikgeschichte
0067-9178 Blick hinter die Fassade
0067-9186 Association for Education and Rehabilitation of the Blind and Visually Impaired. Yearbook
0067-9194 National Museum, Bloemfontein. Memoirs
0067-9208 National Museum, Bloemfontein. Researche
0067-9216 University of the Orange Free State. Opsommings van Proefskrifte en Verhandelinge. Abstracts of Dissertations and Theses
0067-9224 Bloodstock Breeders' Review
0067-9232 Bloomsbury Geographer
0067-9240 Blue Book: Leaders of the English-Speaking World
0067-9267 Blue Book of Europe; European Export Directory
0067-9275 Blue Book of Occupational Education *see* 0360-5434
0067-9283 Blue Book of Optometrists
0067-9321 Boat Owners Buyers Guide *changed to* Yachting's Boat Buyers Guide
0067-933X Boat World
0067-9399 Boating Guide†
0067-9402 B I A Certification Handbook *changed to* N M M A Certification Handbook
0067-9453 Bochumer Universitaetsreden†
0067-9461 Bodendenkmalpflege in Mecklenburg
0067-947X Bydgoskie Towarzystwo Naukowe. Wydzial Nauk Humanistycznych. Prace. Seria D: (Sztuka)
0067-9488 Bodleian Library Record
0067-9496 Boersen- und Wirtschaftshandbuch†
0067-9518 Colombia. Observatorio Astronomico Nacional. Publicaciones
0067-9526 Universidad Nacional de Colombia. Centro de Estudios Folkloriques. Annuario†
0067-9534 Universidad Nacional de Colombia. Centro de Estudios Folkloricos. Monografias
0067-9542 Bois-Chantiers†
0067-9550 Bol og by *changed to* Landbohistorisk Tidsskrift
0067-9585 Boletim Climatologico
0067-9593 Boletim de Ciencias do Mar
0067-9607 Boletim de Engenharia de Producao
0067-9615 Boletim de Industria Animal
0067-9623 Boletim de Zoologia e Biologia Marinha. Nova Serie *see* 0101-3580
0067-9631 Boletim Oficial de Angola
0067-964X Boletim Paranaense de Geociencias†
0067-9666 Boletin de Estudios Medicos y Biologicos
0067-9674 Boletin de Filologia
0067-9690 Boletin de Literatura Argentina e Iberoamericana†
0067-9720 Boletin Genetico
0067-9747 Boletin Hidrologico
0067-9828 Bolivia. Servicio Geologico. Boletin
0067-9836 Bolivia. Servicio Geologico. Circulare
0067-9844 Bolivia. Servicio Geologico. Informe
0067-9852 Bolivia. Servicio Geologico. Serie Mineralogica. Contribucione
0067-9860 B R A D S
0067-9887 Universita degli Studi di Bologna. Osservatorio Astronomico. Notizie e Rassegne†

0067-9895 Universita degli Studi di Bologna. Osservatorio Astronomico. Pubblicazioni†
0067-9909 Bolsilibros
0067-9917 Bombay Labour Journal
0067-9925 Bombay Technologist
0067-9941 Institut "Finanzen und Steuern." Gruene Briefe
0067-995X Institut "Finanzen und Steuern." Schriftenreihe
0067-9968 Rheinisches Landesmuseum, Bonn. Schriften
0067-9976 Rheinisches Landesmuseum in Bonn. Bonner Jahrbuecher
0068-001X Bonner Arbeiten zur Deutschen Literatur
0068-0028 Bonner Beitraege zur Bibliotheks- und Buecherkunde
0068-0036 Bonner Beitraege zur Kunstwissenschaft
0068-0044 Bonner Beitraege zur Soziologie
0068-0052 Bonner Geschichtsblaetter
0068-0087 Station Biologique de Bonnevaux (Doubs). Section de Biologie et d'Ecologie Animales. Publications†
0068-0095 Book Auction Records
0068-0109 Bookdealers in North America *changed to* Sheppard's Bookdealers in North America
0068-0117 Book of Bantams
0068-0125 Book of the States
0068-0133 Bookman's Guide to Americana
0068-0141 Bookman's Price Index
0068-0168 Books about Canada†
0068-0176 Books about Singapore
0068-0184 Books for Secondary School Libraries
0068-0192 Books for the Teen Age
0068-0206 Books from Pakistan
0068-0214 Books in Print
0068-0222 Books of the Theatre Series†
0068-0249 Booksellers Association of Great Britain and Ireland. List of Members *changed to* Booksellers Association of Great Britain and Ireland. Directory of Members
0068-0257 Booksellers Association of Great Britain and Ireland. Trade Reference Book
0068-0265 Bord Iascaigh Mhara. Tuarascail Agus Cuntaisi
0068-0273 Universite de Bordeaux. Collection Sinologique
0068-0281 Boreal Institute, Edmonton. Annual Report *see* 0820-988X
0068-029X Boreal Institute, Edmonton. Miscellaneous Publications
0068-0303 Boreal Institute, Edmonton. Occasional Publications
0068-0338 Boston College. Bureau of Public Affairs. Community Analysis and Action Series. Monograph†
0068-0346 Boston Studies in the Philosophy of Science
0068-0354 Bostwick Paper
0068-0370 Botanica Gothoburgensia
0068-0397 Botany as a Profession *changed to* Careers in Botany
0068-0400 Botanical Society of America. Yearbook *changed to* Botanical Society of America. Directory
0068-0419 Botanical Society of South Africa. Journal *changed to* Veld & Flora
0068-0427 Botanische Studien†
0068-0443 Botschaft des Alten Testaments
0068-0451 Botswana. Annual Statements of Accounts
0068-046X Botswana. Commissioner of the Police. Annual Report
0068-0478 Botswana. Ministry of Agriculture. Annual Report
0068-0494 Bottin International†
0068-0508 Bottlers Year Book
0068-0524 Boundary Historical Society. Report
0068-0532 Boutique†
0068-0540 Bowker Annual
0068-0559 Bowling and Billiard Buyers Guide
0068-0567 Bowling Guide†
0068-0575 Boys Baseball. Blue Book *changed to* Pony Baseball. Blue Book
0068-0605 Boys' Brigade, London. Annual Report
0068-0613 Svenska Riksbyggen. Byggteknisk Information
0068-0621 Braby's Transvaal Directory
0068-063X Bradford's Directory of Marketing Research Agencies and Management Consultants in the United States and the World
0068-0672 Brandeis University. Society of Bibliophiles. Publications
0068-0699 Brasil Industrial *see* 0005-4585
0068-0702 Brassey's Annual - the Armed Forces Year-Book *see* 0305-6155
0068-0710 Brauereien und Maelzereien in Europa
0068-0729 Technische Universitaet Braunschweig. Pharmaziegeschichtlichen Seminar. Veroeffentlichungen *see* 0722-7159
0068-0745 Braunschweigisches Jahrbuch
0068-0761 Technion-Israel Institute of Technology. Braverman Memorial Lecture†
0068-0788 Brazil. Diretoria do Patrimonio Historico e Artistico Nacional. Revista *changed to* Brazil. Patrimonio Historico e Artistico Nacional. Revista
0068-0796 Brazil. Divisao de Pesquisas Ictiologicas. Serie Circular *see* 0374-6658
0068-080X Brazil. Instituto Nacional de Estudos e Pesquisas Educacionais. Conferencia Nacional de Educacao. Anais†
0068-0834 Brazil. Ministerio das Relacoes Exteriores. Biblioteca. Bibliografia Anual *changed to* Brazil. Ministerio das Relacoes Exteriores. Biblioteca. Aquisicoes Bibliograficas
0068-0850 Brazil. Servico de Piscicultura. Publicacao
0068-0877 Breifne
0068-0885 Uebersee-Museum, Bremen. Veroeffentlichungen. Reihe A: Naturwissenschaften
0068-0893 Uebersee-Museum, Bremen. Veroeffentlichungen. Reihe B: Voelkerkunde
0068-0907 Bremer Archaeologische Blaetter
0068-0915 Institut fuer Meeresforschung, Bremerhaven. Veroeffentlichungen†
0068-0931 Brewery Manual *see* 0305-8123
0068-094X Brewing and Malting Barley Research Institute. Annual Report
0068-0958 Brewing Industry Survey†
0068-0982 Bridge†
0068-1008 Brigham Young University. College of Engineering Sciences and Technology. Annual Engineering Symposium. Abstracts
0068-1016 Brigham Young University. Department of Geology. Geology Studies *changed to* Brigham Young University Geology Studies
0068-1032 Bristol and Gloucestershire Archaeological Society, Bristol, England. Transactions
0068-1040 Bristol Naturalists' Society. Proceedings
0068-1075 Britain: An Official Handbook
0068-1105 Britain in the World Today†
0068-113X Britannia
0068-1148 Britannica Atlas
0068-1156 Britannica Book of the Year
0068-1180 A C T F L Annual Review of Foreign Language Education *see* 0147-1236
0068-1199 Britannica Yearbook of Science and the Future *see* 0096-3291
0068-1210 British Aid Statistics; Statistics of U.K. Economic Aid to Developing Countries
0068-1229 Great Britain. British Airports Authority. Annual Report and Accounts
0068-1245 British and Foreign State Papers†
0068-1261 British Antarctic Survey. Scientific Reports†
0068-1288 British Archaeological Association. Journal
0068-1296 Who's Who in Industrial Editing *changed to* B.A.I.E. Membership Directory
0068-130X British Astronomical Association. Handbook
0068-1318 British Astronomical Association. Memoirs†
0068-1326 British Athletics *see* 0267-0267
0068-1334 British Authors Series
0068-1342 British Aviation Year Book
0068-1350 British Books in Print
0068-1377 B B C Annual Report and Handbook
0068-1385 British Bryological Society. Transactions *see* 0373-6687
0068-1407 British Catalogue of Music
0068-1415 British Chamber of Commerce in France. Year Book *changed to* Franco-British Chamber of Commerce and Industry. Year Book
0068-1423 British Columbia. Cancer Foundation. Annual Report *changed to* British Columbia Cancer Research Centre. Annual Report
0068-1431 University of British Columbia. Department of Geophysics and Astronomy. Publications†
0068-144X British Columbia. Ministry of Energy, Mines and Petroleum Resources. Bulletin
0068-1458 British Columbia. Department of Recreation and Conservation. Annual Report†
0068-1466 British Columbia. Department of Human Resources. Annual Report *changed to* British Columbia. Ministry of Social Services and Housing. Services for People. Annual Report (Year)
0068-1490 British Columbia. Forest Service. Annual Report *changed to* British Columbia. Ministry of Forests and Lands. Annual Report
0068-1520 British Columbia. Forest Service. Research Notes *see* 0226-9368
0068-1539 British Columbia. Forest Service. Research Review *changed to* British Columbia. Ministry of Forests and lands. Research Review
0068-1555 British Columbia Fruit Growers Association. Horticultural Conference Proceedings *changed to* British Columbia Fruit Growers Association. Horticultural Forum Proceedings
0068-1563 British Columbia Fruit Growers Association. Minutes of the Proceedings of the Annual Convention
0068-1571 British Columbia Geographical Series: Occasional Papers in Geography
0068-158X British Columbia Hospitals' Association. Proceedings of the Annual Conference *changed to* B. C. Health Association. Proceedings of the Annual Conference
0068-1598 British Columbia Insurance Directory. Insurance Companies, Agents and Adjusters
0068-1601 British Columbia Lumberman's Greenbook†
0068-161X British Columbia Municipal Yearbook
0068-1652 British Columbia Research Council. Annual Report *changed to* B.C. Research. Annual Report
0068-1687 University of British Columbia Library. Asian Studies Division. List of Catalogued Books. Supplement†
0068-1695 University of British Columbia. Center for Continuing Education. Occasional Papers in Continuing Education
0068-1709 University of British Columbia. Department of Civil Engineering. Soil Mechanics Series
0068-1725 University of British Columbia. Department of Geophysics and Astronomy. Annual Report
0068-1733 University of British Columbia. Department of Geology. Report *changed to* University of British Columbia. Department of Geological Sciences. Report
0068-1768 University of British Columbia. Faculty of Education. Journal of Education†
0068-1776 University of British Columbia. Faculty of Forestry. Foresty Bulletin *see* 0318-9171
0068-1784 University of British Columbia. Faculty of Forestry. Research Notes†
0068-1792 University of British Columbia. Faculty of Forestry. Research Papers†
0068-1806 University of British Columbia. Faculty of Forestry. Translations†
0068-1849 University of British Columbia Law Review
0068-1857 University of British Columbia Library. Reference Publication†
0068-1873 British Columbia. Department of Lands, Forests and Water Ressources. Water Resources Service. Report *changed to* British Columbia. Ministry of Environment and Parks. Annual Report
0068-1938 British Cycling Federation. Handbook
0068-1970 British Exports *changed to* British Exports
0068-1989 British Federation of Master Printers. Master Printers Annual *changed to* Printers Yearbook
0068-1997 British Film and T.V. Yearbook *changed to* Screen International Film and T.V. Yearbook
0068-2004 British Film Fund Agency. Annual Report
0068-2012 British Friesian Herd Book
0068-2020 British Glass Industry Research Association. Annual Report
0068-2039 British Goat Society. Herd Book
0068-2047 British Goat Society. Year Book
0068-208X British Hospitals Contributory Schemes Association. Directory of Convalescent Homes Serving the Provinces.
0068-2098 British Hospitals Contributory Schemes Association. Directory of Hospitals Contributory Scheme Benefits
0068-2101 British Hospitals Contributory Schemes Association. Report
0068-211X British Hospitals Home and Overseas†
0068-2128 B H R C A Guide to Hotels and Restaurants *see* 0307-062X
0068-2144 British Initials and Abbreviations†
0068-2152 British Institute in Eastern Africa. Annual Report
0068-2195 British International Law Cases
0068-2217 British Journal of Photography Annual
0068-2268 British Middle Market Directory *changed to* Guide to Key British Enterprises I and II
0068-2292 British Museum (Natural History) Bulletin. Botany
0068-2306 British Museum (Natural History) Bulletin. Historical
0068-2314 British Orthoptic Journal
0068-2322 British Paper and Board Industry Federation. Technical Association. Fundamental Research International Symposia *changed to* Paper Industry Technical Association. Fundamental Research International Symposia
0068-2330 British Paper and Board Industry Federation. Technical Association. Technical Papers
0068-2349 British Paper and Board Industry Federation. Technical Section. Yearbook†
0068-2365 British Petroleum Equipment and Services
0068-2381 Europlastics Year Book *see* 0306-5502
0068-239X British Printer Specification Manual *changed to* British Printer Dataguide
0068-2403 British Pteridological Society. Newsletter *see* 0301-9195
0068-242X British Railways Board. Report and Statement of Accounts
0068-2446 British Rowing Almanack
0068-2454 British School at Athens. Annual

ISSN INDEX 1355

0068-2462 British School at Rome. Papers. Archaeology
0068-2519 British Society for the History of Pharmacy. Transactions
0068-2578 British Standards Year Book *changed to* B S I Catalogue
0068-2586 British Steel Corporation. Annual Report and Accounts
0068-2616 British Tourist Authority. Digest of Tourist Statistics†
0068-2624 B T H A Directory†
0068-2632 British Trades Alphabet *changed to* B T A Studycards
0068-2640 British Transport Commission. Annual Report and Accounts†
0068-2659 British Transport Docks Board. Annual Report and Accounts *changed to* Associated British Ports Holdings PlC. Annual Report and Accounts
0068-2667 British Tourist Authority. Annual Report†
0068-2675 British Trust for Ornithology. Annual Report
0068-2683 British Waterways Board. Annual Report and Accounts
0068-2691 British Year Book of International Law
0068-2705 Univerzita J.E. Purkyne. Filozoficka Fakulta. Sbornik Praci. I: Rada Pedagogicka - Psychologicka
0068-2713 Broadcasting Yearbook *see* 0732-7196
0068-2721 Broadman Comments; International Sunday School Lessons
0068-273X Broads Book†
0068-2748 Broadside (New York, 1940)
0068-2780 Brookfield Bandarlog
0068-2799 Brookhaven Symposia in Biology
0068-2810 Brookings Institution. Reprint *changed to* Brookings Reprint Series
0068-2829 Brookings Research Report Series *changed to* Brookings Reprint Series
0068-2853 Brookside Monographs†
0068-2861 Brown and Haley Lecture Series†
0068-2888 Brown's Directory of North American Gas Companies *see* 0197-8098
0068-290X Brown's Nautical Almanac
0068-2918 Brunei Museum Journal
0068-2926 Bibliotheque Royale Albert 1er. Catalogue Collectif des Periodiques Etrangers†
0068-2934 Discotheque Nationale de Belgique. Catalogue General
0068-2942 Annuaire et Statistique de l'Enseignement Catholique†
0068-2985 Universite Libre de Bruxelles. Institut de Sociologie. Cahiers†
0068-2993 Universite Libre de Bruxelles. Institut d'Etudes Europeennes. Enseignement Complementaire. Nouvelle Serie†
0068-3000 Universite Libre de Bruxelles. Institut d'Etudes Europeennes. Theses et Travaux Economiques†
0068-3019 Universite Libre de Bruxelles. Institut d'Etudes Europeennes. Theses et Travaux Juridiques†
0068-3035 Bryn Mawr-Haverford Review†
0068-3043 Das Buch der Jugend
0068-3051 Buch und Buchhandel in Zahlen
0068-306X Institutul de Geologie si Geofizica. Dari de Seama ale Sedintelor
0068-3078 Muzeul de Istorie Naturala "Gr. Antipa." Travaux
0068-3086 Observatorul Astronomie din Bucuresti. Anuarul *changed to* Centrul de Astronomie si Stiinte Spatiale. Anuarul Astronomic
0068-3094 Observatorul Astronomic din Bucuresti. Observations Solaires *changed to* Centre de l'Astronomie et des Sciences Spatiales. Observations Solaires
0068-3108 Analele Universitatii Bucuresti. Fizica†
0068-3116 Universitatea Bucuresti. Analelf. Acta Logica†
0068-3124 Analele Universitatii Bucuresti. Biologie Animala†
0068-3132 Analele Universitatii Bucuresti. Biologie Vegetala†
0068-3140 Analele Universitatii Bucuresti. Chimie†
0068-3159 Analele Universitatii Bucuresti. Estetica†
0068-3167 Analele Universitatii Bucuresti. Filologie†
0068-3175 Analele Universitatii Bucuresti. Filozofie†
0068-3183 Analele Universitatii Bucuresti. Geologie†
0068-3191 Analele Universitatii Bucuresti. Geografie†
0068-3205 Analele Universitatii Bucuresti. Istorie†
0068-3213 Analele Universitatii Bucuresti. Limbi Clasice†
0068-3221 Analele Universitatii Bucuresti. Limbi Germanice†
0068-323X Analele Universitatii Bucuresti. Limbi Romanice†
0068-3248 Analele Universitatii Bucuresti. Limbi Slave†
0068-3256 Analele Universitatii Bucuresti. Limba si Literatura Romana†
0068-3264 Analele Universitatii Bucuresti. Literatura Universala si Comparata†
0068-3272 Analele Universitatii Bucuresti. Matematica-Mecanica†
0068-3280 Analele Universitatii Bucuresti. Pedagogie†
0068-3299 Analele Universitatii Bucuresti. Psihologie†
0068-3302 Analele Universitatii Bucuresti. Sociologie†
0068-3310 Analele Universitatii Bucuresti. Stiinte Juridice†
0068-3329 Acta Botanica Horti Bucurestiensis
0068-3345 Buddhist Publication Society. Report†
0068-3361 Buecherei des Augenarztes
0068-337X Buecherei des Frauenarztes
0068-3388 Buecherei des Orthopaeden
0068-3396 Ein Buechertagebuch
0068-340X Buenos Aires. Centro de Investigacion de Biologia Marina. Contribucion Cientificia
0068-3418 Buenos Aires. Instituto de Fitotecnia. Boletin Informativo
0068-3485 Universidad del Salvador. Anales
0068-3493 Universidad de Buenos Aires. Instituto Bibliotecologico. Publicacion
0068-3507 B and C J Directory†
0068-3523 Building Board Directory
0068-3531 Building Construction Cost Data
0068-354X Great Britain. Building Research Establishment. Annual Report
0068-3566 Building Societies. Year Book
0068-3612 National Free Library of Rhodesia. Annual Report *changed to* National Free Library of Zimbabwe. Annual Report
0068-3620 Bulgarska Akademiia na Naukite. Arkheologicheski Institut Izvestiia
0068-3639 Astronomicheski Kalendar na Observatoriiata v Sofia
0068-3655 Bulgarska Akademiia na Naukite. Botanicheski Institut. Izvestiia†
0068-3671 Bulgarska Akademiia na Naukite. Tsentralna Biblioteka. Izvestiia†
0068-371X Bulgarska Akademiia na Naukite. Tsentralna Khelmintologichna Laboratoriia. Izvestiia†
0068-3736 Bulgarska Akademiia na Naukite. Geofizichni Institut. Izvestiia *changed to* Balgarskoto Geofizichno Spisanije
0068-3744 Bulgarska Akademiia na Naukite. Geografski Institut. Izvestiia *changed to* Problemi na Geografijata
0068-3787 Bulgarska Akademiia na Naukite. Institut za Bulgarski Ezik. Izvestiia
0068-3817 Bulgarska Akademiia na Naukite. Institut po Morfologiia. Izvestiia†
0068-3841 Bulgarska Akademiia na Naukite. Institut po Obshta i Sravnitelna Patalogiia. Izvestiia†
0068-385X Bulgarska Akademiia na Naukite. Institut po Tekhnicheska Kibernetika. Izvestiia†
0068-3876 Bulgarska Akademiia na Naukite. Institut po Khidrologiia i Meteorologiia. Izvestiia *see* 0018-1331
0068-3884 Bulgarska Akademiia na Naukite. Institut za Pravni Nauki. Izvestiia†
0068-3949 Bulgarian Academy of Sciences, Sofia. Mathematical Institute. Bulletin†
0068-3957 Bulgarska Akademiia na Naukite. Mikrobiologichni Institut. Izvestiia†
0068-3965 Bulgarska Akademiia na Naukite. Institut za Muzikoznanie. Izvestiia†
0068-3973 Bulgarska Akademiia na Naukite. Institut po Filosofiia. Izvestiia†
0068-3981 Bulgarska Akademiia na Naukite, Sofia. Zoologicheski Institut S Muzei. Izvestiia *see* 0324-0770
0068-4007 Institut de Recherches Agronomiques Tropicales et des Cultures Vivrieres. Bulletin Agronomique†
0068-4015 Bulletin d'Archeologie Marocaine
0068-4023 Bulletin de Philosophie Medievale
0068-4031 Bulletin des Jeunes Romanistes†
0068-4058 Bulletin d'Histoire Economique et Sociale de la Revolution Francaise *see* 0766-4516
0068-4066 Bulletin Linguistique et Ethnologique
0068-4090 Bulletin of Sugar Beet Research. Supplement
0068-4104 Bulletin of Suicidology†
0068-4112 Bulletin of Suicidology. Supplements†
0068-4120 Bulletin of the European Communities. Supplement
0068-4139 Bulletin of Thermodynamics and Thermochemistry *see* 0149-2268
0068-4155 Bulletin Socialiste *changed to* Le Poing et la Rose
0068-4171 Institut National des Industries Extractives. Bulletin Technique: Securite et Salubrite†
0068-4198 Bulletins of Marine Ecology†
0068-4201 Bullinger's Postal and Shippers Guide for the United States and Canada
0068-421X Bundesanstalt fuer Pflanzenbau und Samenpruefung, Vienna. Jahrbuch *changed to* Bundesanstalt fuer Pflanzenbau, Vienna. Jahrbuch
0068-4236 Bureau International de l'Heure. Rapport Annuel
0068-4287 Burt Franklin American Classics in History and Social Sciences
0068-4295 Burt Franklin Art History and Art Reference Series
0068-4309 Burt Franklin Bibliography and Reference Series
0068-4317 Burt Franklin Essays in History, Economics, and Social Sciences
0068-4325 Burt Franklin Essays in Literature and Criticism
0068-4333 Monographs in Philosophy and Religious History
0068-4341 Burt Franklin Research and Source Works Series
0068-4376 Buses Annual
0068-4392 West Virginia University. Business and Economic Studies
0068-4406 Business Blue-Book of Southern Africa *changed to* Business Blue Book of S.A.
0068-4414 Business Education Index
0068-4430 University of New Mexico. Bureau of Business and Economic Research. Business Information Series†
0068-4449 Business Monitor: Miscellaneous Series. M2 Cinemas
0068-4457 Business Monitor: Miscellaneous Series. M3 Company Finance
0068-4465 Business Monitor: Miscellaneous Series. M4 Overseas Transactions
0068-4503 Business Who's Who of Australia
0068-4562 Buying and Selling United States Coins†
0068-4570 Bydgoskie Towarzystwo Naukowe. Wydzial Nauk Humanistycznych. Prace. Seria B (Jezyk i Literatura)
0068-4589 Bydgoskie Towarzystwo Naukowe. Wydzial Nauk Humanistycznych. Prace. Seria C (Historia i Archeologia)
0068-4597 Bydgoskie Towarzystwo Naukowe. Wydzial Nauk Technicznych. Prace. Seria Z: (Prace Zbiorowe)
0068-4600 Byers National Industrial Directory
0068-4635 Muzeum Gornoslaskie w Bytomiu. Rocznik. Seria Archeologia
0068-4643 Muzeum Gornoslaskie w Bytomiu. Rocznik. Seria Etnografia
0068-4651 Muzeum Gornoslaskie w Bytomiu. Rocznik. Seria Historia
0068-466X Muzeum Gornoslaskie w Bytomiu. Rocznik. Seria Przyroda
0068-4678 Muzeum Gornoslaskie w Bytomiu. Rocznik. Seria Sztuka
0068-4686 Byzantinobulgarica
0068-4694 C A T V and Station Coverage Atlas and 35-Mile Zone Maps *see* 0193-3639
0068-4708 C. C. Williamson Memorial Lecture†
0068-4716 C E Cost Guide for General Building Construction *see* 0270-1626
0068-4759 C A T V Buyer's Guide†
0068-4767 C A T V Systems Directory and Map Service *see* 0091-1984
0068-4775 Cadastro Brasileiro de Materias-Primas Farmaceuticas, Por Produto, Por Fabricante†
0068-4791 Centre de Geomorphologie, Caen. Bulletin
0068-4805 Universita degli Studi di Cagliari. Istituto di Storia Medioevale. Publicazioni
0068-4813 Economies et Societes. Serie F. Developpement, Croissance, Progres des Pays en Voie de Developpement
0068-4821 Economies et Societes. Serie A B. Economie du Travail
0068-483X Economies et Societes. Serie G. Economie Planifiee
0068-4848 Economies et Societes. Serie L. Economie Regionale†
0068-4856 Economies et Societes. Serie S. Etudes de Marxologie
0068-4864 Economies et Societes. Serie AF. Histoire Quantitative de l'Economie Francaise
0068-4872 Economies et Socieities. Serie T. Information - Recherche Innovation
0068-4880 Economies et Societes. Serie M. Philosophie - Sciences Sociales Economie
0068-4899 Economies et Societes. Serie AG. Progres et Agriculture
0068-4902 Economies et Societes. Serie P. Relations Economiques Internationales
0068-4953 Cahiers Bretons
0068-4961 Cahiers Canadiens Claudel†
0068-4996 Cahiers d'Allemand; Revue de Linguistique et de Pedagogie†
0068-5011 Cahiers de Civilisation Medievale. Supplement
0068-502X Cahiers de Droit d'Auteur†
0068-5038 Cahiers de la Quatrieme Internationale
0068-5046 Cahiers de l'Homme. Nouvelle Serie†
0068-5054 Cahiers de Micropaleontologie
0068-5070 Cahiers de Psychomecanique de Langage
0068-5089 Cahiers de Saint-Michel de Cuxa
0068-5097 Cahiers de Sciences Sociales†
0068-5143 Cahiers du Pacifique *see* 0180-9954
0068-5151 Cahiers du Tourisme
0068-516X Cahiers Ferdinand de Saussure
0068-5194 Cahiers Nepalais
0068-5208 Cahiers O.R.S.T.O.M. Serie Biologie†
0068-5224 Cahiers Rouge. Nouvelle Serie Internationale
0068-5232 Cahiers-Theatre
0068-5259 Cain
0068-5267 Cairngorm Club Journal
0068-5275 Egyptian National Museum. Library. Catalogue *changed to* Egyptian Museum. Library. Catalogue
0068-5283 Societe d'Archeologie Copte. Bibliotheque de Manuscrits
0068-5291 Societe d'Archeologie Copte. Bulletin

1356 ISSN INDEX

0068-5305 Societe d'Archeologie Copte. Textes et Documents
0068-5313 University of Cairo. Herbarium. Publications
0068-5356 Calcutta Management Association. Annual Report
0068-5364 Calcutta Research Series†
0068-5372 School of Tropical Medicine, Calcutta. Bulletin†
0068-5380 University of Calcutta. Centre of Advanced Study in Ancient Indian History and Culture. Lectures
0068-5399 University of Calcutta. Centre of Advanced Study in Ancient Indian History and Culture. Proceedings of Seminars
0068-5402 Calendar of International Film and Television Events *changed to* World Screen Bulletin and Calendar
0068-5410 Calendars of American Literary Manuscripts†
0068-5437 University of Calgary. Archaeological Association. Paleo-Environmental Workshop. Proceedings *changed to* University of Calgary. Archaeological Association. Archaeological Conference. Proceedings
0068-5453 Universidad del Valle Biblioteca. Publicaciones *changed to* Universidad del Valle. Departamento de Biliotecas. Boletin de Adquisiciones
0068-5461 California Academy of Sciences. Occasional Papers
0068-547X California Academy of Sciences. Proceedings
0068-5488 California. Administrative Office of the Courts. Annual Report
0068-5496 California. Air Resources Board. Annual Report
0068-5518 Preservation, Organization and Display of State of California's Historic Documents: Report to the California State Legislature†
0068-5526 Annotated Bibliography of Research in Economically Important Species of California Fish and Game. Supplement†
0068-5550 California. Department of Parks and Recreation. Archaeological Report *changed to* California Archeological Reports
0068-5569 California. Department of Forestry. Range Improvement Studies†
0068-5577 California. Department of Forestry. State Forest Notes *changed to* California Forestry Note
0068-5585 California Environmental Law: A Guide†
0068-5607 California Government Notes†
0068-5615 California Handbook
0068-5631 California Insect Survey. Bulletin
0068-564X California Institute of International Studies. Report *see* 0090-7103
0068-5658 California Institute of Technology. Division of Engineering and Applied Science. Report of Research and Other Activities *changed to* California Institute of Technology. Division of Engineering and Applied Science. Research Report
0068-5682 U.S. National Aeronautics and Space Administration. Jet Propulsion Laboratory. Technical Memorandum†
0068-5720 California Macadamia Society. Yearbook
0068-5739 California Manufacturers Register
0068-5755 California Natural History Guides
0068-5763 California Newspaper Directory *changed to* California Newspaper Publishers Association. Directory and Rate Book
0068-5771 California Public School Directory
0068-5798 California Slavic Studies†
0068-5801 California. State Board of Equalization. Annual Report
0068-581X Taxable Sales in California (Sales and Use Tax)
0068-5836 San Diego State University. Bureau of Business and Economic Research. Monographs
0068-5844 San Diego State University. Bureau of Business and Economic Research. Research Studies and Position Papers
0068-5879 California County Law Library Basic List
0068-5887 California Transportation and Public Works Conference. Proceedings *see* 0192-4117
0068-5895 California Studies in Classical Antiquity *see* 0278-6656
0068-5909 California Studies in the History of Art
0068-5917 California Studies in Urbanization and Environmental Design†
0068-5933 University of California, Berkeley. Archaeological Research Facility. Contributions
0068-5968 University of California, Berkeley. Center for Real Estate and Urban Economics. Reprint Series
0068-5976 University of California, Berkeley. Center for Real Estate and Urban Economics. Research Report *changed to* University of California, Berkeley. Center for Real Estate and Urban Economics. Working Paper
0068-600X University of California. Center for South and Southeast Asia Studies. Occasional Papers
0068-6018 University of California. Center for South and Southeast Asia Studies. Research Monograph Series
0068-6077 University of California. Institute of Business and Economic Research. Publications
0068-6093 University of California, Berkeley. Institute of International Studies. Research Series
0068-6115 University of California, Berkeley. Institute of Transportation Studies. Library References
0068-6123 University of California, Berkeley. Institute of Transportation Studies. Selected List of Recent Acquisitions of the Transportation Library†
0068-6166 University of California, Santa Barbara. Library. Annual Report†
0068-6182 University of California, Los Angeles. Institute of Archaeology. Archaeological Survey. Annual Report†
0068-6190 University of California, Los Angeles. African Studies Center. Occasional Paper†
0068-6204 University of California, Los Angeles. Institute of Archaeology. Archaeological Survey. Special Monograph Series *changed to* University of California, Los Angeles. Institute of Archaeology. Monograph Series
0068-6212 University of California, Los Angeles. Biotechnology Laboratory. Progress Report†
0068-6220 University of California, Los Angeles. Center for Medieval and Renaissance Studies. Publications
0068-6239 University of California, Los Angeles. Center for Medieval and Renaissance Studies. Contributions
0068-6247 University of California, Los Angeles. Center for the Study of Comparative Folklore and Mythology. Publications
0068-6255 University of California, Los Angeles. Institute of Industrial Relations. Monograph Series *see* 0739-439X
0068-6263 University of California, Los Angeles. Latin American Center. Reference Series
0068-628X University of California, Los Angeles. Museum of Cultural History. Occasional Papers
0068-6301 University of California, Davis. Water Resources Center. Contributions
0068-631X University of California Engineering and Physical Sciences Extension Series†
0068-6336 University of California Publications. Anthropological Records
0068-6344 University of California Publications. Classical Studies
0068-6352 University of California Publications. English Studies†
0068-6360 University of California Publications. Folklore Studies *changed to* University of California Publications. Folklore & Mythology Studies
0068-6379 University of California Publications in Anthropology
0068-6387 University of California Publications in Automatic Computation†
0068-6395 University of California Publications in Botany
0068-6409 University of California Publications in Contemporary Music†
0068-6417 University of California Publications in Entomology
0068-6433 University of California Publications in Egyptian Archaeology†
0068-6441 University of California Publications in Geography
0068-645X University of California Publications in Geological Sciences
0068-6468 University of California Publications in History†
0068-6476 University of California Publications in Librarianship†
0068-6484 University of California Publications in Linguistics
0068-6492 University of California Publications in Modern Philology
0068-6506 University of California Publications in Zoology
0068-6514 University of California Publications. Near Eastern Studies
0068-6522 University of California Publications. Occasional Papers†
0068-6530 Californians in Congress
0068-6549 Calwer Hefte†
0068-6557 Calwer Predigthilfen *changed to* Neue Calwer Predigthilfen
0068-659X Cambridge Air Surveys
0068-6603 Cambridge Authors' and Printers' Guides *changed to* Cambridge Authors' and Publishers' Guides
0068-6611 Cambridge Bibliographical Society. Transactions
0068-662X Cambridge Bibliographical Society. Transactions. Monograph Supplements
0068-6638 Cambridge Classical Texts and Commentaries
0068-6654 Cambridge Geographical Studies
0068-6689 Cambridge Latin American Studies
0068-6697 Cambridge Monographs in Experimental Biology
0068-6719 Cambridge Papers in Social Anthropology
0068-6727 Cambridge Papers in Sociology
0068-6735 Cambridge Philological Society. Proceedings
0068-6743 Cambridge Philological Society. Proceedings. Supplement
0068-6751 Cambridge Studies in International and Comparative Law
0068-676X Cambridge Studies in Linguistics
0068-6786 Cambridge Studies in Medieval Life and Thought. Third Series *changed to* Cambridge Studies in Medieval Life and Thought. Fourth Series
0068-6794 Cambridge Studies in Social Anthropology
0068-6808 Cambridge Studies in Sociology
0068-6816 Cambridge Texts and Studies in the History of Education
0068-6824 Cambridge Tracts in Mathematics and Mathematical Physics *changed to* Cambridge Tracts in Mathematics
0068-6832 Cambridge University. Department of Applied Economics. Monographs
0068-6840 Cambridge University. Department of Applied Economics. Occasional Papers
0068-6883 Cambridge University. Institute of Criminology. Bibliographical Series
0068-6891 Cambridge University. Oriental Publications
0068-6905 Camden Fourth Series
0068-693X Campground Guide for Tent and Trailer Tourists†
0068-6948 Camping Caravanning and Sports Equipment Trades Directory
0068-6956 Camping Club of Great Britain and Ireland. Year Book with List of Camp Sites *changed to* Camping Club Handbook and Sites List
0068-6964 Camping Guide†
0068-6980 Camping Sites in Britain and France *changed to* Practical Camper's Sites Guide
0068-7014 Can Manufacturers Institute. Annual Metal Cans Shipment Report *changed to* Can Manufacturers Institute. Annual Cans Shipment Report
0068-7057 Canada. Statistics Canada. Aviation Statistics Centre. Service Bulletin/Bulletin de Service du Centre des Statistiques de l'Aviation
0068-7065 Canada. Grain Commission. Marketings, Distribution and Visible Carry-over of Canadian Grain in and Through Licensed Elevators *see* 0380-8718
0068-7073 Canada. Statistics Canada. Aggregate Productivity Trends/Tendances de la Productivite des Agregats *see* 0317-7882
0068-7103 Canada. Statistics Canada. Crude Petroleum and Natural Gas Industry/Industrie du Petrole Brut et du Gaz Naturel
0068-7111 Canada. Statistics Canada. Dairy Statistics/Statistique Laitiere†
0068-712X Canada. Statistics Canada. Farm Net Income/Revenu Net Agricole
0068-7138 Canada. Statistics Canada. Placer Gold Mines, Gold Quartz Mines and Copper-Gold-Silver Mines/Placers d'Or Mines de Quartz Aurifere et Mines de Cuivre-Or-Argent *see* 0380-4968
0068-7146 Canada. Statistics Canada. Index of Farm Production/Indice de la Production Agricole
0068-7154 Canada. Statistics Canada. Livestock and Animal Products Statistics/Statistique du Betail et des Produits Animaux
0068-7162 Canada. Statistics Canada. Petroleum Refineries/Raffineries de Petrole†
0068-7189 Canada. Statistics Canada. Production of Poultry and Eggs/Production de Volaille et Oeufs
0068-7200 Canada. Statistics Canada. Retail Trade/Commerce de Detail†
0068-7227 Canada. Statistics Canada. System of National Accounts, Domestic Product by Industry/Systeme de Comptabilite Nationale. Produit Interieur par Industric: Releve de la Production *see* 0712-8762
0068-7278 Canada. Department of Agriculture. Analytical Chemistry Research Service. Research Report†
0068-7286 Canada. Agriculture Canada. Economics Branch. Trade in Agricultural Products
0068-7294 Canada. Department of Agriculture. Engineering Research Service, Ottawa. Research Report *changed to* Canada. Agriculture Canada. Engineering & Statistical Research Institute, Ottawa. Research Report
0068-7308 Canada. Agriculture Canada. Food Research Institute, Ottawa. Research Report
0068-7316 Canada. Agriculture Canada. Health of Animals Branch. Bovine Tuberculosis and Brucellosis†
0068-7324 Canada. Agriculture Canada. Livestock Market Review

ISSN INDEX 1357

0068-7375 Canada. Fisheries and Environment Canada. Annual Report *see* 0711-0782
0068-7383 Canada. Department of Insurance. Report. Co-Operative Credit Associations
0068-7391 Canada. Department of Insurance. Report. Trust and Loan Companies
0068-7405 Canada. Department of Insurance. Report of the Superintendent of Insurance
0068-7413 Canada. Department of Insurance. Report. Small Loans Companies and Money-Lenders
0068-743X Canada. Labour Canada. Wage Rates, Salaries and Hours of Labour
0068-7448 Canada. Women's Bureau. Women in the Labour Force: Facts and Figures *changed to* Canada. Women's Bureau. Women in the Labour Force
0068-7456 Canada. Department of National Health and Welfare. Annual Report
0068-7472 Canada. Agriculture Canada. Research Station, Melfort, Saskatchewan. Research Highlights. Annual Publications *changed to* Canada. Agriculture Canada. Research Station, Melfort, Saskatchewan. Research Station Report
0068-7499 Canada. Fisheries & Marine Service Annual. *changed to* Canada. Fisheries Research Board Annual Report
0068-7510 Canada. Fisheries and Marine Service. Biological Station, St. Andrews, New Brunswick. General Series Circular†
0068-7537 Canada. Fisheries Research Board. Bulletin *see* 0706-6503
0068-7545 Canada. Fisheries and Marine Service Review.†
0068-7553 Canada. Fisheries and Marine Service. Technical Report Series *see* 0706-6457
0068-7588 Canada. Department of the Environment. Forest Insect and Disease Survey. Annual Report *changed to* Canada. Canadian Forestry Service. Insect and Disease Conditions in Canada
0068-7626 Canada. Geological Survey. Bulletin
0068-7634 Canada. Geological Survey. Memoir
0068-7642 Canada. Geological Survey. Miscellaneous Report
0068-7650 Canada. Geological Survey. Paper
0068-7669 Canada. Hydrographic Service. Water Levels *see* 0706-2354
0068-7669 Canada. Hydrographic Service. Water Levels *see* 0706-2346
0068-7677 Canada in the Atlantic Economy†
0068-7685 Canada in World Affairs
0068-7693 Canada Land Inventory. Report
0068-7715 Canada. Atmospheric Environment Service. Climatological Studies
0068-7723 Canada. Atmospheric Environment Service. Ice Observations: Canadian Arctic†
0068-7731 Canada. Atmospheric Environment Service. Ice Observations: Canadian Inland Waterways†
0068-774X Canada. Atmospheric Environment Service. Ice Observations: Eastern Canadian Seaboard†
0068-7758 Canada. Atmospheric Environment Service. Ice Summary and Analysis, Canadian Arctic†
0068-7766 Canada. Atmospheric Environment Service. Ice Summary and Analysis, Eastern Canadian Seaboard†
0068-7774 Canada. Atmospheric Environment Service. Ice Summary and Analysis, Hudson Bay and Approaches†
0068-7782 Canada. Atmospheric Environment Service. Meteorological Translations
0068-7790 Canada. Atmospheric Environment Service. Snow Cover Data/Donnees d'Enneigement
0068-7804 Canada. Atmospheric Environment Service. Technical Memoranda
0068-7812 Canada. Mineral Resources Branch. Mineral Information Bulletin. *changed to* Canada. Mineral Policy Sector. Mineral Bulletins
0068-7839 Canada. Mineral Resources Branch. Mineral Survey *see* 0229-8325
0068-7847 Canada. Centre for Mineral and Energy Technology. Information Circular†
0068-7863 Canada. Department of Energy, Mines and Resources. Monographs†
0068-7871 Canada. Mines Branch. Research Report *changed to* Canada. Centre for Mineral and Energy Technology. Technology Series Reports
0068-7898 Canada. Expert Committee on Pesticide Use in Agriculture. Pesticide Research Report
0068-7901 Canada. National Energy Board. Annual Report
0068-7928 Canada. National Harbours Board. Annual Report *changed to* Canada. National Harbours Board. Port Directory
0068-7987 Canada. National Museums, Ottawa. Publications in Botany†
0068-7995 Canada. National Museums, Ottawa. Publications in Biological Oceanography†
0068-8002 Canada. National Museums, Ottawa. Publications in Ethnology†
0068-8010 Canada. National Museums, Ottawa. Publications in History†
0068-8037 Canada. National Museums, Ottawa. Publications in Zoology†
0068-8061 Canada. Oceanographic Data Centre. Data Record Series†
0068-8088 Canada. Public Archives. Register of Post Graduate Dissertations in Progress in History and Related Subjects *changed to* Canada. Register of Post Graduate Dissertations in Progress in History and Related Subjects
0068-8134 Canada Who's Who of the Poultry Industry
0068-8142 Canada Yearbook†
0068-8185 Canadian Agricultural Insect Pest Review
0068-8193 Canadian Almanac and Directory
0068-8207 Canadian Alpine Journal
0068-8215 Canadian Annual Review *see* 0315-1433
0068-8231 Canadian Architecture Yearbook *changed to* Canadian Architect Yearbook
0068-824X Canadian Archivist *see* 0318-6954
0068-8258 C.A.R. Scope *see* 0820-9006
0068-8274 C A A E Annual Report†
0068-8312 Canadian Association of Geographers. Newsletter *see* 0707-3844
0068-8320 Canadian Association of Management Consultants. Annual Report
0068-8347 Canadian Bankruptcy Reports
0068-8398 Canadian Books in Print
0068-8401 C B C Engineering Review
0068-841X Canadian Building Series†
0068-8428 Canadian Bureau for International Education. Bulletin *see* 0827-0678
0068-8436 Canadian Cancer Research Conference. Proceedings†
0068-8444 Canadian Ceramic Society. Journal
0068-8452 Canadian Chemical, Pharmaceutical and Product Directory
0068-8487 Canadian Conference of the Arts. Miscellaneous Reports
0068-8495 Canadian Conference on Research in the Rheumatic Diseases. Proceedings†
0068-8509 Canadian Conference on Social Welfare. Proceedings/Compte Rendu *changed to* Canadian Conference on Social Development. Proceedings/Compte Rendu
0068-8517 Canadian Conference on Uranium and Atomic Energy. Proceedings *changed to* Canadian Nuclear Association. Annual International Conference Proceedings
0068-855X Canadian Correspondence Courses for University Credit *changed to* Canadian University Distance Education Directory
0068-8584 Canadian Council on Social Development. Annual Report/Rapport Annuel
0068-8622 Canadian Dental Association. Directory†
0068-8649 Canadian Depreciation Guide†
0068-8657 C E A Handbook
0068-8665 Canadian Engineering & Industrial Year Book
0068-8681 Canadian Federation of Biological Societies. Newsletter
0068-869X Canadian Federation of Biological Societies. Proceedings *changed to* Canadian Federation of Biological Societies. Programme and Proceedings of the Annual Meeting
0068-8703 Canadian Federation of Biological Societies. Programme of the Annual Meeting *changed to* Canadian Federation of Biological Societies. Programme and Proceedings of the Annual Meeting
0068-8711 Canadian Federation and Municipalities. Annual Conference and Proceedings *see* 0708-9511
0068-872X Canadian Filmography Series†
0068-8746 Canadian Folk Music Journal
0068-8754 Canadian Food and Packaging Directory
0068-8762 Canadian Footwear & Leather Directory
0068-8770 Canadian Fruit Wholesalers' Association. Yearbook
0068-8789 Canadian Furniture & Furnishings Directory
0068-8797 Canadian Gas Association. Manufacturers' Section. Manufacturers Directory†
0068-8800 Canadian Gas Association. Statistical Summary of the Canadian Gas Industry
0068-8819 Canadian Geophysical Bulletin†
0068-8827 Canadian Good Roads Associations. Annual Conference *see* 0826-8193
0068-8835 Canadian Government Series
0068-8843 Canadian Gunner
0068-8851 Canadian Heart Foundation. Annual Report
0068-886X Canadian Historical Association. Historical Booklets. Brochures Historiques
0068-8878 Canadian Historical Association. Historical Papers
0068-8886 Canadian Historical Readings†
0068-8908 Canadian Horticultural Council. Annual Meeting Reports
0068-8916 Canadian Horticultural Council. Committee on Horticultural Research. Annual Reports
0068-8932 Canadian Hospital Directory
0068-8940 Canadian Housing Statistics
0068-8967 Canadian Industry Shows and Exhibitions
0068-8975 Canadian Institute of Actuaries. Yearbook
0068-8983 C I C A Handbook
0068-8991 Canadian Institute of Forestry. Annual Report *issued with* 0015-7546
0068-8991 Canadian Institute of Forestry. Annual Report
0068-9009 C.I.M. Directory
0068-9025 Canadian Insurance. Annual Statistical Issue
0068-9033 Canadian Insurance Law Bulletin Service
0068-9041 Canadian Jewellery & Giftware Directory
0068-905X Canadian Labour Terms
0068-9068 Canadian Library Association. Annual Reports†
0068-9092 Canadian Library Association. Occasional Papers
0068-9106 Canadian Library Association. Proceedings†
0068-9130 C L A Organization Handbook and Membership List *changed to* C L A Directory
0068-9157 Canadian Life and Health Insurance Facts
0068-9165 Canadian Local Histories to 1950. A Bibliography. Histoires Locales et Regionales Canadiennes des Origines A 1950
0068-919X Canadian Mathematical Congress. Proceedings†
0068-9203 Canadian Medical Directory
0068-9211 Canadian Mental Health Association. Annual Report
0068-9246 Canadian Meteorological Memoirs
0068-9254 Canadian Meteorological Society. Annual Congress *changed to* Canadian Meteorological and Oceanographic Society. Annual Congress
0068-9270 Canadian Minerals Yearbook
0068-9289 Canadian Mines Handbook
0068-9297 Canadian Mines Register of Dormant and Defunct Companies
0068-9300 Canadian Mines Register of Dormant and Defunct Companies. Supplement
0068-9319 Canadian Mining Manual *see* 0315-9140
0068-9335 Canadian Music Industry Directory†
0068-9378 Canadian National Institute for the Blind. National Annual Report
0068-9386 Canadian Nurses Association. Biennial Meeting. Folio of Reports†
0068-9424 Canadian Paraplegic Association. Annual Report
0068-9440 Canadian Phytopathological Society. Proceedings†
0068-9459 Canadian Plastics Directory and Buyer's Guide
0068-9505 Canadian Pulp and Paper Association. Pulp and Paper Report
0068-9556 Canada. Radio-Television Commission. Annual Report *changed to* Canada. Canadian Radio-Television and Telecommunications Commission. Annual Report
0068-9564 Canadian Real Estate Annual *changed to* Real Estate Development Annual
0068-9572 Canadian Red Cross Society. Annual Report
0068-9580 Canadian Rehabilitation Council for the Disabled. Annual Report
0068-9610 Canadian Seed Growers Association. Annual Report
0068-9629 Automotive Service Data Book
0068-9637 Canadian Skater†
0068-9645 Canadian Society for Education Through Art. Annual Journal
0068-9653 Canadian Society for Immunology. Bulletin
0068-9688 Canadian Society of Agronomy. Annual Meeting. Proceedings†
0068-9696 Canadian Society of Animal Production. Proceedings†
0068-970X Canadian Society of Biblical Studies. Bulletin
0068-9718 Canadian Society of Rural Extension. Meeting and Convention. Proceedings†
0068-9734 Canadian Special Truck Equipment Manual†
0068-9777 Canadian Studies in Criminology
0068-9793 Canadian Studies in History and Government†
0068-9807 Canadian Studies in Sociology†
0068-9815 Canadian Tax Foundation. Annual Report†
0068-9823 Canadian Tax Foundation. Provincial Finances *see* 0317-946X
0068-984X Canadian Technical Asphalt Association. Proceedings of the Annual Conference
0068-9858 Canadian Textile Directory
0068-9874 Canadian Theses

0068-9882 Canadian Tide and Current Tables
0068-9890 Canadian Toy Fair. Trade Show Directory *see* 0317-9443
0068-9904 Canadian Trade Index
0068-9912 Canada. Transport Commission. Annual Report
0068-9939 Canadian Tuberculosis and Respiratory Disease Association. Annual Report *changed to* Canadian Lung Association. Bulletin
0068-9955 Canadian Variety Merchandise Directory
0068-9963 Canadian Who's Who
0069-0007 Federal-Provincial Wildlife Conference. Transactions
0069-0015 Canadian Wildlife Service. Monograph Series
0069-0023 Canadian Wildlife Service. Progress Notes
0069-0031 Canadian Wildlife Service. Report Series
0069-0058 Canadian Yearbook of International Law
0069-0066 Canals Book†
0069-0082 Australia. National Library. Annual Report of the Council *see* 0313-1971
0069-0104 Canberra Papers on Strategy and Defense†
0069-0147 Cancer Facts and Figures
0069-0155 Cancer Incidence in Sweden
0069-0163 Cancer Institute, Tokyo. Selected Papers†
0069-0171 Cancer Seminar Proceedings
0069-018X Canned Food Pack Statistics†
0069-0198 Canterbury Archaeological Society. Occasional Papers
0069-0201 Canterbury Engineering Journal†
0069-021X Cape Cod Compass†
0069-0228 University of Cape Town. Department of Gynaecology. Annual Report *changed to* University of Cape Town. Department of Obstetrics and Gynaecology. Annual Report
0069-0244 Capuchin Annual†
0069-0260 Car and Driver Yearbook *changed to* Car and Driver Buyers Guide
0069-0309 Caravan Sites and Mobile Home Parks *changed to* Caravan Sites
0069-0317 Caravan & Chalet Sites Guide
0069-0333 Caravan Yearbook *changed to* Caravan Factfinder
0069-035X Cardiff Medical Society. Scientific Proceedings†
0069-0368 Cardinal O'Hara Series†
0069-0384 Cardiovascular Clinics
0069-0392 Cardiovascular Review; a Medical World News Publication†
0069-0406 Cardiovascular Surgery
0069-0422 Careers for School Leavers *changed to* Careers
0069-0430 Careers in Banking, Insurance, Finance†
0069-0449 Careers in Depth
0069-0457 Caribbean Conference Series†
0069-0465 Caribbean Bibliography†
0069-0473 Caribbean Documents†
0069-0481 Caribbean Economic Almanac
0069-0503 Caribbean Islands Research Institute. Annual Report *changed to* Caribbean Research Institute. Report
0069-0511 Caribbean Monograph Series
0069-052X Caribbean Scholars' Conference. Proceedings†
0069-0538 Caribbean Series†
0069-0546 Caridad, Ciencia y Arte *changed to* Nueva Enfermeria
0069-0554 Caritas Internationalis. International Yearbooks†
0069-0570 Caritas; Jahrbuch des Deutschen Caritasverbandes
0069-0597 Carl X Gustaf-Studier†
0069-0600 Carleton Mathematical Series
0069-0619 Carleton University, Ottawa. Department of Geology. Geological Papers†
0069-0635 Carnegie Corporation of New York. Annual Report
0069-0643 Carnegie Endowment for International Peace Report *changed to* Carnegie Endowment for International Peace in the 1970's
0069-0651 Carnegie Foundation for the Advancement of Teaching. Annual Report
0069-066X Carnegie Institution of Washington. Year Book
0069-0694 Carnet des Arts†
0069-0724 Carolina Population Center. Monograph†
0069-0732 Carotenoids Other Than Vitamin A
0069-0740 Carpet and Rug Institute. Directory and Report *changed to* Carpet and Rug Institute. Directory
0069-0767 Carpet Annual
0069-0783 Carson-Newman College, Jefferson City, Tennessee. Faculty Studies
0069-0805 Cartography
0069-0821 Institut des Peches Maritimes. Bulletin
0069-0848 Case Studies in Library Science†
0069-0872 Cases Decided in the Court of Claims of the United States†
0069-0880 Cass Library of African Studies. Africana Modern Library
0069-0899 Cass Library of African Studies. General Studies
0069-0902 Cass Library of African Studies. Researches and Travels
0069-0910 Cass Library of African Studies. South African Studies
0069-0929 Cass Library of African Studies. Travels and Narratives
0069-0937 Cass Library of Industrial Classics
0069-0945 Cass Library of Science Classics
0069-0961 Cassal Bequest Lectures
0069-097X Cassell's Directory of Publishing in Great Britain, The Commonwealth, Ireland and South Africa *changed to* Cassell and Publishers Association Directory of Publishing in Great Britain, the Commonwealth, Ireland, South Africa and Pakistan
0069-0988 Castle's Guide to the Fruit, Flower, Vegetable and Allied Trades
0069-0996 Castle's Town and County Trades Directory
0069-1011 Catalog for College Stores: General Merchandise Buyer's Guide for College Store Managers and Buyers†
0069-102X Catalog of Modern World Coins†
0069-1038 Catalog of Selected Films for Mental Health Education *changed to* Mental Health Media Center Film Catalog
0069-1046 Catalogo de Publicaciones Latinoamericanas Sobre Formacion Profesional
0069-1054 Catalogo dei Libri Italiani in Commercio *changed to* Catalogo dei Libri in Commercio
0069-1062 Catalog of Reprints in Series†
0069-1089 Catalogue de l'Edition Francaise *changed to* Livres Disponibles
0069-1097 Catalogue des Catalogues Automobile
0069-1100 Catalogue des Produits Agrees Par Qualite-France
0069-1135 Catalogue of Reproductions of Paintings Prior to 1860
0069-1143 Catalogue of Reproductions of Paintings, 1860-1973
0069-1151 Catalogue of Indian Chemical Plants *changed to* Guide to Indian Chemical Plants and Equipment
0069-116X Catalogus Musicus
0069-1178 Cataluna Exporta
0069-1186 Universita degli Studi di Catania. Istituto di Storia delle Tradizioni Popolari. Studi e Testi
0069-1194 Catering & Hotel Management Year Book & Diary†
0069-1208 Catholic Almanac
0069-1216 Catholic Central Union of America. Proceedings
0069-1224 Catholic Directory
0069-1232 Catholic Directory for the Clergy and Laity in Scotland *see* 0306-5677
0069-1267 Catholic Theological Society of America. Proceedings
0069-1291 Cavalcade and Directory of Fairs *see* 0361-4255
0069-1305 Cave Research Group of Great Britain. Transactions *see* 0263-760X
0069-1313 Cave Studies†
0069-1321 University of San Carlos. Series A: Humanities
0069-133X University of San Carlos. San Carlos Publications. Series B: Natural Sciences†
0069-1348 University of San Carlos. San Carlos Publications. Series C: Religion†
0069-1356 University of San Carlos. Series D: Occasional Monographs†
0069-1372 Celebrity Service International Contact Book
0069-1399 Celtica
0069-1402 Cement Industry Technical Conference. Record *changed to* I E E E Cement Industry Technical Conference. Record
0069-1429 Census of Industrial Production in Zambia
0069-1437 Census of U.S. Civil Aircraft
0069-1445 Review: Latin American Literature and Arts
0069-1461 Centers of Civilization Series
0069-147X Central African Power Corporation. Annual Report and Accounts
0069-1488 Central Asiatic Studies†
0069-1496 Central Bank of Ceylon. Annual Report
0069-150X Central Bank of China. Annual Report
0069-1518 Central Bank of Cyprus. Annual Report
0069-1526 Central Bank of Egypt. Board of Directors. Report *changed to* Central Bank of Egypt. Annual Report
0069-1534 Central Bank of Iraq, Baghdad. Report
0069-1542 Central Bank of Ireland. Annual Report
0069-1550 Central Bank of Jordan. Annual Report
0069-1569 Central Bank of Kenya. Annual Report
0069-1577 Central Bank of Nigeria. Annual Report and Statement of Accounts
0069-1585 Central Bank of the Philippines. Annual Report
0069-1593 Central Bank of Trinidad and Tobago. Report
0069-1607 Central Conference of American Rabbis. Yearbook
0069-1615 Central Conference of Teamsters. Officers' Report
0069-1623 Central Electric Railfans' Association. Bulletin
0069-1631 Central Institute of Research and Training in Public Cooperation, New Delhi. Publications
0069-164X Central Literary Magazine
0069-1674 Central Naugatuck Valley Regional Planning Agency. Annual Report
0069-1690 Central Road Research Institute, New Delhi. Road Research Paper
0069-1712 Scandinavian Institute of Asian Studies. Monograph Series
0069-1720 Centre Culturel Francais, Alger. Rencontres Culturelles
0069-1739 Centre Culturel International de Cerisy-La-Salle. Decades. Nouvelle Serie†
0069-1747 Centre de Cartographie Phytosociologique. Communications *changed to* Centre d'Ecologie Forestiere et Rurale. Communications
0069-1755 Centre International de Documentation et Sociale Africaine. Enquetes Bibliographiques
0069-1763 Centre International de Documentation Economique et Sociale Africaine. Monographies Documentaires
0069-1771 French-Canadian Civilization Research Center. Cahiers
0069-1798 France. Centre de Recherches sur les Zones Arides. Publications. Serie Geologie *changed to* Centre Geologique et Geophysique de Montpellier. Publications. Serie Geologie
0069-1801 Centre d'Ecologie Forestiere. Notes Techniques *changed to* Centre d'Ecologie Forestiere et Rurale. Notes Techniques. B: Herbageres
0069-1801 Centre d'Ecologie Forestiere. Notes Techniques *changed to* Centre d'Ecologie Forestiere et Rurale. Notes Techniques. A: Forestieres
0069-1836 Centre d'Etude du Sud-Est Asiatique et de l'Extreme-Orient. International Working Sessions. Proceedings†
0069-1844 Centre d'Etudes et de Documentation Europeennes. Cahiers. Annals†
0069-1852 Centre d'Etudes Pratiques d'Informatique et d'Automatique. Collection†
0069-1860 Arts du Spectacle en Belgique†
0069-1879 Centre d'Information des Services Medicaux d'Entreprises et Interentreprises. Annuaire†
0069-1895 Centre Europeen d'Etudes Burgondo-Medianes. Publication
0069-1909 C E L O S Bulletins†
0069-1917 Centre for Environmental Studies, London. Conference Paper†
0069-1925 Centre for Environmental Studies, London. Information Paper†
0069-1968 Centre National de Documentation Scientifique et Technique. Rapport d'Activite
0069-1976 Centre National de la Recherche Scientifique. Colloques Internationaux. Sciences Humaines
0069-1984 Centre National d'Archeologie et d'Histoire du Livre. Publication†
0069-1992 Centre National de Recherches Archeologiques en Belgique. Repertoires Archeologiques. Serie A: Repertoires Bibliographiques
0069-200X Centre National de Recherches Archeologiques en Belgique. Repertoires Archeologiques. Serie B: Repertoires des Collections
0069-2018 Centre National de Recherches Archeologiques en Belgique. Repertoires Archeologiques. Serie C: Repertoires Divers
0069-2026 C R I C Rapport de Recherche
0069-2034 Centre National d'Etudes Spatiales. Rapport d'Activite
0069-2050 Centre Regional de Recherche et de Documentation Pedagogiques de Lyon. Annales
0069-2069 Centre Regional de Documentation Pedagogique de Toulouse. Annales
0069-2077 Centres of Art and Civilization†
0069-2093 Centro Brasileiro de Pesquisas Fisicas. Notas Tecnicas†
0069-2107 Tropical Science Center, Costa Rica. Occasional Paper
0069-214X Centro de Investigaciones en Administracion Publica. Documentos de Trabajo *changed to* Centro de Estudios de Estado y Sociedad. Documentos de Trabajo
0069-2166 Centro de Salud "Max Arias Schreiber", Lima. Congreso Nacional de Tuberculosis y Enfermedades Respiratorias
0069-2204 Centro Studi per la Magna Grecia, Naples. Pubblicazioni Proprie
0069-2212 Center for Agricultural Publishing and Documentation. Agricultural Research Reports†
0069-2220 Ceramic Plants in Canada†
0069-2239 Ceramics and Glass Series *changed to* Ceramics and Glass: Science and Technology Series
0069-2247 Cercle d'Etudes Numismatiques. Travaux
0069-2255 Cerebral Vascular Diseases. Conference *changed to* Princeton Research Conferences on Cerebrovascular Diseases
0069-2263 Ceredigion

ISSN INDEX 1359

0069-228X Ceskoslovenska Akademie Ved. Rozpravy. M P V: Rada Matematickych a Prirodnich Ved
0069-2298 Ceskoslovenska Akademie Ved. Rozpravy. S V: Rada Spolecenskych Ved
0069-2301 Ceskoslovenska Akademie Ved. Rozpravy. T V: Rada Technickych Ved
0069-2328 Ceskoslovenska Pediatrie
0069-2336 Ceskoslovenska Psychiatrie
0069-2344 Ceskoslovenska Radiologie
0069-2352 Sri Lanka. Department of National Museums. Translations Series†
0069-2360 Sri Lanka Export Directory
0069-2379 Ceylon Journal of Science. Biological Sciences
0069-2387 Chain Shoe Stores and Leased Shoe Department Operators
0069-2395 Chain Store Age Supermarket Sales Manual†
0069-2417 Chalmers Tekniska Hoegskola. Handlingar†
0069-2441 Survey of Local Chambers of Commerce
0069-245X Chamber of Mines of South Africa. Research Review†
0069-2476 Chambers Trades Register. Lancashire, Cheshire, and North Wales *see* 0309-5649
0069-2484 Chambers Trades Register. Midlands†
0069-2492 Chambers Trades Register of Scotland *see* 0309-5630
0069-2506 Chambers Trades Register. South Wales and South West England†
0069-2514 Chambers Trades Register. Yorkshire Northumberland and Durham†
0069-2522 Chambre de Commerce d'Agriculture et d'Industrie de Bamako, Mali. Annuaire Statistique *changed to* Mali. Direction Nationale de la Statistique et de L'informatique. Annuaire Statistique
0069-2530 Chambre de Commerce, d'Industrie et des Mines du Cameroun. Rapport Annuel
0069-2549 Chambre de Commerce et d'Industrie d'Alger. Centre d'Etudes Economiques. Publication†
0069-2557 Chambre de Commerce Franco-Asiatique. Annuaire des Membres
0069-2565 Chambre de Commerce Japonaise en France. Annuaire
0069-2581 Chambre Officielle Franco Allemande de Commerce et d'Industrie. Liste des Membres
0069-259X Chambre Syndicale des Mines de Fer de France. Rapport d'Activite
0069-2603 Chambre Syndicale Nationale des Entreprises et Industries de l'Hygiene Publique. Annuaire
0069-2611 Chambre des Ingenieurs-Conseils de France. Annuaire
0069-2646 Champlain Society, Toronto. Report
0069-2654 Chanakya Defence Annual
0069-2662 Chandler and Boatbuilder Trade Directory *changed to* Boat Equipment Buyers' Guide
0069-2697 Charbonnages de France. Rapport *changed to* Charbonnages de France. Rapport d'Activite
0069-2727 Charles E. Merrill Monograph Series in the Humanities and Social Sciences†
0069-2735 Charles F. Kettering Foundation. Annual Report *changed to* Kettering Report
0069-2751 Charles W. Hunt Lecture†
0069-276X Charles Warren Center for Studies in American History. Annual Report†
0069-2778 Chart
0069-2786 Charter
0069-2794 Chartered Insurance Institute, London. Journal *see* 0309-4928
0069-2808 Chartered Insurance Institute, London. Yearbook *see* 0309-4928
0069-2824 Checklists in the Humanities and Education
0069-2840 Chefs-d'Oeuvre de la Science-Fiction†
0069-2859 Chefs-d'Oeuvre Interdits†
0069-2867 Chelates in Analytical Chemistry: A Collection of Monographs†
0069-2875 ChemBooks†
0069-2883 Chemical Analysis
0069-2891 Chemical Buyers Guide
0069-2921 Chemical Engineering Progress. Reprint Manuals†
0069-293X Chemical Engineering Progress. Safety in Air and Ammonia Plants *see* 0149-3701
0069-2948 Chemical Engineering Progress Symposium Series *see* 0065-8812
0069-2956 Chemical Engineering Progress. Technical Manuals *see* 0149-3701
0069-2964 Chemical Guide to Europe†
0069-2972 Chemical Guide to the United States†
0069-2980 Chemical Industry Directory
0069-3022 Chemical Society, London. Annual Reports on the Progress of Chemistry. Section A: General, Physical and Inorganic Chemistry *see* 0260-1818
0069-3030 Royal Society of Chemistry. Annual Reports on the Progress of Chemistry. Section B: Organic Chemistry
0069-3073 Chemie, Physik und Technologie der Kunststoffe in Einzeldarstellungen *see* 0171-709X
0069-3111 Chemistry and Biochemistry of Amino Acids, Peptides, and Proteins
0069-312X Chemistry and Industry Buyers' Guide†
0069-3138 Chemistry and Physics of Carbon: A Series of Advances
0069-3146 Chemistry of Functional Groups
0069-3154 Chemistry of Heterocyclic Compounds
0069-3162 Chemistry of Natural Products
0069-3197 Chess Book List
0069-3219 Chiba University. Faculty of Horticulture. Transactions†
0069-3227 Chiba University. Faculty of Horticulture. Technical Bulletin
0069-3235 Art Institute of Chicago. Museum Studies
0069-3243 Chicago Buyer's Guide *changed to* Buyers' Guide and Industrial Directory of Chicago
0069-3251 Chicago, Cook County and Illinois Industrial Directory
0069-326X Chicago Crime Commission. Annual Report†
0069-3278 Chicago History of American Civilization
0069-3286 Chicago Lectures in Mathematics
0069-3294 Chicago Lectures in Physics
0069-3316 University of Chicago. Center for Health Administration Studies. Research Series†
0069-3324 University of Chicago. Center for Middle Eastern Studies. Publications†
0069-3340 University of Chicago. Department of Geography. Research Papers
0069-3359 University of Chicago. Graduate School of Business. Selected Papers
0069-3367 University of Chicago Oriental Institute. Publications
0069-3375 University of Chicago Studies in Library Science
0069-3391 Chigiana
0069-3405 C A D U Publications *changed to* A R D U Publication
0069-3413 Child Health in Israel
0069-3456 Children Welcome!
0069-3472 Children's Books: Awards and Prizes
0069-3480 Children's Books in Print
0069-3499 Children's Books of the Year†
0069-3502 Suggested as Holiday Gifts *changed to* Children's Books: One Hundred Titles for Reading and Sharing
0069-3510 Chile. Comision de Planeamiento Integral de la Educacion. Bibliografia de Investigaciones y Estudios en Educacion†
0069-3529 Chile. Comision de Planeamiento Integral de la Educacion. Publicacion†
0069-3537 Chile. Servicio Agricola y Ganadero. Division Proteccion Pesquera. Anuario Estadistico *changed to* Chile. Servicio Nacional de Pesca. Anuario Estadistico de Pesca
0069-3545 Chile. Superintendencia de Educacion Publica. Cuadernos†
0069-3553 Universidad de Chile. Departamento de Astronomia. Publicaciones
0069-357X Universidad de Chile. Departamento de Geologia. Serie Communicaciones
0069-3588 Universidad de Chile. Departamento de Geologia. Serie Publicaciones†
0069-3596 Universidad Catolica de Chile. Facultad de Teologia. Anales
0069-3634 Chilton's Auto Repair Manual
0069-3642 Chimes
0069-3677 China Glass and Tableware Red Book Directory
0069-3685 China Medical Board of New York. Annual Report
0069-3715 Chiron
0069-3723 Chittagong Port Trust. Yearbook of Information *changed to* Chittagong Port Authority. Yearbook
0069-3758 Chord and Discord
0069-3774 University of Canterbury. Department of Psychology and Sociology. Research Projects
0069-3790 Lincoln College. Agricultural Economics Research Unit. Research Report
0069-3804 Lincoln College. Agricultural Economics Research Unit. Technical Paper†
0069-3820 Lincoln College. Department of Horticulture. Bulletin
0069-3839 Lincoln College. Farmers' Conference. Proceedings
0069-3855 Christian Camping International Directory *changed to* Guide to Christian Camps & Conference Centers
0069-3863 Christian Endeavour Year Book *changed to* Christian Endeavour Programme Book
0069-3871 Christian Periodical Index
0069-3898 Christian Service Training Series†
0069-391X Handbook for Christian Writers *changed to* Successful Writers and Editors Guidebook
0069-3928 Christmas: An American Annual of Christmas Literature and Art
0069-3936 Chromatographic Science Series
0069-3944 Chromosomes Today†
0069-3952 Chronologie des Communautes Europeennes†
0069-3960 Chronology of the United Nations†
0069-3979 Church and Society Series†
0069-3987 Church of England Yearbook
0069-3995 Church of Scotland. Yearbook
0069-4029 Churchman's Pocket Book and Diary *changed to* Church Pocket Book and Diary
0069-4037 CIBA Foundation. Study Groups†
0069-4045 CIBA Zeitschriften†
0069-4053 Ciencia e Sociedade: Temas e Debates†
0069-4061 Cincinnati Art Museum. Bulletin
0069-4088 Cincinnati Classical Studies. Supplementary Monograph†
0069-410X Excavations of the University of Cincinnati: Guide Book†
0069-4118 Cine Club del Uruguay. Cuadernos
0069-4134 Cineguia
0069-4177 Circe
0069-4215 Circum-Spice
0069-4231 C R F Listing of Contributions of National Level Political Committees to Incumbents and Candidates for Public Offices†
0069-424X C R F Listing of Political Contributiors of Five Hundred Dollars or More†
0069-4258 Civic Municipal Reference Manual and Purchasing Guide *changed to* Civic Public Works Reference Manual and Buyer's Guide
0069-4266 University of Illinois at Urbana-Champaign. Civil Engineering Studies. Construction Research†
0069-4274 University of Illinois at Urbana-Champaign. Civil Engineering Studies. Structural Research Series
0069-4290 Civilisations et Societes
0069-4304 Civilization of the American Indian
0069-4312 Civilta Asiatiche
0069-4339 Civilta Veneziana. Dizionari Dialettali e Studi Linguistici
0069-4347 Civilta Veneziana. Fonti e Testi. Serie Terza
0069-4355 Civilta Veneziana. Fonti e Testi. Serie Prima: Fonti e Testi per la Storia dell'Arte Veneta
0069-4371 Civilta Veneziana. Saggi
0069-438X Civilta Veneziana. Studi
0069-4401 Clark Guidebooks†
0069-441X Clarke Institute of Psychiatry. Monograph Series
0069-4444 Clasicos Colombianos
0069-4452 Classic European Historians†
0069-4460 Classical Association. Proceedings
0069-4487 Classics in Anthropology
0069-4495 Classics in Education†
0069-4509 Classics of British Historical Literature
0069-4525 Classified Directory of Wisconsin Manufacturers
0069-4533 Classiques de la Pensee Politique
0069-4541 Classiques de la Renaissance en France. Premiere Serie†
0069-4592 Clay Resources Bulletin
0069-4606 Clean Air Year Book *see* 0140-6795
0069-4614 Clegg's International Directory of the World's Book Trade†
0069-4630 Poultry Health and Management Short Course. Proceedings†
0069-4649 Clemson University Review of Industrial Management and Textile Science†
0069-4657 Clemson University. Water Resources Research Institute. Report
0069-4665 Catalogue des Theses de Pharmacie Soutenues en France *see* 0758-6922
0069-4681 Universite de Clermont-Ferrand II. Annales Scientifiques. Serie Biologie Animale
0069-469X Universite de Clermont-Ferrand II. Annales Scientifiques. Serie Biologie Vegetale
0069-4703 Universite de Clermont-Ferrand II. Annales Scientifiques. Serie Chemie
0069-4711 Universite de Clermont-Ferrand II. Annales Scientifiques. Serie Geologie et Mineralogie
0069-472X Universite de Clermont-Ferrand 2. Annales Scientifiques. Serie Mathematique
0069-4738 Universite de Clermont-Ferrand II. Annales Scientifiques. Serie Physique
0069-4746 Universite de Clermont-Ferrand II. Annales Scientifiques. Serie Physiologie Animale
0069-4754 Cles de l'Entreprise†
0069-4770 Clin-Alert
0069-4789 University of Illinois at Urbana-Champaign. Clinic on Library Applications of Data Processing. Proceedings
0069-4797 Clinical Approaches to the Problems of Childhood: The Langley Porter Child Psychiatry Series†
0069-4800 Clinical Conference on Cancer. Papers†
0069-4819 Clinical Endocrinology†
0069-4827 Clinical Neurosurgery; Proceedings
0069-4835 Clinics in Developmental Medicine
0069-4843 Closed-Circuit Television and Educational Television; Bibliographical References
0069-4851 Co-Operation†
0069-4886 Coach Tours in Britain and Ireland *changed to* Luxury Coach Tours in Britain & Europe
0069-4894 Coal Mines in Canada†
0069-4916 Coal Traffic Annual
0069-4924 Coates's Herd Book (Beef)
0069-4932 Coates's Herd Book (Dairy)
0069-4967 Coffee Drinking in the United States†
0069-4983 Coins Market Values

ISSN INDEX

0069-4991 Coke Oven Managers' Association. Year Book
0069-5009 Cold Spring Harbor Laboratory. Annual Report
0069-5017 Colecao Filosofia†
0069-5025 Coleccion Aberri ta Azkatasuna†
0069-5033 Coleccion "Aniversarios Culturales"
0069-505X Coleccion Canonica
0069-5068 Coleccion Ciencia Urbanistica
0069-5076 Coleccion Filosofica
0069-5084 Coleccion "Foros y Seminarios." Serie Foros
0069-5092 Coleccion "Foros y Seminarios." Serie Seminarios
0069-5106 Coleccion Historica
0069-5114 Coleccion "Humanism y Ciencia"
0069-5122 Coleccion Juridica
0069-5130 Coleccion Monografica Africana†
0069-5149 Coleccion Pensamiento Argentino†
0069-5165 Collana di Cultura
0069-5203 Collana di Studi e Saggi
0069-5254 Collana Ricciana. Fonti
0069-5262 Collect British Stamps
0069-5270 Collectanea Historiae Musicae
0069-5319 Collected Works on Cardio-Pulmonary Disease
0069-5335 Collection de Sociologie Generale et de Philosophie Sociale†
0069-5343 Collection d'Histoire Contemporaine
0069-5351 Collection Dictionnaires des Idees dans les Litteratures Occidentales. Litterature Francaise†
0069-5378 Collection Etudes et Travaux de la Revue "Mediterranee"†
0069-5386 Figures de Wallonie
0069-5416 Collection "Pilotes"†
0069-5459 Litteratures Anciennes
0069-5513 Collections: Les Idees du Jour
0069-553X College and Adult Reading *changed to* College and Adult Reading
0069-5548 Football Guide
0069-5572 College Blue Book
0069-5580 College de France. Annuaire
0069-5599 College des Medecins et Chirurgiens de la Province de Quebec. Bulletin *see* 0315-2979
0069-5602 Baccalaureate Education in Nursing: Key to a Professional Career in Nursing
0069-5688 College Facts Chart
0069-5696 College Music Symposium
0069-570X College of Dairy Agriculture, Hokkaido. Journal *see* 0388-001X
0069-570X College of Dairy Agriculture, Hokkaido. Journal *see* 0388-0028
0069-5718 College of Insurance. General Bulletin
0069-5726 College of Physicians and Surgeons of British Columbia. Medical Directory
0069-5734 College Placement Annual *changed to* C P C Annual
0069-5777 Collezione di Filosofia
0069-5793 Collier's Yearbook
0069-5807 Colloque de Metallurgie
0069-5815 Colloques Internationaux d'Histoire Maritime. Travaux
0069-5823 Colloquium on Scottish Studies. Proceedings *changed to* Scottish Tradition
0069-5831 Colloquium on the Law of Outer Space. Proceedings
0069-584X Colloquim Series on Transportation. Proceedings *see* 0076-3993
0069-5858 Bibliothekar-Lehrinstitut des Landes Nordrhein-Westfalen. Arbeiten aus dem B L I *see* 0721-7587
0069-5866 Bibliothekar-Lehrinstitut des Landes Nordrhein-Westfalen. Bibliographische Hefte *see* 0721-7587
0069-5874 Universitaet zu Koeln. Geologisches Institut. Sonderveroeffentlichungen
0069-5882 Universitaet zu Koeln. Institut fuer Geophysik und Meteorologie. Mitteilungen
0069-5890 Universitaet Zu Koeln. Jahrbuch
0069-5904 Banco de la Republica Estadisticas Basicas.†
0069-5920 Universidad Nacional de Colombia. Centro de Bibliografia y Documentacion. Boletin Informativo *changed to* Universidad Nacional de Colombia. Biblioteca Central. Boletin de Adquisiciones
0069-5939 Colombo Law Review
0069-5947 Colombo Plan Bureau. Technical Cooperation Under the Colombo Plan. Report *changed to* Colombo Plan Bureau. The Colombo Plan Council Report
0069-5963 Colombo Plan for Co-operative Economic Development in South and South-East Asia. Report of the Consultative Committee *changed to* Colombo Plan for Co-operative Economic and Social Development in Asia and the Pacific. Consultative Committee. Proceedings and Conclusions
0069-5971 Colonial Williamsburg Archaeological Series
0069-598X Coloquio de Estudos Luso Brasileiros. Anais
0069-5998 Color Photography†
0069-6005 Colorado. Cooperative Wildlife Research Unit. Special Scientific Reports. Technical Papers†
0069-6013 Colorado. Department of Highways. Traffic Volume Study *changed to* Colorado State Highway Condition and Volume Report
0069-6048 Colorado Rail Annual
0069-6056 Colorado School of Mines. Professional Contributions
0069-6099 Colorado State University. Fluid Mechanics Papers†
0069-6110 Colorado State University. Hydrology Papers†
0069-6129 Colorado State University. Sanitary Engineering Papers†
0069-6145 University of Colorado. Institute of Arctic and Alpine Research. Occasional Papers
0069-6161 University of Colorado Libraries. Report†
0069-6277 Colston Research Society, Bristol, England. Proceedings of the Symposium. Colston Research Papers
0069-6285 Columbia Biological Series
0069-6293 Columbia County History (Oregon)
0069-6307 Columbia Essays in International Affairs. The Dean's Papers†
0069-6315 Columbia Essays on Modern Writers†
0069-6323 Columbia Essays on the Great Economists
0069-6331 Columbia Studies in Economics
0069-634X Columbia University-Presbyterian Hospital School of Nursing. Alumnae Association. Magazine
0069-6358 Columbia University Studies in International Organization†
0069-6366 Columbia University Studies in Jewish History, Culture, and Institutions†
0069-6412 Comitatus; a Journal of Medieval and Renaissance Studies
0069-6439 Marine Marchand: Etudes et Statistiques *changed to* Transport Maritime: Etudes et Statistiques
0069-6498 Comite International des Poids er Mesures. Comite Consultatif pour la Definition du Metre. Travaux *changed to* Bureau International des Poids et Mesures. Recueil de Travaux
0069-651X Comite National de l'Organisation Francaise. Annuaire
0069-6528 Comite National Francais de Geodesie et Geophysique. Comptes-Rendus†
0069-6536 Comite National Francais de Geodesie et Geophysique. Rapport National Francais a l'U G G I†
0069-6552 Petrole (Year)
0069-6579 Commentationes Biologicae†
0069-6587 Commentationes Humanarum Litterarum
0069-6609 Commentationes Physico-Mathematicae
0069-6617 Commerce Exterieur de la Republique du Chad
0069-6625 Annuaire du Commerce Franco-Italien
0069-6633 Commerce in Nigeria *see* 0189-5036
0069-6676 Commercial Transport Handbook and Buyer's Guide for S.A. *changed to* Transport Manager's Handbook
0069-6692 Commission of the European Communities. Etudes: Serie Aide au Developpement *changed to* Commission of the European Communities. Studies: Development Series
0069-6706 Commission of the European Communities. Etudes: Serie Concurrence-Rapprochement des Legislations *changed to* Commission of the European Communities. Studies: Competition-Approximation of Legislation
0069-6714 Commission of the European Communities. Etudes: Serie Energie *changed to* Commission of the European Communities. Studies: Energy Series
0069-6730 Commission of the European Communities. Etudes: Serie Politique Sociale *changed to* Commission of the European Communities. Studies: Social Policy Series
0069-6749 General Report on the Activities of the European Communities
0069-6757 Commission of the European Communities. Investments in the Community Coal Mining and Iron and Steel Industries. Report on the Survey
0069-6765 Commission of the European Communities. Studies: Agricultural Series†
0069-6773 Commission of the European Communities. Studies: Economic and Financial Series†
0069-679X Commission of the European Communities. Studies: Transport Series†
0069-6811 Commissione Italiana per la Geofisica. Pubblicazioni. Serie I Q S Y†
0069-682X C E D Newsletter
0069-6838 Committee for International Cooperation in Information Retrieval Among Patent Offices. Bulletin.†
0069-6846 Committee for International Cooperation in Information Retrieval Among Patent Offices. Proceedings of Annual Meetings†
0069-6854 Committee on Institutional Cooperation. Annual Report *changed to* Committee on Institutional Cooperation. Biennial Report
0069-6862 Commodity Year Book
0069-6870 Commonwealth Acoustic Laboratories, Sydney. Annual Report *see* 0311-8983
0069-6897 Commonwealth Agricultural Bureaux. List of Research Workers†
0069-6935 Commonwealth Bureau of Nutrition. Annotated Bibliographies *changed to* C.A.B. International Bureau of Nutrition. Annotated Bibliographies
0069-7052 Commonwealth Forestry Bureau Annotated Bibliographies *changed to* C.A.B. International. Forestry Bureau. Annotated Bibliographies
0069-7109 Commonwealth Institute, London. Annual Report
0069-7133 Commonwealth Law Reports
0069-7141 Commonwealth Mycological Institute. Phytopathological Papers *changed to* C.A.B. International. Mycological Institute. Phytopathological Papers
0069-7168 Commonwealth Press Union. Book of Quinquennial Conference†
0069-7184 Commonwealth Scientific and Industrial Research Organization. Annual Report
0069-7192 C S I R O Film Catalogue
0069-7222 Commonwealth Scientific and Industrial Research Organization. Division of Applied Geomechanics. Report†
0069-7249 Commonwealth Scientific and Industrial Research Organization. Division of Geomechanics. Technical Report
0069-7257 Commonwealth Scientific and Industrial Research Organization. Division of Geomechanics. Technical Paper†
0069-7265 Commonwealth Scientific and Industrial Research Organization. Division of Applied Geomechanics. Technical Memorandum†
0069-7273 Commonwealth Scientific and Industrial Research Organization. Division of Animal Health. Annual Report *see* 0812-7336
0069-7281 Commonwealth Scientific and Industrial Research Organization. Division of Animal Physiology. Report. *see* 0155-7742
0069-729X Commonwealth Scientific and Industrial Research Organization. Division of Building Research. Building Study†
0069-732X Commonwealth Scientific and Industrial Research Organization. Division of Entomology. Report
0069-7338 Commonwealth Scientific and Industrial Research Organization. Division of Entomology. Technical Paper
0069-7346 Commonwealth Scientific and Industrial Research Organization. Division of Fisheries and Oceanography. Fisheries Synopsis†
0069-7370 Commonwealth Scientific and Industrial Research Organization. Division of Fisheries and Oceanography. Annual Report *see* 0725-4598
0069-7397 Commonwealth Scientific Industrial Research Organization. Division of Fisheries and Oceanography. Report *see* 0726-4291
0069-7419 Commonwealth Scientific and Industrial Research Organization. Division of Food Research. Report of Research
0069-7427 Commonwealth Scientific and Industrial Research Organization. Division of Food Research. Technical Paper
0069-7435 Commonwealth Scientific and Industrial Research Organisation. Division of Horticultural Research. Report
0069-7443 Commonwealth Scientific and Industrial Research Organization. Division of Irrigation Research. Report†
0069-746X Commonwealth Scientific and Industrial Research Organization. Division of Land Use Research. Technical Paper *see* 0810-4387
0069-7486 Commonwealth Scientific and Industrial Research Organization. Division of Mechanical Engineering. Circular†
0069-7494 Commonwealth Scientific and Industrial Research Organization. Division of Mechanical Engineering. Engineering Development Reports *changed to* Commonwealth Scientific and Industrial Research Organization. Division of Mechanical Engineering. Technical Reports
0069-7508 Commonwealth Scientific and Industrial Research Organization. Division of Mechanical Engineering. Report†
0069-7524 Commonwealth Scientific and Industrial Research Organization. Division of Mathematical Statistics. Technical Paper†

0069-7540 Commonwealth Scientific and Industrial Research Organization. Division of Plant Industry. Annual Report *changed to* Commonwealth Scientific and Industrial Research Organization. Division of Plant Industry. Report
0069-7575 Commonwealth Scientific and Industrial Research Organization. Division of Radiophysics. Report *changed to* Commonwealth Scientific and Industrial Research Organization. Division of Radiophysics. Research Activities
0069-7583 Commonwealth Scientific and Industrial Research Organization. Division of Soils. Biennial Report *see* 0729-4336
0069-7591 Commonwealth Scientific and Industrial Research Organization. Division of Soils. Soil Publications†
0069-7613 Commonwealth Scientific and Industrial Research Organization. Division of Tropical Pastures. Technical Paper *changed to* Commonwealth Scientific and Industrial Research Organization. Division of Tropical Crops and Pastures. Technical Paper
0069-7648 Commonwealth Scientific and Industrial Research Organization. Land Research Series†
0069-7680 Commonwealth Scientific and Industrial Research Organisation. Wheat Research Unit. Report
0069-7699 Commonwealth Secretariat. Commodities Division. Dairy Produce†
0069-7702 Commonwealth Secretariat. Commodities Division. Fruit†
0069-7710 Commonwealth Secretariat. Commodities Division. Meat†
0069-7729 Commonwealth Secretariat. Commodities Division. Plantation Crops†
0069-7737 Commonwealth Secretariat. Commodities Division. Vegetable Oils and Oilseeds†
0069-7745 Commonwealth Universities Yearbook
0069-7761 Annuaire des Communautes d'Enfants
0069-777X Communications Handbook
0069-7788 Communist China Problem Research Series
0069-7796 Communist China Yearbook Series
0069-7818 Community Council of Greater New York. Budget Standard Service. Annual Price Survey and Family Budget Costs†
0069-7842 Community Improvement Corporation. Annual Report
0069-7850 Community Mental Health Journal Monograph Series†
0069-7893 Comparative Juridical Review
0069-794X Comparazione dei Salari e del Costo del Lavoro in Europa†
0069-7958 Compendio Statistico Italiano
0069-7966 Compendium of Pharmaceuticals and Specialties
0069-7974 Complete Book of Engines†
0069-7982 Complete Chevrolet Book†
0069-7990 Complete Ford Book†
0069-8008 Complete Volkswagen Book†
0069-8016 Composers of the Americas
0069-8024 Wilson & Wilson's Comprehensive Analytical Chemistry
0069-8032 Comprehensive Biochemistry *changed to* New Comprehensive Biochemistry
0069-8040 Comprehensive Chemical Kinetics
0069-8067 Comprehensive Media Guide: Korea†
0069-8075 Comptes Nationaux de la Belgique
0069-8091 Compton Yearbook *changed to* Compton's Yearbook
0069-8105 Computer Applications in the Natural and Social Sciences *see* 0308-4221
0069-8121 Computer Index†
0069-8148 Association for Computing Machinery. Annual Computer Personnel Research Conference Proceedings†
0069-8164 Computer Service Buyers Guide†
0069-8180 Computer Yearbook
0069-8202 Comunidad Latinoamericana de Escritores. Boletin *changed to* Comunidad Latinoamericana de Escritores. Revista
0069-8210 Comunidad. Suplementos†
0069-8245 Concise Statistical Yearbook of Greece
0069-8288 The Concrete Year Book
0069-8296 Condon Lectures†
0069-830X Confederation des Industries Ceramiques de France. Annuaire
0069-8326 Confederation Nationale des Groupes Folkloriques Francais. Annuaire†
0069-8350 Conference Board Cumulative Index
0069-8369 Conference Board. Report on Company Contributions *see* 0146-0986
0069-8393 Conference in Reading. Proceedings†
0069-8407 Conference in the Study of Twentieth-Century Literature, Michigan State University. Proceedings†
0069-8415 Conference of Chief Justices. Proceedings†
0069-8474 Conference of State Sanitary Engineers. Report of Proceedings
0069-8490 Advances in X-Ray Analysis
0069-8512 Conference on Biological Sonar and Diving Mammals. Proceedings†
0069-8520 Perugia Quadrennial International Conferences on Cancer. Proceedings
0069-8547 Conference on Frontiers in Education. Digest *see* 0190-5848
0069-8555 Conference on Human Relations in Industry. Proceedings
0069-8563 Conference on Labor, New York University. Proceedings *see* 0193-3418
0069-8571 Conference on Land Surveying, Purdue University. Proceedings†
0069-858X Conference on Laser Engineering and Applications *changed to* Conference on Lasers and Electro-Optics (Publications)
0069-8598 Conference on Latin American History. Publications†
0069-8601 Conference on United Nations Procedures. Report *see* 0743-9180
0069-8636 Conference on Radar Meteorology. Preprints
0069-8644 Conference on Remote Systems Technology. Proceedings
0069-8652 Conference on Research in Income and Wealth *changed to* Studies in Income and Wealth
0069-8679 Conference on Severe Local Storms. Preprints
0069-8687 National Tax Association - Tax Institute of America. Proceedings of the Annual Conference
0069-8695 Conference on Teacher Education in the Eastern Caribbean. Report *changed to* Eastern Caribbean Standing Conference on Teacher Education. Report
0069-8741 Conference on Trace Substances in Environmental Health. Proceedings *see* 0361-5162
0069-875X Conference on Underground Transmission and Distribution. Record *see* 0018-9510
0069-8784 Conferencias de Bioquimica
0069-8792 Conflict Studies
0069-8814 Confluence. Etats des Recherches en Sciences Sociales: Surveys of Research in the Social Sciences†
0069-8830 Zaire. Direction de la Statistique et des Etudes Economiques. Annuaire des Statistiques du Commerce Exterieur *see* 0304-5692
0069-8849 Congregational Church in England and Wales. Congregational Year book *changed to* United Reformed Church in the United Kingdom. United Reformed Church Year Book
0069-8857 Congregational Council for World Mission. Annual Report *changed to* C W M Report
0069-8881 Congres Archeologique de France (Publication.)
0069-8911 Congres National de Speleologie. Actes
0069-892X Congressional Record Digest and Tally of Roll Call Votes
0069-8938 Congressional Staff Directory
0069-8946 Coniectanea Biblica. New Testament Series
0069-8954 Coniectanea Biblica. Old Testament Series
0069-8970 Connecticut Academy of Arts and Sciences. Memoirs
0069-8989 Connecticut Academy of Arts and Sciences. Transactions
0069-8997 Storrs Agricultural Experiment Station. Research Report
0069-9012 Connecticut College Monograph†
0069-9020 Connecticut. Department of Community Affairs Division of Research and Program Evaluation. Construction Activity Authorized by Building Permits. Summary *changed to* Connecticut Housing Production and Permit Authorized Construction
0069-9039 Connecticut Master Transportation Plan
0069-9047 University of Connecticut. Center for Real Estate and Urban Economic Studies. General Series
0069-9055 Connecticut Urban Research Report
0069-9063 University of Connecticut. Institute of Water Resources. Report Series
0069-908X Connolly's Suppressed Writings
0069-9101 U.S. Department of the Interior. Conservation Bulletins†
0069-911X Conservation Directory
0069-9128 Fish and Wildlife Facts†
0069-9136 Conservation of Library Materials
0069-9144 Conservation of Nature and Natural Resources *changed to* Nature and Environment Series
0069-9152 U.S. Department of the Interior. Conservation Yearbook.†
0069-9160 Consortium for the Study of Nigerian Rural Development†
0069-9179 Consortium for the Study of Nigerian Rural Development. C S N R D Working Paper†
0069-9187 Construction in Hawaii
0069-9195 Israel. Central Bureau of Statistics. Construction in Israel
0069-9209 C I R I A. Bulletin *see* 0305-4047
0069-9217 Construction Writers Association. Newsletter
0069-9233 U. S. Federal Trade Commission. Consumer Bulletins†
0069-9241 Consumers' Research Magazine Handbook of Buying†
0069-9276 U.S. National Bureau of Standards. Consumer Information Series†
0069-9284 Consumers Directory
0069-9292 Contabilidad Nacional de Espana
0069-9306 Contact†
0069-9314 Containerization: A Bibliography
0069-9322 Contamination Control Directory†
0069-9330 Contemporary African Monographs
0069-9357 Contemporary American History Series
0069-9381 Contemporary Drama Series
0069-942X Contemporary Issues Series
0069-9446 Contemporary Neurology Series
0069-9454 Contemporary Neurology Symposia†
0069-9527 Continental Camping & Caravan Sites†
0069-9535 Continental Research Series
0069-956X Continuing Engineering Studies Series *changed to* College - Industry Education Conference. Proceedings
0069-9578 Contract Carpeting†
0069-9616 Contributii Botanice
0069-9624 Contributions in Afro-American and African Studies
0069-9640 Texas A & M University. College of Geosciences. Contributions in Oceanography
0069-9667 Contributions to Indian Sociology
0069-9683 Contributions to Library Literature†
0069-9691 Contributions to Marine Science
0069-9705 Contributions to Sensory Physiology
0069-9713 Contributions to the History of Science and Technology in Baltics. *see* 0130-3252
0069-973X Control Magazine
0069-9748 Convegno di Studi Sulla Magna Grecia. Atti†
0069-9764 Convegno Nazionale dei Commercianti de Mobili. Atti e Relazioni†
0069-9772 Convegno Nazionale per la Civilta del Lavoro. Atti.†
0069-9780 Cooper Monographs on English and American Language and Literature
0069-9799 Cooperador Dental
0069-9810 Cooperative Education Association Membership Directory
0069-9829 C I C R I S Directory and Guide to Resources *changed to* C I C R I S Directory
0069-9837 Cooperative Trade Directory for Southeast Asia
0069-9845 Coordination Chemistry
0069-9861 Danmarks Biblioteksskole. Skrifter
0069-987X Geoteknisk Institut, Copenhagen. Bulletin
0069-9896 Denmark. Kongelige Bibliotek. Fund og Forskning
0069-9918 Koebenhavns Universitet. Filosofiska Fakultet. Extracts†
0069-9950 Copyright Law Symposium
0069-9969 Copyright Laws and Treaties of the World. Supplements
0069-9977 Coral Gables Conference on Fundamental Interactions at High Energy. (Proceedings)†
0069-9993 Corn Annual
0070-0002 Cornell Biennial Electrical Engineering Conference
0070-0010 Cornell International Agricultural Development Mimeographs *changed to* Cornell International Agriculture Mimeographs
0070-0029 Cornell International Industrial and Labor Relations Reports
0070-0053 Cornell Studies in Industrial and Labor Relations
0070-0061 Cornell University. Center for Housing and Environmental Studies. Research Reports *changed to* Cornell University. City and Regional Planning Publications. Research Reports
0070-0096 Cornell University. Modern Indonesia Project. Bibliography Series†
0070-0118 Tree Fruit Production Recommendations *changed to* Cornell Recommendations for Commercial Tree-Fruit Production
0070-0126 Cornell University. New York State School of Industrial and Labor Relations. Annual Institute for Training Specialists. (Publication)†
0070-0134 New York State School of Industrial and Labor Relations. Bulletin
0070-0142 Industrial and Labor Relations Bibliography Series
0070-0177 I L R Paperbacks
0070-0185 New York State School of Industrial and Labor Relations. Key Issues Series
0070-0207 Cornell University. New York State School of Industrial and Labor Relations. Technical Monograph Series†
0070-0215 Cornell University. Southeast Asia Program. Data Papers†
0070-0223 Cornell University. Thailand Project. Interim Reports Series†
0070-024X Cornish Archaeology
0070-0282 Corporate Management Tax Conference
0070-0290 Corporate Pension Fund Seminar. Proceedings†
0070-0304 Corporation des Ingenieurs Forestiers du Quebec. Congres Annuel. Texte des Conferences *changed to* Ordre des Ingenieurs Forestiers du Quebec. Congres Annuel. Texte des Conferences
0070-0312 Corpus Antiquitatum Americanensium†

0070-0320 Corpus Catholicorum
0070-0339 Corpus der Romanischen Kunst im Saechsisch-Thueringischen Gebiet†
0070-0347 Corpus Medicorum Graecorum
0070-0355 Corpus Medicorum Latinorum†
0070-0363 Corpus Mensurabilis Musicae
0070-038X Corpus Palladianum
0070-0398 Corpus Scriptorum Christianorum Orientalium: Aethiopica
0070-0401 Corpus Scriptorum Christianorum Orientalium: Arabica
0070-041X Corpus Scriptorum Christianorum Orientalium: Armeniaca
0070-0428 Corpus Scriptorum Christianorum Orientalium: Coptica
0070-0436 Corpus Scriptorum Christianorum Orientalium: Iberica
0070-0444 Corpus Scriptorum Christianorum Orientalium: Subsidia
0070-0452 Corpus Scriptorum Christianorum Orientalium: Syriaca
0070-0460 Corpus Scriptorum de Musica
0070-0479 Corpus Vasorum Antiquorum. Italia
0070-0495 Corpus Vasorum Antiquorum. Poland†
0070-0509 Correctional Literature Published in Canada†
0070-0517 Correspondance d'Orient†
0070-0533 Cosmetic Formulary†
0070-0576 Costa Rica. Ministerio de Hacienda Oficina del Presupesto. Informe
0070-0584 Universidad de Costa Rica. Serie Agronomia†
0070-0592 Universidad de Costa Rica. Serie Bibliotecologia†
0070-0606 Universidad de Costa Rica. Series Ciencias Juridicas y Sociales†
0070-0614 Universidad de Costa Rica. Serie de Filosofia†
0070-0622 Universidad de Costa Rica. Serie Educacion†
0070-0630 Universidad de Costa Rica. Serie Economia y Estadistica†
0070-0649 Universidad de Costa Rica. Serie Economia y Estadistica. Estadistica Universitaria†
0070-0657 Universidad de Costa Rica. Serie Historia y Geografia†
0070-0665 Universidad de Costa Rica. Serie Textos Universitarios†
0070-0673 Cotton International
0070-069X Council for Basic Education. Occasional Papers
0070-072X Council for Old World Archaeology: C O W A Surveys and Bibliographies. Area 1: British Isle†
0070-0738 Council for Old World Archaeology: C O W A Surveys and Bibliographies. Area 2: Scandinavia†
0070-0746 Council for Old World Archaeology: C O W A Surveys and Bibliographies. Area 3: Western Europe: Part 1†
0070-0754 Council for Old World Archaeology: C O W A Surveys and Bibliographies. Area 3: Western Europe: Part 2†
0070-0762 Council for Old World Archaeology: C O W A Surveys and Bibliographies. Area 4: Western Mediterranean†
0070-0770 Council for Old World Archaeology: C O W A Surveys and Bibliographies. Area 5: Central Europe†
0070-0789 Council for Old World Archaeology: C O W A Surveys and Bibliographies. Area 6: Balkans†
0070-0797 Council for Old World Archaeology: C O W A Surveys and Bibliographies. Area 7: Eastern Mediterranean†
0070-0800 Council for Old World Archaeology: C O W A Surveys and Bibliographies. Area 8: European Russia†
0070-0819 Council for Old World Archaeology: C O W A Surveys and Bibliographies. Area 9: Northeast Africa†
0070-0827 Council for Old World Archaeology: C O W A Surveys and Bibliographies. Area 10. Northwest Africa†
0070-0835 Council for Old World Archaeology: C O W A Surveys and Bibliographies. Area 11. West Africa†
0070-0843 Council for Old World Archaeology: C O W A Surveys and Bibliographies. Area 12. Equatorial Africa†
0070-0851 Council for Old World Archaeology: C O W A Surveys and Bibliographies. Area 13. South Africa†
0070-086X Council for Old World Archaeology: C O W A Surveys and Bibliographies. Area 14. East Africa†
0070-0878 Council for Old World Archaeology: C O W A Surveys and Bibliographies. Area 15. Western Asia†
0070-0886 Council for Old World Archaeology: C O W A Surveys and Bibliographies. Area 16. Southern Asia†
0070-0894 Council for Old World Archaeology: C O W A Surveys and Bibliographies. Area 17. Far East†
0070-0916 Council for Old World Archaeology: C O W A Surveys and Bibliographies. Area 18. Northern Asia†
0070-0924 Council for Old World Archaeology: C O W A Surveys and Bibliographies. Area 19. Southeast Asia†
0070-0932 Council for Old World Archaeology: C O W A Surveys and Bibliographies. Area 20. Indonesia†
0070-0940 Council for Old World Archaeology: C O W A Surveys and Bibliographies. Area 21. Pacific Islands†
0070-0959 Council for Old World Archaeology: C O W A Surveys and Bibliographies. Area 22. Australia†
0070-1009 Council of Europe. Consultative Assembly. Documents; Working Papers/Documents de Seance *see* 0252-0656
0070-1017 Council of Europe. Consultative Assembly. Orders of the Day, Minutes of Proceedings/Ordres du Jour, Proces Verbaux *see* 0377-1962
0070-1033 Council of Europe. Consultative Assembly. Texts Adopted by the Assembly/Textes Adoptes Par l'Assemblee *see* 0377-6093
0070-105X Council of Europe. European Treaty Series
0070-1076 Council of Graduate Schools in the United States. Proceedings of the Annual Meeting
0070-1106 Council of Organizations Serving the Deaf. Annual Forum Proceedings†
0070-1114 Council of Organizations Serving the Deaf. Council Membership Directory†
0070-1157 Suggested State Legislation
0070-1173 Council on Legal Education for Professional Responsibility. Newsletter†
0070-1181 Council on Library Resources Report *changed to* Council on Library Resources Annual Report
0070-1211 Councils, Committees and Boards
0070-1238 Countdown: Canadian Nursing Statistics†
0070-1262 Country Dance and Song
0070-1270 Country Life Annual†
0070-1300 County and Municipal Year Book for Scotland *see* 0305-6562
0070-1327 County Louth Archaeological and Historical Journal
0070-136X Course Guide for High School Theatre *changed to* Secondary School Theatre Association Course Guide
0070-1386 Court of Justice of the European Communities. Recueil de la Jurisprudence *changed to* Court of Justice of the European Communities. Report of Cases of the Court
0070-1394 Courtenay Library of Reformation Classics
0070-1408 Courtenay Studies in Reformation Theology
0070-1416 Cranbrook Institute of Science, Bloomfield Hills, Michigan. Bulletin
0070-1424 Cranfield Fluidics Conference. Proceedings†
0070-1467 Credit Manual of Commercial Laws
0070-1475 Cremation Society of Great Britain. Conference Report†
0070-1483 Cri du Peuple
0070-1505 Crime and Delinquency Issues: Monographic Series *changed to* Crime and Delinquency Topics: Monograph Series
0070-1521 Criminal Appeal Reports
0070-153X Critical Essays in Modern Literature
0070-1548 Critical Review Melbourne *changed to* Critical Review
0070-1556 Critiques de Notre Temps Et...
0070-1572 Croissance Urbaine et Progres des Nations
0070-1580 Croner's Reference Book for Employers
0070-1599 Croner's Reference Book for Exporters
0070-1602 Croner's Reference Book for Importers
0070-1610 Croner's Road Transport Operation
0070-1629 Croner's World Directory of Freight Conferences
0070-167X Crystal Structures†
0070-1688 Cuadernos de Historia del Arte
0070-1696 Cuadernos de Historia del Islam. Serie Monografica Islamica Occidentalia *changed to* Cuadernos de Historia del Islam
0070-170X Cuadernos de Orientacion
0070-1718 Cuadernos de Pedagogia
0070-1726 Cuadernos de Sintesis†
0070-1734 Cuadernos de Sociologia†
0070-1750 Cuadernos del Mexico Prehispanico†
0070-1785 Cuadernos para Estudiantes: Los Poetas
0070-1793 Cumulative Index to Nursing Literature, Nursing Subject Headings *see* 0146-5554
0070-1815 Universidade do Parana. Departamento de Historia. Boletim
0070-184X Current Australian Serials†
0070-1858 Current British Directories
0070-1866 Current Caribbean Bibliography
0070-1882 Current Coins of the World†
0070-1904 Current Concerns in Clinical Psychology†
0070-1947 Index of Current Equine Research†
0070-1955 Current European Directories
0070-1971 Current Issues in Higher Education
0070-198X Current Issues in Music Education
0070-1998 Current Legal Problems
0070-2005 Current Medical Information and Terminology
0070-203X Current Practice in Orthopaedic Surgery†
0070-2064 Current Problems in Dermatology
0070-2080 Current Psychiatric Therapies†
0070-2099 Nebraska Symposium on Motivation (Publication)
0070-2110 Current Therapy in Dentistry†
0070-2129 Current Topics in Bioenergetics
0070-2137 Current Topics in Cellular Regulation
0070-2145 Current Topics in Clinical and Community Psychology
0070-2153 Current Topics in Developmental Biology
0070-2161 Current Topics in Membranes and Transport
0070-217X Current Topics in Microbiology and Immunology
0070-2188 Current Topics in Pathology
0070-2196 Current Topics in Surgical Research
0070-2234 Cusanus-Gesellschaft. Buchreihe
0070-2242 Cushman Foundation for Foraminiferal Research. Special Publication
0070-2250 Custom House Guide
0070-2277 Cycle Buyers Guide
0070-2307 Cyprus. Agricultural Research Institute. Annual Report
0070-2315 Cyprus. Agricultural Research Institute. Technical Bulletin
0070-2323 Cyprus. Budget: Estimates of Revenue and Expenditure
0070-2331 Cyprus Chamber of Commerce and Industry Directory
0070-234X Cyprus. Department of Agriculture. Soils and Plant Nutrition Section. Report
0070-2366 Cyprus. Department of Antiquities. Monographs
0070-2374 Cyprus. Department of Antiquities. Annual Report
0070-2390 Cyprus. Ministry of Labour and Social Insurance. Annual Report
0070-2404 Cyprus. Department of Social Welfare Services. Annual Report
0070-2412 Cyprus. Department of Statistics and Research. Economic Report
0070-2420 Cyprus. Department of Statistics and Research. Statistics of Imports and Exports
0070-2439 Cyprus. Department of Statistics and Research. Shipping Statistics†
0070-2447 Cystic Fibrosis: A Bibliography†
0070-2455 Cystic Fibrosis Club Abstracts
0070-2463 Cytobiologie *see* 0171-9335
0070-2471 Czasopismo Prawno-Historyczne
0070-248X Czechoslovakia. Federalni Statisticky Urad. Statisticka Rocenka
0070-2498 D.A.T.A. Book of Discontinued Transistors *see* 0730-4846
0070-251X Dacia; Revue d'Archeologie et d'Histoire Ancienne
0070-2528 Daedalus
0070-2544 Daffodils
0070-2595 Dairy Products and Sugar in Coffee in the United States *changed to* How do Americans Drink Their Coffee?
0070-2617 Institut Fondamental d'Afrique Noire. Catalogues et Documents
0070-2625 Institut Fondamental d'Afrique Noire. Initiations et Etudes Africaines
0070-2633 Institut Fondamental d'Afrique Noire. Memoires
0070-2668 Dana-Report
0070-2676 Dance Directory
0070-2684 Dance Magazine Annual *changed to* Performing Arts Directory
0070-2692 Dance World
0070-2714 Dania Polyglotta
0070-2749 Danish Yearbook of Philosophy
0070-2765 Danmarks Folkeminder†
0070-2781 Danmarks Vareindfoersel og- Udfoersel
0070-279X Dans le Fantastique†
0070-2803 Dansk Elvaerksstatistik *see* 0106-4711
0070-282X Danske Forlaeggerforening. Faelleslagerkatalog
0070-2838 Danske Landmandsbank. Annual Report *changed to* Danske Bank af 1871. Annual Report
0070-2846 Danske Magazin
0070-2854 Oplagstal og Markedstal
0070-2862 Dante Studies
0070-2889 Data Processing in Medicine†
0070-2897 Datos y Cifras de la Ensenanza en Espana
0070-2900 David Davies Memorial Institute of International Studies, London. Annual Memorial Lecture
0070-2927 University of Toronto. David Dunlap Observatory. Publications†
0070-2943 Davison's Knit Goods Trade†
0070-2951 Davison's Textile Blue Book
0070-2986 Davy's Devon Herd Book
0070-2994 Dawn in Central Asia
0070-3001 Dawn Song and All Day
0070-3028 Dayton Art Institute. Annual Report *changed to* Dayton Art Institute. Annual Report and Bulletin
0070-3044 University of Dayton. School of Education. Abstracts of Research Projects
0070-3052 University of Dayton. School of Education. Workshop Proceedings
0070-3060 De Proprietatibus Litterarum. Series Major
0070-3079 De Proprietatibus Litterarum. Series Minor

ISSN INDEX 1363

0070-3087 De Proprietatibus Litterarum. Series Practica
0070-3095 Dead Sea Works, Beersheba, Israel. Report of the Directors
0070-3109 Dealers in Coins
0070-3141 December
0070-315X Dechema Monographien
0070-3176 Decisions of the United States Courts Involving Copyrights
0070-3192 Decorating Contractor Annual Directory
0070-3206 Decorative Art and Modern Interiors†
0070-3222 Deems Lectureship†
0070-3230 Defects in Crystalline Solids *changed to* Defects in Solids
0070-3249 Deiches Fund Studies of Public Library Service†
0070-3257 Dein Kind†
0070-3273 Delaware Geological Survey Bulletins
0070-3281 Delaware Nurse *changed to* Delaware Nurses' Association Reporter
0070-329X Delaware. Department of Highways and Transportation. Traffic Summary
0070-3303 Delegations to the United Nations†
0070-3311 Institute of Economic Growth, Delhi. Census Studies
0070-3338 Delphica†
0070-3346 Democrat
0070-3354 Demographie et Sciences Humaines
0070-3362 Demographie et Societes
0070-3370 Demography
0070-3389 Demokratische Existenz Heute†
0070-3419 Denken, Schauen, Sinnen
0070-3427 Denkmaeler des Rheinlandes†
0070-3435 Denmark. Danmarks Fiskeri- og Havundersoegelser. Meddelelser fra *see* 0106-553X
0070-346X Denmark. Danmarks Statistik. Arbejdsloesheden/Unemployment
0070-3478 Denmark. Danmarks Statistik. Befolkningens Bevaegelser/Vital Statistics
0070-3486 Danmarks Skibe og Skibsfart
0070-3508 Denmark. Danmarks Statistik. Ejendomssalg/Sales of Real Property
0070-3516 Denmark. Danmarks Statistik. Faerdselsuheld/Road Traffic Accidents
0070-3524 Denmark. Danmarks Statistik. Indkomstansaettelser til Staten *see* 0107-105X
0070-3532 Denmark. Danmarks Statistik. Industristatistik/Industrial Statistics
0070-3540 Denmark. Danmarks Statistik. Kriminalstatistik /Crime Statistics
0070-3559 Denmark. Danmarks Statistik. Landbrugsstatistik Herunder Gartneri og Skovbrug *changed to* Denmark. Danmarks Statistik. Landbrugsstatistik/Agricultural Statistics
0070-3567 Denmark. Danmarks Statistik. Statistisk Aarbog/Statistical Yearbook
0070-3583 Denmark. Danmarks Statistik. Statistisk Tiars-Oversigt/Statistical Ten-Year Review
0070-3605 Denmark. Fiskeriministeriet. Forsoegslaboratorium. Aarsberetning/Annual Report
0070-3621 Denmark. Statens Filmcentral. S F C Film *changed to* Denmark. Statens Filmcentral. S F C Catalogue
0070-3648 Dental Delineator
0070-3656 Dental Guide
0070-3664 Dental Images
0070-3672 Dental Laboratorie Bladet
0070-3702 Dental Products Annual Report
0070-3729 Tenth District Dental Society of the State of New York. Bulletin *changed to* Nassau County Dental Society. Bulletin
0070-3737 Dentistry in Japan
0070-3745 Denver Museum of Natural History. Museum Pictorial†
0070-3753 Denver Museum of Natural History. Proceedings†
0070-3788 Derbyshire Archaeological Journal
0070-3826 Description and Analysis of Contemporary Standard Russian
0070-3834 Design and Industries Association. Year Book and Membership List *see* 0306-6185
0070-3869 Dessinateurs, Peintres et Sculpteurs de Belgique *see* 0066-3174
0070-3885 Detroit Studies in Music Bibliography
0070-3893 Deutsch-Slawische Forschungen zur Namenkunde und Siedlungsgeschichte
0070-3907 Deutsche Akademie der Landwirtschaftswissenschaften, Berlin. Jahrbuch†
0070-3915 Akademie fuer Aerztliche Fortbildung der DDR. Bibliographie†
0070-3923 Deutsche Akademie fuer Sprache und Dichtung. Jahrbuch
0070-3931 Bibliographischer Informationsdienst der Deutschen Buecherei
0070-394X Deutsche Bundesbank. Geschaeftsbericht
0070-3958 Deutsche Dendrologische Gesellschaft. Mitteilungen
0070-3966 D F V L R Jahresbericht
0070-3974 Deutsche Forschungsgemeinschaft. Denkschriften zur Lage der Deutschen Wissenschaft
0070-3982 Deutsche Forschungsgemeinschaft. Forschungsberichte
0070-3990 Deutsche Forschungsgemeinschaft. Kommissionenmitteilungen
0070-4016 Deutsche Gaue
0070-4040 Deutsche Gesellschaft fuer Chronometrie. Jahrbuch
0070-4067 Deutsche Gesellschaft fuer Innere Medizin. Verhandlungen
0070-4083 D.G.L.R. Jahrbuecher
0070-4091 Deutsche Gesellschaft fuer Orthopaedie und ihre Grenzgebiete *see* 0044-3220
0070-4105 Deutsche Gesellschaft fuer Ostasienkunde. Koordinierungstelle fuer Gegenwartsbezogene Ostasienforschung Mitteilungen *changed to* Deutsche Gesellschaft fuer Ostasienkunde. Koordinierungsstelle fuer Gegenwartsbezogene Ost- und Suedostasienforschung. Mitteilungen
0070-4113 Deutsche Gesellschaft fuer Pathologie. Verhandlungen
0070-4121 Deutsche Gesellschaft fuer Rheumatologie. Verhandlungen *changed to* Deutsche Gesellschaft fuer Rheumatologie. Fortschritte der Rheumatologie. Verhandlungen
0070-413X Deutsche Gesellschaft fuer Urologie. Verhandlungsbericht *changed to* Deutsche Gesellschaft fuer Urologie. Verhandlungen
0070-4148 German Merchant Fleet
0070-4164 Deutsche Hydrographische Zeitschrift. Ergaenzungsheft. Reihe A
0070-4172 Deutsche Hydrographische Zeitschrift. Ergaenzungsheft. Reihe B
0070-4210 Deutsche Kraftfahrtforschung und Strassenverkehrstechnik
0070-4229 Deutsches Krebsforschungszentrum. Veroeffentlichungen
0070-4237 Die Deutsche Lebensversicherung. Jahrbuch
0070-4245 Deutsche Luft-und Raumfahrt Forschungsberichte *changed to* D F V L R-Forschungsberichte und D F V L R-Mitteilungen
0070-4253 Deutsche Luft- und Raumfahrt. Mitteilungen†
0070-427X Deutsche Ophthalmologische Gesellschaft. Zusammenkunft. Bericht†
0070-4296 Deutsche Papierwirtschaft
0070-430X Deutsche Physikalische Gesellschaft. D P G - Nachrichten†
0070-4318 Deutsche Schiller-Gesellschaft. Jahrbuch
0070-4326 Deutsche Shakespeare-Gesellschaft West. Jahrbuch
0070-4334 Deutsche Texte des Mittelalters
0070-4342 Deutsche Zoologische Gesellschaft. Verhandlungen
0070-4377 Deutscher Kuesten-Almanach
0070-4423 Deutsches Beamten-Jahrbuch; Bundesausgabe
0070-4431 Deutsches Buehnen-Jahrbuch
0070-4458 Deutsches Hydrographisches Institut. Jahresbericht
0070-4490 Deutsches Institut fuer Puppenspiel. Forschung und Lehre†
0070-4504 Deutsches Jahrbuch der Musikwissenschaft *changed to* Jahrbuch Peters
0070-4512 Deutsches Universitaets-Handbuch†
0070-4571 Developments in Sedimentology
0070-458X Developments in Solid Earth Geophysics
0070-4598 Developments in Theoretical and Applied Mechanics†
0070-4628 Central Mining Research Station, Dhanbad. Progress Research *changed to* Central Mining Research Station, Dhanbad. Annual Report
0070-4660 Diagnostische Informationen fuer die aerztliche Praxis *see* 0300-8096
0070-4687 Diatomeenschalen im Elektronenmikroskopischen Bild *changed to* Micromorphology of Diatom Valves
0070-4695 Dichter und Zeichner
0070-4709 Dictionary of African Biography†
0070-4717 Dictionary of Canadian Biography
0070-4725 Dictionary of Dairying. Supplement†
0070-4733 Dictionary of Latin American and Caribbean Biography
0070-475X Dictionnaire des Parfums de France et des Lignes pour Hommes
0070-4768 Dictionnaire des Produits de Beaute et de Cosmetologie *changed to* Dictionnaire des Produits de Soins de Beaute
0070-4776 Dictionnaire des Valeurs des Meubles et Objets d'Art
0070-4792 Didactica Classica Gandensia
0070-4806 Diderot Studies
0070-4814 Diebeners Goldschmiede- und Uhrmacher-Jahrbuch *changed to* Goldschmiede- und Uhrmacher-Jahrbuch
0070-4822 Diesel and Gas Turbine World Wide Catalog
0070-4830 Diesel Locomotive Question & Answer Manual
0070-4849 Digest of Health Statistics for England and Wales *changed to* Health and Personal Social Services Statistics
0070-4857 Digest of Legal Activities of International Organizations and Other Institutions
0070-4865 Digest of Literature on Dielectrics *see* 0018-9367
0070-4873 Digest of World Events
0070-4881 Dimension: Languages
0070-4903 Dine Israel
0070-4938 Diplomatarium Danicum
0070-4946 Diplomatic Corps of Belgrade†
0070-4962 Diplomat's Annual†
0070-4970 Direct Selling: Association Membership Roster Listing Major Companies and Commodities *changed to* Who's Who in Direct Selling
0070-4997 Directories of Science Information Sources, International Bibliography†
0070-5012 Directory for Exceptional Children
0070-5020 Directory for the Nonwoven Fabrics and Disposable Soft Goods Industries *see* 0095-683X
0070-5039 Directory Iron and Steel Plants
0070-5047 Directory of Accredited Camps for Boys and Girls *changed to* Parents' Guide to Accredited Camps. West Edition
0070-5047 Directory of Accredited Camps for Boys and Girls *changed to* Parents' Guide to Accredited Camps. South Edition
0070-5055 Directory of Accredited Private Home Study Schools *changed to* Directory of Accredited Home Study Schools
0070-5063 Directory of American College Theatre†
0070-5071 Directory of American Firms Operating in Foreign Countries
0070-508X Directory of American Philosophers
0070-5098 Directory of American Savings and Loan Associations
0070-5101 Directory of American Scholars
0070-5152 Directory of British Associations
0070-5160 Directory of British Recruitment Services
0070-5179 Directory of Brush and Allied Trades
0070-5187 Directory of Business Schools *changed to* Directory of Educational Institutions
0070-5195 Directory of Buying Offices and Accounts
0070-5217 Directory of Canadian Map Collections
0070-5225 Directory of Canadian Trust Companies
0070-5233 Directory of Catholic Schools and Colleges *changed to* Which School?
0070-5241 Directory of Central Atlantic States Manufacturers. Maryland, Delaware, Virginia, West Virginia, North Carolina, South Carolina
0070-525X Directory of Chemical Engineering Research in Canadian Universities
0070-5268 Directory of Church of England Social Services
0070-5276 Directory of College and University Libraries in New York State
0070-5284 Directory of College Placement Offices *changed to* Directory of Career Planning and Placement Offices
0070-5292 Directory of Communication Organizations *see* 0094-2588
0070-5306 Directory of Community Services in Maryland†
0070-5314 Directory of Companies and Their Subsidiaries in the Wine, Spirit and Brewing Trades *changed to* Off Licence News Directory
0070-5322 Directory of Company Secretaries
0070-5330 Directory of Computerized Information in Science and Technology†
0070-5365 Directory of Corporate Affiliations
0070-5373 Directory of Correctional Institutions and Agencies of the United States of America, Canada, and Great Britain *see* 0190-2555
0070-5381 Directory of Correctional Services in Canada /Repertoire des Services de Correction du Canada *see* 0225-4115
0070-539X Directory of Current Research in Israel: Physical and Life Sciences *see* 0301-4657
0070-5403 Directory of Current Scientific Research Projects in Pakistan†
0070-5411 Directory of Dealers in Secondhand and Antiquarian Books in the British Isles *changed to* Sheppard's Book Dealers in British Isles
0070-542X Directory of Directors
0070-5438 Directory of Directors
0070-5446 Directory of Discount Centers *changed to* Directory of Discount Stores
0070-5454 Directory of Education Studies in Canada
0070-5462 Directory of Engineering College Research and Graduate Study *changed to* Engineering College Research and Graduate Study
0070-5470 Directory of Engineering Societies and Related Organizations
0070-5489 Directory of Engineers *changed to* Institution of Engineers of Ireland. Register of Chartered Engineers and Members
0070-5500 Directory of European Associations. Part 1: National Industrial Trade and Professional Associations *changed to* Directory of European Industrial & Trade Associations
0070-5543 Directory of Foreign Firms Operating in the United States†
0070-556X Directory of Franchising Organizations
0070-5586 Directory of Government Agencies Safeguarding Consumer and Environment†

0070-5594 Directory of Government Production Primecontractors
0070-5616 Directory of Graduate Programs in the Speech Communication Arts and Sciences *see* 0732-2755
0070-5624 Directory of Grant-Making Trusts
0070-5632 Hawaii's Scientific Resources Directory†
0070-5640 Directory of Health, Welfare and Recreation Services of Greater Montreal *see* 0319-258X
0070-5659 Directory of Historical Societies and Agencies in the United States and Canada
0070-5675 Directory of Institutions of Higher Education in Missouri
0070-5691 Directory of Insurance Companies Licensed in New York State
0070-5705 Directory of Israeli Merchants and Manufacturers *changed to* Directory of Israel
0070-5721 Directory of Kansas Manufacturers and Products
0070-573X Directory of Law Teachers
0070-5756 Directory of Lawyer Referral Services, Legal Aid and Defender Offices and Legal Assistance Offices of the Armed Forces†
0070-5772 Directory of Machine Tools and Related Products *changed to* U S Machine Tool Directory
0070-5780 Directory of Magazine Editorial Shopping Sections
0070-5799 Directory of Maryland Exporters-Importers†
0070-5802 Directory of Maryland Manufacturers
0070-5810 Directory of Medical Libraries in New York State
0070-5829 Directory of Medical Specialists
0070-5837 Directory of Mental Health Resources in Florida†
0070-5845 Directory of Michigan Manufacturers *see* 0736-2889
0070-5861 Directory of Mineral Producers in Oklahoma†
0070-5888 Directory of Municipal Officials of New Mexico *changed to* Directory of New Mexico Municipal Officials
0070-5896 Directory of National and International Labor Unions in the United States *see* 0090-4163
0070-5918 Directory of National Trade and Professional Associations of the United States *changed to* National Trade and Professional Associations of the United States and Labor Unions
0070-5926 Directory of Nebraska Manufacturers
0070-5934 Directory of New Mexico Manufacturing and Mining *changed to* New Mexico Manufacturing Directory (Year)
0070-5950 Directory of New York State Public Library Systems *changed to* Directory of Library Systems in New York State
0070-5969 Directory of Oceanographers in the United States *changed to* U S Directory of Marine Scientists
0070-5977 Directory of Official Architects and Planners *changed to* Directory of Official Architecture and Planning
0070-5985 Directory of Ohio Manufacturers *changed to* Harris Ohio Industrial Directory
0070-5993 Directory of Oil Marketing and Wholesale Distributors
0070-6000 Directory of On-Going Research in Smoking and Health
0070-6019 Directory of Opportunities for Graduates
0070-6035 Directory of Organizations and Personnel in Educational Management *changed to* Directory of Organizations and Researchers in Educational Management
0070-6051 Directory of Overseas Summer Jobs
0070-606X Directory of Pakistani Scholars Abroad
0070-6078 Directory of Pakistan's Periodicals in Social Sciences†
0070-6086 Directory of Pathology Training Programs
0070-6094 Directory of Periodicals Publishing Articles on English and American Literature and Language
0070-6124 Directory of Premium and Incentive Buyers *see* 0196-8262
0070-6140 Directory of Professional Photography
0070-6167 Directory of Public Refrigerated Warehouses
0070-6175 Directory of Quarries and Pits†
0070-6183 Directory of Reference and Research Library Resource Systems in New York State *changed to* Directory of Library Systems in New York State
0070-6205 Directory of Regional Councils *changed to* Directory of Regional Councils
0070-6213 Directory of Research Reports Relating to Produce Packaging and Marketing†
0070-623X Directory of Scholarly and Research Publishing Opportunities *see* 0275-3820
0070-6256 Directory of Science Resources for Maryland
0070-6264 Directory of Scientific and Technical Associations and Institutes in Israel *see* 0334-2824
0070-6272 Directory of Scientific Directories
0070-6280 Directory of Scientific Research in Nigeria
0070-6302 Directory of Serials in Pure and Applied Science and Economics Published in Israel†
0070-6310 Directory of Shipowners, Shipbuilders and Marine Engineers
0070-6337 Directory of Singpore Manufacturers *see* 0129-9867
0070-6345 Directory of Service Organizations.†
0070-6396 Directory of Special Libraries in Montreal *changed to* Directory of Special Libraries in the Montreal Area
0070-640X Directory of State and Federal Funds Available for Business Development
0070-6418 Directory of State Arts Councils†
0070-6426 Directory of Steel Foundries in the United States, Canada and Mexico
0070-6442 Tennessee Directory of Manufacturers *see* 0360-5477
0070-6450 Directory of Texas Manufacturers
0070-6477 Directory of the Forest Products Industry
0070-6515 World Directory of Travel Agencies
0070-6523 Directory of United Funds and Community Health and Welfare Councils *changed to* United Way of America. International Directory
0070-6531 Directory of United States Importers
0070-654X Directory of U.S. Institutions of Higher Education *changed to* Education Directory. (School Year): Colleges and Universities
0070-6558 Directory of United States Standardization Activities
0070-6566 Directory of Utah Manufacturers *changed to* Utah Directory of Business and Industry
0070-6574 Directory of Virginia Manufacturing and Mining *changed to* Virginia Industrial Directory
0070-6582 Directory of Visiting Scholars in the United States Awarded Grants Under the Mutual Educational and Cultural Exchange Act (the Fulbright-Hays Act) *changed to* Directory of Visiting Fulbright Scholars and Occasional Lecturers
0070-6604 Directory to the Furnishing Trade
0070-6612 Diretorio Brasileiro da Industria Farmaceutica
0070-6639 D I S A Information. Measurement and Analysis *see* 0900-5579
0070-6655 Disc Collector's Newsletter *see* 0731-843X
0070-6663 Discourse Units in Human Communication for Librarians
0070-668X Discoveries in the Judaean Desert of Jordan
0070-6698 Discovery Reports
0070-6701 Dispersion and Unity *see* 0334-2506
0070-671X Disquisitiones Mathematicae Hungaricae
0070-6728 Dissertationes Botanicae
0070-6736 U S C Annual Distinguished Lecture Series Monographs in Special Education and Rehabilitation
0070-6760 Dix-Huitieme Siecle
0070-6779 Do-It-Yourself. Annual†
0070-6787 Do-It-Yourself Gardening Annual†
0070-6795 Doblingers Verlagsnachrichten†
0070-6809 Doctoral Dissertations on Transportation
0070-6817 Documentologie†
0070-6825 Documenta Romaniae Historica. Serie A: La Moldavie
0070-6833 Documenta Romaniae Historica. Serie B: La Valachie
0070-6841 Documentacion Bibliotecologica
0070-685X Documentatio Didactica Classica
0070-6868 Documentation du Batiment†
0070-6884 Documente Istorice†
0070-6892 Documente si Manuscrise Literare†
0070-6906 Documenti Sulle Arti del Libro
0070-6922 Documentos Latino Americanos†
0070-6957 Documents et Recherches sur l'Economie des Pays Byzantins, Islamiques et Slaves et Leurs Relations Commerciales au Moyen Age†
0070-6973 Documents on American Foreign Relations *changed to* American Foreign Relations-a Documentary Record
0070-7007 Dod's Parliamentary Companion
0070-7015 Dog World Annual
0070-7023 Dokumentation Verschleiss, Reibung und Schmierung *see* 0340-3475
0070-7031 Dokumente zur Deutschlandpolitik
0070-704X Dollars and Cents of Shopping Centers
0070-7058 Domestic Oceanborne and Great Lakes Commerce of the United States *changed to* Domestic Waterborne Trade of the United States
0070-7066 Dominican Republic. Secretaria de Obras Publicas y Comunicaciones. Estadistica *changed to* Dominican Republic Secretaria de Estado de Obras Publicas y Comunicaciones. OPC
0070-7074 Donauschwaebisches Schrifttum
0070-7112 Dorset Natural History and Archaeological Society. Proceedings
0070-7120 Dorset Worthies
0070-7139 Revue Pedagogique et Litteraire *changed to* Ecoles des Lettres
0070-7155 Dossiers du Cinema†
0070-7171 Downdraft
0070-718X Downhill Only Journal
0070-7198 Dramascripts Series
0070-7201 Landesmuseum fuer Vorgeschichte, Dresden. Veroeffentlichungen
0070-721X Medizinische Akademie "Carl Gustav Carus" Dresden. Schriften
0070-7228 Staatliches Museum fuer Mineralogie und Geologie, Dresden. Abhandlungen†
0070-7260 Staatliches Museum fuer Tierkunde in Dresden. Malakologische Abhandlungen
0070-7279 Reichenbachia
0070-7287 Staatliches Museum fuer Tierkunde in Dresden. Zoologische Abhandlungen
0070-7295 Staatliches Museum fuer Voelkerkunde Dresden. Abhandlungen und Berichte
0070-7325 Droit Polonais Contemporain
0070-7333 Drosophila Information Service
0070-7341 Drug Abuse Law Review†
0070-735X Drug Abuse Papers†
0070-7368 Drug Dependence†
0070-7376 Drug Topics Redbook
0070-7392 Drugs in Current Use and New Drugs
0070-7406 Drugs of Choice
0070-7414 Dublin Institute for Advanced Studies. Communications. Series A
0070-7422 Dublin Institute for Advanced Studies. School of Cosmic Physics. Geophysical Bulletin
0070-7430 Dudley, England (West Midlands) Public Libraries. Archives Department. Transcripts†
0070-7457 Universitaet Duesseldorf. Jahrbuch
0070-7473 Duke University. Commonwealth-Studies Center. Publications *changed to* Duke University. Center for International Studies. Publications
0070-7481 Duke University. Cooperative Oceanographic Program. Progress Report†
0070-7546 Dumbarton Oaks Papers
0070-7554 Dumbarton Oaks Studies
0070-7562 Dumbarton Oaks Texts
0070-7597 Dun and Bradstreet Metalworking Directory *see* 0278-8799
0070-7600 Dun and Bradstreet Middle Market Directory *changed to* Million Dollar Directory
0070-7627 Dun and Bradstreet Reference Book of Corporate Managements *changed to* Reference Book of Corporate Managements
0070-7635 Dun and Bradstreet Register *changed to* Dun & Bradstreet Standard Register
0070-7643 Dunsink Observatory. Publications
0070-7694 Duquesne Studies. Philological Series *changed to* Duquesne Studies. Language and Literature Series
0070-7708 Duquesne Studies. Philosophical Series†
0070-7716 Duquesne Studies. Psychological Series†
0070-7732 Duquesne Studies. Theological Series†
0070-7740 University of Durban-Westville. Journal
0070-7759 University of Natal. Institute for Social Research. Annual Report *changed to* University of Natal. Centre for Applied Social Research. Annual Report
0070-7767 Durch Stipendien Studieren
0070-7783 Dutch Studies in Russian Literature†
0070-7791 Dzieje Polskiej Granicy Zachodniej
0070-7805 E D P Conference for Retailers†
0070-7821 E I A Guide
0070-7902 Earth and Extraterrestrial Sciences *see* 0146-2970
0070-7910 Earth Sciences Series
0070-7945 East African Academy. Proceedings *changed to* Kenya National Academy for Advancement of Arts and Sciences. Proceedings
0070-7953 East African Freshwater Fisheries Research Organization. Annual Report *changed to* Uganda Freshwater Fisheries Research Organization. Annual Report
0070-7961 East African Geographical Review
0070-7988 Maktaba
0070-8003 East African Railways. Annual Report†
0070-8011 East African Research Information Centre. E A R I C Information Circular *changed to* Kenya National Academy for Advancement of Arts and Sciences. Research Information Circulars
0070-8038 East African Wildlife Journal *see* 0141-6707
0070-8062 University of Kansas. Center for East Asian Studies. International Studies: East Asian Series. Research Series
0070-8070 University of Kansas. Center for East Asian Studies. International Studies: East Asian Series. Reference Series
0070-8089 East Carolina University Publications in History
0070-8097 East Europe in German Books
0070-8100 East Europe Monographs
0070-8127 East Lakes Geographer
0070-8135 Bangladesh. Education Directorate. Report on Pilot Project on Adult Education

ISSN INDEX

0070-8143 Bangladesh. Directorate of Agricultural Marketing. Agricultural Marketing Series
0070-8151 Bangladesh. Directorate of Agriculture. Season and Crop Report
0070-8178 Bangladesh Research and Evaluation Centre. Report
0070-8186 Bangladesh University of Engineering and Technology, Dacca. Technical Journal
0070-8208 East Yorkshire Local History Series
0070-8224 Eastern Hemisphere Petroleum Directory *see* 0275-3871
0070-8224 Eastern Hemisphere Petroleum Directory *see* 0748-4089
0070-8232 Eastern New Mexico University. Contributions in Anthropology
0070-8259 University of Eastern Philippines. Research Center. Report
0070-8275 Eaton Electronics Research Laboratories. Technical Report†
0070-8305 Echos des Charites de St. Vincent de Paul *see* 0763-5184
0070-8321 Ecole Francaise des Attaches de Presse. Association des Anciens Eleves. Annuaire
0070-833X Tall Timbers Conference on Ecological Animal Control by Habitat Management. Proceedings
0070-8348 Ecological Society of Australia. Proceedings
0070-8356 Ecological Studies; Analysis and Synthesis
0070-8364 Ecologie Marina†
0070-8372 Ecology and Conservation Series†
0070-8399 Economia *changed to* Revista de Economia
0070-8402 Economia e Storia
0070-8437 Economic and Scientific Research Foundation. Annual Report
0070-8453 National Institute of Economic and Social Research, London. Economic and Social Studies
0070-847X Economic Council of Canada. Annual Report
0070-8488 Economic Council of Canada. Annual Review
0070-8518 Economic Development Programme for the Republic of South Africa
0070-8550 Economic Handbook of the Machine Tool Industry
0070-8593 Economic Picture of Japan†
0070-8615 Economic Questions for Illinois Agriculture†
0070-8623 Economic Research Studies†
0070-8631 Economic Review
0070-864X Economic Review of World Tourism
0070-8666 Bank of Japan. Economic Statistics Annual
0070-8674 Economic Studies†
0070-8690 Economic Survey of Asia and the Far East *see* 0252-5704
0070-8704 Bangladesh Economic Survey *changed to* Bamladesa Arthanaitika Jaripa
0070-8712 Economic Survey of Europe
0070-8720 Economic Survey of Latin America *changed to* Economic Survey of Latin America and the Caribbean
0070-8747 Economic Yearbook of Tunisia
0070-8755 Economic and Social Research Institute. Publications Series. Paper
0070-8763 Economics of Fruit Farming
0070-8771 Economie Belge et Internationale†
0070-878X Economie de la Tunisie en Chiffres
0070-8798 Economie et Finances Agricoles
0070-8801 Economie et Societe
0070-881X Luxembourg. Service Central de la Statistique et des Etudes Economiques. Cahiers Economiques. Serie A: Economie Luxembourgeoise
0070-8836 Economisch Instituut voor Het Midden- en Kleinbedrijf. Year Report
0070-8852 Economy and History†
0070-8860 Ecrits Libres
0070-8879 Ecriture
0070-8887 Ecuador. Centro de Desarrollo Industrial. Informe de Labores
0070-8895 Ecuador. Instituto Nacional de Estadistica y Censos. Anuario de Estadisticas Hospitalarias†
0070-8909 Ecuador. Instituto Nacional de Estadistica y Censos. Anuario de Estadisticas Vitales†
0070-8917 Ecuador. Instituto Nacional de Estadistica y Censos. Estadistica del Trabajo
0070-8925 Ecuador Economico
0070-8933 Ecuador. Servicio Nacional de Meteorologia e Hidrologia. Anuario Hidrologico *changed to* Ecuador. Instituto Nacional de Meteorologia e Hidrologia. Anuario Hidrologico
0070-8941 Ecuador. Servicio Nacional de Meteorologia e Hidrologia. Anuario Meteorologico *changed to* Ecuador. Instituto Nacional de Meteorologia e Hidrologia. Anuario Meteorologico
0070-8976 Edgar Brookes Academic and Human Freedom Lecture
0070-8992 University of Edinburgh. Architecture Research Unit. Report
0070-9018 University of Edinburgh. Publications. Language and Literature†
0070-9034 University of Edinburgh. Publications. Science†
0070-9069 Editiones Arnamagnaeanae. Series A
0070-9077 Editiones Arnamagnaeanae. Series B
0070-9085 Editiones Arnamagnaeanae. Supplementum
0070-9093 Editori Librai Cartolibrai e Biblioteche d'Italia†
0070-9107 Editorial Offices in the West†
0070-9115 Education and Science *changed to* Great Britain. Department of Education and Science. Annual Report
0070-9131 Education Authorities' Directory and Annual
0070-9158 Education Committees Year Book *see* 0143-5469
0070-9166 Education for Nursing: The Diploma Way
0070-9182 Education in Europe. Section 1: Higher Education and Research
0070-9204 Education in Europe. Section 3: Out-of-School Education *changed to* Education in Europe and Culture. Section 3: Out-of-School Education
0070-9212 Education in Europe. Section 4 (General)†
0070-9220 Education in Japan; A Graphic Presentation
0070-9239 Education in Large Cities Series†
0070-9263 Educational and Psychological Interactions
0070-931X Educational/Instructional Broadcasting Buyers Guide†
0070-9344 Educational Studies and Documents
0070-9352 Educational Technology Bibliography Series†
0070-9360 Educational Theatre Journal. Supplement†
0070-9379 Educational Therapy†
0070-9387 Educators Grade Guide to Free Teaching Aids
0070-9395 Educators Guide to Free Films
0070-9409 Educators Guide to Free Filmstrips
0070-9417 Educators Guide to Free Guidance Materials
0070-9425 Educators Guide to Free Science Materials
0070-9433 Educators Guide to Free Social Studies Materials
0070-9441 Educators Guide to Free Tapes, Scripts, and Transcriptions *see* 0160-1296
0070-945X Edward Shann Memorial Lecture in Economics†
0070-9468 Egon Ronay's Dunlop Guide to Hotels and Restaurants in the British Isles *changed to* Egon Ronay's Lucas Guide to Hotels, Restaurants and Inns in Great Britain and Ireland
0070-9484 Egyptian Dental Journal
0070-9492 Egyptian Religious Texts and Representation†
0070-9506 Egyptian Society of Endocrinology and Metabolism. Journal
0070-9514 Eidgenoessische Zukunft: Bausteine fuer Die Kommende Schweiz
0070-9522 Einfuehrung in die Information und Dokumentation†
0070-9530 Einkaufsfuehrer durch die Pelz- und Ledermode
0070-9557 Ekologia Polska
0070-9565 El Hi Textbooks in Print *see* 0000-0825
0070-9573 El Paso Archaeological Society. Special Reports
0070-959X Eldridge Reeves Johnson Foundation for Medical Physics. Colloquium. Proceedings
0070-9603 Electeur†
0070-962X Electric Power in Canada
0070-9638 Electrical and Electronic Trader Year Book
0070-9654 Electrical Contractors' Year Book *changed to* E C A Year Book Desk Diary
0070-9662 Electrical Engineering Research Abstracts. Canadian Universities†
0070-9670 Electrical Engineer's Pocket Book†
0070-9689 Electrical Equipment Representatives Association. Directory
0070-9697 Electrical/Electronics Insulation Conference. Record
0070-9719 Electrical Process Heating in Industry. Technical Conference. Record
0070-9735 Electricite de France. Rapport d'Activite
0070-9751 Electricite de France. Statistiques de la Production et de la Consommation
0070-976X Electricity Supply Handbook
0070-9778 Electroanalytical Chemistry: A Series of Advances
0070-9808 Electron, Ion and Laser Beam Technology Conference. Record *changed to* Conference on Lasers and Electro-Optics (Publications)
0070-9816 Electron Technology
0070-9840 Electronic Connection Techniques and Equipment†
0070-9859 Electronic Engineering Association. Annual Report
0070-9867 Electronic Market Data Book
0070-9875 Electronic News Financial Fact Book and Directory
0070-9956 Elektro-Jahr
0070-9964 Elektryfikacja i Mechanizacja Gornictwa i Hutnictwa
0070-9972 Elementa Ad Fontium Editiones
0070-9980 Elementary Teachers Guide to Free Curriculum Materials
0070-9999 Elements de Mathematique†
0071-0008 Elements du Bilan Economique
0071-0016 Elizabethan Bibliographies Supplements
0071-0024 Elizabethan Stamp Catalogue *changed to* Elizabethan Catalogue of Modern Commonwealth Stamps
0071-0032 Elizabethan Theatre†
0071-0067 Elsner; Handbuch fuer Strassenbau und Strassenverkehrstechnik *changed to* Elsners Handbuch fuer Strassenwesen
0071-0075 Elsners Taschenbuch der Eisenbahntechnik
0071-0113 E R E A C Directory *see* 0160-9629
0071-013X Employment and Earnings Statistics for the United States *see* 0271-4787
0071-0148 Employment Opportunities for Advanced Post-Graduate Scientists and Engineers
0071-0156 En Direct Avec l'Histoire
0071-0164 Encore
0071-0180 Encyclopaedia Chimica Internationalis†
0071-0199 Encyclopaedic Dictionary of Physics. Supplement†
0071-0202 Encyclopedia of Associations
0071-0210 Encyclopedia of Business Information Sources
0071-0229 Encyclopedia of Materials Handling. Supplement†
0071-0237 Encyclopedia of Social Work
0071-0288 Engineer Buyers Guide
0071-0318 Engineering Geology and Soils Engineering Symposium. Proceedings
0071-0326 Engineering Geology Case Histories
0071-0334 Engineering in Medicine and Biology Conference. Record *changed to* Conference on Engineering in Medicine and Biology. Record
0071-0342 Engineering Industries Association. Classified Directory and Buyers Guide
0071-0350 Engineering Laboratories Series†
0071-0369 Tennessee Valley Authority. Engineering Laboratory. Research in the Fields of Civil Engineering, Mechanical Engineering, Instrumentation†
0071-0377 Engineering Sciences Data Index *changed to* Engineering Sciences Data Unit Index
0071-0385 Engineers Joint Council. Engineering Manpower Commission. Demand for Engineers and Technicians *changed to* Engineers Joint Council. Engineering Manpower Commission. Demand for Engineers
0071-0393 American Association of Engineering Societies. Engineering Manpower Commission. Engineering and Technology Degrees
0071-0407 American Association of Engineering Societies. Engineering Manpower Commission. Engineering and Technology Enrollments
0071-0415 American Association of Engineering Societies. Engineering Manpower Commission. Engineers' Salaries: Special Industry Report.
0071-0423 American Association of Engineering Societies. Engineering Manpower Commission. Professional Income of Engineers.
0071-0431 Prospects of Engineering and Technology Graduates *changed to* American Association of Engineering Societies. Engineering Manpower Commission. Placement of Engineering and Technology Graduates.
0071-0474 Salaries of Engineering Technicians *changed to* American Association of Engineering Societies. Engineering Manpower Commission. Salaries of Engineering Technicians and Technologists.
0071-0490 English and American Studies in German
0071-0547 English Ceramic Circle. Transactions
0071-0555 English Church Music *changed to* World of Church Music
0071-0571 English Guernsey Herd Book
0071-058X English Historical Documents
0071-0598 English Institute. Selected Essays
0071-0601 English Language and Orientation Programs in the United States
0071-061X English Little Magazines
0071-0628 English Monarch Series
0071-0636 English Place-Name Society
0071-0660 English Translations of German Standards *see* 0174-3805
0071-0679 Ensayo y Testimonio
0071-0687 Ente Nazionale Idrocarburi. Report and Statement of Accounts
0071-0695 Entertainment Industry Series
0071-0709 Entomological Society of Alberta. Proceedings
0071-0717 Entomological Society of America. Miscellaneous Publications
0071-0725 Entomological Society of Australia (N.S.W.) Journal *see* 0158-0760
0071-0733 Entomological Society of British Columbia. Journal
0071-0741 Entomological Society of Canada. Bulletin

0071-075X Entomological Society of Canada. Memoirs
0071-0768 Entomological Society of Ontario. Proceedings
0071-0776 Entomological Society of Pennsylvania. Newsletter
0071-0784 Societe Entomologique du Quebec. Memoires
0071-0792 Entomologicke Problemy
0071-0822 Entretiens sur l'Antiquite Classique
0071-0830 Environment Law Review *see* 0192-8309
0071-0857 Environmental Geology (Montpelier)†
0071-0873 Environmental Health Engineering Series†
0071-092X Environmental Hygiene for the Public Health Inspector *see* 0316-0661
0071-0946 Environmental Wastes Control Manual *see* 0163-9730
0071-0954 Kentron Epistemonikon Ereunon. Epeteris
0071-0962 Ephemeris of the Sun, Polaris and Other Selected Stars with Companion Data and Tables
0071-0989 Epigraphische Studien
0071-1004 Epimeleia: Beitraege zur Philosophie†
0071-1039 Equal Opportunity; the Minority Student Magazine *changed to* Equal Opportunity
0071-1055 Eranos Yearbook. Papers†
0071-1063 Erasmus in English
0071-108X Eretz-Israel. Archaeological, Historical and Geographical Studies
0071-111X Ergebnisse der Inneren Medizin und Kinderheilkunde. New Series
0071-1128 Ergebnisse der Limnologie
0071-1136 Ergebnisse der Mathematik und Ihrer Grenzgebiete. Neue Folge
0071-1160 Erlanger Geologische Abhandlungen
0071-1179 Ernaehrungsforschung
0071-1187 Ernest Bloch Lectures
0071-1195 Ernest Bloch Society. Bulletin *changed to* Ernest Bloch Society. Bulletin
0071-1217 Ernst-Mach-Institut, Freiburg. Wissenschaftlicher Bericht *see* 0340-8833
0071-1233 Ertekezesek a Torteneti Tudomanyok Korebol
0071-125X Erziehung und Unterricht
0071-1268 Esakia
0071-1276 Escola Superior de Agricultura "Luiz de Queiroz". Anais
0071-1284 Universidade de Sao Paulo. Escola Superior de Agricultura "Luis de Queiroz." Boletim Didactico†
0071-1292 Escola Superior de Agricultura "Luiz de Queiroz". Boletim de Divulgacao
0071-1306 Universidade de Sao Paulo. Escola Superior de Agricultura "Luis de Queiroz." Boletim Tecnico-Cientifico†
0071-1314 Escuela Interamericana de Bibliotecologia. Estadisticas
0071-1330 Esprit et Liberte
0071-1349 Essais Philosophiques
0071-1357 Essays and Studies
0071-1365 Essays in Biochemistry
0071-1373 Essays in Chemistry
0071-139X Essays in French Literature†
0071-1411 Essays in History
0071-142X Essays in International Finance
0071-1438 Essays in Physics
0071-1446 Essays in Toxicology
0071-1462 Essener Bibliographie
0071-1470 Essential Articles
0071-1489 Essex Naturalist
0071-1497 Estadistica de la Ensenanza Media en Espana *changed to* Estadistica de la Ensenanza en Espana
0071-1500 Estadistica de la Primaria y de las Escuelas Magisterio en Espana *changed to* Estadistica de la Ensenanza en Espana
0071-1519 Estadistica de la Ensenanza Superior en Espana *changed to* Estadistica de la Ensenanza en Espana
0071-1527 Estadistica del Comercio Exterior de Espana
0071-1543 Mexico. Direccion General de Estadistica. Estadistica Industrial Anual
0071-156X Estadisticas Minera y Metalurgica de Espana
0071-1578 Estate Planning, Quick Reference Outline†
0071-1586 Estates Gazette Digest of Land and Property Cases *changed to* Estates Gazette Law Reports
0071-1594 Mid-Year Estimates of Population of New Mexico Counties†
0071-1616 Current Population Reports: Population Estimates and Projections. Estimates of the Population of the United States and Components of Population Change
0071-1624 Current Population Reports, P-25: Population Estimates and Projections. Estimates of the Population of the United States by Age, Color, and Sex *changed to* Current Population Reports: Population Estimates and Projections. Estimates of the Population of the United States by Age, Race and Sex
0071-1632 Coleccion Estructuras y Formas
0071-1640 Estudios de Arte Moderno†
0071-1659 Estudios de Arte y Estetica
0071-1667 Estudios de Cultura Maya
0071-1675 Universidad Nacional Autonoma de Mexico. Instituto de Investigaciones Historicas. Serie de Cultura Nahuatl. Estudios de Cultura Nahuatl
0071-1683 Estudios de Folklore
0071-1691 Estudios de Literatura
0071-1705 Estudios de Literatura Contemporanea
0071-1713 Estudios Filologicos
0071-1721 Estudios Filologicos. Anejo†
0071-173X Estudios Oceanologicos
0071-1748 Estudios y Fuentes del Arte en Mexico
0071-1772 Ethiopian Publications: Books, Pamphlets, Annuals and Periodical Articles
0071-1837 Ethnographica
0071-1853 Ethnomedizin
0071-1861 Etnografia Polska
0071-187X Etudes Africaines†
0071-1896 Etudes de Cas de Conflits Internationaux†
0071-190X Etudes de Linguistique Appliquee
0071-1918 Etudes de Litterature Etrangere et Comparee *see* 0035-1466
0071-1926 Etudes de Philologie, d'Archeologie et d'Histoire Ancienne
0071-1934 Etudes de Philologie et d'Histoire
0071-1942 Etudes de Pollution Atmospherique a Paris et dans les Departments Peripheriques
0071-1969 Etudes d'Histoire de l'Art
0071-1977 Etudes d'Histoire Economique et Sociale
0071-1993 Etudes d'Histoire Africaine
0071-2027 Etudes et Travaux d'Archeologie Marocaine
0071-2035 Etudes Ethnologiques†
0071-2043 Etudes Europeennes†
0071-2051 Etudes Finno-Ougriennes
0071-206X Etudes Foreziennes
0071-2078 Etudes Gobiniennes†
0071-2086 Etudes Gregoriennes
0071-2108 Etudes Historiques
0071-2116 Etudes Juives†
0071-2124 Etudes Linguistiques
0071-2140 Etudes Picardes†
0071-2175 Cahiers des Etudes Rurales†
0071-2191 Studies on Taxation and Economic Development
0071-2205 Etudes sur l'Histoire, l'Economie et la Sociologie des Pays Slaves†
0071-2213 Etudes Universitaires sur l'Integration Europeenne
0071-2221 Eucarpia
0071-223X Eugenics Society Symposia†
0071-2248 Eureka: the Archimedean's Journal
0071-2264 European Company for the Financing of Railway Rolling Stock. Annual Report
0071-2272 Europa Camping und Caravaning. Internationaler Fuehrer
0071-2299 Europa. Revue de Presse Europeenne
0071-2302 Europa Year Book
0071-2329 Europaeische Schriften
0071-2396 European and Mediterranean Plant Protection Organization. Publications. Series B: Plant Health Newsletter
0071-240X European and Mediterranean Plant Protection Organization. Publications. Series C; Reports of Working Parties *see* 0250-8052
0071-2418 European and Mediterranean Plant Protection Organization. Publications. Series D: Miscellaneous†
0071-2426 European Art Exhibitions. Catalog
0071-2477 European Association for Animal Production. Publications
0071-2485 European Association for Animal Production. Symposia on Energy Metabolism
0071-2493 European Association for Personnel Management. Congress Reports
0071-2507 European Association for Potato Research. Proceedings of the Triennial Conference *changed to* E A P R Abstracts of Conference Papers
0071-2523 European Bookdealers
0071-2531 European Brewery Convention. Proceedings of the International Congress
0071-2558 European Civil Aviation Conference (Report of Session)
0071-2574 Comite Europeen du Beton. Bulletin d'Information *changed to* Comite Euro-International du Beton. Bulletin d'Information
0071-2582 European Companies
0071-2612 European Conference of Local Authorities. Documents *changed to* European Conference of Local and Regional Authorities. Documents
0071-2620 European Conference of Local Authorities. Official Reports of Debates *changed to* European Conference of Local and Regional Authorities. Official Reports of Debates
0071-2639 European Conference of Local Authorities. Texts Adopted *changed to* European Conference of Local and Regional Authorities. Texts Adopted
0071-2647 European Congress on Electron Microscopy
0071-2671 European Congress of Anaesthesiology. Proceedings
0071-2701 European Convention on Human Rights. Yearbook
0071-271X European Coordination Centre for Research and Documentation in Social Sciences. Publications
0071-2728 European Curriculum Studies†
0071-2787 European Federation of Finance House Associations. Annual Report
0071-2795 European Federation of Finance House Associations. Conference Proceedings
0071-2817 Confederation Europeenne pour la Therapie Physique. Congress Reports
0071-2825 European Grassland Federation. Proceedings of the General Meeting
0071-2868 European Investment Bank. Annual Report
0071-2884 European League for Economic Cooperation. Publications
0071-2892 European League for Economic Cooperation. Reports of the International Congress
0071-2906 European Leather Guide *changed to* Leather Guide
0071-2930 European Marketing Data and Statistics
0071-2981 European Organization for Quality Control. Conference Proceedings
0071-3015 Debates of the European Parliament
0071-3023 European Parliament. Documents de Seance *changed to* European Parliament. Working Documents
0071-3074 E S O M A R Handbook
0071-3082 E S O M A R Congress. Proceedings
0071-3104 European Southern Observatory. Bulletin†
0071-3112 International Symposium on Chemical Reaction Engineering. Proceedings
0071-3120 European Passenger Train Timetable Conference Minutes
0071-3139 European Yearbook
0071-3171 E T S Bulletin *see* 0360-8808
0071-321X Evasion†
0071-3236 Everyman's Income Tax†
0071-3244 Everyman's United Nations *changed to* Everyone's United Nations
0071-3252 Evolution de l'Economie des Pays Sud-Americains
0071-3260 Evolutionary Biology
0071-3279 Excavaciones Arqueologicas en Espana
0071-3287 Excavations at Dura-Europos
0071-3295 Exceptional Infant†
0071-3309 Executive Directory of the U.S. Pharmaceutical Industry†
0071-3333 Experiences in Faith†
0071-335X Experientia. Supplementum
0071-3376 Experiment in International Living. President's Report *changed to* Experiment in International Living. Annual Report
0071-3384 Experimental Biology and Medicine
0071-3392 Experimental Botany; An International Series of Monographs
0071-3422 International Congress on Experimental Mechanics. Proceedings
0071-3430 Experimentelle Medizin, Pathologie und Klinik†
0071-3473 Exploration Geophysics†
0071-3481 Explorations in Education
0071-3503 Export-Import Bank of Japan. Annual Report
0071-3511 Export-Import Bank of the United States. Summary of Operations *see* 0270-5109
0071-3546 Exporters' Encyclopaedia-World Marketing Guide *see* 0732-0159
0071-3554 Export Data Exporters Year Book *changed to* Export Data
0071-3570 Fabian Society. Annual Report
0071-3597 Facet Books. Biblical Series†
0071-3600 Facet Books. Historical Series†
0071-3619 Facet Books. Social Ethics Series†
0071-3627 Fachliteratur zum Buch- und Bibliothekswesen
0071-3635 Facts About Israel
0071-3651 Facts about Nursing†
0071-3678 Facts and Figures on Government Finance
0071-3686 Faculty of Actuaries in Scotland. Transactions
0071-3716 Fairchild's Financial Manual of Retail Stores
0071-3724 Fallout in Norway†
0071-3740 Family Holiday Guide
0071-3759 Family Planning Association of Pakistan. Annual Report *changed to* F P A P Biennial Report
0071-3791 Far East and Australasia
0071-3821 Far Eastern Economic Review. Yearbook *changed to* Asia Yearbook
0071-3848 Farm Classification in England and Wales
0071-3864 Farm Credit Corporation Canada. Annual Report
0071-3872 Farm Credit Corporation Canada. Federal Farm Credit Statistics/ Statistiques du Credit Agricole Federal
0071-3880 Farm and Garden Equipment Guide†
0071-3899 Farm Equipment Directory/Annuaire†
0071-3910 Farm Incomes in England and Wales *changed to* Farm Incomes in England
0071-3937 Farm Machinery Yearbook
0071-3945 Farm Management *see* 0311-8665
0071-3961 Farming in the East Midlands

ISSN INDEX   1367

ISSN	Title
0071-397X	Lincoln College. Department of Farm Management and Rural Valuation. Farm Management Papers†
0071-3988	Lincoln College. Department of Farm Management and Rural Valuation. Farm Management Studies†
0071-4003	Farm Real Estate Taxes *changed to* Farm Real Estate Taxes. Recent Trends and Developments
0071-402X	Farnborough Air Show (Public Programme)
0071-4038	Fasciculi Historici
0071-4046	Fastener Standards
0071-4054	Fauna Fennica *see* 0001-7299
0071-4062	Fauna of the Clyde Sea Area†
0071-4070	Fauna Republicii Socialiste Romania†
0071-4089	Fauna Slodkowodna Polski
0071-4097	Fawley Foundation Lectures
0071-4100	Feature Films on 8mm and 16mm *changed to* Feature Films on 8mm, 16mm and Videotape
0071-4119	Federacion Espanola Galguera. Anuario y Memoria Deportiva†
0071-4127	Federal Employees Almanac
0071-4135	Federal Graduated Withholding Tax Tables
0071-4143	Federal Tax Return Manual *changed to* Federal Tax Manual with Monthly Reports
0071-4151	Federatie van Bedrijfsverenigingen. Jaarverslag
0071-416X	Federation d'Associations de Techniciens des Industries des Peintures, Vernis, Emaux et Encres d'Imprimerie de l'Europe Continentale. Annuaire Officiel. Official Yearbook. Amtliches Jahrbuch
0071-4178	Federation des Industries Belges. Rapport Annuel *changed to* Federation des Entreprises de Belgique. Rapport Annuel
0071-4194	Federation Francaise de Natation. Annuaire
0071-4232	Federation Francaise des Sports Equestres. Annuaire Officiel *changed to* Federation Equestre Francaise. Guide Officiel du Cavalier
0071-4240	Federation Francaise et Europeenne du Commerce, de l'Industrie et de l'Epargne. Revue
0071-4259	Federation Horlogere Suisse. Annual Report *changed to* Federation de l'Industrie Horlogere Suisse. Annual Report
0071-4267	Federation Internationale de Rugby Amateur. Annuaire
0071-4283	Federation Internationale Motocycliste. Annuaire
0071-4348	Federation Nationale des Conseils Juridiques et Fiscaux. Cahiers
0071-4356	Annuaire de la Cooperation F.N.C.C.
0071-4364	Federation Nationale des Foyers Ruraux de France. Informations et Liaisons *see* 0180-2410
0071-4380	Federation Nationale du Credit Agricole. Annuaire du Credit Agricole Mutuel
0071-4399	Federation of American Societies for Experimental Biology. Council on Biological Sciences Information. Working Documents†
0071-4402	Federation of European Biochemical Societies. (Proceedings of Meeting)
0071-4410	Federation of Migros Cooperatives. Annual Report
0071-4429	Federation of Pakistan Chambers of Commerce Industry. Brief Report of Activities
0071-4437	Federation of Societies for Paint Technology. Yearbook *changed to* Federation of Societies for Coatings Technology. Yearbook and Annual Membership Directory
0071-4445	Federation Professionelle des Producteurs et Distributeurs d'Electricite de Belgique. Consommation d'Electricite par Provinces et par Regions /Electricitets Verbruik per Provincie en per Streek *changed to* Federation Professionelle des Producteurs et Distributeurs d'Electricite de Belgique. Consommation d'Electricite par Provinces et par Regions/ Elektriciteitsverbruik per Provincie en per Gewest
0071-4453	Federation Professionnelle des Producteurs et Distributeurs d'Electricite de Belgique. Rapport Annuel. Jaarverslag
0071-4461	Federation Professionnelle des Producteurs et Distributeure d'Electricite de Belgique. Repertoire des Enterprises de Production d'Electricite/Repertorium des Ondernemingen van Electriciteitscoorbrenging *changed to* Federation Professionnelle des Producteurs et Distributeurs d'Electricite de Belgique. Repertoire des Centrales Electriques/Repertorium van de Elektrische Centrales
0071-447X	Federation Professionnelle des Producteurs et Distributeurs d'Electricite de Belgique. Statistiques Provisoires. Voorlopige Statistieken
0071-4488	Federation Professionnelle des Producteurs et Distributeurs d'Electricite de Belgique. Secteurs de Distribution
0071-450X	Feed Additive Compendium
0071-4518	Feed Industry Red Book
0071-4542	Universita degli Studi di Ferrara. Istituto di Geologia, Paleontologia e Paleontologia Umana. Annali. Sezione 15. Paleontologia Umana e Paleontologia *changed to* Universita degli Studi di Ferrara. Istituto di Geologia. Annali. Sezione 15. Paleontologia Umana e Paletnologia
0071-4550	Universite degli Studi di Ferrara. Istituto di Geologia, Paleontologia e Paleontologia Umana. Annali. Sezione 9. Scienze Geologiche *changed to* Universita degli Studi di Ferrara. Istituto di Geologia. Annali. Sezione 9. Scienze Geologiche
0071-4569	Universita degli Studi di Ferrara. Istituto di Geologia, Paleontologia e Paleontologia Umana. Memorie Geopaleontologiche†
0071-4577	Universita degli Studi di Ferrara. Istituto di Geologia, Paleontologia e Paleontologia Umana. Pubblicazioni *changed to* Universita degli Studi di Ferrara. Istituto di Geologia. Pubblicazioni
0071-4585	Der Fertighaus-Katalog
0071-4615	Fertilizer Industry Series†
0071-4623	Fertilizer Science and Technology Series
0071-4631	Fertilizer Trends
0071-464X	An Annual Review of World Production, Consumption and Trade *changed to* F A O Fertilizer Yearbook
0071-4658	Festival Film Guide *changed to* American Film and Video Festival Guide
0071-4674	Feuerwehr-Jahrbuch
0071-4682	Fiber Science Series
0071-4690	Fibrinolysis, Thrombolysis, and Blood Clotting; a Bibliography *see* 0360-7607
0071-4704	Fiches Analytiques de la Presse Technique Francaise†
0071-4712	Fiches Typologiques Africaines†
0071-4739	Fieldiana: Anthropology
0071-4763	Fielding's Quick Currency Guide for Europe†
0071-4771	Fielding's Quick Currency Guide for Far, Near and Middle East Including Russia and China†
0071-478X	Fielding's Selective Shopping Guide to Europe
0071-4801	Fielding's Travel Guide to Europe *see* 0192-5326
0071-481X	Figura. Nova Series
0071-4828	Fiji. Bureau of Statistics. Annual Statistical Abstract†
0071-4844	Fiji. Ministry of Agriculture & Fisheries. Annual Report
0071-4852	Filipiniana Book Guild. Publications†
0071-4860	Film: An Anthology by the National Society of Film Critics†
0071-4879	Film-Echo Filmwoche. Verleih-Katalog
0071-4895	Film Product Association of Great Britain. Annual Report
0071-4917	Film Review
0071-4925	Filmarsboken
0071-4933	Spielfilmliste
0071-4941	Filmstatistisches Taschenbuch
0071-495X	Filologia
0071-4968	Filologia e Critica†
0071-4976	Filologos Colombianos
0071-4992	Filozofiai Tanulmanyok
0071-5042	Financial Post Directory of Directors
0071-5050	Financial Post Survey of Industrials
0071-5077	Financial Post Survey of Markets *see* 0227-6038
0071-5085	Financial Post Survey of Mines *see* 0227-1656
0071-5115	Financial Reporting in Canada
0071-5131	Financial Times of Canada. Economic Forecast and Top Hundred *changed to* Top Hundred
0071-5166	Financing Higher Education in Canada.†
0071-5182	Finishing Handbook and Directory
0071-5190	Finnish Meteorological Institute. Contributions
0071-5204	Finland. Ilmatieteen Laitos. Tiedonantoja†
0071-5212	Magnetic Results from Nurmijarvi Geophysical Observatory†
0071-5220	Finnish Meteorological Institute. Observations of Radioactivity†
0071-5239	Finnish Meteorological Institute. Soil Temperature Measurements†
0071-5247	Finland. Kansanelakelaitos. Tilastollinen Vuosikirja
0071-5255	Finland. Kansantalousosasto. Kansantalouden Kehitysarvio. Summary: National Budget for Finland
0071-5271	Finland. Kansantalousosasto. Taloudellinen Katsaus. Economic Survey
0071-528X	Finland. Ulkoasiainministerio. Ulkapolititisija Lausuntoja ja Asiakirjoja
0071-5298	Finland. Posti-ja Lennatinlaitos. Kotimaisten Sanomalehtien Hinnasto. Inhemsk Tidningstaxa
0071-5301	Finland. Posti-ja Lennatinlaitos. Ulkomaisten Sanomalehtien Hinnasto. Utlandsk Tidningstaxa
0071-531X	Finland. Rakennushallitus. Tiedotuksia *changed to* Finland. Rakennushallitus. Tutkimus-ja Kehitystoiminnan. Tiedote
0071-5328	Finland. Sosiaalihallitus. Sosiaalihuoltotilaston Vuosikirja
0071-5336	Finland. Sosiaali- ja Terveysministerio. Tukimusosasto. Sosiaalisia Erikoistutkimuksia
0071-5344	Finland. Tilastokeskus. Teollisuustilasto
0071-5360	Finland. Valtakunnansuunnittelutoimisto. Julkaisuja. Sarja A *see* 0355-8878
0071-5379	Great Britain. Department of the Environment. Fire Research Station. Fire Notes *changed to* Great Britain. Building Research Establishment. Reports
0071-5387	Crime and Fire Prevention *see* 0049-0024
0071-5395	Fire Prevention News
0071-5409	Fire Protection Directory
0071-5417	Fire Protection Handbook
0071-5425	Fire Protection Handbook Study Guide†
0071-5433	Fire Research Annual Reports *see* 0068-354X
0071-545X	Great Britain. Department of the Environment. Fire Research Station. Technical Papers *changed to* Great Britain. Building Research Establishment. Reports
0071-5468	Fire Yearbook
0071-5484	National Bureau of Economic Research. Fiscal Studies†
0071-5492	Fish Disease Leaflets
0071-5522	Fisheries and Wildlife Paper. Victoria†
0071-5530	Fisheries Circular, Victoria†
0071-5549	Fisheries Contribution, Victoria†
0071-5581	Fisheries Statistics of Japan
0071-5603	Fishery Statistics of the United States *changed to* Fisheries of the United States
0071-5611	Fresh Water Fishing Guide†
0071-5638	Fisken og Havet
0071-5654	Fitzgerald/Hemingway Annual
0071-5662	British Librarianship & Information Science *changed to* British Librarianship & Information Work
0071-5670	Fix Your Chevrolet†
0071-5689	Fix Your Ford†
0071-5697	Fix Your Volkswagen†
0071-5735	Flood Damage Prevention; an Indexed Bibliography†
0071-5751	Flora Ecologica de Restingas do Sudeste do Brasil
0071-576X	Flora et Vegetatio Mundi
0071-5786	Flora Malesiana. Series 2: Pteridophyta
0071-5794	Flora Neotropica
0071-5808	Flora of Texas†
0071-5816	Flora Polska; Rosliny Naczyniowe Polski i Ziem Osciennych
0071-5824	Flora Polska: Rosliny Zarodnikowe Polski i Ziem Osciennych
0071-5840	Flora Slodkowodna Polski
0071-5867	Flore du Cambodge, du Laos et du Vietnam
0071-5875	Flore du Cameroun
0071-5883	Flore du Gabon
0071-5948	Florida. Division of Plant Industry. Biennial Report
0071-5999	Florida Requirements for Teacher Certification
0071-6006	Florida Speleological Society. Special Papers
0071-6014	Florida State Documents *see* 0430-7801
0071-6022	Florida Statistical Abstract
0071-6030	University of Florida. Bureau of Economic and Business Research. Population Studies
0071-6065	University of Florida. Department of Accounting. Accounting Series
0071-609X	University of Florida. Institute of Food and Agricultural Sciences. Annual Research Report†
0071-6103	University of Florida. Center for Gerontology. Studies and Programs
0071-6111	Southern Conference on Gerontology Report†
0071-6138	University of Florida. Libraries. Technical Processes Department. Caribbean Acquisitions†
0071-6146	University of Florida. School of Forestry. Cooperative Forest Genetics Research Program. Progress Report *changed to* University of Florida. School of Forest Resources & Conservation. Cooperative Forest Genetics Research Program. Progress Report.
0071-6154	Florida State Museum. Bulletin. Biological Series *changed to* Florida State Museum. Bulletin. Biological Sciences

0071-6162 Florida State Museum. Contributions. Social Sciences *changed to* Florida State Museum. Contributions. Anthropology and History
0071-6189 University of Florida Monographs. Humanities
0071-6197 University of Florida Monographs. Social Sciences
0071-6243 Flour Milling and Baking Research Association. Annual Report and Accounts
0071-6286 Flying Annual and Pilots' Guide *see* 0163-1144
0071-6294 Focus on Dance
0071-6308 Focus (Drink and Gambling) *see* 0260-6429
0071-6316 Focus Series†
0071-6340 Fodor's Austria
0071-6359 Fodor's Belgium and Luxembourg
0071-6367 Fodor's Czechoslovakia†
0071-6383 Fodor's France
0071-6391 Fodor's Germany *changed to* Fodor's Germany
0071-6405 Fodor's Great Britain
0071-6413 Fodor's Greece
0071-6421 Fodor's Hawaii
0071-643X Fodor's Holland
0071-6456 Fodor's Guide to India *see* 0276-5500
0071-6464 Fodor's Ireland
0071-6472 Fodor's Italy
0071-6480 Fodor's Japan and East Asia *changed to* Fodor's Japan
0071-6480 Fodor's Japan and East Asia *see* 0160-8991
0071-6480 Fodor's Japan and East Asia *changed to* Fodor's Korea
0071-6499 Fodor's Mexico
0071-6510 Fodor's Portugal
0071-6529 Fodor's Scandinavia
0071-6537 Fodor's South America
0071-6545 Fodor's Spain
0071-6553 Fodor's Switzerland
0071-6561 Fodor's Guide to the Caribbean, Bahamas and Bermuda *changed to* Fodor's Caribbean
0071-657X Fodor's Yugoslavia
0071-6588 Fodor's Israel
0071-6596 Fodor's London
0071-660X Fodor's Rome: A Companion Guide†
0071-6618 Fodor's Turkey
0071-6634 Foerderungsgemeinschaft fuer Absatz- und Werbeforschung. Schriften *changed to* Aus dem Schrifttum ueber Werbung
0071-6650 Foldrajzi Tanulmanyok
0071-6677 Folia Forestalia Polonica. Series A. Lesnictwo
0071-6685 Folia Forestalia Polonica. Series B. Drzewnictwo
0071-6693 Folia Geographica Danica
0071-6707 Folia Geographica. Geographica-Oeconomica
0071-6715 Folia Geographica. Geographica-Physica
0071-6723 Folia Historiae Artium
0071-6731 Folia Medica Lodziensia†
0071-674X Folia Oeconomica Cracoviensia
0071-6766 Folklivsskildringar och Bygdesstudier
0071-6774 Folklore Americano
0071-6782 Folklore Annual *changed to* University Folklore Association. Folklore Papers
0071-6804 Folktales of the World
0071-6847 Fonds de Developpment Economique et Social. Conseil de Direction. Rapport
0071-6855 Fonetica si Dialectologie†
0071-6863 Fontes Archaeologici Posnanienses
0071-6898 Fontes Rerum Austriacarum. Reihe 3. Fontes Juris
0071-6901 Fonti Sui Comuni Rurali Toscani
0071-6928 Food and Agriculture Organization of the United Nations. Commodity Policy Studies†
0071-6944 Food and Agriculture Organization of the United Nations Conference. Report
0071-6952 Food and Agriculture Organization of the United Nations. Commodity Reference Series†
0071-6960 F A O Agricultural Development Paper
0071-6979 F A O Atomic Energy Series†
0071-6987 F A O Agricultural Studies *changed to* F A O Animal Production and Health Series
0071-7002 F A O Commodity Review and Outlook
0071-7010 F A O Food Additive Control Series†
0071-7029 F A O Forestry Development Papers†
0071-7037 F A O Fisheries Studies *changed to* F A O Fisheries Series
0071-7045 F A O Legislative Series
0071-7061 F A O Manuals in Fisheries Science
0071-707X F A O Nutrition Meetings Report Series†
0071-7088 F A O Nutritional Study *changed to* F A O Food and Nutrition Series
0071-7096 F A O Rice Report†
0071-710X Food and Agriculture Organization of the United Nations. National Grain Policies†
0071-7118 Food and Agriculture Organization of the United Nations. Production Yearbook
0071-7126 Food and Agriculture Organization of the United Nations. Trade Yearbook
0071-7142 Philippines. Food and Nutrition Center. Annual Report *changed to* Philippines. Food and Nutrition Research Institute. Annual Report
0071-7150 Kansas State University. Food and Feed Grain Institute. Technical Assistance in Food Grain Drying, Storage, Handling and Transportation *changed to* Kansas State University. Food and Feed Grain Institute. Technical Assistance in Grain Storage, Processing and Marketing, and Agribusiness Development
0071-7177 Food Industries Manual
0071-7185 Food Industries of S.A. Buyers' Guide *changed to* Food Industries Yearbook and Buyers' Guide
0071-7193 Food Industry Studies†
0071-7207 Food Processing and Packaging Directory *see* 0264-4037
0071-7215 Food Processing Review *see* 0093-0075
0071-7223 Food Science Series
0071-724X Football Association Year Book
0071-7258 Football Register
0071-7274 Ford Foundation Annual Report
0071-7282 Forecast
0071-7312 Foreign Area Studies Series†
0071-7320 Foreign Consular Offices in the United States
0071-7339 Foreign Liabilities, Assets and Foreign Investments in Pakistan†
0071-7355 Foreign Relations of the United States
0071-7371 Annual Foreign Trade Statistics of Bangladesh *changed to* Foreign Trade Statistics of Bangladesh
0071-738X Foreign Trade of Greece *changed to* Commerce Exterieur de la Grece
0071-7398 Foreign Trade Statistics of Africa. Series A: Direction of Trade
0071-7401 Foreign Trade Statistics of Africa. Series B: Trade by Commodity
0071-7436 Foreningen til Norske Fortidsminnesmerkers Bevaring. Aarbok
0071-7444 Forest Engineering Symposium. Proceedings†
0071-7452 Forest Farmer. Manual Edition
0071-7479 U.S. Forest Service. Forest Insect Conditions in the Northern Region *changed to* U.S. Forest Service. Forest Insect and Disease Conditions in the Northern Region
0071-7495 Canada. Forest Management Institute. Program Review *see* 0710-4251
0071-7533 Forest Research in India†
0071-7541 Forest Research News for the South *changed to* U.S. Forest Service. Southern Forest Experiment Station. Recent Publications
0071-7568 Forest Science Monographs
0071-7584 Forestry Abstracts. Leading Article Reprint Series
0071-7614 Etudes Mathematiques en Vue des Applications: Formulaire de Mathematiques a l'Usage des Physiciens et des Ingenieurs†
0071-7622 Formulaire Thera†
0071-7630 Forretnings- og Bedriftslederen
0071-7649 Forschung und Konstruktion im Stahlbau†
0071-7657 Forschungen aus Staat und Recht
0071-7665 Forschungen zur Antiken Sklaverei
0071-7673 Forschungen zur Mittelalterlichen Geschichte
0071-7681 Forschungen zur Romanischen Philologie†
0071-769X F I W - Schriftenreihe
0071-7703 Forschungsprobleme der Vergleichenden Literaturgeschichte
0071-7711 Forschungsstelle fuer Jagdkunde und Wildschadenverhuetung. Schriftenreihe
0071-772X Forstwissenschaftliche Forschungen
0071-7738 Fort Belknap Genealogical Association. Bulletin
0071-7754 Fort Burgwin Research Center. Publications
0071-7762 Fort Hays Studies. New Series. Art†
0071-7770 Fort Hays Studies. New Series. Bibliography†
0071-7789 Fort Hays Studies. New Series. Economics†
0071-7800 Fort Hays Studies. New Series. Literature†
0071-7819 Fort Hays Studies. New Series. Music†
0071-7827 Fort Hays Studies. New Series. Science†
0071-7835 Fortbildung und Praxis
0071-7843 Gastroenterologische Fortbildungskurse fuer die Praxis†
0071-7851 Fortbildungskurse fuer Rheumatologie
0071-786X Fortschritte der Arzneimittelforschung
0071-7878 Fortschritte der Botanik *see* 0340-4773
0071-7886 Fortschritte der Chemie Organischer Naturstoffe
0071-7894 Fortschritte der Chemischen Forschung *see* 0340-1022
0071-7908 Immunology Reports and Reviews†
0071-7924 Fortschritte der Physikalischen Chemie†
0071-7932 Fortschritte der Praktischen Dermatologie und Venerologie
0071-7940 Fortschritte der Psychoanalyse†
0071-7975 Fortschritte der Urologie und Nephrologie
0071-7991 Fortschritte der Zoologie
0071-8009 Fortschritte in der Geologie von Rheinland und Westfalen
0071-8025 Forum der Psychiatrie
0071-8033 Forum des Transports Publics *see* 0397-6521
0071-8041 Forum on Fundamental Surgical Problems
0071-805X Forum on Homemaker-Home Health Aide Service. Report†
0071-8068 Fotogrammetriska Meddelanden
0071-8076 Fotointerpretacja w Geografii
0071-8084 Foulsham's Original Old Moore's Almanack
0071-8092 Foundation Directory
0071-8106 Foundation for the Study of Cycles. Research Bulletin
0071-8122 Foundations of Language Supplementary Series†
0071-8130 Foundry Directory and Register of Forges
0071-8157 Fowler's Mechanical Engineers Pocket Book†
0071-8165 Fowler's Mechanics and Machinists Pocket Book†
0071-8173 Fraenkische Geographische Gesellschaft. Mitteilungen
0071-8181 France-Allemagne
0071-819X France. Archives Nationales. Centre d'Information de la Recherche Historique en France. Bulletin†
0071-8211 France. Service du Traitement de l'Information et des Statistiques Industrielles. Annuaire de Statistique Industrielle *changed to* France. Service d'Etude des Strategies et des Statistiques Industrielles. Annuaire de Statistique Industrielle
0071-822X Annuaire de l'Administration et du Corps des Mines *changed to* Annuaire de l'Administration des Mines
0071-8246 France. Bureau de Recherches Geologiques et Minieres. Memoires
0071-8254 France. Caisse Nationale de Credit Agricole. Rapport sur le Credit Agricole Mutuel
0071-8262 France. Service de Documentation et de Cartographie Geographiques. Memoires et Documents.
0071-8270 Centre National de la Recherche Scientifique. Seminaire d'Econometrie. Monographies
0071-8289 Centre d'Etudes Sociologiques. Travaux et Documents†
0071-8297 France. Centre National de Coordination des Etudes et Recherches sur la Nutrition et l'Alimentation. Cahiers Techniques†
0071-8300 Centre National de la Recherche Scientifique. Colloques Internationaux. Sciences Mathematiques, Physico-Chimiques, Biologiques et Naturelles *changed to* Centre National de la Recherche Scientifique. Colloques Internationaux. Sciences Mathematiques, Physiques, Chimiques, Biologiques et Medicales
0071-8319 France. Centre National de la Recherche Scientifique. Colloques Nationaux
0071-8327 Centre National de la Recherche Scientifique. Rapport d'Activite
0071-8335 Centre National de la Recherche Scientifique. Rapport National de Conjoncture Scientifique†
0071-8343 Centre National de la Recherche Scientifique. Seminaire d'Econometrie. Cahiers
0071-8351 Centre National de la Recherche Scientifique. Annuaire des Chercheurs†
0071-836X Centre National du Commerce Exterieur. Annuaire†
0071-8378 Chambre Syndicale des Commissionaires pour le Commerce Exterieur. Annuaire Officiel†
0071-8386 France-Collectivites: Guide National des Chefs des Services d'Achats et des Fournisseurs de Collectivites
0071-8394 France. Comite des Travaux Historiques et Scientifiques. Bulletin Archeologique.
0071-8416 France. Comite des Travaux Historiques et Scientifiques. Section d'Archeologie. Actes du Congres National des Societes Savantes
0071-8424 Comite des Travaux Historiques et Scientifiques. Section de Geographie. Actes du Congres National des Societes Savantes
0071-8432 France. Comite des Travaux Historiques et Scientifiques. Section de Geographie. Bulletin
0071-8440 France. Comite des Travaux Historiques et Scientifiques. Section d'Histoire Moderne et Contemporaine. Actes du Congres National des Societes Savantes
0071-8459 France. Comite des Travaux Historiques et Scientifiques. Section d'Histoire Moderne et Contemporaine. Bulletin
0071-8467 France. Commissariat a l'Energie Atomique. Annual Report
0071-8483 France. Commission Centrale des Marches. Guide du Fournisseur de l'Etat et des Collectivites Locales

ISSN INDEX 1369

0071-8491 France. Commission Nationale de l'Amenagement du Territoire. Rapport
0071-8505 France. Commission de la Concurrence. Rapports Economiques
0071-8513 France. Conseil National de la Comptabilite. Rapport d'Activite
0071-853X France. Delegation Generale a la Recherche Scientifique et Technique. Recherche dans le Domaine de l'Eau: Repertoire des Laboratoires†
0071-8548 France. Delegation Generale a la Recherche Scientifique et Technique. Repertoire National des Laboratoires; la Recherche Universitaire; Sciences Exactes et Naturelles. Tome 2: Biologie *changed to* France. Ministere de l'Industrie et de la Recherche. Repertoire National des Laboratoires; la Recherche Universitaire. Tome 2: Sciences de la Vie
0071-8556 France. Delegation Generale a la Recherche Scientifique et Technique. Repertoire National des Laboratoires; la Recherche Universitaire; Sciences Exactes et Naturelles. Tome 3: Chimie *changed to* France. Ministere de l'Industrie et de la Recherche. Repertoire National des Laboratoires; la Recherche Universitaire. Tome 3: Sciences Humaines et Sociales
0071-8564 France. Delegation Generale a la Recherche Scientifique et Technique. Repertoire National des Laboratoires; la Recherche Universitaire; Sciences Exactes et Naturelles. Tome 4: Mathematiques, Sciences de l'Espace et de la terre *changed to* France. Ministere de la Recherche et de l'Industrie. Repertoire National des Laboratoires; la Recherche Universitaire; Sciences Exactes et Naturelles. Tome 4: Mathematiques, Sciences de l'Espace et de la Terre
0071-8572 France. Delegation Generale a la Recherche Scientifique et Technique. Repertoire National des Laboratoires; la Recherche Universitaire; Sciences Exactes et Naturelles. Tome 1: Physique *changed to* France. Ministere de l'Industrie et de la Recherche. Repertoire National des Laboratoires; la Recherche Universitaire; Tome 1: Sciences de la Matiere
0071-8629 France. Direction Generale des Douanes et Droits Indirects. Annuaire†
0071-8637 France. Direction Generale des Douanes et Droits Indirects. Annuaire Abrege de Statistiques
0071-8645 France. Direction Generale des Douanes et Droits Indirects. Commentaires Annuels des Statistiques du Commerce Exterieur
0071-8653 France. Direction Generale des Douanes et Droits Indirects. Navigation Maritime Internationale de la France (Tableaux Generaux)†
0071-8661 France. Direction Generale des Douanes et Droits Indirects. Statistiques du Commerce Exterieur. Transit Direct†
0071-8688 France. Direction Generale des Douanes et Droits Indirects. Statistiques du Commerce Exterieur: Importations-Exportations. Nomenclature: N.G.P. (Nomenclature Generale des Produits)
0071-8696 France. Direction Generale des Douanes et Droits Indirects. Statistiques du Commerce Exterieur: Importations-Exportations. Nomenclature C.T.C.I. (Classification Type pour le Commerce International)†
0071-870X France. Direction Generale de la Concurrence et des Prix. Bulletin Officiel des Services des Prix
0071-8718 France. Direction Nationale des Douanes et Droits Indirects. Transport du Commerce Exterieur
0071-8726 France. Direction Nationale des Douanes et Droits Indirects. Tableau General des Transports
0071-8734 France en Poche. Total Guide
0071-8742 France. Inspection Generale des Finances. Annuaire
0071-8793 Annuaire Statistique des Territoires d'Outre Mer†
0071-8823 France. Institut National d'Etudes Demographiques. Cahiers de Travaux et Documents
0071-884X France. Institut Pedagogique National. Dossiers Pedagogiques de la Radio-Television Scolaire†
0071-8866 France. Ministere de la Sante Publique et de la Securite Sociale. Annuaire Statistique de la Sante et de l'Action Sociale *changed to* France. Ministere de la Sante et de la Securite Sociale. Annuaire des Statistiques Sanitaires et Sociales
0071-8882 France. Ministere de la Sante. Note d'Information *changed to* France. Ministere de la Sante et de la Securite Sociale. Notes d'Information
0071-8890 France. Ministere de l'Economie et des Finances. Balance des Paiements Entre la France et l'Exterieur
0071-8904 France. Ministere du Budget. Budget
0071-8912 France. Ministere de l'Economie et des Finances. Rapport du President de la Republique Francaise sur les Operations des Caisses d'Epargne Ordinaires. *changed to* France. Ministere de l'Economie et des Finances. Statistiques et Etudes Financieres. Finance Publique. Serie Bleue
0071-8920 France. Ministere de l'Economie. Rapport du Conseil de Direction du Fonds de Developpement Economique et Social *changed to* France. Ministere de l'Economie, des Finances et du Budget. Rapport du Conseil de Direction du Fond de Developpement Economique et Social
0071-8963 France. Institut National de Recherche et de Documentation Pedagogiques. Repertoire d'Etablissements Publics d'Enseignement et de Services†
0071-8971 France. Ministere des Affaires Etrangeres. Recueil des Traites et Accords de la France
0071-8998 O.R.S.T.O.M. Annales Hydrologiques†
0071-9005 Memoires O.R.S.T.O.M.
0071-9013 O.R.S.T.O.M. Institut Francais de Recherche pour le Developement en Cooperation. Rapport d'Activite
0071-9021 O.R.S.T.O.M. Initiations Documentations Techniques
0071-903X France. Office National d'Immigration. Statistiques de l'Immigration
0071-9048 France-Peinture
0071-9056 France Plastiques
0071-9064 France Prostestante *changed to* Federation Protestante de France. Annuaire
0071-9072 France. Direction Generale de l'Aviation Civile. Annuaire†
0071-9102 France-Sports
0071-9129 Tribunal de Commerce, Paris. Annuaire
0071-917X Franco British Trade Directory
0071-9188 Archiv Ungedruckter Wissenschaftlicher Schriften†
0071-9196 Institut fuer Angewandte Geodaesie. Mitteilungen
0071-920X Nachrichten aus dem Karten- und Vermessungswesen *see* 0469-4236
0071-9218 Frankfurt am Main. Statistisches Amt und Wahlamt. Statistisches Jahrbuch
0071-9226 Frankfurter Beitraege zur Germanistik
0071-9234 Frankfurter Geographische Hefte†
0071-9277 Fraser's Canadian Trade Directory
0071-9285 Frater of Psi Omega
0071-9293 Fraternal Actuarial Association. Proceedings†
0071-9307 Free and Inexpensive Learning Materials†
0071-9315 Free China *see* 0304-1204
0071-9331 Free-World Trends in Passenger-Car Production and Engines *changed to* World Trends in Passenger-Car Production and Engines
0071-934X Freedom from Hunger Campaign. Basic Studies†
0071-9366 Freedom of Speech Yearbook *changed to* S C A Free Speech Yearbook
0071-9374 Freelance Photo Journalist. Yearbook
0071-9382 Freer Gallery of Art, Washington, D.C. Occasional Papers
0071-9390 Freiberger Forschungshefte. Montanwissenschaften: Reihe A. Bergbau und Geotechnik, Arbeitsschutz und Sicherheitstechnik, Grundstoff-Verfahrenstechnik, Maschinen- und Energietechnik
0071-9404 Freiberger Forschungshefte. Montanwissenschaften: Reihe C. Geowissenschaften
0071-9412 Freiberger Forschungshefte. Montanwissenschaften. Reihe D: Economic Sciences.
0071-9420 Freiberger Forschungshefte. Montanwissenschaften: Reihe B. Metallurgie *changed to* Freiberger Forschungshefte. Montanwissenschaften: Reihe B. Metallurgie und Werstofftechnik
0071-9439 Freiburger Geographische Arbeiten†
0071-9447 Freiburger Geographische Hefte
0071-9463 Freies Deutsches Hochstift, Frankfurt am Main. Jahrbuch
0071-9471 Freight Industry Yearbook
0071-948X Fremdenverkehr in Oesterreich
0071-9498 Fremdenverkehrswissenschaftliche Reihe†
0071-9536 Fresh Water and Salmon Fisheries Research (Scotland)†
0071-9544 Fifth District Dental Society. Bulletin *changed to* Thirtieth District Dental Society, Fresno, California. Bulletin
0071-9552 Universite de Fribourg. Paedagogisches Institut. Studien und Forschungsberichte†
0071-9560 F C L Action
0071-9587 Friends Historical Society. Journal
0071-9609 Friends Service Council. Annual Report *see* 0260-9584
0071-9617 American Friends Service Committee. Annual Report
0071-9625 Fringe Benefit Costs in Canada *see* 0701-1539
0071-9641 Frontier Military Series
0071-965X Frontiers of Biology†
0071-9676 Frontiers of Radiation Therapy and Oncology
0071-9684 Frozen Food Factbook and Directory *changed to* National Frozen Food Association Directory
0071-9692 Frozen Foods Year Book *changed to* Frozen and Chilled Foods Year Book
0071-9730 Fuchsia Annual
0071-9749 Fuehrer durch die technische Literatur
0071-9757 Fuehrer zu Archaeologischen Denkmaelern in Deutschland
0071-9765 Fuehrung und Organisation der Unternehmung
0071-9773 Fuentes Indigenas de la Cultura Nahuatl
0071-9781 Fukui University. Faculty of Education. Memoirs. Series 2: Natural Science
0071-979X Fulcrum
0071-982X Fundacion Bariloche. Boletin *changed to* Universitaet Zuerich. Soziologisches Institut. Bulletin
0071-9838 Fundacion Bariloche. Departamento de Sociologia. Documentos de Trabajo *changed to* Fundacion Bariloche. Desarrollos Sinergicos. Publicaciones
0071-9846 Fundacion Bariloche. Programa de Recursos Naturales y Energia. Publicaciones *changed to* Fundacion Bariloche. Instituto de Economia de la Energia. Publicaciones
0071-9862 Fundamentals of Educational Planning
0071-9870 Fundamentals of Educational Planning. Lecture-Discussion Series†
0071-9889 Fundberichte aus Hessen
0071-9897 Fundberichte aus Schwaben, Neue Folge *changed to* Fundberichte aus Baden-Wuerttemberg
0071-9900 Fundheft fuer Arbeitsrecht *see* 0173-1688
0071-9919 Fundheft fuer Oeffentliches Recht
0071-9927 Fundheft fuer Zivilrecht
0071-9943 Funnyworld
0071-9951 Funspots Directory *changed to* Funparks Directory
0071-996X Furnished Holiday Homes and Caravans *changed to* Self-Catering Holiday Homes, Caravans & Boats
0071-9994 Furniture Forum†
0072-0003 Further Aspects of Piaget's Work†
0072-0038 Fysiatricky a Reumatologicky Vestnik
0072-0046 G; Documentation Technique et Commerciale des Vendeurs de Gaz
0072-0062 G Q, Guide to Fashion Sources†
0072-0070 Gabinetto Disegni e Stampe degli Uffizi. Cataloghi.
0072-0089 Galerie Nierendorf, Berlin. Kunstblaetter
0072-0100 Gallia Prehistoire. Supplement
0072-0119 Gallia. Supplement
0072-0127 Galpin Society Journal
0072-0135 Games and Toys Yearbook *changed to* Toys & Games Trader Yearbook
0072-0143 Gandhi Memorial Lectures†
0072-0151 Gann Monographs *changed to* Gann Monographs on Cancer Research
0072-016X Ganterie Francaise†
0072-0178 Gardens' Bulletin, Singapore
0072-0186 Gardens of England and Wales Open to the Public *changed to* Gardens in England and Wales
0072-0208 Gas and Fuel Corporation of Victoria. Annual Report
0072-0216 British Gas Corporation. Report and Accounts
0072-0232 Gas Industry Directory *see* 0307-3084
0072-0240 Gas Journal Directory *see* 0307-3084
0072-0259 Gas Marketing Pocket Book and Diary
0072-0267 Gas Turbine Catalog *see* 0748-0903
0072-0291 Gaster; l'Annuaire de Gastro-Enterologie
0072-0313 Gaz de France. Rapport Annuel†
0072-0321 Gaz de France. Secretariat General. Schema d'Organisation Profor
0072-033X Gazdasagtorteneti Ertekezesek
0072-0348 Gazeteer of India
0072-0356 Gazeto
0072-0364 Politechnika Gdanska. Zeszyty Naukowe. Fizyka
0072-0372 Politechnika Gdanska. Zeszyty Naukowe. Matematyka
0072-0380 Politechnika Gdanska. Zeszyty Naukowe. Mechanika
0072-0402 Uniwersytet Gdanskl. Wydzial Matematyki, Fizyki, Chemii. Zeszyty Naukowe. Matematyka
0072-0410 Gdanskie Towarzystwo Naukowe. Wydzial 1. Nauk Spolecznych i Humanistycznych. Komisja Archeologiczna. Prace
0072-0429 Gdanskie Towarzystwo Naukowe. Wydzial 1. Nauk Spolecznych i Humanistycznych. Seria Popularnonaukowa "Pomorze Gdanskie"
0072-0437 Gdanskie Towarzystwo Naukowe. Wydzial 1. Nauk Spolecznych i Humanistycznych. Seria Zrodel
0072-0445 Gdanskie Towarzystwo Naukowe. Wydzial 3. Nauk Matematyczno-Przyrodniczych. Rozprawy

1370 ISSN INDEX

ISSN	Title
0072-0453	Uniwersytet Gdanski. Wydzial Humanistyczny. Zeszyty Naukowe. Filozofia i Socjologia
0072-0461	Uniwersytet Gdanski. Wydzial Humanistyczny. Zeszyty Naukowe. Historia
0072-047X	Uniwersytet Gdanski. Wydzial Humanistyczny. Zeszyty Naukowe. Pedagogika, Historia Wychowania
0072-0488	Uniwersytet Gdanski. Wydzial Humanistyczny. Zeszyty Naukowe. Prace Historyczno-Literackie
0072-0496	Morski Instytut Rybacki, Gdynia. Prace. Seria A: Oceanograficzno - Ichtiologiczna†
0072-050X	Morski Instytut Rybacki, Gdynia. Prace. Seria B: Technika Rybacka i Technologia Ryb†
0072-0518	Morski Instytut Rybacki, Gdynia. Prace. Seria C: Ekonomika Rybacka†
0072-0526	Gebbie House Magazine Directory *changed to* Internal Publications Directory
0072-0542	Geiriadur Prifysgol Cymru
0072-0550	Geistige Begegnung
0072-0569	Gem State R.N. *see* 0192-298X
0072-0577	Gemeinschaft der Selbst-Verwirklichung. Jahresheft *changed to* Selbst-Verwirklichung: Jahresheft
0072-0585	Genava
0072-0623	General Agreement on Tariffs and Trade. Basic Instruments and Selected Documents Series. Supplement
0072-064X	General Agreement on Tariffs and Trade. International Trade
0072-0658	General Catalogue of Unesco and Unesco-Sponsored Publications
0072-0666	General Conference of the New Church. Yearbook
0072-0674	General Dental Council. Dentists Register
0072-0682	General Dental Council. Minutes of the Proceedings
0072-0690	General Directory of the Press and Periodicals in Jordan and Kuwait
0072-0704	General Directory of the Press and Periodicals in Syria
0072-0720	General Education Reading Material Series
0072-0747	General Fisheries Council for the Mediterranean. Proceedings and Technical Papers. Debats et Documents Techniques
0072-0755	General Fisheries Council for the Mediterranean. Reports of the Sessions
0072-0763	General Medical Council. Medical Register
0072-0771	General Semantics Bulletin
0072-078X	General Stud Book
0072-0798	General Systems Yearbook
0072-0801	Geneseo Studies in Library and Information Science†
0072-081X	Genetics Lectures†
0072-0828	Musee d'Ethnographie de la Ville de Geneve. Bulletin Annuel
0072-0836	Universite de Geneve. Section d'Histoire. Documents
0072-0844	Genie Industriel; Catalogue de l'Ingenierie
0072-0852	Universita degli Studi di Genova. Istituto di Filologia Classica e Medievale. Pubblicazioni
0072-0860	Universita degli Studi di Genova. Istituto di Paleografia e Storia Medievale. Collana. Storica di Fonti e Studi *changed to* Universita degli Studi di Genova. Istituto di Medievistica. Collana. Storica di Fonti e Studi
0072-0879	Gentes Herbarum
0072-0887	Genuine Irish Old Moore's Almanac
0072-0909	Geographer
0072-0917	Geografinis Metrastis
0072-0925	Geographical Observer
0072-0941	Geographische Gesellschaft, Munich. Mitteilungen
0072-095X	Geographisches Jahrbuch
0072-0968	Geographisches Taschenbuch
0072-0984	Geography of New Zealand†
0072-0992	Geologia Colombiana
0072-100X	Geologia Sudetica
0072-1018	Geologica et Palaeontologica
0072-1026	Geologica Ultraiectina
0072-1042	Geological Association of Canada. Special Paper
0072-1050	Geological Journal
0072-1069	Geological Society of America. Memoirs
0072-1077	Geological Society of America. Special Papers
0072-1085	Geological Society of Australia. Special Publication
0072-1107	Geologie des Aires Oceaniques†
0072-1115	Universitaet Hamburg. Geologisch-Palaeontologisches Institut. Mitteilungen
0072-1174	Geophysica Norvegica
0072-1182	Geofizicheskii Byulleten' *see* 0016-7886
0072-1190	George Ernest Morrison Lectures in Ethnology
0072-1204	Georgetown University. Center for Strategic and International Studies. Special Report Series†
0072-1212	Georgetown University. Institute of Languages and Linguistics. Report of the Annual Round Table Meeting on Linguistics and Language Studies *see* 0196-7207
0072-1220	Georgia Congress of Parents and Teachers. Annual Summer Institute. Handbook for P T A Leaders *changed to* Georgia Congress of Parents and Teachers. Annual Leadership Training Conference. Workshop for P T A Leaders
0072-1247	Georgia State University. Hospital Administration Program. Occasional Publication *see* 0093-8041
0072-1255	University of Georgia. Anthropology Curriculum Project. Occasional Paper Series†
0072-1263	University of Georgia. College of Business Administration. Travel Research Series†
0072-1271	University of Georgia. College of Agriculture Experiment Stations. Bulletin
0072-128X	University of Georgia. College of Agriculture Experiment Stations. Research Reports
0072-131X	University of Georgia Libraries. Miscellanea†
0072-1379	Georgia Vital Morbidity Statistics *changed to* Georgia Vital Statistics Data Book
0072-1395	Geoscience and Man *see* 0191-6122
0072-1409	Geoscience Information Society. Proceedings
0072-1417	Geoserials *changed to* Geosources
0072-1433	German Arab Trade
0072-145X	German Motor Tribune
0072-1476	German Research Service
0072-1484	Germanica†
0072-1492	Germanistische Linguistik
0072-1549	D B Report
0072-1573	Germany (Federal Republic, 1949-). Bundesministerium fuer Ernaehrung, Landwirtschaft und Forsten. Jahresbericht. Forschung im Bereich des Bundesministers. *see* 0343-7477
0072-1581	Statistisches Jahrbuch ueber Ernaehrung, Landwirtschaft und Forsten der Bundesrepublik Deutschland
0072-159X	Germany (Federal Republic, 1949-). Sachverstaendigenrat zur Begutachtung der Gesamtwirtschaftlichen Entwicklung. Jahresgutachten
0072-1603	Deutscher Wetterdienst. Seewetteramt. Einzelveroeffentlichungen
0072-1611	Germany (Federal Republic, 1949-). Statistisches Bundesamt Arbeiten *changed to* Survey of German Federal Statistics
0072-162X	Das Arbeitsgebiet der Bundesstatistik
0072-1638	Germany (Federal Republic, 1949-). Statistisches Bundesamt. Alphabetisches Laenderverzeichnis fuer die Aussenhandelsstatistik
0072-1646	Germany (Federal Republic, 1949-) Statistisches Bundesamt. Fachserie 7, Aussenhandel, Reihe 1: Zusammenfassende Uebersichten fuer den Aussenhandel
0072-1654	Germany (Federal Republic, 1949-). Statistisches Bundesamt. Fachserie 7, Aussenhandel, Reihe 2: Aussenhandel nach Waren und Laendern (Spezialhandel)
0072-1662	Germany (Federal Republic, 1949-). Statistisches Bundesamt. Fachserie 7, Aussenhandel, Reihe 3: Aussenhandel Nach Laendern und Warengruppen (Spezialhandel)
0072-1697	Germany (Federal Republic, 1949-). Statistisches Bundesamt. Fachserie 7, Aussenhandel, Reihe 6: Durchfuhr im Seeverkehr und Seeumschlag
0072-1700	Germany (Federal Republic, 1949-). Statistisches Bundesamt. Fachserie 7, Aussenhandel, Reihe 7: Sonderbeitraege.
0072-1719	Germany (Federal Republic, 1949-) Statistisches Bundesamt. Ausgewaehlte Zahlen fuer die Bauwirtschaft
0072-1727	Germany (Federal Republic, 1949-). Statistisches Bundesamt. Fachserie 4, Reihe 5: Beschaeftigung, Umsatz, Investitionen und Kosten Struktur im Baugewerbe *changed to* Germany (Federal Republic, 1949-). Statistisches Bundesamt. Fachserie 4, Produzierendes Gewerbe, Reihe 5
0072-1735	Germany (Federal Republic, 1949-). Statistisches Bundesamt. Fachserie 5, Bautaetigkeit und Wohnungen, Reihe 1: Bautaetigkeit
0072-1743	Germany (Federal Republic, 1949-). Statistisches Bundesamt. Fachserie 5, Bautaetigkeit und Wohnungen, Reihe 2: Bewilligungen im Sozialen Wohnungsbau
0072-1751	Germany (Federal Republic, 1949-). Statistisches Bundesamt. Fachserie 5, Bautaetigkeit und Wohnungen, Reihe 3: Bestand an Wohnungen
0072-1778	Germany (Federal Republic, 1949-). Statistisches Bundesamt. Fachserie 11: Bildung und Kultur
0072-1786	Germany (Federal Republic, 1949) Statistisches Bundesamt. Bevoelkering und Kultur. Reihe 1: Bevoelkerungsstand und Entwicklung *changed to* Germany (Federal Republic, 1949-) Statistisches Bundesamt. Bevoelkering und Erwerbstaetigkeit. Reihe 1: Gebiet und Bevoelkerung
0072-1794	Germany (Federal Republic, 1949-). Statistisches Bundesamt. Fachserie 1, Bevoelkerung und Erwerbstaetigkeit, Reihe 1: Gebiet und Bevoelkerung
0072-1808	Germany (Federal Republic, 1949-) Statistisches Bundesamt. Fachserie 1, Reihe 2.3: Wanderungen†
0072-1832	Germany (Federal Republic, 1949-). Statistisches Bundesamt. Fachserie 1, Bevoelkerung und Erwerbstaetigkeit, Reihe 4: Erwerbetaetigkeit
0072-1840	Germany (Federal Republic, 1949-). Statistisches Bundesamt. Fachserie 12, Gesundheitswesen, Reihe 1: Ausgewaehlte Zahlen fuer das Gesundheitswesen
0072-1859	Germany (Federal Republic, 1949-). Statistisches Bundesamt. Fachserie 10. Rechtspflege
0072-1867	Bevoelkerungsstruktur und Wirtschaftskraft der Bundeslaender
0072-1964	Germany (Federal Republic, 1949-). Statistisches Bundesamt. Fachserie 6, Handel, Gastgewerbe, Reiseverkehr; Reihe 1: Grosshandel
0072-1972	Germany (Federal Republic, 1949-). Statistisches Bundesamt. Fachserie 6, Handel, Gastgewerbe, Reiseverkehr; Reihe 3: Einzelhandel
0072-1980	Germany (Federal Republic, 1949-) Statistisches Bundesamt. Fachserie 6, Handel, Gastgewerbe, Reiseverhr; Reihe 6: Wahrenverkehr mit der Deutschen Demokratischen Republik und Berlin (Ost)
0072-1999	Germany (Federal Republic, 1949-). Statistisches Bundesamt. Fachserie 6, Handel, Gastgewerbe, Reiseverkehr; Reihe 7: Reiseverkehr
0072-2014	Germany (Federal Republic, 1949-). Statistisches Bundesamt. Fachserie 9, Reihe 1: Boden- und Kommunalkreditinstitute†
0072-2022	Germany (Federal Republic, 1949-) Statistisches Bundesamt. Geld und Kredit. Reihe 2: Aktienkurse *changed to* Germany (Federal Republic, 1949-) Statistisches Bundesamt. Fachserie 9, Geld und Kredit, Reihe 2: Aktienmaerkte
0072-2030	Germany (Federal Republic, 1949-). Statistisches Bundesamt. Fachserie 2, Unternehmen und Arbeitsstaetten, Reihe 4: Zahlungsschwierigkeiten
0072-2073	Germany (Federal Republic, 1949-). Statistisches Bundesamt. Fachserie 4, Produzierendes Gewerbe, Reihe 5: Sonderbeitraege
0072-209X	Germany (Federal Republic, 1949-) Statistisches Bundesamt. Fachserie 4, Reihe 2: Indices des Auftragseingangs in Ausgewaehlten Industriezweigen und im Bauhauptgewerbe *changed to* Germany (Federal Republic, 1949-) Statistisches Bundesamt. Fachserie 4, Produzierendes Gewerbe, Reihe 2.2: Indices des Auftragseingangs, des Umsatzes und des Auftragsbestands fuer das Verarbeitende Gewerbe und fuer das Bauhaupt Gewerbe
0072-2103	Germany (Federal Republic, 1949-). Statistisches Bundesamt. Fachserie 4, Produzierende Gastgewerbe, Reihe 7: Handwerk. Beschaeftigte um Umsatz im Handwerk
0072-3673	Germany (Federal Republic, 1949-). Statistisches Bundesamt. Fachserie 3, Land- und Fortswirtschaft, Fischerei; Reihe 4.5: Fischerei
0072-3681	Germany (Federal Republic, 1949-). Statistisches Bundesamt. Fachserie 3, Land- und Fortswirtschaft, Fischerei; Reihe 2: Betriebs-, Arbeits- und Einkommensverhaeltnisse
0072-3754	Germany (Federal Republic, 1949-). Statistisches Bundesamt. Fachserie 13, Reihe 2: Sozialhilfe; Reihe 3: Kriegsopferfuersorge
0072-3762	Germany (Federal Republic, 1949-). Statistisches Bundesamt. Fachserie 13, Sozialleistungen, Reihe 6: Jugendhilfe
0072-3789	Germany (Federal Republic, 1949-). Statistisches Bundesamt. Fachserie 16, Reihe 2: Arbeitnehmerverdienste in Industrie und Handel *changed to* Germany (Federal Republic, 1949-) Statistisches Bundesamt. Fachserie 16, Loehne und Gehaelter, Reihe 1: Arbeiterverdienste in der Landwirtschaft

ISSN INDEX 1371

0072-3797 Germany (Federal Republic, 1949-) Statistisches Bundesamt. Fachserie 16, Loehne und Gehaelten, Reihe 3: Arbeitverdienste im Handwerk
0072-3827 Germany (Federal Republic, 1949-) Statistisches Bundesamt. Fachserie 17, Preise, Reihe 10: Internationaler Vergleich der Preise fuer die Lebenserhaltung
0072-3843 Germany (Federal Republic, 1949-) Statistisches Bundesamt. Fachserie 16, Loehne und Gehaelter, Reihe 4: Tarifloehne und Tarifgehaelter
0072-386X Germany (Federal Republic, 1949-) Statistisches Bundesamt. Fachserie 15, Reihe 1: Wirtschaftsrechnungen *changed to* Germany (Federal Republic, 1949-) Statistisches Bundesamt. Fachserie 15, Wirtschaftsrechnungen, Reihe 1: Einnahmen und Ausgaben Ausgewaehlter Privater Haushalte
0072-3878 Germany (Federal Republic, 1949-) Statistisches Bundesamt. Fachserie 17, Preise, Reihe 3: Index der Grundstoffrpreise
0072-3886 Germany (Federal Republic, 1949-) Statistisches Bundesamt. Fachserie 17, Reihe 2: Preise und Preisindizes fuer Industrielle Produkte. Erzeugerpreise *changed to* Germany (Federal Republic, 1949-) Statistisches Bundesamt. Fachserie 17, Preise, Reihe 2: Preise und Preisindizes fuer Gewerbliche Produkte. Erzeugerpreise
0072-3894 Germany (Federal Republic, 1949-). Statistisches Bundesamt. Fachserie 17, Preise, Reihe 1: Preise und Preisindizes fuer die Land- und Forstwirtschaft
0072-3908 Germany (Federal Republic, 1949-) Statistisches Bundesamt. Preise, Loehne, Wirtschaftsrechnungen. Reihe 5: Preise und Preisindices fuer Bauwerke und Bauland *changed to* Germany (Federal Republic 1949-) Statistisches Bundesamt. Fachserie 17, Preise, Reihe 5: Kaufwerte fuer Bauland
0072-3916 Germany (Federal Republic, 1949-) Statistisches Bundesamt. Fachserie 17, Preise, Reihe 7: Preise und Preisindices der Lebenshaltung
0072-3924 Germany (Federal Republic, 1949-). Statistisches Bundesamt. Fachserie 17, Preise, Reihe 9: Preise fuer Verkehrsleistungen
0072-3940 Germany (Federal Republic, 1949-) Statistisches Bundesamt. Fachserie 17, Preise, Reihe 11: Preise und Preisindizes im Ausland
0072-3967 Studies on Statistics
0072-3975 Germany (Federal Republic, 1949-) Statistisches Bundesamt. Unternehmen und Arbeitsstaetten. Reihe 1: Die Kostenstruktur in der Wirtschaft†
0072-4009 Germany (Federal Republic, 1949-). Statistisches Bundesamt. Fachserie 18, Volkswirtschaftliche Gesamtrechnungen, Reihe 1: Konten und Standardtabellen
0072-4017 Germany (Federal Republic, 1949-) Statistisches Bundesamt. Fachserie 8, Verkehr, Reihe 4: Binnenschiffahrt
0072-4025 Germany (Federal Republic, 1949-) Statistisches Bundesamt. Fachserie 8, Verkehr, Reihe 5: Seeschiffahrt
0072-4033 Germany (Federal Republic, 1949-) Statistisches Bundesamt. Fachserie 8, Verkehr, Reihe 6: Luftverkehr
0072-4041 Germany (Federal Republic, 1949-) Statistisches Bundesamt. Fachserie 8, Verkehr, Reihe 2: Eisenbahnverkehr
0072-405X Germany (Federal Republic, 1949-). Statistisches Bundesamt. Fachserie 8, Verkehr, Reihe 3: Strassenverkehr
0072-4068 Germany (Federal Republic, 1949-). Statistisches Bundesamt. Fachserie 8, Verkehr, Reihe 3.3: Haushaelte und Familien
0072-4092 Germany (Federal Republic, 1949-) Statistisches Bundesamt. Fachserie 8, Verkehr, Reihe 1: Gueterverkehr der Verkehrszweige
0072-4106 Germany (Federal Republic, 1949-) Statistisches Bundesamt. Warenverzeichnis fuer die Aussenhandelsstatistik
0072-4114 Germany (Federal Republic, 1949-) Statistisches Bundesamt. Zahlenkompass
0072-4122 Annalen der Meteorologie. Neue Folge
0072-4130 Deutscher Wetterdienst. Berichte
0072-4149 Deutscher Wetterdienst. Bibliographien
0072-4157 Geron†
0072-4165 Gesamtverzeichnis Oesterreichischer Dissertationen
0072-4173 Geschichte der Ethik†
0072-4203 Geschichtliche Landeskunde
0072-4211 Geselecteerde Agrarische Cijfers van de E E C *changed to* E E G Vademecum
0072-422X Gesellschaft fuer die Geschichte und Bibliographie des Brauwesens. Jahrbuch
0072-4238 Gesellschaft fuer Niedersaechsische Kirchengeschichte. Jahrbuch
0072-4246 Gesellschaft fuer Physiologische Chemie, Mosbach. Colloquium *see* 0366-5887
0072-4254 Gesellschaft fuer Schleswig-Holsteinische Geschichte. Zeitschrift
0072-4270 Gesellschaft pro Vindonissa. Jahresbericht
0072-4289 Gesellschaft pro Vindonissa. Veroeffentlichungen
0072-4327 Geyer's Who Makes It Directory
0072-4335 Ghana. Central Bureau of Statistics. Economic Survey
0072-436X Ghana Law Reports
0072-4378 Ghana National Bibliography
0072-4408 Ghana. Railway and Ports Administration. Report†
0072-4416 University of Ghana. Institute of Statistical, Social and Economic Research. Technical Research Monographs *changed to* University of Ghana. Institute of Statistical, Social and Economic Research. Technical Publication Series
0072-4432 Rijksuniversiteit te Gent. Sterrenkundig Observatorium. Mededelingen
0072-4440 Rijksuniversiteit te Gent. Sterrenkundig Observatorium. Mededelingen: Meteorologie en Geofysica
0072-4459 Giannini Foundation of Agricultural Economics. Research Report
0072-4467 Gids bij de Prijscourant
0072-4475 Gids van de Nederlandse Gasindustrie *changed to* Gids van Produkten en Materialen Voorzien van Het GIVEG-Merk
0072-4483 Universitaetsbibliothek Giessen. Berichte und Arbeiten
0072-4491 Universitaetsbibliothek Giessen. Kurzberichte aus den Papyrus-Sammlungen
0072-4505 Gift and Decorative Accessories Buyers Directory
0072-4513 Gifu University. Faculty of Agriculture. Research Bulletin
0072-4521 Gifu University. School of Medicine. Archives
0072-4548 Gioventu Passionista
0072-4556 Girios Aidas†
0072-4564 Girls School Year Book *changed to* Independent Schools Yearbook: Girls Schools
0072-4610 University of Glasgow. Social and Economic Studies. Occasional Papers†
0072-4629 University of Glasgow. Social and Economic Research Studies†
0072-4637 Glass Containers *changed to* Glass Packaging Institute. Annual Report
0072-4645 Glass/Metal Catalog *see* 0147-300X
0072-4661 Glaxo Volume; an Occasional Contribution to the Science and Art of Medicine†
0072-467X Glenbow-Alberta Institute. Occasional Paper
0072-4688 Politechnika Slaska. Zeszyty Naukowe. Elektryka
0072-4696 Politechnika Slaska. Zeszyty Naukowe. Inzynieria Sanitarna *changed to* Politechnika Slaska. Zeszyty Naukowe. Inzynieria Srodowiska
0072-470X Politechnika Slaska. Zeszyty Naukowe. Matematyka-Fizyka
0072-4718 Politechnika Slaska. Zeszyty Naukowe. Nauki Spoleczne
0072-4742 Global Focus Series†
0072-4750 Glossaria Interpretum†
0072-4769 Glottodidactica; an International Journal of Applied Linguistics
0072-4777 Glove News
0072-4793 Goeteborger Germanistische Forschungen
0072-4807 Acta Regiae Societatis Scientiarum et Litterarum Gothoburgensis. Zoologica
0072-4815 Acta Regiae Societatis Scientiarum et Litterarum Gothoburgensis. Geophysica
0072-4823 Acta Regiae Societatis Scientiarum et Litterarum Gothoburgensis. Humaniora
0072-4831 Goeteborgs Tandlaekare Saellskap. Aarsbok†
0072-484X Goethe-Gesellschaft. Jahrbuch *see* 0323-4207
0072-4858 Goethe-Institut zur Pflege Deutscher Sprache und Kultur im Ausland. Jahrbuch *changed to* Goethe-Institut zur Pflege der Deutschen Sprache im Ausland und zur Foerderung der Internationalen Kulturellen Zusammenarbeit. Jahrbuch
0072-4866 Niedersaechsische Staats- und Universitaetsbibliothek, Goettingen. Arbeiten
0072-4882 Goettinger Jahrbuch
0072-4890 Goff's Guide to Motels in Great Britain and Europe *changed to* Goff's Guide to Motels and Motorways in Great Britain and Ireland
0072-4904 Going-To-College Handbook
0072-4912 Gokhale Institute of Politics and Economics. Studies
0072-4920 Gold†
0072-4939 All-Asia Guide
0072-4947 Golf Course Superintendents Association of America. Proceedings of the International Conference and Show
0072-4955 Golf Guide
0072-4963 Golf Rules Illustrated
0072-498X Golfer's Handbook
0072-4998 Gondwana Newsletter
0072-5005 Good Food Guide
0072-5013 Gornoslaskie Studia Socjologiczne
0072-503X Gothenburg Studies in English
0072-5048 Gothenburg Studies in Philosophy†
0072-5056 Gothenburg Studies in Physics†
0072-5064 Demografiska Forskargruppen, Goeteborg. Reports†
0072-5072 Oceanografiska Institutet, Goeteborg. Meddelanden *changed to* Goeteborgs Universitet. Oceanografiska Institutionen. Reports
0072-5080 Goeteborgs Universitet. Ekonomisk-Historiska Institutionen. Meddelanden
0072-5099 Goeteborgs Universitet. Sociologiska Institutionen. Forsknings-Rapport
0072-5102 Goeteborgs Universitet. Sociologiska Institutionen. Monografier
0072-5110 Goeteborgs Universitet. Statistiska Institutionen. Skriftserie. Publications
0072-5129 Sell's Government and Municipal Contractors Register *see* 0140-5764
0072-5137 Government Contracts Directory
0072-5145 Government Contracts Guide†
0072-5153 Government Contracts Monographs
0072-5161 Government Finance Brief. New Series
0072-517X Government in Hawaii
0072-5188 Government Reference Books
0072-5196 Arizona State University. Governmental Finance Institute. Proceedings *see* 0078-9151
0072-520X Governmental Research Association Directory
0072-5250 Graduate Fellowship Awards Announced by National Science Foundation
0072-5277 Graduate Study in Psychology *changed to* Graduate Study in Psychology and Associated Fields
0072-5285 Graduate Texts in Mathematics
0072-5315 Grafton Fashions for Men†
0072-534X Grain Crops†
0072-5358 Grain Trade of Canada†
0072-5382 Universidad de Granada. Colleccion Monografica
0072-5404 Grandes Figures de la Charite
0072-5439 Grandes Todos
0072-5455 Grands Courants de la Pensee Mondiale Contemporaine†
0072-548X Graphic Arts Japan
0072-5498 Graphic Arts Trade Directory and Register *see* 0147-1651
0072-5501 Graphic Directory†
0072-551X Graphic Guide to Consumer Markets *see* 0072-8314
0072-5528 Graphis Annual
0072-5536 Graphis Packaging†
0072-5544 Grass†
0072-5552 Grassland Research Institute, Hurley, England (Berkshire) Technical Reports *changed to* Animal and Grassland Research Institute, Hurley, England (Berkshire) Technical Reports
0072-5560 Grassland Society of Southern Africa. Proceedings of the Annual Congresses *see* 0256-6702
0072-5579 Great Black Athletes†
0072-5587 Great Britain. Admiralty Advisory Committee Reports: Structural Steel†
0072-5595 Great Britain. Aeronautical Research Council. Current Paper Series
0072-5609 Great Britain. Aeronautical Research Council. Reports and Memoranda Series
0072-5617 Great Britain. Air Transport Licensing Board. Report *see* 0306-3569
0072-5625 Ancient Monuments Board for England. Annual Report
0072-5633 Great Britain. Department of Trade. Bankruptcy: General Annual Report
0072-5641 Great Britain. Civil Aviation Authority. Civil Aviation Publications
0072-565X Great Britain. Department of Trade. Companies: General Annual Report
0072-5668 Great Britain. Department of Trade. Export of Works of Art
0072-5676 Great Britain. Department of Trade. Import Duties Act 1958. Annual Report
0072-5684 Great Britain. Board of Trade. Insurance Business: Annual Report *see* 0308-499X
0072-5692 Great Britain. Department of Trade. Particulars of Dealers in Securities and of Trust Units
0072-5706 Great Britain. Department of Trade. Patents, Design and Trade Marks (Annual Report)
0072-5714 Great Britain. Central Health Services Council. Report†
0072-5722 Great Britain. Central Office of Information. Overseas Publications Division. Reference Pamphlets Series
0072-5730 Great Britain. Central Statistical Office. Annual Abstract of Statistics
0072-5749 Great Britain. Central Statistical Office Abstracts of Regional Statistics *see* 0261-1783

1372 ISSN INDEX

0072-5757 Great Britain. Central Statistical Office. Research Series
0072-5765 Great Britain. Central Statistical Office. Social Trends
0072-5773 Great Britain. Cinematograph Films Council. Annual Report
0072-579X Great Britain. Commission on Industrial Relations. Reports†
0072-5803 Great Britain. Department of the Environment. Committee on Synthetic Detergents. Progress Report†
0072-5811 Great Britain. Committee on Tribology. Report†
0072-582X Great Britain. Department of Education and Science. Computer Board for Universities and Research Councils. Report
0072-5838 Great Britain. Consumer Council. Report†
0072-5846 Annual Statement of the Overseas Trade of the United Kingdom
0072-5870 Great Britain. Department of Education and Science. Building Bulletins
0072-5889 Great Britain. Department of Education and Science. Education Planning Paper†
0072-5897 Great Britain. Department of Education and Science. Education Surveys
0072-5900 Great Britain. Department of Education and Science. Statistics of Education
0072-5919 Great Britain. Department of Education and Science. Science Policy Studies
0072-5927 Great Britain. Department of Employment. Family Expenditure Survey
0072-5935 Great Britain. Department of Employment and Productivity. Safety, Health and Welfare. New Series Booklets†
0072-5943 Great Britain. Department of Employment. Training Information Papers†
0072-5994 Great Britain. Department of Health and Social Security. Hospital Building Bulletins†
0072-6001 Great Britain. Department of Health and Social Security. Hospital Building, England and Wales: Progress Report†
0072-601X Great Britain. Department of Health and Social Security. Hospital Building Notes *changed to* Great Britain. Department of Health and Social Security. Health Building Notes
0072-6028 Great Britain. Department of Health and Social Security. Hospital Equipment Notes *see* 0141-1403
0072-6036 Great Britain. Department of Health and Social Security. Hospital In-Patient Inquiry
0072-6044 Great Britain. Department of Health and Social Security. Hospital Organization and Methods Service Reports†
0072-6052 Great Britain. Department of Health and Social Security. Health Service Design Notes†
0072-6060 Great Britain. Department of Health and Social Security. Hospital Technical Memoranda†
0072-6087 Great Britain. Department of Health and Social Security. On the State of the Public Health
0072-6125 Great Britain. Department of Health and Social Security. Statistical Report Series *changed to* Great Britain. Department of Health and Social Security. Statistical and Research Report Series
0072-6141 Scotland. Directorate of Fisheries Research. Annual Report *see* 0140-5012
0072-615X General Agreement on Tariffs and Trade. G A T T Activities in (Year)
0072-6168 Great Britain. Foreign and Commonwealth Office. Antigua. Report†
0072-6184 Great Britain. Foreign and Commonwealth Office. Bahamas. Report†
0072-6192 Great Britain. Foreign and Commonwealth Office. Bermuda. Report†
0072-6230 Great Britain. Foreign and Commonwealth Office. Colonial Numbered Series†
0072-6249 Great Britain. Foreign and Commonwealth Office. Dominica. Report†
0072-6257 Great Britain. Foreign and Commonwealth Office. Falkland Islands. Report†
0072-6303 Great Britain. Foreign and Commonwealth Office. Montserrat. Report†
0072-632X Great Britain. Foreign and Commonwealth Office. Overseas Research Publications†
0072-6338 Great Britain. Foreign and Commonwealth Office. St. Christopher-Nevis-Anguilla. Report†
0072-6354 Great Britain. Foreign and Commonwealth Office. St. Lucia. Report†
0072-6362 Great Britain. Foreign and Commonwealth Office. Seychelles. Report†
0072-6370 Great Britain. Foreign and Commonwealth Office. St. Vincent. Report†
0072-6397 Great Britain. Foreign and Commonwealth Office. Treaty Series
0072-6400 Great Britain. General Register Office. Studies on Medical and Population Subjects
0072-6419 Great Britain. Herring Industry Board. Annual Report *changed to* Great Britain. Sea Fish Industry Authority. Annual Report and Accounts
0072-6435 Great Britain. Home Office. Research Studies
0072-6443 Great Britain. Home Office. Studies in the Causes of Delinquency and the Treatment of Offenders
0072-6478 Great Britain. Industrial Reorganization Corporation. Report and Accounts†
0072-6486 Great Britain. Pest Infestation Control Laboratory. Report *see* 0261-698X
0072-6486 Great Britain. Pest Infestation Control Laboratory. Report *see* 0261-717X
0072-6486 Great Britain. Pest Infestation Control Laboratory. Report *see* 0261-6963
0072-6486 Great Britain. Pest Infestation Control Laboratory. Report *see* 0261-7161
0072-6486 Great Britain. Pest Infestation Control Laboratory. Report *changed to* Great Britain. Agricultural Science Service. Research and Development Reports: Pesticide Science
0072-6486 Great Britain. Pest Infestation Control Laboratory. Report *changed to* Great Britain. Agricultural Science Service. Research and Development Reports: Storage Pest
0072-6494 Great Britain. Institute of Geological Sciences. Memoirs of the Geological Survey of Great Britain *changed to* Great Britain. British Geological Survey. Memoirs
0072-6508 Great Britain. Iron and Steel Consumers' Council. Report†
0072-6516 Great Britain. Keeper of Public Records. Annual Report of the Keeper of Public Records on the Work of the Public Record Office and the Report of the Advisory Council on Public Records
0072-6524 Great Britain. Laboratory of the Government Chemist. Annual Report of the Government Chemist
0072-6532 Great Britain. Manpower Research Unit. Manpower Studies
0072-6559 Great Britain. Medical Research Council. Monitoring Report Series. Assay of Strontium - 90 in Human Bone in the United Kingdom *changed to* Great Britain. Medical Research Council. Special Report Series
0072-6567 Great Britain. Medical Research Council. Report *see* 0141-2256
0072-6575 Great Britain. Medical Research Council. Special Report Series†
0072-6583 Great Britain. Medical Research Council. Memoranda†
0072-6591 Great Britain. Mercantile Navy List
0072-6605 Great Britain. Meteorological Office. Annual Report
0072-6613 Great Britain. Meteorological Office. Geophysical Memoirs
0072-6621 Great Britain. Meteorological Office. Scientific Paper
0072-6664 Great Britain. Ministry of Agriculture, Fisheries and Food. Animal Disease Surveys†
0072-6680 Great Britain. Ministry of Agriculture. Fisheries and Food. Fishery Investigations. Series II: Sea Fisheries†
0072-6729 Great Britain. Ministry of Agriculture, Fisheries and Food. Technical Bulletin
0072-677X Great Britain. Ministry of Housing and Local Government. Handbook of Statistics†
0072-6796 Great Britain. Ministry of Housing and Local Government. Planning Bulletin *changed to* Great Britain. Department of the Environment. Housing and Construction. Planning Bulletin
0072-680X Great Britain. Ministry of Housing and Local Government. Report†
0072-6818 Great Britain. Department of the Environment. Statistics for Town and Country Planning. Series 1
0072-6826 Great Britain. Department of the Environment. Statistics for Town and Country Planning. Series 2
0072-6842 Great Britain. Department of the Environment. Archaeological Reports
0072-6850 Great Britain. Department of the Environment. Engineering Specifications
0072-6869 Great Britain. Department of the Environment. Metrication in the Construction Industry
0072-6893 Great Britain. Department of the Environment. Highway Statistics *changed to* Transport Statistics Great Britain
0072-6907 Great Britain. National Advisory Council on Art Education. Report†
0072-6923 Great Britain. National Agricultural Advisory Service. Experimental Husbandry Farms and Experimental Horticulture Stations. Progress Report†
0072-694X Great Britain. National Economic Development Office. Monographs†
0072-6958 Great Britain. National Film Finance Corporation. Annual Report
0072-6966 Great Britain National Health Service. Hospital Costing Returns *changed to* England and Wales National Health Service. Health Services Costing Returns
0072-6990 Great Britain. National Savings Committee. Report
0072-7008 Great Britain. Natural Environment Research Council. Report
0072-7016 Great Britain. Public Record Office. Handbooks
0072-7032 Great Britain. Public Works Loan Board. Report
0072-7059 Great Britain. Road Research Laboratory. Technical Papers†
0072-7067 Great Britain. Royal Commission on the Ancient and Historical Monuments and Constructions of England. Interim Report *changed to* Great Britain. Royal Commission on the Historical Monuments of England. Interim Report
0072-7075 Great Britain. Royal Commission on the Ancient and Historical Monuments and Constructions in Wales and Monmouthshire. Interim Report *changed to* Great Britain. Royal Commission on Ancient and Historical Monuments in Wales. Interim Report
0072-7083 Great Britain. Royal Commission on Historical Manuscripts. Commissioners' Reports to the Crown
0072-7091 Great Britain. Royal Commission on Historical Manuscripts. Joint Publication
0072-7105 Great Britain. Royal Mint. Annual Report
0072-7113 Great Britain. Schools Council Publications. Curriculum Bulletins
0072-7121 Great Britain. Schools Council Publications. Examinations Bulletins
0072-713X Great Britain. Schools Council Publications. Working Papers
0072-7148 Great Britain. Science Research Council. Report *see* 0261-7005
0072-7172 Great Britain. Soil Survey of England and Wales. Memoirs†
0072-7180 Great Britain. Soil Survey of England and Wales. Records
0072-7199 Great Britain. Soil Survey of England and Wales. Report
0072-7202 Great Britain. Soil Survey of England and Wales. Special Surveys
0072-7210 Great Britain. Soil Survey of England and Wales. Technical Monographs
0072-7229 Great Britain Specialised Stamp Catalogue
0072-7237 Great Britain. University Grants Committee. Annual Survey
0072-7245 Great Britain. Water Resources Board. Publication
0072-7253 Great Britain. Water Resources Board. Report
0072-7261 Great Gritain. White Fish Authority. Annual Report and Accounts *changed to* Great Britain. Sea Fish Industry Authority. Annual Report and Accounts
0072-727X Great Decisions
0072-7288 Great Ideas Today
0072-7296 Great Lakes Fishery Commission (United States and Canada) Annual Report
0072-730X Great Lakes Fishery Commission (United States and Canada) Technical Report Series
0072-7318 Great Lakes Red Book
0072-7326 Great Lakes Research Checklist
0072-7334 Great Ormond Street Gazette†
0072-7342 Great West and Indian Series
0072-7350 Greater London Papers
0072-7385 Greek National Committee for Astronomy. Annual Reports of the Astronomical Institutes of Greece
0072-7393 Greece. National Statistical Service. Annual Industrial Survey
0072-7407 Greece. National Statistical Service. Annuaire Statistique de l'Enseignement *changed to* Greece. National Statistical Service. Education Statistics
0072-7415 Greece. National Statistical Service. Annual Statistical Survey of Mines, Quarries and Salterns
0072-7423 Greece. National Statistical Service. Shipping Statistics
0072-7431 Greece. National Statistical Service. Statistical Yearbook of Public Finance *changed to* Greece. National Statistical Service. Public Finance Statistics
0072-744X Greek Coins in North American Collections *changed to* Ancient Coins in North American Collections
0072-7458 State of Greek Industry in (Year)
0072-7466 Greek Mathematical Society. Bulletin

ISSN INDEX 1373

0072-7474 Greek, Roman and Byzantine Monographs
0072-7482 Greek, Roman, and Byzantine Studies. Scholarly Aids
0072-7490 Greenwood's Guide to Great Lakes Shipping
0072-7504 Greifswald. Universitaet. Wissenschaftliche Zeitschrift. Gesellschafts- und Sprachwissenschaftliche Reihe *see* 0138-1016
0072-7520 Bibliotheque Universitaire, Grenoble. Publications
0072-7539 Universite des Sciences Sociales de Grenoble. Centre de Recherche d'Histoire Economique, Sociale et Institutionnelle. Collection. Serie Histoire Institutionnelle†
0072-7547 Universite des Sciences Sociales de Grenoble. Centre de Recherche d'Histoire Economique, Sociale et Institutionnelle. Collection. Serie Histoire Sociale†
0072-7555 Universite des Sciences Sociales de Grenoble. Centre de Recherche Economique et Sociale. Collection. Serie Agriculture et Devenir Social†
0072-7563 Universite des Sciences Sociales de Grenoble. Centre de Recherche Economique et Sociale. Collection. Serie Economie du Financement†
0072-7571 Universite des Sciences Sociales de Grenoble. Centre de Recherche Economique et Sociale. Collection. Serie Etudes d'Economie de l'Energie†
0072-758X Universite des Sciences Sociales de Grenoble. Centre de Recherche Economique et Sociale. Collection. Serie Economie du Developpement†
0072-7598 Universite des Sciences Sociales de Grenoble. Centre de Recherche Juridique. Collection. Serie Droit de la Propriete Industrielle†
0072-7601 Universite des Sciences Sociales de Grenoble. Centre de Recherche Juridique. Collection. Serie Droit du Tourisme†
0072-761X Universite des Sciences Sociales de Grenoble. Centre de Recherche Juridique. Collection. Serie Droits Etrangers et Droit Compare†
0072-7628 Universite des Sciences Sociales de Grenoble. Collection Generale†
0072-7636 Universite des Sciences Sociales de Grenoble. Institut d'Etudes Politiques. Serie Essais et Travaux†
0072-7644 Universite des Sciences Sociales de Grenoble. Institut d'Etudes Politiques. Serie Textes et Documents†
0072-7687 Gripper†
0072-7695 Grocer Directory of Multiples and Co-Operatives *changed to* Grocer Marketing Directory
0072-7717 Der Grosse Gartenkatalog
0072-7725 Grosse Heimatbuecher
0072-7741 Grosse Naturforscher
0072-775X Group for the Advancement of Psychiatry. Report *changed to* Group for the Advancement of Psychiatry. Publication
0072-7792 Groupement des Directeurs Publicitaires de France. Annuaire *changed to* Annuaire General de la Publicite
0072-7806 Groupement des Entreprises Francaises dans la Lutte Contre le Cancer. Bulletin National de Liaison
0072-7830 Grundlehren der Mathematischen Wissenschaften in Einzeldarstellungen *changed to* Grundlehren der Mathematischen Wissenschaften
0072-7865 Guam Business Directory
0072-7873 Guam. Department of Revenue and Taxation. Report
0072-7903 Guia de Editores y de Libreros de Espana
0072-7911 Guia Judicial de Lima
0072-792X Guida Camping d'Italia
0072-7954 Guide Analytique du Pharmacien d'Officine†
0072-7962 Guide Annuaire du Commerce Franco-Allemand
0072-7970 Guide de la Papeterie†
0072-7989 Guide de la Parfumerie
0072-8012 Guide des Ports: France, Maghreb, Algerie, Tunisie, Maroc, Afrique Noire
0072-8020 Guide des Prix Litteraires†
0072-8039 Guide des Sports†
0072-8047 Guide du Feu et de la Protection Civile *see* 0337-5781
0072-8055 Guide du Petrole, Gaz, Chimie *changed to* Guide du Petrole, Gaz, Petrochimie
0072-8063 Guide du Show-Business; Guide Professionnel du Spectacle
0072-8071 Guide du Slaviste†
0072-808X Guide Europeen de l'Immobilier†
0072-8098 Guide for Laboratory Animal Facilities and Care *changed to* Guide for the Care and Use of Laboratory Animals
0072-8101 Guide for Planning Educational Facilities
0072-8128 Guide International de l'Energie Atomique et des Etudes Spatiales *changed to* Guide International de l'Energie Nucleare
0072-8136 Guide International des Machines, Appareils, Outils†
0072-8144 Guide Medical et Hospitalier
0072-8209 Guide Rosenwald: Annuaire Medical et Pharmaceutique
0072-8217 Guide Sommaire des Ouvrages de Reference en Sciences Sociales†
0072-8284 Guide to College Courses in Film and Television
0072-8314 Guide to Consumer Markets†
0072-8322 Guide to Correspondence Studies in Colleges and Universities *see* 0733-6020
0072-8330 Guide to Europe†
0072-8403 Guide to Fluorescence Literature
0072-8411 Guide to Foreign Government-Loan Film (16 MM) *changed to* Guide to Free Loan Films About Foreign Lands
0072-842X Guide to Foreign Legal Materials Series†
0072-8438 Guide to Free-Loan Training Films (16 MM)†
0072-8446 Guide to Gas Chromatography Literature
0072-8454 Guide to Government in Hawaii
0072-8462 Guide to Government-Loan Films Volume 1: the Civilian Agencies
0072-8497 Guide to Graduate Departments of Geography in the United States and Canada *changed to* Guide to Departments of Geography in the United States and Canada
0072-8500 Guide to Graduate Study in Botany for the United States and Canada
0072-8519 Guide to Graduate Study: Programs Leading to the Ph.D. Degree†
0072-8551 Guide to Japanese Taxes
0072-8586 Guide to Military-Loan Films *changed to* Guide to Government-Loan Films
0072-8608 Guide to National Bibliographical Information Centres
0072-8616 Guide to New Zealand Income Tax Practice *see* 0111-9370
0072-8624 Guide to Reference Books
0072-8632 Guide to Reference Books. Supplement†
0072-8640 Guide to Reference Material
0072-8659 Guide to Refinery Operating Costs†
0072-8667 Guide to Reprints
0072-8705 Guide to Summer Camps and Summer Schools
0072-8713 Guide to the Coalfields
0072-873X Guide to the Performing Arts†
0072-8748 Guide to the Press of the World *see* 0265-5810
0072-8756 Guide to the Social Services
0072-8764 Guide to the World's Training Facilities in Documentation and Information Work.†
0072-8772 Travel Routes Around the World: Guide to Traveling Around the World by Passenger-Carrying Freighters†
0072-8802 Guidebook of English Coins, Nineteenth and Twentieth Centuries†
0072-8810 Guidebook of Modern United States Currency†
0072-8829 Guidebook of United States Coins
0072-8837 Guidebook to California Taxes
0072-8845 Guidebook to Illinois Taxes
0072-8853 Guidebook to Labor Relations
0072-8861 Guidebook to Massachusetts Taxes
0072-887X Guidebook to Michigan Taxes
0072-8888 Guidebook to New Jersey Taxes
0072-8896 Guidebook to New York Taxes
0072-890X Guidebook to Pennsylvania Taxes
0072-8918 Guidelines for Teachers
0072-8934 Guides to Information Sources in Science and Technology†
0072-8950 Guid'Ouest Africain†
0072-8977 Guild of Prescription Opticians of America. Reference List
0072-8985 Guildhall Miscellany *changed to* Guildhall Studies in London History
0072-9019 Gulf and Caribbean Fisheries Institute. Annual Proceedings
0072-9027 Gulf Research Reports†
0072-906X Guns and Ammo Annual†
0072-9086 Perspectives in Virology†
0072-9094 Gutenberg-Jahrbuch
0072-9108 Guyana. Geological Survey Department. Annual Reports *changed to* Guyana. Geology & Mines Commission. Annual Report
0072-9124 Guyana. Geological Survey Department. Mineral Resources Pamphlet *changed to* Guyana. Geology & Mines Commission. Mineral Resources Pamphlet
0072-9140 H.R. Macmillan Lectureship in Forestry
0072-9159 H. Rowan Gaither Lectures in Systems Science†
0072-9167 H.S.M.A. Hotel-Motel Directory and Facilities Guide *changed to* H.S.M.A. Hotel Facilities Digest
0072-9175 Habelts Dissertationsdrucke. Reihe Alte Geschichte
0072-9183 Habelts Dissertationsdrucke. Reihe Klassische Archaeologie
0072-9191 Habelts Dissertationsdrucke. Reihe Klassische Philologie
0072-9205 Habelts Dissertationsdrucke. Reihe Kunstgeschichte
0072-9213 Habelts Dissertationsdrucke. Reihe Mittelalterliche Geschichte
0072-9221 Hacettepe Fen ve Muhendislik Bilimleri Dergisi
0072-923X Hadassah Medical Organization. Report
0072-9248 Hadassah Vocational Guidance Institute. Report *changed to* Hadassah Vocational Guidance Institute. Annual Report for the Year
0072-9272 Hague Conference on Private International Law. Actes et Documents
0072-9280 Hahn-Meitner-Institut fuer Kernforschung Berlin. Bericht *changed to* Hahn-Meitner-Institut fuer Kernforschung Berlin. Jahresbericht
0072-9302 T.A.E. Report
0072-9310 M E D Report†
0072-9329 Israel Institute of Technology. President's Report and Reports of Other Officers *changed to* Technion - Israel Institute of Technology. President's Report
0072-9345 Addis Ababa University. Geophysical Observatory. Contributions†
0072-9361 Addis Ababa University. Institute of Ethiopian Studies. Qene Collections†
0072-9388 Addis Ababa University. University Testing Center. Technical Report
0072-9396 Hakluyt Society. Works in the Ordinary Series. Second Series
0072-940X Landesmuseum fuer Vorgeschichte, Halle. Veroeffentlichungen
0072-9418 Hals-, Nasen- und Ohrenheilkunde†
0072-9426 Analysen
0072-9469 Hamburgisches Museum fuer Voelkerkunde. Mitteilungen
0072-9493 Forschungstelle fuer Voelkerrecht und Auslaendisches Oeffentliches Recht. Werkhefte *see* 0341-3241
0072-9507 Hamburger Abhandlungen
0072-9515 Hamburger Beitraege fuer Russischlehrer
0072-9523 Hamburger Beitraege zur Numismatik
0072-954X Hamburger Hafen Handbuch†
0072-9558 Hamburger Historische Studien
0072-9566 Hamburger Jahrbuch fuer Wirtschafts- und Gesellschaftspolitik
0072-9574 Hamburger Oeffentlich-Rechtliche Nebenstunden
0072-9582 Hamburger Philologische Studien
0072-9604 Hamburger Studien zur Philosophie
0072-9612 Hamburgisches Zoologisches Museum und Institut. Mitteilungen
0072-9639 Art Gallery of Hamilton. Annual Exhibition *changed to* Art Gallery of Hamilton. Annual Winter Exhibition
0072-9647 Royal Botanical Gardens, Hamilton, Ont. Special Bulletin
0072-9655 Royal Botanical Gardens, Hamilton, Ont. Technical Bulletin
0072-9663 Hammarskjold Forum. Working Paper and Proceedings†
0072-9671 Hampstead Clinic Psychoanalytic Library†
0072-968X Hand *changed to* Journal of Hand Surgery: British Volume
0072-9698 Handball und Faustball in Oesterreich
0072-9728 Handbook of Basic Statistics of Maharashtra State
0072-9736 Handbook of Biochemistry *changed to* C R C Handbook of Biochemistry and Molecular Biology
0072-9760 Handbook of Colleges and Departments of Education *changed to* Handbook of Institutions
0072-9787 Handbook of Denominations in the U.S.
0072-9795 Handbook of Electronic Materials
0072-9817 Handbook of Geochemistry†
0072-9825 Official Handbook of Ghana
0072-9833 Handbook of Latin American Studies: A Selected and Annotated Guide to Recent Publications
0072-9841 Handbook of Medical Treatment
0072-985X Handbook of Ocular Therapeutics and Pharmacology *changed to* Ocular Therapeutics and Pharmacology
0072-9868 Handbook of Papua and New Guinea *changed to* Papua New Guinea Handbook
0072-9876 Handbook of Physiology
0072-9884 Handbook of Private Schools
0072-9892 Handbook of Securities of the United States Government and Federal Agencies and Related Money Market Instruments
0072-9906 Handbook of Sensory Physiology
0072-9914 Handbook of Servicemen's and Veterans' Benefits *changed to* Handbook of Service Members' and Veterans' Benefits
0072-9922 Handbook of the Northern Wood Industries
0072-9930 Handbook of the Universities of Pakistan†
0072-9949 Handbook of United States Coins
0072-9965 Handbook on International Study *see* 0364-1449
0072-9965 Handbook on International Study *changed to* Handbook on U.S. Study for Foreign Nationals
0072-9981 Handbook on U.S. Luminescent Stamps
0073-0009 Handbuch der Analytischen Chemie. Part 2: Qualitative Nachweisverfahren†
0073-0017 Handbuch der Analytischen Chemie. Part 3: Quantitative Bestimmungs- und Trennungsmethoden†

1374   ISSN INDEX

ISSN	Title
0073-0025	Europaeische Volksmusikinstrumente. Handbuch
0073-0068	Handbuch der Grossunternehmen
0073-0076	Handbuch der Internationalen Kautschukindustrie
0073-0084	Handbuch der Internationalen Kunstoffindustrie
0073-0092	Handbuch der Justiz
0073-0106	Handbuch der Klassifikation†
0073-0122	Handbuch der Rationalisierung
0073-0130	Handbuch der Stratigraphischen Geologie
0073-0149	Handbuch der Sudetendeutschen Kulturgeschichte
0073-0165	Handbuch fuer den Werbenden Buch- und Zeitschriftenhandel
0073-0173	Handbuch fuer die Druckindustrie Berlin
0073-0181	Handbuch fuer die Sanitaetsberufe Oesterreich
0073-019X	Handbuch Oeffentlicher Verkehrsbetriebe
0073-0203	Statistik des Hamburgischen Staates
0073-022X	Haney Foundation Series†
0073-0238	Central United States *see* 0273-5229
0073-0254	Hank Seale Oil Directory: Louisiana, Mississippi, Arkansas, Texas Gulf Coast and East Texas *see* 0273-4931
0073-0262	Hank Seale Oil Directory: Texas Including Southeast New Mexico *changed to* Armstrong Oil Directory: Texas Including Southeast New Mexico
0073-0270	Voelkerkundliche Abhandlungen
0073-0289	Technische Universitaet Hannover. Lehrstuhl fuer Stahlbau. Schriftenreihe *changed to* Universitaet Hannover. Institut fuer Stahlbau. Schriftenreihe
0073-0300	Technische Universitaet Hannover. Institut fuer Statik. Mitteilungen *changed to* Universitaet Hannover. Institut fuer Statik. Mitteilungen
0073-0319	Technische Universitaet Hannover. Institut fuer Siedlungswasserwirtschaft. Veroeffentlichungen *changed to* Universitaet Hannover. Institut fuer Siedlungswasserwirtschaft. Veroeffentlichungen
0073-0327	Hansische Geschichtsblaetter
0073-036X	Hardware Merchandising's Hardware Handbook *changed to* Hardware Merchandising's Canadian Hardware Handbook
0073-0394	Harmon Memorial Lectures in Military History
0073-0408	Harpers Directory and Manual of the Wine and Spirit Trade *changed to* Harpers Wine and Spirit Annual
0073-0416	Harpers Guide to Sports Trade
0073-0424	Harry S. Truman Research Institute, Jerusalem. Publications†
0073-0432	Hartford Studies in Linguistics†
0073-0459	Harvard Armenian Texts and Studies
0073-0467	Harvard Books in Biology†
0073-0475	Harvard Books in Biophysics
0073-0483	Harvard East Asian Monographs
0073-0491	Harvard East Asian Series
0073-0505	Harvard Economic Studies
0073-0513	Harvard English Studies
0073-0521	Harvard Historical Monographs
0073-053X	Harvard Historical Studies
0073-0548	Harvard Journal of Asiatic Studies
0073-0564	Harvard Librarian
0073-0572	Harvard Middle Eastern Monographs†
0073-0580	Harvard Middle Eastern Studies
0073-0599	Harvard Oriental Series†
0073-0610	Harvard Papers in Theoretical Geography
0073-0629	Harvard Publications in Music
0073-0637	Harvard Semitic Monographs
0073-0645	Harvard Semitic Series
0073-067X	Harvard Studies in Business History
0073-0688	Harvard Studies in Classical Philology
0073-0696	Harvard Studies in Comparative Literature
0073-070X	Harvard Studies in East Asian Law *changed to* Studies in East Asian Law, Harvard University
0073-0718	Harvard Studies in Romance Languages
0073-0726	Harvard Theological Studies
0073-0734	Harvard University. Center for International Affairs. Annual Report
0073-0742	Harvard University. Center for Studies in Education and Development. Annual Report†
0073-0750	Harvard University. Computation Laboratory. Annals†
0073-0769	Harvard University. Computation Laboratory. Mathematical Linguistics and Automatic Translation; Report to National Science Foundation
0073-0777	Harvard University. Graduate School of Business Administration. Baker Library. Kress Library of Business and Economics. Publications *changed to* Harvard Business School. Baker Library. Kress Library of Business and Economics. Publications
0073-0785	Harvard University. Graduate School of Business Administration. Program for Management Development. Publication
0073-0793	Harvard University. Law School. Library. Annual Legal Bibliography†
0073-0807	Harvard University. Museum of Comparative Zoology. Department of Mollusks. Occasional Papers on Mollusks
0073-0815	Harvard University. Program on Regional and Urban Economics. Discussion Paper†
0073-0831	Harvard University. Russian Research Center. Russian Research Center Studies
0073-084X	Harvard-Yenching Institute. Monograph Series
0073-0858	Harvard-Yenching Institute. Studies
0073-0874	Harvey Lectures
0073-0882	Harz-Zeitschrift
0073-0904	Hat Life Year Book *changed to* Hat Life Yearbook & Directory
0073-0912	Hattori Botanical Laboratory. Journal
0073-0920	Haute Coiffure Francaise
0073-0939	Hautes Etudes du Monde Greco-Romain
0073-0947	Hautes Etudes Islamiques et Orientales d'Histoire Comparee
0073-0955	Hautes Etudes Medievales et Modernes
0073-0963	Hautes Etudes Numismatiques
0073-0971	Hautes Etudes Orientales
0073-1013	Hawaii. Children's Health Services Division. Crippled Children Branch Report *changed to* Hawaii. Family Health Services Division. Crippled Children Services Branch. Report
0073-1021	Hawaii Dental Association. Transactions
0073-1048	Hawaii. Department of Health. Mental Health Statistical Section Psychiatric Outpatient Program *changed to* Hawaii. Department of Health. Mental Health Statistical Section. Psychiatric Outpatient, Inpatient and Community Programs
0073-1056	Hawaii, Department of Health Research and Planning Statistical Office. (Report on) Waimano Training School and Hospital *changed to* Hawaii. Department of Health. Waimano Training School and Hospital Division (Report)
0073-1072	Hawaii. Department of Planning and Economic Development. Annual Report
0073-1080	State of Hawaii Data Book
0073-1102	Hawaii Economic Review. Market Annual†
0073-1110	Hawaii. Insurance Division. Report of the Insurance Commissioner of Hawaii
0073-1129	Hawaii International Conference on System Sciences. Proceedings
0073-1137	Hawaii. Office of the Ombudsman. Report
0073-1145	Hawaii Series
0073-1153	Hawaii Topical Conference in Particle Physics. Proceedings *changed to* Hawaii Conference on High Energy Physics
0073-1226	University of Hawaii. Industrial Relations Center. Occasional Publications
0073-1234	Hawaii Institute of Geophysics. Contributions *changed to* Hawaii Institute of Geophysics. Yearbook
0073-1277	Hawaii. Legislative Reference Bureau. Report
0073-1293	University of Hawaii. Water Resources Research Center. Collected Reprints
0073-1307	University of Hawaii. Water Resources Research Center. Technical Report
0073-1315	Meteorological Monographs†
0073-1331	Hawaii Institute of Marine Biology. Technical Reports
0073-1358	Hawaiian Planters' Record
0073-1366	Hawaiian Sugar Planters' Association Experiment Station. Annual Report
0073-1382	Nathaniel Hawthorne Journal
0073-1404	Hayes Directory of Dental Supply Houses
0073-1412	Hayes Directory of Physician and Hospital Supply Houses *changed to* Hayes Directory of Medical Supply Houses
0073-1420	Hayes Druggist Directory
0073-1439	University of Iowa. Graduate Program in Hospital and Health Administration. Health Care Research Series†
0073-1455	Health Education Monographs *see* 0195-8402
0073-1471	List of Worthwhile Life and Health Insurance Books†
0073-148X	Source Book of Health Insurance Data
0073-1498	Health Physics Society. Newsletter
0073-1501	Health Statistics of India†
0073-151X	Heat Bibliography†
0073-1552	Heating and Ventilating Year Book *see* 0306-3585
0073-1560	Hebbel-Jahrbuecher
0073-1579	Hegel-Jahrbuch†
0073-1587	Hegel-Studien
0073-1595	Heidelberg Science Library
0073-1633	Heidelberger Arbeitsbuecher
0073-1641	Heidelberger Jahrbuecher
0073-165X	Heidelberger Rechtswissenschaftliche Abhandlungen. Neue Folge
0073-1676	Heidelberger Sociologica
0073-1684	Heidelberger Taschenbuecher
0073-1692	Heine-Jahrbuch
0073-1714	Helps for Students of History
0073-1730	Helsingin Yliopisto Keskussairaala. Psykiatrian Klinikka. Julkaisusarja *changed to* Psychiatria Fennica. Reports
0073-179X	University of Helsinki. Department of Education. Research Bulletin
0073-1803	Helvetica Odontologica Acta. Supplementum *changed to* Schweizerische Monatsschrift fuer Zahnmedizin
0073-1811	Helvetica Paediatrica Acta. Supplementum
0073-182X	Helvetia Politica
0073-1846	Henrietta Szold Institute. Report on Activities†
0073-1897	Heraldisch-Genealogische Gesellschaft Adler. Jahrbuch
0073-1900	Heraldo Dental
0073-1927	Herbert Read Series
0073-1943	Herd Book of Hereford Cattle
0073-1951	Hereford Breed Journal
0073-196X	Herforder Jahrbuch; Beitraege zur Geschichte der Stadt und des Stiftes Herford *changed to* Herforder Jahrbuch; Beitraege zur Geschichte der Stadt des Kreises und des Stiftes Herford
0073-1978	Heritage†
0073-1986	Heritage of Sociology
0073-1994	University of Queensland. Great Barrier Reef Committee: Heron Island Research Station. Papers†
0073-2001	Hessisches Jahrbuch fuer Landesgeschichte
0073-201X	Heutiges Deutsch. Reihe I: Linguistische Grundlagen
0073-2044	Hi-Fi Sound Annual *changed to* Which Hi-Fi?
0073-2060	Hi-Fi Year Book†
0073-2095	High Fidelity. Records in Review†
0073-2109	High Polymers†
0073-2141	Highlights of V A Medical Research *changed to* Medical Research in the V.A.
0073-215X	Nation on the Move†
0073-2176	Highway Planning Notes
0073-2184	U.S. Federal Highway Administration. Highway Planning Technical Reports
0073-2206	Highway Research Record *see* 0361-1981
0073-2214	Highway Safety Literature Annual Cumulations†
0073-2222	Highway Safety Literature Indexes†
0073-2230	Hilgardia
0073-2273	Hind Mazdoor Sabha. Report of the Annual Convention
0073-2281	Hindu Astronomical and Mathematical Text Series
0073-229X	Hirosaki University. Faculty of Agriculture. Bulletin
0073-2303	Hiroshima University. Department of Geology. Geological Report
0073-2311	Hiroshima University. Faculty of Engineering. Memoirs
0073-232X	Hiroshima University. Research Institute for Nuclear Medicine and Biology. Proceedings
0073-2338	Histochemische-Methoden†
0073-2354	Histoire de l'Europe†
0073-2362	Histoire de la Pensee
0073-2370	Histoire de la Philosophie Europeenne†
0073-2389	Histoire des Personnages Mysterieux et des Societes Secretes†
0073-2397	Histoire des Idees et Critique Litteraire
0073-2400	Histoire et Civilisation Arabe
0073-2419	Histoire et Civilisation du Livre
0073-2435	Historia
0073-2443	Historia†
0073-2451	Historia del Arte en Mexico†
0073-2486	Historia y Cultura
0073-2494	Historia y Filosofia de la Ciencia. Serie Mayor. Encuadernada
0073-2508	Historia y Filosofia de la Ciencia. Serie Menor. Rustica
0073-2516	Historiae Musicae Cultores Biblioteca
0073-2524	Historiae Naturalis Classica†
0073-2532	Historiae Scientiarum Elementa
0073-2540	Historiallinen Arkisto
0073-2559	Historiallisia Tutkimuksia
0073-2567	Historic Houses, Castles and Gardens *changed to* Historic Houses, Castles and Gardens in Great Britain and Ireland
0073-2591	Historical Association, London. Aids for Teachers†
0073-2605	Teaching of History
0073-2613	Historical Conservation Society. Publications
0073-2621	Historical Problems: Studies and Documents
0073-2648	Historical Society of Ghana. Transactions
0073-2656	Historical Statistics of the Gas Industry
0073-2664	Historical Statistics of the United States
0073-2672	Historical Studies in the Physical Sciences *changed to* Historical Studies in the Physical and Biological Sciences
0073-2680	Historischer Verein der Pfalz. Mitteilungen
0073-2699	Historischer Verein Dillingen an der Donau. Jahrbuch
0073-2702	Historiska och Litteraturhistoriska Studier

ISSN INDEX 1375

0073-2710 History and Structure of Languages
0073-2737 History of Menshevism†
0073-2745 Chicago History of Science and Medicine
0073-2753 History of Science
0073-277X Historyka; Studia Metodologiczne
0073-2788 Hitotsubashi Journal of Arts and Sciences
0073-2796 Hitotsubashi Journal of Law and Politics
0073-280X Hitotsubashi Journal of Social Studies
0073-2818 Hobart Papers
0073-2842 Hochschulbuecher fuer Mathematik
0073-2850 Hochschulbuecher fuer Physik
0073-2877 Hoehnea
0073-2885 E.T.A. Hoffmann-Gesellschaft. Mitteilungen
0073-2893 United States & Canadian Mailing Lists
0073-2907 Hofstra University Yearbook of Business
0073-2915 Hokkaido Dental Association. Journal
0073-2923 Hokkaido National Agricultural Experiment Station. Soil Survey Report
0073-2931 Hokkaido University. Institute of Low Temperature Science. Series A. Physical Science *see* 0439-3538
0073-294X Hokkaido University. Institute of Low Temperature Science. Series B. Biological Science *see* 0439-3546
0073-2958 Holiday Book†
0073-2966 Holiday Camps Directory and Magazine *changed to* Holiday Centres, Chalet and Caravan Parks
0073-2982 Holiday Chalets and Caravans Directory Magazine *changed to* Holiday Centres, Chalet and Caravan Parks
0073-3024 Holidays in Britain
0073-3032 Holland Exports
0073-3059 Hollis Press and Public Relations Annual
0073-3075 U.S. Department of Agriculture. Home and Garden Bulletin
0073-3091 Home Economics Education Association. Bulletin *changed to* Home Economics Educator
0073-3105 Home Economics in Institutions Granting Bachelors or Higher Degrees
0073-3113 U.S. Department of Agriculture. Home Economics Research Report
0073-3148 Home University Library†
0073-3156 Four Things Every Woman Should Know *changed to* Homemaker's Guide
0073-3164 Homing World Stud Book
0073-3180 Homme Face a la Nature†
0073-3199 Hommes et Civilisations
0073-3202 Hommes et la Terre
0073-3210 Hong Kong Catholic Church Directory
0073-3229 Hong Kong. Census and Statistics Department. Annual Departmental Reports†
0073-3237 Hong Kong Library Association. Journal
0073-3245 Hong Kong Manufacturers and Exporters Register
0073-3253 Hong Kong Nursing Journal
0073-3261 Hong Kong Trade Directory†
0073-327X Hontanar
0073-3288 Hood College, Frederick, Maryland. Monograph†
0073-3326 Actualites Nephrologiques
0073-3342 Hoppenstedt Vademecum der Investmentfonds
0073-3350 Hoppenstedt Versicherungs-Jahrbuch
0073-3369 Horace M. Albright Conservation Lectureship
0073-3407 Hornero
0073-3415 Horse and Hound Year Book†
0073-3431 Hoseasons Holiday Boats and Bungalows Hire *changed to* Hoseasons Boating Holidays
0073-3458 Sell's Hospital and Surgical Supplies *see* 0140-5748
0073-3466 Hospital Statistics of New Zealand *see* 0110-1900
0073-3474 Hospitals & Health Services Year Book and Directory of Hospital Suppliers†
0073-3482 Hot Rod Yearbook†
0073-3490 Hotel and Motel Red Book
0073-3504 Sell's Hotel, Restaurant and Canteen Supplies *see* 0142-1824
0073-3512 Hotels and Restaurants in Britain†
0073-3539 Hotels de la France et d'Outre-Mer *changed to* Hotels de la France
0073-3563 House Beautiful's Gardening and Outdoor Living†
0073-3571 House Beautiful's Houses and Plans
0073-3601 Households with Television Sets in the United States†
0073-361X House's Guide to the Building Industry *changed to* House's Guide to the Construction Industry
0073-3644 Housing and Planning Year Book
0073-3741 Howard Journal of Penology and Crime Prevention *see* 0265-5527
0073-375X Hsin-Ya Hsueh Pao†
0073-3768 Atlas of Mammalian Chromosomes†
0073-3776 Hudson Institute. Report to the Members
0073-3792 Hueber Hochschulreihe
0073-3806 University of Hull. Institute of Education. Aids to Research†
0073-3814 University of Hull. Institute of Education. Research Monographs†
0073-3865 Human Resources Research Organization. Bibliography of Publications†
0073-3873 Human Resources Research Organization. Professional Papers
0073-389X Human Resources Research Organization. Technical Report†
0073-3903 European Court of Human Rights. Publications. Series A: Judgments and Decisions
0073-3911 European Court of Human Rights. Publications. Series B: Pleadings, Oral Arguments and Documents
0073-3938 Humanities, Christianity and Culture
0073-3946 Humanities Research Council of Canada. Report *see* 0225-6932
0073-4012 Egeszsegneveles Szakkonyvtara
0073-4020 Hungary. Kozponti Statisztikai Hivatal. Demografiai Evkonyv
0073-4039 Hungary. Kozponti Statisztikai Hivatal. Statisztikai Evkonyv
0073-4055 Magyar Orszagos Leveltar Kiadvanyai. 2. Forraskiadvanyok†
0073-4063 Orszagos Muemleki Felugyeloseg. Kiadvanyok
0073-4071 Huntia
0073-411X Hurricane Annual†
0073-4128 Hvalraadets Skrifter
0073-4136 Hybrid Microelectronics Symposium. (Papers)
0073-4144 National Geophysical Research Institute. Publications
0073-4160 Hydraulic Research in the United States *see* 0094-1832
0073-4179 Hydraulics Conference. Proceedings†
0073-4187 Great Britain. Hydraulics Research Station. Reports†
0073-4217 Hydrological Yearbook of Israel
0073-4268 I F O Institut fuer Wirtschaftsforschung. Studien zu Handelsfragen *see* 0170-5695
0073-4284 I N F A Press and Advertisers Year Book
0073-4292 I N U F A: Internationaler Nutzfahrzeug-Katalog/International Catalogue for Commercial Vehicles *changed to* I N U F A Katalog
0073-4314 University of Ibadan. Institute of Education. Occasional Publications
0073-4322 University of Ibadan. Library. Annual Report
0073-4349 Ibero-Americana†
0073-4365 Ibsen Aarboken
0073-4373 Icefield Ranges Research Project Scientific Results†
0073-4381 J L B Smith Institute of Ichthyology. Ichthyological Bulletin
0073-439X Icones Fungorium Maris†
0073-4403 Icones Plantarum Africanarum
0073-4411 Iconographia Mycologia†
0073-442X Idaho. Bureau of Mines and Geology. Bulletin *see* 0734-3825
0073-4446 Idaho. Bureau of Mines and Geology. Information Circular *changed to* Idaho. Geological Survey. Information Circular
0073-4462 Idaho. Bureau of Mines and Geology. Pamphlet†
0073-4497 Idaho Education Association. Proceedings
0073-4527 Idaho. Department of Fish and Game. Federal Aid Investigation Projects. Progress Reports and Publications
0073-4551 Idaho State University Museum. Occasional Papers *see* 0196-7703
0073-456X Idaho Statistical Abstract†
0073-4586 University of Idaho. Forest, Wildlife and Range Experiment Station, Moscow. Station Bulletin
0073-4594 University of Idaho. Forest, Wildlife and Range Experiment Station, Moscow. Station Note
0073-4608 University of Idaho. Forest, Wildlife and Range Experiment Station, Moscow. Station Paper†
0073-4616 University of Idaho. Water Resources Research Institute. Annual Report
0073-4624 Ideas for Management†
0073-4640 Dictionnaires du Savoir Moderne
0073-4667 Ethnies†
0073-4675 Idesia
0073-4691 Iheringia. Serie Antropologia
0073-4705 Iheringia. Serie Botanica
0073-4713 Iheringia. Serie Geologia
0073-4721 Iheringia. Serie Zoologia
0073-4748 Illinois Biological Monographs
0073-4756 Illinois. Board of Higher Education. Report†
0073-4799 Illinois Directory and Suppliers Listing *changed to* Illinois Dealer Directory and Buyer's Guide
0073-4810 Illinois. Department of Conservation. Technical Bulletin†
0073-4837 Illinois Government. *see* 0195-7783
0073-4853 Illinois. State Geological Survey. Industrial Mineral Notes *see* 0094-9442
0073-487X Illinois Law Enforcement Commission. Annual Report†
0073-490X Illinois. Natural History Survey. Biological Notes
0073-4918 Illinois. Natural History Survey. Bulletin
0073-4926 Illinois. Natural History Survey. Circular
0073-4934 Northern Illinois University. Center for Southeast Asian Studies. Special Report Series
0073-4950 Southern Illinois University, Carbondale. Department of Geography. Discussion Paper
0073-4969 Southern Illinois University, Carbondale. Occasional Paper Series in Geography
0073-4977 Southern Illinois University, Carbondale. University Libraries. Bibliographic Contributions
0073-4985 Southern Illinois University. University Museum Studies
0073-4993 Southern Illinois University, Edwardsville. Center For Urban and Environmental Research and Services. C U E R S Report. *changed to* Southern Illinois University, Edwardsville. Regional Research and Development Services. Report
0073-5051 Illinois. State Geological Survey. Bulletins
0073-506X Illinois. State Geological Survey. Circulars
0073-5078 Illinois. State Geological Survey. Educational Series
0073-5086 Illinois. State Geological Survey. Environmental Geology Notes
0073-5094 Illinois. State Geological Survey. Guidebook Series
0073-5108 Illinois. Environmental Protection Agency. Semi-Annual Report *changed to* Progress (Springfield)
0073-5116 Illinois. State Geological Survey. Mineral Economic Briefs *see* 0094-9442
0073-5124 Illinois. State Geological Survey. Reports of Investigations†
0073-5167 Illinois Studies in Anthropology
0073-5191 University of Illinois at Urbana-Champaign. Center for International Education and Research in Accounting. Monographs
0073-5205 University of Illinois at Urbana-Champaign. College of Agriculture. Special Publication†
0073-5213 University of Illinois at Urbana-Champaign. Department of Agricultural Economics. Agricultural Finance Program Report
0073-5221 University of Illinois at Urbana-Champaign. Department of Agricultureal Economics. Bulletin†
0073-523X University of Illinois at Urbana-Champaign. Department of Agricultural Economics. Research Report
0073-5256 University of Illinois at Urbana-Champaign. Department of Art. Newsletter *changed to* University of Illinois at Urbana-Champaign. School of Art and Design. Newsletter
0073-5264 T & A M Report
0073-5272 University of Illinois at Urbana - Champaign. Engineering Experiment Station. Bulletin
0073-5280 University of Illinois at Urbana - Champaign. Engineering Experiment Station. Summary of Engineering Research
0073-5299 University of Illinois at Urbana-Champaign. College of Agriculture. Agricultural Communications Research Report†
0073-5302 University of Illinois at Urbana-Champaign. Graduate School of Library Science. Monograph Series. *changed to* University of Illinois at Urbana-Champaign. Graduate School of Library and Information Science. Monograph Series
0073-5353 University of Illinois at Urbana-Champaign. Institute of Labor and Industrial Relations. Reprint Series
0073-5361 University of Illinois at Urbana-Champaign. Graduate School of Library Science. Library Research Center. Annual Report. *changed to* University of Illinois at Urbana-Champaign. Graduate School of Library and Information Science. Library Research Center. Annual Report
0073-5396 University of Illinois. Small Homes Council. Building Research Council. Circulars *changed to* University of Illinois. Small Homes Council. Building Research Council. Council Notes
0073-540X University of Illinois. Small Homes Council. Building Research Council. Research Report
0073-5426 University of Illinois. Small Homes Council. Building Research Council. Technical Notes
0073-5434 University of Illinois at Urbana-Champaign. Water Resources Center. Annual Report
0073-5442 University of Illinois at Urbana-Champaign. Water Resources Center. Research Report
0073-5469 I E S Lighting Handbook
0073-5477 Illustrators: The Annual of American Illustration†
0073-5507 Image and Sound in Teaching; Bibliographical References
0073-5515 Image; Illustrierte Zeitschrift fuer Aerzte und Apotheken†

0073-5531 Immunopathology†
0073-5582 Import Car Buyer's Guide†
0073-5604 Importers and Exporters Trade Promotion Guide
0073-5612 Imports into Pakistan under U.S. Economic Aid†
0073-5620 Imprimatur; Jahrbuch fuer Buecherfreunde. Neue Folge *changed to* Imprimatur. Neue Folge
0073-5639 InFact Medical School Information System
0073-5655 In Vitro *see* 0883-8364
0073-5671 Income, Estate and Gift Tax Provisions: Internal Revenue Code *changed to* Income, Employment, Estate and Gift Tax Provisions: Internal Revenue Code
0073-5698 Money Income in (Year) of Families, Unrelated Individuals and Persons in the United States *changed to* Current Population Reports: Consumer Income. Money Income of Households, Families and Persons in the United States (Year)
0073-5701 Incontri e Testimonianze†
0073-571X Restrictive Practices Reports *see* 0306-2163
0073-5728 Incorporated Law Society of Sri Lanka. Annual Report
0073-5736 Incorporated Law Society of Sri Lanka. Journal
0073-5744 Incorporated Society of Organ Builders. Journal
0073-5752 Incunabula Graeca
0073-5779 Independent Schools Association of the Southwest. Membership List
0073-5787 Index Hepaticarum
0073-5817 Index of Articles on Jewish Studies
0073-5825 Index of Graduate Theses in Baptist Theological Seminaries†
0073-5884 Index of Psychoanalytic Writings
0073-5892 Index to Book Reviews in the Humanities
0073-5914 Index to Early American Periodical Literature, 1728-1870†
0073-5930 Index to How to Do It Information
0073-5949 Index to Little Magazines†
0073-5957 Index to New Zealand Periodicals†
0073-5965 Index to Nigeriana in Selected Periodicals
0073-5973 Index to Periodical Articles by and About Negroes *see* 0161-8245
0073-5981 Index to Periodicals of the Church of Jesus Christ of Latter-Day Saints. Cumulative Edition
0073-599X Index to Philippine Periodicals
0073-6007 Index to Plant Chromosome Numbers
0073-6023 Index to Reviews, Symposia Volumes and Monographs in Organic Chemistry†
0073-6031 U.S. Bureau of Outdoor Recreation. Index to Selected Outdoor Recreation Literature†
0073-604X Index to Textile Auxiliaries
0073-6066 Index to Theses Accepted for Higher Degrees in the Universities of Great Britain and Ireland
0073-6074 Index Translationum
0073-6082 Indexes of Output per Person Employed and per Man-Hour in Canada, Commercial Industries *see* 0317-7882
0073-6090 India: a Reference Annual
0073-6120 India. Central Board of Revenue. Central Excise Manual
0073-6139 India. Central Statistical Organization. Annual Survey of Industries
0073-6147 India. Central Statistical Organization. Estimates of National Income *changed to* India. Central Statistical Organization. National Accounts Statistics
0073-6155 India. Central Statistical Organization. Statistical Abstract
0073-6163 India. Central Statistical Organization. Sample Surveys of Current Interest in India. Report *changed to* India. Central Statistical Organization. Annual Report
0073-6171 India. Central Vigilance Commission. Report
0073-618X India. Department of Atomic Energy. Annual Report
0073-6198 India. Khadi and Village Industries Commission. Report *changed to* K V I C Annual Report
0073-6201 India. Ministry of Education and Social Welfare. Department of Education. Report *changed to* India. Ministry of Education and Social Welfare. Department of Education. Report
0073-6236 India. Union Public Service Commission Report
0073-6244 India Who's Who
0073-6252 Indian Adult Education Association. National Seminar. Report†
0073-6260 I A S L I C Technical Pamphlets
0073-6279 I A S L I C Special Publication
0073-6287 Indian Books; Bibliography of Indian Books Published or Reprinted in the English Language *changed to* B E P I
0073-6295 Indian Chemical Directory *issued with* Guide to Indian Chemical Plants and Equipment
0073-6295 Indian Chemical Directory
0073-6309 Indian Council of Medical Research. Annual Report†
0073-6317 Indian Council of Medical Research. Report of the Advisory Committees†
0073-6325 Indian Council of Medical Research. Special Report Series†
0073-6333 Indian Engineering Association. Handbook of Statistics *changed to* Association of Indian Engineering Industry. Handbook of Statistics
0073-6341 C. A. S. N. P. Bulletin†
0073-635X Indian Forest Bulletin (New Series)
0073-6368 Indian Forest Leaflets (New Series)
0073-6376 Indian Forest Records (New Series) Botany
0073-6384 Indian Forest Records (New Series) Composite Wood
0073-6392 Indian Forest Records (New Series) Entomology
0073-6406 Indian Forest Records (New Series) Forest Pathology
0073-6414 Indian Forest Records (New Series) Logging
0073-6422 Indian Forest Records (New Series) Silviculture
0073-6430 Indian Forest Records (New Series) Statistical
0073-6449 Indian Forest Records (New Series) Timber Mechanics
0073-6465 Indian Institute of Advanced Study. Transactions and Monographs
0073-6473 Indian Institute of Foreign Trade. Report
0073-649X Indian Institute of Sugarcane Research, Lucknow. Annual Report
0073-6503 Indian Institute of Technology, Bombay. Series
0073-6511 Indian Institute of Technology, Madras. Annual Report
0073-652X Indian Institute of Technology, Madras. Technical Communications†
0073-6546 I I T C Directory
0073-6554 Indian Journal of Engineers. Annual Foundry Number
0073-6562 Indian Jute Mills Association. Annual Summary of Jute and Gunny Statistics
0073-6570 Indian Jute Mills Association. Loom and Spindle Statistics
0073-6589 Indian Linguistics Monograph Series
0073-6597 I M E Directory: Mines, Minerals, Equipment†
0073-6600 Indian National Science Academy. Proceedings
0073-6619 Indian National Science Academy. Year Book
0073-6627 I N S D O C Union Catalogue Series
0073-6635 Indian Pharmaceutical Guide
0073-6643 Indian Roads Congress. Road Research Bulletin *see* 0376-4788
0073-6651 Indian Rubber Statistics
0073-666X Indian School of International Studies *see* 0075-3548
0073-6678 Indian Society of International Law. Publications
0073-6686 Indian Statistical Institute. Annual Report
0073-6694 Indian Statistical Institute. Econometric and Social Sciences Series. Research Monographs
0073-6708 Indian Statistical Institute. Library. Bibliographic Series
0073-6716 Indian Statistical Institute. Statistics and Probability Series. Research Monographs
0073-6724 Indian Statistical Series
0073-6732 Indian Voice
0073-6759 Indiana Academy of Science. Monograph
0073-6767 Indiana Academy of Science. Proceedings
0073-6775 Indiana. Aeronautics Commission. Annual Report
0073-6783 Indiana. Agricultural Experiment Station. Inspection Report
0073-6791 Indiana. Agricultural Experiment Station. Research Bulletin
0073-6821 Ball State Monographs
0073-6856 Indiana. Civil Rights Commission. Annual Report *changed to* Indiana. Civil Rights Commission. Triennial Report
0073-6880 Indiana Historical Collections
0073-6899 Indiana Historical Society. Prehistory Research Series
0073-6902 Indiana Historical Society. Publications
0073-6910 Indiana Industrial Directory *changed to* Harris Indiana Industrial Directory (Year)
0073-6937 Indiana State University. Department of Geography and Geology. Professional Paper
0073-6945 Indiana Studies in Prediction *changed to* Indiana Studies in Higher Education
0073-6953 Indiana University. Department of Geography. Geographic Monograph Series
0073-6961 Indiana University. Department of Geography. Occasional Publication.
0073-6996 Indiana University. Folklore Institute. Monograph Series†
0073-702X Indiana University Monograph Series in Adult Education†
0073-7062 Indiana University. Research Center for Language and Semiotic Studies. African Series†
0073-7097 Indiana University. Research Institute for Inner Asian Studies. Uralic and Altaic Series.
0073-7127 Indiana University. Sesquicentennial Series on Insurance†
0073-7135 Indianapolis District Dental Society. Journal *changed to* Indianapolis District Dental Society. Newsletter
0073-7151 Indice Agricola Colombiano
0073-7178 Indice General de Publicaciones Periodicas Latinoamericanas. Humanidades y Ciencias Sociales†
0073-7186 Indices of Urban Land Prices and Construction Cost of Wooden Houses in Japan
0073-7194 Indices Verborum Linguae Mongoliae Monumentis Traditorum
0073-7208 Indices zur Deutschen Literatur†
0073-7224 Indo-Iranian Monographs†
0073-7240 Indo-Pacific Mollusca
0073-7275 Industria del Petrolio in Italia
0073-7283 Industria International *see* 0039-7245
0073-7291 Industria Italiana del Ciclo e del Motociclo. Annuario
0073-7305 Industrial Accident Prevention Association. Annual Report
0073-7313 Industrial Accident Prevention Association. Guide to Safety
0073-7321 Industrial Alabama *see* 0145-4048
0073-733X Industrial and Commercial Power Systems and Electrical Space Heating and Air Conditioning Joint Technical Conference. Record *changed to* Industrial and Commercial Power Systems Technical Conference
0073-7356 Industrial Bank of Sudan. Board of Directors. Annual Report
0073-7364 Industrial Catering†
0073-7372 Industrial Development Bank of India. Annual Report
0073-7380 Industrial Development Bank of Israel Limited. Report
0073-7399 Industrial Development Bank of Pakistan. Report
0073-7402 Industrial Development Bank of Turkey. Annual Statement
0073-7410 Foundation for Business Responsibilities. Discussion Paper
0073-7429 Foundation for Business Responsibilities. Occasional Papers
0073-7437 Foundation for Business Responsibilities. Research Paper
0073-7445 Industrial Engineering Conference. Proceedings†
0073-7453 Industrial Fibres†
0073-747X International Finishing Industries Manual *changed to* Finishing Diary
0073-7488 Industrial Health Foundation. Chemical-Toxicological Series. Bulletin
0073-7496 Industrial Health Foundation. Engineering Series. Bulletin
0073-750X Industrial Health Foundation. Legal Series Bulletin.
0073-7518 Industrial Health Foundation. Medical Series. Bulletin
0073-7526 Industrial Hygiene Foundation. Nursing Series. Bulletins *changed to* Industrial Health Foundation. Nursing Series. Bulletins
0073-7542 Industrial Hygiene Highlights *changed to* Industrial Environmental Health
0073-7550 Industrial Intelligence; Industrial Yearbook†
0073-7569 Industrial Locations in Canada
0073-7577 Industrial Planning and Programming Series†
0073-7593 Industrial Relations Research in Canada
0073-7623 Industrial Research Laboratories of the United States *changed to* Directory of American Research and Technology
0073-7658 Industrial South Africa
0073-7666 Industrial Structure of Rajasthan
0073-7682 Industrial Waste Conference, Purdue University, Lafayette, Indiana. Proceedings
0073-7704 Industrie-Adresboek voor Zuid-Holland *changed to* Adreslijst van de Zuid-Hollandse Industrie
0073-7712 Industrie Compass Oesterreich
0073-7720 Industrie de la Manutention dans les Ports Francais
0073-7739 Industrie et Artisanat
0073-7747 Industrie Francaise des Moteurs a Combustion Interne
0073-7755 Industrieabwaesser
0073-7763 Industries Directory, Capitals
0073-7771 Industries Directory, Delhi
0073-7798 Industries Directory, Northern India
0073-7801 Industry - Engineering Education Series *changed to* College - Industry Education Conference. Proceedings
0073-781X Industry in East Africa
0073-7828 Inedits Russes
0073-7836 Informatheque
0073-7844 Information Display Buyers Guide†
0073-7879 Information Processing Association of Israel. National Conference on Data Processing. Proceedings

ISSN INDEX 1377

0073-7887 Information Series on Agricultural Economics *changed to* Giannini Foundation of Agricultural Economics. Information Series
0073-7895 Information Service of the European Communities. Newsletter on the Common Agricultural Policy
0073-7909 Information Service of the European Communities. Trade Union News
0073-7917 Informations Annuelles de Caryosystematique et Cytogenetique
0073-7925 Informations et Etudes Socialistes
0073-7941 Informatique *changed to* Zero-Un Informatique
0073-7984 Informatore Farmaceutico
0073-7992 Ingenieria. Boletin Informativo. *see* 0120-5609
0073-800X Inglis Lecture
0073-8018 Initiation a la Linguistique. Serie A. Lectures
0073-8026 Initiation a la Linguistique. Serie B. Problemes et Methodes
0073-8034 Initiation. Serie Textes, Bibliographies
0073-8042 Inland Printer/American Lithographer Buyer's Guide†
0073-8077 Inorganic Syntheses Series
0073-8085 Chimica Acta Reviews *see* 0020-1693
0073-8093 Canada. Insect Pathology Research Institute. Program Review†
0073-8115 Insects of Micronesia
0073-8123 Insights
0073-8131 Institut Belge de Science Politique. Bibliotheque. Nouvelle Serie *changed to* Institut de Science Politique. Bibliotheque. Nouvelle Serie
0073-814X Institut Belge de Science Politique. Bibliotheque. Serie Documents *changed to* Institut de Science Politique. Bibliotheque. Serie Documents
0073-8158 Institut Belge de Science Politique. Documents *changed to* Institut de Science Politique. Documents
0073-8174 Institute Collegial Europeen. Bulletin *changed to* Institut Collegial Europeen. Actes des Colloques de Loches
0073-8190 Institut de France. Annuaire
0073-8212 Institut de Recherche et d'Histoire des Textes, Paris. Documents, Etudes et Repertoires
0073-8220 Institut Armoricain de Recherches Historiques, Rennes. (Publication) *changed to* Universite de Rennes. Institut Armoricain de Recherches Economiques et Humaines. (Publication)
0073-8239 Institut de Science Economique Appliquee. Rapport d'Activite *changed to* Institut de Sciences Mathematiques et Economiques Appliquees. Rapport d'Activite
0073-8247 Institut d'Emission d'Outre Mer, Paris. Rapport d'Activite
0073-8255 Institut d'Emission Malgache. Rapport d'Activite *changed to* Banque Centrale de la Republique Malgache. Rapport d'Activite
0073-8263 Institut des Etudes Occitanes. Publications
0073-8271 Institut des Hautes Etudes de l'Amerique Latine. Cahiers†
0073-828X Institut des Hautes Etudes de l'Amerique Latine. Centre d'Etudes Politiques, Economiques et Sociales. Publications Multigraphiees.†
0073-8298 Institut des Hautes Etudes de l'Amerique Latine. Travaux et Memoires *changed to* Institut des Hautes Etudes de l'Amerique Latine. Collection des Travaux et Memoires
0073-8301 Institut des Hautes Etudes Scientifiques, Paris. Publications Mathematiques
0073-8336 Institut Francais de Pondichery. Section Scientifique et Technique. Travaux
0073-8344 Institut Francais de Pondichery. Section Scientifique et Technique. Travaux. Hors Serie
0073-8352 Institut Francais d'Indologie. Publications
0073-8360 Institut Francais du Petrole. Collection Colloques et Seminaires
0073-8379 Institut Francais du Petrole. Rapport Annuel
0073-8387 Institut fuer Asienkunde. Schriften
0073-8417 Institut fuer den Wissenschaftlichen Film. Publikationen zu Wissenschaftlichen Filmen. Sektion Biologie
0073-8433 Institut fuer den Wissenschaftlichen Film. Publikationen zu Wissenschaftlichen Filmen. Sektion Technische Wissenschaften, Naturwissenschaften
0073-8441 Publikationen zu Wissenschaftlichen Filmen. Sektion Geschichte, Paedagogik *see* 0341-5937
0073-8468 Institut fuer Gewerbeforschung, Vienna. Taetigkeitsbericht
0073-8484 Institut fuer Oesterreichische Geschichtsforschung. Mitteilungen
0073-8492 Institut fuer Ostrecht. Studien
0073-8522 Institut Historique Belge de Rome. Bibliotheque
0073-8530 Institut Historique Belge de Rome. Bulletin
0073-8549 Institut Historique et Archeologique Neerlandais de Istamboul. Publications
0073-8557 Institut Jules Destree. Etudes et Documents
0073-8565 Institut Michel Pacha. Annales
0073-8573 Institut Pasteur de Lille. Annales†
0073-859X Universite de Geneve. Institut Universitaire de Hautes Etudes Internationales. Etudes et Travaux†
0073-8603 Universite de Geneve. Institut Universitaire de Hautes Etudes Internationales. Publication†
0073-8611 Instituta et Monumenta. Series 1: Monumenta
0073-862X Institute for Balkan Studies. Publications
0073-8638 Institute for Clinical Science. Proficiency Test Service. Report
0073-8654 Institute for Defense Analyses. Papers
0073-8662 Institute for Defense Analyses. Reports
0073-8670 Institute for Defense Analyses. Studies
0073-8697 I D E A Monographs
0073-8700 I D E A Occasional Papers
0073-8751 Institute for Fermentation, Osaka. Research Communications
0073-8778 Institute for Monetary Research. Monographs†
0073-8786 Institute for Palestine Studies. Anthology Series†
0073-8794 Institute for Palestine Studies. Basic Documents Series *changed to* Institute for Palestine Studies. United Nations Resolutions on Palestine and the Arab-Israeli Conflict Series
0073-8808 Institute for Palestine Studies. International Annual Documentary Series
0073-8816 Institute for Palestine Studies. Monograph Series
0073-8832 Institute for Petroleum Research and Geophysics, Holon, Israel. Report
0073-8875 Institute for Psychoanalysis. Report *changed to* Institute for Psychoanalysis. Newsletter
0073-8921 I S M A Papers
0073-893X I S M A Occasional Papers
0073-8948 Institut fuer Iberoamerika-Kunde. Schriftenreihe
0073-8980 Institute of Actuaries. Year Book†
0073-8999 Institute of Bankers in Pakistan. Council. Report and Accounts
0073-9014 Chartered Institute of Building. Year Book and Directory of Members *see* 0260-7727
0073-9030 Institute of Chartered Accountants in England and Wales. Management Information Series
0073-9049 Institute of Chartered Accountants in England and Wales. Practice Administration Series, Exposure Drafts and Statements of Standard Accounting Practice *changed to* Institute of Chartered Accountants in England and Wales. Exposure Drafts and Statements of Standard Accounting Practice
0073-9057 Institute of Chartered Accountants of Scotland. Official Directory
0073-9065 C F A Monograph Series†
0073-9073 Institute of Clerk of Works of Great Britain Incorporated. Year Book
0073-909X Institute of Economic Affairs. Occasional Papers
0073-9103 Institute of Economic Affairs. Research Monographs
0073-9189 I E E E Region 6. Technical Conference. Record *changed to* I E E E Region 6. Conference (Publication)
0073-9197 I E E E Region 5 Conference. Record
0073-9200 Institution of Engineers. Technical Journal
0073-9219 Institution of Engineers. Year Book
0073-9227 Institute of Environmental Sciences. Annual Meeting. Proceedings
0073-9251 Institute of Environmental Sciences. Tutorial Series
0073-926X Institute of European Studies. Announcements
0073-9278 Institute of European Studies. Papers and Addresses of the Annual Conference and Academic Council
0073-9286 I F T World Directory and Buyers' Guide†
0073-9294 Institute of Forest Genetics, Suwon, Korea. Research Report
0073-9308 Great Britain. Institute of Geological Sciences. Annual Report *changed to* Great Britain. British Geological Survey. Annual Report
0073-9316 Great Britain. Institute of Geological Sciences. Geomagnetic Bulletin *changed to* Great Britain. British Geological Survey. Geomagnetic Bulletin
0073-9324 Great Britain. Institute of Geological Sciences. Geophysical Papers†
0073-9332 Great Britain. Institute of Geological Sciences. Overseas Geology and Mineral Resources *changed to* Great Britain. British Geological Survey. Overseas Geology and Mineral Resources
0073-9340 Institute of Geological Sciences, London. Overseas Geology and Mineral Resources. Supplement Series†
0073-9359 Great Britain. Institute of Geological Sciences. Report *changed to* Great Britain. British Geological Survey. Report
0073-9367 Institute of Geological Sciences, London. Statistical Summary of the Mineral Industry *changed to* World Mineral Statistics
0073-9375 Great Britain. Institute of Geological Sciences. Water Supply Papers†
0073-9383 Great Britain. Institute of Geological Sciences. Water Supply Papers. Research Reports†
0073-9391 Great Britain. Institute of Geological Sciences. Water Supply Papers. Technical Communications†
0073-9413 Institute of Judicial Administration. Calendar Status Study†
0073-9421 Institute of Labor and Industrial Relations. Policy Papers in Human Resources and Industrial Relations
0073-943X Institute of Labor and Industrial Relations. Reprint Series
0073-9448 Institute of Medical Laboratory Technology. London. Annual Report *changed to* Institute of Medical Laboratory Sciences. London, Annual Report
0073-9456 Institute of Mennonite Studies Series
0073-9464 Institute of Metals. Monograph and Report Series†
0073-9472 Institute of Nuclear Materials Management. Proceedings of Annual Meeting
0073-9480 Institute of Paper Chemistry. Bibliographic Series
0073-9502 Institute of Pastoral Psychology. Proceedings *see* 0079-0141
0073-9529 Institute of Petroleum, London. Report of the Summer Meeting†
0073-9537 I P C Monographs
0073-9545 I P C Papers
0073-9561 Institute of Psychophysical Research. Proceedings
0073-957X Institute of Public Administration, Dublin. Administrative Procedure Series†
0073-9588 Institute of Public Administration, Dublin. Annual Report
0073-9596 Institute of Public Administration, Dublin. Administration Yearbook and Diary
0073-960X Institute of Public Administration, Dublin. Research Series†
0073-9618 Institute of Public Administration, Khartoum. Occasional Papers
0073-9626 Institute of Public Administration, Khartoum. Proceedings of the Annual Round Table Conference
0073-9650 Institute of Purchasing and Supply. Yearbook†
0073-9677 Institute of Refrigeration, London. Proceedings†
0073-9693 Institute of Social Studies, The Hague. Publications. Paperback Series†
0073-9707 Institute of Social Studies, The Hague. Publications. Series Major†
0073-9723 Institute of Southeast Asian Studies. Library Bulletin
0073-9731 Institute of Southeast Asian Studies. Occasional Paper
0073-9766 I E E Monograph Series†
0073-9782 Institution of Engineers (India). Directory†
0073-9790 Institution of Engineers of Ireland. Transactions
0073-9804 Institution of Municipal Engineers, London. Annual Conference. Proceedings†
0073-9812 Institution of Nuclear Engineers. Year Book†
0073-9839 Institution of Railway Signal Engineers. Proceedings
0073-9847 Institution of Structural Engineers. Yearbook *changed to* Institution of Structural Engineers. Sessional Yearbook and Directory of Members
0073-9855 Instituto Adolfo Lutz. Revista
0073-9863 Instituto Antartico Chileno. Boletin *changed to* Boletin Antartico Chileno
0073-9871 Instituto Antartico Chileno. Contribution. Serie Cientifica
0073-988X Instituto Brasileiro do Cafe. Departamento Economico. Anuario Estatistico do Cafe. *changed to* Instituto Brasileiro do Cafe. Departamento Economico. Anuario Estatistico do Cafe
0073-9901 Instituto Butantan. Memorias
0073-991X Instituto Caro y Cuervo. Serie Bibliografica
0073-9928 Instituto Caro y Cuervo. Serie Minor
0073-9936 Instituto Centro Americano de Investigacion y Tecnologia Industrial. Publicaciones Geologicas
0073-9944 Instituto Centroamericano de Administracion Publica. Serie 100. Aspectos Humanos de la Administracion

ISSN INDEX

0073-9952 Instituto Centroamericano de Administracion Publica. Serie 200. Ciencia de la Administracion
0073-9960 Instituto Centroamericano de Administracion Publica. Serie 300: Investigacion
0073-9979 Instituto Centroamericano de Administracion Publica. Serie 400: Economia y Finanzas
0073-9995 Instituto Centroamericano de Administracion Publica. Serie 600: Informes de Seminarios
0074-0004 Instituto Centroamericano de Administracion Publica. Serie 700: Materiales de Informacion
0074-0012 Instituto Centroamericano de Administracion Publica. Serie 800: Metodologia de la Administracion
0074-0020 Instituto Centroamericano de Administracion Publica. Serie 900: Miscelaneas
0074-0039 Instituto Costarricense de Cultura Hispanica. Publicacion†
0074-0047 Informe de Operacion de las Principales Empresas Productoras y Distribuidoras de Energia Electrica de Costa Rica
0074-0063 Instituto de Ciencia Politica Rafael Bielsa. Anuario
0074-008X Instituto de Investigacao Cientifica de Angola. Bibliograficas Tematicas
0074-0098 Instituto de Investigacao Cientifica de Angola. Memorias e Trabalhos
0074-0144 Instituto de Tecnologia de Alimentos. Instrucoes Praticas
0074-0152 Instituto de Tecnologia de Alimentos. Instrucoes Tecnicas
0074-0195 Instituto Espanol de Oceanografia. Boletin
0074-0209 Instituto Espanol de Oceanografia. Trabajos
0074-0233 Instituto Hondureno de Seguridad Social. Departamento de Estadistica y Procesamiento de Datos. Anuario Estadistico
0074-025X Fundacion Miguel Lillo. Miscelanea
0074-0268 Instituto Nacional de Seguros. Informe Anual *changed to* Instituto Nacional de Seguros Memoria Anual
0074-0276 Instituto Oswaldo Cruz, Rio de Janeiro. Memorias
0074-0284 Instituto Paranaense de Botanica. Revista. Serie: Flora do Parana
0074-0292 I T A Humanidades†
0074-0306 Instituto Tecnologico y de Estudios Superiores. Publicaciones. Serie: Catalogos de Biblioteca†
0074-0330 Instituto Torcuato di Tella. Centro de Estudios Urbanos Regionales. Documentos de Trabajo†
0074-0349 Instituto Torcuato di Tella. Centro de Investigaciones Economicas. Documentos de Trabajo†
0074-0357 Instituto Torcuato di Tella. Centro de Investigaciones Sociales. Documentos de Trabajo†
0074-0373 Institutul de Cercetari Pentru Cultura Cartofului si Sfeclei de Zahar, Brasov. Anale. Cartoful *changed to* Institutul de Cercetari si Productie a Cartofului, Brasov. Anale. Lucrari Stiintifice
0074-0381 Institutul de Cercetari Pentru Cultura Cartofului si Sfeclei de Zahar, Brasov. Anale. Sflecla de Zahar *changed to* Institutul de Cercetari Pentru Cereale si Plante Tehnice. Laborator Sfecla de Zahar. Anale. Lucrari Stiintifice
0074-039X Institutul de Istorie si Arheologie "A.D. Xenopol" - Iasi. Anuarul
0074-0411 Instituut voor Cultuurtechniek en Waterhuishouding. Mededeling *changed to* Instituut voor Cultuurtechniek en Waterhuishouding. Mededeling. Nieuwe Serie
0074-042X Instituut voor Cultuurtechniek en Waterhuishouding. Technical Bulletin *changed to* Instituut voor Cultuurtechniek en Waterhuishouding. Technical Bulletins. New Series
0074-0438 Instituut voor Cultuurtechniek en Waterhuishouding. Verspreide Overdrukken *changed to* Instituut voor Cultuurtechniek en Waterhuishouding. Mededeling. Nieuwe Serie
0074-0446 Instituut voor Plantenziektenkundig Onderzoek. Jaarverslag
0074-0462 Koninklijk Instituut voor Taal-, Land- en Volkenkunde. Bibliographical Series
0074-0470 Koninklijk Instituut voor Taal-, Land- en Volkenkunde. Translation Series
0074-0489 Instituut voor Veevoedingsonderzoek "Hoorn". Jaarverslag *changed to* Instituut voor Veevoedingsonderzoek. Jaarverslag
0074-0527 Standards and Practices for Instrumentation. Instrument Society of America
0074-0551 Instrumentation in the Chemical and Petroleum Industries
0074-056X Instrumentation in the Power Industry
0074-0578 Instruments, Electronics and Automation Purchasing Directory *see* 0267-1441
0074-0586 Instytut Gospodarki Wodnej. Prace
0074-0616 Instytut Slaski. Kommunikaty. Seria Niemcoznawcza†
0074-0632 Instytut Slaski. Wydawnictwa†
0074-0640 Instytut Badan Jadrowych. Zaklad Radiobiologii i Ochrony Zdrowia. Prace Doswiadczaine
0074-0659 Insulation/Circuits Directory/Encyclopedia *see* 0745-4309
0074-0675 Insurance Almanac; Who, What, When and Where in Insurance
0074-0683 Insurance Casebook†
0074-0691 Insurance Directory and Year Book
0074-0705 Israel. Central Bureau of Statistics. Insurance in Israel
0074-0713 Insurance Facts
0074-0721 Insurance Institute of Canada. Report *see* 0225-168X
0074-073X Insurance Periodicals Index
0074-0748 Asociacion Interamericana de Bibliotecarios y Documentalistas Agricolas. Boletin Especial
0074-0756 Asociacion Interamericana de Bibliotecarios y Documentalistas Agricolas. Boletin Tecnico†
0074-0764 Inter-American Commission of Women. Special Assembly. Final Act
0074-0780 Inter-American Commission on Human Rights. Report on the Work Accomplished During Its Special Sessions†
0074-0799 Inter-American Conference of Ministers of Labor on the Alliance for Progress. Final Act†
0074-0802 Inter-American Conference on Community Development. Final Act†
0074-0810 Congresos Indigenistas Interamericanos. Actas
0074-0829 Inter-American Council for Education, Science, and Culture. Final Report
0074-0837 Work Accomplished by the Inter-American Juridical Committee during its Meeting
0074-0861 Inter-American Development Bank. Board of Governors. Proceedings of the Meeting
0074-087X Inter-American Development Bank. Report *changed to* Inter-American Development Bank. Annual Report
0074-0888 Socio-Economic Progress in Latin America; Annual Report *see* 0095-2850
0074-0918 Inter-American Economic and Social Council. Final Report of the Annual Meeting at the Ministerial Level
0074-0926 Inter-American Institute of Agricultural Sciences. Center for Training and Research. Bibliotecologia y Documentacion *see* 0301-438X
0074-0934 Inter-American Music Monograph Series†
0074-0950 Inter-American Port and Harbor Conferences. Final Act†
0074-0969 Inter-American Statistical Conferences. Final Report†
0074-0985 Inter-American Travel Congresses. Final Act†
0074-0993 Inter-American Tropical Tuna Commission. Bulletin
0074-1000 Inter-American Tropical Tuna Commission. Annual Report
0074-1019 Inter-Documentation Company. Newsletter†
0074-1043 Chronicle of Parliamentary Elections *changed to* Chronicle of Parliamentary Elections and Developments
0074-1051 Inter-Parliamentary Union. Conference Proceedings
0074-106X Inter-University Case Program. Case Study
0074-1078 Inter-University Consortium for Political and Social Research. Annual Report
0074-1086 Interamerican Conference on Materials Technology. (Proceedings)†
0074-1116 Interavia A B C
0074-1132 Interdisciplinary Topics in Gerontology
0074-1140 Interferences, Arts, Lettres
0074-1175 Intergovernmental Oceanographic Commission. Technical Series
0074-1191 Design in Greece *changed to* Design and Art in Greece
0074-1205 Internal Revenue Guide to Your Federal Income Tax†
0074-1213 Internal Trade of Iran
0074-123X International Academy of Indian Culture. Satapitaka Series
0074-1248 International Academy of Legal Medicine and of Social Medicine. (Congress Reports)
0074-1256 International Academy of Oral Pathology. Proceedings†
0074-1264 International Actuarial Congress. Transactions
0074-1272 Biennial Survey of Advertising Expenditures Around the World *see* 0568-0301
0074-1329 International Air Transport Association. Bulletin *changed to* International Air Transport Association. Annual General Meeting. Reports and Proceedings
0074-1337 International Air Transport Association. Symposium Papers from the Annual General Meeting†
0074-1353 International Anatomical Congress. Proceedings
0074-137X International Archery Federation. Bulletin Officiel
0074-1388 International Arthurian Society. Bibliographical Bulletin
0074-1396 International Arthurian Society. Report on Congress *see* 0074-1388
0074-140X International Association for Bridge and Structural Engineering. Bulletin/Mitteilungen†
0074-1418 International Association for Bridge and Structural Engineering. Final Report (of Congress) *changed to* I A B S E Congress Report
0074-1434 International Association for Bridge and Structural Engineering. Preliminary Report (of Congress)†
0074-1442 International Association for Bridge and Structural Engineering. Reports of the Working Commissions *changed to* I A B S E Report
0074-1450 International Association for Cereal Chemistry. Working and Discussion Meetings Reports
0074-1469 International Association for Classical Archaeology. Proceedings of Congress
0074-1477 International Association for Hydraulic Research. Congress Proceedings
0074-1507 International Association for Statistics in Physical Sciences. Proceedings (of Meetings)†
0074-1515 I A A E E (International Association for the Advancement of Ethnology and Eugenics). Reprint *changed to* White Paper on Human Ecology
0074-1523 I A A E E (International Association for the Advancement of Ethnology and Eugenics). Monographs *changed to* I C H E International Commission on Human Ecology
0074-154X International Association for the Advancement of Educational Research. Congress Reports *changed to* World Association for Educational Research. Congress Reports
0074-1574 International Association of Applied Psychology. Proceedings of Congress
0074-1582 International Association of Chain Stores. Report of Plenary Session
0074-1604 International Association of Democratic Lawyers. Congress Report
0074-1612 International Association of Engineering Geology. Bulletin
0074-1620 International Association of Gerontology. European Clinical Section Proceedings
0074-1647 International Association of Hail Insurers. Congress Report
0074-1655 International Association of Logopedics and Phoniatrics. Reports of Congress
0074-1663 International Association of Meteorology and Atmospheric Physics. Report of Proceedings of General Assembly
0074-1671 International Association of Milk Control Agencies. Proceedings of Annual Meetings
0074-168X International Association of Museums of Arms and Military History. Congress Reports
0074-1728 International Association of Physical Education and Sports for Girls and Women. Proceedings of the International Congress
0074-1736 International Association of Seed Crushers. Proceedings of the Annual Congress
0074-1744 International Association of State Lotteries. (Reports of Congress)
0074-1752 International Association of Students in Economics and Management. International Compendium. Annual Report
0074-1760 International Association of Thalassotherapy. Congress Reports
0074-1787 International Association of Workers for Maladjusted Children. Congress Reports
0074-1795 International Astronautical Congress. Proceedings *see* 0304-8705
0074-1809 International Astronomical Union. Proceedings of Symposia
0074-1833 International Atomic Energy Agency. Bibliographical Series†
0074-1841 I A E A Laboratory Activities†
0074-185X I A E A Research Contracts†
0074-1868 International Atomic Energy Agency. Legal Series
0074-1876 International Atomic Energy Agency. Panel Proceedings Series
0074-1884 International Atomic Energy Agency. Proceedings Series
0074-1892 International Atomic Energy Agency. Safety Series
0074-1906 International Atomic Energy Agency. Technical Directories
0074-1914 International Atomic Energy Agency. Technical Report Series
0074-1922 International Auction Records
0074-1930 International Audio-Visual Technical Centre. Bibliographical References
0074-1949 International Audio-Visual Technical Centre. Studies and Reports
0074-1973 International Baccalaureate Office. Annual Bulletin

0074-1981 International Badminton Federation. Annual Handbook *see* 0255-4437
0074-199X World Bank Staff Occasional Papers†
0074-2007 International Beekeeping Congress. Reports
0074-2015 International Bibliography of Historical Sciences
0074-2031 International Bibliography of Rice Research
0074-204X International Bibliography of Studies on Alcohol
0074-2066 International Biennial Exhibition of Prints in Tokyo†
0074-2074 I B P Handbooks†
0074-2082 International Biometeorological Congress. Summaries and Reports Presented to the Congress
0074-2090 International Botanical Congress. Abstracts of Papers
0074-2104 International Bureau of Fiscal Documentation. Annual Report
0074-2112 International Bureau of Fiscal Documentation. Publication
0074-2147 International Catalogue of Occupational Safety and Health Films
0074-2155 International Cemetery Directory *changed to* American Cemetery Association. Membership Directory
0074-2163 International Centre for Settlement of Investment Disputes. Annual Report
0074-2171 International Centre of Fertilizers. World Congress. Acts
0074-218X International Ceramic Congress. Proceedings
0074-221X International Civil Aviation Association. Aeronautical Agreements and Arrangements. Annual Supplement
0074-2228 International Civil Aviation Organization. (Panel On) Application of Space Techniques Relating to Aviation. Report of Meeting
0074-2244 International Civil Aviation Organization. Airworthiness Committee. Report of Meeting
0074-2252 International Civil Aviation Organization. Automated Data Interchange Systems Panel. Report of Meeting
0074-2287 International Civil Aviation Organization. Air Navigation Plan. Africa-Indian Ocean Region
0074-2295 International Civil Aviation Organization. Air Navigation Plan. Caribbean and South American Regions *changed to* International Civil Aviation Organization. Air Navigation Plan. Caribbean Region
0074-2309 International Civil Aviation Organization. Air Navigation Plan. European Region†
0074-2317 International Civil Aviation Organization. Air Navigation Plan. Middle East and South East Asia Regions *changed to* International Civil Aviation Organization. Air Navigation Plan. Middle East and Asia Regions
0074-2325 International Civil Aviation Organization. Air Navigation Plan. North Atlantic, North American and Pacific Regions
0074-2333 International Civil Aviation Organization. All-Weather Operations Panel. Report of Meeting
0074-235X International Civil Aviation Organization. Assembly. Resolutions
0074-2368 International Civil Aviation Organization. Assembly. Report and Minutes of the Legal Commission
0074-2376 International Civil Aviation Organization. Assembly. Report of the Economic Commission
0074-2384 International Civil Aviation Organization. Assembly. Report of the Technical Commission
0074-2422 International Civil Aviation Organization. Digests of Statistics. Series AT. Airport Traffic
0074-2430 International Civil Aviation Organization. Digests of Statistics. Series F. Financial Data
0074-2449 International Civil Aviation Organization. Digests of Statistics. Series FP. Fleet, Personnel
0074-2457 International Civil Aviation Organization. Digests of Statistics. Series R. Civil Aircraft on Register
0074-2465 International Civil Aviation Organization. Digests of Statistics. Series T. Traffic
0074-2473 International Civil Aviation Organization. Digests of Statistics. Series TF. Traffic Flow
0074-2481 I C A O Circulars
0074-249X International Civil Aviation Organization. Indexes to I C A O Publications. Annual Cumulation
0074-2503 International Civil Aviation Organization. Legal Committee. Minutes and Documents (of Sessions)
0074-252X International Civil Aviation Organization. Obstacle Clearance Panel. Report of Meeting
0074-2546 International Civil Aviation Organization. Report of the Air Navigation Conference†
0074-2562 International Civil Aviation Organization. Sonic Boom Panel. Report of the Meeting
0074-2570 International Civil Aviation Organization. Technical Panel on Supersonic Transport. Report of Meeting
0074-2589 International Civil Aviation Organization. Visual Aids Panel. Report of Meeting
0074-2597 International Clay Conference. Proceedings†
0074-2600 International College of Dentists. India Section. Newsletter
0074-2627 International Commission for the Northwest Atlantic Fisheries. Annual Proceedings *see* 0704-4798
0074-2635 International Commission for the Northwest Atlantic Fisheries. List of Fishing Vessels *see* 0250-7811
0074-2643 International Commission for the Northwest Atlantic Fisheries. Redbook *see* 0250-6416
0074-2651 International Commission for the Northwest Atlantic Fisheries. Research Bulletin *see* 0250-6408
0074-266X International Commission for the Northwest Atlantic Fisheries. Statistical Bulletin *see* 0250-6394
0074-2694 International Commission of Agricultural Engineering. Reports of Congress
0074-2708 International Commission of Sugar Technology. Proceedings of the General Assembly
0074-2724 International Commission on Illumination. Proceedings
0074-2732 International Commission on Irrigation and Drainage. Congress Reports
0074-2759 International Commission on Radiological Protection. Report
0074-2775 International Organizing Committee of World Mining Congresses. Report *changed to* World Mining Congress. Report
0074-2783 International Committee for Historical Science. Bulletin d'Information
0074-2791 International Committee of Onomastic Sciences. Congress Proceedings
0074-2805 International Committee on Laboratory Animals. Proceedings of Symposium *changed to* International Council for Laboratory Animal Science. Proceedings of the Symposium
0074-2813 International Comparative Literature Association. Proceedings of the Congress
0074-283X International Computer Bibliography†
0074-2856 International Confederation for Agricultural Credit. Assembly and Congress Reports
0074-2872 International Confederation of Free Trade Unions. World Congress Reports
0074-2880 International Confederation of Midwives. Congress Reports
0074-2899 International Confederation of Societies of Authors and Composers
0074-2902 International Conference of Agricultural Economists. Proceedings
0074-2937 International Conference of Educators of Blind Youth. Proceedings *changed to* I C E V H Educator
0074-2945 International Conference of Ethiopian Studies. Proceedings
0074-2961 International Conference of Social Work. Conference Proceedings
0074-297X International Conference for the Sociology of Religion
0074-3011 International Conference on Cloud Physics. Proceedings
0074-3038 International Conference on Congenital Malformations. Proceedings†
0074-3046 International Conference on Cosmic Rays. (Proceedings)
0074-3054 International Conference on Endodontics. Transactions†
0074-3062 International Conference on Engineering in the Ocean Environment. Digest *see* 0197-7385
0074-3089 International Conference on Fluid Sealing. Proceedings
0074-3097 International Conference on Global Impacts of Applied Microbiology. Proceedings
0074-3100 International Conference on Health and Health Education. Proceedings†
0074-3127 World Congresses on Information Processing. Proceedings
0074-3143 International Conference on Phenomena in Ionized Gases. Proceedings†
0074-3151 International Conference on Large High Voltage Electric Systems. Proceedings
0074-316X International Conference on Lead. Proceedings
0074-3178 International Conference on Low Temperature Physics. Reports
0074-3216 International Conference on Oral Biology. Proceedings
0074-3240 International Conference on Physics of Semiconductors. Proceedings *changed to* Physics of Semiconductors
0074-3259 International Conference on Planned Parenthood. Proceedings†
0074-3275 International Conference on Education. Proceedings *changed to* International Conference on Education. Final Report
0074-3305 International Conference on Social Welfare. Proceedings
0074-3313 International Society for Soil Mechanics and Foundation Engineering. Proceedings
0074-333X International Conference on the Physics of Electronic and Atomic Collisions. Papers *changed to* International Conference on the Physics of Electronic and Atomic Collisions. Abstracts of Contributed Papers and Invited Papers
0074-3348 International Conference on the Structural Design of Asphalt Pavements. Proceedings
0074-3356 International Commission on Trichinellosis. Proceedings
0074-3364 International Congress for Analytical Psychology. Proceedings
0074-3380 International Congress for Cybernetics. Proceedings. Actes
0074-3402 International Congress for Logic, Methodology and Philosophy of Science. Proceedings
0074-3429 International Congress for Papyrology. Proceedings
0074-3437 International Congress for Stereology. Proceedings
0074-347X International Congress of Angiology. Proceedings
0074-3488 International Congress of Animal Production. Proceedings†
0074-3496 International Congress of Anthropological and Ethnological Sciences. Proceedings
0074-3526 International Congress of Automatic Control. Proceedings
0074-3534 International Congress of Biochemistry. Proceedings
0074-3542 International Congress for Byzantine Studies. Acts
0074-3615 International Congress of Cybernetic Medicine. Proceedings
0074-364X International Congress of Entomology
0074-3666 International Congress of Food Science and Technology. Proceedings
0074-3682 International Congress of Hematology. Proceedings
0074-3690 International Congress of Histochemistry and Cytochemistry. Proceedings
0074-3704 International Congress of History of Medicine. Proceedings
0074-3712 International Congress of Home Economics. Report
0074-3747 International Congress of Life Assurance Medicine. Proceedings
0074-3755 International Congress of Linguists. Proceedings
0074-3771 International Congress of Nephrology. Abstracts of Reports and Communications
0074-378X International Congress of Nephrology. Proceedings†
0074-3828 International Congress of Occupational Therapy. Proceedings
0074-3844 International Congress of Orthoptists. Transactions
0074-3860 International Congress of Parasitology. Proceedings
0074-3879 International Congress of Pharmaceutical Sciences. Proceedings
0074-3895 International Congress of Primatology. Proceedings
0074-3925 International Congress of Pure and Applied Chemistry. (Lectures)
0074-3933 International Congress of Radiology. (Reports)
0074-3968 International Congress of Sugarcane Technologists. Proceedings
0074-3984 Transplantation Today
0074-3992 International Congress of University Adult Education. Journal *changed to* International Journal of University Adult Education
0074-400X International Conference on Acoustics. Reports
0074-4026 International Congress on Animal Reproduction and Artificial Insemination. Proceedings
0074-4042 International Congress on Clinical Chemistry. Abstracts
0074-4050 International Congress on Clinical Chemistry. Proceedings†
0074-4069 International Congress on Clinical Chemistry. Papers
0074-4077 International Congress on Combustion Engines. Proceedings
0074-4115 International Commission on Large Dams. Transactions
0074-4123 International Congress on Metallic Corrosion. (Proceedings)
0074-4131 International Congress on Occupational Health. Proceedings†
0074-414X International Congress on Phonetic Sciences. Proceedings†
0074-4190 International Congress on the History of Art. Proceedings

0074-4204 International Congress on Underground Techniques and Town-Planning. Reports
0074-4212 International Congresses on Tropical Medicine and Malaria. (Proceedings)
0074-4220 International Convocation on Immunology. Papers
0074-4239 International Cooperation Council. Directory *changed to* Unity-and-Diversity World Directory
0074-4247 International Cooperative Alliance. Congress Report
0074-4255 International Cooperative Alliance. Cooperative Series
0074-4263 International Council for Bird Preservation. British Section. Report
0074-4271 International Council for Bird Preservation. Proceedings of Conferences
0074-428X International Council for Building Research, Studies and Documentation. Congress Reports†
0074-4298 International Council for Philosophy and Humanistic Studies. General Assembly. Compte Rendu *changed to* International Council for Philosophy and Humanistic Studies. Bulletin
0074-4328 I C E S Oceanographic Data Lists *see* 0106-6935
0074-4336 International Council for the Exploration of the Sea. Rapports et Proces-Verbaux des Reunions
0074-4360 International Council of Homehelp Services. Reports of Congress
0074-4387 International Council of Scientific Unions. Year Book
0074-4395 International Council of Voluntary Agencies. Documents Series†
0074-4409 International Council of Voluntary Agencies. General Conference. Record of Proceedings†
0074-4417 I C H P E R Congress Reports *changed to* I C H P E R Congress Proceedings
0074-4425 International Council on Social Welfare. European Symposium. Proceedings
0074-445X International Court of Justice. Yearbook/Annuaire
0074-4468 Credit Union Yearbook
0074-4476 International Customs Journal
0074-4484 International Dairy Federation. Annual Bulletin
0074-4557 S D C E International Die Casting Congress. Transactions
0074-4565 International Directory of Arts
0074-4573 International Directory of Biological Deterioration Research†
0074-4581 International Directory of Computer and Information System Services†
0074-459X International Directory of Marketing Research Houses and Services
0074-4603 International Directory of Philosophy and Philosophers
0074-4611 International Directory of Programs in Business and Commerce†
0074-462X International Directory of 16MM Film Collectors
0074-4638 International District Heating Association. Proceedings
0074-4646 International Economic Association. Proceedings of the Conferences and Congresses
0074-4670 International Electron Devices Meeting. Abstracts *see* 0163-1918
0074-4697 International Electrotechnical Commission. Yearbook/Annuaire
0074-4700 International Encyclopedia of Food and Nutrition *see* 0306-0632
0074-5774 International Engineering Directory
0074-5782 International Eucharist Congress. Proceedings
0074-5790 International Falcon Movement. Conference Reports
0074-5804 F.I.D./C.R. Report Series
0074-5812 International Federation for Documentation. Proceedings of Congress
0074-5820 F I D Annual Report†
0074-5839 F I D Yearbook *see* 0379-3680
0074-5847 International Federation for Medical Psychotherapy. Congress Reports
0074-5863 International Federation of Agricultural Producers. General Conference Proceedings
0074-588X International Federation of Asian and Western Pacific Contractors' Associations. Proceedings of the Annual Convention
0074-5898 International Federation of Associations of Textile Chemists and Colorists. Reports of Congress
0074-5952 International Federation of Fruit Juice Producers. Proceedings of Congress. Compte-Rendu du Congres
0074-5960 I F I Information†
0074-5979 International Federation of Journalists and Travel Writers. Official List/Repertoire Officiel
0074-5987 I F L A Annual
0074-6002 I F L A Directory
0074-6037 International Federation of Medical Students' Associations. Minutes and Reports of the General Assembly
0074-6045 International Federation of Prestressing. Congress Proceedings
0074-6053 International Film Guide
0074-6061 International Finance Corporation. Report
0074-6096 International Folk Music Council Journal *see* 0740-1558
0074-610X International Football Book
0074-6118 International Foundry Congress. Papers and Communications
0074-6126 International Gas Union. Proceedings of Conferences *changed to* International Gas Union. Proceedings of World Gas Conferences
0074-6134 International Geographical Union. Papers
0074-6142 International Geophysics Series
0074-6169 International Graphical Federation. Conference. Proceedings *see* 0018-9782
0074-6177 International Graphical Federation. Report of Activities
0074-6185 International Grassland Congress. Proceedings
0074-6193 International Green Book
0074-6215 International Handbook of Universities and Other Institutions of Higher Education
0074-6223 International Hop Growers Convention. Report of Congress
0074-6231 International Horticultural Congress. Proceedings
0074-624X International Hotel Guide
0074-6258 International Humanist and Ethical Union. Proceedings of the Congress
0074-6274 International Hydrographic Conference. Reports of Proceedings
0074-6282 International Hydrographic Bureau. Yearbook *changed to* International Hydrographic Organization. Yearbook
0074-6320 International Indian Ocean Expedition. Collected Reprints†
0074-6401 I I E P Occasional Papers
0074-641X International Institute for Labour Studies. International Educational Materials Exchange. List of Available Materials†
0074-6428 International Institute for Land Reclamation and Improvement. Annual Report
0074-6436 International Institute for Land Reclamation and Improvement. Bibliography
0074-6444 International Institute for Land Reclamation and Improvement. Bulletin†
0074-6452 International Institute for Land Reclamation and Improvement. Publication
0074-6460 International Institute for Sugar Beet Research. Reports of the Winter Congress
0074-6479 International Institute of Administrative Sciences. Reports of the International Congress
0074-6495 International Institute of Ibero-American Literature. Congress Proceedings. Memoria
0074-6509 International Institute for Labour Studies. Publications
0074-6525 International Institute of Philosophy. Actes
0074-6533 International Institute of Public Finance. Papers and Proceedings
0074-6541 International Institute of Refrigeration. Proceedings of Commission Meetings
0074-655X International Institute of Seismology and Earthquake Engineering. Bulletin
0074-6568 International Institute of Seismology and Earthquake Engineering. Earthquake Report†
0074-6584 International Institute of Seismology and Earthquake Engineering. Lecture Note†
0074-6592 International Institute of Seismology and Earthquake Engineering. Progress Report†
0074-6606 International Institute of Seismology and Earthquake Engineering. Report of Individual Study by Participants to I S E E *changed to* International Institute of Seismology and Earthquake Engineering. Individual Studies by Participants at I I S E E
0074-6614 International Institute of Seismology and Earthquake Engineering. Year Book
0074-6622 International Institute on the Prevention and Treatment of Alcoholism. Selected Papers
0074-6630 International Iron and Steel Institute. Report of Conference Proceedings
0074-6657 International Labor Studies†
0074-6665 International Labour and Industrial Film Triennial. Catalogue of the Participating Films
0074-6673 International Labour Conference. Reports to the Conference and Record of Proceedings
0074-6703 Management Development Series
0074-6738 International Law Association. Reports of Conferences
0074-6746 International League of Liberal Christian Women. Newsletter *changed to* International Association of Liberal Religious Women. Newsletter
0074-6754 International League of Societies for the Mentally Handicapped. World Congress Proceedings *changed to* International League of Societies for Persons With Mental Handicap. World Congress Proceedings.
0074-6762 International Leprosy Congress. Abstracts and Papers *changed to* International Leprosy Congress. Transactions
0074-6797 International Linguistic Association. Monograph
0074-6800 International Linguistic Association. Special Publications
0074-6819 International Literary and Artistic Association. Proceedings and Reports of Congress
0074-6827 International Literary Market Place
0074-6835 International Machine Tool Design and Research Conference. Proceedings
0074-6843 International Magnetics Conference. Digest *changed to* International Magnetics Conference. Digests of the Intermag Conference
0074-6878 International Maize and Wheat Improvement Center. Research Bulletin†
0074-6908 International Market Guide - Continental Europe *see* 0278-6524
0074-6916 International Measurement Conference. Proceedings. Acta IMEKO *see* 0237-028X
0074-6959 International Meeting of Animal Nutrition Experts. Proceedings
0074-6975 International Meeting on Cattle Diseases. Reports
0074-6983 International Metalworkers' Congress. Reports
0074-7009 International Microwave Symposium Digest *see* 0149-645X
0074-7017 International Mineralogical Association. Proceedings of Meetings
0074-7025 International Monetary Fund. Summary Proceedings of the Annual Meeting of the Board of Governors
0074-7033 International Monographs on Advanced Biology and Biophysics
0074-7041 International Monographs on Advanced Chemistry
0074-705X International Monographs on Advanced Mathematics and Physics
0074-7068 International Monographs on Studies in Indian Economics
0074-7084 International Motion Picture Almanac
0074-7114 International Narcotic Conference. Report: Proceedings of Annual Conference *see* 0148-4648
0074-7122 International Naturist Guide
0074-7157 International North Pacific Fisheries Commission. Bulletin†
0074-7165 International North Pacific Fisheries Commission. Annual Report†
0074-7173 International Olive Growers Federation. Congress Reports†
0074-7181 International Olympic Academy. Report of the Sessions
0074-7203 International Organization of Citrus Virologists. Proceedings of the Conference†
0074-722X International P.E.N. Congress. Report
0074-7238 International Pacific Halibut Commission (U.S. and Canada). Annual Report
0074-7246 International Pacific Halibut Commission (U.S. and Canada). Scientific Reports
0074-7254 International Pacific Salmon Fisheries Commission. Annual Report†
0074-7262 International Pacific Salmon Fisheries Commission. Bulletin†
0074-7270 International Pacific Salmon Fisheries Commission. Progress Report†
0074-7289 I P R A Studies in Peace Research†
0074-7297 International Peace Research Association. Proceedings of the Conference†
0074-7300 International Pediatric Association. Proceedings of Congress
0074-7343 International Philatelic Federation. General Assembly. Proces-Verbal
0074-7351 International Photobiological Congress. Proceedings†
0074-7386 International Planned Parenthood Federation. Proceedings of the Conference of the Europe and near East Region†
0074-7394 International Planned Parenthood Federation. Working Papers†
0074-7408 International Association of Plant Breeders for the Protection of Plant Varieties. Congress Reports
0074-7416 I P A Conference Report
0074-7432 International Polar Motion Service. Annual Report
0074-7459 International Political Science Association. Circular *see* 0709-6941
0074-7467 International Political Science Association. World Conference. Proceedings *changed to* International Political Science Association. World Congress
0074-7475 International Poplar Commission. Session Reports†
0074-7483 International Poster Annual†

ISSN INDEX 1381

0074-7491 International Potash Institute. Colloquium. Proceedings
0074-7505 International Potash Institute. Congress Report *changed to* International Potash Institute. Congress Proceedings
0074-7513 International Powder Metallurgy Conference. Proceedings-Modern Developments in Powder Metallurgy
0074-7521 International Pressure Die Casting Conferences. Report *changed to* International Pressure Die Casting Conferences. Proceedings
0074-753X International Psycho-Analytical Association. Bulletin *issued with* 0020-7578
0074-7556 International Publishers Association. Proceedings of Congress
0074-7564 I R T S Gold Medal Annual
0074-7572 International Railway Progress *see* 0309-1465
0074-7580 International Railway Statistics. Statistics of Individual Railways
0074-7599 International Rayon and Synthetic Fibres Committee. Statistical Yearbook
0074-7602 International Rayon and Synthetic Fibres Committee. Technical Conference. Reports†
0074-7610 International Rayon and Synthetic Fibres Committee. World Congress. Report†
0074-7637 International Real Estate Federation. Reports of Congress†
0074-7645 International Reference Annual for Building and Equipment of Sports, Tourism, Recreation Installations
0074-7653 International Reference Handbook of Services, Organizations, Diplomatic Representation, Marketing and Advertising Channels *changed to* International Reference Handbook of Marketing, Management and Advertising Organizations.
0074-7661 International Reinforced Plastics Conference. Papers and Proceedings. *see* 0306-3607
0074-767X International Review of Connective Tissue Research
0074-7688 International Review of Criminal Policy
0074-7696 International Review of Cytology
0074-7718 International Review of Experimental Pathology
0074-7726 International Review of Forestry Research†
0074-7734 International Review of General and Experimental Zoology
0074-7742 International Review of Neurobiology
0074-7750 International Review of Research in Mental Retardation
0074-7777 International Review of Tropical Medicine
0074-7785 International Reviews in Aerosol Physics and Chemistry†
0074-7793 I R R I Annual Report
0074-7815 International Road Congresses. Proceedings
0074-7823 International Rubber Study Group. Summary of Proceedings of the Group Meetings and Assemblies
0074-7858 International School of Physics "Ettore Majorana." Proceedings *changed to* International School of Physics "Enrico Fermi". Italian Physical Society. Proceedings
0074-7874 International Seaweed Symposium. Proceedings
0074-7882 International Society for Performing Arts Libraries and Museums. Congress Proceedings *changed to* International Association of Performing Arts Libraries and Museums. Congress Proceedings
0074-7890 International Security Directory
0074-7904 International Sedimentological Congress. Guidebook
0074-7947 International Series of Monographs in Aeronautics and Astronautics. Division 1. Solid and Structural Mechanics *changed to* International Series in Aeronautics and Astronautics. Division 1. Solid and Structural Mechanics
0074-7955 International Series of Monographs in Aeronautics and Astronautics. Division 2. Aerodynamics *changed to* International Series in Aeronautics and Astronautics. Division 2. Aerodynamics and Astronautics
0074-7963 International Series of Monographs in Aeronautics and Astronautics. Division 3. Propulsion Systems Including Fuels *changed to* International Series in Aeronautics and Astronautics. Division 3. Propulsion Systems Including Fuels
0074-7998 International Series of Monographs in Aeronautics and Astronautics. Division 7. Astronautics *changed to* International Series in Aeronautics and Astronautics. Division 7. Astronautics
0074-8005 International Series of Monographs in Aeronautics and Astronautics. Division 9. Symposia *changed to* International Series in Aeronautics and Astronautics. Division 9. Symposia
0074-8021 International Series on Chemical Engineering†
0074-803X International Series of Monographs in Electrical Engineering
0074-8056 International Series of Monographs in Mechanical Engineering†
0074-8064 International Series in Natural Philosophy†
0074-8080 International Series on Automation and Automatic Control†
0074-8099 International Series on Analytical Chemistry†
0074-8129 International Series on Electronics and Instrumentation†
0074-8137 International Series in Experimental Psychology
0074-820X International Series in Library and Information Sciences†
0074-8234 International Series on Oral Biology†
0074-8242 International Series on Organic Chemistry†
0074-8269 International Series of Monographs on Pure and Applied Biology. Division: Biochemistry *changed to* International Series on Pure and Applied Biology. Biochemistry Division
0074-8277 International Series of Monographs on Pure and Applied Biology. Division: Botany *changed to* International Series on Pure and Applied Biology. Botany Division
0074-8285 International Series of Monographs on Pure and Applied Biology. Division: Modern Trends in Physiological Sciences *changed to* International Series on Pure and Applied Biology. Modern Trends in Physiological Science Division
0074-8293 International Series of Monographs on Pure and Applied Biology. Division: Plant Physiology *changed to* International Series on Pure and Applied Biology. Plant Physiology Division
0074-8307 International Series of Monographs on Pure and Applied Biology. Division: Zoology *changed to* International Series on Pure and Applied Biology. Zoology Division
0074-8315 International Series on Semiconductors†
0074-834X International Shade Tree Conference. Proceedings *changed to* Journal of Arboriculture
0074-8358 International Shipping and Shipbuilding Directory
0074-8404 International Social Science Council. Publications
0074-8439 International Social Security Association. Technical Reports of Assemblies *see* 0251-1339
0074-8447 International Society for Cell Biology. Symposia†
0074-8455 International Society for Labour Law and Social Legislation. Proceedings of Congress
0074-848X International Society for Rock Mechanics. Congress. Proceedings
0074-8498 International Society for Terrain-Vehicle Systems. Proceedings of International Conference
0074-8528 International Society of Blood Transfusion. Proceedings of the Congress
0074-8536 International Society of Geographical Pathology. Proceedings of the Conference†
0074-8544 International Society of Internal Medicine. Congress Proceedings
0074-8552 International Society of Orthopaedic Surgery and Traumatology. Proceedings of Congresses *see* 0341-2695
0074-8560 International Society of Surgery. Comptes-Rendus†
0074-8579 International Society of Urology. Reports of Congress
0074-8587 International Solid State Circuits Conference. Digest *see* 0193-6530
0074-8595 International Spectroscopy Colloquium. Proceedings†
0074-8609 International Statistical Institute. Bulletin. Proceedings of the Biennial Sessions
0074-8617 International Statistical Yearbook of Large Towns†
0074-8684 International Studies in Sociology and Social Anthropology
0074-8692 International Study Week in Traffic Engineering and International Road Safety Congress
0074-8706 International Sugar Organization. Annual Report
0074-8714 International Superphosphate and Compound Manufacturers Association Limited. Technical Meeting. Proceedings
0074-8722 International Symposia on Comparative Law. Proceedings†
0074-8765 International Symposium on Atherosclerosis. Proceedings
0074-8781 International Symposium on Chromatography and Electrophoresis. Proceedings†
0074-8803 International Symposium on Crop Protection. Communications *see* 0368-9697
0074-8811 I E E E International Electromagnetic Compatibility Symposium. Record *changed to* I E E E International Symposium on Electromagnetic Compatibility. (Record)
0074-882X International Symposium on Fault-Tolerant Computing. Digest *see* 0731-3071
0074-8897 International Symposium on Regional Development. Papers and Proceedings
0074-8935 International Symposium on the Reactivity of Solids. Proceedings†
0074-8951 International T N O Conference. (Proceedings)†
0074-9001 List of Cables Forming the World Submarine Network
0074-901X List of Destination Indicators and Telex Identification Codes *changed to* Indicators for the Telegram Retransmission System (TRS) - Telex Identification Codes
0074-9028 List of International Telephone Routes
0074-9044 International Telecommunication Union. List of Telegraph Offices Open for International Service
0074-9052 Table of International Telex Relations and Traffic
0074-9087 International Textile Machinery
0074-9095 International Thyroid Conference. Proceedings†
0074-9109 International Tin Council. Statistical Supplement. Tin, Tinplate Canning *changed to* Tin Statistics
0074-9117 International Tin Council. Statistical Yearbook *changed to* Tin Statistics
0074-9125 International Tin Research Council. Annual Report *changed to* International Tin Research Institute. Annual Report
0074-9133 International Touring Alliance. Minutes of the General Assembly
0074-9141 International Tracts in Computer Science and Technology and Their Application†
0074-915X I T C - Publications. Series A (Photogrammetry)†
0074-9184 International Travel Statistics *changed to* Yearbook of Tourism Statistics
0074-9192 International Union against Cancer. Manual
0074-9214 International Union against Cancer. U I C C Monograph Series†
0074-9222 U I C C Technical Report Series
0074-9230 International Union Against the Venereal Diseases and the Treponematoses. Proceedings of Assemblies *changed to* Genitourinary Medicine
0074-9265 I U C N Yearbook *changed to* I U C N Annual Report
0074-9273 I U C N Publications. New Series†
0074-9281 International Union for Conservation of Nature and Natural Resources. Proceedings and Papers of the Technical Meeting
0074-929X International Union for Conservation of Nature and Natural Resources. Proceedings of the General Assembly
0074-9311 International Union for Inland Navigation. Annual Report
0074-932X International Union for Quaternary Research. Congress Proceedings
0074-9338 International Population Conference. Proceedings
0074-9346 Union Academique Internationale. Compte Rendu de la Session Annuelle du Comite
0074-9362 International Union of Biological Sciences. Reports of General Assemblies *changed to* International Union of Biological Sciences. General Assemblies. Proceedings
0074-9370 International Union of Building Societies and Savings Associations. Congress Proceedings
0074-9389 International Union of Crystallography. Abstracts of the Triennial Congress
0074-9400 International Union of Forestry Research Organizations. Congress Proceedings/Rapports du Congres/Kongressberichte
0074-9419 International Union of Geodesy and Geophysics. Proceedings of the General Assembly
0074-9427 Commission for the Geological Map of the World. Bulletin
0074-9435 International Union of Latin Notaries. Proceedings of Congress
0074-9451 International Union of Official Travel Organizations. Minutes of the IUOTO General Assemblies†
0074-946X International Union of Physiological Sciences. Proceedings of Congress
0074-9486 International Union of Producers and Distributors of Electrical Energy. (Congress Proceedings)
0074-9494 International Union of Public Transport. Reports and Proceedings of the International Congress *changed to* International Union of Public Transport. Proceedings of the International Congress

1382 ISSN INDEX

0074-9508 International Union of Pure and Applied Chemistry. Comptes Rendus of IUPAC Conference†
0074-9516 International Union of Radio Science. Proceedings of General Assemblies
0074-9524 International Union of School and University Health and Medicine. Congress Reports
0074-9532 International Union of Students. Congress Resolutions *changed to* International Union of Students. Congress and Executive Committee Meetings Resolutions
0074-9540 Congres International d'Histoire des Sciences. Actes
0074-9575 International Water Conference. Proceedings
0074-9583 International Water Supply Congress. Proceedings *see* 0735-1917
0074-9591 International Whaling Commission. Report
0074-9613 International Who's Who
0074-9621 International Year Book and Statesmen's Who's Who
0074-963X International Association for Child Psychiatry and Allied Professions. Yearbook
0074-9648 International Yearbook of the Underwater World
0074-9664 International Zoo Yearbook
0074-9672 Internationale Bibliographie der Fachadressbuecher
0074-9729 Internationale Gesellschaft fuer Geschichte der Pharmazie. Veroeffentlichungen. Neue Folge
0074-9737 Internationale Volkskundliche Bibliographie
0074-9745 Internationale Zeitschriftenschau fuer Bibelwissenschaft und Grenzgebiete†
0074-9753 Internationaler Campingfuehrer *changed to* A D A C - Campingfuehrer. Band 1: Suedeuropa
0074-977X Internationaler Spitalbedarf
0074-9796 International Brewer's Directory
0074-9834 Internationales Jahrbuch fuer Geschichts und Geographieunterricht *see* 0172-8237
0074-9850 Internationales Jahrbuch fuer Religionssoziologie†
0074-9877 Internationales Verlagsadressbuch
0074-9907 Internationales Zucker-Jahrbuch
0074-9931 Interscience Monographs and Texts in Physics and Astronomy†
0074-994X Interscience Tracts in Pure and Applied Mathematics *changed to* Pure and Applied Mathematics: A Wiley Interscience Series of Texts, Monographs and Tracts
0074-9958 Interscience Tracts on Physics and Astronomy†
0074-9966 Interstate Commission on the Potomac River Basin. Technical Bulletin *changed to* Interstate Commission on the Potomac River Basin. Technical Reports
0074-9974 North American Conference on Labor Statistics. Selected Papers†
0075-0018 Inventaire General des Monuments et des Richesses Artistiques de la France
0075-0026 Inventari dei Manoscritti delle Biblioteche d'Italia
0075-0034 Inventaria Archaeologica Belgique
0075-0042 Inventaria Archaeologica Ceskoslovensko
0075-0050 Inventaria Archaeologica Denmark
0075-0069 Inventaria Archaeologica Deutschland
0075-0077 Inventaria Archaeologica Espana
0075-0085 Inventaria Archaeologica France
0075-0093 Inventaria Archaeologica Great Britain
0075-0107 Inventaria Archaeologica Italia
0075-0115 Inventaria Archaeologica Jugoslavija
0075-0123 Inventaria Archaeologica Norway
0075-0131 Inventaria Archaeologica Oesterreich
0075-014X Inventaria Archaeologica Pologne
0075-0158 Inventaria Archaeologica Ungarn
0075-0166 Inventaris van Het Kunstpatrimonium van Oost-Vlaanderen
0075-0174 Inventory of Programs in Maryland'S Private and Public Universities and Colleges†
0075-0220 Investigations in Physics†
0075-0247 Investissements Etrangers en Belgique *changed to* Belgium. Ministere des Affaires Economiques. Rapport Annuel sur les Investissements Etrangers en Belique
0075-0255 I B A Occasional Paper†
0075-0263 Securities Industry Association. State and Local Pension Funds†
0075-0271 Investment Companies
0075-028X Investment Dealers' Association of Canada. Canada and Canadian Provinces: Funded Debts Outstanding *see* 0317-607X
0075-0301 Invitation to Photography†
0075-0328 Ion Exchange; a Series of Advances *see* 0092-0193
0075-0336 Ionenaustauscher in Einzeldarstellungen†
0075-0344 I A S Bulletin
0075-0352 Iowa English Yearbook *changed to* Iowa English Bulletin
0075-0360 Iowa Development Commission. Digest†
0075-0379 Directory of Iowa Manufacturers
0075-0387 Iowa Nurses' Association. Bulletin
0075-0409 Iowa State Engineering Research *see* 0149-0605
0075-0425 Iowa State University. Library. Annual Report†
0075-0433 Iowa State University. Engineering Research Institute. Engineering Research Report
0075-045X University of Iowa. Center for Labor and Management. Monograph Series *see* 0578-6371
0075-0468 I P E K†
0075-0476 Iran Almanac and Book of Facts
0075-0484 Iran. Geological Survey. Report
0075-0492 Foreign Trade Statistics of Iran. Yearbook
0075-0506 Iranian Industrial Statistics
0075-0514 Iranian Mineral Statistics
0075-0522 Iranian National Bibliography
0075-0549 Ireland (Eire) Central Statistics Office. Crops and Livestock Numbers. *changed to* Ireland (Eire) Central Statistics Office. Crops and Livestock Enumeration
0075-0557 Ireland (Eire) Central Statistics Office. Estimates of the Quantity and Value of Agricultural Output *changed to* Ireland (Eire) Central Statistics Office. Estimated Output, Input and Income Arising in Agriculture
0075-0565 Ireland (Eire) Central Statistics Office. External Trade Statistics *changed to* Trade Statistics of Ireland
0075-0573 Ireland (Eire) Central Statistics Office. Hire-Purchase and Credit Sales
0075-0581 Ireland (Eire) Central Statistics Office. Inquiry into Advertising Agencies Activities. *changed to* Ireland (Eire) Central Statistics Office. Business of Advertising Agencies
0075-059X Ireland (Eire) Central Statistics Office. Livestock Numbers *changed to* Ireland (Eire) Central Statistics Office. Livestock Enumeration
0075-0603 Ireland (Eire) Central Statistics Office. National Income and Expenditure
0075-0611 Ireland (Eire) Central Statistics Office. Statistics of Wages, Earnings and Hours of Work†
0075-062X Ireland (Eire) Central Statistics Office. Tuarascail Ar Staidreamh Beatha. Report on Vital Statistics
0075-0638 Ireland (Eire) Central Statistics Office. Trend of Employment and Unemployment†
0075-0646 Ireland. Department of Agriculture and Fisheries. Annual Report *changed to* Ireland. Department of Agriculture. Annual Report
0075-0654 Ireland (Eire) Department of Agriculture and Fisheries. Journal†
0075-0662 Ireland Department of Education. Liosta de Iar-Bhunscoileanna Aitheanta. List of Recognised Post-Primary Schools
0075-0670 Ireland (Eire) Department of Finance. Financial Statement of the Minister for Finance
0075-0697 Ireland (Eire) National Industrial Economic Council. Report†
0075-0700 Iris Year Book
0075-0719 Irish Agricultural Organization Society. Annual Report *see* 0790-4568
0075-0727 Irish Baptist Historical Society. Journal
0075-0735 Irish Catholic Directory
0075-0743 Historical Studies
0075-0751 Irish Creamery Managers' Association. Creamery Yearbook and Diary *changed to* Dairy Executive. Directory and Diary
0075-076X Irish Drama Series†
0075-0778 Irish Geography
0075-0816 Irish Play Series
0075-0824 Irodalom - Szocializmus
0075-0832 Irodalomelmelet Klasszikusai
0075-0840 Irodalomtorteneti Fuzetek
0075-0859 Irodalomtorteneti Konyvtar
0075-0867 Iron and Steel. Annual Statistics for the United Kingdom
0075-0875 Iron and Steel Works of the World
0075-0921 Islam in Paperback
0075-093X Islamic Surveys
0075-0948 Islamic World†
0075-0964 Israel. Agricultural and Settlement Planning and Development Center. Statistical Series for the Agricultural Year *changed to* Israel. Rural Planning and Development Authority. Agricultural and Rural Economic Report
0075-0972 Israel Annual Conference on Aviation and Astronautics. Proceedings
0075-0980 Israel. Atomic Energy Commission. IA-Reports
0075-0999 Israel. Central Bureau of Statistics. Causes of Death
0075-1006 Israel. Central Bureau of Statistics. Criminal Statistics
0075-1014 Israel. Central Bureau of Statistics. Diagnostic Statistics of Hospitalized Patients
0075-1022 Israel. Central Bureau of Statistics. Juvenile Delinquency†
0075-1030 Israel. Central Bureau of Statistics. Judicial Statistics
0075-1049 Israel. Central Bureau of Statistics. Labour Force Surveys
0075-1057 Israel. Central Bureau of Statistics. Motor Vehicles
0075-1065 Israel. Central Bureau of Statistics. Schools and Kindergartens
0075-1081 Israel. Central Bureau of Statistics. Students in Academic Institutions *changed to* Israel. Central Bureau of Statistics. Students in Universities
0075-109X Israel. Central Bureau of Statistics. Survey of Housing Conditions
0075-1111 Israel. Central Bureau of Statistics. Vital Statistics
0075-1138 Israel. Department of Surveys. Geodetic Papers
0075-1146 Israel Discount Bank. Report
0075-1154 Israel Export Directory
0075-1162 Israel Film-Making Plus *changed to* Filmmaking in Israel
0075-1189 Israel. Ministry of Agriculture. Department of Fisheries. Israel Fisheries in Figures
0075-1200 Israel. Geological Survey. Bulletin
0075-1219 Israel. Hydrological Service. Hydrological Paper†
0075-1227 Israel Institute of Applied Social Research. Research Report†
0075-1235 Israel Institute of Productivity. Report of Activities†
0075-1243 Israel Journal of Entomology
0075-1251 Israel Medical Bibliography†
0075-126X Israel. Meteorological Service. Series B: Observational Data. Annual Rainfall Summary
0075-1278 Israel. Meteorological Service. Series A (Meteorological Notes)†
0075-1286 Israel. Meteorological Service. Series B: Observational Data. Annual Weather Report
0075-1294 Israel. Agricultural and Settlement Planning and Development Center. Statistical Series of the Budgetary Year *changed to* Israel. Rural Planning and Development Authority. Agricultural and Rural Economic Report
0075-1308 Israel. Ministry of Communications. Statistics
0075-1324 National Insurance Institute, Jerusalem. Full Actuarial Report
0075-1383 Israel Society for Rehabilitation of the Disabled. Annual
0075-1391 Israel Studies in Criminology
0075-1405 Israel Tourist Statistics
0075-1413 Israel Yearbook
0075-1421 Israel. Central Bureau of Statistics. Israel's Foreign Trade
0075-143X Issues†
0075-1472 Studi Etruschi†
0075-1499 Istituto e Museo di Storia della Scienza. Biblioteca
0075-1502 Istituto Ellenico di Studi Bizantini e Postbizantini, Venice. Biblioteca
0075-1529 Istituto Mobiliare Italiano. Annual Report
0075-1537 Istituto Nazionale per l'Assicurazione Contro le Malattie, Rome. Bilancio Consuntivo†
0075-1545 Istituto Siciliano di Studi Bizantini e Neoellenici. Quaderni
0075-1553 Istituto Siciliano di Studi Bizantini e Neoellenici. Testi e Monumenti. Testi
0075-1561 Istituto Storico della Resistenza in Modena e Provincia. Quaderni†
0075-157X Istituto Storico della Resistenza in Modena e Provincia. Rassegna Annuale†
0075-1588 Istituto Universitario Navale, Naples. Annali
0075-160X Istoria Limbii Romane†
0075-1626 Istorie si Civilizatie
0075-1634 Italian Studies
0075-1642 Italy: An Economic Profile†
0075-1650 Italy. Direzione Generale delle Fonti di Energia e delle Industrie di Base. Bilanci Energetici
0075-1669 Italy. Istituto Centrale di Statistica. Annuario di Statistica Agraria
0075-1677 Italy. Istituto Centrale di Statistica. Annuario delle Statistiche Culturali
0075-1685 Italy. Istituto Centrale di Statistica. Annuario di Statistiche Demografiche
0075-1693 Annuario di Statistiche del Lavoro e dell'Emigrazione *see* 0390-6450
0075-1707 Italy. Istituto Centrale di Statistica. Annuario di Statistica Forestale
0075-1715 Italy. Istituto Centrale di Statistica. Annuario di Statistiche Giudiziarie-Tomo 1
0075-1723 Italy. Istituto Centrale di Statistica. Annuario di Statistiche Industriali
0075-1731 Italy. Istituto Centrale di Statistica. Annuario di Statistiche Meteorologiche
0075-1758 Italy. Istituto Centrale di Statistica. Annuario di Statistiche Sanitarie
0075-1774 Italy. Istituto Centrale di Statistica. Annuario Statistiche Zootecniche *see* 0390-6426
0075-1782 Italy. Istituto Centrale di Statistica. Annuario Statistico del Commercio Interno *changed to* Italy. Istituto Centrale di Statistica. Annuario Statistico del Commercio Interno e del Turismo

ISSN INDEX 1383

0075-1790 Italy. Istituto Centrale di Statistica. Annuario Statistico dell'Assistenza e della Previdenza Sociale
0075-1804 Annuario Statistico dell'Attivita Edilizia e delle Opere Pubbliche
0075-1820 Statistiche dei Bilanci delle Amministrazioni Regionali, Provinciali e Comunali
0075-1871 Italy. Istituto Centrale di Statistica. Statistica Annuale del Commercio con l'Estero *see* 0390-6558
0075-1871 Italy. Istituto Centrale di Statistica. Statistica Annuale del Commercio con l'Estero *see* 0390-6566
0075-188X Statistica degli Incidenti Stradali
0075-1898 Italy. Istituto Centrale di Statistica. Annuario Statistico della Navigazione Marittima
0075-1901 Istituto di Fisica dell'Atmosfera, Rome. Bibliografia Generale.
0075-191X Istituto di Fisica dell'Atmosfera, Rome. Contributi Scientifici: Pubblicazioni di Fisica dell'Atmosfera e di Metteorologia.
0075-1928 Istituto di Fisica dell'Atmosfera, Rome. Pubblicazioni Didattiche
0075-1936 Istituto di Fisica dell'Atmosfera, Rome. Pubblicazioni Scientifiche
0075-1944 Istituto di Fisica dell'Atmosfera, Rome. Pubblicazioni Varie.
0075-1952 Istituto di Fisica dell'Atmosfera, Rome. Rapporti Interni Provvisori Adiffusione Limitata
0075-1960 Istituto di Fisica dell'Atmosfera, Rome. Rapporti Scientifici
0075-1979 Istituto di Fisica dell'Atmosfera, Rome. Rapporti Tecnici
0075-1987 Italy. Istituto Nazionale per lo Studio della Congiuntura. Quaderni Analitici
0075-1995 Italy. Ministero del Bilancio e della Programmazione Economica. Relazione Generale Sulla Situazione Economica del Paese
0075-2002 Itinera Romana†
0075-2010 Itsuu Laboratory, Tokyo. Annual Report
0075-2029 Ius Romanum in Helvetia†
0075-2037 Ius Romanum Medii Aevi
0075-2045 J. Anderson Fitzgerald Lecture†
0075-2053 Miller's Sporting Annual and Athletic Record†
0075-2061 J.K. Lasser's Your Income Tax, Professional Ed
0075-207X J. L. B. Smith Institute of Ichthyology. Occasional Paper†
0075-2088 J L B Smith Institute of Ichthyology. Special Publication
0075-2118 Vooraziatisch-Egyptisch Genootschap "Ex Oriente Lux". Jaarbericht
0075-2142 Jacob Blaustein Lectures in International Affairs
0075-2150 Jaeger's Intertravel
0075-2193 Jahrbuch der Auktionspreise *changed to* Jahrbuch der Auktionspreise fuer Buecher, Handschriften und Autographen
0075-2207 Jahrbuch der Berliner Museen
0075-2215 Jahrbuch der Bibliotheken, Archive und Informationstellen der Deutschen Demokratischen Republik
0075-2223 Jahrbuch der Deutschen Bibliotheken
0075-224X Jahrbuch der Export- und Versandtleiter
0075-2266 Graphische Unternehmungen Oesterreichs. Jahrbuch
0075-2274 Jahrbuch der Hamburger Kunstsammlungen†
0075-2282 Jahrbuch des Heeres†
0075-2312 Kunsthistorische Sammlungen in Wien. Jahrbuch
0075-2320 Jahrbuch der Luftwaffe†
0075-2347 Jahrbuch der Oeffentlichen Meinung *changed to* Allensbacher Jahrbuch der Demoskopie
0075-2363 Jahrbuch der Psychoanalyse
0075-2371 Raabe- Gesellschaft. Jahrbuch
0075-238X Jahrbuch der Schiffart†
0075-2398 Jahrbuch der Schleiff-, Hon-, Laepp- und Poliertechnik *changed to* Jahrbuch Schleiffen, Honen, Laeppen und Polieren, Verfahren und Maschinen
0075-2401 Deutscher Turner-Bund. Jahrbuch der Turnkunst
0075-241X Jahrbuch der Wehrmedizin†
0075-2428 Jahrbuch der Wehrtechnik
0075-2436 Jahrbuch des Baltischen Deutschtums
0075-2479 Jahrbuch des Eisenbahnwesens
0075-2487 Jahrbuch des Elektrischen Fernmeldewesens†
0075-2509 Jahrbuch des Kameramanns
0075-2517 Jahrbuch des Oeffentlichen Rechts der Gegenwart
0075-2533 Jahrbuch fuer Amerikastudien *see* 0340-2827
0075-2541 Jahrbuch fuer Antike und Christentum
0075-2568 Jahrbuch fuer Berlin-Brandenburgische Kirchengeschichte
0075-2576 Jahrbuch fuer Bundesbahnbeamte
0075-2584 Jahrbuch fuer Christliche Sozialwissenschaften
0075-2592 Jahrbuch fuer das Textil-Reinigungs-Gewerbe: Waescherei und Chemischreinigung†
0075-2606 Jahrbuch fuer den Oesterreichischen Tierarzt
0075-2622 Erziehungs- und Schulgeschichte Jahrbuch
0075-2630 Exlibriskunst und Graphik *see* 0172-2859
0075-2649 Jahrbuch fuer Fremdenverkehr
0075-2665 Geschichte der Sozialistischen Laender Europas. Jahrbuch
0075-2673 Jahrbuch fuer Geschichte von Staat, Wirtschaft und Gesellschaft Lateinamerikas.
0075-2681 Jahrbuch fuer Liturgik und Hymnologie
0075-269X Jahrbuch der Luftfahrt und Raumfahrt *changed to* Reuss Jahrbuch der Luft- und Raumfahrt
0075-2703 Jahrbuch fuer Musikalische Volks- und Voelkerkunde
0075-2711 Jahrbuch fuer Numismatik und Geldgeschichte
0075-272X Jahrbuch fuer Optik und Feinmechanik
0075-2738 Jahrbuch fuer Ostdeutsche Volkskunde
0075-2746 Jahrbuch fuer Ostrecht
0075-2754 Jahrbuch fuer Salesianische Studien
0075-2762 Jahrbuch fuer Schlesische Kirchengeschichte
0075-2770 Jahrbuch fuer Sozialwissenschaft
0075-2789 Jahrbuch fuer Volksliedforschung
0075-2800 Jahrbuch fuer Wirtschaftsgeschichte
0075-2819 Jahrbuch Oberflaechentechnik (Year)
0075-2827 Jahrbuch zur Alkohol- und Tabakfrage *see* 0170-7337
0075-2835 Jahresbericht der Bayerischen Bodendenkmalpflege
0075-2851 Jahresbericht ueber die Deutsche Fischwirtschaft
0075-286X Deutsche Geschichte. Jahresberichte
0075-2878 Jahresberichte ueber Holzschutz†
0075-2886 Jahresfachkatalog Recht-Wirtschaft-Steuern
0075-2894 Jahreshefte fuer Karst- und Hoehlenkunde *see* 0342-2062
0075-2908 Jahreskatalog Kybernetik, Automation, Informatik *changed to* Kybernetik Jahreskatalog
0075-2916 Jahreskatalog Philosophie *changed to* Katalog Philosophie
0075-2924 Jahreskatalog Psychologie
0075-2932 Jahresschrift fuer Mitteldeutsche Vorgeschichte
0075-2940 Jahresverzeichnis der Deutschen Hochschulschriften *see* 0323-455X
0075-2959 Jahresverzeichnis der Musikalien und Musikschriften
0075-2967 Jahresverzeichnis des Deutschen Schrifttums *see* 0300-8436
0075-2983 Jamaica. Department of Statistics. Annual Abstract of Statistics *changed to* Statistical Institute of Jamaica. Statistical Abstract
0075-2991 Jamaican National Bibliography
0075-3009 James Terry Duce Memorial Series†
0075-3017 Jane's All the World Aircraft
0075-3025 Jane's Fighting Ships
0075-3033 Jane's Freight Containers
0075-305X Jane's Surface Skimmers *changed to* Jane's High-Speed Marine Craft and Air Cushion Vehicles
0075-3068 Jane's Weapon Systems
0075-3084 Jane's World Railways
0075-3092 Janua Linguarum. Series Critica
0075-3106 Janua Linguarum. Series Didactica
0075-3114 Janua Linguarum. Series Major
0075-3122 Janua Linguarum. Series Minor
0075-3130 Janua Linguarum. Series Practica
0075-3157 Japan Annual of Law and Politics†
0075-3165 Japan Anti-Tuberculosis Association. Reports on Medical Research Problems
0075-3173 Japan. Statistics Bureau. Annual Report on Family Income and Expenditures *changed to* Japan. Statistics Bureau. Annual Report on Family Income and Expenditure Survey
0075-319X Japan Chemical Annual
0075-3203 Japan Chemical Directory
0075-3211 Japan Company Directory *see* 0288-9307
0075-322X Japan Directory
0075-3238 Japan Economic Research Center. Center Paper Series
0075-3246 Japan Economic Year Book†
0075-3270 Japan. Ministry of Health and Welfare. Statistics and Information Department. Vital Statistics
0075-3289 Japan Census of Manufactures: Report by Commodities
0075-3300 Japan P.E.N. News *changed to* Japanese Literature Today
0075-3319 Japan Road Association. Annual Report of Roads
0075-3327 Japan Society for Cancer Therapy. Proceedings of the Congress
0075-3343 Japanese Antarctic Research Expedition Data Reports.
0075-336X Japanese Antarctic Research Expedition, 1956-1962. Scientific Reports. Series B: Meteorology *see* 0386-5525
0075-3378 Japanese Antarctic Research Expedition, 1956-1962. Scientific Reports. Series C: Earth Sciences. *see* 0386-5533
0075-3386 Japanese Antarctic Research Expedition, 1956-1962. Scientific Reports. Series D: Oceanography *changed to* National Institute of Polar Research. Memoirs. Series D: Oceanography
0075-3394 Japanese Antarctic Research Expedition, 1956-1962. Scientific Reports. Series E. Biology *see* 0386-5541
0075-3408 Japanese Antarctic Research Expedition, 1956-1962. Scientific Reports. Series F: Logistic *see* 0386-555X
0075-3424 Japanese Journal of Botany†
0075-3432 Japanese Journal of Mathematics†
0075-3440 Japanese Miniature Electronic Components Data†
0075-3459 Japanese Phonograph Records of Folk Songs, Classical and Popular Music
0075-3467 Japanese Progress in Climatology
0075-3475 Japan's Iron and Steel Industry
0075-3491 Jarlibro
0075-3505 Institutul Agronomic Ion Ionescu de la Brad. Lucrari Stiintifice. Seria Agronomie-Horticultura *see* 0379-8364
0075-3505 Institutul Agronomic Ion Ionescu de la Brad. Lucrari Stiintifice. Seria Agronomie-Horticultura *see* 0379-8372
0075-3513 Institutul Agronomic Ion Ionescu de la Brad. Lucrari Stiintifice, Seria Zootechnie - Medicina Veterinaria
0075-3521 Universitatea "Al. I. Cuza" din Iasi. Analele Stiintifice. Sectiunea 2b: Geologie *see* 0379-7902
0075-353X Universitatea "Al. I. Cuza" din Iasi. Analele Stiintifice. Sectiunea 3b: Stiinte Filozofice *see* 0379-7856
0075-3548 Jawaharlal Nehru University. School of International Studies Series
0075-3556 Jazz Catalogue
0075-3572 Jazzforschung
0075-3580 Jean-Paul-Gesellschaft. Jahrbuch
0075-3599 Jefferson Memorial Lecture Series
0075-3602 Jehovah's Witnesses Yearbook
0075-3610 Jerome Lectures
0075-3629 Jersey Herd Book and Directory of the U.K. *changed to* Jersey Herd Book and Members Directory
0075-3637 Hebrew University of Jerusalem. Authority for Research Report. Medicine, Pharmacy, Dental Medicine *see* 0333-6964
0075-3645 Hebrew University of Jerusalem. Authority for Research and Development. Research Report: Humanities, Social Sciences, Law, Education, Social Work, Library *see* 0333-6964
0075-3653 Hebrew University of Jerusalem. Authority for Research and Development. Research Report. Science and Agriculture *see* 0333-6964
0075-3661 Hebrew University of Jerusalem. Folklore Research Center. Studies
0075-3696 Jerusalem Symposia on Quantum Chemistry and Biochemistry
0075-3726 Jewish Book Annual
0075-3734 Jewish Federations, Welfare Funds and Community Councils Directory *see* 0161-2638
0075-3742 Jewish Social Service Yearbook†
0075-3750 Jewish Travel Guide
0075-3769 Jewish Year Book
0075-3777 Jobson's Mining Year Book
0075-3785 Jobson's Year Book of Public Companies
0075-3793 Johannesburg Stock Exchange. Handbook
0075-3807 University of the Witwatersrand, Johannesburg. Library. Annual Report of the University Librarian
0075-3815 John Alexander Monograph Series on Various Phases of Thoracic Surgery
0075-384X John E. Owens Memorial Foundation. Publications†
0075-3858 Johns Hopkins Oceanographic Studies
0075-3866 Johns Hopkins Series in Integration and Community Building in Eastern Europe†
0075-3874 Johns Hopkins Symposia in Comparative History
0075-3890 Johns Hopkins University Studies in Geology
0075-3904 Johns Hopkins University Studies in Historical and Political Science
0075-3912 Johnson Photographic Year Book
0075-3920 Johnsonia
0075-3939 Joint Automatic Control Conference. Record *changed to* American Control Conference. Conference Proceedings
0075-3947 Joint Center for Urban Studies. Publications
0075-3963 Joint F A O/W H O Expert Committee on Food Additives Report†
0075-3971 Joint F A O/W H O Expert Committee on Nutrition. Report†
0075-3998 Joint Railroad Technical Conference. Preprint *changed to* Joint A S M E/I E E E Railroad Conference. I E E E Technical Papers
0075-4005 Ahmedabad Textile Industry's Research Association. Joint Technological Conferences. Proceedings
0075-4013 Jordan. Department of Statistics. Annual Statistical Yearbook
0075-4021 Jordan. Department of Statistics. External Trade Statistics

ISSN INDEX

0075-403X Sweden. Sveriges Geologiska Undersoekning. Jordmagnetiska Publikationer/Geomagnetic Publications
0075-4056 Jouets et Jeux
0075-4072 Journal de Biologie et de Medicine Nucleaires†
0075-4080 Journal des Oiseaux *changed to* Journal des Oiseaux
0075-4099 Journal for the Protection of All Beings†
0075-4102 Journal fuer die Reine und Angewandte Mathematik
0075-4110 Journal of Ancient Indian History
0075-4129 Journal of Animal Science. Supplement
0075-4145 Journal of Behavioural Science *see* 0081-2463
0075-4161 Journal of Byelorussian Studies
0075-417X Journal of Child Psychotherapy
0075-4188 Journal of Civil Procedure
0075-4196 Journal of Commerce Annual Review†
0075-4218 Journal of Croatian Studies
0075-4242 Journal of English Linguistics
0075-4250 Journal of Glass Studies
0075-4269 Journal of Hellenic Studies
0075-4277 Journal of Juristic Papyrology
0075-4285 Journal of Maltese Studies
0075-4293 Journal of Mathematics
0075-4307 Journal of Natural Science
0075-4315 Journal of Nuclear Medicine. Supplement†
0075-4323 Journal of Neuro-Visceral Relations. Supplement *see* 0303-6995
0075-4331 Journal of Periodontal Research. Supplementum
0075-434X Journal of Rhodesian History *changed to* Zimbabwean History
0075-4358 Journal of Roman Studies
0075-4374 Hiroshima University. Journal of Science. Series C. Geology and Mineralogy
0075-4390 Journal of the Warburg and Courtauld Institutes
0075-4404 Journal of Ultrastructure Research. Supplement
0075-4412 Journalism Abstracts
0075-4420 Journee de Reeducation
0075-4439 Journees Annuelles de Diabetologie de l'Hotel Dieu
0075-4447 Journees Biochimiques Latines. Rapports
0075-4455 Journees de Physiologie Appliquee au Travail Humain
0075-4463 Acquisitions Medicales Recentes.†
0075-4471 Journees Parisiennes de Pediatrie
0075-4501 Judean Desert Studies
0075-4528 Jugendherbergs-Verzeichnis
0075-4536 Yugoslovenska Investiciona Banka. Annual Report *changed to* Investbanka. Annual Report
0075-4544 Sir Moses Montefiore Collections des Juifs Celebres
0075-4552 Junior College Directory *changed to* Community, Technical, and Junior College Directory: a Statistical Analysis
0075-4579 Juntendo University, Tokyo. Medical Ultrasonics Research Center. Annual Report
0075-4587 An Interlibrary Loan Service Newsletter *changed to* Just B'twx Us: An Interlibrary Loan Information Bulletin
0075-4609 Universitaet Giessen. Ergebnisse Landwirtschaftlicher Forschung
0075-4617 Justus Liebigs Annalen der Chemie *see* 0170-2041
0075-4625 Jyvaskyla Studies in Education, Psychology and Social Research
0075-4633 Jyvaskyla Studies in the Arts
0075-4641 Jyvaskylan Yliopisto. Matematiikan Laitos. Report
0075-465X Jyvaskylan Yliopisto. Department of Physics. Research Report
0075-4668 Kaiser Foundation Medical Care Program. Annual Report
0075-4684 Kalastuspaikkaopas
0075-4722 Makerere University. Department of Geography. Occasional Paper
0075-4730 Makerere University. Faculty of Agriculture. Handbook
0075-4773 Makerere University. Faculty of Agriculture. Technical Bulletin
0075-4781 Makerere University. Faculty of Law. Handbook
0075-4854 Makerere University. Library. Makerere Library Publications
0075-4900 Kansainvalinen Automatkailu *see* 0355-2896
0075-4919 Kansas Linguistics Conference. Papers *changed to* Mid-America Linguistics Conference. Papers
0075-4927 Kansas Geological Survey. Computer Contribution†
0075-4935 Kansas Geological Survey. Short Papers in Research
0075-4951 Kansas State University. Library Bibliography Series
0075-4986 University of Kansas. Center for Latin American Studies. Graduate Studies on Latin America†
0075-4994 University of Kansas. Department of Geology. Special Publications†
0075-5001 University of Kansas Libraries. Library Series.
0075-501X University of Kansas. Museum of Art. Miscellaneous Publications *changed to* University of Kansas. Spencer Museum of Art. Miscellaneous Publications
0075-5028 University of Kansas. Museum of Natural History. Miscellaneous Publications
0075-5036 University of Kansas. Museum of Natural History. Publications. *changed to* University of Kansas. Museum of Natural History. Museum Series Publications
0075-5044 University of Kansas. Paleontological Contributions. Articles
0075-5052 University of Kansas. Paleontological Contributions. Papers
0075-5060 Kappa Tau Alpha Yearbook†
0075-5079 Karachi. Chamber of Commerce and Industry. Annual Report
0075-5095 Karachi Law Journal†
0075-5109 Karachi Port Trust. Year Book of Information, Port of Karachi, Pakistan
0075-5125 Wyzsza Szkola Ekonomiczna. Zeszyty Naukowe *see* 0208-7944
0075-5133 Staatliche Kunsthalle Karlsruhe. Bildhefte
0075-5141 Staatliche Kunsthalle Karlsruhe. Graphik-Schriftenreihe
0075-515X Karnatak University, Dharwad, India. Journal. Humanities
0075-5168 Karnatak University, Dharwad, India. Journal. Science
0075-5176 Karnatak University, Dharwad, India. Journal. Social Sciences
0075-5184 Karthago. Collection Epigraphique
0075-5192 Kasetsart Journal
0075-5222 Kasmera
0075-5230 Katalog Fauny Pasozytniczej Polski
0075-5257 Katalog Zabytkow Sztuki w Polsce
0075-5265 Katherine Asher Engel Lectures
0075-5281 Wyzsza Szkola Pedagogiczna, Katowice. Zeszyty Naukowe. Sekcja Jezykoznawstwa†
0075-529X Kazakhskii Nauchno-Issledovatel'skii Institut Onkologii i Radiologii. Trudy
0075-5303 Keeping Track, Current News from the Department of Agricultural Economics at Purdue†
0075-5311 Keepsake
0075-532X Keilschrifturkunden aus Boghazkoei
0075-5346 Keio Monographs of Business and Commerce
0075-5354 Kekkaku No Kenkyu. *changed to* Hokkaido University. Institute of Immunological Science. Bulletin
0075-5370 Kelly's Manufacturers and Merchants Directory *changed to* Kelly's Business Directory
0075-5389 Kelly's Post Office London Directory *changed to* Kelly's Post Office London Business Directory
0075-5397 A Kemia Ujabb Eredmenyei
0075-5400 Kempe's Engineers Year-Book
0075-5419 Kemps Directory†
0075-5427 Kemps Film and Television Year Book (International) *changed to* Kemps International Film and Television Year Book
0075-5443 Kemp's Jersey Holiday Guide†
0075-5451 Kemps Music and Record Industry Year Book *changed to* Kemps International Music and Recording Industry Yearbook
0075-546X Kent Studies in Anthropology and Archaeology†
0075-5494 Kentucky Directory of Manufacturers
0075-5508 Kentucky Folklore Series†
0075-5516 Kentucky Industrial Directory *see* 0075-5494
0075-5524 Kentucky Nature Studies†
0075-5532 Kentucky Personal Income *changed to* Kentucky Personal Income Report
0075-5559 Kentucky Geological Survey. Series 11. Bulletin
0075-5567 Kentucky Geological Survey. Series 11. County Report
0075-5575 Kentucky Geological Survey. Guidebook to Geological Field Trips
0075-5583 Kentucky Geological Survey. Series 11. Information Circular
0075-5591 Kentucky Geological Survey. Series 11. Report of Investigations
0075-5605 Kentucky Geological Survey. Series 11. Reprints
0075-5613 Kentucky Geological Survey. Series 11. Special Publication
0075-5621 Kentucky Geological Survey. Series 11. Thesis Series
0075-5761 K I A Occasional Papers
0075-580X Kenya. Mines and Geological Department. Annual Report†
0075-5818 Kenya. Ministry of Economic Planning and Development. Statistics Division. Development Estimates *changed to* Kenya. Central Bureau of Statistics. Development Estimates
0075-5826 Kenya. Ministry of Economic Planning and Development. Estimates of Revenue Expenditures *changed to* Kenya. Central Bureau of Statistics. Estimates of Revenue Expenditures
0075-5834 Kenya. Ministry of Economic Planning and Development. Statistics Division. Estimates of Recurrent Expenditures *changed to* Kenya. Central Bureau of Statistics. Estimates of Recurrent Expenditures
0075-5842 Kenya. Ministry of Economic Planning and Development. Economic Survey *changed to* Kenya. Central Bureau of Statistics. Economic Survey
0075-5850 Kenya. Ministry of Economic Planning and Development. Statistics Division. Statistical Abstract *changed to* Kenya. Central Bureau of Statistics. Statistical Abstract
0075-5869 Kenya. Ministry of Education. Annual Report
0075-5877 Kenya. Ministry of Health and Housing. Annual Report *changed to* Kenya. Ministry of Housing. Annual Report
0075-5885 Kenya. Ministry of Information. Annual Report *changed to* Kenya. Ministry of Information and Broadcasting. Annual Report
0075-5915 Kenya. National Irrigation Board. Reports and Accounts
0075-5923 Kenya. National Library Service Board. Annual and Audit Report
0075-5931 Kenya. Public Accounts Committee. Annual Report
0075-594X Kenya. Public Service Commission. Annual Report
0075-5966 Keswick Week†
0075-5974 Kew Bulletin
0075-5982 Kew Bulletin. Additional Series
0075-5990 Canadian Electronics Engineering Annual Buyers' Guide and Catalog Directory *changed to* Canadian Electronics Engineering Components and Equipment Directory
0075-6008 Keys to Music Bibliography†
0075-6016 Khosla's Industrial and Commercial Directory of India, Afghanistan, Burma, Ceylon, Japan and Foreign
0075-6032 Kierkegaardiana
0075-6040 Kime's International Law Directory
0075-6067 Kinetics and Mechanisms of Polymerization†
0075-6083 Kings of Tomorrow Series
0075-6091 Queen's University at Kingston. Department of Electrical Engineering. Research Report
0075-6113 Queen's University at Kingston. Douglas Library. Occasional Papers
0075-6121 Queen's University. Engineering Society. Proceedings†
0075-613X Queen's University at Kingston. Industrial Relations Centre. Bibliography Series
0075-6148 Queen's University at Kingston. Industrial Relations Centre. Report of Activities
0075-6156 Queen's University at Kingston. Industrial Relations Centre. Reprint Series
0075-6164 Queen's University. Industrial Relations Centre. Research Series *see* 0317-2546
0075-6199 Kirchenmusikalisches Jahrbuch
0075-6202 Kirchenreform†
0075-6210 Kirchliches Jahrbuch fuer die Evangelische Kirche in Deutschland
0075-6229 Kirin Brewery Company, Tokyo. Research Laboratory. Report
0075-6245 Kirtlandia
0075-6261 Kjelberg och SAB Schriften *see* 0039-7083
0075-627X Klasings Bootsmarkt International; Yachten und Boote Zubehoer, Ausruestung, Motoren
0075-6288 Klassieken Nederlandse Letterkunde†
0075-6318 Kleine Deutsche Prosadenkmaeler des Mittelalters
0075-6326 Kleine Museumshefte
0075-6334 Klio
0075-6342 Klucze do Oznaczania Kregowcow Polski†
0075-6350 Klucze do Oznaczania Owadow Polski
0075-6369 Knizcny Zbornik
0075-6385 Knotty Problems of Baseball
0075-6407 Kobe Economic and Business Review
0075-6415 Kobe Economic and Business Research Series
0075-6423 Kobe University Law Review. International Edition
0075-6431 Kobe University. Medical Journal
0075-6458 Koedoe
0075-6466 Koedoe. Monographs
0075-6474 Koehlers Flottenkalender. Jahrbuch fuer Schiffahrt und Haefen
0075-6482 Koeln
0075-6490 Koelner Ethnologische Mitteilungen†
0075-6512 Koelner Jahrbuch fuer Vor- und Fruehgeschichte
0075-6520 Koelner Romanistische Arbeiten
0075-6547 Koleopterologische Rundschau
0075-6555 Kolloid-Gesellschaft. Verhandlungsberichte†
0075-6563 Kolloquium ueber Spaetantike und Fruehmittelalterliche Skulptur
0075-6601 Kommunikation und Kybernetik in Einzeldarstellungen *see* 0340-0034
0075-661X Kompas Danmark *changed to* Kompas Danmark

ISSN INDEX 1385

0075-6628 Kompass Australia *changed to* Kompass Australia
0075-6636 Kompass Belgium/Luxembourg
0075-6644 Kompass Espana
0075-6652 Annuaire Industriel. Repertoire General de la Production Francaise *changed to* La France de l'Industrie et ses Services
0075-6660 Kompass Holland
0075-6679 Kompass Hong Kong†
0075-6687 Kompass Italia
0075-6695 Kompass Maroc
0075-6709 Kompass Norge
0075-6717 Kompass Schweiz/Liechtenstein
0075-6725 Kompass Sverige
0075-6733 Kompass United Kingdom/CBI *changed to* Kompass United Kingdom
0075-6741 Koninklijk Nederlands Geologisch Mijnbouwkundig Genootschap. Verhandelingen
0075-675X Konjunkturberichte ueber das Handwerk *see* 0341-0978
0075-6768 Konstruktionsbuecher
0075-6776 Kontrollraadet foer Betongvaror. Meddelande
0075-6784 Konyvtartudomanyi Tanulmanyok†
0075-6792 Koranyi Sandor Tarsasag. Tudomanyos Ulesek
0075-6806 Korea Development Bank; Its Functions and Activities
0075-6814 Korea Directory
0075-6822 Korea (Republic). National Bureau of Statistics. Annual Report on the Family Income and Expenditure Survey
0075-6830 Korea (Republic). National Bureau of Statistics. Annual Report on the Price Survey
0075-6849 Korea (Republic). National Bureau of Statistics. Report on Mining and Manufacturing Survey
0075-6857 Korea (Republic). National Bureau of Statistics. Wholesale and Retail Trade Census Report
0075-6865 Korea (Republic). Office of Rural Development. Agricultural Research Report *changed to* Korea (Republic). Office of Rural Development. Research Report
0075-6873 Korea Statistical Yearbook
0075-6881 Korean Publications Yearbook
0075-6911 Korosi Csoma Kiskonyvtar
0075-6938 Korrosion†
0075-6946 Korunk Tudomanya
0075-6954 Kosten en Financiering van de Gezondheidzorg in Nederland
0075-6962 Koszen es Koolaj Anyagismereti Monografiak
0075-6970 Kothari's World of Reference Works
0075-6989 Kozgazdasagi Ertekezesek
0075-7004 Akademia Gorniczo-Hutnicza im. Stanislawa Staszica. Zeszyty Naukowe. Hutnictwo
0075-7012 Akademia Gorniczo-Hutnicza im. Stanislawa Staszica. Instytut Ceramiki Specjalnej i Ogniotrwalej. Prace Naukowe *changed to* Akademia Gorniczo-Hutnicza im. Stanislawa Staszica. Zeszyty Naukowe. Ceramika
0075-7020 Krakow Dawniej i Dzis
0075-7039 Muzeum Archeologiczne, Krakow. Materialy Archeologiczne
0075-7047 Obserwatorium Krakowski. Rocznik Astronomiczny. Dodatek Miedzynarodowy
0075-7055 Politechnika Krakowska. Zeszyty Naukowe. Chemia
0075-7071 Krankenhaus-Apotheke *see* 0173-7597
0075-708X Krankenhaus-Probleme der Gegenwart†
0075-7098 Krebsforschung und Krebsbekaempfung†
0075-7101 Beitraege zur Kardiologie und Angiologie†
0075-7136 Kriminologische Gegenwartsfragen
0075-7144 Kriminologie. Abhandlungen ueber abwegiges Sozialverhalten
0075-7152 Kriminologische Abhandlungen†
0075-7160 Kryptadia: Journal of Erotic Folklore
0075-7179 Ksiazka w Dawnej Kulturze Polskiej
0075-7209 Kulturpflanze
0075-7217 Kumamoto University. Institute of Constitutional Medicine. Bulletin. Supplement
0075-7225 University of Science and Technology. Journal
0075-7233 Kungliga Skogs- och Lantbruksakademiens, Tidskrift. Supplement *issued with* 0023-5350
0075-7241 Kunst-Katalog: Auktionen
0075-725X Kunst und Altertum am Rhein
0075-7268 Kunstdenkmaeler des Rheinlandes. Beihefte†
0075-7276 Kunststoff-Industrie und ihre Helfer
0075-7292 Kunststoffe im Lebensmittelverkehr
0075-7306 Kuratorium fuer Verkehrssicherheit. Kleine Fachbuchreihe
0075-7314 Kurtziana
0075-7322 Kurzauszuege Oesterreichischer Dissertationen: Geistes- und Sozialwissenschaften†
0075-7330 Kurzuaszuege Oesterreichischer Dissertationen: Naturwissenschaften und Technik†
0075-7349 Kush
0075-7357 Kyoto University. Institute for Virus Research. Annual Report
0075-7365 Kyoto University. Research Activities in Civil Engineering and Related Fields
0075-7373 Kyoto Prefectural University. Scientific Reports: Agriculture
0075-7381 Kyoto Prefectural University. Scientific Reports: Humanities
0075-739X Kyoto Prefectural University. Scientific Reports: Natural Science, Domestic Science and Social Welfare *changed to* Kyoto Prefectural University. Scientific Reports: Natural Science and Living Science
0075-7403 Universidad Nacional Agraria. Programa Cooperativo de Investigaciones en Maiz. Boletin†
0075-742X Universidad Nacional de la Plata. Instituto de Estudios Sociales y del Pensamiento Argentino. Cuadernos de Extension Universitaria†
0075-7446 Lab World. Labstracts. Annual Reference Guide†
0075-7470 University of Pennsylvania. Wharton School of Finance and Commerce. Labor Relations and Public Policy Series. Reports *changed to* Labor Relations and Public Policy Series
0075-7489 Labor Relations Yearbook†
0075-7500 Laboratory Guide†
0075-756X Labour Literature: A Bibliography
0075-7578 Directory of Labour Organizations in Canada
0075-7586 Labour Standards in Canada. Normes du Travail au Canada
0075-7608 Lafayette Clinic Handbooks in Psychiatry
0075-7616 Lafayette Clinic Monographs in Psychiatry
0075-7624 National Library of Nigeria. Annual Report
0075-7632 National Library of Nigeria. National Library Occasional Publication
0075-7640 Lagos Notes and Records
0075-7659 University of Lagos. Inaugural Lecture Series
0075-7667 University of Lagos. Continuing Education Centre. Occasional Papers
0075-7675 University of Lagos. Humanities Series
0075-7691 University of Lagos. Law Series†
0075-7705 University of Lagos. Library. Annual Report
0075-7713 University of Lagos. Scientific Monograph Series
0075-7721 Universidad de la Laguna. Facultad de Ciencias. Anales
0075-773X Universidad de la Laguna. Facultad de Derecho. Anales
0075-7748 Lake Carriers' Association. Annual Report
0075-7772 Lamar Lecture Series
0075-7780 Lammergeyer
0075-7799 Lancashire Dialect Society. Journal
0075-7810 University of Lancaster. Library. Occasional Papers†
0075-7837 Land Economics Monographs
0075-7853 Landbrukets Aarbok. Jordbruk, Hagebruk, Skogbruk
0075-7861 Landbrukets Aarbok. Skogbruk *see* 0075-7853
0075-787X Landolt-Boernstein, Zahlenwerte und Funktionen aus Naturwissenschaften und Technik. Neue Serie. Group 3: Crystal Physics
0075-7888 Landolt-Boernstein, Zahlenwerte und Funktionen aus Naturwissenschaften und Technik. Neue Serie. Group 1: Nuclear Physics
0075-7896 Landolt-Boernstein, Zahlenwerte und Funktionen aus Naturwissenschaften und Technik. Neue Serie. Group 6: Astronomy
0075-790X Landolt-Boernstein, Zahlenwerte und Funktionen aus Naturwissenschaften und Technik. Neue Serie. Group 5: Geophysics
0075-7918 Landolt-Boernstein, Zahlenwerte und Funktionen aus Naturwissenschaften und Technik. Neue Serie. Group 2: Atomic Physics
0075-7926 Landolt-Boernstein, Zahlenwerte und Funktionen aus Naturwissenschaften und Technik. Neue Serie. Group 4: Macroscopic and Technical Properties of Matter
0075-7942 Landschaftsverband Westfalen-Lippe. Volkskundliche Kommission. Schriften *changed to* Volkskuendlichen Kommission fuer Westfalen. Schriften
0075-7950 Language Monographs†
0075-7969 Language Science Monographs†
0075-7993 Langues et Litteratures de l'Afrique Noire†
0075-8019 Lares. Biblioteca
0075-8027 Laser Focus Buyers' Guide *see* 8755-1616
0075-8035 Lasers: A Series of Advances†
0075-8108 Latin American Monographs
0075-8124 Latin American Political Guide†
0075-8132 University of California, Los Angeles. Latin American Center. Latin American Studies Series
0075-8140 University of Pittsburgh. Center for International Studies: Latin American Studies. Occasional Papers *changed to* University of Pittsburgh. Center for International Studies. Latin American Reprint Series
0075-8159 Latin American Travel and Pan American Highway Guide *changed to* Latin American Travel Guide & Pan American Highway Guide (Mexico-Central-South America)
0075-8167 Latin American Urban Research†
0075-8175 Latin Language Mathematicians Group. Actes et Travaux du Congres†
0075-8191 Universite de Lausanne. Ecole des Sciences Sociales et Politiques. Publications†
0075-8213 World Legal Directory†
0075-8221 Law Books in Print
0075-823X Law in Eastern Europe
0075-8256 Law Reprints. Trade Regulation Series *changed to* Law Reprints: Trade Regulation Series
0075-8264 PreLaw Handbook. Official Law School Guide
0075-8272 Lazy Man's Guide to Holidays Afloat
0075-8310 Leading Advertisers in Business Publications†
0075-8329 Leahy's Hotel-Motel Guide and Travel Atlas†
0075-8337 Learning Disorders†
0075-8345 Leather Buyers Guide and Leather Trade Marks
0075-8353 Lebanese Industrial and Commercial Directory
0075-8361 Year-Book of the Lebanese Joint-Stock Companies
0075-837X Lebanon. Direction Centrale de la Statistique. Comptes Economiques
0075-8388 Lebanon. Direction Centrale de la Statistique. Recueil de Statistiques Libanaises
0075-8396 LeBaron Russell Briggs Prize Honors Essays in English
0075-8418 Lebensdarstellungen Deutscher Naturforscher†
0075-8434 Lecture Notes in Mathematics
0075-8442 Lecture Notes in Economics and Mathematical Systems
0075-8450 Lecture Notes in Physics
0075-8469 Lecture Notes in Pure and Applied Mathematics
0075-8485 Lectures in Applied Mathematics
0075-8493 Lectures in Biblical Studies†
0075-8523 Lectures on Mathematics in the Life Sciences
0075-8531 Lectures on the History of Religions. New Series
0075-854X University of Leeds. Institute of Education. Papers
0075-8558 University of Leeds. Research Institute of African Geology. Annual Report†
0075-8566 Leeds Studies in English
0075-8574 Leeds Texts and Monographs
0075-8582 Legal Almanac Series
0075-8590 Legal Medicine Annual *see* 0197-9981
0075-8612 Lehrer-Briefe zur Verkehrserziehung
0075-8620 Leicester University Geographical Journal *changed to* Confluence
0075-8639 Leidse Geologische Mededelingen†
0075-8647 Leidse Romanistische Reeks
0075-8655 Sportmedizinische Schriftenreihe
0075-8663 Museum fuer Voelkerkunde, Leipzig. Jahrbuch
0075-8671 Museum fuer Voelkerkunde, Leipzig. Veroeffentlichungen
0075-871X Leitende Maenner der Wirtschaft
0075-8728 Stamm Leitfaden Durch Presse und Werbung
0075-8736 Lekarske Prace
0075-8744 Leo Baeck Institute. Year Book
0075-8760 Leonardo
0075-8779 Lepetit Colloquia on Biology and Medicine. Proceedings†
0075-8787 Lepidoptera
0075-8795 Lepidopterists' Society. Memoirs
0075-8809 Leprosy Mission, London. Annual Report
0075-8817 Lesotho. Treasury. Report on the Finances and Accounts
0075-8825 Lessico Intellettuale Europeo
0075-8833 Lessing Yearbook
0075-8841 Letopis Pamatnika Slovenskej Literatury *changed to* Literarno - Muzejny Letopis
0075-8868 Let's Go: The Student Guide to Europe *see* 0163-4585
0075-8892 Lettere Italiane. Biblioteca
0075-8906 La Lettre†
0075-8914 Levant
0075-8922 Lewis Henry Morgan Lectures†
0075-8949 Leybold-Kontakt *changed to* Contact
0075-8957 Liaisons Financieres en France *changed to* Collection Radiographie du Capital - les Liaisons Financieres
0075-8973 Librarians, Censorship and Intellectual Freedom†
0075-8981 Libraries in Nigeria: A Directory
0075-899X Libraries, Museums and Art Galleries Year Book *changed to* Libraries Yearbook
0075-9007 Library and Documentation Journals†
0075-9031 Library Association. Library History Group. Occasional Publication†

0075-904X Library Association of Alberta. Occasional Papers
0075-9058 Library Association. Reference, Special and Information Section. North Western Group. Occasional Papers†
0075-9066 Library Association. Year Book
0075-9074 Library Buildings *see* 0307-9767
0075-9082 Library Journal Book Review†
0075-9104 Library of Exact Philosophy
0075-9120 Library of Law and Contemporary Problems
0075-9201 Libros y Material de Ensenanza
0075-921X Bank of Libya. Balance of Payments
0075-9228 Libya. Census and Statistical Office. External Trade Statistics
0075-9236 Libya. Census and Statistical Office. General Population Census
0075-9244 Libya. Census and Statistical Office. Industrial Census
0075-9252 Libya. Census and Statistical Office. Report of the Annual Survey of Large Manufacturing Establishments
0075-9260 Libya. Census and Statistical Office. Report of the Annual Survey of Petroleum Mining Industry
0075-9279 Libya. Census and Statistical Office. Report of the Survey of Licensed Construction Units
0075-9287 Libya. Census and Statistical Office. Statistical Abstract
0075-9295 Libya. Census and Statistical Office. Wholesale Prices in Tripoli Town
0075-9309 Libyan Travel Series *changed to* Libya Past and Present Series
0075-9325 Lick Observatory. Publications
0075-9333 Universite de Liege. Faculte des Sciences Appliquees. Collection des Publications
0075-9341 Universite de Liege. Institut de Pharmacie. Recueil des Conferences Organisees Par le Cercle A. Gilkinet *changed to* Journee Scientifique de Mars. Conferences et Communications
0075-935X Universite de Liege. Institut de Pharmacie. Travaux Publies†
0075-9368 Universite de Liege. Laboratoire d'Analyse Statistique des Langues Anciennes. Travaux Publies†
0075-9376 Lieux et les Dieux†
0075-9384 Life around Us: A Commercial Directory†
0075-9392 Life Insurance Agency Management Association. Proceedings of the Annual Meeting *changed to* Life Insurance Marketing and Research Association. Proceedings of the Annual Meeting
0075-9406 Life Insurance Fact Book
0075-9414 Life Insurers Conference. Annual Meeting. Proceedings†
0075-9422 Life Sciences and Space Research *see* 0273-1177
0075-9457 Lightweight Concrete Information Sheets
0075-9465 Ligue Antituberculeuse de Quebec. Rapport
0075-9473 Institut de Medecine Legale et de Medecine Sociale. Archives
0075-9481 Lilloa
0075-949X Lilies and Other Liliaceae†
0075-9511 Limnologica
0075-9554 Lindley Lecture
0075-9597 Linguistic Circle of Manitoba and North Dakota. Proceedings
0075-9600 Linguistic Society of America. Meeting Handbooks
0075-9627 Linguistic Society of India. Bulletin
0075-9635 Linguistic Structures†
0075-9643 Academy of the Hebrew Language. Linguistic Studies *changed to* Academy of the Hebrew Language. Texts & Studies
0075-9651 Linguistics in Documentation; Current Abstracts†
0075-9686 Linguistische Reihe
0075-9724 Linzer Hochschulschriften *changed to* Linzer Universitaetsschriften
0075-9732 Linzer Jahrbuch fuer Kunstgeschichte *changed to* Kunstjahrbuch der Stadt Linz
0075-9740 Hebrew University of Jerusalem. Lionel Cohen Lectures
0075-9759 L P-Gas Market Facts
0075-9767 Lisbon. Escola Nacional de Saude de Medicina Tropical. Anais *see* 0303-7762
0075-9775 Lisbon. Universidade. Faculdade de Ciencias. Revista. Serie 2. Seccao B. Ciencias Fisicq-Quimicas†
0075-9813 List Bio-Med; Biomedical Serials in Scandinavian Libraries
0075-9821 L I S T†
0075-983X List of Grants and Awards Available to American Writers *see* 0092-5268
0075-9872 Literarny Archiv
0075-9880 Literary and Library Prizes†
0075-9899 Literary Market Place *see* 0161-2905
0075-9902 Literary Monographs
0075-9929 Literary Prizes in Pakistan
0075-9937 Literatur und Wirklichkeit
0075-9945 Literatura Piekna. Adnotowany Rocznik Bibliograficzny
0075-9961 Literatures of the World in English Translation: A Bibliography†
0075-997X Literaturwissenschaftliches Jahrbuch. Neue Folge
0075-9988 Litomericko
0075-9996 Litterature. Science. Ideologie. *see* 0335-9190
0076-0013 Little Red Book, Classified to All Public Transport Fleet Owners and Operators and Vehicle Manufacturers
0076-003X University of Notre Dame. Department of Theology. Liturgical Studies
0076-0048 Liturgiewissenschaftliche Quellen und Forschungen
0076-0072 Living History of the World†
0076-0080 Living Word Commentary†
0076-0102 Livre Contemporain et les Bibliophiles Francosuisses†
0076-0110 Livre de Langue Francaise - Repertoire des Editeurs *changed to* Repertoire International des Editeurs et Diffuseurs de Langue Francaise
0076-0129 Livre et Societes†
0076-0137 Bulletin Bibliographique Thematique
0076-0145 Livres de l'Annee/BIBLIO†
0076-0153 Livres et Auteurs Quebecois
0076-0188 Llen Cymru
0076-0196 Lloyd's Calendar and Nautical Yearbook *changed to* Lloyd's Nautical Year Book
0076-020X Lloyd's Maritime Atlas
0076-0226 Lloyd's Register of American Yachts *see* 0163-285X
0076-0234 Lloyd's Register of Shipping. Statistical Tables
0076-0242 Local Government Reports of Australia
0076-0269 Locations of Industries in Gujarat State
0076-0277 Lockwood's Directory of the Paper and Allied Trades
0076-0285 Locomotive Maintenance Officers Association. Annual Proceedings
0076-0293 Locomotive Maintenance Officers Association. Preconvention Report
0076-0315 Muzeum Archeologiczne i Etnograficzne, Lodz. Prace i Materialy. Seria Etnograficzna
0076-0323 Politechnika Lodzka. Zeszyty Naukowe. Budownictwo
0076-0331 Politechnika Lodzka. Zeszyty Naukowe. Wlokiennictwo
0076-034X Uniwersytet Lodzki. Prace
0076-0358 Uniwersytet Lodzki. Zeszyty Naukowe. Seria 1. Nauki Humanistyczno-Spoleczne†
0076-0366 Uniwersytet Lodzki. Zeszyty Naukowe. Seria 2: Nauki Matematyczno-Przyrodnicze†
0076-0374 Uniwersytet Lodzki. Zeszyty Naukowe. Seria 3: Nauki Ekonomiczne *changed to* Acta Universitatis Lodziensis. Zeszyty Naukowe. Seria 3: Nauki Ekonomiczne
0076-0382 Lodzkie Studia Etnograficzne
0076-0390 Lodzkie Towarzystwo Naukowe. Rozprawy Komisji Jezykowej
0076-0404 Lodzkie Towarzystwo Naukowe. Prace Wydzialu Jezykoznawstwa, Nauki o Literaturze i Filozofii
0076-0412 Lodzkie Towarzystwo Naukowe. Wydzial III. Nauk Matematyczno-Przyrodniczych. Prace
0076-0420 Lodzkie Towarzystwo Naukowe. Wydzial IV. Nauk Lekarskich. Prace
0076-0439 Lodzkie Towarzystwo Naukowe. Wydzial V. Nauk Technicznych. Prace
0076-0447 Log (Long Beach)
0076-0455 Log of the Star Class
0076-0471 Logos
0076-048X Loi de l'Impot sur le Revenu Canadien *changed to* Loi de l'Impot sur le Revenu du Canada
0076-0501 London and Middlesex Archaeological Society. Transactions
0076-051X London Bibliography of the Social Sciences
0076-0528 London Chamber of Commerce and Industry. Annual Report and Annual Directory *see* 0142-9728
0076-0536 London Divinity Series. New Testament†
0076-0544 London History Studies
0076-0552 London Mathematical Society. Lecture Note Series
0076-0560 L M S Monographs *changed to* London Mathematical Society. Monographs. New Series
0076-0579 London Naturalist
0076-0587 University of Western Ontario. Centre for Radio Science. Annual Report
0076-0595 University of Western Ontario. D.B. Weldon Library. Library Bulletin
0076-0609 University of Western Ontario. Museums. Museum Bulletin†
0076-0633 London Papers in Regional Science
0076-0641 London School of Economics and Political Science. Department of Geography. Geographical Papers
0076-0668 L S E Research Monographs
0076-0684 Stock Exchange Official Year Book
0076-0692 University of London Historical Studies†
0076-0714 University of London Legal Series†
0076-0722 University of London. Institute of Archaeology. Bulletin
0076-0730 University of London. Institute of Classical Studies. Bulletin
0076-0749 University of London. Institute of Classical Studies. Bulletin Supplement
0076-0765 University of London. Institute of Commonwealth Studies. Commonwealth Papers†
0076-0773 University of London. Institute of Commonwealth Studies. Collected Seminar Papers
0076-0781 University of London. Institute of Commonwealth Studies. Annual Report
0076-079X Education Libraries Bulletin Supplements
0076-0803 University of London. Institute of Germanic Studies. Library Publications
0076-0811 London German Studies
0076-082X University of London. Institute of Historical Research Bulletin. Special Supplement *changed to* Historical Research. Special Supplement
0076-0846 University of London. Institute of Latin American Studies. Monographs
0076-0854 University of London. Royal Postgraduate Medical School. Report
0076-0862 Looking for Leisure†
0076-0870 Looking Forward
0076-0889 Looking into Leadership Series
0076-0897 Lorentzia
0076-0900 Natural History Museum of Los Angeles County. Contributions in Science *see* 0459-8113
0076-0927 Natural History Museum of Los Angeles County. Contributions in History†
0076-0935 Science Bulletin *see* 0459-8113
0076-0943 Natural History Museum of Los Angeles County. Science Series
0076-1001 Lost Play Series
0076-101X Lotus; a Review of Contemporary Architecture
0076-1028 Louisiana Directory of Manufacturers *see* 0275-1089
0076-1044 Louisiana Tech University. Division of Life Sciences Research. Research Bulletin
0076-1052 Louisiana State University. Animal Science Department. Livestock Producers' Day Report
0076-1095 Louisiana State University. School of Forestry and Wildlife Management. Annual Forestry Symposium. Proceedings. *changed to* Louisiana State University. School of Forestry, Wildlife, and Fisheries. Annual Forestry Symposium. Proceedings
0076-1109 L S U Wood Utilization Notes
0076-1168 Instituto de Investigacao Cientifica de Mocambique. Memorias. Series A (Ciencias Biologicas)†
0076-1176 Instituto de Investigacao Cientifica de Mocambique. Memorias. Serie B (Ciencias Geograficas-Geologicas)†
0076-1184 Instituto de Investigacao Cientifica de Mocambique. Memorias. Serie C (Ciencias Humanas)†
0076-1192 Centre Belge d'Histoire Rurale. Publications
0076-1206 Universite Catholique de Louvain. Centre d'Etudes Politiques. Working Group "American Foreign Policy." Cahier
0076-1214 Universite Catholique de Louvain. Ecole des Sciences Politiques et Sociales. Collection.
0076-1222 Universite Catholique de Louvain. Faculte de Philosophie et Lettres. Travaux
0076-1230 Universite Catholique de Louvain. Facultes de Theologie et de Droit Canonique. Travaux de Doctorat en Theologie et en Droit Canonique. Nouvelle Serie
0076-1249 Universite Catholique de Louvain. Institut des Langues Vivantes. Cahiers
0076-1265 Universite Catholique de Louvain. Institut Orientaliste. Publications
0076-1273 Universite Catholique de Louvain. Institut Superieur de Philosophie. Cours Publies
0076-1281 Universite Catholique de Louvain. Laboratoire de Pedagogie Experimentale. Cahiers de Recherches†
0076-129X Universite Catholique de Louvain. Section de Philologie Germanique. Serie Microfiches
0076-1303 Universite Catholique de Louvain. Institut de Recherches Economiques, Politiques et Sociales. Publications
0076-1311 Universite Catholique de Louvain. Recueil de Travaux d'Histoire et de Philologie
0076-132X Lovejoy's College Guide
0076-1354 Lovoe Geomagnetic Observatory Yearbook
0076-1370 International Symposium on Atomic, Molecular and Solid-State Theory and Quantum Biology. Proceedings *changed to* International Symposium on Atomic, Molecular and Solid-State Theory, Collision Phenomena and Computational Methods. Proceedings
0076-1389 Lower Paleozoic Rocks of the New World

0076-1400 National Botanic Gardens, Lucknow. Annual Report *changed to* National Botanic Gardens, Lucknow. Progress Report
0076-1419 National Botanical Research Institute, Lucknow. Bulletin
0076-1427 Lucknow Law Journal†
0076-1435 Lud
0076-1443 Lueneburger Blaetter†
0076-1451 Lund Studies in English
0076-146X Lund Studies in Geography. Series A. Physical Geography
0076-1478 Lund Studies in Geography. Series B. Human Geography
0076-1486 Lund Studies in Geography. Series C. General and Mathematical Geography
0076-1494 Lund Studies in International History
0076-1508 Lusitania Sacra
0076-1516 Lustracje Dobr Krolewskich XVI-XVIII Wieku
0076-1524 Lute Society of America. Journal
0076-1532 L E A Yearbook†
0076-1540 Lutheran World Federation. Proceedings of the Assembly
0076-1559 Luxembourg. Ministere des Finances. Budget de l'Etat
0076-1567 Luxembourg. Office National du Travail. Rapport Annuel *changed to* Luxembourg. Administration de l'Emploi. Rapport Annuel
0076-1575 Luxembourg. Service Central de la Statistique et des Etudes Economiques. Annuaire Statistique
0076-1583 Luxembourg. Service Central de la Statistique et des Etudes Economiques. Bulletin du STATEC
0076-1591 Luxembourg. Service Central de la Statistique et des Etudes Economiques. Collection D et M: Definitions et Methodes
0076-1613 Luxembourg. Service Central de la Statistique et des Etudes Economiques. Collection RP: Recensements de la Population
0076-163X Lychnos-Bibliotek. Studies och Kaellskrifter Udgivna av Laerdomshistoriska Samfundet. Studies and Sources Published by the Swedish History of Science Society
0076-1648 Lychnos-Laerdomshistoriska Samfundets Aarsbok. Annual of the Swedish History of Science Society
0076-1656 Universite Claude Bernard. Departement de Mathematiques. Publications
0076-1664 Universite de Lyon. Faculte de Droit et des Sciences Economiques. Annales *changed to* Universite Jean Moulin. Annales
0076-1699 Lyrical Iowa
0076-1710 Sweden. Institute of Marine Research. Series Biology. Reports *see* 0346-8666
0076-1729 M.L. Seidman Memorial Town Hall Lecture Series
0076-1745 Asta-Press
0076-1818 Universita degli Studi di Macerata. Facolta di Lettere e Filosofia. Annali
0076-1842 McGill University, Montreal. Department of Meteorology. Publication in Meteorology†
0076-1850 McGill University, Montreal. Axel Heiberg Island Research Reports
0076-1893 McGill University, Montreal. Centre for Developing-Area Studies. Annual Report
0076-1907 McGill University, Montreal. Centre for Developing-Area Studies. Occasional Paper Series *see* 0702-8431
0076-1915 McGill University, Montreal. Centre for Developing-Area Studies. Reprint Series†
0076-1931 McGill University, Montreal. Department of Geography. Climatological Research Series
0076-194X McGill University, Montreal. Industrial Relations Centre. Annual Conference Proceedings
0076-1966 McGill University, Montreal. Mechanical Engineering Research Laboratories. Report
0076-1974 McGill University, Montreal. Mechanical Engineering Research Laboratories. Technical Note
0076-1982 McGill Sub-Arctic Research Papers
0076-1990 McGoldrick's Handbook of Canadian Customs Tariff and Excise Duties
0076-2016 McGraw-Hill Yearbook of Science and Technology
0076-2032 Machine Intelligence Workshop
0076-2040 Machinery's Annual Buyer's Guide *see* 0305-3121
0076-2059 McMaster University, Hamilton, Ontario. Institute for Materials Research. Annual Report
0076-2067 MacRae's Blue Book *changed to* MacRae's Blue Book
0076-2075 Macromolecular Chemistry (Oxford)
0076-2083 Macromolecular Reviews†
0076-2091 Macromolecular Syntheses
0076-2105 Made in Austria
0076-213X Madison Avenue Europe†
0076-2148 Madison Avenue Handbook
0076-2156 Madison Avenue London†
0076-2164 Madison Avenue Paris†
0076-2180 Madison Avenue West Germany†
0076-2202 University of Madras. Archaeological Series
0076-2210 University of Madras. Endowment Lectures
0076-2229 University of Madras. Historical Series
0076-2237 University of Madras. Kannada Series
0076-2245 University of Madras. Malayalam Series
0076-2253 University of Madras. Philosophical Series
0076-2261 University of Madras. Sanskrit Series
0076-227X University of Madras. Tamil Series
0076-2288 University of Madras. Telugu Series
0076-2296 University of Madras. Urdu Series
0076-230X Casa de Velasquez, Madrid. Melanges
0076-2318 Real Conservatorio Superior de Musica. Anuario†
0076-2326 Maerchen der Europaeischen Voelker†
0076-2342 Magazine of Albemarle County History
0076-2350 Magenta Frog†
0076-2369 Magon. Serie Scientifique
0076-2377 Magon. Serie Technique
0076-2385 Magyar Irodalomtortenetiras Forrasai
0076-2393 Magyar Konyv†
0076-2407 Magyar Kozlony
0076-2415 Magyar Munkasmozgalmi Muzeum. Evkonyv
0076-2423 Magyar Tudomanyos Akademia. Agrartudomanyok Osztalya. Monografiasorozat
0076-2431 Magyar Tudomanyos Akademia. Mikrobiologiai Kutato Intezet. Proceedings
0076-244X Studia Biologica Academiae Scientiarum Hungaricae
0076-2458 Studia Historica Academiae Scientiarum Hungaricae
0076-2466 Studia Philosophica Academiae Scientiarum Hungaricae†
0076-2474 Magyarorszag Allatvilaga
0076-2482 Magyarorszag Kulturfloraja
0076-2490 Magyarorszag Muemleki Topografiaja
0076-2504 Magyarorszag Regeszeti Topografiaja
0076-2512 Magyarorszag Tajfoldrajza
0076-2520 Maharaja Sayajirao University of Baroda. Department of Archaeology and Ancient History. Archaeology Series
0076-2539 An Economic Review *changed to* Economic Survey of Maharashtra
0076-2547 Maharashtra Archives Bulletin
0076-2555 Maharashtra State Budget in Brief
0076-2563 Maharashtra State Financial Corporation. Annual Report
0076-2571 Mahratta
0076-258X Maia†
0076-2636 Maine. Department of Sea and Shore Fisheries. General Bulletin *changed to* Maine. Department of Marine Resources. Fisheries Circulars
0076-2652 Maine Heritage Series
0076-2679 Maine Pocket Data Book *see* 0093-724X
0076-2695 Maine Recreation Authority. Annual Report *changed to* Maine Guarantee Authority. Annual Report
0076-2709 Maine That Was Series†
0076-2717 Maine Writers' Conference Chapbook†
0076-2725 Mainfraenkisches Jahrbuch fuer Geschichte und Kunst
0076-2733 Roemisch-Germanisches Zentralmuseum, Mainz. Ausstellungskataloge†
0076-2741 Roemisch-Germanisches Zentralmuseum, Mainz. Jahrbuch
0076-275X Roemisch-Germanisches Zentralmuseum, Mainz. Kataloge Vor- und Fruehgeschichtlicher Altertuemer
0076-2776 Mainzer Philosophische Forschungen
0076-2784 Mainzer Reihe
0076-2792 Mainzer Zeitschrift
0076-2806 Maison des Sciences de l'Homme. Collection de Reeditions†
0076-2814 Maisons d'Enfants et d'Adolescents de France. Album-Annuaire National
0076-289X Makedonika
0076-2989 Mala Biblioteka Baletowa
0076-2997 Malacologia
0076-3004 Malacological Review
0076-3012 Malawi Year Book *changed to* Malawi Yearbook
0076-3020 Malawi. Accountant General. Report
0076-3047 Malawi. Department of Agriculture. Annual Report *changed to* Malawi. Department of Agricultural Research. Annual Report
0076-3055 Malawi. Department of Civil Aviation. Annual Report
0076-3063 Malawi. Department of Customs and Excise. Annual Report†
0076-3071 Malawi. Department of Forestry and Game. Report
0076-308X Malawi. Police Force. Annual Report
0076-3101 Malawi Economic Report
0076-311X Malawi. Geological Survey Department. Annual Report
0076-3128 Malawi. Geological Survey. Bulletin†
0076-3136 Malawi. Geological Survey. Memoir†
0076-3144 Malawi. Geological Survey. Records†
0076-3152 Malawi. Judicial Department. Annual Report†
0076-3160 Malawi. Ministry of Justice. Annual Report
0076-3179 Malawi. Lands Department. Annual Report†
0076-3195 Malawi. Ministry of Finance. Budget Statement
0076-3225 Malawi. Ministry of Local Government. Annual Report
0076-3233 Malawi. Ministry of Works and Supplies. Annual Report†
0076-3241 Malawi. National Statistical Office. Annual Survey of Economic Activities
0076-325X Malawi. National Statistical Office. Annual Statement of External Trade
0076-3268 Malawi. National Statistical Office. Compendium of Statistics *changed to* Malawi Statistical Yearbook
0076-3276 Malawi. National Statistical Office. Household Income and Expenditure Survey
0076-3284 Malawi. National Statistical Office. National Accounts Report
0076-3292 Malawi. National Statistical Office. National Sample Survey of Agriculture
0076-3306 Malawi. National Statistical Office. Population Census Final Report
0076-3314 Malawi. Office of the Auditor General. Report
0076-3322 Malawi. Post Office Savings Bank. Annual Report
0076-3330 Malawi Railways. Annual Reports and Accounts
0076-3349 Malawi. Registrar of Insurance. Report
0076-3357 Malawi Treaty Series
0076-3365 Malawi. Department of Veterinary Services and Animal Industry. Annual Report
0076-3373 Malaysia Official Year Book
0076-3381 National Archives of Malaysia. Annual Report
0076-339X Malaysia Year Book *changed to* Information Malaysia
0076-3411 Mali. Service de la Statistique Generale, de la Comptabilite Nationale et de la Mecanographie. Annuaire Statistique *changed to* Mali. Direction Nationale de la Statistique et de L'informatique. Annuaire Statistique
0076-342X Malignant Intrigue
0076-3438 University of Lund. School of Dentistry. Faculty of Odontology. Annual Publications
0076-3446 Malta Trade Directory *changed to* Trade Directory (1985-86)
0076-3454 Malta. Office of Statistics. Census of Agriculture *changed to* Malta. Central Office of Statistics. Census of Agriculture and Fisheries
0076-3462 Malta. Central Office of Statistics. Census of Industrial Production Report
0076-3470 Malta. Central Office of Statistics. Demographic Review
0076-3489 Malta. Central Office of Statistics. Education Statistics
0076-3519 Mammalian Species
0076-356X Management Aids Annuals†
0076-3578 Management Aids for Small Manufacturers *see* 0190-3225
0076-3586 Management and Labor Studies. English Series†
0076-3616 Management, Fonctions, Methodes, Experiences†
0076-3624 Management Guide to N C
0076-3640 Management Monographs *changed to* L R I Guides to Management. Monographs
0076-3667 Management Advisory Services Technical Study†
0076-3705 Manchester Association of Engineers. Transactions†
0076-3713 Manchester Guardian Society for the Protection of Trade. Annual Report†
0076-3721 Manchester Literary and Philosophical Society. Memoirs and Proceedings *changed to* Manchester Memoirs
0076-3748 La Mandragore Qui Chante
0076-3756 National Museum of the Philippines. Annual Report
0076-3764 National Museum of the Philippines. Museum Publications (Pamphlet Series) †
0076-3772 National Museum of the Philippines. Monograph Series
0076-3780 Philippine Normal College. Language Study Center. Occasional Paper
0076-3802 Manitoba Cancer Treatment and Research Foundation. Report
0076-3810 Manitoba Entomologist†
0076-3829 Manitoba Historical Society. Transactions†
0076-3853 Manitoba Labour - Management Review Committee. Annual Report
0076-3861 Manitoba Law Journal
0076-387X Manitoba. Mineral Resources Division. Geological Paper *changed to* Manitoba Energy and Mines. Geological Paper
0076-3888 Manitoba Museum of Man and Nature. Biennial Report *changed to* Manitoba Museum of Man and Nature. Annual Report
0076-3896 Manitoba Record Society. Publications
0076-390X Manitoba Trade Directory
0076-3918 University of Manitoba. Center for Settlement Studies. Publication Series†
0076-3926 University of Manitoba. Center for Settlement Studies. Series 1. Annual Reports†

0076-3934 University of Manitoba. Center for Settlement Studies. Series 2. Research Report†
0076-3942 University of Manitoba. Center for Settlement Studies. Series 3. Bibliography and Information†
0076-3950 University of Manitoba. Center for Settlement Studies. Series 4. Proceedings†
0076-3969 University of Manitoba. Center for Settlement Studies. Series 5. Occasional Papers†
0076-3977 University of Manitoba. Center for Transportation Studies. Occasional Paper
0076-3993 University of Manitoba. Center for Transportation Studies. Seminar Series on Transportation. Proceedings
0076-4035 University of Manitoba. Department of Slavic Studies. Readings in Slavic Literature†
0076-4051 University of Manitoba. Faculty of Agriculture. Progress Report on Agricultural Research and Experimentation *changed to* University of Manitoba. Faculty of Agriculture. Annual Progress Review: Agricultural Research, Teaching and Extension
0076-4108 University of Manitoba. Medical Journal *see* 0832-6096
0076-4116 Mankind Quarterly Monograph Series
0076-4124 Manna†
0076-4140 Manpower/Automation Research Notices†
0076-4167 Manual of Materials Handling and Ancilliary Equipment *see* 0142-114X
0076-4175 Mutual Funds Almanac
0076-4205 Manuels Pratiques d'Economie†
0076-4213 MacRae's Manufacturers' Agents Guide *see* 0749-1093
0076-423X Manufacturing Chemists Association. Statistical Summary†
0076-4248 Canada. Statistics Canada. Manufacturing Industries of Canada: Type of Organization and Size of Establishment/Industries Manufacturieres du Canada: Forme d'Organisation et Taille des Etablissements†
0076-4256 Manufacturing Management Series†
0076-4264 Manx Museum, Douglas, Isle of Man. Journal
0076-4280 Maori Education Foundation. Annual Report
0076-4299 Instituto de Biologia Marina. Boletin†
0076-4302 Instituto de Biologia Marina. Serie Contribuciones *see* 0325-6790
0076-4310 Instituto de Biologia Marina. Memoria Anual†
0076-4337 Universidad Nacional del Zulia. Facultad de Humanidades y Educacion. Artes y Letras
0076-4345 Universidad Nacional del Zulia. Facultad de Humanidades y Educacion. Conferencias y Coloquios
0076-4353 Universidad Nacional del Zulia. Facultad de Humanidades y Educacion. Fuera de Serie
0076-4361 Universidad Nacional del Zulia. Facultad de Humanidades y Educacion. Manuales de la Escuela de Educacion
0076-437X Universidad Nacional del Zulia. Facultad de Humanidades y Educacion. Monografias y Ensayos
0076-4418 Marconi's International Register
0076-4434 Marian Library Studies. New Series
0076-4442 Marine Biology; Proceedings of the Interdisciplinary Conference†
0076-4450 Marine Catalog *changed to* Marine Catalog and Buyers Guide
0076-4469 Marine Engineering/Log Annual Maritime Review and Yearbook Issue
0076-4477 Morskaya Geologiya i Geofizika
0076-4493 Marine Research†
0076-4507 Marine Science Affairs *changed to* Reports on Marine Science Affairs
0076-4515 Maritime Bank of Israel. Annual Report
0076-4523 Market Research Society. Yearbook
0076-4531 Market Statistics Key Plant Directory *see* 0098-1397
0076-4582 Marketing Guide to the Chemical Industry *changed to* Kline Guide to the Chemical Industry
0076-4590 Marketing Guide to the Packaging Industries *changed to* Kline Guide to the Packaging Industry
0076-4604 Marketing Guide to the Paint Industry *changed to* Kline Guide to the Paint Industry
0076-4612 Marketing Guide to the Paper and Pulp Industry *changed to* Kline Guide to the Paper and Pulp Industry
0076-4620 Marketing Research Techniques Series†
0076-4647 Markets Year Book
0076-4655 Maroc en Chiffre
0076-4671 Marquette Slavic Studies
0076-4701 Marsyas
0076-471X Martin Classical Lectures
0076-4728 Mary C. Richardson Lecture†
0076-4736 Maryland. Council for Higher Education. Annual Report *see* 0361-140X
0076-4752 Maryland. Department of State Planning. Activities Report†
0076-4779 Maryland. Geological Survey. Bulletin
0076-4787 Maryland. Geological Survey. Educational Series
0076-4795 Maryland. Geological Survey. Information Circular
0076-4809 Maryland. Geological Survey. Report of Investigations
0076-4817 Maryland. Geological Survey. Water Resources Basic Data Report
0076-4833 University of Maryland. College of Library and Information Services. Conference Proceedings
0076-4841 University of Maryland. College of Library and Information Services. Student Contribution Series
0076-4892 Massachusetts Audubon Newsletter *see* 0272-8966
0076-4906 Massachusetts. Department of Mental Health. Newsletter†
0076-4922 Massachusetts. Division of Employment Security. Employment and Wages in Establishments Subject to the Massachusetts Employment Security Law. State Summary
0076-4930 Massachusetts. Division of Employment Security. Annual Planning Report†
0076-4949 Massachusetts. Division of Employment Security. Statistical Digest†
0076-4957 Massachusetts. Division of Fisheries and Game. Annual Report *changed to* Massachusetts. Division of Fisheries and Wildlife. Annual Report
0076-4981 Massachusetts Historical Society. Proceedings
0076-499X Massachusetts Housing Finance Agency. Annual Report
0076-5066 University of Massachusetts. Department of Anthropology. Research Reports
0076-5104 Masters Education; Route to Opportunities in Modern Nursing *changed to* Master's Education: Route to Opportunities in Contemporary Nursing
0076-5112 Master's Theses in Education
0076-5139 Material Culture Monographs (American Indian) *changed to* Material Culture Notes (American Indian)
0076-5147 Materiale si Cercetari Arheologice†
0076-5163 Materiali per Una Storia della Cultura Giuridica
0076-5171 Materialien zur Roemisch-Germanischen Keramik
0076-5201 Materials Science Research
0076-521X Materialy i Prace Antropologiczne
0076-5228 Materialy i Studia do Historii Prasy i Czasopismiennictwa Polskiego†
0076-5236 Materialy Zachodnio-Pomorskie
0076-5244 Materialy Zrodlowe do Dziejow Kosciola W Polsce
0076-5252 Materiaux pour l'Etude de l'Extreme-Orient Moderne et Contemporain. Etudes Linguistiques†
0076-5260 Materiaux pour l'Etude de l'Extreme-Orient Moderne et Contemporain. Textes†
0076-5279 Materiaux pour l'Etude de l'Extreme-Orient Moderne et Contemporain. Travaux†
0076-5287 Materiaux pour l'Histoire du Socialisme International. Serie 2. Essais Bibliographiques†
0076-5295 Materiaux pour l'Histoire du Socialisme International. Serie 1. Textes et Documents†
0076-5333 Mathematical Expositions
0076-5341 University of Notre Dame. Department of Mathematics. Mathematical Lectures†
0076-5376 Mathematical Surveys *changed to* Mathematical Surveys & Monographs
0076-5384 Mathematical Table Series†
0076-5392 Mathematics in Science and Engineering
0076-5406 Mathematiques et Sciences de l'Homme
0076-5414 Mathematische Forschungsberichte†
0076-5430 Mathematische Lehrbuecher und Monographien. Abteilung 2: Mathematische Monographien
0076-5449 Mathematische Schuelerbuecherei
0076-5473 Maurice Falk Center for Economic Research in Israel. Report. *see* 0333-7839
0076-5481 Mauritius. Archives Department. Annual Report
0076-549X Mauritius. Customs and Excise Department. Annual Report
0076-5503 Mauritius. Legislative Assembly. Sessional Paper
0076-5511 Mauritius. Meteorological Services. Report
0076-552X Mauritius. Ministry of Housing, Lands and Town and Country Planning. Annual Reports
0076-5538 Mauritius. Ministry of Social Security. Annual Report *changed to* Mauritius. Ministry of Social Security, National Solidarite and Reform Institutions
0076-5554 Mauritius. Ministry of Works and Internal Communications. Report
0076-5562 Mauritius. Public Accounts Committee. Report
0076-5589 Max C. Fleischmann College of Agriculture. Publications. B (Series)†
0076-5597 Max C. Fleischmann College of Agriculture. Publications. C (Series)†
0076-5600 Max C. Fleischmann College of Agriculture. Publications. R (Series)†
0076-5619 Max C. Fleischmann College of Agriculture. Publications. T (Series)†
0076-5627 Max-Planck-Institut fuer Bildungsforschung, Berlin. Studien und Berichte
0076-5635 Max-Planck-Gesellschaft zur Foerderung der Wissenschaften. Jahrbuch
0076-5643 Max-Planck-Institut fuer Aeronomie. Mitteilungen†
0076-5651 Max-Planck-Institut fuer Auslaendisches Oeffentliches Recht und Voelkerrecht. Fontes *changed to* Max-Planck-Institut fuer Auslaendisches Oeffentliches Recht und Voelkerrecht. Fontes Iuris Gentium
0076-566X Max-Planck-Institut fuer Silikatforschung, Wuerzburg. Veroeffentlichungen†
0076-5678 Mitteilungen aus dem Max-Planck-Institut fuer Stroenmungsforschung und der Aerodynamischen Versuchsansalt *see* 0374-1257
0076-5694 Max-Reger-Institut, Bonn. Mitteilungen†
0076-5716 Meat and Livestock Commission, Bucks., England. Index of Research
0076-5732 Mechanical Engineering Monographs†
0076-5783 Mechanics
0076-5791 Mechanisms of Molecular Migrations†
0076-5805 Politechnika Poznanska. Zeszyty Naukowe. Mechanizacja i Elektryfikacja Rolnictwa *see* 0137-6918
0076-5813 Electro-Radiologiste Qualifie de France. Annuaire *changed to* Medecin Electro-Radiologiste Qualifie de France
0076-5821 Media Scandinavia
0076-583X Medieval Academy of America. Publications *changed to* Medieval Academy Books
0076-5856 Mediaeval Philosophical Texts in Translation
0076-5864 Mediaeval Scandinavia
0076-5872 Mediaeval Studies
0076-5880 Mediaevalia Philosophica Polonorum
0076-5899 Medical Annual
0076-5902 Medical Art *see* 0094-2499
0076-5929 Medical Books in Print *see* 0000-085X
0076-5945 Medical Library Association. Publication†
0076-5953 Medical Physics Series
0076-5961 Medical Protection Society. Annual Report
0076-5988 Medical Research Centre, Nairobi. Annual Report
0076-5996 Medical Research Council (Ireland). Report†
0076-6003 Medical Research Index *changed to* Medical Research Centres
0076-6011 Medical Society of London. Transactions
0076-6038 Medical Ultrasonics†
0076-6046 Medicina
0076-6054 Medicinal Chemistry
0076-6062 Medicinal Research: A Series of Monographs *changed to* Medicinal Research Series
0076-6070 Medicine and Sport *see* 0254-5020
0076-6097 Medieval Archaeology
0076-6100 Medieval Iberian Penninsula
0076-6135 Medium Aevum Monographs†
0076-6143 Medium Industry Bank, Seoul. Report *changed to* Small and Medium Industry Bank, Seoul. Annual Report
0076-6151 Medizinische Laenderkunde. Geomedical Monograph Series
0076-616X Medizinische Praxis†
0076-6178 Medizinische Radiographie und Photographie†
0076-6186 Sozialmedizinische und Paedagogische Jugendkunde
0076-6194 Meet the U. S. A†
0076-6208 Meier-Dudy
0076-6216 Meister des Puppenspiels
0076-6224 Melanderia
0076-6232 Melbourne Historical Journal
0076-6259 Melbourne Monographs in Germanic Studies†
0076-6267 Melbourne Slavonic Studies *changed to* Australian Slavonic and East European Studies
0076-6275 Melbourne Studies in Education
0076-6283 University of Melbourne. Institute of Applied Economic and Social Research. Monographs†
0076-6291 University of Melbourne. Institute of Applied Economic and Social Research. Technical Papers†
0076-6313 Melland Schill Lectures on International Law *changed to* Melland Schill Monographs in International Law
0076-6321 Melsheimer Entomological Series
0076-633X Melville Society Newsletter *see* 0193-8991
0076-6348 Melville Society. Special Publication *see* 0193-8991
0076-6356 Membranes: a Series of Advances†
0076-6364 Memoires de Photo-Interpretation
0076-6372 Memorabilia Zoologica

ISSN INDEX 1389

0076-6380 Junta de Estudios Historicos de Mendoza. Revista
0076-6399 Universidad Nacional de Cuyo. Biblioteca Central. Boletin Bibliografico
0076-6402 Universidad Nacional de Cuyo. Biblioteca Central. Cuadernos de la Biblioteca
0076-6429 Mennonite History Series
0076-6437 Men's Wear Year Book and Diary†
0076-6453 Mental Health Statistics for Illinois
0076-6461 Mental Measurements Yearbook
0076-6518 Merck Index: An Encyclopedia of Chemicals and Drugs
0076-6526 Merck Manual: A Handbook of Diagnosis and Therapy
0076-6542 Merck Veterinary Manual: A Handbook of Diagnosis and Therapy for the Veterinarian
0076-6550 Universidad de los Andes. Facultad de Derecho. Anuario
0076-6569 Universidad de Los Andes. Instituto de Geografia y Conservacion de Recursos Naturales. Cuadernos Geograficos
0076-6577 Merite du Defricheur. Rapport de l'Ordre du Merite du Defricheur *changed to* Merite du Defricheur. Rapport de l'Ordre du Merite Agricole
0076-6607 Mesoamerican Studies†
0076-6615 Mesopotamia
0076-6658 Metal Statistics
0076-6690 Metallurgical Reviews *see* 0950-6608
0076-6704 Metallurgical Works in Canada, Nonferrous and Precious Metals†
0076-6712 Metallurgical Works in Canada, Primary Iron and Steel†
0076-6720 Metaphysische Rundschau
0076-6739 Meteorological Yearbook of Finland. Part 1B: Climatological Data from Jokioinen and Sodankyla Observatories†
0076-6747 Meteorological Yearbook of Finland. Part 1: Climatological Data
0076-6755 Meteorological Yearbook of Finland. Part 2: Precipitation and Snow Cover Data
0076-6763 Meteorological Yearbook of Finland. Part 4: Measurements of Radiation and Bright Sunshine
0076-6771 Methodensammlung der Elektronenmikroskopie
0076-678X Methodes de la Sociologie†
0076-681X Methods and Achievements in Experimental Pathology
0076-6828 Methods and Models in the Social Sciences
0076-6836 Methods and Techniques in Geophysics†
0076-6860 Methods in Computational Physics: Advances in Research and Applications†
0076-6879 Methods in Enzymology
0076-6887 Methods in Free-Radical Chemistry†
0076-6895 Methods in Geochemistry and Geophysics
0076-6909 Methods in Hydroscience *see* 0065-2768
0076-6925 Methods in Neurochemistry†
0076-6933 Methods in Virology
0076-6941 Methods of Biochemical Analysis
0076-695X Methods of Experimental Physics
0076-6984 Metodicke Prirucky Experimentalni Botaniky
0076-700X Metro Building Industry Directory†
0076-7018 METRO; New York Metropolitan Reference and Research Library Agency. METRO Miscellaneous Publications Series
0076-7050 Metropolitan Library Service Agency. Annual Report†
0076-7069 Metropolitan Milwaukee Association of Commerce. Trends in Selected Economic Indicators *changed to* Milwaukee Commerce Hot-line
0076-7077 Metropolitan Milwaukee Association of Commerce. Economic Studies *changed to* Metropolitan Milwaukee Economic Fact Book
0076-7085 Metropolitan Politics†
0076-7093 Metropolitan Toronto
0076-7107 Metropolitan Washington Council of Governments. Annual Report†
0076-7115 Metropolitan Washington Council of Governments. Regional Directory
0076-7131 Instituto Nacional de Cancerologia de Mexico. Revista
0076-7158 Museu Nacional de Antropologia. Cuadernos
0076-7166 Universidad Nacional Autonoma de Mexico. Centro de Estudios Mayas. Cuadernos
0076-7174 Universidad Nacional Autonoma de Mexico. Instituto de Biologia. Anales *see* 0368-8720
0076-7174 Universidad Nacional Autonoma de Mexico. Instituto de Biologia. Anales *changed to* Universidad Nacional Autonoma de Mexico. Instituto de Biologia. Anales: Serie Botanica
0076-7182 Universidad Nacional Autonoma de Mexico. Instituto de Geofisica. Anales†
0076-7204 Universidad Nacional Autonoma de Mexico. Instituto de Geofisica. Monografias
0076-7212 Universidad Nacional Autonoma de Mexico. Instituto de Investigaciones Historicas. Serie de Cultura Nahuatl. Fuentes
0076-7239 Universidad Nacional Autonoma de Mexico. Instituto de Investigaciones Esteticas. Anales
0076-7247 Universidad Nacional Autonoma de Mexico. Instituto de Investigaciones Esteticas. Anales. Suplemento†
0076-7255 Universidad Nacional Autonoma de Mexico. Instituto de Investigaciones Esteticas. Publicaciones Especiales†
0076-7263 Universidad Nacional Autonoma de Mexico. Instituto de Investigaciones Antropologicas. Cuadernos Serie Antropologica *see* 0076-7298
0076-7271 Universidad Nacional Autonoma de Mexico. Instituto de Investigaciones Historicas. Cuadernos Serie Documental
0076-7298 Universidad Nacional Autonoma de Mexico. Instituto de Investigaciones Antropoligicas. Serie Antropologica
0076-7301 Universidad Nacional Autonoma de Mexico. Instituto de Investigaciones Historicas. Serie Bibliografica
0076-731X Universidad Nacional Autonoma de Mexico. Instituto de Investigaciones Historicas. Serie Documental
0076-7328 Universidad Nacional Autonoma de Mexico. Instituto de Investigaciones Historicas. Serie de Culturas Mesoamericanas
0076-7344 Universidad Nacional Autonoma de Mexico. Instituto de Investigaciones Historicas. Serie de Cultura Nahuatl. Monografias
0076-7352 Universidad Nacional Autonoma de Mexico. Instituto de Investigaciones Historicas. Serie de Historia General
0076-7379 Universidad Nacional Autonoma de Mexico. Instituto de Investigaciones Historicas. Serie de Historia Novohispana *see* 0185-2523
0076-7387 Universidad Nacional Autonoma de Mexico. Instituto de Investigaciones Historicas. Serie de Historiadores y Cronistas
0076-7441 Universidad Nacional Autonoma de Mexico. Instituto de Matematicas. Anales
0076-7468 Universidad Nacional Autonoma de Mexico. Seminario de Investigaciones Bibliotecologica. Publicaciones. Serie B. Bibliografia
0076-7476 Instituto Nacional de Energia Nuclear. Publication†
0076-7492 Mexico. Secretaria de Programacion y Presupuesto
0076-7506 Instituto Nacional de Antropologia e Historia. Departamento de Monumentos Coloniales. (Publicaciones)†
0076-7514 Instituto Nacional de Antropologia e Historia. Departamento de Monumentos Prehispanicos. (Publicaciones)†
0076-7557 Instituto Nacional de Antropologia e Historia. Anales†
0076-7565 Instituto Nacional de Antropologia e Historia. Coleccion Breve†
0076-7573 Instituto Nacional de Antropologia e Historia. Investigaciones†
0076-759X Instituto Nacional de Antropologia e Historia. Memorias†
0076-7611 Instituto Nacional de Antropologia e Historia. Coleccion Cientifica
0076-762X Instituto Nacional de Antropologia e Historia. Serie Culturas del Mundo†
0076-7670 Meyers Grosses Jahreslexikon†
0076-7689 Meyniana
0076-7697 Miami Linguistic Series†
0076-7719 University of Miami Hispanic-American Studies†
0076-7727 Michel-Briefmarken-Kataloge
0076-7735 Camping, Caravaning in France
0076-7743 Michelin Red Guide Series: Benelux
0076-7751 Michelin Red Guide Series: Germany
0076-776X Michelin Red Guide Series: Spain & Portugal
0076-7778 Michelin Red Guide Series: France
0076-7786 Michelin Red Guide Series: Italy
0076-7794 Michelin Red Guide Series: Paris
0076-7808 Michigan Abstracts of Chinese and Japanese Works on Chinese History *changed to* Michigan Monographs in Chinese Studies
0076-7824 Michigan Beef Cattle Day Report
0076-7832 Michigan Business Cases†
0076-7840 Michigan Business Papers
0076-7859 Michigan Business Reports
0076-7867 Michigan Business Studies
0076-7875 Michigan. Civil Rights Commission. Report *changed to* Michigan. Civil Rights Commission. Annual Report
0076-7905 Michigan. Department of Natural Resources. Institute for Fisheries Research. Miscellaneous Publication
0076-7913 Michigan. Division of Vocational Education. Report†
0076-7948 Michigan Geographical Publications†
0076-7956 Michigan Governmental Studies
0076-7964 Michigan. Department of Natural Resources. Institute for Fisheries Research. Lake Inventory Summary†
0076-7972 Michigan International Business Studies
0076-7999 Michigan International Labor Studies†
0076-8014 Michigan Municipal League. Municipal Legal Briefs
0076-8057 Michigan Natural Resources Council. Scientific Advisory Committee. Annual Report†
0076-8065 Michigan Papers in Chinese Studies *changed to* Michigan Monographs in Chinese Studies
0076-8073 Michigan. Plant Industry Division. Plant Pest Control Programs†
0076-8081 Michigan Library Directory and Statistics *changed to* Michigan Library Directory
0076-809X Michigan Science in Action *changed to* Futures
0076-8103 Michigan Slavic Contributions
0076-8111 Michigan State Plan for Construction of Community Mental Health Facilities†
0076-812X Michigan State University. Asian Studies Center. Occasional Papers: East Asia Series
0076-8138 Michigan State University. Asian Studies Center. Occasional Papers: South Asia Series
0076-8146 Michigan State University. Department of Physics. Cyclotron Project (Publication) *changed to* Michigan State University. National Superconducting Cyclotron Laboratory (Publication)
0076-8189 Michigan State University. Latin American Studies Center. Monograph Series
0076-8197 Michigan State University.Latin American Studies Center. Occasional Papers†
0076-8200 Michigan State University. Latin American Studies Center. Research Reports
0076-8227 Michigan State University. Museum Publications. Biological Series
0076-8235 Michigan State University. Museum Publications. Cultural Series
0076-8243 Michigan State University. Public Administration Program. Research Report†
0076-8251 Michigan State University. Rural Manpower Center. R M C Mimeograph *changed to* Michigan State University. Center for Rural Manpower & Public Affairs. Mimeograph
0076-826X Michigan State University. Rural Manpower Center. R M C Report *changed to* Michigan State University. Center for Rural Manpower & Public Affairs. Report
0076-8278 Michigan State University. Rural Manpower Center. R M C Special Paper *changed to* Michigan State University. Center for Rural Manpower & Public Affairs. Special Paper
0076-8308 Michigan Statistical Abstract
0076-8332 University of Michigan. Graduate School of Business Administration. Leadership Award Lecture†
0076-8340 University of Michigan. Center for Japanese Studies. Bibliographical Series†
0076-8359 University of Michigan. Center for Japanese Studies. Occasional Papers†
0076-8367 University of Michigan. Museum of Anthropology. Anthropological Papers.
0076-8375 University of Michigan. Museum of Anthropology. Memoirs
0076-8391 University of Michigan. Museum of Art. Bulletin *see* 0270-1642
0076-8405 University of Michigan. Museum of Zoology. Miscellaneous Publications
0076-8413 University of Michigan. Museum of Zoology. Occasional Papers
0076-8421 University of Michigan Observatories. Publications†
0076-843X University of Michigan. School of Dentistry. Alumni Bulletin
0076-8480 Microfiche Foundation. Newsletter
0076-8502 Middle East and North Africa
0076-8510 Middle East Economic Papers†
0076-8529 Middle East Record
0076-8537 Middle Eastern Monographs†
0076-8561 Middle States Association of Colleges and Secondary Schools. Proceedings *changed to* Middle States Association of Colleges and Schools. Proceedings of the Annual Convention
0076-857X University of Chicago. Midwest Administration Center. Monograph Series
0076-8588 Midwest Electrical Buyers' Guide†
0076-8596 Midwest Monographs. Series 1 (Drama) †
0076-860X Midwest Monographs. Series 2 (Poetry)†
0076-8618 Midwest Monographs. Series 3 (Graphic Works)†
0076-8626 Midwest Monographs. Series 4 (Translation)†
0076-8634 Midwest Monographs. Series 5 (Culture and Criticism)†
0076-8642 Mikrochimica Acta. Supplement

0076-8650 Istituto di Ricerche Agrarie, Milan. Contributi†
0076-8669 Universita Cattolica del Sacro Cuore, Milan. Contributi. Serie Terza. Scienze Storiche†
0076-8677 Universita Cattolica del Sacro Cuore, Milan. Contributi. Serie Terza. Scienze Filosofiche†
0076-8685 Universita Cattolica del Sacro Cuore, Milan. Contributi. Serie Terza. Scienze Filologiche e Letteratura†
0076-8693 Universita Cattolica del Sacro Cuore, Milan. Contributi. Serie Terza. Scienze Psicologiche†
0076-8707 Universita Cattolica del Sacro Cuore, Milan. Istituto di Archeologia. Contributi†
0076-8715 Universita Cattolica del Sacro Cuore, Milan. Saggi e Ricerche. Serie Terza. Scienze Filologiche e Letteratura†
0076-8723 Universita Cattolica del Sacro Cuore, Milan. Saggi e Ricerche. Serie Terza. Scienze Filosofiche†
0076-8731 Universita Cattolica del Sacro Cuore, Milan. Saggi e Ricerche. Serie Terza. Scienze Geografiche†
0076-874X Universita Cattolica del Sacro Cuore, Milan. Saggi Ericerche. Serie Terza. Scienze Psicologiche†
0076-8758 Universita Cattolica del Sacro Cuore, Milan. Saggi e Ricerche. Serie Terza. Scienze Storiche†
0076-8766 Mildex Motor Book†
0076-8774 Military Research Series†
0076-8782 Military Year Book
0076-8790 Milla Wa-Milla†
0076-8812 Millesime
0076-8820 Milton Studies
0076-8839 Milu: Wissenschaftliche und Kulturelle Mitteilungen aus dem Tierpark Berlin
0076-8847 M I M S Desk Reference
0076-8855 Brazil. Tribunal Regional do Trabalho. Tercera Regiao. Revista
0076-8863 Universidade Federal de Minas Gerais. Escola de Veterinaria. Arquivos *see* 0102-0935
0076-8871 Universidade Federal de Minas Gerais. Revista†
0076-8901 Mindolo News Letter
0076-891X M W V Jahresbericht
0076-8944 Minerals, Rocks and Inorganic Materials *see* 0343-2181
0076-8952 U.S. Bureau of Mines. Minerals Yearbook
0076-8960 Minerva; Jahrbuch der Gelehrten Welt *changed to* Minerva; Internationales Verzeichnis Wissenschaftlicher Institutionen
0076-8987 Mining in Rhodesia *changed to* Mining in Zimbabwe
0076-8995 Mining Annual Review
0076-9010 Zambia Mining Yearbook
0076-9029 Minkus Austria, Switzerland, Lichtenstein Stamp Catalog
0076-9037 Minkus British Commonwealth Stamp Catalog†
0076-9045 Minkus Germany and Colonies Stamp Catalog†
0076-9053 Minkus Italy, San Marino and Vatican Stamp Catalog
0076-9061 Minkus New American Stamp Catalog
0076-907X Minkus New World Wide Stamp Catalog
0076-9088 Minkus Russia, Poland, Hungary, Romania, Czechoslovakia Stamp Catalog†
0076-9096 Minneapolis Institute of Arts. Annual Report
0076-910X Minneapolis Institute of Arts. Bulletin
0076-9118 Minnesota. Department of Human Rights. Biennial Report
0076-9126 Minnesota. Department of Manpower Services. Annual Report *changed to* Minnesota. Department of Economic Security. Annual Report
0076-9134 Minnesota. Division of Game and Fish. Technical Bulletin *changed to* Minnesota. Division of Fish & Wildlife. Technical Bulletin
0076-9142 Minnesota Drama Editions†
0076-9150 Minnesota Fisheries Investigations
0076-9169 Minnesota. Geological Survey. Bulletin†
0076-9177 Minnesota. Geological Survey. Report of Investigations
0076-9185 Minnesota. Geological Survey. Special Publication Series†
0076-9215 Minnesota Monographs in the Humanities†
0076-9258 Minnesota Studies in the Philosophy of Science
0076-9266 Minnesota Symposia on Child Psychology
0076-9274 University of Minnesota. Audio-Visual Library Service. Educational Resources Bulletin
0076-9282 University of Minnesota. Center for Research in Human Learning. Report *changed to* University of Minnesota. Center for Research in Human Learning. Report and Fellowship Offerings
0076-9290 University of Minnesota. Graduate School Research Center. Inventory of Faculty Research†
0076-9312 University of Minnesota Studies in Economics and Business.†
0076-9347 Miscellanea Byzantina Monacensia
0076-9355 Miscellanea Musicologica†
0076-9371 Mision Arqueologica Espanola en Nubia. Memorias†
0076-9401 Missions to Seamen Handbook *changed to* Missions to Seamen Annual Report
0076-941X Missionswissenschaftliche Abhandlungen und Texte
0076-9428 Missionswissenschaftliche Forschungen
0076-9436 Mississippi Academy of Science. Journal
0076-9460 Mississippi Congress of Parents and Teachers. Proceedings
0076-9479 Mississippi Congress of Parents and Teachers. Yearbook
0076-9509 Mississippi State University. Forest Products Utilization Laboratory. Information Series
0076-9517 Mississippi State University. Christian Student Center. Annual Lectureship
0076-9525 M V C Bulletin†
0076-9533 Mississippi Water Resources Conference. Proceedings†
0076-9541 Missouri Archaeological Society. Memoir Series†
0076-955X Missouri Archaeological Society. Newsletter *see* 0743-7641
0076-9568 Missouri Archaeological Society. Research Series†
0076-9576 Missouri Archaeologist
0076-9584 Missouri Directory of Manufacturing and Mining
0076-9606 Missouri. Division of Geological Survey and Water Resources. Engineering Geology Series
0076-9614 Missouri. Division of Geological Survey and Water Resources. Water Resources Report
0076-9630 Missouri Handbook Series
0076-9649 Missouri Literary Frontiers Series
0076-9657 University of Missouri, St. Louis. Center for International Studies. Monograph†
0076-969X University of Missouri. College of Business and Public Administration. Office of Research, Annual Report†
0076-9703 University of Missouri Studies
0076-9711 University of Missouri, Columbia. Veterinary Medical Diagnostic Laboratory. Annual Report
0076-9754 Mittellateinische Studien und Texte
0076-9762 Mittellateinisches Jahrbuch
0076-9770 Moana; Estudios de Antropologia Oceanica
0076-986X Current Population Reports: Population Characteristics. Mobility of the Population of the United States *changed to* Current Population Reports: Population Characteristics. Geographic Mobility
0076-9878 Moccasin Telegraph *see* 0227-3780
0076-9894 Modern America†
0076-9908 Modern Analytic and Computational Methods in Science and Mathematics†
0076-9916 Modern Approaches to the Diagnosis and Instruction of Multi-Handicapped Children
0076-9924 Modern Aspects of Electrochemistry
0076-9932 Modern Brewery Age Blue Book
0076-9959 Modern Drug Encyclopedia and Therapeutic Index†
0076-9967 Modern Filologiai Fuzetek
0076-9983 Modern Humanities Research Association. Monograph *changed to* Modern Humanities Research Association. Publications
0076-9991 Modern Machine Shop N C Guidebook and Directory *changed to* Modern Machine Shop N C/C I M Guidebook
0077-0000 Modern Materials. Advances in Development and Applications
0077-0027 Modern Middle East Series
0077-0035 Modern Packaging Encyclopedia *changed to* Packaging Encyclopedia
0077-0043 Modern Perspectives in Psychiatry†
0077-0078 Modern Problems in Ophthalmology *see* 0250-3751
0077-0086 Modern Problems in Paediatrics
0077-0094 Modern Problems of Pharmacopsychiatry
0077-0108 Modern Publicity *changed to* World Advertising Review
0077-0167 Modern Vocational Trends Reference Handbook†
0077-0205 Moebel-Industrie und Ihre Helfer
0077-0221 Molecular Biology, Biochemistry and Biophysics
0077-023X Molecular Biology; Proceedings of the International Conference†
0077-0264 University of the West Indies, Jamaica. Department of Geography. Occasional Publications Series†
0077-0272 University of the West Indies, Jamaica. Department of Geography. Research Notes Series†
0077-0280 Monarchist Book Review
0077-0299 Monarchist Press Association. Historical Series
0077-0310 Monde d'Outre-Mer, Passe et Present. 1 Serie: Etudes†
0077-0329 Monde d'Outre-Mer, Passe et Present. 2 Serie: Documents†
0077-0337 Monde d'Outre-Mer, Passe et Present. 3 Serie: Essais†
0077-0345 Monde d'Outre-Mer, Passe et Present. 4 Serie: Bibliographies et Instruments de Travail†
0077-0353 Centre pour l'Etude des Problemes de Monde Musulman Contemporain. Initiations†
0077-0361 Mondo†
0077-0388 Money Market Directory *changed to* Money Market Directory of Pension Funds and Their Investment Advisors
0077-0396 Mongolia Society. Occasional Papers
0077-040X Monitor
0077-0418 Monks Wood Experimental Station. Report *see* 0308-1125
0077-0426 Great Britain. Monks Wood Experimental Station. Symposia *see* 0263-8614
0077-0434 Monnaies, Prix, Conjoncture
0077-0442 Monografias de Filosofia Juridica y Social
0077-0469 Monografias de Psicologia, Normal y Patologica
0077-0485 Monografie Biochemiczne
0077-0493 Monografie di Archeologia Libica
0077-0507 Monografie Matematyczne
0077-0515 Monografie Psychologiczne
0077-0523 Monografie Slaskie Ossolineum
0077-0531 Monografie Slawistyczne
0077-054X Monografie z Dziejow Nauki i Techniki
0077-0558 Monografie z Dziejow Oswiaty
0077-0574 Monograph Series in Probability and Statistics†
0077-0582 Monograph Series in World Affairs
0077-0612 Monograph Series on Languages and Linguistics *see* 0196-7207
0077-0620 Monograph Series on Schizophrenia
0077-0639 Monographiae Biologicae
0077-0647 Monographiae Biologicae Canarienses†
0077-0655 Monographiae Botanicae
0077-0671 Monographien aus dem Gesamtgebiete der Psychiatrie - Psychiatry Series
0077-0698 Monographien zur Angewandten Entomologie
0077-0701 Monographies de l'Industrie et du Commerce en France
0077-071X Monographies Francaises de Psychologie
0077-0728 Monographies Juridiques†
0077-0744 Monographs and Textbooks in Material Science†
0077-0752 Monographs and Texts in the Behavioral Sciences†
0077-0760 Monographs in Allergy
0077-0809 Monographs in Clinical Cytology
0077-0825 Monographs in Developmental Biology
0077-0833 Monographs in Electroanalytical Chemistry and Electrochemistry Series
0077-085X Monographs in Geology and Paleontology
0077-0868 Monographs in Hormone Research *see* 0301-3073
0077-0876 Monographs in Human Genetics
0077-0884 Monographs in Macromolecular Chemistry†
0077-0892 Monographs in Oral Science
0077-0906 Monographs in Organic Functional Group Analysis *changed to* Analysis of Organic Materials: an International Series of Monographs
0077-0914 Monographs in Paediatrics
0077-0930 Monographs in Population Biology
0077-0949 Monographs in Statistical Physics and Thermodynamics†
0077-0965 Monographs in Virology
0077-099X Monographs on Atherosclerosis
0077-1007 Monographs on Education
0077-1015 Monographs on Endocrinology
0077-1023 Monographs on Immunology *see* 0092-6019
0077-1031 Monographs on Linguistic Analysis†
0077-104X Monographs on Oceanographic Methodology
0077-1074 London School of Economics Monographs on Social Anthropology
0077-1090 Montana. Bureau of Mines and Geology. Bulletin
0077-1104 Montana. Bureau of Mines and Geology. Directory of Mining Enterprises
0077-1112 Montana. Bureau of Mines and Geology. Ground Water Reports *see* 0077-1090
0077-1120 Montana. Bureau of Mines and Geology. Memoir
0077-1139 Montana. Bureau of Mines and Geology. Special Publications
0077-1147 Montana Journalism Review†
0077-1155 University of Montana. Forest and Conservation Experiment Station, Missoula. Bulletin.
0077-1163 University of Montana. Forest and Conservation Experiment Station, Missoula. Research Notes.
0077-1198 Montana Vital Statistics
0077-1201 Montana. Water Resources Board. Inventory Series†
0077-1228 Instituto Tecnologico y de Estudios Superiores. Publicaciones. Serie Historia†
0077-1236 Instituto Tecnologico y de Estudios Superiores. Publicaciones. Serie Letras†
0077-1244 Museo Nacional de Historia Natural. Communicaciones Antropologicas
0077-1252 Universidad de Uruguay. Departamento de Literatura Iberoamericana Publicaciones

0077-1260 Universidad de Uruguay. Facultad de Agronomia. Boletin
0077-1279 Universidad de la Republica. Facultad de Agronomia. Publicacion Miscelanea†
0077-1287 Universidad de la Republica. Instituto de Administracion. Cuaderno
0077-1295 Universidad de Uruguay. Instituto de Mathematica y Estadistica. Publicaciones Didacticas†
0077-1309 Montre Suisse. Annuaire
0077-1317 Jardin Botanique de Montreal. Annuelles et Legumes†
0077-1325 Jardin Botanique de Montreal. Memoire†
0077-1341 Universite de Montreal. Ecole de Bibliotheconomie. Publications†
0077-1368 Montreal Women's Liberation Newsletter
0077-1376 Monumenta Aegyptiaca
0077-1384 Monumenta Americana
0077-1392 Monumenta Antiquitatis Extra Fines Hungariae Reperta Quae in Museo Artium Hungarico Aliisque Museis et Collectionibus Hungaricis Conservantur†
0077-1406 Monumenta Artis Romanae
0077-1414 Monumenta Chartae Papyraceae Historiam Illustrantia
0077-1430 Monumenta Historica Budapestinensia
0077-1449 Monumenta Historica Ordinis Minorum Capuccinorum
0077-1457 Monumenta Iuris Canonici
0077-1465 Monumenta Musicae in Polonia *changed to* Polska Akademia Nauk. Instytut Sztuki. Series A: Works by Polish Composers
0077-1465 Monumenta Musicae in Polonia *changed to* Polska Akademia Nauk. Instytut Sztuki. Series B: Fontes Artis Musicae
0077-1465 Monumenta Musicae in Polonia *changed to* Polska Akademia Nauk. Instytut Sztuki. Series C: Tractatus de Musica
0077-1465 Monumenta Musicae in Polonia *changed to* Polska Akademia Nauk. Instytut Sztuki. Series D: Bibliotheca Antiqua
0077-1473 Monumenta Musicae Suecicae
0077-1481 Monumenta Paedagogica
0077-149X Monumenta Serica
0077-1503 Monuments of Renaissance Music
0077-152X Moravske Numismaticke Zpravy
0077-1546 Trends, Financial Statements and Operating Ratios *see* 0278-6567
0077-1554 Moscow Mathematical Society. Transactions
0077-1562 Gosudarstvennyi Muzei Izobrazitel'nykh Iskusstv im. Pushkina. Soobshcheniya
0077-1570 Motocyclo Catalogue
0077-1589 Motor Cycle Diary†
0077-1597 Motor Industry of Great Britain *changed to* Motor Industry of Great Britain (Year) World Automotive Statistics
0077-1600 Motor Manual
0077-1619 Motor Traffic in Sweden
0077-1643 Motor Truck Facts *see* 0146-9932
0077-1678 Motorcycle Buyer's Guide
0077-1694 Motoring in Malaya
0077-1716 Motor Parts & Time Guide
0077-1724 Motor Truck and Diesel Repair Manual *changed to* Motor Light Truck Tuneup & Van Repair Manual
0077-1732 Motorsporten i Tekst og Billeder *changed to* Motorsporten
0077-1740 Mount Zion Hospital and Medical Center, San Francisco. Bulletin
0077-1759 Mountain World†
0077-1767 Movimiento Natural de la Poblacion de Espana
0077-1775 Moyens de la Recherche Scientifique et Technique en Haute-Normandie.†
0077-1791 Instituto de Investigacao Agronomica de Mocambique. Centro de Documentacas Agraria. Memorias
0077-1805 Mozart - Jahrbuch
0077-1813 Muelleria
0077-1864 Muenchner Entomologische Gesellschaft. Mitteilungen
0077-1872 Muenchner Germanistische Beitraege
0077-1880 Muenchener Indologische Studien
0077-1899 Muenchener Jahrbuch der Bildenden Kunst
0077-1902 Muenchener Studien zur Sozial- und Wirtschaftsgeographie
0077-1910 Muenchener Studien zur Sprachwissenschaft
0077-1929 Universitaet Muenster. Astronomisches Institut. Mitteilungen†
0077-1937 Universitaet Muenster. Astronomisches Institut. Sonderdrucke†
0077-1945 Universitaet Muenster. Institut fuer Christliche Sozialwissenschaften. Schriften†
0077-1953 Fontes et Commentationes†
0077-197X Universitaet Muenster. Institut fuer Missionswissenschaft. Veroeffentlichungen
0077-1996 Muenstersche Beitraege zur Deutschen Literaturwissenschaft
0077-2003 Muenstersche Beitraege zur Vor- und Fruehgeschichte
0077-2011 Muensterschwarzacher Studien
0077-202X Multihull International Catalogue Annual†
0077-2046 Multilingual Forestry Terminology Series
0077-2054 Coleccion Mundo Antiguo
0077-2062 Statistisches Jahrbuch Muenchen
0077-2070 Bayerische Staatssammlung fuer Palaeontologie und Historische Geologie. Mitteilungen
0077-2089 Technische Universitaet Muenchen. Jahrbuch†
0077-2100 Universitaet Muenchen. Geophysikalisches Observatorium, Fuerstenfeldbruck. Veroeffentlichungen. Serie B
0077-2119 Westfaelische Wilhelms-Universitaet Muenster. Institut fuer Kreditwesen. Schriftenreihe†
0077-2127 Universitaet Muenchen. Wirtschaftsgeographisches Institut. "W G I"-Berichte zur Regionalforschung
0077-2135 Zoologische Staatssammlung, Muenchen. Veroeffentlichungen *see* 0341-8391
0077-2143 Municipal Association of Victoria. Minutes of Proceedings of Annual Session
0077-2151 Municipal Index
0077-2186 Municipal Year Book
0077-2194 Muse
0077-2208 Museion
0077-2216 Museu Paraense Emilio Goeldi. Boletim. Nova Serie: Botanica *changed to* Museu Paraense Emilio Goeldi. Boletim. Serie Botanica
0077-2224 Museu Paraense Emilio Goeldi. Boletim. Nova Serie: Geologia
0077-2232 Museu Paraense Emilio Goeldi. Boletim. Nova Serie: Zoologia *changed to* Museu Paraense Emilio Goeldi. Boletim. Serie Zoologia
0077-2240 Museu Paraense Emilio Goeldi. Publicacoes Avulsas
0077-2267 Museums and Galleries *see* 0141-6723
0077-2275 Museum Boymans-van Beuningen. Agenda - Diary
0077-2313 Museum Publications†
0077-233X Museums and Monuments Series
0077-2348 Museums Journal of Pakistan
0077-2356 Insects†
0077-2364 Mushroom Science
0077-2372 Music Handbook†
0077-2402 Music Educators National Conference. Selective Music Lists: Vocal Solos and Ensembles
0077-2410 Music in Higher Education†
0077-2429 Music Indexes and Bibliographies†
0077-2445 Music Library Association. Index Series *see* 0094-6478
0077-2453 Music World Year Book
0077-2461 Musica Disciplina
0077-247X Musica Medii Aevi
0077-2488 Musicologica Hungarica
0077-2496 Musicological Studies and Documents
0077-250X Musicology Australia
0077-2518 Musik i Sverige
0077-2526 Musikalische Denkmaeler
0077-2542 Musk-Ox
0077-2577 Muzea Walki
0077-2615 Mystic Seaport Manuscripts Inventory†
0077-2623 N A S A - University Conference on Manual Control (Papers)
0077-2631 N H K Technical Monograph
0077-264X Nagoya University. Research Institute of Atmospherics. Proceedings
0077-2658 Nagyuzemi Gazdalkodas Kerdesei
0077-2666 Nairobi Airport. Annual Report
0077-2690 Names in South Carolina†
0077-2704 Namn och Bygd
0077-2712 Universite de Nancy II. Centre de Recherches et d'Applications Pedagogiques en Langues. Melanges
0077-2720 Universite de Nancy II. Centre Europeen Universitaire. Memoires†
0077-2739 Nanta Mathematica†
0077-2747 Nanyang University Journal†
0077-2755 Napao: A Saskatchewan Anthropology Journal *see* 0829-0547
0077-2763 Istituto Universitario Orientale di Napoli. Annali. Sezione Germanica
0077-2771 Istituto Universitario Orientale di Napoli. Annali. Sezione Slava†
0077-2798 National Bank of Yugoslavia. Annual Report
0077-2801 Narradores de Arca
0077-281X University of Rhode Island. Narragansett Marine Laboratory. Collected Reprints *changed to* University of Rhode Island. Graduate School of Oceanography. Collected Reprints
0077-2828 University of Rhode Island. Narragansett Marine Laboratory. Occasional Publication†
0077-2836 Narragansett Marine Laboratory. Technical Reports *changed to* University of Rhode Island. Graduate School of Oceanography. Marine Technical Reports
0077-2844 Narrativa Latinoamericana
0077-2879 Nassau Review
0077-2887 Nassauische Annalen
0077-2895 Natal Regional Survey. Additional Report†
0077-2925 National Academy of Sciences. Annual Report†
0077-2933 National Academy of Sciences. Biographical Memoirs
0077-2941 National Accounts and Balance of Payments of Rhodesia *changed to* National Accounts of Rhodesia
0077-295X National Accounts of the Maltese Islands
0077-2968 Catalogue of N A L Technical Translations
0077-2976 National Aeronautical Laboratory. Annual Report
0077-300X National Aeronautical Laboratory. Technical Note
0077-3085 National Aeronautics and Space Administration. N A S A Factbook†
0077-3093 N A S A Facts
0077-3115 U.S. National Aeronautics and Space Administration. Research and Technology Program Digest. Flash Index *changed to* U.S. National Aeronautics and Space Administration. Research and Technology Operating Plan (RTOP) Summary
0077-3131 National Aeronautics and Space Administration. Technical Notes
0077-314X National Aeronautics and Space Administration. Technical Reports
0077-3158 National Aeronautics and Space Administration. Technical Translations
0077-3166 List of Accredited Schools of Architecture *changed to* Accredited Programs in Architecture
0077-3174 National Art Education Association. Research Monograph
0077-3204 National Association for Physical Education of College Women. Biennial Record†
0077-3212 N A A C P Annual Report
0077-3220 National Association for the Care and Resettlement of Offenders. Papers and Reprints†
0077-3255 National Association of Animal Breeders. Annual Proceedings
0077-3263 National Association of Boards of Pharmacy. Proceedings
0077-3298 N A E S P Convention Reporter†
0077-3336 N A I A Handbook
0077-3344 N A I A Official Records Book
0077-3352 National Association of Jewish Center Workers. Conference Papers†
0077-3360 N A M F Accounting Manual
0077-3379 N A M F Management Manual
0077-3387 National Association of Regulatory Utility Commissioners. Proceedings
0077-3409 National Association of Schools of Music. Proceedings of the Annual Meeting
0077-3417 N A S S P Convention Reporter†
0077-3425 National Association of State Universities and Land-Grant Colleges. Appropriations of State Tax Funds for Higher Education
0077-3433 National Association of State Universities and Land-Grant Colleges. Proceedings
0077-3441 National Association of Suggestion Systems. Statistical Report
0077-345X National Association of Teachers' Agencies. List of the Accredited Members
0077-3468 Coordinator (New York)†
0077-3476 National Association of Training Schools and Juvenile Agencies. Proceedings
0077-3506 National Bank of Ethiopia. Local Prices†
0077-3514 National Bank of Greece. Annual Report
0077-3522 National Bank of Pakistan. Report and Statement of Accounts
0077-3557 National Bible Society of Scotland. Annual Report
0077-3573 National Budget of Norway
0077-3581 National Building Research Institute. Complete List of N B R I Publications
0077-359X National Building Studies (Great Britain) Research Papers†
0077-3603 National Building Studies (Great Britain) Special Reports†
0077-3611 National Bureau of Economic Research. Annual Report†
0077-3638 National Bureau of Economic Research. General Series†
0077-3654 National Bureau of Economic Research. Technical Papers†
0077-3662 National Cancer Center. Collected Papers
0077-3670 National Cancer Conference. Proceedings
0077-3689 National Cancer Institute of Canada. Annual Report
0077-3719 National Center for Audio Tapes. Catalog *changed to* National Center for Audio Tapes Archive. Catalog
0077-3735 National Civil Service League. Annual Report
0077-376X National Coal Board (Great Britain). Annual Report and Accounts. Vol. 2, Accounts and Statistical Tables *see* 0307-7691
0077-3786 National Coal Board. Report and Accounts
0077-3794 National Collegiate Athletic Association. Annual Reports.
0077-3808 National Collegiate Athletic Association. Convention Proceedings

1392 ISSN INDEX

0077-3816 National Collegiate Athletic Association. Manual
0077-3832 National Colloquium on Oral History. Proceedings *see* 0094-0798
0077-3840 National Committee for Audio-Visual Aids in Education. Experimental Development Unit. Report†
0077-3859 National Committee for Audio-Visual Aids in Education. Occasional Paper†
0077-3913 National Conference on Aerospace Meteorology. Proceedings *changed to* Conference on Atmospheric Environment of Aerospace Systems and Applied Meteorology. Preprints
0077-3956 National Conference on Weather Modification. Preprints *changed to* Conference on Planned and Inadvertent Weather Modification. Preprints
0077-3964 National Conference on Weights and Measures. Report
0077-3980 National Congress of Parents and Teachers. Proceedings of Annual Convention *changed to* National Congress of Parents and Teachers. Convention Digest
0077-4006 National Consumer Credit Counseling Service. Proceedings†
0077-4014 Selected and Annotated Bibliography of Reference Materials in Consumer Credit†
0077-4022 National Cottonseed Products Association. Trading Rules
0077-4030 National Council for Geographic Education. Yearbook *changed to* National Council for Geographic Education. Pacesetter Series
0077-4049 National Council for the Social Studies. Bulletins
0077-4057 National Council for the Social Studies. Social Studies Readings†
0077-4065 N C A E R Occasional Papers†
0077-4073 National Council of Churches. Division of Education and Ministry. Audio-Visual Resource Guide†
0077-4081 National Council of Engineering Examiners. Proceedings
0077-409X National Council of Social Service. Annual Report *changed to* National Council for Voluntary Organizations. Annual Report
0077-4103 National Council of Teachers of Mathematics. Yearbook
0077-4162 National Council on Family Relations. Annual Meeting Proceedings†
0077-4189 National Dahlia Society Annual
0077-4219 National Distribution Directory *changed to* Warehousing/Distribution Directory
0077-4235 U.S. Food and Drug Administration. National Drug Code Directory
0077-4243 National Education Association of the United States. Addresses and Proceedings *changed to* National Education Association of the United States. Proceedings of the Representative Assembly
0077-4413 National Electronics Conference. Proceedings *changed to* National Communications Forum. Proceedings
0077-4421 National Electronics Conference. Record†
0077-443X National Engineering Laboratory, East Kilbridge, Scotland. Annual Report†
0077-4448 National Equine (and Smaller Animals) Defence League. Annual Report
0077-4456 N A L G O Annual Report
0077-4472 National Faculty Directory
0077-4480 National Federation of Plastering Contractors. Year Book
0077-4499 National Federation of Retail Newsagents. National Federation Yearbook†
0077-4510 National Fertilizer Development Center. Annual Report *see* 0730-7322
0077-4529 National Finances: An Analysis of the Revenues and Expenditures of the Government of Canada
0077-4537 National Fire Prevention Gazette†
0077-4545 National Fire Protection Association. National Fire Codes
0077-4553 N F P A Technical Committee. Report
0077-4588 National Football League. Record Manual†
0077-4596 National Foundation for Education Research in England and Wales. Occasional Publication Series†
0077-4618 National Geographic Books (Series)
0077-4626 National Geographic Society Research Reports *see* 8755-724X
0077-4634 National Governors' Conference. Proceedings of the Annual Meeting *see* 0191-3441
0077-4642 National Guild of Piano Teachers. Guild Syllabus
0077-4685 National Heart Foundation of Australia. Research-In-Progress
0077-4707 National Housing and Town Planning Council. Handbook and Year Book
0077-4723 National Income Statistics of Thailand *changed to* National Income of Thailand
0077-4731 National Industrial Fuel Efficiency Service, London Progress Survey with Report and Accounts
0077-474X National Institute for Architectural Education. Yearbook
0077-4758 National Institute for Personnel Research. Annual Report†
0077-4766 National Institute for Personnel Research. List of N I P R Publications†
0077-4774 National Institute Social Services Library
0077-4782 National Institute of Agricultural Botany, Cambridge, England. Annual Report of the Council and Accounts *changed to* National Institute of Agricultural Botany, Cambridge, England. Annual Report and Accounts
0077-4790 National Institute of Agricultural Botany, Cambridge, England. Journal
0077-4804 National Institute of Agricultural Engineering. Reports *changed to* A F R C Institute of Engineering Research. Reports
0077-4812 National Institute of Agricultural Engineering. Translations *changed to* A F R C Institute of Engineering Research. Translations
0077-4820 National Institute of Agricultural Sciences, Tokyo. Bulletin. Series A (Physics and Statistics)†
0077-4839 National Institute of Agricultural Sciences, Tokyo. Bulletin. Series B (Soils and Fertilizers)†
0077-4847 National Institute of Agricultural Sciences, Tokyo. Bulletin. Series C (Plant Pathology and Entomology)†
0077-4855 National Institute of Agricultural Sciences, Tokyo. Bulletin. Series D (Physiology and Genetics)†
0077-4863 National Institute of Agricultural Sciences, Tokyo. Bulletin. Series H (Farm Management, Land Utilization, Rural Life)
0077-4871 National Institute of Agricultural Sciences, Tokyo. Miscellaneous Publication†
0077-488X National Institute of Animal Industry, Chiba, Japan. Bulletin. *changed to* National Institute of Animal Industry, Ibaraki, Japan. Bulletin.
0077-4898 National Institute of Animal Industry, Chiba, Japan. *changed to* National Institute of Animal Industry, Ibaraki, Japan. Bulletin Summaries.
0077-491X National Institute of Economic and Social Research. Annual Report
0077-4928 National Institute of Economic and Social Research, London. Occasional Papers
0077-4936 National Institute of Economic and Social Research, London. Regional Studies *changed to* National Institute of Economic and Social Research, London. Regional Papers
0077-4944 N I F P General Series
0077-4952 N I F P Manual Series
0077-4960 N I F P Monograph Series
0077-4979 N I F P Report Series
0077-4987 N I F P Technical Paper Series
0077-4995 National Institute of Genetics, Mishima, Japan. Annual Report
0077-5002 National Institute of Hygienic Sciences. Bulletin
0077-5010 N I I P Bulletin†
0077-5037 Israeli Life Table
0077-5053 Jamaica. National Insurance Scheme. Annual Reports *changed to* Jamaica. Ministry of Social Security. Report
0077-5061 National Investment Bank, Ghana. Report of the Directors *changed to* National Investment Bank, Ghana. Annual Report
0077-5088 National Junior Horticultural Association. Newsletter
0077-5096 National Kidney Foundation. Annual Report
0077-5118 National League for Nursing. Associate Degree Education for Nursing *changed to* Associate Degree Education for Nursing
0077-5134 National League for Nursing. League Exchange†
0077-5177 National List of Advertisers
0077-5185 National Maritime Board. (Great Britain) Year Book
0077-5193 Sefunim
0077-5223 National Microfilm Association. Proceedings of the Annual Convention *changed to* National Micrographics Association. Proceedings of the Annual Conference
0077-5231 National Minority Business Directory *changed to* Try Us
0077-524X National Observer Index†
0077-5258 N O R C Monographs in Social Research†
0077-5266 National Opinion Research Center. Newsletter
0077-5274 National Opinion Research Center. Report
0077-5282 National Party Platforms. Supplement
0077-5290 National Physical Laboratory, Teddington, England. Annual Report†
0077-5312 National Pig Breeders' Association Herd Book
0077-5320 National Planning Association Center for Development Planning. Planning Methods Series†
0077-5339 National Psychological Association for Psychoanalysis. Bulletin
0077-5347 National Publishing Directory
0077-5355 N R M C A Publication
0077-5371 National Register of Prominent Americans and International Notables
0077-538X National Register of Scholarships and Fellowships†
0077-5401 National Relay Conference. Proceedings
0077-541X National Reprographic Centre for Documentation, Hertford, England. Technical Evaluation Reports *changed to* National Centre for Information Media & Technology (CIMITECH). Technical Evaluation Reports
0077-5428 National Research Council, Canada. Associate Committee on Geotechnical Research. Technical Memorandum
0077-5452 National Research Council, Canada. Division of Building Research. Bulletin†
0077-5460 National Research Council, Canada. Division of Building Research. Building Research Note
0077-5479 National Research Council, Canada. Division of Building Research. Computer Program†
0077-5487 National Research Council, Canada. Division of Building Research. Fire Research Note†
0077-5495 National Research Council, Canada. Division of Building Research. Fire Study†
0077-5509 National Research Council, Canada. Division of Building Research. Housing Note†
0077-5517 National Research Council, Canada. Division of Building Research. Research Program
0077-5525 National Research Council, Canada. Division of Building Research. Research Paper†
0077-5533 National Research Council, Canada. Division of Building Research. Technical Paper†
0077-5541 National Research Council, Canada. National Aeronautical Establishment. Aeronautical Report (L R Series)
0077-555X National Research Council, Canada. National Aeronautical Establishment. Mechanical Engineering Reports
0077-5568 National Research Council, Canada. National Aeronautical Establishment. Publications List and Supplements
0077-5576 National Science Library of Canada. Annual Report *see* 0703-0320
0077-5592 National Research Council, Canada. Space Research Facilities Branch. Report. (SRFB Series)†
0077-5606 National Research Council, Canada. Technical Translation†
0077-5614 National Cooperative Highway Research Program Reports
0077-5622 Highway Research Board Special Publication *see* 0360-859X
0077-5630 Atoll Research Bulletin
0077-5657 National Rural Electric Cooperative Association. Government Relations Department. Research Division. Research Papers and Circulars.
0077-5673 N S G A Circular
0077-5703 National Securities and Research Corporation. Annual Forecast
0077-5711 National Shellfisheries Association. Proceedings *see* 0730-8000
0077-572X National Shorthand Reporters Association. Proceedings of the Annual Convention
0077-5738 National Skeet Shooting Association. Records Annual
0077-5754 National Society for Prevention of Cruelty to Children. Annual Report
0077-5762 National Society for the Study of Education. Yearbook
0077-5770 National Society of Public Accountants. Proceedings of the Annual Professional Institute†
0077-5789 National Soybean Processors Association. Yearbook
0077-5819 National Taiwan University. College of Agriculture. Memoirs
0077-5827 National Taiwan University. College of Engineering. Memoirs†
0077-5835 National Taiwan University. College of Law. Journal of Social Science
0077-5843 National Taiwan University. Department of Archaeology and Anthropology. Bulletin *changed to* National Taiwan University. Department of Anthropology. Bulletin
0077-5851 National Taiwan University Journal of Sociology
0077-586X National Tank Truck Carrier Directory
0077-5886 Tire Dealers Survey *see* 0027-7045
0077-5894 National Trade-Index of Southern Africa
0077-5916 National Trust for Scotland Yearbook
0077-5932 N U S Yearbook *changed to* N U S News

0077-5940 National Union of Teachers. Annual Report
0077-5959 National University Extension Association. Proceedings†
0077-5975 Nationale-Nederlanden. Annual Report
0077-5983 Nationwide Directory of Men's and Boys' Wear Buyers (Exclusive of New York Metropolitan Area)
0077-5991 Nationwide Directory of Women's and Children's Wear Buyers (Exclusive of New York Metropolitan Area)
0077-6009 Nationwide Major Mass Market Merchandisers (Exclusive of New York Metropolitan Area)
0077-6017 Native American Arts†
0077-6025 Natur und Mensch: Jahresmitteilungen der Naturhistorischen Gesellschaft Nuernberg
0077-6033 Natura Jutlandica
0077-6041 Natural Gas Processing Plants in Canada†
0077-6084 Natural Resources Law Newsletter
0077-6092 Natural Resources Research
0077-6106 Naturegraph Ocean Guidebooks†
0077-6114 Mouvement Naturel de la Population de la Grece
0077-6122 Naturforschende Gesellschaft in Basel. Verhandlungen
0077-6130 Naturforschende Gesellschaft in Bern. Mitteilungen
0077-6149 Naturhistorische Gesellschaft Nuernberg. Abhandlungen
0077-6157 Naturwissenschaftliche Rundschau. Buecher der Zeitschrift
0077-6165 Naturwissenschaftlicher Verein fuer Schleswig-Holstein. Schriften
0077-6173 Nauheimer Fortbildungs-Lehrgaenge†
0077-6181 Nauka dla Wszystkich
0077-619X Nautical Almanac
0077-6211 Nautisches Jahrbuch, oder Ephemeriden und Tafeln
0077-6238 U.S. Naval Institute. Naval Review
0077-6262 Navigation
0077-6270 Navis
0077-6289 Maritime Survey†
0077-6297 Nawpa Pacha
0077-6300 Near and Middle East Series
0077-6343 Nebraska Academy of Sciences. Proceedings
0077-6351 Nebraska Academy of Sciences. Transactions
0077-636X Nebraska. Equal Opportunity Commission. Annual Report†
0077-6378 University of Nebraska. School of Journalism. Depth Report
0077-6386 University of Nebraska Studies. New Series
0077-6394 Nebraska Water Resources Research Institute, University of Nebraska. Annual Report of Activities
0077-6408 Nebula Award Stories *see* 0162-3818
0077-6416 Nederlands-Zuidafrikaanse Vereniging. Jaarverslag
0077-6432 Nederlandse Malacologische Vereniging. Correspondentieblad
0077-6467 Negev Institute for Arid Zone Research, Beer-Sheva, Israel. Report for Year *changed to* Ben-Gurion University of the Negev. The Institutes for Applied Research. Scientific Activities.
0077-6475 Negro American Biographies and Autobiographies
0077-6483 Negro in the Congressional Record†
0077-6513 Nelson Gallery and Atkins Museum. Bulletin *changed to* Nelson-Atkins Museum of Art. Bulletin
0077-6521 Neo-Hellenika
0077-653X Neodidagmata
0077-6548 Nepal Industrial Development Corporation. Annual Report
0077-6556 Nepal Industrial Development Corporation. Industrial Digest
0077-6564 Nepal Industrial Development Corporation. Statistical Abstracts
0077-6572 Nepal Law Translation Series *changed to* Nepal Miscellaneous Series
0077-6580 Nepal Rastra Bank. Report of the Board of Directors *changed to* Nepal Rastra Bank. Annual Report
0077-6599 Neprajzi Ertesito
0077-6602 Neprajzi Tanulmanyok
0077-6610 Nerthus†
0077-6637 Nether Press Miscellaneous Series
0077-6645 Jaarstatistiek van de in-en Uitvoer per Land van de Nederlandse Antillen
0077-6653 Jaarstatistiek van de in-en Uitvoer per Goederensoort van de Nederlandse Antillen
0077-6661 Netherlands Antilles. Bureau voor de Statistiek. Statistisch Jaarboek
0077-667X Netherlands Antilles. Bureau voor de Statistiek. Statistiek van de Meteorologische Waarnemingen in de Nederlandse Antillen
0077-6688 Netherlands. Centraal Bureau voor de Statistiek. Bezoek aan Vermakelijkheidsinstellingen. Attendance at Public Entertainments
0077-670X Belastingdruk in Nederland
0077-6777 Sportaccommodatie in Nederland
0077-6785 Netherlands. Centraal Bureau voor de Statistiek. Voorziening in de Behoefte aan Onderwijzers Bij het Lager Onderwijs. Supplying the Need for Teachers in Elementary Education†
0077-6793 Netherlands. Centraal Bureau voor de Statistiek. Faillissementsstatistiek. Bankruptcies
0077-6815 Netherlands. Centraal Bureau voor de Statistiek. Gevangenisstatistiek. Statistics of Prisons
0077-6823 Netherlands. Centraal Bureau voor de Statistiek. Hypotheken en Hypotheekbanken. Statistics of Mortgages *see* 0168-4590
0077-6904 Omvang der Vakbeweging in Nederland *see* 0168-4035
0077-6912 Netherlands. Centraal Bureau voor de Statistiek. Produktiestatistieken. Production Statistics of Individual Industries†
0077-6955 Netherlands. Centraal Bureau voor de Statistiek. Statistiek der Branden. Fire Statistics
0077-6963 Netherlands. Centraal Bureau voor de Statistiek. Statistiek der Lonen in de Landbouw. Statistics of Wages in Agriculture
0077-698X Netherlands. Centraal Bureau voor de Statistiek. Statistiek der Motorrijtuigen *see* 0168-4973
0077-7005 Netherlands. Centraal Bureau voor de Statistiek. Statistiek der Spaarbanken. Statistical View of the Savings Banks†
0077-7048 Netherlands. Centraal Bureau voor de Statistiek. Statistische en Econometrische Onderzoekingen. Statistical and Econometric Studies *changed to* Netherlands. Centraal Bureau voor de Statistiek. Statistische Onderzoekingen
0077-7110 Netherlands. Centraal Bureau voor de Statistiek. Statistiek van de Investeringen in Vaste Activa in de Industrie *see* 0168-7956
0077-7196 Netherlands.Centraal Bureau voor de Statistiek. Statistiek van de Uitgaven der Overheid voor Cultuur en Recreatie *see* 0168-4248
0077-720X Netherlands. Centraal Bureau voor de Statistiek. Statistiek van de Uitgaven der Overheid voor Onderwijs, Wetenschap en Cultuur. Statistics of the Expenditure of the State, the Provinces and the Municipalities on Education, Science and Culture†
0077-7218 Netherlands. Centraal Bureau voor de Statistiek. Statistiek van de Voorlichting Bij Beroepskeuze. Statistics of Vocational Guidance and Selection of Personnel *see* 0168-423X
0077-7226 Netherlands. Centraal Bureau voor de Statistiek. Statistiek van de Gemeentewege per Leerling Beschikbaar Gestelde Bedragenter Bestrijding van de Materiele Exploitatiekosten der Lagere Scholen. Statistics of the Amounts per Pupil Provided by the Municipality to Meet the Material Cost of Elementary Education *see* 0168-5244
0077-7285 Netherlands. Centraal Bureau voor de Statistiek. Statistiek van het Beroepsonderwijs *see* 0168-5457
0077-7293 Netherlands. Centraal Bureau voor de Statistiek. Statistiek van het Internationaal Goederenvervoer. Statistics of the International Goods Traffic *see* 0168-4876
0077-7307 Netherlands. Centraal Bureau voor de Statistiek. Statistiek van het Kunstonderwijs. Statistics on Art Colleges *see* 0168-5503
0077-7315 Netherlands. Centraal Bureau voor de Statistiek. Statistiek van Het Kleuteronderwijs. Statistics of Nursery Schools†
0077-7323 Netherlands. Centraal Bureau voor de Statistiek. Statistiek van het Kweekschoolonderwijs. Statistics on Teacher Training Colleges *changed to* Netherlands. Centraal Bureau voor de Statistiek. Statistiek van het Beroepsonderwijs: Opleidingsscholen Kleuterleidsters en Pedagogische Academies
0077-7331 Netherlands. Centraal Bureau voor de Statistiek. Statistiek van het Land- en Tuinbouwonderwijs. Statistics Concerning Agricultural and Horticultural Education *changed to* Netherlands. Centraal Bureau voor de Statistiek. Statistiek van het Hoger Beroepsonderwijs: Agrarisch Onderwijs
0077-734X Netherlands. Centraal Bureau voor de Statistiek. Statistiek van het Nijverheidsonderwijs *see* 0168-5406
0077-7366 Netherlands. Centraal Bureau voor de Statistiek. Statistiek van het Schriftelijk Onderwijs. Statistics on Correspondence Courses *see* 0168-4906
0077-7374 Netherlands. Centraal Bureau voor de Statistiek. Statistiek van het Sociaal-Pedagogisch Onderwijs. Statistics on Socio-Pedagogic Training *see* 0168-5600
0077-7382 Netherlands. Centraal Bureau voor de Statistiek. Statistiek van Het Toneel. Statistics on Theatre Performances†
0077-7390 Netherlands. Centraal Bureau voor de Statistiek. Statistiek van Het Uitgebreid Lager Onderwijs. Statistics of Continued Elementary Education†
0077-7404 Netherlands. Centraal Bureau voor de Statistiek. Statistiek van het Voorbereidend Hoger en Middelbaar Onderwijs: Leraren. Statistics of Secondary Education: Teachers *see* 0168-5856
0077-7471 Netherlands. Centraal Bureau voor de Statistiek. Toepassing der Kinderwetten. Application of Juvenile Law *changed to* Netherlands. Centraal Bureau voor de Statistiek. Justiciele Kinderbescherming
0077-7501 Vakantiebesteding van de Nederlandse Bevolking *see* 0168-3411
0077-751X Netherlands. Centraal Bureau voor de Statistiek. Winststatistiek der Grotere Naamloze Vennootschappen. Profit-Statistics of the Limited Liability Companies
0077-7528 Netherlands. Centraal Bureau voor de Statistiek. Zuivelstatistiek/Dairy Statistics *see* 0168-518X
0077-7536 Netherlands. Centraal Planbureau. Centraal Economisch Plan
0077-7552 Netherlands. Commissie Zeehavenoverleg. Jaarverslag *changed to* Netherlands. Provisional National Ports Council. Jaarverslag
0077-7560 Netherlands Investment Bank for Developing Countries. Annual Report
0077-7579 Netherlands Journal of Sea Research
0077-7587 Yearbook Geomagnetism: Paramaribo, Surinam†
0077-7595 Netherlands Nitrogen Technical Bulletin *see* 0169-2313
0077-7609 Produktschap voor Siergewassen. Jaarverslag *changed to* Produktschap voor Siergewassen. Jaarverslag/Statistiek
0077-7617 Netherlands. Rijks Geologische Dienst. Jaarverslag
0077-7625 Netherlands. Rijkscommissie voor Geodesie. Publications on Geodesy. New Series
0077-7633 Universite de Neuchatel. Faculte des Lettres. Recueil de Travaux
0077-7641 Universite de Neuchatel. Seminaire de Geometrie. Publications. Serie 1. Courtes Publications *changed to* Centre de Recherches en Mathematiques Pures. Publications. Serie 1. Courtes Publications
0077-765X Universite de Neuchatel. Seminaire de Geometrie. Publications. Serie 2. Monographies *changed to* Centre de Recherches en Mathematiques Pures. Publications. Serie 2. Monographies
0077-7668 Neudrucke Deutscher Literaturwerke
0077-7676 Neudrucke Deutscher Literaturwerke. Sonderreihe
0077-7684 Neue Beitraege zur Englischen Philologie†
0077-7706 Neue Muenstersche Beitraege zur Geschichtsforschung†
0077-7714 Neue Musikgeschichtliche Forschungen
0077-7730 Neues aus der Mariahilfer Strasse†
0077-7749 Neues Jahrbuch fuer Geologie und Palaeontologie. Abhandlungen
0077-7757 Neues Jahrbuch fuer Mineralogie. Abhandlungen
0077-7765 Neues Trierisches Jahrbuch *changed to* Neues Trierisches Jahrbuch fuer Heimatpflege und Heimatgeschichte
0077-7773 Neumanns Jahrbuch der Deutschen Versicherungswirtschaft. Teil 1: Personenversicherung (Lebens- und Krankenversicherung)†
0077-7781 Neumanns Jahrbuch der Deutschen Versicherungswirtschaft. Teil 2: Schaden- und Rueckversicherung†
0077-779X Neumanns Jahrbuch der Deutschen Versicherungswirtschaft. Teil 3: Institutionen, Uebersichten und Anschriften†
0077-7803 Neuro-Ophthalmology†
0077-7838 Neuroradiology Workshop†
0077-7846 Neurosciences Research
0077-7862 Neusser Jahrbuch fuer Kunst, Kulturgeschichte und Heimatkunde
0077-7889 Nevada. Division of Personnel. Biennial Report†
0077-7897 Nevada. State Museum, Carson City. Anthropological Papers
0077-7900 Nevada. State Museum, Carson City. Natural History Publications
0077-7919 Nevada. State Museum, Carson City. Occasional Papers
0077-7927 Nevada. State Museum, Carson City. Popular Series
0077-7935 Nevada Studies in History and Political Science

ISSN INDEX

0077-7943   University of Nevada. Bureau of Business and Economic Research. Research Report
0077-7951   Desert Research Institute Publications in the Social Sciences
0077-796X   University of Nevada. Desert Research Institute. Technical Report
0077-7986   New Acronyms and Initialisms *see* 0148-866X
0077-7994   New African Literature and the Arts†
0077-801X   New Babylon: Studies in the Social Sciences
0077-8036   New Brunswick Department of Fisheries. Annual Report
0077-8052   New Brunswick. Department of Labour. Annual Report *changed to* New Brunswick. Department of Labour and Human Resources. Annual Report
0077-8060   New Brunswick. Department of Municipal Affairs. Report†
0077-8079   New Brunswick. Department of Youth. Report
0077-8087   New Brunswick. Liquor Control Commission. Report†
0077-8109   New Brunswick. Mineral Resources Branch. Report of Investigations
0077-8117   New Brunswick. Research and Productivity Council. Report
0077-8141   University of New Brunswick Law Journal
0077-8168   New Campus†
0077-8206   N D T†
0077-8222   New England Guide *see* 0734-4066
0077-8230   New England Papers on Education†
0077-8281   New England Road Builders Association. N E R B A Annual Directory *changed to* Construction Industries of Massachusetts Directory
0077-832X   New Hampshire. Agricultural Experiment Station, Durham. Research Reports
0077-8338   New Hampshire. Agricultural Experiment Station, Durham. Station Bulletins
0077-8346   New Hampshire Archeologist
0077-8362   New Hampshire. Fish and Game Department. Biennial Report
0077-8370   New Hampshire. Fish and Game Department. Game Management and Research Division. Biological Survey Series
0077-8389   New Hampshire. Fish and Game Department. Game Management and Research Division. Technical Circular Series.
0077-8397   New Hampshire. Fish and Game Department. Game Management and Research Division. Biological Survey Bulletin
0077-8427   New Hampshire Winter Holidays†
0077-8435   New Hebrides. Anglo-French Condominium Geological Survey. Annual Reports *changed to* Vanuatu. Geological Survey. Annual Reports
0077-8443   Vanuatu. Geological Survey. Reports
0077-8451   New Jersey Clean Air Council. Report
0077-846X   New Jersey. Department of Agriculture. Highlights of the Annual Report *changed to* New Jersey Agriculture
0077-8478   New Jersey. Economic Policy Council. Annual Report of Economic Policy Council and Office of Economic Policy
0077-8508   New Jersey Public Employer-Employee Relations†
0077-8516   New Jersey Speech and Hearing Association. Newsletter
0077-8540   New Mexico Agricultural Statistics
0077-8559   New Mexico. Employment Security Commission. Annual Rural Manpower Service Report *changed to* New Mexico. Employment Services Department. Annual Rural Manpower Service Report
0077-8567   New Mexico Geological Society. Guidebook, Field Conference
0077-8575   New Mexico Statistical Abstract
0077-8583   University of New Mexico Art Museum. Bulletin
0077-8591   New Official Guide: Japan
0077-8605   New Orleans Academy of Ophthalmology. Transactions
0077-8613   New Perspectives in Political Science†
0077-8621   New Poetry
0077-8664   New South Wales. Department of Mines. Annual Report *see* 0727-9256
0077-8672   New South Wales. Department of Mines. Chemical Laboratory. Report†
0077-8680   New South Wales. Department of Mines. Coalfields Branch. Reports†
0077-8699   New South Wales. Department of Mines. Memoirs: Palaeontology *changed to* New South Wales. Geological Survey. Memoirs: Palaeontology
0077-8710   New South Wales. Geological Survey. Memoirs: Geology
0077-8729   New South Wales. Geological Survey. Mineral Industry Series
0077-8737   New South Wales. Geological Survey. Mineral Resources Series
0077-8753   New South Wales National Herbarium. Contributions *see* 0312-9764
0077-8788   New South Wales. State Fisheries. Research Bulletin†

0077-8796   University of New South Wales. School of Civil Engineering. U N I C I V Reports. Series I
0077-880X   University of New South Wales. School of Civil Engineering. U N I C I V Reports. Series R
0077-8818   University of New South Wales. Water Research Laboratory, Manly Vale. Laboratory Research Reports
0077-8826   New Teacher
0077-8842   New Testament Tools and Studies
0077-8869   New Trade Names in the Rubber and Plastics Industries
0077-8877   New Trends in Biology Teaching
0077-8885   New Trends in Chemistry Teaching
0077-8893   New Trends in Mathematics Teaching
0077-8907   New Trends in Physics Teaching
0077-8923   New York Academy of Sciences. Annals
0077-8931   New York Botanical Garden. Memoirs
0077-894X   City College Papers†
0077-8958   Metropolitan Museum Journal
0077-8974   New York Crop Reporting Service. Statistics Relative to the Dairy Industry in New York State *see* 0732-9121
0077-9008   New York Psychoanalytic Institute. Kris Study Group. Monographs
0077-9016   New York Public Library. Films†
0077-9024   New York Publicity Outlets
0077-9059   New York State Archeological Association. Occasional Papers†
0077-9067   New York State Archeological Association. Researches and Transactions†
0077-9083   New York State Business Fact Book. Part 1: Business and Manufacturing
0077-9091   New York State Business Fact Book. Part 2: Population and Housing†
0077-9105   New York State Business Fact Book. Supplement
0077-9113   A F R I Research Note†
0077-9148   New York (State) Crime Victims Compensation Board. Report *changed to* New York (State). Crime Victims Board. Report
0077-9156   New York (State) Department of Commerce. Research Bulletin
0077-9172   College and University Degrees Conferred, New York State
0077-9180   College and University Enrollment in New York State *see* 0147-5894
0077-9210   Distribution of High School Graduates and College Going Rate, New York State
0077-9229   Public School Professional Personnel Report, New York State
0077-9245   New York (State) Education Department. Public School Professional Personnel Report *see* 0077-9229
0077-9253   Nonpublic School Enrollment and Staff, New York State
0077-927X   New York (State) Interdepartmental Committee on Indian Affairs. Report†
0077-9296   Checklist of Official Publications of the State of New York
0077-930X   New York. State Library, Albany. Library Development. Excerpts from New York State Education Law, Rules of the Board of Regents, and Regulations of the Commissioner of Education Pertaining to Public and Free Association Libraries, Library Systems, Trustees and Librarians
0077-9318   New York. State Library, Albany. Library Development. Institution Libraries Statistics
0077-9326   New York. State Library, Albany. Library Development. Public and Association Libraries Statistics
0077-9334   New York (State) Division of the Budget. New York State Statistical Yearbook *changed to* New York (State). Rockefeller Institute of Government. New York State Statistical Yearbook
0077-9342   Analysis of School Finances, New York State School Districts
0077-9385   State University of New York, College at Buffalo. Program in Soviet and East Central European Studies. Publications *changed to* State University of New York. College at Buffalo's Program in East European and Slavic Studies. Publications.
0077-9407   New York (State) Upstate Medical Center, Syracuse. Library. Faculty Bibliography†
0077-9415   New York (State) Upstate Medical Center, Syracuse. Library. Library Guide†
0077-9423   New York State Urban Development Corporation. Annual Report
0077-944X   New York University. Comparative Criminal Law Project. Publications *changed to* Wayne State University Law School. Comparative Criminal Law Project. Publications Series
0077-9458   New York University. Criminal Law Education and Research Center. Monograph Series *changed to* Wayne State University Law School. Comparative Criminal Law Project. Monograph Series

0077-9466   New York University Institute of Finance. Bulletin *see* 0276-2021
0077-9490   New York University. Libraries. Bulletin of the Tamiment Library
0077-9504   New York University Studies in Comparative Literature
0077-9520   New Zealand Agricultural Engineering Institute. Annual Report
0077-9539   Lincoln College. New Zealand Agricultural Engineering Institute. Extension Bulletin†
0077-9563   Lincoln College. New Zealand Agricultural Engineering Institute. Research Publication†
0077-9571   New Zealand Business Who's Who
0077-958X   New Zealand. Central Advisory Committee on the Appointments and Promotion of Primary Teachers. Report to the Minister of Education
0077-9601   New Zealand. Department of Scientific and Industrial Research. Annual Report
0077-961X   New Zealand. Department of Scientific and Industrial Research. Bulletin
0077-9628   New Zealand. Department of Scientific and Industrial Research. Geological Survey. Bulletin
0077-9636   New Zealand. Department of Scientific and Industrial Research. Information Series
0077-9644   New Zealand. Soil Bureau. Bulletin†
0077-9652   New Zealand. Department of Statistics. Annual Report of the Government Statistician
0077-9687   New Zealand. Department of Statistics. Population Census: Ages and Marital Status *changed to* New Zealand. Department of Statistics. Population Census: Ages, Marital Status and Fertility
0077-9695   New Zealand. Department of Statistics. Population Census: Dwellings
0077-9709   New Zealand. Department of Statistics. Population Census: Education *changed to* New Zealand. Department of Statistics. Population Census: Education and Training
0077-9717   New Zealand. Department of Statistics. Population Census: General Report
0077-9725   New Zealand. Department of Statistics. Population Census: Households *changed to* New Zealand. Department of Statistics. Population Census: Households and Families
0077-9733   New Zealand. Department of Statistics. Population Census: Incomes *changed to* New Zealand. Department of Statistics. Population Census: Incomes and Social Security Benefits
0077-9741   New Zealand. Department of Statistics. Population Census: Industries and Occupations *changed to* New Zealand. Department of Statistics. Population Census: Labour Force
0077-9768   Provisional Report on Population and Dwellings *changed to* New Zealand. Department of Statistics. Population Census: Provisional Statistics Series. Bulletin One. Local Authority Areas
0077-9776   New Zealand. Department of Statistics. Population Census: Race *changed to* New Zealand. Department of Statistics. Population Census: Birthplaces and Ethnic Origin
0077-9784   New Zealand. Department of Statistics. Population Census: Religious Professions
0077-9792   New Zealand. Department of Statistics. Population Census: Increase and Location of Population *changed to* New Zealand. Department of Statistics. Population Census. Location and Increase of Population. Part A: Population Size and Distribution
0077-9792   New Zealand. Department of Statistics. Population Census: Increase and Location of Population *changed to* New Zealand. Department of Statistics. Population Census. Location and Increase of Population. Part B: Population Density
0077-9806   New Zealand. Department of Statistics. Report and Analysis of External Trade
0077-9822   New Zealand. Department of Statistics. Statistical Report of Farm Production *see* 0110-4624
0077-9865   New Zealand. Department of Statistics. Industrial Production†
0077-9903   New Zealand. Department of Statistics. Statistical Report of Population, Migration and Building. *see* 0112-9155
0077-9911   New Zealand. Department of Statistics. Prices, Wages and Labour *see* 0110-5019
0077-9946   New Zealand Ecological Society. Proceedings *see* 0110-6465
0077-9954   New Zealand Economic Papers
0077-9962   New Zealand Entomologist
0077-9997   New Zealand. Forest Research Institute. Report
0078-0006   New Zealand. Forest Research Institute. Technical Paper†

ISSN INDEX 1395

0078-0022 New Zealand Geographical Society. Miscellaneous Series
0078-0030 New Zealand Geography Conference Proceedings Series
0078-0049 New Zealand Institute of Economic Research. Discussion Paper
0078-0057 New Zealand Institute of Economic Research. Annual Report
0078-0065 New Zealand Institute of Economic Research. Research Paper
0078-0073 New Zealand Institute of Economic Research. Technical Memorandum†
0078-0081 New Zealand Law Register
0078-009X New Zealand Library School, Wellington. Bibliographical Series†
0078-0103 New Zealand Library School, Wellington. Occasional Papers†
0078-0111 New Zealand. Marine Department. Annual Report on Fisheries†
0078-0138 New Zealand. Meat and Wool Boards' Economic Service. Annual Review of the Sheep Industry
0078-0146 New Zealand Medical Records Officers' Association. Conference Proceedings†
0078-0154 New Zealand. National Research Advisory Council. Senior and Post Doctoral Research Fellowship Awards for Research in New Zealand Government Departments†
0078-0170 New Zealand Official Year-Book
0078-0189 New Zealand Pottery and Ceramics Research Association. Technical Report†
0078-0197 New Zealand Poultry Board. Report; and New Zealand Marketing Authority Report and Statement of Accounts
0078-0219 New Zealand Wheat Review
0078-0243 Newcastle History Monographs
0078-0251 University of Newcastle-Upon-Tyne. Philosophical Society. Proceedings
0078-026X University of Newcastle-Upon-Tyne. Department of Geography. Research Series
0078-0278 Newfoundland and Labrador. Department of Education. Statistical Supplement to the Annual Report†
0078-0286 Newfoundland and Labrador Who's Who†
0078-0294 Newfoundland. Department of Social Services. Annual Report
0078-0308 Newfoundland. Mineral Development Division. Geological Survey. Bulletin
0078-0316 Newfoundland Medical Directory
0078-0340 Newfoundland. Mineral Development Division. Information
0078-0359 Newfoundland. Mineral Development Division. Information Circular.
0078-0367 Newfoundland. Mines Branch. Annual Report Series
0078-0383 Newfoundland. Mines Branch. Geological Survey of Newfoundland. Report Series
0078-0421 Newsletters on Stratigraphy
0078-043X Newspaper Press Directory *see* 0269-8358
0078-0448 Israel. Goverment Press Office. Newspapers and Periodicals Appearing in Israel†
0078-0502 Niagara Parks Commission. Annual Report
0078-0510 Nicaragua. Direccion General de Aduanas. Memoria
0078-0537 Niederdeutsche Beitraege zur Kunstgeschichte
0078-0545 Niederdeutsches Wort
0078-0561 Niedersaechsisches Jahrbuch fuer Landesgeschichte *changed to* Niedersachsisches Jahrbuch
0078-057X Nigeria Annual and Trading Directory
0078-0588 Nigeria Assistance Programs of U.S. Non-Profit Organizations†
0078-0596 Nigeria Business Directory
0078-0626 Nigeria. Federal Office of Statistics. Annual Abstract of Statistics
0078-0634 Nigeria. Federal Office of Statistics. Review of External Trade
0078-0642 Nigeria. Federal Office of Statistics. Trade Report†
0078-0650 Nigeria Trade Summary
0078-0677 University of Nigeria. Report on Research†
0078-0685 Nigeria Year Book
0078-0693 Nigerian Books in Print
0078-0707 Nigerian Chamber of Mines. Annual Review
0078-0715 Nigerian Institute for Oil Palm Research. Journal
0078-0723 Nigerian Institute of International Affairs. Digest of Selected Articles on International Questions†
0078-0731 Nigerian Institute of International Affairs. Lecture Series
0078-074X Nigerian Institute of Social and Economic Research. Annual Report
0078-0758 Nigerian Institute of Social and Economic Research. Information Bulletin†
0078-0766 Nigerian Institute of Social and Economic Research. Library. List of Accessions
0078-0774 Nigerian Law Journal†
0078-0782 Nigerian Medical Directory
0078-0804 Nigerian National Advisory Council for the Blind. Annual Report
0078-0812 Current National Bibliography *see* 0331-0019
0078-0820 Nigerian Tobacco Company. Report *changed to* Nigerian Tobacco Company. Annual Report and Accounts
0078-0839 Nippon Veterinary and Zootechnical College. Bulletin
0078-0847 N I B S Bulletin of Biological Research†
0078-0855 Nityanand Universal Series
0078-0863 Nivel de la Economia Argentina
0078-088X N M R
0078-0898 NMR Data Table for Organic Compounds†
0078-0901 Nobel Symposium Series
0078-091X Noble Official Catalog of Canada Precancels
0078-0928 Noble Official Catalog of United States Bureau Precancels
0078-0936 Noctes Romanae
0078-0944 Noda Institute for Scientific Research. Report
0078-0952 Nomenclator Zoologicus
0078-0960 Nomenclature des Entreprises Nationales a Caractere Industriel ou Commercial et des Societies d'Economie Mixte d'Interet National
0078-0979 Nomos
0078-0987 Non-Ferrous Metal Works of the World
0078-0995 Non-Metallic Solids
0078-1029 Nord-Norge Naeringsliv og Oekonomi
0078-1037 Nordelbingen
0078-1045 Nordfriesisches Jahrbuch
0078-1053 Nordicana
0078-1061 Nordisk Medicinhistorisk Aarsbok
0078-107X Nordisk Numismatisk Aarsskrift
0078-1088 Nordisk Statistisk Aarsbok
0078-1096 Nordiske Sjefsstatistikermoete
0078-110X Nordiska Afrikainstitutet. Skriftserie†
0078-1118 Nordic Association for American Studies. Publications†
0078-1126 N K B Skriftserie
0078-1134 Nordistica Gothoburgensia
0078-1150 Norfolk Holiday Handbook *changed to* Holiday Hints Handbook
0078-1169 Norfolk Record Society. Publications
0078-1185 Norges Bank. Report and Accounts
0078-1193 Norges Geotekniske Institutt. Publikasjon
0078-1207 Norwegian Geotechnical Institute. Technical Report†
0078-1215 Norges Handels-Kalender
0078-1223 Norges Landbruksoekonomiske Institutt. Driftsgranskinger i Jordbruket *see* 0333-2500
0078-1231 Norges Teknisk-Naturvitenskapelige Forskningsraad. Aarsberetning
0078-124X Norges Teknisk-Naturvitenskapelige Forskningsraad. Transportoekonomisk Institutt. Aarsberetning *changed to* Transportoekonomisk Institutt. Aarsberetning
0078-1266 Norsk Litteraer Aarbok
0078-1274 North American Association of Alcoholism Programs. Meeting. Selected Papers *changed to* A D P A Selected Papers of Annual Meetings
0078-1282 North American Association of Alcoholism Programs. N A A P Facilities Directory *see* 0092-3826
0078-1304 North American Fauna
0078-1312 North American Flora
0078-1320 North American Forest Soils Conference. Proceedings
0078-1339 North American Protestant Ministries Overseas *see* 0093-8130
0078-1347 North American Radio-T V Guide†
0078-1355 North American Wildlife and Natural Resources Conference. Transactions
0078-1371 North Carolina. Division of Health Services. Public Health Statistics Branch. North Carolina Vital Statistics *changed to* North Carolina. Division of Health Services. State Center for Health Statistics. North Carolina Vital Statistics
0078-138X North Carolina. Department of Revenue. Franchise Tax and Corporate Income Tax Bulletins for Taxable Years *changed to* North Carolina. Department of Revenue. Franchise Tax and Corporate Income Tax Rules and Regulations
0078-1398 North Carolina. Division of Mineral Resources. Special Publication *changed to* North Carolina. Geological Survey Section. Special Publication
0078-141X North Carolina. State Commission on Higher Education Facilities. Facilities Inventory and Utilization Study, for the State of North Carolina
0078-1428 North Carolina State University. Development Council. Report. *changed to* North Carolina State University. Chancellor's Annual Report
0078-1444 North Carolina State University. School of Design. (Student Publication Magazine)
0078-1452 University of North Carolina, Chapel Hill. Graduate School of Business Administration. Technical Papers†
0078-1460 University of North Carolina, Greensboro. Faculty Publications
0078-1495 University of North Carolina, Chapel Hill. Institute of Statistics. Mimeo Series
0078-1525 North Carolina State University. Water Resources Research Institute. Report
0078-1541 North Dakota Crop and Livestock Statistics *changed to* North Dakota Agricultural Statistics
0078-155X North Dakota. Employment Security Bureau. Annual Report *changed to* Job Service North Dakota. Annual Report
0078-1568 North Dakota. Employment Security Bureau. Biennial Report to the Governor *changed to* Job Service North Dakota. Biennial Report to the Governor
0078-1576 North Dakota. Geological Survey. Miscellaneous Series
0078-1592 North-Holland Linguistic Series
0078-1622 North Pacific Fur Seal Commission. Proceedings of the Annual Meeting†
0078-1630 North Queensland Naturalist
0078-1649 North Staffordshire Journal of Field Studies
0078-1665 Northeast Conference on the Teaching of Foreign Languages. Reports of the Working Committees *see* 0733-1169
0078-1681 Northeast Folklore
0078-169X Northeastern University Studies in Rehabilitation†
0078-1703 Northeastern Weed Science Society. Proceedings
0078-1711 Northern Cavern and Mine Research Society. Occasional Publications *changed to* Northern Mine Research Society. Occasional Publications
0078-172X Northern History
0078-1738 Northern House Pamphlet Poets
0078-1746 Northern Ireland. Department of Agriculture. Annual Report on Research and Technical Work
0078-1754 Northern Ireland. Department of Agriculture. Record of Agricultural Research
0078-1762 North-Central State. Ministry of Works. Report *changed to* Kaduna State. Ministry of Works. Report
0078-1770 Northern Virginia Planning District Commission. Annual Report†
0078-1789 Northwest Historical Series
0078-1797 Northwest Wood Products Clinic. Proceedings†
0078-1800 Northwestern-Iowa Dealer Reference Manual *changed to* Northwestern Lumbermens Association Dealer Reference Manual
0078-1835 Norway. Arbeidsdirektoratet. Aarsmelding
0078-1843 Norway. Fiskeridirektoratet. Skrifter. Serie Fiskeri†
0078-186X Norway. Fiskeridirektoratet. Skrifter. Serie Teknologiske Undersoekelser†
0078-1878 Norway. Statistisk Sentralbyraa. Arbeidsmarkedstatistikk / Labour Market Statistics
0078-1886 Norway. Statistisk Sentralbyraa. Industristatistikk / Industrial Statistics *see* 0800-580X
0078-1886 Norway. Statistisk Sentralbyraa. Industristatistikk / Industrial Statistics *see* 0800-5818
0078-1894 Norway. Statistisk Sentralbyraa. Jordbruksstatistikk / Agricultural Statistics
0078-1908 Norway. Statistisk Sentralbyraa. Kredittmarked Statistikk / Credit Market Statistics
0078-1916 Norway. Statistisk Sentralbyraa. Loennsstatistikk / Wage Statistics
0078-1924 Norway. Statistisk Sentralbyraa. Oekonomisk Utsyn / Economic Survey
0078-1932 Norway. Statistisk Sentralbyraa. Statistisk Aarbok / Statistical Yearbook
0078-1940 Norway. Statistisk Sentralbyraa. Utenrikshandel / External Trade
0078-1959 Norway. Statistisk Sentralbyraa. Varehandelsstatistikk / Wholesale and Retail Trade Statistics
0078-1967 Norwegian-American Historical Association. Newsletter
0078-1975 Norwegian American Historical Association. Travel and Description Series
0078-1983 Norwegian-American Studies
0078-1991 Norwegian Studies in English†
0078-2009 Notas de Algebra y Analisis
0078-2017 Notas de Logica Matematica
0078-2025 Notes for Medical Catalogers *see* 0027-9641
0078-2041 Notes in Anthropology†
0078-205X Noticiario Arqueologico Hispanico†
0078-2076 University of Notre Dame. Department of Economics. Union-Management Conference. Proceeding†
0078-2084 Geographical Field Group (Nottingham). Regional Studies
0078-2106 University of Nottingham. School of Agriculture. Report†
0078-2114 Town and Country Planning Summer School; Report of Proceedings
0078-2122 Nottingham Medieval Studies

1396 ISSN INDEX

0078-2130 O.R.S.T.O.M. Recueils des Travaux. Oceanographie *changed to* O.R.S.T.O.M. Resumes des Travaux. Oceanographie
0078-2157 Nouveautes Techniques Maritimes†
0078-2165 Nouvelle Bibliotheque Nervalienne
0078-2211 Nouvelles Economiques
0078-2238 Nova Hedwiga, Beihefte
0078-2246 Nova Kepleriana. Neue Folge
0078-2254 Instituto de Investigacao Agronomica de Angola. Relatorio
0078-2262 Instituto de Investigacao Agronomica de Angola. Serie Cientifica
0078-2270 Instituto de Investigacao Agronomica de Angola. Serie Tecnica
0078-2300 Nova Scotia Community Planning Conference Proceedings†
0078-2319 Nova Scotia. Department of Bacteriology. Annual Report†
0078-2351 Nova Scotia. Department of Pathology. Annual Report†
0078-236X Nova Scotia. Department of Public Health. Nutrition Division. Annual Report
0078-2378 Nova Scotia. Emergency Measures Organization. Report†
0078-2386 Nova Scotia Fruit Growers Association. Annual Report and Proceedings
0078-2459 Nova Scotia Power Corporation. Annual Report
0078-2483 Nova Scotia Research Foundation. Bulletin†
0078-2491 Nova Scotia Technical College. School of Architecture. Report Series *changed to* Technical University of Nova Scotia. School of Architecture. Report Series
0078-2521 Nova Scotian Institute of Science. Proceedings
0078-253X Novarien
0078-2564 Novos Taxa Entomologicos†
0078-2602 Nuclear Medicine Seminar†
0078-2653 Nuernberger Forschungen
0078-2696 Numismatic Chronicle and Journal
0078-270X Numismatic Literature. Supplement†
0078-2718 Numismatic Notes and Monographs
0078-2726 Numismatica Moravica
0078-2734 Numismatiska Meddelanden
0078-2742 Nuntiaturberichte aus Deutschland Nebst Ergaenzenden Aktenstuecken
0078-2769 Nuovi Saggi
0078-2777 Stadtbibliothek Nuernberg. Ausstellungskatalog
0078-2785 Beitraege zur Geschichte und Kultur der Stadt Nuernberg
0078-2807 SIN-Staedtebauinstitut. Schriftenreihe
0078-2815 SIN-Staedtebauinstitut. Studienhefte
0078-2823 SIN-Staedtebauinstitut. Werkberichte
0078-2831 Nursing Education Monographs†
0078-284X Nutrition News in Zambia
0078-2858 Nyelveszeti Tanulmanyok
0078-2866 Nyelvtudomanyi Ertekezesek
0078-2874 O. I. G. G.†
0078-2882 O.P. Market
0078-2890 Oak Ridge Associated Universities. Medical Division. Research Report *changed to* Oak Ridge Associated Universities. Medical and Health Sciences Division. Research Report
0078-2904 Oak Ridge Associated Universities. Report *changed to* Oak Ridge Associated Universities. Annual Report
0078-2920 Oberhessische Gesellschaft fuer Natur- und Heilkunde, Giessen. Berichte
0078-2939 Oberrheinische Geologische Abhandlungen
0078-2947 Oberrheinischer Geologischer Verein. Jahresberichte und Mitteilungen
0078-2955 Objecta
0078-2963 Obraz Literatury Polskiej
0078-3005 Occasional Papers in Anthropology
0078-3013 Occasional Papers in Economic and Social History
0078-303X Occasional Papers in English Local History
0078-3048 Occasional Papers in Estate Management
0078-3056 Occasional Papers in Geography
0078-3064 Occasional Papers in Industrial Relations
0078-3072 Occasional Papers in International Affairs *changed to* Harvard Studies in International Affairs
0078-3080 Occasional Papers in Librarianship†
0078-3099 Occasional Papers in Modern Languages
0078-3129 Occupational Safety and Health Series
0078-3137 Ocean Engineering Information Series
0078-3153 Ocean Technology†
0078-3161 Oceana Docket Classics†
0078-317X Oceana Docket Series†
0078-3188 Oceanic Linguistics. Special Publications
0078-320X Oceanographic Research Institute, Durban. Investigational Report
0078-3218 Oceanography and Marine Biology: an Annual Review
0078-3226 Elsevier Oceanography Series
0078-3234 Oceanologia
0078-3250 Ochrona Przyrody
0078-3269 Octagon Lectures†
0078-3277 Odense University Slavic Studies
0078-3285 Odense University Studies in Art History
0078-3293 Odense University Studies in English
0078-3307 Odense University Studies in History and Social Sciences
0078-3315 Odense University Studies in Linguistics
0078-3323 Odense University Studies in Literature
0078-3331 Odense University Studies in Scandinavian Languages and Literatures
0078-3358 Odontologiska Samfundet i Finland. Aarsbok
0078-3366 Odrodzenie w Polsce†
0078-3374 O'Dwyer's Directory of Public Relations Firms
0078-3390 Oekonometrie und Unternehmensforschung
0078-3404 Oekonomische Studientexte *see* 0233-0946
0078-3412 Oenologie Pratique†
0078-3420 Oerlikon Schweissmitteilungen
0078-3439 Oesterreichisches Ost- und Suedosteuropa Institut. Schriftenreihe
0078-3455 Das Oesterreichische Buch
0078-3463 Oesterreichische Gesellschaft fuer Aussenpolitik und Internationale Beziehungen. Schriftenreihe†
0078-3471 Oesterreichische Gesellschaft fuer Musik. Beitraege
0078-3501 Oesterreichische Komponisten des 20. Jahrhunderts
0078-351X Oesterreichische Moorforschung†
0078-3528 Oesterreichische Nationalbank. Bericht ueber das Geschaeftsjahr mit Rechnungsabschluss
0078-3536 Oesterreichische Schriften zur Entwicklungshilfe
0078-3544 Oesterreichische Schul-Statistik†
0078-3552 Oesterreichische Zeitschrift fuer Oeffentliches Recht. Supplement *see* 0173-1718
0078-3560 Oesterreichischer Buchklub der Jugend. Jahrbuch
0078-3579 Oesterreichisches Archaeologisches Institut. Jahreshefte: Grabungen *changed to* Oesterreichisches Archaeologisches Institut. Jahreshefte
0078-3595 Oesterreichisches Wirtschaftsinstitut fuer Strukturforschung und Strukturpolitik. Schriftenreihe
0078-3617 Oesterreichisches Institut fuer Raumplanung. Taetigkeitsbericht
0078-3625 Oesterreichisches Institut fuer Raumplanung. Veroeffentlichungen *changed to* Oesterreichisches Institut fuer Raumplanung. Oeir-Forum
0078-3692 Offshore Europe†
0078-3706 Off-Shore Technology Conference. Record
0078-3714 Offa-Jahrbuch; Vor- und Fruehgeschichte
0078-3722 Office des Communications Sociales, Montreal. Cahiers d'Etudes et de Recherches
0078-3730 Office des Communications Sociales, Montreal. Selection de Films pour Cine Clubs. *changed to* Office des Communications Sociales, Montreal. Selection de Films en 16 MM
0078-3749 Rydge's Office Equipment Buyers Guide†
0078-3773 France. Office National d'Etudes et de Recherches Aerospatiales. Activities
0078-3781 France. Office National d'Etudes et de Recherches Aerospatiales. Notes Techniques
0078-379X France. Office National d'Etudes et de Recherches Aerospatiales. Publications
0078-3803 Office Universitaire de Recherche Socialiste. Cahiers
0078-382X Official American Basketball Association Guide†
0078-3838 Official Baseball Guide
0078-3846 Official Baseball Rules
0078-3862 Official National Basketball Association Guide
0078-3897 Official Touring Guide to East Africa *changed to* A A Guide to Motoring in Kenya
0078-3900 Official World Series Records†
0078-3919 Official Directory of the Catholic Church of Australia and Papua-New Guinea, New Zealand and the Pacific Islands *changed to* Official Directory of the Catholic Church of Australia and New Zealand
0078-3927 Official Year Book of the Commonwealth of Australia *changed to* Australia. Bureau of Statistics. Year Book Australia
0078-3943 D C C - Camping Fuehrer Europa
0078-3951 Ohio Agricultural Research and Development Center, Wooster. Research Bulletin
0078-396X Ohio Agricultural Research and Development Center, Wooster. Research Circular
0078-3978 Ohio Agricultural Research and Development Center, Wooster. Research Summary†
0078-3986 Ohio Biological Survey. Biological Notes
0078-3994 Ohio Biological Survey. Bulletin. New Series
0078-4001 Ohio. Division of State Personnel. Annual Report
0078-401X Ohio. Division of Mines. Report *changed to* Report on Ohio Mineral Industries
0078-4028 Ohio Fish Monographs *see* 0085-4468
0078-4036 Ohio Game Monographs *see* 0085-4468
0078-4044 Ohio Valley Philosophy of Education Society. Proceedings of the Annual Meeting *see* 0160-7561
0078-4052 Ohio Speech Journal
0078-4087 Ohio State University. College of Administrative Science. Monograph†
0078-4095 Ohio State University. College of Law. Law Forum Series
0078-4109 Ohio State University. Disaster Research Center. D R C - T R *see* 0164-1875
0078-4133 Ohio State University. Disaster Research Center. Report Series *changed to* University of Delaware Disaster Research Center. Report Series
0078-415X Ohio State University. Institute of Polar Studies. Report Series
0078-4184 Kent State University. Center for Business and Economic Research. Comparative Administration Research Institute Series†
0078-4192 Kent State University. Center for Business and Economic Research. Labor and Industrial Relations Series†
0078-4206 Kent State University. Center for Business and Economic Research. Printed Series†
0078-4214 Kent State University. Center for Business and Economic Research. Research Papers†
0078-4222 Kent State University. Libraries. Occasional Paper†
0078-4265 Oikos. Supplementum†
0078-429X Okayama University. Research Laboratory for Surface Science. Reports
0078-4303 Oklahoma Academy of Science. Proceedings
0078-4311 Oklahoma Academy of Science. Annals†
0078-432X Oklahoma Anthropological Society. Bulletin
0078-4338 Oklahoma Anthropological Society. Newsletter
0078-4362 Oklahoma. Department of Institutions, Social and Rehabilitative Services. Annual Report *changed to* Oklahoma. Department of Human Services. Annual Report
0078-4370 Oklahoma. Fishery Research Laboratory, Norman. Bulletin†
0078-4389 Oklahoma. Geological Survey. Bulletin
0078-4397 Oklahoma. Geological Survey. Circular
0078-4400 Oklahoma. Geological Survey. Guidebook
0078-4427 Oklahoma State University. College of Business Administration. Extension Service. Business Papers *changed to* Oklahoma State University. College of Business Administration. Working Papers
0078-4435 University of Oklahoma. Center for Economic and Management Research. Monograph Series†
0078-4508 Oklahoma. Grand River Dam Authority. Annual Report
0078-4516 Old Farmer's Almanac
0078-4540 Old Salem Gleaner
0078-4559 Old Sturbridge Village Booklet Series†
0078-4583 Wyzsza Szkola Rolnicza, Olsztyn. Zeszyty Naukowe *see* 0860-2832
0078-4591 Ombres de l'Histoire
0078-4605 Official Baseball Record Book *changed to* Complete Baseball Record Book
0078-463X Onoma
0078-4648 Onomastica
0078-4664 Ontario. Agricultural Research Institute. Report
0078-4672 Ontario Archaeology
0078-4680 Ontario Association for Curriculum Development. Annual Conference (Report)
0078-4699 Ontario Cancer Treatment and Research Foundation. Annual Report *see* 0315-9884
0078-4702 Ontario Catholic Directory
0078-4745 Ontario. Ministry of Transportation and Communications. Research and Development Division. Research Report†
0078-4753 Ontario. Division of Forests. Research Library. Research Report *see* 0704-2809
0078-4826 Ontario Federation of Labour. Report of Proceedings†
0078-4834 Ontario Field Biologist
0078-4850 Ontario Geography
0078-4869 Ontario Historical Society. Bulletin
0078-4885 Ontario. Ministry of Municipal Affairs and Housing. Annual Report
0078-4893 Ontario. Ministry of the Environment. Industrial Waste Conference. Proceedings
0078-5032 Ontario Joint Highway Research Programme. Report *see* 0078-4745
0078-5059 Ontario. Ministry of Natural Resources. Petroleum Resources Branch. Drilling and Production Report, Oil and Natural Gas *changed to* Ontario. Ministry of Natural Resources. Petroleum Resources Lab. Drilling and Production Report, Oil and Natural Gas

ISSN INDEX

ISSN	Title
0078-5067	Ontario Planning *changed to* Community Ontario
0078-5083	Ontario Research Foundation. Annual Report
0078-5091	Champlain Society. Ontario Series
0078-5105	Ontario Speech and Hearing Association. Journal†
0078-5113	Ontario Statistical Review *changed to* Ontario Statistics
0078-5148	Ontario. Ministry of the Environment. Pollution Control Branch. Research Publication
0078-5156	Ontario. Ministry of the Environment. Ground Water Bulletin
0078-5164	Open Door International for the Emancipation of the Woman Worker. Report of Congress
0078-5172	Open Doors
0078-5237	Opera Botanica
0078-5245	Opera Lilloana
0078-5261	C O R S I Bulletin
0078-5318	Operations Research - Verfahren
0078-5326	Ophelia
0078-5334	Ophthalmological Societies of the United Kingdom. Transactions
0078-5342	Ophthalmological Society of Egypt. Bulletin
0078-5385	Wyzsza Szkola Pedagogiczna, Opole. Zeszyty Naukowe. Seria A. Fizyka
0078-5393	Wyzsza Szkola Pedagogiczna, Opole. Zeszyty Naukowe. Seria A. Historia
0078-5407	Wyzsza Szkola Pedagogiczna, Opole. Zeszyty Naukowe. Seria A. Historia Literatury *see* 0324-9050
0078-5415	Wyzsza Szkola Pedagogiczna, Opole. Zeszyty Naukowe. Seria A. Historia Slaska†
0078-5423	Wyzsza Szkola Pedagogiczna, Opole. Zeszyty Naukowe. Seria A. Jezykoznawstwo
0078-5431	Wyzsza Szkola Pedagogiczna, Opole. Zeszyty Naukowe. Seria A. Matematyka
0078-544X	Wyzsza Szkola Pedagogiczna, Opole. Zeszyty Naukowe. Seria B. Studia i Monografie
0078-5458	Opportunities Abroad for Teachers *changed to* U.S. Department of Education. Opportunities for Teachers Abroad
0078-5466	Optica Applicata
0078-5474	Optical Industry and Systems Directory *see* 0191-0647
0078-5482	Optical Physics and Engineering
0078-5504	Optics and Spectroscopy. Supplement
0078-5512	Optik und Feinmechanik in Einzeldarstellungen†
0078-5520	Opuscula Atheniensia
0078-5539	Opuscula - aus Wissenschaft und Dichtung
0078-5547	Orange Free State. Director of Hospital Services. Report
0078-5555	Orbis Antiquus
0078-5563	Orbis Artium†
0078-5571	Orbis Pictus†
0078-5598	Dictionnaire National des Architectes
0078-5601	Ordre des Geometres-Experts. Annuaire
0078-5644	Oregon Research Institute. Research Bulletins†
0078-5652	Oregon Research Institute. Research Monographs†
0078-5679	Oregon School Directory
0078-5709	Oregon. State Department of Geology and Mineral Industries. Bulletin
0078-5717	Oregon. State Department of Geology and Mineral Industries. G M I Short Papers†
0078-5725	Oregon. State Department of Geology and Mineral Industries. Miscellaneous Papers†
0078-5733	Oregon. State Department of Geology and Mineral Industries. Miscellaneous Publications†
0078-5741	Oregon. State Department of Geology and Mineral Industries. Oil and Gas Investigations
0078-575X	Oregon State Plan for the Construction and Modernization of Hospitals, Public Health Centers and Medical Facilities†
0078-5768	Oregon State Monographs. Bibliographic Series
0078-5776	Oregon State Monographs. Studies in Botany†
0078-5784	Oregon State Monographs. Studies in Economics†
0078-5792	Oregon State Monographs. Studies in Education and Guidance†
0078-5806	Oregon State Monographs. Studies in Entomology†
0078-5814	Oregon State Monographs. Studies in Geology†
0078-5822	Oregon State Monographs. Studies in History†
0078-5830	Oregon State Monographs. Studies in Zoology†
0078-5849	Oregon State University. Water Resources Research Institute. Water Research Summary†
0078-5865	Oregon State University. Forest Research Laboratory. Annual Report *changed to* Oregon State University. Forest Research Laboratory. Biennial Report
0078-5903	Oregon State University. Forest Research Laboratory. Research Bulletin
0078-5911	Oregon State University. Forest Research Laboratory. Research Note
0078-592X	Oregon State University. Forest Research Laboratory. Research Paper
0078-5938	Oregon State University. School of Engineering. Graduate Research and Education†
0078-5946	Oregon State University. School of Engineering. Research Activities†
0078-5962	University of Oregon. Bureau of Business Research. Research Studies†
0078-5970	University of Oregon. Bureau of Governmental Research and Service. Information Bulletin†
0078-5989	University of Oregon. Bureau of Governmental Research and Service. Legal Bulletin†
0078-5997	University of Oregon. Bureau of Governmental Research and Service. Local Government Notes and Information: Policy and Practice Series†
0078-6004	University of Oregon. Center for the Advanced Study of Educationl Administration. Monographs *changed to* University of Oregon. Center for Educational Policy and Management. Monographs
0078-6012	University of Oregon. Center for the Advanced Study of Educational Administration. Occasional Papers *changed to* University of Oregon. Center for Educational Policy and Management. Occasional Papers
0078-6020	University of Oregon. Center for Educational Policy and Management. Technical Reports†
0078-6039	University of Oregon. Library. Occasional Paper†
0078-6047	University of Oregon. Museum of Natural History. Bulletin†
0078-6063	University of Oregon. Bureau of Business Research. Business Publications†
0078-6071	University of Oregon Anthropological Papers
0078-608X	Orestes Brownson Series on Contemporary Thought and Affairs†
0078-6098	Organ Yearbook
0078-611X	Organic Chemistry
0078-6128	Organic Directory†
0078-6136	Organic Electronic Spectral Data
0078-6144	Organic Photochemical Syntheses†
0078-6152	Organic Photochemistry: A Series of Advances
0078-6160	Organic Reaction Mechanisms. Annual Survey
0078-6179	Organic Reactions
0078-6187	Organic Substances of Natural Origin†
0078-6209	Organic Syntheses
0078-6217	Organic Syntheses Collective Volumes†
0078-6225	Organische Chemie in Einzeldarstellungen
0078-6233	Afro-Asian Peoples' Solidarity Organization. Council. Documents of the Session
0078-6241	Review of Fisheries in O.E.C.D. Member Countries
0078-625X	Organization for Economic Cooperation and Development. Nuclear Energy Agency. Activity Report
0078-6276	O E C D High Temperature Reactor Project Dragon†
0078-6284	O.E.C.D. Halden Reactor Project†
0078-6292	List of Research Institutes and Scientists in O. E. C. D. Member Countries†
0078-6306	O A U Review†
0078-6322	Organization of American States. Department of Scientific Affairs. Serie de Fisica: Monografias
0078-6330	Organization of American States. Department of Scientific Affairs. Serie de Matematica: Monografias
0078-6357	Organization of American States. Department of Cultural Affairs. Cuadernos Bibliotecologicos†
0078-6373	Organization of American States. Department of Cultural Affairs. Estudios Bibliotecarios†
0078-6381	Organization of American States. Department of Cultural Affairs. Manuales del Bibliotecario
0078-6403	O A S. General Secretariat. Annual Report
0078-642X	Organization of American States. Official Records. Indice y Lista General
0078-6438	Organization of American States. Permanent Council. Decisions Taken at Meetings (Cumulated Edition)
0078-6489	Organometallic Compounds of the Group IV Elements†
0078-6497	Organometallic Reactions Series *changed to* Organometallic Reactions and Syntheses
0078-6500	Organon
0078-6527	Oriens
0078-6543	Oriental Notes and Studies
0078-6551	Oriental Studies
0078-656X	Orientalia Gothoburgensia
0078-6578	Orientalia Suecana
0078-6586	Original Manuscript Music for Wind and Percussion Instruments†
0078-6594	Ornithological Monographs
0078-6608	Orthodontie Francaise
0078-6624	Orton Society. Bulletin. *see* 0474-7534
0078-6632	Center for Adult Diseases, Osaka. Annual Report
0078-6640	Osaka City University Economic Review
0078-6659	Osaka City University. Faculty of Engineering. Memoirs
0078-6667	Osaka Medical School, Takatsuki. Bulletin. Supplement†
0078-6675	Osaka Museum of Natural History. Bulletin
0078-6683	Osaka Museum of Natural History. Occasional Papers
0078-6691	Osaka University Dental Society. Journal
0078-6705	Osaka University. Institute for Protein Research. Memoirs
0078-6713	Norges Veterinaerhoegskole. Aarsberetning†
0078-6721	Norges Veterinaerhoegskole. Publikasjoner
0078-673X	Norway. Statens Institutt for Alkoholforskning. Skrifter
0078-6748	Universitetet i Oslo. Etnografiske Museum. Aarbok†
0078-6764	Universitetet i Oslo. Institutt for Bibelvitenskap. Smaarskrifter†
0078-6772	Universitetet i Oslo. Institutett for Statsvitenskap. Skrifter†
0078-6780	Physica Mathematica Universitatis Osloensis†
0078-6799	Osram-Gesellschaft. Technisch-Wissenschaftliche Abhandlungen†
0078-6810	Ost-West Paedagogik†
0078-6845	Ostbairische Grenzmarken
0078-687X	Osteuropa Institut, Munich. Veroeffentlichungen. Reihe Geschichte
0078-6888	Osteuropastudien der Hochschulen des Landes Hessen. Reihe 1. Giessener Abhandlungen zur Agrar- und Wirtschaftsforschung des Europaeischen Ostens†
0078-6896	Ostpanorama
0078-690X	Otago Geographer
0078-6918	Otago Law Review
0078-6926	Other Lands, Other Peoples†
0078-6950	Victoria, British Columbia. Dominion Astrophysical Observatory. Publications
0078-6977	National Gallery of Canada. Annual Review *see* 0711-2866
0078-6985	National Gallery of Canada. Library. Canadiana in the Library of the National Gallery of Canada: Supplement†
0078-6993	National Gallery of Canada. Library. Checklist of Canadian Artists Files *changed to* Artists in Canada: Union List of Artists Files
0078-7000	National Library of Canada. Annual Report
0078-7035	Ou Monter a Cheval
0078-7094	Outline of Japanese Tax
0078-7108	Overseas Development Council. Monograph Series†
0078-7116	O D I Review *changed to* Development Policy Review
0078-7124	Overseas Directories, Who's Who, Press Guides, Year Books and Overseas Periodical Subscriptions
0078-7132	Overseas Media Guide *changed to* O P M A Overseas Media Guide
0078-7159	Overseas Newspapers and Periodicals
0078-7167	Owen's Commerce and Travel and International Register *changed to* Owen's Business Directory and Travel Guide
0078-7175	Oxford Bibliographical Society. Occasional Publications
0078-7183	Oxford Bibliographical Society. Publications. New Series
0078-7191	Oxford German Studies
0078-7264	Oxford Studies of Composers
0078-7272	Oxford Theological Monographs
0078-7353	P A S Reporter†
0078-7388	P I/L T; Occasional Papers on Programmed Instruction and Language Teaching†
0078-740X	Pacific Anthropological Records
0078-7418	Pacific Anthropologists†
0078-7426	Pacific Botanists†
0078-7442	Pacific Coast Obstetrical and Gynecological Society. Transactions
0078-7469	Pacific Coast Philology
0078-7507	Pacific History Series†
0078-7515	Pacific Insects Monographs†
0078-7523	Pacific Islands Year Book
0078-7531	Pacific Linguistics. Series A: Occasional Papers
0078-754X	Pacific Linguistics. Series B: Monographs
0078-7558	Pacific Linguistics. Series C: Books
0078-7566	Pacific Linguistics. Series D: Special Publications
0078-7574	Pacific Marine Fisheries Commission. Annual Report
0078-7582	Pacific Marine Fisheries Commission. Bulletin
0078-7590	Pacific Marine Fisheries Commission. Newsletter

1398 ISSN INDEX

0078-7612 Pacific Northwest Conference on Foreign Languages. Proceedings *see* 0277-0598
0078-7620 Pacific Northwest Conference on Higher Education. Proceedings†
0078-7647 Pacific Science Association. Congress Proceedings *changed to* Pacific Science Association. Congress and Inter-Congress Proceedings
0078-7663 Pacific Trollers Association Newsletter
0078-768X Packaging Directory
0078-7698 Packaging Machinery Manufacturers Institute. Official Packaging Machinery Directory
0078-7701 Papua New Guinea. National Statistical Office. Rural Industries
0078-771X Universita degli Studi di Padova. Centro per la Storia della Tradizione Artistotelica nel Veneto. Saggi e Testi
0078-7728 Universita degli Studi di Padova. Facolta di Lettere e Filosofia. Opuscoli Accademici
0078-7736 Universita degli Studi di Padova. Facolta di Lettere e Filosofia. Pubblicazioni
0078-7744 Universita degli Studi di Padova Istituto di Storia Antica. Pubblicazioni
0078-7752 Universita degli Studi di Padova. Istituto per la Storia. Contributi
0078-7760 Universita degli Studi di Padova. Istituto per la Storia. Quaderni
0078-7779 Universita degli Studi di Padova. Scuola di Perfezionamento in Filosofia. Pubblicazioni
0078-7787 Paedagogica Europaea *see* 0141-8211
0078-7795 Paediatrische Fortbildungskurse fuer die Praxis
0078-7809 Paideuma
0078-7817 Polymers Paint and Colour Year Book
0078-7833 Painting Holidays *changed to* Painting, Holidays and Activity
0078-785X Pakistan Annual Law Digest
0078-7868 Pakistan Archaeology
0078-7884 Pakistan Banking Directory
0078-7892 Pakistan Basic Facts
0078-7914 Pakistan. Central Bureau of Education. Educational Statistics Bulletin Series
0078-7922 Pakistan. Central Bureau of Education. Yearbook *see* 0078-8287
0078-7930 Pakistan Central Cotton Committee. Agricultural Survey Report
0078-7949 Pakistan Central Cotton Committee. Technological Bulletin. Series A
0078-7957 Pakistan Central Cotton Committee. Technological Bulletin. Series B
0078-7965 Pakistan. Central Statistical Office. Census of Electricity Undertakings†
0078-7973 Pakistan. Central Statistical Office. Consumer Price Index Numbers for Industrial Workers†
0078-8015 Pakistan. Central Statistical Office. Some Socio-Economic Trends†
0078-804X Pakistan Council of Scientific and Industrial Research. Report†
0078-8058 Pakistan Customs Tariff
0078-8082 Pakistan Economic Survey
0078-8090 Pakistan Export Directory
0078-8104 Pakistan. Export Promotion Bureau. Export Guide Series
0078-8112 Pakistan. Export Promotion Bureau. Fresh Fruits
0078-8139 Pakistan. Food and Agricultural Division. Yearbook of Agricultural Statistics *changed to* Pakistan. Food and Agriculture Division. Agricultural Statistics of Pakistan
0078-8147 Pakistan Forest Institute, Peshawar. Annual Progress Report
0078-8155 Pakistan. Geological Survey. Memoirs; Paleontologia Pakistanica
0078-8163 Pakistan. Geological Survey. Records
0078-8171 Pakistan Historical Society. Memoir
0078-818X Pakistan Historical Society. Proceedings of the Pakistan History Conference
0078-8198 Pakistan Industrial Credit and Investment Corporation. Annual Report
0078-8201 Pakistan Industrial Development Corporation. Report
0078-821X Pakistan Institute of Development Economics. Report
0078-8228 Pakistan Institute of Development Economics. Research Report
0078-8228 Pakistan Development Review
0078-8236 Pakistan Insurance Year Book
0078-8244 Pakistan Journal of Biological and Agricultural Sciences *changed to* Bangladesh Journal of Biological Sciences
0078-8252 Pakistan Leather Year Book†
0078-8287 Pakistan. Ministry of Education. Yearbook
0078-8295 Pakistan. Ministry of Finance. Basic Facts About the Budget *see* 0078-7892
0078-8309 Pakistan. Ministry of Finance. Budget in Brief *changed to* Pakistan. Finance Division. Budget in Brief
0078-8317 Pakistan. Ministry of Finance. Budget of the Central Government *changed to* Budget of the Government of Pakistan. Demands for Grants and Appropriations
0078-8325 Pakistan. Ministry of Finance. Economic Analysis of the Central Government *changed to* Pakistan. Finance Division. Economic Analysis of the Budget
0078-8333 Pakistan. National Assembly. Debates. Official Report
0078-8341 Pakistan National Bibliography
0078-835X Lists of P A N S Doc Bibliographies *changed to* Lists of P A S T I C Bibliographies
0078-8368 P A N S D O C Translations *changed to* P A S T I C Translations
0078-8376 Pakistan Nursing and Health Review
0078-8392 Pakistan. Office of the Economic Adviser. Government Sponsored Corporations and Other Institutions
0078-8406 Pakistan Philosophical Congress. Proceedings
0078-8414 Pakistan. Planning and Development Division. Development Programme
0078-8422 Pakistan Postage Stamps
0078-8430 Pakistan Science Conference. Proceedings
0078-8457 Pakistan Standards Institution. Report†
0078-8473 Pakistan Statistical Association. Proceedings
0078-8481 Pakistan. Survey of Pakistan. General Report
0078-849X Bangladesh Tea Board. Annual Review†
0078-8511 Pakistan Western Railway. Yearbook of Information *changed to* Pakistan Railways. Yearbook of Information
0078-852X Pakistan's Balance of Payments
0078-8538 Palaeoecology of Africa and the Surrounding Islands and Antarctica *see* 0168-6208
0078-8546 Palaeontographica Americana
0078-8554 Palaeontologia Africana
0078-8562 Palaeontologia Polonica
0078-8570 Paleoecologia†
0078-8589 New Zealand Geological Survey. Paleontological Bulletin
0078-8597 Paleontological Society. Memoir
0078-8600 Zentrales Geologisches Institut. Palaeontologische Abhandlungen†
0078-8619 Universita degli Studi di Palermo. Istituto di Entomologia Agraria. Bollettino *changed to* Phytophaga
0078-8627 Universita degli Studi di Palermo. Istituto di Filologia Greca. Quaderni†
0078-866X Pamietnik Slowianski
0078-8686 Universidad de Navarra. Instituto de Ciencias de la Educacion. Coleccion I C E *changed to* Universidad de Navarra. Facultad de Ciencias de la Educacion. Coleccion
0078-8708 Universidad de Navarra. Instituto de Estudios Superiores de la Empresa. Coleccion I E S E. Serie L *changed to* Coleccion la Empresa y su Entorno. Serie L
0078-8716 Universidad de Navarra. Instituto de Estudios Superiores de la Empresas. Coleccion I E S E. Serie AC *changed to* Coleccion la Empresa y Su Entorno. Serie A C
0078-8732 Universidad de Navarra. Escuela de Arquitectura. Coleccion de Arquitectura
0078-8740 Universidad de Navarra. Escuela de Bibliotecarias. Coleccion Bibliotecarias
0078-8759 Universidad de Navarra. Facultad de Derecho Canonico. Manuales: Derecho Canonico
0078-8767 Universidad de Navarra. Manuales: Derecho Notarial Espanol *changed to* Universidad de Navarra. Coleccion Manuales de Derecho
0078-8783 Universidad de Navarra. Facultad de Ciencias de la Informacion. Manuales: Periodismo
0078-8791 Pan American Federation of Engineering Societies. Bulletin
0078-8805 Pan American Highway Congresses. Final Acts†
0078-8813 Pan American Institute of Geography and History. Commission on History. Bibliografias
0078-8821 Pan American Institute of Geography and History. Commission on History. Guias†
0078-883X Pan American Institute of Geography and History. Commission on History. Historiografias Americanas
0078-8848 Pan American Institute of Geography and History. Commission on History. Historiadores de America
0078-8856 Pan American Institute of Geography and History. Commission on History. Monumentos Historicos y Arqueologicos
0078-8864 Pan American Medical Women's Alliance. Newsletter
0078-8899 Panama Canal Company. Meteorological and Hydrographic Branch. Climatological Data: Canal Zone and Panama†
0078-8902 Estadistica Panamena. Seccion 221. Movimento de Poblacion *see* 0378-6749
0078-8937 Panama. Direccion de Estadistica y Censo. Estadistica Panamena. Serie F. Industrias-Encuestas *see* 0378-2557
0078-897X Estadistica Panamena. Estadistica Electoral *see* 0250-4316
0078-8996 Panama en Cifras
0078-9038 Papermakers' and Merchants' Directory of All Nations *see* 0079-158X
0078-9054 Papers in Anthropology†
0078-9062 Papers in Australian Linguistics
0078-9070 Papers in Borneo Linguistics
0078-9100 Papers in International Studies: Africa Series *changed to* Monographs in International Studies: Africa Series
0078-9119 Papers in International Studies: Southeast Asia Series *changed to* Monographs in International Studies: Southeast Asia Series
0078-9127 Papers in Linguistics of Melanesia
0078-9135 Papers in New Guinea Linguistics
0078-9143 Papers in Philippine Linguistics
0078-9151 Papers in Public Administration
0078-916X Papers in Public Administration
0078-9178 Papers in South East Asian Linguistics
0078-9216 Papers on Modern Japan†
0078-9224 London School of Economics Papers in Soviet and East European Law, Economics and Politics†
0078-9232 Papiermusterheft†
0078-9259 Papua New Guinea. National Statistical Office. Statistical Bulletin: Capital Expenditure by Private Businesses
0078-9267 Papua New Guinea. Bureau of Statistics. Workers' Compensation Statistics *changed to* Papua New Guinea. National Statistical Office. Worker's Compensation Claims
0078-9283 Papua New Guinea. Bureau of Statistics. Private Overseas Investment†
0078-9291 Papua New Guinea. Bureau of Statistics. Overseas Trade Statistics *changed to* Papua New Guinea. National Statistical Office. International Trade Statistics
0078-9313 Papua New Guinea. National Statistical Office. Secondary Industries (Factories and Works). Preliminary Statement
0078-9321 Papua New Guinea. National Statistical Office. Rural Industries. Preliminary Statement
0078-933X Papua New Guinea. National Statistical Office. Secondary Industries
0078-9356 Papua New Guinea. Bureau of Statistics. Statistics of Religious Organisations†
0078-9372 Papua New Guinea. National Statistical Office. Taxation Statistics. Preliminary Bulletin
0078-9399 Papua New Guinea. Public Service Board. Report.
0078-9402 Papyrologica Bruxellensia
0078-9410 Papyrologica Coloniensia
0078-9429 Paralogue
0078-9437 Parapsychological Monographs
0078-947X Aeroports de Paris. Service Statistique. Statistique de Trafic
0078-9496 Paris - Bijoux Exportation
0078-950X Bureau Universitaire de Recherche Operationnelle. Cahiers
0078-9518 Societe de l'Ecole des Chartes. Memoires et Documents
0078-9534 Ecole Pratique des Hautes Etudes, Paris. Centre des Etudes Arctiques et Finno-Scandinaves. Contributions *changed to* Ecole des Hautes Etudes en Science Sociales. Centre des Etudes Arctiques et Finno-Scandinaves. Contributions
0078-9577 Sciences Humaines Africanistes
0078-9585 Ecole Pratique des Hautes Etudes, Paris. Centre d'Etudes des Techniques Economiques Modernes. Etudes et Memoires *changed to* Ecole des Hautes Etudes en Sciences Sociales. Centre des Techniques Economiques Modernes. Etudes et Memoires
0078-9593 Ecole Pratique des Hautes Etudes, Paris. Centre de Psychiatrie Sociale. Publications†
0078-9615 Ecole Pratique des Hautes Etudes, Paris. Centre de Sociologie Europeenne. Cahiers†
0078-9631 Ecole Pratique des Hautes Etudes, Paris. Division des Aires Culturelles. Congres et Colloques†
0078-964X Ecole Pratique des Hautes Etudes. Quatrieme Section. Historiques et Philologiques. Annuaire *changed to* Linet de la Quatrieme Section, Ecole Pratique Hautes Etudes
0078-9666 France. Imprimerie Nationale. Annuaire.
0078-9674 Institut de Recherches Agronomiques Tropicales et des Cultures Vivrieres. Bulletin Scientifique.†
0078-9682 Institut Oceanographique. Annales
0078-9704 Musee Guimet, Paris. Bibliotheque d'Etudes
0078-9712 Musee Guimet, Paris. Etude des Collections du Musee
0078-9720 Museum National d'Histoire Naturelle, Paris. Annuaire
0078-9739 Museum National d'Histoire Naturelle, Paris. Archives
0078-9747 Museum National d'Histoire Naturelle, Paris. Memoires. Nouvelle Serie. Serie A. Zoologie
0078-9755 Museum National d'Histoire Naturelle, Paris. Memoires. Nouvelle Serie. Serie B. Botanique

ISSN INDEX 1399

0078-9763 Musee National d'Histoire Naturelle, Paris. Memoires. Nouvelle Serie. Serie C. Sciences de la Terre
0078-9771 Museum National d'Histoire Naturelle, Paris. Memoires. Nouvelle Serie. Serie D. Sciences Physico-Chimiques
0078-9887 Universite de Paris. Faculte des Lettres et Sciences Humaines. Publications. Serie Acta
0078-9895 Universite de Paris. Faculte des Lettres et Sciences Humaines. Publications. Serie Recherches
0078-9909 Universite de Paris VI (Pierre et Marie Curie). Institut Henri Poincare. Seminaire Choquet. Initiation a l'Analyse†
0078-995X Institut d'Etudes Politiques de Paris. Livret†
0078-9968 Institut d'Etudes Slaves, Paris. Annuaire†
0078-9976 Institut d'Etudes Slaves, Paris. Bibliotheque Russe
0078-9984 Institut d'Etudes Slaves, Paris. Collection de Grammaires
0078-9992 Institut d'Etudes Slaves, Paris. Collection de Manuels
0079-0001 Institut d'Etudes Slaves, Paris. Collection Historique
0079-001X Institut d'Etudes Slaves, Paris. Textes
0079-0028 Institut d'Etudes Slaves, Paris. Travaux
0079-0036 Universite de Paris VI (Pierre et Marie Curie). Institut Henri Poincare. Seminaire Lions†
0079-0044 Parker Directory of Attorneys *see* 0196-6138
0079-0052 Parkes Library Pamphlets†
0079-0060 Parkinson's Disease and Related Disorders. Cumulative Bibliography†
0079-0079 Parkinson's Disease and Related Disorders: Citations from the Literature†
0079-0095 Parliament House Book
0079-0117 Partners in Learning
0079-0125 Passaic County Dental Society. Bulletin *changed to* Passaic County Dental Society Newsletter
0079-0133 Passenger Transport in Great Britain *changed to* Transport Statistics Great Britain
0079-0141 Pastoral Psychology Series†
0079-015X Patent and Trademark Institute of Canada. Annual Proceedings
0079-0168 Patent Law Review *see* 0193-4864
0079-0184 Pathology Annual
0079-0206 Patterns of Literary Criticism†
0079-0214 Patterns of Religious Commitment†
0079-0230 Patterson's American Education
0079-0249 Paul Anthony Brick Lectures
0079-0257 Paul Carus Lectures
0079-0265 Universita degli Studi di Pavia. Istituto Botanico. Atti
0079-0273 Paving Conference. Proceedings. *changed to* Paving and Transportation Conference. Proceedings.
0079-0281 Pax Romana
0079-029X Peabody Museum of Archaeology and Ethnology. Memoirs
0079-0303 Peabody Museum of Archaeology and Ethnology. Papers
0079-032X Peabody Museum of Natural History. Bulletin
0079-0338 Peabody Museum of Natural History. Special Publication
0079-0354 Pearce-Sellards Series
0079-0362 Pears Cyclopaedia
0079-0370 Paedagogica Belgica Academica
0079-0400 Pediatrics; a Medical World News Publication†
0079-0435 Marine Research in Indonesia
0079-0451 Penn State Studies
0079-046X Pennsylvania Crop and Livestock Annual Summary
0079-0478 Pennsylvania Crop Reporting Service. C.R.S. *see* 0079-046X
0079-0486 P.E.L. State Bulletin†
0079-0494 Indiana University of Pennsylvania. Annual Research Bulletin†
0079-0508 Pennsylvania School Study Council. Reports
0079-0524 Millersville State College. Contributions to Research: Faculty and Student Publications†
0079-0540 Pennsylvania State University. College of Business Administration. Center for Research. Occasional Papers†
0079-0567 Pennsylvania State University. College of Engineering. Engineering Research Bulletin†
0079-0583 Pennsylvania State University. Council on Research. Research Publications and Other Contributions *see* 0093-7568
0079-0591 Pennsylvania State University. Earth and Mineral Sciences Experiment Station. Bulletin†
0079-0605 Pennsylvania State University. Earth and Mineral Sciences Experiment Station. Bulletin. Mineral Conservation Series. Paper *changed to* Pennsylvania State University. Earth and Mineral Sciences Experiment Station. Technical Papers.
0079-0613 Pennsylvania State University. Earth and Mineral Sciences Experiment Station. Circular†
0079-0621 Pennsylvania State University. Institute for Research on Land and Water Resources. Information Reports†
0079-063X Pennsylvania State University. Institute for Research on Land and Water Resources. Research Publication†
0079-0656 Pennsylvania State University. Libraries. Bibliographical Series
0079-0710 Penrose Annual†
0079-0729 People from the Past Series.
0079-0737 Peoples' Appalachia†
0079-0745 Peoria Academy of Science. Proceedings†
0079-0753 Peptides†
0079-0761 Per Jacobsson Foundation. Proceedings
0079-077X Per Jacobsson Memorial Lecture *see* 0079-0761
0079-0788 Performance Data on Architectural Acoustical Materials *changed to* Acoustical and Board Products. Bulletin
0079-0826 Pergamon Mathematical Tables Series†
0079-0834 Pergamon Series of Monographs in Laboratory Techniques†
0079-0842 Pergamon Series of Monographs on Furniture and Timber†
0079-0869 Pergamon Unified Engineering Series
0079-0877 Periodicals in East African Libraries: a Union List *changed to* Periodicals in Eastern African Libraries: a Union List
0079-0885 Periscope 2000†
0079-0893 Persica
0079-0907 Personal Income in Counties of New York State
0079-0931 Personality and Psychopathology
0079-0958 Perspecta; The Yale Architectural Journal
0079-0966 Perspective†
0079-0982 Perspectives de l'Economique. Serie 1. Fondateurs de l'Economie
0079-1008 Perspectives in Criticism†
0079-1016 Perspectives in Jewish Learning *see* 0196-2183
0079-1032 Perspectives in Powder Metallurgy *changed to* New Perspectives in Powder Metallurgy
0079-1040 Perspectives in Social Work†
0079-1059 Perspectives in Structural Chemistry†
0079-1067 Perth Observatory. Communications
0079-1075 Peru - Problema
0079-1083 Instituto Nacional de Enfermedades Neoplasicas. Trabajos de Investigacion Clinica y Experimental†
0079-1091 Sociedad Geologica del Peru. Boletin
0079-1148 Pesticide Review†
0079-1156 Petersen's Pro Football Annual *see* 0079-5526
0079-1288 Petroleum and Chemical Industry Technical Conference. Record *see* 0090-3507
0079-1296 Petroleum Refineries in Canada†
0079-130X Pets Welcome
0079-1334 Pflanzenschuetzer†
0079-1350 Phaenomenologica
0079-1369 Phanerogamarum Monographiae
0079-1393 Pharmaceutical Historian
0079-1407 Pharmacopeia of the United States of America *changed to* United States Pharmacopeia - National Formulary
0079-1423 Philippine Education Abstracts†
0079-1458 Philippine Men of Science†
0079-1466 Philippine Scientist
0079-1490 Philippines Nuclear Journal
0079-1504 Philippines. Board of Investments. Annual Report
0079-1512 Philippines. Bureau of Agricultural Economics. Crop, Livestock and Natural Resources Statistics *changed to* Philippines. Bureau of Agricultural Economics. Crop and Livestock Statistics
0079-1520 Philippines. Bureau of Agricultural Economics. Report
0079-1539 Philippines. Department of Commerce and Industry. Annual Report *changed to* Philippines. Ministry of Trade. Annual Report
0079-1547 Philippines. National Tax Research Center. Report
0079-158X Phillips' Paper Trade Directory - Europe-Mills of the World
0079-1598 Philologen-Jahrbuch
0079-1628 Philological Monographs
0079-1636 Philological Society Transactions
0079-1644 Philologische Beitraege zur Suedost- und Osteuropaforschung†
0079-1660 Philosophes Contemporains
0079-1679 Philosophes Medievaux
0079-1687 Philosophia Antiqua
0079-1695 Philosophical Society of the Sudan. Proceedings of the Annual Conference
0079-1717 Philosophische Studientexte *see* 0233-089X
0079-1733 Philosophy of Education Society. Proceedings of the Annual Meetings
0079-1768 Phineas L. Windsor Lecture in Librarianship†
0079-1776 Phoenix†
0079-1784 Phoenix. Supplementary Volumes
0079-1806 Photochemistry (Oxford)
0079-1814 Photoelectric Spectrometry Group Bulletin *see* 0144-2317
0079-1830 Photographis
0079-1849 Photography Annual†
0079-1857 Photography Directory and Buying Guide *changed to* Photography Buyers Guide
0079-1865 Photography Year Book
0079-1873 Physical Acoustics: Principles and Methods
0079-1881 Physical Chemistry
0079-189X Physical Education Around the World. Monograph
0079-1903 Physical Education Association of Great Britain and Northern Ireland. Report†
0079-1911 Physical Education Year Book†
0079-1938 Physics and Chemistry in Space
0079-1946 Physics and Chemistry of the Earth
0079-1954 Physics and Chemistry of the Organic Solid State†
0079-1970 Physics of Thin Films; Advances in Research and Development
0079-1989 Physik und Technik†
0079-1997 Physikalisch-Chemische Trenn- und Messmethoden
0079-2004 Physikalisch-Medizinische Sozietaet Erlangen. Sitzungsberichte
0079-2012 Physiologia Plantarum. Supplementum†
0079-2020 Physiological Society. Monographs
0079-2047 Phyton. Annales Rei Botanicae
0079-2055 Pianeta Fresco
0079-2063 Pick's Currency Yearbook *see* 0743-5363
0079-2071 Pilot Studies Approved for State Aid in Public School Systems in Virginia
0079-208X Pion Applied Physics Series
0079-211X Pisarze Slascy 19 i 20 Wieku
0079-2128 Pit and Quarry Handbook and Purchasing Guide *changed to* Pit & Quarry Handbook and Buyers Guide
0079-2144 Pittsburgh Studies in Library and Information Sciences†
0079-2179 L R D C News†
0079-2225 Plant Breeding Institute, Cambridge. Annual Report
0079-2233 Plant Monograph: Reprints†
0079-2241 Plant Physiology. Supplement Abstracts of Annual Meeting
0079-225X Plant Protection Abstracts. Supplement†
0079-2268 Plante et l'Homme
0079-2276 Planung und Kontrolle in der Unternehmung
0079-2284 Planungsstudien
0079-2306 Plastics, Paint and Rubber Buyers' Guide for S.A. *changed to* Plastics and Rubber Yearbook and Buyers' Guide of S.A.
0079-2314 Playfair Cricket Annual
0079-2322 Playfair Football Annual
0079-2349 Playthings Directory
0079-2373 Poche-Couleurs Larousse†
0079-2381 Pocket Book of Transport Statistics of India
0079-239X Australia. Bureau of Statistics. Pocket Compendium of Australian Statistics *see* 0705-0488
0079-2403 Pocket Data Book, USA
0079-2411 Pocket Digest of New Zealand Statistics
0079-242X Pocket Library of Studies in Art
0079-2438 Pocket Poets Series
0079-2446 Pocket Year Book of South Australia
0079-2462 Poesia
0079-2470 Poetes et Prosateurs du Portugal
0079-2500 Poeti e Prosatori Tedeschi
0079-2519 Poetry Eastwest†
0079-2527 Poetyka. Zarys Encyklopedyczny
0079-2535 Points. Films
0079-2543 Points for Emphasis; International Sunday School Lessons in Pocket Size
0079-256X Universite de Poitiers. Centre d'Etudes Superieures de Civilisation Medievale. Publications
0079-2608 Poland. Glowny Urzad Statystyczny. Maly Rocznik Statystyczny. Concise Statistical Yearbook
0079-2616 Poland. Glowny Urzad Statystyczny. Rocznik Demograficzny
0079-2640 Poland. Glowny Urzad Statystyczny. Rocznik Statystyczny Finansow. Yearbook of Finance Statistics
0079-2667 Poland. Glowny Urzad Statystyczny. Rocznik Statystyczny Gospodarki Morskiej. Yearbook of Sea Economy Statistics
0079-2675 Poland. Glowny Urzad Statystyczny. Rocznik Statystyczny Gornictwa. Yearbook of Mining Statistics
0079-2683 Poland. Glowny Urzad Statystyczny. Rocznik Statystyczny Handlu Wewnetrznego/Yearbook of International Trade Statistics
0079-2691 Poland. Glowny Urzad Statystyczny. Rocznik Statystyki Handlu Zagranicznego
0079-2705 Poland. Glowny Urzad Statystyczny. Rocznik Statystyczny Inwestycji i Srodkow Trwalych. Yearbook of Investment and Fixed Assets Statistics
0079-2721 Poland. Glowny Urzad Statystyczny. Rocznik Statystyczny Lesnictwa *changed to* Poland. Glowny Urzad Statystyczny. Rocznik Statystyczny Lesnictwa i Gospodarki Drewnem
0079-273X Poland. Glowny Urzad Statystyczny. Rocznik Statystyki Miedzynarodowej. Yearbook of International Statistics

ISSN INDEX

0079-2748 Poland. Glowny Urzad Statystyczny. Rocznik Statystyczny Ochrony Zdrowia. Yearbook of Public Health Statistics
0079-2756 Poland. Glowny Urzad Statystyczny. Rocznik Statystyczny Powiatow. Statistical Yearbook of Counties
0079-2764 Poland. Glowny Urzad Statystyczny. Rocznik Statystyczny Przemyslu. Yearbook of Industry Statistics
0079-2780 Poland. Glowny Urzad Statystyczny. Rocznik Statystyczny. Statistical Yearbook
0079-2799 Poland. Glowny Urzad Statystyczny. Rocznik Statystyczny Szkolnictwa. Yearbook of Education Statistics
0079-2802 Poland. Glowny Urzad Statystyczny. Rocznik Statystyczny Transportu. Yearbook of Transport Statistics
0079-2810 Poland. Glowny Urzad Statystyczny. Rolniczy Rocznik Statystyczny. Yearbook of Agricultural Statistics *changed to* Poland. Glowny Urzad Statystyczny. Rocznik Statystyczny Rolnictwa i Gospodarki Zywnosciowej. Yearbook of Agricultural Statistics
0079-2829 Poland. Glowny Urzad Statystyczny. Zeszyty Metodyczne
0079-2845 Poland. Glowny Urzad Statystyczny. Studia i Prace Statystyczne *changed to* Poland. Glowny Urzad Statystyczny. Statystyka Polski. Studia i Prace Statystyczne
0079-2861 Poland. Glowny Urzad Statystyczny. Uzytkowanie Gruntow i Powierzchnia Zasiewow Oraz Zwierzeta Gospodarskie *changed to* Poland. Glowny Urzad Statystyczny. Wyniki Spisu Rolniczego. Uzytkowanie Gruntow i Powierzchnia Zasiewow, oraz Zwierzeta Gospodarskie
0079-2896 Poland. Glowny Urzad Statystyczny. Zatrudnienie w Gospodarce Narodowej
0079-290X Poland. Glowny Urzad Statystyczny. Zwierzeta Gospodarskie. Livestock
0079-2918 Polar Notes†
0079-2926 Polemologische Studien†
0079-2950 Police Yearbook
0079-2985 Polish Journal of Soil Science
0079-2993 Polish Psychological Bulletin
0079-3000 Polish Round Table *see* 0208-7375
0079-3027 Politica
0079-3035 Political Handbook and Atlas of the World *changed to* Political Handbook of the World
0079-3043 Political Science Annual†
0079-3051 Maharaja Sayajirao University of Baroda. Political Science Series†
0079-3078 Politics†
0079-3094 Politics of Modernization Series†
0079-3108 Politique Belge†
0079-3116 Pollution Control Review *see* 0090-516X
0079-3124 K-W Probe†
0079-3132 Polonia Typographica Saeculi Sedecimi
0079-3140 Polska Akademia Nauk. Biblioteka, Krakow. Rocznik
0079-3159 Academie Polonaise des Sciences. Centre Scientifique, Paris. Conferences Conferenze
0079-3167 Conferenze
0079-3175 Polska Akademia Nauk. Centrum Obliczeniowe. Prace *changed to* Polish Academy of Sciences. Institute of Computer Science. Reports
0079-3183 Sredniowiecze. Studia o Kulturze†
0079-3205 Polska Akademia Nauk. Instytut Maszyn Przeplywowych. Prace
0079-323X Polish Academy of Sciences. Institute of Fundamental Technological Research. Scientific Activities
0079-3256 Polska Akademia Nauk. Oddzial w Krakowie. Komisja Archeologiczna. Prace
0079-3264 Polska Akademia Nauk. Oddzial w Krakowie. Komisja Ceramiczna. Prace: Ceramika
0079-3272 Polska Akademia Nauk. Oddzial w Krakowie. Komisja Filologii Klasycznej. Prace
0079-3280 Polska Akademia Nauk. Oddzial w Krakowie. Komisja Gorniczo-Geodezyjna. Prace: Gornictwo
0079-3299 Polska Akademia Nauk. Oddzial w Krakowie. Komisja Gorniczo-Geodezyjna. Prace: Geodezja
0079-3310 Polska Akademia Nauk. Oddzial w Krakowie. Komisja Jezykoznawstwa. Prace
0079-3329 Polska Akademia Nauk. Oddzial w Krakowie. Komisja Jezykoznawstwa. Wydawnictwa Zrodlowe
0079-3337 Polska Akademia Nauk. Oddzial w Krakowie. Komisja Mechaniki Stosowanej. Prace: Mechanika
0079-3345 Polska Akademia Nauk. Oddzial w Krakowie. Komisja Metalurgiczno-Odlewnicza. Prace: Metalurgia
0079-3353 Polska Akademia Nauk. Oddzial w Krakowie. Komisja Nauk Ekonomicznych. Prace
0079-3361 Prace Geologiczne
0079-337X Polska Akademia Nauk. Oddzial w Krakowie. Komisja Historycznoliteracka. Rocznik

0079-3388 Polska Akademia Nauk. Oddzial w Krakowie. Komisja Nauk Historycznych. Prace
0079-3396 Polska Akademia Nauk. Oddzial w Krakowie. Komisja Nauk Mineralogicznych. Prace Mineralogiczne
0079-340X Polska Akademia Nauk. Oddzial w Krakowie. Komisja Nauk Pedagogicznych. Prace
0079-3418 Polska Akademia Nauk. Oddzial w Krakowie. Komisja Nauk Pedagogicznych. Rocznik
0079-3426 Polska Akademia Nauk. Oddzial w Krakowie. Komisja Orientalistyczna. Prace
0079-3434 Polska Akademia Nauk. Oddzial w Krakowie. Komisja Slowianoznawstwa. Prace
0079-3442 Polska Akademia Nauk. Oddzial w Krakowie. Komisja Socjologiczna. Prace
0079-3450 Polska Akademia Nauk. Oddzial w Krakowie. Komisja Urbanistyki i Architektury. Teka
0079-3477 Polska Akademia Nauk. Komitet Gospodarki Wodnej. Prace i Studia
0079-3485 Prace Jezykoznawcze
0079-3493 Polska Akademia Nauk. Komitet Przestrzennego Zagospodarowania Kraju. Biuletyn
0079-3507 Polska Akademia Nauk. Komitet Przestrzennego Zagospodarowania Kraju. Studia
0079-3531 Polska Akademia Nauk. Oddzial w Krakowie. Rocznik
0079-354X Polska Akademia Nauk. Oddzial w Krakowie. Komisja Naukowych. Sprawozdania z Posiedzen
0079-3558 Polska Akademia Nauk. Wydzial Nauk Medycznych. Rozprawy
0079-3566 Academie Polonaise des Sciences. Centre d'Archeologie Mediterraneenne. Etudes et Travaux
0079-3574 Polska Akademia Nauk. Instytut Geofizyki. Materialy i Prace *see* 0137-2440
0079-3574 Polska Akademia Nauk. Instytut Geofizyki. Materialy i Prace *see* 0209-0406
0079-3574 Polska Akademia Nauk. Instytut Geofizyki. Materialy i Prace *see* 0208-8525
0079-3574 Polska Akademia Nauk. Instytut Geofizyki. Materialy i Prace *see* 0138-0125
0079-3574 Polska Akademia Nauk. Instytut Geofizyki. Materialy i Prace *see* 0138-0214
0079-3574 Polska Akademia Nauk. Instytut Geofizyki. Materialy i Prace *see* 0208-8061
0079-3574 Polska Akademia Nauk. Instytut Geofizyki. Materialy i Prace *see* 0138-015X
0079-3582 Polska Akademia Nauk. Centrum Badan Naukowych w Wojewodztwie Katowikim. Prace i Studia *see* 0208-4112
0079-3590 Polska Bibliografia Literacka
0079-3612 Polska Piesn i Muzyka Ludowa. Zrodla i Materialy
0079-3620 Polska 2000
0079-3647 Polskie Archiwum Weterynaryjne
0079-3655 Polskie Towarzystwo Cybernetyczne. Biuletyn *see* 0137-3595
0079-3663 Polskie Towarzystwo Geologiczne. Rocznik
0079-3698 Polskie Towarzystwo Matematyczne. Roczniki. Seria II. Wiadomosci Matematyczne
0079-3701 Mechanika Teoretyczna i Stosowana
0079-371X Polskie Towarzystwo Naukowe na Obczyznie. Rocznik
0079-3728 Polymer Engineering and Technology Series†
0079-3736 Polymer Reviews†
0079-3795 Pomologia Republicii Socialiste Romania†
0079-3809 University of Poona. Centre of Advanced Study in Sanskrit. Publications
0079-3825 Poor's Register of Corporations, Directors and Executives
0079-3833 Popes through History†
0079-3841 Popular Lectures in Mathematics Series†
0079-3868 Population Census of Papua New Guinea. Population Characteristics Bulletin Series
0079-3876 Population Council, New York. Country Profiles†
0079-3892 Population Council, New York. Reports on Population/Family Planning†
0079-3906 Population Estimates of Arizona *changed to* Demographic Guide to Arizona (Year)
0079-3914 Population Health Survey Research Bulletin†
0079-3922 University of California, Berkeley. Institute of International Studies. Population Monograph Series†
0079-3957 University of Port Elizabeth. Publications. General Series

0079-3965 University of Port Elizabeth. Publications. Research Papers
0079-3973 University of Port Elizabeth. Publications. Symposia and Seminars *changed to* University of Port Elizabeth. Publications. Symposia, Seminars, and Lectures
0079-3981 Port of Baltimore Handbook *changed to* Port of Baltimore Magazine
0079-399X Port of Piraeus Authority. Statistical Bulletin *changed to* Port of Piraeus Authority. Statistical Report
0079-4007 Port Phillip Authority. Annual Report
0079-4058 Universidade do Rio Grande do Sul. Instituto de Ciencias Naturais. Boletim *see* 0102-597X
0079-4066 Ports of the World†
0079-4082 Portugal. Instituto Nacional de Estatistica. Centro de Estudos Demograficos. Revista
0079-4104 Portugal. Instituto Nacional de Estatistica. Anuario Demografico. *changed to* Portugal. Instituto Nacional de Estatistica. Estatisticas Demograficas. Continente, Acores e Madeira
0079-4112 Portugal. Instituto Nacional de Estatistica. Anuario Estatistico *changed to* Portugal. Instituto Nacional de Estatistica. Anuario Estatistico. Continente, Acores e Madeira
0079-4120 Portugal. Instituto Nacional de Estatistica. Estatisticas das Contribucoes e Impostos *changed to* Portugal. Instituto Nacional de Estatistica. Estatisticas das Contribuicoes e Impostos. Continente, Acores e Madeira
0079-4139 Portugal. Instituto Nacional de Estatistica. Estatisticas Agricolas. Continente, Acores e Madeira
0079-4147 Portugal. Instituto Nacional de Estatistica. Estatisticas do Comercio Externo *changed to* Portugal. Instituto Nacional de Estatistica. Estatisticas do Comercio Externo. Continente, Acores e Madeira
0079-4155 Portugal. Instituto Nacional de Estatistica. Estatisticas de Educacao *changed to* Portugal. Instituto Nacional de Estatistica. Estatisticas de Educacao. Continente, Acores e Madeira
0079-4163 Portugal. Instituto Nacional de Estatistica. Estatisticas das Organizacoes Sindicais *see* 0870-6506
0079-418X Portugal. Estatisticas Industriais: Continente, Acores e Madeira. Volume 2: Industrias Transformadoras
0079-4201 Portugal. Ministerio das Financas. Relatorio do Orcamento Geral do Estado
0079-421X Portugiesische Forschungen der Goerresgesellschaft. Reihe 1: Aufsaetze zur Portugiesischen Kulturgeschichte
0079-4228 Portugiesische Forschungen der Goerresgesellschaft. Reihe 2: Monographien
0079-4236 Post-Medieval Archaeology
0079-4244 Postage Stamps of the United States *changed to* United States Postage Stamps
0079-4252 Postepy Mikrobiologii
0079-4260 Postepy Napedu Elektrycznego
0079-4279 Postepy Pediatrii
0079-4295 Postilla
0079-4309 Potato Marketing Board, London. Annual Report and Accounts
0079-4317 Abstracts of Theses and Dissertations Accepted for Higher Degrees in the Potchefstroom University for Christian Higher Education†
0079-4325 Union Catalogue of Theses and Dissertations of the South African Universities
0079-4333 Potchefstroom University for Christian Higher Education. Wetenskaplike Bydraes. Reeks A: Geesteswetenskappe
0079-4341 Potchefstroom University for Christian Higher Education. Wetenskaplike Bydraes. Reeks B: Natuurwetenskappe. Series
0079-4376 Museum fuer Ur- und Fruehgeschichte der Bezirke Potsdam, Frankfurt/Oder und Cottbus. Veroeffentlichungen
0079-4414 Power Conditioning Specialists Conference. Record *see* 0275-9306
0079-4422 Power Farming Technical Annual
0079-4430 Power Industry Computer Applications Conference. Record *see* 0018-9510
0079-4457 Power Sources Symposium. Proceedings
0079-4465 Powstanie Styczniowe. Materialy i Dokumenty
0079-4473 Politechnika Poznanska. Zeszyty Naukowe. Chemia *changed to* Politechnika Poznanska. Zeszyty Naukowe. Chemia i Inzynieria Chemiczna
0079-4481 Politechnika Poznanska. Materialy Historyczno-Metodyczne. Studia Filozoficzne *changed to* Materialy Historyczno-Metodyczne

ISSN INDEX 1401

0079-449X Politechnika Poznanska. Zeszyty Naukowe. Budownictwo Ladowe *changed to* Politechnika Poznanska. Zeszyty Naukowe. Budownictwo Ladowe
0079-4503 Politechnika Poznanska. Zeszyty Naukowe. Elektryka
0079-4511 Politechnika Poznanska. Zeszyty Naukowe. Fizyka†
0079-452X Politechnika Poznanska. Zeszyty Naukowe. Matematyka *see* 0044-4413
0079-4538 Politechnika Poznanska. Zeszyty Naukowe. Mechanika
0079-4546 Akademia Ekonomiczna, Poznan. Zeszyty Naukowe. Seria 1
0079-4554 Akademia Ekonomiczna, Poznan. Zeszyty Naukowe. Seria 2. Prace Habilitacyjne i Doktorskie
0079-4570 Societe des Amis des Sciences et des Lettres de Poznan. Bulletin. Serie D: Sciences Biologiques
0079-4589 Poznanskie Towarzystwo Przyjaciol Nauk. Komisja Automatyki. Prace *changed to* Studia z Automatyki
0079-4597 Poznanskie Towarzystwo Przyjaciol Nauk. Komisja Budownictwa i Architektury. Prace†
0079-4619 Poznanskie Towarzystwo Przyjaciol Nauk. Komisja Biologiczna. Prace
0079-4627 Poznanskie Towarzystwo Przyjaciol Nauk. Komisja Elektrotechniki. Prace†
0079-4635 Poznanskie Towarzystwo Przyjaciol Nauk. Komisja Filozoficzna. Prace
0079-4651 Poznanskie Towarzystwo Przyjaciol Nauk. Komisja Historyczna. Prace
0079-466X Poznanskie Towarzystwo Przyjaciol Nauk. Komisja Historii Sztuki. Prace
0079-4678 Poznanskie Towarzystwo Przyjaciol Nauk. Komisja Jezykoznawcza. Prace
0079-4708 Poznanskie Towarzystwo Przyjaciol Nauk. Komisja Nauk Rolniczych i Komisja Nauk Lesnych. Prace
0079-4716 Poznanskie Towarzystwo Przyjaciol Nauk. Komisja Nauk Spolecznych. Prace
0079-4724 Poznanskie Towarzystwo Przyjaciol Nauk. Komisja Technologii Drewna. Prace
0079-4740 Lingua Posnaniensis
0079-4759 Prace i Materialy Etnograficzne†
0079-4767 Prace Literackie†
0079-4775 Prace Onomastyczne
0079-4783 Prace Orientalistyczne
0079-4791 Prace Polonistyczne
0079-4805 Prace Popularnonaukowe *changed to* Prace Popularnonaukowe. Zabytki Polski Polnocnej
0079-4805 Prace Popularnonaukowe *changed to* Prace Popularnonaukowe. Biblioteczka Prawnicza
0079-4805 Prace Popularnonaukowe *changed to* Prace Popularnonaukowe. Ekonomia i Organizacja
0079-4821 Practical Table Series†
0079-4848 Praehistorische Zeitschrift
0079-4856 Prague Studies in Mathematical Linguistics†
0079-4872 Prakseologia
0079-4880 Praktische Betriebswirtschaft
0079-4899 Praktische Chirurgie
0079-4902 Prameny Ceske a Slovenske Lingvistiky. Rada Ceska
0079-4929 Pravnehistoricke Studie
0079-4937 Pravoslavny Theologicky Sbornik
0079-4945 Praxis der Klinischen Psychologie†
0079-4953 Prediction Annual
0079-4961 Predigtstudien
0079-497X Prehistoric Society, London. Proceedings
0079-4988 Preparative Inorganic Reactions†
0079-4996 Presbyterian Church in Canada. General Assembly. Acts and Proceedings
0079-502X Press Braille, Adult *see* 0277-5247
0079-5046 Press Radio and T.V. Guide
0079-5062 Pretoria College for Advanced Technical Education. Annual/Jaarblad†
0079-5089 Primary Socialization, Language, and Education†
0079-5100 Primates
0079-5127 Primatologia†
0079-5151 Prince Edward Island. Public Utilities Commission. Annual Report
0079-5178 Princeton-Cambridge Studies in Chinese Linguistics *changed to* Princeton-Cambridge Series in Chinese Linguistics
0079-5186 Princeton Essays in Literature.
0079-5194 Princeton Mathematical Series
0079-5208 Princeton Monographs in Art and Archaeology
0079-5216 Princeton Series in Physics
0079-5240 Princeton Studies in Mathematical Economics
0079-5259 Princeton Studies in Music
0079-5267 Princeton University. Center of International Studies Policy Memorandum
0079-5275 Princeton University. Committee for the Excavation of Antioch. Publications†
0079-5283 Princeton University. Computer Sciences Laboratory. Technical Report *changed to* Princeton University. Department of Computer Science. Technical Report
0079-5291 Princeton University. Econometric Research Program. Research Memorandum
0079-5305 Princeton University. Industrial Relations Section. Research Report
0079-5313 Prindle, Weber and Schmidt Complementary Series in Mathematics†
0079-5321 Printing Historical Society. Journal
0079-533X Printing Magazine Purchasing Guide†
0079-5348 Printing Trades Blue Book. New York Edition
0079-5356 Printing Trades Blue Book. Northeastern Edition
0079-5364 Printing Trades Blue Book. Southeastern Edition
0079-5372 Printing Trades Directory
0079-5399 Private Independent Schools
0079-5402 Private Press Books
0079-5453 Prize Stories; The O. Henry Awards
0079-550X Pro and Senior Hockey Guide *see* 0278-4955
0079-5518 Pro Basketball Guide *changed to* Basketball Guide
0079-5526 Pro Football (Los Angeles)
0079-5550 Pro Helvetia†
0079-5569 N.H.L. Pro Hockey
0079-5577 Pro Hockey Guide†
0079-5593 Pro Mundi Vita. Special Notes *changed to* Pro Mundi Vita Dossiers
0079-5607 Probability and Mathematical Statistics
0079-5615 Probation and Parole *see* 0278-1042
0079-5623 Probau
0079-5631 Probe
0079-564X Probleme der Festkoerperelektronik†
0079-5666 Problemes Actuels d'Endocrinologie et de Nutrition†
0079-5682 Problemi e Ricerche di Storia Antica
0079-5690 Problemi Economici d'Oggi†
0079-5704 Problems behind the Iron Curtain Series†
0079-5739 Problems in Mathematical Analysis Report†
0079-5763 Problems of the Contemporary World
0079-5771 Problems of the North†
0079-578X Problemy Ekonomiczne
0079-5798 Problemy Polonii Zagranicznej *changed to* Biblioteka Polonijna
0079-5801 Problemy Rad Narodowych. Studia i Materialy
0079-581X Problemy Rejonow Uprzemyslawianych
0079-5836 Prodei
0079-5852 Produccion Rural Argentina
0079-5860 Produce Marketing Association. Yearbook *changed to* Produce Marketing Almanac
0079-5879 Production et la Consommation de l'Electricite en Belgique. Annuaire Statistique. Statistisch Jaarboek
0079-5895 Producto Neto de la Agricultura Espanola
0079-5925 Professional and Trade Organisations in India
0079-5933 Professional School Psychology†
0079-595X Profitability of Cotton Growing in Israel
0079-5968 Profitability of Poultry Farming in Israel
0079-5976 Profitability of Sugarbeet Growing in Israel†
0079-5984 Profits†
0079-600X Programmed Learning and Teaching Machines; Bibliographical References
0079-6018 Accredited Programs in Journalism *changed to* Accredited Journalism and Mass Communication Education
0079-6026 Progress in Aeronautical Sciences *see* 0376-0421
0079-6034 Progress in Allergy
0079-6042 Progress in Analytical Chemistry†
0079-6050 Progress in Astronautics and Aeronautics Series
0079-6077 Progress in Bio-Organic Chemistry†
0079-6085 Progress in Biochemical Pharmacology
0079-6107 Progress in Biophysics and Molecular Biology
0079-6115 Progress in Boron Chemistry†
0079-614X Progress in Ceramic Science†
0079-6158 Progress in Chemical Toxicology
0079-6166 Progress in Clinical Cancer
0079-6174 Progress in Clinical Pathology
0079-6182 Progress in Clinical Psychology†
0079-6212 Progress in Control Engineering†
0079-6247 Progress in Elementary Particle and Cosmic Ray Physics†
0079-6255 Progress in Experimental Personality Research
0079-6263 Progress in Experimental Tumor Research
0079-6271 Progress in Gastroenterology†
0079-628X Progress in Geophysics†
0079-6298 Progress in Gynecology†
0079-6301 Progress in Hematology
0079-631X Progress in Heat and Mass Transfer†
0079-6328 Progress in High Temperature Physics and Chemistry†
0079-6336 Progress in Histochemistry and Cytochemistry
0079-6344 Progress in Immunobiological Standardization *see* 0301-5149
0079-6379 Progress in Inorganic Chemistry
0079-6387 Progress in Learning Disabilities†
0079-6409 Progress in Liver Diseases
0079-6417 Progress in Low Temperature Physics
0079-6425 Progress in Materials Science
0079-645X Progress in Medical Virology
0079-6484 Progress in Molecular and Subcellular Biology
0079-6492 Progress in Neurological Surgery
0079-6506 Progress in Neurology and Psychiatry†
0079-6514 Progress in Nuclear Energy. Series 3 - Process Chemistry *see* 0149-1970
0079-6530 Progress in Nuclear Energy. Series 9 - Analytical Chemistry *see* 0149-1970
0079-6565 Progress in Nuclear Magnetic Resonance Spectroscopy
0079-6573 Progress in Nuclear Medicine
0079-6581 Progress in Nuclear Medicine *see* 0163-6170
0079-659X Progress in Nuclear Physics *see* 0146-6410
0079-6603 Progress in Nucleic Acid Research and Molecular Biology
0079-6611 Progress in Oceanography
0079-6638 Progress in Optics
0079-6646 Progress in Pediatric Radiology
0079-6654 Progress in Pediatric Surgery†
0079-6662 Progress in Physical Organic Chemistry
0079-6670 Progress in Physiological Psychology *changed to* Progress in Psychobiology and Physiological Psychology
0079-6689 Progress in Phytochemistry†
0079-6697 Progress in Polarography†
0079-6700 Progress in Polymer Science
0079-6719 Progress in Powder Metallurgy
0079-6727 Progress in Quantum Electronics
0079-6735 Progress in Radiation Therapy†
0079-6743 Progress in Reaction Kinetics
0079-6751 Progress in Respiration Research
0079-6786 Progress in Solid State Chemistry
0079-6794 U.S. Fish and Wildlife Service. Progress in Sport Fishery Research *changed to* Fisheries and Wildlife Research
0079-6808 Progress in Stereochemistry†
0079-6816 Progress in Surface Science
0079-6824 Progress in Surgery
0079-6832 Progress in the Chemistry of Fats and Other Lipids *see* 0163-7827
0079-6840 Progress in the Science and Technology of the Rare Earths†
0079-6859 Progress in Theoretical Biology
0079-6883 Progress Polimernoi Khimii
0079-6891 Progress of Public Education in the United States *changed to* Progress of Education in the United States of America
0079-6913 Progress Report on Clays and Shales of Montana†
0079-6921 Progressive Grocer's Marketing Guidebook
0079-6956 Project Skywater. Annual Report
0079-6980 Proof: The Yearbook of American Bibliographical and Textual Studies†
0079-6999 Proportions†
0079-7014 Prospects for America†
0079-7022 Prospezioni Archeologiche†
0079-7049 Protein Synthesis: a Series of Advances†
0079-7065 Protides of the Biological Fluids
0079-7073 Protoplasmologia; Handbuch der Protoplasmaforschung *see* 0172-4665
0079-7111 Pruefen und Entscheiden
0079-7138 Przeglad Archeologiczny
0079-7154 Przeglad Naukowej Literatury Rolniczej i Lesnej
0079-7170 Przeglad Zagranicznej Literatury Geograficznej
0079-7189 Przeszlosc Demograficzna Polski
0079-7197 Pseudepigrapha Veteris Testamenti Graece
0079-7227 Psychiatria Fennica
0079-726X Psychiatrie de l'Enfant
0079-7278 Psychiatry; a Medical World News Publication†
0079-7286 Psychiatry and Art†
0079-7294 Psychoanalytic Study of Society
0079-7308 Psychoanalytic Study of the Child
0079-7324 Psychologen Adresboek
0079-7332 Psychologia Africana *see* 0081-2463
0079-7340 Psychologia Africana. Monograph Supplement†
0079-7359 Psychological Issues. Monograph
0079-7383 Psychological Studies. Major Series *changed to* Psychological Studies
0079-7391 Psychological Studies. Minor Series†
0079-7405 Psychologie und Person
0079-7421 Psychology of Learning and Motivation: Advances in Research and Theory
0079-743X Psychopharmacology Handbook: Animal Research in Psychopharmacology†
0079-7448 Psychotheque
0079-7456 Pszichologia a Gyakorlatban
0079-7464 Pszichologiai Tanulmanyok
0079-7472 Pubblicita in Italia
0079-7499 Public Administration in Israel and Abroad†
0079-7537 Public and Preparatory Schools. Yearbook *changed to* Independent Schools Yearbook: Boys Schools
0079-7561 Sweden. Riksrevisionsverket. Statens Finanser†
0079-7588 Public Health Conference on Records and Statistics. Proceedings
0079-7596 Public Health Monograph
0079-7618 University of Kansas Libraries. Annual Public Lecture on Books and Bibliography†
0079-7626 Public Papers of the Presidents of the United States
0079-7634 Public Policy Issues in Resource Management

1402 ISSN INDEX

0079-7642 Public Affairs Manual for the Bench and Bar of California†
0079-7650 Public Schools Careers Guide†
0079-7669 S I L Publications on Linguistics and Related Fields *changed to* S I L Publications in Linguistics
0079-7677 Publications in Medieval Studies
0079-7685 Publications in Medieval Science
0079-7707 Publications in Near and Middle East Studies. Series A
0079-7715 Publications in Near and Middle East Studies. Series B
0079-7731 Publications in Psychology
0079-774X Publications in Seismology
0079-7758 Publications in Tropical Geography Savanna Research Series *changed to* McGill University Savanna Research Project - Savanna Research Series
0079-7782 Publications on Asia *changed to* School of International Studies. Publications on Asia
0079-7790 Publications on Russia and Eastern Europe *changed to* School of International Studies. Publications on Russia and Eastern Europe
0079-7804 Publications on Social History†
0079-7812 Publications Romanes et Francaises
0079-7820 Publishers and Printers of Israel; a Select List *see* 0333-6018
0079-7839 Publishers in the United Kingdom and Their Addresses
0079-7847 Publishers International Yearbook†
0079-7855 Publishers' Trade List Annual
0079-7863 Puerto Rico. Negociado del Presupuesto. Resoluciones Conjuntas del Presupuesto General y de Presupuestos Especiales *changed to* Puerto Rico. Oficina de Presupuesto y Gerencia. Resoluciones Conjuntas del Presupuesto General y de Presupuestos Especiales
0079-7871 Puerto Rico. Department of the Treasury. Economy & Finances
0079-788X Universidad de Puerto Rico. Institute of Caribbean Studies. Special Studies *see* 0069-0511
0079-7936 Canada's Pulp and Paper Business Directory *see* 0708-501X
0079-7944 Pulp and Paper Industry Technical Conference. Record *see* 0190-2172
0079-7952 Pulp and Paper Magazine of Canada's Reference Manual and Buyers' Guide *see* 0709-2563
0079-7960 Pulp and Paper Research Institute of Canada. Annual Report
0079-8029 University of the Punjab. Arabic and Persian Society. Journal
0079-8045 University of the Punjab. Department of Zoology. Bulletin. New Series *changed to* Punjab University Journal of Zoology
0079-8061 Pupila: Libros de Nuestro Tiempo
0079-807X Purdue Opinion Panel, Lafayette, Indiana. Report†
0079-8096 Purdue University. Civil Engineering Reprints
0079-810X Purdue University. Engineering Experiment Station. Joint Highway Research Project. Research Reports
0079-8126 Materials Research in Science and Engineering at Purdue University. Progress Report
0079-8134 Purdue University. Office of Manpower Studies. Manpower Report *changed to* Purdue University. Office of Manpower Studies. Manpower & Technical Education Requirements Reports
0079-8142 Purdue University. Road School. Proceedings of Annual Road School
0079-8150 Pure and Applied Cryogenics†
0079-8169 Pure and Applied Mathematics
0079-8177 Pure and Applied Mathematics Series
0079-8185 Pure and Applied Mathematics; a Series of Texts and Monographs *changed to* Pure and Applied Mathematics: A Wiley Interscience Series of Texts, Monographs and Tracts
0079-8193 Pure and Applied Physics
0079-8207 University of Pittsburgh. Pymatuning Laboratory of Ecology. Special Publication
0079-8215 Pyrenae: Cronica Arqueologica
0079-8223 Pyttersen's Nederlandse Almanak
0079-824X Quaderni dei Padri Benedettini di San Giorgio Maggiore†
0079-8258 Quaderni di Archeologia della Libia
0079-8274 Quaderni di Poesia Neogreca
0079-8282 Quaderni e Guide di Archeologia†
0079-8304 Quality of Surface Waters of the United States†
0079-8312 Quarterly Journal of Studies on Alcohol. Supplement *see* 0363-468X
0079-8347 Universite Laval. Centre d'Etudes Nordiques. Travaux et Documents
0079-8355 Universite Laval. Departement d'Exploitation et Utilisation des Bois. Note de Recherches
0079-8363 Universite Laval. Departement d'Exploitation et Utilisation des Bois. Note Technique
0079-838X Universite Laval. Fonds de Recherches Forestieres. Contribution†
0079-8398 Universite Laval. Institut d'Histoire. Cahiers *changed to* Universite Laval. Les Cahiers d'Histoire
0079-8738 Quebec (Province) Department of Natural Resources. Geological Reports
0079-8746 Quebec (Province) Ministere des Richesses Naturelles. Travaux sur le Terrain
0079-8754 Quebec (Province) Marine Biological Station, Grande-Riviere. Rapport *see* 0318-8779
0079-8762 Quebec (Province) Marine Biological Station, Grande-Riviere. Cahiers d'Information *changed to* Quebec (Province) Direction Generale des Peches Maritimes. Cahier d'Information
0079-8770 Quebec (Province) Office de la Langue Francaise. Cahiers
0079-8789 Queen's Medical Review
0079-8797 Queen's Papers in Pure and Applied Mathematics
0079-8800 Geolgical Survey of Queensland Publications
0079-8819 Geological Survey of Queensland. Report†
0079-8827 Queensland Law Almanac *changed to* Queensland Legal Directory
0079-8835 Queensland Museum, Brisbane. Memoirs
0079-8843 Queensland Naturalist
0079-8851 Queensland Society of Sugar Cane Technologists. Proceedings *see* 0726-0822
0079-886X University of Queensland. Computer Centre. Papers†
0079-8878 University of Queensland. Department of Agriculture. Papers†
0079-8886 University of Queensland. Department of Architecture. Papers†
0079-8894 University of Queensland. Department of Accountancy. Papers *changed to* University of Queensland. Department of Commerce. Papers
0079-8908 University of Queensland. Department of Botany. Papers†
0079-8916 University of Queensland. Department of Entomology. Papers†
0079-8924 University of Queensland. Departments of Government and History. Paper†
0079-8932 University of Queensland. Department of Geology. Papers†
0079-8940 University of Queensland. Department of Social Sciences. Papers†
0079-8959 University of Queensland. Department of Zoology. Papers†
0079-8975 University of Queensland. Faculty of Arts. Papers†
0079-8983 University of Queensland. Faculty of Education. Papers†
0079-8991 University of Queensland. Faculty of Law. Papers†
0079-9009 University of Queensland. Faculty of Medicine. Papers†
0079-9017 University of Queensland. Faculty of Veterinary Science. Papers†
0079-9033 University of Queensland Inaugural Lectures†
0079-9041 Queensland'S Health†
0079-905X Quellenkataloge zur Musikgeschichte
0079-9068 Quellen und Forschungen aus Italienischen Archiven und Bibliotheken
0079-9076 Quellen und Forschungen zur Basler Geschichte
0079-9084 Quellen und Forschungen zur Wuerttembergischen Kirchengeschichte
0079-9114 Quellen und Studien zur Geschichte Osteuropas
0079-9130 Quellen und Untersuchungen zur Geschichte der Deutschen und Oesterreichischen Arbeiterbewegung. Neue Folge†
0079-9149 Quellenschriften zur Westdeutschen Vor- und Fruehgeschichte
0079-9157 Quellenwerke zur Alten Geschichte Amerikas
0079-919X Question†
0079-9211 Quetico-Superior Wilderness Research Center, Ely, Minnesota. Annual Report
0079-922X Quetico-Superior Wilderness Research Center, Ely, Minnesota. Technical Notes
0079-9238 University of the Philippines. Asian Center. Monograph Series
0079-9246 University of the Philippines. Community Development Research Council. Study Series
0079-9254 University of the Philippines. Institute of Public Administration. (Publication)
0079-9262 Qui Represente Qui
0079-9270 Qui Vend et Achete Quoi?
0079-9300 R I C
0079-9327 Universidade Federal de Minas Gerais. Corpo Discente. Revista Literaria.
0079-9335 R L S: Regional Language Studies, Newfoundland
0079-9343 R.M. Bucke Memorial Society for the Study of Religious Experience. Newsletter-Review†
0079-9351 R.M. Bucke Memorial Society for the Study of Religious Experience. Proceedings of the Conference
0079-936X Rabbinical Assembly, New York. Proceedings
0079-9386 Rabindranath Tagore Memorial Lectureship†
0079-9394 Raceform Up-to-Date *changed to* Raceform Weekly
0079-9408 Racehorses
0079-9416 Racial Policies of American Industry. Reports†
0079-9424 Racing and Football Outlook: Racing Annual
0079-9440 Radio Amateur's Handbook
0079-9467 Radio Handbook
0079-9483 Radiochemical and Radioanalytical Letters *changed to* Journal of Radioanalytical and Nuclear Chemistry. Articles
0079-9483 Radiochemical and Radioanalytical Letters *changed to* Journal of Radioanalytical Chemistry. Letters
0079-9491 Radner Lectures
0079-9513 Railway Directory and Yearbook
0079-9521 Railway Fuel and Operating Officers Association. Proceedings
0079-9548 Railway Technical Review
0079-9556 Rajasthan, India. Directorate of Economics and Statistics. Budget Study
0079-9564 Rajasthan, India. Directorate of Economics and Statistics. Basic Statistics
0079-9572 Rajasthan Year Book and Who's Who
0079-9580 Incidenca Raka v Sloveniji
0079-9599 Rampenlicht
0079-9602 Ranchi University Mathematical Journal
0079-9610 Rand McNally Campground and Trailer Park Guide *see* 0733-8309
0079-9629 Rand McNally National Park Guide
0079-9637 Rand McNally Discover Historic America
0079-9645 Rand McNally Travel Trailer Guide *see* 0733-8309
0079-967X Ranganathan Series in Library Science†
0079-9688 Rapport Annuel sur l'Economie Arabe†
0079-9696 Rapport Annuel sur l'Economie Syrienne
0079-9726 Rassegna Internazionale del Film Scientifico - Didattico†
0079-9815 Raymond Dart Lectures
0079-9823 Reaction Mechanisms in Organic Chemistry
0079-9831 Reader's Digest Almanac and Yearbook
0079-984X Readex Microprint Publications *changed to* United Nations Documents and Publications. Checklist
0079-9866 Reading University Studies on Contemporary Europe
0079-9874 Readings in Political Economy *see* 0305-814X
0079-9890 Real Estate Reports
0079-9904 Reanimation et Organes Artificiels. Revue Internationale de Physiologie, Medecine, Chirugie et des Techniques Appliquees aux Sciences Biologiques
0079-9912 Recent Advances in Food Science†
0079-9939 Recent Advances in Plasma Diagnostics†
0079-9947 Recent Developments in the Chemistry of Natural Carbon Compounds
0079-9955 Recent Developments of Neurobiology in Hungary
0079-9963 Recent Progress in Hormone Research. Proceedings of the Laurentian Hormone Conference
0079-9971 Recent Progress in Surface Science *changed to* Recent Progress in Surface Membrane Science
0079-998X Recent Publications in the Social and Behavioral Sciences. A B S Guide Supplement†
0080-0015 Recent Results in Cancer Research
0080-0023 Recent Sociology†
0080-0031 Recherches Africaines†
0080-004X Recherches Cooperatives†
0080-0058 Recherches de Psychologie Experimentale et Comparee†
0080-0066 Recherches de Psychopedagogie et de Pedagogie Experimentale†
0080-0074 Recherches et Documents d'Art et d'Archeologie
0080-0090 Recherches Mediterraneennes. Bibliographies†
0080-0104 Recherches Mediterraneennes. Serie 1. Etudes†
0080-0112 Recherches Mediterraneennes. Serie 2 Documents†
0080-0120 Recherches Mediterraneennes. Serie 3: Textes et Etudes Linguistiques†
0080-0139 Recherches sur la Musique Francaise Classique
0080-0155 Recht und Wettbewerb†
0080-0163 Rechts- und Staatswissenschaften
0080-018X Rechtspflege Jahrbuch
0080-0228 Universidade Federal de Pernambuco. Instituto de Antibioticos. Revista
0080-0236 Universidade Federal de Pernambuco. Instituto Oceanografico. Trabalhos *see* 0374-0412
0080-0244 Universidade Federal de Pernambuco. Instituto de Geosciencias. Serie B: Estudos e Pesquisas *changed to* Universidade Federal de Pernambuco. Departamento de Geologia. Serie B. Estudos e Pesquisas
0080-0252 Recommended Wayside Inns of Britain
0080-0260 Reconstruction Surgery and Traumatology

0080-0287 Records of Civilization. Sources and Studies
0080-0295 Records of Oceanographic Works in Japan. New Series†
0080-0309 Recueil Complet des Budgets de la Syrie
0080-0333 Recueil des Instructions Donnees aux Ambassadeurs et Ministres de France
0080-0341 Recurring Bibliography, Education in the Allied Health Professions†
0080-0384 American National Red Cross. Annual Report *changed to* American Red Cross. Annual Report
0080-0392 New Zealand Red Cross Society. Report
0080-0414 Reducing Your Income Tax†
0080-0422 Reed's Nautical Almanac
0080-0449 Reference Book-Argentina
0080-0457 Reference Book-Republic of South Africa
0080-0481 Reformed Church of America. Historical Series
0080-049X Refractory Materials
0080-0503 Refrigeration and Air Conditioning Directory *see* 0305-0777
0080-0511 Refrigeration Annual†
0080-0538 Regency International Directory
0080-0554 Regesta Regum Scottorum
0080-0562 Regi Magyar Dallamok Tara
0080-0570 Regi Magyar Prozai Emlekek
0080-0589 Regional Conference on Water Resources Development in Asia and the Far East. Proceedings†
0080-0619 Regional Science Research Institute. Bibliography Series†
0080-0627 Regional Science Research Institute. Monograph Series†
0080-0643 Regions
0080-066X Registre Aeronautique International
0080-0678 Registre International de Classification de Navires et d'Aeronefs *changed to* Registre Maritime
0080-0686 Registry of Accredited Facilities and Certified Individuals in Orthotics and Prosthetics†
0080-0694 Regnum Vegetabile
0080-0708 Rehabilitation der Entwicklungsgehemmten
0080-0724 Rehabilitation Industries Corporation. Annual Report
0080-0759 Rehovot Conference on Science in the Advancement of New States. (Proceedings)†
0080-0783 Reilly-Lake Shore Graphics. R O P Color Requirements Report *changed to* Newspaper Requirements
0080-0791 Reine und Angewandte Metallkunde in Einzeldarstellungen *changed to* Materials Research and Engineering
0080-0813 Reliability and Maintainability†
0080-0821 Reliability Physics Symposium Abstracts *see* 0735-0791
0080-0848 Religion and Reason; Method and Theory in the Study and Interpretation of Religion
0080-0864 Religion et Sciences de l'Homme
0080-0872 Religion, Wissenschaft, Kultur. Jahrbuch *changed to* Religion, Wissenschaft, Kultur. Schriftenreihe
0080-0880 Chetham Society Publications-Remains, Historical and Literary, Connected with the Palatine Countries of Lancaster and Chester
0080-0899 Remedia Hoechst
0080-0910 Renderers' Yearbook *changed to* Spectrum
0080-0929 Universite de Haute Bretagne. Centre d'Etudes Hispaniques, Hispano-Americanes et Luso-Bresiliennes. Travaux *see* 0761-2397
0080-0937 Commission Belge de Bibliographie, Repertoire des Comptes-Rendus de Congres Scientifiques
0080-0945 Repertoire Complementaire Alphabetique des Valeurs Mobilieres Francaises et Etrangeres Non Cotees en France
0080-0953 Bulletin Signaletique. Part 530: Repertoire d'Art et d'Archeologie. Nouvelle Serie
0080-097X Repertoire des Cooperatives du Quebec
0080-0988 Annuaire des Entreprises du Mali
0080-1003 Repertoire des Livres de Langue Francaise Disponibles *changed to* Livres Disponibles
0080-1011 Repertoire des Principaux Textes Legislatifs et Reglementaires Promulgues en Republique du Mali
0080-102X Repertoire des Productions de l'Industrie Cotonniere Francaise†
0080-1038 France. Delegation Generale a la Recherche Scientifique et Technique. Repertoire des Scientifiques Francais. Tome 3: Biologie†
0080-1046 France. Delegation Generale a la Recherche Scientifique et Technique. Repertoire des Scientifiques Francais. Tome 4: Chimie†
0080-1062 France. Delegation Generale a la Recherche Scientifique et Technique. Repertoire des Scientifiques Francais. Tome 5: Physique†
0080-1070 Repertoire des Societes de Commerce Exterieur Francaises
0080-1089 Repertoire Dictionnaire Industriel
0080-1097 Repertoire du Marketing et du Management
0080-1100 Syndicat National de la Librairie Ancienne et Moderne. Repertoire *changed to* Guide a l'Usage des Amateurs de Livres
0080-1119 Repertoire Francais du Commerce Exterieur
0080-1127 Repertoire General Alphabetique des Valeurs Cotees en France et des Valeurs Non Cotees
0080-1135 Repertoire General des Clubs Sportifs de France
0080-1151 Repertoire International des Medievistes
0080-116X France. Delegation Generale a la Recherche Scientifique et Technique. Repertoire National des Chercheurs: Sciences Sociales et Humaines. Tome 1: Ethnologie, Linguistique, Psychologie, Psychologie Sociale, Sociologie†
0080-1186 France. Delegation Generale a la Recherche Scientifique et Technique. Repertoire Permanent de l'Administration Publique *changed to* Repertoire Permanent de l'Administration Francaise
0080-1194 Repertoire Pratique de la Publicite
0080-1216 Repertorio delle Industrie Siderurgiche Italiane
0080-1224 Repertorium van Werken, in Vlaanderen Uitgegeven, of Door Monopoliehouders Ingevoerd
0080-1240 Report and Studies in the History of Art *see* 0091-7338
0080-1267 Report of Milk Utilization in Montana *changed to* Recap of Milk Receipts and Utilization in Montana
0080-1283 Fisheries of Scotland Report
0080-1305 Zambia. Central Statistical Office. Agricultural and Pastoral Production *changed to* Zambia. Central Statistical Office. Agricultural and Pastoral Production (Commercial and Non-Commercial)
0080-1305 Zambia. Central Statistical Office. Agricultural and Pastoral Production *changed to* Zambia. Central Statistical Office. Agricultural and Pastoral Production (Non-Commercial)
0080-1305 Zambia. Central Statistical Office. Agricultural and Pastoral Production *changed to* Zambia. Central Statistical Office. Agricultural and Pastoral Production (Commercial Farms)
0080-1313 Israel. Ministry of Labour. Registrar of Cooperative Societies. Report on the Cooperative Movement in Israel
0080-1321 Development of Education in Pakistan
0080-133X Reportages Fantastiques
0080-1348 Reports and Papers in the Social Sciences
0080-1356 Reports and Papers on Mass Communications
0080-1364 Reports of Patent, Design, Trade Mark and Other Cases
0080-1372 International Astronomical Union. Transactions
0080-1380 Reprints in International Finance
0080-1429 Requirements for Certification of Teachers, Counselors, Librarians, Administrators for Elementary Schools, Secondary Schools, Junior Colleges
0080-1437 Requirements for Teaching Certificates in Canada
0080-1453 Research and Clinical Studies in Headache *see* 0255-3910
0080-1461 Research and Development Directory
0080-147X Register of Research and Investigation in Adult Education†
0080-1488 Research and Publications in New York State History†
0080-1518 Research Centers Directory
0080-1526 Alberta Research Council. Annual Report
0080-1534 Alberta Research Council. Contribution Series
0080-1542 Alberta Research Council. Hail Studies Reports *changed to* Alberta Research Council. Atmospheric Sciences Reports
0080-1550 Alberta Research. Highways and River Engineering Reports *changed to* Alberta Research Council. River Engineering and Surface Hydrology Reports
0080-1569 Alberta Research Council. List of Publications
0080-1577 Alberta Research Council. Memoirs†
0080-1593 Alberta Research Council. Preliminary Reports. Soil Surveys†
0080-1607 Research Council of Alberta. Report *changed to* Alberta Research Council. Reports
0080-1623 Research Group for European Migration Problems. Publications
0080-1631 Research in Economics/Business Administration†
0080-1658 Research in Protozoology†
0080-1666 Research in Surface Forces
0080-1674 Research in the History of Education: A List of Theses for Higher Degrees in the Universities of England and Wales
0080-1704 Research Relating to Children. Bulletins
0080-1739 Research Studies in Library Science†
0080-1763 Resena de Literatura, Arte, y Espectaculos
0080-1771 Reserve Bank of Australia. Annual Report
0080-178X Reserve Bank of Australia. Occasional Papers
0080-1801 Reserve Bank of India. Annual Report
0080-181X Residue Reviews
0080-1828 Resources of Music
0080-1836 Restaurator. Supplement†
0080-1844 Results and Problems in Cell Differentiation
0080-1852 Retail Credit Federation Membership Directory *changed to* Consumer Credit Association of the United Kingdom. Membership Directory
0080-1860 Retail Wages and Salaries in Canada *changed to* Retail Council of Canada. Retail Wages
0080-1933 Review of Accidents on Indian Government Railways
0080-1992 Review of the Economy of Rhodesia *changed to* Annual Economic Review
0080-2018 Reviews in Engineering Geology
0080-2026 U.S. National Science Foundation. Reviews of Data on Science Resources†
0080-2050 Reviews of Plasma Physics
0080-2069 Revista Agronomica del Noroeste Argentino
0080-2085 Revista Cartografica
0080-2093 Revista Chilena de Historia Y Geografia
0080-2107 Revista de Administracao
0080-2115 Revista de Biologia Marina
0080-2123 Revista de Ciencias Agronomicas. Serie A†
0080-2131 Revista de Ciencias Agronomicas. Serie B†
0080-214X Revista de Ciencias Biologicas. Serie A†
0080-2158 Revista de Ciencias Biologicas. Serie B†
0080-2166 Revista de Ciencias do Homem. Serie A†
0080-2174 Revista de Ciencias do Homen. Serie B†
0080-2182 Revista de Ciencias Geologicas. Serie A†
0080-2190 Revista de Ciencias Geologicas. Serie B†
0080-2204 Revista de Ciencias Matematicas. Serie A†
0080-2212 Revista de Ciencias Matematicas. Serie B†
0080-2220 Revista de Ciencias Medicas. Serie A†
0080-2239 Revista de Ciencias Medicas. Serie B†
0080-2247 Revista de Ciencias Veterinarias. Serie A†
0080-2255 Revista de Ciencias Veterinarias. Serie B†
0080-2263 Revista de Fisica, Quimica e Engenharia. Serie A†
0080-2271 Revista de Fisica, Quimica e Engenharia. Serie B†
0080-228X Revista de Humanidades†
0080-2360 Revista de Matematica y Fisica Teorica. Serie A
0080-2387 Revista Humanidades†
0080-2425 Revista Peruana de Entomologia
0080-2433 Revista Portuguesa de Filologia
0080-2441 Revista Scriitorilor Romani
0080-2476 Revolutionary Cuba: A Bibliographical Guide†
0080-2484 Revue Bibliographique de Sinologie
0080-2506 Revue Francaise de Cooperation Economique Avec Israel
0080-2530 Revue des Archeologues et Historiens d'Art de Louvain
0080-2557 Revue des Etudes Slaves
0080-2581 Revue Economique de Madagascar†
0080-259X Egyptian Review of International Law
0080-2603 Revue Hittite et Asiatique†
0080-2611 Revue Internationale d'Histoire de la Banque
0080-262X Revue Roumaine d'Histoire de l'Art. Serie Beaux-Arts
0080-2638 Revue Roumaine d'Histoire de l'Art. Serie Theatre, Musique, Cinematographie
0080-2646 Revue Roumaine des Sciences Sociales. Serie de Sociologie
0080-2654 Revue Theologique de Louvain
0080-2662 Rhein-Mainische Forschungen†
0080-2670 Rheinische Lebensbilder
0080-2689 Rheinische Schriften
0080-2697 Rheinisches Jahrbuch fuer Volkskunde
0080-2700 Rheumatism Review†
0080-2719 Rheumatismus†
0080-2727 Rheumatology
0080-2743 Rhode Island Directory of Manufacturers and List of Commercial Establishments *changed to* Rhode Island Directory of Manufacturers
0080-2751 National Education Association. Journal *changed to* National Education Association Rhode Island. Newsline
0080-2778 University of Rhode Island. Bureau of Government Research. Information Series†
0080-2786 University of Rhode Island. Bureau of Government Research. Metropolitan Series†
0080-2794 University of Rhode Island. Bureau of Government Research. Research Series†
0080-2808 University of Rhode Island. Law of the Sea Institute. Occasional Paper Series†

0080-2832 Zimbabwe. Ministry of Water Resources and Development. Hydrological Summaries *changed to* Zimbabwe. Ministry of Energy and Water Resources and Development. Hydrological Summaries
0080-2840 Zimbabwe. Ministry of Water Resources and Development. Hydrological Year Book†
0080-2859 Zimbabwe. Ministry of Education. African Education Report
0080-2875 Zimbabwe-Rhodesia. Tobacco Research Board. Annual Report and Accounts *changed to* Zimbabwe. Tobacco Research Board. Annual Report and Accounts
0080-2883 Rhodesian Nurse†
0080-2891 Rhododendrons, with Magnolias and Camellias
0080-2905 Rhododendron Information†
0080-293X Ricerche di Storia della Lingua Latina
0080-2948 Ricerche Filosofiche†
0080-2964 Ricerche Sulle Dimore Rurali in Italia
0080-2972 Richard J. Gonzalez Lecture†
0080-3006 University of Richmond. Institute for Business and Community Development. Newsletter†
0080-3014 Rickia
0080-3022 Rickia. Suplemento†
0080-3065 Instituut voor Rassenonderzoek van Landbouwgewassen. Mededelingen *changed to* Rijksinstituut voor het Rassenonderzoek van Cultuurgewassen. Mededelingen
0080-3073 Rinascimento
0080-309X A List of Ring Systems Used in Organic Chemistry. Supplement *see* 0742-5996
0080-3103 Colegio Militar do Rio de Janeiro. Revista Didactica
0080-3111 Museu Nacional, Rio de Janeiro. Arquivos
0080-312X Museu Nacional, Rio de Janeiro. Boletim. Nova Serie. Zoologia
0080-3138 Observatorio Nacional, Rio de Janeiro. Relatorios Preliminares†
0080-3146 Observatorio Nacional, Rio de Janeiro. Servico Astronomico. Publicacoes†
0080-3154 Observatorio Nacional, Rio de Janeiro. Servico Gravimetrico. Publicacoes†
0080-3162 Observatorio Nacional, Rio de Janerio. Servico Magnetico. Publicacoes†
0080-3189 Museu Nacional, Rio de Janeiro. Boletim. Nova Serie. Antropologia
0080-3197 Museu Nacional, Rio de Janeiro. Boletim. Nova Serie. Botanica
0080-3200 Museu Nacional, Rio de Janeiro. Boletim. Nova Serie. Geologie
0080-3227 River Bend Library System. Report of the Director
0080-3235 Rivista Archeologica dell'Antica Provincia e Diocesi di Como
0080-3243 Rivista di Chirurgia della Mano
0080-3251 Rivista di Cultura Classica e Medioevale. Quaderni
0080-3278 Road Builder's Clinic. Proceedings
0080-3286 Road Facts India†
0080-3294 Road Notes *changed to* Transport and Road Research Laboratory. Research Reports
0080-3308 Road Research *changed to* Transport and Road Research Laboratory. Research Reports
0080-3316 Roadmasters and Maintenance of Way Association of America. Proceedings
0080-3324 Roads and Transportation Association of Canada. Proceedings *see* 0826-8193
0080-3340 R M A Annual Statement Studies
0080-3375 Rock Mechanics/Felsmechanik/Mechanique des Roches. Supplement
0080-3383 Rockbridge Historical Society, Lexington, Virginia. Proceedings
0080-3405 Rockefeller University, New York. Annual Report *changed to* Rockefeller University, New York. Scientific and Educational Programs
0080-3413 Rocket and Space Science Series†
0080-3421 Rocznik Bialostocki
0080-343X Rocznik Ekonomiczny
0080-3448 Rocznik Elektrycznosci Atmosferycznej i Meteorologii
0080-3456 Rocznik Gdanski
0080-3464 Rocznik Grudziadzki
0080-3472 Rocznik Historii Sztuki
0080-3480 Rocznik Jeleniogorski
0080-3499 Rocznik Krakowski
0080-3502 Rocznik Lodzki
0080-3510 Rocznik Lubelski
0080-3537 Rocznik Olsztynski
0080-3545 Rocznik Orientalistyczny
0080-3561 Rocznik Sadecki
0080-357X Polskie Towarzystwo Botaniczne. Sekcja Dendrologiczna. Rocznik
0080-3588 Rocznik Slawistyczny
0080-3618 Rocznik Wroclawski
0080-3626 Roczniki Biblioteczne
0080-3634 Roczniki Dziejow Spolecznych i Gospodarczych
0080-3642 Roczniki Gleboznawcze
0080-3650 Roczniki Nauk Rolniczych. Seria A. Produkcja Roslinna
0080-3669 Roczniki Nauk Rolniczych. Seria B. Zootechniczna
0080-3677 Roczniki Nauk Rolniczych. Seria C. Technika Rolnicza
0080-3685 Roczniki Nauk Rolniczych. Seria D. Monografie
0080-3693 Roczniki Nauk Rolniczych. Seria E. Ochrona Roslin
0080-3707 Roczniki Nauk Rolniczych. Seria F. Melioracji i Vzytkow Zielonych
0080-3715 Roczniki Nauk Rolniczych. Seria G. Ekonomika Rolnictwa
0080-3723 Roczniki Nauk Rolniczych. Seria H. Rybactwo
0080-3731 Roczniki Socjologii Wsi. Studia i Materialy
0080-374X Roczniki Technologii i Chemii Zywnosci *see* 0137-1495
0080-3758 Rodd's Chemistry of Carbon Compounds
0080-3782 Roemische Bronzen aus Deutschland
0080-3790 Roemische Historische Mitteilungen
0080-3820 Romance Languages and Their Structures. First Series. F: (French)†
0080-3839 Romance Languages and Their Structures. First Series. R: (Rumanian) †
0080-3847 Romance Languages and Their Structures. First Series. S: (Spanish)†
0080-3855 Romanica Gandensia
0080-3863 Romanica Gothoburgensia
0080-3871 Romanica Helvetica
0080-388X Romanische Bibliographie
0080-3898 Romanistisches Jahrbuch
0080-391X Istituto Giapponese di Cultura, Rome. Annuario.
0080-3928 Istituto Giapponese di Cultura, Rome. Notiziario.
0080-3936 Museo dell'Impero Romano. Studi e Materiali *changed to* Museo della Civilta Romana. Studi e Materiali
0080-3960 Pontificia Universita Gregoriana. Istituto di Scienze Sociali Studia Socialia.
0080-3979 Pontificia Universita Gregoriana. Miscellanea Historiae Pontificiae
0080-3987 Pontificia Universita Gregoriana. Studia Missionalia
0080-4010 Universita degli Studi di Roma. Istituto di Economia Politica. Collana di Studi†
0080-4045 U.P. Irrigation Research Institute. General Annual Report
0080-4053 U.P. Irrigation Research Institute. Technical Memorandum
0080-4088 Rothmans Football Yearbook
0080-4134 Royal Agricultural Society of England. Journal
0080-4185 Royal Architectural Institute of Canada. Allied Arts Catalogue. Catalogue des Arts Connexes†
0080-4193 Royal Astronomical Society of Canada. Observer's Handbook
0080-4274 Notes from the Royal Botanic Garden, Edinburgh
0080-4282 Royal Caledonian Curling Club. Annual
0080-4290 Royal Canadian Academy of Arts. Annual Exhibition. Catalogue†
0080-4304 Royal Canadian Institute. Proceedings†
0080-4312 Royal Canadian Institute. Transactions†
0080-4320 Royal College of Organists. Year Book
0080-4339 Royal Dublin Society. Scientific Proceedings Series A†
0080-4347 Royal Dublin Society. Scientific Proceedings. Series B†
0080-4355 Royal Entomological Society of London. Proceedings *see* 0140-1890
0080-4363 Royal Entomological Society of London. Symposia
0080-4371 Great Britain. Royal Greenwich Observatory. Annals†
0080-4398 Royal Historical Society. Guides and Handbooks
0080-4401 Royal Historical Society. Transactions. Fifth Series
0080-441X R.H.S. Gardener's Diary
0080-4428 Royal Society of Chemistry. Monographs for Teachers
0080-4436 Royal Institute of Philosophy. Lectures
0080-4444 Royal Institute of the Architects of Ireland. Yearbook *changed to* R I A I Architects Yearbook
0080-4452 Royal Musical Association, London. Proceedings *changed to* Royal Musical Association. Journal
0080-4460 Royal Musical Association. R.M.A. Research Chronicle
0080-4479 Royal National Institute for the Blind. Information Leaflets
0080-4487 Royal Numismatic Society. Special Publications
0080-4495 Royal School of Mines, London. Journal
0080-4509 R S P B Annual Report and Accounts *see* 0006-3665
0080-4517 Royal Society of Canada. Proceedings
0080-4541 Royal Society of Edinburgh. Proceedings. Section A. Mathematical and Physical Sciences *see* 0308-2105
0080-455X Royal Society of Edinburgh. Proceedings. Section B. Biology *changed to* Royal Society of Edinburgh. Proceedings. (Biological Sciences)
0080-4576 Royal Society of Edinburgh. Year Book
0080-4606 Royal Society of London. Biographical Memoirs of Fellows of the Royal Society
0080-4614 Royal Society of London. Philosophical Transactions. Series A. Mathematical and Physical Sciences
0080-4622 Royal Society of London. Philosophical Transactions. Series B. Biological Sciences
0080-4630 Royal Society of London. Proceedings. Series A. Mathematical and Physical Sciences
0080-4649 Royal Society of London. Proceedings. Series B. Biological Sciences
0080-4673 Royal Society of London. Year Book
0080-469X Royal Society of Queensland, St. Lucia. Proceedings
0080-4703 Royal Society of Tasmania, Hobart. Papers and Proceedings
0080-4711 Royal Society of Tropical Medicine and Hygiene, London. Yearbook
0080-472X Royal Society of Ulster Architects. Year Book
0080-4738 Early Days
0080-4746 Rozell'S Complete Lessons†
0080-4754 Rozprawy z Dziejow Oswiaty
0080-4762 Rubber and Plastics Industry Technical Conference. Record *see* 0272-4685
0080-4789 Rudolf Steiner Publications
0080-4797 Rudolf Virchow Medical Society in the City of New York. Proceedings
0080-4800 Ruestungsbeschraenkung und Sicherheit†
0080-4819 Ruff's Guide to the Turf and the Sporting Life Annual
0080-4827 Rugby Football League Official Guide
0080-4835 Rumanian Journal of Sociology†
0080-4843 Runa: Archivo para las Ciencias del Hombre†
0080-4851 Rural Development Research Paper
0080-4878 Russian and East European Series†
0080-4886 Russian and East European Studies
0080-4916 Russian Series on Social History
0080-4924 Rutgers Banking Series†
0080-4940 Rutgers Series on Systems for the Intellectual Organization of Information†
0080-4967 Rutgers University. Bureau of Biological Research. Research Conference. Research Conferences of the Bureau of Biological Research (Proceedings)†
0080-4975 Rutgers University. Bureau of Engineering Research. Annual Report
0080-4983 Rutgers University. Center of Alcohol Studies. Monograph *changed to* Rutgers Center of Alcohol Studies. Monograph
0080-5009 Rutherglen, Australia. Research Station. Digest of Recent Research *see* 0814-4990
0080-5033 Rwanda. Direction Generale de la Documentation et de la Statistique. Rapport Annuel *changed to* Rwanda. Direction Generale de la Statistique. Rapport Annuel
0080-505X Ryland's Directory
0080-5076 South African Fishing Industry Handbook and Buyer's Guide
0080-5084 S I A M - A M S Proceedings
0080-5092 S.J. Hall Lectureship in Industrial Forestry
0080-5122 S W A T H†
0080-5130 S.A. Mechanised Handling Equipment Buyer's Guide†
0080-5149 Saab Technical Notes
0080-5165 Annales Universitatis Saraviensis. Reihe: Mathematisch-Naturwissenschaftliche Fakultaet†
0080-5173 Universitaet des Saarlandes. Jahresbibliographie
0080-5181 Saarbruecker Beitraege zur Altertumskunde
0080-519X Saarbruecker Studien zur Musikwissenschaft
0080-5203 Sabah. Department of Statistics. Annual Bulletin of Statistics
0080-5211 Sabah. Forest Department. Annual Report
0080-522X Sabah. Marine Department. Annual Report
0080-5246 Sacred Books of the East†
0080-5262 Saechsische Akademie der Wissenschaften, Leipzig. Jahrbuch
0080-5270 Saechsische Akademie der Wissenschaften, Leipzig. Mathematisch-Naturwissenschaftliche Klasse. Sitzungsberichte
0080-5297 Saechsische Akademie der Wissenschaften, Leipzig. Philologisch-Historische Klasse. Abhandlungen
0080-5319 Saeculum
0080-5335 Sagamore Army Materials Research Conference. Proceedings
0080-5343 Sage Professional Papers in Comparative Politics†
0080-5351 Sage Readers in Cross-National Research†
0080-536X Sage Research Progress Series on War, Revolution and Peacekeeping†
0080-5378 Sage Series on Armed Forces and Society†
0080-5386 Sage Series on Politics and the Legal Order†
0080-5394 Saggi e Memorie di Storia dell'Arte
0080-5408 Sagittarius *changed to* Schuetz-Jahrbuch
0080-5416 Sahitya Akademi, New Delhi. Report

ISSN INDEX 1405

0080-5432 Saint Bonaventure University. Franciscan Institute. Philosophy Series
0080-5440 Saint Bonaventure University. Franciscan Institute. Text Series
0080-5459 Franciscan Studies
0080-5467 Saint Bonaventure University. Science Studies†
0080-5483 St. Louis University. Pius XII Library. Publications†
0080-5513 Science Museum of Minnesota. Museum Observer†
0080-5521 Science Museum of Minnesota. Scientific Publications *see* 0161-4452
0080-5548 Salaries, Wages, and Fringe Benefits in Michigan Municipalities over 4,000 Population *changed to* Salaries and Wages for Michigan Municipalities over 1,000 Population
0080-5572 Saling Aktienfuehrer
0080-5661 El Salvador. Direccion General de Estadistica y Censos. Anuario Estadistico
0080-567X Salvation Army Year Book
0080-5696 Salzburger Jahrbuch fuer Philosophie
0080-570X Salzburger Patristische Studien†
0080-5718 Salzburger Studien zur Anglistik und Amerikanistik†
0080-5726 Salzburger Studien zur Philosophie
0080-5734 Salzburger Universitaetsreden
0080-5769 Samaru Miscellaneous Paper
0080-5777 Samaru Research Bulletin
0080-5793 Sammlung Chemischer und Chemisch-Technischer Beitraege. Neue Folge†
0080-5807 Sammlung Dalp
0080-5815 Sammlung Dialog†
0080-5823 Sammlung Geltender Staatsangehoerigkeitsgesetze
0080-5831 Sammlung Lebensmittelrechtlicher Entscheidungen
0080-584X Sammlung Meusser†
0080-5858 Sammlung Wissenschaft und Gegenwart†
0080-5866 Samos
0080-5882 San Diego Business Survey†
0080-5890 San Diego Museum of Man. Ethnic Technology Notes
0080-5904 San Diego Museum of Man. Papers
0080-5920 San Diego Society of Natural History. Memoirs
0080-5939 San Diego Society of Natural History. Occasional Papers *see* 0080-5947
0080-5947 San Diego Society of Natural History. Transactions
0080-5955 Instituto y Observatorio de Marina. Observaciones Meteorologicas, Magneticas y Sismicas. Anales
0080-5971 Instituto y Observatorio de Marina. Efemerides Astronomicas
0080-598X San Mateo County Dental Society. Bulletin
0080-6013 Water Quality Conference. Proceedings *changed to* Public Water Supply Engineers Conference (Proceedings)
0080-6021 Sanitation Industry Yearbook *changed to* World Wastes Equipment Catalog
0080-603X Hochschule St. Gallen fuer Wirtschafts- und Sozialwissenschaften. Forschungsinstitut fuer Absatz und Handel. Schriftenreihe
0080-6048 Sankt Galler Beitraege zum Fremdenverkehr und zur Verkehrswirtschaft: Reihe Verkehrswirtschaft
0080-6056 Sankt Gallische Naturwissenschaftliche Gesellschaft. Bericht ueber Die Taetigkeit
0080-6064 Sankyo Kenkyusho Nempo
0080-6099 Santa Fe. Centro de Documentacion e Informacion Educativa. Boletin de Informacion Educativa†
0080-6137 Santakuti Vedic Research Series
0080-6145 Universidad Internacional Menendez Pelayo. Publicaciones
0080-6153 Santiago de Chile. Instituto de Fomento Pesquero Publicacion *changed to* Instituto de Fomento Pesquero. Informes Pesquero
0080-6234 Universidade de Sao Paulo. Escola de Enfermagem. Revista
0080-6250 Universidade de Sao Paulo. Faculdade de Direito. Revista
0080-6374 Universidade de Sao Paulo. Museu Paulista. Anais
0080-6382 Museu Paulista. Colecao *changed to* Universidade de Sao Paulo. Museu Paulista. Colecao. Serie de Etnologia
0080-6382 Museu Paulista. Colecao *changed to* Universidade de Sao Paulo. Museu Paulista. Colecao. Serie de Historia
0080-6382 Museu Paulista. Colecao *changed to* Universidade de Sao Paulo. Museu Paulista. Colecao. Serie de Numismatica
0080-6382 Museu Paulista. Colecao *changed to* Universidade de Sao Paulo. Museu Paulista. Colecao. Serie de Mobiliario
0080-6382 Museu Paulista. Colecao *changed to* Universidade de Sao Paulo. Museu Paulista. Colecao. Serie de Geografia
0080-6382 Museu Paulista. Colecao *changed to* Universidade de Sao Paulo. Museu Paulista. Colecao. Serie de Arqueologia
0080-6390 Universidade de Sao Paulo. Museu Paulista. Revista
0080-6412 Sao Paulo, Brazil (State). Observatorio. Anuario Astronomico *changed to* Universidade de Sao Paulo. Instituto Astronomico e Geofisico. Anuario Astronomico
0080-6420 Sarawak. Department of Agriculture. Research Branch. Annual Report
0080-6439 Annual Statistical Bulletin Sarawak
0080-6447 Sarawak Vital Statistics
0080-6455 Sarawak External Trade Statistics
0080-6471 Sarvadanand Universal Series
0080-648X Saskatchewan. Department of Agriculture. Family Farm Improvement Branch. Technical Bulletin
0080-6498 Saskatchewan. Department of Industry and Commerce. Report for the Fiscal Year
0080-6501 Saskatchewan. Department of Mineral Resources. Core Index†
0080-6536 Saskatchewan Manufacturers Guide
0080-6544 Saskatchewan. Medical Care Insurance Commission. Annual Report
0080-6552 Saskatchewan Natural History Society. Special Publications
0080-6560 Saskatchewan Poetry Book
0080-6579 Saskatchewan Professional Engineer
0080-6587 Saskatchewan Research Council. Annual Report
0080-6595 Saskatchewan Research Council. Geology Division. Circular†
0080-6609 Saskatchewan. Research Council. Geology Division. Report†
0080-6633 Saskatchewan Telecommunications. Annual Report
0080-665X University of Saskatchewan. Institute for Northern Studies. Annual Report†
0080-6676 Saskatchewan Economic and Financial Position
0080-6684 Sather Classical Lectures
0080-6706 Scandinavian Institute of African Studies. Annual Seminar Proceedings *see* 0281-0018
0080-6714 Scandinavian Institute of African Studies. Research Report
0080-6722 Scandinavian Journal of Haematology. Supplementum
0080-6730 Scandinavian Journal of Respiratory Diseases. Supplementum *see* 0106-4347
0080-6757 Scandinavian Political Studies
0080-6765 Scando-Slavica
0080-6773 Scavi di Spina. *changed to* Scavi di Luni
0080-679X Schiffahrtmedizinisches Institut der Marine, Kiel. Veroeffentlichungen
0080-6803 Schiffbautechnischen Gesellschaft. Jahrbuch
0080-6811 Embroidery Directory
0080-6838 Schoenste Schweizer Buecher
0080-6854 Scholae Adriani de Buck Memoriae Dicatae†
0080-6897 Schools *changed to* Which School?
0080-6900 Schools Abroad
0080-6919 Schools of England, Wales, Scotland and Ireland
0080-6927 Schools of English in Great Britain *see* 0143-2214
0080-6935 Schopenhauer-Jahrbuch
0080-6943 Schowalter Memorial Lecture Series†
0080-6951 Monumenta Germaniae Historica. Schriften
0080-696X Schriften und Quellen der Alten Welt
0080-6994 Schriften zur Geschichte und Kultur des Alten Orients
0080-7001 Schriften zur Handelsforschung
0080-701X Schriften zur Jugendlektuere
0080-7028 Schriften zur Kooperationsforschung. Berichte
0080-7036 Schriften zur Kooperationsforschung. Studien
0080-7044 Schriften zur Kooperationsforschung. Vortraege
0080-7052 Schriften zur Kunstgeschichte†
0080-7060 Schriften zur Rechtslehre und Politik†
0080-7079 Schriften zur Sozialpsychologie†
0080-7087 Schriftenreihe zur Theoretischen und Angewandten Betriebswirtschaftslehre†
0080-7117 Schriftenreihe des Buchklubs der Jugend†
0080-7125 Deutsch-Auslaendische Beziehungen. Schriftenreihe
0080-7133 Schriftenreihe fuer Laendliche Sozialfragen
0080-7141 Schriftenreihe fuer Sportwissenschaft und Sportpraxis *see* 0342-457X
0080-715X Schriftenreihe Neurologie/Neurology Series
0080-7176 Schrifttum zur Deutschen Kunst
0080-7192 Schrijvers Prentenboek
0080-7214 Schweizer Anglistische Arbeiten
0080-7230 Schweizer Buchhandels-Adressbuch
0080-7249 Publicus
0080-7257 Switzerland. Schweizerische Anstalt fuer das Forstliche Versuchswesen. Mitteilungen *changed to* Switzerland. Eidgenoessische Anstalt fuer das Forstliche Versuchswesen. Mitteilungen
0080-7273 Schweizerische Beitraege zur Altertumswissenschaft
0080-7281 Schweizerische Botanische Gesellschaft. Berichte *see* 0253-1453
0080-729X Schweizerische Geisteswissenschaftliche Gesellschaft. Schriften†
0080-732X Schweizerische Gesellschaft fuer Volkskunde. Schriften
0080-7338 Schweizerische Meteorologische Anstalt. Annalen
0080-7346 Schweizerische Meterologische Zentralanstalt. Veroeffentlichungen *changed to* Schweizerische Meteorologische Anstalt. Veroeffentlichungen
0080-7354 Schweizerische Musikforschende Gesellschaft. Publikationen. Serie 2
0080-7389 Schweizerische Palaeontologische Abhandlungen
0080-7400 Schweizerisches Medizinisches Jahrbuch
0080-7419 Schweizerisches Sozialarchiv
0080-7427 T.M.
0080-7451 Science and Technology (San Diego) *see* 0278-4017
0080-746X Science and Technology (Pittsburgh)
0080-7478 Science Council of Canada. Annual Report *see* 0228-6246
0080-7540 Science Nouvelle
0080-7559 Science of Advanced Material and Process Engineering Series
0080-7591 Science Policy Studies and Documents
0080-7605 Science Record†
0080-7613 Science Surveys†
0080-7621 Science Year
0080-763X Sciences
0080-7648 Sciences de l'Education†
0080-7672 Sciences Secretes†
0080-7680 Scientific and Learned Societies of Great Britain†
0080-7702 Scientific and Technical Periodicals Published in South Africa†
0080-7710 Scientific and Technical Societies in South Africa
0080-7737 Scientific Horticulture
0080-7745 Scientific Research in British Universities and Colleges†
0080-7753 Israel. National Council for Research and Development. Scientific Research in Israel
0080-7761 Scientific Research Organizations in South Africa
0080-7788 Scotland by Road†
0080-7796 Great Britain. Department of Agriculture and Fisheries for Scotland. Advisory Bulletins†
0080-7826 Scotland for Coarse Fishing *changed to* Angler's Guide to Scottish Waters
0080-7834 Scotland for Fishing *changed to* Angler's Guide to Scottish Waters
0080-7842 Scotland-Home of Golf†
0080-7850 Scotland. Red Deer Commission. Annual Report
0080-7869 Scotland. Registrar General. Annual Report
0080-7877 Great Britain. Scottish Health Services Planning Council. Annual Report
0080-7885 Scotland. Scottish Home and Health Department. Hospital Design in Use†
0080-7915 Great Britain. Scottish Law Commission. Annual Report
0080-7923 Scotland Tomorrow *see* 0266-5441
0080-7931 Scottish Castles and Historic Houses *changed to* Scotland: 1001 Things to See
0080-7966 Scottish Agricultural Economics; Some Studies of Current Economic Conditions in Scottish Farming *changed to* Economic Report on Scottish Agriculture
0080-7974 Scottish Bakers' Year Book
0080-8008 Scottish Council for Research in Education. Publications
0080-8024 Scottish Gaelic Studies†
0080-8059 Scottish Hardware and Drysalters Association. Yearbook
0080-8075 Scottish Journal of Science
0080-8083 Scottish Law Directory
0080-8091 Scottish Libraries
0080-8105 Scottish Licensed Trade Association. Annual Handbook†
0080-8113 Scottish Licensed Trade Directory†
0080-8121 S. M. B. A. Collected Reprints†
0080-813X Scottish Mountaineering Club. Journal
0080-8148 Scottish National Register of Classified Trades *changed to* Sell's Scottish Directory
0080-8164 Scottish Postmark Group. Handbook
0080-8202 Scottish Sea Fisheries Statistical Tables
0080-8210 Scottish Society for Prevention of Vivisection. Annual Pictorial Review
0080-8229 Scottish Sports Holidays *changed to* Scotland for Youth
0080-8245 Scottish Typographical Annual Report†
0080-8288 Screen World
0080-830X Scripps Clinic and Research Foundation. Annual Report
0080-8318 Scripps Institution of Oceanography. Bulletin
0080-8326 Scripps Institution of Oceanography. Contributions *changed to* Scripps Institution of Oceanography. Contributions. New Series
0080-8334 Scripps Institution of Oceanography. Deep Sea Drilling Project. Initial Reports.
0080-8350 Scripta Artis Monographia
0080-8369 Scripta Hierosolymitana
0080-8377 Scripta Mongolica†
0080-8385 Scriptores Byzantini†
0080-8393 Scriptores Latini

0080-8415 Seabird Report *see* 0267-9310
0080-8423 Seaports and the Shipping World. Annual Issue
0080-8474 Securities Law Review
0080-8482 Sediment Data for Selected Canadian Rivers
0080-8504 Seed Trade Buyer's Guide
0080-8512 Seeker's Guide
0080-8539 Kihara Seibutsugaku Kenkyusho. Seiken Ziho
0080-8547 Seishin-Igaku Institute of Psychiatry, Tokyo. Bulletin
0080-858X Selected Documents of the International Petroleum Industry
0080-8628 Selected Studies on Indonesia†
0080-8636 Selected Topics in Solid State Physics
0080-8644 Selected Trade and Professional Associations in Texas *changed to* Texas Trade and Professional Associations and Other Selected Organizations
0080-8660 Selective Organic Transformations†
0080-8695 Sell's British Aviation *see* 0143-1145
0080-8709 Sell's British Exporters *changed to* Sell's British Exporters
0080-8717 Sell's Building Index
0080-8725 Sell's Directory of Products & Services *see* 0261-5584
0080-875X Selysia
0080-8768 Semainier Beaux Pays de France
0080-8792 Seminaire Belge de Perfectionnement aux Affaires. Exposes
0080-8806 Seminar de Fizica Teoretica†
0080-8814 Seminar on Canadian-American Relations (Papers) *see* 0384-1103
0080-8830 Seminar on Integrated Surveys of Environment. Proceedings *changed to* I T C-U N E S C O International Seminar. Proceedings
0080-8849 Seminar on the Acquisition of Latin American Library Materials. Final Report and Working Papers *changed to* Seminar on the Acquisition of Latin American Library Materials. Papers
0080-8857 Seminar on the Acquisition of Latin American Library Materials. Microfilming Projects Newsletter
0080-8881 Semitic Texts with Translations†
0080-889X Senckenbergiana Maritima. Zeitschrift fuer Meeresgeologie und Meeresbiologie
0080-8903 Sennacieca Revuo
0080-8938 Serie Afrique Noire
0080-8946 Universidad de Costa Rica Serie Ciencias Naturales†
0080-8954 Series Entomologica
0080-8962 Series in Decision and Control†
0080-8997 Series on Company Approaches to Industrial Relations†
0080-9004 Series on Rock and Soil Mechanics
0080-9012 Series Paedopsychiatrica†
0080-9020 Service de la Carte Geologique d'Alsace et de Lorraine. Memoires *see* 0302-2684
0080-9039 Service d'Echange d'Informations Scientifiques. Serie A: Bibliographies†
0080-9047 Service d'Echange d'Informations Scientifiques. Serie B: Guides et Repertoires†
0080-9055 Service d'Echange d'Informations Scientifiques. Serie C: Catalogues et Inventaires†
0080-9063 Service d'Echange d'Informations Scientifiques. Serie D: Methodes et Techniques†
0080-9071 Servitor di Piazza†
0080-9098 Seto Marine Biological Laboratory. Special Publications *see* 0389-6609
0080-9101 Universidad de Sevilla. Seminario de Antropologia Americana. Publicaciones
0080-911X Seyd's Commercial Lists *changed to* Dun & Bradstreet Standard Register
0080-9128 Shakespeare - Jahrbuch
0080-9152 Shakespeare Survey
0080-9160 Shalom
0080-9209 University of Sheffield. Metallurgical Society. Journal†
0080-9233 Shepard's Acts and Cases by Popular Names, Federal and State
0080-9241 Sherborn Fund Facsimiles
0080-9268 Shipping and Aviation Statistics of the Maltese Islands
0080-9284 Shipping Marks on Timber
0080-9292 Ships and Aircraft of the United States Fleet
0080-9314 Shivaji University, Kolhapur, India. Journal. Humanities and Sciences
0080-9322 Shri Chhatrapati Shivaji University. Report
0080-9330 Shoe Buyers Guide†
0080-9349 Shoe Trades Directory
0080-9365 Shooter's Bible
0080-9381 Shop Equipment and Shopfitting Directory *see* 0143-0971
0080-9403 Short Play Series
0080-9411 Short Studies in Political Science†
0080-9446 Shuttle Craft Guild. Monographs
0080-9497 Siemens-Entwicklungsberichte *see* 0370-9736
0080-9519 Sierra Club Exhibit Format Series†
0080-9527 Chamber of Commerce of Sierra Leone. Journal
0080-9535 Sierra Leone in Figures
0080-9551 Sierra Leone. Ministry of Education. Report
0080-956X Sigma†
0080-9578 Sigma Zetan
0080-9594 Silesia Antiqua
0080-9608 Sinclair Lewis Newsletter†
0080-9616 University of Sind. Research Journal. Arts Series: Humanities and Social Sciences
0080-9624 University of Sind. Research Journal. Science Series
0080-9640 Singapore Accountant
0080-9659 Singapore Book World
0080-9667 University of Singapore. Chinese Society. Journal
0080-9675 Singapore. Department of Statistics. Report on the Census of Industrial Production
0080-9683 Singapore. Economic Development Board. Annual Report
0080-9691 Singapore Facts and Pictures
0080-9705 Singapore Law Review
0080-973X Singapore. National Library. Board Report†
0080-9748 Sinologica†
0080-9756 Sinopsis Dun - Brazil
0080-9772 Sintesis Bibliografica
0080-9780 Sir George Earle Memorial Lecture on Industry and Government
0080-9799 Sir Thomas Browne Instituut. Publications. General Series *changed to* Sir Thomas Browne Instituut. Publications. General Series and Special Series
0080-9810 Site Selection Handbook
0080-9829 Situation Economique de Cote d'Ivoire
0080-9837 Situation Economique de l'Algerie†
0080-9845 Situation Economique du Maroc
0080-9853 Situation Economique du Senegal
0080-9888 Sjoefartshistorisk Aarbok
0080-9918 Skier's Guide†
0080-9950 Skolens Aarbok
0080-9985 S L A M: Trade Year Book of Africa†
0080-9993 Slavia Antiqua
0081-0002 Slavia Occidentalis
0081-0010 Slavica Gothoburgensia
0081-0029 Slavistic Printing and Reprintings
0081-0045 Sloan-Kettering Institute for Cancer Research. Progress Report
0081-0053 Slog-Europa†
0081-0061 Slovaci v Zahranici
0081-007X Slovanske Historicke Studie
0081-0088 Slovenska Numizmatika
0081-0118 Small Business Management Series†
0081-0126 Small Business Research Series†
0081-0142 Family Hotel and Guest House†
0081-0169 Small Marketers Aids†
0081-0177 Small Marketers Aids Annuals†
0081-0193 Smith College Studies in History
0081-0207 Smithsonian Annals of Flight†
0081-0223 Smithsonian Contributions to Anthropology
0081-0231 Smithsonian Contributions to Astrophysics
0081-024X Smithsonian Contributions to Botany
0081-0258 Smithsonian Studies in History and Technology
0081-0266 Smithsonian Contributions to Paleobiology
0081-0274 Smithsonian Contributions to the Earth Sciences
0081-0282 Smithsonian Contributions to Zoology
0081-0304 International Astronomical Union. Central Bureau for Astronomical Telegrams. Circular
0081-0312 International Association of Geodesy. Central Bureau for Satellite Geodesy. Information Bulletin
0081-0320 Smithsonian Institution. Astrophysical Observatory. S A O Special Report
0081-0339 Smithsonian Opportunities for Research and Study in History Art Science
0081-0355 Smoker's Handbook *changed to* Tobacco Trade Marketing Directory
0081-0363 Smoking and Health Bulletin
0081-038X Soccer Year Book for Northern Ireland
0081-0398 Sociaal-Geografische Studien†
0081-0401 Sociaal-Historische Studien
0081-041X Social and Economic Studies. New Series†
0081-0444 Great Britain. Social Science Research Council. Report *see* 0266-2043
0081-0452 Social Science Research Council of Canada. Report *changed to* Social Science Federation of Canada. Annual Report
0081-0460 Social Science Studies†
0081-0487 Social Scientist
0081-0495 Social Security Handbook
0081-0533 Zambia. Department of Social Welfare. Social Welfare Research Monographs
0081-055X Social Work and Social Issues
0081-0568 Social Work Practice†
0081-0584 Denmark. Socialforskningsinstituttet. Beretning om Socialforskningsinstituttets Virksomhed
0081-0606 Socialist Register
0081-0630 Sociedad Rural Argentina. Memoria
0081-0649 Sociedad Uruguaya
0081-0657 Sociedade Broteriana. Boletim
0081-0665 Sociedade Broteriana. Memorias
0081-0681 Societa di Studi Romagnoli. Guide
0081-0703 S.I.S.F. Documenti
0081-0711 Societatis Scientiarum Lodziensis. Acta Chimica†
0081-072X Societe Academique des Arts Liberaux de Paris. Anthologie des Societaires *changed to* Societe Academique des Arts Liberaux de Paris. Collection
0081-0738 Societe Astronomique de Bordeaux. Bulletin
0081-0746 Societe Belge d'Ophtalmologie. Bulletin
0081-0754 Societe Chateaubriand. Bulletin. Nouvelle Series
0081-0770 Societe de Chimie Physique. Annuaire†
0081-0789 Societe de Geographie de Marseille. Bulletin
0081-0797 Societe de l'Industrie Minerale. Annuaire
0081-0819 Societe d'Emulation Historique et Litteraire d'Abbeville. Bulletin
0081-0835 Societe d'Ergonomie de Langue Francaise. Actes du Congres
0081-0843 Societe des Auteurs, Compositeurs, Editeurs pour la Gerance des Droits de Reproduction Mecanique. Bulletin
0081-086X Societe des Explorateurs et des Voyageurs Francais. Annuaire General
0081-0878 Societe des Francs-Bibliophiles. Annuaire
0081-0886 Societe des Ingenieurs Civils de France. Annuaire *changed to* Societe des Ingenieurs et Scientifiques de France. Annuaire
0081-0894 Societe des Oceanistes. Publications
0081-0908 Societe des Poetes Francais. Annuaire
0081-0916 Societe des Professeurs Francais en Amerique. Bulletin Annuel
0081-0924 Bulletin S.E.D.E.I.S†
0081-0940 Societe d'Histoire de France. Annuaire
0081-0959 Societe d'Histoire et d'Archaeologie de Geneve. Bulletin
0081-0967 Societe d'Histoire et d'Archeologie de la Goele. Bulletin d'Information
0081-0975 Societe d'Histoire Moderne. Annuaire
0081-0983 Societe Entomologique d'Egypte. Bulletin
0081-0991 Societe Entomologique d'Egypte. Bulletin. Economic Series
0081-1033 Societe Francaise de Chirurgie Orthopedique et Traumatologique. Conferences d'Enseignement
0081-1068 Societe Francaise de Microbiologie. Annuaire
0081-1076 Societe Francaise de Physique. Annuaire
0081-1084 Societe Francaise des Ingenieurs d'Outre-Mer. Annuaire†
0081-1106 Societe Franco-Japonaise de Biologie. Bulletin†
0081-1114 Societe Generale de Belgique. Rapport/Report
0081-1122 Bulgarsko Istorichesko Druzhestvo. Izvestiia†
0081-1130 Societe Historique de Quebec. Textes†
0081-1157 Societe Mouvements Sociaux et Ideologies. 1 Serie: Etudes†
0081-1165 Societe Mouvements Sociaux et Ideologies. 2 Serie: Documents et Temoignages†
0081-1173 Societe Mouvements Sociaux et Ideologies. 3 Serie: Bibliographies†
0081-1181 Societe Nationale des Antiquaires de France. Bulletin
0081-119X Societe Nationale des Chemins de Fer Belges. Rapport Annuel
0081-1203 Societe Odonto-Stomatologique du Nord-Est. Revue Annuelle
0081-1211 Mededelingen "Ex Oriente Lux" *changed to* Vooraziatisch-Egyptisch Genootschap "Ex Oriente Lux". Mededelingen en Verhandelingen
0081-122X Societe Phycologique de France. Bulletin *see* 0181-1568
0081-1238 Bibliotheque de la S E L A F
0081-1262 Federation Nationale des Societes d'Economie Mixte de Construction, d'Amenagement et de Renovation. Annuaire
0081-1270 Societe d'Ophtalmologie de France. Bulletin
0081-1297 Society for African Church History. Bulletin†
0081-1300 Society for American Archaeology. Memoirs†
0081-1319 Asian Music Publications. Series A: Bibliographic and Research Aids
0081-1327 Asian Music Publications. Series B. Translations
0081-1335 Asian Music Publications. Series C: Reprints
0081-1343 Asian Music Publications. Series D: Monographs
0081-136X Society for Endocrinology (Great Britain) Memoirs
0081-1386 Society for Experimental Biology. Symposia
0081-1394 Society for General Microbiology. Symposium
0081-1416 Society for International Development. World Conference Proceedings†
0081-1424 Society for Italian Historical Studies. Newsletter
0081-1432 Society for New Testament Studies. Monograph Series
0081-1440 Society for Old Testament Study. Book List

0081-1475 Society for Psychical Research. Proceedings
0081-1483 Society for the Advancement of Food Service Research. Proceedings
0081-1491 Society for the History of Technology. Monograph Series
0081-1513 Society for the Promotion of Nature Reserves. Technical Publications *see* 0261-7358
0081-153X Society for the Study of Human Biology. Symposia
0081-1556 National S A M P E Technical Conference Series. N S T C Preprint Series *changed to* International S A M P E Technical Conference Series. N S T C Preprint Series
0081-1564 Society of Antiquaries of Scotland. Proceedings
0081-1572 Society of Chemical Industry, London. Reports on the Progress of Applied Chemistry†
0081-1580 Society of Cypriot Studies. Bulletin
0081-1599 Society of Exploration Geophysicists. Yearbook†
0081-1602 Society of Glass Decorators. Papers Presented at Annual Seminar *changed to* Society of Glass Decorators. Seminar Proceedings
0081-1629 Society of Logistics Engineers. Proceedings
0081-1637 Society of Manufacturing Engineers. Collected Papers and Technical Papers Presented at Southeastern Engineering and Tool Exposition†
0081-1645 Society of Manufacturing Engineers. Collected Papers and Technical Papers Presented at Western Metal and Tool Exposition and Conference†
0081-1653 Society of Manufacturing Engineers. Technical Papers
0081-1661 Society of Naval Architects and Marine Engineers. Transactions
0081-1688 Society of Petroleum Engineers of American Institute of Mining, Metallurgical and Petroleum Engineers. Petroleum Transactions Reprint Series *changed to* Society of Petroleum Engineers. Reprint Series
0081-1696 Society of Petroleum Engineers. Transactions
0081-170X Society of Plant Protection of North Japan. Annual Report
0081-1718 Society of Professional Well Logging Analysts. S P W L A Annual Logging Symposium Transactions
0081-1734 Sociologia I†
0081-1742 Sociologia II
0081-1750 Sociological Methodology
0081-1769 Sociological Review. Monograph
0081-1777 Sociological Yearbook of Religion in Britain†
0081-1807 Sociologist
0081-1823 Sofiiski Universitet. Biologicheski Fakultet. Godishnik
0081-1831 Sofiiski Universitet. Fakultet po Slavianska Filologiia. Godishnik
0081-184X Sofiiski Universitet. Filosofski Fakultet. Godisnik
0081-1858 Sofiiski Universitet. Fakultet po Matematika i Mekhanika. Godishnik
0081-1866 Sofiiski Universitet. Juridiheski Fakultet. Godisnik
0081-1882 Soil Conservation Society of America. Proceedings of the Annual Meeting†
0081-1890 Books in Soils and the Environment Series
0081-1904 S S S A Special Publication Series
0081-1912 Soils and Land Use Series
0081-1939 Preparation and Properties of Solid State Materials†
0081-1947 Solid State Physics; Advances in Research and Applications
0081-1963 Solid State Physics Literature Guides
0081-1971 Solid State Surface Science†
0081-203X Some Statistics on Baccalaureate and Higher Degree Programs in Nursing *changed to* N L N Nursing Data Review
0081-2048 Somerset Birds
0081-2056 Somerset Archaeology and Natural History
0081-2080 Soundings: A Music Journal
0081-2110 Sources in Ancient History†
0081-2129 Sources of Supply/Buyers Guide
0081-2137 S A B S Yearbook *see* 0259-3602
0081-2145 Department of Agricultural Technical Services. Agricultural Research *changed to* South Africa. Department of Agriculture. Agricultural Research
0081-2153 South Africa. Department of Agricultural Technical Services. Report of the Secretary for Agricultural Technical Services *changed to* South Africa. Department of Agriculture. Report of the Chief for Agriculture and Water Supply
0081-2161 South Africa. Department of Agricultural Technical Services. Special Publication *changed to* South Africa. Department of Agriculture. Special Publications
0081-217X South Africa. Department of Agricultural Technical Services. Technical Communication *changed to* South Africa. Department of Agriculture. Technical Communication
0081-2188 South Africa. Department of Bantu Education. Annual Report *changed to* South Africa. Department of Education and Training. Annual Report
0081-2196 South Africa. Department of Customs and Excise. Foreign Trade Statistics *changed to* South Africa. Commissioner for Customs and Excise. Foreign Trade Statistics
0081-220X South Africa. Department of Higher Education. Annual Report
0081-2218 South Africa. Division of Sea Fisheries. Annual Report *changed to* South Africa. Sea Fisheries Research Institute. Marine Development Branch. Annual Report
0081-2234 South Africa. Sea Fisheries Institute. Investigational Report *changed to* South Africa. Sea Fisheries Research Institute. Investigational Report
0081-2250 University of South Africa. Communications†
0081-2307 South Africa. Weather Bureau. Notos†
0081-2315 South Africa. Weather Bureau. Radiosonde Rawin Data†
0081-2323 South Africa. Weather Bureau. Report on Meteorological Data of the Year/ Verslag Oor Weerkundige Data van die Jaar†
0081-2331 South Africa. Weather Bureau. W.B. Series
0081-234X South African Association for Marine Biological Research. Bulletin†
0081-2390 C S I R O Organisation and Activities
0081-2412 Report to S C A R on South African Antarctic Research Activities
0081-2420 S.A. Engineer and Electrical Review *changed to* Current
0081-2439 South African Institute of International Affairs. Annual Report *changed to* South African Institute of International Affairs. Biennial Report of the National Chairman
0081-2455 South African Journal of Antarctic Research
0081-2463 South African Journal of Psychology
0081-2471 South African Speech and Hearing Association. Journal *changed to* South African Journal of Communication Disorders
0081-248X South African Medical Research Council. Annual Report
0081-2498 South African Mining and Engineering Yearbook
0081-2501 S A N T A Annual Report
0081-251X South African Pollen Grains and Spores†
0081-2528 South African Reserve Bank. Annual Economic Report
0081-2536 South African Society of Animal Production. Proceedings. Handelinge *see* 0375-1589
0081-2544 South African Statistics
0081-2552 S A F T O Annual Report
0081-2560 S A W T R I Technical Report
0081-2579 South American Handbook
0081-2587 South and Southeast Asia Urban Affairs Bi-Annuals†
0081-2595 South Asia Church Aid Newsletter *changed to* South Asia Church Aid Association. Annual
0081-2633 South Australia. Libraries Board. Annual Report
0081-2641 South Australia. Libraries Board. Books for Young People†
0081-2676 South Australian Museum, Adelaide. Records
0081-2684 South Carolina Arts Commission. Annual Report
0081-2706 University of South Carolina. Libraries. Report of the Director of Libraries
0081-2714 University of South Carolina. School of Education. Proceedings of the Reading Conference†
0081-2722 South Central Research Library Council. Library Directory *changed to* Directory of Libraries and Library Resources in the South Central Research Library Council Region
0081-2773 South Dakota State Historical Society. Collections *changed to* South Dakota Historical Collections
0081-2803 South London Field Studies Society. Journal
0081-2811 South Pacific Commission. Handbook
0081-282X South Pacific Commission. Information Circular
0081-2838 South Pacific Commission. Information Document
0081-2846 South Pacific Commission. Report of S P C Fisheries Technical Meetings
0081-2854 South Pacific Commission. South Pacific Report *changed to* South Pacific Commission. Annual Report
0081-2862 South Pacific Commission. Technical Paper
0081-2889 South Seas Society. Journal
0081-2897 South Seas Society. Monograph
0081-2935 University of Southampton. Library. Automation Project Report
0081-2943 Southeastern Association of Game and Fish Commissioners. Proceedings of the Annual Conference *changed to* Southeastern Association of Fish and Wildlife Agencies. Proceedings
0081-2951 S E C O L A S Annals
0081-296X Southeastern Geology. Special Publication†
0081-2986 Southern Angler's and Hunter's Guide
0081-2994 Southern Anthropological Society. Proceedings
0081-3001 Southern Baptist Convention. Annual
0081-301X Southern Baptist Convention. Historical Commission. Microfilm Catalogue
0081-3028 Southern Baptist Periodical Index†
0081-3036 Southern Historical Publications†
0081-3044 Southern Illinois Studies†
0081-3052 Southern Journal of Agricultural Economics
0081-3060 Southern Regional Education Board. Annual Report
0081-3079 S R E B Research Monograph Series†
0081-3087 Southern Regional Education Board. State Legislation Affecting Higher Education in the South *changed to* Southern Higher Education Legislative Report
0081-3109 Southern Water Resources and Pollution Control Conference. Proceedings†
0081-3141 Southwestern Profiles†
0081-315X Southwestern Studies. Monographs
0081-3192 Sovietica. Monographs *changed to* Sovietica. Publications and Monographs
0081-3206 Sovietica. Publication *changed to* Sovietica. Publications and Monographs
0081-3222 Soybean Digest Blue Book *see* 0275-4509
0081-3249 Soziale Sicherheit†
0081-3257 Textausgaben zur Fruehen Sozialistischen Literatur in Deutschland
0081-3265 Soziologische Gegenwartsfragen. Neue Folge
0081-3338 Spain. Instituto Nacional de Estadistica. Estadistica del Movimento de Viajeros en Alojamientos Hoteleros y Acampamentos Turisticos *changed to* Estadisticas de Turismo
0081-3346 Spain. Instituto Nacional de Estadistica. Estadistica de Transporte†
0081-3354 Spain. Instituto Nacional de Estadistica. Estadistica Industrial
0081-3362 Spain. Instituto Nacional de Estadistica. Industrias Derivadas de la Pesca
0081-3370 Spain. Instituto Nacional de Estadistica. Informe sobre la Distribucion de las Rentas *changed to* Spain. Instituto Nacional de Estadistica. La Renta Nacional en (Year) y Su Distribution
0081-3389 Spain. Instituto Nacional de Estadistica. Poblacion Activa *changed to* Spain. Instituto Nacional de Estadistica. Encuesta de la Poblacion Activa
0081-3397 Informes J.E.N.
0081-3435 Spain. Ministerio de Hacienda. Informacion Estadistica
0081-3443 Spain. Ministerio de Hacienda. Memoria *changed to* Spain. Ministerio de Economia y Hacienda. Direccion General de Seguros. Balances y Cuentas
0081-3451 Spain. Instituto de Credito Oficial. Memoria del Credito Oficial
0081-346X Spain. Ministerio de Informacion y Turismo. Estadisticas de Turismo *changed to* Spain. Ministerio de Comercio y Turismo. Estadisticas de Turismo
0081-3478 Spain. Servicio de Extension Agraria. Serie Tecnica†
0081-3494 Spanische Forschungen der Goerresgesellschaft. Reihe 2: Monographien
0081-3532 Special Education and Rehabilitation Monograph Series *changed to* Syracuse Special Education and Rehabilitation Monograph Series
0081-3540 Special Libraries Association. Washington D.C. Chapter. Chapter Notes
0081-3559 Special Papers in International Economics
0081-3567 Specification
0081-3575 Specola Astronomica Vaticana, Castel Gandolfo, Italy. Annual Report†
0081-3583 Specola Astronomica Vaticana, Castel Gandolfo, Italy. Miscellanea Astronomica†
0081-3591 Specola Astronomica Vaticana, Castel Gandolfo, Italy. Ricerche Astronomiche†
0081-3605 Specola Astronomica Vaticana, Castel Gandolfo, Italy. Ricerche Spettroscopiche†
0081-3648 Speech Communication Association. Directory *see* 0190-2075
0081-3656 Speech Index
0081-3672 Spezial
0081-3680 Spezialbibliographien zu Fragen des Staates und des Rechts

1408 ISSN INDEX

0081-3699 Spezielle Pathologische Anatomie
0081-3702 Spiegel Deutscher Buchkunst *changed to* Die Schoensten Buecher der Deutschen Demokratischen Republik
0081-3729 Spirituosen-Jahrbuch
0081-3745 Spolia Zeylanica
0081-3761 Raceform "Horses in Training"
0081-377X Raceform Up-to-Date Form Book Annual *changed to* Raceform Flat Annual
0081-3788 Sporting News' National Football Guide *see* 0732-1902
0081-3818 Sprache und Denken; Finnische Beitrage zur Philosophie und Sprachwissenschaft†
0081-3826 Sprache und Dichtung. Neue Folge
0081-3834 Sprawozdania Archeologiczne
0081-3842 Sprechplatten Katalog†
0081-3850 Sprenger Instituut. Jaarverslag/Annual Report
0081-3869 Springer Tracts in Modern Physics
0081-3877 Springer Tracts in Natural Philosophy
0081-3885 Squash Rackets Association. Handbook *changed to* Squash Rackets Association. Annual
0081-3907 Sri Venkateswara University. Oriental Journal
0081-3915 Sri Venkateswara University. Department of Sanskrit. Symposium
0081-394X Srpska Akademija Nauka i Umetnosti. Odeljenje Drustvenih Nauka. Glas
0081-3958 Srpska Akademija Nauka i Umetnosti. Odeljenje Jezika i Knjizevnosti. Glas
0081-3966 Srpska Akademija Nauka i Umetnosti. Odeljenje Medicinskih Nauka. Glas
0081-3974 Srpska Akademija Nauka i Umetnosti. Odeljenje Tehnickih Nauka. Glas
0081-3982 Srpska Akademija Nauka i Umetnosti. Odeljenje Drustvenih Nauka. Posebna Izdanja
0081-3990 Srpska Akademija Nauka i Umetnosti. Odeljenje Jezika i Knjizevnosti. Posebna Izdanja
0081-4008 Srpska Akademija Nauka i Umetnosti. Odeljenje Likovne i Muzicke Umetnosti. Posebna Izdanja
0081-4016 Srpska Akademija Nauka i Umetnosti. Odeljenje Medicinskih Nauka. Posebna Izdanja
0081-4024 Srpska Akademija Nauka i Umetnosti. Odeljenje Prirodno-Matematickih Nauka. Posebna Izdanja
0081-4032 Srpska Akademija Nauka i Umetnosti Spomenica
0081-4040 Srpska Akademija Nauka i Umetnosti. Odeljenje Tehnickih Nauka. Posebna Izdanja
0081-4059 Srpska Akademija Nauka i Umetnosti. Odeljenje Drustvenih Nauka. Spomenik
0081-4067 Srpski Etnografski Zbornik. Naselja i Poreklo Stanovnistva
0081-4075 Srpski Etnografski Zbornik. Rasprave i Gradja
0081-4083 Srpski Etnografski Zbornik. Srpske Narodne Umotvorine
0081-4091 Srpski Etnografski Zbornik. Zivot i Obicaji Narodni
0081-4105 Staat und Politik
0081-4113 Staatliche Mathematisch-Physikalische Salons, Dresden. Veroeffentlichungen
0081-4148 Stadler Genetics Symposium. Proceedings
0081-4172 Stahl und Form†
0081-4180 Stahleisen Kalender *see* 0724-8482
0081-4210 Stamps of the World
0081-4229 Standard Directory of Advertisers
0081-4237 Standard Education Almanac†
0081-4245 Standard Lesson Commentary
0081-427X Standard Nomenclature of Athletic Injuries†
0081-430X Standards Engineering Society. Proceedings of Annual Meeting
0081-4318 National Conference of Standards Laboratories. Proceedings *changed to* National Conference of Standards Laboratories. Newsletter.
0081-4326 Stanford Journal of International Studies *see* 0731-5082
0081-4342 Stanford Studies in Germanics and Slavics†
0081-4350 Stanford University. Publications. Geological Sciences
0081-4369 Stanstead County Historical Society. Journal
0081-4377 Star Almanac for Land Surveyors
0081-4407 Stars and Stellar Systems†
0081-4415 Starting and Managing Series
0081-4423 State-Approved Schools of Nursing - L.P.N./L.V.N.
0081-4431 State-Approved Schools of Nursing - R.N.
0081-444X State Bank of Pakistan. Annual Report†
0081-4458 State Bank of Pakistan. Department of Research. Report on Currency and Finance†
0081-4466 State Bank of Pakistan. Index Numbers of Stock Exchange Securities
0081-4474 State Constitutional Convention Studies†
0081-4482 State Court Systems†
0081-4504 State Government Undertakings in Gujarat†
0081-4520 State of British Agriculture†
0081-4539 State of Food and Agriculture
0081-4563 State of Nevada Wage Report *changed to* Nevada Wage Survey
0081-4571 State of the Air Transport Industry *changed to* I A T A Annual Report
0081-4598 State Tax Handbook
0081-4601 Statesman's Year Book
0081-461X Stationery Trade Reference Book and Buyers Guide
0081-4636 Statistical Abstract of Ceylon *changed to* Statistical Abstract of the Democratic Socialist Republic of Sri Lanka
0081-4644 Statistical Abstract of Higher Education in North Carolina
0081-4652 Statistical Abstract of Iceland
0081-4660 Statistical Abstract of Ireland
0081-4679 Israel. Central Bureau of Statistics. Statistical Abstract of Israel
0081-4687 Statistical Abstract of Latin America
0081-4709 Statistical Abstract of Maharashtra State
0081-4717 Statistical Abstract of Rajasthan
0081-4725 Syria. Central Bureau of Statistics. Statistical Abstract
0081-4733 Malta. Central Office of Statistics. Annual Abstract of Statistics
0081-4741 Statistical Abstract of the United States
0081-475X Statistical Abstract of Virginia†
0081-4768 Statistical Analysis of World's Merchant Fleets Showing Age, Size, Speed and Draft by Frequency Groupings†
0081-4776 Statistical and Social Inquiry Society of Ireland. Journal
0081-4784 Statistical Guides in Educational Research†
0081-4792 Statistical Handbook of Japan
0081-4806 Korea Statistical Korea
0081-4814 Statistical Handbook of Sarawak†
0081-4822 Statistical Handbook of Thailand
0081-4857 Statistical Office of the European Communities. Associes Statistique du Commerce Exterieur. Annuaire†
0081-4865 Statistical Office of the European Communities. Balances of Payments Yearbook *changed to* Statistical Office of the European Communities. Balances of Payments. Quarterly Data
0081-4873 Statistical Office of the European Communities. Basic Statistics
0081-4881 Statistical Office of the European Communities. Commerce Exterieur: Products C E C A
0081-489X Statistical Office of the European Communities. Energy Statistics. Yearbook
0081-4903 Statistical Office of the European Communities. Foreign Trade: Standard Country Classification
0081-4911 Statistical Office of the European Communities. National Accounts. Yearbook
0081-492X Statistical Office of the European Communities. Overseas Associates. Annuaire Statistiques des Etats Africains et Malgache†
0081-4938 Statistical Office of the European Communities. Recettes Fiscales. Annuaire†
0081-4946 Statistical Office of the European Communities. Statistique Agricole
0081-4954 Statistical Office of the European Communities. Siderurgie Annuaire
0081-4962 Statistical Office of the European Communities. Statistiques des Transports. Annuaire
0081-4970 Statistical Office of the European Communities. Statistiques Industrielles Annuaire
0081-4989 Statistical Office of the European Communities. Statistiques Sociales. Annuaire†
0081-4997 Statistical Office of the European Communities. Yearbook of Regional Statistics
0081-5012 Statistical Pocket Book: India
0081-5020 Statistical Research Monographs†
0081-5039 Statistical Review of the World Oil Industry *changed to* B P Statistical Review of World Energy
0081-5047 Statistical Survey of Economy of Japan
0081-5063 Suomen Tilastollinen Vuosikirja
0081-5071 Statistical Yearbook of Greece
0081-508X Statisticians and Others in Allied Professions *see* 0278-405X
0081-5098 Statistics - Africa
0081-5101 Statistics - Europe
0081-511X Statistics for Iron and Steel Industry in India
0081-5128 Statistics of Farmer Cooperatives
0081-5136 Statistics of Foreign Trade of Syria
0081-5144 India (Republic) Ministry of Shipping and Transport. Statistics of Water Transport Industries *changed to* Water Transport Statistics of India
0081-5152 Statistics of Indiana Libraries
0081-5160 Statistics of Road Traffic Accidents in Europe
0081-5179 Statistics of the Communications Industry in the United States
0081-5195 Statistics of World Trade in Steel
0081-5217 Statistics on Social Work Education *see* 0091-7192
0081-5225 Statistiek van de Gasvoorziening in Nederland
0081-5233 Austria. Statistisches Zentralamt. Statistik der Aktiengesellschaften in Oesterreich
0081-5241 Statistik der Kommunalen Oeffentlichen Bibliotheken der Bundesrepublik†
0081-525X Switzerland. Directorate General of Customs. Annual Statistics
0081-5268 Statistique Criminelle de la Belgique
0081-5276 Statistiques du Commerce Exterieur de Cote d'Ivoire
0081-5292 Statistiques du Commerce Exterieur de la Tunisie
0081-5306 Statistiques du Commerce Exterieur de Madagascar
0081-5314 Statistisches Handbuch fuer die Republik Oesterreich
0081-5322 Statistisches Jahrbuch Berlin
0081-5330 Statistisches Jahrbuch der Schweiz
0081-5357 Statistisches Jahrbuch fuer die Bundesrepublik Deutschland
0081-5365 Statistisches Jahrbuch der Eisen- und Stahlindustrie
0081-5381 Statistisk Aarsbok foer Sverige
0081-539X Statni Banka Ceskoslovenska. Bulletin
0081-5403 Statsvetenskapliga Foereningen i Uppsala. Skrifter†
0081-5411 Steam-Electric Plant Factors *changed to* Steam-Electric Plant Factors (1978)
0081-542X Steam Passenger Service Directory
0081-5438 Steklov Institute of Mathematics. Proceedings
0081-5446 Stellenbosch, South Africa. University. Bureau for Economic Research. Economic Prospects. Ekonomiese Vooruitsigte†
0081-5454 University of Stellenbosch. Bureau for Economic Research. Survey of Contemporary Economic Conditions and Prospects *changed to* University of Stellenbosch. Bureau for Economic Research. Economic Prospects
0081-5462 Steppenwolf†
0081-5470 Stereo/Hi-Fi Directory *changed to* Stereo Review's Stereo Buyers Guide
0081-5519 Steuerberater-Jahrbuch
0081-5535 Der Stickstoff
0081-5551 Stifterverband fuer die Deutsche Wissenschaft. Jahrbuch *changed to* Stifterverband fuer die Deutsche Wissenschaft. Taetigkeitsbericht
0081-5586 Still: Yale Photography Annual
0081-5594 Stille Schar
0081-5608 Stimmen Indianischer Voelker†
0081-5624 Stock Values and Dividends for Tax Purposes
0081-5632 Ethnographical Museum of Sweden. Monograph Series
0081-5640 Flygtekniska Foersoeksanstalten. Meddelande/Report
0081-5659 Ingenioersvetenskapsakademien. Transportforskningskommissionen. Meddelanden†
0081-5667 Ingenioersvetenskapsakademien. Transportforskningskommissionien. Utredningsrapporter†
0081-5675 Musikhistoriska Museet. Skrifter *changed to* Musikmuseets Skrifter
0081-5683 Sweden. Nationalmuseum. Skriftserie *changed to* Sweden. Nationalmusei Skriftserie
0081-5691 Museum of Far Eastern Antiquities. Bulletin
0081-5705 Statens Geotekniska Institut. Proceedings *see* 0348-0755
0081-573X Tekniska Nomenklaturcentralen Publikationer
0081-5772 Stone and Cox General Insurance Year Book *changed to* Stone and Cox General Insurance Register
0081-5780 Stone and Cox Life Insurance Tables
0081-5799 Stones of Pittsburgh†
0081-5802 Storage Battery Manufacturing Industry Yearbook†
0081-5810 Stores and Shops Retail Directory *changed to* Retail Directory
0081-5829 Stores of the World Directory *changed to* Directory of European Retailers & International Buying Agents
0081-5837 Storia, Costumi e Tradizioni
0081-5845 Storia della Miniatura. Studi e Documenti
0081-5861 Stories from the Hills
0081-5896 Strahovska Knihovna
0081-590X Observatoire de Strasbourg. Publication *changed to* Journees de Strasbourg
0081-5918 Universite de Strasbourg II. Centre de Philologie et Litteratures Romanes. Actes et Colloques
0081-5926 Universite de Strasbourg. Centre de Recherche et de Documentation des Institutions Chretiennes. Bulletin du CERDIC†
0081-5934 Universite de Strasbourg II. Institut de Phonetique. Travaux
0081-5942 Strategy for Peace Conference. Report *see* 0748-9641
0081-5950 Stratford International Film Festival†
0081-5977 Street and Highway Manual *see* 0163-9730
0081-5985 Strikes and Lockouts in Canada
0081-5993 Structure and Bonding
0081-6027 Structurist
0081-6043 Stubbs Buyers Guide *changed to* Stubbs Directory

ISSN INDEX 1409

0081-6051 Stubs (Metro N.Y.)
0081-606X Student Guide: North America†
0081-6086 Student London†
0081-6116 Studi Albanesi. Studi e Testi
0081-6124 Studi Classici e Orientali
0081-6140 Studi d'Architettura Antica
0081-6159 Studi di Metrica Classica
0081-6175 Studi e Materiali di Storia delle Religioni. Quaderni†
0081-6205 Studi Romagnoli
0081-6213 Studi Romagnoli. Estratti di Sezione
0081-6221 Studi Romagnoli. Quaderni
0081-6248 Studi Secenteschi
0081-6256 Studi Tassiani
0081-6264 Studi Veneziani
0081-6272 Studia Anglica Posnaniensia
0081-6280 Studia Archaeologica
0081-6299 Studia Archaeologica
0081-6302 Studia Archeologiczne
0081-6310 Studia Aristotelica
0081-6337 Studia Biophysica
0081-6353 Studia Celtica
0081-637X Studia Estetyczne
0081-6388 Studia et Documenta Historiae Musicae: Bibliotheca
0081-6396 Studia Francisci Scholten Memoriae Dicata
0081-640X Studia Geograficzne
0081-6418 Studia Geograficzno-Fizyczne z Obszaru Opolszczyzny†
0081-6426 Studia Geologica Polonica
0081-6434 Studia Geomorphologica Carpatho-Balcanica
0081-6442 Studia Germanica Gandensia
0081-6450 Studia Graeca et Latina Gothoburgensia
0081-6469 Studia Grammatica
0081-6477 Studia Hibernica
0081-6485 Studia Historiae Oeconomica
0081-6493 Studia Historica
0081-6507 Studia Historica
0081-6515 Studia Historica Gothoburgensia†
0081-6523 Studia Historica Jyvaskylaensia
0081-6531 Studia Historica Upsaliensia
0081-654X Studia i Materialy do Dziejow Wielkopolski i Pomorza
0081-6566 Studia i Materialy do Teorii i Historii Architektury i Urbanistyki
0081-6574 Studia i Materialy z Dziejow Nauki Polskiej. Seria A. Historia Nauk Spolecznych
0081-6582 Studia i Materialy z Dziejow Nauki Polskiej. Seria B. Historia Nauk Biologicznych i Medycznych
0081-6590 Studia i Materialy z Dziejow Nauki Polskiej. Seria C. Historia Nauk Matematycznych, Fizyko-Chemicznych i Geologiczno-Geograficznych
0081-6604 Studia i Materialy z Dziejow Nauki Polskiej. Seria D. Historia Techniki i Nauk Technicznych
0081-6612 Studia i Materialy z Dziejow Nauki Polskiej. Seria E. Zagadnienia Ogolne
0081-6620 Studia i Materialy z Dziejow Polski w Okresie Oswiecenia†
0081-6647 Studia i Materialy z Dziejow Teatru Polskiego *see* 0208-404X
0081-6663 Studia Irenica
0081-6671 Studia Iuridica
0081-668X Studia Judaica†
0081-6698 Studia Juridica
0081-6701 Studia Copernicana
0081-6736 Studia Moralia
0081-6744 Studia Musicologica Upsaliensia. Nova Series
0081-6752 Studia nad Zagadnieniami Gospodarczymi i Spolecznymi Ziem Zachodnich
0081-6760 Studia Naturae *changed to* Studia Naturae. Seria A. Wydawnictwa Naukowe
0081-6760 Studia Naturae *see* 0551-4193
0081-6779 Studia Numismatica et Medailistica
0081-6787 Studia Palmyrenskie
0081-6795 Studia Pedagogiczne
0081-6809 Studia Philologiae Scandinavicae Upsaliensia
0081-6817 Studia Philologica†
0081-6825 Studia Philosophica†
0081-6833 Studia Philosophica Gandensia *see* 0379-8402
0081-6841 Studia Prawno-Ekonomiczne
0081-685X Studia Psychologiczne
0081-6884 Studia Rossica Posnaniensia
0081-6892 Studia Scientiae Paedagogicae Upsaliensia *see* 0347-1314
0081-6906 Studia Scientiarum Mathematicarum Hungarica
0081-6914 Studia Semitica Neerlandica
0081-6922 Studia Slovenica. Special Series
0081-6930 Studia Spoleczno-Ekonomiczne
0081-6949 Studia Staropolskie
0081-6957 Studia Theodisca
0081-7015 Studia Uralica et Altaica Upsaliensia
0081-7023 Studia Warszawskie†
0081-704X Studia z Dziejow Gornictwa i Hutnictwa†
0081-7058 Studia z Dziejow Osadnictwa†
0081-7082 Studia z Dziejow ZSRR i Europy Srodkowej
0081-7090 Studia z Filologii Polskiej i Slowianskiej
0081-7104 Studia z Historii Sztuki
0081-7112 Studia z Okresu Oswiecenia
0081-7120 Studia z Teorii Filmu†
0081-7139 Studia z Zakresu Budownictwa *see* 0137-5393
0081-7147 Studia Zrodloznawcze
0081-7155 Studiecentrum voor Kernenergie. Annual Scientific Report *changed to* S C K Annual Report
0081-7163 Centre d'Etude de l'Energie Nucleaire. Index of S.C.K. /C.E.N. Papers†
0081-718X Studien zu Religion, Geschichte und Geisteswissenschaften†
0081-7198 Studien zur Agrarwirtschaft
0081-721X Studien zur Begabungsforschung und Bildungsfoerderung†
0081-7228 Studien zur Deutschen Kunstgeschichte
0081-7236 Studien zur Deutschen Literatur
0081-7244 Studien zur Englischen Philologie, Neue Folge
0081-7252 Studien zur Europaeischen Geschichte
0081-7260 Studien zur Evangelischen Ethik†
0081-7279 Studien zur Finanzpolitik
0081-7287 Studien zur Geschichte Asiens, Afrikas und Lateinamerikas. *see* 0138-5550
0081-7295 Studien zur Geschichte der Katholischen Moraltheologie
0081-7309 Studien zur Geschichte des Neunzehnten Jahrhunderts
0081-7317 Studien zur Geschichte Osteuropas
0081-7325 Studien zur Kunst des Neunzehnten Jahrhunderts
0081-7333 Studien zur Medizingeschichte des Neunzehnten Jahrhunderts
0081-7341 Studien zur Musikgeschichte des Neunzehnten Jahrhunderts
0081-735X Studien zur Philosophie und Literatur des Neunzehnten Jahrhunderts
0081-7368 Studien zur Rhetorik des Neunzehnten Jahrhunderts†
0081-7376 Studien zur Wissenschaftstheorie im Neunzehnten Jahrhundert†
0081-7384 Studienbuecherei
0081-7392 Studienhefte Psychologie in Erziehung und Unterricht
0081-7406 Studientage fuer Die Pfarrer†
0081-7414 Studier i Nordisk Arkeologi
0081-7449 Studies and Reports in Hydrology Series
0081-7465 University of Texas, Austin. Bureau of Business Research. Studies in Accounting†
0081-7481 Studies in African History†
0081-749X Studies in African History, Anthropology, and Ethnology†
0081-7503 Studies in American History†
0081-7511 Studies in American Jewish History
0081-752X Studies in American Literature†
0081-7538 Studies in Anabaptist and Mennonite History
0081-7546 Studies in Ancient History
0081-7554 Studies in Ancient Oriental Civilization
0081-7562 Studies in Art†
0081-7570 University of Texas, Austin. Bureau of Business Research. Studies in Banking and Finance†
0081-7589 Studies in Biblical Theology†
0081-7597 Studies in Biblical Theology. Second Series†
0081-7600 Studies in Bibliography
0081-7619 Studies in British History and Culture†
0081-7627 University of New Mexico. Bureau of Business and Economic Research. Studies in Business and Economics†
0081-7635 Studies in Business and Society
0081-7643 Studies in Business Cycles†
0081-766X Studies in Capital Formation and Financing†
0081-7694 Studies in Chinese Government and Politics†
0081-7724 Studies in Classical Literature
0081-7732 Studies in Communism, Revisionism and Revolution†
0081-7767 Studies in Comparative Literature (Los Angeles)†
0081-7775 Studies in Comparative Literature (Chapel Hill)
0081-7783 Studies in Compulsory Education†
0081-7791 Studies in Consumer Instalment Financing†
0081-7805 Studies in Corporate Bond Financing†
0081-7813 Studies in Development Progress†
0081-7821 Studies in Early English History *changed to* Studies in the Early History of Britain
0081-783X Finnish Meteorological Institute. Studies on Earth Magnetism†
0081-7856 Studies in Economics
0081-7872 Studies in Economics and Business Administration†
0081-7880 University of Mississippi Studies in English
0081-7899 Studies in English Literature†
0081-7902 Studies in Ethnomusicology†
0081-7910 Studies in European History
0081-7929 Studies in Federal Taxation. Tax Study *changed to* Studies in Federal Taxation
0081-7937 Studies in French Literature
0081-7945 Studies in General and Comparative Literature
0081-7953 Studies in General Anthropology
0081-7961 Studies in Geography in Hungary
0081-797X Studies in German Literature
0081-7988 Studies in Higher Education in Canada
0081-7996 Studies in Historical and Political Science. Extra Volumes
0081-8011 Studies in Industrial Economics†
0081-802X Studies in International Affairs (Baltimore)
0081-8054 Studies in International Communism†
0081-8062 Studies in International Economic Relations†
0081-8070 Studies in International Finance
0081-8097 Studies in Irish History†
0081-8100 Studies in Irish History. Second Series†
0081-8119 Studies in Italian Literature
0081-8127 Studies in Japanese Culture†
0081-8135 University of Texas, Austin. Bureau of Business Research. Studies in Latin American Business†
0081-8143 Studies in Latin Literature and Its Influence *changed to* Greek and Latin Studies Series
0081-8151 Studies in Librarianship†
0081-8178 Studies in Manuscript Illumination
0081-8186 University of Texas, Austin. Bureau of Business Research. Studies in Marketing†
0081-8194 Studies in Mathematical and Managerial Economics
0081-8208 Studies in Mathematics (Washington)
0081-8224 Studies in Medieval and Renaissance History
0081-8232 Studies in Mediterranean Archaeology. Monograph Series
0081-8240 Studies in Money in Politics†
0081-8259 Studies in Museology
0081-8267 Studies in Music
0081-8275 Studies in Mycenaean Inscriptions and Dialect
0081-8291 New York University. Studies in Near Eastern Civilization
0081-8305 Studies in Neuro-Anatomy†
0081-8313 Great Britain. Central Statistical Office. Studies in Official Statistics
0081-8321 Studies in Oriental Culture
0081-8348 University of Texas, Austin. Bureau of Business Research. Studies in Personnel and Management†
0081-8364 Studies in Personnel Psychology†
0081-8380 Studies in Philosophy
0081-8399 Studies in Philosophy
0081-8402 Studies in Political Development†
0081-8437 University of Pennsylvania. Wharton School of Finance and Commerce. Studies in Quantitative Economics
0081-8453 Studies in Rural Land Use
0081-8461 Studies in Semitic Languages and Linguistics
0081-8496 Studies in Social Anthropology
0081-850X Studies in Social History†
0081-8518 Studies in Social Life
0081-8534 Studies in Spanish Literature†
0081-8542 Studies in Statistical Mechanics
0081-8569 Studies in the Economic Development of India†
0081-8577 Studies in the Foundations, Methodology and Philosophy of Science
0081-8585 Studies in the Geography of Israel
0081-8593 Studies in the Germanic Languages and Literatures
0081-8607 Studies in the History of Christian Thought
0081-8615 Studies in the History of Discoveries†
0081-8623 Studies in the Humanities†
0081-8631 Studies in the Modern Russian Language
0081-864X Studies in the National Income and Expenditure of the United Kingdom
0081-8658 Studies in the Renaissance *see* 0034-4338
0081-8666 Studies in the Romance Languages and Literatures *changed to* North Carolina Studies in the Romance Languages and Literatures.
0081-8674 Studies in the Social Sciences
0081-8682 West Georgia College Studies in the Social Sciences
0081-8690 Studies in the Structure of Power: Decision Making in Canada
0081-8704 Studies in the Theory of Science†
0081-8720 Studies in Tropical Oceanography
0081-8747 Studies in Vermont Geology†
0081-8771 Studies of Developing Countries
0081-878X Studies of Negro Employment†
0081-8798 Studies of Northern Peoples†
0081-8801 Studies of Urban Society
0081-8844 Studii Clasice
0081-8852 Studii de Literatura Universala si Comparata†
0081-8860 Studii de Slavistica†
0081-8879 Studii si Cercetari de Bibliologie. Serie Noua†
0081-8887 Studii si Cercetari de Numismatica
0081-8909 Studium Biblicum Franciscanum. Analecta
0081-8917 Studium Biblicum Franciscanum. Collectio Maior
0081-8925 Studium Biblicum Franciscanum. Collectio Minor
0081-8933 Studium Biblicum Franciscanum. Liber Annuus
0081-8941 Studium Niemcoznawcze
0081-895X Study Abroad
0081-8992 Bibliothek fuer Zeitgeschichte, Stuttgart. Jahresbibliographie
0081-900X Bibliothek fuer Zeitgeschichte, Stuttgart. Schriften

1410 ISSN INDEX

0081-9050 Sudan. National Planning Commission. Economic Survey *changed to* Sudan. Ministry of Finance and National Economy. Economic and Financial Research Section. Economic Survey
0081-9077 Suedost-Forschungen
0081-9085 Suedostdeutsches Archiv
0081-9093 Suedostdeutsches Kulturwerk, Munich. Kleine Suedostreihe
0081-9107 Suedostdeutsches Kulturwerk, Munich. Schriftenreihen. Reihe A. Kultur und Dichtung
0081-9115 Suedostdeutsches Kulturwerk, Munich. Schriftenreihen. Reihe B. Wissenschaftliche Arbeiten
0081-9123 Suedostdeutsches Kulturwerk, Munich. Schriftenreihen. Reihe C. Erinnerungen und Quellen
0081-9131 Suedosteuropa - Bibliographie
0081-914X Suedosteuropa - Jahrbuch
0081-9158 Suedosteuropa-Schriften†
0081-9166 Suedosteuropa - Studien
0081-9174 Suesswaren Jahrbuch
0081-9204 Sugar Technology Reviews
0081-9212 Sugar y Azucar Yearbook
0081-9220 Suid-Afrikaanse Guernsey
0081-9255 Sulphur Institute. Technical Bulletin†
0081-9271 Sumer
0081-928X Sumitomo Bulletin of Industrial Health
0081-9301 Summary of Floods in the United States†
0081-931X Summary of State Laws and Regulations Relating to Distilled Spirits
0081-9352 Summer Employment Directory of the United States
0081-9379 Summer Study Abroad *changed to* Vacation Study Abroad
0081-9387 Summer Theatre Directory†
0081-9395 Suomen Aikakauslehti-Indeksi†
0081-9417 Suomen Historiallinen Seura. Kasikirjoja
0081-9425 Suomen Historian Laehteitae
0081-9433 Suomen Naishammaslaakarit Ryhma. Julkaisu
0081-9441 Suomen Osallistuminen Yhdistyneiden Kansakuntien Toimintaan *see* 0781-2442
0081-945X Bank of Finland. Annual Statement
0081-9468 Bank of Finland. Yearbook
0081-9476 Suomen Pankki Taloustieteellinen Tutkimuslaitos. Julkaisuja. Series A: Taloudellisia Selvityksia *see* 0355-6034
0081-9484 Suomen Pankki. Taloustieteellinen Tutkimuslaitos. Julkaisuja. Series B *see* 0357-4776
0081-9492 Suomen Pankki. Julkaisuja. Sarja C
0081-9506 Suomen Pankki. Taloustieteellinen Tutkimuslaitos. Series D. Mimeographed Series *see* 0355-6042
0081-9514 Suomen Pankki. Taloustieteellinen Tutkimuslaitos. Julkaisuja. Series Kasvututkimuksia *see* 0355-6050
0081-9522 Facts About New Supermarkets *see* 0732-233X
0081-9530 Supermarket Industry Speaks *see* 0190-3349
0081-9557 Supreme Court Review
0081-9573 Surface and Colloid Science†
0081-9581 Surface Water Supply of the United States†
0081-959X Surface Water Year Book of Great Britain
0081-9603 Surfactant Science Series
0081-9611 Surfboard Builder's Yearbook *see* 0276-6582
0081-9638 Surgery Annual
0081-9646 Ackerman's Surgical Pathology
0081-9654 Surgical Trade Buyers Guide *changed to* Health Industry Buyers Guide
0081-9662 Surplus Dealers Directory
0081-9670 Surrey Papers in Economics
0081-9697 Survey of Biological Progress
0081-9727 Survey of Consumer Finances *see* 0085-3410
0081-9743 Israel. Ministry of Commerce and Industry. Surveys and Development Plans of Industry in Israel
0081-9751 Survey of London
0081-976X Survey of Progress in Chemistry
0081-9778 Survey of Race Relations in South Africa
0081-9794 Svensk Foersaekrings-Aarsbok
0081-9808 Svensk Geografisk Aarsbok
0081-9816 Svensk Tidskrift foer Musikforskning
0081-9867 Svenska Filminstitutet. Dokumentationsavdelningen. Skrifter†
0081-9905 Cement- och Betonginstitutet. Utredningar. Applied Studies†
0081-9913 Svenska Handelsbanken. Annual Report
0081-9921 Svenska Institutet i Athen. Skrifter
0081-993X Svenska Institutet i Rom. Skrifter. Acta Series Prima
0081-9956 Kungl Vetenskapsakademien. Bidrag till Kungliga Vetenskapsakademiens Historia
0081-9964 Sveriges Jaernvaegar
0081-9980 Swansea Geographer
0081-9999 Swaziland. Geological Survey and Mines Department. Annual Report
0082-0008 Swaziland. Geological Survey and Mines Department. Bulletin
0082-0016 Sweden. Sveriges Geologiska Undersoekning. Serie Ca. Avhandlingar och Uppsatser i Kvarto/Notices in Quarto and Folio
0082-0024 Sweden. Sveriges Geologiska Undersoekning. Serie C. Avhandlingar och Uppsatser/Memoirs and Notices
0082-0032 Institute of Freshwater Research, Drottningholm. Report
0082-0040 Kungliga Skogshoegskolan. Institutionen foer Virkeslaera. Rapporter *see* 0348-4599
0082-0059 Kungliga Skogshoegskolan. Institutionen foer Virkeslaera. Uppsatser *changed to* Sveriges Lantbruksuniversitet. Institutionen foer Virkeslaera. Uppsatser
0082-0067 Sweden. Konjunkturinstitutet. Occasional Paper
0082-0075 Sweden. Riksfoersaekringsverket. Allmaen Foersaekring
0082-0083 Swedish Social Security Scheme†
0082-0091 Riksgaeldskontoret. Aarsbok *changed to* Riksgaeldkontoret. Statistisk Aarsbok
0082-0105 Sweden. Sjukvaardens och Socialvaardens Planerings- och Rationaliseringsinstitut. S P R I Specifikationer
0082-0113 Sweden. Sjukvaardens och Socialvaardens Planerings- och Rationaliseringsinstitut. S P R I Raad
0082-0121 Sweden. Statens Institut foer Konsumentfraagor. Meddelar *see* 0035-7235
0082-0156 Sweden. Statistiska Centralbyraan. Befolkningsfoeraendringar
0082-0164 Sweden. Statistiska Centralbyraan. Folkmaengd
0082-0172 Sweden. Statistiska Centralbyraan. Industri
0082-0180 Sweden. Statistiska Centralbyraan. Information i Prognosfragor/Forecasting Information†
0082-0199 Sweden. Statistiska Centralbyraan. Jordbruksstatistisk Aarsbok
0082-0202 Sweden. Statistiska Centralbyraan. Kommunal Personal
0082-0210 Sweden. Statistiska Centralbyraan. Loener
0082-0229 Sweden. Statistiska Centralbyraan. Meddelanden i Samordningsfraagor
0082-0237 Sweden. Statistiska Centralbyraan. Statistiska Meddelanden. Subgroup Am (Labor Market)
0082-0245 Sweden. Statistiska Centralbyraan. Statistiska Meddelanden. Subgroup Be (Population)
0082-0261 Sweden. Statistiska Centralbyraan. Statistiska Meddelanden. Subgroup H (Trade)
0082-027X Sweden. Statistiska Centralbyraan. Statistiska Meddelanden. Subgroup I (Manufacturing)
0082-0288 Sweden. Statistiska Centralbyraan. Statistiska Meddelanden. Subgroup J (Agriculture)
0082-0296 Sweden. Statistiska Centralbyraan. Statistiska Meddelanden. Subgroup N (National Accounts and Finance)
0082-030X Sweden. Statistiska Centralbyraan. Statistiska Meddelanden. Subgroup P (Prices and Price Indices)
0082-0318 Sweden. Statistiska Centralbyraan. Statistiska Meddelanden. Subgroup R (Judicial Statistics. Law and Social Welfare)
0082-0326 Sweden. Statistiska Centralbyraan. Statistiska Meddelanden. Subgroup S (Social Welfare Statistics)
0082-0334 Sweden. Statistiska Centralbyraan. Statistiska Meddelanden. Subgroup T (Transport and Other Forms of Communication)
0082-0342 Sweden. Statistiska Centralbyraan. Statistiska Meddelanden. Subgroup U (Education and Research)
0082-0350 Sweden. Statistiska Centralbyraan. Urval Skriftseries/Selection Series
0082-0369 Sweden. Statistiska Centralbyraan. Utrikeshandel/Foreign Trade
0082-0377 Sweden. Universitetskanslersaembetet. *see* 0283-7692
0082-0393 Swedish Budget
0082-0415 Swedish Nutrition Foundation. Symposia
0082-0423 Swedish Theological Institute, Jerusalem. Annual†
0082-0431 Sweet's Canadian Construction Catalogue File
0082-044X Swiatowit
0082-0458 Rocznik Magnetyczny
0082-0490 Switching and Automata Theory Conference. Record *see* 0272-5428
0082-0504 Switzerland. Bundesamt fuer Sozialversicherung. Spezialitaeten-Liste/Liste des Specialites/Elenco delle Specialita
0082-0512 Sydney Law Review
0082-0520 Sydney Studies in Literature†
0082-0547 University of Sydney. Basser Department of Computer Science. Technical Report
0082-0555 University of Sydney. Department of Agriculture Economics. Mimeographed Report. *see* 0817-8771
0082-0563 University of Sydney. Department of Agricultural Economics. Research Bulletin†
0082-0571 University of Sydney. Department of Architectural Science. Reports†
0082-0598 Sydowia: Annales Mycologici
0082-0601 Syesis†
0082-061X Sylloge Nummorum Graecorum Deutschland *changed to* Sylloge Nummorum Graecorum Deutschland. Staatliche Muenzsammlung Muenchen
0082-0644 Symbolae Botanicae Upsalienses
0082-0660 Symbolon
0082-0695 Symposia Biologica Hungarica
0082-0725 Symposia Mathematica
0082-0733 Symposia on Fundamental Cancer Research. Papers
0082-0741 Symposia on Naval Structural Mechanics. Proceedings†
0082-075X Symposia on Theoretical Physics and Mathematics
0082-0768 Symposia Series in Immunobiological Standardization *see* 0301-5149
0082-0776 International Television Symposium and Technical Exhibition, Montreux. (Papers)
0082-0784 Symposium (International) on Combustion
0082-0806 Symposium on Advanced Propulsion Concepts. Proceedings†
0082-0830 Symposium on Information Display. Digest of Technical Papers *see* 0097-966X
0082-0849 Symposium on Naval Hydrodynamics. Proceedings
0082-0857 Symposium on Nondestructive Evaluation of Components and Materials in Aerospace, Weapons Systems and Nuclear Applications *changed to* Proceedings on Nondestructive Evaluation
0082-0865 Symposium on Nondestructive Testing of Aircraft and Missile Components *changed to* Proceedings on Nondestructive Evaluation
0082-0873 Symposium on Ocular Therapy†
0082-089X Symposium on Particleboard. Proceedings
0082-0903 Symposium on Physics and Nondestructive Testing, San Antonio. Proceedings *changed to* Symposium on Nondestructive Evaluation. Proceedings
0082-0911 Institute of Management Sciences. Symposium on Planning. Proceedings†
0082-092X Symposium on Reliability. Proceedings *see* 0149-144X
0082-0954 Symposium on Special Ceramics, Stoke-On-Trent, England. Special Ceramics, Proceedings
0082-0970 Symposium on the Nondestructive Testing of Wood. Proceedings†
0082-1012 Symposium on Water Resources Research. Proceedings†
0082-1020 Syndicat des Industries de Material Professionnel Electronique et Radioelectrique. Annuaire *changed to* S P E R Annuaire
0082-1047 Syndicat General de l'Industrie Cotonniere Francaise. Annuaire
0082-1055 Syndicat General des Impots. Guide National de l'Enregistrement et des Domaines *changed to* Syndicat General des Impots. Guide Foncier
0082-1098 Syndromes de la Douleur†
0082-1101 Synopses of the British Fauna
0082-111X Synthese Historical Library
0082-1128 Synthese Library
0082-1144 Synthetic Organic Chemicals, United States Production and Sales
0082-1152 Synthetic Procedures in Nucleic Acid Chemistry†
0082-1160 Syracuse Geographical Series†
0082-1179 Syracuse University Publications in Continuing Education. Occasional Papers
0082-1195 System of Ophthalmology
0082-1209 Systemes-Decisions. Section II. Gestion Financiere et Comptabilite
0082-1217 Systems Engineering of Education Series
0082-1241 Szczecinskie Towarzystwo Naukowe. Sprawozdania
0082-125X Szczecinskie Towarzystwo Naukowe. Wydzial Nauk Lekarskich. Prace
0082-1268 Szczecinskie Towarzystwo Naukowe. Wydzial Nauk Matematyczno Technicznych. Prace†
0082-1276 Szczecinskie Towarzystwo Naukowe. Wydzial Nauk Przyrodniczo-Rolniczych. Prace
0082-1284 Szczecinskie Towarzystwo Naukowe. Wydzial Nauk Spolecznych. Prace *see* 0082-1292
0082-1292 Szczecinskie Towarzystwo Naukowe. Wydzial Nauk Spolecznych
0082-1306 Szilikatkemiai Monografiak
0082-1322 Szociologiai Tanulmanyok
0082-1330 T.B. Davie Memorial Lecture
0082-1357 T V Feature Film Source Book
0082-1365 T V - Film Filebook
0082-1373 T V Film Source Book. Series, Serials and Packages *changed to* Series, Serials, and Packages
0082-1381 T V "Free" Film Source Book†

ISSN INDEX 1411

0082-139X T V in Psychiatry Newsletter
0082-1411 Tables of Constants and Numerical Data†
0082-1438 Tableware and Pottery Gazette Reference Book *changed to* European Tableware Buyers Guide
0082-1446 Taccuino dell'Azionista
0082-1454 Tagore Studies†
0082-1470 Taiwan Buyers' Guide
0082-1489 Taiwan. Fisheries Research Institute, Keelung. Bulletin
0082-1497 Taiwan. Fisheries Research Institute, Keelung. Laboratory of Fishery Biology. Report
0082-1519 Talking Books, Adult (Large Print Edition)
0082-1527 Tall Timbers Fire Ecology Conference. Proceedings *changed to* Tall Timbers Ecology and Management Conference. Proceedings
0082-156X Tamagawa University. Faculty of Agriculture. Bulletin
0082-1578 Tamil Nadu. Department of Statistics. Annual Statistical Abstract
0082-1586 Tamil Nadu. Department of Statistics. Season and Crop Report
0082-1594 Tamil Nadu. Legislative Council. Quinquennial Review†
0082-1608 Tamworth Annual
0082-1624 Universite de Madagascar. Annales. Serie Sciences de la Nature et Mathematiques†
0082-1632 Tanulmanyok a Nevelestudomany Korebol
0082-1659 Review of the Mineral Industry in Tanzania
0082-1675 National Museum of Tanzania. Annual Report
0082-1705 Tappert
0082-1713 Tarbell's Teacher's Guide
0082-173X Tariff Schedules of the United States Annotated
0082-1748 Tarsadalomtudomanyi Kismonografiak
0082-1764 Taschenbuch der Fernmelde-Praxis
0082-1772 Taschenbuch der Giesserei-Praxis
0082-1799 Taschenbuch der Pflanzenarztes
0082-1802 Taschenbuch der Werbung *changed to* Deutscher Werbekalender
0082-1829 Taschenbuch des Oeffentlichen Lebens
0082-1837 Taschenbuch des Textileinzelhandels
0082-1845 Taschenbuch fuer Agrarjournalisten
0082-1853 Taschenbuch fuer den Buchhalter *changed to* Jahrbuch fuer Praktiker des Rechnungswesens
0082-1861 Taschenbuch fuer den Fernmeldedienst†
0082-187X Taschenbuch fuer Liturgie und Kirchenmusik *see* 0344-1407
0082-1888 B A T: Taschenbuch fuer den Oeffentlichen Dienst
0082-1896 Taschenbuch fuer die Textil-Industrie
0082-190X Taschenbuch der Post- und Fernmelde-Verwaltung
0082-1918 Taschenbuch fuer Ingenieure und Techniker im Industrie und Wirtschaft†
0082-1926 Taschenbuch fuer Ingenieure und Techniker im Oeffentlichen Dienst†
0082-1934 Taschenbuch fuer Kriminalisten
0082-1942 Taschenbuch fuer Logistik†
0082-1950 Taschenbuch Geschichte
0082-1969 Taschenbuecher zur Musikwissenschaft
0082-1985 Information about Investment in Tasmania†
0082-1993 Tasmania. Department of Agriculture. Annual Report
0082-2043 Tasmania. Department of Mines. Geological Survey Bulletins
0082-2051 Tasmania. Department of Mines. Geological Survey Record†
0082-206X Tasmania. Department of Mines. Geological Survey Reports†
0082-2078 Tasmania. Department of Mines. Technical Reports†
0082-2086 Tasmania. Department of Mines. Underground Water Supply Papers†
0082-2094 Tasmania. Metropolitan Water Board. Report. *changed to* Tasmania. Hobart Regional Water Board. Report.
0082-2108 University of Tasmania Law Review
0082-2116 Australia. Bureau of Statistics. Tasmanian Office. Tasmanian Year Book
0082-2124 Tatura, Australia. Horticultural Research Station. Annual Research Report *changed to* Tatura, Australia. Irrigation Research Institute. Biennial Report
0082-2132 Tatzlil†
0082-2159 Tax Foundation. Research Publications. New Series
0082-2167 Taxation in Western Europe†
0082-2175 Taxation Tables
0082-2183 Taylor's Encyclopedia of Government Officials. Federal and State
0082-2191 Tbilisskii Universitet. Institut Prikladnoi Matematiki. Seminar. Annotatsii Dokladov
0082-2205 Teacher Education
0082-2213 Teachers' Associations. Associations d'Enseignants. Asociaciones de Personal Docente†
0082-223X Teaching
0082-2256 Teatro Clasico de Mexico. Boletin. Notas y Comentarios†
0082-2264 Technical Aids for Small Manufacturers†
0082-2272 Technical and Scientific Books in Print†
0082-2299 T A G A Proceedings
0082-2310 Technical Papers in Hydrology Series
0082-2329 Technical Service Data (Automotive)
0082-2353 Technician Education Yearbook *changed to* Technician Education Directory
0082-2361 Technikgeschichte in Einzeldarstellungen
0082-240X Technique of Organic Chemistry *see* 0082-2531
0082-2418 Techniques and Applications in Organic Synthesis Series
0082-2434 Techniques and Methods of Polymer Evaluation†
0082-2442 Techniques Artisanales Modernes
0082-2450 Techniques Avancees†
0082-2469 Techniques d'Aujourd'Hui
0082-2477 Techniques Economiques Modernes. Analyse Economique
0082-2485 Techniques Economiques Modernes. Espace Economique†
0082-2493 Techniques Economiques Modernes. Histoire et Pensee Economique†
0082-2507 Techniques Economiques Modernes. Production et Marches†
0082-2515 Techniques in Pure and Applied Microbiology
0082-2523 Techniques of Biochemical and Biophysical Morphology†
0082-2531 Techniques of Chemistry
0082-254X Techniques of Electrochemistry†
0082-2558 Techniques of Metals Research†
0082-2566 Technische Fortschrittsberichte†
0082-2590 Technische Physik in Einzeldarstellungen
0082-2604 Technology and Democratic Society *changed to* Organisations, People, Society/O P S
0082-2612 Etudes Teilhardiennes
0082-2620 Museum of Antiquities of Tel-Aviv-Yafo. Publications
0082-2639 Tel Aviv-Yafo. Research and Statistical Department. Special Surveys *changed to* Tel Aviv-Yafo. Center for Economic and Social Research. Research and Surveys Series
0082-2647 Telemetry Journal Buyers Guide†
0082-2655 Telephone Engineer and Management Directory
0082-2663 Telephone Tickler for Insurance Men and Women *changed to* New York Telephone Tickler for Insurance Men and Women
0082-2671 Telephony's Directory of the Telephone Industry *changed to* Telephony's Directory & Buyer's Guide for the Telecommunications Industry
0082-268X Television Factbook *see* 0732-8648
0082-2698 Television for the Family†
0082-2701 Coleccion Temas de Arquitectura Actual
0082-2744 East Tennessee State University. Research Development Committee. Publications†
0082-2752 Tennessee. State Planning Office. State Planning Office Publication†
0082-2760 Tennessee Statistical Abstract
0082-2779 Tennessee Tech Journal
0082-2795 Tennessee Valley Authority. Power Annual Report *see* 0730-4889
0082-2809 Tennessee Valley Authority. Technical Monographs
0082-2817 Tennessee Valley Authority. Technical Reports
0082-2825 Tennis for Travelers†
0082-2833 Tennis Guide†
0082-2841 Tennyson Research Bulletin
0082-285X Tennyson Society, Lincoln, England. Monographs
0082-2868 Tennyson Society, Lincoln, England. Report
0082-2884 Terrae Incognitae
0082-2930 Texas Archeological Society. Bulletin
0082-2949 Texas Archeology
0082-2957 Texas Archeology Salvage Project. Papers†
0082-2973 Texas Christian University Monographs in History and Culture†
0082-2981 Texas. Coordinating Board. Texas College and University System. C B Annual Report *changed to* Texas. Coordinating Board. Texas College and University System. C B Annual Report and Statistical Supplement
0082-299X Texas. Coordinating Board. Texas College and University System. C B Policy Paper
0082-3007 Texas. Coordinating Board. Texas College and University System. C B Study Paper
0082-3015 Texas Folklore Society. Paisano Series†
0082-3023 Texas Folklore Society. Publications
0082-3031 Texas. Forest Service. Cooperative Forest Tree Improvement Program. Progress Report
0082-304X Texas Forestry Papers
0082-3058 Texas. Governor's Committee on Aging. Biennial Report *changed to* Texas. Department on Aging. Biennial Report
0082-3066 Texas Industry Series†
0082-3074 Texas Memorial Museum. Bulletin
0082-3082 Texas Memorial Museum. Miscellaneous Papers
0082-3090 Texas Memorial Museum. Notes Series†
0082-3104 Texas Mineral Producers†
0082-3120 Texas Public Library Statistics
0082-3139 Texas Research Foundation, Renner. Contributions†
0082-3163 Texas Special Libraries Directory
0082-318X Stephen F. Austin State University. School of Forestry. Bulletin
0082-3198 Texas Tech University. Graduate Studies
0082-3201 University of Texas. African and Afro-American Research Institute. Occasional Publication *changed to* African and Afro-American Studies and Research Center. Occasional Publication
0082-3228 University of Texas, Austin. Bureau of Business Research. Area Economic Survey†
0082-3236 University of Texas, Austin. Bureau of Business Research. Bibliography†
0082-3244 University of Texas, Austin. Bureau of Business Research. Business Guide†
0082-3279 University of Texas, Austin. Bureau of Business Research. Research Monograph *changed to* University of Texas, Austin. Bureau of Business Research. Research Report Series
0082-3287 University of Texas, Austin. Bureau of Economic Geology. Annual Report
0082-3295 University of Texas. Bureau of Economic Geology. Guidebook *see* 0363-4132
0082-3309 University of Texas, Austin. Bureau of Economic Geology. Geological Circular
0082-3333 University of Texas, Austin. Bureau of Economic Geology. Mineral Resource Circulars
0082-335X University of Texas, Austin. Bureau of Economic Geology. Report of Investigations
0082-3384 University of Texas, Austin. Natural Fibers Economic Research. Research Report†
0082-3392 Texas Cotton Review†
0082-3406 University of Texas, Austin. County Auditors' Institute. Proceedings†
0082-3414 University of Texas, Austin. Department of Anthropology. Anthropology Series†
0082-3422 University of Texas, Austin. Governmental Accounting and Finance Institute. Proceedings†
0082-3430 University of Texas, Austin. Institute for Tax Assessors. Proceedings†
0082-3449 University of Texas. Institute of Marine Science. Contributions *changed to* Contributions in Marine Science
0082-3554 Texas. Water Development Board. Biennial Report†
0082-3562 Texas. Water Development Board. Report *changed to* Texas. Water Development Board. Report
0082-3570 Texas. Water Quality Board. Biennial Report†
0082-3589 Texte und Untersuchungen zur Geschichte der Altchristlichen Literatur
0082-3597 Texte zur Kirchen- und Theologiegeschichte†
0082-3600 Textes Sociologiques *changed to* Textes de Sciences Sociales
0082-3627 Textil-Industrie und ihre Helfer
0082-3635 Textile Chemistry†
0082-3651 Textile Industry Technical Conference. Record *see* 0094-9884
0082-366X Textile Japan
0082-3708 Textiles Suisses/Interieur
0082-3732 Texts and Studies in the History of Mediaeval Education
0082-3759 Texts from Cuneiform Sources
0082-3767 Textus
0082-3775 Textus Patristici et Liturgici
0082-3783 Thai Investment Review†
0082-3791 Thailand. National Statistical Office. Statistical Bibliography
0082-3805 Thames Book
0082-3821 Theatre Annual
0082-3848 Theatre Student Series
0082-3856 Theatre World
0082-3880 Theodor-Storm-Gesellschaft. Schriften
0082-3899 Theokratia; Jahrbuch des Institutum Judaicum Delitzschianum
0082-3902 Theologische Dissertationen
0082-3945 Theoretical and Experimental Biology
0082-3953 Theoretical and Experimental Biophysics: A Series of Advances†
0082-3961 Theoretical Chemistry
0082-3988 Theorie de la Production
0082-3996 Theory, Technique and Functional Use of Film; Bibliographical References
0082-4003 Theriaca
0082-4011 Thermal Analysis Series†
0082-402X Thermodynamics Research Center. Data Project. Selected Values of Properties of Chemical Compounds. Category B. Selected Infrared Spectral Data
0082-4038 Thermodynamics Research Center. Data Project. Selected Values of Properties of Chemical Compounds. Category D. Selected Raman Spectral Data *changed to* Thermodynamics Research Center. Hydrocarbon Project. Selected Values of Properties of Hydrocarbons and Related Compounds. Category D: Selected Raman Spectral Data

0082-4046 Thermodynamics Research Center. Data Project. Selected Values of Properties of Chemical Compounds. Category A. Tables of Selected Values of Physical and Thermodynamic Properties of Chemical Compounds
0082-4054 Thermodynamics Research Center Data Project. Selected Values of Properties of Chemical Compounds. Category C. Selected Ultraviolet Spectral Data†
0082-4062 Thermodynamics Research Center Data Project. Selected Values of Properties of Chemical Compounds. Category E. Selected Mass Spectral Data†
0082-4070 Thermodynamics Research Center Data Project. Selected Values of Properties of Chemical Compounds. Category F. Selected Nuclear Magnetic Resonance Spectral Data *changed to* Thermodynamics Research Center. Data Project. Selected Values of Properties of Chemical Compounds. Category F. Selected 1H Nuclear Magnetic Resonance Spectral Data
0082-4089 Akademiya Nauk Litovskoi S.S.R. Silumine Fizika
0082-4097 Thesaurismata†
0082-4100 Theses and Dissertations Accepted for Higher Degrees in Nigerian Universities
0082-4119 Theses in Germanic Studies†
0082-4127 University of London. Institute of Germanic Studies. Theses in Progress at British Universities *see* 0260-5929
0082-4151 Thomas Grocery Register
0082-416X Thomas Hardy Year Book
0082-4178 Thomas Jefferson Center for Political Economy. Research Monographs.†
0082-4186 Thomas Mann Gesellschaft. Blaetter
0082-4208 St. Thomas More Lectures
0082-4216 Thomas Register of American Manufacturers *changed to* Thomas Register of American Manufacturers and Thomas Register Catalog File
0082-4224 Thom's Commercial Directory
0082-4232 Thoresby Society, Leeds, England. Publications
0082-4240 Thoroughbred Racing Associations. Directory and Record Book
0082-4283 Thunder Bay Historical Museum Society. Papers and Records
0082-4305 Tierwelt Deutschlands
0082-4313 Tijdschrift voor Privaatrecht
0082-433X Timber and Plywood. Board News Annual
0082-4364 Timber Trades Journal. Annual Special Issue
0082-4372 Timber Trades Directory
0082-4399 Times Guide to the House of Commons
0082-4429 Times 1000
0082-4445 Times of India Directory and Yearbook Including Who's Who
0082-4453 Universitatea din Timisoara. Analele. Stiinte Fizico-Chimice *changed to* Universitatea din Timisoara. Analele. Stiinte Fizice
0082-4461 Universitatea din Timisoara. Analele. Stiinte Filologice
0082-4496 Tire and Rim Association. Standards Year Book
0082-450X Tiryns
0082-4518 Tissue Culture Studies in Japan: The Annual Bibliography†
0082-4526 Titles in Series†
0082-4534 Titles of Dissertations and Theses Completed in Home Economics
0082-4542 Tjaenstemaennens Central Organisation. Aarsrapport *changed to* Aaret som Gaatt
0082-4550 Tlatoani†
0082-4569 Tlatoani. Suplemento†
0082-4585 Sources of Contemporary Jewish Thought
0082-4593 Tobacco Associates. Annual Report
0082-4607 Tobacco Research Council. Research Papers†
0082-4615 Tobacco Research Council. Review of Activities†
0082-4623 Tobacco Science Yearbook
0082-4631 Tobaco Trade Year Book and Diary *changed to* Tobacco Trade Marketing Directory
0082-464X Tohoku University. Institute of Geology and Paleontology. Science Reports. Second Series
0082-4658 Tohoku University. Institute of Geology and Paleontology. Contributions
0082-4666 Tohoku University. Research Institutes. Science Reports. Series D: Agriculture *changed to* Tohoku University. Institute for Agricultural Research. Reports
0082-4674 Tokai-Kinki National Agricultural Experiment Station, Tsu, Japan. Bulletin†
0082-4690 Tokyo Astronomical Bulletin
0082-4704 Tokyo Astronomical Observatory. Annals
0082-4712 Tokyo Astronomical Observatory. Reprints
0082-4720 Tokyo Metropolitan Agricultural Experiment Station, Itsukaichi Office. Forestry Experimental Bulletin
0082-4739 Tokyo Medical and Dental University. Institute for Medical and Dental Engineering. Reports
0082-4747 Tokyo Metropolitan University. Faculty of Technology. Memoirs
0082-4755 National Science Museum. Memoirs
0082-4763 Snow Brand Milk Products Company. Research Laboratory. Reports
0082-4771 Tokyo Metropolitan Research Laboratory of Public Health, Annual Report
0082-478X University of Tokyo. Department of Geography. Bulletin
0082-4798 University of Tokyo. Institute for Solid State Physics. Technical Report. Series A
0082-4801 University of Tokyo. Institute for Solid State Physics. Technical Report. Series B
0082-481X University of Tokyo. Institute of Applied Microbiology. Reports
0082-4828 University of Tokyo. Institute of Space and Aeronautical Science. Report
0082-4836 Tokyo University of Fisheries Journal. Special Edition /Tokyo Suisan Daigaku Tokubetu Kenkyu Honoku
0082-4844 Tokyo University of Foreign Studies. Summary
0082-4895 Tonga. Minister of Health. Report
0082-495X Topics in Inorganic and General Chemistry
0082-4968 Topics in Lipid Chemistry†
0082-4992 Topics in Phosphorous Chemistry†
0082-500X Topics in Stereochemistry
0082-5018 Art Gallery of Ontario. Annual Report
0082-5034 Hospital for Sick Children, Toronto. Research Institute. Annual Report
0082-5042 Toronto Medieval Bibliographies
0082-5050 Toronto Mediaeval Latin Texts
0082-5077 Royal Ontario Museum. Art and Archaeology. Occasional Papers *changed to* Royal Ontario Museum. Archaeology Occasional Papers
0082-5093 Royal Ontario Museum. Life Sciences. Miscellaneous Publications
0082-5107 Royal Ontario Museum. Life Sciences. Occasional Papers
0082-5115 Royal Ontario Museum. Annual Report
0082-5123 Toronto Semitic Texts and Studies
0082-514X University of Toronto. Department of Electrical Engineering. Research Report
0082-5158 University of Toronto. Department of English. Studies and Texts†
0082-5166 Natural Hazard Research Working Papers
0082-5174 University of Toronto. Department of Geography. Research Publications
0082-5182 University of Toronto. Department of Mechanical Engineering. Technical Publication Series
0082-5190 University of Toronto. Faculty of Forestry. Technical Reports†
0082-5239 University of Toronto. Institute for Aerospace Studies. Progress Report
0082-5247 University of Toronto. Institute for Aerospace Studies. Review
0082-5255 University of Toronto. Institute for Aerospace Studies. Report
0082-5263 University of Toronto. Institute for Aerospace Studies. Technical Note
0082-5271 University of Toronto. Institute for the Quantitative Analysis of Social and Economic Policy. News Letter *changed to* University of Toronto. Institute for Policy Analysis. Annual Report
0082-5298 University of Toronto. Institute for the Quantitative Analysis of Social and Economic Policy. Reprint Series *changed to* University of Toronto. Institute for Policy Analysis. Reprint Series
0082-5301 University of Toronto. Institute for the Quantitative Analysis of Social and Economic Policy. Working Paper Series *see* 0829-4909
0082-531X University of Toronto. Library. Annual Report†
0082-5328 Pontifical Institute of Mediaeval Studies. Studies and Texts
0082-5336 University of Toronto Romance Series
0082-5344 Torquay Natural History Society. Transactions and Proceedings
0082-5352 Torry Research Station, Aberdeen, Scotland. Annual Report
0082-5360 Tottori University. Faculty of Agriculture. Journal
0082-5379 Tottori University Forests. Bulletin *changed to* Tottori Universty Forests. Research Bulletin
0082-5395 Universite de Toulouse-le Mirail. Faculte des Sciences. Annales†
0082-5409 France-Iberie Recherche. Etudes et Documents
0082-5417 France-Iberie Recherche. These et Documents *changed to* France-Iberie Recherche. Theses et Recherches
0082-5441 Touring with Towser
0082-545X Tourism in Greece†
0082-5468 Tourist Bibliography *changed to* Tourism Compendium
0082-5484 Toute la Boisson. International
0082-5506 Towarzystwo Naukowe w Toruniu. Fontes
0082-5514 Towarzystwo Naukowe w Toruniu. Komisja Historii Sztuki. Teka
0082-5522 Towarzystwo Naukowe w Toruniu. Roczniki
0082-5530 Studia Societatis Scientiarum Torunensis. Sectio B (Chemia)†
0082-5549 Studia Societatis Scientiarum Torunensis. Sectio C (Geografia et Geologia)
0082-5557 Studia Societatis Scientiarum Torunensis. Sectio D. Botanica
0082-5565 Studia Societatis Scientiarum Torunensis. Sectio E. Zoologia
0082-5573 Studia Societatis Scientiarum Torunensis. Sectio F. Astronomia
0082-5581 Studia Societatis Scientiarum Torunensis. Sectio G. Physiologia
0082-5611 Toy Trader Year Book
0082-562X Oriental Library. Research Department. Memoirs
0082-5638 Trabajos de Prehistoria. Nueva Serie
0082-5662 Tractocatalogue
0082-5689 Trade Associations and Professional Bodies of the United Kingdom
0082-5697 Trade Directory of Malta†
0082-5735 Trade Directory of the Republic of the Sudan
0082-5743 Trade Directory Wine and Spirit *changed to* Off Licence News Directory
0082-5778 Trade of China
0082-5786 Trademark Register of the United States
0082-5808 Trades Register of London *changed to* London Directory of Industry and Commerce
0082-5824 Trado; Asian-African Directory of Exporters, Importers and Manufacturers
0082-5859 Traffic Laws Commentary
0082-5867 Traffic Report of the St. Lawrence Seaway
0082-5891 Railway World Annual
0082-5913 Transit Fact Book *see* 0821-2996
0082-5921 Transition Metal Chemistry: A Series of Advances†
0082-593X Translations and Reprints from the Original Sources of European History *changed to* Middle Ages
0082-5948 Transplantation Reviews *see* 0105-2896
0082-5956 Transportation Statistics in the United States
0082-5964 Transportieren Umschlagen Lagern†
0082-5980 Transtelel; Transmissions, Telecommunications, Electronique en France
0082-6006 Trattati di Architettura
0082-6022 Travaux de Droit, d'Economique de Sociologie et de Sciences Politiques
0082-6049 Travaux de Linguistique
0082-6057 Travaux de Linguistique et de Litterature
0082-6073 Travaux d'Histoire Ethico-Politique
0082-6081 Travaux d'Humanisme et Renaissance
0082-609X Travaux sur les Pecheries du Quebec
0082-6103 Travel Abroad: Frontier Formalities
0082-612X Canadian Tourist Association. Proceedings *changed to* Tourism Industry Association of Canada. Convention Report
0082-6146 Travel Industry Personnel Directory
0082-6197 Travel Research Journal†
0082-6200 Travel Trends in the United States and Canadian Provinces *changed to* Travel Trends in the United States and Canada
0082-6219 Travel World Year Book and Diary†
0082-6243 Treatise on Analytical Chemistry. Part 1: Theory and Practice of Analytical Chemistry
0082-6251 Treatise on Analytical Chemistry. Part 2: Analytical Chemistry of the Elements; Analytical Chemistry of Inorganic and Organic Compounds
0082-626X Treatise on Analytical Chemistry. Part 3: Analytical Chemistry in Industry
0082-6278 Treatise on Coatings†
0082-6286 Trends in Developing Countries†
0082-6316 Trends in Southeast Asia
0082-6324 Trends in the International Petroleum-Refining Industry†
0082-6340 Treubia
0082-6367 T R I U M F Annual Report *changed to* T R I U M F Annual Report Scientific Activities
0082-6391 Tribolium Information Bulletin
0082-6405 Tribology Convention. Proceedings†
0082-6413 Tribus
0082-643X Trierer Grabungen und Forschungen
0082-6448 Istituto Sperimentale Talassografico, Trieste. Annuario.
0082-6456 Instituto Sperimentale Talassografico, Trieste. Pubblicazione
0082-6464 Universita di Trieste. Istituto di Chimica Biologica. Publicazioni†
0082-6472 Universita degli Studi di Trieste. Istituto di Chimica Farmaceutica. Pubblicazioni†
0082-6480 Universita degli Studi di Trieste. Istituto di Pedagogia. Quaderni
0082-6502 Trinidad and Tobago. Central Statistical Office. Annual Statistical Digest

ISSN INDEX 1413

0082-6510 Trinidad and Tobago. Central Statistical Office. Digest of Statistics on Education†
0082-6529 Trinidad and Tobago. Central Statistical Office. Financial Statistics
0082-6537 Trinidad and Tobago. Central Statistical Office. International Travel Report
0082-6545 Trinidad and Tobago. Central Statistical Office. Overseas Trade. Annual Report
0082-6553 Trinidad and Tobago. Central Statistical Office. Population and Vital Statistics; Report
0082-6561 Trinidad and Tobago Today†
0082-657X Trinidad and Tobago Trade Directory
0082-6588 Trinitarian Bible Society. Annual Report
0082-6596 Trinity University Studies in Religion†
0082-6618 Universitet i Trondheim. Norges Tekniske Hoegskole. Vassdrags-og Havnelaboratoriet. Meddlelelse *changed to* Norwegian Hydrotechnical Laboratory. Bulletin
0082-6642 Tropical Pesticides Research Institute. Annual Report
0082-6669 Tuberkulose-Jahrbuch†
0082-6677 Tuberkulose und ihre Grenzgebiete in Einzel-Arstellungen†
0082-6693 Universidad Nacional de Tucuman. Instituto de Ingenieria Electrica. Revista
0082-6707 Tudomanyszervezesi Fuzetek
0082-6715 Tudomanytorteneti Tanulmanyok
0082-6731 Tuebinger Rechtswissenschaftliche Abhandlungen
0082-674X Tufting Year Book *changed to* Carpet Manufacturer International
0082-6758 Tulane Studies in English *changed to* T S E: Tulane Studies in English
0082-6774 Tulane Studies in Political Science
0082-6782 Tulane Studies in Zoology and Botany
0082-6790 Howard-Tilton Memorial Library. Report†
0082-6812 University of Tulsa. Department of English. Monograph Series *changed to* University of Tulsa. Monograph Series
0082-6820 Tunisia. Ministere du Plan. Budget Economique
0082-6839 Tunisia. Institut National de la Statistique. Statistiques Industrielles *changed to* Tunisia. Institut National de la Statistique. Recensement des Activites Industrielles
0082-6847 Turcica; Revue d'Etudes Turques
0082-6855 Institut Universitaire d'Etudes Europeennes de Turin. Annuaire†
0082-6871 Universita di Torino. Facolta di Agraria. Annali
0082-688X Universita degli Studi di Torino. Istituto di Storia. Collana†
0082-6898 Turkish Review of Ethnography
0082-6901 Turkey. Devlet Istatistik Enstitusu. Dis Ticaret Yillik Istatistik/Statistique Annuelle du Commerce Exterieur/ Annual Foreign Trade Statistics
0082-691X Turkiye Istatistik Yilligi
0082-6928 Turkey. Devlet Istatistik Enstitusu. Tarim Istatistikleri Ozeti/Summary of Agricultural Statistics
0082-6936 Turkey. Devlet Istatistik Enstitusu. Tarimsal Yapi ve Uretim/Agricultural Structure and Production
0082-6944 Turkey. Devlet Planama Teskilati. Yili Programi Ucuncu Bes Yil/Annual Program of the Five Year Development Plan
0082-6952 Turkish Trade Directory & Telex Index
0082-6979 Turun Yliopisto. Julkaisuja. Sarja A. II. Biologica- Geographica- Geologica
0082-6987 Turun Yliopisto. Julkaisuja. Sarja B. Humaniora
0082-6995 Turun Yliopisto. Julkaisuja. Sarja C. Scripta Lingua Fennica Edita
0082-7002 Turun Yliopisto. Julkaisuja. Sarja A. I. Astronomica-Chemica-Physica-Mathematica
0082-7010 Turun Yliopisto. Kirjasto. Julkaisuja
0082-7029 Turun Yliopisto. Klassillisen Filologian Laitos. Opera Ex Instituto Philologiae Classicae Universitatis Turkuensis Edita
0082-7037 Turun Yliopisto. Psykologian Laitos. Reports *see* 0359-0216
0082-7037 Turun Yliopisto. Psykologian Laitos. Reports *see* 0356-8741
0082-7088 Twentieth Century Legal Philosophy Series
0082-710X St. Paul, Minnesota. Metropolitan Transit Commission. Annual Report *changed to* St. Paul, Minnesota. Twin Cities Area Metropolitan Transit Commission. Annual Report
0082-7118 Tyndale Bulletin
0082-7126 U C L A Business Forecast for the Nation and California
0082-7134 U C L A Forum in Medical Sciences
0082-7142 U K Trade Names
0082-7150 Ub'†
0082-7169 Uganda. Geological Survey and Mines Department. Memoirs†
0082-7177 Uganda. Forestry Department. Annual Report
0082-7185 Uganda. Forestry Department. Bulletins†
0082-7193 Uganda. Forestry Department. Technical Notes
0082-7215 Uganda. Geological Survey and Mines Department. Annual Report
0082-724X Uganda. Ministry of Planning and Economic Development. Statistics Division. Enumeration of Employees
0082-7282 Uhrmacher-Jahrbuch†
0082-7290 Uhrmacher - Jahrbuch fuer Handwerk und Handel
0082-7312 Uj Magyar Nepkoltesi Gyujtemeny
0082-7347 Ulster Folklife
0082-7355 Ulster Journal of Archaeology
0082-7363 Ulster-Scot Historical Series†
0082-7371 Ulster Year Book
0082-7444 Underwater Acoustics†
0082-7452 Underwriting Results in Canada†
0082-7460 Unesco Bibliographical Handbooks *changed to* Documentation, Libraries and Archives: Bibliographies and Reference Works
0082-7479 Unesco Earthquake Study Missions
0082-7487 Unesco Handbook of International Exchanges†
0082-7495 Unesco Manuals for Libraries *changed to* Documentation, Libraries and Archives: Studies and Research
0082-7509 Unesco. Records of the General Conference. Proceedings
0082-7517 Unesco. Records of the General Conference. Resolutions
0082-7525 Unesco. Report of the Director-General on the Activities of the Organization
0082-7533 Unesco Statistical Reports and Studies
0082-7541 Unesco Statistical Yearbook
0082-755X Ungarn - Jahrbuch
0082-7568 Uniatec Congress. Records
0082-7576 Uniespana-Cine Espanol
0082-7584 International Conference of Building Officials. Uniform Building Code
0082-7592 Uniform Crime Reports for the United States
0082-7630 Union List of Publications in Opaque Microforms†
0082-7649 Union List of Scientific and Technical Periodicals Held in the Principal Libraries of East Africa†
0082-7657 Union List of Scientific Serials in Canadian Libraries
0082-7681 Union List of Serials in the Wayne State University Libraries *changed to* Union List of Selected Serials of Michigan
0082-7711 Union Nationale de l'Enseignement Agricole Prive. Annuaire
0082-7738 Union Nationale des Oenologues. Annuaire
0082-7762 Union of Nova Scotia Municipalities. Proceedings of the Annual Convention
0082-7770 Union Professionnelle Feminine. Annuaire
0082-7789 Index to Titles of English News Releases of Hsinhua News Agency
0082-7797 Unitarian and Free Christian Churches. Yearbook of the General Assembly *changed to* Unitarian and Free Christian Churches. Handbook and Directory of the General Assembly
0082-7800 Unitarian Historical Society, London. Transactions
0082-7819 Unitarian Historical Society. Proceedings *changed to* Unitarian Universalist Historical Society. Proceedings
0082-7827 Unitarian Universalist Directory
0082-7835 Egypt. Service des Antiquites. Annales
0082-7843 United Baptist Convention of the Atlantic Provinces. Yearbook
0082-786X United Church of Canada. Committee on Archives. Bulletin. Records and Proceedings
0082-7878 United Church of Canada. General Council. Record of Proceedings
0082-7886 United Church of Canada. Year Book
0082-7894 United Community Funds and Councils of America. Addresses Delivered at the United Way Staff Conference†
0082-7908 United Free Church of Scotland. Handbook
0082-7916 United Graphic Guide *changed to* United & Babson Graphic Guide
0082-7932 Travel Trade Directory, U K and Ireland
0082-7940 United Kingdom Atomic Energy Authority. Annual Report
0082-7959 United Kingdom Fire and Loss Statistics *see* 0260-3098
0082-7967 Meat Trade Yearbook *changed to* Meat Trade Yearbook & Diary
0082-7983 United Methodist Church (United States) Division of Education. Adult Planbook *see* 0149-998X
0082-8009 United Nations and What You Should Know about It†
0082-8025 United Nations Congress on the Prevention of Crime and the Treatment of Offenders. Report
0082-8041 Demographic Yearbook
0082-805X Population Studies
0082-8076 United Nations. Disarmament Commission. Official Records *changed to* United Nations Disarmament Yearbook
0082-8084 United Nations. Economic and Social Council. Index to Proceedings
0082-8092 United Nations. Economic and Social Council. Official Records
0082-8106 United Nations Economic and Social Commission for Asia and the Pacific. Development Programming Techniques Series†
0082-8114 United Nations. Economic and Social Commission for Asia and the Pacific. Mineral Resources Development Series
0082-8122 United Nations Economic and Social Commission for Asia and the Pacific. Regional Economic Cooperation Series†
0082-8130 United Nations. Economic and Social Commission for Asia and the Pacific. Water Resources Development Series
0082-8157 Index to Proceedings of the General Assembly of the United Nations
0082-8211 Resolutions of the General Assembly of the United Nations *see* 0082-8157
0082-8289 International Law Commission. Yearbook *changed to* International Law Commission Yearbook
0082-8297 United Nations Juridical Yearbook
0082-8300 United Nations Legislative Series
0082-8319 United Nations. Multilateral Treaties in Respect of Which the Secretary-General Performs Depository Functions *changed to* United Nations. Multilateral Treaties Deposited with the Secretary-General
0082-8327 Estimated World Requirements of Narcotic Drugs. Supplement
0082-8335 Estimated World Requirements of Narcotic Drugs
0082-8343 United Nations. Permanent Central Opium Board. Report to the Economic and Social Council on the Work of the Permanent Central Narcotics (Opium) Board *see* 0257-3717
0082-836X United Nations Regional Cartographic Conference for Asia and the Far East. Proceedings of the Conference and Technical Papers *changed to* United Nations Regional Cartographic Conference for Asia and the Pacific. Report of the Conference
0082-8408 United Nations. Security Council. Index to Proceedings
0082-8416 United Nations. Security Council. Official Records
0082-8459 United Nations. Statistical Yearbook
0082-8475 United Nations. Trade and Development Board. Official Records *changed to* United Nations. Conference on Trade and Development. Trade and Development Board. Official Records
0082-8483 United Nations. Trade and Development Board. Official Records. Supplements
0082-8491 United Nations. Trusteeship Council. Index to Proceedings
0082-8505 United Nations. Trusteeship Council. Official Records
0082-8513 United Nations. Trusteeship Council. Official Records. Supplements
0082-8521 United Nations. Yearbook
0082-8548 United Presbyterian Church in the United States of America. Minutes of the General Assembly
0082-8556 U S O Annual Report
0082-8564 United Society for Christian Literature. Annual Report *changed to* U S C L Bulletin
0082-8599 U S A Oil Industry Directory
0082-8602 U S College-Sponsored Programs Abroad. Academic Year *changed to* Academic Year Abroad
0082-8637 U. S. Agency for International Development. Proposed Foreign Aid Program, Summary Presentation to Congress†
0082-8661 Tables on Hatchery and Flock Participation in the National Poultry Improvement Plan
0082-867X U.S. Agricultural Research Service. Animal Science Research Division. Tables on Hatchery and Flock Participation in the National Turkey Improvement Plan *see* 0082-8661
0082-8688 U.S. Air Force Academy Assembly. Proceedings
0082-8696 U.S. Air Force Academy Library. Special Bibliography Series
0082-870X U.S. Air Force Cambridge Research Laboratories. A F C R L (Series) *changed to* U.S. Air Force Geophysics Laboratory. A F G L (Series)
0082-8742 United States and Canadian Publications on Africa†
0082-8750 United States Animal Health Association. Proceedings of the Annual Meeting
0082-8769 U.S. Arms Control and Disarmament Agency. Annual Report to Congress
0082-8793 World Military Expenditures and Related Data *changed to* World Military Expenditures and Arms Transfers
0082-8815 U. S. Atomic Energy Commission. Annual Report to Congress†
0082-8823 U. S. Atomic Energy Commission. Annual Report to Congress. Supplement. Atomic Energy Research Reports†

ISSN INDEX

0082-8831 — U. S. Atomic Energy Commission. Division of Plans and Reports. Fundamental Nuclear Energy Research†
0082-884X — U. S. Atomic Energy Commission. Safety and Fire Protection Technical Bulletins†
0082-8904 — U.S. Bureau of Commercial Fisheries. Special Scientific Report *changed to* U.S. National Marine Fisheries Service. Technical Report
0082-8939 — U.S. Bureau of International Commerce. Annual Reports
0082-8947 — Export Control Regulations *see* 0094-8411
0082-8963 — U.S. Bureau of International Commerce. Trade Lists *changed to* U.S. Department of Commerce. Trade Lists
0082-9013 — U.S. Bureau of Labor Statistics. Analysis of Work Stoppages†
0082-9021 — U.S. Bureau of Labor Statistics. Bulletins
0082-903X — U.S. Bureau of Labor Statistics. B L S Staff Paper†
0082-9048 — U.S. Bureau of Labor Statistics. Employment and Earnings Statistics for States and Areas *changed to* U.S. Bureau of Labor Statistics. Employment and Earnings: States and Areas
0082-9056 — U.S. Bureau of Labor Statistics. Handbook of Labor Statistics
0082-9064 — U.S. Bureau of Labor Statistics. Industry Wage Surveys
0082-9099 — U.S. Bureau of Labor Statistics. Union Wages and Hours Surveys†
0082-9102 — U.S. Bureau of Labor Statistics. Wage Chronologies†
0082-9110 — U.S. Bureau of Land Management. Public Land Statistics
0082-9129 — U.S. Bureau of Mines. Bulletin
0082-9137 — U.S. Bureau of Mines. Commodity Data Summaries *see* 0160-5151
0082-9250 — U. S. Bureau of Radiological Health. Seminar Paper Series†
0082-9307 — U.S. Bureau of the Census. Annual Survey of Manufactures
0082-9315 — U.S. Bureau of the Census. Census of Agriculture
0082-9323 — U.S. Bureau of the Census. Census of Business *changed to* U.S. Bureau of the Census. Census of Retail Trade
0082-9323 — U.S. Bureau of the Census. Census of Business *changed to* U.S. Bureau of the Census. Census of Wholesale Trade
0082-9323 — U.S. Bureau of the Census. Census of Business *changed to* U.S. Bureau of the Census. Census of Service Industries
0082-934X — U.S. Bureau of the Census. Census of Construction Industries
0082-9358 — U.S. Bureau of the Census. Census of Governments
0082-9366 — U.S. Bureau of the Census. Census of Housing
0082-9374 — U.S. Bureau of the Census. Census of Manufactures
0082-9382 — U.S. Bureau of the Census. Census of Mineral Industries
0082-9390 — U.S. Bureau of the Census. Census of Population
0082-9404 — U.S. Bureau of the Census. Census of Transportation
0082-9412 — U.S. Bureau of the Census. Census Tract Manual†
0082-9420 — U.S. Bureau of the Census. Recurrent Reports on Governments. Chart Book on Government Finances and Employment *see* 0360-2508
0082-9439 — Current Governments Reports: City Government Finances
0082-9447 — U.S. Bureau of the Census. Congressional District Data Book
0082-9455 — U.S. Bureau of the Census. County and City Data Book
0082-9463 — U.S. Bureau of the Census. County Business Patterns
0082-9471 — Current Population Reports
0082-9498 — International Population Reports *changed to* International Population Data
0082-9501 — Current Population Reports: Population Characteristics. Marital Status and Family Status *changed to* Current Population Reports: Population Characteristics. Marital Status and Living Arrangements
0082-951X — U.S. Bureau of the Census. Current Population Reports: Negro Population *changed to* Current Population Reports: Population Characteristics. Social and Economic Characteristics of the Black Population
0082-9528 — U.S. Bureau of the Census. Current Population Reports: School Enrollment: October (Year) *changed to* Current Population Reports: Population Characteristics. School Enrollment: Social and Economic Characteristics of Students
0082-9536 — U.S. Bureau of the Census. Technical Notes†
0082-9544 — U.S. Bureau of the Census. Technical Paper

0082-9552 — U.S. Bureau of the Census. Working Papers
0082-9560 — United States Catholic Missionary Personnel Overseas *changed to* Mission Handbook
0082-9609 — U.S. Civil Aeronautics Board. Aircraft Operating Cost and Performance Report†
0082-9625 — U.S. Coast Guard. Oceanographic Reports (CG-373 Series)
0082-9641 — U.S. Commission on Civil Rights. Clearinghouse Publications
0082-965X — World Refugee Report†
0082-9706 — United States Cross-Country and Distance Running Coaches Association. Proceedings *changed to* United States Cross-Country Coaches Association. Annual Business Meeting. Minutes
0082-9714 — U.S. Department of Agriculture. Agricultural Statistics
0082-9722 — Hatcheries and Dealers Participating in the National Poultry Improvement Plan
0082-9765 — U.S. Department of Agriculture. Farmer Cooperative Service. Information (Series) *changed to* U.S. Department of Agriculture. Agricultural Cooperative Service. Cooperative Information Report
0082-9781 — U.S. Department of Agriculture. Marketing Research Report
0082-979X — U.S. Department of Agriculture. Production Research Reports
0082-9803 — U.S. Department of Agriculture. Report of the Secretary of Agriculture
0082-9811 — U.S. Department of Agriculture. Technical Bulletin
0082-9846 — U.S. Bureau of Domestic and International Business Administration. Overseas Business Reports
0082-9862 — U.S. Department of Defense. Defense Program and Defense Budget
0082-9889 — U. S. Department of Health, Education, and Welfare. Catalog of H E W Assistance Providing Financial Support and Service to States, Communities, Organizations, Individuals†
0082-9897 — U. S. Department of Health, Education and Welfare. Health, Education and Welfare Trends†
0082-9900 — U.S. National Center for Juvenile Justice. Juvenile Court Statistics†
0082-9935 — U.S. Department of Health, Education and Welfare. Statistics on Public Institutions for Delinquent Children *changed to* Children in Custody
0082-9943 — U.S. Department of Justice. Annual Report of the Attorney General of the United States
0082-9951 — U.S. Department of Justice. Opinions of Attorney General
0083-0003 — U.S. Department of State. African Series
0083-002X — U.S. Department of State. Commercial Policy Series
0083-0038 — U.S. Department of State. Department and Foreign Service Series
0083-0054 — U.S. Department of State. East Asian and Pacific Series
0083-0062 — U.S. Department of State. Economic Cooperation Series
0083-0070 — U.S. Department of State. European and British Commonwealth Series
0083-0089 — Far Eastern Series *see* 0083-0054
0083-0097 — U.S. Department of State. General Foreign Policy Series
0083-0100 — U.S. Department of State. Geographic Bulletins†
0083-0119 — U.S. Department of State. International Information and Cultural Series
0083-0127 — U.S. Department of State. International Organization and Conference Series
0083-0135 — U.S. Department of State. International Organization Series
0083-0143 — U.S. Department of State. Inter-American Series
0083-0151 — U.S. Department of State. Near and Middle Eastern Series *changed to* U.S. Department of State. Near East and South Asian Series
0083-016X — U.S. Department of State. Office of the Geographer. Geographic Notes
0083-0186 — U.S. Department of State. Treaties and Other International Acts Series
0083-0194 — U.S. Department of State. Treaties in Force
0083-0208 — United States Participation in the United Nations
0083-0305 — U.S. Army. Corps of Engineers. Port Series
0083-0313 — U.S. Army. Corps of Engineers. Technical Reports, T R (Series)
0083-0321 — U.S. Department of the Interior. Annual Report *see* 0069-9152
0083-0364 — U. S. Department of the Interior. Safety Conference Guides†
0083-0380 — U.S. Department of Transportation. Bibliographic Lists
0083-0399 — U.S. Department of Transportation. Annual Report on High Speed Ground Transportaion Act *changed to* U.S. Department of Transportation. Report on the High Speed Ground Transportation Act of 1965

0083-0429 — United States Dispensatory and Physicians Pharmacology *changed to* United States Dispensatory
0083-0445 — U.S. Department of Agriculture. Agricultural Economics Report
0083-050X — Sewage Facilities Construction†
0083-0518 — U.S. Environmental Protection Agency. Pesticides Enforcement Division. Notices of Judgement under Federal Insecticide, Fungicide, and Rodenticide Act
0083-0526 — U.S. Equal Employment Opportunity Commission. Annual Report
0083-0534 — U S Excise Tax Guide
0083-0542 — U.S. Farm Credit Administration. Annual Report of the Farm Credit Administration on the Work of the Cooperative Farm Credit System *changed to* Farm Credit Administration. Annual Report
0083-0607 — U.S. Federal Communications Commission. I N F Bulletins
0083-0631 — U. S. Federal Council for Science and Technology. Interdepartmental Committee for Atmospheric Sciences. I C A S Reports†
0083-0658 — U.S. Federal Deposit Insurance Corporation. Annual Report
0083-0666 — U.S. Federal Deposit Insurance Corporation. Bank Operating Statistics
0083-0674 — U.S. Federal Deposit Insurance Corporation. Changes Among Operating Banks and Branches
0083-0682 — U. S. Federal Fire Council. Federal Fire Experience for Fiscal Year†
0083-0690 — U. S. Federal Fire Council. Minutes of Annual Meeting†
0083-0704 — U. S. Federal Fire Council. Recommended Practices†
0083-0720 — U.S. Federal Home Loan Bank Board. Report
0083-0747 — U.S. Federal Home Loan Bank Board. Trends in the Savings and Loan Field
0083-0755 — U.S. Federal Maritime Commission. Annual Report
0083-0771 — U.S. Federal Mediation and Conciliation Service. Annual Report
0083-078X — U. S. Federal Power Commission. Annual Report†
0083-0828 — Statistics of Electric Utilities in the United States. Classes A and B Privately Owned Companies *changed to* Financial Statistics of Selected Electric Utilities
0083-0852 — Steam Electric Plant Construction Cost and Annual Production Expenses *changed to* Historical Plant Cost and Annual Production Expenses for Selected Electric Plants
0083-0887 — U.S. Federal Reserve System. Annual Report
0083-0917 — U.S. Federal Trade Commission. Annual Report
0083-0925 — U.S. Federal Trade Commission. Federal Trade Commission Decisions, Findings, Orders and Stipulations
0083-0933 — U.S. Federal Trade Commission. Statutes and Court Decisions Pertaining to the Federal Trade Commission. Supplements *changed to* U.S. Federal Trade Commission. Court Decisions Pertaining to the Federal Trade Commission
0083-0941 — U.S. Fish and Wildlife Service. Research Reports
0083-0968 — United States Foamed Plastic Markets and Directory *changed to* U S Foamed Plastics Markets and Directory
0083-0976 — U.S. Foreign Agricultural Service. Food and Agricultural Export Directory
0083-0984 — Foreign Agriculture Reports†
0083-0992 — U.S. Foreign Agricultural Service. Miscellaneous Reports†
0083-1018 — U.S. Forest Service. Forest Products Laboratory, Madison, Wisconsin. Report of Research at the Forest Products Laboratory.†
0083-1093 — U.S. Geological Survey. Bulletin
0083-1107 — U.S. Geological Survey. Circular *see* 0364-6017
0083-1131 — U.S. Geological Survey. Water Supply Papers
0083-1166 — U. S. Government Films for Public Educational Use†
0083-1174 — United States Government Organization Manual *see* 0092-1904
0083-1220 — U.S. Immigration and Naturalization Service. Administrative Decisions under Immigration and Nationality Laws
0083-1239 — U.S. Immigration and Naturalization Service. Administrative Decisions under Immigration and Nationality Laws. Interim Decisions of the Department of Justice
0083-1247 — U.S. Immigration and Naturalization Service. Annual Report
0083-1263 — United States Import Duties Annotated†
0083-128X — United States in World Affairs *changed to* American Foreign Relations-a Documentary Record

ISSN INDEX

0083-1298 United States Independent Telephone Association. Annual Statistical Volume *changed to* United States Telephone Association. Annual Statistical Volume
0083-1328 U.S. Industrial College of the Armed Forces. Monographs. R Series
0083-1344 U.S. Industrial Outlook *changed to* U.S. Industrial Outlook (Year)
0083-1425 U.S. Institute of Tropical Forestry. Annual Report†
0083-1468 U.S. Forest Service. Annual Report *changed to* U.S. Forest Service. Intermountain Forest and Range Experiment Station. Recent Reports.
0083-1476 U.S. Internal Revenue Service. Annual Report
0083-1484 U.S. Internal Revenue Service. Tax Guide for Small Business
0083-1506 U.S. Interstate Commerce Commission. Advance Bulletin of Interstate Commerce Acts Annotated†
0083-1514 U.S. Interstate Commerce Commission. Annual Report
0083-1522 U.S. Interstate Commerce Commission. Interstate Commerce Acts Annotated
0083-1530 U.S. Interstate Commerce Commission. Interstate Commerce Commission Reports. Decisions of the Interstate Commerce Commission of the United States
0083-1557 United States Lawn Tennis Association. Yearbook
0083-1565 U.S. Library of Congress. Annual Report of the Librarian of Congress
0083-1573 Dewey Decimal Classification Additions, Notes and Decisions
0083-1603 U.S. Library of Congress. Library of Congress Publications in Print
0083-1611 U.S. Library of Congress. Manuscript Division. Registers of Papers
0083-1646 Newspapers Currently Received and Permanently Retained in the Library of Congress *changed to* Newspapers Received Currently
0083-1670 U.S. Maritime Administration. Annual Report
0083-1697 U.S. Maritime Administration. Technical Report Index, Maritime Administration Research and Development†
0083-1700 U S Master Tax Guide
0083-1786 U.S. National Bureau of Standards. Applied Mathematics Series
0083-1794 U.S. National Bureau of Standards. Building Science Series
0083-1808 U.S. National Bureau of Standards. Commercial Standards *changed to* U.S. National Bureau of Standards. Voluntary Product Standards
0083-1840 U.S. National Bureau of Standards. National Standard Reference Data Series
0083-1859 U.S. National Bureau of Standards. Product Standards *changed to* U.S. National Bureau of Standards. Voluntary Product Standards
0083-1905 Technical Highlights of the National Bureau of Standards *changed to* U.S. National Bureau of Standards. Annual Report
0083-1913 U.S. National Bureau of Standards. Technical Notes
0083-1921 U.S. National Cancer Institute. Monograph *changed to* N C I Monographs
0083-1956 U.S. National Center for Health Statistics. Health Resources Statistics†
0083-1964 U.S. National Center for Health Care Statistics. Vital and Health Statistics. Series 12. Data from the Institutional Population Surveys *changed to* U.S. National Center for Health Statistics. Vital and Health Statistics. Series 13. Data on Health Resources Utilization
0083-1972 U.S. National Center for Health Statistics. Vital and Health Statistics. Series 10. Data from the Health Interview Survey
0083-1980 U.S. National Center for Health Statistics. Vital and Health Statistics. Series 11. Data from the Health Examination Survey *changed to* U.S. National Center for Health Statistics. Vital and Health Statistics. Series 11. Data from the Health and Nutrition Examination Survey
0083-1999 U.S. National Center for Health Statistics. Vital and Health Statistics. Series 14. Data on Health Resources: Manpower and Facilities
0083-2006 U.S. National Center for Health Care Statistics. Vital and Health Statistics. Series 13. Data from the Hospital Discharge Survey *changed to* U.S. National Center for Health Statistics. Vital and Health Statistics. Series 13. Data on Health Resources Utilization
0083-2014 U.S. National Center for Health Statistics. Vital and Health Statistics. Series 1. Programs and Collection Procedures
0083-2022 U.S. National Center for Health Statistics. Vital and Health Statistics. Series 20. Data on Mortality
0083-2030 U.S. National Center for Health Statistics. Vital and Health Statistics. Series 21. Data on Natality, Marriage, and Divorce
0083-2049 U.S. National Center for Health Statistics. Vital and Health Statistics. Series 22. Data on Natality and Mortality Surveys *see* 0083-2022
0083-2049 U.S. National Center for Health Statistics. Vital and Health Statistics. Series 22. Data on Natality and Mortality Surveys *see* 0083-2030
0083-2057 U.S. National Center for Health Statistics. Vital and Health Statistics. Series 2. Data Evaluation and Methods Research
0083-2065 U.S. National Center for Health Statistics. Vital and Health Statistics. Series 3. Analytical Studies
0083-2073 U.S. National Center for Health Statistics. Vital and Health Statistics. Series 4. Documents and Committee Report
0083-209X N C R P Report
0083-2103 U.S. National Endowment for the Arts. Annual Report
0083-2111 National Endowment for the Humanities. Annual Report
0083-2162 U. S. National Institute of Neurological Diseases and Stroke. N I N D S Research Profiles; Summary of Research†
0083-2200 U.S. National Labor Relations Board. Annual Report
0083-2219 U.S. National Labor Relations Board. Court Decisions Relating to the National Labor Relations Act
0083-2243 U.S. National Library of Medicine. Annual Report *see* 0093-0393
0083-2251 National Library of Medicine. Literature Search Series
0083-2278 U.S. National Mediation Board. (Reports of Emergency Boards)
0083-2286 U.S. National Mediation Board. Annual Report
0083-2294 National Medical Audiovisual Center. Catalog†
0083-2308 U.S. National Park Service. Archaeological Research Series *see* 0270-1308
0083-2316 U.S. National Park Service. Historical Handbook Series
0083-2324 U.S. National Park Service. Source Books Series†
0083-2332 U.S. National Science Foundation. Annual Report *see* 0565-825X
0083-2359 U.S. National Science Foundation. Federal Funds for Science *changed to* U.S. National Science Foundation. Federal Funds for Research Development
0083-2375 U.S. National Science Foundation. N S F Factbook†
0083-2383 U.S. National Science Foundation. Research and Development in Industry
0083-2405 U.S. National Science Foundation. Surveys of Science Resources Series
0083-2421 Astronomical Phenomena
0083-243X U.S. Naval Observatory. Astronomical Papers Prepared for Use of American Ephemeris and Nautical Almanac
0083-2448 U.S. Naval Observatory. Publications. Second Series
0083-2472 U.S. Forest Service. North Central Forest Experiment Station, St. Paul, Minnesota. Annual Report *changed to* U.S. Forest Service. North Central Forest Experiment Station. List of Publications
0083-2480 U.S. Forest Service. General Technical Report NE
0083-2618 U. S. Office of Education. Accredited Higher Institutions†
0083-2634 U.S. National Center for Education Statistics. Digest of Educational Statistics *changed to* U.S. National Center for Education Statistics. Digest of Education Statistics
0083-2677 Education Directory. Public Schools Systems *see* 0273-4346
0083-2715 U. S. Office of Education. Guide to Organized Occupational Curriculums in Higher Education†
0083-2723 U. S. Office of Education. International Teacher Development Program. Annual Report to Bureau of Education and Cultural Affairs, Department of State†
0083-2758 Opening Fall Enrollment in Higher Education *changed to* U.S. National Center for Education Statistics. Fall Enrollment in Higher Education
0083-2774 U. S. Office of Education. Public School Finance Program†
0083-2790 U. S. Office of Education. Residence and Migration of College Students, Analytic Report†
0083-2855 U. S. Office of Education. Studies in Comparative Education. Education in (Country)†
0083-288X U. S. Office of Education. Title VII: New Educational Media News and Reports†
0083-2898 U. S. Office of Education. Vocational and Technical Education, Annual Report†
0083-2901 U. S. Office of Saline Water. Desalting Plants Inventory Report†
0083-291X U. S. Office of Saline Water. Saline Water Conversion Report†
0083-2979 U.S. Office of the Federal Register. Guide to Record Retention Requirements†
0083-2987 U.S. Forest Service. Pacific Northwest Forest and Range Experiment Station. Annual Report†
0083-2995 U.S. Forest Service. Pacific Southwest Forest and Range Experiment Station. Annual Report†
0083-3002 U.S. Patent and Trademark Office. Annual Report of the Commissioner of Patents
0083-3010 U.S. Patent and Trademark Office. Classification Bulletins
0083-3029 General Information Concerning Trademarks
0083-3037 U.S. Patent Office. Index of Patents Issued from the United States Patent Office *see* 0362-0719
0083-3045 Index of Trademarks Issued from the United States Patent Office *see* 0099-0809
0083-3088 U.S. Peace Corps. Annual Report
0083-3118 United States Polo Association. Yearbook
0083-3134 U. S. Renewal Assistance Administration. Technical Guides†
0083-3142 U. S. Renewal Assistance Administration. Urban Renewal Project Characteristics†
0083-3150 U. S. Renewal Assistance Administration. Urban Renewal Service Bulletins†
0083-3169 U.S. Rocky Mountain Forest and Range Experiment Station. Annual Report of Research at the Station†
0083-3177 U.S. Rural Electrification Administration. Annual Statistical Report. Rural Electrification Borrowers
0083-3185 U.S. Rural Electrification Administration. Annual Statistical Report. Rural Telephone Program
0083-3193 U.S. Rural Electrification Administration. Report of the Administrator of the Rural Electrification Administration
0083-3207 U.S. Saint Lawrence Seaway Development Corporation. Annual Report
0083-3215 U.S. Securities and Exchange Commission. Annual Report
0083-3223 U.S. Securities and Exchange Commission. Decisions and Reports
0083-3231 U.S. Securities and Exchange Commission. Judicial Decisions
0083-3258 United States Ski Association. Directory
0083-3266 U.S. Small Business Administration. Administrative Management Course Program. Topics
0083-3274 U.S. Small Business Administration. Annual Report
0083-3282 S B I C Industry Review *see* 0149-2500
0083-3304 U.S. Soil Conservation Service. National Engineering Handbook
0083-3320 U.S. Soil Conservation Service. Soil Survey Investigation Reports
0083-3339 U.S. Soil Conservation Service. Technical Publications
0083-3398 United States Squash Racquets Association. Official Year Book
0083-3401 United States Statutes at Large
0083-3428 U.S. Tariff Commission. Annual Report *changed to* U.S. International Trade Commission. Annual Report
0083-3436 U.S. International Trade Commission. Imports of Benzenoid Chemicals and Products
0083-3444 U.S. International Trade Commission. Operation of the Trade Agreements Program
0083-3479 United States Tobacco and Candy Journal Supplier Directory
0083-3487 United States Treaties and Other International Agreements
0083-3495 Sires and Dams *changed to* U S T A Sires and Dams
0083-3509 Trotting and Pacing Guide
0083-3517 U S T A Year Book
0083-3533 U.S. Veterans Administration. Annual Report
0083-355X U.S. Veterans Administration. Medical Research Program.
0083-3576 U.S. Veterans Administration. V A Fact Sheets *changed to* Federal Benefits for Veterans and Dependents, IS-1 Fact Sheet
0083-3592 United States Volleyball Association. Official Volleyball Guide and Rule Book
0083-3622 Handbook of Women Workers *changed to* Time of Change: Handbook on Women Workers
0083-3665 United Way of America. Directory *changed to* United Way of America. International Directory
0083-3673 Univers Historique

0083-3681 Univers Politique; Relations Internationales
0083-369X Universal Business Directories, Brisbane and Suburban Business and Trade Directory *changed to* Universal Business Directories, Brisbane and Suburban Business and Street Directory
0083-3703 Universal Business Directories Combined Central and Southern New South Wales Business and Trade Directory†
0083-3746 Universal Business Directories, Melbourne and Suburban Business and Trade Directory
0083-3754 Universal Business Directories North Territory Business and Trade Directory†
0083-3789 Universal Business Directories, Perth and Fremantle and Suburbs Business and Trade Directory
0083-3797 Universal Business Directories, Adelaide and South Australia Country Trade and Business Directory *changed to* Universal Business Directories, Adelaide Business and Street Directory
0083-3819 Universal Business Directories, Sydney and Suburban Business and Trade Directory *changed to* Universal Business Directories, Sydney and Suburban Business and Street Directory
0083-3827 Universal Business Directories, Tasmania Business and Trade Directory *changed to* Universal Business Directories, Tasmania Business and Street Directory
0083-3835 Universal Business Directories West Victoria Country Business and Trade Directory†
0083-3843 Universal Business Directories Western Australia Country Business and Trade Directory
0083-3851 Kongresa Libro
0083-3878 Universal Postal Union. Documents du Congres *changed to* Union Postale Universelle. Actes
0083-3886 Universalist Historical Society. Journal†
0083-3932 Universities and Colleges of Canada *see* 0706-2338
0083-3940 Universities-National Bureau Conference Series†
0083-3967 U C E A Case Series in Educational Administration†
0083-3975 University Geographer
0083-4025 University of Kansas Law Review
0083-4041 University of Queensland Law Journal
0083-405X University of Singapore Science Journal†
0083-4068 University of West Los Angeles Law Review
0083-4106 Univerzita Komenskeho. Filozoficka Fakulta. Zbornik: Ethnologia Slavica
0083-4114 Univerzita Komenskeho. Filozoficka Fakulta. Zbornik: Graecolatina et Orientalia
0083-4122 Univerzita Komenskeho. Filozoficka Fakulta. Zbornik: Historica
0083-4130 Univerzita Komenskeho. Filozoficka Fakulta. Zbornik: Musaica
0083-4165 Univerzita Komenskeho. Filozoficka Fakulta. Zbornik: Paedagogica
0083-4173 Univerzita Komenskeho. Filozoficka Fakulta. Zbornik: Philologica
0083-4181 Univerzita Komenskeho. Filozoficka Fakulta. Zbornik: Philosophica
0083-419X Univerzita Komenskeho. Filozoficka Fakulta. Zbornik: Psychologica
0083-4211 Univerzita Komenskeho. Oddelenie Liecebnej a Specialnej Pedagogiky. Zbornik: Paedagogica Specialis
0083-422X Univerzita Komenskeho. Filozoficka Fakulta. Zbornik: Zurnalistika
0083-4238 Uniwersytet im. Adama Mickiewicza w Poznaniu. Wydzial Biologii i Nauk of Ziemi. Prace. Seria Geologia
0083-4246 Uniwersytet im. Adama Mickiewicza w Poznaniu. Wydzial Filozoficzno-Historyczny. Prace. Seria Filozofia-Logika *changed to* Filozofia-Logika
0083-4254 Uniwersytet im. Adama Mickiewicza w Poznaniu. Wydzial Historyczny. Prace. Seria Psychologia-Pedagogika *changed to* Psychologia-Pedagogika
0083-4262 Uniwersytet im. Adama Mickiewicza w Poznaniu. Wydzial Prawa. Prace *changed to* Prawo
0083-4270 Historia Sztuki
0083-4289 Uniwersytet Jagiellonski. Zeszyty Naukowe. Prace Geograficzne. Prace z Geografii Ekonomicznej†
0083-4300 Uniwersytet Jagiellonski. Zeszyty Naukowe. Prace Archeologiczne
0083-4319 Uniwersytet Jagiellonski. Zeszyty Naukowe. Prace Chemiczne
0083-4327 Uniwersytet Jagiellonski. Zeszyty Naukowe. Prace Etnograficzne
0083-4335 Uniwersytet Jagiellonski. Zeszyty Naukowe. Prace Fizyczne
0083-4343 Uniwersytet Jagiellonski. Zeszyty Naukowe. Prace Geograficzne
0083-4351 Uniwersytet Jagiellonski. Zeszyty Naukowe. Prace Historyczne
0083-436X Uniwersytet Jagiellonski. Zeszyty Naukowe. Prace Historycznoliterackie
0083-4378 Uniwersytet Jagiellonski. Zeszyty Naukowe. Prace Jezykoznawcze
0083-4386 Uniwersytet Jagiellonski. Zeszyty Naukowe. Prace Matematyczne *changed to* Uniwersytet Jagiellonski. Zeszyty Naukowe. Acta Matematica
0083-4394 Uniwersytet Jagiellonski. Zeszyty Naukowe. Prace Prawnicze
0083-4408 Uniwersytet Jagiellonski. Zeszyty Naukowe. Prace Psychologiczno-Pedagogiczne
0083-4416 Uniwersytet Jagiellonski. Zeszyty Naukowe. Prace Zoologiczne
0083-4424 Uniwersytet Jagiellonski. Zeszyty Naukowe. Prace z Historii Sztuki
0083-4432 Uniwersytet Jagiellonski, Krakow. Zeszyty Naukowe. Prace z Logiki *see* 0137-2904
0083-4467 Uniwersytet Mikolaja Kopernika, Torun. Nauki Humanistyczno-Spoleczne. Archeologia *see* 0137-6616
0083-4475 Uniwersytet Mikolaja Kopernika, Torun. Nauki Humanistyczno-Spoleczne. Filozofia *see* 0208-564X
0083-4483 Uniwersytet Mikolaja Kopernika, Torun. Nauki Humanistyczno-Spoleczne. Filologia Polska *see* 0208-5321
0083-4491 Uniwersytet Mikolaja Kopernika, Torun. Nauki Humanistyczno-Spoleczne. Historia *see* 0137-5830
0083-4513 Uniwersytet Mikolaja Kopernika, Torun. Nauki Humanistyczno-Spoleczne. Prawo *see* 0208-5283
0083-4521 Uniwersytet Mikolaja Kopernika, Torun. Nauki Matematyczno-Przyrodnicze. Biologia *see* 0208-4449
0083-453X Unternehmensforschung fuer die Wirtschaftspraxis†
0083-4548 Unternehmung und Unternehmungsfuehrung
0083-4564 Untersuchungen zur Deutschen Literaturgeschichte
0083-4572 Untersuchungen zur Deutschen Staats- und Rechtsgeschichte. Neue Folge†
0083-4580 Untersuchungen zur Sprach- und Literaturgeschichte der Romanischen Voelker
0083-4610 Upper Midwest Economic Study. Progress Report *changed to* Upper Midwest Council. (Reports)
0083-4637 Upper Midwest Economic Study. Technical Paper *changed to* Upper Midwest Council. (Reports)
0083-4645 Upper Midwest Economic Study. Urban Report *changed to* Upper Midwest Council. (Reports)
0083-4661 Uppsala Universitet. Institutionen foer Nordiska Spraak. Skrifter†
0083-4688 Urban Affairs Annual Reviews
0083-4696 Urban Environment†
0083-470X Urban Land Institute. Research Report†
0083-4718 Urban Land Institute. Technical Bulletin†
0083-4726 Urban Planning/Development Series *changed to* University of Washington. College of Architecture and Urban Planning. Development Series
0083-4769 Uro-Nephro; Annuaire de l'Urologie et de la Nephrologie
0083-4785 Universidad de la Republica. Facultad de Odontologia. Anales
0083-4793 Uruk-Warka: Abhandlungen der Deutschen Orient-Gesellschaft *changed to* Deutsche Orient-Gesellschaft. Abhandlung
0083-4807 Used Book Price Guide
0083-4823 Utah Academy of Science, Arts, and Letters. Proceedings *see* 0196-9110
0083-484X Utah Geological Association. Annual Guidebook
0083-4858 Utah State University of Agriculture and Applied Science. Monograph Series†
0083-4947 University of Utah Anthropological Papers
0083-4963 Utrecht Micropaleontological Bulletins
0083-4998 Disputationes Rheno-Trajectinae†
0083-5013 Uttar Pradesh, India. Scientific Research Committee Monograph Series
0083-5021 V W Z
0083-5072 Vade-Mecum
0083-5080 Vademecum Deutscher Lehr- und Forschungsstaetten
0083-5102 Vaikunth Mehta National Institute of Cooperative Management. Publications
0083-5137 Value Engineering Association. Proceedings†
0083-5145 Van Nostrand Mathematical Studies†
0083-5161 Vancouver Art Gallery. Annual Report
0083-517X Vancouver Board of Trade. Annual Report
0083-5196 Vancouver Neurological Centre. Annual Reports
0083-520X Vancouver Stock Exchange. Annual Report
0083-5218 Vanderbilt Rubber Handbook
0083-5226 Vanderbilt Sociology Conference. Proceedings†
0083-5242 Varia†
0083-5250 VARTA Fuehrer durch Deutschland, Westlicher Teil und Berlin
0083-5269 Vascular Flora of Ohio
0083-5277 Vaskohaszati Enciklopedia†
0083-5293 Vatican Observatory Publications
0083-5307 Vegetable Growers Association of Manitoba. Technical and Scientific Papers Presented at the Annual Meeting *changed to* Vegetable Growers Association of Manitoba. Technical and Scientific Papers Presented at Horticultural Industry Days
0083-5315 Vegetarian Handbook *changed to* International Vegetarian Handbook
0083-5323 Die Vegetation Ungarischer Landschaften
0083-5331 Vehicle Builders and Repairers Association. Yearbook *changed to* Vehicle Builders & Repairers Association. Directory of Members & Buyers Guide
0083-534X Veiligheidsjaarboek *changed to* Arbo Jaarboek
0083-5358 Vejtransporten i Tal og Tekst
0083-5366 Venezuela. Ministerio de Agricultura y Cria. Direccion de Economica y Estadistica Agropecuaria. Anuario Estadistico Agropecuario
0083-5374 Venezuela. Ministerio de Minas e Hidrocarburos. Memoria y Cuenta *changed to* Venezuela. Ministerio de Energia y Minas. Memoria y Cuenta
0083-5382 Venezuela. Ministerio de Minas e Hidrocarburos. Oficina de Economia Minera. Hierro y Otros Datos Estadisticos *changed to* Hierro
0083-5390 Venezuela. Ministerio de Minas e Hidrocarburos. Oficina de Economia Petrolera. Petroleo y Otros Datos Estadisticos *changed to* Venezuela. Ministerio de Energia y Minas. Petroleo y Otros Datos Estadisticos
0083-5412 Universidad Central de Venezuela. Facultad de Derecho. Coleccion Tesis de Doctorado†
0083-5420 Universidad Central de Venezuela. Instituto de Estudios Politicos. Cuadernos†
0083-5439 Universidad Central de Venezuela. Consejo de Desarrollo Cientifico y Humanistico. Bibliografia de Humanidades y Ciencias Sociales y Bibliografia de Ciencia y Tecnologia del Profesorado
0083-5447 Musei Civici Veneziani. Bollettino
0083-5455 Venture Capital†
0083-5471 Verband der Automobilindustrie. Taetigkeitsbericht *changed to* Verband der Automobilindustrie. Jahresbericht
0083-548X Tatsachen und Zahlen aus der Kraftverkehrswirtschaft
0083-5501 Verband der Versicherungsunternehmungen Oesterreichs. Bericht ueber das Geschaeftsjahr *changed to* Verband der Versicherungsunternehmungen Oesterreichs. Geschaeftsbericht
0083-5536 Varbergs Museum. Aarsbok
0083-5544 Verdensmarkedet og Danmark†
0083-5560 V D I - Berichte
0083-5579 Verein fuer Geschichte der Stadt Nuernberg. Mitteilungen
0083-5587 Verein fuer Hamburgische Geschichte. Zeitschrift
0083-5609 Verein fuer Luebeckische Geschichte und Altertumskunde. Zeitschrift
0083-5617 Jahrbuch des Vereins fuer Niederdeutsche Sprachforschung
0083-5625 Verein zum Schutze der Alpenpflanzen und Tiere. Jahrbuch *changed to* Verein zum Schutz der Bergwelt. Jahrbuch
0083-5633 Vereinigte Evangelisch-Lutherische Kirche Deutschlands. Amtsblatt†
0083-5641 Vereinigung Pro Sihltal. Blaetter
0083-565X Vereinigung Freunde der Universitaet Mainz. Jahrbuch†
0083-5676 Verfassung und Verfassungswirklichkeit
0083-5684 Verhandlungen des Deutschen Geographentages
0083-5692 Verified Directory of Manufacturers' Representatives *changed to* MacRae's Verified Directory of Manufacturers' Representatives
0083-5706 Vermont. Agricultural Experiment Station, Burlington. Research Report
0083-5714 Vermont. Agricultural Experiment Station, Burlington. Station Bulletin Series
0083-5722 Vermont. Agricultural Experiment Station, Burlington. Station Pamphlet Series
0083-5730 Vermont. Commissioner of Banking and Insurance. Annual Report of the Bank Commissioner
0083-5757 Vermont. Geological Survey. Bulletin
0083-5765 Vermont. Geological Survey. Special Publication†
0083-5781 Vermont Year Book
0083-579X Vermont's Game Annual†
0083-5803 Verpackungs-Magazin†
0083-5811 Verpackungsfolien/Verpackungspapiere†
0083-582X Verse Speaking Anthology†
0083-5846 Verstaendliche Wissenschaft
0083-5862 Veterinaer-Medizinische Nachrichten
0083-5870 Veterinary Annual
0083-5889 Vetus Testamentum. Supplements

ISSN INDEX 1417

ISSN	Title
0083-5897	Viator
0083-5900	Great Britain. Victoria and Albert Museum. Illustrated Booklets *changed to* Great Britain. Victoria and Albert Museum. Illustrated Books
0083-5919	Great Britain. Victoria and Albert Museum. Monographs
0083-5927	Victoria and Albert Museum, South Kensington. Yearbook†
0083-5935	Victoria, Australia. Department of Agriculture. Agricultural Economics Branch. Contract Rates†
0083-5943	Victoria, Australia. Department of Agriculture. Agricultural Economics Branch. Farm Credit (Sources and Terms)†
0083-5951	Victoria, Australia. Department of Agriculture. Pig Industry Branch. Pig Farm Management Study†
0083-596X	Victoria, Australia. Department of Agriculture. Poultry Branch. Poultry Farm Management Study†
0083-5978	Victoria, Australia. Forests Commission. Forestry Technical Papers†
0083-5986	National Museum of Victoria. Memoirs *changed to* Museum of Victoria. Memoirs
0083-601X	Victoria League for Commonwealth Friendship. Annual Report
0083-6036	Victoria University of Wellington. Awards Handbook
0083-6079	Victorian Society. Annual
0083-6087	Victorian Society. Conference Reports†
0083-6095	Vie des Affaires
0083-6109	Vie Musicale en France Sous les Rois Bourbons. Serie 1: Etudes
0083-6117	Vie Musicale en France Sous les Rois Bourbons. Serie 2: Recherches sur la Musique Classique Francaise
0083-6125	Informationen zu Aktuellen Fragen der Sozial- und Wirtschaftpolitik
0083-6133	Naturhistorisches Museum in Wien. Annalen
0083-6141	Naturhistorisches Museum in Wien. Flugblatt†
0083-6168	Universitaet Wien. Institut fuer Statistik. Schriftenreihe. Neue Folge†
0083-6176	Vienna. Universitaet. Institut fuer Theaterwissenschaft. Wissenschaftliche Reihe *changed to* Wiener Forschungen zur Theater und Medienwissenschaft
0083-6184	Assemblees de Dieu de France. Annuaire
0083-6230	Viewpoints in Biology†
0083-6249	Viking Fund Publications in Anthropology†
0083-6257	Viking Society for Northern Research. Text Series
0083-6265	Vilagtortenet
0083-6273	Villa Guide
0083-6281	Vincentian Studies†
0083-629X	Virgil Society. Proceedings
0083-6311	Virginia Baptist Register
0083-632X	Virginia. Division of Mineral Resources. Information Circular *changed to* Virginia. Division of Mineral Resources. Reports
0083-6338	Virginia. Division of Mineral Resources. Resources Report *changed to* Virginia. Division of Mineral Resources. Reports
0083-6346	Virginia. Division of Mineral Resources. Report of Investigations *changed to* Virginia. Division of Mineral Resources. Reports
0083-6354	Virginia Educational Directory
0083-6370	Virginia Highway Conference. Proceedings *changed to* Virginia Highway and Transportation Conference. Proceedings
0083-6389	Virginia Historical Society. Documents
0083-6397	Virginia Institute of Marine Science, Gloucester Point. Translation Series.
0083-6427	Virginia Institute of Marine Science, Gloucester Point. Educational Series
0083-6435	Virginia Institute of Marine Science, Gloucester Point. Marine Resources Advisory Series
0083-6443	Virginia Institute of Marine Science, Gloucester Point. Special Scientific Report
0083-6451	Virginia Military Institute, Lexington. Publications, Theses, and Dissertations of the Staff and Faculty
0083-6508	Virginia Polytechnic Institute and State University. Wood Research and Wood Construction Laboratory. Special Report *changed to* Virginia Polytechnic Institute and State University. Pallet and Container Research Laboratory. Special Report
0083-6516	Virginia Port Authority. Foreign Trade Annual Report: The Ports of Virginia†
0083-6524	Virginia. State Library. Publications†
0083-6532	Virginia Port Authority. Board of Commissioners. Annual Report†
0083-6575	Virginia's Supply of Public School Instructional Personnel
0083-6591	Virology Monographs
0083-6613	Vishveshvaranand Indological Paper Series
0083-6621	Vishveshvaranand Indological Series
0083-6656	Vistas in Astronomy
0083-6672	Visti Iz Sarseliu
0083-6680	Visual Education Yearbook†
0083-6710	Vital Statistics of the United States
0083-6729	Vitamins and Hormones: Advances in Research and Applications
0083-6737	Kungliga Vitterhets-, Historie- och Antikvitets Akademien. Antikvariskt Arkiv
0083-6745	Kungliga Vitterhets-, Historie- och Antikvitets Akademien. Filologiskt Arkiv
0083-6753	Kungliga Vitterhets-, Historie- och Antikvitets Akademien. Historiskt Arkiv
0083-6761	Kungliga Vitterhets-, Historie- och Antikvitets Akademien. Handlingar. Antikvariska Serien
0083-677X	Kungliga Vitterhets-, Historie- och Antikvitets Akademien. Handlingar. Filologisk-Filosofiska Serien
0083-6788	Kungliga Vitterhets-, Historie- och Antikvitets Akademien. Handlingar. Historiska Serien
0083-6796	Kungliga Vitterhets-, Historie- och Antikvitets Akademien. Aarsbok
0083-6826	Voix dans le Monde
0083-6842	Agricultural Research Organization, Rehovot. Bulletin *changed to* Agricultural Research Organization. Pamphlet
0083-6877	Volkstum der Schweiz
0083-6893	Vollschlank†
0083-6907	Voluntary Social Services *changed to* Voluntary Agencies
0083-6915	Vom Wasser
0083-6923	Vorreformationsgeschichtliche Forschungen
0083-6931	Vortraege aus der Praktischen Chirurgie *see* 0079-4899
0083-694X	Vulkaniseur - Jahrbuch
0083-6982	Waermelehre und Waermewirtschaft in Einzeldarstellungen†
0083-6990	Landbouwhogeschool, Wageningen. Miscellaneous Papers
0083-7016	Tasmanian Almanac†
0083-7024	Walden's A B C Guide and Paper Production Yearbook
0083-7059	Walia
0083-7067	Walker's Old Moore's Almanac
0083-7075	Wall Street Journal Index
0083-7091	Wallace Wurth Memorial Lecture†
0083-7105	Wallraf-Richartz-Jahrbuch; Westdeutsches Jahrbuch fuer Kunstgeschichte *changed to* Wallraf-Richartz-Jahrbuch; Westdeutsches Jahrbuch fuer Kunstgeschichte. Neue Folge
0083-7113	Wirtschaftswissenschaftliche und Wirtschaftsrechtliche Untersuchungen
0083-7121	Walter Lynwood Fleming Lectures in Southern History
0083-7148	Walter W.S. Cook Alumni Lecture
0083-7156	Walters Art Gallery. Journal
0083-7172	Wanderlust†
0083-7199	Warburg Institute. Studies
0083-7202	Warburg Institute. Surveys *see* 0266-1772
0083-7210	Ward - Phillips Lectures in English Language and Literature
0083-7229	Ward's Automotive Yearbook
0083-7261	Biblioteka Narodowa. Rocznik
0083-7288	Akademia Rolnicza, Warsaw. Zeszyty Naukowe. Ogrodnictwo *see* 0208-5747
0083-7296	Akademia Rolnicza, Warsaw. Zeszyty Naukowe. Seria Historyczna†
0083-730X	Szkola Glowna Planowania i Statystyki. Zeszyty Naukowe†
0083-7326	Uniwersytet Warszawski. Instytut Geograficzny. Prace i Studia.†
0083-7334	Uniwersytet Warszawski. Katedra Klimatologii. Prace i Studia†
0083-7342	Uniwersytet Warszawski. Roczniki†
0083-7350	Warwick Economic Research Papers
0083-7369	Warwick Research Industrial and Business Studies *changed to* Warwick Papers in Management
0083-7393	Washington (Year)
0083-7407	Textile Museum Journal
0083-7431	Washington State Dental Journal
0083-744X	Washington (State). Department of Fisheries. Fisheries Research Papers†
0083-7466	Washington (State). Department of Fisheries. Research Bulletin†
0083-7474	Washington (State) Department of Fisheries. Technical Report
0083-7482	Washington (State) Office of Program Planning and Fiscal Management. Population and Enrollment Section. Population Trends *changed to* Washington (State) Office of Financial Management. Policy Analysis and Forecasting. Population Trends
0083-7512	Washington State University. College of Engineering. Annual Report *see* 0033-6327
0083-7520	University of Washington. Department of Oceanography. Contribution†
0083-7539	University of Washington. Department of Oceanography. Fishery Report†
0083-7547	University of Washington. Department of Oceanography. Special Report†
0083-7555	Research in Fisheries
0083-7563	Washington. State University, Pullman. Library Staff Association. L S A Open Stacks
0083-7571	University of Washington Publications in Biology†
0083-758X	Washington (State) Utilities and Transportation Commission. Transportation Report†
0083-761X	Waste Management Research Abstracts
0083-7628	Watchmaker, Jeweller and Silversmith Directory of Trade Names and Punch Marks *changed to* Jewellers' Reference Book
0083-7636	Water
0083-7644	Water Engineer's Handbook *changed to* Water Services Year Book
0083-7652	Water in Biological Systems†
0083-7660	Water Pollution Research†
0083-7679	Water Pollution Research Laboratory, Stevenage, England. Technical Papers†
0083-7717	Water Works Manual *see* 0163-9730
0083-7725	Waterborne Commerce of the United States
0083-7733	Waterloo Historical Society. Report
0083-775X	Wayne State University. Medical Library. Report *changed to* Wayne State University, Detroit. Medical School Library. Report
0083-7776	Wealth and Welfare of Andhra Pradesh Series *changed to* Social Sciences Research Series
0083-7822	Wehrwissenschaftliche Berichte *changed to* Bernard und Graefe Aktuell
0083-7849	Weizmann Institute of Science, Rehovot, Israel. Scientific Activities
0083-789X	New Zealand Oceanographic Institute. Collected Reprints
0083-7903	New Zealand Oceanographic Institute. Memoir
0083-7911	Welsh Bibliographical Society. Journal
0083-7938	Welsh Soils Discussion Group. Report
0083-7946	Welsh Studies in Education Series
0083-7954	Weltstaedte der Kunst. Edition Leipzig†
0083-7989	Wenner Gren Center International Symposium Series
0083-7997	Wenner - Gren Foundation for Anthropological Research. Report *changed to* Wenner - Gren Foundation for Anthropological Research. Annual Report
0083-8012	Werbung in Deutschland *see* 0344-712X
0083-8047	Werken und Wohnen
0083-8055	Werkstattbuecher fuer Betriebsfachleute Konstrukteure und Studenten *see* 0171-5062
0083-811X	Wessex Cave Club Occasional Publication
0083-8136	Wessex Geographical Year
0083-8144	West Africa Annual
0083-8160	West African Journal of Archaeology
0083-8187	West African Religion
0083-8217	West Coast Reliability Symposium
0083-8292	Pakistan. Directorate of Livestock Farms. Report
0083-8306	Pakistan. Directorate of Rural Works Programme. Evaluation Report
0083-8322	Pakistan. Official Language Committee. Urdu Translation of Official Terms and Phraseology
0083-8349	Pakistan. Water and Power Development Authority. Report
0083-8381	West Virginia. Agricultural Experiment Station, Morgantown. Current Report *changed to* West Virginia. Agricultural and Forestry Experiment Station. Current Report
0083-8403	West Virginia University. Center for Appalachian Studies and Development. Information Series†
0083-8411	West Virginia University. Center for Appalachian Studies and Development. Research Series *changed to* West Virginia University. Center for Extension and Continuing Education. Research Series
0083-842X	West Virginia Coal Mining Institute. Proceedings
0083-8438	West Virginia. Commission on Aging. Annual Progress Report
0083-8446	West Virginia. Commission on Mental Retardation. Annual Report†
0083-8462	West Virginia. Department of Mines. Directory of Mines *changed to* West Virginia. Department of Energy. Annual Report and Directory
0083-8470	West Virginia Geological Survey Newsletter *see* 0163-2825
0083-8489	West Virginia Geological Survey. Archaeological Series†
0083-8497	West Virginia Geological Survey. Basic Data Reports *changed to* West Virginia River Basin Basic Data Reports
0083-8500	West Virginia Geological Survey. Bulletin†
0083-8519	West Virginia Geological Survey. Circulars†
0083-8527	West Virginia Geological Survey. Geological Publications. Volumes†
0083-8535	West Viginia Geological Survey. Archaeological Investigations *changed to* West Virginia Reports of Archaeological Investigations

0083-8543 West Virginia Geological Survey. Reports of Investigations *changed to* West Virginia Reports of Geologic Investigations
0083-856X West Virginia Geological Survey. River Basin Bulletins *changed to* West Virginia River Basin Bulletins
0083-8578 West Virginia Geological Survey. State Park Bulletins *changed to* West Virginia State Park Geology Bulletins
0083-8586 West Virginia Government†
0083-8594 West Virginia. Human Rights Commission. Report
0083-8608 West Virginia University. Bureau for Government Research. Publications†
0083-8640 West Virginia University. Engineering Experiment Station. Bulletin†
0083-8659 West Virginia University. Engineering Experiment Station. Report†
0083-8675 Western Australia. Department of Agriculture. Technical Bulletin
0083-8683 Western Australia. Fisheries and Fauna Department. Bulletin *see* 0155-9435
0083-8691 Western Australia. Office of Director General of Transport. Annual Report†
0083-8705 University of Western Australia. Institute of Agriculture. Research Report: Agricultural Economics†
0083-8713 University of Western Australia. Library. Report on the Library†
0083-8721 Western Australia Museum, Perth. Report of the Museum Board *changed to* Western Australian Museum, Perth. Annual Report
0083-873X Western Australian Museum, Perth. Special Publication†
0083-8748 Western Australian Naturalists' Club, Perth. Handbook *see* 0726-9609
0083-8756 Western Australian Pocket Yearbook
0083-8764 Western Australian Reports
0083-8772 Western Australian Yearbook. New Series
0083-8799 Western Canada Water and Sewage Conference. Papers Presented at Annual Convention *changed to* Western Canada Water and Waste Water Association. Bulletin
0083-8810 Western Canadian Society for Horticulture . Report of Proceedings of Annual Meeting
0083-8829 Western Canadian Studies in Modern Languages and Literature†
0083-8853 Assembly of Western European Union. Proceedings
0083-887X Western Frontier Library
0083-8888 Western Frontiersmen Series
0083-8918 Western Highway Institute. Research Committee. Report
0083-8934 Western Lands and Waters Series
0083-8942 Western Market Almanac†
0083-8950 Western Ontario Law Review *see* 0703-900X
0083-8969 Western Pharmacology Society. Proceedings
0083-8977 W P S Professional Handbook Series
0083-8985 Western Reserve Historical Society, Cleveland. Publications *changed to* Western Reserve Historical Society News
0083-9019 Westernlore Ghost Town Series
0083-9027 Westfaelische Forschungen
0083-9043 Westfaelische Zeitschrift
0083-906X Westminster Series†
0083-9078 Weyers Flottentaschenbuch
0083-9086 Whales Research Institute, Tokyo, Japan. Scientific Reports
0083-9094 University of Pennsylvania. Wharton School of Finance and Commerce. Industrial Research Unit Studies *changed to* Major Industrial Research Unit Studies
0083-9108 What Every Veteran Should Know
0083-9116 What Research Says to the Teacher Series
0083-9132 What You Should Know about Taxes in Puerto Rico
0083-9167 Where America's Large Foundations Make Their Grants
0083-9175 Where to Buy
0083-9213 Where to Golf in Europe *see* 0017-1735
0083-9221 Where to Stay in Scotland *changed to* Scotland: Where to Stay, Hotels and Guest Houses
0083-9221 Where to Stay in Scotland *changed to* Scotland: Where to Stay, Bed and Breakfast
0083-923X Which University *changed to* Which Degree
0083-9256 Whitaker's Almanack
0083-9272 White Paper on Japan's Forest Industries
0083-9299 Wer Baut Maschinen
0083-9302 Who Owns Whom. Continental Europe
0083-9310 Who Owns Whom, North America
0083-9329 Who Owns Whom. United Kingdom *see* 0140-4040
0083-9337 Who Represents Whom†
0083-937X Who's Who
0083-9396 Who's Who in America
0083-9477 Who's Who in Communist China
0083-9485 Who's Who in Consulting
0083-9493 Who's Who in East Africa†
0083-9507 Who's Who in Electronics
0083-9515 Who's Who in Europe
0083-9523 Who's Who in Finance and Industry
0083-9531 Who's Who in France
0083-9558 Who's Who in Indian Engineering and Industry
0083-9566 Who's Who in Indian Science
0083-9574 Who's Who in Insurance
0083-9590 Who's Who in Israel
0083-9612 Who's Who in Lebanon
0083-9620 Who's Who in Malaysia and Singapore
0083-9639 Who's Who in Movies†
0083-9647 Who's Who in Music and Musicians' International Directory *see* 0307-2894
0083-9655 Who's Who in New Zealand†
0083-9671 Who's Who in Pakistan
0083-9701 Who's Who in Soviet Science and Technology†
0083-971X Who's Who in Soviet Social Sciences, Humanities, Art and Government†
0083-9728 Who's Who in Space†
0083-9736 Who's Who in Switzerland
0083-9752 Who's Who in the Arab World
0083-9760 Who's Who in the East
0083-9779 Who's Who in the Gas Industry *see* 0307-3084
0083-9787 Who's Who in the Midwest
0083-9809 Who's Who in the South and Southwest
0083-9817 Who's Who in the West
0083-9825 Who's Who in the World
0083-9833 Who's Who in the Theatre *see* 0749-064X
0083-9841 Who's Who of American Women
0083-985X Who's Who of British Engineers†
0083-9868 Who's Who of Rhodesia, Mauritius, Central and East Africa *changed to* Who's Who of Southern Africa Including Mauritius, South West Africa, Zimbabwe and Neighboring Countries
0083-9876 Who's Who of Southern Africa *changed to* Who's Who of Southern Africa Including Mauritius, South West Africa, Zimbabwe and Neighboring Countries
0083-9892 Widener Library Shelflist†
0083-9906 Wiener Arbeiten zur Deutschen Literatur
0083-9914 Wiener Beitraege zur Englischen Philologie
0083-9922 Wiener Beitraege zur Kulturgeschichte und Linguistik
0083-9930 Wiener Beitraege zur Theologie†
0083-9957 Wiener Geographische Schriften
0083-9973 W I S T-Informationen
0083-9981 Wiener Jahrbuch fuer Kunstgeschichte
0083-999X Wiener Jahrbuch fuer Philosophie
0084-0009 Wiener Katholische Akademie. Studien†
0084-0017 Wiener Musikhochschule. Publikationen
0084-0025 Wiener Rechtswissenschaftliche Studien
0084-0033 Wiener Romanistische Arbeiten
0084-0041 Wiener Slavistisches Jahrbuch
0084-005X Wiener Studien. Zeitschrift fuer Klassische Philologie und Patristik
0084-0068 Wiener Voelkerkundliche Mitteilungen
0084-0076 Wiener Zeitschrift fuer die Kunde des Morgenlandes
0084-0084 Wiener Zeitschrift fuer die Kunde Suedasiens und Archiv fuer Indische Philosphie
0084-0092 Wiener Zeitschrift fuer Nervenheilkunde und deren Grenzgebiete. Supplement†
0084-0106 Wijsgerige Teksten en Studies
0084-0114 Wilderness Report†
0084-0122 Wildlife Behavior and Ecology
0084-0130 Alaska. Department of Fish and Game. Wildlife Booklet Series
0084-0149 Wildlife Circular, Victoria†
0084-0157 Victoria, Australia. Fisheries and Game Department. Wildlife Contributions *changed to* Wildlife Contribution, Victoria
0084-0165 U.S. Fish and Wildlife Service. Wildlife Leaflets
0084-0173 Wildlife Monographs
0084-0181 Wiley American Republic Series†
0084-019X Wiley Series on Systems Engineering and Analysis
0084-0203 Wiley Series on the Science and Technology of Materials†
0084-0238 William-Frederick Poets Series†
0084-0246 William K. McInally Lecture
0084-0254 William Morris Society. Journal
0084-0297 Williamsburg in America Series
0084-0300 Williamsburg Research Studies
0084-0327 Wilmington Society of the Fine Arts. Report *changed to* Delaware Art Museum. Annual Report
0084-0335 Wiltshire Archaeological and Natural History Magazine *changed to* Wiltshire Archaeological and Natural History Magazine (1982)
0084-0343 Wine and Spirit Trade Review Directory *changed to* Off Licence News Directory
0084-0351 Wines and Vines - Annual Directory of the Wine Industry *changed to* Wines and Vines: Directory of the Wine Industry in North America
0084-036X Child Guidance Clinic of Winnipeg. Annual Report†
0084-0386 Winter Sports in Scotland†
0084-0394 Winter's Tales
0084-0408 Winterthur Conference Report *see* 0084-0416
0084-0416 Winterthur Portfolio: A Journal of American Material Culture
0084-0424 Wire Industry Yearbook
0084-0432 Wire Review *changed to* Wire Industry Machinery Guide
0084-0440 Wireless Pioneer *changed to* Sparks (Santa Rosa)
0084-0459 Wireless World Diary†
0084-0467 Wirkung der Literatur†
0084-0483 Wirtschaft im Ostseeraum *see* 0720-4868
0084-0505 Wisconsin Academy of Sciences, Arts and Letters. Transactions†
0084-0513 Wisconsin Business Monographs
0084-0521 Wisconsin Business Papers†
0084-053X Wisconsin China Series
0084-0548 Wisconsin. Commissioner of Securities. Annual Report *changed to* Wisconsin. Commissioner of Securities. Biennial Report
0084-0564 Wisconsin. Department of Natural Resources. Technical Bulletin
0084-0572 Wisconsin. Department of Transportation. Division of Planning and Budget. Highway Mileage Data
0084-0580 Wisconsin. Department of Transportation. Division of Planning. Highway Traffic
0084-0599 Wisconsin Economy Studies
0084-0602 Wisconsin. Governor's Advocacy Committee on Children and Youth Annual Report†
0084-0610 Wisconsin Project Reports†
0084-0629 Wisconsin Research and Development Center for Cognitive Learning. Practical Papers *changed to* Wisconsin Research and Development Center for Individualized Schooling. Practical Papers
0084-0637 Wisconsin Research and Development Center for Cognitive Learning. Theoretical Papers *changed to* Wisconsin Research and Development Center for Individualized Schooling. Theoretical Papers
0084-0645 Wisconsin Research and Development Center for Cognitive Learning. Technical Reports *changed to* Wisconsin Research and Development Center for Individualized Schooling. Technical Reports
0084-067X Wisconsin State Historical Society. Urban History Group. Newsletter†
0084-0734 University of Wisconsin, Madison. Applied Population Laboratory. Population Notes
0084-0742 University of Wisconsin, Madison. Applied Population Laboratory. Population Series
0084-0769 University of Wisconsin, Madison. Institute for Research on Poverty. Reprint Series
0084-0785 Land Tenure Center. Newsletter†
0084-0793 Land Tenure Center. Paper
0084-0807 University of Wisconsin, Madison. Land Tenure Center. Reprint†
0084-0815 Land Tenure Center. Research Paper
0084-0823 University of Wisconsin, Madison. Land Tenure Center. Training and Methods Series†
0084-0831 University of Wisconsin, Milwaukee. Language and Area Center for Latin America. Discussion Papers *changed to* University of Wisconsin-Milwaukee. Center for Latin America. Discussion Paper Series
0084-084X University of Wisconsin-Milwaukee. Center for Latin America. Essay Series
0084-0858 University of Wisconsin, Milwaukee. Language and Area Center for Latin America. Special Studies Series *changed to* University of Wisconsin-Milwaukee. Center for Latin America. Bibliographic Series
0084-0904 Wisdom†
0084-0912 Wissenschaftliche Alpenvereinshefte
0084-0939 Wissenschaftliche Gesellschaft fuer Personenstandswesen und Verwandte Gebiete. Schriftenreihe. Neue Folge
0084-0947 Wissenschaftliche Normung†
0084-0955 Die Wissenschaftliche Redaktion†
0084-0963 Wissenschaftliche Taschenbuecher. Reihe Biologie
0084-0971 Wissenschaftliche Taschenbuecher. Reihe Chemie
0084-098X Wissenschaftliche Taschenbuecher. Reihe Mathematik, Physik
0084-1005 Wissenschaftliche Vereinigung der Augenoptiker. Fachvortraege der Jahrestagungen *changed to* Wissenschaftliche Vereinigung fuer Augenoptik und Optometrie. Fachvortraege des WVAO - Jahreskongresses
0084-1013 Wistar Institute Symposium Monograph†
0084-103X Wolfman Report on the Photographic Industry in the United States
0084-1056 Women's Accessories Directory; New York Metropolitan Area
0084-1064 Women's Coats and Suits Directory: New York Metropolitan Area *changed to* Women's, Misses & Jr. Coats and Suits Buyers Directory; New York Metropolitan Area

ISSN INDEX 1419

0084-1072 Woningbouwstudies *changed to* R.I.W. Publicaties
0084-1080 Wood & Wood Products Reference Data/Buying Guide *changed to* Wood & Wood Products Reference Buying Guide
0084-1102 Woodall's Mobile-Modular Living *see* 0731-6526
0084-1110 Woodall's Trailering Parks and Campgrounds *changed to* Woodall's Campground Directory. North American Edition
0084-1110 Woodall's Trailering Parks and Campgrounds *see* 0162-7406
0084-1137 Woodrow Wilson National Fellowship Foundation. Newsletter
0084-1145 Woodrow Wilson National Fellowship Foundation. Report
0084-117X Woodstock Papers: Occasional Essays for Theology†
0084-1188 Woodworker *changed to* Woodworker Projects & Techniques
0084-1196 Woodworker Annual *see* 0043-776X
0084-120X Woodworking Industry /Directory *changed to* Woodworking Industry / Buyers' Guide
0084-1218 Wool Review
0084-1226 Woolhope Naturalists' Field Club, Herefordshire. Transactions
0084-1234 Knitovations
0084-1242 Woolner Indological Series
0084-1250 Words: Wai-Te-Ata Studies in Literature†
0084-1285 Work of Aslib: Annual Report *changed to* Aslib Annual Report
0084-1307 Working Conditions in Canadian Industry
0084-1323 Working Press of the Nation
0084-1358 World Agricultural Situation
0084-1366 World Air Transport Statistics
0084-1374 World Airline Record
0084-1382 World Almanac and Book of Facts
0084-1404 World Association for the Advancement of Veterinary Parasitology. Proceedings of Conference†
0084-1412 World Association of Girl Guides and Girl Scouts. Report of Conference
0084-1439 World Book Year Book
0084-1455 WorldBusiness Perspectives†
0084-1463 World Cars
0084-1471 World Cartography
0084-148X World Coal Trade *changed to* International Coal
0084-1498 World Collectors Annuary
0084-1501 World Commerce Annual
0084-151X World Confederation for Physical Therapy. Proceedings of the Congress
0084-1528 W C O T P Annual Report *changed to* W C O T P Report
0084-1544 Trade Unions International of Chemical, Oil and Allied Workers. International Trade Conference. Documents
0084-1552 World Conference on Animal Production. Proceedings
0084-1560 World Conference on Earthquake Engineering. Proceedings†
0084-1609 World Congress of Psychiatry. Proceedings
0084-1625 World Congress of the Deaf. Lectures and Papers *changed to* World Congress of the W F D. Proceedings
0084-1641 World Congress on Fertility and Sterility. Proceedings
0084-165X World Congress on the Prevention of Occupational Accidents and Diseases. Proceedings
0084-1668 World Council of Churches. Commission on World Mission and Evangelism. Research Pamphlets†
0084-1676 World Council of Churches. General Assembly. Assembly-Reports
0084-1684 World Council of Churches. Minutes and Reports of the Central Committee Meeting
0084-1692 World Council of Churches. World Council Studies†
0084-1706 World Crafts Council. General Assembly. Proceedings of the Biennial Meeting
0084-1714 World Economic Survey
0084-1722 World Energy Conference. Plenary Conferences. Transactions
0084-1730 World Energy Conference. Survey of Energy Resources
0084-1749 World Energy Supplies *changed to* Energy Statistics Yearbook
0084-1781 World Fellowship of Buddhists. Book Series
0084-179X World Food Problems
0084-1811 World Forestry Congress. Proceedings
0084-182X World Grain Trade Statistics†
0084-1854 World Jersey Cattle Bureau. Conference Reports
0084-1862 World Jute Directory
0084-1870 World List of Social Science Periodicals
0084-1889 World List of Universities, Other Institutions of Higher Education and University Organizations
0084-1897 World Medical Association. General Assembly. Proceedings†
0084-1900 World Meteorological Association. Regional Associations. Abridged Final Reports *changed to* World Meteorological Organization. Reports of Sessions of Regional Associations
0084-1919 World Meteorological Association. Technical Commissions Abridged Final Reports *changed to* World Meteorological Organization. Reports of Sessions of Technical Commissions
0084-1927 World Meteorological Congress. Abridged Report with Resolutions
0084-1935 World Meteorological Congress. Proceedings
0084-1943 World Meteorological Organization. Basic Documents, Records and Reports *changed to* World Meteorological Organization. Basic Documents
0084-196X Abridged Reports with Resolutions *changed to* World Meteorological Organization. Executive Council Session. Abridged Final Reports with Resolutions
0084-1978 Global Atmospheric Research Programme. Publication Series†
0084-1986 Global Atmospheric Research Programme. G A R P Special Reports†
0084-1994 World Meteorological Organization. Annual Reports
0084-2001 World Meteorological Organization. Reports on Marine Science Affairs
0084-201X World Meteorological Organization. Technical Notes
0084-2028 World Money Guide†
0084-2036 World Motor Vehicle Production and Registration†
0084-2044 World Movement of Mothers. Reports of Meetings
0084-2052 World Muslim Conference. Proceedings
0084-2060 World Muslim Gazetteer
0084-2117 World of Learning
0084-2141 World Peace through Law Center. Pamphlet Series†
0084-2184 World Ploughing Contest. Official Handbook
0084-2206 World Psychiatric Association. Bulletin†
0084-2214 World Record Marine Fishes *see* 0194-3340
0084-2230 World Review of Nutrition and Dietetics
0084-2257 U.S. Department of State. World Strength of the Communist Party Organizations. Annual Report.†
0084-2273 World Tobacco Directory
0084-2281 World Today Series: Africa
0084-229X World Today Series: Far East and Southwest Pacific *changed to* World Today Series: East Asia and the Western Pacific
0084-2311 World Today Series: Middle East and South Asia
0084-2338 World Today Series: Western Europe
0084-2346 World Touring and Automobile Organization. Documentation for Traffic Engineering and Safety Study Weeks
0084-2370 World Trade Union Congress. Reports†
0084-2400 World Union of Organizations for the Safeguard of Youth *changed to* World Union for the Safeguard of Youth. Conference Proceedings
0084-2419 World University Service. Annual Report†
0084-2427 World University Service. Programme of Action†
0084-2443 World Veterinary Congress. Proceedings
0084-2451 World Weather Watch Planning Reports
0084-2478 World Wide Chamber of Commerce Directory
0084-2486 Worldwide Register of Adult Education
0084-2494 World Wildlife Series†
0084-2508 World Yearbook of Education
0084-2516 World Zionist Organization. General Council. Addresses, Debates, Resolutions
0084-2532 World's Poultry Science Association. Report of the Proceedings of International Congress
0084-2540 World's Woman's Christian Temperance Union. Convention Report *changed to* World's Woman's Christian Temperance Union. Triennial Report
0084-2559 Worldview†
0084-2567 Worldwide Directory of National Technical Information Services†
0084-2575 Worldwide Offshore Contractors Directory *changed to* Offshore Contractors and Equipment Worldwide Directory
0084-2583 Worldwide Petrochemical Directory
0084-2605 Wormley, England (Surrey) National Institute of Oceanography. Collected Reprints *see* 0309-7463
0084-2613 Der Wormsgau
0084-2621 Wormsloe Foundation. Publications
0084-263X Woytinsky Lectures
0084-2648 Wrightia†
0084-2664 Writers' and Artists' Yearbook
0084-2680 Writers' and Photographers' Marketing Guide; Directory of Australian and New Zealand Literary and Photo Markets
0084-2699 Writers Directory†
0084-2702 Writer's Guide
0084-2710 Writer's Handbook
0084-2729 Writer's Market
0084-2737 Writer's Yearbook
0084-2745 Writing (San Francisco)
0084-2753 Writings on British History *see* 0308-4558
0084-277X Akademia Medyczna we Wroclawiu. Prace Naukowe
0084-2788 Instytut Automatyki Systemow Energetycznych. Prace
0084-2796 Muzeum Etnograficzne, Wroclaw. Zeszyty Etnograficzne
0084-280X Politechnika Wroclawska. Instytut Technologii Elektronowej. Prace Naukowe. Monografie
0084-2818 Politechnika Wroclawska. Instytut Chemii i Technologii Nafty i Wegla. Prace Naukowe. Studia i Materialy
0084-2826 Politechnika Wroclawska. Instytut Energoelektryki. Prace Naukowe. Studia i Materialy
0084-2834 Politechnika Wroclawska. Instytut Geotechniki. Prace Naukowe. Monografie
0084-2842 Politechnika Wroclawska. Instytut Geotechniki. Prace Naukowe. Studia i Materialy
0084-2850 Politechnika Wroclawska. Instytut Inzynierii Chemicznej i Urzadzen Cieplnych. Prace Naukowe. Monografie
0084-2869 Politechnika Wroclawska. Instytut Inzynierii Ochrony Srodowska. Prace Naukowe. Monografie
0084-2877 Politechnika Wroclawska. Instytut Inzynierii Ochrony Srodowiska. Prace Naukowe. Studia i Materialy
0084-2885 Politechnika Wroclawska. Instytut Technologii Elektronowej. Prace Naukowe. Studia i Materialy
0084-2893 Politechnika Wroclawska. Instytut Technologii Nieorganicznej i Nawozow Mineralnych. Prace Naukowe. Konferencje
0084-2907 Politechnika Wroclawska. Instytut Technologii Nieorganicznej i Nawozow Mineralnych. Prace Naukowe. Monografie
0084-2915 Politechnika Wroclawska. Instytut Technologii Nierorganicznej i Nawozow Mineralnych. Prace Naukowe. Studia i Materialy
0084-294X Politechnika Wroclawska. Instytut Ukladow Elektromaszynowych. Prace Naukowe. Studia i Materialy
0084-2958 Politechnika Wroclawska. Instytut Metrologii Elektrycznej. Prace Naukowe. Studia i Materialy
0084-2974 Wroclawski Rocznik Ekonomiczny
0084-2982 Wroclawskie Towarzystwo Naukowe. Komisja Historii Sztuki. Rozprawy
0084-2990 Wroclawskie Towarzystwo Naukowe. Komisja Jezykowa. Rozprawy
0084-3008 Litteraria
0084-3016 Wroclawskie Towarzystwo Naukowe. Prace. Seria A. Humanistyka
0084-3024 Wroclawskie Towarzystwo Naukowe. Prace. Seria B. Nauki Scisle
0084-3032 Wspolczesne Malarstwo Wroclawskie†
0084-3040 Wuerttembergischer Pferdeuchtverband. Mitteilungen†
0084-3067 Wuerttembergisch Franken
0084-3083 Wuerzburger Wehrwissenschaftliche Abhandlungen
0084-3091 Technische Akademie Wuppertal. Berichte†
0084-3113 Wykeham Science Series
0084-3121 Wykeham Technological Series
0084-3164 Wyoming Nurses Newsletter *changed to* Wyoming Nurse
0084-3180 University of Wyoming. Natural Resources Research Institute. Information Circular†
0084-3210 University of Wyoming. Water Resources Research Institute. Water Resources Series†
0084-3229 Xavier University. Museum and Archives Publications
0084-3237 Yachting Belge
0084-3253 Yachting World Handbook†
0084-3261 Yachtsman's Guide to the Caribbean
0084-327X Yachtsman's Guide to the Great Lakes
0084-3288 Yad Vashem News†
0084-3296 Yad Vashem Studies on the European Jewish Catastrophe and Resistance *changed to* Yad Vashem Studies
0084-330X Yale Classical Studies
0084-3318 Yale College Series
0084-3326 Yale Fastbacks
0084-3334 Yale Germanic Studies
0084-3342 Yale Historical Publications (Manuscripts and Edited Texts)†
0084-3350 Yale Historical Publications (Miscellany)
0084-3369 Yale Judaica Series
0084-3377 Yale Mathematical Monographs†
0084-3385 Yale Near Eastern Researches
0084-3393 Yale Publications in American Studies
0084-3407 Yale Publications in Religion
0084-3415 Yale Publications in the History of Art
0084-3423 Yale Romanic Studies. Second Series
0084-3431 Yale Russian and East European Studies
0084-344X Yale Scene; University Series
0084-3458 Yale Series of Younger Poets
0084-3466 Yale Southeast Asia Studies
0084-3482 Yale Studies in English

0084-3490 Yale Studies in Political Science
0084-3504 Yale Studies in the History of Music†
0084-3512 Yale Studies in the History of Science and Medicine†
0084-3520 Yale Studies of the City
0084-3539 Yale University Art Gallery. Bulletin
0084-3555 Yale Western Americana Paperbounds†
0084-3563 Yale Western Americana Series
0084-358X Yearbook and Directory of Osteopathic Physicians *changed to* A O A Yearbook and Directory of Osteopathic Physicians
0084-3601 Yearbook of Adult Education *changed to* Yearbook of Adult Continuing Education
0084-3628 U.S. Department of Agriculture. Yearbook of Agriculture
0084-3644 Yearbook of American and Canadian Churches
0084-3652 Year Book of Anesthesia
0084-3679 Year Book of Cancer
0084-3687 Yearbook of Cardiovascular Medicine and Surgery *see* 0145-4145
0084-3695 Yearbook of Comparative and General Literature
0084-3709 Yearbook of Comparative Criticism
0084-3717 Year Book of Dentistry
0084-3733 Year Book of Drug Therapy
0084-3741 Year Book of Endocrinology
0084-375X Yearbook of Fishery Statistics
0084-3768 Yearbook of Forest Products
0084-3784 Yearbook of Higher Education†
0084-3806 Yearbook of International Congress Proceedings
0084-3814 Yearbook of International Organizations
0084-3822 International Trade Statistics Yearbook
0084-3830 Yearbook of Israel Ports Statistics
0084-3857 Year Book of Labour Statistics.
0084-3865 Manitoba Agriculture Yearbook
0084-3873 Year Book of Medicine
0084-3881 Yearbook of National Account Statistics *changed to* United Nations. National Accounts Statistics
0084-3903 Year Book of Nuclear Medicine
0084-3911 Year Book of Obstetrics and Gynecology
0084-392X Year Book of Ophthalmology
0084-3938 Year Book of Orthopedics and Traumatic Surgery *see* 0276-1092
0084-3946 Year Book of Pathology and Clinical Pathology
0084-3954 Year Book of Pediatrics
0084-3962 Year Book of Plastic and Reconstructive Surgery
0084-3970 Year Book of Psychiatry and Applied Mental Health
0084-3989 Year Book of Radiology *see* 0098-1672
0084-4020 Yearbook of Technical Education and Training for Industry *see* 0309-5290
0084-4047 Yearbook of the Commonwealth
0084-4055 Year Book of the Ear, Nose and Throat *changed to* Year Book of Otolaryngology
0084-4071 Year Book of Urology
0084-408X Yearbook of World Affairs†
0084-4098 Yearbook on Human Rights
0084-4101 Yearbook on International Communist Affairs
0084-411X Yearbook on Jute
0084-4128 Yearbooks in Christian Education
0084-4144 Year's Work in English Studies
0084-4152 Year's Work in Modern Language Studies
0084-4160 Yeats Centenary Papers *changed to* New Yeats Papers
0084-4179 Yerkes Regional Primate Research Center. Newsletter†
0084-4195 Yeshiva University. Belfer Graduate School of Science. Monographs†
0084-4209 Yivo Annual of Jewish Social Science
0084-4217 Yivo Bleter
0084-4225 Finnish Broadcasting Company. Section for Long-Range Planning. Research Reports *changed to* Finnish Broadcasting Company. Planning and Research Department. Research Reports
0084-4241 York University. Toronto. Institute of Behavioural Research. Bulletin *changed to* York University, Toronto. Institute for Behavioural Research. Newsletter
0084-4268 York University, Toronto. Molecular Psycho-Biology Laboratory. Report†
0084-4276 Yorkshire Archaeological Journal
0084-4292 Y M C A Yearbook and Official Roster
0084-4306 Young Women's Christian Association of the United States of America. The Printout
0084-4314 J.K. Lasser's Your Income Tax
0084-4322 Your United Nations
0084-4349 Yugoslav Export - Import Directory
0084-4357 Demografska Statistika
0084-4365 Yugoslavia. Savezni Zavod za Statistiku. Statisticki Bilten
0084-4373 Statistika Spoljne Trgovine SFR Jugoslavije
0084-439X Yuval
0084-4411 Z Dziejow Form Artystycznych w Literaturze Polskiej
0084-442X Z Dziejow Muzyki Polskiej
0084-4438 Dziejow Stosunkow Polsko-Radziechich *see* 0137-6381
0084-4446 Zagadnienia Rodzajow Literackich
0084-4454 Zagadnienia Eksploatacji Maszyn
0084-4462 Zahnaerztliche Fortbildung†
0084-4489 Zambia. Central Statistical Office. Annual Statement of External Trade
0084-4497 Zambia. Office of the Auditor-General. Report of the Auditor-General
0084-4500 Zambia. Central Statistical Office. Employment and Earnings
0084-4519 Zambia. Central Statistical Office. Financial Statistics of Public Corporations
0084-4527 Zambia. Central Statistical Office. Government Sector Accounts (Economic and Functional Analysis) *changed to* Zambia. Central Statistical Office. Financial Statistics of Government Sector (Economic and Functional Analysis)
0084-4535 Zambia. Central Statistical Office. Insurance Statistics†
0084-4543 Zambia. Central Statistical Office. Migration Statistics
0084-4551 Zambia. Central Statistical Office. Statistical Year Book
0084-456X Zambia. Central Statistical Office. Vital Statistics
0084-4586 Zambia. Commission for the Preservation of Natural and Historical Monuments and Relics. Annual Report
0084-4608 Zambia. Department of Community Development. Report
0084-4616 Zambia. Department of Forestry. Report
0084-4632 Zambia. Department of Labour. Report
0084-4659 Zambia. Prisons Department. Report
0084-4667 Zambia. Department of Social Welfare. Report
0084-4675 Zambia. Department of Taxes. Annual Report of the Commissioner of Taxes
0084-4683 Zambia. Department of the Administrator-General and Official Receiver. Report
0084-4705 Zambia. Department of Water Affairs. Report
0084-4713 Fisheries Research Bulletin of Zambia
0084-473X Zambia. Geological Survey. Annual Reports
0084-4748 Zambia. Geological Survey. Economic Reports
0084-4756 Zambia. Geological Survey. Occasional Papers
0084-4764 Zambia. Geological Survey. Reports
0084-4802 Zambia. Immigration Department. Report
0084-4810 Zambia. Information Services. Annual Report
0084-4853 Zambia. Ministry of Agriculture. Annual Report
0084-487X Zambia. Ministry of Education. Annual Report
0084-4896 Zambia. Ministry of Finance. Annual Report *changed to* Zambia. Ministry of Planning and Finance. Annual Report
0084-4942 National Archives of Zambia. Annual Report
0084-4950 Zambia. National Council for Scientific Research. Annual Report
0084-4969 Zambia. National Food and Nutrition Commission. Annual Report
0084-4977 Zambia. National Museums Board. Report
0084-4993 Zambia. Natural Resources Board. Annual Report *changed to* Zambia. Natural Resources Department. Annual Report
0084-5000 Zambia. Pneumoconiosis Medical and Research Bureau and Pneumoconiosis Compensation Board. Annual Reports
0084-5019 Zambia. General Post Office. Annual Report of the Postmaster-General *changed to* Zambia. Posts and Telecommunications Corporation. Annual Report
0084-5035 Zambia. Public Service Commission. Report
0084-506X Zambia. Sports Directorate. Report
0084-5078 Zambia. Survey Department. Report
0084-5086 Zambia. Teaching Service Commission. Annual Report
0084-5108 University of Zambia. Institute for African Studies. Communication
0084-5116 Zambian Industrial Directory.†
0084-5124 Zambian Papers
0084-5132 Escuela de Gerentes de Cooperativas. Cartillas de Cooperacion
0084-5159 Escuela de Gerentes de Cooperativas. Coleccion Textos
0084-5167 Escuela de Gerentes de Cooperativas. Cuadernos de Practicas
0084-5175 Escuela de Gerentes de Cooperativas. Serie Especial
0084-5183 Zbornik Istorije Knjizevnosti
0084-5191 Zbornik za Istoriju, Jezik i Knjizevnost Srpskog Naroda. Fontes Rerum Slavorum Meridionalium
0084-5205 Zbornik za Istoriju, Jezik i Knjizevnost Srpskog Naroda. Spomenici na Srpskom Jeziku
0084-5213 Zbornik za Istoriju, Jezik i Knjizevnost Srpskog Naroda. Spomenici na Tudjim Jezicima
0084-5221 Ze Skarbca Kultury
0084-523X Zeichenwerk
0084-5264 Savigny-Stiftung fuer Rechtsgeschichte. Zeitschrift. Germanistische, Romanistische und Kanonistische Abteilung
0084-5272 Zeitschrift fuer Alternsforschung. Supplementbaende
0084-5280 Zeitschrift fuer Angewandte Baeder- und Klimaheilkunde†
0084-5299 Zeitschrift fuer Assyriologie und Vorderasiatische Archaeologie
0084-5302 Zeitschrift fuer Celtische Philologie
0084-5310 Zeitschrift fuer die Gesamte Strafrechtswissenschaft
0084-5337 Zeitschrift fuer Ernaehrungswissenschaft. Supplementa†
0084-5345 Zeitschrift fuer Klinische Psychologie - Forschung und Praxis
0084-5353 Zeitschrift fuer Krebsforschung und Klinische Onkologie *see* 0171-5216
0084-5361 Zeitschrift fuer Meteorologie
0084-5388 Zeitschrift fuer Papyrologie und Epigraphik
0084-5396 Zeitschrift fuer Romanische Philologie. Beihefte
0084-5442 Zenith *changed to* Zenith Science Magazine
0084-5477 Zeszyty Problemowe Postepow Nauk Rolniczych
0084-5485 Ziegeleitechnisches Jahrbuch
0084-5493 Ziema Kozielska. Studia i Materialy†
0084-5507 Ziemie Zachodnie. Studia i Materialy
0084-5515 Jimbun
0084-5523 Zionism; Studies in the History of the Zionist Movement and of the Jews in Palestine/Ha-Tsiyonut *see* 0334-1771
0084-5531 Zionist Year Book
0084-554X Zonarida
0084-5558 Zondervan Pastor's Annual
0084-5566 Zoning Digest *see* 0094-7598
0084-5574 ZooBooks†
0084-5582 Zoologia†
0084-5590 Zoologica Gothoburgensia†
0084-5604 Zoological Record
0084-5612 Zoological Society of London. Symposia
0084-5620 Zoological Society of London. Transactions *changed to* Zoological Society of London. Journal of Zoology. Series B
0084-5639 Zoologisch-Botanische Gesellschaft, Vienna. Abhandlungen
0084-5647 Zoologisch-Botanische Gesellschaft, Vienna. Verhandlungen
0084-5655 Zoology of Iceland
0084-5663 Zoophysiology and Ecology *see* 0720-1842
0084-5671 Shipbuilding Yearbook†
0084-568X Zrodla do Dziejow Bydgoszczy
0084-5698 Zrodla do Dziejow Mysli Pedagogicznej†
0084-5701 Zrodla do Dziejow Nauki i Techniki†
0084-571X Zrodla do Historii Muzyki Polskiej
0084-5736 Zuckerwirtschaftliches Taschenbuch
0084-5744 Eidgenoessische Technische Hochschule Zuerich. Mitteilungen. Aerodynamik
0084-5752 Eidgenoessische Technische Hochschule Zuerich. Mitteilungen. Photoelastizitaet
0084-5779 Eidgenoessische Technische Hochschule Zuerich. Institut fuer Geophysik. Schweizerische Erdbebendienst. Jahresbericht†
0084-5809 Zur Lage der Schweiz
0084-5817 Zweisprachige Reihe†
0084-5825 Zwierzeta Laboratoryjne†
0084-5833 A D C A: American Directory of Collection Agencies and Attorneys
0084-5841 A M A
0084-585X Aarboeger for Nordisk Oldkyndighed og Historie
0084-5876 Academie d'Architecture, Paris. Annuaire
0084-5884 Accountancy Research Foundation, Melbourne. Accounting and Auditing Research Committee. Research Studies *changed to* Australian Accounting Research Foundation. Research Studies
0084-5892 Achter het Boek
0084-5906 Acta Botanica Venezuelica
0084-5914 Acta Phytogeographica Suecica
0084-5922 Adelaide City Council Municipal Yearbook *changed to* Adelaide City Council Municipal Reference Book
0084-5930 Advances in Cyclic Nucleotide Research *changed to* Advances in Cyclic Nucleotide Research and Protein Phosphorylation Research
0084-5949 Advances in Cytopharmacology
0084-5957 Advances in Nephrology from the Necker Hospital *changed to* Advances in Nephrology
0084-5965 Adventure Trip Guide *changed to* Adventure Travel North America
0084-5981 African and Oriental Holiday *changed to* African, Mediterranean and Oriental Travel
0084-6015 Agence pour la Securite de la Navigation Aerienne en Afrique et a Madagascar. Direction de l'Exploitation Meteorologique. Publications. Serie 2
0084-6023 Agenda Memento des Cadres et Maitrises de l'Imprimerie, de l'Edition et des Industries Graphiques *changed to* Agenda Memento des Protes
0084-6031 Agricultural Technologist†
0084-6066 Agricultural Wages in India

ISSN INDEX 1421

0084-6082 Akademie der Wissenschaften, Goettingen. Jahrbuch
0084-6090 Bayerische Akademie der Wissenschaften. Jahrbuch
0084-6104 Akademie der Wissenschaften und der Literatur, Mainz. Jahrbuch
0084-6112 Alabama Linguistic and Philological Series†
0084-6120 Alaska Science Conference. Proceedings *changed to* Arctic Science Conference. Proceedings
0084-6139 Alaska. State Library, Juneau. Historical Monographs
0084-6147 University of Alaska. Institute of Marine Science. Occasional Publication
0084-6163 Alberta. Department of Health and Social Development. Annual Report *see* 0381-4327
0084-6171 Alberta Motor Transport Directory
0084-618X University of Alberta. Department of Animal Science. Annual Feeders' Day Report
0084-6198 ALGOL Bulletin
0084-6201 All Sports International
0084-621X University of Allahabad. Education Department. Researches and Studies
0084-6236 Almanaque Salvadoreno
0084-6244 Aloha Aina†
0084-6252 Altern und Entwicklung†
0084-6260 Alternatives Newsmagazine *see* 0199-9346
0084-6279 Aluminium Development Council of Australia. Technical Papers
0084-6287 A A R Studies in Religion
0084-6317 A B F Research Reporter *changed to* American Bar Foundation Research Reporter
0084-6325 A C I Bibliography
0084-6333 American Council on Industrial Arts Teacher Education. Yearbook
0084-6341 American Educational Research Association. Annual Meeting Paper and Symposia Abstracts†
0084-635X American Frozen Food Institute. Membership Directory *see* 0361-0888
0084-6368 American Institute for Marxist Studies. Occasional Papers
0084-6376 American Institute of Chemists. Membership Directory *changed to* American Institute of Chemists. Professional Directory
0084-6384 A I G A Children's Books Show†
0084-6406 A L A Handbook of Organization
0084-6414 National Formulary *changed to* United States Pharmacopeia - National Formulary
0084-6422 American Philosophical Quarterly. Monograph Series†
0084-6430 American Philosophical Society. Library Publications†
0084-6449 American Society of Hospital Pharmacists. Membership Directory†
0084-6465 Anderseniana
0084-6473 Annee Balzacienne
0084-6481 Annuaire de la Photographie Professionnelle
0084-6511 Annuaire des Institutions d'Enseignement Secondaire *see* 0066-8990
0084-652X Annuaire National des Industries de la Conserve *see* 0245-1301
0084-6538 Annuaire National du Lait
0084-6546 Annual Fertilizer Review *changed to* F A O Fertilizer Yearbook
0084-6554 Annual Report on Dental Auxiliary Education
0084-6570 Annual Review of Anthropology
0084-6589 Annual Review of Biophysics and Bioengineering *see* 0883-9182
0084-6597 Annual Review of Earth and Planetary Sciences
0084-6600 Annual Review of Materials Science
0084-6619 Annuario Amministrativo Italiano
0084-6627 Annuario Generale Italiano
0084-6635 Annuario Italiano delle Imprese Assicuratrici
0084-6651 Apartment Building Income-Expense Analysis *see* 0194-1941
0084-666X Apocalypse†
0084-6678 Apparel Plant Wages and Personnel Policies *see* 0275-8873
0084-6678 Apparel Plant Wages and Personnel Policies *changed to* Personnel Policies and Benefits for the Apparel Industry
0084-6708 Architects, Builders, and Contractors Blue-Book†
0084-6716 Buildings of the Year
0084-6724 Archiv fuer Religionspsychologie
0084-6732 Armidale and District Historical Society. Journal and Proceedings
0084-6740 University of New England. Bulletin *see* 0156-1006
0084-6759 University of New England. Faculty of Agricultural Economics. Farm Case Study†
0084-6767 University of New England. Faculty of Agricultural Economics. Farm Management Report†
0084-6775 Arquivos Brasileiros de Nutricao
0084-6783 Art at Auction; the Year at Sotheby's and Parke-Bernet
0084-6805 Asia in the Modern World Series†
0084-6813 Asian Institute Translations†
0084-6821 Asian Population Programme News *see* 0252-3639
0084-683X A T A V E Boletin Informativo
0084-6848 Asociacion Venezolano Britanica de Comercio e Industria. Anuario *changed to* Camara Venezolano Britanica de Comercio e Industria. Anuario
0084-6864 Association for Supervision and Curriculum Development. Curriculum Materials *changed to* Association for Supervision and Curriculum Development. Curriculum Materials Digest
0084-6899 Association of Consulting Engineers of Canada. Specialization Typical Projects *see* 0317-6525
0084-6902 Center for Chinese Research Materials. Bibliographical Series
0084-6929 Revista del Ateneo Paraguayo†
0084-6953 Australasian Bandsman
0084-6961 Australasian Commercial Teachers' Association. Journal
0084-697X A.I.J. Manual of Australasian Life Assurance
0084-6988 Australasian Methodist Historical Society. Journal and Proceedings *changed to* Church Heritage
0084-6996 Australasian Society of Engineers. Engineers Handbook
0084-7011 Australia. Bureau of Agricultural Economics. Beef Situation *see* 0311-0885
0084-702X Australia. Bureau of Agricultural Economics. Coarse Grains and Oilseeds Situation *see* 0311-0788
0084-702X Australia. Bureau of Agricultural Economics. Coarse Grains and Oilseeds Situation *see* 0311-8789
0084-7038 Australia. Bureau of Agricultural Economics. Dairy Situation *see* 0311-8843
0084-7046 Australia. Bureau of Agricultural Economics. Egg Situation *changed to* Australia. Bureau of Agricultural Economics. Eggs: Situation and Outlook
0084-7054 Australia. Bureau of Agricultural Economics. Mutton and Lamb Situation *see* 0311-0885
0084-7089 Australia. Bureau of Mineral Resources, Geology and Geophysics. Bulletin
0084-7097 Australia. Bureau of Mineral Resources, Geology and Geophysics. Petroleum Search Subsidy Acts. Publications†
0084-7100 Australia. Bureau of Mineral Resources, Geology and Geophysics. Reports
0084-7135 Australia. Department of Foreign Affairs. International Treaties and Conventions *see* 0519-5950
0084-7208 Australian and New Zealand Hospitals and Health Services Yearbook *see* 0312-5599
0084-7216 A.A.T.E. Guide to English Books
0084-7224 Australian Association of Neurologists Proceedings *see* 0158-1597
0084-7232 Australian Aviation Yearbook†
0084-7259 Australian Catholic Historical Society. Journal
0084-7267 Australian Coin Catalogue†
0084-7275 Australian Communist
0084-7283 A C F Newsletter
0084-7291 Australian Cricket Yearbook
0084-7305 Australian Directory of Exports *changed to* Australian Exports
0084-7348 Australian Economy; Business Forecast *see* 0816-2484
0084-7356 Australian Fisheries Paper†
0084-7364 Australian Gliding Yearbook
0084-7402 Australian Horse Racing Annual
0084-7410 Australian Hospital Newsletter *changed to* Hospital Brief
0084-7429 Australian House and Garden Annual†
0084-7445 Australian Industrial Law Review
0084-7453 Australian Insurance Institute. Journal *see* 0314-8580
0084-747X Australian Journal of Biblical Archaeology†
0084-7488 Australian Mineral Industry. Annual Review
0084-7496 Australian National University, Canberra. Department of Engineering Physics. Publication Ep-Rr
0084-750X Australian National University, Canberra. Geology Department. Publication
0084-7518 Australian National University, Canberra. Research School of Physical Sciences. Research Paper
0084-7526 Australian Packaging and Materials Handling Yearbook and Buyers Guide *changed to* Australian Packaging Buyers Guide
0084-7534 A.P.E.A. Journal
0084-7550 Australian Poetry†
0084-7593 Australian Ski Yearbook
0084-7607 Australian Society for Limnology. Bulletin†
0084-7623 Australian Welder *changed to* Australian and New Zealand Welder
0084-764X Australian Wool Corporation. Statistical Analysis *see* 0311-9882
0084-7658 Australian Yearbook of International Law
0084-7674 Automobile Year
0084-7682 Bach-Jahrbuch
0084-7690 Forststatistisches Jahrbuch
0084-7704 Band Music Guide
0084-7712 Battelle Memorial Institute. Published Papers and Articles
0084-7720 Baurat
0084-7739 Baustatistisches Jahrbuch
0084-7747 Bean Improvement Cooperative. Annual Report
0084-7763 Beecham Society Bulletin
0084-7771 Belgica Selecta; Nouveau Livres Belges†
0084-778X University of Bergen. Department of Applied Mathematics. Report
0084-7798 Musikwissenschaftliche Arbeiten in der DDR. Bericht†
0084-7801 Beyond the Age Barrier: Newsletter for Adult Students at Iowa State University *changed to* Adult Students
0084-781X Indian Agriculture in Brief
0084-7828 Bibliografia Internationala Cinema†
0084-7836 Bibliographia Internationalis Spiritualitatis
0084-7844 Bibliographia Musicologica
0084-7852 Bibliographical Society of Australia and New Zealand. Bulletin
0084-7860 Bibliographie de la Cote d'Ivoire
0084-7879 Bibliography of Electrical Recordings in the CNS and Related Literature†
0084-7887 Bibliography on the Hypothalamic-Pituitary-Gonadal System†
0084-7909 Black Position
0084-7925 Blantyre Water Board. Annual Report and Statement of Accounts
0084-7941 Federacion Nacional de Cafeteros de Colombia. Boletin de Informacion Estadistica Sobre Cafe
0084-7968 Bolsa de Cereales. Revista Institucional. Numero Estadistico
0084-7976 Bornholmske Samlinger
0084-7984 Borough of Twickenham Local History Society. Papers
0084-7992 Bowdoin College. Museum of Art. Occasional Papers
0084-800X Bradea
0084-8018 B B C Music Guides
0084-8026 British Building Products Catalogue
0084-8034 British Columbia. Library Development Commission. Public Libraries, Statistics *changed to* British Columbia Public Libraries, Statistics
0084-8050 University of British Columbia Library. Serial Holdings†
0084-8069 University of British Columbia. Research Forest Annual Report
0084-8085 Checklist of British Official Serial Publications
0084-8107 Bromeliads
0084-8115 Bruce County Historical Society. Year Book
0084-8123 Brunei Annual Report†
0084-8131 Brunei Museum. Special Publication
0084-814X Building and Engineering Review
0084-8182 Bulletin of Zoo Management
0084-8204 Buyer's Guide to Microfilm Equipment, Products, and Services *see* 0362-0131
0084-8212 By og Bygd
0084-8220 Cahiers Amitie Franco-Vietnamienne
0084-8239 Cahiers Paul-Louis Courier
0084-8263 California. Department of Water Resources. Bulletin
0084-8271 California Government & Politics Annual
0084-828X California Savings and Loan Data Book†
0084-8298 University of California, Davis. Institute of Governmental Affairs. Environmental Quality Series†
0084-8328 Cambrian Law Review
0084-8336 Cambridge Studies in Early Modern History
0084-8352 Camena†
0084-8379 Canada. Department of Agriculture. Library. Current Periodicals. Periodiques en Cours†
0084-8387 Canada. Earth Physics Branch. Seismological Series
0084-8425 Canadian Catholic Conference. National Bulletin on Liturgy *changed to* Canadian Conference of Catholic Bishops. National Bulletin on Liturgy
0084-8565 Canadian Ladies' Golf Association. Year Book
0084-8573 Canadian Law List
0084-859X Caracterologie†
0084-8603 Cardiologisches Bulletin *see* 0179-7166
0084-862X Catalog of Dealers' Prices for Marine Shells
0084-8638 Catholic International Education Office. Bulletin Trimestriel *see* 0770-1683
0084-8646 Universidade Federal do Ceara. Escola de Agronomia. Departamento de Fitotecnia. Relatoria Tecnico
0084-8654 Center for Consumer Education Services. Monographs†
0084-8662 Central Valley Project (California) Annual Report *changed to* U.S. Bureau of Reclamation. Mid-Pacific Region. Report
0084-8689 Circular C I A T
0084-8697 Centro de Investigaciones Agricolas de Tamaulipas. Informe Anual de Labores
0084-8700 Channel Islands Annual Anthology *changed to* Channel Islands Anthology

1422 ISSN INDEX

0084-8719 Chapel Hill Conference on Combinatorial Mathematics and Its Applications. Proceedings†
0084-8727 Charles C. Moskowitz Lectures *changed to* Joseph I. Lubin Memorial Lectures
0084-8735 Chiasma
0084-8743 Chilton's Import Car Repair Manual *changed to* Chilton's Import Car Repair Manual
0084-8751 Chitty's Ontario Annual Practice *changed to* Ontario Annual Practice
0084-8786 Ciba Collection of Medical Illustrations
0084-8794 Ciencia
0084-8808 Coburger Landesstiftung. Jahrbuch
0084-8816 Cold-Drill
0084-8824 Cold Spring Harbor Laboratory. Abstracts of Papers Presented at Meetings
0084-8859 C.T.T.S. Annual
0084-8875 Colorado. Division of Wildlife. Special Report
0084-8883 Colorado. Division of Wildlife. Technical Publication
0084-8891 Colorado Ski and Winter Recreation Statistics
0084-8905 Colorado State University Libraries. Publication
0084-893X Comentarios Bibliograficos Americanos. Anuario *changed to* Anuario - C B A - Yearbook
0084-8948 Comitato Glaciologico Italiano. Bollettino†
0084-8956 Commentary
0084-8964 Committee for Economic Development. Supplementary Paper†
0084-8972 Council of Ontario Universities Biennial Review *changed to* Council of Ontario Universities Quadrennial Review
0084-8999 Commonwealth Scientific and Industrial Research Organization. Minerals Research Laboratories. Investigation Report *see* 0726-1780
0084-9014 Commonwealth Scientific and Industrial Research Organization. Division of Animal Physiology. Technical Report *changed to* Commonwealth Scientific and Industrial Research Organization. Division of Animal Production Technical Report
0084-9073 Commonwealth Scientific and Industrial Research Organization. Division of Wildlife Research. Technical Memorandum *see* 0813-0493
0084-909X Company of Master Mariners of Australia. Journal
0084-9103 Texas Tech University. Interdepartmental Committee on Comparative Literature. Proceedings of the Comparative Literature Symposium
0084-9138 Conference for College and University Leaders in Continuing Education. Proceedings†
0084-9146 Conference on Artifical Insemination of Beef Cattle. Proceedings *changed to* Conference on Artificial Insemination and Embryo Transfer of Beef Cattle. Proceedings.
0084-9154 Conference on Bank Structure and Competition. Proceedings
0084-9162 Conference on Electrical Insulation and Dielectric Phenomena. Annual Report
0084-9189 Conimbriga
0084-9197 Conseil Superieur du Livre. Annuaire *changed to* Societe de Developpement du Livre et du Periodique. Annuaire
0084-9219 Contributions in American History
0084-9227 Contributions in American Studies
0084-9235 Contributions in Economics and Economic History
0084-9243 Contributions in Librarianship and Information Science
0084-9251 Contributions in Military History *see* 0883-6884
0084-926X Contributions in Philosophy
0084-9278 Contributions in Sociology
0084-9294 Convenience Store Industry Report
0084-9308 Denmark. Nationalmuseet. Arbejdsmarkt
0084-9324 Cosmetics Handbook†
0084-9332 COSPAR Technique Manual†
0084-9340 C O S P A R Transactions†
0084-9359 Costs and Curves†
0084-9405 Cover
0084-9413 Cowles Foundation for Research in Economics at Yale University. Monographs *changed to* Cowles Foundation Monographs
0084-943X Criminal Justice Review†
0084-9456 Criticism and Interpretation
0084-9499 Current Biography Yearbook
0084-9502 Curtain, Drapery and Bedspread National Buyers Guide *changed to* Interior Textiles National Buyers Guide
0084-9510 Cyprus. Development Estimates
0084-9529 Dacotah Territory†
0084-9537 Dada/Surrealism
0084-9553 Danforth News and Notes†
0084-957X Biblioteksaarbog
0084-9588 Dansk Medicinhistorisk Aarbog
0084-9596 Dansk Periodicafortegnelse. Supplement†
0084-960X University of Dar es Salaam. Bureau of Resource Assessment and Land Use Planning. Annual Report
0084-9626 University of Dar es Salaam. Bureau of Resource Assessment and Land Use Planning. Research Paper
0084-9634 University of Dar es Salaam. Bureau of Resource Assessment and Land Use Planning. Research Report
0084-9642 Delaware. Department of Natural Resources and Environmental Control. Annual Report
0084-9650 Delaware Museum of Natural History. Monograph Series
0084-9669 Delaware Museum of Natural History. Reproduction Series
0084-9677 Delaware Museum of Natural History. Special Publications†
0084-9685 Delaware. State Treasurer. Annual Report
0084-9693 Denmark Exports†
0084-9715 Denmark. Rigsbibliotekarembedet. Accessionskatalog
0084-9723 Dental Register of Ireland
0084-9731 Descent
0084-974X Designers in Britain†
0084-9758 Deutsche Gesellschaft fuer Hygiene und Mikrobiologie. Berichte ueber Tagungen†
0084-9766 Deutsche Messen und Ausstellungen - Ein Zahlenspiegel *see* 0724-0554
0084-9774 Gezeitentafeln
0084-9782 Institut der Deutschen Wirtschaft. Gewerkschaftsreport
0084-9790 Deutschlandfunk. Jahrbuch
0084-9804 Dialectic
0084-9812 Dickens Studies Annual
0084-9820 Dimensions of Radio†
0084-9839 Dimensions of Television†
0084-9855 Directory of Bankers Schools
0084-9863 Directory of Canadian Community Funds and Councils *changed to* United Way of Canada. Directory of Members
0084-988X Directory of College Stores
0084-9898 Directory of Colorado Manufacturers
0084-9901 Directory of Data Processing Service Organizations *changed to* A D A P S O Membership Directory
0084-991X Directory of Educational Institutions in New Mexico
0084-9936 Directory of Fulbright Alumni
0084-9944 Directory of Governments in Metropolitan Toronto†
0084-9952 Directory of Incorporated (Registered) Companies in Nigeria†
0084-9960 Directory of Iranian Periodicals
0084-9979 Directory of Little Magazines, Small Presses and Underground Newspapers *see* 0092-3974
0084-9987 Directory of National Organizations Concerned with Land Pollution Control
0084-9995 Directory of Pakistan Commerce and Industry†
0085-0004 Directory of Registered Dentists and Registered Dental Hygienists in Connecticut†
0085-0012 Directory of Social and Health Agencies of New York City
0085-0020 Directory of the College Student Press in America
0085-0039 Directory of the Public Aquaria of the World†
0085-0071 Drexel Research Conference. Summary Report *changed to* Drexel Faculty Publication
0085-008X Drexel University Research Review†
0085-0128 Earth's Wild Places†
0085-0144 Economic Aspects of Public Education in Pennsylvania†
0085-0160 Economic Survey of Indian Agriculture *changed to* India. Ministry of Agriculture. Bulletin on Commercial Crops Statistics
0085-0187 Edubba
0085-0225 Elizabethan Club Series
0085-025X English around the World†
0085-0268 Enterprise
0085-0276 Enzyklopaedie der Rechts- und Staatswissenschaft. New Series. Staatswissenschaft†
0085-0284 Universidade Federal do Espirito Santo. Comissao de Planejamento. Documentario Estatistico sobre a Situacao Educacional
0085-0292 Universidade Federal do Espirito Santo. Comissao de Planejamento. Documentario Estatistico sobre a Situacao Educacional. Supplemento
0085-0306 Universidade Federal do Espirito Santo. Comissao de Planejamento. Vestibulandos†
0085-0314 Estimates of Area and Production of Principal Crops in India. Summary Tables *changed to* Area and Production of Principal Crops in India. Summary Tables
0085-0322 Etudes Haguenoviennes†
0085-0330 Eurail Guide
0085-0349 Europa Handbuch der Werbegesellschaften
0085-0365 Excerpta Historica Nordica *see* 0346-8755
0085-0373 Explore Canada *changed to* Guide to Canada
0085-039X Expression
0085-042X Universidade Federal do Rio Grande do Sul. Faculdade de Medicina. Anais
0085-0438 Farm and Ranch Vacation Guide *see* 0195-8437
0085-0462 Federal Law Reports
0085-0489 Federation des Industries Chimiques de Belgique. Rapport Annuel
0085-0497 Federation Nationale des Chambres de Commerce, d'Industrie et d'Agriculture de la Republique du Zaire. Circulaire d'Information *changed to* Association Nationale des Entreprises du Zaire. Circulaire d'Information
0085-0500 Felix Ravenna; Rivista di Antichita Ravennati, Cristiane e Bizantine
0085-0519 Fer-Blanc en France et dans le Monde
0085-0527 Ferdinand Roten Galleries. Catalog of Original Graphic Art
0085-0535 Film and TV Festival Directory†
0085-0543 Financial Aids to Illinois Students
0085-0551 Financial Stock Guide Service. Directory of Obsolete Securities
0085-0586 Flinders Asian Studies Lecture
0085-0608 Florida. Bureau of Geology. Geological Bulletins
0085-0616 Florida. Bureau of Geology. Information Circulars
0085-0624 Florida. Bureau of Geology. Map Series
0085-0640 Florida. Bureau of Geology. Special Publications
0085-0659 Florida. Bureau of Historic Sites and Properties. Bulletin†
0085-0683 Memoirs of the Hourglass Cruises
0085-0748 Folia Mendeliana *changed to* Acta Musei Moraviae. Scientia Naturales 3: Folia Mendeliana
0085-0756 Folk; Dansk Etnografisk Tidsskrift
0085-0764 Folklivsstudier
0085-0802 Foreign Investment Opportunities in the Philippines
0085-0829 Foreign Medical School Catalogue†
0085-0845 Fra Als og Sundeved
0085-0853 Fra Viborg Amt. Aarbog
0085-0861 Frantsia
0085-0888 French 20 Bibliography; Critical and Biographical References for the Study of French Literature since 1885
0085-0896 Frodskaparrit; Annales Societatis Scientiarum Faeroensis
0085-090X Fruit World Annual and Orchardists Guide†
0085-0918 Fynske Aarboeger
0085-0934 Genealogisches Handbuch des Bayerischen Adels
0085-0942 Observatoire de Geneve. Publications. Serie A
0085-0950 Universita degli Studi di Genova. Bolletino dei Musei e degli Istituti Biologici
0085-0969 Geographical Education
0085-0977 Geography Teachers Association of Queensland. Journal *see* 0314-3457
0085-0985 Geological Survey of Ireland. Bulletin
0085-0993 Geological Survey of Ireland. Information Circulars
0085-1019 Geological Survey of Ireland. Special Papers
0085-1027 Geology, Exploration, and Mining in British Columbia *changed to* Exploration in British Columbia
0085-1043 Georgia Statistical Abstract
0085-106X Gesellschaft zur Foerderung Tiefenpsychologischer und Psychotherapeutischer Forschung und Weiterbildung, Munich. Beitraege und Berichte†
0085-1078 Rijksuniversiteit te Gent. Laboratorium voor Experimentele, Differentiele en Genetische Psychologie. Mededelingen en Werkdocumenten
0085-1108 Goettinger Universitaetsreden
0085-1124 Good Health†
0085-1132 Graduate Careers Directory *see* 0311-4201
0085-1140 Grain†
0085-1167 Great Britain. Commission of Inquiry on Small Firms. Research Report†
0085-1191 Great Britain. Ministry of Housing and Local Government. Design Bulletin *changed to* Great Britain. Department of the Environment. Housing and Construction. Design Bulletin
0085-1205 University of Northern Colorado. Museum of Anthropology. Occasional Publications in Anthropology. Ethnology Series
0085-1213 University of Northern Colorado. Museum of Anthropology. Occasional Publications in Anthropology. Miscellaneous Series
0085-1221 University of Northern Colorado. Museum of Anthropology. Occasional Publications in Anthropology. Archaeology Series
0085-123X University of Northern Colorado. Museum of Anthropology. Occasional Publications in Anthropology. Linguistics Series

ISSN INDEX 1423

0085-1264 Universite de Grenoble. Institut de Phonetique. Manuels. Serie A *changed to* Universite de Grenoble III. Institut de Phonetique. Travaux: Serie A: Manuals
0085-1272 Universite de Grenoble III. Institut de Phonetique. Travaux. Serie B: Etudes Linguistiques
0085-1280 Growth
0085-1299 Grundbegriffe der Modernen Biologie.
0085-1302 Gruppenpsychotherapie und Gruppendynamik. Beihefte
0085-1310 Guam Statistical Annual Report
0085-1329 University of Guelph. Department of Land Resource Science. Progress Report
0085-1337 Guia de los Caballos Verificadas en Espana
0085-1353 Guide to Biomedical Standards
0085-1361 Hafnia; Copenhagen Papers in the History of Art
0085-140X Handbuch der Physik†
0085-1418 Handels- og Soefartsmuseet paa Kronborg. Aarbog
0085-1442 Harris Survey Yearbook of Public Opinion†
0085-1450 Health Physics Research Abstracts
0085-1469 Hefte zur Unfallheilkunde
0085-1477 Herald Caravanning Guide
0085-1485 Herald Motel Guide
0085-1493 Here and Now
0085-1523 Higher Education Monograph Series†
0085-1531 California Senior Citizen News *changed to* California Senior Citizen
0085-154X History Teacher
0085-1558 History Teachers Association of New South Wales. Newsletter
0085-1566 Hockey Association. Official Handbook
0085-1574 Home Appliance Blue Book *changed to* Home Appliance Trade-in Blue Book
0085-1647 How to Avoid Financial Tangles: Section C. The Harvest Years Financial Plan†
0085-1663 Hunter Valley Research Foundation. Monographs
0085-1671 Hypomnemata
0085-1698 Icographic†
0085-1728 Illinois Labor History Society Reporter
0085-1736 Illustrated Human Embryology†
0085-1760 Index of Art in the Pacific Northwest
0085-1779 India. Department of Science & Technology. Annual Report
0085-1787 Indian Agricultural Statistics†
0085-1795 F M U Occasional Lectures
0085-1809 Indian Livestock Census†
0085-1817 Indian Science Congress Association. Proceedings
0085-1876 Informator Archeologiczny
0085-1884 Inlet
0085-1892 Institut Royal de Patrimoine Artistique. Bulletin
0085-1914 Instituto Boliviano del Petroleo. Boletin†
0085-1922 Instituto de la Patagonia. Anales *changed to* Instituto de la Patagonia. Anales. Social Sciencias
0085-1930 Insurance Life/Non-Life Annual Statistics *see* 0910-5719
0085-1930 Insurance Life/Non-Life Annual Statistics *see* 0910-5727
0085-1949 Inter-American Institute of Agricultural Sciences. Bibliografias *see* 0301-438X
0085-1965 S T P Notes†
0085-1981 Intergovernmental Council for Automatic Data Processing. Proceedings of Conference *changed to* International Council for Automatic Data Processing in Government Administration. Proceedings of Conference
0085-199X I A T A News Review *see* 0376-642X
0085-2007 International Association for Scientific Study of Mental Deficiency. Proceedings of International Congress
0085-2015 I A S L Newsletter
0085-2023 International Atomic Energy Agency. Annual Report
0085-204X International Bibliography of the Social Sciences. Economics
0085-2058 International Bibliography of the Social Sciences. Political Science
0085-2066 International Bibliography of the Social Sciences. Sociology
0085-2074 International Bibliography of the Social Sciences. Social and Cultural Anthropology
0085-2082 I B M Research Symposia Series
0085-2090 International Clean Air Congress. Proceedings
0085-2104 International Conference on Chemical Vapor Deposition. Proceedings†
0085-2112 International Congress of Psychology. Proceedings
0085-2120 International Council for Scientific Management. Proceedings of World Congress
0085-2147 International Court of Justice. Bulletin†
0085-2163 International Monetary Fund. Annual Report on Exchange Restrictions *see* 0250-7366
0085-2171 International Monetary Fund. Annual Report of the Executive Directors *see* 0250-7498
0085-218X International Percussion Reference Library. Catalog†
0085-2198 International Press Institute. Survey
0085-2201 International Telecommunication Union. Report on the Activities
0085-221X Memento de l'O.I.V.
0085-2236 Iowa Academy of Science. Proceedings
0085-2252 Iowa State Archaeologist. Report
0085-2260 Iraq Natural History Museum. Publication *changed to* Iraq Natural History Museum. Publication
0085-2295 Italia Dialettale
0085-2309 Italy. Consiglio Nazionale delle Ricerce. Nota di Bibliografia e di Documentazione Scientifica *changed to* Italy. Istituto di Studi sulla Ricerca e Documentazione Scientifica. Note di Bibliografia e Documentazione Scientifica
0085-2325 Iwate University. Faculty of Engineering. Technology Reports
0085-2341 Jahrbuch fuer Regionalgeschichte
0085-2368 Jewish Boston
0085-2376 Journal of Arabic Literature
0085-2384 Journal of Astrological Studies
0085-2392 Journal of Development Planning
0085-2406 Journal of Drug Research of Egypt
0085-2414 Journal of Northwest Semitic Languages†
0085-2430 Juvenile Court Digest *see* 0279-2257
0085-2449 Kalamies
0085-2457 University of Kansas. Department of Anthropology. Publications in Anthropology
0085-2465 University of Kansas. Museum of Natural History. Monographs
0085-2473 University of Kansas Humanistic Studies
0085-2481 Karate International Annual
0085-249X Kariba Studies†
0085-2503 Kerry Archaeological and Historical Society. Journal
0085-2511 Key to Finland†
0085-2538 Kidney International
0085-2546 King's Gazette
0085-2554 Kirkon Nuoriso-Pistis *see* 0356-794X
0085-2562 Knitting Times Yearbook
0085-2570 Kobe University. School of Business Administration. Annals
0085-2589 Kongelig Dansk Hof- og Statskalender; Statshaandbog for Kongeriget Danmark
0085-2597 Kontrast
0085-2600 Kultaseppien Lehti
0085-2619 Kyrkohistorisk Aarsskrift
0085-2627 Kyushu University. Faculty of Science. Memoirs Series B: Physics†
0085-2635 Kyushu University. Faculty of Science. Memoirs. Series C: Chemistry
0085-2643 France. Laboratoires des Ponts et Chausees. Rapport de Recherche
0085-266X Land Laws Service†
0085-2678 Langue et Cultures
0085-2686 Langue Internationale
0085-2694 Latin American Studies in the Universities of the United Kingdom
0085-2708 Latin American Studies in the Universities of the United Kingdom. Staff Research in Progress or Recently Completed in the Humanities and the Social Sciences
0085-2724 L I R I Research Bulletin
0085-2740 Report by the Auditor General on the Accounts of Lesotho
0085-2759 Louisiana State University. Library. Library Lectures
0085-2767 Library Lit
0085-2775 Light Age Directory; The Buyers Guide to Lamps. Lighting Fixtures, Accessories and Shades†
0085-2783 Centre International de Documentation Arachnologiques. Liste des Travaux Arachnologiques
0085-2805 Livestock and Poultry in Latin America. Annual Conference *changed to* International Conference on Livestock and Poultry in the Tropics (Proceedings)
0085-2813 Lloyds Australian and New Zealand Trade Register
0085-2821 Local Government Finances in Maryland
0085-283X London Record Society. Occasional Publications†
0085-2848 London Record Society. Publications
0085-2856 University of London. School of Oriental and African Studies. Contemporary China Institute. Publications
0085-2899 Lozania
0085-2902 Luksave†
0085-2910 Lyman's Canada-British North America Standard Postage Stamp Retail Catalogue *see* 0227-1699
0085-2945 Madras. Government Museum. Bulletin. New Series
0085-2953 Mail Order Business Directory
0085-297X Maine. Soil and Water Conservation Commission. Biennial Report†
0085-2988 Malacological Society of Australia. Journal
0085-3003 Malawi. National Statistical Office. Balance of Payments
0085-3011 Malawi. National Statistical Office. Compendium of Agricultural Statistics *see* 0076-3292
0085-302X Malawi. National Statistical Office. Tourist Report *changed to* Malawi Tourism Report
0085-3038 University of Malawi Libraries. Report to the Senate on the University Libraries
0085-3046 Malaysia. Department of Statistics. Survey of Construction Industries: Peninsular Malaysia
0085-3054 Management Monographs (New York)†
0085-3070 Manitoba. Mines Branch. Publication *changed to* Manitoba Energy and Mines. Geological Report
0085-3100 Mario Negri Institute for Pharmacological Research. Monographs
0085-3119 Marken-Handbuch der Werbung und Etatbetreuung
0085-3135 Maryland. Police Training Commission. Annual Report *changed to* Maryland. Police and Correctional Training Commissions. Report to the Governor, the Secretary of Public Safety and Correctional Services, and Members of the General Assembly
0085-3178 Mathematics Annual *see* 0711-2521
0085-3186 Matrix (North Hollywood)†
0085-3194 Mauritius Directory of the Diplomatic Corps
0085-3208 Ny Carlsberg Glyptotek. Meddelelser
0085-3224 Melbourne Journal of Politics
0085-3232 Melbourne Notes on Agricultural Extension†
0085-3240 University of Melbourne. Department of Civil Engineering. Departmental Report
0085-3259 University of Melbourne. Department of Electrical Engineering. Research Report
0085-3267 University of Melbourne. Faculty of Agriculture and Forestry. Agricultural Economics Report†
0085-3275 University of Melbourne. Gazette
0085-3283 Melbourne University Magazine†
0085-3291 Memo of Current Books in the Brain Sciences†
0085-3321 M.T.I.A. Annual Report
0085-3356 Michigan. Department of Education. Bulletin†
0085-3364 Michigan. Geological Survey Division. Miscellany†
0085-3372 Michigan Mineral Producers Annual Directory:†
0085-3380 Michigan Police Journal *changed to* Michigan Police Chiefs Newsletter
0085-3410 Surveys of Consumers†
0085-3429 Michigan's Oil and Gas Fields: Annual Statistical Summary
0085-3445 Mineral Industry of Michigan Annual Statistical Summary†
0085-3453 Mine and Quarry Mechanisation
0085-3461 Ministerialtidende for Kongeriget Danmark: Section A & B
0085-3488 Minority Student Opportunities in United States Medical Schools
0085-3496 Missouri. Department of Conservation. Annual Report
0085-350X Missouri Journal of Research in Music Education
0085-3518 Modern Plastics Encyclopedia
0085-3526 Modern Teaching†
0085-3534 Monmouth Reviews: Journal of the Literary Arts *changed to* Monmouth Review
0085-3542 Monographs in Modern Concepts of Philosophy†
0085-3550 Montana. Governor's Annual Report†
0085-3577 Movie/T V Marketing Global Motion Picture Year Book
0085-3585 Municipal Association of Tasmania. Session. Minutes of Proceedings
0085-3607 Music and Life
0085-3623 Musikalier i Danske Biblioteker
0085-364X N U M U S Numismatica, Medalhistica, Argueologia
0085-3658 NADA†
0085-3674 Natalia
0085-3682 National Civic Council. Facts
0085-3690 National Council for the Social Studies. Curriculum Series†
0085-3704 National Council for the Social Studies. Crisis Series†
0085-3712 National Council for the Social Studies. How to Do It Series
0085-3720 National Council for the Social Studies. Yearbook†
0085-378X National Institute for Educational Research. Research Bulletin
0085-3798 National Institute for Research in Dairying. Biennial Report *see* 0302-0851
0085-3801 National Institute for Research in Dairying. Biennial Reviews†
0085-381X National Opera Association. Membership Directory
0085-3828 National Research Council, Canada. Division of Building Research. Bibliography
0085-3836 National Science Council (Ireland). Register of Scientific Research Personnel
0085-3860 Nature/Science Annual†
0085-3887 Nemouria: Occasional Papers of the Delaware Museum of Natural History
0085-3909 Network (New York, 1970)†
0085-3917 Neue Hefte fuer Philosophie

ISSN INDEX

ISSN	Title
0085-3925	University of Nevada. Anthropology Department. Student Papers in Anthropology†
0085-3933	N E H T A Newsletter see 0028-4912
0085-395X	New Jersey. Department of Transportation. Report of Operations changed to New Jersey. Department of Transportation. Annual Report
0085-3968	University of New Mexico. Institute of Meteoritics. Special Publication
0085-3976	New South Wales. Department of Education. School Management Bulletin†
0085-3984	New South Wales. Forestry Commission. Research Notes
0085-400X	New South Wales. Law Reform Commission. Report
0085-4018	University of New South Wales. Metallurgical Society. Metallurgical Review
0085-4026	New South Wales Veterinary Proceedings
0085-4042	New York Pro Musica Instrumental Series
0085-4077	Annual Educational Summary, New York State
0085-4093	Racial/Ethnic Distribution of Public School Students and Staff, New York State
0085-414X	New Zealand. Water and Soil Division. Hydrological Research Annual Report & Series†
0085-4158	University of Newcastle. Department of Electrical Engineering. Technical Report EE changed to University of Newcastle. Department of Electrical and Computer Engineering. Technical Report EE
0085-4166	News from the Rare Book Room
0085-4174	Newsletter on Contemporary Japanese Prints
0085-4190	Nigerian Office and Quarters Directory see 0331-0973
0085-4204	Nimrod†
0085-4212	Nordisk Ekumenisk Aarsbok
0085-4220	Nordiske Domme i Sjofartsanliggender
0085-4247	Universitetet i Trondheim. Norges Tekniske Hoegskole. Biblioteket. Literaturliste†
0085-4263	N I B R Rapport
0085-4271	Norsk Polarinstitutt. Aarbok
0085-428X	North Carolina Communicable Disease Morbidity Statistics
0085-4301	Norway. Forsvaret forskningsinstitutt. N D R E Report see 0800-4412
0085-431X	Norway. Statistisk Sentralbyraa. Artikler/Articles
0085-4344	Norway. Statistisk Sentralbyraa. Samfunnsoekonomiske Studier/Social Economic Studies
0085-4352	Norwegian-American Historical Association. Topical Studies
0085-4387	Noticiero Tuberosas
0085-4395	Nova Scotia. Fire Marshal. Annual Report
0085-4409	Nucleus†
0085-4417	Nuytsia
0085-4433	Oesterreichs Volkseinkommen
0085-4441	New South Wales Year Book
0085-445X	Oficina; Revista de Equipos para Oficinas
0085-4468	Ohio Fish and Wildlife Report†
0085-4484	Oklahoma Art Center. Annual Eight State Exhibition of Painting and Sculpture Catalog†
0085-4506	Oondoona†
0085-4514	Opera Slavica changed to Opera Slavica. Neue Folge
0085-4522	Orientalia Lovaniensia Periodica
0085-4530	Der Orthopaede
0085-4557	Osler Library Newsletter
0085-4565	Oslo Boers. Beretning
0085-4573	Ostracodologist†
0085-4581	P I E
0085-459X	Pacific Islands Studies and Notes
0085-4603	Paedagogica†
0085-4611	Palaeontographica. Supplementbaende
0085-4638	Pan American Health Organization. Bulletin
0085-4662	Papers on Islamic History†
0085-4670	Papers on the History of Bourke
0085-4689	Papua and New Guinea Law Reports
0085-4697	Papua New Guinea Scientific Society. Annual Report and Proceedings see 0310-4303
0085-4700	Papua and New Guinea Scientific Society. Transactions
0085-4719	Papua New Guinea. Department of Labour. Industrial Review.†
0085-4735	University of Papua New Guinea. Department of Physics. Technical Paper
0085-4743	Paraguay. Ministerio de Industria y Comercio. Division de Registro y Estadistica Industrial. Encuesta Industrial
0085-476X	Museum National d'Histoire Naturelle, Paris. Bibliotheque Centrale. Liste des Periodiques Francais et Etrangers. Supplement
0085-4778	Cartes Synoptiques de la Chromosphere Solaire changed to Cartes Synoptiques de la Chromosphere Solaire et Catalogues des Filaments et des Centres d'Activite
0085-4786	Documents de Linguistique Quantitative
0085-4794	Partiojohtaja
0085-4816	Pennsylvania. Department of Education. Our Colleges and Universities Today†
0085-4824	Pennsylvania. Office of the Budget. Program Budget
0085-4840	Peru. Oficina Regional de Desarrollo del Norte. Analisis General de Situacion de la Region Norte
0085-4859	Petroleum Search in Australia†
0085-4867	Phi Sigma Iota News Notes changed to Phi Sigma Iota Forum
0085-4875	Philippine Mining and Engineering Journal. Mining Annual and Directory
0085-4883	Philippines Today†
0085-4905	Plumbers Friend
0085-4956	Teki Historyczne
0085-4980	Politique de la Science
0085-4999	Polk's World Bank Directory. International Edition
0085-5006	Population Profile see 0146-7646
0085-5014	P R B Selection see 0146-7646
0085-5022	University of Port Elizabeth. Publications. Inaugural and Emeritus Addresses
0085-5030	Port of New Orleans Annual Directory
0085-5073	Praxis der Kinderpsychologie und Kinderpsychiatrie. Beihefte
0085-5103	Prescriber's Journal changed to Australian Prescriber
0085-512X	Prince Edward Island. Department of Labour. Annual Report
0085-5138	Prince Edward Island. Department of the Environment Annual Report changed to Prince Edward Island. Department of Community and Cultural Affairs. Annual Report
0085-5154	Privates Bausparwesen
0085-5170	Progress and Growth of Papua New Guinea†
0085-5189	Progress in Atomic Medicine see 0163-6170
0085-5219	International Personnel Management Association. Annual Report†
0085-5227	Publications in the American West
0085-5235	Quaternaria†
0085-5243	Universite Laval. Archives de Folklore
0085-526X	Queen Alexandra Solarium for Crippled Children Annual Report changed to Queen Alexandra Hospital for Children. Annual Report
0085-5278	Queen Victoria Museum and Art Gallery. Launceston, Tasmania. Records
0085-5286	Queensland. Bureau of Sugar Experiment Stations. Technical Communication†
0085-5308	Queensland Historical Review†
0085-5316	Queensland Pocket Yearbook
0085-5324	Queensland Police Journal
0085-5332	Queensland Primary Producers' Co-Operative Association. Primary Producers' Guide†
0085-5359	Queensland Yearbook
0085-5367	Quellen und Studien zur Geschichte der Pharmazie†
0085-5375	Quirindi and District Historical Notes†
0085-5383	Randschriften; a Newsletter for the Guild of Carilloneurs see 0827-5955
0085-5391	Readings in Literary Criticism†
0085-5405	Real Estate Trends in Metropolitan Vancouver changed to MetroTrends
0085-5413	Notas e Comunicacoes de Matematica
0085-5421	Record Houses†
0085-543X	Recueil des Films
0085-5456	Register of Companies in New South Wales†
0085-5499	Repertoire Bibliographique des Livres Imprimes en France
0085-5510	Report on Australian Universities†
0085-5529	Report on the World Health Situation
0085-5545	Research and Development in Ireland
0085-5553	Research in Phenomenology
0085-5561	Respiratory Therapy Buyers Guide and Ordering Catalog†
0085-5596	Review of Economic Situation of Air Transport
0085-560X	Review of Maritime Transport
0085-5626	Revista Brasileira de Entomologia
0085-5642	Revistero
0085-5650	Revolver/Tijdschrift voor Hedendragse Poezie
0085-5677	Rhodesia National Bibliography changed to Zimbabwe National Bibliography
0085-5693	Zimbabwe. Department of Meteorological Services. Rainfall Report
0085-5707	Zimbabwe. Department of Meteorological Services. Report of the Director
0085-5715	Riddell's Australian Purchasing Yearbook see 0311-5070
0085-5723	Rivista di Antropologia
0085-5731	Rivista di Etnografia
0085-5774	Royal Asiatic Society. Hong Kong Branch. Journal
0085-5782	Royal Automobile Association of South Australia. Accommodation Guide changed to Australian Accommodation Guide
0085-5790	Royal Geographical Society of Australasia. South Australian Branch. Proceedings see 0811-6504
0085-5804	Royal Historical Society of Queensland. Journal
0085-5812	Royal Society of South Australia. Transactions
0085-5820	Royal Zoological Society of New South Wales. Proceedings changed to Koolewong
0085-5839	Rural Africana
0085-5855	St. John's University, Collegeville, Minnesota. Monastic Manuscript Microfilm Library. Project Progress Report†
0085-588X	Sammlung Musikwissenschaftlicher Abhandlungen
0085-5898	San Francisco Bay Conservation and Development Commission. Annual Report
0085-5901	Universidade Federal de Santa Maria. Centro de Ciencias Rurais. Revista
0085-591X	Scandinavian Journal of Clinical and Laboratory Investigation. Supplement
0085-5928	Scandinavian Journal of Gastroenterology. Supplement
0085-5936	Scandinavian Studies in Criminology
0085-5944	Scandinavian Studies in Law
0085-5952	Schmankerl
0085-5960	Schriftenreihe fuer Vegetationskunde
0085-5979	Science Fiction Book Review Index
0085-5995	Scientific, Technical and Related Societies of the United States†
0085-6002	Scottish Building & Civil Engineering Year Book
0085-6010	Search†
0085-6029	Seminario Matematico Garcia de Galdeano. Publicaciones†
0085-6037	Semitica
0085-6045	Setting National Priorities. the (Year) Budget†
0085-6053	Seychelles. Labour Department. Annual Report†
0085-6061	Shaw's Directory of Courts in England and Wales see 0264-312X
0085-607X	Sheller's Directory of Clubs, Books, Periodicals and Dealers
0085-6118	Singapore Libraries
0085-6126	Skandinavisk Tidskrift for Faerg och Lack. Aarsbok
0085-6134	Slovenski Jezuiti V Kanade. Year Book
0085-6142	Center for Short Lived Phenomena. Annual Report†
0085-6169	Snoeck's Almanach
0085-6177	Snoeck's; Literatuur Kunst Film Toneel Mode Reizen
0085-6193	Social, Economic and Political Studies of the Middle East
0085-6207	Social History of Canada
0085-6223	Sociedad Mexicana de Micologia. Boletin changed to Revista Mexicana de Micologia
0085-6231	Societa Storica Valtellinese. Bollettino
0085-624X	Societe d'Etude du Vingtieme Siecle. Bulletin†
0085-6266	Societe Historique et Archeologique dans le Limbourg. Publications
0085-6282	Societe Royale des Sciences de Liege. Memoires in 8†
0085-6304	Society for the Study of Midwestern Literature. Newsletter
0085-6312	Real Estate Agents & Valuers Society. Land and Building
0085-6339	Soelleroedbogen
0085-6347	Source (Ann Arbor)†
0085-6355	Investment Sources and Ideas changed to S I E Guide to Investment Services
0085-6363	South African Biographical and Historical Studies
0085-6371	South African Jewish Frontier†
0085-638X	South African Journal of African Affairs see 0256-2804
0085-6398	South African Journal of Photogrammetry changed to South African Journal of Photogrammetry, Remote Sensing and Cartography
0085-6401	South Asia: Journal of South Asian Studies
0085-641X	South Australian Road Transport Year Book
0085-6428	South Australian Yearbook
0085-6436	South Carolina. Alcoholic Beverage Control Commission. Annual Report changed to South Carolina. Commission on Alcoholism and Drug Abuse. Annual Report
0085-6452	University of South Carolina. Institute of International Studies. Essay Series
0085-6460	South Dakota. Department of Revenue. Annual Statistical Report
0085-6479	South Dakota Geological Survey. Bulletin
0085-6487	South Dakota Geological Survey. Circular
0085-6495	South Dakota Geological Survey. Reports of Investigation
0085-6509	Southeast Asian Archives

0085-6517 Southeast Asian Seminar on Parasitology and Tropical Medicine. Proceedings *changed to* TropMed Seminars on Tropical Medicine. Proceedings
0085-6525 Southern Indian Studies
0085-6533 Soviet Affairs Symposium†
0085-6541 Spain. Direccion General de Capacitacion y Extension Agrarias Resumen de Actividades†
0085-655X Spain. Direccion General de Trafico. Anuario Estadistico de Accidentes. Boletin Informativo
0085-6592 S F I Bulletin
0085-6606 Standard Australian Coin Catalogue†
0085-6614 Standard Directory of Advertising Agencies
0085-6622 Standard Directory of Newsletters†
0085-6630 Standard Periodical Directory
0085-6657 Standards for Australian Aluminium Mill Products
0085-6665 Stanford Museum
0085-6673 Stanford Occasional Papers in Linguistics†
0085-6703 New South Wales State Reports *see* 0312-1674
0085-6711 Statistical Yearbook for Asia and the Far East *see* 0252-3655
0085-672X Statistics on the Developing South *changed to* Southeastern Historical Statistics
0085-6738 Status
0085-6746 Steinbeck Monograph Series
0085-6770 Stratford Festival
0085-6800 Student Mathematics
0085-6819 Studi Americani
0085-6827 Studi e Saggi Linguistici
0085-6835 Studia Fennica
0085-6843 Studies in Anthropology†
0085-6851 University of Texas, Austin. Bureau of Business Research. Studies in Insurance and Actuarial Science†
0085-686X Studies in Jewish Jurisprudence†
0085-6878 Studies in Medieval Culture
0085-6886 Studies in Polish Civilization†
0085-6894 Studies in Romance Languages *changed to* Studies in Romance Languages & Literatures
0085-6908 Studies on Selected Development Problems in Various Countries in the Middle East
0085-6916 Universitaet Stuttgart. Institut fuer Steuerungstechnik der Werkzeugmaschinen und Fertigungseinrichtungen. i S W Berichte
0085-6932 Suomen Geodeettisen Laitoksen. Julkaisuja
0085-6940 Suomen Kalatalous
0085-6967 Cement- och Betonginstitutet. Handlingar. Proceedings†
0085-6975 Cement- och Betonginstitutet. Meddelanden. Bulletins†
0085-6983 Svenska Traeforskningsinstitutet. Meddelande. Series A *see* 0348-2650
0085-6991 Sweden. Statistiska Centralbyraan. Statistiska Meddelanden. Subgroup Bo (Housing and Construction)
0085-7009 Sydney Observatory Papers†
0085-7017 Sydney Speleological Society. Communications *changed to* Sydney Speleological Society. Occasional Paper
0085-7025 University of Sydney Economics Society. Economic Review
0085-7033 University of Sydney. Institute of Criminology. Proceedings
0085-7041 University of Sydney Medical Journal†
0085-7068 Symposium on Coal Mine Drainage Research. Papers
0085-7076 Symposium on the Physiology and Pathology of Human Reproduction *changed to* Harold C. Mack Symposium. Proceedings
0085-7092 University of Texas, Austin. Tarlton Law Library. Legal Bibliography Series
0085-7106 Tasmanian State Reports
0085-7114 Teachers of History in the Universities of the United Kingdom *see* 0268-6732
0085-7130 Telektronikk
0085-7149 Television Blue Book *changed to* Television Trade-in Blue Book
0085-7157 Television News Index and Abstracts
0085-7165 Tennessee Civilian Work Force Estimates *changed to* Tennessee Annual Average Labor Force Estimates
0085-7246 Thailand. Division of Agricultural Chemistry. Report on Fertilizer Experiments and Soil Fertility Research
0085-7262 Thorvaldsens Museum. Meddelelser
0085-7270 Today's House
0085-7289 Nankyoku Shiryo
0085-7297 Topics in Ocean Engineering†
0085-7327 Transport och Hanteringsekonomi *see* 0346-2773
0085-7335 Travaux Linguistiques de Prague†
0085-7351 Better Homes and Gardens Travel Ideas†
0085-7378 Treewell
0085-7386 Trilobite News
0085-7408 True to Life†
0085-7416 T R U K-P A C T
0085-7432 Turkiyat Mecmuasi
0085-7440 Turun Historiallinen Arkisto
0085-7467 Annuaire U N I T†
0085-7475 United Nations Association of Australia. K U R U N A†
0085-7491 United Nations. Division of Narcotic Drugs. Information Letter
0085-7513 United Nations Economic and Social Commission for Asia and the Pacific. Social Development Division. Social Work Training and Teaching Materials Newsletter *see* 0252-452X
0085-7580 Dairy Herd Improvement *changed to* Dairy Herd Improvement Letter
0085-7602 Union Postale Universelle. Statistique des Services Postaux
0085-7629 University of Newcastle Historical Journal†
0085-7645 Vendsyssel Aarbog
0085-7653 Venezuela. Ministerio de Agricultura y Cria. Direccion de Economia y Estadistica Agropecuaria. Division de Estadistica. Plan de Trabajo
0085-7661 Verbaende, Behoerden, Organisationen der Wirtschaft
0085-767X Museo Civico di Storia Naturale, Verona. Memorie *see* 0392-0062
0085-770X Victoria, Australia. Department of Agriculture. Technical Bulletin†
0085-7718 Vegetable Growers Digest†
0085-7726 Victoria, Australia. Education Department. Curriculum and Research Branch. Research Reports
0085-7742 Victoria, Australia. Forest Commission. Bulletin *changed to* Victoria, Australia. Department of Conservation, Forests and Lands. Bulletin
0085-7750 Victoria, Australia. Geological Survey. Bulletin
0085-7769 Victoria, Australia. Geological Survey. Memoirs
0085-7823 Vietnamese Studies
0085-7831 Viridian Starfire *changed to* Square Balloon
0085-784X Vocational Training in New York City. . Where to Find It†
0085-7858 Wagga Wagga and District Historical Society. Journal
0085-7866 Waigani Seminar. Papers
0085-7882 W R I Newsletter
0085-7904 Washington Center for Metropolitan Studies. Metropolitan Bulletin†
0085-7920 University of Washington Publications in Anthropology†
0085-7939 University of Washington Publications in Fisheries
0085-7947 University of Washington Publications on Language and Literature†
0085-798X Washington University. Institute for Urban and Regional Studies. Working Paper†
0085-8013 Water Research Foundation of Australia. Bulletin *see* 0085-8021
0085-8021 Water Research Foundation of Australia. Reports
0085-803X Weed Society of New South Wales. Proceedings†
0085-8048 Welcome to Finland
0085-8056 Welcome to Greenland *changed to* North Atlantic
0085-8064 Welcome to Iceland *changed to* North Atlantic
0085-8072 Welcome to the Faroes *changed to* North Atlantic
0085-8080 West Malaysia Annual Statistics of External Trade
0085-8099 West Virginia Education Directory
0085-8102 Western Association of State Game and Fish Commissioners. Proceedings *changed to* Western Association of Fish and Wildlife Agencies. Proceedings
0085-8110 Western Australia. Aboriginal Affairs Planning Authority. Newsletter *changed to* Western Australia. Department of Aboriginal Affairs. Newsletter
0085-8129 Western Australia. Forest Department. Bulletin *changed to* Western Australia. Department of Conservation and Land Management. Bulletin
0085-8137 Western Australia. Geological Survey. Bulletin
0085-8145 Western Australia. Geological Survey. Report
0085-8153 Western Australia. Government Chemical Laboratories. Report of Investigations
0085-8161 Western Australia Law Almanac
0085-8188 Western Canadian Steam Locomotive Directory
0085-8196 Wheat Australia
0085-8196 Wheat Australia *see* 0814-9267
0085-820X Whiteacre
0085-8226 Wisconsin. Department of Administration. Annual Fiscal Report
0085-8242 Wisconsin Women Newsletter *changed to* Wisconsin Women and Public Policy
0085-8250 Witchcraft Digest
0085-8285 World Health Organization. Work of W H O
0085-8307 World Motor Vehicle Data
0085-8315 World Population Data Sheet
0085-8331 Wyoming Work Injury Report *see* 0093-1241
0085-834X Yamagata University. Bulletin
0085-8366 Yokohama National University. Science Reports. Section 1: Mathematics, Physics, Chemistry
0085-8374 York Journal of Convocation
0085-8382 Your Australian Garden
0085-8412 Zeitschrift fuer Psychosomatische Medizin und Psychoanalyse. Beihefte
0085-8420 Eidgenoessische Sternwarte, Zurich. Astronomische Mitteilungen†
0088-7714 Materiali e Documenti Ticinesi
0090-0036 American Journal of Public Health
0090-0044 National Union Catalog of Manuscript Collections
0090-0079 MEDI-KWOC Index†
0090-0087 Monthly List of State Publications *see* 0027-0288
0090-0117 U.S. Library of Congress. Legislative Reference Service. Digest of Public General Bills *changed to* U.S. Library of Congress. Congressional Research Service. Digest of Public General Bills and Resolutions
0090-0125 U.S. Library of Congress. Legislative Reference Service. Digest of Public General Bills and Selected Resolutions *changed to* U.S. Library of Congress. Congressional Research Service. Digest of Public General Bills and Resolutions
0090-0141 Directory of Dental Educators *changed to* Directory of Dental Educators
0090-0176 Japanese Studies in the History of Science *changed to* Historia Scientiarum
0090-0214 Nuclear Data Tables *see* 0092-640X
0090-0222 Great Lakes Entomologist
0090-0311 J O G N Nursing *see* 0884-2175
0090-0443 Current Concepts in Nutrition
0090-046X Medical Communicator *changed to* A M W A Journal
0090-0486 Environment Film Review†
0090-0494 Obesity & Bariatric Medicine†
0090-0508 Current Contents/Agriculture, Biology & Environmental Sciences
0090-0559 Clinical Trends in Family Practice†
0090-0575 International Bibliography on Burns
0090-0591 C T F A Cosmetic Journal†
0090-0613 N O A A National Weather Service. Climate Analysis Center. Average Monthly Weather Outlook *changed to* N O A A National Weather Service. Climate Analysis Center. Monthly and Seasonal Weather Outlook
0090-0656 Fishery Bulletin
0090-0664 North Carolina State University. School of Forest Resources. Technical Report.
0090-0672 Union Catalog of Medical Periodicals *see* 0276-7570
0090-0702 Maternal-Child Nursing Journal
0090-0710 Hospital Medical Staff *changed to* Medical Staff News
0090-0737 Pennsylvania Crop Reporting Service. Pennsylvania Orchard and Vineyard Survey†
0090-0753 Index of Tissue Culture†
0090-077X New Jersey. Developmental Disabilities Council. Annual Report
0090-0818 Pro and Amateur Hockey Guide *see* 0278-4955
0090-0834 Optical Management†
0090-0842 Consensus†
0090-0869 O A G Travel Planner & Hotel/Motel Guide *see* 0193-3299
0090-0877 Immunological Communications *see* 0882-0139
0090-0893 N F A I S Newsletter
0090-0907 Chemical Marketing Reporter
0090-0923 Family Planning/Population Reporter†
0090-0931 New Mexico. State Records Center and Archives. Publications Filed *changed to* New Mexico. State Records Center & Archives. Annual Publications List
0090-0958 Institute for the Development of Indian Law. Education Journal *see* 0145-7993
0090-1032 Harvard Political Review
0090-1059 Oregon. Department of Education. Racial and Ethnic Survey†
0090-1083 Annual Review of Allergy *see* 0278-9566
0090-1091 Journal of Clinical Computing
0090-1156 U.S. Center for Disease Control. Brucellosis Surveillance: Annual Summary
0090-1164 Current Citations on Strabismus, Amblyopia, and Other Diseases of Ocular Motility
0090-1180 Administration in Mental Health
0090-1210 A S T M Standardization News
0090-1229 Clinical Immunology and Immunopathology
0090-1237 Claudel Studies
0090-1245 Index of Dermatology†
0090-1326 Recurring Bibliography of Hypertension
0090-1377 Cumulated Abridged Index Medicus
0090-1407 Cerebrovascular Bibliography†
0090-1423 Cumulated Index Medicus
0090-144X Psychotherapy *changed to* Psychotherapy
0090-1482 Journal of Alcohol and Drug Education
0090-1520 Florida. Legislature. Joint Legislative Management Committee. Summary of General Legislation

0090-1601 Foundation Grants Index; Subjects on Microfiche *changed to* Comsearch: Subjects
0090-161X Bio-Medical Insight†
0090-1652 Biology of Brain Dysfunction†
0090-1660 Committee of Interns and Residents Bulletin *changed to* C I R News
0090-1741 National Roster of Realtors *changed to* National Roster of Realtors Directory
0090-1830 Marine Fisheries Review
0090-1881 American Psychiatric Association. Scientific Proceedings in Summary Form
0090-1903 Norda Briefs
0090-1911 Vibrational Spectra and Structure
0090-192X Key Systems Guide†
0090-1938 Journal of Erie Studies
0090-1954 Symposium on Creation†
0090-1989 Directory: North Dakota City Officials
0090-1997 Florida Symposium on Automata and Semigroups†
0090-2047 Oui
0090-2055 U.S. Environmental Protection Agency. Office of Research and Development. Bibliography of Water Quality Research Reports *changed to* U.S. Environmental Protection Agency. Office of Research and Development. Indexed Bibliography
0090-2063 Photographica *changed to* Photographica Journal
0090-2071 Proteus†
0090-208X Official Associated Press Almanac *changed to* Hammond Almanac: One-Volume Encyclopedia of a Million Facts & Records (year)
0090-2136 Q P Herald *see* 0146-5023
0090-2209 Newspaper Guild. Annual T.N.G. Convention Officers' Report
0090-2225 In-Service Training and Education *see* 0160-7006
0090-2233 Hawaii. Commission on Aging. Report of Achievements of Programs for the Aging
0090-225X Foreign Newspaper Report *see* 0190-9819
0090-2268 Lectures in Heterocyclic Chemistry
0090-2292 Hockey Register
0090-2381 I E E E Power Processing and Electronics Specialists Conference. Record *see* 0275-9306
0090-2411 A.E. Legal Newsletter
0090-2446 Field and Stream Camping on Wheels *changed to* Field & Stream Guide to Camping on Wheels
0090-2454 Product Management *see* 0278-1530
0090-2500 Adit†
0090-2519 Contamination Control/Biomedical Environments†
0090-2535 Guidebook of Catholic Hospitals *changed to* Catholic Health Association of the United States. Guidebook
0090-2578 Sunset Christmas Ideas and Answers†
0090-2586 Journal for the Study of Consciousness
0090-2594 Vanderbilt Journal of Transnational Law
0090-2616 Organizational Dynamics
0090-2756 Connecticut. Department of Correction. Publications
0090-2810 World Currency Charts
0090-2845 U.S. Copyright Office. Annual Report of the Register of Copyrights
0090-2861 Microfilm Source Book *see* 0272-0310
0090-287X Annual Review of the Schizophrenic Syndrome†
0090-2918 Public Health Reports
0090-2934 Dialysis & Transplantation
0090-2942 American Journal of Chinese Medicine *see* 0192-415X
0090-2969 Alcohol and Health Notes *see* 0364-0531
0090-2977 Neurophysiology
0090-2985 Carnival & Circus Booking Guide
0090-2993 Cavalcade and Directory of Acts and Attractions *changed to* Cavalcade of Acts & Attractions
0090-3000 Cinemagic
0090-3019 Surgical Neurology
0090-3116 Association of Hospital and Institution Libraries. Quarterly *see* 0270-6717
0090-3159 Contemporary Ob/Gyn
0090-3167 Learning
0090-3191 United Way of America. Information Center. Digest of Current Reports *changed to* United Way of America. Information Center. Digest of Selected Reports
0090-3213 Planetarian
0090-3221 State of Nebraska Uniform Crime Report
0090-3248 Illinois. Housing Development Authority. Annual Report
0090-3256 Good Sam Club's Recreational Vehicle Owners Directory *changed to* Trailer Life's Recreational Vehicle Campground and Services Directory
0090-3272 Communications in Statistics *see* 0361-0926
0090-3272 Communications in Statistics *see* 0361-0918
0090-3280 Non-G P O Imprints Received in the Library of Congress†
0090-3329 American Dental Association. Annual Reports and Resolutions *changed to* American Dental Association. Transaction Series: Annual Reports and Resolutions, Supplements One and Two, Transactions
0090-3353 Rock Scene
0090-3361 Keyboard Arts
0090-337X Countryside and Small Stock Journal *see* 8750-7595
0090-3477 Journal of Non-Metals *see* 0309-5991
0090-3485 Engage/Social Action *see* 0164-5528
0090-3493 Critical Care Medicine
0090-3507 Petroleum and Chemical Industry Conference. Record of Conference Papers
0090-3515 A R L I S/N A Newsletter *see* 0730-7187
0090-3531 Minority Group Employment in the Federal Government *changed to* Affirmative Employment Statistics
0090-3558 Journal of Wildlife Diseases
0090-3604 American Academy of Psychoanalysis. Journal
0090-3612 Puerto Rico Official Industrial Directory
0090-3647 American Bar Association. Section of Administrative Law. Annual Reports of Committees†
0090-3655 Semiconductor Application Notes D.A.T.A. Book *see* 0732-5894
0090-3663 Music World Magazine†
0090-3671 Year Book of Surgery
0090-371X U.S. Library of Congress. Accessions List: Eastern Africa
0090-3736 U.S. Library of Congress. Accessions List: Sri Lanka†
0090-3744 U.S. Library of Congress. Accessions List: Nepal†
0090-3752 Nuclear Data Sheets
0090-3779 Appalachian Journal
0090-3809 Montana State Plan for Alcohol Abuse and Alcoholism Prevention, Treatment and Rehabilitation *changed to* Montana Comprehensive Chemical Dependency Plan
0090-3825 Management World *changed to* Management Success
0090-3833 Destination: Philadelphia
0090-3841 Recreational Vehicle Retailer *changed to* R V Business
0090-3868 World Today Series: Soviet Union and Eastern Europe
0090-3884 Steam Electric Fuels *changed to* Steam-Electric Plant Factors (1978)
0090-3906 Oregon. Mass Transit Division. Annual Report *changed to* Public Transportation in Oregon
0090-3914 American Society of Civil Engineers. Environmental Engineering Division. Journal *see* 0733-9372
0090-3949 Cross-Talk†
0090-3957 Group Therapy *see* 0276-5594
0090-3965 National Association of College Admissions Counselors. Membership Directory
0090-3973 Journal of Testing and Evaluation
0090-3981 High Fidelity's Test Reports†
0090-399X Realty Bluebook
0090-4007 Country Music
0090-4023 Successful Ventures in Contemporary Education in Oklahoma†
0090-4058 Franklin Mint. Numismatic Issues *changed to* Franklin Mint. Limited Editions
0090-4066 Directory of Corporate Urban Affairs Officers†
0090-4074 National Directory of Providers of Psychiatric Services to Religious Institutions†
0090-4082 Outstanding Elementary Teachers of America†
0090-4104 Journal of Soviet Mathematics
0090-4112 Critiques†
0090-4155 Behaviorism
0090-4163 Directory of National Unions and Employee Associations†
0090-4171 Stations†
0090-418X Who's Who in the Securities Industry
0090-4201 Journal of Sports Medicine *see* 0363-5465
0090-4236 Annual Editions: Readings in Sociology *see* 0277-9315
0090-4244 Mountain Plains Journal of Adult Education
0090-4260 Literature/Film Quarterly
0090-4295 Urology
0090-4309 Annual Editions: Business/Management
0090-4325 Montana. Office of the Legislative Auditor. Department of Institutions Reimbursements Program; Report on Audit
0090-4341 Archives of Environmental Contamination and Toxicology
0090-4368 G.H.S. Foot-Notes
0090-4376 Cable Tech
0090-4384 Annual Editions: Readings in Biology *changed to* Annual Editions: Biology
0090-4392 Journal of Community Psychology
0090-4406 Photography Year†
0090-4414 Amateur Athletic Union of the United States. Official A A U Basketball Handbook†
0090-4422 Economics: Encyclopedia *changed to* Encyclopedia of Economics
0090-4430 Annual Editions: Readings in Economics *changed to* Annual Editions: Economics
0090-4449 Evaluation and Change†
0090-4473 American Association of Zoological Parks and Aquariums. Proceedings. Annual A A Z P A Conference
0090-4481 Pediatric Annals
0090-449X Clark County History
0090-4511 Annual Editions: Readings in American History
0090-452X Catskills†
0090-4546 Virginia Woolf Quarterly†
0090-4570 Rag Times
0090-4589 Job Safety and Health†
0090-4600 Tax Management International Journal
0090-466X Journal of Pharmacokinetics and Biopharmaceutics
0090-4716 New York (State) Department of Social Services. Bureau of Data Management and Analysis. Program Analysis Report
0090-4759 Soviet Journal of Particles and Nuclei
0090-4848 Human Resource Management
0090-4872 Directory - Juvenile Adult Correctional Institutions and Agencies of the United States of America, Canada, and Great Britain *see* 0190-2555
0090-4910 Retirement Living *see* 0163-2027
0090-4937 Junior American Modeler *changed to* Sport Modeler
0090-4945 Directory of Consulting Specialists†
0090-4961 Sunday Clothes†
0090-4996 Animal Learning & Behavior
0090-502X Memory and Cognition
0090-5038 National Trade and Professional Associations of the United States and Labor Unions *changed to* National Trade and Professional Associations of the United States and Labor Unions
0090-5046 Physiological Psychology *see* 0889-6313
0090-5054 Psychonomic Society. Bulletin
0090-5070 Groundwater Newsletter
0090-5089 K A F P Journal
0090-5119 Health, Physical Education and Recreation Microform Publications Bulletin
0090-5143 Iowa Summary of Vital Statistics *see* 0161-8695
0090-5151 Woodall's Campground Directory. Florida Campgrounds Edition *changed to* Woodall's Campground Directory. Florida Edition
0090-516X Pollution Technology Review
0090-5178 Heavy Duty Equipment Maintenance/Management *see* 0733-3056
0090-5224 Poe Studies
0090-5232 L C Science Tracer Bullet
0090-5259 Scene†
0090-5267 Control and Dynamic Systems: Advances in Theory and Applications
0090-5291 Electronics Buyers' Guide
0090-5305 Pocket Playboy†
0090-5348 Annual Editions: Readings in Human Development
0090-5364 Annals of Statistics
0090-5380 Symphony News *see* 0271-2687
0090-5402 Paint Red Book
0090-5461 Journal of Non-White Concerns in Personnel and Guidance *see* 0883-8534
0090-547X Annual Editions: Readings in American Government *changed to* Annual Editions: American Government
0090-5488 Biomaterials, Medical Devices, and Artificial Organs *see* 0890-5533
0090-5496 Oregon. State Board of Education. ESEA Title III State Plan†
0090-5526 Small Group Behavior
0090-5542 Basic Life Sciences
0090-5550 Rehabilitation Psychology
0090-5569 Selected Abstracts on Animal Models for Biomedical Research†
0090-5577 Directory of North Dakota Manufacturers
0090-5593 California. Teachers Retirement Board. State Teacher's Retirement System; Annual Report to the Governor and the Legislature
0090-5607 Ultrasonics Symposium. Proceedings
0090-5631 Meat Science Institute. Proceedings
0090-5674 Paideuma
0090-5720 Journal of Behavioral Economics
0090-5747 Sage Urban Studies Abstracts
0090-5895 Current Governments Reports: State Government Finances
0090-5917 Political Theory
0090-5968 California State Water Project
0090-5992 Nationalities Papers
0090-600X Wheelers Trailer Resort and Campground Guide *changed to* Wheelers R V Resort and Campground Guide: North American Edition
0090-6034 Cricket
0090-6077 Connecticut. Department on Aging. Report to the Governor and General Assembly
0090-6093 Cowan Clan United. Newsletter
0090-6107 Maine. Law Enforcement Planning & Assistance Agency. Progress Report *changed to* Maine. Criminal Justice Planning & Assistance Agency. Progress Report

ISSN INDEX

0090-6263 Annual Report of Federal Civilian Employment by Geographic Area *changed to* Federal Civilian Workforce Statistics. Biennial Report of Employment by Geographic Area
0090-628X Nebraska. Accounting Division. Annual Report of Receipts and Disbursements *changed to* Nebraska. Department of Administrative Services. Annual Fiscal Report
0090-6352 Assessment and Valuation Legal Reporter
0090-6360 Atomic Physics
0090-6409 Oregon. Department of Forestry. Biennial Report of the State Forester *see* 0015-7449
0090-6425 Minnesota. State Board of Health. Biennial Report†
0090-6433 Better Homes and Gardens Hundreds of Ideas†
0090-645X Billboard International Tape Directory *changed to* Billboard's Audio/Video/Tape Sourcebook
0090-6484 Directory of Executive Recruiters
0090-6514 Telos
0090-6557 Tennessee Pocket Data Book†
0090-6581 Cosmetics and Perfumery *see* 0361-4387
0090-6611 Popular Computing (Calabasas)†
0090-662X Yearbook of Drug Abuse *see* 0273-3722
0090-6638 American Druggist Merchandising *see* 0190-5279
0090-6662 Hospital Statistics; Data from American Hospital Association Annual Survey *changed to* Hospital Statistics (Year)
0090-6689 Medical Instrumentation
0090-6700 Official Museum Directory
0090-6735 Oregon. State Board of Accountancy. Certified Public Accountants, Public Accountants, Professional Corporations, and Accountants Authorized to Conduct Municipal Audits in Oregon *changed to* Oregon. State Board of Accountancy. Certified Public Accountants, Public Accountants, and Accountants Authorized to Conduct Municipal Audits in Oregon
0090-6743 Montana. Department of Public Instruction. Descriptive Report of Program Activities for Vocational Education†
0090-6778 I E E E Transactions on Communications
0090-6786 Stereo Directory and Buying Guide *changed to* Stereo Review's Stereo Buyers Guide
0090-6808 U.S. Environmental Protection Agency. Office of Research and Development. Selected Irrigation Return Flow Quality Abstracts†
0090-6816 U S A N and the U S P Dictionary of Drug Names
0090-6883 Synthesis (Cambridge)
0090-6905 Journal of Psycholinguistic Research
0090-6913 Letters in Applied and Engineering Sciences *see* 0020-7225
0090-693X Community-Clinical Psychology Series†
0090-6964 Annals of Biomedical Engineering
0090-6980 Prostaglandins
0090-7103 World Affairs Report
0090-7111 Census of Maine Manufactures
0090-7227 Federal Civilian Manpower Statistics. Monthly Release *changed to* Federal Civilian Workforce Statistics. Employment and Trends
0090-7235 L O M A Literature on Modern Art *see* 0300-466X
0090-7286 Topical New Issues
0090-7324 R S R
0090-7383 Conference on Data Systems Languages. Data Base Task Group. Report
0090-7421 Journal of Allied Health
0090-7480 Best's Safety Directory
0090-760X Missouri Life
0090-7618 U.S. National Center for Education Statistics. Expenditures and Revenues for Public Elementary and Secondary Education *see* 0149-2497
0090-7634 B and P - Brass & Percussion *changed to* Woodwind, Brass & Percussion
0090-7782 A H M E Journal†
0090-7790 Black Perspective in Music
0090-7812 Directory of Missouri's Regional Planning System *changed to* Directory of Missouri's Regional Planning Commissions
0090-7820 Bonnes Feuilles
0090-7847 Railroad History
0090-7855 P A A B S Revista†
0090-7863 U.S. National Credit Union Administration. N C U A Quarterly†
0090-788X Let's Go: The Student Guide to the United States and Canada *changed to* Let's Go: U S A
0090-791X Environment Index
0090-7944 Columbia Human Rights Law Review
0090-7987 Children's Book Review Service
0090-7995 Rhodes Directory of Black Dentists Registered in the United States
0090-8002 U.S. Emergency Loan Guarantee Board. Annual Report†
0090-8029 Auto Racing Digest
0090-8118 National Society for Programmed Instruction. Newsletter *changed to* Performance & Instruction Journal
0090-8142 Western Society of Weed Science. Research Progress Report
0090-8177 Minnesota. Department of Natural Resources. Biennial Report
0090-8185 Dirt Bike Buyer's Guide†
0090-8207 Graphic Arts Literature Abstracts
0090-8223 Urban Mass Transportation Abstracts
0090-8258 Gynecologic Oncology
0090-8266 Graduate & Professional School Opportunities for Minority Students†
0090-8274 Hawaii Literary Review *see* 0093-9625
0090-8282 Insect World Digest†
0090-8290 Canadian-American Slavic Studies
0090-8304 U.S. Library of Congress. Accessions List. Bangladesh†
0090-8312 Energy Sources
0090-8320 Ocean Development and International Law
0090-8339 Coastal Zone Management Journal
0090-8347 Energy Systems and Policy
0090-8363 Chemical Abstracts - Applied Chemistry and Chemical Engineering Sections
0090-8371 U.S. Copyright Office. Catalog of Copyright Entries. Third Series. Parts 12-13. Motion Pictures and Filmstrips *see* 0163-7320
0090-838X Alcohol Health and Research World
0090-8401 Michigan. Employment Security Commission. Labor Market Analysis Section. Annual Manpower Planning Report: Detroit Labor Market Area *changed to* Michigan. Employment Security Commission. Annual Planning Report
0090-8479 Venereal Disease Bibliography†
0090-8517 Connecticut River Valley Covered Bridge Society. Bulletin
0090-8541 U.S. National Bureau of Standards. Methods of Measurement for Semiconductor Materials, Process Control, and Devices; Quarterly Report *changed to* U.S. National Bureau of Standards. Semiconductor Measurement Technology
0090-8584 Current Topics in Comparative Pathobiology
0090-8592 Behavior of Nonhuman Primates: Modern Research Trends†
0090-8614 A L A Sights to See Book
0090-8630 Family Circle's Home Decorating Guide *changed to* Decorating Remodeling
0090-8649 Southern Regional Education Board. State and Local Revenue Potential *changed to* Southern Regional Education Board. State and Local Tax Performance
0090-8649 Southern Regional Education Board. State and Local Revenue Potential *changed to* Issues in Higher Education
0090-8657 Tire Science and Technology†
0090-8673 Ohio College Library Center. Annual Report *see* 0730-5125
0090-8711 Cuttin' Hoss Chatter
0090-8738 Bromeliad Society. Journal
0090-8746 Library Scene *see* 0735-8571
0090-8762 Practical Horseman
0090-8800 Contemporary Topics in Molecular Immunology
0090-8843 Alabama Marine Resources Bulletin
0090-8878 Household & Personal Products Industry *changed to* H A P P I: Household & Personal Products Industry
0090-8886 Infectious Diseases
0090-8932 Render
0090-8967 Illinois Institute for Environmental Quality. Annual Report†
0090-8991 New York Mercantile Exchange Statistical Yearbook†
0090-9033 Buyer's Guide to the World of Tape *see* 0161-4371
0090-905X Iowa Genealogical Society. Surname Index
0090-9076 American Psychological Association. Biographical Directory *see* 0196-6545
0090-9084 Journal of Police Science and Administration
0090-9092 Art Psychotherapy *see* 0197-4556
0090-9114 Americana
0090-9130 Index of American Periodical Verse
0090-919X Corporation Finance and New Issue Weekly *changed to* Corporate Financing Week
0090-9203 H I S S News-Journal†
0090-9211 Art Investment Report *see* 0161-1232
0090-9300 Maryland Geographer†
0090-9319 Woman's Day 101 Gardening & Outdoor Ideas†
0090-9327 Penny Stock Handbook
0090-9386 Maine. Criminal Justice Planning & Assistance Agency. Criminal Justice Internship Program. Report and Evaluation
0090-9416 Latin American Index
0090-9440 Hawaii. Department of Education. Office of Business Services. Report on Federally Connected Pupils: Hawaii Public Schools†
0090-9467 Foreign Economic Trends and Their Implications for the United States
0090-9475 Exporter's Encyclopedia-United States Marketing Guide†
0090-9491 Stochastics
0090-9521 Architecture Plus†
0090-9556 Drug Metabolism and Disposition
0090-9580 International Journal of Cooperative Development†
0090-9599 R F Illustrated *changed to* R F
0090-9661 F L I R T Newsletter *see* 0273-1061
0090-9688 U.S. Department of Agriculture. Food and Home Notes†
0090-9718 Focus: Technical Cooperation†
0090-9742 Private Investors Abroad
0090-9785 M R I S Bulletin *see* 0147-572X
0090-9815 North Dakota Crop and Livestock Reporting Service. Wheat Varieties, North Dakota†
0090-9866 Clergy's Federal Income Tax Guide *see* 0163-1241
0090-9882 Journal of Applied Communication Research
0090-9912 Montana. Office of the Legislative Auditor. State of Montana Board of Investments. Report on Examination of Financial Statements
0090-9955 Directory of Polish Officials
0090-9963 Maryland. Correctional Training Commission. Annual Report *changed to* Maryland. Police and Correctional Training Commissions. Report to the Governor, the Secretary of Public Safety and Correctional Services, and Members of the General Assembly
0090-9971 Executive Compensation Service. Reports on International Compensation. Puerto Rico
0090-998X Audio Journal Review: General Surgery†
0091-0031 U.S. Centers for Disease Control. Morbidity and Mortality Weekly Report
0091-004X Pediatric Conferences with Sydney Gellis†
0091-0120 Current Packaging Abstracts
0091-0155 Enzyme Technology Digest†
0091-018X Food Management
0091-0198 Grain and Farm Service Centers *changed to* Grain & Feed Journals
0091-0260 Public Personnel Management
0091-0279 Veterinary Clinics of North America *see* 0195-5616
0091-0279 Veterinary Clinics of North America *see* 0196-9846
0091-0287 Yale Scientific
0091-0376 Prairie Naturalist
0091-0392 Bank Protection Bulletin *changed to* Banking Insurance and Protection Bulletin
0091-0406 Nebraska State Publications Checklist
0091-0430 Lawyer-to-Lawyer Consultation Panel†
0091-0449 D M G - D R S Journal: Design Research and Methods *see* 0147-1147
0091-0457 Montana. Environmental Quality Council. Annual Report *changed to* Montana. Environmental Quality Council. Biennial Report
0091-0465 Annual Guide to Undergraduate Study *see* 0737-3163
0091-0538 A P L A Quarterly Journal
0091-0546 Oregon. Public Utility Commissioner. Statistics of Electric, Gas, Steam Heat, Telephone, Telegraph and Water Companies
0091-0554 Space Age News†
0091-0562 American Journal of Community Psychology
0091-0600 International Journal of Psychoanalytic Psychotherapy†
0091-0627 Journal of Abnormal Child Psychology
0091-0651 Field & Stream Sportsman†
0091-0678 Maine. State Planning Office. Annual Report†
0091-0716 Guide to Nebraska State Agencies
0091-0724 Annual Causes and Conditions of Poverty in South Dakota *changed to* Poverty in South Dakota
0091-0732 Idaho. Department of Employment. Annual Farm Labor Report *changed to* Idaho. Department of Employment. Annual Rural Employment Report
0091-0759 Maine. State Library. Special Subject Resources in Maine
0091-0775 Kentucky School Directory
0091-0791 Public Continuing and Adult Education Almanac†
0091-0848 Texas. Water Quality Board. Agency Publication†
0091-0899 Dairy Scope†
0091-0988 Western Economic Indicators†
0091-0996 Montana. Department of Social and Rehabilitation Services. Annual Report†
0091-1003 Directory. Diocesan Agencies of Catholic Charities. United States, Puerto Rico and Canada *changed to* Directory. Diocesan Agencies of Catholic Charities and Catholic Charities U S A Member Institutions. United States, Puerto Rico and Canada
0091-1054 Oklahoma Pontotoc County Quarterly
0091-1062 S A M P E Journal
0091-1097 Missouri Annual Highway Safety Work Program *changed to* Missouri. Division of Highway Safety. Highway Safety Plan
0091-1186 Guidebook to North Carolina Taxes
0091-1305 FarmFutures

1428 ISSN INDEX

0091-1372 Soap/Cosmetics/Chemical Specialties
0091-1402 Statehouse Observer
0091-1410 Transportation. Current Literature
0091-1429 United States Earthquakes
0091-1461 Ski Racing Redbook
0091-1488 Bachy†
0091-1518 A Report on the Work and Programs of Scripps Institution of Oceanography *changed to* Scripps Institution of Oceanography. Annual Report
0091-1526 Wall Street Review of Books
0091-1550 Texas Livestock Statistics
0091-1607 A-Ki-Ki *changed to* The-A-KiKi
0091-1615 Working Papers for a New Society *changed to* Modern Times
0091-1658 American Statistics Index
0091-1666 Chicago Dental Society Review
0091-1674 Clinical Social Work Journal
0091-1682 Clinical Trends in Urology†
0091-1704 Current Contents/Clinical Pratice *changed to* Current Contents/Clinical Medicine
0091-1712 Environmental Education Report *changed to* Environmental Education Report and Newsletter
0091-1720 Public Science Newsletter†
0091-1747 Syndrome Identification†
0091-1798 Annals of Probability
0091-181X Marine Behaviour and Physiology
0091-1887 Underwater Photographer†
0091-1909 Journal of Urban Analysis *changed to* Journal of Urban Analysis and Public Management
0091-1984 C A T V Systems Directory, Map Service and Handbook†
0091-2026 Atmospheric Technology†
0091-2085 Documents to the People
0091-2131 Ethos
0091-2166 Hearing Aid Journal *changed to* Hearing Journal
0091-2174 International Journal of Psychiatry in Medicine
0091-2182 Journal of Nurse-Midwifery
0091-2220 Best Editorial Cartoons of the Year
0091-2263 Population and the Population Explosion: a Bibliography†
0091-2271 U.S. Army Infantry Center. History; Annual Supplement *changed to* U.S. Army Infantry School. History; Annual Supplement
0091-231X Missouri. Division of Mental Health. Annual Report *changed to* Missouri. Department of Mental Health. Progress Notes
0091-2328 Investment Adviser Directory
0091-2360 Today's Chiropractic
0091-2379 Nursing Care *changed to* Licensed Practical Nurse
0091-2387 National Spokesman
0091-2395 National Drug Reporter†
0091-2468 Transportation Research Forum. Proceedings: Annual Meeting
0091-2476 A C T F L Review of Foreign Languages Education *see* 0147-1236
0091-2484 News Citizen *changed to* Scholastic News: News Citizen
0091-2492 U.S. Executive Office of the President. International Economic Report of the President†
0091-2573 Potomac Review†
0091-2611 Corrective and Social Psychiatry and Journal of Applied Behavior Therapy *see* 0093-1551
0091-262X Iowa. Department of Job Service. Research and Statistics Division. Annual Manpower Planning Report†
0091-2646 U.S. Labor-Management Services Administration. Decisions and Reports on Rulings of the Assistant Secretary of Labor for Labor-Management Relations
0091-2662 Drug Abuse Council. Public Policy†
0091-2700 Journal of Clinical Pharmacology
0091-2700 Journal of Clinical Pharmacology
0091-2743 Baptist Missionary Association of America. Directory and Handbook
0091-2751 Journal of Clinical Ultrasound
0091-2786 American Gas Association. Research and Development†
0091-2859 Regional Institute of Social Welfare Research. Annual Report
0091-2948 Lost Generation Journal
0091-3057 Pharmacology, Biochemistry and Behavior
0091-3065 Review of Child Development Research
0091-3103 Medicaid Statistics: Medical Assistance (Medicaid) Financed Under Title 19 of the Social Security Act
0091-3154 Who's Who in Ecology†
0091-3219 Journal of Ethnic Studies
0091-3235 Directory of Latin Americanists *changed to* Directory of A S U Latin Americanists
0091-3243 Directory of Secondary Schools with Occupational Curriculums, Public and Nonpublic *changed to* Occupational Education: Enrollments and Programs in Noncollegiate Postsecondary Schools
0091-3251 New York (State). Department of Audit and Control. Index to the Public Schools†
0091-3286 Optical Engineering
0091-3294 Films and Other Materials for Projection *changed to* National Union Catalog. Audiovisual Materials
0091-3367 Journal of Advertising
0091-3383 American SquareDance
0091-3391 Amateur Athletic Union of the United States. Athletic Library. Official A A U Gymnastics Handbook†
0091-3405 Amateur Athletic Union of the United States. Official Handbook of the A A U Code
0091-3421 Contemporary Literary Criticism Series
0091-3448 Georgia. State Economic Opportunity Office. Annual Report†
0091-3464 Georgia Manpower Trends *changed to* Georgia Labor Market Trends
0091-3472 Robert Wood Johnson Foundation. Annual Report
0091-3499 Building Cost File *changed to* Berger Building & Design Cost File. Unit Prices. Vol. 1: General Construction Trades
0091-3499 Building Cost File *changed to* Berger Building & Design Cost File. Unit Prices. Vol. 2: Mechanical and Electrical Trades
0091-3502 U.S. Department of Agriculture. Economics, Statistics, and Cooperatives Service. Agricultural Finance Statistics†
0091-3553 U.S. Community Services Administration. Federal Outlays in Summary
0091-3588 State of Iowa Scholarships, Tuition Grants. Biennium Report *changed to* Iowa. College Aid Commission. Biennium Report
0091-3634 Deeds and Data†
0091-3642 Fruit Varieties Journal
0091-3669 Mosquito Systematics
0091-3685 National Journal Reports *see* 0360-4217
0091-3707 Social Sciences Citation Index
0091-3715 Political Science Reviewer
0091-3723 Journal of Chinese Linguistics
0091-3731 Print Review†
0091-3774 Motorcycle Blue Book
0091-3782 Northwest Missouri State University Studies†
0091-3804 American Bankers Association. Committee on Uniform Security Identification Procedures. C U S I P Directory: Corporate Directory *changed to* C U S I P Corporate Directory
0091-3839 U S P Guide to Select Drugs†
0091-3847 Physician and Sportsmedicine
0091-3855 Cost of Personal Borrowing in the United States.
0091-3901 Illustrated Digest of Baseball†
0091-391X International Symposium on Silicon Materials Science and Technology. Proceedings
0091-3952 Advances in Neurology
0091-3960 American Journal of Acupuncture
0091-3979 Dental Hygiene
0091-3995 S I E C U S Report
0091-4010 Guidebook to Ohio Taxes
0091-4029 Hofstra Law Review
0091-4037 International Journal of Polymeric Materials
0091-4045 Nutritional Update *changed to* Your Good Health
0091-4061 S E C Docket
0091-407X U S /Japan Outlook†
0091-4118 Pennsylvania. Crime Commission. Report
0091-4150 International Journal of Aging & Human Development
0091-4169 Journal of Criminal Law & Criminology
0091-4185 Wisconsin Dental Association. Journal
0091-4266 History of Childhood Quarterly *see* 0145-3378
0091-4347 Lietuviu Tautos Praeitis
0091-4371 American Horseman
0091-4428 Cutter and Chariot Racing World *see* 0194-8814
0091-4452 Journal of Color and Appearance†
0091-4460 M A F E S Research Highlights
0091-4479 Association of Research Libraries. University Library Management Studies Office. Occasional Paper *changed to* Association of Research Libraries. Office of Management Studies. Occasional Paper
0091-4487 Western Society of Weed Science. Proceedings
0091-4509 Contemporary Drug Problems
0091-4576 Consumer Guide Photographic Equipment Test Reports Quarterly *changed to* Consumer Guide Photo Annual
0091-4630 U.S. Office of Minority Business Enterprise. Minority Enterprise Progress Report†
0091-4665 Lawn & Garden Marketing
0091-4673 Texas Small Grains Statistics
0091-4711 Louisiana Labor Market
0091-4738 C V P: Journal of Cardiovascular and Pulmonary Technology *changed to* Cardiology Management
0091-4789 Colorado County and City Retail Sales by Standard Industrial Classification *see* 0732-071X
0091-4800 Worldwide Projects
0091-4835 Governmental Finance *changed to* Government Finance Review
0091-4843 Milling & Baking News
0091-4916 Journal of Nuclear Medicine Technology
0091-4924 Flannery O'Connor Bulletin
0091-4932 U.S. Federal Housing Administration. F H A Homes
0091-4975 Corporate Reports on File†
0091-5041 Geological Society of America. Memorials
0091-5114 Pennsylvania State Plan for the Administration of Vocational - Technical Education Programs
0091-5122 American Association of State Highway and Transportation Officials. Sub-Committee on Computer Technology. National Conference. Proceedings
0091-5173 Health Care Engineering *see* 0098-8219
0091-519X Criminal Justice News†
0091-5203 Gravure Environmental and O S H A Newsletter *see* 0271-1699
0091-5254 Wisconsin Population Projections
0091-5270 C A L L
0091-5300 Veterinary Toxicology *see* 0145-6296
0091-536X Conservation Foundation Letter
0091-5440 University of Baltimore Law Review
0091-5459 Union Labor Report
0091-5513 West Virginia Coal Facts
0091-5521 Community College Review
0091-553X A D & D; Tax Interpretations†
0091-5564 Delaware Reporter
0091-5572 Railroad Car Journal
0091-5599 Survey of Salaries and Employee Benefits of Private and Public Employers in Arizona. *changed to* Joint Governmental Salary Survey: Arizona
0091-5610 American Universities Field Staff. Population: Perspective†
0091-5629 Illinois. Governor's Office of Human Resources. Annual Report†
0091-5637 Journal of South Asian Literature
0091-5645 Coda: Poets and Writers Newsletter *see* 0891-6136
0091-5653 Monthly Checklist of Kentucky State Publications
0091-5661 Personal Income Tax in Oregon†
0091-5688 Access (Washington)†
0091-5696 Quality of Life in Iowa
0091-5793 Motorcycle Facts
0091-5823 Colorado. Department of Social Services. Research and Statistics Section. Research Report AFDC†
0091-584X University of Alaska. State Wide Bulletin†
0091-5858 Multi Media Reviews Index *see* 0363-7778
0091-5882 Idaho. State Board for Vocational Education. Annual Descriptive Report of Program Activities for Vocational Education
0091-5939 Housing and Development Reporter
0091-6080 Wisconsin. Department of Transportation. Traffic Planning Section. Automatic Recorder Station Traffic Data *see* 0098-0323
0091-6102 West Virginia Research League. Statistical Handbook
0091-6129 Pennsylvania Manufacturing Exporters *see* 0360-8859
0091-6137 Magazine of New York Business *see* 0148-0146
0091-6145 Progress in Extractive Metallurgy†
0091-6188 Delaware. Department of Public Instruction. Educational Personnel Directory
0091-6196 West Virginia's State System of Higher Education; Annual Report, Current Operating Revenues and Expenditures†
0091-620X Saturday Review
0091-6234 U.S. General Accounting Office. Social Development Activities in Latin America Promoted by the Inter-American Foundation: Report to the Congress by the Comptroller General of the United States†
0091-6242 U.S. General Services Administration. Management Report
0091-6269 A O A Newsbriefs†
0091-6277 Surgical Team *see* 0161-9721
0091-6315 Mental Retardation and Developmental Disabilities
0091-6323 Soul Journey†
0091-6331 Exercise and Sport Sciences Reviews
0091-634X American Academy of Psychiatry and the Law. Bulletin
0091-6358 Astronomy
0091-6390 Northwestern and Mississippi Valley Lumberman *changed to* Building Material Retailer
0091-6439 Midwest Genealogical Society. Surname Index *see* 0271-8685
0091-6471 Journal of Psychology and Theology
0091-6501 California Mosquito Control Association. Proceedings and Papers of the Annual Meeting *changed to* California Mosquito and Vector Control Association. Proceedings and Papers of the Annual Meeting
0091-6528 Society for Neuroscience. Annual Meeting. Conference Report†

ISSN INDEX 1429

0091-6536 C R C Critical Reviews in Clinical Radiology and Nuclear Medicine *see* 0147-6750
0091-6544 Family Therapy
0091-6595 Annual Review of Behavior Therapy: Theory & Practice *changed to* Review of Behavior Therapy: Theory & Practice
0091-6617 Fiber Producer Buyer's Guide *changed to* Fiber World
0091-6633 Missouri State Government Publications
0091-6641 Studio Potter
0091-6676 Irvine Humanities Review†
0091-6684 Navajo Historical Publications. Biographical Series†
0091-6706 Wood - Woods Family Magazine
0091-6722 Radiation Data and Reports†
0091-6730 Nebraska Medical Journal
0091-6749 Journal of Allergy and Clinical Immunology
0091-6765 E H P
0091-6773 Behavioral Biology *see* 0163-1047
0091-679X Methods in Cell Biology
0091-6811 Research Futures†
0091-6846 Strategic Review
0091-6854 Spectrum One: Stock Holdings Survey *changed to* Spectrum 1: U S and European Investment Company Stock Holdings Survey
0091-6862 Spectrum Two: Investment Company Portfolios *changed to* Spectrum 2: U S and European Investment Company Portfolios
0091-6900 Kansas Agriculture Report *changed to* Kansas. State Board of Agriculture. Annual Report with Farm Facts
0091-6919 U.S. Department of Defense. Defense Department Report
0091-6943 Vintage Airplane
0091-6978 New Jersey Airport Directory
0091-7036 International Journal of Computer and Information Sciences
0091-7052 Guide to Graduate Departments of Sociology
0091-7176 Ancient Times
0091-7192 Statistics on Social Work Education in the United States
0091-7206 E D P Performance Review
0091-7214 Mathematics International†
0091-7222 National Gallery of Art. Annual Report
0091-7257 Vertex (Los Angeles)†
0091-7265 Washington (State). Department of Social and Health Services. Jail Inspection Report†
0091-7281 Learning Today†
0091-729X Admission Requirements of U S and Canadian Dental Schools
0091-7311 Washington Report on Long Term Care *changed to* Long Term Care Management
0091-732X Review of Research in Education
0091-7338 Studies in the History of Art
0091-7346 Index to Literature on the American Indian†
0091-7354 U.S. Department of Transportation. Office of Policy Review. Working Paper†
0091-7370 Annals of Clinical and Laboratory Science
0091-7389 American Psychopathological Association. Proceedings of the Annual Meeting
0091-7397 Current Topics in Experimental Endocrinology
0091-7419 Journal of Supramolecular Structure *see* 0730-2312
0091-7435 Preventive Medicine
0091-7443 Association for Research in Nervous and Mental Disease. Research Publications
0091-7451 Cold Spring Harbor Laboratory. Symposia on Quantitative Biology
0091-746X Institute of Medicine of Chicago. Proceedings
0091-7516 Quarter Racing Record
0091-7605 Food Purity Perspectives
0091-7613 Geology (Boulder)
0091-7648 Wildlife Society Bulletin
0091-7664 Whiskey, Women, And...†
0091-7699 Instrument Society of America. I S A Final Control Elements Symposium. Final Control Elements; Proceedings†
0091-7710 Journal of Anthropological Research
0091-7729 Science-Fiction Studies
0091-7737 Technical Association of the Pulp and Paper Industry. Directory
0091-780X Colorado. Department of Social Services. Research and Statistics Section. Research Report W P M†
0091-7818 Colorado. Department of Social Services. Research and Statistics Section. Research Report W I N†
0091-7842 Colorado. Department of Social Services. Research and Statistics Section. Research Report A D M†
0091-7885 Technology Book Guide *see* 0360-2761
0091-7907 Conference Publications Guide *see* 0360-2729
0091-7915 Government Publications Guide *see* 0360-2796
0091-7958 University of Kansas. Museum of Natural History. Occasional Papers.
0091-8059 Headlights
0091-8075 Statistical Profile of the U.S. Exchange Program†
0091-8083 Studies in American Fiction
0091-8105 Food Fish Market Review and Outlook†
0091-8172 Psychotherapy and Behavior Change *see* 0360-0696
0091-8180 Colorado. Department of Social Services. Research and Statistics Section. Report A D C†
0091-8245 Guidelines for Improving Practice. Architects and Engineers Professional Liability
0091-8253 Washington (State) Legislature. Pictorial Directory
0091-8261 U.S. Bureau of Labor Statistics. Employee Compensation in the Private Nonfarm Economy†
0091-8296 Missiology
0091-830X Best's Recommended Independent Insurance Adjusters *changed to* Best's Directory of Recommended Insurance Adjusters
0091-8369 Journal of Homosexuality
0091-8377 Industrial Machinery and Equipment Pricing Guide
0091-8385 Techniques of Marriage and Family Counseling†
0091-8393 U S Medical Directory
0091-8415 Fixed Income Investor *see* 0731-1974
0091-844X Nebraska. Department of Roads. Traffic Analysis Unit. Continuous Traffic Count Data and Traffic Characteristics on Nebraska Streets and Highways
0091-8601 Industrial Education
0091-861X Cooking for Profit
0091-8644 U.S. Department of Transportation. Climatic Impact Assessment Program Office. Technical Abstract Report†
0091-8660 Ebony Jr†
0091-8695 Report on Federal Funds Received in Iowa
0091-8725 U.S. National Weather Service. Data Acquisition Division. Marine Surface Observations†
0091-8733 Muleskinner News *see* 0161-1747
0091-8784 Oregon Education Biennial Report†
0091-8792 Arizona. State Advisory Council for Vocational Education. Annual Report *changed to* Arizona. State Advisory Council for Vocational Technical Education. Annual Report
0091-8806 Cincinnati. Division of Police. Annual Report
0091-8822 Motor Sport Yearbook†
0091-8830 Southwest Art Magazine *see* 0192-4214
0091-8857 Watauga Association of Genealogists. Upper East Tennessee. Bulletin
0091-8873 Alaska State Chamber of Commerce. Membership Directory†
0091-8938 Student Enrollment Report; West Virginia Institutions of Higher Education†
0091-8954 Product Safety Up To Date
0091-8962 Iowa. Department of Public Instruction. Summary of Federal Programs
0091-8970 Indiana. State University Council for Vocational Technical Education. Annual Report *changed to* Indiana. Council on Vocational Education. Annual Report
0091-8989 Educational Testing Service Annual Report
0091-9004 North Dakota. Geological Survey. Educational Series
0091-9039 U.S. Department of Commerce. Publications; a Catalog and Index Supplement *see* 0277-7207
0091-9047 Michigan Business and Economic Research Bibliography
0091-908X K-Bar-T Country Roundup *changed to* Country Music Roundup
0091-9101 Election Laws of Hawaii *changed to* Election Laws of Hawaii Handbook
0091-9128 Nebraska. Commission on Law Enforcement and Criminal Justice. Criminal Justice Comprehensive Plan†
0091-9144 Centrum
0091-9152 Chain Store Guide Directory: Food Service Distributors *see* 0271-7662
0091-9187 New Jersey. Office of Demographic and Economic Analysis. Population Estimates for New Jersey
0091-9195 Nebraska. Commission on Law Enforcement and Criminal Justice. Criminal Justice Action Plan†
0091-9209 Current Governments Reports: City Employment
0091-9217 Best Science Fiction†
0091-9225 Air Defense Trends *changed to* Air Defense Artillery
0091-9233 Puerto Rico. Department of Labor. Bureau of Labor Statistics. Employment Hours and Earnings in the Manufacturing Establishments Promoted by the Economic Development Administration of the Puerto Rican Industrial Development Company
0091-9276 Johns Hopkins University. Population Information Program. Population Reports. Series G. Prostaglandins†
0091-9284 Johns Hopkins University. Population Information Program. Population Reports. Series F. Pregnancy Termination†
0091-9322 Temperature: Its Measurement and Control in Science and Industry
0091-9357 American Book Prices Current
0091-9381 American Baptist Churches in the U.S.A. Directory
0091-9403 U.S. Bureau of Labor Statistics. Employment and Wages.†
0091-9446 North Dakota. Milk Stabilization Board. Annual Report of Administrative Activities
0091-9489 Lawrence Berkeley Laboratory. Research Highlights
0091-9500 U.S. National Oceanographic Data Center. Key to Oceanographic Records Documentation
0091-9519 Electronic Industries Association. Trade Directory and Membership List
0091-9527 Catholic Schools in the United States *see* 0147-8044
0091-956X Report from N J D A†
0091-9578 Plastics Engineering
0091-9586 Kansas Country Living
0091-9632 Guide to Graduate Study in Political Science.
0091-9659 Northwest Journal of African and Black American Studies†
0091-9675 Semiconductor Diode D.A.T.A. Book *see* 0271-0803
0091-9683 To the World's Oboists *changed to* Double Reed
0091-9748 U. S. Advisory Council on Historic Preservation. Newsletter *see* 0098-4035
0091-9756 Metropolitan Atlanta Business Directory *changed to* Terminus Business Directory
0091-9772 Journal of Primal Therapy *changed to* Primal Institute Newsletter
0091-9780 Art Dealer & Framer *see* 0273-5652
0091-9837 Environmental Defense Fund. Annual Report
0091-9845 Hawaii Observer†
0091-9918 Conference Board. Monthly Business Review *see* 0362-5435
0091-9942 Florida. Governor. Annual Report on State Housing Goals†
0091-9977 Street & Smith's Official Yearbook: College Football
0091-9993 No-Till Farmer
0092-0002 International Decade of Ocean Exploration. Progress Report†
0092-0037 Ag Chem and Commercial Fertilizer *see* 0092-0053
0092-0053 Farm Chemicals
0092-0150 Modern Pharmacology *see* 0098-6925
0092-0177 Florida. Division of Motor Vehicles. Tags and Revenue
0092-0193 Ion Exchange and Solvent Extraction
0092-0258 Stanford Review†
0092-0290 University of California, Berkeley. Office of Institutional Research. Campus Statistics *changed to* University of California, Berkeley. Campus Statistics
0092-0320 U.S. Coast Guard. Polluting Incidents in and Around U.S. Waters
0092-0371 A A M C Curriculum Directory
0092-038X Current Business Reports: Monthly Selected Services Receipts†
0092-0436 Disc and That
0092-0444 Apartment Life *see* 0273-2858
0092-0479 Powder Coating Conference†
0092-0487 Faxon Librarians' Guide to Periodicals *see* 0275-8466
0092-0495 Carpet and Rug Institute. Review-State of the Industry *changed to* Carpet and Rug Industry Review
0092-0509 Powder Diffraction File Search Manual. Alphabetical Listing. Inorganic
0092-0517 Journal of Country Music
0092-0525 Jazz Digest
0092-0541 Solid Waste Management: Abstracts from the Literature†
0092-055X Teaching Sociology
0092-0576 Powder Diffraction File Search Manual. Organic
0092-0606 Journal of Biological Physics.
0092-0614 Directory of Louisiana Cities, Towns and Villages
0092-0622 Aqueduct
0092-0673 Louisiana Annual Rural Manpower Report†
0092-0681 Northwestern Lumberman *changed to* Building Material Retailer
0092-0703 Academy of Marketing Science. Journal
0092-0711 A.D. United Church Herald Edition *changed to* United Church of Christ A.D.
0092-072X Christian Association for Psychological Studies. Proceedings *see* 0147-7978
0092-0908 World Directory of Environmental Organizations†
0092-0940 A E L E Law Enforcement Legal Liability Reporter *changed to* Law Enforcement Liability Reporter
0092-0959 Baldwin's Ohio Legislative Service
0092-1009 Air Pollution Effects Surveillance Network Data Report *changed to* Air Quality Data for Arizona.
0092-1025 Outstanding Secondary Educators of America†
0092-105X Soviet Aerospace
0092-1068 American Hunter

ISSN INDEX

0092-1084 Nevada. Commission on Crime, Delinquency and Corrections. Comprehensive Law Enforcement Plan†
0092-1122 Battelle Memorial Institute. Research Outlook *see* 0145-8477
0092-1149 Monograph Abstracts (Ann Arbor) *see* 0362-7535
0092-1157 Journal of Biological Standardization
0092-1270 Virgin Islands Register
0092-1289 Camp Fire Leadership
0092-1297 Commercial Directory of Puerto Rico-Virgin Islands *changed to* Commercial Buyer's Guide Puerto Rico-Virgin Islands
0092-1300 Powder Diffraction File Search Manual. Fink Method. Inorganic
0092-1319 Powder Diffraction File Search Manual. Hanawalt Method. Inorganic
0092-1335 Annual Reports in Inorganic and General Syntheses
0092-1343 California Enviromental Yearbook and Directory *see* 0148-0324
0092-1386 Current World Leaders - Speeches, Reports and Position Papers *see* 0192-6802
0092-1416 Directory of Women Attorneys in the United States *changed to* Directory of Women Law Graduates and Attorneys in the U.S.A.
0092-1424 M A T Y C Journal *see* 0730-8639
0092-1432 Employment Relations Abstracts: Subject Heading List *changed to* Work Related Abstracts Subject Heading List
0092-1459 New Jersey Covered Employment Trends by Geographical Areas of the State *changed to* Covered Employment Trends in New Jersey
0092-1483 Directory-Hardware and Home Improvement Center Chains, Auto Supply Chains *see* 0736-0452
0092-1491 National Defense
0092-1505 Nebraska. Commission on Law Enforcement and Criminal Justice. Legislative Reporter†
0092-153X Texas Field Crop Statistics
0092-1548 Brookhaven Highlights
0092-1599 U.S. National Credit Union Administration. Research Report†
0092-1602 New Jersey. Division of Water Resources. Special Report†
0092-1645 U.S. Federal Railroad Administration. Office of Safety. Accident Bulletin *see* 0163-4674
0092-1661 Symposium on Incremental Motion Control Systems and Devices. Proceedings
0092-1696 Nebraska. Fisheries Production Division. Annual Report
0092-1726 North Carolina. Secretary of State. North Carolina Elections†
0092-1734 New Fishing
0092-1777 Hawaii. Department of Education. Educational Directory: State & District Office
0092-1785 U.S. Agricultural Research Service. A R S - N C
0092-1793 Fremontia
0092-1807 Twentieth Century *see* 0272-1635
0092-1815 International Journal of Instructional Media
0092-1858 Alaska Blue Book
0092-1866 Intercultural Studies Information Service†
0092-1874 Directory of Registered Federal and State Lobbyists *see* 0146-0323
0092-1904 United States Government Manual (1973)
0092-1912 Fiction International
0092-1920 Incentive Travel Manager *changed to* Sales Motivation
0092-1939 U.S. Agricultural Research Service. A R S-S†
0092-198X South Dakota. Department of History. Report and Historical Collections *changed to* South Dakota Historical Collections
0092-2013 Teaching Political Science
0092-2056 U.S. National Oceanic and Atmospheric Administration. Interdepartmental Committee for Meteorological Services and Supporting Research. National Hurricane Operations Plan
0092-2102 Interfaces
0092-2145 California and Western States Grape Grower
0092-2242 University of California, Los Angeles. Latin American Center. Latin American Activities and Resources†
0092-2293 Verdict Reports *changed to* Verdict Review
0092-2307 H I S S Titles and Review†
0092-2315 American Journal of Criminal Law
0092-2323 Journal of Indo-European Studies
0092-2358 Tri-State Regional Planning Commission. Annual Regional Report *changed to* Tri-State Planning Commission. Annual Report
0092-2374 Utah Export Directory†
0092-2382 Journal of World Education *changed to* Association for World Education. Journal
0092-2463 New Times (New York)†
0092-2471 Chicagoan†
0092-2498 Criminal Justice (Washington, 1973)†
0092-2528 Oklahoma Water Resources Research Institute. Annual Report
0092-2552 A.E.L.E. Law Enforcement Legal Defense Manual *see* 0191-877X
0092-2560 Weekly California Citator
0092-2633 National Peach Council. Proceedings
0092-2684 Colorado Water Resources Circulars†
0092-2765 U.S. Postal Service. Support Group. Revenue and Cost Analysis *changed to* U.S. Postal Service. Revenue and Cost Analysis Report
0092-2803 Rand Paper Series *changed to* Rand Report Series
0092-2811 American Coin-Op
0092-282X Pickup, Van and 4WD *see* 0747-1971
0092-2838 Music, Books on Music and Sound Recordings
0092-2846 Review of Public Data Use *changed to* Journal of Economic & Social Measurement
0092-2870 Air Freight Directory
0092-2889 Arkansas Average Covered Employment and Earnings by County and Industry *changed to* Arkansas Covered Employment and Earnings
0092-2900 Perspectives in Nephrology and Hypertension
0092-2935 National Roster of Black Elected Officials *see* 0882-1593
0092-2986 Midwest History of Education Society. Journal
0092-3052 Homosexual Counseling Journal†
0092-3060 Oregon. Office of Community Health Services. Local Health Services Annual Summary†
0092-3079 New Jersey. Violent Crimes Compensation Board. Annual Report†
0092-3117 U.S. Department of Transportation. Fiscal Year Budget in Brief
0092-3206 U.S. Bureau of East-West Trade. Office of Export Administration. Export Administration Report *changed to* U.S. International Trade Administration. Export Administration Annual Report
0092-3214 Street & Smith's Official Yearbook: Pro Football
0092-3257 Directory of Facilities for the Learning Disabled *changed to* Directory of Services and Facilities for the Learning Disabled
0092-3281 Illinois Air Sampling Network Report *changed to* Illinois. Division of Air Pollution Control. Annual Air Quality Report
0092-3311 New Jersey. Department of Environmental Protection. Annual Report
0092-332X U.S. Geological Survey. Water Resources Investigations
0092-3362 Massachusetts. Division of Mineral Resources. Annual Report†
0092-3419 Native American Rights Fund. Catalogue *changed to* National Indian Law Library. Catalogue
0092-3427 Tennessee Thrusts†
0092-3435 Occupational Safety and Health Decisions
0092-346X N A S A Report to Educators
0092-3478 American Baptist Churches in the U.S.A. Yearbook
0092-3486 Annual Index to Popular Music Record Reviews†
0092-3524 Iustitia (Bloomington)†
0092-3540 Texscope: U S A Textile Industry Overview
0092-3559 Texas Southern University Law Review
0092-3591 Overview of the F A A Engineering & Development Programs
0092-3761 Data on Iowa's Area Schools
0092-380X Washington State†
0092-3818 Illinois Services Directory
0092-3826 Alcoholism Treatment Facilities Directory: United States and Canada†
0092-3850 Woman's Day Gifts You Can Make for Christmas *changed to* Woman's Day Best Ideas for Christmas
0092-3877 Bar†
0092-394X Newsletter for Research in Mental Health & Behavioral Sciences
0092-3974 International Directory of Little Magazines and Small Presses
0092-4032 Medical Challenge†
0092-4067 Directory of Missouri Libraries
0092-4091 Present Tense
0092-4113 W.P.A.S. Museletter
0092-4148 World Today Series: Latin America
0092-4164 Where the Trails Cross
0092-4180 Better Homes and Gardens Crafts & Sewing†
0092-4199 Day Care and Early Education
0092-4202 Directory of Private Business Correspondence Schools *changed to* Directory of Private Schools
0092-4210 Investment Statistics: Capital Investment Conditions *see* 0195-8313
0092-4229 Speed†
0092-4245 Wesleyan Theological Journal
0092-4261 Woodrow Wilson International Center for Scholars. Annual Report
0092-427X Arctic Bulletin†
0092-4288 University of Nevada. Seismological Laboratory. Bulletin
0092-430X Pepperdine Law Review
0092-4318 Platte Valley Review
0092-4326 American Society for Engineering Education. Review and Directory *changed to* A S E E Profile
0092-4334 B I S Conference Report†
0092-4407 Managers†
0092-4415 Primitive Baptist Yearbook
0092-4423 Resource Guide to Reading & Language Arts Programs & Materials†
0092-444X Intercom (Washington) *see* 0749-2448
0092-4466 Hearing Instruments
0092-4555 U.S. Federal Aviation Administration. National Aviation System Policy Summary *changed to* U.S. Federal Aviation Administration. National Aviation System: Development and Capital Needs
0092-4563 Syntax and Semantics
0092-4571 Border States
0092-4598 Who's Who in Training and Development
0092-4601 N.A.D.A. Recreation Vehicle Appraisal Guide
0092-461X Facts About Maryland Public Education *changed to* Fact Book
0092-4652 Criminal Justice Plan for New Jersey
0092-4679 National Security Traders Association. Traders' Annual
0092-4695 Soviet Business and Trade
0092-4725 Browning Institute Studies
0092-4733 Michigan State University. Institute for Community Development and Services. Population Report. Community Development Series†
0092-4768 American Institute of Certified Public Accountants. Committee on Minority Recruitment and Equal Opportunity. Report†
0092-4857 M E I Marketing Economics Guide
0092-4865 R E I T Handbook of Member Trusts†
0092-489X Artes Visuales
0092-4954 Credit Union Directory and Buyers' Guide
0092-4962 Classified Index of National Labor Relations Board Decisions and Related Court Decisions *changed to* Classified Index of N.L.R.B. and Related Court Decisions
0092-4970 Directory of Electric Light and Power Companies
0092-4989 International Directory of Executive Recruiters
0092-5039 Franklin Mint Almanac
0092-5055 Annual of Psychoanalysis
0092-508X D.A.T.A. Book of Discontinued Thyristors *changed to* Thyristor Discontinued Devices D.A.T.A. Book
0092-511X Street and Smith's College and Pro Official Basketball Yearbook *see* 0149-7103
0092-5144 Vermont Facts and Figures†
0092-5187 N E M A Bulletin
0092-5268 Grants and Awards Available to American Writers
0092-5322 Fusilier (La Puente)†
0092-5349 Michigan. State Library Services. Catalog of Books on Magnetic Tape†
0092-542X Safety Science Abstracts *see* 0160-1342
0092-5438 Youth Reporter†
0092-5462 Data Resources Review *see* 0197-6966
0092-5470 Developments in Human Services Series†
0092-5489 National Directory of Women's Athletics *changed to* National Directory of College Athletics (Women)
0092-5535 Panjandrum Poetry Journal
0092-5543 Washington (State). Vocational Rehabilitation Services Division. State Facilities Plan *changed to* Washington (State). Vocational Rehabilitation Services Division. State Facilities Development Plan
0092-5594 U.S. Centers for Disease Control. Congenital Malformations Surveillance
0092-5632 American Journal of Roentgenology and Radium Therapy *see* 0361-803X
0092-5659 American Lung Association. Bulletin†
0092-5667 Healthnews†
0092-5675 Academy Awards Oscar Annual
0092-5756 Bibliography of Noise†
0092-5764 Connecticut Walk Book
0092-5799 O.S.H.A. Compliance Letter *changed to* Safety Compliance Letter
0092-5810 Vermont's Fisheries Annual†
0092-5845 Food Service Marketing *see* 0746-1887
0092-5853 American Journal of Political Science
0092-5896 U.S. Department of Agriculture. Bimonthly List of Publications and Visuals *changed to* U.S. Department of Agriculture. Quarterly List of Publications
0092-590X American History and Culture†
0092-5934 Attorneys and Agents Registered to Practice Before the U.S. Patent Office *see* 0361-3844
0092-5950 N M R I Compensation in Mass Retailing, Salaries and Incentives
0092-5969 Popular Sports Face-off†
0092-6000 Current Literature in Family Planning

0092-6019 Immunology: An International Series of Monographs and Treatises
0092-606X Degrees Conferred by West Virginia Institutions of Higher Education†
0092-6086 Inter Alia
0092-6108 Title Varies†
0092-6132 Directory of the Mutual Savings Banks of the United States *changed to* National Council of Savings Institutions Directory
0092-6175 Transportation and Products Legal Directory
0092-6213 Circulatory Shock
0092-6221 High School Behavioral Science†
0092-623X Journal of Sex & Marital Therapy
0092-6248 Lawrence Berkeley Laboratory. Inorganic Materials Research Division. Annual Report *changed to* Lawrence Berkeley Laboratory. Materials and Molecular Research Division. Annual Report
0092-6256 Aurora A F X Road Racing Handbook
0092-6280 Association for Educational Data Systems. Handbook and Directory†
0092-6299 Iowa. Bureau of Labor. Occupational Injuries and Illnesses Survey
0092-6302 Semiconductor Heat Sink, Socket & Associated Hardware D.A.T.A. Book†
0092-6345 Iowa State Journal of Research
0092-6353 HorsePlay
0092-6361 Current Contents/Social & Behavioral Sciences
0092-640X Atomic Data and Nuclear Data Tables
0092-6426 Limits in the Seas
0092-6442 Nebraska. Natural Resources Commission. State Water Plan Publication (Lincoln) *changed to* Nebraska. Natural Resources Commission. State Water Planning and Review Process
0092-6485 American Medical Technologists. Official Journal *see* 0741-5397
0092-6507 Auerbach Annual: Best Computer Papers†
0092-6531 Federal Estate and Gift Taxes Explained, Including Estate Planning
0092-654X Illustrated Digest of Pro Football†
0092-6558 Interdenominational Theological Center, Atlanta. Journal
0092-6566 Journal of Research in Personality
0092-6639 Women's Organizations & Leaders Directory
0092-6647 Foreign Newspaper and Gazette Report *see* 0190-9819
0092-6655 Personal Income Tax Analysis *changed to* Analysis of Oregon Personal Income
0092-6736 Alaska. Department of Revenue. State Investment Portfolio
0092-6752 Pesticides (Sacramento)
0092-6841 Nevada. Office of Fiscal Analyst. Annual Report *changed to* Nevada. Office of Legislative Auditor. Biennial Report
0092-6868 Aspen Leaves *changed to* Aspen Journal of the Arts
0092-6876 Automatic Taxfinder and Tax Preparer's Handbook†
0092-6884 Daily Tax Report
0092-7023 Journal of Physical and Colloid Chemistry *see* 0022-3654
0092-7082 Sports Afield Almanac *see* 0190-1249
0092-7147 Daily Bread
0092-718X Letters & Papers on the Social Sciences: an Undergraduate Review†
0092-7201 Linear Integrated Circuits and M.O.S. Devices†
0092-721X R C A Corporation. Solid State Division. R. F. Power Devices†
0092-7228 Thyristors, Rectifiers, and Diacs†
0092-7287 U.S. National Center for Health Statistics. Current Listing and Topical Index to the Vital and Health Statistics Series *see* 0278-4912
0092-735X Continuing Education for the Family Physician
0092-7384 I A B C Journal *changed to* Communication World
0092-7392 Index to the Contemporary Scene†
0092-7422 American Defense Preparedness Association. Annual Directory. *see* 0092-1491
0092-7449 Direction (Alexandria)
0092-7481 Urban Institute. Annual Report
0092-749X Walker's Manual of Western Corporations
0092-7643 Overseas Development Council. Annual Report
0092-7651 Archives of Podiatric Medicine and Foot Surgery†
0092-7678 Asian Affairs: an American Review
0092-7686 Booklegger
0092-7694 Cason Quarterly
0092-7708 Conch Review of Books
0092-7724 Past and Likely Future of 58 Research Libraries, 1951-1980: a Statistical Study of Growth and Change†
0092-7732 Product Safety & Liability Reporter
0092-7759 Social and Rehabilitation Record *changed to* U.S. Health Care Financing Administration Forum
0092-7767 Predicasts Source Directory
0092-7783 Illinois. Junior College Board. Annual Report *changed to* Illinois Community College Board. Biennial Report
0092-7813 Children's Hospital National Medical Center. Clinical Proceedings†
0092-7821 World Association for Christian Communication. Journal *changed to* Media Development
0092-7856 Architecture Schools in North America
0092-7872 Communications in Algebra
0092-7899 Mississippi Educational Directory
0092-7929 Annual of New Art and Artists†
0092-7937 Pennsylvania. Citizens Advisory Council to the Department of Environmental Resources. Annual Report
0092-7945 Missouri River Basin Commission. Annual Report *changed to* Missouri Basin States Association. Annual Report
0092-7953 Genealogical Society of Old Tryon County. Bulletin
0092-7961 Better Homes and Gardens Furnishings and Decorating Ideas *see* 0731-7441
0092-797X Keeping Up with Orff Schulwerk in the Classroom†
0092-7996 Texas Yearbook†
0092-8003 Save On Shopping *see* 0276-6701
0092-8089 Adsorption and Adsorbents†
0092-8208 Children's Literature (New Haven)
0092-8216 Cord Sportfacts: Hunting
0092-8240 Bulletin of Mathematical Biology
0092-8313 Prairie Scout
0092-833X Libraries of Maine; Directory and Statistics
0092-8364 District of Columbia. City Council. Annual Report†
0092-8372 Disciple (St. Louis)
0092-8380 Encyclopedia of Governmental Advisory Organizations
0092-8410 N.A.C.D.S. Lilly Digest†
0092-8437 Physics *changed to* Physics News
0092-847X University of Wisconsin, Madison. Institute for Research on Poverty. Research Report†
0092-8526 Directory Listing Curriculums Offered in the Community Colleges of Pennsylvania†
0092-8550 U.S. General Accounting Office. Office of the General Counsel. Quarterly Digest of Unpublished Decisions of the Comptroller General of the United States; Procurement Law†
0092-8577 Health Affairs†
0092-8593 A P C D Digest
0092-8607 Biomedical Communications†
0092-8615 Drug Information Journal
0092-8623 Journal of Mental Health Administration
0092-8631 St. Luke's Hospital. Medical Staff Journal
0092-8658 A P S A Directory of Department Chairmen *changed to* A P S A Directory of Department Chairpersons
0092-8666 Bell Tower
0092-8674 Cell
0092-8704 Jacksonville Genealogical Society. Magazine. *see* 0149-6867
0092-881X College Football Modern Record Book *see* 0735-5475
0092-8828 P B X Systems Guide
0092-8836 Reference Data on Socioeconomic Issues of Health *see* 0198-7399
0092-8887 Creative Guitar International†
0092-8917 U.S. National Oceanic and Atmospheric Administration. Manned Undersea Science and Technology Program; Report
0092-8933 Police and Law Enforcement
0092-9018 Inspiration Three†
0092-914X American Real Estate and Urban Economics Association. Journal
0092-9158 California. Department of Water Resources. Inventory of Waste Water Production and Waste Water Reclamation Practices in California
0092-9166 Creation Research Society Quarterly
0092-9174 Directory of San Francisco Attorneys
0092-9190 Hawaii. State Commission on the Status of Women. Annual Report
0092-9212 Michigan State Employees' Retirement System Financial and Statistical Report
0092-9301 Memory and Learning - Neural Correlates in Animals *changed to* Memory and Learning - Research in the Nervous System
0092-9336 Osteopathic Annals
0092-9395 G P S A Journal *see* 0730-2177
0092-9425 Schist†
0092-9433 U.S. Environmental Protection Agency. Clean Water; Report to Congress
0092-9441 Urban Telecommunications Forum†
0092-945X C & P Warrant Analysis†
0092-9476 Maryland. Department of Human Resources. Information Pamphlet
0092-9492 U.S. Department of State. Foreign Affairs Research Documentation Center. Foreign Affairs Research Papers Available†
0092-9506 Fielding's Selected Favorites: Hotels and Inns, Europe *see* 0191-0329
0092-9522 Abortion Bibliography
0092-9530 U.S. Department of Agriculture. Economics, Statistics and Cooperatives Service. Cost of Storing and Handling Cotton at Public Storage Facilities†
0092-9549 Oswego County Historical Society. Journal†
0092-9565 Current Geological and Geophysical Studies in Montana
0092-9638 Utah. Forestry and Fire Control. R C and D Release†
0092-9654 U.S. Forest Service. General Technical Report INT
0092-9662 U.S. Forest Service. General Technical Report PSW *see* 0196-2094
0092-9670 National Air Monitoring Program Air Quality and Emissions Trends. Report *changed to* National Air Quality and Emissions Trends Report
0092-9727 Popular Periodical Index
0092-9751 Nuclear Industry Status *changed to* Worldwide Uranium Producer Profiles
0092-9778 National Issues Outlook *see* 0360-4217
0092-9794 Massachusetts Agricultural Statistics
0092-9824 F A S Public Interest Report
0092-9832 Bergen County Dental Society. Journal
0092-9867 Toxicological and Environmental Chemistry Reviews *see* 0277-2248
0092-993X Nuclear Fuel Status and Forecast *changed to* N A C - Update
0092-9948 Nuclear Powerplant Performance†
0093-0040 Utah. State Office of Education. Opinions of the Utah State Superintendent of Public Instruction
0093-0075 Food Technology Review†
0093-0083 Clemson University. Department of Forestry. Forestry Bulletin
0093-0164 Lyons Teacher-News
0093-0237 American Association of Psychiatric Services for Children. Newsletter *see* 0027-6022
0093-0245 Business Radio/Action *see* 0746-8911
0093-0261 Energy Users Report *changed to* Energy Report
0093-0288 N U Quarter Notes
0093-0296 R C A Corporation. Solid State Division. Power Transistors and Power Hybrid Circuits†
0093-0334 Hastings Center Report
0093-0393 National Library of Medicine. Programs and Services
0093-0407 Sleep Research
0093-0415 Western Journal of Medicine
0093-0431 Children's Literary Almanac *changed to* International Directory of Children's Literature
0093-044X Crime Prevention Review†
0093-0458 Dimensions (Washington)†
0093-0466 Automobile Insurance Losses, Collision Coverages, Variations by Make and Series
0093-0482 Meetings & Expositions†
0093-0512 Energy Pipelines and Systems *changed to* Chilton's Oil & Gas Energy
0093-0520 Maryland. State Department of Legislative Reference. Synopsis of Laws Enacted by the State of Maryland
0093-0539 Summary of Ground Water Data for Tennessee†
0093-0563 U.S. Library of Congress. Library of Congress Name Headings with References†
0093-0571 Monographic Series†
0093-061X Government Publications Review *changed to* Government Publications Review
0093-0679 Landslide (Eureka)
0093-0687 Louisiana Fairs and Festivals
0093-0709 Syracuse Journal of International Law & Commerce
0093-0717 Arizona Business
0093-0741 Missouri. Public Service Commission. Regulated Electric Study†
0093-0776 Something Else Yearbook†
0093-0938 Better Homes and Gardens Building Ideas
0093-1004 Biological Psychology Bulletin†
0093-1039 Alaska Bar Brief *changed to* Alaska Bar Rag
0093-1047 Harris Auction Galleries. Collectors' Auction
0093-1063 Florida Law Revision Commission. Annual Report *changed to* Florida Law Revision Council. Annual Report.
0093-1071 Florida. State Board of Independent Colleges and Universities. Report
0093-1098 New Jersey Public Libraries. Statistics *changed to* New Jersey Public Library Statistics For (Year)
0093-111X Pretrial Justice Quarterly†
0093-1160 Association of Trial Lawyers of America. Newsletter *see* 0364-8125
0093-1179 Atlanta Constitution: a Georgia Index
0093-1195 Official Motor Home Trade-in Guide *changed to* Motor Home & Truck Camper Trade-in Guide
0093-1241 Wyoming. Department of Labor and Statistics. Survey of Occupational Injuries and Illnesses†
0093-1284 American Annals of the Deaf and Dumb *see* 0002-726X
0093-1314 Medical Meetings†
0093-1330 American Bell Association. Directory
0093-1365 Photo Information Almanac

0093-1454 American Marketing Association. Directory of Marketing Services and Membership Roster *changed to* American Marketing Association. International Membership Directory and Marketing Services Guide
0093-1535 Employment Safety and Health Guide
0093-1551 Corrective and Social Psychiatry and Journal of Behavioral Technology Methods and Therapy
0093-156X Journal of Numerical Control *changed to* I M Report
0093-1659 Purchasing World†
0093-1713 Excited States
0093-173X Hospital Topics and Buyer's Guide *see* 0018-5868
0093-1799 Official Port of Detroit World Handbook
0093-1853 Journal of Psychiatry and Law
0093-1861 American Artist Business Letter†
0093-1888 Librarians' Handbook
0093-1896 Critical Inquiry
0093-190X Babson's Investment Digest†
0093-1918 Classic Collector†
0093-1926 I.R.C.A. Foreign Log
0093-2094 American Indian Media Directory†
0093-2124 On Scene
0093-2132 Product Digest *see* 0146-5023
0093-2205 International Journal of Occupational Health & Safety *see* 0362-4064
0093-2213 Pavlovian Journal of Biological Science
0093-2302 Minicomputer Review†
0093-2310 Serials Updating Service†
0093-2329 Serials Updating Service Quarterly†
0093-2388 U.S. Federal Railroad Administration. Bibliography of Published Research Reports *see* 0097-0042
0093-2485 Economic Books: Current Selections
0093-2515 Drug Abuse Bibliography
0093-2531 McLean Guide to Kennels of America†
0093-254X Photographic Historical Society of New York. Membership Directory
0093-2558 Minnesota Alcohol Programs for Highway Safety†
0093-2582 St. Croix Review
0093-2825 For Younger Readers, Braille and Talking Books (Large Print Edition)
0093-2914 Applied Anthropology *see* 0018-7259
0093-304X Columbia Law Alumni Observer
0093-3058 Duquesne Law Review
0093-3066 American Chemical Society. Division of Environmental Chemistry. Preprints of Papers.
0093-3074 U.S. National Park Service. Public Use of the National Park System; Fiscal Year Report
0093-3082 Montana. Animal Health Division. Statistical Data *changed to* Montana. Animal Health Division. Statistical Summary
0093-3090 Southern California Business Directory and Buyers Guide
0093-3104 Theory and Research in Social Education
0093-3139 College Literature
0093-3155 Forest H. Belt's Yearbook of Consumer Electronics†
0093-3163 Grants and Awards Available to Foreign Writers†
0093-3171 Journal of Family Counseling *see* 0192-6187
0093-318X Monday *see* 0145-1677
0093-3236 E C & M's Electrical Products Yearbook
0093-3252 Hastings Center Studies *see* 0093-0334
0093-3279 Alcoholism Digest Annual
0093-3287 Environment Abstracts
0093-3295 Pesticides Abstracts
0093-3317 Studies on the Development of Behavior and the Nervous System
0093-3414 College and University Employees, New York State
0093-3430 U.S. Department of Health, Education and Welfare. Annual Report to the Congress of the United States on Services to Handicapped Children in Project Head Start *changed to* U.S. Department of Health and Human Services. Annual Report to the Congress of the United States on Services Provided to Handicapped Children in Project Head Start
0093-3465 Opportunities in Iowa's Area Schools†
0093-3481 Hawaii. Department of Health. Research and Statistics Office. R & S Report
0093-3503 Your Business and the Law *changed to* You and the Law
0093-3546 Cardiovascular Diseases *see* 0730-2347
0093-3589 Industrial Pharmacology†
0093-3619 Year Book of Dermatology
0093-3627 Yearbook of Dermatology and Syphilology *see* 0093-3619
0093-3643 N E C Newsletter *changed to* Campus Activities Programming
0093-3651 Sea Technology
0093-366X U.S. Civil Service Commission. Personnel Research and Development Center. Technical Study
0093-3686 Studies in Jazz Discography *see* 0731-0641
0093-3708 Metric News†
0093-3716 U. S. Department of the Interior. Office of Personnel Management. Annual Manpower Personnel Statistics†
0093-3813 I E E E Transactions on Plasma Science
0093-3821 List of Journals Indexed in Index Medicus
0093-3864 Land Use Planning Report
0093-3929 Southern Horseman
0093-3945 U. S. Office of Saline Water. Catalog of Research Projects†
0093-3961 Journal of Financial Education
0093-397X Legal Notes for Education†
0093-3996 Pacific Tropical Botanical Garden. Bulletin
0093-4038 California and Western Medicine *see* 0093-0415
0093-4054 Contemporary Topics in Immunobiology
0093-4062 American Automobile Association. Digest of Motor Laws
0093-4089 Florida Senate
0093-416X Computer Review
0093-4240 New School for Social Research. Philosophy Department. Graduate Faculty Philosophy Journal
0093-4267 Battelle Memorial Institute. Columbus Laboratories. Report on National Survey of Compensation Paid Scientists and Engineers Engaged in Research and Development Activities†
0093-4283 Trailer Life's Recreational Vehicle Campground and Services Guide *changed to* Trailer Life's Recreational Vehicle Campground and Services Directory
0093-433X Cotton Ginnings in the United States *changed to* Cotton Ginnings by States
0093-4429 Peanut Market News
0093-4437 Anesthesiology Review
0093-4445 Journal of Long-Term Care Administration
0093-4461 Physicians' Desk Reference
0093-447X Physicians' Desk Reference to Pharmaceutical Specialties and Biologicals *see* 0093-4461
0093-4518 American Society for Preventive Dentistry Journal†
0093-4526 Journal of Zoo Animal Medicine
0093-4585 Guide to the Recommended Country Inns of New England
0093-4593 Leisure Home Living†
0093-4615 Council on Foreign Relations. President's Report *see* 0192-236X
0093-4623 University of Michigan. Graduate School of Business Administration. Proceedings of the Annual Business Conference†
0093-4631 U.S. Fish and Wildlife Service. Selected List of Federal Laws and Treaties Relating to Sport Fish and Wildlife
0093-4658 Journal of Coated Fabrics
0093-4666 Mycotaxon
0093-4674 Criminal Law Commentator (New York) †
0093-4682 Family Law Commentator (New York)†
0093-4690 Journal of Field Archaeology
0093-4712 American Journal of Pharmacy *see* 0730-7780
0093-4720 Benchmark Papers in Animal Behavior *changed to* Benchmark Papers in Behavior
0093-4755 Evolutionary Theory
0093-4763 Groups: a Journal of Group Dynamics and Psychotherapy
0093-4771 Methods in Membrane Biology *changed to* Cell Membranes, Methods and Reviews
0093-4909 Lackawanna-Wayne-Pike-Susquehanna Farm & Home News
0093-4992 Energy Resources Report *see* 0278-5099
0093-500X Energy Today
0093-5018 Europe Basic Oil Law & Concession Contracts
0093-5026 Good News of Tomorrow's World *see* 0032-0420
0093-5034 New York (State) Department of Labor. Division of Research and Statistics. Labor Research Report
0093-5050 Skeptic *see* 0160-4929
0093-5069 U.S. Division of Wildlife Services. Annual Report†
0093-5107 Journal of Real Estate Taxation
0093-5166 Contemporary Problems in Cardiology†
0093-5220 Insiders' Guide to the Colleges†
0093-5239 U. S. Bureau of Sport Fisheries and Wildlife. Report to the Fish Farmer†
0093-5255 Business Week Letter *changed to* Personal Finance Letter
0093-5263 Creativity in Action
0093-5271 Doane's Agricultural Report
0093-5301 Journal of Consumer Research
0093-531X Perspectives in Religious Studies
0093-5328 Phi Kappa Phi Newsletter
0093-5336 Recon
0093-5352 Retirement Letter
0093-5387 Undersea Biomedical Research
0093-5417 Budd Gore Media Mix Newsletter
0093-5530 Wyoming. Division of Planning, Evaluation and Information Services. Statistical Report Series
0093-5557 Benchmark Papers in Human Physiology
0093-5603 Population Analysis of the Illinois Adult Prison System†
0093-5654 U. S. Bureau of Radiological Health. Research Grants Program†
0093-5700 Geothermal Energy Magazine *see* 0146-3675
0093-5794 Word Processing World *see* 0279-7992
0093-5816 Directory of Published Proceedings. Series P C E : Pollution Control & Ecology
0093-5891 Toxic Materials News
0093-6049 Foresight (Washington)†
0093-609X Origins, N C Documentary Service
0093-6138 Florida Speech Communication Journal
0093-6235 North American Society for Sport History. Proceedings
0093-6332 Vanderbilt University. Department of Environmental and Water Resources Engineering. Technical Reports
0093-6383 Civil Liberties Review†
0093-6391 Endocrine Research Communications *see* 0743-5800
0093-6405 American Society of Civil Engineers. Geotechnical Engineering Division. Journal *see* 0733-9410
0093-6413 Mechanics Research Communications
0093-6472 Montana Advisory Council for Vocational Education. Annual Report *changed to* Montana Council on Vocational Education. Annual Report
0093-6502 Communication Research
0093-6510 Findings and Forecasts†
0093-6553 Cost of Picking and Hauling Florida Citrus Fruits
0093-6626 Biography News†
0093-6642 Monographs on Music in Higher Education†
0093-6693 Washington (State). Attorney General's Office. Directory of Charitable Organizations and Trusts Registered with the Office of Attorney General *changed to* Washington (State). Attorney General's Office. Charitable Trust Directory
0093-6715 Florida. Division of Family Services. Annual Statistical Report *changed to* Florida. Department of Health and Rehabilitative Services. Annual Statistical Report
0093-674X Federal Telephone Directory†
0093-6758 Film Literature Index
0093-6766 International Bonds *changed to* International Bond Guide
0093-6774 Michigan. Department of Social Services. Public Assistance Statistics *see* 0093-7835
0093-6782 Motorboat *see* 0006-5374
0093-6901 Oceanic Abstracts
0093-691X Theriogenology
0093-6987 Ridge Runners†
0093-6995 Tax Management Executive Compensation Journal *see* 0747-8607
0093-7002 American Journal of Optometry and Physiological Optics
0093-7053 Modern Healthcare (Long-Term Care) *see* 0160-7480
0093-7061 Modern Healthcare (Short-Term Care) *see* 0160-7480
0093-707X Persimmon Hill
0093-7134 Idaho's Comprehensive Plan for Criminal Justice†
0093-7142 Montana Manual of State and Local Government†
0093-7223 Idaho. State Superintendent of Public Instruction. Annual Report. State of Idaho Johnson-O'Malley Program
0093-7231 Juvenile Justice *see* 0161-7109
0093-724X Maine Economic Data Book†
0093-7274 Woodall's Directory of Mobile Home Communities *see* 0731-6526
0093-7282 Audio Journal of Podiatric Medicine†
0093-7290 Data Channels
0093-7347 New Jersey Dental Association. Journal
0093-7355 Lab Animal
0093-7363 National Medical Audiovisual Center Motion Picture and Videotape Catalog *see* 0083-2294
0093-7398 Population Sciences: Index of Biomedical Research†
0093-7436 University of Alaska Museum. Annual Report
0093-7487 Multinational Executive Travel Companion
0093-7495 Origins (Loma Linda)
0093-7525 California. Department of Industrial Relations. Division of Labor Statistics and Research. Building Trades Wage Rates†
0093-7568 Pennsylvania State University. Research Publications and Professional Activities†
0093-7630 F E P Guidelines
0093-7657 Energy Report
0093-7673 People (New York) *changed to* People Weekly
0093-7703 Directory of Educational Facilities for the Learning Disabled *changed to* Directory of Services and Facilities for the Learning Disabled
0093-7711 Immunogenetics
0093-7754 Seminars in Oncology
0093-7797 American Bar Association. Special Committee on Environmental Law. Quarterly Newsletter *changed to* Environmental Law (Washington)
0093-7800 Compliance and Legal Seminar. Proceedings†
0093-7835 Michigan. Department of Social Services. Program Statistics

ISSN INDEX 1433

0093-7843 North Dakota State Plan for Rehabilitation Facilities and Workshops
0093-7851 Petroleo Internacional
0093-786X Deseret News Church Almanac
0093-7886 Maine. Bureau of Labor and Industry of Labor and Industry. Occupational Wage Survey *changed to* Maine. Department of Labor. Occupational Wage Survey
0093-7924 U.S. National Advisory Council on Indian Education. Annual Report to the Congress of the United States
0093-8025 Basebook
0093-8041 Georgia State University. Institute of Health Administration. Occasional Publication†
0093-8076 Clinical Laboratory Reference
0093-8130 Mission Handbook: North American Protestant Ministries Overseas
0093-8149 Public Telecommunications Review (PTR)†
0093-8157 Reviews in Anthropology
0093-8203 North Dakota. Department of Agriculture. Annual Report *changed to* North Dakota. Department of Agriculture. Biennial Report
0093-8246 Montana. Department of Business Regulation. Annual Report
0093-8262 Federal Reserve Bank of San Francisco. Business Review *see* 0363-0021
0093-8270 C O S/M O S Digital Integrated Circuits†
0093-8297 E S Q
0093-8327 Industrial Fishery Products; Market Review and Outlook†
0093-8343 Engineering Issues *see* 0733-9380
0093-8394 Energy Conservation Abstracts†
0093-8408 Energy Abstracts
0093-8416 Energy Conversion Abstracts *see* 0093-8408
0093-8440 Soldiers
0093-8475 Folklore Feminists Communication†
0093-8505 Railway History Monograph
0093-8548 Criminal Justice & Behavior
0093-8572 National Patterns of R. & D. Resources; Funds & Manpower in the United States *changed to* National Patterns of Science and Technology
0093-8599 U.S. National Clearinghouse for Drug Abuse Information. Report Series *changed to* U.S. National Institute on Drug Abuse. Report Series
0093-8610 Criminal Defense†
0093-8637 Guidebook to Florida Taxes
0093-8645 Guidebook to Wisconsin Taxes
0093-8653 Annual Public Defenders' Workshop. Handbook†
0093-8688 Journal of College and University Law
0093-8696 Learning and the Law†
0093-870X Minnesota. Department of Education. Biennial Report†
0093-8726 Industrial Fishery Products. Annual Summary†
0093-8742 Educational Research Service. Salaries Scheduled for Administrative and Supervisory Personnel in Public Schools†
0093-8750 Executive Compensation Service. Technician Report
0093-8769 Clinical Dentistry†
0093-8785 U.S. Health Resources Administration. Health Resources News†
0093-8823 Direct Levies on Gaming in Nevada†
0093-8831 Fact Book and Report of the West Virginia State System of Higher Education†
0093-884X Physical Facilities at Institutions of Higher Education in West Virginia†
0093-8858 Pro Se†
0093-8874 Teaching English to the Deaf *changed to* Teaching English to Deaf and Second Language Students
0093-8912 California. Council on Criminal Justice. Comprehensive Plan for Criminal Justice
0093-8920 Latvija Sodien
0093-8939 Illinois. Judicial Inquiry Board. Report
0093-8955 Utah. State Archives and Records Service. Administrative Rule Making Bulletin *see* 0882-4738
0093-9021 National Environmental Research Center. Annual Report†
0093-9048 Montana Law Enforcement Academy. Annual Report to the Governor of Montana†
0093-9102 Missouri. Air Conservation Commission. Annual Report†
0093-9137 Michigan. Advisory Council for Vocational Education. Annual Report
0093-9161 Public Sector Arbitration Awards
0093-9188 Alternatives in Print†
0093-9277 Education Bulletin (Missoula)†
0093-9285 Sociology of Work and Occupations *see* 0730-8884
0093-9293 Southern Voices†
0093-934X Brain and Language
0093-9374 Leica Manual†
0093-9382 United Methodists Today†
0093-9390 Michigan. Office of Criminal Justice. Comprehensive Law Enforcement and Criminal Justice Plan†
0093-9404 Overview of Blood†
0093-9447 International Media Guide. Newspapers: Worldwide
0093-9501 Directory of Special Programs for Minority Group Members; Career Information Services, Employment Skills, Banks, Financial Aid Sources
0093-951X Directory of Trust Institutions
0093-9552 Illinois State and Regional Economic Data Book
0093-9579 Semiotext(e)
0093-9595 Nevada. Advisory Council for Manpower Training and Career Education. Annual Evaluation Report *changed to* Nevada. Advisory Council for Vocational-Technical Education. Annual Evaluation Report
0093-9625 Hawaii Review
0093-9633 U S Export Weekly *see* 0748-0172
0093-9692 U.S. Department of Commerce. Effects of Pollution Abatement on International Trade†
0093-9706 Guide to Dental Materials and Devices *changed to* Dentist's Desk Reference
0093-9714 Research Advances in Alcohol & Drug Problems
0093-9722 Urology Times
0093-9730 North Carolina. Council on State Goals and Policy. Annual Report *changed to* North Carolina. State Goals and Policy Board. Annual Report
0093-9811 Parrott Talk
0093-982X E M Bibliography for Consumers†
0093-9854 Heart of Texas Records
0093-9889 Tennessee. State Board for Vocational Education. Information Series
0093-9897 U.S. Department of Transportation. Year-End Report†
0093-9951 Roster of Black Elected Officials in the South
0093-996X Tape Recording and Buying Guide *changed to* Stereo Review's Tape Recording & Buying Guide
0093-9978 Noise Control Engineering *see* 0736-2501
0093-9986 New Jersey. Legislature. Office of Fiscal Affairs. Annual Report†
0093-9994 I E E E Transactions on Industry Applications
0094-0003 Physical Review/Index
0094-002X American Indian Law Review
0094-0089 U S China Business Review *see* 0163-7169
0094-0100 Advanced Biomedical Technology *see* 0147-2682
0094-0119 Biomedical Inventions Reporter *see* 0147-2682
0094-0127 Government Documents Review *see* 0147-2682
0094-0135 Health Care Statistics Report *see* 0147-2682
0094-0143 Urologic Clinics of North America
0094-0151 Reference Guide and Comprehensive Catalog of International Serials *see* 0742-3985
0094-0178 Old-House Journal
0094-0186 Off-Lead
0094-0194 New York Culture Review
0094-0208 N A E P Newsletter
0094-0216 Library Security Newsletter *see* 0196-0075
0094-0224 Lawyer's Newsletter *changed to* Law Office Management Digest
0094-0232 Imprint: Oregon†
0094-0240 First Friday
0094-0259 Alfantics
0094-0267 Addictive Diseases *see* 0276-5608
0094-0283 Genealogy†
0094-0291 Hiking (Highland Park)†
0094-0305 McCall's Cooking School
0094-033X New German Critique
0094-0348 Population Mobility in Hawaii *see* 0145-9643
0094-0364 Multitype Library Cooperative News
0094-0372 Cockshaw's Construction Labor News & Opinion
0094-0399 Your School and the Law
0094-0402 Biennial Report of the Arts Activities in Alabama *see* 0096-1388
0094-0488 Arkansas Nurse†
0094-0496 American Ethnologist
0094-050X S C A G Annual Report†
0094-0526 Blair & Ketchum's Country Journal
0094-0534 Consumers Index
0094-0585 Journal of Carbohydrates, Nucleosides, Nucleotides *see* 0732-8311
0094-0585 Journal of Carbohydrates, Nucleosides, Nucleotides *see* 0732-8303
0094-0593 Journal of Corporate Taxation
0094-0607 Journal of Voluntary Action Research
0094-0615 Law & Liberty†
0094-0623 Legal Notes for Insurance
0094-064X Planning Review (Oxford)
0094-0658 Sage International Yearbook of Foreign Policy Studies
0094-0712 Arizona. Department of Economic Security. Annual Report *changed to* D E S Activities Report
0094-0763 Huber Law Survey†
0094-0771 Middle School Journal
0094-078X Northwestern Tour Book *see* 0363-2695
0094-0798 Oral History Review
0094-0801 University of Florida. Growth Conference. Prepared Papers†
0094-0836 Student Advocate *see* 0746-3545
0094-0844 Thorny Trail
0094-0852 Explorations in Economic Research†
0094-0887 Far-Western Forum†
0094-0895 Biofeedback Society of America. Proceedings of the Annual Meeting
0094-0968 University of Chicago. Law School. Law Alumni Journal†
0094-100X Directory of Municipal Bond Dealers of the United States
0094-1050 Curriculum Improvement
0094-1069 Michigan. Office of Highway Safety Planning. Annual Highway Safety Work Plan *see* 0731-1966
0094-1093 Administrative Law Newsletter†
0094-1115 Basic Economic Data for Idaho
0094-1123 Nevada State Plan for Vocational Education *changed to* Nevada State Plan for Occupational Education
0094-114X Mechanism and Machine Theory
0094-1182 Civil War Collectors' Dealer Directory
0094-1190 Journal of Urban Economics
0094-1204 National Investor Relations Institute. Proceedings of the Annual National Conference *changed to* National Investor Relations Institute. Executive Summary of the Annual National Conference
0094-1220 Social Services in North Dakota
0094-1247 Nebraska. State Patrol. Annual Report
0094-1255 Book of Names†
0094-1271 Idaho Agricultural Statistics.
0094-128X Northeast Pacific Pink and Chum Salmon Workshop. Proceedings
0094-1298 Clinics in Plastic Surgery
0094-1344 Country Music World
0094-1352 IndustriScope
0094-1360 Jeffersonian Review†
0094-1409 Minnesota. Office of Ombudsman for Corrections. Annual Report
0094-1417 Astrograph
0094-1468 Florida. Department of Education. Florida Statewide Assessment Program: Capsule Report *changed to* Florida. Department of Education. Florida Statewide Assessment Program: State, District and Regional Report of Statewide Assessment Results
0094-1476 Philadelphia Association for Psychoanalysis. Journal†
0094-1484 Magyar Evkonyv
0094-1492 Materials Performance
0094-1506 Michigan State Plan for Vocational Education
0094-1514 Motor Handbook
0094-1522 N.C.F.A. Office Manual *see* 0276-783X
0094-1557 Georgia. Department of Education. Statistical Report
0094-1565 University of Toledo. Business Research Center. Working Papers in Operations Analysis *changed to* University of Toledo. Business Research Center. Working Papers
0094-162X Tenth Muse†
0094-1638 Sociology: Reviews of New Books†
0094-1646 Industrial Energy *see* 0194-2468
0094-1670 Conservation in Kansas
0094-1689 American Cartographer
0094-1697 Minnesota. Governor. Annual Report on the Quality of the Environment *changed to* Minnesota. Governor. Governor's Report on Environmental Quality
0094-1700 Journal of Sport History
0094-1719 Academy of Sciences of the Lithuanian S.S.R. Mathematical Transactions *see* 0363-1672
0094-1727 Minnesota Statutes. Supplement
0094-1735 International Monetary Fund. Selected Decisions of the International Monetary Fund and Selected Documents
0094-176X W V E A School Journal *see* 0274-8606
0094-1786 Alaska. State Board of Registration for Architects, Engineers and Land Surveyors. Directory of Architects, Engineers and Land Surveyors
0094-1794 Estate Planning (Boston)
0094-1824 Society of Pharmacological and Environmental Pathologists. Bulletin *see* 0192-6233
0094-1832 Hydraulic Research in the United States and Canada†
0094-1840 International Contact Lens Clinic *changed to* International Eyecare
0094-1859 Journal of Afro-American Issues†
0094-1875 National Traffic Law News
0094-1891 Woodall's Mobile Home Park Directory *see* 0731-6526
0094-1921 Campaign Law Reporter
0094-1948 Forum (Baltimore) *changed to* Law Forum
0094-1956 Journal of Instructional Psychology
0094-1964 Paintbrush
0094-1972 Review of Applied Urban Research
0094-2006 University of Washington Medicine
0094-2057 California School Law Digest
0094-2065 Communio

1434 ISSN INDEX

0094-2073 Minnesota. Governor's Commission on Crime Prevention and Control. Comprehensive Plan *changed to* Minnesota. Crime Control Planning Board. Comprehensive Plan
0094-209X Directories of Hawaii
0094-2200 South Dakota. Department of Labor. Research and Statistics. Annual Report on State and Area Occupational Requirements for Vocational Education†
0094-2227 American College Testing Program. Handbook for Financial Aid Administrators
0094-2235 Illinois Student Lawyer†
0094-2243 Cincinnati Bar Association. Journal†
0094-2251 Virginia State Bar. Younger Members Conference. Newsletter *changed to* Docket Call (Richmond)
0094-226X Newsletter & Digest of Selected Opinions of State Attorneys General†
0094-2278 Railway Passenger Car Annual
0094-2294 Florida. Mental Health Program Office. Statistical Report of Hospitals
0094-2308 Supply and Demand: Educational Personnel in Delaware
0094-2316 World of Politics
0094-2324 Community Development Digest
0094-2332 Criminal Justice Digest†
0094-2367 Everyman†
0094-2375 Fantasiae (Los Angeles)
0094-2383 Journal of Abstracts in International Education
0094-2391 Journal of Agronomic Education
0094-2405 Medical Physics
0094-2413 Juvenile Justice Digest
0094-2421 Celebration: a Creative Worship Service
0094-243X A I P Conference Proceedings
0094-2448 Bead Journal *see* 0148-3897
0094-2464 Small Businessman's Clinic
0094-2499 Journal of Biocommunication
0094-2502 Business Regulation Law Report†
0094-2510 Marketing California Dried Fruits: Prunes, Raisins, Dried Apricots & Peaches
0094-2553 United States Judicial Reporter
0094-2561 Disclosure Record
0094-257X Weekly Record (New York)
0094-2588 Communication Directory†
0094-260X A A B C Newsletter
0094-2626 Library Statistics of Illinois Colleges and Universities: Institutional Data†
0094-2634 Index to Foreign Market Reports†
0094-2677 Ohio Juvenile Court Statistics†
0094-2715 Inscape (Pasadena)
0094-2758 South Dakota Manufacturers & Processors Directory.
0094-2766 Monthly Summary of Texas Natural Gas
0094-2782 New Mexico Forest Products Directory *changed to* Wood Industries of New Mexico
0094-2790 Movement of California Fruits and Vegetables by Rail, Truck, and Air
0094-2820 Washington Geologic Newsletter
0094-2855 Southwestern Camping *see* 0731-8103
0094-2863 Soviet Union
0094-2871 U.S. Environmental Protection Agency. Office of Air Quality Planning and Standards. State Air Pollution Implementation Plan Progress Report†
0094-288X Russian History
0094-2898 Southeastern Symposium on System Theory. Proceedings
0094-291X Rhode Island. Department of Mental Health, Retardation and Hospitals. Mental Health, Retardation and Hospitals
0094-2987 Illinois. Department of Public Instruction. Publications Resource Manual†
0094-3002 Broker-Dealer Directory
0094-3029 Carnegie Endowment for International Peace. Financial Report
0094-3037 East Central Europe
0094-3061 Contemporary Sociology
0094-3096 American Metric Journal *changed to* A M J-S I Metricpac
0094-310X Barrister Bulletin *see* 0162-2900
0094-3134 Probe Directory of Foreign Direct Investment in the United States
0094-3142 U.S. Environmental Protection Agency. Summaries of Foreign Government Environmental Reports†
0094-3231 Environmental Information Systems Directory†
0094-324X International Academy of Preventive Medicine. Journal
0094-3320 13th Moon
0094-3339 East-West Markets†
0094-3347 Eutrophication†
0094-3355 Horse and Horseman
0094-3452 Places†
0094-3479 Michigan. Department of Commerce. Annual Report Summary *changed to* Michigan. Department of Commerce. Annual Report
0094-3495 Journal of Social Welfare†
0094-3509 Journal of Family Practice
0094-3517 I C T A Roster *changed to* I C T A Directory
0094-3568 Arts in Alaska *changed to* Alaska. State Council on the Arts. Bulletin
0094-3576 Arkansas. Bureau of Vital Statistics. Annual Report of Births, Deaths, Marriages and Divorces as Reported to the Bureau of Vital Statistics
0094-3584 American Bar - The Canadian Bar - The International Bar
0094-3614 Southern Europe Travel Guide *changed to* Travel Guide to Europe
0094-3630 Missouri. Division of Fisheries. Abstracts of Fishery Research Reports†
0094-3649 Drum Corps Review
0094-3657 Central Europe and Scandinavia Travel Guide *changed to* Travel Guide to Europe
0094-3673 Behavior Science Research
0094-3681 Chem Sources - Europe†
0094-372X South Dakota Indian Recipients of Social Welfare†
0094-3738 Journal of Peace Science *changed to* Conflict Management and Peace Science
0094-3746 Glass Dealer *changed to* Glass Magazine
0094-3754 Michigan. Department of Education. College Admissions and Financial Assistance Handbook *changed to* Michigan Postsecondary Admissions & Financial Assistance Handbook
0094-3770 American Bibliography of Slavic and East European Studies
0094-3800 California Plant Pathology
0094-3894 Recipe Index Series†
0094-3924 Wyoming. State of Wyoming Annual Report
0094-3932 Advances in Fire Retardants†
0094-3975 Fundamentals of Aerospace Instrumentation.
0094-3983 Minnesota Pocket Data Book†
0094-3991 Narcotics and Drug Abuse A-Z
0094-4033 Union Catalog of Maps†
0094-4076 Emory Law Journal
0094-4084 International Directory of Behavior and Design Research†
0094-4114 Nantucket Review
0094-422X American Society of Pension Actuaries. Transcribings. Annual Conference†
0094-4246 Arizona Legislative Service
0094-4262 Facts About South Dakota†
0094-4270 I.C.C. Supplemental Reports†
0094-4289 Journal of Engineering Materials and Technology
0094-4327 California. State Board of Cosmetology. Rules and Regulations.
0094-4335 Statistics for Water Utilities Including Water Authorities in Pennsylvania
0094-4424 U.S. Centers for Disease Control. Family Planning Services: Annual Summary
0094-4459 National Collegiate Athletic Association. Proceedings of the Special Convention
0094-4467 Southeastern Europe
0094-4491 Maryland Manual
0094-4505 Guide to American Scientific and Technical Directories
0094-4548 Letters in Heat and Mass Transfer *see* 0735-1933
0094-4610 Visual Merchandising *see* 0745-4295
0094-4629 Maryland. Bureau of Air Quality Control. State-Local Cooperative Air Sampling Program Yearly Data Report. *changed to* Maryland Air Management Administration. Data Report
0094-467X Securities Investor Protection Corporation. Annual Report
0094-4742 World Environmental Directory†
0094-4831 Bibliography of Society, Ethics and the Life Sciences†
0094-484X Dental Research in the United States, Canada, and Great Britain *see* 0147-264X
0094-4858 Fresh Fruit and Vegetable Market News: Weekly Summary, Shipments, Unloads *changed to* Fresh Fruit and Vegetable Market News: Weekly Summary, Shipments-Arrivals
0094-4904 Canine Practice
0094-4920 Social Sciences Index
0094-5048 Maine. Department of Transportation. Annual Report†
0094-5056 Eastern Economic Journal
0094-5072 Inter Dependent
0094-5080 Journal of Forest History
0094-5099 Music Library Association. Technical Reports
0094-5102 Journal of Marriage and Family Counseling *see* 0194-472X
0094-5129 New Human Services Review†
0094-5145 Journal of Community Health
0094-5196 U.S. National Oceanic and Atmospheric Administration. Report to the Congress on Ocean Dumping and Other Man-Induced Changes to Ocean Ecosystems *see* 0098-4922
0094-5218 Official Railway Guide. North American Passenger Travel Edition *see* 0273-9658
0094-5226 Official National Collegiate Athletic Association Football Rules and Interpretations *see* 0736-5160
0094-5234 Official National Collegiate Athletic Association Basketball Rules *changed to* N C A A Men's Basketball Rules and Interpretations
0094-5242 Official Meeting Facilities Guide
0094-5277 Barrister
0094-5307 Advances in Satellite Meteorology†
0094-5323 Augustinian Studies
0094-534X Ohio Northern University Law Review
0094-5358 Solid Waste Systems *see* 0190-7808
0094-5366 Bilingual Review
0094-5404 Essays in Literature
0094-5420 Judicial Education News†
0094-5439 Maine Prosecutor Bulletin†
0094-5447 Metallurgy - Materials Education Yearbook
0094-5455 North Dakota Academic Library Statistics. *changed to* North Dakota Library Statistics
0094-5463 Product Safety & the Law†
0094-5471 Directory of Women Physicians in the U.S.†
0094-5498 Journal of Altered States of Consciousness *see* 0276-2366
0094-5528 Agricultural Situation in Africa and West Asia *changed to* World Agriculture Regional Supplement: Middle East and North Africa
0094-5587 Community Leaders and Noteworthy Americans *changed to* Community Leaders of America
0094-5617 Hastings Constitutional Law Quarterly
0094-5633 Measuring Mormonism
0094-5641 Minnesota Health Statistics
0094-5668 Ohio Journal of Religious Studies *see* 0193-3604
0094-5676 Oppositions†
0094-5714 Synthesis and Reactivity in Inorganic and Metalorganic Chemistry
0094-5749 Indiana. Environmental Management Board. Annual Report
0094-5765 Acta Astronautica
0094-579X Stone Soup
0094-5803 University of Wisconsin, Madison. Bureau of Business Research and Service. Research in the School of Business†
0094-582X Latin American Perspectives
0094-5846 Fundamentals of Cosmic Physics
0094-5870 Dine Bizaad Manil'iih
0094-5897 Arnold Newsletter *see* 0160-4848
0094-5900 Syracuse University. Libraries. Annual Report†
0094-5978 Illinois. Cities and Villages Municipal Problems Commission. Annual Report to the Session of the General Assembly *changed to* Illinois. Cities and Villages Municipal Problems Commission. Biennial Report to the Session of the General Assembly
0094-601X Annual Handbook for Group Facilitators *changed to* University Associates, Inc. Annual
0094-6028 Computer Medicine†
0094-6109 Ohio Higher Education. Basic Data Series
0094-615X L A C U N Y Journal *see* 0276-9298
0094-6176 Seminars in Thrombosis and Hemostasis
0094-6184 Serial Handbook of Modern Psychiatry†
0094-6192 Continuing Education in Nursing Home Administration *see* 0160-6980
0094-6206 Origins of Behavior Series†
0094-6230 Oklahoma. Department of Highways. Sufficiency Rating Report and Needs Study: Oklahoma State Highways *changed to* Oklahoma. Department of Transportation. Sufficiency Rating Report and Needs Study: Oklahoma State Transportation
0094-6249 Chemical Reference Manual
0094-6265 Maryland. State Highway Administration. Traffic Trends
0094-6281 Energy Index
0094-6303 Global Directory of Gas Companies†
0094-6338 South Carolina Vital and Morbidity Statistics
0094-6354 A A N A Journal
0094-6427 Susquehanna River Basin Commission. Annual Report
0094-6435 Florida. Division of Corrections. Financial Report *changed to* Florida. Department of Corrections. Annual Report
0094-6451 Economics Working Papers
0094-6478 Music Library Association. Index and Bibliography Series
0094-6494 Illinois. Department of Public Health. Poison Control Program Report†
0094-6516 Legal Bibliographic Data Service Weekly Subject Listing *see* 0360-7151
0094-6532 Early Years *changed to* Early Years/K-8
0094-6575 Emergency Medical Services
0094-6591 Orthopaedic Review
0094-6648 Graduate School Programs in Public Affairs and Public Administration *changed to* Graduate Programs in Public Affairs and Public Administration
0094-6745 Institutions/Volume Feeding *see* 0273-5520
0094-6761 Current Topics in Molecular Endocrinology†
0094-6818 International Index to Multi Media Information†
0094-6842 Systems and Management Annual†
0094-6893 Federal Reserve Bank of Richmond. Economic Review

ISSN INDEX 1435

0094-6907 Cantwell Tapestry
0094-6915 Backtracker
0094-6923 International Telex Book. Americas Edition
0094-6958 Sage Public Administration Abstracts
0094-7008 U.S. National Marine Fisheries Service. Grant-in-Aid for Fisheries: Program Activities
0094-7024 S S I E Science Newsletter†
0094-7032 Advances in Image Pickup and Display
0094-7040 Aldine Crime and Justice Annual†
0094-7091 Geokhimiya Translations†
0094-7148 Report of Cases Determined in the Supreme Court and Court of Appeals of the State of New Mexico
0094-7156 Federal Home Loan Mortgage Corporation. Report
0094-7172 Research in Parapsychology
0094-727X Connecticut. Commission to Study and Investigate the Problems of Deaf and Hearing-Impaired Persons. Annual Report *changed to* Connecticut. Commission on the Deaf and Hearing-Impaired. Annual Report
0094-7288 Engineering and Society Series†
0094-7296 Federal Aid Fact Book†
0094-730X Journal of Fluency Disorders
0094-7326 New Mexico. Veterans' Service Commission. Report
0094-7342 Journal of Mormon History
0094-7393 Highway User Quarterly†
0094-7466 International Symposium on Transport and Handling of Minerals. Proceedings†
0094-7474 Summer Computer Simulation Conference. Proceedings
0094-7482 Status of the Market Nuclear Fuel Fabrication†
0094-7504 Annual Statistical Report of the Colorado Judiciary
0094-7512 Directory of Counseling Services†
0094-7520 Foreign Trade Reports. General Imports of Cotton Manufactures *changed to* Foreign Trade Reports. General Imports of Cotton, Wool and Manmade Fiber Manufactures
0094-7547 New York (City) Mayor. Schedules Supporting the Executive Budget
0094-7555 Banking Legislation in the Congress†
0094-7571 Crime and Social Justice
0094-7598 Land Use Law and Zoning Digest
0094-7628 New Hampshire Comprehensive Law Enforcement Plan *changed to* New Hampshire Comprehensive Criminal Justice Plan
0094-7660 Illinois Insurance
0094-7679 Journalism History
0094-7687 New Hampshire Annual Rural Manpower Report†
0094-7695 National Federation of Independent Business. Quarterly Economic Report *see* 0362-3548
0094-7733 Society of General Physiologists Series
0094-775X Folk Mass and Modern Liturgy *see* 0363-504X
0094-7768 International Studies Notes
0094-7776 U.S. Occupational Safety and Health Review Commission. Administrative Law Judge and Commission Decisions
0094-7814 Inventory of Marriage and Family Literature
0094-7822 Theatre/Drama and Speech Index *changed to* Theatre/Drama Abstracts
0094-7857 U.S. National Science Foundation. Division of Environmental Systems and Resources. Summary of Awards†
0094-7881 U.S. National Science Foundation. Graduate Science Education Student Support and Postdoctorals
0094-789X Executive Compensation Journal *see* 0747-8607
0094-792X C P A Letter
0094-7954 A P S A Departmental Services Program Survey of Departments
0094-7962 University of California, Davis. Food Protection and Toxicology Center. Summary Report†
0094-7989 Bergen County History†
0094-8012 Firelands Arts Review *changed to* Firelands Review
0094-8039 Journal of Muscle Shoals History
0094-8055 Peace Science Society (International). Papers†
0094-8063 Energy Review
0094-8071 Flammability Institute. News Bulletin *changed to* Flammability News Bulletin
0094-8101 Outboard Boating Handbook†
0094-8128 Combustion Toxicology *see* 0362-1669
0094-8136 Yachting Year Book of Northern California
0094-8187 Surgery Update†
0094-8233 Alloys Index
0094-8268 Summary of Expenditure Data for Michigan Public Schools
0094-8276 Geophysical Research Letters
0094-8284 National Trade and Professional Associations of the United States and Canada and Labor Unions *changed to* National Trade and Professional Associations of the United States and Labor Unions
0094-8306 North Dakota. State Advisory Council for Vocational Education. Annual Evaluation Report
0094-8314 Utah. State Office of Education. Annual Report of the State Superintendent of Public Instruction
0094-8322 Illinois. Board of Higher Education. Directory of Higher Education
0094-8373 Paleobiology
0094-8381 Air Force Law Review
0094-8403 Directory of Colorado Libraries
0094-8411 U.S. Bureau of East-West Trade. Export Administration Regulations
0094-8454 Official Southern California Ports Maritime Directory and Guide
0094-8470 Progress in Radiation Protection†
0094-8500 Enzyme Engineering
0094-8519 American Society for Microbiology. Abstracts of the Annual Meeting
0094-8543 American Arabic Speaking Community Almanac†
0094-8551 Florida. Bureau of Local Government Finance. Annual Local Government Financial Report
0094-8594 Journal of Purchasing & Materials Management
0094-8616 U.S. Bureau of Labor Statistics. Consumer Price Index *see* 0095-926X
0094-8632 Eastern Europe Travel Guide *changed to* Travel Guide to Europe
0094-8667 Directory: Home Centers and Hardware Chains, Auto Supply Chains *see* 0736-0452
0094-8667 Directory: Home Centers and Hardware Chains, Auto Supply Chains *see* 0272-0167
0094-8675 Homeowners Handbook *see* 0195-2196
0094-8705 Journal of the Philosophy of Sport
0094-873X Montana Library Directory, with Statistics of Montana Public Libraries
0094-8764 Association of American Plant Food Control Officials. Official Publication
0094-8829 Library Development in Alaska: Long Range Program
0094-8837 Selected Tables in Mathematical Statistics.
0094-8845 St. Lawrence University. Conference on the Adirondack Park (Proceedings)†
0094-8853 Council of Better Business Bureaus. Annual Report
0094-890X New Jersey. State Library. Union List of Serials†
0094-8934 Folk Harp Journal
0094-8950 Monographs in Lipid Research
0094-8969 American Hospital Association. Guide to the Health Care Field
0094-8985 Los Angeles Institute of Contemporary Art. Journal *changed to* Journal: A Contemporary Art Magazine
0094-9000 Theory of Probability and Mathematical Statistics
0094-9019 Wyoming. Department of Revenue and Taxation. Annual Report
0094-9027 Young Students Encyclopedia Yearbook†
0094-9043 Ohio Geographers: Recent Research Themes
0094-9086 Hopkins Quarterly
0094-9108 Physical Fitness Research Digest†
0094-9183 Annual Editions: Readings in Social Problems *see* 0272-4464
0094-9191 A.P.C.A. Directory and Resource Book *changed to* A P C A Government Agencies Directory
0094-9205 University of Georgia. Institute of Ecology. Annual Report
0094-9264 Principles and Techniques of Human Research and Therapeutics†
0094-9302 Concise Clinical Neurology Review†
0094-9329 Modern Sawmill Techniques†
0094-9337 International Journal of Sulfur Chemistry. Part A. Original Articles, Notes and Communications *see* 0308-664X
0094-9345 International Journal of Sulfur Chemistry. Part B. Quarterly Reports *see* 0308-664X
0094-9353 International Journal of Sulfur Chemistry. Part C. Mechanisms of Reactions of Sulfur Compound *see* 0308-664X
0094-9426 Book Forum
0094-9442 Illinois Minerals Notes
0094-9477 Previews of Heat and Mass Transfer
0094-9515 Joint Federal-State Land Use Planning Commission for Alaska. Annual Report *changed to* Alaska's Land
0094-9531 Shepard's Federal Law Citations in Selected Law Reviews
0094-9582 U.S. National Institute of Neurological Diseases and Stroke. Research Program Reports†
0094-9604 Medical Group Management Association. International Directory *changed to* Medical Group Management Association. Directory
0094-9620 American Optometric Association News
0094-9655 Journal of Statistical Computation and Simulation *changed to* Statistical Computation and Simulation
0094-9671 Conference on Ground Water. Proceedings
0094-9701 Ha-Mesivta
0094-9744 Basenji
0094-9779 Geothermal World Directory
0094-9787 Olympian (Colorado Springs)
0094-9841 Chemical Engineering. Equipment Buyer's Guide Issue *see* 0272-4057
0094-9884 Textile Industry Technical Conference (Publication)
0094-9914 Your Highway Department, Arkansas
0094-9922 Transportation USA
0094-9930 Journal of Pressure Vessel Technology
0094-9973 Best's Agents Guide to Life Insurance Companies
0095-0025 Job Corps Happenings†
0095-0033 Data Base (New York)
0095-0084 Business Digest†
0095-0092 Business Monthly *changed to* Managing (New York)
0095-0106 Communique (Boston)†
0095-0149 Environmental Quality Abstracts†
0095-0157 Florida Marine Research Publications
0095-0165 Homegrown†
0095-019X Osiris
0095-0203 Personal Finance Letter†
0095-0211 Real Estate Investor *see* 0734-5860
0095-0262 U.S. National Heart and Lung Advisory Council. Annual Report *see* 0161-1917
0095-036X Texas Nursing
0095-0386 Mort's Guide to Low-Cost Vacations & Lodgings on College Campuses
0095-0475 Practical Psychology for Physicians *see* 0162-6957
0095-0491 Catfish Farmer and World Aquaculture News *see* 0199-1388
0095-053X National Library Reporter†
0095-0556 Car Classics *see* 0164-5552
0095-0564 Wisconsin. Division of Corrections. Bureau of Planning, Development and Research. Work Release-Study Release Program *changed to* Wisconsin. Division of Corrections. Office of Information Management. Work Release-Study Release Program
0095-0580 Hospital/Health Care Training Media Profiles *see* 0740-1892
0095-0629 L C Foreign Acquisitions Newsletter†
0095-0637 Fact Book. Alabama Institutions of Higher Education, Universities and Colleges *changed to* Fact Book. Higher Education in Alabama
0095-0645 Minnesota. Department of Revenue. Biennial Report
0095-0653 Collegiate Woman's Career Magazine *see* 8755-9218
0095-067X WoodenBoat
0095-0688 Manhattan Directory of Commercial & Industrial Properties
0095-0696 Journal of Environmental Economics and Management
0095-0726 Commerce Reporter†
0095-0750 Doctoral Scientists and Engineers in the United States. Profile *changed to* Science, Engineering, and Humanities Doctorates in the United States: Profile
0095-0777 Instrumentation in the Food Industry
0095-084X Electrical Installation & Repair Projects†
0095-0858 Social Psychiatry†
0095-0866 Western Pennsylvania Genealogical Quarterly *see* 0278-7431
0095-0874 Symbols of American Libraries
0095-0890 Foreign Trade Reports. U.S. Waterborne Exports and General Imports
0095-0963 Automedica
0095-0971 Bio-Medical Scoreboard†
0095-0998 Medical School Rounds†
0095-1005 Search and Seizure Law Report
0095-1013 Lifestyle†
0095-1021 I. F. T. Journal†
0095-1048 Footwear Manual
0095-1072 U.S. Library of Congress. Chinese Cooperative Catalog†
0095-1080 Africana Journal
0095-1102 New Hampshire Occupational Outlook†
0095-1137 Journal of Clinical Microbiology
0095-1145 Psychology†
0095-1188 Women Law Reporter†
0095-1250 Water Resources Research in Virginia, Annual Report†
0095-1269 Alabama World Trade Directory *changed to* Alabama International Trade Directory
0095-1285 Alabama. Commission on Higher Education. Biennial Report to the Governor and the Legislature *changed to* Alabama. Commission on Higher Education. Annual Report
0095-134X CoEvolution Quarterly *see* 0749-5056
0095-1358 Fodor's Soviet Union
0095-1374 R.E.I.T. Fact Book
0095-1382 Vermont. Department of Employment Security. Statistical Tables. *changed to* Vermont. Department of Employment & Training Security. Statistical Tables
0095-1390 Albion
0095-1404 American Hairdresser/Salon Owner *changed to* American Salon
0095-1420 Artbibliographies Current Titles
0095-1439 Central Kentucky Researcher
0095-1447 Cinefan†
0095-1455 National Association of Regional Councils. Directory *changed to* Directory of Regional Councils
0095-148X American Venereal Disease Association. Journal *see* 0148-5717
0095-1498 Kentucky Local Debt Report

0095-1528 Urban Planning Quarterly†
0095-1536 Women (Washington)†
0095-1544 Journal of Cyclic Nucleotide Research *changed to* Journal of Cyclic Nucleotide and Protein Phosphorylation Research
0095-1579 British Isles and Ireland Travel Guide *changed to* Travel Guide to Europe
0095-1587 Foster Natural Gas Report
0095-1625 Rider
0095-1633 North Dakota. Social Service Board. Statistics†
0095-165X El Dorado
0095-1684 American Poetry and Poetics
0095-1692 Civil Engineering Report Series *changed to* Water Resources Report Series
0095-1714 Imprint†
0095-1730 Seems
0095-1811 American Clean Car
0095-182X American Indian Quarterly
0095-1846 Virginia. Law Enforcement Officers Training Standards Commission. Biennial Report *changed to* Virginia. Criminal Justice Services Commission. Annual Report
0095-1870 Industrial Contact List for North Carolina Communities†
0095-1897 Monthly Energy Indicators *see* 0095-7356
0095-1900 Texas. Department of Corrections. Research and Development Division. Research Report
0095-1978 Virginia. State Water Control Board. Annual Report
0095-1994 Tennessee. Department of Safety. Annual Report
0095-2060 Florida. Department of Transportation. Annual Report†
0095-2087 I M P Directory *see* 0148-6942
0095-2109 U.S. Office of Technology Assessment Annual Report to the Congress
0095-2117 Comptroller General's Procurement Decisions
0095-2125 Energy: a Continuing Bibliography with Indexes†
0095-2141 U.S. Bureau of Health Resources Development. Division of Nursing. Special Project Grants and Contracts Awarded for Improvement in Nurse Training†
0095-2184 Integrity: Gay Episcopal Forum *changed to* Integrity Forum
0095-2214 Chromatography Newsletter
0095-2222 Consumers' Research *changed to* Consumers' Research Magazine
0095-2257 Russian Orthodox Greek-Catholic Church of America. Yearbook *see* 0145-7950
0095-2265 New York State Society of Anesthesiologists. Bulletin *see* 0095-2273
0095-2273 N Y S S A Sphere
0095-2338 Journal of Chemical Information and Computer Sciences
0095-2346 Drugs in Health Care†
0095-2354 Southeastern Drug/Southern Pharmaceutical Journal *see* 0192-5792
0095-2397 Advent Review and Sabbath Herald *see* 0161-1119
0095-2427 Harvard Magazine
0095-2443 Journal of Elastomers and Plastics
0095-2583 Economic Inquiry
0095-2591 International Netsuke Collectors Society Journal
0095-2605 Keeping up with Experimental Music in the Schools†
0095-2613 Orff Echo
0095-263X Rare Coin Review
0095-2648 Transportation Research Abstracts†
0095-2656 Transportation Research News *changed to* T R News
0095-2664 Tunneling Technology Newsletter
0095-2699 Agricultural Libraries Information Notes
0095-2702 Serials Updating Service Annual†
0095-2737 Computers & Society
0095-2788 Vogue Patterns
0095-280X Studies in American Humor
0095-2826 American Society for Personnel Administration. Personnel and Industrial Relations Colleges†
0095-2850 Economic and Social Progress in Latin America; Annual Report
0095-2869 Directory of American Book Specialists†
0095-2893 Illinois. State Museum. Inventory of the Collections
0095-2907 Dickson Mounds Museum Anthropological Studies†
0095-2915 Illinois. State Museum. Research Series. Papers in Anthropology
0095-2923 Insurance Forum
0095-2931 Alan Shawn Feinstein Insiders Report
0095-294X Forecaster
0095-2958 Biology Digest
0095-2966 Resources†
0095-2974 New World Communications†
0095-2982 Nurses Association of A.C.O.G. Bulletin *see* 0884-2175
0095-2990 American Journal of Drug and Alcohol Abuse
0095-3024 Minnesota. Department of Revenue. Petroleum Division. Annual Report
0095-3075 Virginia. Employment Commission. Manpower Research Division. Economic Assumptions†
0095-3105 Nebraska Statistical Report of Abortions
0095-3113 National Directory of State Agencies
0095-3121 Family Planning Programs in Oklahoma
0095-313X Epidemiologic Notes and Communicable Disease Morbidity Report†
0095-3237 Occupational Safety & Health Reporter
0095-3245 Fleet Maintenance and Specifying *changed to* Fleet Equipment
0095-327X Armed Forces and Society
0095-3318 Alaska. Office of Alcoholism. Report
0095-3326 Nation's Schools and Colleges *see* 0194-2263
0095-3342 Federal Funding Guide for Elementary and Secondary Education *changed to* Guide to Federal Funding for Education
0095-3369 Digest of the United States Practice in International Law
0095-3415 Alaska. Violent Crimes Compensation Board. Annual Report
0095-3423 Commerce Business Daily
0095-3431 Alabama's Vital Events
0095-3482 Summary and Analysis of International Travel in the U.S.
0095-3490 Statistics of Virginia Public Libraries *see* 0731-8464
0095-3547 Geological Society of America. Yearbook *see* 0277-5816
0095-3555 West Coast Review of Books *changed to* Books/100 Reviews
0095-3563 Vinifera Wine Growers Journal
0095-3601 Cal-Neva Wildlife; Transactions
0095-361X Alabama. Public Library Service. Basic State Plan and Annual Program *changed to* Alabama. Public Library Service. Annual Report
0095-3628 Microbial Ecology
0095-3679 Peanut Science
0095-3741 Current Governments Reports: Governmental Finances
0095-3784 Abstracts of Instructional and Research Materials in Vocational and Technical Education *see* 0160-2004
0095-3814 Topics in Health Care Financing
0095-3830 Economic Outlook U.S.A.
0095-3865 Alaska. Legislature. Budget and Audit Committee. Annual Report.
0095-389X Wyoming. Employment Security Commission. Research and Analysis Section. Farm Labor Report†
0095-3903 Foreign Trade Annual Report. Virginia Ports *see* 0083-6516
0095-3911 St. Clair County Historical Society. Journal
0095-392X State University of New York at Buffalo. Law Library. Law Library Periodicals†
0095-3962 Sales Training & Development *see* 0193-2136
0095-3997 Administration and Society
0095-4004 Wisconsin. Division of Corrections. Bureau of Planning, Development, and Research. Adult Probation Admissions†
0095-4012 American Journal of I.V. Therapy *changed to* Intravenous Therapy News
0095-4020 Massachusetts. Department of Public Welfare. State Advisory Board. Annual Report†
0095-4047 New York (State). Division of Criminal Justice Service. Annual Report
0095-4063 Communications World†
0095-4101 Popular Music Periodicals Index†
0095-411X Production and Marketing California Grapes, Raisins and Wine *see* 0527-2181
0095-4144 Executive Compensation Service. Reports on International Compensation. Argentina
0095-4152 State Tax Collections *see* 0270-0808
0095-4209 Hawaii. State Law Enforcement and Juvenile Delinquency Planning Agency. Annual Action Program†
0095-4225 Power Semiconductors *see* 0164-0038
0095-4241 S M/Successful Meetings *see* 0148-4052
0095-425X Christianity Applied†
0095-4306 Wisconsin. Division of Corrections. Office of Information Management. Juvenile Probation Admissions†
0095-4314 Wisconsin Trails
0095-4322 World Mines Register†
0095-4330 Washington Agricultural Statistics
0095-4365 U.S. National Climatic Center. Climatological Data; National Summary†
0095-4403 American Society for Information Science. Bulletin
0095-4411 Northwestern Camping *changed to* Northwestern Campbook
0095-442X Oklahoma. Conservation Commission. Biennial Report
0095-4438 Columban Mission
0095-4470 Journal of Phonetics
0095-4489 Studies in Browning and His Circle
0095-4519 Innovations†
0095-4527 Cytology and Genetics
0095-4535 Advances in Environmental Sciences *see* 0065-2563
0095-4543 Primary Care: Clinics in Office Practice
0095-4551 International Bibliography of Research in Marriage and the Family *see* 0094-7814
0095-4594 Corrections Magazine†
0095-4608 Byzantine Studies
0095-4616 Applied Mathematics and Optimization
0095-4624 Connecticut. Council on Environmental Quality. Annual Report
0095-4632 A.D.F.& G. Technical Data Report
0095-4640 Benchmark Papers in Ecology
0095-4659 West Virginia. Department of Natural Resources. Annual Report on the Comprehensive Water Resources Plan†
0095-4667 Alaska Medicaid Status Report†
0095-4675 Alaska. Division of Medical Assistance. Medicaid Annual Status Report *see* 0095-4667
0095-4683 Airline Handbook
0095-4721 L.S.C.A. Annual Program, Hawaii State Library System
0095-4748 National Treasury Employees Union. Bulletin
0095-4772 Pensions & Investments *see* 0273-5466
0095-4829 Advances and Technical Standards in Neurosurgery
0095-4837 U.S. Bureau of Labor Statistics. Chartbook on Prices, Wages, and Productivity†
0095-4853 I R M *see* 0739-9049
0095-4861 Clinical and Biochemical Analysis
0095-4888 Directory of Minnesota's Area Mental Health, Mental Retardation, Inebriety Programs†
0095-490X Intercollegiate Bibliography. New Cases in Administration. *changed to* H B S Case Bibliography
0095-4918 Journal of Portfolio Management
0095-4942 North Carolina. Department of Human Resources. Annual Plan of Work
0095-4977 Curriculum Materials Clearinghouse. Index and Curriculum Briefs†
0095-4993 Journal of African Studies
0095-5086 Public Utilities Law Anthology
0095-5108 Clinics in Perinatology
0095-5175 Florida. Office of the Governor. Budget in Brief
0095-5183 Drug Development Communications *see* 0363-9045
0095-5191 Directory of Investor-Owned Hospitals, Hospital Management Companies and Health Systems
0095-5213 Kaleidoscope (Boston)†
0095-5221 Interest-Adjusted Index†
0095-5248 New Frontiers (Seattle)†
0095-5264 Nevada. Bureau of Mines and Geology. Report
0095-5299 U S Auto Reports *see* 0148-9410
0095-5310 Arizona. Department of Education. Annual Report of the Superintendent of Public Instruction
0095-5329 Consolidated Report on Elementary and Secondary Education in Colorado
0095-537X Weighing & Measurement
0095-5388 Voyages to the Inland Sea†
0095-5396 American Bankers Association. National Operations & Automation Conference. Proceedings
0095-5418 Strictly U.S.†
0095-5434 Catalog of World Bank Publications
0095-5493 Foreign Trade Reports. U.S. General Imports - Schedule A - Commodity by Country
0095-5523 New Hampshire Vital Statistics
0095-5558 Country Place *see* 0147-4928
0095-5574 Kentucky Manpower Development. Annual Report
0095-5582 Annual Editions: Readings in Anthropology *changed to* Annual Editions: Anthropology
0095-5590 New York (State) Consumer Protection Board. Annual Report
0095-5655 Gallaudet Almanac†
0095-5663 New York Times School Microfilm Collection Index by Reels *changed to* New York Times School Microfilm Collection Index
0095-5698 Access: The Supplementary Index to Periodicals
0095-571X Semeia
0095-5744 Viking
0095-5760 Alaska Hunting Guide†
0095-5787 Annual Editions: Readings in Education
0095-5833 Criminal Victimization in the United States
0095-585X Montana Federal Grants-in-Aid Report†
0095-5876 San Diego Biomedical Symposium. Proceedings
0095-5884 Louisiana. State Board of Nurse Examiners. Report *changed to* Louisiana. State Board of Nursing. Report (Calendar Year)
0095-5892 Training
0095-5930 N A C L A's Latin America and Empire Report *see* 0149-1598
0095-5981 Humanities Index
0095-599X Drug Interactions†
0095-6120 North Dakota. Judicial Council. Statistical Compilation and Report *changed to* North Dakota. Judicial Conference. Annual Report
0095-6139 Ethnicity†
0095-6155 Annual Editions: Readings in Marriage and Family *see* 0272-7897

0095-6201 Georgia Archive *changed to* Provenance
0095-6236 Rangeman's Journal *see* 0190-0528
0095-6317 Technical Education Reporter†
0095-635X Military Media Review
0095-6384 Kentucky Law Enforcement Council. Annual Report†
0095-6406 Fielding's Low-Cost Europe *see* 0739-0785
0095-6414 Directory of Small Magazine/Press Editors and Publishers
0095-6422 Delaware. Department of Health and Social Service. Annual Report
0095-6430 State of Florida Comprehensive Manpower Plan
0095-6449 Computer Design's Data Sheet Directory of Digital Electronics†
0095-6457 Carpet Specifier's Handbook
0095-6465 California Historical Courier
0095-6481 National Conference on Power Transmission. Proceedings†
0095-6538 N.A.D.A. Mobile Home Appraisal Guide
0095-6562 Aviation, Space, and Environmental Medicine
0095-6570 State-Approved Schools of Practical and Vocational Nursing *see* 0081-4423
0095-6619 Hawaii. Legislative Reference Bureau. Digest and Index of Laws Enacted†
0095-6627 Pet Mass Marketing *see* 0162-8666
0095-6694 O.S.S.C. Bulletin
0095-6708 Impact (Ann Arbor)†
0095-6716 U.S. National Center for Education Statistics. Financial Statistics of Institutions of Higher Education
0095-6740 Blue Cross Association. Research Series†
0095-6775 Damon Runyon-Walter Winchell Cancer Fund. Annual Report
0095-6783 Mississippi Marine Resources Council. Annual Report
0095-683X International Directory of the Nonwoven Fabrics Industry
0095-6848 Journal of Japanese Studies
0095-6880 National Computer Conference and Exposition (Proceedings) *changed to* National Computer Conference (Proceedings)
0095-6910 Homegrown†
0095-6937 V.D. Fact Sheet *changed to* S T D Fact Sheet
0095-6945 Intersections
0095-6953 N.A.D.A. Motorcycle Appraisal Guide
0095-697X Juvenile Law Newsletter†
0095-702X Rendezvous of Western Art†
0095-7089 Mathematics Student†
0095-7100 B N A Pension Reporter
0095-7119 Best Science Fiction of the Year
0095-7151 Convenience Store Merchandiser
0095-7186 Election Index†
0095-7216 Hip
0095-7232 Reviews in European History†
0095-7240 World Almanac Guide to Pro Hockey
0095-7267 California. Office of Criminal Justice Planning. Bulletin
0095-7275 Electronics and Equipment Market Abstracts *see* 0161-8032
0095-7291 Foreign Tax Law Bi-Weekly Bulletin
0095-733X Michigan. Department of Management and Budget. Annual Report†
0095-7348 Minnesota and Environs Weather Almanac *changed to* Minnesota Weather Guide Calendar
0095-7356 Monthly Energy Review
0095-7364 New England Journal on Prison Law *changed to* New England Journal on Criminal and Civil Confinement
0095-7437 Alaska. Division of Geological Survey. Miscellaneous Paper *see* 0065-5783
0095-7550 Reviews of Neuroscience
0095-7577 Journal of Space Law
0095-7607 European Parliament Digest†
0095-7615 Grumman Aerospace Horizons *changed to* Grumman Horizons
0095-7755 Software Briefs†
0095-7771 Foreign Trade Reports. U.S. Airborne Exports and General Imports
0095-781X National Savings and Loan League Journal *see* 0740-5464
0095-7895 Cancer Therapy Abstracts†
0095-7917 Current Contents/Engineering, Technology & Applied Sciences
0095-795X U.S. Library of Congress. Accessions List: Brazil
0095-7976 Materials Performance Buyer's Guide
0095-7984 Journal of Black Psychology
0095-8107 New Harbinger; a Journal of the Cooperative Movement *see* 0190-2741
0095-8115 Discography Series
0095-8123 Interface Journal†
0095-8131 Information Times *changed to* Information Times
0095-8174 Virginia. Department of Labor and Industry. Division of Research and Statistics. Occupational Injuries and Illnesses by Industry†
0095-8247 Illinois. Fire Protection Personnel Standards and Education Commission. Annual Report†
0095-8301 Diabetes Forecast
0095-8514 Earth Science Digest *see* 0012-8228
0095-8891 Journal of Consulting Psychology *see* 0022-006X
0095-8948 Engineering & Mining Journal
0095-8956 Journal of Combinatorial Theory. Series B.
0095-8964 Journal of Environmental Education
0095-8972 Journal of Coordination Chemistry
0095-9065 Journal of Medicinal and Pharmaceutical Chemistry *see* 0022-2623
0095-9197 Electrical Engineering *see* 0018-9235
0095-926X U.S. Bureau of Labor Statistics. C P I Detailed Report
0095-9286 New Silver Technology
0095-9294 National Center for the Study of Collective Bargaining in Higher Education. Annual Conference Proceedings *see* 0742-3667
0095-9308 Mortgage Banking: Financial Statements and Operating Ratios *see* 0278-6567
0095-9618 Journal of Oral Surgery, Anesthesia and Hospital Dental Service *see* 0278-2391
0095-9626 Journal of Morphology and Physiology *see* 0362-2525
0095-9650 American Society of Agronomy. Journal *see* 0002-1962
0095-9782 Journal of Solution Chemistry
0095-9820 Journal of the Aerospace Sciences *see* 0001-1452
0095-9952 Cement-Mill and Quarry *see* 0032-0293
0095-9960 Ceramic Abstracts
0096-0179 Connecticut State Medical Journal *see* 0010-6178
0096-025X American Public Works Association. Yearbook *see* 0360-6899
0096-0322 American Physics Teacher *see* 0002-9505
0096-0349 American Professional Pharmacist *see* 0003-0627
0096-0365 American Rabbit Journal
0096-0381 American Review of Tuberculosis *see* 0003-0805
0096-039X American Review of Tuberculosis and Pulmonary Diseases *see* 0003-0805
0096-0489 Florida. Bureau of Geology. Report of Investigations
0096-0551 Computer Languages
0096-0586 Group Psychotherapy and Psychodrama *see* 0731-1273
0096-0640 Journal of Engineering Education (Washington) *see* 0022-0809
0096-0764 Fluid Mechanics - Soviet Research
0096-0772 Foote Prints
0096-0799 Government Reports Announcements *see* 0097-9007
0096-0802 Heat Transfer - Japanese Research
0096-0810 I S A Journal *see* 0192-303X
0096-0845 American Society of Brewing Chemists. Proceedings *see* 0361-0470
0096-0896 American Perfumer(1960) *see* 0361-4387
0096-090X American Paper Converter *see* 0031-1138
0096-0918 American Painter and Decorator *see* 0003-0325
0096-1043 Reviews of Modern Physics *see* 8755-1209
0096-1159 Graphic Arts Technical Foundation. Research Project Report
0096-1191 Journal of Foraminiferal Research
0096-1221 International Pacific Halibut Commission. Report *see* 0579-3920
0096-1248 Tennessee Valley Authority. Division of Land and Forest Resources. Technical Note
0096-1337 Journal of Undergraduate Psychological Research†
0096-1345 Index and Cumulative List of Papers on Radiation Chemistry *see* 0164-5315
0096-1353 Ford's Deck Plan Guide
0096-1388 Annual Report of the Arts Activities in Alabama
0096-140X Aggressive Behavior
0096-1442 Journal of Urban History
0096-1469 Ashleys of America Quarterly *changed to* Ashleys Addenda Annual
0096-1507 A I D Research and Development Abstracts
0096-1515 Journal of Experimental Psychology: Human Learning and Memory *see* 0278-7393
0096-1523 Journal of Experimental Psychology: Human Perception and Performance (JEP: HPP)
0096-1736 J O M: Journal of Occupational Medicine *see* 0022-3212
0096-221X Eastman Organic Chemical Bulletin *see* 0270-4986
0096-2279 Colorado-Wyoming Academy of Sciences Journal
0096-2333 Rubber Age and Tire News *see* 0146-0706
0096-2341 U.S. Library of Congress. Accessions List: Southeast Asia
0096-2651 Fieldiana: Geology
0096-2686 Journal of Gas Chromatography *see* 0021-9665
0096-2708 Horizons in Biochemistry and Biophysics
0096-2716 Contact Lens Journal†
0096-2732 Journal of Preventive Dentistry *see* 0163-9633
0096-2740 Perspective on Aging
0096-3003 Applied Mathematics and Computation
0096-3070 Florida State University Law Review
0096-3089 Geochimica†
0096-3135 Politeia†
0096-3143 Orange County Bar Journal†
0096-3216 Karter News
0096-3224 Current Governments Reports: Finances of Employee Retirement Systems of State and Local Governments
0096-3259 Translator Referral Directory†
0096-3291 Yearbook of Science and the Future
0096-3364 Current Aviation Statistics†
0096-3380 American Baptist Convention. Directory *see* 0091-9381
0096-3402 Bulletin of the Atomic Scientists
0096-3445 Journal of Experimental Psychology: General (JEP: GEN)
0096-3518 I E E E Transactions on Acoustics, Speech and Signal Processing
0096-3917 Cancer Letter
0096-3925 Moscow University Biological Sciences Bulletin
0096-3941 Eos (Washington)
0096-3984 Operations Research Society of America. Journal *see* 0030-364X
0096-4077 Tulane Studies in Geology *see* 0041-4018
0096-414X South Carolina Academy of Science. Bulletin
0096-4417 American Horticulturist
0096-4484 Industrial and Analytical Chemistry. Analytical Edition *see* 0003-2700
0096-4859 Mines Directory
0096-5022 Michigan. Department of Conservation. Geological Survey Division. Progress Report *changed to* Michigan. Geological Survey Division. Report of Investigation
0096-5154 American Machinist/Metalworking Manufacturing *changed to* American Machinist & Automated Manufacturing
0096-5278 American Manufacturer *see* 0019-8889
0096-5294 Journal of Hygiene *see* 0002-9262
0096-5332 Advances in Carbohydrate Chemistry *see* 0065-2318
0096-591X Textile Colorist and Converter *see* 0002-8266
0096-6320 Water Works and Wastes Engineering *see* 0273-2238
0096-6347 American Journal of Orthodontics *changed to* American Journal of Orthodontics and Pentofacial Orthodontics
0096-6746 American Journal of Tropical Medicine *see* 0002-9637
0096-686X American Therapeutic Society. Transactions *see* 0002-8614
0096-6894 A.M.A. Archives of Otolaryngology *see* 0003-9977
0096-7033 Lying-in *see* 0024-7758
0096-7238 Instrumentation in the Aerospace Industry.
0096-736X S A E Transactions
0096-7394 American Ceramic Society. Transactions *changed to* American Ceramic Society Journal/Communications
0096-7408 American Institute of Chemical Engineers. Transactions *see* 0360-7275
0096-7750 Academy of Natural Sciences of Philadelphia. Monographs
0096-7807 Soviet Journal of Ecology
0096-7955 Nondestructive Testing (Chicago) *see* 0025-5327
0096-820X American Industrial Hygiene Association Quarterly *see* 0002-8894
0096-848X Yearbook of Physical Anthropology (Washington)
0096-8684 Begonian
0096-8692 Bell Telephone Magazine
0096-8765 Systems-Computers-Control *see* 0882-1666
0096-8803 U.S. Library of Congress. Subject Catalog†
0096-882X Journal of Studies on Alcohol
0096-8846 Italian Americana
0096-8870 Gas Processors Association. Annual Convention. Proceedings
0096-8994 A M A American Journal of Diseases of Children *see* 0002-922X
0096-9117 Society of Vertebrate Paleontology. News Bulletin
0096-9168 Plastics Industry *see* 0032-1273
0096-9222 Pennsylvania Academy of Science. Proceedings
0096-9419 Navy Civil Engineer
0096-9842 Wyoming Mineral Yearbook
0096-9877 U.S. Bureau of the Census. Data User News
0096-9907 International Economic Indicators and Competitive Trends *changed to* International Economic Indicators
0097-0042 Railroad Research Bulletin†
0097-0050 Health Education
0097-0085 Medicolegal News *see* 0277-8459
0097-0247 Journal of Fire & Flammability/Fire Retardant Chemistry *see* 0362-1693
0097-0255 National University Extension Association. Handbook and Directory *changed to* National University Continuing Education Association. Directory
0097-0492 Sport Fishing Institute. Bulletin *see* 0085-6592
0097-0549 Neuroscience and Behavioral Physiology
0097-0638 American Fisheries Society. Special Publication

ISSN INDEX

0097-0905 Connecticut. Agricultural Experiment Station, New Haven. Bulletin
0097-109X Progress in Cardiology
0097-1138 Absolute Sound
0097-1146 Anima
0097-1154 Indian Law Reporter
0097-1162 Journal of Fire & Flammability/Consumer Product Flammability Supplement see 0362-1677
0097-1170 Journal of Physical Education and Recreation see 0730-3084
0097-1189 State O'Maine Facts†
0097-1324 Association of Official Seed Analysts. Proceedings see 0146-3071
0097-1510 Virginia Polytechnic Institute and State University. Research Division. Report see 0731-9649
0097-1936 Air Quality Instrumentation†
0097-2126 American Power Conference. Proceedings.
0097-2509 International Pulp & Paper Directory
0097-2533 Modern Hi-Fi & Music
0097-2762 Eugenics Quarterly see 0037-766X
0097-3033 Industrial Development
0097-3157 Academy of Natural Sciences of Philadelphia. Proceedings
0097-3165 Journal of Combinatorial Theory. Series A
0097-3254 Academy of Natural Sciences of Philadelphia. Special Publications
0097-3297 American Photo-Engraver changed to GraphiCommunicator
0097-3416 Iowa Agriculture and Home Economics Experiment Station. Research Bulletin
0097-3491 Arkansas Agricultural Experiment Station. Bulletin
0097-3599 Journal of Medical Research see 0002-9440
0097-4056 A R S Journal see 0001-1452
0097-4080 Converter see 0031-1138
0097-4145 American Concrete Institute. Proceedings
0097-4382 Gulf Coast Research Laboratory. Publications of the Museum†
0097-4455 Conference Board of the Mathematical Sciences. Regional Conference Series in Applied Mathematics
0097-4463 Carnegie Museum of Natural History. Annals of (the) Carnegie Museum
0097-4536 Cross Ties
0097-4706 J.C.C.: Journal of Clinical Chiropractic
0097-4714 Journal of Clinical Chiropractic. Archives see 0097-4706
0097-4730 Statistics of Paper and Paperboard see 0731-8863
0097-4773 Chilton's Motor-Age Service Handbook see 0363-2393
0097-4854 Dental Research in the United States and Canada see 0147-264X
0097-4862 From the State Capitals. Drug Abuse Control Report see 0734-0877
0097-4943 Computers & Mathematics with Applications
0097-496X Pembroke Magazine
0097-5125 Iowa Agriculture and Home Economics Experiment Station. Special Report
0097-5184 Nineteenth Century†
0097-5192 Official Airline Guide. International Edition see 0364-3875
0097-5206 Randax Education Guide
0097-5222 Shale Country†
0097-5230 Cold Spring Harbor Conferences on Cell Proliferation†
0097-5257 Pediatric Nephrology†
0097-5370 Arkansas Agricultural Experiment Station. Report Series
0097-5397 S I A M Journal on Computing
0097-5419 Southern Medicine†
0097-5427 Wadley Medical Bulletin see 0162-9360
0097-5877 Photoengravers Bulletin see 8750-2224
0097-5982 Pediatric Conferences†
0097-5990 Q R B
0097-6008 Sonix†
0097-6024 Middle East Newsletter
0097-6059 California Historical Quarterly see 0162-2897
0097-6075 Creativity
0097-6083 Directory of Law Enforcement and Criminal Justice Education changed to Law Enforcement and Criminal Justice Education Directory
0097-6156 A C S Symposium Series
0097-6164 Advocate (Springfield) changed to I E A/N E A Advocate
0097-6172 America: History and Life. Part B: Index to Book Reviews
0097-6180 American Congress on Surveying and Mapping. Bulletin
0097-6199 Current Awareness in Real Estate and Planning†
0097-6237 Florida Journal of Commerce/American Shipper see 0160-225X
0097-627X American Dance Therapy Association. Monographs†
0097-6288 Principal International Businesses
0097-6326 Federal Register
0097-6482 Analog Sounds†
0097-6512 National Braille Club. Bulletin see 0550-5666
0097-6539 Hype†
0097-6555 Issues in Ego Psychology
0097-6563 Sigma Phi Epsilon Journal
0097-6687 Railway Engineering and Maintenance see 0033-9016
0097-6830 North American Wildlife Conference. Transactions see 0078-1355
0097-7004 Modern China
0097-7039 Amtrak Annual Report
0097-711X S A E Journal of Automotive Engineering see 0098-2571
0097-7136 Directory of Nature Centers and Related Environmental Education Facilities†
0097-7144 Audubon Field Notes see 0004-7686
0097-7209 Crystal Mirror
0097-7268 North Cal-Neva Resource Conservation and Development Project. Annual Work Plan
0097-7314 International Tax Journal
0097-7330 Magnetic Resonance Review: A Quarterly Literature Review changed to Magnetic Resonance Review
0097-7357 Pulpwood Production and Timber Harvesting see 0160-6433
0097-7373 Ski Magazine's Guide to Cross Country Skiing changed to Cross Country Ski Magazine
0097-739X Wyoming Area Manpower Review†
0097-7403 Journal of Experimental Psychology: Animal Behavior Processes (JEP: ABP)
0097-7519 Water Quality Monitoring Data for Georgia Streams
0097-7721 G T E Journal of Research and Development†
0097-7764 Study of Employment of Women in the Federal Government changed to Affirmative Employment Statistics
0097-7799 U.S. Office of Management and Budget. Catalog of Federal Domestic Assistance
0097-7829 Copper see 0163-4186
0097-7977 U.S. Administrative Office of the United States Courts. Report on Applications for Orders Authorizing or Approving the Interception of Wire or Oral Communications
0097-7985 U.S. Library of Congress. Accessions List: Pakistan†
0097-8035 Paid My Dues†
0097-8043 Restaurant Business
0097-8051 San Jose Studies
0097-8078 Water Resources
0097-8124 Babe Ruth Baseball's Athletes of the Year†
0097-8132 Broadcasting Cable Sourcebook see 0732-7196
0097-8140 Creative Computing†
0097-8159 Energy Communications†
0097-8167 Washington Post. Newspaper Index see 0195-6361
0097-8175 Gebbie Press All-In-One Directory changed to Gebbie Press All-in-One Media Directory
0097-8213 New Settler's Guide for Washington, D.C. and Communities in Nearby Maryland and Virginia
0097-8221 Occasional Review†
0097-8256 Record and Tape Reviews Index†
0097-8299 Transit Journal†
0097-8329 Consumer Electronics Product News
0097-8337 Consumer Guide Magazine
0097-8345 Credit (Washington)
0097-8388 I & S M changed to Iron and Steelmaker
0097-8396 I C P Software Directory see 0272-1171
0097-840X Journal of Human Stress
0097-8418 S I G C S E Bulletin
0097-8434 New Jersey Municipal Bond News
0097-8485 Computers & Chemistry
0097-8493 Computers & Graphics
0097-8507 Language (Baltimore)
0097-8515 Transportation Research Circular
0097-8523 European Labor and Working Class History Newsletter see 0147-5479
0097-8620 Current Prescribing†
0097-8663 Estreno
0097-8779 O A G Worldwide Cruise & Shipline Guide
0097-8884 Bittersweet†
0097-8892 Journal of Developmental Disabilities†
0097-8930 Computer Graphics (New York)
0097-8949 American Blade see 0744-6179
0097-8957 Consumer Guide Magazine: Stereo & Tape Equipment Test Reports†
0097-8965 International Studies Newsletter see 0020-8817
0097-899X American Medical Association. Directory of Approved Residencies changed to Directory of Residency Training Accredited by the Accreditation Council for Graduate Medical Education
0097-9007 Government Reports Announcements and Index
0097-9015 Government Reports Index see 0097-9007
0097-9031 J N M see 0161-5505
0097-9112 Montana State Board of Health. Annual Statistical Supplement see 0077-1198
0097-9120 Montana. State Department of Health. Annual Statistical Supplement see 0077-1198
0097-9171 Wisconsin. Employment Relations Commission. Reporter
0097-921X Annual Index of Rheumatology†
0097-9325 Nebraska Statistical Handbook
0097-9376 U.S. Mining Enforcement and Safety Administration. Informational Report
0097-9473 Ohio. Division of Geological Survey. Guidebook
0097-952X Cultural Information Service
0097-9546 Orchid Advocate
0097-9554 Securities Regulation Law Journal
0097-9562 Soroptimist of the Americas
0097-9627 Newspapers in Microform†
0097-9643 National District Attorneys Association. Economic Crime Project. Annual Report†
0097-966X S I D International Symposium. Digest of Technical Papers
0097-9708 Tennessee Valley Historical Review changed to Historical Review & Antique Digest
0097-9716 Journal of Dermatologic Surgery see 0148-0812
0097-9732 Medoc: Index to U S Government Publications in the Medical and Health Sciences
0097-9740 Signs: Journal of Women in Culture and Society
0097-9759 Cooperative Housing Bulletin
0097-9783 Human Life Review
0097-9791 Middle East Review
0097-9805 Pediatric Nursing
0097-9813 Litigation
0097-9953 Arizona. Governor's Commission on Arizona Environment. Annual Report changed to Arizona. Commission on the Arizona Environment. Annual Report
0098-0005 List of Legal Investments for Savings Banks in Connecticut†
0098-0110 Missouri. State Board of Training Schools. Annual Report changed to Missouri. Division of Youth Services. Annual Report
0098-0129 Transportation Focus†
0098-0137 Advances in Sex Hormone Research†
0098-0242 Foreign Trade Reports. U.S. Exports - Schedule B - Commodity by Country see 0190-499X
0098-0269 Illinois. Department of Public Instruction. Annual State of Education Message see 0147-2860
0098-0285 New Jersey. Department of Labor and Industry. Division of Planning and Research. Commercial and Industrial Construction Plans Approved; Annual Summary†
0098-0307 Michigan Labor Market Review
0098-0323 Wisconsin Traffic Data - Automatic Traffic Recorder
0098-0331 Journal of Chemical Ecology
0098-0366 Somatic Cell Genetics
0098-0404 Air Carrier Traffic Statistics see 0731-3411
0098-0471 Film Review Digest†
0098-051X North Carolina. Division of Social Services. Statistical Journal†
0098-0579 Human Rights Organizations & Periodicals Directory
0098-0668 Keeping up with Kodaly Concepts in Music Education†
0098-0714 Railfan (Newton) see 0163-7266
0098-0722 Remote Computing Directory†
0098-0757 Alcohol, Tobacco and Firearms Bulletin
0098-079X Maine Prosecutor, Criminal Legislation Manual†
0098-0846 Wyoming. Water Quality Division. Wyoming State Plan
0098-0889 Radioassay News changed to Radioassay - Ligand Assay News
0098-0897 Resources in Education
0098-0900 Center for Hermeneutical Studies in Hellenistic and Modern Culture. Protocol Series of the Colloquies
0098-0919 H U L Notes see 0017-8136
0098-096X Directory of Occupational Education Programs in New York State†
0098-1109 Directory of U.S. Government Audiovisual Personnel†
0098-1133 Official Gazette of the United States Patent and Trademark Office. Patents
0098-1176 Chicago Tribune. Newspaper Index see 0195-6353
0098-1184 Index to the Christian Science Monitor
0098-1192 Los Angeles Times. Newspaper Index see 0195-6418
0098-1206 New Orleans Times-Picayune. Newspaper Index see 0195-640X
0098-1214 Asia Society. Annual Report
0098-1222 Insects of Virginia
0098-1230 Bicycle Bibliography see 0193-8584
0098-1273 Journal of Polymer Science. Polymer Physics Edition
0098-1354 Computers & Chemical Engineering
0098-1389 Social Work in Health Care
0098-1397 Marketing Economics Key Plants
0098-1435 California Employer
0098-1451 National Directory of Summer Internships for Undergraduate Students†
0098-1486 American Nurse changed to American Nurse Newspaper
0098-1508 Directory of Visiting Fulbright Scholars in the United States changed to Directory of Visiting Fulbright Scholars and Occasional Lecturers
0098-1516 Emergency Nurse Legal Bulletin

ISSN INDEX 1439

0098-1524 Emergency Physician Legal Bulletin
0098-1532 Medical and Pediatric Oncology
0098-1540 Microbiology (Washington)
0098-1575 Practical Guide to Individual Income Tax Return Preparation *changed to* 1040 Preparation
0098-1605 Anthropology Newsletter
0098-1613 Fodor's Japan and Korea *changed to* Fodor's Japan
0098-1613 Fodor's Japan and Korea *changed to* Fodor's Korea
0098-1648 Library of Congress Professional Association. Newsletter
0098-1664 Student Activities Programming *changed to* Campus Activities Programming
0098-1672 Year Book of Diagnostic Radiology
0098-1702 B O C A Basic Plumbing Code *changed to* B O C A Basic-National Plumbing Code
0098-1745 Motor's Auto Repair Manual *changed to* Motor Auto Repair Manual
0098-1753 Pension World
0098-1761 Pickin' *see* 0162-0401
0098-180X Hospital Infection Control
0098-1818 U.S. Bureau of Labor Statistics. Monthly Labor Review
0098-1850 Abstracts of Doctoral Dissertations in Anthropology†
0098-1923 University of Michigan Business Review†
0098-1974 Missouri Vital Statistics
0098-2067 Policy Analysis *see* 0276-8739
0098-2091 National Basic Intelligence Factbook *see* 0277-1527
0098-2113 Currents in Theology and Mission
0098-2121 De-Acquisitions Librarian *see* 0146-2679
0098-213X Forecast (Somerville)
0098-2164 Academy of Sciences of the U.S.S.R. Biology Bulletin
0098-2180 Emergency Product News *see* 0162-5942
0098-2199 John Berryman Studies†
0098-2202 Journal of Fluids Engineering
0098-2210 Metal Distribution
0098-2245 F & O S *see* 0160-4570
0098-2318 Beverage World (English Edition)
0098-2326 Hebert's Catalogue of Used Plate Number Singles *changed to* Hebert's Catalogue of Plate Number Singles
0098-2342 American Journal of Therapeutics & Clinical Reports - Cases & Comments†
0098-2377 American Group Practice Association Directory
0098-2393 International Bibliography of the Forensic Sciences
0098-2423 Sexual Law Reporter†
0098-2431 Institute for the Certification of Computer Professionals. Annual Report
0098-2466 Dun & Bradstreet's Guide to Your Investments
0098-2474 Explorations in Renaissance Culture
0098-2512 Washington Report on Health Legislation *changed to* Health Legislation
0098-2547 Fodor's Caribbean, Bahamas and Bermuda *changed to* Fodor's Caribbean
0098-2571 Automotive Engineering Magazine
0098-2601 Eighteenth Century Life
0098-261X Justice System Journal
0098-2644 Yearbook of Herpetology†
0098-2741 M G World *changed to* M G International
0098-275X Studies in Modern European History and Culture
0098-2784 Bibliography and Index of Geology
0098-2806 Fate of Drugs in the Organism; a Bibliographic Survey†
0098-2814 A-Ph-Armacy Weekly *changed to* Pharmacy Weekly
0098-2822 Art and Architecture Book Guide *see* 0360-2699
0098-2830 Federal Home Loan Bank of San Francisco. Annual Report.
0098-2857 National Bar Examination Digest
0098-2865 N A H B Journal-Scope *see* 0744-1193
0098-2873 Estate Planning Review
0098-2881 Council on Anthropology and Education Quarterly *see* 0161-7761
0098-2997 Molecular Aspects of Medicine
0098-3004 Computers & Geosciences
0098-3039 Urban Life *changed to* Journal of Contemporary Ethnography
0098-3063 I E E E Transactions on Consumer Electronics
0098-308X U.S. National Capital Planning Commission. Quarterly Review of Commission Proceedings
0098-311X Health Consequences of Smoking
0098-3209 Annual Report on Highway Safety Improvement Programs *see* 0277-2310
0098-3276 Fire Independent
0098-3292 Hospitality, Restaurant *see* 0147-9989
0098-3322 Yellow Book of Funeral Directors & Services
0098-3365 Phaedrus
0098-3381 New England Musician's Guide *see* 0362-2959
0098-342X Science Books & Films
0098-3446 Medical Electronics & Data *changed to* Medical Electronics
0098-3462 Health and Rehabilitative Library Services News *see* 0270-6717
0098-3470 Drug Enforcement
0098-3497 Current Governments Reports: Local Government Employment in Selected Metropolitan Areas and Large Counties†
0098-3500 A C M Transactions on Mathematical Software
0098-3519 Cruising World
0098-3527 Dulcimer Players News
0098-3543 American Association of Veterinary Laboratory Diagnosticians. Proceedings of Annual Meeting
0098-3551 I E E E Vehicular Technology Conference. Record
0098-356X Schwann-1, Records and Tapes *see* 0160-1571
0098-3608 Labor Rates for the Construction Industry
0098-3616 Medicaid Recipient Characteristics and Units of Selected Medical Services
0098-3624 Motor Truck Repair Manual *changed to* Motor Light Truck Tuneup & Van Repair Manual
0098-3675 Urban Anthropology Newsletter†
0098-3721 American College of Nurse-Midwifery. Bulletin *see* 0091-2182
0098-3748 American Medical Association Auxiliary. Bulletin *see* 0163-0512
0098-3772 Allegheny County Medical Society. Bulletin
0098-3780 A A A M Bulletin *changed to* A A A M Quarterly Journal
0098-3810 Academy of General Dentistry. Bulletin *see* 0363-6771
0098-3888 U.S. Department of Defense. Report of Secretary of Defense to the Congress
0098-3896 U.S. Treasury Department. Bureau of Government Financial Operations. Report on Foreign Currencies Held by the U.S. Government
0098-3942 Federal Communications Commission Reports
0098-4000 Agricultural Situation in Eastern Europe *changed to* World Agriculture Regional Supplement: Eastern Europe
0098-4027 United States. Defense Property Disposal Service. Annual Historical Summary†
0098-4035 U. S. Advisory Council on Historic Preservation. Report†
0098-4094 I E E E Transactions on Circuits and Systems
0098-4108 Journal of Toxicology and Environmental Health
0098-4132 State Directory of Higher Education Institutions and Agencies in Maryland†
0098-4485 Doctoral Dissertations on Asia
0098-4507 Sav-on-Hotels (Year)
0098-4558 J O M *see* 0148-6608
0098-4574 Woodwind World-Brass and Percussion *changed to* Woodwind, Brass & Percussion
0098-4582 Columbia Journal of Environmental Law
0098-4590 Florida Scientist
0098-4604 Index to U.S. Government Periodicals
0098-4612 Journal of Political Science (Clemson)
0098-4752 Condition of Education
0098-4760 Old Fort Log
0098-4779 Equipment Market Abstracts *see* 0161-8032
0098-4825 Utah Geological and Mineral Survey. Bulletin
0098-4833 Medical Law Letter for Physicians, Surgeons & Health Professionals
0098-4841 Copper State Bulletin
0098-4922 U.S. National Oceanic and Atmospheric Administration. Report to the Congress on Ocean Pollution, Overfishing, and Offshore Development
0098-4981 American Portuguese Society. Journal
0098-5058 Wyoming. Governor's Office of Highway Safety. Annual Report†
0098-5104 Energy Abstracts for Policy Analysis
0098-5139 Ohio. Advisory Council for Vocational Education. Annual Report
0098-5147 California Private School Directory
0098-5244 Joint Center for Urban Studies of M I T and Harvard University. Review *changed to* Joint Center for Housing Studies of M I T and Harvard University. Joint Center Review
0098-5252 Medical Bulletin (New York)
0098-5279 Data Book on Illinois Higher Education
0098-5368 Pennsylvania Chamber of Commerce. Directory of State, Regional and Commercial Organizations *changed to* Pennsylvania Chamber of Commerce. State & Regional Directory
0098-5376 Equipment & Technology International†
0098-5422 Spur
0098-5430 American Paint & Coatings Journal
0098-5449 Faith & Reason
0098-5481 Backstage T V Film/Tape & Syndication Directory
0098-5554 Current Christian Books. Authors and Titles *see* 0270-2347
0098-5562 Current Christian Books. Titles, Authors, and Publishers *see* 0270-2347
0098-5570 United States National Student Association. N S A Magazine†
0098-5589 I E E E Transactions on Software Engineering
0098-5597 Review of Education
0098-5619 A S T D Consultant Directory *changed to* A S T D Buyers Guide and Consultants Directory
0098-5651 Oklahoma Health Statistics
0098-5708 Hawaii. Criminal Injuries Compensation Commission. Annual Report.
0098-5716 Idaho. Department of Agriculture. Annual Report†
0098-5805 Medical College of South Carolina Bulletin *changed to* Auctus
0098-5910 Society of Wireless Pioneers. Yearbook†
0098-5929 Working Papers on Language Universals†
0098-5961 Law and Psychology Review
0098-597X Journal of Computer-Based Instruction
0098-5988 Basketball Digest
0098-6054 Romanian Sources
0098-6062 Index to St. Louis Newspapers†
0098-6070 A C R Bulletin
0098-6089 Advances in Neurochemistry
0098-6097 American Association of Industrial Nurses Journal *changed to* American Association of Occupational Health Nurses Journal
0098-6127 Artery
0098-6151 J A O A: Journal of the American Osteopathic Association
0098-616X Psychopharmacology Communications†
0098-6186 Connecticut State Industrial Directory *see* 0740-2937
0098-6194 Maine State Industrial Directory *see* 0740-2945
0098-6216 New Hampshire State Industrial Directory *see* 0740-2945
0098-6224 New Jersey State Industrial Directory *see* 0733-3684
0098-6232 Delaware Valley Regional Planning Commission. Biennial Report *changed to* Delaware Valley Regional Planning Commission. Annual Report
0098-6240 Medical Tribune and Medical News *see* 0279-9340
0098-6267 A W I S Newsletter *see* 0160-256X
0098-6275 S A L A L M Newsletter
0098-6283 Teaching of Psychology
0098-6291 Teaching English in the Two-Year College
0098-6305 E N R Directory of Design Firms
0098-6399 New Jersey. Department of Human Services. Community Mental Health Projects Summary Statistics†
0098-6445 Chemical Engineering Communications
0098-6453 E N R Directory of Contractors
0098-6461 Mideast Markets†
0098-647X Research Opportunities in Renaissance Drama
0098-6569 Catheterization and Cardiovascular Diagnosis
0098-6615 Ecology U S A
0098-6623 U.S. Center for Disease Control. Foodborne & Waterborne Disease Outbreaks. Annual Summary
0098-6631 Golden Gate Law Review *see* 0363-0307
0098-664X Directory of Music Faculties in Colleges & Universities U S and Canada
0098-6658 Microelectronics *see* 0363-8529
0098-6739 Kentucky Vital Statistics *changed to* Kentucky. Cabinet for Human Resources. Vital Statistics Report
0098-6755 Delaware State Minority Business Directory†
0098-678X Current Governments Reports: County Government Finances
0098-681X U.S. Federal Trade Commission. Quarterly Financial Report for Manufacturing, Mining and Trade Corporations
0098-6909 Hospital Formulary
0098-6925 Modern Pharmacology-Toxicology Series
0098-6976 Wisconsin Journal of Public Instruction†
0098-6984 Wyoming. Department of Health and Social Services. Annual Report
0098-7077 New Mexico. Bureau of Mines and Mineral Resources. Progress Report
0098-7093 Coldspring Journal†
0098-7107 Michigan State Dental Association *see* 0026-2102
0098-7115 Southern California State Dental Association. Journal *see* 0008-0977
0098-7174 Pennsylvania Police Criminal Law Bulletin
0098-7182 Flight Safety Facts and Reports *changed to* Flight Safety Digest
0098-7239 Issues in Media Management†
0098-7298 Journal of Applied Photographic Engineering *see* 0747-3583
0098-7301 Perspectives on Contemporary Literature
0098-7336 Bankruptcy Court Decisions
0098-7387 Arizona Commission on the Arts. Report to the Governor
0098-7409 New Jersey. Division of Banking. Annual Report *changed to* New Jersey. Department of Banking. Annual Report
0098-7484 J A M A: the Journal of the American Medical Association
0098-7522 Michigan State Medical Society. Journal *see* 0026-2293

1440 ISSN INDEX

0098-7530 Product Safety Letter
0098-7549 It's Happening
0098-7557 Downtown Malls *see* 0364-586X
0098-7565 Creative Child and Adult Quarterly
0098-7573 Devices & Diagnostics Letter
0098-7611 B A R-B R I Bar Review. Torts
0098-762X B A R - B R I Bar Review. Contracts
0098-7638 B A R - B R I Bar Review. Constitutional Law
0098-7689 Genealogy Digest
0098-7719 International Law Perspective
0098-7735 National Urban League Progress Report *changed to* National Urban League Annual Report
0098-7778 Package Printing and Diecutting *see* 0163-9234
0098-7786 Modern Paint and Coatings
0098-7840 Mississippi. State Game and Fish Commission. Annual Report to the Regular Session of the Mississippi Legislature *see* 0733-2017
0098-7875 Michigan. State Court Administrator. Annual Report.
0098-7913 Serials Review
0098-7921 Population and Development Review
0098-793X Allied Landscape Industry Member Directory *changed to* American Association of Nurserymen Directory for the Nursery Industry and Related Associations
0098-7956 Historical Evaluation and Research Organization. Combat Data Subscription Service†
0098-7972 L A D Newsletter (Library Administration Division) *see* 0888-4463
0098-7980 Bay Area Review Course. Legal Ethics *changed to* B A R - B R I Bar Review. Professional Responsibility
0098-7999 B A R - B R I Bar Review. Remedies
0098-8014 Shellfish Market Review and Outlook†
0098-8030 Michigan Germanic Studies
0098-8049 B A R-B R I Bar Review. Criminal Law
0098-8073 New Jersey. Division of Savings and Loan Associations. Annual Report *changed to* New Jersey. Department of Banking. Annual Report
0098-809X Center for the Study of the Presidency. Center House Bulletin *see* 0360-4918
0098-8111 U.S. President's Committee on Mental Retardation. Mental Retardation and the Law†
0098-8138 Connecticut. Judicial Department. Report
0098-8162 N C C C Chronicles†
0098-8170 Fish and Wildlife Reference Service Newsletter
0098-8219 Health Care Facilities†
0098-8227 Photographic Applications in Science, Technology and Medicine *see* 0360-7216
0098-8235 World Environment Report
0098-8243 Comprehensive Therapy
0098-826X Nebraska. Governor's Conference on Human Resource Development Report†
0098-8278 I A S S W Directory; Member Schools and Associations
0098-8332 California. Employment Data and Research Division. Taxable and Total Wages, Regular Benefits Paid, Employer Contributions Earned, and Average Covered Employment, by Industry†
0098-8340 Canto Libre†
0098-8359 Export-Import Bank of the United States. Cumulative Records†
0098-8383 Marine Science Communications *see* 0890-5460
0098-8421 American Medical Women's Association. Journal
0098-8448 Association for Physical and Mental Rehabilitation. Journal *see* 0002-8088
0098-8472 Environmental and Experimental Botany
0098-8510 Pennsylvania. Department of Public Welfare. Public Welfare Annual Statistics†
0098-8529 Rental Age
0098-8537 Homicide in California
0098-8553 Multidisciplinary Research
0098-8561 Idaho. Department of Health and Welfare. Bureau of Research and Statistics. Research Report *changed to* Idaho. Department of Health and Welfare. Research and Statistics Section. Quarterly Welfare Statistical Bulletin
0098-857X Scandinavian Review
0098-8588 American Journal of Law & Medicine
0098-8596 Biocharacterist *see* 0098-8618
0098-860X Birth and the Family Journal *see* 0730-7659
0098-8618 Health Evaluation Review†
0098-8642 Aquatic World†
0098-8650 Bike World†
0098-8669 Down River *see* 0161-052X
0098-8677 Gymnastics World†
0098-8685 Nordic World *see* 0273-642X
0098-8693 Self-Defense World†
0098-8707 Soccer World†
0098-8731 North Carolina Review of Business and Economics
0098-874X Florida Administrative Weekly
0098-8847 Earthquake Engineering and Structural Dynamics
0098-8855 Alternatives†
0098-8863 Exposure (New York)
0098-8871 Court Crier *changed to* Court Manager
0098-8898 Employee Relations Law Journal
0098-8901 Land Use Planning Abstracts†
0098-891X Lending Law Forum
0098-8928 Marketing California Pears for Fresh Market
0098-8936 Real Estate Directory of Manhattan
0098-8944 Savings Association Annals†
0098-8952 School Student and the Courts *see* 0164-3851
0098-8960 Upshaw Family Journal
0098-9010 73 Magazine for Radio Amateurs *see* 0883-234X
0098-9037 Country Music News
0098-9053 Linguistic Analysis
0098-9061 Quarterly Survey of Judicial Salaries in State Court Systems *changed to* Survey of Judicial Salaries
0098-907X Optics News
0098-910X U.S. International Trade Commission. Quarterly Report to the Congress and the East-West Foreign Trade Board on Trade Between the United States and the Nonmarket Economy Countries
0098-9134 Journal of Gerontological Nursing
0098-9142 R C Respiratory Care *see* 0730-8418
0098-9169 Assets Protection *see* 0749-1484
0098-9207 Qualified Remodeler
0098-9215 Radio Control Buyers Guide†
0098-924X Centerpoint†
0098-9258 Advances in Consumer Research
0098-9282 Zion's Herald (1976)
0098-9355 French Forum
0098-9363 Ascent (Urbana)
0098-9371 Children's Book Showcase. Catalog†
0098-9398 Media Guide International. Business Publications Edition *changed to* International Media Guides. Business/Professional Publications Edition
0098-9444 Biblical Archaeology Review
0098-9452 Chariton Review
0098-9487 I.A.J.R.C. Journal
0098-9495 Journal of Education Finance
0098-9509 Marxism and the Mass Media
0098-9517 Sabbath Watchman
0098-9533 National Journal of Criminal Defense†
0098-9541 New Jersey Orchard and Vineyard Survey
0098-955X Quest (Washington)
0098-9568 Real Estate Valuation Cost File†
0098-9576 Washington Energy Directory†
0098-9584 Journal of School Social Work†
0098-9665 Index to Scientific Reviews. Guide and Journal Lists†
0098-9673 Special Project Grants Awarded for Improvement in Nurse Training *see* 0095-2141
0098-972X U.S. National Institute of Mental Health. Mental Health Statistical Notes†
0098-9738 Aha'Ilono
0098-9770 Kentucky. Council on Public Higher Education. Origin of Enrollments, Accredited Colleges and Universities *changed to* Kentucky. Council on Higher Education. Origin of Kentucky College & University Enrollments
0098-9819 Current Physics Index
0098-9827 Educational opportunity Program Notes†
0098-9835 Guide to Professional Development Opportunities for College and University Administrators: Seminars, Workshops, Conferences, and Internships *see* 0197-128X
0098-9886 International Journal of Circuit Theory & Applications
0098-9983 California State Plan for Hospital and Health Center Construction *changed to* California State Health Plan
0099-0027 Professional Safety
0099-0035 National Bluegrass News
0099-0043 Engravers Journal
0099-0051 Bowling-Fencing Guide *changed to* N A G W S Guide. Bowling - Golf
0099-006X Council of State Governments. Southern Legislative Conference. Summary, Annual Meeting†
0099-0086 College and Research Libraries News *changed to* C & R L News
0099-0094 Environmental Geology *changed to* Environmental Geology and Water Sciences
0099-0108 Connecticut. Treasury Department. Annual Report
0099-0159 Goldenseal
0099-0167 Schwann-2, Records and Tapes *see* 0271-5783
0099-0205 N A A Where to Stay Book
0099-0213 Grant Information System†
0099-0248 C R C Critical Reviews in Food Science and Nutrition
0099-0256 Accreditation
0099-0264 Moons and Lion Tailes†
0099-0280 Moment
0099-0299 Nebraska Library Commission. Annual Report *changed to* Nebraska Library Commission. Library Directory
0099-0302 Pennsylvania. Department of Education. Special Education Programs-Services†
0099-0310 Professional Decorating and Coating Action *see* 0735-9713
0099-0329 Western Society for French History. Proceedings of the Annual Meeting
0099-0353 Commercial Fish Farmer and Aquaculture News *see* 0199-1388
0099-0361 Indian America†
0099-037X Progress in Behavior Modification
0099-0418 Bay Area Review Course. Conflicts of Law†
0099-0442 State and Local Construction Mileage *changed to* Nebraska. Department of Roads. Nebraska Selected Statistics
0099-0450 Plastics Manufacturing Capabilities in Mississippi†
0099-0604 Harmony (Harmony)
0099-0612 Guide to Occupational Safety Literature†
0099-0809 Index of Trademarks Issued from the U.S. Patent and Trademark Office
0099-085X Southeastern Library Network. Annual Report *changed to* Solinet. Annual Report
0099-0868 Common Ground (Hanover)†
0099-0876 Index to Pravda†
0099-0914 P I M S Monthly Petroleum Report *see* 0095-7356
0099-0973 Survey of Business†
0099-1015 County Year Book†
0099-1023 Indiana Public Management *changed to* Indiana University. School of Public and Environmental Affairs Review
0099-1031 Bar Leader
0099-1058 State Bar of Arizona. Newsletter *changed to* Arizona Bar Briefs
0099-1066 Agricultural Outlook
0099-1090 I F P A Communicator *changed to* Communicator (South Pasadena)
0099-1112 Photogrammetric Engineering and Remote Sensing
0099-1147 Advances in Pathobiology†
0099-118X Public Health Statistics, State of Oklahoma *see* 0098-5651
0099-121X I E E E/O S A Conference on Laser Engineering and Applications. Digest of Technical Papers *changed to* Conference on Lasers and Electro-Optics (Publications)
0099-1236 B A R - B R I Bar Review. Corporations
0099-1244 B A R - B R I Bar Review. Civil Procedure
0099-1260 Oregon. Employment Division. Annual Report†
0099-1279 Wyoming. Department of Environmental Quality. Annual Report
0099-1333 Journal of Academic Librarianship
0099-135X Detroit College of Law Review
0099-1414 Sage Annual Reviews of Communication Research
0099-1465 Southern University Law Review
0099-152X Internal Medicine News *see* 0274-5542
0099-1546 Progress in Anesthesiology
0099-1554 Training Directory of the Rehabilitation Research and Training Centers†
0099-166X Defense Reference
0099-1694 Desarrollo Nacional - Servicios Publicos
0099-1708 Journal of Design Automation and Fault-Tolerant Computing *see* 0888-224X
0099-1716 A/E Concepts in Wood Design†
0099-1759 Faith for the Family†
0099-1767 J E N
0099-1791 Luptonian
0099-1821 N C R R Bulletin *changed to* Journal of Resource Management and Technology
0099-183X Social Thought†
0099-1848 Collier Bankruptcy Cases
0099-1864 Martin Family Quarterly
0099-1872 Industrial Growth in Tennessee, Annual Report
0099-1929 Louisiana. Department of Agriculture. Analysis of Official Pesticide Samples; Annual Report
0099-2011 Meat Industry *changed to* Meat and Poultry Magazine
0099-2100 State Health Benefits Program of New Jersey. Annual Report
0099-2224 Management Research (Amherst)†
0099-2232 Lutheran New Yorker†
0099-2240 Applied and Environmental Microbiology
0099-2267 U.S. Department of Transportation. Office of University Research. Awards to Academic Institutions by the Department of Transportation
0099-2305 South Dakota. State Department of Public Welfare. Research and Statistics Annual Report
0099-2313 Sunset Ideas for Improving Your Home†
0099-2356 Mid-South Folklore *see* 0275-6013
0099-2364 Applied Radiology and Nuclear Medicine *see* 0160-9963
0099-2372 Cancer News Journal
0099-2399 Journal of Endodontics
0099-2410 Public Documents - State of Louisiana *changed to* State of Louisiana Public Documents
0099-2445 Financial Analysis of the Motor Carrier Industry
0099-2453 Human Resources Abstracts
0099-4480 Illuminating Engineering Society. Journal

ISSN INDEX 1441

0099-5010 Arkansas Agricultural Experiment Station. Research Series
0099-5851 Iowa State University Veterinarian
0099-6335 Research & Development Associates for Military Food and Packaging Systems. Activities Report
0099-8400 McIlvainea
0099-8745 Na Okika O Hawaii
0099-9059 Raptor Research *changed to* Journal of Raptor Research
0100-0039 Cientifica
0100-0195 Revista Medica do Estado do Rio de Janeiro
0100-0217 Revista Pernambucana de Desenvolvimento
0100-0233 Revista Baiana de Saude Publica
0100-039X Perspectiva Economica
0100-0551 Pesquisa e Planejamento Economico
0100-0705 Bibliografia Brasileira de Engenharia
0100-0756 Bibliografia Brasileira de Quimica e Quimica Tecnologica
0100-0829 Universidade Federal de Minas Gerais. Escola de Biblioteconomia. Revista
0100-0845 Centro de Pesquisas do Cacau. Boletin Tecnico
0100-0888 Revista Letras
0100-0977 Amazonia - Bibliografia
0100-123X Brazil. Servico Nacional de Levantamento e Conservacao de Solos. Boletim Tecnico
0100-1248 Navigator
0100-1299 Anuario Estatistico do Brasil
0100-1345 Sinopse Estatistica do Brasil
0100-1574 Cadernos de Pesquisa
0100-1876 Brazil. Biblioteca Nacional. Boletim Bibliografico
0100-1922 Brazil. Biblioteca Nacional. Anais
0100-1949 Bahia, Brazil (State). Centro de Pesquisas e Desenvolvimento. Boletim Tecnico†
0100-1965 Ciencia da Informacao
0100-204X Pesquisa Agropecuaria Brasileira
0100-2228 Sistemas†
0100-2538 Estudos Juridicos
0100-2716 Periodicos Brasileiros de Cultura *see* 0100-2767
0100-2767 Periodicos Brasileiros de Ciencias e Tecnologia†
0100-2910 Brazilian Economic Studies
0100-3143 Educacao e Realidade
0100-3151 Instituto Florestal. Boletim Tecnico
0100-3232 Revista Brasileira de Clinica e Terapeutica
0100-3283 Hansenologia Internationalis
0100-3364 Informe Agropecuario
0100-3399 Calendario de Eventos Tecnico-Cientificos Realizados no Brazil *changed to* Eventos em Politica Cientifica e Tecnologica
0100-350X Instituto de Tecnologia de Alimentos. Coletanea
0100-3593 Energia Nuclear e Agricultura
0100-3941 Rede Ferroviaria Federal. Lista de Artigos Selecionados
0100-3984 Radiologia Brasileira
0100-4158 Fitopatologia Brasileira
0100-4204 Fitossanidade
0100-4298 Agroanalysis
0100-4409 Sao Paulo, Brazil (State). Instituto de Economia Agricola. Informacoes Economicas *changed to* Informacoes Economicas
0100-4557 I P E F Publicacao Semestral
0100-4670 Ecletica Quimica
0100-4700 Natureza em Revista
0100-4743 Index Medicus Latinoamericano
0100-4859 Sociedade Brasileira de Zootecnia. Revista
0100-4948 Sao Paulo. Biblioteca Mario de Andrade. Boletim Bibliografico
0100-4964 Instituto de Tecnologia de Alimentos. Estudos Economicos. Alimentos Processados
0100-5065 Centro de Pesquisas do Cacau. Informe Tecnico
0100-5146 Universidade de Sao Paulo. Instituto Oceanografico. Publicacao Especial
0100-5162 Precos Medios do Boi Gordo e La
0100-5197 Universidade de Sao Paulo. Instituto Oceanografico. Relatorio de Cruzeiros
0100-5219 Precos Recebidos Pelos Agricultores
0100-5243 Universidade de Sao Paulo. Instituto Oceanografico. Relatorio Interno
0100-526X Prognostico
0100-5316 Prognostico Regiao Centro-Sul
0100-5405 Summa Phytopathologica
0100-560X Acompanhamento da Situacao Agropecuaria do Parana
0100-6045 Manuscrito
0100-6142 Data News
0100-6266 Bibliografia Brasileira de Odontologia
0100-655X Literatura Economica
0100-6800 Bibliografia Brasileira de Agricultura *changed to* Bibliografia Brasileira de Agricultura (year)
0100-7025 Novos Estudos C E B R A P
0100-7076 Revista de Cultura Vozes
0100-7157 Revista de Biblioteconomia de Brasilia
0100-7173 Informe Demografico
0100-722X Bibliografia de Publicacoes Oficiais Brasileiras
0100-7238 Brazil. Fundacao Nacional do Livro Infantil e Juvenil. Boletim Informativo
0100-7475 Brazil. Museu do Indio. Boletim. Etno-Historia
0100-7912 Geografia
0100-8064 Brazil. Centro Nacional de Pesquisa de Mandioca e Fruticultura. Circular Tecnica
0100-8102 Centro de Pesquisa Agropecuaria do Tropico Umido. Boletim de Pesquisa
0100-8153 Africa
0100-8161 Pesquisa em Andamento
0100-8226 Hanseniasis Letter†
0100-8404 Revista Brasileira de Botanica
0100-8455 Brazilian Journal of Genetics
0100-8501 Pesquisa Agropecuaria Pernambucana
0100-8633 Annuario Brasileiro de Ceramica
0100-8730 Anuario Estatistico do Estado de Sao Paulo
0100-879X Revista Brasileira de Pesquisas Medicas e Biologicas
0100-8854 Brazil. Centro Nacional de Pesquisa de Mandioca e Fruticultura. Comunicado Tecnico
0100-9591 Forum Educacional
0101-0352 Universidade Federal do Parana. Centro de Estudos Portugueses. Arquivos
0101-0484 Brazil. Museu do Indio. Boletim. Documentacao
0101-0530 Brazil. Museu do Indio. Boletim. Linguistica
0101-059X Didatica
0101-0646 Banco do Brasil. Annual Report
0101-0697 Banco de Bibliografias
0101-0794 C & I
0101-0972 Universidade Federal do Rio Grande do Sul. Instituto Central de Biociencias. Boletim *see* 0102-597X
0101-1049 Laudo
0101-1138 Tecnicouro
0101-1693 Sao Paulo. Coordenadoria de Saude Mental. Arquivos
0101-1774 Universidade Estadual Paulista. Revista de Odontologia
0101-1944 Naturalia
0101-2223 Nordeste; Analise Conjuntural
0101-2304 Som
0101-3173 Trans/Form/Acao
0101-322X Revista de Ciencias Biomedicas
0101-3300 Estudos C E B R A P *see* 0100-7025
0101-3459 Perspectivas
0101-3505 Revista de Letras
0101-3580 Boletim de Zoologia
0101-3645 Brazil Comercio e Industria
0101-3793 Revista de Ciencias Farmaceuticas
0101-4064 Estudos Ibero-Americanos *changed to* Revista de Estudos Ibero-Americanos
0101-4110 Estudos Economicos *see* 0101-4161
0101-4161 Revista Estudos Economicos
0101-4331 Informacao Psiquiatrica†
0101-4781 Revista do Medico†
0101-4854 Documentacao Amazonica
0101-5117 Boletim de Pesquisa
0101-5303 Estudos Tecnologicos
0101-5354 Acta Biologica Leopoldensia
0101-5400 Universidade Federal do Rio Grande do Norte. Departamento de Geologia. Boletim
0101-563X Revista Brasiliera de Mandioca
0101-5680 Brazil. Departamento Nacional de Obras Contra as Secas. Relatorio
0101-5818 Cadernos de Seguro
0101-6261 Micro Mundo
0101-630X C T A A. Boletim de Pesquisa
0101-6377 Informe Conjuntural
0101-658X Destaques†
0101-6636 Balanco Energetico Nacional
0101-6903 Camara Brasileira do Livro. Centro de Catalogaco na Fonte. Oficina de Livros: Novidades Catalogadas na Fonte
0101-7217 Revista DocPop
0101-7284 Revista do Exercito Brasileiro
0101-7616 Roessleria
0101-8353 Indicadores I B G E
0101-8469 Revista Brasileira de Neurologia
0101-9074 Historia
0101-9082 Geociencias
0101-9112 Antenna - Eletronica Popular
0101-9236 Centro Brasileiro de Pesquisas Fisicas. Monografias†
0101-9457 Revista de Geografia
0101-9635 Leopoldianum
0101-9872 Revista Ibero-Latino-Americana de Dermatologia
0102-0145 Mundo Mecanico
0102-0471 Associacao Mineira de Acao Educacional. Revista
0102-0692 Bahia, Brazil (State). Centro de Planejamento. Comercio Exterior da Bahia: Exportacao Segundo as Firmas e Mercadorias
0102-0811 Revista de Matematica e Estatistica
0102-0935 Arquivo Brasileiro de Medicina Veterinaria e Zootecnia
0102-129X Faculdade de Odontologia de Ribeirao Preto. Revista
0102-1397 Universidade Federal dc Uberlandia. Curso de Direito. Revista
0102-2253 Congresso Brasileiro de Economia e Sociologia Rural. Anais
0102-2636 Convivium
0102-3225 Guia Panrotas
0102-3292 Sociedade Paranaense de Matematica. Monografias
0102-3772 Psicologia: Teoria e Pesquisa
0102-4930 R F F S A. Anuario Estatistico
0102-5694 Sintese Ferroviaria Brasileira
0102-597X Universidade Federal do Rio Grande do Sul. Instituto de Biociencias. Boletim
0102-700X Acervo
0102-7085 Revista Analise & Conjuntura
0105-001X Acta Linguistica *see* 0374-0463
0105-0141 Odontologi
0105-0168 Automatik
0105-0192 Arv og Eje
0105-0257 Kopenhagener Beitraege zur Germanistischen Linguistik†
0105-0281 Stambog over Kvaeg af Roed Dansk Malkerace
0105-032X L O-Bladet
0105-0370 Dansk Psoriasis Tidsskrift
0105-0516 Veterinaermedicinsk Tidsskrift Information†
0105-0532 I E F Information
0105-0621 Odense University Studies in Psychiatry and Medical Psychology
0105-063X Danmarks Geologiske Undersoegelse. Aarbog
0105-0648 Danske Fysioterapeuter
0105-0656 Acta Pathologica et Microbiologica Scandinavica. Section B: Microbiology. Supplementum *see* 0108-0199
0105-0788 Denmark. Danmarks Statistik. Arbejdsmarkedsstatistik: Kvartalsvis Regionalstatistik
0105-0826 Mark og Montre
0105-0834 Dansk Pelsdyrblad *see* 0011-6424
0105-0877 Denmark. Danmarks Statistik. Maanedlig Ordre- og Omsaetningsstatistik for Industri
0105-0885 Groenlands Befolkning
0105-0907 Danmarks Tekniske Hoejskole. Fysisk Laboratorium 1. Report
0105-0982 Kontakt
0105-1024 Folk og Kultur†
0105-1040 Dansk Geologisk Forening. Meddelelser *see* 0011-6297
0105-1083 Denmark. Danmarks Statistik. Maanedlig Beskaeftigelses- og Loenstatistik for Industri
0105-1113 Rajneesh *see* 0107-7996
0105-1121 Retfaerd
0105-1164 Denmark. Danmarks Statistik. Skatter og Afgifter/Taxes and Duties. Oversigt
0105-1245 Dansk Dragesport *see* 0109-5595
0105-1377 Boernefilmkataloget
0105-1385 N O R D I C O M
0105-1393 Psykologisk Litteratur i Danske Forskningsbiblioteker
0105-1423 Historia Medicinae Veterinariae
0105-1466 Convivium (Copenhagen)†
0105-1504 Alrune
0105-1660 Harja
0105-1830 Almindelige Danske Laegeforening *changed to* Laegeforeningens Vejviser
0105-1873 Contact Dermatitis
0105-189X Odont *see* 0107-8097
0105-1903 Kommunistisk Tidsskrift *see* 0109-890X
0105-192X Teknisk Videnskabelig Forskning
0105-1938 Carlsberg Research Communications
0105-2071 Blixeniana†
0105-208X D S L Praesentationshaefte
0105-2233 Arbejderbevaegelsen i Danmark. Historisk og Aktuelt. Tilvaekst
0105-2373 Aktuel Elektronik
0105-2454 Welcome to Norway†
0105-2543 Denmark. Kungl Veterinaer og Landbohoejskole. Meddelelser
0105-2608 Vendsyssel Nu og Da
0105-2616 Information for Forskningsbiblioteker
0105-2691 Udkast
0105-2853 Danmarks Tekniske Hoejskole. Laboratoriet for Akustik. Publikation
0105-2861 Aarhus Universitet. Psykologisk Skriftseri
0105-287X Laegemiddelkataloget
0105-2896 Immunological Reviews
0105-3027 Technical University of Denmark. Acoustics Laboratory Report
0105-3035 Bidrag†
0105-3051 Kritiske Historikere
0105-3094 Miljoe-Projekter
0105-3167 Kongelige Bibliotek. Publikumsorienteringer
0105-3191 Dansk Teologisk Tidsskrift
0105-3213 International Council for the Exploration of the Sea. Cooperative Research Reports
0105-3507 Groenlands Geologiske Undersoegelse. Bulletin
0105-3531 Sociologisk Litteratur i Danske Forskningsbiblioteker
0105-4058 Handelshoejskolen i Aarhus. Institut for Finansiering og Kreditvaesen. Kompendium D
0105-4066 Denmark. Statens Planteavlsforsoeg. Sorter af Groensager†
0105-4090 Tidsskriftindeks for Skolebiblioteker
0105-4112 Aarhus Universitet. Slavisk Institut. Arbejdspapirer
0105-4120 Forest Tree Improvement
0105-4139 Koebenhavns Universitet. Institut for Social Medicin. Publikation
0105-4201 V og S Priser. Husbygning
0105-421X V og S Priser *changed to* V og S Priser. Anleg
0105-4236 Aarhus University. Botanical Institute. Reports

1442 ISSN INDEX

0105-4244 Landbrugets Samraad for Forskning og Forsoeg. Kortlaegning
0105-4260 Forsikring
0105-4503 I W G I A Documents
0105-452X Denmark. Planlaegningsraadet for Forskingen-Statens 6 Forskningsraed. Beretning *changed to* Denmark. Planlaegningsraadet for Forskningen Dandok-Statens 6 Forskningsraed. Beretning
0105-4538 Allergy
0105-4554 Danske Statslaan
0105-4570 Landinspektoeren
0105-4821 Koebenhavns Universitet. Institut for Religionshistorie. Skrifter
0105-4856 Danmarks Laererhoejskole. Geografisk Institut. Skrifter
0105-4880 Ny Elektronik
0105-5003 S T S Information *see* 0108-2655
0105-5046 Kongelige Bibliotek. Fagbibliografer
0105-5070 Denmark. Statens Filmcentral. Statistik over Udlejning af 16mm Film i Finansaaret
0105-5100 Nordisk Kulturelt Samarbejde
0105-5119 Technical University of Denmark. Institute of Roads, Transport and Town Planning. Papers and Reports
0105-5151 Sundhedsstyrelsen. Aarsberetning
0105-5194 Danmarks Tekniske Hoejskole. Instituttet for Landmaaling og Fotogrammetri. Meddelelse
0105-5216 Humaniora†
0105-533X Handelshoejskolen i Aarhus. Institut for Markedsoekonomi. Skriftserie E
0105-5399 Socialpaedagogen
0105-5526 Denmark. Statens Filmcentral. S F C, 16mm Film
0105-564X Roskilde Universitetsbibliotek. Skriftserie
0105-5801 Forteana
0105-5836 Denmark. Nyt fra Miljoestyrelsen
0105-5933 Fajabefa Nyt
0105-5992 Erhvervfremmende og Forbrugerpolitiske Foranstaltninger
0105-6077 Folkebiblioteksstatistik, Budgetter, Virksomhed
0105-614X Akademiet for de Tekniske Videnskaber. Lydteknisk Institut. Rapport
0105-6239 Pas Paa
0105-6255 Acta Campanologica
0105-6263 International Journal of Andrology
0105-6336 Hvide Lotus *see* 0108-9145
0105-6387 I W G I A Newsletter
0105-6433 Byhornet
0105-6441 Modelflyve nyt
0105-6492 N A A
0105-6514 Statens Planteavlsforsoeg. Meddelelse
0105-6603 D P A
0105-6611 Nordisk Tidsskrift for Rensning og Vask
0105-6654 Levnedsmiddelbladet-Supermarkedet
0105-6662 Erhvervsnoeglen
0105-6867 Episkopet
0105-6883 Denmark. Statens Husdyrbrugsforsog. Beretning
0105-6956 Rapport fra S T I K K
0105-709X Boernebladets Jul *changed to* Alle Boerns Jul
0105-7154 Historiske Studier fra Fyn†
0105-7162 Haandbog for Provinsens Distriksblade
0105-7340 Asien-Studier i Skandinavien *see* 0109-4203
0105-7405 Serie om Videnskabsforskning
0105-7421 Aalborg Universitetscenter. Instituttet for Bygningsteknik. Rapport
0105-7456 Kommunal Litteratur
0105-7480 Danske Laegemiddelstandarder
0105-7502 Forskning i Groenland-Tusaat
0105-7510 Orbis Litterarum
0105-7618 Sfinx
0105-7669 Contact with Denmark
0105-7723 Doeves Jul
0105-7855 Flygtning Bladet *see* 0108-1837
0105-7871 Danmarks Ingenioerakademi. Bygningsafdelingen. Dialog
0105-7936 Panda-Nyt *see* 0108-7991
0105-8010 Nordisk Kunst og Design†
0105-8045 Dansk Musikfortegnelse
0105-8118 Hikuin
0105-8134 Goer det Selv Indeks
0105-8185 Aalborg Universitetscenter. Instituttet for Bygningsteknik. Note
0105-8215 Kongelige Bibliotek. Specialhjaelpmidler
0105-824X Aarhus Universitet. Geologisk Institut. Geoskrifter
0105-8258 Aarhus Universitet. Geologisk Institut. Geokompendier
0105-8266 Aarhus Universitet. Geologisk Institut. Georapporter
0105-8282 Ergoterapeuten
0105-8339 Roskilde Kommune. Statistikken
0105-8347 Jeg Arbejder Med
0105-8355 Zise
0105-8401 Currero International de Interlingua
0105-8509 Amstkommunernes Oekonomi
0105-8517 Aarhus Universitet. Matematisk Institut. Datalogisk Afdeling. DAIMI PB
0105-8525 Aarhus Universitet. Matematisk Institut. Datalogisk Afdeling. DAIMI MD
0105-8533 Aarhus Universitet. Matematisk Institut. Datalogisk Afdeling. DAIMI FN
0105-8541 Danmarks Tekniske Hoejskole. Instituttet for Teleteknik. Rapport I T
0105-8630 Zoneterapeut Forening af 28. Februar 1976 *see* 0109-0895
0105-8738 Trae og Industri
0105-8819 Nyt fra Nationalmuseet
0105-8827 Roskilde Universitetscenter. Institut for Samfundsoekonomi og Planlaegning. Research Report
0105-8924 Lovbibliotek
0105-9041 Grafiske Funktionaerers Landesforening. Medlemsblad *see* 0109-0879
0105-9068 Kvindestudier†
0105-9106 Nordisk Julemaerke Katalog
0105-9122 Forbrugerindeks
0105-9173 Register over Autoriserede Laboratorier
0105-9211 Fisk og Hav
0105-9254 Koebstadsmuseet Den Gamle By
0105-9289 Dansk Paediatrisk Selskab. Aarbog
0105-9327 Holarctic Ecology
0105-936X Koebenhavns Bymuseum†
0105-9386 Kemisk Analyse af Mineraler og Bjergarter
0105-9416 Haandvaerket and Maskinen
0105-9459 Urban and Regional Research in Danmark
0105-9475 Select Bibliography of Danish Works on the History of Towns Published
0105-9483 D U E Notat†
0105-9556 Skolebiblioteket
0105-9602 Denmark. Planstyrelsen. Regionplanorientering
0105-9629 Installations Nyt
0105-9645 Universitetets Statistiske Institut. Research Report
0105-9696 Geodaetisk Institut. Meddelelse
0105-9785 Hjerteforeningen
0105-9807 Denmark. Statens Husdyrbrugsforsoeg. Indeks
0105-9815 Dansk Amator Astronomi *see* 0107-2862
0105-9858 Frederiksborgmuseet. Aarsskrift
0105-9882 Landsudvalget for Fjerkrae. Meddelelse
0105-9963 Anglica et Americana
0105-9998 New Religious Movements Up-Date *see* 0108-7029
0106-0031 Danske Hedeselskab. Forsoegsvirksomheden. Beretning
0106-0104 Produktions Nyt
0106-0104 Produktions Nyts Leverandoerregister
0106-0120 Dansk Fagpresse
0106-0147 Danmarks Tekniske Hoejskole. Afdelingen for Baerende Konstruktioner. Forelaesningsnotat F†
0106-0279 Hjemkundskab
0106-035X Novelleregister
0106-0392 Haandbog i Dansk Politik†
0106-0406 Dansk Betonforening. Publikation†
0106-0430 Loegumkloster-Studier
0106-0449 Filosofiske Studier
0106-0465 Aarbog for Folkeskolen
0106-0473 Auto Nyt
0106-0473 Auto Nyts Leverandoerregister
0106-0481 Kongelige Danske Videnskabernes Selskab. Historisk-Filosofiske Meddelelser
0106-0546 Ugeskrift for Jordbrug
0106-0627 1066 Tidsskrift for Historisk Forskning
0106-0724 Danmarks Transport-Tidende
0106-0805 C D R Project Paper
0106-0821 Roskilde Universitetscenter. Lingvistgruppen. Rolig-Papir
0106-0864 Denmark. Jordbrugsoekonomisk Institut. Undersoegelse†
0106-0872 G I P
0106-0880 Anthropological Analyses
0106-0899 Groenland i Tal
0106-0953 Paedagogik†
0106-1003 International Council for the Exploration of the Sea. Annales Biologiques
0106-102X Mediaeval Scandinavia Supplements
0106-1046 Meddelelser om Groenland, Geoscience
0106-1054 Meddelelser om Groenland, Bioscience
0106-1062 Meddelelser om Groenland, Man & Society
0106-1100 Kompass Select Export. Business Services
0106-1119 Kompass Select Export. Chemical Industry
0106-1135 Kompass Select Export. Building Construction, Contractors
0106-1143 Kompass Select Export. Electrical and Electronic Equipment
0106-1151 Kompass Select Export. Food Industry
0106-116X Kompass Select Export. Furniture
0106-1178 Kompass Select Export. Scientific and Industrial Instruments, Watch Industry
0106-1186 Kompass Select Export. Machine Industry
0106-1194 Kompass Select Export. Metal Products
0106-1208 Kompass Select Export. Paper Industry, Graphic Arts
0106-1216 Kompass Select Export. Rubber Industry, Plastics Industry
0106-1224 Kompass Select Export. Textiles, Clothing and Footwear
0106-1232 Kompass Select Export. Transport Equipment
0106-1240 Kompass Select Export. Wood Industry
0106-1275 Laegeforeningens Medicinfortegnelse
0106-1283 Varnaes Birk
0106-1291 Denmark. Jordbrugsoekonomisk Institut. Landbrugets Oekonomi
0106-1313 Slavica Othiniensia
0106-1348 ICO-Iconographisk Post
0106-1356 Ny Korea *see* 0108-8467
0106-1372 Commission for Scientific Research in Greenland. Newsletter
0106-147X Dansk Artikelindeks: Aviser og Tidsskrifter
0106-1488 Dansk Anmeldelsesindeks
0106-1585 Plast Nyt
0106-1607 International Journal of Andrology. Supplement
0106-164X Elektronik Nyt
0106-1658 Agro Nyt†
0106-1666 Virksomheds Nyt
0106-1720 Plast Panorama Scandinavia
0106-1763 Reproduction & Emancipation *changed to* Gloder
0106-1852 Trafikoekonomiske Enhedspriser
0106-1860 Antikvariske Studier
0106-1887 Denmark. Statens Husholdningsraad. Pjecer
0106-1895 Denmark. Statens Husholdningsraad. Tekniske Meddelelser
0106-1917 Moelposen
0106-1925 Touring Nyt
0106-1941 Danske Byggemarkeder
0106-1968 Tropical Bands Survey
0106-1992 Serie om Fremmedsprog
0106-2085 Fortegnelse over Danske Aktieselskaber, Anpartsselskaber, Filialer af Udenlandske Selskaber samt over Foreninger
0106-2093 Forsvar: Militaer Kritisk Magasin
0106-2107 Information om Skolan i Norden *see* 0109-8985
0106-214X Romansk Filmklub. Medlemsblad *see* 0109-0631
0106-2212 Odense Universitet. Laboratorium for Folkesproglig Middelalderlitteratur. Mindre Skrifter
0106-2220 Aarbog for Svendborg e Omegns Museum
0106-2301 Scandinavian Psychoanalytic Review
0106-2328 Forbrugerombudsmanden. Beretning
0106-2344 Statistik for Hovedstadsregionen
0106-2484 Sekvens
0106-2530 Folkeskolen i de Enkelte Kommuner
0106-2557 Forsoegsanlaeg Risoe. Aarsberetning *changed to* Forskningscenter Risoe. Aarsberetning
0106-2573 Forskningslaboratoriet for Frugt og Groentindustri. Aarsberetning
0106-259X Denmark. Statens Planteavlsudvalg. Sorter af Landbrugsplanter†
0106-2689 Denmark. Jordbrugsoekonomisk Institut. Meddelelse†
0106-2697 Skive-egnens Jul
0106-2735 Dansk Forsikrings Aarbog
0106-2778 Roskilde Universitetscenter. Department of Geography, Social Economics and Computer Science. Meddelelser
0106-2840 Denmark. Forsoegsanslaeg Risoe. Risoe-R
0106-2875 Greenland in Figures
0106-2891 Denmark. Ministeriet for Groenland. Statistisk Kontor. Meddelelser *see* 0900-2510
0106-2905 Statens og Kommunernes Budgetter
0106-2956 Krigsplan
0106-3006 Denmark. Finansministeriet. Budgetdepartmentet. Budgetredegoerelse
0106-3014 U Vejviser
0106-3022 Guide i Jylland
0106-3030 Architectura
0106-3081 Atomkraft†
0106-312X Denmark. Statens Vejlaboratorium. Laboratorierapport
0106-3278 Film†
0106-3324 Fabrik og Bolig
0106-343X M S T Luft. A
0106-3537 Roskilde Universitetscenter. Department of Geography, Social Economics and Computer Science. Research Reports
0106-3545 Roskilde Universitetscenter. Department of Geography, Social Economics and Computer Science. Kompendium
0106-357X Combined Simulation
0106-3618 Koebenhavns Universitet. Geografisk Centralinstitut. Laboratorium for Geomorfologi
0106-3626 Denmark. Bibliotekstilsynet Informerer
0106-3642 Denmark. Jordbrugsoekonomisk Institut. Memorandum†
0106-3677 Vandteknik
0106-3715 Bygningsstatiske Meddelelser
0106-3812 Landbrugseksporten
0106-3839 Kobenhavns Statistiske Aarbog
0106-3871 Scandinavian Institute of Asian Studies. Annual Newsletter
0106-3952 U T *changed to* Eksport
0106-4002 Korrosionscentralen. Rapport†
0106-407X Environmental Radioactivity in Denmark
0106-4177 Hvem, Hvad, Hvor
0106-4339 European Journal of Respiratory Diseases
0106-4347 European Journal of Respiratory Diseases. Supplementum
0106-4355 Gas-Teknik
0106-4363 Handelshoeskolen i Aarhus. Institute for Erhvervs- og Samfundsbeskrivelse. Skriftserie C
0106-441X A R K
0106-4428 Biophon†
0106-4452 Soenderjyske Arboeger
0106-4479 Moeldrup Kommunes Lokalhistoriske Arkiv. Aarsskrift
0106-4487 Dolphin

ISSN INDEX 1443

0106-4517 Faerdselsorientering
0106-4622 Dansk Udsyn
0106-4711 Dansk Elforsyning
0106-4762 Denmark. Forskningenssekretariatet. Forskning og Samfund
0106-4819 Actualitates *see* 0901-2273
0106-4878 Kroghs Register *see* 0108-7878
0106-4908 Denmark. Statsskattedirektoratet og Ligningsraadet. Meddelelser 1. Haefte: Indkomst- og Formueansaettelser
0106-4932 Forbrugerklagenaevnet. Aarsberetning
0106-4940 Hymnologiske Meddelelser
0106-4967 Denmark. Jordbrugsoekonomisk Institut. Aarsberetning
0106-4991 Historisk Tidsskrift (Copenhagen)
0106-5017 Souvenir Normand *changed to* Annuaire Souvenir Normand
0106-5076 Is- og Besejlingsforholdene i de Danske Farvande i Vinteren
0106-5114 Herefordbladet *see* 0108-9692
0106-5122 Marinehistorisk Tidsskrift
0106-519X Denmark. Jordbrugsoekonomisk Institut. Beretning†
0106-5327 Rougsoe Lokalhistoriske Forening. Aarsskrift
0106-5343 Dansk Presse
0106-5351 Lokalhistorisk Journal
0106-5440 Helsingoer som Fotografen saa det
0106-553X Dana
0106-5726 Dansk Natur-Dansk Skole
0106-5815 Classica et Mediaevalia
0106-5823 Undervisningsmidler for Folkeskolen. Oversigtskatalog
0106-5866 Kulturgeografiske Haefter
0106-5912 Aarbog for Arbejderbevaegelsens Historie
0106-5920 Roskilde Universitetscenter. Department of Geography, Social Economics and Computer Science. Working Papers
0106-5955 Undervisningsmidler for Gymnasiet og Hf
0106-5963 Undervisningsmidler for Erhvervsuddannelserne
0106-5971 Undervisningsmidler for Ungdoms- og Voksenundervisning
0106-6072 Brandvaern
0106-6137 Fra Vestsjaellands Museer†
0106-6145 Noerre-Alslev Kommune. Lokalhistorisk Arkiv. Aarsskrift
0106-6218 Praesteforeningens Blad
0106-6234 Fjernvarmen
0106-6242 Tekster fra I M F U F A
0106-6366 D C A M M Report
0106-6463 Meteorologisk Aarbog
0106-648X Udenlandske Tidsskriftanalyser
0106-6579 Pressens Arbog
0106-6625 Udenlandske Litteratur i Danske Folkebiblioteker. Boerneboger
0106-6633 Udenlandsk Litteratur i Danske Folkebiblioteker Faglitteratur
0106-6641 Udenlandsk Litteratur i Danske Folkebiblioteker. Skoenlitteratur
0106-665X Skuespilregister
0106-6668 Filosofi og Videnskabsteori paa Roskilde Universitetscenter
0106-6706 D S I Notat
0106-6714 Opdraettervejviseren
0106-6838 Denmark. Arbejdstilsynet. Rapport
0106-6927 Sporvejsmuseet Skjoldenaesholm. Aarsberetning
0106-6935 I C E S Oceanographic Data Lists and Inventories
0106-7052 Beretning over Arbejdsmiljoefondets Virksomhed
0106-7125 Orienting om Skoleaaret
0106-7222 University of Copenhagen. Physics Labortory II. Report
0106-7265 Nordeuropaeisk Mejeri-Tidsskrift *see* 0109-3207
0106-729X Boernebibliotekskatalog. Grammofonplader Kassetteband
0106-7338 Svineavl og -Produktion i Danmark
0106-7362 Kommuneplanorientering
0106-7389 Denmark. Vejdirektoratet. Trafikrapport *changed to* Denmark. Vejdirektoratet. Oekonomisk-Statistisk Afdeling. Trafikrapport
0106-7451 Svampe
0106-7478 Askov Laerlinge
0106-7508 Fred og Sikkerhed *see* 0109-2855
0106-7540 Stopinterviewanalyse
0106-7575 Katalog for Skolebiblioteker. Forfatterkatalog *see* 0106-7591
0106-7583 Katalog for Skolebiblioteker. Titelkatalog
0106-7591 Katalog for Skolebiblioteker. Emnekatolog
0106-7672 Teater i Danmark
0106-7699 Gallup Media & Marketing Index. Konsumentvaremarkedet *changed to* Gallup Media & Marketing Index
0106-7729 Statistik om Praevention og Aborter
0106-7737 Landscentralen for Undervisningsmidler. Baandcentralen. Baandkatalog
0106-7745 Undervisningsmidler til Specialundervisning
0106-7753 A V Katalog
0106-7826 Arbejdsmarkedsoversigt
0106-7990 Boernefilmkataloget. Supplement
0106-8024 Skatten
0106-8113 Planteavlsarbejdet i de Landoekonomiske Foreninger
0106-8172 Anmeldelser i Paedagogiske Tidsskrifter
0106-8180 Filmregistret
0106-8199 Boernebogsserier Tegneserier
0106-8229 Fra Bov Museum
0106-8237 Kongelige Veterinaer- og Landbohoejskole. Jordbrugsteknisk Institut. Meddelelse
0106-8253 Romanserier og Selvbiografiske Serier
0106-8261 Kongelige Veterinaer og Landbohoejskole. Skovbruginstitutet. Meddelelser
0106-8334 Tidevandstabeller for Danmark
0106-8342 Tidevandstabeller for Faeroerne
0106-8377 Fauna Entomologica Scandinavica
0106-8393 Gartner Tidende
0106-8490 Handelshoejskolen i Aarhus. Skriftserie
0106-8539 Skoven
0106-8563 Koebenhavns Universitet. Institut for Anvendt og Matematisk Lingvistik. Skrifter
0106-8598 Statsfroekontrollen. Beretning
0106-8628 Institut for Graenseregionsforskning. Arbejdspapir
0106-8709 Odense Universitet. Erhvervoekonomisk Institut. Skrifter†
0106-8725 Brandmanden
0106-8822 Faaborg-Aarbogen
0106-8857 Statens Husdyrbrugsforsoeg. Meddelelse
0106-8881 V V S Installatoeren
0106-8911 Roskilde Universitetscenter. Institut for Socialvidenskab. Instituttets Skriftserie†
0106-8989 Liber Academiae Kierkegaardiensis Annuarius
0106-8997 Aarhus Universitet. Matematisk Institut. Elementaerafdeling
0106-9039 Denmark. Nordisk Statistisk Sekretariat. Tekniske Rapporter
0106-9047 Aarhus Universitet. Geografisk Institut. Notat
0106-9128 Dansk Biavl *see* 0108-3139
0106-9136 Toget *see* 0107-6310
0106-925X Dans
0106-9276 Kartoffel-Nyt
0106-9306 Danmarks Tekniske Hoejskole. Matematisk Institut. Mat - P R
0106-9411 Deruda *see* 0109-3851
0106-9446 Tvaerfagligt Forum for Sundhedspaedagogik og -Politik. Nyhedsbrev *see* 0107-3575
0106-9535 Driftsoekonomi
0106-9543 Liver
0106-9551 Seminariehaandbogen
0106-9586 Gospel Time
0106-9616 Raethinge-Posten
0106-9683 Arbejdsulykker. Aarsstatistik
0106-9691 Boernebibliotekskatalog. Boeger z Tidsskrifter Forfatterkatalog
0106-9705 Boernebibliotekskatalog. Boeger z Tidsskrifter Titelkatalog
0106-9713 Boernebibliotekskatalog. Boeger z Tidsskrifter Emnekatalog
0106-9748 Lokalhistorisk Forening for Sejlflod Kommune
0106-9780 Udenrigshandelen Fordelt paa Varer og Lande/External Trade by Commodities and Countries
0106-9802 Denmark. Danmarks Statistik. Kommunale Finanser /Local Government Finance
0106-9918 Aestetik
0106-9969 Aarhus Universitet. Matematisk Institut. Datalogisk Afdeling. DAIMI IR
0106-9977 Danmarks 200 Stoerste Virksomheder
0106-9985 Danmarks 2000 Stoerste Virksomheder
0107-0061 Endelig Betaekning over Statsregnskabet for Finansaaret
0107-0134 Danmarks Tekniske Hoejskole. Institutet for Veje, Trafik og Byplan. Notat
0107-0258 U F O Aspekt *see* 0108-3503
0107-0304 Aarsskrift for Toender Landbrugsskole
0107-0363 Selskabet for Dansk Fotografi. Aarskatalog†
0107-0371 Denmark. Danmarks Statistik. Valgene til de Kommunale og Amtskommunale Raad
0107-0398 Tidevandstabeller for Groenland
0107-0436 Dansk Historisk Aarsbibliografi
0107-0452 Copenhagen Political Studies Abstracts
0107-0479 Blickpunkt Daenemark†
0107-0487 Dansk Udenrigspolitisk Aarbog
0107-0517 Denmark. Statens Levnedsmiddelinstitut. Publikation
0107-0525 M T M
0107-0533 Data Center - Nyt *see* 0109-4157
0107-055X Nordic Journal of Botany
0107-0606 M C Revyen
0107-0614 Vejdatalaboratoriet. Rapport
0107-0665 Civilforsvar
0107-072X Bjerg-Posten. Medlemsblad
0107-0851 Dansk Arbejdsgiverforening. Statistikken
0107-0886 D I F Flyaarbog
0107-0894 Nye Boeger om Film/TV
0107-0908 D D Bulletin *changed to* D D Bulletin
0107-0916 Litteraturtolkninger
0107-0932 Denmark. Jordfordelingssekretariatet. Aarsberetning†
0107-0940 Filmatiserede Boeger
0107-0967 Denmark. Danmarks Statistik. Varestatistik for Industri. Series A
0107-0975 Denmark. Danmarks Statistik. Varestatistik for Industri. Series B
0107-0983 Denmark. Danmarks Statistik. Varestatistik for Industri. Series C
0107-0991 Denmark. Danmarks Statistik. Varestatistik for Industri. Series D
0107-1033 Filmsaesonen: Dansk Filmfortegnelse
0107-105X Denmark. Danmarks Statistik. Indkomster og Formuer /Income and Property Assessments
0107-1076 Social Aarbog†
0107-1165 Laegestillinger og Sengepladser paa Institutioner
0107-1173 Personale- og Oekonomistik for Sygehusvaesenet
0107-1181 Tal og Data, Medicin og Sundhedsvaesen
0107-119X Bygge- og Boligpolitiske Oversigt
0107-122X Haandbog for D J V K: Agronomer, Forstkandidater, Hortonomer, Licentiater
0107-1238 Lyboen
0107-1270 Take Off-Trafik og Turisme
0107-1300 Landboforeningernes Driftsoekonomiske Virksomhed, Regnskabresultater, Kalenderaar
0107-136X Vore Kunstnere
0107-1378 Odense University Classical Studies
0107-1475 Arnamagnaean Institute and Dictionary. Bulletin
0107-1491 Forlagsseriekatalog for Boerne- og Skolebiblioteker
0107-1572 Almennyttige Boligselskabers Regnskaber
0107-1629 Uddannelse Institutioner over Grundskoleniveau
0107-1637 Danmarks Laererhoeskole. Institut for Paedagogik og Psykologi. Testsamling
0107-1742 Odense Universitetsbibliotek. Specialer og Prisopgaver
0107-1769 Haandarbejdets Fremme
0107-1777 Kaelvningsstatistik†
0107-1815 Denmark. Miljoestyrelsen. Oversigt over Godkendte Bekaempelsesmidler
0107-184X Soemaendenes Idraets Klub
0107-1866 Byggeri
0107-1971 Slaegtsbladet
0107-2013 Vedroerende Udviklingen i de Europaeiske Faellesskaber. Beretning
0107-2064 Organisatoriske Fragmenter
0107-2072 Spansk Skandinavisk Forening. Medlemsinformation
0107-2188 Nordschleswig
0107-2242 Dansk Squash
0107-2366 Romanske Stenarbejder
0107-2390 Modersmaal Selskabet. Aarbog
0107-2412 Oversaettelser af Dansk Lovgivning med Alfabetisk Register. Fortegnelse
0107-2455 Havneguide for Fritidssejlere
0107-248X Teaterraadets Indstilling
0107-2560 A S F-Dansk Folkehjaelp. Aarsskrift
0107-2587 Internationalen
0107-2668 Epilepsi
0107-2676 Themata
0107-2692 K M D-Plannyt
0107-2722 Denmark. Orientering fra Miljoestyrelsen
0107-2757 Fra Bjerringbro Kommune
0107-2854 Jysk Arkaeologisk Selskabs. Skrifter
0107-2862 Astronomi & Rumfart
0107-2900 Skeptika *see* 0901-201X
0107-2951 Denmark. Statens Kunstfond. Beretning
0107-301X D S - Kontakt
0107-3028 Skolestart
0107-3052 Race Walking World Statistics
0107-3060 Psykologisk Laboratorium. Forskningsrapport
0107-3095 Denmark. Danmarks Statistik. Kreditmarkedsstatistik. *see* 0108-5476
0107-3109 Kontaktudvalget for Dansk Maritim Historie- og Samfundsforskning. Aarsbibliografi
0107-3117 Faellesraadet Vedroerende Mineraliske Raastoffer i Groenland. Beretning
0107-3168 Dags Data
0107-3265 Koebenhavns Universitets Slaviske Institut. Rapporter
0107-3362 Fodplejeren
0107-3435 Uddannelsesnoeglen
0107-3532 Project†
0107-3575 Hel
0107-3591 Kultur og Samfund
0107-363X Arken
0107-3680 Profil
0107-3699 K G Orientering *see* 0107-3680
0107-3702 Jernbanen
0107-3729 Fugle
0107-3737 Emballageinstituttets Leverandoerhaandbog *changed to* Leverandoerhaandbogen (Skovlunde)
0107-3761 Teknologi og Effektivitet
0107-377X Undervisningsmaterialer til Begynder- og Specialundervisning
0107-3796 Vandrerhjem
0107-380X Oplagsbulletin
0107-3818 Stambog
0107-3885 Skatten. Erhverv
0107-3893 Politihistorisk Selskab. Aarsskrift
0107-3931 El & Energi
0107-3982 Luftskibet†
0107-4148 Fodspecialisten *see* 0107-3362
0107-4156 Befolkningens Forbrug af Psykiatriske Sengepladser
0107-4172 Broken Strings *see* 0109-2480
0107-4202 O - Posten
0107-4229 Dansk Massekommunikationsforskning†
0107-4237 Shan
0107-4296 Undervisningsmidler for Folkeskolen. Nyhedskatalog
0107-430X Specifications of Mineral Concessions and Licenses in Greenland

ISSN INDEX

ISSN	Title
0107-4350	Adresseloese Postforsendelser
0107-4369	Adresserede Brevforsendelser
0107-4393	Danskerne
0107-4415	Bio-Nyt
0107-4431	Dansk Digtregister
0107-444X	Arbejdsformidlingsstatistik for Erhvervshaemmede
0107-4458	Handelshoejskolen i Koebenhavn. Institut for Organisation og Arbejdssociologi. H D Studiet i Organisation
0107-4466	D E K Haandbog
0107-4504	Folkehoejskoler
0107-4520	Arken-Tryk
0107-4539	Danske Vinselskab see 0109-5684
0107-4547	D A F i Tal
0107-4598	Kursuskoordineringsudvalgets Oversigt over Kurser for Medarbejdere i den Sociale Sektor†
0107-4601	Small Investors' Newsletter
0107-461X	Landbrugets Maskinoversigt
0107-4628	Arbejderbevaegelsens Bibliotek og Arkiv. Bibliografiske Serie
0107-4636	Laes om
0107-4652	Denmark. Statens Paedagogiske Forsoegscenter. Arbejdsbeskrivelse
0107-4733	Specialarbejderkurser
0107-4806	Navigatoer
0107-4849	Fra Bornholms Museum
0107-4857	Dansk Orgelaarbog
0107-4911	Skulptur Veksoelund
0107-492X	Monopoltilsynets Aarsberetning
0107-4946	Matieres see 0109-2820
0107-4954	Sygehusvaesenet
0107-4989	Paedagogisk Bibliograf
0107-4997	Oversigt over Rapporter m.m. Vedroerende Vandkraftundersoegelser i Groenland
0107-5047	Sociale Ydelser, Hvem, Hvad, og Hvornaar
0107-5055	Aalborg Stiftsbog
0107-5071	Befolkningen i Koebenhavn i Januar
0107-508X	Sygehusklassifikation og Kommunekoder
0107-5098	Kommunal Budgetredegoerelse
0107-511X	Denmark. Direktoratet for Kriminalforsorgen. Kriminalforsorgen changed to Kriminalforsorgens Aarsberetning
0107-5144	Biologiske Udvikling i Utterslev Mose, Koebenhavn med Henblik Specielt paa Fuglebestandene†
0107-5152	Denmark. Statens Uddannelsesstoette. Regelsamling for Stoetteaaret
0107-5179	Sikkerhedsmaessig Vurdering og Prioritering af Mindre Anlaegsarbejder paa Hovedlandeveje
0107-5187	Bog og Baand
0107-5209	Gode Lydboeger
0107-5217	Computerworld
0107-5225	Nye Verdener
0107-5233	Instituttet for Matematisk Statistik og Operationsanalyse. Working Paper
0107-5276	Ikkevold
0107-5330	Modelbanen
0107-5357	Denmark. Jordbrugsoekonomisk Institut. Rapport
0107-5373	Teknisk Tidsskrift for Textil og Beklaedning
0107-539X	Slaegt og Stavn
0107-5403	D D V - Analysen
0107-5411	Effektiv Kontoradministration
0107-5446	Jul i Frederikssund
0107-5462	Odense Universitetsbibliotek. Tidsskriftkatalog
0107-535X	I W G I A Boletin
0107-5586	Casesamling
0107-5608	D P B's Litteratur om Boerns og Unges Laesning
0107-5624	Euro Laerer Nyt
0107-5675	Denmark. Jordbrugsoekonomisk Institut. Serie A: Landbrugets Regnskabsstatistik
0107-5683	Denmark. Jordbrugsoekonomisk Institut. Serie B: Oekonomien i Landbrugets Driftsgrene
0107-5691	Denmark. Jordbrugsoekonomisk Institut. Serie C: Landbrugets Prisforhold
0107-5705	Denmark. Jordbrugsoekonomisk Institut. Serie D: Gartneri-Regnskabsstatistik
0107-590X	Register over Danske Patenter Udstedt
0107-5993	Margrethe og Vi Andre†
0107-6094	Blicheregnens Museumsforening. Aarsskrift
0107-6108	Jordbrug Oestjylland (Midt): Samtlige Landbrug, Skovbrug og Gartnerier
0107-6116	Twist
0107-6167	Plant Diseases and Pests in Denmark
0107-6183	Factsheet Denmark
0107-6264	Danmarks Eksportmarkeder†
0107-6280	Rytme
0107-6299	Patient
0107-6310	Modeltoget
0107-6329	Objektiv
0107-6345	Daginstitutionen
0107-6353	Vore Daginstitutioner see 0107-6345
0107-6396	Dansk Japansk Venskabsforenings Blad
0107-6418	Dansk Joedisk Historie
0107-6531	Aarhus Universitet. Romansk Institut. Romansk Afdelingen. Information
0107-654X	Musikplader og -baand. Klassisk Musik
0107-6582	Stikord
0107-6612	Folkefronten
0107-6663	Zoneterapi og Sundhed
0107-6701	Krejl
0107-6744	Statistisk Tiaars-Oversigt for Koebenhavns Kommune
0107-6752	Holstebro Museum. Aarsskrift
0107-6760	Peru Information
0107-6779	B T B
0107-6787	Skibstilsynets Godkendelsesbog
0107-6795	Kaleidoscope
0107-6841	Kunst i Dag†
0107-6868	Historisk Samfund for Praesto Amt. Aarbog
0107-6876	Goer-det-Selv changed to Goer det Selv i Hjemmet
0107-6922	Fortegnelse over Anerkendte Avlscentre, Aspirantbesaetninger, Opformeringsbesaetninger
0107-6930	Hitchcock's Krimi Magasin
0107-6949	Paa Jobbet
0107-6957	Kunstavisen
0107-7031	Denmark. Danmarks Statistik. Varestatistik for Industri
0107-7074	Folkemusikhusringen
0107-7090	Recipientundersoegelse ved Marmorilik
0107-7104	F L's Medlemsavis
0107-7112	Dansk Grafia
0107-7120	Aarhus Kommunes Statistiske Kontor. Information
0107-7139	Danmark i Tal
0107-7163	Landoekonomisk Oversigt
0107-721X	Historisk Aarbog for Skive og Omegn
0107-7279	Lyrik†
0107-7295	Ud med Kirken
0107-7325	Slaa Igen
0107-7333	Joedisk Plevy
0107-7384	Odense University Studies in Philosophy
0107-7392	Universite d'Odense. Etudes Romanes
0107-7430	Denmark. Miljoestyrelsen. Havforureningslaboratorium. Report of the Marine Pollution Laboratory
0107-7449	Kulturkampen
0107-7481	Display
0107-749X	Sundhedsstyrelsen Vitalstatistik
0107-7503	Forebyggende
0107-752X	Nippon Nyt
0107-7546	Avisteknisk Information†
0107-7554	Motor-Bladet
0107-7597	Medicinsk Foedselsstatistik
0107-7619	Aktiviteten i Sygehusvaesenet
0107-7627	Forbruget af Somatiske Sengepladser
0107-766X	Badminton Revy
0107-7716	Fagligt Forsvar
0107-7724	Harvard Boersen
0107-7767	Boernenes Aarbog†
0107-7783	Ungdomskalender
0107-7805	Cykle-Jul
0107-783X	Historisk Aarbog for Roedding Kommune
0107-7902	Kosmos
0107-7988	Maelkeproducenten
0107-7996	Rajneesh Buddhafelt Dansk Newsletter†
0107-8003	Denmark Bibliotekstilsynet. Beretning
0107-8011	Dansk Illustreret Skibsliste
0107-8054	Connaisseur
0107-8097	Infodont
0107-8119	Smalfilm og Video
0107-8135	Voksenuddannelse
0107-8216	D M C Information
0107-8224	Danske Bank af 1871. Orientering
0107-8232	Naar Lampen Taendes. Fortaellinger
0107-8240	Danske Bank af 1871. Danish Bulletin
0107-8275	E G V Information
0107-8283	Koebenhavns Universitet. Datalogisk Institut. Rapport
0107-8305	Markeds-bog
0107-8313	I Byen's Spiseguide
0107-8348	Denmark. Forsoegsanlaeg Risoe. Fysikafdelingen. Annual Progress Report
0107-8356	Folk i Fuglebjerg
0107-8372	Grenaa og Noerre Djurs Foer og Nu
0107-8380	Sygdomsmoensteret ved Somatiske Sygehusafdelingen
0107-8399	Fyens Stiftsbog
0107-8437	Sygesikringsstatistik
0107-8453	Skole- og Laereboeger
0107-8496	Feltbiologen
0107-8518	Arbejderbladet Deruda see 0109-3851
0107-8534	Fremtiden i Vore Haender. Nyhedsbrev see 0107-8542
0107-8542	F I V H-Nyt
0107-8550	Miljoevaern
0107-8585	Langhaars-Nyt
0107-8623	Radio Denmark changed to Baereboelgen
0107-8631	Aarhus Universitet. Institut for Litteraturhistorie. Skrifter
0107-8666	Rapport om Kontrollen med Konsummaelkprodukter
0107-8690	Musikplader og -baand. Rytmisk Musik
0107-8720	Deutscher Volkskalender Nordschleswig
0107-8747	Rasp
0107-8755	Psykologi†
0107-8771	Denmark. Danmarks Statistik. Loen- og Indkomststatistik
0107-8798	Lolland-Falsters Historiske Samfund. Aarbog
0107-8801	Oversigt over de Meteorologiske Forhold paa Forsoegsstationerne
0107-8860	Kristelig Fagforening og K F O see 0109-1131
0107-8860	Kristelig Fagforening og K F O see 0109-2057
0107-8879	Hippokraten
0107-8887	Julehilsen
0107-8917	Uddannelse og Arbejde i Udlandet
0107-8925	Viborg Stifts Aarbog
0107-8933	Kunstmuseets Aarsskrift
0107-8941	Novelle Magasinet
0107-895X	Fra Kvangaard til Humlekule
0107-8976	Motionsgang
0107-8984	D M C see 0109-3649
0107-900X	S B I Aarsberetning
0107-9018	Arbejderbevaegelsens Bibliotek og Arkiv
0107-9042	Discinform
0107-9069	Environmental Radioactivity in the Faroes
0107-9077	Forsoegsanlaeg Risoe. changed to Forskningscenter Risoe. Energi Systems Gruppen. Annual Progress Report
0107-9085	Kulturpolitisk Redegoerelse†
0107-9107	Effektiv Butiksdrift
0107-9123	Kirkegaardslederen
0107-9131	Jagt
0107-9166	Erhverssprog
0107-9190	Manuel Medicin
0107-928X	Romu
0107-931X	Koege Museum
0107-9352	Universitetets Statistiske Institut. Computer Programmes
0107-9387	D F 3 Formning
0107-9417	Aulisarnermit Nutarsiagssat
0107-9476	Frederiksvaerkegnens Museumsforening. Aarsskrift
0107-9522	Film U V
0107-9530	Sparekassen
0107-9573	Humanist
0107-959X	Inspiration
0107-9611	Haandarbejdets Fremme. Aarets Korssting
0107-962X	Elnyt
0107-9646	Dansk Windsurfing
0107-9654	Audio-Visuelle Materialer: Skolebiblioteket
0107-9670	Folketingets Haandbog
0107-9735	Arbejdsmarkedet og Arbejdsmarkedspolotik
0107-9743	Arbejdsmarkedets Regelsamling†
0107-976X	Koebenhavnerliv Foer og Nu
0107-9786	Centrale Videnskabsetiske Komite. Beretning
0107-9794	Corner
0107-9816	Dansk Lydfortegnelse
0107-9824	Kirkefondets Aarbog
0107-9840	Grenzland
0107-9948	Greenland Newsletter
0107-9980	Datajournalen
0107-9999	Plovfuren
0108-0016	Foto-Revyen
0108-0024	Nyt om Arbejdsmiljoe†
0108-0032	Galten Egnsarkiv. Annales
0108-0040	Musikbranchens Aarbog
0108-0075	Arusia. Historiske Skrifter
0108-0105	Ny Torsdag
0108-0164	Acta Pathologica, Microbiologica et Immunologica Scandinavica. Section A: Pathology
0108-0172	Acta Pathologica, Microbiologica et Immunologica Scandinavica. Section A: Pathology. Supplementum
0108-0180	Acta Pathologica, Microbiologica et Immunologica Scandinavica. Section B: Microbiology
0108-0199	Acta Pathologica, Microbiologica et Immunologica Scandinavica. Section B: Microbiology. Supplementum
0108-0202	Acta Pathologica, Microbiologica et Immunologica Scandinavica. Section C: Immunology
0108-0210	Acta Pathologica, Microbiologica et Immunologica Scandinavica. Section C: Immunology. Supplementum
0108-0229	V og S Priser. Bygningsdele
0108-0253	A S E A N Business Club of Denmark. Newsletter†
0108-0261	Artikler i Boeger
0108-027X	Nyt om Euro-Forskning
0108-0296	Filatelistisk Katalog-Noegle
0108-0326	Bryozoa
0108-0342	Skanderborg Museum. Aarsskrift
0108-0385	V D L Nyt
0108-0393	Helsingoer Kommunes Museer. Aarbog
0108-0458	Serigrafen
0108-0466	Spildevandsteknisk Tidsskrift
0108-0504	Denmark. Geografisk Magasin†
0108-0571	Danmarks Tekniske Hoejskole. Afdelingen B
0108-058X	Danmarks Tekniske Hoejskole. Afdelingen for Baerende Konstruktioner. Serie I
0108-0598	Heraldo de Interlingua
0108-061X	Billedterapi
0108-0687	Laegemiddelforbruget i Danmark
0108-0695	Design from Scandinavia
0108-0717	D S A M Orientering see 0109-2235
0108-0768	Danmarks Tekniske Hoejskole. Afdelingen for Baerende Konstruktioner. Serie R.
0108-0806	Ribe Stiftsbog
0108-0814	Danske Reklamefotografer
0108-0822	Profiler i Dansk Erhvervsliv†
0108-0830	H S G's Aarbog
0108-0849	Lovnoegle
0108-0857	Plejehjemshaandbogen
0108-0903	Stambog over Koeer af Roed Dansk Malkerace
0108-092X	Restauratoeren
0108-0962	Environmental Radioactivity in Greenland

ISSN INDEX 1445

0108-1012 Stofskifte
0108-1020 Studenterhaandbogen
0108-1098 Trav & Galop Journalen
0108-1101 Studenteravisen
0108-1195 Nyt fra Dansk P E N†
0108-1217 D A L Forum†
0108-1225 D S T S - Nyt
0108-1233 Rugby Nyt
0108-1306 Detailforskrifter for Koeretoejer
0108-1314 Brugskunst Skandinavien
0108-1349 Lyrikbogklubben†
0108-1357 Gamle Evangelium er Lige Nyt i Dag
0108-142X Faeroesk Lovregister
0108-1489 Institut for Afsaetningsoekonomi. Nyt
0108-1497 New Products from Denmark
0108-1527 Lev Bedre
0108-1586 Arab Studies in Scandinavia see 0801-2067
0108-1594 Prima Vista†
0108-1608 Print
0108-1632 Philosophia
0108-1683 Meddelelser fra Sortsafproevningen
0108-1756 Blaa Kors Familieaarbog see 0108-1764
0108-1764 Blaa Kors' Aarbog†
0108-1780 Zinx
0108-1810 Aarets Bogarbejde
0108-1829 New United Nations Publications
0108-1837 Flygtninge†
0108-1845 Nyt om Flygtninge changed to Flygtninge Nyt
0108-1888 Kvinder, Kvinder
0108-190X D T Forum
0108-1934 Historie (Ballerup)
0108-1942 Biologi
0108-1969 I F U's Participation in Joint Ventures see 0901-6171
0108-1993 Religionsvidenskabeligt Tidsskrift
0108-2019 Boghvedegryn
0108-2027 Fagpresenoeglen
0108-2051 Videofilm
0108-2086 Pesticidrester i Danske Levnedsmidler
0108-2108 Chef-Nyt
0108-2124 Ascolta
0108-2132 Socialpaedagogernes Landsforbund. T R Information
0108-2191 Annoncoerforenings Bureaufortegnelse
0108-2205 Roskilde Universitetscenter. Institut for Samfundsoekonomi og Planlaegning. Arbejdspapir.
0108-2272 Dansk Sangindeks
0108-2299 Dansk Literaturhistorisk Bibliografi†
0108-2302 Vore Kirkegaarde
0108-2329 Investering i Produktion
0108-2388 Nyrenyt
0108-2396 Akvariebladet
0108-240X Fredsmeddelelser fra Samarbejdskomiteen see 0109-2855
0108-2418 F I C E Information
0108-2426 Ungdomsskolen i Tal
0108-2442 Russisklaererforeningen. Meddelelser
0108-2450 Trigon
0108-2469 Studies in Labor Market Dynamics
0108-2477 O S - Information see 0108-2485
0108-2485 O S - Nyt
0108-2515 Danske Tegneserier Ekstra
0108-2531 Redningshistorisk Forening. Information see 0108-254X
0108-254X Redningshistorisk Forenings Information
0108-2558 Selskabet for Dansk Fotografi. Kontaktblad changed to Dansk Fotografi
0108-2604 A F I D-Dialog
0108-2612 Kina Information
0108-2655 S T S Debat
0108-2671 Skole & Landbrug
0108-2698 Ejendomsinformation
0108-2701 Acta Crystallographica. Section C: Crystal Structure Communications.
0108-271X Nordisk Sexologi
0108-2736 Samojeden
0108-2744 Landbrug Fyn
0108-2779 Dialyse og Transplantation see 0108-2388
0108-2787 Aarsskrift for Sottrup Sogn
0108-2795 Zibaldone
0108-2833 Stemmer fra Oldtiden
0108-2841 Nyt om Gigt
0108-285X Danmarks Journalisthoejskoles Aarskrift
0108-2868 Mariager Aarbog
0108-2884 Store Glaede
0108-2922 Occurrences of the Polar Slant E Condition, SEC at Narssarssuag, Godhavn, Thule†
0108-2957 Nyt fra Tyrkiet
0108-2965 Jul i Lejre
0108-3023 Nemalah
0108-3082 Danmarks Folkehoejskoler
0108-3104 International Kierkegaard Newsletter
0108-3139 Dansk-Biavl og Miljoe
0108-321X Gymnasiemusik
0108-3236 Libyen Bulletin
0108-3244 Lokalhistorien for Torslunde Ishoej og Tranegilde
0108-3279 Forum
0108-3309 Forskellighed
0108-3333 Nouvelles Scientifiques Franco-Danoises
0108-3376 Politiets Aarsberetning
0108-3422 Naturgas Nyt
0108-3430 Specialarbejderskolen
0108-3449 Dansk i Dag†
0108-3457 L V S Bladet see 0108-3430
0108-3503 Nyt Aspekt
0108-3511 Omkring et Kunstvaerk

0108-3562 Teknik-Samfund
0108-3589 Arilds Lokaltidende
0108-3627 D J OE F - Haandbogen
0108-3643 F R A M
0108-366X Vidar see 0108-3678
0108-3678 Gymnastik
0108-3708 Datalogi O
0108-3759 Revisorhaandbogen
0108-3775 Erhvervslejeren
0108-3783 Israelske Ambassade. Information
0108-3791 Gamle Loejt
0108-3805 Thorslunde Ishoej Lokalhistoriske Forening see 0108-3244
0108-3813 Power
0108-3821 Race Walking World Statistics - Women
0108-3856 S L F Information
0108-3864 Alt om Video†
0108-3872 Skole og Fremtid
0108-3880 Slaegten Fisker
0108-3910 Danmark Export: Food & Beverages
0108-3945 Kulturgeografiske Haefters Skriftserie
0108-3953 Supplement til Skattelovsamling†
0108-3961 Kvindestudier ved A U C. Aarbog
0108-397X Skaeppen
0108-4003 Landbrugets Organisationshaandbog
0108-4011 Denmark. Energiministeriet. Energiforskningsprogram
0108-402X Uddrag af Energilitteratur paa Danmarks Tekniske Bibliotek, Soenderborg Tekniske Bibliotek, Aarhus Tekniske Bibliotek changed to Danmarks Tekniske Bibliotek. Uddrag
0108-4054 Gymnasieskolernes Musiklaererforening Medlemsorientering see 0108-321X
0108-4089 Frimaerkens Verden
0108-4100 Historisk Aarbog fra Randers Amt
0108-4135 Living Architecture
0108-4151 Oversigt over By- og Regionforskning
0108-4232 V S R Kommunikation see 0108-3279
0108-4259 Friskoler og Private Grundskoler
0108-4291 Kontaktkalender
0108-4321 Nyere Dansk Faglitteratur. Supplement
0108-433X Sprog og Samfund
0108-4380 Oestnyt
0108-4402 Skolemusikhaandbogen
0108-4429 Dansk Isolering z Energihaandbog
0108-4453 Chaos
0108-4496 Gralen
0108-450X Centra Bulteno see 0108-3759
0108-4518 Landbrugets Samraad for Forskning og Forsoeg. Rammeplaner
0108-4542 Teater og Bevaegelse
0108-4550 Luft og Rumfartsaarbogen
0108-4577 Energi Information
0108-4585 D A B Information
0108-4593 Skole-Bladet
0108-4615 Varmeforsyningsplanlaegning: Status
0108-4631 Bridgeaarbogen†
0108-464X Journal of Danish Archaeology
0108-4658 Hi-Fi and Video Revyen
0108-4666 Focus Damefodbold
0108-4690 Lokal Historie i Skoerping Kommune
0108-4712 Tidsskrift for Oplysningens Tidsalder
0108-4739 Autoriserede Laeger, Tandlaeger, Dyrlaeger i Danmark
0108-4755 Groent Miljoe
0108-4763 Denmark. Statens Levnedsmiddelinstitut. Centrallaboratoriet. Arbejdsprogrammer†
0108-4844 Danmarks Fiskeri- og Havunersoegelser. Ferskvandsfiskerilaboratoriet. Meddelelser. changed to Meddelelser fra Ferskvandsfiskerilaboratoriet
0108-4887 Plantebeskyttelsemidler
0108-4925 C B N
0108-4968 Sejlsport
0108-4976 B U M
0108-4992 Toyo Spiseguide
0108-5018 Bilens Aarsrevy
0108-5077 Fodboldens Aarsrevy
0108-5115 Sportens Aarsrevy†
0108-5174 Barbara Cartland's Verden af Romantik
0108-5190 Kontakt
0108-5212 Nyt fra Brasilien
0108-5220 Visuelt
0108-5255 Discountbutikker (Year)
0108-528X Uddrag af Energilitteratur paa Danmarks Tekniske Bibliotek changed to Danmarks Tekniske Bibliotek. Uddrag
0108-5328 Music Management & International Promotion
0108-5344 Oftalmolog
0108-5352 Dagpleje-Hemmet
0108-5409 Hej see 0901-4500
0108-5417 S D A - Nyt
0108-5476 Denmark. Danmarks Statistik. Penge og Kapitalmarked.
0108-5506 Denmark. Danmarks Statistik. Udenrigshandel/External Trade
0108-5557 Faroerne og Groenland
0108-562X Human Settlements Situation and Related Trends and Policies
0108-5646 Doedsaarsagerne
0108-5697 L B Levende Billeder
0108-5727 Markedsdata†
0108-6022 Skattelove
0108-6103 Socialraadgiveren
0108-6251 Teater, Film og TV see 0900-0119
0108-6391 Vestfynsk Hjemstavn
0108-6464 Oekonomiske Udvikling paa Faeroerne
0108-6510 El Salvador Nyt changed to Mellemamerika Nyt
0108-6596 C D R Research Reports

0108-6618 Boernetandplejen i Danmark
0108-6626 Radiobranchen
0108-6634 Nyt om Naturgas†
0108-6650 Sikkerhed
0108-6669 Aktuelt om Byggelitteratur
0108-6707 Driftsteknikerbogen
0108-6715 Forum Fabulatorum
0108-6758 Trailer
0108-6804 Historisk Forening for Vaerloese Kommune. Arsskrift
0108-6812 Rejsebogen (Year)
0108-688X Skatteberegningen
0108-6898 Inuit
0108-6901 Denmark. Miljoeministeriet. Miljoeministerens Redegoerelse om Landsplanlaegning
0108-691X Vulkanen: Ren L A V A
0108-6944 Studie- og Erhvervsvalget
0108-6952 Unge Laeser Om
0108-6979 Danmarks Nationalbank. Beretning og Regnskab (Dansk Udgave)
0108-6987 Handleren
0108-6995 Danmarks Nationalbank. Report and Accounts for the Year (Year)
0108-7029 Update (Aarhus)
0108-7142 Allesoe, Broby, Naesby Lokalarkiv
0108-7150 Arbejdsretligt Tidsskrift
0108-7169 Anklagemyndighedens Aarsberetning
0108-7177 Bank
0108-7193 Denmark. Forsvarsministeriet. Forsvarsministerens Aarlige Redegoerelse
0108-7207 P P P
0108-7215 Litteratur paa Indvandrersprog i Danske Folkebiblioteker
0108-7231 Landshavneplanbidrag
0108-724X Social Revy
0108-7258 U K-Modelinformation see 0900-470X
0108-7266 Sikkerhed og Nedrustning
0108-7274 Normtal for Koebmaend†
0108-7282 Fugle i Nordjylland
0108-7290 Aktiv Islam
0108-7304 Forsikringstilsynet. Beretning om Tilsynets Virksomhed
0108-7320 D I M S Bulletin
0108-7355 Camping Danmark
0108-7371 Polen-Nyt
0108-738X Denmark. Danmarks Statistik. Regnskabsstatistik for Industrien / Industrial Accounts Statistics
0108-7460 Philosophus see 0109-4831
0108-7487 Denmark. Miljoekreditraadet. Beretning
0108-7495 Denmark. Energistyrelsen. Nyt fra Energistyrelsen
0108-7509 Eksportkredit, Eksportfremme: Aarsberetninger
0108-7517 Dansk E D B Bibliografi
0108-7568 Denmark. Danmarks Statistik. Bygningsopgoerelsen /Stock of Building
0108-7584 Sail Surfing
0108-7622 Andelsbanken Boersoversigt
0108-7630 Andelsbanken Erhvervsorientering changed to Konsekvens
0108-7649 Andelsbanken Handelskontakter†
0108-7657 Geografi
0108-7665 Samtidsorientering
0108-7673 Acta Crystallographica. Section A: Foundations of Crystallography
0108-7681 Acta Crystallographica. Section B: Structural Science
0108-7711 L A N A Nyt
0108-772X Film Magasinet
0108-7738 Fjordhesten
0108-7746 Focus paa Undervisning
0108-7754 Reportaget†
0108-7789 Nordisk Tidsskrift for Fagsprog og Terminologi
0108-7800 Psykisk Forum see 0108-3503
0108-7819 Beretning for Psykiatriske Institutioner i Danmark
0108-7843 Mer om Koenssygdomme changed to Sex og Sundhed
0108-7851 Mer om Sex og Sikkerhed changed to Sex og Sundhed
0108-786X Husholdningsarbejdet
0108-7878 Kroghs Lovinformation
0108-7886 Udviklingstendenserne paa de Langvarigt Uddannedes Arbejdsmarked
0108-7908 Socialistisk Folkeparti. Status see 0902-1612
0108-7924 Nyt fra S S F
0108-7991 Levende Natur
0108-8017 Herning-Bogen
0108-8025 Ord & Sag
0108-805X Landsdelslaboratorierne†
0108-8068 Dansk Energi Tidsskrift
0108-8076 Befolkningen i Kommunerne / Populations of Municipalities
0108-8149 Elektronik Indkoebsbogen
0108-8157 Transport (Aarlig)
0108-8165 Odense Universitet. Institut for Virksomhedsledelse. Skrifter
0108-8173 Denmark. Danmarks Statistik. Nationalregnskabsstatistik /National Accounts Statistics
0108-8203 Miljoeundersoegelser ved Ivigtut
0108-822X Selskab for Nordisk Filologi. Aarsberetning
0108-8238 Biblioteksvejviser over Storkoebenhavns Folkebiblioteker
0108-8262 Efterskoler. Fortegnelse
0108-8297 Nye Aar

ISSN INDEX

ISSN	Title
0108-8300	Gartneriets Informationstjeneste. Planteskoleinfo *changed to* Groensagsinfo
0108-8335	Kraks TransportKatalog
0108-8343	Dansen's Blad
0108-8351	Bistandshaandbogen
0108-836X	L U Information
0108-8378	Eleven
0108-8416	N O W E L E
0108-8440	Horisont
0108-8459	Agrologisk Tidsskrift Marken
0108-8467	Korea Bulletin
0108-8491	Radisen
0108-8513	Teledata Nyt
0108-853X	Rakettidende
0108-8572	Dansk Kunstnerraad
0108-8580	Dayanisma
0108-8599	Risoe International Symposium on Metallurgy and Materials Science. Proceedings
0108-8602	Murerhaandbog
0108-8629	Fiskeriet ved Groenland & Groenlands Fiskeriundersoegelsers Aktivitet
0108-8653	Hednos Daneses
0108-867X	Vendsyssel Historiske Museum
0108-8688	Commercial Times
0108-8718	D M U - Nyt
0108-873X	Turistfoerer
0108-8777	Frederiksberg Gennem Tiderne
0108-8785	Sprint
0108-8793	Familieplanlaegning
0108-8815	F S Bulletin
0108-884X	Jordbrug
0108-8858	Museumsavisen
0108-8866	Standpunkt *see* 0108-8874
0108-8874	Liberal Debat
0108-8904	Hjertenyt
0108-8912	Shipping-Bladet
0108-8920	Groenne Fag
0108-8939	T F-Nyhedsbrev *see* 0109-3169
0108-8963	B U K S
0108-898X	Nyt fra Bibelselskabet
0108-8998	Dansk Atlet Union, Landdsorganisation for Brydning *see* 0108-9013
0108-9013	D A U Bladet
0108-9048	F A T - Bladet
0108-9072	Huset Ude og Inde *changed to* Interieur
0108-9102	Love og Bekendtgoerelser m.v.
0108-9129	Banker og Sparekasser
0108-9145	Factum Humanum
0108-9161	Westcoast Offshore Guide *changed to* Danish Offshore Guide and Yearbook
0108-917X	Museet for Holbaek og Omegn. Aarsberetning
0108-9188	D M P F Medlemmer
0108-9196	Revisor Posten
0108-9218	Tracking
0108-9242	BoersenData
0108-9307	Lokomotivet
0108-9315	Sandeviften
0108-934X	Helses Boerneblad
0108-9358	E S O Foelgeforskning
0108-9412	Kommunernes Institutions. Haandbog
0108-9439	Ren Energi
0108-9463	Skat
0108-948X	Undersoegelse over Apotekernes Driftsforhold
0108-9625	Arbejderbevaegelsens Erhvervsraad. Beretning
0108-9633	Litteratur paa Indvandrersprog i Danske Folkebiblioteker. Serbokroatisk
0108-9641	Litteratur paa Indvandrersprog i Danske Folkebiblioteker. Tyrkisk
0108-965X	Litteratur paa Indvandrersprog i Danske Folkebiblioteker. Urdu
0108-9668	Three Year Art Book
0108-9684	Photodermatology
0108-9692	Hereford
0108-9714	Statistik om Sundhedsplejerskernes Virksomhed
0108-9722	Opgavesamling i Skat 1
0108-9730	Opgavesamling i Skat 2 og Erhvervsjura
0108-9773	E K-Bladet
0108-9781	Denmark. Sundhedsstyrelsen. Kursusoversigt
0108-979X	Denmark. Indenrigsministeriet. Indenrigsministeriets Afgoerelser og Udtalelser om Kommunale Forhold
0108-9803	Denmark. Boligministeriet. Building Regulations
0108-9811	Koebenhavns Universitet. Retsvidenskabeligt Institut B. Studier
0108-982X	Danish Contract
0108-9846	Alle Tiders Odsherreds
0108-9862	Vinyl
0108-9870	Facet for Frihed *changed to* Facet
0108-9900	E D B - Kursuskatalog
0108-9935	Piranesi
0108-9943	Presseblomster
0108-996X	Facts om Danmark
0109-0003	Treklang
0109-002X	Lokalhistorie: Hadsund Kommune
0109-0054	Niels Bohr International Gold Medal†
0109-0062	Verden Rundt
0109-0070	Denmark. Teknologistyrelsen. Nyhedsbrev
0109-0089	T I
0109-0097	Gaffa
0109-0100	Vaernskontakt
0109-0119	Druiden *changed to* D R U Nytt
0109-0135	Avis 81
0109-0178	Langaa
0109-0194	Egnshistorisk Forening i Grundsoe. Aarsskrift
0109-0208	Nyt for Bogvenner
0109-0259	Sund og Rask†
0109-0291	Maskinstationen og Landbrugslederen
0109-0305	Emneregister, Selskabs- og Hovedaktionaerforhold m.v.
0109-0321	Denmark. Statens Byggeforskningsinstitut. Program Resumeer
0109-033X	Andels-Boligen
0109-0356	Kvinder paa Tinder
0109-0364	Musikalier i Danske Biblioteker
0109-0372	Fructus
0109-0402	Amazonerne
0109-0429	Samspil
0109-0453	Vesttyskland i Bevaegelse
0109-0461	Gryden
0109-047X	Kerteminde Museum. Aarsskrift *changed to* Cartha
0109-0518	Nyt fra D U K
0109-0526	D F L†
0109-0534	D U K
0109-0550	New Foundland Information
0109-0631	R F Medlemsblad
0109-064X	Landskomiteen Sydafrika-Aktion. Nyhedsbrev†
0109-0674	Historisk Arkiv for Broerup og Omegn. Aarsskrift
0109-0690	Motionsbladet
0109-0704	Hjerteforeningens Motionsblad *see* 0109-0690
0109-0712	Ledoeje-Smoerum Historisk Forening og Arkiv
0109-0720	Focus paa Mellemoesten†
0109-0747	Lokalhistorisk Orientering Hvidovre
0109-0755	Buteo *see* 0109-257X
0109-0763	Hurtigmetode-nyt *changed to* Mikrobiologi-Nyt
0109-0778X	Harmonika Folder
0109-0828	P & I
0109-0852	Stof
0109-0860	Grafiske Funktionaerers Landsforening. Orientering *see* 0109-0879
0109-0879	Grafiske Funktionaerer
0109-0895	Fagblad for Zoneterapeuter
0109-0917	Fremtider
0109-0925	F A K E-Nyt *changed to* K C-Nyt
0109-095X	Bios
0109-0968	Dansk Fagpresskatalog
0109-0976	Odense Universitet. Institut for Offentlig Oekonomi og Politik. Occasional Paper
0109-0984	Rue-Revue
0109-0992	Andelsbanken Danebank. Newsletter
0109-100X	Retspolitik
0109-1026	D O N G Orientering *changed to* Dansk Olie & Naturgas. Orientering
0109-1085	D S S -Nyt
0109-1107	Ankenaevnet for Arbejdsloeshedsforsikringen. Beretning
0109-1115	E S A Foelgeforskning
0109-1131	Kristelig Funktionaer-Organisation. Medlemsblad
0109-1158	Arbejdermuseet. Aarbog
0109-1174	Film Premierer†
0109-1190	Dyr i Natur og Museum
0109-1212	Liste over Rytmiske Spillesteder i Danmark
0109-1239	Vaabenkaploeb og Vaabenkontrol
0109-1247	Opgavesaet til Dansk Skr. Fremstilling, Folkeskolens Udvidede Afgangsproeve *see* 0109-1255
0109-1255	Opgavesaet til Dansk Skriftlig Fremstilling, Folkeskolens Afgangsproeve
0109-1271	Denmark. Danmarks Statistik. Konjunkturtendenser i Udvalgte Lande
0109-128X	Transportnyt
0109-1328	Uddelerbladet
0109-1417	Engelsk Fodbold
0109-1425	Fortvivl
0109-1441	Fynboer og Arkaeologi
0109-145X	Danske Assurandoeren *see* 0109-1875
0109-1468	Tidsskrift for Danske Assurandoeren *see* 0109-1875
0109-1476	D K K F - Nyt
0109-1492	Kvindeliv†
0109-1514	Arbejdsdirektoratet Beretning om Arbejdsformidligen og Arbejdsloeshedsforsikringen
0109-1549	P S
0109-1565	Arbejdsmiljoe og Samfund
0109-1573	Normtal
0109-1581	Fisk & Fri
0109-159X	Sport paa Bornholm
0109-1646	T V Aarbogen†
0109-1700	Rambukken
0109-1727	Skipper Clement
0109-1743	Advance
0109-1751	Detail-Bladet
0109-176X	Folkets Roest
0109-1816	Gamle Maane
0109-1875	Assurandoeren
0109-1913	Denmark. Miljoeministeriet. Miljoeministeriets Lovregister
0109-193X	Boernebibliotekskatalog. Lydboeger, Bog & Baand
0109-2014	International Society for Strategic Studies (Africa). Newsletter
0109-2030	Boernebibliotekskatalog. Dias, Film, Video
0109-2049	Vind - Nyt
0109-2057	Kristelig Fagforening. Medlemsblad
0109-2073	Groenlands Geologiske Undersoegelse. Gletscher-hydrologiske Meddelelser
0109-2111	Gyden
0109-2138	Historisk Aarbog for Felsted Sogn
0109-2146	Sport
0109-2162	Lokalhistorisk Arkiv Stubbekoebing. Aarsskrift
0109-2170	Brorfelde, Magnetic Results
0109-2235	Practicus
0109-2251	Loevens Gab
0109-2278	Europa
0109-2294	Kliniske Tandteknikere
0109-2308	Travsport for Fagfolk
0109-2316	Thomson Nyt†
0109-2324	Gartneren
0109-2359	Elteknik
0109-2367	D G U Information
0109-2375	Soendagsskolekontakt
0109-2383	Tidsskrift for Skatteret
0109-2391	S & P
0109-2405	Denmark. Vejdirektoratet. Aarsberetning
0109-2421	Indvendreren
0109-2456	Illustreret Videnskab
0109-2472	Vadehavsrapport
0109-2480	Lydhullet
0109-2499	Antikvitetsudstilling, Odd-Fellow Palaeet
0109-2502	Endodontics & Dental Traumatology
0109-2510	Fiches d'Identification des Maladies et Parasites des Poissons, Crustaces et Mollusques
0109-2529	Fiches d'Identification du Plancton
0109-257X	Bladsmutten
0109-2588	Star
0109-2596	U F O Forskning
0109-260X	Schultz Medicinalbibliotek. Publikation
0109-2618	Musikhistorisk Museum og Carl Claudius Samling. Meddelelser
0109-2669	Dansk-Fransk Handelsunion. Bulletin
0109-2707	Skolernes Indkoebshaandbog
0109-274X	Stigsnaes
0109-2766	Folk og Liv paa Roendeegnen-. Dengang
0109-2774	Film
0109-2774	Film Aarbogen
0109-2820	Poetica et Analytica
0109-2839	Lokalhistorisk Forening for Hoerup Sogn. Aarsskrift
0109-2847	Alt om Data: Special
0109-2855	Fredsavisen
0109-2863	Soenderjyllands Erhvervsorientering: Produktion, Handel, Kontakt
0109-291X	Beton- og Konstruktionsinstituttet. Rapport
0109-2936	Kristelig Fagforening, Kristelig Funktionaer-Organisation. Medlemsblad *see* 0109-1131
0109-2936	Kristelig Fagforening, Kristelig Funktionaer-Organisation. Medlemsblad *see* 0109-2057
0109-2944	Historisk Samfund for Hoeje-Taastrup Kommune. Meddelelser
0109-2952	Roedderne
0109-2979	C C Orientering
0109-2995	Naturligvis
0109-3002	Statistik om Hjemmesygeplejerkevirksomheden
0109-3061	Heraldiske Studier
0109-307X	Spanskaererforeningen. Informationer
0109-3118	Grafisk Kontakt†
0109-3142	Danske Datavaernskonference
0109-3169	Nyhedsbrev
0109-3177	Apoteket†
0109-3207	North European Dairy Journal
0109-3290	Ernaeringsnyt
0109-3304	Eftersyn
0109-3312	Plantevaern i Landbruget
0109-3339	Danske Illustratorer
0109-3347	Munksgaards Social Aarbog
0109-3363	Teaterseminar
0109-3371	D K
0109-3401	Copenhagen School of Economics and Business Administration. Marketing Institute. Working Papers
0109-3460	Samlernyt
0109-3479	Charlottenborg Foraarsudstillingen
0109-3487	Informationskilder for Social- og Sundhedssektor
0109-3509	Traeets Arbejdsgivere
0109-3525	Jaeger-Nyt†
0109-3533	Konsulentordningen
0109-3541	P C World
0109-355X	Firezfirs
0109-3592	D B D Bat
0109-3649	D M C - Bladet
0109-3738	Dansk Filatelistisk Tidsskrift
0109-3762	Aksel
0109-3770	Aalborg Universitetsdatacenter. Publikation
0109-3797	Serie Kureren
0109-3800	Kalveproducenten
0109-3851	Arbejderbladet
0109-3878	Komiteen mod Dyreforsoeg, Fonden til Sygdomsbekaempelse uden Dyreforsoeg
0109-3886	K S Bulletin
0109-3916	Olieberetning
0109-3967	Nordica
0109-3975	Nordafrika
0109-4017	Lokalhistorisk Forening for Soenderhald Kommune. Aarsskrift
0109-4033	D M V Nyt
0109-405X	Forlagsvejviser
0109-4076	Denmark. Statens Filmcentral. Information og Beretning
0109-4106	Child Care International†

ISSN INDEX 1447

0109-4130 Vand og Miljoe
0109-4149 Befolkningens Energisparebestraebelser
0109-4157 A U D - Nyt
0109-4165 Dansk Kunst†
0109-4203 C I N A - Nytt
0109-4211 Cyklen
0109-4262 Organisationer og Tal i Gartneriet
0109-4289 Rude Skov Magnetic Results†
0109-4300 Godhavn Magnetic Results
0109-4319 Indsatsen mod Ungdomsarbejdsloesheden
0109-4378 Afghanistan Bulletin
0109-4432 Danmarks Fiskeri og Havundersoegelser. Rapport
0109-4440 Aarets Pressefoto
0109-4475 D Bat *see* 0109-3592
0109-4505 Ide - nyt til Lejligheder
0109-4564 Haandvaerkshistorisk Tidsskrift
0109-4599 Muldvarpen
0109-4718 Ask
0109-4777 Horse Holidays in W. Europe
0109-4831 P S
0109-4939 Tennis Jul
0109-4955 Fortegnelse over Dansk Udviklingsforskning
0109-4998 Kongelige Veterinaer og Landbohoejskole. Haandbog
0109-5013 Data om Markedet
0109-5021 Doeveforsorgens Historiske Selskab
0109-503X Raastofproduktionsopgoerelse *see* 0109-7474
0109-5072 Nu *changed to* Magasinet Nu
0109-5110 Danish Hydraulics
0109-5129 Fravaer ved Anmeldte Arbejdsulykker
0109-5196 R F Avisen
0109-5234 Danske Statsskoves Udbytte af Ved og Penge
0109-5250 A S - Bogen
0109-5277 Kvartalsvis Statistik for Koebenhavnsomraadet
0109-534X Pladeanmeldelser, Rytmisk Musik
0109-5358 Dansk-Tjekkoslovakisk Selskab. Kvartalsnyt
0109-5366 I F L A Communications
0109-5390 L Ae S
0109-5439 Laegekredsforeningen Fyns Amt
0109-548X R D F Bulletin†
0109-5498 Fortegnelse over Fabrikanter og Importoerer af Goedninger og Grundforbedringsmidler
0109-5536 Dansk Idraet
0109-5544 Ny Abstraktion
0109-5579 Penge
0109-5587 Handelshoejskolen i Koebenhavn. H A-Center. Rapport
0109-5595 Dragesport
0109-5641 Dental Materials
0109-565X Gerodontics
0109-5668 Cancer Reviews
0109-5684 Danske Vinblad
0109-5692 Bygningskonstruktoerernes Medlemsorientering
0109-5781 Hele Fyns Erhvervsliv
0109-5811 Farvandvaesenets Trafikanalyse
0109-582X Odense Universitet. Arabisk Informationscenter. Nyhedsbrev *changed to* Den Arabisk Verden. Maanedsoversigt
0109-5846 Danske Bibelselskabs Aarbog
0109-5854 Museumsforeningen for Laesoe. Litterature
0109-5994 Dansk Golfhaandbog
0109-6044 Laengden af Offentlige Veje
0109-6060 T L Aarbog
0109-6109 Edb Nyt
0109-6125 Danmarks Turist Vejviser
0109-6311 Politikens Computer Aarbog†
0109-6389 D S U -Nyt *see* 0109-6397
0109-6397 En Tern. Informations og Debatblad
0109-6486 Dansk Faellesrejse Forening. Medlemsblad
0109-6605 Dansk Rumforskninginstitut. Publikationer
0109-6656 Gilleleje Museum
0109-6664 Fysiktips
0109-6672 Denmark. Direktoratet for Toldvaesenet. Toldvaesenets Aarsberetning
0109-6699 Lokalhistorisk Arkiv, Aalestrup. Aarsskrift
0109-6702 Feature fra Danmark
0109-6761 Bordtennis Aarbogen
0109-6796 Dannebrog Comics†
0109-6966 Alt om Mad
0109-7172 Vaern om Danmark
0109-7202 Pulsen
0109-7318 Windpower Monthly *changed to* Windpower Monthly Newsmagazine
0109-7458 Raastofproduktionen, Landomraadet. Produktionsmaengden af Geologiske Raastoffer Fordelt paa Antskommuner og Kommuner
0109-7466 Raastofproduktionen, Havomraadet
0109-7474 Raastofproduktionen, Landomraadet. Handelsvarer og Anvendelse, Gravforhold, Arealforhold
0109-7598 Managements Erhvervspolitiske Forum. Rapport
0109-7644 Dagens Danmark
0109-7679 Landscentralen for Undervisningsmidler. Teknisk Information
0109-7687 Cielo dei Vichinghi
0109-7695 Denmark. Miljoeministeriet. Miljoeministeriet Publikationsregister.
0109-7709 Barn og Kultur i Norden†
0109-7717 Video. Vaerd at Se
0109-7725 Oekonomisk Analyse, Sommerregnskaber
0109-7733 Vente Journalen
0109-7814 Vision
0109-7822 Amternes Oekonomi
0109-792X Erhvervslederen
0109-8047 Aktuell Nordisk Statistik
0109-8071 Telex Danmark
0109-8314 Denmark. Danmarks Statistik. Vejviser i Statistiken
0109-8330 Veteranfly Klubben
0109-8365 Folk Fortaeller
0109-8411 Dansk Artist Forbund. Show Guide
0109-8438 Samfundet til Udgivelse af Dansk Musik. Bulletin
0109-8489 Bangsbomuseet. Aarbog
0109-8551 Lokalhistorisk Arkiv, Roedby. Aarsskrift
0109-856X Feltundersoegelse
0109-8586 Dansk Textil Exportguide
0109-8608 Du-Bladet
0109-8640 Bibliotek og Uddannelse
0109-8667 Hele Aarhus Amts Erhvervsliv
0109-8691 Dansk Karate Forbund *see* 0109-8705
0109-8705 Dansk Karate Forbund. Medlemsblad
0109-8829 Vestsjaellands Erhvervsavis
0109-8845 V F *see* 0109-8861
0109-8853 Folkebibliotekernes Udenlanske Boernebogssamling. Katalog
0109-8861 Vegetarisk Tidsskrift
0109-887X Q - Avisen
0109-890X K T
0109-8985 Skolan i Norden
0109-9019 Videofilm der er og for Boern†
0109-9035 Aarhus Universitet. Center for Latinamerikastudier. Nyhedsbrev
0109-9043 Exportoeren
0109-9051 Grusavisen
0109-906X Lyrik & Prosa
0109-9078 Fuglelivet ved Roskilde Fjord
0109-9108 Freinet Nyt
0109-9140 Homeservice Stations Outside the Tropical Bands
0109-9167 A-Kasse Information
0109-923X Bibliotekshistorie
0109-9264 Historisk Samfund for Soenderjylland. Skrifter
0109-9280 Jyske Historiker
0109-9299 Leder. Kursuskatalog
0109-9310 Erhvervs-Orientering Stat Amt, Kommune
0109-9426 Investeringsforeninger Tilsynet
0109-9442 G L B
0109-9450 Dialog
0109-9485 Om Gymnasiet, Studenterkursus og Hoejre Forberedelseseksamen
0109-9531 Soft Special
0109-9639 Ingenioer
0109-9779 Datalogiske Skrifter
0109-9787 Sporten
0109-9876 Fodbold, Danske Kampe
0109-9892 Fodbold, Udenlandse Kampe
0109-9914 Om Laerlinge og Efg Uddannelserne
0109-9930 Denmark. Sundhetsstyrelsen. Laegemiddelafdelningen. Aarsberetning
0109-9957 Operationsmoensteret paa Danske Sygehuse
0109-9973 Aarhus Universitet. Socialmedicinsk Institut. Rapport
0110-0068 Miorita
0110-0076 New Quarterly Cave *changed to* Crosscurrent
0110-0084 Outrigger†
0110-022X N.Z. Family Physician
0110-0246 New Zealand Tax Reports
0110-0262 New Zealand International Review
0110-036X Noumenon
0110-0483 Country Side of Music
0110-070X Butterworths Current Law
0110-0831 New Zealand Annual *changed to* Weekly News Annual
0110-084X Farming Statistics
0110-0858 Islands
0110-0890 New Zealand Nursing Forum
0110-1048 What's New in Forest Research
0110-1145 Spiral
0110-1153 Horticulture in N.Z.
0110-1242 New Zealand Wool Board. Statistical Handbook
0110-1277 New Zealand Administrative Reports
0110-1390 New Zealand Town Planning Appeals
0110-1447 National Museum of New Zealand. Miscellenaneous Series
0110-1625 Turnbull Library Record
0110-165X New Zealand. Soil Bureau. Bibliographic Report
0110-1668 New Zealand Energy Journal *see* 0111-5839
0110-1749 New Zealand. Ministry of Agriculture and Fisheries. Fisheries Research Division. Bulletin.
0110-1765 New Zealand. Ministry of Agriculture and Fisheries. Fisheries Research Division. Occasional Publication
0110-1900 New Zealand. Department of Health. Hospital Management Data
0110-1951 New Zealand. Ministry of Foreign Affairs. United Nations Handbook
0110-2079 New Zealand. Soil Bureau. Soil Survey Reports
0110-2184 New Zealand. Department of Statistics. Exports
0110-2192 University of Waikato. Antarctic Research Unit. Report
0110-3458 New Zealand. Department of Statistics. Transport Statistics
0110-3466 New Zealand. Department of Statistics. Local Authority Statistics
0110-3474 New Zealand. Department of Statistics. Insurance Statistics
0110-3482 New Zealand. Department of Statistics. Justice Statistics *see* 0112-4447
0110-3490 New Zealand. Department of Statistics. Building Statistics
0110-3563 Engineering Management & Equipment Digest
0110-3741 New Zealand. Department of Statistics. Imports
0110-375X New Zealand. Department of Statistics. Population and Migration. Part A: Population *see* 0112-9155
0110-3768 New Zealand. Department of Statistics. Population and Migration. Part B: External Migration *see* 0112-6709
0110-3776 New Zealand. Department of Statistics. Incomes and Income Tax Statistics
0110-392X New Zealand Household Survey *see* 0112-6601
0110-3970 Pacific Quarterly Moana *changed to* Crosscurrent
0110-3989 Camera
0110-4004 Whakatane & District Historical Society. Monographs
0110-4055 New Zealand. Department of Statistics. Quarterly Population Bulletin *see* 0111-8102
0110-4152 University of Auckland. Department of Mathematics. Report Series
0110-4373 Library Life
0110-4519 New Zealand. Ministry of Agriculture and Fisheries. Fisheries Research Division: Information Leaflet
0110-4527 Entomological Society of New Zealand. Bulletin
0110-4578 Patient Management
0110-4586 New Zealand. Department of Statistics. Vital Statistics
0110-4616 New Zealand. Department of Statistics. Balance of Payments *see* 0112-5117
0110-4624 New Zealand. Department of Statistics. Agricultural Statistics
0110-4640 New Zealand. Department of Statistics. Census of Building and Construction
0110-4772 New Zealand Economist *see* 0111-8021
0110-4802 New Zealand. Ministry of Foreign Affairs. Development
0110-4969 New Zealand Environmental Health Inspector *see* 0112-0212
0110-5019 New Zealand. Department of Statistics. Part A: Prices.
0110-5027 New Zealand. Department of Statistics. Part B: Wages and Labour†
0110-5124 New Zealand Antarctic Record
0110-5132 Book Trade Monthly *see* 0111-8781
0110-5191 Public Sector
0110-5205 N Z O I Oceanographic Field Report
0110-5221 D S I R Discussion Paper
0110-523X Reserve Bank of New Zealand. Research Papers
0110-5337 N.Z.A.R.T. Amateur Radio Callbook
0110-540X New Zealand Journal of Archaeology
0110-5493 Aviation Historical Society of New Zealand. Journal
0110-571X New Zealand Speech-Language Therapists Journal
0110-5760 Royal New Zealand Institute of Horticulture. Annual Journal
0110-5787 New Zealand Listener
0110-585X English in New Zealand
0110-5892 Canterbury Botanical Society. Journal
0110-6007 New Zealand Cartographic Journal
0110-604X Wildlife - a Review
0110-6112 New Zealand. Department of Scientific and Industrial Research. Geophysics Division. Report
0110-6155 Rails
0110-618X N Z O I Records
0110-6260 Orchardist of New Zealand
0110-6287 New Zealand Environment
0110-6295 Automation and Control
0110-6376 S E T: Research Information for Teachers
0110-6392 New Zealand Operational Research
0110-6465 New Zealand Journal of Ecology
0110-6589 Agronomy Society of New Zealand. Proceedings
0110-6619 Continuing Education in New Zealand *see* 0112-224X
0110-6635 New Zealand Justices' Quarterly
0110-666X Directory of Australian Associations
0110-6872 New Zealand. Ministry of Transport. Traffic Research Report
0110-7011 Blue Water
0110-7089 New Zealand. Department of Scientific and Industrial Research. Geophysics Division. Technical Note
0110-7720 Lincoln College. Agricultural Economics Research Unit. Discussion Paper
0110-7844 Forest Industries Review *changed to* Forest Industries
0110-8085 Celluloid Strip
0110-8247 People & Planning
0110-8603 Broadsheet
0110-8700 New Zealand. Department of Statistics. Population Census: Internal Migration
0110-943X National Museum of New Zealand Records

0110-9464 National Museum of New Zealand. Bulletin
0110-9510 New Ethicals Catalogue
0110-9944 New Zealand. Department of Health. Environmental Radioactivity Annual Report
0111-0225 New Zealand. Department of Statistics. New Zealand Life Tables
0111-0470 New Zealand Planning Council. Planning Paper
0111-0489 Youth Studies in New Zealand
0111-0756 New Zealand. Road Research Unit. Occasional Paper
0111-0829 New Zealand Agricultural Engineering Institute. Current Publications
0111-0950 Technical Papers on New Zealand Wool *see* 0112-2932
0111-1108 Economic Review of New Zealand Agriculture†
0111-1302 N Z O I Oceanographic Summary
0111-1485 New Zealand Society of Periodontology. Journal
0111-1957 Alpha
0111-2473 Agricultural Economist
0111-2821 N Z C E R Newsletter
0111-3364 New Zealand Pottery and Ceramics Research Association. Annual Report†
0111-378X N.Z.A.E.I. Newsletter
0111-3895 Royal Society of New Zealand. Miscellaneous Series
0111-395X Nat Ed Newsletter
0111-4123 Planning Research Index†
0111-4239 New Zealand. District Court Reports
0111-5251 New Zealand. Ministry of Foreign Affairs. Project Profiles
0111-5308 Centrepoint
0111-5383 Fauna of New Zealand
0111-5499 Weather and Climate
0111-5774 Pacific Arts Newsletter
0111-5782 New Zealand Times
0111-5839 Energy Journal†
0111-6142 New Zealand Diplomatic Corps and Consular and Other Representatives
0111-6355 New Zealand School Journal
0111-6606 Food Technologist
0111-672X New Zealand Science Abstracts
0111-6770 Mazengarb's Industrial Law Bulletin
0111-686X New Zealand. Nature Conservation Council. Newsletter
0111-7122 Ionospheric Data, New Zealand†
0111-7351 New Zealand Social Work
0111-7416 Quality Assurance. New Zealand
0111-7874 Massey University. Department of Accounting & Finance. Discussion Paper Series
0111-8021 New Zealand Financial Review
0111-8102 New Zealand. Department of Statistics. Demographic Bulletin
0111-8129 New Zealand. F R I Bulletin
0111-834X New Zealand Publishing News
0111-8358 New Zealand Family Law Reports
0111-8587 D S I R Industrial Information Series
0111-8617 New Zealand. National Health Statistics Centre. Fetal and Infant Deaths
0111-8676 Parallax†
0111-8781 New Zealand Bookseller & Publisher
0111-8854 Mentalities
0111-915X New Zealand Dairy Exporter
0111-9176 New Zealand Statistician
0111-9370 Staples' Guide to New Zealand Income Tax Practice
0111-9435 New Zealand Planning Institute. Planning Quarterly
0112-0212 New Zealand Journal of Environmental Health
0112-0395 N Z O I Hydrology Station Data
0112-0433 N Z Micro
0112-0603 Massey University. Centre for Agricultural Policy Studies. Discussion Paper†
0112-109X New Zealand Journal of Psychology
0112-1170 New Zealand Institute of Economic Research. Medium Term Review
0112-1545 University of Auckland. Department of Geography. Occasional Publication
0112-1642 Sports Medicine
0112-2061 New Zealand. Economic Monitoring Group Report
0112-224X New Zealand Journal of Adult Learning
0112-2320 AgLink Index and Catalogue
0112-2339 New Zealand. Department of Scientific and Industrial Research. Social Science Series
0112-2479 Collected Papers from the Journal of the Royal Society of New Zealand
0112-255X Hospital Therapeutics
0112-2584 Annual Returns of Production from Quarries and Mineral Production Statistics
0112-2851 Wool Research Organisation of New Zealand Reports
0112-2908 Wool Research Organisation of New Zealand Communications
0112-2932 Wool Research Organisation of New Zealand Technical Papers
0112-3629 New Zealand Census of Transport, Storage & Communication
0112-3890 New Zealand Journal of Technology
0112-3939 New Zealand. Department of Statistics. Statistics of Incomes and Income Tax of Persons
0112-3998 New Zealand. Department of Statistics. Statistics of Incomes and Income Tax of Companies
0112-4048 New Zealand Dairy Research Institute Annual Report *changed to* New Zealand Dairy Research Institute Biennial Review
0112-4447 New Zealand. Department of Statistics. Justice Statistics: Part A
0112-4501 New Zealand. Department of Statistics. Justice Statistics: Part B
0112-4951 Dance News
0112-5117 New Zealand. Department of Statistics. Overseas Balance of Payments
0112-5842 Business Keynote†
0112-6261 New Zealand Family Law Bulletin
0112-6601 New Zealand Household Expenditure and Income Survey
0112-6709 New Zealand. Department of Statistics. External Migration Statistics
0112-8388 C P Newsletter Monthly
0112-8949 New Zealand Flight Safety
0112-9155 New Zealand. Department of Statistics. Demographic Trends Bulletin
0112-9597 New Zealand Forestry
0115-0022 Sylvatrop
0115-0243 Philippine Quarterly of Culture and Society
0115-0405 C L S U Journal of the Arts†
0115-0456 Forpride Digest *changed to* F P R D I Journal
0115-0464 Private Development Corporation of the Philippines. Monthly Economic Letter
0115-0529 Monitor
0115-0553 Kalikasan
0115-0693 Countryside Banking
0115-0820 Araneta Research Journal
0115-0944 International Rice Research Newsletter
0115-0960 Canopy *changed to* Canopy International
0115-1126 Santo Tomas Journal of Medicine
0115-1142 I R R I. Research Highlights
0115-1169 P S S C Social Science Information
0115-1207 Philippine Astronomical Handbook
0115-1304 N R C P Research Bulletin
0115-1312 Construction & Engineering
0115-138X Integrated Bar of the Philippines. Journal
0115-1401 C B Review
0115-1541 P C A Coconut Farmers Bulletin†
0115-1746 Philippine Business Review
0115-1843 Builder of Progress†
0115-1851 Philippines. Labor Statistics Service. Year Book of Labor Statistics
0115-2106 Philippine Biota
0115-2130 Kimika
0115-2157 Trends in Technology
0115-2173 Philippine Journal of Veterinary and Animal Sciences
0115-2351 Philippine Textile Digest
0115-2394 Trade Post
0115-2408 Journal of Northern Luzon
0115-2467 I R R I Reporter
0115-2521 University of Baguio Journal†
0115-2645 L W U A Quarterly
0115-2661 Social Development News
0115-2742 Mindanao Journal
0115-2777 N S T A Technology Journal
0115-2971 Homelife
0115-3110 Graduate School Journal
0115-3307 Table of Sunrise, Sunset, Twilight, Moonrise and Moonset
0115-3676 Evergreen *see* 0115-9259
0115-3757 Atomedia
0115-3773 S M A R C Monitor
0115-3862 I R R I Research Paper Series
0115-3994 Balikaton Newsletter
0115-4141 I C L A R M Translations
0115-4249 Philippines. Ministry of Education, Culture and Sports. National Scholarship Center. Annual Report
0115-4389 I C L A R M Studies and Reviews
0115-4419 Private Development Corporation of the Philippines. Industry Digest
0115-4435 I C L A R M Conference Proceedings.
0115-4575 I C L A R M Newsletter *changed to* N A G A: I C L A R M Quarterly
0115-4729 Abstract Bibliography on Coconut†
0115-4931 C M U Journal of Agriculture, Food and Nutrition
0115-4990 Habitat Philippines†
0115-5032 Ang Tagamasid
0115-5490 P F N P Newsletter†
0115-5547 I C L A R M Technical Reports
0115-5814 Ang Tala
0115-5997 I C L A R M Bibliographies
0115-6012 Kinaadman
0115-625X Scientia Filipinas
0115-6373 Philippines. Journal of Industrial Relations
0115-6403 Philippine Biochemical Society. Bulletin
0115-6853 Mindanao Art & Culture
0115-690X Journal of Fisheries & Aquaculture†
0115-6950 Arts & Sciences Journal
0115-7000 Development Administration Journal
0115-7205 Philippine Law Report
0115-7329 Mindanao State University. U R C Professional Papers
0115-7809 Science Diliman
0115-8341 S L U-E I S S I Newsletter
0115-835X Likas-Yaman
0115-8473 N F E/W I D Exchange - Asia. Occasional Paper
0115-8724 Philippine Science and Technology Abstracts Bibliography
0115-9259 Bagong Sibol
0116-0516 Studies in Philippine Linguistics
0116-2993 Asian Environment
0116-3426 Philippine Revenue Journal
0120-0011 Universidad Nacional de Colombia. Facultad de Medicina. Revista
0120-0216 Aleph
0120-0283 Universidad Industrial de Santander. Boletin de Geologia
0120-033X Revista E A F I T - Temas Administrativos *changed to* Revista Universidad E A F I T
0120-0534 Revista Latinoamericana de Psicologia
0120-0631 Revista de las Fuerzas Armadas
0120-0747 Estudios Rurales Latinoamericanos
0120-0798 Revista Acodal
0120-0852 Universidad Industrial de Santander. Revista - Investigaciones
0120-0887 C E R L A L: Noticias sobre el Libro y Bibliografia
0120-0909 Universidad Industrial de Santander. Revista - Medicina
0120-0933 Universidad de Antioquia. Facultad de Ciencias Economicas. Administracion de Empresas. Tecnologia Administrativa
0120-095X Universidad Industrial de Santander. Revista - Humanidades
0120-0976 Revista Interamericana de Bibliotecologia
0120-0992 Universidad de los Andes. Cuadernos de Filosofia y Letras
0120-100X Revista Ion
0120-1034 Neurologia Colombia
0120-1085 Museo de Arte Moderno. Boletin Informativo†
0120-1131 Resumenes de la Literatura Medica Colombiana†
0120-1158 Noticias C E R L A L *see* 0120-0887
0120-1182 Sociedad Colombiana de Endocrinologia. Revista
0120-1204 Boletin Bibliografico C E R L A L *see* 0120-0887
0120-1263 Escritos
0120-1344 Memorias Martes del Paraninfo
0120-1425 Boletin Geologico
0120-1468 Franciscanum
0120-1484 Pastos Tropicales. Boletin Informativo *changed to* Pasturas Tropicales. Boletin
0120-1492 Universidad de Caldas. Facultad de Filosofia. Revista
0120-1557 Revista de Egresados
0120-1603 Revista Universidad Tecnologica
0120-1794 Revista Temas Economicos *see* 0120-2596
0120-1824 Cassava Bulletin *changed to* Cassava Newsletter
0120-1875 Informativo Juridico
0120-1921 Informativo Fasecolda
0120-1972 Revista Fasecolda
0120-2073 Instituto Colombiano para el Fomento de la Educacion Superior. Boletin Bibliografico†
0120-2235 International Center for Tropical Agriculture. Bean Program Annual Report
0120-2278 Revista Cafetera de Colombia
0120-2391 Informe Anual del Programa de Pastos Tropicales
0120-2480 Hojas de Frijol para America Latina
0120-2499 Centro Interamericano de Fotointerpretacion. Revista
0120-2561 Universidad Nacional de Colombia. Facultad Nacional de Minas. Anales
0120-2596 Lecturas de Economia
0120-2669 Universidad Nacional de Colombia. Facultad de Arquitectura. Revista
0120-2758 Colombia. Observatorio Astronomico Nacional. Anuario
0120-2812 Acta Agronomica
0120-2839 Universidad Pedagogica Nacional. Centro de Investigaciones. Boletin Informativo
0120-2855 Revista Odontologia
0120-2898 Abstracts on Cassava
0120-2928 Abstracts on Field Beans
0120-2944 Resumenes Analiticos sobre Pastos Tropicales
0120-3053 Universidad Pedagogica y Tecnologica de Colombia. Centrode Estudios Economicos. Apuntes del C E N E S
0120-3169 C I A T Report
0120-3215 Familia y Sociedad
0120-324X Revista Comercio Exterior de Colombia
0120-3347 Revista Colombiana de Anestesiologia
0120-338X Forma y Funcion
0120-3479 Lenguaje
0120-3576 Coyuntura Economica
0120-3584 Desarrollo y Sociedad
0120-3754 Administracion y Desarrollo
0120-3797 Avances en Psicologia Clinica Latinoamericana
0120-3819 Educacion Superior y Desarrollo
0120-3878 Perspectivas en Psicologia
0120-4017 Colombia. Superintendencia Bancaria. Revista
0120-4084 C I A T International
0120-4092 C I A T Internacional
0120-4114 Revista Veterinaria y Zootecnica de Caldas
0120-4165 Controversia
0120-422X Semillas
0120-4289 Camara de Comercio de Bogota. Revista
0120-4351 Flora de Colombia

0120-5056	Directorio de la Educacion Superior en Colombia
0120-5102	Camara Colombiana de la Construccion. Revista
0120-5226	Bancos y Bancarios de Colombia
0120-5455	Texto e Contexto
0120-5595	Colombia: Ciencia y Tecnologia
0120-5609	Ingenieria e Investigacion
0120-6281	Colombia. Direccion General de Estadistica. Boletin Mensual de Estadistica *see* 0010-1370
0120-6311	Revista Internacional de Pediatria
0120-677X	Educacion Fisica y Deporte
0120-6907	Colombia su Gentes y Regiones
0125-0000	Thai Abstracts, Series A. Science and Technology
0125-0019	Quarterly Bulletin of Statistics for Asia and the Pacific
0125-0027	Sample Surveys in the ESCAP Region
0125-0140	Business in Thailand
0125-0191	Thai-American Business
0125-0981	Thailand Business
0125-1074	Bank of Thailand. Monthly Report
0125-1759	Journal of Ferrocement
0125-1767	A G E News
0125-2186	Environmental Sanitation Abstracts - Low Cost Options
0125-2488	P A S A A Journal
0125-3719	Renewable Energy Review Journal
0125-4529	Scientific Serials in Thai Libraries
0125-4537	List of Scientific and Technical Literature Relating to Thailand
0125-5606	N I D A Bulletin
0125-5827	Index to Thai Periodical Literature
0125-5983	Chiang Mai Medical Bulletin
0125-605X	Bank of Thailand. Quarterly Bulletin
0125-7978	Kasetsart University, Bangkok, Thailand. Faculty of Fisheries. Notes
0125-9008	Baca
0125-9156	Berita L.I.P.I.
0125-9229	Warta Ekonomi Maritim Review for Entrepreneurs
0125-9318	Menara Perkebunan
0125-9555	Indonesia. Badan Tenaga Atom Nasional. Majalah B A T A N *see* 0303-2876
0125-9687	Hukum dan Pembangunan
0125-9830	Oseanologi di Indonesia
0126-0057	Trubus
0126-0561	Badan Meteorologi dan Geofisika. Laporan Evaluasi Hujan dan Perkiraan Hujan
0126-057X	Foto Indonesia
0126-0758	BioIndonesia
0126-0812	Indonesia. National Scientific Documentation Center. Annual Report
0126-1282	Indeks Berita Surat Kabar†
0126-1312	Journal of the Medical Sciences
0126-1568	Atom Indonesia
0126-1584	Atma Jaya Research Centre. Newsletter
0126-1630	Atma Jaya Research Centre. Library Bulletin
0126-2319	Indonesia. Central Bureau of Statistics. Economic Indicator Bulletin
0126-270X	Prisma (1983)
0126-2874	N U S A
0126-2912	Statistical Year Book of Indonesia
0126-3595	Statistical Pocketbook of Indonesia
0126-3714	Indonesia. Export by Commodity, Country of Destination and Port of Export
0126-4273	Tempo
0126-4419	Indonesia. Import by Commodity and Country of Origin
0126-5024	Masalah Pendidikan
0126-5040	Malaysian Periodicals Index
0126-5105	Development Forum
0126-5156	Foram Pembangunan
0126-5210	Malaysian National Bibliography
0126-527X	Malaysian Panorama
0126-5415	Pemberita†
0126-5504	Malayan Business
0126-5520	U M B C Economic Review†
0126-5539	Geological Society of Malaysia Newsletter *changed to* Warta Geologi
0126-5547	Timah
0126-5652	Malaysian Veterinary Journal
0126-5709	M A R D I Research Bulletin
0126-575X	Planter
0126-5806	Siaran Pekebun
0126-5849	Rubber Research Institute of Malaysia. Planters Conference Proceedings
0126-5865	Malaysian Rubber Producers' Council. Monthly Statistical Bulletin
0126-6039	Sains Malaysiana: Jernal Sains Alam Semula
0126-6128	Pertanika
0126-6136	Jurnal Sains Institut Penyelidikan Getah Malaysia
0126-6187	Geological Society of Malaysia. Bulletin
0126-6209	A B U Technical Review
0126-625X	Accounting Journal
0126-6330	Malaysia. Directory of Timber Trade
0126-6403	Asian Defence Journal
0126-6705	Malaysian Mathematical Society. Bulletin
0126-690X	Foreign Affairs Malaysia
0126-7000	Ilmu Alam
0126-7191	Suara Buruh
0126-7558	Kuala Lumpur Stock Exchange. Companies Handbook
0126-7590	Southeast Asian Ministers of Education Organisation. Regional Centre for Education in Science and Mathematics. Library Accession List
0126-7612	R E C S A M News
0126-7663	Journal of Science and Mathematics Education in Southeast Asia
0126-771X	Maskayu
0126-7809	Majallah Perpustakaan Malaysia
0126-8031	Concern†
0126-8104	Malaysia. National Population and Family Development Board. Buletin Keluarga
0126-8155	Southeast Asian-Ministers of Education Organisation. Regional Centre for Education in Science and Mathematics. Governing Board Meeting. Final Report
0126-818X	Malaysia. Department of Mines. Statistics Relating to the Mining Industry of Malaysia
0126-8198	Forest Research Institute: Research Pamphlet
0126-8279	Rubber Research Institute of Malaysia. Annual Report
0126-8309	Malaysian Rubber Producers' Council. Annual Report
0126-8392	National Productivity Centre, Malaysia. Annual Report
0126-8856	Malaysia. Ministry of Agriculture. Fisheries Division. Annual Fisheries Statistics
0126-8864	Malaysia. Meteorological Service. Summary of Observations for Malaysia *changed to* Malaysia. Meteorological Service. Annual Summary of Meteorological Observations
0126-8872	Monthly Abstract of Meteorological Observations of Malaysia
0126-8937	Usahaluan
0126-9003	Menemui Matematik
0126-9046	District Memoir
0126-9062	Indeks Suratkhabar Malaysia
0126-9410	Rubber Research Institute of Malaysia. Technology Bulletin
0126-9437	Kajian Veterinar Malaysia
0127-0001	Business Conditions Malaysia
0127-0559	Malaysia. Geological Survey. Annual Report
0127-144X	Sarawak Electricity Supply Corporation. Annual Report
0127-1474	Malaysian Journal of Tropical Geography
0127-1555	Current Malaysian Serials (Non-Government)
0127-1962	Jurnal Ekonomi Malaysia
0127-4880	Index to Malaysian Conferences
0127-4937	Surveyor
0127-6441	Malaysian Technologist
0129-2056	Asian Mass Communications Bulletin
0129-279X	Singapore. National Statistical Commission. Statistical News†
0129-2900	A S E A N Business Quarterly
0129-2951	Singapore Business
0129-3109	Singapore Government Directory
0129-3117	Singapore Literature†
0129-315X	Singapore National Bibliography
0129-3184	Planews
0129-3214	Shaonian Yuekan†
0129-3621	Singapore Banking & Finance
0129-4024	Asian Journal of Infectious Diseases
0129-4172	Asian Journal of Pharmaceutical Sciences
0129-4423	Singapore Business Yearbook
0129-4776	Singapore Journal of Education
0129-5020	Singapore Travel
0129-508X	Students' Literature†
0129-5276	Singapore International Chamber of Commerce. Investor's Guide *changed to* Singapore International Chamber of Commerce. Investors Guide to the Economic Climate of Singapore
0129-5780	Singapore Chinese Chamber of Commerce and Industry. Economic Quarterly
0129-606X	Silver Kris
0129-6256	Singapore Standards Yearbook
0129-6310	Singapore. Ministry of Labour. Annual Report
0129-6485	Singapore Journal of Primary Industries
0129-6531	Engineering Journal of Singapore
0129-6612	Media Asia
0129-6639	Young Generation
0129-6736	Harapan†
0129-6760	Singapore. Department of Statistics. Report on the Census of Wholesale, Retail Trades, Restaurants & Hotels
0129-6787	New Worker†
0129-6884	Singapore Arts
0129-7414	Singapore Monthly Trade Statistics: Imports & Exports
0129-7457	Singapore Community Health Bulletin
0129-7619	Singapore Journal of Tropical Geography
0129-766X	Singapore
0129-7716	R E L C Annual Report
0129-7767	R E L C Guidelines
0129-797X	Contemporary Southeast Asia
0129-8194	Decor Guide
0129-8372	Mimar
0129-8828	Institute of Southeast Asian Studies. Research Notes and Discussion Series
0129-8844	R E L C Occasional Papers
0129-9239	N B D C S News
0129-9786	Singapore. Department of Statistics. Report on the Survey of Services
0129-9867	Tradelink - S M A Annual Directory (Year)
0130-0172	Lietuviu Kalbotyros Klausimai
0130-1128	Geokhimiya i Rudoobrazovanie
0130-1519	Zashchitnye Pokrytiya na Metallakh
0130-1802	Izobretatel' i Ratsionalizator
0130-2663	Kriobiologiya i Kriomeditsina†
0130-3104	Detskaya Literatura
0130-3252	Contributions to the History of Natural Sciences and Technology in the Baltic
0130-3686	Materialy Glyatsiologicheskikh Issledovanii
0130-5247	Ukrains'kyi Istorychnyi Zhurnal
0130-5395	Upravlyayushchie Sistemy i Mashiny
0130-5719	Filosofs'ka Dumka
0130-6774	Itogi Nauki i Tekhniki: Tekhnicheskaya Kibernetika
0130-6782	Itogi Nauki i Tekhniki: Tekhnologiya i Oborudovanie Mekhanosborochnogo Proizvodstva†
0130-6804	Itogi Nauki i Tekhniki: Elektrosvyaz'
0130-6936	Narodna Tvorchist' ta Etnografiya
0130-6995	Narody Azii i Afriki: Istoriya, Ekonomika, Kul'tura
0130-9404	Matematicheskie Metody v Ekonomike
0130-9420	Matematicheskie Metody i Fiziko-mekhanicheskie Polya
0131-0194	Radyans'ke Literaturoznavstvo
0131-0208	Ekspress-Informatsiya. Kvantovaya Radiotekhnika
0131-0224	Ekspress-Informatsiya. Kontrol'no-Izmeritel'naya Tekhnika
0131-0232	Ekspress-Informatsiya. Korroziya i Zashchita Metallov
0131-0275	Ekspress-Informatsiya. Nadezhnost' i Kontrol' Kachestva
0131-0321	Ekspress-Informatsiya. Podvodno-Tekhnicheskie, Vodolaznye i Sudopod'emnye Raboty. *changed to* Ekspress-Informatsiya. Podvodno-Tekhnicheskie, Vodolaznye i Sudopod'emnye Raboty. Gidrotekhnicheskie Sooruzheniya
0131-0356	Ekspress-Informatsiya. Porshnevye i Gazoturbinnye Dvigateli
0131-0380	Ekspress-Informatsiya. Pribory i Elementy Avtomatiki i Vychislitel'noi Tekhniki
0131-0402	Ekspress-Informatsiya. Promyshlennyi Transport
0131-0437	Ekspress-Informatsiya. Radiotekhnika Sverkhvysokikh Chastot
0131-0445	Ekspress-Informatsiya. Rezhushchie Instrumenty†
0131-047X	Ekspress-Informatsiya. Sinteticheskie Vysokopolimernye Materialy
0131-0488	Ekspress-Informatsiya. Sistemy Avtomaticheskogo Upravleniya
0131-0526	Ekspress-Informatsiya. Tara i Upakovka. Konteinery
0131-0577	Ekspress-Informatsiya. Tekhnicheskaya Kibernetika
0131-0593	Ekspress-Informatsiya. Tekhnologiya i Oborudovanie Liteinogo Proizvodstva†
0131-0607	Ekspress-Informatsiya. Tekhnologiya i Oborudovanie Mekhanosborochnogo Proizvodstva†
0131-0615	Ekspress-Informatsiya. Tekhnologiya i Oborudovanie Kuznechno-Shtampovochnogo Proizvodstva†
0131-0747	Ekspress-Informatsiya. Elektronika
0131-1611	Problemy Spetsial'noi Elektrometallurgii†
0131-176X	Fizika Molekul *see* 0206-3166
0131-2413	Mukomol'no-elevatornaya i Kombikormovaya Promyshlennost'
0131-2596	Okhota i Okhotnich'e Khozyaistvo
0131-2669	Pomniki Histor'ii Kul'tury Belarusi
0131-2928	Problemy Mashinostroeniya
0131-3525	Referativnyi Zhurnal. Svarka
0131-3533	Referativnyi Zhurnal. Korroziya i Zashchita ot Korrozii
0131-3541	Referativnyi Zhurnal. Biofizika†
0131-355X	Referativnyi Zhurnal. Radiatsionnaya Biologiya
0131-3568	Sadovodstvo
0131-3843	Akademiya Nauk Litovskoi S.S.R. Trudy. Seriya A. Obshchestvennye Nauki
0131-3851	Akademiya Nauk Litovskoi S.S.R. Trudy. Seriya C. Biologicheskie Nauki
0131-6265	Sovetskaya Bibliografiya
0131-6397	Sel'skokhozyaistvennaya Biologiya
0131-6451	Signal'naya Informatsiya. Avtomatika i Telemekhanika†
0131-646X	Signal'naya Informatsiya. Vychislitel'naya Tekhnika†
0131-6478	Signal'naya Informatsiya. Poluprovodnikovye Pribory†
0131-6508	Signal'naya Informatsiya. Teoreticheskaya Radiotekhnika - Radiosvyaz' - Radioizmereniya†
0131-6516	Signal'naya Informatsiya. Tekhnicheskaya Kibernatika†
0131-6532	Signal'naya Informatsiya. Virusologiya†
0131-6540	Signal'naya Informatsiya. Neirofiziologiya - Vysshaya Nervnaya Deyatel'nost' - Obshchaya i Eksperimental'naya Psikhologiya - Nervnomyshechnaya Sistema†

ISSN INDEX

ISSN	Title
0131-6559	Signal'naya Informatsiya. Fiziologiya Cheloveka i Zhivotnykh: Krov' i Limfa *see* 0233-6618
0131-6567	Signal'naya Informatsiya. Fiziologiya Endokrinnoi Sistemy: Razmnozhenie - Laktatsiya†
0131-6656	Smena
0131-6672	Rybovodstvo i Rybolovstvo
0131-7105	Tekhnika v Sel'skom Khozyaistve
0131-7377	Sem'ya i Shkola
0131-7393	Sel'skii Mekhanizator
0131-7962	Ekspress-Informatsiya. Gorodskoi Transport
0131-7970	Ekspress-Informatsiya. Detali Mashin
0131-7997	Ekspress-Informatsiya. Ispytatel'nye Pribory i Stendy
0132-0793	Model's Season
0132-1226	Sovetskii Krasnyi Krest
0132-1331	Radyans'ke Pravo
0132-165X	Ekspress-Informatsiya. Avtomaticheskie Linii i Metallorezhushchie Stanki†
0132-1668	Ekspress-Informatsiya. Astronavtika i Raketodinamika
0132-2729	Akademiya Nauk Litovskoi S.S.R. Trudy. Seriya B. Khimiya, Tekhnika, Fizicheskaya Geografiya
0132-2818	Akademiya Nauk Litovskoi S.S.R. Litovskii Matematicheskii Sbornik
0132-4160	Avtomatika i Vychislitel'naya Tekhnika (Riga)
0132-5639	Referativnyi Zhurnal. Organizatsiya Upravleniya
0132-6058	Sak'art'velos S.S.R. Mec'nierebat'a Akademiis Mac'ne. Istoriis Ark'eologiis, Et'nograp'iisa da Xelovnebis Istoriis Seria
0132-6414	Fizika Nizkikh Temperatur
0132-6422	Akademiya Nauk Latviiskoi S.S.R. Izvestiya
0132-6457	Darzs un Drava
0132-6503	Baltistica
0132-6732	Signal'naya Informatsiya. Plazma†
0132-7348	Obshchestvennye Nauki za Rubezhom. Seriya 9: Vostokovedenie i Afrikanistika
0132-7356	Obshchestvennye Nauki za Rubezhom. Seriya 3: Filosofiya i Sotsiologiya
0132-7372	Obshchestvennye Nauki za Rubezhom. Seriya 2: Ekonomika
0132-9030	Signal'naya Informatsiya. Zoologiya Nazemnykh Pozvonochnykh†
0133-011X	Baromfitenyesztes es Feldolgozas
0133-0152	Magyar Kozgazdasagi Irodalom
0133-0276	Hungarian Journal of Industrial Chemistry
0133-0284	Szovetkezeti Ipar
0133-0365	Hungarian Economy
0133-0373	Muszaki Lapszemle. Elektrotechnika/Technical Abstracts. Electrical Engineering *see* 0231-0783
0133-0381	Tarsadalomtudomanyi Kozlemenyek
0133-0438	Kulfoldi Magyar Nyelvu Folyoiratok Repertoriuma *see* 0133-333X
0133-056X	Forras
0133-0616	Kulpolitika
0133-0748	Soproni Szemle
0133-090X	Magyar Hirek
0133-0918	Gabonaipar
0133-1167	Tiszataj
0133-1353	Uj Elet
0133-1531	Ars Hungarica
0133-1655	Tajekoztato a Kulfoldi Kozgazdasagi Irodalomrol. Series B, Bibliografia *changed to* Kulfoldi Kozgazdasagi Irodalmi Szemle. Series B
0133-168X	Filateliai Szemle
0133-1736	Reaction Kinetics and Catalysis Letters
0133-1779	Teologia
0133-2074	Szociologiai Informacio
0133-2368	Literatura
0133-2449	Budapesti Statisztikai Tajekoztato
0133-2465	Szabolcs-Szatmari Szemle
0133-2813	Szakszervezeti Szemle
0133-2929	Publications of the Technical University for Heavy Industry. Series D: Natural Sciences
0133-297X	Publications of the Technical University for Heavy Industry. Series C, Machinery
0133-3046	Studia Comitatensia
0133-3305	Vizgazdalkodas es Kornyezetvedelem
0133-3321	Hungarian Building Marketing
0133-333X	Kulfoldi Magyar Nyelvu Kiadvanyok
0133-3356	Alkohologia
0133-3399	Alkalmazott Matematikai Lapok
0133-3461	Szociologia
0133-3496	Magyar Konyveszet (Budapest. 1961)
0133-3720	Cereal Research Communications
0133-3755	Kincskereso
0133-381X	Szoleszet es Boraszat†
0133-3844	Biologia
0133-3852	Analysis Mathematica
0133-4387	Vizminosegi es Viztechnologiai Kutatasi Eredmenyek†
0133-4611	Magyar Konyveszet. Tankonyvek†
0133-4751	Eletunk
0133-4875	Mezogazdasagi es Elelmiszeripari Konyvtarosok Tajekoztatoja
0133-5162	Marx Karoly Kozgazdasagtudomanyi Egyetem Oktatoinak Szakirodalmi Munkassaga
0133-543X	Hungary. Kozponti Statisztikai Hivatal. Foglalkoztatottsag es Kereseti Aranyok
0133-5464	Magyar Belorvosi Archivum
0133-5502	Hungarian Academy of Sciences. Central Research Institute for Physics. Yearbook
0133-5545	Bulletin du Musee Hongrois des Beaux-Arts
0133-5707	Muszaki es Gazdasagi Fejlodes Fo Iranyai†
0133-5782	Magyar Nemzeti Bibliografia. Zenemuvek Bibliografiaja
0133-5847	Magyar Statisztikai Zsebkonyv
0133-5944	Studio Sound & Broadcast Engineering
0133-6193	Keleti Tanulmanyok
0133-6436	Epitesugyi Ertesito
0133-6452	Ipargazdasagi Szemle
0133-6622	Folia Historica
0133-6673	Ars Decorativa
0133-6843	Magyar Nemzeti Bibliografia. Konyvek Bibliografiaja
0133-6894	Magyar Nemzeti Bibliografia. Idoszaki Kiadvanyok Repertoriuma
0133-6924	Antaeus
0133-7084	Cartinform *see* 0008-7009
0133-736X	Magyar Konyvtari Szakirodalom Bibliografiaja
0133-7505	Hungarika Irodalmi Szemle
0133-7564	Hevesi Szemle
0133-7599	Theologiai Szemle
0133-7769	Trends in World Economy
0133-7890	SZOVOSZ Tajekoztato
0133-8684	Hungary. Kozponti Statisztikai Hivatal. Ipari Zsebkonyv
0133-8862	Magyar Tudomanyos Akademia Konvytaranak Kiadvanyai
0133-9060	Debreceni Orvostudomanyi Egyetem Evkonyve
0133-9133	Hungary. Kozponti Statisztikai Hivatal. Kozlekedesi es Hirkozlesi Evkonyv *changed to* Hungary. Kozponti Statisztikai Hivatal. Kozlekedesi Posta es Tavkozlesi
0133-9214	Ludas Matyi Evkonyve
0133-9559	Szamitastechnikai Evkonyve *see* 0139-3286
0133-9966	Gyorsindex - Szamitastechnika, Automatizalas
0134-0050	Historisch-Demographische Mitteilungen
0134-0247	Kurrens Idoszaki Kiadvanyok *see* 0231-4592
0134-0719	Journal of Radioanalytical Chemistry *changed to* Journal of Radioanalytical and Nuclear Chemistry. Articles
0134-1103	Nemzetkozi Szemle
0134-1138	Hungary. Kozponti Statisztikai Hivatal. Belkereskedelmi Evkonyv
0134-1464	Magyar Irodalom es Irodalomtudomany Bibliografiaja
0134-1510	Informacio a Konyvtari es Informacios Munka Eszkozeirol es Berendezeseirol†
0134-2673	Itogi Nauki i Tekhniki: Fiziologiya Cheloveka i Zhivotnykh
0134-272X	Novaya Sovetskaya Literatura po Obshchestvennym Naukam. Ekonomika
0134-2738	Novaya Sovetskaya Literatura po Obshchestvennym Naukam. Gosudarstvo i Pravo
0134-2746	Novaya Sovetskaya Literatura po Obshchestvennym Naukam. Istoriya - Arkheologiya - Etnografiya
0134-2754	Novaya Sovetskaya Literatura po Obshchestvennym Naukam. Naukovedenie
0134-2762	Novaya Sovetskaya Literatura po Obshchestvennym Naukam. Yazykoznanie
0134-2770	Novaya Sovetskaya Literatura po Obshchestvennym Naukam. Literaturovedenie
0134-2789	Novaya Sovetskaya Literatura po Obshchestvennym Naukam. Filosofskie Nauki
0134-2797	Novaya Inostrannaya Literatura po Obshchestvennym Naukam. Literaturovedenie
0134-2800	Novaya Inostrannaya Literatura po Obshchestvennym Naukam. Naukovedenie
0134-2819	Novaya Inostrannaya Literatura po Obshchestvennym Naukam. Yazykoznanie
0134-2827	Novaya Inostrannaya Literatura po Obshchestvennym Naukam. Istoriya - Arkheologiya - Etnografiya
0134-2835	Novaya Inostrannaya Literatura po Obshchestvennym Naukam. Ekonomika
0134-2843	Novaya Inostrannaya Literatura po Obshchestvennym Naukam. Gosudarstvo i Pravo
0134-2851	Novaya Inostrannaya Literatura po Obshchestvennym Naukam. Filosofiya i Sotsiologiya
0134-2916	Novaya Sovetskaya i Inostrannaya Literatura po Obshchestvennym Naukam. Blizhnii i Srednii Vostok - Afrika
0134-2924	Novaya Sovetskaya i Inostrannaya Literatura po Obshchestvennym Naukam. Pol'skaya Narodnaya Respublika
0134-2932	Novaya Sovetskaya i Inostrannaya Literatura po Obshchestvennym Naukam. Problemy Ateizma i Religii
0134-2940	Novaya Sovetskaya i Inostrannaya Literatura po Obshchestvennym Naukam. Mezhdunarodnoe Rabochee Dvizhenie
0134-2959	Novaya Sovetskaya i Inostrannaya Literatura po Obshchestvennym Naukam. Yuzhnaya i Yugo-Vostochnaya Aziya - Dal'nii Vostok
0134-2967	Novaya Sovetskaya i Inostrannaya Literatura po Obshchestvennym Naukam. Chekhoslovatskaya Sotsialisticheskaya Respublika
0134-2975	Novaya Sovetskaya i Inostrannaya Literatura po Obshchestvennym Naukam. Germanskaya Demokraticheskaya Respublika
0134-2983	Novaya Sovetskaya i Inostrannaya Literatura po Obshchestvennym Naukam. Evropeiskie Sotsialisticheskie Strany
0134-2991	Novaya Sovetskaya i Inostrannaya Literatura po Obshchestvennym Naukam. Narodnaya Respublika Bolgariya
0134-3009	Novaya Sovetskaya i Inostrannaya Literatura po Obshchestvennym Naukam. Sotsialisticheskaya Federativnaya Respublika Yugoslaviya
0134-3017	Novaya Sovetskaya i Inostrannaya Literatura po Obshchestvennym Naukam. Vengerskaya Narodnaya Respublika
0134-3033	Novaya Sovetskaya i Inostrannaya Literatura po Obshchestvennym Naukam. Strany Azii i Afriki
0134-3041	Novaya Sovetskaya i Inostrannaya Literatura po Obshchestvennym Naukam. Problemy Slavyanovedeniya i Balkanistiki
0134-3823	Polutehniline Instituut Tallinn. Raschet i Proektirovanie Priborov, Ustroistv i Sistem Tekhnicheskoi Kibernetiki
0134-580X	Referativnyi Zhurnal. Farmakologiya. Obshchaya Farmakologiya Nervnoi Sistemy
0134-7683	Ekspress-Informatsiya. Put' i Stroitel'stvo Zheleznykh Dorog. Problemy B.A.M.
0134-7772	Referativnyi Zhurnal. Elektrosvyaz'
0134-7799	Itogi Nauki i Tekhniki: Organizatsiya Upravleniya Transportom (VINITI)
0134-9236	Morskoi Sbornik
0135-0536	Patma-Banasirakan Handes
0135-0609	Voprosy Informatsionnoi Teorii i Praktiki
0135-0617	Vsesoyuznyi Institut Nauchno-Tekhnicheskoi Informatsii. Deponirovannye Nauchnye Raboty
0135-0633	Signal'naya Informatsiya. Radiofizika i Fizicheskie Osnovy Elektroniki
0135-0870	Signal'naya Informatsiya. Atomy i Molekuly
0135-0889	Signal'naya Informatsiya. Gazy i Zhidkosti. Termodinamika i Statisticheskaya Fizika
0135-0897	Signal'naya Informatsiya. Optika
0135-0919	Signal'naya Informatsiya. Tekhnicheskii Analiz v Metallurgii†
0135-0927	Signal'naya Informatsiya. Teoriya Metallurgicheskikh Protsessov†
0135-0935	Signal'naya Informatsiya. Kompozitsionnye Materialy
0135-0986	Signal'naya Informatsiya. Metallurgiya Poluprovodnikov†
0135-1281	Analogo-Diskretnye Preobrazovaniya Signalov
0135-1419	Atmosferos Fizika
0135-2164	Geologiya i Geokhimiya Goryuchikh Iskopaemykh
0135-2202	Istorychni Doslidzhennya. Istoriya Zarubizhnykh Krayin
0135-2210	Istorychni Doslidzhennya. Vitchyznyana Istoriya
0135-2253	Problemy Kontrolya i Zashchita Atmosfery ot Zagryazneniya
0135-8375	Signal'naya Informatsiya. Struktura i Svoistva Chuguna, Stali, Splavov i Kompozitsionnykh Materialov na Osnove Zheleza†
0135-8383	Signal'naya Informatsiya. Poroshkovaya Metallurgiya†
0135-8405	Signal'naya Informatsiya. Fizicheskie Svoistva. Prochnost' i Plastichnost' Metallov i Splavov†
0135-8537	Semiotika i Informatika
0135-857X	Signal'naya Informatsiya. Svarka†
0136-0612	Signal'naya Informatsiya. Magnitnye Svoistva Tverdykh Tel
0136-1732	Adgeziya Rasplavov i Paika Materialov
0136-3549	Polutehniline Instituut Tallinn. Avtomatizatsiya Tekhnologicheskogo Proyektirovaniya Protsessov Mekhanicheskoi Obrabotki.
0136-3557	Polutehniline Instituut Tallinn. Svoistva i Tekhnologiya Izgotovleniya Iznosostoikikh Materialov
0136-9377	Biokhimiya Zhivotnykh i Cheloveka
0137-0251	Itogi Nauki i Tekhniki: Organicheskaya Khimiya
0137-1096	Acta Universitatis Wratislaviensis. Prace Pedagogiczne
0137-1126	Studies on Fascism and Hitlerite Crimes
0137-1215	Politechnika Wroclawska. Prace Naukoznawcze i Prognostyczne

ISSN INDEX

ISSN	Title
0137-1223	Systems Science
0137-1339	Materials Science
0137-1363	Politechnika Krakowska. Zeszyty Naukowe. Budownictwo Wodne i Inzynieria Sanitarna
0137-1371	Politechnika Krakowska. Zeszyty Naukowe. Architektura
0137-138X	Politechnika Krakowska. Zeszyty Naukowe. Podstawowe Nauki Techniczne
0137-1398	Politechnika Wroclawska. Instytut Technologii Organicznej i Tworzyw Sztucznych. Prace Naukowe. Konferencje
0137-141X	Nauki Polityczne
0137-1428	Nauki Ekonomiczne
0137-1444	Jezykoznawstwo Stosowane
0137-1460	Antropologia
0137-1479	Fruit Science Reports
0137-1495	Acta Alimentaria Polonica
0137-1657	Instytut Zootechniki. Roczniki Naukowe Zootechniki
0137-169X	Akademia Rolnicza, Poznan. Roczniki. Algorytmy Biometryczne i Statystyczne
0137-1703	Akademia Rolnicza, Poznan. Roczniki. Archeozoologia
0137-1711	Akademia Rolnicza, Poznan. Roczniki. Ekonomika i Organizacja Rolnictwa
0137-172X	Akademia Rolnicza, Poznan. Roczniki. Lesnictwo
0137-1738	Akademia Rolnicza, Poznan. Roczniki. Ogrodnictwo
0137-1746	Akademia Rolnicza, Poznan. Roczniki. Ornitologia Stosowana
0137-1754	Akademia Rolnicza, Poznan. Roczniki. Rolnictwo
0137-1762	Akademia Rolnicza, Poznan. Rocznik. Technologia Rolno-Spozywcza *changed to* Akademia Rolnicza, Poznan. Roczniki. Technologia Zywnosci
0137-1770	Akademia Rolnicza, Poznan. Roczniki. Zootechnika
0137-1797	Akademia Rolnicza, Poznan. Rocznik. Technologia Drewna *changed to* Akademia Rolnicza, Poznan. Roczniki. Chemiczna Technologia Drewna
0137-1800	Akademia Rolnicza, Poznan. Roczniki. Mechaniczna Technologia Drewna
0137-1819	Annales Universitatis Mariae Curie-Sklodowska. Sectio AA. Physica et Chemica *see* 0137-6861
0137-1983	Annales Universitatis Mariae Curie-Sklodowska. Sectio B. Geographia, Geologia, Mineralogia et Petrographia
0137-2025	Annales Universitatis Mariae Curie-Sklodowska. Sectio I. Philosophia-Sociologia
0137-2033	Annales Universitatis Mariae Curie-Sklodowska. Sectio F. Humaniora *changed to* Annales Universitatis Mariae Curie-Sklodowska. Sectio F. Historia
0137-219X	Eksploatacya Kolei
0137-2351	Uniwersytet Jagiellonski. Zeszyty Naukowe. Prace z Biologii Molekularnej
0137-2378	Uniwersytet Jagiellonski. Zeszyty Naukowe. Prace z Nauk Politycznych
0137-2440	Polish Academy of Sciences. Institute of Geophysics. Series A. Physics of the Earth's Interior
0137-2459	Papers and Studies in Contrastive Linguistics
0137-2467	Studia Germanica Posnaniensia
0137-2564	Politechnika Lodzka. Zeszyty Naukowe. Fizyka
0137-2572	Politechnika Lodzka. Zeszyty Naukowe. Matematyka
0137-2599	Politechnika Lodzka. Zeszyty Naukowe. Organizacja i Zarzadzanie
0137-2602	Politechnika Lodzka. Zeszyty Naukowe. Inzynieria Chemiczna
0137-2661	Politechnika Lodzka. Zeszyty Naukowe. Cieplne Maszyny Przeplywowe
0137-284X	Drogi Kolejowe
0137-2858	Automatyka Kolejowa
0137-2904	Reports on Mathematical Logic
0137-2939	Polska Akademia Nauk. Oddzial w Krakowie. Osrodek Dokumentacji Fizjograficznej. Studia
0137-2963	Trakcja i Wagony
0137-2998	Kwartalnik Historii Prasy Polskiej
0137-3013	Humanizacja Pracy
0137-303X	Przeglad Poloniny
0137-3080	Estudios Latinoamericanos
0137-3099	Kronika Warszawy
0137-3102	Kronika Wielkopolski
0137-3218	Nasza Przeszlosc
0137-3234	Pamietnikarstwo Polskie
0137-3250	Poznanskie Towarzystwo Przyjaciol Nauk. Komisja Archeologiczna. Prace
0137-3277	Historia i Wspolczesnosc
0137-3390	Studia Historyczne (Bydgoszcz)†
0137-3404	Studia o Ksiazce
0137-3471	Wolnosc i Lud
0137-3501	Rocznik Kaliski
0137-3544	Polska Akademia Nauk. Instytut Krajow Socjalistycznych. Biuletyn Informacyjny
0137-3587	Studia Maritima
0137-3595	Postepy Cybernetyki
0137-3609	Prezentacje
0137-3935	Pagine
0137-3943	Paideia
0137-4079	Ethnologia Polona
0137-4354	Studia Kieleckie
0137-4370	Studia Polonistyczne
0137-4389	Studia Polono-Slavica Orientalia. Acta Litteraria
0137-4435	Transport Museums
0137-4761	Przeglad Lubuski
0137-477X	Quaestiones Geographicae
0137-4885	Polish Archaeological Abstracts
0137-4990	Ergonomia
0137-5059	Biblioteka Fizyki
0137-5083	Polish Journal of Chemistry
0137-5156	Radomskie Towarzystwo. Naukowe. Biuletyn Kwartalny
0137-5164	Zeszyty Gorzowskie†
0137-5172	Z Badan Nad Polskimi Ksiegozbiorami Historycznymi
0137-5253	Instytut Baltycki Gdansk. Komunikaty
0137-5288	Polska Klasa Robotnicza. Studia Historyczne
0137-530X	Studia i Materialy do Dziejow Zup Solnych w Polsce
0137-5326	Szkice Legnickie
0137-5393	Studia z Zakresu Inzynierii
0137-5415	Przestepczosc na Swiecie
0137-5431	Biuletyn Slawistyczny
0137-544X	Przeglad Glottodydaktyczny
0137-5482	Kras i Speleologia
0137-5733	Studia do Dziejow Dawnego Uzbrojenia i Ubioru Wojskowego
0137-5806	Oeconomica Polona
0137-5830	Acta Universitatis Nicolai Copernici. Historia
0137-5881	Acta Physiologiae Plantarum
0137-589X	Instytut Metali Niezelaznych. Prace
0137-5911	Czasopismo Techniczne. Series B: Budownictwo
0137-592X	Czasopismo Techniczne. Series M: Mechanika
0137-6217	Politechnika Wroclawska. Biblioteka Glowna i Osrodek Informacji Naukowo-Technicznej. Prace Naukowe. Konferencje†
0137-6225	Politechnika Wroclawska. Biblioteka Glowna i Osrodek Informacji Naukowo-Technicznej. Prace Naukowe. Studia i Materialy
0137-6233	Politechnika Wroclawska. Instytut Architektury i Urbanistyki. Prace Naukowe. Konferencje
0137-6241	Politechnika Wroclawska. Instytut Budownictwa. Prace Naukowe. Studia i Materialy
0137-625X	Politechnika Wroclawska. Instytut Fizyki. Prace Naukowe. Konferencje
0137-6268	Politechnika Wroclawska. Instytut Matematyki. Prace Naukowe. Konferencje
0137-6284	Politechnika Wroclawska. Instytut Ukladow Elektromaszynowych. Prace Naukowe. Monografie
0137-6292	Politechnika Wroclawska. Instytut Ukladow Elektromaszynowych. Prace Naukowe. Przemysl†
0137-6306	Politechnika Wroclawska. Osrodek Badan Prognostycznych. Prace Naukowe. Konferencje
0137-6314	Politechnika Wroclawska. Osrodek Badan Prognostycznych. Prace Naukowe. Monografie
0137-6322	Politechnika Wroclawska. Osrodek Badan Prognostycznych. Prace Naukowe. Studia i Materialy
0137-6330	Politechnika Wroclawska. Osrodek Badan Prognostycznych. Prace Naukowe. Wspolpraca.
0137-6349	Politechnika Wroclawska. Studium Praktycznej Nauki Jezykow Obcych. Prace Naukowe. Studia i Materialy
0137-6365	Studia Geotechnica et Mechanica
0137-6381	Dziejow Stosunkow Polsko Radzieckich i Rozwoju Wspolnoty Panstw Socjalistycznych
0137-6462	Fluid Dynamics Transactions
0137-6535	Akademia Gorniczo-Hutnicza im. Stanislawa Staszica. Zeszyty Nukowe. Metalurgia i Odlewnictwo
0137-6608	Studia Semiotyczne
0137-6616	Acta Universitatis Nicolai Copernici. Archeologia
0137-6667	Acta Universitatis Nicolai Copernici. Nauki Polityczne
0137-6683	Badania Fizjograficzne nad Polska Zachodnia. Seria C. Zoologia
0137-6853	Annales Universitatis Mariae Curie-Sklodowska. Sectio AA. Chemia
0137-6861	Annales Universitatis Mariae Curie-Sklodowska. Sectio AAA. Physica
0137-6896	Politechnika Poznanska. Zeszyty Naukowe. Chemia Techniki Zastosowan *changed to* Politechnika Poznanska. Zeszyty Naukowe. Chemia i Inzynieria Chemiczna
0137-690X	Politechnika Poznanska. Zeszyty Naukowe. Ekonomika i Organizacja Przemyslu *changed to* Politechnika Poznanska. Zeszyty Naukowe. Organizacja i Zarzadzanie
0137-6918	Politechnika Poznanska. Zeszyty Naukowe. Maszyny Robocze i Pojazdy
0137-6934	Polish Academy of Sciences. Mathematical Institute. Banach Center Publications
0137-6969	Politechnika Czestochowska. Zeszyty Naukowe. Nauki Techniczne. Mechanika
0137-6977	Politechnika Czestochowska. Zeszyty Naukowe. Nauki Techniczne. Elektrotechnika
0137-7183	Problemy Szkolnictwa i Nauk Medycznych
0137-7310	Zycie Szkoly
0137-7566	Geografia w Szkole
0137-7612	Hotelarz
0137-7647	Jezyk Rosyjski
0137-8015	Poland. Urzad Patentowy. Biuletyn
0137-8082	Wychowanie w Przedszkolu
0137-8171	Szkola Zawodowa
0137-818X	Szkola Specjalna
0137-8848	Matematyka
0137-8996	Poznanskie Towarzystwo Przyjaciol Nauk. Komisja Matematyczno-Przyrodnicza. Prace
0137-9585	Rocznik Pedagogiczny
0137-9704	Studia Ubezpieczeniowe
0137-9712	Polonica
0137-9771	Poznanskie Towarzystwo Przyjaciol Nauk. Komisja Geograficzno-Geologiczna. Prace
0137-9860	Studies on the Developing Countries†
0138-0125	Polish Academy of Sciences. Institute of Geophysics. Series D. Physics of the Atmosphere
0138-015X	Polish Academy of Sciences. Institute of Geophysics. Series M. Miscellanea
0138-0214	Polish Academy of Sciences. Institute of Geophysics. Series F. Planetary Geodesy
0138-032X	Archiwum Nauki o Materialach
0138-0389	Instytut Geologiczny. Biuletyn. Geology of Poland
0138-0532	Science of Science
0138-063X	Uniwersytet Gdanski. Wydzial Humanistyczny. Zeszyty Naukowe. Studia Scandinavica
0138-0796	Instytut Techniki Budowlanej. Prace *changed to* Prace Instytutu Techniki Budowlanej. Kwartalnik
0138-0990	Akademia Gorniczo-Hutnicza im. Stanislawa Staszica. Zeszyty Naukowe. Gornictwo. Kwartalnik
0138-1016	Ernst-Moritz-Arndt-Universitaet Greifswald. Wissenschaftliche Zeitschrift. Gesellschaftswissenschaftliche Reihe
0138-1059	Akademie der Wissenschaften der DDR. Abhandlungen. Abteilung Mathematik, Naturwissenschaften, Technik
0138-1067	Ernst-Moritz-Arndt-Universitaet Greifswald. Wissenschaftliche Zeitschrift. Medizinische Reihe
0138-1105	Meteorologischen Dienstes der D D R. Veroeffentlichungen
0138-1245	Boxring
0138-127X	Wissenschaftliche Taschenbuecher. Reihe Texte und Studien
0138-1296	Handball
0138-1377	Paedagogische Hochschule Liselotte Herrmann Guestrow. Philosophische Fakultaet. Wissenschaftliche Zeitschrift
0138-1385	Bibliographie Staat und Recht
0138-1393	Radsportler
0138-144X	Sportkegler
0138-1482	Tanz
0138-1520	Paedagogische Hochschule Karl Friedrich Wilhem Wander. Wissenschaftliche Zeitschrift *changed to* Paedagogische Hochschule Karl Friedrich Wilhelm Wander. Wissenschaftliche Zeitschrift. Paedogogische Reihe
0138-1520	Paedagogishe Hochschule Karl Friedrich Wilhem Wander. Wissenschaftlihe Zeitschrift *changed to* Paedagogische Hochschule Karl Friedrich Wilhelm Wander. Wissenschaftliche Zeitschrift. Gesellschaftswissenschaftliche Reihe
0138-1520	Paedagogische Hochschule Karl Friedrich Wander. Wissenschaftliche Zeitschrift *changed to* Paedagogische Hochschule Karl Friedrich Wilhelm Wander. Wissenschaftliche Zeitschrift. Mathematisch-naturwissenschaftliche Reihe
0138-1539	Zauberkunst
0138-1555	Arbeitsschutz, Arbeitshygiene
0138-1563	Paedagogische Hochschule Liselotte Herrmann Guestrow. Wissenschaftliche Zeitschrift *see* 0138-1377
0138-1563	Paedagogische Hochschule Liselotte Herrmann Guestrow. Wissenschaftliche Zeitschrift *see* 0138-1768
0138-1601	Visier
0138-1644	Deutsche Demokratische Republik. Gesetzblatt
0138-1652	Friedrich-Schiller-Universitaet Jena. Wissenschaftliche Zeitschrift
0138-1768	Paedagogische Hochschule Liselotte Herrmann Guestrow. Paedagogische Fakultaet. Wissenschaftliche Zeitschrift
0138-1989	Informationen fuer die Museen in der DDR
0138-2004	Fundgrube

1452 ISSN INDEX

0138-2055 Informationsbulletin. Aktuelle Probleme der Philosophie der U.d.S.S.R.
0138-208X Nahrung und Ernaehrung der Menschen. Bibliographie F.G. - Ernaehrung
0138-2101 Betontechnik
0138-2136 Nahrung und Ernaehrung der Menschen. Bibliographie F.G. - Lebensmittelwissenschaft
0138-2144 Thematische Information Philosophie
0138-2225 Bibliographie Aktuell
0138-2233 Zeitschriftenschau Keramik
0138-2357 Geophysik und Geologie
0138-242X Informationsbulletin
0138-2543 Katolski Posol
0138-2578 Referateblatt Philosophie. Reihe A: Dialektischer un Historischer Materialismus, Philosophie Probleme des Sozialismus *see* 0232-8798
0138-2586 Gemeinsam
0138-2691 Gewerkschaftsleben
0138-2721 Referateblatt Philosophie. Reihe E. Aktuelle Probleme und Kritik der Buergerlichen Philosophie
0138-2764 Wohnen im Gruenen
0138-2802 Nordeuropa Studien
0138-2810 Wohnen
0138-2853 Ernst-Moritz-Arndt-Universitaet Greifswald. Wissenschaftliche Zeitschrift. Mathematisch-Naturwissenschaftliche Reihe
0138-290X Paedagogische Hochschule "Karl Liebnecht" Potsdam. Wissenschaftliche Zeitschrift
0138-3019 Mathematische Forschung. Schriftenreihe
0138-3027 Literaturschau Polymere und Chemiefaserstoffe
0138-3116 Quartaerpalaeontologie
0138-3167 Veroeffentlichungen zur Volkskunde und Kulturgeschichte
0138-3213 Werte Unserer Heimat
0138-3280 Industriemaessige Gemueseproduktion
0138-3337 Industriemaessige Rinderproduktion
0138-3361 Schriften zur Ur- und Fruehgeschichte
0138-3388 Industriemaessige Schweineproduktion
0138-340X Referatedienst zur Literaturwissenschaft
0138-3418 Schriften zur Philosophie und ihrer Geschichte
0138-3469 Akademie der Wissenschaften der D.D.R. Zentralinstitut fuer Wirtschaftswissenschaften. Schriften
0138-3566 Akademie der Wissenschaften der DDR. Zentralinstitut fuer Geschichte. Schriften
0138-3604 Jenaer Beitraege zur Parteiegeschichte
0138-3612 Kritik der Buergerlichen Ideologie
0138-3655 Referatedienst Jugendforschung
0138-3663 Meroitica
0138-3914 Zentralinstituts fuer Alte Geschichte und Archaeologie. Veroeffentlichen
0138-3957 Saechsische Akademie der Wissenschaften, Leipzig. Philologisch-Historische Klasse. Sitzungsberichte
0138-3973 Der Tourist
0138-4074 Common Name - Kartei Pflanzenschutz- und Schaedlingsbekaempfungsmittel
0138-4112 Akademie der Wissenschaften der DDR. Studien der Geschichte
0138-4228 Berliner Turfantexte
0138-4279 Beitraege zur Ur- und Fruehgeschichte der Bezirke Rostock, Schwerin und Neubrandenburg
0138-435X Jahrbuch fuer Soziologie und Sozialpolitik
0138-4414 Schuetzen und Helfen
0138-4422 Beitraege zur Geographie
0138-4449 Vorderasiatische Schriftdenkmaler der Staatlichen Mussen zu Berlin
0138-4503 Jahrbuch fuer Volkskunde und Kulturgeschichte. Neue Folge
0138-4600 Forschungsbereichs fuer Geo- und Kosmoswissenschaften. Veroeffentlichen
0138-4821 Beitraege zur Algebra und Geometrie
0138-4988 Acta Biotechnologica
0138-5003 Erkrankungen der Zootiere
0138-5011 Neue Zeit
0138-502X Teubner-Texte zur Mathematik
0138-5038 Bibliographie Soziologie
0138-5100 Forschungen zur Wirtschaftsgeschichte
0138-5208 Staats- und Rechtstheoretische Studien
0138-5410 German Democratic Republic. Consumer Co-operative Societies. Magazine
0138-547X Bienen
0138-550X Sammlung Akademie-Verlag: Sprache
0138-5518 Der Lustige Grillenfaenger
0138-5550 Studien ueber Asien, Afrika und Lateinamerika
0138-5569 Kunterbunt
0138-5615 Denkspiegel
0138-5658 Germany (Democratic Republic, 1949-). Meteorologischer Dienst. Abhandlungen
0138-5666 Steckenpferd
0138-5739 Information und Dokumentation: Annotierte Titelliste
0138-5755 Wissenschaft und Gesellschaft
0138-5836 Referatblatt Soziologie
0138-5852 Sprache und Gesellschaft
0138-595X Schriften zur Geschichte und Kultur der Antike
0138-6093 Ciencia y Tecnica en la Agricultura. Serie: Cafe y Cacao
0138-6107 Revista de Informacion Cientifica y Tecnica Cubana
0138-6352 Revista Cubana de Ciencia Avicola
0138-6409 Revista Avicultura
0138-6441 Revista Forestal Baracoa
0138-6492 Revista Plantas Medicinales
0138-6700 Revista Cubana de Reproduccion Animal
0138-6735 Informacion Express. Serie: Forestales
0138-6786 Informacion Express. Serie: Pastos y Forrajes
0138-6832 Informacion Express. Serie: Genetica y Reproduccion
0138-7030 Informacion Express. Serie: Suelos y Agroquimica
0138-7081 Informacion Express. Serie: Rumiantes
0138-7103 Hospital Psiquiatrico de la Habana. Revista
0138-7138 Informacion Express. Serie: Tabaco
0138-7154 Ciencias Biologicas
0138-7170 Problemas de Organizacion de la Ciencia
0138-7189 Informacion Express. Serie: Viandas, Hortalizas y Granos
0138-7235 Informacion Express. Serie: Veterinaria
0138-7251 Ciencias de la Agricultura
0138-7286 Informacion Express. Serie: Proteccion de Plantas
0138-7324 Academia de Ciencias de Cuba. Instituto de Documentacion e Informacion Cientifica y Tecnica. Actualidades de la Informacion Cientifica y Tecnica
0138-7332 Informacion Express. Serie: Mechanizacion Agropecuaria
0138-7383 Informacion Express. Serie: Avicultura
0138-743X Informacion Express. Serie: Citricos y Otros Frutales
0138-7480 Informacion Express. Serie: Economia y Organizacion del Trabajo Agropecuario
0138-7537 Informacion Express. Serie: Ganado Equino
0138-7588 Informacion Express. Serie: Ganado Porcino
0138-7634 Informacion Express. Serie: Cafe y Cacao
0138-7685 Informacion Express. Serie: Apicultura
0138-7731 Informacion Express. Serie: Arroz
0138-7782 Cuba. Centro de Informacion y Documentacion Agropecuario. Boletin de Resenas. Serie: Forestales
0138-7839 Cuba. Centro de Informacion y Documentacion Agropecuario. Boletin de Resenas. Serie: Pastos y Forrajes
0138-788X Cuba. Centro de Informacion y Documentacion Agropecuario. Boletin de Resenas. Serie: Riego y Drenaje
0138-7936 Cuba. Centro de Informacion y Documentacion Agropecuario. Boletin de Resenas. Serie: Suelos y Agroquimica
0138-8037 Cuba. Centro de Informacion y Documentacion Agropecuario. Boletin de Resenas. Serie: Plantas Medicinales
0138-8088 Cuba. Centro de Informacion y Documentacion Agropecuario. Boletin de Resenas. Serie: Proteccion de Plantas
0138-8134 Cuba. Centro de Informacion y Documentacion Agropecuario. Boletin de Resenas. Serie: Veterinaria
0138-8185 Ciencia y Tecnica en la Agricultura. Serie: Tabaco
0138-8231 Cuba. Centro de Informacion y Documentacion Agropecuario. Boletin de Resenas. Serie: Hortalizas, Papas, Granos y Fibras
0138-8339 Cuba. Centro de Informacion y Divulgacion Agropecuario. Boletin de Resenas. Serie: Citricos
0138-838X Cuba. Centro de Informacion y Documentacion Agropecuario. Boletin de Resenas. Serie: Arroz
0138-8436 Cuba. Centro de Informacion y Documentacion Agropecuario. Boletin de Resenas. Serie: Cafe y Cacao
0138-8452 Revista Cubana de Investigaciones Pesqueras *changed to* Revista Cubana de Investigaciones Pesqueras. Boletines Bibliograficos
0138-8487 Ciencia y Tecnica en la Agricultura. Serie: Riego y Drenaje
0138-8533 Ciencia y Tecnica en la Agricultura. Serie: Pastos y Forrajes
0138-8584 Ciencia y Tecnica en la Agricultura. Serie: Economia Agropecuaria
0138-8630 Ciencia y Tecnica en la Agricultura. Serie: Hortalizas, Papas, Granos y Fibras
0138-8681 Ciencia y Tecnica en la Agricultura. Serie: Mecanizacion
0138-8738 Ciencia y Tecnica en la Agricultura. Serie: Ganado Porcino
0138-8789 Ciencia y Tecnica en la Agricultura. Serie: Arroz
0138-8835 Ciencia y Tecnica en la Agricultura. Serie: Citricos y Otros Frutales
0138-8886 Ciencia y Tecnica en la Agricultura. Serie: Viandas Tropicales
0138-8932 Ciencia y Tecnica en la Agricultura. Serie: Proteccion de Plantas
0138-8983 Ciencia y Tecnica en la Agricultura. Serie: Suelos y Agroquimica
0138-9130 Scientometrics
0138-9157 Technical Film Cards/International Selection†
0138-9289 Gyogyszerterapias Dokumentacios Szemle
0139-035X Hungarian Machinery†
0139-1305 Konyv es Konyvtar
0139-1682 Heti Vilaggazdasag
0139-2026 Revue de Droit Hongrois
0139-2409 Historia (Budapest)
0139-2751 Opuscula Byzantina *see* 0567-7246
0139-3006 Acta Alimentaria
0139-3286 Hungary. Kozponti Statisztikai Hivatal. Szamitastechnikai Statisztikai Evkonyv
0139-3510 Hungary. Kozponti Statisztikai Hivatal. Beruhazasi, Epitoipari, Lakasepitesi Zsebkonyv
0139-3634 Hungary. Kozponti Statisztikai Hivatal. Kulkereskedelmi Statisztikai Evkonyv
0139-4045 Marx Karoly Kozgazdasagtudomanyi Egyetem. Egyetemi Szemle. University Review
0139-4533 Hungary. Kozponti Statisztikai Hivatal. Belkereskedelmi es Idegenforgalmi Adatok†
0139-4649 Artes Populares
0139-4932 International Basketball
0139-5009 Heraldika
0139-5106 Novinky Literatury: Biologie†
0139-5203 Novinky Literatury: Ekonomie
0139-5335 Knihovna
0139-5351 Novinky Literatury: Chemie†
0139-5378 Slovenske Narodne Muzeum. Zbornik Etnografia
0139-5408 Novinky Literatury: Matematika. Fyzika†
0139-5459 Novinky Literatury: Novinky Knihovnicke Literatury
0139-5505 Novinky Literatury. Politika
0139-5548 Univerzita Komenskeho Trnave. Pedagogicke Fakulta. Zbornik. Spolocenske Vedy. Historia
0139-5602 Novinky Literatury: Umeni†
0139-617X Krajske Vlastivedne Muzeum v Olomouci. Zpravy
0139-6587 Zdravotnicka Dokumentace
0139-6595 Pedagogicka Fakulta v Ostrave. Sbornik Praci. Radi C: Dejepis-Zemepis
0139-6765 Vodni Sporty
0139-7346 Pedagogicka Fakulta v Plzni. Sbornik. Dejepis
0139-7605 Tesinsko
0139-7915 Zakladni a Rekreacni Telesna Vychova
0139-8539 Bibliografie Ceskeho Knihovnictvi. Bibliografie a V T I
0139-8571 Biologizace a Chemizace Zivocisne Vyroby-Veterinaria
0139-8741 Geneologicka a Heraldicka Spolecnost Prague. Zpravodaj. Acta Geneologica ac Heraldica
0139-9446 Novinky Literatury: Marxismus-Leninismus. Spolecenske Vedy†
0139-9462 Vlastivedny Sbornik Okresu Novy Jicin
0140-0053 Emergency Services News†
0140-0061 Economic and Social History Surveys
0140-0096 Conservator
0140-0118 Medical & Biological Engineering & Computing
0140-0142 Chartered Institute of Public Finance and Accountancy. Waste Disposal Statistics. Estimates
0140-0150 Chartered Institute of Public Finance and Accountancy. Waste Disposal Statistics. Actuals
0140-038X Staffordshire Guide Industry and Commerce
0140-0428 Educational Administration and History Monographs
0140-0525 Hazards Bulletin *see* 0267-7296
0140-0649 International Communist†
0140-0673 Creativity Network *see* 0263-2926
0140-072X International Advances in Nondestructive Testing†
0140-0789 Royal College of Psychiatrists. Bulletin
0140-0835 Topics in Enzyme and Fermentation Biotechnology
0140-0991 Kingsman
0140-1017 Local Government Manpower
0140-1149 Coin Hoards
0140-1165 Sepia
0140-1270 Labour Review
0140-1599 Acoustics Letters
0140-1750 Journal of Social and Biological Structures
0140-1769 International Symposium on Dredging Technology. Proceedings
0140-1785 British Hydromechanics Research Association. Proceedings of Pneumotransport
0140-1874 Arab Business Yearbook
0140-1890 Antenna
0140-1963 Journal of Arid Environments
0140-1971 Journal of Adolescence
0140-2080 International Conference on Pressure Surges. Proceedings
0140-2099 Fluid Power Symposium. Proceedings
0140-2129 European Conference on Mixing and Centrifugal Separation. Proceedings
0140-2145 British Pump Manufacturers Association. Technical Conference Proceedings
0140-2188 C B I News
0140-2285 Jazz Journal International
0140-2382 West European Politics
0140-2390 Journal of Strategic Studies
0140-2447 New Literature on Old Age
0140-2498 Marine Stores International†
0140-2722 British Medicine

0140-2773 Interlending Review: Journal of the British Library Lending Division *see* 0264-1615
0140-2889 B A P I P Bulletin
0140-2935 Envoy International†
0140-2986 Health and Hygiene
0140-3028 Medical Laboratory World
0140-315X Concetto
0140-3206 London Shop Surveys
0140-3230 Education Equipment, Primary & Middle School Edition *see* 0262-5717
0140-3273 Health Education Index
0140-3281 Knight's Local Government Reports
0140-332X Historic Society of Lancashire and Cheshire. Transactions
0140-3397 Quinquereme
0140-3435 Which Computer?
0140-3494 Browne Records
0140-3524 P H L S Library Bulletin
0140-3664 Computer Communications
0140-3826 Zero†
0140-3990 Leicestershire Archaeological and Historical Society. Transactions
0140-4040 Who Owns Whom. United Kingdom and Republic of Ireland
0140-4059 Milling Feed and Fertiliser *changed to* Milling Feed and Farm Supplies
0140-4067 Nuclear Energy
0140-4113 British Library of Political and Economic Science. Quarterly List of Additions in Russian and East European Languages
0140-4156 R A P R A Recent Literature on Hazardous Environments in Industry†
0140-4199 National Institute of Agricultural Botany, Cambridge, England. Technical Leaflets
0140-4202 Birmingham & Warwickshire Archaeological Society. Transactions
0140-4229 Whitaker's Cumulative Book List
0140-4237 International Building Services Abstracts
0140-4253 C R U S News
0140-427X Map Collector
0140-4288 IMS Pharmaceutical Marketletter *changed to* Marketletter
0140-4296 World Pharmaceutical Introductions
0140-4415 M I M S Africa
0140-4539 Treasure Hunting
0140-4547 Bike
0140-4563 Association of National Health Service Supplies Officers. Reference Book & Buyer's Guide
0140-458X Climate Monitor
0140-4741 IMS Monitor Report: Europe *changed to* Marketletter
0140-4768 Rural Development Abstracts
0140-4776 Rural Extension, Education and Training Abstracts
0140-4784 Forest Products Abstracts
0140-4822 Agricultural Supply Industry
0140-4857 Bio-Medical Applications of Polymers†
0140-489X Economic Outlook
0140-4903 Library Management News†
0140-492X European Bibliography of Soviet, East European and Slavonic Studies
0140-4962 People's Dispensary for Sick Animals. Guild News†
0140-4989 Sheffield and North Derbyshire Topic *changed to* Sheffield & South Yorkshire Topic
0140-5004 Scotland. Department of Agriculture and Fisheries. Freshwater Fisheries Triennial *changed to* Department of Agriculture and Fisheries for Scotland. Freshwater Fisheries Laboratory. Triennial Review of Research
0140-5012 Scotland. Department of Agriculture and Fisheries. Marine Laboratory. Triennial Review of Research
0140-5039 E A R
0140-5047 Fairplay World Shipping Year Book
0140-511X Journal of Audiovisual Media in Medicine
0140-5136 Alembic
0140-5179 Sales Management *see* 0264-3200
0140-525X Behavioral and Brain Sciences
0140-5268 Offshore Petroleum Exploration Service *changed to* Weekly Exploration Service
0140-5284 European Journal of Science Education
0140-5365 Toxicology Abstracts
0140-5373 Aquatic Sciences & Fisheries Abstracts. Part 1: Biological Sciences & Living Resources
0140-5381 Aquatic Sciences & Fisheries Abstracts. Part 2: Ocean Technology, Policy and Non-Living Resources
0140-542X Rally Sport
0140-5500 International Accounting and Financial Report†
0140-5578 Shoe Retailers Manual *see* 0080-9349
0140-5721 Country Music Round up
0140-5748 Health Service Buyers Guide
0140-5764 Government and Municipal Contractors
0140-5772 British Exporters *changed to* Sell's British Exporters
0140-5810 Scottish Women's Liberation Journal
0140-5977 Gem Craft *see* 0144-2937
0140-6000 Darts World
0140-6078 Musica Asiatica
0140-6116 Afrique†
0140-6337 British Furniture for the World†
0140-6450 World Airline Fleets Monthly *see* 0263-3272
0140-654X Stonehenge Viewpoint
0140-6566 Molecular Crystals and Liquid Crystals. Letters *changed to* Molecular Crystals and Liquid Crystals
0140-6647 Pension Funds & Their Advisers
0140-6701 Fuel and Energy Abstracts
0140-671X Journal of Sources in Educational History
0140-6728 Westminster Studies in Education
0140-6736 Lancet
0140-6795 N.S.C.A. Reference Book
0140-6981 Leicester Topic
0140-7007 International Journal of Refrigeration
0140-7260 University of London. School of Slavonic and East European Studies. Library. Bibliographical Guides
0140-7430 National Gallery, London. Technical Bulletin
0140-7503 Essex Family Historian
0140-7554 International Association of Orientalist Librarians. Newsletter *see* 0161-7397
0140-7562 Kevren
0140-7597 Iron
0140-7635 Economics Selections *see* 0884-8335
0140-766X British Electrotechnical Approvals Board. Annual List of Approved Electrotechnical Equipment
0140-7694 Gay Christian
0140-7708 Physical Education Review
0140-7724 Postgraduate Doctor: Middle East
0140-7732 School Technology
0140-7740 Animations
0140-7767 Pellison's Researcher
0140-7775 Journal of Fish Diseases
0140-7783 Journal of Veterinary Pharmacology and Therapeutics
0140-7791 Plant, Cell and Environment
0140-7805 Books in the Earth Sciences
0140-7813 British Geological Literature
0140-7821 Zapis
0140-7880 Archaeology Abroad Bulletin
0140-7953 Middle East Living Costs
0140-7961 Matter of Degree
0140-797X Future Studies Centre Newsletter *changed to* Common Futures
0140-8003 Private Post
0140-8011 Arab Business
0140-8046 Reed's Special Ships†
0140-8089 Leeds Medieval Studies
0140-8186 Coventry Chamber of Commerce & Industry Directory†
0140-8291 Chartered Institute of Public Finance and Accountancy. Probation Statistics. Actuals
0140-8313 Middle East Transport *changed to* Middle East Transport & Telecommunications
0140-8321 Middle East Travel
0140-833X New African
0140-8399 Minor Metals Survey
0140-8402 Iron & Manganese Ores Survey
0140-8410 Revealer Cassettes†
0140-8429 Flintshire Historical Society. Publications, Journal and Record Series
0140-8445 Powder Coatings Bulletin
0140-8453 Chief Executive
0140-8461 Maritime Management *changed to* Shipcare & Maritime Management
0140-8488 Building with Steel†
0140-8623 Banyan Tree
0140-8763 British Art and Antiques Yearbook *changed to* British Art & Antiques Directory
0140-878X Plastics in Retail Packaging Bulletin *changed to* Food, Cosmetics and Drugs Packaging
0140-8798 Waterborne & High Solids Coatings Bulletin
0140-895X Irish Literary Studies
0140-9050 World Water
0140-9069 Rabies Magazine
0140-9115 Annual Reports on Fermentation Processes
0140-9131 Northamptonshire Past and Present
0140-9158 Medicine Digest
0140-9174 Management Research News
0140-9220 Aerial Archaeology
0140-9247 Forecasts of Exchange Rate Movements (Dollar Edition) *see* 0143-0769
0140-9255 Forecasts of Exchange Rate Movements (Overseas Edition) *see* 0143-0769
0140-9301 Leicestershire Family History Circle. Newsletter *see* 0262-7574
0140-9352 Aggie Weston's
0140-9360 Machine Tool Enterprise
0140-9506 New Equals
0140-9719 Henley Centre for Forecasting. Director's Guide *changed to* Henley Centre for Forecasting. Director's Guide to the U.K. Economy
0140-9727 Modern Chess Theory†
0140-9743 General Review of the World Coal Industry. Progress Report†
0140-976X Municipal Entertainment *see* 0143-8980
0140-9816 Business Location File *changed to* Project Search File
0140-9883 Energy Economics
0140-9948 Clothing Research Journal†
0141-0008 University of Nottingham. Department of Adult Education. Bulletin of Local History, East Midlands Region
0141-0121 Aquarian Arrow
0141-0156 Collected Papers on South Asia
0141-0164 Rice Abstracts
0141-0172 Soyabean Abstracts
0141-0180 Seed Abstracts
0141-0229 Enzyme and Microbial Technology
0141-0288 National Association of Plumbing, Heating and Mechanical Services Contractors Yearbook
0141-0296 Engineering Structures
0141-030X Studies in Welsh History
0141-0342 Midland Macromolecular Monographs†
0141-0423 Journal of Research in Reading
0141-0547 Harpers & Queen
0141-0555 Cosmopolitan: English Edition
0141-0571 Current Literature on Health Services *changed to* Health Service Abstracts
0141-061X Electronic Technology
0141-0644 Medicine in Society
0141-0660 W E A Southern District Journal
0141-0687 Cargo Handling Abstracts
0141-0768 Royal Society of Medicine. Journal
0141-0784 Building Refurbishment and Maintenance
0141-0792 Liszt Society. Journal
0141-0806 World Stainless Steel Statistics
0141-0814 Society for Underwater Technology. Journal *changed to* Underwater Technology
0141-0822 Veterinary Review†
0141-0857 Practical Wireless
0141-0962 Forensic Photography
0141-1020 American Business Overseas†
0141-1039 Overseas American
0141-1047 European and Middle East Tax Report†
0141-1063 Tax Haven & Shelter Report *changed to* Tax Haven & Investment Report
0141-108X Durham and Newcastle Research Review
0141-1128 Monographs on Astronomical Subjects
0141-1136 Marine Environmental Research
0141-1144 Company
0141-1152 Oxford Theatre Texts
0141-1179 Dramau'r Byd
0141-1187 Applied Ocean Research
0141-1195 Advances in Engineering Software
0141-1241 Global Tapestry Journal
0141-1268 National Maritime Museum. Occasional Lectures Series
0141-1314 I D S Research Report
0141-1381 Diesel Engines for the World†
0141-1403 Great Britain. Department of Health and Social Security. Health Equipment Notes
0141-142X Harpers Sports and Camping *see* 0263-8134
0141-1594 Phase Transitions
0141-1667 State Research
0141-1748 International Broadcasting Systems & Operation
0141-1772 Benn's Press Directory *see* 0269-8358
0141-1780 Queen's Award Magazine
0141-187X Chartered Institute of Public Finance and Accountancy. Leisure and Recreation Statistics. Estimates
0141-1896 Journal of Musicological Research
0141-1918 International Power Generation
0141-1926 British Educational Research Journal
0141-2116 National Institute for Medical Research. Report
0141-2140 General and Synthetic Methods
0141-2159 Direction Line
0141-2175 Planned Innovation
0141-2183 Publications Review-Management & Technology Policy *changed to* Publications Review-Innovation & Management
0141-2256 Great Britain. Medical Research Council. Annual Report
0141-2264 Excavation of the Roman Forts of the Classis Britannica at Dover 1970-1977
0141-2361 Gardens Open to the Public in England and Wales *changed to* Gardens in England and Wales
0141-2388 B I M H Mental Handicap Bulletin
0141-2442 Socialist Review *changed to* Socialist Worker Review
0141-2604 Great Britain. Departments of the Environment and Transport. Library Services. Annual List of Publications
0141-2698 Stanley Link in Design and Craft Education *changed to* Stanley Link in Design and Technology
0141-2701 Thomas Cook International Timetable (1980) *see* 0144-7467
0141-2701 Thomas Cook International Timetable *see* 0144-7475
0141-2728 Education Journal
0141-2760 Journal of Clinical & Laboratory Immunology
0141-2779 Planning for Social Change
0141-2817 C I R I A News
0141-2876 British Tax Report†
0141-2930 B C I R A Abstracts of International Foundry Literature *see* 0268-3393
0141-2949 Police Studies
0141-299X Cell Nucleus
0141-3228 Financial Times International Year Books: Oil and Gas
0141-3236 Financial Times International Year Books: Who's Who in World Oil and Gas
0141-3244 Financial Times International Year Books: Mining
0141-3279 Great Britain. Warren Spring Laboratory. Annual Review

1454 ISSN INDEX

0141-3287 Natural Energy & Living
0141-3325 British Antarctic Survey. Annual Report
0141-3376 Prospecting in Areas of Glaciated Terrain
0141-3406 Information Privacy *see* 0261-4103
0141-3473 Behavioural Psychotherapy
0141-3511 Leicester Literary & Philosophical Society. Transactions
0141-3589 Talbotania
0141-3619 Open Earth
0141-3635 Factotum
0141-3899 Nursing Research Abstracts
0141-3910 Polymer Degradation and Stability
0141-3929 African Business
0141-4100 Scan
0141-4143 Register of Offshore Units, Submersibles and Diving Systems
0141-4151 Seatrade Guide to Arab Shipping *changed to* Arab Shipping
0141-4305 Know More About Oil World Statistics
0141-4348 London Bird Report
0141-4437 Petroleum Times (1981)
0141-447X Free!
0141-4607 Agricultural Wastes
0141-4690 Ferro Alloys: A World Survey†
0141-4704 Falmer
0141-4836 International Environment and Safety
0141-4909 Lloyd's Register of Ships
0141-4925 Development Research Digest†
0141-5050 Writers of Wales
0141-5077 S C I M P
0141-5085 Grainger Society Journal
0141-5107 Clocks
0141-5204 Kennington News†
0141-5263 Industrial Minerals Directory *see* 0269-1701
0141-5298 Stainless Steel World Guide†
0141-531X Aluminum World Survey†
0141-5352 Quaker Peace & Service *see* 0265-7848
0141-5387 European Journal of Orthodontics
0141-5425 Journal of Biomedical Engineering
0141-5433 Practical Computing
0141-5492 Biotechnology Letters
0141-5530 International Journal of Materials in Engineering Applications *see* 0264-1275
0141-5689 Department of Energy. Publications in Print
0141-5743 Commercial Vehicle Buyer's Guide *changed to* Commercial Vehicle & Buyer's Guide
0141-5867 Law Notes
0141-5956 Aspects of Educational Technology
0141-5972 British Qualifications
0141-5999 Construction Today
0141-6014 Decanter
0141-6022 Primary Education Review
0141-6197 British Insurance Broker
0141-6200 British Journal of Religious Education
0141-6251 A B C Hotel Guide *changed to* A B C Worldwide Hotel Guide
0141-6278 A B C Guide to International Travel
0141-6340 Nomina
0141-6359 Precision Engineering
0141-6383 A.S.L.G. Newsletter *see* 0265-3389
0141-6391 The Hermetic Journal
0141-6405 Scoltock Family Bulletin
0141-6413 B A S R A Journal
0141-6421 Journal of Petroleum Geology
0141-6456 Bibliofem†
0141-6464 Great Britain. Institute of Terrestrial Ecology. Statistical Checklist
0141-6529 A B C Air Cargo Guide
0141-6561 Library and Information Research News
0141-6707 African Journal of Ecology
0141-6723 Museums and Galleries in Great Britain and Ireland
0141-6782 Plastics Today
0141-6790 Art History
0141-6936 B Q S F Review†
0141-6952 New Ecologist *see* 0261-3131
0141-7258 Commercial Laws of Europe
0141-7266 European Commercial Cases
0141-7282 Educare
0141-7436 Quest (London)†
0141-7533 Monitor (London, 1976)
0141-7568 Occupational Hygiene Monographs
0141-7592 Engineering Employers' Federation Directory
0141-7681 Journal of Epidemiology & Community Health
0141-7711 Neurosciences Abstracts
0141-772X Pharmacology Abstracts†
0141-7789 Feminist Review
0141-7835 Chartered Institute of Public Finance and Accountancy. Water Services Charges Statistics
0141-8009 Glasgow & West of Scotland Family History Society. Newsletter
0141-8017 International Security Review
0141-8033 Journal of Social Welfare Law
0141-8106 Advances in Environmental Science and Engineering
0141-8130 International Journal of Biological Macromolecules
0141-8149 Oxford German Studies Book Supplement†
0141-8181 C F I Occasional Papers *changed to* O F I Occasional Papers
0141-8211 European Journal of Education
0141-8246 Health & Safety at Work
0141-8327 Extel Dividend & Interest Record
0141-8335 Extel Capital Gains Tax Service
0141-8505 University of London. Institute of Archaeology. Occasional Publication
0141-8513 Commonwealth Currents
0141-8688 Rank & File Teacher
0141-8696 Cheshire History
0141-8734 Combustion Research Digest†
0141-8912 Association of Clinical Biochemists. News Sheet
0141-8955 Journal of Inherited Metabolic Disease
0141-8963 Laboratory Equipment Directory
0141-8971 Archaeological Reports
0141-898X Rural Technology Guide
0141-9056 British Theatrelog
0141-9072 Scottish Educational Review
0141-917X Booksellers Association of Great Britain and Ireland. Charter Group. Economic Survey
0141-9307 Social Work Service†
0141-9331 Microprocessors & Microsystems
0141-9382 Displays
0141-9412 International Theatrelog
0141-9471 Broadcast Engineering Notes
0141-948X M/F
0141-9498 Great Britain. Civil Aviation Authority. Library Bulletin
0141-9501 International Distribution & Handling Review
0141-9536 Africa Health
0141-9544 North Middlesex Family History Society. Journal
0141-9684 B N F Nutrition Bulletin
0141-9803 H S L Abstracts†
0141-9811 Electric Vehicle Developments
0141-982X Teaching Statistics
0141-9838 Parasite Immunology
0141-9846 Journal of Developmental Physiology
0141-9854 Clinical and Laboratory Haematology
0141-9862 Fisheries Management *see* 0266-996X
0141-9870 Ethnic and Racial Studies
0141-9889 Sociology of Health and Illness
0141-9897 In Fact *see* 0950-0014
0141-9927 Buses Extra
0141-9935 Trains Illustrated/Express Trains *changed to* Steam Train
0141-9943 Sequel†
0142-0011 Motor Caravan World
0142-0097 Craft and Hobby Trade Directory
0142-0100 Rural Wales
0142-0232 Personal Computer World
0142-0356 Journal of Chemical Technology and Biotechnology *see* 0268-2575
0142-0364 Command
0142-0372 Nursing
0142-0399 Ecologist Quarterly *see* 0261-3131
0142-0453 Journal of Automatic Chemistry
0142-0461 E I P R: European Intellectual Property Review
0142-0496 Computer Fraud and Security Bulletin
0142-050X Product Liability Bulletin *see* 0143-1587
0142-0534 Clothing and Footwear Journal *see* 0263-1008
0142-0569 Agrospray†
0142-0615 Electrical Power and Energy Systems
0142-064X Journal for the Study of the New Testament
0142-0674 B E C A N
0142-0755 Publican
0142-0798 Hali
0142-095X International Journal of Cement Composites *see* 0262-5075
0142-0968 International Journal of Lightweight Concrete *see* 0262-5075
0142-0976 International Journal of Wood Preservation†
0142-1042 Click
0142-1050 Current
0142-1085 Light Hovercraft
0142-1123 International Journal of Fatigue
0142-114X Materials Handling Buyers Guide
0142-128X Urbane Gorilla
0142-1468 Chartered Institute of Public Finance and Accountancy. Water and Sewage Treatment and Disposal Statistics. Actuals†
0142-1484 Chartered Institute of Public Finance and Accountancy. Charges for Leisure Services
0142-1557 I C L Technical Journal
0142-1581 Pharmaceutical Medicine
0142-159X Medical Teacher
0142-162X Financial Times World Business Weekly
0142-1670 Outcome†
0142-1794 Sports Documentation Monthly Bulletin
0142-1824 Hotel, Restaurant and Catering Supplies
0142-1832 Caves & Caving
0142-1875 University of London. Institute of Latin American Studies. Occasional Papers
0142-1883 Fruit and Tropical Products
0142-1891 Hides and Skins
0142-1913 Tobacco Quarterly
0142-193X Tsetse and Trypanosomiasis Information Quarterly
0142-1972 C H E C Points
0142-2081 Fashion Index
0142-209X British Airports World†
0142-2146 N H R National Newsletter
0142-2154 General Teaching Council for Scotland. Bulletin
0142-2197 Employment Report
0142-2324 Earth Science Conservation
0142-2367 Royal Society of Medicine. International Congress and Symposium Series
0142-2383 Network†
0142-2391 Resource Management and Optimization
0142-2405 Radioactive Waste Management *see* 0739-5876
0142-2413 Surveys in High Energy Physics
0142-2421 S I A-Surface and Interface Analysis
0142-2448 Radiation Effects Letters
0142-2456 Community Medicine
0142-2464 I U C C Bulletin *see* 0265-4385
0142-2472 Research in British Universities Polytechnics and Colleges. Vol.1: Physical Sciences *see* 0267-1948
0142-2499 Great Britain. Ministry of Agriculture, Fisheries and Food. Directorate of Fisheries Research. Aquatic Environment Monitoring Report
0142-2529 Industrial Relations News†
0142-2545 Food Books Review
0142-2693 C C E T S W News *changed to* C C E T S W Reporting
0142-2774 Journal of Occupational Behaviour
0142-2782 Biopharmaceutics & Drug Disposition
0142-3215 Metal Detecting *see* 0140-4539
0142-3304 Historical Metallurgy
0142-3312 Institute of Measurement and Control. Transactions
0142-3363 Board of Celtic Studies. Bulletin
0142-3371 Efrydiau Athronyddol
0142-3401 Chemical Physics of Solids and Their Surfaces†
0142-3460 Family History Newsletter *changed to* Lincolnshire Family Historian
0142-3479 Msprint
0142-3517 Public Health Laboratory Service Board. Annual Report
0142-3525 Czechout
0142-3630 Building Services Journal *changed to* Building Services
0142-4319 Journal of Muscle Research and Cell Motility
0142-4602 Great Britain. Department of Employment. Work Research Unit. Information System Abstract *see* 0267-873X
0142-4645 Language for Learning
0142-4688 Southern History
0142-4696 Armed Forces
0142-4742 Caribbean Insight
0142-4769 Directory of Export Buyers in the U.K.
0142-4807 Studies in Design, Education Craft and Technology
0142-4823 Currency Forecasting Service *changed to* Currency Confidential
0142-484X Key Reports in Cell and Molecular Biology *changed to* I R C S Medical Science: Cell and Molecular Biology
0142-4858 I R C S Medical Science: Key Reports in Human and Animal Physiology *see* 0305-6880
0142-4866 E O C Research Bulletin
0142-4874 International Education Newsletter†
0142-4904 Ciba-Geigy Technical Notes†
0142-4963 Pictorial Education Special *changed to* Junior Projects
0142-498X Year Book of Agricultural Co-Operation
0142-4998 Agricultural Co-Operation in the United Kingdom: Summary of Statistics *changed to* Agricultural Co-Operatives in the United Kingdom. Statistics
0142-5005 Plunkett Foundation for Co-Operative Studies. Study Series
0142-5056 Seatrade U.S. Yearbook
0142-5064 Seatrade Guide to Latin American Shipping *changed to* Turkish Shipping
0142-5072 City of London Directory & Livery Companies Guide
0142-5080 Society for Seventeenth Century French Studies. Newsletter *see* 0265-1068
0142-5145 A S R A Journal
0142-5196 Chartered Quantity Surveyor
0142-5218 British Alternative Theatre Directory
0142-5242 Grass and Forage Science
0142-5285 World Alcohol Project
0142-5307 Paper and Packaging Bulletin
0142-5374 A B C Nordic Air Guide†
0142-5382 Actions (London)†
0142-5455 Employee Relations
0142-5463 International Journal of Cosmetic Science
0142-5471 Information Design Journal
0142-5498 Arena
0142-5587 Narrow Gauge
0142-5595 Narrow Gauge News
0142-5625 Channel Islands Specialised Catalogue
0142-5641 Coins and Medals†
0142-5692 British Journal of Sociology of Education
0142-5854 Communication Technology Impact
0142-5862 Hazards Review†
0142-5919 International Journal of Solar Energy
0142-5927 Practical Approach to Patents, Trademarks and Copyrights†
0142-5935 Go Teach Primaries
0142-5943 Teen-Search
0142-5951 Journal Contents in Quantitative Methods
0142-596X African Construction†
0142-5978 Good Camps Guide
0142-6001 Applied Linguistics
0142-601X London Studies on South Asia
0142-6028 Studies on Asian Topics
0142-6044 Exchange Rate Outlook
0142-6168 Highways and Public Works *changed to* Highways
0142-6184 Defence

0142-6222 Warship
0142-6230 Hi-Fi News and Record Review
0142-6265 Insurance Age
0142-6338 Journal of Tropical Pediatrics
0142-6354 Investment - U S A
0142-6397 Landscape Research
0142-6419 C B I Members Bulletin *see* 0140-2188
0142-6427 C B I Education and Training Bulletin
0142-6435 C B I Industrial Trends Survey *changed to* C B I Quarterly Industrial Trends Survey
0142-646X West European Living Costs
0142-6494 Dragon's Teeth
0142-6540 Oxford Art Journal
0142-6575 Socialist Challenge†
0142-6591 Animal Health Trust. Annual Report
0142-6699 Air Cushion Review†
0142-6702 Art Monthly
0142-6761 Scottish Sports Council. Bulletin
0142-694X Design Studies
0142-7008 Horse and Driving *see* 0268-8999
0142-7024 Atlantic Review (London) *see* 0264-6773
0142-7067 I P R A Review
0142-7113 C A A T Newsletter
0142-7164 Applied Psycholinguistics
0142-7210 Computing Today
0142-7229 Electronics Today International
0142-7237 First Language
0142-7245 Minerals and the Environment *changed to* Environmental Geochemistry and Health
0142-7253 Archaeoastronomy
0142-727X International Journal of Heat and Fluid Flow
0142-7318 Aliphatic and Related Natural Product Chemistry†
0142-7326 Live Rail
0142-7377 Hull Papers in Politics
0142-7466 T V World
0142-7474 Conference Britain
0142-7490 Lawyer's Remembrancer
0142-7547 Society for General Microbiology Quarterly
0142-7555 Welsh Medieval Pottery Research Group. Bulletin
0142-761X Fast Food *changed to* Popular Foodservice
0142-7628 Book Report
0142-7660 Bonny Moor Hen
0142-7830 Commonwealth Catalogue of Queen Elizabeth Stamps†
0142-7849 Third World Planning Review
0142-7865 Photography/Politics†
0142-7873 Journal of Plankton Research
0142-7946 Postgraduate Doctor: Africa
0142-7954 U H Stamp Digest
0142-8004 Biological Rhythms
0142-8020 Cell Calcium (Sheffield)
0142-8039 Cell Contact Phenomena
0142-8047 Cell Membranes
0142-8055 Cyclic Amp
0142-8071 Enzyme Regulation
0142-8098 Gastric Secretion
0142-8101 Gastrointestinal Hormones
0142-8128 Immunoassay
0142-8136 Immunohistochemistry
0142-8144 Insulin and Glucagon
0142-8160 Leucocytes
0142-8179 Lymphocytes
0142-8195 Macrophages
0142-8209 Microfilaments and Microtubules *changed to* Cytoskeleton
0142-8217 Mitochondria
0142-8225 Nerve Cell Biology
0142-8233 Neuropeptides (Sheffield)
0142-8241 Neurophysiology
0142-825X Pancreatic and Salivary Secretion
0142-8268 Platelets
0142-8284 Prostaglandins - Biology
0142-8292 Protein Phosphorylation
0142-8314 Releasing Hormones
0142-8322 Ribosomes
0142-8330 Steroid Receptors
0142-8349 Thyroid Hormones
0142-8357 Renal Transplantation and Dialysis
0142-8543 Vision (Sheffield)
0142-8810 Tissue Culture
0142-8853 Graphics World
0142-8950 Hampshire Field Club and Archaeological Society Proceedings
0142-8977 Royal Observatory, Edinburgh. Communications†
0142-9094 What's New in Building
0142-9124 South West Review†
0142-9132 Arts Alert†
0142-9191 Committee of Vice-Chancellors and Principals of the Universities of the United Kingdom. Newsletter†
0142-9256 Quantitative Sociology Newsletter†
0142-9272 Nigeria Newsletter
0142-9310 Egypt Newsletter†
0142-9353 Rubber and Plastics Fire and Flammability Bulletin *changed to* Fire & Flammability
0142-9361 Simulation/Games for Learning *changed to* Perspectives on Academic Gaming & Simulation
0142-937X Great Britain. Sea Fish Industry Authority. European Supplies Bulletin
0142-9388 Parley Papers
0142-9418 Polymer Testing
0142-9469 Rolls-Royce Magazine
0142-9523 Book Dealers' and Collectors' Year-Book and Diary†
0142-9612 Biomaterials
0142-9663 Ten.8
0142-9671 Mackintosh European Electronics Companies File *changed to* Macintosh European Electronics Companies File
0142-968X Journal of Plant Foods
0142-971X Runnymede Trust Bulletin
0142-9728 London Chamber of Commerce and Industry. Directory
0142-9752 British Commonwealth Stamp Catalogue
0142-9760 Austria & Hungary Stamp Catalogue
0142-9779 Balkans Stamp Catalogue
0142-9787 Benelux Stamp Catalogue
0142-9795 Czechoslovakia & Poland Stamp Catalogue
0142-9809 France Stamp Catalogue
0142-9817 Germany Stamp Catalogue
0142-9825 Italy & Switzerland Stamp Catalogue
0142-9833 Portugal & Spain Stamp Catalogue
0142-9841 Russia Stamp Catalogue
0142-985X Scandinavia Stamp Catalogue
0142-9868 Africa Since Independence Stamp Catalogue
0142-9876 Central America Stamp Catalogue
0142-9884 Central Asia Stamp Catalogue
0142-9892 China Stamp Catalogue
0142-9906 Japan & Korea Stamp Catalogue
0142-9914 Middle East Stamp Catalogue
0142-9922 South America Stamp Catalogue
0142-9930 South-East Asia Stamp Catalogue
0142-9949 United States Stamp Catalogue
0142-9981 Journal of Morphanalysis†
0143-0009 University of St. Andrews. Library. Current Serials
0143-0076 Y Cylchgrawn Efengylaidd
0143-0084 Res Mechanica
0143-0106 Plantsman
0143-0122 Reality Studios
0143-0149 Pope Teaches
0143-0181 Revelation
0143-0211 O P T: One Parent Times
0143-0238 Cycling World
0143-0246 Argo (Oxford)
0143-0262 Popular Archaelogy *changed to* Archaeology Today
0143-0270 Bookdealers in India, Pakistan and Sri Lanka
0143-0297 Nottinghamshire Industrial Archaeological Society Journal
0143-0343 School Psychology International
0143-036X New Magic Lantern Journal
0143-0378 Nature Conservancy Council. Chief Scientist Team Reports
0143-0386 Research Report Digest
0143-0394 Soviet Scientific Reviews. Section A: Physics Reviews
0143-0408 Soviet Scientific Reviews. Section B: Chemistry Reviews
0143-0416 Soviet Scientific Reviews. Section C: Mathematical Physics Reviews
0143-0424 Soviet Scientific Reviews. Section D: Biological Reviews
0143-0432 Soviet Scientific Reviews. Section E: Astrophysics & Space Physics Reviews
0143-053X U K S T U Newsletter
0143-0599 U.K.I.R.T. Newsletter
0143-0602 International Journal of Masonry Construction†
0143-0645 Far East Health
0143-0661 Archaeolog
0143-067X Auto Export
0143-0688 Annual Art Sales Index (1979) *changed to* Art Sales Index: Oil Paintings, Drawings, Water Colours and Sculpture
0143-0696 Mackintosh European Electronics Companies Bulletin *changed to* Macintosh European Electronics Companies File
0143-0734 Research in British Universities Polytechnics and Colleges. Vol.2: Biological Sciences *see* 0267-1956
0143-0742 Research in British Universities Polytechnics and Colleges. Vol.3: Social Sciences *see* 0267-1964
0143-0750 International Journal of Ambient Energy
0143-0769 Currency Profiles
0143-0793 Journal of Advertising History
0143-0807 European Journal of Physics
0143-0815 Clinical Physics and Physiological Measurement
0143-0831 Involve
0143-084X Journal of Industrial Affairs
0143-0963 Cleaning Maintenance and Big Buildings Management *changed to* Cleaning Maintenance
0143-0971 Shop Equipment Display & Shopfitting Directory
0143-1005 Helicopter Magazine *changed to* Helicopter International Magazine
0143-103X Return of Outstanding Debt *see* 0263-2985
0143-1064 Syzygy
0143-1080 European Medical Ultrasonics†
0143-1102 D P International†
0143-1145 Aviation Europe
0143-1153 Sell's Marine Market
0143-1161 International Journal of Remote Sensing
0143-1218 Journal of Biodynamic Psychology
0143-1234 Scottish Wildlife
0143-1250 Transactions of the Monumental Brass Society
0143-1269 Elgar Society. Journal
0143-1285 Books in Scotland
0143-1307 West African Farming and Food Processing *see* 0266-8017
0143-1366 Ur
0143-1374 Mind Your Own Business
0143-1404 Bio-Control News & Information
0143-1412 Slow Dancer
0143-1455 Process Engineering Directory
0143-1471 Environmental Pollution. Series A: Ecological and Biological
0143-148X Environmental Pollution. Series B: Chemical and Physical
0143-1536 N P L News
0143-1560 Cement & Concrete Association. Development Report
0143-1587 Product Liability International
0143-1722 N C C Information and Library Services. Bibliography Series†
0143-1749 Secondary Education Journal
0143-1927 Ambassador†
0143-1935 British Alternative Press Index†
0143-2028 Cosmos Newsletter†
0143-2044 Cryo-Letters
0143-2060 Environmental Technology Letters
0143-2087 Optimal Control Applications and Methods
0143-2095 Strategic Management Journal
0143-2192 Labels and Labelling International
0143-2214 Where to Learn English in Great Britain†
0143-2257 Airfinance Journal
0143-2389 Worcestershire Archaeological Society. Transactions
0143-2443 Water Research Centre. Annual Report *changed to* Water Research Centre. Annual Review
0143-2516 Tourism Management
0143-2532 Cambridge Economic Policy Review†
0143-2680 Bargaining Report
0143-2729 Ireland Socialist Review
0143-2745 Worker Writer
0143-2796 Architectural Association Annual Review *changed to* Architectural Annual Review
0143-280X Rowland's Tax Guide *see* 0267-8829
0143-2885 International Endodontic Journal
0143-294X Tolley's Practical Tax
0143-2958 European Electronic Component Distributor Directory
0143-2974 Local Population Studies
0143-3083 Research and Clinical Forums
0143-3105 Latin American Newsletters. Book News†
0143-3164 Directory of Crematoria
0143-3180 Journal of Clinical and Hospital Pharmacy
0143-3245 Block
0143-3253 Action Newsletter
0143-3296 Ecology Abstracts
0143-330X Biochemistry Abstracts, Part 1: Biological Membranes
0143-3318 Biochemistry Abstracts, Part 2: Nucleic Acids
0143-3326 Biochemistry Abstracts, Part 3: Amino Acids, Peptides & Proteins
0143-3334 Carcinogenesis
0143-3369 International Journal of Vehicle Design
0143-3385 A L L C Journal *changed to* Literary and Linguistic Computing
0143-3415 Quarterly Review of South African Gold Shares
0143-3490 Directory of Summer Jobs in Britain
0143-3512 Business Matters
0143-3555 L R D G Bulletin *see* 0268-2125
0143-3563 Nova Hrvatska
0143-3598 Fouling Prevention Research Digest
0143-3601 Footprints (Northampton)
0143-3628 Geriatric Medicine†
0143-3636 Nuclear Medicine Communications
0143-3679 Habitat Europe†
0143-3709 Marine Propulsion International
0143-3725 Science Fiction Media News
0143-3768 Landscape History
0143-3784 Medieval English Theatre
0143-3792 Journal of Microcomputer Applications
0143-3857 Ergodic Theory and Dynamical Systems
0143-4004 Placenta
0143-4020 Measurement and Inspection Technology *changed to* Quality Today
0143-4128 International Society for the Study of Church Monuments. Bulletin *see* 0268-7518
0143-4136 National Association for the Teaching of English. Newsletter
0143-4144 Conserver
0143-4160 Cell Calcium (Edinburgh)
0143-4179 Neuropeptides (Edinburgh)
0143-4187 Municipal and Public Services Journal
0143-4233 Membrane Proteins
0143-4241 Transmitters Receptors & Synapses
0143-4276 Neurohypophysical Hormones
0143-4284 Renin, Angiotensin & Kinnins
0143-4381 Vending International Manual
0143-4500 Aberdeen and North East Scotland Family History Society. Newsletter *changed to* Aberdeen and North East Scotland Family History Society. Journal
0143-4519 Arts Council of Great Britain. Education Bulletin

0143-4632 Journal of Multilingual & Multicultural Development
0143-4659 Worcestershire Archaeology and Local History Newsletter
0143-4748 Youth Service Scene
0143-4780 Smaller Business Management Abstracts†
0143-4861 R L J: Roskill's Letter from Japan
0143-4918 Plainsong & Mediaeval Music Society. Journal
0143-5000 Drydock
0143-5019 Current Affairs Bibliographies†
0143-5051 Social Biology and Human Affairs
0143-5094 European Monographs in Health Education Research
0143-5108 Journal for the Study of the New Testament. Supplement Series
0143-5124 Library Management
0143-5140 International Labmate
0143-5183 Microprocessors at Work *changed to* Automated Manufacturing Strategy
0143-5205 Institute of Chartered Accountants in England and Wales. Quarterly Taxation Bulletin
0143-5221 Clinical Science
0143-523X Latin America Regional Reports - Caribbean
0143-5248 Latin America Regional Reports - Andean Group
0143-5256 Latin America Regional Reports - Southern Cone
0143-5264 Latin America Regional Reports - Mexico & Central America
0143-5272 Latin America Regional Reports - Brazil
0143-5280 Latin America Weekly Report
0143-5329 Credit Control
0143-5345 Industry/Education View
0143-537X Aspects
0143-5418 Sut Anubis
0143-5426 Fight Racism! Fight Imperialism!
0143-5442 Stainless Steel: An International Directory *changed to* Stainless Steel: An International Survey and Directory
0143-5469 Education Year Book
0143-5485 Coin *changed to* Coin Monthly (1980)
0143-554X Home Miniaturist
0143-5590 Torquay Pottery Collectors Society. Newsletter *changed to* Torquay Pottery Collectors Society. Magazine
0143-5663 International Index to Television Periodicals
0143-5671 Fiscal Studies
0143-5698 International Tree Crops Journal
0143-5744 Voluntary Action
0143-5833 B A R B S
0143-5906 Hereford's North America
0143-6058 Educational Computing
0143-6082 Guides to Practice in Corrosion Control
0143-6090 Newsagent
0143-6112 Contraceptive Delivery Systems
0143-6147 Tropical Pest Management
0143-6228 Applied Geography
0143-6236 Social Science Information Studies *see* 0268-4012
0143-6244 Building Services Engineering Research & Technology
0143-6260 Popular Technology
0143-6279 Process Economics International
0143-6287 Coal Calendar
0143-6295 Business Law Review
0143-6333 James Joyce Broadsheet
0143-6368 Arid Land Abstracts†
0143-6392 Which Word Processor?
0143-6481 Noise and Vibration Control-Worldwide
0143-6503 Oxford Journal of Legal Studies
0143-6538 Tibet News Review
0143-6554 Sudan Texts Bulletin
0143-6570 M D E-Managerial and Decision Economics
0143-6597 Third World Quarterly
0143-6619 WestIndian Digest
0143-6643 Air Infiltration Review
0143-6694 Oilman
0143-683X Historical Geography Research Series
0143-6864 Hazardous Cargo Bulletin
0143-6961 Recent Advances in Radiology and Medical Imaging
0143-6996 Peatain Family History Newsletter†
0143-7011 Stamps *changed to* Stamps and Foreign Stamps
0143-702X I E E Proceedings Part A: Covering Reviews, Physical Science, Measurement and Instrumentation, Management and Education
0143-7038 I E E Proceedings Part B: Electric Power Applications
0143-7046 I E E Proceedings Part C: Generation, Transmission and Distribution
0143-7054 I E E Proceedings Part D: Control Theory and Applications
0143-7062 I E E Proceedings Part E: Computers and Digital Techniques
0143-7070 I E E Proceedings Part F: Communications, Radar and Signal Processing
0143-7089 I E E Proceedings Part G: Electronic Circuits and Systems
0143-7097 I E E Proceedings Part H: Microwaves, Optics and Antennas *changed to* I E E Proceedings Part H: Microwaves, Antennas & Propagation
0143-7100 I E E Proceedings Part I: Solid-State and Electron Devices
0143-7127 Journal of Oil and Petrochemical Pollution *changed to* Oil and Petrochemical Pollution
0143-7208 Dyes and Pigments
0143-7216 Anglo-Japanese Economic Institute. Bulletin
0143-7240 Aeroplane Monthly
0143-7267 Thoroughbred and Classic Cars *changed to* Classic Cars
0143-7283 University of Strathclyde. Department of Architecture & Building Science. Research Bulletin
0143-7364 C I E News *changed to* C I T E News
0143-7380 Labour Party. Economic Review†
0143-7402 British Music Society. Journal
0143-7410 Reports Index
0143-7429 Glasgow Directory of Voluntary Organizations
0143-7453 International Bar News
0143-7488 Academus Poetry Magazine
0143-7496 International Journal of Adhesion and Adhesives
0143-7518 Christian Fellowship
0143-7526 Sensory Perception and Information Processing
0143-7585 Reactive Personal Distress
0143-7607 Metal Traders of the World
0143-7690 Scrip - World Pharmaceutical News
0143-7704 Community Studies Series
0143-7720 International Journal of Manpower
0143-7739 Leadership and Organisation Development Journal
0143-7755 Tableware International
0143-778X Coal International
0143-7798 Steel Times International
0143-781X History of Political Thought
0143-7844 Sheet Metal Industries International†
0143-7852 Bulk Systems International *see* 0269-381X
0143-7895 Conference World
0143-7917 Family Life
0143-7925 Focus (Grantham)
0143-7941 Tax Management International Forum
0143-795X Hereford's Air Cargo
0143-7976 International Travel Catering *changed to* Tax Free Marketing
0143-7984 Wellcome Unit for the History of Medicine. Research Publications
0143-800X Abstracts. Histopathology, Cytopathology *see* 0268-4993
0143-8018 Great Britain. Ministry of Agriculture, Fisheries and Food. Directorate of Fisheries Research. Laboratory Leaflet
0143-8115 Numerical Engineering
0143-8123 Comments on Molecular and Cellular Biophysics
0143-8131 Artistes and Their Agents
0143-814X Journal of Public Policy
0143-8158 West Midlands Archives Newsletter
0143-8166 Optics and Lasers in Engineering
0143-8174 Reliability Engineering
0143-8190 Countryside Planning Yearbook *changed to* International Yearbook of Rural Planning
0143-8247 One Earth
0143-8263 International Authors and Writers Who's Who
0143-831X Economic and Industrial Democracy
0143-8352 F R A M E Technical News *see* 0268-4306
0143-8425 Drawing Paper
0143-8441 Food: Flavouring Ingredients Processing & Packaging
0143-8484 Plunkett Development Series
0143-8557 Solids Handling
0143-8565 Yesteryear Transport†
0143-859X N I M L A
0143-8611 Electronics Engineer
0143-8654 School of Agriculture, Aberdeen. Annual Report
0143-8689 Curriculum
0143-8697 Kent Review
0143-8743 Miniature Book World *see* 0142-9523
0143-8786 Outlook (Milton Keynes)†
0143-8859 Strays
0143-8875 Platform (Keighley)
0143-8883 Prospect (Edinburgh)
0143-8921 Centre for the Study of Islam and Christian Muslim Relations. Newsletter
0143-8972 Scottish Planning Appeal Decisions
0143-8980 Entertainment and Arts Management
0143-8999 Planning Exchange Information Bulletin
0143-9014 Pig News & Information
0143-9030 N C V O Information Service†
0143-9073 Ecos
0143-909X Books for Keeps
0143-9111 British Business
0143-912X Interim (Birmingham)
0143-9138 Waifarers
0143-9162 Bus Fayre
0143-9170 Fare Stage *see* 0143-9162
0143-926X Cosmatom
0143-9308 War on Wants Outlook†
0143-9359 Administrative Accounting *changed to* Administrative Accountant
0143-9405 China Business Report†
0143-9529 Consumer Credit Bulletin
0143-9553 Keyword Index to Serial Titles
0143-9561 Communications Engineering International
0143-9596 What's New in Farming
0143-960X I W P C Newsletter
0143-9634 Nature in Devon
0143-9642 Computer Performance†
0143-9669 Re Report†
0143-9677 Tax Haven & Shelter Report-North American Edition†
0143-9685 Historical Journal of Film, Radio and Television
0143-9693 Sussex Genealogist and Local Historian
0143-9715 European Muslims and Christian-Muslim Relations. Abstracts†
0143-974X Journal of Constructional Steel Research
0143-9758 Institute of Chartered Accountants in England and Wales. Technical Bulletin *changed to* Institute of Chartered Accountants in England and Wales. Update
0143-9774 News of Muslims in Europe
0143-9782 Journal of Time Series Analysis
0143-9855 Multiracial School *see* 0260-0226
0143-9863 Ramp†
0143-991X Industrial Robot
0144-0004 Jane's Military Communications
0144-0101 Scottish Business Education Council. Business Education Guide *changed to* Scottish Vocational Education Council. Handbook
0144-025X Online Notes
0144-0292 Modern Railways Pictorial *changed to* Motive Power Monthly
0144-0322 Society of Leather Technologists and Chemists. Journal
0144-0365 Journal of Legal History
0144-0373 Journal of Media Law and Practice
0144-039X Slavery & Abolition
0144-0403 Medicine International. U K Edition
0144-0411 Medicine International. Quarterly Edition
0144-042X Medicine International. Irish Edition†
0144-0438 Medicine International. Middle Eastern Edition
0144-0462 Scope: A Review of Voluntary and Community Work in Northern Ireland
0144-0470 Jane's Defence Review *see* 0265-3818
0144-0497 Middle Thames Naturalist
0144-0543 Franchise World
0144-056X Library Association. University, College and Research Section. Newsletter
0144-0586 Northamptonshire Natural History Society and Field Club Journal
0144-0640 Social Services Research Group. Journal *see* 0264-519X
0144-0675 Farm Contractor
0144-0683 Nottinghamshire Link
0144-073X Christian Statesman
0144-0764 Stirling Technical Reports in Education
0144-0810 Netball
0144-0888 British Journal of Language Teaching
0144-0918 Politics and Power
0144-0969 Social Work Information Bulletin
0144-1019 Seaways
0144-1027 Company Lawyer
0144-1078 Recent Advances in Infection
0144-123X Northern Bibliography
0144-1248 Camera *changed to* Creative Photography
0144-1302 Scottish Pottery Historical Review
0144-1396 A Y R S Airs
0144-1647 Transport Reviews
0144-1655 Modern Tramway and Light Rail Transit
0144-1671 European Digest
0144-1752 Socialist Librarians Journal†
0144-1779 Radical Bookseller
0144-1787 Arts South West *changed to* Arts West
0144-1795 Journal of Autonomic Pharmacology
0144-1825 Ceramic Review
0144-1973 Societe Guernesiaise. Report and Transactions
0144-2015 Hambro Company Guide
0144-2066 Word Processing Now *changed to* Word & Information Processing
0144-2147 British Ceramic Research. Special Publications
0144-221X Natural History Society of Northumbria. Transactions
0144-2317 U.V. Spectrometry Group. Bulletin†
0144-235X International Reviews in Physical Chemistry
0144-2368 Beacon House Bulletin
0144-2376 Felt and Damaging Earthquakes
0144-2384 Refer
0144-2449 Zeolites
0144-2457 Logos
0144-2481 Great Britain. Civil Aviation Authority. General Aviation Airmisses *changed to* Great Britain. Civil Aviation Authority. General Aviation Airmiss Bulletin
0144-249X Stanley Gibbons Postcard Catalogue
0144-252X Magnetic Fluids†
0144-2570 U K C I S Newsletter *changed to* Royal Society of Chemistry. Database Newsletter
0144-2600 Institute of Energy. Journal
0144-2694 Walk
0144-2708 Tiddly Dyke
0144-2740 Major Companies of Nigeria
0144-2767 Business Yearbook of Brazil, Mexico & Venezuela†
0144-2791 History Journal
0144-2813 Business Education
0144-2821 Scottish Arts Council. Bulletin†
0144-2848 T O P S: The Old Police Station
0144-2872 Policy Studies
0144-2880 Polymer Photochemistry
0144-2902 Christian Jewish Relations
0144-2910 Model Boats

ISSN INDEX 1457

0144-2937 Popular Crafts
0144-2988 Macromolecular Chemistry (London)
0144-2996 Croydon Chamber of Commerce and Industry Directory *changed to* Southern Home Counties Chamber of Commerce Directory
0144-3054 E C L R: European Competition Law Review
0144-3070 Occasional Papers in Modern Dutch Studies
0144-3127 Studies in Language Disability and Remediation
0144-3194 Navy International
0144-3313 University of Edinburgh. Department of Archaeology. Occasional Papers
0144-333X International Journal of Sociology and Social Policy
0144-3356 School of Agriculture, Aberdeen. Research Investigations and Field Trials†
0144-3399 Context (Leeds)
0144-3410 Educational Psychology
0144-3453 Transport (London)
0144-3461 Caprice†
0144-3488 Interchange
0144-3577 International Journal of Operations and Production Management
0144-3585 Journal of Economic Studies
0144-3593 Statute Law Review
0144-3615 Journal of Obstetrics and Gynaecology
0144-3631 British Ceramic Research Association. Technical Notes
0144-364X Birdwatcher's Yearbook *changed to* Birdwatcher's Yearbook and Diary
0144-3674 Computer Age (London)
0144-3704 Hospitality
0144-3720 Management Confidential *changed to* Management Success
0144-3755 Hovercraft Bulletin
0144-3828 Gardening World†
0144-3879 Animal Disease Occurrence - Data Tables
0144-3968 Haverhill and District Archaeological Group. Journal
0144-3976 Aviation Postcard Collector
0144-4018 Kent Recusant History
0144-4034 Boat Technology International†
0144-4077 Journal of Local Studies *changed to* Journal of Regional and Local Studies
0144-4212 P S L G
0144-4220 Annual Monetary Review *see* 0266-7339
0144-4247 Energy R & D Summary and Sources
0144-4271 Medeconomics
0144-4298 World Studies Journal
0144-4301 S P A I D News
0144-4360 Literary Review and Quarto
0144-4379 Paper Bag
0144-4425 Paint Titles
0144-4476 I C B P Newsletter
0144-4484 Co-Operative Fishermen's Bulletin†
0144-4492 Solar System Today
0144-4514 Chartered Institute of Public Finance and Accountancy. Homelessness Statistics
0144-4549 Lloyd's Shipping Index
0144-4557 Lloyd's Voyage Record
0144-4565 Biomass
0144-4581 State Enterprise
0144-459X Doncaster Ancestor
0144-4611 Awards for Commonwealth University Academic Staff
0144-462X Grants for Study Visits by University Administrators and Librarians
0144-4646 Communication Research Trends
0144-4751 Venezuela (London)
0144-4778 Midlands Homoeopathy Research Group. Research Letter *changed to* British Homoeopathy Research Group. Communications
0144-4816 Essex Review of Children's Literature
0144-4948 Health Now
0144-5014 B I P Plastics Review
0144-5073 University of Bath. Centre for Catalogue Research. Newsletter
0144-5081 Community Service Statistics: Scotland
0144-5138 History of Universities
0144-5154 Assembly Automation
0144-5170 Journal of Garden History
0144-5243 Miltronics
0144-5251 Dairyman's Yearbook†
0144-5324 International Investment Guide *changed to* World Markets Service
0144-5340 History and Philosophy of Logic
0144-5359 Wessex Studies in Special Education
0144-557X Analytical Proceedings
0144-5596 Social Policy and Administration
0144-5618 Royal Society of Medicine. Forum Series *see* 0268-3091
0144-574X About Books for Children
0144-5774 Sounds
0144-5804 Record Mirror *changed to* R M
0144-5847 Other Poetry
0144-5863 Anglo-Catalan Society. Occasional Publications
0144-5871 High Performance Textiles
0144-5898 Lookback†
0144-5952 Human Toxicology
0144-5960 Wolff's Guide to the London Metal Exchange
0144-5979 Clinical Physiology
0144-5987 Energy Exploration and Exploitation
0144-5995 Termite Abstracts
0144-6002 Orbit (London)†
0144-6010 Video Today
0144-6037 Sound International *see* 0133-5944
0144-6045 Plastics and Rubber Processing and Applications
0144-6088 Cue
0144-610X Chartered Institute of Public Finance and Accountancy. Personal Social Services Estimate Statistics
0144-6118 Enterprise
0144-6126 B R A D Advertiser & Agency List
0144-6169 Farm Animal Welfare Co-ordinating Executive. Newsletter
0144-6193 Journal of Construction Industry Economics and Management *changed to* Construction Management and Economics
0144-624X Recreation Management Handbook
0144-6258 Ecology & Conservation Studies
0144-6266 Recent Advances in Crosslinking & Curing
0144-6274 Grow Together†
0144-6282 Surgery Today
0144-6304 Insurance Index
0144-6320 What Camera Weekly *changed to* Camera Weekly
0144-6339 Arthritis News
0144-6347 B S H S Newsletter
0144-6355 G.D.R. Monitor
0144-6363 Heritage and Destiny†
0144-6371 Quest (Cardiff)†
0144-6398 A R V A C Pamphlet†
0144-6428 Slade Magazine†
0144-6436 Loot
0144-6487 English Magazine
0144-6517 Property Law Bulletin
0144-6525 R I P A Report
0144-6533 Legion
0144-655X Dine Out
0144-6576 B A R G Review *see* 0263-1091
0144-6592 Recent Advances in Nursing
0144-6622 Soviet Engineering Research
0144-6630 New Age†
0144-6649 Computerworld UK†
0144-6657 British Journal of Clinical Psychology
0144-6665 British Journal of Social Psychology
0144-6673 Lloyd's Shipping Economist
0144-6681 Lloyd's Loading List
0144-672X Brentford and Chiswick Local History Society. Journal
0144-6738 Warwick Statistics Service. Occasional Review *changed to* University of Warwick Business Information Service. Occasional Review
0144-6800 I C O Library Monthly Entries - Coffeeline
0144-6827 L A Trade Union News
0144-6843 National Council for Educational Standards. Bulletin
0144-686X Ageing and Society
0144-6878 Sussex Yesterdays†
0144-6894 Timepiece *changed to* Timepiece Register
0144-6916 Midland Bonsai Society Journal
0144-6967 N A C C Newsletter
0144-6991 National College of Agricultural Engineering News *changed to* Silsoe College News
0144-7106 Trade Union Studies Journal
0144-7114 Music and Video *see* 0261-4200
0144-7122 Assyrian Observer
0144-7130 Textile News†
0144-7149 Chronicle (London)
0144-7165 YF: Yours Financially *changed to* Stockmarket Confidential
0144-7181 Sport and Leisure
0144-719X N A M E *see* 0260-0226
0144-7203 British Equestrian Directory
0144-7211 Inquisition *changed to* North West Societies. Combined Register of Members' Interests
0144-7238 Wood Based Panels International
0144-7262 Rock Drill
0144-7327 Youth Exchange News
0144-7394 Teaching Public Administration
0144-7416 Ritz Newspaper
0144-7424 Arrowhead
0144-7440 Political Studies Association of the United Kingdom. Newsletter
0144-7459 Directory of Arts Centres
0144-7467 Thomas Cook Continental Timetable (1980)
0144-7475 Thomas Cook Overseas Timetable
0144-7505 Printing Historical Society Bulletin
0144-7521 African Textiles
0144-7548 Republican Englishman
0144-7556 British Reports, Translations and Theses
0144-7564 Comparative Criticism
0144-7572 Heatline†
0144-7580 H C I M A Quarterly Bibliography of Hotel and Catering Management
0144-7602 British Plant Growth Regulator Group. News Bulletin
0144-7637 Traveller's Guide to North Africa
0144-7645 Traveller's Guide to West Africa
0144-7653 Traveller's Guide to East Africa and the Indian Ocean
0144-7661 Traveller's Guide to Central and Southern Africa
0144-7777 Clinica
0144-7831 Res Mechanica Letters†
0144-784X Bucks Advertiser
0144-7866 London Drinker
0144-8005 New Celtic Review
0144-8048 Great Britain. Department of Education and Science. Assessment of Performance Units. Summaries of Reports
0144-8072 Early Music Record Services. Monthly Review
0144-8099 Tourism†
0144-8129 Slimming
0144-8153 Evangelical Review of Theology
0144-817X Information Technology: R & D†
0144-8188 International Review of Law and Economics
0144-8196 Scottish Planning Law & Practice
0144-8218 Far Eastern Technical Review
0144-8234 Africa Economic Digest
0144-8242 British Shipbuilder†
0144-8250 Car Parts & Accessories†
0144-8285 Catholic Commission for Racial Justice. Notes & Reports†
0144-8315 Staffordshire Post
0144-8331 Organ Player and Keyboard Review
0144-8374 Baking Today†
0144-8404 Spon's Landscape Pricebook *changed to* Spon's Landscape & External Works Pricebook
0144-8412 Artery
0144-8420 Radiation Protection Dosimetry
0144-8439 Conduit
0144-8447 Science for People
0144-8455 Postgraduate Doctor: Asia†
0144-8463 Bioscience Reports
0144-8471 Insight (London)†
0144-8498 Quarterly Energy Review: Far East & Australasia
0144-8560 Running
0144-8579 Hampshire Field Club and Archaeological Society. Local History Newsletter *see* 0265-9190
0144-8587 Chartered Institute of Building. Construction Papers†
0144-8609 Aquacultural Engineering
0144-8617 Carbohydrate Polymers
0144-8625 British Journal of Family Planning
0144-8676 Royal Society of Medicine. Annual Report of the Council
0144-8684 Current Topics in Anaesthesia
0144-8692 Management of Malignant Disease Series
0144-8722 Sobornost
0144-8757 Quarterly Journal of Experimental Physiology and Cognate Medical Sciences
0144-8765 Biological Agriculture and Horticulture
0144-8773 Heterocyclic Chemistry
0144-8781 Far East Shipping
0144-879X British Journal of Intravenous Therapy *changed to* Intensive Therapy & Clinical Monitoring
0144-8803 British Journal of Pharmaceutical Practice
0144-8994 Quarterly Energy Review: Middle East
0144-9036 B M P Monthly Statistical Bulletin
0144-9052 B M P Information
0144-9060 B M P Forecasts
0144-9117 O R C Notes
0144-9206 Quarterly Energy Review: North America
0144-9214 Quarterly Energy Review: Latin America & the Caribbean
0144-9222 Quarterly Energy Review: Western Europe
0144-9230 Quarterly Energy Review: U.S.S.R. & Eastern Europe
0144-9249 Quarterly Energy Review: Africa
0144-9281 Environmental Education and Information
0144-929X Behavior and Information Technology
0144-9311 Transmission
0144-932X Liverpool Law Review
0144-9346 Tried & Tested
0144-9451 Liverpool Latin Texts *see* 0951-7391
0144-946X Purvadesh
0144-9486 University College of Swansea. Centre for Development Studies. Monograph Series†
0144-9494 University College of Swansea. Centre for Development Studies. Occasional Papers Series†
0144-9508 United Society for the Propagation of the Gospel. Annual Report/Review *changed to* United Society for the Propagation of the Gospel. Yearbook
0144-9524 Production Management and Control
0144-9613 Association Management
0144-9621 B A S C A News
0144-9745 A R C News†
0144-9753 Asian Digest *changed to* Asian Times
0144-9761 British Naturalist
0144-9818 Western Buddhist
0144-9826 Conchological Society Special Publication
0144-9842 Not Poetry†
0144-9850 University of London. Institute of Germanic Studies. Bithell Memorial Lectures
0144-9877 Chelmer Working Papers in Environmental Planning
0144-9885 Chartered Institute of Public Finance and Accountancy. Police Statistics. Estimates
0144-9893 Corporate Crime *changed to* Corporate Crime & Security
0144-9907 Security Report *changed to* Corporate Crime & Security

0144-9915 Chartered Institute of Public Finance and Accountancy. Police Statistics. Actuals
0144-9931 Catalyst
0144-9958 British Library. Reference Division Newspaper Library. Newsletter *changed to* British Library. Newspaper Library. Newsletter
0144-9966 Bibliography in Socio-Legal Studies†
0144-9974 Pippin in Playland *changed to* Pippin
0145-0034 Abstract Newsletter: Behavior and Society
0145-0085 Electronic Connector Study Group. Annual Connector Symposium. Proceedings
0145-0093 Kansas State University. Center for Energy Studies. Report†
0145-0344 Weekly Government Abstracts. Civil and Structural Engineering *see* 0163-1454
0145-0379 Berkeley Papers in History of Science
0145-062X Public Documents Highlights†
0145-0689 River Currents
0145-0743 American Society of Civil Engineers. Water Resources Planning and Management Division. Journal *see* 0733-9496
0145-1014 Aviation Monthly
0145-1022 Real Estate Investing Letter
0145-1030 Money Management Digest†
0145-1065 U.S. National Institute on Drug Abuse. Statistical Series D. Client Oriented Data Acquisition Process. Quarterly Report *see* 0161-603X
0145-1073 Surface Warfare
0145-109X Boating Safety Newsletter *see* 0198-1501
0145-1146 Vessel Safety Review
0145-1227 Fireword†
0145-1391 Epoch (Ithaca)
0145-1405 Atlanta Historical Bulletin *see* 0162-5721
0145-1413 Museum Notes (New York)
0145-1421 East-West Technology Digest
0145-1456 Soviet Journal of Marine Biology
0145-1472 College Student and the Courts
0145-1499 Authors in the News
0145-160X Washington Spectator/Between the Lines *see* 0887-428X
0145-1642 Ayer Directory of Publications *changed to* Gale Directory of Publications
0145-1677 First Monday
0145-1715 Downtown Planning & Development Annual†
0145-1731 Caligrafree Scribe *changed to* Calligranews
0145-1847 Tax Facts on Life Insurance *changed to* Tax Facts 1
0145-188X Industrial Relations Law Journal
0145-191X Guide to Catholic Literature *see* 0008-8285
0145-2029 And It Is Divine *changed to* Elan Vital
0145-2037 Educational Commission for Foreign Medical Graduates. Annual Report
0145-2061 Thrust (Sacramento)
0145-207X Engineering Index. Notes and Comment *changed to* Notes & Comment
0145-2096 Diplomatic History
0145-210X Songsmith's Journal†
0145-2118 Design Abstracts International†
0145-2126 Leukemia Research
0145-2134 Child Abuse & Neglect
0145-224X Nuclear Track Detection *changed to* International Journal of Radiation Applications and Instrumentation. Part D: Nuclear Tracks and Radiation Measurements
0145-2258 African Economic History
0145-2355 Sources: A Guide to Print and Nonprint Materials Available from Organizations, Industry, Government Agencies, and Specialized Publishers *see* 0738-1522
0145-2363 Anales de la Novela de Posguerra *see* 0272-1635
0145-2371 Alpine Information†
0145-2517 Music & Musicians: Instructional Disc Recordings Catalog (Large Print Edition)
0145-2525 Music & Musicians: Instructional Cassette Recordings Catalog (Large Print Edition)
0145-2584 International Countermeasures Handbook
0145-2681 De Colores
0145-2711 Society of Biblical Literature. Seminar Papers (Year)
0145-2843 Jazz
0145-3017 Corporate Buyers of Design Services/U S A
0145-3041 Social Services U.S.A.†
0145-305X Developmental and Comparative Immunology
0145-3068 Journal of Bioengineering *see* 0090-6964
0145-3076 State Court Journal
0145-3084 Bibliography Newsletter
0145-3130 Music & Musicians: Braille Scores Catalog - Piano (Large Print Edition)
0145-3149 Music & Musicians: Braille Scores Catalog - Organ (Large Print Edition)
0145-3157 Music & Musicians: Braille Scores Catalog - Voice *changed to* Music & Musicians: Braille Scores Catalog - Vocal (Large Print Edition)
0145-3165 Music & Musicians: Braille Scores Catalog - Instrumental
0145-3173 Music & Musicians: Braille Scores Catalog - Choral (Large Print Edition)
0145-319X N A S A Tech Briefs *see* 0889-8464
0145-3351 Association for the Care of Children in Hospitals. Journal *see* 0273-9615
0145-3378 Journal of Psychohistory
0145-3416 Immigration Newsletter
0145-3432 Southern Illinois University Law Journal
0145-3483 Cinegram
0145-3505 Professional Liability Reporter
0145-3513 International Trombone Association. Journal
0145-370X International Ophthalmological Reporter
0145-3718 Advances in Modern Nutrition†
0145-3726 Progress in Cancer Research and Therapy
0145-3793 National New Health Practitioner Program Profile *changed to* Physician Assistant Programs, A National Directory
0145-3815 Environmental Periodicals Bibliography: Indexed Article Titles *changed to* Environmental Periodicals Bibliography
0145-3831 Swimming and Diving Case Book *changed to* Swimming and Diving and Water Polo Rulebook
0145-3939 Extra
0145-3963 Cornell Executive†
0145-4013 Visual Arts Program *see* 0277-0490
0145-403X Cardiovascular Medicine *see* 0363-5104
0145-4048 Alabama Directory of Mining and Manufacturing
0145-4064 Firehouse
0145-4072 Exchange (Columbia)†
0145-4129 Health Lawyers News Report
0145-4145 Year Book of Cardiology
0145-417X Coal Data
0145-4250 American Handgunner
0145-4455 Behavior Modification
0145-4471 Powder
0145-448X New York Law School Law Review
0145-4498 Current Concepts in Emergency Medicine†
0145-4560 C B Radio/S 9
0145-4676 U.S. National Bureau of Standards. Semiconductor Measurement Technology. Quarterly Report *changed to* U.S. National Bureau of Standards. Semiconductor Measurement Technology
0145-4692 Evaluation Quarterly *see* 0193-841X
0145-479X Journal of Bioenergetics and Biomembranes
0145-482X Journal of Visual Impairment & Blindness
0145-4927 Current Industrial Reports: Manufacturers' Export Sales and Orders of Durable Goods†
0145-5028 Current Industrial Reports: Woven Fabrics. Production, Inventories, and Unfilled Orders *changed to* Current Industrial Reports: Finished Fabrics. Production, Inventories, and Unfilled Orders
0145-5125 Radio Free Jazz *see* 0272-572X
0145-5168 Current Industrial Reports: Fats and Oils. Oilseed Crushings
0145-5176 Current Industrial Reports: Fats and Oils. Production, Consumption, and Factory and Warehouse Stocks
0145-5273 Package Development and Systems *see* 0274-4996
0145-5281 Circus Maximus†
0145-529X Milton and the Romantics *see* 0733-6519
0145-5303 Phantasm
0145-5311 Recently Published Articles
0145-5338 Benchmark Papers in Analytical Chemistry
0145-5397 Library Developments
0145-5400 G. P. U. News
0145-5419 Music America *see* 0733-5253
0145-546X Mountain Review†
0145-5508 Journal of Pedodontics
0145-5532 Social Science History
0145-5575 Thorndyke File
0145-5605 Earth Resources: A Continuing Bibliography with Indexes
0145-5613 Ear, Nose and Throat Journal
0145-5664 Current Business Reports: Canned Food†
0145-5672 I U P A C Information Bulletin *see* 0193-6484
0145-5680 Cellular & Molecular Biology
0145-5699 Communications in Psychopharmacology†
0145-5702 Mazingira
0145-5753 Rohmer Review
0145-5761 Working Woman
0145-5788 Teaching Philosophy
0145-5818 Criminal Justice Periodical Index
0145-5869 Foodservice Distributor Salesman†
0145-5885 Florida Environmental and Urban Issues
0145-5958 Symposium on Engineering Problems of Fusion Research. Proceedings *changed to* Symposium on Fusion Engineering. Proceedings
0145-5982 R I L A
0145-5990 Kentucky. Department for Human Resources. Selected Vital Statistics and Planning Data *changed to* Kentucky. Cabinet for Human Resources. Vital Statistics Report
0145-6008 Alcoholism: Clinical and Experimental Research
0145-6016 Hobby Artist News†
0145-6024 Country Messenger†
0145-6032 Cinefantastique
0145-6059 English Genealogist
0145-6075 White Book of U S Ski Areas *see* 0163-9684
0145-6105 American Historical Society of Germans from Russia. Work Paper *see* 0162-8283
0145-613X Daiwa Fishing Annual
0145-6180 M P L A Newsletter
0145-6202 Federal Yellow Book
0145-6210 Body Forum
0145-6237 Guitar Foundation of America Soundboard *changed to* Soundboard
0145-6261 Feed/back (San Francisco)
0145-627X Book Talk
0145-6288 International Plant Protection Center. Infoletter
0145-6296 Veterinary and Human Toxicology
0145-6318 China Exchange Newsletter *see* 0272-0086
0145-6334 Assur
0145-6342 A L I-A B A Course Materials Journal
0145-6431 Orlando-Land *see* 0279-1323
0145-644X Washington Watch†
0145-6466 Indian Opinion†
0145-6571 Law Officer's Bulletin
0145-6601 N A G W S Guide. Soccer, Speedball, Flag Football *see* 0163-4747
0145-6636 Pastoral Music Notebook
0145-6644 Fund Sources in Health and Allied Fields†
0145-6776 Auto Index
0145-6792 Glassworks
0145-6822 A C T News *see* 0163-7908
0145-6830 Society for Slovene Studies Newsletter *see* 0193-1075
0145-6857 Alabama's Health
0145-6873 C N L/Quarterly World Report
0145-692X Corporate Profiles for Executives & Investors
0145-7071 Business People in the News†
0145-7233 Concordia Journal
0145-7241 Artnewsletter
0145-7322 Criminal Law Outline
0145-7365 Christian Science Quarterly (Inkprint Edition)
0145-7616 Computed Axial Tomography *see* 0149-936X
0145-7624 Death Education *see* 0748-1187
0145-7632 Heat Transfer Engineering
0145-7659 Privacy Journal
0145-7667 Liberty Bell
0145-7675 Other Side (Philadelphia)
0145-7683 Significant Advances in Science†
0145-7780 Graham House Review
0145-7861 Society for South India Studies. Newsletter *changed to* South Asia News
0145-7888 Studies in Twentieth Century Literature
0145-7918 Blaisdell Institute. Journal.†
0145-7950 Orthodox Church in America. Yearbook and Church Directory
0145-7969 New Pulpit Digest *see* 0160-838X
0145-7985 W I N News
0145-7993 American Indian Journal
0145-8035 Guide to Graduate and Professional Study†
0145-8043 Student Aid Manual *see* 0190-339X
0145-8116 International Review of African American Art
0145-8124 Election Administration Reports
0145-8256 Needlepoint News
0145-8264 Journal of the Milking Shorthorn and Illawarra Breeds
0145-8302 Grantechs
0145-8310 Cathartic
0145-8361 Seeker Newsletter *changed to* Emerging
0145-837X Pharmaceutical Trends†
0145-8388 New Laurel Review
0145-8396 Institute for Studies in American Music. Newsletter
0145-840X Korean Studies
0145-8418 Eastern Electrical Buyers' Guide†
0145-8426 Southern Electrical Buyers' Guide†
0145-8442 Customer Service Newsletter
0145-8477 Battelle Today
0145-8493 American Academy and Institute of Arts and Letters. Proceedings
0145-871X Consultant's Coin Report *changed to* Consultant's Certified Coin Report
0145-8752 Moscow University Geology Bulletin
0145-8779 Marianne Moore Newsletter†
0145-8787 Pulp†
0145-8795 Joint Conference†
0145-8809 Astrology Now†
0145-8825 Greater Llano Estacado Southwest Heritage†
0145-8833 Vantage Conference Report *see* 0748-0571
0145-8841 Stanley Foundation. Policy Paper
0145-885X Gnostica†
0145-8868 Llewellyn's Astrological Calendar
0145-8876 Journal of Food Process Engineering

0145-8884 Journal of Food Biochemistry
0145-8892 Journal of Food Processing and Preservation
0145-8930 Hospital Libraries
0145-8973 Chasqui
0145-899X Combinations
0145-9007 Maine Marketing Directory *changed to* Maine Manufacturing Directory
0145-9023 VideoNews
0145-9031 Carnegie Museum of Natural History. Special Publication
0145-904X Racing Cars†
0145-9058 Carnegie Museum of Natural History. Bulletin
0145-9074 Business Law Review†
0145-9090 World Coin News
0145-9104 Gaysweek
0145-9112 Northeast Improver
0145-918X Ski Competition East†
0145-9198 American Oil & Gas Reporter
0145-9244 Materials and Components in Fossil Energy Applications and E R D A Newsletter *changed to* Materials and Components in Fossil Energy Applications
0145-9317 Near East and North Africa Report *changed to* Near East/South Asia Report
0145-935X Child & Youth Services
0145-9376 Florida Vocational Journal
0145-9392 Oklahoma Farmer-Stockman
0145-9406 Security Management
0145-9457 B P Report
0145-9473 Joyer Travel Report *see* 0741-5826
0145-9481 Sahel Bibliographic Bulletin/Bulletin Bibliographique.†
0145-949X Chairman's Chat *see* 0163-0253
0145-952X U.S. Social Security Administration. Office of Research and Statistics. Public Assistance Statistics *changed to* Quarterly Public Assistance Statistics
0145-9546 Horological Times
0145-9570 Coach: Women's Athletics *see* 0160-2624
0145-9635 Independent School
0145-9643 Population Reports
0145-9651 Media Report to Women
0145-9678 Clements' International Report
0145-9686 Clements' Encyclopedia of World Governments
0145-9740 Medical Anthropology (Pleasantville)
0145-9759 Film/Psychology *changed to* Film/Psychology Review
0145-9767 N A G W S Guide. Team Handball, Racquetball, Orienteering *changed to* N A G W S Guide. Team Handball, Orienteering
0145-9791 Horse Illustrated
0145-983X Weid: the Sensibility Revue†
0145-997X Bulletin: Open Court Newsletter *changed to* Educator: Open Court Newsletter
0146-0005 Seminars in Perinatology
0146-0013 Quarterly Review of Film Studies
0146-0021 Sundance Community Dream Journal†
0146-0072 Pay T V Newsletter
0146-0080 Cablecast *see* 0731-0250
0146-0099 Multicast
0146-0102 Cable TV Regulation *see* 0731-0269
0146-0110 Broadcast Investor
0146-0129 In a Nutshell†
0146-0137 Technical Education News
0146-0145 International Flash†
0146-0153 Photomethods
0146-0196 South Carolina Baptist Historical Society Journal
0146-0234 Internationsal Society for Labor Law and Social Legislation. United States National Committee. Bulletin *see* 0147-9202
0146-0269 Graves Family Newsletter
0146-0315 Santa Clara Law Review
0146-0323 Directory of Registered Lobbyists and Lobbyist Legislation†
0146-0404 Investigative Ophthalmology & Visual Science
0146-0412 Journal of Energy†
0146-0463 Xanadu
0146-0471 Ear (San Francisco)
0146-0498 Indiana Speech Journal†
0146-0501 Pesticide & Toxic Chemical News
0146-0595 Real Estate Issues
0146-0609 New Review of Books and Religion *see* 0890-0841
0146-0625 B M W E Railway Journal
0146-0641 Journal of Solid-Phase Biochemistry *see* 0273-2289
0146-0706 Elastomerics
0146-0722 Advances in Pain Research and Therapy
0146-0749 Microbiological Reviews
0146-0781 American Motor Carrier Directory: Illinois-Missouri Edition†
0146-079X American Motor Carrier Directory: Southeastern Edition†
0146-0803 American Motor Carrier Directory: Middle Atlantic Edition†
0146-0811 American Motor Carrier Directory: New England Edition†
0146-0838 Checklist of Official New Jersey Publications
0146-0846 Series in Clinical and Community Psychology
0146-0854 Series in Thermal and Fluids Engineering
0146-0862 Issues in Comprehensive Pediatric Nursing
0146-0889 Sporting Goods Business
0146-0897 Catalog Showroom Business *changed to* C S M
0146-0900 Bank Systems & Equipment
0146-0919 Multi Housing News
0146-0935 Trademark Design Register†
0146-0951 National Purchasing Review†
0146-0978 Conservative Digest
0146-0986 Conference Board. Annual Survey of Corporate Contributions
0146-0994 Japanese Philately
0146-1001 Alternative Sources of Energy
0146-1044 Sexuality and Disability
0146-1052 Journal of Population *see* 0199-0039
0146-1079 Biblical Theology Bulletin
0146-1087 New Jersey Poetry Monthly *changed to* New Jersey Poetry
0146-1095 Channel D L S
0146-1109 Midcontinental Journal of Archaeology
0146-1117 Council Notes
0146-1133 Women's Coaching Clinic†
0146-1141 International Foundation of Employee Benefit Plans. Digest
0146-115X Career Education Workshop†
0146-1168 Guidance Clinic
0146-1176 Reading Clinic
0146-1184 Slow Learner Workshop†
0146-1214 Technology & Conservation
0146-132X North American Metalworking Research Conference. Proceedings *changed to* North American Manufacturing Research Conference. Proceedings
0146-1362 Woodall's Campground Directory. North American/Canadian Edition *changed to* Woodall's Campground Directory. North American Edition
0146-1397 Stone Country
0146-1559 Tox-Tips
0146-1672 Personality and Social Psychology Bulletin
0146-1710 Yale Italian Studies†
0146-1737 Production Engineering
0146-1745 International Review of Natural Family Planning
0146-1788 Educom Networking†
0146-1842 News for South Carolina Libraries
0146-1869 Rio Grande History
0146-1885 Rockingchair: The Review Newsletter for Librarians and Popular Music Fans Who Buy Records *see* 0160-4201
0146-1907 Summary of Rate Schedules of Natural Gas Pipeline Companies as Filed with the Federal Power Commission *changed to* Summary of Rate Schedules of Natural Gas Pipeline Companies
0146-194X Geothermal Energy Update *see* 0736-6620
0146-1990 Bryant Backtrails
0146-2059 Structural Mechanics Software Series
0146-2067 Stony Hills
0146-2075 Pimienta
0146-2083 Tuumba†
0146-2091 Media Digest
0146-2105 Star-Web Paper
0146-2113 Affirmative Action Register
0146-2156 Summary of Congress
0146-2199 Cape Rock
0146-2202 J'adoube!†
0146-2229 Utah Genealogical Association. Genealogical Journal
0146-2237 P L A Report
0146-2334 Lilith
0146-2350 E D C News†
0146-2377 Konglomerati†
0146-2520 In Situ
0146-2539 Senior World *changed to* Senior World of California
0146-2547 Second Republic Newsletter *changed to* Rangel's Reports
0146-2555 G S M Quarterly†
0146-2571 University of California, Los Angeles. Graduate School of Management. Annual Report†
0146-258X University of Wisconsin, Milwaukee. Center for Latin America. Discussion Papers *changed to* University of Wisconsin-Milwaukee. Center for Latin America. Discussion Paper Series
0146-2598 University of Wisconsin-Milwaukee. Center for Latin America. Special Papers Series *changed to* University of Wisconsin-Milwaukee. Center for Latin America. Community Resources Series
0146-2628 Super Chevy
0146-2644 1001 Truck and Van Ideas *see* 0195-0509
0146-2660 Faxon Librarians' Guide *see* 0275-8466
0146-2679 Collection Management
0146-2725 L B L Newsmagazine†
0146-275X Long-Term Care Administrator
0146-2768 Health in Wisconsin
0146-2806 Current Problems in Cardiology
0146-2857 Factory Outlet Newsletter
0146-2970 Comments on Astrophysics
0146-2989 Bulletin of Medieval Canon Law. New Series
0146-2997 Arizona Mining and Manufacturing†
0146-3071 Journal of Seed Technology
0146-308X Audio Journal Review: Ophthalmology†
0146-3128 PharmChem Newsletter
0146-3136 Poets On:
0146-3160 Mystery Fancier†
0146-3225 Chowder Review†
0146-3284 Soccer Corner†
0146-3349 Worldwide Pipelines and Contractors Directory†
0146-3365 C A O Times
0146-3373 Communication Quarterly
0146-3381 Teachers & Writers Magazine
0146-339X Off Belay†
0146-3403 Optical Index
0146-3411 Heresies
0146-3489 Relix
0146-3527 Pulp, Paper and Board *see* 0164-095X
0146-3535 Progress in Crystal Growth and Characterization
0146-3586 Studies in Human Rights
0146-3608 Contributions in Labor History
0146-3640 Older American Reports
0146-3659 Plants Alive
0146-3667 Electro-Technology Newsletter
0146-3675 Geothermal Energy
0146-3721 American Journal of Dance Therapy
0146-3756 Improving Human Performance Quarterly *changed to* Performance & Instruction Journal
0146-3764 L.S.B. Leakey Foundation News *changed to* Anthroquest
0146-3772 Hang Glider Weekly *see* 0164-3452
0146-3799 Copy Cornucopia *changed to* Creative Forum
0146-3810 Advances in General and Cellular Pharmacology†
0146-3861 Law Book Guide *see* 0360-2745
0146-390X World Issues†
0146-3934 College Student Journal
0146-3942 Institute of Mathematical Statistics. Bulletin
0146-3977 International Institute of Synthetic Rubber Producers. Annual Meeting Proceedings
0146-4094 Hebrew Studies
0146-4108 Soviet Meteorology and Hydrology
0146-4116 Automatic Control and Computer Sciences
0146-4124 Topology Proceedings
0146-4140 Journal of Ballistics
0146-4167 Colloquia in Anthropology
0146-423X Columbia Today *see* 0162-3893
0146-4299 Fossil Energy Update
0146-4329 School Universe Data Book *see* 0162-9646
0146-437X New York History
0146-4558 Distribution of Physicians in the U S *see* 0731-0315
0146-4566 International Solar Energy Society. American Section. Annual Meeting. Proceedings *changed to* American Solar Energy Society. Annual Meeting
0146-4574 Polo
0146-4582 Red Book of Ophthalmology
0146-4604 Radiation Curing
0146-4639 Product Safety Watchdog Service *see* 0275-0902
0146-4647 I T A News Digest†
0146-4671 Petersen's Hunting
0146-4701 Audio Critic
0146-4744 Business Assistance Monograph Series
0146-4752 High Solids Coatings
0146-4760 Journal of Analytical Toxicology
0146-4779 Journal of Environmental Pathology and Toxicology *see* 0731-8898
0146-4817 Noise Control Report
0146-4825 D.A.T.A. Book of Discontinued Integrated Circuits *changed to* Digital & Audio-Video Discontinued Devices D.A.T.A. Book
0146-4833 Computer Communication Review
0146-485X S E C Accounting Report
0146-4906 Federal Civilian Work Force Statistics. Occupations of Federal White-Collar Workers *changed to* Federal Civilian Work Force Statistics. Occupations of Federal White-Collar and Blue-Collar Workers
0146-4930 New Letters
0146-4965 African Literature Association Newsletter *changed to* African Literature Association. Bulletin
0146-4981 International Journal of Fusion Energy
0146-5007 Basketball Clinic
0146-5015 Salaries of Scientists, Engineers and Technicians
0146-5023 Motion Picture Product Digest†
0146-5031 U V Curing Buyer's Guide *see* 0197-8039
0146-5090 Journal of Cybernetics and Information Science†
0146-5104 Handbook for Recruiting at the Historically Black Colleges *changed to* Handbook for Recruiting Minority College Students
0146-521X Regional Anesthesia
0146-5376 Contemporary China†
0146-5414 Harvest Book Series
0146-5422 Online (Weston)
0146-5473 Public Works News
0146-5481 N A I C Malpractice Claims†
0146-5511 American Jewish Historical Society. Publications *see* 0164-0178
0146-5546 Jump Cut
0146-5554 Cumulative Index to Nursing & Allied Health Literature (C I N A H L)
0146-5562 Interracial Books for Children Bulletin

1460 ISSN INDEX

0146-5643 Idaho Heritage†
0146-5678 Nonferrous Castings
0146-5716 New Periodicals Index†
0146-5724 Radiation Physics and Chemistry *changed to* International Journal of Radiation Applications and Instrumentation. Part C: Radiation Physics and Chemistry
0146-5759 Crime in Virginia
0146-5783 Association for Gravestone Studies. Newsletter
0146-5813 C B Report
0146-5856 Arnold Schoenberg Institute. Journal
0146-5864 Solar Thermal Energy Utilization *changed to* Solar Energy Utilization: a Bibliography. Vol. 1. Solar Power Generation
0146-5864 Solar Thermal Energy Utilization *see* 0148-4397
0146-5864 Solar Thermal Energy Utilization *see* 0160-368X
0146-5872 American Board of Medical Specialties. Annual Report *see* 0272-9741
0146-5945 Policy Review
0146-5996 Home Improvement Contractor *see* 0746-2344
0146-6119 E M S A Bulletin
0146-6143 Dixie Gun Works Muzzleloaders' Annual
0146-6178 Group Psychotherapy, Psychodrama and Sociometry *see* 0731-1273
0146-6216 Applied Psychological Measurement
0146-6283 Cereal Foods World
0146-6291 Deep-Sea Research *see* 0198-0149
0146-6305 Oceanographic Abstracts and Bibliography *see* 0198-0149
0146-6321 A H C A Weekly Notes *changed to* A H C A Notes
0146-6364 Chinese Astronomy *see* 0275-1062
0146-6372 Journal of Enterprise Management†
0146-6380 Organic Geochemistry
0146-6399 Materials and Society
0146-6402 Advances in Behavior Research and Therapy
0146-6410 Progress in Particle and Nuclear Physics
0146-6429 Society of Vector Ecologists. Bulletin
0146-6453 International Commission on Radiological Protection. Annals
0146-6518 International Journal for Housing Science and Its Applications
0146-6534 Dow Jones-Irwin Business Almanac *changed to* Dow Jones-Irwin Business and Investment Almanac
0146-6607 Crafts 'n Things
0146-6615 Journal of Medical Virology
0146-6623 Journal of Aquatic Plant Management
0146-6631 Journal of Medical Entomology. Supplement
0146-664X Computer Graphics and Image Processing *see* 0734-189X
0146-678X Oriental Institute Communications
0146-6798 Materials and Studies for Kassite History
0146-6801 Toll Free Business
0146-6917 Princeton Conference on Cerebrovascular Diseases *changed to* Princeton Research Conferences on Cerebrovascular Diseases
0146-695X Monthly Poetry Anthology *changed to* Realities
0146-7042 Big Deal†
0146-7085 Directory Information Service
0146-7123 Design Automation Conference. Proceedings *changed to* A C M/I E E E Design Automation Conference. Proceedings
0146-7158 California. Division of Mines and Geology. Preliminary Report†
0146-7166 Christian Science Bible Lessons (Braille Edition)
0146-7190 Powell Monetary Analyst
0146-7204 Powell Gold Industry Guide & International Mining Analyst
0146-7220 Eudora Welty Newsletter
0146-7239 Motivation and Emotion
0146-728X Washington Drug Review *see* 0744-2823
0146-7336 Directory of Research Grants
0146-7352 Administration of the Employee Retirement Income Security Act *see* 0271-1567
0146-7581 Value Line Option & Convertible Survey
0146-7611 Investigative and Cell Pathology *see* 0022-3417
0146-7638 Keeping Abreast Journal *see* 0164-7083
0146-7646 P R B Report†
0146-7743 Insight (New York)
0146-7751 Minnesota State Register
0146-776X Sea Grant Law Journal *see* 0197-9906
0146-7824 Well-Being
0146-7832 New Thought (Scottsdale)
0146-7883 Music-in-Print Series
0146-7891 Nineteenth Century French Studies
0146-7921 Christopher Street
0146-7980 I L Z R O Lead Research Digest
0146-7999 I L Z R O Zinc Research Digest *changed to* I L Z R O Zinc/Cadium Research Digest
0146-8006 Struggle *see* 0742-9940
0146-8022 Medical and Healthcare Marketplace Guide
0146-8030 Fiber and Integrated Optics
0146-809X Southern Exposure (Durham)
0146-8170 New Thought Bulletin *see* 0146-7832
0146-8197 International Series on Biomechanics†
0146-8227 Developmental Neurobiology†
0146-8251 Southern Golf - Landscape and Turf Industry *changed to* Southern Golf - Landscape & Resort Management
0146-8286 National Federation of State High School Associations. Softball Rules *see* 0732-2844
0146-8294 Artist's and Photographer's Market *see* 0161-0546
0146-8510 Uroboros
0146-8537 Comentarios Sobre el Desarrollo Internacional†
0146-8588 Advances in Modern Toxicology†
0146-860X Video Bluebook *see* 0731-454X
0146-860X Video Bluebook *changed to* General Interest and Education Videolog
0146-8677 Queens College Studies in Librarianship
0146-8685 Rhode Island Library Association. Bulletin
0146-8693 Journal of Pediatric Psychology
0146-8812 Fighting Woman News
0146-8901 C O M P Newsletter *changed to* Local Government Performance
0146-8936 L C Acquisition Trends†
0146-8995 Canto†
0146-9061 Universitas
0146-9096 Kettering Abstracts of Available Literature on the Biological and Related Aspects of Lead and Its Compounds
0146-9126 Ocean Resources Engineering†
0146-9177 Criminal Justice Abstracts
0146-9223 Market Scope†
0146-924X Leningrad University. Vestnik. Mathematics†
0146-9282 Educational Considerations
0146-9290 Coatings Adlibra *see* 0891-1886
0146-9304 Foods Adlibra
0146-9312 Sea History
0146-9339 Mythlore
0146-9347 Mythprint
0146-9398 Ala-Arts
0146-9428 Journal of Food Quality
0146-9436 M A S K C Komondor News
0146-9487 Homemaker†
0146-9517 N S S Bulletin
0146-9568 Toledot
0146-9576 San Francisco Theatre Magazine
0146-9584 Journal of Legislation
0146-9592 Optics Letters
0146-9606 American Artist Directory of Art Schools & Workshops
0146-9673 Employment and Training Reporter
0146-9738 Dental Lab Products
0146-9770 A I C P A Washington Report
0146-9819 Auditing Research Monographs
0146-9924 Circuit Rider (Nashville)
0146-9932 M V M A Motor Vehicle Facts and Figures
0146-9959 Meteor News
0146-9967 Longest Revolution†
0146-9975 N S O A Bulletin
0146-9983 Postal History U.S.A
0146-9991 Colorado Express
0147-0019 Brown Family
0147-0035 Data Entry Digest and Distributed Processing *changed to* Data Entry Digest
0147-0051 Fire & Movement
0147-006X Annual Review of Neuroscience
0147-0078 Recent Researches in American Music
0147-0086 Recent Researches in the Music of the Classical Era
0147-0108 Collegium Musicum: Yale University
0147-0272 Current Problems in Cancer
0147-0302 Motor Skills: Theory into Practice†
0147-0310 Association of American Publishers. Exhibits Directory
0147-0353 Health Values: Achieving High Level Wellness
0147-0396 Rebis Chapbook Series
0147-0493 C C L P: Contents of Current Legal Periodicals *see* 0279-5787
0147-0515 N I A A A - R U C A S Alcoholism Treatment Series
0147-0590 Regulation (Washington, 1977)
0147-0604 Michigan State University. Library. Africana: Select Recent Acquisitions
0147-0612 Michigan State University. Library. Latin America: Select Recent Acquisitions†
0147-0620 Michigan State University. Library. Asia: Select Recent Acquisitions†
0147-0639 Maine Antique Digest
0147-0655 Human Sexuality *changed to* Annual Editions: Human Sexuality
0147-071X Advances in Behavioral Pharmacology
0147-0728 Gay Community News
0147-0779 Modern Greek Society: A Social Science Newsletter
0147-0787 Books at Brown
0147-0833 Journal of Equine Medicine and Surgery
0147-0906 Linguistics in Literature *changed to* Language and Literature
0147-0981 Fletcher Forum
0147-1015 Ukrainian Orthodox Word. English Edition
0147-1023 Contributions in Family Studies
0147-1031 Contributions in Intercultural and Comparative Studies
0147-104X Contributions in Women's Studies
0147-1058 Contributions in Medical History
0147-1066 Contributions in Political Science
0147-1074 Contributions in Legal Studies
0147-1082 Contemporary Problems of Childhood
0147-1090 New Directions in Librarianship
0147-1104 Studies in Population and Urban Demography
0147-1112 Dax Money-Maker Newsletter
0147-1120 Association of College Unions-International. Proceedings of the Annual Conference
0147-1139 Dignity
0147-1147 Design Methods and Theories
0147-1155 Cancer Focus
0147-1201 M A I N
0147-121X Light†
0147-1228 Hoosier Journal of Ancestry
0147-1236 A C T F L Foreign Language Education Series
0147-1260 Child Protection Report
0147-1465 Washington Review of Strategic and International Studies *see* 0163-660X
0147-1481 Offshore Rig Newsletter
0147-149X Cottonwood Review *changed to* Cottonwood
0147-1503 Thermodynamics Research Center. International Data Series. Selected Data on Mixtures. Series A. Thermodynamic Properties of Non-reacting Binary Systems of Organic Substances
0147-152X Ocean Construction Report
0147-1570 CompFlash
0147-1597 Opus Two
0147-1627 Calyx
0147-1635 Journal of Basic Writing
0147-1651 Graphic Arts Green Book
0147-1678 Directory of Fee-Based Information Services
0147-1686 Floating Island
0147-1694 Contemporary Jewry
0147-1740 Urban League Review
0147-1759 Women & Literature
0147-1767 International Journal of Intercultural Relations
0147-1775 International Journal of Family Counseling *see* 0192-6187
0147-1783 Washington (State). Division of Geology and Earth Resources. Information Circular
0147-1821 Graduate Programs: Physics, Astronomy, and Related Fields
0147-1902 Georgia Museum of Art. Bulletin
0147-1937 Real Analysis Exchange
0147-1961 Banking Today
0147-197X Current Problems in Anesthesia and Critical Care Medicine†
0147-1988 Current Problems in Obstetrics and Gynecology *see* 8756-0410
0147-1996 Year Book of Family Practice
0147-2003 Southwest Regional Conference for Astronomy and Astrophysics. Proceedings†
0147-2011 Society
0147-2135 A R L Statistics
0147-216X Directory of Washington Representatives of American Associations and Industry *see* 0192-060X
0147-2208 Laventhol and Horwath Perspective
0147-2275 Seriatim
0147-2313 Screen Achievement Records Bulletin *see* 0163-5123
0147-2399 Travel Research Bulletin *see* 0047-2875
0147-2410 Western Investor
0147-2429 Plastics in Building Construction
0147-2453 Curriculum Review
0147-2461 Art and Crafts Market *see* 0161-0554
0147-2461 Art and Crafts Market *see* 0161-0546
0147-247X Photographer's Market
0147-2488 Richardson Family Researcher and Historical News
0147-2496 E R *changed to* Environmental Review
0147-250X Bibliography of Books for Children
0147-2526 Dance Chronicle
0147-2542 Ohio Documents
0147-2550 Massachusetts Music News
0147-2593 Lion & the Unicorn
0147-2615 Abstracts of Popular Culture†
0147-2631 Hollow Spring Review of Poetry
0147-264X Dental Research in the United States and Other Countries†
0147-2682 Biomedical Technology Information Service
0147-2704 Seventh Ray
0147-2747 N S P I Journal (1976) *changed to* Performance & Instruction Journal
0147-281X West Point Museum Bulletin†
0147-2828 Black Press Information Handbook†
0147-2860 Illinois. State Board of Education. Annual Report
0147-2917 Comparative Medicine East and West *see* 0192-415X
0147-2992 Interface Age *changed to* Computing for Business
0147-300X International Glass/Metal Catalog
0147-3077 Periodical Guide for Computerists†
0147-3085 Celestinesca
0147-3158 Research Libraries Group. Newsletter *see* 0196-173X
0147-3204 I E E E Transactions on Cable Television†
0147-3247 Nuestro
0147-328X Liquid Chromatography Literature - Abstracts and Index

ISSN INDEX 1461

0147-3301 Cablelines
0147-3328 G T E Automatic Electric Technical Journal *see* 0273-141X
0147-3379 Product Marketing *see* 0278-1530
0147-345X Eastman Notes
0147-3522 Ocean Engineering *see* 0146-9126
0147-3565 Porsche Panorama
0147-3646 A.P.S. Writers Unit Number Thirty News Bulletin *changed to* Philatelic Communicator
0147-3654 Scienceland
0147-3700 Mental Disability Law Reporter *see* 0883-7902
0147-3743 Safety Sadistics†
0147-3751 Americans Abroad†
0147-3786 Quest (Year)†
0147-3867 Country Vacations U.S.A. *see* 0195-8437
0147-3964 Multivariate Experimental Clinical Research
0147-4006 Carcinogenesis
0147-4022 Journal of Divorce
0147-4030 How to Fly for Less†
0147-4049 Bright Lights†
0147-4057 Newsounds
0147-409X Export Grafics U S A
0147-4243 Economic Analysis of North American Ski Areas
0147-4308 Israel Securities Review Monthly Magazine *see* 0147-4316
0147-4316 Israel Securities Review
0147-4367 Voice of Washington Music Educators
0147-4375 A A E S P H Review (American Association for the Education of the Severely-Profoundly Handicapped) *changed to* Association for Persons with Severe Handicaps. Journal
0147-4391 B I A Education Research Bulletin†
0147-4413 American Liszt Society. Journal *changed to* J A L S
0147-4502 West Coast Plays
0147-4529 Government-Supported Research on Foreign Affairs *see* 0194-8660
0147-4642 Communication Yearbook
0147-4650 Checklist of Official Publications of the State of Oregon†
0147-4693 On the Line Magazine (New York)
0147-4707 Chicago Library System Communicator *see* 0277-8955
0147-4804 World Wide Printer
0147-4820 A A S H T O Quarterly Magazine
0147-4871 Feedback
0147-4928 Country Gentleman
0147-4936 Invisible City
0147-507X First World
0147-510X Us (New York, 1977)
0147-5118 Toxic Substances Sourcebook†
0147-5185 American Journal of Surgical Pathology
0147-5207 Mon-Khmer Studies
0147-5231 Somatics
0147-5363 Project Management Quarterly *changed to* Project Management Journal
0147-538X New York Times Index
0147-5401 Industrial Hygiene News
0147-5428 West Coast Writer's Conspiracy
0147-5436 Aloha
0147-5452 Telephone†
0147-5460 Journal of Hispanic Philology
0147-5479 International Labor and Working Class History
0147-5533 Billboard's International Disco Sourcebook *changed to* Billboard's International Club and Disco Equipment Sourcebook
0147-5622 Psychosocial Rehabilitation Journal
0147-5630 Index to Free Periodicals
0147-572X M R I S Abstracts†
0147-5754 Intermedia Magazine†
0147-5762 Alive & Kicking
0147-5770 Finders International Newsletter
0147-5789 Scintilation *see* 0162-0126
0147-5851 E M T Journal†
0147-5894 College and University Admissions and Enrollment, New York State
0147-5916 Cognitive Therapy and Research
0147-5924 Info Franchise Newsletter
0147-5967 Journal of Comparative Economics
0147-5975 Experimental Mycology
0147-6165 Roaring Twenties, Gay Nineties†
0147-619X Plasmid
0147-6254 Bedside Care†
0147-6297 Contemporary Art - Southeast *see* 0278-1441
0147-6335 Korean Studies Forum
0147-6491 Bibliographic Guide to North American History
0147-6513 Ecotoxicology and Environmental Safety
0147-6521 Energy Information Abstracts
0147-6521 Energy Information Abstracts Annual *changed to* Energy Information Index/Abstracts Annual
0147-6548 New Atlantean Journal†
0147-6580 Federal Reserve Bank of New York. Quarterly Review
0147-6629 Seattle Review
0147-6726 Journal for Medicaid Management *changed to* Perspectives on Medicaid and Medicare Management
0147-6742 Medical Ultrasound
0147-6750 C R C Critical Reviews in Diagnostic Imaging
0147-6793 Orthopaedic Survey *see* 0738-2278
0147-6874 Moscow University Soil Science Bulletin
0147-6882 Scientific and Technical Information Processing
0147-6890 Fiscal Observer†
0147-6939 Fatal Accident Reporting System. Annual Report *see* 0732-9792
0147-698X Journal of Powder & Bulk Solids Technology
0147-6998 D E/Domestic Engineering
0147-7013 Moravian Music Foundation. Bulletin *see* 0278-0763
0147-7129 Attic Press
0147-7137 Urban Futures Idea Exchange *see* 0732-8265
0147-7188 Managing the Leisure Facility
0147-720X Outdoors in Georgia†
0147-7218 Law and Behavior†
0147-7226 Hope Reports Perspective†
0147-7285 Mideastern Camping *see* 0734-2705
0147-7307 Law and Human Behavior
0147-7366 International Review of Biochemistry†
0147-7439 Satellite Communications
0147-7447 Orthopedics (Thorofare)
0147-7463 Human Nature†
0147-7471 Adventure Travel (Seattle)†
0147-7544 Dialogue in Instrumental Music Education
0147-7625 New Realities
0147-7633 Chilton's Review of Optometry
0147-7668 Aerophile
0147-7676 High Fidelity's Buying Guide to Speaker Systems *see* 0278-1387
0147-7684 Car Care Handbook†
0147-7706 Short Story International
0147-782X International Psychic Register
0147-7862 Hart Crane Newsletter *changed to* Visionary Company: A Magazine of the Twenties
0147-7870 U.S. Department of Housing and Urban Development. Statistical Yearbook
0147-7889 A S C Newsletter
0147-7927 Perinatology/Neonatology
0147-7927 Perinatology-Neonatology Buyers Guide
0147-7943 District Lawyer *changed to* Washington Lawyer
0147-7951 Dressage and Combined Training *see* 0147-796X
0147-796X Dressage & C T
0147-7978 Journal of Psychology and Christianity
0147-8001 Urban Systems *see* 0198-9715
0147-8044 N C E A Ganley's Catholic Schools in America
0147-8087 Pharmaceutical Technology
0147-8168 Southern Review of Public Administration *see* 0734-9149
0147-8176 Fodor's Egypt
0147-8222 Illinois Journal of Pharmacy *see* 0195-2099
0147-8257 Harvard Environmental Law Review
0147-8265 Who's Who in Chiropractic, International
0147-829X Social Psychology *see* 0190-2725
0147-8311 Conditions
0147-832X Kitchens & Baths *see* 0270-305X
0147-8354 Adult Literacy and Basic Education
0147-8389 P A C E
0147-8451 Peterson's Annual Guide to Undergraduate Study *see* 0737-3163
0147-8451 Peterson's Annual Guide to Undergraduate Study *see* 0737-3171
0147-8478 U.S. Geological Survey. Annual Report *see* 0162-9484
0147-8591 Gardens *see* 0270-3041
0147-8613 North Central Campbook
0147-8648 Update on Law-Related Education
0147-8656 Fodor's Southwest†
0147-8680 Fodor's South
0147-8745 Fodor's U S A
0147-877X Business Officer
0147-8818 Ham Radio Horizons *see* 0148-5989
0147-8869 Cuba Review *changed to* Cubatimes
0147-8885 Journal of Histotechnology
0147-8893 Diagnostic Medicine†
0147-8907 Video
0147-8923 Marine Business *see* 0006-5404
0147-9024 Journal of New World Archaeology
0147-9156 Contemporary French Civilization
0147-9202 Comparative Labor Law
0147-9245 Digital Design
0147-9253 Intermedia Arts and Communication Resource Newsletter†
0147-9288 American Alpine News
0147-9296 Association for Educational Data Systems. Annual Convention Proceedings
0147-9415 Computer Terminals Review
0147-9466 Directory of African and Afro-American Studies in the United States *changed to* Directory of Third World Studies in the United States
0147-9512 Global Political Assessment†
0147-9563 Heart and Lung
0147-9571 Comparative Immunology, Microbiology and Infectious Diseases
0147-958X Clinical and Investigative Medicine
0147-9695 Vintage Triumph
0147-9725 Maryland Birdlife
0147-9733 Colorado Libraries
0147-9741 Center on Evaluation, Development and Research. Quarterly†
0147-992X McElroy Family Newsletter†
0147-9970 Litigation News
0147-9989 Restaurant Hospitality
0148-0057 Measurements and Control
0148-0065 Directory of East Asian Collections in North American Libraries
0148-012X Contract Interiors *see* 0164-8470
0148-0146 Manhattan Business†
0148-0162 Raccoon
0148-0170 Transportation Engineering *see* 0162-8178
0148-0227 J G R: Journal of Geophysical Research *changed to* J G R: Journal of Geophysical Research: Oceans and Atmospheres
0148-0227 J G R: Journal of Geophysical Research *see* 0196-6928
0148-0227 J G R: Journal of Geophysical Research *changed to* J G R: Journal of Geophysical Research: Solid Earth and Planets
0148-0243 American Go Journal
0148-0324 California Environmental Directory
0148-0375 International Petroleum Encyclopedia
0148-0537 Fusion (New York)
0148-0545 Drug and Chemical Toxicology
0148-0561 Kxe6s Verein Newsletter
0148-057X Kxe6s Verein Chess Society. Advisory Board Record
0148-0650 Illinois Health Sciences Libraries Serials Holdings List†
0148-0685 Women's Studies (Oxford) *see* 0277-5395
0148-0731 Journal of Biomechanical Engineering
0148-0766 Lodging Hospitality
0148-0812 Journal of Dermatologic Surgery and Oncology
0148-0847 Social Work Research and Abstracts
0148-0863 Public Revenues from Alcohol Beverages†
0148-1037 Minority Voices†
0148-1045 Media Law Reporter
0148-1061 Education Libraries
0148-107X Employment Discrimination Digest
0148-1096 Zetetic *see* 0194-6730
0148-1150 N A G W S Rules. Skiing†
0148-1177 Pacific Almanac. Pacific Northwest and Alaska *see* 0276-8771
0148-1789 Thomas Wolfe Newsletter *see* 0276-5683
0148-1827 Ore Bin *see* 0164-3304
0148-186X Administration of the Marine Mammal Protection Act of 1972 *see* 0196-4690
0148-1878 Moody's Bond Record
0148-1886 Massachusetts Archaeological Society. Bulletin
0148-1940 I R S Letter Rulings
0148-1959 Interdisciplinary Perspectives *see* 0890-9792
0148-2009 Lonergan Workshop
0148-2033 Specialty Advertiser†
0148-2041 Event
0148-2076 19th Century Music
0148-2092 Freebies
0148-2114 Journeyman Barber and Beauty Culture†
0148-2165 Lifelong Learning: The Adult Years *see* 0740-0578
0148-2181 Journal of Pension Planning and Compliance
0148-2203 Spinoff
0148-2548 Radio Liberty Research Bulletins *changed to* Radio Liberty Research Bulletins on the Soviet Union
0148-2963 Journal of Business Research
0148-3161 Homeowners How To Handbook *see* 0195-2196
0148-3218 Best's Insurance Report: Property-Casualty
0148-3250 Louisville Review
0148-3277 Directory of Women in Philosophy†
0148-3331 Christianity and Literature
0148-3366 Municipal Law Docket
0148-3390 Illinois Magazine
0148-3471 Surgical Techniques Illustrated†
0148-3641 Directory of Washington Manufacturers *see* 0148-5687
0148-3706 Golf Business†
0148-382X Refrigeration Service & Contracting
0148-3838 University of Michigan. Museum of Paleontology. Papers on Paleontology
0148-3846 Journal of Rehabilitation Administration
0148-3897 Ornament
0148-3900 Journal of Interdisciplinary Modeling and Simulation†
0148-3919 Journal of Liquid Chromatography
0148-3927 Clinical and Experimental Hypertension *see* 0730-0077
0148-396X Neurosurgery
0148-3994 Parke Society News Letter
0148-4001 Modern Salon
0148-4036 Pennsylvania Mennonite Heritage
0148-4052 Successful Meetings
0148-4079 Job Safety and Health (Silver Spring) *changed to* Workplace Health
0148-4087 Public Transit Report *changed to* Urban Transport News
0148-4109 Federal Research Report
0148-4125 Sludge Newsletter
0148-415X New International Review
0148-4184 Accounting Historians Journal
0148-4214 Missouri Area Labor Trends
0148-4265 Current Nephrology
0148-432X American Educator
0148-4397 Solar Energy Utilization: a Bibliography. Vol. 2. Solar Thermal Components†
0148-4419 Southern Journal of Applied Forestry
0148-4443 Pipeline (Houston)

0148-4451 Serials in Transition†
0148-446X Abstract Newsletter: Energy
0148-4478 Chilton's Food Engineering International
0148-4508 National Directory of Educational Programs in Gerontology
0148-4532 Yale Lit *see* 0148-4605
0148-4605 Yale Literary Magazine (1977)
0148-4648 International Drug Report
0148-477X Special Education Report†
0148-4818 U S Pharmacist
0148-4834 J N E. Journal of Nursing Education *see* 0022-3158
0148-4958 Foodservice Equipment Specialist *changed to* Foodservice Equipment & Supplies Specialist
0148-5008 Inquiry (Washington)†
0148-5016 Archives of Andrology
0148-5032 Mayflower Quarterly
0148-5040 Wisconsin. Department of Public Instruction. Newsletter *changed to* Education Forward
0148-5059 Wisconsin Public School Directory
0148-5113 Geographical Survey†
0148-5164 Journal of Continuing Education in Obstetrics & Gynecology *see* 0198-9197
0148-5172 Journal of Continuing Education in Urology *see* 0197-7709
0148-5180 Journal of Continuing Education in O.R.L. & Allergy *see* 0198-7038
0148-5199 Journal of Continuing Education in Cardiology *changed to* Cardiology Digest (1979)
0148-530X U.S. Bureau of Labor Statistics. Publications†
0148-5407 Disabled U S A
0148-5431 D M: Data Management *changed to* Data Management
0148-5482 Mandolin Notebook *see* 0270-9325
0148-5512 Federal Index Monthly *changed to* C S I Federal Index
0148-558X Journal of Accounting Auditing & Finance†
0148-5598 Journal of Medical Systems
0148-561X Degre Second: Studies in French Literature
0148-5628 Climatological Data for Amundsen-Scott, Antarctica†
0148-5644 U.S. Library of Congress. Accessions List: Afghanistan†
0148-5652 Delaware State Industrial Directory *changed to* MacRae's Maryland/D.C./Delaware State Industrial Directory
0148-5660 Maryland State Industrial Directory *changed to* MacRae's Maryland/D.C./Delaware State Industrial Directory
0148-5679 Rhode Island State Industrial Directory *see* 0740-4689
0148-5687 Washington Manufacturers Register
0148-5717 Sexually Transmitted Diseases
0148-5733 Pacific Information Service on Street-Drugs†
0148-5741 Yale Forest School News
0148-5792 Jobber/Retailer
0148-5806 E C & T J
0148-5865 Arabesque
0148-5881 Nevada Review of Business and Economics
0148-5903 American Bookseller
0148-5989 Ham Radio Magazine†
0148-6039 Accident Facts
0148-6055 Journal of Rheology
0148-6071 Parenteral and Enteral Nutrition. Journal *changed to* J P E N: Journal of Parenteral and Enteral Nutrition
0148-6101 R I P E H The Review of Iranian Political Economy & History
0148-6128 W P I Journal
0148-6179 Black American Literature Forum
0148-6187 Beverage Industry
0148-6195 Journal of Economics and Business
0148-6225 Association for Asian Studies. Committee on East Asian Libraries. Bulletin
0148-6373 Electronic, Electro-Optic and Infrared Countermeasures *see* 0164-4076
0148-6381 Who's Who Among Vocational and Technical Students in America
0148-639X Muscle & Nerve
0148-6403 Head & Neck Surgery
0148-6411 I E E E Transactions on Components, Hybrids and Manufacturing Technology
0148-642X Catalog of Fossil Spores and Pollen
0148-6489 Public Land & Resources Law Digest
0148-6543 Studies in History and Philosophy. Pamphlet Series†
0148-6551 Studies in Law†
0148-656X Studies in Social Theory†
0148-6578 Teacher *changed to* Instructor
0148-6586 Index to Mormonism in Periodical Literature†
0148-6608 Journal of Metals (1977)
0148-6616 Genealogical Society of Okaloosa County, Florida. Journal
0148-6659 Roots
0148-6675 Fire Technology Abstracts†
0148-6705 Funeral Service Insider
0148-6713 Leisure Beverage Insider Newsletter
0148-6721 Car Dealer Insider Newsletter
0148-673X Trumpeter
0148-6748 Europe Today (Augusta)
0148-6802 Invest Yourself
0148-6845 Violin Society of America. Journal
0148-690X Compensation Planning Journal *see* 0747-8607
0148-6934 E E O Review
0148-6942 Mime Directory†
0148-6985 State of Black America
0148-7043 Annals of Plastic Surgery
0148-7078 Motel/Hotel Insider Newsletter
0148-7094 Africa and West Asia Agricultural Situation *changed to* World Agriculture Regional Supplement: Middle East and North Africa
0148-7132 Wallace Stevens Journal
0148-7175 Afro-American Journal†
0148-7191 S A E Technical Papers
0148-7280 Gamete Research
0148-7299 American Journal of Medical Genetics
0148-7442 Directory of Michigan Municipal Officials
0148-7469 Air Cargo Magazine *see* 0745-5100
0148-7558 Massachusetts State Industrial Directory *see* 0740-4689
0148-7566 Get Ready Sheet
0148-7604 D.A.T.A. Book of Discontinued Semiconductor Diodes *changed to* Diode Discontinued Devices D.A.T.A. Book
0148-7639 A D F L Bulletin
0148-7655 Louisiana Genealogical Register
0148-7671 Polar Geography *see* 0273-8457
0148-771X Grass Roots Perspectives on American History
0148-7736 Texas Monthly
0148-7760 U.S.S.R. Facts & Figures Annual
0148-7795 Panhandle-Plains Historical Review
0148-7868 Africana Libraries Newsletter *changed to* Africana Libraries Newsletter
0148-7876 Texas. Department of Water Resources. Library. Bulletin *changed to* Texas. Water Commission. Library. Bulletin.
0148-7922 Family Law Reporter
0148-7930 Retail/Services Labor Report *see* 0891-4141
0148-7949 Government Manager
0148-7957 Noise Regulation Reporter
0148-7965 B N A's Patent, Trademark & Copyright Journal
0148-7973 Chemical Regulation Reporter
0148-7981 Labor Relations Reporter
0148-799X Dynamic Years†
0148-8066 Association of Departments of Foreign Languages. Bulletin *see* 0148-7639
0148-8139 United States Law Week
0148-8147 Affirmative Action Compliance Manual for Federal Contractors
0148-8155 Daily Report for Executives
0148-8279 Lithuanian Mathematical Transactions *see* 0363-1672
0148-8287 Journal of Thermal Insulation
0148-8309 Stack Sampling News
0148-8317 Environmental Impact News†
0148-8325 South Dakota. Department of Social Services. Annual Medical Report†
0148-8376 Journal of Social Service Research
0148-8384 International Journal of Family Therapy *changed to* Contemporary Family Therapy: An International Journal
0148-8414 American Spectator
0148-8430 Press
0148-8465 M R I S Current Awareness Service†
0148-849X National Research Council. Transportation Research Board. Bibliography
0148-8597 Federal Civilian Workforce Statistics. Annual Report of Employment by Geographic Area *changed to* Federal Civilian Workforce Statistics. Biennial Report of Employment by Geographic Area
0148-8619 U S Journal of Drug and Alcohol Dependence
0148-8627 Ensayistas
0148-866X New Acronyms, Initialisms and Abbreviations
0148-8732 Sailboat & Equipment Directory
0148-8740 Motorboat & Equipment Directory†
0148-8821 Marriage and Divorce Today
0148-883X Sexuality Today
0148-8848 United States Banker
0148-8899 Professional Agent
0148-8996 Biblioscan Q-Z
0148-9011 Biblioscan H-L
0148-902X Plainswoman
0148-9038 Fungicide and Nematicide Tests
0148-9062 International Journal of Rock Mechanics and Mining Sciences & Geomechanics Abstracts
0148-9100 American Art and Antiques *see* 0195-8208
0148-9119 Plastics Compounding
0148-9127 Crafts
0148-9143 Florida Monthly†
0148-9151 Jackson Magazine *see* 0164-6699
0148-916X International Journal of Leprosy and Other Mycobacterial Diseases
0148-9232 Indiana. Office of Community Services Administration. Annual Report†
0148-9267 Computer Music Journal
0148-9364 Fanfare (Tenafly)
0148-9410 Auto Reports†
0148-9437 Gift and Tableware Reporter. Gift Guide
0148-9496 Federation of American Hospitals. Review *changed to* Federation of American Health Systems Review
0148-9526 Outlook for U.S. Agricultural Exports
0148-9542 Jax Fax *changed to* Jax Fax Travel Marketing Magazine
0148-9585 Higher Education Review *see* 0162-5748
0148-9607 Tech
0148-9615 I E E E Communications Society Magazine *see* 0163-6804
0148-9666 Driftwood East *see* 0190-2253
0148-9798 National Collegiate Championships Record Book *see* 0190-4329
0148-9801 Fueloil & Oil Heat & Solar Systems
0148-9836 Northeast Gulf Science
0148-9895 American Society of Civil Engineers. Waterway, Port, Coastal and Ocean Division. Journal *see* 0733-950X
0148-9909 American Society of Civil Engineers. Technical Councils. Journal *see* 0733-9461
0148-9917 Journal of Ambulatory Care Management
0149-015X Studies in the American Renaissance
0149-0214 Gambling Times
0149-0257 Holiday Homes International *changed to* Homes International
0149-0265 Journal of Continuing Education in Psychiatry *see* 0278-4602
0149-0273 Journal of Continuing Education in Family Medicine *changed to* Medical Digest (1979) Education in Family Medicine
0149-0281 Who Audits America
0149-0354 Barataria
0149-0370 E E: Evaluation Engineering
0149-0389 Terrorism
0149-0397 Marine Mining
0149-0400 Leisure Sciences
0149-0419 Marine Geodesy
0149-0427 Acoustical Imaging and Holography *see* 0732-6726
0149-0451 Geomicrobiology Journal
0149-046X Membrane Biochemistry
0149-0478 Expenditure and Employment Data for the Criminal Justice Systems *changed to* Justice Expenditure and Employment in the U.S.
0149-0508 Peace & Change
0149-0516 Pequod
0149-0532 Women's Agenda†
0149-0605 Engineering Research Highlights†
0149-0672 Equus
0149-0699 Self (New York)
0149-0729 Mahogany
0149-0737 News Media and the Law
0149-0796 African Index
0149-080X Manpower and Human Resources Studies
0149-0818 Multinational Industrial Relations Series
0149-0907 Bioresearch Today: Pesticides
0149-0915 Bioresearch Today: Population, Fertility & Birth Control
0149-0923 Bioresearch Today: Industrial Health & Toxicology
0149-0931 Bioresearch Today: Human Ecology
0149-094X Bioresearch Today: Human and Animal Parasitology
0149-0958 Bioresearch Today: Food Additives & Residues
0149-0966 Bioresearch Today: Human & Animal Aging
0149-0974 Bioresearch Today: Food Microbiology
0149-0982 Bioresearch Today: Birth Defects
0149-0990 Bioresearch Today: Bio Engineering & Instrumentation
0149-1008 Bioresearch Today: Addiction
0149-1016 Bioresearch Today: Cancer A-Carcinogenesis
0149-1024 Bioresearch Today: Cancer B-Anticancer Agents
0149-1032 Bioresearch Today: Cancer C-Immunology
0149-1040 New York Literary Forum
0149-1083 Guide to Independent Study Through Correspondence Instruction *see* 0733-6020
0149-1091 O'Dwyer's Directory of Corporate Communications
0149-1172 Washington Journalism Review
0149-1199 A C M Guide to Computing Literature
0149-1202 Bibliography and Subject Index of Current Computing Literature *see* 0149-1199
0149-1210 33 Metal Producing
0149-1237 Kastlemusick Exchange *see* 0276-0606
0149-1288 Fodor's Paris
0149-1342 Urethane Abstracts
0149-1423 A A P G Bulletin
0149-144X Reliability and Maintainability Symposium. Proceedings
0149-1482 Reading Today International†
0149-1563 Russian & East European Studies Indexed Journal Reference Guide†
0149-1598 N A C L A Report on the Americas
0149-1644 Organizational Communications
0149-1695 Legal Briefs for Editors, Publishers and Writers†
0149-1717 Pharmacy and Law Digest
0149-175X Texas Tech University. Museum. Occasional Papers
0149-1768 Texas Tech University. Museum. Special Publications
0149-1776 Glaciological Data
0149-1784 Journal of South Asian and Middle Eastern Studies
0149-1830 Velvet Light Trap

ISSN INDEX 1463

0149-1911 Avanti Owners Association Newsletter
0149-192X Quantitative Applications in the Social Sciences
0149-1938 Sunworld
0149-1946 Off P'tree
0149-1970 Progress in Nuclear Energy (New Series)
0149-1997 Allegheny Ludlum Horizons†
0149-2004 Aletheia
0149-2047 Community Health Studies
0149-2063 Journal of Management (Lubbock)
0149-2136 J P T. Journal of Petroleum Technology
0149-2268 Bulletin of Chemical Thermodynamics (1977)
0149-2276 Competitivedge
0149-2357 Modern Electronics
0149-2365 Soccer Digest
0149-2373 Strike
0149-2381 Chemical Times & Trends
0149-2438 Tufts Kinsmen
0149-2446 A C S A News
0149-2462 Georgia. Water Resources Survey. Hydrologic Report†
0149-2489 A F L-C I O American Federationist†
0149-2497 U.S. National Center for Education Statistics. Revenues and Expenditures for Public Elementary and Secondary Education
0149-2500 U.S. Small Business Administration. S B I C Digest
0149-2578 Washington Social Legislation Bulletin
0149-2616 U.S. Center for Disease Control. Tuberculosis in the United States
0149-2632 Hospital Peer Review
0149-2683 Fair Employment Practices
0149-2705 Payroll Compensation *see* 0005-3228
0149-2926 Sexual Medicine Today
0149-3361 Indiana Writes *see* 0738-386X
0149-337X American City & County
0149-3442 Tack 'n Togs Merchandising
0149-3450 ElHi Funding Sources Newsletter†
0149-3574 NuclearFuel
0149-3582 Securities Week
0149-3701 Ammonia Plant Safety and Related Facilities
0149-3701 C E P Technical Manuals†
0149-3752 Illinois Issues Annual†
0149-3922 Powder Metallurgy in Defense Technology
0149-399X Asia Mail†
0149-4147 Turbomachinery International
0149-4228 Grub Street†
0149-4236 Chaplaincy†
0149-4244 New Oxford Review
0149-4252 Chaplaincy Letter†
0149-4260 Journal of Continuing Education in Ophthalmology *see* 0048-1955
0149-435X Michigan Librarian Newsletter *changed to* Michigan Librarian
0149-4465 Diesel and Gas Turbine Progress Worldwide *see* 0278-5994
0149-4473 Viva†
0149-449X Iowa. Department of Job Service. Annual Report
0149-4511 American Transportation Builder
0149-4600 Industrial Development's Site Selection Handbook *see* 0080-9810
0149-4635 Hustler
0149-466X Players
0149-4740 National N O W Times
0149-4856 Airline Executive
0149-4880 Papers in International Studies: Latin American Series *changed to* Monographs in International Studies: Latin America Series
0149-4899 Plastics Machinery and Equipment *changed to* Plastics Machinery and Equipment Sourcebook for Extruders
0149-4902 M O T A
0149-4910 N A C T A Journal
0149-4929 Marriage & Family Review
0149-4996 Western Railroader and Western Railfan
0149-5011 Overtones
0149-5046 Heard Heritage
0149-5054 Computer Peripherals Review
0149-5070 Western New York Magazine
0149-5135 Sufi Times *see* 0161-6331
0149-516X Southern Accents
0149-5240 Equipment Guide News *changed to* Equipment Today
0149-5283 Mine Productivity Report *changed to* Coal Week International
0149-5348 Current Bibliography of Plastic & Reconstructive Surgery
0149-5364 Federal Reserve Bank of Dallas. Economic Review
0149-5372 Checklist of Human Rights Documents†
0149-5380 W W D *changed to* Women's Wear Daily
0149-5437 Olson†
0149-5534 Industry Mart†
0149-5585 International Construction Week
0149-5682 Textile Booklist†
0149-5712 Maarav
0149-5720 Numerical Heat Transfer
0149-5739 Journal of Thermal Stresses
0149-5747 Advanced Lighter-Than-Air Review†
0149-5771 Electrical Marketing Newsletter
0149-578X Coal Week *changed to* Coal Week International
0149-5879 Sewage Treatment Construction Grants Manual
0149-5887 Tiger Report†
0149-5895 Food, Drug & Cosmetic Manufacturing†
0149-5917 Inspiration (Los Angeles)†
0149-5925 Vans & Pickups†
0149-5933 Comparative Strategy
0149-5941 Conflict
0149-5968 Drug Abuse and Alcoholism Review *see* 0270-3106
0149-5976 Monthly Detroit
0149-5992 Diabetes Care
0149-6018 Routes
0149-6026 Inner Paths
0149-6085 Journal of Food Safety
0149-6093 Good Ideas for Decorating *changed to* Good Ideas
0149-6115 Geotechnical Testing Journal
0149-6123 Cement, Concrete, and Aggregates
0149-614X Together (New York) *see* 0199-7149
0149-6158 Together Sexology *see* 0199-7149
0149-6166 Index to Federal Tax Articles (Supplement)
0149-6212 S G A Journal
0149-6352 Hospital Week†
0149-6395 Separation Science and Technology
0149-6425 Rodeo News
0149-6441 West Branch
0149-645X I E E E/M T T - S International Microwave Symposium. Digest
0149-6492 Voluntary Action Leadership
0149-6549 Health Practitioner *changed to* Physician Assistant
0149-6573 Environmental Comment†
0149-6581 Directory of Companies Required to File Annual Reports with the Securities and Exchange Commission Under the Securities Exchange Act of 1934
0149-6646 Alaska. Department of Natural Resources. Annual Report†
0149-6700 Studies in History of Biology
0149-6719 Cardiopulmonary Medicine
0149-6727 Medical Imaging†
0149-6743 Nutrition Planning
0149-676X American Wine Society Manual
0149-6778 American Wine Society. Bulletin
0149-6832 V U Marketplace *changed to* Video Manager
0149-6840 Folklife Center News
0149-6859 Cross Reference†
0149-6867 Jacksonville Genealogical Society Quarterly
0149-6891 Unearth†
0149-6948 Case Analysis in Social Science and Social Therapy
0149-6956 Crain's Chicago Business
0149-6964 International Review of Food & Wine *see* 0279-6740
0149-6972 Far West†
0149-6980 Media & Values
0149-7014 On Location Magazine
0149-7081 Women Artists News
0149-709X R F D
0149-7103 Street & Smith's Official Yearbook: Basketball
0149-7111 Symposium on Computer Architecture. Conference Proceedings
0149-712X Journal of Reform Judaism
0149-7162 Down's Syndrome
0149-7189 Evaluation and Program Planning
0149-7197 Retired Military Almanac
0149-7219 Yearbook of Romanian Studies
0149-7316 Runner
0149-7324 Impresario†
0149-7332 Somos
0149-7421 Developments in Marketing Science
0149-7448 Regulators†
0149-7499 Floral Underawl & Gazette Times
0149-7510 Job Safety & Health (Washington)
0149-7537 Who's Who in Engineering
0149-7545 Engineers of Distinction *see* 0149-7537
0149-7634 Neuroscience and Biobehavioral Reviews
0149-7642 Red Book of Housing Manufacturers
0149-7677 Dance Research Journal
0149-7790 Mariah *see* 0278-1433
0149-7820 Beehive†
0149-7847 Directory of Conservative and Libertarian Serials, Publishers, and Freelance Markets
0149-7863 Pushcart Prize: Best of the Small Presses
0149-7898 Silicon Gulch Gazette
0149-7901 Journal of Applied Management†
0149-791X New Mexico Studies in the Fine Arts
0149-7936 Washington Dossier
0149-7944 Current Surgery
0149-7952 German Studies Review
0149-7995 Arizona Manpower Review†
0149-8029 OpFlow
0149-8037 Willing Water (Denver) *see* 0273-3218
0149-8045 Quilt World
0149-8061 Humane Education *changed to* Children and Animals
0149-8088 Index to Scientific & Technical Proceedings
0149-810X Subject Guide to Reprints†
0149-8118 Dun and Bradstreet Exporters' Encyclopaedia - World Marketing Guide *see* 0732-0159
0149-8142 Dunsworld Marketing Management†
0149-8231 New York Business Change Service†
0149-824X New Jersey Business Change Service†
0149-8274 U.S. Federal Deposit Insurance Corporation. Trust Assets of Insured Commercial Banks *see* 0278-5692
0149-8347 Adult Bible Studies
0149-838X A E I Defense Review *see* 0163-9927
0149-8398 Ecolibrium†
0149-8428 Religion Index One: Periodicals
0149-8436 Religion Index Two: Multi-Author Works
0149-8444 Keystone Folklore
0149-8452 Status Report (Stamford)
0149-8487 Gratz College Annual of Jewish Studies†
0149-8606 Encyclopedia of Food Technology and Food Science Series†
0149-8681 Marxist Perspectives†
0149-8703 Work in America Institute: Highlights of the Literature
0149-8711 Omni
0149-8738 International Environment Reporter
0149-8797 Public Administration Times
0149-8851 River Styx
0149-886X Journal of Optometric Vision Development
0149-8924 Sourcebook of Equal Educational Opportunity†
0149-8932 Interview (New York)
0149-8991 Geothermal Resources Council. Special Report
0149-9017 A T Q
0149-9106 Architecture Minnesota
0149-9114 Kansas History
0149-9157 Public Opinion (Washington)
0149-9262 Access (Washington, 1975)
0149-9289 Ningas-Cogon *changed to* Ningas
0149-9300 Micrographics Today *changed to* Inform (Silver Spring)
0149-936X C T: The Journal of Computed Tomography
0149-9386 Energy Magazine
0149-9408 American Book Review
0149-9483 Advances in Nutritional Research
0149-953X Prana Yoga Life
0149-9556 Data/Comm Industry Report
0149-9572 Minority Group Media Guide *see* 0730-5141
0149-9580 Disciplinary Law and Procedure Advance Sheets *see* 0273-2122
0149-9602 Health Foods Business
0149-970X Chicago Catholic
0149-9785 A E I Economist
0149-9807 Immigration and Nationality Law Review
0149-9815 Inland Shores†
0149-9858 Slavic and European Education Review *changed to* East-West Education
0149-9912 Physician's Guide to Practical Gastroenterology *see* 0277-4208
0149-9939 National Library of Medicine. Audiovisuals Catalog
0149-9963 American Statistical Association. Statistical Computing Section. Proceedings (of the Annual Meeting)
0149-9971 Review of International Broadcasting
0149-998X Adult Planbook
0150-0112 Dossiers de l'Elevage
0150-1011 Israel & Palestine
0150-1399 Bibliographie de la France. Supplement 1: Publications en Serie
0150-1402 Bibliographie de la France. Livres *see* 0294-0000
0150-2441 Confluent
0150-4428 Lys Rouge
0150-536X Journal of Optics/Nouvelle Revue d'Optique
0150-5467 Feuillet Rapide Fiscal Social
0150-5505 Geostandards Newsletter
0150-5602 Medica Gestion
0150-5955 Bibliographie de la France. Publications Officielles
0150-5971 Bibliographie de la France. Supplement 3: Musique
0150-5998 Bibliographie de la France. Supplement 4: Atlas, Cartes et Plans
0150-6404 Foret - Entreprise
0150-6463 Petrole Informations International
0150-651X Maille Informations *see* 0750-4764
0150-7214 Revue Moto Technique
0150-7230 Auto Expertise
0150-7516 Revue des Ingenieurs
0150-7540 Toutes les Nouvelles de l'Hotellerie et du Tourisme
0150-7745 France. Institut National de la Statistique et des Etudes Economiques. Courrier des Statistiques
0150-8695 Bulletin Signaletique. Part 528: Bibliographie Internationale de Science Administrative
0150-9861 Journal of Neuroradiology /Journal de Neuroradiologie
0151-0479 Cahiers C E R T-C I R C E†
0151-0509 Academie des Sciences. Comptes Rendus Hebdomadaires des Seances. Serie 1: Mathematiques
0151-0592 B.O.P.I. Abreges *see* 0750-7674
0151-0827 Documents
0151-1335 Academie d'Agriculture de France. Comptes Rendus des Seances
0151-1408 Demographie Africaine: Bulletin de Liaison
0151-1475 France. Institut National de la Statistique et des Etudes Economiques. Informations Rapides
0151-1793 Economie Champenoise
0151-1998 Sante de l'Homme
0151-2137 Psychologie et Education
0151-2943 Indicateur Bertrand
0151-3605 Visages du Vingtieme Siecle
0151-4016 Renaitre 2000
0151-4695 Jardineries
0151-5772 Royaliste
0151-5845 Psychomotricite

0151-685X Sciences et Tecniques Biomedicales
0151-6973 Techniques et Sciences Municipales Eau *changed to* Techniques -Sciences - Methodes. Genie Urbain Rural
0151-6981 Aquarama
0151-7163 Al Islam
0151-7341 Alsace Historique
0151-7791 Fou Parle
0151-783X Phot 'argus (Edition Professionnelle)
0151-7848 Phot 'argus (Edition Generale)
0151-8720 Societe Generale pour Favoriser de Developpement du Commerce et de l'Industrie en France. Bulletin†
0151-9107 Annales de Chimie: Science des Materiaux
0151-9638 Annales de Dermatologie et de Venereologie
0151-9808 Ethnopsychiatrica *see* 0762-6819
0152-5425 Petrole et Techniques
0152-7886 Phreatique
0153-162X France. Ministere de l'Agriculture. Informations Rapides. Situation Agricole
0153-1999 France. Ministere de l'Agriculture. Informations Rapides Commerce Exterieur Agro-Alimentaire
0153-226X Energie Solaire Actualites†
0153-3320 Cahiers de Linguistique Asie Orientale
0153-3401 Al Mostakbal
0153-3428 Watan al-Arabi
0153-3614 L'Argus International
0153-3657 Association pour l'Etude des Problemes d'Outre Mer. Documentation-Developpement
0153-3673 Monuments Historiques
0153-4157 Maghreb Selection
0153-4270 Mediatheques Publiques
0153-4351 Histoire pour Tous
0153-4602 Escargot Folk?†
0153-4742 Lettre Medicale
0153-5021 Etudes sur l'Egypte et le Soudan Anciens *changed to* Habitats et Societes Urbaines en Egypte et au Soudan
0153-5048 Cahiers de Philologie
0153-5196 C.T.N.E.R.H.I. Recherches†
0153-6133 Association Francaise des Amis d'Albert Schweitzer. Cahiers
0153-6184 Institut d'Amenagement et d'Urbanisme de la Region d'Ile de France. Cahiers
0153-6540 France. Bureau de Recherches Geologiques et Minieres. Bulletin. Section 2: Geologie des Gite Mineraux *changed to* France. Bureau de Recherches Geologiques et Minieres. Agence Francaise pour la Maitrise de l'Energie. Geothermie/Actualities
0153-8446 Geochronique
0153-9019 Marche de l'Innovation
0153-9396 Electro-Negoce
0153-9442 Enerpresse
0153-9604 Moules et Modeles *changed to* Moules, Modeles et Maquettes
0153-9620 Vagabondages
0153-985X Courrier du C N R S
0153-9884 Interets Prives
0153-9930 Institut Europeen de Formation des Techniciens des Circuits Imprimes. Informations
0153-999X Catalogue National du Genie Climatique-Chauffage et Conditionnement d'Air
0154-0009 Tequi Electricite Electronique†
0154-0033 Bulletin Officiel du Ministere de l'Environnement et du Cadre de Vie et du Ministere des Transports
0154-0157 Institut d'Etudes Slaves. Lexiques
0154-0165 Plan de Classement P A S C A L
0154-0238 Groupe d'Etudes des Rythmes Biologiques. Bulletin
0154-1757 Alpinisme et Randonnee *changed to* Alpirando
0154-4101 Pulsar
0154-5604 Interference
0154-6902 Semiotique et Bible
0154-7283 Amis de l'Oeuvre et la Pensee de Georges Migot. Bulletin d'Information
0154-7313 Drovers Journal (Australia)
0154-7550 France Clima†
0154-8840 Juri-Social
0155-0144 C I S Newsletter *see* 0814-9321
0155-0195 University of New South Wales. Library. Information Bulletin†
0155-0306 Social Alternatives
0155-0438 Corella
0155-0489 Development News Digest *see* 0815-9424
0155-0543 Musicological Society of Australia. Newsletter
0155-0659 Classicvm
0155-0837 Dairy Topics†
0155-0918 Australia. Department of Primary Industries. Marketing Newsletter
0155-1108 New South Wales. Department of Education. School Magazine
0155-1264 Trolley Wire
0155-2090 C A I News
0155-218X Reading Time
0155-252X Communique
0155-2589 Industrial Arbitration Reports, New South Wales
0155-2856 Labyrinth
0155-2880 Quaver
0155-2899 Clean Air Clarion
0155-297X Australian Legal Directory
0155-3070 A.A.P.A. Newsletter
0155-3089 A.A.P.A. Technitopics *see* 0727-0003
0155-3372 New South Wales. Geological Survey. Records
0155-3380 Australian Gourmet
0155-3410 New South Wales. Geological Survey. Quarterly Notes
0155-4425 Labor Forum
0155-4786 Fisherman's Journal
0155-4980 Opera Australia
0155-5561 New South Wales. Geological Survey. Bulletin
0155-5588 Australian Scientific and Technological Reports†
0155-560X Library Association of Australia. Handbook
0155-5936 Sydney Gay Guide
0155-6002 Australasian Corrosion Association. Annual Conference Proceedings
0155-6215 Pocket Australian Stamp Catalogue
0155-6223 Research Development in Higher Education. Publications
0155-624X Australian National University. Research School of Physical Sciences. Annual Report
0155-6282 Monash University. Department of Civil Engineering. Civil Engineering Research Report
0155-6320 New South Wales, Australia, Government Gazette
0155-6894 Word in Life
0155-7009 Australian Imports
0155-7742 Commonwealth Scientific and Industrial Research Organization. Division of Animal Production Report
0155-7785 Speculations in Science and Technology
0155-8498 Australasian Stamp Catalogue
0155-8560 Galleries and Craft Shops in Australia
0155-8862 A.C.P.C. Forum
0155-9044 Helix
0155-9060 Australian National University. Development Studies Centre. Pacific Research Monograph
0155-9222 Primary Industry Newsletter
0155-9397 S W A N S
0155-9419 Australian Mineral Industry. Quarterly
0155-9435 Western Australia. Department of Fisheries and Wildlife. Fisheries Research Bulletin
0155-9443 Australian Renewable Energy Resources Index *see* 0816-1070
0155-9508 Annual Review of the Residential Property Market
0155-9567 National Directory of Internships, Residencies & Registrarships
0155-9648 Truckin' Life Magazine
0155-9664 Queensland. Department of Forestry. Technical Paper
0155-977X Social Analysis
0155-9982 Accounting Forum
0156-0107 Australian Youth Hostels Handbook
0156-0115 Hostel Yarn *changed to* Y H A Hostel Yarn
0156-0182 Asian Studies Association of Australia. Conference Papers
0156-0301 Australian Journal of Reading
0156-0352 Food and Liquor Retailer
0156-0417 Australian Journal of Clinical and Experimental Hypnosis
0156-0433 P S
0156-0905 New Education
0156-0972 Australasian Plant Pathology
0156-0999 Australian Early Childhood Research Booklets
0156-1006 U N E Convocation Bulletin & Alumni News
0156-1103 Links
0156-1383 Bird Behaviour
0156-1596 Inside Asean†
0156-160X A N S O L Bibliography Series *see* 0725-2803
0156-1650 Religious Traditions
0156-191X Bulletin of Christian Affairs†
0156-1987 V I S E Handbook *changed to* V C A B Handbook
0156-2126 Civil Engineering Working Papers
0156-2444 Commonwealth Scientific and Industrial Research Organization. Division of Tropical Crops and Pastures. Research Report
0156-2681 Australian Meat Industry Bulletin
0156-2703 Inpharma
0156-2878 Community Education Newsletter
0156-3394 Australia. Bureau of Industry Economics. Research Report
0156-3491 Forceps *changed to* Forceps, Snippets & Acorn News
0156-3548 Fintas
0156-3661 Hotel, Motel Index
0156-3688 Hospitality Buyers Guide
0156-370X Metal and Engineering Industry Handbook *see* 0314-1586
0156-3726 Pacific Aviation Yearbook
0156-403X Professional Fisherman
0156-4374 Public Libraries of Victoria. Annual Statistical Bulletin
0156-4420 Studies in Society
0156-4579 Freewheeling
0156-4714 Health Education News and Views
0156-4919 Pursuit
0156-5842 Great Barrier Reef Marine Park Authority Workshop Series
0156-5907 Australian Pork Journal
0156-594X Australian Marc Record Service
0156-6148 Western Intelligence Report
0156-6555 Exceptional Child
0156-6717 Guidelines
0156-7365 Australian Journal of Chinese Affairs
0156-7373 Australia. Sea Transport Statistics. Trade and Cargo Review†
0156-7381 Australia. Sea Transport Statistics. Stevedoring Labour Review
0156-742X Australian International U.F.O. Flying Saucer Research
0156-7446 Australia. Bureau of Agricultural Economics. Quarterly Review of the Rural Economy
0156-7594 The Rationalist News
0156-7799 Reflections
0156-7918 Australia. Bureau of Statistics. Tasmanian Office. Motor Vehicle Census†
0156-8124 Island Magazine
0156-8698 The Great Circle
0156-8760 New South Wales. Department of Technical and Further Education. T A F E Quarterly†
0156-904X Human Resource Management Australia
0156-9732 Australia. Bureau of Statistics. Victorian Office. The Labour Force - Victoria
0156-9945 Commonwealth Scientific and Industrial Research Organization. Institute of Earth Resources. Technical Communication. *see* 0726-1772
0156-9953 Commonwealth Scientific and Industrial Research Organization. Institute of Earth Resources. Investigation Report. *see* 0726-1780
0157-0919 V I S E Circular†
0157-0994 Push On
0157-1079 University of Queensland. Undergraduate Degree Handbook
0157-1133 University of Queensland. Higher Degree Handbook.
0157-1532 Australian Journal of Audiology
0157-1729 Guns Australia
0157-177X A.C.T.-S.T.A. Journal *see* 0818-2019
0157-1826 HERDSA News
0157-1923 New South Wales. Department of Decentralisation. Regional Developer†
0157-2024 Register of Australian Drug and Alcohol Research†
0157-2083 A M P L A Yearbook
0157-2431 Railway Digest
0157-244X Australian Science Education Research Association. Research in Science Education
0157-258X South Australia. State Library. Monthly List of Publications
0157-2601 Organic Grower (Wembly)
0157-2784 Directory of Internships, Residencies and Registrarships Available in Victorian Hospitals
0157-2849 University of Queensland. Calendar
0157-2938 Tasmanian Tramp
0157-3039 Australian Canegrower
0157-308X Australian Littoral Society. Bulletin
0157-3136 Veterinary Prescribers Index
0157-3357 Practising Administrator
0157-3381 Mulga Wire
0157-3470 Release
0157-3705 C R N L E Reviews Journal
0157-3942 Infocus Newsletter
0157-3977 Hosteller
0157-4159 Melbourne Papers on Australian Defence
0157-4310 A.D.A. Journal *see* 0811-6407
0157-4566 Australian Coal Report
0157-5295 Fun Runner
0157-5767 Australian National University. Development Studies Centre. Monograph
0157-5783 Community and Real Estate News
0157-6054 Australia. Sea Transport Statistics. Report of Manhours Lost by Operational Employees of Stevedoring Companies Due to Industrial Disputes
0157-6178 Australia. Public Service Board. Bulletin
0157-6224 A A E C Nuclear News
0157-6232 Australian National University. Development Studies Centre. Demography Teaching Notes
0157-6321 Australian Social Welfare: Impact
0157-6402 Directory of Australian Music Organisations
0157-6429 Australian Marine Sciences Association. Bulletin *changed to* Australian Marine Science Bulletin
0157-650X Riv Lib File *see* 0812-7352
0157-7204 C S I R O Directory
0157-7271 Reactions
0157-7662 New Zealand Books in Print
0157-7786 Queensland Agricultural Journal
0157-7794 Queensland Journal of Agricultural and Animal Sciences
0157-8081 Commonwealth Scientific and Industrial Research Organization. Marine Laboratories. Fishery Situation Report
0157-809X Queensland. Department of Forestry. Research Paper
0157-8103 Western Australia (Perth, 1979)†
0157-8200 Australia. National Information Service on Drug Abuse. Technical Information Bulletin
0157-8243 Australia. Department of Primary Production. Agnote
0157-8464 Southern Caver

ISSN INDEX

0157-8804 FitzHardinge's Nobiliary
0157-9169 Ozarts
0157-9509 E T C H
0157-9630 Australia. Department of Primary Industry. Australian Fishing Industry Directory
0157-9711 Commonwealth Scientific and Industrial Research Organization. Division of Tropical Crops and Pastures. Tropical Agronomy Technical Memorandum
0157-9762 Chemical Engineering in Australia
0158-0140 Interdom Christian Referdex *changed to* Christian Referdex
0158-0655 Australian Penthouse
0158-0760 General and Applied Entomology
0158-0809 New South Wales. Energy Authority. Annual Report
0158-0876 Incite
0158-099X Lowdown
0158-1090 Sower
0158-1309 Australia. Department of Primary Industry. Annual Report
0158-1570 Royal Australasian College of Dental Surgeons. Annals
0158-1589 Victorian Government Directory
0158-1597 Clinical and Experimental Neurology
0158-1953 S E A R M G Newsletter
0158-202X Australia. Bureau of Statistics. Victorian Office. Monthly Summary of Statistics, Victoria
0158-2658 Australian Camera Craft
0158-2720 Petty Sessions Review
0158-3026 Literacy Link
0158-3158 P E News
0158-3301 Western Australian Institute of Technology. Department of Biology. Bulletin *changed to* Western Australian Institute of Technology. School of Biology. Bulletin
0158-3778 Filmviews
0158-3921 Victorian Fiction Research Guides
0158-3999 Australian Standard
0158-4154 Cantrills Filmnotes
0158-4197 Emu
0158-4243 Comet
0158-4960 Australian Journal of Medical Laboratory Science
0158-5126 Words and Visions†
0158-5231 Biochemistry International
0158-538X Commonwealth Scientific and Industrial Research Organization. Division of Tropical Crops and Pastures. Annual Report
0158-5460 Link-Up
0158-5711 Federation News
0158-572X Australian Angler's Fishing World
0158-6041 South East Asian Monograph Series
0158-6262 World Missions Update
0158-6289 School Mathematics Journal
0158-6602 A I M M Bulletin *see* 0817-2668
0158-6610 Auchmuty Library Publication
0158-6912 Home Economics Association of Australia. Journal
0158-698X Cinema Papers Yearbook
0158-7048 Craft Victoria
0158-7285 Australia. Bureau of Mineral Resources. Geology and Geophysics. Yearbook
0158-7374 Period Building Restoration Trades & Suppliers Directory
0158-7382 Commonwealth Scientific and Industrial Research Organization. Bureau of Scientific Services. Annual Report†
0158-7390 Commonwealth Scientific and Industrial Research Organization. Institute of Animal and Food Sciences. Annual Report
0158-7412 Commonwealth Scientific and Industrial Research Organization. Institute of Earth Resources. Annual Report. *see* 0729-056X
0158-7447 Australian Administrator
0158-7765 Zinc Today
0158-779X Unesco Review
0158-7919 Distance Education
0158-9172 School Libraries in Australia
0158-9830 Research Discussion Papers
0158-9911 Nature and Health
0158-9938 Australasian Physical & Engineering Sciences in Medicine
0159-0030 Australian Hi-Fi
0159-0073 Butterworths Trade Practices†
0159-0219 Commonwealth Scientific and Industrial Research Organization. Division of Atmospheric Research. Research Report
0159-0340 Guiding in Australia
0159-060X National Union Catalogue of Library Materials for the Handicapped
0159-1088 Instep†
0159-1096 Contact (Sydney)
0159-110X Now†
0159-1428 South Australia. Department of Agriculture. Rural Marketing and Policy†
0159-1487 Australian Journal of Sex, Marriage and Family
0159-2033 Lab-Talk
0159-2068 Institution of Engineers, Australia. Transactions. Civil Engineering
0159-2319 Australian Lithographer, Printer, and Packager
0159-2947 Australian Electronics Directory
0159-2955 Australian Engineering Directory
0159-3641 South Australia. Department of Environment and Planning. Directory of Non-Government Environmental Groups in South Australia†
0159-3803 Quest
0159-3935 Process Engineering News
0159-396X Australia. Air Transport Statistics. Domestic Air Transport
0159-5709 Australian Health Review
0159-6012 Crane Australasia
0159-6071 Commonwealth Scientific and Industrial Research Organization. Division of Tropical Crops and Pastures. Genetic Resources Communication
0159-6306 Discourse
0159-6330 Dance Australia
0159-6845 Commonwealth Regional Renewable Energy Resources Index *see* 0816-1070
0159-7027 Coiffure†
0159-7043 South Australia. Department of Mines and Energy. Annual Report
0159-7132 Chalkface
0159-7345 News Digest - International
0159-7485 Regional Information Series
0159-7531 Australian Law News
0159-7841 Matilda Literary Magazine *changed to* Matilda Magazine: Literary and Art Magazine
0159-8090 Australian Association of Clinical Biochemists. Newsletter
0159-818X Nomen Nudum
0159-8821 Northern Territory. Conservation Commission. Annual Report
0159-8872 Challenge (Petersham North)
0159-8880 Professional Photography in Australia
0159-8910 Australian Journal of Geodesy, Photogrammetry & Surveying
0159-897X Scout Magazine
0159-9011 Australian Journal of Developmental Disabilities *see* 0726-3864
0159-9143 Institute of Family Studies *see* 0818-0229
0159-9178 Commonwealth Scientific and Industrial Research Organization. Institute of Energy and Earth Resources. Minerals & Energy Bulletin
0159-9321 Pocket Yearbook of New South Wales
0159-9399 Hume News
0159-950X Monash Review
0159-9585 Photoworld Buyer's Guide. Index†
0159-9593 Photoworld Buyer's Guide. Darkrooms†
0159-9607 S W R C Reports and Proceedings
0159-9615 S W R C Newsletter
0159-9976 It's a Math Math World
0160-001X Washington Report (Washington, 1966)†
0160-0028 Drug Abuse and Alcoholism Newsletter
0160-0036 U.S. Health Care Financing Administration Record *changed to* U.S. Health Care Financing Administration Forum
0160-0168 Bulletin of Research in the Humanities
0160-0176 International Regional Science Review
0160-0281 American Journal of Trial Advocacy
0160-0303 Graphic Communications Marketplace
0160-0311 Military Journal†
0160-0338 Texas Woman†
0160-0346 Logging Management†
0160-0354 Spiritual Community Guide
0160-0362 Professional Marketing Report
0160-0419 French-American Review†
0160-063X Face the Nation (Annual)†
0160-0664 Collections (Buffalo)
0160-0680 Sulphur in Agriculture
0160-0699 Umbrella (Glendale)
0160-0850 Fiddle and a Bow†
0160-0885 United Methodist Church. Curriculum Plans
0160-0893 Cornell Review†
0160-0923 Helios (Lubbock)
0160-0974 Colorado. Water Conservation Board. Ground Water Series. Circular *see* 0092-2684
0160-1040 I A
0160-1059 Electric Vehicle/Battery Technology
0160-1067 Society for Industrial Archeology Newsletter
0160-1075 New Directions for Women
0160-1083 Growth Industry News *changed to* Industries in Transition
0160-1148 Electronates
0160-127X Interface (Carmel)
0160-1296 Educators Guide to Free Audio and Video Materials
0160-1342 Safety Science Abstracts Journal
0160-1504 D I S C U S Facts Book†
0160-1512 International Energy Biweekly Statistical Review *see* 0163-3724
0160-1571 Schwann-1 Record & Tape Guide
0160-1644 Motor Early Model Crash Estimating Guide
0160-1725 Historical Geography Newsletter
0160-1741 U.S. National Bureau of Standards. Journal of Research
0160-1792 Arise†
0160-1830 Sports Afield Deer
0160-1857 Left Curve
0160-2004 Resources in Vocational Education†
0160-2047 Log
0160-2071 Micropaleontology Special Publications
0160-208X Journal of Jewish Art
0160-2098 Journal of Juvenile Law
0160-2144 Great River Review
0160-2179 Advances in Polyamine Research
0160-2217 New Brooklyn
0160-225X American Shipper
0160-2365 American Musical Instrument Society. Newsletter
0160-2373 Gleanings (Cambridge)†
0160-242X Comprehensive Endocrinology
0160-2438 E E G Interpretation†
0160-2446 Journal of Cardiovascular Pharmacology
0160-2454 M.D. Anderson Clinical Conferences on Cancer
0160-2462 Membrane Transport Processes
0160-2470 Nutrition in Health and Disease
0160-2489 Seminars in Neurological Surgery
0160-2500 Case Western Reserve University. Warner Swasey Observatory. Publications
0160-2527 International Journal of Law and Psychiatry
0160-2543 Cynegeticus
0160-2551 Critical Care Quarterly *changed to* Critical Care Nursing Quarterly
0160-256X Association for Women in Science. Newsletter
0160-2578 American Bench-Judges of the Nation
0160-2624 Coaching: Women's Athletics†
0160-2659 Kansas Water Resources Research Institute. Annual Report
0160-2675 Policy Grants Directory
0160-2713 Journal of African-Afro-American Affairs†
0160-2748 Neurotoxicology
0160-2780 Urbanism Past and Present *see* 0703-0428
0160-2853 Georgetown University Papers on Languages and Linguistics†
0160-287X Wassaja *see* 0199-9052
0160-2896 Intelligence (Norwood)
0160-3000 Woodall's Trailer & R V Travel†
0160-3027 University of Illinois at Urbana-Champaign. Department of Agricultural Economics. Landlord and Tenant Shares
0160-3078 University of Oklahoma. Archaeological Research and Management Center. Project Report Series
0160-3086 University of Oklahoma. Archaeological Research and Management Center. Research Series
0160-3094 Public Accounting Report
0160-323X State and Local Government Review
0160-3248 Special Children *see* 0741-9325
0160-3280 Boys Gymnastics Rulebook
0160-3302 Illinois Manufacturers Directory
0160-3329 Backpacker (1973) *see* 0277-867X
0160-3345 Alaska Economic Trends
0160-3361 Rockefeller University. Institute for Comparative Human Development. Quarterly Newsletter†
0160-337X Enhanced Oil-Recovery Field Reports
0160-3450 American Pharmacy
0160-3469 Sociological Forum *see* 0273-2173
0160-3477 Journal of Post Keynesian Economics
0160-3493 Hispano-Italic Studies†
0160-3515 Pulpit Preaching *see* 0160-838X
0160-3566 Black Sociologist†
0160-3574 S P E C Flyer *see* 0160-3582
0160-3582 S P E C Kit
0160-3604 Energy Research Abstracts
0160-3671 Solar Thermal Power Generation *changed to* Solar Energy Utilization: a Bibliography. Vol. 1. Solar Power Generation
0160-368X Solar Energy Utilization: a Bibliography. Vol. 3. Solar Thermal Heating and Cooling†
0160-371X Tabs†
0160-3728 Who's Who in Religion†
0160-3779 Mineral Economics Abstracts†
0160-3787 Isozymes: Current Topics in Biological and Medicine Research
0160-3817 Weaver's Journal
0160-3825 Student Press Law Center Report
0160-3876 Musical Heritage Review Magazine
0160-3906 Fodor's Canada
0160-3914 Fodor's Cruises Everywhere†
0160-3930 N I T A
0160-4074 Industrial Research & Development *see* 0746-9179
0160-4090 Zip *changed to* Zip Target Marketing
0160-4112 Fatigue of Engineering Materials and Structures *changed to* Fatigue and Fracture of Engineering Materials and Structures
0160-4120 Environment International
0160-4139 Progress in Analytical Atomic Spectroscopy *changed to* Progress in Analytical Spectroscopy
0160-4147 Downtown Implementation Guide†
0160-4163 Conference of Insurance Legislators†
0160-4198 Journal of Health and Human Resources Administration
0160-4201 Voice of Youth Advocates
0160-4309 Exceptional Child Education Resources
0160-4317 Freshwater and Marine Aquarium
0160-4341 Humboldt Journal of Social Relations
0160-449X Labor Studies Journal
0160-4570 F & O S Motor Carrier Annual Report
0160-4635 Handbook of International Sociometry *see* 0731-1273
0160-4651 Travel Outlook Forum Proceedings *changed to* Outlook for Travel and Tourism
0160-4724 Chief Executive Magazine
0160-4767 Pizzazz†

0160-4848 The Arnoldian
0160-4872 Weekly Insiders Poultry Report
0160-4880 Fiction Catalog
0160-4910 Weekly Insiders Turkey Letter
0160-4929 Politics Today (Santa Barbara)
0160-4953 Collection Building
0160-5119 Florida Friends of Bluegrass Society. Newsletter
0160-5151 U.S. Bureau of Mines. Mineral Commodity Summaries
0160-5305 Idaho (Moscow)
0160-5402 Journal of Pharmacological Methods
0160-5429 International Education
0160-5534 Perekrestki *see* 0888-5257
0160-5569 School Psychology Digest *see* 0279-6015
0160-5607 Construction News
0160-564X Artificial Organs
0160-5682 Operational Research Society. Journal
0160-5704 Horse, of Course!†
0160-5720 M L A Newsletter (New York)
0160-5739 Florida Retirement Living
0160-5852 Organizational Communications Abstracts *see* 0149-1644
0160-5895 House & Garden Decorating Guide†
0160-5976 Humanity & Society
0160-5992 In These Times
0160-6042 Lawn Care Industry
0160-6077 Directory of Library Reprographic Services
0160-6107 Van Life and Family Trucking *see* 0744-074X
0160-6123 Information Manager†
0160-6131 McCall's Working Mother *see* 0278-193X
0160-614X Made in U S A
0160-6158 Standard (New York)
0160-6166 Club Living
0160-6174 Diamond Report
0160-6271 School Food Service Journal
0160-628X Blake: an Illustrated Quarterly
0160-6352 P T J. Passenger Train Journal *see* 0160-6913
0160-6360 Chemical New Product Directory†
0160-6379 Family and Community Health
0160-6433 Timber Harvesting
0160-6476 National Zip Code Directory *see* 0731-9185
0160-6557 N J E B: Nebraska Journal of Economics and Business *see* 0747-5535
0160-6565 Guest Author
0160-659X Common Law Lawyer
0160-6662 National Conference on Individual Onsite Wastewater Systems. Proceedings†
0160-6689 Journal of Clinical Psychiatry
0160-6719 American Peanut Research and Education Association. Proceedings *see* 0197-8748
0160-6824 Golf Industry
0160-6840 Wide Angle
0160-6891 Research in Nursing & Health
0160-6913 Passenger Train Journal
0160-6980 Continuing Education for Health Care Providers†
0160-7006 Health Care Education†
0160-7014 Year in Hematology *see* 0197-3649
0160-7049 Conference of Presidents of Major American Jewish Organizations. Annual Report *see* 0160-7057
0160-7057 Conference of Presidents of Major American Jewish Organizations. Annual Report
0160-7065 Diesel Car Digest
0160-7081 Foundation of Thanatology. Archives
0160-7146 Jacob Marschak Interdisciplinary Colloquium on Mathematics in the Behavioral Sciences
0160-7219 Perinatal Press
0160-7227 Health Law Newsletter *changed to* N H E L P Health Advocate
0160-7243 Stone in America
0160-7278 Army/Navy Store & Outdoor Merchandiser
0160-7308 Trial Diplomacy Journal
0160-7332 Amateur Boxer
0160-7340 Guide to Manufactured Homes†
0160-7375 Frank Lloyd Wright Newsletter
0160-7383 Annals of Tourism Research
0160-7391 West Virginia State Industrial Directory *see* 0740-4328
0160-7413 Compost Science/Land Utilization *see* 0276-5055
0160-7472 International Telephone Directory of the Deaf *changed to* International Telephone Directory of T D D Users
0160-7480 Modern Healthcare (1977)
0160-7499 Irrigation Association. Technical Conference Proceedings
0160-7545 Ellen Glasgow Newsletter
0160-7553 I D O C/International Documentation†
0160-7561 Philosophical Studies in Education
0160-757X Infusion
0160-7618 Health and Medical Care Services Review *see* 0735-9683
0160-7626 Infertility
0160-7650 Crafts Report *changed to* Working Craftsman
0160-7677 Slackwater Review†
0160-7685 Journal of Continuing Education in Dermatology *see* 0198-6643
0160-7693 Journal of Continuing Education in Pharmacy *changed to* Journal of Continuing Education in Hospital and Clinical Pharmacy
0160-7707 Journal of Continuing Education in Orthopedics *see* 0198-6376
0160-7715 Journal of Behavioral Medicine
0160-7731 Bill of Rights in Action
0160-7766 Journal of Continuing Education in Pediatrics *see* 0198-6341
0160-7774 Journal of Supervision and Training in Ministry
0160-7782 Geothermal Resources Council. Bulletin
0160-7790 Billboard's International Recording Equipment & Studio Directory
0160-7847 Fundamenta Scientiae
0160-788X Reclamation Review†
0160-791X Technology in Society
0160-7952 Metals Forum
0160-7960 Counseling and Values
0160-7987 Medical Anthropology *see* 0277-9536
0160-7995 Medical Economics *see* 0277-9536
0160-8002 Medical Geography *see* 0277-9536
0160-8010 Toys, Hobbies & Crafts†
0160-8029 U.S. Library of Congress. Cataloging Service Bulletin
0160-8037 Developing Country Courier†
0160-8045 Latin American Indian Literatures *see* 0888-5613
0160-8053 Food, Nutrition & Health Newsletter
0160-8061 Journal of Organizational Behavior Management
0160-807X Research Resources Reporter
0160-8126 Public Education Directory
0160-8134 Executive Female Digest *see* 0199-2880
0160-8177 Practical Law Books Review
0160-8223 Market & Credit Interchange Report
0160-8266 A P A Planning Advisory Service Reports
0160-8320 Athletic Training
0160-8347 Estuaries
0160-8371 I E E E Photovoltaic Specialists Conference. Conference Record
0160-838X Pulpit Digest (1978)
0160-8398 Viewpoints in Teaching and Learning†
0160-8401 Solar Age *changed to* Progressive Builder
0160-8428 National Conference on Fluid Power. Proceedings
0160-8460 Annotation
0160-8495 Pennsylvania Law Journal *changed to* Pennsylvania Law Journal Reporter
0160-8533 Cleveland Magazine
0160-8584 Laboratory and Research Methods in Biology and Medicine
0160-8592 I A S Annual Meeting. Conference Record *see* 0197-2618
0160-8665 Mime, Mask & Marionette†
0160-8673 World of Opera†
0160-8703 Literary Onomastics Studies
0160-8746 Oklahoma. Geological Survey. Educational Publication
0160-8754 Remote Sensing of Natural Resources: A Quarterly Literature Review
0160-8770 Lexington Theological Quarterly
0160-8797 Master's Theses in the Arts and Social Sciences
0160-8819 Bibliography of Corporate Social Responsibility†
0160-8843 American Association of Stratigraphic Palynologists. Contributions Series
0160-8894 Grocers Report
0160-8908 Claude Hall's International Radio Report
0160-8916 Computer Dealer
0160-8932 Key: The Newsletter that Helps you Make Money with Mail Order Classified Advertising
0160-8991 Fodor's Southeast Asia
0160-9009 Frontiers: a Journal of Women Studies
0160-9203 Update (Washington)
0160-9211 U.S. Library of Congress. National Library for the Blind and Physically Handicapped. News *changed to* U.S. Library of Congress. National Library Service for the Blind and Physically Handicapped. News
0160-9289 Clinical Cardiology
0160-9300 Chronicle College Counseling for Transfers *see* 0276-0363
0160-9327 Endeavour
0160-9394 Folia Slavica
0160-9416 Newsfront International†
0160-9459 Drug Therapy (Hospital Edition) *changed to* Hospital Therapy
0160-9475 Spina Bifida Therapy
0160-9513 Social Work with Groups
0160-9572 Seybold Report on Office Systems
0160-9580 National Beverage Marketing Directory (Year)
0160-9602 Northeastern Nevada Historical Society Quarterly
0160-9629 E-R-C Directory
0160-9645 Ancient World
0160-967X Addiction and Substance Abuse Report *changed to* Substance Abuse Report
0160-9688 Criminal Justice and the Public†
0160-9696 Success with Youth Report†
0160-970X Book Industry Trends
0160-9734 Grants Magazine
0160-9742 Network Planning Paper
0160-9769 High Performance
0160-9807 Unexplored Deviance†
0160-9815 Annual Editions: Urban Society
0160-984X Palestine-Israel Bulletin
0160-9939 Marathoner†
0160-9947 Future Life†
0160-9963 Applied Radiology (1976)
0160-998X Index to Audio Visual Serials in the Health Sciences†
0161-0007 O H Osteopathic Hospitals *changed to* Osteopathic Hospital Leadership
0161-0155 Broward Life
0161-0287 Practice Digest†
0161-0295 T I M S/O R S A Bulletin
0161-0325 Highway & Vehicle/Safety Report
0161-0333 Together (Washington, 1975) *see* 0193-3922
0161-035X Solid Wastes Management/Refuse Removal Journal and Liquid Wastes Management *see* 0745-6921
0161-0376 Analytical & Enumerative Bibliography
0161-0384 Business International Money Report
0161-0457 Scanning
0161-0511 Sons of the American Revolution Magazine
0161-052X River World†
0161-0546 Artist's Market
0161-0554 Craftworker's Market†
0161-0562 Current Career and Occupational Literature
0161-0619 Housing†
0161-0627 Iran Economic News
0161-0694 O T C Review
0161-0708 University of Puget Sound Law Review
0161-0724 American Universities Field Staff Reports *see* 0743-9644
0161-0775 Theater (New Haven)
0161-0902 Population and Family Planning Programs
0161-0945 American Congress on Surveying and Mapping. Proceedings of Annual Meeting *see* 0277-2876
0161-0996 Eighteenth Century: A Current Bibliography
0161-1054 Ski X-C
0161-1089 State and Mind *changed to* Issues in Radical Therapy
0161-1119 Adventist Review
0161-1127 Government R and D Report†
0161-1135 A M R Reporter: Managing Without Interference†
0161-1178 American Family
0161-1186 Cum Notis Variorum
0161-1194 Cryptologia
0161-1232 Art/Antiques Investment Report
0161-1259 P G A Magazine
0161-1267 Bottom Line
0161-1364 P I M A Magazine
0161-1372 Surgical Rounds
0161-1380 Integral Yoga
0161-1402 A S I L S International Law Journal
0161-1461 Language, Speech and Hearing Services in Schools
0161-1496 Modern Recording's Buyer's Guide *see* 0276-9239
0161-1577 Brilliant Corners†
0161-1593 C R C Critical Reviews in Solid State & Materials Sciences
0161-164X New Women's Times
0161-1674 U.S. Department of Energy. Office of State and Local Programs. Annual Report to the President and the Congress on the State Energy Conservation Program
0161-1704 Music O C L C Users Group. Newsletter
0161-1712 International Journal of Mathematics and Mathematical Sciences
0161-1747 Music Country
0161-1755 Airline and Travel Food *changed to* Airline, Ship & Catering Onboard Services Magazine
0161-178X Taxation for Lawyers
0161-1798 Velo-news
0161-1801 Socialist Review (San Francisco)
0161-181X Asante Seminar *see* 0272-8419
0161-1828 Overseas Outlook (Large Print Edition)
0161-1836 Birding
0161-1895 I.D.E.A.S.
0161-1917 U.S. National Heart, Lung, and Blood Advisory Council. Report
0161-1933 Parenteral Drug Association. Journal *see* 0279-7976
0161-1941 Petroleum Market Shares: Report on Sales of Refined Petroleum Products†
0161-1976 Agenda *see* 0735-1755
0161-1992 Bride's
0161-2018 Street & Smith's Official Yearbook: Baseball
0161-2042 Successful Business†
0161-2085 Whole Earth Papers
0161-2115 N C J W Journal
0161-2131 Outlook (Alexandria)
0161-2158 International Association of Fire Chiefs. Official Publication *changed to* International Fire Chief
0161-2190 Vogue Beauty & Health Guide
0161-2328 Analog Science Fiction-Science Fact
0161-2336 House & Garden Plans Guide†
0161-2387 Federal Reserve Bank of Kansas City. Economic Review
0161-2395 Delta Nu Alphian *changed to* Transportation Worldwide
0161-2425 Personnel Consultant
0161-2433 New York Times Biographical Service

0161-245X Equal Employment Opportunity Statistics *changed to* Affirmative Employment Statistics
0161-2492 Callaloo
0161-2506 Bloodroot (Grand Forks)
0161-2514 Aging and Work†
0161-2549 Gallimaufry
0161-259X Chemical Industry Products News *see* 0747-0398
0161-2638 Directory of Jewish Federations, Welfare Funds and Community Councils
0161-2654 Music Clubs Magazine
0161-2719 Tull Tracing†
0161-2778 Journal of Personality and Social Systems†
0161-2786 Earnshaw's Infants, Girls and Boys Wear Review
0161-2832 Boston College International and Comparative Law Journal *see* 0277-5778
0161-2840 Issues in Mental Health Nursing
0161-2875 World Meetings: Medicine
0161-2905 Literary Market Place
0161-2972 Weekly Regulatory Monitor†
0161-3065 American Journal of Intravenous Therapy *changed to* Intravenous Therapy News
0161-3081 Tune up
0161-3162 Social Sciences Citation Index Journal Citation Reports
0161-3170 Science Citation Index Journal Citation Report
0161-3189 Mississippi Pharmacist
0161-3243 University of Alaska. Biological Papers. Special Reports
0161-326X A J O T: The American Journal of Occupational Therapy *see* 0272-9490
0161-3308 Journal of Psychoanalytic Anthropology
0161-3332 International Association of Fish and Wildlife Agencies. Proceedings of the Convention
0161-3340 General Social Surveys
0161-3448 Satellite News
0161-3464 Dax Dynamic Showcase
0161-3499 Veterinary Surgery
0161-3561 Water, Woods & Wildlife
0161-357X McGraw-Hill's Construction Contracting *see* 0270-1588
0161-3626 Analog Dialogue
0161-3650 N A G W S Guide. Basketball, Volleyball†
0161-3871 Tennessee Sportsman
0161-4010 Copyright Management
0161-4029 Index to Reviews of Bibliographical Publications
0161-4126 Communication Outlook
0161-4169 National Science Foundation. Summaries of Projects Completed†
0161-4193 Parents' Magazine *see* 0195-0967
0161-4223 Lightworks
0161-4274 National Food Review
0161-4282 Seminars
0161-4312 Racquetball Illustrated *see* 0161-7966
0161-4339 Farm Industry News/West *see* 0199-6924
0161-4347 Farm Industry News/South *see* 0199-6924
0161-4355 Asia†
0161-4363 Bacon's International Publicity Checker
0161-4371 High Fidelity's Buying Guide to Tape Systems†
0161-4428 Focus on Alcohol and Drug Issues *changed to* Focus on Family and Chemical Dependence
0161-4452 Science Museum of Minnesota. Scientific Publications, New Series
0161-4479 Treteaux
0161-4576 Journal of Sex Education and Therapy
0161-4622 Italian Culture
0161-4630 Prostaglandins and Medicine *see* 0262-1746
0161-4681 Teachers College Record
0161-4703 Horn of Africa
0161-472X Report on Survival Studies of Patients With Cystic Fibrosis *see* 0197-7423
0161-4738 North Carolina State Industrial Directory *changed to* MacRae's North Carolina/South Carolina/Virginia
0161-4754 Journal of Manipulative and Physiological Therapeutics
0161-4835 Death
0161-4843 Casino-East
0161-4851 Gas Digest
0161-486X Columbia: A Magazine of Poetry and Prose
0161-4878 Ohio Industrial Directory *changed to* Harris Ohio Industrial Directory
0161-4886 Denver Magazine
0161-4908 Asian Theatre Reports *see* 0742-5457
0161-4924 Annual New Mexico Water Conference. Proceedings
0161-4932 Florida Genealogist
0161-4940 Catalysis Reviews: Science and Engineering
0161-5092 Impact (Sunnyvale)
0161-5114 Re-View
0161-522X Marine Recreational Fisheries
0161-5238 Brethren Missionary Herald
0161-5246 Issues in Health Care of Women *changed to* Health Care for Women, International
0161-5262 Income-Expense Analysis. Apartments, Condominiums and Cooperatives *see* 0194-1941
0161-5262 Income-Expense Analysis. Apartments, Condominiums and Cooperatives *see* 0191-2208
0161-5319 Frontiers of Power Technology Conference. Proceedings
0161-5378 Highlander
0161-5386 Taxation with Representation Newsletter†
0161-5394 A M A Management Digest†
0161-5408 Ag Alert
0161-5440 Historical Methods
0161-5491 Journal of Holistic Health†
0161-5505 Journal of Nuclear Medicine (1978)
0161-5556 Book-Mart†
0161-5653 School Social Work Journal
0161-5661 Graduate Woman
0161-570X Alternative Lifestyles *see* 0882-3391
0161-5785 Printing Paper†
0161-5807 U.S. Energy Information Administration. Annual Report to Congress
0161-5815 Prorodeo Sports News
0161-5823 Broadcasting and the Law
0161-5866 Money Business: Grants and Awards for Creative Artists
0161-5874 Health Science *see* 0883-8216
0161-5882 National Association of Realtors. Existing Home Sales
0161-5890 Molecular Immunology
0161-5947 Chorister *changed to* Young Chorister
0161-5971 Songwriter's Market
0161-5998 Academy of Management Newsletter
0161-6005 A P I C Journal *see* 0196-6553
0161-603X U.S. National Institute on Drug Abuse. Statistical Series D. Data from the Client Oriented Data Acquisition Process. Quarterly Report. Provisional Data
0161-6048 Energy Technology Conference. Proceedings
0161-6072 I C U I S Justice Ministries
0161-6080 Successful Dealer
0161-6129 Police Magazine†
0161-6234 Linn's Stamp News
0161-6277 U.S. Environmental Protection Agency. Grants Administration Division. Awards Register, Grants Assistance Programs†
0161-6293 B P C (Building Products Catalog) *changed to* Hutton's Building Products Catalog
0161-6315 Cost Engineering (1978) *see* 0274-9696
0161-6323 American Seaport *changed to* W W S/World Wide Shipping
0161-6331 Wings†
0161-6412 Neurological Research
0161-6420 Ophthalmology
0161-6439 Journal of Otolaryngology and Head and Neck Surgery *see* 0194-5998
0161-6447 Michigan Restaurateur
0161-6463 American Indian Culture and Research Journal
0161-651X Mine Safety & Health†
0161-6528 Atlas World Press Review *see* 0195-8895
0161-6536 Encore American & Worldwide News
0161-6544 Friends of George Sand Newsletter
0161-6587 Boston College Law Review
0161-6595 Energy Conservation News
0161-6668 Connoisseurs Guide to California Wine
0161-6684 Human Rights and the U.S. Foreign Assistance Program†
0161-6706 Sports 'n Spokes
0161-6730 Virginia Road Builder
0161-6749 Interaction (Washington, 1977)†
0161-6765 Health, Safety & Education†
0161-6773 Long Term Care and Health Services Administration Quarterly†
0161-6781 Health Manpower Report *see* 0736-9077
0161-682X Romantist
0161-6838 Teacher Information Exchange†
0161-6846 Public Library Quarterly
0161-6854 American Photographer
0161-6862 Computer Products
0161-7001 Best Buys in Print†
0161-7095 University of Detroit Journal of Urban Law *changed to* University of Detroit Law Review
0161-7109 Juvenile & Family Court Journal
0161-7133 Missionary Monthly
0161-715X Sibyl-Child
0161-7184 Travel *changed to* Travel-Holiday
0161-7222 Studia Mystica
0161-7230 Research in Political Economy
0161-7249 Research in Philosophy and Technology
0161-7257 Current Construction Costs
0161-7303 Literature of Liberty†
0161-7311 Producer Prices and Price Indexes *changed to* Producer Price Indexes
0161-7338 New York Running News
0161-7346 Ultrasonic Imaging
0161-7354 Journal of Applied Biochemistry *see* 0885-4513
0161-7362 Sierra
0161-7370 Popular Science
0161-7389 U S A Today
0161-7397 International Association of Orientalist Librarians. Bulletin†
0161-7400 School Social Work Quarterly†
0161-7419 Fairfield County Executive
0161-7427 Microelectronic Manufacturing and Testing
0161-7435 George Herbert Journal
0161-7443 National Passive Solar Conference. Proceedings. *changed to* American Solar Energy Society. Passive Conference. Annual Meeting
0161-746X Florida Pharmacy Journal
0161-7478 Forum on Medicine†
0161-7486 Harvard Medical School Health Letter
0161-7494 Public Employee (Washington)
0161-7508 Datacomm and Distributed Processing Report *changed to* Distributed Processing Product Reports
0161-7516 Radiology/Nuclear Medicine International
0161-7567 Journal of Applied Physiology: Respiratory, Environmental and Exercise Physiology *changed to* Journal of Applied Physiology
0161-7605 CableLibraries†
0161-7648 Towson State University Journal of Psychology
0161-7672 World Smoking & Health
0161-7710 Bflo†
0161-7729 Scholars' Facsimiles & Reprints
0161-7745 Best's Review. Property-Casualty Insurance Edition
0161-7753 Arkansas Educator
0161-7761 Anthropology & Education Quarterly
0161-777X Sludge Magazine†
0161-7796 U.S. Environmental Protection Agency. Radiation Protection Activities†
0161-780X Current Neurology
0161-7818 Current Radiology
0161-7826 D Magazine
0161-7885 Illinois Horizons†
0161-7915 Pacific Search *see* 0199-6363
0161-7966 National Racquetball
0161-7982 N Y E A Advocate *changed to* N E A New York
0161-8032 Predicasts Overview of Markets and Technologies
0161-8105 Sleep
0161-8113 Zoning and Planning Law Report
0161-813X Neurotoxicology (Park Forest South)
0161-8229 Sales Training *see* 0193-2136
0161-8237 American Agriculturist
0161-8245 Index to Periodical Articles by and About Blacks
0161-8318 Assembling *changed to* Assembling Annual
0161-8342 Antique Trader Weekly
0161-8369 University of North Carolina. Sea Grant College Newsletter *changed to* Coastwatch
0161-8415 Pharmaceutical Representative
0161-8423 Theodore Roosevelt Association Journal
0161-8458 Journal of Mechanical Design *see* 0739-3717
0161-8458 Journal of Mechanical Design *see* 0738-0666
0161-8490 E P A Activities Under the Resource Conservation and Recovery Act of 1976†
0161-8555 Cosmic Search
0161-8571 Georgia State Industrial Directory *see* 0733-4982
0161-8644 Bilalian News *changed to* A M Journal
0161-8660 New Roots *changed to* Renewable Energy News: Northeast
0161-8695 Vital Statistics of Iowa
0161-8741 Dallas-Fort Worth Home & Garden
0161-8784 Realites (Horsham)
0161-8792 Perspectives in Ophthalmology†
0161-8938 Journal of Policy Modeling
0161-8954 Advances in Aquatic Microbiology
0161-9004 Statistics of Privately Owned Electric Utilities in the United States *changed to* Financial Statistics of Selected Electric Utilities
0161-9055 Home Video Report *see* 0748-0792
0161-9152 Age
0161-9225 I & L
0161-9241 California Lawyer
0161-9268 Advances in Nursing Science
0161-9276 Clergy Tax Tips
0161-9284 The Magazine Antiques
0161-9292 Union Leader *see* 0019-3291
0161-9330 In Public Service
0161-9373 Maritime Newsletter
0161-9500 Executive Educator
0161-9543 Musician, Player and Listener *see* 0733-5253
0161-9640 Clinical Chemistry News
0161-9705 Chinese Literature: Essays, Articles, Reviews
0161-9721 Journal of Surgical Practice
0161-973X RetailWeek†
0161-987X Notre Dame Magazine
0161-9896 Highlands Voice
0161-990X Construction Labor News
0162-0029 Garcia Lorca Review
0162-0045 Food Monitor
0162-0061 Pawn Review†
0162-007X Physical Education/Sports Index
0162-0088 World Wide Shipping Guide
0162-0126 Cinemonkey
0162-0134 Journal of Inorganic Biochemistry
0162-0169 Red M(irage)
0162-0177 C R: Centennial Review
0162-0223 Media Index *see* 0199-9273
0162-0266 Hit Parader

ISSN INDEX

0162-0290 Directory and Statistics of Oregon Libraries
0162-0304 Greenhouse Review *changed to* Greenhouse Review Press Chapbook Series
0162-0363 Catholic Sentinel (Diocese of Baker)
0162-0401 Frets Magazine
0162-0436 Qualitative Sociology
0162-0444 Significant Decisions of the Supreme Court
0162-0517 Swift River†
0162-0525 Journal of Juvenile and Family Courts *see* 0161-7109
0162-0533 Builder (Washington) *see* 0744-1193
0162-0606 E E Report *changed to* Environmental Education Report and Newsletter
0162-069X X, a Journal of the Arts *see* 0195-7848
0162-0789 China Geographer†
0162-0800 Olmste/ad's Genealogy Recorded†
0162-0843 Health Sciences Serials
0162-0878 South Carolina State Industrial Directory *see* 0733-4931
0162-0886 Reviews of Infectious Diseases
0162-0894 Tamarack
0162-0908 Year Book of Sports Medicine
0162-0916 Where to Write for Marriage Records: United States and Outlying Areas†
0162-0932 Verbatim
0162-1017 Tamarisk
0162-1025 Fleet Owner: Small Fleet Edition
0162-1041 El Paso Business Review *see* 8750-6033
0162-105X Personnel Alert†
0162-1149 Gargoyle (Washington)
0162-1211 Bar Journal (Trenton) *see* 0195-0983
0162-122X Products Liability Reporter
0162-1238 Pollution Control Guide†
0162-1262 Texas Business and Texas Parade *see* 0164-7628
0162-1289 Seven Days†
0162-1300 Impact Journal
0162-1327 Peninsula Magazine
0162-1343 Play Meter
0162-1378 Mode
0162-1394 Once *changed to* Young Once
0162-1408 Residential and Community Child Care Administration *changed to* Residential Treatment for Children & Youth
0162-1416 Child Behavior Therapy *see* 0731-7107
0162-1424 Home Health Care Services Quarterly
0162-1432 A S A I O Journal†
0162-1440 Tree Tracers
0162-1459 J A S A. Journal of the American Statistical Association
0162-153X American Shotgunner
0162-1564 T L, Tennessee Librarian
0162-1599 New England States Limited
0162-1602 N A R D Newsletter *see* 0027-5972
0162-1718 Utilities Law Reports
0162-1815 Tax Court Reports
0162-1831 National Forum (Ann Arbor)
0162-184X Center for Southern Folklore Newsletter *see* 0195-4903
0162-1858 Exchange: the Organizational Behavior Teaching Journal *changed to* Organizational Behavior Teaching Review
0162-1866 S T T H
0162-1890 Evangel
0162-1904 Zone
0162-1912 Western Journal of Agricultural Economics
0162-1939 Illinois. State Museum. Guidebooklet Series
0162-1955 Planning Helps
0162-1963 General Science Index
0162-2048 Serial Sources for the Biosis Data Base
0162-2102 Catholic Sentinel (Archdiocese of Portland, Oregon)
0162-2110 World of Rodeo and Western Heritage
0162-217X Charles Redd Monographs in Western History
0162-2188 Isaac Asimov's Science Fiction Magazine
0162-220X Cancer Nursing
0162-2226 Professional Remodeling†
0162-2234 Assemblies of God Home Missions†
0162-2242 SportStyle
0162-2250 Journal of Commerce & Industry
0162-2269 Clinical Behavior Therapy Review†
0162-2285 Medical Self-Care
0162-234X Philosopher's Annual†
0162-2404 Soviet World Outlook†
0162-2412 Iowa R E C News
0162-2439 Science, Technology & Human Values
0162-2471 News and Views from Federally Employed Women *changed to* F E W's News and Views
0162-2498 Book Collector's Market *see* 0196-5654
0162-2617 Tennessee Farm Bureau News
0162-2641 Journal of Instructional Development
0162-2692 Young Spartacus†
0162-2706 Society of Chartered Property and Casualty Underwriters. Journal
0162-2714 Coal Outlook
0162-2730 Fuel Oil Week†
0162-2749 International Family Planning Perspectives and Digest *see* 0190-3187
0162-2757 Detroit in Perspective†
0162-2765 Goodfellow Review of Crafts†
0162-2773 L A E Journal†

0162-2811 Communication Abstracts
0162-2846 P E R Report†
0162-2870 October
0162-2889 International Security
0162-2897 California History (San Francisco)
0162-2900 Los Angeles Lawyer
0162-296X Orpheus
0162-2978 Adobe Today *changed to* Solar Earthbuilder International
0162-2994 Washington Drug and Device Letter *see* 0194-1291
0162-3036 Engineering Index Monthly and Author Index
0162-3052 L A E News
0162-3095 Ethology and Sociobiology
0162-3109 Immunopharmacology
0162-3125 Bacon's Publicity Checker
0162-3141 U.S. Army Recruiting and Re-Enlisting Journal *changed to* Recruiter Journal
0162-315X Weimaraner Magazine
0162-3168 Construction Contractor
0162-3176 Construction Briefings
0162-3192 Journal of Guidance and Control *see* 0731-5090
0162-3206 National Security Record
0162-3214 Petersen's 4 Wheel & Off-Road
0162-3230 Flower and Garden. Southern Edition *see* 0162-3249
0162-3249 Flower and Garden
0162-3257 Journal of Autism and Developmental Disorders
0162-3273 Computer Graphics (Eugene) *see* 0271-4159
0162-3281 Related Patent Index†
0162-329X Dual Dictionary to Petroleum Abstracts†
0162-3338 Professional Woman
0162-3346 Perspectives (Pittsburgh) *changed to* Managing (Pittsburgh)
0162-3354 Periodical Update†
0162-3362 Prep
0162-3370 Better Living
0162-3389 Actuator Systems†
0162-3397 American Lawyer
0162-3400 Savor†
0162-3451 Moneytree
0162-3494 Standard Federal Tax Reports
0162-3532 Journal for the Education of the Gifted
0162-3559 P S B A Bulletin
0162-3567 Unity
0162-3583 Rifle
0162-3591 A A A Traveler Magazine (Madison)
0162-3605 Health Policy & Biomedical Research: The Blue Sheet
0162-3613 B S C S Journal†
0162-3621 Annual Editions. Focus: Aging *see* 0272-3808
0162-3656 Agency Sales Magazine
0162-3664 Young World *see* 0009-3971
0162-3737 Educational Evaluation & Policy Analysis
0162-3745 Communique (Washington)†
0162-3753 Crystal Structure†
0162-3761 Contemporary Pharmacy Practice†
0162-3788 Charge, Spin and Momentum Density†
0162-3796 Campground Management
0162-3818 Nebula Winners
0162-3885 Business Communications Review
0162-3893 Columbia (New York)
0162-3907 American Physical Therapy Association. Progress Report
0162-3958 Energy Resources and Technology *see* 0278-5099
0162-3974 Neighbors
0162-4024 Continuum (Washington) *changed to* Continuing Higher Education Review
0162-4040 Financial Review (New York)†
0162-4067 World Naturopathic Journal†
0162-4075 Concrete International: Design & Construction
0162-4083 E P O†
0162-4105 Database (Weston)
0162-4148 Advanced Bible Study
0162-4156 Adult Bible Study
0162-4164 Adult Bible Teacher
0162-4172 Adult Leadership
0162-4180 Baptist Adults
0162-4199 Baptist Youth
0162-4202 Bible Book Study for Adult Teachers
0162-4237 Cemetery Business & Legal Guide†
0162-4245 Family Heritage
0162-4253 Living (Nashville)
0162-4261 Living with Teenagers
0162-427X Mature Living
0162-4288 More (Nashville)
0162-4296 Open Windows
0162-430X Opus One
0162-4318 Sunday School Leadership
0162-4326 Proclaim
0162-4334 Southern Baptist Convention. Sunday School Board. Quarterly Review
0162-4342 Interprete
0162-4350 Living with Preschoolers
0162-4369 Look and Listen
0162-4377 Music Makers
0162-4385 On the Wing
0162-4393 Preschool Leadership
0162-4407 Sunday School Lesson Illustrator *see* 0195-4407
0162-4415 Exploring A *changed to* Exploring 1
0162-4423 Exploring A for Leaders *changed to* Exploring 1 for Leaders
0162-4458 Exploring C *changed to* Exploring 2
0162-4466 Exploring C for Leaders *changed to* Exploring 2 for Leaders

0162-4474 Guide A for Preschool Teachers *changed to* Preschool Bible Teacher A
0162-4482 Guide B for Preschool Teachers *changed to* Preschool Bible Teacher B
0162-4490 Guide C for Preschool Teachers *changed to* Preschool Bible Teacher C
0162-4512 Growing (Nashville)
0162-4539 Care for Leaders†
0162-4547 Encounter!
0162-4571 Collegiate Bible Study†
0162-458X Come Alive†
0162-4598 Come Alive for Leaders†
0162-4601 Church Training
0162-461X Children's Leadership
0162-4644 Simplified Bible Study *changed to* Bible Study-Special Ministries
0162-4660 Bible Learners. Teacher
0162-4679 Bible Learners
0162-4687 Bible Discoverers: Teacher
0162-4695 Bible Discoverers
0162-4709 Youth Leadership
0162-4717 Bible Reader's Guide
0162-4733 Senior Adult Bible Study
0162-4741 Bible Study Pocket Commentary
0162-475X Bible Study Leaflet (Life and Work Series)
0162-4768 Youth in Discovery. Teacher
0162-4784 Youth in Action
0162-4792 Youth in Action. Teacher
0162-4806 Baptist Young Adults
0162-4814 Young Adult Bible Study
0162-4822 Bible Book Study for Youth
0162-4830 Bible Book Study for Youth Teachers
0162-4849 Bible Book Study for Adults
0162-4857 Bible Lesson Digest
0162-4865 Youth Teacher *changed to* Sunday School Youth - Teacher
0162-4873 Sunday School Lessons Simplified *changed to* Sunday School Lessons Special Ministries
0162-4881 Sunday School Youth A *changed to* Sunday School Youth
0162-489X Sunday School Youth B†
0162-4903 Sunday School Young Adults
0162-4911 Sunday School Adults
0162-4962 Biography (Honolulu)
0162-4989 Impact (Washington)
0162-5039 Journal of Aerospace Education *see* 0164-5269
0162-5047 Livestock Weekly
0162-5055 Juvenile Law Digest *see* 0279-2257
0162-5098 Crops and Soils Magazine
0162-5136 Candy Wholesaler
0162-5144 Eagle (Champaign)†
0162-5152 Insiders' Chronicle
0162-5160 Pennsylvania Township News
0162-5217 R-A-D-A-R
0162-5233 Washington Food Report *see* 0745-4503
0162-5241 Profile (Omaha)
0162-5284 New Hampshire Audubon
0162-5306 Action Line (Memphis)
0162-5322 Bibliographic Guide to Soviet and European Studies
0162-5330 Ceramic Mold Mart†
0162-5381 Planbook for Leaders of Children
0162-5403 Alaska Review of Social and Economic Conditions
0162-5411 Official Baseball Dope Book†
0162-542X Official Baseball Register
0162-5446 Dermatology *see* 0273-2254
0162-5454 Seminars in Infectious Disease†
0162-5519 Hadronic Journal
0162-5586 World Agricultural Supply and Demand Estimates
0162-5594 Intercontinental Press Combined with Imprecor *changed to* Intercontinental Press
0162-5616 Florida Folk Arts Directory *changed to* Florida Folklife Resource Directory
0162-5632 Miniature Magazine *see* 0146-6607
0162-5667 Hearing & Speech Action†
0162-5683 B N A's Washington Memorandum *see* 0886-0475
0162-5691 Corporate Practice Series
0162-5721 Atlanta Historical Journal
0162-573X Daisy†
0162-5748 Review of Higher Education
0162-5764 Licensing Law and Business Report
0162-5810 Alembic†
0162-5837 Who
0162-5853 Computer Business News *see* 0746-6765
0162-5861 Dining In & Out†
0162-5896 Chilton's Hardware Age *see* 8755-254X
0162-5918 Alpha
0162-5934 S W L
0162-5942 Emergency
0162-5950 On-Your-Own Guide to Asia
0162-5977 C S P Directory of Suppliers of Educational Foreign Language Materials†
0162-5993 D I S C U S Newsletter†
0162-6019 Message Magazine *see* 0026-0231
0162-6108 Frozen Fishery Products. Annual Summary
0162-6175 Monthly Coke Report *changed to* U.S. Energy Information Administration. Quarterly Coal Report
0162-6191 Constructor
0162-6205 Highway Safety Highlights
0162-6221 Metro (Redondo Beach)

0162-6272 Opiniones Latinoamericanas *changed to* Opiniones
0162-6280 Folklore and Mythology Studies
0162-6302 New York (State) Department of Social Services. Bureau of Data Management and Analysis. Program Brief
0162-6329 Defenders of Wildlife Magazine *see* 0162-6337
0162-6337 Defenders
0162-6345 Footwear Focus†
0162-6353 Carolinas Companies†
0162-637X Chemical Worker
0162-6396 Sexology (1978) *see* 0199-7149
0162-6418 20th Century Christian
0162-6426 Library of Congress
0162-6434 Journal of Special Education Technology
0162-6493 Infectious Disease Practice
0162-654X United States Hockey and Arena Biz *see* 8756-3789
0162-6566 American Journal of Proctology, Gastroenterology & Colon & Rectal Surgery
0162-6574 Journal of Experiential Learning and Simulation†
0162-6604 Aftermarket Executive†
0162-6612 A L S C Newsletter
0162-6620 Action in Teacher Education
0162-6639 Index of N L M Serial Titles†
0162-6663 Handy Andy Magazine *see* 0195-0967
0162-6671 Primroses
0162-6728 American Fisheries Directory and Reference Book†
0162-6760 Spirituality Today
0162-6795 Journal of Asian Culture
0162-6817 Market Logic
0162-6825 Dimension (Birmingham)
0162-6833 Aware Contents
0162-6841 Start (Birmingham)
0162-6876 Sharing (Rockville)
0162-6906 Monographs in Developmental Pediatrics†
0162-6957 Behavioral Medicine†
0162-6973 Cadence (Redwood)
0162-6981 Skyline†
0162-704X Conference Papers Index
0162-7082 R, D & A
0162-7090 Ceramic Teaching Projects and Trade News *changed to* Ceramic Projects
0162-7104 Indiana Prairie Farmer
0162-7139 Decade
0162-7155 Journal of Nursing Care *changed to* Licensed Practical Nurse
0162-7163 L A C M A Physician
0162-7171 Synopsis of Family Therapy Practice
0162-7201 Contemporary Quarterly
0162-7295 Legal Times *changed to* Legal Times
0162-7317 Dental Dealer International Product News
0162-7325 National Law Journal
0162-7333 New York Theatre Annual *see* 0195-945X
0162-7341 Journal of Sport Behavior
0162-735X O A G Travel Planner & Hotel/Motel Guide. European Edition
0162-7376 Woodall's Campground Directory. Texas Edition *changed to* Woodall's Campground Directory. Texas/Mexico Edition
0162-7384 Woodall's Campground Directory. Arizona Edition *changed to* Woodall's Campground Directory. Arizona/New Mexico Edition
0162-7392 Woodall's Campground Directory. California Edition *changed to* Woodall's Campground Directory. California/Nevada/Mexico Directory
0162-7406 Woodall's Campground Directory. Eastern Edition
0162-7414 Woodall's Campground Directory. Western Edition
0162-7422 Bank Loan Officers Report
0162-7430 Bank Marketing Report
0162-7449 Bank Personnel Report
0162-7457 Bank Security Report
0162-7465 Bank Tax Report
0162-7473 Bank Teller's Report
0162-7481 Branch Banker's Report
0162-7503 Executive Compensation Report *changed to* Employee Benefits Report
0162-7511 Kess Tax Practice Report†
0162-752X Real Estate Law Report
0162-7538 Real Estate Tax Ideas
0162-7546 Reviews of Chemical Intermediates†
0162-7570 Washington University Magazine
0162-7635 Yachtsman's Guide to the Greater Antilles
0162-766X Middle East: Abstracts and Index
0162-7880 Who's Who in American Law
0162-7899 Groundswell
0162-7902 El Quetzal
0162-7910 A A H E Bulletin
0162-7929 Concordia Commentator†
0162-7937 A L S A Forum *changed to* Legal Studies Forum
0162-7961 Social Work in Education
0162-7996 Antitrust
0162-8003 Advances in Archaeological Method and Theory
0162-8046 U F O Annual†
0162-816X Medical Equipment Classified
0162-8178 I T E Journal
0162-8208 Altadena Review
0162-8216 Communication Theory in the Cause of Man *changed to* Communication Theory in the Cause of Humanity
0162-8267 Heritage Review
0162-8283 American Historical Society of Germans from Russia. Journal
0162-8291 Sea World†
0162-8305 Galileo (Boston)
0162-833X Journal of the New Alchemists†
0162-8356 Confluencia†
0162-8372 University of Arkansas at Little Rock Law Journal
0162-8402 Hydrogen Progress†
0162-8410 Nashville!
0162-8445 Arts & Humanities Citation Index
0162-8453 Journal of Curriculum Theorizing
0162-8488 Pre-Raphaelite Review *see* 0271-1435
0162-8496 Mail Order Product Newsletter†
0162-8534 Electrical Business†
0162-8585 American Hispanist
0162-8623 Wind Energy Report
0162-8658 Small Business Tax Control
0162-8666 Pets/Supplies/Marketing
0162-8712 California Sociologist
0162-8739 A Different Drummer
0162-8763 Santa Clara County Business Magazine
0162-8771 New England Printer and Publisher
0162-8801 Home and Auto *changed to* Aftermarket Business
0162-8801 Home & Auto Buyer's Guide *changed to* Aftermarket Business Buyer's Guide
0162-881X Flooring
0162-8828 I E E E Transactions on Pattern Analysis and Machine Intelligence
0162-8836 Housewares
0162-8887 Standard Rate and Data Service. Community Publication Rates and Data
0162-8895 Standard Rate and Data Service. Weekly Newspaper and Shopping Guide Rates and Data *see* 0162-8887
0162-8917 Sassy†
0162-8933 Character *see* 0883-1718
0162-8941 Equine Practice
0162-895X Political Psychology
0162-8968 Inc.
0162-8976 Prairie Sun
0162-8984 Practical Politics
0162-9050 New Issues
0162-9069 Nursing Job Guide to Over 7000 Hospitals *changed to* Nursingworld Journal Nursing Job Guide
0162-9077 Home Lighting & Accessories
0162-9085 Nahuatzen†
0162-9093 Communications and the Law
0162-9107 Januz Direct Marketing Letter
0162-9123 Workbasket
0162-9131 Energy User News
0162-9158 H F D - Retailing Home Furnishings
0162-9166 Southeastern Camping *see* 0731-5112
0162-9174 University of Dayton Law Review
0162-9182 Journal of International Relations *see* 0191-8028
0162-9301 Bible and Spade *changed to* Archaeology and Biblical Research
0162-9360 Journal of Clinical Hematology and Oncology†
0162-9379 Orthopaedic Transactions
0162-945X Update (Alexandria)
0162-9468 Textile Products and Processes
0162-9484 U.S. Geological Survey. Yearbook
0162-9506 Spokane†
0162-9646 C I C's State School Directories
0162-9689 Bus World
0162-9700 Journal of Applied Metalworking
0162-9719 Journal of Materials for Energy Systems
0162-976X A A B S Newsletter
0162-9778 Journal of Baltic Studies
0162-9794 Forum on Taxing and Spending *see* 0272-7595
0162-9816 TravLtips
0162-9824 Nathaniel Hawthorne Society. Newsletter *see* 0890-4197
0162-9832 World Refugee Survey Report *see* 0197-5439
0162-9867 International Gymnast *see* 0276-1041
0162-9875 Extension Review
0162-9883 A's and B's of Merit Scholarships *changed to* A's & B's: Your Guide to Academic Scholarship
0162-9905 Restoration: Studies in English Literary Culture, 1660-1700
0162-9972 Hotel and Travel Index
0162-9999 Group for the Use of Psychology in History. Newsletter *see* 0363-891X
0163-0008 Ohio Monthly Record
0163-0016 Working Papers in Applied Linguistics *changed to* Ohio University. Working Papers in Linguistics and Language Teaching
0163-0040 American Hungarian Educator
0163-0067 Information World†
0163-0075 Cincinnati Medicine
0163-0083 Woodall's Campground Directory. New England States Edition
0163-0105 Woodall's Campground Directory. Wisconsin Edition *changed to* Woodall's Campground Directory. Minnesota/Wisconsin Edition
0163-0113 Woodall's Campground Directory. New Jersey/New York Edition *changed to* Woodall's Campground Directory. New York Edition
0163-0121 Woodall's Campground Directory. Michigan Edition
0163-0172 Focus (Seattle)†
0163-0180 Research in Sociology of Knowledge, Science and Art *see* 0278-1557
0163-0229 Korean Review
0163-0253 Life Lines†
0163-030X Chilton's I A M I Iron Age Metalworking International†
0163-0334 Diet and Exercise *changed to* Better Homes and Gardens Low-Calorie Recipes
0163-0350 Latin American Music Review
0163-0369 New Farm
0163-0415 Dieciocho
0163-0423 Identity†
0163-0458 Health Devices Alerts
0163-0466 Index to New England Periodicals
0163-0504 Genealogical Forum of Portland, Oregon. Bulletin *see* 0433-3179
0163-0512 Facets
0163-0539 Genealogical Society of Portland, Oregon. Monthly Bulletin *see* 0433-3179
0163-0547 Computers and Medicine (Glencoe)
0163-0563 Numerical Functional Analysis and Optimization
0163-0571 Journal of Immunopharmacology
0163-0628 Fodor's Brazil
0163-0644 Sulphur Research & Development†
0163-0652 Limited Partners Letter
0163-0660 Allergy Information Exchange *see* 0192-995X
0163-0679 Chilton's Control Equipment Master†
0163-0741 Wind Technology Journal†
0163-075X Kenyon Review
0163-0768 Forum Linguisticum
0163-0784 Massachusetts Nurse
0163-0911 Antiques World†
0163-092X Portfolio
0163-0938 Fashion Rage
0163-0946 Odyssey (Milwaukee)
0163-0954 Icarus(Baltimore)†
0163-0989 Earth's Daughters
0163-1004 Fuego de Aztlan†
0163-1020 U S News Washington Letter†
0163-1047 Behavioral and Neural Biology
0163-108X Policy Studies Review Annual
0163-1101 Shepard's Military Justice Citations
0163-1128 Bookwoman
0163-1144 Flying Annual & Buyers' Guide
0163-1152 Maine Historical Society Quarterly
0163-1187 Chronicles of Culture *changed to* Chronicles: A Magazine of American Culture
0163-1209 Cumberlands†
0163-1241 Abingdon Clergy Income Tax Guide
0163-1268 Small Business Computers†
0163-1276 New York Production Manual *see* 0732-6653
0163-1284 Platt's Oilgram News
0163-1306 Family Circle's Great Ideas
0163-1314 Acupuncture Letter
0163-1322 Hospital Purchasing Management *changed to* Hospital Materials Management
0163-1365 American Jewish Congress. Congress Monthly
0163-1373 L A M P Occasional Newsletter *changed to* Legal Assistance Newsletter
0163-1411 Massachusetts Law Review
0163-1438 Abstract Newsletter: Natural Resources & Earth Sciences
0163-1446 Abstract Newsletter: Physics
0163-1454 Abstract Newsletter: Civil Engineering
0163-1462 Abstract Newsletter: Electrotechnology
0163-1489 Procurement Systems Digest *changed to* Federal Computer Market Report
0163-1497 Abstract Newsletter: Biomedical Technology & Human Factors Engineering
0163-1500 Abstract Newsletter: Building Industry Technology
0163-1519 Abstract Newsletter: Chemistry
0163-1527 Abstract Newsletter: Transportation
0163-1535 Abstract Newsletter: Urban and Regional Technology and Development
0163-1578 Advances in Asthma & Allergy†
0163-1586 N Y State Pharmacist
0163-1608 American Revenuer
0163-1640 18 Almanac
0163-1667 Texas. Department of Health Resources. Biennial Report
0163-1675 Cardiology Update
0163-1691 Dermatology Update
0163-1721 Psychiatric Medicine Update
0163-1748 Professional Salesman's Letter *changed to* Creative Selling
0163-1756 Children's Books International. Proceedings
0163-1780 World Traveling
0163-1799 Today's Christian Woman
0163-1810 Institute of Industrial Engineers. Fall Industrial Engineering Conference. Proceedings *changed to* Institute of Industrial Engineers. Industrial Engineering Conference. Proceedings
0163-1829 Physical Review B (Condensed Matter)
0163-1853 Polamerica *changed to* Poland Today
0163-1861 Kent Collector
0163-1918 International Electron Devices Meeting. I E D M Technical Digest
0163-1926 Cat World

0163-1942 American Journal of Forensic Psychiatry
0163-1950 Woodall's Campground Directory. Ohio/Pennsylvania Editions *changed to* Woodall's Campground Directory. New Jersey/Ohio/Pennsylvania Editions
0163-1977 Mobile-Modular Housing Dealer *changed to* M H Business
0163-2027 50 Plus
0163-206X Data Resources Steel Industry Review
0163-2078 Judicial Newsletter *changed to* Tennessee Judicial Newsletter
0163-2116 Digestive Diseases and Sciences
0163-2124 National Contract Management Quarterly Journal *changed to* National Contract Management Journal (1980)
0163-2183 Synerjy
0163-2205 L I N K S
0163-2213 C A R C H News
0163-223X Nursing Job News *changed to* Nursingworld Journal
0163-2248 New England Senior Citizen
0163-2280 Censored *see* 0883-282X
0163-2388 R L I N Newsletter (Research Libraries Information Network) *see* 0196-173X
0163-2396 Studies in Symbolic Interaction
0163-240X Woodall's Campground Directory. Ontario Edition
0163-2418 Quality Control Reports: The Gold Sheet
0163-2426 Medical Devices, Diagnostics & Instrumentation Reports: The Gray Sheet
0163-2469 Milford Series
0163-2485 Woodall's Campground Directory. Illinois/Indiana Edition
0163-2493 Woodall's Campground Directory. Idaho/Oregon/Washington Edition *changed to* Woodall's Campground Directory. Idaho/Oregon/Washington/British Columbia Edition
0163-2566 E D F Letter
0163-2574 Current Contents/Physical, Chemical & Earth Sciences
0163-2582 Physical Fitness/Sports Medicine *changed to* Physical Fitness/Sports Medicine Bibliography
0163-2590 Allied Medical Education Directory *see* 0194-3766
0163-2647 Universal Human Rights *see* 0275-0392
0163-2655 Psychiatric Opinion†
0163-2728 Patterson's American Educational Directory *see* 0079-0230
0163-2787 Evaluation and the Health Professions
0163-2795 Handbook for Recruiting at Minority Colleges *changed to* Handbook for Recruiting Minority College Students
0163-2809 Children's Language
0163-2817 Official National Collegiate Athletic Association Basketball Rules and Interpretations *changed to* N C A A Men's Basketball Rules and Interpretations
0163-2825 Mountain State Geology
0163-2833 S A R Statistics
0163-2841 Modern Psychotherapy
0163-285X North American Yacht Register
0163-2884 Swimming and Diving Rules *changed to* Swimming and Diving and Water Polo Rulebook
0163-2914 State Laws and Regulations†
0163-2922 Urban, State, and Local Law Newsletter
0163-2965 Studia Africana
0163-299X Today's Professionals
0163-3007 Black Stars†
0163-3015 Boston Phoenix
0163-3023 Commonsense†
0163-3031 Corporate Finance Sourcebook
0163-3058 Magill's Literary Annual
0163-3066 New Hampshire Times
0163-3139 Sonshine Times
0163-3155 Current Contents/Arts & Humanities
0163-3171 Global Tectonics and Metallogeny
0163-321X R F Design
0163-3228 Diagnosis
0163-3252 Journal of Studies in Technical Careers
0163-3287 Employment Information in the Mathematical Sciences
0163-3295 Urthkin
0163-3341 Entrepreneur (Los Angeles)
0163-3392 Current Issues and Research in Advertising
0163-3449 Organic Gardening *see* 0884-3252
0163-3457 E D A Research Review†
0163-3562 Dynamite
0163-3570 Scholastic Action
0163-3589 Scholastic Sprint
0163-3597 Scholastic Search *changed to* Scholastic Update
0163-3651 Art Teacher *see* 0004-3125
0163-366X West Virginia University Alumni Quarterly *changed to* West Virginia University Alumni Magazine
0163-3716 Palestine Perspectives
0163-3724 International Energy Statistical Review
0163-3767 Semiconductor International
0163-3813 Contributions in Comparative Colonial Studies
0163-3821 Contributions in Drama and Theatre Studies
0163-3848 Edward Sapir Monograph Series in Language, Culture, and Cognition
0163-3856 Fusion Energy Update
0163-3864 Journal of Natural Products (LLOYDIA)
0163-3872 Porch†
0163-3929 Historical Journal of Western Massachusetts *see* 0276-8313
0163-3937 Books of the Times†
0163-3945 National Guard
0163-3996 Health Law Project Library Bulletin†
0163-4070 Soccer America
0163-4089 American Demographics
0163-4100 Chronicle Annual Vocational School Manual *see* 0276-0371
0163-4119 Feed and Grain Times
0163-4143 Studies in Contemporary Satire
0163-416X ZooGoer
0163-4186 Copper: Quarterly Report†
0163-4267 N A G W S Guide. Synchronized Swimming†
0163-4275 Environmental Ethics
0163-4313 Woodall's Florida and Southern States Retirement and Resort Communities Directory *see* 0731-6526
0163-433X Journal of Sport Psychology
0163-4348 Science Fiction and Fantasy Book Review *see* 0747-234X
0163-4356 Therapeutic Drug Monitoring
0163-4372 Journal of Gerontological Social Work
0163-4399 Formed Fabrics Industry *see* 0163-4429
0163-4429 Nonwovens Industry
0163-4437 Media Culture and Society
0163-4445 Journal of Family Therapy
0163-4453 Journal of Infection
0163-4461 Humanities in Society†
0163-447X B C & T News
0163-4488 Supermarket Trends *see* 0278-6346
0163-4518 Farm Show Magazine
0163-4526 Journal of Water Borne Coatings
0163-4534 Polyphony *see* 0884-4720
0163-4542 Powder Coatings†
0163-4585 Let's Go: The Budget Guide to Europe.
0163-4593 Next†
0163-4615 Handbook of Business Finance and Capital Sources
0163-4631 Precisely
0163-464X Pharmacy Management *see* 0730-7780
0163-4674 U.S. Federal Railroad Administration. Office of Safety. Accident/Incident Bulletin
0163-4712 Florida State Industrial Directory *see* 0740-4697
0163-4747 N A G W S Guide. Soccer
0163-4763 National Federation of State High School Associations. Soccer Rules *see* 0731-9541
0163-4828 Weekly Reader Eye *changed to* Weekly Reader, Edition 5
0163-4844 Know Your World Extra
0163-4852 Senior Weekly Reader *changed to* Weekly Reader, Senior Edition
0163-4860 Weekly Reader News Parade *changed to* Weekly Reader, Edition 4
0163-4879 Weekly Reader News Patrol *changed to* Weekly Reader, Edition 3
0163-4887 Weekly Reader Surprise *changed to* Weekly Reader, Edition K
0163-4895 Buddy's Weekly Reader *changed to* Weekly Reader, Edition 1
0163-4909 Weekly Reader News Hunt *changed to* Weekly Reader, Edition 2
0163-4917 Medicaid Management Reports†
0163-4941 Aeronautical Engineering; a Special Bibliography with Indexes
0163-495X American Petroleum Institute. Refining Department. Proceedings
0163-4976 Iowa. Crop and Livestock Reporting Service. Planting to Harvest. Weather and Field Crops *changed to* Iowa Agricultural Statistics
0163-4984 Biological Trace Element Research
0163-4992 Cell Biophysics: an International Journal
0163-5026 Impact Two†
0163-5069 Film Criticism
0163-5077 Labor Relations and Employment *see* 0193-5739
0163-5085 World Development Report
0163-5093 Information Moscow *changed to* Information Moscow, Western Edition
0163-5107 Health Policy Quarterly†
0163-5123 Annual Index to Motion Picture Credits†
0163-514X Journal of Prevention *see* 0278-095X
0163-5158 Ageing International
0163-5182 Human Factors Society Annual Meeting. Proceedings
0163-5255 Rockford Papers†
0163-5271 Mixed Pickles
0163-528X Folk Dance Directory
0163-5298 Journal of Continuing Education in Radiology
0163-531X Business (Atlanta)
0163-5328 Woodall's Campground Directory. Arkansas/Missouri Edition
0163-5336 Woodall's Campground Directory. Kentucky/Tennessee Edition
0163-5344 Woodall's Campground Directory. Colorado Edition
0163-5352 Woodall's Campground Directory. North Carolina/South Carolina Edition
0163-5379 Advances in Instructional Psychology
0163-5387 Persuasion at Work
0163-5425 Focus: Teaching English Language Arts
0163-5433 Wyoming Issues†
0163-545X Environmental Law Newsletter
0163-5468 Field & Stream Bass Fishing Annual
0163-5476 Middle East Contemporary Survey
0163-5484 Northeastern Agricultural Economics Council. Journal *changed to* Northeastern Journal of Agricultural Economics and Resource Economics
0163-5506 Public Libraries
0163-5514 Federal Controls†
0163-5530 Writing (La Mesa)†
0163-5549 Journal of Integral Equations†
0163-5573 American Institute of Industrial Engineers. Proceedings of the Spring Annual Conference *see* 0278-8012
0163-5581 Nutrition and Cancer
0163-559X International Society of Magnetic Resonance. Bulletin†
0163-5662 Energy Guidebook *changed to* Power's Energy Systems Guidebook
0163-5689 Progress in Communication Sciences
0163-5727 S I G C A P H Newsletter
0163-5778 S I G N U M Newsletter
0163-5808 S I G M O D Record
0163-5824 S I G S A M Bulletin
0163-5905 Nordic
0163-5948 S I G S O F T Software Engineering Notes
0163-5964 S I G A R C H Computer Architecture News
0163-5980 Operating Systems Review
0163-6006 A P L Quote Quad
0163-6065 Directory of Blood Establishments Registered Under Section 510 of the Food, Drug, and Cosmetic Act *changed to* Directory of Blood Service Establishments
0163-6111 Peterson's Annual Guides/Graduate Study. Graduate Programs in the Physical Science and Mathematics. *changed to* Peterson's Graduate Programs in the Physical Sciences and Mathematics (Year)
0163-6170 Recent Advances in Nuclear Medicine
0163-6197 Electronic Business
0163-6200 Football Case Book
0163-626X Voice of Z - 39
0163-6278 Current Chemical Reactions
0163-6359 Wildlifer
0163-6383 Infant Behavior and Development
0163-6391 Canada-United States Law Journal
0163-6413 Durak†
0163-6480 Moral Education Forum†
0163-6499 Urban Innovation Abroad *see* 0887-4468
0163-6529 Urban Transit Abroad *see* 0887-4468
0163-6537 Directory of Personal Image Consultants
0163-6545 Radical History Review
0163-657X Stanford French Review
0163-6588 Research in Law and Sociology *changed to* Research in Law, Deviance and Social Control
0163-660X Washington Quarterly
0163-6618 P/S/R/O Reports *see* 0277-8548
0163-6626 Interface: the Computer Education Quarterly
0163-6642 Family Practice Recertification
0163-6650 Eberly's Michigan Journal
0163-6693 F and S Index of Corporate Change *see* 0744-2785
0163-6715 Gospel Teacher†
0163-6766 Biomass Digest *changed to* Bioprocessing Technology
0163-6774 Acronyms
0163-6782 Savings and Loan Market Study†
0163-6804 I E E E Communications Magazine
0163-6812 I E E E Circuits and Systems Magazine†
0163-6855 Eastern Finance Association. Proceedings of the Annual Meeting *see* 0732-8516
0163-6952 People and Energy†
0163-7010 Oxbridge Directory of Newsletters
0163-7029 Modern Technics in Surgery. Cardiac/Thoracic Surgery
0163-7037 Modern Technics in Surgery. Neurosurgery
0163-7088 Notes on Teaching English
0163-710X Family Advocate
0163-7134 Sawyer's Gas Turbine International *see* 0149-4147
0163-7169 China Business Review
0163-7193 Industrial Gas and Energy Utilization *see* 0164-4262
0163-7207 Boating Registration Statistics
0163-7258 Pharmacology and Therapeutics
0163-7266 Railfan & Railroad
0163-7274 Purpose
0163-7282 Exetasis
0163-7290 U.S. Copyright Office. Catalog of Copyright Entries. Fourth Series. Part 1: Nondramatic Literary Works
0163-7304 U.S. Copyright Office. Catalog of Copyright Entries. Fourth Series. Part 2: Serials and Periodicals
0163-7312 U.S. Copyright Office. Catalog of Copyright Entries. Fourth Series. Part 3: Performing Arts
0163-7320 U.S. Copyright Office. Catalog of Copyright Entries. Fourth Series. Part 4: Motion Pictures and Filmstrips
0163-7339 U.S. Copyright Office. Catalog of Copyright Entries. Fourth Series. Part 5: Visual Arts Excluding Maps

0163-7347 U.S. Copyright Office. Catalog of Copyright Entries. Fourth Series. Part 6: Maps
0163-7355 U.S. Copyright Office. Catalog of Copyright Entries. Fourth Series. Part 7: Sound Recordings
0163-7363 U.S. Copyright Office. Catalog of Copyright Entries. Fourth Series. Part 8: Renewals
0163-7428 Women's Sports *see* 8750-653X
0163-7452 Board & Sail Magazine
0163-7460 Art Product News
0163-7479 Texas International Law Journal
0163-7517 S and M M Sales and Marketing Management *changed to* Sales & Marketing Management
0163-7525 Annual Review of Public Health
0163-755X M E L U S
0163-7584 Medicaid Statistics *see* 0277-5611
0163-7606 Federal Communications Law Journal
0163-7622 Milwaukee History
0163-7665 Federal Personnel Guide
0163-7673 Reviews in Biochemical Toxicology
0163-769X Endocrine Reviews
0163-7770 Haiti Report
0163-7789 Bulletin Exterieur
0163-7800 Current Pulmonology†
0163-7827 Progress in Lipid Research
0163-7843 Pacific Horticulture
0163-7851 Horticultural Reviews
0163-786X Research in Social Movements, Conflicts and Change
0163-7878 Research in Population Economics
0163-7894 Primary Care Physician's Guide to Practical Gastroenterology *see* 0277-4208
0163-7908 Re: Act†
0163-7916 Untitled
0163-8130 Attenzione - USA
0163-8211 American Rag
0163-822X Illinois School Research and Development
0163-8238 Puerto Rico. Agricultural Experiment Station. Bulletin
0163-8246 N M A L: Notes on Modern American Literature
0163-8262 Impact (Syracuse)†
0163-8270 Federal Civilian Workforce Statistics. Monthly Release *changed to* Federal Civilian Workforce Statistics. Employment and Trends
0163-8289 Congressional Record Index†
0163-8297 Public Welfare Directory
0163-8300 American Public Welfare Association. W - Memo
0163-8343 General Hospital Psychiatry
0163-836X Annual Editions: Readings in Human Sexuality *changed to* Annual Editions: Human Sexuality
0163-8386 Guide to Microforms in Print. Subject
0163-8440 Commercial Remodeling *changed to* Commercial Renovation
0163-8459 Topics
0163-8475 Community Review
0163-8483 World Higher Education Communique†
0163-8491 Holistic Health Review *see* 0195-5977
0163-8505 Sociological Practice
0163-853X Discourse Processes
0163-8548 Human Studies
0163-8602 President's National Urban Policy Report
0163-8653 Convention of the International Association of Fish and Wildlife Agencies *see* 0161-3332
0163-8971 Group (Loveland)
0163-898X O C L C Newsletter
0163-8998 Annual Review of Nuclear and Particle Science
0163-903X Washington Review
0163-9048 Human Rights Internet Newsletter *see* 0275-049X
0163-9056 Criminology Review Yearbook
0163-9153 Colorado School of Mines Quarterly
0163-9218 Massachusetts Institute of Technology. Research Laboratory of Electronics. R L E Progress Report
0163-9226 M S I-L S I Memory D.A.T.A. Book *see* 0195-5853
0163-9234 Package Printing
0163-9242 Chronicle College Chart *see* 0191-3670
0163-9250 Darkroom Photography
0163-9269 Behavioral & Social Sciences Librarian
0163-9277 Goodstay: Your Hospital Stay Magazine
0163-9285 Southeast Optician
0163-9293 Southwest Optician
0163-9307 Far West Optician
0163-9323 Great Lakes Optician
0163-9366 Journal of Nutrition for the Elderly
0163-9374 Cataloging & Classification Quarterly
0163-9404 Feature†
0163-9412 Advertising World *see* 0885-3363
0163-948X Inside F.E.R.C. (Federal Energy Regulatory Commission)
0163-9498 Open Chain†
0163-9501 Current Cardiology
0163-9528 Supermarket Shopper†
0163-9536 Impact American Distilled Spirits Market Review and Forecast
0163-9544 Impact the American Wine Market Review and Forecast
0163-9552 Friends of Photography. Newsletter *see* 0891-5326
0163-9587 Mossbauer Effect Reference and Data Journal
0163-9609 U.S. National Diabetes Advisory Board. Annual Report†
0163-9617 AmStat News
0163-9625 Deviant Behavior
0163-9633 Clinical Preventive Dentistry
0163-9641 Infant Mental Health Journal
0163-9684 White Book of Ski Areas. U S and Canada
0163-9706 View (Oakland)
0163-9730 Public Works Manual
0163-9803 Bioethics Quarterly *changed to* Journal of Medical Humanities and Bioethics
0163-9811 E M M S
0163-9897 Gay Insurgent
0163-9900 Herb Quarterly
0163-9927 A E I Foreign Policy and Defense Review
0163-9951 Clan MacNeil Association of America. Galley
0163-996X Federal Tax Coordinator 2d. Weekly Alert
0163-9986 Research Institute of America. Estate Planners Alert
0163-9994 Research Institute Lawyers Tax Alert
0164-002X Optoelectronics D.A.T.A. Book
0164-0038 Power Semiconductors D.A.T.A. Book
0164-0046 Advances in Space Exploration *see* 0273-1177
0164-0070 Carolina Planning
0164-0089 Chilton's Instruments and Control Systems *see* 0746-2395
0164-0119 Interface I Cs D.A.T.A. Book
0164-0135 Microwave Tubes *see* 0271-0773
0164-0143 Short Stories in Spanish†
0164-016X National Center Reporter *see* 0190-1168
0164-0178 American Jewish History
0164-0186 Better Homes and Gardens Bedroom and Bath Decorating Ideas†
0164-0259 Knowledge: Creation, Diffusion, Utilization
0164-0267 Law and Policy Quarterly *see* 0265-8240
0164-0275 Research on Aging
0164-0283 Sage Family Studies Abstracts
0164-0291 International Journal of Primatology
0164-0305 Journal of Behavioral Assessment
0164-0313 Journal of Fusion Energy
0164-0356 50 State Legislative Review
0164-0364 American Criminal Law Review
0164-0372 Probate and Property
0164-0496 Missouri Union List of Serial Publications
0164-0534 Topics in Clinical Nursing *changed to* Holistic Nursing Practice
0164-0542 Group Health News *see* 0887-9087
0164-0593 Associated Equipment Distributors. Rental Rates Compilation
0164-0674 Catholic Near East Magazine
0164-0682 Economic Perspectives
0164-0712 National Wetlands Newsletter
0164-0720 Running Times Yearbook†
0164-0739 Microforms in Print. Supplement *changed to* Guide to Microforms in Print. Supplement
0164-0747 Guide to Microforms in Print. Author, Title
0164-0763 Library Research *see* 0740-8188
0164-0771 Philosophy Research Archives
0164-078X Psychotherapy Digest
0164-0828 Bank Note Reporter (Iola)
0164-0836 Car Exchange†
0164-0917 A E E Directory of Energy Professionals
0164-0925 A C M Transactions on Programming Languages and Systems
0164-0941 Fishing in Maryland
0164-095X Forest Products Review†
0164-0968 Task Force on Environmental Cancer and Heart and Lung Disease. Annual Report to Congress
0164-1085 Silverfish Review
0164-1093 Science Fiction Voices
0164-1212 Journal of Systems and Software
0164-1220 Futurics
0164-1239 Annals of the History of Computing
0164-1247 Comparative Studies in Sociology *see* 0195-6310
0164-1255 Fundamental Concepts of Estate Administration†
0164-1263 Pediatric Dentistry
0164-1298 Artpark
0164-1336 Michigan Health Educator
0164-1352 Checklist of State Publications *see* 0197-5668
0164-1360 Notes on Modern American Literature *see* 0163-8246
0164-1433 South Jersey
0164-1441 Bostonia
0164-145X Higginson Journal
0164-1484 Periodically Speaking†
0164-1492 Dickinson Studies
0164-1514 Washington Health Record
0164-1522 Collaboration
0164-1530 California Work Injuries and Illnesses
0164-1662 Florida Journal of Anthropology
0164-1670 American Medical Association. Directory of Accredited Residencies *changed to* Directory of Residency Training Accredited by the Accreditation Council for Graduate Medical Education
0164-1689 Transportation Law Seminar. Papers and Proceedings *see* 0271-4396
0164-1689 Transportation Law Seminar. Papers and Proceedings *see* 0271-437X
0164-1697 Occupational Injuries and Illnesses in California *see* 0164-2707
0164-1743 Media Guide International. Business/Professional Publications Edition *changed to* International Media Guides. Business/Professional Publications Edition
0164-176X P I P E R
0164-1867 D R C Historical and Comparative Disasters Series
0164-1875 D R C Book & Monograph Series
0164-1883 Trouser Press†
0164-1905 Artes Graficas U S A
0164-2049 Geoscience Wisconsin
0164-2103 Cosecha/Harvest *see* 0145-2681
0164-2111 Fantastica *changed to* Fangoria
0164-212X Occupational Therapy in Mental Health
0164-2340 Topics in Emergency Medicine
0164-2472 Social Text
0164-2502 Journal of Career Education *changed to* Journal of Career Development
0164-2537 Karikazo
0164-2707 Work Injuries and Illnesses in California. Quarterly†
0164-2790 Analysis of Jewish Policy Issues
0164-2839 Design News. Materials *changed to* Design News Materials Directory
0164-2847 National Association of Schools of Music. Handbook
0164-2863 Air Gun
0164-2871 Design News. Fluid Power *changed to* Design News Fluid Power Directory
0164-288X Forum (College Park) *changed to* Forum International
0164-3010 Springfield/Hartford
0164-3037 Bird Watcher's Digest
0164-3150 American Organist
0164-3169 Perspectiva Mundial
0164-3177 New England Review *see* 0736-2579
0164-3207 Democratic Left
0164-3223 Drum Corps World
0164-324X Fiberarts
0164-3290 Nutshell News
0164-3304 Oregon Geology
0164-3371 M S N Microwave Systems News *changed to* Microwave Systems News & Technology
0164-3452 Hang Glider Magazine†
0164-3495 Emmy
0164-3525 Economic World
0164-3533 New England Business
0164-3576 Michigan Bar Journal
0164-3622 Louisiana Municipal Review
0164-3746 Gulf Coast Fisherman
0164-3754 South-West Foodservice
0164-3762 Electronic Field Engineer
0164-3835 Barclays Law Monthly
0164-3851 Schools and the Courts
0164-386X Sheet Music *see* 0197-3495
0164-3959 K E A News
0164-3967 New Age Magazine *changed to* New Age Journal
0164-4076 Military Electronics Countermeasures†
0164-4092 Aviation Engineering and Maintenance *changed to* Military Science and Technology
0164-4114 Woodsmith
0164-4211 Verona Missions *changed to* Comboni Missions
0164-4238 Surgical Technologist
0164-4262 Modern Industrial Energy†
0164-4289 Kennel Review
0164-4297 Arizona State Law Journal
0164-4327 Reproductions Review and Methods *changed to* In-Plant Reproductions & Electronic Publishing
0164-4335 Meat, Poultry & Seafood Digest†
0164-4343 Marketing Communications
0164-4386 Nephrology Nurse†
0164-4483 Siberian World
0164-4556 Southwest Magazine
0164-4645 Glaucoma
0164-4742 Words
0164-4777 Jordan (Washington)
0164-4858 Spa and Sauna Trade Journal
0164-4882 Joyful Woman
0164-4904 Automotive Design & Development
0164-503X Motorhome Life *see* 0744-074X
0164-5048 Dromenon
0164-5080 American Auditory Society. Journal *see* 0196-0202
0164-5137 Chilton's Iron Age *changed to* Chilton's Iron Age: Manufacturing Management
0164-5137 Chilton's Iron Age *changed to* Chilton's Iron Age: Metals Producer
0164-517X Dun and Bradstreet Reports *see* 0746-6110
0164-5196 Police Product News
0164-5218 Black Odyssey
0164-5226 Rainbow (Minneapolis)†
0164-5242 Specifying Engineer *changed to* Consulting/Specifying Engineer
0164-5269 Aviation/Space
0164-5315 Biweekly List of Papers on Radiation Chemistry and Photochemistry
0164-5331 California - Arizona Farm Press
0164-534X Cause/Effect Magazine
0164-5382 Small Business Report (Monterey)
0164-5390 Law Office Information Service
0164-5412 Michigan Real Estate Magazine†
0164-5420 A P A News†

1472 ISSN INDEX

0164-5455 Compendium on Continuing Education for the Small Animal Practitioner *see* 0193-1903
0164-5463 International Motorcycle Trade Journal†
0164-5528 E/S A
0164-5552 Car Collector and Car Classics
0164-5560 Classic Film/Video Images *see* 0275-8423
0164-5595 City Weekly *see* 0164-5935
0164-5609 Council of Biology Editors. Newsletter *changed to* C B E Views
0164-5617 Motor Inn Journal *see* 0018-6082
0164-5706 Paint Horse Journal
0164-5749 Flotation Sleep Industry
0164-5757 A L I Reporter
0164-5765 Laundry News
0164-582X Ideal Beef Memo
0164-5846 Recreational Computing†
0164-5854 G S A News & Information
0164-5889 Subway
0164-5897 Pizza Maker
0164-5919 Tidewater Life
0164-5935 Nation's Cities Weekly
0164-5951 O W N
0164-6028 Update (Minneapolis)†
0164-6044 Muffler Digest
0164-6060 Co-Op News (Berkeley)
0164-6079 Human Services Reporter
0164-6117 Cuisine†
0164-6168 Texas Thoroughbred
0164-6184 Possessions
0164-6214 House Beautiful's Colonial Homes *see* 0195-1416
0164-6249 Real Estate Washington *changed to* Washington Regardie's Business
0164-6257 Federal Veterinarian
0164-632X Ocean World†
0164-6338 Pro Sound News
0164-6346 Motor Imported Car Crash Estimating Guide
0164-6397 Fire and Police Personnel Reporter
0164-646X J O H: Journal of Housing *see* 0272-7374
0164-6486 Dairymen's Digest: Southern Region Edition
0164-6532 Twin Cities
0164-6540 Snowmobile West
0164-6559 Shelter
0164-6605 Stanford Business School Magazine
0164-6613 Evener
0164-6656 Quarter Horse Journal
0164-6699 Mississippi Magazine
0164-6753 Expo (Philadelphia) *see* 0199-7602
0164-6761 North Carolina Tar Heel Coast
0164-6796 New Mexico Business Journal
0164-6834 Audio Visual Product News *see* 0747-1335
0164-6850 North Carolina State Bar Quarterly
0164-694X Jogger *changed to* Running & Fitnews
0164-7016 Investigative Reporters & Editors Journal
0164-7059 Business Viewpoint†
0164-7083 Keeping Abreast Journal of Human Nurturing†
0164-7164 Inform†
0164-7172 Ohio Magazine
0164-7202 Nutrition Health Review
0164-7253 Mountain Movers
0164-730X Fly Tyer
0164-7318 Deer & Deer Hunting
0164-7415 National Right to Life News
0164-7547 National Knife Collector *changed to* National Knife Magazine
0164-7628 Texas Business
0164-7695 Hardware Retailing *changed to* Do-it-Yourself Retailing
0164-7709 Insights (Springfield)
0164-7725 Issues in Bank Regulation
0164-7741 Science-Ciencia
0164-775X Communique (Kent)
0164-7768 Personal Finance: The Inflation Survival Letter
0164-7792 Muscle Digest†
0164-7822 Pennsylvania Naturalist
0164-7830 Calculators/Computers Magazine†
0164-7857 Current Concepts in Hospital Pharmacy Management
0164-7881 Shooting Sportsman†
0164-7954 International Journal of Acarology
0164-7970 New Directions for Student Services
0164-7989 New Directions for Program Evaluation
0164-8047 Arena News
0164-8071 Atlanta Business Chronicle
0164-8098 New York Theatre Review†
0164-8128 Internews International Bulletin
0164-8136 American Firearms Industry
0164-8152 New Hampshire Business Review
0164-8195 Denver Monthly†
0164-8233 Specialty Salesman and Business Opportunities *see* 0738-4211
0164-8241 National Wood Stove and Fireplace Journal *see* 0279-4357
0164-8276 Texas & Southern Quarter Horse Journal
0164-8314 Deke Quarterly
0164-8330 Alaska Fisherman's Journal
0164-8470 Interiors: for the Contract Design Professional
0164-8489 T V C *see* 0745-2802
0164-8497 Vegetarian Times
0164-8500 In League
0164-8527 Child Care Information Exchange
0164-856X Solidarity (Detroit)
0164-8578 Rural Missouri
0164-8675 Irish Wolfhound Quarterly
0164-8683 Mississippi Educator
0164-8756 Computer/Law Journal
0164-8780 Ranch & Coast
0164-8942 Skateboarder *see* 0279-8689
0164-8985 Audio & Electronics Digest
0164-9175 VocEd *changed to* Vocational Education Journal
0164-9183 Bowlers Journal
0164-9191 Craft Horizons with Craft World *see* 0194-8008
0164-923X United States Specialist
0164-9248 Circus Weekly *changed to* Circus (1979)
0164-9256 Motorcyclist's Post
0164-9345 Kentucky Bench & Bar
0164-9353 United Caprine News
0164-9442 Oklahoma Dental Association Journal
0164-9515 Woman Executive's Bulletin
0164-9531 Animal Keepers' Forum
0164-9566 Library P R News
0164-9612 Diving World
0164-9620 Electronics Test
0164-9655 Millimeter
0164-9698 Financial Planning Today *changed to* Journal of Financial Planning Today
0164-9728 G/C/T (Gifted/Creative/Talented Children) *changed to* Gifted Child Today
0164-9760 C T A/N E A Action *changed to* C T A Action
0164-9787 Houston Engineer
0164-985X Clinical Cancer Letter
0164-9876 Marketing Bestsellers *see* 0744-3102
0164-9914 Chain Drug Review
0164-9922 Spray *see* 0273-7892
0164-9930 Oregon Magazine
0164-9957 Mix
0164-9981 Computer Systems News
0164-999X Broadcast Communications *changed to* Television Broadcast
0165-0009 Climatic Change
0165-0025 Praktijkgids
0165-005X Culture, Medicine and Psychiatry
0165-0068 Urban Law and Policy
0165-0076 Proces
0165-0106 Erkenntnis
0165-0114 Fuzzy Sets and Systems
0165-0122 Tijdschrift voor de Politie
0165-0157 Linguistics and Philosophy
0165-0165 Journal of Comparative Corporate Law and Securities Regulation *changed to* Journal of Comparative Business and Capital Market Law
0165-0173 Brain Research Reviews
0165-019X Z T
0165-0203 Natural Resources Forum
0165-0211 Zenit
0165-022X Journal of Biochemical and Biophysical Methods
0165-0254 International Journal of Behavioral Development
0165-0262 Outlook on Science Policy
0165-0270 Journal of Neuroscience Methods
0165-0300 Review of Socialist Law
0165-0327 Journal of Affective Disorders
0165-0378 Journal of Reproductive Immunology
0165-0386 Marge†
0165-0424 Aquatic Insects
0165-0475 Journal of Clinical Neuropsychology *changed to* Journal of Clinical and Experimental Neuropsychology
0165-0505 Bijdragen en Mededelingen Betreffende de Geschiedenis der Nederlanden
0165-0513 Recueil des Travaux Chimiques des Pays-Bas
0165-0521 Studies on Neotropical Fauna and Environment
0165-0572 Resources and Energy
0165-0610 Instituut voor Cultuurtechniek en Waterhuishouding. Jaarverslag
0165-0629 International Review of Social History
0165-0653 International Journal for the Advancement of Counselling
0165-0750 Common Market Law Review
0165-0807 Moon and the Planets *see* 0167-9295
0165-0890 Tikker
0165-1005 Core Journals in Ophthalmology
0165-1048 Bibliotheek en Samenleving
0165-1056 Core Journals in Clinical Neurology
0165-1072 Hartmans Tijdschrift voor Studerenden Openbaar Bestuur
0165-1153 Itinerario
0165-1269 International Journal of Invertebrate Reproduction *changed to* International Journal of Invertebrate Reproduction and Development
0165-1404 Hydrobiological Bulletin
0165-1439 Tijdschrift voor Marketing
0165-148X Overzicht-Internationale Universitaire Samenwerking *changed to* Overzicht Onderwijs, Onderzoek en Ontwikkeling
0165-1587 European Review of Agricultural Economics
0165-1625 Beleid en Maatschappij
0165-1633 Solar Energy Materials
0165-1676 Sociodrome
0165-1684 Signal Processing
0165-1730 Current Bibliography of Agriculture in China†
0165-1765 Economics Letters
0165-1773 Kennis en Methode
0165-1781 Psychiatry Research
0165-182X Tijdschrift voor Criminologie
0165-1838 Journal of the Autonomic Nervous System
0165-1854 Current Topics in Materials Science
0165-1889 Journal of Economic Dynamics and Control
0165-2079 Air Law
0165-2125 Wave Motion
0165-2176 Veterinary Quarterly
0165-2222 Excerpta Medica. Section 51: Leprosy and Related Subjects
0165-2273 Geo-Processing
0165-2281 Health Policy and Education *changed to* Health Policy
0165-232X Cold Regions Science and Technology
0165-2370 Journal of Analytical and Applied Pyrolysis
0165-2427 Veterinary Immunology and Immunopathology
0165-2478 Immunology Letters
0165-2516 International Journal of the Sociology of Language
0165-2524 Esperanto-Dokumentoj. Nova Serio
0165-2575 Esperanto Documents
0165-2583 N B L C Info Bulletin
0165-2672 Lingvaj Problemoj Kaj Lingvo-Planado *see* 0272-2690
0165-2818 Outlook on Research Libraries
0165-2826 Intertax
0165-2966 Fiscale en Administratieve Praktijkvragen
0165-2974 Sjow *changed to* Tijdschriften voor Jeugdhulpverlening
0165-3806 Developmental Brain Research
0165-4055 International Journal of Psycholinguistics†
0165-4101 Journal of Accounting and Economics
0165-4438 Trend-Boutique
0165-4543 Meubel
0165-4608 Cancer Genetics & Cytogenetics
0165-4748 Key to Economic Science
0165-4772 Wereld van het Jonge Kind
0165-4888 Text
0165-4896 Mathematical Social Sciences
0165-537X Trend
0165-5426 Tendens
0165-5477 Koeltechniek
0165-5515 Journal of Information Science
0165-5523 Klimaatbeheersing
0165-5701 International Ophthalmology
0165-5728 Journal of Neuroimmunology
0165-5752 Systematic Parasitology
0165-5817 Philips Journal of Research
0165-5876 International Journal of Pediatric Otorhinolaryngology
0165-5949 H B Modelbouw & Techniek
0165-604X Trends in Pharmacological Sciences
0165-6074 Microprocessing and Microprogramming
0165-6090 Thymus
0165-6473 Centraal Bureau voor Genealogie. Mededelingen
0165-6546 Moesson
0165-716X Amsterdam Studies in the Theory and History of Linguistic Science. Series 2: Classics in Psycholinguistics
0165-7224 Documentatiegroep 40-45. Maandorgaan *see* 0920-3958
0165-7267 Amsterdam Studies in the Theory and History of Linguistic Science. Series 5: Library and Information Sources in Linguistics
0165-7380 Veterinary Research Communications
0165-7569 Lingvisticae Investigationes: Supplementa
0165-7666 Vicus Cuadernos: Linguistica†
0165-7712 Linguistic & Literary Studies in Eastern Europe
0165-7747 Systems, Objectives, Solutions *see* 0378-7206
0165-7763 Studies in Language Companion Series
0165-7836 Fisheries Research
0165-8042 Lover
0165-8107 Neuro-Ophthalmology
0165-8182 Zeewezen
0165-8220 Nu
0165-8379 Welzijn
0165-8573 Zuivelzicht
0165-859X Marine Biology Letters†
0165-8646 Photobiochemistry and Photobiophysics
0165-8654 Beeldenaar
0165-8743 Purdue University Monographs in Romance Language
0165-8794 Science of Religion
0165-8867 Pen en Toets
0165-9227 Grazer Philosophische Studien
0165-9367 Bulletin Antieke Beschaving
0165-9375 C S M Informatie
0165-9545 Milieudefensie
0165-9677 Finish
0165-988X Wereld en Zending
0165-9936 Trends in Analytical Chemistry
0166-0012 Journal of Italian Linguistics†
0166-0268 Netherlands. Centraal Bureau voor de Statistiek. Maandschrift
0166-0373 Amandla
0166-0462 Regional Science & Urban Economics
0166-0535 Muziek en Dans
0166-0616 Studies in Mycology
0166-0667 Volkskundig Bulletin
0166-0829 Linguistik Aktuell
0166-0934 Journal of Virological Methods
0166-137X Betoniek
0166-1426 Boogie Woogie and Blues Collector
0166-1922 R A I Actueel
0166-2031 Metamedicine *see* 0167-9902

ISSN INDEX 1473

0166-218X Discrete Applied Mathematics
0166-2481 Developments in Psychiatry
0166-2694 Documentatieblad: The Abstracts Journal of the African Studies Centre Leiden
0166-3097 Resources and Conservation
0166-3178 Molecular Physiology†
0166-3488 Clamavi
0166-3542 Antiviral Research
0166-3615 Computers in Industry
0166-3704 Kleine Aarde
0166-4298 Raakpunt
0166-4328 Behavioral Brain Research
0166-4360 In Search
0166-445X Aquatic Toxicology
0166-4786 Aarde en Kosmos/D J O
0166-4972 Technovation
0166-5162 International Journal of Coal Geology
0166-5316 Performance Evaluation
0166-5324 Journal of Pipelines
0166-5618 Diepzee
0166-5677 Van Horen Zeggen
0166-574X Demografie *see* 0169-1473
0166-5855 Pedagogisch Tijdschrift
0166-5960 Developments in Neurology
0166-6002 Verbum
0166-610X Penitentiaire Informatie
0166-6231 Criminology & Penology Abstracts
0166-6258 Pragmatics and Beyond
0166-6282 Police Science Abstracts
0166-6444 Buenteelt
0166-6584 Notulae Odonatologicae
0166-6622 Colloids and Surfaces
0166-6789 Registratie†
0166-6797 Bericht over Rassenkeuze *changed to* Rassenbericht
0166-6851 Molecular and Biochemical Parasitology
0166-6983 Structure Reports. Section A
0166-7033 Structure Reports. Section B
0166-7688 Analyse
0166-8595 Photosynthesis Research
0166-8641 Topology and Its Applications
0166-9087 Netherlands. Centraal Bureau voor de Statistiek. Conjunctuurtest
0166-9222 Beleidsanalyse
0166-9281 Netherlands. Centraal Bureau voor de Statistiek. Maandstatistiek van de Binnenlandse Handel en Dienstverlening
0166-932X Berichten aan Zeevarenden
0166-9435 Netherlands. Centraal Bureau voor de Statistiek. Maandstatistiek Politie, Justitie en Brandweer
0166-9680 Netherlands. Centraal Bureau voor de Statistiek. Statistisch Bulletin
0166-9834 Applied Catalysis
0166-9966 Bibliografie van Nederlandse Proefschriften
0167-0115 Regulatory Peptides
0167-093X Linksaf
0167-1200 Concilium
0167-1340 Databus
0167-1618 Oncodevelopmental Biology and Medicine *see* 0289-5447
0167-1731 Fertilizer Research
0167-174X I F O R Report *changed to* Reconciliation International
0167-1839 French-Language Psychology†
0167-188X Engineering Costs and Production Economics
0167-1936 Material Flow
0167-1987 Soil and Tillage Research
0167-2088 Tijdschrift voor de Geschiedenis der Geneeskunde, Natuurwetenschappen, Wiskunde en Techniek
0167-2185 Deutsche Buecher
0167-2231 Carnegie-Rochester Conference Series on Public Policy
0167-224X Speleo Nederland
0167-2533 Human Systems Management
0167-2681 Journal of Economic Behavior & Organization
0167-2738 Solid State Ionics
0167-2746 Chemisch Magazine
0167-2878 Dutch Birding
0167-3157 Pharmacy International
0167-319X Sponsorbulletin
0167-3696 Ins and Outs
0167-3890 Durability of Building Materials
0167-3998 Nederlandsche Bank N.V. Annual Report
0167-4048 Computers & Security
0167-4110 Natural Resources Forum Library†
0167-420X Large Scale Systems: Theory and Applications
0167-4366 Agroforestry Systems
0167-4412 Plant Molecular Biology
0167-4544 Journal of Business Ethics
0167-4730 Structural Safety
0167-4749 Paedo Alert News Magazine
0167-4757 Selected Annotated Bibliography of Population Studies in the Netherlands
0167-4765 Boekblad
0167-4773 T T T Interdisciplinair Tijdschrift voor Taal- en Tekstwetenschap
0167-479X Spartacus Magazine *changed to* Spartacus Travel Magazine
0167-482X Journal of Psychosomatic Obstetrics and Gynaecology
0167-4870 Journal of Economic Psychology
0167-4919 Immunology Today
0167-4994 Caert-Thresoor
0167-5036 Japan Annual Reviews in Electronics, Computers & Telecommunications. Amorphous Semiconductor Technologies & Devices
0167-5087 Nuclear Instruments and Methods in Physics Research *see* 0168-9002
0167-5133 Journal of Semantics
0167-5249 Law and Philosophy
0167-5265 Information Services & Use
0167-5273 International Journal of Cardiology
0167-5303 Buut
0167-5311 Spanish-Language Psychology†
0167-5419 Engineering Management International
0167-5427 Aquatic Mammals
0167-5516 Tijdschrift voor Theaterwetenschap
0167-5567 Handbook of Inflammation
0167-5583 Uranium
0167-5710 Office: Technology and People
0167-5729 Surface Science Reports
0167-577X Materials Letters
0167-580X Sociology of Leisure and Sport Abstracts
0167-5826 Energy in Agriculture
0167-5850 Justitiele Verkenningen
0167-5877 Preventive Veterinary Medicine
0167-594X Journal of Neuro-Oncology
0167-5966 Zien Magazine
0167-6059 Behavior Research of Severe Developmental Disabilities†
0167-6105 Journal of Wind Engineering and Industrial Aerodynamics
0167-6164 Journal of African Languages and Linguistics
0167-6172 Plan and Action
0167-6245 Information Economics and Policy
0167-6296 Journal of Health Economics
0167-6318 Linguistic Review
0167-6369 Environmental Monitoring and Assessment
0167-6377 Operations Research Letters
0167-6393 Speech Communication
0167-6423 Science of Computer Programming
0167-644X Reclamation and Revegetation Research
0167-6636 Mechanics of Materials
0167-6644 Netherlands. Ministerie van Onderwijs en Wetenschappen. Onderwijsliteratuur
0167-6679 Studies in Classical Antiquity
0167-6687 Insurance: Mathematics & Economics
0167-6695 Isotope Geoscience
0167-6784 Ophthalmic Paediatrics and Genetics
0167-6806 Breast Cancer Research and Treatment
0167-6830 Orbit
0167-6857 Plant Cell, Tissue and Organ Culture
0167-6865 International Journal of Microcirculation: Clinical & Experimental
0167-6903 Plant Growth Regulation
0167-6911 Systems and Control Letters
0167-6962 Transnational Data Report
0167-6989 Reactive Polymers, Ion Exchangers, Sorbents
0167-6997 Investigational New Drugs
0167-7012 Journal of Microbiological Methods
0167-7055 Computer Graphics Forum
0167-7063 Journal of Neurogenetics
0167-7136 Computer Compacts
0167-7152 Statistics & Probability Letters
0167-7187 International Journal of Industrial Organization
0167-7322 Journal of Molecular Liquids
0167-739X Future Generations Computer Systems
0167-7411 Topoi
0167-7659 Cancer Metastasis Reviews *changed to* Cancer and Metastasis Reviews
0167-7764 Journal of Atmospheric Chemistry
0167-7861 Journal of Inclusion Phenomena
0167-7888 T R W Series of Software Technology
0167-8019 Acta Applicandae Mathematicae
0167-8043 Annals of Global Analysis and Geometry
0167-8051 Computers and Standards *see* 0920-5489
0167-806X Natural Language and Linguistic Theory
0167-8094 Order
0167-8116 International Journal of Research in Marketing
0167-8140 Radiotherapy & Oncology
0167-8191 Parallel Computing
0167-8299 Reviews in Chemical Engineering
0167-8329 Education for Information
0167-8396 Computer-Aided Geometric Design
0167-8442 Theoretical and Applied Fracture Mechanics
0167-8493 Robotics
0167-8507 Multilingua
0167-8558 Insurance Abstracts and Reviews†
0167-8590 Kema Scientific & Technical Reports
0167-8655 Pattern Recognition Letters
0167-871X Effective Health Care
0167-8760 International Journal of Psychophysiology
0167-899X Nuclear Engineering and Design
0167-9031 Mining Science and Technology
0167-9104 Perspektief
0167-9236 Decision Support Systems
0167-9260 Integration
0167-9287 Education & Computing
0167-9295 Earth, Moon and Planets
0167-9317 Microelectronic Engineering
0167-9368 Space Communication and Broadcasting
0167-9473 Computational Statistics and Data Analysis
0167-9554 Dia Regno
0167-9708 Eindhoven University of Technology. Research Reports
0167-9848 Husserl Studies
0167-9856 European Environmental Science Synopses. Part A: Water Pollution†
0167-9899 International Journal of Cardiac Imaging
0167-9902 Theoretical Medicine
0167-9945 International Journal of Clinical Monitoring and Computing
0168-0072 Annals of Pure and Applied Logic
0168-0102 Neuroscience Research
0168-1168 Pluimvee Documentatie
0168-1605 International Journal of Food Microbiology
0168-1656 Journal of Biotechnology
0168-1699 Computers and Electronics in Agriculture
0168-1702 Virus Research
0168-1850 Leidraad
0168-1923 Agricultural and Forest Meteorology
0168-2563 Biogeochemistry
0168-2857 Maandblad Aktiviteitensektor
0168-2997 Andon
0168-3330 Netherlands. Centraal Bureau voor de Statistiek. Statistiek van de Spaargelden. Statistics of Savings
0168-3381 Netherlands. Centraal Bureau voor de Statistiek. Beleggingen van Institutionele Beleggers. Investments of Institutional Investors *changed to* Netherlands. Centraal Bureau voor de Statistiek. Institutionele Beleggers. Institutional Investors
0168-3411 Netherlands. Centraal Bureau voor de Statistiek. Vakantieonderzoek
0168-3462 Netherlands. Centraal Bureau voor de Statistiek. Statistiek van de Openbare Bibliotheken
0168-3489 Netherlands. Centraal Bureau voor de Statistiek. Nationale Rekeningen. National Accounts
0168-3519 Netherlands. Centraal Bureau voor de Statistiek. Muziek en Theater
0168-3659 Journal of Controlled Release
0168-3667 Netherlands. Centraal Bureau voor de Statistiek. Statistiek Werkzame Personen
0168-3705 Netherlands. Centraal Bureau voor de Statistiek. Statistisch Zakboek. Pocket Yearbook
0168-373X Statistiek der Rijksfinancien
0168-3748 Allicht
0168-3853 Population of the Municipalities of the Netherlands
0168-3888 Netherlands. Centraal Bureau voor de Statistiek. Vermogensverdeling. Regionale Gegevens. Distribution of Personal Wealth. Regional Data
0168-3918 Netherlands. Centraal Bureau voor de Statistiek. Statistiek van de Land- en Tuinbouw. Statistics of Agriculture
0168-4000 Netherlands. Centraal Bureau voor de Statistiek. Jaarstatistiek van de Bevolking. Population Statistics
0168-4035 Statistiek der Vakbeweging in Nederland
0168-4086 Netherlands. Centraal Bureau voor de Statistiek. Statistiek van de Algemene Bijstand. Statistics of Public Assistance
0168-4094 Netherlands. Centraal Bureau voor de Statistiek. Naamlijsten voor de Statistiek van de Buitenlandse Handel. Supplement. List of Goods for the Statistics of Foreign Trade. Supplement
0168-4108 Netherlands. Centraal Bureau voor de Statistiek. Diagnosestatistiek Bedrijfsverenigingen (Omslagleden). Social Insurance Sickness Statistics
0168-4167 Netherlands. Centraal Bureau voor de Statistiek. Statistiek van de Visserij. Statistics of Fisheries
0168-423X Netherlands. Centraal Bureau voor de Statistiek. Statistiek van de Voorlichting Bij Scholen en Beroepskeuze. Statistics of Vocational Guidance
0168-4248 Netherlands. Centraal Bureau voor de Statistiek. Statistiek van de Inkomsten en Uitgaven der Overheid voor Cultuur en Recreatie. Statistics of Government Expenditure on Culture and Recreation
0168-4280 Netherlands. Centraal Bureau voor de Statistiek. Criminele Statistiek. Criminal Statistics
0168-4361 Netherlands. Centraal Bureau voor de Statistiek. Produktiestatistieken: Papier- en Kartonindustrie
0168-4388 Netherlands. Centraal Bureau voor de Statistiek. Toepassing der Wegenverkeerswet. Statistics of the Application of the Road Traffic Act
0168-4590 Netherlands. Centraal Bureau voor de Statistiek. Hypotheken. Statistics of Mortgages
0168-468X Speur- en Ontwikkelingswerk in Nederland
0168-4809 Nederlandse Jeugd en Haar Onderwijs
0168-4825 Netherlands. Centraal Bureau voor de Statistiek. Statistiek van Aan-, Af- en Doorvoer. Goederenvervoer per Goederensoort van en naar de Zeehavens van Rotterdam en Amsterdam
0168-485X Netherlands. Centraal Bureau voor de Statistiek. Voortgezet Onderwijs Regionaal Bezien

1474 ISSN INDEX

0168-4876 Netherlands. Centraal Bureau voor de Statistiek. Statistiek van de Aan-, Af- en Doorvoer. Goederenvervoer van en naar Nederland. Statistics of the International Goods Traffic
0168-4884 Netherlands. Centraal Bureau voor de Statistiek. Statistiek der Verkiezingen. Gemeenteraden. Election Statistics. Municipal Councils
0168-4906 Netherlands. Centraal Bureau voor de Statistiek. Statistiek van het Erkende Schriftelijk Onderwijs. Statistics on Correspondence Courses
0168-4973 Netherlands. Centraal Bureau voor de Statistiek. Statistiek der Motorvoertuigen. Statistics of Motor Vehicles
0168-5023 Netherlands. Centraal Bureau voor de Statistiek. Statistiek van de Verkeersongevallen op de Openbare Weg. Statistics of Road-Traffic Accidents
0168-5058 Netherlands. Centraal Bureau voor de Statistiek. Statistiek van Het Wetenschappelijk Onderwijs. Statistics of University Education
0168-5074 Netherlands. Centraal Bureau voor de Statistiek. Statistiek van het Personenvervoer. Statistics of Passenger Transport
0168-518X Netherlands. Centraal Bureau voor de Statistiek. Productie Statistiek van de Zuivelindustrie/Production Statistics of the Dairy Industry
0168-5236 Netherlands. Centraal Bureau voor de Statistiek. Nederlandse Energiehuishouding
0168-5244 Netherlands. Centraal Bureau voor de Statistiek. Per Leerling Beschikbaar Gestelde Bedragen voor het Lager Onderwijs. Amounts per Pupil Provided for Primary Education
0168-5287 Netherlands. Centraal Bureau voor de Statistiek. Produktiestatistieken: Suikerfabrieken
0168-5325 Netherlands. Centraal Bureau voor de Statistiek van het Binnenlands Goederenvervoer. Statistics of Internal Goods Transport in the Netherlands
0168-5333 Netherlands. Centraal Bureau voor de Statistiek. Produktiestatistieken: Veevoederindustrie
0168-5376 Netherlands. Centraal Bureau voor de Statistiek. Statistiek van de Internationale Binnenvaart. Statistics of the International Inland Shipping
0168-5406 Netherlands. Centraal Bureau voor de Statistiek. Statistiek van het Beroepsonderwijs: Huishoud- en Nijverheidsonderwijs
0168-5422 Netherlands. Centraal Bureau voor de Statistiek. Statistiek van de Zeevaart. Statistics of Seaborne Shipping
0168-5457 Netherlands. Centraal Bureau voor de Statistiek. Statistiek van het Beroepsonderwijs: Technisch en Nautisch Onderwijs. Statistics on Vocational Training
0168-549X Netherlands. Centraal Bureau voor de Statistiek. Sociaal-Economische Maandstatistiek
0168-5503 Netherlands. Centraal Bureau voor de Statistiek. Statistiek van het Beroepsonderwijs: Kunstonderwijs. Art Colleges
0168-552X Netherlands. Centraal Bureau voor de Statistiek. Statistiek van de Luchtvaart. Civil Aviation Statistics
0168-5538 Netherlands. Centraal Bureau voor de Statistiek. Statistiek Vreemdelingenverkeer. Tourism Statistics
0168-5600 Netherlands. Centraal Bureau voor de Statistiek. Statistiek van het Beroepsonderwijs: Sociaal-Pedagogisch Onderwijs
0168-5686 Netherlands. Centraal Bureau voor de Statistiek. Statistiek der Verkiezingen. Tweede Kamer der Staten-Generaal. Election Statistics. Second Chamber of the States-General
0168-5708 Netherlands. Centraal Bureau voor de Statistiek. Statistiek van het Beroepsonderwijs: Beroepsbegeleidend Onderwijs Leerlingwezen
0168-5732 Netherlands. Centraal Bureau voor de Statistiek. Statistiek der Verkiezingen. Provinciale Staten. Election Statistics. Provincial Councils
0168-5767 Netherlands. Centraal Bureau voor de Statistiek. Produktiestatistieken: Alcoholfabrieken, Bierbrouwerijen en Mouterijen, Distilleerderijen en Frisdrankenindustrie
0168-583X Nuclear Instruments & Methods in Physics Research. Section B. Beam Interactions with Materials and Atoms
0168-5856 Netherlands. Centraal Bureau voor de Statistiek. Statistiek van het W V O, H A V O en M A V O: Instroom, Doorstroom en Uitstroom van Leerlingen
0168-5864 Netherlands. Centraal Bureau voor de Statistiek. Produktiestatistieken: Rijwiel- en Motorrijwielindustrie
0168-5988 Netherlands. Centraal Bureau voor de Statistiek. Bibliografie van Regionale Onderzoekingen Op Sociaalwetenschappelijk Terrein. Bibliography of Regional Studies in the Social Sciences
0168-6054 Annales de Readaptation et de Medecine Physique
0168-6151 Modern Quaternary Research in Southeast Asia
0168-6208 Paleoecology of Africa
0168-6259 Indo-Malayan Zoology
0168-6291 Irrigation and Drainage Systems
0168-6577 European Journal of Population Demography
0168-6674 Delft Hydroscience Abstracts
0168-7166 Export Magazine
0168-7336 Reactivity of Solids
0168-7433 Journal of Automated Reasoning
0168-7565 Veeteelt
0168-7697 New in Chess Yearbook
0168-7778 Journal of Management Consulting
0168-7840 Elektronica
0168-7905 Netherlands. Centraal Bureau voor de Statistiek. Statistiek van de Uitgaven der Overheid voor Onderwijs. Statistics of the Expenditure of the State, the Provinces and the Municipalities on Education
0168-7956 Netherlands. Centraal Bureau voor de Statistiek. Statistiek van de Investeringen in Vaste Activa in de Nijverheid. Statistics on Fixed Capital Formation in Industry
0168-8162 Experimental & Applied Acarology
0168-8227 Diabetes Research and Clinical Practice
0168-8278 Journal of Hepatology
0168-8472 Nederlandse Vereniging voor Klinische Chemie. Tijdschrift
0168-8626 Tijdschrift voor Agologie
0168-874X Finite Elements in Analysis and Design
0168-8782 New in Chess Magazine
0168-9002 Nuclear Instruments & Methods in Physics Research. Section A. Accelerators, Spectrometers, Detectors, and Associated Equipment
0168-9444 Harvard Holland Review
0168-9452 Plant Science
0168-9479 Trends in Genetics
0168-9673 Acta Mathematicae Applicatae Sinica
0168-9770 Forschungsberichte zur D D R-Literatur
0168-9843 Instituut voor Rassenonderzoek van Landbouwgewassen. Jaarverslag *changed to* Rijksinstituut voor het Rassenonderzoek van Cultuurgewassen. Jaarverslag
0168-9959 Tijdschrift voor Theologie
0169-0124 Studies in Slavic and General Linguistics
0169-0175 Studies in Slavic Literature and Poetics
0169-0221 Amsterdamer Publikationen zur Sprache und Literatur
0169-023X Data & Knowledge Engineering
0169-0272 Amsterdam Studies in Theology
0169-0337 H I V O S - Projectbericht
0169-037X Indices Zum Altdeutschen Schrifttum
0169-0426 Quellen und Forschungen zur Erbauungsliteratur des Spaeten Mittelalters und der Fruehen Neuzeit†
0169-0477 Beschreibende Bibliographien
0169-1007 Agrarisch Onderwijs *changed to* Netherlands. Centraal Bureau voor de Statistiek. Statistiek van het Hoger Beroepsonderwijs: Agrarisch Onderwijs
0169-1112 Pain Clinic
0169-1317 Applied Clay Science
0169-1422 Population and Family in the Low Countries
0169-1473 Demos
0169-2070 International Journal of Forecasting
0169-2313 Netherlands Fertilizer Technical Bulletin
0169-2607 Computer Methods & Programs in Biomedicine
0169-2763 Infomediary
0169-2801 Groniek
0169-281X Leidinggeven & Organiseren
0169-2895 Soviet Journal of Numerical Analysis and Mathematical Modelling
0169-328X Molecular Brain Research
0169-3298 Surveys in Geophysics
0169-3816 Journal of Cross-Cultural Gerontology
0169-3867 Biology and Philosophy
0169-3913 Transport in Porous Media
0169-4146 Journal of Industrial Microbiology
0169-4332 Applied Surface Science
0169-4839 Nederlandse Geografische Studies
0169-4901 Agricultural Science in the Netherlands
0169-5126 Kerngetallen/Testbeeloen
0169-5150 Agricultural Economics
0169-5401 De Spaarbank
0169-5606 Visible Religion
0169-5614 Volkscultuur
0169-5983 Fluid Dynamics Research
0169-6009 Bone and Mineral
0169-6076 Trend Piccolo
0169-6165 Bochumer Anglistische Studien
0169-6289 C B S Newsletter
0169-6459 Molens
0169-6726 Nederlands Kunsthistorisch Jaarboek
0169-7269 Opstap
0169-7439 Chemometrics and Intelligent Laboratory Systems
0169-7471 Zelfbestuur
0169-7722 Journal of Contaminant Hydrology
0169-796X Contributions to Asian Studies *changed to* Journal of Developing Societies
0169-8141 International Journal of Ergonomics
0170-0189 Bacillaria†
0170-026X Zeitschrift fuer Arabische Linguistik
0170-0413 Zeitschrift fuer Deutsches und Internationales Baurecht
0170-0456 Die Chemische Produktion
0170-0499 Fleisch-Lebensmittel-Markt
0170-0510 Welt der Modell- und Eisenbahn
0170-0553 Bioscience Journal†
0170-0561 Genetik.Grundlagen und Perspektiven†
0170-060X Praxis der Psychomotorik
0170-0618 Columbus
0170-0839 Polymer Bulletin
0170-0847 Oesterreichisches Jahrbuch fuer Politik
0170-0863 Biologica Didactica†
0170-0944 Sachunterricht und Mathematik in der Grundschule
0170-1320 Specimina Philologiae Slavicae
0170-1452 Jura
0170-1509 Deutsche Volleyball Zeitschrift
0170-1533 Freie Universitaet Berlin. Osteuropa-Institut. Balkanologische Veroeffentlichungen
0170-1541 Mathematica Didactica
0170-155X Technica Didactica *changed to* Didaktik-Arbeit, Technik, Wirtschaft
0170-1665 Berliner Kunstblatt
0170-1703 E T Z Archiv
0170-1711 Elektrotechnische Zeitschrift *changed to* E T Z Zeitschrift fuer Elektrische Energietechnik
0170-1754 Media Perspektiven
0170-1916 Bochumer Materialen zur Entwicklungsforschung und Entwicklungspolitik
0170-2025 Jahrbuch fuer Westdeutsche Landesgeschichte
0170-2033 Elektrische Energie Technik
0170-2041 Liebigs Annalen der Chemie
0170-219X Semiosis
0170-236X Germany (Federal Republic, 1949-) Bundesaufsichtsamt fuer das Versicherungswesen. Veroeffentlichen
0170-2408 Hiersemanns Bibliographische Handbuecher
0170-2416 Uebersee-Museum, Bremen. Veroeffentlichungen. Reihe E: Human-Oekologie
0170-2653 Ahnenlisten Kartei
0170-2793 Ersatzkassen-Report
0170-284X Deutsche Branchen-Fernsprechbuch
0170-2971 Spektrum der Wissenschaft
0170-3013 Modern German Studies
0170-303X Technique du Roulement
0170-3056 Tecnica de los Rodamientos
0170-3080 Deutsche Handelsakten des Mittelalters und der Neuzeit
0170-3099 Universitaet Frankfurt. Seminar fuer Voelkerkunde. Arbeiten
0170-3102 Bibliotheca Islamica
0170-3137 Beitraege zur Suedasienforschung
0170-3153 Deutsche Sprache in Europa und Uebersee
0170-3188 Erdwissenschaftliche Forschung
0170-3196 Aethiopistische Forschungen
0170-3218 Beitraege zur Aegyptischen Bauforschung und Altertumskunde
0170-3226 Frankfurter Historische Abhandlungen
0170-3242 Alt- und Neu-Indische Studien
0170-3250 Geoecological Research
0170-3285 Freiburger Islamstudien
0170-3293 Frankfurter Historische Vortraege
0170-3307 Freiburger Altorientalische Studien
0170-3315 Beitraege zur Literatur des 15.-18. Jahrhunderts
0170-334X Materialfluss
0170-3447 Veroeffentlichungen zur Geschichte des Glases und der Glashuetter in Deutschland
0170-3455 Glasenapp-Stiftung
0170-3463 Industriegewerkschaft Druck und Papier. Schriftenreihe fuer Betriebsrate
0170-348X Uebersetzungen Auslaendischer Arbeiten zur Antiken Sklaverei
0170-3544 Studien zur Kulturkunde
0170-3560 Mainzer Studien zur Sprach- und Volksforschung
0170-3579 Wissenschaftliche Paperbacks
0170-3595 Quellen und Studien zur Geschichte des Oestlichen Europa
0170-3617 I F O Spiegel der Wirtschaft
0170-3633 Verschollene und Vergessene
0170-365X Institut fuer Europaeische Geschichte, Mainz. Veroeffentlichungen. Abteilung Universalgeschichte. Beihefte
0170-3668 Muenchener Ostasiatische Studien
0170-3676 Muenchener Ostasiatische Studien. Sonderreihe
0170-3684 Studien zur Ostasiatischen Schriftkunst
0170-3692 Universitaet zu Koeln. Kunsthistorisches Institut. Abteilung Asien. Publikationen
0170-3706 Sinologica Coloniensia
0170-3730 Hermannstrase 14†
0170-3846 Lutherische Theologie und Kirche
0170-4044 Oberflaeche und J O T
0170-4214 Mathematical Methods in the Applied Sciences
0170-4249 Esoterik und Wissenschaft
0170-4478 Betriebswirtschaftlicher Informationsdienst†

ISSN INDEX 1475

0170-4621 L O K Report Reisefuehrer
0170-4761 Kritik†
0170-4818 Englera
0170-5091 Basler Afrika Bibliographien. Mitteilungen
0170-5105 Buchhandelsgeschichte. Zweite Folge
0170-5253 Roll on Roll off in Europe
0170-5261 Zeitschrift fuer Vegetationstechnik
0170-5288 Eisenbahn-Kurier
0170-5334 Anaesthesiologie und Intensivmedizin
0170-5598 Arbeitsgemeinschaft der Parlaments-und Behoerdenbibliotheken. Mitteilungen
0170-5652 Studien zur Verkehrswirtschaft
0170-5660 Studien zur Industriewirtschaft
0170-5679 Ciret Studien
0170-5687 Studien zur Bauwirtschaft
0170-5695 I F O Institut fuer Wirtschaftsforschung. Studien zu Handels- und Dienstleistungsfragen
0170-5725 Ur und Fruehzeit
0170-5768 Schrifttums fuer den Bereich Haushalt und Verbauch. Bibliographie
0170-5792 Motorik
0170-5822 Hoppenstedt Kurstabellen - Kursanalysen
0170-5946 Sprache und Geschichte in Afrika
0170-6012 Informatik-Spektrum
0170-608X Daten und Dokumente Zum Umweltschutz†
0170-6136 Weg und Wahrheit
0170-6225 Kunst und Unterricht
0170-6233 Berichte zur Wissenschaftsgeschichte
0170-6241 Zeitschrift fuer Semiotik
0170-625X Kindheit
0170-6632 Chip
0170-6659 Bankfachklasse
0170-6802 An Rems und Murr
0170-6845 Steuer-Training
0170-6977 Wissenschaft und Umwelt
0170-6993 Instandhaltung
0170-7213 Who's Who at the Frankfurt Book Fair
0170-723X Marktforschung
0170-7302 Katholisches Leben und Kirchenreform im Zeitalter der Glaubensspaltung
0170-7337 Jahrbuch zur Frage der Suchtgefahren
0170-7353 Wer und Was in der Deutschen Fleisch- Fisch- und Feinkost-Industrie
0170-7434 Physics Briefs/Physikalische Berichte
0170-7558 Quickborn
0170-7663 I F O Digest
0170-7671 Agrarsoziale Gesellschaft. Kleine Reihe
0170-7779 Studien zur Energiewirtschaft
0170-7787 South Asian Digest of Regional Writing
0170-7809 Z M P Bilanz Getreide-Futtermittel
0170-7922 Schulleiter Handbuch
0170-8007 Balkan-Archiv Neue Folge
0170-8090 Landschaftsverband Westfalen-Lippe *changed to* Volkskuendlichen Kommission fuer Westfalen. Schriften
0170-8287 E E G Labor
0170-8309 Technische Universitaet Berlin. Institut fuer Sozialoekonomie der Agrarentwicklung. Annual Report (Abridged Version)
0170-8376 Technische Universitaet Berlin. Institut fuer Sozialoekonomie der Agrarentwicklung. Jahresbericht
0170-8406 Organization Studies
0170-8643 Lecture Notes in Control and Information Sciences
0170-866X W & M
0170-8791 N Z: Neue Zeitschrift fuer Musik
0170-8864 Monographien zur Indischen Archaeologie, Kunst und Philologie
0170-8929 Muenchener Zeitschrift fuer Balkankunde
0170-8988 Archiv fuer das Post - und Fernmeldewesen
0170-902X Das Band
0170-9135 Mainzer Studien zur Amerikanistik
0170-9291 European Patent Office. Annual Report
0170-9364 Die Alte Stadt
0170-9496 Siemens Energietechnik *changed to* Siemens Energie und Automation
0170-950X Siemens Power Engineering *changed to* Siemens Energy and Automation
0170-9526 V D I Informationsdienst. Blechbearbeitung
0170-9550 V D I Informationsdienst. Kaltmassivumformung
0170-9569 V D I Informationsdienst. Elektrisch Abtragende Fertigungsverfahren
0170-9615 B M F T Journal
0170-9690 V G A Nachrichten
0170-9739 Zeitschrift fuer Physik. Section C: Particles and Fields
0170-9771 Consulting
0170-9828 Allgemeine Fleischer Zeitung
0170-9925 Archives of Gynecology
0170-9933 Metal Statistics (Years)
0171-0079 Atalanta
0171-0087 Basler Afrika Bibliographien. Nachrichten
0171-0125 Bibliographien zur Romanistik
0171-0826 Lexikon des Steuer- und Wirtschaftsrechts
0171-0834 Kodikas
0171-1091 Urologic Radiology
0171-1555 B B A Planen und Bauen
0171-1660 Beitraege zur Afrikakunde
0171-1687 Geomethodica
0171-1741 European Journal of Applied Microbiology and Biotechnology *see* 0175-7598
0171-1814 Anaesthesiologie und Intensivmedizin
0171-1873 Springer Series in Solid State Sciences
0171-1970 Briefmarkenwelt
0171-2004 Handbook of Experimental Pharmacology
0171-2063 Humboldtiana *changed to* Bibliographia Humboldtiana
0171-2160 Topics in Infectious Diseases
0171-2268 Uni Hannover
0171-290X Portugiesische Forschungen der Goerresgesellschaft. Reihe 3: Vieira-Texte und Vieira-Studien
0171-2985 Zeitschrift fuer Immunitaetsforschung. Immunobiology
0171-3183 Perspektiven
0171-3191 Kernforschungszentrum Karlsruhe. Ergebnisbericht ueber Forschung und Entwicklung
0171-3302 Berliner Wissenschaftlicher Gesellschaft. Jahrbuch
0171-3434 Psychosozial
0171-3469 Reformationsgeschichtliche Studien und Texte
0171-3604 Prisma
0171-3647 V D I Informationsdienst. Schmieden und Pressen
0171-3655 Projektbereich Auslaendische Arbeiter. Materialien†
0171-3698 Marxistische Studien
0171-3736 Provinzialinstitut fuer Westfaelische Landes- und Volkforschung. Veroeffentlichungen *changed to* Provinzialinstitut fuer Westfaelische Landes- und Volksforschung des Landschaftsverbandes Westfalen-Lippe. Veroeffentlichungen
0171-3876 Medikament & Meinung
0171-4090 Articulata
0171-4163 Test-Index
0171-4171 Lebendige Katechese
0171-4341 Wer und Was in der Deutschen Koerperpflege-, Wasch- und Reinigungsmittel-Industrie
0171-4449 Wer und Was in der Deutschen Pharmazeutischen-Industrie
0171-4457 Wer und Was in der Deutschen Getraenke-Industrie
0171-4511 M P T - Metallurgical Plant and Technology
0171-4538 Sozialpsychiatrische Informationen
0171-4996 Italienisch
0171-5038 W E M A Bezugsquellenverzeichnis
0171-5046 V K G Jahrbuch
0171-5062 Fertigung und Betrieb
0171-5216 Journal of Cancer Research and Clinical Oncology
0171-5410 Arbeiten aus Anglistik und Amerikanistik
0171-5445 Bauphysik
0171-5747 Atomkernenergie/Kerntechnik
0171-5860 Analyse & Kritik
0171-6026 Homosexuelle Emanzipation
0171-6042 Made in Europe. Furniture and Interiors
0171-6204 Erneuerung in Kirche und Gesellschaft
0171-6425 Thoracic and Cardiovascular Surgeon
0171-645X Beitraege zur Hochschulforschung
0171-6468 Operations Research - Spektrum
0171-6530 Aurora-Buchreihe
0171-6794 Studies in Descriptive Linguistics
0171-6913 Information
0171-709X Polymers-Properties and Applications
0171-712X Recht der Elektrizitaetswirtschaft
0171-7243 Amusement-Industrie
0171-7383 Angler Rinderzucht
0171-7456 I F O A M
0171-7634 Extracta Otorhinolaryngologica
0171-791X Praxis der Psychotherapie und Psychosomatik
0171-7936 Offenbacher Verein fuer Naturkunde. Abhandlungen
0171-7952 Bauen fuer die Landwirtschaft
0171-7995 Ballett Info *see* 0722-6268
0171-8096 Technisches Messen - T M
0171-8177 Entomologia Generalis
0171-838X B T E Marketing-Berater
0171-8495 B L L V Bayerische Schule
0171-8630 Marine Ecology-Progress Series
0171-8649 Geographie und Schule
0171-8819 Arbeit und Soziales
0171-8932 Zeitschriften-Datenbank
0171-9262 Wirtschaftsschutz *changed to* Wirtschaftsschutz und Sicherheitstechnik
0171-9289 Freibeuter
0171-9327 Sozial Paediatrie
0171-9335 European Journal of Cell Biology
0171-9378 Studien zu Nichteuropaeischen Rechtstheorien
0171-9386 Junges Forum
0171-9599 Contactologia
0171-9629 Sonderschulmagazin
0171-967X Calcified Tissue International
0171-9718 Behindertenhilfe Durch Erziehung, Unterricht und Therapie
0171-9750 Archives of Toxicology. Supplement
0172-0015 Photorin
0172-0171 Bildung und Wissenschaft.
0172-0457 Literarisches Arbeitsjournal
0172-0473 Blumen
0172-049X Wettbewerb in Recht und Praxis
0172-0554 Blickpunkt D B
0172-0570 Agrarmeteorologischer Wochenhinweis fuer das Gebiet Bundesrepublik Deutschland
0172-0589 Brauerei Journal
0172-0643 Pediatric Cardiology
0172-0686 Steuern in der Elektrizitaetswirtschaft
0172-0929 Priesterjahrheft
0172-1232 Current Diagnostic Pediatrics
0172-1518 Forschung
0172-1526 German Research
0172-1623 Wechselwirkung
0172-1631 Natur und Recht
0172-1895 Buergerrechte und Polizei
0172-200X Bau & Heimwerker Markt
0172-2115 Materialen zur Kunst des Neunzehnten Jahrhunderts
0172-2131 Akademie fuer Oeffentliches Gesundheitswesen. Schriftenreihe
0172-2182 Made in Europe Buyers' Guide
0172-2190 World Patent Information
0172-2255 Der Chorsaenger
0172-2476 Handballtraining
0172-2514 Wuerttembergische Bau-Berufsgenossenschaft. Mitteilungen
0172-2530 Vorteilhafte Geldanlagen
0172-2611 Process Automation-P A†
0172-2751 Arbeitsmarkt in Hessen
0172-2859 Exlibriskunst und Graphik. Jahrbuch
0172-2867 D L W Nachrichten
0172-2875 Zeitschrift fuer Berufs- und Wirtschaftspaedagogik
0172-3146 Internationale Aufgaben der D G D
0172-3227 Diplomatic Observer
0172-3510 Bielefelder Beitraege zur Sprachlehrforschung
0172-3790 Hygiene & Medizin
0172-3960 Bibliographie Linguistischer Literatur
0172-4207 Advanced Series in Agricultural Sciences
0172-4568 Applications of Mathematics
0172-4606 Aktuelle Endokrinologie und Stoffwechsel
0172-4614 Ultraschall in der Medizin
0172-4622 International Journal of Sports Medicine
0172-4665 Cell Biology Monographs
0172-4770 Beitraege Zum Auslaendischen Oeffentlichen Recht und Voelkerrecht
0172-4827 Comprehensive Manuals of Surgical Specialities
0172-4843 Comprehensive Manuals in Radiology
0172-5076 Crystals: Growth, Properties and Applications
0172-5203 Fachberichte Messen - Steuern - Regeln
0172-5238 Fachschwester - Fachpfleger
0172-5300 Vox Latina
0172-5505 Musiktherapeutische Umschau
0172-5564 Zentralblatt fuer Bakteriologie, Mikrobiologie und Hygiene *see* 0723-2020
0172-570X Studies in the History of Mathematics and Physical Sciences
0172-5726 Springer Series in Computational Physics
0172-5734 Springer Series in Electrophysics
0172-5742 Studies of Brain Function
0172-5939 Universitexts
0172-5963 Wirtschaftspolitische Studien
0172-5998 Texts and Monographs in Physics
0172-603X Texts and Monographs in Computer Science
0172-6056 Undergraduate Texts in Mathematics
0172-6099 Acta Medico Technica†
0172-6153 Elektronik Entwicklung
0172-6161 Springer Series on Environmental Management
0172-6188 Springer Series in Experimental Entomology
0172-620X Springer Series in Language and Communication
0172-6218 Springer Series in Chemical Physics
0172-6226 Springer Advanced Texts in Life Sciences
0172-6315 Sources in the History of Mathematics and Physical Sciences
0172-6323 Springer Advanced Texts in Chemistry
0172-6331 Springer Series in Microbiology
0172-6374 Kunststoffberater
0172-6390 Hepato-Gastroenterology
0172-6404 Historical Social Research
0172-6412 Rehabilitation und Praevention
0172-6625 Proceedings in Life Sciences
0172-6641 Perspectives in Mathematical Logic
0172-665X Schriftenreihe des Bayer. Landesamtes fuer Wasserwirtschaft
0172-7028 European Photography
0172-7117 Industriebedarf
0172-7249 Der Allgemeinarzt
0172-7311 Arbeitsgemeinschaft fuer Klinische Nephrologie. Mitteilungen
0172-732X O L B G Info
0172-7389 Springer Series in Synergetics
0172-7397 Springer Series in Statistics
0172-7400 Kreditpraxis
0172-7419 Anlagepraxis
0172-7478 Praxis in der Gemeinde
0172-7699 Human Genetics. Supplement
0172-7788 Lecture Notes in Medical Informatics
0172-780X Neuroendocrinology Letters†
0172-7966 Inorganic Chemistry Concepts
0172-8008 Ingenieurbauten
0172-8083 Current Genetics
0172-8113 Der Pathologe
0172-8172 Rheumatology International
0172-8237 Internationale Schulbuchforschung
0172-8261 Audiologisch Akustik
0172-8296 Educacion, Sociedad y Politica. Anuario†
0172-8512 Jahrbuch Ueberblicke Mathematik
0172-8539 Marineforum

0172-8563 Mannheimer Hefte fuer Schriftvergleichung
0172-8865 E W W
0172-9039 Experimental Brain Research. Supplementa
0172-9047 Lohn und Gehalt
0172-908X Magnesium Bulletin
0172-9160 Medica *changed to* Medica Report
0172-9179 Facies
0172-9209 Komparatistische Hefte
0172-9314 Cargoworld
0172-9624 Kongressbericht Bundesschulmusikwoche
0172-9683 Gitarre & Laute
0172-9721 Animation
0173-007X Diskurs†
0173-0274 Ingenieurwissenschaftliche Bibliothek
0173-0282 International Boehringer Mannheim. Symposia
0173-0290 Blickpunkt Strassenbahn
0173-0339 Religionspaedagogische Beitraege
0173-0614 Lernen in Deutschland
0173-0665 I D - Informationsdienst fuer die Personalabteilung
0173-0835 Electrophoresis
0173-0843 Dokumente zum Hochschulsport
0173-0851 A Q†
0173-0967 Beitraege zur Psychologie und Soziologie des Kranken Menschen
0173-0975 Studienreihe Paedagogische Psychologie
0173-1629 Extracta Gastroenterologica
0173-1637 Bibliographie zur Kunstgeschichtlichen Literatur in Ost- und Suedosteuropaeischen Zeitschriften
0173-1688 Fundheft fuer Arbeits- und Sozialrecht
0173-170X Disorders of Human Communication
0173-1718 Oesterreichische Zeitschrift fuer Oeffentliches Recht und Voelkerrecht. Supplement
0173-1726 Siemens Components
0173-1831 Bibliographien zur Philosophie
0173-184X Peripherie
0173-1890 Pharmazeutische Verfahrenstechnik Heute
0173-1904 Abhandlungen des Deutschen Palaestinavereins
0173-1955 Von Deutschland Nach Amerika
0173-2110 Das Schaufenster (Stuttgart)
0173-2153 Historisch Sozialwissenschaftliche Forschungen†
0173-2307 Arbeiten und Text zur Slavistik
0173-2323 G D S-Zeitung
0173-2358 Goettinger Orientforschungen. Reihe II: Studien zur Spaetantiken und Fruehchristlichen Kunst
0173-2412 Feuerverzinken†
0173-2471 Ruhr-Universitaet. Institut zur Geschichte der Arbeiterbewegung. Mitteilungsblatt
0173-2595 Z P A
0173-2803 Makromolekulare Chemie. Rapid Communications
0173-2986 Abstracts in German Anthropology
0173-3524 Werkstattschriften zur Sozialpsychiatrie
0173-363X U - das Technische Umweltmagazin *see* 0341-1206
0173-3842 Materialien aus der Bildungsforschung
0173-430X Dr. Med. Mabuse
0173-4415 W S T Knitting Technik *see* 0177-4875
0173-458X Suizidprophylaxe
0173-4784 Kirche im Sozialismus
0173-4911 Journal of Optical Communication
0173-4970 Film und Fernsehen in Forschung und Lehre
0173-5187 Forum Musikbibliothek
0173-5322 Journal fuer Mathematik-Didaktik
0173-539X Geschichte mit Pfiff
0173-5500 Seifen, Oele, Fette, Wachse
0173-5543 Fraenkischer Hauskalender und Caritaskalender
0173-5896 Statistical Software Newsletter
0173-6388 Bayerische Staatsbibliothek. New Contents Slavistics. Inhaltsverzeichnisse Slavistischer Zeitschriften - ISZ
0173-6507 Zahlentafeln der Physikalisch-Chemischen Untersuchungen des Rheinwassers
0173-6582 Brasilien Nachrichten
0173-6612 Industriekaufmann
0173-7058 Zeitschrift fuer das Gesamte Sachverstaendigenwesen
0173-7074 Berliner Naturschutzblaetter
0173-7260 Deutsches Gewaesserkundliches Jahrbuch. Rheingebiet Teil 2: Main
0173-7481 Naturwissenschaftlicher Verein in Hamburg. Verhandlungen
0173-749X Naturwissenschaftlicher Verein in Hamburg. Abhandlungen und Verhandlungen *changed to* Naturwissenschaftlicher Verein in Hamburg. Abhandlungen
0173-749X Naturwissenschaftlicher Verein in Hamburg. Abhandlungen und Verhandlungen *see* 0173-7481
0173-7597 Krankenhauspharmazie
0173-7600 Jahrbuch fuer Regionalwissenschaft
0173-783X Beitraege zur Tabakforschung International
0173-7872 Z S Magazin
0173-7937 Psychotherapie - Psychosomatik - Medizinische Psychologie
0173-8046 A I T
0173-8062 Zeitschrift fuer Logistik
0173-8585 Bausteine Kindergarten
0173-8593 International Journal of Biological Research in Pregnancy *changed to* Biological Research in Pregnancy and Perinatology
0173-8607 Piano-Jahrbuch
0173-8720 Umwelt und Energie
0173-9565 Marine Ecology
0173-9573 Geistige Behinderung
0173-9832 Bio-land
0173-9913 Ceramic Forum International
0173-9980 Bulk Solids Handling
0174-0156 Rechtspfleger - Studienhefte
0174-0202 Zeitschrift fuer Rechts-soziologie
0174-0431 Dresdner Bank. Economic Quarterly
0174-0601 Literatur aus der Bildungsforschung *changed to* Literaturinformationen aus der Bildungsforschung
0174-0652 Ural-Altaische Jahrbuecher. Neue Folge
0174-0830 Zeitschrift fuer Berufs und Wirtschaftspaedagogik. Beihefte
0174-1098 Zeitschrift fuer Laermbekaempfung
0174-1551 Cardiovascular and Interventional Radiology
0174-173X Collagen and Related Research
0174-1764 L F B Documentation. Report
0174-1837 Anaesthesie - Intensivtherapie - Notfallmedizin
0174-1985 Baubedarf Manager *changed to* Baubedarf Einkaufen, Beraten, Verkaufen
0174-2108 Informationsbrief Auslaenderrecht
0174-2132 Schreibheft
0174-2450 Colo-Proctology
0174-2477 Berliner Islamstudien
0174-2655 Blitz Magazin *changed to* Blitz-Terminal
0174-2795 Zentralinstitut fuer Versuchstierzucht. Jahresbericht
0174-2809 Deutscher Studienkreis
0174-3015 Zentralblatt fuer Bakteriologie, Parasitenkunde, Infektionskrankheiten und Hygiene. Series B: Krankenhaushygiene-Praeventive Medizin-Betriebshygiene
0174-3031 Zentralblatt fuer Bakteriologie, Parasitenkunde, Infektionskrankheiten und Hygiene. Series A; Medizinische Mikrobiologie und Parasitologie
0174-304X Neuropediatrics
0174-3058 Bauspar-Journal
0174-3082 Zeitschrift fuer Kinderchirurgie
0174-3120 W Z B - Mitteilungen
0174-3163 F L F
0174-3279 Airport Forum News
0174-3384 Braunschweiger Naturkundliche Schriften
0174-3465 Die Eule
0174-352X Kunstpreis-Jahrbuch
0174-3538 V T F-Post
0174-3597 Helgolaender Meeresuntersuchungen
0174-3805 English Translations of German Standards. Catalogue
0174-4704 Human Rights Law Journal
0174-4747 Analysis
0174-478X Gesetzblatt fuer Baden-Wuerttemberg
0174-4879 International Journal of Clinical Pharmacology, Therapy and Toxicology
0174-4895 Schmerz *changed to* Schmerz Pain Douleur
0174-5395 Betriebspruefung
0174-5522 E I
0174-559X Transportrecht
0174-5735 Magazin fuer Heimwerker
0174-5832 Stafette
0174-6170 Wirtschaft und Erziehung
0174-6200 Basistexte Personalwesen
0174-6227 Fussballtraining
0174-7207 Melos
0174-7215 Industrie-Ausruestungs-Magazin
0174-7312 K E M - European Design Engineering
0174-7371 Trace Elements in Medicine
0174-738X Verdauungs-Krankheiten
0174-8726 Alt-Offenbach
0175-0038 Neue Kunst in Europa *changed to* N I K E
0175-0143 Pilot und Flugzeug
0175-1344 Segelsport
0175-3053 Medizinische Kongresse
0175-3851 Intensivmedizin und Notfallmedizin
0175-4548 F & W - Fuehren und Wirtschaften im Krankenhaus
0175-4750 Micro
0175-4815 Deutsches Polizeiblatt
0175-5161 K A B
0175-5293 Dokumentation Deutsche Finanzrechtsprechung
0175-5811 Aerzte Zeitung
0175-5854 Behindertenzeitschrift
0175-6206 Lexicographica
0175-6486 Wissenschaft und Gegenwart. Geisteswissenschaftliche Reihe
0175-6508 Philosophische Abhandlungen
0175-6524 Lansky: Bibliotheksrechtliche Vorschriften
0175-6532 Max-Planck-Institute fuer Europaische Rechtsgeschichte. Veroeffentlichungen. JusCommune. Sonderhefte
0175-6575 F T B-Handel
0175-6796 Bibliotheken der Bundesrepublik Deutschland. Datierte Handschriften
0175-7024 Israel und Palaestina
0175-7571 European Biophysics Journal
0175-758X European Archives of Psychiatry and Neurological Sciences
0175-7598 Applied Microbiology and Biotechnology
0175-7601 Das Logbuch
0175-7784 Zeitschrift fuer Stomatologie
0175-825X Badminton - Report
0175-8292 Vitis - Viticulture and Enology Abstracts
0175-8314 Alles Ueber Wein
0175-8659 Journal of Applied Ichthyology
0175-9531 Das Auto-International-in Zahlen
0175-9698 Markt fuer Klassische Automobile und Motorraeder
0176-036X Uni Ulm Intern
0176-0599 Deutsche Tennis Zeitung
0176-0750 P D S
0176-0882 Tennis Aktuell
0176-0947 Sozialistische Praxis
0176-1625 Gummi, Asbest, Kunstoffe *changed to* Gummi, Fasern, Kunststoffe
0176-1633 Fernerkundung in Raumordung und Stadtebau
0176-1714 Social Choice and Welfare
0176-1900 Goldmann-Nachrichten
0176-2265 Particle Characterization
0176-2494 Bio Garten
0176-2680 European Journal of Political Economy
0176-2710 Ministranten Post
0176-3539 Maueranker
0176-3679 Pharmacopsychiatry
0176-3717 Arbeiten & Lernen
0176-3946 Soester Zeitschrift
0176-3997 Carolinea
0176-4225 Diachronica
0176-4268 Journal of Classification
0176-4276 Constructive Approximation
0176-4594 Spektrum Film
0176-490X Pferde Heute
0176-5035 Lecture Notes in Engineering
0176-5248 Presse-Portraets
0176-540X Exporama
0176-5493 Katholischer Arbeitskreis fuer Zeitgeschichtliche Fragen. Informationsdienst.
0176-604X Neue Politische Literatur. Beihefte.
0176-6058 Werkstoffe-Betriebsleitung Technik
0176-6449 Zentralblatt fuer Jugendrecht
0176-6511 Tibia
0176-7437 Handarbeiten und Hauswirtschaft
0176-781X Dokumentationsdienst Bibliothekswesen
0176-7836 Blind/Sehbehindert
0176-8220 Buchreport
0176-8522 Archaeologie in Deutschland
0176-8530 Atelier
0176-859X Ideen Archiv
0176-8654 Unix/Mail
0176-8700 Betrifft Sport
0176-8816 Besseres Leben
0176-9146 Familienpolitische Informationen
0176-9243 Heim und Anstalt
0176-9383 World UNIX & Co.
0176-943X Geschichte Betrifft Uns
0176-9448 Politik Betrifft Uns
0176-9707 Journalisten Jahrbuch
0177-0667 Engineering with Computers
0177-1116 Schiffsbetriebstechnik Flensburg
0177-1531 Du Darfst
0177-1612 Bonsai-Magazin
0177-1647 Bulletin of the Middle Eastern Culture
0177-1965 Zivildienst
0177-2074 Literatur im Historischen Prozess (Neue Folge)
0177-2392 Tropical Medicine and Parasitology
0177-3348 Fortschritte der Zahnaertzliche Implantologie *changed to* Zeitschrift fuer Zahnaerztliche Implantologie
0177-350X Musikpsychologie
0177-3542 Alpin-Magazin
0177-4247 Jugendbuchmagazin
0177-4476 Neuland Ansaetze zur Musik der Gegenwart†
0177-4557 Eurokunst Magazin Reisen *changed to* Eurokunst: Besser Reisen & Mehr Erleben
0177-4565 K E S
0177-462X Evangelium-Gospel
0177-4743 Turcologica
0177-4875 Knitting Technique
0177-5014 T A S P O - Magazin
0177-5251 W I K
0177-5855 Magazin fuer Technik und Unterricht
0177-5944 Concerto
0177-6355 Koelner Statistische Nachrichten
0177-6487 Wuerttembergische Blaetter fuer Kirchenmusik
0177-6657 I N P R E K O R R
0177-6738 Neue Gesellschaft/Frankfurter Hefte
0177-7173 Marktforschungsreport
0177-7351 Frankfurter Statistische Berichte
0177-7459 Konstruktion & Elektronik
0177-7491 Maerkte im Saarland
0177-7955 Neuro-Orthopedics
0177-7963 Few-Body Systems. Acta Physica Austriaca. New Series
0177-7971 Meteorology and Atmospheric Physics
0177-8285 Bulldok Bauschaeden
0177-8358 Arbeitsgemeinschaft Katholisch-Theologischer Bibliotheken. Mitteilungsblatt
0177-8390 Live
0177-8706 Evangelikale Missiologie
0177-9303 Entscheiden zum Wirtschaftsrecht-Ewir
0177-9540 Contrapunct†
0177-9656 Steuer-Seminar

ISSN INDEX 1477

0177-9664 Steuer-Lexikon Teil II
0177-9761 V K G - Nachrichten
0177-9788 Wettbewerbe
0178-0026 Robotersysteme
0178-0530 Personal und Vorlesungsverzeichnis der Universitaet zu Wuerzburg
0178-1448 Betriebsecho†
0178-1723 Beitraege zur Phonetik und Linguistik
0178-1928 Meerestechnik *changed to* Meerestechnik
0178-1944 Praxis Sonderschule
0178-2010 R F L - Runsdschau Fleischhyiene und Lebensmittelueberwachung
0178-2223 Interbrick
0178-269X Cq Dl
0178-2762 Biology and Fertility of Soils
0178-2789 Visual Computer
0178-2983 Handball Magazin
0178-4218 Museen der Stadt Koeln. Bulletin
0178-4226 Niedersaechsischer Staedtetag
0178-4536 Hoergeraete-Akustiker
0178-4757 Johannes gutenberg-Universitaet Mainz. Forschungsmagazin
0178-5028 Quick Sport *changed to* Sportshop Hotline
0178-5109 Grauer Panther
0178-515X Bioprocess Engineering
0178-6768 Wissenschaften in der D.D.R.
0178-7128 Aufklaerung
0178-7276 Deutsche Zeitschrift fuer Biologische Zahn-Medizin
0178-7578 Kurzberichte aus der Bauforschung
0178-7586 Hard and Soft
0178-7667 Forum der Psychoanalyse
0178-7675 Computational Mechanics
0178-7683 Zeitschrift fuer Physik. Section D: Atoms, Molecules and Clusters
0178-8051 Probability Theory and Related Fields
0178-837X Der Staudengarten
0178-9287 International Listening Guide
0178-9945 Swingtrend
0178-9953 Der Punkt
0179-0374 Applied Agricultural Research
0179-0404 Medizin Heute
0179-0463 Informatik und Recht
0179-051X Dysphagia
0179-0811 V D I/V D E Dokumentation Regelungstechnik *changed to* V D I. Informationsdienst Regelungstechnik
0179-1133 Praxis Computer
0179-1419 Berg (Year)
0179-1591 Schloss & Beschlag & Markt
0179-1613 Ethology
0179-1621 Mediterranean Language and Culture Monograph Series
0179-1796 Fertilitaet, Sterilitaet, In-Vitro Fertilisation, Sexualitaet, Kontrazeption
0179-1869 Hoeruebersicht International
0179-1958 International Journal of Colorectal Disease
0179-3063 That's Yugoslavia
0179-3187 Erdoel - Erdgas - Kohle
0179-3551 Glaube und Lernen
0179-499X Materialwirtschaft im Unternehmen
0179-5376 Discrete and Computational Geometry
0179-5988 Druck
0179-647X Art Aurea
0179-6755 Universitaet Goettingen. Veroeffentlichungen des Seminars fuer Indologie
0179-6844 Textcontext
0179-714X Deutsche Zeitschrift fuer Biologische Veterinaer-Medizin
0179-7158 Strahlentherapie und Onkologie
0179-7166 Cardiologische-Angiologisches Bulletin
0179-7360 Prima Vita
0179-7409 Natur - Umwelt und Medizin
0179-7581 Hufeland-Journal
0179-7603 Agrarsoziale Gesellschaft. Laendlicher Raum Rundbriefe
0179-7743 Binnenschiffahrts-Nachrichten
0179-8669 Theoretical Surgery
0179-9541 Plant Breeding
0180-0817 Urgence
0180-2410 Federation Nationale des Foyers Ruraux de France. Bulletin d'Information
0180-3344 Palais de la Decouverte. Revue
0180-3905 Demeures et Chateaux en France *see* 0291-1191
0180-4103 Notes Bibliographiques Caraibes
0180-5738 Chirurgie Pediatrique
0180-7307 Revue d'Economie Regionale et Urbaine
0180-7897 Europ
0180-8214 Commentaire
0180-8567 Amitie Charles Peguy. Bulletin d'Informations et de Recherches
0180-9210 Bulletin de Mineralogie
0180-9237 Plastiques Flash
0180-9261 Cahiers du Memontois
0180-9296 Bulletin Signaletique. Part 527: Histoire et Sciences des Religions
0180-9350 Andre Gide
0180-9385 Arthur Rimbaud
0180-9555 Documents Pedozoologiques
0180-961X Parc National de La Vanoise. Travaux Scientifiques
0180-9741 Education Menagere†
0180-9822 Voies†
0180-9849 Revue de Droit Immobilier
0180-989X Annuaire des Marees pour l'An. Tome 1. Ports de France
0180-9938 Avis aux Navigateurs
0180-9954 Cahiers de l'Indo-Pacifique†
0180-9962 Annuaire des Marees pour l'An. Tome 2. Ports d'Outre Mer
0180-9970 Recueil des Corrections de Cartes (Year)
0180-9989 Bulletin Signaletique. Part 361: Reproduction. Embryologie. Endocrinologie *changed to* P A S C A L Folio. Part 54: Reproduction des Vertebres. Embryologie des Vertebres et des Invertebres
0181-0006 Bulletin Signaletique. Part 364: Protozoaires et Invertebres. Zoologie Generale et Appliquee *changed to* P A S C A L Thema. Part 260: Zoologie Fondamentale et Appliquee des Invertebres (Milieu Terrestre, Eaux Douces)
0181-0014 Bulletin Signaletique. Part 365: Zoologie des Vertebres. Ecologie Animale. Physiologie Appliquee Humaine *changed to* P A S C A L Folio. Part 64: Anatomie et Physiologie des Vertebres
0181-0014 Zoologie des Vertebres. Ecologie Animale. Physiologie Appliquee Humaine *changed to* P A S C A L Folio. Part 56: Ecologie Animale et Vegetale
0181-0030 Bulletin Signaletique. Part 380: Produits Alimentaires†
0181-0146 Promethee
0181-0197 Archistra: Archives-Histoire-Traditions
0181-0804 France. Caisse Nationale des Allocations Familiales. Statistiques Action Sociale
0181-0839 Cahiers Geographiques de Rouen
0181-110X Informatique et Sciences Juridiques
0181-1223 Lettre d'Information Metaux
0181-1304 Universite Rene Descartes. Bulletin†
0181-1347 Alpes - Region†
0181-1525 Musee National d'Art Moderne. Cahiers
0181-1568 Cryptogamie: Algologie
0181-1576 Cryptogamie: Bryologie et Lichenologie
0181-1584 Cryptogamie: Mycologie
0181-1789 Actualites Botaniques
0181-1797 Lettres Botaniques
0181-1835 Artus
0181-1878 Le Rail et le Monde
0181-1894 Bulletin Signaletique. Part 525: Prehistoire et Protohistoire
0181-1916 Reproduction, Nutrition, Developpement
0181-2874 Action Juridique (Paris, 1978)
0181-3048 Connaissance des Temps
0181-4095 Langage et Societe
0181-4141 Filmechange
0181-513X Dossiers de l'Etudiant *see* 0766-6330
0181-5210 Paris Voices
0181-5334 Systeme d'Information sur les Transports de Marchandises: Resultats Generaux, Trafic Interieur et International
0181-5512 Journal Francais d'Ophtalmologie
0181-561X Universite de Haute Bretagne. Centre d'Etudes Irlandaises. Cahier
0181-687X 4 Taxis
0181-7582 Revue de Cytologie et de Biologie Vegetales-la Botaniste
0181-7671 Centre Protestant d'Etudes et de Documentation. Bulletin
0181-8120 Entretien des Textiles
0181-9224 Champion d'Afrique
0181-9445 Intellect
0181-9801 Feuillets de Radiologie
0181-995X Agriculture et Cooperation
0182-0176 Moyen-Orient Selection
0182-0230 Argus de la Miniature
0182-0346 Grands Reportages
0182-0745 Oceanis
0182-1377 Medecine et Troisieme Age *changed to* Practiciens et 3eme Age
0182-1598 France. Caisse Nationale des Allocations Familiales. Statistiques Prestations Familiales. Resultats Generaux: Recettes, Depenses, Beneficiaires
0182-2322 Afrique Defense
0182-2411 Histoire
0182-2705 Cahiers de l'Avenir de la Bretagne
0182-3329 Batiment International
0182-4295 Fondation Louis de Broglie. Annales
0182-564X Chronique de la Recherche Miniere
0182-5887 Verbum
0182-7103 Philosophie
0182-8843 C.T.N.E.R.H.I. Etudes†
0183-0139 Le Van et le Camping-Car
0183-3189 Pour la Danse
0183-3634 Philatelie Francaise
0183-3898 Tout le Tricot - le Crochet et le Tricot d'Art *changed to* Crochet d'Art
0183-3901 Tout le Tricot
0183-391X Tout le Tricot - Ouvrages au Crochet *changed to* Ouvrages au Crochet
0183-3928 Tout le Tricot - Tricot d'Art
0183-3944 Toute la Broderie - Point de Croix
0183-4037 Chambre de Commerce et d'Industrie d'Auxerre. Documentation Economique
0183-4150 Dossiers Histoire de la Mer
0183-4568 Generaliste
0183-4738 Tous les Ouvrages - Toute la Broderie
0183-5173 Journal d'Agriculture Traditionnelle et de Botanique Appliquee
0183-5688 Societe de Biometrie Humaine. Revue *see* 0758-2714
0183-5742 L'Ivre de Pierres
0183-5807 Depeche Mode - Consumer
0183-6242 Centre Genealogique de l'Ouest. Revue Trimestrielle
0183-7516 Officiel de l'Equipement Menager
0183-7591 Etudes sur Pezenas et l'Herault *see* 0249-1664
0183-8490 Cartes Postales et Collections
0183-8636 Revue Francaise des Telecommunications
0183-9187 Revue de Nematologie
0183-973X Etudes Irlandaises
0184-0584 Journal du Travail Temporaire et des Services
0184-0932 Cahiers de Combat pour la Paix
0184-5055 Annee Bateaux Magazine
0184-6469 France. Caisse Nationale des Allocations Familiales. Statistiques Prestations de Logement
0184-6892 France. Ministere de l'Urbanisme et du Logement. Statistiques et Etudes Generales
0184-7589 Geographie et Recherche
0184-7678 Cahiers Elisabethains
0184-7783 Population et Societes
0184-8895 Banc-Titre/Animation Stand†
0184-9662 Agri-Afrique
0184-9670 Afrique Informations
0184-9697 Equip-Afric
0184-9719 Banque Afrique
0185-0008 Ciencia y Desarrollo
0185-0059 Boletin I I E
0185-0113 Dialogos†
0185-013X Foro Internacional
0185-0148 Demografia y Economia†
0185-0164 Estudios de Asia y Africa
0185-0172 Historia Mexicana
0185-0261 Informacion Cientifica y Tecnologica
0185-027X Cuadernos Politicos
0185-0326 Biotica
0185-0369 I N I R E B Informa
0185-0431 Palabra y el Hombre
0185-0547 Educacion (Mexico)
0185-058X Mexico Indigena
0185-0601 Comercio Exterior
0185-061X Cuadernos de Marcha
0185-075X Ciencia
0185-0814 Relaciones Internacionales
0185-0830 Universidad Veracruzana. Centro de Investigaciones Linguistico-Literarias. Texto-Critico
0185-0903 C L A S E
0185-0962 Universidad Nacional Autonoma de Mexico. Instituto de Geologia. Revista
0185-1004 Periodica. Indice de Revistas Latinoamericanas en Ciencias
0185-1012 Revista Mexicana de Anestesiologia
0185-1136 Centro de Estudios Monetarios Latinoamericanos. Monetaria
0185-125X K I N A M
0185-1268 Mercado de Valores
0185-1284 Revista Latinoamericana de Estudios Educativos
0185-1322 Universidad Nacional Autonoma de Mexico. Anuario de Geografia
0185-1357 Naturaleza
0185-1578 Bibliografia Historica Mexicana
0185-1594 Ensenanza e Investigacion en Psicologia
0185-1616 Estudios Politicos
0185-1659 Cuicuilco
0185-1918 Revista Mexicana de Ciencias Politicas y Sociales
0185-1934 Compendium de Investigaciones Clinicas Latinoamericanas
0185-1977 Universidad Nacional Autonoma de Mexico. Instituto de Geografia. Boletin
0185-2248 Nuestra America
0185-2310 Instituto Nacional de Investigaciones Forestales. Boletin Tecnico
0185-2361 Instituto Nacional de Investigaciones Forestales. Boletin Divulgativo
0185-2418 Instituto Nacional de Investigaciones Forestales. Ciencia Forestal
0185-2426 Caribe Contemporaneo
0185-2493 C N I D A Informa
0185-2523 Estudios de Historia Novohispana
0185-2558 Universidad Nacional Autonoma de Mexico. Instituto de Investigaciones Filosoficas. Cuadernos
0185-2566 Instituto Nacional de Investigaciones Forestales. Publicacion Especial
0185-2604 Cuadernos de Critica (Mexico)
0185-2698 Perfiles Educativos
0185-2876 Historia Obrera
0185-2884 Bibliografia Latinoamericana
0185-3082 Acta Poetica
0185-3198 Asociacion Latinoamericana de Psicologia Social. Revista†
0185-3295 Anuario Juridico
0185-3309 Revista Mexicana de Fitopatologia
0185-3597 Docencia Postsecondaria
0185-3929 Relaciones
0185-4003 Sociedad Mexicana de Mecanica de Suelos. Boletin
0185-4011 Nabor Carrillo Lecture Series. Proceedings
0185-402X Mexican Society for Soil Mechanics Meeting. Proceedings
0185-4038 Dermatologia
0185-4399 Informe
0185-4534 Revista Mexicana de Analisis de la Conducta
0185-4968 Nacional Financiera. Annual Report
0185-6235 Atencion Medica
0186-0445 Cuaderno de Informacion Oportuna

1478 ISSN INDEX

0186-0496 Estadisticas del Comercio Exterior de Mexico
0186-1166 Muebletecnic
0186-3401 Pemex. Boletin Bibliografico
0186-5757 El Correo Fronterizo
0186-7180 Universidad Autonoma de Yucatan. Revista
0189-0514 Nigeria. National Animal Production Research Institute. Journal
0189-0816 Nigeria Forum
0189-0913 Nigerian Journal of Nutritional Sciences
0189-3319 Nigerian Journal of Financial Management
0189-5036 Nigerian Business Journal
0189-5117 Tropical Journal of Obstetrics and Gynaecology
0189-6709 African Journal of Academic Librarianship
0189-8892 Newswatch
0190-0005 City Hall Digest
0190-0013 Philosophy and Literature
0190-0226 Boarding Kennel Proprietor†
0190-0234 Inklings
0190-0242 Children's Rights Report†
0190-0250 E I S Cumulative
0190-0331 Allied Health and Behavioral Sciences†
0190-0412 Gestalt Journal
0190-0447 Cross-Reference on Human Resources Management *see* 0740-9982
0190-0471 Analytical and Quantitative Cytology *changed to* Analytical and Quantitative Cytology and Histology
0190-0528 Rangelands
0190-0536 Philosophical Investigations
0190-0684 Journal of Civil Engineering Design *see* 0730-8213
0190-0692 International Journal of Public Administration
0190-0870 St. Louis Labor Tribune
0190-0943 I T E M
0190-1028 Behavioral Counseling Quarterly *see* 0749-1301
0190-1052 American Society for Engineering Education. Annual Conference Proceedings
0190-1168 New Spirit†
0190-1192 Community Association Law Reporter
0190-1206 Cancer Clinical Trials *see* 0277-3732
0190-1249 Sports Afield Outdoor Almanac†
0190-1281 Research in Economic Anthropology
0190-129X Louisiana State Industrial Directory *see* 0733-3234
0190-1311 Tennessee State Industrial Directory *see* 0740-4646
0190-1338 Michigan State Industrial Directory *see* 0733-4958
0190-1346 Mississippi State Industrial Directory *see* 0740-4654
0190-1354 Kentucky State Industrial Directory *see* 0740-4328
0190-1362 Indiana State Industrial Directory *see* 0740-6045
0190-1370 Electrical Apparatus
0190-1397 Forge
0190-1400 Photoletter
0190-1427 A J S Update *changed to* Update (Chicago)
0190-1435 Dr. Dobb's Journal of Computer Calisthenics and Orthodontia *changed to* Dr. Dobb's Journal of Software Tools
0190-1451 Laser Focus with Fiberoptic Communications *see* 8755-1853
0190-1486 Current Topics in Hematology†
0190-1494 I E E E International Symposium on Electromagnetic Compatibility. Symposium Record *changed to* I E E E International Symposium on Electromagnetic Compatibility. (Record)
0190-1559 Banjo Newsletter
0190-1567 Free Stock Photography Directory
0190-1575 International Advances in Surgical Oncology†
0190-1737 Street Magazine
0190-1761 Earthwise
0190-1788 Poetry in Motion†
0190-1796 Professional Women and Minorities
0190-1966 Penny Power
0190-1974 Learning Resources (Washington)†
0190-1982 C B S News Review
0190-1990 New York Times Current Events Edition
0190-2008 Journal of Caribbean Studies
0190-2040 Patient Counselling and Health Education *see* 0738-3991
0190-2067 History of Sociology: An International Review
0190-2075 Speech Communication Directory
0190-2148 Experimental Lung Research
0190-2172 Pulp and Paper Industry Technical Conference. Conference Record
0190-2180 Humanities Report†
0190-2199 Counselor Education Directory: Personnel and Programs *see* 0271-5368
0190-2210 State Consumer Action†
0190-2229 Pacific Coast Council on Latin American Studies. Proceedings
0190-2253 Gusto†
0190-2261 Journal of Fee-Based Information Services
0190-2288 Design News Fastening Directory *changed to* Design News Fastening Directory
0190-2296 Design News. Fastening *changed to* Design News Fastening Directory
0190-230X Family and Child Mental Health Journal *changed to* Child and Adolescent Social Work Journal
0190-2318 Obesity and Metabolism *see* 0731-4361
0190-2334 Regional Council Directory *changed to* Directory of Regional Councils
0190-2350 Legal Aspects of Medical Practice
0190-2369 Modern Chinese Literature
0190-2377 Tennessee Out-of-Doors
0190-2407 Studies in the Age of Chaucer
0190-2423 Agri-Fieldman and Consultant *changed to* Ag Consultant
0190-2458 In Business
0190-2482 White Cloud Journal
0190-2555 Juvenile and Adult Correctional Departments, Institutions, Agencies, and Paroling Authorities of the United States and Canada
0190-2563 Corrections Today
0190-2571 On the Line (College Park)
0190-2709 Academy of Sciences of the U S S R. Special Astrophysical Observatory-North Caucasus. Bulletin
0190-2717 Academy of Sciences of the U S S R. Crimean Astrophysical Observatory. Bulletin
0190-2725 Social Psychology Quarterly
0190-2733 Examiner (Dayton)
0190-2741 Co-Op (Ann Arbor)†
0190-275X H U D Statistical Yearbook *see* 0147-7870
0190-2911 MidAmerica (East Lansing)
0190-292X Policy Studies Journal
0190-2946 Academe (New York, 1983)
0190-2954 U.S. Office of Consumer Affairs. Directory: Federal, State, County, and City Government Consumer Offices *see* 0190-2962
0190-2962 U.S. Office of Consumer Affairs. Directory: Federal, State, and Local Government Consumer Offices†
0190-2970 Current Topics in Eye Research
0190-2989 Health Sciences Audiovisual Resource List *changed to* Nursing Audiovisual Resource List
0190-2997 Summary of Rate Schedules of Natural Gas Pipeline Companies as Filed with the Federal Energy Regulatory Commission and the National Energy Board of Canada *changed to* Summary of Rate Schedules of Natural Gas Pipeline Companies
0190-3012 Northern New England Review
0190-3055 Rhode Island Genealogical Register
0190-3071 Encyclopedia of American Associations *see* 0071-0202
0190-3101 Truck & Van Buyer's Guide†
0190-3136 World Food Situation *see* 0084-1358
0190-3160 Community and Junior College Journal *changed to* Community, Technical, and Junior College Journal
0190-3187 International Family Planning Perspectives
0190-3225 Management Aids for Small Business Annual†
0190-3233 Review (Charlottesville)
0190-3241 Future Survey
0190-325X Policy Report *changed to* Cato Policy Report
0190-3276 Copley Mail Order Advisor
0190-3284 Zero
0190-3292 N A S A Activities
0190-3306 Faceplate
0190-3314 Green Feather
0190-3330 Thinking
0190-3349 Food Marketing Industry Speaks
0190-3357 Foundation Center. Annual Report
0190-3373 Anthropological Literature
0190-339X Chronicle Student Aid Annual
0190-3586 Bostonian Society. Proceedings.
0190-3632 A R R L Repeater Directory
0190-3640 Sez
0190-3659 Boundary 2
0190-3705 Video Register
0190-373X U.S. Community Services Administration. Annual Report of Community Services Administration
0190-3748 Food Topics *see* 0196-5700
0190-3799 National Municipal Review *see* 0027-9013
0190-3845 Live (Springfield)
0190-3896 U.S. Administration on Aging. Elderly Population: Estimates by County†
0190-3918 International Conference on Parallel Processing. Proceedings
0190-4019 American Journal of Clinical Biofeedback *see* 0827-1038
0190-406X Museums New York
0190-4094 Chemical, Biomedical and Environmental Instrumentation *see* 0743-5797
0190-4132 International Conference of Lasers. Proceedings
0190-4167 Journal of Plant Nutrition
0190-4175 Electric Vehicle Progress
0190-4183 Practical Parenting
0190-4205 St. Louis Home/Garden
0190-4213 Peterson's Annual Guide to Careers and Employment for Engineers, Computer Scientists and Physical Scientists *see* 0730-0980
0190-4329 National Collegiate Championships
0190-4361 Journal of Jewish Lore and Philosophy *see* 0360-9049
0190-4523 Duke Divinity School Bulletin *see* 0012-7078
0190-4655 Cooperative Education Quarterly
0190-4663 Chronicle Career Index Annual *see* 0276-0355
0190-4701 Furman Studies
0190-4752 Paragraph†
0190-4817 Advances in Cancer Chemotherapy
0190-485X Counter Pentagon†
0190-4876 Energy Research Reports
0190-4906 Black Review
0190-4914 Business Owner
0190-4922 Contributions to Music Education
0190-4981 Combined Cumulative Index to Pediatrics
0190-499X Foreign Trade Reports. U.S. Exports - Schedule E - Commodity by Country
0190-5066 Same-Day Surgery
0190-5074 International Psoriasis Bulletin
0190-5104 Sage Annual Reviews of Drug and Alcohol Abuse
0190-521X Political Science Discussion Papers
0190-5244 What's New in Collective Bargaining Negotiations & Contracts
0190-5252 Law Week's Summary and Analysis of Current Law *changed to* United States Law Week Summary and Analysis
0190-5260 Union Labor Report Weekly Newsletter
0190-5279 American Druggist
0190-535X Oncology Nursing Forum
0190-5422 U.S. National Arthritis Advisory Board. Annual Report
0190-5570 Telescope Making
0190-5589 Semi-Annual Electric Power Survey *changed to* Electric Power Annual Report
0190-5600 Annual Electric Power Survey *changed to* Electric Power Annual Report
0190-5619 Electric Power Survey *changed to* Electric Power Annual Report
0190-5724 Carnivore
0190-5821 I L A Newsletter
0190-5848 Frontiers in Education Conference. Proceedings
0190-5856 Baptist Review and Expositor *see* 0034-6373
0190-5872 Meeting Site Selector
0190-5961 Center for Cuban Studies. Newsletter *see* 0197-5277
0190-597X SciQuest†
0190-6003 International Directory of Research and Development Scientists *changed to* Current Contents Address Directory-Science & Technology
0190-6011 Journal of Orthopaedic and Sports Physical Therapy
0190-602X China Facts and Figures Annual
0190-6100 Wesleyan Methodist *see* 0043-289X
0190-6275 Business America
0190-647X Culture and Language Learning Newsletter *changed to* East-West Culture Learning Institute Report
0190-6526 Flying Yearbook†
0190-6569 Light' n' Heavy†
0190-6577 Folk Music Magazine
0190-6585 DataWorld
0190-6593 Western New England Law Review
0190-6607 Administrative Directory of College and University Computer Science Departments and Computer Centers *changed to* A C M Administrative Directory of College and University Computer Science/Data Processing Programs and Computer Facilities
0190-6623 State Government Research Checklist
0190-6631 A C H Newsletter
0190-6690 Official Intermodal Equipment Register
0190-6704 Official Railway Guide. North American Freight Service Edition
0190-6739 R V Aftermarket†
0190-6798 Speedy Bee
0190-7034 Boston College Environmental Affairs Law Review
0190-731X Scriblerian and Kit-Cats
0190-7409 Children and Youth Services Review
0190-745X Bulletin of Bibliography
0190-7476 National Directory of Children & Youth Services†
0190-7492 Marketing California Ornamental Crops
0190-7654 Financial Education *see* 0093-3961
0190-7662 National Education Association of the United States. Proceedings of the Annual Meeting *changed to* National Education Association of the United States. Proceedings of the Representative Assembly
0190-7808 National Waste News†
0190-7956 Yacht Racing and Cruising *changed to* Sailing World
0190-8049 National Arts Guide
0190-8189 Folk and Kinfolk of Harris County†
0190-8197 New Information Systems and Services
0190-8227 Applewood Journal†
0190-8294 American Society of Civil Engineers. Energy Division. Journal *see* 0733-9402

ISSN INDEX 1479

0190-8340 A P I C S International Technical Conference Proceedings *changed to* American Production and Inventory Control Society. Annual International Conference Proceedings
0190-8553 Commercial Kitchen & Institutional Dining Room†
0190-8715 Reports on Research Assisted by the Petroleum Research Fund
0190-8766 ProFile
0190-9177 Journal of Heat Treating
0190-9185 Monitoring the Future
0190-9320 Political Behavior
0190-9363 N A G W S Guide. Flag Football, Speedball, Speed-a-Way†
0190-9452 Restaurant Operations *changed to* Restaurant Industry Operations Report
0190-9622 American Academy of Dermatology. Journal
0190-9649 Billboard's International Talent Directory *see* 0732-0124
0190-9797 U.S. Civil Service Commission. Annual Report
0190-9819 National Preservation Report†
0190-9827 Audiovisual Materials *changed to* National Union Catalog. Audiovisual Materials
0190-9835 White Walls
0190-986X Lens' on Campus†
0190-9940 Archaeoastronomy
0191-0051 O'Dwyer's Directory of Public Relations Executives
0191-0132 Asian Wall Street Journal Weekly
0191-0310 Statistical Abstract of Oklahoma
0191-0329 Fielding's Favorites: Hotels & Inns, Europe†
0191-040X Catalyst (New York)
0191-0574 Index to Social Sciences & Humanities Proceedings
0191-0647 Optical Industry and Systems Purchasing Directory
0191-0760 Gravida
0191-0833 C N I Weekly Report *see* 0736-0096
0191-0914 Reading Research. Advances in Theory and Practice
0191-0930 Texas Journal of Political Studies
0191-0965 Yoga Journal
0191-1031 Kentucky Review
0191-1058 Illinois. State Library, Springfield. Publications of the State of Illinois.
0191-118X Analysis of Workers' Compensation Laws
0191-1295 Library Computer Equipment Review *see* 0278-260X
0191-135X Sealift†
0191-1422 Congressional Yellow Book
0191-1503 A R M A Records Management Quarterly
0191-1538 O A G North American Pocket Flight Guide *changed to* O A G Pocket Flight Guide North American Edition
0191-1554 Performing Woman
0191-1562 Minnesota Statutes
0191-1600 Developmental Disabilities Abstracts†
0191-1619 Official Airline Guide. North American Edition
0191-1643 Fact Book on Higher Education in the South
0191-1686 Nuclear Science Applications *changed to* Nuclear Science Applications - Section A - Short Reviews, Research Papers, and Comments
0191-1686 Nuclear Science Applications *changed to* Nuclear Science Applications - Section B - in Depth Reviews
0191-1759 National Health
0191-1767 Foundry World *see* 0273-9607
0191-1783 American Production and Inventory Control Society. Annual Conference Proceedings *changed to* American Production and Inventory Control Society. Annual International Conference Proceedings
0191-183X Florida Business Publications Index
0191-1872 Update in Clinical Dentistry†
0191-1937 Research in Corporate Social Performance and Policy
0191-1953 Full Blast†
0191-1961 Missouri Review
0191-2151 Science in Alaska *changed to* Arctic Science Conference. Proceedings
0191-2186 Focus on Poverty Research *see* 0195-5705
0191-2208 Expense Analysis: Condominiums, Cooperatives and Planned Unit Developments
0191-2216 I E E E Conference on Decision and Control, Including the Symposium on Adaptive Processes. Proceedings *changed to* I E E E Conference on Decision and Control. Proceedings
0191-2259 Black Box†
0191-2283 High/Low Report
0191-2291 Nurses' Drug Alert
0191-2321 Fodor's Australia, New Zealand and the South Pacific
0191-2453 Current Topics in Nutrition and Disease
0191-2607 Transportation Research. Part A: General
0191-2615 Transportation Research. Part B: Methodological
0191-2682 Bricker's International Directory of University-Sponsored Executive Development Programs *see* 0361-1108
0191-2690 Ballet News†
0191-2763 Loss Prevention and Control
0191-2771 Metabolic and Pediatric Ophthalmology *see* 0277-9382
0191-278X Nuclear Tracks *changed to* International Journal of Radiation Applications and Instrumentation. Part D: Nuclear Tracks and Radiation Measurements
0191-2836 Arthritis Foundation Annual Report
0191-2917 Plant Disease
0191-2925 Stamp Show News & Philatelic Review
0191-2933 Plants, Sites & Parks
0191-2941 Nature and System†
0191-295X Bubblegum Gazette, Summer Weekly Reader *changed to* D.J.'s Summer Weekly Reader
0191-2968 Peppermint Press *see* 0745-9130
0191-2976 Jellybean Jamboree *changed to* Zip's Summer Weekly Reader
0191-3026 Research in Marketing
0191-3034 Jewish Civilization: Essays and Studies
0191-3085 Research in Organizational Behavior
0191-3123 Ultrastructural Pathology
0191-328X Alaska Today
0191-3352 Agni Review
0191-3379 International Forum for Logotherapy
0191-3387 Pacific Basin Quarterly†
0191-3417 Audiovisual Instruction with Instructional Resources *see* 8756-3894
0191-3441 National Governors' Association. Annual Meeting. Proceedings†
0191-345X Restaurant Design *see* 0745-4929
0191-3468 Sunset Western Travel Adventures†
0191-3522 Man at Arms
0191-3530 Venture (New York)
0191-3557 Journal of California and Great Basin Anthropology
0191-3581 Neurobehavioral Toxicology *see* 0275-1380
0191-359X National Librarian
0191-3654 Turtle
0191-3662 Chronicle Two-Year College Databook
0191-3670 Chronicle Four-Year College Databook
0191-3700 East West Journal *changed to* East West: The Journal of Natural Health and Living
0191-3727 How to Evaluate Health Programs†
0191-3794 Cancer Control Journal
0191-3867 Almanac for Computers
0191-3875 Desert Tortoise Council. Proceedings of Symposium
0191-3883 Hammond Almanac of a Million Facts, Records, Forecasts *changed to* Hammond Almanac: One-Volume Encyclopedia of a Million Facts & Records (year)
0191-3905 Draper Fund Report
0191-3913 Journal of Pediatric Ophthalmology and Strabismus
0191-3999 Garden
0191-4006 Business Library Newsletter
0191-4030 Stereo World
0191-4138 Man in the Northeast
0191-4146 University Publishing
0191-4219 Studying Adult Life and Work Lessons
0191-426X Argosy (1979)†
0191-4294 Christian Single
0191-4502 Oxbridge Directory of Religious Periodicals†
0191-4537 Philosophy and Social Criticism
0191-4545 Europe (Luxembourg)
0191-4588 Quick Printing
0191-4618 Florida Forum
0191-4626 Starlog
0191-4634 Web†
0191-4650 Iowa Beverage Journal *see* 0747-3214
0191-4685 Missouri Beverage Journal *see* 0747-3192
0191-4766 Pet Business
0191-4847 Radical Teacher
0191-4898 Broadcast Programming and Production†
0191-491X Studies in Educational Evaluation
0191-5096 Journal of Sociology and Social Welfare
0191-5142 South Bay†
0191-5207 Truth Consciousness Journal
0191-5215 Enterprise (Washington, 1977)
0191-524X Virginia Federation of Business and Professional Women's Clubs. Federation Notes†
0191-5258 Georgia Disabled American Veterans†
0191-5320 Alaska Beverage Analyst
0191-5355 West Virginia State Firemen's Association Journal†
0191-5371 Ion-Selective Electrode Reviews
0191-538X Advances in Earth-Oriented Applications of Space Technology *see* 0277-4488
0191-5398 Environmental Professional
0191-5401 Behavioral Assessment
0191-541X Lighting Dimensions
0191-5428 Communications Engineering and Design
0191-5592 Colorado Woman†
0191-5606 MobileTimes†
0191-5614 Live and Invest
0191-5622 Solubility Data Series
0191-5657 High Country News
0191-5665 Mechanics of Composite Materials
0191-5681 Behavioral Group Therapy†
0191-5738 Lawman†
0191-5835 Racquetball Industry
0191-5851 Tennis Industry
0191-586X Florida Grocer
0191-5886 Journal of Nonverbal Behavior
0191-5959 Grain & Feed Review (Des Moines)
0191-5967 Magnolia L P N
0191-5975 Maryland's Highlights†
0191-5983 Palmetto Licensed Practical Nurse
0191-5991 Senior Circle
0191-6017 Spyglass†
0191-6025 Tennessee Fireman
0191-6084 T.L.P.N.A. Bulletin†
0191-6122 Palynology
0191-6181 Food Production/Management
0191-6394 Pharmacy West
0191-6408 Rotor & Wing International
0191-6505 Maryland Magazine of Genealogy *see* 0025-4258
0191-6521 Africa News
0191-6599 History of European Ideas
0191-6734 Handicapped Rights and Regulations *see* 0276-2889
0191-6750 Mental Health Reports
0191-6769 C I R A Scope (Chicago and Illinois Restaurant Association) *changed to* Illinois Food Service News
0191-6777 Heavy-Duty Distribution
0191-6785 Hurdy Gurdy
0191-6793 N/C Commline *see* 0744-2386
0191-6807 Northern Hardware Trade *changed to* Northern Hardware
0191-6815 Outlook *see* 0273-9968
0191-6823 Professional Car Washing *changed to* Professional Car Washing & Detailing
0191-6904 Model Retailer
0191-6912 Miniatures and Doll Dealer *changed to* Miniatures Dealer
0191-6939 Generations (Baltimore)
0191-6963 Drawing
0191-6971 National Zip Code and Post Office Directory *see* 0731-9185
0191-7390 Nethula Journal of Contemporary Art & Literature
0191-7579 American Logger and Lumberman
0191-7587 Drug Store News
0191-765X Evaluation in Education/International Progress *changed to* International Journal of Educational Research
0191-7706 Equine Events†
0191-7714 Eastern-Western Quarter Horse Journal
0191-7757 Harvard Medical Alumni Bulletin
0191-7870 Clinical Biomechanics
0191-8028 International Security Review†
0191-8036 E N. Evaluation News *changed to* Evaluation Practice
0191-8087 United Nations Documents *changed to* United Nations Documents and Publications. Checklist
0191-8095 Snow Goer *changed to* Snowmobile
0191-8133 National Dean's List
0191-8141 Journal of Structural Geology
0191-815X Nuclear and Chemical Waste Management
0191-8176 Wisconsin Trillium†
0191-8206 Latitude 20
0191-8257 Urban Health *changed to* Urban Practice
0191-8273 Printing Journal
0191-8397 Pacific Goldsmith *see* 0274-7456
0191-8427 Archery Retailer *changed to* Archery Business
0191-8443 Design Professional Product Bulletin Directory†
0191-8508 Fastener Technology *see* 0746-2441
0191-8575 Ocean Yearbook
0191-8591 Panorama (New York)†
0191-8699 Sojourner
0191-8745 Landscape West and Irrigation News *changed to* Landscape & Irrigation
0191-8753 World of Golf-Tennis & Resorts
0191-877X Defense Manual
0191-8796 Sacramento Magazine
0191-880X Stockton's Port Soundings
0191-8818 Connecticut Beverage Journal
0191-8826 Apartment Owner
0191-8834 Pig International. Europe, Africa and Asia/Pacific
0191-8869 Personality and Individual Differences
0191-8877 Substance and Alcohol Actions/Misuse *changed to* Alcohol and Drug Research
0191-8923 Westchester Illustrated†
0191-9016 North Central Journal of Agricultural Economics
0191-9040 Insect Science and Its Application
0191-9059 Physicochemical Hydrodynamics
0191-9067 Space Power Review *changed to* Space Power
0191-9075 Electronic Distributing *changed to* Electronic Purchaser
0191-9113 Alabama & Gulf Coast Retailing News
0191-9121 Georgia Retailing News
0191-913X Population Research Center Papers
0191-9199 French 17
0191-9202 Physical Education Index
0191-9210 Coffee Break†
0191-9237 Purchasor - New York State
0191-9245 Syracuse Magazine†
0191-927X General Aviation News: the Green Sheet
0191-9288 Hudson Valley Magazine
0191-9318 Susquehanna *see* 0279-9855

1480 ISSN INDEX

0191-9334 Feed Industry Review†
0191-9458 Administrative Officials Classified by Functions *see* 0561-8630
0191-9474 Greater Salt Lake Builder
0191-9482 Mountainwest Magazine
0191-9512 Ozone
0191-9601 Pediatrics in Review
0191-961X Rx Home Care
0191-961X Rx Home Care Buyer's Guide
0191-9679 U.S. Department of Housing and Urban Development. Office of International Affairs. International Review†
0191-975X Field Artillery Journal
0191-9768 Mobile/Manufactured Home Merchandiser†
0191-9776 Computer and Information Systems Abstract Journal
0191-9792 Working Arts†
0191-9822 Willamette Law Review
0191-9873 Contemporary Administrator *changed to* Contemporary Long-Term Care
0192-0030 Apartment Age
0192-0103 G A T N *changed to* German American Trade
0192-0227 Design Cost and Data for the Construction Industry *see* 0739-3946
0192-0359 National Utility Contractor
0192-0561 International Journal of Immunopharmacology
0192-0596 Training and Development Alert
0192-060X Washington Representatives
0192-0618 c/o: Journal of Alternative Human Services†
0192-0790 Journal of Clinical Gastroenterology
0192-0812 Research in Community and Mental Health
0192-0839 F R E S Newsletter (Federal Regulation of Employment Service) *changed to* Employment Coordinator
0192-0855 Business Atlanta
0192-0863 Pecan South *changed to* Pecan South Including Pecan Quarterly
0192-0871 Undercurrent
0192-091X New Consultants
0192-0944 Diplomat International Calendar
0192-0952 Fodor's Germany: West and East *changed to* Fodor's Germany
0192-0995 Automotive Body Repair News
0192-1118 Plant Energy Management *changed to* Energy Management Technology
0192-1193 Journal of Clinical and Experimental Gerontology
0192-1207 Keltica
0192-1223 N A P S A C News
0192-1266 Biomedical Products
0192-1274 C E E
0192-1290 Engineer's Digest
0192-1304 20/20
0192-1312 Development Communication Report
0192-1347 Fastfacts European Hotel Locator
0192-1371 College Administrator and the Courts
0192-1460 MacNeil/Lehrer Report
0192-1487 Designers West
0192-1533 Equal Opportunity Forum†
0192-1541 Electronic Engineering Times
0192-1622 American Inventor†
0192-1630 Southeast Real Estate News
0192-1657 Installation & Cleaning Specialist
0192-1703 Sun/Coast Architect-Builder
0192-1711 Plumbing Engineer
0192-1746 Solid State Power Conversion *see* 0885-0259
0192-1878 Apparel Industry
0192-1975 Leisure Cooking
0192-2238 Petersen's Pro Basketball†
0192-2262 Hospital Materiel Management Quarterly
0192-2270 Rocky Mountain Magazine
0192-2289 First Class
0192-2297 Directory of Architects for Health Facilities
0192-2319 New Magazine Review
0192-2327 Restaurant Employee
0192-236X Council on Foreign Relations. Annual Report
0192-2378 Fodor's People's Republic of China
0192-2394 Nursing (Year) Career Directory
0192-2408 New Pacific *changed to* Pacific Magazine
0192-2467 Ohio Valley Retailer
0192-2475 Retail Reporter
0192-2505 Park Maintenance and Grounds Management
0192-2521 Environmental Mutagenesis
0192-253X Developmental Genetics
0192-2718 Military Clubs & Recreation
0192-2807 Meat Plant Magazine
0192-2815 Livestock†
0192-2858 Annals of Scholarship
0192-2874 Book Production Industry and Magazine Production *see* 0273-8724
0192-2882 Theatre Journal (Baltimore)
0192-2890 Dreamworks†
0192-2912 Conservation Administration News
0192-2920 Let's Go: The Budget Guide to Italy
0192-2963 Physician East
0192-298X R. N. Idaho
0192-3021 I D: Industrial Design Magazine
0192-303X InTech
0192-3048 Golf Course Management
0192-3056 Missouri Beef Cattleman
0192-3064 Industry and Commerce
0192-3072 Simmental Shield
0192-3080 Topeka Magazine
0192-3102 Bay Views (San Rafael)
0192-3137 Direct Marketing Market Place
0192-3145 Forensic Services Directory
0192-3153 Renews (Deerfield)
0192-3161 Animal Hospital Product News†
0192-3196 PhotographiConservation†
0192-320X Naval Abstracts†
0192-3250 Farmerage
0192-3293 Construction Equipment Maintenance†
0192-3307 College Union *changed to* College Union & On-Campus Hospitality
0192-3315 A A I I Journal
0192-3323 Criminal Law Review
0192-334X Discographies
0192-3404 Oil Pollution Reports *see* 0270-4315
0192-3412 Fodor's New England
0192-3420 Kite Tales *see* 0192-3439
0192-3439 KiteLines
0192-3498 Florida Hotel and Motel News *see* 8750-6807
0192-3595 Eastern Aftermarket Journal
0192-3641 Hunt Institute for Botanical Documentation. Journal *changed to* Hunt Institute for Botanical Documentation. Bulletin
0192-3706 Decorating and Craft Ideas *changed to* Creative Ideas for Living
0192-3730 Fodor's Far West
0192-3749 Chinese Music
0192-3757 Black Collegian (New Orleans)
0192-382X Port of New Orleans. Weekly Bulletin
0192-3838 Louisiana Pharmacist
0192-3846 Marina Management/Marketing
0192-3951 Rocky Mountain Construction (South Edition)
0192-396X Buddhist Research Information *see* 0888-5869
0192-3978 Construction Equipment
0192-3994 I T S Review
0192-401X O R T E S O L Journal†
0192-4036 International Journal of Comparative and Applied Criminal Justice
0192-4044 Journal of Superstition & Magical Thinking†
0192-4117 California Transportation and Public Works Conference. Selected Papers†
0192-415X American Journal of Chinese Medicine†
0192-4168 Southern Tier Town & Country Living
0192-4176 Bradford-Tioga-Sullivan-Potter-Wyoming Farm & Home News
0192-4184 Seven County Farm and Home News
0192-4214 Southwest Art
0192-429X Journal of Electronic Defense
0192-4311 Purchasing Administration *see* 0279-4799
0192-432X Medical Products Salesman *see* 0279-4802
0192-4389 Gulf Coast Lumberman
0192-4397 Year Book of Pediatrics Newsletter†
0192-4400 Griffin Report
0192-4486 Carpet & Rug Industry
0192-4575 Kilobaud Microcomputing *see* 0744-4567
0192-4583 Kilobaud *see* 0744-4567
0192-4699 American Association of Textile Chemists and Colorists. National Technical Conference. Book of Papers
0192-4729 Music-in-Print Annual Supplement
0192-4745 Mine Safety & Health Reporter
0192-477X Transatlantic Perspectives
0192-4788 Activities, Adaptation & Aging
0192-4893 New Homes Magazine
0192-4907 Twin Cities Woman
0192-4923 Minicomputer News *changed to* Computer Times
0192-4974 Urban Interest
0192-5059 Plantation Society in the Americas
0192-5067 A S L A Members Handbook
0192-5083 Lincoln Review
0192-5121 International Political Science Review
0192-513X Journal of Family Issues
0192-5148 Epigraphic Society. Occasional Publications
0192-5164 Senior Profile
0192-5199 Truck Tracks
0192-5210 Yankee Horsetrader
0192-5237 Farm and Ranch
0192-5245 Antiques Observer
0192-527X Capital District Business Review
0192-5326 Fielding's Europe
0192-5482 Athletic Purchasing and Facilities *see* 0747-315X
0192-5490 Personal Computing *changed to* Personal Computing
0192-5539 Friendscript
0192-5571 Fodor's Midwest†
0192-558X Advances in the Economics of Energy and Resources
0192-5709 American Tool, Die & Stamping News
0192-5717 Ann Arbor Observer
0192-5725 Ann Arbor Scene Magazine
0192-5776 Amicus *see* 0276-7201
0192-5784 Official (Los Angeles)
0192-5792 Southern Pharmacy Journal
0192-5857 American Mathematical Society. Abstracts of Papers Presented.
0192-592X T.H.E. Journal
0192-6071 All Volunteer *changed to* Recruiter Journal
0192-6152 Legal Memorandum
0192-6160 N A S S P Practitioner
0192-6179 Mineral & Energy Resources†
0192-6187 American Journal of Family Therapy
0192-6233 Toxicologic Pathology
0192-6365 N A S S P Bulletin
0192-6411 Kentucky Sports World
0192-642X Kentucky Business Ledger
0192-6438 Southern Advertising/Markets *see* 0270-8302
0192-6551 Progress in Biomass Conversion
0192-6667 Daily Planet
0192-6675 Healthways Magazine Digest *changed to* Health Perspective
0192-6756 Texas Child Care Quarterly
0192-6764 Brahman Journal
0192-6772 National Home Center News
0192-6802 Current World Leaders
0192-6845 W A A *changed to* Agricultural Aviation
0192-6918 Studies in the Anthropology of Visual Communications *see* 0276-6558
0192-6942 Ohio Media Spectrum
0192-6950 Metropolitan Museum of Art. Notable Acquisitions
0192-6985 Biological Abstracts/R R M (Reports, Reviews, Meetings)
0192-7000 N O O N *changed to* Outside Magazine
0192-7027 My Little Salesman
0192-7051 Journal of Prison Health *see* 0731-8332
0192-7116 Chef Institutional
0192-7124 Logger and Lumberman
0192-7132 Processed Prepared Foods *see* 0747-2536
0192-7140 Stockman Farmer
0192-7159 Pacific Coast Nurseryman and Garden Supply Dealer
0192-7175 Electronic Technician/Dealer *see* 0278-9922
0192-7256 Graphics (Kissimmee) *see* 0274-774X
0192-7272 American Association of Stratigraphic Palynologists. Abstracts of Papers Presented at the Annual Meetings.
0192-7299 American Association of Stratigraphic Palynologists. Newsletter
0192-7310 Health Practitioner, Physician Assistant *changed to* Physician Assistant
0192-7329 National Independent Coal Leader
0192-7345 Voice (Honolulu)
0192-7361 Skydiving
0192-737X American Association of Stratigraphic Palynologists Foundation. Field Trip Guide
0192-7396 Small Boat Journal
0192-740X Gerontopics†
0192-7469 Exhaust News
0192-7507 Accent
0192-7590 Building Construction News
0192-7639 Domestic and International Commercial Loan Charge-Offs *changed to* Report on Domestic and International Commercial Loan Charge-Offs
0192-7663 Media Management Monographs
0192-7922 Ad East
0192-7973 Metropolitan Purchasor
0192-7981 Club and Food Service *see* 0886-8832
0192-799X Furniture Manufacturing Management
0192-8015 Gas Phase Molecular Structure†
0192-804X New Orleans
0192-8058 F D M - Furniture Design & Manufacturing
0192-818X Music Retailer *changed to* Music Video Retailer
0192-8198 Patent Law Handbook
0192-8201 Industrial Maintenance and Plant Operation *see* 8755-2523
0192-8228 National Jail and Adult Detention Directory
0192-8287 Fodor's Budget Travel in America *changed to* Fodor's American Cities on a Budget
0192-8309 Land Use & Environment Law Review
0192-8325 Industrial Safety Product News *see* 8755-2566
0192-8333 Carbide and Tool Journal
0192-8430 Entertainment Bits
0192-8457 Insulator's Guide *see* 0273-5954
0192-8473 Accent/Grand Rapids *changed to* West Michigan Magazine
0192-8481 Porsche ueber Alles
0192-8562 American Journal of Pediatric Hematology/Oncology
0192-8651 Journal of Computational Chemistry
0192-8694 Fairfield County
0192-8716 Pikestaff Forum
0192-8724 Pikestaff Review†
0192-8732 Stores of the Year
0192-8740 Air Traffic Control Association. Fall Conference Proceedings
0192-8929 Wind Sock
0192-8953 Iowa Snowmobiler†
0192-8961 Minnesota Snowmobiler†
0192-8988 Sunflower (Fargo)
0192-8996 Applied Geography Conferences
0192-9062 Interface. Banking Industry
0192-9143 Houston Living
0192-9186 Southwest Floor Covering
0192-9194 Southwest Real Estate News
0192-9216 Texas Contractor
0192-9240 Detroit Industrial Market News
0192-9259 Chevy 4 x 4
0192-9275 Printing History
0192-9453 Land & Water
0192-9488 Baltimore Purchaser *changed to* Maryland Purchasing & Material Management
0192-9496 Drug Update†

ISSN INDEX 1481

0192-950X Midwest Dairyman†
0192-9526 Agri-Equipment and Chemical
0192-9550 Tile and Decorative Surfaces
0192-9593 Oklahoma Business
0192-9607 Purchasing Professional
0192-9755 Seminars in Respiratory Medicine
0192-9763 American Journal of Otology
0192-9828 Chinese Studies in Archeology†
0192-9917 Journal of Magic History
0192-9925 Fodor's California
0192-9933 American Printer and Lithographer *see* 0744-6616
0192-995X Living with Allergies
0193-0176 Utility Specifier Engineer†
0193-0184 Gothic Chapbook Series *changed to* Gothic
0193-0257 Michigan Banking & Business News
0193-0265 New England Sportsman
0193-0281 Progress (Framingham)
0193-032X Ophthalmology Times
0193-0400 Hardhat
0193-0451 L A M A Newsletter (Library Administration and Management Association) *see* 0888-4463
0193-0486 Hospital Management Systems Society. Annual Conference Proceedings
0193-0516 Insurance Conference Planner
0193-0540 Law Enforcement Communications *see* 0747-3680
0193-0559 Luggage and Travelware *changed to* Travelware
0193-0648 What's New in Plant Physiology
0193-0818 Research Communications in Substance Abuse
0193-0826 Journal of Library Administration
0193-0834 Shenandoah Valley *changed to* Virginian
0193-0869 New Ventures†
0193-0885 M U G Quarterly
0193-0915 Fashion Accessories (East Norwalk) *changed to* Accessories
0193-0982 Special Topics in Endocrinology and Metabolism†
0193-1075 Slovene Studies
0193-1091 American Journal of Dermatopathology
0193-1105 American Journal of Diagnostic Gynecology and Obstetrics *see* 0196-9617
0193-113X Volunteers Who Produce Books
0193-1199 Chain Store Age Executive with Shopping Center Age *see* 0731-1303
0193-1202 Dance Magazine College Guide
0193-1229 F and S Europe *see* 0270-4536
0193-1350 Chain Store Age General Merchandise Group *changed to* Chain Store Age General Merchandise Trends
0193-1369 Chain Store Age Supermarkets†
0193-1466 Sikh Religious Studies Information *see* 0888-5869
0193-1504 Whole Foods
0193-1709 Academic Psychology Bulletin
0193-1814 News Circle
0193-1830 A M H C A Journal
0193-1849 American Journal of Physiology: Endocrinology and Metabolism
0193-1857 American Journal of Physiology: Gastrointestinal and Liver Physiology
0193-1865 Registered Representative
0193-189X Mideast Business Exchange†
0193-1903 Compendium on Continuing Education for the Practicing Veterinarian
0193-1954 Mechanical and Electrical Cost Data *see* 0748-2698
0193-1962 Aircraft Owners Bulletin. Kansas-Missouri-Southern Illinois Edition†
0193-1997 Heart of America Aquarium Society News
0193-2012 Horses Unlimited
0193-2020 Kansas City Magazine
0193-2039 Mid-Continent Purchaser
0193-2047 Mid-America Commerce & Industry
0193-2055 Modern Jeweler. South-East†
0193-2063 Modern Jeweler. North Central†
0193-2071 Modern Jeweler. South-Central†
0193-208X Modern Jeweler. National Executive
0193-2098 Modern Jeweler. Western†
0193-2101 Modern Jeweler. North-East†
0193-211X Pilot News
0193-2128 Service Reporter
0193-2136 Training World
0193-2276 Graduating Engineer
0193-2284 Cigar Magazine†
0193-2306 Research in Experimental Economics
0193-2381 Fodor's Budget Britain *changed to* Fodor's Budget Travel Britain
0193-239X Connecticut Honey Bee
0193-2551 Giftware News
0193-2586 Inside Contracting *see* 0888-0387
0193-2683 Home Health Review *see* 0738-467X
0193-2691 Journal of Dispersion Science and Technology
0193-2713 Operant Subjectivity
0193-273X S O L I N E W S
0193-2748 Studies in Formative Spirituality
0193-2799 Truck Stop Management†
0193-2861 Satellite Week
0193-2993 Rancho Bernardo
0193-3086 O D L Source
0193-3108 New Florida
0193-3140 Aquaculture Digest
0193-3221 Business Opportunities Journal
0193-323X Chilton's Food Engineering
0193-3248 Chilton's Distribution Worldwide *see* 0273-6721
0193-3264 Chilton's Automotive Marketing
0193-3299 O A G Travel Planner & Hotel/Motel Guide. North American Edition
0193-3329 World Opinion Update
0193-3396 Science and Nature
0193-3418 Annual National Conference on Labor at New York University. Proceedings
0193-3434 Speech and Language: Advances in Basic Research and Practice
0193-3442 Ukrainian American Index: The Ukrainian Weekly†
0193-3450 Fish Kills Report *see* 0193-3558
0193-3469 Communist†
0193-3477 Clear Track
0193-3485 Revolutionary Worker
0193-3507 Pacific Boating Almanac. Southern California, Arizona, Baja
0193-3515 Pacific Boating Almanac. Northern California & Nevada
0193-3558 U.S. Environmental Protection Agency. Fish Kills Caused by Pollution†
0193-3604 Journal of Religious Studies
0193-3612 Revolution
0193-3639 Cable and Station Coverage Atlas and 35-Mile Zone Maps
0193-3655 Early Warning Report
0193-3663 Public Broadcasting Report
0193-3736 Advances in Agricultural Technology†
0193-3760 Agricultural Reviews and Manuals†
0193-3817 Agricultural Research Results†
0193-3876 Coal Industry News†
0193-3892 Coronica
0193-3906 Military Law Reporter
0193-3914 Pulpit Helps
0193-3922 Journal for Specialists in Group Work
0193-3949 Printing Trades Blue Book. Delaware Valley-Ohio Edition
0193-3973 Journal of Applied Developmental Psychology
0193-4066 C E P Newsletter
0193-4120 Test Engineering & Management
0193-418X Schools & Civil Rights News†
0193-4201 Significant Issues Facing Directors
0193-421X Greyledge Review†
0193-4279 Directorship
0193-4287 New Special Libraries
0193-4295 Digital I Cs D.A.T.A. Book
0193-4309 Tar Heel Libraries
0193-4406 Brimleyana
0193-4414 Business Advocate *changed to* Business Counsel
0193-4457 Advertising-Communications Times
0193-4503 Navajo Education Newsletter *changed to* Navajo Area Newsletter
0193-4511 Science (Year)†
0193-4600 Blue Chip Economic Indicators
0193-4716 Ways & Means
0193-4783 Across the Seas†
0193-4791 Hudson Forum
0193-4864 Intellectual Property Law Review
0193-4872 Harvard Journal of Law and Public Policy
0193-4953 Towers Club U S A Newsletter
0193-497X Wine Spectator
0193-5011 American Chemical Society. Directory of Graduate Research
0193-502X Focus-Metropolitan Philadelphia's Business Newsweekly
0193-5135 P R N Radio Guide
0193-5151 American Petroleum Institute. Central Abstracting and Indexing Service. Thesaurus
0193-5186 Neurochemical Transmitters and Modulators†
0193-5216 Hillside Journal of Clinical Psychiatry
0193-5321 St. Louis Bowling Review
0193-533X Gazette (New York)
0193-5356 New Mexico Independent
0193-5364 Recent Researches in the Music of the Nineteenth and Early Twentieth Centuries
0193-5372 American Suzuki Journal
0193-5380 Eighteenth Century: Theory and Interpretation
0193-5488 Cognition and Brain Theory†
0193-550X Legislative Manual *see* 0886-7402
0193-5615 Anthropology and Humanism Quarterly
0193-5712 Louisiana Business Survey
0193-5739 Labor & Employment Law†
0193-5755 Smoloskyp
0193-5771 Tax Angles†
0193-578X A I T Newsletter
0193-5798 Enclitic
0193-5895 Research in Law and Economics
0193-5933 Geothermal Resources Council. Transactions
0193-5941 Journal of Social and Political Studies *see* 0278-839X
0193-600X International Association of Buddhist Studies. Journal
0193-6093 A C S U S Newsletter *see* 0272-2011
0193-6131 Junior Eagle†
0193-614X Chilton's Electronic Component News
0193-6174 Chilton's Instrument and Apparatus News *changed to* Chilton's I A N (Instrumentation & Control News)
0193-628X Chilton's C C J *see* 0734-1423
0193-6301 Black Warrior Review
0193-6336 By Valor & Arms†
0193-645X Lighting Supply & Design
0193-6468 Econoscope View
0193-6484 Chemistry International
0193-6530 I E E E International Solid State Circuits Conference. Digest of Technical Papers
0193-6794 Neighborhood and Rehab Report *changed to* Economic Growth and Revitalization Report
0193-6808 Managing Housing Letter
0193-6832 Buss
0193-6840 Directory of Online Databases
0193-6859 American Popular Culture
0193-6867 Art Reference Collection
0193-6875 Contributions to the Study of Science Fiction and Fantasy
0193-6883 Denominations in America
0193-6913 Robotics Today
0193-693X C L E Register
0193-6956 Artspace (Albuquerque)
0193-7022 Chilton's Motor Age
0193-7103 Mary Wollstonecraft Journal *see* 0147-1759
0193-7146 American Humor *see* 0095-280X
0193-7189 Policy Analysis and Information Systems *see* 0195-9301
0193-7235 Journal of Sport and Social Issues
0193-726X Brake and Front End
0193-7308 A I P R (American Industrial Properties Report) *see* 0746-0023
0193-7367 Judicial Conduct Reporter
0193-7375 Counseling and Human Development
0193-7383 Editorial Eye
0193-7391 Publishing in the Output Mode†
0193-7405 Central Serials Record
0193-7421 Child Behavior and Development
0193-7472 Builder Architect-Contractor Engineer *changed to* Builder Architect
0193-7480 Arizona Business/Industry
0193-757X Zoning Law Anthology
0193-7626 Extracts *see* 0193-8991
0193-7677 Travel Marketing *changed to* Travel Market Yearbook (1980)
0193-7758 I R B: a Review of Human Subjects Research
0193-7774 C H I N O P E R L Papers
0193-7782 A F T A
0193-7812 New England Report *changed to* First National Bank of Boston. Economic Review
0193-7871 World Eagle
0193-7901 Agrow-Marketer *see* 0886-4780
0193-791X Neighborhood Works
0193-7928 Health Funds Development Letter
0193-7944 South America (New York)
0193-8010 Gilbert Law Summaries. Criminal Procedure
0193-8037 Growing Parent Newsletter
0193-8061 Phoebus
0193-8118 American Romanian Review
0193-8207 American Indian Libraries Newsletter
0193-8274 Sharing the Practice
0193-8312 Women's Track World
0193-8320 Gospel in Context *see* 0272-6122
0193-8339 Contemporary Poetry *changed to* Poesis: A Journal of Criticism
0193-8355 Natural Hazards Observer
0193-8371 City & Town (North Little Rock)
0193-841X Evaluation Review
0193-8452 Contemplative Review *see* 0890-5568
0193-8487 Farm and Garden Index
0193-855X Anthropology
0193-8568 Modern Technics in Surgery. Urologic Surgery
0193-8576 Electron Device Letters *see* 0741-3106
0193-8584 Bicycle Resource Guide†
0193-8622 Educational Resources Directory
0193-8630 Hub Rail
0193-869X Synthesis (San Francisco) *see* 0193-8703
0193-8703 Contemporary Marxism
0193-8738 Latin American Petroleum Directory†
0193-8991 Melville Society Extracts
0193-9025 Food Research Institute Studies
0193-9033 Fodor's Budget Germany *changed to* Fodor's Budget Travel Germany
0193-9041 Contributions to the Study of Music and Dance
0193-905X Index to International Public Opinion
0193-9106 Green Markets Fertilizer Price Handbook†
0193-9122 Fodor's Budget Caribbean *changed to* Fodor's Budget Travel Caribbean
0193-919X Convenience Stores *see* 0274-869X
0193-9211 Word & Spirit
0193-922X Criminal Practices *see* 0193-8010
0193-9270 International Petroleum Finance
0193-9297 Consumer Complaint Contact System, Annual Report
0193-936X Epidemiologic Reviews
0193-9416 New Directions for Mental Health Services
0193-9459 Western Journal of Nursing Research
0193-953X Psychiatric Clinics of North America
0193-9556 Fodor's Florida
0193-9564 Worcester Art Museum. Journal
0193-9599 Videolog: Programs for Business and Technology *see* 0731-454X
0193-9602 Programs for General Interest and Entertainment *changed to* General Interest and Education Videolog
0193-9629 University of Wisconsin, Madison. Engineering Experiment Station. Annual Report
0193-970X Public Administration Series: Bibliography
0193-9777 Irish Renaissance Annual†

0193-9866 Military Images Magazine
0193-9920 Directory of Top Computer Executives
0193-9939 Hospital Fund Raising Newsletter
0194-0090 Nephrology Reviews
0194-0104 NoLoad Fund X
0194-0139 Refundle Bundle
0194-0147 Water Pollution Control
0194-0236 Focus on Learning†
0194-0252 Inside N.R.C. (Nuclear Regulatory Commission)
0194-0287 Environmental Science and Technology: a Wiley-Interscience Series of Texts and Monographs
0194-0406 B I N California Goldbook†
0194-0430 Journal of Contemporary Business†
0194-0449 Unite (Chicago)
0194-0465 Seminars in Family Medicine†
0194-049X Rutgers Art Review
0194-0538 Biochemistry: Series of Monographs
0194-0546 Conference Papers Annual Index
0194-0694 Information Intelligence Online Newsletter
0194-0767 National Employment Listing Service for the Criminal Justice System. Bulletin *changed to* National Employment Listing Service for the Criminal Justice System and Social Services. Bulletin
0194-0775 National Employment Listing Service for Human Services. Bulletin *changed to* National Employment Listing Service for the Criminal Justice System and Social Services. Bulletin
0194-0805 National Employment Listing Service for the Criminal Justice System. Special Edition: Education Opportunities
0194-0813 National Employment Listing Service for the Criminal Justice System. Police Employment Guide
0194-083X Green Book of Home Improvement Contractors†
0194-0902 S I S T M Quarterly Incorporating Brain Theory Newsletter (Society for the Interdisciplinary Study of the Mind) *see* 0193-5488
0194-0910 National Hardwood Magazine
0194-0929 Rice Farming and Rice Industry News
0194-0937 Southeast Farm Press
0194-0953 Criminal Justice History
0194-0988 Transfer Credit Practices of Designated Educational Institutions
0194-1038 Risk Management News
0194-1062 Not Man Apart
0194-1070 Art/World
0194-1089 Hudson Home Magazine *see* 0278-2839
0194-1135 American Institute of Industrial Engineers. Health Services Division. Annual Conference Proceedings *changed to* Institute of Industrial Engineers. Health Services Division. Annual Conference Proceedings
0194-1194 Water Equipment News
0194-1240 Tennessee Journal
0194-1259 Tennessee Attorneys Memo
0194-1291 Washington Drug Letter (Washington, 1979)
0194-1305 American Arts *changed to* Vantage Point: Issues in American Arts
0194-1313 Mickle Street Review
0194-1321 Home Center Magazine
0194-1356 Architecture Series: Bibliography
0194-1380 Pool News Directory *changed to* Pool & Spa News Directory
0194-1410 Chilton's Truck and Off-Highway Industries *changed to* Truck & Off-Highway Industries
0194-1429 Specialty Food Merchandising
0194-1445 Catalyst for Environment/Energy
0194-1453 Northeastern Geology
0194-1461 Measurements & Control News
0194-150X Log Trucker
0194-1526 Film News Omnibus
0194-1607 Media Science Newsletter *changed to* Media Science Reports
0194-1658 Journal of Intravenous Therapy
0194-1666 Commentaries on Research in Breast Disease†
0194-1682 California Correctional News
0194-1690 Visions (Arlington)
0194-1704 National Employment Listing Service for the Criminal Justice System. Federal Employment Information Directory†
0194-1720 Seminars in Ultrasound *changed to* Seminars in Ultrasound, CT and MR
0194-178X Directory of Nightclubs, Hotels, Theatres, Lounges & Discotheques
0194-1879 Houston Journal of International Law
0194-1895 Annual Microprogramming Workshop. Proceedings *changed to* Microprogramming Workshop. Proceedings
0194-1941 Income-Expense Analysis: Conventional Apartments
0194-195X Data Communications Buyers' Guide
0194-2158 Journal of Community Communications
0194-2174 Dispensing Optician
0194-2212 Student Aid News
0194-2247 Federal Grants & Contracts Weekly
0194-2255 Education of the Handicapped
0194-2263 Nation's Schools Report
0194-2271 School Law News
0194-228X Tax Exempt News
0194-231X Education and Work *changed to* Vocational Training News
0194-2344 Equal Opportunity in Higher Education
0194-2352 Health Grants & Contracts Weekly
0194-2360 Labor Relations in Education *changed to* Employee Relations in Education
0194-2387 Executive Golfer
0194-2468 Gas Industries
0194-2484 Home Video†
0194-2492 Babcox's Importcar *see* 0735-7877
0194-2506 Magazine Age *changed to* Inside Print
0194-2514 Diagnostic Imaging
0194-2557 Cardiac Alert
0194-2581 Savvy
0194-2603 Los Angeles Business Journal
0194-262X Science & Technology Libraries
0194-2638 Physical & Occupational Therapy in Pediatrics
0194-2670 University of New Mexico. Division of Government Research. Monograph Series
0194-2816 Scripps Institution of Oceanography (Year) *changed to* Scripps Institution of Oceanography. Annual Report
0194-2859 Teacher Update
0194-2875 Industrial Organization Review
0194-2883 Cincinnati Historical Society Bulletin *see* 0746-3472
0194-2905 Chilton's Jewelers' Circular-Keystone
0194-2913 California Communities†
0194-2948 Puppetry in Education News
0194-2972 Price Trends of Food Ingredients Newsletter
0194-2980 Food Packaging and Labeling Newsletter
0194-2999 Watermark *changed to* Letter to Libraries
0194-3022 Catalog Showroom Merchandiser *changed to* C S M
0194-3030 Wilderness Record
0194-3057 Research in Labor Economics
0194-3073 C P E R
0194-3081 New Directions for Community Colleges
0194-3243 Presstime
0194-3294 Vette'n U S A
0194-3340 World Record Game Fishes
0194-3359 Technology & Society
0194-3405 Desert
0194-3413 Archaeological News
0194-3448 American Journal of Theology & Philosophy
0194-3502 Crossroad
0194-3510 Leaders
0194-357X Compute!
0194-3588 D M News
0194-360X Furniture/Today
0194-3650 Harvard Architecture Review
0194-3766 Allied Health Education Directory
0194-3790 Handbook of the Nations
0194-3812 Dog Groomers Gazette *changed to* Groomers Gazette
0194-3847 Nielsen's New Products Bulletin *see* 0738-0690
0194-388X Mississippi Libraries
0194-3901 Hall Radio Report *see* 0273-3056
0194-3936 T A P†
0194-3944 Wet
0194-3960 Research in Human Capital and Development
0194-4053 Congressional Studies *see* 0734-3469
0194-4096 Comments from C A S T
0194-410X Association of Collegiate Schools of Architecture. Proceedings of the Annual Meeting
0194-4118 Newscribes
0194-4134 Computer Law Monograph Series†
0194-4150 Fodor's Budget France *changed to* Fodor's Budget Travel France
0194-4185 Critical Mass Energy Journal *changed to* Connections (Washington)
0194-4193 Stumpwork Society Chronicle
0194-4282 Beefmaster Cowman
0194-4312 Lifetimes
0194-4320 North American Hunter
0194-4339 Filmmakers' Monthly
0194-4347 Dental Graduate *see* 0199-736X
0194-4363 American Planning Association. Journal
0194-4371 Mariah/Outside *see* 0278-1433
0194-438X New Wine
0194-4444 Fluid and Lubricant Ideas *changed to* Practical Lubrication & Maintenance
0194-4495 Seeds
0194-4517 Earth Shelter Digest and Energy Report *changed to* Earth Shelter Living. Newsletter
0194-4525 Midlands Business Journal
0194-4533 Modern Drummer
0194-4584 Africa Update
0194-4592 Fashions Magazine†
0194-4622 Great Lakes Sailing Scanner
0194-4665 P.R.O.'s Magazine
0194-472X Journal of Marital and Family Therapy
0194-4746 Electrical Energy Management†
0194-4800 Florida Administrative Law Reports
0194-4851 TypeWorld
0194-4908 Abstracts of Health Care Management Studies
0194-5017 National Mall Monitor
0194-5025 68 Micro Journal
0194-5041 Nostalgia World
0194-5068 Midwest Flyer Magazine
0194-5092 Air Progress Aviation Review
0194-5181 Today's O R Nurse
0194-5246 Emphasis on Faith and Living
0194-5254 Eastern Grape Grower and Winery News *changed to* Vineyard & Wine Management
0194-5297 Saluki Quarterly
0194-5343 Health Foods Communicator
0194-5351 Pool & Spa News
0194-5386 Earthton†
0194-5408 Intermountain Golf News†
0194-5416 Washington Actions on Health
0194-5467 Photographer's Forum
0194-5475 Writing (Highland Park)
0194-5483 Air Trails Classic Flying Models
0194-5572 Current Energy and Ecology *changed to* Biology Bulletin Monthly
0194-567X Kentucky Pharmacist
0194-570X Van, Pickup and Offroad World†
0194-5785 Civitan
0194-5823 Retriever International
0194-5874 H P M (Heating and Plumbing Merchandiser) *changed to* Heating, Air Conditioning & Plumbing Products
0194-5955 Timber Mart-South
0194-598X Missouri Police Chief
0194-5998 Otolaryngology - Head and Neck Surgery
0194-603X Handling & Shipping Management
0194-6161 World Meetings: Social & Behavioral Sciences, Human Services and Management
0194-6196 Payroll Exchange
0194-6218 Propeller
0194-6226 Solar Engineering Magazine *see* 0148-382X
0194-6277 Michigan Food & Beverage†
0194-6404 Old Cars Price Guide
0194-6420 I C C A's Newsletter *see* 0885-6788
0194-6455 Thermophysics and Electronics Newsletter
0194-6498 A W P Newsletter
0194-6536 American Chiropractor
0194-6552 Inside Running
0194-6587 B I D Service Weekly
0194-6595 International Journal of the Sociology of Law
0194-6625 AgReview
0194-6706 Dog Sports
0194-6730 Skeptical Inquirer
0194-6900 Real Estate Intelligence Report
0194-6919 People & Taxes
0194-7060 Southern California Contractor
0194-7079 Model Builder
0194-7176 A H E A Action
0194-7206 Newf-Tide
0194-7249 Bobina
0194-7257 Landscape Contractor
0194-729X A G D Impact
0194-7419 Heavy Duty Aftermarket Exchange *see* 0198-6678
0194-7435 Arizona Professional Engineer
0194-7648 Journal of Legal Medicine
0194-7818 Handicapped Requirements Handbook
0194-7869 Comics Journal
0194-7885 Electronic Warfare/Defense Electronics *see* 0278-3479
0194-7958 Sophia
0194-7990 Amerikai Magyar Szo
0194-8008 American Craft
0194-8032 Heartbeat (White Plains)
0194-8075 OnComputing *see* 0279-4721
0194-813X New Mexico Beverage Analyst
0194-8261 C A H P E R Journal/Times *see* 0273-6896
0194-827X Aircraft Owners Bulletin. Eastern Nebraska-Iowa-Western Illinois Edition†
0194-8431 Pittsburgh
0194-844X Medical Device & Diagnostic Industry
0194-8652 A/C Flyer
0194-8660 Government-Sponsored Research on Foreign Affairs
0194-8814 Horse & Chariot†
0194-8822 Tax, Financial and Estate Planning for the Owner of a Closely-Held Corporation
0194-8849 A E A Advocate
0194-8857 Florida Gulf Coast Living
0194-8903 Construction Dimensions Magazine
0194-9039 Flight Reports
0194-9071 A I Art Insight *changed to* Art Insight/Southwest
0194-9098 Tennis Week
0194-9101 Mercer Business Magazine (Trenton)
0194-911X Hypertension
0194-9144 Fashionews
0194-9225 News Front Business Trends†
0194-9268 N A H R O Monitor
0194-9314 Surfing (San Clemente)
0194-939X National Bus Trader
0194-9535 Esquire (1979)
0194-9543 Angus Journal
0194-9756 Dog (Chippewa Falls)
0194-9772 Cotton Grower
0194-9845 Impact: Information Technology *see* 0739-8182
0194-9888 Choppers & Big Bike Magazine†
0194-9977 Space Gamer†
0195-0118 Textile Rental
0195-0207 Phillips Exeter Bulletin
0195-0223 Eastern Basketball Magazine
0195-0282 American Journal of Intravenous Therapy and Clinical Nutrition *changed to* Intravenous Therapy News
0195-0304 International Federation of Organic Agriculture Movements. Bulletin

ISSN INDEX 1483

0195-038X Muzzleloading Artilleryman *changed to* Artilleryman
0195-0495 Specialty Advertising Business
0195-0509 Sport Trucking†
0195-0673 Washington Agricultural Record
0195-072X Gallery
0195-0738 Journal of Energy Resources Technology
0195-0819 Chicago Apparel News
0195-0967 Parents
0195-0983 New Jersey Lawyer
0195-1017 Film News (1979) *changed to* Film & Video News (1979)
0195-1157 Community Jobs (Washington)
0195-1386 Garden Supply Retailer
0195-1386 Garden Supply Retailer Green Book
0195-1416 Colonial Homes
0195-1513 N F I B
0195-153X S N E A Impact: The Student Voice of the United Teaching Profession
0195-1548 Pulpit Resource
0195-1564 Automotive Executive
0195-1599 New Gun Week
0195-1661 Corvette Fever Magazine
0195-1688 Women's Political Times
0195-1696 Obscenity Law Bulletin
0195-1718 Soundview Executive Book Summaries
0195-1777 A A R Times
0195-1785 Solar Law Reporter†
0195-1793 Minnesota (St. Paul)†
0195-1858 Insurance Litigation Reporter
0195-1874 Home Energy Digest & Wood Burning Quarterly†
0195-198X Southwest Business and Economic Review *see* 8750-6033
0195-2056 Asian Week
0195-2064 Journal of Retail Banking
0195-2099 Illinois Pharmacist (1979)
0195-2137 Teens' and Boys' Magazine†
0195-2196 Homeowner
0195-2242 New Directions for Continuing Education
0195-2250 Global Communications
0195-2269 New Directions for Child Development
0195-2358 Informer (Washington)†
0195-2366 Material Handling Product News
0195-2390 Equal Employment News
0195-2617 Federal Grants Management Handbook
0195-2633 British Heritage
0195-265X Christian Crusade
0195-2692 Lost Treasure
0195-2781 P T A Today
0195-282X Carolina Lifestyle†
0195-2889 Journal Francais d'Amerique
0195-2900 Indianapolis Monthly
0195-2986 A A P G Explorer
0195-3036 Cosmetic Technology†
0195-3117 True Story
0195-315X Internal Medicine Alert
0195-3346 F C X Carolina Cooperator
0195-3354 Nursing Abstracts
0195-3370 Technology Tomorrow†
0195-3389 Education Tomorrow†
0195-3397 Business Tomorrow†
0195-3419 Friends of the Library National Notebook *changed to* Friends of Libraries U S A National Notebook
0195-3443 Maryland Documents
0195-3478 Inside Sports
0195-3508 Channel (Los Angeles)
0195-3516 Exit
0195-3524 Oil Spill Intelligence Report
0195-3532 San Francisco Business Journal
0195-3567 Computer Law Bibliography†
0195-3591 C F T C Databook†
0195-3613 Journal of Labor Research
0195-363X A L L-O-Grams
0195-3729 Giustizia†
0195-3737 Justicia
0195-3761 Checklist of Congressional Hearings and Committee Prints *changed to* Congress in Print
0195-377X L A C U S Forum
0195-3842 Current Clinical Topics in Infectious Diseases
0195-3869 H R A F Newsletter
0195-3974 World Trade & Business Digest
0195-3982 Griffith Observer
0195-3990 College and University Administrators Directory
0195-4016 Finger Lakes Library System. Newsletter
0195-4024 Environmental Nutrition Newsletter
0195-4121 County Lines
0195-4156 Careers (Saratoga)
0195-4202 Oxbridge Directory of Ethnic Periodicals†
0195-4210 Symposium on Computer Applications in Medical Care. Proceedings
0195-4296 Marketing & Media Decisions
0195-4326 Design Directory
0195-4342 Hellenic American Society. Journal *see* 0364-2976
0195-4350 Journal of Digital Systems *see* 0888-224X
0195-4407 Biblical Illustrator
0195-4474 Energy Conservation Digest
0195-4490 Daily Traffic World
0195-4636 Workbook
0195-4865 Association of Food and Drug Officials. Quarterly Bulletin
0195-4903 Center for Southern Folklore Magazine†
0195-5241 National Center for State Courts. Report
0195-5314 Pennmarva
0195-5365 Science Fiction Chronicle
0195-5373 Atomic Spectroscopy
0195-539X Who's Who in California Business and Finance†
0195-5616 Veterinary Clinics of North America: Small Animal Practice
0195-5632 Army Motors
0195-5705 Focus (Madison)
0195-5764 Landscape Architecture Technical Information Series
0195-5810 Massachusetts Directory of Manufacturers
0195-5853 Memory I Cs D.A.T.A. Book
0195-590X Canadian Oil Industry Directory†
0195-5926 Pediatric Social Work
0195-5969 Stepfamily Bulletin†
0195-5977 Journal of Holistic Medicine
0195-6000 Journal of Public and International Affairs†
0195-6051 Journal of Popular Film and Television
0195-6108 A J N R
0195-6116 Journal of Offender Counseling, Services & Rehabilitation
0195-6124 Outdoor Writers Association of America. Directory
0195-6140 People's Computers *see* 0164-5846
0195-6167 Music Theory Spectrum
0195-6183 Woman Poet
0195-623X International Symposium on Multiple-Valued Logic. Proceedings
0195-6310 Comparative Social Research
0195-6353 Index to the Chicago Tribune†
0195-6361 Index to Washington Post†
0195-6396 Index to the San Francisco Chronicle
0195-640X Index to the New Orleans Times-Picayune
0195-6418 Index to the Los Angeles Times
0195-6426 Bell and Howell Newspaper Index to the American Banker *changed to* Index to the American Banker
0195-6434 Index to the Denver Post
0195-6442 Index to the Chicago Sun-Times†
0195-6450 Defense Monitor
0195-6515 Pacific Fishing
0195-654X Home Fashion Textiles
0195-6574 Energy Journal
0195-6582 Rodale's New Shelter *changed to* Rodale's Practical Home Owner
0195-6612 Communications and Information Handling Equipment & Services: Semi-Annual Directory/Index†
0195-6639 State Legislative Leadership, Committees and Staff
0195-6663 Appetite
0195-6671 Cretaceous Research
0195-668X European Heart Journal
0195-6698 European Journal of Combinatorics
0195-6701 Journal of Hospital Infection
0195-6728 Discotheque Magazine
0195-6744 American Journal of Education
0195-6752 Journal of Historical Review
0195-6760 Swim Swim
0195-6779 Media History Digest
0195-6787 International Journal of Oral History
0195-6817 New Jersey Media Directory *see* 0883-9778
0195-6876 Engineering Times
0195-6884 Eton Journal of Real Estate Investment†
0195-6981 Association of Executive Recruiting Consultants. Directory†
0195-7031 C I S Highlights†
0195-7074 Louisiana Contractor
0195-7082 Arizona State Industrial Directory *see* 0739-8476
0195-7112 Minnesota State Industrial Directory *see* 0740-6061
0195-7120 Montana State Industrial Directory *see* 0740-6088
0195-7139 Nevada State Industrial Directory *see* 0740-6126
0195-7147 Oregon State Industrial Directory *see* 0740-610X
0195-7155 Wisconsin State Industrial Directory *see* 0740-6053
0195-7163 Arcadia Bibliographica Virorum Eruditorum
0195-7244 Chilton's Distribution *see* 0273-6721
0195-7260 Papers in Romance†
0195-7279 Pleasures of Cooking
0195-7287 E F T Report
0195-7295 Videolog: Programs for the Health Sciences *see* 0731-5945
0195-7384 Je Me Souviens
0195-7430 C M J Progressive Media *changed to* C M J New Music Report
0195-7449 Research in Race and Ethnic Relations
0195-7473 Political Communication and Persuasion
0195-749X Federal Regulatory Directory
0195-7554 International Journal for the Study of Animal Problems†
0195-7589 U S Import Weekly *see* 0748-0172
0195-7597 Journal for Vocational Special Needs Education
0195-7600 New Roots; for the Northeast *changed to* Renewable Energy News: Northeast
0195-7619 Directory of New England Newspapers, College Publications, Periodicals, and Radio and Television Stations *see* 0883-9999
0195-7678 Comparatist
0195-7708 Sexually Transmitted Diseases. Abstracts & Bibliography
0195-7716 Volumes: The Jewish Book Report†
0195-7732 Women & Politics
0195-7740 National Council on Radiation Protection and Measurements. Proceedings of the Annual Meeting
0195-7783 Illinois Government Research
0195-7791 Social Science Monitor
0195-7848 Cumberland Journal†
0195-7910 American Journal of Forensic Medicine and Pathology
0195-7988 Social Planning, Policy & Development Abstracts
0195-8011 A M S Studies in the Renaissance
0195-802X Hofstra University Cultural and Intercultural Studies†
0195-8054 Silver and Gold Report
0195-8062 Air California Magazine *changed to* AirCal
0195-8100 Sports Literature Index
0195-8127 Journal of Psychiatric Treatment and Evaluation†
0195-8178 Alarm Installer & Dealer
0195-8186 Interloop†
0195-8194 Mobility (Washington)
0195-8208 Art & Antiques
0195-8267 American Classic Screen
0195-8313 Manufacturing Investment Statistics: Capital Appropriations and Capital Investment and Supply Conditions
0195-8402 Health Education Quarterly
0195-8437 Farm, Ranch and Country Vacations
0195-8445 Adventure Travel (New York) *changed to* Adventure Travel North America
0195-8453 Rocky Mountain Medieval and Renaissance Association. Journal
0195-8461 Blue Book of Major Home Builders
0195-847X Gold Book of MultiHousing
0195-8488 Annual Review of Clinical Biochemistry *changed to* Annual Review of Clinical Biochemistry
0195-8496 Plumbers Ink†
0195-8550 Economic Forum (Salt Lake City)
0195-8569 Electric Vehicle Council Newsletter†
0195-8631 Health Care Financing Review
0195-8682 Metas
0195-8690 National Cancer Institute. Annual Report
0195-878X Advances in Shock Research
0195-8895 World Press Review
0195-8933 Human Sexuality Update†
0195-8941 Hudson Home Products Directory†
0195-895X Best Newspaper Writing
0195-9085 Horizons in Biblical Theology
0195-9107 Hazardous Materials Management Journal†
0195-9131 Medicine and Science in Sports and Exercise
0195-914X Abraham Lincoln Association. Papers
0195-9204 Leadership
0195-9212 Baha'i News
0195-9255 Environmental Impact Assessment Review
0195-9263 Hyperbaric Oxygen Review†
0195-9271 International Journal of Infrared and Millimeter Waves
0195-928X International Journal of Thermophysics
0195-9298 Journal of Nondestructive Evaluation
0195-9301 International Journal of Policy Analysis and Information Systems†
0195-931X Western Wood Products Association. Statistical Yearbook
0195-9336 Destination of Shipments of Western Wood Species by State
0195-9344 Western Wood Products Association. Quarterly Injury & Illness Incidence Report
0195-9379 Starship *see* 0195-5365
0195-9387 Christian Anti-Communism Crusade. Newsletter
0195-9395 Lumber Price Index. Inland Index
0195-9409 Western Wood Products Association. Monthly F.O.B. Price Summary, Past Sales. Inland Mills
0195-9417 Infection Control
0195-9425 Journal of Security Adminstration
0195-945X American Theatre Annual†
0195-9468 Spenser Studies
0195-9492 Index to Government Regulation
0195-9611 Pacific Skipper *see* 0274-905X
0195-9646 Packet
0195-9700 Education's Federal Funding Alert†
0195-9735 Contest Hotline
0195-9743 Woman in History
0195-9883 E T Journal *see* 0270-1170
0195-9948 Journal of Financial Planning *changed to* Journal of Financial Planning Today
0196-0016 F T C: Watch
0196-0040 Facts on File. Yearbook
0196-0075 Library & Archival Security
0196-0091 E P A Publications Bibliography Quarterly Abstracts Bulletin
0196-0148 New Book of Knowledge Annual
0196-0172 Encyclopedia Year Book
0196-0180 Americana Annual
0196-0202 Ear and Hearing
0196-0229 Recombinant D N A Technical Bulletin
0196-0253 Coffee Market *changed to* Mercadeo de Cafe nos Estados Unidos e no Canada
0196-0555 Directory of World Chemical Producers
0196-058X Occupational Health & Safety Letter
0196-0598 Environmental Health Letter
0196-0644 Annals of Emergency Medicine
0196-0660 Franchise Adviser
0196-0695 Freedom Appeals *see* 0016-0520

0196-0709 American Journal of Otolaryngology
0196-0717 Southwest & Texas Water Works Journal
0196-0768 Smithsonian Contributions to the Marine Sciences
0196-0784 Congressional Insight
0196-0806 U.S. Federal Highway Administration. Monthly Motor Gasoline Reported by States
0196-0830 Cuba Update
0196-0873 Mission (Washington)†
0196-0881 Mapline
0196-0903 Book Publishers Directory *see* 0742-0501
0196-0911 Equipping Youth
0196-1004 C P C Salary Survey
0196-1063 Northern Social Science Review
0196-108X Seminars in Speech, Language and Hearing *see* 0734-0478
0196-1098 Georgia. Office of Planning and Budget. State Investment Plan
0196-1152 Research in Social Problems and Public Policy
0196-125X Arms Control Today
0196-1276 Overseas Private Investment Corporation. Annual Report
0196-1292 Consultants and Consulting Organizations Directory
0196-1306 Columns (Madison)
0196-1349 Federal Income Tax Guide
0196-1365 International Journal of Therapeutic Communities
0196-1373 Revista Interamericana *see* 0360-7917
0196-1446 On the Rock
0196-1454 Platt's C H A Digest *see* 0278-226X
0196-1489 Northrop University Law Journal of Aerospace, Energy and the Enviornment *see* 0887-4301
0196-1683 Small Town
0196-1721 National Humanities Center Newsletter
0196-173X Research Libraries Group. News
0196-1748 Journal of Climatology
0196-1756 Compendium of Continuing Education in Dentistry
0196-1772 Sulfur Reports
0196-1780 Current Law Index
0196-1799 L I T A Newsletter
0196-1810 Retailer Owned Cooperative Chains, Voluntary Chains and Wholesale Grocers *see* 0277-1969
0196-1829 Fodor's Budget Mexico *changed to* Fodor's Budget Travel Mexico
0196-1845 Directory of Supermarket, Grocery & Convenience Store Chains
0196-1853 Sinister Wisdom
0196-1918 Modern Technics in Surgery. Abdominal Surgery
0196-1942 Association Trends
0196-1969 Challenge (Washington)†
0196-1977 Library Insights, Promotion & Programs
0196-2000 Journal of Social Reconstruction†
0196-2035 Denver Journal of International Law and Policy
0196-2043 Oregon Law Review
0196-206X Journal of Development and Behavioral Pediatrics *changed to* J D B P: Journal of Development and Behavioral Pediatrics
0196-2094 U.S. Forest Service. Pacific Southwest Forest and Range Experiment Station. General Technical Report P S W
0196-2116 Corporate Director *see* 0746-8652
0196-2183 Solomon Goldman Lectures
0196-2213 Gaming Business *changed to* Gaming & Wagering Business
0196-2221 Anthology of Magazine Verse and Yearbook of American Poetry
0196-2256 J G R: Journal of Geophysical Research: Oceans and Atmospheres. C/D *changed to* J G R: Journal of Geophysical Research: Oceans and Atmospheres
0196-2280 University of Hartford Studies in Literature
0196-2418 Cystic Fibrosis G A P Conference Reports
0196-2434 Cost and Production Survey Report
0196-2604 Moody Street Irregulars
0196-2701 Dentists Medical Digest
0196-2787 Neuroimmunology†
0196-2809 Countries of the World and Their Leaders Yearbook
0196-2884 San Fernando Poetry Journal
0196-2892 I E E E Transactions on Geoscience and Remote Sensing
0196-3031 J Q. Journalism Quarterly
0196-3171 N A R D A's Costs of Doing Business Survey
0196-3228 Northwestern Journal of International Law & Business
0196-3309 C M L E A Journal
0196-3341 Organization of American Historians Newsletter
0196-335X Government Publications Review. Part A: Research Articles *changed to* Government Publications Review
0196-3368 Acquisitions Guide to Significant Government Publications at All Levels *changed to* Government Publications Review
0196-3422 N A R A S Institute Journal
0196-3538 Arab-Asian Affairs
0196-3546 Gold & Silver Survey
0196-3554 China Economic Report
0196-3597 Armed Forces Journal International
0196-3627 Veterinary Radiology
0196-3635 Journal of Andrology
0196-3643 Information Chicago
0196-3716 Genetic Engineering
0196-3767 Hazardous Substance Advisor
0196-3821 Research in Finance
0196-3929 New Mexico Blue Book *see* 0732-3093
0196-3988 Pacific Basin Economic Indicators†
0196-4003 National Association of Regional Councils. Washington Report
0196-4151 Applied Social Psychology Annual
0196-4186 Arts Reporting Service *see* 0270-8159
0196-4240 Native Self-Sufficiency
0196-4283 Journal of Foodservice Systems
0196-4305 Industrial & Engineering Chemistry Process Design and Development *changed to* Industrial & Engineering Chemistry Research
0196-4313 Industrial & Engineering Chemistry Fundamentals *changed to* Industrial & Engineering Chemistry Research
0196-4321 Industrial & Engineering Chemistry Product Research and Development *changed to* Industrial & Engineering Chemistry Research
0196-433X Ovation
0196-4399 Clinical Microbiology Newsletter
0196-4402 Guide to Recognized Accrediting Agencies *changed to* Guide to C O P A Recognized Accrediting Bodies
0196-4429 Video Marketing Newsletter
0196-4445 Computer Consultant†
0196-4453 Community Property Journal
0196-447X Index to Book Reviews in the Sciences†
0196-4542 Readings in Environment *see* 0272-9008
0196-4690 Marine Mammal Protection Act of 1972 Annual Report
0196-4801 Social Anarchism
0196-4984 Basic Education
0196-5069 U S Publicity Directory. Radio & TV†
0196-5093 U S Publicity Directory. Business & Finance†
0196-5107 U S Publicity Directory. Communication Services†
0196-514X Financial Freedom Report
0196-5204 S I A M Journal on Scientific and Statistical Computing
0196-5212 S I A M Journal on Algebraic and Discrete Methods
0196-5530 Quarterly Index to Current Contents/ Life Sciences†
0196-5549 3 - Wheeling
0196-5581 Biological Oceanography Journal
0196-559X Digital Systems for Industrial Automation†
0196-5603 Institute Scholar
0196-5654 American Book Collector
0196-5700 Supermarket Business
0196-5816 E D A M Newsletter
0196-5875 Art Ink
0196-5905 Video Week
0196-5913 Pudding Magazine
0196-5921 Zymurgy
0196-5964 Engineering Thermophysics in China†
0196-5972 Annual Report on Medicare
0196-6006 SciTech Book News
0196-612X Current American Government
0196-6138 Parker Directory of California Attorneys
0196-6146 S S P Proceedings *changed to* Society of Scholarly Publishing. Proceedings of Annual Meetings
0196-6219 Ceramic Engineering and Science Proceedings
0196-6227 Cashflow Magazine
0196-626X G M P Letter
0196-6286 William Carlos Williams Review
0196-6316 Awards, Honors and Prizes
0196-6324 American Journal of Mathematical and Management Sciences
0196-6332 Group Health Journal *see* 0888-4250
0196-6456 Northeastern Camping *see* 0732-7315
0196-6545 American Psychological Association. Directory
0196-6553 American Journal of Infection Control
0196-6561 A M S Studies in the Eighteenth Century
0196-657X A M S Studies in the Nineteenth Century
0196-6677 In Common *see* 0271-9592
0196-6693 Synfuels Week *changed to* Coal-Synfuels Technology
0196-6707 Pittsburgh Regional Library Center. Newsletter
0196-6715 Education Law and the Public Schools. Bulletin and Update Subscription Service†
0196-674X American Society of Photogrammetry Fall Convention. Proceedings *changed to* American Society for Photogrammetry and Remote Sensing Fall Convention. Technical Papers
0196-6774 Journal of Algorithms
0196-6790 Nurse, the Patient and the Law
0196-6871 New York Medical Quarterly
0196-691X Artful Dodge
0196-6928 J G R: Journal of Geophysical Research: Space Physics
0196-6936 J G R: Journal of Geophysical Research: Solid Planets. B *changed to* J G R: Journal of Geophysical Research: Solid Earth and Planets
0196-6960 Exceptional Education Quarterly *see* 0741-9325
0196-6979 Instructional Innovator *see* 8756-3894
0196-7053 Contributions to the Study of Religion
0196-707X Contributions to the Study of Education
0196-7088 Contributions in Ethnic Studies
0196-7150 Air Pollution Control
0196-7207 Georgetown University Round Table on Languages and Linguistics
0196-7223 B R S Bulletin
0196-7304 Survey of Judicial Salaries in State Court Systems *changed to* Survey of Judicial Salaries
0196-7355 Nevada Public Affairs Review
0196-7428 S P E A H R Head *see* 8756-0844
0196-7495 Peterson's Annual Guide to Independent Secondary Schools *changed to* Peterson's Guide to Independent Secondary Schools
0196-7525 Chicago M B A
0196-755X List of Serials and Monographs Indexed for Online Users *changed to* List of Serials Indexed for Online Users
0196-7622 Belgian American Chamber of Commerce in the United States. Directory
0196-7703 Idaho Museum of Natural History. Occasional Papers
0196-786X Professional Educator
0196-7967 Sonneck Society Newsletter *changed to* Sonneck Society Bulletin
0196-7975 Guidebook to Fair Employment Practices
0196-8009 Who's Who in American Jewry (Los Angeles)
0196-8017 Mass Communication Review Yearbook
0196-8092 Lasers in Surgery and Medicine
0196-8203 Disclosure
0196-8211 Materials Management & Physical Distribution Abstracts
0196-822X Practices of the Wind
0196-8238 Cottonboll
0196-8262 Directory of Premium, Incentive and Travel Buyers
0196-8432 Magic Changes
0196-8599 Journal of Communication Inquiry
0196-8602 Business and Trade *see* 0092-4695
0196-8602 Business and Trade *see* 0731-7700
0196-8696 Advances in Data Processing Management
0196-870X Advances in Computer Programming Management
0196-8718 Advances in Data Base Management
0196-8858 Advances in Applied Mathematics
0196-8882 Tax Alert for Management
0196-8904 Energy Conversion and Management
0196-8998 Byron Society Newsletter
0196-903X Interpretations *changed to* Arthurian Interpretations
0196-9110 Encyclia
0196-9323 Peter Dag Investment Letter
0196-9358 Official National Collegiate Athletic Association Track and Field Guide *see* 0736-7783
0196-9455 Management Update
0196-9536 Revenue Sharing Bulletin
0196-9617 Diagnostic Gynecology and Obstetrics†
0196-9668 Youth-Serving Organizations Directory
0196-9722 Cybernetics and Systems
0196-9781 Peptides (New York, 1980)
0196-979X A.L.S. Forum and Newsletter†
0196-9846 Veterinary Clinics of North America: Large Animal Practice†
0197-0062 Electric Company Magazine
0197-0070 Journal of Adolescent Health Care
0197-0100 Journal of Jewish Music and Liturgy
0197-0127 Goldsmith's Journal *see* 0270-1146
0197-0178 I D P Report
0197-0186 Neurochemistry International
0197-0208 Stolen Art Alert *see* 8756-7172
0197-0216 Bulletin of Alloy Phase Diagrams
0197-0348 Chronicle of the Catholic Church in Lithuania
0197-0364 Antiquarian Trade List Annual
0197-0380 M L A Directory of Periodicals
0197-0542 Annual Editions: Readings in Psychology *see* 0272-3794
0197-0690 Research in Health Economics *see* 0731-2199
0197-0747 Acquisitive Librarian†
0197-0771 Campaigns and Elections
0197-0798 Christian Family Chronicles
0197-1042 Philosophy Teacher's Handbook†
0197-1077 Marine Management Letter†
0197-1085 Portage
0197-1093 Art & Auction
0197-1115 Inland Towboat Newsletter†
0197-1212 Universitas (Albany)†
0197-1220 Maine, Vermont and New Hampshire Directory of Manufacturers
0197-128X Guide to Leadership Development Opportunities for College and University Administrators†
0197-1387 West Virginia Forestry Notes
0197-1433 Advances in Distributed Processing Management
0197-1441 Comuniunea Romaneasca
0197-1468 Genealogist (New York)
0197-1476 Advances in Data Communications Management
0197-1484 Psycscan: Clinical Psychology
0197-1492 Psycscan: Developmental Psychology
0197-1506 Pipeline Digest
0197-1514 Advances in Computer Security Management

ISSN INDEX 1485

0197-1522 Journal of Immunoassay *changed to* Journal of Immunoassay
0197-1816 Manufactured Housing Newsletter
0197-1859 Clinical Immunology Newsletter
0197-1867 Chrysalis
0197-1905 Robotics Age *changed to* Robotics Engineering
0197-2030 Solar Collector Manufacturing Activity
0197-2103 Connecticut Ancestry
0197-212X Older Boat Price Guide *changed to* Used Boat Price Guide
0197-2138 Psi - M
0197-2146 Literary Voices
0197-2219 Rubber & Plastics News II
0197-2227 Classical and Modern Literature: A Quarterly
0197-2243 Information Society
0197-2251 Annual Review of Rehabilitation
0197-2340 Texas Natural Resources Reporter
0197-2359 Advertising Age/Europe *changed to* Advertising Age's Focus
0197-2367 Collector-Investor†
0197-2375 Crain's Cleveland Business
0197-2456 Controlled Clinical Trials
0197-2510 J E M S
0197-2588 Bar Bulletin *see* 0162-2900
0197-260X Chess Life
0197-2618 Industry Applications Society. I E E E - I A S Annual Meeting. Conference Record
0197-2669 National Conference of Referees in Bankruptcy. Journal *see* 0027-9048
0197-2715 Gospel Music *changed to* Gospel Music Offical Directory
0197-2839 Reviews in Pure and Applied Pharmacological Sciences *changed to* Reviews in Clinical and Basic Pharmacology
0197-3045 Bride of Christ
0197-3096 Human Development
0197-3118 Cardiovascular Reviews and Reports
0197-3177 Hazardous Materials Transportation
0197-3355 C R C Critical Reviews in Immunology
0197-3371 Helicon Nine
0197-3401 Index/Directory of Women's Media
0197-3428 Tributaries†
0197-3444 Workshop on Color Aerial Photography in the Plant Sciences. Proceedings
0197-3460 Sea Grant Today†
0197-3479 Ski Industry Letter
0197-3495 Sheet Music. Standard Organ Edition
0197-3533 Basic and Applied Social Psychology
0197-3592 Ostaro's Market Newsletter
0197-3606 Free-Lance West
0197-3649 Contemporary Hematology/Oncology
0197-3657 House Ear Institute. Progress Report
0197-3681 International Journal of Clinical Neuropsychology
0197-369X United States Imports and Exports of Natural Gas†
0197-3738 Health Care Labor Manual
0197-3746 International Museum of Cultures. Publication
0197-3762 Visual Resources
0197-3800 Arkansas State Industrial Directory *see* 0740-4670
0197-3827 North Dakota State Industrial Directory *see* 0739-8468
0197-3835 Nebraska State Industrial Directory *see* 0740-428X
0197-3851 Prenatal Diagnosis
0197-3975 Habitat International
0197-3991 Paper Industry *see* 0161-1364
0197-4009 Poetry East
0197-4017 Aging Research & Training News
0197-4025 Aging Services News
0197-4041 Ligand Review
0197-4084 Potpourri From Herbal Acres
0197-4106 Propagation & Distribution of Fishes from National Fish Hatcheries for the Fiscal Year
0197-4254 Atlantic Economic Journal
0197-4327 Western Journal of Black Studies
0197-4556 Arts in Psychotherapy
0197-4564 U C Davis Law Review
0197-4572 Geriatric Nursing
0197-4580 Neurobiology of Aging
0197-4637 Multinational Monitor
0197-467X Police Beat†
0197-4696 Gas Phase Ion-Molecule Reactions†
0197-4777 Waterways
0197-4998 Fodor's Budget Europe
0197-5056 Horizons (Chicago)
0197-5072 Inside Track†
0197-5080 Research in Sociology of Education and Socialization
0197-5110 Journal of Receptor Research
0197-5129 International Reading Association. Summary of Investigations Relating to Reading *see* 0034-0553
0197-5277 Cuba in Focus†
0197-5323 Journal for Special Educators *see* 0741-9325
0197-534X Catalysis in Organic Syntheses†
0197-5374 Education Times
0197-5382 Managed Accounts Reports
0197-5390 Future Industry
0197-5439 World Refugee Survey
0197-5579 C A A S Newsletter
0197-5587 Library Imagination Paper
0197-5617 Farm Bureau News
0197-5668 State Publications Index†
0197-5676 Response (Solana Beach)
0197-5684 Pesticide Handbook *see* 0553-8521
0197-5897 Journal of Public Health Policy
0197-5919 Annual Review of Research in Religious Education†
0197-5927 Bread & Roses
0197-596X Lymphokine Reports *see* 0277-013X
0197-5986 Modern Photography's Guide to the World's Best Cameras†
0197-6044 Highroller *changed to* High Roller
0197-6052 Reporter's Report†
0197-6060 Ragan Report
0197-6338 Poets in the South
0197-6524 Information Management (Sioux City)
0197-6656 Student Guide to Summer Law Study Programs
0197-6664 Family Relations
0197-6672 Missouri. Emergency Management Agency. Newsletter
0197-6729 Journal of Advanced Transportation
0197-6753 T M R Travel Marketing Report
0197-677X International Videotex Teletext News
0197-6788 Soviet Mathematics-Doklady
0197-6796 Contact 2
0197-680X Phantasmagoria†
0197-6818 Snippets†
0197-6826 Pastiche†
0197-6931 North American Archaeologist
0197-6966 Data Resources Review of the U.S. Economy
0197-7016 Blue Unicorn
0197-7024 Polygraph (Severna Park)
0197-7032 National Right to Work Newsletter
0197-7040 Anderson Report *changed to* Anderson Report on Computer Graphics
0197-7075 Cash Manager
0197-7083 Donoghue's Moneyletter
0197-7091 Donoghue's Money Fund Report of Holliston, MA 01746
0197-713X Physician Assistant/Health Practitioner *changed to* Physician Assistant
0197-7156 Soviet Mathematics-Iz. V U Z
0197-7164 Directive Teacher
0197-7261 Lithic Technology
0197-7296 Aura
0197-7342 Keywords
0197-7385 Oceans. Conference Record
0197-7393 International Goat and Sheep Research
0197-7423 Report of the Patient Registry
0197-744X California. Department of Education. Annual Report on Publicly Subsidized Child Care Services
0197-7520 Society of Petroleum Engineers Journal†
0197-7547 California Weekly Explorer
0197-7709 Urology Digest (1979)
0197-7717 Behavioral Medicine Abstracts
0197-7792 Fortune World Business Directory
0197-7830 Africa-Middle East Petroleum Directory *see* 0748-4089
0197-7873 Stanford Environmental Law Annual *see* 0892-7138
0197-7903 Art Hazards News
0197-7997 Replacement Parts Guide†
0197-8004 New York Times Annual Review†
0197-8039 Radiation Curing Buyer's Guide
0197-8071 Society for the Study of Southern Literature. Newsletter
0197-8098 Brown's Directory of North American and International Gas Companies
0197-8101 Human Rights Directory *see* 0270-2282
0197-8160 Human Genetics, Informational and Educational Materials. Supplement
0197-8322 Advances in Inflammation Research
0197-8357 Journal of Interferon Research
0197-8381 Upton Sinclair Quarterly
0197-8454 Clinical Lab Letter
0197-8462 Bioelectromagnetics
0197-8497 Images and Issues Magazine
0197-8527 Hawaii on 25 Dollars a Day *changed to* Hawaii on 35 Dollars a Day
0197-8748 A P R E S Proceedings
0197-8896 Witness
0197-890X Tendril
0197-9035 Public Policy Book Forecast *see* 0190-3241
0197-9140 Water Pollution Research Journal of Canada
0197-9175 Migration Today *changed to* Migration World
0197-9183 International Migration Review
0197-9191 University of Illinois at Urbana-Champaign. Civil Engineering Studies. Transportation Engineering Series
0197-9272 Sage Annual Reviews of Studies in Deviance
0197-9280 Industrial Robots International *changed to* Advanced Manufacturing Technology
0197-9299 Pennsylvania Library Association. Bulletin
0197-9337 Earth Surface Processes and Landforms
0197-9353 Journal of Preventive Psychiatry
0197-937X Corporate 500: the Directory of Corporate Philanthropy
0197-9388 ScriptWriter *see* 0279-9596
0197-9426 Annual National Conference on Recreation Planning and Development. Proceedings†
0197-9477 Fastfacts U S A Hotel Motel Locator
0197-9906 New York Sea Grant Law and Policy Journal†
0197-9930 Early Man†
0197-9973 Resources in Education Annual Cumulation
0197-9981 Legal Medicine
0198-0068 Banbury Reports
0198-0092 Modeling and Simulation
0198-0106 M A S C A Journal
0198-0149 Deep-Sea Research with Oceanographic Literature Review
0198-0211 Foot & Ankle
0198-0238 D N A
0198-0246 Food for Thought (Los Angeles)
0198-0254 Oceanographic Literature Review *see* 0198-0149
0198-1021 Carta Abierta
0198-103X Advances in the Management of Cardiovascular Disease†
0198-1056 Cinefex
0198-1064 Cinemacabre
0198-1080 Purser's Magazine†
0198-1501 Safe Boating†
0198-6171 Farmer *changed to* Farmer/Dakota Farmer
0198-6201 Beginning (Nashville)
0198-6325 Medicinal Research Reviews
0198-6341 Pediatrics Digest (1979)†
0198-635X Urdun
0198-6376 Orthopedics Digest (1979)†
0198-6473 Cancer Biology Reviews
0198-6503 Federal Reporter
0198-6511 Bread for the World
0198-6597 Sports Collectors Directory
0198-6643 Dermatology Digest (1979)†
0198-666X Grace Theological Journal
0198-6678 Heavyduty Marketing†
0198-6686 Thrust-Science Fiction in Review *changed to* Thrust-Science Fiction & Fantasy Review
0198-683X Ohio Underwriter
0198-6856 Theological Educator
0198-6880 Chemical Technology Review†
0198-6945 Just Pulp
0198-697X Online Terminal-Microcomputer Guide and Directory *see* 0734-5097
0198-7038 O.R.L. & Allergy Digest†
0198-7089 Advances in Behavioral Pediatrics *changed to* Advances in Developmental and Behavioral Pediatrics
0198-7097 Radiology Management
0198-7100 Simplicity Today Incorporating Home Catalog *changed to* Simplicity Sewing for Today
0198-7194 North American Society for Oceanic History. Proceedings
0198-7208 Ohio Monitor
0198-7224 High Fidelity's Buying Guide to Stereo Components†
0198-7275 Melliand Textilberichte (English Edition)
0198-7356 Bartonia
0198-7399 Socioeconomic Issues of Health†
0198-7429 Behavioral Disorders Journal
0198-7518 Annual Editions: Educating Exceptional Children
0198-7542 South Texas Journal of Research and the Humanities *see* 0276-9220
0198-7569 International Journal of Periodontics and Restorative Dentistry
0198-7593 Journal of Heat Recovery Systems
0198-7607 Objectivist Forum
0198-7992 Thai Philately
0198-8085 Current Gastroenterology
0198-8107 Writ
0198-8190 Sportsguide for Team Sports†
0198-8212 Handwoven
0198-8239 Spin-Off
0198-831X Colorado Shakespeare Festival Annual *changed to* On-Stage Studies
0198-8344 R A S D Update
0198-8360 U.S. Nuclear Regulatory Commission. Occupational Radiation Exposure, Annual Report
0198-8379 Scholastic Math
0198-8387 Fiberscope†
0198-8425 Fact Book for Academic Administrators *changed to* Fact Book for Higher Education
0198-8433 California Academic Libraries List of Serials
0198-8549 Northern Kentucky Law Review
0198-8557 Management (Washington, 1979)
0198-8611 N E A Advocate
0198-8700 U.S. National Science Foundation. Federal Funds for Research, Development, and other Scientific Activities *changed to* U.S. National Science Foundation. Federal Funds for Research Development
0198-8719 Political Power and Social Theory
0198-8778 Specialty Law Digest: Health Care
0198-8786 Society for the Right to Die. Handbook *see* 0886-7402
0198-8794 Annual Review of Gerontology & Geriatrics
0198-8816 American Chianina Journal
0198-8840 C O I N T Reports
0198-8859 Human Immunology
0198-9006 Quarterly Strategic Bibliography
0198-9014 Index to the Code of Federal Regulations
0198-9065 In-Plant Reproductions *changed to* In-Plant Reproductions & Electronic Publishing
0198-9103 Compendium Newsletter
0198-912X Annual Editions: Personal Growth and Behavior
0198-9197 Ob/Gyn Digest (1979)†

1486 ISSN INDEX

0198-9375 Gateway Heritage
0198-9391 Amie†
0198-9405 Medieval Prosopography
0198-9456 Videodisc/Teletext *changed to* Optical Information Systems Magazine
0198-9561 International Bonsai
0198-9618 Mariner's Catalog†
0198-9634 Contact Quarterly
0198-9715 Computers, Environment and Urban Systems
0198-9731 Annual Review of Family Therapy†
0198-9855 Sing Heavenly Muse!
0198-9871 Contributions to the Study of Popular Culture
0198-9901 Blueline
0198-9936 Powell Alert
0198-9952 Impact American Beer Market Review and Forecast
0198-9987 Sportsguide for Individual Sports†
0199-0012 True Experience
0199-0020 True Romance
0199-0039 Population and Environment
0199-0071 Z P G Reporter
0199-0152 Richmond LifeStyle *see* 0010-3365
0199-0187 Journal of Veterinary Orthopedics†
0199-0217 Christmas Trees Magazine
0199-0330 City Limits
0199-0349 Hispanic Business Magazine
0199-0462 Glos Polek
0199-0497 Shooting Commericials and Industrials *see* 0273-2246
0199-0586 Alaskafest *changed to* Alaska Airlines Magazine
0199-0640 International Cat Fancy *see* 0892-6514
0199-0683 Financial Accounting Reporter
0199-0691 Information Systems News *changed to* Information Week
0199-0802 Civil Litigation Reporter
0199-0837 Nautical Quarterly
0199-0918 Ohio P T A News
0199-1035 80-U.S. *changed to* Basic Computing
0199-1272 Medical Liability Advisory Service
0199-1329 Office Products Dealer *changed to* Office Products Dealer Buying Guide and Directory
0199-137X University of Hawaii. Sea Grant College Program. Sea Grant Quarterly
0199-1388 Aquaculture Magazine
0199-1531 Austin Homes & Gardens
0199-1574 Atlanta Skier
0199-1604 Pattern World†
0199-1639 Wisconsin Master Plumber
0199-1795 Dance Teacher Now
0199-1833 Medical Liability Reporter
0199-1876 Advocate (Los Angeles)
0199-1884 Power Conversion International *see* 0885-0259
0199-1892 Woodworker's Journal
0199-1914 Model Railroading
0199-2066 Chicago Nurse
0199-2139 Bicycle U S A
0199-2155 Northeast Optician
0199-2333 Kind†
0199-2376 Kliatt Young Adult Paperback Book Guide
0199-2414 C A L Underwriter
0199-2511 Word Processing Systems *see* 0279-7992
0199-2678 Afghan Quarterly
0199-2686 Commuter Air
0199-2716 Biological Therapies in Psychiatry Newsletter
0199-2805 Southeast Food Service News
0199-2864 Adweek
0199-2880 Executive Female
0199-2899 Long Island Jewish World
0199-3054 Shepherd
0199-3097 Backpacker Including Wilderness Camping *see* 0277-867X
0199-3100 Benefits News Analysis
0199-3151 Fantasy Newsletter *see* 0747-234X
0199-3178 Toxic Substances Journal
0199-3186 Director
0199-3313 Keyboard World
0199-3372 Southern Outdoors
0199-3410 Oil and Gas Regulation Analyst *changed to* Natural Gas
0199-350X People (Palo Alto)
0199-3607 Kansas Business News
0199-3704 I U D Digest
0199-378X Music World†
0199-3933 House & Garden Building & Remodeling Guide†
0199-3941 Nit & Wit
0199-3992 Texas Homes
0199-4220 American Cowboy†
0199-4239 Holstein World
0199-4328 Decorative Products World
0199-4336 Grain Storage and Handling
0199-4433 Mission Journal
0199-4441 Jewish World (Albany)
0199-4514 Tole World
0199-4557 New Jersey Interact†
0199-4581 Insurance Sales
0199-4743 Adweek/West
0199-4913 Petersen's Photographic
0199-5014 Indian River Life
0199-5103 Group Practice Journal
0199-5111 Cruise Travel
0199-5197 Cobblestone
0199-5219 F and S Index Europe *see* 0270-4536
0199-5243 M A P A Log
0199-5278 Sportswear Graphics†
0199-5421 Mainline Modeler
0199-5456 Bovine Practice *see* 0745-452X
0199-5510 Nutrition Action *changed to* Nutrition Action Healthletter
0199-5529 Western Office Dealer
0199-5553 Museum Magazine
0199-5650 Energy Management†
0199-5707 Chevron U S A *changed to* Chevron U S A/Odyssey
0199-5723 Network (Washington, 1971)
0199-5820 International Fiber Optics and Communications†
0199-5847 Environmental Regulation Analyst *see* 0732-7927
0199-5855 Whitchappel's Herbal†
0199-5979 Bird World
0199-6096 Bus Tours Magazine
0199-6134 Municipal Finance Journal
0199-6231 Journal of Solar Energy Engineering
0199-6290 Back Home in Kentucky
0199-6304 Employee Health and Fitness
0199-6312 Hospital Risk Management
0199-6363 Pacific Northwest
0199-6460 Ag Consultant and Fieldman *changed to* Ag Consultant
0199-6487 Chinmaya Mission West Newsletter
0199-6495 Terrier Type
0199-6509 Management Digest (Chicago)†
0199-6584 M D A Journal *changed to* Missouri Dental Journal
0199-6614 Journal of Cardiovascular Medicine *see* 0363-5104
0199-6649 InfoWorld
0199-669X California Business Law Reporter
0199-6738 Setter Quarterly
0199-6789 80 Microcomputing *see* 0744-7868
0199-6835 Alarm Signal†
0199-686X C B I A News
0199-6916 Environmental Education Report *changed to* Environmental Education Report and Newsletter
0199-6924 Farm Industry News
0199-6991 A A U News *see* 0279-9863
0199-7114 Program Manager
0199-7149 Sexology Today†
0199-7173 Lake Superior Port Cities *see* 0890-3050
0199-7211 Military Police Law Enforcement Journal *see* 0884-0024
0199-7238 Cape Cod Life
0199-7297 American Brittany
0199-7335 Pet Gazette†
0199-7343 Colorado Medicine
0199-736X Dental Practice†
0199-7424 Israel Scene
0199-7602 Inside (Philadelphia)
0199-7610 Specialist (Radnor)†
0199-7661 Leadership (Carol Stream)
0199-7696 Foodservice Product News
0199-770X Hispanic Times Magazine
0199-7793 County (Des Moines)
0199-7890 Vette
0199-7920 Speaker Builder
0199-7947 Senior Citizen Sentinel
0199-7955 Microsystems†
0199-8013 Plant Services
0199-8196 Current Consumer *see* 0745-0265
0199-820X Current Health
0199-8218 Current Lifestudies *see* 0745-0265
0199-8226 Farmstead Magazine
0199-8285 Wittenburg Door
0199-8323 Contact High *see* 0747-3818
0199-8366 Groom & Board
0199-8501 Inside Kung Fu
0199-8536 Powerlifting U S A
0199-8595 Energy Engineering
0199-865X V F W Auxiliary
0199-8668 Southern Struggle†
0199-8730 Biz
0199-8765 Bema
0199-8838 M I S Week
0199-8854 Southwest Homefurnishings News *changed to* Home Furnishings
0199-8951 Systems User
0199-8994 N C E E Registration Bulletin
0199-9052 Wassaja/The Indian Historian†
0199-9060 Soil and Water Conservation News
0199-9230 Crossroads (Evanston)†
0199-9249 Internos *see* 0744-1223
0199-9257 Prevue
0199-9273 Media Review
0199-929X Collector Editions Quarterly *see* 0733-2130
0199-9303 Los Angeles Home and Garden Magazine†
0199-9346 Communities
0199-9370 Sunshine Artists U S A
0199-9419 Asia Record†
0199-9435 A R C
0199-9664 Nebraska State Historical Society. Historical Newsletter
0199-9788 Games
0199-9796 New Books on Asia Announced for Publication in the Soviet Union
0199-9818 American Academy of Arts and Sciences. Proceedings *see* 0011-5266
0199-9869 Solutions
0199-9885 Annual Review of Nutrition
0199-9915 Retail Automation Report†
0199-994X Geographical Perspectives
0199-9974 Weekly Government Abstracts. Health Planning and Health Services Research *changed to* Abstract Newsletter: Health Planning & Health Services Research
0200-0156 Hungarica Kulfoldi Folyoiratszemle *see* 0133-7505
0200-0679 Magyar Zenemuvek Bibliografiaja *see* 0133-5782
0200-2396 Weekly Bulletin *see* 0024-8495
0200-5344 Zalai Tukor
0200-5352 Magyar Nepmuveszet Evszazadai†
0201-419X Kul'tura Slova
0201-5307 Signal'naya Informatsiya. Kvantovaya Radiotekhnika - Kriogennaya Radioehlekrtronika†
0201-5315 Signal'naya Informatsiya. Antenny - Volnovody - Ob'emnye Rezonatory - Rasprostranenie Radiovoln†
0201-5323 Signal'naya Informatsiya. Ehlektrosvyaz†
0201-5331 Signal'naya Informatsiya. Radiolokatsiya - Radionavigatsiya - Televidenie - Impul'snaya Tekhnika†
0201-7369 Akademiya Meditsinskikh Nauk S.S.S.R. Vsesoyuznyi Kardiologicheskii Nauchnyi Tsentr. Byulleten'
0201-7474 Khimiya Drevesiny
0201-7563 Anesteziologiya i Reanimatologiya
0201-8446 Akademiya Nauk Ukrainskoi S.S.R. Doklady. Seriya A. Fiziko-Matematicheskie i Tekhnicheskie Nauki
0201-8454 Akademiya Nauk Ukrainskoi S.S.R. Doklady. Seriya B. Geologicheskie, Khimicheskie i Biologicheskie Nauki
0201-8462 Mikrobiologichnyi Zhurnal
0201-8470 Ukrain'skyi Biokhimichnyi Zhurnal
0201-8489 Geologicheskii Zhurnal
0202-0726 Itogi Nauki i Tekhniki: Geodeziya i Aeros'emka
0202-0734 Itogi Nauki i Tekhniki: Issledovanie Kosmicheskogo Prostranstva
0202-0742 Itogi Nauki i Tekhniki: Astronomiya
0202-0769 Itogi Nauki i Tekhniki: Radiotekhnika
0202-2001 Lituanistika v S.S.S.R. Filosofiya i Psikhologiya
0202-201X Lituanistika v S.S.S.R. Yazykoznanie
0202-2028 Lituanistika v S.S.S.R. Pravo
0202-2036 Obshchestvennye Nauki v S.S.S.R. Seriya 1: Problemy Nauchnogo Kommunizma
0202-2044 Obshchestvennye Nauki v S.S.S.R. Seriya 2: Ekonomika
0202-2052 Obshchestvennye Nauki v S.S.S.R. Seriya 3: Filosofskie Nauki
0202-2060 Obshchestvennye Nauki v S.S.S.R. Seriya 4: Gosudarstvo i Pravo
0202-2079 Obshchestvennye Nauki v S.S.S.R. Seriya 5: Istoriya
0202-2087 Obshchestvennye Nauki v S.S.S.R. Seriya 6: Yazykoznanie
0202-2095 Obshchestvennye Nauki v S.S.S.R. Seriya 7: Literaturovedenie
0202-2109 Obshchestvennye Nauki za Rubezhom. Seriya 4: Gosudarstvo i Pravo
0202-2117 Obshchestvennye Nauki za Rubezhom. Seriya 7: Literaturovedenie
0202-2125 Obshchestvennye Nauki za Rubezhom. Seriya 1: Problemy Nauchnogo Kommunizma
0202-2133 Obshchestvennye Nauki za Rubezhom. Seriya 6: Yazykoznanie
0202-2141 Obshchestvennye Nauki za Rubezhom. Seriya 8: Naukovedenie
0202-2540 Novaya Sovetskaya i Inostrannaya Literatura po Obshchestvennym Naukam. Sotsialisticheskaya Respublika Rumyniya
0202-327X Geografija ir Geologija
0202-3296 Literatura
0202-330X Kalbotyra
0202-4098 Referativnyi Zhurnal. Avtomatika, Telemekhanika i Vychislitel'naya Tekhnika *changed to* Referativnyi Zhurnal. Avtomatika i Vychislitel'naya Tekhnika
0202-5132 Referativnyi Zhurnal. Farmakologiya Effektornykh Sistem. Khimioterapevticheskie Sredstva
0202-5140 Referativnyi Zhurnal. Ekologiya Cheloveka
0202-7003 Itogi Nauki i Tekhniki: Biofizika *see* 0234-2979
0202-702X Itogi Nauki i Tekhniki: Zoologiya Pozvonochnykh
0202-7070 Itogi Nauki i Tekhniki: Molekulyarnaya Biologiya
0202-7127 Itogi Nauki i Tekhniki: Onkologiya
0202-716X Itogi Nauki i Tekhniki: Rastenievodstvo
0202-7208 Itogi Nauki i Tekhniki: Geografiya Zarubezhnykh Stran
0202-7216 Itogi Nauki i Tekhniki: Geografiya SSSR†
0202-7240 Itogi Nauki i Tekhniki: Kartografiya
0202-7275 Itogi Nauki i Tekhniki: Geomagnetizm i Vysokie Sloi Atmosfery
0202-7321 Itogi Nauki i Tekhniki: Okhrana Prirody i Vosproizvodstvo Prirodnykh Resursov
0202-7348 Itogi Nauki i Tekhniki: Geokhimiya - Mineralogiya - Petrografiya
0202-7356 Itogi Nauki i Tekhniki: Gidrogeologiya. Inzhenernaya Geologiya
0202-7372 Itogi Nauki i Tekhniki: Obshchaya Geologiya
0202-7380 Itogi Nauki i Tekhniki: Rudnye Mestorozhdeniya
0202-7410 Itogi Nauki i Tekhniki: Razrabotka Mestorozhdenii Tverdykh Poleznykh Iskopaemykh

ISSN INDEX 1487

0202-7429 Itogi Nauki i Tekhniki: Razrabotka Neftyanykh i Gazovykh Mestorozhdenii
0202-7437 Itogi Nauki i Tekhniki: Obogashchenie Poleznykh Iskopaemykh
0202-7445 Itogi Nauki i Tekhniki: Algebra - Topologiya - Geometriya
0202-7453 Itogi Nauki i Tekhniki: Matematicheskii Analiz
0202-7461 Itogi Nauki i Tekhniki: Problemy Geometrii
0202-747X Itogi Nauki i Tekhniki: Sovremennye Problemy Matematiki†
0202-7488 Itogi Nauki i Tekhniki: Teoriya Veroyatnostej - Matematicheskaya Statistika-Teoreticheskaya Kibernetika
0202-7542 Itogi Nauki i Tekhniki: Dvigateli Vnutrennego Sgoraniya
0202-7585 Itogi Nauki i Tekhniki: Metrologiya i Izmeritel'naya Tekhnika†
0202-7739 Itogi Nauki i Tekhniki: Metallovedenie i Termicheskaya Obrabotka
0202-7747 Itogi Nauki i Tekhniki: Metallurgiya Tsvetnykh Metallov
0202-7755 Itogi Nauki i Tekhniki: Metallurgicheskaya Teplotekhnika
0202-778X Itogi Nauki i Tekhniki: Svarka
0202-7798 Itogi Nauki i Tekhniki: Teoriya Metallurgicheskikh Protsessov†
0202-781X Itogi Nauki i Tekhniki: Mekhanika Zhidkosti i Gaza
0202-7836 Itogi Nauki i Tekhniki: Obshchaya Mekhanika†
0202-7844 Itogi Nauki i Tekhniki: Avtomobil'nyi i Gorodskoi Transport
0202-7879 Itogi Nauki i Tekhniki: Vodnyi Transport
0202-7887 Itogi Nauki i Tekhniki: Vozdushnyi Transport
0202-7909 Itogi Nauki i Tekhniki: Promyshlennyi Transport
0202-7917 Itogi Nauki i Tekhniki: Truboprovodnyi Transport
0202-795X Itogi Nauki i Tekhniki: Biologicheskaya Khimiya
0202-7968 Itogi Nauki i Tekhniki: Kinetika. Kataliz
0202-7976 Itogi Nauki i Tekhniki: Korroziya i Zashchita ot Korrozii
0202-7984 Itogi Nauki i Tekhniki: Kristallokhimiya
0202-8018 Itogi Nauki i Tekhniki: Protsessy i Apparaty Khimicheskoi Tekhnologii
0202-8050 Itogi Nauki i Tekhniki: Khimicheskaya Termodinamika i Ravnovesiya†
0202-8069 Itogi Nauki i Tekhniki: Khimiya i Tekhnologiya Vysokomolekulyarnykh Soedinenii
0202-8093 Itogi Nauki i Tekhniki: Elektrokhimiya
0202-8190 Itogi Nauki i Tekhniki: Kotel'nye Ustanovki i Vodopodgotovka†
0202-8247 Itogi Nauki i Tekhniki: Teplo- i Massoobmen†
0202-8301 Itogi Nauki i Tekhniki: Elektricheskie Apparaty
0202-831X Itogi Nauki i Tekhniki: Elektricheskie Mashiny i Transformatory†
0202-8328 Itogi Nauki i Tekhniki: Elektricheskie Stantsii, Seti i Sistemy *changed to* Itogi Nauki i Tekhniki: Elektricheskie Stantsii i Seti
0202-8387 Signal'naya Informatsiya. Genetika Cheloveka†
0202-8395 Signal'naya Informatsiya. Ikhtiologiya†
0202-8425 Signal'naya Informatsiya. Obmen Veshchestv, Pitanie i Pishchevarenie†
0202-8433 Signal'naya Informatsiya. Obshchaya Genetika†
0202-8441 Signal'naya Informatsiya. Obshchaya Mikrobiologiya†
0202-845X Signal'naya Informatsiya. Obshchie Problemy Biologii†
0202-8468 Signal'naya Informatsiya. Obshchie Problemy Fiziologii Cheloveka i Zhivotnykh. Prikladnaya Fiziologiya†
0202-8476 Signal'naya Informatsiya. Onkologiya: Opukholi u Cheloveka†
0202-8484 Signal'naya Informatsiya. Onkologiya: Terapiya Opukholei†
0202-8492 Signal'naya Informatsiya. Onkologiya: Eksperimental'naya†
0202-8506 Signal'naya Informatsiya. Prikladnaya Mikrobiologiya†
0202-8514 Signal'naya Informatsiya. Toksikologiya *see* 0233-6588
0202-8522 Signal'naya Informatsiya. Farmakologiya: Khimioterapevticheskie Sredstva†
0202-8530 Signal'naya Informatsiya. Fiziologiya Krovoobrashcheniya i Dykhaniya: Pochki†
0202-8549 Signal'naya Informatsiya. Tsitologiya - Tsitogenetika†
0202-8565 Signal'naya Informatsiya. Analiticheskaya Khimiya-Oborudovanie Laboratorii *see* 0234-9744
0202-8638 Signal'naya Informatsiya. Vysokomolekulyarnye Soedineniya†
0202-8646 Signal'naya Informatsiya. Zhiry, Masla, Moyushchie Sredstva i Dushistye Veshchestva†
0202-8662 Signal'naya Informatsiya. Kinetika - Kataliz - Fotokhimiya - Radiatsionnaya Khimiya†
0202-8670 Signal'naya Informatsiya. Korroziya i Zashchita ot Korrozii
0202-8689 Signal'naya Informatsiya. Kristallokhimiya i Kristallografiya†
0202-8697 Signal'naya Informatsiya. Laki - Kraski - Organicheskie Pokrytiya
0202-8727 Signal'naya Informatsiya. Natural'nyi Kauchuk-Rezina†
0202-8735 Signal'naya Informatsiya. Neorganicheskaya Khimiya-Kompleksnye Soedineniya-Radiokhimiya†
0202-8743 Signal'naya Informatsiya. Obshchie Voprosy Khimii†
0202-8751 Signal'naya Informatsiya. Obshchie i Teoreticheskie Voprosy Organicheskoi Khimii†
0202-876X Signal'naya Informatsiya. Osnovy Khimicheskoi Tekhnologii†
0202-8778 Signal'naya Informatsiya. Pererabotka Tverdykh Goryuchikh Iskopaemykh, Nefti, Gazov, Drevesiny†
0202-8786 Signal'naya Informatsiya. Pestitsidy†
0202-8794 Signal'naya Informatsiya. Pishchevaya, Brodil'naya i Sakharnaya Promyshlennost'†
0202-8808 Signal'naya Informatsiya. Plastmassy i Ionoobmennye Materialy†
0202-8816 Signal'naya Informatsiya. Poverkhnostnye Yavleniya - Khimiya Kolloidov†
0202-8824 Signal'naya Informatsiya. Prirodnye Soedineniya i Ikh Sinteticheskie Analogi†
0202-8832 Signal'naya Informatsiya. Promyshlennyi Organicheskii Sintez i Sintez Krasitelei†
0202-8840 Signal'naya Informatsiya. Silikatnye Materialy†
0202-8859 Signal'naya Informatsiya. Sinteticheskaya Organicheskaya Khimiya†
0202-8867 Signal'naya Informatsiya. Sinteticheskie i Prirodnye Lekarstvennye Veshchestva†
0202-8875 Signal'naya Informatsiya. Stroenie Molekul i Khimicheskaya Svyaz'†
0202-8883 Signal'naya Informatsiya. Struktura i Svoistva Vysokomolekulyarnykh Soedinenii†
0202-8891 Signal'naya Informatsiya. Termodinamika - Termokhimiya - Ravnovesiya - Rastvory†
0202-8905 Signal'naya Informatsiya. Tekhnika Bezopasnosti - Sanitarnaya Tekhnika
0202-8921 Signal'naya Informatsiya. Tekhnologiya Neorganicheskikh Veshchestv†
0202-893X Signal'naya Informatsiya. Khimicheskie Volokna - Tekstil - Kozha - Mekh†
0202-8948 Signal'naya Informatsiya. Khimiya Vody
0202-8956 Signal'naya Informatsiya. Khimiya Tverdogo Tela - Gazy - Zhidkosti - Amorfnye Tela†
0202-8980 Signal'naya Informatsiya. Enzimologiya
0202-8999 Signal'naya Informatsiya. Razrabotka Neftyanykh i Gazovykh Mestorozhdenii†
0202-912X Referativnyi Zhurnal. Bionika - Biokibernetika - Bioinzheneriya
0202-9138 Referativnyi Zhurnal. Genetika i Selektsiya Vozdelyvaemykh Rastenii
0202-9146 Referativnyi Zhurnal. Genetika Cheloveka
0202-9154 Referativnyi Zhurnal. Immunologiya - Allergologiya
0202-9162 Referativnyi Zhurnal. Klinicheskaya Farmakologiya
0202-9170 Referativnyi Zhurnal. Molekulyarnaya Biologiya†
0202-9189 Referativnyi Zhurnal. Obshchie Voprosy Patologii *changed to* Referativnyi Zhurnal. Obshchie Voprosy Patologicheskoi Anatomii
0202-9197 Referativnyi Zhurnal. Onkologiya
0202-9200 Referativnyi Zhurnal. Rastenievodstvo (Biologicheskie Osnovy)
0202-9219 Referativnyi Zhurnal. Toksikologiya
0202-9227 Referativnyi Zhurnal. Farmakologiya. Khimioterapevticheskie Sredstva. Toksikologiya†
0202-9235 Referativnyi Zhurnal. Fitopatologiya
0202-9332 Referativnyi Zhurnal. Okhrana Prirody i Vosproizvodstvo Prirodnykh Resursov
0202-9898 Referativnyi Zhurnal. Pozharnaya Okhrana
0202-9952 Referativnyi Zhurnal. Organizatsiya i Bezopasnost' Dorozhnogo Dvizheniya
0203-1272 Mekhanika Kompozitnykh Materialov
0203-3100 Geofizicheskii Zhurnal
0203-3119 Sverkhtverdye Materialy
0203-3275 Kompositsionnye Polimernye Materialy
0203-3933 Soviet Shipping
0203-4646 Ekologiya Morya
0203-4654 Fizika i Tekhnika Vysokikh Davlenii
0203-5189 Referativnyi Zhurnal. Electrotekhnika i Elektroenergetika *changed to* Referativnyi Zhurnal. Elektrotekhnika
0203-5308 Referativnyi Zhurnal. Energetika
0203-5405 Itogi Nauki i Tekhniki: Obshchie Problemy Biologii
0203-5413 Signal'naya Informatsiya. Metallurgiya Blagorodnykh, Redkikh, Redkozemel'nykh i Radioaktivnykh Metallov i Splavov. Proizvodstvo Tsvetnykh Metallov i Splavov iz Vtorichnogo Syr'ya†
0203-5421 Signal'naya Informatsiya. Metallurgiya Legkikh i Tyazhelykh Metallov i Splavov†
0203-543X Signal'naya Informatsiya. Metallurgicheskaya Teplotekhnika†
0203-5448 Signal'naya Informatsiya. Metodika Issledovanii Metallov i Splavov i Laboratornoe Oborudovanie. Termicheskaya i Khimiko-Termicheskaya Obrabotka Metallov i Splavov†
0203-5456 Signal'naya Informatsiya. Obshchie Voprosy Metallovedenya i Termicheskoi Obrabotki. Fazovye Ravnovesiya Metallov i Splavov. Fazovye i Strukturnye Prevrashcheniya v Metallakh i Splavakh†
0203-5464 Signal'naya Informatsiya. Obshchie Voprosy Prokatnogo Proizvodstva. Teoriya Prokatki Metallov. Proizvodstvo Blyumov, Slyabov, Zagotovok i Profilei Prokata Chernykh Metallov†
0203-5472 Signal'naya Informatsiya. Obshchie Voprosy Tsvetnoi Metallurgii. Obogashchenie Rud Tsvetnykh Metallov†
0203-5480 Signal'naya Informatsiya. Obshchie Voprosy Chernoi Metallurgii. Obshchezavodskoe Khozyaistvo Chernoi Metallurgii†
0203-5499 Signal'naya Informatsiya. Podgotovka Syr'evykh Materialov Chernoi Metallurgii. Proizvodstvo Chuguna i Ferrosplavov. Pryamoe Poluchenie Zheleza i Stali†
0203-5502 Signal'naya Informatsiya. Proizvodstvo Listov Chernykh Metallov†
0203-5510 Signal'naya Informatsiya. Proizvodstvo Zagotovok, Profilei, Katanki, Listov i Fol'gi iz Tsvetnykh Metallov i Splavov. Volochil'noe i Metiznoe Proizvodstvo. Proizvodstvo Trub†
0203-5529 Signal'naya Informatsiya. Proizvodstvo Stali†
0203-5537 Signal'naya Informatsiya. Struktura i Svoistva Tsvetnykh Metallov i Splavov i Kompozitsionnykh Materialov na Ikh Osnove. Metally i Splavy v Atomnoi i Termoyadernoi Ehnergetike†
0203-5545 Signal'naya Informatsiya. Atomnoe Yadro
0203-5553 Signal'naya Informatsiya. Nelineinaya Optika i Kvantovaya Elektronika
0203-5561 Signal'naya Informatsiya. Struktura i Dinamika Reshetki Tverdykh Tel
0203-6223 Referativnyi Zhurnal. Ekonomika Promyshlennosti
0203-6436 Referativnyi Zhurnal. Teplo i Massobmen
0203-6495 F I D/R I Series on Problems of Information Science
0203-7343 Polutehniline Instituut Tallinn. Teoriya i Raschet Tonkostennykh i Prostranstvennykh Konstruktsii
0203-8889 Ekspress-Informatsiya. Informatika
0203-9494 Problemy Slov'iyanoznavstva
0203-9699 Polutehniline Instituut Tallinn. Narodonaselenie i Rabochaya Sila
0203-9702 Polutehniline Instituut Tallinn. Neustanovivsheesya Dvizheniya Zhidkosti v Trubakh
0203-9710 Polutehniline Instituut Tallinn. Teoriya i Tekhnologiya Polucheniya Stroitel'nykh Materialov iz Zol Tverdykh Topliv
0203-9737 Polutehniline Instituut Tallinn. Problemy Podzemnoi i Otkrytoi Razrabotki Goryuchikh Slantsev i Nerudnykh Materialov
0203-9745 Polutehniline Instituut Tallinn. Optimal'nye Sistemy i Algoritmy
0203-9788 Polutehniline Instituut Tallinn. Voprosy Povysheniya Kachestva Pishchevykh Produktov
0204-3548 Mineralogicheskii Zhurnal
0204-3556 Khimiya i Tekhnologiya Vody
0204-3564 Eksperimental'naya Onkologiya
0204-3572 Elektronnoe Modelirovanie
0204-3580 Metallofizika
0204-3599 Tekhnicheskaya Elektrodinamika
0204-3602 Promyshlennaya Teplotekhnika
0204-4005 Sofiiski Universitet. Istoricheski Fakultet. Godishnik.
0204-4013 Izvestiya na Muzeite v Severozapadna Bulgariya
0204-4021 Palaeobulgarica
0204-403X Izvestiya na Muzeite ot Iugoiztochna Bulgariya
0204-4048 Godishnik na Muzeite ot Severna Bulgariia
0204-4056 Otechestvo
0204-4072 Izvestiya na Muzeite ot Iuzhna Bulgariya
0204-4080 Voenno Istoricheski Sbornik
0204-4099 Natsionalen Muzei na Revoliutsionnogo Dvizhenie v Bulgariya. Godishnik†
0204-4110 Serdika; Bulgarsko Matematichesko Spisanie
0204-4684 Statisticeski Danni za Bibliotekite v Bulgaria
0204-5109 Neftena i Vuglistna Geologiia

ISSN INDEX

0204-5265 Abstracts of Bulgarian Scientific Literature. Industry, Building and Transport
0204-5311 Rudoobrazuvatelni Protsesi i Mineralni Nakhodishta
0204-5931 Zentralblatt der Bulgarischen Wissenschaftlichen Literatur. Geschichte, Archaeologie und Ethnographie
0204-5958 Fiziko-Khimicheska Mekhanika
0204-6032 Abstracts of Bulgarian Scientific Literature. Economics and Law
0204-6989 Iaderna Energiia
0204-7373 Bibliografiia na Bulgarskata Bibliografiia
0204-7438 Bibliotekar
0204-7535 Materialoznanie i Tekhnologiia
0204-7594 Biomekhanika
0204-7667 Bulletin d'Analyses de la Litterature Scientifique Bulgare. Linguistique et Litterature
0204-7675 Ekologiia
0204-7934 Inzenerna Geologiia i Khidrogeologiia
0204-8248 Vodni Problemi
0204-8728 Tantsovo Izkustvo
0204-8809 Acta Microbiologica Bulgarica
0204-8892 Bulgarian Foreign Trade
0204-8906 Bulgarian Historical Review
0204-9384 Abstracts of Bulgarian Scientific Literature. Biology and Biochemistry *changed to* Abstracts of Bulgarian Scientific Literature. Biology
0204-9406 Abstracts of Bulgarian Scientific Literature. Nauki za Zemiata
0204-9449 Abstracts of Bulgarian Scientific Literature. Mathematical and Physical Sciences
0204-9619 Sofiiski Universitet. Katedra po Nauchen Komunizm. Godishnik
0204-9627 Sofiiski Universitet. Katedra po Politiceska Ikonomiya. Godisnik
0204-9848 Problemi na Tekhnicheskata Kibernetika i Robotika
0205-0617 Naselenie
0205-0625 Uspehi na Moleculiarnata Biologia
0205-194X Rodoliubie
0205-9606 Voprosy Istorii Estestvoznanya i Tekhniki
0206-3131 Nadezhnost' i Dolgovechnost' Mashin i Sooruzhennii
0206-3166 Fizika Mnogochastichnykh Sistem
0206-3441 Khemoretseptsiya Nasekomykh
0206-4952 Immunologiya
0206-538X Signal'naya Informatsiya. Radioveshchanie - Ehlektroakustika - Zapis' i Vosproizvedenie Ehlektricheskikh Signalov†
0206-5398 Signal'naya Informatsiya. Tekhnologiya Proizvodstva Radioapparatury†
0206-5401 Signal'naya Informatsiya. Ehlektrovakuumnye Pribory i Ustroistva†
0206-541X Signal'naya Informatsiya. Materialy Elektronnoi Tekhniki†
0206-5428 Signal'naya Informatsiya. Optoehlektronnye Pribory†
0206-5452 Referativnyi Zhurnal. Elektronika
0206-5525 Referativnyi Zhurnal. Veterinariya
0206-5533 Referativnyi Zhurnal. Zhivotnovodstvo
0206-572X Mekhanizatsiya i Elektrifikatsiya
0206-6130 Referativnyi Zhurnal. Tekhnologicheskie Aspekty Okhrany Okruzhayushchei Sredy
0206-6149 Referativnyi Zhurnal. Sistemy, Pribory i Metody Kontrolya Kachestva Okruzhayushchei Sredy
0206-6157 Referativnyi Zhurnal. Okhrana i Uluchshenie Gorodskoi Sredy
0207-0111 Gibridnye Vychislitel'nye Mashiny i Kompleksy
0207-1266 Lituanistika v S.S.S.R. Ekonomika
0207-1274 Lituanistika v S.S.S.R. Literaturovedenie
0207-1371 Referativnyi Zhurnal. Raketostroenie *changed to* Referativnyi Zhurnal. Raketostroenie i Kosmicheskaya Tekhnika
0207-141X Referativnyi Zhurnal. Fiziologiya i Morfologiya Cheloveka i Zhivotnykh
0207-2165 Maslichnye Kul'tury
0207-5008 Ekspress-Informatsiya. Aviastroenie
0207-5016 Ekspress-Informatsiya. Organizatsiya Perevozok, Avtomatizirovanie, Telemekhanika i Svyaz' na Zheleznykh Dorogakh *changed to* Ekspress-Informatsiya. Organizatsiya Perevozok. Avtomatizirovannie Sistemy Upravlenia Transportom
0207-5024 Ekspress-Informatsiya. Protsessy i Apparaty Khimicheskikh Proizvodstv i Khimicheskaya Kibernetika
0207-5032 Ekspress-Informatsiya. Pryamoe Preobrazovanie Teplovoi i Khimicheskoi Energii v Elektricheskuyu
0208-0052 Novaya Sovetskaya Literatura po Obshchestvennym Naukam. Nauchnyi Kommunizm
0208-0613 Molekulyarnaya Genetika, Mikrobiologiya i Virusologiya
0208-0656 Signal'naya Informatsiya. Poverkhnost'
0208-404X Studia i Materialy do Dziejow Teatru Polskiego
0208-4082 Pomorskie Monografie Toponomastyczne
0208-4112 Polska Akademia Nauk. Instytut Podstaw Inzynierii Srodowiska. Prace i Studia
0208-4147 Probability and Mathematical Statistics
0208-4198 Archiwum Combustionis
0208-421X Studia i Materialy Oceanologiczne
0208-4228 Linguistica Silesiana
0208-4252 Bibliografia Prac Magisterkich, Doktoskich i Habilitacyjnych Przyjetych w S G G W - A R w Warszawie
0208-4260 Bibliografia Publikacji Pracownikow S G G W - A R w Warszawie
0208-4325 Gazeta Obserwatora I M G W
0208-4333 Bibliotekarz
0208-4449 Acta Universitatis Nicolai Copernici. Biologia
0208-4562 Uniwersytet Gdanski. Wydzial Humanistyczny. Zeszyty Naukowe. Psychologia
0208-4589 Prace i Studia Geograficzne
0208-4678 Uniwersytet Gdanski. Wydzial Humanistyczny. Zeszyty Naukowe. Filologia Rosyjska
0208-4732 Uniwersytet Gdanski. Wydzial Humanistyczny. Zeszyty Naukowe. Nauki Polityczne
0208-4740 Uniwersytet Gdanski. Wydzial Humanistyczny. Zeszyty Naukowe. Slawistyka
0208-4775 Uniwersytet Gdanski. Wydzial Ekonomiki Produkcji. Zeszyty Naukowe. Zagadnienia Finansowe
0208-4783 Uniwersytet Gdanski. Wydzial Ekonomiki Produkcji. Zeszyty Naukowe. Zagadnienia Ekonomiki Przemyslu
0208-4791 Uniwersytet Gdanski. Wydzial Ekonomiki Produkcji. Zeszyty Naukowe. Organizacja Pracy i Zarzadzanie
0208-4805 Uniwersytet Gdanski. Wydzial Ekonomiki Produkcji. Zeszyty Naukowe. Cybernetyka Ekonomiczna i Informatyka
0208-4813 Uniwersytet Gdanski. Wydzial Ekonomiki Transportu. Zeszyty Naukowe. Instytut Ekonomii Politycznej. Prace i Materialy
0208-4821 Uniwersytet Gdanski. Wydzial Ekonomiki Transportu. Zeszyty Naukowe. Ekonomika Transportu Ladowego
0208-483X Uniwersytet Gdanski. Wydzial Ekonomiki Transportu. Zeszyty Naukowe. Ekonomika Transportu Morskiego
0208-4864 Uniwersytet Gdanski. Wydzial Ekonomiki Transportu. Zeszyty Naukowe. Ekonomika Handlu Zagranicznego. Prace i Materialy
0208-4872 Uniwersytet Gdanski. Wydzial Matematyki, Fizyki i Chemii. Zeszyty Naukowe. Problemy Dydaktyki Fizyki
0208-4910 Uniwersytet Gdanski. Wydzial Prawa i Administracji. Zeszyty Naukowe. Prawo
0208-4929 Uniwersytet Gdanski. Wydzial Prawa i Administracji. Zeszyty Naukowe. Prace Instytutu Administracji i Zarzadzania
0208-4937 Uniwersytet Gdanski. Wydzial Biologii i Nauk o Ziemi. Zeszyty Naukowe. Geografia *changed to* Uniwersytet Gdanski. Wydzial Biologii, Geografii i Oceanologii. Zeszyty Naukowe. Geografia
0208-4961 Uniwersytet Gdanski. Wydzial Biologii i Nauk o Ziemi. Zeszyty Naukowe. Biologia *changed to* Uniwersytet Gdanski. Wydzial Biologii, Geografii i Oceanologii. Zeszyty Naukowe. Biologia
0208-4996 Lubelskie Towarzystwo Naukowe. Wydzial Humanistyczny. Prace. Monografie
0208-5003 Z Problematyki Prawa Pracy i Polityki Socjalnej
0208-5011 Z Teorii i Praktyki Dydaktycznej Jezyka Polskiego
0208-502X Studia Iuridica Silesiana
0208-5038 Rusycystyczne Studia Literaturoznawcze
0208-5046 Acta Biologica *see* 0860-2441
0208-5054 Geographia
0208-5062 Muzeum Archeologiczne i Etnograficzne, Lodz. Prace i Materialy. Seria Numizmatyczna i Konserwatorska
0208-5240 Uniwersytet Gdanski. Wydzial Humanistyczny. Zeszyty Naukowe. Filologia Angielska
0208-5259 Acta Universitatis Nicolai Copernici. Filologia Germanska
0208-5267 Acta Universitatis Nicolai Copernici. Socjologia Wychowania
0208-5283 Acta Universitatis Nicolai Copernici. Prawo
0208-5291 Acta Universitatis Nicolai Copernici. Geografia
0208-5305 Acta Universitatis Nicolai Copernici. Ekonomia
0208-5321 Acta Universitatis Nicolai Copernici. Filologia Polska
0208-533X Acta Universitatis Nicolai Copernici. Zabytkoznawstwo i Konserwatorstwo
0208-5348 Acta Universitatis Nicolai Copernici. Prace Limnologiczne
0208-5402 Uniwersytet Slaski w Katowicach. Prace Wydzialu Techniki
0208-5410 Uniwersytet Slaski w Katowicach. Prace Matematyczne *changed to* Uniwersytet Slaski w Katowicach. Annales Mathematicae Silesianae
0208-5429 Uniwersytet Slaski w Katowicach. Prace Pedagogiczne
0208-5437 Uniwersytet Slaski w Katowicach. Prace z Nauk Spolecznych
0208-5445 Uniwersytet Slaski w Katowicach. Prace Jezykoznawcze
0208-5488 Problemy Prawne Gornictwa
0208-5496 Problemy Prawne Handlu Zagranicznego
0208-550X Problemy Prawa Wynalazczego i Patentowego
0208-5518 Problemy Prawa Przewozowego
0208-5526 Pedagogika Pracy Kulturalno-Oswiatowej
0208-5534 Uniwersytet Slaski w Katowicach. Geology
0208-5550 Neophilologica
0208-5569 Psychologiczne Problemy Funkcjonowania Czlowieka w Sytuacji Pracy
0208-564X Acta Universitatis Nicolai Copernici. Filozofia
0208-5704 Warsaw Agricultural University. S G G W-A R. Annals. Forestry and Wood Technology
0208-5712 Warsaw Agricultural University. S G G W - A R. Annals. Agriculture
0208-5720 Warsaw Agricultural University. S G G W - A R. Annals. Agricultural Economics and Rural Sociology
0208-5739 Warsaw Agricultural University. S G G W A R. Annals. Animal Science
0208-5747 Warsaw Agricultural University. S G G W-A R. Annals. Horticulture
0208-5755 Warsaw Agricultural University. S G G W-A R. Annals. Food Technology and Nutrition
0208-5763 Warsaw Agricultural University. S G G W-A R. Annals. Veterinary Medicine
0208-5771 Warsaw Agricultural University. S G G W - A R. Annals. Land Reclamation
0208-578X Fizyka i Chemia Metali
0208-5925 Instytut Sadownictwa i Kwiaciarstwa w Skierniewicach. Prace. Seria B: Rosliny Ozdobne
0208-5933 Instytut Sadownictwa i Kwiaciarstwa w Skierniewicach. Seria A: Prace Doswiadczalne z Zakresu Sadownictwa
0208-6077 Acta Universitatis Lodziensis: Folia Linguistica
0208-6093 Acta Universitatis Lodziensis: Folia Paedagogica et Psychologica
0208-6107 Acta Universitatis Lodziensis: Folia Philosophica
0208-6123 Acta Universitatis Lodziensis: Folia Geographica
0208-614X Acta Universitatis Lodziensis: Folia Biochimica et Biophysica
0208-6190 Acta Universitatis Lodziensis: Folia Physica
0208-6204 Acta Universitatis Lodziensis: Folia Mathematica
0208-6263 Instytut Meteorologii i Gospodarki Wodnej. Wiadomosci
0208-6336 Problemy Prawa Karnego
0208-6425 Inzynieria Chemiczna *changed to* Inzynieria Chemiczna i Procesowa
0208-645X Instytut Geologiczny. Prace
0208-6573 Functiones et Approximatio Commentarii Mathematici
0208-7286 Politechnika Slaska. Zeszyty Naukowe. Informatyka
0208-7375 Polish Political Science
0208-7596 Archiwum Tlumaczen z Teorii Literatury i Metodologii Badan Literackich
0208-7944 Akademia Ekonomiczna, Krakow. Zeszyty Naukowe
0208-8061 Polish Academy of Sciences. Institute of Geophysics. Series G. Numerical Methods in Geophysics
0208-8371 Politechnika Wroclawska. Studium Praktycznej Nauki Jezykow Obcych. Prace Naukowe. Monografie
0208-841X Planetary Geodesy
0208-8428 Space Physics
0208-8436 Akademia Rolnicza, Poznan. Roczniki. Rozprawy Naukowe
0208-8525 Polish Academy of Sciences. Institute of Geophysics. Series C. Geomagnetism
0208-8932 Akademia Rolnicza, Poznan. Rocznik. Melioracje Wodne *changed to* Akademia Rolnicza, Poznan. Roczniki. Melioracje
0208-8940 Akademia Rolnicza, Poznan. Roczniki. Fizyka, Chemia
0208-9564 Wyzsza Szkola Pedagogiczna, Opole. Zeszyty Naukowe. Seria A. Psychologia
0208-9963 Biblioteka Res Facta
0209-0112 Zbiorcza Szkola Gminna
0209-0260 Polish Engineering
0209-0406 Polish Academy of Sciences. Institute of Geophysics. Series B. Seismology
0209-1593 Prace Naukowo-Badawcze Instytutu Maszyn Matematycznych
0209-164X Zywienie Czlowieka

0209-1674 Akademia Ekonomiczna, Krakow. Zeszyty Naukowe. Seria Specjalna: Monografie
0209-2077 Etnografia
0209-2573 Politechnika Wroclawska. Instytut Sterowania i Techniki Systemow. Prace Naukowe. Monografie
0209-3324 Politechnika Slaska. Zeszyty Naukowe. Transport
0209-4002 Hungary. Kozponti Statisztikai Hivatal. Iparstatisztikai Evkonyv
0209-4010 Hungary. Kozponti Statisztikai Hivatal. Beruhazasi-Epitoipari Adatok†
0209-4401 Made in Hungary Yearbook
0209-4541 Oxidation Communications
0209-4819 Idegenforgalmi Statisztika *see* 0230-4414
0209-5033 Muszaki Lapszemle. Gepeszet-Gepgyartastechnologia *see* 0231-0694
0209-5327 Hazai es Kulfoldi Roplapok, Prospektusok, Kulonlenyomatok, Szabvanyok es Szabadamak az Agroinform Allomanyaban
0209-5386 Hungarian Digest
0209-5513 Hungary. Kozponti Statisztikai Hivatal. Lakasepites es Megszunes *see* 0236-9524
0209-584X Jelkep
0209-6919 Hungary. Kozponti Statisztikai Hivatal. Agazati Kapcsolatok Merlege
0209-7915 Hungary. Kozponti Statisztikai Hivatal. Vizgazdalkodasi Statisztikai Zsebkonyv
0209-9403 Studia Poetica
0209-9543 Acta Universitatis Szegediensis de Attila Jozsef Nominatae. Sectio Ethnographica et Linguistica
0209-9578 Textil- es Textilruhazati Ipari Szakirodalmi Tajekoztato
0209-9683 Combinatorica
0209-9853 Gyorsindex - Epites
0210-0002 Revistas Espanolas en Curso de Publicacion†
0210-0045 Awrag *changed to* Awraq Yadida
0210-0118 Novamaquina 2000
0210-0177 Actualidad Bibliografica Iberoamericana
0210-0223 Sistema
0210-024X Petrogas
0210-0266 Spain. Consejo Superior de Investigaciones Cientificas. Cuadernos de Economia
0210-0274 Batik
0210-0320 Yate y Motonautica
0210-0347 Boletin Informativo de Medio Ambiente†
0210-0363 Estudios Trinitarios
0210-0398 Ciencia Tomista
0210-0436 Perspectiva Social
0210-0479 Cimbra
0210-0487 Ciudad y Territorio
0210-055X Metales y Maquinas
0210-0576 Revista Espanola de Ortodoncia
0210-0592 Sumario Actual de Revistas
0210-0614 Revista Espanola de Documentacion Cientifica
0210-0630 Cuadernos de Pedagogia
0210-069X Spain. Servicio Social de Higiene y Seguridad del Trabajo. Boletin Bibliografico *see* 0212-2359
0210-0711 Colectanea de Jurisprudencia Canonica
0210-0738 Confederacion Espanola de Cajas de Ahorros. Fundacion Fondo para la Investigacion Economica y Social. Coyuntura Economica
0210-0746 Cuadernos de Filologia Clasica
0210-0762 Maestria Industrial
0210-0770 Embalajes *see* 0210-1084
0210-0800 Revista de la Industria Textil
0210-0819 Ciencia e Industria Farmaceutica
0210-0827 Instituto de Investigaciones Pesqueras. Datos Informativos†
0210-0835 Nueva Estafeta†
0210-0851 Moralia
0210-086X Cuadernos de Geografia
0210-0975 Instituto de Estudios de Administracion Local. Secretariado Iberoamericano de Municipios. Boletin de Informacion *changed to* Instituto de Estudios de Administracion Local. Oficina Tecnica de la O I C I. Boletin de Informacion
0210-1017 Panorama Veterinario
0210-1025 Revista Espanola de Economia
0210-1084 Embalajes & Plasticos y Manufacturas
0210-1122 Boletin del Mutualismo Laboral†
0210-1173 Hacienda Publica Espanola
0210-1203 Edicion
0210-122X Proceso de Datos
0210-1297 Escuela Tecnica Superior de Ingenieros de Montes. Biblioteca. Boletin Bibliografico y Documental *see* 0212-226X
0210-1343 Anuario de Filologia
0210-1432 Comentario Sociologico
0210-1475 Sociedad Castellonense de Cultura. Boletin
0210-1513 Manipulacion de Materiales en la Industria
0210-1580 Boletin de Estadistica y Coyuntura
0210-1602 Teorema
0210-1610 Estudios Eclesiasticos
0210-1688 Banca Espanola
0210-1718 Laboreo
0210-1742 Revista de Extension Agraria
0210-1785 Anuario de Sociologia y Psicologia Juridicas
0210-1793 Facultad de Medicina de Barcelona. Departamento de Psiquiatria. Revista
0210-1815 Industria Internacional
0210-1831 Boletin Merksa de Estudios de Mercado
0210-184X M I
0210-1874 Revista Espanola de Linguistica
0210-1912 Cunicultura
0210-1920 Confiteria Espanola
0210-1963 Arbor
0210-2056 Energia
0210-2064 Ingenieria Quimica
0210-2137 Gaceta Numismatica
0210-2153 Luz y Fuerza
0210-2196 Revista Quirurgica Espanola
0210-220X Jano "Medicina y Humanidades"
0210-2307 Industria Minera
0210-2315 Boletin de la Normalizacion Espanola
0210-2331 Perspectiva Escolar
0210-2404 Revista de Economia y Hacienda Local *changed to* Revista de Hacienda Autonomica y Local
0210-2412 Revista Espanola de Financiacion y Contabilidad
0210-2420 Revista Jurisdiccion Contencioso - Administrativa
0210-2463 Spain. Instituto Nacional de Investigaciones Agrarias. Anales. Serie: General†
0210-2471 Spain. Instituto Nacional de Investigaciones Agrarias. Anales. Serie: Recursos Naturales *see* 0211-9102
0210-2498 Spain. Instituto Nacional de Investigaciones Agrarias. Anales. Serie: Higiene y Sanidad Animal *see* 0211-4674
0210-2501 Spain. Instituto Nacional de Investagaciones Agronomicas. Anales *see* 0211-4682
0210-251X Instituto de Investigacion Textil y de Cooperacion Industrial. Boletin *changed to* Instituto de Investigacion Textil y de Cooperacion Industrial. Boletin INTEXTAR
0210-2536 Estacion Central de Ecologia. Boletin
0210-2560 Spain. Instituto Nacional de Investigaciones Agrarias. Comunicaciones. Serie: Tecnologia Agraria
0210-2579 Comercio Industria†
0210-2595 Comercio e Industria. Suplemento Quicenal *changed to* Comercio e Industria
0210-2692 Zona Abierta
0210-282X Tecnica Topografica
0210-2854 Revista de Estudios Extremenos
0210-2870 Dialogo Ecumenico
0210-2897 Revista de Derecho Publico
0210-2919 Cronica Tributaria
0210-2943 Memorias de Historia Antigua
0210-3168 Alforja
0210-3206 Informacion Economica Mundial
0210-3214 Camp de l'Arpa
0210-329X Spain. Instituto Nacional de Investigaciones Agrarias. Comunicaciones. Serie: Produccion Vegetal
0210-3303 Spain. Instituto Nacional de Investigaciones Agrarias. Comunicaciones. Serie: Produccion Animal
0210-3311 Spain. Instituto Nacional de Investigaciones Agrarias. Comunicaciones. Serie: General
0210-332X Spain. Instituto Nacional de Investigaciones Agrarias. Comunicaciones. Serie: Economia y Sociologia Agrarias
0210-3338 Spain. Instituto Nacional de Investigaciones Agrarias. Comunicaciones. Serie: Recursos Naturales
0210-3397 Avances en Terapeutica
0210-3419 Spain. Ministerio de Justicia. Secretaria General Tecnica. Documentacion Juridica
0210-3516 Letras de Deusto
0210-3559 Pastoral Misionera
0210-3605 Vida Silvestre
0210-3680 Revista de Acustica
0210-3761 T G
0210-3869 Delta (Barcelona) *see* 0011-2453
0210-4083 Monsalvat
0210-4105 Astrum
0210-4113 Fomento Social *see* 0015-6043
0210-4148 Fundacion Juan March. Boletin Informativo
0210-4164 A N A B A D Boletin
0210-4245 Nueva Estetica
0210-4261 Eikonos
0210-4296 Revista Juridica de Cataluna
0210-4326 Parapsicologia†
0210-4334 Quimica Analitica
0210-4466 Asclepio
0210-4547 Anales de Literatura Hispanoamericana
0210-4563 C.A.U.
0210-461X Clinica Hematologica†
0210-4628 Clinica Gastroenterologica†
0210-4636 Clinica Endocrinologica†
0210-4644 Clinica Radiologica†
0210-4660 Clinica Anestesiologica
0210-4687 Revista de Bachillerato
0210-4822 Real Academia Espanola. Boletin
0210-4857 Cuadernos Salmantinos de Filosofia
0210-489X Informacion Arqueologica
0210-4903 Universidad de Murcia. Miscelanea Medieval Muriciana
0210-4911 Universidad de Murcia. Estudios Romanicos
0210-492X Universidad de Murcia. Didactica Geografica
0210-4938 Clinica Ginecologica
0210-5004 Mediterranea
0210-508X I.Q.S.
0210-5187 Medicina Cutanea Ibero-Latino-Americana
0210-5233 Revista Espanola de Investigaciones Sociologicas
0210-539X Universidad de Murcia. Anales de Derecho
0210-5454 Universidad de Antioquia. Revista
0210-5454 Universidad de Granada. Boletin
0210-5462 Cuadernos Geograficos
0210-5489 Euromueble
0210-5527 Universidad de Oviedo. Facultad de Medicina. Archivos
0210-5535 Panorama Harinero
0210-5578 Diario de Congresos Medicos
0210-5608 Ethnica
0210-5616 Tria
0210-5632 Consulta
0210-5659 Nuestra Cabana
0210-5705 Gastroenterologia y Hepatologia
0210-5713 American Journal of Medicine (Spanish Edition)†
0210-5721 Pediatrics (Spanish Edition)
0210-573X Clinica e Investigacion en Ginecologia y Obstetricia
0210-5810 Anuario de Estudios Americanos
0210-5845 Federacion Espanola de Natacion. Anuario.†
0210-5888 Poesia
0210-5977 Presupuesto y Gasto Publico
0210-6086 Estudios Filosoficos
0210-6302 Actualidad Electronica
0210-637X Anuario Hortofruticola Espanol
0210-6485 Rotacion de la Tierra
0210-6493 Boletin Astronomico
0210-6566 Cuadernos de Historia de la Farmacia
0210-6825 Alerta Informativa. Serie B: Fisica Aplicada†
0210-6833 Diputacio Provincial. Biblioteca Catalunya Cataleg la Produccion Editorial Barcelonesa
0210-685X Deformacion Metalica
0210-6868 Piscinas
0210-7007 Alerta Informativa. Serie D: el Mundo Rural†
0210-7023 Alerta Informativa. Serie E: Economia de la Empresa†
0210-7074 Estudios Josefinos
0210-7171 Avances en Obstetricia y Ginecologia
0210-7295 Tribuna Cooperativa
0210-7309 O.R.L.- D I P S
0210-735X Almanaque Nautico
0210-7570 Faventia†
0210-7597 Acta Botanica Barcinonensia
0210-7678 Anales de la Universidad Hispalense. Serie: Filosofia y Letras
0210-7686 Anales de la Universidad Hispalense. Serie: Derecho
0210-7694 Habis
0210-7732 Anuario de Eusko-Folklore
0210-7775 Medios Audiovisuales
0210-7953 Estudios de Filologia Inglesa
0210-7988 Revista de Ferreteria
0210-8046 Almanaque Nautico Reducido para Uso con Maquinas de Calcular
0210-8119 Ocultaciones de Estrellas por la Luna
0210-8127 Fenomenos Astronomicos
0210-8291 Quaderns de Treball
0210-8348 Psiquis
0210-8356 Revista de Minas
0210-8372 Bibliografia Espanola. Suplemento de Publicaciones Periodicas
0210-8488 Indice Espanol de Humanidades
0210-8623 Centro De Edafologia y Biologia Aplicada. Anuario
0210-8852 F A C: Revista Practica de Medicina
0210-9107 Papeles de Economia Espanola
0210-9220 Spain. Direccion General de Trafico. Boletin Informativo.
0210-9522 Miscelanea Comillas
0210-9603 Anuario de Historia Moderna y Contemporanea
0210-9743 Universidad Complutense de Madrid. Centro de Calculo. Boletin†
0211-030X Agrishell
0211-0334 Boletin de Estudios y Documentacion de Servicios Sociales†
0211-0547 Cuadernos de Investigacion Filologica
0211-0768 D'Art
0211-1268 Boletin de Coyuntura y Estadistica del Pais Vasco†
0211-1284 Coyuntura Industrial y Utilizacion de la Capacidad Productiva de Alava
0211-1314 Spain. Instituto Nacional de Investigaciones Agrarias. Comunicaciones. Serie: Higiene y Sanidad
0211-1322 Jardin Botanico de Madrid. Anales
0211-1373 Indice Espanol de Ciencias Sociales
0211-1578 Comercio Industria y Navegacion
0211-1748 Noticiario Arqueologico Hispanico: Arqueologia
0211-1993 Revistas Espanolas con ISSN
0211-2299 Endocrinologia
0211-2329 Instituto de Estudios Gerundenses. Anales

1490 ISSN INDEX

0211-2477 Instituto de Estudios Gerundenses. Serie Monografica
0211-2892 Rotacion
0211-2930 Cambus
0211-304X Sernaval
0211-3465 Ciencia Pediatrika
0211-4046 Boletin de Traducciones
0211-4143 Actualidad Bibliografica de Filosofia y Teologia
0211-4410 Guia de Centros Educativos Catolicos
0211-4526 Persona y Derecho
0211-4569 Sal Terrae
0211-4674 Spain. Instituto Nacional de Investigaciones Agrarias. Anales. Serie: Ganadera†
0211-4682 Spain. Instituto Nacional de Investigaciones Agrarias. Anales. Serie: Agricola†
0211-4704 Campo y Mecanica
0211-5379 Coyuntura Comercial. Alava
0211-5581 Revista Politica Comparada
0211-5611 Anthropos
0211-6057 Nutricion Clinica: Dietetica Hospitalaria
0211-6243 Real Sociedad Espanola de Fisica y Quimica. Anales de Fisica
0211-6529 Miscellanea Zoologica
0211-6561 Mensajero
0211-6820 Cuadernos de Investigacion Geografica
0211-6839 Cuadernos de Investigacion Historia
0211-6901 Gine Dips
0211-7142 Banco Central. Boletin Informativo
0211-8173 Tecnologia del Agua
0211-8335 B I B E Bulletin
0211-8335 B I B E Annual Summary
0211-8734 Informe Economico Regional
0211-8866 Region Exporta
0211-8998 Institucion Fernan-Gonzalez. Boletin
0211-9102 Spain. Instituto Nacional de Investigaciones Agrarias. Anales. Serie: Forestal†
0211-9323 Coyuntura Industrial de la Region Valenciana
0211-9536 Dynamis
0211-9749 Vida Religiosa
0211-9897 Spain. Ministerio de Agricultura, Pesca y Alimentacion. Boletin Mensual de Estadistica
0212-0151 Lancet (Edicion en Espanol)
0212-0208 Pensamiento Iberoamericano
0212-033X Spain. Ministerio de Relaciones con las Cortas y de la Secretaria de Estado. Boletin Oficial del Estado
0212-0542 Gaseta Sanitaria de Barcelona
0212-0550 Cuadernos de Traduccion e Interpretacion
0212-159X Andalucia Islamica. Textos y Estudios
0212-2146 Campo
0212-226X Escuela Tecnica Superior de Ingenieros de Montes. Biblioteca. Boletin Bibliografico y Documental. Informacion Forestal. Seria A: Monografias
0212-2278 Escuela Tecnica Superior de Ingenieros de Montes. Biblioteca. Boletin Bibliografico y Documental. Informacion Forestal. Serie B: Publicaciones Periodicas
0212-2359 Instituto Nacional de Seguridad e Higiene en el Trabajo. Boletin Bibliografico
0212-3215 Sociedad de Estudios Vascos. Cuadernos de Seccion. Artes Plasticas y Monumentales
0212-3223 Sociedad de Estudios Vascos. Cuadernos de Seccion. Hizkuntza Eta Literatura
0212-3231 Poder y Libetad
0212-324X Vindicacion Feminista
0212-3754 Revista de Robotica
0212-3800 Infectologika
0212-4173 Sociedad de Estudios Vascos. Cuadernos de Seccion. Ciencias Naturales
0212-4696 C Q Radio Amateur
0212-5226 Equipack
0212-5382 Nursing (Year) (Edicion en Espanol)
0212-5625 Caza y Pesca
0212-5765 Inmunologia
0212-5919 Thalassas
0212-5978 Razon Espanola
0212-5994 Suplementos Sobre el Sistema Financiero de Papeles de Economia Espanola
0212-6052 Ciencia Medica
0212-6109 Historia Economica
0212-6559 Universidad de Murcia. Anales de Historia Contemporanea
0212-6818 Electro-Ocio
0212-7202 Industrias Pesqueras
0212-7512 Tribuna Medica
0212-7547 Sociedad de Estudios Vascos. Cuadernos de Seccion. Folklore
0212-8322 Universidad de Murcia. Anales de Pedagogia
0212-8519 Instalaciones Deportivas
0212-8977 Universidad de Oviedo. Revista de Biologia
0212-9108 Ruizia
0212-9248 Museu Arxiu de Santa Maria. Fulls
0212-9698 Universidad de Murcia. Anales de Filosofia
0212-9728 Universidad de Murcia. Anales de Psicologia
0212-9744 Geriatrika
0213-005X Enfermedades Infecciosas
0213-0157 Revista de Farmacologia Clinica y Experimental
0213-0289 Sociedad de Estudios Vascos. Cuadernos de Seccion. Medios de Comunicacion
0213-0297 Sociedad de Estudios Vascos. Cuadernos de Seccion. Antropologia-Etnografia
0213-0483 Sociedad de Estudios Vascos. Cuadernos de Seccion. Derecho
0213-0602 Spain. Ministerio de Agricultura, Pesca y Alimentacion. Informacion Extranjero. Boletin
0213-0815 Sociedad de Estudios Vascos. Cuadernos de Seccion. Musica
0213-0823 Nueva Ferreteria
0213-120X Joyas & Joyeros
0213-1781 Universidad de Murcia. Papeles de Geografia
0213-2257 Miscelanea de Texos Medievales *changed to* Miscel-lania de Textos Medievals
0213-2273 Situacion. Suplemento de Coyuntura
0213-2699 Estudios Economicos
0213-2958 Universidad de Murcia. Anales de Filologia Francesa
0213-3024 Sociedad de Estudios Vascos. Cuadernos de Seccion. Prehistoria y Arqueologia
0213-3091 Inter-Transport
0213-3601 Sociedad de Estudios Vascos. Cuadernos de Seccion. Medicina
0213-3636 Sociedad de Estudios Vascos. Cuadernos de Seccion. Educacion
0213-392X Universidad de Murcia. Imafronte. Departmento de Historia del Arte
0213-3938 Universidad de Murcia. Anales de Biologia. Seccion Especial
0213-3954 British Medical Journal. Edicion Espanola
0213-3997 Universidad de Murcia. Anales de Biologia. Seccion Biologia Animal
0213-4004 Universidad de Murcia. Anales de Biologia. Seccion Biologia Ambiental
0213-4144 Archivos de Odonto Estomatologia
0213-4365 Universidad de Murcia. Anales de Filologia Hispanica
0213-5434 Universidad de Murcia. Anales de Veterinaria
0213-5442 Universidad de Murcia. Anales de Biologia. Seccion Biologia General
0213-5450 Universidad de Murcia. Anales de Biologia. Seccion Biologia Vegetal
0213-5469 Universidad de Murcia. Anales de Ciencias
0213-5477 Universidad de Murcia. Contrastes: Revista de Historia Moderna
0213-5485 Universidad de Murcia. Cuadernos de Filologia Inglesa
0213-571X Productronica
0213-635X Spain. Instituto Nacional de Investigaciones Agrarias. Investigacion Agraria: Economia
0213-6449 Saber Leer
0216-0269 Kabar
0216-0412 Ekonomi Indonesia (English Edition)
0216-1052 Indonesian Importers
0216-1265 University of Indonesia. Institute of Management. Newsletter
0216-1273 Berita Bibliografi
0216-3217 Indonesia. Lembaga Pertahanan Nasional. National Resilience
0216-3527 Indonesian Public Health Association. Journal
0216-4000 Jepara. Shrimp Culture Research Centre. Bulletin *changed to* Brackishwater Aquaculture Development Centre. Bulletin
0216-4027 Mantap: Majalah Ilmaih P K M I
0216-4167 Sari Karangan Indonesia
0216-4760 Buletin Penelitian Hutan *changed to* Forest Research Bulletin
0216-6216 Index of Indonesian Learned Periodicals
0216-7204 Indonesian Journal of Bioanthropology
0217-0590 Social Dimension
0217-104X Management Abstracts of Singapore *changed to* A S E A N Management Abstracts
0217-1058 Her World Annual
0217-1546 Singapore. National Library. Annual Report
0217-2992 Contributions to Southeast Asian Ethnography
0217-3077 R E L C Newsletter
0217-3476 Singapore Stock Exchange Journal
0217-3891 Telecommunication Authority of Singapore. Telecoms Annual Report
0217-4456 Singapore Accountant (Singapore, 1984)
0217-4472 A S E A N Economic Bulletin
0217-6009 Times Business Directory of Singapore
0217-6998 Mabuhay
0217-717X Malaysian Accountant
0217-7528 Singapore Trade News
0217-7587 Politeia
0217-765X Go
0217-7668 S I A Yearbook
0217-7706 Creative Homes
0217-7757 Singapore This Week†
0217-8311 Directory of Certified Products in Singapore
0217-913X University of Singapore. History Society. Journal
0219-5550 Commodities *see* 0746-2468
0220-0546 Lettre d'Intergeo
0220-2425 Campos
0220-2476 Information Cardiologique
0220-276X Gwechall
0220-3294 Industrie du Petrole - Gaz - Chimie
0220-5157 Plume Limousine
0220-5270 Revue de l'Offshore†
0220-5424 Bulletin des Consommateurs
0220-5610 Cahiers Victoriens et Edouardiens
0220-6102 Tiers-Monde Engineering *changed to* Tiers Monde Ingenierie
0220-6137 Carrousel
0220-6617 Revue Archeologique du Centre de la France
0220-6668 Ecole Buissonniere
0220-6862 International Executive Search Newsletter *see* 0752-4676
0220-746X Collection Oralites-Documents
0220-8156 Ville de Paris
0220-9535 L C I E-Informations
0220-9896 Revue de la Concurrence et de la Consommation
0220-9926 Realites Familiales
0221-0142 U N S S. Sport Scolaire
0221-0436 Mondes et Cultures
0221-0665 Annales Francaises des Chronometrie et de Microtechniques *see* 0294-1228
0221-2536 France. Bureau de Recherches Geologiques et Minieres. Documents
0221-2781 Politique Internationale
0221-301X Presse du Vin-Vinetec
0221-5780 Cote-d'Ivoire Selection
0221-7945 Societe Theophile Gautier. Bulletin
0221-8747 Metabolic Bone Disease and Related Research *changed to* Bone
0222-0377 Charcuterie et Gastronomie
0222-1543 Russkoe Vozrozhdenie
0222-3856 Audition et Parole†
0222-4275 N R S
0222-447X Minis Autos
0222-4828 Jeux d'Afrique
0222-4844 Connaissance du Rail
0222-5069 International Journal of Microsurgery
0222-5220 France. Ministere de l'Agriculture. Situation Agricole en France. Conjoncture Generale
0222-593X Bamerkhav†
0222-5956 Cahiers Confrontation
0222-6618 Commerce et Cooperation
0222-6766 Cercle Genealogique et Heraldique de Normandie *see* 0294-7382
0222-6782 Revue Francaise de Genealogie
0222-7762 Institut de Recherches Marxistes. Issues *changed to* S E P I R M Issues
0222-8394 France. Laboratoire Central des Ponts et Chaussees. Rapport de Recherche
0222-9714 Cahiers Evangile
0223-0100 Sigma
0223-0127 Videoglyphes
0223-0135 Revue Technique Machinisme Agricole
0223-1077 A B C D
0223-1603 Galerie des Arts
0223-3290 Hommes et Migrations
0223-3398 B.O.P.I. Dessins & Modeles
0223-3401 B.O.P.I. Marques
0223-341X Bulletin Signaletique. Part 520: Sciences de l'Education
0223-3843 Medieviste et l'Ordinateur
0223-4092 B.O.P.I. Listes
0223-4238 Bulletin Signaletique. Part 381: Sciences Agronomiques. Productions Vegetales†
0223-4246 Bulletin Signaletique. Part 891: Industries Mecaniques *changed to* P A S C A L Folio. Part 10: Mecanique et Acoustique
0223-4254 Bulletin Signaletique. Part 892: Batiment. Travaux Publics. Transports *changed to* P A S C A L Thema. Part 195: Batiment. Travaux Publics
0223-4254 Bulletin Signaletique. Part 892: Batiment. Travaux Publics. Transports *changed to* P A S C A L Folio. Part 25: Transports Terrestres et Maritimes
0223-4335 Societe Francaise du Vide. Comptes Rendus des Travaux des Congres et Colloques
0223-4637 Semaine Sociale Lamy
0223-4696 Flash-Informations
0223-4718 Revue Fiduciaire
0223-4726 Legi-Social
0223-4734 Croire Aujourd'hui
0223-4866 Enjeux
0223-4912 France. Ministere de l'Agriculture. Informations Rapides. Production Animale
0223-4920 France. Ministere de l'Agriculture. Informations Rapides. Secteur Avicole
0223-4939 France. Ministere de l'Agriculture. Informations Rapides. Statistique Laitiere
0223-5137 Neuroptera International
0223-5145 Entreprise et Formation Permanente
0223-534X Instructions Nautiques
0223-5358 Feux et Signaux de Brume
0223-5420 Accueillir
0223-5714 Proletariat†
0223-5730 Realities Franc-Comtoises
0223-5749 Reforme
0223-5773 Cahiers D'Action Francaise *changed to* Aspects de la France
0223-5838 Questions de Securite Sociale
0223-5846 Hommes et Commerce
0223-5854 Eglise Aujourd'hui
0223-5986 Enseignement Public
0223-7237 Genealogies Bourbonnaises et du Centre
0223-9159 Bibliographie Internationale des Industries Agro-Alimentaires
0223-9353 Masques
0223-9434 Lettre du Psychiatre

ISSN INDEX 1491

0223-9469 Universite de Saint Etienne. Centre Jean Palerne. Memoires
0224-1196 Special Motoculteurs et Tondeuses a Gazon *changed to* L'Officiel Jardin-Motoculture
0224-2265 Semaine de l'Energie
0224-2435 Syndicat General des Commerces et Industries du Caoutchouc et des Plastiques. Guide
0224-2478 Annuaire Repertoire de la Motoculture de Plaisance Jardinage
0224-2680 Asie du Sud-Est et Monde Insulindien
0224-4365 Travail et Emploi
0224-4772 Geopolitique du Petrole†
0224-5027 Boulanger-Patissier, Confiseur, Glacier
0224-7232 Casse-Tete Magazine
0224-8042 C.T.N.E.R.H.I. Documents†
0225-0233 Bonne Nouvelle
0225-0500 Canadian Journal of Netherlandic Studies
0225-0608 Canadian Taxpayer
0225-1205 Minjoong Shinmoon
0225-1485 Canadian Heritage
0225-1507 Canada. Statistics Canada. Coastwise Shipping Statistics
0225-1574 Canadiana Authorities
0225-168X Insurance Institute of Canada. Newsletter
0225-1701 Insurance Institute of Ontario. Newsletter
0225-1760 U T L A S Newsletter
0225-2112 Feuillet Biblique
0225-2279 Canadian Native Law Reporter
0225-2287 Legal Information Service Reports
0225-2910 Banque Nationale du Canada. Revue Economique
0225-3216 Canadiana on Microfiche
0225-3550 S P E A Q Journal
0225-3895 Medicine North America
0225-4115 Justice - Directory of Services
0225-4190 Handbook of Canadian Consumer Markets
0225-4212 Plasmapheresis and Plasma Exchange†
0225-4484 Boreal Institute for Northern Studies. Library Bulletin
0225-4530 Quebec (Province) Pension Board. Supplemental Pension Plans-Characteristics and Membership Statistics†
0225-4565 Agent West Weekly *see* 0834-0471
0225-4700 Ma Caisse
0225-4913 Horses All
0225-509X British Columbia. Housing Management Commission. Annual Report
0225-5170 A S T I S Occasional Publications
0225-5189 Canadian Journal of Development Studies
0225-5316 Ontario. Geological Survey. Geoscience Research Grant Program. Summary of Research
0225-5383 Moving to Saskatchewan
0225-5642 Canada. Statistics Canada. List of Canadian Hospitals and Special Care Facilities/Liste des Hopitaux Canadiens et des Etablissements de Soins Speciaux
0225-5804 Resilog
0225-5847 Canadian Legislative Report†
0225-6002 Canadian Earthquakes
0225-6320 C T M: the Human Element
0225-6363 Coatings
0225-6398 Landscape Trades
0225-6843 Broadside
0225-686X Musicworks
0225-6932 Canadian Federation for the Humanities. Annual Report
0225-7068 Mandate
0225-7165 Atlantic Salmon Newsletter
0225-7270 Theodolite
0225-7351 Chess Canada Echecs *see* 0822-5672
0225-7459 Canadian News Index
0225-7572 Logging & Sawmilling Journal
0225-8013 Economic Council of Canada. Discussion Papers
0225-851X Professional Engineer
0225-9036 Index to Commonwealth Legal Periodicals†
0225-9044 Spirale
0225-9435 Canadian Music Trade
0225-9591 Medecin Veterinaire du Quebec
0225-9958 Canadian Review of Physical Anthropology
0226-0336 Canada Mortgage and Housing Corporation. Annual Report
0226-0344 Cottager Magazine†
0226-0786 Forintek Canada Corp., Western Laboratory. Review Reports†
0226-0840 Pottersfield Portfolio
0226-093X Canadian Homeowner
0226-1472 International Journal of Energy Systems
0226-1480 M I M I
0226-1510 Healthsharing
0226-1537 Index of Industrial Relations Literature
0226-157X Canadian Railway Club. Newsletter
0226-1685 A S T I S Bibliography
0226-1928 Ethnocultural Directory of Ontario†
0226-210X Quebecensia
0226-2169 Le Sagamien
0226-224X Economic Council of Canada. Au Courant
0226-2320 Canada. Statistics Canada. Restaurant, Caterer and Tavern Statistics
0226-3068 Zapad
0226-3440 U.C. Review
0226-3491 Studies in Aboriginal Rights
0226-3882 Negotiated Working Conditions from Collective Agreements in Nova Scotia
0226-3890 Nova Scotia. Department of Labour and Manpower. Compendium of Grievance Arbitration Decisions *changed to* Nova Scotia. Department of Labour. Compendium of Grievance Arbitration Decisions
0226-4781 Ici Radio Canada Television†
0226-5036 Manitoba History
0226-5125 Canadian Theatre Checklist†
0226-5419 Directory of Long-Term Care Centres in Canada
0226-5664 Canadian Collector
0226-5702 Ontario Water Skier
0226-5761 Theatre History in Canada
0226-577X Canadian Amateur Softball Association. Facts & Figures†
0226-5923 C H A C Review
0226-6105 Generations
0226-6156 Brayon *changed to* Societe Historique du Madawska. Revue
0226-6245 Entraide Genealogique
0226-6326 Guelph This Week
0226-6342 Canada. Environment Canada. Information Reports Digest
0226-661X Inter-Church Committee on Human Rights in Latin America. Newsletter
0226-6776 Moving to Houston†
0226-6881 Dialogues et Cultures
0226-7004 Summer Breezes†
0226-7063 Cahiers d'Histoire de Deux-Montagnes
0226-7101 Kingston Business Review†
0226-7209 Toronto Historical Board. Year Book
0226-7276 Moving to Vancouver & B.C.
0226-7365 Quality of Working Life†
0226-7454 Universites
0226-7462 Whiskey Jack†
0226-7470 Canadian Nuclear Society. Transactions *see* 0227-0129
0226-7527 Carleton University. Library. Serials List†
0226-7551 Shopping Centre Canada
0226-7586 McGill University. Register
0226-7616 Centre for Resources Studies. Working Papers
0226-7705 Quebec Farmers Association. Newsletter *changed to* Quebec Farmers Advocate
0226-773X Federation of Canadian Archers. Rules Book
0226-7829 Moving to Toronto and Area *see* 0713-8377
0226-7837 Moving to Ottawa/Hull
0226-8043 Quaderni d'Italianistica
0226-8086 Fuse
0226-8264 Canadian Real Estate Journal†
0226-8361 Marine Affairs Bibliography
0226-854X I P Sharp Newsletter
0226-8922 Conventions & Meetings-Canada
0226-8965 Coaching Science Update†
0226-9031 Freelance Editors' Association of Canada. Directory of Members
0226-9317 Indian Life
0226-9368 British Columbia. Ministry of Forests and Lands. Research Notes
0226-9686 Suburban
0226-9708 Photo Selection
0226-9759 Canada. Environment Canada. Insect and Disease Conditions in Canada *changed to* Canada. Canadian Forestry Service. Insect and Disease Conditions in Canada
0226-9902 Femmes d'Action
0227-0072 University of Manitoba Anthropology Papers
0227-0129 Canadian Nuclear Society. Annual Conference Summaries
0227-017X Canada. Statistics Canada. Retail Chain and Department Stores
0227-034X Service
0227-0382 Communications Week *see* 0825-3021
0227-0390 Federal Court of Appeal Decisions
0227-0579 Alberta Wild Rose Quarter Horse Journal
0227-0595 Buildcore Index
0227-0773 Island (Lantzville)
0227-0994 Family Genealogies
0227-1001 Wood Technology Notes *see* 0821-1841
0227-1192 Chronicle
0227-1230 Juice & Cookie
0227-1265 Tax Principles to Remember
0227-1311 Conflict Quarterly
0227-1362 Trends in Collective Agreement Settlement Wage Rate Changes in Nova Scotia†
0227-1370 Gaspesie
0227-1397 Ontario Business
0227-1400 Annual Bibliography of Victorian Studies
0227-1524 North American Anarchist *see* 0712-1539
0227-1532 Newfoundland T V Topics
0227-1559 U F O Update
0227-1656 Financial Post Survey of Mines and Energy Resources
0227-1699 Lyman's Standard Catalogue of Canada-B N A Postage Stamps
0227-1796 Canada. Statistics Canada. Estimation of Population by Marital Status, Age and Sex, Canada and Provinces/ Estimations de la Population Suivant l'Etat Matrimonial, l'Age et le Sexe, Canada et Provinces†
0227-1834 Soccer Canada
0227-1907 Canadian Nuclear Society. Annual Conference Proceedings
0227-2083 Professional Circle *see* 0227-2091
0227-2091 Circle
0227-2199 University of Waterloo Courier
0227-227X Liaison
0227-2393 F A M L I
0227-2636 L M G Report on Data and Word Processing
0227-2652 Cross-Canada Writers' Quarterly
0227-2865 National Bank of Canada. Economic Review
0227-289X Quebec (Province) Centrale des Bibliotheques. Services et Publications *changed to* Quebec (Province) Centrale des Bibliotheques. Produits et Services Documentaires
0227-3020 Transport-Action
0227-3160 Helicopters in Canada *changed to* Helicopters Magazine Canada
0227-3268 Ontario. Federal Cabinet. Orders-in-Council
0227-3330 Canadian Pool & Spa Marketing
0227-3357 Alberta Drilling Progress and Pipeline Receipts, Weekly Report
0227-3748 Canadian Health Record Association. Bulletin *changed to* C C H E A/C H R A. Bulletin.
0227-3780 School Libraries in Canada
0227-3802 British Columbia. Ministry of Agriculture and Food. Agricultural Aid to Developing Countries
0227-437X Provincial Results in Canada of General Insurance Companies
0227-4752 Nova Scotia Historical Review
0227-5090 Scrivener
0227-5317 Family Newsletter Directory *see* 0828-4466
0227-5910 Crisis
0227-6038 Financial Post Canadian Markets
0227-6178 Court Cases of Interest to the Ombudsman Institution
0227-7506 British Columbia. Ministry of Environment. Annual Report *changed to* British Columbia. Ministry of Environment and Parks. Annual Report
0227-7514 Saskatchewan Archaeology Society Newsletter
0227-7883 Alberta Hospitals and Medical Care. Annual Report
0227-7980 Canadian Pest Management Society Proceedings
0227-809X Canadian Business Management Developments
0227-8332 Informatique & Bureautique
0227-8642 EcoAlert
0227-8669 Canadian Business Index
0227-8731 Micro-Scope†
0227-9363 Journal de Radiologie
0227-9916 Ontario Hydro Research Review
0228-0620 J A M
0228-0736 Canada. Petawawa National Forestry Institute. Information Report
0228-0906 Victorian Order of Nurses for Canada. National Office. Newsletter†
0228-0914 Canadian School Executive
0228-1082 Alberta Motorist
0228-1244 Ennui
0228-1635 Journal of Ukrainian Studies
0228-1686 Producteur de Lait Quebecois
0228-1821 C R S Perspectives
0228-2194 Nicola Indian†
0228-2356 Aspen†
0228-250X Tricolorul
0228-2518 In Summary
0228-2984 Westminster Institute Review†
0228-3344 Potboiler Magazine
0228-3530 La Plongee
0228-359X GATT-Fly Report
0228-4642 Ontario Science Centre. Newscience
0228-491X Canadian Philosophical Reviews
0228-5134 Canada. Statistics Canada. Listing of Supplementary Documents
0228-5215 Media Editorial Profile Edition
0228-5452 La Barrique
0228-5479 La Vie en Rose
0228-5584 Agriweek
0228-5819 Canada. Statistics Canada. Current Economic Analysis *see* 0828-0851
0228-5819 Canada. Statistics Canada. Current Economic Analysis *see* 0828-086X
0228-5819 Canada. Statistics Canada. Current Economic Analysis *see* 0828-0878
0228-5843 Noticias do Canada
0228-5851 Regina Geographical Studies
0228-586X Alive
0228-6033 Baseball America
0228-6157 Wine Tidings
0228-6203 International Journal of Modelling & Simulation
0228-6211 B.C. Business Bulletin *see* 0821-0020
0228-6246 Science Council of Canada. Annual Review†
0228-6637 Arpenteur-Geometre
0228-6726 Video Guide
0228-6963 Landscape Architectural Review
0228-7153 Moving to & Around Maritimes & Newfoundland
0228-7404 Moosehead Review
0228-7587 Drillsite
0228-7730 Association des Colleges du Quebec Annuaire

0228-7781 Sound Heritage Series†
0228-7951 Ecriture Francaise dans le Monde†
0228-8117 Ministry of Agriculture. Field Crop Production Guide *changed to* British Columbia. Ministry of Agriculture and Food. Field Crop Production Guide
0228-8397 Canadian Association of African Studies. Bulletin
0228-8605 Papers in Mediaeval Studies
0228-863X Directory of Alcohol and Drug Treatment Resources in Ontario
0228-8648 Substance Abuse Book Review Index†
0228-877X Ontario Medical Technologist
0228-9806 Science Express
0228-9989 Canada. Environment Canada. Forestry Service Research Notes†
0229-0243 Royal Bank Letter†
0229-0413 Plastics Business (Toronto)
0229-0421 Health Law in Canada
0229-1320 Ontario Craft
0229-1916 Quaker Concern
0229-1932 New Canadian Fandom
0229-2181 International Ombudsman Institute. Newsletter
0229-2548 Canadian Parliamentary Review
0229-2947 Projection
0229-3099 Alberta Science Teacher
0229-3196 Toronto Clarion
0229-3455 Champion
0229-3803 Vie Ouvriere
0229-3811 Quebec (Province) Department of Recreation, Fish and Game. Annual Report
0229-4435 Artisan†
0229-4931 Source *see* 0832-9354
0229-4958 Collective Agreement Expiration in Nova Scotia†
0229-4966 Athletics
0229-5024 Birdfinding in Canada
0229-5032 Moving to Washington, D.C.†
0229-5040 Moving to Dallas/Fort Worth
0229-527X British Columbia Genealogical Society. Newsletter
0229-5385 Hysteria
0229-5679 R I A Digest†
0229-6098 Canada. Statistics Canada. Mineral Wool: Including Fibrous Glass Insulation
0229-6373 Clan Suibhne Association. Newsletter†
0229-7094 Fifth Column
0229-7108 Alberta Insurance Report
0229-7175 His Dominion
0229-7256 Canadian Research Institute for the Advancement of Women. Newsletter/Bulletin
0229-7345 Canadian Nurses Association. Nursing Programs and Entrance Requirements at Canadian Universities.
0229-737X Sugar World
0229-7876 Producteur de Porc Quebecois
0229-8090 Grainews *changed to* Grainews and Cattlemans Corner
0229-8104 O P S E U News
0229-8325 Canada. Mineral Policy Sector. Mineral Survey†
0229-8546 Alberta's Reserve of Gas: Complete Listing
0229-8651 R S S I
0229-8910 Bedford Institute of Oceanography Review
0229-9119 Varsity Student Handbook
0230-1202 Ez a Divat
0230-2241 Szolotermesztes es Boraszat
0230-2780 Acta Universitatis de Attila Jozsef Nominatae. Papers in English and American Studies
0230-3337 A Testnevelesi Foiskola Kozlemenyei
0230-4066 Hungary. Kozponti Statisztikai Hivatal. Mezogazdasagi Statisztikai Evkonyv/Yearbook of Agricultural Statistics
0230-4414 Hungary. Kozponti Statisztikai Hivatal. Idegenforgalmi Evkonyv
0230-5348 Anyagmozgatasi es Csomagolasi Szakirodalmi Tajekoztato
0230-581X Magyar Korhazak es Klinikak Evkonyve
0230-5828 Magyarorszag
0230-7065 Geologiai es Geofizikai Szakirodalmi Tajekoztato
0230-8452 Monumenta Linguae Mongolicae Collecta
0230-9718 Public Finance in Hungary
0231-0643 Automatizalasi, Szamitastechnikai es Merestechnikai Szakirodalmi Tajekoztato
0231-0651 Banyaszati Szakirodalmi Tajekoztato
0231-066X Elektronikai es Hiradastechnikai Szakirodalmi
0231-0678 Energiaipari es Energiagazdalkodasi Tajekoztato
0231-0686 Gepeszeti Szakirodalmi Tajekoztato
0231-0694 Gepgyartastechnologiai es Szerszamgepipari Szakirodalmi Tajekoztato
0231-0708 Kohaszati es Onteszeti Szakirodalmi Tajekoztato
0231-0716 Kornyezetvedelmi Szakirodalmi Tajekoztato
0231-0724 Kozuti Kozlekedesi Szakirodalmi Tajekoztato
0231-0732 Melyepitesi es Vizepitesi Szakirodalmi Tajekoztato
0231-0740 Papiripari es Nyomdaipari Szakirodalmi Tajekoztato
0231-0759 Vallalatszervezesi es Ipargazdasagi Szakirodalmi Tajekoztato
0231-0767 Vasuti Kozlekedesi Szakirodalmi Tajekoztato
0231-0775 Vegyipari Szakirodalmi Tajekoztato
0231-0783 Elektrotechnikai Szakirodalmi Tajekoztato
0231-1941 Hajozasi Szakirodalmi Tajekoztato
0231-195X Ipari Formatervezesi Szakirodalmi Tajekoztato
0231-2379 Audio-Vizualis Kozlemenyek
0231-2522 Tarsadalomkutatas
0231-2662 Finommechanika, Mikrotechnika
0231-2670 Acta Universitatis Szegediensis de Attila Jozsef Nominatae. Section Philosophica - Filozofia
0231-3146 Acta Chimica Hungarica
0231-3316 Szamitogepes Muszaki Tervezes
0231-3928 Repulesi Szakirodalmi Tajekoztato
0231-424X Acta Physiologica Hungarica
0231-441X Acta Paediatrica Hungarica
0231-4428 Acta Physica Hungarica
0231-4592 Magyar Nemzeti Bibliografia. Idoszaki Kiadvanyok Bibliografiaja
0231-4614 Acta Chirurgica Hungarica
0231-4622 Acta Microbiologica Hungarica
0231-4932 Technical and Scientific Films *see* 0236-9702
0231-5025 Univerzita J. E. Purkyne. Filozoficka Fakulta. Sbornik Praci. F: Rada Uminovedna
0231-522X Univerzita J. E. Purkyne. Filozoficka Fakulta. Sbornik Praci. H: Rada Hudebnevedna
0231-5335 Acta Dendrobiologica
0231-5351 Univerzita J. E. Purkyne. Filozoficka Fakulta. Sbornik Praci. K: Rada Germanisticko - Anglisticka
0231-5823 Archaeologia Historica
0231-5882 General Physiology and Biophysics
0231-5955 Acta Comeniana. Archiv pro Badani o Zivote a Dile Jana Amose Komenskeho
0231-6005 Acta Historiae Rerum Naturalium nec non Technicarum
0231-6153 Sbornik k Dejinam 19 a 20 Stoleti
0231-620X Sbornik k Problematice Dejin Imperialismu
0231-7494 Folia Historica Bohemica
0231-7532 Univerzita J. E. Purkyne. Filozoficka Fakulta. Sbornik Praci. L: Rada Romanistica
0231-7540 Hospodarske Dejiny
0231-7567 Univerzita J. E. Purkyne. Filozoficka Fakulta. Sbornik Praci. A: Rada Jazykovedna
0231-7664 Univerzita J. E. Purkyne. Filozoficka Fakulta. Sbornik Praci. B: Rada Filozoficka
0231-7710 Univerzita J. E. Purkyne. Filozoficka Fakulta. Sbornik Praci. C: Rada Historicka
0231-7818 Univerzita J. E. Purkyne. Filozoficka Fakulta. Sbornik Praci. D: Rada Literarnevedna
0231-7915 Univerzita J. E. Purkyne. Filozoficka Fakulta. Sbornik Praci. E: Rada Archeologicko-Klasicka
0231-9136 Monographia Historica Bohemica
0232-0150 Dejiny Socialistickeho Ceskoslovenska
0232-041X Bibliograficky Katalog C S S R: Ceske Knihy. Zvlastni Sesit. Ceske Disertace
0232-1300 Crystal Research and Technology
0232-1351 Informatik - Kybernetic - Rechentechnik. Schriftenreihe
0232-1459 Corpus Vitrearum Medii Aevi
0232-1513 Experimental Pathology
0232-1556 Beitraege zur Alexander-von Humboldt-Forschung
0232-2064 Zeitschrift fuer Analysis und Ihre Anwendungen
0232-2609 Restaurierung und Museumstechnik
0232-265X Weimarer Monographien zur Ur- und Fruehgeschichte
0232-2714 Beitraege zur Erforschung der Deutschen Sprache
0232-2765 Baustoffindustrie. Ausgabe A. Primaerbaustoffe
0232-2803 Beitraege zur Kritik der Buergerlichen Ideologie und des Revisionismus
0232-2900 Griechischen Christlichen Schriftsteller der ersten Jahrhunderte
0232-3001 Hilprecht: Sammlung
0232-315X Literatur und Gesellschaft
0232-3257 Papyri aus den Staatlichen Museen zu Berlin
0232-346X Kleine Naturwissenschaftliche Bibliothek
0232-3516 Biographien Hervorragender Naturwissenschaftler, Techniker und Mediziner
0232-3702 Volksmaerchen
0232-3869 Technische Mechanik
0232-3907 Thuringen-Bibliographie
0232-4393 Zentralblatt fuer Microbiologie
0232-4768 Die Wirtschaft
0232-4865 Bibliographie zur Archaeo-Zoologie und Geschichte der Haustiere
0232-489X Gnadauer Mitteilungen
0232-5160 Arbeitsmedizininformation
0232-5381 Altenburger Naturwissenschaftliche Forschungen
0232-5446 Landesmuseum fuer Vorgeschichte, Dresden. Kleine Schriften
0232-5616 Saechsische Landesbibliothek. Bibliographie Illustrierte Buecher der Deutschen Demokratischen Republik
0232-5780 Trade and Technical Review
0232-5810 Bibliographie Bildende Kunst
0232-6086 Adventgemeinde
0232-6310 Evangelische Kirche der Kirchenprovinz Sachsen. Amtsblatt
0232-6833 E D V-Aspekte
0232-7546 Dienstleistungen. Ausgabe A: Fachzeitschrift fuer Theorie und Praxis der Haus- und Stadtwirtschaftlichen Dienstleistungen
0232-766X Biomedica Biochimica Acta
0232-7678 Bibliographie Musik
0232-8399 Dienstleistungen. Ausgabe B: Fuer Testilreinigung und Hauswirtschaftliche Dienstleistungen
0232-8410 Asien - Afrika - Lateinamerika. Jahrbuch
0232-8461 Altorientalische Forschungen
0232-8798 Referateblatt Philosophie
0232-9298 Systems Analysis Modelling Simulation
0232-9387 Zeitgenoessisches Musikschaffen in der Deutschen Demokratischen Republik. Urauffuehrungen
0233-0105 Beitraege zur Bachforschung
0233-0741 Korrosion
0233-089X Philosophiehistorische Texte
0233-0911 Teubner-Texte zur Physik
0233-0946 Oekonomiehistorische Texte
0233-0962 Teubner-Archiv zur Mathematik
0233-1063 Mathematik und ihre Anwendungen in Physik und Technik
0233-1098 Saechsische Landesbibliothek. Neuerwerbungen und Nachrichten
0233-111X Journal of Basic Microbiology
0233-1608 Zeitschrift fuer Klinische Medizin
0233-173X Mauritiana (Altenburg)
0233-1934 Series Optimization
0233-2655 Agroselekt. Reihe 1: Landtechnik
0233-2701 Agroselekt. Reihe 2: Pflanzenproduktion
0233-2752 Agroselekt. Reihe 3: Tierproduktion
0233-2809 Agroselekt. Reihe 4. Veterinaermedizin
0233-2892 Mikroprozessortechnik
0233-6588 Signal'naya Informatsiya. Toksikologiya Lekarstvennaya
0233-6618 Signal'naya Informatsiya. Fiziologiya i Morfologiya Cheloveka i Zhivotnykh: Krov' i Limfa
0234-2979 Itogi Nauki i Tekhniki: Biofizika Membran
0234-4483 Ionnye Rasplavy i Tverdye Electrolity
0234-7059 Referativnyi Zhurnal. Environment Management Abstracts
0234-9647 Referativnyi Zhurnal. Volokonno-opticheskie Systemy
0234-968X Signal'naya Informatsiya. Khimiya Vysokikh Energii
0234-9698 Signal'naya Informatsiya. Sorbenty i Poverkhnostno-Aktivnye Veshchestva
0234-9701 Signal'naya Informatsiya. Ochistika i Utilizatsiya Otkhodov Khimicheskikh Proizvodstv
0234-971X Signal'naya Informatsiya. Napolnennye i Armirovannye Plastiki
0234-9736 Signal'naya Informatsiya. Kataliz i Ktalizatory
0234-9744 Signal'naya Informatsiya. Analiticheskaya Khimiya
0234-9752 Signal'naya Informatsiya. Neiropeptidy
0234-9760 Signal'naya Informatsiya. Ishemicheskaya Bolezn' Serdtsa
0236-5278 Acta Geologica Hungarica
0236-5286 Acta Medica Hungarica
0236-5294 Acta Mathematica Hungarica
0236-5391 Acta Morphologica Hungarica
0236-5731 Journal of Radioanalytical and Nuclear Chemistry *changed to* Journal of Radioanalytical and Nuclear Chemistry. Articles
0236-5731 Journal of Radioanalytical and Nuclear Chemistry *changed to* Journal of Radioanalytical Chemistry. Letters
0236-6134 Magyar Elektronika
0236-6290 Acta Veterinaria Hungarica
0236-6495 Acta Botanica Hungarica
0236-6568 Hungarian Studies
0236-705X Elelmiszertudomanyi es Elelmiszeripari Szakirodalmi Tajekoztato
0236-7130 Acta Zoologica Hungarica
0236-8722 International Agrophysics
0236-9524 Hungary. Kozponti Statisztikai Hivatal. Lakasstatisztikai Evkonyv
0236-9702 Scientific Films and Videocassettes
0237-0115 Biotechnology Information
0237-028X Acta I M E K O
0237-0298 Hungary. Kozponti Statisztikai Hivatal. Epitoipari Arak Alakulasa
0237-0808 Hungarian R and D Abstracts. Science and Technology
0237-2215 International Symposium of the Technical Committee on Photon-Detectors
0238-969X Polish Export-Import *see* 0032-2881
0239-0094 Politechnika Poznanska. Instytut Nauk Ekonomicznych i Spolecznych. Prace Naukowe *see* 0239-9423
0239-3182 Politechnika Wroclawska. Instytut Konstrukcji i Eksploatacji Maszyn. Prace Naukowe. Wspolpraca
0239-3204 Politechnika Wroclawska. Instytut Nauk Ekonomiczno-Spolecznych. Prace Naukowe. Monografie

ISSN INDEX 1493

0239-3212 Politechnika Wroclawska. Instytut Nauk Ekonomiczno-Spolecznych. Prace Naukowe. Studia i Materialy

0239-3433 Politechnika Wroclawska. Instytut Sterowania i Techniki Systemow. Prace Naukowe. Konferencje

0239-4243 Annales Universitatis Mariae Curie-Sklodowska. Sectio EE. Zootechnika

0239-4421 Bibliografia Wydawnictw Ciaglych

0239-488X Politechnika Poznanska. Zeszyty Naukowe. Geometria

0239-5274 Akademia Gorniczo-Hutnicza im. Stanislawa Staszica. Zeszyty Naukowe. Elektrotechnika. Kwartalnik

0239-5312 Akademia Gorniczo-Hutnicza im. Stanislawa Staszica. Zeszyty Naukowe. Elektrotechnika

0239-5320 Akademia Gorniczo-Hutnicza im. Stanislawa Staszica. Zeszyty Naukowe. Mechanika

0239-541X Przeglad Dokumentacyjny z Zakresu Handlu Wewnetrznego i Uslug

0239-622X Bibliografia Gospodarki i Inzynierii Wodnej

0239-6238 Materialy Badawcze. Seria: Gospodarka Wodna i Ochrona Wod

0239-6246 Bibliografia Hydrologii i Oceanologii

0239-6254 Materialy Badawcze. Seria: Inzynieria Wodna

0239-6262 Materialy Badawcze. Seria: Meteorologia

0239-6270 Bibliografia Meteorologii

0239-7277 Polish Academy of Sciences. Bulletin. Earth Sciences

0239-751X Polish Academy of Sciences. Bulletin. Biological Sciences

0239-7528 Polish Academy of Sciences. Bulletin. Technical Sciences

0239-8931 Centralny Katalog Zagranicznych Wydawnictw Ciaglych w Bibliotekach Polskich. Alfabetyczny Wykaz Tytulow

0239-9148 Szkice o Kulturze Muzycznej XIX Wieku. Studia i Materialy

0239-9253 Informator dla Kandydaton na Studia Podyplomowe i Doktoranckie

0239-9423 Politechnika Poznanska. Instytut Nauk Ekonomicznych i Spolecznych. Zeszyty Naukowe

0239-958X Bibliografia Agrometeorologii

0239-9679 Budownictwo Weglowe. Projekty-Problemy

0240-0154 Francaise Frisonne

0240-1568 Alternative

0240-2041 Langues et Civilisations a Tradition Orale

0240-2955 Universite de Toulouse. Faculte des Sciences. Annales

0240-3803 Special Scies a Moteur et Accessoires *changed to* Special Scies a Moteur et Techniques Forestieres

0240-396X Echange-Travail

0240-4656 Celebrer

0240-5024 Jardin Familial de France

0240-5407 Tour de l'Orle d'Or

0240-6411 Avenir et Sante

0240-642X Acta Endoscopica

0240-7418 Chroniques d'Histoire Maconnique

0240-7426 Commerce et Industrie†

0240-7914 Journal Francais d'Orthoptique

0240-8368 Epimenides

0240-8376 Epidecides Lunaires

0240-8465 Chimie *changed to* P A S C A L Folio. Part 17: Chimie Generale, Minerale et Organique

0240-8473 Bulletin Signaletique. Part 172: Chimie Analytique *changed to* P A S C A L Folio. Part 16: Chimie Analytique Minerale et Organique

0240-8481 Bulletin Signaletique. Part 173: Chimie Minerale et Organique *changed to* P A S C A L Folio. Part 17: Chimie Generale, Minerale et Organique

0240-849X Bulletin Signaletique. Part 120: Astronomie - Physique Spatiale - Geophysique *changed to* P A S C A L Explore. Part 48: Environnement Cosmique Terrestre, Astronomie et Geologie Extraterrestre

0240-849X Bulletin Signaletique. Part 120: Astronomie - Physique Spatiale - Geophysique *changed to* P A S C A L Explore. Part 49: Meteorologie

0240-8503 Bulletin Signaletique: Bibliographie des Sciences de la Terre. Section 225: Tectonique Geophysique Interne *changed to* P A S C A L Folio. Part 45: Tectonique. Geophysique Interne.

0240-8546 Bulletin Signaletique. Part 370: Biologie et Physiologie Vegetales. Sylviculture *changed to* P A S C A L Folio. Part 55: Biologie Vegetale

0240-8554 Eldoc-Electronique *changed to* P A S C A L Explore. Part 20: Electronique et Telecommunications

0240-8562 Eldoc-Electrotechnique. *changed to* P A S C A L Folio. Part 21: Electrotechnique

0240-8740 Bulletin Signaletique. Part 401: Congres. Rapports. Theses *changed to* P A S C A L Explore. Part 99: Congres. Rapports. Theses

0240-8783 Revue d'Hydrobiologie Tropicale

0240-8813 Sciences des Aliments

0240-8864 Pouvoir dans la Litterature et la Pensee Anglaises

0240-8910 Abstracta Iranica

0240-8937 Museum National d'Histoire Naturelle. Bulletin.

0240-902X Alta Nizza

0240-9542 Industrie Minerale. Techniques

0240-9925 Inter Regions

0241-0702 Tricot Prestige

0241-1407 Revue de Geologie Dynamique et de Geographie Physique

0241-2640 Infotecture

0241-2799 Cahiers Philosophiques

0241-6794 Cahiers Techniques du Batiment

0241-7375 Info Dechets. Environment et Technique

0241-8185 A-YA

0241-8622 Moteurs Loisirs

0242-1283 Commutation et Transmission

0242-2085 Graph-Agri

0242-3502 Hudson Letter

0242-3782 Agence Telegraphique Juive. Bulletin

0242-4002 Association Nationale d'Etude et de Lutte Contre les Fleaux Atmospheriques. Rapport de Campagne

0242-5017 Annales de Virologie *see* 0769-2617

0242-5823 Argus du Livre Ancien et Moderne *changed to* Argus du Livre de Collection et de l'Autographe

0242-6277 R G S

0242-6498 Annales de Pathologie

0242-6536 Observatoire de Strasbourg. Centre de Donnees Stellaires. Information Bulletin

0242-6862 Tonus Dentaire

0242-7818 Economie Prospective Internationale

0242-9284 Auto-Loisirs

0242-9616 Psychoanalistes

0243-1181 Revue de l'Artisan Electricien *see* 0761-0076

0243-1203 Journal Europeen de Radiotherapie

0243-1947 C.E.P.I.I. Lettre

0243-5314 Institut Appert. Bulletin Analytique Cie

0243-6108 France. Ministere de l'Agriculture. Informations Rapides. Fruits

0243-6140 France. Ministere de l'Agriculture. Informations Rapides. Legumes

0243-6167 France. Ministere de l'Agriculture. Informations Rapides. Statistiques des Entreprises

0243-6175 France. Ministere de l'Agriculture. Situation Agricole en France. Note de Conjoncture Production Porcine

0243-6183 France. Ministere de l'Agriculture. Situation Agricole en France. Note de Conjoncture Production Avicole

0243-6248 France. Ministere de l'Agriculture. Situation Agricole en France. Note de Conjoncture Production Vegetale

0243-6280 France. Ministere de l'Agriculture. Situation Agricole en France. Note de Conjoncture Production Bovine

0243-6345 France. Ministere de l'Agriculture. Situation Agricole en France. Note de Conjoncture Production Animale

0243-6450 M O T S: Mots, Ordinateurs, Textes, Societes

0243-6558 France. Ministere de l'Agriculture. Series "S". Production Vegetale *see* 0755-3218

0243-6566 France. Ministere de l'Agriculture. Series "S". Production Animale

0243-6574 France. Ministere de l'Agriculture. Series "S". Departements d'Outre-Mer

0243-6639 France. Ministere de l'Agriculture. Series "S". Structures et Environnement des Exploitations

0243-6647 France. Ministere de l'Agriculture. Series "S". Industries Agricoles et Alimentaires

0243-6655 France. Ministere de l'Agriculture. Series "S". Statistique Forestiere *see* 0755-3218

0243-7090 Afram Newsletter

0243-7651 Acta Oecologica-Oecologia Plantarum

0243-766X Acta Oecologica-Oecologia Generalis

0243-7678 Acta Oecologica-Oecologia Applicata

0243-8283 France. Ministere de l'Agriculture. Situation Agricole en France. Commerce Exterieur Bois et Derives

0243-8585 France. Ministere de l'Agriculture. Series "S". Methodes et Applications Scientifiques

0244-0008 Amina

0244-2019 Isolation

0244-5271 France. Ministere de l'Agriculture. Series "S". Synthese Statistique Comptes et Revenus

0244-6014 Societe Francaise de Photogrammetrie et de Teledetection. Bulletin

0244-710X Francexport

0244-7118 France. Service d'Etude des Strategies et des Statistiques Industrielles. Collections: Traits Fondamentaux du Systeme Industriel Francais

0244-7878 Nouvel Humanisme

0244-9358 Revue Trimestrielle de Droit Commercial et du Droit Economique

0244-9870 Traitement de Texte

0245-0283 French Engineering Catalog

0245-1301 Annuaire National de la Conserve

0245-5552 Journal d'Echographie et de Medecine Ultrasonore

0245-5919 Motricite Cerebrale: Readaptation Neurologie du Developpement.

0245-6001 Messages des P T T

0245-761X Banque de l'Union Europeenne. Chiffres et Commentaires

0245-8756 Aeroports de Paris. Bulletin Mensuel de Statistiques

0245-8977 France. Education Physique et Sportive au 1er Degre

0245-9132 Economie et Humanisme

0245-9310 Guide Offshore

0245-9337 International Pediatric Association. Bulletin

0245-9345 France. Bureau de Recherches Geologiques et Minieres. Manuels et Methodes

0245-9418 Oceanographie Tropicale

0245-954X Bulletin Signaletique. Part 215: Biotechnologies (French Edition) *changed to* P A S C A L Thema. Part 215: Biotechnologies (Edition Francaise)

0245-9558 Bulletin Signaletique. Part 233: Medicine Tropicale *changed to* P A S C A L Thema. Part 235: Medecine Tropicale

0245-9868 Bulletin Signaletique. Part 215: Biotechnology (English Edition) *changed to* P A S C A L Thema. Part 216: Biotechnology (English Edition)

0245-9884 Bulletin Signaletique. Part 361: Reproduction. Gynecologie. Obstetrique. Embryologie. Endocrinologie *changed to* P A S C A L Folio. Part 54: Reproduction des Vertebres. Embryologie des Vertebres et des Invertebres

0245-9884 Bulletin Signaletique. Part 361: Reproduction. Gynecologie. Obstetrique. Embryologie. Endocrinologie *changed to* P A S C A L Explore. Part 64: Endocrinologie Humaine et Experimentale. Endocrinopathies

0245-9884 Bulletin Signaletique. Part 361: Reproduction. Gynecologie. Obstetrique. Embryologie. Endocrinologie *changed to* P A S C A L Explore. Part 82: Gynecologie. Obstetrique. Andrologie

0245-9981 Bureaux d'Etudes

0246-1528 Hydrologie Continentale

0246-2303 Institut d'Elevage et de Medecine Veterinaire des Pays Tropicaux. Rapport d'Activite

0246-2346 Debat

0246-5957 Magic Crochet

0246-9715 Innovation et Produits Nouveaux *changed to* Telecommunications, Innovation et Produits Nouveaux

0246-9731 Institut de Recherches Marxistes. Cahiers d'Histoire *changed to* Cahiers d'Histoire (Paris)

0247-1086 Centre d'Entraide Genealogique de Franche-Compte. Bulletin

0247-1132 Jeux et Strategie

0247-1906 Neige Magazine

0247-3518 Informations du Caoutchouc et des Plastiques

0247-381X Criticon

0247-400X Annuaire des Pays de l'Ocean Indien

0247-4352 Videotex

0247-4468 France. Ministere de la Cooperation. Services des Etudes et Questions Internationales. Etudes et Documents *changed to* France. Ministere des Relations Exterieures. Sous-Directions des Etudes et Developpement. Etudes et Documents

0247-4751 Temps Reel *changed to* Resources Informatiques. Temps Reel

0247-5421 Profils Economiques

0247-6355 Mutu

0247-7181 Chausser

0247-8277 Eco 3

0247-8315 Gabon Selection

0247-8390 Cartonnages & Emballages Modernes

0247-8633 D'onte Ses

0247-915X Contrastes

0248-0018 Journal d'Urologie

0248-1758 Psychiatrie du Praticien *changed to* Pratique Medicale

0248-3165 Feuille de Route

0248-4684 Cahiers d'Information Therapeutique†

0248-5516 Sources et Travaux d'Histoire Haut-Pyreneenne

0248-8663 Revue de Medecine Interne

0249-1605 Rayons Jardin

0249-1664 Etudes sur l'Herault

0249-1729 E L F - Aquitaine News

0249-3136 Fonderie, Fondeur d'Aujourd'hui

0249-3446 Alea

0249-4744 Economie et Prevision

0249-4779 C E M A G R E F Bulletin d'Information†

0249-4787 C E M A G R E F Etudes†

0249-5570 Cahiers de Recherche en Gestion des Entreprises

0249-5619 Recherches d'Histoire et de Sciences Sociales

0249-5635 Universite de Bordeaux II. Cahiers Ethnologiques

0249-5686 C E M A G R E F Nouvelles

0249-5740 France. Centre de Recherche Zootechnique. Departement de Genetique Animale. Bulletin Technique

0249-5805 Societe Sciences Nat. Bulletin

1494 ISSN INDEX

0249-5902 Centre d'Histoire Economique et Sociale de la Region Lyonnaise. Bulletin
0249-6208 Journal de Medecine Legale Droit Medicale
0249-6216 Journal de Toxicologie Medicale *changed to* Journal de Toxicologie Clinique et Experimentale
0249-6267 Modeles Linguistiques
0249-6402 Toxicological European Research
0249-6550 Journal d'Ergotherapie
0249-6704 Fils-Tubes-Bandes & Profils
0249-6739 Orientation Scolaire et Professionnelle
0249-7069 Societe d'Etudes Linguistiques et Anthropologiques de France. Numeros Speciaux
0249-7271 Recueil des Decisions du Conseil d'Etat
0249-7344 Bibliotheque Nationale Revue
0249-7522 Association pour le Developpement International de l'Observatoire de Nice. Bulletin
0249-7549 Societe Geologique de France. Memoires
0249-7557 Reunion Annuelle des Sciences de la Terre
0249-9185 Cahiers de Psychologie Cognitive
0250-0019 Dyers Dyegest *changed to* Textile Industries Dyegest Southern Africa
0250-0027 Dynamica
0250-0116 Africa Seminar: Collected Papers
0250-0167 Communicatio
0250-0213 Cormorant
0250-0418 Electron Microscopy Society of Southern Africa. Proceedings
0250-054X Architecture S.A. (Cape Town)
0250-104X Cripple Care News
0250-1163 Johannesburg Historical Foundation. Journal
0250-1236 N T K - Nuus
0250-1325 South African Laundry and Cleaning Review
0250-1333 South African Shoemaker and Leather Review
0250-152X Educamus
0250-1619 Centre d'Etudes et de Documentation Africaines. Cahiers
0250-1651 National Science Council Monthly
0250-1910 Informa
0250-1961 I S S U P Strategic Review
0250-2003 Contacts
0250-216X University of Cape Town. Department of Geology. Precambrian Research Unit. Annual Report
0250-2399 Bibliography of Foreign Publications About South Africa†
0250-2402 Barclays Business Brief
0250-2887 Sugar Industry Abstracts *changed to* Tate and Lyle's Sugar Industry Abstracts
0250-2992 Cookeia
0250-300X Smithersia
0250-3018 Zimbabwea
0250-3190 Revista A I B D A
0250-3212 Beitraege zur Urologie
0250-3220 Contributions to Oncology
0250-3328 Asian Medical News
0250-362X Kuwait Bulletin of Marine Science
0250-3654 Pakistan Hotel Guide
0250-3662 Pakistan Hotel and Travel Review
0250-3689 Gesundheit
0250-3697 Societe pour le Developpement Minier de la Cote d'Ivoire. Rapport Annuel
0250-3751 Developments in Ophthalmology
0250-3778 Khanya Theological Education by Extension Newsletter†
0250-3786 Aeronautical Society of South Africa. Journal *see* 0257-8573
0250-3794 World Health Statistics Annual
0250-3891 E I B - Information
0250-4057 Social Security Documentation: Asian Series
0250-4065 Kuwait Institute for Scientific Research. Annual Research Report
0250-4162 Scopus
0250-4197 Advances in Clinical Enzymology
0250-4316 Estadistica Panamena. Situacion Politica, Administrativa y Justicia. Seccion 611. Estadistica Electoral
0250-4324 Estadistica Panamena. Situacion Economica. Seccion 312. Siembra y Cosecha de Hortilizas
0250-4340 Pakistan Hotel and Restaurant Guide
0250-4367 Medicinal and Aromatic Plants Abstracts
0250-4421 Blues Life
0250-443X Wiener-Goethe-Verein. Jahrbuch
0250-4731 Hjukrun
0250-474X Indian Journal of Pharmaceutical Sciences
0250-4928 Transnational Associations
0250-4952 Therapie Familiale
0250-4960 Nephrologie
0250-4987 Revue Celinienne
0250-5193 Gujarat Agricultural University Research Journal
0250-524X Indian Journal of Forestry
0250-5266 Indian Veterinary Medical Journal
0250-5363 Journal of Science
0250-5371 Legume Research
0250-538X Maadini
0250-541X National Academy of Sciences, India. Science Letters
0250-5584 U N D O C: Current Index
0250-5592 University of Dar es Salam. University Science Journal *changed to* Tanzania Journal of Science
0250-5657 Zambian Geographical Journal
0250-5673 Bibliographie der Berner Geschichte
0250-5754 E P News
0250-5789 Euronet Diane News *changed to* Information Market
0250-5886 Green Europe
0250-5940 Rechtsbibliographie
0250-5959 I I C A in the Americas
0250-5983 Indian Academy of Sciences. Proceedings (Engineering Sciences) *changed to* Indian Academy of Sciences. Sadhana Proceedings in Engineering Sciences
0250-5991 Journal of Biosciences
0250-6009 Indian Institute of Tropical Meteorology. Research Report *see* 0252-1075
0250-6017 Indian Institute of Tropical Meteorology. Annual Report
0250-6068 Pharmanual†
0250-6114 Chiefs of State and Cabinet Ministers of the American Republics
0250-6130 Educacion
0250-6173 Juventud†
0250-6211 Organization of American States. Directory
0250-6270 Inter-American Review of Bibliography
0250-6289 Organization of American States. Statistical Bulletin
0250-6327 Bulletin of Materials Science
0250-6335 Journal of Astrophysics and Astronomy
0250-6386 Arnoldia Zimbabwe
0250-6394 N A F O Statistical Bulletin
0250-6408 Journal of Northwest Atlantic Fishery Science
0250-6416 N A F O Scientific Council Meeting Reports
0250-6432 N A F O Scientific Council Studies
0250-6440 Der Gesellschafter
0250-6459 Zeitschrift fuer Neuere Rechtsgeschichte
0250-6505 Regional Development Dialogue
0250-6521 Universidad de la Republica. Facultad de Humanidades y Ciencias. Revista. Serie Ciencias de la Tierra
0250-653X Universidad de la Republica. Facultad de Humanidades y Ciencias. Revista. Serie Ciencias Biologicas
0250-6548 Universidad de la Republica. Facultad de Humanidades y Ciencias. Revista. Serie Linguistica
0250-6556 Universidad de la Republica. Facultad de Humanidades y Ciencias. Revista. Serie Letras
0250-6564 Universidad de la Republica. Facultad de Humanidades y Ciencias. Revista. Serie Ciencias Antropologicas
0250-6793 Stem Cells *see* 0254-7600
0250-6807 Annals of Nutrition and Metabolism
0250-6874 Sensors and Actuators
0250-6971 Revue de Theologie et de Philosophie. Cahiers
0250-6998 Cinema Vision India
0250-7005 Anticancer Research
0250-7013 Fauna & Flora
0250-7102 Naturopa
0250-7161 Revista Latinoamericana de Estudios Urbano Regionales
0250-7188 Hamdard Medicus
0250-7196 Hamdard Islamicus
0250-7242 Fiji. Mineral Resources Division. Bulletin *see* 0379-1580
0250-7269 Fiji Mineral Resources Division. Memoir *see* 0252-2497
0250-7277 Fiji. Mineral Resources Department. Geothermal Report
0250-7366 International Monetary Fund. Annual Report on Exchange Arrangements and Exchange Restrictions
0250-7374 International Monetary Fund. Government Finance Statistics Yearbook
0250-7463 International Financial Statistics Yearbook
0250-7498 International Monetary Fund. Annual Report of the Executive Board
0250-7609 Geosur
0250-7617 Carindex: Social Sciences and Humanities
0250-7633 I D O C Monthly Bulletin†
0250-7730 International Designs Bulletin
0250-7757 P C T Gazette
0250-7765 Petroleum News
0250-7781 European Parliament's Official Handbook†
0250-779X Unesco Yearbook on Peace and Conflict Studies
0250-7811 N A F O List of Fishing Vessels
0250-7862 Science Bulletin
0250-7935 Industry and Development
0250-801X United Nations Industrial Development Organization. Development and Transfer of Technology Series
0250-8052 E P P O Bulletin
0250-8060 Water International
0250-8079 Polymer Engineering. Journal†
0250-8087 Pseudo-Allergic Reactions
0250-8095 American Journal of Nephrology
0250-8109 Z G A Occasional Studies
0250-8117 Z G A School Supplement
0250-8125 Z G A Bibliographic Series
0250-8133 Zambia Geographical Association. Regional Handbook
0250-8257 Kenya Journal of Science and Technology. Series A: Physical and Chemical Sciences
0250-8281 Tourism Recreation Research
0250-829X Indian Journal of Botany
0250-8346 Journal of Himalayan Studies and Regional Development
0250-8710 Euro Reports and Studies
0250-944X International Fruit World
0250-9555 I A R C Monographs on the Evaluation of the Carcinogenic Risk of Chemicals to Humans
0250-961X Inside China Mainland
0250-9628 Journal of Combinatorics, Information & System Sciences
0250-9636 Indian Society of Statistics and Operations Research. Journal
0250-9660 I C S S R Journal of Abstracts and Reviews: Political Science
0250-9679 Indian Psychological Abstracts
0250-9687 I C S S R Journal of Abstracts and Reviews: Geography
0250-9695 I C S S R Journal of Abstracts and Reviews: Economics
0250-9709 Indian Dissertation Abstracts
0250-9717 Asian Banking and Corporate Finance *changed to* AsiaBanking
0250-9725 Biblioteek voor Hedendaagse Dokumentatie. Bulletin
0250-975X Bhashavimarsa
0250-9784 Mechanical and Corrosion Properties *changed to* Key Engineering Materials
0250-9784 Mechanical and Corrosion Properties *changed to* Single Crystal Properties
0250-9792 Resumen Semanal
0250-9806 QueHacer
0250-9814 Serie Praxis
0250-9989 Ecoforum
0251-0006 Mikro-Klein Computer
0251-0081 Annual Bulletin of Trade in Chemical Products
0251-012X Indian Musicological Society. Journal
0251-0146 I S P T Journal of Research in Educational & Psychological Measurement
0251-0154 Luso
0251-0170 Experimental Hematology Today†
0251-0332 Executive
0251-0480 Pakistan Journal of Agricultural Research
0251-0944 Revue de l'Ingenieur Industriel
0251-0952 Seed Science and Technology
0251-1088 Environmentalist
0251-1118 Institution of Engineers (India). Interdisciplinary Panels Journal
0251-1223 Geobios
0251-1339 International Social Security Association. Reports of the General Assemblies of the ISSA
0251-1495 Training for Agriculture and Rural Development
0251-1630 Indian Institute of World Culture. Bulletin
0251-1711 Portugal. Biblioteca Nacional. Revista
0251-172X Odonto-Stomatologie Tropicale
0251-1746 Shree Hari Katha
0251-1762 Schweizerischer Medizinalkalender
0251-1770 Journal of Engineering Production
0251-1789 Invasion and Metastasis
0251-1924 Nyala
0251-2017 C B M-Pet News *see* 0251-0006
0251-2068 Concepts in Pediatric Neurosurgery
0251-2408 De Franse Nederlanden
0251-2432 World Health Forum
0251-2440 Agricultural Abstracts for Tanzania
0251-2459 Industrial Abstracts for Tanzania
0251-2467 Child Health and Development
0251-2483 Estudios Paraguayos
0251-2491 Andean Report
0251-2513 Bulletin A I O S P/I A E V G/I V S B B
0251-2645 D S T C Newsletter *changed to* New Technologies. Innovation Policy
0251-2661 Bunadarrit
0251-3056 Journal of Government and Political Studies
0251-317X Development Policy and Administrative Review
0251-348X Social Sciences Research Journal
0251-3609 Francia†
0251-3625 D I S P
0251-401X World Bank. Commodity Trade and Price Trends
0251-4141 Associacao Portuguesa de Bibliotecarios Arquivistas e Documentalistas. Noticia
0251-4265 United Nations Commission on International Trade Law. Yearbook
0251-4796 China, Republic. National Central Library. Bulletin
0251-5342 Frontiers in Diabetes
0251-5350 Neuroepidemiology
0251-6365 International Monetary Fund. Occasional Papers
0251-6616 United Nations Library. Monthly Bibliography: Part 1
0251-6624 United Nations Library. Monthly Bibliography: Part 2
0251-6802 Bulletin on Aging
0251-6810 International Colloquium on Prospective Biology (Proceedings)†
0251-7329 U N Chronicle
0251-7396 Hey *changed to* S O H-Info
0251-7434 Pacific

0251-7493 Oesterreichische Geologische Gesellschaft. Mitteilungen
0251-7604 Population Bulletin of the United Nations
0251-9461 International Trade and Development Statistics. Handbook
0252-0397 Journal of Higher Education
0252-0508 European Information Centre for Nature Conservation. Newsletter. Nature
0252-0591 Council of Europe. Documentation Centre for Education in Europe. Newsletter/Faits Nouveaux
0252-063X International Exchange of Information on Current Criminological Research Projects in Member States
0252-0648 Exchange of Information on Research in European Law
0252-0656 Council of Europe. Parliamentary Assembly. Documents; Working Papers/Documents de Seance
0252-0664 Council of Europe. Parliamentary Assembly. Official Report of Debates.
0252-0869 Cultural Policy
0252-0877 Council of Europe. Directorate of Legal Affairs. Information Bulletin on Legislative Activities
0252-0958 Council of Europe Forum
0252-1024 Asian Banking Directory *changed to* Asiabanking Almanac
0252-1032 Acta de Odontologia Pediatrica
0252-1059 Mechanical and Corrosion Properties. Series A. Key Engineering Materials *changed to* Key Engineering Materials
0252-1067 Mechanical and Corrosion Properties. Series B. Single Crystal Properties *changed to* Single Crystal Properties
0252-1075 Indian Institute of Tropical Meteorology. Contributions
0252-1105 Information Resources Annual
0252-1121 Bulletin Celinien
0252-1156 Magnesium
0252-1164 Clinical Physiology and Biochemistry
0252-1172 Applied Pathology
0252-1865 Apuntes
0252-1962 Revista de Investigaciones Marinas
0252-2462 Fiji. Mineral Resources Department. Annual Report
0252-2470 Fiji. Department of Lands, & Mineral Resources. Annual Report *see* 0252-2462
0252-2489 Fiji. Geological Survey. Annual Report *see* 0252-2462
0252-2497 Fiji. Mineral Resources Department. Memoir
0252-2659 Weekly Analysis of Ecuadorian Issues/Analisis Semanal
0252-2667 Journal of Information & Optimization Sciences
0252-2683 Informations Recentes sur les Comptes Nationaux des Pays en Developpment
0252-2969 Schweizerischen Naturforschenden Gesellschaft. Jahrbuch†
0252-3051 International Monetary Fund. Balance of Payments Statistics
0252-306X Direction of Trade Statistics
0252-3353 Date Palm Journal
0252-337X Academia de Geografia e Historia de Guatemala. Anales
0252-3639 Population Headliners
0252-3647 United Nations Economic and Social Commission for Asia and the Pacific. Statistical Newsletter
0252-3655 Statistical Yearbook for Asia and the Pacific
0252-4392 Transport & Communications Bulletin for Asia & the Pacific
0252-4406 Electric Power in Asia and the Pacific
0252-4422 A D O P T
0252-4457 Statistical Indicators for Asia and the Pacific
0252-4481 Industy and Technology Development News - Asia and the Pacific
0252-452X United Nations Economic and Social Commission for Asia and the Pacific. Social Development Division. Social Work Education and Development
0252-4538 Foreign Trade Statistics of Asia and the Pacific. Series A
0252-4546 Foreign Trade Statistics of Asia and the Pacific. Series B
0252-5216 Trade and Development: an U N C T A D Review
0252-5348 Mekong Bulletin
0252-5704 Economic and Social Survey of Asia and the Pacific
0252-7308 Interfaces in Computing *see* 0920-5489
0252-7979 Guide to Current Literature in Environmental Health Engineering and Science
0252-8088 Conditions of Work *see* 0257-3512
0252-8150 Zygos (1982)
0252-8169 Journal of Comparative Literature and Aesthetics
0252-8177 N S C Symposium Series
0252-8274 Ernstia
0252-8290 Revue d'Etudes Palestiniennes
0252-8347 Papua New Guinea National Bibliography
0252-8398 Bibliography of the Geology of Fiji
0252-841X Boletin de Antropologia Americana
0252-8479 Repertorio Americano
0252-855X C E D E F O P News
0252-8584 Economia y Desarrollo
0252-8754 Inforpress Centroamericana
0252-8843 Revista de Critica Literaria Latinoamericana
0252-9114 European Commission of Human Rights. Annual Review/Compte Rendu Annual†
0252-9416 Mausam
0252-9505 Transnational Perspectives
0252-9521 Ciencias Economicas
0252-9564 Survey of Immunologic Research *see* 0257-277X
0252-9602 Acta Mathematica Scientia
0252-9610 Cargonews Asia
0252-9629 Travelnews Asia
0252-9769 Revista Geofisica
0252-9920 Indian Review of Life Sciences
0252-9939 Caribbean Geography
0252-9963 Mesoamerica
0252-9971 Centro de Investigaciones Regionales de Mesoamerica. Serie Monografica
0252-998X Educacion Especial
0253-0015 Boletin de Lima
0253-004X Phonographic Bulletin
0253-035X Schweizerische Gesellschaft fuer Klinische Chemie. Bulletin
0253-0538 Carib-Latin Energy Consultant
0253-0910 Family and School
0253-1062 Geotermia
0253-1216 Universite d'Ankara. Faculte des Sciences. Communications. Serie C1. Geologie
0253-1321 F I O D S Revue
0253-1445 Refugee Abstracts
0253-1453 Botanica Helvetica
0253-1496 Agricultural Reviews
0253-150X Agricultural Science Digest
0253-1933 O.I.E. Revue Scientifique et Technique
0253-1941 Pakistan and Gulf Economist
0253-195X Unir Cinema
0253-1968 Regional and Local Affairs News†
0253-200X Synthetic Methods of Organic Chemistry
0253-2069 Biology International: I U B S Newsmagazine
0253-2093 Advances in Pharmacotherapy
0253-2492 Consejo Nacional de Investigaciones Cientificas y Tecnologicas, Costa Rica. Informe Anual
0253-2859 World Debt Tables
0253-2948 Revista Costarricense de Ciencias Medicas
0253-3073 Korean Journal of Pharmacognosy
0253-3219 Nuclear Techniques
0253-3316 Acta Academiae Medicinae Wuhan
0253-3340 Geobios New Reports
0253-3367 Electricidade, Energia, Electronica *see* 0870-5364
0253-3413 Boletim de Bibliografia Portuguesa. Monografias
0253-3421 Boletim de Bibliografia Portuguesa. Publicacoes em Serie
0253-343X Boletim de Bibliografia Portuguesa. Documentos nao Textuais
0253-3634 Acta Physica Temperaturae Humilis Sinica
0253-3715 Internationale Berg- und Seilbahn-Rundschau
0253-3804 Journal of Civil and Hydraulic Engineering
0253-3839 Chinese Institute of Engineers. Journal
0253-4177 Chinese Journal of Semiconductors
0253-4290 Acta Academiae Medicinae Sichuan
0253-438X Survey and Synthesis of Pathology Research *see* 0257-2761
0253-4398 Survey of Digestive Diseases *see* 0257-2753
0253-4533 Sprache & Kognition
0253-4754 International Journal of Structures
0253-4770 King Faisal Specialist Hospital Medical Journal *see* 0256-4947
0253-4843 Survey of Drug Research in Immunologic Disease
0253-4851 Tropical Veterinarian†
0253-4886 Digestive Surgery
0253-4894 I C M E News
0253-5033 Boletin S I N I C Y T
0253-505X Acta Oceanologica Sinica
0253-5068 Blood Purification
0253-5076 Complement
0253-5092 Anthropologika
0253-5106 Chemical Society of Pakistan. Journal
0253-5114 Current Practices in Environmental Engineering *changed to* Current Practices in Environmental Science and Engineering
0253-5122 Current Practices in Geotechnical Engineering
0253-519X Discourse
0253-5416 Bangladesh Journal of Botany
0253-5696 Jardin Botanico Nacional. Revista
0253-5823 Science in China Part B
0253-5831 Science in China Part A
0253-584X Unir: Echo de Saint Louis
0253-5858 Unir Cine Media
0253-5904 Die Makromolekulare Chemie. Supplement
0253-6005 A R P E L. Boletin Tecnico
0253-6269 Archives of Pharmacal Research
0253-6544 Supreme Court Cases (Criminal)
0253-6552 Supreme Court Cases (L & S) *changed to* Supreme Court Cases (Labour)
0253-6560 Supreme Court Cases (Taxation)
0253-6579 Current Central Legislation
0253-6587 Uttar Pradesh Services Cases†
0253-6595 Asian Journal of Dairy Research
0253-665X Progress in Ecology
0253-6730 Revue de Paleobiologie
0253-6749 Cyprus. Agricultural Research Institute. Miscellaneous Reports
0253-6757 N I H F W Technical Reports
0253-682X Arogya
0253-7141 Indian Journal of Environmental Protection
0253-7206 International Bio-Sciences Monographs
0253-7222 Journal of Dharma
0253-7230 Journal of Scientific Research
0253-7249 Journal of Scientific Research in Plants & Medicines
0253-7257 Acoustical Society of India. Journal
0253-7273 Journal of Zoological Research
0253-7370 West Indian Law Journal
0253-7397 Ciencias Tecnicas Fisicas y Matematicas
0253-7400 Archiv der Geschichte der Naturwissenschaften
0253-7419 Medequip
0253-7427 Eurosocial Newsletter
0253-7435 Oberoesterreich
0253-7583 Physics News
0253-7605 Journal of Cytology and Genetics
0253-7613 Indian Journal of Pharmacology
0253-8083 News from Iceland
0253-8296 Speleological Abstracts
0253-8539 Industriearchaeologie
0253-8555 Cyprus. Department of Statistics and Research. Economic Indicators
0253-8563 Tourism, Migration and Travel Statistics
0253-858X Cyprus. Department of Statistics and Research. Imports and Exports Statistics
0253-8598 Cyprus. Department of Statistics and Research. Services Survey
0253-8601 Health Statistics†
0253-8628 Hospital Statistics†
0253-8636 Sales of Vine Products Manufactured in Cyprus†
0253-8660 Cyprus. Department of Statistics and Research. Wages, Salaries and Hours of Work†
0253-8687 Cyprus. Department of Statistics and Research. Analysis of Wholesale and Retail Trade†
0253-8695 Cyprus. Department of Statistics and Research. Criminal Statistics
0253-8709 Cyprus. Department of Statistics and Research. Tourism, Migration and Travel Statistics
0253-8725 Cyprus. Department of Statistics and Research. Construction and Housing Report
0253-8733 Statistics of Education in Cyprus
0253-8741 Cypriot Students Abroad†
0253-875X Cyprus. Department of Statistics and Research. Statistical Abstract
0253-8776 J I S T A
0253-9071 Language Forum
0253-9268 Revista Cubana de Fisica
0253-9276 Tecnologia Quimica
0253-9306 Research Journal: Science
0253-9365 Bangalore Theological Forum
0253-9403 United Nations. International Narcotics Control Board. Statistics on Psychotropic Substances Furnished by Governments in Accordance with the Convention of 1971 on Psychotropic Substances *changed to* International Narcotics Control Board. Statistics on Psychotropic Substances for (Year)
0253-9454 Greece. National Statistical Service. Social Welfare and Health Statistics
0253-9527 Third World International
0253-9810 Recht
0253-9950 Journal of Nuclear Chemistry and Radio Chemistry
0254-0126 International Journal of Tropical Plant Diseases
0254-0185 Studies in Education and Teaching Techniques
0254-0193 Series in English Language and Literature
0254-0207 Language Forum Monograph Series
0254-0215 Series in Sikh History and Culture
0254-0819 Acute Care
0254-0886 N I M H A N S Journal
0254-105X Progress in Reproductive Biology and Medicine
0254-1106 Revista Critica de Ciencias Sociais
0254-1157 Asian Sources Gifts & Home Products
0254-1173 Asian Sources Timepieces
0254-1270 Karger Continuing Education Series
0254-1300 Review of Tropical Plant Pathology
0254-1521 Samisdat
0254-1858 South African Journal of Zoology
0254-217X Asian Computer Monthly
0254-2234 Polyscope Computer und Elektronik
0254-2412 Development Information Abstracts
0254-2471 Central America Report
0254-3028 Ariel
0254-3036 I F D A Dossier
0254-3052 Physica Energiae Fortis et Physica Nuclearis
0254-3060 Acta Mechanica Sinica
0254-4059 Chinese Journal of Oceanology and Limnology
0254-4105 Indian Journal of Veterinary Surgery
0254-4296 Annales Aequatoria
0254-4318 Elektronikschau
0254-4326 O E G A I Journal
0254-4334 Christliche Demokratie
0254-4377 Glaube in der 2. Welt

0254-4474	Language Research
0254-4962	Psychopathology
0254-5020	Medicine and Sport Science
0254-5047	P R O S I
0254-5195	Progress in Applied Microcirculation
0254-5233	Prison Information Bulletin
0254-5241	J B I Journal
0254-5268	Business India
0254-5292	Reiseland Oesterreich
0254-5306	Output Oesterreich
0254-5330	Annals of Operations Research
0254-5373	Karger Biobehavioral Medicine Series
0254-5586	Asian Sources Computer Products
0254-6183	Asian Literary Market Review
0254-6221	Daseinsanalyse
0254-623X	Progress in Critical Care Medicine
0254-6299	South African Journal of Botany
0254-6426	Evergreen
0254-6493	Aquiculture
0254-7147	Consulting Medical Laboratories. Bulletin
0254-7600	Natural Immunity and Cell Growth Regulation
0254-7694	Short Book Reviews
0254-7848	V A C News
0254-7856	Counselor
0254-797X	Garabato
0254-8186	Revue Internationale d'Histoire Militaire
0254-8275	Beitraege zur Intensiv- und Notfallmedizin
0254-8305	Dryland Resources and Technology *changed to* Current Practices in Dryland Resources and Technology
0254-8356	Neotestamentica
0254-8704	Journal of Environmental Biology
0254-8739	Concepts in Toxicology
0254-8747	Advances in Audiology
0254-8755	International Journal of Tropical Agriculture
0254-8798	Environmental Awareness
0254-8801	Agrindex
0254-881X	Diagnostic Imaging in Clinical Medicine†
0254-8852	Discussions in Neurosciences
0254-8860	Indian Journal of Gastroenterology
0254-9166	Touche Ross European Commentary
0254-9204	Pakistan Journal of Applied Economics
0254-9212	Anthropologica (Lima)
0254-9239	Lexis
0254-9247	Revista de Psicologia
0254-9433	Geobotanisches Institut ETH, Stiftung Ruebel, Zurich. Veroeffentlichungen
0254-9441	Praxis des Bundesgerichts
0254-945X	Zeitschrift fuer Schweizerisches Recht
0254-9492	Arab Medical Bulletin
0254-9522	Manual Medicine
0254-9549	New Voices
0254-962X	Caricom Perspective
0254-9662	Youth of the 21
0254-9670	Experimental and Clinical Immunogenetics
0254-9743	Earthscan Bulletin
0254-9794	Calcutta Historical Journal
0254-9808	Tibetan Bulletin
0255-0008	I L C A Bulletin
0255-0024	I L C A Newsletter
0255-0040	I L C A Annual Report
0255-0067	Bermuda National Bibliography
0255-0172	Transvaal Museum. Monographs
0255-0695	Zambia Educational Review
0255-0776	Social Europe
0255-0849	International Bibliography of Historical Demography
0255-0903	Groupe International d'Etude de la Ceramique Egyptienne. Bulletin de Liaison
0255-0962	Institut Francais d'Archeologie Orientale du Caire. Bulletin
0255-271X	U N C H S. Habitat News
0255-2760	International Whaling Commission. Special Issues
0255-2779	Literary Endeavour
0255-2809	Litterae Numismaticae Vindobonenses
0255-3139	International Council on Archives. Committee on Conservation and Restauration. Committee on Archival Reprography (Bulletin)
0255-3627	Organization for Economic Cooperation and Development. Quarterly Labour Statistics/Statistiques Trimestrielles de la Population Active
0255-3678	Kriminalsoziologische Bibliographie
0255-3813	N A T O Review
0255-3910	Pain and Headache
0255-4062	Eye Care
0255-4291	Annual Review of the Chemical Industry
0255-4429	World Badminton
0255-4437	International Badminton Federation. Annual Statute Book
0255-5018	Disaster Management
0255-5476	Materials Science Forum
0255-5484	Documentation Indian National Affairs
0255-6472	Lesotho Law Journal
0255-6588	National Science Council, Republic of China. Proceedings. Part A: Physical Science and Engineering
0255-6596	National Science Council, Republic of China. Proceedings. Part B: Life Sciences
0255-6715	Studien zur Kinderpsychoanalyse. Jahrbuch
0255-6715	Studien zur Kinderpsychoanalyse
0255-6766	Statistical Yearbook of China
0255-6863	Tamkang Journal of Management Sciences
0255-7010	Agricultural Research Seoul National University
0255-7312	Business Traveller
0255-7320	Asia Travel Trade
0255-7460	Central Bank of Barbados. Economic Review
0255-755X	C E D E Department des Sciences Sociales. Bulletin
0255-769X	Managment Forum
0255-7924	Boletin de Biotecnologia
0255-7975	Pediatric Neuroscience *see* 0256-7040
0255-7983	Concepts in Immunopathology
0255-8033	Dirasat
0255-8165	National Buildings Construction Corporation. Bulletin
0255-8173	I C R A F Newsletter
0255-8203	Nyam News
0255-8246	Swiss Review of International Competition Law
0255-8254	Stamps World
0255-8432	Central Bank of Barbados. Balance of Payments
0255-8440	Central Bank of Barbados. Annual Statistical Digest
0255-8858	Theologia Evangelica
0255-8866	Travel Business Analyst
0255-9293	Annual Review of Engineering Industries and Automation
0255-9587	Zoological Survey of India. Bulletin
0255-9870	Free China Journal
0255-9900	E C Index
0255-9994	Olivae
0256-002X	Scenaria
0256-0038	Chromium Review
0256-0054	Ecquid Novi
0256-0070	Jagger Journal
0256-0100	South African Journal of Education
0256-0119	G A T T Focus
0256-0240	Frontline
0256-0356	Odyssey
0256-0550	S.A. Motorscene
0256-0569	South African Runner
0256-064X	Weekend Workshop
0256-0666	Hit
0256-0909	Vikalpa
0256-1042	International Bibliography: Publications of Intergovernmental Organizations
0256-1069	Cyprus Time Out
0256-1530	Advances in Atmospheric Sciences
0256-1565	University of Lausanne. Department des Langues et des Sciences du Langage. Cahiers
0256-159X	Book People
0256-1654	Bulletin of Electrochemistry
0256-1824	Falkland Islands Journal
0256-2332	O E C D Energy Prices and Taxes
0256-2456	U N E P News
0256-2480	Hamlet Studies
0256-2715	Einzelhandel - Verkaufsindex
0256-2804	Africa Insight
0256-2901	Papua New Guinea Institute of Medical Research. Monograph Series
0256-3061	Estudios de Ciencias y Letras
0256-307X	Chinese Physics Letters
0256-3096	S C A D Bulletin
0256-310X	Myclogia Helvetica
0256-355X	Haiti. Bureau National d'Ethnologie. Bulletin
0256-3576	Greece. National Statistical Service. Labour Force Survey
0256-3584	Greece. National Statistical Service. Results of Sea Fishery Survey by Motor Vessels
0256-3592	Greece. National Statistical Service. Statistical Bulletin of Public Finance
0256-3614	Greece. National Statistical Service. Employment Survey Conducted in Urban and Semi-Urban Areas *see* 0256-3576
0256-3665	Greece. National Statistical Service. Statistics on Civil, Criminal and Reformatory Justice
0256-4017	Indian Architects Directory
0256-4025	Directory of Interior Designers
0256-4106	Informat
0256-4203	Travel Directory
0256-4246	Universitaet fuer Bodenkultur in Wien. Dissertationen
0256-436X	Journal of Plant Anatomy and Morphology
0256-4513	I A W P R C Newsletter *changed to* Water Quality International
0256-4548	Arab Gulf Journal of Scientific Research *see* 0259-8930
0256-4637	Journal of Pure and Applied Ultrasonics
0256-4653	Walter Roth Museum of Anthropology. Journal
0256-4726	Go
0256-4947	Annals of Saudi Medicine
0256-4971	Maktabat al-Idarah
0256-5374	Ciencias Matematicas
0256-5935	H C J Communications Report
0256-6044	Semitics
0256-6524	Journal of Agricultural Engineering
0256-6575	Lebensmittel Technologie
0256-6672	International Quarterly of Entomology
0256-6702	Grassland Society of Southern Africa. Journal
0256-6710	S A I L I S Newsletter
0256-6974	Lighting Review
0256-6990	Studies in Marxism
0256-7040	Child's Nervous System
0256-7121	Commission of the European Communities. Monthly Catalogue. Part A: Publications
0256-730X	Safety Evaluation and Regulation of Chemicals
0256-7423	University of Durban-Westville. Bulletin for Academic Staff
0256-7431	South African Yachting, Sail, Power & Waterski
0256-7512	Bulletin of Agricultural Research in Botswana
0256-7822	International Defense Directory
0256-7865	Universite d'Ankara. Faculte des Sciences. Communications Serie C. Biologie
0256-8314	Cyprus. Ministry of Labour and Social Insurance. Labour Review
0256-856X	Melanesian Journal of Theology
0256-8837	Musicus
0256-8853	Progressio
0256-8861	South African Journal of Library and Information Science
0256-8896	U N I S A Psychologia
0256-9043	Sinorama
0256-971X	Uttar Pradesh Journal of Zoology
0256-9728	Insight *changed to* Zimbabwe Insight
0257-1420	International Angler
0257-1625	Artesanias de America
0257-1749	Tecnologica
0257-1862	South African Journal of Plant and Soil
0257-1870	Yearbook of International Commodity Statistics
0257-1994	Meson
0257-2028	Pharmaceutical and Cosmetic Review
0257-2036	Ensovoort
0257-2117	South African Journal of African Languages
0257-2222	I S D S Register
0257-2753	Digestive Diseases
0257-2761	Pathology and Immunopathology Research
0257-277X	Immunologic Research
0257-2788	Fetal Therapy
0257-3199	Allgemeinmedizin
0257-3229	I A S L Conference Proceedings
0257-3431	Institution of Engineers (India). Agricultural Engineering Journal
0257-344X	Institution of Engineers (India). Architectural Engineering
0257-3512	Conditions of Work Digest
0257-3717	International Narcotics Control Board. Report for (Year)
0257-3822	Medien und Recht International
0257-4284	Tidal Gravity Corrections
0257-4292	Tipografia
0257-4306	Universidad de la Habana. Direccion de Informacion Cientifica y Tecnica. Investigacion Operacional
0257-442X	Institution of Engineers (India). Mining Engineering Division. Journal
0257-540X	Transkei Official Gazette *see* 0257-5418
0257-5418	Transkei Government Gazette Index
0257-5426	Wiel
0257-6406	I J A. Research Reports
0257-6430	Studies in History (New Delhi)
0257-6457	Cuadernos de Poetica
0257-7046	Paiperlek
0257-7305	Manushi
0257-7348	South Asian Anthropologist
0257-7364	South East Asian Review
0257-7739	Message of the Library
0257-7747	Tydskrif vir die Suid-Afrikaanse Reg
0257-7860	Special United Nations Services
0257-8034	Fertiliser Marketing News
0257-8069	A S C I Journal of Management
0257-8166	Taiwan Electronics Industry
0257-8174	Taiwan Electronics Industry Components
0257-8573	Aeronautica Meridiana
0257-859X	Rubber Reporter
0257-8700	Water Sewage and Effluent
0257-8972	Surface and Coating Technology
0258-0136	South African Journal of Philosophy
0258-0144	South African Journal of Sociology
0258-0284	Telecoms Technical Quarterly
0258-0357	Acta Anthropogenetica
0258-0365	Aligarh Journal of English Studies
0258-0381	New Quest
0258-0446	Man & Environment
0258-0772	Arbido-R
0258-1698	Studies in History (Sahibabad)†
0258-1701	Review Journal of Philosophy and Social Science
0258-2171	Turk Mikrobiyologi Cemiyeti Dergisi
0258-3038	Mechanical & Electronic Industries Yearbook of China
0258-3046	China's Customs Statistics
0258-3054	China Market Monthly
0258-3062	China Coal Industry Yearbook
0258-3240	Maritime China
0258-3259	China Transport
0258-3267	Medical China
0258-3321	South African Journal of Dairy Science
0258-3690	I C S I D Review: Foreign Investment Law Journal
0258-4476	Tea Research Foundation of Central Africa. Annual Report
0258-5812	Pesca y Marina
0258-5901	Seoul Journal of Psychiatry
0258-655X	Ploutarkhos
0258-6746	Abstracts of Chinese Geological Literature
0258-7173	Growth

ISSN INDEX 1497

0258-719X Momentum
0258-7211 Staffrider Magazine
0258-7262 Gold Patent Digest
0258-7270 International Affairs Bulletin
0258-8536 Instituto de Estudios Aymaras. Boletin
0258-8900 Bulletin of Volcanology
0258-9052 Tshiingamo
0258-9079 Xihondzo Xo Rindza
0258-9281 Truck & Bus, South Africa
0258-9680 Journal of European Studies
0258-977X China Sources
0259-0026 Vitae
0259-0034 Vitae Yearbook
0259-0654 Beihefte zur Wiener Zeitschrift fuer die Kunde des Morgenlandes
0259-0662 Beitraege zur Sprachinselforschung
0259-0670 Conceptus-Studien
0259-0689 Johannes-Kepler-Universitaet Linz. Dissertationen
0259-0697 Technische Universitaet Wien. Dissertationen
0259-0700 Universitaet Salzburg. Dissertationen
0259-0719 Wirtschaftsuniversitaet Wien. Dissertationen
0259-0727 Kanon
0259-0735 Kirche und Recht
0259-0743 Klagenfurter Beitraege zur Philosophie
0259-0751 Leobener Gruene Hefte. Neue Folge
0259-076X Musik und Gesellschaft
0259-0786 Quellen zur Theatergeschichte
0259-0794 Salzburger Beitraege zur Paracelsusforschung
0259-0808 Studia Uralica
0259-0816 Law & Anthropology
0259-0824 Polyaisthesis
0259-0972 Institute of Medicine. Journal
0259-1146 Directory of Chinese External Economic Organizations & Industrial/Commercial Enterprises
0259-1162 Anaesthesia Essays and Researches
0259-1235 Electronic News for China
0259-188X Indicator South Africa
0259-207X Education Journal
0259-3238 Commercial Agriculture in Zimbabwe
0259-3602 S A B S Catalogue
0259-4382 Central American Historical Institute. Update
0259-5796 Africa Press Clips
0259-7349 Photographia
0259-7373 Bulletin Critique des Annales Islamologiques
0259-8264 World Translation Index
0259-8272 Asian Journal of Public Adminstration
0259-8388 International Quarterly of Analytical Chemistry
0259-8396 International Quarterly of Antibiotic Research
0259-840X International Quarterly of Cancer Research
0259-8418 International Quarterly of Materials Science
0259-8426 International Quarterly of Virology
0259-8930 Arab Gulf Journal of Scientific Research. Section A: Mathematical & Physical Sciences
0259-8949 Arab Gulf Journal of Scientific Research. Section B: Agricultural & Biologi
0259-9171 Economic Review (Year)
0259-9791 Journal of Mathematical Chemistry
0259-9805 Muon Catalyzed Fusion
0260-0005 Serials in the British Library
0260-0099 Butterworths International Medical Reviews: Clinical Pharmacology and Therapeutics†
0260-0137 Butterworths International Medical Reviews: Neurology
0260-0218 Scottish Council of Social Service. News Bulletin†
0260-0226 Multiracial Education
0260-0234 Printers Pie†
0260-0250 Clwyd Historian
0260-0293 Cityscope
0260-0315 Bookmark
0260-0366 Museum Ethnographers Group. Newsletter
0260-0374 Lincolnshire Dragon
0260-0382 Shepherd
0260-0439 English Horizon†
0260-0447 Current Transnational Corporations Bibliography†
0260-0463 Geologist's Directory
0260-0471 Great Britain. Department of Education and Science. Architects and Building Branch. Broadsheets
0260-0498 Eurovet Bulletin†
0260-0544 Castle Lodge News and Views
0260-0552 Alternative Alternative
0260-0587 North West England Industrial Classified Directory *changed to* North West England Directory of Industry and Commerce
0260-0595 Paperback Inferno
0260-0617 Scottish Episcopal Church Yearbook
0260-0625 I S T C Banner *changed to* I S T C Phoenix
0260-0684 University of Liverpool. Research Report†
0260-0706 Graduate Careers in Sales and Marketing for Graduates and Postgraduates *changed to* Dog Volume 3. Administration, Management, Marketing and Sales
0260-0749 Financial Aid for First Degree Study at Commonwealth Universities
0260-0765 I B I D
0260-0781 Qarch
0260-082X B A A F Discussion Series
0260-0854 Oxford Reviews of Reproductive Biology
0260-0935 Technical Papers for the Bible Translator
0260-0943 Practical Papers for the Bible Translator
0260-0951 British Shipper *changed to* British Shipper and Forwarder
0260-096X Business Review of Burton upon Trent and District *changed to* Business Review for the Burton-on-Trent and Surrounding Areas
0260-0986 Popular D I Y†
0260-0994 Educational Analysis *changed to* Contemporary Analyses in Education
0260-1001 Estate Agent
0260-101X Retail Security & Fire Prevention†
0260-1036 Leeds Naturalists' Club and Scientific Association. Newsletter
0260-1044 Herefordshire Family History Society. Journal
0260-1060 Nutrition and Health
0260-1079 Journal of Interdisciplinary Economics
0260-1087 International Bulk Journal
0260-1117 A C T H & Related Peptides
0260-1141 Purines
0260-115X Energy Review†
0260-1168 Greenfly
0260-1176 Finance Director's Review†
0260-1265 Yearbook and Philatelic Societies' Directory
0260-1362 School Organization
0260-1370 International Journal of Lifelong Education
0260-146X Barclays U.K. Financial Survey
0260-1508 Exhibitor's Handbook†
0260-1532 British Telecom Journal
0260-1559 Focus on Tourism†
0260-1656 Electrical Products
0260-1664 Current Topics in Infection
0260-1729 Trent Papers in Education
0260-1745 Kitchens
0260-1753 Hel Achau
0260-180X Bus News
0260-1818 Royal Society of Chemistry. Annual Reports on the Progress of Chemistry. Section A: Inorganic Chemistry
0260-1826 Royal Society of Chemistry. Annual Reports on the Progress of Chemistry. Section C: Physical Chemistry
0260-1842 Phototrain Express
0260-1869 Manpower: Glass Industry
0260-194X Business News Index
0260-1974 Food World News
0260-2067 Irish Slavonic Studies
0260-2105 Review of International Studies
0260-2113 Ecuatorial
0260-2199 The Conference Green Book
0260-2202 Cubit
0260-2288 Sensor Review
0260-2334 Medicine International. Southern African Edition
0260-2342 Medicine in Practice†
0260-2350 Palestine Report†
0260-2377 Brazilian Agriculture & Commodities
0260-2385 Brokers' Monthly & Insurance Adviser
0260-2393 Fur Review
0260-2407 Nationalism Today
0260-2415 North of Scotland Visitor
0260-2423 Radio Advertisers' Guide
0260-2431 The Conference Blue Book
0260-2474 Aspis
0260-2504 Grampian English Views
0260-2547 Poole - Commercial Users Handbook 1983/4 *changed to* Poole Handbook
0260-2563 Student Nationalist
0260-261X Barclays Commodities Survey
0260-2695 N B A Technical Note†
0260-2725 Royal Society News
0260-2776 Writer (Penzance)
0260-2784 Marine Biological Association of the United Kingdom. Occasional Papers *changed to* Marine Biological Association of the United Kingdom. Occasional Publications
0260-2806 S.I.S. Workshop
0260-2814 Society for Radiological Protection. Journal
0260-2911 Practical Classics
0260-2938 Assessment and Evaluation in Higher Education
0260-2946 Physiological Principles in Medicine
0260-2954 Avon Past
0260-2970 Locomotives Large & Small
0260-3004 Smash Hits
0260-3020 Atomic Energy News†
0260-3055 Annals of Glaciology
0260-3063 Muslim World Book Review
0260-3098 Fire Statistics United Kingdom
0260-311X Educational Drama Association. Newsletter
0260-3233 Vegetarian
0260-3241 North Herts Medical Journal
0260-3268 New Tolkien Newsletter
0260-3306 Great Britain. Advisory Council for Adult and Continuing Education. Annual Report
0260-3330 New Gandy Dancer
0260-3403 World Copper Survey
0260-3438 International Directory of Software
0260-3594 Comments on Inorganic Chemistry
0260-3667 American Trust for the British Library. Newsletter
0260-3675 Transit Packaging†
0260-3683 Fuel Poverty News
0260-3691 W E F Communications Report†
0260-373X Institute of Management Consultants. Yearbook
0260-3756 Local Authority Specifiers' Reference Book and Buyers Guide
0260-3772 Centre for the Study of Islam and Christian-Muslim Relations. Research Papers *changed to* Research Papers: Muslims in Europe
0260-3810 Labour Party. Campaign Briefing
0260-3837 Cats
0260-3853 Conspectus For...Of Further Education in the Inner and Outer London Region†
0260-387X World Poultry Industry†
0260-3888 B A A F News
0260-390X Clarinet and Saxophone
0260-3926 Whillans's Tax Tables
0260-3934 Edinburgh Medicine
0260-3985 British-Israel Trade
0260-3993 Vive la Difference
0260-4000 Arclight *see* 0144-9745
0260-4019 Intercede (Manchester)
0260-4027 World Futures
0260-4043 Ultrasound Patents & Papers
0260-406X Chartered Institute of Public Finance and Accountancy. Housing Rents. Statistics
0260-4078 Chartered Institute of Public Finance and Accountancy. Housing Revenue Accounts. Actuals Statistics
0260-4086 Chartered Institute of Public Finance and Accountancy. Housing Estimate Statistics *changed to* Chartered Institute of Public Finance and Accountancy. Housing Revenue Account Estimate Statistics
0260-4094 Housing Corporation. Quarterly Review
0260-4116 Traditional Kent Buildings
0260-4140 Royal Society of Chemistry. Information Services. Newsletter *changed to* Royal Society of Chemistry. Database Newsletter
0260-4256 Textile Digest
0260-4272 Arabia: The Islamic World Review
0260-4299 International Coal Report
0260-437X Journal of Applied Toxicology
0260-4388 Manchester Training Handbooks
0260-440X Carnivorous Plant Society Journal
0260-4426 West of Scotland Visitor
0260-4515 Stock Car Reporter
0260-4531 Spindrift
0260-454X Afrosport
0260-4604 International Who's Who in Water Supply *changed to* I W S A Year Book
0260-4620 Company Law Digest
0260-4639 Clinics in Immunology and Allergy *see* 0889-8561
0260-4698 Expired British Patents & Licences of Right
0260-471X Short Stories Magazine
0260-4736 Sandgrouse
0260-4752 Practical English Teaching
0260-4779 International Journal of Museum Management and Curatorship
0260-4817 N M I News *changed to* British Maritime Technology News
0260-4833 I E S Proceedings
0260-4868 European Human Rights Reports
0260-4876 I. P. Reports from Socialist Countries†
0260-4884 Dozenal Journal
0260-4892 Threshing Floor
0260-4906 Top Fruit Times†
0260-4914 London and Middlesex Genealogical Directory†
0260-4922 Engineering Distributor
0260-4930 Graphics World. Services and Supplies Directory†
0260-4957 Heritage
0260-4965 Fighters Monthly *changed to* Fighters
0260-5007 Directory of Land and Hydrographic Survey Services in the United Kingdom
0260-504X Wind and Water Mills
0260-5058 F E R N Journal
0260-5090 Movie News†
0260-5112 Free Life
0260-5120 B J-Builder's Journal *see* 0263-7936
0260-5139 Gloucestershire Local History Newsletter
0260-5163 Student Update *changed to* Trainee
0260-5171 Business History Newsletter
0260-518X O T C Medication
0260-5236 Finders Keepers (Wellingborough) *changed to* New Collecting Lines
0260-5244 Community View
0260-5252 Mental Health Statistics for Wales
0260-5295 Home Care Services, Day Care Establishments, Day Services - Scotland
0260-5317 European Rubber Journal
0260-5325 School Nurse
0260-5333 Period Piece & Paperback
0260-535X British National Formulary
0260-5414 Extro
0260-5503 Manchester Geographer
0260-5511 Abstracts on Hygiene and Communicable Diseases

0260-5546 Chartered Institute of Public Finance and Accountancy. Rate Collection Statistics. Actuals
0260-5554 Problem-Solving News
0260-5562 Phase Two *changed to* Micros in Scottish Education
0260-5570 Handbooks in Maritime Archaeology
0260-5597 Scottish Society for the Conservation and Restoration of Historic and Artistic Works. Newsletter *see* 0264-9039
0260-5600 Cambridge Medieval Celtic Studies
0260-5619 Catalogue of British Official Publications Not Published by H.M.S.O.
0260-5627 Labrador Retriever Club of Wales. Yearbook
0260-5716 Light and Design International
0260-5724 Business Computing
0260-5732 Shetland Life
0260-5759 Market Assessment
0260-5783 Hot Shoe *changed to* Hot Shoe International
0260-5805 British Herpetological Society. Bulletin
0260-5813 Clapham Omnibus *changed to* Consumer Voice
0260-5821 C T O
0260-5848 Royal College of Midwives. Current Awareness Service
0260-5872 Clinical Cytogenetics
0260-5880 Haemic and Lymphatic Cell Culture†
0260-5902 Plant Biotechnology
0260-5910 Development of Social Skills†
0260-5929 University of London. Institute of Germanic Studies. Research in Germanic Studies
0260-597X Turner Studies
0260-5988 Timecraft
0260-5996 British Acupuncture Association. Newsletter
0260-6003 Bicycle Trade Times
0260-6054 Kelly's Directory of British Industry & Services in Eastern England†
0260-6097 Bicycle Times
0260-6127 Workers Education Association. Women's Studies Newsletter
0260-6151 Kelly's Directory of British Industry & Services in Northern England†
0260-6186 Guide to Banks & Other Financial Institutions in Asia (Including Iran & the Arab Region)
0260-6194 Kelly's Directory of British Industry & Services in The Midlands†
0260-6208 Bulletin of Scottish Politics
0260-6216 B C I S Quarterly Review of Building Prices
0260-6267 International Journal of Pharmaceutical Technology & Product Manufacture
0260-6275 Journal of Separation Process Technology
0260-6313 Crosscurrent
0260-6321 Glass and Glazing News
0260-633X Kelly's Directory of British Industry & Services in Scotland and Northern Ireland†
0260-6348 Lyle Official Books Review†
0260-6356 Homeopathic Alternative†
0260-6364 L S A Quarterly *changed to* L S A Newsletter
0260-6372 Trading Standards and Consumer Protection Statistics. Actuals
0260-6399 Steel Industry Monitor†
0260-6402 Minority Rights Group. Newsletter
0260-6410 C P A G Newsletter
0260-6429 C O A D Words
0260-6445 P.S. (London)
0260-647X Adverse Drug Reactions and Acute Poisoning Reviews
0260-6488 A - Z of U.K. Marketing Data
0260-6496 Institute of Chartered Accountants in England and Wales. Tax Digest
0260-650X Irish in Britain Directory
0260-6518 Textile Horizons
0260-6526 Large Stores Directory
0260-6534 Home Entertainment *changed to* Television: the New Era
0260-6542 Euromonitor Reports on D I Y and Home Improvement Markets *see* 0263-5437
0260-6550 Bulletin of Northern Ireland Law
0260-6593 Current Technology Index
0260-6615 Labour & Ireland
0260-664X Austin Healey Year Book
0260-6658 Electronic Publishing Review *changed to* Electronic and Optical Publishing Review
0260-6674 Sheffield Studies in Japanese
0260-6704 People's Power†
0260-6739 Philatelist and Philatelic Journal of Great Britain
0260-6747 Euromoney Syndication Guide *changed to* Euromoney Capital Markets Guide
0260-6755 Parliaments, Estates & Representation
0260-6771 Rabbits *changed to* Fur & Feather
0260-6801 Arts London Review
0260-681X Cephalopod Newsletter
0260-6844 Terminus
0260-6879 Information and Library Manager
0260-6887 Workshop Equipment News *see* 0267-307X
0260-6917 Nurse Education Today
0260-6925 Great Britain. Institute of Terrestrial Ecology. Bangor Occasional Paper
0260-6941 Scientific & Technical Books†
0260-695X Newth-Nuth Family History Society. Newsletter
0260-6976 South
0260-7050 Computer Price Guide for Large Computers†
0260-7069 Micrographics Year Book *changed to* Micrographics and Optical Storage Buyer's Guide
0260-7123 Combat (Cleckheaton)
0260-714X Black Country Geologist
0260-7174 Wiltshire Family History Society. Journal
0260-7212 Marxist Humanism
0260-7247 Infomatics
0260-728X Sea Angling Monthly
0260-7336 Socialist Youth
0260-7387 List of Shipowners
0260-7409 International Packaging Abstracts
0260-7417 Journal of Educational Television
0260-7425 Tonic
0260-745X Cranes Today Handbook
0260-7468 European Racehorse
0260-7476 Journal of Education for Teaching
0260-7492 Wild Cat
0260-7522 I C S A Bulletin
0260-7530 What Video?
0260-7549 Twirling Times
0260-7557 Liverpool Family History Society *see* 0260-759X
0260-7565 Oxfordshire Local History
0260-759X Liverpool Family Historian
0260-7603 Chartered Institute of Public Finance and Accountancy. Waste Collection Statistics. Actuals
0260-762X Model Cars
0260-7638 Liverpool Software Gazette
0260-7654 Zip
0260-7727 Chartered Institute of Building. Year Book
0260-7735 National Council on Inland Transportation. Newsletter
0260-7743 London Federation of Museum and Art Galleries. Newsletter
0260-7751 P.P.A. North West Region Newsletter
0260-776X Conferences Meetings & Exhibitions Welcome
0260-7786 Hong Kong Handbook
0260-7794 Darlington Astronomical Society. Newsletter
0260-7808 Early Childhood†
0260-7816 Family Links: Past and Present *changed to* Irish Family Links
0260-7840 Modern Power Systems
0260-7883 Agricultural Administration Network. Newsletter *see* 0951-1865
0260-7891 Union Fact Sheet
0260-7921 Fellowship in Prayer†
0260-7948 New Hope International
0260-7964 Irish Drama Selections
0260-7972 Scottish Pottery Studies
0260-8049 Shearsman *see* 0264-6773
0260-8065 Strathclyde's Budget *changed to* Strathclyde Regional Council. Annual Report & Financial Statement
0260-8081 Fairfield Experimental Horticulture Station. Summary Annual Review
0260-809X Energy Matters
0260-8103 Equi†
0260-8111 Equestrian Year
0260-8154 Irish Studies in Britain
0260-8189 Probe Report
0260-8235 Manchester Papers on Development
0260-8251 Fantasy Macabre
0260-8278 Creative Mind
0260-8294 Nottingham Licensed Taxi Owners & Drivers Association. Newsletter
0260-8308 Everything Has a Value†
0260-8316 Conferences and Exhibitions International
0260-8359 Journal of Economic Affairs *see* 0265-0665
0260-8367 Clinical Research Reviews†
0260-8391 Caraher Family History Society. Journal
0260-8405 Lincolnshire Population
0260-8448 Praxis International
0260-8456 Faba Bean Abstracts
0260-8464 Lentil Abstracts
0260-8472 Microcomputer News International *see* 0263-6522
0260-8480 Irish Studies†
0260-8499 Reflections
0260-8502 Manchester Polytechnic. Department of Library and Information Studies. Occasional Papers
0260-8537 Studio Sound's Pro-Audio Yearbook *changed to* Studio Sound's Pro-Audio Directory
0260-8553 Knitting Industry Technical Review†
0260-8634 Business News†
0260-8642 Chartered Institute of Public Finance and Accountancy. Planning and Development Statistics. Actuals
0260-8677 Epoxy Resins & Plastics†
0260-8685 Head and Hand
0260-8693 Handgunner
0260-8707 Historic House
0260-8723 Arts Report (Birmingham)
0260-8774 Journal of Food Engineering
0260-8790 Correlation
0260-8804 Clydesdale Bank Scottish Football League Review
0260-8812 Forecast of Shop Rents
0260-8820 Directory of Private Hospitals and Health Services
0260-8839 London Port Handbook 1984
0260-8855 Knitstats
0260-8944 ComLon
0260-8952 Bradford Center Occasional Papers
0260-8979 Euroednews
0260-9061 Weekender
0260-907X Rent Review *see* 0263-7499
0260-9088 Soil Survey and Land Evaluation
0260-9096 British Journal of Administrative Management
0260-910X Visit California with Fyfe Robertson
0260-9126 Journal of Education in Museums
0260-9150 New Computer Careers
0260-9169 Barbour Compendium Building Products
0260-9177 Pelham Golf Year†
0260-9215 British Pirandello Society. Yearbook
0260-924X Ireland Ports & Shipping Handbook
0260-9282 Falmouth Port and Industry Handbook 1984
0260-9290 City Handbook
0260-9339 Poetry and Little Press Information
0260-9355 Edmonton Hundred Historical Society. Chronicle
0260-9363 Instant Record
0260-938X F O L K Magazine *changed to* F O L K Newsletter
0260-9398 Stereotype
0260-9428 A L P S P Bulletin
0260-9436 Polymicros†
0260-9452 Boating Business
0260-9460 Biblical Creation
0260-9517 Great Yarmouth Port and Industry Handbook
0260-9541 Archives of Natural History
0260-955X Annual Register of Pharmaceutical Chemists
0260-9584 Quaker Peace & Service. Annual Report
0260-9592 London Review of Books
0260-9762 Chartered Institute of Public Finance and Accountancy. Local Government Comparative Statistics
0260-9770 Multicultural Education Abstracts
0260-9819 Communist Affairs†
0260-9827 Political Geography Quarterly
0260-9835 T.E. Lawrence Studies Newsletter
0260-986X Irish Hare
0260-9886 Chartered Institute of Public Finance and Accountancy. Highways and Transportation. Actuals
0260-9894 Chartered Institute of Public Finance and Accountancy. Highways and Transportation Statistics. Estimates
0260-9924 Canterbury Diocesan News Service
0260-9959 Chartered Institute of Public Finance and Accountancy. Cemeteries Statistics. Actuals *see* 0263-2969
0260-9967 Chartered Institute of Public Finance and Accountancy. Local Authority Airports. Accounts and Statistics *changed to* Chartered Institute of Public Finance and Accountancy. Local Authority Airports. Accounts and Statistics. Actuals Statistics
0260-9975 Chartered Institute of Public Finance and Accountancy. Airport Financial Statistics. Estimates†
0260-9983 U.K.I.R.T. Report
0260-9991 Journal of Art & Design Education
0261-0094 Anbar Management Publications Joint Index
0261-0108 Anbar Management Publications Bibliography
0261-0124 Aireings
0261-0140 Progress in Obstetrics and Gynaecology
0261-0159 Equal Opportunities International
0261-0183 C S P: Critical Social Policy
0261-0191 C A T N I
0261-023X Bulletin of Inventions and Summary of Patent Specifications
0261-0272 Reviewing Sociology
0261-0302 Average Prices of British Academic Books
0261-0310 International Who's Who in the Arab World
0261-0329 Glazed Expressions
0261-0337 Training Action†
0261-0345 Diesel Engineers and Users Association. Transactions *changed to* Institution of Diesel and Gas Turbine Engineers. Transactions
0261-0353 Bradford Occasional Papers
0261-0388 Afghan Voice
0261-0426 Company Car (London, 1980) *changed to* Executive Car
0261-0450 Commercial Vehicle and P S V Buyer's Guide *changed to* Commercial Vehicle & Buyer's Guide
0261-0477 New Growth *see* 0264-4614
0261-0558 Curious Woman
0261-0604 Nucleus (Cambridge)†
0261-0655 Property Guide: Homes in Beds/Bucks/Berks & Oxon†
0261-0663 Estuaries and Coastal Waters of the British Isles
0261-068X I A M S Newsletter
0261-0752 Lincolnshire, Housing
0261-0760 Resources
0261-0795 Poetry into Print
0261-0833 Independent Retailer and Caterer *changed to* Convenience Store
0261-0868 Magpie
0261-0876 Majalla
0261-0884 Insist
0261-0892 Popular Astronomy

0261-099X Strathclyde Modern Language Studies
0261-1023 Okikiolu Scientific and Industrial Organization. Bulletin of Mathematics
0261-1066 Literary Drivel Society. Transactions
0261-1104 Cronicl Powys
0261-1139 Greentrees
0261-1171 Crimp Journal
0261-1252 Chartered Institute of Public Finance and Accountancy. Public Money
0261-1260 Telegram (London) *see* 0264-6773
0261-1279 Early Music History
0261-1309 Electrical Contracting News
0261-1325 I S Annual
0261-1341 Moz-Art†
0261-135X Shropshire Family History Journal
0261-1376 Explorations in Knowledge
0261-1384 Home Economist
0261-1392 Leisure, Recreation and Tourism Abstracts
0261-1430 Popular Music
0261-1465 Benn's Hardware Directory & D-I-Y Buyers Guide
0261-1473 Middle East Industry and Transport *changed to* Middle East Transport & Telecommunications
0261-152X International Federation of Library Associations and Institutions. Section of Art Libraries. Newsletter
0261-1538 Liverpool Monographs in Hispanic Studies
0261-1589 Fire Research News
0261-1600 Beatles Book
0261-1635 Westgate Tax Planner's Letter
0261-1686 Zerb
0261-1708 Network (London, 1965)
0261-1724 R L C: Roskill's Letter from China†
0261-1732 Information Technology and People†
0261-1783 Great Britain. Central Statistical Office. Regional Trends
0261-1791 Great Britain. Central Statistical Office. Guide to Official Statistics
0261-1813 Space Education
0261-1821 Appendix *see* 0264-6420
0261-1899 Stamp and Postal History News *see* 0265-8216
0261-1902 Pop Puzzles
0261-1910 International Video Yearbook *see* 0266-2256
0261-1929 Alternatives to Laboratory Animals: A T L A
0261-1953 S O A P
0261-1961 Unexplained
0261-197X T P A S Notes
0261-1988 Heritage Outlook
0261-2038 Fried Fish Caterer
0261-2089 Scottish Anti-Vivisection Society. Newsletter
0261-2127 Electricity Consumers Council. Annual Report
0261-2135 Craftsman's Directory
0261-2143 Somerset Mines Research Group. Newsletter *changed to* Somerset Mines Research Group. Journal
0261-2178 British Library Research Reviews
0261-2194 Crop Protection
0261-2208 Countryside Monthly†
0261-2275 Mid Glamorgan Industrial Directory
0261-2305 Barclays U.K. Economic Survey
0261-2313 African Air Transport
0261-233X Defense Latin America *changed to* Defensa Latino Americana
0261-2356 Fairplay World Ports Directory
0261-2364 T E S T Bureau. Technical Reports
0261-2399 World Airnews
0261-2429 Cancer Surveys
0261-2437 Current Fluid Engineering Titles†
0261-2445 Devon County Planning Department. Tourism and Recreation. Annual Report *changed to* Devon Tourism Review
0261-2453 Devon County Planning Department. Conservation and Primary Industries. Annual Report *changed to* Devon. Property Department. Conservation and Primary Industries. Annual Report
0261-250X Record Collector (London)
0261-2534 Good 6500 *changed to* Good Food
0261-2550 Collectors Items
0261-2593 Library Science Book Distribution Service. Quality Monitor *changed to* Library Science Book Distribution Service. Library and Information Science Update
0261-2607 Protect and Survive Monthly and British Civil Defence News *see* 0264-4525
0261-2631 Northern Ireland Council for Educational Research. Research Unit. Staffing Needs of Post-Primary Schools†
0261-264X True Crime Monthly
0261-2666 Electrosonic World
0261-2674 English Hops
0261-2712 Casualty Return Statistical Summary of Merchant Ships Totally Lost, Broken Up, Etc *see* 0268-0815
0261-2720 Annual Summary of Merchant Ships Completed in the World
0261-2747 European Information Service
0261-2755 School Organisation & Management Abstracts
0261-281X Medway Ports Shipping Handbook
0261-2828 Homoeopathy Today
0261-2836 Pennine Magazine
0261-2909 Nueva Historia
0261-2917 Laboratory Hazards Bulletin
0261-2925 Arab Banker
0261-2933 B M C I S Building Maintenance Price Book
0261-2992 C A B L I S
0261-300X Pelham Horse Year†
0261-3018 Scottish Society of Composers. Newsletter *changed to* Stretto
0261-3042 Riverside Interviews
0261-3050 Bulletin of Latin American Research
0261-3069 Materials in Engineering *see* 0264-1275
0261-3107 Philatelic Magazine *see* 0265-8216
0261-3131 Ecologist (1979)
0261-314X C E C T A L Conference Papers Series
0261-3182 Software and Microsystems *see* 0268-6961
0261-3212 Studies of Meaning, Language & Change
0261-3220 National Galleries of Scotland. News
0261-3247 Oil Spot
0261-3263 Video Review†
0261-331X Computer Applications (Bradford)†
0261-3344 Risk Measurement Service
0261-3409 Archaeologia
0261-3425 A N: Artists Newsletter
0261-3468 Wagner News
0261-3492 What Computer?
0261-3506 Japan Electronics Today News
0261-3514 Living Sunday
0261-3530 Journal of Area Studies
0261-3646 Medical Forum
0261-3654 I B M User
0261-3697 Computer & Video Games
0261-3735 America Latina Informe Economico *see* 0263-5372
0261-3743 America Latina Informe Politico *see* 0263-5372
0261-3751 America Latina Informe de Mercados *see* 0263-5372
0261-3786 Barclay's Industrial Survey†
0261-3794 Electoral Studies
0261-3816 Garden Trade News
0261-3824 Council of Civil Service Unions. Bulletin
0261-3867 Problem Solver†
0261-3875 Legal Studies
0261-3883 Petroleum Times Price Report
0261-3921 Scottish Medicine
0261-3948 International Dollmaking & Collecting
0261-3956 Wining & Dining
0261-3964 City News (Newcastle upon Tyne)
0261-4014 Links (Oxford)
0261-4022 Kampuchea Bulletin
0261-4049 Welfare & Social Services Journal
0261-4057 Scottish Theatre News
0261-4065 Trailer World†
0261-4073 Product Finder: Swift-Sasco Buyers Guide
0261-409X S T O R M
0261-4103 Information Age
0261-4146 Beauty Salon *changed to* Health & Beauty Salon
0261-4170 Lloyd's European Loading List†
0261-4189 E M B O Journal
0261-4200 Popular Video
0261-4227 Book Choice
0261-426X European and North American Scrap Directory
0261-4286 Journal of World Forest Resource Management
0261-4294 Gifted Education International
0261-4316 Catholic Archives
0261-4324 Medical News Weekly†
0261-4332 Archaeological Review from Cambridge
0261-4340 Italianist
0261-4367 Leisure Studies
0261-4375 Family Law Reports
0261-4391 World Book News†
0261-4413 International Agricultural Development
0261-4448 Language Teaching
0261-4499 Microcomputer Printout
0261-4707 High Performance Liquid Chromatography
0261-4952 Invertebrate Neurobiology
0261-4960 Monoclonal Antibodies
0261-4979 Recombinant D N A
0261-4987 Catecholamines and Adrenergic Receptors *see* 0950-0502
0261-4995 Intestinal Function
0261-5002 Micronutrient News
0261-5010 Manganese in Agriculture
0261-5045 Molybdenum in Agriculture
0261-5061 Retrospect (Burnley)
0261-5088 Pre-School Playgroups Association. Crewe and Nantwich Branch. Newsletter
0261-5096 Northumbrian Pipers' Society Magazine
0261-510X British Journal of Developmental Psychology
0261-5118 Municipal Review and A M A News
0261-5142 Microdecision
0261-5150 Arab Gulf Journal†
0261-5169 Pims Media Directory
0261-5207 Guide to In-Career Training Courses for Civil Engineers
0261-5223 Trackwise†
0261-5282 London Theatre Record
0261-5304 Building Society News
0261-5312 Coarse Fishing Monthly†
0261-5339 Fraud Report
0261-5355 Aquatechnic International
0261-5363 New Bookbinder
0261-5436 Copper in Agriculture
0261-5444 Boron in Agriculture
0261-5452 Zinc in Agriculture
0261-5487 I R P I: International Reinforced Plastics Industry
0261-5495 Scandinavian Contact
0261-5525 Lincolnshire Bird Report
0261-5576 Gregory Awards
0261-5584 Sell's Directory
0261-5606 Journal of International Money and Finance
0261-5614 Clinical Nutrition
0261-5622 European Journal of Sexually Transmitted Diseases†
0261-5630 Agape
0261-5649 Ruskin College, Oxford. Library. Occasional Publication
0261-5657 Electro Optics Newsletter
0261-5665 Sports Industry
0261-5703 Schools of Prayer
0261-5711 Welsh Books & Writers†
0261-5746 Paint and Resin
0261-5754 W.E.A. Arts Newsletter†
0261-5770 World Hi-Fi Guide†
0261-5789 World Fertilizer News Summary
0261-586X Fort
0261-5878 Fluids Handling *changed to* Fluids Handling Technology
0261-5886 International Freighting Management†
0261-5894 Copperplate
0261-5916 C A S T M E Journal
0261-5924 Activity Holidays in Britain
0261-5932 Angus District Council. Housing Plans and Programmes
0261-6025 Childrens Clothing International
0261-6033 Alternative Times
0261-6386 B S A European Bulletin
0261-6394 B S A Bulletin
0261-6408 Building Societies in (Year) *see* 0266-4828
0261-6416 Building Societies Association. Monthly Figures Press Release
0261-6491 Inner City Focus
0261-6505 Richmond Collage
0261-6513 Airports International Directory
0261-653X Society (London)
0261-6548 Stand To!
0261-6688 Lloyd's Register of Classed Yachts
0261-6777 Ocean Voice
0261-6793 Arabian Government and Public Services
0261-6823 A A Files
0261-6866 Coin Slot Location†
0261-6912 New Socialist
0261-6920 C A D-C A M International
0261-6939 2D: Drama, Dance
0261-6963 Great Britain. Agricultural Science Service. Research and Development Reports: Crop and Pest Diseases
0261-698X Great Britain. Agricultural Science Service. Research and Development Reports: Animal Science
0261-7005 Science and Engineering Research Council. Report
0261-7048 Artefact/Pin Up†
0261-7099 Mediscope
0261-7102 Small Computer Program Index†
0261-7110 Consumer Education Newsletter
0261-7161 Great Britain. Agricultural Science Service. Research and Development Reports: Mammal and Bird Pests
0261-717X Great Britain. Agricultural Science Service. Research and Development Reports: Crop Nutrition and Soil Science
0261-7188 Mechanical Engineering Technology
0261-7226 Sarawak Journal
0261-7277 Soil Dynamics and Earthquake Engineering
0261-7358 Natural World
0261-7374 European Energy Profile†
0261-7382 Latin American Markets
0261-7404 Message to the Anglo-Saxon and Celtic Peoples *changed to* National Message
0261-7412 Process Equipment News
0261-7420 Quilters Guild. Newsletter
0261-7633 World Energy Business Centre Reference Book and Buyers' Guide
0261-7641 Institution of Engineering Designers Official Reference Book and Buyers Guide
0261-7943 Fishing Handbook
0261-7951 Gardening Handbook
0261-796X Business Location Handbook
0261-8028 Journal of Materials Science Letters
0261-8044 Flesh and Blood
0261-8222 Fender Musician†
0261-8230 Executive Health Club
0261-8249 European Review
0261-8273 B E C A N. Instrumentation and Techniques in Cardiology
0261-8281 B E C A N. Electrodes for Medicine and Biology
0261-8451 Office Automation Report†
0261-8567 Wholistic Health†
0261-863X European Policies and Legislative Proposals†
0261-8648 Institute of Grocery Distribution. Economic Bulletin *changed to* Institute of Grocery Distribution. Economics and Finance. Bulletin
0261-8664 Touche Ross & Company. Tax Newsletter
0261-8761 Building Products
0261-880X Norwich and Norfolk Chamber of Commerce and Industry. Directory

0261-8818 Poynton Local History Society Newsletter
0261-8834 Rajneesh Buddafield European Newsletter†
0261-8850 Aspects of Edenbridge
0261-8877 Falkirk Central Community Council. News Letter
0261-8966 Education in the Royal County of Berkshire
0261-8982 D & B Creditnews
0261-9180 High Temperature Technology
0261-9253 Industrial Chemistry Bulletin†
0261-9288 Immigrants and Minorities
0261-9296 Orchard Lodge Studies of Deviancy
0261-9768 European Journal of Teacher Education
0261-9776 Personnel Executive†
0261-9784 Quaternary Studies
0261-9873 Hematology - Oncology Clinics of North America
0261-9881 Clinics in Anaesthesiology *see* 0889-8537
0261-989X Life Support Systems
0261-9903 Journal of Advertising *see* 0265-0487
0261-9911 Facts about Lewisham†
0261-9962 Brazil, Land of the Present†
0261-9970 Library Association. Local Studies Group. Newsletter *see* 0263-0273
0261-9997 Mental Handicap
0262-0022 Microfilm & Video Systems†
0262-0030 Food Law Monthly
0262-0057 N E I News
0262-0073 Middle East Hospital†
0262-0081 A I A Education Newsletter
0262-0200 Maternal & Child Health
0262-0219 Top 2,000 Directories and Annuals: A Guide to the Major Titles Used in British Libraries *changed to* Top 3,000 Directories and Annuals: A Guide to the Major Titles Used in British Libraries
0262-0227 Plant & Works Engineering
0262-0251 Media in Education & Development
0262-0278 British Library. Bibliographic Services Division. Cataloguing Practice Notes for UKMARC Records
0262-0308 British Tourism Yearbook†
0262-0383 Northern Economic Review
0262-0413 Theatre International†
0262-0448 Helicopter World
0262-0456 East European Markets
0262-0782 T H S: Times Health Supplement†
0262-0812 Gramophone Spoken Word & Miscellaneous Catalogue
0262-0820 Fish Farming International
0262-0839 Resources Supplement†
0262-0847 Geophysics and Tectonics Abstracts *see* 0268-7941
0262-0855 International Development Abstracts
0262-0898 Clinical and Experimental Metastasis
0262-0995 International Directory of Laboratory Accreditation Systems and other Schemes of Testing Laboratories *changed to* International Directory of Testing Arrangements and Testing Laboratory Accreditation Systems
0262-1010 G P Guide to Emergency & Medical Services
0262-1037 Creative Review
0262-1045 Schooling & Culture†
0262-1053 Scottish Tyndale Bulletin *changed to* Scottish Bulletin of Evangelical Theology
0262-1061 White Fathers-White Sisters
0262-1150 Solvent News
0262-1169 Southern Arts Bulletin
0262-1193 Themes in Family Planning
0262-1215 Rothamsted Experimental Station. Report
0262-1452 Lincolnshire Information. Employment
0262-1460 Robot News International *see* 0950-5113
0262-1533 Metamorphic Association. Newsletter *changed to* Metamorphosis
0262-1622 Goole Port Handbook
0262-1630 Associated British Ports Handbook
0262-1657 Airline Fleets
0262-1673 Electronics Locations File
0262-1703 Journal of International Marketing†
0262-1711 Journal of Management Development
0262-172X H V A Current Awareness Bulletin
0262-1746 Prostaglandins, Leukotrienes and Medicine
0262-1819 Footloose
0262-1940 Badminton Association of England. Annual Handbook
0262-2203 Conservation Education
0262-2238 Animal Pharm
0262-2254 What's New in Electronics
0262-236X Behavioural Abstracts†
0262-2394 Agricultural Statistics, England
0262-2513 Better Business†
0262-2556 R E News
0262-2564 Chemical Engineering Bulletin†
0262-2572 Radio & Electronics World
0262-2726 Traveller
0262-2734 What's New in Computing
0262-2742 What's New in Interiors
0262-2750 French Studies Bulletin
0262-2793 C O S P E N News
0262-2874 Good News (Birmingham)
0262-2955 Laboratory Microcomputer
0262-2963 Biotech Quarterly†
0262-298X Book World Advertiser *changed to* Book World
0262-3080 London Housing
0262-3099 A A E News
0262-3102 Small Business
0262-3110 British Association for Behavioural Psychotherapy. Newsletter
0262-3145 Hospital Doctor
0262-3153 Directory of Social Action Programmes *changed to* Action Stations: The Directory of Social Action Programmes
0262-3161 Industrial Planning & Development
0262-3196 E C I: Electronic Components and Instruments
0262-3226 Industrial Safety Data File
0262-3234 Anthony and Berryman's Magistrates' Court Guide
0262-3242 Fire World
0262-3358 Hospital Acquired Infection†
0262-3439 Travel and Leisure (Belfast)
0262-3447 L R D Book of Wage Rates, Hours and Holidays *see* 0143-2680
0262-3579 I-D
0262-3765 Commercial Grower Weekly†
0262-3781 Briefing Paper on Southern Africa
0262-3803 Oxfam News
0262-3943 Guide to Steam Trains in the British Isles
0262-4001 Popular Caravan
0262-401X British Telecommunications Engineering
0262-4087 British Psychological Society. Education Section. Review
0262-4109 Behavioural Approaches with Children
0262-4206 Scoop Sport Annual
0262-4230 Manufacturing Chemist
0262-4249 Air Travel and Interline News *changed to* Air Travel
0262-4257 Investment Opportunities
0262-4354 Logistics Today
0262-4389 Scottish Archaeological Review
0262-4427 Peterborough & District Family History Society Journal
0262-4435 Leithead Family Newsletter
0262-4451 Fire News (London)
0262-4478 Keyways
0262-4508 International Road Haulage by British Registered Vehicles *see* 0262-6195
0262-4540 Practical Alternatives
0262-4559 Livestock Farming
0262-4583 Tolley's Tax Data (Year)
0262-4591 Searchlight
0262-4605 Scoop (London)†
0262-4648 Cash & Carry Wholesaler
0262-4672 Gwent Family History Society. Journal
0262-4710 Pace Motor Racing Directory†
0262-4737 Nigerian Criminal Reports†
0262-4745 Rothmans Rugby League Yearbook
0262-4753 Grass-roots (Poole)
0262-4842 Journal of One-Name Studies
0262-4850 Rothmans F.A. Non-League Football Yearbook†
0262-4885 S N H A T News Bulletin *see* 0950-5458
0262-4893 Cellular Polymers
0262-4907 Enterprise (Oxford)
0262-4923 Archive (Air-Britain)
0262-4966 Churchscape
0262-5008 Camera Counter
0262-5016 Best of London Eating
0262-5024 British Journal of Geriatric Nursing *changed to* Geriatric Nursing & Home Care
0262-5032 British Journal of Psychiatric Nursing†
0262-5075 International Journal of Cement Composites and Lightweight Concrete
0262-5091 Nuclear Engineer
0262-5113 Atholl & Breadalbane Community Comment
0262-5156 E C J R: European Court of Justice Reporter
0262-5245 Music Analysis
0262-5253 Oxford Journal of Archaeology
0262-5288 Technology Week
0262-5296 Energy Action Bulletin
0262-5326 Buttons
0262-5334 Commercial and Industrial Floorspace Statistics
0262-5342 Bygone Kent
0262-5377 Psychiatry in Practice
0262-5407 Asia and Pacific *changed to* Asia & Pacific Review
0262-5415 Latin America and Caribbean *changed to* Latin America & Caribbean Review
0262-5458 Sinclair User
0262-5474 Epilepsy Now!
0262-5504 Dermatology in Practice
0262-5512 Rheumatology in Practice
0262-5547 Cardiology in Practice
0262-5636 Cognitive Development Abstracts†
0262-5644 Studies on Women Abstracts
0262-5695 Finance Confidential
0262-5717 Primary & Middle School Equipment
0262-575X L T P
0262-5768 Adventure Sports & Travel†
0262-5849 Pet Product Marketing
0262-5873 Construction Plant and Equipment
0262-5881 Chemist & Druggist Directory
0262-5938 Coffee & Cocoa International
0262-5946 Gifts International
0262-5954 O S E A P Journal
0262-5997 Lifeskills Teaching Magazine†
0262-6004 Suffolk Institute of Archaeology and History. Proceedings
0262-6063 Builders & Timber Merchant
0262-6071 Timber Trades Journal and Wood Processing
0262-6101 Print Buyer
0262-6195 International Road Haulage by United Kingdom Registered Vehicles
0262-6373 Newstime (London)
0262-6381 Black Insight
0262-642X Welding Review
0262-6438 Chemical Engineering Abstracts
0262-6454 Metal Bulletin Handbook *see* 0269-1698
0262-6470 Television & Radio
0262-6489 Fur and Feather *changed to* Fur & Feather
0262-6497 Insuror
0262-6616 Impulse Foods
0262-6624 Kerrang!
0262-6659 Highland Family History Society Journal
0262-6667 Hydrological Sciences Journal
0262-6756 IMS Monitor Report *changed to* Marketletter
0262-6845 Monitor Weekly
0262-6853 I A P A Bulletin
0262-6896 C A S Newsletter
0262-6942 Bowls International
0262-6950 Flypast
0262-6969 International Financial Law Review
0262-6993 Radical Scotland
0262-7043 Respiratory Disease in Practice
0262-7051 A X 5
0262-706X Community Education Network
0262-7078 Collusion
0262-7108 Energy Economist
0262-7116 Hazards, Pollution and Legislation in the Coatings Field
0262-7140 Crested Circle
0262-7159 C B S Newsletter (Glasgow) *changed to* Community Business News
0262-7183 Biotech Business Bulletin†
0262-7221 N A T T A Newsletter
0262-723X Calder Voice
0262-7280 South Asia Research
0262-7299 Abortion Review
0262-7310 International Tax and Duty Free Buyers' Index
0262-7507 Child Education Special *changed to* Infant Projects
0262-7515 Junior Education Special *changed to* Junior Projects
0262-754X Schools Council Project, Art and the Built Environment. Working Parties Project. Bulletin†
0262-7574 Leicestershire Family History Society. Newsletter
0262-7612 Enlightenment and Dissent
0262-7620 Industry, Commerce, Development†
0262-7647 Law & Tax Review
0262-7655 Cheshire Ornithological Association. Bird Report
0262-7663 Exchange Rate Movements Year Book†
0262-7671 S E R C Bulletin
0262-7701 Captive Insurance Company Review
0262-7760 B E C A N. Equipment for the Disabled Population
0262-7779 B E C A N. Biomechanics & Orthopaedics
0262-7795 O S E A P Centre Update
0262-7841 Library Micromation News
0262-785X S C A D Newsheet†
0262-7884 Practical Biotechnology
0262-7922 End Papers
0262-7965 Mines and Mining Equipment Companies Worldwide *changed to* Mines & Mining Equipment and Service Companies Worldwide (Year)
0262-8015 Ditchley Newsletter
0262-8023 Today (London) *changed to* Leadership Today
0262-804X Gamer†
0262-8074 Computer Business Europe†
0262-8090 Tractor & Farm Machinery Trader
0262-8104 Waterlines
0262-8155 Building Societies Association. Report of the Council
0262-8163 N I C E R Bulletin
0262-818X Mideast File
0262-8201 Flying M
0262-8236 G E C Journal for Industry *changed to* G E C Review
0262-8260 Music & Automata
0262-8279 Electric Living Journal
0262-8295 Digest of Welsh Statistics
0262-8309 Welsh Economic Trends
0262-8317 Statistics of Education in Wales
0262-8376 Futures World *changed to* Futures & Options World
0262-8406 Scale Trains *changed to* Scale Model Trains
0262-8481 What C B†
0262-852X Smoke
0262-8597 Business South East
0262-8600 P I R A Annual Review of Research & Services
0262-8643 Northern Ireland Local Studies *changed to* Local Studies: A Bibliography of Recent Books & Articles Relating to Life in Northern Ireland
0262-8759 Community Outlook
0262-8805 Railpower
0262-8856 Image and Vision Computing
0262-8880 Forth Ports Handbook 1984
0262-8937 Dowry
0262-9003 Uren There†
0262-9070 Body Shop News†
0262-9208 Girl Annual
0262-9216 E D C Newsletter

0262-9232 Your Health
0262-9283 Psychiatric Developments
0262-9356 Share It
0262-9380 E E C Information Services
0262-9488 Foreign Exchange Outlook
0262-9577 Chart Watch
0262-9615 Fish Farmer
0262-9763 British Paperbacks in Print†
0262-9771 Directory of International Broadcasting
0262-9798 Youth and Policy
0262-9828 B A A R G Bulletin
0262-9860 Shakti
0262-9909 Water Bulletin
0263-0001 Initiatives
0263-0052 Bedford Operator†
0263-0060 Brazing & Soldering
0263-0079 Bulletin of Archaeology for Schools *changed to* Education Bulletin
0263-0095 Green Drum
0263-0125 Blastpipe
0263-015X County Border Times
0263-0249 Liszt Saeculum
0263-0257 Civil Engineering Systems
0263-0273 Local Studies Librarian†
0263-0338 African Archaeological Review
0263-0346 Laser and Particle Beams
0263-0354 Association of Football Statisticians. Annual
0263-0362 Cardiff Working Papers in Welsh Linguistics
0263-0664 Education Social Worker
0263-080X Structural Survey
0263-0869 Multicultural Teaching
0263-0885 Your Computer
0263-0915 Wind Engineering Abstracts
0263-0923 Journal of Low Frequency Noise & Vibration
0263-0974 Accountants' & Administrators' Handbook
0263-0982 Computers in Schools
0263-1008 Apparel International
0263-1040 Brad Directories and Annuals
0263-1067 Business in Yorkshire
0263-1083 V B R A Directory of Members
0263-1091 Bristol and Avon Archaeology
0263-1229 Expatriate's Guide to Savings and Investment
0263-1385 Civil Aircraft Registrations†
0263-1407 C J A and H S A Newsletter
0263-1474 Electronic Product Design
0263-1644 Gadfly (Retford)†
0263-175X Business Information Technology†
0263-1768 Approved Courses for Accountancy Education
0263-1776 Wellsian
0263-1911 Media Project News *changed to* On Air/Off Air
0263-1989 African National Congress of South Africa. Newsbriefings
0263-2012 Aerospace Dynamics
0263-2039 I C R News†
0263-2047 British Institute of Interior Design Members' Reference Book
0263-211X Educational Management & Administration
0263-2128 Pi
0263-2136 Family Practice
0263-2187 On Line (Sunbury-on-Thames)
0263-2268 Journal of African Marxists
0263-2276 Chartered Institute of Public Finance and Accountancy. Financial General & Rating Statistics
0263-2322 London Theatre Index (Year)
0263-2373 European Management Journal
0263-2381 Scottish Criminal Case Reports
0263-242X Britain's Top 1000 Foreign-Owned Companies
0263-2438 British Chemical Industry
0263-2446 Britain's Top 500 Electronic Companies
0263-2462 British Newspaper Industry†
0263-2500 North West European Continental Shelf Oil & Gas Field Development Survey *changed to* North West Europe Offshore Development
0263-2543 Blitz Magazine
0263-2632 Chorleywood Digest
0263-2659 A S M Translations Index *see* 0278-4238
0263-2764 Theory Culture & Society
0263-2926 Creativity & Innovation Network
0263-2942 Parnasse
0263-2969 Chartered Institute of Public Finance and Accountancy. Cemeteries & Crematoria Statistics. Actuals
0263-2977 Chartered Institute of Public Finance and Accountancy. Direct Labour Statistics. Actuals
0263-2985 Capital Expenditure and Debt Financing Statistics
0263-3094 Health and Safety: Quarries
0263-3183 Classic & Sportscar
0263-3191 Society of Antiquaries of Scotland. Monograph Series
0263-3213 Black Beauty & Hair
0263-3221 Ditchley Conference Reports
0263-323X Journal of Law and Society
0263-3248 Computers in Genealogy
0263-3272 Airline Data News
0263-3396 Table Tennis
0263-3515 British Rate and Data
0263-3523 British Economy Survey
0263-3604 C L W Contents†
0263-3612 Library Link
0263-3620 Reed's Mediterranean Navigator
0263-3639 Nationwide Building Society. House Prices
0263-3655 British Security Companies
0263-3671 Britain's Top 1000 Private Companies *changed to* Britain's Privately Owned Companies: The Top 2000
0263-368X British Hotel Industry
0263-3698 British Distilling Industry†
0263-3701 C O M E C O N Data
0263-3809 Sponsorship News
0263-3817 S B B Tax News *see* 0262-3102
0263-3868 Administrator
0263-404X East Midlands Chambers of Commerce Regional Directory
0263-4066 Golf - Where to Play and Where to Stay
0263-4228 Large Mixed Retailing
0263-4236 Carpet & Floorcoverings Review
0263-4260 Panama Handbook 1983
0263-4368 International Journal of Refractory & Hard Metals
0263-4384 Offset Printing & Reprographics
0263-4430 Busy Solicitors' Digest
0263-4457 Journal of Applied Language Study†
0263-4503 Marketing Intelligence & Planning
0263-4538 Current Research in French Studies at Universities and University Colleges in the United Kingdom *changed to* Current Research in French Studies at Universities and Polytechnics in the United Kingdom
0263-4635 Litmus
0263-466X Christian Brethren Review
0263-4759 Engineering Computers
0263-4929 Journal of Metamorphic Geology
0263-4937 Central Asian Survey
0263-497X Ink & Print
0263-502X B I S F A Magazine
0263-5038 Spon's Plant and Equipment Price Guide
0263-5046 First Break
0263-5054 Aberdeen Petroleum Report
0263-5062 Defence Helicopter World
0263-5070 Oil & Gas: Law and Taxation Review
0263-5100 Human Potential Resources
0263-5143 Research in Science & Technological Education
0263-5372 Informe Latinoamericano
0263-5402 Institute of Development Studies. Commissioned Studies
0263-5437 Do-It-Yourself Report
0263-547X Recent Polar and Glaciological Literature
0263-5488 International Tax-Free Trade Buyers Guide & Directory
0263-5569 F T London Policy Guide
0263-5720 P C User
0263-5739 Refrigeration, Air Conditioning & Heat Recovery
0263-5747 Robotica
0263-5798 Papers in Slavonic Linguistics
0263-5917 Critical Reports on Applied Chemistry
0263-5933 Royal Society of Edinburgh. Transactions. (Earth Sciences)
0263-5976 Warwick Papers in Industry, Business and Administration *changed to* Warwick Papers in Management
0263-6050 World Cement
0263-6085 Beauty Counter & Perfumery & Toiletries Buyer
0263-6115 Australian Mathematical Society. Journal. Series A
0263-614X P I T C O M *see* 0266-8513
0263-6166 Public Relations
0263-6174 Adsorption Science and Technology
0263-6182 Postgraduate Courses in United Kingdom Universities *changed to* British Universities' Guide to Graduate Studies
0263-6190 C A D/C A M Digest
0263-6212 Keyboards and Music Player
0263-6263 Truck and Bus Builder
0263-6271 Science in Parliament
0263-6336 Robotics in Japan†
0263-6395 International Media Law
0263-6484 Cell Biochemistry and Function
0263-6506 North West Kent Family History
0263-6522 Integrated Circuits International
0263-6530 D E C User
0263-6565 Fiction Magazine
0263-6697 Compass Sport/Orienteer
0263-6700 Policy Market
0263-6727 Atlantic Quarterly†
0263-6735 Information Technology Training
0263-6751 Anglo-Saxon England
0263-676X Themes in Drama
0263-6778 Abstracts in BioCommerce
0263-6786 Vox Evangelica
0263-6794 Tube International
0263-6832 A C O L A M Newsletter
0263-6921 Young Farmer
0263-7022 James Hogg Society. Newsletter
0263-7057 Golfing Handbook†
0263-7073 Canary Islands Shipping Handbook 1983/4
0263-7081 Wheels & Tracks
0263-709X Art Book Review
0263-7103 British Journal of Rheumatology
0263-7138 Institution of Mechanical Engineers. Proceedings. Part A: Power and Process Engineering
0263-7146 Institution of Mechanical Engineers. Proceedings. Part B: Management and Engineering Manufacture
0263-7154 Institution of Mechanical Engineers. Proceedings. Part C: Mechanical Engineering Science
0263-7243 Cardiovascular Pharmacology
0263-7383 Annales Benjamin Constant
0263-7472 Property Management
0263-7480 Journal of Valuation
0263-7499 Rent Review and Lease Renewal
0263-7553 Picture House
0263-7561 Beebug
0263-760X Cave Science: Transactions of the British Cave Research Association
0263-7707 The Medal
0263-774X Environment and Planning C: Government & Policy
0263-7758 Environment and Planning D: Society & Space
0263-7774 Leisure Futures
0263-7855 Journal of Molecular Graphics
0263-7863 International Journal of Project Management
0263-7928 Partnership Management
0263-7936 Professional Builder & House Remodeller
0263-7952 Industrial Research in United Kingdom
0263-7960 Built Environment†
0263-8029 Biotech News
0263-8134 Harpers Sports & Leisure
0263-8223 Composite Structures
0263-8231 Thin-Walled Structures
0263-8371 Changes
0263-8614 Great Britain. Institute of Terrestrial Ecology. Symposia
0263-8894 Orbit†
0263-8908 Microcomputer Newsletter *changed to* Computer Newsletter (Bracknell)
0263-9114 European Journal of Chiropractic
0263-9181 Public Library Expenditure in Scotland
0263-9203 Middle East Computing
0263-9254 Current Research in Library & Information Science
0263-9327 Computer-Aided Engineering Journal
0263-9432 Whitaker's Classified Monthly Book List
0263-9459 Cruciferae Newsletter
0263-9475 Circa Art Magazine
0263-953X What Investment
0263-9661 World Precious Metals Survey
0263-9688 Hampstead Clinic. Bulletin *see* 0267-3061
0263-9696 National Association of Inspectors and Educational Advisors. Journal
0263-9777 F M S Magazine
0263-9874 Information on TV Directory *changed to* Professional T V & Radio Media Directory
0263-9904 Romance Studies
0263-9947 V A T Intelligence
0264-0155 Euro-Asia Business Review
0264-0201 International Council for Distance Education. Bulletin
0264-0236 Concrete Plant and Production
0264-0295 G E C Engineering *changed to* G E C Review
0264-0325 Royal Society of Health. Papers
0264-0414 Journal of Sports Sciences
0264-0422 Glasgow Magazine†
0264-0449 Sinclair Projects†
0264-0473 Electronic Library
0264-0643 A D I U Report
0264-0724 Mackintosh Yearbook of International Electronics Data
0264-0732 World Leasing Yearbook
0264-0775 World Ports and Harbours Abstracts
0264-0783 World Ports and Harbours News†
0264-0821 Land Development Studies
0264-083X World of Interiors
0264-0856 Cencrastus
0264-1011 Templar†
0264-1062 Model Flyer†
0264-1127 Law Reports: Queen's Bench Division
0264-1240 Fish Stock Record *see* 0308-0935
0264-1259 Antwerp Handbook 1984
0264-1275 Materials & Design
0264-1283 British Micro Software News
0264-1291 Horticultural Trades Association Members' Reference Book
0264-1356 Bulletin on Islam and Christian-Muslim Relations in Africa
0264-1615 Interlending and Document Supply: Journal of the British Library
0264-1674 Current Military Literature
0264-1771 P M International Newsletter *changed to* P M Environmental Newsletter
0264-1828 Arts & the Islamic World
0264-1887 Technology
0264-2212 Signal Review *changed to* Signal Selection of Children's Books
0264-2220 Model Shipwright
0264-2247 International Pharmaceutical Technology & Product Manufacture Abstracts
0264-2425 Reading in a Foreign Language
0264-2441 U A P Newsletter
0264-2506 Finishing
0264-2549 Health and Fitness
0264-2557 Amateur Radio
0264-2751 Cities
0264-2875 Dance Research
0264-312X Shaw's Directory of Courts in the United Kingdom
0264-3200 Sales and Marketing Management
0264-3219 Book Marketing News
0264-3227 What's on & Where to Go
0264-3294 Cognitive Neuropsychology
0264-3340 Asian Electricity

1502 ISSN INDEX

0264-3375 Journal of Semicustom ICs
0264-3383 Music and Video Week Directory *changed to* Music Week Directory
0264-3405 British Cactus & Succulent Journal
0264-3413 Journal of Chemical Technology and Biotechnology. Part A: Chemical Technology *see* 0268-2575
0264-3421 Biotechnology *see* 0268-2575
0264-357X Fashion Buyers Diary
0264-3596 Interzone
0264-3642 Modern Railways Pictorial Profile†
0264-3693 Bookplate Journal
0264-3707 Journal of Geodynamics
0264-3758 Journal of Applied Philosophy
0264-3898 Society for Italic Handwriting. Bulletin
0264-3944 Pastoral Care in Education
0264-4002 Rural Viewpoint
0264-4037 Food Industry Directory
0264-4088 Community Currents
0264-410X Vaccine
0264-4134 Asian Timber Trades Journal
0264-4169 Electrical and Mechanical Executive Engineer (EMEE) *see* 0266-2450
0264-4193 Computer Systems
0264-4479 Computer Answers
0264-4509 Video Retailer†
0264-4525 Journal of Practical Civil Defence
0264-4606 B O C A A D
0264-4614 Maladjustment and Therapeutic Education
0264-4649 Combat Craft *see* 0144-3194
0264-4703 Precision Toolmaker
0264-4754 Animal Technology
0264-4770 Texas Personal Injury Law Reporter
0264-4924 Archives of Emergency Medicine
0264-4932 Industry Northwest
0264-5181 Housing Year Book
0264-519X Research, Policy and Planning
0264-522X Regionalist
0264-5378 Coffee International Directory
0264-5394 Tobacco Directory and Diary *changed to* Tobacco Trade Marketing Directory
0264-5408 Middle East Agribusiness Buyers Guide
0264-5467 Research and Development in Agriculture
0264-5483 C P N A Journal *see* 0265-7007
0264-5505 Probation Journal
0264-553X Microprocessor Software Quarterly†
0264-5564 Vinaver Studies in French
0264-5572 Scottish Church History Society. Records
0264-5629 Microprofile
0264-5637 British Book News Children's Books
0264-5661 Vancouver Port Handbook
0264-567X Sydney Ports Handbook (Year)
0264-5688 Scottish Health Education Group Bulletin
0264-5807 Society for Environmental Therapy. Newsletter
0264-5890 Formaos
0264-598X Christian Arena
0264-5998 Iron in Agriculture
0264-6021 Biochemical Journal
0264-6137 Bare Nibs
0264-6196 British Journal of Visual Impairment
0264-6307 Texas Insurance Law Reporter
0264-6358 Videodisc Newsletter
0264-6412 Rad for Radiographers, Radiologists and Radiotherapists
0264-6420 Maritime Guide
0264-6501 Uncensored Poland News Bulletin
0264-6544 Chartered Institute of Public Finance and Accountancy. Probation. Estimates
0264-6552 Chartered Institute of Public Finance and Accountancy. Administration of Justice. Estimates
0264-6706 Euromoney Trade Finance Report
0264-6714 Key Statistical Indicators for National Health Service Management in Wales
0264-6773 Ninth Decade
0264-6781 Imprint (York)
0264-682X Engineering Analysis
0264-6838 Journal of Reproductive and Infant Psychology
0264-6854 Construction Computing
0264-6900 Cerebral Circulation and Metabolism
0264-6943 Graduate Management Research
0264-7125 Chartered Institute of Public Finance and Accountancy. Education Statistics. Unit Costs
0264-7249 Fibre Optics Newsletter
0264-729X Physics and Chemistry of Materials Treatment
0264-7303 Metallic Materials
0264-7419 Technology and Science of Informatics
0264-7540 Devon Archaeology
0264-7664 Travel Management International
0264-7699 Arts Yorkshire *changed to* Yorkshire Artscene
0264-7753 High Performance Plastics
0264-7761 Temporary Occupations and Employment *changed to* Jobs in the 'Gap' Year
0264-7877 Conference Papers in Applied Physical Sciences
0264-8059 Marine Pollution Research Titles
0264-8121 New Law for General Practice Surveyors
0264-8148 Designers' Journal
0264-8156 Designing & Making
0264-8164 Asian Building & Construction
0264-8172 Marine and Petroleum Geology
0264-8199 Trading in Metals
0264-8296 Media Information - UK†
0264-8334 Paragraph
0264-8342 Pater Newsletter
0264-8377 Land Use Policy
0264-8466 Training and Education
0264-8555 Fashion Extras
0264-8563 Housewares
0264-8571 Society for Renaissance Studies. Bulletin
0264-858X Comeback
0264-861X Oxford Surveys of Plant Molecular and Cell Biology
0264-8717 S C O L A G
0264-8725 Biotechnology and Genetic Engineering Reviews
0264-8768 Primary Teaching and Micros
0264-9039 Scottish Society for Conservation and Restoration. Bulletin
0264-9152 I T Focus *changed to* I T Focus
0264-9187 G E C Journal of Research
0264-9314 Trade U S A†
0264-9373 British Journal of Sports History *changed to* International Journal of the History of Sport
0264-9381 Classical and Quantum Gravity
0264-9586 Lymphokines
0264-9659 Liposomes
0264-9780 Fireworks
0264-9993 Economic Modelling
0265-0215 European Journal of Anaesthesiology
0265-0231 Railways Today
0265-024X Sea Fishing Today
0265-0266 Great Britain. Civil Aviation Authority. C A A Monthly Operating and Traffic Statistics *changed to* Great Britain. Civil Aviation Authority. U.K. Airlines Monthly Operating & Traffic Statistics
0265-0266 Great Britain. Civil Aviation Authority. C A A Monthly Operating and Traffic Statistics *changed to* Great Britain. Civil Aviation Authority. U.K. Airports Monthly Statements of Movements, Passengers and Cargo
0265-041X Library Conservation News
0265-0487 International Journal of Advertising
0265-0495 Woodworking Crafts
0265-0517 British Journal of Music Education
0265-0525 Social Philosophy and Policy
0265-0665 Economic Affairs
0265-0673 Pharmaceutical Medicine (Houndmills)
0265-0681 Good Beer Guide
0265-069X Benn's Hardware Price List
0265-0711 Oxford Survey in Information Technology
0265-072X Oxford Surveys in Evolutionary Biology
0265-0738 Oxford Surveys on Eukaryotic Genes
0265-0746 I M A Journal of Mathematics Applied in Medicine & Biology
0265-0754 I M A Journal of Mathematical Control & Information
0265-0762 Mircen - Journal of Applied Microbiology & Biotechnology
0265-0916 International Journal of Rapid Solidification
0265-0924 Journal of Arts Policy and Management
0265-0940 Abstracts on Productivity, Technology and Training *changed to* Productivity Insights
0265-0959 Benn Electronics Executive
0265-0975 I P C S Bulletin
0265-0983 Metals & Minerals International
0265-1025 Spon's Civil Engineering Price Book
0265-1068 Seventeenth Century French Studies
0265-1076 Historian
0265-1084 Fashion Update
0265-1092 Design International
0265-1165 Dover Port Handbook
0265-1173 Mersey Ports Handbook (Year)
0265-1181 Tees and Hartlepool Ports
0265-1211 Law Reports: Chancery and Family Division
0265-122X Law Reports: Appeal Cases
0265-1270 Fiesta
0265-1289 Knave
0265-1327 Survival International News
0265-1335 International Marketing Review
0265-1351 Microbiological Sciences
0265-1432 Third World Book Review
0265-1459 Childright
0265-1513 Stock Exchange Fact Sheet Monthly
0265-1521 London. Stock Exchange. Stock Exchange Companies
0265-1548 Music Week
0265-1602 Education and Health
0265-1610 Guidance and Assessment Review
0265-1653 Property Business†
0265-1734 Energy Focus
0265-1785 Society of Antiquaries of Newcastle Upon Tyne. Monograph Series
0265-184X Lisbon Letter†
0265-1858 W F S A Lectures *see* 0267-0003
0265-1904 Institution of Mechanical Engineers. Proceedings. Part D: Transport Engineering
0265-1947 B U F O R A Bulletin
0265-2021 Health and Healing
0265-203X Food Additives and Contaminants
0265-2048 Journal of Microencapsulation
0265-2072 Purchasing and Supply Management
0265-2099 Credit Management
0265-2196 Medical Association for Prevention of War. Journal *see* 0748-8009
0265-2455 Lloyd's Ship Manager
0265-2501 Independent Solicitor
0265-2609 Theatrephile
0265-2722 Metals Society World *see* 0026-0940
0265-2730 Guide to Postgraduate Degrees, Diplomas and Courses in Medicine
0265-2897 Buddhist Studies Review
0265-2900 Buddhist Forum†
0265-2927 Satellite and Cable Television News†
0265-3028 Hybrid Circuits
0265-3273 Scottish Slavonic Review
0265-3389 American Studies Library Newsletter
0265-3400 P H L S Microbiology Digest
0265-3443 New Materials/Japan
0265-3656 B B C Wildlife
0265-3664 Heritage Interpretation
0265-377X Cubism
0265-3818 Jane's Defence Weekly
0265-3842 Kew Magazine
0265-3877 International Biotechnology Directory *changed to* Biotechnology Directory
0265-3990 Pipelines Abstracts
0265-4024 A B C Air Asia
0265-4040 Micro User
0265-4245 Methods in Organic Synthesis
0265-4385 University Computing
0265-4415 Thomas Cook Airport Links *see* 0266-9404
0265-444X Mauritian International
0265-4490 Database and Network Journal
0265-4504 Commuter World
0265-4601 Thomas Callander Memorial Lectures
0265-4792 Safety Practitioner
0265-4822 Afghan Studies *see* 0266-6030
0265-4881 Salisbury Review
0265-5039 North Sea Oil & Gas Directory
0265-5071 Industrial Heritage Magazine
0265-5136 Irrigation News
0265-5217 British Journal of Healthcare Computing
0265-5241 Intensive & Critical Care Digest
0265-5292 Middle East Education & Training
0265-5322 Language Testing
0265-5373 Farm Buildings and Engineering
0265-539X Community Dental Health
0265-5500 Rock Garden
0265-5527 Howard Journal of Criminal Justice
0265-5683 O'Neill Clan News
0265-5691 Maguire Bulletin
0265-5705 Crawford Chronicle
0265-5721 Chemical Hazards in Industry
0265-5802 Adventure Education
0265-5810 Little Red Book
0265-5918 International Journal of Bulk Solids Storage in Silos
0265-5942 Journal of Newspaper and Periodical History
0265-5985 Diabetes Research
0265-6000 I L A M Journal *changed to* Leisure Manager
0265-6027 European Semiconductor Design & Production
0265-6159 Scottish Current Law Year Book
0265-6183 Performance Car
0265-6248 Venture Capital Report
0265-6272 World: Quarterly Energy Review
0265-637X Urethanes Technology
0265-640X Oil and Gas Industry *changed to* Oil and Oil Field Equipment & Service Companies Worldwide
0265-6434 Asian Agribusiness
0265-6442 Security Times
0265-6469 Middle East Food Trade & Catering Equipment
0265-6582 Journal of Synthetic Lubrication
0265-6590 Child Language Teaching and Therapy
0265-6647 Health Libraries Review
0265-671X International Journal of Quality & Reliability Management
0265-6736 International Journal of Hyperthermia
0265-6760 Mini Micro Software
0265-6817 B U F V C Newsletter
0265-6922 Greek Orthodox Calendar
0265-6930 New Home Economics
0265-6957 Social Services Research
0265-6981 Malpas History
0265-7007 Community Psychiatric Nursing Journal
0265-7015 Potato World
0265-7066 16 Bit Computing
0265-7260 B A I E Magazine
0265-7295 North Wind
0265-766X All England Law Reports. Annual Review
0265-7759 Motorcycle Enthusiast
0265-7848 Q P S Reporter
0265-7937 Road Traffic Law Bulletin
0265-8038 Durham Archaeological Record *changed to* Durham Archaeological Journal
0265-8062 Phonology Yearbook
0265-8119 Swedish Book Review
0265-8178 British Columbia Ports Handbook 1984
0265-8186 Montreal Port and Shipping Handbook (Year)
0265-8194 Turkey Port and Shipping Handbook 1984
0265-8216 Stamp News
0265-8240 Law & Policy
0265-8275 Directory of British Biotechnology
0265-8291 Shipyard Orders. Weekly Report
0265-8305 Print Quarterly
0265-833X Asian Agriculture Buyers Guide *changed to* Asian Agribusiness Buyers Guide
0265-8399 Small Business Confidential
0265-8429 Outwrite Women's Newspaper

ISSN INDEX 1503

0265-8445 Commons, Open Spaces and Footpaths Preservation Society. Annual Report *see* 0010-3322
0265-8569 Aerogram
0265-8739 R I B A Product Selector
0265-9190 Hampshire Field Club and Archaeological Society. Section Newsletters
0265-9220 Contents Pages in Education
0265-9239 Electronic Banking & Finance
0265-9247 Bioessays
0265-928X Biosensors
0265-931X Journal of Environmental Radioactivity
0265-9646 Space Policy
0265-9786 Landscape Issues
0265-9883 British Journal of Psychotherapy
0265-9999 Senior Nurse
0266-0016 Folio Poetry Magazine
0266-0032 Soil Use and Management
0266-0180 Index to Business Reports
0266-0210 Publishing and Bookselling Directory *changed to* Professional Publishing Media Directory
0266-0512 Risk in Society
0266-0644 Los Angeles Port and Shipping Handbook
0266-0652 New South Wales Ports Handbook
0266-0776 Welsh Hospital Waiting List Bulletin
0266-0784 English Today
0266-0806 Texas Health Law Reporter
0266-0814 Texas Evidence Reporter
0266-0962 British Isles Airlines Schedule†
0266-1144 Geotextiles and Geomembranes
0266-1233 Information from the Volunteer Centre Media Project
0266-1241 Social Action and the Media
0266-1322 Perspectives in American History
0266-139X Civil Engineering Surveyor
0266-1500 Linen Hall Review
0266-1616 Inspec Matters
0266-1640 Pteridologist
0266-1713 B P I C S Control
0266-1772 Warburg Institute. Surveys and Texts
0266-2043 Great Britain. Economic and Social Research Council. Report
0266-206X Scandinavian Institute of Asian Studies. Occasional Papers
0266-2078 Medical Textiles
0266-2094 Middle East Financial Directory
0266-2132 Airfinance Annual
0266-2140 International Labour Reports
0266-2159 Great Britain. Economic and Social Research Council. Research Supported by the Economic and Social Research Council
0266-2256 Professional Video International Yearbook
0266-2329 British Music Education Yearbook
0266-2426 International Small Business Journal
0266-2450 Electrotechnical News
0266-2493 Control Systems
0266-2639 E S R C Newsletter
0266-2922 International Powder & Bulk Solids Abstracts
0266-2930 International Process Technology Abstracts
0266-2949 Chartered Institute of Public Finance and Accountancy. School Meals Statistics
0266-2957 Ghana Studies Bulletin
0266-299X What Telephone & Communication News *changed to* Communications Now
0266-3082 Bioengineering and the Skin
0266-3112 Offshore Fleet Economics
0266-3147 International Banking & Financial Law Bulletin
0266-3198 Ferro Alloy Directory
0266-321X P C Review†
0266-3368 Educational Technology Abstracts
0266-3481 Atomisation and Spray Technology
0266-349X Journal of Micronutrient Analysis
0266-3503 Journal of Shoreline Management
0266-3511 Space Structures
0266-352X Computers and Geotechnics
0266-3538 Composites Science and Technology
0266-3597 Hazell's Guide to the Judiciary and the Courts with the Holborn Law Society's List of Barristers by Chambers *changed to* Hazell's Guide to the Judiciary & the Courts with the Holborn Law Society's Bar List by Chambers
0266-366X Peter Warlock Society Newsletter
0266-3821 Business Information Review
0266-3848 Port Rashid: Dubai Shipping Handbook
0266-3856 Port Kelang Shipping Handbook
0266-3880 Biology and Society
0266-397X B.R.M.A. Directory Rubber and Polyurethane
0266-3988 International Cargo Crime Prevention
0266-3996 International Cargo Handling Coordination Association. Buyers' Guide to Manufacturers
0266-4194 Economic Development Digest
0266-4208 Booknews
0266-4232 Children's Books of the Year
0266-4356 British Journal of Oral and Maxillofacial Surgery
0266-4380 Architectural Periodicals Index
0266-4429 Holiday Parks
0266-4623 International Journal of Technology Assessment in Health Care
0266-4631 Computer Newsletter (Cambridge)
0266-464X New Theatre Quarterly
0266-4666 Econometric Theory
0266-4674 Journal of Tropical Ecology
0266-4720 Expert Systems
0266-4755 Report on British Palaeobotany & Palynology
0266-4763 Journal of Applied Statistics
0266-4771 Harvest
0266-4828 Building Society Factbook (Year)
0266-4909 Journal of Computer Assisted Learning
0266-5433 Planning Perspectives
0266-5441 Scotlink
0266-5611 Inverse Problems
0266-5905 Middle East Agribusiness
0266-6030 South Asian Studies
0266-6073 Dental Annual
0266-612X Intensive Care Nursing
0266-6138 Midwifery
0266-6154 Physiotherapy Practice
0266-6189 Lloyd's Monthly List of Laid up Vessels
0266-6197 Lloyd's Ports of the World
0266-6200 Across Architecture
0266-6278 A C E Bulletin
0266-6286 Word & Image
0266-6294 Blood Coagulation Factors
0266-6308 D N A Probes
0266-6650 Postgraduate Doctor: Pakistan
0266-6669 Information Development
0266-6677 African Technical Review
0266-6731 Africa Bibliography
0266-6960 Information Media & Technology
0266-6979 Geology Today
0266-7037 Intensive Care World
0266-7061 Computer Applications in the Biosciences
0266-707X Who's Who in Arts Management
0266-7142 Optical & Electron Microscopy†
0266-7177 Modern Theology
0266-7207 Future Computing Systems
0266-7215 European Sociological Review
0266-7223 Yearbook of European Law
0266-7274 Virginia Ports and Shipping Handbook
0266-7320 Progress of Rubber and Plastics Technology
0266-7339 City University Business School. Economic Review
0266-7347 World Wrought Copper Statistics
0266-7363 Educational Psychology in Practice
0266-7398 Cricketer International
0266-7401 Cricketer Quarterly Facts and Figures
0266-7428 Scottish Industrial History
0266-7452 Trolleybus Magazine
0266-7460 Television and Video Production
0266-7525 Third World Women's News
0266-7800 European Paint and Resin News
0266-7835 New Ground
0266-7878 Camping & Trailer
0266-7932 University of London. Institute of Germanic Studies. Bithell Series of Dissertations
0266-7991 Promotions and Incentives
0266-8017 African Farming & Food Processing
0266-8025 Far Eastern Agriculture
0266-8033 Memory Lane
0266-8068 National Trust
0266-8394 Knitting International
0266-8459 Directory of Postgraduate and Post-Experience Courses
0266-8467 Directory of First Degree and Diploma of Higher Education Courses
0266-8505 Machine Knitting News
0266-8513 Information Technology and Public Policy
0266-8521 Altrive Chapbooks
0266-8548 Quarterly Journal of Social Affairs
0266-867X World Marxist Review
0266-8688 Media International
0266-8750 Liverpool Link
0266-8769 Lampada
0266-8920 Probabilistic Engineering Mechanics
0266-898X Japanese Motor Business
0266-9013 Chartered Institute of Public Finance and Accountancy. Block Grant Statistics
0266-9021 Hannah Research
0266-903X Oxford Review of Economic Policy
0266-9064 City of Birmingham Directory of Industry & Commerce
0266-9102 Leisure Management
0266-9129 Network (London, 1984)
0266-9404 Thomas Cook Airports Guide Europe
0266-9412 U S Business Briefing
0266-9455 Landscape Industry International
0266-9463 Microsoftware for Engineers
0266-9536 Anti-Cancer Drug Design
0266-9544 E.I.D.C.T.- C.D.T. Year Book
0266-9552 Chartered Institute of Public Finance and Accountancy. Environmental Health Statistics. Actuals
0266-9560 Chartered Institute of Public Finance and Accountancy. Leisure Usage. Actuals
0266-9838 Environmental Software
0266-9870 River and Flood Control Abstracts
0266-996X Aquaculture and Fisheries Management
0267-0003 Lectures in Anaesthesiology
0267-0054 Housing Information Digest
0267-0267 Athletics Coach
0267-0275 Postgraduate Doctor: Caribbean
0267-033X Sesame
0267-0348 Selected Bibliographies on Ageing
0267-0372 C E G B Abstracts
0267-064X British Library. Lending Division Newsletter *see* 0269-1175
0267-0739 Policing
0267-0763 Advertising Law and Practice *changed to* Advertising and Marketing Law & Practice
0267-078X Professional Negligence
0267-0801 R I B A Interior Design Product Selector
0267-0836 Materials Science and Technology
0267-0844 Surface Engineering
0267-0879 Fairplay Marine Computing Guide
0267-0887 Free Associations
0267-1166 Golf Club Management & Equipment News
0267-1174 Chartered Institute of Public Finance and Accountancy. Teaching Hospital Statistics. Actuals
0267-1182 Chartered Institute of Public Finance and Accountancy. Non-Teaching Hospital Costs. Statistics
0267-1247 Protostar
0267-1263 London Energy News
0267-1344 Delawarr Laboratories Information Service Newsletter†
0267-1395 Communications Systems Worldwide
0267-1441 Directory of Electronics, Instruments & Computers
0267-145X Butterworths Company Law Cases
0267-1468 Britain's Best Holidays - A Quick Reference Guide
0267-1506 Food Manufacture International
0267-1522 Research Papers in Education
0267-1530 London. Stock Exchange. Stock Exchange Quarterly
0267-1611 British Psychological Society. Division of Educational and Child Psychology. Papers
0267-1689 Institution of Electronic and Radio Engineers. Journal
0267-1700 Religion Today
0267-1719 Management Digest†
0267-1891 Pelargonium News
0267-1913 Worldwide Tanker Nominal Freight Scale
0267-1948 Current Research in Britain. Physical Sciences
0267-1956 Current Research in Britain. Biological Sciences
0267-1964 Current Research in Britain. Social Sciences
0267-1972 Current Research in Britain. Humanities
0267-1980 Computer Applications in Social Work and Allied Professions
0267-2006 Institute of Chartered Shipbrokers. Reference Book and List of Members (Year)
0267-2014 Health and Safety Officer's Handbook
0267-2022 Local Government Administrators' Official Source Book
0267-2030 Institute of Maintenance and Building Management. Reference Book and List of Members
0267-2049 Plant Manager's Directory (Year)
0267-2073 Journal of Paediatric Dentistry
0267-2103 Recreation Managers' Association of Great Britain Year Book
0267-2243 Boston Sea and Air Port Handbook
0267-2316 Sharjah Ports Handbook
0267-2502 Start *changed to* Start Magazine of Literature and the Arts
0267-2537 S I P R I Chemical & Biological Warfare Studies
0267-2618 N E M S News
0267-2669 Bulletin of Islamic Studies
0267-2871 Farm Holiday Guide (England Edition) *changed to* Farm Holiday Guide (England, Wales & Ireland)
0267-288X Farm Holiday Guide (Scotland Edition)
0267-2898 Farm Holiday Guide (Wales Edition) *changed to* Farm Holiday Guide (England, Wales & Ireland)
0267-2987 Maize Abstracts
0267-3037 Housing Studies
0267-3053 Third Sector
0267-3061 Anna Freud Centre. Bulletin
0267-307X O E M Newsletter
0267-3304 Sport and Recreation Information Group Bulletin
0267-3355 Guide to Caravan and Camping Holidays
0267-3363 Bed & Breakfast Stops
0267-3371 Heritage Britain. Where to Visit: Where to Stay
0267-338X Scotland's Best Holidays
0267-3398 England's Best Holidays
0267-3401 Holidays in Wales *changed to* Wales Best Holidays
0267-341X Mini-Break Holidays in Britain *changed to* Recommended Short Break Holidays
0267-3428 Recommended Country Hotels of Britain
0267-3436 Bed and Breakfast in Britain
0267-3460 Root
0267-3517 Bulletin of Forthcoming Anglo-Hellenic Events
0267-3673 Institute of Insurance Consultants. Reference Book and List of Members (Year)
0267-3762 International Journal of High Technology Ceramics
0267-3843 International Journal of Adolescence and Youth
0267-3851 Catering and Health

1504 ISSN INDEX

0267-3878 International Journal of Social Gerontology
0267-3932 I E E Proceedings Part J: Optoelectronics
0267-3991 Art and Design
0267-4009 Advances in Special Electrometallurgy
0267-4319 Canada - U.K. Link *changed to* Can - U.K. Link
0267-4343 Preservation in Action
0267-4394 Food Marketing
0267-4424 Financial Accountability & Management
0267-4599 Self-Catering and Furnished Holidays
0267-4645 Disability, Handicap & Society
0267-4653 Sexual and Marital Therapy
0267-484X Atlas
0267-4874 Advances in Contraception
0267-4890 Bulletin sur l'Islam et les Relations Islamo-Chretiennes en Afrique
0267-5080 Women's Review
0267-5307 Technical Review. Middle East
0267-5374 Employment Affairs Report
0267-5439 Biomedical Polymers
0267-5447 Data Storage Report
0267-5471 National Institute of Agricultural Engineering. Divisional Notes *changed to* A F R C Institute of Engineering Research. Divisional Notes
0267-5498 Linguistics Abstracts
0267-5501 Micromath
0267-5528 Professional Promotion Media Directory
0267-565X Broadcast Systems Engineering
0267-5730 International Journal of Technology Management
0267-5900 Chemtronics
0267-5943 Railwatch
0267-6192 Computer Systems Science and Engineering
0267-6222 Acid Rain Update
0267-6230 Social and Economic Impact of New Technology
0267-6281 Royal Observatory. Research and Facilities
0267-629X Energy Shipping
0267-6303 E I U Business Update
0267-6362 Africa Events
0267-6583 Second Language Research
0267-6591 Perfusion
0267-6605 Clinical Materials
0267-6672 Edinburgh Review
0267-6761 Libertarian Alliance. Foreign Policy Perspectives
0267-677X Libertarian Alliance. Cultural Notes
0267-6788 Libertarian News
0267-6796 Libertarian Reprints
0267-7059 Libertarian Alliance. Political Notes
0267-7067 Libertarian Alliance. Scientific Notes
0267-7083 Libertarian Alliance. Legal Notes
0267-7091 Libertarian Alliance. Philosophical Notes
0267-7105 Libertarian Alliance. Historical Notes
0267-7113 Libertarian Alliance. Sociological Notes
0267-7121 Libertarian Alliance. Background Briefings
0267-7156 Libertarian Alliance. Personal Perspectives
0267-7164 Libertarian Alliance. Economic Notes
0267-7172 Libertarian Alliance. Psychological Notes
0267-7180 Libertarian Alliance. Study Guides
0267-7199 Libertarian Student
0267-7253 Piano Journal
0267-7296 Hazards
0267-7350 Melbourne Port and Shipping Handbook
0267-7369 Penang Port Handbook
0267-7377 Aberdeen Port Handbook
0267-7385 Planning Information Digest
0267-744X International Property Review
0267-7563 Geofile
0267-7717 International Executive Transfers
0267-8071 O P A L Journal
0267-8128 England. Economic and Social Research Council. Research Programme Bulletin
0267-8136 Manpower Policy & Practice
0267-8225 International Motor Business
0267-8233 European Motor Business
0267-8349 Joint Association of Classical Teachers. Bulletin
0267-8470 Orthodox News
0267-8519 Company Car (Redhill)
0267-873X Great Britain. Advisory Conciliation Arbitration Service. Work Research Unit. Information Service News and Abstracts
0267-8829 Moores & Rowland's Tax Guide
0267-8853 Oils & Fats International
0267-8896 Texas Real Estate Law Reporter
0267-8926 Pumps and Turbines†
0267-9264 International Journal for Artificial Intelligence in Engineering
0267-9299 International Electronics for China
0267-9310 Seabird
0267-9469 Comments & Criticisms
0267-9477 Journal of Analytical Atomic Spectrometry
0267-9515 Online Business Information
0267-954X Space (Burnham)
0267-9612 Finnegans Wake Circular
0267-9698 Directory of Museums & Living Displays
0267-9981 I S C O Careers Bulletin
0268-0033 Clinical Biomechanics
0268-005X Food Hydrocolloids
0268-0106 International Journal of Estuarine and Coastal Law
0268-0181 J A C T Review
0268-0432 African Concord
0268-0491 Carbon & High Performance Fibres Directory
0268-053X Scottish Ambassador
0268-0599 Personal Investor
0268-0645 Postgraduate Study at the University of Liverpool
0268-0661 South America, Central America and the Caribbean
0268-067X Sinclair Q L World
0268-070X Lloyd's Non-Marine Insurance
0268-0750 Making Better Movies
0268-0815 Casualty Return
0268-0858 Articles in Hospitality and Tourism
0268-1056 Polin
0268-1064 Mind & Language
0268-1072 New Technology, Work & Employment
0268-1080 Health Policy and Planning
0268-1099 Health Promotion
0268-1102 Information Technology for Development
0268-1110 Dynamics and Stability of Systems
0268-1129 I M A Journal of Mathematics in Management
0268-1153 Health Education Research
0268-1161 Human Reproduction
0268-117X The Seventeenth Century
0268-1188 Automated Manufacturing Directory
0268-1218 Journal of Medical & Veterinary Mycology
0268-1242 Semiconductor Science and Technology
0268-1358 Laboratory Science and Technology
0268-1390 Poetry World
0268-1552 Peptide Hormone Receptors
0268-1579 Inositides and Diacylglyserols
0268-1595 Growth Factors
0268-1617 Extracellular Matrix
0268-1633 Bioelectronics
0268-1641 Atrial Natriuretic Factors
0268-1900 International Journal of Materials & Product Technology
0268-1935 Insurance Systems Bulletin
0268-2117 Pims Financial Directory
0268-2125 Learning Resources Journal
0268-2141 Support for Hearing
0268-2184 Economic Development Briefing
0268-2222 Arab Commercial Law Review
0268-2230 Business Finance Review
0268-2257 Asian Living Costs
0268-2265 Budget Representations to the Chancellor
0268-2273 C B I Annual Report
0268-2281 North American Living Costs
0268-2311 Major Energy Companies of Europe
0268-232X Major Banks, Finance & Investment Companies of Continental Europe
0268-2338 Major Companies of the United States of America
0268-2362 University of Liverpool Prospectus
0268-2400 British Bulletin of Publications on Latin America, the Caribbean, Portugal and Spain
0268-246X Bookselling News
0268-2494 Topical Issues
0268-2575 Journal of Chemical Technology and Biotechnology
0268-2664 Urban Wildlife News
0268-3091 Royal Society of Medicine. Round Table Series
0268-3253 Lloyd's Marine Equipment Guide
0268-327X Lloyd's Maritime Directory
0268-3296 British Gas Corporation. Monitor *changed to* British Gas Plc. Monitor
0268-330X R & D Digest
0268-3369 Bone Marrow Transplantation
0268-3393 B C I R A Abstracts of International Literature on Metal Castings Production
0268-3539 University Library Expenditure Statistics
0268-3830 Verse
0268-3903 International Journal of Retailing
0268-3911 Industrial Marketing & Purchasing
0268-392X International Review of Economics & Ethics
0268-3946 Journal of Managerial Psychology
0268-3954 I T Intelligence
0268-3962 J I T
0268-4012 International Journal of Information Management
0268-4020 Papers in the Administration of Development
0268-4306 F R A M E News
0268-4594 Mobile & Holiday Homes
0268-4764 Textile Outlook International
0268-4861 Arab Medicare
0268-4993 Abstracts: Cellular Pathology
0268-5000 Jennings Magazine
0268-5124 R I B A Computer Software Selector
0268-5418 Thomas Hardy Journal
0268-5485 Optometry Today
0268-5531 Netlink
0268-5655 Simplified Spelling Society Newsletter *changed to* Simplified Spelling Society. Journal
0268-5663 Catering Manager's Buyer's Guide (Year)
0268-5671 International Meeting Place
0268-568X British Security Industry Buyer's Guide (Year)
0268-5795 Countryside Campaigner
0268-5809 International Sociology
0268-5949 Electricity for China
0268-5973 Health Information Service
0268-5981 Rialto
0268-6309 Marine Money
0268-6376 Radical Statistics Newsletter
0268-6384 Business
0268-6481 Oakland Port and Shipping Handbook
0268-649X Cherbourg Port Handbook
0268-6503 Darwin Port Handbook
0268-6511 Southampton Port Handbook
0268-6716 Historical Research for Higher Degrees in the United Kingdom. Part 1: Theses Completed
0268-6724 Historical Research for Higher Degrees in the United Kingdom. Part 2: Theses in Progress
0268-6732 Teachers of History in the Universities and Polytechnics of the United Kingdom
0268-6856 Hydrosoft
0268-6902 Managerial Auditing Journal
0268-6961 Software Engineering Journal
0268-702X Rouen Port and Shipping Handbook
0268-7518 Church Monuments
0268-7615 Airline Business
0268-7836 Hornsey Historical Society. Bulletin
0268-7844 Weekly Petroleum Argus
0268-7879 Geographical Abstracts A (Landforms and the Quaternary)
0268-7887 Geographical Abstracts B (Climatology and Hydrology)
0268-7895 Geographical Abstracts C (Economic Geography)
0268-7909 Geographical Abstracts D (Social & Historical Geography)
0268-7917 Geographical Abstracts E (Sedimentology)
0268-7925 Geographical Abstracts F (Regional and Community Planning)
0268-7933 Geographical Abstracts G (Remote Sensing Photogrammetry and Cartography)
0268-7941 Geological Abstracts: Geophysics and Tectonics
0268-800X Geological Abstracts: Economic Geology
0268-8018 Geological Abstracts: Palaeontology and Stratigraphy
0268-8026 Geological Abstracts: Sedimentology *changed to* Geological Abstracts: Sedimentary Geology
0268-8050 Condition Monitor
0268-8336 Law Library Information Reports
0268-8697 British Journal of Neurosurgery
0268-8921 Lasers in Medical Science
0268-893X Public Library Journal
0268-8999 Horse International
0268-9146 Animal Genetics
0268-9235 Journal of Management in Medicine
0268-9650 B M T Abstracts
0268-9707 British Library. Bibliographic Services. Newsletter
0268-9847 Advanced Ceramics Report
0269-0225 Diagnostic Engineering
0269-0500 International Review of Children's Literature and Librarianship
0269-0543 Agricultural Zoology Reviews
0269-056X C L W Contents Monthly
0269-1175 British Library. Document Supply Centre. Newsletter
0269-1191 French History
0269-1213 Renaissance Studies
0269-1698 Metal Bulletin Prices & Data Book
0269-1701 Industrial Minerals Directory - World Guide to Producers and Processors
0269-1760 Centre for South-East Asian Studies. Bibliography and Literature Series
0269-1779 Centre for South-East Asian Studies. Occasional Papers
0269-2139 Protein Engineering
0269-2155 Clinical Rehabilitation
0269-2163 Palliative Medicine
0269-2171 International Review of Applied Economics
0269-2619 Princess Grace Irish Library
0269-2694 Butterworths Journal of International Banking and Financial Law
0269-2716 Ipswich & Suffolk Directory of Industry & Commerce
0269-2805 Butterworths Trading Law Cases
0269-2848 Surfacing Journal International
0269-3046 Office Magazine
0269-3291 County Court Practice
0269-3658 Paterson's Licensing Acts
0269-3682 Stone's Justices' Manual
0269-3712 Yearbook of Law Computers and Technology
0269-3720 Tax Practitioner's Diary
0269-3747 International Tourism Reports
0269-3755 Travel & Tourism Analyst
0269-381X CoalTrans
0269-4565 Epithelia
0269-4735 Pro Sound News (Europe)
0269-4824 Tuba
0269-4999 London Energy Group Data Book and Diary
0269-5006 France & Colonies Philatelic Society of Great Britain. Journal
0269-7513 Electricity Council Abstracts Bulletin
0269-8358 Benn's Media Directory
0269-8641 Journal of the Academic Proceedings of Soviet Jewry
0269-8803 Journal of Psychophysiology
0269-8811 British Association for Psychopharmacology. Journal
0269-8951 Medical Science Research
0269-9710 L S E Quarterly
0269-9931 Cognition and Emotion

ISSN INDEX 1505

0269-9982 Canoeist
0270-0069 Deer Hunting (Los Angeles)
0270-0255 Mathematical Modelling
0270-031X Annual Directory of Vegetarian Restaurants†
0270-0352 F M I Monthly Index Service *changed to* Reference Point: Food Industry Abstracts
0270-0360 Wildlife News
0270-045X International Economic Scoreboard
0270-0476 Frontiers in Immunoassay *changed to* Frontiers in Immunoassay and Biotech Update
0270-059X University of Tennessee. Library Lectures
0270-0662 News from the Hill (Washington)
0270-0751 Enviroline User's Manual
0270-0794 Advances in Cellular Neurobiology
0270-0808 Current Governments Reports: State Government Tax Collections
0270-1146 Metalsmith
0270-1170 Journal of Enterostomal Therapy
0270-1197 Building Standards
0270-1200 Policy Research Centers Directory
0270-1235 Asia-Pacific Petroleum Directory *see* 0748-4089
0270-1308 Publications in Archaelogy
0270-1316 American Association of Stratigraphic Palynologists. Proceedings of the Annual Meeting *see* 0191-6122
0270-1367 Research Quarterly for Exercise and Sport
0270-1421 Kentucky Economy: Review & Perspective
0270-1448 Readings on Equal Education
0270-1456 Harvard Women's Law Journal
0270-1480 Annual Student Symposium on Marine Affairs. Proceedings
0270-1588 Construction Contracting†
0270-160X Who's Who in the Fish Industry
0270-1618 Korean Culture
0270-1626 Engelsman's General Construction Cost Guide†
0270-1642 University of Michigan. Museums of Art and Archaeology. Bulletin
0270-1707 Philatelic Literature Review
0270-1715 Accredited Institutions of Postsecondary Education
0270-174X Nouvelles *see* 0047-4576
0270-1812 Sport Scene
0270-1847 Cold Spring Harbor Monograph Series
0270-1960 Gerontology & Geriatrics Education
0270-1987 Review of Personality and Social Psychology
0270-2010 Journal of Soviet Laser Research
0270-2029 Girls Gymnastics Rules *changed to* Girls Gymnastics Rules and Manual
0270-207X Outreach (Chicago)†
0270-2088 Controversies in Nephrology†
0270-2150 Western Reserve Law Review *see* 0008-7262
0270-2282 North American Human Rights Directory
0270-2304 Family Practice Research Journal
0270-2347 Current Christian Books
0270-238X Kentucky. Council of Economic Advisors. Annual Report *changed to* Commonwealth of Kentucky. Annual Economic Report (Year)
0270-2398 Travelore Report
0270-2460 Commercial News U S A. New Products Annual Directory
0270-2487 Government Union Review
0270-2495 Journal of African Civilizations
0270-2525 Andy Awards
0270-2592 Journal of Financial Research
0270-2614 Skenectada
0270-2703 Prison Decisions
0270-2711 Reading Psychology
0270-272X William Mitchell Law Review
0270-2738 International Data Networks News *see* 0735-1844
0270-2746 Cycle World Test Annual and Buyers Guide
0270-2894 Continental Birdlife
0270-2975 House and Garden Building Guide *see* 0199-3933
0270-2983 A M S Studies in Modern Literature
0270-2991 A M S Studies in Criminal Justice
0270-3041 Gardening
0270-305X House & Garden Kitchen & Bath Guide†
0270-3092 Applied Research in Mental Retardation
0270-3106 Advances in Alcohol & Substance Abuse
0270-3114 Prevention in Human Services
0270-3122 Journal of Aged Care *see* 0731-7115
0270-3149 Women & Therapy
0270-3157 Special Collections
0270-3173 Resource Sharing and Library Networks *see* 0737-7797
0270-3181 Physical & Occupational Therapy in Geriatrics
0270-319X Legal Reference Services Quarterly
0270-3211 Teratogenesis, Carcinogenesis, and Mutagenesis
0270-322X Pediatric Pharmacology†
0270-3416 Behind the Scenes *see* 0278-467X
0270-3424 Legal Connection: Corporations and Law Firms
0270-3513 Sportsmans Book of U.S. Records
0270-3521 Mississippi Valley Review
0270-353X Political Finance/Lobby Reporter *changed to* P A Cs & Lobbies
0270-3580 Gizeh
0270-3653 Borgo Reference Library
0270-370X United States Foreign Policy
0270-3718 Foster Oil Pipeline Report from Washington†
0270-3750 Dictionary, Encyclopedia, Handbook Review†
0270-3777 Dangerous Properties of Industrial Materials Report
0270-3793 Laurels
0270-3807 I E E E Power Engineering Society. Discussions and Closures of Abstracted Papers from the Winter Meeting†
0270-3831 Entertainment Law Reporter
0270-3866 Year Book of General Therapeutics *see* 0084-3733
0270-3904 Anthology of Magazine Verse *see* 0196-2221
0270-3920 Advances in School Psychology
0270-3963 Insulation Outlook
0270-4013 Advances in Special Education
0270-4021 Advances in Early Education and Day Care
0270-403X Air Force Journal of Logistics
0270-4048 Jazz Rag
0270-4056 Advances in Myocardiology†
0270-4110 Artists/Prints
0270-4137 Prostate
0270-4145 Journal of Craniofacial Genetics and Developmental Biology
0270-4153 Weekly Insiders Dairy & Egg Letter
0270-4161 Restaurant Buyers Guide *changed to* Hotel, Restaurant, Institutional Buyers Guide
0270-417X Seafood Price-Current
0270-4218 Baseball Case Book
0270-4226 Basketball Officials Manual
0270-4234 National Society to Prevent Blindness. Report
0270-4315 Oil Pollution Abstracts
0270-4331 Kansas. Legislative Research Department. Report on Kansas Legislative Interim Studies
0270-434X Federal Government and Cooperative Education *see* 0277-7002
0270-4374 M I B Mineral Industries Bulletin *see* 0192-6179
0270-4390 Reverse Acronyms, Initialisms and Abbreviations Dictionary
0270-4404 Acronyms, Initialisms and Abbreviations Dictionary
0270-4447 Safety News (Denver)
0270-448X Commuter Air Carrier Traffic Statistics *changed to* Air Carrier Industry Schedule Service Traffic Statistics. Medium Regional Carriers
0270-451X Light (Brooklyn)
0270-4528 Predicasts F & S Index International
0270-4536 Predicasts F & S Index Europe
0270-4544 Predicasts F & S Index United States
0270-4684 Analysis and Intervention in Developmental Disabilities
0270-4757 Signcraft
0270-4811 Government Research Centers Directory *changed to* Government Research Directory
0270-4846 Computer Literature Index
0270-4862 California International Trade Register†
0270-4870 Directory of Communications Management†
0270-4889 American Bar Association. Section of Labor and Employment Law. Committee Reports.†
0270-4919 Historical Intelligencer
0270-4986 Kodak Laboratory Chemicals Bulletin
0270-5036 One Hundred and One Electronics Projects†
0270-5052 C B Yearbook†
0270-5060 Journal of Freshwater Ecology
0270-5087 Export-Import Bank of the United States. Statement of Conditions *see* 0270-5109
0270-5109 Export-Import Bank of the United States. Annual Report
0270-5117 Acoustical Imaging: Recent Advances in Visualization and Characterization
0270-5133 International Symposium on Cartography and Computing. Proceedings *changed to* International Symposium on Computer-Assisted Cartography. Proceedings
0270-515X Kentucky. Council of Economic Advisors. Policy Papers Series
0270-5168 Kentucky. Council of Economic Advisors. Studies in Applied Economics†
0270-5176 International Air Safety Seminar Proceedings *changed to* International Air Safety and Corporate Aviation Safety Seminar Proceedings
0270-5184 Export-Import Markets
0270-5206 Bender's Dictionary of 1040 Deductions
0270-5214 Johns Hopkins A P L Technical Digest
0270-5222 Southern Pulp & Paper
0270-5230 Topics in Health Record Management
0270-5257 International Conference on Software Engineering. Proceedings
0270-5281 Cemetery Management
0270-529X Shepard's Texas Briefcase
0270-532X Constantian
0270-5338 Stokvis Studies in Historical Chronology & Thought
0270-5346 Camera Obscura
0270-5354 Edmund's Auto-Pedia *changed to* Edmund's Car Savvy
0270-5370 Alaska Almanac: Facts About Alaska
0270-5443 Ohio Biological Survey. Informative Circular
0270-5451 Geological Society of the Oregon Country. Geological Newsletter
0270-5494 Tax Notes
0270-5508 Szivarvany
0270-5524 Sea Heritage News
0270-5540 Energy News Digest
0270-5664 International Studies in Philosophy
0270-5672 Farmline Magazine
0270-6229 A I Ch E M I Modular Instruction. Series A: Process Control†
0270-6253 A M S Studies in Social History
0270-6261 A M S Studies in the Middle Ages
0270-6296 Journal of Soviet Oncology†
0270-630X Journal of Soviet Cardiovascular Research†
0270-6334 Anales de la Narrativa Espanola Contemporanea *see* 0272-1635
0270-6377 Recombinant D N A
0270-6636 Nursing Law and Ethics *see* 0277-8459
0270-6644 Clinical Psychiatry News
0270-6679 Feminist Issues
0270-6687 Corona
0270-6717 Interface (Chicago)
0270-675X Toxic Substances Reporter†
0270-6776 P C A S Newsletter
0270-6822 M U F O N - U F O Journal
0270-6881 N A E N Bulletin
0270-7012 New Directions in Middle East Studies Newsletter†
0270-7284 S N A Perspective
0270-7306 Molecular and Cellular Biology
0270-7314 Journal of Futures Markets
0270-7446 China International Business†
0270-7454 Pat-Ab: U S Patent Abstracts & Background, Solar Thermal Energy†
0270-7497 Great Issues of the Day
0270-7527 Resume (Denver)
0270-7543 Directors Encyclopedia of Newspapers
0270-756X U.S. Department of Energy. Annual Report to Congress on the Automotive Technology Program
0270-7624 A I Ch E M I Modular Instruction. Series B: Stagewise and Mass Transfer Operations†
0270-7632 A I Ch E M I Modular Instruction. Series C: Transport
0270-7640 A I Ch E M I Modular Instruction. Series D: Thermodynamics†
0270-7659 A I Ch E M I Modular Instruction. Series E: Kinetics†
0270-7667 A I Ch E M I Modular Instruction. Series F: Material and Energy Balances†
0270-7780 Virginia Nurse
0270-787X Fodor's Budget Italy *changed to* Fodor's Budget Travel Italy
0270-7888 Fodor's Budget Spain *changed to* Fodor's Budget Travel Spain
0270-790X Trends in History†
0270-7950 N C I Fact Book
0270-7969 Business Traveler's Report
0270-7993 Woman's Art Journal
0270-8027 Small-Scale Master Builder†
0270-8159 Charles Christopher Mark's Arts Reporting Service
0270-8183 Fodor's Central America
0270-8191 National Directory of Health/Medicine Organizations
0270-823X Energy Research Digest *changed to* Coal-Synfuels Technology
0270-8248 Improving Urban Mobility *see* 0270-8264
0270-8264 Directory of Research, Development and Demonstration Projects
0270-8302 Adweek/Southeast Advertising News
0270-8388 Art of Negotiating Newsletter
0270-8531 High-Performance Liquid Chromatography
0270-854X John Marshall Law Review
0270-8663 Audio-Cassette Newsletter
0270-8841 Cable T V Security†
0270-885X Cable T V Advertising
0270-8973 Public Sector: Health Care Risk Management
0270-8981 Dance Films Association. Bulletin
0270-899X Sixteen
0270-9015 Command Policy†
0270-9031 Weather Guide Calendar *changed to* Minnesota Weather Guide Calendar
0270-904X Review of Afro-American Issues and Culture†
0270-9074 Archives of Family Practice†
0270-9139 Hepatology (Baltimore)
0270-9155 Energy Technology Review†
0270-9163 Energy Law Journal
0270-9171 Dancer's Digest *changed to* Dancer's Digest & Off Broadway
0270-9228 Advances in Family Intervention, Assessment and Theory
0270-9287 United Methodist Board of Higher Education and Ministry. Quarterly Review
0270-9295 Seminars in Nephrology
0270-9325 Guitar and Mandolin
0270-935X National Center for a Barrier Free Environment. Report†
0270-9368 Shaker Messenger
0270-9384 U.S. Foreign Broadcast Information Service. Daily Reports: Middle East and North Africa *changed to* U.S. Foreign Broadcast Information Service. Daily Reports: Middle East & Africa

1506 ISSN INDEX

0270-9392 Conference on Modern Jewish Studies Annual *see* 0270-9406
0270-9406 Modern Jewish Studies Annual
0270-9465 Discontinued Diodes D.A.T.A. Book *changed to* Diode Discontinued Devices D.A.T.A. Book
0270-9635 Telephone Marketing Report†
0270-9872 Dataguide†
0270-9899 House and Garden Gardening Guide *see* 0270-3041
0270-9937 Ethnic Racial Brotherhood *see* 0736-6086
0270-9988 Linear I Cs D.A.T.A. Book
0271-0129 Discontinued Integrated Circuit D.A.T.A. Book *changed to* Digital & Audio-Video Discontinued Devices D.A.T.A. Book
0271-0137 Journal of Mind and Behavior
0271-0269 U.S. Foreign Broadcast Information Service. Daily Reports: Western Europe
0271-0315 Oil Shale Symposium Proceedings
0271-0323 E E R C Reports
0271-0498 Middle East Executive Reports
0271-0552 New Directions for Methodology of Behavioral Science *see* 0271-1249
0271-0560 New Directions for Higher Education
0271-0579 New Directions for Institutional Research
0271-0587 New Directions for Institutional Advancement†
0271-0595 New Directions for Experiential Learning†
0271-0609 New Directions for Testing and Measurement†
0271-0617 New Directions for College Learning Assistance†
0271-0625 New Directions for Exceptional Children†
0271-0633 New Directions for Teaching and Learning
0271-0641 Arizona State University Anthropological Research Papers
0271-065X A O P A's Airports U.S.A.
0271-0668 American Land†
0271-0706 Nuclear Index†
0271-0722 Discontinued Transistors D.A.T.A. Book *see* 0730-4846
0271-0730 Arba Sicula
0271-0749 Journal of Clinical Psychopharmacology
0271-0773 Microwave D.A.T.A. Book
0271-079X D.A.T.A. Books Master Type Locator *changed to* International Directory I Cs & Semiconductors D.A.T.A. Book
0271-0803 Diode D.A.T.A. Book
0271-0811 Response: The New Sexuality
0271-0838 Photograph Collector
0271-0927 Best's Directory of Recommended Independent Insurance Adjusters *changed to* Best's Directory of Recommended Insurance Adjusters
0271-0951 VideoPrint
0271-0986 Hispanic Journal
0271-0994 New Publications for Architecture Libraries
0271-1052 National Weather Digest
0271-1079 N C ShopOwner†
0271-1206 Topics in Hospital Pharmacy Management
0271-1214 Topics in Early Childhood Special Education
0271-1222 Topics in Health Care Planning and Marketing Quarterly *changed to* H C P and M: Health Care Planning and Marketing
0271-1249 New Directions for Methodology of Social & Behavioral Science†
0271-1265 Audio-Digest Anesthesiology
0271-1273 Audio-Digest Surgery
0271-1281 Audio-Digest Ophthalmology
0271-129X Audio-Digest Obstetrics-Gynecology
0271-1303 Audio-Digest Internal Medicine
0271-1311 Audio-Digest Psychiatry
0271-132X Audio-Digest Orthopaedics
0271-1338 Audio-Digest Urology
0271-1346 Audio-Digest Pediatrics
0271-1354 Audio-Digest Otolaryngology-Head and Neck Surgery
0271-1362 Audio-Digest Family Practice
0271-1400 Advertising Research Foundation. Yearbook *changed to* Advertising Research Foundation. Annual Report and Yearbook
0271-1427 Southwest Folklore
0271-1435 Pre-Raphaelite Studies. Journal
0271-1443 Weekly Reader Funday *changed to* Weekly Reader, Pre-K Edition
0271-1478 Chemical Substances Control
0271-1494 Topics in Learning and Learning Disabilities *see* 0741-9325
0271-1567 U.S. Department of Labor. Employee Retirement Income Security Act. Report to Congress
0271-1575 Journal of Neurological and Orthopaedic Surgery *see* 0890-6599
0271-1591 Vegetarian Voice
0271-1699 Gravure Environmental Newsletter
0271-1702 Learning Traveler. Vacation Study Abroad *changed to* Vacation Study Abroad
0271-1761 Index: Foreign Broadcast Information Service Daily Reports: China
0271-1966 Classical Calliope
0271-1990 Kobrin Letter
0271-2040 Johnson Outboards Boating
0271-2067 Cost Data for Landscape Construction
0271-2075 Public Administration and Development
0271-2083 Atlanta Art Papers *see* 0278-1441
0271-2091 International Journal for Numerical Methods in Fluids
0271-2199 N A G W S Guide. Competitive Swimming and Diving†
0271-2202 Transnational Immigration Law Reporter
0271-2229 A A A S Publication
0271-2334 Advances in Transport Processes
0271-2482 T A T Journal
0271-2512 Space and Time
0271-2555 U S M A Newsletter
0271-258X Real Estate Appraiser and Analyst
0271-2601 Hazardous Waste Report
0271-2636 Petersen's Pro Hockey†
0271-2679 International Journal of Family Psychiatry
0271-2687 Symphony Magazine
0271-2709 Dispute Resolution
0271-2776 Fodor's Alaska
0271-2792 Survey of Law†
0271-2849 St. Louis Law Review *see* 0043-0862
0271-2938 Glass Science and Technology
0271-2946 Ocean Thermal Energy Conversion Workshop. Workshop Proceedings
0271-3012 Seven
0271-3020 Design & Management for Resource Recovery†
0271-3136 Theatre Directory
0271-3179 Key Issues†
0271-3225 Stepparent News *changed to* Stepfamilies & Beyond
0271-3241 Key, Lock and Lantern
0271-3276 Alaska Journal of Commerce & Pacific Rim Reporter
0271-3284 Immunology Tribune
0271-3306 Library Management Quarterly
0271-3462 Discipline and Grievances: White Collar Edition
0271-3489 Licensing Law and Business Institute. Annual *changed to* Licensing Law and Business Institute. Seminar
0271-3519 Arab Studies Quarterly
0271-3586 American Journal of Industrial Medicine
0271-3659 Executive Speaker
0271-3683 Current Eye Research
0271-3829 Photograph†
0271-3977 England and Scotland on Twenty Dollars a Day *changed to* England and Scotland on Twenty-Five Dollars a Day
0271-3993 Sylloge Nummorum Graecorum
0271-4043 American Society of Photogrammetry Fall Convention. Technical Papers *changed to* American Society for Photogrammetry and Remote Sensing Fall Convention. Technical Papers
0271-4132 Contemporary Mathematics
0271-4159 Computer Graphics World
0271-4299 Columbia Road Review†
0271-437X Eastern Transportation Law Seminar Papers and Proceedings
0271-4396 Western Transportation Law Seminar. Papers and Proceedings
0271-4450 American Railway Engineering Association. Proceedings, Technical Conference *changed to* American Railway Engineering Association. Proceedings
0271-4655 I E E E International Symposium on Information Theory. Abstracts of Papers
0271-4760 Fodor's Caribbean and Bahamas *changed to* Fodor's Caribbean
0271-4760 Fodor's Caribbean and Bahamas *changed to* Fodor's Bahamas
0271-4779 Cardiovascular Review
0271-4787 Employment and Earnings: United States
0271-4795 C R I Communications Update Service
0271-5023 En Passant/Poetry
0271-5031 Scottish-American Genealogist
0271-5090 Woodstove, Coalstove, Fireplace & Equipment Directory *changed to* Woodheat
0271-5147 Northern Ohio Live
0271-5198 Clinical Hemorheology
0271-521X I B R O Neuroscience Calendar
0271-5287 Federal Reserve Bank of Minneapolis. Quarterly Review
0271-5309 Language & Communication
0271-5317 Nutrition Research
0271-5333 Radiographics
0271-535X Insider's Guide to Prep Schools†
0271-5368 Counselor Preparation (Year)
0271-5376 Coastal Research
0271-5384 Medical Psychology *see* 0277-9536
0271-5430 Telephone News
0271-5481 Liability Reporter *changed to* Law Enforcement Liability Reporter
0271-5783 Schwann-2 Record & Tape Guide
0271-5848 Labor Unity
0271-5880 Co-Op Directory
0271-5902 A S E E Computers in Education Division. Application Notes *see* 0736-8607
0271-5945 Repair and Remodeling Cost Data
0271-5988 Children in Crisis *changed to* Children & Teens Today
0271-6062 Principal (Alexandria)
0271-6100 Florida Keys Magazine
0271-6194 Resource and Environmental Science Series
0271-6283 New York State Criminal Law Review
0271-6437 Brooklyn Engineer
0271-6445 U.S. Library of Congress. Accessions List: South Asia
0271-6518 Admission Requirements of American Medical Colleges, Including Canada *see* 0066-9423
0271-6585 Cell Motility
0271-6607 French Literature Series
0271-6615 California Services Register
0271-6623 Micropolitics†
0271-6712 Importcar *see* 0735-7877
0271-6771 A V S Biomedical Bulletin *changed to* Biomedical Bulletin
0271-678X Journal of Cerebral Blood Flow and Metabolism
0271-6798 Journal of Pediatric Orthopedics
0271-6801 Journal of Molecular and Applied Genetics†
0271-6925 Ripley P. Bullen Monographs in Anthropology and History
0271-7085 Enhanced Energy Recovery News
0271-7107 Applied Genetics News
0271-7123 Social Science and Medicine. Part A: Medical Sociology *see* 0277-9536
0271-7190 C A R D Report
0271-7220 Old-House Journal Catalog
0271-7352 American Journal of Reproductive Immunology *changed to* American Journal of Reproductive Immunology and Microbiology
0271-7506 Psycscan: Applied Psychology
0271-7514 N A G W S Guide. Bowling-Fencing *changed to* N A G W S Guide. Archery-Fencing
0271-7557 Naropa Institute Journal of Psychology
0271-7565 Police and Security Bulletin
0271-759X Country Magazine *changed to* Mid-Atlantic Country Magazine
0271-7662 Directory of Food Service Distributors
0271-7735 Little Balkans Review
0271-7751 Money Market Fund Survey
0271-7794 Masters of Science Fiction
0271-7808 Fantasy Voices
0271-7956 Year Book of Clinical Pharmacy†
0271-7964 Year Book of Emergency Medicine
0271-8006 Directory of Retailer Owned Cooperative Chains, Wholesaler Sponsored Voluntary Chains, Wholesale Grocers *see* 0277-1969
0271-8014 Entertainment Industry Directory
0271-8057 Journal of Tissue Culture Methods
0271-8170 Sporting News National Basketball Association Register *see* 0739-3067
0271-8189 Best of Micro†
0271-8197 New Pages
0271-8200 Journal of Precision Teaching
0271-8219 Modern Technics in Surgery. Head and Neck Surgery
0271-8227 Iowa Woman
0271-8235 Seminars in Neurology
0271-8294 Topics in Language Disorders
0271-8472 News on Tests
0271-8510 A A P G Studies in Geology Series
0271-860X N C A A Water Polo Rules *see* 0734-0508
0271-8677 Directory of Dental and Allied Dental Educators *changed to* Directory of Dental Educators
0271-8685 Midwest Historical and Genealogical Register. Quarterly
0271-8707 Drug Interactions Newsletter
0271-8987 Alaska Shippers Guide
0271-9002 Micro
0271-9029 Alternate Energy Transportation Newsletter
0271-9045 Business Law Memo *changed to* Business Lawyer Update
0271-9061 I.O. Evans Studies in the Philosophy & Criticism of Literature
0271-9126 Landscaping, Lawns and Gardens
0271-9142 Journal of Clinical Immunology
0271-9150 National Consultor
0271-9347 Wistar Symposium Series
0271-9479 Graphic Arts Research Center. G A R C Newsletter *changed to* T & E News
0271-9487 American Man†
0271-9509 Greenwood Encyclopedia of American Institutions
0271-9517 N A C A D A Journal
0271-955X Frontiers in Aging Series
0271-9592 Common Cause Magazine
0271-9800 Annual of Armenian Linguistics
0271-9894 B I N Merchandiser
0271-9940 Dance Book Forum
0271-9983 Clinical Respiratory Physiology†
0272-0035 Arthur Frommer's Dollarwise Guide to Germany *see* 0731-4442
0272-0051 Appraisal Manual *see* 0732-815X
0272-0086 China Exchange News
0272-0108 Nuclear Medicine Annual
0272-0116 Construction Lawyer
0272-0167 Home Center Operators & Hardware Chains (Year)
0272-0264 Greenwood Encyclopedia of Black Music
0272-0299 Corporate E F T Report
0272-0310 International Micrographics Source Book
0272-037X D L A Bulletin
0272-0396 Entrepreneurial Manager's Newsletter
0272-0426 Ancestoring

ISSN INDEX 1507

0272-0485 Metals Daily†
0272-0493 Wise Giving Bulletin†
0272-0515 Women & Health Roundtable Reports
0272-0558 Enterprise (Cincinnati)†
0272-0582 Psychological Cinema Register
0272-0590 Fundamental and Applied Toxicology
0272-0639 Graphics Today *see* 0274-5828
0272-0671 Policy Publishers and Associations Directory
0272-068X Advances in Human Psychopharmacology
0272-0701 Free Inquiry
0272-0817 Rental House & Condo Investor†
0272-0825 National Fund Raiser
0272-0868 Forecasts & Strategies
0272-0884 Technicalities
0272-0906 American Institute of Architects. International Directory
0272-1015 Irish-American Genealogist
0272-1074 George D. Hall's New York Manufacturers Directory
0272-1082 Century
0272-1104 Directory of Apparel Specialty Stores. Women's and Children's *see* 0277-9617
0272-1112 Directory of Men's and Boy's Specialty Stores *see* 0277-9625
0272-1155 Heritage Lectures
0272-1163 American Export Register
0272-1171 I C P Directory
0272-1236 Video Programs Index†
0272-1406 Tampa Bay History
0272-1570 Northwest Discovery
0272-1589 East Asian Executive Reports
0272-1635 Anales de la Literatura Espanola Contemporanea
0272-1708 I E E E Control Systems Magazine
0272-1716 I E E E Computer Graphics and Applications
0272-1724 I E E E Power Engineering Review
0272-1732 I E E E Micro
0272-1740 Advances in Substance Abuse: Behavioral and Biological Research
0272-1775 International Golf Directory
0272-1902 New Hearer
0272-1961 Legal Assistants Update
0272-197X Falconer's Current Drug Handbook
0272-1988 Reference Book Review
0272-1996 W L W Journal
0272-2011 American Review of Canadian Studies
0272-2046 Marijuana and Health: Annual Report to the U.S. Congress from the Secretary of Health, Education and Welfare†
0272-2062 International Banjo
0272-2089 Family Journal
0272-2135 Directory of College Recruiting Personnel†
0272-2275 Moped and Economy Motorcycle Buyer's Guide†
0272-2348 Journal of Refugee Resettlement†
0272-2380 E S P Journal
0272-2410 Pace Law Review
0272-247X National Directory of Landscape Architecture Firms
0272-2488 Contemporary Concepts in Physics
0272-2631 Studies in Second Language Acquisition
0272-2666 Perfumer & Flavorist
0272-2690 Language Problems and Language Planning
0272-2712 Clinics in Laboratory Medicine
0272-2720 Hollywood Drama-Logue
0272-2801 Research in the Interweave of Social Roles
0272-2836 U.S. National Toxicology Program. Annual Report on Carcinogens
0272-3271 Bank Personnel News
0272-3328 N R D C Newsletter†
0272-3387 Directory of Professional Genealogists and Related Services *changed to* Association of Professional Genealogists. List of Professional Genealogists and Related Services
0272-3417 Farming Uncle
0272-3425 Mobius
0272-3433 Public Historian
0272-3530 Drug-Nutrient Interactions
0272-3565 Benzene Magazine
0272-3573 Today's Education. General Edition *see* 0737-1888
0272-3581 Today's Education: Social Studies Edition†
0272-359X Today's Education: Elementary Edition†
0272-3646 Physical Geography
0272-3727 American Institute for Conservation of Historic and Artistic Works. Preprints of Papers Presented at the Annual Meeting
0272-3751 Pets and People of the World
0272-3794 Annual Editions: Psychology
0272-3808 Annual Editions: Aging
0272-3816 Annual Editions: Criminal Justice
0272-3875 Index: Foreign Broadcast Information Service Daily Reports: Asia and Pacific
0272-3913 T S F Bulletin
0272-3921 Nuclear Technology/Fusion *see* 0748-1896
0272-4057 Chemical Engineering Equipment Buyer's Guide
0272-4065 Directory of Corporate Counsel†
0272-4103 Today's Education: Vocational-Career Education Edition†
0272-4111 Today's Education: Mathematics-Science Edition†
0272-4154 Better Homes and Gardens Brides Book†
0272-4294 Seafood America
0272-4308 International Journal of Partial Hospitalization
0272-4316 Journal of Early Adolescence
0272-4324 Plasma Chemistry & Plasma Processing
0272-4332 Risk Analysis
0272-4340 Cellular & Molecular Neurobiology
0272-4359 Another Chicago Magazine
0272-4367 Freedom Socialist
0272-4383 American Kennel Club. Show, Obedience and Field Trial Awards
0272-4391 Drug Development Research
0272-4464 Annual Editions: Social Problems
0272-4499 McCall's Country Decorating
0272-4537 Faxon Librarians' Guide to Continuations†
0272-4553 Computer and Communications Buyer
0272-4561 Construction Claims Monthly
0272-457X Hybridoma
0272-4588 Monoclonal Antibody News
0272-4626 European Applied Research Reports-Environmental and Natural Resources Section
0272-4634 Journal of Vertebrate Paleontology
0272-4685 Conference of Electrical Engineering Problems in the Rubber and Plastics Industries. I E E E Conference Record
0272-4715 Simulation Symposium. Record of Proceedings
0272-4782 British Defence Directory
0272-4790 Advances in Drying
0272-4804 Series in Computational Methods in Mechanics and Thermal Sciences
0272-4847 Annual Symposium on Switching and Automata Theory. Proceedings *see* 0272-5428
0272-4855 Office Automation Conference Digest
0272-4936 Annals of Tropical Paediatrics
0272-4944 Journal of Environmental Psychology
0272-4952 Power Industry Research†
0272-4960 I M A Journal of Applied Mathematics
0272-4979 I M A Journal of Numerical Analysis
0272-4987 Quarterly Journal of Experimental Psychology. Section A: Human Experimental Psychology
0272-4995 Quarterly Journal of Experimental Psychology. Section B: Comparative and Physiological Psychology
0272-5045 American Society of International Law. Proceedings of the Annual Meeting
0272-5231 Clinics in Chest Medicine
0272-5355 Nelson Directory of Securities Research *see* 0886-0521
0272-5371 Western Bank Directory
0272-5428 Symposium on Foundations of Computer Science. Proceedings
0272-5436 Archaeoastronomy Bulletin *see* 0190-9940
0272-5444 Small Systems World *changed to* Systems /3X World
0272-5460 Internships
0272-5495 OncoLogic†
0272-5541 Masson Today†
0272-5657 Me
0272-5665 Journal of Therapeutic Humor†
0272-569X Travel Expense Management
0272-572X Jazz Times (Washington)
0272-5754 N C A A Illustrated Basketball Rules *changed to* N C A A Men's Illustrated Basketball Rules
0272-5827 Search (Miami)
0272-5959 Libertarian Digest
0272-5967 Maize†
0272-6017 Changing Public Attitudes on Governments and Taxes
0272-6122 International Bulletin of Missionary Research
0272-6300 C B O Management Report *see* 0747-6086
0272-6319 Childbirth Alternatives Quarterly
0272-6343 Electromagnetics
0272-6351 Particulate Science and Technology
0272-636X Director of Nursing Labor Alert
0272-6378 Mark Twain Society Bulletin
0272-6386 American Journal of Kidney Diseases
0272-6440 Journal of Research in Singing *changed to* Journal of Research in Singing and Applied Vocal Pedagogy
0272-6513 Connections (New York)†
0272-6742 Woodrose
0272-6750 Democracy†
0272-6807 Sculpture *changed to* Sculpture Review
0272-684X International Quarterly of Community Health Education
0272-6904 Colorado Homes & Lifestyles
0272-6939 Tentmaker's Journal
0272-6955 Your Patient and Cancer *see* 0743-8176
0272-7064 Osteopathic Physician's Compendium of Drug Therapy
0272-7145 Children's Digest (1980)
0272-717X Mid-Hudson Language Studies
0272-720X S I G Small Newsletter
0272-7250 Albanian Catholic Bulletin
0272-7331 F T Fastener Technology *see* 0746-2441
0272-7358 Clinical Psychology Review
0272-7374 Journal of Housing
0272-7404 Comedy
0272-7595 Journal of Contemporary Studies†
0272-7625 Nedrud: the Criminal Law *see* 0278-1816
0272-765X Social Action and the Law
0272-7714 Estuarine, Coastal and Shelf Science
0272-7730 Starmont Reader's Guides
0272-7749 Diagnostic Histopathology *see* 0022-3417
0272-7757 Economics of Education Review
0272-7838 U S Woman Engineer
0272-7846 S E C Monthly Statistical Review
0272-7870 Chemical Briefs Report
0272-7897 Annual Editions: Marriage and Family
0272-7900 Pulmonary Disease Reviews
0272-7919 International Journal of Turkish Studies
0272-7951 Accent on Liturgy *see* 0276-2358
0272-8060 Houston Monthly Magazine
0272-8079 Speechwriter's Newsletter
0272-8087 Seminars in Liver Diseases
0272-8095 N C A A Swimming *see* 0736-5128
0272-8117 Delaware Directory of Commerce and Industry
0272-8141 I S A Directory of Instrumentation
0272-8362 Setting Municipal Priorities
0272-8370 American Association of Petroleum Landmen. Membership Directory
0272-8397 Polymer Composites
0272-8419 Asantesem†
0272-8443 Health Facilities Energy Report
0272-846X Journal of Clinical Neuro-Ophthalmology
0272-8486 Bulletin on Training
0272-8494 Folklore Bibliography for (Year)†
0272-8532 Base Line
0272-8540 Chicago History
0272-8559 Professional Consultant and Seminar Business Report
0272-8583 Minnesota Industrial Minerals Directory
0272-863X N A G W S Guide. Tennis
0272-8761 Life Insurance Index†
0272-880X International Centre for Heat and Mass Transfer. Proceedings
0272-8826 New Trade Names
0272-8842 Ceramics International
0272-8850 Periodicals Digest in Dentistry
0272-8869 Bibliography of Fossil Vertebrates
0272-8893 Focus on Learning Problems in Mathematics
0272-8907 Colorado Heritage News
0272-8923 Cycle Street and Touring Guide
0272-8931 Capstone Journal of Education
0272-8958 Consultation on Church Union. Official Record *changed to* Consultation on Church Union. Digest
0272-8966 Sanctuary
0272-8974 U.S. Urban Initiatives Anti-Crime Program. Annual Report to Congress
0272-9008 Annual Editions: Environment
0272-9016 University of Southern California. School of Social Work. Social Work Papers
0272-9032 Genetic Technology News
0272-9075 University of California. Lawrence Berkeley Laboratory. Biology and Medicine Division. Annual Report
0272-9377 Colorado Heritage
0272-9490 American Journal of Occupational Therapy
0272-9504 Advances in Plastics Technology *see* 0730-6679
0272-9520 Tarakan Music Letter
0272-9598 RiverSedge
0272-9601 Prooftexts
0272-9660 Telematics†
0272-9709 Promoting Health
0272-9741 American Board of Medical Specialties. Annual Report & Reference Handbook
0272-9784 Evaluation Notes†
0272-9873 South Carolina Geology
0272-9881 Clinical Biochemistry Reviews *changed to* Annual Review of Clinical Biochemistry
0272-989X Medical Decision Making
0272-9903 Selecta Mathematica Sovietica
0273-0200 Harris Postage Stamp Price Index†
0273-0227 Linda Hall Library. Miscellany
0273-0278 Postgraduate Radiology
0273-0324 Source (Jamaica)
0273-0340 Henry James Review
0273-043X Holly Society of America. Proceedings *see* 0738-2421
0273-0685 Securities and Federal Corporate Law Report
0273-0693 Scotia
0273-0839 Alternatives *see* 0361-6908
0273-0979 American Mathematical Society. Bulletin.
0273-0995 Brief (Chicago)
0273-1037 Harris Survey
0273-1061 Federal Librarian
0273-1134 National Academy of Sciences of the United States of America. Proceedings. Biological Sciences
0273-1177 Advances in Space Research
0273-1223 Water Science and Technology
0273-1231 Studies in Freedom
0273-124X Contributions to the Study of Childhood and Youth
0273-1266 World Faiths Insight
0273-1398 Fine Homebuilding
0273-141X G T E Automatic Electric World-Wide Communications Journal†
0273-1428 Country Music Sourcebook
0273-1576 Sesame Street Parents' Newsletter†
0273-1665 Plum Magazine
0273-1673 E E R Energy Price Forecast
0273-1800 Gulf Solidarity

0273-1916 Alaska. Oil and Gas Conservation Commission. Statistical Report
0273-2017 Survival Tomorrow
0273-2041 B H M Support†
0273-2068 Association of Graduate Dance Ethnologists U.C.L.A. Journal *changed to* U.C.L.A. Journal of Dance Ethnology
0273-2076 California Alcohol Program Plan *changed to* California Alcohol Program: Report to the Legislature (Year)
0273-2122 National Center for Professional Responsibility Advance Sheets†
0273-2157 Directory of Special Opportunities for Women
0273-2173 Sociological Spectrum
0273-2238 Water/Engineering and Management
0273-2246 Shooting Commercials (White Plains)
0273-2254 Dermatology & Allergy†
0273-2289 Applied Biochemistry and Biotechnology
0273-2297 Developmental Review
0273-2300 Regulatory Toxicology and Pharmacology
0273-2335 Los Chihuahuas
0273-2343 S H A R E†
0273-2351 Research Libraries in O C L C: A Quarterly
0273-236X Employee Benefit Cases
0273-2378 Energy Purchasing Report
0273-2696 Syntax
0273-270X New Jersey Monthly
0273-2726 Kerr Report *changed to* Mobilehome Parks Report
0273-2858 Metropolitan Home
0273-2866 Dairy and Food Sanitation
0273-2904 Biofuels Report *see* 6377-9137
0273-2920 Song of Zion
0273-298X Current Energy Patents
0273-3013 Benchmark Soils News†
0273-3048 Asbestos Litigation Reporter
0273-3056 RadioNews†
0273-3072 Cato Journal
0273-3080 S C A N Newsletter
0273-3102 Energy Clearinghouse
0273-3145 Action (Winona Lake)
0273-3188 Defense Week
0273-3196 Initiative News Report†
0273-320X Nursing (Year) Drug Handbook
0273-3218 A W W A Mainstream
0273-3226 Biotechnology News
0273-3234 Work Related Abstracts
0273-3242 Resophonic Echoes *see* 0733-8759
0273-3250 Cooling Tower Institute. Journal
0273-3315 C C L M News
0273-3323 Central Park
0273-3382 Journal of International Student Personnel
0273-3463 Missouri Dental Association Journal *changed to* Missouri Dental Journal
0273-3579 Psychology Information Guide Series
0273-3617 Risk Management Report: Medical Records *see* 0883-6671
0273-3706 Extractive and Process Metallurgy *see* 0882-7508
0273-3722 Yearbook of Substance Use and Abuse
0273-3951 Virginia Librarian Newsletter *changed to* Virginia Librarian
0273-3994 Predicasts Index of Corporate Change *see* 0744-2785
0273-4079 Dial
0273-4125 Findex
0273-4257 Professional Practice Management
0273-429X Chinese Physics
0273-4346 Education Directory. Local Education Agencies
0273-4419 Whalewatcher
0273-4435 Federal Funding Guide
0273-4443 Education Funding News
0273-4451 Local Government Funding Report *see* 0741-3173
0273-446X Rural Educator
0273-4494 Revenue Enhancement Reporter *see* 0892-3612
0273-4605 A L A Handbook of Organization and Membership Directory *see* 0084-6406
0273-4613 Consulting Opportunities Journal
0273-4621 Perspectives in Computing
0273-4699 West Coast Sailors
0273-4753 Journal of Marketing Education
0273-480X World's Fair
0273-4931 Armstrong Oil Directory: Louisiana, Mississippi, Arkansas, Texas Gulf Coast and East Texas
0273-4958 Radiology Letter *see* 0741-160X
0273-4974 National Report on Computers and Health
0273-5016 Producer's Price Current (West Coast Edition) *changed to* Urner Barry's Price Current (West Coast Edition)
0273-5024 Journal of Teaching in Physical Education
0273-5032 U.S. Bureau of Alcohol, Tobacco and Firearms. Explosives Incidents
0273-5229 Armstrong Oil Directories: Rocky Mountain and Central United States
0273-5326 Performance and Instruction *changed to* Performance & Instruction Journal
0273-5415 Precancel Forum
0273-5466 Pension & Investment Age
0273-5520 Restaurants and Institutions†
0273-5636 On Cable†
0273-5652 Art Business News
0273-5695 Wood 'n Energy
0273-5865 Discipleship Journal
0273-5954 Contractor's Guide
0273-5970 National Comment†
0273-6160 Better Living
0273-6187 Intermountain Catholic
0273-6225 Builder Developer West
0273-6241 S Gaugian
0273-625X Locksmith Ledger/Security Guide & Directory
0273-6357 Mergers and Corporate Policy
0273-642X Skier's World†
0273-6462 Sheet Music Magazine. Standard Piano-Guitar Edition
0273-6519 Appaloosa World
0273-6535 Contemporary Dialysis *changed to* Contemporary Dialysis & Nephrology
0273-656X Chilton's Automotive Industries *changed to* Automotive Industries
0273-6624 Nelson Survey of Industry Research *see* 0740-5103
0273-6691 Gray's Sporting Journal
0273-6721 Chilton's Distribution
0273-6748 V W & Porsche Etc
0273-6837 Wall Paper
0273-6896 C A H P E R D Journal/Times
0273-6950 Arizona Business Gazette
0273-7000 Annual Energy Litigation Institute. Effective Strategies and Techniques
0273-7027 Estate Planning and California Probate Reporter
0273-7086 Housewares Retailing
0273-7124 Nursing Careers
0273-7175 Brandeis Quarterly *changed to* Brandeis Review
0273-7183 Global Church Growth Bulletin *see* 0731-1125
0273-7485 I S
0273-7574 Kick Illustrated *changed to* Inside Karate
0273-7582 Children's Digest and Children's Playcraft *see* 0272-7145
0273-7590 Humpty Dumpty's Magazine
0273-7612 Executive Compensation & Taxation Coordinator
0273-7620 Common Faith†
0273-7639 Avionics
0273-7655 Surgical Practice News
0273-768X Employee Benefits Compliance Coordinator
0273-7752 Low Priced Stock Survey
0273-7884 B G R Newsletter†
0273-7892 Spray's Water Ski Magazine
0273-7930 Indiana Business
0273-7973 Winning Negotiator†
0273-8023 Alliance Update
0273-804X California Optometry
0273-8139 Pharmaceutical Engineering
0273-8147 South Penn Traveler *changed to* A A A Traveler (York, 1983)
0273-8163 Alternative Energy Retailer
0273-8236 S R E A Briefs
0273-8333 Lhasa Apso Reporter
0273-835X Outlook (Palo Alto)
0273-8414 Lambda *changed to* V L S I Systems Design
0273-8457 Polar Geography and Geology
0273-8481 Journal of Burn Care and Rehabilitation
0273-8546 Brain/Mind Bulletin
0273-8562 Taegliche Andachten
0273-8570 Journal of Field Ornithology
0273-8589 Diver
0273-8724 Book and Magazine Production†
0273-8910 E A P Digest
0273-9046 Executive Compensation and Employee Benefits Report *changed to* Employee Benefits Report
0273-9097 R U R: Rural and Urban Roads *changed to* Roads
0273-9240 Creative Products News
0273-9267 Credit Union Management
0273-9313 Industrial Chemical News
0273-9380 Leading Edge†
0273-9399 Specialist (New York)
0273-9526 Keyboard Classics
0273-9569 Compliance Management Report†
0273-9607 Casting Engineering and Foundry World
0273-9615 Children's Health Care Journal
0273-9658 Official Railway Guide. North American Travel Edition
0273-9712 West Plains Gazette
0273-9747 Florida Funeral Director
0273-978X Stamp Dealer
0273-9836 New Times Weekly
0273-9917 Education in Photojournalism. Journal†
0273-9968 Corporate Report-Kansas City
0273-9976 American Medical Record Association. Journal
0273-9992 Producers' Price-Current *changed to* Urner Barry's Price-Current
0274-4791 Good Housekeeping's Country Living *see* 0732-2569
0274-4805 Bottom Line/Personal
0274-4929 Indianapolis Business Journal
0274-497X Journal of Biological Photography
0274-4996 Packaging Technology
0274-5046 Goucher Quarterly *changed to* Goucher Quarterly
0274-5097 Prints (Alton)
0274-5437 Motorcycle Industry Shopper *changed to* Motorcycle Industry Magazine
0274-5453 Seattle Business Journal *changed to* Puget Sound Business Journal
0274-547X Indiana Beverage Journal
0274-5496 Greater Washington Board of Trade News
0274-5526 Plexus
0274-5542 Internal Medicine News & Cardiology News
0274-5828 Today's Art and Graphics
0274-5852 William Winter Comments
0274-5887 This Is Arkansas *changed to* Arkansas Journal
0274-5925 New England Fashion Retailer *changed to* Fashion Retailer
0274-5933 San Francisco Focus
0274-5968 Resource Management Journal
0274-600X Prayers for Worship
0274-6050 Big Farmer Entrepreneur†
0274-6107 Corporate Controllers Report
0274-631X Computers in Hospitals *see* 0745-1075
0274-6328 Ad Forum *changed to* Adweek: National Marketing Edition
0274-6441 Second Boat
0274-645X Supervisory Sense
0274-6506 Personnel Manager's Legal Reporter
0274-6549 Oregon Optometry
0274-6662 Volleyball
0274-6816 Living Alternatives Magazine
0274-6905 Beatlefan
0274-7057 Franchising Today
0274-712X Quilter's Newsletter Magazine
0274-7138 Grain Journal
0274-7154 Hawaiian Church Chronicle
0274-7170 Skateboarder's Action Now *see* 0279-8689
0274-726X Contraceptive Technology Update
0274-7286 Siberian Quarterly
0274-7405 Wings of Gold
0274-7456 Goldsmith
0274-7472 Wisconsin Restaurateur
0274-7529 Discover
0274-774X Southern Graphics
0274-7766 Premiere *see* 0279-0041
0274-8096 Printed Circuit Fabrication
0274-8193 Jewelry Making, Gems and Minerals
0274-8282 Alaska Outdoors
0274-8525 Mid-South Business *see* 0747-167X
0274-855X Perspectives: A Civil Rights Quarterly *changed to* New Perspectives
0274-8606 West Virginia School Journal
0274-8614 Equitable Distribution Reporter
0274-8622 Minnesota Sportsman
0274-8630 Softside
0274-869X C-Store Business†
0274-8800 Southwest Purchasing†
0274-8843 Metal Construction News
0274-8916 Association for the Care of Children's Health. Journal *see* 0273-9615
0274-8983 Florida Homefurnishings
0274-9041 B I N of California
0274-905X Sea & Pacific Skipper
0274-9076 Lakeland Boating Incorporating Sea *see* 0744-9194
0274-9149 Northwest Skier and Northwest Sports
0274-9394 New England Offshore *changed to* Offshore (Needham)
0274-9483 Association for the Severely Handicapped. Journal (JASH) *changed to* Association for Persons with Severe Handicaps. Journal
0274-9491 Tennessee Realtor
0274-9513 Soldier Support Journal
0274-9629 Softalk for Apple Computers†
0274-9696 Cost Engineering (Morgantown, 1980)
0274-9777 Student Press Service
0274-984X Regardie's Business and Real Estate Washington *changed to* Washington Regardie's Business
0274-9874 A P I C S News *changed to* Production and Inventory Management Review with A P I C S News
0274-9912 Kansas Citian
0275-0031 Wise Giving Guide
0275-004X Retina
0275-0066 Cardiology (Year)
0275-0147 Radix (Berkeley)
0275-0155 University of Chicago. Division of Biological Sciences and Pritzker School of Medicine. Report
0275-0198 Chopper Noise *see* 0271-9029
0275-0201 Moody's Commercial Paper Record
0275-0236 Infection Control Digest†
0275-0244 Hazardous Waste Litigation Reporter
0275-0260 Successful Woman
0275-0392 Human Rights Quarterly
0275-0430 Inteltrade†
0275-0457 Fiber Optics and Communications
0275-0473 International Telecommunications Energy Conference. Proceedings
0275-049X Human Rights Internet Reporter
0275-0503 Professional Liability†
0275-0589 Gamut
0275-0686 ViewText (Bethesda)
0275-0732 Sporting News Baseball Yearbook
0275-0740 American Review of Public Administration
0275-0759 Chapter I Handbook: Understanding and Implementing the New Regulations *see* 0737-2094
0275-0902 Regulatory Watchdog Service
0275-0929 Oklahoma. Geological Survey. Special Publication Series
0275-0945 Best Sellers and Best Choices (Year) *see* 8755-9633
0275-1062 Chinese Astronomy and Astrophysics
0275-1089 Directory of Louisiana Manufacturers
0275-1100 Public Budgeting and Finance

0275-1275 Journal of the Early Republic
0275-1356 American Council on Consumer Interests. Proceedings of the Annual Conference
0275-1364 Joyful Noise†
0275-1380 Neurobehavioral Toxicology and Teratology
0275-1399 Laser Focus with Fiberoptic Technology *see* 8755-1853
0275-1410 Threepenny Review
0275-1429 Journal of Cardiac Rehabilitation *see* 0883-9212
0275-1569 American Society of Bookplate Collectors and Designers. Year Book
0275-1607 Raritan
0275-1739 Poetry/L A
0275-1836 MacRae's New Mexico State Industrial Directory *see* 0739-8476
0275-1852 MacRae's Wyoming State Industrial Directory *see* 0740-6088
0275-1879 Special Care in Dentistry
0275-1895 Alaska Directory of Attorneys
0275-1909 Rhode Island Media Directory†
0275-2069 Communication and the Human Condition
0275-2107 Specialty Law Digest: Education
0275-2123 Fiction Writer's Market
0275-2220 Ocean Science and Engineering *see* 0890-5460
0275-2271 State/E P A Agreements. Annual Report
0275-2484 Centaur (Gaithersburg)†
0275-2565 American Journal of Primatology
0275-2581 Current Topics in Environmental and Toxicological Chemistry
0275-2743 Cornerstone (Chicago)
0275-276X Year-End Regulatory Review
0275-2786 American Land Forum
0275-2832 Employers Guide to A B A Approved N A L P Member Law Schools *changed to* Employers Guide to Law Schools
0275-2883 Caribbean/American Directory
0275-2905 Energy Executive Directory†
0275-3030 Volunteering
0275-3049 Advances in Developmental Psychology
0275-3065 Hoosharar-Mioutune
0275-3073 Day Tonight/Night Today
0275-3081 Industrial Relations Research Association. Proceedings of Annual Winter Meeting *changed to* Industrial Relations Research Association. Proceedings of the Annual Meeting
0275-309X Covert Action Information Bulletin
0275-3502 Source (Boca Raton)
0275-3510 Series in Death Education, Aging, and Health Care
0275-3545 Travel Marketing and Agency Management Guidelines
0275-3588 Journal of Arab Affairs
0275-3596 Pacific Studies
0275-360X Modern Aging Research
0275-3618 Prostaglandin and Related Lipids†
0275-3650 Journal of Library History, Philosophy and Comparative Librarianship
0275-3677 P R Casebook
0275-3685 McGraw-Hill's Biotechnology Newswatch
0275-3707 Radioactive Waste Management (Oak Ridge)
0275-3715 Aurora (Madison)
0275-3723 Journal of Supramolecular Structure and Cellular Biochemistry *see* 0730-2312
0275-374X Hazardous Waste News
0275-3758 U S Rail News
0275-3766 Toxic Materials Transport
0275-3774 Minerals Report *see* 0278-5099
0275-3782 Emergency Preparedness News
0275-3812 Art Express
0275-3820 Directory of Publishing Opportunities in Journals and Periodicals†
0275-3871 European Petroleum Directory
0275-3901 U V/E B News†
0275-391X Car Care
0275-3987 Psychomusicology
0275-3995 A A G Newsletter
0275-4002 Policy Studies Personnel Directory
0275-4088 Legal Looseleafs in Print
0275-410X Lamar Journal of the Humanities
0275-4177 Microcirculation†
0275-4207 BioEngineering News
0275-4347 Journal of Educational Equity and Leadership
0275-4401 Plain Speaking†
0275-4452 Labor Notes
0275-4479 New York Stock Exchange. Statistical Highlights
0275-4487 Sporting News Super Bowl Book
0275-4509 Soya Bluebook
0275-4592 Interstate Compact for Education *see* 0736-7511
0275-4657 Wind Power Digest
0275-4681 Cosmetic Insider's Report
0275-469X New Glass Review
0275-4770 Real Times
0275-4797 Medical Detective†
0275-4819 How to Get Help for Kids
0275-4924 Focus: on the Center for Research Libraries
0275-4959 Research in the Sociology of Health Care
0275-5122 Planned Parenthood Review
0275-519X Pandora
0275-5203 Sonora Review
0275-522X Inform Reports
0275-5270 Word & World
0275-5289 Energy and the Environment
0275-5319 Research in International Business and Finance
0275-5351 Trialogue†
0275-5408 Ophthalmic and Physiological Optics
0275-5416 Advances in Tunnelling Technology and Subsurface Use
0275-5580 Directory of Directories
0275-5599 Washington Report on the Hemisphere
0275-5629 Maenad
0275-5637 Inspirational Review†
0275-5696 A A P T Announcer
0275-5742 Advances in Medical Social Science: Health and Illness as Viewed by Anthropology, Geography, History, Psychology and Sociology
0275-5777 Polymer Monographs
0275-5823 Military Operations Research
0275-584X Perspectives on the American South
0275-5874 Economic Handbook of the World†
0275-5947 North American Journal of Fisheries Management
0275-5971 Theatre Communications†
0275-598X Soviet Sports Review
0275-6013 Mid-America Folklore
0275-6064 Guide to Federal Energy Development and Assistance Programs†
0275-6072 Journal of Law and Education
0275-6080 Bravo
0275-6099 Fiber/Laser News *see* 8756-2049
0275-6145 First Catholic Slovak Union of America. Minutes of Annual Meeting
0275-634X In Defense of the Alien
0275-6358 Advances in Cell Culture
0275-6587 Bear & Company†
0275-6595 Microwave News
0275-6617 System Development
0275-6625 Alabama Forests
0275-6633 Mono Lake Committee Newsletter
0275-665X Obstetric Anesthesia Digest
0275-6668 Journal of Business Strategy
0275-6692 A I D Bulletin
0275-6706 We Proceeded On
0275-6722 Small Computers in Libraries
0275-6757 Sapphic Touch
0275-682X Reprint Bulletin Book Reviews
0275-6870 Typography *changed to* Typography 7
0275-6889 Manhattan Review
0275-6919 Saguaroland Bulletin
0275-6935 Re-Vision Journal *changed to* Revision
0275-6951 Tax Regulation Series *changed to* Law Reprints: Tax Law Series
0275-696X B N A's Law Reprints: Securities Regulation Series *changed to* Law Reprints: Securities Regulation Series
0275-6978 B N A's Law Reprints: Trade Regulation Series *changed to* Law Reprints: Trade Regulation Series
0275-6986 B N A's Law Reprints: Criminal Law Series *changed to* Law Reprints: Criminal Law Series
0275-6994 B N A's Law Reprints: Labor Law Series *changed to* Law Reprints: Labor Law Series
0275-7001 B N A's Law Reprints: Patent, Trademark and Copyright Series *changed to* Law Reprints: Patent, Trademark & Copyright Series
0275-7184 Commercial Food Patents†
0275-7206 History and Anthropology
0275-7214 Mathematical Reports
0275-7257 Remote Sensing Reviews
0275-7427 Top 1,500 Private Companies *changed to* Trinet Directory of Leading U S Companies: Top 1,500 Private
0275-7435 Top 1,500 Companies *changed to* Trinet Directory of Leading U S Companies: Top 1,500
0275-7443 Second 1,500 Companies *changed to* Trinet Directory of Leading U S Companies: Second 1,500
0275-746X Congressional District Business Patterns†
0275-7478 Northern Great Plains Research Center. Annual Research Report†
0275-7540 Chemistry and Ecology
0275-7567 C1 Molecule Chemistry
0275-7656 Tanner Lectures on Human Values
0275-7664 Great Plains Quarterly
0275-7672 Vanderbilt Review†
0275-777X Indiana Libraries
0275-7893 Soviet Technology Reviews. Section A: Energy Reviews
0275-7915 Advances in Irrigation
0275-7966 Energy Economics, Policy and Management *changed to* Strategic Planning and Energy Management
0275-7982 Studies in Communications
0275-8032 New Poetic Drama†
0275-8059 F M I Issues Bulletin
0275-8113 Milkweed Chronicle
0275-8148 Pioneer
0275-8210 U.S. Department of Health, Education and Welfare. Catalog of Publications *see* 0278-0143
0275-8393 Guide to Federal Funding for Education *changed to* Guide to Federal Funding for Education
0275-8407 A M S Studies in Modern Society
0275-8423 Classic Images
0275-844X Trace Analysis
0275-8466 Faxon Librarians' Guide to Serials
0275-8539 J P S Bookmark *see* 0006-7407
0275-8555 Mississippi Geology
0275-858X Index to the St. Louis Post-Dispatch (Wooster)
0275-8598 Journal of Offender Counseling
0275-8709 Science, Technology and American Diplomacy (Washington)†
0275-8717 Progress in Cybernetics and Systems Research
0275-8873 Apparel Plant Wages Survey
0275-889X Annual of American Architecture†
0275-8911 Georgia Journal of Accounting
0275-9098 Current Topics of Contemporary Thought
0275-911X Soviet Journal of Remote Sensing
0275-9128 Geophysical Journal
0275-9136 Electronic Modeling
0275-9144 Physics of Metals
0275-9187 Rock Yearbook
0275-9306 I E E E Power Electronics Specialists Conference. Record
0275-9314 Swedish American Genealogist
0275-9322 Public Eye
0275-9381 Symphony Gold Book
0275-939X Applied Research Summary of Awards
0275-9470 A I G A Graphic Design U S A
0275-9489 Commodities Magazine Reference Guide to Futures Markets *see* 0746-2468
0275-9527 South Asian Review
0275-9594 Demographic Monographs
0275-9616 U.S. Library of Congress. Manuscript Division. Acquisitions
0275-9624 Journal of Somatic Experience
0275-9667 Ages 3-4 Church and Home Leaflets
0275-973X World Jazz Calendar of Festivals & Events *changed to* Jazz Festivals International Directory
0275-9802 Himalayan *see* 0891-6144
0275-9926 Journal of Energy Law and Policy
0275-9942 Journal of Linguistic Research†
0275-9993 Hebrew Union College Annual Supplements
0276-0037 Journal of Telecommunication Networks *see* 0888-2223
0276-0045 Review of Contemporary Fiction
0276-0142 Journal of Freshwater
0276-0290 Nous Letter *see* 0090-2586
0276-0347 Cosmetic Surgery†
0276-0355 Chronicle Career Index
0276-0363 Chronicle Guide for Transfers†
0276-0371 Chronicle Vocational School Manual
0276-0401 Research and Invention
0276-0436 Pulpsmith (1981)
0276-0444 Mananam
0276-0460 Geo-marine Letters
0276-0606 Kastlemusick Monthly Bulletin†
0276-072X Rural/Regional Education News *see* 0036-0023
0276-0738 Fodor's Europe on a Budget *see* 0197-4998
0276-0770 Journal of Religious Education of the African Methodist Episcopal Church *changed to* Journal of Christian Education of the African Methodist Episcopal Church
0276-0843 Public Affairs Review†
0276-086X Psi News†
0276-0916 Leisure Industry Digest
0276-0959 Modern's Market Guide
0276-1017 N C A A Basketball
0276-1041 International Gymnast Magazine
0276-1076 Interferon
0276-1092 Year Book of Orthopedics
0276-1106 University of Texas Publications in Astronomy
0276-1114 Modern Judaism
0276-1416 Byelorussian Times
0276-1440 Computer Graphics News
0276-1459 Multiphase Science and Technology
0276-1491 Federation Reports *see* 0882-5793
0276-1505 Bench & Bar of Minnesota
0276-1564 Bloomsbury Review
0276-1572 Channels of Communications
0276-1599 Occupational Therapy Journal of Research
0276-1610 Psychic Studies
0276-1653 Research in Domestic and International Agribusiness Management
0276-1696 Drivers License Guide *changed to* I D Checking Guide (Year)
0276-170X Farm & Ranch Living
0276-1858 Energy Newsletter Index
0276-1866 Datapro Directory of Small Computers
0276-1882 Genetic Engineering Letter
0276-2021 Salomon Brothers Center for the Study of Financial Institutions. Monograph Series
0276-203X Center for Law and Education. Newsnotes
0276-2056 I S T F News
0276-2072 Fat Tuesday
0276-2080 Philosophical Topics
0276-2110 New Hampshire Marketing Directory *changed to* New Hampshire Manufacturing Directory
0276-2129 Petersen's College Football†
0276-2226 A R C Bulletin†
0276-2285 Journal of Rural Community Psychology
0276-2293 National Reye's Syndrome Foundation
0276-2307 Sporting News Pro Football Yearbook
0276-2323 Hospital Safety Information Service
0276-2358 Accent on Worship
0276-2366 Imagination, Cognition and Personality
0276-2374 Empirical Study of the Arts

1510 ISSN INDEX

0276-2552 Fodor's Budget Japan *changed to* Fodor's Budget Travel Japan
0276-2560 Fodor's Rome
0276-2870 State Regulation Report
0276-2889 Handicapped Americans Reports
0276-2897 Nuclear Waste News
0276-2900 U S Census Report *changed to* American Marketplace
0276-2919 Fusion Power Report
0276-2935 Yacht Racing *changed to* Sailing World
0276-3052 Interval
0276-3095 BIOSIS/CAS Selects: Allergy and Antiallergy
0276-3109 BIOSIS/CAS Selects: Biochemistry of Fermented Foods
0276-3117 BIOSIS/CAS Selects: Biological Clocks†
0276-3125 BIOSIS/CAS Selects: Cancer Immunology
0276-3133 BIOSIS/CAS Selects: Endorphins
0276-3141 BIOSIS/CAS Selects: Geriatric Pharmacology
0276-315X BIOSIS/CAS Selects: Histochemistry and Cytochemistry†
0276-3168 BIOSIS/CAS Selects: Immunochemical Methods
0276-3176 BIOSIS/CAS Selects: Interferon
0276-3184 BIOSIS/CAS Selects: Mammalian Birth Defects
0276-3192 BIOSIS/CAS Selects: Pediatric Pharmacology
0276-3206 BIOSIS/CAS Selects: Plant Genetics
0276-3214 BIOSIS/CAS Selects: Schizophrenia†
0276-3222 BIOSIS/CAS Selects: Transplantation†
0276-3338 Old Mill News
0276-3362 Hemingway Review
0276-3397 The Tamarind Papers
0276-3427 Children's Leader
0276-3435 Ages 4-6 Church and Home Leaflets
0276-3478 International Journal of Eating Disorders
0276-3494 Moving Image†
0276-3508 Advances in Ophthalmic Plastic & Reconstructive Surgery
0276-3516 Moody's Handbook of O T C Stocks
0276-3559 Tennis Directory
0276-3621 Proletarian Internationalism†
0276-363X Workers' Advocate
0276-3656 Insecticide and Acaricide Tests
0276-3680 Ocean Construction Locator
0276-3737 Poe Messenger
0276-3850 Journal of Social Work & Human Sexuality
0276-3869 Medical Reference Services Quarterly
0276-3877 Reference Librarian
0276-3885 Women & History
0276-3893 Journal of Housing for the Elderly
0276-3915 Community & Junior College Libraries
0276-3923 Business Management *see* 0090-4309
0276-4148 Himalayan International Institute/ Eleanor N. Dana Laboratory. Research Bulletin
0276-4156 Wisconsin Preservation: National Register of Historic Places. Newsletter
0276-4164 Palmetto
0276-4245 Broadcast Databook†
0276-4253 Bank Compliance *changed to* A B A Bank Compliance
0276-4318 Family Physician's Compendium of Drug Therapy
0276-4342 Internist's Compendium of Drug Therapy
0276-4415 Housing Finance Review
0276-461X N A P E H E Proceedings
0276-4644 Costa Rica Report
0276-4679 Fulness
0276-4695 Cold Spring Harbor Reports in the Neurosciences†
0276-4741 Mountain Research and Development
0276-4792 Real Estate Investment Digest
0276-4806 B I S G Bulletin†
0276-4849 U.S. National Ocean Survey Hydrographic Conference. Annual Meeting. Proceedings *changed to* U.S. National Ocean Service Hydrographic Conference. Annual Meeting. Proceedings
0276-4857 Knox County, Kentucky Kinfolk
0276-4865 Worldwide Hunting Annual†
0276-489X Municipal Year Book Directories
0276-4954 Estandarte Obrero
0276-5047 Arteriosclerosis *changed to* Arteriosclerosis
0276-5055 BioCycle
0276-5098 Microcomputer Systems D.A.T.A. Book
0276-5101 Consumer I C's D.A.T.A. Book *changed to* Audio-Video I Cs D.A.T.A. Book
0276-511X Microprocessor I C's D.A.T.A. Book
0276-5276 National Recreational, Sporting and Hobby Organizations of the United States
0276-5284 Nursing and Health Care
0276-5330 Critical Perspectives on Contemporary Psychology†
0276-5349 Association of American Publishers. Annual Report
0276-5365 Directory of Legal Aid and Defender Offices in the United States
0276-539X O P D Chemical Buyers Directory
0276-5497 Clinical and Experimental Dialysis and Apheresis *see* 0886-022X
0276-5500 Fodor's India & Nepal
0276-5519 American Register of Printing and Graphic Arts Services
0276-556X Export Documentation Handbook†
0276-5594 Group and Family Therapy†
0276-5608 Chemical Dependencies: Behavioral & Biomedical Issues†
0276-5624 Research in Social Stratification and Mobility
0276-5675 D E S Litigation Reporter
0276-5683 Thomas Wolfe Review
0276-5713 Cable T V Technology
0276-5721 Data Base Monthly
0276-5756 Computing Resources for the Professional
0276-606X Health of Kansas Chart Book
0276-6256 Journal of Children in Contemporary Society
0276-6264 Children in Contemporary Society *see* 0276-6256
0276-6345 Syracuse Scholar
0276-6353 Operating Room Research Institute. Journal†
0276-6469 U.S. International Development Cooperation Agency. Congressional Presentation, Fiscal Year
0276-6493 Georgia Genealogical Survey†
0276-6515 Richmond Quarterly
0276-6558 Studies in Visual Communications†
0276-6566 U.S. Bureau of the Census. State and Metropolitan Area Data Book
0276-6574 Computers in Cardiology
0276-6582 Surfboard
0276-6701 S.O.S. Directory
0276-6744 Yearbook of Podiatric Medicine and Surgery†
0276-6779 Let's Go: The Budget Guide to Greece, Israel and Egypt *changed to* Let's Go: The Budget Guide to Greece, Israel and Egypt - Including Cyprus & Turkish Coast
0276-6795 Ex Tempore
0276-6949 Bibliography of the English-Speaking Caribbean
0276-6965 Probation and Parole Law Reports
0276-7031 New on the Charts
0276-7074 Driving Digest Magazine
0276-7120 Q C: The Magazine of Queens County
0276-7155 Southwestern Review
0276-7163 State Executive Directory
0276-718X Education Law Bulletin
0276-7201 Amicus Journal
0276-721X Cost Engineering Magazine *see* 0274-9696
0276-7244 United States Postal Card Catalog
0276-7309 Television and Children *changed to* Television & Families
0276-7317 Industria Internacional
0276-7333 Organometallics
0276-7430 European Review *changed to* Data Resources European Review
0276-7449 Journal of the Alleghenies
0276-7473 Recycling News†
0276-749X Computer Aided Design Report
0276-7511 New England Society of Allergy. Proceedings *changed to* New England and Regional Allergy Proceedings
0276-752X Client Counseling Update
0276-7546 National Law Review Reporter
0276-7554 Motions in Proteins, Peptides & Amino Acids†
0276-7562 Phase-Transfer Reactions†
0276-7570 U C M P Quarterly
0276-7589 Effective Speech Writer's Newsletter
0276-7597 Airbrush Digest
0276-7651 State Laws and Published Ordinances, Firearms
0276-7783 M I S Quarterly
0276-7805 Directory of Faculty Contracts and Bargaining Agents in Institutions of Higher Education
0276-783X Directory of Consumer Finance Companies†
0276-7856 Chimeres, a Journal of French and Italian Literature
0276-7872 Burrelle's Pennsylvania Media Directory
0276-7899 Second Century
0276-7945 Baptist Reformation Review *see* 0739-2281
0276-7953 Journal of Industrial Fabrics†
0276-7961 Microwave World
0276-7988 Women's Annual
0276-8038 Clinical Management in Physical Therapy
0276-8135 Short-Timer's Journal
0276-8151 Peter W. Rodino Institute of Criminal Justice. Annual Journal†
0276-8186 National Parks (Washington, 1981)
0276-8208 Florida Builders and Contractors Directory
0276-8259 Technology (Boulder)†
0276-8267 Computer State of the Art Reports
0276-8275 Washington Tariff & Trade Letter
0276-8283 C P T
0276-8291 Abbey Newsletter
0276-8313 Historical Journal of Massachusetts
0276-8429 Chemical Engineering Catalog
0276-8577 Comments on Geochemistry and Cosmochemistry†
0276-8585 Journal of Ecological and Life Chemistry†
0276-8593 Multichannel News
0276-8631 Specialized Transportation Planning and Practice
0276-864X U C L A Historical Journal
0276-8704 Protein Semisynthesis†
0276-8712 Current Awareness Profile on Chemical Information†
0276-8739 Journal of Policy Analysis and Management
0276-8747 Op
0276-8771 Pacific Boating Almanac. Oregon, Washington, British Columbia & Southeastern Alaska
0276-8798 New York Agricultural Statistics
0276-8836 Institutions, Etc. *changed to* Augustus
0276-8860 Journal of Clinical Laboratory Automation†
0276-8895 Sports Afield Hunting Annual
0276-8968 Travel and Tourism Research Association. Proceedings of the Annual Conference
0276-8976 Applications of Management Science
0276-900X Worldwide Government Directory
0276-9018 Fodor's Colorado
0276-9220 Borderlands Journal
0276-9239 Modern Recording & Music's Buyer's Guide†
0276-928X Journal of Staff Development
0276-9298 Urban Academic Librarian
0276-9387 Modern Technics in Surgery. Plastic Surgery
0276-959X Directory of Government Document Collections and Librarians
0276-9603 Juvenile Law Reports
0276-9611 T and E Center Newsletter *changed to* T & E News
0276-9719 Johannesburg Quarterly Gold Stock Report *changed to* Johannesburg Gold & Metal Mining Advisor
0276-9751 Advertising Age Yearbook
0276-9883 Crime Digest†
0276-9891 Guide to Federal Procurement *changed to* Doing Business with the Federal Government: A Procurement Guide
0276-9905 In - Fisherman
0276-9913 Advances in Descriptive Psychology
0276-993X Tennessee Williams Review
0276-9948 University of Illinois Law Review
0276-9956 Enfo
0276-9964 Sunspeak
0276-9972 Computer Publicity News
0277-0008 Pharmacotherapy
0277-0059 Micro Moonlighter
0277-0113 Dallas Civic Opera Magazine *see* 0731-8529
0277-013X Lymphokines
0277-0156 Pulp & Paper Week Price/Export-Import Databoook†
0277-0180 O P E C Review
0277-0288 Library Systems Newsletter
0277-0296 Sportsguide *changed to* Sports Market Place
0277-0326 Seminars in Anesthesia
0277-0342 Cityguide - The San Francisco Bay Area and Northern California
0277-0385 National Women's Health Network Newsletter
0277-0393 Clinical Engineering Information Service
0277-0407 C C A N (Construction Computer Applications Newsletter) *changed to* C P M in Construction
0277-0415 Platt's Oil Marketing Bulletin
0277-044X Scripta Series in Geography
0277-0474 Biblical Scholarship in North America
0277-0490 Visual Arts
0277-0598 Selecta (Corvallis)
0277-0628 Uncoverings
0277-0679 Communications Daily
0277-0687 Advances in Disease Prevention†
0277-0709 Window Energy Systems *changed to* Window Fashions Magazine
0277-0717 Fantasy Book
0277-0725 Knives (Year)
0277-0768 Science Fiction Digest†
0277-0784 Access: Microcomputers in Libraries
0277-0792 Keynotes (New Orleans)
0277-0814 U.S. Department of Agriculture. Poultry and Egg Outlook and Situation *changed to* U.S. Department of Agriculture. Livestock and Poultry Outlook and Situation
0277-0865 Computer Security Journal
0277-0903 Journal of Asthma (Ossining)
0277-0938 Pediatric Pathology
0277-0946 Mexico Report
0277-0954 Land Drilling and Oilwell Servicing Contractors Directory†
0277-0962 Worldwide Refining and Gas Processing Directory
0277-0970 National Parking Association Newsletter *changed to* Parking World
0277-1047 A A A World (St. Paul)
0277-1071 A A R Academy Series
0277-108X Group Headquarters Directory†
0277-1098 Play the Red
0277-1152 Mississippi College Law Review
0277-1233 Engineer of California
0277-1292 Country Song Roundup Yearbook
0277-1314 Massachusetts Political Almanac
0277-1322 Res
0277-1330 I C B P Parrot Working Group Meeting. Proceedings
0277-1349 Hindu Text Information *see* 0888-5869
0277-1357 High Performance Review
0277-1446 Continuity
0277-1470 A's and B's of Academic Scholarships *changed to* A's & B's: Your Guide to Academic Scholarship

ISSN INDEX 1511

0277-1497 Loans Closed and Servicing Volume for the Mortgage Banking Industry
0277-1527 World Factbook
0277-1535 La Palabra
0277-1551 Best's Directory of Recommended Insurance Attorneys
0277-1659 A-E-C Automation Newsletter
0277-1667 Executive's Personal Health Advisor *changed to* Executive Productivity
0277-1683 Personal Tax Strategist
0277-1705 Journal of Community Action
0277-1926 Ground Water Monitoring Review *changed to* Journal of Ground Water
0277-1942 Water and Power Era *see* 0733-6446
0277-1950 Apple Orchard†
0277-1969 Directory of Cooperatives, Voluntaries and Wholesale Grocers
0277-1985 Directory of General Merchandise, Mail Order Firms and Family Centers *see* 0731-6925
0277-2027 Business & Professional Ethics Journal
0277-2086 Champaign County Genealogical Society Quarterly
0277-2094 American Society of Photogrammetry. Technical Papers from the Annual Meeting *changed to* American Society for Photogrammetry and Remote Sensing. Technical Papers from the Annual Meeting
0277-2108 O A G Frequent Flyer
0277-2116 Journal of Pediatric Gastroenterology and Nutrition
0277-2132 Washington Book Review
0277-2140 Wind Energy Abstracts
0277-2159 Pipes & Filters *see* 0742-1206
0277-2248 Toxicological and Environmental Chemistry
0277-2272 Voice (Newark)
0277-2302 Instauration
0277-2310 U.S. Department of Transportation. Highway Safety Stewardship Report
0277-2361 American Bar Association. Section of Taxation. Newsletter.
0277-2418 Alternative Source†
0277-2426 Landscape Journal
0277-2442 International Living
0277-2469 Psychology and Social Theory
0277-2736 Discussions on Teaching
0277-2833 Research in the Sociology of Work
0277-2876 American Congress on Surveying and Mapping. Technical Papers
0277-2922 Iranian Assets Litigation Reporter
0277-2981 High Technology (Boston)
0277-299X Technology Illustrated†
0277-3015 New Methods: The Journal of Animal Health Technology
0277-3074 U.S. Department of Energy. Patents Available for Leasing *changed to* U.S. Department of Energy. D.O.E. Patents Available for Licensing
0277-3082 New E R A Newsletter *changed to* I R F Newsletter
0277-3171 Rabbits
0277-318X Rutgers Law Journal
0277-3236 G A L A Review *changed to* G A L A
0277-3317 Video Source Book
0277-3325 Federal Civilian Work Force Statistics. Work Years and Personnel Costs. Executive Branch, United States Government
0277-335X South Atlantic Review
0277-3368 Stamp World†
0277-3376 National Health Practitioner Program Profile *changed to* Physician Assistant Programs, A National Directory
0277-3538 Design Solutions
0277-3619 A S D A Handbook
0277-3627 A S D A News (1981)
0277-3635 Dentistry (Year)
0277-3678 Broadcasting/Cable Yearbook *see* 0732-7196
0277-3708 Colorado Legislative Almanac
0277-3716 Drug Store Market Guide
0277-3732 American Journal of Clinical Oncology
0277-3740 Cornea
0277-3775 Civil Engineering for Practicing & Design Engineers
0277-3791 Quaternary Science Reviews
0277-3813 Journal of Wood Chemistry and Technology
0277-3899 Stamp Collector
0277-3945 Rhetoric Society Quarterly
0277-4178 Problems of Industrial Psychiatric Medicine Series
0277-4208 Practical Gastroenterology
0277-4232 Education Week
0277-4240 Rutgers Professional Psychology Review
0277-4275 Wire Journal International
0277-433X Plymouth Colony Genealogist†
0277-4356 Letras Femeninas
0277-4461 Dawn (Honesdale)
0277-447X Swift Kick
0277-4488 Earth-Oriented Applications of Space Technology
0277-450X University of Texas at Austin. General Libraries. Library Bulletin
0277-4720 St. John's Review
0277-4933 Defense & Foreign Affairs
0277-5166 Negative Capability
0277-5247 Braille Books (Large Print Edition)
0277-5263 COMEXAZ: News Monitoring Service
0277-5271 Survive *changed to* Guns & Action
0277-5379 European Journal of Cancer & Clinical Oncology
0277-5387 Polyhedron
0277-5395 Women's Studies International Forum
0277-5476 Federal Reserve Chart Book
0277-5565 Lottery Players Magazine
0277-559X Official Read-Easy Basketball Rules
0277-5611 National Monthly Medicaid Statistics†
0277-5727 Search
0277-576X Popular Woodworking
0277-5778 Boston College International and Comparative Law Review
0277-5816 Geological Society of America. Membership Directory
0277-5891 CineFan
0277-5913 Genealogical Computing
0277-593X Ismael Reed and Al Young's Quilt
0277-5948 Recommended Reference Books for Small & Medium-Sized Libraries and Media Centers
0277-5956 Connecticut News Handbook
0277-5980 Jazz Echo *changed to* Jazz World
0277-6030 Space News
0277-609X Naturalists' Directory International *changed to* Naturalists' Directory and Almanac International
0277-612X For Parents
0277-6146 Telescope (Baltimore)†
0277-6189 Community Service Newsletter
0277-6197 U.S. National Weather Service. Oceanographic Monthly Summary
0277-6294 Municipal Attorneys' Opinions *see* 0148-3366
0277-6308 Arkansas Archeological Survey. Publications on Archeology. Research Reports
0277-6448 Family Festivals *changed to* Festivals
0277-6456 Passive Solar Journal: Heating, Cooling, Hybrid Technologies and Strategies for Sustainable Design†
0277-6464 Family Therapy News
0277-6626 Annual American Music Export Buyers Guide
0277-6693 Journal of Forecasting
0277-6707 Human Learning *see* 0888-4080
0277-6715 Statistics in Medicine
0277-6723 Cover
0277-674X I E E E International Symposium on Circuits and Systems. Proceedings
0277-6766 Lymphokine Research
0277-6774 Community/Junior College: Quarterly of Research and Practice
0277-6782 Colleccion Vortex
0277-6812 International Oil Scouts Association. Official Publication
0277-6863 Crit
0277-6944 Energy Stocks Handbook *changed to* Oil & Gas Stocks Handbook
0277-6987 Don't Miss Out
0277-6995 Cervantes
0277-7002 Earn & Learn: Cooperative Education Opportunities Offered by the Federal Government
0277-7010 Individual Psychology
0277-7037 Mass Spectrometry Reviews
0277-7053 Art on the Line
0277-707X Recreation, Sports and Leisure
0277-710X Kairos
0277-7126 American Journal of Semiotics
0277-7207 U.S. Department of Commerce. Publications Catalog
0277-7223 Chiricu
0277-724X Directory of Nonprofit Immigration Counseling Agencies
0277-7312 Bricker's International Directory of University Executive Development Programs *see* 0361-1108
0277-7347 Industrial Relations Research Association. Proceedings of the Annual Winter Meeting *changed to* Industrial Relations Research Association. Proceedings of the Annual Meeting
0277-7398 Managing the Human Climate
0277-7436 Fisheries Research Review *see* 0588-4462
0277-7460 National Senior Citizens Law Center Weekly
0277-7533 Big Mama Rag†
0277-7738 Joy of Travel *see* 0741-5826
0277-7770 Connecticut Poetry Review
0277-7789 Writing Instructor
0277-7800 Threshold of Fantasy
0277-7835 Puns Upon a Time†
0277-7983 Solid-State Circuits Conference. Digest of Technical Papers *see* 0193-6530
0277-7991 World Food Problems and United States Food Politics and Policies†
0277-8033 Journal of Portein Chemistry
0277-8041 Contemporary Psychiatry
0277-805X Medical Grand Rounds†
0277-8068 Journal of Crystallographic and Spectroscopal Research
0277-8114 Soul Teen
0277-8173 American Journal of Social Psychiatry
0277-8181 Blatant Image†
0277-8254 Federal Grants Handbook Annual†
0277-8270 International Journal for Hybrid Microelectronics
0277-8300 Transmission Digest
0277-8343 Directory of Securities Research *see* 0886-0521
0277-836X Better Homes and Gardens Window & Wall Ideas
0277-8416 Discovericard Directory of Cities and Hotels
0277-8432 Imprimis
0277-8459 Law, Medicine & Health Care
0277-8491 Housing Law Bulletin
0277-8548 Washington Health Costs Letter
0277-8556 National Productivity Review
0277-8610 Means Historical Cost Indexes
0277-867X Backpacker
0277-8688 American Mining Congress Journal
0277-8696 Mine Regulation and Productivity Report *changed to* Coal Week International
0277-870X International Solid Fuel Buyer's Guide Directory
0277-8726 Markers
0277-8750 N A P C A E Exchange†
0277-8939 Library School Review Newsletter *changed to* Gleanings (Emporia)
0277-8955 Communicator (Chicago)†
0277-9048 Airpower Historian *see* 0001-9364
0277-9110 Astro Annual *changed to* New Age Astrology Guide (Year)
0277-9137 Petro Engineering News *see* 6377-9137
0277-9196 Lauriston S. Taylor Lecture Series
0277-9250 Information Intelligence Online Hotline *see* 0889-6119
0277-9269 Journal of Musicology
0277-9277 Market Watch
0277-9315 Annual Editions: Sociology
0277-9366 Clinical Immunology Reviews *see* 0882-0139
0277-9374 Applied Physics Communications
0277-9382 Metabolic, Pediatric, and Systemic Ophthalmology†
0277-9390 Government Publications Review Including Acquisitions Guide *changed to* Government Publications Review
0277-9536 Social Science & Medicine
0277-9609 Apparel World
0277-9617 Directory of Women's & Children's Wear Specialty Stores
0277-9625 Directory of Men's and Boys' Wear Specialty Stores
0277-9668 Yellowjacket
0277-9714 Drug Facts and Comparisons *changed to* Facts and Comparisons
0277-9722 Packaging Letter
0277-9730 Pediatric Infectious Disease
0277-9781 Wind Industry News Digest
0277-979X FineScale Modeler
0277-9803 CinemaScore
0277-9846 Electronic Publisher†
0277-9870 International Guide to Psi-Periodicals *see* 0734-9033
0277-9897 Post Script (Jacksonville)
0277-9900 U.S. Department of Agriculture. Vegetable Outlook and Situation
0277-9935 Journal of Christian Education *changed to* Christian Education Journal
0277-9943 Advertising Compliance Service Newsletter
0277-9951 Modern Applications News
0277-996X New England Journal of Human Services
0277-9986 Directory of Real Estate Investors
0278-002X P S F Q†
0278-0038 Going Public - The I P O Reporter
0278-0046 I E E E Transactions on Industrial Electronics
0278-0062 I E E E Transactions on Medical Imaging
0278-0070 I E E E Transactions on Computer-Aided Design of Integrated Circuits and Systems
0278-0097 I E E E Technology and Society Magazine
0278-0119 Directory of Industry Data Sources, U.S. and Canada
0278-0127 U.S. Department of Agriculture. Feed Outlook and Situation
0278-0135 Predicasts Forecasts
0278-0143 U.S. Department of Health and Human Services. Publication Catalog
0278-016X Social Cognition
0278-0178 J L A G Review†
0278-0224 Parity
0278-0232 Hematological Oncology
0278-0240 Disease Markers
0278-0372 Journal of Crustacean Biology
0278-0410 S A C Movie News†
0278-047X Wine Country
0278-0569 N.A.S.S.P. Newsleader
0278-0585 American Sentinel
0278-0763 Moravian Music Journal
0278-0771 Journal of Ethnobiology
0278-0801 Cargo Facts
0278-0828 Passages North
0278-0844 1001 Home Ideas
0278-0879 Attorney's Directory of Forensic Psychiatrists in the United States and Canada
0278-0895 Nondestructive Testing Communications
0278-0933 Lips
0278-095X Journal of Primary Prevention
0278-0984 Advances in Applied Microeconomics
0278-0992 Compensation in Manufacturing - Engineers and Managers
0278-1018 Soviet Christian Prisoner List *changed to* Christian Prisoners in the U.S.S.R.
0278-1042 Journal of Probation and Parole
0278-1077 Complex Variables
0278-1093 Congress Watcher
0278-1174 Catholic New York

1512 ISSN INDEX

0278-1190 Mendocino Review†
0278-1204 Current Perspectives in Social Theory
0278-1336 Home Video Yearbook *see* 0735-469X
0278-1360 Index: Foreign Broadcast Information Service Daily Reports: Latin America
0278-1387 Speakers†
0278-1409 Parents Home *see* 0195-0967
0278-1425 Professional Surveyor
0278-1433 Outside (Chicago, 1980)
0278-1441 Art Papers
0278-145X Seminars in Dermatology
0278-1506 A M S Guide to Management Compensation
0278-1530 Product Marketing and Cosmetic and Fragrance Retailing
0278-1557 Knowledge and Society
0278-1565 American Bus Association. Report
0278-159X Robotics Industry Directory *changed to* International Robotics Industry Directory
0278-1603 Wildrows†
0278-1808 Focal Points
0278-1816 Criminal Law Monthly†
0278-1859 State (Washington)
0278-1891 Pynchon Notes
0278-1913 Competition Report *changed to* Financial Services Week
0278-193X Working Mother (New York)
0278-1980 B Y U Studies
0278-2219 A S A News
0278-2227 Inside Energy With Federal Lands
0278-226X Platt's Energy Litigation Report†
0278-2308 International Social Science Review
0278-2316 I D N - Infectious Diseases Newsletter
0278-2324 Conjunctions
0278-2340 B I H E P
0278-2359 Advances in the Psychology of Human Intelligence
0278-2367 Advances in Personality Assessment
0278-2383 Information and Referral
0278-2391 Journal of Oral and Maxillofacial Surgery
0278-2448 International Construction Week: Asia Construction Business Report
0278-2456 International Construction Week: Latin America Construction Business Report
0278-2464 International Construction Week: Mideast Construction Business Report
0278-260X Computer Equipment Review
0278-2618 Washington Letter on Latin America†
0278-2626 Brain and Cognition
0278-2634 Software Review (Westport) *see* 0742-5759
0278-2642 Quality Circle Digest
0278-2677 Clinical Pharmacy
0278-2693 Sports Collectors Digest
0278-2715 Health Affairs
0278-2723 Heart Transplantation
0278-2731 International Research Centers Directory
0278-2774 Computer Graphics Marketplace
0278-2839 Home
0278-2863 Community Animal Control
0278-2871 Rock Art
0278-2898 I S I Atlas of Science *changed to* I S I Atlas of Science: Vol. 1: Biochemistry and Molecular Biology
0278-2901 Journal of Photoacoustics†
0278-291X Rocky Mountain Symposium on Microcomputers: Systems, Software, Architecture. Proceedings†
0278-3118 Nautilus Magazine
0278-3134 Smith Papers
0278-3177 New Hampshire Media Directory†
0278-3258 Electronic Learning
0278-3274 Novitates Arthropodae
0278-3282 Spring (Emmaus)†
0278-3428 Los Angeles Business and Economics *see* 0733-2408
0278-3452 Health Devices Sourcebook
0278-3479 Defense Electronics
0278-355X Property & Liability Insurance Index†
0278-3649 International Journal of Robotics Research
0278-3819 Transportation Studies
0278-3916 Law/Technology
0278-4017 Science and Technology Series
0278-4033 Association for Jewish Studies Newsletter†
0278-405X Directory of Statisticians
0278-4114 Loose Change
0278-4149 Legal Systems Letter†
0278-4165 Journal of Anthropological Archaeology
0278-4173 Hot Water Review
0278-419X Hollywood Reporter Studio Blu-Book Directory
0278-4238 Translations Index
0278-4246 Ruralamerica†
0278-4254 Journal of Accounting and Public Policy
0278-4262 Astrology for the 80's†
0278-4270 E M C Technology & Interference Control News
0278-4289 Annals of Public Administration
0278-4297 Journal of Ultrasound in Medicine
0278-4300 Ecology of Disease†
0278-4319 International Journal of Hospitality Management
0278-4327 Progress in Retinal Research
0278-4335 World Language English *changed to* World Englishes
0278-4343 Continental Shelf Research
0278-436X J A P O S Bulletin
0278-4378 Source I
0278-4386 Source II
0278-4408 Northern Sun News
0278-4416 Policy Studies Review
0278-4424 Manufacturing Technology Horizons
0278-4432 Mendy and the Golem
0278-4440 Organizing Notes†
0278-4491 Environmental Progress
0278-4513 Plant/Operations Progress
0278-4521 Energy Progress
0278-4602 Psychiatry Digest (1979)†
0278-4653 Annual Editions: Health
0278-467X Tours and Visits Directory
0278-4726 Construction Industry Litigation Reporter
0278-4750 Problems of Desert Development
0278-4807 Rehabilitation Nursing
0278-4823 School Library Media Quarterly
0278-4858 Washington State Library News
0278-4882 Occasional Papers in Middle Eastern Librarianship
0278-4912 U.S. National Center for Health Statistics. Catalog of Publications
0278-4920 Handbook of Trade and Technical Careers and Training
0278-4947 What's Cooking in Congress?
0278-4955 Hockey Guide
0278-4998 Pediatric Mental Health
0278-5013 Video Age International
0278-503X Cable T V Programming
0278-5048 Sales Rep's Advisor
0278-5099 Energy & Minerals Resources†
0278-5161 Lab Report for Physicians
0278-520X I E E E Technical Activities Guide
0278-5277 Criminal Justice Career Digest†
0278-5293 Electronic Education
0278-5307 Libertas Mathematica
0278-5374 U.S. National Institutes of Health. Division of Research Resources. Program Highlights
0278-551X Axios
0278-5633 Rutgers Journal of Computers, Technology, and the Law *see* 0735-8938
0278-565X Pockets
0278-5676 Microwave Discontinued Devices D.A.T.A. Book
0278-5692 U.S. Federal Deposit Insurance Corporation. Trust Assets of Banks and Trust Companies
0278-5706 Job Catalog
0278-5846 Progress in Neuro-Psychopharmacology and Biological Psychiatry
0278-5854 U S Law Library Alert *see* 0883-1297
0278-5919 Clinics in Sports Medicine
0278-5927 Journal of American Ethnic History
0278-5943 American Classical Studies
0278-5994 Diesel & Gas Turbine Worldwide
0278-6052 California Journal of Teacher Education *see* 0737-5328
0278-6060 Psychoenergetics
0278-6079 Nightsun
0278-6087 Journal of Business Forecasting Methods and Systems
0278-6117 Sulfur Letters
0278-6125 Journal of Manufacturing Systems
0278-6133 Health Psychology
0278-6265 Chemical Industry Institute of Toxicology Series
0278-6273 Laser Chemistry
0278-6281 Life Chemistry Reports
0278-632X Kidstuff
0278-6346 Trends: Consumer Attitudes and the Supermarket Update
0278-6419 Moscow University Computational Mathematics and Cybernetics
0278-6508 Dr. Dobb's Journal for the Experienced in Microcomputing *changed to* Dr. Dobb's Journal of Software Tools
0278-6524 Market Guide Continental Europe
0278-6532 Babcox's ImportCar (Akron, 1980) *see* 0735-7877
0278-6567 Financial Statements and Operating Ratios for the Mortgage Banking Industry
0278-663X Terrorism
0278-6648 I E E E Potentials
0278-6656 Classical Antiquity
0278-6664 W W S/World Ports *changed to* W W S/World Wide Shipping
0278-6702 A E Airline Executive *see* 0149-4856
0278-6745 Legal Notes and Viewpoints Quarterly
0278-6826 Aerosol Science and Technology
0278-6850 PharmAlert
0278-6915 Food and Chemical Toxicology
0278-694X Statistical Reference Index
0278-7016 Raise the Stakes
0278-7024 Cleveland Electrical/Electronics Conference and Exposition. Conference Record
0278-7032 I E E E Symposium on Security and Privacy. Proceedings
0278-7067 Welding and Fabricating Data Book
0278-7121 Publishing Abstracts†
0278-7261 Critica Hispanica
0278-7288 Literatura Chilena en el Exilio *see* 0730-0220
0278-7334 Parks & Recreation Resources†
0278-7393 Journal of Experimental Psychology: Learning, Memory, and Cognition (JEP: LMC)
0278-7407 Tectonics
0278-7431 Western Pennsylvania Genealogical Society Quarterly
0278-7504 Better Homes and Gardens 100's of Needlework & Craft Ideas
0278-7601 Growth Capital
0278-7857 Directory of Library Resources for the Blind and Physically Handicapped *see* 0364-1236
0278-7946 O M S Annual Report
0278-8012 Institute of Industrial Engineers. Proceedings of the Spring Annual Conference†
0278-8020 Batteries Today *changed to* I B D B Bulletin
0278-8063 World Agricultural Regional Supplement: Africa and the Middle East *changed to* World Agriculture Regional Supplement: Middle East and North Africa
0278-8217 Safety Products News *see* 8755-2566
0278-8322 Phenomenology Information Bulletin *see* 0885-3886
0278-839X Journal of Social, Political and Economic Studies
0278-842X Who's Who in Special Libraries
0278-8799 Dun's Industrial Guide/Metalworking Directory
0278-8888 Annual Insider Index to Public Policy Studies†
0278-8896 Bondweek (1972)
0278-8969 Afro-Hispanic Review
0278-906X Handbook of Food Preparation
0278-9078 Ethnic Forum
0278-9175 Computing Teacher
0278-9183 Videodisc/Videotex *changed to* Optical Information Systems Magazine
0278-9213 Cross Country Skier
0278-923X U.S. Department of Agriculture. Livestock and Meat Outlook and Situation *changed to* U.S. Department of Agriculture. Livestock and Poultry Outlook and Situation
0278-9353 Secured Lender
0278-937X Washington Papers
0278-940X C R C Critical Reviews in Biomedical Engineering
0278-9434 Transportation Quarterly
0278-9469 PaLiNet News
0278-9485 Livability Digest
0278-9493 Psychiatric Aspects of Mental Retardation Newsletter *changed to* Psychiatric Aspects of Mental Retardation Reviews
0278-9507 American Ceramics
0278-9523 Journal of Bioethics *changed to* Journal of Medical Humanities and Bioethics
0278-954X Siddha Path *see* 0892-130X
0278-9566 Bi-Annual Review of Allergy
0278-9612 Wrestling's Main Event
0278-9647 Computer Technology Review
0278-9671 Literature & Medicine
0278-9698 Directory of Convenience Store Companies *changed to* Directory of Convenience Stores
0278-9728 Biotechnology Law Report
0278-9736 Agricultural Genetics Report
0278-9744 University of Kansas. Paleontological Contributions. Monographs
0278-9752 Borgo Political Scenarios
0278-9760 Fit *changed to* Ujena Girl
0278-9841 Informs
0278-9922 Electronic Servicing & Technology
0278-999X Management (Los Angeles)
0279-0041 American Premiere
0279-0106 Arbor Age
0279-0327 Typographer
0279-0424 Charisma
0279-0432 Picture Magazine *see* 0732-1511
0279-0491 Illinois Vocational Education Journal
0279-067X Essex Genealogist
0279-0688 Education and Psychological Research
0279-070X Computers and Programming†
0279-0726 Food Development
0279-0734 Media General Financial Weekly
0279-0742 M D A News *see* 8750-2321
0279-0750 Pacific Philosophical Quarterly
0279-0785 Chamber Today
0279-0815 Uncle Sam
0279-0858 Clavier's Piano Explorer
0279-0882 Rhode Island Lawyers Weekly
0279-0998 Sporting Classics
0279-1021 C P A Marketing Report
0279-103X Objector
0279-1072 Journal of Psychoactive Drugs: A Multidisciplinary Forum
0279-1102 Construction Litigation Reporter
0279-1110 Toiletries, Fragrances and Skin Care: The Rose Sheet
0279-1196 Communicare
0279-120X N A T O News & Views
0279-1323 Orlando Magazine†
0279-134X Swimming Pool Age and Spa Merchandiser
0279-1420 Buying for the Farm
0279-1447 Robb Report
0279-151X Radio World
0279-1536 Survey of Wall St. Research *see* 0740-5103
0279-1552 Buildings Journal
0279-165X Texas Farmer-Stockman
0279-1706 Amazing Stories
0279-2125 New Health
0279-2176 Truck & Equipment Salesman†
0279-2230 Federal Career Opportunities
0279-2257 Juvenile and Family Law Digest
0279-2435 G W Times
0279-246X Epic Illustrated†

0279-2508 National Dairy News *changed to* Cheese Market News
0279-2664 Interact
0279-2680 Your Life and Health *see* 0749-3509
0279-2737 On Track
0279-2834 V L S I Design *changed to* V L S I Systems Design
0279-2893 Non-Store Marketing Report
0279-3040 Dun's Business Month *changed to* Business Month
0279-3083 National Motorist
0279-3091 Nursing Life
0279-3156 Oregon Outdoors
0279-3180 Indianapolis Magazine
0279-3369 Instructor and Teacher *changed to* Instructor
0279-3415 B'nai B'rith International Jewish Monthly
0279-3547 Health
0279-3563 Fire Service Today *see* 0746-9586
0279-358X American Cocker Magazine
0279-3695 Journal of Psychosocial Nursing and Mental Health Services
0279-375X State Bar of New Mexico. News and Views *changed to* State Bar of New Mexico. Bulletin and Advance Opinions
0279-3768 California (Los Angeles)
0279-3857 Georgia Business and Economic Conditions
0279-4004 Cable Age
0279-4039 Dynamic Business
0279-4071 Contracting Business
0279-408X Directions (Lawrenceville)
0279-4160 Acquisition/Divestiture Weekly Report
0279-4187 Converting Product News *see* 0746-7141
0279-4268 Gung-Ho: The Magazine for the International Military Man
0279-4357 National Energy Journal
0279-4462 Lutheran Perspective
0279-4470 American Import/Export Management *changed to* Global Trade Executive
0279-4527 New Orleans CityBusiness
0279-4691 Federal Bar News/Journal
0279-4705 Concrete
0279-4721 Popular Computing (Peterborough)†
0279-473X New Dimensions (Reston)
0279-4756 Gifted Children Newsletter *changed to* Gifted Children Monthly
0279-4799 Hospital Purchasing News
0279-4802 Medical Products Sales
0279-4896 New York's Inside Design†
0279-490X Childbirth Educator
0279-4918 Draperies & Window Coverings
0279-4969 Coltsfoot
0279-4977 Metropolis (New York, 1981)
0279-5027 Modern Textile Business†
0279-5051 S E M A News
0279-5086 Gun Dog
0279-5272 Pharmacy Student
0279-5337 Western City
0279-5345 Missions U S A
0279-5353 Consumers Union News Digest
0279-5442 Critical Care Nurse
0279-5523 Will Eisner's Spirit
0279-5590 Whole Life Times
0279-5647 Orthopedics Today
0279-568X Dialogue: an Art Journal
0279-5701 Sync†
0279-5787 Legal Contents
0279-585X Science and Electronics *see* 0279-070X
0279-5957 Rural Sociologist
0279-6015 School Psychology Review
0279-6058 Format (Minneapolis)
0279-6163 Coordinator
0279-6198 Watch and Clock Review
0279-6309 Realtor News
0279-6368 Builder-Dealer
0279-6430 A E D C Journal†
0279-6481 New Jersey Tax Court. Reports
0279-6503 Land Line Magazine
0279-6570 Pharmaceutical Executive
0279-6678 Sports Retailer
0279-6694 GyroScope
0279-6740 Monthly Magazine of Food & Wine
0279-6791 Lousiana Life
0279-6848 Amazing Science Fiction Stories *see* 0279-1706
0279-6910 Clinical Prosthetics and Orthotics
0279-7798 Northeast Oil Reporter *changed to* Northeast Oil World
0279-7801 Oil Price Information Service
0279-7844 New York Apparel News
0279-7976 Journal of Parenteral Science and Technology
0279-7992 Word Processing and Information Services†
0279-8085 Empire for the S F Writer *changed to* Waystation for the S F Writer
0279-8123 Hardcopy
0279-8174 Mid-South Business Journal
0279-8301 Napa Valley Magazine's Wine Country *see* 0278-047X
0279-8344 MassBay Antiques
0279-8468 Destinations (Washington)
0279-8484 Kiplinger Texas Letter
0279-8557 New Jersey Education Law Report
0279-8611 New York Holstein News
0279-8689 Action Now†
0279-8743 Legislative Monitor *changed to* Professional Monitor
0279-8824 Louisiana Market Bulletin
0279-8891 Cable Marketing
0279-8905 Vital†
0279-9030 Kansas Wildlife
0279-9138 Swarthmore College Bulletin
0279-9162 New England Farm Bulletin
0279-9308 Flying Safety
0279-9316 A S M E News
0279-9340 Medical Tribune (1980)
0279-9456 Groundwater Digest
0279-9529 American College of Physicians Observer
0279-9588 Religious Book Review†
0279-9596 ScriptWriter News†
0279-960X Marple's Business Newsletter
0279-9626 County Bar Update
0279-9766 Staten Island
0279-9782 Software News (Westborough)
0279-9855 Susquehanna Monthly Magazine
0279-9863 Info A A U
0280-1078 Kungliga Tekniska Hoegskolan. Flygteknisk Institutionen. K T H Aero Memo F I
0280-1183 Transportraadet Rapport
0280-185X Ekonomisk Dokumentation
0280-2171 Current African Issues
0280-2791 Scandinavian Journal of Development Alternatives
0280-3038 Cykling
0280-3046 Riksarkivets Rapporter
0280-378X New Swedish Technology
0280-3984 Slaekthistoriskt Forum
0280-4026 Chalmers University of Technology. Department of Sanitary Engineering
0280-4131 Sweden. Statens Planverk. Plan o Bygg Aktuellt
0280-4239 Bergsmannen med Jernkontorets Annaler
0280-4557 L K B News with Science Tools *changed to* L K B News
0280-4638 Hjaerta Kaerl Lungor
0280-4743 Wages and Total Labour Costs for Workers: International Survey
0280-6347 Din Fastighet
0280-6495 Tellus. Series A: Dynamic Meteorology and Oceanography
0280-6509 Tellus. Series B: Chemical and Physical Meteorology
0280-6983 Socialt Arbete
0280-7610 Sweden. Statistiska Centralbyraans Bibliotek. Statistik Fran Enskilda Laender
0280-7629 Sweden. Statistiska Centralbyraan Bibliotek. Internationella Organ. Statistik *changed to* Sweden. Statistiska Centralbyraan Bibliotek. Statistik fraan Internationella Organ
0280-7637 Sweden. Statistiska Centralbyraans Bibliotek. Nyfoervaerv
0280-7815 Nya Byggnormer *see* 0281-7276
0280-8234 Loggen
0280-8463 Kattegat-Skagerrak-Projectet. Meddelelser
0280-8633 Studia Anthroponymica Scandinavica
0280-8773 Invandrarfraagor. Aarsbok
0280-896X V T I Topics
0280-9060 Sindikalne Novosti
0281-0018 Scandinavian Institute of African Studies. Seminar Proceedings
0281-0557 Sindikalistika Nea
0281-0891 Skola och Vuxenutbilning *see* 0282-4736
0281-1278 Kloeverbladet
0281-286X Kyrkomusikernas Tidning
0281-2932 Ute-Magasinet
0281-3408 Swedish Research on Higher Education *see* 0283-7692
0281-3432 Scandinavian Journal of Primary Health Care
0281-4447 Swedish Road Safety Office. Analysis Section Report
0281-5737 Scandinavian Housing and Planning Research
0281-658X Building and Technic
0281-6776 Pedagogiska Rapporter/Educational Reports
0281-6881 Sweden Sjukvaardens och Socialvaardens Planerings och Rationaliseringsins
0281-7276 Nya Byggregler
0281-7446 Arbetarhistoria
0281-8515 Energy, Environment and Development in Africa
0282-0080 Glycoconjugate Journal
0282-0145 Goeteborg. Stadskansli. Boersmeddelanden†
0282-0196 Acid Magazine
0282-0595 Kyrkogarden
0282-1001 S S R Tidningen
0282-1540 Acidification: Research in Sweden
0282-423X Journal of Official Statistics
0282-4485 Landstingsvarlden
0282-4736 Skolvux-soe
0282-5902 Kulturens Vaerld
0282-6283 C B I Informerar
0282-7581 Scandinavian Journal of Forest Research
0282-7654 Buss-Svensk Omnibustidning
0282-8677 Studies in Plant Ecology
0283-1155 Brand och Raeddning
0283-1686 Kiruna Geophysical Institute. Annual Report
0283-1694 Kiruna Geophysical Institute. Scientific Report
0283-2380 Acta Philosophica Gothoburgensia
0283-2399 Goeteborg Women's Studies
0283-2852 Faaglar i Kvismaren
0283-2925 Communidad
0283-5452 Skydd och Saekerhet
0283-7692 Studies of Higher Education and Research
0285-0303 Nippondenso Technical Disclosure. Journal
0285-0494 Enerugi Shigen
0285-0508 Journal of Dental Hygiene
0285-0516 Journal of Dental Office†
0285-0796 Immuno-Advance
0285-0850 Raiken
0285-0877 Yobo Igaku Journal
0285-1350 National Rehabilitation Center for the Disabled. Research Bulletin
0285-1601 African Study Monographs
0285-1806 Hokkaido Eiyo Syokuryo Gakkaishi
0285-2608 I H J Bulletin
0285-2926 Jisuberi
0285-2969 Kyowa Engineering News
0285-3167 Denki Tetsudo
0285-3809 Tradescope
0285-3817 Tohoku Institute of Technology. Memoirs. Series 1: Science and Engineering
0285-3825 Tohoku Institute of Technology. Memoirs. Series 2: Humanities and Social Science
0285-3833 Japan Electronic Materials Society. Bulletin
0285-4333 Waseda University. Science and Engineering Research Laboratory. Report
0285-4600 Nikkei Biotechnology
0285-4619 Nikkei Computer
0285-4937 Pharma Japan
0285-5518 Isotope News
0285-6018 Doro to Konkurito
0285-6425 Micomlife
0285-7960 National Research Institute of Police Science. Report. Research on Forensic Science
0285-9394 Data Communications and Processing
0286-0376 Go World
0286-0406 Science and Technology in Japan
0286-0619 Earthquake Prediction Research
0286-0635 Japan Aviation Directory
0286-0651 Newton
0286-4215 Keio Science and Technology Reports
0286-4312 Kuruma No Techyo
0286-4568 Reichorui Kenkyujo Nenpo
0286-4932 St. Marianna University School of Medicine. Bulletin
0286-522X Bulletin of Informatics and Cybernetics
0286-6102 Shokuchu Shokubutsu Kenkyukai Kaishi
0286-6722 Radiation Chemistry
0286-715X Recent Progress of Natural Sciences in Japan†
0286-7427 Marine Technology Research Abstracts & Index
0286-8210 Japan Semiconductor Technology News†
0286-9667 African Study Monographs. Supplementary Issue
0286-9810 Entomological Review of Japan
0287-0185 Arerugia
0287-0517 Environmental Medicine *see* 0469-4759
0287-0916 Oita University. Research Institute of Economics. Bulletin
0287-1254 Fukuoka-Ken Eisei Kogai Senta Nenpo
0287-2404 L T C B Research
0287-5012 Abstracts on Science and Technology in Japan: Renewable Energy
0287-5128 Japan Shipbuilding Information Notes
0287-5594 Mediya Sakaru
0287-7007 Waseda Journal of Political Science and Economics
0287-7775 Seicho
0287-7791 Kagoshima Daigaku. Nankanen Shiryo Senta. Hokoku
0287-9506 Nikkei Personal Computing
0287-9530 Japan Directory of Professional Associations
0287-9549 Nara Women's University. Health Administration Center. Archives of Health Care
0288-1829 Donan Igakukai
0288-2043 Radiation Medicine
0288-3317 Matsumoto Dental College Research Bulletin
0288-3635 New Generation Computing
0288-5026 Nikkei New Media
0288-5530 Tokyo Denki University. Faculty of Engineering. General Education. Research Reports
0288-6340 Kokugakuin University Economic Review
0288-7622 Local Government Review in Japan
0288-9307 Japan Company Handbook
0288-9315 Second Section Firms
0288-9617 Kanagawa-ken Seishin Igakkaishi
0289-0003 Zoological Science
0289-0011 Biotronics
0289-0755 Research and Practice in Forensic Medicine
0289-0968 Japanese Journal of Child & Adolescent Psychiatry
0289-1239 Cross Currents
0289-1522 Financial Statistics of Japan
0289-1956 Japan Times
0289-3606 Friends of Music
0289-3614 Record Art
0289-3622 Stereo
0289-3630 Musica Nova
0289-3649 Weekly F M
0289-3657 Study of Musical Education

1514 ISSN INDEX

0289-3673 M A Journal
0289-405X Japan Comparative Education Society. Bulletin
0289-4238 National Institute of Animal Industry, Ibaraki, Japan. Annual Report
0289-4947 Journal of Practical Diabetes
0289-5447 Tumour Biology
0289-6508 Nikkei Byte
0289-6516 Nikkei Venture
0289-7806 Doboku Gakkai Ronbunshu
0289-842X Riken. Accelerator Progress Report
0289-9841 Nikkei Aerospace
0289-9922 Drug Approval and Licensing Procedures in Japan
0290-7747 Tchad Nouvelles
0290-8271 International Silk Association. Monthly Newsletter
0291-1191 Demeures et Chateaux
0291-1981 Journal de Pharmacie Clinique
0291-2430 Bio
0291-5871 France. Ministere de l'Education Nationale. Bulletin Officiel
0291-6207 France. Ministere de l'Education. Bulletin Officiel Complementaire
0291-8099 Neo Restauration Hotellerie Collectivites
0291-8102 France. Ministere de l'Agriculture. Series "S". Reseau d'Information Comptable Agricole
0291-8404 Cahiers de l'Animation
0291-8692 Tableaux Economiques de Midi-Pyrenees
0291-8706 Dossiers Antilles Guyane. Etudes Diverses
0291-8897 France. Direction des Affaires Economiques et Internationales. Informations Rapides
0292-1782 E C O D O C
0292-3238 Mot Pour Mot†
0292-7292 Cinema Francais Production
0292-7357 Journal de l'Economie Africaine
0292-7616 Groupe de Demographie Africaine. Etudes et Documents†
0292-7934 Magyar Fuzetek
0292-8418 Bio-Sciences
0293-0773 Amis de Ramuz. Bulletin
0293-3055 Lettre du SolAgrAl
0293-3489 Officiel de la Caravane et du Camping-Car
0293-5090 Arteres et Veines
0293-6852 Lien Horticole
0293-9274 Connaissance des Arts
0293-9320 Ecrit du Temps
0293-9339 Archipelago†
0293-9436 Michelin Green Guide Series: Jura
0293-9614 Bulletin Signaletique d'Information Administrative
0293-9908 Comptes Rendus de Therapeutique et de Pharmacologie Clinique
0293-9932 Voix d'Afrique
0293-9967 Annuaire Officiel de la Charcuterie
0294-0000 Livres Hebdo
0294-0051 Perspectives (Paris)†
0294-0701 Guide Europeen des Progiciels
0294-0736 Journal d'Economie Medicale
0294-0957 Filmo
0294-1228 Annales Francaises des Microtechniques et de Chronometrie
0294-1449 Institut Henri Poincare. Annales: Analyse Non Lineaire
0294-1759 Vingtieme Siecle: Revue d'Histoire
0294-1805 Philosophie
0294-2623 Revue de Parapsychologie
0294-2925 International Viewpoint
0294-3069 Recherches Internationales
0294-3506 Biofutur
0294-4030 Nouvelle Tour de Feu
0294-4081 Cahiers de la Photographie
0294-4480 O R A C L
0294-5495 Societe Speleologique et Prehistorique de Bordeaux. Memoire
0294-6475 Indian Ocean Newsletter
0294-6939 Cahiers de la Guitare
0294-7382 Revue Genealogique Normande
0294-7544 Infotecture
0294-8141 Intersocial
0294-8281 Dirigeant
0294-8303 Cooperation-Distribution-Consommation
0294-8397 C F D T Aujourd'hui
0294-8400 France. Centre d'Etudes de l'Emploi. Bulletin d'Information
0294-8508 Marine Marchande
0295-5717 Centre Technique du Bois et de l'Ameublement. Revue Documentaire
0296-3353 France Peche International
0296-6867 Societe des Poetes Francais. Bulletin Trimestriel
0298-2900 Association des Medecins Israelites de France. Revue Medicale
0300-0087 Annali di Ostetricia Ginecologia Medicina Perinatale
0300-0109 Archivio e Rassegna Italiana di Ottalmologia
0300-0214 Canada. Statistics Canada. Rubber Products Industries
0300-0249 Canada. Statistics Canada. Tobacco Products Industries/Industrie du Tabac
0300-0265 Canada. Statistics Canada. Wool Production and Supply/Production et Stocks de Laine
0300-0273 Canadian Statistical Review. Weekly Supplement/Supplement Hebdomadaire de la Revue Statistique du Canada†
0300-0443 Psychological Reader's Guide†
0300-0486 Society of Biological Chemists. Proceedings
0300-0508 Physiotherapy Canada
0300-0524 Rendiconti Romani di Gastro-Enterologia *see* 0300-0877
0300-0583 Caraibe Medical
0300-0605 Journal of International Medical Research
0300-0621 Steroids and Lipids Research *see* 0301-0163
0300-0664 Clinical Endocrinology
0300-0672 Rassegna Italiana d'Ottalmologia *see* 0300-0109
0300-0702 Mises a Jour Cardiologiques
0300-0729 Rhinology
0300-0877 Rendiconti di Gastroenterologia†
0300-0893 Biomedecine *see* 0753-3322
0300-0923 W H O Food Additives Series†
0300-0958 Flora of New South Wales.†
0300-0990 Arbeitsgemeinschaft fuer Juristisches Bibliotheks- und Dokumentationswesen. Mitteilungen
0300-1016 Versuchstierkunde
0300-1067 Studia Phonologica
0300-1156 Norwegian Journal of Botany *see* 0107-055X
0300-1164 Bulletin Mensuel de la Normalisation Francaise *see* 0223-4866
0300-1172 Banque du Zaire. Rapport Annuel
0300-1199 Canada. Statistics Canada. Household Furniture Manufacturers/Industrie des Meubles de Maison†
0300-1202 Canada. Statistics Canada. Wool Yarn and Cloth Mills/Filature et Tissage de la Laine†
0300-1237 European Journal of Forest Pathology
0300-1245 Pediatrician
0300-1261 Chemoreception Abstracts
0300-1342 New Zealand Journal of Dairy Science and Technology
0300-1385 Cocoa Research Institute. Annual Report
0300-1407 Carbohydrate Chemistry and Metabolism Abstracts†
0300-1547 Annual Reports on competition in O E C D Member Countries *changed to* Competition Policy in O E C D Countries
0300-1555 South Africa. Prisons Department. Report of the Commissioner of Prisons/Verslag van die Kommissaris van Gevangenisse
0300-1628 International Tax Report
0300-1652 Nigerian Medical Journal
0300-1679 Guinness Book of Records *changed to* Guinness Book of World Records
0300-1695 Pilot
0300-1725 Current Problems in Clinical Biochemistry
0300-1881 Nigeria. Federal Ministry of Trade. Quarterly Information Bulletin†
0300-2012 Wolfenbuettler Beitraege
0300-208X Who's Notable in Mexico
0300-211X Radical Philosophy
0300-2144 Management Journal
0300-2233 European Law Newsletter *changed to* Business Law Brief
0300-2241 Liberia. Department of State. Newsletter
0300-225X World Peace
0300-2373 Kenya. Central Bureau of Statistics. Agricultural Census (Large Farm Areas)
0300-2446 Literarni Mesicnik
0300-2497 Neki Pokazatelji Tehnickog Razvoja Privrede Jugoslavije
0300-2519 U N I S I S T Newsletter
0300-2527 Drustveni Proizvod i Narodni Dohodak
0300-2535 Licni Dohoci
0300-2594 Institut d'Etudes Slaves, Paris. Documents Pedagogiques
0300-2608 Enseignement du Russe
0300-2659 Prevent
0300-2667 Management Information Service
0300-2713 Oriental Insects Supplements Series†
0300-2721 Insaat Muhendisleri Odasi. Teknik Bulten†
0300-2772 Austria. Bundesministerium fuer Wissenschaft und Forschung. Bericht der Bundesregierung an den Nationalrat
0300-2829 Arable Farming
0300-287X Bibliothekspraxis
0300-2896 Archivos de Bronoconeumologia
0300-3000 I S D S Bulletin *see* 0257-2222
0300-306X Nippon Steel Technical Report
0300-3094 Nordisk Statutsamling
0300-3108 Travelgram *see* 0041-204X
0300-3124 Teollisuussanomat *see* 0358-7673
0300-3132 Tavola Rotonda†
0300-3159 Tekawennake
0300-3167 Umformtechnik
0300-3175 Valori Umani
0300-3183 Vida Hospitalar†
0300-3205 Voice of Malta
0300-3213 Voxair
0300-3221 Work-Environment-Health *see* 0355-3140
0300-3256 Zoologica Scripta
0300-3264 Young Soldier
0300-3272 Talyllyn News
0300-3280 Swing *changed to* On the Agenda
0300-3299 Nepal Science Magazine *changed to* Nepalese Journal of Science
0300-3302 Sun Yat-Sen Cultural Foundation Bulletin/Chung Shan Hsueh Shu Wen Hua Chi Kan
0300-3310 Skip
0300-3329 Sicherheitsingenieur
0300-3337 Sicherheitsbeauftragter
0300-3361 Science Chelsea
0300-337X Scottish Genealogist
0300-3388 Salamandra
0300-3396 Rheumatology and Rehabilitation *see* 0263-7103
0300-340X Rivista Storica dell'Antichita
0300-3434 Renal Physiology
0300-3442 Hospital Career†
0300-3450 Rechentechnik-Datenverarbeitung
0300-3469 Reader
0300-3477 Razza Bovina Piemontese
0300-3485 Rassegna di Diritto, Legislazione e Medicina Legale Veterinaria
0300-3493 Foreign Compound Metabolism in Mammals†
0300-3507 Rank & File *see* 0141-8688
0300-3515 Rally†
0300-3523 Protee
0300-3531 Processeans *changed to* Founders
0300-3558 Prison Service Journal
0300-3566 Prezzi dei Materiali e delle Opere Edili in Ferrara
0300-3574 Pollustop
0300-3582 Plastics and Polymers *see* 0309-4561
0300-3604 Photosynthetica
0300-3612 University of the Philippines. Institute of Library Science. Newsletter
0300-3620 Philippines. Civil Service Commission. Civil Service Reporter
0300-3639 Phenix
0300-3655 Personalhistorisk Tidsskrift
0300-3663 Periodex *changed to* Point de Repere
0300-368X Nigerian Agricultural Journal
0300-3701 Orquidea (Mexico)
0300-371X Notes on the Science of Building
0300-3728 Nova Scotia Historical Quarterly
0300-3736 New Spectator *see* 0314-6200
0300-3752 New Linguist†
0300-3779 Muchachas†
0300-3787 Mundo Electronico
0300-3809 Natun Thikana
0300-3817 Magyar Tortenelmi Szemle
0300-3825 Medico†
0300-3868 Medical Technician *see* 0309-2666
0300-3884 Mundo Financiero
0300-3906 Mindanao Mail
0300-3914 Mitsubishi Bank Review
0300-3922 Multinational Business
0300-3930 Local Government Studies
0300-3957 Kerala Homoeo Journal
0300-3965 Interdit *changed to* Les Diplomes
0300-3973 Informazione Radio/TV
0300-3981 Informationen zur Orts-, Regional- und Landesplanung *see* 0251-3625
0300-4007 Indranil
0300-4015 Korean Journal of Physiology
0300-4023 Indochina
0300-4031 In Terris
0300-4058 International Law Reporter
0300-4074 Kanara Chamber of Commerce & Industry Journal
0300-4112 Forstarchiv
0300-4139 Germinal
0300-4155 Impact
0300-4163 I P P F - S E A O R News *see* 0126-8031
0300-4171 I D E
0300-418X Hong Kong Monthly Digest of Statistics
0300-421X British Baking Industries Research Association. Abstracts *see* 0430-7941
0300-4228 Fleet Street Letter
0300-4236 Evangelische Kommentare
0300-4252 European Federation of Finance House Associations. Newsletter
0300-4260 English Golf Union. News and Fixtures *changed to* English Amateur Golf
0300-4279 Education Three-Thirteen
0300-4287 Economics
0300-4309 Dhandha
0300-4317 Desarrollo del Tropico Americano†
0300-4325 British Clayworker *see* 0305-7623
0300-4333 University of Calgary Gazette
0300-4341 Business Japan
0300-435X Canadian Guider
0300-4368 Charadista
0300-4384 Concord
0300-4414 Dejiny Ved a Techniky
0300-4422 Deputazione di Storia Patria per l'Umbria. Bollettino
0300-4430 Early Child Development and Care
0300-4465 Cooperator†
0300-4473 Cidade†
0300-4481 Cerveza y Malta
0300-449X Transport and Tourism Journal
0300-4503 Case Studies in Atomic Physics *see* 0370-1573
0300-4511 Canada Rides
0300-452X Camouflage Air Journal
0300-4538 Cahiers de la Presse Francaise†
0300-4546 Society and Commerce
0300-4554 B I P
0300-4562 British Lichen Society Bulletin
0300-4570 British Ceramic Abstracts
0300-4589 Bollettino di Collegamento
0300-4600 Athletic Echo

ISSN INDEX 1515

0300-4619 Brewing Industry Research Foundation. Bulletin of Current Literature *changed to* Brewing Research Foundation. Bulletin of Current Literature
0300-4627 Blatt fuer Sortenwesen
0300-4651 Odini
0300-466X Artbibliographies Modern
0300-4678 Action
0300-4686 Acrida
0300-4708 A M A Gazette *see* 0729-9745
0300-4716 Canada Manpower Review *see* 0318-4099
0300-4732 Dansk Forsikrings Tidende/Assurandoeren *see* 0105-4260
0300-4740 Cayman Islands. Legislative Assembly. Minutes
0300-483X Toxicology
0300-4864 Journal of Neurocytology
0300-4880 Public Health in Europe
0300-4910 Annales d'Immunologie *see* 0769-2625
0300-4937 Medecine et Armees
0300-4953 Artes de Mexico
0300-4961 Rocky Mountain Social Science Association. Newsletter *changed to* Western Social Science Association Newsletter
0300-4988 Chester Zoo News *changed to* Chez Nous Chester Zoo News
0300-5038 I A R C Scientific Publications
0300-5062 Actas Luso-Espanolas de Neurologia Psiquiatria y Ciencias Afines
0300-5089 Clinics in Gastroenterology *see* 0889-8553
0300-5127 Biochemical Society, London. Transactions
0300-5143 Clean Air
0300-5186 Monographs in Neural Sciences
0300-5194 Excerpta Medica. Section 46: Environmental Health and Pollution Control
0300-5224 Nieren- und Hochdruckkrankheiten
0300-5232 Society of Chemical Industry. Bulletin
0300-5275 Ontario Dentist
0300-5283 Medical Journal of Malaysia
0300-5305 Architektura C S R
0300-5321 Excerpta Medica. Section 36: Health Economics and Hospital Management
0300-533X Institute of Child Health, Calcutta. Annals†
0300-5356 Arhitectura
0300-5364 British Journal of Audiology
0300-5372 Excerpta Medica. Section 29: Clinical Biochemistry
0300-5402 Acta Universitatis Carolinae: Geographica
0300-5410 Annales de Microbiologie *see* 0769-2609
0300-5429 Environmental Physiology & Biochemistry†
0300-5453 New Al-Hoda
0300-5461 Hospital and Health Service Purchasing
0300-5488 Studies on the Fauna of Suriname and Other Guyanas
0300-550X Agricultural Association of China. Journal
0300-5526 Intervirology
0300-5534 Natuurwetenschappelijke Studiekring voor Suriname en de Nederlandse Antillen. Uitgaven
0300-5550 Revista Espanola de Lecheria
0300-5577 Journal of Perinatal Medicine
0300-5607 Courses et Elevage
0300-5623 Urological Research
0300-5658 Eperon†
0300-5704 Aktuelle Gerontologie *see* 0044-281X
0300-5712 Journal of Dentistry
0300-5720 Hospital Development
0300-5747 South Africa. Maize Board. Report on Grain Sorghum and Buckwheat for the Financial Year†
0300-5755 Alimentaria
0300-5763 Biological Membrane Abstracts *see* 0143-330X
0300-5771 International Journal of Epidemiology
0300-581X Arbeitsmedizin, Sozialmedizin, Praeventivmedizin
0300-5852 Behavioural Biology Abstracts, Section A: Animal Behaviour *see* 0301-8695
0300-5860 Zeitschrift fuer Kardiologie
0300-5879 Medical Technologist *see* 0309-2666
0300-5925 Public Health Engineer
0300-595X Clinics in Endocrinology and Metabolism *see* 0889-8529
0300-5992 Terpenoids and Steroids†
0300-600X Venture Management†
0300-6018 New Dimensions in Legislation *see* 0146-9584
0300-6026 Trends in Housing
0300-6034 Consumer Credit and Truth-In-Lending Compliance Report
0300-6050 Texas State and Region Newsletter†
0300-6069 New Jersey Register
0300-6077 Under Twenty-Five Newsletter
0300-6107 California Teachers Association. Chapter News Service†
0300-6115 New Jersey Savings League Guide *changed to* New Jersey Savings League News
0300-6123 Rubber & Plastics News
0300-6131 San Diego County. Planning Department. Population and Housing *changed to* Info Bulletin-Population and Housing Estimates
0300-6158 Miesiecznik Franciszkanski
0300-6166 T A A Newsletter *changed to* Sister City News
0300-6182 South Dakota Municipalities
0300-6190 Tube Topics
0300-6204 Business & Government Insider Newsletter†
0300-6212 Svithiod Journal
0300-6239 Southern Tobacco Journal
0300-6247 Talking Leaf
0300-6271 Pregled Review
0300-6298 Teacher Advocate *changed to* I S T A Advocate
0300-6301 Motor North
0300-6328 Rawhide Press
0300-6336 Union W.A.G.E.†
0300-6379 Rainbow (Jersey City)
0300-6387 Sports Car†
0300-6409 N A H R O Letter *see* 0194-9268
0300-6425 Recovering Literature
0300-6433 T E P S A Journal
0300-6441 Regional Plan Association Library Acquisitions *changed to* Regional Plan Association Selected Library Acquisitions
0300-645X Virginia Genealogist
0300-6468 Rhode Island Statewide Planning Program Monthly Progress Report
0300-6484 Palestine Digest†
0300-6506 Transportation Business Report†
0300-6514 Pan-American Trader
0300-6530 West Virginia Record and West Virginia Merchant
0300-6549 Walker's Manual Supplements
0300-6557 Trailer Boats
0300-6565 Whispering Wind
0300-6573 Whitmore Investment Letter†
0300-659X Womanpower *see* 0195-2390
0300-6603 Twin Cities Courier
0300-6611 Women's Advocate†
0300-662X Western Mining News
0300-6638 Voluntary Action News *see* 0149-6492
0300-6646 National On-Campus Report
0300-6654 R H G H Vital Signs
0300-6662 N Y D H I C Improver *see* 0145-9112
0300-6670 N S A A Newsletter *changed to* N S A A News
0300-6689 N A T E News
0300-6700 Technology and Human Affairs *changed to* I I T Technology and Human Affairs
0300-6727 North Carolina Agribusiness†
0300-6743 Noticiero Obrero Norteamericano†
0300-676X Oshkosh Advance-Titan
0300-6778 Nichols Alumnus *changed to* Nichols News
0300-6786 Post Eagle
0300-6794 Nostalgia Newsletter†
0300-6816 P A A Affairs
0300-6824 Northwest Investment Review *see* 0886-3768
0300-6832 North Dakota Publisher†
0300-6840 Northwest Investment Tablistics *see* 0147-2410
0300-6859 Urban Affairs Abstracts
0300-6867 W E A L Washington Report
0300-6883 I A L News
0300-6891 A.D. Presbyterian Life Edition *changed to* United Presbyterian A.D.
0300-6905 Highway Safety Literature†
0300-6921 Chicago Reporter
0300-6948 Arts in Common *changed to* Vantage Point: Issues in American Arts
0300-6956 Current Programs *see* 0162-704X
0300-6964 Augsburg College Now
0300-6972 Abortion Surveillance *changed to* U.S. Centers for Disease Control. Abortion Surveillance. Annual Summary
0300-6999 Federation Forum *changed to* Planning and Action
0300-7006 World Education Reports
0300-7014 Feminist Art Journal†
0300-7022 A D R I S Newsletter
0300-7030 Concerned Business Students' Report†
0300-7057 Video Publisher *see* 0748-0792
0300-7065 A C A Word from Washington *changed to* A C A Update
0300-7073 Family Practice News
0300-7081 Chicago. Municipal Reference Library. Recent Additions
0300-7103 Essecondsex†
0300-7111 Fashion Newsletter
0300-712X Chicago. Municipal Reference Library. Checklist of Publications Issued by the City of Chicago
0300-7138 Du Pont Context†
0300-7154 Michael Reese Hospital & Medical Center. Medical Staff Newsletter *changed to* Rounds
0300-7162 Diacritics
0300-7170 Environmental Pollution Control Journal†
0300-7197 Drywall Newsmagazine *see* 0194-8903
0300-7200 Medic Alert Newsletter
0300-7219 American Challenge
0300-7227 Bibliography and Index of Micropaleontology
0300-7235 Bay View†
0300-7243 Clyde LaMotte's Washington Energy Memo
0300-7278 American Indian News†
0300-7308 Metric Association Newsletter *see* 0271-2555
0300-7316 Discovery (Richmond)
0300-7324 Dow Theory Forecasts
0300-7340 D C A T Bulletin
0300-7359 Media Ecology Review†
0300-7367 Commodity Exchange Bulletin
0300-7375 Consumer Newsweek *changed to* Consumer Newsweekly
0300-7391 Contents of Current Legal Periodicals *see* 0279-5787
0300-7405 Intermountain Logging News†
0300-7421 American University Report *changed to* American
0300-743X C O R E Magazine
0300-7448 American Dance Guild Newsletter
0300-7472 Afterimage
0300-7499 Buffalo Spree
0300-7502 Maryland Travel Scene
0300-7510 Bnai Yiddish†
0300-7529 Connecticut Business Journal
0300-7553 Margins†
0300-7561 Crab
0300-757X Inside R & D
0300-7588 Inter-Society Color Council Newsletter *see* 0731-2911
0300-7618 Poblacion†
0300-7626 American White Water
0300-7634 Correio Operario Norteamericano†
0300-7669 Your Clipping Analyst
0300-7677 Indian Legal Information Development Service Legislative Review *see* 0145-7993
0300-7685 Industrial Television News *changed to* International Television News
0300-7693 Performance Guide Publications. Mutual Funds and Timing
0300-7707 M A S C D Newsletter *changed to* Focus Magazine (Detroit)
0300-7715 Payment Systems Newsletter†
0300-7723 Photo Industry Newsletter
0300-7766 Popular Music & Society
0300-7782 Headlines
0300-7804 Live Steam Magazine *see* 0364-5177
0300-7812 Goddard Journal†
0300-7820 Suomi-Opiston Viesti†
0300-7839 Human Ecology (New York)
0300-7898 New York (State) University. Division of Continuing Education. Newsletter†
0300-7901 Know News Service†
0300-7928 Ripon College Magazine
0300-7936 Robinson Jeffers Newsletter
0300-7952 Kitchen Planning *see* 0744-1916
0300-7960 Shmuessen mit Kinder Un Yugent
0300-7995 Current Medical Research and Opinion
0300-8002 Junior High-Middle School Bulletin†
0300-8029 Inforasia†
0300-8037 Scandinavian Journal of Social Medicine
0300-8053 International Jugglers Association Newsletter *changed to* Juggler's World Magazine
0300-807X Geographia Medica
0300-8096 D T. I†
0300-810X Italian Heritage Newsletter†
0300-8126 Infection
0300-8134 Journal of Human Ergology
0300-8169 Medicina e Historia†
0300-8177 Molecular and Cellular Biochemistry
0300-8185 Pakistan Journal of Biochemistry†
0300-8207 Connective Tissue Research
0300-8258 Connecticut Fireside
0300-8274 Actualites Psychiatriques
0300-8282 E D V in Medizin und Biologie
0300-8320 Helminthological Abstracts. Series B: Plant Nematology
0300-8339 Helminthological Abstracts. Series A: Animal and Human Helminthology
0300-8347 Health & Social Service Journal
0300-8355 Gem City News *changed to* Idaho Cities
0300-8371 Neue Muenchner Beitraege zur Geschichte der Medizin und Naturwissenschaften. Medizinhistorische Serie
0300-838X Microbiology Abstracts. Section A. Industrial & Applied Microbiology
0300-8398 Microbiology Abstracts. Section B. Bacteriology
0300-8428 Basic Research in Cardiology
0300-8436 Jahresverzeichnis der Verlagsschriften und Einer Auswahl der Ausserhalb des Buchhandels Erschienenen Veroeffentlichungen der D.D.R., der B.R.D. und Westberlins Sowie der Deutschsprachigen Werke Anderer Laender†
0300-8452 Forecast FM *changed to* Forecast (Silver Spring)
0300-8495 Australian Family Physician
0300-8509 Fore
0300-8533 Oyo Yakuri Kenkyukai
0300-8584 Medical Microbiology and Immunology
0300-8592 Roentgen Blaetter
0300-8622 Leber Magen Darm
0300-8630 Klinische Paediatrie
0300-8665 Verein fuer Wasser-, Boden- und Lufthygiene. Schriftenreihe
0300-869X Zeitschrift fuer Klinische Psychologie und Psychotherapie
0300-8703 Studebaker Story
0300-8711 Zentralblatt fuer Veterinaermedizin. Series A. *see* 0721-0981
0300-872X Zeitschrift fuer Immunitaetsforschung, Experimentelle und Klinische Immunologie *see* 0171-2985
0300-8754 Housing and Community Development News *see* 0194-2913
0300-8819 Neurobiology†

1516 ISSN INDEX

0300-8827 Acta Orthopaedica Scandinavica. Supplementum
0300-8835 Acta Obstetrica et Gynecologica Scandinavica. Supplement
0300-8851 Herold der Wahrheit
0300-8908 Nevada Planner†
0300-8924 Acta Vitaminologica et Enzymologica
0300-8932 Revista Espanola de Cardiologia
0300-8959 New Alaskan
0300-8967 Acta Psychiatrica Belgica
0300-9009 Acta Neurologica Belgica
0300-9033 Acta Gastroenterologica Latinoamericana
0300-9084 Biochimie
0300-9092 Akusherstvo i Ginekologiya
0300-9130 Research in Experimental Medicine
0300-922X Royal Society of Chemistry. Journal: Perkin Transactions 1
0300-9238 Royal Society of Chemistry. Journal: Faraday Transactions 2
0300-9246 Royal Society of Chemistry. Journal: Dalton Transactions
0300-9254 National Science Council of Sri Lanka. Journal
0300-9262 Bulletin Signaletique: Bibliographie des Sciences de la Terre. Section 220. Mineralogie. Geochimie. Geologie Extraterrestre *changed to* P A S C A L Folio. Part 40: Mineralogie. Geochimie. Geologie Extraterrestre
0300-9270 Bulletin Signaletique: Bibliographie des Sciences de la Terre. Section 221. Cahier B. Gitologie, Economie Miniere *changed to* P A S C A L Folio. Part 41: Gisements Metalliques et Non-Metalliques. Economie Miniere
0300-9289 Bulletin Signaletique: Bibliographie des Sciences de la Terre. Section 222: Roches Cristallines *changed to* P A S C A L Folio. Part 42: Roches Cristallines
0300-9297 Bulletin Signaletique: Bibliographie des Sciences de la Terre. Section 223. Roches Sedimentaires. Geologie Marine *changed to* P A S C A L Folio. Part 43: Roches Sedimentaires. Geologie Marine
0300-9300 Bulletin Signaletique. Bibliographie des Sciences de la Terre. Section 224. Stratigraphie, Geologie, Regionale et Geologie Generale. *changed to* P A S C A L Folio. Part 44: Stratigraphie. Geologie Regionale. Geologie Generale
0300-9319 Bulletin Signaletique-Bibliographie des Sciences de la Terre. Section 225. Tectonique *changed to* P A S C A L Folio. Part 45: Tectonique. Geophysique Interne.
0300-9327 Bulletin Signaletique: Bibliographie des Sciences de la Terre. Section 226: Hydrologie. Geologie de l'Ingenieur. Formations Superficielles *changed to* P A S C A L Folio. Part 46: Hydrologie. Geologie de l'Ingenieur. Formations Superficielles
0300-9335 Bulletin Signaletique: Bibliographie des Sciences de la Terre. Section 227: Paleontologie *changed to* P A S C A L Folio. Part 47: Paleontologie
0300-9351 France. Bureau de Recherches Geologiques et Minieres. Bulletin. Section 2. Geologie Appliquee-Chronique des Mines *changed to* France. Bureau de Recherches Geologiques et Minieres. Agence Francaise pour la Maitrise de l'Energie. Geothermie/Actualities
0300-936X France. Bureau de Recherches Geologiques et Miniere. Bulletin. Section 3: Hydrologie-Geologie de l'Ingenieur *changed to* France. Bureau de Recherches Geologiques et Minieres. Hydrogeologie
0300-9432 Forensic Science *see* 0379-0738
0300-9467 Chemical Engineering Journal
0300-9475 Scandinavian Journal of Immunology
0300-9483 Boreas
0300-9513 Revue Francaise d'Histoire d'Outre-Mer
0300-9556 Paediatrie und Paedologie. Supplement
0300-9564 Journal of Neural Transmission
0300-9572 Resuscitation
0300-9580 Royal Society of Chemistry. Journal: Perkin Transactions 2
0300-9599 Royal Society of Chemistry. Journal: Faraday Transactions 1
0300-9629 Comparative Biochemistry and Physiology. Part A: Comparative Physiology
0300-9637 Biochemistry, General and Molecular *see* 0024-3205
0300-9653 Life Sciences. Part 1: Physiology and Pharmacology *see* 0024-3205
0300-967X Zeitschrift fuer Geburtshilfe und Perinatologie
0300-970X Acta Hepato-Gastroenterologica *see* 0172-6390
0300-9718 Revista de Quimica Textil
0300-9734 Uppsala Journal of Medical Sciences
0300-9742 Scandinavian Journal of Rheumatology
0300-9750 Acta Endocrinologica Congress. Advance Abstracts
0300-9777 Journal of Oral Pathology
0300-9785 International Journal of Oral Surgery *see* 0901-5027
0300-9815 Revue d'Odonto-Stomatologie
0300-9823 O.I.E. Bulletin
0300-9831 Internationale Zeitschrift fuer Vitamin- und Ernaehrungsforschung
0300-984X Archiv fuer Genetik†
0300-9858 Veterinary Pathology
0300-9920 Journal of Tropical Pediatrics and Environmental Child Health *see* 0142-6338
0300-9947 Nursing Bibliography
0300-9963 Selected Annual Reviews of the Analytical Sciences†
0300-9998 International Journal of Chronobiology†
0301-0015 Journal of Physics A-Mathematical, Nuclear and General *see* 0305-4470
0301-0023 Society of Occupational Medicine. Journal
0301-0066 Perception
0301-0074 Organometallic Chemistry
0301-0082 Progress in Neurobiology
0301-0104 Chemical Physics
0301-0112 Abstracts on Police Science *see* 0166-6282
0301-0139 Pigment Cell
0301-0147 Haemostasis
0301-0155 Frontiers of Matrix Biology
0301-0163 Hormone Research
0301-0171 Cytogenetics and Cell Genetics
0301-018X Australasian Nurses Journal†
0301-0244 Polish Journal of Pharmacology and Pharmacy
0301-0260 Presence Croix-Rouge
0301-0279 Revue des Maladies Respiratoires
0301-0287 Psychiatries
0301-0295 Biochimie. Biophysique Moleculaire *changed to* P A S C A L Folio. Part 52: Biochimie. Biophysique Moleculaire. Biologie Moleculaire et Cellulaire
0301-0309 Bulletin Signaletique. Part 101: Sciences de l'Information. Documentation *changed to* P A S C A L Thema. Part 205: Sciences de l'Information. Documentation
0301-0333 Kenya Nursing Journal
0301-035X Bangladesh Medical Journal
0301-0368 Asian Archives of Anaesthesiology and Resuscitation
0301-0376 Modern Medicine of Asia†
0301-0384 Health of the People
0301-0422 Public Health Reviews
0301-0430 Clinical Nephrology
0301-0449 Pediatric Radiology
0301-0457 Behring Institute Mitteilungen
0301-0481 Zeitschrift fuer Hautkrankheiten H und G
0301-049X Food Irradiation Information†
0301-0503 Journal of Maxillofacial Surgery
0301-0511 Biological Psychology
0301-0546 Allergologia et Immunopathologia
0301-0554 Malaysian Journal of Science
0301-0597 Ceskoslovenska Neurologie a Neurochirurgie
0301-0635 Sciences Pharmaceutiques et Biologique de Lorraine†
0301-0643 Epoch (Croydon)
0301-0708 Biosynthesis†
0301-0716 Radiochemistry†
0301-0724 Folia Veterinaria Latina†
0301-0732 South African Veterinary Association. Journal
0301-0740 World Health Organization. World Health Assembly and the Executive Board. Handbook of Resolutions and Decisions. *changed to* World Health Organization. Handbook of Resolutions and Decisions of the World Health Assembly and the Executive Board.
0301-0791 Cahiers de Chirurgie†
0301-0813 F.N.I.B.
0301-0821 Queen's Nursing Journal†
0301-0864 Anaesthesia, Resuscitation and Intensive Therapy†
0301-0902 Aichi Medical University Association. Journal
0301-0996 Goeteborg Psychological Reports
0301-102X John Rylands University Library of Manchester. Bulletin
0301-1208 Indian Journal of Biochemistry and Biophysics
0301-133X Bulletin Signaletique. Part 349: Anesthesie. Reanimation *changed to* P A S C A L Explore. Part 83: Anesthesie et Reanimation
0301-1402 Klassische Homoeopathie
0301-1445 Giornale di Batteriologia, Virologia ed Immunologia ed Annali dell'Ospedale Maria Vittoria di Torino. Parte 2. Sezione Clinica *see* 0390-5454
0301-1453 Giornale di Batteriologia, Virologia ed Immunologia ed Annali dell'Ospedale Maria Vittoria di Torino. Parte 1. Microbiologia *see* 0390-5462
0301-150X Electromyography and Clinical Neurophysiology
0301-1518 La Presse Medicale
0301-1526 Vasa
0301-1569 O R L
0301-1607 Z W R - Zahnaerztliche Welt, Zahnaerztliche Rundschau *see* 0044-166X
0301-1623 International Urology and Nephrology
0301-2115 European Journal of Obstetrics, Gynecology and Reproductive Biology
0301-2123 Acta Biologica Paranaense
0301-2190 Hospital and Health Administration *changed to* Australian Hospital
0301-2204 Gynecologie
0301-2212 Social Behavior and Personality
0301-2255 Anali Klinicke Bolnice "Dr. M. Stojanovic"
0301-228X British Journal of Orthodontics
0301-2328 Microbiology Abstracts. Section C. Algology, Mycology & Protozoology
0301-2425 Biofizika Zhivoi Kletki
0301-2514 Acta Universitatis Palackianae Olomucensis. Facultatis Medicae
0301-2662 Josai Shika Daigaku Kiyo
0301-2689 Berichte ueber Landwirtschaft. Sonderhefte
0301-2719 Gaertnerische Berufspraxis
0301-2727 Advances in Plant Breeding
0301-2735 Advances in Agronomy and Crop Science
0301-2743 Fortschritte in der Tierphysiologie und Tierernaehrung
0301-276X Monumenta Venatoria†
0301-2778 Mammalia Depicta
0301-2794 Advances in Verterinary Medicine
0301-2808 Advances in Ethology
0301-2891 Calendar of Congresses of Medical Sciences
0301-2980 Datenverarbeitung im Recht
0301-2999 Vierteljahresschrift fuer Sozialrecht
0301-3006 Analytische Psychologie
0301-3057 Monographs on Drugs†
0301-3073 Frontiers of Hormone Research
0301-3081 Contributions to Microbiology and Immunology
0301-3154 International Symposium on the Pharmacology of Thermoregulation
0301-3243 Infusionstherapie und Klinische Ernaehrung *see* 0378-0791
0301-326X European Ophthalmological Society. Congress Acta
0301-3294 Zeitschrift fuer germanistische Linguistik
0301-3308 Electrotechnique *changed to* P A S C A L Folio. Part 21: Electrotechnique
0301-3316 Electronique *changed to* P A S C A L Explore. Part 20: Electronique et Telecommunications
0301-3324 Bulletin Signaletique. Part 346: Ophtalmologie *changed to* P A S C A L Explore. Part 71: Ophtalmologie
0301-3332 Bulletin Signaletique. Part 160: Physique de l'Etat Condense *changed to* P A S C A L Explore. Part 12: Etat Condense
0301-3340 Bulletin Signaletique. Part 161. Cristallographie *changed to* P A S C A L Explore. Part 13: Structure des Liquides et des Solides. Cristallographie
0301-3359 Atomes et Molecules. Physiques des Fluides et Plasmas *changed to* P A S C A L Explore. Part 11: Physique Atomique et Moleculaire. Plasmas
0301-3375 Bulletin Signaletique. Part 347: Oto-Rhino-Laryngologie, Stomatologie, Pathologie Cervicofaciale *changed to* P A S C A L Explore. Part 72: Otorhinolaryngologie. Stomatologie. Pathologie Cervicofaciale
0301-3383 Bulletin Signaletique. Part 348: Dermatologie - Venerologie *changed to* P A S C A L Explore. Part 73: Dermatologie. Maladies Sexuellement Transmissibles
0301-3391 Bulletin Signaletique. Part 362: Maladies de l'Appareil Respiratoire du Coeur et des Vaisseaux. Chirurgie Thoracique et Vasculaire *changed to* P A S C A L Explore. Part 74: Pneumologie
0301-3405 Bulletin Signaletique. Part 354: Maladies de l'Appareil Digestif. Chirurgie Abdominale *changed to* P A S C A L Explore. Part 76: Gastroenterologie, Foie, Pancreas, Abdomen
0301-3413 Bulletin Signaletique. Part 355: Maladies des Reins et des Voies Urinaires. Chirurgie *changed to* P A S C A L Explore. Part 77: Nephrologie. Voies Urinaires
0301-3421 Bulletin Signaletique. Part 356: Maladies du Systeme Nerveux Myopathies-Neurochirurgie *changed to* P A S C A L Explore. Part 78: Neurologie
0301-343X Bulletin Signaletique. Part 357: Maladies des Os et des Articulations. Chirurgie Orthopedique. Traumatologie *changed to* P A S C A L Explore. Part 79: Pathologie et Physiologie Osteoarticulaires
0301-3448 Bulletin Signaletique. Part 359: Maladies du Sang *changed to* P A S C A L Explore. Part 80: Hematologie
0301-3456 Bulletin Signaletique. Part 360. Biologie Animale. Physio-Pathologie des Invertebres. Ecologie *changed to* P A S C A L Thema. Part 260: Zoologie Fondamentale et Appliquee des Invertebres (Milieu Terrestre, Eaux Douces)
0301-3464 Bulletin Signaletique. Part 363: Genetique *changed to* P A S C A L Explore. Part 60: Genetique

ISSN INDEX 1517

0301-3472 Bulletin Signaletique. Part 365. Physiologie des Vertebres *changed to* P A S C A L Folio. Part 64: Anatomie et Physiologie des Vertebres
0301-3480 Bulletin Signaletique. Part 745: Soudage, Brasage et Techniques Connexes *changed to* P A S C A L Thema. Part 245: Soudage, Brasage et Techniques Connexes
0301-3499 Bulletin Signaletique. Part 885: Nuisances *changed to* P A S C A L Explore. Part 36: Pollution de l'Eau, de l'Air et du Sol
0301-3537 Bulletin Signaletique. Part 110: Informatique-Automatique-Recherche Operationnelle-Gestion-Economie *changed to* P A S C A L Explore. Part 34: Robotique. Automatique et Automatisation des Processus Industrieis
0301-3693 Nuovo Archivo Italiano di Otologia, Rinologia e Laringologia *changed to* Otorinolaringologica
0301-374X New Techniques in Biophysics and Cell Biology†
0301-3782 Basel Institute for Immunology. Annual Report
0301-3901 Institut d'Hygiene des Mines. Revue†
0301-391X Itogi Nauki i Tekhniki: Genetika Cheloveka
0301-3952 Journal de Biologie Buccale
0301-4150 A G E Current Awareness Series
0301-4169 Asian Geotechnical Engineering Abstracts
0301-4185 Digital Processes†
0301-4193 Contributions to Human Development
0301-4207 Resources Policy
0301-4215 Energy Policy
0301-4223 New Zealand Journal of Zoology
0301-4231 Contributions to Primatology
0301-4347 Zimbabwe. National Archives. Annual Report
0301-4355 Instituto Interamericano de Ciencias Agricolas de la O E A. Documentos Oficiales *changed to* Instituto Interamericano de Cooperacion para la Agricultura - O E A. Documentos Oficiales
0301-438X Inter-American Centre for Agricultural Documentation and Information. Documentacion e Informacion Agricola
0301-4428 Theoretical Linguistics
0301-4436 R & D Projects in Documentation and Librarianship
0301-4444 Annales de Medecine de Reims Champagne- Ardennes†
0301-4460 Annals of Human Biology
0301-4495 Annee Therapeutique et Clinique en Ophtalmologie
0301-4606 Bangladesh Pharmaceutical Journal
0301-4614 Bibliographie der Bibliographien
0301-4622 Biophysical Chemistry
0301-4657 Current Research and Development Projects in Israel: Natural Sciences and Technology†
0301-4665 Deutsche Bibliographie. Hochschulschriften-Verzeichnis
0301-4681 Differentiation
0301-469X Eastern Archives of Ophthalmology
0301-4703 Essays in Fundamental Immunology†
0301-4711 European Journal of Cardiology *see* 0167-5273
0301-472X Experimental Hematology
0301-4738 Indian Journal of Ophthalmology
0301-4746 Industrial Safety Chronicle
0301-4797 Journal of Environmental Management
0301-4800 Journal of Nutritional Science and Vitaminology
0301-4827 Kerala Medical Journal
0301-4835 Die Krankenversicherung
0301-4843 Kupat-Holim Yearbook
0301-4851 Molecular Biology Reports
0301-486X Mycopathologia
0301-5017 Revue Internationale du Trachome et de Pathologie Tropicale et Subtropicale
0301-5068 Egyptian Journal of Pharmaceutical Sciences
0301-5076 United Arab Republic Journal of Pharmaceutical Sciences *see* 0301-5068
0301-5092 Veterinaria Mexico
0301-5106 Who's Who in India (Calcutta)
0301-5149 Developments in Biological Standardization
0301-5165 Chinese National Bibliography
0301-536X Frontiers of Oral Physiology
0301-5521 New Zealand Journal of Experimental Agriculture
0301-5548 European Journal of Applied Physiology and Occupational Physiology
0301-5556 Advances in Anatomy, Embryology and Cell Biology
0301-5564 Histochemistry
0301-5572 British Journal of Sexual Medicine
0301-5599 Major Problems in Anaesthesia
0301-5629 Ultrasound in Medicine & Biology
0301-5645 People
0301-5661 Community Dentistry and Oral Epidemiology
0301-567X Tropische Landwirtschaft und Veterinaermedizin. Beitraege
0301-5696 Faraday Symposia
0301-5718 Update
0301-5769 Schmuck†
0301-5785 Australian Outlook
0301-584X Kongresszentralblatt fuer die Gesamte Innere Medizin. Sektion A: Zentralblatt Praktische Innere Medizin und Grenzgebiete/Internal Medicine *changed to* Zentralblatt Innere Medizin
0301-5912 Biotelemetry *see* 0254-0819
0301-6129 Acta Diurna Historica†
0301-6145 C S I R Publications
0301-620X Journal of Bone and Joint Surgery: British Volume
0301-6226 Livestock Production Science
0301-6242 Petroleum International
0301-6269 Indonesian Indicator *see* 0126-270X
0301-6315 Hannah Research Institute. Report *see* 0266-9021
0301-634X Radiation and Environmental Biophysics
0301-6366 Mensuel du Medecin Acupuncteur
0301-6374 N G M
0301-6404 North-Eastern Affairs
0301-6412 Neurolinguistics
0301-6420 Studia Historica Slavo-Germanica
0301-6528 Rockville International
0301-6536 Building Services Engineer *changed to* Building Services
0301-6587 Anthropologica
0301-6625 Central Bank of Yemen. Annual Report
0301-6722 Universidade Federal do Para. Revista†
0301-679X Tribology International
0301-6811 Zeitschrift fuer Kinder- und Jugendpsychiatrie
0301-6897 Matematicheskie Problemy Geofiziki
0301-6900 Lingvisticheskie Issledovaniya
0301-6919 Voprosy Fiziki Tverdogo Tela
0301-7028 Water Services
0301-7036 Problemas del Desarrollo
0301-7095 Malaysia in Brief
0301-7214 Guitar *changed to* Guitar International
0301-7230 Financas Publicas
0301-7249 Faraday Discussions
0301-7257 Byron Journal
0301-7265 Community Medicine†
0301-7303 Revue Roumaine de Medecine. Serie Neurologie et Psychiatrie
0301-7338 Revista de Igiena, Bacteriologie, Virusologie, Parazitologie, Pneumoftiziologie. Bacteriologie, Virusologie, Parazitologie, Epidemiologie
0301-7362 Istanbul Medical Faculty. Medical Bulletin
0301-7443 Anuario Financiero y de Sociedades Anonimas de Espana
0301-7478 Survey of Construction Activities of the Private Sector in Urban Areas of Iran
0301-7516 International Journal of Mineral Processing
0301-7524 Greater London Council. Housing Facts and Figures†
0301-7559 Financial Statistics of Education in Cyprus†
0301-7567 Guia de Reuniones Cientificas y Tecnicas en la Argentina
0301-7575 Electron Spin Resonance Spectroscopy Abstracts
0301-7605 Critique
0301-7621 Almanak Jakarta
0301-7729 Universidade Federal de Minas Gerais. Faculdade de Medicina. Anais
0301-7737 Annales Universitatis Mariae Curie-Sklodowska. Sectio DD. Medicina Veterinaria
0301-7753 Cameroon Year Book
0301-7761 Daily Mail Year Book
0301-7788 Iter†
0301-7796 Facts and Figures
0301-7818 Argentina. Biblioteca del Congreso. Boletin Legislativo
0301-7850 Magyar Belorovosi Archivum es Ideggyogyaszati Szemle *see* 0133-5464
0301-7877 Finish Digest†
0301-8059 Sociedade Entomologica do Brasil. Anais
0301-8105 South Africa. Department of Statistics. Census of Electricity, Gas and Steam *changed to* South Africa. Central Statistical Service. Census of Electricity, Gas and Steam
0301-8156 Rio Grande do Sul, Brazil. Fundacao de Economia e Estatistica. Indicadores Sociais†
0301-8407 National Dairy Research Institute. Annual Report
0301-8423 Gambia. Produce Marketing Board. Annual Report
0301-8520 Afrique Industrie Infrastructures
0301-861X Contraception-Fertilite-Sexualite
0301-8636 Archives Belges de Dermatologie†
0301-8660 Egyptian Journal of Physiological Science
0301-8695 Animal Behavior Abstracts
0301-8768 Intergeo *see* 0396-5880
0301-8849 Egyptian Journal of Bilharziasis
0301-8881 Let's Square Dance
0301-8938 Fluorocarbon and Related Chemistry†
0301-9004 In
0301-9020 Botswana Handbook
0301-9039 Clean Air Conference (Gt. Brit.)
0301-9047 Democratic World
0301-9055 Democratic Forum
0301-9063 Derecho
0301-908X Finnish Fisheries Research
0301-9101 Ideas
0301-9195 British Pteridological Society. Bulletin
0301-9217 Exports of the Republic of China
0301-9225 Handbuch der Oeffentlichen Bibliotheken
0301-9233 Ironmaking and Steelmaking
0301-9268 Precambrian Research
0301-9322 International Journal of Multiphase Flow
0301-9349 Confederacion General de la Industria. Memoria y Balance General
0301-9780 National Food Research Institute. Report
0302-0231 Japan Map Center News
0302-0282 Nihon No Minken Kyoiku
0302-0479 Kanazawa University. College of Liberal Arts. Annals of Science
0302-0622 Euro Cooperation; Economic Studies on Europe
0302-0665 Bibliotheca Gastroenterologica *changed to* Frontiers of Gastrointestinal Research
0302-0681 South Africa. Official Yearbook of the Republic of South Africa
0302-069X Geological Correlation
0302-072X Journal de Physique - Lettres†
0302-0738 Journal de Physique
0302-0762 Hot Buttered Soul†
0302-0797 Chemical Engineer
0302-0851 National Institute for Research in Dairying. Report†
0302-086X Mauri Ora
0302-1114 Greece. National Statistical Service. Statistics on the Declared Income of Physical Persons and Its Taxation
0302-1122 Anthropines Scheseis
0302-1173 Koinonike Epitheoresis†
0302-1254 Big Beat†
0302-1289 Energy Conservation
0302-1319 Journal of Indian Writing in English
0302-1416 Greece. National Statistical Service. Statistics on the Declared Income of Legal Entities and Its Taxation
0302-1440 Study of Nursing Care: Research Project Series
0302-1475 Sign Language Studies
0302-1599 Himalangue
0302-1610 Indian Journal of Psychiatric Social Work
0302-167X P T A Heute
0302-1688 Origins of Life *changed to* Origins of Life and Evolution of the Biosphere
0302-1742 Crystal Structure Communications
0302-184X Ocean Management
0302-1998 National Children's Bureau. Annual Review
0302-2013 Bank Indonesia. Data Kredit Perbankan†
0302-203X Forest Products Trade Statistics of Indonesia *changed to* Indonesian Statistics on Trade of Forest Products
0302-2048 Schweizerische Gesellschaft fuer Marktforschung. Geschaeftsbericht
0302-2056 National Accounts of Botswana
0302-2129 Industrie Minerale
0302-2137 Medical Biology
0302-217X Universidade Federal do Rio Grande do Sul. Instituto de Filosofia e Ciencias Humanas. Revista†
0302-2196 Internationales Verzeichnis der Wirtschaftsverbaende
0302-2226 Hungary. Kozponti Statisztikai Hivatal. Tudomanyos Kutatas es Feolesztes
0302-2277 Observatorio Astronomico Municipal de Rosario. Boletin
0302-2293 Monographs on Standardization of Cardioangiological Methods
0302-2315 Uniwersytet Gdanski. Wydzial Humanistyczny. Zeszyty Naukowe. Filologia Polska. Prace Jezykoznawcze
0302-2358 Archives Internationales Claude Bernard
0302-2366 Advances in Neurosurgery
0302-2374 Statistical Yearbook of Bangladesh
0302-2404 Postgraduate Institute of Medical Education and Research. Bulletin
0302-2420 Estudios Interdisciplinarios
0302-2439 Universidade de Sao Paulo. Departamento de Botanica. Boletim de Botanica
0302-2447 Budkavlen
0302-2471 Chemical Senses and Flavour *see* 0379-864X
0302-248X Archiv for Pharmaci og Chemi. Scientific Edition
0302-2528 Siemens Zeitschrift
0302-2536 Revue Siemens†
0302-2587 G E C Journal of Science and Technology *see* 0264-9187
0302-2684 Sciences Geologiques - Memoires
0302-2692 Sciences Geologiques. Bulletin
0302-2706 R A D I A L S Bulletin *see* 0263-9254
0302-2773 Applied Neurophysiology
0302-2781 Biosciences Communications *see* 0378-9845
0302-2803 Child's Brain *see* 0256-7040
0302-2811 Mental Health and Society†
0302-282X Neuropsychobiology
0302-2838 European Urology
0302-2846 British Book Design & Production
0302-2870 Pumps and Other Fluids Machinery Abstracts
0302-2927 Annals of Nuclear Science and Engineering *see* 0306-4549
0302-2935 Malaysian Forester
0302-2951 Goeteborg. Stadskontor. Statistiska Meddelanden *see* 0282-0145
0302-3052 Mondes en Developpment

0302-3060 Chancellor College. Journal of Social Science *changed to* Malawi Journal of Social Science
0302-3125 Uniwersytet Gdanski. Wydzial Biologii, i Nauk o Ziemi. Zeszyty Naukowe. Oceanografia
0302-3176 Ayrshire Collections
0302-3184 Baptist Union Directory
0302-3249 Institute of Trading Standards Administration Monthly Review
0302-329X Civil Service Year Book
0302-3338 Human Experimentation & Toxicology Abstracts†
0302-3354 Liquid Scintillation Counting.†
0302-3427 Science and Public Policy
0302-3451 Audiovisual Librarian
0302-3478 Underwater Information Bulletin†
0302-3494 Summary of Postgraduate Diplomas and Courses in Medicine *see* 0265-2730
0302-3524 Estuarine and Coastal Marine Science *see* 0272-7714
0302-4091 Who Owns Whom. Australasia and Far East
0302-4148 Merseyside Chamber of Commerce and Industry. Directory
0302-4172 M I M S Middle East
0302-4180 Paper Review of the Year
0302-4261 East African Journal of Medical Research
0302-427X Annales de Kinesitherapie
0302-4326 Maternidade Dr. Alfredo da Costa, Lisbon. Arquivo Clinico†
0302-4342 Anales Espanoles de Pediatrica
0302-4350 Aktuelle Neurologie
0302-4369 Acta Chemica Scandinavica. Series B: Organic Chemistry and Biochemistry
0302-4377 Acta Chemica Scandinavica. Series A: Physical and Inorganic Chemistry
0302-4466 Acta Dermatovenerologica Iugoslavica
0302-4520 Egyptian Journal of Animal Production
0302-4555 Sugar Technologists' Association of Trinidad and Tobago. Proceedings.
0302-4598 Bioelectrochemistry and Bioenergetics
0302-4601 Aktuelle Literaturinformationen aus dem Obstbau
0302-4717 Rivista di Patologia e Clinica della Tubercolosi e di Pneumologia
0302-4725 Stomatologie der D D R
0302-4814 Universite de Brazzaville. Annales
0302-4822 Mexico. Comision Nacional de los Salarios Minimos. Informe de Labores
0302-4881 Rajasthan State Tanneries Limited. Annual Report
0302-4946 Landbrugsaarbog
0302-5004 Mexico. Secretaria del Trabajo y Prevision Social. Subdireccion de Documentacion. Resena Laboral
0302-5047 Zambia. Meteorological Department. Totals of Monthly and Annual Rainfall
0302-5063 Quarto Potere
0302-508X N C E R T Newsletter
0302-5128 Sleep†
0302-5144 Contributions to Nephrology
0302-5160 Historiographia Linguistica
0302-5195 Precos Pagos Pelos Agricultores
0302-5233 Ecuador. Instituto Nacional de Estadistica y Censos. Encuesta Anual de Manufactura y Mineria†
0302-5268 Investigacion e Informacion Textil y de Tensioactivos
0302-5349 Dansk Maskinhandlerforening. Handbog
0302-5403 Kongeriget Danmarks Handels-Kalender
0302-542X Itogi Nauki i Tekhniki: Mestorozhdeniya Goryuchikh Poleznykh Iskopaemykh
0302-5489 We Represent in Israel and Abroad.
0302-5608 Germany (Federal Republic, 1949-). Bundesaufsichtsamt fuer das Versicherungswesen. Geschaeftsbericht
0302-5640 Cultures au Zaire et en Afrique
0302-5691 Antartida
0302-5705 Argentina. Servicio Nacional de Parques Nacional. Anales
0302-5756 L E M I T. Anales†
0302-5802 Timber Trade Review
0302-6248 Karka
0302-6256 Vedere-International
0302-6329 Arbeitskreis Zweiter Weltkrieg. Bulletin
0302-6477 Galvano-Organo *changed to* Galvano-Organo-Traitements de Surface
0302-6574 Review of Economics and Business
0302-6604 Management in Enterprises and Management Education in Universities
0302-6620 States of Malaya Chamber of Mines. Council Report
0302-6655 Revista Juridica Panamena†
0302-6671 Management Heute und Marktwirtschaft
0302-668X Management Heute *see* 0302-6671
0302-6701 Egyptian Journal of Soil Science
0302-671X Bonner Zoologische Monographien
0302-6736 Makerere Institute of Social Research. Research Abstracts and Newsletter†
0302-6744 Indian Records
0302-6795 Bank Ekspor Impor Indonesia. Annual Report/Laporan Tahunan
0302-6809 Barclays National Review *see* 0250-2402
0302-6957 Anales de Ciencias Humanas
0302-6965 Anuario del Arte Espanol
0302-6973 National Debate
0302-6981 Yuva Bharati
0302-7104 Agroanimalia†
0302-7112 Agrochemophysica†
0302-7120 Phytophylactica
0302-7139 Agroplantae†
0302-7368 Magyar Tudomanyos Akademia. Acta Alimentaria *see* 0139-3006
0302-7384 Symbolae Philologorum Posnaniensium
0302-7406 Instituto Antituberculoso Francisco Moragas. Publicaciones
0302-7481 University of the North. Department of Bantu Languages. Communications
0302-7503 Deutsche Wochen-Zeitung
0302-752X Folclorica
0302-7546 I C S S R Journal of Abstracts and Reviews *changed to* I C S S R Journal of Abstracts and Reviews: Sociology & Social Anthropology
0302-7554 Indian Biologist
0302-7562 Indian Journal of Zoology
0302-7600 Praktische Anaesthesie *see* 0174-1837
0302-7651 C I S Abstracts
0302-766X Cell and Tissue Research
0302-7678 Chemical Industry Developments
0302-7724 Cuadernos de Realidades Sociales
0302-7775 Ingegneria Ambientale Inquinamento e Depurazione
0302-7902 World Transport Data
0302-8003 Revista E A C
0302-8070 Balneologia Bohemica
0302-8127 Immanuel
0302-8143 Adrikhalut *changed to* A-A
0302-8178 Bay Zikh
0302-8186 Folk, Velt un Medine
0302-8194 Biaf - Israel Aviation and Space Magazine
0302-8267 Israel. Ministry of the Interior. City and Region
0302-833X Mejeribrugets Uge-Nyt
0302-8429 Academie des Sciences. Comptes Rendus Hebdomadaires des Seances. Serie A. Sciences Mathematiques *see* 0151-0509
0302-8437 Academie des Sciences. Comptes Rendus Hebdomadaires des Seances. Serie B. Sciences Physiques *see* 0151-0509
0302-847X Muzykal'noe Vospitanie v Shkole
0302-8585 Uniwersytet Jagiellonski. Zeszyty Naukowe. Prace Botaniczne
0302-8755 Spain. Instituto Nacional de Investigaciones Agrarias. Comunicaciones. Serie: Proteccion Vegetal
0302-8844 Addab Journal
0302-8852 Revisor
0302-8933 Archives of Microbiology
0302-8984 Psychotherapie und Medizinische Psychologie *see* 0173-7937
0302-9069 Liteinoe Proizvodstvo, Metallovedenie i Obrabotka Metallov Davleniem
0302-9085 Issledovania po Teorii Algorifmov i Matematicheskoi Logike
0302-9263 Mediterranee Medicale
0302-9336 Jamaica. Department of Statistics. Consumer Price Indices *changed to* Statistical Institute of Jamaica. Consumer Price Indices
0302-9379 Laryngologie, Rhinologie, Otologie und ihre Grenzgebiete *changed to* Laryngologie, Rhinologie, Otologie
0302-9417 Tropische und Subtropische Pflanzenwelt
0302-9468 B G S
0302-9530 Archives of Oto-Rhino-Laryngology
0302-9611 Banco de la Republica. Registros de Exportacion e Importacion†
0302-9697 Etesia Statistike. Erevna tou Karkinou
0302-9743 Lecture Notes in Computer Science
0302-9794 Novum Gebrauchsgraphik
0302-9840 Vincent†
0303-111X Sovetskie Ljudi Segodnja
0303-1179 Asterisque
0303-1187 Institut Henri Poincare and Societe Mathematique de France. Circulaire d'Informations†
0303-1241 Betriebs- und Marktwirtschaft im Gartenbau
0303-125X One World
0303-1268 Euromicro Journal *see* 0165-6074
0303-1276 Bulletin de Liaison de la Recherche en Informatique et Automatique
0303-1705 Portugal. Instituto Nacional de Estatistica. Delegacao do Funchal. Boletim Trimestral de Estatistica - Arquipelago de Madeira *changed to* Madeira. Servico Regional de Estatistica. Boletim Trimestral de Estatistica
0303-1829 Centro Latinoamericano de Demografia. Notas de Poblacion
0303-190X Philippine National Bibliography
0303-1969 Data-Data Iklim di Indonesia
0303-2019 Muszaki Lapszemle. Hiradastechnika/ Technical Abstracts. Telecommunication *see* 0231-066X
0303-2221 C S S R. Kronika Vnitropolitickych Udalosti
0303-223X Bilten Dokumentacije. Savremena Organizacaija i Ekonomija Radnih Organizacija *see* 0351-4048
0303-2361 Itogi Nauki i Tekhniki: Tekhnologiya Organicheskikh Veshchestv†
0303-240X Revue de l'Energie
0303-2434 I T C Journal
0303-2485 Kuukausikatsaus Suomen Ilmastoon
0303-2493 Informationen zur Raumentwicklung
0303-2515 South African Museum. Annals
0303-2582 Indian Journal of Clinical Psychology
0303-2590 Roentgen Technology
0303-2647 Biosystems
0303-2728 Ahram Index
0303-2876 Majalah B A T A N
0303-2884 Berita Hasil Hutan *changed to* Forestry in Indonesia
0303-2906 Prayasa
0303-2949 Gunakesari†
0303-3007 International Journal of Korean Studies
0303-3074 Sarvotkrushta Marathi Katha
0303-3171 Man and Society
0303-321X Sangkakala Peradilan
0303-3309 I S O Catalogue
0303-3317 I S O Annual Review†
0303-3848 Brass Bulletin
0303-3856 Revolutionary World†
0303-3899 Educational Documentation and Information/Documentation et Information Pedagogiques *changed to* International Bureau of Education. Bulletin
0303-3902 Interface
0303-3910 Irish Journal of Psychology
0303-3929 Mathematical Programming Studies
0303-3937 Orbis Musicae
0303-4011 Plasticos Universales
0303-402X Colloid and Polymer Science
0303-4097 Indian Journal of Mycology and Plant Pathology
0303-4100 Finnish Chemical Letters
0303-4135 Academiae Medicae Gedanensis. Annales
0303-4151 International Commission for the Northwest Atlantic Fisheries. Annual Report *see* 0704-4798
0303-4178 Poetica
0303-4208 Tropenmedizin und Parasitologie *see* 0177-2392
0303-4216 Topics in Applied Physics
0303-4240 Reviews of Physiology, Biochemistry and Experimental Pharmacology
0303-4259 Psychiatrische Praxis
0303-4283 Leben und Umwelt
0303-4305 Innere Medizin
0303-4461 Oesterreichische Krankenpflegezeitschrift
0303-4534 Zeitschrift fuer Geologische Wissenschaften
0303-4550 Bulletin of Reprints†
0303-4569 Andrologia
0303-4577 I M B I S
0303-4879 Economic Titles/Abstracts
0303-4992 Indonesia. Lembaga Pertahanan Nasional. Ketahanan Nasional
0303-5220 Reproduccion†
0303-5344 Hungary. Kozponti Statisztikai Hivatal. Teruleti Statisztikai Evkonyv
0303-5395 Uttar Pradesh
0303-5476 Chiba Medical Journal
0303-5980 Studia Leibnitiana. Supplementa
0303-5999 Bibliographie der Deutschsprachigen Psychologischen Literatur
0303-6200 Intensivmedizinische Praxis†
0303-6251 Intensivmedizin *see* 0175-3851
0303-6448 Statistical Yearbook of the Netherlands
0303-6510 Sweden. Sjukvaardens och Socialvaardens Planerings- och Rationaliseringsinstitut. S P R I Raad 5
0303-6529 Sweden. Sjukvaardens och Socialvaardens Planerings- och Rationaliseringsinstitut. S P R I Raad 6
0303-6537 Sweden. Sjukvaardens och Socialvaardens Planerings- och Rationaliseringsinstitut. S P R I Raad 7
0303-6545 Sweden. Sjukvaardens och Socialvaardens Planerings-och Rationaliseringsinstitut. S P R I Raad 4
0303-6553 Sweden. Sjukvaardens och Socialvaardens Planerings-och Rationaliseringsinstitut. S P R I Raad 1.
0303-6634 Geography of World Agriculture
0303-6758 Royal Society of New Zealand. Journal
0303-6812 Journal of Mathematical Biology
0303-6847 Blood Vessels
0303-6898 Scandinavian Journal of Statistics
0303-691X West African Journal of Pharmacology and Drug Research
0303-6936 Hydrological Sciences Bulletin *see* 0262-6667
0303-6979 Journal of Clinical Periodontology
0303-6987 Journal of Cutaneous Pathology
0303-6995 Journal of Neural Transmission. Supplement
0303-7002 Kerrygold International†
0303-7169 Singapore Bulletin
0303-7207 Molecular and Cellular Endocrinology
0303-7339 Tijdschrift voor Psychiatrie
0303-7479 Groupement International Pour la Recherche en Stomatologie et Odontologie. Bulletin
0303-7584 Instituto de Tonantzintla. Boletin *changed to* Instituto Nacional de Astrofisica, Optica y Electronica. Boletin
0303-7657 Revista Brasileira de Saude Ocupacional
0303-7762 Instituto de Higiene e Medicina Tropical. Anais
0303-7819 Encyclopaedia Judaica Year Book
0303-7932 Majalah Kedokteran Surabaya
0303-7940 Archifacts
0303-805X I S O Bulletin
0303-8106 Audiology Japan
0303-8122 Science Society of Thailand. Journal

0303-8157 Poznan Studies in the Philosophy of the Sciences and the Humanities
0303-8173 Acta Medica Austriaca
0303-8246 Southeast Asian Journal of Social Sciences
0303-8300 Social Indicators Research
0303-8432 Folia Allergologica et Immunologica Clinica
0303-8459 Excerpta Medica. Section 50: Epilepsy
0303-8467 Clinical Neurology and Neurosurgery
0303-853X Economic Survey of Liberia
0303-8688 Belize Institute of Social Research and Action. National Studies *changed to* Belizean Studies
0303-8874 Anales Otorrinolaringologicos Ibero-Americanos
0303-8971 Institut Economique Agricole. Cahiers†
0303-9021 Vlaams Diergeneeskundig Tijdschrift
0303-903X Belgium. Rijksstation voor Sierplantenteelt. Mededelingen
0303-9056 Belgium. Rijksstation voor Landbouwtechniek. Mededelingen
0303-9072 Belgium. Rijksstation voor Zeevisserij. Mededelingen
0303-9099 Annales de Gembloux
0303-9102 Rijksuniversiteit te Gent. Mededelingen van de Fakulteit Diergeneeskunde†
0303-9145 Institut Royal Belge pour l'Amelioration de la Betterave. Publication Trimestrielle
0303-9153 Jardin Botanique National de Belgique. Bulletin
0303-9382 M E R A D O News
0303-9676 Estudios Sociales Centroamericanos
0303-9889 Revista de Estudios Sociales
0303-9919 Anales de Economia
0303-9927 Spain. Ministerio de Justicia. Secretaria General Tecnica. Informacion Juridica *see* 0210-3419
0303-9951 Indian Journal of Politics
0304-0003 L I A S; Sources and Documents Relating to the Early Modern History of Ideas.
0304-0062 U N I S I S T Boletin de Informacion
0304-0089 Yearbook of World Problems and Human Potential
0304-0100 I I C A en America†
0304-0119 Indice Agricola de America Latina y el Caribe†
0304-0313 Patologia e Clinica Ostetrica e Ginecologica
0304-0550 Istituto Sperimentale per la Floricoltura. Annali
0304-0593 Rivista di Ingegneria Agraria
0304-0658 Laboratorio di Entomologia Agraria. Bollettino
0304-0704 Planeur
0304-0712 Amsterdam Studies in the Theory and History of Linguistic Science. Series 1: Amsterdam Classics in Linguistics, 1800-1925
0304-0720 Amsterdam Studies In the Theory and History of the Linguistic Science. Series 3: Studies In the History of Linguistics *changed to* Amsterdam Studies in the Theory and History of Linguistic Science. Series 3: Studies in the History of the Language Sciences
0304-0763 Amsterdam Studies in the Theory and History of Linguistic Science. Series 4: Current Issues in Linguistic Theory
0304-078X Cultures†
0304-0798 Natal Museum. Annals
0304-0941 Decision
0304-095X Bangladesh Development Studies
0304-100X Services Law Cases
0304-1042 Japanese Journal of Religious Studies
0304-1131 Agriculture and Environment *changed to* Agriculture, Ecosystems and Environment
0304-1158 Indian School of Mines. Annual Report
0304-1166 Chemical India Annual
0304-1190 Ghana
0304-1204 Free China Today†
0304-1263 Iceland Review
0304-1298 Bulletin Signaletique. Part 161: Structure de l'Etat Condense. Cristallographie *changed to* P A S C A L Explore. Part 13: Structure des Liquides et des Solides. Cristallographie
0304-1301 Bulletin Signaletique: Bibliographie des Sciences de la Terre. Section 221. Gisements Metalliques et Non Metalliques *changed to* P A S C A L Folio. Part 41: Gisements Metalliques et Non-Metalliques. Economie Miniere
0304-131X Acta Pathologica et Microbiologica Scandinavica. Section B: Microbiology *see* 0108-0180
0304-1328 Acta Pathologica et Microbiologica Scandinavica. Section C: Immunology *see* 0108-0202
0304-1409 Atheist
0304-162X Times of India. Index
0304-1646 Industry and Society *see* 0007-5116
0304-1735 New Zealand. Soil Bureau. Scientific Report
0304-1743 Norwegian Maritime Research
0304-176X Planning and Administration
0304-1786 Prospect†
0304-2138 Fundacao Servicos de Saude Publica. Revista
0304-2146 Japanese Journal of Tropical Medicine and Hygiene
0304-2154 Akademie der Wissenschaften der DDR. Jahrbuch
0304-2162 Mois Economique et Financier
0304-2170 Indonesian Quarterly
0304-2251 Royal Asiatic Society. Malaysian Branch. Journal
0304-2286 University of Bombay. Journal
0304-2308 Pesquisa e Planejamento *see* 0100-0551
0304-2421 Theory and Society
0304-243X Trabalhos de Antropologia e Etnologia
0304-2499 Tecnica Pesquera
0304-2502 Pastizales
0304-2529 Actividades en Turrialba
0304-2553 Bangladesh Economic Review *see* 0304-095X
0304-2634 Boletin de Estudios Latinoamericanos y del Caribe
0304-2685 Ciencia & Tropico
0304-2839 Documentacion e Informacion para el Desarrollo Agricola†
0304-2847 Facultad Nacional de Agronomia Medellin
0304-2863 Colloquium Internationale†
0304-2871 European Organization for Nuclear Research. Liste des Publications Scientifiques/List of Scientific Publications
0304-288X C E R N Courier
0304-2898 C E R N School of Computing. Proceedings
0304-2901 C E R N Annual Report
0304-324X Gerontology
0304-3282 Organization for Economic Cooperation and Development. Guide to Legislation on Restrictive Business Practices. Supplements
0304-3312 Organization for Economic Cooperation and Development. Labour Statistics/ Statistiques de la Population Active *see* 0255-3627
0304-3320 Research on Transport Economics/ Recherche en Matiere d'Economie des Transports
0304-3371 O E C D Financial Statistics
0304-341X Nuclear Law Bulletin
0304-3460 Goodwin Series. Occasional Papers
0304-3479 Russian Literature
0304-3487 Russian Linguistics
0304-3568 Experimental Cell Biology
0304-3584 Actualidades Biologicas
0304-3606 Irrinews
0304-3622 International Association for Shell and Spatial Structures. Bulletin
0304-3681 Extern†
0304-3703 Vinculos
0304-3711 Brenesia
0304-3738 Organization for Economic Cooperation and Development. Quarterly National Accounts Bulletin/Bulletin des Comptes Nationaux Trimestriels
0304-3746 Agro-Ecosystems
0304-3754 Alternatives
0304-3762 Applied Animal Ethology *changed to* Applied Animal Behaviour Science
0304-3770 Aquatic Botany
0304-3797 European Journal of Engineering Education
0304-3800 Ecological Modelling
0304-3835 Cancer Letters
0304-3843 Hyperfine Interactions
0304-3851 Journal of Applied Science and Engineering Section A. Electrical Power and Information Systems†
0304-386X Hydrometallurgy
0304-3878 Journal of Development Economics
0304-3886 Journal of Electrostatics
0304-3894 Journal of Hazardous Materials
0304-3908 Journal of Industrial Aerodynamics *see* 0167-6105
0304-3924 Landscape Planning
0304-3932 Journal of Monetary Economics
0304-3940 Neuroscience Letters
0304-3959 Pain
0304-3967 Resource Recovery and Conservation *see* 0166-3097
0304-3975 Theoretical Computer Science
0304-3991 Ultramicroscopy
0304-4009 Urban Ecology
0304-4017 Veterinary Parasitology
0304-4025 Wave Electronics†
0304-4033 Revista Centroamericana de Nutricion y Ciencias de Alimentos†
0304-4041 Excerpta Medica. Section 40: Drug Dependence
0304-405X Journal of Financial Economics
0304-4068 Journal of Mathematical Economics
0304-4076 Journal of Econometrics
0304-4084 Excerpta Medica. Section 47: Virology
0304-4092 Dialectical Anthropology
0304-4114 Mass Emergencies†
0304-4130 European Journal of Political Research
0304-4149 Stochastic Processes and Their Applications
0304-4157 B B A - Reviews on Biomembranes
0304-4165 B B A - General Subjects
0304-4173 B B A Reviews on Bioenergetics
0304-4181 Journal of Medieval History
0304-419X B B A - Reviews on Cancer
0304-4203 Marine Chemistry
0304-4211 Plant Science Letters *see* 0168-9452
0304-422X Poetics
0304-4238 Scientia Horticulturae
0304-4246 Contributions to Gynecology and Obstetrics
0304-4254 Pediatric and Adolescent Endocrinology
0304-4262 Progress in Reproductive Biology *see* 0254-105X
0304-4270 INSEAD Address Book
0304-4289 Pramana
0304-4297 European Research
0304-4319 Anuario de Historia del Derecho Espanol
0304-4556 Iranian Journal of Public Health
0304-4602 Academy of Medicine, Singapore. Annals
0304-4815 Revista Espanola de Reumatologia
0304-4858 Gaceta Medica de Bilbao
0304-5013 Progresos de Obstetricia y Ginecologia
0304-5056 Revista Espanola de Cirugia Osteoarticular
0304-5102 Journal of Molecular Catalysis
0304-5188 Institutul Politehnic Iasi. Buletinul. Sectia I: Matematica, Mecanica Teoretica, Fizica.
0304-5242 Journal of Plantation Crops
0304-5250 Indian Journal of Ecology
0304-5293 Academia Sinica. Institute of Physics. Annual Report
0304-5307 National Museums and Monuments of Rhodesia. Occasional Papers. Series A: Human Sciences. *changed to* National Museums and Monuments Administration. Occasional Papers. Series A: Human Sciences
0304-5315 National Museums and Monuments of Rhodesia. Occasional Papers. Series B: Natural Sciences *see* 0250-300X
0304-5323 Museum Memoir†
0304-534X I N S D O C. Russian Scientific and Technical Publications. Accessions List
0304-5358 Contents List of Soviet Scientific Periodicals
0304-5374 Comparative Animal Nutrition
0304-5439 C I M M Y T Report on Wheat Improvement†
0304-5447 C I M M Y T Today†
0304-5463 C I M M Y T Review†
0304-548X C I M M Y T Report on Maize Improvement†
0304-551X C I M M Y T Information Bulletin†
0304-5579 Investigacion y Progreso Agricola *changed to* Investigacion y Progreso Agropecuario. La Platina
0304-5609 Ciencia e Investigacion Agraria
0304-5617 Investigacion Agricola†
0304-5692 Zaire. Institut National de la Statistique. Annuaire des Statistiques du Commerce Exterieur†
0304-5714 Institut Oceanographique. Memoires
0304-5722 Institut Oceanographique. Bulletin
0304-5757 Conjonction
0304-5765 Tropical Grain Legume Bulletin
0304-582X F A O Documentation-Current Bibliography
0304-5935 Abstracts of Geochronology and Isotope Geology†
0304-5951 Abstracts on Tropical Agriculture
0304-5978 G E R V Activiteitsverslag†
0304-6125 Afghanistan Journal†
0304-6133 Afghanistan Republic Annual
0304-615X Africanus
0304-6184 Madhya Pradesh. Directorate of Agriculture. Agricultural Statistics
0304-6214 A I I S Quarterly Newsletter
0304-6257 Amsterdamer Beitraege zur Neueren Germanistik
0304-6451 Association of Urban Authorities. Annual Bulletin
0304-6729 Arab Fund for Economic and Social Development. Annual Report
0304-6796 Central Bank of Barbados. Annual Report
0304-6818 Central Sericultural Research and Training Institute. Annual Report
0304-6907 Cotton Corporation of India. Annual Report
0304-6966 Deposit Insurance Corporation. Annual Report: Directors' Report, Balance Sheet and Accounts
0304-7032 Indian Council of Historical Research. Annual Report
0304-7067 Indian Veterinary Research Institute. Annual Report
0304-7083 Institute of Secretariat Training and Management. Annual Report
0304-7091 International Centre for Theoretical Physics. Annual Report
0304-7164 Jammu & Kashmir Minerals Limited. Annual Report
0304-7245 Madhya Pradesh State Agro-Industries Development Corporation Ltd. Annual Report
0304-727X Liberia. Ministry of Finance. Annual Report
0304-7296 Liberia. Ministry of Lands and Mines. Annual Report *changed to* Liberia. Ministry of Lands, Mines and Energy. Annual Report
0304-730X Liberia. Ministry of Local Government, Rural Development & Urban Reconstruction. Annual Report
0304-7326 Liberia. Ministry of Public Works. Annual Report
0304-7350 Singapore. National Statistical Commission. Annual Report†
0304-7423 Israel Oceanographic and Limnological Research. Biennial Report
0304-7628 Focus on Rhodesia

1520 ISSN INDEX

0304-8101 Punjab National Bank. Annual Report
0304-8152 Salar Jung Museum. Annual Report
0304-8179 Shellac Export Promotion Council. Annual Report
0304-8349 United Planting Association of Malaysia. Annual Report
0304-8594 Architects Trade Journal
0304-8608 Archives of Virology
0304-8616 Archivos de Farmacologia y Toxicologia
0304-8624 Armenian Studies
0304-8632 Art Spectrum *see* 0004-3230
0304-8675 Asian Profile
0304-8683 Asiryada
0304-8705 Astronautical Research†
0304-8713 Austria Today
0304-8721 Automobil
0304-8845 P T L†
0304-8853 Journal of Magnetism and Magnetic Materials
0304-8942 Food and Nutrition
0304-9191 Spain. Direccion General de Trafico. Anuario Estadistico General.
0304-9272 Brahmana-Gaurava
0304-9523 Astronomical Society of India. Bulletin
0304-9558 Indian Institute of History of Medicine. Bulletin (New Delhi)
0304-9566 Osmania Medical College. Institute of History of Medicine. Bulletin *see* 0304-9558
0304-9620 Societe des Naturalistes Luxembourgeois. Bulletin
0304-968X Buy from India
0304-9701 International Forum on Information and Documentation
0304-971X Revista de Biologia del Uruguay
0304-9841 C S I O Communications
0304-985X Delft Progress Report
0304-9884 Indian Journal of Engineering Mathematics
0305-0009 Journal of Child Language
0305-0017 Geocom Programs *see* 0098-3004
0305-0033 Aslib Information
0305-0041 Cambridge Philosophical Society. Mathematical Proceedings.
0305-005X Emergency Post
0305-0068 Comparative Education
0305-0076 Review of Applied Entomology. Series A: Agricultural
0305-0084 Review of Applied Entomology. Series B: Medical and Veterinary
0305-0122 Bulk Carrier Register
0305-0130 Local Government Companion
0305-0165 Current Clinical Chemistry
0305-0270 Journal of Biogeography
0305-0297 Labour Leader†
0305-0319 Cosmetic World News
0305-0351 C I P Descriptions of Plant-Parasitic Nematodes
0305-036X Arabian Studies
0305-0424 News from Victoria (Australia) *changed to* Economic Review
0305-0440 Historical Breechloading Smallarms Association. Journal
0305-0467 Freezer Foods†
0305-0483 Omega (Elmsford)
0305-0491 Comparative Biochemistry and Physiology. Part B: Comparative Biochemistry
0305-0513 Offshore Abstracts
0305-0548 Computers & Operations Research
0305-0629 International Interactions
0305-0637 Classified World
0305-0653 Work Study & O and M Abstracts
0305-0661 Marketing & Distribution Abstracts
0305-067X Personnel & Training Abstracts
0305-0718 Commonwealth Law Bulletin
0305-0734 The Middle East
0305-0777 Refrigeration and Air Conditioning Year Book
0305-0785 Scottish Literary Journal
0305-0904 Thomas Cook News *changed to* Internationally Speaking
0305-0920 Appropriate Technology
0305-0963 Radical Science Journal *see* 0950-5431
0305-0998 Norwegian Chamber of Commerce. Year Book and Directory of Members
0305-103X Urban Abstracts *changed to* Urban Abstracts
0305-1048 Nucleic Acids Research
0305-1129 Stock Exchange, London. Members and Firms of the Stock Exchange
0305-1277 National Institute of Agricultural Botany, Cambridge, England. Farmers Leaflets
0305-1471 N M M News†
0305-1498 Oxford Literary Review *changed to* Oxford Literary Review: A Post-Structuralist Journal
0305-1536 Home and School
0305-1668 Systems International
0305-1706 Film Dope
0305-1781 C I R I A Technical Note
0305-179X Tanker Register
0305-1803 Liquid Gas Carrier Register
0305-1811 Journal of Immunogenetics
0305-182X Journal of Oral Rehabilitation
0305-1838 Mammal Review
0305-1846 Neuropathology and Applied Neurobiology
0305-1862 Child: Care, Health and Development
0305-1870 Clinical and Experimental Pharmacology and Physiology
0305-1897 Geo Abstracts A (Landforms and the Quaternary) *see* 0268-7879
0305-1900 Geo Abstracts B (Climatology and Hydrology) *see* 0268-7887
0305-1919 Geo Abstracts C (Economic Geography) *see* 0268-7895
0305-1927 Geo Abstracts D (Social and Historical Geography) *see* 0268-7909
0305-1935 Geo Abstracts E (Sedimentology) *see* 0268-7917
0305-1943 Geo Abstracts F (Regional and Community Planning) *see* 0268-7925
0305-1951 Geo Abstracts G (Remote Sensing Photogrammetry and Cartogrpaphy) *see* 0268-7933
0305-196X Ecological Abstracts
0305-1978 Biochemical Systematics and Ecology
0305-2001 Royal Observatory, Edinburgh. Publications†
0305-2044 Association of County Councils. Yearbook
0305-2109 Communications International
0305-215X Engineering Optimization
0305-2176 I C E Abstracts *see* 0332-4095
0305-2230 Incentive Marketing and Sales Promotion *see* 0266-7991
0305-2249 Audio Visual
0305-2257 National Electronics Review
0305-2303 South East Hampshire Geneaological Society. Journal *see* 0306-6843
0305-2346 Institute of Physics, London. Conference Series. Proceedings
0305-2524 Commonwealth Bureau of Soils. Annotated Bibliographies *changed to* C.A.B. International Bureau of Soils. Annotated Bibliographies
0305-2680 Descriptions of Plant Viruses
0305-3040 Applied Ecology Abstracts *see* 0143-3296
0305-3091 Electrocomponent Science & Technology†
0305-3105 Water *see* 0262-9909
0305-3121 Machinery Buyers' Guide
0305-3199 Adhesives Directory
0305-3210 Middle East Review
0305-3253 Higher Education Exchange *changed to* Educational International
0305-3342 Medical Directory
0305-3504 Mintel *changed to* Market Intelligence
0305-3555 Fabian Research Series
0305-3601 Communication & Broadcasting
0305-3679 Essex Union List of Serials
0305-3695 Corporate Planning Journal *changed to* Local Government Policy Making
0305-3709 Bulk: Storage, Movement, Control *changed to* Bulk Handling: Storage, Movement, Control
0305-3717 Zambezi Press International
0305-3849 Par Golf
0305-3873 Surface and Defect Properties of Solids *see* 0142-3401
0305-4012 Stores, Shops, Hypermarkets Retail Directory *changed to* Retail Directory
0305-4039 Bale Catalogue of Palestine and Israel Stamps *changed to* Bale Catalogue of Israel Postage Stamps
0305-4047 C I R I A Annual Report
0305-408X C I R I A Report
0305-411X Council of Legal Education. Calendar
0305-4136 Hospital Update
0305-4179 Burns
0305-4233 Communication
0305-4284 Offshore Drilling Register†
0305-4322 Ditchley Journal *see* 0262-8015
0305-4349 Druglink
0305-439X Processing
0305-4403 Journal of Archaeological Science
0305-4438 Music and Liturgy
0305-4470 Journal of Physics A: Mathematical and General
0305-4543 Spon's Mechanical & Electrical Services Price Book
0305-4608 Journal of Physics F: Metal Physics
0305-4616 Journal of Physics G: Nuclear Physics
0305-4624 Physics in Technology
0305-4659 Northamptonshire Archaeology
0305-4756 Camden History Review
0305-4829 Heat Treatment of Metals
0305-4934 Ornamental Horticulture
0305-4985 Oxford Review of Education
0305-5000 Dental Update
0305-5167 British Library Journal
0305-5183 British Library. Lending Division. Index of Conference Proceedings Recieved *changed to* British Library. Document Supply Centre. Index of Conference Proceedings Received
0305-5280 Current Archaeological Offprints and Reports *changed to* British Archaeological News
0305-5426 Programming Index†
0305-5574 University of Strathclyde. Annual Report
0305-5620 Framework Forecasts for the United Kingdom
0305-5698 Educational Studies
0305-5728 Vine
0305-5752 Property Studies in the U.K. and Overseas
0305-5795 Devon Archaeological Society. Proceedings
0305-5892 Register of Thoroughbred Stallions†
0305-5914 Geographical Papers
0305-5973 B S R I A Application Guides
0305-5981 Omnibus
0305-6104 Independent Broadcasting†
0305-6139 British Society for Middle Eastern Studies. Bulletin
0305-6147 Radical Education
0305-6155 R. U. S. I. and Brassey's Defence Yearbook†
0305-6198 Saturated Heterocyclic Chemistry†
0305-6244 Review of African Political Economy
0305-6252 Minority Rights Group. Reports
0305-635X Office Equipment Index
0305-6473 Civil Engineering
0305-6481 I R C S Journal of Medical Science†
0305-649X I R C S Medical Science: Classified List†
0305-6503 B L L Review *see* 0264-1615
0305-652X Pick
0305-6562 Scotlands Regions
0305-6589 Laxton's Building Price Book *changed to* Laxton's National Building Price Book
0305-6651 I R C S Medicai Science: Library Compendium *changed to* I R C S Medical Science: Full Edition
0305-666X I R C S Medical Science: Immunology and Allergy†
0305-6678 I R C S Medical Science: Alimentary System *changed to* I R C S Medical Science: Gastroenterology
0305-6686 I R C S Medical Science: Anatomy and Human Biology†
0305-6694 I R C S Medical Science: Anesthetics†
0305-6708 I R C S Medical Science: Biochemistry†
0305-6716 I R C S Medical Science: Biomedical Technology†
0305-6724 I R C S Medical Science: Cancer†
0305-6732 I R C S Medical Science: Cardiovascular System†
0305-6740 I R C S Medical Science: Cell and Membrane Biology *changed to* I R C S Medical Science: Cell and Molecular Biology
0305-6759 I R C S Medical Science: Clinical Pharmacology and Therapeutics†
0305-6767 I R C S Medical Science: Connective Tissue, Skin and Bone†
0305-6775 I R C S Medical Science: Dentistry and Oral Biology†
0305-6783 I R C S Medical Science: Endocrine System†
0305-6791 I R C S Medical Science: The Eye *changed to* I R C S Medical Science: The Eye and Visual System
0305-6805 I R C S Medical Science: Hematology†
0305-6813 I R C S Medical Science: Kidneys and Urinary System *changed to* I R C S Medical Science: Nephrology and Urology
0305-6821 I R C S Medical Science: Metabolism and Nutrition†
0305-683X I R C S Medical Science: Microbiology, Parasitology and Infectious Diseases†
0305-6848 I R C S Medical Science: Neurobiology and Neurophysiology†
0305-6856 I R C S Medical Science: Neurology and Neurosurgery†
0305-6864 I R C S Medical Science: Pediatrics†
0305-6872 I R C S Medical Science: Pharmacology†
0305-6880 I R C S Medical Science: Physiology†
0305-6899 I R C S Medical Science: Psychiatry and Clinical Psychology†
0305-6902 I R C S Medical Science: Psychology†
0305-6910 I R C S Medical Science: Radiology and Nuclear Medicine†
0305-6929 I R C S Medical Science: Reproduction, Obstetrics and Gynecology†
0305-6937 I R C S Medical Science: Respiratory System *changed to* I R C S Medical Science: Respiratory System and Otorhinolaryngology
0305-6945 Social and Occupational Medicine *changed to* I R C S Medical Science: Environmental and Social Medicine
0305-6953 Surgery and Transplantation *changed to* I R C S Medical Science: Clinical Medicine and Surgery
0305-6961 I R C S Medical Science: Veterinary Science†
0305-697X Inorganic Chemistry of the Main Group Elements†
0305-6996 B K S T S Journal *see* 0950-2114
0305-7046 Clothing Machinery Times
0305-7054 Consumer Bulletin *see* 0265-6930
0305-7070 Journal of Southern African Studies
0305-7100 Kemps Music and Record Industry Year Book International *changed to* Kemps International Music and Recording Industry Yearbook
0305-716X Journal of Flour and Animal Feed Milling *changed to* Milling Feed and Farm Supplies
0305-7194 C E G B Research
0305-7224 Psychoenergetic Systems *see* 0278-6060
0305-7232 Cancer Biochemistry - Biophysics
0305-7240 Journal of Moral Education
0305-7259 Mathematics in School
0305-7291 Education for Development *changed to* Welsh Journal of Education
0305-7321 Brushes International *changed to* Brushmaking International
0305-733X Blinds and Shutters
0305-7348 Ideas†
0305-7356 Psychology of Music

ISSN INDEX 1521

0305-7364 Annals of Botany
0305-7372 Cancer Treatment Reviews
0305-7399 Clinical Oncology *changed to* European Journal of Surgical Oncology
0305-7402 Containerisation International Yearbook
0305-7429 Modern China Studies. International Bulletin†
0305-7445 International Journal of Nautical Archaeology and Underwater Exploration
0305-7453 Journal of Antimicrobial Chemotherapy
0305-7488 Journal of Historical Geography
0305-7496 Educational Administration *see* 0263-211X
0305-750X World Development
0305-7518 Leprosy Review
0305-7593 Modern Languages in Scotland
0305-7615 Applied Health Physics Abstracts and Notes
0305-7623 Ceramic Industries Journal
0305-7631 British Journal of In-Service Education
0305-764X Cambridge Journal of Education
0305-7658 Conference *changed to* Conference & Common Room
0305-7666 Studies in Design, Education and Craft *see* 0142-4807
0305-7682 British Exports. Export Services. *changed to* British Exports
0305-7704 Reaction Kinetics *see* 0309-6890
0305-7712 Environmental Chemistry
0305-7755 Teaching English
0305-7798 Sheet Metal Industries Year Book
0305-781X Association of British Theological and Philosophical Libraries. Bulletin
0305-7828 Aether
0305-7860 Therapeutic Education *see* 0264-4614
0305-7879 Vocational Aspect of Education
0305-7887 British Library. Annual Report
0305-7925 Compare
0305-795X Scottish Journal of Adult Education
0305-7984 University of Manchester. School of Education. Gazette†
0305-7992 Proof
0305-8018 Teaching Geography
0305-8077 A B C Air/Rail Europe *changed to* American Express SkyGuide Europe/Middle East
0305-8107 Journal of Occupational Psychology
0305-8123 Brewery Manual and Who's Who in British Brewing†
0305-8131 B C R A Review†
0305-814X Reading in Political Economy
0305-8174 Offshore Fishing†
0305-8182 Jabberwocky
0305-8190 University of Oxford. School of Geography. Research Papers
0305-8204 Current Topics in Immunology
0305-8220 Regular Savings Plans *changed to* Unit-Linked Regular Savings Plans
0305-8255 Inorganic Reaction Mechanisms†
0305-8298 Millennium
0305-8336 N E R C News Journal
0305-8344 New Review†
0305-8441 Coombe Lodge Report
0305-8468 Focus on International and Comparative Librarianship
0305-8476 European Law Digest
0305-8549 Devon Historian
0305-859X British Cave Research Association. Transactions *see* 0263-760X
0305-862X African Research and Documentation
0305-8646 University of Glasgow. Institute of Latin American Studies. Occasional Papers
0305-8670 Common Market News
0305-8689 Background Data on the Common Market
0305-8697 Awards for Commonwealth University Staff *see* 0144-4611
0305-8751 Home and Freezer Digest
0305-876X Offshore Engineer
0305-8913 British Journal of Teacher Education *see* 0260-7476
0305-8921 Tolley's Income Tax (Year)
0305-8964 Tropical Storage Abstracts *see* 0041-3291
0305-8972 M I R A Abstracts *see* 0309-0817
0305-8980 Glasgow Archaeological Journal
0305-9006 Progress in Planning
0305-9014 Public Finance and Accountancy
0305-9049 Oxford Bulletin of Economics and Statistics
0305-9154 Plant Growth Regulator Abstracts
0305-9162 Maize Quality Protein Abstracts *see* 0267-2987
0305-9189 State Librarian
0305-9219 Viking Society for Northern Research. Saga Book
0305-9227 University of Liverpool Calendar
0305-9235 Fluid Flow Measurement Abstracts
0305-9243 Omnibus Magazine
0305-9251 Theatrefacts *changed to* Theatrefacts/Theatrelogs
0305-926X Housman Society Journal
0305-9308 Writer (Zennor)†
0305-9324 Fellowship for Freedom in Medicine. Newsletter
0305-9332 Industrial Law Journal
0305-9340 Health and Welfare Libraries Quarterly
0305-9367 Insurance†
0305-9421 Quarry Management and Products *changed to* Quarry Management
0305-9456 Civil Engineering Hydraulics Abstracts
0305-9499 Applecon†
0305-9529 New Internationalist
0305-9537 Handbook and Directory of Crematoria *see* 0143-3164
0305-9545 Carbonization Research Report†
0305-9553 Standard Chartered Review†
0305-9561 Eurolaw Commercial Intelligence†
0305-960X Religious Books in Print
0305-9669 Family Practitioner Services
0305-9707 Alkaloids†
0305-9715 Aromatic and Heteroaromatic Chemistry†
0305-9723 Colloid Science
0305-9731 Chemical Thermodynamics†
0305-974X Dielectric and Related Molecular Processes†
0305-9758 Electron Spin Resonance
0305-9774 Inorganic Chemistry of the Transition Elements†
0305-9782 Molecular Spectroscopy†
0305-9790 Molecular Structure by Diffraction Methods†
0305-9804 Nuclear Magnetic Resonance
0305-9812 Organic Compounds of Sulphur, Selenium and Tellurium
0305-9839 Hard Cheese
0305-9855 A L L C Bulletin *changed to* Literary and Linguistic Computing
0305-9863 Buying Antiques
0305-988X Modern Purchasing†
0305-9898 Borthwick Institute Bulletin
0305-9928 Henley Centre for Forecasting. Costs & Prices
0305-9936 Framework Forecast for the E E C Economies
0305-9944 Forecasts of Exchange Rate Movements
0305-9960 Statistical Mechanics†
0305-9979 Electrochemistry
0305-9987 Mass Spectrometry
0306-0004 Amino-Acids, Peptides, and Proteins
0306-0012 Royal Society of Chemistry. Reviews
0306-0020 Mantatoforos†
0306-0039 I S M E C Bulletin
0306-0128 Dance Gazette
0306-0152 Great Britain. Property Services Agency. Construction References
0306-0160 Leicestershire, Northamptonshire & Rutland Farmer
0306-0179 Engineering Capacity
0306-0195 Poetry Post
0306-0209 Naval Architect
0306-0225 Sub Cellular Biochemistry
0306-0233 Health Services Manpower Review
0306-0241 Dundee Tayside
0306-0284 Bibliography of Insecticide Materials of Vegetable Origin†
0306-0314 C I P A
0306-0322 African Book Publishing Record
0306-0349 Airtrade
0306-0357 Organ Club Journal
0306-0373 Delius
0306-0381 O E M Design
0306-039X Pharmacology and Therapeutics. Part B. General and Systematic Pharmacology *see* 0163-7258
0306-0403 Swimming Teacher
0306-042X B M S - Biomedical Mass Spectrometry *changed to* Biomedical & Environmental Mass Spectrometry
0306-0438 T A A-Thermal Analysis Abstracts
0306-0462 Craft Teacher News *changed to* Craft, Design & Technology News
0306-0497 Self & Society
0306-0519 Furniture Manufacturer
0306-056X Street Research Bulletin
0306-0586 High-Speed Ground Transportation and Urban Rapid Transit Systems Bibliography Service†
0306-0594 Air-Cushion and Hydrofoil Systems Bibliography Service†
0306-0624 University of York. Institute of Advanced Architectural Studies. Research Papers
0306-0632 Progress in Food & Nutrition Science
0306-0659 Stable Management
0306-0691 Screen Education†
0306-0713 Organophosphorus Chemistry
0306-0748 Textiles
0306-0772 Facts
0306-0837 Llafur
0306-0845 Urban History Yearbook
0306-087X Theological and Religious Index *changed to* Theological and Religious Bibliographies
0306-0896 Pacifica
0306-090X Civic Trust News *see* 0261-1988
0306-0942 Service Point
0306-0985 Cargo Systems International
0306-1000 B A I E News
0306-1043 Great Britain. Departments of the Environment and Transport. Library. Library Bulletin *changed to* Great Britain. Department of the Environment and Department of Transport. Library. Library Bulletin.
0306-1051 Antiques Trade Gazette
0306-1078 Early Music
0306-1108 University of Sussex. Centre for Continuing Education. Occasional Paper
0306-1124 Commonwealth Bibliographies
0306-1132 Football News
0306-1140 Romford Record
0306-1159 Audio Arts
0306-1256 Gallery
0306-1264 A B L C News *changed to* Textile Services
0306-1280 Lancashire
0306-1353 Annual Reports on Analytical Atomic Spectroscopy
0306-1396 Chemical Society. Analytical Division. Proceedings *see* 0144-557X
0306-140X Pennine Platform
0306-1426 Women's Report†
0306-1450 B I A S Journal
0306-1477 Voices of North Devon†
0306-1485 Hoversport†
0306-1493 Hovercraft Contact Book and International ACV Directory†
0306-1531 Public Health Laboratory Service Board. Year Book *see* 0142-3517
0306-154X After the Battle
0306-1582 Poultry Abstracts
0306-1604 Clockwork
0306-1620 S W *changed to* Arts West
0306-1639 Digest of English-Language Textile Literature *see* 0260-4256
0306-1647 Motorcycle Rider
0306-1655 Verifact†
0306-1701 Emigrante
0306-1728 Schedule of Postgraduate Courses in United Kingdom Universities *changed to* British Universities' Guide to Graduate Studies
0306-1736 Scholarships Guide for Commonwealth Postgraduate Students
0306-1744 Higher Education in the United Kingdom
0306-1841 EuroClay
0306-1884 New Towns Bulletin†
0306-1892 Workers' Control Bulletin†
0306-1914 Current Information in the Construction Industry
0306-1922 Procurement Weekly
0306-1973 Literature & History
0306-1981 I L E A Contact
0306-2015 Children's Literature Abstracts
0306-204X European Glass Directory and Buyer's Guide
0306-2074 Spore Research†
0306-2082 Music and Man *see* 0141-1896
0306-2090 Experimental Embryology and Teratology†
0306-2104 Liquid Chromatography Abstracts
0306-2163 Industrial Cases Reports
0306-2201 Sussex Business Times
0306-2252 Transport News Digest
0306-2279 European Industrial & Commercial Review†
0306-2295 Outlook *changed to* Newscan
0306-2309 Offshore Services *changed to* Offshore Services & Technology
0306-2317 Gloucester and Avon Life *changed to* Somerset and Avon Life
0306-2392 Undercurrents *see* 0034-5970
0306-2406 Certified Accountant
0306-2414 Natural Gas for Commerce†
0306-2465 A T L A Abstracts *see* 0261-1929
0306-2473 Yearbook of English Studies
0306-2481 Sociological Analysis & Theory
0306-252X Paper Technology and Industry
0306-2538 Staff and Welfare Caterer†
0306-2597 Liquid Crystals Abstracts†
0306-2619 Applied Energy
0306-2643 International Review of Psycho-Analysis
0306-2686 Plant Foods for Man *see* 0142-968X
0306-2708 Society for General Microbiology Proceedings *see* 0142-7547
0306-2732 International Symposium on Jet Cutting Technology. Proceedings
0306-2740 Queen Mary College. Department of Geography. Occasional Papers *changed to* Queen Mary College. Department of Geography and Earth Science. Occasional Papers
0306-283X Quaker Service *see* 0265-7848
0306-2856 Quality Assurance
0306-2864 Diagnostics Index†
0306-2880 Reprographics Quarterly *see* 0266-6960
0306-2910 I B C A M Journal
0306-2945 Lloyd's Maritime & Commercial Law Quarterly
0306-2988 Stainless Steel Industry
0306-3003 Intestinal Absorption *see* 0261-4995
0306-3046 Spon's Architects' & Builders' Price Book
0306-3054 Spon's Landscape Handbook *changed to* Spon's Landscape & External Works Pricebook
0306-3062 Recreation Management Yearbook *see* 0144-624X
0306-3070 Journal of General Management
0306-3089 Financial Times Tax Newsletter
0306-3127 Social Studies of Science
0306-3151 Gwynedd Archives Service. Bulletin†
0306-316X Scotia Review
0306-3208 International Journal of Criminology and Penology *see* 0194-6595
0306-3216 Building Trades Journal
0306-3224 Contents Pages in Management
0306-3240 District Councils Review
0306-3275 Molecular Aspects *see* 0264-6021
0306-3283 Biochemical Journal. Part 1: Cellular Aspects *see* 0264-6021
0306-3291 Current Advances in Ecological Sciences
0306-3313 N.A.P.V. Newsletter
0306-3321 Guerrilheiro†
0306-333X Electronic Production

1522 ISSN INDEX

0306-3348 Guardian Gazette
0306-3356 Clinics in Obstetrics and Gynaecology *see* 0889-8545
0306-3380 British Geomorphological Research Group. Technical Bulletin
0306-3410 Jane's Infantry Weapons
0306-3437 Footwear World†
0306-3461 Meridian†
0306-347X Marine Week†
0306-3534 European Plastics News
0306-3542 Progress of Rubber Technology *see* 0266-7320
0306-3550 Accidents to Aircraft on the British Register
0306-3569 Great Britain. Civil Aviation Authority. Annual Report and Accounts
0306-3577 Great Britain. Civil Aviation Board. C A A Monthly Statistics *changed to* Great Britain. Civil Aviation Authority. U.K. Airlines Monthly Operating & Traffic Statistics
0306-3585 Heating, Ventilating and Air Conditioning Year Book
0306-3593 Boatbuilders' and Chandlers' Directory of Suppliers *changed to* Boat Equipment Buyers' Guide
0306-3607 Reinforced Plastics Congress
0306-3623 General Pharmacology
0306-3631 Journal of Commonwealth & Comparative Politics
0306-364X Renewable Energy Bulletin
0306-3666 Men of Achievement
0306-3674 British Journal of Sports Medicine
0306-3704 British Journal of Law and Society *see* 0263-323X
0306-3712 Brass Band Review†
0306-3763 N C A V A E. E D U. Technical Reports *see* 0261-2364
0306-3860 St. Thomas's Gazette
0306-3879 Double Glazing - Domestic, Industrial and Commercial *changed to* Window Industries
0306-3895 Business Graduate
0306-3909 Creative Camera International Year Book *changed to* Creative Camera Collection
0306-3933 Hambro Euromoney Directory
0306-395X Petroleum Economist
0306-3968 Race and Class
0306-3992 Equals *see* 0140-9506
0306-400X International Water Power and Dam Construction
0306-4034 University of Birmingham. Centre for Urban and Regional Studies. Research Memorandum
0306-4069 Hydraulic Pneumatic Mechanical Power
0306-4077 Bindery Data Index†
0306-4107 British Theatre Directory
0306-4123 Board Manufacture & Processing
0306-4190 International Journal of Mechanical Engineering Education
0306-4212 Foundry Yearbook
0306-4220 Index on Censorship
0306-428X S R L News *changed to* S R I S News
0306-4336 International Tourism Quarterly *see* 0269-3747
0306-4379 Information Systems
0306-4395 Harpsichord Magazine
0306-4409 Recorder and Music Magazine
0306-4484 Current Advances in Plant Science
0306-4492 Comparative Biochemistry and Physiology. Part C: Comparative Pharmacology *changed to* Comparative Biochemistry and Physiology. Part C: Comparative Pharmacology & Toxicology
0306-4522 Neuroscience
0306-4530 Psychoneuroendocrinology
0306-4549 Annals of Nuclear Energy
0306-4565 Journal of Thermal Biology
0306-4573 Information Processing and Management
0306-4603 Addictive Behaviors
0306-462X Life and Health†
0306-4824 World Trade Union Movement
0306-4832 Electrochemistry in Industrial Processing & Biology
0306-4859 Society for Lincolnshire History and Archaeology. Annual Report and Statement of Accounts
0306-4867 Motor Cycle and Cycle Trader Year Book
0306-4964 Foundation
0306-4980 I D F Bulletin
0306-5030 Manchester Free Press
0306-5065 British Mensa Newsletter *changed to* Mensa
0306-5103 Collect Channel Islands Stamps *changed to* Collect Channel Islands and Isle of Man Stamps
0306-512X New Humanist
0306-5154 Shirley Institute Publications. S: Series
0306-5162 European Market Report†
0306-5197 Chigwell Local History Society. Transactions
0306-5251 British Journal of Clinical Pharmacology
0306-526X Metallurgist and Materials Technologist *see* 0026-0940
0306-5278 Northern Scotland
0306-5286 Road Traffic Reports
0306-5332 Museums Association Information Sheets
0306-543X Who's Who in Football
0306-5456 British Journal of Obstetrics & Gynaecology
0306-5480 H.G. Wells Society Newsletter
0306-5499 Institute of United States Studies Monographs†
0306-5502 European Plastics Buyers Guide†
0306-5529 Prospect *changed to* Swansea Review
0306-5537 Key Abstracts - Solid State Devices *see* 0950-4850
0306-5553 Key Abstracts - Systems Theory *see* 0950-477X
0306-5561 Key Abstracts - Power Transmission and Distribution *see* 0950-4834
0306-557X Key Abstracts - Electronic Circuits
0306-5588 Key Abstracts - Communications Technology *see* 0950-4877
0306-5596 Key Abstracts - Industrial Power and Control Systems *see* 0950-4842
0306-5618 Sales Engineering *see* 0264-3200
0306-5634 Air International
0306-5650 North West Business Monthly
0306-5677 Catholic Directory for Scotland
0306-5693 Esperanto News
0306-5707 Challenge†
0306-5723 Outdoors *see* 0007-120X
0306-5758 Manchester Chamber of Commerce and Industry. Yearbook
0306-5766 References to Scientific Literature on Fire *changed to* Fire Science Abstracts
0306-5774 Mackintosh Yearbook of West European Electronics Data
0306-5790 Anglesey Antiquarian Society Transactions
0306-5839 Mobile Home and Holiday Caravan *see* 0268-4594
0306-5928 British Music Yearbook
0306-6045 International Tax-Free Trader & Duty-Free World
0306-6061 Political Social Economic Review
0306-610X Crafts
0306-6118 Security Surveyor
0306-6142 C A T M O G
0306-6150 Journal of Peasant Studies
0306-6185 D I A Yearbook - Design Action
0306-6193 Educational Yearbook†
0306-624X International Journal of Offender Therapy and Comparative Criminology
0306-6266 Natural Food Trade Journal *changed to* Natural Food Retailer
0306-6274 Motor Report International
0306-6304 Language Teaching and Linguistics Abstracts *see* 0261-4448
0306-6312 750 Bulletin
0306-6398 East Malling Research Station. Annual Report
0306-6444 Gas Engineering & Management
0306-6479 New Law Journal
0306-6495 Practical Hi-Fi & Audio *changed to* Hi-Fi Today
0306-6509 Solid Wastes *changed to* Wastes Management
0306-6517 International Flavours and Food Additives *see* 0143-8441
0306-6541 Pram and Nursery Trader Year Book *see* 0082-5611
0306-6568 Sea Angler
0306-6614 Bucks and Berks Countryside *see* 0306-672X
0306-6649 W R C Information *see* 0748-2531
0306-6673 Personnel and Training Management Yearbook *changed to* Personnel and Training Databook
0306-672X Hertfordshire Countryside
0306-6746 Progress in Water Technology *see* 0273-1223
0306-6800 Journal of Medical Ethics
0306-6843 Hampshire Family Historian
0306-686X Journal of Business Finance & Accounting
0306-6886 Computer Report
0306-6908 Middle East Week†
0306-6916 British Hydromechanics Research Association. Proceedings of Hydrotransport
0306-7041 British Airways Executive
0306-7068 Monotype Pictorial†
0306-7076 British Ceramic Review
0306-719X Farm Business Review†
0306-7262 Reform
0306-7297 Journal of Human Movement Studies
0306-7319 International Journal of Environmental and Analytical Chemistry
0306-7327 Irrigation and Drainage Abstracts
0306-7335 Challenger Society. Newsletter
0306-7351 Ocean Energy†
0306-7408 University of Strathclyde, Fraser of Allander Institute for Research on the Scottish Economy. Research Monograph
0306-7432 Association of Teachers of Russian. Newsletter
0306-7440 Traditional Music
0306-7475 Antiquarian Book Monthly Review
0306-7556 Crop Physiology Abstracts
0306-7564 Dynamica *see* 0883-7066
0306-7580 Small Animal Abstracts
0306-7645 JustPeace
0306-7696 International Newsletter on Chemical Education
0306-770X Oil World Statistics *see* 0141-4305
0306-7734 International Statistical Review
0306-7858 Tape Teacher†
0306-7866 University of Strathclyde. Fraser of Allander Institute for Research on the Scottish Economy. Quarterly Economic Commentary
0306-7912 Beermat Magazine
0306-7920 Lawn Tennis *changed to* Tennis
0306-7947 British Model Soldier Society. Bulletin
0306-7963 L A G Bulletin *changed to* Legal Action
0306-7971 Spare Rib
0306-798X B U F O R A Journal *see* 0265-1947
0306-7998 Jewish Historical Society of England. Annual Report and Accounts for the Session
0306-8099 Opera North†
0306-8129 Forestry and Home Grown Timber *see* 0308-7638
0306-8145 Canada Today *changed to* Canada Today/D'Aujourd'hui
0306-817X Art Design Photo†
0306-8234 Paper
0306-8285 Industrial Pollution Control Yearbook†
0306-8293 International Journal of Social Economics
0306-8374 Asian Affairs
0306-8404 Bandersnatch
0306-8412 Africa Currents†
0306-8463 Postal History International†
0306-8471 Eugenics Society Bulletin *see* 0266-3880
0306-848X Radnorshire Society. Transactions
0306-8536 Manxman†
0306-8552 Electrotechnology
0306-8560 Livestock International *changed to* Agriculture International
0306-8765 Intermusik
0306-8781 Amon Hen
0306-879X Italiano†
0306-882X Flora
0306-8838 Bradwell Abbey Field Centre for the Study of Archaeology, Natural History & Environmental Studies. Occasional Papers†
0306-8919 Optical and Quantum Electronics
0306-8927 Hostelling News *changed to* Y H A Magazine
0306-8943 Stainless
0306-9001 Northamptonshire & Bedfordshire Life
0306-9028 Window
0306-9079 Cornish Banner
0306-9192 Food Policy
0306-9206 North Cheshire Family Historian
0306-9338 Bangor Occasional Papers in Economics
0306-9346 B B C Modern English†
0306-9389 Tabs
0306-9397 Conferences and Exhibitions *see* 0260-8316
0306-9400 Law Teacher
0306-9419 International Journal of Forensic Dentistry
0306-9427 Welding Research International†
0306-9435 Transport Manager's Handbook
0306-9516 African Books in Print
0306-9524 Index Islamicus
0306-9532 Chartered Mechanical Engineer
0306-9540 M E N (Mechanical Engineering News) *changed to* Engineering News
0306-9559 Chartered Institute of Transport. Handbook
0306-9575 Contact Lens Journal
0306-9699 Midwife, Health Visitor and Community Nurse
0306-977X Ilkeston and District Local History Society. Occasional Paper†
0306-9788 City of London Law Review *changed to* City of London. Law Faculty. Journal
0306-9796 Cambria: A Welsh Geographical Review
0306-9869 Electron Microscopy Abstracts
0306-9877 Medical Hypotheses
0306-9885 British Journal of Guidance and Counselling
0306-9915 U F O Research Review *changed to* Anomalous Phenomenon Review
0307-0018 Cranes Today
0307-0026 E S N-European Spectroscopy News
0307-0042 University of Wales. Board of Celtic Studies. Social Science Monographs
0307-0131 Byzantine and Modern Greek Studies
0307-0158 Birmingham & West Midlands Chambers of Commerce Directory
0307-0220 Fairplay International Shipping Weekly
0307-0255 F A S Journal†
0307-0298 Harrington Family Miscellany
0307-0360 London Currency Report
0307-0379 International Economic Data Service
0307-0387 Middle East Currency Reports
0307-0395 Young Drama†
0307-0409 Anbar Yearbook
0307-0417 Greater London Arts Association. Annual Report and Yearbook *see* 0309-1945
0307-0441 Local Government Trends
0307-0468 Chartered Institute of Public Finance and Accountancy. Housing Maintenance & Management. Actuals Statistics
0307-0484 Azania Combat
0307-0506 Chartered Institute of Public Finance and Accountancy. Local Health and Social Services Statistics *see* 0309-653X
0307-0514 Chartered Institute of Public Finance and Accountancy. Education Estimates Statistics

ISSN INDEX 1523

0307-0522 Chartered Institute of Public Finance and Accountancy. Public Library Statistics. Estimates
0307-0565 International Journal of Obesity
0307-0573 Chartered Institute of Public Finance and Accountancy. Fire Service Statistics. Estimates
0307-0603 Digest of United Kingdom Energy Statistics
0307-062X Official Guide to Hotels & Restaurants in Great Britain, Ireland and Overseas
0307-0654 University of Durham. Centre for Middle Eastern and Islamic Studies. Occasional Papers Series.
0307-0697 Power and Works Engineering†
0307-0719 University College London. Institute of Jewish Studies. Bulletin†
0307-076X National Institute for Medical Research. Scientific Report *see* 0141-2116
0307-0778 Paper and Board Abstracts
0307-0786 Ostrich
0307-0794 Marketing Abstracts *see* 0308-2172
0307-0808 Studies in Library Management
0307-0832 Navin Weekly
0307-093X Social Services Yearbook
0307-0980 New Humanity Journal
0307-1006 Discourse Analysis Monographs
0307-1022 Social History
0307-109X Theses in Latin American Studies at British Universities in Progress and Completed *changed to* Theses in Latin American Studies at British Universities in Progress or Recently Completed
0307-112X Immunology Abstracts
0307-1146 Great Britain. Electricity Council. Annual Report and Accounts
0307-1154 Garage and Transport *changed to* Garage and Automotive Retailer
0307-1189 About Wine Newsletter
0307-1243 Garden History
0307-1308 Chartered Institute of Public Finance and Accountancy. Housing Part 1: Rents. Actuals Statistics *see* 0260-406X
0307-1316 Chartered Institute of Public Finance and Accountancy. Housing Part 2: Revenue Accounts. Actuals Statistics *see* 0260-4078
0307-1375 Arboricultural Journal
0307-1391 S S R C Survey Archive Bulletin *changed to* E S R C Data Archive Bulletin
0307-1448 Donizetti Society. Journal
0307-1456 S A L G Newsletter
0307-1596 Food Machinery and Ingredients Export News†
0307-1634 E A A Review
0307-1642 Thomas Hardy Society. Review *see* 0268-5418
0307-1677 Industrial Past *see* 0265-5071
0307-174X International Polymer Science and Technology
0307-1782 Water Services Handbook *changed to* Water Services Year Book
0307-1790 Youth in Society
0307-1804 Locomotives Illustrated
0307-1847 R U S I Journal
0307-188X Intelligence Digest Weekly Review *changed to* Intelligence Digest (Cheltenham)
0307-1901 E S S R A Magazine†
0307-191X Pensions World
0307-1936 Contact (London, 1973)†
0307-2029 Calgacus
0307-2053 Home Economics *see* 0265-6930
0307-2061 British National Association for Soviet and East European Studies. Information Bulletin
0307-2118 Fitech
0307-2169 Black Music & Jazz Review
0307-2274 Association of Commonwealth Universities. Annual Report of the Council Together with the Accounts of the Association
0307-2312 Teaching over 13s†
0307-2363 Retail and Distribution Management
0307-2401 Electronics Industry
0307-2444 Studies for Trade Unionists
0307-2460 East Anglian Archaeology. Report
0307-2517 Knitting World & Textile Manufacturer†
0307-2525 Museums Bulletin
0307-2576 Soil Association. Quarterly Review
0307-2606 Locke Newsletter
0307-2614 S E E Journal
0307-2630 U K Plant Hire Guide *changed to* Contract Journal (1979)
0307-2649 Journal of A T E *changed to* Test-Cadmat
0307-2657 B S B I Abstracts
0307-2770 New German Studies
0307-2827 C H E C News *changed to* C H E C Journal
0307-2851 Midland Ancestor
0307-2894 International Who's Who in Music and Musicians' Directory
0307-2916 Fireweed†
0307-2991 What Car?
0307-3084 Gas Directory and Who's Who
0307-3149 Jane's Ocean Technology†
0307-3262 Iberian Studies
0307-3289 Institute of Health Education. Journal
0307-3319 Great North Review
0307-3408 Bard
0307-3424 Tass Journal *changed to* Tass News and Journal
0307-3513 Youth Social Work Bulletin *see* 0307-1790
0307-353X Insight: Soviet Jews
0307-3572 Tennyson Society, Lincoln, England. Occasional Papers
0307-3580 Management Review & Digest
0307-4293 New Fiction
0307-4331 Austria
0307-434X British Directory of Little Magazines and Small Presses†
0307-4358 Managerial Finance
0307-4412 Biochemical Education
0307-4463 Population Trends
0307-4536 Greek Review *changed to* Greek Institute Review
0307-4552 Barclays Country Reports
0307-4617 Screen International
0307-4625 Centerpiece†
0307-4722 Art Libraries Journal
0307-4730 British Journal of Clinical Equipment†
0307-4757 Policy Publications Review *changed to* Publications Review-Innovation & Management
0307-4803 New Library World
0307-4811 Vegan
0307-4870 Journal of Planning and Environment Law
0307-5036 Royal Scottish Museum Information Series: Natural History†
0307-5044 Royal Scottish Museum Information Series: Technology†
0307-5052 Royal Scottish Museum Information Series: Geology†
0307-5079 Studies in Higher Education
0307-5087 Contrebis
0307-5095 Journal of Electrophysiological Technology
0307-5133 Journal of Egyptian Archaeology
0307-5281 Watford and District Industrial History Society. Journal
0307-5354 S P E L
0307-5400 European Law Review
0307-5451 History of Technology
0307-546X Tangent
0307-5494 Microbios Letters
0307-5508 Community Care
0307-5583 Cromwelliana
0307-5591 Industrial Relations Law Reports
0307-5656 Institute of Medical Laboratory Sciences. Gazette *changed to* I M L S. Gazette
0307-580X Jeweller†
0307-5826 Library Association. Rare Books Group. Newsletter
0307-5966 Journal of Meteorology
0307-5974 Religion in Communist Lands
0307-5982 Together
0307-6008 India Office Library and Records Newsletter
0307-6032 Who's Who in Finance†
0307-6067 Community Work
0307-6075 Dissertation Abstracts International. Section C: European Abstracts
0307-6091 Federation of Children's Book Groups. Yearbook *see* 0144-574X
0307-6113 International Directory of Current Research in the History of Cartography and in Carto-Bibliography
0307-6164 British Plastics and Rubber
0307-6202 Sheffield University Calendar
0307-6334 Church Music Quarterly
0307-6474 Wedding and Home
0307-6490 Automotive Engineer
0307-6539 Commonwealth Magistrates' Conference. Report
0307-6547 Great Britain. Department of Energy. Report on Research and Development†
0307-6571 Coin Yearbook
0307-6628 Cheshire Archaeological Bulletin
0307-6652 Notes on Water Research†
0307-6679 Stamp Magazine
0307-6687 Tolley's Tax Tables (Year)
0307-6695 New Aspects of Breast Cancer†
0307-6717 Criminal Statistics, Scotland.
0307-6741 Toy Retailing News†
0307-6768 Management Services
0307-6776 R A I N: Royal Anthropological Institute News *changed to* Anthropology Today
0307-6784 Lewisletter
0307-6792 Society for the Social History of Medicine. Bulletin
0307-6822 Road Accidents in Great Britain
0307-6857 International Planned Parenthood Federation. Annual Report *changed to* I P P F Annual Report
0307-689X Directory of Agricultural Co-Operatives in the United Kingdom
0307-6903 S C O C L I S News
0307-692X Australian Journal of Ecology
0307-6938 Clinical and Experimental Dermatology
0307-6946 Ecological Entomology
0307-6962 Physiological Entomology
0307-6970 Systematic Entomology
0307-7004 Triticale Abstracts *changed to* Wheat, Barley and Triticale Abstracts
0307-7039 Politics Today
0307-7098 Collect Isle of Man Stamps†
0307-7144 Lore and Language
0307-7195 Printing Industries
0307-7225 Church of England. General Synod. Report of Proceedings
0307-7233 German Political Studies†
0307-7276 Weyfarers
0307-7349 Soviet Non-Ferrous Metals Research
0307-7365 Surfacing Journal *see* 0269-2848
0307-7411 Air Extra†
0307-742X Clinics in Rheumatic Diseases *see* 0889-857X
0307-7497 Occasional Papers in German Studies
0307-7535 Fabian Tract
0307-7543 Trade Union Register†
0307-7640 Medical Informatics
0307-7667 Quarterly Review of Marketing
0307-7675 Museums Yearbook
0307-7683 New Civil Engineer
0307-7691 National Coal Board Statistical Tables†
0307-7713 Civil Engineering Technician *changed to* Civil Engineering Technology
0307-7772 Clinical Otolaryngology and Allied Sciences
0307-7780 Securitech
0307-7861 Accountants Weekly†
0307-7896 Metal Construction
0307-7942 Energy World
0307-7950 Heating and Air Conditioning Journal
0307-7969 Key Abstracts - Physical Measurements and Instrumentation *see* 0950-4818
0307-7977 Key Abstracts - Electrical Measurements and Instrumentation *see* 0950-480X
0307-8000 Comparison *changed to* New Comparison
0307-8051 Courtauld Institute Illustration Archives. Archive 1
0307-806X Courtauld Institute Illustration Archives. Archive 2
0307-8078 Courtauld Institute Illustration Archives. Archive 3
0307-8086 Courtauld Institute Illustration Archives. Archive 4
0307-8108 Football *changed to* Football Monthly
0307-8140 Northumberland & Durham Family History Society. Journal
0307-823X Sussex Anthropology
0307-8329 Chartered Institute of Public Finance and Accountancy. Planning Estimates Statistics. Actuals *changed to* Chartered Institute of Public Finance and Accountancy. Planning and Development Statistics. Estimates
0307-8329 Chartered Institute of Public Finance and Accountancy. Planning Estimates Statistics. Actuals *see* 0260-8642
0307-8337 English Language Teaching Journal
0307-8353 Institution of Civil Engineers. Proceedings. Part 1: Design and Construction
0307-8361 Institution of Civil Engineers. Proceedings. Part 2: Research and Theory
0307-8388 Themelios
0307-8477 Newscheck
0307-8515 Clothing Institute Year Book and Membership Register *changed to* Clothing and Footwear Institute Year Book and Membership Register
0307-8531 Rare Earth Bulletin
0307-8558 Management Services in Government *changed to* Management in Government
0307-8590 Maritime Monographs and Reports
0307-8604 Coop Marketing & Management
0307-8612 New Universities Quarterly *see* 0951-5224
0307-8647 Bar Quarterly†
0307-8698 Ringing and Migration
0307-8833 Theatre Research International
0307-8884 Seed
0307-8957 Robert Burns Chronicle
0307-8965 Computing Europe *changed to* Computing
0307-9007 N R Technology
0307-9023 Research Intelligence *see* 0141-1926
0307-904X Applied Mathematical Modelling
0307-9058 Great Britain. Centre for Overseas Pest Research. Miscellaneous Report†
0307-9066 Mining Department Magazine
0307-9074 Stream
0307-9082 Great Britain. Centre for Overseas Pest Research. Report†
0307-9112 London Mystery Selection†
0307-9163 Association of Art Historians. Bulletin
0307-9201 Sage Race Relations Abstracts
0307-9244 Le Nurb
0307-9252 Communicator†
0307-9341 Lakeland Dialect Society. Journal *changed to* Lakeland Dialect
0307-9457 Avian Pathology
0307-9481 British Library News
0307-9562 Thames Poetry†
0307-9570 Moonshine†
0307-9589 Great Britain. Civil Service Department. Report
0307-9597 Scottish Social Work Statistics *see* 0260-5295
0307-9708 School and Community
0307-9732 International Yearbook of Educational & Instructional Technology
0307-9767 New Library Buildings†
0307-9813 Gay Left
0307-9821 Halsbury's Laws of England Monthly Review
0307-9864 Annual Bibliography of Scottish Literature
0307-9929 Under-5
0308-003X Tape and Hi-Fi Test†

ISSN INDEX

ISSN	Title
0308-0110	Medical Education
0308-0129	English Philological Studies
0308-0137	Rural Recreation and Tourism Abstracts see 0261-1392
0308-0161	Pressure Vessels and Piping changed to International Journal of Pressure Vessels and Piping
0308-017X	Thomas Hardy Society. Newsletter†
0308-0188	I S R - Interdisciplinary Science Reviews
0308-0226	British Journal of Occupational Therapy
0308-0234	Hospital and Health Services Review
0308-0404	Enthusiasm†
0308-0455	Business Graduates Association Address Book
0308-0501	F A M-Fire and Materials
0308-051X	Pharmatherapeutica
0308-0528	Middle East Construction
0308-0587	Modern English Teacher
0308-0617	Catholic Life†
0308-0633	Contact (London, 1961)
0308-0676	Warfare
0308-0765	Human Rights Review†
0308-082X	Town and Country Planning Association. Annual Report
0308-0838	Fern Gazette
0308-0862	British Plumbing and Heating changed to Plumbing and Heating
0308-0889	Four Decades†
0308-0900	London Facts and Figures
0308-0935	Great Britain. Ministry of Agriculture, Fisheries and Food. Directorate of Fisheries Research. Fishing Prospects
0308-0943	Skinner's British Textile Register†
0308-0951	Charles Lamb Bulletin
0308-1060	Transportation Planning and Technology
0308-1079	International Journal of General Systems
0308-1087	Linear and Multilinear Algebra
0308-1125	Great Britain. Institute of Terrestrial Ecology. Report
0308-1206	Comments on Solid State Physics see 0885-4483
0308-1222	Energy Trends
0308-1230	On Target
0308-1273	Netherlands-British Trade Directory
0308-129X	Royal Society of Edinburgh. Communications, Physical Sciences†
0308-1400	International Dredging Abstracts see 0264-0775
0308-1419	Great Britain. Department of Employment. New Earnings Survey
0308-1443	Printing Industries Annual changed to Printers Yearbook
0308-1451	Royal Institution of Chartered Surveyors Year Book†
0308-146X	Great Britain. Central Statistical Office. Regional Statistics see 0261-1783
0308-1656	Akhbar-e-Watan Urdu Newsweekly
0308-1699	New African Yearbook changed to New African Yearbook: West and Central
0308-1699	New African Yearbook changed to New African Yearbook: East and South
0308-1729	Savings Market
0308-1745	Great Britain. Department of the Environment. Local Government Financial Statistics: England and Wales
0308-1796	National Review
0308-180X	Natural History Book Reviews
0308-1907	N A T F H E Journal
0308-1958	Impact of Tax Changes on Income Distribution†
0308-1990	Footnote
0308-2024	Writing
0308-2075	Occasional Papers in Linguistics and Language Learning
0308-2091	Artefact see 0261-7048
0308-2105	Royal Society of Edinburgh. Proceedings. (Mathematics)
0308-2113	Royal Society of Edinburgh. Proceedings. (Natural Environment) changed to Royal Society of Edinburgh. Proceedings. (Biological Sciences)
0308-2164	Environment and Planning B: Planning & Design
0308-2172	Management and Marketing Abstracts
0308-2199	British Mining
0308-2261	Clinics in Haematology see 0889-8588
0308-230X	British Library. Bibliographic Services Division. Newsletter see 0268-9707
0308-2342	Journal of Chemical Research
0308-244X	British Journal of Music Therapy
0308-2636	P N Review
0308-2741	Society for Lincolnshire History and Archaeology. Newsletter
0308-275X	Critique of Anthropology
0308-2776	Prospice
0308-2792	New Age Concern Today see 0144-6630
0308-2857	Survival International Review
0308-2881	Christian Educator†
0308-2938	International Marketing Data and Statistics
0308-2962	Tropical Oil Seeds Abstracts
0308-2970	Sorghum and Millets Abstracts
0308-2997	Feeding-Weight and Obesity Abstracts†
0308-3047	Market Research Great Britain
0308-308X	Elektor changed to Elektor Electronics
0308-3217	International†
0308-3233	Issues in Race and Education
0308-3268	Horticulture Industry see 0262-3765
0308-3276	S.I.S. Review
0308-3306	Farming Industry†
0308-3322	Great Britain. Royal Greenwich Observatory. Annual Report
0308-3381	Bananas
0308-342X	Surrey Archaeological Society. Research Volumes
0308-3446	Market Research Europe
0308-3535	Royal College of Art, Journal changed to Ark (1978)
0308-356X	Teaching 10-13's
0308-3586	Focus on Political Repression in Southern Africa
0308-3594	Local Council Review
0308-3616	Medical Laboratory Sciences
0308-3675	Great Britain. Institute of Terrestrial Ecology. Merlewood Research and Development Paper
0308-3705	Consuming Interest
0308-3713	Japanese Patents Gazette. Part 1: Chemical changed to Japanese Patents Gazette. Unexamined
0308-373X	Plumbing and Heating Equipment News
0308-3756	Pali Buddhist Review see 0265-2897
0308-3764	Court†
0308-4035	South East Asia Library Group Newsletter
0308-4086	Journal of Crystal and Molecular Structure see 0277-8068
0308-4094	B L L D Announcement Bulletin see 0144-7556
0308-4159	I C E Yearbook changed to I C E List of Members
0308-4183	Bristol and Avon Family History Society. Journal
0308-4205	Professional Printer
0308-4213	Cable Television Engineering
0308-4221	Computer Applications
0308-423X	I B A Technical Review
0308-4272	Radiological Protection Bulletin
0308-4329	Journal of Human Nutrition changed to Human Nutrition
0308-4353	Consumer Europe
0308-4388	Halsbury's Laws of England Annual Abridgment
0308-4426	Journal of Maternal and Child Health see 0262-0200
0308-4450	West African Journal of Sociology and Political Science
0308-4469	International Cocoa Organization. Quarterly Bulletin of Cocoa Statistics
0308-4485	Offset Data Index†
0308-4507	Carpet Review Weekly see 0263-4236
0308-4531	Stella Polaris
0308-454X	Television (London, 1928)
0308-4558	Royal Historical Society. Annual Bibliography of British and Irish History
0308-4574	Bracton Law Journal
0308-4590	International Metals Review see 0950-6608
0308-4620	World Patents Index Gazette. Section P: General changed to World Patents Index Gazette Service. Section P: General
0308-4639	World Patents Index Gazette. Section Q: Mechanical changed to World Patents Index Gazette Service. Section Q: Mechanical
0308-4647	World Patents Index Gazette. Section R: Electrical changed to World Patents Index Gazette Service. Section R: Electrical
0308-4655	World Patents Index Gazette. Section Ch: Chemical changed to World Patents Index Gazette Service. Section Ch: Chemical
0308-4698	British Country Music Association. Yearbook
0308-4752	Omens
0308-4787	Limestone Literary Magazine see 0263-4635
0308-4795	Diesel Engineering†
0308-4809	Northumbriana
0308-4892	Committee on Invisible Exports. Annual Report changed to British Invisible Exports Council. Annual Report
0308-4922	British Paedodontic Society. Proceedings see 0267-2073
0308-4930	A and S changed to Architect & Surveyor
0308-4949	Royal British Legion. Journal.†
0308-499X	Great Britain. Department of Trade. Insurance Business: Annual Report
0308-5074	Great Britain. Royal Greeenwich Observatory. Bulletin
0308-5082	Great Britain. Institute of Geological Sciences. Seismological Bulletins changed to Great Britain. British Geological Survey. Seismological Bulletins
0308-5090	United Kingdom Mineral Statistics
0308-5147	Economy and Society
0308-518X	Environment and Planning A
0308-5198	Defence Materiel
0308-5201	Maritime Defence International changed to Maritime Defence
0308-521X	Agricultural Systems
0308-5252	C W I Herald
0308-5279	Bank of England. Report and Accounts
0308-5325	Great Britain. Institute of Geological Sciences. Overseas Memoirs changed to Great Britain. British Geological Survey. Overseas Memoirs
0308-5333	Great Britain. Institute of Geological Sciences. Mineral Assessment Report changed to Great Britain. British Geological Survey. Mineral Assessment Report
0308-5376	B U F C Newsletter see 0265-6817
0308-5384	Biological Structure and Function
0308-5414	Pollution Monitor changed to P M Environmental Newsletter
0308-5457	Royal Horticultural Society. Garden Journal
0308-5473	Librarians' Christian Fellowship Newsletter
0308-5538	Documents on International Affairs†
0308-5554	Sounding Brass changed to Brass International
0308-5562	Oxoniensia
0308-5570	Great Britain. Ministry of Agriculture, Fisheries and Food. Directorate of Fisheries Research. Report of the Director of Fisheries Research
0308-5589	Great Britain. Ministry of Agriculture, Fisheries and Food. Directorate of Fisheries Research. Fisheries Research Technical Report
0308-5597	A A R P Journal see 0393-5183
0308-5651	Buildings Maintenance & Services changed to Cleaning Maintenance
0308-5694	Imago Mvndi
0308-5732	Agricultural Engineer
0308-5759	Adoption and Fostering
0308-5791	British Flower
0308-5864	I D S Discussion Paper
0308-5872	I D S Bulletin
0308-5899	Fortean Times
0308-5910	Oil Paintings, Drawings and Watercolours changed to Art Sales Index: Oil Paintings, Drawings, Water Colours and Sculpture
0308-5953	Microprocessors see 0141-9331
0308-5961	Telecommunications Policy
0308-597X	Marine Policy
0308-6003	Chemical Society. Annual Reports on the Progress of Chemistry. Section A: Physical and Inorganic Chemistry see 0260-1818
0308-602X	Chest, Heart and Stroke Journal†
0308-6100	Craft & Hobby Dealer
0308-6119	University of London. Contemporary China Institute. Research Notes and Studies
0308-6135	Portsmouth Magazine
0308-616X	Housing Outlook†
0308-6194	Christian Parapsychologist
0308-6224	B S R I A Statistics Bulletin
0308-6259	Commercial Food Information
0308-6283	New Poetry†
0308-6348	Nottinghamshire Historian
0308-6380	Marfleet Society Newsletter
0308-650X	General Engineer
0308-6534	Journal of Imperial and Commonwealth History
0308-6569	Anglo-American Law Review
0308-6577	Cotton and Tropical Fibres Abstracts
0308-6593	Journal of Clinical Pharmacy see 0143-3180
0308-6631	Mining Magazine
0308-664X	Phosphorus and Sulfur and the Related Elements
0308-6666	Great Britain. Central Statistical Office. Monthly Digest of Statistics
0308-6674	Mallorn
0308-6712	British Toys and Hobbies changed to British Toys & Hobbies Briefing
0308-6739	Freshwater Biological Association. Occasional Publications
0308-6747	Architecture West Midlands
0308-678X	Africa Guide changed to Africa Review
0308-6801	J C A T S changed to C.A.T.S. Reports
0308-6852	Red Letters
0308-6860	Ethnic Groups
0308-6887	Amnesty International Newsletter
0308-6895	A T P A S Printing Education & Training Journal
0308-6909	C O R E
0308-6917	Engineering Materials and Design
0308-6925	Communicator of Scientific and Technical Information changed to Communicator (Hatfield)
0308-6992	Geographers
0308-7018	Cassell's Directory of Publishing in Great Britain, The Commonwealth, Ireland, South Africa and Pakistan changed to Cassell and Publishers Association Directory of Publishing in Great Britain, the Commonwealth, Ireland, South Africa and Pakistan
0308-7026	Gas Marketing
0308-7107	Sell's Health Service Buyers Guide see 0140-5748
0308-7123	Directory of Summer Jobs Abroad
0308-7174	Electrical Contractor
0308-7212	In Touch (London)
0308-7298	History of Photography
0308-731X	Cherwell
0308-7344	Potato Abstracts
0308-7379	Scottish Diver
0308-7387	Extel Book of Prospectuses and New Issues changed to Extel Prospectuses and New Issues Fiche Service
0308-7395	Quarterly Index Islamicus

0308-7417 Historical Research for University Degrees in the United Kingdom. Part 1: Theses Completed *see* 0268-6716
0308-7425 Historical Research for University Degrees in the United Kingdom. Part 2: Theses in Progress *see* 0268-6724
0308-745X Partners
0308-7484 Registered Accountant†
0308-7506 Tertiary Research Group. Special Papers *changed to* Tertiary Research Special Papers
0308-7565 Canoeing†
0308-762X International Newsletter
0308-7638 Forestry and British Timber
0308-7646 Gifts *see* 0262-5946
0308-7654 Gas World
0308-7670 Scottish Ophthalmic Practitioner
0308-7751 Planning Consumer Markets
0308-7786 European Scrap Directory *see* 0261-426X
0308-7794 Metallurgical Plantmakers of the World
0308-7808 Therapy Weekly
0308-7816 Residential Social Work†
0308-7840 Community Home Schools Gazette *changed to* Community Homes Gazette
0308-7883 Income Tax Digest and Accountants' Review
0308-7948 Whillan's Tax Tables and Tax Reckoner *see* 0260-3926
0308-7999 Gazelle Review of Literature on the Middle East
0308-8006 Steel Traders of the World
0308-8022 Scottish Fisheries Research Reports
0308-8030 Simon's Tax Cases
0308-8049 Simon's Tax Intelligence
0308-8073 Chartered Institute of Building. Estimating Information Service *changed to* Technical Information Service-T I S
0308-8081 Chartered Institute of Building. Site Management Information Service *changed to* Technical Information Service-T I S
0308-812X Ley Hunter
0308-8146 Food Chemistry
0308-8197 Dairy Industries International
0308-8219 Bar List of the United Kingdom†
0308-8227 Rights *changed to* Civil Liberty
0308-8359 Materials Handling Index *changed to* Manufacturing and Materials Handling Index
0308-8367 Laboratory Equipment Index
0308-8375 Electronic Engineering Index
0308-8383 Engineering Components and Materials Index
0308-8391 Chemical Engineering Index *changed to* Process Engineering Index
0308-8405 Manchester United Football Book†
0308-8456 Archaeology in Britain (Year)
0308-8464 Financial Times International Year Books: World Hotel Directory
0308-8480 C A B News†
0308-8499 Extel Issuing House Year Book
0308-8537 Bectis Bulletin
0308-8561 Domestic Heating Plus Plumbing: Bathrooms-Kitchens *changed to* Domestic Heating Plus Plumbing: Bathrooms
0308-8669 Labour Weekly
0308-8677 L A N S A
0308-8766 Society of Osteopaths. Journal†
0308-8774 Latest Literature in Family Planning
0308-8839 Maritime Policy and Management
0308-8855 World Cement Technology *see* 0263-6050
0308-8863 Agricultural Engineering Abstracts
0308-888X Essays in Poetics
0308-8987 Kitchin's Road Transport Law
0308-9002 Interest Rate Service
0308-9037 Kent Family History Society. Record Publication
0308-9053 C A S S News *see* 0260-390X
0308-9088 City Directory
0308-9126 N D T International
0308-9134 Security and Protection
0308-9142 Iron and Steel International *see* 0143-7798
0308-9274 A G M Service
0308-9290 Research Fields in Physics at United Kingdom Universities and Polytechnics
0308-9304 A B C Freight Guide
0308-9347 Music Master *changed to* Music Master Catalogue
0308-9398 Footwear Industry Statistical Review
0308-9533 Highways and Road Construction International *changed to* Highways
0308-9541 Journal of Applied Systems Analysis
0308-9568 L A C News†
0308-9584 Agent's Hotel Gazetteer: Tourist Cities *changed to* Agent's Hotel Gazetteer: Cities of Europe
0308-9614 Domestic Heating and Air Conditioning
0308-9649 Tertiary Research
0308-9665 Building Management Abstracts *changed to* Technical Information Service-T I S
0308-9673 Extel Handbook of Market Leaders
0308-9703 Epilepsy News *see* 0262-5474
0308-9762 Classical Music Weekly *changed to* Classical Music
0308-9770 Iron and Steel Industry: Monthly Statistics†
0308-9789 I M M Bulletin
0308-9819 Great Britain. Department of the Environment. Housing and Construction Statistics
0308-9886 Body Lines
0309-0019 Performing Right News
0309-0078 National Association of Pension Funds. Annual Survey
0309-0108 Royal Observatory, Edinburgh. Annual Report†
0309-0132 Great Britain. Medical Research Council. Handbook
0309-0167 Histopathology
0309-0175 Independent Broadcasting Authority. Annual Report and Accounts
0309-0191 University of Sheffield. Newsletter Diary *changed to* University of Sheffield. Diary of Events
0309-0191 University of Sheffield. Newsletter Diary *changed to* University of Sheffield. Newsletter
0309-023X Soil and Water
0309-0248 B S R I A Technical Notes
0309-0256 Media Reporter
0309-0264 Food Trades Directory & Food Buyer's Yearbook
0309-0329 Canada-U.K. Year Book
0309-0388 Commonwealth Diary of Coming Events *see* 0141-8513
0309-0396 Shaw Newsletter
0309-040X Offshore Service Vessel Register
0309-0531 Nutrition Information Centre. Bulletin†
0309-0558 Managerial Law
0309-0566 European Journal of Marketing
0309-0574 Recommended Recordings
0309-0582 Management Bibliographies and Reviews
0309-0590 Journal of European Industrial Training
0309-0655 British Library. Lending Division. Current Serials Received *changed to* British Library. Document Supply Centre. Science Reference and Information Service. Current Serials Received
0309-0698 Monographs on Physical Biochemistry
0309-0728 Industrial Archaeology Review†
0309-0787 Journal for the Study of the Old Testament. Supplement Series
0309-0809 Milk Bulletin
0309-0817 M I R A Automobile Abstracts
0309-0884 Performing Right Year Book
0309-0892 Journal for the Study of the Old Testament
0309-099X Royal Observatory. Occasional Reports
0309-1031 Dog News and Family Pets
0309-1082 Great Britain. Land Resources Development Centre. Progress Report
0309-1112 Family Planning Today
0309-1139 Cadmium Abstracts *changed to* Cadscan
0309-118X InterMedia
0309-1252 Bristow's Book of Yachts
0309-1287 Protozoological Abstracts
0309-1295 Nutrition Abstracts and Reviews. Series A: Human and Experimental
0309-1309 Mervyn Peake Review
0309-1317 International Journal of Urban and Regional Research
0309-1325 Progress in Human Geography
0309-1333 Progress in Physical Geography
0309-135X Nutrition Abstracts and Reviews. Series B: Livestock Feeds and Feeding
0309-1376 Meccano Magazine
0309-1384 Planner
0309-1414 Police Review
0309-1422 Waterways World
0309-1449 British Quarrying & Slag Federation. Technical Review *see* 0141-6936
0309-1465 Developing Railways
0309-1473 I R C S Medical Science: Environmental Biology *changed to* I R C S Medical Science: Environmental and Social Medicine
0309-1481 I R C S Medical Science: Clinical Biochemistry†
0309-149X I R C S Medical Science: Developmental Biology and Medicine†
0309-1503 I R C S Medical Science: Drug Metabolism and Toxicology†
0309-1511 I R C S Medical Science: Pathology†
0309-152X I R C S Medical Science: Psychology and Psychiatry†
0309-1546 I R C S Medical Science: Clinical Medicine *changed to* I R C S Medical Science: Clinical Medicine and Surgery
0309-1554 I R C S Medical Science: Nervous System†
0309-1562 I R C S Medical Science: Experimental Animals†
0309-1600 Institution of Water Engineers and Scientists. Journal
0309-1619 Powys Review
0309-1627 Faith & Worship
0309-1635 British Journal of Alcohol and Alcoholism *see* 0735-0414
0309-1643 Land Resource Bibliography†
0309-1651 Cell Biology International Reports
0309-166X Cambridge Journal of Economics
0309-1708 Advances in Water Resources
0309-1740 Meat Science
0309-1783 Hobart Paperbacks
0309-1813 Atomic Absorption & Emission Spectrometry Abstracts
0309-1821 Guinea-Pig News Letter†
0309-1848 Rat News Letter
0309-1902 Journal of Medical Engineering & Technology
0309-1929 Geophysical and Astrophysical Fluid Dynamics
0309-1945 Greater London Arts Association. Annual Report†
0309-1953 Heat Transfer & Fluid Flow Digest
0309-1961 Lectures in Commercial Diplomacy *see* 0378-5920
0309-2003 Middle East Health
0309-2097 O E Report
0309-2143 Converter Directory
0309-2178 University of London King's College. Department of Geography. Occasional Paper
0309-2216 International Copper Information Bulletin
0309-2224 Conservation News
0309-2232 Library Research Occasional Paper *see* 0143-5124
0309-2275 Oxfordshire Family Historian
0309-233X Vision†
0309-2356 U K Chemical Industry Statistics Handbook†
0309-2402 Journal of Advanced Nursing
0309-2445 Publishing History
0309-2534 Advances in Raman Spectroscopy†
0309-2658 Action (Horsham) *changed to* Action Research
0309-2666 Medical Technologist and Scientist
0309-2984 History Workshop
0309-300X Latin America Commodities Report
0309-3018 Finishing Industries *see* 0264-2506
0309-3077 L P Gas Review
0309-3093 Berkshire Archaeological Journal
0309-3115 United Kingdom Temperance Alliance. Alliance News
0309-314X Online Review
0309-3204 Council for British Archaeology. Newsletter and Calendar of Excavations *changed to* British Archaeological News
0309-3247 Journal of Strain Analysis for Engineering Design
0309-3263 Reading Geographer†
0309-3298 In the Making
0309-331X Coffee International *see* 0262-5938
0309-3328 Counterpoint†
0309-3336 What Hi-Fi?
0309-345X African Environment Special Reports
0309-3468 Wiltshire Natural History Magazine *changed to* Wiltshire Archaeological and Natural History Magazine (1982)
0309-3476 Wiltshire Archaeological Magazine *changed to* Wiltshire Archaeological and Natural History Magazine (1982)
0309-3484 Junior Education
0309-3492 Third Way
0309-3557 Recycling and Waste Disposal†
0309-3573 A E P Journal *see* 0266-7363
0309-3646 Prosthetics and Orthotics International
0309-3654 Messenger
0309-3700 Liverpool Classical Monthly
0309-3786 G L A D Journal
0309-3891 Journal of Consumer Studies & Home Economics
0309-3913 African Journal of Medicine & Medical Sciences
0309-393X Royal Scottish Museum Information Series: Art & Archaeology†
0309-3948 Institute of Marine Engineers Technical Reports
0309-3980 Free Nation
0309-4073 Leveller†
0309-409X Chelsea Spelaeological Society. Records
0309-4170 Christian Librarian
0309-426X Advances in Infrared and Raman Spectroscopy†
0309-4332 Geophysical Abstracts *see* 0268-7941
0309-4359 Gramophone Popular Catalogue
0309-4367 Gramophone Classical Catalogue
0309-4405 Elgar Society. Newsletter *see* 0143-1269
0309-4413 Directory for Disabled People
0309-4472 Institute of Oceanographic Sciences. Annual Report
0309-4545 Fertility and Contraception†
0309-4561 Plastics and Rubber International
0309-457X Maghreb Review
0309-4693 Social Service Abstracts
0309-4707 Middle East Electricity
0309-474X European Bulletin and Press
0309-4898 Style Pattern Book *changed to* Style Magazine
0309-4928 C I I Journal
0309-4944 International Petroleum Abstracts
0309-4960 Worldwide Marketing Opportunities Digest
0309-4979 Coal Abstracts
0309-4995 Employment Digest
0309-510X Practical Self-Sufficiency *changed to* Home Farm
0309-5118 Hatcher Review
0309-5134 Daily Mail Skier's Holiday Guide *changed to* Audi/Daily Mail Skier's Holiday Guide
0309-5150 Optics Abstracts†
0309-5207 Journal of Beckett Studies
0309-524X Wind Engineering
0309-5258 Leasing Digest *changed to* Asset Finance and Leasing Digest
0309-5290 Directory of Technical and Further Education
0309-5304 L G O R U Transportation News†

1526 ISSN INDEX

0309-5312 X-Ray Diffraction Abstracts
0309-5320 Laser Raman & Infrared Spectroscopy Abstracts
0309-5339 Directory of European Associations. Part 2: National Learned, Scientific & Technical Societies
0309-5355 Popular Hi-Fi and Sound *changed to* New Hi-Fi Sound
0309-5371 Statistics - Asia & Australasia: Sources for Market Research
0309-5398 Waste Management Information Bulletin
0309-5444 Microcomputer Analysis *see* 0263-6522
0309-5452 Statistics - America
0309-5495 Newsrelease
0309-5541 ARCA
0309-5606 Quarry and Mining News
0309-5614 Chartered Institute of Public Finance and Accountancy. Education Statistics. Actuals
0309-5630 Chambers Trades Register of Scotland and North East England†
0309-5649 Chambers Trades Register of the Wirral to the Wash†
0309-5703 Tenders and Contracts Journal
0309-5770 Catalysts in Chemistry
0309-586X Agricultural Administration
0309-5991 Semiconductors and Insulators
0309-6149 Croydon Natural History & Scientific Society. Bulletin
0309-6157 A B C World Airways Guide
0309-622X Chartered Institute of Public Finance and Accountancy. Fire Service Statistics. Actuals
0309-6254 Nautical Review *see* 0265-2455
0309-6270 Logophile: the Cambridge Journal of Words and Language
0309-653X Chartered Institute of Public Finance and Accountancy. Personal Social Services Statistics. Actuals
0309-6629 Chartered Institute of Public Finance and Accountancy. Public Library Statistics. Actuals
0309-667X Great Britain. Civil Aviation Authority. General Aviation Safety Information Leaflets
0309-6858 International Association of Dentistry for Children. Journal
0309-6866 Fire Prevention
0309-6890 Gas Kinetics and Energy Transfer†
0309-6904 I P P F Co-operative Information Service
0309-703X Company Secretary's Review
0309-7234 European Industrial Relations Review
0309-7242 Purchasing and Supply *see* 0265-2072
0309-7285 Cienfuegos Press Anarchist Review
0309-7323 Scottish Opera News
0309-7374 North West Industrial Development Association. Newsletter†
0309-7463 Institute of Oceanographic Sciences. Collected Reprints
0309-7498 Hospital Engineering
0309-751X Financial Times International Year Books: World Insurance
0309-7552 Science Bulletin†
0309-7560 Forth Naturalist and Historian
0309-7676 International Business Lawyer
0309-7684 International Legal Practitioner
0309-7714 Journal of Environmental Planning and Pollution Control†
0309-7765 Bronte Society Transactions
0309-7773 British Psychological Society. Annual Report
0309-7803 Surrey Archaeological Collections
0309-7846 Hydrographic Journal
0309-7854 Economic Bulletin (London)
0309-7900 Tax Planning International Review
0309-7935 Bookplate Society Newsletter
0309-7951 Texture of Crystalline Solids *see* 0730-3300
0309-7978 Breaking Chains
0309-7986 Cumberland and Westmorland Antiquarian and Archaeological Society. Transactions
0309-7994 Devonshire Association for the Advancement of Science, Literature and Art. Report and Transactions
0309-8036 Theatre Papers
0309-8044 British Federation of Music Festivals. Yearbook
0309-8079 Handicapped Children
0309-8168 Capital and Class
0309-8230 Noise Control, Vibration and Insulation *see* 0143-6481
0309-8249 Journal of Philosophy of Education
0309-8265 Journal of Geography in Higher Education
0309-8273 East Coast Digest *changed to* Coast and Country
0309-8338 Cumbria Guide Industry and Commerce
0309-8346 Huguenot Society of London. Proceedings
0309-8354 Huguenot Society of London. Quarto Series
0309-8389 Kirklees Chamber of Commerce. Member's Directory
0309-8397 Bradford and Halifax Chambers of Commerce Members Directory
0309-8486 Northamptoniana
0309-8524 Tourism International Research/ Caribbean†
0309-8559 Family History News and Digest
0309-8567 Tourism International Policy†
0309-8575 Tourism International History†
0309-8591 Croydon Bibliographies for Regional Survey
0309-8613 Tourism International Research/Pacific†
0309-8621 Tourism International Airletter†
0309-8648 Dozenal Review *see* 0260-4884
0309-8656 Croydon Natural History & Scientific Society. Proceedings and Transactions
0309-8710 Israel Physical Society. Annals
0309-8729 Infuse†
0309-877X Journal of Further and Higher Education
0309-8885 Computing Journal Abstracts
0309-8907 University of Leeds English Society Paper *see* 0144-3399
0309-8990 Trent Law Journal
0309-9105 Scottish Fisheries Information Pamphlets
0309-9113 Higher Education Current Awareness Bulletin†
0309-913X Hertfordshire People
0309-9156 Ideology and Consciousness *changed to* I & C
0309-9210 Thoroton Society of Nottinghamshire. Transactions
0309-9253 New Vegetarian *see* 0260-3233
0309-9334 Business Traveller
0310-0014 Australian Law Reports
0310-0049 Australian Mammalogy
0310-0081 Droughtmaster Digest
0310-0103 New South Wales. Higher Education Board. Higher Education Handbook†
0310-0111 Hunter's Hill Trust Journal
0310-0138 Massada Quarterly *changed to* Kivun
0310-0189 Space
0310-0294 Eco Info *changed to* Queensland Conservation Council Newsletter
0310-0308 F.A.A. Journal
0310-0316 Impact
0310-0367 Water
0310-0391 Bookmark
0310-0405 Australian Weed Control Handbook
0310-0537 Agriscene Australia
0310-057X Anaesthesia and Intensive Care Journal *changed to* Anaesthesia and Intensive Care
0310-0634 Audio Visual Australia†
0310-0677 Australia†
0310-0685 Australia. Bureau of Agricultural Economics. Meat Situation *see* 0311-0885
0310-0871 Australia. Bureau of Statistics. South Australian Office. Manufacturing Establishments *changed to* Australia. Bureau of Statistics. South Australian Office. Manufacturing Establishments, Details of Operations by Industry
0310-1010 Autosafe†
0310-1029 Australian Acoustical Society. Bulletin *changed to* Acoustics Australia
0310-1045 Australian Association of Permanent Building Societies. National Newsletter
0310-1053 Australian Business Law Review
0310-1118 Australian Family Circle
0310-1258 Australian Pipeliner
0310-1304 Australian Shell News
0310-1347 Australian Superannuation and Employee Benefits Planning in Action *changed to* Australian Superannuation and Employee Benefits Guide
0310-138X Australian Veterinary Practitioner
0310-1398 Australian Wool Corporation. Bi-Monthly Market Report *changed to* Australian Wool Corporation. Wool Market News: Monthly Perspective
0310-1444 Bell Bryant News
0310-1452 Belle
0310-1584 Cabbages and Kings
0310-1649 Canberra Papers in Continuing Education
0310-1797 Cleo
0310-186X New South Wales. Department of Agriculture. Commodity Bulletin
0310-1878 C C E A Newsletter
0310-1886 Commonwealth Police Officers' Association Journal
0310-1894 Commonwealth Scientific and Industrial Research Organization. Division of Geomechanics. Abstracts of Published Papers
0310-1908 Commonwealth Scientific and Industrial Research Organization. Division of Atmospheric Physics. Annual Report *see* 0159-0219
0310-1967 Comworks Technical Bulletin *changed to* Australia. Department of Housing and Construction. Technical Bulletin
0310-2076 Cosmopolitan
0310-2084 Australia. Department of Agriculture. Marketing Division. Cotton Market News *changed to* Australia. Department of Primary Industry. Cotton Market News
0310-2157 Deed†
0310-2165 Digger
0310-222X Earth Garden
0310-2246 Economic Newsletter†
0310-2467 Bronze Swagman Book of Bush Verse
0310-270X Environmental Control†
0310-2890 Grass Roots
0310-2920 Guide to Book Outlets in Australia†
0310-2939 Habitat Australia
0310-2971 Herd Book for Angora Goats in Australia
0310-3064 Australian Council of Employers Federation. Economic Newsletter *see* 0155-2090
0310-3137 Jaguar Journal of Australia†
0310-3145 Keep Australia Beautiful News†
0310-320X Landline in Australia
0310-3242 Learning Exchange†
0310-334X Manifest
0310-3439 Metropolitan Speleological Society. Newsletter
0310-3471 Minie News
0310-3625 National Water Well Association. Journal *changed to* W M D Journal
0310-3684 New South Wales. Attorney-General. Bureau of Crime Statistics and Research. Statistical Report
0310-3706 New South Wales Clayworker
0310-3714 New South Wales Dairyman *see* 0810-4115
0310-3773 Niugini Caver
0310-3781 N. A. G. Newsletter†
0310-3811 Australia. Chamber of Industries, Northern Territory. Northern Territory Business Journal *changed to* Australia. Chamber of Industries, Northern Territory. N.T. Business Journal
0310-4036 Priorities†
0310-4044 Probe†
0310-4079 Queensland. Department of Education. Research and Curriculum Branch. Curriculum Paper
0310-4087 Queensland. Department of Education. Research and Curriculum Branch. Document *changed to* Queensland. Department of Education. Information and Publications Branch. Document
0310-4095 Queensland. Department of Education. Research and Curriculum Branch. Reporting Research *changed to* Queensland. Department of Education. Research Branch. Reporting Research
0310-4141 R. M. C. Historical Journal†
0310-4168 Refractory Girl
0310-4184 P E X: Australia's Petroleum Exploration Newsletter
0310-4257 Rydge's C C E M Industry Report and Buyers Guide†
0310-4273 Saturday Club Book of Poetry *see* 0313-685X
0310-4303 Science in New Guinea
0310-4389 Something on Paper
0310-4540 Syntec
0310-4575 Tasmanian Chamber of Industries. Service Bulletin *changed to* T.C.I. News
0310-4591 Tasmanian Official Publications†
0310-4605 Teaching Religion Today†
0310-463X Tok Tok Bilong Haus Buk
0310-4664 Training and Development in Australia
0310-4729 University of Sydney. Archives Record
0310-4923 Rural Reconstruction Authority of Western Australia. Annual Report *changed to* Rural Adjustment and Finance Corporation of Western Australia. Annual Report
0310-5083 Ploughman's Lunch *see* 0310-6837
0310-5121 Queensland. Department of Education. Research and Curriculum Branch. Information Statement *changed to* Queensland. Department of Education. Information and Publications Branch. Information Statement
0310-5202 South Australia. Department of Education. School Libraries Branch. Review†
0310-5296 Australian Labor Party (NSW Branch). Labor Year Book†
0310-5415 Current Australian and New Zealand Legal Literature Index
0310-544X Australian Department of Social Security. Social Security Quarterly *changed to* Australian Department of Social Security. Social Security Journal
0310-5466 Sydney Town Express
0310-5504 A. C. A. P. Newsletter
0310-5571 International Association for the Evaluation of Educational Achievement (Australia). Newsletter†
0310-558X I. E. A. (Australia) Report†
0310-5601 Urbanology
0310-5652 Feedback†
0310-5695 Monash University. Higher Education Advisory and Research Unit. Notes on Higher Education†
0310-5709 Developing Education
0310-5725 Environment Control News†
0310-5814 Ancient Society; Resources for Teachers
0310-5822 Aboriginal Child at School
0310-5857 Ekstasis†
0310-5865 Australian Computer Weekly *changed to* Pacific Computer Weekly
0310-589X National Greyhound News
0310-5903 Australian Weight Lifting Journal†
0310-5938 Gredzens
0310-5946 New South Wales Horizons†
0310-5989 Australian Disc and Tape Review
0310-6012 Australia. National Drug Information Service. Technical Information Bulletin *see* 0157-8200
0310-6020 Filter: a Paper for Secondary Science Teachers
0310-608X Association of Teachers of English as a Foreign Language. Bulletin
0310-6152 Australia's External Aid *changed to* Australia's Overseas Development Assistance. Budget Paper

ISSN INDEX 1527

0310-6217 Tube
0310-6276 Australia. Environment Housing and Community Development. Farm Holidays†
0310-6330 Western Australia. Main Roads Department. Technical Report†
0310-6357 Mathnews *changed to* P R I M E
0310-6381 Australian Theatre Review†
0310-639X Gentle Folk and Other Creatures
0310-6403 Australasian Stud and Stable *see* 0311-8215
0310-6411 Video-Tronics
0310-6462 M.C.B. Newsletter *changed to* M.C.B. News
0310-6500 Australian Comparative Education Society. Newsletter
0310-6578 Cities Commission Bulletin†
0310-6632 Newsletter on Soviet and East European Studies in Australia and New Zealand†
0310-6659 Indonesian Acquisitions List
0310-6721 Meatworker
0310-6748 Ball Bearing Journal
0310-6756 Parks and Wildlife†
0310-6810 Australian Journal of Hospital Pharmacy
0310-6837 Ploughman†
0310-6861 St. Thomas More Society. Journal
0310-687X Queensland Architect
0310-6969 Welcare
0310-7078 South Australian Canine Journal
0310-7108 Travel News from Victoria, Australia
0310-7175 Independent Education
0310-7213 Wedgwood News
0310-723X Aboriginal News†
0310-7299 Albury/Wodonga†
0310-7345 Official Publications of Western Australia†
0310-740X Serbian Bulletin
0310-7442 Spectrum†
0310-7531 Tasmanian Transport Bulletin *changed to* Tasmanian Transport Statistics
0310-7582 Steel Spiel
0310-7787 W A P E T Journal†
0310-7809 W E L Spoken
0310-7817 Australian Federal Tax Reporter
0310-7833 Australian Wildlife Research
0310-7841 Australian Journal of Plant Physiology
0310-7949 Interaction (Clayton North)
0310-8031 International Telex Directory. International Service
0310-8147 Papua New Guinea. Department of Social Development and Home Affairs. Social Science Research†
0310-8163 C. S. I. R. O. Sheep and Wool Research†
0310-818X Scout Association of Australia. Review of Progress *changed to* Scout Association of Australia. Annual Report
0310-8198 News Exchange†
0310-8228 Consequences†
0310-8252 Australian Marxist Review
0310-8279 Cattle *changed to* Australian Cattle Magazine
0310-8341 Aboriginal Medical Service. Newsletter
0310-8368 Australian Speedway Yearbook *changed to* Peter Webster's International Speedway Review
0310-8465 Interprobe *changed to* Business Week
0310-8546 Victoria, Australia. Directory of Government Departments and Authorities *see* 0158-1589
0310-8554 Graduate Careers Council of Australia. Digest of Research†
0310-8562 Australian Estate and Gift Duty Reporter†
0310-8651 Executive Briefing†
0310-8740 J E T R O Information Bulletin *changed to* J E T R O News Digest
0310-8813 Australian Corporate Affairs Reporter *see* 0726-6065
0310-8856 Australian Advisory Council on Bibliographical Services. Library Services for Australia *see* 0812-6267
0310-8880 Irrigation Farmer
0310-8902 Australian Hi-Fi Annual
0310-8937 Informed Opinion†
0310-897X Western Australia. Department of Agriculture. Rangeland Management Section. Rangeland Bulletin†
0310-9011 Landscape Australia
0310-9054 A. P. E. A. News†
0310-9070 C S I R O Food Research Quarterly
0310-9100 Science and Technology†
0310-9143 Retrieval
0310-916X Institute of Economic Democracy. Information Bulletin
0310-9178 Artificial Breeding News *changed to* T H I O News!
0310-9186 Iris and Res Novissimae
0310-9267 Art Dialogue
0310-933X Australian Process Engineering *see* 0159-3935
0310-9348 On the Move
0310-9356 Cricket Quadrant
0310-9399 Soaring in the A.C.T.†
0310-9534 B.N.I.A. *changed to* Build
0310-9569 A.C.E.S. Review
0310-9593 Tariff Insight
0310-964X Liberation
0310-9658 Ecology Action Newsletter
0310-9666 Murray Grey World
0310-9674 M.L.T.A. News
0310-9704 Marine Board of Hobart. Newsletter†
0310-9879 Australian and Pacific Book Prices Current†
0310-9917 Australia. Bureau of Agricultural Economics. Wheat: Situation and Outlook†
0310-9968 Gegenschein
0311-0001 Caspa *changed to* Pool & Spa Review
0311-0079 National Bottle Review
0311-0095 Artviews
0311-015X Steel Fabrication Journal
0311-0184 Pharmaceutical Society of Victoria. Bulletin *changed to* Pharmaceutical Society of Australia (Victorian Branch). Bulletin
0311-0192 Insurance and Banking Record *see* 0725-4644
0311-0222 Pivot†
0311-0230 Electronics News
0311-0265 Australian Securities Law Reporter
0311-0273 Mitsui News
0311-029X Credit Scene *changed to* Credo
0311-0311 I F A P News *changed to* I F A P Bulletin
0311-032X Moonbi
0311-0346 Australian Racing Drivers Club Journal
0311-0362 Garamut *see* 0158-6262
0311-0370 Agribusiness Decision
0311-0389 Company Directors Association of Australia. Directors Law Reporter
0311-0400 Australian Golf Instructional *changed to* Australian Golf (1978)
0311-0419 Kabar
0311-046X Craft Australia
0311-0478 Society for Mass Media and Resource Technology. Journal
0311-0486 Challenge
0311-0559 Flautist
0311-0567 Impact†
0311-0621 I M U Canberra Circular
0311-0699 Dental Anaesthesia and Sedation†
0311-0702 South Australia. Department of Labour. Guide to Legislation
0311-0710 University of Sydney. Department of Architectural Science. General Reports†
0311-0729 Australian Mathematical Society Gazette
0311-0737 Checkpoint
0311-0745 Nature Conservation Council of N.S.W. Bulletin *changed to* Nature Conservation Council of N.S.W. Newsletter
0311-0753 Plain Turkey
0311-0761 Dane Digest
0311-0788 Australia. Bureau of Agricultural Economics. Coarse Grains: Situation and Outlook†
0311-0826 Pacific Travel Directory
0311-0842 A.M.R.C. Review†
0311-0850 Canberra Bulletin†
0311-0885 Australia. Bureau of Agricultural Economics. Meat: Situation and Outlook†
0311-0931 Australian and New Zealand Environmental Report†
0311-094X Australian Tax Review
0311-0982 C A T Newsletter†
0311-1008 Engineering Associate *changed to* Engineers Australia
0311-1016 Nurungi
0311-1032 A.B.O.A. Newsletter (Australian Bank Officials Association) *changed to* A.B.E.U. Newsletter
0311-1172 Your Chamber Reporting†
0311-1180 Concrete Masonry Association of Australia. Project Review†
0311-1199 Australian Speedway†
0311-1229 Caesarian
0311-1237 Australia. Department of Manufacturing Industry. Technical Newsletter†
0311-1245 Cor Serpentis
0311-1253 A I M L S Newsletter
0311-127X V.C.M. File *changed to* File
0311-1342 Primary Journal *changed to* Primary Journal K-7
0311-1385 Baker and Miller's Journal *changed to* Australasian Baking
0311-1431 Farming Forum
0311-175X Big League
0311-1784 Words and Windmills
0311-1806 Modern Cleaning *see* 0813-4804
0311-1822 Prod†
0311-1873 Nexus†
0311-1881 Australian Entomological Magazine
0311-1903 Chartered Builder†
0311-1911 Power Farming
0311-1938 South Australia. Department of Agriculture. Agricultural Record
0311-1946 Country Shows Annual *changed to* Agricultural Shows Annual
0311-1954 Australian Journal of Remedial Education
0311-1962 Polycom†
0311-2152 Australia. Patent Office. Annual Report of Activities
0311-2160 Manufacturing News in Australia *changed to* Factory Management
0311-2179 Travel Consultant†
0311-2195 Tourism Australia†
0311-2209 Australia. Department of Manufacturing Industry. Bulletin *changed to* Australia. Department of Industry and Commerce. Bulletin
0311-2217 Sound News
0311-2225 Adbrief
0311-2233 Studium
0311-2349 Q I E R Journal *see* 0818-545X
0311-2373 Serials in Education in Australian Libraries: a Union List
0311-2381 New Products Bulletin†
0311-2497 Cordell's Building Cost Book and Estimating Guide. New South Wales *changed to* Cordell's Building Cost Guide. Commercial and Industrial
0311-2519 Business Outlook†
0311-2527 Action Report
0311-2543 Education Research and Perspectives
0311-2659 Gay Liberation Press *see* 0312-7915
0311-2667 Australian Key Business Directory
0311-2764 Australian Composer
0311-2772 Teacher Feedback *see* 0013-1156
0311-2780 Mitchell Business Review†
0311-2810 Poets of Australia
0311-290X Southeast Asian Research Materials Group. Newsletter *see* 0158-1953
0311-2926 Ark
0311-2934 Australian Copyright Council. Bulletin
0311-2950 Australia. Bureau of Agricultural Economics. Fibre Review†
0311-2969 Hospitality Yearbook *see* 0156-3688
0311-3000 Australian Council on Awards in Advanced Education. Bulletin†
0311-306X Cancer Forum
0311-3078 South Australia. State Library. Reference Services Branch. Reference Services Bibliographies†
0311-3140 Monash University Law Review
0311-323X Australian Audio-Visual Reference Book
0311-3248 A N Z H E S Journal *changed to* History of Education Review
0311-3531 Earth Science and Related Information
0311-354X Municipal Engineering in Australia
0311-3558 Waste Disposal and Water Management in Australia
0311-3655 Chart Book of the Melbourne Share Price Index†
0311-368X Community†
0311-3760 Migration Action
0311-3930 Globe
0311-4015 Goodwill†
0311-4023 Impact†
0311-4031 Play
0311-404X Splashdown†
0311-4074 Australia. Department of Aboriginal Affairs. Western Australian Office. Newsletter†
0311-4198 Hecate
0311-4201 Graduate Careers†
0311-4511 Administration for Development
0311-4546 Ecos
0311-4627 Canberra Linguist
0311-4775 Unicorn
0311-4805 South Australia. Department of Environment and Planning. Coastline†
0311-5070 Business Who's Who Australian Buying Reference
0311-5518 Alcheringa
0311-5836 C S I R O Index
0311-5984 Australian Law Librarians' Group. Newsletter
0311-628X Australian Transport
0311-6336 Australian Bulletin of Labour
0311-6603 Australian Institute of Criminology. Information Bulletin *changed to* Information Bulletin of Australian Criminology
0311-6875 Australian Education Review
0311-6999 Australian Educational Researcher
0311-7057 Scarlet Letter
0311-7189 Australia. Environment Housing and Community Development. Annual Report†
0311-7731 Modern Office and Data Management *changed to* Modern Office
0311-7839 Australian Sea Spray
0311-7979 A W R C Activities†
0311-7987 Australian Water Resources Council. Water Resources Newsletter *changed to* Australian Water Resources Council. Water News
0311-7995 Australian Foreign Affairs Record
0311-8150 Australian Birds
0311-8215 Stud and Stable
0311-8223 Australian Parks & Recreation
0311-8347 Thoroughbred Breeders' Handbook
0311-8576 New South Wales. Department of Agriculture. Technical Bulletin
0311-8665 Australian Farm Management Society Newsletter
0311-8754 Right to Choose
0311-8789 Australia. Bureau of Agricultural Economics. Oilseeds: Situation and Outlook†
0311-8835 Australia. Bureau of Agricultural Economics. Situation and Outlook (Year). Cotton†
0311-8843 Australia. Bureau of Agricultural Economics. Dairy Products: Situation and Outlook†
0311-8924 Historical Journal
0311-8959 Australia. Department of Primary Industry. Fishing Industry Research Committee. Annual Report
0311-8975 Australia. Bureau of Statistics. Mineral Production, Australia
0311-8983 National Acoustic Laboratories, Sydney. Annual Report†
0311-905X Current Therapeutics

1528 ISSN INDEX

0311-9300 University of New England. Management Forum
0311-9319 Overseas Map Acquisitions
0311-9491 Queensland. Department of Local Government. Conference of Local Authority Engineers. Proceedings†
0311-9629 Australian Directory of Services for Alcoholism and Drug Dependence†
0311-9882 Australian Wool Sale Statistics. Statistical Analysis. Part A & B
0312-0007 University of Wollongong. Calendar *see* 0726-4844
0312-0007 University of Wollongong. Calendar *see* 0726-0717
0312-0007 University of Wollongong. Calendar *changed to* University of Wollongong. Postgraduate Handbook
0312-004X Stereo Buyer's Guide. Directory†
0312-0058 Stereo Buyer's Guide. Manual *see* 0819-0216
0312-0066 Stereo Buyer's Guide. Turntables *see* 0819-0208
0312-0074 Stereo Buyer's Guide. Speakers†
0312-0104 Stereo Buyer's Guide. Cassettes†
0312-0112 Australasian Small Press Review†
0312-0325 Australian Women's Wear†
0312-1356 Australia. Bureau of Statistics. Tasmanian Office. Public Justice†
0312-1372 Chain Reaction
0312-1437 Australia. Bureau of Statistics. Trade Union Statistics, Australia
0312-1658 Queensland Lawyer
0312-1674 New South Wales Law Reports
0312-200X C H O M I-Das
0312-2115 Australian Road Index
0312-2417 Australian Archaeology
0312-259X Australia. National Library. Acquisitions Newsletter†
0312-2654 Metro
0312-3162 Western Australian Museum. Records
0312-3480 Working Kelpie Council. National Stud Book
0312-3685 Mathematical Scientist
0312-4029 Industrial Arbitration Service
0312-407X Australian Social Work
0312-4134 A F C O Quarterly†
0312-455X Work and People
0312-4681 Fleetline
0312-4738 Endocrine Society of Australia. Proceedings
0312-4746 Official Year Book of Australia *changed to* Australia. Bureau of Statistics. Year Book Australia
0312-5033 Australian Journal of Early Childhood
0312-5041 Humanities Research Centre Bulletin
0312-5211 Commonwealth Scientific and Industrial Research Organization. C S I R O Textile News
0312-5327 Australian Giftguide Magazine
0312-5467 Australia. Working Papers in Language and Linguistics
0312-5599 Australian Hospitals and Health Services Yearbook
0312-5807 Australian Naval Institute. Journal
0312-5963 Clinical Pharmacokinetics
0312-620X Rebuild
0312-6242 Australia. Bureau of Statistics. Value of Primary Production, Excluding Mining, and Indexes of Quantum and Unit Gross Value of Agricultural Production *changed to* Australia. Bureau of Statistics. Value of Agricultural Commodities Produced, Australia
0312-6250 Australia. Bureau of Statistics. Australian National Accounts - National Income and Expenditure
0312-6447 Australia. Bureau of Statistics. Dairying Industry *changed to* Australia. Bureau of Statistics. Dairying and Dairy Products, Australia
0312-6994 Australia. Law Reform Commission. Annual Report
0312-7559 Nepean Review†
0312-7850 Australia. Bureau of Statistics. Tasmanian Office. Local Government Finance
0312-7915 Working Papers in Sex, Science and Culture†
0312-7923 Royal Australian College of Dental Surgeons. Annals *see* 0158-1570
0312-8059 A N Z A A S Congress Papers
0312-827X Australian Journal for Health, Physical Education and Recreation *see* 0813-2283
0312-875X Modern Medicine
0312-8997 West Australian Nut and Tree Crop Association Yearbook
0312-9217 Australia's Overseas Development Assistance *changed to* Australia's Overseas Development Assistance. Budget Paper
0312-9225 Commonwealth Scientific and Industrial Research Organization. Division of Chemical Technology. Research Review *changed to* Commonwealth Scientific and Industrial Research Organization. Division of Chemical & Wood Technology. Research Review
0312-9608 B M R Journal of Australian Geology and Geophysics
0312-9616 Media Information Australia
0312-9764 Telopea
0312-9837 Petroleum Newsletter
0312-9888 Luna
0313-0096 University of New South Wales Law Journal
0313-0568 Thomson's Liquor Guide
0313-122X Western Australian Museum. Records. Supplement
0313-1459 Span
0313-153X Reform
0313-1971 Australia. National Library. Annual Report
0313-2080 Theatre Australia
0313-2153 New Doctor
0313-2463 Victorian Government Publications
0313-251X Ancestral Searcher
0313-2781 Australia. Department of Primary Industry. Australian Plague and Locust Commission. Annual Report
0313-2919 Health Action†
0313-3192 Australian Plant Introduction Review
0313-3249 Instead
0313-3311 Australian Computer Society. Conference Proceedings†
0313-363X Skysailor
0313-4075 Ports of New South Wales Journal
0313-4083 Adelaide Botanic Gardens. Journal
0313-4245 Brunonia
0313-4253 Queensland Law Society Journal
0313-427X University of New South Wales. Library. Annual Report
0313-4288 L I P
0313-4334 Pedal Power
0313-4393 Industrial and Commercial Photography
0313-4504 Rhombus
0313-4954 Skindiving *changed to* Sportdiving
0313-5047 Tomorrow's Business Decisions *see* 0313-5055
0313-5055 McCabe-McMiles Letter
0313-5136 Commonwealth Record
0313-5519 Institution of Engineers, Australia. Transactions. Mechanical Engineering
0313-5780 Australia. Environmental Studies Working Papers
0313-5977 Canberra Historical Journal
0313-6086 Mineral Industry Quarterly
0313-6221 Parergon
0313-6620 Australian Citizen Limited *changed to* Interaction (Canberra)
0313-6647 Australian Journal of Public Administration
0313-6728 Queensland. Department of Education. Division of Special Education. Special Education Bulletin
0313-6744 Tableaus
0313-6825 Function
0313-685X S C O P P
0313-6906 University of Wollongong. Annual Report
0313-704X A E S I S Quarterly
0313-7384 Australian Society of Endodontology. Newsletter
0313-7414 Australian National University. Centre for Resource and Environmental Studies. Working Papers
0313-766X Powerboat
0313-7864 Enterprise: Western Australia†
0313-7872 Beach Conservation
0313-8143 Queensland Education Digest†
0313-8410 Monash University. Publications in Geography
0313-8445 Australian Company Law Reports
0313-8461 Australian Film, Television and Radio School Handbook
0313-8704 University of Sydney. Department of Agricultural Economics. Agricultural Extension Bulletin†
0313-8747 Explore
0313-8860 Western Geographer
0313-895X Australian Road Research Board. Technical Manual
0313-9050 Australian Computer Bulletin†
0313-9549 Environment W.A.
0313-9603 Australian Commonwealth Specialists' Catalogue†
0313-9611 Australian Banknote Catalogue†
0313-9727 Australia/Israel Review
0313-9921 University of Wollongong. Research Bulletin†
0313-9948 Australia. National Capital Development Commission. Technical Papers
0313-9980 Australian National University. National Centre for Development Studies. Newsletter
0314-0377 Australasian Shipping Record
0314-1004 Nutrition Society of Australia. Proceedings
0314-1039 Defence Force Journal
0314-111X National Rehabilitation Digest *see* 0728-490X
0314-1160 Criminal Law Journal
0314-1306 Wool Outlook†
0314-1357 Research Laboratories Review of Activities
0314-1438 Australian Forest Resources
0314-1578 D P Index and Software Register
0314-1586 Metal & Engineering Industry Year Book
0314-1608 Salssah on Com†
0314-1640 Australia. Bureau of Statistics. Tasmanian Office. Pocket Year Book of Tasmania
0314-1659 Australia. Bureau of Statistics. Tasmanian Office. Agricultural Industry *changed to* Australia. Bureau of Statistics. Tasmanian Office. Agriculture, Tasmania
0314-1667 Australia. Bureau of Statistics. Tasmanian Office. Fruit Production *see* 0810-9176
0314-1705 Australia. Bureau of Statistics. Tasmanian Office. Education†
0314-1888 Australia. Australian Bureau of Statistics. Tasmanian Office. Mining Tasmania
0314-2094 Australia. Bureau of Statistics. Tasmanian Office. Monthly Summary of Statistics Tasmania
0314-2531 Panorama (Hobart)
0314-254X Commonwealth Scientific and Industrial Research Organization. Division of Protein Chemistry. Annual Report
0314-285X Inprint
0314-2868 Australian Council of Trade Unions. Bulletin
0314-2876 Australian Society of Exploration Geophysicists. Bulletin
0314-2981 Helen Vale Foundation. Journal†
0314-3058 Trust News
0314-3171 Australian Institute of Petroleum. Annual Report
0314-3457 Queensland Geographer
0314-3767 Australian Society of Indexers Newsletter
0314-4224 Earthmover and Civil Contractor
0314-4240 Chemistry in Australia
0314-4321 Monitor *see* 0725-2986
0314-4607 Mining Review
0314-464X Australian Musician
0314-5204 Victorian Statutes Cumulative Supplement
0314-5514 Life: Be in It /Y S R News†
0314-6162 Howard Florey Institute of Experimental Physiology & Medicine. Annual Report and Notice of Meeting
0314-6200 Church & Nation
0314-660X Patient Management (Australia)
0314-6677 Science Fiction
0314-6820 Statistical Society of Australia. Newsletter
0314-7134 Victoria, Australia. Women's Bureau. Women and Work Newslettter *changed to* Women & Work
0314-724X V I S E News†
0314-7320 Currency
0314-7487 Energy
0314-7495 New Literature Review
0314-7533 Asian Studies Association of Australia. Review
0314-755X Monthly Summary of Australian Conditions *changed to* National Australia Bank Monthly Summary
0314-7592 Journal of Industry and Commerce
0314-7606 Sigma
0314-7762 Australian Mining Year Book
0314-7894 Candy Family History Newsletter†
0314-8009 Compass
0314-8580 A I I Journal
0314-8769 Aboriginal History
0314-9099 Canberra Anthropology
0315-0003 Accessible *see* 0027-9633
0315-0054 Dalhousie University. School of Library Service. Newsletter
0315-0062 Canadian Frontier†
0315-0097 Encounter
0315-0143 Urban Focus†
0315-0208 Spear
0315-0380 Eco/Log Week
0315-0496 Stuffed Crocodile†
0315-0518 Recreation Property *changed to* Ontario Cottager
0315-0534 Montreal Calendar Magazine *changed to* Montreal Magazine
0315-0542 Outdoor Canada
0315-0550 Cuttings and Comments†
0315-0607 Articles et Commentaires†
0315-0623 Lodgistiks†
0315-0631 Directory of Community Services in Metropolitan Toronto
0315-0720 Titmouse Review *changed to* Titmouse Annual
0315-0771 Ottawa Ethnic Groups Directory
0315-0836 Canadian Theatre Review
0315-0860 Historia Mathematica
0315-0879 Canadian Key Business Directory
0315-0887 Volleyball Technical Journal†
0315-0895 Guide to Departments of Sociology and Anthropology in Canadian Universities *see* 0316-1854
0315-0909 Canadian Amateur Boxing News
0315-0917 Beale's Letter
0315-0941 Geoscience Canada
0315-095X Y Canada
0315-1042 On Continuing Practice
0315-1174 T. S. Eliot Newsletter *see* 0704-5700
0315-1182 AudioScene Canada *changed to* Sound & Vision
0315-1204 Cooperateur Agricole
0315-1298 Heritage Canada *see* 0225-1485
0315-1301 Cosmetics
0315-1409 Canadian and International Education
0315-1433 Canadian Annual Review of Politics and Public Affairs
0315-1468 Canadian Journal of Civil Engineering
0315-162X Journal of Rheumatology
0315-1654 Energy Analects
0315-1700 World Directory of Historians of Mathematics
0315-1808 T A S A
0315-1840 L S M News†
0315-1859 Charlatan
0315-1867 Le Consommateur Canadien

ISSN INDEX 1529

0315-1972 Civic Public Works
0315-2022 Western Geographical Series
0315-2081 Eau du Quebec *see* 0823-0269
0315-2138 Bivoie
0315-2146 Entomological Society of Manitoba. Proceedings
0315-2154 Country Estate Magazine
0315-2227 Focus (Edmonton)
0315-2235 Venture Forth
0315-226X Corporation Professionnelle des Medecins du Quebec. Annuaire Medical
0315-2286 Canadian Bar National
0315-2316 R A D A R *changed to* Point de Repere
0315-2340 Documentation et Bibliotheques
0315-2359 Beaux-Arts
0315-2456 File
0315-2464 Canadian Police Chief *see* 0713-4517
0315-2561 Information North
0315-257X C P I Management Service *changed to* Corpus Chemical Report
0315-260X Quebec Chasse et Peche
0315-2685 Jewish Dialogue
0315-2804 Raincoast Chronicles
0315-2979 Corporation Professionnelle des Medecins du Quebec. Bulletin
0315-3010 Westwater†
0315-3037 Ego
0315-3088 Where to Eat in Canada
0315-310X Hellenic View
0315-3118 Skimania†
0315-3223 Biomass Energy Institute. Newsletter *changed to* Bio-Joule Magazine
0315-3290 Creative Canada
0315-3339 Accelerator (Ottawa)
0315-3371 History Collection: Canadian Catholic Church†
0315-3452 Canadian Layman
0315-3495 Canadian Defence Quarterly
0315-3509 Alberta Teachers' Association. Special Education Council. Newsletter
0315-3525 Canadian Rehabilitation Council for the Disabled. Employment Bulletin†
0315-3541 Canadian Association of University Schools of Music. Journal. *see* 0710-0353
0315-355X Alberta-Westmorland-Kent Regional Library. Extension Department. News†
0315-3584 Pathfinder Travel Parks Directory
0315-3606 Body Politic
0315-3630 Northern Journey†
0315-369X Reporting Classroom Research
0315-3770 Event
0315-3819 E D P In-Depth Reports
0315-3835 British Columbia Genealogist
0315-3843 C R E A Reporter *changed to* Canadian Real Estate
0315-3932 Waves
0315-3959 Canadian Dancers News
0315-3967 Cahiers Linguistiques d'Ottawa
0315-3975 Video-Presse
0315-4025 Cahier de Linguistique *see* 0710-0167
0315-4114 Concern International
0315-4149 International Fiction Review
0315-4254 C B Newsletter†
0315-4297 Journal of Canadian Art History
0315-4351 Comment on Education
0315-4459 Forgotten People
0315-4661 Computernews
0315-467X Chien d'Or
0315-4785 Arctic and Northern Development Digest *see* 0824-4952
0315-4793 Better Vending & Catering†
0315-484X Actrascope News†
0315-4874 Landscape/Paysage Canada†
0315-4998 Ligne Directe *see* 0823-5651
0315-5064 Manitoba Nature†
0315-5153 Vie Medicale au Canada Francais†
0315-5226 Vanguard (Vancouver)
0315-5463 Canadian Institute of Food Science and Technology. Journal
0315-5943 Repertoire de l'Edition au Quebec†
0315-5986 I N F O R Journal
0315-6168 Canadian Parliamentary Guide
0315-6230 Canadian Banker and I C B Review *see* 0822-6830
0315-6621 C P P A Newsletter
0315-6877 Canadian Society for Horticultutral Science. Journal *changed to* Canadian Society for Horticultural Science. Newsletter
0315-6915 Shaver Focus
0315-6923 Newsletter Called Fred
0315-694X Mark II *see* 0708-6024
0315-6966 Motion
0315-7083 Corpus Almanac & Canadian Sourcebook
0315-727X C S S E Yearbook†
0315-7288 Guide to Periodicals and Newspapers in the Public Libraries of Metropolitan Toronto
0315-7326 Sixteen Mm Films Available in the Public Libraries of Metropolitan Toronto
0315-7423 Grain
0315-7466 Atlantic Sport News†
0315-758X Next Year Country *changed to* Next Year Country Journal
0315-758X Next Year Country *changed to* Next Year Country News
0315-7601 Canada: an Historical Magazine†
0315-761X Canadian Archaeological Association. Bulletin *see* 0705-2006
0315-7725 Pakistan Forum *see* 0888-0328
0315-7784 Black Images†
0315-7911 City Magazine
0315-7997 Historical Reflections
0315-8020 Kateri
0315-8098 Corporate Insurance in Canada *see* 0008-3879
0315-8101 Mennonite Mirror
0315-811X Digest, Business & Law Journal
0315-8179 Ascent
0315-8233 Canadian Gas Association. Membership Directory
0315-8349 Directory of Gas Utilities *changed to* Canadian Gas Association Directory
0315-8527 Horizon
0315-8691 Foreign Focus†
0315-8705 Canadian Ethnic Studies Association. Bulletin
0315-8748 A I M E†
0315-8756 Log House
0315-8888 Emergency Librarian
0315-8934 Automatic Control: Theory and Applications *see* 0730-9538
0315-8977 Canadian Society for Mechanical Engineering. Transactions
0315-9000 Council of Ontario Universities. Annual Review *changed to* Council of Ontario Universities Quadrennial Review
0315-9027 Discovery Through Art
0315-906X Classmate
0315-9116 Manitoba Social Science Teacher
0315-9124 Manitoba School Library Audio Visual Association Journal
0315-9140 Canadian Mining Journal's Reference Manual & Buyers' Guide
0315-9159 Manitoba Science Teacher
0315-9183 Plant Management and Engineering
0315-9337 Canadian Micrographic Society. Micro Notes
0315-9353 Business Ed. News *see* 0833-062X
0315-9388 Educational Planning
0315-9396 Digger's Digest
0315-940X Universities Art Association of Canada. Journal
0315-9566 Humanities Research Council of Canada. Bulletin *see* 0707-8048
0315-9590 Council of Ontario Universities Triennial Review *changed to* Council of Ontario Universities Quadrennial Review
0315-9655 M I C Mission News
0315-985X Canadian Chemical Register†
0315-9884 Cancer in Ontario
0315-9906 R A C A R
0315-9922 About Unions
0315-9930 Argus (Montreal)
0315-9981 I D R C Reports
0316-0033 Probe *changed to* Saskatchewan Environmental Society. Newsletter
0316-0041 Criminologie
0316-0068 Centre for Urban and Community Studies. Research Papers
0316-0114 National Research Council, Canada. Associate Committee on Scientific Criteria for Environmental Quality. Status Report
0316-0173 British Columbia English Teachers' Association. Journal
0316-0297 Directory of Federally Supported Research in Universities
0316-0300 Essays on Canadian Writing
0316-0343 Canadian Plains Bulletin
0316-0386 Notes on Unions†
0316-0602 Lifeline *changed to* Writer's Lifeline
0316-0661 Environmental Management for the Public Health Inspector†
0316-0688 Dalhousie Labour Institute for the Atlantic Provinces. Proceedings†
0316-0696 Canadian Essay and Literature Index†
0316-0734 Directory of Associations in Canada
0316-0769 Subsidia Mediaevalia
0316-0874 Mediaeval Sources in Translation
0316-0955 Association pour l'Avancement des Sciences et des Techniques de la Documentation. Rapport
0316-0963 Association pour l'Avancement des Sciences et des Techniques de la Documentation. Nouvelles de l'A S T E D
0316-1218 Canadian Journal of Higher Education
0316-1226 Directory of Accredited Camps
0316-1234 Cours de Perfectionnement du Notariat
0316-1269 Royal Ontario Museum. History, Technology and Art Monographs
0316-1277 Royal Ontario Museum. Ethnography Monograph
0316-1285 Royal Ontario Museum. Archaeology Monographs
0316-1323 Canadian Theatre Review Yearbook *changed to* Canadian Theatre Review
0316-1544 British Columbia Art Teachers' Association. Journal
0316-1552 Alberta History
0316-1609 Room of One's Own
0316-1617 Ontario Government Publications, Monthly Checklist
0316-1854 Guide to Departments of Sociology, Anthropology and Archaeology in Universities and Museums in Canada
0316-1862 Canada. National Museum of Man. Mercury Series. Canadian Ethnology Service. Papers
0316-1897 Canada. National Museum of Man. Mercury Series. Canadian Centre for Folk Culture Studies. Papers
0316-1900 Canada. National Museum of Man. Mercury Series. History Division. Papers
0316-1919 Canada. National Museum of Man. Mercury Series. Canadian War Museum. Papers
0316-2281 Mining in Canada - Facts & Figures
0316-2494 Tailspinner
0316-2508 Vexillum
0316-2516 Sound Heritage *see* 0228-7781
0316-2540 Talespinner *see* 0316-2494
0316-2672 Etudes Francaises dans le Monde *see* 0226-7454
0316-2702 Grand Manan Historian
0316-280X Canadian Camper
0316-2907 Canadian Gideon
0316-2915 Torch and Trumpet *see* 0316-2907
0316-2923 Philosophiques
0316-3040 Come and See
0316-313X Social Development *changed to* Social Development Overview
0316-327X PSST†
0316-3334 Perspectives
0316-3350 Wildland News
0316-3393 L A W G Letter
0316-3423 Profitable Outdoor Occupations *see* 0316-3431
0316-3431 Outdoor Careers†
0316-3458 Winnipeg Industrial Topics†
0316-3547 Canadian Gas Facts
0316-3571 Canadian Tax Foundation. Tax Conference. Report of Proceedings
0316-3768 Writ
0316-3903 O T F/F E O Interaction
0316-3938 Canadian Locations of Journals Indexed in Index Medicus *see* 0707-7629
0316-4004 Pulp & Paper Canada
0316-4047 National Research Council of Canada. Annual Report on Scholarships and Grants in Aid of Research *changed to* Natural Sciences and Engineering Research Council of Canada. List of Scholarships and Grants in Aid of Research
0316-4055 Ontario Review
0316-4241 Canadian Pulp and Paper Association. Annual Newsprint Supplement
0316-4357 Genetics Society of Canada Bulletin
0316-4454 Rehabilitation Institute of Montreal. Bulletin *changed to* Institut de Readaptation de Montreal. Bulletin
0316-4543 Canadian Association of University Business Officers. Bulletin
0316-4608 Profile Index to Canadian and Municipal Government Publications *see* 0707-3135
0316-4616 Royal Society of Canada. Proceedings and Transactions
0316-4675 University of Western Ontario. Department of Psychology. Research Bulletin†
0316-4683 University of Alberta. Department of Computing Science. Technical Reports
0316-4691 Centre for Urban and Community Studies. Bibliographic Series
0316-473X Alberta Catholic Directory
0316-4853 Pulp and Paper Research Institute of Canada. Logging Research Reports†
0316-4969 History and Social Science Teacher
0316-5000 Index of Feature Length Films *see* 0316-5019
0316-5019 Index of 16 mm & 35 mm Feature Length Films Available in Canada†
0316-5078 Queen's University. Institute for Economic Research. Discussion Paper
0316-5310 Law Society of Upper Canada. Special Lectures
0316-5329 Nineteenth Century Theatre Research *changed to* Nineteenth Century Theatre
0316-5345 Science et Esprit
0316-5515 Canadian Film Digest Yearbook†
0316-5973 Modernist Studies: Literature and Culture, 1920-1940†
0316-5981 Atlantic Provinces Book Review
0316-599X Chuchoteries
0316-6260 International Corner *see* 0829-4976
0316-6325 Nova Scotia Law News
0316-6368 Universite de Moncton. Revue
0316-6546 Institute of Chartered Accountants of Alberta. Monthly Statement
0316-6570 McGill University, Montreal. Centre for Developing-Area Studies. Bibliography Series
0316-6597 Serials Holdings in the Libraries of Memorial University of Newfoundland, St. John's Public Library and College of Trades and Technology *see* 0709-0536
0316-6600 Memorial University of Newfoundland. Library. Serials Holdings in the Libraries of Memorial University of Newfoundland and St. John's Public Library *see* 0709-0536
0316-6724 Charlottes
0316-7437 Books in Bengali
0316-7518 New Canadian Stories *see* 0703-9476
0316-7631 Canadian Export Association. Export News Bulletin
0316-7739 Grand News

1530 ISSN INDEX

0316-7771 Canadian Sporting Goods & Playthings. Directory
0316-7828 Boreal Institute, Edmonton. Report of Activities *see* 0820-988X
0316-7917 Canadian Journal of Research in Semiotics *see* 0229-8651
0316-7933 Canadian Urban Transit Association. Proceedings
0316-7941 Canadian Transit Association. Proceedings *see* 0316-7933
0316-7984 University of Manitoba. Center for Transportation Studies. Research Report
0316-800X Lutheran Churches in Canada. Directory
0316-8131 Canadian and Provincial Golf Records
0316-8212 Royal Canadian Golf Association. National Tournament Records *see* 0316-8131
0316-8484 Canadian Children's Annual
0316-8549 Ontario Directory of Education
0316-8565 Canadian Journal of Social Work Education *changed to* Canadian Social Work Review
0316-859X Canadian Logger & Pulpwood Contractor†
0316-8603 German-Canadian Yearbook
0316-8670 Words from Inside†
0316-8743 Canadian Religious Conference. Bulletin
0316-8840 Revolting Librarian†
0316-8913 My Brother and I
0316-8956 Canadian Information Processing Society. Computer Census
0316-9014 Humane Viewpoint
0316-9200 Ordre des Architectes du Quebec. Bulletin
0316-9235 Art & Literary Review *see* 0316-9243
0316-9243 Muskeg Review†
0316-9375 Canadian Construction Association. Documentation de Reference
0316-9448 Current Canadian Books
0316-9537 Blue Book of Food Store Operators & Wholesalers
0317-0209 Journal of Orthomolecular Psychiatry *changed to* Journal of Orthomolecular Medicine
0317-0349 Ontario Education Dimensions†
0317-0403 All About Boating†
0317-0500 Chesterton Review
0317-056X From the Ground Up
0317-0659 Third World Forum
0317-0713 Cahiers de Psychologie et de Reeducation†
0317-0802 English Studies in Canada
0317-0845 Repository†
0317-0861 Canadian Public Policy
0317-0926 C I M Bulletin
0317-1272 Insurance Marketer†
0317-1280 R T A C News
0317-1485 Dogs in Canada
0317-1493 Consensus (Winnipeg)†
0317-1655 Jewish Historical Society of Western Canada. Annual Publication
0317-1663 Dalhousie Law Journal
0317-1671 Canadian Journal of Neurological Sciences
0317-1817 Fisheries Fact Sheet.†
0317-1892 Canadian Grain Commission Grain Research Laboratory. Annual Report
0317-2023 Canadian Fisherman *changed to* Canadian Fisherman
0317-2031 Arts Victoria†
0317-204X Canadian American Review of Hungarian Studies *changed to* Hungarian Studies Review
0317-2147 Chelsea Journal†
0317-2244 Canada. National Museum of Man. Mercury Series. Archaeological Survey of Canada. Papers
0317-2317 Journal of Leisurability
0317-2333 Cinema Quebec
0317-2473 Population Research Laboratory. Discussion Paper Series
0317-2481 Flypaper
0317-2546 Queen's University. Industrial Relations Centre. Research and Current Issues Series
0317-266X Evangelical Baptist Churches in Canada. Fellowship Yearbook
0317-2678 Guide de Reussite dans la Carriere d'Assureur-Vie
0317-2686 Guide d'Une Carriere a Succes *see* 0317-2678
0317-2716 Canada. National Museum of Man. Mercury Series. Communications Division. Papers†
0317-2775 Canadian Urban Sources *see* 0707-3135
0317-2791 Canadian Pool and Patio†
0317-2937 Voix de l'Ancai
0317-2961 Vernon's City of Guelph (Ontario) Directory
0317-297X British Columbia Provincial Judges' Association. Annual Conference†
0317-3100 Population Research Laboratory. Population Reprint Series
0317-3119 University of Alberta. Department of Sociology. Population Research Laboratory. Alberta Series Report†
0317-3348 University of Waterloo Biology Series
0317-3445 Canada. Statistics Canada. Railway Freight Traffic/Trafic Marchandises Ferroviaire†
0317-3518 Emergency Planning Digest
0317-3526 Nova Scotia. Environmental Control Council. Annual Report
0317-3550 Pulp and Paper Canada Business Directory *see* 0708-501X
0317-3720 Canada. Statistics Canada. Surgical Procedures and Treatments/ Interventions Chirurgicales et Traitements
0317-3739 Administration Hospitaliere et Sociale
0317-3798 Autosport Canada
0317-3925 Alberta Statistical Review
0317-3992 Ontario School Counsellors' Association. Newsletter *see* 0383-9931
0317-4018 Svetovy Kongres Slovakov. Bulletin.
0317-4026 Canadian Business Review
0317-4085 Canada. Energy, Mines and Resources Canada. Indian and Northern Affairs. Canada Oil and Gas Lands Administration Released Geophysical/ Geological Data
0317-4336 Social Services in Nova Scotia *changed to* Social Services for Nova Scotians
0317-4344 Saskatchewan. Department of Culture and Youth. Annual Report *changed to* Saskatchewan. Department of Culture and Recreation. Annual Report
0317-4514 In Search†
0317-4522 Living†
0317-4530 Prince Edward Island. Department of Health. Annual Report *changed to* Prince Edward Island. Department of Health and Social Services. Annual Report
0317-4611 Saskatchewan. Department of the Environment. Annual Report
0317-4654 Canadian Materials *changed to* C M: A Reviewing Journal of Canadian Materials for Young People
0317-4670 British Columbia. Ministry of Human Resources. Services for People *changed to* British Columbia. Ministry of Social Services and Housing. Services for People. Annual Report (Year)
0317-4697 Canada. Department of Manpower and Immigration. Strategic Planning and Research. Supply, Demand and Salaries: New Graduates of Universities and Community Colleges. Offre, Demande et Salaires.: Nouveaux Diplomes d'Universites et de Colleges.†
0317-4808 Incite Magazine
0317-4859 Reports of Family Law
0317-4921 Public Libraries in Canada†
0317-4956 Germano-Slavica
0317-5006 A C M C Forum
0317-5065 Cahiers des Etudes Anciennes
0317-5375 Canada. Statistics Canada. Exports-Merchandise Trade/Exportations-Commerce de Merchandises
0317-543X Canadian Society for Legal History. Newsletter†
0317-5545 Krzyk
0317-5642 National Museum of Natural Sciences. Natural History Series†
0317-5685 Canadian Communications Research Information Centre. Newsletter†
0317-5693 Canadian Commission for Unesco. Annual Report
0317-5766 National Science Library. Health Sciences Resources Centre. Conference Proceedings in the Health Sciences Held by the National Science Library/ Comptes Rendus des Conferences sur les Sciences de la Sante Qui Se Trouvent a la Bibliotheque Scientifique Nationale†
0317-5839 Conservation News *see* 0383-6479
0317-5979 Tournees de Spectacles *see* 0715-755X
0317-6045 C M A Gazette/A M C Gazette *see* 0820-0165
0317-607X Bond Record
0317-6126 Ahoy
0317-6193 Captain George's Penny Dreadful
0317-6207 Dairy Facts and Figures at a Glance
0317-6282 Prairie Forum
0317-6436 Ontario. Ministry of Education. Report
0317-6525 Consulting Engineers-Canada-Ingenieurs-Conseils
0317-6649 Canada Business Corporations Act with Regulations
0317-6673 Conservation Canada†
0317-6738 Canada. Statistics Canada. Travel Between Canada and Other Countries/ Voyages Entre le Canada et les Autres Pays
0317-6789 Economic Council of Canada. Economic and Social Indicators†
0317-6878 C A Magazine
0317-6908 Canada. Forestry Service. Bi-Monthly Research Notes *see* 0228-9989
0317-6983 Maltese Directory: Canada, United States
0317-7076 Decks Awash
0317-7114 University of Waterloo. Solid Mechanics Division. Reports
0317-7130 University of Waterloo. Solid Mechanics Division. Papers
0317-7173 Cartographica
0317-7254 Carleton Germanic Papers
0317-7262 Manitoba. Horse Racing Commission. Annual Report
0317-7335 Saskatchewan Labour Report
0317-7645 Dimensions in Health Service
0317-7785 Canadian Rodeo News
0317-7882 Canada. Statistics Canada. Aggregate Productivity Measures/Mesures Globales de Productivite
0317-7904 Canadian Review of Studies in Nationalism
0317-7920 Canadian Art Auction Record†
0317-8064 Chess Federation of Canada. Bulletin *see* 0822-5672
0317-8161 Ontario. Ministry of Consumer and Commercial Relations. Statistical Review†
0317-8196 Canada. Road and Motor Vehicle Traffic Safety Branch. Road Safety Annual Report. Rapport Annuel, Securite Routiere
0317-8382 Papers on European and Mediterranean Societies
0317-851X En Eglise
0317-8536 Directory of Libraries in Manitoba
0317-8552 Free Press Report on Farming†
0317-8579 Alberta Teachers' Association. Mathematics Monograph *see* 0711-2521
0317-8625 Contact (Waterloo) *see* 0711-6780
0317-8633 University of Waterloo. Division of Environmental Studies. Occasional Paper *changed to* University of Waterloo. Faculty of Environmental Studies. Occasional Paper
0317-8668 Lawyer's Phone Book (Year)
0317-8765 Anglican Year Book
0317-8781 Scott's Industrial Directory. Western Provinces *see* 0317-879X
0317-879X Scott's Industrial Directories - Western
0317-882X Canadian Pulp and Paper Association. Technical Section. Transactions *changed to* Journal of Pulp & Paper Science
0317-9044 Canadian Drama
0317-9311 U F O - Quebec†
0317-9443 Toy and Decoration Fair Directory
0317-946X Canadian Tax Foundation. Provincial and Municipal Finances
0317-9508 Mining - What Mining Means to Canada
0317-9575 Long Point Bird Observatory Newsletter
0317-9656 Universite de Sherbrooke. Revue de Droit
0317-9672 Canada. Statistics Canada. Production and Value of Maple Products/ Production et Valeur des Produits de l'Erable
0317-9737 Dance in Canada
0317-9893 University of Toronto. Department of Geography. Discussion Paper Series
0318-000X Indian Education Newsletter†
0318-0069 Cable Communications Magazine
0318-0077 Learning Resources
0318-0107 Gargoyle
0318-0123 Donum Dei
0318-0220 Courier
0318-0247 O L A Focus *changed to* Focus (Toronto)
0318-0344 Fraser's Construction & Building Directory†
0318-0433 H P E C Runner *see* 0707-3186
0318-0468 Water and Pollution Control. Directory and Handbook *changed to* Water & Pollution Control. Directory and Buyers' Guide
0318-0492 Quebec Astronomique
0318-0522 Canadian Structural Engineering Conference. Proceedings
0318-0646 Professional Institute of the Public Service of Canada. Communications
0318-0743 Ontario. Provincial-Municipal Affairs Secretariat. Municipal Directory
0318-0794 Canadian Environmental Control Newsletter
0318-0859 Canadian Process Equipment & Control News
0318-0867 Canadian Amateur
0318-0913 Simmental Scene *changed to* Simmental Country
0318-0948 Reviewing Librarian
0318-1006 Nursing Papers/Perspectives en Nursing
0318-1049 Meetings & Incentive Travel
0318-1235 University of Toronto-York University Joint Program in Transportation. Newsletter†
0318-1251 University of Toronto-York University. Joint Program in Transportation. Annual Report
0318-1340 Liaison†
0318-1693 Quebec Construction
0318-1723 N A P E News *changed to* Communicator (St. John's)
0318-1766 Mining Exploration and Development Review *see* 0711-3277
0318-1944 Canadian Information Processing Society. Canadian Salary Survey†
0318-1960 C A H P E R News *changed to* In Touch
0318-2037 Current Soviet Leaders†
0318-2096 Canadian Psychological Review *see* 0708-5591
0318-2118 Manitoba Spectra
0318-2126 Association of New Brunswick Land Surveyors. Annual Report

ISSN INDEX

ISSN	Title
0318-2274	Canada. Statistics Canada. Private and Public Investment in Canada. Outlook/Investissements Prives et Publics au Canada. Perspectives *see* 0823-065X
0318-2460	Windsor This Month
0318-2592	Stereo Guide *see* 0833-9570
0318-2789	Canadian Conservation Directory
0318-2851	Association of Canadian Map Libraries. Bulletin
0318-2967	Dairy Policy
0318-3122	University of Waterloo. Solid Mechanics Division. Studies Series
0318-3270	Introductions from an Island *see* 0826-5909
0318-3319	Erasmus Studies
0318-3610	Matrix
0318-3661	Ministry of Agriculture. Vegetable Production Guide *changed to* British Columbia. Ministry of Agriculture and Food. Vegetable Production Guide
0318-3742	Captain Lillie's Coast Guide and Radiotelephone Directory
0318-3874	Canada. Statistics Canada. Salaries and Qualifications of Teachers in Public, Elementary and Secondary Schools/Traitements et Qualifications des Enseignants des Ecoles Publiques, Primaires et Secondaires
0318-3912	Manitoba. Water Services Board. Annual Report
0318-3971	Alberta Opportunity Company. Annual Report
0318-4099	Canada Manpower and Immigration Review
0318-4137	Recherches Amerindiennes au Quebec
0318-4277	Canadian Forest Industries
0318-434X	Annals of Good St. Anne
0318-4390	Touring & Travel
0318-4552	Housing Ontario *changed to* Community Ontario
0318-4684	Saskatchewan. Parks and Renewable Resources Annual Report
0318-4757	Alberta. Department of Transportation. Annual Report *see* 0702-7702
0318-4854	Quebec (Province). Curatelle Publique. Rapport Annuel du Curateur Public
0318-4943	Alberta Fishing Guide
0318-5036	Canadian Association of Administrative Sciences. Proceedings, Annual Conference *changed to* Administrative Sciences Association of Canada. Proceedings, Annual Conference
0318-5133	Canadian Society of Environmental Biologists Newsletter
0318-5176	Alberta Modern Language Journal
0318-5184	Canada. Statistics Canada. Survey of Canadian Nursery Trades Industry/Enquete sur l'Industrie des Pepinieres Canadiennes
0318-5273	Canada. Statistics Canada. Household Facilities and Equipment/L'Equipment Menager
0318-5303	Quebec (Province). Commission des Transports. Rapports des Activites de la Commission des Transports du Quebec *see* 0702-0996
0318-5311	Issues in Canadian Science Policy†
0318-5729	Amigo
0318-5737	Amisol
0318-5753	Amber
0318-6075	Cross Country
0318-6210	Training Aids Action Service†
0318-6229	Careers for Graduates
0318-6342	T.S. Eliot Review *see* 0704-5700
0318-6385	Metric Message
0318-6415	Manitoba Community Reports *changed to* Manitoba. Economic Development Network. Community Profile Information System
0318-658X	Agronews
0318-6644	Artmagazine
0318-6717	Canadian Business Periodicals Index *see* 0227-8669
0318-675X	Canadian Government Publications: Catalogue†
0318-6954	Archivaria
0318-7020	Parachute (Montreal)
0318-708X	Canada. Statistics Canada. National Income and Expenditure Accounts/Comptes Nationaux des Revenus et des Depenses *changed to* Canada. Statistics Canada. System of National Accounts, National Income and Expenditure Accounts/Systeme de Comptabilite Nationale. Comptes Nationaux des Revenus et des Depenses
0318-7128	Canada. Statistics Canada. Sawmills and Planing Mills and Shingle Mills/Scieries et Ateliers de Rabotage et Usines de Bardeaux *see* 0828-9867
0318-7179	University and College Libraries in Canada†
0318-7306	Action Canada France
0318-7403	Dalhousie University. School of Library Service. Occasional Papers *changed to* Dalhousie University. University Libraries and School of Library Service. Occasional Papers
0318-742X	C G A Magazine
0318-7446	Land *see* 0700-1770
0318-7454	Forestalk *see* 0700-1770
0318-7489	Fine
0318-7500	Fotoflash
0318-7527	Ontario Municipal Board Reports
0318-7551	Eskimo
0318-7632	Hiballer Magazine *see* 0708-2169
0318-7888	Canada. Statistics Canada. Report on Fur Farms/Rapport sur les Fermes a Fourrure
0318-7985	Italian Chamber of Commerce Bulletin *changed to* Italcommerce
0318-8116	L U A C Monitor
0318-8140	Urban Forum†
0318-8272	Huxley Institute - C S F Newsletter *changed to* Health and Nutrition Update
0318-8329	Inventory of Research into Higher Education in Canada†
0318-8647	Indian-Ed *see* 0710-1481
0318-8701	Fashion Textiles Mode
0318-871X	Fem Ego
0318-8752	Franchise Annual
0318-8779	Quebec (Province) Direction Generale des Peches Maritimes. Direction de la Recherche. Rapport Annuel
0318-8787	Canada. Statistics Canada. Selected Financial Statistics of Charitable Organizations/Certaines Statistiques Financieres des Ouevres de Charite†
0318-8809	Canada. Statistics Canada. Building Permits/Permis de Batir
0318-8841	Canada. Statistics Canada. Contract Drilling for Petroleum and Other Contract Drilling/Forage de Puits de Petrole a Forfait et Autre Forage a Forfait†
0318-8868	Canada's International Investment Position/Bilan Canadien des Investissements Internationaux *changed to* Canada. Statistics Canada. System of National Accounts, Canada's International Investment Position/Systeme de Comptabilite Nationale Bilan Canadien des Investissements Internationaux
0318-8876	Canada. Statistics Canada. Provincial Government Finance: Assets, Liabilities, Sources and Uses of Funds *see* 0710-1023
0318-8914	Canada. Statistics Canada. Shipping Report. Part 1: International Seaborne Shipping (by Country) /Transport Maritime. Partie 1: Transport Maritime International (Par Pays)†
0318-8930	Canada. Statistics Canada. Shipping Report. Part 3: Coastwise Shipping/Transport Maritime. Partie 3: Navigation Nationale†
0318-8949	Canada. Statistics Canada. Shipping Report. Part 5: Origin and Destination for Selected Commodities/Transport Maritime. Partie 5: Origine et Destination de Certaines Marchandises†
0318-9007	Canada. Statistics Canada. Estimates of Labour Income/Estimations du Revenu du Travail
0318-9090	Canadian Journal of University Continuing Education
0318-9171	University of British Columbia. Faculty of Forestry. Bulletin†
0318-9201	Voix et Images
0318-9236	Poumons
0318-9244	Metropolitan Toronto Library Board. News
0318-9392	Vie Oblate
0318-9422	Gold Book of Snowmobile Data and Used Prices
0318-952X	Current Industrial Relations Scene in Canada
0318-9600	Canadian Aural/Oral History Association. Bulletin *see* 0383-6576
0318-9651	Apartment & Building
0318-9937	American Society for Information Science, Western Canada Chapter. Annual Meeting Proceedings
0319-003X	Atlantic Canada Economics Association. Annual Conference: A C E A Papers
0319-0080	Canadian Children's Literature
0319-0161	Computing Canada
0319-0188	Sphinx
0319-0358	North Shore Numismatic Society. Bulletin *see* 0380-8866
0319-0382	Canada. Epidemiology Division. Venereal Disease in Canada *changed to* Venereal Diseases in Canada
0319-0404	British Columbia. Labour Relations Board. Annual Report
0319-0412	British Columbia Economic Outlook Survey *changed to* Economic Review and Outlook
0319-051X	Canadian Review of Comparative Literature
0319-0552	York Dance Review†
0319-0595	Harlequin†
0319-0684	B C S T A Convention Reporter *see* 0703-766X
0319-0994	Women Can *see* 0319-1001
0319-1001	Pedestal
0319-1095	Interuniversity Centre for European Studies. Bulletin
0319-1362	Bull & Bear Financial Newspaper
0319-1443	Family Involvement
0319-1648	Kabalarian Courier
0319-1915	Canadian Gladiolus Society. Annual
0319-1974	Canadian Research
0319-2008	Uncertified Human *see* 0711-7388
0319-2121	Forum (Toronto)
0319-2148	Canadian Office†
0319-2156	Connection†
0319-2431	Canadian Tax News
0319-2571	Canadian Archer *changed to* F C A Official Newsletter
0319-258X	Directory of Community Services of Greater Montreal
0319-2636	Order of Nurses of Quebec. News and Notes *changed to* Nursing Quebec
0319-2644	Canadian Public Health Association. Proceedings of the Annual Meeting†
0319-2709	Mart
0319-2822	Cycle Canada
0319-2865	Moto Journal
0319-2962	Canada News *changed to* Korea Times Toronto
0319-3098	Jardin Botanique de Montreal. Annuelles et Legumes: Resultats des Cultures d'Essai
0319-3101	Jardin Botanique de Montreal. Annuelle *see* 0319-3098
0319-3225	Canadian Funeral Director
0319-3233	Canadian Export Association. Review and Digest Bulletin *see* 0713-0376
0319-3322	Canadian Business Law Journal
0319-3403	Canadian Energy News
0319-3535	Alberta Hail and Crop Insurance Corporation. Annual Report
0319-3578	Saskatchewan. Department of Agriculture. Annual Report
0319-3608	Environment News *see* 0701-9637
0319-3799	Canada. Statistics Canada. Honey Production/Production de Miel *see* 0829-3163
0319-3896	CanPara
0319-4019	Monarchy Canada
0319-4027	Industrial Manager *see* 0045-5156
0319-423X	Alberta. Alcoholism and Drug Abuse Commission. Annual Report *changed to* Alberta. Alcohol and Drug Abuse Commission. Annual Report
0319-4264	Alberta Economic Accounts
0319-4434	Canadian Journal of Radiography, Radiotherapy, Nuclear Medicine *changed to* Canadian Journal of Radiography, Radiation Therapy, Nuclear Medicine
0319-4477	Canadian Newsletter of Research on Women *see* 0707-8412
0319-4558	A P T Communique
0319-4604	R N A N S Bulletin
0319-4620	Centre for Urban and Community Studies. Major Report Series
0319-4639	Cape Breton's Magazine
0319-4728	Centre Stage†
0319-4787	Canadian Nurses Association. Entrance Requirements for Diploma Schools of Nursing and Schools of Practical Nursing.
0319-485X	Religious Studies Review
0319-4930	Canada. Statistics Canada. Labour Costs in Canada: Finance, Insurance and Real Estate/Couts de la Main-d'Oeuvre au Canada: Finances, Assurances, et Immeuble†
0319-4957	Canada. Statistics Canada. Feldspar and Quartz Mines/Mines de Feldspath et de Quartz†
0319-5023	Action *changed to* P M A C News
0319-5082	Summer in Canada†
0319-5147	Polish Canadian Courier
0319-5376	Canadian Association of Law Libraries. Newsletter
0319-5724	Canadian Journal of Statistics
0319-5759	Energy Processing/Canada
0319-583X	Canada North Almanac
0319-5864	Canada. National Museums of Canada. Journal†
0319-616X	Floor Covering News
0319-6267	Canadian Premiums and Incentives *changed to* Marketing Magazine
0319-6348	Canadian Quarter Horse Journal *see* 0702-9071
0319-6356	Canadian Music Teacher
0319-6771	Environmental Health Review
0319-681X	Cegepropos
0319-6879	C V 2
0319-6887	Bharati
0319-6984	Alerte au Quebec
0319-7018	Building Management Maintenance News *changed to* Building Operating Manager
0319-7093	Canadian Travel News Weekly
0319-7107	Canadian Travel News
0319-7336	Hume Studies
0319-7387	Canadian Co-operative Wool Growers Magazine
0319-7468	Communique
0319-7549	Common Sense Economics
0319-7581	Corinthian *changed to* Corinthian Horse Sport in Canada
0319-7697	Manitoba Moods†
0319-7778	Communications *see* 0827-0678
0319-7832	CraftNews
0319-7840	Craftsman *see* 0229-1320
0319-7980	Alberta Decisions, Civil and Criminal Cases
0319-7999	Saskatchewan Decisions, Civil and Criminal Cases

1532 ISSN INDEX

0319-8014 Canada. Statistics Canada. Hospitals Section. List of Canadian Hospitals and Related Institutions and Facilities/ Liste des Hopitaux Canadiens et des Etablissements et Installations Connexes *see* 0225-5642
0319-8227 Canada. Statistics Canada. Statistics of Criminal and Other Offences/ Statistique de la Criminalite†
0319-8251 Canada. Statistics Canada. Construction Price Statistics. Quarterly Report/ Statistiques des Prix de la Construction Rapport Trimestriel†
0319-8278 Canada. Statistics Canada. Housing Starts and Completions/Logements Mis en Chantier et Paracheves
0319-8294 Industrial Business Management *changed to* Technology Transfer
0319-8316 Library Selections *see* 0705-517X
0319-8367 Delta-K
0319-8413 Design Product News
0319-8480 Discovery
0319-8499 Saskatchewan Registered Nurses' Association. Bulletin
0319-8561 Cross Trail News
0319-8588 Dome *changed to* Common Ground
0319-8650 Envers du Decor
0319-8693 Asia Times
0319-8715 Canadian India Star
0319-8774 Quebec (Province). Conseil de la Protection du Consommateur. Rapport Annuel
0320-0108 Pis'ma v Astronomicheskii Zhurnal
0320-0647 Naryzy z Istoriyi Pryrodoznavstva i Tekhniky *changed to* Ocherki po Istorii Estestvoznaniya i Tekhniki
0320-1058 Ekspress-Informatsiya. Peredacha Informatsii
0320-2372 Inozemna Filolohija
0320-3123 Signal'naya Informatsiya. Akustika
0320-314X Signal'naya Informatsiya. Fizika Yadernykh Reaktorov
0320-3166 Signal'naya Informatsiya. Elektricheskie Svoistva Tverdykh Tel
0320-3182 Signal'naya Informatsiya. Chastitsy i Polya
0320-3336 Polutehniline Instituut Tallinn. Issledovanie Elektromagnitnykh i Elektromashinnykh Ustroistv Upravleniya i Kontrolya Spetsial'nogo Naznacheniya
0320-3344 Polutehniline Instituut Tallinn. Trenie i Iznos v Mashinakh
0320-3352 Polutehniline Instituut Tallinn. Issledovanie Dvumernogo Vozmushchennogo Polya Napryazheniya
0320-3379 Polutehniline Instituut Tallinn. Neorganicheskaya Khimiya i Tekhnologiya
0320-3433 Polutehniline Instituut Tallinn. Teoreticheskoe i Eksperimental'noe Issledovanie Avtomobil'nykh Dorog i Avtomobil'nogo Transporta Estonskoi S.S.R. v Usloviyakh Intensivnoi Avtomobilizatsii
0320-3468 Polutehniline Instituut Tallinn. Sintez i Primenenie Polikondensatsionnykh Kleev
0320-5223 Referativnyi Zhurnal. Ekonomika, Organizatsiya, Tekhnologiya i Oborudovanie Poligraficheskogo Proizvodstva
0320-7218 Absorbtsiya i Absorbenty†
0320-8907 Voprosy Istorii K.P.S.S.
0320-930X Astronomicheskii Vestnik
0320-9407 Arkheologiya
0320-9695 Biologiya Morya *see* 0203-4646
0321-0359 Belaruski Dziarzhauny Universitet. Vesnik. Seryia 3; Historiya, Filosofiya, Navukovy Kamunism, Ekanomika, Prava
0321-1576 Zhurnal Mod
0321-1649 Akademiya Navuk Belarusskai S.S.R. Vestsi. Seryya Gramadskikh Navuk
0321-1657 Akademiya Navuk Belarusskai S.S.R. Vestsi. Seryya Sel'skagaspadarchykh Navuk
0321-1673 Akademiya Nauk Latviiskoi S.S.R. Izvestiya. Seriya Fizicheskikh i Tekhnicheskikh Nauk
0321-1738 Akademiyai Fanhoi R.S.S. Tojikiston. Shu'Bai Fanhoi Jam'iiati. Akhboroti
0321-186X Leningradskii Universitet. Vestnik. Seriya Biologiya
0321-1975 Mekhanika Tverdogo Tela
0321-2068 S.SH.A.
0321-3056 Severo-Kavkazskii Nauchnyi Tsentr Vysshei Shkoly. Obshchestvennye Nauki. Izvestiya
0321-3668 Ekspress-Informatsiya. Promyshlennyi Organicheskii Sintez
0321-3900 Teoriya Sluchainykh Protsessov
0321-4508 Kosmicheskie Issledovaniya na Ukraine *changed to* Kosmicheskaya Nauka i Tekhnika
0321-5040 Kosmicheskaya Biologiya i Aviakosmicheskaya Meditsina
0322-7243 Metodicky Zpravodaj Cs. Soustavy Vedeckych, Technickych a Ekonomickych Informaci
0322-807X Kniznice a Vedecke Informacie
0322-8959 Novinky Literatury: Geologie-Geografie†
0322-9378 Novinky Literatury: Jazykoveda. Literarni Veda†
0322-9564 Prumyslove Informace†
0322-9653 Financni Zpravodaj
0323-0287 Folia Facultatis Scientiarum Naturalium Universitatis Purkynianae Brunensis: Physica
0323-0465 Acta Physica Slovaca
0323-052X Casopis Matice Moravske
0323-0562 Universita Karlova. Acta Universitatis Carolinae. Historia Universtatis Carolinas Pragensis
0323-0570 Moravske Muzeum Brno. Casopis
0323-0678 Slezske Muzeum. Casopis. Serie B. Vedy Historicke
0323-0937 Historicka Demografie
0323-0988 Historicka Geografie
0323-1119 Anthropologie
0323-1283 Hudebni Nastroje
0323-1313 Ceskoslovenska Akademie Ved. Archivni Zpravy
0323-1364 Atletika
0323-1445 Lyzarstvi
0323-1569 Bibliograficky Katalog C S S R: Ceske Hudebniny a Gramofonove Desky
0323-1615 Bibliograficky Katalog C S S R: Ceske Knihy
0323-164X Marxismus a Soucasnost
0323-1666 Bibliograficky Katalog C S S R. Ceske Knihy. Zvlastni Sesit. Bibliografie a V T I *see* 0139-8539
0323-1712 Bibliograficky Katalog C S S R. Ceske Knihy. Zvlastni Sesit. Ceska Grafika a Mapy v Roce
0323-1763 Bibliograficky Katalog C S S R: Ceske Knihy. Zvlastni Sesit. Ceskoslovenske Disertace *see* 0232-041X
0323-1860 Bibliograficky Katalog C S S R. Ceske Knihy. Zvlastni Sesit. Soupis Ceskych Bibliografii
0323-214X Myslivost
0323-2581 Vlastivedny Vestnik Moravsky
0323-3022 Neue Erziehung im Kindergarten
0323-312X Modellbau Heute
0323-3154 Bibliographie Fremdsprachiger Germanica
0323-3162 Landschaftsarchitektur
0323-3189 Federball
0323-3227 Film und Fernsehen
0323-326X Forschung, Lehre, Praxis
0323-3308 Agrartechnik
0323-3413 Architektur der D.D.R.
0323-3472 Deutscher Angelsport
0323-3499 Wissenschaftliche Mitteilungen
0323-3545 Handelshochschule Leipzig. Wissenschaftliche Zeitschrift
0323-3553 D E T†
0323-357X Der Falke
0323-3596 Deutsche Nationalbibliographie. Reihe A: Neuerscheinungen des Buchhandels
0323-3642 Deutsche Nationalbibliographie. Reihe B: Neuerscheinungen Ausserhalb des Buchhandels
0323-3677 Ganztaegige Bildung und Erziehung
0323-3715 Sprachpraxis
0323-374X Deutsches Buecherverzeichnis
0323-3766 Literarisches Sonderheft
0323-3790 Asien, Afrika, Lateinamerika
0323-3804 Textiltechnik
0323-3847 Biometrical Journal
0323-3901 I P W Forschungshefte
0323-3944 Series Statistics
0323-410X Frisur und Kosmetik
0323-4134 Leichtathlet
0323-4207 Goethe-Jahrbuch
0323-4290 Zidis-Information *changed to* Zidis Standpunkt
0323-4304 Standpunkt
0323-4320 Acta Hydrochimica et Hydrobiologica
0323-4347 Folia Haematologica
0323-4355 Bibliographie Geschichte der Technik
0323-438X Musik-Information
0323-4444 Leopoldina
0323-455X Jahresverzeichnis der Hochschulschriften der DDR, der BRD und Westberlins
0323-4568 Arbeit und Arbeitsrecht
0323-4614 D D R - Medizin-Report
0323-4630 Wilhelm-Pieck-Universitaet Rostock. Wissenschaftliche Zeitschrift
0323-4657 Nachrichtentechnik-Elektronik
0323-4681 Rostock Wilhelm-Pieck-Universitaet. Wissenschaftliche Zeitschrift. Naturwissenschaftliche Reihe
0323-4711 Forschung der Sozialistischen Berufsbildung
0323-4762 Gastronomie
0323-4797 Bau
0323-4916 Koerpererziehung
0323-4932 Folia Ophthalmologica
0323-4967 Kultur im Heim
0323-4983 Anaesthesiologie und Reanimation
0323-5017 Kultur und Freizeit
0323-5033 H N O - Praxis
0323-5084 Fortschritte der Onkologie
0323-5106 Musikforum
0323-5130 Beitraege zur Forschungstechnologie
0323-5270 Technische Hochschule Carl Schorlemmer Leuna-Merseburg. Wissenschaftliche Zeitschrift.
0323-5297 Theorie und Praxis
0323-5386 Medizin Aktuell
0323-5394 Warenzeichen- und Musterblatt
0323-5408 Archiv fuer Phytopathologie und Pflanzenschutz
0323-5610 Aquarien - Terrarien
0323-5637 Zeitschrift fuer Medizinische Laboratoriumsdiagnostik
0323-5750 F D G B. Rundschau
0323-5815 Neues Leben
0323-5947 Fuer Dich
0323-598X Journal of Information Recording Materials
0323-5998 Rundfunk- und Fernsehprogramm
0323-6471 Bauern-Echo
0323-7117 C L G-Information
0323-7168 Handelswoche/Konsum-Genossenschafter
0323-7648 Acta Polymerica
0323-7982 Zeitschrift fuer Germanistik
0323-8202 Glaube und Heimat
0323-8253 Landschaftspflege und Naturschutz in Thueringen
0323-830X Around the World
0323-8407 Fuwo
0323-8474 Journal of Information Processing
0323-8490 Bauinformation Wissenschaft und Technik
0323-8628 Deutsches Sportecho
0323-8776 Z F I - Mitteilungen
0323-8946 Schriftenreihe fuer Geologische Wissenschaften
0323-8962 Numismatische Beitraege
0323-9004 Narodnostopanski Arkhiv
0323-9217 Bulgarian Journal of Physics
0323-9268 Bulgarska Etnografiia
0323-9365 Bulgarski Gramofonni Plochi
0323-9411 Bulgarski Disertacii
0323-956X Bulgarski Zhurnalist
0323-9578 Dukhovna Akademiya SV. Kliment Okhridski. Godishnik
0323-9667 Bulgarski Knigopis. Seriia 2: Sluzhebni Izdaniia i Disertatsii
0323-9748 Istoricheski Pregled
0323-9764 Bulgarski Periodichen Pechat
0323-9780 Izvestiya na Darzhavnite Arkhivi
0323-9799 Istoriya i Osnovi na Komunizma
0323-9861 Bulgarski Folklor
0323-9950 Acta Physiologica et Pharmacologica Bulgarica
0323-9969 Bulgaria v Chuzhdata Literatura
0323-9985 Bulgarska Akademiia na Naukite. Institut za Istoriia. Izvestiia
0324-0037 Sofiya
0324-024X Filosofska Misul
0324-0282 Institut po Istoriia na B K P. Izvestiia
0324-0290 Fiziologiia na Rasteniiata
0324-0347 Letopis na Statiite ot Bulgarskite Vestnitsi
0324-0398 Letopis na Statiite ot Bulgarskite Spisaniia i Sbornitsi
0324-0495 Literaturna Misal
0324-0525 Sofiiski Universitet. Geologo-Geografski Fakultet. Geografiia. Godisnik.
0324-0770 Acta Zoologica Bulgarica
0324-0835 Natsionalen Voennoistoricheski Muzei, Sofia. Izvestiya
0324-0878 Okeanologiia
0324-0894 Geologica Balcanica
0324-0924 Hydrobiology
0324-0967 Vekove
0324-0975 Fitologija
0324-1092 Mezhdunarodni Otnosheniya
0324-1114 Vissha Geodeziia
0324-1130 Izvestiia po Khimiia
0324-119X M B I
0324-1203 Arkheologiia
0324-1459 Astrofizicheskie Issledovaniia
0324-1491 Pneumologia i Ftiziatria
0324-1572 Sociologiceski Problemi
0324-1653 Linguistique Balkanique
0324-1661 Geotektonika, Tektonofizika i Geodinamika
0324-1718 Geokhimiia, Mineralogiia i Petrologiia
0324-1793 Muzei i Pametnitsi na Kulturata
0324-1858 Bibliotekoznanie, Bibliografiia, Knigoznanie, Nauchna Informatsiia
0324-1998 Obsta i Sravnitelna Patologiia
0324-3044 Fortnightly Bulletin *see* 0024-8495
0324-3451 Hungarian Book Review
0324-4202 Kulgazdasag
0324-4628 Publications of the Technical University for Heavy Industry. Series A, Mining
0324-4652 Neohelicon
0324-4679 Publications of the Technical University for Heavy Industry. Series B, Metallurgy
0324-5268 Attila Jozsef University. Acta Geographica
0324-542X Alba Regia
0324-5454 Acta Universitatis Debreceniensis de Ludovico Kossuth Nominatea. Series Historica. Magyar Torteneti Tanulmanyok
0324-5934 Studia Iuridica Auctoriatate Universitatis Pecs Publicata
0324-6051 Periodica Polytechnica. Mechanical Engineering
0324-6256 Acta Marxistica Leninistica. Politikai Gazdasagtan Tanulmanyok
0324-6302 Acta Marxistica Leninistica. Filozofiai Tanulmanyok
0324-6353 Acta Marxistica Leninistica. Tudomanyos Szocializmus Tanulmanyok
0324-6817 Severni Morava
0324-6965 Acta Universitatis de Attila Jozsef Nominatae. Acta Historica
0324-7171 Allam es Igazgatas

ISSN INDEX 1533

0324-721X Attila Jozsef University. Acta Cybernetica
0324-7228 Valosag
0324-7260 Acta Universitatis Szegediensis de Attila Jozsef Nominatae. Sectio Paedagogica et Psychologica
0324-7341 Modszertani Kiadvanyok
0324-7473 New Hungarian Exporter
0324-7627 Honismeret
0324-7961 Spolecenske Vedy ve Skole
0324-8003 Kartkowy Katalog Nowosci
0324-802X Politechnika Slaska. Zeszyty Naukowe. Hutnictwo
0324-8038 Politechnika Slaska. Zeszyty Naukowe. Jezyki Obce†
0324-8046 Politechnika Slaska. Zeszyty Naukowe. Organizacja
0324-8208 Teksty†
0324-8240 Szpitalnictwo Polskie†
0324-8283 Studies on International Relations†
0324-8291 Studies in Physical Anthropology
0324-833X Postepy Biologii Komorki
0324-8429 Annales Societatis Mathematicae Polonae. Seria 4: Fundamenta Informaticae
0324-8453 Magazyn Fotograficzny FOTO
0324-8461 Archiwum Ochrony Srodowiska
0324-850X Fotografia
0324-8534 Immunologia Polska
0324-8569 Control and Cybernetics
0324-8739 Prace Przemyslowego Instytutu Maszyn Rolniczych
0324-8747 Foundations of Control Engineering
0324-8763 Polish Ecological Studies
0324-8828 Environment Protection Engineering
0324-8844 Plastyka w Szkole
0324-8895 Uniwersytet Gdanski. Wydzial Humanystyczny. Zeszyty Naukowe. Studium Praktycznej Nauki Jezykow Obcych
0324-8925 Muzeum Literatury im. Adama Mickiewicza. Blok-Notes
0324-8976 Uniwersytet Slaski w Katowicach. Prace Fizyczne†
0324-8992 Wyzsza Szkola Pedagogiczna, Opole. Zeszyty Naukowe. Seria A. Nauki Techniczne
0324-9034 Wyzsza Szkola Pedagogiczna, Opole. Zeszyty Naukowe. Seria A. Chemia
0324-9050 Wyzsza Szkola Pedagogiczna, Opole. Zeszyty Naukowe. Filologia Polska
0324-9166 Ekonomika *see* 0860-2948
0324-9174 Geodezja i Urzadzenia Rolne *see* 0860-262X
0324-9182 Mechanika i Budownictwo Ladowe *see* 0860-2956
0324-9190 Ochrona Wod i Rybactwo Srodladowe *see* 0860-2611
0324-9204 Adademia Rolniczo-Techniczna. Zeszyty Naukowe *see* 0860-2832
0324-9212 Technologia Zywnosci *see* 0860-2859
0324-9220 Weterynaria *see* 0860-2840
0324-9239 Zootechnika *see* 0860-2603
0324-931X Politechnika Wroclawska. Instytut Ukladow Elektromaszynowych. Prace Naukowe. Konferencje
0324-9328 Politechnika Wroclawska. Instytut Telekomunikacji i Akustyki. Prace Naukowe. Monografie
0324-9336 Politechnika Wroclawska. Instytut Telekomunikacji i Akustyki. Prace Naukowe. Studia i Materialy
0324-9344 Politechnika Wroclawska. Instytut Telekomunikacji i Akustyki. Prace Naukowe. Konferencje
0324-9352 Politechnika Wroclawska. Instytut Technologii Budowy Maszyn. Prace Naukowe. Monografie
0324-9360 Politechnika Wroclawska. Instytut Technologii Budowy Maszyn. Prace Naukowe. Studia i Materialy
0324-9379 Politechnika Wroclawska. Instytut Technologii Budowy Maszyn. Prace Naukowe. Konferencje
0324-9387 Politechnika Wroclawska. Instytut Techniki Cieplnej i Mechaniki Plynow. Prace Naukowe. Monografie
0324-9395 Politechnika Wroclawska. Instytut Techniki Cieplnej i Mechaniki Plynow. Prace Naukowe. Konferencje
0324-9409 Politechnika Wroclawska. Instytut Techniki Cieplnej i Mechaniki Plynow. Prace Naukowe. Studia i Materialy
0324-9441 Politechnika Wroclawska. Instytut Podstaw Elektrotechniki i Elektrotechnologii. Prace Naukowe. Konferencje
0324-945X Politechnika Wroclawska. Instytut Podstaw Elektrotechniki i Elektrotechnologii. Prace Naukowe. Monografie
0324-9468 Politechnika Wroclawska. Instytut Organizacji i Zarzadzania. Prace Naukowe. Studia i Materialy
0324-9484 Politechnika Wroclawska. Instytut Organizacji i Zarzadzania. Prace Naukowe. Konferencje
0324-9492 Politechnika Wroclawska. Instytut Organizacji i Zarzadzania. Prace Naukowe. Monografie.
0324-9506 Politechnika Wroclawska. Instytut Nauk Spolecznych. Prace Naukowe. Monografie *see* 0239-3204
0324-9514 Politechnika Wroclawska. Instytut Nauk Spolecznych. Prace Naukowe. Studia i Materialy *see* 0239-3212
0324-9530 Politechnika Wroclawska. Instytut Metrologii Elektrycznej. Prace Naukowe. Przemysl†
0324-9549 Politechnika Wroclawska. Instytut Metrologii Elektrycznej. Prace Naukowe. Monografie
0324-9557 Politechnika Wroclawska. Instytut Metrologii Elektrycznej. Prace Naukowe. Konferencje
0324-9565 Politechnika Wroclawska. Instytut Materialoznawstwa i Mechaniki Technicznej. Prace Naukowe. Monografie
0324-9573 Politechnika Wroclawska. Instytut Materialoznawstwa i Mechaniki Technicznej. Prace Naukowe. Konferencje
0324-9603 Politechnika Wroclawska. Instytut Matematyki. Prace Naukowe. Monografie
0324-9611 Politechnika Wroclawska. Instytut Matematyki. Prace Naukowe. Studia i Materialy
0324-962X Politechnika Wroclawska. Instytut Konstrukcji i Eksploatacji Maszyn. Prace Naukowe. Monografie
0324-9638 Politechnika Wroclawska. Instytut Konstrukcji i Eksploatacji Maszyn. Prace Naukowe. Studia i Materialy
0324-9646 Politechnika Wroclawska. Instytut Konstrukcji i Eksploatacji Maszyn. Prace Naukowe. Konferencje
0324-9654 Politechnika Wroclawska. Instytut Historii Architektury, Sztuki i Techniki. Prace Naukowe. Studia i Materialy
0324-9662 Politechnika Wroclawska. Instytut Historii Architektury, Sztuki i Techniki. Prace Naukowe. Monografie
0324-9670 Politechnika Wroclawska. Instytut Gornictwa. Prace Naukowe. Konferencje
0324-9689 Politechnika Wroclawska. Instytut Gornictwa. Prace Naukowe. Monografie
0324-9697 Politechnika Wroclawska. Instytut Fizyki. Prace Naukowe. Studia i Materialy
0324-9719 Politechnika Wroclawska. Instytut Inzynierii Ochrony Srodowiska. Prace Naukowe. Konferencje
0324-9727 Politechnika Wroclawska. Instytut Inzynierii Ladowej. Prace Naukowe. Monografie
0324-9743 Politechnika Wroclawska. Instytut Inzynierii Ladowej. Prace Naukowe. Konferencje
0324-9751 Politechnika Wroclawska. Instytut Inzynierii Chemicznej i Urzadzen Cieplnych. Prace Naukowe. Studia i Materialy
0324-976X Politechnika Wroclawska. Instytut Energoelektryki. Prace Naukowe. Monografie
0324-9778 Politechnika Wroclawska. Instytut Energoelektryki. Prace Naukowe. Konferencje
0324-9786 Politechnika Wroclawska. Instytut Cybernetyki Technicznej. Prace Naukowe. Monografie
0324-9794 Politechnika Wroclawska. Instytut Cybernetyki Technicznej. Prace Naukowe. Konferencje
0324-9808 Politechnika Wroclawska. Instytut Cybernetyki Technicznej. Prace Naukowe. Studia i Materialy
0324-9816 Politechnika Wroclawska. Instytut Chemii Organicznej i Fizycznej. Prace Naukowe. Monografie
0324-9824 Politechnika Wroclawska. Instytut Chemii Organicznej i Fizycznej. Prace Naukowe. Konferencje
0324-9832 Politechnika Wroclawska. Instytut Chemii Nieorganicznej i Metalurgii Pierwiastkow Rzadkich. Prace Naukowe. Konferencje
0324-9840 Politechnika Wroclawska. Instytut Chemii Nieorganicznej i Metalurgii Pierwiastkow Rzadkich. Prace Naukowe. Monografie
0324-9859 Politechnika Wroclawska. Instytut Chemii i Technologii Nafty i Wegla. Prace Naukowe. Monografie
0324-9867 Politechnika Wroclawska. Instytut Chemii i Technologii Nafty i Wegla. Prace Naukowe. Konferencje
0324-9875 Politechnika Wroclawska. Instytut Budownictwa. Prace Naukowe. Monografie
0324-9883 Politechnika Wroclawska. Instytut Budownictwa. Prace Naukowe. Konferencje
0324-9891 Politechnika Wroclawska. Instytut Architektury i Urbanistyki. Prace Naukowe. Studia i Materialy
0324-9905 Politechnika Wroclawska. Instytut Architektury i Urbanistyki. Prace Naukowe. Monografie
0325-0075 Archivos Argentinos de Pediatria *see* 0325-3767
0325-0210 Ceramica y Cristal *see* 0325-0229
0325-0229 Ceramica y Cristal
0325-0245 Tesis Presentadas a la Universidad de Buenos Aires†
0325-0253 Asociacion Argentina de Mineralogia, Petrologia y Sedimentologia. Revista
0325-0288 Anales de Arqueologia y Etnologia
0325-0326 Industria Azucarera
0325-0342 Physis
0325-0407 Noticiero del Plastico-Elastomeros
0325-0415 Envasamiento
0325-0431 C L A C S O Boletin *changed to* David y Goliath
0325-0474 Revista Latinoamericana de Ingenieria Quimica y Quimica Aplicada
0325-058X Revista de la Union Industrial†
0325-0598 Liberacion y Derecho†
0325-0601 Revista de Ciencias Juridicas Sociales
0325-0679 Indice de la Literatura Dental Periodica en Castellano
0325-0725 Revista Latinoamericana de Filosofia
0325-0806 Revista de Ciencias Economicas. Temas de Administracion *see* 0325-0814
0325-0814 Administracion
0325-0822 Revista de Ciencias Economicas. Temas de Economia *see* 0325-0830
0325-0830 Economia
0325-1071 Universidad Nacional de Cordoba. Facultad de Odontologia. Revista
0325-1209 Universidad de Buenos Aires. Instituto de Historia Antigua Oriental. Revista
0325-1276 Revista de la Bolsa de Cereales *see* 0045-2467
0325-1306 Centro de Investigacion y Accion Social. Revista
0325-1675 Integracion Latinoamericana
0325-1772 Instituto Nacional de Tecnologia Agropecuaria. Estacion Experimental Regional Agropecuaria. Boletin de Divulgacion Tecnica
0325-1799 Estacion Experimental Region Agropecuaria Pergamino. Informe Tecnico
0325-1888 Revista Argentina de Relaciones Internacionales *changed to* Ceinar
0325-1950 Argentina. Instituto Nacional de Estadistica y Censos. Boletin de Estadistica y Censos
0325-1969 Argentina. Instituto Nacional de Estadistica y Censos. Boletin Estadistico Trimestral
0325-223X Mendeliana
0325-2280 Patristica et Mediaevalia
0325-2345 Quiron
0325-2388 Economic Information on Argentina
0325-2698 Sociedad Argentina de Estudios Geograficos Boletin
0325-2809 Asociacion de Ciencias Naturales del Litoral. Revista
0325-2868 Archivo General de la Nacion. Revista
0325-3147 Argentina. Congreso. Biblioteca. Serie Bibliografica
0325-3228 Rassegna. Revista de Informacion Medica y Cultural
0325-3732 Hickenia
0325-3767 Pediatria†
0325-383X Argentina. Ministerio de Economia, Hacienda y Finanzas. Boletin Semanal de Economia
0325-3856 Argentina. Museo Provincial de Ciencias Naturales. Comunicaciones. Nueva Serie
0325-3899 Anuario Interamericano de Archivos
0325-4194 Argos
0325-4216 F A C E N A
0325-4453 Nudos en la Cultura Argentina
0325-4615 Summa
0325-5182 Acta Oceanographica Argentina
0325-5387 Ethos
0325-6146 S C A R Boletin
0325-6251 Bibliotecologia y Documentacion Argentina
0325-6278 Argentina. Instituto Nacional de Tecnologia Industria. Boletin Tecnico
0325-6375 Instituto Nacional de Investigacion y Desarrollo Pesquero. Revista
0325-6448 Summarios
0325-6502 Psychologica
0325-6790 Instituto Nacional de Investigacion y Desarrollo Pesquero. Serie Contribuciones
0325-6987 Instituto Nacional de Investigacion y Desarrollo Pesquero. Memoria
0325-7479 Circulo Argentino de Odontologia. Revista
0325-7541 Revista Argentina de Microbiologia
0325-7592 Limnobios
0325-7622 Instituto de Numismatica e Historia de San Nicolas de los Arroyos. Boletin
0325-7657 Cuadernos de Numismatica y Ciencias Historicas
0325-8203 Interdisciplinaria
0325-8238 Folia Historica del Nordeste
0325-8815 Boletin de Educacion y Cultura†
0325-9064 Instituto para el Desarrollo de Ejecutivos en la Argentina. Revista
0325-9153 Encuesta de Expectativas Agropecurias
0325-9161 Situacion Coyuntural del Sector Agropecuario
0325-9293 Aeronavegacion Comercial Argentina
0325-934X I N T I
0325-9404 Documentos de Geohistoria Regional
0325-9676 Critica y Utopia
0325-9781 Argentina. Direccion de Investigaciones Forestales. Folleto Tecnico Forestal†

1534 ISSN INDEX

0326-0011 Rey
0326-0690 Instituto de Matematica Beppo Levi. Cuadernos
0326-0992 Gaceta Agronomica
0326-1336 Notas de Matematica Discreta
0326-1352 Historia
0326-1417 Centro de Estudios Urbanos y Regionales. Cuadernos
0326-1956 Comunicaciones Biologicas
0326-1980 Bimestre†
0326-226X L E A
0326-2928 Letras de Buenos Aires
0326-3142 Microscopia Electronica and Biologia Celular
0326-3169 Ciencia del Suelo
0326-3193 Slovensky Zivot
0326-386X Ideas en Ciencias Sociales
0326-3878 Ideas en Arte y Tecnologia
0326-4629 Veterinaria Argentina
0326-6400 Revista Argentina de Linguistica
0326-6672 Actividad Minera
0326-6680 Bibliografia Teologica Comentada del Area Iberoamericana
0326-677X Plural
0326-6982 Hueso Perdido
0326-7296 Revista Agronomica de Manfredi
0326-7857 Boletin de Medio Ambiente y Urbanizacion
0326-7997 Studia Croatica
0326-8470 Centro de Estudios Urbanos y Regionales. Boletin
0330-8987 Revue d'Histoire Maghrebine
0330-9290 Guide Economique de la Tunisie
0331-0019 National Bibliography of Nigeria
0331-0086 Barrister
0331-0094 Nigerian Journal of Entomology
0331-0124 Journal of Medical and Pharmaceutical Marketing
0331-0361 Nigerian Economic Society. Proceedings of the Annual Conference
0331-0388 Association for Teacher Education in Africa. Western Council. Report of the Annual Conference
0331-0515 West African Journal of Educational and Vocational Measurement
0331-0531 West African Journal of Modern Languages
0331-0566 Okike
0331-0604 Journal of Pharmaceutical and Medical Sciences
0331-0973 Nigerian Yellow Pages
0331-1481 Nsukka Library Notes
0331-2151 Nigeria Bulletin on Foreign Affairs†
0331-3468 Muse
0331-3646 Nigerian Journal of International Affairs
0331-3735 Nigerian Society of Physiotherapy. Journal
0331-4340 International Institute of Tropical Agriculture. Research Highlights
0331-4448 Nigerian Nurse
0331-4782 Medipharm
0331-6254 Nigerian Institute of International Affairs. Monograph Series
0331-6742 Noma
0331-7285 Samaru Journal of Agricultural Research
0331-8109 School Libraries Bulletin
0331-8400 Marketing in Nigeria
0331-8494 Healthy Living†
0331-8508 Third World First *see* 0794-3415
0331-8524 Nigerian Journal of Political Science
0331-8583 Journal of Business & Social Studies
0331-9911 Positive Review
0332-0006 Dublin. National Library of Ireland. Council of Trustees Report
0332-0111 Irish Birds
0332-0189 Progressive Farmer†
0332-0197 Irish Computer
0332-0235 Glasra
0332-0375 Irish Journal of Food Science and Technology
0332-0510 Irish Journal of Psychiatric Nursing
0332-0561 Irish Rod & Gun
0332-1150 Scripture in Church
0332-1274 Gaelic World
0332-1312 In Touch (Dublin) *see* 0332-4036
0332-1428 Milltown Studies
0332-1460 Irish Studies in International Affairs
0332-1541 Soundpost†
0332-1568 Aontas Review
0332-1584 Irish Council for Civil Liberties. Bulletin *see* 0790-2743
0332-1592 Peritia
0332-1649 Compel
0332-1665 Irish Journal of Environmental Science
0332-1673 Gaelic Games Monthly
0332-1711 Engineers Journal
0332-1800 Royal Dublin Society. Journal of Life Sciences†
0332-1851 Royal Dublin Society. Journal of Earth Sciences
0332-2262 Farm Machinery†
0332-236X Irish Veterinary News
0332-2408 Irish Farmers Monthly
0332-253X Blazes
0332-2599 Central Bank of Ireland. Quarterly Statistical Bulletin *see* 0332-2645
0332-2629 Sherkin Island. Journal
0332-2645 Central Bank of Ireland. Quarterly Bulletin
0332-2696 Central Bank of Ireland. Irish Economic Statistics
0332-2742 Central Bank of Ireland. Statistical Supplement to the Quarterly Bulletin *see* 0790-3979
0332-2793 Central Bank of Ireland. Statistical Tables of the Quarterly Bulletin *see* 0790-3979
0332-317X Irish Stamp News
0332-3633 Irish History Workshop
0332-4036 Identity (Dublin)†
0332-4095 International Civil Engineering Abstracts
0332-4117 Cathair na Mart
0332-4273 Moorea
0332-4338 Fisheries Bulletin
0332-4427 Irish Biblical Association. Proceedings
0332-4869 Maynooth Review
0332-4893 Irish Economic and Social History
0332-5024 Studia Musicologica Norvegica
0332-5040 Vaeret
0332-5121 Gyldendals Aktuelle Magasin†
0332-5229 Jord og Myr
0332-5237 Northern Offshore *see* 0305-876X
0332-5326 Plan og Bygg *changed to* Byggaktuelt
0332-5334 Scandinavian Oil-Gas Magazine
0332-5415 Fokus paa Familien
0332-544X Noroil
0332-5466 Norsk Advokatblad *changed to* Advokatbladet
0332-5474 Norsk Landbruk
0332-5512 Tidsskrift om Edruskapsspoersmaal
0332-5520 Tekstilforum
0332-5547 Ur
0332-558X Skipsnytt *changed to* Skipsrevyen
0332-5598 Penger og Kreditt
0332-5652 N I P H Annals
0332-5709 Norsk Institutt for Skogforskning. Meddelelser
0332-5733 Mur
0332-5768 N G U Bulletin
0332-5814 Videregaaende Opplaering
0332-5865 Nordic Journal of Linguistics
0332-5938 Teknikk og Miljoe
0332-5997 Tradisjon
0332-611X Ingenioer - Nytt
0332-6128 Moderne Transport
0332-6136 Norsk Plast
0332-6144 North Sea Observer
0332-6152 Byggherren
0332-6179 Miljoemagasinet
0332-6306 A M S - Varia
0332-6411 A M S - Smaatrykk
0332-6470 Norsk Psykologforening. Tidsskrift
0332-6497 Propaganda *see* 0025-3502
0332-6527 Nordisk Statistisk Skriftserie
0332-656X Synopsis
0332-6578 Norske Arkitektkonkurranser
0332-6756 Bergen Banks Kvartalsskrift
0332-6802 Personal-Opplaering
0332-6934 Fly-Nytt
0332-6942 Doeves Tidsskrift
0332-7094 Mot Brann *changed to* Brann og Sikkerhet
0332-7124 Arbeidervern
0332-7167 Skoleforum
0332-7205 Fortidsvern
0332-7299 Norsk Utenrikspolitisk Aarbok
0332-7434 Sunnhetsbladet
0332-7566 Svineavlsnytt
0332-7590 Juristkontakt
0332-768X Fauna Norvegica Series A. Norwegian Fauna except Entomology and Ornithology
0332-7698 Fauna Norvegica Series B. Norwegian Journal of Entomology
0332-7701 Fauna Norvegica Series C. Norwegian Journal of Ornithology
0332-7795 Revisjon og Regnskap
0332-7841 Hjelpepleieren
0332-7906 Norway. Statistisk Sentralbyraa. Helsestatistikk/Health Statistics
0332-7957 Norway. Statistisk Sentralbyraa. Familie Statistikk/Family Statistics†
0332-7965 Norway. Statistisk Sentralbyraa. Alkohol og Andre Rusmidler/Alcohol and Drugs†
0332-8015 Norway. Statistisk Sentralbyraa. Framskriving Av Folkemengden: Regionale Tall/Population Projections: Regional Figures
0332-8023 Norway. Statistisk Sentralbyraa. Kommune og Fylkestings Valget/Municipal and County Elections
0332-8090 Kongelige Norske Videnskabers Selskab Museet. Rapport. Botanisk Serie
0332-8171 Norsk Datatidende
0332-8201 Kontor og Datateknikk
0332-8244 Forum for Utviklingsstudier
0332-8554 Gunneria
0332-8678 Norges Apotekerforenings Tidsskrift
0332-8821 El-Installasjon og Handel
0332-883X Politiembetsmennenes Blad
0332-8988 Samferdsel
0332-9038 Sivilforsvarsbladet
0332-9062 Forsvarets Forum
0332-9410 Hold Pusten
0332-9666 Friidrett
0332-9798 Cockpit Forum
0333-001X Norsk Institutt for Skogforskning. Rapport
0333-0141 Kroppsoeving
0333-0192 Norsk Maskin-Tidende
0333-0249 Norsk Bedriftshelsetjeneste
0333-0451 Avis- og Bladlista†
0333-0656 Stavanger Museum. Aarbok
0333-0664 Stavanger Museum. Skrifter
0333-0796 Fysiokjemikeren
0333-1024 Cephalagia
0333-1342 Nordisk Sosialt Arbeid
0333-1423 Norsk Skattelovsamling
0333-144X Stoffmisbruk
0333-1512 Acta Ad Archaeologiam et Artium Historiam Pertinentia (Miscellaneous)
0333-1555 Utemiljoe
0333-208X Norway. Statistisk Sentralbyraa. Reiselivstatiskk/Statistics on Travel
0333-2217 Forming i Skolen
0333-2241 I C L A S Bulletin
0333-2314 Universitetet i Trondheim. Norges Tekniske Hoegskole. Biblioteket. Meldinger og Boklister†
0333-2500 Norges Landbruksoekonomiske Institutt. Driftsgranskinger i Jord- og Skogbruk
0333-273X European Political Data Newsletter
0333-2810 Skatterett
0333-3124 Kristiansand Museum. Aarbok
0333-3302 Automatisering
0333-3329 Huseierens Magasin
0333-354X Moebelhandleren
0333-3620 I A S P Newsletter
0333-3825 Spraaknytt
0333-3914 Norway. Statistisk Sentralbyraa. Kriminalstatistikk/Criminal Statistics
0333-4112 Norges Geologiske Undersoekelse. Arsmelding
0333-4325 University of Bergen. Institute of Psychology. Psychological Report Series
0333-5151 Dapim Licheker Tikufat Hashoah
0333-5194 I O L R Collected Reports
0333-5275 Geographical Research Forum *changed to* Geography Research Forum
0333-533X English Teachers' Journal (Israel)
0333-5372 Poetics Today
0333-5526 United States-Israel Binational Science Foundation. Project-Report Abstracts†
0333-5666 Yeda Lemeida
0333-5690 H S L *changed to* H S L A
0333-5771 Israel. Atomic Energy Commission. Annual Report
0333-5879 Technion - Israel Institute of Technology. Faculty of Agricultural Engineering. Publications
0333-5895 Isra/Counter-Source
0333-5925 Israel Yearbook on Human Rights
0333-600X Israel. Central Bureau of Statistics. Staff in Universities
0333-6018 Israel Book Trade Directory
0333-6131 Calendar of Scientific and Technological Meetings in Israel
0333-6166 Books from Israel†
0333-6190 Israel Academy of Sciences and Humanities. Section of Sciences. Proceedings
0333-6271 Out of Jerusalem
0333-6298 B'Or ha'Torah
0333-6387 Nogah
0333-6425 Israel. Geological Survey. Current Research
0333-6514 Israel Public Council for Soviet Jewry. Scientists' Committee. News Bulletin†
0333-6697 Sivevot
0333-676X Voices - Israel
0333-6867 Israel - Land and Nature
0333-6875 Holy Land Postal History
0333-6948 Pi Haatom
0333-6964 Hebrew University of Jerusalem. Authority for Research and Development. Current Research
0333-7286 A.B.
0333-7308 Israel Journal of Psychiatry and Related Sciences
0333-7499 Israel Museum Journal
0333-7588 Khadarim
0333-7618 Jerusalem Cathedra *see* 0334-4657
0333-7839 Maurice Falk Institute for Economic Research in Israel. Report and Discussion Paper Series
0333-7936 Israel. Meteorological Service. Monthly Agroclimatological Report
0333-8347 Jewish Language Review
0333-838X Identity
0333-8428 I D F Journal
0333-8487 Herodote
0333-8584 Koloat
0333-8886 Alon Hanotea
0333-9270 Oraita
0333-9521 Technologies
0333-953X Israel Book News
0333-9661 Studies in Jewish Education
0333-9688 Lamed Leshonkha
0333-9815 Pamphlet for Biology Teachers
0333-9831 Jerusalem Institute for Israel Studies. Discussion Papers
0333-9858 Current Contents of Periodicals on the Middle East
0333-9874 Integrated Rural Development. Publications
0333-9971 Tnuah Vetachbora
0334-0082 International Journal of Turbo and Jet Engines
0334-0139 International Journal of Adolescent Medicine and Health
0334-018X Journal of Pediatric Endocrinology
0334-0236 Journal of Orthopedic Surgical Techniques
0334-0554 Yedion
0334-0740 Metov Tiberia
0334-0899 Apereyon
0334-0953 Jews of the Soviet Union
0334-1003 Yalkut Lemachshava Sotzialistit
0334-1100 Interface (Rehovot)
0334-1151 Weizmann Institute of Science. Research

ISSN INDEX 1535

0334-1186	Perspectives in Drug Abuse
0334-133X	Israel Social Science Research
0334-1380	Barkai
0334-1704	High Temperature Materials and Processes
0334-1763	Reviews in the Neurosciences
0334-1771	Studies in Zionism
0334-1798	Yisrael-Am Ve'Eretz
0334-181X	Composite Materials Science
0334-1860	Journal of Intelligent Systems
0334-200X	Yad la-Kore
0334-2026	Israel Studies in Musicology
0334-2050	Environment in Israel. Selected Papers†
0334-2093	Bank of Israel. Israel's Banking System
0334-2123	Phytoparasitica: Israel Journal of Plant Protection Sciences
0334-2166	Dor le-Dor
0334-2182	Kibbutz (Tel Aviv)
0334-2190	Reviews on Drug Metabolism and Drug Interactions
0334-2212	Kidma
0334-2263	Hed Hagan
0334-2301	Israel Dance
0334-2336	Da'at
0334-2344	Reviews on Powder Metallurgy *see* 0379-0002
0334-2425	Trade Marks Journal
0334-2468	Current Research in Behavioral Sciences in Israel
0334-2476	Statistics of Travel and Tourism/Tayarut v'Sherutei ha-Araha
0334-2506	Forum
0334-2514	State, Government and International Relations
0334-2565	Iyunim Bi-Hinukh
0334-2573	Israel. Central Bureau of Statistics. Agricultural Statistics Quarterly
0334-2581	Hebrew University of Jerusalem. News
0334-2700	Australian Mathematical Society. Journal. Series B
0334-2719	Ariel
0334-2751	Sapanut
0334-2786	Jerusalem Papers on Peace Problems
0334-2808	Mid-East and World Shipping News(Information Paper) *changed to* Mediterranean and World Shipping News (Information Paper)
0334-2816	Divrei ha-Akademia ha-Leumit ha-Yisraelit Lemadaim
0334-2824	Directory of Scientific and Technical Associations in Israel
0334-2867	Maagalai Kareya
0334-2875	Directory of Research Institutes and Industrial Research Units in Israel *see* 0334-3197
0334-2948	Journalism Yearbook
0334-3057	Israel Electronics
0334-3065	Rivon ha-Yisraeli l'Misim
0334-309X	Bibliography of Modern Hebrew Literature in Translation
0334-3162	Israel. Environmental Protection Service. Ekhut ha-Svivah be-Yisrael. Luakh Shnati
0334-3170	Baeretz Yisrael
0334-3197	Directory of Research Institutes and Industrial Laboratories in Israel†
0334-3251	Siah
0334-326X	Argamon
0334-3278	Israel. Central Bureau of Statistics. New Statistical Projects and Publications in Israel
0334-3510	Israel. Geological Survey. Current Bibliography of Middle East Geology
0334-357X	Halochame
0334-3626	Leshonenu
0334-3650	Tarbiz
0334-3715	Levantina
0334-3774	Horizons
0334-3804	Israel Environment Bulletin
0334-3847	Innovation
0334-3863	Babniyah Building Centre of Israel Quarterly *changed to* Building Centre of Israel Bulletin
0334-3871	Assia
0334-3898	Israel Business
0334-3928	Eytanim
0334-3952	Maasef
0334-4029	Society and Welfare
0334-4088	Pe'amim
0334-4096	Jerusalem Letter
0334-4142	Soviet Union and the Middle East
0334-4150	Michael
0334-4169	Maeda Lerofei
0334-4258	Gal-ed
0334-4266	Modern Hebrew Literature
0334-4347	Reviews in Inorganic Chemistry
0334-4355	Tel Aviv Journal of Archaeology
0334-4401	Israel Oriental Studies
0334-4479	Salit
0334-4525	Crime and Social Deviance
0334-4541	Bank of Israel. Annual Statistics of Israel's Banking System
0334-4568	Hachenuch Hamishutaf
0334-4649	Crossroads (Jerusalem)
0334-4657	Cathedra
0334-4754	Alai Sefer
0334-4762	Social Research Review
0334-4770	Studies in Educational Administration and Organization
0334-4800	Jerusalem Quarterly
0334-4827	Alai Siach
0334-4975	Proza
0334-5076	Alon Lamorah Lesifrut
0334-5084	Alim
0334-5831	Free Man
0334-5904	Yearbook for Jewish Communities and Organizations
0334-5963	Assaph. Section C. Studies in the Theatre
0334-6080	Israel Quarterly of Psychology
0334-648X	Kulanu
0334-701X	Jewish History
0334-7532	Michkar Chaklaei Beyisrael
0334-7559	Jewish-Contemporary and Eternal Questions. Journal
0334-794X	Adrichalut
0334-889X	Semana
0334-8903	Dispersion y Unidad
0334-8954	Aurora
0334-9160	Leumi Review
0334-9594	Yerusholaimer Almanakh.
0335-0274	I N R S Bulletin de Documentation
0335-0290	Association Francaise d'Amitie et de Solidarite avec les Peuples d'Afrique. Bulletin d'Information *see* 0339-9958
0335-0894	Migrants Formation
0335-1653	Association Francaise pour l'Etude du Sol. Bulletin/Science du Sol
0335-1971	Numismatique & Change
0335-2013	Relations Internationales
0335-2021	Construction Neuve et Ancienne
0335-2927	Theatre Public
0335-2986	Gymnastique Volontaire
0335-3559	Repertoire de Materiaux et Elements Controles du Batiment
0335-3710	Abeilles et Fleurs
0335-377X	Pulp and Paper/Pates et Papiers†
0335-394X	Guide de l'Acheteur NF†
0335-3958	Quercy Recherche
0335-4024	Reunion. Service de Statistique Agricole. Notes de Conjoncture *see* 0758-7244
0335-4105	Council of Europe. Information Bulletin on Social Policy/Bulletin d'Information sur la Politique Sociale†
0335-5012	Assemblee Nouvelle
0335-5047	Droit et Pratique du Commerce International
0335-5233	Archeologie en Bretagne
0335-5276	Courrier de l'Industriel du Bois et de l'Ameublement *changed to* C T B Info
0335-5322	Actes de la Recherche en Sciences Sociales
0335-5330	Documents de Cartographie Ecologique
0335-5985	Archives de Sciences Sociales des Religions
0335-6280	Cinema Politique
0335-6469	Calao
0335-6566	Mineraux et Fossiles
0335-704X	Escargot *see* 0153-4602
0335-7163	Centre de Promotion de la Presse Industrielle et Scientifique Francaise. Revue des Sommaires†
0335-7368	Nouvelle Revue d'Optique *see* 0150-536X
0335-752X	Nouvelles du Livre Ancien
0335-7619	Tribune Medicale
0335-8259	France. Centre National pour l'Exploitation des Oceans. Colloques. Actes *see* 0761-3962
0335-9190	L.S.I.
0335-9255	Sciences de la Terre: Serie Informatique Geologique
0335-9395	Combat pour la Paix *see* 0184-0932
0335-9956	Officiel
0336-030X	Heimdal
0336-1357	Universite de Lyon III. Faculte de Droit. Annales *changed to* Universite Jean Moulin. Annales
0336-1438	Ethnographie
0336-1454	France. Institut National de la Statistique et des Etudes Economiques. Economie et Statistique
0336-1470	Centre d'Etude des Revenus et des Couts. Documents
0336-1578	Revue des Sciences Sociales de la France de l'Est
0336-1667	Architecture Mouvement Continuite *see* 0336-1675
0336-1675	A M C
0336-1721	Pluriel
0336-2086	A G E C O P Liaison
0336-2698	Archontes†
0336-3112	France. Centre National pour l'Exploitation des Oceans. Centre Oceanologique de Bretagne. Recueil des Travaux *changed to* France. I.F.Re.Mer. Centre de Brest. Recueil des Travaux
0336-335X	Solidaires
0336-3686	International Copyright Information Centre. Information Bulletin†
0336-3945	New Caledonia. Institut Territorial de la Statistique et des Etudes Economiques. Informations Statistiques
0336-4402	Ingenieurs des Villes de France *see* 0336-4410
0336-4410	I V F - Ingenieurs des Villes de France
0336-4437	A.F.C. *see* 0395-2096
0336-4895	Recherche, Pedagogie et Culture†
0336-5522	Travaux et Documents de Geographie Tropicale
0336-5638	France. Ministere de l'Agriculture. Collections de Statistique Agricole
0336-5697	Annuaire de Statistique Agricole du Departement de la Reunion
0336-626X	Aeroports Magazine
0336-6324	Maghreb, Machrek, Monde Arabe
0336-6979	France. Institut National de la Statistique et des Etudes Economiques. Documents Divers
0336-8300	Societe Versaillaise des Sciences Naturelles. Bulletin
0336-8424	Bouliste
0336-9331	Fiches du Cinema
0336-9420	Combat Socialiste†
0336-9455	Connaissance du Pays d'Oc
0336-9609	Revue Sexpol
0336-9730	Traverses
0336-9749	Babillard *see* 0338-5922
0336-9919	France. Ministere de l'Agriculture. Service Central des Enquetes et Etudes Statistiques. Bulletin de Statistique Agricole
0336-9943	France. Ministere de l'Agriculture. Cahiers de Statistiques Agricoles
0336-9994	Societe Geologique de Normandie et des Amis du Museum du Havre. Bulletin Trimestriel
0337-1883	Haut - Parleur
0337-1891	Hifi Stereo
0337-2014	Paradoxes
0337-2219	Industrie du Petrole dans le Monde - Gaz - Petrochimie *see* 0220-3294
0337-2731	Ingenierie-Information
0337-274X	Ingeniere-Edition Regionale, Sud-Ouest de la France
0337-307X	Futuribles
0337-3126	Connexions Psychosociologie Sciences Humaines
0337-4084	C E N A D D O M Bulletin d'Information *see* 0769-3478
0337-4092	Actualite, Combustibles, Energie†
0337-5714	Repertoire General de la Production Francaise *changed to* La France de l'Industrie et ses Services
0337-5781	Guide du Feu
0337-5927	Annuaire National M.K.D.E. France *see* 0337-5935
0337-5935	Annuaire National des Masseurs Kinesitherapeutes
0337-5978	Mots en Liberte, Bulletin d'Etudes Lexicales†
0337-5986	Lexique Dernier†
0337-6176	Universite de la Reunion. Cahier
0337-6680	Union Genealogique du Centre. Informations Genealogiques
0337-6729	Informatique Nouvelle *changed to* Informatique Professionnelle
0337-7091	Regards sur l'Actualite
0337-7393	Revue de Jurisprudence Fiscale
0337-8659	Eclats de Rire
0337-8888	Nostra
0337-9353	Loisirs Service-Sports Europe
0337-9515	Afrique Agriculture
0337-9736	Revue d'Orthopedie Dento-Faciale
0337-9965	Technicien Biologiste *see* 0766-5725
0338-0181	Khamsin
0338-0548	Bulletin d'Informations Proustiennes
0338-1439	Cahiers Medicaux†
0338-1552	Nouveau Pouvoir Judiciaire
0338-1684	Diabete & Metabolisme
0338-1757	Solidaires (Paris)
0338-1900	Oeuvres et Critiques
0338-2079	Revue du Magnetisme-Etude du Psychisme Experimental
0338-2397	Psychanalyse a l'Universite
0338-2842	H *changed to* H L M Aujourd'hui
0338-3423	France. Ministere de la Sante et de la Securite Sociale. Sante, Securite Sociale. Statistiques et Commentaires *changed to* Solidarite/Sante
0338-4187	D F Actualites
0338-4241	France. Direction de la Prevision. Rationalisation des Choix Budgetaires†
0338-4446	Bibliotheque Nationale Bulletin *see* 0249-7344
0338-4535	Revue Francaise de Transfusion et Immuno-Hematologie
0338-5922	France. Secretariat d'Etat aux Universities. Service des Bibliotheques. Division de la Cooperation et de l'Automatisation. Bulletin de la DICA†
0338-6473	Propriete Industrielle Bulletin Documentaire
0338-7070	Centre Lyonnais d'Acupuncture de Saint-Luc. Bulletin de Liaison
0338-7208	Cahiers Bleus
0338-8190	Inconnu
0338-9529	Handicapes Mechants
0339-0047	Secrets de l'Histoire†
0339-0055	Presence de l'Enseignement Agricole Prive
0339-0462	Foi et Developpement
0339-0608	Collections et Monnaies *see* 0183-8490
0339-0713	Sapho
0339-0934	Citoyen
0339-1116	Centre Auvergne Gadz'arts. Bulletin Trimestriel des Ingenieurs Arts et Metiers de la Region Auvergne
0339-1493	Photoroman d'Amour
0339-1507	Sol et Murs Magazine
0339-1531	50 Millions de Consommateurs
0339-154X	Consommateurs Actualites
0339-1558	Composants Mecaniques, Electriques et Electroniques *see* 0245-9981
0339-1744	Purushartha
0339-2171	Cahiers d'Etudes et de Recherche Victoriennes *see* 0220-5610

0339-2899 France. Centre National pour l'Exploitation des Oceans. Publications. Serie: Rapports Scientifiques et Techniques *see* 0761-3970
0339-2902 France. Centre National pour l'Exploitation des Oceans. Publications. Serie: Resultats des Campagnes a la Mer *see* 0761-3989
0339-2910 France. Centre National pour l'Exploitation des Oceans. Publications. Serie: Rapports Economiques et Juridiques *see* 0761-3938
0339-2945 France. Departement d'Economie et de Sociologie Rurales. Bulletin d'Information†
0339-3070 Faire
0339-3097 Cahiers de l'Analyse des Donnees
0339-3275 Interfolk
0339-4212 I N E S Informations *see* 0980-3637
0339-5081 Unites Petrochimiques en Europe de l'Ouest†
0339-6460 Notes d'Informations Communautaires
0339-6851 Actes
0339-686X Champ Social
0339-6886 Revoltes Logiques
0339-722X S T A L
0339-7238 Association des Techniciens d'Animaux de Laboratoire. Bulletin Trimestriel *see* 0339-722X
0339-7963 Cuisine Chez Sol
0339-8390 Fleurs de France
0339-8498 Belisane
0339-8617 Dossiers de Puericulture Information
0339-8811 Universite de Paris VII. Groupe de Linguistique Japonaise. Travaux *changed to* Travaux de Linguistique Japonaise
0339-8943 Cinema Different
0339-8978 Changer le Cinema
0339-9052 Cheval Hebdo
0339-9702 Mecanisation Forestiere
0339-9958 Aujourd'hui l'Afrique
0340-000X Bibliotheksforum Bayern
0340-0026 International Journal of Clinical Pharmacology and Biopharmacy *see* 0174-4879
0340-0034 Communication and Cybernetics
0340-0050 International Classification
0340-0077 Technische Universitaet Hannover. Franzius-Institut fuer Wasserbau und Kuesteningenieurwesen. Mitteilungen *changed to* Franzius-Institut fuer Wasserbau und Kuesteningenierurwesen. Mitteilungen
0340-0093 Medizinische Psychologie†
0340-0123 Beitraege zur Psychodiagnostik des Kindes
0340-0131 International Archives of Occupational and Environmental Health
0340-0158 Communications
0340-0174 Zeitschrift fuer Historische Forschung
0340-0204 Journal of Non-Equilibrium Thermodynamics
0340-0220 Exakt†
0340-0255 Friedens-Warte
0340-031X Wissenschaftliche Forschungsberichte. Reihe 1. Grundlagenforschung und Grundlegende Methodik. Abt. C. Psychologie†
0340-0352 I F L A Journal
0340-0409 Bibliographia Cartographica
0340-0425 Leviathan
0340-0441 Scala
0340-045X International Journal of Law Libraries *see* 0731-1265
0340-0476 Materialien zur Politischen Bildung
0340-0522 International Bulletin for Research on Law in Eastern Europe.†
0340-0603 Epitaph
0340-062X Journal of Geophysics
0340-0700 Staatsbibliothek Preussischer Kulturbesitz. Ausstellungskataloge
0340-0727 Psychological Research
0340-0751 Deutsche Forschungsberichte *see* 0343-5520
0340-076X Zeitschrift fuer klinische Chemie und klinische Biochemie
0340-0778 Stereo
0340-0794 Roux' Archives of Developmental Biology
0340-0824 Zeitschrift fuer Archaeologie des Mittelalters
0340-0840 Funktionsanalyse Biologischer Systeme
0340-0905 Waking and Sleeping†
0340-0921 Frontal
0340-0956 Sportwissenschaftliche Dissertationen
0340-1022 Topics in Current Chemistry
0340-1057 Biophysics of Structure and Mechanism *see* 0175-7571
0340-112X Graue Literatur zur Orts Regional- und Landesplanung
0340-1162 Immunitaet und Infektion
0340-1170 Kommunalwissenschaftliche Dissertationen
0340-1200 Biological Cybernetics
0340-1227 Virchows Archiv. Section A: Pathological Anatomy and Histology. *changed to* Virchows Archiv. Section A: Pathological Anatomy and Histopathology
0340-1294 Bergwelt
0340-1324 Cleveland *see* 0160-8533
0340-1332 Handbuch der Internationalen Dokumentation und Information
0340-1502 Rassegna Tecnica A E G-Telefunken†
0340-1545 Online
0340-1553 Datenverarbeitung A E G-Telefunken *see* 0040-1447
0340-1588 Laryngologie, Rhinologie, Otologie und ihre Grenzgebiete Vereinigt mit Monatsschrift fuer Ohrenheilkunde *changed to* Laryngologie, Rhinologie, Otologie
0340-160X Die Dritte Welt†
0340-1618 RoeFo. Fortschritte auf dem Gebiete der Roentgenstrahlen und der Nuklearmedizin
0340-1650 WISt
0340-1669 Monatsschrift fuer Unfallheilkunde *see* 0341-5694
0340-1677 Psychologie Heute
0340-1707 Deutsches Institut fuer Wirtschaftsforschung. Vierteljahrshefte zur Wirtschaftsforschung
0340-174X Suedosteuropa-Mitteilungen
0340-1758 Zeitschrift fuer Parlamentsfragen
0340-1766 Der Freie Zahnarzt
0340-1774 Informationen zur Modernen Stadtgeschichte (I M S)
0340-1790 Bayerisches Staatsministerium fuer Arbeit und Sozialordnung. Amtsblatt.
0340-1804 Zeitschrift fuer Soziologie
0340-1812 Monatsschrift fuer Deutsches Recht
0340-1855 Zeitschrift fuer Rheumatologie
0340-1898 Deutsches Tieraerzteblatt
0340-1901 Aktuelle Probleme der Intensivmedizin†
0340-1952 F und M, Feinwerktechnik und Messtechnik
0340-1960 Current Topics in Nutritional Sciences†
0340-2002 C. I. I. A. Symposia†
0340-2037 Divice†
0340-2061 Anatomy and Embryology
0340-2088 Chimica Didactica
0340-2096 Anatomia, Histologia, Embryologia. Series C
0340-210X Aktuelle Probleme der Polymer-Physik†
0340-2118 European Journal of Applied Microbiology *see* 0175-7598
0340-2134 Physica Didactica
0340-2150 Praxis der Sozialpsychologie†
0340-2185 B T†
0340-2193 Zeitschrift fuer Physik. Section A: Atomic and Nuclei
0340-2207 Der Fremdsprachliche Unterricht
0340-2215 Studien zur Altaegyptischen Kultur
0340-224X Zeitschrift fuer Physik. Section B. Quanta and Matter *see* 0722-3277
0340-2258 Der Deutschunterricht
0340-2266 Entomologica Germanica *see* 0171-8177
0340-2274 Staatsbibliothek Preussischer Kulturbesitz. Jahresbericht
0340-2304 Sozialwissenschaftliche Informationen fuer Unterricht und Studium
0340-2355 Suedwestdeutsche Schulblaetter
0340-241X Veroeffentlichungen aus der Pathologie
0340-2444 Zeitschrift fuer Arbeitswissenschaft
0340-2452 Fortschritte im Integrierten Pflanzenschutz†
0340-2479 Zeitschrift fuer Unternehmens- und Gesellschaftsrecht
0340-2495 Denkmalpflege in Baden-Wuerttemberg
0340-2509 Spezielle Anorganische Chemie†
0340-2541 Aktuelle Dermatologie
0340-255X Progress in Colloid and Polymer Science
0340-2592 Der Urologe. Section A
0340-2649 Unfallchirurgie
0340-2657 Der Chemieunterricht
0340-269X Phytocoenologia
0340-2703 Wissenschaftliche Forschungsberichte. Reihe 2. Anwendungstechnik und Angewandte Wissenschaft†
0340-2827 Amerikastudien
0340-2924 Surface and Vacuum Physics Index†
0340-2940 Technik in der Medizin†
0340-2967 F und I-Bau
0340-3017 Zahnaerzteblatt Baden-Wuerttemberg
0340-305X Phlebologie und Proktologie
0340-3068 Ibero-Amerikanisches Archiv
0340-3130 Akupunktur: Theorie und Praxis
0340-3157 Acta Pharmaceutica Technologica
0340-3238 Dokumentation Arbeitsmedizin/Documentation Occupational Health *changed to* Beruf und Gesundheit
0340-3254 Mitteilungen aus der Arbeitsmarkt- und Berufsforschung
0340-3270 Landesversicherungsanstalt Wuerttemberg. Mitteilungen
0340-3289 Der Versorgungsbeamte
0340-3297 Dokumentation Ostmitteleuropa
0340-3343 Chemiefasern /Textil-Industrie
0340-3440 A B T Informationen†
0340-3475 Dokumentation Tribologie
0340-3491 Das Rationelle Buero
0340-3505 Baden - Wuerttembergische Verwaltungspraxis
0340-3513 Elektrowaerme International. Part A: Elektrowaerme im Technischen Ausbau
0340-3521 Elektrowaerme International. Part B: Industrielle Elektrowaerme
0340-3572 Fernwaerme International
0340-3602 Das Krankenhaus
0340-3637 Der Gemeindetag†
0340-3645 Der Gemeindehaushalt
0340-367X Sozialversicherungs-Beamte und -Angestellte BSBA *changed to* G D S-Zeitung
0340-3696 Archives of Dermatological Research
0340-3718 Bonner Energie-Report
0340-3734 Naturwissenhistorischer Verein Augsburg. Bericht *see* 0720-3705
0340-3793 Applied Physics *see* 0721-7250
0340-3793 Applied Physics *see* 0721-7269
0340-3858 D G S
0340-3912 Architektur und Wohnwelt *see* 0173-8046
0340-3955 Dokumentation Regelungstechniktechnik *changed to* V D I. Informationsdienst Regelungstechnik
0340-398X K I *changed to* K I Klima, Kaelte, Heizung
0340-3998 Forschung im Strassenwesen
0340-403X Vogelkundliche Berichte aus Niedersachsen
0340-4099 Unterrichtswissenschaft
0340-4137 Management Wissen
0340-4145 Goettinger Floristische Rundbriefe
0340-4242 Germany(Federal Republic, 1949-). Bundesanstalt fuer Gewaesserkunde. Hydrologische Bibliographie†
0340-4277 Beitraege zur Naturkunde Niedersachsens
0340-4285 Transition Metal Chemistry†
0340-434X Regelungstechnik *changed to* Automatisierungstechnik
0340-4439 Sanitaer-Installateur und Heizungsbauer *see* 0931-7775
0340-448X Die Neue Hochschule
0340-4528 Internationales Archiv fuer Sozialgeschichte der Deutschen Literatur
0340-4536 Verkehr und Technik
0340-4544 Werkstattstechnik- W T
0340-4552 Promet
0340-4560 Zeitschrift fuer Vermessungswesen
0340-4684 Blood Cells
0340-4730 Regelungstechnik *changed to* Automatisierungstechnische Praxis
0340-4749 Referate Organ: Schweissen und Verwandte Verfahren
0340-4773 Progress in Botany
0340-4781 Osnabruecker Naturwissenschaftliche Mitteilungen
0340-4803 Stahl und Eisen
0340-4811 Zeitschrift fuer Naturforschung. Section A: Physics, Physical Chemistry, Cosmic Physics
0340-4838 Hafenbautechnische Gesellschaft. Jahrbuch
0340-4897 Mathematisch-Physikalische Semesterberichte *see* 0720-728X
0340-4900 Literaturberichte ueber Wasser, Abwasser, Luft und Feste Abfallstoffe
0340-4951 Zeitschriften- und Buecherschau "Stahl und Eisen"
0340-5044 Die Bautechnik. Ausgabe B
0340-5060 Thyssen Technische Berichte
0340-5087 Zeitschrift fuer Naturforschung. Section B: Inorganic and Organic Chemistry
0340-5109 Zentralblatt fuer Geologie und Palaeontologie. Teil I: Allgemeine, Angewandte, Regionale und Historische Geologie
0340-5133 Sprechsaal fuer Keramik, Glas, Baustoffe *see* 0341-0676
0340-5141 Vermessungswesen und Raumordnung (VR)
0340-5176 Deutsches Gewaesserkundliches Jahrbuch. Donaugebiet
0340-5184 Deutsches Gewaesserkundliches Jahrbuch. Kuestengebiet der Nord- und Ostsee
0340-5214 Zentralblatt Hals-, Nasen- und Ohrenheilkunde, Plastische Chirurgie an Kopf und Hals
0340-5303 Schwester/Der Pfleger
0340-5354 Journal of Neurology
0340-5362 Bremer Aerzteblatt
0340-5370 Betriebswirtschaftliche Forschung und Praxis
0340-5389 Electromedica
0340-5400 Research in Molecular Biology
0340-5419 Karl-August-Forster-Lectures
0340-5443 Behavioral Ecology and Sociobiology
0340-5508 Medizinisch-Orthopaedische Technik
0340-5532 Arzt- und Arzneimittelrecht
0340-5559 Dokumentation Impfschaeden-Impferfolge†
0340-5613 Zeitschrift fuer Psychosomatische Medizin und Psychoanalyse
0340-5664 Chirurgia Plastica *changed to* European Journal of Plastic Surgery
0340-5672 Deutsche Zeitschrift fuer Onkologie
0340-5702 Aerztliche Kosmetologie
0340-5710 Deutschland in Geschichte und Gegenwart
0340-5745 A.G.T. Dokumentation
0340-5753 Die Rentenversicherung
0340-5761 Archives of Toxicology
0340-577X Modernes Leben-Natuerliches Heilen
0340-5796 Afrika
0340-580X Hauptschulmagazin *changed to* Lehrerjournal Hauptschulmagazin
0340-5818 Welt der Schule†
0340-5826 Blaetter fuer Lehrerfortbildung
0340-5869 Politik und Kultur
0340-5877 Der Kinderarzt
0340-5923 Bouvier Disputanda†
0340-594X Studien zur Germanistik, Anglistik und Komparatistik
0340-5958 Studien zur Franzoesischen Philosophie des Zwanzigsten Jahrhunderts

ISSN INDEX 1537

0340-5982 Kybernetik - Datenverarbeitung - Recht†
0340-5990 Studien zur Literatur- und Sozialgeschichte Spaniens und Lateinamerikas
0340-6008 Studien zur Englischen Literatur†
0340-6040 Stahl-Report Lernen und Leisten
0340-6075 Virchows Archiv. Section B: Cell Pathology
0340-6083 Goettinger Predigtmeditationen
0340-6091 Frohe Botschaft
0340-6121 Bibliographie der Wirtschaftswissenschaften
0340-613X Geschichte und Gesellschaft
0340-6199 European Journal of Pediatrics
0340-6210 Luther
0340-6229 Die Welt des Orients
0340-6245 Thrombosis and Haemostasis
0340-6253 Match
0340-6261 Freiburger Beitraege zur Indologie
0340-627X Enchoria
0340-6318 Wolfenbuetteler Barock-Nachrichten
0340-6326 Goettinger Orientforschungen. Reihe I: Syriaca
0340-6342 Goettinger Orientforschungen. Reihe IV: Aegypten
0340-6369 Giorgio Levi della Vida Conferences. Reports of the Conference.
0340-6377 Bonner Orientalistische Studien†
0340-6385 Neuindische Studien
0340-6393 Codices Arabici Antiqui
0340-6407 Oriens Christianus
0340-6423 Societas Uralo-Altaica. Veroeffentlichungen
0340-644X Saarlaendisches Aerzteblatt
0340-6490 Schriften zur Geistesgeschichte des Oestlichen Europa
0340-6628 Materialien zur Psychoanalyse und Analytisch Orientierten Psychotherapie
0340-6652 Universitaet Frankfurt am Main. Ostasiatischen Seminars. Veroeffentlichunge
0340-6679 Submarin†
0340-6687 Ruhr-Universitaet Bochum. Ostasien Institut. Veroeffentlichungen
0340-6695 European Journal of Behavioural Analysis and Modification *changed to* Behavioural Analysis and Modification
0340-6717 Human Genetics
0340-6725 Zoomorphologie *see* 0720-213X
0340-6792 Studies in Oriental Religions
0340-6989 Kieler Studien
0340-6997 European Journal of Nuclear Medicine
0340-7004 Cancer Immunology, Immunotherapy
0340-7047 Zentralblatt fuer Arbeitsmedizin, Arbeitsschutz und Prophylaxe
0340-7063 Die Schaltung†
0340-7071 Strassenbahn Magazin
0340-7217 Soziale Forschung und Praxis†
0340-7322 Anzeiger fuer Schaedlingskunde, Pflanzen- und Umweltschutz *see* 0340-7330
0340-7330 Anzeiger fuer Schaedlingskunde, Pflanzenschutz, Umweltschutz
0340-7349 Public International Law
0340-739X Eurosport and Freizeitmode *changed to* Sportshop
0340-7403 Kritische Berichte
0340-7462 Propellants and Explosives *see* 0721-3115
0340-7489 Baurecht
0340-7497 Zeitschrift fuer Miet- und Raumrecht
0340-7519 Strom Praxis
0340-7551 Amts- und Mitteilungsblatt der Bundesanstalt fuer Materialpruefung
0340-7586 Bayerische Akademie der Wissenschaften. Mathematisch-Naturwissenschaftliche Klasse. Sitzungberichte
0340-7594 Journal of Comparative Physiology. A: Sensory, Neural, and Behavioral Physiology
0340-7616 Journal of Comparative Physiology. B. Systematic, and Environmental Physiology *changed to* Journal of Comparative Physiology. B: Biochemical, Systematic, and Environmental Physiology
0340-7632 Current Contents Africa†
0340-7691 Bayerische Kommission fuer die Internationale Erdmessung. Veroeffentlichungen
0340-7756 Informationen Jugendliteratur und Medien-Jugendschriften-Warte
0340-7810 V D L-Nachrichten
0340-7829 Die Pirsch - der Deutsche Jaeger
0340-7837 Land Aktuell
0340-7845 Psycho
0340-7853 Bibliothek der Griechischen Literatur
0340-7888 Literarischer Verein in Stuttgart. Bibliothek
0340-7896 Glueckauf
0340-7918 Betriebs-Berater
0340-7926 Recht der Internationalen Wirtschaft
0340-7969 Allgemeine Zeitschrift fuer Philosophie
0340-7993 Paepste und Papsttum
0340-8035 Monumenta Germaniae Historica. Staatsschriften des Spaeteren Mittelalters
0340-8043 Fachberichte Huettenpraxis Metallweiterverarbeitung
0340-8051 Bibliothek des Buchwesens (B B)
0340-806X Dermatologen-Mitteilungsblatt *see* 0340-8078
0340-8078 Der Deutsche Dermatologe
0340-8094 Indices Naturwissenschaftlich-Medizinischer Periodica bis 1850
0340-8140 Mendelssohn Studien
0340-8175 Giesserei-Kalender
0340-8183 M M G
0340-8280 Renovatio
0340-8329 Zeitschrift fuer Luft- und Weltraumrecht
0340-8361 Z I D
0340-837X Technisches Messen - A T M *see* 0171-8096
0340-8388 Dokumentation Rheologie
0340-8396 Deutsches Mittelalter, Kritische Studientexte der Monumenta Germaniae Historica
0340-840X Agrarrecht
0340-8434 Arbeit und Sozialpolitik
0340-8442 Kunststoffberater, -Rundschau, -Technik *see* 0172-6374
0340-8450 Records of the Ancient Near East
0340-8485 Zeitschrift fuer das Gesamte Kreditwesen
0340-8515 Physik und Didaktik
0340-8590 Demokratie und Recht
0340-8604 Deutsche Notar-Zeitschrift
0340-8671 Biologische Medizin
0340-8728 Vierteljahrschrift fuer Sozial- und Wirtschaftsgeschichte
0340-8744 Empirica
0340-8825 Manuscripta Geodaetica
0340-8833 Ernst-Mach-Institut, Freiburg. Bericht
0340-8906 Grundrechte; die Rechtsprechung in Europa *see* 0341-9800
0340-8973 Forschungsdokumentation zur Arbeitsmarkt- und Berufsforschung
0340-9023 Studien zur Literatur der Moderne
0340-9031 Die Wirtschaftspruefung
0340-9058 Zeitschrift fuer Sportpaedagogik *changed to* Sportpaedagogik
0340-9066 Fisch und Umwelt†
0340-9120 Sel'skoe Khozyaistvo za Rubezhom
0340-918X Soziologie
0340-9201 Sozialisation und Kommunikation
0340-9244 Politikwissenschaftliche Forschung†
0340-9260 Neues Steuerrecht von A bis Z
0340-9279 Betriebliches Vorschlagswesen
0340-9341 Deutsche Sprache
0340-9422 Z O R - Zeitschrift fuer Operations Research
0340-949X Beitraege zur Umweltgestaltung. Reihe B.
0340-9503 Die Steuerliche Betriebspruefung
0340-9511 Medizin im Recht und Ethik
0340-952X Die Tiefbauberufsgenossenschaft
0340-9716 Beitraege zur Umweltgestaltung. Reihe A
0340-9767 Kritikon Litterarum
0340-9783 Hohenheimer Arbeiten
0340-9821 Veroeffentlichungen der Astronomischen Institut der Universitaet Bonn
0340-983X Materialiensammlung Staedtebau
0340-9929 Suedkurs†
0340-9961 Chemie-Technik
0340-997X Hospital-Hygiene†
0341-0056 Historia. Einzelschriften
0341-0064 Hermes-Einzelschriften
0341-0099 Beitraege zur Geschichte der Pharmazie
0341-0110 Apotheker und Kunst
0341-0137 Deutsche Morgenlaendische Gesellschaft. Zeitschrift
0341-0218 Max-Planck-Gesellschaft. Jahrbuch
0341-0331 A K Holz
0341-0331 Holz-kunststoff-Moebelfertigung
0341-0382 Zeitschrift fuer Naturforschung. Section C: Biosciences
0341-0412 D L G - Mitteilungen
0341-0455 Altenpflege
0341-0463 Archiv fuer Eisenbahntechnik
0341-0498 Grundlagen und Fortschritte der Lebensmitteluntersuchung und Lebensmitteltechnologie
0341-0501 Aktuelle Ernaehrungsmedizin
0341-051X Aktuelle Rheumatologie
0341-0528 Germany (Federal Republic, 1949-). Bundesanstalt fuer Materialpruefung. Jahresbericht
0341-0544 Referateorgan: Zerstoerungsfreie Pruefung
0341-0552 Z I International
0341-0595 Informationsdienst Krankenhauswesen
0341-0609 Kopfklinik†
0341-0668 Rundschau fuer Fleichuntersuchung und Lebensmittelueberwachung *see* 0178-2010
0341-0676 Sprechsaal
0341-0730 Medizin in Unserer Zeit†
0341-0765 Studia Leibnitiana. Sonderhefte
0341-0773 Sudhoffs Archiv. Beihefte
0341-0781 Melliand Textilberichte /International Textile Reports
0341-079X Archiv fuer Rechts- und Sozialphilosophie. Beihefte
0341-0803 Deutsche Morgenlaendische Gesellschaft. Zeitschrift. Supplementa
0341-0811 Zeitschrift fuer Franzoesische Sprache und Literatur. Beihefte. Neue Folge
0341-082X Wort in der Welt *changed to* Die Weltmission
0341-0838 Zeitschrift fuer Dialektologie und Linguistik. Beihefte
0341-0846 Vierteljahrschrift fuer Sozial- und Wirtschaftsgeschichte. Beihefte
0341-0854 Acta Pharmaceutica Technologica. Supplementa†
0341-0862 Hamburger Hafen-Nachrichten
0341-0935 Betriebsverpflegung†
0341-0943 Kritische Medizin im Argument
0341-0951 Forschung Stadtverkehr†
0341-0978 Die Konjunktur im Handwerk†
0341-0986 Internationales Jahrbuch fuer Kartographie
0341-101X Haerterei-Technische Mitteilungen (HTM)
0341-1052 Die Bautechnik. Ausgabe A
0341-1060 Braunkohle
0341-1184 Acta Praehistorica et Archaeologica
0341-1206 Umweltmagazin
0341-1222 Archaeologische Ausgrabungen
0341-1230 Aurora
0341-1281 Aerokurier
0341-1362 Electrotechnische Zeitschrift E T Z *changed to* E T Z Zeitschrift fuer Elektrische Energietechnik
0341-1869 I K O - Innere Kolonisation - Land und Gemeinde†
0341-1915 Neue Juristische Wochenschrift
0341-1982 Niedersaechsische Wirtschaft
0341-2040 Lung
0341-2091 Deutscher Gartenbau
0341-2172 Wuppertaler Schriftenreihe Literatur
0341-2210 Verkehrsunfall *changed to* Verkehrsunfall und Fahrzeugtechnik
0341-2253 Wolfenbuetteler Notizen zur Buchgeschichte
0341-2261 Eildienst: Bundesgerichtliche Entscheidungen
0341-2334 Zeitschrift fuer Verkehrserziehung
0341-2350 Klinikarzt
0341-2377 Reactivity and Structure: Concepts of Organic Chemistry
0341-2431 Dokumentation zur Raumentwicklung†
0341-244X Forschungen zur Raumentwicklung
0341-2458 Aerztin
0341-2474 Denkmaeler der Buchkunst
0341-2512 Referateblatt zur Raumentwicklung
0341-2520 Agraringenieur und Agrarmanager
0341-2601 C C B†
0341-261X Lohnunternehmen in Land- und Forstwirtschaft
0341-2679 Wasser, Luft und Betrieb
0341-2695 International Orthopaedics
0341-2709 Aquarium
0341-2717 Baumarkt
0341-275X Vereinigung von Afrikanisten in Deutschland. Schriften
0341-2784 Architektur und Wettbewerbe *changed to* Architecture & Competitions
0341-2792 Personal-Buero in Recht und Praxis
0341-2903 Notfallmedizin
0341-2911 Medizin *see* 0344-5836
0341-2954 Steuer und Wirtschaft
0341-2970 Europaeischer Wetterbericht
0341-3055 Atemwegs- und Lungenkrankheiten
0341-3063 Intensivbehandlung
0341-3071 Jugendscala
0341-311X Fenno-Ugrica
0341-3136 Universitaet Bonn. Institut fuer Kommunikationsforschung und Phonetik. Forschungsberichte
0341-3144 Forum Phoneticum
0341-3152 Hamburger Beitraege zur Archaeologie
0341-3179 Hamburger Juristische Studien
0341-3187 Hamburger Phonetische Beitraege *see* 0178-1723
0341-3195 Papiere zur Textlinguistik
0341-3209 Romanistik in Geschichte und Gegenwart
0341-3217 Bibliotheca Russica
0341-3225 Linguarum Minorum Documenta Historiographica
0341-3233 Universitaet Hamburg. Institut fuer Internationale Angelegenheiten. Veroeffentlichungen
0341-3241 Universitaet Hamburg. Institut fuer Internationale Angelegenheiten. Werkhefte
0341-3276 Dokumente zur Deutschlandpolitik. Beihefte
0341-339X Wirtschaft und Berufs-Erziehung
0341-3403 Atem und Mensch
0341-3624 Baum-Zeitung
0341-3659 Bau- und Moebelschreiner
0341-3667 Bank und Markt
0341-3675 Deutsch Lernen
0341-3772 Scripta Geobotanica
0341-3780 Goettinger Geographische Abhandlungen
0341-3810 Bauwirtschaft. Ausgabe A
0341-3861 Praxis Geographie
0341-3896 B I
0341-3918 Bayerische Vorgeschichtsblaetter
0341-4000 Bau-Zentralblatt *changed to* B Z Bauzentralblatt
0341-4027 Geologisches Jahrbuch Hessen
0341-4035 Nachrichten-Elektronik *changed to* Nachrichten-Elektronik & Telematik
0341-4043 Geologische Abhandlungen Hessen
0341-406X Drosera
0341-4159 Kunst & Antiquitaeten
0341-4175 Elo
0341-4183 Bibliothek Forschung und Praxis
0341-4191 Studien zur Indologie und Iranistik
0341-4213 A T W News
0341-440X R A K - Riechstoffe, Aromen, Kosmetica
0341-4434 Arzt und Auto
0341-4477 Betrieb und Meister
0341-4507 Beschaffung Aktuell

0341-4558 Fleischbeschau und Lebensmittelkontrolle
0341-468X Kraftfahrt-Bundesamt. Statistische Mitteilungen
0341-471X Schulbibliothek Aktuell
0341-4728 Schnellstatistik Allgemeiner Oeffentlicher Bibliotheken†
0341-4817 Haustechnik†
0341-5104 Modell Fan
0341-5112 Mobil
0341-5163 Nachrichten aus Chemie, Technik und Laboratorium
0341-5244 Bus-Fahrt
0341-5279 Geographie Heute
0341-5309 Lebensmittel und Gerichtliche Chemie *changed to* Lebensmittelchemie und Gerichtliche Chemie
0341-5376 Monographs on Theoretical and Applied Genetics
0341-5406 Die Computer Zeitung
0341-5449 D S W R
0341-5457 D D R Report
0341-549X D F Z Wirtschaftsmagazin
0341-5570 Techno-Tip
0341-5589 Elektronikpraxis
0341-5600 Werbeartikel-Berater
0341-5694 Unfallheilkunde
0341-5724 Textilkunst
0341-5759 Du und das Tier
0341-5775 Maschinenmarkt
0341-5783 Europa Industrie Revue†
0341-5872 Forschungsarbeiten aus dem Strassenwesen. Schriftenreihe
0341-5910 Institut fuer den Wissenschaftlichen Film. Publikationen zu Wissenschaftlichen Filmen. Sektion Ethnologie
0341-5929 Institut fuer den Wissenschaftlichen Film. Publikationen zu Wissenschaftlichen Filmen. Sektion Medizin
0341-5937 Institut fuer den Wissenschaftlichen Film. Publikationen zu Wissenschaftlichen Filmen. Sektion Geschichte, Publizistik
0341-6097 Export-Markt
0341-6151 Law and State
0341-616X Institute for Scientific Co-operation with Developing Countries. Economics
0341-6208 Bankhistorisches Archiv
0341-633X Lecture Notes in Biomathematics
0341-6399 Geologisches Jahrbuch. Reihe A: Allgemeine und Regionale Geologie B.R. Deutschland und Nachbargebiete, Tektonik, Stratigraphie, Palaeontologie
0341-6402 Geologisches Jahrbuch. Reihe B: Regionale Geologie Ausland
0341-6410 Geologisches Jahrbuch. Reihe C: Hydrogeologie. Ingenieurgeologie
0341-6429 Geologisches Jahrbuch. Reihe D: Mineralogie. Petrographie, Geochemie, Lagerstaettenkunde
0341-6437 Geologisches Jahrbuch. Reihe E: Geophysik
0341-6445 Geologisches Jahrbuch. Reihe F: Bodenkunde
0341-6569 Components Report *see* 0173-1726
0341-6593 D T W - Deutsche Tieraerztliche Wochenschrift
0341-6615 Konstruieren und Giessen
0341-6631 China Aktuell
0341-6771 Deike Gedenktage
0341-6836 Meeresforschung
0341-6860 Medien & Erziehung
0341-6879 Gruppe und Spiel
0341-695X Agrartechnik International *changed to* Agrartechnik
0341-7115 Brauindustrie
0341-7158 Was & Wie?
0341-7190 Kindergottesdienst/Lass mich Hoeren
0341-7212 Aesthetik und Kommunikation
0341-7301 Behindertenpaedagogik
0341-7387 Leistungssport
0341-7492 Beiheft zu Leistlingssport†
0341-759X Meister - Zeitung
0341-7603 Schule und Museum†
0341-7638 Journal of Literary Semantics
0341-7727 M P G Spiegel
0341-7743 Musikbibliothek Aktuell†
0341-7778 Max-Planck-Gesellschaft zur Foerderung der Wissenschaften Berichte und Mitteilungen
0341-7816 Finnisch-ugrische Mitteilungen
0341-7840 Germany (Federal Republic, 1949-). Bundesministerium fuer Arbeit und Sozialordnung. Hauptergebnisse der Arbeits- und Sozialstatistik
0341-7948 Praxis des Rechnungswesens
0341-8022 Dokumentation Gefaehrdung durch Alkohol, Rauchen, Drogen, Arzneimittel
0341-8057 Geographie im Unterricht
0341-8073 Presse Report (PR)
0341-8235 Schul-Management
0341-8243 Lehrmittel Aktuell
0341-826X Diakonie
0341-8324 Archiv fuer Frankfurts Geschichte und Kunst
0341-8332 Archiv fuer Angewandte Sozialpaedagogik
0341-8340 Arbeitsinformationen ueber Studienprojekte auf dem Gebiet der Geschichte des Deutschen Judentums und des Antisemitismus
0341-8383 Anzeiger des Germanischen Nationalmuseums
0341-8391 Spixiana Journal of Zoology
0341-8413 Schuhtechnik A B C
0341-8448 Iconographia Ecclesiae Orientalis†
0341-8510 Praxis der Naturwissenschaften. Biologie im Unterricht der Schulen
0341-8588 Ost-West Commerz
0341-8634 Museum
0341-8642 Indiana
0341-8669 Umsatzsteuer-Rundschau
0341-8685 International Journal of Physical Education
0341-8707 Schleswig-Holsteinisches Aerzteblatt
0341-8723 Wissenschaftlicher Literaturanzeiger
0341-8766 Deutsche Verkehrsteuer-Rundschau
0341-8812 Diabetes-Journal
0341-8960 Religionsunterricht an hoeheren Schulen
0341-8995 Zahnaerztliche Mitteilungen
0341-907X Mineralien Magazin†
0341-910X Beitraege Archaeologie des Romischen Rheinlands
0341-9142 Istanbuler Mitteilungen
0341-9150 Bayerische Denkmalpflege. Jahrbuch
0341-9177 Jahrbuch der Historischen Forschung in der Bundesrepublik Deutschland
0341-9185 Beitraege zur Archaeologie des Mittelalters
0341-9193 Beitraege zur Urgeschichte des Rheinlandes
0341-9258 Geographie *changed to* Uebersee-Museum, Bremen. Veroeffentlichungen. Reihe C: Geographie
0341-9274 Uebersee-Museum, Bremen. Veroeffentlichungen. Reihe D: Voelkerkundliche Monographien
0341-9312 Romisch-Germanischen Kommission. Berichte
0341-9363 Bibliographie der Deutschen Sprach- und Literaturwissenschaft
0341-938X Psychologie und Gesellschaft†
0341-9452 Blaetter fuer Pfaelzische Kirchengeschichte und Religioese Volkskunde
0341-9622 Bremisches Jahrbuch
0341-9665 Pollichia. Mitteilungen
0341-9681 K F Z Anzeiger
0341-9738 Spektrum der Psychiatrie und Nervenheilkunde
0341-9746 H N O
0341-9754 Arzt und Krankenhaus†
0341-9762 Libertas
0341-9770 Bunte Tierwelt
0341-9789 Rasen - Turf - Gazon
0341-9797 Garten als Jungborn *changed to* Der Garten Drinnen und Draussen
0341-9800 Europaeische Grundrechtte Zeitschrift
0341-9835 Zeitschrift fuer Allgemeinmedizin
0342-0019 Duesseldorfer Jahrbuch
0342-0078 Frankfurter Judaistische Beitraege
0342-0124 Stiftung Preussische Kulturbesitz. Jahrbuch
0342-0175 Jugend Beruf Gesellschaft
0342-0221 Bayerische Staatsbibliothek, Munich. Jahresbericht
0342-0329 Aktueller Informationsdienst Moderner Orient
0342-037X Dokumentationsdienst Lateinamerika
0342-0388 Spiegel der Lateinamerikanischen Presse
0342-0396 Aktueller Informationsdienst Afrika
0342-0477 Sprache - Stimme - Gehoer
0342-0493 S B Warenhaus†
0342-0523 Orgadata
0342-0671 Erziehung und Wissenschaft
0342-068X Zeitschrift fuer Flugwissenschaften und Weltraumforschung
0342-0736 Kunde
0342-0752 Verein fuer Niederdeutsche Sprachforschung. Korrespondenzblatt.
0342-0787 Kieler Arbeitspapiere
0342-0795 Dokumentation Medizin im Umweltschutz
0342-0809 Kompass
0342-0817 Betriebskrankenkasse
0342-0884 Linguistica Biblica
0342-0930 Der Langfristige Kred1t
0342-0957 D M I - Die Medizinische Information†
0342-0965 Geschichtsblaetter fuer Waldeck
0342-1058 Spanische Forschungen der Goerresgesellschaft. Reihe 1: Gesammelte Aufsaetze zur Kulturgeschichte Spaniens
0342-1104 Hannoversche Geschichtsblaetter
0342-1120 Algological Studies
0342-118X Deutsche Orient-Gesellschaft. Mitteilungen
0342-1341 Beitraege zur Geschichte des Alten Moenchtums und des Benediktinerordens
0342-1406 Nachrichten aus Niedersachsens Urgeschichte
0342-1422 Nietzsche-Studien
0342-1430 Theologische Quartalschrift
0342-1511 Neues Archiv fuer Niedersachsen
0342-1589 Diskussion Deutsch
0342-1643 Diakonie Report
0342-1694 Archiv fuer Arzneitherapie†
0342-1716 Kultur Vorschau Europa
0342-1724 Sport-Vorschau
0342-1732 Deike-Press
0342-1783 Zeitschrift fuer Wirtschafts- und Sozialwissenschaften
0342-1791 Physics and Chemistry of Minerals
0342-1805 Rheinische Heimatpflege
0342-1821 Rechtsprechung zum Wiedergutmachungsrecht†
0342-183X Psychologie in Erziehung und Unterricht
0342-1864 Iberoamericana
0342-1945 Recht der Arbeit
0342-1953 Fraunhofer-Gesellschaft. Berichte
0342-202X Forum Staedte-Hygiene
0342-2062 Karst und Mozlen Neue Forschungen und Berichte†
0342-2119 Z P F
0342-2216 Textil Report *changed to* Fashion
0342-2259 Der Landkreis
0342-2372 Theologische Beitraege
0342-2380 Sportwissenschaft
0342-2402 Sportunterricht
0342-2410 Verkuendigung und Forschung
0342-2461 Lehrhilfen fuer den Sportunterricht
0342-2534 Verwaltungsprechsprechung in Deutschland *changed to* Neue Zeitschrift fuer Verwaltungsrecht
0342-2747 Familiendynamik
0342-2801 Extracta Gynaecologica
0342-281X Extracta Paediatrica
0342-2828 Extracta Dermatologica
0342-2852 Zeitschrift fuer Unternehmensgeschichte
0342-2895 Franzoesisch Heute
0342-2968 Kosmetik Journal
0342-2976 Kosmetik International
0342-3026 Laboratoriums Medizin
0342-3042 Fracht Management
0342-3158 Graphische Kunst
0342-3247 Mikrofauna des Meeresbodens
0342-328X Z F A
0342-3476 Z L R -Zeitschrift fuer das Gesamte Lebensmittelrecht
0342-3484 Zeitschrift fuer Zoelle und Verbrauchsteuern
0342-3557 Gesetz und Verordnungsblatt fuer das Land Hessen
0342-3573 Bindereport
0342-3689 Mode im Verkauf
0342-376X G V - Praxis mit Tiefkuehlpraxis *changed to* G V - Praxis
0342-3875 Beihefte zur Internationalen Wissenschaftlichen Korrespondenz zur Geschichte der Deutschen Arbeiterbewegung
0342-393X Zeitschrift fuer Individualpsychologie
0342-3956 Zeitschrift fuer Unternehmensgeschichte. Beihefte
0342-3964 Bibliographie Sozialisation und Sozialpaedagogik
0342-4022 Abwassertechnik mit Abfalltechnik *changed to* Abwassertechnik-Abfalltechnik und Recycling
0342-4030 Universitaetssternwarte zu Wien. Annalen†
0342-4103 Medizinische Informatik und Statistik
0342-4111 Springer Series in Optical Sciences
0342-4162 Geolit
0342-4316 Zeitschrift fuer Bayerische Kirchengeschichte
0342-4340 Wolfenbuetteler Renaissance Mitteilungen
0342-4553 Schauspielfuehrer
0342-457X Sportwissenschaft und Sportpraxis
0342-4634 I S B N Review
0342-4642 Intensive Care Medicine
0342-4774 Fremdenverkehr und das Reisebuero *changed to* Der Fremdenverkehr-Tourismus & Kongress
0342-4839 Schriften des Oesterreichischen Kulturinstituts Kairo. Archaeologisch-Historische Abteilung
0342-4871 Bibliotheca Nostratica
0342-4898 Hoergeschaedigten-Paedagogik
0342-4901 Lecture Notes in Chemistry
0342-491X Schiffahrt International
0342-4960 Informationsdienst fuer den K F Z-Zubehoer Fachhandel und -Ersatzteile
0342-507X Halbjaehrliches Verzeichniss Taschenbuecher
0342-5088 Hauswirtschaftliche Bildung
0342-5142 Glas und Rahmen
0342-5258 Unsere Jugend
0342-5282 International Journal of Rehabilitation Research
0342-5487 Naturwissenschaften im Unterricht. Biologie
0342-5622 Oil Gas European Magazine
0342-5665 Energy Developments
0342-5746 Politik-Aktuell fuer den Unterricht
0342-5789 Antimilitarismus Information
0342-5800 Confructa
0342-5843 Journal of Consumer Policy
0342-5991 Bayerische Akademie der Wissenschaften. Philosophisch-Historische Klasse. Sitzungsberichte
0342-6017 Wirtschaft und Gesellschaft im Unterricht
0342-6173 Zielsprache Englisch
0342-6203 Zielsprache Franzoesisch
0342-6300 Jahrbuch Deutsch Als Fremdsprache
0342-6319 I W - Report
0342-6335 Weltkonjunkturdienst
0342-6378 Wort und Antwort
0342-6513 Ja, Das Wort Fuer Alle
0342-6521 Der Zimmermann
0342-6610 Uebersee-Museum Bremen. Veroeffentlichungen. Reihe G: Bremer Suedpazifik-Archiv
0342-6777 Politische Didaktik†
0342-6785 Alexander von Humboldt Foundation. Annual Report

ISSN INDEX 1539

0342-6793 Topics in Current Physics
0342-6831 Integrative Therapie
0342-6866 Metamed *see* 0167-9902
0342-6904 Zur Zeit
0342-6947 European Petroleum Yearbook
0342-7064 Die Betriebswirtschaft
0342-7099 K-Plastic und Kautschuk Zeitung
0342-7102 Konstruktion Elemente Methoden
0342-7145 Theorie und Praxis der Sozialpaedagogik
0342-7161 Teddy
0342-7188 Irrigation Science
0342-7196 Cardiovascular Radiology *see* 0174-1551
0342-7269 Fussboden Forum
0342-734X Archaeologisches Korrespondenzblatt
0342-7358 Textilarbeit & Unterricht
0342-7439 Arnes Journal fuer Guten Geschmack
0342-7471 Schiedsmanns Zeitung
0342-7498 Praxis und Klinik der Pneumologie
0342-7609 Koelner Aerztliche Nachrichten†
0342-7706 Staedte- und Gemeindebund
0342-7722 Schwartzsche Vakanzen-Zeitung
0342-7757 Unsere Katze
0342-7978 Zeitschrift fuer Plastische Chirurgie *see* 0722-1819
0342-801X D I N - Taschenbuecher
0342-8095 Bimbo
0342-815X Sozialpaedagogische Blaetter
0342-8184 S B Z - Sanitaer, Heizungs- und Klimatechnik
0342-8206 S B Z-monteur
0342-8281 Rudersport
0342-829X Die Realschule
0342-8699 Altfraenkische Bilder und Wappenkalender
0342-8729 Praxis der Naturwissenschaften
0342-8745 Praxis der Naturwissenschaften. Chemie im Unterricht der Schulen
0342-8834 Und-oder-nor und Steuerungstechnik
0342-8893 Cancer Campaign
0342-8974 Wochenschau fuer politische Erziehung, Sozial- und Gemeinschaftskunde. Ausgabe fuer Sekundarstufe II
0342-8982 Studium Linguistik
0342-8990 Wochenschau fuer politische Erziehung, Sozial- und Gemeinschaftskunde. Ausgabe fuer Sekundarstufe I
0342-9148 Nachrichtentechnik
0342-9423 Zeitschrift fuer Mission
0342-9512 Lebensmittel Zeitung
0342-958X Microscopica Acta. Supplementa
0342-9601 Medizinische Monatsschrift fuer Pharmazeuten
0342-9857 Neue Praxis
0343-0170 Lernzielorientierter Unterricht
0343-0200 Die Milchpraxis und Rindermast
0343-043X Maschinen Anlagen Verfahren
0343-0510 Bergbau-Berufsgenossenschaft. Geschaeftsbericht *changed to* Bergbau-Berufsgenossenschaft. Jahresbericht
0343-0642 M D
0343-0987 Beitraege zur Hydrologie
0343-1002 Medizin Bibliothek Dokumentation
0343-1088 Kleine Aegyptische Texte
0343-1401 Publik-Forum
0343-1657 Literatur fuer Leser
0343-1711 Bergische Handwerk
0343-1762 Althaus Modernisierung
0343-2009 Saecula Spiritalia
0343-2092 Gas
0343-2181 Minerals and Rocks
0343-2246 K K - die Kaelte und Klimatechnik
0343-2319 Office Management
0343-2432 Dermatosen in Beruf und Umwelt
0343-2521 GeoJournal
0343-267X Controller Magazin
0343-2734 Suesswaren-Markt *changed to* Suesswaren-Wirtschaft
0343-2793 Offenbacher Verein fuer Naturkunde. Bericht
0343-3005 Informatik-Fachberichte
0343-3048 Zentralblatt fuer Haut- und Geschlechtskrankheiten Sowie Deren Grenzgebiete/Dermatology-Venerology-Andrology *changed to* Zentralblatt Haut- und Geschlechtskrankheiten/Dermatology
0343-3129 Kunststoffe im Bau†
0343-3137 Deutsche Zeitschrift fuer Mund, Kiefer- und Gesichtschirurgie
0343-317X Rechenzentrum *see* 0930-5157
0343-3218 Diaconia XP *changed to* Diaconia Christi
0343-3226 Selbstbedienung-Dynamik im Handel *see* 0722-6950
0343-3277 Duisburger Journal
0343-334X I P E
0343-3366 Lady International
0343-3420 Dokumentation Neusprachlicher Unterricht
0343-3463 Elektro Boerse
0343-3528 Primate Report
0343-3560 Schadenprisma
0343-3587 Progress in Orthopaedic Surgery†
0343-382X Dachdeckermeister
0343-3838 Der Deutsche Badebetrieb
0343-3846 Deutsche Bauern-Korrespondenz
0343-3919 Getraenke Revue
0343-3935 Contrapunkt
0343-4052 Handwerk Aktuell†
0343-4060 Accessories
0343-4079 Das Maler- und Lackiererhandwerk
0343-4109 Soziologische Revue
0343-4117 Bibliographie zur Geschichte der deutschen Arbeiterbewegung
0343-4125 Contributions to Sedimentology
0343-4192 Links und Rechts der Autobahn
0343-4206 HiFi und TV
0343-4346 Deutsche Handwerks-Zeitung
0343-4494 Schrifttum Bauwesen: Gesamtausgabe *see* 0722-060X
0343-4648 Geschichte, Politik und ihre Didaktik
0343-4842 Drug Development and Evolution
0343-5156 Winzer Kurier *changed to* Weinwirtschaft Anbau
0343-5202 Sprache und Datenverarbeitung
0343-5334 Didaktik der Mathematik
0343-5377 Zeitschrift fuer Energiewirtschaft
0343-5385 Datenschutz und Datensicherung Zugleich der Datenschutzbeauftragte *see* 0724-4371
0343-5520 Forschungsberichte aus Technik und Naturwissenschaften
0343-5539 German Chemical Engineering *changed to* Chemical Engineering and Technology
0343-5563 Deutsche Universitaetszeitung *changed to* Universitaetszeitung das Deutsche Hochschulmagazin
0343-5571 Film und TV Kameramann
0343-5598 D N V
0343-5881 Einkaufs 1x1 der Deutschen Industrie
0343-589X Deutsches Bundes-Adressbuch: Industrie, Gross- und Aussenhandel, Dienstleistungen, Organisationen
0343-6098 Anatomica Clinica *see* 0930-312X
0343-6462 Entwicklung und Laendlicher Raum
0343-6691 Erfolg
0343-6993 Mathematical Intelligencer
0343-7051 Abhandlungen aus dem Gebiet der Auslandskunde. Series B & C
0343-7140 Alte Uhren
0343-7167 Zeitschrift fuer Umweltpolitik
0343-7183 Packung und Transport in der Chemischen Industrie
0343-7256 Geographie und ihre Didaktik
0343-7477 Germany (Federal Republic, 1949-). Bundesministerium Fuer Ernaehrung, Landwirtschaft und Forsten. Jahresbericht. Forschung im Geschaeftsbereich des Bundesministers fuer Ernaerungland, Wirtschaft und Forsten
0343-7493 Universitaet Muenchen. Geophysikalisches Observatorium, Fuerstenfeldbruck. Veroeffentlichungen. Serie A
0343-754X Economic Bulletin (Aldershot)
0343-7647 A Z-Nachrichten
0343-7744 Forum Religion
0343-785X Ozean und Technik
0343-7868 Informationen - Bildung, Wissenschaft
0343-7892 Deutschen Gemmologischen Gesellschaft. Zeitschrift
0343-7906 Stuttgarter Geographische Studien
0343-835X Freie Universitaet Berlin. Osteuropa-Institut. Rechtswissenschaftliche Veroeffentlichungen
0343-8651 Current Microbiology
0343-8732 Gottesdienst
0343-8740 Geldinstitute
0343-9003 Junge Radio- Fernseh- und Industrie-Elektroniker
0343-9011 K F Z Zeitschrift fuer den Nachwuchs des Kraftfahrzeuhandwerks
0343-9321 P K V Informationdienst
0343-9429 Klinische Psychologie und Psychopathologie
0343-9496 Deutsche Verwaltungspraxis
0343-9771 Recht und Schaden
0344-015X Liste Pharmindex
0344-0249 Wirtschafts-Nachrichten fuer den Linken Niederrhein *changed to* Wirtschafts-Nachrichten
0344-0338 Pathology, Research and Practice
0344-0354 Alexander von Humboldt-Stiftung. Mitteilungen
0344-0397 Agrarmeteorologischer Wochenbericht fuer Norddeutschland
0344-0591 Sammlung Groos
0344-1369 Marketing
0344-1407 Taschenbuch fuer Liturgie Kirchenmusik und Musikerziehung
0344-1415 Die Frauenfrage in Deutschland. Bibliographie
0344-1733 LaborPraxis
0344-1741 Aerztekammer Nordrhein. Bezirksstelle Duesseldorf. Mitteilungsblatt†
0344-1857 Bonner Akademische Reden
0344-208X Advances in Animal Breeding and Genetics
0344-2292 Geschaeftsidee
0344-239X Arbeit und Sicherheit
0344-242X Gulliver
0344-2667 Anschlaege
0344-2934 Deutscher Hugenotten-Verein E.V. Geschichtsblaetter
0344-3094 German Yearbook of International Law
0344-3418 Zeitschrift fuer Siebenbuergische Landeskunde
0344-385X Goettinger Miszellen
0344-4201 Internistische Welt
0344-4317 Uebersee-Museum, Bremen. Veroeffentlichungen. Reihe F: Bremer Afrika-Archiv
0344-4325 Springer Seminars in Immunopathology
0344-4376 Kueche
0344-4422 Restaurant and Hotel Management
0344-4430 Informationsaufnahme und Informationsverarbeitung im Lebenden Organismus
0344-449X Materialia Turcica
0344-4686 Backtechnik *changed to* Brot-und Backwaren
0344-4724 Telecom Report
0344-4910 Berlin
0344-5038 Extracta Urologica
0344-5062 Allergologie
0344-5089 Berliner Beitraege zur Archaeometrie
0344-5259 Internationale Hydrologisches Programm: Operationelles Hydrologisches Programm: Jahrbuch Bundesrepublik Deutschland und Berlin (West)
0344-5372 D G D Schriftenreihe
0344-5399 Jazz Index
0344-5542 Tungusica
0344-5550 Staat und Wirtschaft in Hessen
0344-5607 Neurosurgical Review
0344-5631 Der Mann Magazin
0344-5690 Kultur and Technik
0344-5704 Cancer Chemotherapy and Pharmacology
0344-5712 Agrarsoziale Gesellschaft. Materialsammlung
0344-5836 Moderne Medizin
0344-5909 Germanistische Mitteilungen
0344-5925 Deutsche Zeitschrift fuer Sportmedizin
0344-5933 Klinikarzt mit Medizinstudent. Ausgabe B†
0344-6034 Konstruktion und Design *changed to* Konstruktion, Entwicklung & Design
0344-6379 Versicherungsbetriebe
0344-6492 Sport- Baeder- Freizeitbauten
0344-6581 Jahrbuch fuer das Elektrohandwerk
0344-6727 Linguistische Arbeiten
0344-676X Romanistische Arbeitshefte
0344-6816 Doemensianer
0344-7006 Prager Nachrichten
0344-7030 Ost-Wirtschaftsreport
0344-7103 Deutsche Optikerzeitung
0344-712X Jahrbuch der Werbung
0344-7138 H R C & C C
0344-7146 L O K Report
0344-7154 Pharmakotherapie
0344-7596 Moderne Fertigung
0344-7758 Informationsdienst Laerm
0344-7871 Recht und Politik
0344-8029 Computing Supplementa
0344-824X Studien ueber Wirtschaft-und Systemvergleiche
0344-8266 Anglistik und Englischunterricht
0344-8274 Wunderblock
0344-8444 Archives of Orthopaedic and Traumatic Surgery
0344-8614 Sielmanns Tierwelt†
0344-8622 Curare
0344-8657 Zuckerindustrie
0344-8711 Stuckgewerbe *changed to* Das Stukkateur
0344-8843 Markt & Technik
0344-9092 Liturgie Konkret
0344-9130 Germany (Federal Republic, 1949-). Deutscher Bundestag. Wissenschaftliche Dienste. Materialien
0344-9270 Die Voliere
0344-9416 Medizintechnik
0344-9696 Technologie-Nachrichten - Management-Informationen
0344-9750 Technologie-Nachrichten - Programm-Informationen
0344-9777 Zeitschrift fuer Oeffentliche und Gemeinwirtschaftliche Unternehmen
0344-9823 Transnational
0344-984X Schiefertafel
0345-0074 Striae
0345-0112 Text
0345-0139 Stockholms Universitet. Psykologiska Institutionen. Report Series
0345-0155 Umeaa Studies in the Humanities
0345-0171 Sweden. Socialstyrelsen. Legitimerade Laekare/Authorized Physicians
0345-021X Stockholms Universitet. Psykologiska Institutionen. Reports. Supplement Series
0345-0295 Aneks
0345-049X Aktiespararen
0345-0635 Aktuellt i Politiken
0345-0732 Alkohol och Narkotika
0345-0759 Allas Veckotidning
0345-1097 Bibliotekariesamfundet Meddelar
0345-1135 B i S
0345-1402 Scandinavian Journal of Behaviour Therapy
0345-1453 Biblicum
0345-1593 Blaaklint - Livlinan
0345-178X Bryggan
0345-1798 Bridge
0345-181X Broed-Konditorn
0345-1941 Byggreferat
0345-200X Clinical Chemistry Lookout
0345-2131 Dans†
0345-2212 Daa och Nu
0345-2328 Development Dialogue
0345-2409 Djurens Raett
0345-2417 Djurfront
0345-2581 Entre
0345-2719 Svenska Bankfoereningen. Ekonomiska Meddelanden
0345-3251 Fasader
0345-3278 Fastighetsmaeklaren

0345-3286 F B R Aktuellt†
0345-3685 Frihetlig Socialistisk Tidskrift
0345-3766 Affaersvaerlden
0345-3979 Golv till Tak
0345-4347 Hockey
0345-4495 Handelskammartidningen
0345-4630 Hemmets Veckotidning
0345-4789 Haeften foer Kritiska Studier
0345-4843 Haent i Veckan
0345-4983 Invandrartidningen Information *see* 0349-554X
0345-4991 Invandrartidningen (Weekly)
0345-5068 I C A - Kuriren
0345-5300 Information-Ekonomi och Miljoe, Vetenskap och Humanism
0345-5440 International Union of Tenants. International Information
0345-5505 Invandrarrapport
0345-5564 Journal of Traffic Medicine
0345-5653 Jefferson
0345-6005 Kvaekartidskrift
0345-6471 Kontakten
0345-6706 Kustbon
0345-696X Tidskriften Laboratoriet
0345-7001 Lantbruksnytt
0345-7044 Ledarbladet Samspel
0345-7133 Leveranstidningen Entreprenad
0345-7389 Luthersk Barntidning
0345-7605 Arkivet foer Folkets Historia. Meddelanden *see* 0349-6279
0345-7656 Modern Elektronik
0345-7699 Musiktidningen
0345-7737 Moebler och Miljoe
0345-7788 MaskinKontakt†
0345-780X Mat foer Millioner†
0345-7842 Laerarnas Missionsfoerening. Meddelande till L M F.
0345-7982 Bygd och Natur
0345-8199 M S-Brevet *see* 0348-8071
0345-8202 Munskaenken
0345-830X Nordisk Mejeriindustri
0345-8326 Nord Refo
0345-8539 Nordisk Posttidsskrift
0345-8660 Ny i Sverige
0345-8768 Nysvenska Studier
0345-9225 Pensionaeren
0345-9616 P S O Aktuellt
0346-0479 Skandinavisk Numismatik *changed to* Skandinaviska Mynt Magasinet
0346-0762 S C C News†
0346-0827 Scout
0346-1025 Ship Abstracts
0346-1238 Scandinavian Actuarial Journal
0346-1300 Skohandlaren
0346-1351 Skorstensfejarmaestaren
0346-1386 Skraedderi
0346-1602 Sparbankerna
0346-2099 Svensk Froetidning
0346-2250 Svensk Veterinaertidning
0346-2471 Svinskoetsel
0346-251X System
0346-2765 Tobakshandlaren
0346-2773 Transport och Hantering
0346-2846 Traeindustrin
0346-3001 Teratology Lookout†
0346-329X Tonfallet
0346-3605 Undervisningsteknologi†
0346-363X Ung Vaerld†
0346-3788 Utsikt
0346-3869 Verdandisten
0346-4229 Vi Baataegare
0346-4687 Vaar Ponny
0346-4997 Vaextskydds - Kuriren
0346-5020 Didakometry and Sociometry
0346-5365 Sveriges Socialfoerbunds Tidskrift
0346-5578 Sverige-E G
0346-5764 Sweden. Statens Lantmaeteriverk. L M V Information†
0346-5799 Sweden. Socialstyrelsen. Redovisar
0346-5837 Sweden. Medicinalvaesendet. Foerfattningssamling *see* 0346-6000
0346-5837 Sweden. Medicinalvaesendet. Foerfattningssamling *see* 0346-6019
0346-6000 Sweden. Socialstyrelsen. Foerfattningssamling: Medical
0346-6019 Sweden. Socialstyrelsen. Foerfattningssamling: Social
0346-6159 Paa Fritid *see* 0347-5484
0346-6175 Educational Development *see* 0283-7692
0346-6310 Elteknik med Aktuell Elektronik
0346-640X Dagens Industri
0346-6493 Uppsala Studies in Economic History
0346-6620 Stockholm Studies in Politics
0346-6728 Norna - Rapporter
0346-6868 Swedish Natural Science Research Council. Ecological Bulletins
0346-6906 C B I Forskning/Research
0346-7090 Svenska Traeskyddsinstitutet. Meddelanden
0346-7236 Lantbrukshoegskolan Institutionen foer Vaextodling. Rapporter och Arhandlingar *changed to* Sveriges Lantbruksuniversitet. Institutionen foer Vaextodling. Rapporter och Avhandlingar
0346-7341 Vaar Foeda. Supplement
0346-735X Vaextekologiska Studier *see* 0282-8677
0346-8186 Eastern Business Magazine
0346-8240 C B I Rapporter/Reports
0346-8445 Sweden. Sjukvaardens och Socialvaardens Planerings- och Rationaliseringsinstitut. S P R I Informerar
0346-8488 Skrifter Utgivna av Svenska Riksarkivet
0346-8666 Sweden. Fishery Board. Institute of Marine Research. Report
0346-8712 Slavica Lundensia
0346-8755 Scandinavian Journal of History
0346-895X L O-Tidningen
0346-9158 Afrikabulletinen
0346-9212 Antik & Auktion
0346-9468 Current Business in Sweden
0346-9670 Foereningsbankerna†
0346-9735 Historiska Institutionens Tidskrift
0347-030X Railway Scene†
0347-0342 S A C O/S R-Tidningen
0347-0520 Scandinavian Journal of Economics
0347-0547 Saagrevyn
0347-0989 Motpol
0347-1314 Uppsala Studies in Education
0347-1748 Kullagertidningen
0347-2205 World Armaments and Disarmament: S I P R I Yearbook *changed to* S I P R I Yearbook: World Armaments and Disarmament
0347-2787 Bible Researcher
0347-3139 Skandinaviska Enskilda Banken Quarterly Review
0347-3198 Sveriges Riksbank. Foervaltningsberaettelse
0347-3236 Vaextskyddsrapporter
0347-3449 Registreringstidning foer Varumaerken. Part A (Publications for Opposition) *see* 0348-324X
0347-3457 Registreringstidning foer Varumaerken. Part C (Renewals, Changes of Ownership) *see* 0348-3266
0347-3465 Registreringstidning foer Varumaerken. Part B (Publications of Registrations) *see* 0348-3258
0347-3899 Praktiskt Butiksarbete
0347-4135 Tidningsteknik
0347-416X Kyrkosaangsfoerbundet *see* 0281-286X
0347-4178 Svensk Kyrkomusik (Edition B for Choir Members)†
0347-4240 A I C A R C Bulletin
0347-4275 Yrkesfiskaren
0347-4585 R A-Nytt
0347-4917 Acta Regiae Societatis Scientiarum et Litterarum Gothoburgensis. Botanica
0347-4925 Acta Regiae Societatis Scientiarum et Litterarum Gothoburgensis. Interdisciplinaria
0347-4976 R & D for Higher Education *see* 0283-7692
0347-5387 Svenska Barnboksinstitutet. Skrifter
0347-5484 Kommun-Aktuelt
0347-5719 Documenta
0347-6030 Sweden. V T I Rapport
0347-6049 V T I Meddelande
0347-6057 Sweden. Statens Vaeg- och Trafikinstitut. Verksamhetsberaettelse
0347-6154 Konsumentraett och Ekonomi
0347-6405 Kiruna Geophysical Institute. Report *see* 0283-1694
0347-6820 Utlaendska Nyfoervaerv till Stoerre Svenska Folkbibliotek
0347-7169 Sweden. Finansdepartmentet. Regeringens Budgetfoerslag
0347-724X Sweden. Statens Arbetsgivarverk. Foerfattningar om Statligt Reglerade Tjaenster: F S T
0347-8173 Sweden. Statens Naturvaardsverk. Naturvaardsverkets Aarsbok
0347-8785 Svenskt Raattsforum
0347-884X Goeteborgs Universitet. Universitetsbibliotek. Aarsberaettelse
0347-9331 Lill-Allers†
0347-9706 University of Agricultural Sciences. Report
0347-9994 Swedish Dental Journal
0348-0356 Aakeri och Transport
0348-0755 Statens Geotekniska Institut. Rapport
0348-1093 Scripta Academica
0348-1964 Studies of Law in Social Change and Development†
0348-2219 Goeteborgs Universitet. Institutionen foer Praktisk Pedagogik. Rapport
0348-2251 Sweden. Luftfartsverket. Aarsbok
0348-243X S K R-Meddelanden†
0348-2456 Lunds Universitet. Vaextekologiska Institutionen. Meddelanden
0348-2480 Accessionskatalog over Utlaendsk Litteratur i Svenska Forskningsbibliotek
0348-2626 S A R E C Report
0348-2650 S T F I Meddelande. Series A
0348-2790 C B I Rekommendationer/Recommendations *see* 0282-6283
0348-3118 Transport-Journalen
0348-324X Svensk Varumaerkestidning/Swedish Trademark Journal. Part A (Publications for Opposition)
0348-3258 Svensk Varumaerkestidning/Swedish Trademark Journal. Part B (Publications of Registrations)
0348-3266 Svensk Varumaerkestidning/Swedish Trademark Journal. Part C (Renewals, Changes of Ownership)
0348-3304 Svenska Motor-Magasinet
0348-4076 Gothenburg Studies in Social Anthropology
0348-4114 Gothenburg Studies in Art and Architecture
0348-4386 Striolae
0348-4599 Sveriges Lantbruksuniversitet. Institutionen foer Virkeslaera. Rapporter
0348-4769 Folkhoegskolan
0348-4998 Datornytt, med Maskin- och Programvara
0348-5099 Uppsala Studies in Cultural Anthropology
0348-5153 Sveriges Riksbank. Kredit- och Valutaoeversikt
0348-5242 Personal
0348-5676 Centre for Development Research. Publications†
0348-6087 Civilingenjoeren
0348-6133 Samlaren
0348-6508 Sweden Business Report
0348-6516 Nordisk Foersaekringstidskrift
0348-6613 Foeredrag vid Pyroteknikdagen
0348-6788 Gothenburg Studies in the History of Science and Ideas
0348-7032 Tidskrift foer Frukt- och Baerodling
0348-7148 Byggnadsstyrelsens Tidskrift†
0348-7342 Sveriges Riksbank. Statistisk Aarsbok
0348-7369 Energy Technology
0348-7377 Qufo
0348-7962 Ny Litteratur om Kvinnor: En Bibliografi
0348-7997 Tvaersnitt
0348-8071 Handikapp-Reflex
0348-811X Sweden. Statistiska Centralbyraan. Statsanstaelllda†
0348-8691 Africana in the Library of the Scandinavian Institute of African Studies
0348-8799 Annual Report on Results of Treatment in Gynecological Cancer
0348-9078 Revisionist History
0348-9221 Byggnormindex *changed to* Byggregler (Year)
0348-9388 Pedagogiska Rapporter Umeaa *see* 0281-6776
0348-9698 Ethnologia Scandinavica
0348-971X Fataburen
0349-0068 International Meteorological Institute in Stockholm. Annual Report
0349-0297 Soermlandsbygden
0349-0505 Arkiv, Samhaelle och Forskning
0349-0564 Acta Wexionensia. Serie 1: History & Geography
0349-0823 Fauna Norrlandica
0349-0874 S A R E C Annual Report
0349-1048 Foereningen Armemusei Vaenner. Meddelande: Kungliga Armemuseum *changed to* Meddelande Armemuseum. Yearbook
0349-1714 Svenska Antavlor
0349-2559 Till Tjaenst: Tidskrift foer Ledare
0349-2656 Kiruna Geophysical Institute. Preprint
0349-2664 Kiruna Geophysical Institute. Software Report
0349-2672 Kiruna Geophysical Institute. Technical Report
0349-2680 Uppsala Ionospheric Observatory. Technical Reports
0349-2699 Uppsala Ionospheric Observatory. Scientific Reports
0349-2702 Uppsala Ionospheric Observatory. Administrative Reports†
0349-2710 E I S C A T Technical Note
0349-2737 Duty & Tax-Free Shop World Guide Series. Vol. 1: Best "N" Most in Wines & Spirits
0349-2737 Duty & Tax-Free Shop World Guide Series. Vol. 3: Best "N" Most in Cigarettes, Cigars and Tobacco
0349-2737 Duty & Tax-Free Shop World Guide Series. Vol. 2: Best "N" Most in Perfumes & Cosmetics
0349-3210 Nytt Fraan D F I
0349-3733 Byggindustrin
0349-5264 Sveriges Natur
0349-5426 Kommunal Litteratur
0349-554X Invandrartidningen (Monthly)
0349-5612 Educational Reports Umeaa†
0349-6244 Nordicom Review of Nordic Mass Communication Research
0349-6279 Folkets Historia
0349-6287 Raw Materials Report
0349-652X Acta Radiologica. Series 2: Oncology, Radiation Therapy, Physics and Biology
0349-6740 S A F-Tidningen
0349-7038 Nordiskt Lantbruk
0349-764X Tjustbygden
0349-9375 Social Debatt
0349-9464 Svensk Handel *see* 0346-640X
0349-988X Musical Interpretation Research
0350-0012 Wissenschaftliche Mitteilungen des Bosnisch-Herzegowinischen Landesmuseums. Naturwissenschaft
0350-0020 Akademija Nauka i Umjetnosti Bosne i Hercegovine. Centar za Balkanoloska Ispitivanja. Godisnjak
0350-0039 Akademija Nauka i Umjetnosti Bosne i Hercegovine. Odeljenje Drustvenih Nauka. Radovi
0350-0055 Bilten Dokumentacije. Zavarivanje†
0350-0063 Zdravstveni Vestnik
0350-0071 Akademija Nauka i Umjetnosti Bosne i Hercegovine. Odeljenje Medicinskih Nauka. Radovi†
0350-0101 Bilten Dokumentacije. Analiticka Hemija
0350-011X Naucni i Strucni Skupovi u Jugoslavii i u Inostranstvu

0350-0144 Survey Sarajevo
0350-0152 Bilten Dokumentacije. Otpadne Vode i Zagadjenje Vazduha†
0350-0179 Balcanoslavica
0350-0209 Bilten Dokumentacije. Iskoriscenje Otpadaka *see* 0352-1036
0350-0233 Folia Anatomica Iugoslavica
0350-0241 Starinar
0350-025X Bilten Tehnickih Informacija Iz Oblasti Industrije Gume†
0350-0306 Bilten Dokumentacije. Zastita na Radu
0350-0349 Bibliografija Jugoslavije. Serijske Publikacije
0350-0357 Bilten Dokumentacije. Informatika
0350-0365 Institut za Javno Upravo. Vestnik
0350-0403 O A P. Automatika Obrada Podataka. Bibliografija *see* 0351-3548
0350-0411 Katalog Stranih Serijskih Publikacija u Bibliotekama Jugoslavije
0350-0454 Bilten Dokumentacije. Drzavni Organi. Drustvene Politicke Zajednice. Privreda. Drustvene Sluzbe. Pravo†
0350-0470 Zbornik za Slavistiku
0350-0578 Vojnoekonomski Pregled *changed to* Pozadina
0350-0594 Tehnicka Fizika
0350-1019 Komercijalist
0350-1094 Vaspitanje i Obrazovanje
0350-1272 Dijalektika
0350-140X Univerzitet u Novom Sadu. Prirodno-Matematicki Fakultet. Zbornik Radova. Serija za Matematiku
0350-1418 Gazi Husrevbegova Biblioteka. Anali
0350-1442 Zavod za Mentalno Zdravlje. Anali *see* 0350-2538
0350-1450 Bibliografija Domacih i Stranih Knjiga
0350-1531 Organizacija in Kadri
0350-154X Revija za Sociologiju
0350-1558 Bulletin Scientifique. Section A: Sciences Naturelles, Techniques et Medicales
0350-1604 Bulletin Scientifique. Section B: Sciences Humanies
0350-1698 Makedonska Akademija na Naukite i Umetnostite. Oddelenie za Opstestveni Nauki. Prilozi
0350-1701 Gradjevinski Fakultet. Institut za Materijale i Konstrukcije. Zbornik Istrazivackih Radova
0350-1728 Makedonski Arhivist
0350-1892 Diabetologia Croatica
0350-1914 Makedonska Akademija na Naukite i Umetnostite. Oddelenie za Lingvistika i Literaturna Nauka. Prilozi
0350-2104 Medjunarodni Radnicki Pokret
0350-2155 Jugoslovensko Vocarstvo
0350-2252 Yugoslav Law
0350-2457 Veterinarski Glasnik
0350-2538 Psihijatrija Danas
0350-2562 Bibliografija Zvanicnih Publikacija S F R J
0350-2619 Nase Gradevinarstvo
0350-2627 Rudarstvo - Geologija - Metalurgija
0350-2643 Acta Biologica Iugoslavica. Serija G: Biosistematika
0350-2651 Kinematografija u Srbiji *changed to* Kinematografija u Srbiji - Uporedo SFRJ
0350-2856 Arhivist
0350-2929 Goriski Letnik
0350-2953 Savremena Poljoprivredna Tehnika
0350-3089 Macedonian Review
0350-3097 Sveuciliste u Zagrebu. Fakultet Strojarstva i Brodogradnje. Zbornik Radova
0350-3283 University of Belgrade. Faculty of Sciences. Department of Astronomy. Publications
0350-3569 Narodna in Univerzitetna Knjiznica. Zbornik
0350-3577 Obvestila Republiske Maticne Knjiznice *changed to* Obvestila Republiske Maticne Sluzbe
0350-3585 Slovenska Bibliografija
0350-3615 Fragmenta Herbologica Jugoslavica
0350-3658 Acta Parasitologica Iugoslavica†
0350-3666 Arhitektura
0350-414X Latina et Graeca
0350-4158 Letunk
0350-4247 Mesecni Statisticki Pregled
0350-4484 National Bank of Yugoslavia. Quarterly Bulletin
0350-4697 Slovenski Cebelar
0350-4778 Spone
0350-5510 Acta Entomologica Jugoslavica
0350-5537 Koncar Strucne Informacije
0350-5723 Primorska Srecanja
0350-5774 Zgodovinski Casopis
0350-6134 Collegium Antropologicum
0350-6525 Mostovi
0350-6541 Nastava Povijesti
0350-6584 Odzivi
0350-6746 Centro di Ricerche Storiche, Rovigno. Quaderni
0350-7130 Vestnik Koroskih Partizanov
0350-7165 Arheoloski Muzej u Zagrebu. Vjesnik
0350-7483 Sam
0350-7696 Komisija za Ispitivanje S-Uredjaja. Bilten
0350-820X Science of Sintering
0350-8498 Zbornik Obcine Grosuplje
0350-9370 Muzejski Vjesnik
0350-9400 Obelezja
0350-9419 Povijest Sporta
0350-9494 Varstvo Spomenikov
0350-9508 Yugoslav Information Bulletin
0350-9974 Bibliografija Prevoda U S F R J
0351-0085 Yugoslav Chemical Papers
0351-0123 I R C I H E Bulletin
0351-0174 Informativni Bilten Urbanisticnega Instituta SR Slovenije. Sporocila
0351-0697 Revija Obrazovanja
0351-0999 Zito Hleb
0351-1030 Naucni Podmladak: Tehnicke Nauke
0351-1375 Sahovski Informator
0351-1871 Polimeri
0351-1898 Suvremeni Promet
0351-2045 Annales Forestales
0351-2177 Beogradski Univerzitet. Elektrotehnicki Fakultet. Publikacije. Serija: Elektronika, Telekomunikacije, Automatika
0351-2312 Bilten Dokumentacije. Poljoprivreda. Biljna Proizvodnja
0351-2320 Bilten Dokumentacije. Poljoprivreda-Stocna Proizvodnja
0351-238X Bilten Dokumentacije. Elektroprivreda
0351-2398 Bilten Dokumentacije. Elektrotehnika i Elektronika *changed to* Bilten Dokumentacije. Elektrotehnika i Elektronika. Proizvodnja Elektricnih Masina i Aparata. Ptt Usluge
0351-2479 Bilten Dokumentacije. Proizvodnja Prehrambenih Proizvoda. Proizvodnja Pica
0351-2509 Bilten Dokumentacije. Prerada Nemetalnih Minerala-Proizvodnja Gradjevinskog Materijala
0351-2576 Bilten Dokumentacije. Gradjevinarstvo - Niskogradnja i Hidrogradnja
0351-2592 Bilten Dokumentacije. Urbanizam i Arhitektura
0351-2800 Institute of International Law and International Relations. Contributions to the Study of Comparative and International Law
0351-286X Economic Analysis and Workers Management
0351-3246 Makedonska Akademija na Naukite i Umetnostite. Oddelenie za Matematicki i Tehnicki Nauki
0351-3254 Makedonska Akademija na Naukite i Umetnostite. Oddelenie za Bioloski i Medicinski Nauki. Prilozi
0351-3297 Jugoslavenske Akademije Znanosti i Umjetnosti. Razred za Prirodne Znanosti. Rad
0351-3548 A O P. Bibliografija
0351-3947 Obnovljeni Zivot
0351-4048 Bilten Dokumentacije. Savremena Organizacija i Ekonomija Organizacija Udruzenog Rada
0351-4501 Mediterranean Journal of Social Psychiatry
0351-4706 Filozofska Istrazivanja†
0351-5699 Naucni Podmladak: Drustvene Nauke i Filozofija
0351-580X Acta Stereologica
0351-6245 Vesnik
0351-6768 Mikrografija u Informacionim Sistemima
0351-689X Nuklearna Tehnologija
0351-8906 Bilten Dokumentacije. Metalopreradjivacka Delatnost. Proizvodnja Raznovrsnih Proizvoda
0351-8949 Nasa Knjiga
0351-9430 Bilten za Hmelj, Sirak i Lekovito Bilje
0352-1028 Bilten Dokumentacije. Gradjevinarstvo-Visokogradnja i Zavrsni Radovi u Gradjevinarstvu
0352-1036 Bilten Dokumentacije. Zastita Covekove Okoline i Iskoriscenje Otpadaka
0352-1168 Centar za Drustvena Istrazivanja Slavonije i Baranje. Zbornik *see* 0352-8650
0352-1427 Centro di Ricerche Storiche, Rovigno. Atti
0352-1605 Revija za Psihologiju
0352-1613 Naucni Podmladak: Medicinske Nauke
0352-2873 Start
0352-3055 Filoloski Fakultet. Katedra za Istocnoslovenski i Zapadnoslovenski Jazici i Knizeunosti. Slavisticki Studii
0352-3659 Geofizika
0352-4000 Crkva u Svijetu
0352-4973 Luca
0352-5740 Academie Serbe des Sciences et des Arts. Classe des Sciences Mathematiques et Naturelles. Bulletin. Sciences Naturelles
0352-8650 Slavonski Povijesni Zbornik
0355-001X Suomen Kirjallisuus
0355-0036 Signum
0355-0044 Kansallis-Osake-Pankki. Taloudellinen Katsaus
0355-0079 Yearbook of Finnish Foreign Policy
0355-0087 Annales Academiae Scientiarum Fennicae. Series A, I: Mathematica Dissertationes
0355-0133 Union Bank of Finland. Annual Report
0355-0206 N I F Newsletter
0355-0214 Suomalais-Ugrilaisen Seuran. Aikakauskirja
0355-0303 Kanava
0355-0311 Kalevalaseuran Vuosikirja
0355-0346 Business Contacts in Finland
0355-0451 Maamies
0355-0532 Mejeritidskrift foer Finlands Svenskbygd
0355-0648 Riista- ja Kalatalouden Tutkimuslaitos. Kalantutkimusosasto. Tiedonantoja
0355-0729 Koneviesti
0355-0982 Finland. Vestientutkimuslaitos. Julkaisuja
0355-1008 International Peat Society. Bulletin
0355-1059 Musiikki
0355-113X Annales Academiae Scientiarum Fennicae. Dissertationes Humanarum Litterarum
0355-1253 Finnisch-Ugrische Forschungen
0355-1350 Helsingin Yliopiston Kirjaston. Julkaisuja
0355-1393 Keski-Suomi
0355-1466 Valokuva
0355-1628 Kemia-Kemi
0355-1644 Aarni
0355-1717 Finland. Ilmatieteen Laitos. Tutkimusseloste†
0355-1733 Finnish Meterological Institute. Technical Report†
0355-1784 Ylioppilasaineita
0355-1792 Acta Philosophica Fennica
0355-1806 Suomen Museo
0355-1814 Finskt Museum
0355-1822 Suomen Muinaismuistoyhdistyksen Aikakauskirja
0355-1830 Kansatieteellinen Arkisto
0355-1849 Paasikivi-Society. Mimeograph Series
0355-1865 Pientalo-Omakoti†
0355-1873 Tee Itse†
0355-189X Suur-Seura *changed to* Seura (1979)
0355-1903 T H-Kotilaakari
0355-1911 Non Stop†
0355-192X Muoti & Kauneus
0355-1962 Suomen Geodeettisen Laitoksen. Tiedonantoja
0355-2004 Finnish Meteorological Institute. Observations of Satellites. Visual Observations of Artificial Earth Satellites in Finland†
0355-2063 Finland. Tilastokeskus. Kasikirjoja
0355-2071 Finland. Tilastokeskus. Tutkimuksia
0355-208X Finland. Tilastokeskus. Tilastollisia Tiedonantoja *changed to* Finland. Tilastokeskus. Tilastollisia Tiedonantoja. Kotitaloustiedustelu
0355-2098 Suuri Kasityokerho
0355-2101 Aku Ankka
0355-211X Finland. Tilastokeskus. Tulo- ja Omaisuustilasto *see* 0780-9352
0355-2128 Finland. Tilastokeskus. Kuolleisuus- Ja Eloonjaamistauluja *changed to* Finland. Tilastokeskus. Kuolleisuus. Kuolleisuus- Ja Eloonjaamistauluja
0355-2136 Finland. Tilastokeskus. Vaestolaskenta *changed to* Finland. Tilastokeskus. Vaesto- ja Asuntolaskenta
0355-2144 Finland. Tilastokeskus. Kuolemansyyt
0355-2152 Finland. Tilastokeskus. Asuntotuotanto
0355-2160 Finland. Tilastokeskus. Rikollisuus. Poliisin Tietoon Tullut Rikollisuus
0355-2179 Finland. Tilastokeskus. Rikollisuus. Tuomioistuinten Tutkimat Rikokset
0355-2187 Finland. Tilastokeskus. Tuomioistuinten Toiminta
0355-2195 Finland. Tilastokeskus. Valtiolliset Vaalit. Tasavallan Presidentin Vaalit Valisijamiesten
0355-2209 Finland. Tilastokeskus. Kansanedustajain Vaalit *changed to* Finland. Tilastokeskus. Valtiolliset Vaalit. Kansanedustajain Vaalit
0355-2217 Finland. Tilastokeskus. Kunnallisvaalit
0355-2225 Finland. Tilastokeskus. Korkeakoulut
0355-2233 Finland. Tilastokeskus. Tutkimustoiminta
0355-2276 Finland. Tilastokeskus. Tilastotiedotus KT. Kansantalouden Tilinpito/National Raekenskaper/National Accounts
0355-2284 Finland. Tilastokeskus. Tieliikenneonnettomuudet
0355-2381 Finland. Tilastokeskus. Indeksitiedotus KH. Kuluttajahintaindeksi
0355-239X Finland. Tilastokeskus. Indeksitiedotus RK. Rakennuskustannusindeksi/Byggnadskostnadsindex/Building Cost Index
0355-2403 Finland. Tilastokeskus. Indeksitiedotus TH. Tuottajahintaiset Indeksit
0355-2411 Finland. Tilastokeskus. Indeksitiedotus TR. Tienrakennuskustannusindeksi
0355-2446 Finland. Tilastokeskus. Yleissivistavat Oppilaitokset
0355-2454 Finland. Tilastokeskus. Pankit
0355-256X Commentationes Scientiarum Socialium
0355-2624 Vaasan Kauppakorkeakoulu. Julkaisuja. Opetusmonisteita *see* 0358-9110
0355-2632 Vaasan Kauppakorkeakoulu. Julkaisuja. Tutkimuksia *see* 0358-9080
0355-2667 Acta Wasaensia
0355-2691 Suomen Autolehti
0355-2705 Acta Polytechnica Scandinavica. Civil Engineering and Building Construction Series
0355-2713 Acta Polytechnica Scandinavica. Mathematics and Computer Science Series
0355-2721 Acta Polytechnica Scandinavica. Applied Physics Series
0355-2764 Jermu
0355-2772 Seksi
0355-2896 Autolla Ulkomaille
0355-2950 Avotakka
0355-2969 Katso
0355-2977 Elamani Tarina†
0355-2985 Eeva
0355-2993 Nakke
0355-3000 Ravi ja Ratsastus†
0355-3027 Eevaneule

1542   ISSN INDEX

ISSN	Title
0355-3035	Anna
0355-3043	U M: Uusi Maailma†
0355-3051	Apu
0355-3078	Kauppias *changed to* Kehittyvae Kauppa
0355-3086	Rautaviesti
0355-3108	Iskos
0355-3140	Scandinavian Journal of Work, Environment & Health
0355-3221	Acta Universitatis Ouluensis. Series D. Medica
0355-3256	Myyntineuvoja
0355-337X	Technical Research Centre of Finland. Publication. Building Technology and Community Development†
0355-3388	Technical Research Centre of Finland. Publication. Materials and Processing Technology†
0355-3396	Technical Research Centre of Finland. Publication. Electrical and Nuclear Technology†
0355-3434	Valtion Teknillinen Tutkimuskeskus. Kojetekniikan Labboratorio. Tiedonanto†
0355-3450	Valtion Teknillinen Tutkimuskeskus. Geotekniikan Laboratorio. Tiedonanto†
0355-3477	Valtion Teknillinen Tutkimuskeskus. Maankayton Laboratorio. Tiedonanto†
0355-3485	Valtion Teknillinen Tutkimuskeskus. Palotekniikan Laboratorio. Tiedonanto†
0355-354X	Valtion Teknillinen Tutkimuskeskus. Biotekniikan Labboratorio. Tiedonanto†
0355-3558	Valtion Teknillinen Tutkimuskeskus. Elintarvikelabboratorio. Tiedonanto†
0355-3566	Valtion Teknillinen Tutkimuskeskus. Graafinen Labboratorio. Tiedonanto†
0355-3574	Valtion Teknillinen Tutkimuskeskus. Kemian Laboratorio. Tiedonanto†
0355-3590	Valtion Teknillinen Tutkimuskeskus. Polttl- ja Voiteluainelaboratorio. Tiedonanto†
0355-3639	Valtion Teknillinen Tutkimuskeskus. Tekstiililaboratorio. Tiedonanto†
0355-3663	Valtion Teknillinen Tutkimuskeskus. Reaktorilaboratorio. Tiedonanto†
0355-3671	Valtion Teknillinen Tutkimuskeskus. Sahkotekniikan Laboratorio. Tiedonanto†
0355-368X	Valtion Teknillinen Tutkimuskeskus. Teletekniikan Laboratorio. Tiedonanto†
0355-3698	Valtion Teknillinen Tutkimuskeskus. Ydinvoimatekniikan Laboratorio. Tiedonanto†
0355-3701	Valtion Teknillinen Tutkimuskeskus. Teknillinen Informaatiopalvelulaitos. Tiedonanto†
0355-3736	Lapset Ja Yhteiskunta
0355-3752	Tuottavuus
0355-3779	Siirtolaisuus
0355-3930	Suomen Antropologi
0355-3949	Help!†
0355-3957	Joensuun Korkeakoulu. Julkaisuja. Sarja B *see* 0355-6832
0355-3965	Opettaja
0355-4031	Aabo Akademi. Statsvetenskapliga Fakulteten. Meddelanden. Serie A *changed to* Aabo Akademi. Statsvetenskapliga Fakulteten. Meddelanden
0355-4074	Suomen Sanomalehtien Mikrofilmit
0355-4201	J P Joka Poika *see* 0781-7177
0355-4236	Jaana†
0355-4465	Aabo Akademi. Statsvetenskapliga Fakulteten. Meddelanden. Serie B *changed to* Aabo Akademi. Statsvetenskapliga Fakulteten. Meddelanden
0355-4481	Finland. Patentti- ja Rekisterihallitus. Mallioikeuslehti/Moensterraettstidning/Design Gazette
0355-4503	Electroniikka *changed to* Elektroniikka & Automaatio
0355-4651	Suomen Hammaslaakariseura. Toimituksia. Supplementa
0355-4759	Finland. Sosiaalihallitus. Huoltoapu
0355-4767	Finland. Sosiaalihallitus. Kodinhoitoapu.
0355-4813	Finland. Kansanelakelaitos. Julkaisuja. Sarja AL
0355-4821	Finland. Kansanelakelaitos. Julkaisuja. Sarja M
0355-483X	Finland. Kansanelakelaitos. Julkaisuja. Sarja ML
0355-4848	Finland. Kansanelakelaitos. Julkaisuja. Sarja E
0355-4856	Finland. Kansanelakelaitos. Julkaisuja. Sarja EL
0355-5003	Finland Kansanelakelaitos. Toimintakertomus
0355-5011	Tuberculosis and Respiratory Diseases Yearbook
0355-502X	Philatelia Fennica
0355-5054	Rondo
0355-550X	Rakentajain Kalenteri
0355-5526	Rakennustuotanto
0355-5534	Rakennusalan Suomalaisen Kirjallisuuden Kuukausikatsaus *changed to* Rakennustieto
0355-5615	Numismaatikko
0355-578X	Acta Academiae Aboensis. Series A: Humaniora†
0355-5798	Aabo Akademi. Aarsskrift
0355-6034	Suomen Pankki. Julkaisuja. Sarja A
0355-6042	Suomen Pankki. Julkaisuja. Sarja D
0355-6050	Suomen Pankki. Julkaisuja. Kasvututkimuksia
0355-6093	Finlands Kommunaltidskrift
0355-6395	Valtion Teknillinen Tutkimuskeskus. Metallilaboratorio. Tiedonanto†
0355-6654	Liikenneturva. Reports
0355-6735	Radiokauppias
0355-6832	Joensuun Korkeakoulu. Julkaisuja. Sarja B2†
0355-6999	Kenkalusikka
0355-7073	Liikuntakasvatus
0355-7227	Et-Lehti
0355-7235	Koiranne - Vaara Hundar
0355-726X	Toimiupseeri
0355-7286	Ammattiautoilija
0355-7294	Forsakringstidning
0355-7421	Kotiteollisuus
0355-7596	Metsanhoitaja
0355-7693	Psychiatria Fennica. Julkaisusarja *changed to* Psychiatria Fennica. Reports
0355-7707	Psychiatria Fennica. Monografiasarja
0355-7839	Muoviuutiset†
0355-7855	Tie ja Liikenne
0355-7871	Navigator
0355-7898	Teksi
0355-8878	Finland. Valtioneuvoston Kanslian. Julkaisuja
0355-8991	Tekstiiliopettaja-Textillaren
0355-9076	Valtion Teknillinen Tutkimuskeskus. Sairaalatekniikan Laboratorio. Tiedonanto†
0355-9106	Narinkka
0355-9378	Y V O
0355-9483	Turun Yliopisto. Julkaisuja. Sarja D. Medica-Odontologica
0355-9521	Annales Chirurgiae et Gynaecologiae
0355-953X	Puumies
0355-9610	Aja
0355-9912	Uudistuva Konttori
0356-0023	Meri
0356-004X	Valtion Teknillinen Tutkimuskeskus. A T K-Palvelutoimisto. Tiedonanto†
0356-0732	Veckan med Radio och TV
0356-0805	Leirinta ja Retkeily *see* 0359-0607
0356-0910	Nordenskiold-Samfundets Tidskrift
0356-1062	Biological Research Reports from the University of Jyvaskyla
0356-1364	University of Helsinki. Department of Cooperative Studies. Publications
0356-1496	Historiska Samfundet i Abo. Skrifter Utgivna
0356-1704	Vapaa-Aika-Eurosport†
0356-178X	Fink-S
0356-276X	Savon Luonto
0356-2913	Finland. Tilastokeskus. Maatilatalous
0356-3014	Mallas ja Olut
0356-3081	Syopa
0356-3189	Savonia
0356-3316	Finland. Tilastokeskus. Tyovoimatiedustelu *see* 0781-5611
0356-343X	Metsatilastollinen Vuosikirja
0356-3472	P.S.†
0356-4096	Projektio
0356-4827	Auto ja Liikenne *see* 0359-7636
0356-5092	Hinnat ja Kilpailu
0356-5327	Tehokas Yritys *see* 0358-4208
0356-5629	Faravid
0356-6110	Rakennusviesti *changed to* Meidantalo
0356-6927	Academia Scientiarum Fennica. Yearbook
0356-7133	Aqua Fennica
0356-7753	Finnish Boatbuilding Industry
0356-780X	Institute for Migration, Turku. Migration Studies *changed to* Migration Institute. Migration Studies
0356-7818	Kemistin Kalenteri
0356-7826	Suomen Vakuutusvuosikirja
0356-7842	Laeraren
0356-7850	Liikearkisto
0356-7869	Maankaytto
0356-7893	Current Research on Peace and Violence
0356-7915	Markkinointi *changed to* Mark Markkinoinnin Ammattilenti
0356-7923	Muusikko
0356-7931	Osto
0356-794X	Pistis†
0356-8067	Tahti
0356-8075	Valokuvauksen Vuosikirja
0356-8083	Vaatturi
0356-8091	Valtionyhtiot
0356-8105	Formerly; U I T B B Information *changed to* U I T B B Bulletin
0356-8156	A Fin L A Yearbook
0356-8164	Helsingin Kauppakorkeakoulu. Julkaisusarja D. Laitosjulkaisuja
0356-8199	Studia Historica Septentrionalia
0356-8202	Makasiini
0356-827X	Finland. Tilastokeskus
0356-8741	Turun Yliopisto. Psykologian Tutkimuksia
0356-9489	Helsingin Kaupungin Tilastollinen Vuosikirja
0356-9624	Nordinfo-Nytt
0357-0614	Finland. Tilastokeskus. Valtion Tilastojulkaisut
0357-0738	Hifi
0357-1076	Finnish Marine Research
0357-1831	Valtion Teknillinen Tutkimuskeskus. Metallurgian ja Mineraalitekniikan Laboratorio. Tiedonanto†
0357-2498	Bibliografia Eritysiryhmien Liikunnan Tutkimuksesta
0357-2625	Finland. Tilastokeskus. Ammatilliset Oppilaitokset
0357-2714	Koululainen
0357-2862	Mark Uusi Markkinointilehti *changed to* Mark Markkinoinnin Ammattilenti
0357-2943	Kuva ja Aani *see* 0780-4199
0357-3362	Helsingin Kaupungin Tilastokeskuksen Neljannesvuosikatsaus
0357-3486	Vaasa School of Economics. Proceedings. Discussion Papers *see* 0358-870X
0357-3737	Valtion Teknillinen Tutkimuskeskus. Betoni- ja Silikaattitekniikan Laboratorio. Tiedonanto†
0357-3796	R T - Uutiset *changed to* Rakennustieto
0357-4121	Prosessori
0357-4776	Suomen Pankki. Julkaisuja. Sarja B
0357-5632	Scandinavian Journal of Sports Sciences
0357-7031	Valtion Teknillinen Tutkimuskeskus. Rakennetekniikan Laboratorio. Tiedonanto†
0357-7201	Finland. Tilastokeskus. Indeksitiedotus AT. Palkansaajien Ansiotasoindeksi
0357-749X	Vitriini
0357-816X	Sotahistoriallinen Aikakauskirja
0357-8747	Elainmaailma
0357-8755	Roope-Seta
0357-9387	V T T Symposium
0357-9492	Sukuviesti
0357-9921	Jyvaskyla Studies in Computer Science, Economics and Statistics
0358-0628	Kehittyva Yritys
0358-1039	Tiede 2000
0358-2019	Finland. Tilastokeskus. Energiatilastot
0358-2671	Finland. Ilmatieteen Laitos. Ilmansahkohavaintoja†
0358-2825	Finland. Tilastokeskus. Tulonjakotilasto
0358-2973	Helsingin Kauppakorkeakoulu. Julkaisusarja F. Tyopapereita
0358-3414	Arx Tavastica
0358-3511	Muoto
0358-4208	Yritystalous (1981)
0358-495X	Finland. Kehittaemistiedote *changed to* Finland. Rakennushallitus. Tutkimus-ja Kehitystoiminnan. Tiedote
0358-5069	Technical Research Centre of Finland. Publications
0358-5077	Valtion Teknillinen Tutkimuskeskus. Tutkimuksia
0358-5085	Valtion Teknillinen Tutkimuskeskus. Tiedotteita
0358-5581	Opusculum
0358-562X	Fakta
0358-6758	Walter and Andree de Nottbeck Foundation Scientific Reports
0358-7045	N O R D I N F O Publikation
0358-7088	S S I D Liaison Bulletin
0358-710X	Scripta Historica
0358-7673	Teollisuusviikko
0358-7711	V R - Express
0358-8424	Helsingfors Slaktforskare. Skrifter Utgivna
0358-870X	University of Vaasa. Proceedings. Discussion Papers
0358-9080	Vaasan Korkeakoulu. Julkaisuja. Tutkimuksia
0358-9110	Vaasan Korkeakoulu. Julkaisuja. Opetusmonisteita
0358-9609	Communicationes Instituti Forestalis Fenniae
0359-0216	University of Turku. Psychological Research Reports
0359-0267	Sinamina
0359-0607	Suomen Matkailu
0359-081X	Finland. Tilastokeskus. Kuntien Talous
0359-3223	Historiallinen Kirjasto
0359-4947	Tietokone
0359-6079	Prima
0359-7008	Technik aus Finnland *changed to* Technik aus Finnland
0359-7601	Nordisk Komite for Transportoekonomisk Forskning. Publikation
0359-7636	Moottori (Year)
0359-9329	Kuluttajatietoa
0360-0017	Multiple Sclerosis Indicative Abstracts†
0360-0025	Sex Roles: A Journal of Research
0360-005X	Maine Fish and Wildlife
0360-0114	Florida Bar News
0360-0157	Young Socialist
0360-0181	New Conversations
0360-0270	Illinois. State Museum. Reports of Investigations
0360-0289	Illinois. State Museum. Story of Illinois Series
0360-0297	Illinois. State Museum. Popular Science Series
0360-0300	A C M Computing Surveys
0360-0319	Street Drug Survival *see* 0739-4683
0360-0327	Soviet Astronomy Letters
0360-0335	Soviet Journal of Low Temperature Physics
0360-0343	Soviet Journal of Plasma Physics
0360-0467	Areito†
0360-0521	U.S. Department of Agriculture. Economic Research Service. Sugar and Sweetener Situation *see* 0362-9511
0360-0556	Civil Engineering A S C E
0360-0564	Advances in Catalysis
0360-0572	Annual Review of Sociology
0360-0637	Ebsco Bulletin of Serials Changes
0360-0661	Index to Scientific Reviews
0360-067X	Rhode Island Medical Journal

0360-0696 Behavior Change†
0360-0726 Rehabilitation/World
0360-0815 National Panorama of American Youth
0360-0939 A C A Bulletin
0360-0971 Information Reports and Bibliographies
0360-1005 Mandate Magazine
0360-1013 Ohio Review
0360-1021 Archaeology of Eastern North America
0360-1048 New Mexico Almanac *changed to* New Mexico Digest
0360-1056 North Carolina Genealogical Society Journal
0360-1102 Needlework Guild of America. Annual Report
0360-120X Soviet Technical Physics Letters
0360-1218 Journal of Structural Mechanics *see* 0890-5452
0360-1226 Journal of Environmental Science and Health. Part A: Environmental Science and Engineering
0360-1234 Journal of Environmental Science and Health. Part B: Pesticides, Food Contaminants, and Agricultural Wastes
0360-1250 Current Book Review Citations†
0360-1269 Earth Surface Processes *see* 0197-9337
0360-1277 Educational Gerontology
0360-1285 Progress in Energy and Combustion Science
0360-1307 Iranian Journal of Science and Technology†
0360-1315 Computers & Education
0360-1323 Building and Environment
0360-1358 Contact and Intraocular Lens Medical Journal *see* 0733-8902
0360-1390 Suicide *see* 0363-0234
0360-1420 Journal of Christian Reconstruction
0360-1439 Legal Economics
0360-1455 New River Review†
0360-151X Brigham Young University Law Review
0360-1560 Lumberman and Wood Industries *see* 0015-7430
0360-1579 Ballots Newsletter *see* 0196-173X
0360-1676 Florida Dental Journal
0360-1684 National Association of Chiropodists. Journal *changed to* American Podiatric Medical Association. Journal
0360-1722 Ongoing Current Bibliography of Plastic and Reconstructive Surgery *see* 0149-5348
0360-1757 E I A Electronics Multimedia Handbook†
0360-1765 Leviathan and Kinnikinnik
0360-1773 Market Chronicle
0360-1846 Great Lakes Review *changed to* Michigan Historical Review
0360-1862 TeleSystems Journal†
0360-1889 Astrologia†
0360-1897 Pacific Theological Review
0360-1927 Journal of Latin American Lore
0360-1935 Main Title†
0360-1943 Music Book Guide *see* 0360-2753
0360-1978 Richmond Historian†
0360-1986 Women's Work (Washington)
0360-2044 Forum Law Journal *changed to* Law Forum
0360-2087 Houston Home & Garden
0360-2109 Paul's Record Magazine
0360-2133 Metallurgical Transactions A - Physical Metallurgy and Materials Science
0360-2141 Metallurgical Transactions B - Process Metallurgy
0360-215X Dictionary of Contemporary Quotations
0360-2184 U.S. Department of Agriculture. Economics Management Staff. Cotton and Wool Situation *see* 0744-2890
0360-2206 Balkanistica†
0360-2230 Plymouth Colony Genealogical Helper *see* 0277-433X
0360-2265 E P A Reports Bibliography Quarterly *see* 0196-0091
0360-2273 Popular Mechanics Do-It-Yourself Yearbook
0360-2397 Harper's Weekly†
0360-2400 Management Contents
0360-2508 Current Governments Reports: Chart Book on Government Data. Organization, Finances and Employment
0360-2516 Billboard Index†
0360-2532 Drug Metabolism Reviews
0360-2540 Separation and Purification Methods
0360-2559 Polymer- Plastics Technology and Engineering
0360-2672 Scree
0360-2699 Bibliographic Guide to Art and Architecture
0360-2710 Bibliographic Guide to Black Studies
0360-2729 Bibliographic Guide to Conference Publications
0360-2737 Bibliographic Guide to Dance
0360-2745 Bibliographic Guide to Law
0360-2753 Bibliographic Guide to Music
0360-2761 Bibliographic Guide to Technology
0360-277X Bibliographic Guide to Psychology
0360-2788 Bibliographic Guide to Theatre Arts
0360-2796 Bibliographic Guide to Government Publications
0360-280X Bibliographic Guide to Government Publications-Foreign
0360-2834 Maryland Register
0360-2834 Maryland Register. State Contract Supplement
0360-2877 Concrete Pipe Industry Statistics
0360-2915 Trinity Studies *see* 0360-3032
0360-3016 International Journal of Radiation: Oncology - Biology - Physics
0360-3024 Family Motor Coaching
0360-3032 Trinity Journal
0360-3059 Vermont. Agency of Environmental Conservation. Biennial Report†
0360-3083 Wood Industry Abstracts†
0360-3091 Portland Review *changed to* Portland Review Magazine
0360-3164 Plating and Surface Finishing
0360-3180 Yale Art Gallery Bulletin *see* 0084-3539
0360-3199 International Journal of Hydrogen Energy
0360-3245 U.S. Federal Bureau of Investigation. Bomb Summary
0360-3326 New York State Sea Grant Program. Annual Report *changed to* New York Sea Grant Institute. Annual Report
0360-3334 Calendar of Folk Festivals and Related Events†
0360-3342 Liberty, Then and Now†
0360-3350 L A D O C
0360-3385 Tristania
0360-3520 Body Fashions/Intimate Apparel
0360-3571 E R D A Energy Research Abstracts *see* 0160-3604
0360-3598 Family in Historical Perspective *see* 0363-1990
0360-3601 Genesis III†
0360-361X A.D. United Church of Christ Edition *changed to* United Church of Christ A.D.
0360-3628 A.D. United Presbyterian Edition *changed to* United Presbyterian A.D.
0360-3636 Arithmoi†
0360-3679 Institutes of Religion and Health. Institutes Reporter†
0360-3687 A I I S Annual Report *changed to* American Institute of Indian Studies. Biennial Report
0360-3695 Film & History
0360-3709 American Poetry Review (Philadelphia)
0360-3725 A.M.E. Church Review
0360-3733 Theological Currents†
0360-3741 Black Church†
0360-3768 Candler Review†
0360-3784 E F T S Report *changed to* E F T S Industry Report
0360-3814 Performing Arts Resources
0360-3857 Virginia Bar Association Journal
0360-3881 Alaska. Division of Geological and Geophysical Surveys. Special Report
0360-389X Adventist Heritage
0360-392X U.S. National Transportation Safety Board. Briefs of Accidents Involving Midair Collisions, U.S. General Aviation†
0360-3938 Business Outlook†
0360-3954 U. S. National Transportation Safety Board. Listing of Aircraft Accidents-Incidents by Make and Model, U.S. Civil Aviation†
0360-3989 Human Communication Research
0360-3997 Inflammation
0360-4012 Journal of Neuroscience Research
0360-4020 Association of Military Dermatologists. Journal
0360-4039 Nursing (Year) (Springhouse)
0360-4055 C S Journal
0360-4071 Quality Rock Reader
0360-4098 Agricultural Situation in the Soviet Union *changed to* World Agriculture Regional Supplement: U S S R
0360-4152 B O C A Basic Mechanical Code *changed to* B O C A Basic-National Mechanical Code
0360-4209 Notre Dame Journal of Legislation *see* 0146-9584
0360-4217 National Journal (1975)
0360-4225 Visual Dialog†
0360-4233 A S P A News and Views *see* 0149-8797
0360-4357 D P I Yellow Pages *changed to* Directory of Nebraska Services
0360-4365 In Theory Only
0360-4381 River City
0360-439X Tobacco Stocks
0360-4411 Who's Where in Music
0360-4438 Appalachian Notes
0360-4497 Soviet Journal of Bioorganic Chemistry
0360-4500 Scottish Genealogical Helper *see* 0271-5031
0360-4519 Irish Genealogical Helper *see* 0272-1015
0360-4527 Fleet Specialist *see* 0199-7610
0360-4543 U.S. Department of the Interior. Oil Shale Environmental Advisory Panel. Annual Report†
0360-4594 U.S. Food and Nutrition Service. Food and Nutrition Programs
0360-4608 Record (Nashville)
0360-473X Directions (Somerville)
0360-487X U.S. Social and Rehabilitation Service. Annual Report of Welfare Programs†
0360-4918 Presidential Studies Quarterly
0360-4969 American Health Care Association. Journal
0360-4985 Environmental Report Data System *changed to* Electric Power Industry Abstracts
0360-4993 Budget Decorating & Remodeling
0360-5027 Journal of Teaching and Learning *see* 0887-9486
0360-5043 Soviet Journal of Glass Physics and Chemistry
0360-506X Retailing Today
0360-5094 Midwestern Advocate *changed to* Hamline Law Review
0360-5108 Looking Back to Those Wonderful Days Gone by†
0360-5132 Official Gazette of the United States Patent and Trademark Office. Trademarks Supplements
0360-5159 Metal Industry (New York) *see* 0026-0576
0360-5167 American Hospital Association. House of Delegates. Proceedings
0360-523X Conference Board. Utility Investment Statistics. Utility Appropriations
0360-5248 Who's Who Among Students in American Vocational and Technical Schools *see* 0148-6381
0360-5272 Rail Transit Directory†
0360-5280 Byte
0360-5302 Communications in Partial Differential Equations
0360-5310 Journal of Medicine and Philosophy
0360-5361 N A D L Journal
0360-5388 Ais-Eiri *changed to* An Gael
0360-5434 Occupational Education
0360-5442 Energy (Oxford)
0360-5450 Vertica
0360-5477 Tennessee Manufacturers Directory†
0360-5485 Affiliate (Chicago)
0360-5531 Old Northwest
0360-554X Uniformed Services Almanac. Special Reserve Forces Edition *see* 0363-860X
0360-5558 Alaska. Department of Natural Resources. Division of Oil and Gas. Statistical Report *see* 0273-1916
0360-5590 Texas Tech Journal of Education†
0360-5612 Loon†
0360-5701 Freeing the Spirit†
0360-5779 Chronicle (Greensburg) *changed to* American Baptist Quarterly
0360-5809 Information News and Sources *see* 0360-5817
0360-5817 Information Hotline
0360-5825 Financial Corporate Bond Transfer Service *changed to* Financial Corporate Municipal Bond Transfer Service
0360-5892 American Machinist (1877) *changed to* American Machinist & Automated Manufacturing
0360-5906 R T S D Newsletter
0360-5949 American Philological Association. Transactions
0360-5973 Journal of Psychiatric Nursing and Mental Health Services *see* 0279-3695
0360-6031 Yearbook of Cardiovascular Medicine *see* 0145-4145
0360-6058 Bricklayers', Masons' and Plasterers' International Union of America. Journal *see* 0362-3696
0360-6112 Buddhist Text Information
0360-618X Center for Process Studies. Newsletter
0360-6244 Living Worship *see* 0276-2358
0360-6325 L D & A
0360-6333 African Economic History Review *see* 0145-2258
0360-6376 Journal of Polymer Science. Polymer Chemistry Edition
0360-6384 Journal of Polymer Science. Polymer Letters Edition
0360-6503 Process Studies
0360-6511 Personal Growth
0360-652X Patristics
0360-6538 Annotated Bibliography of New Publications in the Performing Arts†
0360-6724 Obsidian II: Black Literature in Review
0360-683X Nebraska. Indian Commission. Report
0360-6848 U.S. Social Security Administration. Applications and Case Dispositions for Public Assistance *changed to* Quarterly Public Assistance Statistics
0360-6864 Columbia River Water Management Report
0360-6899 American Public Works Association. Directory
0360-6929 American Society for Quality Control. Annual Technical Conference Transactions
0360-6945 Lutheran Journal
0360-697X A A C S B Newsline†
0360-6996 A R T B A Officials and Engineers Directory, Transportation Agency Personnel
0360-7046 M S U U Newsletter *changed to* M S U U Newsletter: Gleanings
0360-7100 American Institute for Decision Sciences. Southeast Section. Proceedings
0360-7119 Reporter (St. Louis. 1975)
0360-7135 Creative World†
0360-7151 Legal Bibliographic Data Service: Weekly Listing†
0360-716X Navy Supply Corps Newsletter
0360-7178 A A M O A Reports
0360-7216 Functional Photography (Heampstead)
0360-7275 Chemical Engineering Progress
0360-7283 Health and Social Work
0360-7348 Replay
0360-7372 Survey of Law Reviews *see* 0279-5787

1544 ISSN INDEX

0360-7410 Renaissance Two; Journal of Afro-American Studies
0360-7437 A A M C Directory of American Medical Education
0360-7453 Violations of Human Rights in Soviet Occupied Lithuania
0360-7461 Arizona. Water Commission. Bulletin *changed to* Arizona. Department of Water Resources. Report
0360-7496 Canoe
0360-750X U. S. Urban Mass Transportation Administration Report to Congress Concerning the Demonstration of Fare-Free Mass Transportation†
0360-7569 Current Concepts in Psychiatry
0360-7607 Hemostasis and Thrombosis; a Bibliography†
0360-7690 Nuclear Regulation Reports
0360-7739 Amicus Curiae *changed to* Friend of the Court
0360-7860 Revista Chicano - Riquena *changed to* Americas Review
0360-7887 Rackham Literary Studies *see* 0731-4817
0360-7917 Revista/Review Interamericana
0360-7941 National Development - Modern Government
0360-795X Journal of Corporation Law
0360-800X Utah. Division of Wildlife Resources. Biennial Report†
0360-8085 Best in Posters *changed to* Best in Covers and Posters
0360-814X American Water Works Association. Proceedings, A W W A Annual Conference
0360-8166 U.S. National Advisory Council on Extension and Continuing Education. Annual Report *changed to* U.S. National Advisory Council on Continuing Education. Annual Report
0360-8174 I S I's Who Is Publishing in Science *changed to* Current Contents Address Directory-Science & Technology
0360-8182 Uniquest *see* 0191-3379
0360-8212 Radical Religion
0360-8247 People Soup *changed to* Synapse (Boston)
0360-8263 Best in Advertising Campaigns *changed to* Best in Advertising
0360-8271 Best in Environmental Graphics
0360-8298 Cumberland Law Review
0360-8301 Massachusetts. Division of Employment Security. Employment and Wages in Establishments Subject to the Massachusetts Employment Security Law *see* 0076-4922
0360-8352 Computers & Industrial Engineering
0360-8360 Current Advances in Genetics†
0360-8409 ICarbS
0360-8417 International Defense Business *changed to* Defense & Economy World Report
0360-8425 American Foreign Service Journal *see* 0015-7279
0360-845X S P: Sociological Practice *see* 0163-8505
0360-8476 Search at the State University of New York†
0360-8484 Matthay News
0360-8557 Engineering Index Annual
0360-8581 I E E E Engineering Management Review
0360-859X Transportation Research Board Special Report
0360-862X C A S E Currents *changed to* Currents (Washington)
0360-8654 Guide to Micrographic Equipment†
0360-8662 United Business and Investment Report *changed to* United & Babson Investment Report
0360-8670 Aviation Quarterly†
0360-8689 Best in Packaging
0360-8727 R I d I M - R C M I Newsletter
0360-8743 Best in Annual Reports
0360-8751 Stream Improvement Technical Bulletin *changed to* National Council of the Paper Industry for Air and Stream Improvement. Technical Bulletin
0360-8778 Atmospheric Quality Improvement Technical Bulletin *changed to* National Council of the Paper Industry for Air and Stream Improvement. Technical Bulletin
0360-8786 Current Register of American Leaders†
0360-8808 Evangelical Theological Society. Journal
0360-8816 Northeast Rising Sun†
0360-8832 International Symposium on Atomic, Molecular and Solid-State Theory and Quantum Statistics. Proceedings *changed to* International Symposium on Atomic, Molecular and Solid-State Theory, Collision Phenomena and Computational Methods. Proceedings
0360-8840 American Accounting Association. Southeast Regional Group. Collected Papers of the Annual Meeting
0360-8859 Pennsylvania Exporters Directory†
0360-8867 Marine Geotechnology
0360-8905 Journal of Polymer Science. Polymer Symposia Edition
0360-8913 International Conference on Cybernetics and Society. Proceedings *changed to* I E E E International Conference on Systems, Man, and Cybernetics. Proceedings
0360-8921 Argus F C & S Chart
0360-8980 U.S. Department of Transportation. Summary of National Transportation Statistics *changed to* U.S. Department of Transportation. National Transportation Statistics. Annual
0360-8999 Foundry Management & Technology
0360-9006 Hastings Center. Recent Activities†
0360-9030 Historical Footnotes (St. Louis)
0360-9049 Hebrew Union College Annual
0360-9081 American Archivist
0360-912X Shocks†
0360-9146 Uniform Crime Report for the State of Michigan
0360-9154 Alaska Accident Statistics†
0360-9162 Illinois Air Quality Report *changed to* Illinois. Division of Air Pollution Control. Annual Air Quality Report
0360-9170 Language Arts
0360-9197 American Association of Blood Banks. Bulletin *see* 0041-1132
0360-9235 Lodging
0360-9278 Hearing Rehabilitation Quarterly
0360-9286 Highlights *see* 0360-9278
0360-9294 American Audiology Society. Journal *see* 0196-0202
0360-9316 Survey of Hospital Charges *changed to* Hospital Statistics (Year)
0360-9421 Pope Family Register†
0360-9553 Non-Ferrous Metal Data
0360-9588 Adherent†
0360-9642 N I D A Supported Drug Treatment Programs†
0360-9669 Horizons (Villanova)
0360-9693 Military Chaplains' Review
0360-9731 Nevada Government Today
0360-9766 Readings in Health *see* 0278-4653
0360-9774 Short Story Index
0360-9782 United Church of Christ. Pension Boards (Annual Report)
0360-9790 Lektos†
0360-991X Z.C.L.A. Journal *changed to* Zen Writings
0360-9928 Marathon Handbook†
0360-9936 Quality (Wheaton)
0360-9960 Advances in Bioengineering
0360-9987 Directory of Diesel Fuel Stations Coast to Coast *changed to* Diesel Fuel Guide
0361-0004 Modern Recording *changed to* Modern Recording & Music
0361-0020 Retailing in Tennessee
0361-0047 Foreign Trade Reports. Summary of U.S. Export and Import Merchandise Trade
0361-0128 Economic Geology and the Bulletin of the Society of Economic Geologists
0361-0144 American Humanities Index
0361-0152 Newspaper and Gazette Report *see* 0190-9819
0361-0160 Sixteenth Century Journal
0361-0179 Aging (New York)
0361-0195 Health Systems Management
0361-0209 Journal of Electrophysiological Techniques
0361-0233 Progress in Chemical Fibrinolysis and Thrombolysis
0361-025X Tests in Print
0361-0268 T C A Manual *see* 0271-8057
0361-0365 Research in Higher Education
0361-0438 Commerce America *see* 0190-6275
0361-0462 International Brain Research Organization Monograph Series
0361-0470 American Society of Brewing Chemists. Journal
0361-0489 Kroc Foundation Series†
0361-0519 Ohio. Division of Geological Survey. Miscellaneous Report
0361-0527 Perspectives in Cardiovascular Research
0361-0551 Theoretical Chemistry: Advances and Perspectives
0361-056X Campaign Practices Reports
0361-0640 Rubber Red Book
0361-073X Experimental Aging Research
0361-0748 Society of Photo-Optical Instrumentation Engineers. Proceedings
0361-0772 American Nurses' Association. House of Delegates. Summary Proceedings†
0361-0802 Pilgrimage: The Journal of Pastoral Psychotherapy *changed to* Pilgrimage: The Journal of Psychotherapy and Personal Exploration
0361-0845 Coin World Almanac
0361-0853 Manufacturing Engineering
0361-0861 Southern School Law Digest
0361-0888 American Frozen Food Institute. Membership Directory and Buyers' Guide
0361-0896 Celebrate; the Annual for Cake Decorators *changed to* Wilton Yearbook of Baking and Cake Decorating
0361-090X Cancer Detection and Prevention
0361-0918 Communications in Statistics. Part B: Simulation and Computation
0361-0926 Communications in Statistics. Part A: Theory and Methods
0361-0942 Video Systems
0361-0977 Formal Linguistics†
0361-1043 Motorhome Life and Camper Coachman *see* 0744-074X
0361-1108 Bricker's International Directory of University Executive Programs
0361-1116 Abortion Research Notes
0361-1124 J A C E P *see* 0196-0644
0361-1175 Western Society of Malacologists. Annual Report
0361-1205 Labor-Management Alcoholism Journal†
0361-1213 Microstructural Science†
0361-1299 Rocky Mountain Review of Language and Literature
0361-1302 Samizdat Bulletin
0361-1353 Alaska Geographic
0361-1361 Milepost
0361-137X Selected Alaska Hunting & Fishing Tales†
0361-140X Maryland. Council for Higher Education. Annual Report and Recommendations†
0361-1434 I E E E Transactions on Professional Communication
0361-1442 Computers and People
0361-1493 Directory of Drug Information and Treatment Organizations†
0361-1507 National Institute of Education. Career Education Program: Program Plan
0361-1515 Grassroots (Madison)
0361-1582 Federal Grant-in-Aid Activity in Florida: a Summary Report
0361-1612 Council for Tobacco Research--U.S.A. Report
0361-1647 School Media Quarterly *see* 0278-4823
0361-1663 Abraxas
0361-1671 Milwaukee County Historical Society. Historical Messenger *see* 0163-7622
0361-168X New Boston Review *see* 0734-2306
0361-1817 Nurse Practitioner: The American Journal of Primary Health Care
0361-1833 American Association for the Advancement of Science. Meeting Program.
0361-185X Selbyana
0361-1906 Journal of Theology
0361-1981 Transportation Research Record
0361-204X New York Folklore
0361-2066 Best in Covers *changed to* Best in Covers and Posters
0361-2090 Massachusetts Municipal Directory
0361-2112 Dress
0361-2120 Wisconsin. Educational Communications Board. Biennial Report
0361-2147 Antique Phonograph Monthly
0361-2147 A P M Monograph Series
0361-2163 Micro Proceedings *changed to* Microprogramming Workshop. Proceedings
0361-218X Worldwide Lodging Industry *changed to* Worldwide Hotel Industry
0361-2198 U S Lodging Industry
0361-221X Baton Twirling Rules and Regulations *changed to* Baton Twirling Handbook
0361-2228 Directory of Physics & Astronomy Staff Members *changed to* Directory of Physics & Astronomy Staff (Year)
0361-2279 National Research Council. Committee on Polar Research. Report on United States Antarctic Research Activities
0361-2295 North Carolina Governor's Highway Safety Program. Summary of Activities *changed to* North Carolina. Department of Transportation. Office of Highway Safety. Summary of Activities
0361-2309 Corporate Examiner
0361-2317 Color Research and Application
0361-2325 Political Intelligence†
0361-2333 Prospects
0361-2376 Congregational Journal
0361-2422 Post American *see* 0364-2097
0361-2449 U.S. Forest Service. Research Note N C
0361-2481 Wind
0361-249X Ophthalmic Seminars†
0361-2562 Resources Recovery/Energy Review†
0361-2570 Sales and Marketing Management *changed to* Sales & Marketing Management
0361-2597 Texas. Industrial Commission. Annual Report
0361-2635 Micropublishers' Trade List Annual
0361-2643 U.S. Social and Rehabilitation Service. Office of Management. Quality Control, States' Corrective Action Activities†
0361-2651 U.S. Department of the Army. Projects Recommended for Deauthorization, Annual Report
0361-2678 Viewpoint (Columbus) *changed to* Artspace (Columbus)
0361-2759 History: Reviews of New Books
0361-2767 Empirical Research in Theatre *changed to* Empirical Research in Theatre Annual
0361-2783 Auerbach Guide to Computing Equipment Specifications†
0361-2791 C T A Quarterly
0361-2805 U.S. National Ocean Survey. Collected Reprints *changed to* U.S. National Ocean Service. Collected Reprints
0361-2821 Mechanical Properties *changed to* Key Engineering Materials
0361-2848 Wisconsin Library Service Record
0361-2929 Health Facilities Directory (Sacramento)
0361-2961 Advances in Holography†
0361-297X Alabama. Department of Industrial Relations. Annual Manpower Planning Report *changed to* Alabama. Department of Industrial Relations. Annual Planning Information

ISSN INDEX 1545

0361-2988 Complete Handbook of Pro Football
0361-2996 Directory of Manufacturers in Arkansas *changed to* Directory of Arkansas Manufacturers
0361-3011 Field & Stream Hunting Annual
0361-3038 N.E.S.F.A. Index: Science Fiction Magazines and Anthologies
0361-3046 Selected Studies in Medical Care and Medical Economics†
0361-3054 Scripps Clinic and Research Foundation. Scientific Report *changed to* Scripps Clinic and Research Foundation. Research Institute. Scientific Report
0361-3062 Germanic Genealogical Helper *see* 0363-9169
0361-3070 Instrumentation in the Mining and Metallurgy Industries
0361-3232 Showcase (New York)
0361-3313 Electronics and Communications Abstracts Journal
0361-3321 Science Research Abstracts Journal. Superconductivity; Magnetohydrodynamics and Plasmas; Theoretical Physics *changed to* Solid State Abstracts Journal
0361-333X Western Reserve Magazine
0361-3372 Practical Cardiology
0361-3399 I J A L Native American Texts Series†
0361-3410 Toxicology Annual†
0361-3445 Directory of State Government Energy-Related Agencies†
0361-3453 Fine Woodworking
0361-3488 International Journal of Powder Metallurgy & Powder Technology
0361-3496 Environmental Psychology and Nonverbal Behavior *see* 0191-5886
0361-3550 Maine. Bureau of Property Taxation. Biennial Report *changed to* Maine. Bureau of Property Taxation. Annual Report
0361-3577 Loblolly
0361-3593 Southwest Directory of Advertising and Public Relations Agencies
0361-3658 Conservation & Recycling
0361-3666 Disasters
0361-3674 Metabolic Ophthalmology *see* 0277-9382
0361-3682 Accounting, Organizations and Society
0361-3690 Habitat (Oxford) *see* 0197-3975
0361-3712 Arlington Catholic Herald
0361-3747 Welding & Joining Digest
0361-3763 A B A Lawyers' Title Guaranty Funds Newsletter
0361-3771 Directory of Psychosocial Investigators†
0361-3798 Mental Retardation and Developmental Disabilities Abstracts *see* 0191-1600
0361-3801 Fine Print
0361-381X Bicycle Dealer Showcase
0361-3828 Breast: Diseases of the Breast†
0361-3836 Annual Editions: Readings in Personality and Adjustment *see* 0198-912X
0361-3844 Attorneys and Agents Registered to Practice Before the U.S. Patent and Trademark Office
0361-3852 B & P A
0361-3895 National Income and Product Accounts of the United States: Statistical Tables
0361-3968 Asian Thought and Society: an International Review
0361-3976 Women's International Bowling Congress. Playing Rules
0361-3984 Alaska Fishing Guide†
0361-4018 New York State Medical Care Facilities Finance Agency. Annual Report
0361-4034 Grocery Distribution
0361-4050 Employee Benefits Journal
0361-4166 Rehabilitation Gazette
0361-4190 Xerox Disclosure Journal
0361-4204 U.S. Federal Highway Administration. Federally Coordinated Program of Highway Research and Development
0361-4220 International Guild Guide
0361-4239 Conference Board. Manufacturing Investment Statistics. Capital Appropriations *see* 0195-8313
0361-4247 Buyer's Directory of Suppliers for General Merchandise Buyers†
0361-4255 Directory of North American Fairs and Expositions
0361-4336 Children Today
0361-4344 F D A Drug Bulletin
0361-4387 Cosmetics and Toiletries
0361-4425 Yale University. School of Forestry. Bulletin
0361-4433 Geodesy, Mapping and Photogrammetry *changed to* Mapping Sciences & Remote Sensing
0361-4441 Cuban Studies
0361-4468 Health, United States
0361-4476 Journal of Energy and Development
0361-4506 California. State Water Resources Control Board. Annual State Strategy *changed to* California. State Water Resources Control Board. Program Guide
0361-4514 U.S. Office of Education. Determination of Basic Grant Eligibility Index†
0361-4522 U.S. Food and Drug Administration. Pesticide-P C B in Foods Program. Evaluation Report
0361-4530 U.S. Solicitor for the Department of the Interior. Solicitor's Review†
0361-4565 Wire Technology *changed to* Wire Tech
0361-4646 Behavioral Sciences Newsletter
0361-4654 A A U Junior Olympic Handbook
0361-4662 Bottomline†
0361-4670 European Skinny†
0361-4689 R & D Review (Schenectady)†
0361-4719 Instrumentation in the Pulp and Paper Industry
0361-4735 Current Biographies of Leading Archaeologists
0361-4751 American Film Magazine (Washington) *changed to* American Film
0361-476X Contemporary Educational Psychology
0361-4794 Current Mathematical Publications
0361-4921 Fiber Producer *changed to* Fiber World
0361-4948 Tourbook: Alabama, Louisiana, Mississippi
0361-4956 Tourbook: Georgia, North Carolina, South Carolina
0361-4964 Tourbook: Kentucky, Tennessee
0361-4972 Electrical Consultant (Atlanta)
0361-4999 Ithacagun Hunting & Shooting Annual†
0361-5006 Annual Symposium on Pulmonary Diseases†
0361-5030 Flight Operations
0361-5049 Educational Catalyst†
0361-5057 College Recruiting Report
0361-5065 Buoyant Flight
0361-5162 Trace Substances in Environmental Health
0361-5170 Victimology
0361-5219 Solid Fuel Chemistry
0361-5227 Modern Psychoanalysis
0361-5235 Journal of Electronic Materials
0361-526X Serials Librarian
0361-5294 Doors and Hardware
0361-5316 Professional Builder and Apartment Business *changed to* Professional Builder
0361-5359 Drug Survival News *see* 0739-4683
0361-5367 New York's Food and Life Sciences Quarterly
0361-5383 Billboard's on Tour *see* 0732-0124
0361-5391 Wisconsin Secondary School Administrators Association. Bulletin *changed to* Association of Wisconsin School Administrators. Bulletin
0361-5405 Helicopter Safety Bulletin
0361-5413 History in Africa
0361-5421 M P, the Microprocessor†
0361-5499 National Geographic World
0361-5502 Hispanic American Periodicals Index
0361-5537 North Carolina Medical Society. Transactions
0361-5545 C B S News Almanac *changed to* Hammond Almanac: One-Volume Encyclopedia of a Million Facts & Records (year)
0361-5553 Clarinet
0361-5561 Journal of Commerce and Commercial
0361-5634 Essays in Arts and Sciences
0361-5669 A R L Annual Salary Survey
0361-5685 Dance Life in New York *changed to* Dance Life
0361-5693 Western Tobacco Journal *changed to* Tobacco Reporter
0361-574X Historic Madison. Journal
0361-5782 Journal of Management (Tucson) *see* 0149-7901
0361-5820 Contemporary Keyboard *see* 0730-0158
0361-5855 Recorder Review†
0361-5871 Tax Guide
0361-591X Kentucky Deskbook of Economic Statistics *changed to* Kentucky Economic Statistics
0361-5952 Advances in Prostaglandin and Thromboxane Research
0361-5960 Cancer Treatment Reports
0361-5995 Soil Science Society of America. Journal
0361-6029 American Schools of Oriental Research. Newsletter
0361-6061 Face-to-Face (New York)
0361-607X Artist's Market *see* 0161-0546
0361-6118 Reading Abstracts
0361-6193 East Tennessee Historical Society's Publications
0361-6207 South Carolina Historical Association. Proceedings
0361-6215 West Tennessee Historical Society. Papers
0361-6266 Abstracts in Human Evolution†
0361-6274 Health Care Management Review
0361-6290 W W II Journal†
0361-6347 New Titles in Bioethics
0361-638X Woman's Day Home Decorating Ideas
0361-6428 Journal of Radiation Curing
0361-6436 New York (State) Department of Social Services. Bureau of Research. Program Brief. *see* 0162-6302
0361-6479 South Carolina State Library. Annual Report
0361-6525 Sociobiology
0361-6576 Journal of Economics (Vermillion)
0361-6584 Kronos
0361-6606 O O B A Guidebook to Theatres *see* 0732-300X
0361-6622 Selected Reports in Ethnomusicology
0361-6657 Comprehensive Dissertation Index. Supplement†
0361-6665 Wage-Price Law & Economics Review
0361-6673 U.S. Environmental Protection Agency. Office of General Counsel. a Collection of Legal Opinions†
0361-6681 Public Productivity Review
0361-6797 U.S. Civil Service Commission. Bureau of Personnel Management Evaluation. Evaluation Methods Series
0361-6843 Psychology of Women Quarterly
0361-6851 Alternative Higher Education *see* 0742-5627
0361-686X Abba†
0361-6878 Journal of Health Politics, Policy and Law
0361-6886 Acta Geologica Sinica (English Edition) †
0361-6908 Continuation Education
0361-6916 Bibliography, Corporate Responsibility for Social Problems *see* 0160-8819
0361-6959 World of Work Report
0361-6967 Electric Machines and Electromechanics *see* 0731-356X
0361-6975 Community/Junior College Research Quarterly *see* 0277-6774
0361-6983 Detroit News. Newspaper Index *changed to* Index to the Detroit News
0361-7025 California Optometrist *see* 0273-804X
0361-7092 Notes on Urban-Industrial Mission, Literature and Training†
0361-7122 South Central Research Library Council. Reports
0361-7149 Soviet Geology and Geophysics
0361-7157 English Genealogical Helper *see* 0145-6059
0361-7165 Family Heritage Series†
0361-7173 Jewish Arts Quarterly†
0361-7181 Journal of California Anthropology *see* 0191-3557
0361-719X N A G W S Guide. Aquatics *see* 0271-2199
0361-7203 Computer Law & Tax Report
0361-722X Film Reader
0361-7238 Modern Plywood Techniques†
0361-7246 Journal of Historical Studies (Washington)†
0361-7300 Army Administrator *see* 0274-9513
0361-7440 U.S. National Commission for Manpower Policy. Annual Report to the President and the Congress *changed to* U.S. National Commission for Employment Policy. Annual Report
0361-7467 P P F Survey
0361-7483 World Coal *changed to* World Mining Equipment
0361-7491 Acta (Binghamton)
0361-7491 Acta (Albany)
0361-753X R & D Management Digest
0361-7629 Iowa. Geological Survey. Annual Report of the State Geologist to the Geological Board *changed to* Iowa. Geological Survey. Annual Report of the State Geologist to the Governor
0361-7653 Business and Public Administration Student Review†
0361-7688 Programming and Computer Software
0361-7734 Operative Dentistry
0361-7742 Progress in Clinical and Biological Research
0361-7823 Facts About Alaska *see* 0270-5370
0361-7858 Population Council Annual Report
0361-7874 American Association for the Advancement of Science. Handbook; Officers, Organization, Activities
0361-7882 International Journal of African Historical Studies
0361-7947 Theatre Profiles
0361-8013 Federal Reserve Bank of Minneapolis. Annual Report
0361-8021 Harvard Teachers Record *see* 0017-8055
0361-803X A J R
0361-8242 Sky *see* 0037-6604
0361-8269 Southern Speech Communication Journal
0361-8382 Fire Protection Reference Directory
0361-8412 Malpractice Lifeline *see* 0732-9636
0361-8528 Schoharie County Historical Review
0361-8552 Yellow Brick Road†
0361-8560 South Dakota State Library Newsletter†
0361-8587 Perfumer and Flavorist International *see* 0272-2666
0361-8609 American Journal of Hematology
0361-865X Mass Media Bi-Weekly Newsletter *changed to* Mass Media Newsletter
0361-8668 Keeping You Posted
0361-8676 South Dakota History
0361-8714 Federal Reserve Bank of Boston. Conference Series
0361-8773 J C T, Journal of Coatings Technology
0361-8854 Context
0361-8862 Congregation
0361-8927 Guide to Four-Year College Databook *see* 0191-3670
0361-8935 Loyola Lawyer†
0361-8994 Career World *changed to* Career World-Real World
0361-9001 Chinese Science
0361-9095 California Livestock Statistics
0361-9117 Women Artist Newsletter *see* 0149-7081
0361-915X Bell Journal of Economics *see* 0741-6261
0361-9168 American Society of Magazine Photographers. Bulletin
0361-9230 Brain Research Bulletin
0361-9249 Current Practice in Obstetric and Gynecological Nursing†
0361-9257 Current Practice in Pediatric Nursing†

1546 ISSN INDEX

0361-9273 Guidebook of U.S. & Canadian Postdoctoral Dental Programs†
0361-929X M C N: American Journal of Maternal Child Nursing
0361-9362 Accredited Institutions of Postsecondary Education and Programs *see* 0270-1715
0361-9397 Chilton's Motor-Age Professional Labor Guide and Parts Manual *see* 0749-5579
0361-9451 Wisconsin Sportsman
0361-946X Mediaevalia
0361-9478 W I L C O Newsletter†
0361-9486 American Bar Foundation. Research Journal
0361-9591 Means Construction Cost Indexes
0361-9613 Society for the Study of Pre-Han China. Newsletter *see* 0362-5028
0361-9621 Explicacion de Textos Literarios
0361-9737 U.S. National Park Service. Public Use of the National Park System; Calendar Year Report
0361-9885 Health and Education *see* 0161-6765
0361-9966 Seminar on the Acquisition of Latin American Library Materials. Resolutions and Lists of Commitees†
0362-0034 Nuclear Materials Management *changed to* Journal of Nuclear Materials Management
0362-0050 Notebook of Empirical Petrology†
0362-0069 New York's Food and Life Sciences Bulletin
0362-0085 Theologia 21
0362-0131 Buyer's Guide to Micrographic Equipment, Products, and Services†
0362-0212 Fodor's India *see* 0276-5500
0362-0247 Four Zoas
0362-028X Journal of Food Protection
0362-0298 Behavioral Engineering†
0362-0344 Trail Breakers
0362-0395 Automation in Housing/Systems Building News *see* 0740-3534
0362-0409 Choral Praise
0362-0417 Gospel Choir
0362-0425 Ironcaster *changed to* Metalcaster
0362-0506 Highway and Heavy Construction
0362-0522 Spring (Dallas)
0362-0557 Pilgrim State Newsletter *changed to* Pilgrim State News
0362-0565 Underground Space
0362-0581 Gettysburg Seminary Bulletin *changed to* Lutheran Theological Seminary Bulletin
0362-0603 Theological Markings
0362-062X Journal of Reprints of Documents Affecting Women
0362-0662 Georgia Vital and Health Statistics *changed to* Georgia Vital Statistics Data Book
0362-0689 Dow Jones Commodities Handbook†
0362-0697 Economic Crime Digest†
0362-0700 Sport Fishery and Wildlife Research *changed to* Fisheries and Wildlife Research
0362-0719 Index of Patents Issued from the United States Patent and Trademark Office
0362-0794 N I C M Journal for Jews and Christians in Higher Education *changed to* Religion and Intellectual Life
0362-0808 M S S
0362-0816 Associate Reformed Presbyterian
0362-0824 Bioethics Northwest *changed to* Journal of Medical Humanities and Bioethics
0362-0867 Explor
0362-0875 Film & Broadcasting Review†
0362-0905 Focus Chicago *changed to* Facets Features
0362-0913 Quintessence of Dental Technology
0362-0964 Theatre Studies
0362-0999 Microform Market Place
0362-1006 Micrographics Equipment Review *changed to* Micrographics and Optical Storage Equipment Review
0362-1014 Microlist *changed to* Guide to Microforms in Print. Supplement
0362-1057 A J S Joint Enterprise *changed to* Update (Chicago)
0362-1065 Abstracts of Book Reviews in Current Legal Periodicals
0362-1138 Nebraska. Department of Economic Development. Annual Economic Report†
0362-1146 New West *see* 0279-3768
0362-1162 Audiovideo International
0362-1170 Foundation Center Source Book *changed to* Foundation Center Source Book Profiles
0362-1197 Human Physiology
0362-1219 Gone Soft *changed to* Soundings East
0362-1235 University of Missouri, Columbia. Museum of Anthropology. Museum Briefs
0362-1243 California. Division of Oil and Gas. Annual Report of the State Oil and Gas Supervisor
0362-1251 Compact New York Times Magazine†
0362-1278 Financial Industry
0362-1294 Literary Research Newsletter
0362-1324 Electric Comfort Conditioning News†
0362-1332 F D A Consumer
0362-1340 S I G P L A N Notices
0362-1383 Massachusetts Advocacy Center. Annual Report†
0362-1391 Georgia Genealogist†
0362-1405 Financial Industry Number Standard Directory
0362-1421 Arizona. Department of Health Services. Annual Report
0362-1472 Association of Theological Schools in the United States and Canada. Bulletin
0362-1510 News from the Congregational Christian Historical Society
0362-1529 Traditio
0362-1537 Transactional Analysis Journal
0362-1561 Michigan Foundation Directory
0362-1588 Houston Journal of Mathematics
0362-1596 Parabola
0362-1618 N E L B Link†
0362-1626 Annual Review of Energy
0362-1642 Annual Review of Pharmacology and Toxicology
0362-1650 Atherosclerosis Reviews
0362-1669 Journal of Combustion Toxicology†
0362-1677 Journal of Consumer Product Flammability†
0362-1693 Journal of Fire Retardant Chemistry†
0362-1715 American Fisheries Society Monograph
0362-188X Air Force Engineering & Services Quarterly
0362-191X Commodity Drain Report of Florida's Primary Forest Industries
0362-1952 Deer Sportsman
0362-1979 J. Paul Getty Museum Journal
0362-2428 Research Communications in Psychology, Psychiatry and Behavior
0362-2436 Spine
0362-2452 Body Fashions/Intimate Apparel Directory
0362-2487 Enjine!-Enjine!
0362-2525 Journal of Morphology (1931)
0362-2606 Merchandising 2 - Way Radio *changed to* Personal Communications
0362-2622 Occasional Papers in Entomology
0362-2630 American Indian Art Magazine
0362-2711 B & M Bulletin
0362-2746 Teaching Language through Literature
0362-2770 Options (Wayne)
0362-2800 San Francisco Bay Area Rapid Transit District. Annual Report
0362-2827 Tab†
0362-2843 Southern California Rapid Transit District. Annual Report
0362-2908 Association of Feminist Consultants. Directory of Members†
0362-2916 Carrier Case Reports†
0362-2959 Musician's Guide
0362-2967 New Jersey Area Library Directory†
0362-2983 Study of Federal Tax Law. Income Tax Volume: Business Enterprises
0362-3122 Transportation Terminal Techniques†
0362-3165 Health Planning and Manpower Report *see* 0736-9077
0362-3173 Lactation Review
0362-3211 Toxicology Research Projects Directory†
0362-3238 C B S News Index
0362-3246 Survey of Sources Newsletter†
0362-3254 N A G W S Guide. Basketball†
0362-3270 Official Field Hockey Rules for School Girls *changed to* International Field Hockey Rules
0362-3289 Idaho. Department of Water Resources. Annual Report†
0362-3300 American Musical Instrument Society. Journal
0362-3416 E P R I Journal
0362-3432 Tennessee Valley Authority. Operations: Municipal and Cooperative Distributors of T.V.A. Power *see* 0730-4889
0362-3459 Guide to Minority Business Directories *changed to* Guide to Obtaining Minority Business Directories
0362-3475 Southeast Michigan Council of Governments. Annual Report
0362-3513 Indiana. Geological Survey. Annual Report of the State Geologist
0362-3548 N F I B Quarterly Economic Report for Small Business
0362-3572 Recent Researches in the Music of the Middle Ages and Early Renaissance
0362-3599 Tourbook: Arizona, New Mexico
0362-3602 Tourbook: Western Canada and Alaska
0362-3610 Understanding Financial Support of Public Schools†
0362-3637 Afroasiatic Linguistics
0362-3688 New York Times Film Reviews
0362-3696 International Union of Bricklayers and Allied Craftsmen. Journal
0362-370X M E S A†
0362-3718 Massachusetts. Bureau of Regional Planning. Regional Profiles†
0362-3750 Who's Who Among Music Students in American High Schools
0362-3777 Corvette, the Sensuous American *changed to* Corvette, Sportscar of America
0362-3793 Labor Force Status of Indiana Residents
0362-3815 Transport 2000 *changed to* Transport 2000 and Intermodal World
0362-3823 Woodall's Campground Directory *changed to* Woodall's Campground Directory. North American Edition
0362-3823 Woodall's Campground Directory *see* 0162-7414
0362-3823 Woodall's Campground Directory *see* 0162-7406
0362-3890 Facts and Figures on Footwear *see* 0095-1048
0362-3904 Georgia. State Data Center. City Population Estimates *changed to* Georgia Descriptions in Data
0362-3912 Idaho. Department of Labor and Industrial Services. Annual Report
0362-3920 Merchandising *changed to* Dealerscope Merchandising
0362-3955 Sound Image
0362-4021 Group
0362-403X Issues in Child Mental Health *changed to* Child and Adolescent Social Work Journal
0362-4048 American Rehabilitation
0362-4064 Occupational Health & Safety
0362-4102 Photo-Image†
0362-4110 California. Department of the Youth Authority. Affirmative Action Statistics
0362-4129 California. Department of Industrial Relations. Annual Report
0362-4145 Children's Literature Review
0362-4196 Alaska. Employment Security Division. Labor Force Estimates by Industry and Area.†
0362-420X Guide to Two-Year College Majors and Careers *see* 0191-3662
0362-4250 Bestways Magazine
0362-4285 Federal Funding Guide for Local Governments *see* 0273-4435
0362-4293 Lost in Canada?
0362-4366 Directory: Community Development Education and Training Programs Throughout the World†
0362-4439 Pharmaceutical News Index
0362-4447 Bonsai
0362-4455 Code & Symbol
0362-4463 Southern Weed Science Society. Proceedings
0362-448X L J Special Reports†
0362-4498 International Microfilm Source Book *see* 0272-0310
0362-451X D, the Magazine of Dallas *see* 0161-7826
0362-4528 Discothekin'
0362-4536 I E E E Student Papers
0362-4544 Journal Holdings in the Washington-Baltimore Area
0362-4552 M I M C Microforms Annual *changed to* Microforms Annual
0362-4595 Chicago
0362-4641 Moslem World *see* 0027-4909
0362-4668 Interdependence
0362-4706 University of Chicago Record
0362-4722 Consumer Electronics
0362-4730 D R I European Review *changed to* Data Resources European Review
0362-4749 Gun World Hunting Guide *changed to* Gun World Annual
0362-4765 Political Science Utilization Directory
0362-4781 Texas Register
0362-4803 Journal of Labelled Compounds and Radiopharmaceuticals
0362-4846 Three Rivers Poetry Journal
0362-4889 Low Vision Abstracts
0362-4994 American Gas Association. Operating Section. Proceedings
0362-5001 A M J†
0362-501X Corporate Systems†
0362-5028 Early China
0362-5044 French Periodical Index
0362-5079 Population and Occupied Dwelling Units in Southeast Michigan†
0362-5214 Pig Iron
0362-5230 Study of Federal Tax Law. Income Tax Volume *changed to* Study of Federal Tax Law. Income Tax Volume: Individuals
0362-5249 Supreme Court Historical Society. Yearbook
0362-5354 Wisconsin. Department of Natural Resources. Annual Water Quality Report to Congress
0362-5419 Gloria Vanderbilt Designs for Your Home
0362-5435 Conference Board. Quarterly Business Review†
0362-5451 Rx: R I A for Physicians†
0362-546X Nonlinear Analysis
0362-5478 Pharmacology and Therapeutics. Part A. Chemotherapy, Toxicology and Metabolic Inhibitors *see* 0163-7258
0362-5486 Pharmacology and Therapeutics. Part C. Clinical Pharmacology and Therapeutics *see* 0163-7258
0362-5524 Illinois. Board of Higher Education. Statewide Space Survey
0362-5567 Fishing Guide†
0362-5664 Clinical Neuropharmacology
0362-5699 Reviews in Perinatal Medicine
0362-5710 Directory of Delaware Schools
0362-5737 Truck Broker Directory
0362-5745 Army Communicator
0362-5753 Who's Who Among Black Americans
0362-580X Journal of Social and Political Affairs *see* 0278-839X
0362-5818 E E O Today *see* 0745-7790
0362-5834 Youth Magazine†
0362-5850 Plants & Gardens: Brooklyn Botanic Garden Record
0362-5907 A G O Times *see* 0164-3150

0362-5915 A C M Transactions on Database Systems
0362-5923 Activity Programmers Sourcebook†
0362-5931 Georgia Legislative Review
0362-594X Geographic Origin and Distribution of Students, Missouri Institutions of Higher Education†
0362-5958 New Jersey. Department of Education. Educational Assessment Program State Report
0362-5982 South
0362-6016 Policy Studies Directory
0362-6059 Accent†
0362-6075 Andover Review†
0362-613X American Journal of Computational Linguistics *changed to* Computational Linguistics
0362-6148 Chicago Daily Law Bulletin
0362-6180 Buyers' Guide for the Mass Entertainment Industry
0362-6199 Data Resources U.S. Long-Term Bulletin *changed to* Data Resources U S Long-Term Review
0362-6245 U & L C
0362-6288 Utah Geological and Mineral Survey. Survey Notes
0362-6296 Hawaii. Department of Health. Mental Health Services for Children and Youth
0362-6369 Washington (State). Department of Ecology. Water Quality Assessment Report†
0362-6385 Field & Stream Fishing Annual
0362-6415 Red River Valley Historical Review†
0362-6466 Food and Drug Letter
0362-6474 Threads in Action Monograph
0362-6490 Virginia. Agricultural Opportunities Development Program. Annual Report†
0362-6520 Hudson Home Guides *see* 0278-2839
0362-6547 Red River Valley Historical Journal of World History†
0362-6563 California Department of Parks and Recreation. a Stewardship Report†
0362-6644 Your Good Health Review & Digest†
0362-6660 Kids Fashions Magazine
0362-6679 Summary of Kentucky Education Statistics *changed to* Information on Education
0362-6741 United States Investor/Eastern Banker *see* 0148-8848
0362-6784 Curriculum Inquiry
0362-6830 Monthly Catalog of United States Government Publications
0362-6881 Bentley Historical Library Annual Report
0362-6911 Frontiers of Economics†
0362-6962 Alaska. Division of Game. Annual Report of Survey - Inventory Activities
0362-7047 Latvju Maksla
0362-708X Academy
0362-7098 Louisiana. Division of Mental Health. Annual Performance Report and Continuation of the State Plan for Drug Abuse Prevention
0362-7152 Country Scene†
0362-7179 Directory of Services for Migrant Families
0362-7284 Alaska. Criminal Investigation Bureau. Annual Report
0362-7330 Gospel Music Association. Annual Directory and Yearbook *changed to* Gospel Music Offical Directory
0362-7373 Songwriter Magazine
0362-742X Public Welfare in California†
0362-7462 Washington (State). Department of Revenue. Forest Tax Report *changed to* Washington (State). Department of Revenue. Forest Tax Section. Forest Tax Annual Report
0362-7470 Wisconsin. Division of Corrections. Bureau of Planning, Development and Research. Releases from Juvenile Institutions *changed to* Wisconsin. Division of Corrections. Office of Information Management. Releases from Juvenile Institutions
0362-7535 Research Abstracts (Ann Arbor)
0362-7705 Schoolhouse *changed to* E F L Reports
0362-7772 Demolition Age
0362-7799 Petroleum Marketer
0362-7888 Harvest *changed to* Connecticut Writer
0362-7926 Texas Pharmacy
0362-7942 F A A General Aviation News
0362-7969 Painted Bride Quarterly
0362-8078 Harvard Ukrainian Research Institute. Minutes of the Seminar in Ukrainian Studies
0362-8205 S A E Handbook
0362-823X Business Research Bulletin†
0362-8302 Jam to-Day
0362-8337 Health Careers†
0362-8353 Criminal Justice Plan (Richmond)
0362-837X Los Angeles Bar Journal *see* 0162-2900
0362-8396 Provincetown Poets *changed to* Provincetown Magazine
0362-8493 Across the Table
0362-8507 U.S. Advisory Commission on Intergovernmental Relations. Intergovernmental Perspective
0362-8523 Poor Joe's Pennsylvania Almanac†
0362-854X University of Texas at Austin. General Libraries. Newsletter
0362-8558 Journal of Dialysis *see* 0886-022X
0362-8566 Self Reliance†
0362-8671 Index to Book Reviews in Historical Periodicals†
0362-868X Massachusetts Tax Primer
0362-8701 Best's Insurance Securities Research Service
0362-8736 Inter-University Consortium for Political and Social Research. Guide to Resources and Services.
0362-8744 New York Metropolitan Reference and Research Agency. Directory of Members *changed to* Metro Handbook and Directory of Members (Year)
0362-8787 Delaware. State Board of Education. Report of Educational Statistics
0362-8809 Journal on Political Repression†
0362-8817 Insurance Industry *see* 0745-0419
0362-8833 N R E C A - A P P A Legal Reporting Service
0362-8841 Mother Jones
0362-885X Manufacturing and Engineering *see* 0744-7698
0362-8868 Louisiana. Health and Human Resources Administration Comprehensive Annual Services Program Plan for Social Services Under Title 20
0362-8914 American Journal of Ancient History
0362-8922 Gnostica News *see* 0145-885X
0362-8930 School Library Journal
0362-8973 Information Processing Journal *see* 0191-9776
0362-9066 F P S: a Magazine of Young People's Liberation
0362-9074 History of Anthropology Newsletter
0362-9090 Human Factor
0362-9163 U.S. Office of Management and Budget. Special Analysis: Budget of the United States Government
0362-9198 Maryland. Division of Correction. Report
0362-9279 Idaho. Department of Health and Welfare. Annual Summary of Vital Statistics
0362-9287 Directory - Juvenile and Adult Correctional Departments, Institutions, Agencies, and Paroling Authorities of the United States and Canada *see* 0190-2555
0362-9368 Packard Cormorant
0362-9376 Plastics Design Forum
0362-9406 School Security†
0362-9457 American Society of Arms Collectors. Bulletin
0362-9473 Iowa Detailed Report of Vital Statistics *see* 0161-8695
0362-9481 N A G W S Guide. Track and Field†
0362-9511 U.S. Department of Agriculture. Sugar and Sweetener Outlook and Situation
0362-9554 Aspen Anthology *changed to* Aspen Journal of the Arts
0362-9651 Brand Guide and Directory
0362-9708 Manufacturing Investment Statistics: Capital Investment and Supply Conditions *see* 0195-8313
0362-9716 Ohio Inventory of Business and Industrial Change†
0362-9783 Humanistic Educator *see* 0735-6846
0362-9791 Journal of Educational Statistics
0362-9805 Legislative Studies Quarterly
0362-9821 Tourbook: Colorado, Utah
0362-9902 C.F.O. Journal
0362-9910 Fortitudine
0362-9945 American Philological Association. Proceedings†
0363-0021 Federal Reserve Bank of San Francisco. Economic Review
0363-0048 Preview of United States Supreme Court Cases
0363-0129 S I A M Journal on Control and Optimization
0363-0153 Archives of Pathology & Laboratory Medicine
0363-0161 Bibliography of Bioethics
0363-0188 Current Problems in Diagnostic Radiology
0363-020X Health Services Manager†
0363-0234 Suicide and Life-Threatening Behavior
0363-0242 Women & Health
0363-0250 Action for Libraries
0363-0269 Hemoglobin
0363-0277 Library Journal
0363-0307 Golden Gate University Law Review
0363-0358 National Association of Insurance Commissioners. Proceedings
0363-0366 Medical and Health Annual
0363-0404 Journal of Products Liability
0363-0447 First Principles
0363-0471 Hispamerica
0363-0617 Parks
0363-065X Access: the Index to Little Magazines†
0363-0781 Health Sciences Video Directory *see* 0731-5945
0363-079X Shout in the Street†
0363-0889 C P P R
0363-0927 Guide to External and Continuing Education†
0363-0978 Shepard's Criminal Justice Citations
0363-0994 Unified World
0363-1001 Videography
0363-101X Tennessee Valley Authority. Annual Report
0363-1028 Whistle Stop
0363-1079 Indochina Chronicle *see* 0738-050X
0363-1095 Washington Academy of Sciences. Proceedings *see* 0043-0439
0363-1133 Women's Studies Newsletter *see* 0732-1562
0363-1168 Virgin Islands Archaeological Society. Journal
0363-1192 Utah Geology†
0363-1230 Webster Review
0363-1249 America: History and Life. Part C: American History Bibliography
0363-1257 METRO C A P Catalog
0363-129X California Worker's Compensation Reporter
0363-1370 Sunstone
0363-1540 Tourbook: New York
0363-1605 Community Mental Health Review *see* 0270-3114
0363-1621 Contact Lens Forum
0363-1664 Laughing Man
0363-1672 Lithuanian Mathematical Journal
0363-1699 Matchbox†
0363-1710 Mortgage Banking: Loans Closed and Servicing Volume *see* 0277-1497
0363-1788 Tourbook: Atlantic Provinces and Quebec
0363-1818 Consumer Life†
0363-1850 Eureka Review
0363-1869 Harris Michigan Manufacturers Industrial Directory *changed to* Harris Michigan Industrial Directory
0363-1877 Headmaster U.S.A. *changed to* Private School Quarterly
0363-1907 Journal of Psychiatric Education
0363-1915 CableFile
0363-1923 Illinois Classical Studies
0363-194X Pennsylvania Illustrated†
0363-1990 Journal of Family History†
0363-2024 Urban Anthropology†
0363-2067 Vermont Industrial Development Authority. Annual Report
0363-2083 E M Complaint Directory for Consumers *see* 0732-0485
0363-2091 Eastern Canada Campbook
0363-2148 University of Dayton Intramural Law Review *see* 0162-9174
0363-2164 Laughing Bear
0363-2237 Sea Grant Publications Index†
0363-2245 Sean O'Casey Review†
0363-2318 Appalachian Heritage
0363-2369 Kidney Disease and Nephrology Index†
0363-2377 Allegorica
0363-2393 Chilton's Motor-Age Professional Automotive Service Manual
0363-2407 Executive's Tax Review†
0363-2415 Fisheries
0363-2423 Glendale Law Review
0363-2431 T F News
0363-2504 N A G W S Guide. Softball
0363-2512 North Dakota. Geological Survey. Oil and Gas Production Statistics†
0363-2539 American Bankers Association. Operations and Automation Division. Results of the National Operations & Automation Survey
0363-2547 Audiotapes Reprints Publications†
0363-258X Electronic Warfare *see* 0278-3479
0363-2598 Improving College and University Teaching Yearbook†
0363-2601 Innovative Graduate Programs Directory
0363-2636 Lens Magazine†
0363-2644 Metric Bulletin†
0363-2679 Oklahoma Journal of Forensic Medicine *changed to* Medicolegal-Gram
0363-2695 Tourbook: Idaho, Montana, Wyoming
0363-2717 Historical Abstracts. Part A: Modern History Abstracts, 1450-1914
0363-2725 Historical Abstracts. Part B: Twentieth Century Abstracts, 1914 to the Present
0363-2792 Image *changed to* Image: The Journal of Nursing Scholarship
0363-2822 Access: the Index to Little Magazines microform edition of 0363-065X
0363-2830 Downtown Promotion Reporter
0363-2849 International Trumpet Guild. Journal *changed to* I T G Journal
0363-2857 I T G Newsletter†
0363-2865 Jerusalem Journal of International Relations
0363-2873 Journal of Libertarian Studies
0363-2903 Arete
0363-2911 Art and Cinema *changed to* Art & Cinema
0363-2970 Algae, Bacteria, Bacteriophages, Fungi and Protozoa *changed to* American Type Culture Collection. Catalogue of Recombinant D N A Collections
0363-2989 American Type Culture Collection. Catalogue of Viruses, Rickettsiae, Chlamydiae *changed to* American Type Culture Collection. Catalogue of Cell Lines and Hybridomas
0363-308X Technos†
0363-311X Tibet Society Newsletter *see* 0883-7732
0363-3195 Social Indicators Newsletter *see* 0885-6729
0363-3268 Research in Economic History
0363-3276 Wilson Quarterly
0363-3519 Virginia Museum of Fine Arts Bulletin
0363-3551 Virginia Business Report
0363-3586 Biofeedback & Self Regulation
0363-3624 Nurse Educator
0363-3640 Journal of Library & Information Science

1548 ISSN INDEX

0363-3659	Maledicta: the International Journal of Verbal Aggression
0363-3705	Tequesta
0363-373X	Better Schools (Chicago) see 0194-2468
0363-3764	Bus Ride: Bus Industry Directory
0363-3780	En Passant Poetry Quarterly see 0271-5023
0363-3799	Sensory Processes†
0363-3810	Union of American Hebrew Congregations. State of Our Union
0363-3918	International Review of Physiology†
0363-4132	University of Texas, Austin. Bureau of Economic Geology. Guidebook
0363-4140	Astrology Annual Reference Book changed to Astrology Reference Book
0363-4183	California. Department of Housing and Community Development. Annual Report†
0363-4205	Journal of New Jersey Poets
0363-4396	C C H Tax Planning Review
0363-440X	Carolinas Genealogical Society. Bulletin
0363-4426	Multinational Marketing & Employment Directory
0363-4507	Iowa Comprehensive State Plan for Drug Abuse Prevention: Annual Performance Report changed to Iowa Comprehensive State Plan for Substance Abuse (Year)
0363-4523	Communication Education
0363-454X	Brass Research Series
0363-4558	Edward H. Tarr Series
0363-4566	Texas School Directory
0363-4574	Cornfield Review
0363-4590	Seeker (Pittsburg)
0363-4639	Hemming's Vintage Auto Almanac
0363-4655	Pharmacopeial Forum
0363-468X	Journal of Studies on Alcohol. Supplement
0363-471X	A S A Refresher Courses in Anesthesiology
0363-4744	Housing Market Report
0363-4779	T.U.B.A. Newsletter see 0363-4787
0363-4787	T.U.B.A. Journal
0363-4795	World Military and Social Expenditures
0363-4817	Pacific Area Destination Handbook changed to Pacific Destinations Handbook
0363-4833	Western School Law Digest†
0363-4841	Encomia
0363-4922	Security Letter
0363-4965	N A S B O Newsletter†
0363-5023	Journal of Hand Surgery
0363-504X	Modern Liturgy
0363-5058	In Common
0363-5104	Primary Cardiology
0363-5120	Fast Service see 0744-0405
0363-5155	Inventory of Population Projects in Developing Countries Around the World
0363-5171	Great Lakes Fisherman
0363-5198	Kentucky Directory of Selected Industrial Services
0363-5236	Bye Cadmos
0363-5244	Pro Musica Magazine†
0363-5252	Davison's Salesman's Book
0363-5260	American National Metric Council. Annual Report†
0363-5341	Minnesota. Division of Fish and Wildlife, Environment Section. Special Publication†
0363-535X	American Executive Travel Companion†
0363-5376	Alaska. Office of Ombudsman. Report of the Ombudsman
0363-5406	Window and Wall Decorating Ideas see 0277-836X
0363-5414	Dikta
0363-5422	Federal Budget: Focus and Perspective changed to Federal Budget (Year)
0363-5430	Foreign Exchange Rates and Restrictions†
0363-5465	American Journal of Sports Medicine
0363-552X	Fishing in the Mid-Atlantic changed to Fishing in New Jersey
0363-5538	Bob Zwirz' Fishing Annual changed to Fishing and Boating Illustrated
0363-5570	Harvard Ukrainian Studies
0363-566X	American Business
0363-5694	American Society for Church Architecture. Journal†
0363-5708	International Trombone Association Series
0363-5732	Abstract Journal in Earthquake Engineering
0363-5767	Casting & Jewelry Craft†
0363-5775	Los Angeles County Department of Regional Planning. Quarterly Bulletin†
0363-5783	Gavel
0363-5872	Recent Advances in Studies on Cardiac Structure and Metabolism see 0270-4056
0363-5880	House & Garden Guide to American Tradition†
0363-5910	Gay Nineties see 0147-6165
0363-5937	National/International Sculpture Conference. Proceedings
0363-6003	Solar Engineering see 0148-382X
0363-6100	American Journal of Physiology: Endocrinology, Metabolism and Gastrointestinal Physiology see 0193-1849
0363-6100	American Journal of Physiology: Endocrinology, Metabolism and Gastrointestinal Physiology see 0193-1857
0363-6119	American Journal of Physiology: Regulatory, Integrative and Comparative Physiology
0363-6127	American Journal of Physiology: Renal, Fluid and Electrolyte Physiology
0363-6135	American Journal of Physiology: Heart and Circulatory Physiology
0363-6143	American Journal of Physiology: Cell Physiology
0363-6275	Braddock's Federal-State-Local Government Directory
0363-6291	Change in Higher Education see 0009-1383
0363-6380	Invention Management changed to Technology Management World
0363-6399	Data Communications
0363-6437	Paperworker
0363-6445	Systematic Botany
0363-647X	Annals of Phenomenological Sociology changed to Phenomenology and the Human Sciences
0363-6488	Philadelphia Photo Review changed to Photo Review
0363-650X	Connecticut. Advisory Council on Vocational and Career Education. Vocational Education Evaluation Report
0363-6526	Current Concepts in Gastroenterology
0363-6542	1869 Times
0363-6550	Midwest Studies in Philosophy
0363-6569	Pastoral Music
0363-6690	Western Wildlands
0363-6712	Sea Boating Almanac. Southern California, Arizona, Baja see 0193-3507
0363-6720	Fact Book on Higher Education changed to Fact Book for Higher Education
0363-6771	General Dentistry
0363-678X	Commercial News for the Foreign Service changed to Commercial News U S A
0363-6798	Foreign Trade Reports. Bunker Fuels
0363-6828	U.S. Geological Survey. Board on Geographic Names. Decisions of Geographic Names in the United States
0363-6836	Current Population Reports: Population Characteristics
0363-6895	Catholic Periodical Index see 0008-8285
0363-6941	J E G P. Journal of English and Germanic Philology
0363-6968	New Life
0363-700X	Manufacturing Engineering. Engineering Transactions changed to North American Manufacturing Research Conference. Proceedings
0363-7107	Harvard Library Notes see 0017-8136
0363-7123	International Organisations in World Politics Yearbook†
0363-7158	Tennessee Public Library Statistics
0363-7166	Federal Programs, State of Arizona†
0363-7190	Empire State Report see 0747-0711
0363-7204	World Military Expenditures changed to World Military Expenditures and Arms Transfers
0363-7220	Geophysics, Astronomy, and Space changed to U S S R Report: Space
0363-7239	U.S. Congress. Congressional Record
0363-7360	Osteopathic Medicine†
0363-7417	Weekly Government Abstracts. Urban Technology see 0163-1535
0363-745X	C U Directory
0363-7476	C C H Compliance Guide for Plan Administrators changed to Compliance Guide for Plan Administrators
0363-7492	History News (Nashville)
0363-7530	Texas State Directory
0363-7565	Monumenta Archaeologica (Los Angeles)
0363-7700	Sea Boating Almanac. Northern California and Nevada see 0193-3515
0363-7719	American Journal of Health Planning
0363-7751	Communication Monographs
0363-7778	Media Review Digest
0363-7816	San Francisco Chronicle. Newspaper Index see 0195-6396
0363-7824	Houston Post. Newspaper Index changed to Index to the Houston Post
0363-7867	Colorado Lawyer
0363-7891	Soviet Physics - Collection
0363-7905	Mini-Micro Computer Report
0363-7972	Doll Castle News
0363-7980	Central School Law Digest†
0363-7999	Sea Boating Almanac. Pacific Northwest and Alaska see 0276-8771
0363-8006	Recent Developments in Maryland Law†
0363-8057	Gradiva
0363-8065	Abrasive Engineering Society. Abrasive Usage Conference. Proceedings
0363-8111	Public Relations Review
0363-8138	Custom Bike changed to Custom Bike-Choppers
0363-8197	Texas Business see 0164-7628
0363-8200	Diplomatic World Bulletin and Delegates World Bulletin
0363-8219	Aerospace Propulsion†
0363-8227	Helicopter News
0363-8235	Computerized Tomography see 0730-4862
0363-826X	Gayellow Pages
0363-8286	Current Housing Reports: Market Absorption of Apartments
0363-8294	Current Construction Reports: Value of New Construction Put in Place
0363-8332	Current Topics in Early Childhood Education
0363-8340	National Property Law Digests
0363-8391	Pacific Northwest Council on Foreign Languages. Proceedings see 0277-0598
0363-8448	Monthly Retail Trade, Sales and Accounts Receivable changed to Current Business Reports: Monthly Retail Trade, Sales and Inventories
0363-8464	U.S. Department of Defense. Index of Specifications and Standards
0363-8472	Music and Musicians: Large Print Scores and Books Catalog for the Blind and Physically Handicapped changed to Music & Musicians: Large-Print Scores and Books Catalog (Large Print Edition)
0363-8480	Recent Advances in Tobacco Science
0363-8529	Soviet Microelectronics
0363-8537	Current Construction Reports: New One Family Homes Sold and for Sale
0363-8553	Current Business Reports: Monthly Wholesale Trade: Sales and Inventories
0363-8561	U.S. Crop Reporting Board. Crop Production
0363-8588	Uniformed Services Almanac. National Guard Edition see 0363-8618
0363-860X	Reserve Forces Almanac
0363-8618	National Guard Almanac
0363-8642	Cements Research Progress
0363-8715	Journal of Computer Assisted Tomography
0363-8723	Countryside (Waterloo) see 8750-7595
0363-874X	Educational Directory of Mississippi Schools see 0092-7899
0363-8774	Rhode Island State Council on the Arts. Newsnotes
0363-8782	Texas Speech Communication Journal
0363-8790	Current Construction Reports: Housing Units Authorized by Building Permits and Public Contracts changed to Current Construction Reports: Housing Units Authorized by Building Permits
0363-8812	Federal Design Matters†
0363-8820	Energy Reporter
0363-8855	Journal of Clinical Engineering
0363-8898	Fishing in Maryland and Virginia see 0164-0941
0363-891X	Psychohistory Review
0363-8928	International Symposium on Fault-Tolerant Computing. Proceedings see 0731-3071
0363-8960	Old Time Songs and Poems (Seabrook)†
0363-8987	Financial Studies of the Small Business
0363-9029	Cassette Books
0363-9037	Maledicta Press Publications
0363-9045	Drug Development and Industrial Pharmacy
0363-9061	International Journal for Numerical and Analytical Methods in Geomechanics
0363-907X	International Journal of Energy Research
0363-910X	B A I Index of Bank Performance†
0363-9169	Germanic Genealogist
0363-9185	Help (Washington)
0363-9207	Ohio. Commission on Aging. Annual Report changed to Ohio. Department of Aging. Annual Report
0363-9282	N A G W S Guide. Gymnastics
0363-9290	Republican Almanac
0363-9347	International League for Human Rights. Annual Report
0363-9401	S.C.A., State & County Administrator†
0363-9428	American Journal of Small Business
0363-9444	Impact: Wine and Spirits Newsletter changed to Impact (New York)
0363-9452	Grand Jury Report†
0363-9460	Confrontation-Change Review
0363-9479	C L S I Newsletter changed to C L S I Newsletter of Library Automation
0363-9487	T V Season†
0363-9509	Community College Frontiers†
0363-9525	37 Design & Environment Projects†
0363-9568	Nursing Administration Quarterly
0363-972X	Directory of Dance Companies
0363-9762	Clinical Nuclear Medicine
0363-9797	Human Factors Society. Proceedings of the Annual Meeting see 0163-5182
0363-9819	U.S. Environmental Protection Agency. Radiological Quality of the Environment in the United States†
0363-9835	New York (State). Department of Social Services. Annual Report
0363-9843	New York (State). Board of Social Welfare. Annual Report see 0363-9835
0363-9991	Interstate
0364-0000	Cutting Edge†
0364-0078	Country Style
0364-0086	Tourbook: Mid-Atlantic
0364-0094	A J S Review
0364-0116	E D I S†
0364-0175	Smithsonian Institution Research Reports
0364-0205	Monthly Petroleum Statistics Report†
0364-0213	Cognitive Science

0364-023X Flea Market Trader
0364-0302 Libertarian Review†
0364-0337 Missouri. Disaster Operations Office. Newsletter *see* 0197-6672
0364-0396 U.S. National Center for Health Statistics. Monthly Vital Statistics Report
0364-040X U.S. Social Security Administration. Monthly Benefit Statistics
0364-0426 Advisor, Navy Civilian Manpower Management†
0364-0531 N I A A A Information and Feature Service†
0364-071X Colt American Handgunning Annual
0364-0728 Arkansas Vital Statistics
0364-0736 Farmer Cooperatives
0364-0752 Financial Stock Guide Service. Directory of Active Stocks
0364-0760 Charities U S A
0364-0779 Institute for Socioeconomic Studies. Journal
0364-0868 Biweekly Cryogenics Current Awareness Service†
0364-0930 U.S. Department of Housing and Urban Development. Office of International Affairs. Foreign Publications Accessions List†
0364-0981 U.S. Coast Guard Marine Safety Council. Proceedings
0364-099X Grain Market News *changed to* Grain and Feed Market News
0364-1066 Correspondent
0364-1074 E I S: Key to Environmental Impact Statements *changed to* E I S: Digests of Environmental Impact Statements
0364-1082 Group & Organization Studies
0364-1112 Stress and Anxiety
0364-118X E L C†
0364-1198 Female Patient
0364-1228 Current Index to Statistics
0364-1236 Library Resources for the Blind and Physically Handicapped (Large Print Edition)
0364-1287 Army Lawyer
0364-1414 U.S. Federal Supply Service. Index of Federal Specifications and Standards
0364-1449 Handbook on International Study for U.S. Nationals. Vol. 1: Study in Europe†
0364-152X Environmental Management (New York)
0364-1538 Stereopus
0364-1546 Dirt Bike
0364-1554 New Baby Talk *changed to* Baby Talk Magazine
0364-1597 A L A Yearbook
0364-1678 Federal Government†
0364-1708 Glyph
0364-1724 Law Enforcement News
0364-1732 Simplicity Home Catalog *changed to* Simplicity Sewing for Today
0364-1988 Journal of Marine Science *see* 0148-9836
0364-2003 Fusion Energy Foundation Newsletter *see* 0148-0537
0364-2011 E T A Interchange†
0364-202X U.S. Crop Reporting Board. Cattle on Feed
0364-2046 Feed Market News *changed to* Livestock, Meat and Wool Market News
0364-2097 Sojourners
0364-2151 Environment Midwest†
0364-216X Aesthetic Plastic Surgery
0364-2178 Occasional Bulletin of Missionary Research *see* 0272-6122
0364-2194 Barbeque Planet†
0364-2216 Journal of the Graduate Music Students at the Ohio State University
0364-2232 Voice for the Defense
0364-2267 U.S. Securities and Exchange Commission. Official Summary of Security Transactions and Holdings
0364-2313 World Journal of Surgery
0364-2321 Soviet Physics - Lebedev Institute Reports
0364-2348 Skeletal Radiology
0364-2356 Gastrointestinal Radiology
0364-2410 M E L A Notes
0364-2429 Money Digest†
0364-2437 Afro-Americans in New York Life and History
0364-2569 Monographs in Pharmacology and Physiology†
0364-2577 Guidelines to Metabolic Therapy†
0364-2615 Tennessee Valley Perspective†
0364-264X Children's Book International. Proceedings and Book Catalog *see* 0163-1756
0364-2801 P A A B S Symposium Series *changed to* Pan American Association of Biochemical Societies Symposium
0364-2968 Journal of Germanic Philology *see* 0363-6941
0364-2976 Journal of the Hellenic Diaspora
0364-3093 Offender Rehabilitation *see* 0195-6116
0364-3107 Administration in Social Work
0364-3115 Grantsmanship Center News†
0364-3190 Neurochemical Research
0364-3263 Combat Fleets of the World
0364-3301 Corrosion Prevention/Inhibition Digest
0364-3344 Box 749
0364-3352 Current Bibliographic Survey of National Defense *see* 0198-9006
0364-3379 Artists of the Rockies and the Golden West *see* 0883-8992
0364-3409 T P G A Journal
0364-345X Passenger Transport
0364-3484 Mass Transit
0364-3549 English Literature in Transition (1880-1920)
0364-359X Dragonfly
0364-3670 International CODEN Directory
0364-3735 Private Higher Education *see* 0734-6735
0364-3824 Taste
0364-3875 Official Airline Guide. World Wide Edition
0364-3921 Nevada Public Affairs Report *see* 0196-7355
0364-3999 Micropublishing of Current Periodicals *see* 0743-9636
0364-4006 A L A Bulletin *see* 0002-9769
0364-4014 Spirit That Moves Us
0364-4022 Poesie-U.S.A.
0364-4529 Ninth District Quarterly *see* 0271-5287
0364-4626 Soviet Journal of Coordination Chemistry
0364-474X Electric Perspectives
0364-4782 Journal of Human Services Abstracts
0364-491X U.S. Bureau of Labor Statistics. Employment Situation
0364-4928 Weekly Government Abstracts. Materials Sciences *changed to* Abstract Newsletter: Materials Sciences
0364-4936 Weekly Government Abstracts. Environmental Pollution and Control *changed to* Abstract Newsletter: Environmental Pollution & Control
0364-4944 Weekly Government Abstracts. Communication *changed to* Abstract Newsletter: Communication
0364-4952 Weekly Government Abstracts. Biomedical Technology and Engineering *see* 0163-1497
0364-4979 Weekly Government Abstracts. Natural Resources *see* 0163-1438
0364-5134 Annals of Neurology
0364-5177 Live Steam
0364-5193 Bioethics Digest
0364-5215 U S B E News
0364-5274 Energy Daily
0364-5479 Informer (Los Angeles)
0364-5487 Peters Notes†
0364-5517 Seybold Report *see* 0736-7260
0364-5533 Infosystems
0364-5541 Journal of Mental Imagery
0364-555X Russian-English Translators Exchange†
0364-5568 Professional Translator†
0364-5711 Standard & Poor's International Stock Report†
0364-586X Downtown Mall Annual & Urban Design Report†
0364-5916 CALPHAD
0364-5924 Hayes Historical Journal *changed to* Hayes Historical Journal: A Journal of the Gilded Age
0364-6017 Geological Survey Circular
0364-6408 Library Acquisitions: Practice and Theory
0364-6424 Weekly Government Abstracts. Ocean Technology and Engineering *changed to* Abstract Newsletter: Ocean Technology & Engineering
0364-6432 Weekly Government Abstracts. Medicine and Biology *changed to* Abstract Newsletter: Medicine & Biology
0364-6440 Weekly Government Abstracts. N A S A Earth Resources Survey Program *changed to* Abstract Newsletter: N A S A Earth Resources Survey Program
0364-6459 Weekly Government Abstracts. Problem-Solving Information for State and Local Governments *changed to* Abstract Newsletter: Problem-Solving Information for State and Local Governments
0364-6467 Weekly Government Abstracts. Library and Information Sciences *changed to* Abstract Newsletter: Library & Information Sciences
0364-6475 N E I S S News *changed to* N E I S S Data Highlights
0364-6483 Weekly Government Abstracts. Industrial and Mechanical Engineering *changed to* Abstract Newsletter: Industrial & Mechanical Engineering
0364-6491 Weekly Government Abstracts. Government Inventions for Licensing *changed to* Abstract Newsletter: Government Inventions for Licensing
0364-6505 Edebiyat
0364-6521 Telesis *see* 0277-6863
0364-6610 Physician Distribution and Medical Licensure in the U S *see* 0731-0315
0364-6645 Harvard Business School. Baker Library. Working Papers in Baker Library
0364-6653 Transportation Topics for Consumers *changed to* Transportation Consumer
0364-6696 U.S. Office of the Secretary of the Treasury. Treasury Papers†
0364-6718 S E C News Digest
0364-6742 International Notices to Airmen
0364-6807 U.S. Navy Medicine
0364-6866 Nuclear Reactors Built, Being Built, or Planned in the United States
0364-698X American Wine Society Journal
0364-6998 Solar Energy Update
0364-7064 U.S. National Cartographic Information Center. Newsletter
0364-7072 U.S. National Earthquake Information Service. Preliminary Determination of Epicenters, Monthly Listing
0364-7129 U.S. Railroad Retirement Board. Monthly Benefit Statistics
0364-7145 Maintenance†
0364-7161 South Central Camping *changed to* South Central Campbook
0364-717X Minnesota. Department of Employment Services. Annual Report *changed to* Minnesota. Department of Economic Security. Annual Report
0364-720X Lake Superior Review†
0364-7234 World Economic Conditions in Relation to Agricultural Trade†
0364-7358 Manpower Planning *see* 0733-0332
0364-7390 Evaluation Studies Review Annual
0364-7471 American Druggist Blue Book
0364-7501 Musical Mainstream (Large Print Edition)
0364-7609 Primavera (Chicago)
0364-7625 Access Reports *changed to* Access Reports/Freedom of Information
0364-765X Mathematics of Operations Research
0364-7668 Rising Tide
0364-7692 Harvard University Gazette
0364-7714 Water Supply and Management†
0364-7722 Progress in Neuro-Psychopharmacology *see* 0278-5846
0364-7811 Directory of Geoscience Departments, United States and Canada
0364-796X Weekly Government Abstracts. Computers, Control and Information Theory *changed to* Abstract Newsletter: Computers, Control & Information Theory
0364-7978 Weekly Government Abstracts. Business and Economics *changed to* Abstract Newsletter: Business & Economics
0364-7986 Weekly Government Abstracts. Administration *changed to* Abstract Newsletter: Administration and Management
0364-7994 Abstract Newsletter: Agriculture & Food
0364-8117 Soviet Aeronautics - Iz. V U Z
0364-8125 A T L A Law Reporter
0364-815X Marquee (Norwalk)
0364-8184 New Horizon-Polish American Review
0364-8265 U.S. General Accounting Office. Monthly List of GAO Reports
0364-8303 International and Comparative Public Policy†
0364-8389 R I F Newsletter
0364-8591 Old Testament Abstracts
0364-8664 Kentucky Romance Quarterly *changed to* Romance Quarterly
0364-8877 Financial Aids for Higher Education
0364-8893 Associated Equipment Distributors. Rental Compilation *see* 0164-0593
0364-8958 International Fire Chief *changed to* International Fire Chief
0364-8966 Directory of U.S. and Canadian Marketing Surveys and Services†
0364-9008 Defense Business *changed to* Defense & Economy World Report
0364-9024 Journal of Graph Theory
0364-9059 I E E E Journal of Oceanic Engineering
0364-9156 Directors & Boards
0364-9210 Ethnodisc Journal of Recorded Sound
0364-9229 Astronomy Quarterly
0364-9237 Speedhorse
0364-9253 Estates, Gifts and Trusts Journal *changed to* Tax Management Estates, Gifts and Trusts Journal
0364-930X Alfa Owner
0364-9342 Mini-Micro Systems
0364-9369 E E-Electrical Equipment *changed to* E E-Electronic/Electrical Product News
0364-9407 Th-Bao Ga *changed to* Vietnam Quarterly
0364-9474 Friends of Wine
0364-9490 Delaware Journal of Corporate Law
0364-9539 National Distribution Directory of Local Cartage-Short Haul Carriers Warehousing *changed to* Warehousing/Distribution Directory
0364-9733 Saturday Evening Post microform edition of 0048-9239
0364-9857 Research Quarterly for Exercise and Sport microform edition of 0270-1367
0364-9865 American Artist microform edition of 0002-7375
0364-9873 American Anthropologist microform edition of 0002-7294
0364-989X America microform edition of 0002-7049
0364-9911 Adult Education Quarterly microform edition of
0364-9962 A S H R A E Journal microform edition of 0001-2491
0365-0138 Astronomy and Astrophysics Supplement Series
0365-0340 Archiv fuer Acker- und Pflanzenbau und Bodenkunde
0365-0375 Asociacion Quimica Argentina. Anales
0365-0502 Universita degli Studi di Bari. Facolta di Agraria. Annali

1550 ISSN INDEX

0365-0596 Anais Brasileiros de Dermatologia
0365-0723 Arquivos Brasileiros de Medicina
0365-0979 Arquivos de Biologia e Tecnologia
0365-1029 Annales Universitatis Mariae Curie-Sklodowska. Sectio A. Mathematica
0365-1118 Annales Universitatis Mariae Curie-Sklodowska. Sectio E. Agricultura
0365-1789 Advanced Energy Conversion *see* 0196-8904
0365-1800 Estacion Experimental de Aula Dei. Anales
0365-2017 Annales de l'Est
0365-2181 Universidade de Sao Paulo. Faculdade de Farmacia. Anais *see* 0581-6866
0365-2181 Universidade de Sao Paulo. Faculdade de Farmacia. Anais *changed to* Universidade de Sao Paulo. Revista de Farmacia e Bioquimica
0365-2459 Arkiv for Det Fysiske Seminar i Trondheim
0365-2726 Agronomico
0365-2807 Chile. Instituto de Investigaciones Agropecuarias. Agricultura Tecnica
0365-3927 Alluminio
0365-4184 Acta Pathologica et Microbiologica Scandinavica. Section A: Pathology *see* 0108-0164
0365-4389 Museo Civico di Storia Naturale "Giacomo Doria," Genoa. Annali
0365-4478 Acta Medica Medianae
0365-4850 Acta Naturalia Islandica
0365-4877 Analusis
0365-5237 Acta Oto-Laryngologica. Supplement
0365-5377 Ateneo Parmense. Collana di Monografie
0365-5563 Acta Pathologica et Microbiologica Scandinavica *see* 0108-0180
0365-5571 Acta Pathologica et Microbiologica Scandinavica. Section B: Microbiology and Immunology *see* 0108-0180
0365-5571 Acta Pathologica et Microbiologica Scadinavica. Section B: Microbiology and Immmunology *see* 0108-0202
0365-5814 Institut Phytopathologique Benaki. Annales
0365-6233 Archiv der Pharmazie
0365-6470 Saechsische Akademie der Wissenschaften, Leipzig. Mathematisch-Naturwissenschaftliche Klasse. Abhandlungen
0365-6527 Societe Belge de Medecine Tropicale. Annales
0365-723X Commonwealth Scientific and Industrial Research Organization. Division of Soils. Technical Papers
0365-8066 Acta Universitatis de Attila Jozsef Nominatae. Acta Mineralogica - Petrographica
0365-8406 Archiv fuer Zuechtungsforschung
0365-8414 Atomwirtschaft - Atomtechnik
0365-9356 British Columbia. Ministry of Energy, Mines and Petroleum Resources. Annual Report
0365-9429 Biochemical Reviews
0365-9445 Bromatologia i Chemia Toksykologiczna
0365-9542 Deutsche Keramische Gesellschaft. Berichte *see* 0173-9913
0365-9615 Byulleten' Eksperimental'noi Biologii i Meditsiny
0365-9623 Cancer Research Campaign. Annual Report
0365-9631 Deutsche Botanische Gesellschaft. Berichte
0365-9844 Naturhistorische Gesellschaft Hannover. Berichte
0365-9860 Okayama University. Berichte des Ohara Instituts fuer Landwirtschaftliche Biologie.
0366-0281 Instituto de Tecnologia de Alimentos. Boletin
0366-077X British Journal of Dermatology. Supplement
0366-1326 Societe Linneenne de Lyon. Bulletin Mensuel
0366-1644 Sociedad Chilena de Quimica. Boletin
0366-2284 Bios
0366-2381 Boletin de Patologia Vegetal y Entomologia Agricola *see* 0211-4682
0366-2403 Bollettino di Zoologia Agraria e di Bachicoltura
0366-3221 Denmark. Statens Mejerifrosoeg. Beretning
0366-3345 Institut Textile de France. Bulletin Scientifique
0366-3469 Societe Neuchateloise des Sciences Naturelles. Bulletin
0366-3612 Kongelige Danske Videnskabernes Selskab. Biologiske Skrifter
0366-4198 Great Britain. Institute of Geological Sciences. Bulletin of the Geological Survey of Great Britain†
0366-5232 Caldasia
0366-5526 Chimika Chronika. General Edition
0366-5690 C E R N-H E R A Reports
0366-5887 Colloquium Mosbach
0366-600X Cuadernos de Geologia
0366-6123 Chagyo Gijutsu Kentyu†
0366-6778 Clinica
0366-6824 Collective Phenomena
0366-6913 Ceramica
0366-693X Chimika Chronika. New Series
0366-7022 Chemistry Letters
0366-7154 Chemie Mikrobiologie Technologie der Lebensmittel
0366-757X CODATA Bulletin
0366-7588 Coelum†
0366-8258 Academie Internationale d'Histoire des Sciences. Collection des Travaux
0366-8681 Academie Bulgare des Sciences. Comptes Rendus
0366-8819 Electronic Engineering
0366-9092 Electrotechnical Laboratory. Bulletin
0366-9424 Deutsche Molkerei-Zeitung
0367-0244 Ecology of Food and Nutrition
0367-0449 Estudios Geologicos
0367-0643 Eksperimentalna Medicina i Morfologija
0367-0708 Elektrotechnika
0367-1119 Energy Digest
0367-150X Environmental Pollution Management†
0367-1887 Freshwater Biological Association. Scientific Publications
0367-2174 Forstlige Forsoegsvaesen i Danmark
0367-2387 Meijeritieteellinen Aikakauskirja
0367-2409 Fiziko-Khimicheskaya Mekhanika i Liofilnost' Dispersnykh Sistem
0367-2476 Folia Limnologica Scandinavica
0367-2530 Flora
0367-2921 Fizika Plazmy
0367-3014 Farmatsiya
0367-326X Fitoterapia
0367-3812 Gaceta Veterinaria *see* 0326-4629
0367-4061 Gunma Journal of Liberal Arts and Sciences
0367-4088 Gidromekhanika
0367-4223 Gesunde Pflanzen
0367-4444 Glasnik Hemicara i Tehnologa Bosne i Hercegovine
0367-4983 Prirodnjacki Muzej u Beogradu. Glasnik. Serija A: Minerologija, Geologija, Paleontologija
0367-5807 Korean Journal of Animal Sciences
0367-5939 Hokkaido University of Education. Journal. Section 2 A. Mathematics, Physics, Chemistry and Engineering
0367-598X Hemijska Industrija
0367-6439 Hirosaki University. Faculty of Science. Science Reports
0367-6447 Houtim
0367-6722 Indian Journal of Animal Research
0367-7257 Indian Chemical Manufacturer
0367-7370 Iwate University. Faculty of Education. Annual Report
0367-777X Informacion de Quimica Analitica Pura y Aplicada a la Industria *see* 0210-4334
0367-7850 Institution of Gas Engineers. Proceedings
0367-8229 Indian Journal of Agricultural Chemistry
0367-8245 Indian Journal of Agricultural Research
0367-8377 International Journal of Peptide and Protein Research
0367-8393 Indian Journal of Radio & Space Physics
0367-9012 Indian Journal of Medical Research. Supplement
0367-939X Industrielle Obst- und Gemueseverwertung
0367-973X Indian Phytopathology
0368-0762 Irish Veterinary Journal
0368-0770 International Association of Theoretical and Applied Limnology. Proceedings
0368-1327 Agricultural Society of Trinidad & Tobago. Journal†
0368-1416 Jornal Brasileiro de Ginecologia
0368-2048 Journal of Electron Spectroscopy and Related Phenomena
0368-2145 Hokkaido University. Faculty of Science. Journal. Series 5: Botany
0368-2188 Hokkaido University. Faculty of Science. Journal. Series 6: Zoology
0368-2196 University of Tokyo. Faculty of Science. Journal. Section 3: Botany
0368-220X University of Tokyo. Faculty of Science. Journal. Section 4: Zoology
0368-2307 Gesellschaft fuer Naturkunde in Wuerttemberg. Jahreshefte
0368-2315 Journal de Gynecologie Obstetrique et Biologie de la Reproduction
0368-2323 Geochemical Society of India. Journal
0368-2595 Institution of Nuclear Engineers. Journal *see* 0262-5091
0368-265X Japan Pesticide Information
0368-2781 Japanese Journal of Antibiotics
0368-3141 Japan Congress on Materials Research. Proceedings
0368-4636 Textile Association (India). Journal
0368-492X Kybernetes
0368-5039 Kyoto University. Institute of Atomic Energy. Bulletin
0368-5063 Kagoshima Daigaku Igaku Zasshi
0368-5365 Fermentation Research Institute. Report
0368-556X Khimicheskaya Tekhnologiya
0368-5829 Kyorin Igakkai Zasshi
0368-5969 Kobe Kaiyo Kishodai Iho
0368-6302 Kongelige Norske Videnskabers Selskab
0368-6310 Kongelige Norske Videnskabers Selskab. Skrifter
0368-7066 Kurortologija i Fizioterapija
0368-7155 Kvantovaya Elektronika
0368-7171 Kongelige Veterinaer- og Landbohoejskole. Aarskrift†
0368-7201 Kongelige Danske Videnskabernes Selskab. Oversigt over Selskabets Virksomhed. Annual Report
0368-7368 Lab Instrumenten
0368-7708 Long Ashton Research Station. Report
0368-8720 Universidad Nacional Autonoma de Mexico. Instituto de Biologia. Anales: Serie Zoologia
0368-945X Metallurgia and Metal Forming *changed to* Metallurgia: the Journal of Metals Technology, Metal Forming and Thermal Processing
0368-9689 Kyoto University. Faculty of Science. Memoirs. Series of Physics, Astrophysics, Geophysics and Chemistry
0368-9697 International Symposium on Crop Protection. Proceedings
0369-0369 Osaka University. Institute of Scientific and Industrial Research. Memoirs
0369-0512 Kyushu Institute of Technology. Memoirs: Engineering
0369-061X Metallurgical Engineer
0369-1233 Monatsschrift fuer Brauerei *changed to* Brauerei-Forum
0369-1527 Medicinski Podmladak
0369-1632 Mine and Quarry
0369-1829 Royal Astronomical Society, England. Memoirs†
0369-1950 Waseda University. School of Science and Engineering. Memoirs
0369-2345 Metallgesellschaft Aktiengesellschaft. Review of the Activities
0369-3228 Nagasaki Igakkai Zasshi
0369-3627 Niigata University. Faculty of Science. Science Reports. Series E: Geology and Mineralogy
0369-4097 Societa Italiana di Fisica. Nuovo Cimento A
0369-4100 Societa Italiana di Fisica. Nuovo Cimento B
0369-4313 Nihon University. Research Institute of Science and Technology. Journal
0369-4577 Chemical Society of Japan. Chemistry and Industrial Chemistry. Journal
0369-5255 Norsk Pelsdyrblad
0369-5387 Nippon Kagaku Zasshi *see* 0369-4577
0369-5611 Nagoya City University. Faculty of Pharmaceutical Science. Annual Report
0369-576X Niigata University. Faculty of Science. Science Reports. Series A: Mathematics
0369-5867 New South Wales. Department of Agriculture. Science Bulletin
0369-6367 Ultragarsas
0369-6464 Nutrition News
0369-7649 Onkologija
0369-7827 Osiris
0369-8203 National Academy of Sciences, India. Proceedings. Section A. Physical Sciences
0369-8211 National Academy of Sciences, India. Proceedings. Section B. Biological Sciences
0369-8599 Institution of Chemists (India). Proceedings
0369-8629 Pchelovodstvo
0369-9420 Pigment and Resin Technology
0369-9560 Photographe
0369-979X Pharmazie Heute
0370-0089 Indian Academy of Sciences. Proceedings (Chemical Science, Earth and Planetary Sciences, Mathematical Sciences)
0370-0097 Indian Academy of Sciences. Proceedings. (Plant Sciences, Animal Sciences)
0370-0291 Poljoprivredna Znanstvena Smotra
0370-0755 Politechnika Wroclawska. Instytut Chemii Nieorganicznej i Metalurgii Pierwiastkow Rzadkich. Prace Naukowe. Studia i Materialy
0370-0798 Politechnika Wroclawska. Instytut Gornictwa. Prace Naukowe. Studia i Materialy
0370-081X Politechnika Wroclawska. Instytut Chemii Organicznej i Fizycznej. Prace Naukowe. Studia i Materialy
0370-0828 Politechnika Wroclawska. Instytut Fizyki. Prace Naukowe. Monografie
0370-0836 Politechnika Wroclawska. Instytut Geotechniki. Prace Naukowe. Konferencje
0370-0844 Politechnika Wroclawska. Instytut Inzynierii Ladowej. Prace Naukowe. Studia i Materialy
0370-0852 Politechnika Wroclawska. Instytut Podstaw Elektrotechniki i Elektrotechnologii. Prace Naukowe. Studia i Materialy
0370-0879 Politechnika Wroclawska. Instytut Technologiii Organicznej i Tworzyw Sztucznych. Prace Naukowe. Studia i Materialy
0370-0887 Politechnika Wroclawska. Instytut Technologii Elektronowej. Prace Naukowe. Konferencje
0370-0917 Politechnika Wroclawska. Instytut Materialoznawstwa i Mechaniki Technicznej. Prace Naukowe. Studia i Materialy
0370-1093 Oregon Academy of Science. Proceedings
0370-1158 Polymers Paint and Colour Journal
0370-1573 Physics Reports
0370-1859 Process Engineering
0370-1972 Physica Status Solidi (B). Basic Research
0370-2030 Agricultural Society of Trinidad & Tobago. Proceedings *see* 0368-1327
0370-226X Petroleum and Petrochemical International *see* 0301-6242

ISSN INDEX 1551

0370-2529 Problems of Control and Information Theory
0370-2731 New Zealand Society of Animal Production. Proceedings
0370-372X Revista Brasileira de Farmacia
0370-4246 University of the Ryukyus. College of Agriculture. Science Bulletin
0370-4475 Revue d'Electroencephalographie et de Neurophysiologie Clinique
0370-4726 Revista de Farmacia e Bioquimica
0370-5048 Revue Generale des Colloides *see* 0021-7689
0370-5331 High-Temperature Materials and Processes
0370-5943 Revista Latinoamericana de Quimica
0370-6559 Royal Society of New Zealand. Bulletin Series
0370-7288 Sociedad Geologica Argentina. Revista *see* 0004-4822
0370-7857 Revista Electrotecnica
0370-7962 Revista Theobroma
0370-8063 Referativnyi Zhurnal. Fotokinotekhnika
0370-8098 Referativnyi Zhurnal. Khimicheskoe, Neftepererabatyvayuschchee i Polimernoe Mashinostroenie
0370-8179 Serbian Archives of General Medicine
0370-8314 Southern African Museums Association. Bulletin
0370-8454 C S I R Annual Report
0370-923X Studia Botanica
0370-9531 Seitai No Kagaku
0370-9612 Physiology and Ecology Japan
0370-9736 Siemens Forschungs- und Entwicklungsberichte
0371-0165 Heidelberger Akademie der Wissenschaften. Mathematisch-Naturwissenschaftliche Klasse. Sitzungsberichte
0371-0580 Textile Machinery Society of Japan. Journal (Japanese Edition).
0371-2222 Studia Pneumologica et Phtiseologica Cechoslovaca
0371-232X Space Research *see* 0273-1177
0371-2672 Niigata University. Faculty of Science. Science Reports. Series D: Biology
0371-2885 Societas Scientiarum Fennica. Aarsbok Vuosikirja
0371-3172 Studi Sassaresi
0371-3385 Shiga Prefectural Junior College. Scientific Reports
0371-375X Towarzystwo Naukowe w Toruniu. Sprawozdania
0371-4098 Suomen Kemistilehti A *see* 0355-1628
0371-4101 Suomen Kemistilehti B *see* 0303-4100
0371-4756 Wroclawskie Towarzystwo Naukowe. Sprawozdania. Seria A
0371-5167 Takeda Research Laboratories. Journal
0371-6813 Tokyo Gakugei University. Bulletin
0371-7208 South-African Journal of Geology
0371-7453 Institution of Mining and Metallurgy. Transactions. Section B: Applied Earth Sciences
0371-750X Indian Ceramic Society. Transactions
0371-7682 Formosan Medical Association. Journal
0371-7844 Institution of Mining and Metallurgy. Transactions. Section A: Mining Industry
0371-9553 Institution of Mining and Metallurgy. Transactions. Section C: Mineral Processing & Extractive Metallurgy
0371-9588 Mining, Geological and Metallurgical Institute of India. Transactions
0372-0187 Newcomen Society for the Study of the History of Engineering and Technology. Transactions
0372-2112 Acta Electronica Sinica
0372-4123 Ukrains'kyi Botanichnyi Zhurnal
0372-5480 Veterinarski Arhiv
0372-5715 V G B Kraftwerkstechnik,
0372-6053 Politekhnichnyi Instytut Kiev. Vestnik. Seriya Mashinostroeniya
0372-6436 Visnyk Akademiyi Nauk Ukrainskoi S.S.R.
0372-7025 Vojenske Zdravotnicke Listy
0372-7181 Waseda University. Science and Engineering Research Laboratory. Bulletin
0372-7610 Technische Hochschule Karl-Marx-Stadt. Wissenschaftliche Zeitschrift
0372-8854 Zeitschrift fuer Geomorphologie
0372-9311 Zhurnal Mikrobiologii, Epidemiologii i Immunobiologii
0372-9400 Akademia Gorniczo-Hutnicza im. Stanislawa Staszica. Instytut Gornictwa Podziemnego. Prace
0372-9427 Akademia Gorniczo-Hutnicza im. Stanislawa Staszica. Zeszyty Naukowe. Geologia. Kwartalnik
0372-9443 Akademia Gorniczo-Hutnicza im. Stanislawa Staszica. Zeszyty Naukowe. Metelurgia i Odlewnictwo. Kwartalnik
0372-9486 Politechnika Krakowska. Zeszyty Naukowe. Mechanika
0372-9494 Politechnika Slaska. Zeszyty Naukowe. Chemia
0372-9508 Politechnika Slaska. Zeszyty Naukowe. Gornictwo
0372-9699 Politechnika Czestochowska. Zeszyty Naukowe. Nauki Techniczne. Hutnictwo
0372-9796 Politechnika Slaska. Zeszyty Naukowe. Energetyka
0372-9893 Zernovoe Khozyaistvo
0373-0204 Zucker- und Suesswaren Wirtschaft
0373-0468 Bonner Geographische Abhandlungen
0373-0514 Bulletin Francais de Pisciculture *changed to* Bulletin Francais de la Peche et de la Pisciculture
0373-0956 Universite Scientifique et Medicale de Grenoble. Institut Fourier. Annales
0373-0999 Revista Mathematica Hispano-Americana
0373-1006 Seppyo
0373-1537 Bedi Kartlisa
0373-1766 Magyar Nemzeti Bibliografia *see* 0133-6894
0373-1766 Magyar Nemzeti Bibliografia *see* 0133-5782
0373-1766 Magyar Nemzeti Bibliografia *see* 0133-6843
0373-1766 Magyar Nemzeti Bibliografia *see* 0231-4592
0373-1944 Travail et Securite
0373-1987 Bibliografia Geologiczna Polski
0373-2029 Archives of Mechanics
0373-2045 International Council for the Exploration of the Sea. Bulletin Statistique
0373-2061 Bulletin Scientifique de Bourgogne
0373-2134 Prirodnjacki Muzej u Beogradu. Glasnik. Serija B: Bioloske Nauke
0373-2266 Ardea
0373-241X Glasgow Naturalist
0373-2525 Saussurea
0373-2568 Pirineos
0373-2630 Revue d'Economie Politique
0373-2746 Tidsskrift for Praktisk Laegegering
0373-2916 Strade
0373-3033 Accademia delle Scienze di Torino. Memorie. Part 1. Classe di Scienze Fisiche, Matematiche e Naturali
0373-3165 Buecherei des Paediaters
0373-3297 Societe Languedocienne de Geographie. Bulletin
0373-353X Vsesoyuznoe Geograficheskoe Obshchestvo. Izvestiya
0373-3629 Annales Hydrographiques
0373-3874 Dansk Naturhistorisk Forening. Videnskabelige Meddelelser
0373-403X Chmelarstvi
0373-4064 Metal Bulletin Monthly
0373-4137 Bollettino di Zoologia
0373-4250 Associated Scientific and Technical Societies of South Africa. Annual Proceedings
0373-4285 Recherche et Architecture†
0373-4331 Betonwerk und Fertigteil-Technik
0373-4447 Library and Information Science
0373-4633 Journal of Navigation
0373-4854 Auroral Observatory. Magnetic Observations
0373-5125 Observatorio Astronomico de Madrid. Anuario
0373-529X Royal Institution of Naval Architects. Supplementary Papers
0373-5346 Railway Gazette International
0373-5354 Tudomanyos Tajekoztatas Elmelete es Gyakorlata
0373-5478 Archives d'Histoire Doctrinale et Litteraire du Moyen Age
0373-5524 Universidade de Sao Paulo. Instituto Oceanografico. Boletim
0373-5796 Spain. Instituto Nacional de Investigaciones Agrarias. Anales. Serie: Economia y Sociologia Agrarias
0373-580X Sociedad Argentina de Botanica. Boletin
0373-5893 Zoological Society, Calcutta. Proceedings
0373-5982 Postepy Astronautyki
0373-6067 Universite de Grenoble. Laboratoire d'Hydrologie et de Pisciculture. Travaux†
0373-6121 Institute of Electronics and Communication Engineers of Japan. Journal
0373-6245 South African Geographical Journal
0373-6369 Bibliografija Jugoslavije. Serija A. Drustvene Nauke
0373-6377 Bibliografija Jugoslavije. Serija C. Umetnost, Sport, Filologija, Knjizevnost i Muzikalije
0373-6385 Kyushu University. Faculty of Science. Memoirs. Series A: Mathematics
0373-6407 Referativnyi Zhurnal. Aviatsionnye i Raketnye Dvigateli
0373-6415 Referativnyi Zhurnal. Gornoe i Neftepromyslovoe Mashinostroenie
0373-6547 Polska Akademia Nauk. Instytut Geografii i Przestrzennego Zagospodarowania. Prace Geograficzne
0373-6687 Journal of Bryology
0373-6873 Societas pro Fauna et Flora Fennica. Memoranda
0373-7101 Spain. Observatorio Astronomico Nacional. Boletin Astronomico
0373-7187 Arbeiten zur Rheinischen Landeskunde
0373-7349 Association Nationale de Lutte Contre les Fleaux Atmospheriques. Rapport de Campagne *see* 0242-4002
0373-7632 Floristisch-Soziologische Arbeitsgemeinschaft. Mitteilungen *see* 0722-494X
0373-7640 Bayerische Botanische Gesellschaft. Berichte
0373-7772 Condizionamento dell'Aria *changed to* Condizionamento dell'Aria, Riscaldamento, Refrigerazione
0373-7837 Institut Hodowli i Aklmatyzacji Roslin. Biuletyn
0373-7896 Geobotanisches Institut ETH, Stiftung Ruebel, Zurich. Berichte
0373-8299 Polskie Towarzystwo Matematyczne. Roczniki. Seria 1: Commentationes Mathematicae. Prace Matematyczne
0373-8493 Mitteilungen aus dem Zoologischen Museum in Berlin
0373-8663 Politechnika Gdanska. Zeszyty Naukowe. Budownictwo Wodne
0373-8671 Politechnika Gdanska. Zeszyty Naukowe. Budownictwo Ladowe
0373-868X Politechnika Gdanska. Zeszyty Naukowe. Budownictwo Okretowe
0373-8809 Revue Pratique de Controle Industriel
0373-8981 Staatliches Museum fuer Tierkunde in Dresden. Entomologische Abhandlungen
0373-9066 Museo Argentino de Ciencias Naturales "Bernardino Rivadavia." Instituto Nacional de Investigacion de las Ciencias Naturales. Revista. Zoologia
0373-9465 Folia Entomologica Hungarica
0373-9627 Zitteliana
0374-0412 Universidade Federal de Pernambuco. Departamento de Oceanografia. Centro de Tecnologia. Trabalhos Oceanograficos
0374-0463 Acta Linguistica Hafniensia
0374-0676 Information Bulletin on Variable Stars
0374-1257 Mitteilungen aus dem Max-Planck-Institut fuer Stroemungsforschung
0374-1338 Reumatizam
0374-1842 Acta Geodaetica, Geophysica et Montanistica Hungarica
0374-2105 Ophthalmologia
0374-2261 Le Trefile
0374-2385 Rechentechnik-Datenverarbeitung. Beiheft *see* 0232-6833
0374-2466 Astronomical Herald
0374-2490 Aviation Review *changed to* Aerospace & Defence Review
0374-2636 Bauelemente der Elektrotechnik *see* 0172-6153
0374-2806 Comments on Plasma Physics and Controlled Fusion
0374-289X Data Report *changed to* Siemens-Magazin COM
0374-3098 Elektron-International
0374-3101 Electro-Revue
0374-3225 Fluid: Apparecchiature Idrauliche e Pneumatiche
0374-3268 Geos
0374-3535 Journal of Elasticity
0374-356X Society of Environmental Engineers. Journal
0374-3659 Kent Technical Review†
0374-387X Universita degli Studi di Roma. Istituto di Automatica. Notiziario†
0374-3896 Naukovedenie i Informatika
0374-4256 Revue Polytechnique
0374-4329 Nagoya University. Faculty of Engineering. Automatic Control Laboratory. Research Reports
0374-4353 Research Disclosure
0374-4361 Radio & Electronics Constructor†
0374-4493 Systemes Logiques†
0374-4639 Tokyo Astronomical Observatory. Report
0374-4663 Takenaka Gijutsu Kenkyu Hokoku
0374-4760 Akademiya Navuk Belarusskai S.S.R. Vesti. Seryya Fizika-Energetycznych Havuk
0374-4779 Vrashchenie i Prilivnye Deformatsii Zemli†
0374-4795 Works Management
0374-4809 X-Ray Focus†
0374-4965 Acta Anaesthesiologica Italia
0374-5295 Aichi Cancer Center Research Institute. Annual Report
0374-5791 Istituto Sperimentale per l'Enologia Asti. Annali
0374-5880 Anales de la Universidad Hispalense. Serie: Ciencias
0374-6003 Ecole Nationale Superieure d'Agronomie et des Industries Alimentaires. Bulletin
0374-6038 Societe Royale Belge d'Entomologie. Bulletin et Annales
0374-6054 Naturhistorische Gesellschaft Hannover. Beihefte zu den Berichten
0374-6224 Instituto Bacteriologico de Chile. Boletin *changed to* Instituto de Salud Publica de Chile. Boletin
0374-6232 Institut Royal de Sciences Naturelles de Belgique. Bulletin. Serie Entomologie
0374-6240 Florida Genealogical Society Journal
0374-6291 Institut Royal des Sciences Naturelles de Belgique. Bulletin. Serie Sciences de la Terre
0374-633X British Journal of Mental Subnormality
0374-6569 Bionika
0374-6607 Botanical Society of Edinburgh Transactions
0374-6658 Brazil. Departamento Nacional de Obras Contra as Secas. Boletim Tecnico
0374-6852 Ceskoslovenska Gynekologie
0374-7115 Central Plantation Crops Research Institute. Annual Report
0374-7344 Danish Review of Game Biology
0374-7646 Freshwater Biological Association. Annual Report
0374-776X Family Physician
0374-7999 Gayana: Miscelanea
0374-8014 Health Bulletin
0374-8030 Havsfiskelaboratoriet. Meddelande

1552 ISSN INDEX

0374-8189 Instituto de Economia y Producciones Ganaderas del Ebro. Comunicaciones
0374-826X Indian Journal of Heredity
0374-8278 Inmersion y Ciencia†
0374-8731 Kanagawa Horticultural Experiment Station. Bulletin
0374-8774 Kerala Journal of Veterinary Science
0374-8804 Kagawa Prefective Agricultural Experiment Station. Bulletin
0374-9061 Geographische Gesellschaft in Hamburg. Mitteilungen
0374-9096 Mikrobiyologi Bulteni Supplement
0374-9118 Istituto Italiano di Idrobiologia. Memorie
0374-9444 Monitore Zoologico Italiano. Supplemento
0374-955X Natuurhistorisch Genootschap in Limburg. Publicaties
0374-9665 National Museum. Memoirs
0374-9800 National Centre for Occupational Health. Annual Report
0374-9851 Nihon Contact Lens Gakkaishi
0374-9894 Nature Canada
0375-0183 Odonatologica
0375-0191 Osaka Institute of Technology. Memoirs. Series A: Science and Technology
0375-0299 Palaeontographica. Abt. B: Palaeophytologie
0375-0442 Palaeontographica. Abt. A: Palaeozoologie - Stratigraphie
0375-1589 South African Journal of Animal Science
0375-1651 Sellowia
0375-2038 Svenska Linne-Sallskapet Aarsskrift
0375-2062 Scottish Marine Biological Association. Annual Report
0375-2135 Staatliches Museum fuer Tierkunde in Dresden. Faunistische Abhandlungen
0375-2682 South African Sugar Association Experiment Station. Annual Report
0375-2909 Steentrupia
0375-3220 College of Medicine of South Africa. Transactions
0375-3417 Instituto de Economia y Producciones Ganaderas del Ebro. Trabajos
0375-4588 University of New England. Annual Report
0375-5363 Victoria University of Wellington Zoology Publications
0375-5452 Acta Humboldtiana. Series Geologica, Palaeontologica et Biologica
0375-605X Canadian Rock Mechanics Symposium. Proceedings†
0375-6505 Geothermics
0375-6742 Journal of Geochemical Exploration
0375-7471 Quartaer
0375-7587 Scripta Geologica
0375-8338 Acta Medica Yugoslavica
0375-8869 Europa Medica *see* 0014-2565
0375-8990 Gidrobiologicheskii Zhurnal
0375-9210 Journal of Applied Chemistry and Biotechnology *see* 0268-2575
0375-9229 Journal of Bone and Joint Surgery *see* 0021-9355
0375-930X Lettere al Nuovo Cimento†
0375-9415 Molekulyarnaya Biologiya (Kiev)†
0375-9504 Banyaszati es Kohaszati Lapok - Ontode
0375-9660 Problemy Endokrinologii
0375-9717 Referativnyi Zhurnal. Geodeziya i Aeros'emka
0376-0073 Vestnik Sel'skohoziaistvennoi Nauki
0376-0421 Progress in Aerospace Sciences
0376-0456 Universidad Nacional del Litoral. Facultad de Ingenieria Quimica. Revista
0376-0898 Chemia Stosowana
0376-1185 T U Sicherheit und Zuverlaessigkeit in Betrieb und Verkehr *changed to* T U - Technische Ueberwachung. Sicherheit Zuverlaessigheit und Umweltschutz in Wirtschaft und Verkehr
0376-1843 Produccion Animal *see* 0211-4674
0376-1851 Spain. Instituto Nacional de Investigaciones Agrarias. Anales. Serie: Produccion Vegetal *see* 0211-4682
0376-2599 Visindafelag Islendinga RIT
0376-2793 Museo Argentino de Ciencias Naturales "Bernardino Rivadavia." Instituto Nacional de Investigacion de las Ciencias Naturales. Revista. Botanica.
0376-4001 Utrechtse Geografische Studies†
0376-4087 S C I M A
0376-4109 Indian Philosophical Annual.
0376-415X Indian Philosophical Quarterly
0376-4206 I C S S R Research Abstracts Quarterly
0376-4230 Contributions to Vertebrate Evolution
0376-4249 Current Topics in Critical Care Medicine†
0376-4265 E S A Bulletin
0376-4699 Indian Journal of Chemistry. Section B: Organic and Medicinal Chemistry
0376-4710 Indian Journal of Chemistry. Section A: Inorganic, Physical, Theoretical and Analytical Chemistry
0376-4761 Pneumonologia Polska
0376-4788 Indian Roads Congress. Highway Research Board Bulletin
0376-4796 Indian Journal of Meteorology, Hydrology and Geophysics *see* 0252-9416
0376-480X Advances in Pollen Spore Research
0376-4818 University of Kuwait. Journal (Science)
0376-4826 Steirische Beitraege zur Hydrogeologie
0376-4842 Current Awareness in Particle Technology
0376-5016 O P T I M A Newsletter
0376-5024 Asociacion de Escribanos del Uruguay. Revista
0376-5032 Print Letter
0376-5040 Core Journals in Pediatrics
0376-5059 Core Journals in Obstetrics/Gynecology
0376-5067 Trends in Biochemical Sciences
0376-5075 Computer Networks *changed to* Computer Networks and I S D N Systems
0376-5083 I R R I C A B: Current Annotated Bibliography of Irrigation
0376-5091 Excerpta Medica. Section 37: Drug Literature Index
0376-5156 Geophytology
0376-5423 Meghalaya Industrial Development Corporation. Annual Report
0376-5466 India. Department of Space. Annual Report
0376-5490 Bahamas. Ministry of Works. Annual Report *changed to* Bahamas. Ministry of Works and Utilities. Annual Report
0376-5512 Andhra Pradesh State Trading Corporation Limited. Annual Report
0376-5725 Reserve Bank of Malawi. Financial and Economic Review
0376-5776 Congress Marches Ahead
0376-6039 Books Ireland
0376-6128 France. Ministere de la Sante et de la Famille. Bulletin de Statistiques et Sante *changed to* Solidarite/Sante
0376-6349 Journal of Occupational Accidents
0376-6357 Behavioural Processes
0376-6381 World Index of Scientific Translations and List of Translations Notified to the International Translation Centre *see* 0259-8264
0376-6411 Terra et Aqua
0376-642X I A T A Review
0376-6438 Organization for Economic Cooperation and Development. Economic Surveys: New Zealand
0376-6608 Masihi Avaza
0376-6772 Personenvervoer
0376-7213 Construction and Property News
0376-7221 Irish Motor Industry
0376-7272 Vaare Veger
0376-7329 Advances in Research and Technology of Seeds
0376-7388 Journal of Membrane Science *changed to* Membrane Science and Desalination
0376-7426 S M Archives
0376-7604 Current Management Literature
0376-7655 Cajanus
0376-7701 Caribbean Journal of Education
0376-7787 C C A I Monthly News Letter
0376-7809 C E N C U S: Central Excise and Customs Journal
0376-7833 Cerrahpasa Medical Faculty. Journal
0376-7868 Chartered Secretary
0376-7965 Conservation of Cultural Property in India
0376-8090 Damilica
0376-8546 Directory of Public Enterprises in India
0376-8554 Directory of Scientific Research in Indian Universities
0376-8600 Directory of Special Libraries in Indonesia *changed to* Directory of Special Libraries and Information Sources
0376-8716 Drug and Alcohol Dependence
0376-8791 Economic Survey of Singapore
0376-8929 Environmental Conservation
0376-9569 Highlander
0376-9682 I C H R Newsletter
0376-9836 Indian Historical Review
0376-9844 Indian Journal of Criminology
0376-9852 Indian Journal of Engineers
0376-9879 Indian Journal of Social Sciences
0376-9887 Indian Miller
0376-9909 Indian Railways Yearbook
0376-9976 Indonesian Shipping Directory
0376-9984 Indonesia Statistics
0377-0001 Indonesian Commercial Newsletter
0377-0036 Industrial Herald
0377-0044 Industrial Property, Statistics B/ Propriete Industrielle, Statistiques B
0377-0087 Inkworld
0377-0141 International Journal of Critical Sociology
0377-015X International Journal of Ecology and Environmental Sciences
0377-0168 International Journal of Zoonoses†
0377-0257 Journal of Non-Newtonian Fluid Mechanics
0377-0273 Journal of Volcanology and Geothermal Research
0377-0400 Journal of Applied Medicine
0377-0427 Journal of Computational and Applied Mathematics
0377-0443 Journal of Kerala Studies
0377-046X Journal of Molecular Medicine†
0377-0486 J R S-Journal of Raman Spectroscopy
0377-0494 Journal of Shipping, Customs, and Transport Law
0377-0508 Journal of Social and Economic Studies
0377-0648 Jawaharal Nehru University. School of Languages. Journal
0377-0737 Labor in Perspective *changed to* Labor and Development
0377-0745 Wiener Gesellschaft fuer Theaterforschung. Jahrbuch
0377-077X Labour in the Public Sector Undertakings: Basic Information
0377-0850 Law and Progress
0377-0907 Legal History
0377-0974 Libros Espanoles I S B N
0377-1083 Lore
0377-1261 Meghalaya Chronicle
0377-144X Barbados. Legislature. House of Assembly. Minutes of Proceedings
0377-1458 Barbados. Legislature. Senate. Minutes of Proceedings
0377-1482 M M T C News
0377-1490 Modern Fibres
0377-1741 New Botanist
0377-1792 Norsk Sykehustidende *changed to* Helsetjenesten. Fagtidsskriftet
0377-1962 Council of Europe. Parliamentary Assembly. Orders of the Day, Minutes of Proceedings/Ordres du Jour, Proces Verbaux
0377-2012 Molecular Structures and Dimensions
0377-2063 Institution of Electronics and Telecommunication Engineers. Journal
0377-2063 Institution of Electronics and Telecommunication Engineers. Journal *changed to* I E T E Technical Review
0377-2152 Portugal. Instituto Nacional de Estatistica. Boletim Mensal das Estatisticas da Agricultura e da Pesca. Continente, Acores e Madeira†
0377-2179 Portugal. Instituto Nacional de Estatistica. Boletim Mensal das Estatisticas Industrias. Continente, Acores e Madeira†
0377-2187 Portugal. Instituto Nacional de Estatistica. Boletim Trimestral das Estatisticas Monetarias e Financeiras. Continente, Acores e Madeira†
0377-2217 European Journal of Operational Research
0377-2233 Portugal. Estatisticas da Energia: Continente, Acores e Madeira
0377-225X Portugal. Instituto Nacional de Estatistica. Estatisticas Agricolas *see* 0079-4139
0377-2276 Portugal. Instituto Nacional de Estatistica. Estatisticas das Financas Publicas *changed to* Portugal. Instituto Nacional de Estatistica. Estatisticas das Financas Publicas. Continente, Acores e Madeira
0377-2284 Portugal. Instituto Nacional de Estatistica. Estatisticas Demograficas Continente e Ilhas Adjacentes *changed to* Portugal. Instituto Nacional de Estatistica. Estatisticas Demograficas. Continente, Acores e Madeira
0377-2292 Portugal. Instituto Nacional de Estatistica. Servicos Centrais. Estatisticas dos Transportes e Communicacoes: Continente, Acores e Madeira
0377-2306 Portugal. Instituto Nacional de Estatistica. Estatisticas do Turismo. Continente, Acores e Madeira
0377-2314 Portugal. Estatisticas Industriais: Continente, Acores e Madeira. Volume 1: Industrias Extractivas, Electricidade, Gas, Agua
0377-2470 Portugal (Year)
0377-2586 Pakistan Pictorial
0377-2713 People's Power
0377-2772 Philosophy and Social Action
0377-2969 Pakistan Academy of Sciences. Proceedings.
0377-3132 Psycho-Lingua
0377-3205 Qualitas Plantarum
0377-3302 Rajasthan Forest Statistics
0377-3310 Rajasthan Journal of English Studies†
0377-3426 Reading Journal
0377-3450 R E C S A M Annual Report
0377-3574 Contributions to Epidemiology and Biostatistics
0377-368X International Commission for the Conservation of Atlantic Tunas. Report
0377-3744 National Institute of Nutrition. Annual Report
0377-449X Singapore International Chamber of Commerce. Annual Report
0377-4902 Homeopathic Herald
0377-4910 I C M R Bulletin
0377-5135 Sciences, Techniques, Informations C R I A C
0377-5380 Social and Labour Bulletin
0377-5437 Institute of Southeast Asian Studies. Annual Review
0377-5445 Southern Africa Record
0377-547X Spices Newsletter
0377-6093 Council of Europe. Parliamentary Assembly. Texts Adopted by the Assembly/Textes Adoptes Par l'Assemblee
0377-628X Revista de Filologia y Linguistica†
0377-6352 Uplift
0377-6360 Vedic Light
0377-6549 Warta Kesehatan *changed to* Warta Dinas Kesehatan
0377-6611 Working Class
0377-6719 Yearly All India Criminal Digest.
0377-6832 Data India
0377-6883 Diffusion and Defect Data
0377-7154 Egyptian Computer Journal
0377-7243 I A B S E Periodica
0377-7251 I A B S E Surveys *see* 0377-7243
0377-726X I A B S E Journal *see* 0377-7243

ISSN INDEX 1553

0377-7278 I A B S E Proceedings *see* 0377-7243
0377-7286 I A B S E Structures *see* 0377-7243
0377-7294 I A B S E Bulletin *see* 0377-7243
0377-7308 Gedrag *changed to* Gedrag & Gezondheid
0377-7316 Anuario de Estudios Centroamericanos
0377-7332 Empirical Economics
0377-7340 Indian Electronics Directory
0377-7359 Indian Films
0377-7367 Indian Library Movement
0377-7391 Industrial Welder
0377-743X Jijnasa
0377-757X Municipalities and Corporation Cases
0377-7669 North Atlantic Treaty Organization. Expert Panel on Air Pollution Modeling. Proceedings
0377-7774 Family Planning Association of India. Report
0377-7928 Singapore Periodicals Index
0377-7936 Space Science Instrumentation *see* 0004-640X
0377-8002 Tamil Nadu Journal of Co-operation
0377-8053 Water Resources Journal
0377-8231 Academie Royale de Medecine de Belgique. Bulletin et Memoires
0377-8282 Drugs of the Future
0377-8320 Psicodeia
0377-8398 Marine Micropaleontology
0377-8401 Animal Feed Science and Technology
0377-841X Engineering and Process Economics *see* 0167-188X
0377-8436 Indian Journal of Textile Research (CSIR)
0377-8487 Vignana Bharathi
0377-8592 Safety Management
0377-8657 Purchasing South Africa†
0377-8711 Corrosion and Coatings
0377-8886 Norway. Statistisk Sentralbyraa. Legestatistikk *see* 0800-403X
0377-8894 N G U Skrifter
0377-8967 Review of Population Reviews
0377-9017 Letters in Mathematical Physics
0377-919X Journal of Palestine Studies
0377-9238 Bangladesh Medical Research Council Bulletin
0377-9254 Journal of Engineering Sciences
0377-9335 Entomon
0377-9378 Karnataka Medical Journal
0377-9408 Tool and Alloy Steels
0377-9424 Agronomia Costarricense
0377-9688 Limnological Society of Southern Africa. Journal
0377-9890 Journal of Educational Media Science *changed to* Journal of Educational Media and Library Science
0378-0112 Index to Chinese Periodicals
0378-0392 Mineral and Electrolyte Metabolism
0378-0473 Kanina
0378-052X Ciencia y Tecnologia
0378-0643 Poesie
0378-0651 Muziek en Onderwijs
0378-066X Entretiens d'Actualite†
0378-0759 Indian Linguistics
0378-0791 Infusionstherapie und Klinische Ernaehrung - Forschung und Praxis
0378-0856 Indo-Iranica
0378-0864 Geologische Bundesanstalt, Vienna. Abhandlungen
0378-0880 Communication and Cognition
0378-1070 C O M L A Newsletter
0378-1097 F E M S-Microbiology Letters
0378-1100 Contemporary Crises
0378-1119 Gene
0378-1127 Forest Ecology and Management
0378-1135 Veterinary Microbiology
0378-1186 Gerontologie *changed to* Tijdschrift voor Gerontologie en Geriatrie
0378-1240 Garcia de Orta: Serie de Geologia
0378-1291 Arbeitsgemeinschaft fuer Elektrische Nachrichtentechnik. Mitteilungen
0378-178X Central Bank of Barbados. Economic and Financial Statistics
0378-181X Pedofauna
0378-1844 Interciencia
0378-1909 Environmental Biology of Fishes
0378-195X Metro: A Bibliography
0378-1968 International Statistical Handbook of Urban Public Transport
0378-1976 Congres de l'U I T P. Rapports Techniques
0378-2158 Kenya Uhuru Yearbook
0378-2166 Journal of Pragmatics
0378-2395 Journal of Maharashtra Agricultural Universities
0378-2409 Journal of Root Crops
0378-2484 I J D L
0378-2522 Estadistica Panamena. Situacion Economica. Seccion 351. Indice de Precios al por Mayor y al Consumidor
0378-2530 Estadistica Panamena. Situacion Economica. Seccion 351. Precios Pagados por el Productor Agropecuario
0378-2557 Estadistica Panamena. Situacion Economica. Seccion 314, 321, 323, 324, 325. Industria
0378-2565 Estadistica Panamena. Situacion Economica. Seccion 312. Superficie Sembrada y Cosecha de Arroz, Maiz y Frijol de Bejuco
0378-2573 Estadistica Panamena. Situacion Economica. Seccion 312. Superficie Sembrada y Cosecha de Cafe, Tabaco y Cana de Azucar
0378-2581 Estadistica Panamena. Situacion Economica. Seccion 312. Produccion Pecuaria
0378-259X Estadistica Panamena. Situacion Politica, Administrativa y Justicia. Seccion 631. Justicia
0378-2603 Estadistica Panamena. Situacion Economica. Seccion 342. Cuentas Nacionales
0378-2611 Estadistica Panamena. Situacion Economica: Seccion 351-Precios Recibidos por el Productor Agropecuario
0378-262X Estadistica Panamena. Situacion Social. Seccion 431. Asistencia Social
0378-2654 Industrial Development Abstracts
0378-2662 Balance of Payments Yearbook *see* 0252-3051
0378-2689 University of Hong Kong. Centre of Asian Studies. Occasional Papers and Monographs
0378-2697 Plant Systematics and Evolution
0378-2808 Archivum Ottomanicum
0378-3073 Oesterreichische Zeitschrift fuer Oeffentliches Recht und Voelkerrecht
0378-309X Biotelemetry and Patient Monitoring *see* 0254-0819
0378-3227 Portugal. Instituto Nacional de Estatistica. Serie Estatisticas Regionais
0378-3316 Rocas y Minerales
0378-3340 Revista del Pensamiento Centroamericano
0378-3472 Euro Abstracts Section II. Coal and Steel
0378-3588 Statistical Office of the European Communities. Crop Production
0378-3758 Journal of Statistical Planning and Inference
0378-3766 North-Holland/T I M S Studies in the Management Sciences
0378-3774 Agricultural Water Management
0378-3782 Early Human Development
0378-3790 Inorganic Perspectives in Biology and Medicine†
0378-3804 Journal of Mechanical Working Technology
0378-3812 Fluid Phase Equilibria
0378-3820 Fuel Processing Technology
0378-3839 Coastal Engineering
0378-3928 Hindustani Zaban
0378-4029 Geological Survey of India. News
0378-4037 International Bulletin of Sports Information
0378-4045 Progress in Clinical Neurophysiology
0378-4053 Calendar - Scientific and Technical Meetings in South Africa†
0378-407X Gereformeerde Vroueblad
0378-4088 Imbongi Yenkosi
0378-410X Molaetsa-Molaetsa
0378-4126 Murumiwa
0378-4134 Umthombo Wamandla
0378-4150 German Language and Literature Monographs†
0378-4169 Lingvisticae Investigationes
0378-4177 Studies in Language
0378-4207 Eurostat News
0378-4266 Journal of Banking and Finance
0378-4274 Toxicology Letters
0378-4282 Animal Regulation Studies†
0378-4290 Field Crops Research
0378-4304 Analytica Chimica Acta-Computer Technique and Optimization *see* 0003-2670
0378-4312 Veterinary Science Communications *see* 0165-7380
0378-4320 Animal Reproduction Science
0378-4339 Protection Ecology *changed to* Agriculture, Ecosystems and Environment
0378-4347 Journal of Chromatography-Biomedical Applications
0378-4371 Physica
0378-4487 Advances in Molecular Relaxation and Interaction Processes *see* 0167-7322
0378-4509 Avances en Produccion Animal
0378-4525 Zambian Ornithological Society. Bulletin†
0378-4533 Zambian Ornithological Society. Newsletter
0378-455X Economic Bulletin for Asia and the Pacific
0378-4568 Anvesak
0378-469X Balafon
0378-4754 Mathematics and Computers in Simulation
0378-4770 Women at Work
0378-4789 Independent Journal of Philosophy
0378-4797 Africa Index *changed to* Africa Index to Continental Periodical Literature
0378-4827 Synthetic
0378-4835 Oncologia/80
0378-4843 F C T L
0378-4940 Estadistica Panamena. Indicadores Economicos y Sociales. Seccion 011. Indicadores Economicos y Sociales
0378-4967 Estadistica Panamena. Situacion Cultural. Seccion 511. Educacion
0378-4975 Estadistica Panamena. Situacion Demografica. Seccion 231. Migracion Internacional
0378-4983 Estadistica Panamena. Situacion Economica. Seccion 331. Comercio Exterior (Preliminary Report)
0378-4991 Estadistica Panamena. Situacion Economica. Seccion 352. Hoja de Balance de Alimentos
0378-5068 Vocational Training *see* 0252-855X
0378-5122 Maturitas
0378-5165 International Journal of Political Education†
0378-5173 International Journal of Pharmaceutics
0378-5254 Dietetics & Home Economics
0378-5327 South African Geographer
0378-5378 D O C P A L Resumenes Sobre Poblacion en America Latina
0378-5386 Centro Latinoamericano de Demografia. Boletin Demografico
0378-5408 Labour and Society
0378-5424 Travail et Societe
0378-5467 Labour Education
0378-5726 Etudes Mesoamericaines
0378-584X Onkologie
0378-5858 Renal Physiology
0378-5866 Developmental Neuroscience
0378-5882 International Labour Office. Official Bulletin. Series A
0378-5890 International Labour Office. Official Bulletin. Series B
0378-5904 I L O Publications
0378-5912 Trends in Neurosciences
0378-5920 World Economy
0378-5939 Journal of Research Communication Studies *see* 0138-9130
0378-5947 Terotechnica *changed to* Maintenance Management International
0378-5955 Hearing Research
0378-5963 Applications of Surface Science *see* 0169-4332
0378-6196 N I H A E Bulletin *changed to* Health and Population: Perspectives and Issues
0378-620X Integral Equations and Operator Theory
0378-6218 Results in Mathematics
0378-6242 Indian National Science Academy. Bulletin
0378-6307 Geophysical Research Bulletin
0378-651X Financial Market Trends
0378-6536 Organization for Economic Cooperation and Development. Quarterly Oil Statistics *changed to* Organization for Economic Cooperation and Development. Quarterly Oil and Gas Statistics
0378-6714 Statistical Office of the European Communities. Selling Prices of Vegetables Products. *changed to* Statistical Office of the European Communities. Agricultural Prices
0378-6722 Statistical Office of the European Communities. Selling Prices of Animal Products *changed to* Statistical Office of the European Communities. Agricultural Prices
0378-6730 Estadistica Panamena. Situacion Economica. Seccion 343-344. Hacienda Publica y Finanzas
0378-6749 Estadistica Panamena. Situacion Demografica. Seccion 221. Estadisticas Vitales - Cifras Preliminares
0378-6757 Estadistica Panamena. Situacion Fisica. Seccion 121-Clima. Meteorologia *changed to* Estadistica Panamena. Situacion Fisica. Seccion 121. Meteorologia
0378-6765 Estadistica Panamena. Situacion Social. Seccion 451. Accidentes de Transito
0378-6803 World Transindex *see* 0259-8264
0378-6900 Advances in Cardiovascular Physics
0378-6919 Schweizer Foerster
0378-6927 Plusminus 20
0378-6935 Dialog *changed to* Theaterzytig
0378-7192 EUDISED R & D Bulletin
0378-7206 Information and Management
0378-7346 Gynecologic and Obstetric Investigation
0378-7354 Advances in Biological Psychiatry
0378-7362 I L O Judgements of the Administrative Tribunal
0378-7389 Estadistica Panamena. Situacion Economica. Seccion 333 y 334. Transporte y Comunicaciones
0378-7397 Estadistica Panamena. Situacion Economica. Seccion 341. Balanza de Pagos
0378-746X I R E B I†
0378-7478 Research in Tourism
0378-7494 Creative Book Selection Index
0378-7508 Library History Review
0378-7516 Asian Journal of European Studies
0378-7524 History of Agriculture
0378-7532 Management Development
0378-7540 Current Trends in Life Sciences
0378-7656 International Federation for Documentation. P-Notes
0378-7680 Ciencia y Sociedad
0378-7699 Instituto del Mar del Peru. Boletin
0378-7702 Instituto del Mar del Peru. Informe.
0378-7710 Swaziland National Bibliography
0378-7753 Journal of Power Sources
0378-7761 Fire Research *see* 0379-7112
0378-777X Environmental Policy and Law
0378-7788 Energy and Buildings
0378-7796 Electric Power Systems Research
0378-7818 Luz†
0378-7931 Deviance et Societe
0378-7966 European Journal of Drug Metabolism and Pharmacokinetics
0378-7974 Revista de Estudios Hispanicos
0378-8024 Journal of Turkish Phytopathology

0378-8032 Garcia de Orta: Serie de Estudos Agronomicos
0378-8059 Sudanow
0378-8148 A T I R A Technical Digest
0378-8156 Indian Journal of Physical Anthropology and Human Genetics
0378-8350 Langues et Terminologies†
0378-8407 Tempo Medical
0378-8490 Karger Highlights: Nephrology†
0378-8512 Korean Journal of Biochemistry
0378-8644 Oesterreichische Akademie der Wissenschaften. Almanach
0378-8652 Oesterreichische Akademie der Wissenschaften. Philosophisch-Historische Klasse. Anzeiger
0378-8660 Oesterreichische Byzantinistik. Jahrbuch
0378-8679 Beitraege zu Infusionstherapie und Klin. Ernaehrung
0378-8717 Science Teacher
0378-8733 Social Networks
0378-8741 Journal of Ethnopharmacology
0378-8873 Barbados. Statistical Service. Monthly Digest of Statistics
0378-892X Instituut voor Hygiene en Epidemiologie. Reseau Soufre-Fumee/Zwavel-Rook Meetnet
0378-9098 South African Journal of Business Management
0378-9144 Boardroom
0378-9179 Braby's Cape Province Directory
0378-9217 Braby's East London Directory
0378-9268 Ladysmith Directory
0378-9292 Braby's Orange Free State Directory
0378-9454 Vistas in Plant Sciences
0378-9519 Journal of Entomological Research
0378-9535 Urja
0378-956X Instituto Tecnologico de Santo Domingo. Documentos
0378-9608 Universidade de Coimbra. Faculdade de Farmacia. Boletim
0378-9721 Inter-African Bureau for Animal Resources. Bulletin of Animal Health and Production in Africa
0378-9837 Diagnostic Imaging *see* 0254-881X
0378-9845 Health Communications and Informatics†
0378-9853 Karger Highlights: Cardiology†
0378-9861 Human Gene Mapping
0378-9896 Universidad Catolica Nuestra Senora de la Asuncion. Centro de Estudios Antropologicos. Suplemento Antropologico
0378-9942 Bibliographie du Senegal
0378-9977 International Background†
0378-9993 Industry and Environment
0379-0002 Reviews on Powder Metallurgy & Physical Ceramics
0379-0010 Monthly Bulletin of Statistics (FAO)
0379-0037 Indian Journal of Applied Linguistics
0379-0207 Oesterreichische Akademie der Wissenschaften, Vienna. Mathematisch-Naturwissenschaftliche Klasse. Denkschriften
0379-0258 Automatic Data Processing Information Bulletin
0379-0290 Current Research in Social Security
0379-0347 U N C R D Newsletter
0379-0355 Methods and Findings in Experimental and Clinical Pharmacology
0379-038X National Academy of Medical Sciences. Annals
0379-0436 Comparative Physiology and Ecology
0379-0479 Indian Journal of Cryogenics
0379-055X Tobacco Research
0379-0568 Indian Society of Desert Technology and University Centre of Desert Studies. Transactions
0379-0584 Index to South African Periodicals
0379-0622 Zambezia: The Journal of the University of Zimbabwe
0379-0649 Penpals
0379-072X Estadistica Panamena. Situacion Social. Seccion 441. Estadisticas del Trabajo
0379-0738 Forensic Science International
0379-0754 Estadistica Panamena. Situacion Economica. Seccion 323. Produccion Manufacturera *changed to* Estadistica Panamena. Situacion Economica. Seccion 323. Indice de Volumen Fisico de la Produccion Industrial
0379-0797 International Rehabilitation Medicine *changed to* International Disability Studies
0379-0827 Cyprus. Agricultural Research Institute. Agricultural Economics Report
0379-0916 Cyprus. Meteorological Service. Summary of the Weather in Cyprus
0379-0924 Cyprus. Department of Statistics and Research. Agricultural Statistics
0379-0932 Cyprus. Agricultural Research Institute. Technical Paper†
0379-1041 E U L A R Bulletin
0379-1068 Karger Highlights: Gerontology†
0379-122X Unesco Journal of Information Science, Librarianship and Archives Administration†
0379-1424 Universitaet Wien. Dissertationen
0379-1564 Bibliographical Series on Coconut
0379-1580 Fiji. Mineral Resources Department. Bulletin
0379-1734 I L O Information
0379-1815 Belgian Environmental Research Index
0379-1998 Karger Highlights: Oncology†
0379-2005 Karger Highlights: Oral Science†
0379-2218 Unisist Newsletter - General Information Programme
0379-2269 Children in the Tropics
0379-2285 E S A Journal
0379-2463 Siren
0379-248X Information
0379-2501 Output
0379-2528 Unterhaltungs-Elektronik
0379-2811 I A L A Bulletin
0379-2862 China Letter
0379-2870 Philippine Letter
0379-2889 Japan Letter
0379-2897 Sinet
0379-2927 Journal for the History of Arabic Science
0379-296X Fiji. Mineral Resources Division. Economic Investigation *changed to* Fiji. Mineral Resources Department. Economic Investigation
0379-3133 European File
0379-3168 Pure and Applied Mathematika Sciences
0379-3338 World Union for the Safeguard of Youth. Bulletin
0379-3400 Teacher Education
0379-3486 European Communities Trade with ACP States and the South Mediterranean States†
0379-3532 Q R Journal
0379-3540 Zoological Survey of India. Memoirs
0379-3621 Codices Manuscripti
0379-363X Paracelsus†
0379-3664 Schweizerische Zeitschrift fuer Soziologie
0379-3680 F I D Directory
0379-3885 Journal of Indian Psychology
0379-3915 Studies in History of Medicine *changed to* Studies in History of Medicine and Science
0379-3982 Tecnologia en Marcha
0379-3990 Thesis Abstracts
0379-4008 Haryana Agricultural University. Journal of Research
0379-4016 Trinidad Naturalist *changed to* Naturalist
0379-4032 Islam and the Modern World
0379-4040 Agri-Week
0379-4121 Annual Drug Data Report *changed to* Drug Data Report
0379-4229 European Applied Research Reports-Nuclear Science and Technology Section
0379-4237 Estadistica Panamena. Situacion Demografica. Seccion 221. Estadisticas Vitales
0379-4245 Estadistica Panamena. Situacion Economica. Seccion 321 y 325. Industria Encuesta
0379-4261 Estadistica Panamena. Situacion Economica. Seccion 331-Comercio. Comercio Exterior (Annual) *changed to* Estadistica Panamena. Situacion Economica. Seccion 331-Comercio. Anuario de Comercio Exterior
0379-4296 Bangladesh Journal of Agricultural Sciences
0379-4350 South African Journal of Chemistry
0379-4369 South African Journal of Wildlife Research
0379-4377 South African Journal of Physics
0379-4415 Recht der Schule
0379-4423 Rundfunkrecht
0379-4474 Karger Highlights: Medical Imaging†
0379-4504 Current Literature on Science of Sciences
0379-4636 Caravan and Outdoor Life
0379-4792 Transport and Road Digest
0379-4857 Acta Medica Dominicana
0379-508X Acta Botanica Indica
0379-5101 Himalayan Geology
0379-511X Indian Geological Index
0379-5128 Indian Journal of Earth Sciences
0379-5136 Indian Journal of Marine Sciences
0379-5179 Kavaka
0379-5187 Mineral Research
0379-525X Pacific Perspective
0379-5268 Mana
0379-5411 Acta Ciencia Indica
0379-542X Cheiron
0379-5446 Indian Foundry Journal
0379-5489 Journal of Nuclear Agriculture and Biology
0379-556X Pharmstudent
0379-5578 Plant Biochemical Journal
0379-5594 Seed Research
0379-5608 Soaps, Detergents & Toiletries Review
0379-5721 Food and Nutrition Bulletin
0379-5853 HongKongiana
0379-6027 South African Journal of Dairy Technology *see* 0258-3321
0379-606X Revue A T E E Journal *see* 0261-9768
0379-6078 South Africa. Government Gazette Index
0379-6086 University of Stellenbosch. Bureau for Economic Research. Consumer Survey *changed to* University of Stellenbosch. Bureau for Economic Research. Trade and Commerce
0379-6124 National Institute for Transport and Road Research. Annual Report
0379-6175 South African Journal of Physiotherapy
0379-6191 University of Stellenbosch. Bureau for Economic Research. Trends
0379-6205 Journal for Studies in Economics and Econometrics
0379-6477 Armed Forces
0379-6485 Ars Nova
0379-654X Animal Anti-Cruelty League. Chairman's Report
0379-6736 South Africa. Weather Bureau. Technical Paper/Tegniese Verhandelinge
0379-6779 Synthetic Metals
0379-6787 Solar Cells
0379-6922 Mundo Nuevo
0379-6930 African Journal of Plant Protection
0379-7007 Portugal. Instituto Nacional de Estatistica. Centro de Estudos Demograficos. Caderno
0379-704X Social Security Documentation: African Series
0379-7074 African News Sheet
0379-7082 Revista de Educacion†
0379-7104 Universiteit van Pretoria. Biblioteekdiens. Verslagreeks
0379-7112 Fire Safety Journal
0379-7368 Chinese Biochemical Society. Journal
0379-7651 Chemie Magazine
0379-7724 Higher Education in Europe
0379-7783 Brief
0379-7856 Universitatea "Al. I. Cuza" din Iasi. Analele Stiintifice. Sectiunea 3b: Filozofie
0379-7864 Universitatea "Al. I. Cuza" din Iasi. Analele Stiintifice. Sectiunea 3c: Stiinte Economice
0379-7872 Universitatea "Al. I. Cuza" din Iasi. Analele Stiintifice. Sectiunea 3d: Stiinte Juridice
0379-7880 Universitatea "Al. I. Cuza" din Iasi. Analele Stiintifice. Sectiunea 3e: Lingvistica
0379-7899 Universitatea "Al. I. Cuza" din Iasi. Analele Stiintifice. Sectiunea 3f. : Literatura
0379-7902 Universitatea "Al. I. Cuza" din Iasi. Analele Stiintifice. Geologie-Geografie
0379-797X Behavioural Sciences and Rural Development *changed to* Journal of Rural Development
0379-8070 World Health Statistics Quarterly
0379-8097 Biological Memoirs
0379-8151 Hahnemannian Homoeopathic Sandesh
0379-8194 Journal of Sikh Studies
0379-8305 Developmental Pharmacology and Therapeutics
0379-8321 Iraqi Chemical Society. Journal
0379-8364 Institutul Agronomic Ion Ionescu de la Brad. Lucrari Stiintifice. Seria Agronomie
0379-8372 Institutul Agronomic Ion Ionescu de la Brad. Lucrari Stiintifice. Seria Horticultura
0379-8402 Philosophica
0379-8461 European Commission of Human Rights. Decisions and Reports
0379-8577 Curationis *changed to* Nursing R S A Verpleging
0379-8585 Architecture & Behaviour
0379-8607 Schweizerische Akademie der Medizinischen Wissenschaften. Bulletin†
0379-864X Chemical Senses
0379-8658 Greenhill Journal of Administration
0379-8674 World Bank. Monthly Operational Summary
0379-8836 Stats - Statistical Review *changed to* STATS - Monthly Statistical and Marketing Digest
0379-8860 South African Journal of Ethnology
0379-8895 South African Yearbook of International Law
0379-9506 Garcia de Orta: Serie de Botanica
0379-9514 Garcia de Orta: Serie de Geografia
0379-9549 Asia Monitor†
0379-9786 Christian Education Advance†
0379-9867 Contree
0379-9921 Custos
0380-0008 Manitoba Decisions, Civil and Criminal Cases
0380-0067 Eastern Ontario Farmer *changed to* Ontario Farmer (Eastern Edition)
0380-0121 Mennonite Reporter
0380-013X Canadian Mennonite Reporter *see* 0380-0121
0380-0180 Marketing Social
0380-0199 Media Message *see* 0710-4340
0380-0326 L B M A O Reporter
0380-0334 Canada. Statistics Canada. Communications Service Bulletin/Communications-Bulletin de Service
0380-0342 Canada. Statistics Canada. Water Transportation/Transport Par Eau
0380-0482 Expression†
0380-0547 Canada. Statistics Canada. Infomat
0380-0741 Canada. Statistics Canada. Consumer Credit/Credit a la Consummation†
0380-1020 Canada. Department of Insurance. List of Securities
0380-1039 Vintage Canada†
0380-1098 Education Today†
0380-1306 Alberta Learning Resources Journal
0380-1314 Consensus (Ottawa)
0380-1330 Journal of Great Lakes Research
0380-1349 Canada. Statistics Canada. Imports-Merchandise Trade/Importations-Commerce de Marchandises
0380-1446 Critical List
0380-1462 Teaching Positions Available†
0380-1470 Trellis

ISSN INDEX 1555

0380-1489 Canadian Studies in Population
0380-1616 Ontario Genealogy Society. Newsleaf
0380-1721 Cahiers Quebecois de Demographie
0380-1799 Orchestra Canada
0380-1861 Registered Nursing Orderly
0380-1888 Ontario Society of Medical Technologists. Newsletter *see* 0228-877X
0380-1969 Ontario Technologist
0380-2019 C T M Weekly Bulletin *changed to* Travelweek Bulletin
0380-2051 Journal du Nord-Ouest
0380-2108 Canada. Statistics Canada. Labour Costs in Canada: Education, Libraries and Museums/Couts de la Main d'Oeuvre au Canada. Enseignement, Bibliotheques et Musees†
0380-2221 Canadian Financial E-Z Directory
0380-2264 Canadian Association Executive
0380-2361 Canadian Journal of Education
0380-2469 Anglican Chiurch of Canada. General Synod. Journal of Proceedings *changed to* Anglican Church of Canada. General Synod. Journal
0380-2531 Mayday
0380-2604 Tab International
0380-2639 F M Compilation of the Statutes of Canada
0380-2795 Ontario Campus Culture Association. Newsletter†
0380-2817 NeWest Review
0380-2841 N.E.R.L.S. Newsletter *see* 0708-9066
0380-285X Onion
0380-2892 In a Nutshell†
0380-2906 M P A News *see* 0380-2892
0380-2914 Adagio
0380-2973 Talking Books in the Public Library Systems of Metropolitan Toronto
0380-3147 L U A C Forum
0380-321X Foret-Conservation
0380-3333 Greenmaster
0380-352X Feather Fancier
0380-3554 Jr. Rider
0380-3651 Hog Marketplace Quarterly
0380-3945 I.F.†
0380-3988 Institute of Public Administration of Canada. Bulletin
0380-4011 Institute of Chartered Accountants of Guyana. Newsletter
0380-4194 Adaptation (Montreal)
0380-4208 Land Compensation Reports
0380-4275 Reserves of Coal, Province of Alberta
0380-4305 Schedule of Wells Drilled for Oil and Gas in Alberta
0380-4321 Alberta Coal Industry, Annual Statistics
0380-4496 Conservation in Alberta†
0380-450X Alberta. Environment Conservation Authority. Annual Report†
0380-4623 Museogramme
0380-4852 Manitoba Highway News
0380-4933 International Commission for the Northwest Atlantic Fisheries. Selected Papers *see* 0250-6432
0380-4968 Canada. Statistics Canada. Gold Quartz and Copper-Gold-Silver Mines/Mines de Quartz Aurifere et Mines de Cuivre-Or-Argent†
0380-5107 Manpower and Immigration Review: Quebec Region
0380-5131 Music Scene
0380-5352 Notre Langue et Notre Culture *see* 0831-5825
0380-5476 Voice of Tourism†
0380-5522 Northern Perspectives
0380-562X Alberta Wilderness Association. Newsletter *see* 0830-8284
0380-5689 Nova Scotia. Department of Labour. Annual Report
0380-5735 Notes on Agriculture
0380-5921 Canadian Mathematical Congress. Research Committee. Report
0380-5948 Canada. Statistics Canada. Urban Transport *see* 0829-1756
0380-6197 Thunder Bay Camping Guide
0380-6294 Canada. Statistics Canada. Motion Picture Theatres and Film Distributors/Cinemas et Distributeurs de Films
0380-6308 Canada. Statistics Canada. Railway Carloadings/Chargements Ferroviaires
0380-6367 P T I C Bulletin†
0380-6375 P T I C Newsletter
0380-6642 Peterborough Historical Society Bulletin
0380-6693 Sift
0380-6804 Canada. Statistics Canada. The Labour Force/La Population Active
0380-6847 Canada. Statistics Canada. Coal and Coke Statistics/Statistique du Charbon et du Coke
0380-691X Canada. Statistics Canada. Consumer Prices and Price Indexes/Prix a la Consommation et Indices des Prix
0380-6928 Canada. Statistics Canada. Commercial Failures/Faillites Commerciales†
0380-6936 Canada. Statistics Canada. Employment, Earnings and Hours/Emploi, Gaines et Duree du Travail
0380-6952 Canada. Statistics Canada. Miscellaneous Non-Metal Mines/Mines Non Metalliques Diverses†
0380-6979 Makara†
0380-6987 Canadian Automobile Association. Communique†
0380-6995 Studies in Canadian Literature
0380-7053 Canada. Statistics Canada. Investment Statististics Service Bulletin/Bulletin de Service sur la Statistique des Investissements†
0380-7150 Q L A Bulletin
0380-7177 Canada. Statistics Canada. Merchandising Inventories/Stocks Commerciaux
0380-7223 Canada. Statistics Canada. Gypsum Products/Produits de Gypse
0380-7525 Canada. Statistics Canada. Industrial Corporations Financial Statistics/Societes Industrielles Statistique Financiere
0380-7533 Canada. Statistics Canada. Causes of Death, Provinces by Sex and Canada by Sex and Age/Causes de Deces, Par Provinces Selon le Sexe et le Canada Selon le Sexe et l'Age
0380-7541 Canada. Statistics Canada. Index Numbers of Farm Prices of Agricultural Products/Nombres-Indices des Prix des Produits Agricoles
0380-7797 Canada. Statistics Canada. Canada's Mineral Production: Preliminary Estimate/Production Minerale du Canada, Calcul Preliminaire
0380-7835 Canada. Statistics Canada. Telephone Statistics: Preliminary Report on Large Telephone Systems†
0380-7851 Canada. Statistics Canada. Primary Iron and Steel
0380-7878 Canada. Statistics Canada. Retail Chain Stores/Magasins de Detail a Succursales *see* 0227-017X
0380-7894 Canada. Statistics Canada. Wholesale Trade/Commerce de Gros
0380-7967 Post *see* 0709-1370
0380-7975 Perceptual Post *see* 0709-1370
0380-8025 Publisher
0380-8041 S L I S Newsletter†
0380-8068 Georgian Bay Regional Library System. Directory-Member Libraries
0380-8114 Random Thoughts
0380-8238 Canada. Statistics Canada. Scrap Iron and Steel/Dechets de Fer et d'Acier†
0380-8297 Saskatchewan. Advisory Council on the Status of Women. Publication
0380-8475 Catholic Hospital Association of Canada. Directory *see* 0828-5748
0380-8491 Learning Resources Council Newsletter
0380-8505 Alberta Teachers' Association. School Library Council. Newsletter *see* 0380-1306
0380-8513 Alberta Teachers' Association. Audio-Visual Council. Newsletter *see* 0380-1306
0380-8599 N B C/N F C News
0380-8688 Canadian Scout Executive *changed to* Scout Executive
0380-8718 Canada. Grain Commission. Economics and Statistics Division. Visible Grain Supplies and Disposition
0380-8823 Repertoire des Theses de Doctorat Soutenues Devant les Universites de Langue Francaise†
0380-8858 Toronto News†
0380-8866 Shore Line
0380-8890 Ecornifleux†
0380-8920 A T A News Bulletin *see* 0709-4272
0380-903X Imperial Oil Limited. Review *see* 0700-5156
0380-9056 Direction (Downsview)
0380-9099 Business Life
0380-9102 A T A Magazine
0380-9218 Canadian Journal of Information Science
0380-9242 Nova Scotian Surveyor
0380-9366 Neologie en Marche. Serie A. Langue Generale
0380-9420 Canadian Journal of Political & Social Theory
0380-9455 Canada on Stage: Canadian Theatre Review Yearbook *changed to* Canada on Stage: The National Theatre Yearbook
0380-951X Canada. Statistics Canada. Electric Power Statistics Volume 1: Annual Electric Power Survey of Capability and Load/Statistique de l'Energie Electrique. Volume 1: Enquete Annuelle sur la Puissance Maximale et sur la Charge des Reseaux
0380-9544 Vancouver's Leisure Magazine *see* 0380-9552
0380-9552 Vancouver
0380-9633 Megadrilogica
0380-9668 B.C. Hotelman
0380-9676 University of Saskatchewan. Library. Notable Works and Collections
0380-9773 Orienteering *see* 0382-8255
0380-979X Manitoba. Environmental Council. Studies
0380-9803 Manitoba. Environmental Council. Annual Report
0380-9854 C C I Journal†
0381-0100 Conference Board of Canada. Quarterly Provincial Forecast *see* 0827-5785
0381-0380 Eglise de Montreal
0381-0410 University of British Columbia. Department of Economics. Resources Paper
0381-0569 Interlude†
0381-0925 Continuum
0381-095X Communicator (Springhill)
0381-0976 Canada. Information Canada. Municipal Report
0381-0984 Journal of Natural Resource Management and Interdisciplinary Studies†
0381-1352 F C M Forum
0381-1387 Learning
0381-1603 Political Economy Series†
0381-1638 University of Toronto. Faculty of Law. Review
0381-1794 Society
0381-1905 Circuit†
0381-2022 Newfoundland and Labrador Provincial Libraries. Newsletter
0381-2049 Legal Aid New Brunswick Annual Report
0381-209X Newfoundland and Labrador Regional Libraries. Newsletter *see* 0381-2022
0381-2146 Canada. Environmental Protection Service. Canada-Ontario Agreement Research Report†
0381-2278 Saskatchewan. Alcoholism Commission. Annual Report *changed to* Saskatchewan. Alcohol and Drug Abuse Commission. Annual Report
0381-2294 Alberta. Utilities Division. Annual Report *changed to* Alberta. Department of Utilities. Annual Report
0381-2421 Farmers' Market
0381-2472 Grain Facts
0381-2510 British Columbia. Law Reform Commission. Annual Report
0381-2561 Canada Health Manpower Inventory
0381-260X British Columbia Institute of Technology. Annual Report *changed to* B C I T Annual Report
0381-2669 Chalk River Nuclear Laboratories. Chemistry and Materials Division. Progress Report†
0381-2677 Chalk River Nuclear Laboratories. Biology and Health Physics Division. Progress Report *changed to* Chalk River Nuclear Laboratories. Health Sciences Division. Progress Report
0381-2898 British Columbia. Department of Labour. Annual Report *see* 0705-9698
0381-2995 Canada. Environment Canada. Environment Protection Service. Annual Summary: National Air Pollution Surveillance *changed to* Canada. Environment Canada. Conservation and Protection Service. Annual Summary: National Air Pollution Surveillance
0381-3134 New Brunswick
0381-3142 Nouveau-Brunswick Aujourd'hui *see* 0381-3134
0381-3215 Manitoba. Pension Commission. Annual Report *changed to* Manitoba. Pension Commission. Update Study
0381-3223 Saskatchewan Farmers' Markets Annual Report†
0381-3258 Trends in Collective Bargaining Settlements in Nova Scotia†
0381-3711 Employers of New Community College Graduates: Directory
0381-372X Employers of New University Graduates: Directory
0381-3738 Directory of Employers Offering Employment to New University Graduates *see* 0381-372X
0381-3746 This Magazine
0381-3886 Heartline†
0381-3924 Ontario. Ministry of Natural Resources. Forest Research Report *see* 0704-2809
0381-3932 Clover Leaflet
0381-4319 National Research Council, Canada. Division of Building Research. D B R Paper
0381-4327 Alberta. Department of Social Services and Community Health. Annual Report
0381-4432 Canada. Statistics Canada. New Surveys/Nouvelles Enquetes†
0381-4459 Spill Technology Newsletter
0381-4556 Telephone Echo
0381-4831 Bedford Institute of Oceanography. Computer Note†
0381-4890 International Perspectives
0381-5013 Canadian Oldtimers' Hockey News *changed to* Oldtimers' Hockey News
0381-5250 H R I Observations *see* 0826-9947
0381-5447 Canadian Spectroscopic News
0381-5528 Outdoor Power Products†
0381-565X Computing Services Bulletin
0381-5730 Canadian Music Directory
0381-5765 Canadian Hotel, Restaurant, Institution & Store Equipment Directory
0381-5781 Association des Traducteurs et Interpretes de l'Ontario. Information
0381-579X Yes, There Is Canadian Music†
0381-5900 Maritime Psychological Association. Bulletin *see* 0004-6833
0381-5919 Information *see* 0707-7793
0381-5927 Agricultural Science *see* 0707-7793
0381-5951 Alberta Counselletter
0381-596X Brasier†
0381-5978 British Columbia School Trustees Association. Newsletter
0381-6036 B.C. Science Teacher

1556 ISSN INDEX

ISSN	Title
0381-6060	Anglican Church of Canada. Division of National and World Program. Bulletin *see* 0381-6079
0381-6079	Anglican Church of Canada. Bulletin†
0381-6109	Them Days
0381-6133	Canadian Association of Slavists Newsletter
0381-6206	Brome County Historical Society. Publication
0381-6303	Alberta Wilderness Arts and Recreation *see* 0705-3150
0381-646X	Environment Probe *changed to* Saskatchewan Environmental Society. Newsletter
0381-6486	C-Core News
0381-6524	Journal of Our Time
0381-6532	Guide to a Successful Life Insurance Career
0381-6591	Poetry Toronto Newsletter *changed to* Poetry Toronto
0381-6605	Journal of Otolaryngology
0381-6745	Beverage Canada
0381-6826	N A P E Journal *changed to* Communicator (St. John's)
0381-6834	Beef Today *changed to* Canadian Livestock Journal
0381-6885	Harrowsmith
0381-6907	Quebec (Province) Centrale des Bibliotheques. Bulletin de Bibliographie†
0381-7024	Dalhousie University. Institute of Public Affairs. Occasional Papers
0381-7032	Ars Combinatoria
0381-7059	Canadian Amateur Photographer†
0381-730X	Tidings *see* 0228-6157
0381-7369	Canada Quilts
0381-7377	Conference Board of Canada. Survey of Consumer Buying Intentions *see* 0827-5831
0381-7547	Philatelie au Quebec *changed to* Philatelie Quebec
0381-7717	Native Perspective†
0381-7946	Maria
0381-7962	Public Employees Journal
0381-7970	New Brunswick Public Employees Association. News Letter
0381-8004	Ontario Industrial Arts Association. Bulletin
0381-8012	O I A A Bulletin *see* 0381-8004
0381-8047	Crucible
0381-8160	Farm Equipment Quarterly
0381-8179	Sanford Evans Gold Book of Used Car Prices
0381-8187	Scope†
0381-8225	Revue des Fermieres
0381-8284	Transportation R & D in Canada *changed to* Surface Transportation R & D in Canada
0381-8357	Archaic Notes *changed to* Ottawa Archaeologist
0381-8454	Revue d'Histoire du Bas Saint Laurent
0381-8535	Fur Trade Journal
0381-856X	Caledonian
0381-8632	O C S Nouvelles
0381-873X	S I E C C A N Newsletter
0381-8802	Canada. Statistics Canada. Hospital Statistics: Preliminary Annual Report/Statistique Hospitaliere: Rapport Annuel Preliminaire†
0381-8845	Canada. Statistics Canada. Tuberculosis Statistics. Volume 2: Institutional Facilities, Services and Finances/La Statistique de la Tuberculose, Volume 2: Installations, Services et Finance des Etablissements†
0381-8888	Estates and Trusts Quarterly
0381-8950	Deutsche Katholik in Kanada
0381-8977	Sporting Goods Canada†
0381-9000	S T O P Newsletter *see* 0705-1212
0381-9027	Silahis
0381-9035	Speaking of Mime
0381-9043	International Yoga Life and Yoga Vacations *changed to* Yoga Life
0381-9116	Special Education *see* 0826-4716
0381-9124	Special Education in Canada *see* 0826-4716
0381-9132	Olifant
0381-9159	Canadian Band Directors Association. Newsletter
0381-9175	C B C: Coiffure-Beaute-Charme *see* 8750-0477
0381-9191	Herstory†
0381-9256	Canada. Statistics Canada. Miscellaneous Non-Metallic Mineral Products Industries/Industries des Produits Mineraux Non-Metalliques Divers†
0381-9280	Sporting Goods Trade *changed to* Sports Trade Canada
0381-9345	Atlantic Provinces Transportation Commission. Tips & Topics
0381-9361	Teiresias
0381-9388	Societe Historique Nicolas Denys. Revue d'Histoire
0381-9418	Status of Women News†
0381-9507	Canadian L P & Tape Catalogue
0381-9515	Artviews
0381-9612	Trust
0381-9663	Alberta Construction and Resource Industries Directory. Purchasing Guide†
0381-9825	Montreal Special Libraries Association. Bulletin *see* 0824-7749
0381-9833	Special Libraries Association. Montreal Chapter. Bulletin *see* 0824-7749
0381-9868	Motive Power International†
0381-9884	Jewish Public Library Bulletin†
0381-9930	Toys & Games
0381-9957	Association des Traducteurs et Interpretes de l'Ontario. Bulletin de l'A T I O *see* 0381-9965
0381-9965	Association des Traducteurs et Interpretes de l'Ontario. Translatio†
0382-0068	Voice of United Senior Citizens of Ontario
0382-0130	Ishtar Newsletter *see* 0382-0149
0382-0149	Ishtar News
0382-0157	Western Ontario Historical Notes†
0382-0203	Village Squire
0382-0262	Vie Francaise
0382-0289	Vista
0382-0327	Voice of Radom
0382-0335	Jeu
0382-036X	View *see* 0700-4400
0382-0424	Vision
0382-0467	Arctic in Colour†
0382-0718	Vector
0382-0726	British Columbia Association of Mathematics Teachers. Newsletter *see* 0382-0718
0382-0734	Hollinger Mines Limited. Annual Report
0382-0750	Transition†
0382-0769	I D E E S
0382-0831	Westmorland Historical Society. Newsletter
0382-084X	Lettres Quebecoises
0382-0912	Town and Country Librarian
0382-0920	Canada. Statistics Canada. Enrollment in Community Colleges/Effectifs des Colleges Communautaires
0382-0939	Canada. Statistics Canada. For-Hire Trucking Survey/Enquete sur le Transport Routier de Marchandises pour Compte d'Autrui†
0382-0971	Canada. Statistics Canada. Concrete Products Manufacturers/Fabricants de Produits en Beton†
0382-098X	Canada. Statistics Canada. Principal Taxes and Rates: Federal, Provincial and Local Governments *see* 0382-0998
0382-0998	Canada. Statistics Canada. Principal Taxes in Canada†
0382-1005	Computers
0382-1048	Novia Scotia. Department of Labour and Manpower. Monthly Summary of Activities-Industrial Relations Division†
0382-1102	Current Labour Force Statistics for Nova Scotia†
0382-1161	Canada. Commissioner of Official Languages. Annual Report
0382-1242	Wage Rates, Salaries and Hours of Labour in Nova Scotia
0382-1315	Education Nova Scotia†
0382-1463	Canada. Law Reform Commission. Annual Report
0382-1587	Canada. Pension Review Board. Reports
0382-1773	Trends in Collective Agreement Base Rate Changes in Nova Scotia *see* 0227-1362
0382-1838	Saskatchewan Universities Commission. Annual Report
0382-1889	Labour Research Bulletin†
0382-2028	Manitoba Grassland Projects†
0382-2273	C F D C Annual Report *changed to* Telefilm Canada Annual Report
0382-232X	Canada Diseases Weekly Report
0382-2788	Environment Ontario Legacy†
0382-2834	Ontario Hydro. Statistical Yearbook
0382-3814	Education Quebec†
0382-4012	Canada. Statistics Canada. Manufacturing Industries of Canada: Sub-Provincial Areas/Industries Manufactures du Canada: Niveau Infraprovincial
0382-4020	Canada. Statistics Canada. Manufacturing Industries Division. Potash Mines/Mines de Potasse†
0382-4039	Young Communist *changed to* Rebel Youth
0382-4047	Young Worker *changed to* Rebel Youth
0382-408X	Teacher
0382-411X	Canada. Statistics Canada. Educational Staff in Community Colleges/Personnel d'Enseignement des Colleges Communautaires†
0382-4128	Canada. Statistics Canada. Statistical Profiles of Educational Staff in Community Colleges/Profiles Statistiques sur le Personnel d'Enseignement des Colleges Communautaires *see* 0382-411X
0382-4306	Anglican Crusader *see* 0382-4314
0382-4314	Crusader (Toronto)
0382-4365	Avec "Lui"
0382-4373	Aim
0382-4438	Athletica†
0382-4500	Arrow†
0382-4527	Action
0382-4535	Swim Signals *see* 0382-4527
0382-4543	Red Cross Youth *see* 0382-4527
0382-4551	Volunteer *see* 0382-4527
0382-456X	Advocate
0382-4624	Canadian Living
0382-4756	Banque de Commerce Canadienne Imperiale. Lettre Commerciale†
0382-4764	Canadian Historical Association. Newsletter
0382-4926	Vie Montante. Edition Canadienne
0382-5027	Current Index to Commonwealth Legal Periodicals *see* 0225-9036
0382-5078	Criteria†
0382-5124	Ateliers†
0382-5167	Alberta Counsellor
0382-5175	Alberta English Notes†
0382-5191	Alberta English
0382-5205	Urban Reader†
0382-5264	Branching out
0382-5272	British Columbia Monthly
0382-5302	Bulletin - S V P *changed to* Environnement
0382-5310	Societe pour Vaincre la Pollution. Bulletin de Liaison *changed to* Environnement
0382-5493	Teaching Mathematics†
0382-5507	B. C. A. M. T. Journal *see* 0382-5493
0382-5566	N B A R N News *see* 0382-5574
0382-5574	Info (Fredericton)
0382-5604	Bousqueil†
0382-5655	Blue Bill
0382-5728	Miners' Voice†
0382-5795	Canadian Hackney Stud Book
0382-5868	Long Time Coming†
0382-5876	Canadian Funeral News
0382-5906	Ontario Real Estate Law Guide
0382-5914	Repertoire des Cours d'Ete†
0382-5949	Contact *see* 0410-3882
0382-6031	Canadian Manhood†
0382-6384	Beacon
0382-6406	Canadian Jersey Herd Record
0382-6414	Canadian Jersey Cattle Club. Record *see* 0382-6406
0382-6627	Owl
0382-6996	Heating, Plumbing, Air Conditioning Buyers' Guide
0382-7038	C L U Comment (English Edition)
0382-7046	Commentaires (Don Mills)
0382-7054	United Cooperatives of Ontario. News *changed to* Co-Op Cornerstone
0382-7062	United Co-operatives of Ontario. Directors' Newsletter *changed to* Co-Op Communicator
0382-7070	U C O Leader *changed to* Co-Op Communicator
0382-7305	Dan Sha News
0382-7437	Canadian Practitioner *see* 0382-7453
0382-7453	Canadian Practitioner and Review
0382-7518	Powell River Progress
0382-7577	Big Country Voice
0382-7658	Canadian Friend
0382-7712	Canadian Mining and Financial News
0382-7798	Communication Information
0382-7879	School Calendar/Calendrier Scolaire
0382-7887	Calgary Chamber of Commerce. Business News *see* 0707-8064
0382-7976	A C E H I Journal
0382-8042	Canadian Miner *see* 0029-3164
0382-8115	Canada Crafts†
0382-8255	C O F Newsletter
0382-8409	Challenge (Winnipeg)
0382-8476	Nurscene
0382-8522	South of Tuk *changed to* Sequel
0382-8565	Brick
0382-8727	Christian Bus Driver
0382-876X	Iconomatrix†
0382-8824	Laomedon Review
0382-8832	Cultural Horizons of the Deaf in Canada†
0382-8980	Deaf Herald†
0382-909X	Descant
0382-912X	Council of Ontario Universities. Research Division. Application Statistics
0382-9251	Abaka
0382-9391	Diocesan Times
0382-9812	Historical Society of Alberta Newsletter
0383-008X	Canada. Statistics Canada. Fruit and Vegetable Production/Production de Fruits et de Legumes
0383-0101	Canadian Nurses Association. Library. Periodical Holdings†
0383-0152	Rythme de Notre Eglise *changed to* Actualite Diocesaine
0383-0187	Guide to Film and Television Courses in Canada *changed to* Guide to Film, Television and Communications Studies in Canada
0383-0470	Cite Libre *see* 0009-7489
0383-056X	Revue de Modification du Comportement
0383-0640	Stationery & Office Products†
0383-090X	Metalworking Production & Purchasing
0383-1280	Canadian Music Library Association. Newsletter *see* 0383-1299
0383-1299	C A M L Newsletter
0383-1310	Catholic Dutch Canadian Association. C D C A Nieuws *see* 0383-1329
0383-1329	Nieuwe Weg (Montreal)
0383-1418	Eastern Light
0383-1620	Catholic Register
0383-1825	Microscopical Society of Canada. Bulletin
0383-2031	Waters
0383-2058	Western Livestock & Agricultural News *changed to* Western Beef Producers News
0383-2244	Farm Trends†
0383-2368	Guide Camping *see* 0705-8314
0383-2406	Canadian Campus Career Directory†

ISSN INDEX 1557

0383-2430 Building Supply Dealers Association. Survey *see* 0829-559X
0383-2538 Ievanhel's'kyi Holos
0383-2759 International Migration Newsletter *see* 0383-2767
0383-2767 International Newsletter on Migration
0383-283X Squatchberry Journal
0383-2848 Carleton University, Ottawa. Norman Paterson School of International Affairs. Bibliography Series
0383-2945 Canadian Weekly Stock Charts: Industrials
0383-2953 Canadian Weekly Stock Charts: Mines & Oils
0383-2961 Nouvelle Revue Canadienne *see* 0547-0749
0383-3003 Living Places†
0383-3372 Labour Legislation in Nova Scotia
0383-3402 Electricity Today†
0383-3437 Labour Organizations in Nova Scotia
0383-3585 Rural Real Estate Values in Alberta *see* 0701-7502
0383-3615 Alberta. Health Care Insurance Commission. Annual Report *changed to* Alberta. Health Care Insurance Plan. Annual Report
0383-3712 Alberta. Legislature Library. Annual Report
0383-3739 Alberta. Department of the Environment. Annual Report
0383-3925 Manitoba. Health Services Commission. Annual Report
0383-3933 Manitoba. Health Services Commission. Statistical Supplement to the Annual Report *changed to* Manitoba. Health Services Commission. Annual Statistics
0383-414X Canada. National Farm Products Marketing Council. Annual Report
0383-4239 Costume Society of Ontario. Newsletter
0383-4352 Saskatchewan Trading Corporation. Annual Report
0383-4379 Canada. Correctional Investigator. Annual Report
0383-4417 Grain Matters
0383-4514 Documents in the History of Canadian Art
0383-4638 Canada. Department of National Defence. Defence (Year)
0383-4654 Cooperation Canada†
0383-4778 Ontario. Labour Relations Board. Reports. A Monthly Series of Decisions
0383-5154 Canada. Department of Industry, Trade and Commerce. Annual Report.†
0383-5391 Masterpieces in the National Gallery of Canada
0383-5405 Canadian Artists Series
0383-5472 Water Quality Data for Ontario Streams & Lakes
0383-5588 Manitoba. Human Rights Commission. Annual Report
0383-5766 Canada. Statistics Canada. Passenger Bus and Urban Transit Statistics/Statistique du Transport des Voyageurs Par Autobus et du Transport Urbain
0383-6061 Intercom
0383-6096 Manitoba Educational Research Council. Newsletter *changed to* Manitoba Educational Research Council. Research Bulletin
0383-6207 Dairy Contact
0383-6266 Artswest
0383-6304 Importfile
0383-6312 Smallholder
0383-6347 S O S Press *see* 0705-1212
0383-6355 A.D.A. News Information
0383-641X Comeback†
0383-6436 Countdown
0383-6479 Ontario Conservation News
0383-6509 Caledonia Diocesan Times
0383-6576 Canadian Oral History Association. Bulletin†
0383-6649 Canadian Appraiser
0383-669X Revue du Barreau
0383-6894 Canadian Oral History Association. Journal
0383-6908 Sound Canada *changed to* Sound & Vision
0383-7114 Country Guide
0383-7300 Gift Magazine
0383-7521 Derives
0383-7645 Presbyterian Comment *changed to* Channels
0383-7653 Prairie Harvester
0383-7920 Canadian Rental Service
0383-7939 Bluenose Magazine *changed to* Earth & Tide
0383-8021 Condominium
0383-8358 Directory of Law Teachers
0383-8447 Ecole de Medecine Veterinaire, Saint-Hyacinthe, Quebec. Annuaire *see* 0383-8455
0383-8455 Universite de Montreal. Faculte de Medecine Veterinaire. Annuaire
0383-8528 Dialect
0383-8536 Nuclear Canada. Yearbook
0383-8544 Shepherd†
0383-8714 L'Actualite
0383-9133 Lillooet District Historical Society. Bulletin†
0383-9168 Newslitter
0383-9184 Metric Fact Sheets
0383-9230 Ontario Credit Union News†
0383-9257 Landscape Ontario
0383-9338 Broadcast Equipment Today *see* 0709-9797
0383-9494 Criminal Reports (Third Series)
0383-9567 Nova Scotia Bird Society. Newsletter *changed to* Nova Scotia Birds
0383-9737 Commerce Journal†
0383-9745 Southam Business†
0383-9931 O S C A Reports
0384-0174 Critere
0384-0298 Le Colombien
0384-0360 Financial Post Magazine *changed to* Financial Post Moneywise Magazine
0384-0417 Parapet
0384-0425 Simgames†
0384-0433 Contemporary Poetry of British Columbia†
0384-0581 B C Business
0384-059X McGill University, Montreal. Centre for Developing-Area Studies. Working Papers *see* 0821-6452
0384-0816 Mon Bebe
0384-093X Marsh and Maple
0384-0999 Canadian Yachting
0384-1014 Norman Mackenzie Art Gallery. Newsletter *changed to* Vista
0384-1022 N M A G Review *changed to* Vista
0384-1103 Annual Canadian-American Seminar. Proceedings
0384-1367 North-South Canadian Journal of Latin American Studies *see* 0826-3663
0384-1405 Todays Generation *changed to* Teen Generation
0384-1480 Canadian Wolf Defenders. Newsletter
0384-1642 Newspacket
0384-1677 Canadian Power Engineer†
0384-1820 Canadian Medical and Biological Engineering Society. Newsletter
0384-1839 Canadian Review of Art Education Research
0384-1898 Newfoundland and Labrador Engineer†
0384-191X Calgary Archaeologist
0384-2126 Discussion†
0384-2282 Noticiario de Canada
0384-2304 Hebdo Canada
0384-2312 Canada Weekly
0384-2355 Who's Who: A Guide to Federal and Provincial Departments and Agencies, Their Funding Programs and the People Who Head Them *see* 0832-865X
0384-2843 Canada. Statistics Canada. Cane and Beet Sugar Processors/Traitement du Sucre de Canne et de Betteraves
0384-2967 Canada. Statistics Canada. Foundation Garment Industry/Industrie des Corsets et Soutiens-Gorge†
0384-3300 Canada. Statistics Canada. Leather Glove Factories/Fabriques de Gants en Cuir†
0384-3343 Canada. Statistics Canada. Knitting Mills/Bonneterie†
0384-3378 Canada. Statistics Canada. Jewellery and Silverware Industry *see* 0828-9832
0384-3696 Canada. Statistics Canada. Miscellaneous Food Processors/Traitment des Produits Alimentaires Divers
0384-3769 Canada. Statistics Canada. Miscellaneous Clothing Industries/Industries Diverses de l'Habillement
0384-3912 Canada. Statistics Canada. Manufacturers of Soap and Cleaning Compounds/Fabricants de Savon et de Produits de Nettoyage†
0384-4080 Canada. Statistics Canada. Office Furniture Manufacturers/Industrie des Meubles de Bureau†
0384-4161 Canada. Statistics Canada. Electric Lamp and Shade Manufacturers/Industrie des Lampes Electriques et des Abat-Jour†
0384-4242 Canada. Statistics Canada. Scientific and Professional Equipment Industries/Fabrication de Materiel Scientifique et Professionnel
0384-4420 Canada. Statistics Canada. Fruit and Vegetable Processing Industries/Preparation de Fruits et de Legumes
0384-4498 Canada. Statistics Canada. Women's and Children's Clothing Industries/Industries des Vetements pour Dames et pour Enfants
0384-4633 Canada. Statistics Canada. Pulp and Paper Mills/Usines de Pates et Papiers
0384-465X Canada. Statistics Canada. Corrugated Box Manufacturers/Fabricants de Boites en Carton Ondule†
0384-4811 Canada. Statistics Canada. Miscellaneous Leather Products Manufacturers/Fabricants d'Articles Divers en Cuir†
0384-4935 Canada. Statistics Canada. Smelting and Refining/Fonte et Affinage
0384-4951 Canada. Statistics Canada. Slaughtering and Meat Processors/Abattage et Conditionnement de la Viande†
0384-5052 Ontario Folkdancer
0384-5060 Computers and Medieval Data Processing
0384-5087 Conference Catholique Canadienne. Bulletin National de Liturgie *changed to* Conference des Eveques Catholiques du Canada. Bulletin National de Liturgie
0384-5133 Musique Liturgique†
0384-5184 Canadian Children's Magazine†
0384-5753 Canadian Bar Association. British Columbia Branch. Program Report
0384-5958 Foresight
0384-661X Communicate (Beaverlodge)†
0384-6628 Focus on Winnipeg Schools *see* 0384-6636
0384-6636 Our Schools
0384-6903 Canadian Directory of Railway Museums and Displays†
0384-6970 Rapports de Pratique de Quebec *changed to* Revue de Droit Judiciaire
0384-7322 Fraser's Potato Newsletter
0384-7411 University of Ottawa. Vanier Library. List of Serials†
0384-7446 Livre Canadien *changed to* Nos Livres
0384-7500 Pulse for Jaycee Executives *see* 0008-3895
0384-756X O V C Bulletin *see* 0384-7578
0384-7578 Ontario Veterinary College. Alumni Association. Alumni Bulletin†
0384-7802 Blue Book of C B S Stock Reports
0384-7810 Plein Soleil
0384-8116 Dalhousie University. Computer Centre. Newsletter *see* 0829-5425
0384-8159 Royal Ontario Museum. Life Sciences. Contributions
0384-8167 Revista Canadiense de Estudios Hispanicos
0384-8175 Island Magazine
0384-8523 Alchemist
0384-868X Versus
0384-8701 Contact C I L *changed to* Perspectives C I L
0384-8744 Canadian Journal of Public and Cooperative Economy
0384-8833 Essence†
0384-9120 Regards sur Israel
0384-9147 New Directions
0384-9252 Canada Report
0384-9627 Ontario Museum News
0384-9694 Journal of Religious Ethics
0384-9813 Publicat Index to Canadian Federal Publications *see* 0707-3135
0384-9821 Urban Canada *see* 0707-3135
0384-983X Canadian Newspaper Index *see* 0225-7459
0384-9856 Camping Canada
0384-9864 Congressus Numerantium
0385-0005 Tokai Journal of Experimental and Clinical Medicine
0385-0110 Japanese Association of Periodontology. Journal
0385-0145 Nihon University. Journal of Oral Science
0385-0188 Semmon Toshokan
0385-0234 Kawasaki Medical Journal
0385-0447 A E U
0385-1036 Maku
0385-1109 Shima Marineland. Science Report
0385-1176 J A F S A Library News *see* 0286-7427
0385-1311 Iwate Medical University. Dental Journal
0385-1443 Kanagawa Dental College. Bulletin
0385-1478 Studies in Information and Behavioral Sciences
0385-1559 Journal of Pesticide Science
0385-1613 Matsumoto Shigaku
0385-1621 Japanese Society of Soil Mechanics and Foundation Engineering. Journal
0385-1699 Nikkei Medical
0385-1982 Shinshu University. School of Allied Medical Sciences. Treatises and Studies
0385-2156 Jin To Toseki
0385-230X Kokusai Koryu
0385-2318 Japan Foundation Newsletter
0385-2342 Asian Folklore Studies
0385-2350 D K B Economic Report
0385-2423 National Science Museum. Bulletin. Series A: Zoology
0385-2431 National Science Museum. Bulletin. Series B: Botany
0385-244X National Science Museum. Bulletin. Series C: Geology & Paleontology
0385-2520 Rock Magnetism and Paleogeophysics
0385-2687 Kaiyo Jiho
0385-3039 National Science Museum. Bulletin. Series D: Anthropology
0385-325X Japan. National Diet Library. Annual Report
0385-3284 Japanese National Bibliography
0385-3292 Japanese National Bibliography Weekly List
0385-3330 Monthly List of Selected Atomic Energy Publications *see* 0454-1944
0385-3780 Hydraulics and Pneumatics
0385-3985 Sennke
0385-4000 Library Journal
0385-4035 Hokkaido Mathematical Journal
0385-406X Tohoku Gakuin University Review
0385-4132 Iwate Medical University School of Liberal Arts & Sciences. Annual Report
0385-4418 J E O L News - Analytical Instruments/Application *changed to* J E O L News: Analytical Instrumentation
0385-4426 J E O L News - Electron Optics Instruments/Application *changed to* J E O L News: Electron Optics Instrumentation
0385-4507 J E E
0385-4515 J E I
0385-5023 Dokkyo Journal of Medical Sciences
0385-5082 Journal of Law and Political Science
0385-5414 Heterocycles

0385-549X Kango Tenbo
0385-5600 Microbiology and Immunology
0385-5694 Geijutsu Shunju
0385-5988 Kango Gakusei
0385-6003 Current Bibliography on Science and Technology: Chemistry and Chemical Engineering (Japanese)
0385-6011 Current Bibliography on Science and Technology: Environmental Pollution
0385-6151 Hakkokogaku
0385-6186 Saga University. Faculty of Science and Engineering. Reports
0385-6305 Shoni Naika
0385-6321 Soka Gakkai News
0385-6380 Journal of Fermentation Technology
0385-6402 Asian Culture
0385-6437 J A E R I Reports Abstracts
0385-6658 Computer Report
0385-6747 Contents
0385-6763 Kumamoto Journal of Science. Mathematics
0385-7042 Chosa Shiryo
0385-7298 Society of Automotive Engineers of Japan. Journal
0385-7360 Diamond's Industria *changed to* Diamond's Economic Journal Industria
0385-7530 Japan Indexers Association. Journal
0385-7638 Hyogo Ika Daigaku Igakkai Zasshi
0385-7832 Research Laboratory of Precision Machinery and Electronics. Bulletin
0385-8278 Kyushu University. Department of Geology. Science Reports
0385-8286 Shimabara Earthquake and Volcano Observatory. Sciences Reports
0385-8545 Chishitsugaku Ronshu
0385-8634 Niigata University. Faculty of Agriculture. Bulletin
0385-8863 A.I.P.P.I.
0385-8960 Descriptive and Applied Linguistics. Annual Reports
0385-9282 Japan Welding Society. Transactions
0385-969X Japan. Ministry of Health and Welfare. Statistics and Information Department. Monthly Report on Vital Statistics
0385-9932 Japanese Journal of Animal Reproduction
0386-037X Process: Architecture
0386-0744 National Institute of Polar Research. Memoirs. Special Issue.
0386-0752 Kyoto University. Institute of Atomic Energy. Research Activities
0386-1112 I A T S S Research
0386-1198 Institute for Sea Training. Journal
0386-1430 Atomu Fukushima
0386-1465 Furusato Tembo†
0386-2062 Pharmaceutical Library Bulletin
0386-2143 Chemical Abstracts
0386-2186 Kobunshi Ronbunshu
0386-250X Vegetable and Ornamental Crops Research Station. Bulletin. Series B
0386-2755 Thought
0386-300X Acta Medica Okayama
0386-3425 Snake
0386-3980 Japanese Journal of Leprosy
0386-4103 Osaka City Medical Journal
0386-4243 Sendai Radio Technical College. Research Reports *changed to* Sendai National College of Technology. Research Reports
0386-4251 Young East
0386-426X Tohokai
0386-4294 Gunma University. Faculty of Education. Annual Report: Cultural Science Series
0386-4472 Hokkaido University of Education. Journal. Section 1 A. Humanities
0386-4480 Hokkaido University of Education. Journal. Section 1 B. Social Science
0386-4499 Hokkaido University of Education. Journal. Section 1 C. Education
0386-4901 Hokkaido University of Education. Journal. Section 2 C. Home Economics, Teacher Training for School Health and Physical Education
0386-5096 Mitsubishi Electric Advance
0386-5444 Solar Terrestrial Environmental Research in Japan
0386-5452 Japanese Antarctic Research Expedition, 1956-1962. Scientific Reports. Special Issue *see* 0386-0744
0386-5517 National Institute of Polar Research. Memoirs. Series A: Aeronomy.
0386-5525 National Institute of Polar Research. Memoirs. Series B: Meteorology.
0386-5533 National Institute of Polar Research. Memoirs. Series C: Earth Sciences.
0386-5541 National Institute of Polar Research. Memoirs. Series E: Biology and Medical Science
0386-555X National Institute of Polar Research. Memoirs. Series F: Logistics.
0386-5924 Kawasaki Igakkai Shi
0386-5959 Shimane Journal of Medical Science
0386-5991 Kodai Mathematical Journal
0386-6076 Dentsu Japan Marketing/Advertising Yearbook
0386-6092 Acta Medica Kinki University
0386-6157 Society of Powder Technology, Japan. Journal.
0386-6165 Japan Petroleum Weekly
0386-6688 Pollen Science
0386-7196 Cell Structure and Function
0386-720X Nanzan Institute for Religion and Culture. Bulletin
0386-7285 Far Seas Fisheries Research Laboratory. Bulletin
0386-7293 Current Contents of Academic Journals in Japan
0386-8044 Infrared Society of Japan. Proceeding
0386-8141 Seitai Kagaku
0386-8176 Ogasawara Research Committee. Publications
0386-8362 World Livestock Industry
0386-8435 Research and Clinical Center for Child Development. Annual Report
0386-846X Journal of Pharmacobio-Dynamics
0386-8710 Tokyo Metropolitan University. Department of Geography. Geographical Reports
0386-9571 Hospital Administration
0386-9962 Administrative Management
0387-0766 Micro Computer & Electronics†
0387-1045 Machine Design
0387-1061 Konkuriito Kogaku
0387-1207 Gastroenterological Endoscopy
0387-172X Tohoku National Agricultural Experiment Station. Miscellaneous Publication
0387-2432 Mitsubishi Juko Giho
0387-2793 Journal of Population Problems
0387-2815 American Review
0387-2882 Journal of Law and Politics
0387-3005 Katorikku Kenkyu
0387-3021 Doshisha University Economic Review
0387-3242 Journal of Agricultural Economics
0387-3404 Waseda Commercial Review
0387-3528 National Institute of Special Education. Bulletin
0387-3544 Press Working
0387-382X Japan Marine Science and Technology Center. Technical Reports
0387-3870 Tokyo Journal of Mathematics
0387-3927 J P G Letter
0387-3935 Japan English Magazine Directory *see* 0910-7908
0387-4001 Current Bibliography on Science and Technology: Energy
0387-4095 Orthopaedic and Traumatic Surgery
0387-4141 Research Committee of Essential Amino Acids. Reports
0387-4753 Seijo University Economic Papers
0387-480X Osaka University. Faculty of Pharmaceutical Sciences. Memoirs
0387-5245 O E P
0387-5857 Standard Frequency and Time Service Bulletin
0387-7000 Periodicals in Print in Japan
0387-7019 Media Data Japan
0387-7604 Brain and Development
0387-7647 Hiroshima Daigaku Seibutsu Seisan Gakubu Kiyo
0387-821X University of Occupational and Environmental Health. Journal
0387-8503 Japanese Periodicals Index. Medical Sciences and Pharmacology†
0387-8805 Journal of Light & Visual Environment
0387-8961 Plankton Society of Japan. Bulletin
0387-9348 Heron
0387-9844 Tokyo Metropolitan University. Annual Report of Research on the Ogasawara (Bonin) Islands
0388-0001 Language Sciences
0388-001X College of Dairying. Journal; Natural Science
0388-0028 College of Dairying. Journal; Cultural and Social Sciences
0388-0079 Marine Engineering Society in Japan. Bulletin
0388-0117 Sado Marine Biological Station. Annual Report *changed to* Sado Marine Biological Station. Report
0388-0311 Focus Japan
0388-0494 Japan Computer Quarterly
0388-0508 Journal of Intercultural Studies
0388-0532 Kyoto Review
0388-0605 Monthly Finance Review
0388-0664 Nippon Tungsten Review
0388-0966 Tokyo University of Fisheries. Transactions
0388-1032 Wing Newsletter
0388-1423 A M J Newsletter
0388-1865 World Traders
0388-2403 Japan. National Institute of Animal Health. Bulletin
0388-3051 Marine Engineering Society in Japan. Journal
0388-3213 Japan. National Chemical Laboratory for Industry. Journal
0388-4201 Japan English Books in Print *see* 0910-7908
0388-5267 Energy Forum
0388-5585 Kurinikaru Sutadi
0388-5593 Asian Book Development
0388-5607 Tohoku University. Science Reports. Series 8: Physics and Astronomy
0388-7081 Patents and Licensing
0388-7367 Aichi Kyoiku Daigaku Kenkyu Hokoku
0388-7405 Japan Institute of Navigation. Journal
0388-7421 Japan. National Veterinary Assay Laboratory. Annual Report
0388-7448 Neurosciences
0388-7480 Educational Music, Elementary School
0388-7502 Educational Music, High School
0388-886X Kansai University Review of Law and Politics
0388-9459 Kankyo Gijutsu
0388-9475 Kawasaki Steel Technical Report
0389-0473 Kochi University. Agricultural Science. Research Reports
0389-1313 Nihon Seikisho Gakkai Zasshi
0389-1887 Medical Technology
0389-1895 Journal of Dental Technics
0389-3081 Tokai University. Foreign Language Center. Bulletin
0389-4088 Kochi Gakuen College. Bulletin
0389-4304 J S A E Review
0389-5483 Japan Society of Lubrication Engineers. Journal. International Edition
0389-5610 Neurotraumatology
0389-5696 Medical Apparatus *see* 0289-3673
0389-5858 National Research Institute of Aquaculture. Bulletin
0389-617X Tokyo Denki University. Faculty of Engineering. Research Reports
0389-6609 Seto Marine Biological Laboratory. Special Publication Series
0389-7389 Abstracts of the Current Literature on Respiratory Diseases and T B
0389-8105 Osaka Museum of Natural History. Annual Report
0389-8237 Ionospheric Data at Syowa Station (Antarctica)
0389-8326 Japanese Journal of Nursing
0389-9004 Japan Statistical Yearbook
0389-9047 Osaka Museum of Natural History. Special Publications
0389-9128 Institute of Nature Education in Shiga Heights. Bulletin
0389-9136 Research Institute of Brewing. Report
0389-9403 Shokaki Naishikyo No Shinpo
0390-0037 Chronobiologia
0390-0355 Terzo Occhio
0390-0444 Colture Protette
0390-0460 Micologia Italiana
0390-0479 VigneVini
0390-0487 Zootecnica e Nutrizione Animale
0390-0517 Oncologia Clinica†
0390-0541 Industrie delle Bevande
0390-0711 Medioevo Romanzo
0390-0916 Archivio Trimestrale
0390-1009 Archivio Storico Civico e Biblioteca Trivolziana. Libri & Documenti
0390-1106 Giornale di Astronomia
0390-1246 Ambiente Naturale e Urbano
0390-1807 Cronorama
0390-1815 C S E L T Rapporti Tecnici *see* 0393-2648
0390-2153 Forme del Significato
0390-217X Il Futuro dell'Uomo
0390-2358 I C P
0390-2439 Informatica & Documentazione
0390-346X Psicologia Contemporanea
0390-492X Memorie di Biologia Marina e di Oceanografia
0390-5179 Saggi
0390-5381 Rivista degli Ospedali†
0390-5454 Annali dell'Ospedale Maria Vittoria di Torino
0390-5462 Giornale di Batteriologia, Virologia ed Immunologia
0390-5489 Italian Journal of Orthopaedics and Traumatology
0390-5748 La Ricerca in Clinica e in Laboratorio
0390-6035 Materials Chemistry and Physics
0390-6078 Haematologica
0390-640X Compendio Statistico *see* 0069-7958
0390-6426 Italy. Istituto Centrale di Statistica. Annuario Statistico della Zootecnia, della Pesca e della Caccia
0390-6434 Italy. Istituto Centrale di Statistica. Bolletino Mensile di Statistica. Supplementi
0390-6450 Italy. Istituto Centrale di Statistica. Annuario di Statistiche del Lavoro
0390-6531 Annuario di Contabilita Nazionale Tomo 2
0390-654X Annuario di Contabilita Nazionale Tomo 1
0390-6558 Italy. Istituto Centrale di Statistica. Statistica Annuale del Commercio con l'Estero. Tomo 1
0390-6566 Italy. Istituto Centrale di Statistica. Statistica Annuale del Commercio con l'Estero. Tomo 2
0390-6574 Conti degli Italiani
0390-6582 Annuario Statistico dell'Istruzione-Tomo 1
0390-6590 Annuario Statistico dell'Istruzione-Tomo 2
0390-6620 Italy. Istituto Centrale di Statistica. Indicatori Mensili
0390-6663 Clinical and Experimental Obstetrics and Gynecology
0390-668X Rivista di Informatica
0390-6736 Montanaro d'Italia-Monti e Boschi *changed to* Monti e Boschi
0390-6779 Cooperation in Education†
0390-7783 Accademia delle Scienze di Siena Detta de Fisiocritici. Atti
0390-8542 Diritto e Societa (Naples)
0391-108X Rocca
0391-1527 Cronache Pompeiane
0391-1535 Cronache Ercolanesi
0391-1551 Rivista di Biologia Normale e Patologica
0391-1632 Monitore Zoologico Italiano. Monografie
0391-1926 Contributi di Sociologia
0391-1934 Capitalismo e Socialismo
0391-1942 Strumenti Linguistici
0391-1950 Romanica Neapolitana
0391-2019 H P Trasporti
0391-2035 Clinica e Laboratorio

ISSN INDEX 1559

0391-2043 Medicina Illustrata†
0391-2515 Giornale Storico di Psicologia Dinamica
0391-2639 Otto-Novecento
0391-3104 Quaderni del Vittoriale
0391-3163 Anthropos
0391-3171 Contributi di Sociologia. Readings
0391-321X Istituzioni Culturali†
0391-3228 Le Lingue e le Civilta Straniere Moderne
0391-3236 Quaderni di Analisi Matematica
0391-3244 Scienze della Materia
0391-3252 Serie di Matematica e Fisica
0391-3260 Societa e Diritto di Roma
0391-3279 Collana di Storia Moderna e Contemporanea
0391-3295 Teorie Economiche
0391-3457 Dossier Europa-Emigrazione
0391-3848 Refrattari e Laterizi
0391-3953 T I M *see* 0393-599X
0391-3988 International Journal of Artificial Organs
0391-4089 Italian Journal of Sports Traumatology
0391-4097 Journal of Endocrinological Investigation
0391-4127 Ricerche Slavistiche
0391-4186 Verifiche
0391-4259 Stazione Sperimentale del Vetro. Rivista
0391-4380 Musica Domani
0391-4631 I.M.E.
0391-464X Carte d'Acquisto†
0391-4887 Societa Italiana di Scienza dell'Alimentazione. Rivista
0391-500X Universita degli Studi di Firenze. Facolta di Architettura. Biblioteca. Bollettino di Segnalazioni e Notizie Bibliografiche†
0391-5018 Doc; Documentazione *changed to* Doc Italia
0391-5026 Economic Notes
0391-5115 Journal of European Economic History
0391-5360 Energie Alternative: Habitat, Territorio, Energia
0391-5379 C S E L T Infotel
0391-5425 Armonia di Voci
0391-5433 Catechesi
0391-5468 Dimensioni Nuove
0391-5476 Espressione Giovani†
0391-5484 Mondo Erre
0391-5492 Migranti-Press
0391-5506 Presenza Nuova degli Anziani†
0391-5514 Progetto (Turin)
0391-5522 Apitalia
0391-5603 Urology
0391-5646 Archivio Giuridico
0391-5859 Gortania
0391-5891 Lamiera
0391-5905 Giornale di Fisica. Quaderni†
0391-5972 Istituto Centrale per la Patologia del Libro "Alfonso Gallo." Bollettino
0391-6030 Forme Materiali ed Ideologie del Mondo Antico
0391-6049 Nuovo Medioevo
0391-6065 Dossier di le Monde Diplomatique†
0391-609X Societa e la Scienza
0391-6103 Studi d'Economia
0391-6162 Rivista Aeronautica
0391-6200 Educazione Sanitaria e Medicina Preventiva
0391-6367 E D P Telematica Notizie
0391-6391 Elettronica Oggi
0391-6510 International Journal of Pediatric Nephrology
0391-674X Cooperazione
0391-7029 Archivio di Chirurgia Toracica e Cardiovascolare
0391-7045 Sviluppo e Organizzazione
0391-7096 Castelli Romani
0391-7231 Medicina Ospedaliera Romana
0391-7258 Basic and Applied Histochemistry
0391-7290 V G Vendogiocattoli
0391-7312 Quaderni Terzo Mondo
0391-7339 A E S
0391-7347 E D I†
0391-7363 I M U *see* 0393-599X
0391-7398 Market-Espresso
0391-7401 Plast
0391-741X Progetto (Milan)
0391-7452 Isto Cito Patologia
0391-7487 Ottagono
0391-7525 Giornale Italiano di Diabetologia
0391-769X Fiuggi
0391-7754 Giornale del Maiscoltore
0391-7789 Studi Musicali
0391-7797 Prospettiva Sindacale
0391-7819 Santo
0391-7983 Spezia Oggi
0391-8211 Istituto Storico Artistico Orvietano. Bollettino
0391-822X Bollettino del Lavoro *changed to* Bollettino del Lavoro e del Tributi
0391-8289 Note Economiche
0391-836X Prospettive Settanta
0391-8394 Quaderni Sardi di Economia
0391-8440 International Journal of Transport Economics
0391-8505 Cultura
0391-8513 Informazioni Librarie
0391-8521 Qualita della Vita
0391-853X Religione e Societa
0391-8548 Nuova Universale Studium
0391-8564 Verba Seniorum
0391-8580 I C U Papers†
0391-8599 S I P E
0391-8645 Oleodinamica - Pneumatica - Lubrificazione
0391-8718 Samnium
0391-898X Pediatria Oggi Medica e Chirurgica
0391-8998 Clinica Oculistica e Patologia Oculare
0391-9013 Giornale Italiano di Ostetricia e Ginecologia
0391-9056 Giornale Italiano di Senologia
0391-9064 Artibus et Historiae
0391-9293 Museo Archeologico di Tarquinia. Materiali
0391-9706 Acta Embryologiae et Morphologiae Experimentalis (1980)
0391-9749 Nematologia Mediterranea
0391-9757 Fisica e Tecnologia
0391-9854 Bollettino d'Arte
0391-9889 Giornale Italiano di Medicina del Lavoro
0391-9994 Actum Luce
0392-0038 Archeografo Triestino
0392-0062 Museo Civico di Storia Naturale, Verona. Bolletino
0392-0100 Nuova Polizia e Riforma dello Stato
0392-0143 Centro di Riferimento Italiano Diane. Notiziario
0392-0208 Journal of Nuclear Medicine and Allied Sciences
0392-047X Folia Oncologica
0392-0550 Biblioteca Statale e Libreria Civica di Cremona. Annali
0392-0658 Eta Evolutiva
0392-0879 Collezioni e Musei Archeologici del Veneto
0392-0887 Kokalos
0392-0895 Rivista di Archeologia
0392-0909 Sikelika. Serie Archeologica
0392-0917 Sikelika. Serie Storica
0392-0925 Novita Bibliografiche: Antichita Greca e Romana
0392-1212 Economia del Lavoro (Rome)
0392-128X Giornale Italiano di Oncologia
0392-131X Largo Consumo
0392-1344 Clinica & Terapia Cardiovascolare
0392-1360 Rivista Italiana di Otorinolaringologia, Audiologia e Foniatria
0392-1387 Giornale Italiano di Angiologia
0392-1395 Dermatologia Clinica
0392-1417 Ortopedia e Traumatologia Oggi
0392-162X Ricerche Storiche (Naples)
0392-1875 Quaderni Medievali
0392-1913 Obiettivi e Documenti Veterinari
0392-1948 Studi di Storia dell'Educazione
0392-2049 Acta Mediterranea di Patologia Infettiva e Tropicale
0392-209X Psichiatria e Cultura
0392-2111 Cultura e Mass Media
0392-2146 Studi sull'Educazione
0392-2154 Teorie e Oggetti
0392-2219 Accademia Ligure di Scienze e Lettere. Atti
0392-2227 Giornale Italiano di Chimica Clinica
0392-2294 Automazione Navale
0392-2308 Astronomia (Naples)
0392-2332 Nouvelles de la Republique des Lettres
0392-2510 Biologi Italiani
0392-2715 Bagno Oggi e Domani
0392-2723 Bagno e Accessori
0392-2790 Professionalita
0392-2804 Animazione ed Espressione
0392-2812 Direzione e Scuola
0392-2847 Am Albergo Moderno
0392-2863 Aquarium
0392-2936 European Journal of Gynecological Oncology
0392-2960 C I News (Ceramics International) *changed to* Industrial Ceramic-C I News
0392-3002 Aggiornamento del Medico
0392-3134 Bollettino Informativo Fiscale†
0392-3452 Technologie Chimiche
0392-3460 Tecnologie Elettriche Iternational
0392-3479 Commercio Elettrico
0392-3487 Tecnologie Meccaniche International
0392-3568 Italia Contemporanea
0392-3614 Giornale degli Apparecchi Domestici
0392-3622 Il Giornale della Subfornitura
0392-3630 Giornale dell'Installatore Elettrico
0392-3673 Monthly Review
0392-3711 Notizario Bibliografico di Audiologia
0392-3800 Interplastics
0392-3886 Il Bolscevico
0392-3983 Meccanizzazione Agricola
0392-4173 Naturismo
0392-4270 Cooperativa Centro di Documentazione. Notiziario
0392-4416 Rivista di Pediatria Preventiva e Sociale-Nipiologia
0392-4424 Societa Italiana di Fotogrammetria e Topografia. Bollettino
0392-4564 Memoria
0392-4599 Recuperare: Edilizia, Design, Impianti
0392-4602 Treni Oggi
0392-4629 N U A International Journal of Nephrology, Urology, Andrology
0392-4653 Bank of Italy. Economic Papers†
0392-4661 Banca d'Italia. Contributi alla Ricerca Economica *changed to* Banca d'Italia. Contributi alla Analisi Economica
0392-467X Banca d'Italia. Bollettino Statistico
0392-4718 Pasticceria Internazionale
0392-4815 Meccanica Pratica *see* 0393-5558
0392-4823 Progettista Industriale
0392-4831 Tecnica Ospedaliera
0392-4874 Gruppo Micologico "G. Bresadola". Bollettino
0392-4890 Ceramica per l'Edilizia International
0392-5080 Riscontri
0392-517X Radiotecnica TV, Hi-Fi, Elettronica Professionale *changed to* Radiotecnica TV - Elettronik'Consumo
0392-5404 Schede Medievali
0392-5439 Medaglia
0392-5544 Musica
0392-5730 Ambiente Cucina
0392-5773 Amici della Pipa
0392-5803 Cronache Castellane
0392-5978 Annuario dei Fornitori
0392-6036 Controlli Numerici Macchine a C N Robot Industriali *see* 0393-3911
0392-6044 Energia Solare e Fonti Alternative†
0392-6052 Export†
0392-6060 Latte
0392-6079 Mondo dei Gioielli
0392-6087 R C I
0392-6095 Inventario
0392-6192 Arredo Tessile *see* 0393-4454
0392-629X Instituta et Monumenta. Series 2. Instituta
0392-6567 Utensil
0392-6648 Notiziario Informativo
0392-6699 Eos
0392-6702 Immunologia Clinica e Sperimentale
0392-6737 Societa Italiana di Fisica. Nuovo Cimento D
0392-6788 Studi per l'Ecologia del Quaternario
0392-6796 Le Grandi Automobili
0392-7199 Medical Tribune
0392-7296 Giornale Italiano di Entomologia
0392-7326 Studi Settecenteschi
0392-7334 Centro di Studi Vichiani. Bollettino
0392-7342 Elenchos
0392-7423 Elenchus Bibliographicus Biblicus
0392-7512 Alimentazione Nutrizione Metabolismo
0392-7571 Istituto per la Documentazione Giuridica. Bibliografia. Diritto Civile
0392-758X Museo Regionale di Scienze Naturali, Torino. Bollettino
0392-7733 Fisiopatologia della Riproduzione
0392-7903 Conservazione degli Alimenti
0392-7911 Energia
0392-792X Imbottigliamento
0392-7938 Panis
0392-7946 Scienzasocieta
0392-7954 Tecnologie del Filo
0392-8225 Ceramica Moderna
0392-8306 Agora (Rome)
0392-8535 Dialoghi di Archeologia
0392-8586 Biblioteche Oggi
0392-8764 Heat and Technology
0392-8829 Automazione Oggi
0392-8926 Storia della Storiografia
0392-9043 Il Solidale
0392-9108 Indicatore Cartario *see* 0008-8765
0392-9116 Algologia
0392-9353 Chip
0392-9507 Journal of Foetal Medicine
0392-9590 International Angiology
0392-9698 Acta Cardiologica Mediteranea
0392-9884 Circolo Culturale B.G. Duns Scoto di Roccarainola. Atti
0393-0483 A M U
0393-0505 Junior Dental e Bocca Nuda†
0393-0726 Antologia Medica Italiana
0393-0882 Alta Fedelta
0393-0890 Tennis Italiano
0393-098X E D A V
0393-1218 Uccelli d'Italia
0393-1358 Federalist
0393-1412 Universita Cattolica. Istituto di Storia Antica. Ricerche
0393-1471 Chirurgia Epatobiliare
0393-196X Bollettino di Oceanologia
0393-2095 Kos
0393-2214 Florence Journal of Surgery
0393-2648 C S E L T Technical Reports
0393-2664 Anteprima Libri
0393-2702 Universitas
0393-2729 International Spectator
0393-2842 Match-Ball†
0393-2850 Super Football†
0393-330X Datalignum
0393-3318 Ferrarissima
0393-3415 Rivista di Storia Economica
0393-3571 Istituto Ricerche Pesca Marittima. Quaderni
0393-3598 Cristianesimo nella Storia
0393-361X Psichiatria dell'Infanzia e dell'Adolescenza
0393-3687 Studi Ecumenici
0393-3849 Ricerche Storiche Salesiane
0393-3911 Automazione Integrata
0393-4195 La Favilla
0393-4217 Rivista della Montagna
0393-4330 Zoom (Italian Edition)
0393-439X Aerte e Cornice
0393-4403 Informobili
0393-4411 Riabita
0393-4454 Arredo-Biancheria Casa
0393-4462 Arredo Tessili-Complementi
0393-4470 Interfaccia
0393-4489 Casa Classica†
0393-4500 Giornale dell'Arredamento
0393-4551 Savings and Development
0393-487X Clot and Hematologic Malignancies
0393-4977 Cittanova
0393-5132 Arredostile Middle East
0393-5140 Casarredo Middle East
0393-5167 Forwood International
0393-5183 A A R P Environment Design
0393-5418 Fogli di Informazione
0393-5442 Centauro

1560 ISSN INDEX

0393-5469 Itinerario
0393-5558 Meccanica Moderna
0393-5957 Giornale Italiano di Ricerche Cliniche e Terapeutiche
0393-5981 Brevetti & Invenzioni
0393-599X Industria Mercato
0393-6147 Vesuvio
0393-6368 Universita e Istituti di Studio e Ricerca in Italia. Annuario DEA
0393-6376 Acta Chirurgica Mediterranea
0393-6384 Acta Medica Mediterranea
0393-6392 Acta Pediatrica Mediterranea
0393-6457 Lettera dall'Italia
0393-652X Selezione Chimica Tintoria
0393-6740 Comunismo
0393-6775 Donne e Politica
0393-7445 Lanternino
0393-7526 Ruotaspring
0393-7534 Tribuna del Collezionista
0393-7569 Le Basi Razionali della Terapia
0393-7623 La Medicina di Laboratorio
0393-7631 Odontoiatria Oggi
0393-764X Progressi Clinici: Chirurgia
0393-7658 Progressi Clinici: Medicina
0393-7666 Motori
0393-7844 Politica Meridionalista
0393-7984 Comunita Sportiva
0393-800X J D
0393-8050 Fiere
0393-8077 Vie e Trasporti
0393-8204 Tecno Show
0393-8212 Nuovo Governo Locale
0393-8263 Arsenale
0393-8387 Auto e Design
0393-876X Marmor
0393-8875 Natura e Societa
0393-9243 Economia e Banca
0393-9383 International Journal of Anthropology
0393-9413 Pubblico Esercizio
0393-9480 Steve
0394-0616 Studi e Ricerche sull'Oriente Cristiano
0395-000X Ordinaire du Psychanalyste
0395-0026 Cle des Mots†
0395-0530 Afro Music
0395-0840 Animation et Education
0395-1294 France Transports†
0395-160X Maisons et Decors de l'Est *changed to* Maisons & Decors. Alsace, Lorraine, Champagne
0395-1618 Maisons de l'Est *changed to* Maisons & Decors. Alsace, Lorraine, Champagne
0395-1766 En Equipe au Service de l'Evangile
0395-2061 Guide Europeen des Produits Logiciels *see* 0294-0701
0395-2096 Forum Chirurgical
0395-2126 Hetero
0395-2673 Conseils Sols et Murs
0395-269X Ex Libris Francais
0395-2894 Specialement Votre
0395-3203 Universite de Nantes. Centre de Recherches sur l'Histoire de la France Atlantique. Enquetes et Documents *changed to* Universite de Nantes. Centre de Recherches sur l'Histoire du Monde Atlantique. Enquetes et Documents
0395-3491 Sports Equestres†
0395-3599 Courses Hippiques
0395-367X Technic Hebdo
0395-3890 Bulletin Europeen de Physiopathologie Respiratoire *see* 0271-9983
0395-403X Societe Francaise de Cardiologie. Bulletin d'Informations
0395-4366 Autohebdo
0395-4374 Bulletin de Medecine Legale, Urgence Medicale, Centre Anti-Poisons *see* 0249-6208
0395-4382 Karate Cinema
0395-451X Bulletin Rapide de Droit des Affaires
0395-5494 Marches Europeens des Fruits et Legumes *changed to* Fruits et Legumes Actualites
0395-5621 C F D T Magazine
0395-6601 France. Centre National de Documentation Pedagogique. Textes et Documents pour la Classe.
0395-7276 France. Ministere de l'Economie et des Finances. Bulletin de Liaison et d'Information *changed to* France. Ministere de l'Economie. Bulletin de Liaison et d'Information
0395-7349 Medecine, Sciences et Documents
0395-7519 Centre de Recherches Zootechniques et Veterinaires de Theix. Bulletin Technique
0395-7594 Federation Francaise de Sports pour Handicaps Physiques. Informations *changed to* Handisport Magazine
0395-7691 Education Rurale
0395-773X Traduire
0395-7837 Chantiers de Pedagogie Mathematique
0395-7845 Chants des Peuples
0395-8086 Universite d'Aix-Marseille 3. Centre des Hautes Etudes Touristiques. Collection "Essais"
0395-8175 Cahiers du Credit Mutuel
0395-8183 Charolais
0395-8507 Foret - Loisirs et Equipements de Plein Air†
0395-8531 Horticulture Francaise
0395-8876 Journal de l'Ile de la Reunion
0395-9066 Sport de l'Esprit *changed to* Bouquet
0395-9279 Journal de Microscopie et de Spectroscopie Electroniques
0395-9295 A.D.M.A.: la Vie Musicale en Aquitaine†
0395-9317 Cahiers de la Mediterranee
0395-9481 Actuel Developpement
0396-0382 Syndicat General des Industries Medico-Chirurgicales et Dentaires. Annuaire†
0396-0595 Courrier de l'Exploitant et du Scieur *changed to* C T B Info
0396-0625 Annuaire des Fournisseurs de Laboratoires Pharmaceutiques et Cosmetiques
0396-1214 Catalogue National du Traitement des Surfaces de l'Anticorrosion et des Traitements Thermiques
0396-2024 Connaissance de l'Ouest
0396-2156 Annuaire du Tiers Monde
0396-2318 Annuaire des Avocats
0396-2393 Union des Superieures Majeurs de France. Annuaire
0396-2458 Promotion
0396-2644 Unites Petrochimiques dans les Pays de l'OPEC et de l'OPAEP†
0396-2679 Caribbean Archives
0396-2687 Bulletin des Centres de Recherches Exploration-Production ELF Aquitaine
0396-3128 Relais - Statistiques de l'Economie Picarde
0396-3640 Revue Fiduciaire Comptable
0396-3683 Comite d'Organisation des Recherches Appliquees sur le Developpement Economique et Social. Recherches Economiques et Sociales *changed to* Nouvelles Recherches Economiques et Sociales
0396-437X Chroniques d'Actualite de la S E D E I S
0396-4388 Port Autonome du Havre. Bulletin Analytique de Documentation Generale
0396-4396 Port Autonome du Havre. Bulletin Analytique de Documentation Technique
0396-4914 Mes Premieres Grilles
0396-4957 Encyclopedie d'Utovie
0396-5015 Semaine Veterinaire
0396-5791 Courrier de la Microcopie
0396-5880 Intergeo-Bulletin
0396-6666 Achats et Entretien-Equipement Industriel
0396-7107 Therapeutiques Naturelles
0396-7115 Groupement National pour l'Organisation de la Medecine Auxiliaire. Bulletin de Liaison *see* 0396-7107
0396-714X Commerce Moderne
0396-7360 Jeunesse du Quart Monde
0396-7891 Alimentation Moderne *see* 0761-3652
0396-8235 Chasseur d'Images
0396-8863 Association des Services Geologiques Africains. Bulletin d'Information et de Liaison. Information and Liaison Bulletin *changed to* Geologie Africaine
0396-8936 Federation Nationale des Agriculteurs Multiplicateurs de Semences. Bulletin
0396-9657 Recherches Geographiques a Strasbourg
0396-969X Esprit Saint
0396-9975 Informations d'Ile de France
0397-006X Ciments, Betons, Platres, Chaux
0397-0280 Unions Sexuelles
0397-0736 Echanges
0397-1511 Journal du Mineur
0397-2836 Biologie et Ecologie Mediterraneene
0397-2844 Geologie Mediterraneenne
0397-3816 Manutention *changed to* Logistiques Magazine
0397-3999 Techniques Orthopediques
0397-4715 Expomat Actualites†
0397-474X Transport Public
0397-5754 Marches Agricoles-l'Echo des Halles
0397-6424 Hi Fi Magazine†
0397-6491 Science Film†
0397-6505 Secretaires d'Aujourd'hui†
0397-6513 T E C
0397-6521 Transports Urbains
0397-7153 Biologie du Comportement
0397-7757 Bulletin Signaletique. Part 130: Physique Mathematique, Optique, Acoustique, Mechanique, Chaleur *changed to* P A S C A L Folio. Part 10: Mecanique et Acoustique
0397-7757 Bulletin Signaletique. Part 130: Physique Mathematique, Optique, Acoustique, Mechanique, Chaleur *changed to* P A S C A L Explore. Part 27: Methodes de Formation et Traitement des Images
0397-7757 Bulletin Signaletique. Part 130: Physique Mathematique, Optique, Acoustique, Mechanique, Chaleur *changed to* P A S C A L Explore. Part 32: Metrologie et Appareillage en Physique et Physicochimie
0397-7870 Revue Francaise d'Etudes Americaines
0397-8060 Progres Technique
0397-8079 Revue de l'Embouteillage et des Industries du Conditionnement, Traitement, Distribution Transport *changed to* Conditionnement des Liquides-Embouteillage
0397-8249 Annuaire de l'U R S S et des Pays Socialistes Europeens
0397-8389 Economie Familiale
0397-8435 Centre National de la Cinematographie. Bulletin d'Information
0397-8702 Film Francais
0397-9180 Pediatre (Paris)
0397-944X Migrants Nouvelles
0397-9873 Revue Trimestrielle de Droit Civil
0398-0006 Paris Madame
0398-0049 Theatre et Animation
0398-0499 Journal des Maladies Vasculaires
0398-074X Astrolab
0398-1851 Electronique et Applications Industrielles
0398-3145 Cadres C F D T
0398-3218 Geophysique *see* 0766-5105
0398-3765 Centre International de Documentation Occitane. Serie Etudes
0398-4346 Revue Arachnologique
0398-7515 Argus du Petrole
0398-7620 Revue d'Epidemiologie et de Sante Publique
0398-8287 Institut Technique de l'Aviculture. Tendances des Marches
0398-8341 Sport Bowling
0398-8384 Revue des Livres pour Enfants
0398-8716 Service 2000
0398-9089 Soul Bag
0398-9372 Nouveau Photocinema *changed to* Photomagazine
0398-9453 Biza Neira (Bise Noire)
0398-9682 Nouvelles de France
0398-9771 Journal Francais d'Oto-Rhino-Laryngologie
0398-9836 Nouveau Journal de Chimie
0398-9941 Bulletin Signaletique. Part 310: Genie Biomedical. Informatique Biomedicale. Physique Biomedicale *changed to* P A S C A L Explore. Part 84: Genie Biomedical. Informatique Biomedicale
0398-995X Bulletin Signaletique. Part 890: Industries Mecaniques-Batiment-Travaux Public-Transports *changed to* P A S C A L Folio. Part 10: Mecanique et Acoustique
0398-9968 Bulletin Signaletique. Part 165: Atomes et Molecules. Plasmas *changed to* P A S C A L Explore. Part 11: Physique Atomique et Moleculaire. Plasmas
0399-0087 Septentrion
0399-0265 Services d'Aide Medicale Urgente. Revue
0399-0281 France. Ministere de l'Amenagement du Territoire, de l'Equipement, du Logement et des Transports. Bulletin Officiel
0399-0346 Journal des Africanistes
0399-0370 Afrique et l'Asie Modernes
0399-0435 Journal Francais de Biophysique et Medecine Nucleaire *changed to* Journal de Biophysique et Medecine Nucleaire
0399-0443 Universite de Bordeaux III. Centre de Recherches sur l'Amerique Anglophone. Annales
0399-0516 R A I R O Analyse Numerique/ Numerical Analysis
0399-0524 R A I R O Automatique/Systems Analysis and Control
0399-0532 R A I R O Informatique/Computer Science
0399-0540 R A I R O Informatique Theorique/ Theoretical Informatics
0399-0559 R A I R O Recherche Operationnelle/ Operations Research
0399-0575 Revue Bryologique et Lichenologique *see* 0181-1576
0399-0648 Thesindex Medical†
0399-0656 Thesindex Dentaire†
0399-0842 Journal de Mecanique Appliquee
0399-0966 Planification, Habitat, Information
0399-0974 Cybium
0399-1121 Amitie Henri Bosco. Cahiers *see* 0753-4590
0399-1148 Revue Pratique de Droit Social
0399-1156 Vie des Collectivites Ouvrieres *changed to* Revue des Comites d'Entreprise
0399-1164 Vie Ouvriere
0399-1245 Analyses de la S.E.D.E.I.S.
0399-1253 Peuples Mediterraneens - Mediterranean Peoples
0399-127X Universite Scientifique et Medical de Grenoble. Institut des Sciences Nucleaires. Rapport Annuel *changed to* Institut des Sciences Nucleaires Grenoble. Rapport
0399-1415 Cahiers Leopold Delisle
0399-1563 Bulletin Signaletique. Part 110: Informatique-Automatique-Recherche Operationnelle-Gestion-Economie *changed to* P A S C A L Explore. Part 34: Robotique. Automatique et Automatisation des Processus Industrieis
0399-1563 Bulletin Signaletique. Part 110: Informatique-Automatique-Recherche Operationnelle-Gestion Economie *changed to* P A S C A L Explore. Part 33. Informatique
0399-1571 G A P H Y O R. Atomes, Molecules, Gaz Neutres Et Ionises. *changed to* G A P H Y O R. Base de Donnees
0399-1784 Oceanologica Acta
0399-1989 Recherches Germaniques
0399-2322 Bella (Milan, 1975)
0399-3752 Revue Culturelle Reunionnaise†

ISSN INDEX 1561

0399-5070 Actuels
0399-7014 Brud Nevez
0399-7081 Dico - Plus
0399-7189 Dependable's List Marketing Newsletter
0399-7715 Caravanier
0399-8223 Nouveau Guide Gault-Millau
0399-8320 Gastro-Enterologie Clinique et Biologique
0399-855X Techniques de l'Energie *see* 0755-5202
0399-8975 C N P R Revue des Entreprises
0399-9505 France U.R.S.S. Magazine
0399-9726 France. Comite des Travaux Historiques et Scientifiques. Section d'Histoire Moderne et Contemporaine (Depuis 1610). Bulletin *see* 0071-8459
0399-9734 Bulletin du Bibliophile et du Bibliothecaire *see* 0399-9742
0399-9742 Bulletin du Bibliophile†
0400-0439 A C E I Newsletter *see* 0732-5371
0400-132X A.M.I.F. *see* 0298-2900
0400-1559 A P R O Bulletin
0400-163X A R E O Quarterly *see* 0003-0791
0400-227X Aarbok for den Norske Kirke
0400-4043 Acta Humboldtiana.
0400-471X Actualites Sociales Hebdomadaires
0400-5104 Adesso†
0400-5880 Adult Teacher
0400-7719 Agricoltore di Terra di Lavoro
0400-8111 Agronomia Sulriograndense
0400-8510 Air Currents
0401-3174 Alfold
0401-331X Algemeen Werkloosheidsfonds. Jaarverslag
0401-3689 Alhambra
0401-3956 Printing Times
0401-5576 Aluminum Light *changed to* Glass Workers News
0401-6351 American Association for Automotive Medicine. Proceedings
0402-4249 Angolite
0402-4621 Annales de Medecine Physique *see* 0168-6054
0402-5563 Anregung
0402-6233 Antoinette
0402-6802 Anwaltsverzeichnis†
0402-7493 Arab Horse Society News
0402-7817 Arbeits und Forschungsberichte zur Saechsischen Bodendenkmalpflege
0402-852X Archaeologia Japonica
0402-9054 Archivos de Pediatria
0402-9283 Arena
0403-0133 Argentina. Ministerio de Trabajo y Seguridad Social. Boletin de Biblioteca†
0403-0699 Arizona. State. State Land Department. Water Resources Report *changed to* Arizona. Department of Water Resources. Report
0403-1792 Arkansas Highways
0403-3884 Arzt und Christ†
0403-4457 Asiatic Society. Annual Report
0403-5542 Aspas de la Patata
0403-8894 Atomic Energy Guideletter *changed to* Washington Atomic Energy Report
0403-9114 Chalk River Nuclear Laboratories. Physics Division. Progress Report†
0403-9319 Atoms in Japan
0404-181X Australia. Department of Primary Industry. Tobacco Industry Trust. Account Annual Report
0404-3529 Automobil
0404-6811 Balik ve Balikcilik
0404-6919 Ballroom Dancing Year Book *changed to* Dancing Year Book
0404-8997 Bar North *changed to* North Dakota Stockman
0404-9462 Bollettino di S. Nicola
0405-1033 Der Beamten-Bund
0405-1157 Beauty & Barber Dealers World
0405-119X Beauty School World
0405-6485 Betriebs- und Arbeitswirtschaft in der Praxis
0405-6590 Better Homes and Gardens Christmas Ideas
0405-668X Better Nutrition
0405-6701 Betteravier Francais
0405-721X Bibliografia Brasileira de Quimica Tecnologia *see* 0100-0756
0405-9212 Biblioteca Promocion del Pueblo
0406-3317 Biologie in der Schule
0406-3597 Plant Protection Bulletin
0406-3678 Bitumes Actualites
0406-5948 Boletin de Londres†
0406-6987 Tata Institute of Fundamental Research. Lectures on Mathematics and Physics. Mathematics *changed to* Tata Institute Lectures on Mathematics
0406-9765 Brazil. Fundacao Instituto Brasileiro de Geografia e Estatistica. Boletim Bibliografico
0407-2294 University of British Columbia. Forest Club. Research Note†
0407-5439 Buchwissenschaftliche Beitraege *see* 0724-7001
0407-5501 Bucks County Law Reporter
0407-7202 Building and Allied Trades Official Handbook *changed to* Building and Allied Industries Official Handbook
0407-8985 B D I-Mitteilungen†
0407-923X Bunte Illustrierte *changed to* Bunte
0408-0904 Japanese Hospital Directory
0408-2133 Bahrain News
0408-215X Bahrain Trade Directory
0408-3075 Banca y Seguros
0408-3164 Banco Central de Costa Rica. Informacion de Estadistica Mensual *changed to* Banco Central de Costa Rica. Boletin Estadistico
0408-3172 Banco Central de Costa Rica. Informacion Economica Semanal
0408-4284 Bank for International Settlements. Monetary and Economic Department. International Commodity Position. General Survey†
0408-4632 Bank Pembangunan Indonesia. Annual Report
0408-5655 Bardsey Observatory Report
0408-568X Bargain Paradises of the World *changed to* Retirement Paradises of the World
0408-6104 Baseball Guidebook
0408-6392 Bastions de Geneve
0408-8107 Beitraege zum Buch- und Bibliothekswesen
0408-8344 Beitraege zur Geschichte der Reichskirche in der Neuzeit
0408-8379 Beitraege zur Geschichte der Universitaet Mainz
0408-8492 Beitraege zur Landeskunde
0408-8514 Beitraege zur Mittelamerikanischen Voelkerkunde
0408-9006 Commission Belge de Bibliographie. Bulletin
0408-9189 Belgium. Ministere de l'Emploi et du Travail. Bibliotheque. Bulletin Bibliographique Mensuel
0408-9235 Belgium. Ministere des Affaires Economiques. Direction Generale des Etudes et de la Documentation. Apercu de l'Evolution Economique *changed to* Belgium. Ministere des Affaires Economiques. Direction Generale des Etudes et de la Documentation. Lettre de Conjoncture
0408-9936 Saopstenja
0409-0179 Belgrade. Univerzitet. Elektrotehnicki Fakultet. Publikacije. Serija: Telekomunikacije i Elektronika *see* 0351-2177
0409-0314 Zavod za Zdravstvenu Zastitu S R Srbije. Glasnik
0409-1132 La Berio
0409-1477 Freie Universitaet Berlin. Osteuropa-Institut. Berichte
0409-2163 Bermuda Historical Society. Occasional Publications
0409-2570 Best Jewish Sermons†
0409-2694 Beton-Litteratur Referater
0409-2740 Betontechnische Berichte
0409-2791 Betriebstechnik
0409-3453 Bibliografia Pomorza Zachodniego
0409-3739 Bibliografski Vjesnik
0409-3747 Bibliographia Belgica
0409-6568 C A F Bulletin Mensuel *changed to* C A F Revue
0409-7734 Cactus
0409-8757 Cahiers Medico-Sociaux
0409-9192 Caja de Ahorros y Monte de Piedad de las Baleares. Memoria
0410-2894 California F P
0410-3556 California Teacher
0410-3882 Calvinist Contact
0410-5389 Canada. Statistics Canada. Grain Milling Statistics/Statistiques de Mouture des Grains†
0410-5869 Canada. Statistics Canada. Road and Street Mileage and Expenditure/Voies Publiques: Longueur et Depenses *see* 0706-3105
0410-5877 Canada. Statistics Canada. Sales Financing/Financement des Ventes†
0410-904X Canadian Jewish Congress. Information and Comment, Social and Economic Studies: Fundamental Rights and Freedoms in Canada. Progress Reports†
0411-129X Carnuntum Jahrbuch
0411-275X Catholic Truth
0411-5023 Centro de Historia del Tachira. Boletin
0411-5562 Cercle Ernest Renan. Cahiers
0411-7085 Directory of Chain Restaurant Operators
0411-8634 Chemia w Szkole
0411-8871 Chemical Spotlight
0411-8987 Chemische Gesellschaft der DDR. Mitteilungsblatt
0412-2658 Chirugia Generale†
0412-2968 Christ in Our Home
0412-3131 Christian Librarian
0412-4553 Church Administration
0412-5568 Cineromanzo
0412-5878 Cirugia, Ginecologia y Urologia *see* 0009-739X
0412-6300 Citrus Engineering Conference. Transactions
0412-7994 Clinical Medicine *changed to* Journal of Continuing Education in Rural and Community Medicine
0413-7647 Colorado's Annual Highway Report†
0413-8384 Columbia University. Bureau of Applied Social Research. Bureau Reporter†
0413-9593 Comite du Folklore Champenois. Bulletin
0414-1105 Communes d'Europe
0414-2713 Concretezza†
0414-4406 Congress International Medical de Pays de Langue Francaise de l'Hemisphere Americain. Rapports et Communications
0414-7790 Contemporary Philosophy Series
0414-8126 Contractor *changed to* Builder & Contractor
0414-8681 Enquette Restreinte sur les Salaries
0415-1798 Deine Gesundheit
0415-3200 Musashino Electrical Communication Laboratory. Technical Journal
0415-3693 Samling af Bekendtgoerelser *see* 0108-9102
0415-3944 Danish Plant Protection Service. Annual Report
0415-6102 Deutsche Ostkunde
0415-6412 D Z A
0415-7508 B D I Deutschland Liefert
0415-8407 Digest of Chiropractic Economics
0415-9241 Directory of Blood Transfusion Facilities and Services *see* 0419-2206
0415-9764 Directory of Oil Well Drilling Contractors
0415-9772 Directory of Oil Well Supply Companies
0416-0371 Discussione
0416-2706 Donaldson's Port Elizabeth , Uitenhage and Despatch Directory
0416-6906 Dansk Dendrologisk Arsskrift
0416-6981 Dansk Teknisk Litteraturselskab. Skriftserie
0416-7309 Politechnika Gdanska. Zeszyty Naukowe. Chemia
0416-833X Decheniana-Beihefte (Bonn)
0416-928X Delpinoa
0416-9336 Delta Pi Epsilon. Research Bulletin
0416-9565 Democrazia e Diritto
0417-0164 Denmark. Danmarks Statistik. Detailpriser
0417-0296 Denryoku to Tetsudo
0417-0792 Dermatologia i Venerologia
0417-2051 Deutsche Gesellschaft fuer Musik des Orients. Mitteilungen
0417-2957 Z D
0417-3635 Deutsches Soldatenjahrbuch
0417-3937 Dharmayug
0417-5190 Dirasat Arabiyat
0417-5522 Directory of American Horticulture *changed to* North American Horticulture: A Reference Guide
0417-5662 British Commonwealth Collections of Micro-Organisms. Directory of Collections and List of Species Maintained in Australia†
0417-5751 Directory of Conventions
0417-5905 Directory of Geophysical and Oil Companies Who Use Geophysical Service†
0417-5964 Directory of Indian Engineering Exporters
0417-6383 Directory of Professional Electrologists
0417-6766 Diritto e Pratica nell'Assicurazione
0417-9382 Dominica. Ministry of Finance and Development. Annual Overseas Trade Report
0417-9927 Doriana
0417-9994 Dortmunder Beitraege zur Zeitungsforschung
0418-1263 Duesseldorf in Zahlen
0418-1379 Dukes County Intelligencer
0418-2057 Dwarf Iris Society Portfolio
0418-2642 Quaternary Research
0418-2693 Daily Labor Report
0418-3304 Danish Films
0418-3614 Politechnika Gdanska. Zeszyty Naukowe. Elektronika
0418-3746 University of Dar es Salaam. Economic Research Bureau. Papers
0418-3770 Dar es Salaam University Law Journal
0418-3975 Geography Publications at Dartmouth†
0418-4297 Daugavas Vanagu Menesraksts
0418-453X Universitatis Scientiarum Debreceniensis. Acta Classica
0418-4556 Acta Universitatis Debreceniensis de Ludovico Kossuth Nominatea. Series Historica. Egyetemes Torteneti Tanulmanyok
0418-4572 Sudia Romanica Universitatis Debreceniensis de Ludovico Kossuth Nominatae. Series Litteraria
0418-4580 Nemet Filologiai Tanulmanyok
0418-5013 Defense Indicators†
0418-5021 Defense Industry Bulletin *see* 0011-7595
0418-5633 I.A.M.R. Reports
0418-582X Documentation List: Africa
0418-6303 Denki Kagaku Newsletter *changed to* Electrochemistry and Industrial Physical Chemistry
0418-6435 Risoe-M
0418-6443 Denmark. Atomenergikomissionens Forsoegsanslaeg, Risoe. Risoe Report *see* 0106-2840
0418-6559 Groenlands Geologiske Undersoegelse. Rapport
0418-6745 Denmark Review
0418-694X Dental Outlook
0418-7598 Desert Bighorn Council. Transactions
0418-761X Desert Locust Control Organization for Eastern Africa. Annual Report
0418-7717 Designed in Finland *changed to* Design in Finland
0418-7830 Detalle
0418-8381 Das Deutsche Firmen-Alphabet
0418-842X Deutsche Forschungsgemeinschaft. Mexiko-Projekt
0418-8802 Der Deutsche Lehrer im Ausland
0418-9140 Deutsche Studien†
0418-9698 Baghdader Mitteilungen

0418-9779 Germanische Denkmaeler der Voelkerwanderungszeit
0419-005X Deutschsprachige Zeitschriften Deutschland - Oesterreich - Schweiz
0419-0254 Developments in Geotectonics
0419-0432 Hukerikar Memorial Lecture Series
0419-0637 Dialog der Gesellschaft
0419-0890 Dianoia
0419-1137 Dictionary of International Biography
0419-1153 Dictionnaire Vidal
0419-1188 Didaskalos†
0419-1218 Didattica delle Scienze
0419-1285 Digest of Commercial Laws of the World
0419-1293 Digest of Current Industrial and Labour Law
0419-1854 Direction (Washington)
0419-2052 Directors Guild of America. Directory of Members
0419-2109 Directory of Alcoholism Treatment Facilities, Domiciliary Houses and State and Provincial Alcoholism *see* 0092-3826
0419-2141 American Medical Association. Directory of Approved Internships and Residencies *changed to* Directory of Residency Training Accredited by the Accreditation Council for Graduate Medical Education
0419-2206 Directory of Blood Banking and Transfusion Facilities and Services†
0419-2281 C I B Directory of Building Research Information and Development Organizations *changed to* International Directory of Building Research, Information and Development Organizations
0419-2370 Directory of Collections and List of Species Maintained in Canada†
0419-2400 Directory of Communicators in Agriculture†
0419-2443 Directory of Cooperative Organisations in South-East Asia†
0419-2508 Directory of Department Stores
0419-2559 Directory of Educational Opportunities in Georgia *changed to* Directory: A Guide to Colleges, Vocational-Technical Schools & Special Purpose Institutions
0419-2648 Directory of Fire Research in the United States *changed to* Directory of Fire Research
0419-2818 Directory of Jewish Health and Welfare Agencies
0419-2923 Directory of Mailing List Houses
0419-3040 Directory of Music Faculties in American Colleges and Universities *see* 0098-664X
0419-3253 Directory of Physics and Astronomy Facilities in North American Colleges and Universities *changed to* Directory of Physics & Astronomy Staff (Year)
0419-3733 Directory of the Cultural Organizations of the Republic of China
0419-3806 Directory of the Turf
0419-3857 Directory of Washington State Manufacturers, Products, Industry, Location *see* 0148-5687
0419-3865 Directory of Water Pollution Research Laboratories†
0419-3903 Direktor
0419-3911 Dirigente Municipal
0419-4187 Dispatch
0419-4209 Dissertation Abstracts International. Section A: Humanities and Social Sciences
0419-4217 Dissertation Abstracts International. Section B: Physical Sciences and Engineering
0419-4241 Dissertationes Archaeologicae Gandenses
0419-4357 Distribution of Physicians, Hospital, Hospital Beds in the U S *see* 0731-0315
0419-4632 Dizionario Bibliografico delle Riviste Giuridiche Italiane
0419-5345 Documentation on Asia
0419-5361 Documentation Photographique
0419-537X Documentation sur l'Europe Centrale†
0419-5612 Review of International Affairs
0419-5728 Documents pour la Carte de la Vegetation des Alpes *see* 0335-5330
0419-5736 Documents pour Servir a l'Histoire de l'Afrique Equatoriale Francaise. Deuxieme Serie. Brazza et la Fondation du Congo Francaise†
0419-7305 Saechsische Bibliographie
0419-747X Droit de l'Espace†
0419-764X Drug Topics Health & Beauty Aids Directory†
0419-7674 Drum (South Africa)
0419-7682 Drum (Nigerian Edition)
0419-7925 Dubrovacki Horizonti
0419-8050 Duke Endowment. Annual Report
0419-8093 Duke University. Council on Aging and Human Development. Proceedings of Seminars†
0419-8735 Dwon Lwak
0419-8816 Dzieje Lublina
0419-8824 Dzieje Najnowsze
0419-9081 Diagramm
0419-9154 Directory of Textile Plant Processes†
0419-9472 Danmarks 500 Stoerste Virksomheder *see* 0106-9985
0420-0098 Design Automation Workshop. Proceedings *changed to* A C M/I E E E Design Automation Conference. Proceedings
0420-0152 Deutsche Bibliothek
0420-0195 Deutsche Physikalische Gesellschaft. Verhandlungen
0420-0632 Directory of Law Enforcement Professors†
0420-0918 Doshisha American Studies
0420-0942 Test Yourself for Science†
0420-1078 Dutch Archaeological and Historical Society. Studies
0420-1132 Dansk Geologisk Forening. Aarsskrift
0420-2155 Directory of Engineers and Land Surveyors Registered in South Carolina
0420-2384 Dydaktyka Szkoly Wyzszej
0420-2392 Dziko
0420-3690 Eastern Indiana Farmer *changed to* Farmweek
0420-8870 Einst und Jetzt
0420-9397 Electric Power Industry in Japan
0420-9885 Der Elektrofachmann
0421-0670 Elternhaus und Schule
0421-2835 Entisaikain Helsinki
0421-2991 Entscheidungen der Finanzgerichte
0421-4226 E S O P E
0421-4935 Est Industriel et Commercial†
0421-4986 Estadisticas de la Aviacion Civil en Espana
0421-5370 Estudios Internacionales *see* 0185-1616
0421-6423 Europe Service†
0421-7527 European Congress of Cardiology. Abstracts of Papers
0421-9090 Exile
0421-9724 Extension *see* 0020-4919
0421-9910 Analysis of Public Utility Financing
0422-017X ERB-Dom†
0422-0943 East Anglia Life
0422-1001 East-European Spokesman
0422-1494 Eastern Europe Agricultural Situation *changed to* World Agriculture Regional Supplement: Eastern Europe
0422-1540 Eastern Industrial World *changed to* Northeastern Industrial World
0422-2482 Echoes from the East Tennessee Historical Society *changed to* Newsline (Knoxville)
0422-2504 Echos des Communications†
0422-2555 Eco
0422-2628 Eco Motori
0422-2784 Economia Industrial
0422-2954 Economic Research Institute. Economic Bulletin†
0422-5740 Edinburgh Tatler
0422-6186 Editur
0422-6690 Educational Council for Foreign Medical Graduates. Annual Report *see* 0145-2037
0422-6739 Educational Quest†
0422-7727 Ehime University. Memoirs. Serie: Natural Science
0422-9053 Electronic Industry Telephone Directory
0422-9304 Der Elektriker
0422-9576 Elelmiszervizsgalati Kozlemenyek
0422-9878 Elsevier Lexica†
0422-9932 Elu Local
0423-104X Endokrynologia Polska†
0423-1082 Energetica
0423-1163 Energiewirtschaft
0423-4243 Espresso
0423-4596 Financial and Estate Planners Quarterly
0423-4847 Estudios de Deusto
0423-5037 Estudios Turisticos
0423-5509 Etnoloski Pregled
0423-5673 Etudes Eburneennes
0423-5975 Eulenspiegel
0423-6645 E A A S Newsletter
0423-6777 European Bureau of Adult Education. Notes & Studies†
0423-6831 European Coal and Steel Community. Consultative Committee. Yearbook
0423-6955 Commission of the European Communities. Collection du Droit du Travail†
0423-7242 European Congress of Cardiology. (Proceedings)
0423-7269 European Cotton Industry Statistics
0423-7781 European Organization for Nuclear Research. Repertoire des Communications Scientifiques. Index of Scientific Publications *see* 0304-2871
0423-7846 European Parliament. Bulletin
0423-8044 European Purchasing Conference. (Proceedings)
0423-8346 Evangelisch-Lutherische Landeskirche Sachsens. Amtsblatt
0423-9938 E E M
0424-0227 E U M E N Action†
0424-0928 East African Studies
0424-1088 East Midland Archaeological Bulletin *changed to* East Midlands Archaeology
0424-1401 East Pakistan Medical Journal *see* 0301-035X
0424-1851 Eastern Nigerian School Libraries Association. Bulletin *see* 0331-8109
0424-2033 Eau Pure
0424-2238 Ecole des Parents
0424-2483 Economia Politica
0424-2513 Economic Affairs
0424-2769 How to Avoid Financial Tangles
0424-3145 Economie Agricole
0424-3331 E I U World Outlook
0424-3374 Economista Mexicano†
0424-480X Year-End Summary of the Electric Power Situation in the United States *changed to* Electric Power Annual Report
0424-4923 Editor & Publisher International Year Book
0424-5059 Edmund's Used Car Prices
0424-5393 Education des Adultes *see* 0018-8891
0424-5407 Education Development Center. Annual Report
0424-5504 Education in the Americas Information Series; Bulletin†
0424-5512 Education in the North
0424-6241 Educators Guide to Free Health, Physical Education & Recreation Materials
0424-6268 E D U C O M Bulletin
0424-7086 Japanese Journal of Sanitary Zoology
0424-7116 Eiszeitalter und Gegenwart
0424-7558 Ekonomski Pregled
0424-7701 Electra
0424-7760 Electrical Engineering in Japan
0424-8201 Electron Microscopy Society of America. Proceedings
0424-8287 Electronic Production Aids Catalog *changed to* Electronic Packaging and Production Vendor Selection Issue
0424-8368 Electronics and Communications in Japan
0424-8384 Electronics Hobbyist†
0424-8562 Das Elektrofach
0424-8775 Elements de Bibliographie†
0424-8848 Elet es Irodalom
0424-9283 Empirical Research in Accounting, Selected Studies *changed to* Journal of Accounting Research. Supplement
0424-9402 Commercial Bank of Greece. Report of the Chairman of the Board of Directors
0424-9674 Encuentro
0425-0494 English in Education
0425-0508 English in Africa
0425-0575 English Miscellany
0425-1067 Entomological Society of Nigeria. Bulletin *see* 0331-0094
0425-1466 Ephemerides Mariologicae
0425-1482 Epidemiologija, Mikrobiologija i Infekciozni Bolesti
0425-1644 Estomatologia e Cultura
0425-1741 Erdkundliches Wissen
0425-2772 Espanol Actual
0425-340X Estudio Agustiniano
0425-3442 Estudios Agrarios
0425-3485 Estudios Cooperativos
0425-3698 Estudios Empresariales
0425-3752 Estudios Lulianos
0425-4082 Estudos Universitarios
0425-4309 Ethiopia. Customs Head Office. External Trade Statistics
0425-4414 Ethiopian Journal of Education
0425-4597 Ethnologia Europaea
0425-4791 Revue des Lettres Modernes. Etudes Bernanosiennes
0425-4937 Commission of the European Communities. Collection Physiologie et Psychologie du Travail†
0425-497X Conseil Oecumenique des Eglises. Etudes†
0425-5054 Etudes et Sports Sous-Marins
0425-5089 F A O Nutrition Meeting for Europe. Report.†
0425-5291 F I S Bulletin
0425-5860 Fact Finder *see* 0260-6429
0425-676X Family Economics Review
0425-7111 Far East Film News *see* 0047-8288
0425-7170 Far East Reporter (Tokyo) *changed to* Far East Traveler
0425-9076 Federation des Industries Chimiques de Belgique. Annuaire
0426-2700 Shobo Kenkyujo Hokuku
0426-3383 Fizyka w Szkole
0426-7230 Fontes Iuris Gentium. Section 2
0426-8261 Footprints
0426-844X For Men Only†
0426-9373 Forestal
0426-9918 Forschungsgesellschaft fuer das Strassenwesen. Arbeitsgruppe Asphalt-und Teerstrassen. Schriftenreihe *changed to* Forschungsgesellschaft fuer Strassen-und Verkehrswesen. Arbeitsgruppe Asphalt-und Teerstrassen. Schriftenreihe
0427-0576 Foto
0427-2218 Institut Geographique National. Bulletin d'Information
0427-5217 Freie Welt
0427-7554 Fundacao Getulio Vargas. Boletim Informativo *changed to* Fundacao Getulio Vargas. Informativo
0427-7783 Der Fuss
0427-7945 Fynske Minder
0427-8070 F A O Regional Conference for Asia and the Far East. Report *changed to* F A O Regional Conference for Asia and the Pacific. Report
0427-8089 F A O Regional Conference for the Near East. Report
0427-8321 F I F A Official Bulletin *changed to* F I F A News
0427-8879 Facts

0427-8968 Yugoslav Facts and Views
0427-9107 Faerg och Fernissa
0427-9522 Familiengeschichtliche Blaetter
0427-959X Family Fare†
0427-9638 Family Law Newsletter *see* 0163-710X
0427-9824 Fantasmagie
0428-0296 Farmatsia
0428-061X Fauna Japonica†
0428-1039 Federacion Sudamericana de Asociaciones Cristianas de Jovenes. Noticias *changed to* Confederacion Latinoamericana de Asociaciones Cristianas de Jovenes. Carta
0428-1128 Federal Economic Review *see* 0254-9204
0428-1276 Economic Commentary
0428-1365 Federal Savings and Loan Insurance Corporation. List of Member Institutions *changed to* Federal Home Loan Bank System. List of Member Institutions
0428-1659 Federation Internationale de Gymnastique. Bulletin
0428-1845 Federation of Kenya Employers. Newsletter
0428-2779 Feuillets de Biologie
0428-304X Field Studies
0428-3279 Fiji. Geological Survey. Economic Investigation *changed to* Fiji. Mineral Resources Department. Economic Investigation
0428-3341 Filatelia
0428-4666 Fire Control Notes†
0428-4836 First Days
0428-4879 Citibank. Foreign Information Service. Annual Summary of Exchange and Foreign Trade Regulations†
0428-5018 Fischwirt
0428-5190 Fishing Guidebook
0428-5387 Museum of Northern Arizona Glen Canyon Series†
0428-5395 Museum of Northern Arizona Technical Series†
0428-5670 Flexographic Technical Association. Report of the Proceedings: Annual Meeting and Technical Forum
0428-6766 Florida State University. Publications of the Faculty
0428-7738 Fluid Power Handbook & Directory
0428-819X Foldrajzi Monografiak
0428-8211 Folger Shakespeare Library Annual Report
0428-8254 Folia Antropologica
0428-8386 Folison†
0428-903X Fontes Iuris Gentium *see* 0426-7230
0428-9374 Food and Agriculture Organization of the United Nations. Forestry Occasional Paper†
0428-9390 Food and Agriculture Organization of the United Nations. Index of Agricultural Institutions in Europe†
0428-9447 Nutrition Newsletter *see* 0304-8942
0428-9552 Food and Agriculture Organization of the United Nations. Animal Health Branch. Animal Health Monograph†
0428-9625 F A O Papers on Demand Analysis†
0428-9749 Food and Agricultural Organization of the United Nations. Plant Protection Committee for Southeast Asia and Pacific Region. Quarterly Newsletter *changed to* Food and Agriculture Organization of the United Nations. Asia and Pacific Plant Protection Commission. Quarterly Newsletter
0428-9765 Food and Agricultural Organization of the United Nations. Plant Protection Committee for Southeast Asia and Pacific Region. Technical Document *changed to* Food and Agriculture Organization of the United Nations. Asia and Pacific Plant Protection Commission. Technical Document
0429-0208 Footwear News Fact Book
0429-0550 Forefront: News from New Zealand†
0429-0917 Forest Products News
0429-1050 Form & Zweck
0429-1573 Forschungen zur Innsbrucker Universitaetsgeschichte
0429-1816 Forschungsgesellschaft fuer das Strassenwesen. Arbeitsgruppe Betonstrassen. Schriftenreihe *changed to* Forschungsgesellschaft fuer Strassen-und Verkehrswesen. Arbeitsgruppe Betonstrassen. Schriftenreihe
0429-2405 P I D C Journal *changed to* Civil Aviation in Pakistan: Half-Yearly Newsletter
0429-2871 Fragmenta Coleopterologica
0429-288X Fragmenta Entomologica
0429-3843 France. Direction du Gaz et de l'Electricite. Statistiques Officielles de l'Industrie Gaziere en France *changed to* Statistiques de l'Industrie Gaziere en France
0429-4092 Bulletin Mensuel de Statistiques Industrielles
0429-5412 France-Horizon
0429-7539 Frodskaparrit; Annales Societatis Scientiarum Faeronsis. Supplementa
0429-7725 Frontiers in Physics
0429-7857 Fruits et Abeilles
0429-8284 Fuji Electric Review
0429-8357 Fujikura Technical Review
0429-8764 Centro de Estudios Sociales de la Santa Cruz del Valle de los Caidos. Boletin *see* 0303-9889
0429-8918 Fundamenty
0429-8950 Fundidor
0429-9159 Furukawa Review
0429-9329 F A O Fisheries Circulars
0429-9337 F A O Fisheries Reports
0429-9345 F A O Fisheries Technical Paper
0429-9353 F A O Regional Conference for Africa
0429-9388 F A O/W H O Expert Panel on Veterinary Education. Report of the Meeting†
0429-9442 F D A Clinical Experience Abstracts
0429-9574 Faba
0429-9639 Fabulous Mexico
0429-9655 Fachbibliographischer Dienst Bibliothekswesen†
0430-0440 Familienkundliches Jahrbuch Schleswig-Holstein
0430-0610 Far East Scouting Bulletin *changed to* Asia-Pacific Scouting
0430-0661 Far Western Philosophy of Education Society. Proceedings *see* 0094-1050
0430-0750 Farm Chemicals Handbook
0430-084X Farm Management Notes for Asia and the Far East
0430-1188 Faulkner Facts and Fiddlings
0430-1536 Federacion Latinoamericana de Bancos. Revista *changed to* Revista FeLaBan
0430-1692 Federal Employees' News Digest
0430-1919 Federal Reserve Bank of Chicago. Seventh District Statistics†
0430-1943 Federal Reserve Bank Reviews†
0430-2222 Congress F A T I P E C
0430-2419 Federation Internationale des Syndicats Chretiens d'Ouvriers Agricoles. Travailleur de la Terre†
0430-2583 Federation of Insurance Counsel. Quarterly *changed to* Federation of Insurance and Corporate Counsel. Quarterly
0430-2990 Femina
0430-327X Fertiliser Association of India. Fertiliser Statistics
0430-3288 Fertiliser Associaion of India. Annual Review of Fertiliser. Consumption and Production *see* 0015-0266
0430-3938 Fiji. Geological Survey. Memoir *see* 0252-2497
0430-4055 Fikr-o-Nazar
0430-4497 Filmoteca Ultramarina Portuguesa. Boletim
0430-4578 Il Filo Metallico
0430-4748 Financial Aid News†
0430-5205 Finland. Kansanelakelaitos. Julkaisuja. Sarja A
0430-5272 Finland. Tilastokeskus. Liikennetilastollinen Vuosikirja
0430-5280 Finland. Tyovoimaministerio. Tyovoimakatsaus
0430-5299 Finland. Laakintohallitus. Laakarit, Hammaslaakarit, Sairaalat *changed to* Finland. Laakintohallitus. Laakarit, Hammaslaakarit/Lakare, Tandlaekare
0430-5329 Finland. Board of Agriculture. Statistical Office. Monthly Review of Agricultural Statistics
0430-5566 Finland. Tilastokeskus. Kuntien Finanssitilasto *see* 0359-081X
0430-5604 Finland. Tilastokeskus. Talonrakennustilasto
0430-5612 Finland. Tilastokeskus. Vaestonmuutokset *changed to* Finland. Tilastokeskus. Vaesto
0430-5809 Schriften aus dem Finnland-Institut Koeln
0430-5817 Finsk Palstidskrift
0430-6155 Fitopatologia
0430-6252 Fiziko-Khimicheskaya Mekhanika Materialov
0430-635X Museum of Northern Arizona Ceramic Series†
0430-6457 Fleet Street Patent Law Reports *changed to* Fleet Street Reports
0430-666X Flore de la Nouvelle Caledonie et Dependances
0430-6953 Florida Tourist Study *changed to* Florida's Visitors
0430-7291 Florida State University. Slavic Papers *changed to* Florida State University. Center for Yugoslav-American Studies, Research, and Exchanges. Proceedings and Reports of Seminars and Research
0430-7313 Florida State University. Educational Media Center. Educational Motion Pictures *changed to* Florida State University. Instructional Support Center. Film and Video
0430-7658 Florida Economic Indicators†
0430-7690 Florida F L Reporter†
0430-7801 Florida Public Documents
0430-7941 Flour Milling and Baking Research Association Abstracts
0430-8247 Focus (Waterloo)†
0430-8603 Folia Entomologica Mexicana
0430-862X Folia Linguistica
0430-8751 Folk Dance Scene
0430-8778 Folk Life
0430-9928 Galloway Journal
0431-1930 GeoChile
0431-1981 Geografia nelle Scuole
0431-6045 Economic Situation in the Federal Republic of Germany
0431-8315 Ghana. Meteorological Department. Monthly Summary of Rainfall
0431-8323 Ghana. Meteorological Department. Monthly Weather Report
0431-8943 Gioventu al Lavoro
0431-915X Glades Star
0431-9168 Gladio Grams
0432-1251 Arstryck
0432-2924 R E M E Journal
0432-6105 Greece
0432-7454 Grundlagen und Fortschritte der Lebensmitteluntersuchung *see* 0341-0498
0432-9120 Guida Nazionale del Commercio Con l'Estero
0433-0730 Gaceta Bibliotecaria del Peru
0433-0854 Gaceta Indigenista
0433-0919 Garden Life
0433-230X Gdanskie Towarzystwo Naukowe. Wydzial 1. Nauk Spolecznych i Humanistycznych. Seria Monografii
0433-2733 Gelderse Bloem
0433-3179 Genealogical Forum of Portland, Oregon. Quarterly Bulletin
0433-3519 General Fisheries Council for the Mediterranean. Studies and Reviews
0433-4035 Nuclear Engineering
0433-4515 Geographical Outlook *see* 0046-5712
0433-5015 Australia. Bureau of Mineral Resources, Geology and Geophysics. Geophysical Observatory Group. Report
0433-5473 Georgia. Geological Survey. Information Circular
0433-6305 German Business Weekly
0433-6844 Statistiches Taschenbuch der DDR
0433-6933 Zentralinstitut fuer Bibliothekswesen. Mitteilungen und Materialien
0433-7484 Wirtschaftliche Lage in der Bundesrepublik Deutschland
0433-7603 Weltwirtschaft am Jahreswechsel
0433-8251 Jahresbericht des Deutschen Wetterdienstes
0433-8456 Geschied- en Oudheidkundige Kring voor Leuven en Omgeving. Jaarboek
0433-860X Gesellschaft fuer Bibliothekswesen und Dokumentation des Landbaues. Mitteilungen
0433-969X Ghana Year Book†
0434-0035 Giessener Schriftenreihe Tierzucht und Haustiergenetik
0434-0094 Gifu Pharmaceutical University. Annual Proceedings
0434-0299 Giornalino
0434-040X Giurisprudenza Agraria Italiana
0434-0760 Politechnika Slaska. Zeszyty Naukowe. Automatyka
0434-0779 Politechnika Slaska. Zeszyty Naukowe. Budownictwo
0434-0817 Politechnika Slaska. Zeszyty Naukowe. Mechanika
0434-1066 Glyndebourne Festival Programme Book
0434-2151 Gospodarka i Administracja Terenowa *changed to* Rada Narodowa, Gospodarka, Administracja
0434-2410 Goeteborgs Universitet. Nationalekonomiska Institutionen. Ekonomiska Studier
0434-2593 Government Contracts Citator
0434-3336 Le Grand Baton
0434-3581 Grands Naturalistes Francais†
0434-3883 Steiermaerkisches Landesarchiv. Mitteilungen
0434-5975 Greater Minneapolis *changed to* Guide to Leading Twin Cities Companies
0434-6785 Instituut voor Bodemvruchtbaarheid. Jaarverslag
0434-6793 Instituut voor Bodemvruchtbaarheid. Rapport
0434-8850 Guide to Employment Abroad†
0434-9245 Guild of Book Workers Journal
0435-1096 Gamma Field Symposia
0435-1312 Gas Turbine International *see* 0149-4147
0435-1339 Gastroenterologia Japonica
0435-1568 Gdanski Rocznik Kulturalny *changed to* Rocznik Kulturalny Ziemi Gdanskiej
0435-1754 Gekkan Shakaito
0435-1835 Geldgeschichtliche Nachrichten
0435-1924 Geltende Seekriegsrecht in Einzeldarstellungen *changed to* Das Geltende Seevoelkerrecht in Einzeldarstellungen
0435-2033 Bulletin des Recherches Agronomiques de Gembloux
0435-219X Gendai no Me
0435-2866 Studies on Voltaire and the Eighteenth Century
0435-2874 I I L S Bulletin *see* 0378-5408
0435-2939 Observatoire de Geneve. Publications. Serie B
0435-3048 Universita degli Studi di Genova. Facolta di Giurisprudenza. Annali
0435-3676 Geografiska Annaler. Series A. Physical Geography
0435-3684 Geografiska Annaler. Series B. Human Geography
0435-3730 Geographia Medica Hungarica *see* 0300-807X
0435-382X Aardrijkskunde/Geographie *changed to* Aardrijkskunde
0435-3870 Geologia Applicata e Idrogeologia
0435-3951 Geological Journal - Special Issues
0435-401X Geological Society of Jamaica Journal
0435-4311 Geonews

1564 ISSN INDEX

0435-5113 University of Georgia. Geography Curriculum Project Publications
0435-5253 Georgia Advocate
0435-5261 Georgia Alert
0435-5385 Georgia Genealogical Magazine
0435-5482 Georgia Manufacturing Directory
0435-5601 Geos
0435-7183 Bundesinstitut fuer Ostwissenschaftliche und Internationale Studien. Berichte
0435-7329 Germany (Federal Republic, 1949-). Bundesministerium fuer das Post- und Fernmeldewesen. Jahresrechnung, Nachweisung ueber die Einnahmen und Ausgaben der Deutschen Bundespost
0435-7442 Gesamtstatistik der Kraftfahrtversicherung
0435-7965 Deutscher Wetterdienst. Monatlicher Witterungsbericht
0435-8406 Gesher
0435-8600 Gewerblicher Rechtsschutz und Urheberrecht. Internationaler Teil
0435-8805 External Trade Statistics of Ghana
0435-8864 Ghana. Central Bureau of Statistics. Quarterly Digest of Statistics
0435-9348 Ghana Commercial Bank. Annual Report
0435-9380 Ghana Journal of Sociology
0435-9437 Ghana Radio and Television Times *changed to* G B C Radio and T V Times
0435-950X Rijksuniversiteit te Gent. Centrum voor Onkruidonderzoek. Mededeling
0436-0257 Giving U.S.A. Bulletin *changed to* Fund-Raising Review
0436-0265 Gizi Indonesia
0436-029X Gladius
0436-0524 Glasshouse Crops Research Institute. Annual Report
0436-0605 Glenbow Foundation. Archives Series *changed to* Glenbow Museum. Archives Series
0436-0664 Globusfreund
0436-1024 Godesberger Heimatblaetter
0436-1121 Goeteborg Studies in Educational Sciences
0436-113X Goeteborgs Kungliga Vetenskaps- och Vitterhets-Samhaelle. Aarsbok
0436-1202 Universitaet Goettingen. Jahresbericht
0436-1326 Gokhale Institute Mimeograph Series
0436-1474 Golf Course Superintendents Association of America. Membership Directory
0436-1571 Good Tidings *changed to* East Asian Pastoral Review
0436-2020 Goeteborgs Etnografiska Museum. Aarstryck
0436-2225 U S/R & D
0436-2616 Gradina
0436-2624 Gradinarska i Lozarska Nauka
0436-7316 Handbook of the Indian Cotton Textile Industry
0437-133X Heating and Ventilating Research Association. Technical Notes *see* 0309-0248
0437-3014 Herbergen der Christenheit
0437-5602 Hispania Antiqua Epigraphica†
0437-7168 Die Holzzucht
0438-1629 Human Factors Society Bulletin
0438-2013 Hungarian Travel Magazine†
0438-2242 Budapest Statisztikai Zsebkonyve
0438-4385 Martin-Luther-Universitaet Halle-Wittenberg. Wissenschaftliche Zeitschrift
0438-4415 Universitaets- und Landesbibliothek Sachsen-Anhalt. Arbeiten
0438-4555 Protokolle zur Fischereitechnik
0438-5004 Handakten fuer die Standesamtliche Arbeit
0438-5403 Handel Wewnetrzny
0438-8887 Heating and Ventilating Research Association. Laboratory Reports *see* 0305-5973
0438-895X Hebrew Abstracts *see* 0146-4094
0439-1284 High-Way
0439-1292 Highway
0439-1365 Comparative Law Journal
0439-1551 Das Himmelsjahr
0439-1705 Hirosaki University. Faculty of Literature and Science. Science Reports *see* 0367-6439
0439-2116 Historia Junior *changed to* Gister en Vandag
0439-2183 Historian Aitta
0439-2248 Historic Nantucket
0439-237X Historical Society of Michigan. Review
0439-2795 Hitachi Zosen News
0439-3465 Hokkaido University. Research Institute of Applied Electricity. Monograph Series
0439-3511 Hokkaido University. Faculty of Fisheries. Data Record of Oceanographic Observations and Exploratory Fishing
0439-3538 Low Temperature Science. Series A. Physical Science
0439-3546 Low Temperature Science. Series B. Biological Science
0439-3678 Holiday Time in Thailand
0439-4208 Homiletica
0439-4216 Homme
0439-4291 Homo Faber
0439-5530 Horisont
0439-6162 Hospitalisation Privee
0439-9056 Hungarian Co-operation
0439-9080 Hungarian P.E.N
0439-9285 Hungary. Kozponti Statisztikai Hivatal. Haztartasstatisztika
0439-9714 Husserliana
0440-0607 Haematologie und Bluttransfusion
0440-1352 Hallmark†
0440-1719 Hamburger Mittel-Ostdeutsche Forschungen
0440-1875 Handboek van de Nederlandse Pers en Publiciteit
0440-193X Handbook on International Study: for Foreign Nationals *changed to* Handbook on U.S. Study for Foreign Nationals
0440-1948 Handbook on International Study for U.S. Nationals *see* 0364-1449
0440-2103 Handbuch des Oeffentlichen Lebens in Oesterreich
0440-2278 Handjuawg
0440-2316 Hanging Loose
0440-2863 Hans-Pfitzner-Gesellschaft. Mitteilungen
0440-3428 Harvard Germanic Studies†
0440-3452 Harvard Monographs in Applied Science†
0440-4122 Haskins & Sells. Selected Papers†
0440-4947 Directory of State, County, and Federal Officials
0440-5145 Hawaiian Journal of History
0440-5234 Hawkeye Heritage
0440-5323 Haydn-Studien
0440-548X Health Education Abstracts†
0440-5609 Health Organizations of the U.S., Canada and the World
0440-5730 Heartbeat†
0440-5749 Heat Transfer - Soviet Research
0440-5757 Heather Society. Yearbook
0440-5927 Hegel-Studien Beihefte
0440-601X Universitaet Heidelberg. Suedasien-Institut. Schriftenreihe
0440-6230 Heimatgruss
0440-6826 Hemijski Pregled
0440-7180 Hermeneutische Untersuchungen zur Theologie
0440-7881 Higher Education in New England *changed to* Connection (Boston)
0440-8152 Hillside Hospital Journal *see* 0193-5216
0440-9078 Acta Universitatis Upsaliensis. Historia Litterarum
0440-9213 Historical Archaeology
0440-9221 Historical Arms Series
0440-9264 Historical Association of Tanzania. Papers
0440-9426 Chronicle (Ann Arbor)
0440-9515 Historicke Studie
0440-9558 Historische Forschungen
0440-9728 Historiches Jahrbuck der Stadt Graz
0440-9736 Historisches Jahrbuch der Stadt Linz
0440-9809 Historisk-Topografisk Selskab for Gladsaxe Kommune. Arsskrift
0440-9884 History of Economic Thought Newsletter
0441-067X Hokkaido University. Faculty of Science. Journal. Series 7: Geophysics
0441-0734 Japan. Government Industrial Development Laboratory, Hokkaido. Reports
0441-0785 Geological Survey of Hokkaido. Report
0441-084X Hokkaido Fisheries Experimental Station. Scientific Reports
0441-1196 Almanakh Gomonu Ukrainy
0441-1900 University of Hong Kong. Centre of Asian Studies. Bibliographies and Research Guides
0441-2044 Honolulu
0441-2370 Hornbill
0441-2516 Radioactivity Survey Data in Japan
0441-2613 Hospital and Nursing Yearbook of Southern Africa
0441-2745 Hospital Medicine
0441-389X Hudson's Washington News Media Contacts Directory
0441-4004 University of Hull. Department of Geography. Miscellaneous Series in Geography
0441-4128 Affirmation
0441-4144 Humanidad
0441-4195 Humanistic Judaism
0441-4411 Hungarian Law Review
0441-4438 Hungarian Medical Bibliography
0441-4446 Hungarian Musical Guide†
0441-4675 Hungary. Kozponti Statisztikai Hivatal. Mezogazdasagi Adatok†
0441-4683 Hungary. Kozponti Statisztikai Hivatal. Mezogazdasagi Statisztikai Zsebkonyu
0441-4713 Hungary. Kozponti Statisztikai Hivatal. Nemzetkozi Statisztikai Evkonyv
0441-5302 Hydronymia Germaniae
0441-537X Hyogo-ken Gan Senta Nenpo *changed to* Hyogo Cancer Hospital. Bulletin
0441-5833 Hi Fi Aarbogen
0441-5973 Hungarian Music News
0441-6058 Hacettepe Bulletin of Social Sciences and Humanities†
0441-6619 Heraldry in Canada
0441-6651 Herpetological Association of South Africa. Journal
0441-6813 Hofmannsthal-Blaetter
0441-6910 Huguenot Trails
0441-7410 Hokudai Economic Papers
0441-7445 Home Study
0441-7461 Horticultural Research International
0441-7895 Honolulu's Annual Area Manpower Review *changed to* Hawaii. Department of Labor and Industrial Relations. Labor Market Review
0441-7933 Health and Physical Education Bulletin for Teachers in Secondary Schools *changed to* Physical Education and Health
0441-9057 International Recreation Association. Bulletin *changed to* World Leisure and Recreation
0442-1744 University of Illinois at Urbana-Champaign. Civil Engineering Studies. Hydraulic Engineering Research Series
0442-3054 Illustrierter Motorsport
0442-6827 Indian Forest Records Wood Anatomy
0442-736X Indian Silk and Rayon *changed to* Indian Synthetic & Rayon
0442-8102 Indiana Rural News *changed to* Electric Consumer
0443-1243 Information fuer die Truppe
0443-2460 Insel-Almanach
0443-3173 Institut Geographique du Zaire. Rapport Annuel
0443-9155 Fiches d'Identification du Zooplancton *see* 0109-2529
0444-0978 International Office of Cocoa and Chocolate and the International Sugar Confectionary Manufacturers' Association. Periodic Bulletin *changed to* International Office of Cocoa and Chocolate and the International Sugar Confectionary Manufacturers' Association. Annual Statistical Bulletin
0444-4566 Iowa Documents†
0444-4736 Iowa School Board Bulletin *see* 0021-0668
0444-6801 Israel. Meteorological Service. Series C: Miscellaneous Papers†
0445-0485 I C E A News *see* 0887-8625
0445-0698 I F C A T I Directory *changed to* I T M F Directory
0445-1821 Ich Schreibe
0445-2216 Ideas and Action Bulletin
0445-2429 Igaku Toshokan
0445-2577 Kleine Ikonenbuecherei†
0445-3387 Illinois. State Museum. Handbook of Collections
0445-3395 Illinois. State Museum. Scientific Papers Series
0445-4529 Imagen y Sonida *see* 0210-4261
0445-5150 Incontri Con la Pubblicita†
0445-6289 Trade Unions in India
0445-6653 Press in India
0445-6831 India. Parliament. Public Accounts Committee. Report on the Accounts
0445-7706 Indian Journal of Occupational Therapy
0445-7722 Indian Journal of Sericulture
0445-7854 Indian Machine Tools Journal
0445-7897 Indian Minerals Year Book
0445-801X Indian Press
0445-8192 Indian Tobacco *changed to* Tobacco News
0445-8206 Town and Country Planning Association Quarterly Journal
0446-0243 Industria dei Farmaci
0446-1266 Industries of Japan
0446-2378 Ingenieria
0446-2424 Ingenieria Sanitaria
0446-2491 Ingenioeren Indkoebsbog
0446-3161 Installation Specialist *see* 0192-1657
0446-3943 Jahrbuch fuer Fraenkische Landesforschung
0446-4648 Geological Society of Egypt. Annual Meeting. Abstracts of Papers
0446-5059 Japan. Meteorological Agency. Seismological Bulletin
0446-5458 Japan. Ministry of Agriculture and Forestry. Annual Report
0446-6217 Japan Hotel Guide
0446-6667 Japan's Bicycle Guide
0446-7310 Jersey at Home
0446-7965 Jezyki Obce w Szkole
0446-9283 Jordan Medical Journal
0446-9577 Joseph Haas Gesellschaft. Mitteilungensblatt
0446-9739 Journal du Fermier et du Metayer
0447-2276 J L C News *changed to* J L C Review
0447-2462 Jacksonville Seafarer *changed to* Seafarer
0447-2500 Jagriti
0447-2624 Jahrbuch der Wittheit zu Bremen
0447-2713 Jahrbuch fuer die Gefluegelwirtschaft
0447-3086 Jamaica. Department of Statistics. Quarterly Abstract of Statistics†
0447-3280 Jamaica Annual
0447-3728 Japan. Maritime Safety Agency. Hydrographic Department. Notices to Mariners
0447-3892 Japan. Meteorological Agency. Volcanological Bulletin
0447-5240 Japan Agricultural Coop News
0447-5321 Japan Cotton Statistics and Related Data
0447-5933 Japanese Society of Grassland Science. Journal
0447-6425 Jelenkor
0447-6441 Jemna Mechanika a Optika
0447-6719 Jerusalem Chamber of Commerce. Bulletin†
0447-7227 Jibi to Rinsho *changed to* Otologia Fukuoka/Jibi to Rinsho
0447-8053 Information Processing Society of Japan. Journal

ISSN INDEX 1565

0447-8452 Joint Meeting of the Members of the Consultative Assembly of the Council of Europe and of the Members of the European Parliamentary Assembly. Official Report of Debates†
0447-8819 Jornal do Exercito
0447-9181 Transportation Telephone Tickler
0447-922X Journal of Economic Behavior
0447-953X Journal of Sports Philately
0447-9645 Journalismus†
0447-9823 Association Internationale pour l'Histoire du Verre. Bulletin
0448-0147 Prirodoslovna Istrazivanja: Acta Biologica
0448-0155 Prirodoslovna Istrzivanja: Acta Geologica
0448-021X News-Jugoslavija Film
0448-1054 Jabalpur Law Journal
0448-1143 Jadavpur Journal of Comparative Literature
0448-116X Jaderna Energie
0448-150X Jahrbuch fuer den Kreis Pinneberg
0448-1518 Jahrbuch fuer Geologie
0448-1526 Jahrbuch fuer Geschichte
0448-1690 Rajasthan University Studies in English
0448-1712 University of Rajasthan. Studies in Sanskrit and Hindi
0448-2174 Jamaica Library Association. Annual Bulletin *changed to* Jamaica Library Association. Bulletin
0448-2433 Jammu and Kashmir. Legislative Council. Committee on Privileges. Report
0448-3294 Annual Statistics of Maritime Safety
0448-3758 Japan. Meteorological Agency. Annual Report
0448-4703 Science Council of Japan. Annual Report
0448-6072 Finance
0448-858X Japan Chemical Review†
0448-8709 Japan Science Review: Economic Sciences
0448-8806 Japanese Annual of International Law
0448-8938 Japanese Railway Engineering
0448-8954 Japanese Religions
0448-9144 Jaszkunsag
0448-9241 Jazykovedne Studie
0448-9497 Jena Review
0449-0193 Local Government Review *see* 0288-7622
0449-0436 Jizni Morava
0449-0495 Job/Scope†
0449-0576 Jokull
0449-0738 Johari za Kiswahili
0449-122X Joint F A O/W H O Codex Alimentarius Commission. Report of the Session
0449-1343 J I L A Information Center. Report *changed to* J I L A Data Center. Report
0449-1483 Jordan. Department of Statistics. External Trade Statistics and Shipping Activities in Aqaba Port†
0449-1491 Jordan Economy in Figures
0449-1513 Jordan. Department of Statistics. National Accounts
0449-1602 Jordan Lectures in Comparative Religion†
0449-1750 Jornal Portugues de Economia e Financas
0449-1971 Journal des Agreges†
0449-2099 Journal Mondial de Pharmacie†
0449-2145 Journal of African and Asian Studies†
0449-2153 Journal of Alabama Archaeology
0449-2285 Egyptian Journal of Chemistry
0449-2544 Journal of Foot Surgery
0449-2560 Journal of Geosciences
0449-2722 Journal of Long Island History†
0449-2986 Journal of Polymer Science. Part B Polymer Letters *see* 0360-6384
0449-2994 Journal of Polymer Science. Part C Polymer Symposia *see* 0360-8905
0449-3060 Japan Radiation Research Society. Journal *changed to* Journal of Radiation Research
0449-3109 Journal of Schizophrenia *changed to* Journal of Orthomolecular Medicine
0449-3168 Journal of Social Sciences
0449-3362 Journalism Scholarship Guide *changed to* Journalism Career and Scholarship Guide
0449-3540 Judaisme Sephardi†
0449-3648 Jugoslavenska Akademija Znanosti i Umjetnosti. Historijski Institut, Dubrovnik. Anali.
0449-4156 Japan Society of Lubrication Engineers. Journal
0449-4342 Juristische Abhandlungen
0449-4555 Juventud Tecnica
0449-4733 Journal de l'Annee
0449-4741 Journal of Contemporary Revolutions†
0449-4830 Japan Atomic Energy Commission. Annual Report
0449-4881 Jerusalem Historical Medical Publications *changed to* Koroth
0449-5225 Jahrbuch der Wirtschaft Osteuropas
0449-5314 Japan. Statistics Bureau. News Bulletin
0449-5705 Journal of Bioenergetics *see* 0145-479X
0449-5721 Journal of Plant and Machinery
0449-752X Japanese Journal of Nursing Arts
0449-7554 Kansai University Economic Review
0449-7732 Kansas. Department of Health and Environment. Monthly Summary of Vital Statistics†
0449-7953 Kansas. State Department of Public Instruction. Bulletin *changed to* Kansas. State Department of Education. Bulletin
0450-0261 Kemps Harrow and District Local Directory†
0450-2167 Chirurgia
0450-3171 Kirkehistoriske Samlinger
0450-609X Kobe University of Mercantile Marine. Review. Part 2. Maritime Studies, and Science and Engineering
0450-6219 Kochi University. Faculty of Agriculture. Memoirs
0450-6235 Kochpraxis und Gemeinschaftsverpflegung
0450-660X Navigation
0450-7169 Kommunalwirtschaft
0451-0887 Kunsterziehung
0451-1476 Kyoto University. Research Institute for Food Science. Bulletin
0451-1611 Kyushu Hematological Society. Journal
0451-1646 K-Mitteilungen
0451-1980 National Research Institute of Police Science. Report *see* 0285-7960
0451-1999 National Research Institute of Police Science. Report. Research on Prevention of Crime and Deliquency
0451-2006 National Research Institute of Police Science. Report. Research on Traffic Safety and Regulation
0451-2030 Chemical Factory†
0451-243X K V Convertible Fact Finder Service†
0451-3371 Kansa Taisteli - Miehet Kertovat†
0451-3991 Kansas City Genealogist
0451-4041 Kansas Farmer-Stockman *changed to* Kansas Farmer
0451-5978 Management Science (Keiei- Kagaku) *changed to* Operations Research
0451-6001 Light Metal Statistics in Japan
0451-6109 National Research Laboratory of Metrology. Bulletin
0451-6222 Economic Theory *changed to* Wakayama Economic Review
0451-7059 Kentucky Economic Outlook *see* 0270-1421
0451-9396 Mechanical Engineering
0451-9930 Kirkia
0452-2370 Kobe University. Faculty of Agriculture. Science Reports
0452-2834 Engineering Materials
0452-2907 Testimonia Siciliae Antiqua
0452-3687 Norway. Komite for Romforskning. N.S.R.C. Report *changed to* Space Research in Norway
0452-4918 Konstanzer Blaetter fuer Hochschulfragen
0452-5914 Korean Stamps
0452-621X Kosmos Bibliothek†
0452-6457 Akademia Gorniczo-Hutnicza im. Stanislawa Staszica. Zeszyty Naukowe. Geodezja
0452-7208 Kristofer Lehmkuhl Forelesning
0452-7739 Die Kueste
0452-9650 Annual Report of Educational Psychology in Japan
0452-9995 Kyoto University. Research Institute for Food Science. Memoirs†
0453-0047 Kyoto Technical University. Faculty of Industrial Arts. Memoirs: Science and Technology *see* 0911-0305
0453-0314 Kyushu University. Contributions from the Department of Fisheries and the Fishery Research Laboratory
0453-0349 Kyushu Institute of Technology. Bulletin: Humanities, Social Sciences
0453-0357 Kyushu Institute of Technology. Bulletin: Science and Technology
0453-0535 Japan. National Institute of Animal Health. Annual Report†
0453-0578 Kacic
0453-0667 National Research Institute of Police Science. Annual Report
0453-0675 National Research Institute of Police Science. Data†
0453-0691 Japan Association for Philosophy of Science. Annals
0453-0853 Kagoshima University. Faculty of Agriculture. Memoirs
0453-1388 Kalmia
0453-1515 Yearbook of Pulp and Paper Statistics
0453-1981 Kanazawa University. Faculty of Law and Literature. Studies and Essays
0453-2198 Kansai University Technology Reports
0453-2384 Kansas. State Conservation Commission. Conservation in Kansas *see* 0094-1670
0453-2406 Library School Review *changed to* Great Plains Libraries
0453-2805 Kansas Sportsman
0453-3283 Karlsruher Juristische Bibliographie
0453-3402 Karstenia
0453-3429 Karthago
0453-3585 Kataliz i Katalizatory
0453-3623 Katalog Fauny Polski
0453-4387 Keats-Shelley Journal
0453-4395 Keats-Shelley Memorial Bulletin
0453-4484 Keidanren Geppo
0453-4514 Operations Research Society of Japan. Journal
0453-4557 Keio Business Review
0453-4611 Keiryo Kokugogaku
0453-4662 Society of Instrument and Control Engineers Journal
0453-4778 Economic Journal
0453-4867 Kellogg World *changed to* Kelloggram
0453-4972 B R I Research Papers
0453-512X Kennedy Quarterly†
0453-5146 Kensetsu Kogaku KenKyushyo Hokoku
0453-5677 Kentucky City
0453-5723 Kentucky Genealogist
0453-5944 Kenya. Dairy Board. Annual Report
0453-6002 Kenya Statistical Digest
0453-6525 Kenya, Uganda, Tanzania, Zambia, Malawi and Ethiopia Directory; Trade and Commercial Index *changed to* Kenya, Uganda, Tanzania, East African Community Directory; Trade Commerce Index
0453-7440 Kerala; an Economic Review
0453-767X Kernkraft Zentrale, Gundremmingen. Jahresberichte†
0453-7831 Kevo Subarctic Research Institute. Reports
0453-8129 Sudan Research Information Bulletin
0453-8854 Kingston Law Review
0453-9222 National Research Institute for Metals. Transactions
0453-9249 Kiplinger California Letter
0453-9478 Kiruna Geophysical Data
0453-9842 Klaus-Groth-Gesellschaft. Jahresgaben
0454-1111 Kobe University Economic Review
0454-1383 Koepfe des 20. Jahrhunderts
0454-1723 Kokugakuin University. Faculty of Law and Politics. Journal
0454-191X Foreign Aero-Space Literature
0454-1944 Japan. National Diet Library. Monthly List of Foreign Scientific and Technical Publications
0454-2029 National Institute for Leprosy Research. Annual Report
0454-2150 Asian Cultural Studies
0454-3491 Konyvtari es Dokumentacios Szakirodalom
0454-4196 Korean Trade Unions
0454-448X Kosmosophie
0454-4544 Kotai Butsuri
0454-4617 Kovcezic
0454-4773 Akademia Gorniczo-Hutnicza im. Stanislawa Staszica. Zeszyty Naukowe. Automatyka
0454-4862 Politechnika Krakowska. Zeszyty Naukowe. Budownictwo Ladowe
0454-5265 Kriminalwissenschaftliche Abhandlungen
0454-5478 K R S Jugoslavije
0454-5508 Krugozor
0454-577X Kulkereskedelem *see* 0324-4202
0454-6059 Cultuurpatronen†
0454-6245 Kuml†
0454-6520 Kunst og Museum
0454-7330 Kwartalnik Historii Ruchu Zawadowego
0454-7543 Korea (Republic). Economic Planning Board. Annual Report on the Economically Active Population
0454-7586 Mutual Aid Association. Medical Journal
0454-7659 Kyoto University. Abuyama Seismological Observatory. Seismological Bulletin
0454-7675 Kyoto University. Disaster Prevention Research Institute. Bulletin
0454-7802 Kyoto University. Faculty of Science. Memoirs. Series of Biology
0454-7810 Kyoto University. Faculty of Science. Memoirs. Series of Geology and Mineralogy
0454-7845 Kyoto University. Research Institute for Mathematical Sciences. Publications: Series A *see* 0034-5318
0454-7985 Kyoto University African Studies†
0454-8086 Kytoesavut
0454-8132 Kyushu American Literature
0454-8221 Kyushu Institute of Technology. Bulletin: Mathematics, Natural Science
0454-8302 Kanagawa Shigaku
0454-9244 Kyoto University. Research Reactor Institute. Annual Reports
0454-949X Kenya Newsletter
0454-9910 Kibernetika i Vychislitel'naya Tekhnika
0455-0374 Kernenergie Forschungsschiff "Otto Hahn". Jahresbericht†
0455-0463 Knjizevna Smotra
0455-2342 Landarbeit und Technik
0456-3271 Living with Children
0456-3867 Canadian Hardware, Electrical & Building Supply Directory
0456-4804 Ramsay Society of Chemical Engineers. Journal
0456-5339 Look Japan
0456-7463 Louisiana English Journal
0456-9814 Laboratorio *changed to* Il Nuovo Laboratorio
0457-0715 Landeskundliche Luftbildauswertung im Mitteleuropaeischen Raum *see* 0176-1633
0457-1320 Langues et Styles
0457-1673 Universidad Nacional de la Plata. Instituto de la Produccion. Serie Contribuciones
0457-3633 Legislative Trends
0457-3897 Neujahrsgabe der Deutschen Buecherei
0457-3900 Sonderbibliographien der Deutschen Bucherei
0457-3919 Deutsche Hochschule fuer Koerperkultur. Wissenschaftliche Zeitschrift

0457-4184 Lejeunia
0457-5792 Letecky Obzor
0457-6047 Leveltari Szemle
0457-7019 County Newsletter†
0457-7817 South Staffordshire Archaeological and Historical Society. Transactions
0457-8910 Lilly Endowment. Report†
0457-9976 Liste des Societes Savantes et Litteraires
0458-063X Liturgy
0458-1520 Muzeum Archeologiczne i Etnograficzne, Lodz. Prace i Materialy. Seria Archeologiczna
0458-1547 Politechnika Lodzka. Zeszyty Naukowe. Zeszyt Specjalny†
0458-1555 Politechnika Lodzka. Zeszyty Naukowe. Chemia
0458-1563 Politechnika Lodzka. Zeszyty Naukowe. Mechanika
0458-1822 Lok Magazin
0458-2314 Memorial Hospital of Long Beach. Quarterly Bulletin *changed to* Memorial Mercury
0458-4201 Lower Cape Fear Historical Society. Bulletin
0458-4317 Annales Universitatis Mariae Curie-Sklodowska. Sectio G. Ius
0458-4767 Lund Universitet. Historiska Museum. Meddelanden
0458-497X Lutheran Digest
0458-5143 Lutte de Classe
0458-5674 L P V-Listos para Vencer
0458-5747 Labo - Pharma Problems et Techniques *see* 0758-6922
0458-5860 France. Laboratoires des Ponts et Chaussees. Bulletin de Liaison
0458-5933 Laboratory Animal Handbooks
0458-595X Laboratory Guide to Instruments, Equipment and Chemicals *see* 0003-2700
0458-6026 Labour Law Cases†
0458-6123 Ladenbau *changed to* Architektur und Ladenbau
0458-6506 Lalit Kala
0458-6573 Washington Energy Memo *see* 0300-7243
0458-6859 Landbauforschung Voelkenrode
0458-6972 Landmark
0458-7014 Landscape Research News *see* 0142-6397
0458-7073 Landslaget for Bygde og Byhistorie. Skrifter *changed to* Landslaget for Lokalhistorie
0458-7367 Language Research in Progress†
0458-7871 Laser and Unconventional Optics Journal
0458-7944 Lateinamerika
0458-8460 Law and Legislation in the German Democratic Republic
0458-8592 Law in Society
0458-8711 Law Society of Scotland. Journal
0458-8983 Leads
0458-9564 Legal Bulletin
0458-9599 Legal-Legislative Reporter. News Bulletin
0458-9971 Leidse Germanistische en Anglistische Reeks
0458-998X Leidse Historische Reeks
0458-9998 Leidse Juridische Reeks
0459-0007 Leidse Wijsgerige Reeks†
0459-004X Deutsche Buecherei. Jahrbuch
0459-0805 Leningradskii Universitet. Uchenye Zapiski. Seriya Geologicheskikh Nauk
0459-0953 Lens and Speaker†
0459-1801 Rijksmuseum van Natuurlijke Historie. Zoologische Bijdragen
0459-2182 Liberia. Ministry of Planning and Economic Affairs. Annual Report to the Session of the Legislature of the Republic of Liberia *changed to* Liberia. Ministry of Planning and Economic Affairs. Annual Report to the People's Redemption Council
0459-2298 Liberian Naturalist *changed to* U L Science Magazine
0459-2476 Y L G News†
0459-3030 Libyca†
0459-3650 American Council of Life Insurance. Economic and Investment Report†
0459-3774 Life Sciences†
0459-3871 Ligue Internationale Contre la Concurrence Deloyale. Annuaire
0459-388X Ligue Internationale Contre la Concurrence Deloyale. Communication
0459-4487 Lincolnshire History and Archaeology
0459-4541 Lines Review
0459-4835 Lipunan Journal
0459-4851 Repertorio das Publicacoes Periodicas Portuguesas†
0459-5009 List of Current Periodical Publications in Ethiopia†
0459-5084 Liszt Society, London. Newsletter *see* 0141-0792
0459-6137 Living Bird *see* 0732-9210
0459-6404 University E. Kardelja in Ljubljana. Biotechnical Faculty. Research Reports
0459-6730 Lock Haven Review†
0459-6803 Locusta
0459-682X Politechnika Lodzka. Zeszyty Naukowe. Elektryka
0459-6854 Societe des Sciences et des Lettres de Lodz. Bulletin
0459-7222 Military Balance
0459-7230 Strategic Survey
0459-7354 University of London Classical Studies†

0459-7400 Bartlett Society. Transactions†
0459-8113 Contributions in Science
0459-8474 Louisiana. Geological Survey. Water Resources Bulletin
0459-8881 Louisiana Bar Journal
0459-889X Louisiana Cancer Reporter
0459-8962 Louisiana Folklore Miscellany
0459-9586 Annales Universitatis Mariae Curie-Sklodowska. Sectio H. Oeconomia
0459-9756 Lucknow Law Times
0460-007X Lute Society Journal
0460-024X Lutheran Church in America. Western Canada Synod. Minutes of the Annual Convention†
0460-0274 Lutheran Historical Conference Newsletter
0460-1297 Little Lamp
0460-1327 Locator
0460-1424 Denmark. Landoekonomiske Driftsbureau. Meddelelse *see* 0106-2689
0460-2048 Leidse Kunsthistorische Reeks
0460-2099 Lesotho. Ministry of Foreign Affairs. Diplomatic and Consular List
0460-2374 Luftverunreinigung
0460-2390 M & B Pharmaceutical Bulletin†
0460-3060 Resultados das Observacoes Meteorologicas de Macau
0460-5047 Das Magazin
0460-6736 Maine Geological Survey. Mineral Resources Index Series†
0461-0040 Manual of Excellent Management†
0461-2531 Masinstvo
0461-5298 Denmark. Rigsbibliotekaren. Meddelelser *see* 0901-7496
0461-6308 Medicinsk Aarbog
0461-6529 Medizinstudent *see* 0344-5933
0461-7185 Melodias†
0461-7398 Men and Women of Hawaii
0462-1069 Mexico News
0462-3134 Advocacy Institute. Proceedings
0462-4874 Military Digest
0462-9086 Heimatkundliches Beiblatt *changed to* Heimat im Weinland
0463-1536 Monitor de la Farmacia y de la Terapeutica
0463-1935 Monographien zur Rheinisch-Westfaelischen Kunst der Gegenwart†
0463-6457 Motor Club News
0463-6635 Motor Vehicle Statistics of Japan
0463-9847 Universidad de Murcia. Anales de Ciencias *see* 0213-5489
0463-9863 Universidad de Murcia. Anales de Letras
0464-1973 M P S A Newsletter
0464-2147 Ma'arachot
0464-3755 Escuela Diplomatica. Cuadernos†
0464-476X Parttorteneti Kozlemenyek
0464-5030 Maharaja Sayajirao University of Baroda. Department of History Series
0464-5820 Maine Historical Society. Newsletter *see* 0163-1152
0464-591X Mainly Marketing
0464-7734 Male†
0464-7777 Der Maler und Lackierermeister
0464-8072 Mammillaria Journal
0464-882X Manual Azucarero Mexicano
0464-9567 March of the Nation†
0464-9605 Marche Financier de Paris
0464-9680 Marian Studies
0464-9974 Market Bulletin
0465-0166 Marktforscher *see* 0170-723X
0465-031X Marriage Guidance
0465-1499 Commerce Digest†
0465-2592 Maszyny i Ciagniki Rolnicze
0465-3750 Mathematik in der Schule
0465-3769 Mathematisch-Naturwissenschaftliche Bibliothek
0465-4773 Universidad de Medellin. Facultad de Ciencias Administrativas. Revista
0465-5818 Revue de Politique Internationale
0465-5893 Medycyna Pracy
0465-7004 N R A News *changed to* Restaurants U S A
0466-1478 Official National Collegiate Athletic Association Baseball Guide *see* 0736-5209
0466-1761 N.C.A.I. News Bulletin *changed to* Sentinel/Bulletin - N C A I News
0466-3276 National Institute of Sciences of India. Mathematical Tables *changed to* Indian National Science Academy. Mathematical Tables
0466-499X Safety Newsletter: Occupational Health Nursing Section *changed to* Occupational Health Nursing Newsletter
0466-5007 Safety Newsletter: Public Utilities Section *changed to* Public Utilities Newsletter
0466-6054 Nature in Wales
0466-7530 Netherlands Federation of Trade Unions. Information Bulletin *changed to* F N V News
0467-006X Rijksdienst voor het Oudheidkundig Bodemonderzoek te Amersfoort. Berichten
0467-1872 New Caducean†
0467-6769 New York (State). Insurance Department. Loss and Expense Ratios
0467-8966 New Zealand Civil Aviation Statistics
0468-1746 Der Niedergelassene Arzt
0468-1835 Nielsen Newscast

0468-3390 Norddeutsche Familienkunde *changed to* Nordeutsche Familienkunde in Verbindung mit der Zeitschrift fuer Niederdeutsche Familienkunde
0468-5067 Groundwater Bulletin
0468-6853 Northeastern Tour Book *changed to* Tourbook: Connecticut, Massachusetts, Rhode Island
0468-6853 Northeastern Tour Book *changed to* Tourbook: Maine, New Hampshire, Vermont
0468-8147 Norway. Statistisk Sentralbyraa. Samferdselsstatistikk/Transport and Communication Statistics
0468-8155 Norway. Statistisk Sentralbyraa. Skogstatstikk/Forestry Statistics
0469-0281 Nova Trgovina
0469-2071 Nukada Institute for Medical and Biological Research. Reports
0469-2454 Nuova Rivista Pedagogica
0469-323X N A S B I C News
0469-337X N B S Publications Newsletter†
0469-4007 N U S A S Newsletter *changed to* Dissent
0469-4236 Nachrichten aus dem Karten- und Vermessungswesen. Reihe I: Originalbeitraege
0469-4244 Nachrichten aus dem Karten- und Vermessungswesen. Reihe II: Uebersetzungen
0469-4759 Nagoya University. Research Institute of Environmental Medicine. Annual Report
0469-4783 Nagoya Port Statistics Annual
0469-5550 Nara Medical Association. Journal
0469-8029 National Automotive Directory†
0469-8592 National Collegiate Athletic Association. Official Skiing Rules *changed to* N C A A Men's and Women's Skiing Rules
0469-9130 National Council for Geographic Education. Do It This Way†
0470-0384 National Forest Products Association. Fingertip Facts & Figures†
0470-0929 National Geographer
0470-1321 National Institute of Agricultural Botany, Cambridge, England. Vegetable Growers Leaflets
0470-1380 National Institute of Sciences of India. N I S I Monographs *changed to* Indian National Science Academy. Monographs
0470-2824 Safety Newsletter: Aerospace Section *changed to* Aerospace Newsletter
0470-2832 Safety Newsletter: Air Transport Section *changed to* Air Transport Newsletter
0470-2840 Safety Newsletter: Public Employee Section *changed to* Public Employee Newsletter
0470-3219 National Stripper Well Survey
0470-3901 Naturkundliches Jahrbuch der Stadt Linz
0470-5017 Proceedings of the Section of Mathematics, Natural Science and Medicine *changed to* Naukove Tovarystvo Imeni Shevchenka. Proceedings of the Section of Mathematics and Physics
0470-5017 Proceedings of the Section of Mathematics, Natural Sciences and Medicine *changed to* Naukove Tovarystvo Imeni Shevchenka. Proceedings of the Section of Chemistry, Biology and Medicine
0470-5106 Navajo Times *changed to* Navajo Times Today
0470-5661 Nebraska Optometric Association. Journal *changed to* N O A Journal
0470-6021 Nederlandse Chemische Industrie†
0470-6684 Netherlands. Centraal Bureau voor de Statistiek. Maandstatistiek van de Industrie
0470-6978 Netherlands. Centraal Bureau voor de Statistiek. Sociale Maandstatistiek *see* 0168-549X
0470-7427 Synoptic and Upper Air Observations in the Netherlands†
0470-8105 Neurologia Medico-Chirurgica
0471-0320 Odziez
0471-1424 Office Equipment Exporter
0471-380X Oil & Gas Directory
0471-3850 Oil Directory of Alaska†
0471-3877 Oil Directory of Houston, Texas
0471-492X Oklahoma Employment Security Review
0471-7376 Orafo Italiano
0471-7708 Ordine dei Medici. Bollettino *changed to* Piemonte Medico
0471-8356 State Board of Accountancy. Roster of Accountants Authorized to Conduct Municipal Audits *changed to* Oregon. State Board of Accountancy. Certified Public Accountants, Public Accountants, and Accountants Authorized to Conduct Municipal Audits in Oregon
0471-9174 Oregon Cattleman
0471-9336 Oregon Psychological Association. Newsletter *changed to* Oregon Psychology
0472-0490 Orient
0472-0601 Orientacion Medica
0472-0784 Orientamenti Pastorali

ISSN INDEX 1567

0472-0989 Orissa, India. Finance Department. White Paper on Departmental Activities, Government of Orissa *changed to* Orissa, India. Finance Department. White Paper on the Economic Conditions and the Developmental Activities in Orissa
0472-190X Ostdeutsche Familienkunde
0472-2191 Oswiata Doroslych
0472-2744 Ouranos
0472-397X Ob-Gyn Collected Letters
0472-5263 Oeil
0472-5859 Oesterreichisches Forschungsinstitut fuer Sparkassenwesen. Schriftenreihe
0472-6685 Ohio. Division of Geological Survey. Educational Leaflet
0472-7584 Oil and Australia†
0472-7711 Oil Directory of Companies Outside the U.S. and Canada
0472-8637 Olam Hadash
0472-8807 Oleo-Semenal
0472-8874 Oljyposti
0472-948X Ondas
0472-9986 Ontario. Labour Relations Board. Decisions *see* 0383-4778
0473-0062 Ontario Cancer Treatment and Research Foundation. Clinical Conference. Proceedings†
0473-0658 Instituto de Botanica "Dr. Goncalo Sampaio". Publicacoes. 3 Serie†
0473-0917 Optique†
0473-1034 Opuscula Zoologica
0473-1174 Orafo Italiano nel Mundo
0473-3657 Organization of African Unity. Health, Sanitation and Nutrition Commission. Proceedings and Report†
0473-4351 Ortnamnssallskapet i Uppsala. Aarsskrift
0473-4378 Ortopedia i Traumatologia
0473-4548 Osaka Daigaku Keizaigaku *changed to* Osaka Daigaku Keizaigaku - Osaka Economic Papers
0473-4580 Osaka University. Laboratory of Nuclear Studies. Annual Report
0473-4637 University of Osaka Prefecture. Bulletin. Series D: Sciences of Economy, Commerce and Law
0473-5277 Frankfurter Abhandlungen zur Slavistik
0473-5587 Automation
0473-5609 Otorinolaringologija
0473-6788 Organization for Economic Cooperation and Development. Reviews of Manpower and Social Policies
0473-7490 Occasional Papers in Political Science†
0473-7733 Ochrona Przed Korozja
0473-8063 Osterbotten
0473-8322 Oesterreichische Papier *changed to* Papier aus Oesterreich
0473-8624 Oesterreichisches Volksliedwerk. Jahrbuch
0473-8837 Studies on Current Health Problems
0473-9442 Game Research in Ohio *see* 0085-4468
0473-9787 O C W R U Quarterly Report†
0474-0114 Oil Directory of Canada
0474-0157 Oita University Economic Review
0474-0696 Oklahoma Anthropological Society. Memoir
0474-070X Oklahoma Economic Indicators†
0474-0750 Oklahoma Ornithological Society. Bulletin
0474-1382 On View†
0474-1560 Ontario. Ministry of Agriculture and Food. Seasonal Fruit and Vegetable Report
0474-2125 O L A Newsletter *changed to* Focus (Toronto)
0474-2389 Open Places
0474-2893 Opolskie Roczniki Ekonomiczne
0474-2966 Wyzsza Szkola Pedagogiczna, Opole. Zeszyty Naukowe. Seria A. Ekonomia
0474-2974 Wyzsza Szkola Pedagogiczna, Opole. Zeszyty Naukowe. Seria A. Filologia Rosyjska
0474-3253 Oral History Association. Newsletter
0474-3326 Orbit (New York)
0474-3342 Orchadian
0474-4039 Public Welfare in Oregon *changed to* Adult and Family Services in Oregon
0474-4535 Oregon Historical Society. News
0474-4616 Oregon Recreation Briefs
0474-4829 Organisation of European Aluminum Smelters. Economic Situation of the Aluminum Smelters in Europe *changed to* Aluminum Smelters
0474-5086 Organization for Economic Cooperation and Development. Catalogue of Publications
0474-5124 Organization for Economic Cooperation and Development. Economic Surveys: Austria
0474-5132 Organization for Economic Cooperation and Development. Economic Surveys: Belgium-Luxembourg Economic Union
0474-5140 Organization for Economic Cooperation and Development. Economic Surveys: Canada
0474-5159 Organization for Economic Cooperation and Development. Economic Surveys: Denmark
0474-5167 Organization for Economic Cooperation and Development. Economic Surveys: France
0474-5175 Organization for Economic Cooperation and Development. Economic Surveys: Germany
0474-5183 Organization for Economic Cooperation and Development. Economic Surveys: Greece
0474-5191 Organization for Economic Cooperation and Development. Economic Surveys: Iceland
0474-5205 Organization for Economic Cooperation and Development. Economic Surveys: Ireland
0474-5213 Organization for Economic Cooperation and Development. Economic Surveys: Italy
0474-5221 Organization for Economic Cooperation and Development. Economic Surveys: Japan
0474-523X Organization for Economic Cooperation and Development. Economic Surveys: Netherlands.
0474-5248 Organization for Economic Cooperation and Development. Economic Surveys: Norway
0474-5256 Organization for Economic Cooperation and Development. Economic Surveys: Portugal
0474-5264 Organization for Economic Cooperation and Development. Economic Surveys: Socialist Federal Republic of Yugoslavia
0474-5272 Organization for Economic Cooperation and Development. Economic Surveys: Spain
0474-5280 Organization for Economic Cooperation and Development. Economic Surveys: Sweden
0474-5299 Organization for Economic Cooperation and Development. Economic Surveys. Switzerland
0474-5302 Organization for Economic Cooperation and Development. Economic Surveys: Turkey
0474-5310 Organization for Economic Cooperation and Development. Economic Surveys: United Kingdom
0474-5329 Organization for Economic Cooperation and Development. Economic Surveys: United States
0474-5337 Organization for Economic Cooperation and Development. Employment of Special Groups†
0474-5353 Organization for Economic Cooperation and Development. Survey of Electric Power Equipment. Enquete sur l'Equipment Electrique†
0474-537X Food Consumption in the O.E.C.D. *changed to* Food Consumption Statistics in the O.E.C.D. Countries
0474-5388 Organization for Economic Cooperation and Development. Statistics of Foreign Trade. Series A: Monthly Bulletin/ Statistiques du Commerce Exterieur. Serie A: Bulletin Mensuel *changed to* Organization for Economic Cooperation and Development. Monthly Foreign Trade Statistics/ Statistiques Mensuel du Commerce Exterieur.
0474-5396 Organization for Economic Cooperation and Development. Statistics of Foreign Trade. Series B: Tables by Reporting Countries /Statistiques du Commerce Exterieur. Serie B: Tableaux Par Pays Declarants†
0474-540X Organization for Economic Cooperation and Development. Foreign Trade by Commodities
0474-5434 Geographical Distribution of Financial Flows to Less Developed Countries. (Disbursements) *changed to* Geographical Distribution of Financial Flows to Developing Countries. (Disbursement)
0474-5442 Organization for Economic Cooperation and Development. Historical Statistics. Statistiques Retrospectives *changed to* Organization for Economic Cooperation and Development. Main Economic Indicators. Historical Statistics. Statistiques Retrospectives
0474-5450 Organization for Economic Cooperation and Development. Industrial Production. Production Industrielle†
0474-5469 Organization for Economic Cooperation and Development. Industrial Statistics. Statistiques Industrielles†
0474-5477 Organization for Economic Cooperation and Development. Electricity Supply Industry. l'Industrie de l'Electricite†
0474-5485 Pulp and Paper Industry in the O.E.C.D. Member Countries and Finland†
0474-5493 Organization for Economic Cooperation and Development. Cement Industry. Industrie du Ciment†
0474-5515 Organization for Economic Cooperation and Development. Labour Force Statistics (Yearbook) /Statistiques de la Population Active
0474-5523 O E C D Main Economic Indicators/ Principaux Indicateurs Economiques
0474-5574 O E C D Economic Outlook
0474-5620 Organization for Economic Cooperation and Development. Wages and Labour Mobility Supplement†
0474-5655 Organization for Economic Cooperation and Development. Council. Code de la Liberation des Mouvements de Capitaux. Code of Liberalisation of Capital Movements
0474-5663 Organization for Economic Cooperation and Development. Development Cooperation
0474-585X Hides, Skins and Footwear Industry in O E C D Countries.†
0474-5868 Organization for Economic Cooperation and Development. Library. Special Annotated Bibliography: Automation. Bibliographie Speciale Analytique
0474-5876 Organization for Economic Cooperation and Development. Machinery Committee. Engineering Industries in North-America-Europe-Japan†
0474-5884 Organization for Economic Cooperation and Development. Maritime Transport Committee. Maritime Transport
0474-5892 Organization for Economic Cooperation and Development. Social Affairs Division. Developing Job Opportunities†
0474-5922 Organization for Economic Cooperation and Development. Social Affairs Division. Employment of Special Groups†
0474-5973 Organization for Economic Cooperation and Development. Special Committee for Iron and Steel. Iron and Steel Industry
0474-6007 Organization for Economic Cooperation and Development. Special Committee for Oil. Oil Statistics. Supply and Disposal
0474-6023 Textile Industry in O.E.C.D. Countries
0474-6171 Organization of African Unity. Scientific Technical and Research Commission. Publication
0474-6279 Organization of the Petroleum Exporting Countries. Bulletin
0474-6317 Organization of the Petroleum Exporting Countries. Annual Review and Record *changed to* Organization of the Petroleum Exporting Countries. Annual Report.
0474-635X Organizzarsi
0474-6376 Organo
0474-7534 Annals of Dyslexia
0474-781X Osaka University. College of General Education. Science Reports
0474-7844 University of Osaka Prefecture. Bulletin. Series A: Engineering and Natural Sciences
0474-7852 University of Osaka Prefecture. Bulletin. Series B: Agriculture and Biology
0474-7879 Osaka (Prefecture). Radiation Center, Annual Report
0474-8042 Norsk Polarinstitutt. Polarhaandbok
0474-8328 Osteuropastudien der Hochschulen des Landes Hessen. Reihe 2†
0474-8530 Osttiroler Heimatblaetter
0474-8603 Otago Museum. Records. Anthropology†
0474-8611 Otago Museum. Records. Zoology†
0474-8662 Otbor i Peredacha Informatsii *changed to* Otbor i Obrabotka Informatsii
0474-9030 Our Heritage
0474-9588 Trabajos de Geologia
0474-9847 Oyo Kikai Kogaku
0475-0071 Okayama University. School of Engineering. Memoirs
0475-0209 One World
0475-0608 Organization of the Petroleum Exporting Countries. Annual Statistical Bulletin
0475-0926 Oklahoma. Attorney General's Office. Opinions of the Attorney General
0475-0942 Ontario. Ministry of the Environment. Water Resources Branch. Water Resources Report
0475-1310 Offshore Contractors and Equipment Directory *changed to* Offshore Contractors and Equipment Worldwide Directory
0475-1388 Old Athlone Society Journal
0475-1671 Oyez
0475-171X Oceans
0475-1876 Old Car Value Guide
0475-1906 Optimum
0475-2015 Organizational Directory of the Government of Thailand
0475-2058 Osaka Dental University. Journal
0475-2112 Owner Operator
0475-2953 P S, The Preventive Maintenance Monthly
0475-4816 Palabra Diaria
0475-9141 Patre
0476-0069 Pediatria Internazionale†
0476-1103 Pennsylvania Statistical Abstract
0476-3475 Die Personalvertretung
0476-5532 Philippine Government Rulings
0476-9465 Plana†
0477-2008 Police & Constabulary Almanac
0477-244X Politica dei Trasporti
0477-5449 Poodle Review
0477-6801 Ports and Dredging and Oil Report *changed to* Ports and Dredging
0477-7166 Boletim Actinometrico *see* 0870-4740
0477-7255 Portugal Illustrado
0477-8685 Pozemni Stavby
0478-1376 Presenza
0478-1392 Preservation Progress
0478-1546 Presse

1568 ISSN INDEX

0478-1805 Previdenza Sociale nell'Agricoltura
0478-3166 Pro Austria Romana
0478-4049 Asbestos Producer
0478-4251 Products Finishing Directory
0478-6378 Proyeccion
0478-6726 Przemysl Drzewny
0479-0790 Pacific Hotel Directory and Travel Guide *see* 8750-8672
0479-1290 Padova
0479-1363 Beihefte Paedagogik
0479-2327 Pakistan Cotton Bulletin *see* 0030-9699
0479-3013 Pan
0479-4346 Panorama Economico
0479-480X Magyar Grafika
0479-7337 Pays de Bruxelles *changed to* Action Bruxelloise et le Pays de Bruxelles
0479-7876 Pediatria
0479-8244 Pembrokeshire Historian†
0479-8775 Pennsylvania. Department of Public Welfare. Public Welfare Report *see* 0098-8510
0479-9828 Pentecostes *see* 0210-0851
0480-0257 Performing Arts Magazine (San Francisco Edition)
0480-0516 Permanent International Association of Navigation Congresses. Bulletin
0480-2160 Petroleum Intelligence Weekly
0480-2780 Philadelphia Association for Psychoanalysis. Bulletin *see* 0094-1476
0480-2853 Philanthropic Digest
0480-3981 Series of Philippine Scientific Bibliographies†
0480-7898 Quill
0480-8207 Quotidiano Minerva Medica
0480-9653 Queensland. Department of Forestry. Annual Report
0481-0023 Quellen zur Geschichte des Islamischen Aegyptens
0481-0112 Quelques Donnees Statistiques sur l'Industrie Francaise des Pates, Papiers, Cartons *changed to* Statistiques de l'Industrie Francaise des Pates. Papiers et Cartons
0481-1275 Quantum Physics and Its Applications†
0481-2085 Quarterly Journal of Engineering Geology
0481-2158 Quarterly Medical Review
0481-2786 Quebec (Province) Department of Tourism, Fish and Game. Annual Report *see* 0229-3811
0481-2875 Quebec (Province). Liquor Board. Rapport Annuel *changed to* Societe des Alcools du Quebec. Rapport Annuel
0481-3219 Research Note
0481-3375 Queensland. Registrar of Co-Operative and Other Societies. Report
0481-4118 Quimica e Derivados
0481-5084 R F D News
0481-5475 Rachunkowosc
0481-6684 Revista de Chirurgie, Oncologie, O.R.L., Radiologie, Oftalmologie, Stomatologie. Radiologie
0481-6722 Radionic Quarterly
0481-9306 Recht der Jugend *see* 0034-1312
0482-0819 Reform Judaism
0482-1319 Register of Registrars
0482-2803 Report on Credit Unions
0482-430X Retreader's Journal
0482-5020 Revista Cailor Ferate Romane†
0482-5276 Revista de Ciencias Sociales
0482-5527 Revista de Educacao e Cultura
0482-5772 Revista de Ingenieria
0482-640X Revista Nacional de Oncologia
0482-6876 Revista Mexicana de Seguridad Social†
0482-7678 Revue de Droit Familial *changed to* Cahiers de Droit Familial
0482-8062 Revue du Travail
0483-142X Rivista del Lavoro
0483-2027 Robotnik
0483-3686 Rose Annual *changed to* Rose
0483-7738 R P A Bulletin *changed to* Regional Plan News
0483-9218 Rajshahi University Studies
0483-9889 Rating and Valuation
0484-0305 Readaptation
0484-0828 Recent Researches in the Music of the Baroque Era
0484-1506 Recording for the Blind. Catalog of Recorded Books
0484-1689 Redbook of Used Gun Values†
0484-2286 Referativnyi Zhurnal. Kommunal'noe, Bytovoe i Torgovoe Oborudovanie
0484-2480 Referativnyi Zhurnal. Stroitel'nye i Dorozhnye Mashiny
0484-2502 Referativnyi Zhurnal. Teploenergetika†
0484-2545 Referativnyi Zhurnal. Vodnyi Transport
0484-2561 Referativnyi Zhurnal. Vozdushnyi Transport
0484-2596 Referativnyi Zhurnal. Zheleznodorozhnyi Transport
0484-2650 Reflection (Spokane)
0484-6796 Revista de Ciencias Economicas: Economia, Financas, Administracao, Estatistica *changed to* Ciencias Economicas
0484-6885 Revista de Derecho Financiero y de Hacienda Publica
0484-6923 Revista de Derecho Social Ecuatoriano
0484-8578 Revue de Mycologie *see* 0181-1584
0484-8594 Revue de Podologie
0484-8764 Revue Francaise de Comptabilite
0484-8934 Revue Metapsychique
0484-8942 Revue Numismatique
0484-9019 Rit Fiskideildar
0485-1412 Japanese Journal of Clinical Nutrition
0485-2044 Rio Grande Valley Horticultural Society. Journal
0485-2400 Rivista di Istochimica Normale e Patologica *see* 0391-7258
0485-2435 Rivista Giuridica dell' Edilizia
0485-2877 Rocket News
0485-3091 Rocznik Pilski *see* 0557-2088
0485-3504 Rodzina i Szkola
0485-5175 Roving Commissions
0485-6724 Old Sturbridge Visitor
0485-8182 R I S S; National Magazine for Residents, Interns, and Senior Students *see* 0018-5795
0485-8255 Regional Science Research Institute. Discussion Paper Series†
0485-893X Radiologia Iugoslavica
0485-9561 Rajasthan Medical Journal
0485-9790 Rand Corporation. Index of Selected Publications *see* 0037-1343
0485-9960 Random Lengths Yearbook
0486-0306 Rassegna Geriatrica
0486-0349 Rassegna Italiana di Sociologia
0486-0373 Rassegna Parlamentare
0486-0748 Reactive Intermediates in Organic Chemistry†
0486-0845 University of Reading. Department of Agricultural Economics and Management. Miscellaneous Studies
0486-1019 Realidade†
0486-106X Realites Gabonaises
0486-123X Recent Researches in the Music of the Renaissance
0486-1426 Recherches Voltaiques†
0486-1493 Recht und Geschichte
0486-2236 Referativnyi Zhurnal. Astronomiya
0486-2252 Referativnyi Zhurnal. Avtomobil'nye Dorogi
0486-2260 Referativnyi Zhurnal. Biologicheskaya Khimiya *see* 0034-2300
0486-2279 Referativnyi Zhurnal. Dvigateli Vnutrennego Sgoraniya
0486-2287 Referativnyi Zhurnal. Elektronika i ee Primenenie *see* 0206-5452
0486-2309 Referativnyi Zhurnal. Geologiya
0486-2325 Referativnyi Zhurnal. Khimiya
0486-2333 Referativnyi Zhurnal. Kibernetika *changed to* Referativnyi Zhurnal. Tekhnicheskaya Kibernetika
0486-235X Referativnyi Zhurnal. Informatika
0486-252X Reformed Journal
0486-2902 Regional Science Association. Papers
0486-3720 Renaissance and Modern Studies
0486-3739 Renaissance Drama
0486-3887 Renewal of Town and Village†
0486-400X Rentgenologija i Radiologija
0486-4271 Repertorium Plantarum Succulentarum
0486-4514 Diplomatic Corps and Consular and Other Representatives in Canada
0486-4689 Res Facta
0486-4700 Res Publica
0486-4867 Research Corporation Quarterly Bulletin *see* 0276-0401
0486-5111 Research Progress in Organic, Biological and Medicinal Chemistry†
0486-5383 Reserve Bank of Malawi. Report and Accounts
0486-5588 Responsa Meridiana
0486-5642 Restoration Quarterly
0486-6134 Review of Radical Political Economics
0486-6460 Revista Camoniana
0486-8234 Saechsische Heimatblaetter
0486-8323 Safe Driver
0487-1596 I C A P Lista de Nuevas Adquisiciones
0487-2088 St. Hedwigsblatt
0487-3750 Guida Sardegna d'Oggi
0487-4013 Saskatchewan. Geodata Statistics and Research Branch. Weekly Drilling and Land Report *see* 0707-9788
0487-6830 School Sister of Notre Dame
0487-8965 Scientific Meetings
0488-2644 Sempex Pharmaceutique
0488-3721 Servex
0488-6720 Shipmate
0488-7115 Show Business Who's Where *see* 0508-6795
0488-728X Free Albanian
0488-8812 Simplicity School Catalog†
0489-1376 Literarny Almanach Slovaka V Amerike†
0489-2089 Norsk Etnologisk Gransking. Smaaskrifter†
0489-2313 Smithsonian Institution. Annual Symposia Publications†
0489-5606 Engineering Know-How in Engine Design
0489-5967 Socijalizam
0489-8567 South African Licensee's Guardian
0490-0200 Southern Illinois Labor Tribune
0490-1274 Soviet Export
0490-1606 Soziale Arbeit
0490-2270 Instituto de Aclimatacion. Archives†
0490-3323 Spain. Ministerio de la Vivienda. Boletin Oficial
0490-334X Spain. Ministerio de Obras Publicas. Boletin de Informacion *changed to* Obras Publicas
0490-4176 Spex Speaker
0490-4788 Spoletium
0490-5113 Sport Universitario
0490-5326 Sports Afield Gun Annual†
0490-5474 Sports Turf Bulletin
0490-5687 Sportaube
0490-6381 Sri Lanka
0490-6659 Srpska Akademija Nauka i Umetnosti. Odeljenje Likovne i Muzicke Umetnosti. Muzicka Izdanja
0490-9348 Steirischer Burgenverein. Mitteilungen
0491-0869 Stockholm Studies in History of Literature
0491-0877 Stockholm Studies in Philosophy
0491-0982 Stomatologija
0491-1245 Strafvollzug in der Schweiz
0491-1520 Street and Smith's Baseball Yearbook *see* 0161-2018
0491-2705 Studia Ethnographica Upsaliensia
0491-3310 Studies in Public Opinion†
0491-3418 Studii de Muzicologie†
0491-4481 Sudan Medical Journal
0491-6204 Surmach
0491-6441 Svarochnoe Proizvodstvo
0492-004X Transportarbetaren
0492-0716 T V Star Annual†
0492-1283 Tag des Herrn
0492-1712 Taiwan Sugar
0492-1755 Tajekoztato a Kulfoldi Kozgazdasagi Irodalomrol *changed to* Kulfoldi Kozgazdasagi Irodalmi Szemle. Series A
0492-1755 Tajekoztato a Kulfoldi Kozgazdasagi Irodalomrol *changed to* Kulfoldi Kozgazdasagi Irodalmi Szemle. Series B
0492-3901 Taylor Talk
0492-4134 Teachers of the World
0492-4851 Technik Wlokienniczy
0492-5408 Teen Talk†
0492-6471 Temas Sociales
0492-6749 Tempo Medico
0492-746X Tennessee Magazine
0493-4091 Tokyo Keizai University. Journal
0493-4253 University of Electro-Communications. Report
0493-4334 University of Tokyo. Faculty of Science. Misaki Marine Biological Station. Contributions
0493-5284 Torch: U.S.
0493-5306 Torino Motori *see* 0393-7666
0493-6779 Trade Times
0493-8348 Trelleborgs Nyheter†
0493-9042 Tribune
0494-2884 Turkey Today†
0494-3880 T A C Attack
0494-4739 Korean Journal of Dermatology
0494-5336 Taiwan Exports
0494-612X Taminga *changed to* S.A. Geographer Bulletin
0494-6944 Tap Roots
0494-7061 Tareas
0494-8203 Source References for Facts and Figures on Government Finance†
0494-8343 Taxation in Australia
0494-8440 Te Reo
0494-9390 Technische Mitteilungen Krupp
0494-9501 Technica e Metodologia Economale *changed to* Sintesi
0494-9870 Tehran Economist
0495-0127 Tele (English Edition)
0495-0615 Temas Economicos
0495-0658 Temi Romana
0495-1328 Tennessee Lawyer *see* 0497-2325
0495-145X Industrial Development in the T.V.A. Area
0495-257X Texas Vital Statistics
0495-2634 University of Texas, Austin. Bureau of Business Research. Publications
0495-2944 Texas Archeological Society. Special Publication
0495-369X Textile World Buyer's Guide/Fact File
0495-5773 Tierras de Leon
0495-7199 Tohogaku
0495-7601 Tokushima University. Journal of Gakugei
0495-7725 Maison Franco-Japonaise. Bulletin
0495-7814 University of Tokyo. Institute for Nuclear Study. INS-J
0495-7822 University of Tokyo. Institute for Nuclear Study. Report
0495-8012 Journal of Humanities and Natural Sciences
0495-8020 Tokyo Institute of Technology. Bulletin†
0495-8055 Tokyo Institute of Technology. Research Laboratory of Resources Utilization. Report
0495-8667 Toomey J Gazette *see* 0361-4166
0495-9728 Town & Country Planning Association. Planning Bulletin
0496-1021 Transportes
0496-1102 Transvaal Museum. Bulletin
0496-1803 Tri-City Genealogical Society. Bulletin
0496-3547 Tsuda Review
0496-4845 Turista
0496-6201 Two and a Bud
0496-6457 T.A.
0496-7046 Taiwan Financial Statistics Monthly *changed to* Financial Statistics Monthly, Taiwan District, Republic of China
0496-7631 Tall Timbers Research Station. Bulletin
0496-764X Tall Timbers Research Station. Miscellaneous Publication
0496-8018 Universite de Madagascar. Centre d'Etudes des Coutumes. Cahiers *changed to* Cahiers d'Histoire Juridique et Politique

ISSN INDEX 1569

0496-8026 Tane
0496-8360 C A F R A D News†
0496-8492 Appropriation Accounts, Revenue Statements, Accounts of the Funds and Other Public Accounts of Tanzania†
0496-8859 Taraxacum
0496-8913 Tar Heel Junior Historian
0496-9472 Tata Institute of Fundamental Research. Lectures on Mathematics and Physic. Physics *changed to* Tata Institute Lectures on Mathematics
0496-974X Tax Foundation's Research Bibliography
0496-9936 Teachers & Writers Collaborative Newsletter *see* 0146-3381
0496-9944 Teacher's Arts & Crafts Workshop†
0497-0489 Technical Translation Bulletin
0497-0527 Technicon International Congress. Papers†
0497-1000 University of Teheran. Central Library. Library Bulletin
0497-1035 Tehnika Podmazivanja i Primjena Goriva *changed to* Goriva i Maziva
0497-137X Telecommunication Journal
0497-1388 Telecommunications
0497-1507 Television Digest *see* 0497-1515
0497-1515 Television Digest with Consumer Electronics
0497-1817 Temenos (Turku)
0497-2007 France. Institut National de la Statistique et des Etudes Economiques. Tendances de la Conjoncture
0497-2325 Tennessee Bar Journal
0497-2384 Tennessee Studies in Literature
0497-2627 Teoreticheskaya i Eksperimental'naya Khimiya
0497-9400 Asian Bibliography
0498-2002 U.S. Agricultural Marketing Service. Dairy Division. Federal Milk Order Market Statistics
0498-7667 Wholesale Prices and Price Indexes *changed to* Producer Price Indexes
0498-7845 U.S. Bureau of Mines. Mineral Industry Surveys
0498-8442 Current Construction Reports: Housing Starts
0498-8450 Current Housing Reports: Housing Characteristics
0498-8469 Current Housing Reports: Housing Vacancies
0498-8477 Current Industrial Reports
0498-8485 Current Population Reports: Special Studies
0499-0994 U.S. Department of Commerce. Publications. Supplement *see* 0277-7207
0499-9320 National Aeronautics and Space Administration. Technical Memorandum
0500-1951 U.S. Office of Naval Research. Annual Task Summary: Contract Research Program
0500-5922 Universitas Belgica. Communication/ Mededeling *changed to* Universitas Belgica
0500-7720 Utah Vital Statistics Annual Report
0501-0659 Ulkopolitiikka
0501-1213 International Conference of Building Officials. Uniform Housing Code
0501-1590 Union of European Football Associations. Bulletin
0501-3615 Race Question in Modern Science†
0501-4697 U S D A-D H I A Cow Performance Index List†
0501-7041 U.S. Bureau of Labor Statistics. National Survey of Professional, Administrative, Technical and Clerical Pay
0501-7467 U.S. Bureau of Reclamation. Engineering and Research Center. Research Reports *changed to* U.S. Bureau of Reclamation. Engineering and Research Center. Research Reports
0501-7718 Current Governments Reports: Quarterly Summary of State and Local Tax Revenue
0501-8390 U.S. Centers for Disease Control. Malaria Surveillance Report
0501-9117 Agricultural Finance Outlook *changed to* Agricultural Finance Outlook and Situation
0501-9257 Agricultural Situation in the Western Hemisphere *changed to* World Agriculture Regional Supplement: Western Hemisphere
0501-9664 Employees of Diplomatic Missions
0501-9966 Background Notes on the Countries of the World
0502-0034 International Boundary Study
0502-3238 World Marketing†
0502-4994 U.S. Forest Service. Research Note RM
0502-5001 U.S. Forest Service. Research Paper RM
0502-5842 United States-Italy Trade Directory
0502-6660 Latinamericanist†
0502-6938 Unsere Heimat (Vienna)
0502-7179 Up-To-Date
0502-9392 U A W Ammunition *changed to* U A W Ammo
0502-949X Universidad Nacional de Colombia. Direccion de Divulgacion Cultural. Revista
0502-9554 Unesco Source Books on Curricula and Methods
0502-9767 U S Oil Week
0503-1001 Ukrainian Academy of Arts and Sciences in the U S. Annals
0503-1036 Komitet' Ukrainstsiv Kanady. Biuleten'
0503-1265 Ukrainskii Fizicheskii Zhurnal
0503-146X Hauma
0503-1540 Mer (Tokyo)
0503-1966 Uniform Commercial Code Law Letter
0503-1982 Uniformed Services Almanac
0503-2032 Unima France *changed to* U N I M A - France Marionnettes
0503-2334 Union Mondiale des Organisations Syndicales sur Bases Economique et Sociale Liberales. Conferences: Rapport
0503-2407 Collection of Documents for the Study of International Non-Governmental Relations
0503-2628 Unit Trust Yearbook
0503-3551 United Methodist Church. General Minutes of the Annual Conferences
0503-356X United Methodist Directory
0503-3772 Half-Yearly Bulletin of Electric Energy Statistics for Europe†
0503-3934 United Nations. Regional Centre for Demographic Training and Research in Latin America. Serie A
0503-3942 United Nations. Regional Centre for Demographic Training and Research in Latin America. Serie C
0503-3950 United Nations. Regional Centre for Demographic Training and Research in Latin America. Serie D
0503-4299 Unesco Technical Papers in Marine Science
0503-440X Selected List of Catalogues for Short Films and Filmstrips†
0503-4434 Unesco. Regional Office for Science and Technology for Africa. Bulletin
0503-4442 Unesco. Regional Centre for the Training of Educational Planners, Administrators and Supervisors in Asia. Publication†
0503-4450 Unesco. Regional Office for Education in Asia. Bulletin. *changed to* Unesco. Regional Office for Education in Asia and the Pacific. Bulletin
0503-4469 Unesco. Regional Office for Education in Asia. Regional Conference Reports *changed to* Population Education in Asia and the Pacific Newsletter and Forum
0503-4663 United Schools International. Documents of the Biennial Conference
0503-5422 Appalachian Regional Commission. Annual Report
0504-0523 Veselye Kartinki
0504-0779 Veterans' Voices
0504-4251 Virginia Engineer
0504-426X Virginia English Bulletin
0504-6556 Voix des Jeunes
0504-7250 Voordrachten Gehouden voor de Gelderse Leergangen te Arnhem†
0505-0146 Vanidades Continental
0505-0332 Vasi Szemle
0505-0448 Vector
0505-2904 V D E W die Oeffentliche Elektrizitaetsversorgung
0505-3838 Vesitalous
0505-4753 Vidya
0505-5164 Naturhistorisches Museum in Wien. Veroeffentlichungen. Neue Folge
0505-5849 Vilagossag
0505-7523 Vishva Jyoti
0505-8813 Voice of the Tennessee Walking Horse
0505-9259 Volksarmee
0505-9461 Voluntad Hidraulica
0506-2772 Vatrechni Bolesti
0506-306X V D G S A News
0506-337X Vaabenhistorisk Tidsskrift
0506-3590 Yearbook of Population Research in Finland
0506-3876 Finnish State Railways†
0506-3973 Vancouver Historical Journal†
0506-4252 Varstvo Narave
0506-4406 Veckans Affaerer
0506-4414 Vector Genetics Information Service†
0506-5283 Venezuelan Petroleum Industry
0506-5291 Venezuela. Division de Estadistica Vital. Informe Especial *changed to* Venezuela. Departamento de Estadistica Vital. Informe Especial
0506-6913 Verde Olivo
0506-7286 Verfassung und Recht in Uebersee
0506-7294 Vergilius
0506-7472 Vermont Labor Force *changed to* Vermont Labor Market
0506-7847 Vertebratologicke Zpravy
0506-7936 Verzeichnis der Orientalischen Handschriften in Deutschland
0506-7944 Verzeichnis der Orientalischen Handschriften in Deutschland. Supplementbaende
0506-8339 Vi i Norden
0506-872X Vida Escolar
0507-0252 Viola da Gamba Society of America. Journal
0507-102X Virginia State Publications in Print
0507-1259 Virginia Polytechnic Institute and State University. Department of Geological Sciences. Geological Guidebooks.
0507-1410 Vishveshvaranand Indological Journal
0507-1577 Vista
0507-1690 Vita Evangelica
0507-1887 Vizgazdalkodas
0507-1925 Vjesnik Bibliotekara Hrvatske
0507-2298 Voice of P S E A
0507-3758 Voprosy Onkologii
0507-3952 Voprosy Teatra
0507-4088 Voprosy Virusologii
0507-570X Universidad Central de Venezuela. Instituto de Ciencias Penales y Criminologicas. Anuario.
0507-6714 Verein Deutscher Zementwerke. Forschungsinstitut der Zementindustrie. Taetigkeitsbericht
0507-6773 Vertebrate Pest Conference. Proceedings
0507-6986 Vajra Bodhi Sea
0507-7184 Vida Pastoral
0508-0924 Washington Report on Legislation for Children and What You Can do About It *changed to* Washington Report on Federal Legislation for Children
0508-0959 Washington Spectator *see* 0887-428X
0508-1254 Wasserrecht und Wasserwirtschaft
0508-2404 Weinberg und Keller
0508-2757 Welt der Arbeit
0508-461X Westerheem
0508-6795 Who's Where†
0508-7104 Wiadomosci Tytoniowe
0508-8445 Wir vom Konsum
0509-0652 Wochenpost
0509-5166 W.C.J. Meredith Memorial Lectures
0509-5190 W E M A Directory *changed to* American Electronics Association Directory
0509-5832 Waksman Foundation of Japan. Report
0509-6057 Walter E. Edge Lectures†
0509-6413 Bibliografia Bibliografii i Nauki o Ksiazce
0509-6529 Centralny Osrodek Badan i Rozwoju Techniki Drogowej. Prace *changed to* Instytut Badawczy Drog i Mostow. Prace
0509-6839 Biuletyn Warzywniczy
0509-6936 Muzeum Narodowe w Warszawie. Rocznik
0509-7053 Przemyslowy Instytut Elektroniki. Prace
0509-7134 Szkolna Glowna Gospodarstwa Wiejskiego. Zeszyty Naukowe. Zootechnika *see* 0208-5739
0509-769X Environmental Radiation Surveillance in Washington State. Annual Report
0509-7703 Washington (State). Department of Institutions. Jail Inspection Report *see* 0091-7265
0509-7967 Washington State Traffic Accident Facts†
0509-8262 Manufacturers and Distributors Directory of the Washington, D.C. Area†
0509-8858 Das Wassertriebwerk
0509-9498 Weekly Crusader *see* 0195-265X
0509-9773 Hochschule fuer Architektur und Bauwesen Weimar. Wissenschaftliche Zeitschrift
0510-0054 N Z O I Miscellaneous Publications
0510-1492 West Virginia Geological Survey. Educational Series *changed to* West Virginia Geologic Education Series
0510-2014 Western Australia. Geological Survey. Mineral Resources Bulletin†
0510-2332 Western Express
0510-243X Western Material Handling/Packaging/ Shipping
0510-3517 Kihara Institute for Biological Research. Wheat Information Service
0510-3746 Belaruski Instytut Navuki Mactatstva. Zapisy
0510-4130 Who's Who in the Egg and Poultry Industries
0510-4262 Wiadomosci Melioracyjne i Lekarskie
0510-4270 Wiadomosci Naftowe†
0510-4882 William Nelson Cromwell Foundation. Legal Studies†
0510-5315 Die Wirbelsaeule in Forschung und Praxis
0510-5528 Bilanz
0510-5609 Wirtschaftszahl
0510-6966 Wissenschaft und Fortschritt
0510-7350 Women's Comfort†
0510-7385 Women's Household
0510-8055 World Branches Conference of the English Speaking Unions. Principal Addresses and Summary of the Proceedings†
0510-8225 World Congress in Public Park Administration. Reports *changed to* Congress in Park and Recreation Administration. Reports
0510-8233 World Congress in Public Park Administration. Programme *changed to* Congress in Park and Recreation Administration. Programme
0510-8284 World Congress of Sodalities of Our Lady. Proceedings†
0510-8292 World Congress of the Deaf. Proceedings.
0510-8837 World Health Organization. Regional Office for Africa. Report of the Regional Director
0510-8845 World Health Organization. Regional Office for the Western Pacific. Report on the Regional Seminar on the Role of the Hospital in the Public Health Programme
0510-9744 Wspotczesnosc *changed to* Literatura
0510-9833 Wuerzburger Geographische Arbeiten
0510-9868 Wychowanie Fizyczne i Higiena Szkolna
0510-9884 Wychowanie Techniczne w Szkole
0511-0440 Wyoming Trucker
0511-0653 Waelzlagertechnik

0511-0726 A A G Bijdragen
0511-084X Wakayama Medical Reports
0511-1145 Warehouse Distributor News†
0511-1196 Ruch Wydawniczy w Liczbach
0511-1927 Waseda University. Casting Research Laboratory. Report
0511-196X Waseda Political Studies
0511-2141 Washington (State) Department of Fisheries. Information Booklet†
0511-2400 Washington Economic Indicators†
0511-2834 University of Washington. College of Business Administration. Occasional Paper†
0511-3040 University Resources in the United States for Linguistics and the Teaching of English as a Foreign Language *changed to* Directory of Programs in Linguistics
0511-3172 Washington Financial Reports *see* 0891-0634
0511-3180 Washington Highway News *changed to* Transpo News
0511-3202 Washington Library Letter†
0511-3520 Wasser-Kalender
0511-3555 Water & Pollution Control Directory *changed to* Water & Pollution Control. Directory and Buyers' Guide
0511-392X Selected List of Biomedical Serials in Metropolitan Detroit *changed to* Union List of Selected Serials of Michigan
0511-4063 Wedgwood Society. Proceedings
0511-411X Weed Control Manual and Herbicide Guide
0511-4144 Weed Society of America. Abstracts *changed to* Weed Science Society of America. Abstracts
0511-4187 U.S. Office of the Federal Register. Weekly Compilation of Presidential Documents
0511-4365 Welding Data Book *see* 0278-7067
0511-4934 Wesleyan Poetry Program
0511-5493 West Bengal. Bureau of Applied Economics and Statistics. Statistical Handbook
0511-568X West-European Symposia on Clinical Chemistry†
0511-6147 West Pakistan Cooperative Review *changed to* Punjab Cooperative Union. Review
0511-6775 West Virginia Statistical Handbook
0511-6848 Western Association of Graduate Schools. Proceedings of the Annual Meeting
0511-6910 Western Australia. Major Investment Projects, Public and Private, Current and Proposed†
0511-6996 Western Australia. Geological Survey. Annual Report†
0511-750X Western Forest Fire Committee. Proceedings *changed to* Western Forestry Conference. Proceedings
0511-7518 Western Forest Pest Committee. Proceedings *changed to* Western Forestry Conference. Proceedings
0511-7526 Western Reforestation Coordinating Committee. Proceedings *changed to* Western Forestry Conference. Proceedings
0511-7542 Western Foundation of Vertebrate Zoology. Occasional Papers
0511-7666 W I C H E Reports
0511-7704 Western Lumber Facts
0511-8255 Barometer (Portland)
0511-8298 Western Wood Products Association. Monthly F.O.B. Price Summary, Past Sales. Coast Mills
0511-8484 Westpreussen-Jahrbuch
0511-8654 What's New in Chemical Processing Equipment *see* 0747-0398
0511-8662 What's New in Forensic Sciences *see* 0022-1198
0511-8719 Where to Retire on a Small Income
0511-8794 Whitmark Directory
0511-8824 Whitney Review
0511-8832 Whittier Newsletter
0511-8891 Who's Who Among Students in American Junior Colleges
0511-8905 Who's Who in Advertising
0511-8948 Who's Who in California
0511-8964 Who's Who in Floriculture
0511-9022 Who's Who in Public Relations (International)
0511-9162 Wiadomosci Historyczne
0511-9510 Wildlife Review†
0511-9618 Willdenowia
0511-9715 William L. Bryant Foundation American Studies. Report†
0511-9723 William L. Hutcheson Memorial Forest. Bulletin
0512-0624 Wisconsin. Division of Highways. System Planning Section. Highway Traffic in Wisconsin Cities *see* 0084-0580
0512-0640 Wisconsin. Geological and Natural History Survey. Information Circulars
0512-0659 Wisconsin. Geological and Natural History Survey. Special Report
0512-0918 University of Wisconsin. Bureau of Business Research and Service. Monographs *see* 0084-0513
0512-1175 Wisconsin Academy Review
0512-1213 Wisconsin English Journal
0512-1523 Universitaet Frankfurt. Wissenschaftliche Gesellschaft. Sitzungsberichte
0512-1817 Women of Korea
0512-1825 Women of Vietnam
0512-2368 World Airline Record Newsletter *see* 0002-2748
0512-2457 World Bank Atlas
0512-2511 World Confederation of Organizations of the Teaching Profession. Occasional Papers†
0512-252X W C O T P Theme Study†
0512-2589 Faith and Order Papers
0512-2740 World Directory of Mathematicians
0512-2953 World Fertilizer Atlas
0512-3011 Vaccination Certificate Requirements for International Travel *changed to* Vaccination Certificate Requirements and Health Advice for International Travel
0512-3038 World Health Organization. Monograph Series
0512-3054 W H O Technical Report Series
0512-3070 World Health Organization. Regional Office for Africa. Report of the Regional Committee. Minutes of the Plenary Session *changed to* World Health Organization. Regional Office for Africa. Report of the Regional Committee.
0512-3089 World Health Organization. Regional Office for the Eastern Mediterranean. Annual Report of the Regional Director *changed to* World Health Organization. Regional Office for the Eastern Mediterranean. Biennial Report of the Regional Director
0512-3135 World Hospitals
0512-3186 World Land Use Survey. Occasional Papers†
0512-3194 World Land Use Survey. Regional Monograph†
0512-3453 World Peace Through Law Center. Report of the Director-General†
0512-350X Estatistica Brasileira de Energia
0512-3739 World Trade Annual
0512-3747 World Trade Annual Supplement
0512-3844 World Wheat Statistics
0512-4077 Wrangler
0512-4255 Wychowanie Myzyczne w Szkole
0512-4263 Wychowanie Obywatelskie
0512-4395 Wyoming Statistical Review†
0512-4409 Wyoming Labor Force Trends
0512-4638 W.A. Cargill Memorial Lectures in Fine Art†
0512-4743 West Virginia Union List of Serials
0512-4921 World Health Organization. Regional Office for the Western Pacific. Annual Report of the Regional Director to the Regional Committee for the Western Pacific
0512-5030 Wasser und Abwasser in Forschung und Praxis
0512-5235 Western Catholic Reporter
0512-5278 What's Happening on the Chinese Mainland
0512-5405 Wire Journal Directory/Catalog *changed to* Wire Journal International Directory/Catalog
0512-5456 Wisconsin Studies in Vocational Rehabilitation. Monographs†
0512-5472 Works in Progress†
0512-5804 What They Said
0512-5898 Eutrophication Abstracts *see* 0094-3347
0512-5901 Woman's Day Christmas Ideas for Children†
0512-6355 Occupational Opportunities Information for Wisconsin†
0512-9575 Youth Planbook
0513-0794 Yugoslavia. Savezni Zavod za Statistiku. Saobracaj i Veze
0513-0832 Yugoslavia. Savezni Zavod za Statistiku. Ucenici u Privredi
0513-0883 Yugoslavia. Savezni Zavod za Statistiku. Zaposleno Osoblje
0513-0891 Yugoslavia. Savezni Zavod za Statistiku. Zaposlenost
0513-1405 Yale Law School Studies
0513-1545 Western Historical Series†
0513-1715 Yamaguchi University. Faculty of Agriculture. Bulletin
0513-1812 Yamaguchi Medical School. Bulletin
0513-2088 Yearly Digest of Criminal Cases
0513-2592 Yokohama National University. Faculty of Engineering. Bulletin
0513-2711 York Pioneer
0513-2762 Yorkshire Dialect Society. Summer Bulletin
0513-3297 Youth *see* 0013-1482
0513-417X Yadoriga
0513-4242 Pharmaceutical Society of Korea. Journal
0513-4412 Yale Linguistic Series *changed to* Yale Language Series
0513-4501 Yale Southeast Asia Studies. Monograph Series
0513-5303 Yeni Yayinlar
0513-5389 Yessis Review of Soviet Physical Education and Sports *see* 0275-598X
0513-5613 Yokohama National University. Science Reports. Section 2: Biological Sciences *changed to* Yokohama National University. Science Reports. Section 2: Biological and Geological Sciences
0513-5621 Yokohama National University. Humanities. Section 1: Philosophy and Social Sciences
0513-5656 Yokohama National University. Educational Sciences
0513-5710 Yonago Acta Medica
0513-5796 Yonsei Medical Journal
0513-5982 Young Fabian Pamphlet
0513-6032 World Alliance of Y M C A's Directory
0513-6121 Young Socialist Forum *see* 0044-0884
0513-6261 Yrke och Framtid
0513-7926 Zahntechnik
0513-8809 Zdrowie i Trzezwosc
0513-9147 Zeitschrift fuer Theologie und Kirche
0513-9295 Zeleznicni Technika
0513-9481 Zena
0513-9856 Zhinochyi Svit
0514-0668 Eidgenoessische Technische Hochschule Zuerich. Bibliothek. Schriftenreihe
0514-2253 Japanese Periodicals Index. Science and Technology *see* 0387-8503
0514-2482 Zeal
0514-2571 Zeitschrift fuer Beamtenrecht
0514-2733 Zeitschrift fuer Philosophische Forschung. Beihefte
0514-275X Zeitschrift fuer Rechtsvergleichung
0514-2938 Zement-Taschenbuch
0514-3292 Genealogisches Jahrbuch
0514-342X Zeszyty "Argumentow"
0514-3446 Zeszyty Gliwickie
0514-3993 Zoo Review *see* 0736-2676
0514-4795 Zygos
0514-5090 Zavod za Slavensku Filologiju. Radovi†
0514-5236 Zambezia: A Journal of Social Studies in Southern and Central Africa *see* 0379-0622
0514-5392 Zambia. Central Statistical Office. Transport Statistics
0514-5430 Zambia. Department of Cooperatives. Annual Report
0514-5457 Zambia. Educational and Occupational Assessment Service. Annual Report
0514-5724 Zane Grey Collector†
0514-6151 Zbornik za Istoriju Skolstva i Prosvete
0514-616X Zbornik Zastite Spomenika Kulture
0514-6321 Zeitschrift fuer Allgemeine und Textile Marktwirtschaft†
0514-6364 Zeitschrift fuer Bibliothekswesen und Bibliographie. Sonderhefte
0514-6496 Zeitschrift fuer Rechtspolitik
0514-6658 Acta Biologica Iugoslavica. Serija A: Zemljiste i Biljka
0514-7115 Zentralblatt fuer Mineralogie. Teil I: Kristallographie, Mineralogie
0514-7123 Zentralblatt fuer Mineralogie. Teil II: Petrographie, Technische Mineralogie, Geochemie und Lagerstaettenkunde
0514-7166 Zentralblatt fuer Veterinaermedizin. Series B *see* 0721-1856
0514-7352 Zeri i Rinise
0514-7441 Zivotnovadni Nauki
0514-7905 Zoning Bulletin
0514-7972 Zoonosis†
0514-809X Z M P D. Kwartalny Biuletyn Informacyjny
0514-8294 Zur Politik und Zeitgeschichte
0514-8561 Zeitschrift fuer Hohenzollerische Geschichte
0514-857X Zentralasiatische Studien
0514-8731 Zambia. Central Statistical Office. Fisheries Statistics (Natural Waters)
0514-8782 Zeitschrift fuer Militaermedizin
0514-8863 American Crystallographic Association. Monographs
0514-9061 A D L Nachrichten *see* 0340-1545
0514-9142 A E G Newsletter
0514-9193 Arte Fotografico
0514-9797 A N A P
0514-9886 A O K Gesundheitsblatt *changed to* A O K Aktuell
0515-0272 A S L A Newsletter
0515-2003 Academy of American Poets. Lamont Poetry Selections *changed to* Academy of American Poets. Lamont Poetry Selection and Walt Whitman Selection
0515-2089 Academy Reporter *see* 0360-3679
0515-2178 Accademia Italiana di Scienze Forestali. Annali
0515-2712 Acta Albertina Ratisbonensia
0515-2720 Acta Anaesthesiologica Scandinavica. Supplementum
0515-2925 Acta Medica et Sociologica
0515-3085 Acta Politecnica Mexicana
0515-3700 Actualites Pharmaceutiques
0515-4510 Advance
0515-4987 Advocate
0515-6327 Afro-Asian Publications
0515-6610 Aggiornamenti Su Malattie Infettive Ed Immunologia
0515-6912 Agricoltore Bresciano
0515-698X Agricultura†
0515-7935 Aile et Roue
0515-8125 Air Freight Directory of Points in the United States Served Directly by Air and by Pick-up and Delivery Service and by Connecting Motor Carriers *see* 0092-2870
0515-8672 Agriculture Asia
0516-3145 Akademiska Dzive
0516-4303 Alaska. Department of Fish and Game. Informational Leaflet
0516-4850 Alaska Farm Production *see* 0065-5694

ISSN INDEX 1571

0516-5504 Albuquerque Bar Journal†
0516-5644 Alemannisches Jahrbuch†
0516-5849 Alexandria Medical Journal
0516-6950 Cotton Textile Statistics†
0516-8635 Amateur Hockey Association of the United States. Official Guide
0516-866X Amateur Skating Union of the United States. Offical Handbook
0516-8856 American Academy of Orthopaedic Surgeons. Directory
0516-9313 American Association of Colleges for Teacher Education. Directory
0516-9445 Reference Book of Highway Personnel
0516-9518 A A V S O Bulletin *changed to* A A V S O Bulletin--Predicted Dates of Maxima and Minima of Long Period Variable Stars
0516-9593 American Astronautical Society. Proceedings of the Annual Meeting
0516-9623 American Atheist
0516-9674 Tourbook: Florida
0516-9968 A B A Washington Letter
0517-0648 American College Public Relations Association. Newsletter†
0517-0680 American College Testing Program. Annual Report
0517-0745 American Concrete Institute. Compilation
0517-1024 Facts About States for the Dentist Seeking a Location
0517-3833 American Montessori Society. Proceedings of the National Seminar†
0517-3868 Anthropological Handbook†
0517-404X Numismatic Studies
0517-4252 American Perfumer and Aromatics *see* 0361-4387
0517-5178 American Society of Clinical Hypnosis. Directory
0517-5208 American Society of Clinical Pathologists. Summary Report
0517-564X American Trade Schools Directory
0517-5666 Truck Taxes by States†
0517-6298 Ammo House Bulletin *changed to* C.A.C. Sporting Bulletin
0517-6735 Analecta Praemonstratensia
0517-6816 Anales de Medicina. Cirugia *changed to* Anales de Medicina
0517-6824 Anales de Medicina. Medicina *changed to* Anales de Medicina
0517-6832 Anales de Medicina. Especialidades *changed to* Anales de Medicina
0517-6956 Analisis de la Situacion Agricola de Sinaloa
0517-7731 Anglican
0517-8045 Ancient Iranian Cultural Society. Publication
0517-8452 Annales Bogorienses
0517-855X Annales des Antilles
0517-8991 Annuaire des Fournisseurs de Laboratoires Pharmaceutiques *see* 0396-0625
0517-9130 Annuaire Professionnel de l'Horticulture et des Pepinieres *changed to* Annuaire Federal de l'Horticulture et des Pepinieres
0518-0147 Handbuch Holz
0518-0937 Anuario dos Criadores
0518-1259 L'Apicoltore Moderno
0518-1852 Arab World
0518-2220 Arbeitsgemeinschaft der Parlaments- und Behoerdenbibliotheken. Arbeitshefte
0518-2840 Arche
0518-3138 Politechnika Gdanska. Zeszyty Naukowe. Architektura
0518-3618 Archivo
0518-3979 Arena, Auditorium, Stadium Guide *see* 0067-0537
0518-4614 Argentina. Direccion General de Parques Nacionales. Anales de Parques Nacionales *see* 0302-5705
0518-4673 Argentina. Direccion Nacional de Estadistica y Censos. Boletin Mensual de Estadistica *see* 0325-1950
0518-5327 Arhiv za Rudarstvo i Geologiju
0518-6242 Arizona Statistical Review
0518-6374 Water Resources Summary
0518-6544 University of Arkansas. Industrial Research and Extension Center. Annual Report
0518-6617 Arkansas Amateur
0518-7648 Art et Poesie
0518-794X Arthritis Foundation. Conference Series†
0518-8857 Asian Conference on Occupational Health. Proceedings†
0518-8881 Asian News Sheet
0518-8989 Asian Textile Workers Conference. Proceedings†
0518-9519 Asociacion Latinoamericana de Libre Comercio. Informe de las Actividades†
0519-1505 Association of Private Camps. Buyers Guide and Camp Directory *changed to* Association of Independent Camps. Buyers Guide and Camp Directory
0519-1572 Bank Holding Company Facts
0519-2048 Associazione Italiana Biblioteche. Quaderni del Bollettino d'Informazioni
0519-3125 Atlantic Mail
0519-3273 Atlas Histoire *changed to* Atlas - Air France
0519-3389 Atomic Energy Clearinghouse
0519-4997 Australia. Bureau of Statistics. Installment Credit for Retail Sales, Australia†
0519-5659 Commonwealth Scientific and Industrial Research Organization. Division of Fisheries and Oceanography *see* 0726-4275
0519-5950 Australia. Department of Foreign Affairs. Select Documents on International Affairs
0519-6035 Australia. Department of the Treasury. Taxation Branch. Taxation Statistics
0519-7201 Biblioteca Romanica Hispanica. Estudios y Ensayos *changed to* Biblioteca Romanica Hispanica
0519-8356 Biblioteka Matematyczna
0519-8631 Biblioteka Pisarzow Polskich. Seria A
0519-8658 Biblioteka Pisarzy Reformacyjnych
0519-9514 Bibliotekovedenie i Bibliografiya za Rubezhom
0519-9603 Bibliotheca Archaeologica
0520-1373 Bildnerisches Volksschaffen
0520-1810 Biological Journal of Okayama University†
0520-1985 Biophysical Society. Symposium Proceedings *see* 0067-8910
0520-2795 Bliss Classification Bulletin
0520-2949 Blue Book, Inboard/Outdrive Boat Trade-in Guide
0520-2973 Blue Book of Junior College Athletics *changed to* Blue Book of Junior & Community College Athletics
0520-3015 Bluebell News
0520-3325 Bodhi Leaves
0520-4895 Bollettino delle Ricerche Sociali†
0520-5441 Bombay Cooperator†
0520-626X Borsodi Szemle
0520-6790 Bourne Society Local History Records
0520-6804 Bouwmarkt
0520-7002 Brabantica†
0520-7010 Braby's Bloemfontein Directory
0520-7037 Braby's Pietermaritzburg Directory
0520-9048 Brennstoffstatistik der Waermekraftwerke fuer die Oeffentliche Elektrizitaetsversorgung in Oesterreich
0520-9404 Breve†
0520-9455 Breviora Geologica Asturica
0521-1573 British Schools Exploring Society. Report
0521-4211 Marx Karoly Kozgazdasagtudomanyi Egyetem: Doktori Ertekezesek
0521-4602 Temadokumentacios Kiadvanyok
0521-4882 Budapest Statisztikai Evkonyve
0521-517X Hospital de Ninos. Revista
0521-6680 Bulgarski Tiutiun
0521-7091 Federation Belgo-Luxembourgeoise des Industries du Tabac. Bulletin F E D E T A B
0521-713X Bulletin Historique et Artistique du Calais
0521-7237 Bulletin of Brewing Science†
0521-7903 Journal of Cultural Sciences
0521-8195 Burgense
0521-9477 British Broadcasting Corporation. B B C Lunchtime Lectures†
0521-9590 Library Association of Trinidad and Tobago. Bulletin
0521-9744 Babel
0521-9884 Kommission fuer Geschichtliche Landeskunde in Baden-Wuerttemberg. Veroeffentlichungen. Reihe B: Forschungen
0522-0033 Der Baer von Berlin
0522-0629 Ball and Roller Bearing Engineering
0522-0653 Ballet Review
0522-0777 Banaras Hindu University. Darshana Series†
0522-0939 Banco Central de Bolivia. Boletin Estadistico
0522-098X Banco Central de Costa Rica. Estadisticas Economicas
0522-1153 Banco Central de Venezuela. Seccion A.L.A.L.C. Algunas Estadisticas de los Paises de A.L.A.L.C.
0522-1315 Banco de Bilbao. Informe Economico
0522-1986 Banco Nacional de Panama. Cuadernos
0522-2079 Banco Regional de Desenvolvimento do Extremo Sul. Relatorio da Directoria *changed to* Banco Regional de Desenvolvimento do Extremo Sul. Annual Report
0522-246X Bank of Sudan. Foreign Trade Statistical Digest
0522-2478 Bank Auditing and Accounting Report
0522-2494 Bank Director's Report
0522-2508 Bank Executive's Report
0522-2818 Bank of New South Wales Review *see* 0812-3470
0522-3199 Banque de France. Direction de la Conjoncture. Structure et Evolution Financiere des Regions de Province *changed to* Banque de France. Direction de la Conjoncture. Situation Financiere des Regions En (Year)
0522-327X Banque Marocaine du Commerce Exterieur. Monthly Bulletin of Information *changed to* B M C E Information Review
0522-3806 Boletin Estadistico Coyuntural *see* 0210-1580
0522-3822 Colegio de Agentes de Cambio y Bolsa de Barcelona. Servicio de Estudios e Informacion. Boletin Financiero
0522-4314 Burqab†
0522-4497 International Peace Research Institute. Basic Social Science Monographs†
0522-4810 Battelle Research Outlook *see* 0145-8477
0522-4950 Bauingenieur-Praxis†
0522-5078 Letopis. Reihe B. Geschichte
0522-5086 Letopis. Reihe C. Volkskunde
0522-5337 Bayerische Verwaltungsblaetter
0522-5949 Beethoven-Jahrbuch
0522-604X Behoerden und Organisationen der Land- Forst- und Ernaehrungswirtschaft
0522-6201 Beitraege zum Buechereiwesen. Reihe B: Quellen und Texte†
0522-6562 Beitraege zur Geschichte der Universitaet Erfurt (1392-1816)
0522-6570 Beitraege zur Geschichte der Wissenschaft und der Technik
0522-6643 Beitraege zur Geschichte des Parlementarismus und der Politischen Parteien
0522-6759 Beitraege zur Japanologie
0522-6848 Beitraege zur Kolonial und Ueberseegeschichte
0522-7216 Beitraege zur Wirtschaftspolitik
0522-7232 Bekesi Elet
0522-7291 Museu Paraense Emilio Goeldi. Boletim. Nova Serie: Antropologia *changed to* Museu Paraense Emilio Goeldi. Boletim. Serie Antropologia
0522-7496 Belgium. Commission Royale des Monuments et des Sites. Bulletin
0522-764X Belgium. Institut National de Statistique. Statistiques du Commerce et des Transports *changed to* Belgium. Institut National de Statistique. Statistique du Commerce
0522-7690 Annuaire Statistique de la Sante Publique
0522-8557 Zavod za Fiziku. Radovi *see* 0350-0594
0522-8603 Belize. Weekly Newsletter†
0522-8670 Bellman Memorial Lecture *changed to* Bellman Lecture
0522-8883 Benedictine Yearbook
0522-8948 Benelux Economic Union. Conseil Consultatif Economique et Social Rapport du Secretaire Concernant les Activites du Conseil *changed to* B E N E L U X Economic Union. Conseil Central de l'Economie. Rapport du Secretaire sur l'Activite du Conseil
0522-8980 Patrika *changed to* Bamla Ekademi Gabeshana Patrika
0522-9170 Bergen. Universitetet. Aarbok†
0522-9804 Archiv der Hauptstadt der Deutschen Demokratischen Republik. Beitraege Dokumente, Informationen
0522-9863 Humboldt-Universitaet zu Berlin. Wissenschaftliche Zeitschrift
0522-9898 Humboldt-Universitaet zu Berlin. Universitaetsbibliothek. Schriftenreihe
0523-1051 Better Beef Business
0523-1159 Bevolking en Gezin
0523-1469 Besadeh Chemed
0523-1639 Bibliografi Nasional Indonesia
0523-1698 Bibliografia Argentina de Psicologia
0523-1760 Bibliografia Espanola (Annual)
0523-218X Bibliografija Jugoslavije. Serija B. Prirodne i Primenjene Nauke
0523-2201 Bibliografija Jugoslavije. Knjige, Brosure i Muzikalije
0523-2392 Bibliographie de l'Algerie
0523-2465 Bibliographie der Franzoesischen Literaturwissenschaft
0523-2678 Bibliographie Paedagogik
0523-2767 Bibliographien zur Deutschen Literatur des Mittelalters
0523-2988 Bibliography of Seismology
0523-302X Bibliography on Irrigation, Drainage, River Training and Flood Control
0523-5154 Biblische Untersuchungen
0523-5774 Bijdrage tot de Geschiedenis van het Zeewezen
0523-6150 Bilten za Hematologiju i Transfuziju
0523-7238 Black Panther†
0523-7688 Blue Shield (Chicago)†
0523-7785 Boarding School Directory of the United States†
0523-8226 Boethius
0523-8587 Bohemia: Zeitschrift fuer Geschichte und Kultur der Bohemischen Laender
0523-9095 Boletin del Cemento Portland
0523-9141 C E N D E S Boletin Industrial
0523-9478 Museo Risorgimento. Bolletino
0524-0166 Bomaby Civic Journal *changed to* Brihanmumbai Mahanagarpalika Patrika
0524-0182 Bombay Hospital Journal
0524-045X Bonner Mathematische Schriften
0524-0476 Bonplandia
0524-0581 Book Review Index: Annual Clothbound Cumulations
0524-0654 Books and Articles on Oriental Subjects Published in Japan
0524-0913 Borthwick Institute of Historical Research. Borthwick Papers
0524-1014 Bosques *changed to* Bosques y Fauna
0524-112X Boston College Studies in Philosophy
0524-1448 Botswana. Estimates of Revenue and Expenditure
0524-1561 Bottin Europe†
0524-2444 Braunschweiger Geographische Studien

0524-2533 Brazil. Comissao Central de Levantamento e Fiscalizacao das Safras Triticolas. Annuario Estatistico do Trigo: Producao Nacional
0524-4714 Briefs (Lexington)†
0524-5141 British Ceramic Society. Proceedings
0524-5168 British Club Year Book
0524-5370 British Columbia. Department of Economic Development. Monthly Bulletin of Business Activity *see* 0821-0020
0524-5508 Schedule of Wells Drilled for Oil and Natural Gas in British Columbia
0524-5672 British Columbia Energy Board. Annual Report *changed to* British Columbia. Utilities Commission. Annual Report
0524-5826 British Fern Gazette *see* 0308-0838
0524-6431 British Museum (Natural History). Bulletin. Entomology
0524-6474 British Museum (Natural History) Bulletin *changed to* British Museum (Natural History) Report
0524-7403 Acta Universitatis Agriculturae. Ser. Facultas Agronomica
0524-7438 Acta Universitatis Agriculturae. Ser. Facultas Silviculturae
0524-7446 Acta Universitatis Agriculturae. Ser. Facultas Agroeconomica
0524-7624 Bibliotheque Royale Albert 1er. Acquisitions Majeures†
0524-7632 Bibliotheque Royale de Belgique. Bulletin *see* 0770-4372
0524-7764 Belgium. Institut Royal Meteorologique. Annuaire: Magnetisme Terrestre/ Jaarboek: Aardmagnetisme
0524-7780 Belgium. Institut Royal Meteorologique. Annuaire: Rayonnement Solaire/ Jaarboek: Zonnestraling
0524-8655 Eotvos Lorand Geophysical Institute of Hungary. Annual Report
0524-8868 Orszagos Szechenyi Konyvtar Evkonyve
0524-8906 Petofi Irodalmi Muzeum Evkonyve
0524-904X Acta Facultatis Politico-Juridicae Universitatis Scientiarum Budapestiensis de Rolando Eotvos Nominatae
0524-9481 Museo Argentino de Ciencias Naturales "Bernardino Rivadavia." Instituto Nacional de Investigacion de las Ciencias Naturales. Revista. Ecologia
0524-949X Museo Argentino de Ciencias Naturales "Bernardino Rivadavia." Instituto Nacional de Investigacion de las Ciencias Naturales. Revista. Entomologia
0524-9503 Museo Argentino de Ciencias Naturales "Bernardino Rivadavia." Instituto Nacional de Investigacion de las Ciencias Naturales. Revista. Hidrobiologia
0524-9511 Museo Argentino de Ciencias Naturales "Bernardino Rivadavia." Instituto Nacional de Investigacion de las Ciencias Naturales. Revista. Paleontologia
0524-952X Museo Argentino de Ciencias Naturales "Bernardino Rivadavia." Instituto Nacional de Investigacion de las Ciencias Naturales. Revista. Parasitologia
0524-9864 Buenos Aires (Province). Archivo Historico. Publicaciones. Sexta Serie
0525-0110 B O C A Basic Housing-Property Maintenance Code *changed to* B O C A Basic-National Existing Structures Code
0525-0846 Etudes Historiques
0525-1443 Bulletin of Epizootic Diseases of Africa *see* 0378-9721
0525-1524 Bulletin of Volcanic Eruptions
0525-1931 Bunseki Kagaku
0525-2156 Bulletin to Management
0525-2539 Burundi. Ministere du Plan. Departement des Statistiques. Bulletin de Statistique *changed to* Burundi. Departement des Etudes et Statistiques. Bulletin Trimestriel.
0525-2989 Buss Handbuch Europaeischer Produktenboersen†
0525-3063 Butterworths Budget Tax Tables
0525-3306 Byzantinische Forschungen
0525-3675 Bibliografia Espanola (Monthly)
0525-3772 University of Birmingham. Faculty of Commerce and Social Science. Discussion Papers: Series F: Birmingham Society and Politics†
0525-4205 British National Committee on Large Dams. News and Views
0525-4507 Byzantina Neerlandica
0525-4620 Bank Administration Institute. Personnel Administration Commission. Biennial Survey of Bank Officer Salaries
0525-4663 Basketball Case Book
0525-4736 Beitraege zur Landesentwicklung
0525-4752 Belgium. Administration des Mines. Service: Statistiques. Siderurgie, Houille, Agglomeres, Cokes *changed to* Belgium. Administration des Mines. Statistiques: Houille, Cokes, Agglomeres Metallurgie, Carrieres/ Statistieken: Steenkolen, Cokes, Agglomeraten, Metaalnijverheid, Groeven
0525-5090 Botswana Notes and Records
0525-6402 Cooperative News Digest
0525-8693 Accidentes de Transito en Costa Rica†
0525-9282 Report on the Activities of the Council of Europe†
0526-4375 Current and Forthcoming Offprints on Archaeology in Great Britain and Ireland *changed to* British Archaeological News
0526-5053 Analysis of Cyprus Foreign Trade†
0526-5096 Cyprus. Department of Statistics and Research. Statistical Summary†
0526-6122 C A T C Electronic News
0526-6513 C.I.C.A.E. Bulletin d'Information
0526-7994 Cahiers de la Resistance
0526-8133 Cahiers des Explorateurs
0526-8443 Cahiers Percherons
0526-9288 California State Plan for Hospitals and Related Health Facilities *changed to* California State Health Plan
0526-9970 California. Division of Forestry. Conservation Camp Program†
0527-0014 California. Division of Mines and Geology. Special Report
0527-0189 California Property Tax Laws Annotated, Including Regulations
0527-2181 California Fruit and Nut Acreage
0527-3277 California Tomato Grower
0527-446X Camping Journal (New York)†
0527-4834 Canada. Statistics Canada. Boatbuilding and Repair/Construction et Reparation d'Embarcations†
0527-4869 Canada. Statistics Canada. Breweries/ Brasseries†
0527-4893 Canada. Statistics Canada. Carpet, Mat and Rug Industry/Industrie des Tapis, des Carpettes et de la Moquette
0527-4915 Canada. Statistics Canada. Coffin and Casket Industry/Industrie des Cercueils†
0527-494X Canada. Statistics Canada. Communications Equipment Meanufacturers/Fabricants d'Equipement de Telecommunication *see* 0828-9824
0527-4974 Canada. Statistics Canada. Construction in Canada/Construction au Canada
0527-4990 Canada. Statistics Canada. Cordage and Twine Industry /Corderie et Ficellerie (Fabrication)†
0527-5016 Canada. Statistics Canada. Cotton Yarn and Cloth Mills/Filature et Tissage du Coton†
0527-5024 Canada. Statistics Canada. Distilleries†
0527-5148 Canada. Statistics Canada. Federal Government Employment in Metropolitan Areas/Emploi dans l'Administration Federale Regions Metropolitaines
0527-5172 Canada. Statistics Canada. Fish Products Industry/Industrie de la Transformation du Poisson
0527-5318 Canada. Statistics Canada. Gas Utilities (Transport and Distribution Systems) / Services de Gaz (Reseaux de Transport et de Distribution)
0527-5504 Canada. Statistics Canada. Manufacturers of Electric Wire and Cable/Fabricants de Fils et de Cables Electriques *see* 0833-2002
0527-5539 Canada. Statistics Canada. Manufacturers of Industrial Chemicals/ Fabricants de Produits Chimiques Industriels†
0527-5679 Canada. Statistics Canada. Men's Clothing Industries/Industrie des Vetements pour Hommes
0527-5822 Canada. Statistics Canada. Motor Vehicle, Part 1, Rates and Regulations/ Vehicules a Moteur, Partie 1, Charges Fiscales et Reglementation†
0527-5830 Canada. Statistics Canada. Motor Vehicle. Part 2. Motive Fuel Sales/ Vehicules a Moteur. Partie 2. Ventes des Carburants *see* 0703-654X
0527-5849 Canada. Statistics Canada. Motor Vehicle, Part 4, Revenues/Vehicules a Moteur, Partie 4, Recettes†
0527-5865 Canada. Statistics Canada. Motor Vehicle Traffic Accidents/Accidents de la Circulation Routiere†
0527-5881 Canada. Statistics Canada. New Manufacturing Establishments in Canada/Nouveaux Etablissements Manufacturiers au Canada†
0527-5911 Canada. Statistics Canada. Oils and Fats/Huiles et Corps Gras
0527-5997 Canada. Statistics Canada. Ornamental and Architectural Metal Industry/ Industrie des Produits Metalliques d'Architecture et d'Ornement *see* 0828-9921
0527-608X Canada. Statistics Canada. Provincial Government Employment/L'Emploi dans les Administrations Provinciales *see* 0825-9224
0527-6144 Canada. Statistics Canada. Shipbuilding and Repair/Construction et Reparation de Navires†
0527-6160 Canada. Statistics Canada. Shipping Statistics/Statistiques Maritime†
0527-6179 Canada. Statistics Canada. Shorn Wool Production/Production de Laine Tondue
0527-6403 Canada. Statistics Canada. Vegetable Oil Mills/Moulins a Huile Vegetale
0527-6411 Canada. Statistics Canada. Vending Machine Operators/Exploitants de Distributeurs Automatiques
0527-6497 Canadian Civil Aircraft Register
0527-6624 Marketing Boards in Canada
0527-687X Canada. Department of Finance. Small Business Loans Act. Annual Report *changed to* Canada. Department of Industry, Trade and Commerce. Small Business Loans Act. Annual Report
0527-7892 Martin's Annual Criminal Code
0527-9275 Directory of Canadian Chartered Accountants
0528-1458 Carl Newell Jackson Lectures
0528-1865 Carta Economica del Ecuador
0528-2152 Case Studies of International Conflict†
0528-2438 Guia del Comercio y de la Industria de Madrid *changed to* Guia del Comercio y de la Industria (Year)
0528-2594 Catalogus Translationem et Commentatorium
0528-2950 Catholic International Education Office. Bulletin Documentaire†
0528-3280 Revista Caucho
0528-4252 Centralna Rada Zwiazkow Zawodowych w Polsce. Biuro Historyczne. Biuletyn *see* 0454-7330
0528-4465 Centre d'Etudes et de Recherches Scientifiques de Biarritz. Bulletin
0528-4759 Centre International de Liaison des Ecoles de Cinema et de Television. Bulletin d'Informations
0528-5984 Cerberus Alarm
0528-757X Ceylon Economist
0528-7618 Ceylon Journal of Social Work
0528-7820 National Research Institute of Tea. Bulletin *changed to* National Research Institute of Vegetables, Ornamental Plants and Tea. Bulletin
0528-8231 Chambre Francaise de Commerce et d'Industrie du Maroc. Revue de Conjoncture
0528-8592 Char-Koosta News
0528-9254 Politechnika Lodzka. Zeszyty Naukowe. Technologia I. Chemia Spozywcza
0528-9432 Chemicke Vlakna
0528-953X Chemmunique†
0529-0775 Institute of Gas Technology. Technical Reports†
0529-0937 University of Chicago. Industrial Relations Center. Occasional Papers *changed to* University of Chicago. Human Resources Center. Occasional Papers
0529-1607 Current Publications: Serials *changed to* Catalogue of Japanese Periodicals
0529-1674 Child Welfare League of America. Directory of Member Agencies and Associates *changed to* Child Welfare League of America. Directory of Member And Associate Agencies
0529-4975 Chroniques de Port-Royal
0529-7028 Church Recreation *changed to* Church Recreation Magazine
0529-7451 Cina
0529-8016 Cites Unies
0529-9160 Classroom Teacher Series in Health, Education, Recreation and Safety†
0529-9675 Clinical Trends in Ophthalmology, Otolaryngology, Allergy†
0529-9853 Club Filatelico de Caracas. Revista *changed to* Fila Nova
0530-0495 Coir
0530-0657 Colecao de Estudos Juridicos
0530-749X Commission of the European Communities. Collection d'Hygiene et de Medecine du Travail†
0530-8836 Collection Panorama†
0530-9794 Collegium Carolinum. Veroeffentlichungen
0530-9867 Istituto Internazionale di Studi Liguri. Collezione di Monografie Preistoriche Ed Archeologiche
0531-0008 Colligite†
0531-0318 Universitaet zu Koeln. Institut fuer Handelsforschung. Mitteilungen. Sonderhefte
0531-1926 Etudes Orientales
0531-1934 Etudes Philosophiques et Litteraires *changed to* Interdisciplinarite Etudes Philosophiques et Litteraires
0531-1950 Etudes Preliminaires aux Religions Orientales dans l'Empire Romain
0531-2051 Etudes Togolaises
0531-206X Etudes Vietnamiennes
0531-2159 Eulenspiegel-Jahrbuch
0531-2248 Eurocontrol†
0531-2485 Europarecht
0531-2612 European Academy of Allergy. Proceedings
0531-2663 European Aspects, Social Studies Series
0531-2671 European Aspects, Law Series
0531-2701 E A A A Newsletter
0531-2728 European Association of Exploration Geophysicists. Constitution and By-Laws, Membership List.
0531-2922 European Coal and Steel Community. Organe Permanent pour la Securite dans les Mines de Houille. Rapport *see* 0588-702X

ISSN INDEX 1573

0531-3015 Commission of the European Communities. Collection d'Economie du Travail†
0531-3023 Commission of the European Communities. Collection d'Economie et Politique Regionale†
0531-304X Commission of the European Communities. Conjoncture Energetique dans la Communaute *changed to* Commission of the European Communities. Energy Situation in the Community
0531-3120 Fontes et Aciers†
0531-3198 Commission of the European Communities. Collection Objectifs Generaux Acier†
0531-3724 Commission of the European Communities. Expose sur l'Evolution Sociale dans la Communaute *changed to* Commission of the European Communities. Report on the Social Situation
0531-4119 E F T A Trade
0531-4127 European Free Trade Association. Annual Report
0531-4283 C E R N School of Physics. Proceedings
0531-4321 European Parliament News *see* 0250-5754
0531-4496 European Southern Observatory. Annual Report
0531-4518 European Space Research Organization. General Report†
0531-4526 European Space Research Organization. Report†
0531-4798 Evangelische Mission Jahrbuch *changed to* Jahrbuch Mission
0531-495X Everyman's Science
0531-5174 European Council of Jewish Community Services. Exchange Information Service *changed to* European Council of Jewish Community Services. Exchange
0531-531X Exercise Exchange
0531-5360 Exhibits Schedule
0531-5565 Experimental Gerontology
0531-5824 Herold Export-Adressbuch von Oesterreich
0531-5980 Chemicals and Allied Products Export Promotion Council. Exporters Directory
0531-6723 Egyptian Library Journal
0531-674X Ehe- und Familienrechtliche Entscheidungen
0531-6847 I E E E Electromagnetic Compatibility Symposium. Record. *changed to* I E E E International Symposium on Electromagnetic Compatibility. (Record)
0531-6863 E A S C O N. Electronics and Aerospace Systems Convention. Record *changed to* I E E E/E A S C O N. Electronics and Aerospace Conference. (Record)
0531-7436 European League for Economic Cooperation. Report of the Secretary General on the Activities of E.L.E.C.
0531-7444 European Organisation for Civil Aviation Electronics. General Assembly. Annual Report
0531-7452 European Space Research Organization. Scientific Memorandum†
0531-7460 European Space Research Organization. Scientific Note†
0531-7479 Europhysics News
0531-755X Explotacion Agraria†
0531-786X Ecumene†
0531-7886 Edmund's Foreign Car Prices
0531-8203 Economia Politica
0531-8327 Educating the Disadvantaged *see* 0270-1448
0531-8432 Ecology *see* 0096-7807
0531-8955 Economic Review
0531-9110 Acta Biologica Iugoslavica. Serija D: Ekologija
0531-9153 Ele e Ela
0531-9218 Der Elektroniker
0531-9315 E R I C Clearinghouse for Junior Colleges. Topical Paper Series
0531-9323 Statistische Studien
0531-9455 Etudes Baudelairiennes
0531-9684 Folk Music Journal
0532-0194 Food and Agriculture Organization of the United Nations. Agricultural Planning Studies
0532-0208 Food and Agriculture Organization of the United Nations. Basic Texts
0532-0283 F A O Forestry and Forest Products Studies *changed to* F A O Forestry Studies
0532-0291 F A O Library List of Recent Accessions†
0532-0305 F A O Nutrition Special Reports†
0532-0313 F A O Terminology Bulletin
0532-0348 Food and Agriculture Organization of the United Nations. Interamerican Meeting on Animal Production and Health. Report†
0532-0402 Meeting of International Organizations for the Joint Study of Programs and Activities in the Field of Agriculture in Europe. Report.†
0532-0437 Food and Agriculture Organization of the United Nations. Soils Bulletins
0532-0488 Food and Agriculture Organization of the United Nations. World Soil Resources Reports
0532-0623 F A O African Regional Meeting on Animal Production and Health. Report of the Meeting.†
0532-0666 Food and Agriculture Organization of the United Nations. Forest Tree Seed Directory†
0532-0690 Food and Agriculture Organization of the United Nations. Forestry and Forest Products Division. World Forest Products Statistics†
0532-0747 Forestry Newsletter of the Asia-Pacific Region
0532-0941 Food Quality Control *changed to* F D C Control Newsletter
0532-0968 Food Science
0532-1042 Footwear and Leather Abstracts†
0532-1360 Udenrigs Handelskalenderen for Danmark
0532-2189 Forschungen zur Kunstgeschichte und Christlichen Archaeologie
0532-2731 Fortschritte der Verfahrenstechnik†
0532-3010 Fotomuveszet
0532-5781 Francis Thompson Society. Journal *changed to* Eighteen Nineties Society. Journal
0532-596X Veroeffentlichungen des Ostasiatischen Seminars der Johann-Wolfgang-Goethe-Universitaet, Frankfurt. Reihe A. Suedostasienkunde
0532-6370 Freedom from Hunger Campaign. F F H C Report†
0532-7091 F C L Newsletter
0532-7334 From the Sourdough Crock†
0532-7466 Frontiers in Neuroendocrinology
0532-7776 Real Estate Research
0532-8942 Furniture Production
0532-9140 F F Dabei
0532-9175 A.A.'s Far East Businessman's Directory
0532-9396 E I F A C Newsletter†
0532-9841 Film Special
0533-005X Foundry Catalog File *changed to* Foundry Databook & Catalog File
0533-0327 Federacion Panamericana de Associaciones de Facultades de Medicina. Boletin
0533-0386 Universita degli Studi di Ferrara. Annali. Sezione 14. Fisica Sperimentale e Teorica
0533-0653 All of Mexico at Low Cost
0533-070X Forum foer Ekonomi och Teknik
0533-0793 France. Institut National de la Statistique et des Etudes Economiques. Collections. Serie C, Comptes et Planification
0533-0807 France. Institut National de la Statistique et des Etudes Economiques. Collections. Serie D, Demographie et Emploi
0533-0815 France. Institut National de la Statistique et des Etudes Economiques. Collections. Serie E, Enterprises
0533-0823 France. Institut National de la Statistique et des Etudes Economiques. Collections. Serie M, Menages
0533-0831 France. Institut National de la Statistique et des Etudes Economiques. Collections. Serie R, Regions
0533-0866 France - Pays Arabes
0533-0939 Family Findings
0533-0963 Federal Aviation Regulations for Pilots
0533-1072 Barron's Profiles of American Colleges. Vol. 2: Index to Major Areas of Study
0533-1153 Fiziologicheski Aktivnye Veshchestva
0533-196X Great Lakes Commission. Report to the States†
0533-2869 Greyfriar/Siena Studies in Literature
0533-3164 Group Analysis: International Panel and Correspondence *changed to* Group Analysis
0533-3180 Colloques A M P E R E†
0533-3431 Grundschule
0533-4179 Instituto de Nutricion de Centro America y Panama. Informe Anual
0533-4500 Guia de la Industria del Caucho
0533-4675 Turismo, Guia Peuser *changed to* Guia Peuser de Turismo Argentina y Sudamericana
0533-5248 Guide to American Directories
0533-5388 Guide to Microreproduction Equipment *see* 0360-8654
0533-540X Guide to Radio Electronics & Components Trade and Industry in India *changed to* Guide to Electronics Industry in India
0533-5426 Guide to Scientific Instruments
0533-5450 Guide to Hotels in South Africa *changed to* C V R Hotel Guide to Southern Africa
0533-5469 Guide to the Mexican Markets
0533-5485 Guide to Traffic Safety Literature†
0533-5620 Guides to Jewish Subjects in Social and Humanistic Research†
0533-5701 Journal Officiel de Guinee
0533-649X Gujarat State Financial Corporation. Annual Report
0533-6627 Gunma University, Faculty of Education. Annual Report: Art, Technology, Health & Physical Education, and Science of Human Living Series
0533-6724 Gumma Symposia on Endocrinology
0533-7291 Generation (Windsor)
0533-7526 German Patents Gazette. Section 1: Chemical
0533-7534 German Patents Gazette. Section 2: Electrical
0533-7542 German Patents Gazette. Section 3: Mechanical and General
0533-7712 Giornale Italiano di Dermatologia e Venereologia
0533-8301 Geological Society of Iraq. Journal
0533-8387 Georgia Welcome Center. Research Report†
0533-8646 University of Ghana. Institute of African Studies. Local Studies Series
0533-8859 Govor†
0533-9235 Gaudeamus Information. English Edition
0533-9286 Geografia Urbana
0533-9685 Great Britain. Royal Commission on Historical Manuscripts. Secretary's Report to the Commissioners
0533-991X Guyana. Statistical Bureau. Annual Account Relating to External Trade
0534-0012 Acta Biologica Iugoslavica. Serija F: Genetika
0534-042X Laerarhoegskolan i Goeteborg. Pedagogiska Institutionen. Rapport *see* 0348-2219
0534-0489 G R I Newsletter
0534-0500 Great Britain. Department of Employment. Changes in Rates of Wages and Hours of Work *changed to* Great Britain. Department of Employment. Statistics Division. Time Rates of Wages and Hours of Work
0534-2104 Chartered Institute of Public Finance and Accountancy. Crematoria Statistics. Actuals *see* 0263-2969
0534-3364 Instituto de Estudios Tarraconenses Ramon Berenguer IV. Publicacion
0534-3844 Spain. Instituto Nacional de Industria. Direccion Financiera. Boletin de Informacion Financiera†
0534-4050 Kjeller Report†
0534-4697 Inter-African Conference on Co-Operative Societies Meeting. Reunion
0534-4700 Inter-African Conference on Food and Nutrition. Programa e Informacoes
0534-4727 Inter-African Conference on Industrial Commercial and Agricultural Education Meeting
0534-4735 Inter-African Conference on Medical Co-Operation. Meeting
0534-4751 Inter-African Conference on Social Science Meeting
0534-476X Inter-African Conference on Social Science Rapports
0534-4794 Inter-African Conference of the Mechanisation of Agriculture Meeting
0534-4816 Inter-African Conference on the Treatment of Offenders. Meetings. Reunion
0534-4824 Inter-African Forestry Conference. Conference Forestiere Interafricaine (Communications)
0534-607X Intercity Truck Tonnage *changed to* Motor Carrier Statistical Summary
0534-6509 International Aeronautic Federation. General Conference Minutes (of the) Business Meetings *changed to* International Aeronautic Federation. Annual Information Bulletin
0534-655X International African Seminar. Studies Presented and Discussed†
0534-6622 International Amateur Basketball Federation. Official Report of the World Congress *changed to* International Basketball Federation. Official Report of the World Congress
0534-669X International Association for Dental Research. Abstracts of the General Meeting
0534-7319 I A E A Library Film Catalog
0534-7793 International Cargo Handling Coordination Association. Rapports des Comites Nationaux†
0534-8021 International Children's Centre. Paris. Travaux et Documents
0534-8242 International Commission of Jurists. Bulletin *see* 0020-6393
0534-8293 International Commission on Large Dams. Bulletin
0534-8587 International Conference of Human Genetics. (Rapports et des Communications)†
0534-8676 International Conference on Electron and Ion Beam Science and Technology. Abstracts
0534-8803 International Conference on Science and World Affairs. Proceedings
0534-8811 International Conference on Shielding Around High Energy Accelerators. Papers†
0534-9044 International Congress of Graphoanalysts. Proceedings
0534-9168 International Congress of Psychopathological Art. Program. Programme
0534-9257 International Congress on Canned Foods. Texts of Papers Presented and Resolutions
0534-9710 International Design Conference in Aspen. Report
0534-9869 International Egg Marketing Conference. Proceedings

1574 ISSN INDEX

0534-9907 International Electrotechnical Commission. Central Office Report *see* 0074-4697
0535-0182 International Federation of Fruit Juice Producers. Proceedings. Berichte. Rapports *changed to* International Federation of Fruit Juice Producers. Rapport Annuel d'Activite
0535-0492 International Financial Statistics. Supplement†
0535-1405 International Medical News
0535-1588 International North Pacific Fisheries Commission. Statistical Yearbook†
0535-1626 International Office of Cocoa and Chocolate and the International Sugar Confectionary Manufacturers' Association. Report of the General Assembly
0535-1774 World List of Family Planning Agencies
0535-2479 International Skating Union. Minutes of Congress
0535-3076 International Symposium on Nervous Inhibition. Proceedings†
0535-3114 International Symposium on Submarine and Space Medicine. Proceedings†
0535-4358 Internationales Handbuch fuer Rundfunk und Fernsehen
0535-4676 Interstate Commission on the Potomac River Basin. Proceedings
0535-5079 Inventare Nichtstaatlicher Archive
0535-5133 Investigacion Clinica
0535-5729 Iowa Archeological Society. Journal
0535-899X Istruzione Tecnica e Professionale
0535-9821 Italy. Istituto Centrale di Statistica. Statistica Mensile del Commercio con l'Estero
0536-1095 I A G A News
0536-1184 I B M Medical Symposium. Proceedings†
0536-132X I C S U Bulletin *changed to* I C S U Newsletter
0536-1362 I D
0536-1486 I E E E International Conference on Communications. Conference Record
0536-1966 I R C D Bulletin†
0536-2008 I S A Aerospace Instrumentation Symposium. Proceedings *see* 0096-7238
0536-2008 I S A Aerospace Instrumentation Symposium. Proceedings *see* 0568-0204
0536-2067 I S O Memento
0536-2113 I T C Information Booklets†
0536-2121 I T V Guide to Independent Television *see* 0262-6470
0536-2512 Ibero-American Bureau of Education. Information and Publications Department Series V: Technical Seminars and Meetings
0536-2571 I C A C H
0536-2733 Idaho Employment
0536-3055 Idaho Farm Labor Bulletin†
0536-3683 Japanese Journal of Breeding
0536-3713 Illinois. Administrative Office of Illinois Courts. Annual Report to the Supreme Court of Illinois
0536-4604 University of Illinois at Urbana-Champaign. Graduate School of Library Science. Allerton Park Institute. Papers. *changed to* University of Illinois at Urbana-Champaign. Graduate School of Library and Information Science. Allerton Park Institute. Papers
0536-5139 Illinois Teacher for Contemporary Roles *changed to* Illinois Teacher of Home Economics
0536-6518 Index of Reviews in Organic Chemistry
0536-7506 India. Office of the Comptroller and Auditor-General. Report: Union Government (Posts and Telegraphs)
0536-8014 Quarterly Statistics of the Working of Capital Issues Control
0536-9029 India (Republic). Meteorological Department Report on Seismology *changed to* National Report for India: Seismology and Physics of the Earth's Interior
0536-9061 Import Trade Control Policy
0536-9290 India. Ministry of Finance. Budget *changed to* India. Finance Department. Budget of the Central Government
0536-9657 Bulletin for Metalliferous Mines in India†
0536-9983 Import Trade Control: Handbook of Rules and Procedures
0537-0035 India. Office of the Registrar General. Newsletter *changed to* India. Ministry of Home Affairs. Vital Statistics Division. Sample Registration Bulletin
0537-0744 India. Zoological Survey. Annual Report
0537-0922 India Today
0537-1120 Survey of India's Exports
0537-1546 Indian Ephemeris and Nautical Almanac *changed to* Indian Astronomical Ephemeris
0537-166X Indian Foreign Affairs
0537-197X Indian Journal of Agronomy
0537-1996 Indian Journal of Extension Education
0537-2003 Indian Journal of Fisheries
0537-202X Indian Journal of Homoeopathy *see* 0019-5243
0537-2410 Indian Phytopathological Society. Bulletin
0537-2429 Indian Police Journal
0537-2666 Indian Textile Annual & Directory
0537-2704 Indian Yearbook of International Affairs
0537-3131 Folklore Institute. Journal *see* 0737-7037
0537-3522 Indice Historico Espanol
0537-3638 Indo-Iranian Reprints†
0537-3654 Indo-Pacific Fisheries Council. Regional Studies
0537-4715 Indus
0537-5126 Industrial Development in Arizona: Manufacturing *see* 0146-2997
0537-5215 Industrial Hygiene Foundation. Chemical-Toxicological Series. Bulletin *see* 0073-7488
0537-5223 Industrial Hygiene News Report
0537-5355 Industrial Relations Aspects of Manpower Policy†
0537-5452 Industrial Review of Japan *changed to* Japan Economic Almanac
0537-6149 Information and Systems Theory†
0537-6173 Information Circular on Insecticide Resistance. Insect Behaviour and Vector Genetics†
0537-6211 Societe Saint-Jean-Baptiste de Montreal. Information Nationale
0537-6246 Information Processing in Japan†
0537-6297 Documentation Europeenne - Serie Agricole
0537-667X Informator Nauki Polskiej
0537-7137 Journal of Humanistic Studies
0537-779X Institut Francais d'Archeologie d'Istanbul. Bibliotheque Archeologique et Historique†
0537-7919 Institut fuer Europaeische Geschichte, Mainz. Veroeffentlichungen. Abteilung Universitaetsgeschichte und Abteilung fuer Abendlaendische Religionsphilosophie *changed to* Institut fuer Europaeische Geschichte, Mainz. Veroeffentlichungen. Abteilung Universalgeschichte und Abteilung fuer Abendlaendische Religionsgeschichte
0537-7927 Institut fuer Europaeische Geschichte, Mainz. Vortraege. Abteilung Universalgeschichte und Abteilung fuer Abendlaendische Religionsphilosophie *changed to* Institut fuer Europaeische Geschichte, Mainz. Vortraege. Abteilung Universalgeschichte und Abteilung fuer Abendlaendische Religionsgeschichte
0537-9024 Studies in Biology
0537-9202 I.D.E. Occasional Papers Series
0537-9679 Institute of Town Planners, India. Journal
0537-9768 University of Miami, Coral Gables. Law Center. Annual Institute on Estate Planning
0537-9989 I E E Conference Publication Series
0538-0022 British Institution of Radio Engineers. Journal *see* 0267-1689
0538-0057 Institution of Engineers, Malaysia. Journal
0538-009X Institution of Surveyors. Journal *changed to* Indian Surveyor
0538-0391 Instituto Colombiano Agropecuario. Boletin Tecnico
0538-0898 Instituto de Investigacion de Recursos Naturales. Publicacion
0538-1126 Instituto Forestal Latinoamericano de Investigacion y Capitacion. Boletin *changed to* Revista Forestal Latinoamericana
0538-1347 Instituto Latinoamericano de Mercadeo Agricola. I L M A - RR†
0538-1355 Instituto Latinoamericano de Mercadeo Agricola. Information Bulletin†
0538-1428 Instituto Mexicano del Petroleo. Revista
0538-2351 Instrument Maintenance Management†
0538-2629 Insurance Marketplace
0538-2769 Organization of African Unity. Inter-African Bureau for Soils. Bibliographie
0538-2785 Inter-African Conference on Food and Nutrition. Report
0538-2807 Inter-African Labour Conference Reports, Recommendations and Conclusions
0538-2912 Inter-American Commission of Women. News Bulletin
0538-2920 Inter-American Commission of Women. Noticiero
0538-3048 Inter-American Council of Commerce and Production. Uruguayan Section. Publicaciones
0538-3110 Inter-American Development Bank. Institute for Latin American Integration. Annual Report
0538-3277 Inter-American Institute of Agricultural Sciences. Informe Anual *changed to* Inter-American Institute for Cooperation on Agriculture. Informe Anual
0538-3579 Inter-American Statistical Institute. Committee on Improvement of National Statistics. Report
0538-3609 Inter-American Tropical Tuna Commission. Data Report
0538-3641 Interbank
0538-4028 Intermediate Technology Development Group. Bulletin *see* 0305-0920
0538-4141 I A A World Directory of Marketing Communications Periodicals†
0538-4168 International Advertising Association. United Kingdom Chapter. Concise Guide to International Markets
0538-4281 International Animated Film Association. Bulletin
0538-4400 International Association for Shell Structures. Bulletin *see* 0304-3622
0538-4427 International Association for the Exchange of Students for Technical Experience. Annual Report
0538-4524 International Association of Law Libraries. Bulletin *see* 0731-1265
0538-4680 International Association of Theoretical and Applied Limnology. Communications
0538-4850 International Atomic Energy Agency. Radiation Data for Medical Use; Catalogue *changed to* Radiation Dosimetry Data; Catalogue
0538-4893 International Atomic Energy Agency. Law Library. Books and Articles in the I A E A Law Library. List†
0538-4915 International Audiology *see* 0020-6091
0538-5342 International Centre for African Social and Economic Documentation. (Bibliographical Index Cards)†
0538-5415 International Centre for Theoretical Physics. Report *see* 0304-7091
0538-5466 International Chamber of Commerce. United States Council. Report *changed to* United States Council for International Business. Newsletter
0538-5482 International Children's Center. Courrier
0538-5490 International Children's Centre. Paris. Report of the Director-General to the Executive Board
0538-5504 International China Painting Teachers Organizations. News
0538-5520 International Christian Democratic Study and Documentation Center. Bulletin International *changed to* Christian Democratic International. Information Bulletin
0538-5539 International Christian Democratic Study and Documentation Center. Cahiers d'Etudes *changed to* Christian Democratic Study and Documentation Center. Cahiers d'Etudes
0538-5555 International Christian Democratic Study and Documentation Center. Informations *changed to* Panorama Democrate Chretien
0538-5644 International Colloquium on Rapid Mixing and Sampling Techniques Applicable to the Study of Biochemical Reactions. Proceedings†
0538-5687 International Commission for the Scientific Exploration of the Mediterranean Sea. Bulletin de Liaison des Laboratoires†
0538-5768 International Commission on Irrigation and Drainage. Report
0538-5865 International Committee on Urgent Anthropological and Ethnological Research. Bulletin
0538-5946 International Confederation of Free Trade Unions. Features†
0538-6012 International Conference of Orientalists in Japan. Transactions
0538-6039 International Conference of Social Work. Japanese National Committee. Progress Report *changed to* Japanese Report to the International Council on Social Welfare
0538-611X International Conference on Liquefied Natural Gas. Proceedings *changed to* International Conference on Liquefied Natural Gas. Papers
0538-6128 International Conference on Lighthouses and Other Aids to Navigation. (Reports)
0538-6381 International Congress for the Study of Pre-Columbian Cultures of the Lesser Antilles. Proceedings
0538-6527 International Congress of Libraries and Museums of the Performing Arts. Acts
0538-6586 International Congress of Radiation Research. Proceedings†
0538-6772 International Congress Science Series
0538-6829 International Cotton Industry Statistics
0538-6918 C O D A T A Newsletter
0538-7043 International Crop Improvement Association. Production Publication *changed to* Association of Official Seed Certifying Agencies. Production Publication
0538-7051 International Cryogenics Monograph Series
0538-7078 International Dairy Federation. Annual Memento
0538-7086 International Dairy Federation. Catalogue of I D F Publications. Catalogue des Publications de la F I L
0538-7094 International Dairy Federation. International Standard
0538-7159 International Directory of Antiquarian Booksellers
0538-7191 International Directory of Prisoners' Aid Agencies
0538-7302 F I D Publications Catalogue†
0538-7353 I A G Communications†

ISSN INDEX 1575

0538-740X International Federation of Film Archives. Annuaire. Yearbook†
0538-7442 International Federation of Operational Research Societies. Airline Group (A G I F O R S) Proceedings
0538-7477 International Federation of Plantation, Agricultural and Allied Workers. Report of the Secretariat to the I F P A A W World Congress
0538-7590 Gas and Liquid Chromatography Abstracts
0538-7639 International Geographical Union. Newsletter *see* 0018-9804
0538-7736 International Histological Classification of Tumours†
0538-7779 Internationale Hydrologische Dekade: Yearbook of the Federal Republic of Germany *see* 0344-5259
0538-7965 Worldwide Bibliography of Space Law and Related Matters†
0538-8066 International Journal of Chemical Kinetics
0538-8082 International Journal of Comparative Sociology
0538-8295 Cost of Social Security
0538-8325 Labour-Management Relations Series
0538-8333 International Labour Office. Special Report of the Director-General on the Application of the Declaration Concerning the Policy of Apartheid of the Republic of South Africa
0538-8643 International Maritime Committee. Documentation *changed to* C M I News Letter
0538-8643 International Maritime Committee. Documentation *changed to* C M I Year Book
0538-8732 International Military Sports Council Academy. Technical Brochure *changed to* International Military Sports Council. Technical Brochure
0538-8759 International Monetary Fund. Pamphlet Series
0538-8783 I M Z Information *see* 0019-0071
0538-8791 International Music Council. German Committee. Referate Informationen
0538-8821 International Narcotic Enforcement Officers Association. Annual Conference Report
0538-8880 International Oceanographic Tables
0538-8988 International Organization of Consumers Unions. Proceedings
0538-9089 Family Planning in Five Continents
0538-9275 International Quantum Electronics Conference. Digest of Technical Papers
0538-933X International Reading Association. Annual Report†
0538-9461 International Rescue Committee Annual Report
0538-9550 International Rice Commission. Newsletter
0538-9771 International Sedimentary Petrographical Series
0538-978X International Seismological Centre. P-Nodal Solutions for Earthquakes†
0538-9887 International Series on Civil Engineering†
0538-9895 International Series on Heating, Ventilation and Refrigeration
0538-9968 International Series on Cerebrovisceral and Behavioral Psychology and Conditioned Reflexes†
0538-9984 International Series on Earth Sciences
0538-9992 International Series on Electromagnetic Waves†
0539-0125 International Series in Pure and Applied Mathematics
0539-0133 International Series in Solid State Physics
0539-0168 International Skating Union. Ice Dancing Regulations
0539-0230 I E S A Information
0539-0281 International Society for Rock Mechanics. News
0539-032X International Society of Criminology. Bulletin
0539-0338 International Society of Food Service Consultants. Directory†
0539-0346 International Society of Plant Morphologists. Yearbook
0539-0613 International Symposium on Rarefied Gas Dynamics. Proceedings†
0539-0761 International Television Almanac *changed to* International Television & Video Almanac
0539-0788 International Textile Bulletin Dyeing/Finishing Edition
0539-0796 International Textile Bulletin Spinning Edition *changed to* International Textile Bulletin Yarn Forming Edition
0539-080X International Textile Bulletin Weaving Edition
0539-0893 I T C Publications. Series B. Photo-Interpretation†
0539-0915 International Transport Workers' Federation Report on Activities
0539-0990 Commission on Crystallographic Apparatus†
0539-1016 International Union of Geodesy and Geophysics. Monograph
0539-1113 International Union of Physiological Sciences. Newsletter
0539-113X International Union of Public Transport. Transports Publics dans les Principales Villes du Monde *see* 0378-1968
0539-1148 International Union of Pure and Applied Chemistry. Information Bulletin *see* 0193-6484
0539-1296 International Wheat Council. Report for Crop Year *changed to* International Wheat Council. Annual Report
0539-130X International Wheat Council. Record of Operations of Member Countries
0539-1318 International Wheat Council. Review of the World Grains Situation *changed to* Review of the World Wheat Situation
0539-1326 International Wheat Council. Secretariat Papers
0539-1342 International Who's Who in Poetry†
0539-1512 Internationale Gesellschaft fuer Urheberrecht. Yearbook
0539-1539 Zahlentafeln der Physikalisch-Chemischen Untersuchungen des Rheins sowie der Mosel *see* 0173-6507
0539-2047 Potomac River Water Quality Network *changed to* Potomac River Basin Water Quality Reports
0539-2063 Legal Report of Oil and Gas Conservation Activities
0539-2306 Inventaria Archaeologica Roumanie†
0539-242X Academia Nacional de la Historia. Investigaciones y Ensayos
0539-3728 Mercado Mundial
0539-3876 Merchandise Mart Directory *changed to* Merchandise Mart Buyers Guide
0539-3973 Mereni a Regulace†
0539-421X Meshek Haofote
0539-5429 Metropolitan Washington Council of Governments. Regional Report *changed to* Region (Washington)
0539-6115 Hospital Infantil de Mexico. Boletin Medico
0539-6387 Mexico (City). Universidad Nacional. Observatorio Astronomico, Tacubaya. Boletin de los Observatorios Tonantzintla y Tacubaya *changed to* Instituto Nacional de Astrofisica, Optica y Electronica. Boletin
0539-7413 Michigan Health Statistics
0539-8703 Michigan Aviation
0539-8908 Michigan Sportsman
0539-998X Mie Prefectural University. Faculty of Fisheries. Bulletin *changed to* Mie University. Faculty of Fisheries. Journal
0540-0694 Milford Historical Society Newsletter
0540-0961 Milton Society of America. Proceedings
0540-3847 Mississippi State University Abstracts of Theses *changed to* Mississippi State University Abstracts of Theses and Dissertations
0540-3995 Mississippi Genealogical Exchange
0540-410X Mississippi's Health†
0540-4193 Missouri's New and Expanding Industries
0540-4517 Missouri Veterinarian *changed to* Veterinary Medical Review
0540-4568 Misul Charyo
0540-469X Mitsubishi Technical Bulletin
0540-4924 Miyazaki University. Faculty of Engineering. Memoirs
0540-5556 Modern Surgical Monographs†
0540-6471 Mongol Nyelvemlektar *see* 0230-8452
0540-6722 Monografie Parazytologiczne
0540-8962 Mortgage Market†
0541-2404 Muehlviertler Heimatblaetter
0541-2439 Muemlekvedelem
0541-4385 Musizi
0541-4393 Muskeg Research Conference. Proceedings†
0541-4873 Mwana Shaba
0541-5357 M B I's Indian Industries Annual
0541-5462 M.I.I. Series
0541-5489 M L A News
0541-5632 Mitzion Tetzeh Torah. M.T.T.
0541-5896 Maccabi News Bulletin *changed to* Maccabi World Union. Newsletter
0541-6159 McGill Journal of Business
0541-623X Keith Callard Lecture Series†
0541-6256 Canadian Meteorological and Oceanographic Society. Climatological Bulletin
0541-6299 McGill University. Marine Sciences Centre. Annual Report *changed to* McGill University. Institute of Oceanography. Biennial Report
0541-6388 Machine Building Industry
0541-6434 Machine Tool Engineer
0541-6507 Mackinac History†
0541-8836 Magazin Polovnika
0541-8933 Technische Hochschule Otto von Guericke. Wissenschaftliche Zeitschrift
0541-9093 Magyar Bibliografiak Bibliografiaja†
0541-9220 Magyar Kulpolitikai Evkonyv
0541-9298 Magyar Nyelvjarasok
0541-9344 Magyar Szo Naptara
0541-9417 Research Institute for Agricultural Economics. Bulletin
0541-9492 Magyar Tudomanyos Akademia Konyvtara Kezirattaranak Katalogusai
0541-9522 Nepi Kultura-Nepi Tarsadalom
0542-0938 Mahasagar
0542-0997 Mail-Coach
0542-1136 Maine Geological Survey. Special Economic Studies Series†
0542-1462 Mainstream
0542-1470 Maintenant†
0542-1551 Mainzer Romanistische Arbeiten
0542-1594 Maison de Marie Claire
0542-1748 Egyptian Statistical Journal
0542-2108 Makedonski Folklor
0542-3570 Malaysia. Department of Statistics. Annual Bulletin of Statistics
0542-3686 Monthly Statistical Bulletin of West Malaysia
0542-397X Malaysian Chinese Association. Annual Report
0542-4550 Malta Yearbook
0542-5395 Manitoba Crop Insurance Corporation. Annual Report
0542-559X Manitoba Library Association Bulletin
0542-5794 Manpower Information Service *see* 0146-9673
0542-5808 Manpower Journal
0542-6243 Map Collectors Circle†
0542-626X Maps†
0542-6375 Universidad del Zulia. Facultad de Medicina. Revista
0542-6480 Marburger Abhandlungen zur Politischen Wissenschaft†
0542-6669 Marche Romane
0542-6685 Marches Publics
0542-6685 Revue des Marches Publics
0542-6758 Mare Balticum
0542-6766 International Association of Geodesy. Commission Permanente des Marees Terrestres. Marees Terrestres Bulletin d'Information
0542-6820 Lolland-Falsters Stiftsmuseums Aarskrift
0542-7029 Marine Resources of the Atlantic Coast†
0542-7363 Marketing Forum *see* 0307-7667
0542-7770 Marxistische Blaetter
0542-8343 Maryland English Journal
0542-8351 Maryland Genealogical Society Bulletin
0542-836X Maryland Lawyer's Manual
0542-9943 Mishua
0542-9951 Informatyka
0542-9986 Matematicheskaya Fizika *changed to* Matematicheskaya Fizika i Nelineinaya Mekhanika
0543-0313 Materials Management Journal of India
0543-0941 Mathematics and Its Applications
0543-100X Mathematik fuer Naturwissenschaft und Technik
0543-1042 Mathematische Monographien
0543-1077 Iseljenicki Kalendar
0543-1433 Mauritania. Direction de la Statistique et des Etudes Economiques. Bulletin Mensuel Statistique
0543-1565 Mauritius. Director of Audit. Report
0543-1719 Max Freiherr von Oppenheim-Stiftung. Schriften
0543-1735 Veroeffentlichungen des Max-Reger-Institutes
0543-1786 Ma'yanot
0543-1972 Measurement Techniques
0543-2146 Med-Events†
0543-2243 Medecine de l'Homme
0543-2499 Medical Anthropology Newsletter *changed to* Medical Anthropology Quarterly
0543-3657 Medjunarodna Politika
0543-3770 Meeting on Soil Correlation for North America. (Report)†
0543-3789 Meeting on Soil Survey Correlation and Interpretation for Latin America. Report†
0543-4726 Der Mensch als Soziales und Personales Wesen
0543-5056 Merchant Explorer
0543-5099 Mercurius†
0543-5838 Metalurgiya
0543-5900 Meteor Forschungsergebnisse. Reihe A. Allgemeines, Physik und Chemie des Meeres *see* 0721-8761
0543-5927 "Meteor" Forschungsergebnisse. Reihe C. Geologie und Geophysik
0543-5935 "Meteor" Forschungsergebnisse. Reihe D. Biologie†
0543-6095 Methodology and Science
0543-615X Metmenys
0543-6206 Metodistkyrkans i Sverige. Aarsbok
0543-6915 Principales Indicadores Economicos de Mexico
0543-758X Anuario de Letras
0543-7741 Mexico
0543-8497 Michigan. Geological Survey Division. Bulletin
0543-9833 Michigan Jewish History
0543-9930 Michigan Slavic Materials
0544-0327 Mid-Atlantic Industrial Waste Conference Proceedings
0544-0424 Middle East Economic Survey
0544-1153 Migraine News
0544-1188 Migration Today
0544-1374 Fondazione Giangiacomo Feltrinelli. Annali
0544-2540 Mineralogical Journal
0544-3105 Minnesota. Geological Survey. Information Circulars
0544-3512 Minnesota Economic Data: Countries and Regions†
0544-3520 Minnesota English Newsletter
0544-358X Minnesota History News
0544-4020 Singapore Mirror *changed to* Mirror
0544-408X Miscelanea de Estudios Arabes y Hebraicos
0544-4136 Miscellanea Musicologica

1576 ISSN INDEX

0544-439X Missions Digest and Year Book *see* 0317-266X
0544-5396 U M R Journal†
0544-5779 Mitsubishi Electric Engineer†
0544-6511 Modern Concepts of Medical Virology, Oncology and Cytology†
0544-7526 Momento
0544-8417 Monographs in Semiconductor Physics†
0544-8433 Monographs in the Economics of Development
0544-845X Monographs on American Art
0544-8794 Directory of Montana Manufacturers *changed to* Montana Manufacturers & Products Directory
0544-9189 Uruguay. Biblioteca Nacional. Revista
0545-0209 Moody's Handbook of Corporate Managements *changed to* Reference Book of Corporate Managements
0545-0217 Moody's Industrial Manual
0545-0233 Moody's Municipal & Government Manual
0545-0241 Moody's Public Utility Manual
0545-0373 Morgannwg
0545-0489 Morocco. Direction de la Statistique. Bulletin Mensuel des Statistiques
0545-1604 New Hampshire Archeological Society Newsletter
0545-2252 New Jersey. Division of Water Resources. Water Resources Circulars†
0545-6061 New York City Trade Union Handbook
0545-7041 New Zealand. Dairy Production and Marketing Board. Annual Report and Statement of Accounts *changed to* New Zealand. Dairy Board. Annual Report and Statement of Accounts
0545-7157 New Zealand. Department of Statistics. External Trade. Country Analyses†
0545-7297 New Zealand. Lottery Board of Control. Report *changed to* New Zealand Lottery Board. Report
0545-7572 New Zealand Current Taxation
0545-7785 New Zealand News Review
0545-7866 New Zealand Shipping Directory
0545-7904 New Zealand Soil News
0545-9249 Universidad Nacional Autonoma de Nicaragua. Biblioteca Central. Boletin†
0545-9516 Niger. Service de la Statistique. Bulletin Trimestriel de Statistique *changed to* Niger. Direction de la Statistique et des Comptes Nationaux. Bulletin Trimestriel de Statistique
0545-9532 Niger: Fraternite-Travail-Progres
0545-9923 Nigeria. Meteorological Service. Agrometeorological Bulletin
0546-0719 Japan Printing Art Annual
0546-0786 Commodity Classification for Foreign Trade Statistics: Japan *changed to* Export Statistical Schedule of Japan (Year)
0546-0786 Commodity Classification for Foreign Trade Statistics: Japan *changed to* Import Statistical Schedule of Japan (Year)
0546-093X Japanese National Railways. Facts and Figures
0546-109X Science Council of Japan. Annual Report of the Development of Agriculture in Japan *see* 0911-8012
0546-126X Japan Steel Works Technical Review
0546-1324 Studies in the Field of Social Labour
0546-2347 Noise and Smog News
0546-2851 Nordisk Arkivnyt
0546-3432 Norman Ford's Florida
0546-4552 E S E Notes
0546-5001 North Dakota. Geological Survey. Bulletin
0546-5370 Northeast Folklore Society Newsletter
0546-5559 Northern Dog News *see* 0164-4483
0546-6210 Northwest Ruralite *changed to* Ruralite
0546-8051 Nove Obzory
0546-9112 Nuernberger Wirtschafts-und Sozialgeographische Arbeiten
0546-9414 Numismaticky Sbornik
0546-9937 Nutmeg Shelf *changed to* Provisioner
0547-034X N A S S P Newsletter *see* 0278-0569
0547-051X N E C Research and Development
0547-0730 N P A News
0547-0749 N R C - Nouvelle Revue Canadienne†
0547-1435 Collected Papers on Sciences of Atmosphere and Hydrosphere
0547-1567 Nagoya University. Institute of Plasma Physics. Annual Review
0547-1788 University of Nairobi. Institute for Development Studies. Discussion Papers
0547-1796 University College, Nairobi. Institute for Development Studies. Occasional Papers *changed to* University of Nairobi. Institute for Development Studies. Occasional Paper
0547-2075 Napjaink
0547-2504 Narodna Umjetnost
0547-3101 Nase Gospodarstvo
0547-3128 Nase Snahy
0547-3144 Nase Teme
0547-3578 I E E E National Aerospace and Electronics Conference. Proceedings
0547-3616 National Agricultural Society of Ceylon. Journal *changed to* National Agricultural Society of Sri Lanka. Journal
0547-4175 National Association of Schools of Music. Directory
0547-4205 National Association of Secondary School Principals. Curriculum Report
0547-4728 National Business Education Yearbook
0547-485X National Catholic Educational Association. Calendar of Meetings of National and Regional Educational Associations†
0547-5090 National Committee for the Defence of Peace in the Socialist Republic of Romania. Information Bulletin
0547-5554 National Cooperative Highway Research Program Research Results Digest
0547-5570 National Cooperative Highway Research Program Synthesis of Highway Practice
0547-5619 C O S E R V Newsletter (National Council for Community Services to International Visitors) *changed to* N C I V Newsletter
0547-616X National Directory of College Athletics (Men's Edition)
0547-6232 National Directory of Newsletters and Reporting Services *changed to* National Newsletters, Directory and Reporting Services
0547-6658 National Endowment for the Arts. Guide to Programs *changed to* Guide to National Endowment for the Arts
0547-6844 Birth Defects Original Article Series
0547-7115 National Guild of Catholic Psychiatrists. Bulletin
0547-7204 Consumer Attitudes and Buying Plans
0547-7212 Consumer Market Indicators†
0547-7271 National Industrial Conference Board. Investment Statistics. Capital Appropriations *see* 0195-8313
0547-7301 Conference Board. Investment Statistics. Utility Appropriations *see* 0360-523X
0547-7557 National Institute of Sciences of India. Biographical Memoirs of Fellows *changed to* Indian National Science Academy. Biographical Memoirs of Fellows
0547-7573 National Institute of Sciences of India. Yearbook *see* 0073-6619
0547-7794 Legal Bulletin (Washington) *changed to* Legal Update
0547-8804 Financial and Operating Results of Department and Specialty Stores
0547-8847 N R E C A Legal Reporting Service *see* 0362-8833
0547-888X Fleet Safety Newsletter
0547-9665 Nature and Resources
0547-9789 Naturwissenschaftlicher Verein Wuppertal. Jahresberichte
0548-0442 Politechnika Krakowska. Zeszyty Naukowe. Nauki Ekonomiczne
0548-0523 Nautologia
0548-1163 Nederlandse Entomologische Vereniging. Monographs
0548-1384 Need a Lift?
0548-1406 Neftepererabotka i Neftekhimiya
0548-1422 Negocios
0548-1643 Annual of Advertising Art in Japan
0548-1910 Netherlands. Centraal Bureau voor de Statistiek. Maandcijfers van de Invoer, Uitvoer en Assemblage van Motorrijtuigen.
0548-1937 Netherlands. Centraal Bureau voor de Statistiek. Maandstatistiek Politie en Justitie *see* 0166-9435
0548-2674 Neue Arzneimittel und Spezialitaeten *see* 0724-567X
0548-2682 Neue Ausgrabungen und Forschungen aus Niedersachsens Urgeschichte
0548-2801 Neue Heimat
0548-2836 Neue Landschaft
0548-3093 Neues von Rohde und Schwarz
0548-4065 New Brunswick Development Corporation. Annual Report†
0548-4162 New Canadian Film†
0548-4340 New Directions in Psychology†
0548-4456 New England Electrical Blue Book
0548-4537 New Era *changed to* Nave Parva
0548-5924 New Management
0548-5967 New Mexico. Agricultural Experiment Station. Research Report
0548-5975 New Mexico. Bureau of Mines and Mineral Resources. Memoir
0548-6599 New River News
0548-6793 New South Wales District Court Reports†
0548-6831 University of New South Wales, Kensington. Research and Publications
0548-7269 Foundation Center. Report *see* 0190-3357
0548-7390 New York Stock Exchange Monthly Review *see* 0275-4479
0548-7900 School Business Management Handbook†
0548-9040 New York State English Council. Monograph Series
0548-9067 New York State Industrial Directory *see* 0740-2953
0548-9415 Cancer Data: Deaths and Cases Reported *changed to* Cancer Data: New Registrations and Deaths
0548-944X New Zealand. Department of Health. Special Report Series
0548-9911 Mortality and Demographic Data
0548-992X Mental Health Data
0548-9938 Hospital and Selected Morbidity Data
0548-9962 New Zealand. Customs Department. Customs Bulletin
0549-0014 New Zealand. Road Research Unit. Newsletter
0549-0030 New Zealand. Road Research Unit. Bulletin
0549-0219 New Zealand Concrete Construction
0549-0294 New Zealand Federation of Labour. Bulletin
0549-0618 New Zealand Universities Law Review
0549-110X News from the Ukraine
0549-2351 Nigeria. Federal Ministry of Labour. Quarterly Review.
0549-2513 Nigeria. Federal Department of Petroleum Resources. Monthly Petroleum Information *changed to* Nigerian National Petroleum Corporation. Monthly Petroleum Information
0549-2629 Nigeria and the Classics *changed to* Museum Africum
0549-2734 Nigerian Industrial Development Bank. Annual Report and Accounts
0549-2998 Nihon University. Research Institute of Science and Technology. Report
0549-317X Bank of Japan. Japan's Balance of Payments. Summary Report
0549-3811 Japan Society for Aeronautical and Space Sciences. Transactions
0549-4192 Japanese Political Science Association. Yearbook†
0549-4540 Mathematical Society of Japan. Publications
0549-4680 Monthly Statistics of Japan
0549-4826 Niigata University. Faculty of Agriculture. Memoirs
0549-5245 Nippon Dental University. Annual Publications
0549-6179 Norddeutsche Studentenzeitung
0549-6233 Nordisk Handels Kalender: Skandinavisk Addressebog
0549-6330 Scandinavian Institute of African Studies. Newsletter
0549-6896 Norsk Skogbruksmuseum. Aarbok
0549-7000 Norske Veritas Classification and Registry of Shipping. Publication†
0549-7078 North American Mentor Magazine
0549-7175 N A T O Handbook
0549-7191 North Atlantic Treaty Organization. Advisory Group for Aerospace Research and Development. A G A R D Conference Proceedings
0549-7728 North Carolina State Library Newsletter *see* 0193-4309
0549-8333 North Dakota Securities Bulletin
0549-8368 North Dakota Growth Indicators
0549-8899 Northeast Asia Journal of Theology†
0550-0532 Norway. Statistisk Sentralbyraa. Sivilrettsstatistikk/Civil Judicial Statistics
0550-0567 Norway. Statistisk Sentralbyraa. Statistisk Ukehefte/Weekly Bulletin of Statistics
0550-0842 Notatki Ornitologiczne
0550-0850 Ukrainian Art Digest
0550-0923 Notes et Documents Voltaiques
0550-0958 Notes from Eastman *see* 0147-345X
0550-0990 Notes on Cardiovascular Diseases
0550-1067 Noticias de Galapagos
0550-1091 Noticias Sobre Reforma Agraria†
0550-1105 Noticiero del Cafe
0550-1156 Notiziario Chimico e Farmaceutico
0550-1326 Nouveau Commerce
0550-1555 Nova Americana†
0550-1741 Nova Scotia. Department of Labour. Economics and Research Division. Wage Rates, Salaries and Hours of Labour in Nova Scotia
0550-2241 Prirodni Vedy. Rada Biologicka *see* 0139-5106
0550-225X Prirodni Vedy. Rada Chemicke *see* 0139-5351
0550-3205 Nuclear Physics†
0550-3213 Nuclear Physics, Section B
0550-3248 Nuclear Science Abstracts of Japan *see* 0029-5620
0550-4082 Nuttall Ornithological Club. Publications
0550-4112 Nya Perspektiv
0550-4333 National Association of Real Estate Investment Funds N A R E I F Handbook of Member Trusts *see* 0092-4865
0550-4376 N.C.A.I. Sentinel *changed to* Sentinel (Washington, D.C.)
0550-4791 N E I W P C C Aqua News *changed to* N E I W P C C Water Connection
0550-5054 New York University Education Quarterly†
0550-5666 National Braille Association. Bulletin
0550-5682 N C E A Notes
0550-5755 Classroom Practices in Teaching English†
0550-6565 New York Botanical Garden Newsletter†
0550-6638 New York (State). Department of Labor. Statistics on Operations. Annual Report.
0550-6743 New Zealand National Society for Earthquake Engineering. Bulletin
0550-6891 Niger
0550-712X Northian Newsletter†
0550-7138 Northland Newsletter†
0550-7170 Norway. Statistisk Sentralbyraa. Folkemengden Etter Alder og Ekteskapelig Status/Population by Age and Marital Status

ISSN INDEX 1577

0550-7421 National Association of Independent Schools. Annual Report
0550-7448 National Bibliography of Cases in Business Administration†
0550-824X Trends in Health and Health Services
0550-8398 Non-Ionizing Radiation
0550-8401 Non-Profit Organization Tax Letter
0550-8452 North Atlantic Treaty Organization. Advisory Group for Aerospace Research and Development. A G A R D Annual Meeting
0550-8525 North of Scotland College of Agriculture, Aberdeen. Annual Report *see* 0143-8654
0550-8754 Ny Teknik
0550-8843 N A F A Conference Brochurand and Reference Book *changed to* N A F A Annual Reference Book
0550-9483 New Mexico Labor Market Trends *changed to* New Mexico Labor Market Review
0550-9955 Nova Scotia Labour-Management Study Conference. Proceedings†
0551-0503 Plastics Age
0551-0910 Plunkett Foundation for Co-Operative Studies. Occasional Papers†
0551-2050 Pokolenia
0551-3464 Politisk Revy
0551-3707 Polonistyka
0551-3790 Biblioteka Kornicka. Pamietnik
0551-4193 Studia Naturae. Seria B. Wydawnictwa Popularno-Naukowe
0551-4932 University of Poona Science and Technology. Journal
0551-651X Politechnika Poznanska. Zeszyty Naukowe. Bibliografia
0551-6625 Uniwersytet im. Adama Mickiewicza w Poznaniu. Wydzial Matematyki, Fizyki i Chemii. Prace. Seria Matematyka *changed to* Matematyka
0551-9039 Pravnicke Studie
0551-9276 Predi-Briefs
0552-2005 Problems of the Baltic†
0552-2080 Problemy Gematologii i Perelivaniya Krovi *changed to* Gematologiya i Transfusiologiya
0552-2188 Problemy Opiekunczo- Wychowawcze
0552-2234 Problemy Rodziny
0552-4199 Przeglad Kolejowy Przewozowy *see* 0137-219X
0552-4245 Przeglad Zachodnio - Pomorski
0552-4466 Psychologische Achtergronden†
0552-5276 Census of Manufacturing Industries of Puerto Rico
0552-5934 Pulsen†
0552-6426 Pure Life Society. Annual Report
0552-6450 Push Pin Graphic†
0552-6981 Publizistikwissenschaftlicher Referatedienst
0552-7252 Pacific Coast Archaeological Society Quarterly
0552-7325 Pacific Dairyman *changed to* Utah Farmer-Stockman
0552-7333 Pacific Geology
0552-7635 Packaging Machinery Catalog *changed to* Package Engineering Annual Buyers Guide
0552-7775 Pedagogische Studien
0552-8100 World Peace Through Law Center. Bulletin†
0552-9034 Pakistan Journal of Agricultural Sciences
0552-9050 Pakistan Journal of Scientific Research
0552-9115 Pakistan Petroleum Limited. Annual Report
0552-9352 Palaeontologia Jugoslavica
0552-9395 Palante
0552-9506 Osservatorio Regionale per le Malattie della Vite. Osservazioni di Meteorologia, Fenologia e Patologia della Vite
0552-9638 Palingenesia
0552-9913 Pan American Development Foundation. Annual Report
0553-0067 Pan American Highway Congress. Boletin Informativo†
0553-013X Pan American Institute of Geography and History. Commission on History. Bulletin†
0553-0237 Studies in Export Promotion†
0553-027X Pan American Union. Department of Educational Affairs. Bulletin of Information *changed to* Organization of American States. Department of Educational Affairs. Bulletin of Information
0553-0296 Pan American Union. Department of Educational Affairs. Resena Analitica *changed to* Organization of American States. Department of Educational Affairs. Resena Analitica
0553-0326 Pan American Associations in the United States; A Directory with Supplementary Lists of Other Associations. Inter-American and General†
0553-0334 Pan American Union. Department of Scientific Affairs. Report of Activities. *changed to* Organization of American States. Department of Scientific Affairs. Report of Activities
0553-0342 Organization of American States. Department of Scientific Affairs. Serie de Biologia: Monografias
0553-0377 Organization of American States. Department of Scientific Affairs. Serie de Quimica: Monografias
0553-0385 Estudio Social de America Latina†
0553-0407 Pan American Union. Department of Social Affairs. Studies and Monographs†
0553-058X Inter-American Briefs†
0553-0644 University of Malaya. Chinese Language Society. Journal
0553-0946 Panchayati Raj (New Delhi) *see* 0023-5660
0553-2361 Materiaux pour le Manuel de l'Histoire des Song†
0553-237X Ecole Pratique des Hautes Etudes, Paris. Section des Sciences Economiques et Sociales. Memoires et Travaux *changed to* Ecole des Hautes Etudes en Sciences Sociales. Section des Sciences Economiques et Sociales. Memoires et Travaux
0553-2507 Musee de l'Homme, Paris. Catalogues. Serie B: Afrique Blanche et Levant†
0553-2515 Musee de l'Homme, Paris. Catalogues. Serie G: Arctiques†
0553-3066 Park News
0553-3104 Parking Progress *see* 0362-3122
0553-3864 Patent Law Annual-Southwestern Legal Foundation
0553-4054 Patterson's Schools Classified
0553-4283 Peace Research Reviews
0553-4917 Penguin Modern Poets†
0553-5743 Foreign Policy Research Institute. Research Monograph Series *changed to* Philadelphia Policy Papers
0553-5816 University of Pennsylvania. Population Studies Center. Analytical and Technical Report†
0553-6065 Pennsylvania State Industrial Directory *see* 0740-4298
0553-6499 Percussionist *changed to* Percussive Notes
0553-6626 Periodica Polytechnica. Civil Engineering
0553-6812 Permanent International Committee of Linguists. Committe on Linguistic Statistics. Publication†
0553-6855 General Treaty for Central American Economic Integration. Permanent Secretariat. Carta Informativa
0553-6863 Convenios Centroamericanos de Integration Economica.
0553-6898 General Treaty for Central American Economic Integration. Permanent Secretariat. Newsletter
0553-6979 Peparimi
0553-738X Perspective†
0553-8467 Pesquisas: Publicacoes de Antropologia
0553-8475 Pesquisas: Publicacoes de Botanica
0553-8491 Pesquisas: Publicacoes de Historia
0553-8505 Pesquisas: Publicacoes de Zoologia
0553-8521 Pesticide Handbook (Entoma)†
0553-8572 Pet Dealer
0553-9196 Pharmaceutical Chemistry Journal
0553-9323 Pharmacien Biologiste *changed to* Biologiste
0553-9978 Philippine Atomic Energy Commission. Annual Report
0554-0186 Philippines. National Census and Statistics Office. Vital Statistical Report
0554-2537 Planiranje i Analiza Poslovanja
0554-2626 Planning News†
0554-2693 Plant Engineering Directory & Specifications Catalog
0554-2731 Plant Location
0554-291X Plasticos†
0554-3037 Play Index
0554-3045 Plays. A Classified Guide to Play Selection
0554-341X Pochvoznanie i Agrokhimiia *changed to* Pochvoznanie, Agrokhimiia i Rastitelna Zashtita
0554-3983 Poetry Pilot
0554-4084 Poeziya (Kiev)
0554-4246 Pointer
0554-498X Polish Yearbook of International Law
0554-5196 Political Science Review
0554-5455 Politische Bildung†
0554-5749 Polska Akademia Nauk. Instytut Geografii. Prace Geograficzne *see* 0373-6547
0554-579X Polska Akademia Nauk. Oddzial w Krakowie. Komisja Historycznoliteracka. Prace
0554-6222 Poluprovodnikovaya Tekhnika i Mikroelektronika†
0554-7040 Poreditsa Balkani
0554-7342 Porta Linguarum Orientalium
0554-7555 Ports and Harbors
0554-7598 Portsmouth Papers
0554-8039 Akustyka
0554-811X Biologia
0554-8128 Geografia
0554-8136 Zoologia
0554-8144 Filologia Angielska
0554-8160 Filologia Klasyczna
0554-8195 Archeologia (Poznan)
0554-8233 Astronomia
0554-8241 Chemia
0554-825X Fizyka
0554-873X Pount
0554-890X Power Transmission and Bearing Handbook *changed to* Power Transmission Design Handbook
0554-9221 Rocenka Povetrnostnich Pozorovani Observatore Karlov†
0554-9256 Naprstkovo Muzeum Asijskych, Africkych a Americkych Kultur. Annals
0554-9264 Acta Faunistica Entomologica
0554-9884 Prajna
0554-9906 Prakit Jain Institute Research Publication Series
0555-0025 Zeszyty Prasoznawcze
0555-0572 Presbyterian Layman
0555-1099 Prikladnaya Biokhimiya l Mikrobiologiya
0555-1501 Princeton University. Center of International Studies. Research Monograph Series
0555-1838 Prispevki za Zgodovino Delavskega Gibanja *changed to* Prispevki za Novejso Zgodovino
0555-3121 Producteur Agricole Francais *changed to* Le Nouvel Agriculteur
0555-3121 Producteur Agricole Francais†
0555-3407 Professional Pilot Magazine
0555-3989 Progress in Industrial Microbiology
0555-4276 Progress in Solid Mechanics†
0555-4349 Progress of Medical Parasitology in Japan†
0555-4810 Prospettive dell'Industria Italiana
0555-5027 Protokolle
0555-5264 Przemysl Fermentacyjny i Rolny
0555-5620 Psychological Research Bulletin
0555-5795 Psychopathology and Pictorial Expression†
0555-5914 Public Affairs
0555-6015 Public Health Papers
0555-6023 Public Library Abstracts†
0555-6031 Public Library Reporter
0555-6392 Publishing, Entertainment and Advertising and Allied Fields Law Quarterly
0555-6511 Puerto Rico. Division of Demographic Registry and Vital Statistics. Annual Vital Statistics Report
0555-6562 Puerto Rico. Planning Board. Statistics Coordination Section. Programas Estadisticos†
0555-6635 Empleo y Desempleo en Puerto Rico
0555-6945 Pulse
0555-7666 University of the Punjab. Journal of Research: Humanities
0555-7860 Puranam
0555-8158 Pushto
0555-8581 Pacific Southwest Directory
0555-8786 Pakistan. Ministry of Finance Estimates of Foreign Assistance *changed to* Pakistan. Finance Division. Estimates of Foreign Assistance
0556-0136 Philosophia Aarhusiensis *see* 0108-1632
0556-0152 Phyllis Schlafly Report
0556-056X Police Research Bulletin
0556-0691 Pomorania Antiqua
0556-1183 Universita Karlova. Pedagogicky Fakulta. Sbornik. Historie
0556-1442 Pressure Research Notes†
0556-1515 Printing Historical Society Newsletter *see* 0144-7505
0556-171X Problemy Prochnosti
0556-1906 Progress of Science in India
0556-2791 Physical Review A (General Physics)
0556-2805 Physical Review B (Solid State) *see* 0163-1829
0556-2813 Physical Review C (Nuclear Physics)
0556-2821 Physical Review D (Particles and Fields)
0556-3100 Problems in Education and Nation Building†
0556-3321 Pakistan Journal of Botany
0556-3488 Partio
0556-350X Pasquim
0556-3585 Exports by Pennsylvania Manufacturers
0556-3593 Pennsylvania. Department of Commerce. Bureau of Statistics. Statistics by Industry and Size of Establishment†
0556-3615 Pennsylvania. Department of Commerce. Bureau of Statistics, Research and Planning. Statistics for Manufacturing Industries†
0556-3860 Photochemistry (London)
0556-431X Psychosocial Process *changed to* Child and Adolescent Social Work Journal
0556-5006 Photofact Annual Index *changed to* Photofact/Computerfacts Annual Index
0556-5367 Antique Trader. Price Guide to Antiques and Collectors' Items
0556-543X Produktschap voor Siergewassen. Statistiek *changed to* Produktschap voor Siergewassen. Jaarverslag/ Statistiek
0556-5693 Revista de Derecho
0556-5987 Revista de Historia de las Ideas
0556-5995 Revista de Historia de Rosario
0556-6177 Revista de Medicina
0556-655X Revista Espanola de Micropaleontologia
0556-6630 Revista Geografica
0556-6703 Revista Interamericana de Ciencias Sociales†
0556-6835 Revista Mexicana de Fianzas
0556-6908 Revista Paraguaya de Microbiologia
0556-6916 Revista Paranaense de Desenvolvimento†

1578 ISSN INDEX

0556-7238 Revue Bibliographique des Ouvrages de Droit, de Jurisprudence, d'Economie Politique, de Science Financiere, de Sociologie, d'Histoire et de Philosophie†
0556-7262 Revue Camerounaise de Pedagogie
0556-7297 Revue d'Economie et de Droit Immobilier†
0556-7335 Revue Annuelle d'Histoire du Quatorzieme Arrondissement de Paris
0556-7343 Revue d'Histoire et de Civilisation du Maghreb
0556-7734 Acta Technica Belgica. Revue E P E: Energie Primaire
0556-7793 Revue Francaise de Dietetique
0556-7807 Revue Francaise de Pedagogie
0556-7963 Revue Juridique Themis
0556-8099 Revue Roumaine de Geologie, Geophysique et Geographie. Geographie
0556-8102 Revue Roumaine de Geologie, Geophysique et Geographie. Geologie
0556-8110 Revue Roumaine de Geologie, Geophysique et Geographie. Geophysique
0556-8218 Rheinisch-Westfaelische Zeitschrift fuer Volkskunde
0556-8587 Rhode Island Audubon Report *changed to* Audubon Society of Rhode Island. Report
0556-8609 Rhode Island Jewish Historical Notes
0556-8692 Zimbabwe. Registrar of Insurance. Report
0556-8706 Zimbabwe. Central Statistical Office. Monthly Digest of Statistics
0556-9605 Rhodesiana *changed to* Heritage
0557-0352 Japan. Government Forest Experiment Station, Tokyo. Annual Report *changed to* Japan. Forestry and Forest Products Research Institute. Annual Report
0557-0395 Japan. Government Forest Experiment Station. Kyushu Branch. Annual Report
0557-0506 Bolsa de Valores do Rio de Janeiro. Resumo Anual
0557-109X Economic Studies Quarterly
0557-1391 Rivista Italiana di Diritto e Procedura Penale
0557-1464 Rivista Trimestrale di Diritto Pubblico
0557-1480 Revon Lebankaut
0557-1693 Rocenka Odborara
0557-2088 Rocznik Nadnotecki†
0557-2282 Rodna Gruda
0557-2614 Romanfuehrer
0557-3122 Universita degli Studi di Roma. Seminario di Archeologia e Storia dell'Arte Greca e Romana. Studi Miscellanei
0557-319X Central Building Research Institute. Building Digest *changed to* Central Building Research Institute. Building Research Note
0557-322X Central Building Research Institute. List of Publications
0557-3254 University of Roorkee Research Journal†
0557-4161 Royal Society of New Zealand. Proceedings
0557-4242 Royal Western Australian Historical Society. Newsletter
0557-4250 Rozhlad
0557-465X Institutul Agronomic Cluj-Napoca. Buletinul. Seria Agricultura
0557-4668 Institutul Agronomic Cluj-Napoca. Buletinul. Seria Zootehnie si Medicina Veterinara
0557-532X Russian Orthodox Greek Catholic Church of America. Yearbook and Church Directory *see* 0145-7950
0557-5737 Fer de Lance
0557-6601 Royal New Zealand Institute of Horticulture. Journal *see* 0110-5760
0557-661X R Y A News
0557-6644 Rural Reconstruction
0557-6911 University of Reading. Department of Agricultural Economics and Management. Farm Business Data
0557-6989 Recherches Anglaises et Americaines
0557-7330 Research into Disease
0557-7527 Review of Plant Protection Research†
0557-7705 Revue Archeologique Narbonnaise
0557-7713 Revue d'Acoustique
0557-7853 Rheinische Ausgrabungen
0557-8019 Rivista di Studi Salernitani†
0557-8051 Rocky Mountain Mineral Law Newsletter *changed to* Rocky Mountain Mineral Law Foundation
0557-8280 Readings in Development Economics
0557-8558 Revista Interamericana de Sociologia
0557-8639 University of Rhode Island. Law of the Sea Institute. Special Publications†
0557-9147 Record Exchanger
0557-9414 Revue Libanaise des Sciences Politiques
0557-9430 Riabilitazione
0558-0293 S I A M Series in Applied Mathematics†
0558-0439 Norsk Senter for Informatikk. Artikkel Indeks
0558-1257 Safn til Soegu Islands og Islenzkra Bokmenta
0558-1613 Shakhs
0558-1931 St. Lawrence County Historical Association. Quarterly
0558-2431 Saitama University. Science Reports. Series A: Mathematics, Physics and Chemistry *changed to* Saitama University. Science Reports. Series A: Mathematics
0558-244X Saitama University. Science Reports. Series B: Biology and Earth Sciences†
0558-3918 San Diego Economic Bulletin *changed to* Economic Bulletin (San Diego)
0558-4477 San Marino (Repubblica). Segretaria di Stato per gli Affari Esteri. Notiziario *changed to* San Marino (Repubblica). Segretaria di Stato per gli Affari Esteri. Notizia
0558-4639 Suomen Kielen Seuran Vuosikirja *changed to* Sananjalka
0558-4779 Industry and Commerce†
0558-6208 Saobracaj
0558-6976 Saskatchewan Economic Review
0558-7220 Saudi Arabian Monetary Agency. Annual Report
0558-9274 Schriften zur Phonetik, Sprachwissenschaft und Kommunikationsforschung
0558-9746 Schriftenreihe fuer Raumforschung und Raumplanung.
0559-1414 Scientia et Praxis
0559-1422 Scientia Iuridica
0559-1791 Scottish Fisheries Bulletin
0559-2674 Sedar
0559-3840 Semaine Internationale d'Etudes Superieures des Methodes Physiques d'Analyse. (Papers)
0559-4065 Seminar of African Christian Students in Europe. Report
0559-5258 Serial Slants *see* 0024-2527
0559-698X Social Development Research Institute. Organization and Activities
0559-8540 Shinrin Boeki Nyusu *changed to* Forest Pests
0559-8621 Shinshu University. Faculty of Textile Science and Technology. Journal. Series C: Chemistry
0559-9091 Shopping Center Newsletter
0559-9822 Sieboldia Acta Biologica
0560-0391 Silence
0560-0871 Sind University Journal of Education
0560-1894 Skalk
0560-3641 Sociaal-Economische Raad. Jaarverslag
0560-4168 Boletin de la Sociedad Cientifica del Paraguay y del Museo Etnografico
0560-5296 Societe des Etudes Juives. Memoires†
0560-5466 Societe Geologique et Mineralogique de Bretagne. Bulletin, Serie C *changed to* Hercynica
0560-6152 Society of Archer-Antiquaries. Journal
0560-8325 Songwriter's Annual Directory†
0560-9208 South Africa. Geological Survey. Handbook
0560-9941 South African Wool and Textile Research Institute. Annual Report
0561-015X Checklist of South Carolina State Publications
0561-1784 Southwestern Legal Foundation. Annual Report
0561-3590 Instituto de Estudios Giennenses Boletin
0561-3663 Anejos de Archivo Espanol de Arqueologia
0561-4619 Spain. Ministerio de Educacion y Ciencia. Junta Nacional Contra el Analfabetismo. Boletin†
0561-4902 Spain. Ministerio de la Vivienda. Estadistica de la Industria de la Construccion
0561-5062 Evolucion de la Economia Espanola†
0561-5313 Spain-U.S. Trade Bulletin
0561-6832 Sports Turf Research Institute. Journal
0561-7383 Srpska Akademija Nauka i Umetnosti. Predavanja†
0561-7855 Stahlbau-Rundschau
0561-7979 Stamford Genealogical Society. Bulletin *see* 0197-2103
0561-8630 State Administrative Officials (Classified by Functions)
0561-8738 State Bank of Pakistan. State Bank News
0561-922X Statistical Notes of Japan
0561-9998 University of Stellenbosch. Bureau for Economic Research. Opinion Survey *changed to* University of Stellenbosch. Bureau for Economic Research. Manufacturing Survey
0562-0031 Stepping Stones
0562-0953 Statens Geotekniska Institut. Saertryck och Preliminaera Rapporter *see* 0348-0755
0562-1887 Strojarstvo
0562-2719 Studia Anglistica Upsalienses
0562-2786 Studia i Materialy do Historii Wojskowosci
0562-2867 Studia Litteraria
0562-3022 Studia Romanica Upsaliensia
0562-4649 Subsidia Scientifica Franciscalia
0562-5033 Sudan Cotton Bulletin
0562-5068 Sudan Cotton Review
0562-5092 Sudan News Agency. English Daily Bulletin *changed to* SUNA
0562-5130 Sudan Society
0562-5297 Suedostdeutsche Vierteljahresblaetter
0562-6048 Sunrise
0562-7087 Survivre *see* 0384-7810
0562-7192 Savremenna Medicina
0562-7451 Svenska Arkivsamfundet Skrifterie *see* 0349-0505
0562-8490 Sweden. Fisheries Board. Series Hydrography. Reports *see* 0346-8666
0562-861X Arbetsskador
0562-9020 Nouvelles Economiques de Suisse
0563-0355 Systemation Letter†
0563-0592 Acta Universitatis de Attila Jozsef Nominatae. Acta Biologica
0563-0606 Acta Universitatis de Attila Jozsef Nominatae. Acta Iuridica et Politica
0563-0614 Acta Universitatis de Attila Jozsef Nominatae. Acta Climatologica
0563-0622 Acta Universitatis Szegediensis de Attila Jozsef Nominatae. Sectio Oeconomico-Politica. Politikai Gazdasagtan
0563-0657 Acta Universitatis Szegediensis de Attila Jozsef Nominatae. Sectio Scientiae Socialismi. Tudomanyos Szocializmus
0563-0924 S C A U L Newsletter *see* 0189-6709
0563-1491 Universitaet des Saarlandes. Geographisches Institut. Arbeiten
0563-1637 Terre Malgache
0563-1742 Archives d'Ethnographie *changed to* Musee Royal de l'Afrique Centrale. Archives d'Anthropologie
0563-1874 Test Collection Bulletin *see* 0271-8472
0563-2153 Teva Va-Aretz
0563-2595 University of Texas. Humanities Research Center. Tower Bibliographical Series†
0563-2625 Texas Biannual of Electronics Research *changed to* Texas Annual of Electronics Research
0563-3400 Thai Chamber of Commerce. Business Directory
0563-3737 Thailand Year Book†
0563-4040 Theatre News (Washington)
0563-4245 Au Coeur de l'Afrique
0563-4407 Theorie des Systemes†
0563-4458 Theorie und Praxis der Koerperkultur
0563-4660 Things *see* 0440-2316
0563-4725 33 Magazine *see* 0149-1210
0563-4784 This Is Malawi
0563-4806 This Week in Public Health†
0563-5446 Timber Tax Journal
0563-5489 Timeless Fellowship
0563-587X Tiscia
0563-6140 Tobacco Bibliography
0563-6191 Tax Burden on Tobacco
0563-6523 Tohoku University. Science Reports. Series 7: Geography†
0563-6590 Tohoku University. Research Institute for Strength and Fracture of Materials. Reports
0563-685X Institute of Statistical Mathematics. Proceedings
0563-7848 University of Tokyo. Institute for Nuclear Study. INS-PT
0563-7856 University of Tokyo. Institute for Nuclear Study. INS-TCA†
0563-7864 University of Tokyo. Institute for Nuclear Study. INS-TCB†
0563-7872 University of Tokyo. Institute for Nuclear Study. INS-TH
0563-7880 University of Tokyo. Institute for Nuclear Study. INS-TL
0563-7902 Strong-Motion Earthquake Records in Japan
0563-7929 University of Tokyo. Electrical and Electronic Engineering Department. Bulletin
0563-7937 University of Tokyo. Faculty of Engineering. Journal: Series B
0563-8054 University of Tokyo. Institute of Social Science. Annals
0563-8186 Institute for Comparative Studies of Culture. Annals
0563-8313 Tokyo University of Agriculture & Technology. Annual Report
0563-8372 Tokyo University of Fisheries. Report
0563-8887 Tools and Tillage
0563-8895 Top Companies
0563-9425 Torreia
0563-9727 Universite des Sciences Sociales de Toulouse. Annales
0563-9743 Homo
0563-9751 Litteratures
0563-9786 Via Domitia
0563-9794 Universite de Toulouse II (le Mirail). Institut d'Art Prehistorique. Travaux
0564-0334 Trabajo
0564-0342 Trabalho
0564-0482 Trade Directories of the World
0564-0490 Trade Directory and Guide Book to Ethiopia
0564-089X Training Research Abstracts *changed to* Training and Development Journal (1978)
0564-108X Ch'indaba
0564-1373 Transports
0564-1632 Travel Market Yearbook *changed to* Travel Market Yearbook (1980)
0564-2159 Tribal Research and Development Institute. Bulletin
0564-2477 Universita degli Studi di Trieste. Istituto di Storia dell'Arte (Pubblicazioni)
0564-2612 Trinidad and Tobago. Central Statistical Office. Continuous Sample Survey of Population
0564-3287 Trooper
0564-3295 Tropical Ecology
0564-3325 Tropical Stored Products Information *see* 0041-3291
0564-3392 Truck Data Book
0564-3783 Tsitologiya i Genetika

ISSN INDEX 1579

0564-4070 Universidad Nacional de Tucuman. Facultad de Filosofia y Letras. Cuadernos de Humanitas
0564-4232 Tuebinger Geographische Studien
0564-4402 Tulane Tax Institute
0564-5093 Turk Kulturu Arastirmalari
0564-5409 Handelshoegeskolan vid Aabo Akademi. Ekonomisk-Geografiska Institutionen. Meddelanden *changed to* Aabo Akademi. Ekonomisk-Geografiska Institutionen. Meddelanden
0564-5654 Twentieth Century Series†
0564-6103 Tavkozlesi Kutato Intezet Evkonyve†
0564-6170 Teplofizika i Teplotekhnika *see* 0204-3602
0564-6294 Topics in Astrophysics and Space Physics†
0564-6545 Tanzania. Central Statistical Bureau. Survey of Industrial Production *changed to* Tanzania. Bureau of Statistics. Survey of Industrial Production
0564-6723 Tea Research Association. Tocklai Experimental Station. Scientific Annual Report
0564-6758 Tecnologia de Alimentos
0564-6855 University of Texas. Humanities Research Center. Bibliographical Monograph Series†
0564-6898 University of Tokyo. Ocean Research Institute. Bulletin
0564-7169 T A I U S†
0564-724X Tanzania Directory of Trades
0564-7630 University of Tokyo. Research Institute of Logopedics and Phoniatrics. Annual Bulletin
0564-7975 C E R E S Cahiers. Serie Linguistique
0564-836X Report on Tourism Statistics in Tanzania
0564-8602 Memphis State University. Anthropological Research Center. Occasional Papers
0564-8742 University of Tokyo. Computer Center. Report†
0564-9048 25 Weekend Build-It Projects†
0565-0704 U.S. Fish and Wildlife Service. Investigations in Fish Control
0565-0828 U.S. Bureau of the Census. Census Bureau Methodological Research
0565-0909 Monthly Retail Trade *changed to* Current Business Reports: Monthly Retail Trade, Sales and Inventories
0565-0917 Current Population Reports: Federal-State Cooperative Program for Population Estimates *changed to* Current Population Reports: Local Population Estimates
0565-0933 U.S. Bureau of the Census. Guide to Foreign Trade Statistics
0565-0941 Foreign Trade Reports. Highlights of U.S. Export and Import Trade
0565-1034 Current Business Reports: Monthly Department Store Sales for Selected Areas†
0565-1190 Foreign Trade Reports. U.S. Imports for Consumption and General Imports; Tariff Schedules Annotated by Country *changed to* Foreign Trade Reports. U.S. Imports for Consumption and General Imports-T S U S A Commodity by Country of Origin: Annual (Year)
0565-1204 Foreign Trade Reports. U.S. Trade with Puerto Rico and U.S. Possessions
0565-1530 U.S. Coast Guard Boating Statistics *changed to* Boating Statistics
0565-1603 U.S. Coastal Engineering Research Center. Bulletin and Progress Reports†
0565-1980 Poultry Market Statistics
0565-2820 U.S. Department of Housing and Urban Development. Annual Report
0565-4866 Flight Standards Information Manual†
0565-5560 U.S. Foreign Broadcast Information Service. Daily Reports: Soviet Union
0565-6311 U S I T T Newsletter
0565-6567 U.S. Law Enforcement Assistance Administration. Annual Report†
0565-7024 National Advisory Council on the Education of Disadvantaged Children. Annual Report to the President and the Congress
0565-7199 Management (Baltimore)
0565-744X U.S. National Center for Education Statistics. Earned Degrees Conferred
0565-7717 U.S. National Highway Traffic Safety Administration. Motor Vehicle Safety Defect Recall Campaigns
0565-811X Medical Subject Headings
0565-825X U.S. National Science Foundation. Grants and Awards†
0565-8454 Where to Write for Divorce Records: U.S. and Outlying Areas†
0565-8462 Where to Write for Marriage Records *see* 0162-0916
0565-8543 Gulfstream *see* 0277-6197
0565-8721 U.S. Forest Service. Research Paper N C
0565-873X U.S. Forest Service. Resource Bulletin N C
0565-9442 U.S. Office of Water Resources Research. Annual Report *changed to* U.S. Office of Water Research and Technology. Annual Report
0565-9582 Directory of Registered Patent Attorneys and Agents *see* 0361-3844
0566-0327 U.S. Social Security Administration. O R S I P Notes
0566-0963 United Steelworkers of America. Information
0566-201X Universite de Yaounde. Faculte des Sciences. Annales
0566-2389 University of Richmond Law Review
0566-263X Unsere Kunstdenkmaeler
0566-2680 Untei
0566-3628 Monthly Price Review
0566-4152 Utah. Juvenile Court. Annual Report
0566-6201 Unesco Asian Fiction Series
0566-7038 U.S. National Institute of Mental Health. Report Series on Mental Health Statistics. Series C: Methodology Reports†
0566-7631 Census of Traffic on Main International Traffic Arteries *changed to* Census of Motor Traffic on Main International Traffic Arteries
0566-7658 United Nations. International Narcotics Control Board. Statistics on Narcotic Drugs Furnished by Governments in Accordance with the International Treaties and Maximum Levels of Opium Stocks *changed to* International Narcotics Control Board. Statistics on Narcotic Drugs for (Year)
0566-8549 Selected United States Government Publications†
0566-8654 Univers des Sciences et Techniques†
0566-8719 University of Kentucky Research Foundation. Annual Report *changed to* Odyssey (Lexington)
0566-9197 Music News Bulletin
0567-1469 Handelsrechtliche Entscheidungen
0567-168X Austrian Trade Bulletin *changed to* Made in Austria
0567-2317 Automotive Rebuilder
0567-2392 Autopista
0567-2848 Avicultura Tecnica
0567-4069 A Ph A Newsletter *changed to* Pharmacy Weekly
0567-4263 A T A Professional Services Directory *changed to* Translation Services Directory
0567-428X A U C A
0567-4492 Alborg-Bogen
0567-4565 Aarets Fotboll
0567-4573 Aarets Idrott
0567-4980 Abhandlungen fuer die Kunde des Morgenlandes
0567-4999 Abhandlungen zur Kunst-, Musik- und Literaturwissenschaft
0567-5782 Academia de Ciencias de Cuba. Instituto de Oceanologia. Serie Oceanologica†
0567-5871 Academia Dominicana de la Historia. Publicaciones
0567-6029 Academia Provincial de la Historia. Boletin
0567-6304 Revista de Istorie
0567-6541 Academie des Sciences. Comptes Rendus Hebdomadaires des Seances. Series C: Sciences Chimiques *changed to* Academie des Sciences. Comptes Rendus Hebdomadaires des Seances. Series 2: Mecanique, Physique, Chimie, Sciences de la Terre, Sciences de l'Univers
0567-655X Academie des Sciences. Comptes Rendus Hebdomadaires des Seances. Series D: Sciences Naturelles *changed to* Academie des Sciences. Comptes Rendus Hebdomadaires des Seances. Series 3: Sciences de la Vie
0567-6576 Academie et Societe Lorraines de Sciences. Bulletin
0567-6584 Academie Royale de Langue et de Litterature Francaises. Annuaires
0567-6592 Academie Royale des Sciences d'Outre Mer. Revue Bibliographique†
0567-6630 Academy of American Franciscan History. Bibliographical Series
0567-672X Acarologie
0567-7246 Acta Universitatis de Attila Jozsef Nominatae. Acta Antiqua et Archaeologica
0567-7254 Acta Asiatica
0567-7289 Acta Baltica
0567-7327 Acta Biologica Debrecina
0567-7394 Acta Crystallographica. Section A: Crystal Physics, Diffraction, Theoretical and General Crystallography *see* 0108-7673
0567-7408 Acta Crystallographica. Section B: Structural Crystallography and Crystal Chemistry *see* 0108-7681
0567-7416 Acta Embryologiae et Morphologiae Experimentalis *see* 0391-9706
0567-7475 Acta Geographica Dedrecina
0567-7505 Acta Geologica Hispanica
0567-7513 Acta Geologica Lilloana
0567-753X Acta Herediana
0567-7572 Acta Horticulturae
0567-7599 Acta Humboldtiana. Series Historica
0567-7661 Academia Scientiarum Hungarica. Acta Litteraria
0567-7734 Acta Medica et Biologica
0567-7785 Acta Mexicana de Ciencia y Tecnologia
0567-784X Acta Neophilologica
0567-7874 Acta Organologica
0567-7912 Acta Paedagogica Debrecina
0567-7920 Acta Palaeontologica Polonica
0567-7947 Acta Physica et Chimica Debrecina
0567-8056 Acta Radiologica. Series 1: Diagnosis
0567-8064 Acta Radiologica. Series 2: Therapy, Physics, Biology *see* 0349-652X
0567-8099 Acta Universitatis de Attila Jozsef Nominatae. Acta Romanica
0567-8250 Acta Universitatis Carolinae: Medica
0567-8293 Universita Karlova. Acta Universitatis Carolinae. Philosophica et Historica
0567-8412 Action *see* 0746-8911
0567-8587 Organization of American States. Department of Educational Affairs. Actualidades†
0567-932X Adelphi Papers
0567-9494 Administrative Law News
0567-9907 Advances in Electrochemistry and Electrochemical Engineering
0568-0204 Advancement in Test Measurement. Proceedings
0568-0301 World Advertising Expenditures
0568-0352 Advertising Research Foundation. Conference Proceedings†
0568-0476 Aegyptologische Abhandlungen
0568-0530 Aero West†
0568-0581 University of Illinois at Urbana-Champaign. Department of Electrical Engineering. Aeronomy Laboratory. Aeronomy Report
0568-062X Aerosol Review
0568-0743 Die Berliner Aerztekammer
0568-1138 Africa Institute of South Africa. Bulletin *changed to* Africa Institute Bulletin
0568-1278 African Christian Student Seminar in Europe. Papers
0568-1308 African Development Bank. Report by the Board of Directors
0568-1332 African Historian
0568-1499 African Student Christian Seminar (Report)†
0568-2517 Agricultura Tecnica en Mexico
0568-2622 Agricultural Digest
0568-2800 Index of Current Research on Pigs
0568-3025 Agrociencia
0568-3114 Agrotecnia de Cuba
0568-3343 Ailleurs
0568-3424 Air Canada. Annual Report
0568-3653 Air Quality Monograph Series†
0568-3866 Airplane, Missile and Spacecraft Structure Series†
0568-3939 Aisthesis
0568-4447 Akademie der Wissenschaften und der Literatur, Mainz. Orientalische Kommission. Veroeffentlichungen
0568-465X Rastenievadni Nauki
0568-5230 Academy of Sciences of the U S S R. Division of Chemical Sciences. Bulletin
0568-6245 Rezul'taty Issledovanii po Mezhdunarodnym Geofizicheskim Proektam. Glyatsiologicheskie Issledovaniya
0568-6776 Akademiya Nauk S.S.S.R. Sibirskoe Otdelenie. Ural'skii Nauchnyi Tsentr. Institut Elektrokhimii. Trudy†
0568-6989 Geofizicheskii Sbornik *see* 0203-3100
0568-7276 Der Akademiker in Wirtschaft und Verwaltung
0568-7306 Achsav
0568-7594 Aktuelle Fragen des Landbaues†
0568-7632 Aktuelle Schaufenster *see* 0173-2110
0568-8442 Alaska. State Library, Juneau. State and Local Publications Received-Alaska
0568-8604 University of Alaska. Biological Papers
0568-8876 Economia Alavesa
0568-9074 University of Alberta. Faculty of Agriculture. Agriculture Bulletin *see* 0705-3983
0568-9848 Revue Algerienne du Travail
0569-0196 All India Central Land Development Bank Cooperative Union. Journal *changed to* Land Bank Journal
0569-0838 Almanac for Geodetic Engineers
0569-1346 Altamura
0569-1451 Altnuernberger Landschaft. Mitteilungen
0569-163X Am ve Adamato
0569-1796 Amateur Wrestling News
0569-1966 America by Car
0569-2229 American Antiquarian Society. News-Letter
0569-2245 American Assembly. Report
0569-230X School Nursing Monographs†
0569-2393 American Association for the Advancement of Science. Committee on Desert and Arid Zone Research. Contributions
0569-2482 Report of Credit Given by Educational Institutions *see* 0194-0988
0569-2628 A A F M Proceedings of Annual Meeting
0569-2679 American Association of Medical Clinics. Directory *see* 0098-2377
0569-2857 Eastern Canada Tour Book *see* 0363-1788
0569-292X American Bank Directory
0569-2954 American Bankers Association. Committee on Uniform Security Identification Procedures. C U S I P Directory *changed to* C U S I P Master Directory
0569-3098 American Bar Association. Section of Administrative Law. Annual Reports of Divisions and Committees *see* 0090-3647
0569-3160 Docket Call (Chicago) *see* 0741-9066
0569-3314 Public Contract Newsletter

1580 ISSN INDEX

0569-3349 American Bar Association. Utility Section. Newsletter
0569-3357 American Bar Association. Section of Real Property, Probate and Trust Law. Newsletter *see* 0164-0372
0569-3667 American Chamber of Commerce in Italy. Directory
0569-3845 American Christmas Tree Journal
0569-3993 A C T Research Report
0569-4043 Industrial Ventilation; a Manual of Recommended Practice
0569-4108 American Council of Polish Cultural Clubs. Quarterly Review *changed to* Polish Heritage
0569-4221 American Crystallographic Association. Program & Abstracts
0569-4353 American Educational Research Association. Directory of Members†
0569-4450 American Entomological Institute. Contributions
0569-4833 American Foundation for the Study of Man. Publications
0569-5341 A I A Emerging Techniques†
0569-5376 Research Problems in Biology†
0569-5457 A I Ch E Workshop Series
0569-5473 A I Ch E Equipment Testing Procedures
0569-5503 Electronic Components Conference. Proceedings
0569-5554 A I I E Transactions *changed to* I I E Transactions
0569-5716 Physics Manpower - Education and Employment Statistics
0569-5961 American Italian Historical Association. Newsletter
0569-6275 Financial Assistance for Library Education
0569-6348 American Lutheran Church. Yearbook *changed to* Lutheran Church in America. Yearbook
0569-6356 American Motor Carrier Directory: National Edition *changed to* American Motor Carrier Directory: North American Edition
0569-6364 American Motor Carrier Directory: Specialized Services Edition *changed to* American Motor Carrier Directory: North American Edition
0569-6534 American Medical Association. Directory of Officials and Staff *see* 0748-5557
0569-6666 American Musicological Society. Greater New York Chapter. Publications†
0569-6720 American Numismatic Society. Annual Report
0569-6763 A O A News Review *see* 0091-6269
0569-6852 American Petroleum Institute. Division of Statistics and Economics. Annual Statistical Review *changed to* Basic Petroleum Data Book
0569-6909 American Petroleum Institute. Division of Refining. Proceedings. *see* 0163-495X
0569-6992 American Phytopathological Society. Monographs
0569-714X American Psychological Association. Membership Register
0569-7344 American Review of Art and Science†
0569-7468 Symposium on the Art of Glassblowing Proceedings.
0569-776X American Society for Training and Development. Membership Directory *see* 0092-4598
0569-7832 American Society of Animal Science. Western Section Proceedings
0569-7840 A S A Monograph
0569-7859 American Society of Appraisers. Appraisal and Valuation Manual†
0569-7891 Transportation Engineering Journal *see* 0733-947X
0569-7948 American Society of Civil Engineers. Construction Division. Journal *see* 0733-9364
0569-8030 American Society of Civil Engineers. Power Division. Journal *see* 0733-9402
0569-8057 Reinforced Concrete Research Council. Bulletins
0569-8073 American Society of Civil Engineers. Surveying and Mapping Division. Journal *see* 0733-9453
0569-8081 American Society of Civil Engineers. Urban Planning and Development Division. Journal *see* 0733-9488
0569-8154 American Society of Dowsers. Quarterly Digest *changed to* American Dowser
0569-8219 American Society of Mammalogists. Special Publications
0569-8243 Reports on Diesel and Gas Engines Power Costs†
0569-8553 A S H A Reports
0569-8561 A S H A Directory (American Speech and Hearing Association) *changed to* American Speech - Language - Hearing Association. Directory
0569-9053 American Wedgwoodian†
0569-9460 Amministrazione della Difesa†
0569-9479 Amministrazione Tributi e Finanze
0569-9495 Amnesty International Annual Report *changed to* Amnesty International Report
0569-9665 Netherlands. Rijksmuseum Amsterdam. Bulletin
0569-9789 Analecta Calasanctiana
0569-9827 Analecta Musicologia
0569-9843 Analecta Praehistorica Leidensia
0569-986X Analecta Romanica
0569-9894 Anales de Anatomia
0569-9908 Anales del Desarrollo
0570-023X Ancient Peoples and Places†
0570-0655 Andhra Pradesh
0570-0973 Angol Filologiai Tanulmanyok
0570-1538 Annales Agriculturae Fenniae
0570-1597 Annales de l'Abeille *see* 0044-8435
0570-1619 Invertebres *see* 0753-3969
0570-1627 Annales de Paleonotologie: Vertebres *see* 0753-3969
0570-1716 Annales Islamologiques
0570-1724 Annales Malgaches. Droit *changed to* Universite de Madagascar. Annales. Serie Droit
0570-1791 Annals of Arid Zone
0570-1864 Annals of Regional Science
0570-2070 Union of European Football Associations. Handbook of U E F A
0570-2194 Geneva International Year Book†
0570-2658 Annual Survey of Commonwealth Law†
0570-2666 Annual Survey of Indian Law
0570-2674 Annual Survey of Massachusetts Law
0570-2976 Anthropological Studies†
0570-3697 Antropologia Social†
0570-393X Anuario Bibliografico Colombiano
0570-3956 Anuario Brasileiro de Propaganda
0570-3980 Anuario Comercial Iberoamericano
0570-4006 Anuario Cultural del Peru
0570-4022 Anuario da Provincia de Mocambique *changed to* Anuario do Estado de Mocambique
0570-4200 Anuario del Desarrollo de la Educacion, la Ciencia y la Cultura en America Latina†
0570-4251 Anuario Ecuatoriano de Derecho Internacional
0570-426X Anuario Estadistico Centroamericano de Comercio Exterior
0570-4324 Anuario Iberoamericano
0570-4359 Anuario Latinoamericano
0570-4723 Die Apothekenhelferin
0570-4839 Applied Economic Papers
0570-4898 Journal of Applied Polymer Science. Symposia
0570-4928 Applied Spectroscopy Reviews
0570-4979 Approach
0570-5029 Approdo Letterario†
0570-507X Aqlam Journal
0570-5169 Aquilo. Ser. Botanica
0570-5177 Aquilo. Ser. Zoologica
0570-5258 Arab Observer†
0570-5398 Arabica
0570-5886 Arbeitsmethoden der Medizinischen und Naturwissenschaftlichen Kriminalistik
0570-6068 Archaeologia Zambiana
0570-6084 Archaeological Reports *issued with* 0075-4269
0570-6262 Archenhold-Sternwarte. Vortraege und Schriften
0570-6270 Archeologia
0570-6483 Architectural Index
0570-6602 Architektur Aktuell
0570-6769 Archiv fuer Musikwissenschaft. Beihefte
0570-6793 Archiv fuer Vergleichende Kulturwissenschaft†
0570-6955 Archives Medicales de l'Ouest†
0570-7242 Archivum Bibliographicum Carmelitanum
0570-7293 Arco
0570-734X Arctos; Acta Philologica Fennica
0570-7439 Arena†
0570-751X Areopag
0570-8621 Argentine Republic. Mercado Nacional de Hacienda. Memoria *changed to* Argentina. Mercado Nacional de Hacienda. Anuario
0570-8834 Argentina. Instituto Forestal Nacional. Anuario de Estadistica Forestal
0570-8869 Argo
0570-8915 L'Argus de la Legislation Libanaise
0570-8966 Arheoloski Vestnik
0570-9520 Arizona. Oil & Gas Conservation Commission. Oil, Gas & Helium Production
0570-9601 Arizona State University. Faculty of Industrial Engineering. Industrial Engineering Research Bulletin†
0571-0111 Arizona Political Almanac†
0571-0189 Arkansas Agricultural Experiment Station. Special Report
0571-0278 Arkansas. Geological Commission. Water Resources Circulars
0571-0456 Arkansas Almanac
0571-0731 Arkivinformation
0571-1223 Arquivo de Bibliografia Portuguesa
0571-1371 Ars Orientalis
0571-1509 Art de Basse Normandie
0571-1924 Artes Textiles: Bijragen tot de Geschiedenis van de Tapijt
0571-205X Artificial Satellites *see* 0208-841X
0571-205X Artificial Satellites *see* 0208-8428
0571-2742 Asian and African Studies
0571-2912 A.P.D.S.A. Journal†
0571-2920 Asian Peoples' Anti-Communist League. China. Pamphlet
0571-2939 Asian Peoples' Anti-Communist League. Charts About Chinese Communists on the Mainland
0571-3005 Asian Productivity Organization. Review of Activities of National Productivity Organizations *changed to* Directory of the National Productivity Organizations in A P O Member Countries
0571-3161 Asiatic Society, Calcutta. Journal
0571-320X Asiatische Forschungen
0571-3218 Asilomar Conference on Circuits and Systems. Conference Record *changed to* Asilomar Conference on Circuits, Systems and Computers. Conference Record
0571-3609 Asociacion de Investigacion Textil Algodonera. Coleccion de Manuales Tecnicos
0571-3692 Asociacion Espanola de Orientalistas. Boletin
0571-3846 Anuario de los Paises de A L A L C *see* 0066-5118
0571-3854 Asociacion Latinoamericana de Libre Comercio. Boletin Bibliografico†
0571-3870 Asociacion Latinoamericana de Libre Comercio. Comercio Exterior. Argentina. Exportacion *changed to* Asociacion Latinoamericana de Libre Comercio. Estadisticas de Comercio Exterior - Serie A: Exportaciones
0571-3889 Asociacion Latinoamericana de Libre Comercio. Comercio Exterior Argentina. Importacion *changed to* Asociacion Latinoamericana de Libre Comercio. Estadisticas de Comercio Exterior-Serie B-Importaciones
0571-3919 Asociacion Latinoamericana de Libre Comercio. Documentacion A L A L C†
0571-3927 Asociacion Latinoamericana de Libre Comercio. Indice Alfabetico de Mercaderias†
0571-3935 Asociacion Latinoamericana de Libre Comercio. Lista Consolidada de Concesiones†
0571-396X Asociacion Latinoamericana de Libre Comercio. Lista Nacional de Brasil†
0571-3978 Asociacion Latinoamericana de Libre Comercio. Lista Nacional de Chile†
0571-3986 Asociacion Latinoamericana de Libre Comercio. Lista Nacional de Colombia†
0571-3994 Asociacion Latinoamericana de Libre Comercio. Lista Nacional de Ecuador†
0571-4001 Asociacion Latinoamericana de Libre Comercio. Lista Nacional de la Republica Argentina *changed to* Asociacion Latinoamericana de Libre Comercio. Lista Nacional de Argentina
0571-401X Asociacion Latinoamericana de Libre Comercio. Lista Nacional de Mexico†
0571-4028 Asociacion Latinoamericana de Libre Comercio. Lista Nacional de Paraguay†
0571-4036 Asociacion Latinoamericana de Libre Comercio. Lista Nacional de Peru†
0571-4044 Asociacion Latinoamericana de Libre Comercio. Lista Nacional de Uruguay†
0571-4052 Asociacion Latinoamericana de Libre Comercio. Listas de Concesiones Arancelarias para Ecuador y Paraguay†
0571-4079 Asociacion Latinoamericana de Libre Comercio. Serie Estadistica†
0571-4087 Asociacion Latinoamericana de Libre Comercio. Serie Instrumentos†
0571-5288 Association Canadienne-Francaise pour l'Avancement des Sciences. Interface
0571-5520 Association for Asian Studies. Committee on East Asian Libraries. Newsletter *see* 0148-6225
0571-5644 A R E Journal†
0571-5857 International Association for Byzantine Studies. Bulletin d'Information et de Coordination
0571-5865 International Association of French Studies. Cahiers
0571-5873 Association Internationale du Droit Commercial. Et du Droit Affaires. Groupe Francais. Travaux *see* 0074-6738
0571-5962 Association of American Geographers. Handbook-Directory *changed to* Association of American Geographers. Directory
0571-6241 Association of Commonwealth Universities. Report of the Council Together with the Accounts of the Association *see* 0307-2274
0571-625X Compendium of University Entrance Requirements for First Degree Courses in the United Kingdom
0571-6322 Association of Institutes for European Studies. Annuaire
0571-6330 Association of Institutes for European Studies. Year-Book
0571-6357 A I L/Doc†
0571-6373 Abstracts of Supreme Court Decisions Interpreting the Interstate Commerce Act
0571-6519 Academic Library Statistics *see* 0147-2135
0571-7760 Crisis Papers†
0571-7795 Atlantic Papers
0571-7817 Atlantic Provinces Checklist†
0571-7868 Atlantic Series†
0571-8236 Attakapas Gazette

ISSN INDEX 1581

0571-8597 Attack†
0571-8619 Audio-Digest General Practice *see* 0271-1362
0571-8678 Audio-Technik
0571-8724 Audiology *see* 0303-8106
0571-8759 Audio-Visual Equipment Directory *changed to* Equipment Directory of Audio-Visual, Computer and Video Products
0571-9291 Australasian Conference on Hydraulics and Fluid Mechanics. Proceedings
0571-9518 Australia. Bureau of Statistics. Life Insurance, Australia†
0571-964X Australia. Bureau of Statistics. Seasonally Adjusted Indicators
0571-9844 Australia. Bureau of Statistics. Tasmanian Office. Wool Production Statistics *changed to* Australia. Bureau of Statistics. Tasmanian Office. Wool Production and Disposal
0572-0125 Geological Survey of South Australia. Explanatory Notes
0572-0400 Australia. Department of Civil Aviation. Civil Aviation Report *see* 0311-628X
0572-0451 Australia. Department of Primary Industry. Wheat Industry Research, A.C.T. Annual Report
0572-0494 Australia. Department of Territory of Norfolk Island. Report *changed to* Australia. Department of Home Affairs. Norfolk Island Annual Report
0572-1431 Australian Road Research Board. Proceedings
0572-144X Australian Road Research Board. Special Report
0572-192X Oberoesterreichisches Landesarchiv. Mitteilungen
0572-2241 Automatika
0572-2691 Avtomatika
0572-2969 Cuaderno Literario Azor
0572-2993 Aarets Storsta Handelser i Bilder
0572-3221 Agricultural Science Hong Kong *changed to* Agriculture Hong Kong
0572-3590 American Bar Association. Section of Individual Rights and Responsibilities. Newsletter *changed to* American Bar Association. I.R.R. Section Newsletter
0572-4171 Asian Industrial Development News *see* 0252-4481
0572-4198 Asian Institute of Technology. Research Summary
0572-4295 Association of American Geographers. Proceedings†
0572-4325 Association of Southeast Asian Institutions of Higher Learning. Newsletter
0572-4562 Aarbok for Hadeland
0572-4953 American Association of Law Libraries. Newsletter
0572-5534 Brazil. Superintendencia da Borracha. Annuario Estatistico. Mercado Estrangeiro
0572-5860 Baas Becking Geobiological Laboratory. Annual Report
0572-5933 Bank Automation Newsletter
0572-5941 National Income of Iran
0572-595X Bank Marketing Management *changed to* Bank Marketing
0572-5968 Bank of Jamaica. Statistical Digest
0572-6042 Barbados Nursing Journal
0572-6557 Biology and Behavior Series†
0572-6654 Bochumer Schriften zur Entwicklungsforschung und Entwicklungspolitik
0572-6921 Brigham Young University. Center for Thermochemical Studies. Contributions
0572-7146 Bruecke-Archiv
0572-7529 Bureau International des Societes Gerant les Droits d'Enregistrement et de Reproduction Mecanique. Bulletin
0572-7545 Business Asia
0572-7669 Colorado School Law Review
0572-7820 Columbia College Today
0572-9750 Common Market Reports
0572-9912 Trade Regulation Reports
0573-0473 Committee of the Professional Photographers of Europe. General Assembly. Report of Proceedings
0573-0872 Commonwealth Space-Flight Symposium. Proceedings†
0573-0910 Communes de France
0573-2646 International Art Treasures Exhibition
0573-3022 Conference Internationale sur les Phenomenes d'Ionisation dans les Gaz. Comptes Rendus
0573-4347 Conferencia de Facultades Latinoamericanas de Derecho. (Documentos Oficiales)
0573-4843 Congres International Aeronautique. Compte Rendu des Travaux
0573-5661 Congress of International Congress Organizers and Technicians. Proceeding
0573-665X Connecticut Market Data
0573-715X Conservation Topics†
0573-8555 Contributions to Economic Analysis
0573-8636 Control de Publicidad y Ventas
0573-9195 Analyse Economique et Fonctionelle du Budget de l'Etat des Pays du Benelux
0573-9209 Analyse Economique et Fonctionelle des Depenses de l'Etat en Belgique, aux Pays Bas et au Luxembourg
0573-9233 Etude Comparative des Budgets Belges, Neerlandais et Luxembourgeois
0573-9543 Cooperation Mediterraneenne pour l'Energie Solaire. Bulletin *changed to* Revue Internationale d'Heliotechnique
0573-9799 Koebenhavn Boligkommissionen. Aarsberetning
0573-9985 Computer Aided Design i Danmark
0574-0045 Koebenhavns Universitet. Oekonomiske Institut. Memo
0574-0681 Cornell University. Modern Indonesia Project. Translations†
0574-1181 Corporate Diagrams and Administrative Personnel of the Chemical Industry
0574-1602 Corriere Nuova Europa
0574-2315 Cotton and Allied Textile Industries *changed to* International Textile Manufacturing
0574-2323 Cotton Farming
0574-2374 Cotton Statistics Monthly
0574-248X Calendar of Regional Congresses of Medical Sciences *see* 0301-2891
0574-3370 Courrier Consulaire du Burkina Faso
0574-3680 Covered Wagon
0574-3842 Anthropologia Hungarica
0574-475X Cronache e Opinioni
0574-5101 Cruzada Espanol
0574-6132 Anuario Estadistico de Cuba
0574-7120 Curious Naturalist†
0574-8135 Cycle
0574-8259 Cyprus. Geological Survey Department. Memoirs
0574-8267 Cyprus. Geological Survey Department. Annual Report
0574-8305 Cyprus. Loan Commissioners. Accounts and Statistics for the Year
0574-8399 Cyprus. Department of Statistics and Research. Motor Vehicles and Road Accidents†
0574-9069 Politechnika Czestochowska. Zeszyty Naukowe. Nauki Podstawowe
0574-9077 Politechnika Czestochowska. Zeszyty Naukowe. Nauki Spoleczno-Ekonomiczne
0574-9468 C.I.A. Revue
0574-9549 C I S
0575-0075 Cadernos de Folclore
0575-0415 Cahiers Charles du Bos
0575-0466 Cahiers d'Analyse Textuelle
0575-0547 Cahiers d'Histoire des Prix
0575-0563 Cahiers de Biotherapie
0575-0571 Cahiers de Bruges
0575-0970 Cahiers du Sart Tilman
0575-108X Cahiers Ligures de Prehistoire et d'Archeologie *changed to* Cahiers Ligures de Prehistoire et de Protohistoire
0575-1632 Caisse Centrale de Cooperation Economique. Rapport d'Activite *changed to* Caisse Centrale de Cooperation Economique. Rapport Annuel
0575-206X University of Calgary. Department of Mathematics and Computing Science. Research Papers *changed to* University of Calgary. Department of Mathematics and Statistics. Research Papers
0575-2124 Caliban
0575-2221 California State Plan for Hospitals *changed to* California State Health Plan
0575-2426 California Economic Indicators
0575-2906 Characteristics of the California Youth Authority Parole Caseload†
0575-3368 Administrative Law Bulletin†
0575-4208 Giannini Foundation of Agricultural Economics. Monograph
0575-4941 California Water Resources Center. Contribution
0575-4968 California Water Resources Center. Annual Report *changed to* California Water Resources Center. Report
0575-6316 California Trial Lawyers Journal *see* 0889-7751
0575-6863 Cambridge South Asian Studies
0575-6871 Cambridge Studies in the History and Theory of Politics
0575-7258 Activites Minieres au Cameroun
0575-7894 Canada. Statistics Canada. Annual Report of Notifiable Diseases/Rapport Annuel sur les Maladies a Declaration Obligatoire†
0575-7975 Canada. Statistics Canada. Building Permits. Annual Summary/Permis de Batir
0575-8254 Canada. Statistics Canada. Consolidated Government Finance: Fiscal Year Ended Nearest to December 31/ Finances Publiques Consolidees: Annee Financiere Terminee le Plus Pres de 31 Decembre
0575-8262 Canada. Statistics Canada. Corporation Financial Statistics
0575-8440 Canada. Statistics Canada. Estimates of Production and Disappearance of Meats/Estimation de la Production et de la Disparition des Viandes†
0575-8491 Canada. Statistics Canada. Federal Government Employment/Emploi dans l'Administration Publique Federale
0575-8521 Canada. Statistics Canada. Federal Government Finance: Revenue and Expenditure, Assets and Liabilities/ Finances Publiques Federales: Recettes and Depenses, Actif et Passif
0575-8548 Canada. Statistics Canada. Field Crop Reporting Series/Serie de Rapports sur les Grandes Cultures
0575-8645 Canada. Statistics Canada. General Review of the Mineral Industries/ Revue Generale sur les Industries Minerales
0575-8661 Canada. Statistics Canada. Glass and Glass Products Manufacturers/ Fabricants de Verre et d'Articles en Verre *changed to* Canada. Statistics Canada. Glass and Glass Products Industries/Industries du Verre et d'Articles en Verre
0575-8807 Canada. Statistics Canada. Industrial Research and Development Expenditures in Canada/Depenses au Titre de la Recherche et du Developpement Industriels au Canada†
0575-884X Canada. Statistics Canada. Iron and Steel Mills/Siderurgie†
0575-9021 Canada. Statistics Canada. Miscellaneous Manufacturing Industries/Industries Manufacturieres Diverses
0575-9048 Canada. Statistics Canada. Miscellaneous Metal Mines/Mines Metalliques Diverses.†
0575-9072 Canada. Statistics Canada. Motor Carriers Freight Quarterly/ Entrepreneurs en Camionnage†
0575-9137 Canada. Statistics Canada. Moving and Storage Household Goods†
0575-917X Canada. Statistics Canada. Murder Statistics/Statistique de l'Homicide *see* 0825-432X
0575-9331 Canada. Statistics Canada. Police Administration Statistics/Statistique de l'Administration Policiere†
0575-934X Population Estimates by Marital Status, Age & Sex, Canada and Provinces/ Estimations de la Population Suivant l'Etat Matrimonial, l'Age et le Sexe, Canada et Provinces *see* 0227-1796
0575-9412 Canada. Statistics Canada. Printing, Publishing and Allied Industries
0575-9455 Canada. Statistics Canada. Products Shipped by Canadian Manufacturers/ Produits Livres Par les Fabricants Canadiens
0575-9463 Canada. Statistics Canada. Provincial Government Enterprise Finance: Income and Expenditure, Assets, Liabilities and Net Worth/Revenus et Depenses, Actif, Passif et Valeur Nette
0575-9501 Canada. Statistics Canada. Provincial Government Finance, Revenue and Expenditure (Estimates) /Finances Publiques Provinciales, Revenus et Defenses (Previsions)†
0575-9560 Canada. Statistics Canada. Radio and Television Broadcasting/Radiodiffusion et Television
0575-9633 Sales of Toilet Preparations in Canada†
0575-9757 Canada. Statistics Canada. Shipping Report. Part 4: Origin and Destination for Selected Ports/Transport Maritime. Partie 4: Orgine et Destination pour Certains Ports†
0575-979X Canada. Statistics Canada. Sporting Goods and Toy Industries/Fabrication d'Articles de Sport et de Jouets
0575-9846 Canada. Statistics Canada. Stone Quarries/Carrieres†
0575-996X Canada. Statistics Canada. Training Schools/Etablissements de Protection de la Jeunesse†
0575-9978 Canada. Statistics Canada. Trusteed Pension Plans-Financial Statistics/ Regimes de Pensions en Fiducie Statistique Financiere
0576-0046 Canada. Statistics Canada. Urban Transit/Transport Urbain†
0576-0062 Canada. Statistics Canada. Wire and Wire Products Manufacturers *see* 0828-9913
0576-0070 Canada. Statistics Canada. Wooden Box Factories/Fabriques de Boites en Bois†
0576-0097 Canada. Statistics Canada. Mechanical Contracting Industry/Les Entrepreneurs d'Installations Mecaniques
0576-0100 Canada. Statistics Canada. Credit Unions
0576-0119 Canada. Statistics Canada. Corporation Taxation Statistics
0576-016X Canada. Statistics Canada. Health Manpower Section. Annual Salaries of Hospital Nursing Personnel/ Traitements Annuels du Personnel Infirmier des Hopitaux†
0576-1174 Canada. Department of Manpower and Immigration. Quarterly Immigration Bulletin†
0576-1999 Gazetteer of Canada
0576-2286 Canada. Immigration Division. Immigration Statistics *changed to* Canada. Immigration and Demographic Policy Group. Immigration Statistics
0576-4157 Unemployment Insurance Canada. Annual Report
0576-4300 Canada Council Annual Report and Supplement

0576-5161 Canadian Electrical Association. Engineering and Operating Division. Transactions
0576-5234 Canadian Folk Music Society Newsletter *changed to* Canadian Folk Music Bulletin
0576-5269 Canadian Gas Utilities Directory *changed to* Canadian Gas Association Directory
0576-5528 Canadian Jewish Archives (New Series)
0576-5803 Canadian Notes & Queries
0576-6176 Canadian Symposium on Water Pollution Research. Water Pollution Research in Canada. Proceedings *see* 0197-9140
0576-6370 Canadian Wildlife Service. Occasional Papers
0576-6621 Cancer Cytology†
0576-6885 University of Cape Town. Libraries. Statistical Report
0576-6931 Capilla Alfonsina. Boletin
0576-7172 Carbohydrate Chemistry *changed to* Carbohydrate Chemistry. Part 1: Mono-, Di-, & Tri-saccharides & Their Derivatives
0576-7172 Carbohydrate Chemistry *changed to* Carbohydrate Chemistry. Part 2: Macromolecules
0576-7296 Career Index *see* 0276-0355
0576-7547 Caribbean Congress of Labour. Report
0576-7598 Caribbean Monthly Bulletin
0576-7954 Carnegie Quarterly
0576-808X Carolina Comments
0576-8519 Casa, Arredamento e Giardino *changed to* Casa & Giardino
0576-8861 Catalogo Bolaffi d'Arte Moderna *changed to* Catalogo dell'Arte Moderna Italiana
0576-8888 Catalogo Bolaffi del Cacciatore e delle Armi†
0576-8942 Catalogo de Filmes Brasileiros *changed to* Brasil Cinema
0576-9280 Catgut Acoustical Society Newsletter *see* 0882-2212
0576-9787 Cellulose Chemistry and Technology
0576-9922 C R I Abstracts
0577-0335 C E N T O Newsletter†
0577-036X Central Africa Historical Association. Local Series Pamphlets *changed to* Historical Association of Zimbabwe. Local Series Pamphlets
0577-0653 Central Bank of Malta. Annual Report
0577-084X Central Marine Fisheries Research Institute. Bulletin
0577-1056 C E B E D E A U. Tribune
0577-1331 Centre d'Etudes Ethnologiques. Publications *changed to* Centre d'Etudes Ethnologiques Bandundu. Publications
0577-1730 Centre International d'Etude des Problems Humains. Bulletins
0577-1765 Universite Catholique de Louvain. Centre International de Dialectologie Generale. Travaux
0577-179X Centre Interuniversitaire d'Histoire Contemporaine. Cahiers
0577-1935 Centrepoint
0577-2168 Centro Camuno di Studi Preistorici. Bollettino
0577-2176 Centro Camuno di Studi Preistorici. Publicazioni†
0577-2451 Centro de Estudios Monetarios Latinoamericanos. Ensayos
0577-2907 Centro Interamericano de Investigacion y Documentacion Sobre Formacion Profesional. Boletin
0577-2915 C I N T E R F O R - Documentacion
0577-2931 C I N T E R F O R Estudios y Monografias
0577-3334 Ceramica de Cultura Maya
0577-3490 Ceska Bibliografie
0577-3725 Sbornik Historicky
0577-4691 Ceylon Historical Journal
0577-4772 Ceylon Rationalist Ambassador
0577-5000 Annuaire Statistique du Tchad
0577-5132 Challenge (Armonk)
0577-5183 Analysis of Workmen's Compensation Laws *see* 0191-118X
0577-5574 Charioteer
0577-571X Capital Investments of the World Petroleum Industry
0577-5728 Chases' Calendar of Annual Events
0577-6848 Chiba University. Faculty of Engineering. Journal
0577-7240 Chicago Linguistic Society. Papers from the Regional Meetings
0577-7259 Chicago Mercantile Exchange Yearbook
0577-750X Plant Protection Bulletin (Taiwan)
0577-781X Children's Books in Print
0577-800X Chile. Instituto Nacional de Estadisticas. Sintesis Estadistica *changed to* Chile. Instituto Nacional de Estadisticas. Informativo Estadistico
0577-8131 Chile. Servicio de Impuestos Internos. Memoria†
0577-8832 China Informatie *see* 0920-203X
0577-9065 Chinese Historical Society of America. Bulletin
0577-9081 Chinese Journal of Physics†
0577-9294 Chip Chats
0577-9316 Malacological Society of Japan. Newsletter
0578-0152 Christian Science Monitor. Cumulated Index *see* 0098-1184
0578-0160 Christiana Albertina
0578-0594 Chrzescijanskie Stowarzyszenie Spoleczne. Information Bulletin
0578-2228 Chuo University. Faculty of Science and Engineering. Bulletin
0578-3097 Circle K Magazine *see* 0745-1962
0578-3283 Citizen (Jackson)
0578-3364 Citizens Conference on State Legislatures. Research Memorandum†
0578-3747 Civil Engineering in Japan
0578-3755 University of Illinois at Urbana-Champaign. Civil Engineering Studies. Photogrammetry Series
0578-3828 Civil Service Digest *see* 0381-7962
0578-3917 Civilisation Malgache
0578-4131 Clanky v Slovenskych Casopisoch *changed to* Slovenska Narodna Bibliografia Seria C: Clanky
0578-4182 Claretianum
0578-4247 Clark University (Worcester, Mass.) Dissertations and Theses *changed to* Clark University Bulletin (Worcester, Mass.)
0578-4565 Classification Society Bulletin†
0578-4573 Classified Bibliography on Graph Theory†
0578-5294 Clothing Institute Journal *see* 0263-1008
0578-5464 Studia Universitatis "Babes-Bolyai" Iurisprudentia
0578-5472 Studia Universitatis "Babes-Bolyai." Oeconomica.
0578-5480 Studia Universitatis "Babes-Bolyai". Philosophia
0578-5502 Studia Universitatis Babes-Bolyai. Psychologia-Pedagogia *see* 0578-5480
0578-5634 Coastal Engineering in Japan
0578-5677 Coastal Research Notes *see* 0271-5376
0578-6371 University of Iowa. Center for Labor and Management. Research Series.†
0578-6533 Iowa Advocate
0578-655X Iowa Archeological Society. Newsletter
0578-6959 Iran. Ministry of Economy. Report on Commencement and Operation Permits for Industrial Establishments
0578-6967 Iran
0578-7483 Irish Journal of Agricultural Research
0578-8056 Islamic Education
0578-8250 Israel. Department of Customs and Excise. Yalkut *changed to* Israel. Department of Customs and V A T. Yalkut
0578-9230 Israel Academy of Sciences and Humanities. Section of Humanities. Proceedings
0578-9427 Israels Aussenhandel
0578-9761 Sarkiyat Mecmuasi
0578-9923 Istituto Italiano di Numismatica. Annali
0579-174X Itogi Nauki: Stratigrafiya. Paleontologiya *changed to* Itogi Nauki i Tekhniki: Stratigrafiya, Paleontologiya
0579-1766 Itogi Nauki: Tekhnologiya Organicheskikh Veshchestv *see* 0303-2361
0579-2290 Ittihad
0579-2428 Max-Planck-Institute fuer Europaische Rechtsgeschichte. Veroeffentlichungen. Ius Commune
0579-2983 Izvestiya Vysshikh Uchebnykh Zavedenii. Seriya Energetika
0579-3238 India. Department of Labour and Employment. Annual Report *changed to* India. Ministry of Labour. Annual Report
0579-3599 Instituto Argentino de Ciencias Genealogicas. Boletin Interno
0579-3718 Sociedad Interamericana de Planificacion. Correo Informativo/Newsletter *changed to* Revista Interamericana de Planificacion. Correo Informativo/Newsletter
0579-3742 International Association for Mass Communications Research. Letter from the President
0579-3769 International Conference of Building Officials. Code Changes Committee. Annual Report
0579-3866 International Federation of Catholic Universities. General Assembly. (Report)
0579-3912 International Organization for Medical Cooperation. General Assembly. Report *changed to* International Organization for Cooperation in Health Care. General Assembly. Report
0579-3920 International Pacific Halibut Commission (U.S. and Canada). Technical Reports
0579-4005 Introduktsiya ta Aklimatyzatsiya Rozlyn na Ukrayini *changed to* Introduktsiya i Aklimatyzatsiya Rastenii
0579-4234 I E E E International Symposium on Circuit Theory. Symposium Digest. Summaries of Papers *see* 0277-674X
0579-4374 Immigration History Newsletter
0579-4757 Indian Agricultural Index†
0579-5109 Institut Maurice Thorez. Conferences†
0579-5192 Instituto Latinoamericano de Mercadeo Agricola. Actividades del I L M A†
0579-5206 Instituto Latinoamericano de Mercadeo Agricola. Informes Sobre Comercializacion†
0579-5214 Instituto Latinoamericano de Mercadeo Agricola. Sistemas de Mercadeo de Productos Agricolas en Medellin†
0579-529X Insurance Stock Review *changed to* Insurance and Financial Review
0579-5362 International Association of Volcanology and Chemistry of the Earth's Interior. Newsletter†
0579-5400 International Cellular Plastics Conference. Proceedings
0579-5427 I C I D Bulletin
0579-5486 Management Datamatics†
0579-5567 International Police Association. Meeting of the International Executive Council
0579-5613 I S O Information *changed to* Organ Building Periodical
0579-5621 U.I.A.M.S. Bulletin Trimestriel
0579-6059 Index to the Science Fiction Magazines *see* 0361-3038
0579-6105 India. Ministry of Education and Social Welfare. Provisional Statistics of Education in the States
0579-6407 Ingenieur Digest
0579-6695 Inter American Press Association. Committee on Freedom on the Press. Report
0579-6733 International Association of Hydrogeologists. Memoires
0579-6881 International Police Association. Travel Scholarships
0579-6903 I P T C Newsletter *changed to* I P T C News
0579-692X International Union of Official Travel Organizations. Technical Bulletin *changed to* World Tourism Organization. Collection of Technical Bulletins
0579-6938 Internationaler Weltkongress der U F O-Forscher. Dokumentarbericht
0579-7152 Acta Biologica Iugoslavica. Serija E: Ichthyologia
0579-7195 University of Ife. Faculty of Agriculture. Annual Research Report *changed to* Ife Journal of Agriculture
0579-7772 Universitaet Innsbruck. Medizinische Fakultaet. Arbeiten
0579-7780 Universitaet Innsbruck. Theologische Fakultaet. Studien und Arbeiten
0579-7918 International Institute for the Unification of Private Law. Rapport sur l'Activite de l'Institute†
0579-7926 Tunisia. Institut National Scientifique et Technique d'Oceanographie et de Peche. Bulletin
0579-8108 International Conference on World Politics. Conference Papers
0579-8140 International Directory of Occupational Safety and Health Services and Institutions
0579-8256 Through Europe by Train
0579-8299 International Union of Food and Allied Workers' Associations. Meeting of the Executive Committee. I. Documents of the Secretariat. II. Summary Report
0579-8302 International Union of Food and Allied Workers' Associations. Tobacco Workers' Trade Group Board. Meeting†
0579-8337 Inter-Parliamentary Union. Series: "Reports and Documents"
0579-8388 Inventor
0579-9406 Moskovskii Universitet. Vestnik. Seriya 4: Geologiya
0580-0412 Motion Picture, TV & Theatre Directory
0580-0420 Motive†
0580-0714 Mountain-Plains in Books *see* 0145-6180
0580-0943 Mowia Wieki
0580-1540 Westfaelische Wilhelms-Universitaet Muenster. Slavisch-Baltisches Seminar†
0580-1737 Multiple Sclerosis Abstracts *see* 0360-0017
0580-2652 Museums Calendar *see* 0307-7675
0580-289X Music Library Association. Newsletter
0580-2954 Musica Britannica
0580-308X Musical America Annual Directory Issue *changed to* Musical America International Directory of the Performing Arts
0580-3403 Musteranlagen der Energiewirtschaft
0580-3594 Muveltseg es Hagyomany
0580-3713 Muzica
0580-373X Muzikoloski Zbornik
0580-3896 Myotis
0580-4396 Mysore Orientalist
0580-4485 Minoseg es Megbizhatosag
0580-468X Universidad de Madrid. Departamento de Botanica y Fisiologia Vegetal. Trabajos
0580-4787 Magyar Tudomanyos Akademia Fold-es Banyaszati Tudomanyok Osztalyanak Kozlemenyei†
0580-4795 Gazdasag es Jogtudomany *see* 0231-2522
0580-4981 Makedonska Akademija na Naukite i Umetnostite. Oddelenie za Prirodno-Matematicki Nauki. Prilozi. *see* 0351-3246
0580-535X Agassiz Center for Water Studies. Research Report
0580-6097 University of Michigan. Herbarium. Contributions
0580-6712 Universidad de Murcia. Monteagudo

ISSN INDEX 1583

0580-7727 Massachusetts. Division of Employment Security. Quarterly Survey of Unfilled Job Openings - Boston *changed to* Massachusetts. Division of Employment Security. Survey of Unfilled Job Openings - Boston
0580-8162 Modern Photography Annual†
0580-8421 M D†
0580-8537 Reporter (Montreal)
0580-8650 Universidad de Madrid. Seminario de Metafisica. Anales
0580-8898 Manager and Entrepreneur†
0580-9320 Medicina Termale e Climatologia
0580-9746 Michigan State University. Institute of Water Research. Technical Report
0581-0000 Mineral Statistics of India
0581-0086 Minnesota Genealogist
0581-0205 M L A Newsletter *see* 0884-2205
0581-0558 Musicologica Slovaca
0581-0892 Malawi Housing Corporation. Annual Report and Accounts
0581-0906 Malawi. National Library. Annual Report *changed to* Malawi. National Library Service Board. Annual Report
0581-1023 Marketing
0581-1058 Marxist Miscellany
0581-1155 Mathematical Chronicle
0581-1538 Acta Biologica Iugoslavica. Serija B: Mikrobiologija
0581-2011 Mujeres
0581-2674 Safaho-Monographs
0581-2739 Safety†
0581-2801 Saga University. Faculty of Agriculture. Bulletin
0581-295X Saguenayensia
0581-2984 Sahifat al-Takhtit al-Tarbawi fi al-Bilad al-Arabiyah
0581-3018 Sahitya Sahakar†
0581-3115 Sailboat Directory *see* 0148-8732
0581-3263 Information Veterinaire
0581-3298 Saint Lawrence Seaway Authority. Annual Report
0581-3808 Universidad de Salamanca. Seminario de Derecho Politico. Boletin Informativo†
0581-3999 Salt Research & Industry *changed to* Salt Inorganic and Bio-inorganic Chemistry
0581-4111 El Salvador. Ministerio de Planificacion y Coordinacion del Desarrollo Economico y Social. Indicadores Economicos y Sociales
0581-4448 Sami Aellin†
0581-4480 Samiske Samlinger
0581-4758 Sanskriti
0581-4766 Samuel H. Kress Foundation. Annual Report
0581-4790 Samvadadhvam
0581-572X Sankhya
0581-5738 Sankhya. Series B
0581-5908 Sericultural Experiment Station. Annual Report
0581-6076 Universidade Federal de Santa Catarina. Museu de Antropologia. Anais
0581-6106 Santa Clara Lawyer *see* 0146-0315
0581-6866 Universidade de Sao Paulo. Faculdade de Odontologia. Revista
0581-7501 Zemaljski Muzej Bosne i Hercegovine. Glasnik. Arheologija
0581-751X Zemaljski Muzej Bosne i Hercegovine. Glasnik. Etnologija
0581-7528 Zemaljski Muzej Bosne i Hercegovine. Glasnik. Prirodne Nauke
0581-8079 Travel on Saskatchewan Highways
0581-8109 Saskatchewan. Department of Mineral Resources. Annual Report *changed to* Saskatchewan Energy & Mines. Annual Report
0581-8389 Saskatchewan Fur Marketing Service. Annual Report
0581-8435 Saskatchewan Municipal Directory
0581-8443 Saskatchewan Natural History Society Newsletter *changed to* Blue Jay News
0581-8532 Satapitaka. Indo-Asian Literatures
0581-8672 Saudi Arabian Monetary Agency. Statistical Summary
0581-8761 Savings and Loan Fact Book *changed to* Savings and Loan Yearbook
0581-8761 Savings and Loan Fact Book *see* 0731-0935
0581-8850 Savremena Poljoprivreda
0581-9172 Sbornik Geologickych Ved: Geologie
0581-9180 Sbornik Geologickych Ved: Loziskova Geologie, Mineralogie
0581-9423 Scandinavian Building Research†
0581-9431 Scandinavian Corrosion Congress. Proceedings
0581-9911 School Activities and the Library†
0582-0421 Beitraege zur Politischen Wissenschaft†
0582-138X Schrifttumnachweis Bau-, Wohnungs- und Siedlungswesen†
0582-1487 Schwann Artist Catalog
0582-1592 Societe Suisse des Americanistes. Bulletin
0582-1673 Biblische Beitraege
0582-2343 Scientia Agriculturae Bohemoslovaca
0582-2351 Scientia Paedagogica Experimentalis
0582-2637 Scissortail
0582-3226 Scripta Instituti Donneriani Aboensis
0582-3234 Scripta Islandica
0582-3692 Secondary Education *see* 0013-1482
0582-3978 Segnalazioni Assofarma
0582-4001 Seguridad Social
0582-4192 Seikei Ronso/Faculty of Politics, Law, and Economics. Journal *see* 0288-6340
0582-4206 Japan Society of Precision Engineering. Bulletin
0582-4524 Journal of Classical Studies
0582-4532 World
0582-4656 Japan Petroleum Institute. Bulletin
0582-4761 Selbstbedienung und Supermarkt *see* 0722-6950
0582-4788 Selden Society, London. Supplementary Series
0582-4818 Selecciones Avicolas
0582-4877 Selecta
0582-5164 Sel'skaya Nov'
0582-6314 Seminarium
0582-6802 Seoul Journal of Medicine
0582-7094 Cerro Tololo Interamerican Observatory (La Serena, Chile). Contributions†
0582-8198 Astrometriya i Astrofizika†
0582-8759 Sestante†
0582-8929 Universidad de Sevilla. Instituto Garcia Oviedo. Publicaciones
0582-9399 Shakespeare Studies
0582-9402 Shakespeare Studies
0582-9836 Shamativ
0582-9860 Victorious
0582-9887 Shepard's Law Review Citations
0582-9909 Shepard's United States Administrative Citations
0582-9917 Shepard's United States Patents and Trademarks Citations
0583-0362 Shimane Law Review
0583-0648 Shinshu University. Faculty of Textile Science and Technology. Journal. Series A: Biology
0583-0664 Shinshu University. Faculty of Textile Science and Technology. Journal. Series D: Arts
0583-0923 Shizuoka University. Faculty of Science. Reports
0583-1024 Shock and Vibration Digest
0583-1180 Shoni Igaku
0583-1296 Shout
0583-1776 Siberian Husky Club of America Newsletter
0583-2268 Sierra Leone. Library Board. Report
0583-239X Sierra Leone Geographical Journal
0583-2594 Signpost *changed to* Signpost for Northwest Trails
0583-3132 Silvicultura Em Sao Paulo
0583-3655 Singapore Yearbook of Statistics
0583-3736 Singapore International Chamber of Commerce. Report *see* 0377-449X
0583-4279 Sino-British Trade Review
0583-4449 Siskiyou Pioneer and Yearbook
0583-4570 Sixties *changed to* Eighties
0583-4961 Institut za Nacionalna Istorija, Skopje. Glasnik
0583-5356 Universitatis Debreceniensis de Ludovico Kossuth Nominatae. Instituti Philologiae Slavicae. Annales. Slavica
0583-5429 Slavistische Beitraege
0583-5445 Slavistische Studienbuecher
0583-5623 Slovakia
0583-564X Slovanske Studie
0583-6263 Slovo na Storozhi
0583-6948 Great Britain. Social Science Research Council. Research Supported by the Social Science Research Council *see* 0266-2159
0583-7065 Social Work Forum
0583-712X Denmark. Socialforskningsinstitutt. Publikation
0583-7200 Socialist Thought and Practice
0583-7405 Societat d'Historia Natural de Baleares. Boletin
0583-7480 Sociedad Espanola de Historia de la Medicina. Boletin
0583-7693 Sociedad Quimica de Mexico. Revista
0583-7731 Sociedad Venezolana de Espeleologia. Boletin
0583-774X Guacharo
0583-7774 Sociedad Venezolana de Planificacion. Cuadernos
0583-8045 Limba si Literatura
0583-8177 Societe Botanique de Geneve. Travaux *see* 0373-2525
0583-8193 Societe d'Archeologie et d'Histoire de la Manche. Departement de la Manche. Revue.
0583-8266 Societe d'Histoire de la Guadeloupe. Bulletin
0583-8452 Societe des Amis de Marcel Proust et des Amis de Combray. Bulletin
0583-8894 Analytical Sciences Monographs
0583-8975 S C E H Newsletter
0583-9009 Society for Developmental Biology. Symposium
0583-9181 Society for the Preservation of Long Island Antiquities. Newsletter
0583-9246 Water Treatment and Examination†
0583-9270 S.A.W.E. Journal *changed to* Weight Engineering
0583-9572 S P I E Seminar Proceedings *see* 0361-0748
0583-9750 Sociologia
0584-0007 Narodna Biblioteka Kiril i Metodii. Izvestiya
0584-0252 Sofiiski Universitet. Fakultet po Zapadni Filologii. Godisnik *changed to* Sofiiski Universitet. Fakultet po Klasiceski i Novi Filologii. Godisnik
0584-0651 Solar Energy Progress in Australia and New Zealand†
0584-0821 O Solo
0584-1070 Something
0584-1739 Textile Information Sources and Resources†
0584-195X South Africa. Department of Statistics. Road Traffic Accidents *changed to* South Africa. Central Statistical Service. Road Traffic Accidents
0584-2166 South Africa. Department of Coloured Relations and Rehoboth Affairs. Annual Report†
0584-2352 South Africa. Geological Survey. Annals
0584-2360 Bibliography and Subject Index of South African Geology
0584-3073 South African Reserve Bank. Monthly Release of Money and Banking Statistics
0584-3170 South Asian Studies
0584-3219 Quarterly Geological Notes
0584-4088 Southeast Asia Treaty Organization. Secretary General. S E A T O Report†
0584-4118 S E C A C Review and Newsletter *changed to* Southeastern College Art Conference Review
0584-4266 S E W R P C Newsletter
0584-6374 Instituto de Estudios Madrilenos. Anales
0584-6544 Spain. Direccion General de Aduanas. Informe Mensuel Sobre el Comercio Exterior
0584-7109 Documentacion Iberoamericana
0584-8016 Span
0584-8024 Span (Slough)
0584-8067 Spanner (London, 1974)
0584-8164 Speaker and Gavel
0584-8539 Spectrochimica Acta. Part A: Molecular Spectroscopy
0584-8547 Spectrochimica Acta. Part B: Atomic Spectroscopy
0584-8555 Spectroscopic Properties of Inorganic & Organometallic Compounds
0584-8652 Speculum Juris
0584-9217 Sport Parachutist
0584-9365 Spotlight on Africa
0584-9667 Springs
0585-0444 Standard Trade Index of Japan
0585-086X Stapp Car Crash Conference Proceedings
0585-0991 State Bank of India. Report of the Central Board of Directors *changed to* State Bank of India. Annual Report
0585-1009 State Bank of Pakistan. Export Receipts
0585-1289 State of South Africa†
0585-1432 Statistical Compendium of the Americas†
0585-1580 Statistical Office of the European Communities. Quarterly Bulletin of Energy Statistics
0585-1777 Statistical Pocket Book of Ceylon *changed to* Statistical Pocket Book of the Democratic Socialist Republic of Sri Lanka
0585-198X Statistics Sources
0585-2471 Stephen Wilson Annual Pharmacy Seminar. Report†
0585-2544 Stereophile
0585-2730 Great Britain. Warren Spring Laboratory. Investigation of Air Pollution: National Survey, Smoke and Sulphur Dioxide *changed to* Great Britain. Warren Spring Laboratory. U K Smoke and Sulphur Dioxide Monitoring Networks
0585-3214 Medelhavsmuseet. Bulletin
0585-3273 Studia Missionalia Upsaliensia†
0585-3400 Sweden. Statens Raad foer Byggnadsforskning. Informationsblad†
0585-3923 Straits Times Annual *changed to* Times Annual
0585-3931 Straits Times Directory of Malaysia and Singapore *changed to* N S T Directory of Malaysia
0585-3931 Straits Times Directory of Malaysia and Singapore *see* 0217-6009
0585-4172 Stredocesky Sbornik Historicky†
0585-4393 Struktura i Rol' Vody v Zhivom Organizme *changed to* Molekulyarnaya Fizika i Biofizika Vodnykh Sistem
0585-4555 Student Aid Annual *see* 0190-339X
0585-4768 Studi di Letteratura Francese
0585-4911 Studi Genuensi
0585-492X Studi Ispanici
0585-5098 Studia Entomologica†
0585-5462 Studia Philologica Jyvaskylaensia
0585-5500 Studia Post-Biblica
0585-5543 Studia Slovenica
0585-5578 Studia Sumiro-Hungarica
0585-5721 Studiecentrum voor Jeugdmisdadigheid. Publikatie†
0585-5837 Studien und Texte zur Geistesgeschichte des Mittelalters
0585-5853 Studien zu den Bogazkoey-Texten
0585-6094 Studien zur Japanologie
0585-6175 Studien zur Publizistik. Bremer Reihe
0585-6515 Studies in Anglesey History
0585-6523 Studies in Anthropological Method
0585-6833 Studies in Judaica†
0585-6884 Studies in Managerial Economics†
0585-6914 Studies in Medieval and Reformation Thought
0585-6965 Studies in Philosophy & the History of Philosophy

ISSN INDEX

0585-7023 Studies in Pre-Columbian Art and Archaeology
0585-7031 Studies in Public Communication
0585-718X Studies in Speleology
0585-7260 Studies in the History of Religions *changed to* Numen Supplements
0585-7449 Studies on the Left *see* 0161-1801
0585-7694 Study Centre for Yugoslav Affairs. Review
0585-7856 Universitaet Stuttgart. Institut fuer Geologie und Palaeontologie Arbeiten Neue Folge
0585-8127 National University of Singapore. Economics & Statistics Society. Journal
0585-8488 Sudan. Department of Statistics. Foreign Trade Statistics
0585-8631 Sudan Law Journal and Reports
0585-9328 Sunday School Senior Adults
0585-9581 Suomen Obligaatiorkirja *see* 0781-4437
0585-9794 Supreme Court Monthly Review
0585-9840 Surfaces (Paris)
0585-9980 Surrey Archaeological Society. Bulletin
0586-0431 Svensk Tidskriftsfoerteckning
0586-0709 Svenskt Musikhistoriskt Arkiv. Bulletin
0586-1357 Swaziland. Central Statistical Office. Annual Statistical Bulletin
0586-1691 Sweden. Sjukvaardens och Socialvaardens Planerings- och Rationaliseringsinstitut. S P R I Rapport
0586-1926 Sweden. Televerket. Annual Report *changed to* Swedish Telecom. Annual Report
0586-2000 Swedish Archaeological Bibliography *changed to* Swedish Archaeology
0586-3031 U S Symposium on Rock Mechanics. Proceedings
0586-3260 Synteza *changed to* Ekonomika Prace
0586-3414 Syracuse University. Program of East African Studies. East African Bibliographic Series†
0586-3422 Syracuse University. Program of East African Studies. Occasional Bibliographies†
0586-3430 Syracuse University. Program of East African Studies. Occasional Papers†
0586-3708 Acta Universitatis de Attila Jozsef Nominatae. Acta Historiae Litterarum Hungaricarum
0586-3724 Acta Universitatis Szegediensis. Sectio Philosophica *see* 0231-2670
0586-3732 Acta Universitatis Szegediensis de Attila Jozsef Nominatae. Dissertationes Slavicae *changed to* Acta Universitatis Szegediensis de Attila Jozsef Nominatae. Dissertationes Slavicae. Sectio Linguistica
0586-3732 Acta Universitatis Szegediensis de Attila Jozsef Nominatae. Dissertationes Slavicae *changed to* Acta Universitatis Szegediensis de Attila Jozsef Nominatae. Sectio Historiae Litterarum
0586-3783 Szep Versek
0586-4496 Sieg's Moentkatalog. Danmark, Dansk Vestindien, Faeroeerne, Groenland, Island
0586-4534 Sinteticheskie Almazy *see* 0203-3119
0586-4607 Slovenska Akademia Vied. Geofyzikalny Ustav. Contributions
0586-4925 Statistical Office of the European Communities. Aussenhandel: Analitische Ubersichten. Foreign Trade: Analytical Tables
0586-4941 University of Stellenbosch. Bureau for Economic Research. Building and Construction
0586-500X Strictly Wholesaling†
0586-5050 Studies in Accounting Research
0586-5107 Studies in Urban Geography†
0586-5344 Sadakichi Hartmann Newsletter†
0586-5360 Saga och Sed
0586-5395 Saisons de la Danse
0586-5581 Scanning Electron Microscope Symposium. Proceedings *changed to* Scanning Electron Microscopy
0586-5751 Scientific Directory of Hong Kong
0586-6235 Social Studies Professional
0586-6766 Sweden. Statens Raad foer Byggnadsforskning. Document
0586-6898 Studies and Documents on Cultural Policies
0586-6928 Studies in Language and Linguistics
0586-7282 Salt Lake City Messenger
0586-7606 Schema et Schematisation
0586-7614 Schizophrenia Bulletin
0586-7746 Scientific and Technical Societies of Canada
0586-8440 Forest Products Research Institute. Annual Report
0586-8491 Southern Wholesalers' Guide *changed to* National Hardware Wholesalers' Guide
0586-9145 Symposia Otorhinolaryngologica Iugoslavica
0586-9668 Science and Archaeology
0586-9889 Serie Vie Locale
0586-9919 Anales de la Universidad Hispalense. Serie: Medicinas
0587-0631 Southeast Asia Treaty Organization. Secretary General. Record of Progress *see* 0584-4088
0587-1131 Storia dell'Arte
0587-1514 Szamitastechnika
0587-1689 Arbeitsmarkt Politik
0587-1948 Association for Institutional Research. Annual Forum on Institutional Research. Proceedings *changed to* A I R
0587-1956 A R S C Bulletin *see* 0004-5438
0587-2006 Journalists' International Association for Studying Problems of Overseas Peoples. Annuaire†
0587-2138 Australasian Tax Reports
0587-2871 American Animal Hospital Association Journal
0587-2936 American Bar Association. Section of Local Government Law. Committee Reports.†
0587-3053 A N A in Action *changed to* American Nurse Newspaper
0587-3452 Arch Plus
0587-3460 Archaeographie†
0587-3533 Arkansas Archeological Survey. Publications on Archeology. Popular Series
0587-3584 Art - Language
0587-3606 Asia Foundation. President's Review *changed to* Asia Foundation. Annual Report
0587-3746 Assure Social
0587-4076 Aarbok for Telemark
0587-4246 Acta Physica Polonica. Series A: General Physics, Physics of Condensed Matter, Optics and Quantum Electronics, Atomic and Molecular Physics, Applied Physics
0587-4254 Acta Physica Polonica. Series B: Elementary Particle Physics, Nuclear Physics, Theory of Relativity, Field Theory
0587-4300 Actualidad Pastoral
0587-4394 Advances in Metabolic Disorders. Supplements *see* 0065-2903
0587-4793 All India Architects Directory *see* 0256-4017
0587-503X American Peanut Research and Education Association. Journal *see* 0197-8748
0587-5196 Anuario del Cuento Costarricense
0587-5234 Angewandte Sozialforschung
0587-5277 Archiv der Deutschen Jugendbewegung. Jahrbuch
0587-5447 Arte y Arqueologia
0587-5455 Arti Musices
0587-5471 Asian Pacific Congress of Cardiology. Symposia
0587-5560 Bulletin de l'ANECLA†
0587-565X Astronomie und Raumfahrt
0587-5846 Australian Conservation Foundation. Annual Report
0587-5943 Pesticide Residues in Food
0587-5994 Co-Existence
0587-6435 Colecao de Estudos Filologicos
0588-2583 Collectionneur Francais
0588-2990 Colleges Classified†
0588-3253 Colloquium Geographicum
0588-4462 Colorado Fisheries Research Review†
0588-4543 Colorado. State Department of Public Health. Annual Progress Report. State Migrant Plan for Public Health Services†
0588-5094 Colour Society. Journal
0588-5477 Columbia University. Russian Institute. Studies
0588-621X Comite International des Poids et Mesures. Comite Consultatif de Photometrie et Radiometrie.(Rapport et Annexes)
0588-6228 Comite International des Poids et Mesures. Comite Consultatif pour la Definition de la Seconde. (Rapport et Annexes)
0588-6236 Comite International des Poids et Mesures. Comite Consultatif pour la Definition du Metre (Rapport et Annexes)
0588-6244 Comite International des Poids et Mesures. Comite Consultatif pour les Etalons des Mesure des Radiations Ionisantes(Rapport et Annexes) *changed to* Comite International des Poids et Mesures. Comite Consultatif pour les Etalons des Mesure des Rayonnements Ionisants (Rapport et Annexes)
0588-6414 Commentationes Balticae
0588-649X Euromarket News†
0588-6694 Commercial Bank of Ethiopia. Annual Report
0588-6783 Commission for Technical Co-Operation in Africa. Joint Project†
0588-6953 Commission of the European Communities. Expose Annuel sur les Activities d'Orientation Professionnelle dans la Communaute†
0588-702X Mines Safety and Health Commission. Report
0588-7356 C O R D News *see* 0149-7677
0588-7445 Common Market Law Reports
0588-7712 Abstracts of Papers on Geology of the United Kingdom *changed to* Abstracts of Current Information on Geology and Mineral Resources
0588-7720 Commonwealth Geological Liaison Office. Liaison Report†
0588-7739 Commonwealth Geological Liaison Office. Newsletter *changed to* Earth Sciences Programme Newsletter
0588-7755 Commonwealth Geological Liaison Office. Report (on) Resources of the British Commonwealth†
0588-7763 Commonwealth Geological Liaison Office. Special Publication
0588-7933 Commonwealth Trade†
0588-8018 Communications
0588-8093 Communicator†
0588-8360 Community
0588-8611 Easter Commemoration Digest†
0588-9049 Comparative Education Society in Europe. Proceedings of the General Meeting
0588-912X Compendio Estadistico Centroamericano
0588-9278 Comprehensive Education
0588-9405 Computer Programs for Chemistry†
0588-9545 Comunicaciones - Revista Tecnica†
0588-9979 Confederacao Nacional do Comercio. Divisao de Divulgacao. Carta Mensal *changed to* Confederacao Nacional do Comercio. Conselho Tecnico Consultivo. Carta Mensal
0589-1019 Alliance for Engineering in Medicine and Biology. Proceedings of the Annual Conference
0589-2813 Congreso Latinamericano de Siderurgia. Memoria Tecnica
0589-3267 Congresso Europeo di Storia Ospitaliera. Atti
0589-3305 Congresso Latinamericano de Hidraulica (Papers)
0589-3496 Connaissance de l'Orient. Collection Unesco d'Oeuvres Representatives
0589-400X Connecticut Water Resources Bulletin.
0589-4069 Conscientia
0589-4301 Consejo Superior Universitario Centroamericano. Actas de la Reunion Ordinaria
0589-4360 Consejo Superior Universitario Centroamericano. Publicaciones†
0589-4522 Conservative Journal
0589-4735 Construction-Amenagement
0589-4859 Consultants and Consulting Organizations *see* 0196-1292
0589-4867 Consultation on Church. Digest *changed to* Consultation on Church Union. Digest
0589-5065 Contact Lens Society of America Journal *see* 0096-2716
0589-5081 Contacto
0589-5286 Contemporary Music Newsletter†
0589-574X Contrast
0589-6355 Cooperative Housing Journal
0589-6665 Denmark. Statens Byggeforskningsinstitut. Landbrugsbyggeri
0589-6681 University of Copenhagen. Institute of Phonetics. Annual Report
0589-686X Corax
0589-7300 Cornell University. Modern Indonesia Project Publications. Monographs, Translations, Bibliographies
0589-7351 Cornell University. Library. Wason Collection. Southeast Asia Accessions List *changed to* Cornell University. Library. John M. Echols Collection on Southeast Asia. Accessions List
0589-7688 Ecuador. Comision de Valores. Corporacion Financiera Nacional. Memoria *changed to* Ecuador. Corporacion Financiera Nacional. Memoria
0589-7742 Corporacion Nacional de Fertilizantes. Memoria Anual
0589-7920 Corporate Report Fact Book
0589-8056 Corpus Hispanorum de Pace
0589-8218 Correctional Psychologist *see* 0093-8548
0589-8366 Corriere Africano
0589-8447 Cosmetic World
0589-8544 Costa Rica. Direccion General de Estadistica y Censos. Inventario de las Estadisticas Nacionales
0589-8617 Costa Rica. Ministerio de Transportes. Memoria *changed to* Costa Rica. Ministerio de Obras Publicas y Transportes. Memorias
0589-8765 Costruttori Italiani nel Mondo
0589-9028 C B A Annual Report
0589-915X Calendar of International Congresses of Medical Sciences *see* 0301-2891
0589-9362 Council of Europe. Exchange of Information Between the Member States on Their Legislative Activity and Regulations (New Series)†
0589-9478 Council of Europe. Council for Cultural Cooperation. Annual Report†
0589-9508 Council of Europe. Concise Handbook†
0589-9575 European Co-Operation
0589-9591 Council of Europe Film Weeks†
0589-9788 State Headlines†
0590-0239 Courrier des Pays de l'Est
0590-0727 Creditanstalt-Bankverein. Wirtschaftsberichte†
0590-1111 Cronache Meridionali†
0590-1243 Crop Protection Courier (International)
0590-1545 Cuadernos Bibliograficos
0590-1871 Cuadernos de Etnologia y Etnografia de Navarra
0590-2568 Cuadernos Uruguayos de Filosofia†
0590-2916 Cuba Azucar

ISSN INDEX

ISSN	Title
0590-3343	Universidad de Oriente. Instituto Oceanografico Biblioteca. Boletin Bibliografico
0590-3351	Universidad de Oriente. Instituto Oceanografico. Cuadernos Oceanograficos
0590-4102	Current Primate References
0590-417X	Current Research in British Studies by American and Canadian Scholars
0590-4846	Cyprus. Department of Statistics and Research. Demographic Report
0590-4854	Cyprus. Department of Statistics and Research. Annual Industrial Production Survey *changed to* Cyprus. Department of Statistics and Research. Industrial Production Survey
0590-5001	Czechoslovak Economic Papers
0590-501X	Dokumentacni Prehled C T K
0590-5214	Veterinarni Medicina
0590-5702	Canada. Statistics Canada. Direct Selling in Canada/Vente Directe au Canada
0590-580X	Canada. Department of Indian Affairs and Northern Development. Mines and Minerals, Activities *changed to* Canada. Indian and Northern Affairs Canada. Mines and Mineral Activities (Year)
0590-5966	Casopis za Zgodovino in Narodpisje
0590-6008	Catholic International Education Office. Etudes et Documents†
0590-6105	Informes Latinoamericanos de Fisica†
0590-630X	Chronicle College Charts *see* 0191-3662
0590-6334	Cicindela
0590-6342	Cimbebasia. Series A: Natural History
0590-6563	Commission of the European Communities. Community Law
0590-6571	Commission of the European Communities. Financial Report
0590-6776	Cord Sportfacts Guns Guide
0590-711X	C P D A News
0590-7225	Cours et Documents de Biologie†
0590-7233	Bibliographie de Jurisprudence Europeenne Concernant les Decisions Judiciaires Relatives aux Traites Institutant les Communautes Europeennes†
0590-7853	Canada West *see* 0829-5026
0590-8191	C R C Critical Reviews in Clinical Laboratory Sciences
0590-8434	Cleveland and Teesside Local History Society. Bulletin
0590-8760	Consumer Communique *changed to* Consumer Contact
0590-8876	Costume
0590-9325	Canada. Statistics Canada. Market Research Handbook
0590-9597	Casopis za Suvremenu Povijest
0590-9775	British Shipping Statistics†
0590-9783	Charities Digest
0590-9945	Coin Bulletin
0591-0110	Commission of the European Communities. Expose Annuel sur les Activities des Services de Main-d'Ouvre des Etats Membres de la Communaute†
0591-0129	Committee for Economic Development of Australia. C E D A Occasional Papers†
0591-017X	Concern
0591-0188	Comentarios Economico†
0591-0358	Koebenhavns Universitet. Institut du Moyen-Age Grec et Latin. Cahier
0591-0471	Courrier de l'Extreme-Orient
0591-0633	Cahiers Marxistes
0591-0986	Catalogue of Little Press Books in Print Published in the UK
0591-1036	Centrale Nucleare Garigliano. Relazione Annuale†
0591-1044	Centrale Elletronucleare Latina. Relazione Annuale†
0591-1133	Geschied- en Oudheidkundige Kring van Ronse en het Tenement van Inde. Annalen
0591-1281	Chips and Ships†
0591-1710	Commerce Yearbook of Public Sector
0591-1737	Commission of the European Communities. Etudes: Serie Industrie *changed to* Commission of the European Communities. Studies: Industry Series
0591-1745	Commission of the European Communities. Directory
0591-2237	Country Music People
0591-2296	Crux of the News
0591-2334	Custom Car
0591-2369	Zycie Literackie
0591-2377	Zycie Szkoly Wyzszej
0591-2385	Zygon
0591-2628	Panorama
0640-3603	Zeitschrift fuer Unfallchirurgie, Versicherungsmedizin und Berufskrankheiten
0700-0278	Canada. Statistics Canada. Canvas Products and Cotton and Jute Bag Industries/Industrie des Articles en Grosse Toile et des Sacs de Coton et de Jute†
0700-0324	Canada. Statistics Canada. Flour and Breakfast Cereal Products Industry/Meunerie et Fabrication de Cereales de Table
0700-0731	Canada. Statistics Canada. Felt and Fibre Processing Mills/Industrie du Feutre et du Traitement des Fibres†
0700-138X	Canada. Statistics Canada. Therapeutic Abortions/Avortements Therapeutiques†
0700-141X	Canada. Statistics Canada. Continuing Education: Universities/Education Permanente: Universites†
0700-1444	Canada. Statistics Canada. Continuing Education: Elementary-Secondary/Education Permanente: Niveau Elementaire-Secondaire†
0700-1681	Quebec (Province) Ministere du Travail et de la Main d'Oeuvre. Jurisprudence en Droit du Travail: Tribunal du Travail
0700-1770	ForesTalk(1978)†
0700-205X	Canada. Statistics Canada. Quarterly Estimates of Trusted Pension Funds/Estimations Trimestrielles Relatives aux Caisses de Pensions en Fiducie
0700-2092	Public Sector
0700-2181	Canada. Statistics Canada. University Financial Statistics/Universites Statistiques Financieres†
0700-2211	Canada. Statistics Canada. Railway Transport. Service Bulletin *see* 0828-2897
0700-2408	Metric Monitor/Moniteur Metrique *changed to* Metric
0700-2645	Alberta. Department of Energy and Natural Resources. Annual Report†
0700-2661	A Guide to National Associations, Service Organizations and Unions Operating in the Arts *see* 0832-865X
0700-284X	Coal in Canada, Supply and Demand *changed to* Statistical Review of Coal in Canada
0700-2866	Canada. Grains Council. Annual Report
0700-2971	Manitoba Statistical Review
0700-3048	Dialogue (Ottawa)
0700-3226	Korean Journal
0700-3269	Kodaly Institute of Canada. Notes *changed to* Kodaly Society of Canada. Notes
0700-3617	Overview
0700-365X	Estuaire
0700-3684	Manitoba Library Association. Newsline
0700-3722	Information-Status of Women†
0700-3749	Quebec (Province) Ministere des Terres et Forets. Conseil Consultatif des Reserves Ecologiques. Rapport Annuel *changed to* Quebec (Province). Conseil Consultatif sur les Reserves Ecologiques. Rapport Annuel
0700-3838	Music Research News
0700-3862	Labour
0700-3900	A l'Ecoute
0700-3986	U S Activities Report *changed to* U S A C Communique
0700-4192	Missions des Franciscans
0700-432X	Equipement et Methodes
0700-4400	International View†
0700-4532	Metropolitan Toronto Library Board. Annual Report
0700-463X	Intralogue†
0700-4745	Musicanada
0700-480X	Sources Directory
0700-4982	London Community Services Directory
0700-5008	Marquee
0700-5032	Angler and Hunter in Ontario *changed to* Angler and Hunter
0700-5040	Habitabec
0700-5105	Laurier Campus
0700-5156	Imperial Oil Review (1982)
0700-5199	Szamadas
0700-5202	Slavna Nadele
0700-5245	Conseil Canadien de Protection des Animaux, Ressource
0700-5296	Book Trade in Canada
0700-5318	Opus
0700-5350	World Literacy of Canada. Newsletter *see* 0820-6686
0700-5369	Literacy
0700-5482	Quest for a Common Denominator *see* 0702-7575
0700-5539	Canadian Business Service Investment Reporter
0700-558X	Eureka *see* 0705-0348
0700-5768	Aerospace Canada
0700-5989	Association of Ontario Land Surveyors. Annual Report
0700-6004	Reseau
0700-6365	Glenbow Foundation. Occasional Paper *see* 0072-467X
0700-6500	Notre Dame du Cap. Revue
0700-6802	Scarboro Missions
0700-7388	Boating News
0700-7426	Sphere
0700-8007	Purchasing Management Digest
0700-9070	Federation of C.P.T.A. Associations of Ontario. Newsletter
0700-9216	Canadian Electrical Engineering Journal
0700-9224	Applied Mathematics Notes
0700-9275	Sea Pen
0700-9283	Records of Early English Drama Newsletter
0700-9712	Community Information Service. Newsletter
0700-9771	A R C Arabic Journal
0700-9801	Journal of Psychology and Judaism
0700-9828	Canadian Red Cross Society. Manitoba Division. News and Views
0700-9844	Ontario Safety League. News *changed to* Safety Update
0700-9895	Outdoor Crest Newsletter *see* 0700-9909
0700-9909	Outdoor Crest
0700-9976	Gastown and Vancouver Today†
0700-9992	Upstream
0701-001X	Coach *see* 0705-7504
0701-0028	Gestion
0701-0184	Culture & Tradition
0701-0192	Posol
0701-0214	Draudzes Vestis
0701-0400	Connections Newsletter
0701-0419	Bookings†
0701-0524	University of Toronto. Centre of Criminology Library. Acquisitions List
0701-0605	Black Dial Directory
0701-0710	C I M Reporter
0701-0745	Grand Slam
0701-0788	Catholic Quote
0701-080X	Engineering Forum†
0701-0826	Periodical Writers Association. National Newsletter
0701-1008	Etudes Inuit Studies
0701-1024	Alberta Science Education Journal
0701-1156	About Women (Regina) *changed to* A. E. & M. Network
0701-1237	Alberta Teachers' Association. Religious Studies & Moral Education Council. Newsletter
0701-1245	Equipment Trader†
0701-130X	Curling News *see* 0701-1318
0701-1318	British Columbia Curling News
0701-1369	Wings Magazine of Canada *changed to* Wings Newsmagazine of Canada
0701-144X	County Magazine
0701-1539	Employee Benefit Costs in Canada
0701-1547	Action (Winnipeg)
0701-158X	Annals of Air and Space Law
0701-161X	Committee on Canadian Labour History. Journal†
0701-1687	Produits pour l'Industrie Quebecoise
0701-1733	Canadian Cases on the Law of Torts
0701-1776	Alberta Archaeological Review
0701-1784	Canadian Water Resources Journal
0701-1792	Journal of Ukrainian Graduate Studies *see* 0228-1635
0701-1865	Antenne
0701-1989	Revue 2
0701-2748	Periodics†
0701-4309	Canadian Council of Churches. Record of Proceedings
0701-4945	Phenomena†
0701-5208	National Research Council, Canada. Division of Building Research. Special Technical Publication
0701-5216	National Research Council, Canada. Division of Building Research. Building Practice Note
0701-5372	British Columbia. Department of Health. Annual Report *see* 0706-4810
0701-5488	Canada. Statistics Canada. Pension Plans in Canada/Regimes de Pensions au Canada
0701-5666	Quebec (Province) Regie de l'Assurance-Depots du Quebec. Rapport Annuel
0701-6557	Quebec (Province) Ministere de l'Agriculture. Rapport Annuel: Merite Agricole
0701-6786	Canada. Hydrographic Service. Activity Report
0701-6794	Study of Saskatchewan Collective Bargaining Agreements *see* 0830-0763
0701-6956	Prince Edward Island. Department of Community Affairs. Annual Report *changed to* Prince Edward Island. Department of Community and Cultural Affairs. Annual Report
0701-7243	Inter-National
0701-7391	Canada. Ministry of State for Science and Technology. Federal Science Programs *see* 0706-2206
0701-7502	Agricultural Real Estate Values in Alberta
0701-7758	Ontario Science Centre. Centre News *see* 0228-4642
0701-7928	Canada. Statistics Canada. Air Carrier Traffic at Canadian Airports
0701-7995	Neologie en Marche. Serie B. Langues de Specialites
0701-8002	Natural Life†
0701-8185	Hunter Training and Conservation. Instructor Newsletter†
0701-8533	Ontario Business News†
0701-8681	C I P S Review
0701-8746	Lutte Ouvriere *changed to* Combat Socialiste
0701-8878	Relatively Speaking
0701-8894	Dalhousie University. School of Library Service. Y-A Hotline
0701-8983	Canadian Industrial Health & Safety News *changed to* Canadian Occupational Health & Safety News
0701-9637	Environment Views
0701-9858	Ministry of Agriculture. Grape Production Guide *changed to* British Columbia. Ministry of Agriculture and Food. Grape Production Guide
0702-0007	Memorial University of Newfoundland. Occasional Papers in Biology
0702-0333	Canada-Japan, the Export-Import Picture

1586 ISSN INDEX

0702-0465 Canada. Statistics Canada. Quarterly Report on Energy Supply. Demand in Canada/Bulletin Trimestriel. Disponibilite et Ecoulement d'Energie au Canada
0702-0481 International Journal of Mini and Microcomputers
0702-0538 Ontario. Human Rights Commission. Annual Report
0702-0627 Monitor (Ottawa)†
0702-0759 Labour Directory (Victoria) *see* 0703-0878
0702-0996 Quebec (Province). Commission des Transports du Quebec. Rapport Annuel
0702-1003 B.C. Regular Baptist *changed to* B.C. Fellowship Baptist
0702-1437 Bakka Magazine†
0702-2735 Independent Forester†
0702-3138 Alberta Disaster Services News and Notes *changed to* Alberta Public Safety Services News & Notes
0702-3162 Canadian Coin News
0702-3855 Hrvatski Put
0702-4894 Wee Giant†
0702-5459 On-Site
0702-5785 In the Driver's Seat
0702-6005 Foreign Investment Review†
0702-634X Basilian Historical Bulletins†
0702-6587 Canada. Statistics Canada. Security Transactions with Non-Residents/ Operations avec des Non-Residents sur des Valeurs Mobilieres
0702-6633 Economic Council of Canada. Bulletin *see* 0226-224X
0702-6641 British Columbia. Ministry of Municipal Affairs. Municipal Statistics, Including Regional Districts
0702-6803 Magook
0702-6943 Quebec at a Glance†
0702-7001 Atlantic Issues†
0702-701X Ski Canada
0702-7060 Industrial Management
0702-7206 Municipal and Planning Law Reports
0702-7222 Progressive Conservative Party of Canada. Leader's Report
0702-732X N.S. Conservation
0702-7354 Alberta Square and Round Dance Federation. Newsletter†
0702-7524 Boating Business
0702-7532 New Literature and Ideology
0702-7575 Mamashee†
0702-7583 C S A Information Update
0702-7702 Alberta Transportation. Annual Report
0702-7818 Atlantis
0702-7842 Ontario. Ministere des Affaires Culturelles et des Lois de l'Ontario. Rapport Annuel
0702-7958 C.S.P. World News
0702-8075 B.C. Market News *changed to* Talking Business
0702-8083 Canada. Statistics Canada. Electrical Contracting Industry/Entrepreneurs d'Installations Electriques
0702-8091 Canada. Statistics Canada. Law Enforcement, Judicial and Correctional Statistics Service Bulletin/La Statistique Policiere, Judiciaire, et Correctionnelle, Bulletin de Service†
0702-8210 Ottawa Letter
0702-8318 Automotive Marketer
0702-8393 Fugue
0702-8431 McGill University, Montreal. Centre for Developing-Area Studies. Occasional Monograph Series
0702-844X End-Time News
0702-8458 Edmonton Revival Centre. News *see* 0702-844X
0702-8466 University of Ottawa. Psychiatric Journal
0702-8520 Dime Bag: Fiction Issue†
0702-8571 Revue Independantiste
0702-858X Monde des Loisirs
0702-8865 Alternate Routes
0702-8881 Sheep Canada
0702-9012 Music McGill
0702-9071 Canadian Rider
0702-9179 Moving to Toronto *see* 0713-8377
0702-9187 Moving to Vancouver/Victoria *see* 0226-7276
0702-9233 Jewish Historical Society of Canada. Journal *see* 0706-3547
0702-9284 Recreation Research Review
0702-9659 Alberta. Alberta Culture. Annual Report
0702-9829 Nova Scotia. Department of Labour and Manpower. Bulletin†
0702-987X Collective Agreement Settlements in Nova Scotia†
0702-9888 Selected Labour Statistics for Nova Scotia†
0703-0169 Saskatchewan. Department of Labour. Policy Planning & Research Division. Wage Adjustments in Collective Bargaining Agreements†
0703-0312 EnRoute
0703-0320 Canada Institute for Scientific and Technical Information. Annual Report
0703-0428 Urban History Review
0703-0606 New Brunswick Museum. Journal†
0703-0665 British Columbia. Ministry of Labour. Negotiated Working Conditions
0703-0827 Manitoba. Lotteries Commission. Annual Report *changed to* Manitoba Lotteries Foundation. Annual Report
0703-086X British Columbia. Energy Commission. Annual Report *changed to* British Columbia. Utilities Commission. Annual Report
0703-0878 B.C. Labour Directory†
0703-0940 Quebec (Province) Ministere des Richesses Naturelles. Rapport
0703-1157 Chem Thirteen News
0703-1319 Weekly Criminal Bulletin
0703-1440 Big Country Cariboo Magazine
0703-1459 Canadian Journal of Irish Studies
0703-1599 Canadiana Germanica
0703-1831 Cicada†
0703-184X Ukulele Yes!†
0703-1874 Europa: a Journal of Interdisciplinary Studies†
0703-1890 Bois Ouvre†
0703-1920 Conference Board of Canada. Survey of Business Attitudes and Investment Spending Intentions *see* 0827-6277
0703-2048 Saskatchewan Reporter†
0703-2226 Wage Changes in Collective Agreement Settlements in Nova Scotia†
0703-2633 Canada. Statistics Canada. Annual Report/Rapport Annuel
0703-2684 Canada. Statistics Canada. Historical Labour Force Statistics, Actual Data, Seasonal Factors, Seasonally Adjusted Data/Statistiques Chronologiques sur la Population Active, Chiffres Reels, Facteurs Saisonniers et Donnees Desaisonnalisees
0703-2749 Canada. Statistics Canada. Local Government Finance: Revenue and Expenditure, Assets and Liabilities, Actual/Finances Publiques Locales: Revenus et Depenses, Actif et Passif, Chiffres Reels
0703-3052 Studies in Music
0703-3060 British Columbia Law Reports (2nd Series)
0703-3117 Alberta Law Reports (2nd Series)
0703-3249 Canadian Conference on Information Science. Proceedings *see* 0380-9218
0703-4520 Forge
0703-4563 Review Ottawa†
0703-4598 Centre
0703-4660 National Museum of Natural Sciences. Natural History Notebook Series†
0703-4687 Real Property Reports
0703-4857 Canada. Statistics Canada. Farm Income and Prices Section. Farm Cash Receipts/Recettes Monetaires Agricoles†
0703-4873 Canada. Statistics Canada. Employment, Earnings and Hours. Seasonally-Adjusted Series/Emploi, Remunerations et Heures; Series Desaisonnalisees†
0703-489X Material History Bulletin
0703-5330 International Review of Slavic Linguistics
0703-5357 Atlantic Co-Operator
0703-5365 Postal History Society of Canada. Journal *see* 0714-8305
0703-5411 International Atlantic Salmon Foundation. Newsletter *see* 0225-7165
0703-5500 Victorian Studies Association of Western Canada. Newsletter
0703-5527 P C L A Newsletter
0703-5551 Business Law Reports
0703-5608 Aviation Quebec
0703-5624 C P H A Health Digest
0703-5640 Theatre Canada. Special Bulletin
0703-5748 Antiques and Art *changed to* Fine Art & Auction Review
0703-5764 Diabetes Dialogue
0703-5861 Canadians for a Democratic Workplace. Newsletter
0703-6078 Canada Council. Touring Office. Bulletin†
0703-6337 Revue d'Integration Europeenne
0703-6507 Dawson and Hind
0703-6523 Canada. Atmospheric Environment Service. Daily Soil Temperature Data/ Donnees Quotidiennes sur la Temperature du Sol
0703-654X Canada. Statistics Canada. Road Motor Vehicles-Fuel Sales/Vehicules Automobiles-Ventes de Carburants
0703-6566 New Brunswick. Department of Tourism. Annual Report
0703-6892 E & M Newsletter
0703-7007 Link (Mississauga)
0703-7090 R T A C Forum *see* 0826-8193
0703-7139 Possibles
0703-7228 Katimavik†
0703-7244 Canada. Statistics Canada. Cable Television/Teledistribution
0703-7252 Canada. Statistics Canada. Telecommunications Statistics/ Statistique des Telecommunications
0703-7295 Canada. Statistics Canada. Non-Residential General Building Contracting Industry/Industrie des Entreprises Generales en Construction Non Domiciliaire
0703-7333 Canada. Statistics Canada. Stocks of Frozen Meat Products/Stocks de Viandes Congelees
0703-7368 Canada. Statistics Canada. Family Incomes (Census Families) /Revenus des Famille (Familles de Recensement)
0703-7384 Corpus Administrative Index
0703-7406 Canada. Statistics Canada. Silver-Cobalt Mines and Silver-Lead-Zinc Mines/ Mines d'Argent-Cobalt et Mines d'Argent-Plomb-Zinc†
0703-766X A G M Reporter
0703-7732 Benefits Canada
0703-8240 International Journal of Women's Studies†
0703-8372 Canadian Association of Pathologists. Newsletter
0703-8763 Edmonton Area Series Report
0703-895X Canadian Token
0703-8968 Briarpatch
0703-8984 Electronics Today
0703-900X University of Western Ontario Law Review
0703-9018 Arab Review†
0703-9085 A I B C Forum†
0703-9115 Promises *see* 0831-0254
0703-9158 Dairy Goat Gazette and Lively Vivid Escapades *see* 0708-6164
0703-9328 Canada. Statistics Canada. Financial Statistics of Education/Statistiques Financieres de l'Education
0703-9409 New Brunswick Anglican
0703-9468 Artisan News *see* 0229-4435
0703-9476 Best Canadian Stories
0703-9484 Auxiliaire *changed to* Infirmiere Auxiliaire
0703-9492 Scientific Policy, Research and Development in Canada†
0703-9514 Furniture Production and Design Meubles *changed to* Furniture Production & Design
0703-9905 Marketing Voyages
0704-0059 Antiques *see* 0704-0067
0704-0067 Antique News (Toronto)†
0704-0288 Advocates Quarterly
0704-0407 Hospital Trustee
0704-0547 Silangan
0704-0598 N G R C Forum†
0704-061X Cineclube†
0704-0652 Maritimer
0704-0717 Canadian Workshop
0704-0733 Trot
0704-0857 Canadian Community Law Journal
0704-0873 Bulletin sur les Relations du Travail
0704-0970 New Brunswick. Forest Products Commission. Progress Report†
0704-1217 L A R U Studies
0704-1225 Canadian Journal of Family Law
0704-1349 Palliser Wheat Growers Association. Newsletter *changed to* Wheatgrower
0704-1543 Commission d'Energie du Nord Canadien. Revue de l'Exploitation *changed to* Northern Canada Power Commission. Annual Report
0704-1551 Northern Canada Power Commission. Annual Review *changed to* Northern Canada Power Commission. Annual Report
0704-173X Your Home†
0704-2582 Ontario. Geological Survey. Report *changed to* Ontario. Geological Survey. Geological Report
0704-2590 Ontario. Geological Survey. Study
0704-2671 Education Manitoba
0704-2701 Ocean Dumping Report†
0704-2728 Information C.B. *changed to* Actualites C B
0704-2752 Ontario. Geological Survey. Miscellaneous Paper
0704-2809 Ontario. Ministry of Natural Resources. Forest Research
0704-3015 Canada. Earth Physics Branch. Geomagnetic Series
0704-3139 Canada. Hydrographic Service. Annual Report *see* 0701-6786
0704-3147 Canada. Service Hydrographique. Rapport Annuel *see* 0701-6786
0704-3694 Canadian Industry Report of Fisheries and Aquatic Sciences
0704-3724 Canadian Occupational Safety & Health Law
0704-4062 E C O/L O G Information Services†
0704-4550 Gazette des Femmes
0704-4771 N A F O Meeting Proceedings†
0704-4798 N A F O Annual Report
0704-4836 Northern Development *see* 0824-4952
0704-4860 Hearsay, for Dalhousie Law Graduates *changed to* Hearsay
0704-5263 Perception
0704-5352 Voix Sepharade
0704-5387 Canada. Statistics Canada. Public Warehousing/Entreposage Public†
0704-5522 Concerned Canadian
0704-5646 Canadian Poetry (London, Ont.)
0704-5697 Y E R Monograph Series
0704-5700 Yeats Eliot Review
0704-576X National Museum of Natural Sciences. Syllogeus
0704-5824 Occasional
0704-5905 Targumic and Cognate Studies. Newsletter
0704-6138 A C M E Newsletter
0704-6286 Germination
0704-6359 L'Hospitalite
0704-6383 Image des Laurentides†
0704-6391 Canadian Firefighter
0704-6588 Crosscurrents
0704-6596 Canada. Statistics Canada. Elementary-Secondary School Enrollment/Effectifs des Ecoles Primaires et Secondaires

ISSN INDEX 1587

0704-6766 Construction Safety Journal
0704-6804 Airforce
0704-6839 Northern Titles: K W I C Index
0704-6936 Issues, Events & Ideas
0704-7002 Polyphony
0704-7223 Taxipresse
0704-7517 Apprentissage et Socialisation *see* 0827-1844
0704-7576 Grande Replique
0704-7584 International Development Research Centre. Annual Report
0704-7673 Canada. Northern Forestry Centre. Information Report
0704-769X Canada. Maritimes Forest Research Centre, Fredericton, New Brunswick. Information Report M-X *see* 0834-406X
0704-772X Forest Pest Management Institute. Information Report Series
0704-7886 Lundi
0704-7916 Arts Atlantic
0704-7924 Cahiers de Recherches en Sciences de la Religion†
0704-7940 Repertoire des Produits Fabriques au Quebec
0704-7975 Gardenland
0704-8017 Edmonton Chamber of Commerce. Commerce News
0704-8025 Reports on Separatism†
0704-8475 Virus Montreal
0704-8874 Labour Topics
0704-9056 Alberta Art Foundation. Annual Report
0704-9145 Alberta Genealogical Society. Surnames Register *changed to* Alberta Genealogical Society. Ancestor Index
0704-9153 Ovo Magazine
0704-9226 Halton Farm News
0704-9471 Hamilton-Burlington Month
0704-9528 Administrateur Hospitalier†
0704-9536 Film Edmonton
0704-9641 Ontario. Advisory Committee on Confederation. Report†
0704-9722 Canadian Journal of Criminology
0705-0038 Childrens Book News
0705-0348 Crux Mathematicorum
0705-0488 Australia. Bureau of Statistics. Pocket Year Book, Australia
0705-0496 Australia. Bureau of Statistics. Social Indicators
0705-0518 Australia. Bureau of Statistics. Overseas Trade, Australia, Part 1: Exports and Imports *changed to* Australia. Bureau of Statistics. Foreign Trade, Australia, Part 1: Exports and Imports
0705-0526 Australia. Bureau of Statistics. Foreign Trade, Australia. Part 2: Comparative and Summary Tables
0705-0534 Australia. Bureau of Statistics. Australian Exports, Country by Commodity
0705-0542 Australia. Bureau of Statistics. Australian Imports, Country by Commodity†
0705-0550 Australia. Bureau of Statistics. Commonwealth Government Finance
0705-0585 Decor a Coeur†
0705-064X Development Directions†
0705-0852 Journal de la Majorite *changed to* Quebec Etudiant
0705-0992 Adsum
0705-1026 Federation des Associations de Parents et Instituteurs Langues Francaise de l'Ontario. Liaison
0705-1093 Decoration Chez-Soi
0705-1123 Echo (Ottawa)
0705-114X Alberta Teachers' Association. Council on School Administration. Newsletter
0705-1166 I N D E C Communicator
0705-1212 S T O P Press
0705-1328 Journal of Canadian Poetry
0705-1360 All Canada Weekly Summaries - National
0705-1433 Canadian Footwear Journal
0705-1530 Canadian Stereo Guide *see* 0833-9570
0705-1727 Canadian Weightlifting Journal/Journal Candien d'Halterophilie *see* 0832-8196
0705-176X Canadian Wrestler
0705-1867 Vani
0705-1883 Books in Finnish
0705-1905 Saint John Today
0705-1913 Review of Architecture and Landscape Architecture
0705-1980 Shearwater Warrior *see* 0707-8056
0705-2006 Canadian Journal of Archaeology
0705-2030 Motorcycle Dealer and Trade
0705-2103 Committee for Justice and Liberty. Newsletter *see* 0824-2062
0705-212X Lawn & Garden Trade
0705-2146 Australia. Bureau of Statistics. Western Australian Office. Fisheries
0705-2162 Canadian Federation of Film Societies. Newsletter
0705-2294 Books in Dutch
0705-2316 Going On
0705-2332 Books in Danish
0705-2367 Coal Miner
0705-243X Quebec Yachting *changed to* Quebec Yachting Voile & Moteur
0705-2669 Manitoba Archaeological Quarterly
0705-288X Water Pollution Research in Canada *see* 0197-9140
0705-3002 Canadian Journal of Italian Studies
0705-3045 Eastern Ontario Construction Industry Directory and Purchasing Guide†
0705-3150 Wilderness Arts and Recreation
0705-3193 Canadian Controls & Instruments *changed to* Canadian Controls & Instrumentation (1983)
0705-3215 C'est pour Quand
0705-3355 Northwest Travel Guide - Alaska - Yukon *changed to* Northwest Travel Guide - Alaska - Yukon - British Columbia
0705-3371 Northwest Travel Guide - British Columbia *changed to* Northwest Travel Guide - Alaska - Yukon - British Columbia
0705-3428 Tam Ti Delam
0705-3436 Loisir et Societe
0705-3657 Canadian Journal of Communication
0705-369X Injured Athlete
0705-372X Directory of Social Services in the A.C.T.†
0705-3754 Crescent International
0705-3797 Episodes
0705-3851 Femmes d'Ici
0705-3878 Canadian Water Well
0705-3894 Free Throw†
0705-3932 Canadian Renewable Energy News *changed to* Renewable Energy News
0705-3983 University of Alberta. Agriculture and Forestry Bulletin
0705-4009 Music Magazine
0705-4157 Alumi-News
0705-4165 Incidences (1979)†
0705-4297 Canada. Statistics Canada. International Air Charter Statistics†
0705-4319 Canada. Statistics Canada. Control and Sale of Alcoholic Beverages in Canada/Controle et la Vente des Boissons Alcooliques au Canada
0705-4343 Canada. Statistics Canada. Air Passenger Origin and Destination. Canada-United States Report/Origine et Destination des Passagers Aeriens. Rapport sur le Trafic Canada-Etat Unis
0705-436X Canada. Statistics Canada. Coal Mines/Mines de Charbon
0705-4572 Chinook
0705-4580 Canadian Journal of Regional Science
0705-470X Ministry of Agriculture. Tree Fruit Production Guide *changed to* British Columbia. Ministry of Agriculture and Food. Tree Fruit
0705-470X New South Wales. Department of Agriculture. Soil Survey Bulletin
0705-4831 Nova Scotia Trappers Newsletter
0705-503X Canada. Great Lakes Forest Research Centre. Survey Bulletin *changed to* Canada. Great Lakes Forestry Centre. Survey Bulletin
0705-5064 Checklist of Canadian Theatres *see* 0226-5125
0705-5137 Canadian Report
0705-517X Ontario. Ministry of Labour. Library. Library Bulletin
0705-5196 C A N M E T Report
0705-520X Canada. Great Lakes Forest Research Centre. Forestry Research Newsletter *changed to* Canada. Great Lakes Forestry Centre. Forestry Newsletter
0705-5242 Canada. Statistics Canada. Report on Livestock Surveys: Cattle, Sheep/Rapport des Enquetes sur le Betail: Bovins, Moutons†
0705-5331 Canada: Official Handbook of Present Conditions and Recent Progress†
0705-548X Canadian Film Series
0705-5587 Canada Addictions Foundation. Directory
0705-5617 Coaching Review†
0705-5757 Ministry of Agriculture. Nursery Production Guide *changed to* British Columbia. Ministry of Agriculture and Food. Nursery Production Guide
0705-5765 Canada. Statistics Canada. Canadian Statistical Review. Annual Supplement to Section 1/Revue Statistique du Canada. Supplement Annuel de la Section 1.†
0705-5773 Australia. Bureau of Statistics. Tasmanian Office. Divorces Tasmania
0705-5838 Australian Geomechanics News
0705-5870 German Journal of Psychology
0705-5900 Atmosphere - Ocean
0705-5935 Gay Counselling
0705-596X Alberta. Office of the Superintendent of Insurance and Real Estate. Annual Report *see* 0229-7108
0705-6028 Canada. Advisory Council on the Status of Women. Annual Report
0705-6095 Sport and Recreation Index *see* 0882-553X
0705-6109 Misleading Advertising Bulletin
0705-6249 Directory of Canadian Orchestras and Youth Orchestras
0705-6257 Australia. Bureau of Statistics. Victorian Office. Estimated Population in Local Government Areas, Victoria *changed to* Australia. Bureau of Statistics. Victorian Office. Estimated Resident Population In Local Government Areas, Victoria
0705-6311 Physician's Management Manuals
0705-6494 Books in Hungarian
0705-6591 Canadian Society for the Prevention of Cruelty to Children. Journal *see* 0825-7531
0705-6605 Televiews†
0705-6672 Court Judgement Report
0705-6680 Canadian Perspective
0705-6702 Newfoundland Medical Association Journal†
0705-6931 Leadline†
0705-7091 Financial Post Survey of Energy Resources *see* 0227-1656
0705-7113 A J A S: Australian Journal of American Studies
0705-7156 Books in Spanish
0705-7172 Books in Arabic
0705-7199 Geographie Physique et Quaternaire
0705-7377 Criminal Law in New South Wales. Volume 1: Indictable Offences
0705-7385 Criminal Law in New South Wales. Volume 2: Summary Offences
0705-7423 University of Wollongong. Handbook for Undergraduates†
0705-7504 Canadian Soccer Association. Technical Manual
0705-7520 Gite
0705-7814 Wise Owl News (Toronto)†
0705-7822 Nayer Dor
0705-7830 Alberta Teachers' Association. Journal of Home Economics Education
0705-7970 Liban au Canada
0705-8063 Vandance
0705-8160 Directory of Courses/Tourism/Hospitality/Recreation
0705-8209 Books in Armenian
0705-825X Books in Urdu
0705-8292 Conseil de la Jeunesse Scientifique. Bottin
0705-8314 Guide du Camping
0705-8330 Canadian Business Economics†
0705-8373 Books in Hindi
0705-8454 A S T I S Current Awareness Bulletin
0705-856X Facts
0705-8594 Middle East Focus
0705-8616 Algonkian's *see* 0707-3143
0705-8748 Farm Gate
0705-8764 Great Barrier Reef Marine Park Authority Bulletin
0705-8799 Trade News North
0705-8802 British Columbia School Counsellors' Association. Newsletter
0705-8829 World Literacy of Canada, News and Views *see* 0820-6686
0705-887X City of Toronto Planning Board. City Planning *changed to* City of Toronto Planning and Development Department. City Planning
0705-8993 Marine Trades
0705-906X Western Grocer Magazine
0705-9094 Canadian Association for the Prevention of Crime. Bulletin/Societe Canadienne pour la Prevention du Crime. Bulletin *see* 0823-9436
0705-9191 Ryerson Rambler
0705-9213 Australian Road Research in Progress
0705-9272 Environment Systems and Industries *see* 0017-9418
0705-9698 British Columbia. Ministry of Labour. Annual Report
0706-0203 About Arts and Craft/Art et l'Artisanat *see* 0822-7217
0706-0262 Insight (Regina)
0706-0300 Bicycling News Canada†
0706-0661 Canadian Journal of Plant Pathology
0706-067X Canada. Statistics Canada. Road Motor Vehicles-Registrations/Vehicules Automobiles-Immatriculations
0706-0955 Northward Journal
0706-1005 Concordia University Magazine
0706-1021 Annuaire Franco-Ontarien
0706-1064 Book Times *see* 0705-0038
0706-1293 Canadian Nuclear Association. Annual International Conference. Summaries *changed to* Canadian Nuclear Association. Annual International Conference Proceedings
0706-1420 Alberta Electric Industry, Annual Statistics
0706-151X Input
0706-1706 Labour, Capital and Society
0706-1889 Writing
0706-1897 Passing Show†
0706-2168 Canadian Geographic
0706-2176 Western Australian Economic Review
0706-2206 Canada. Ministry of State for Science and Technology. Federal Science Activities†
0706-2249 Quebec (Province) Centrale des Bibliotheques. Choix: Documentation Imprimee
0706-2257 Quebec (Province) Centrale des Bibliotheques. Choix: Documentation Audiovisuelle
0706-2265 Quebec (Province) Centrale des Bibliotheques. Choix Jeunesse: Documentation Imprimee
0706-2273 Quebec (Province) Centrale des Bibliotheques. Choix Jeunesse: Documentation Audiovisuelle *see* 0706-2257
0706-2338 Directory of Canadian Universities
0706-2346 Canada. Hydrographic Service. Water Levels. Vol. 2: Tidal Highs and Lows
0706-2354 Canada. Hydrographic Service. Water Levels. Vol. 1: Daily Means
0706-2362 Photoworld Buyer's Guide. Cameras†
0706-2419 Parlure†

ISSN INDEX

ISSN	Title
0706-2451	Canada. Statistics Canada. Highway, Road, Street and Bridge Contracting Industry/Entrepreneurs de Grande Route, Chemin, rue et Pont
0706-246X	Institute of Man and Resources Reports†
0706-2788	Canada. Statistics Canada. Homicide Statistics/Statistique de l'Homicide see 0825-432X
0706-280X	Canadian Jewish Herald
0706-2893	British Columbia Police Journal†
0706-2907	School Library Association Newsletter see 0706-2915
0706-2915	School Library Newsletter
0706-2966	Canada. Statistics Canada. Annual Review of Science Statistics†
0706-3105	Canada. Statistics Canada. Road and Street Length and Financing/Voies Publiques, Longueur et Financement†
0706-3202	Australian Institute of Pharmacy Management Newsletter
0706-3253	Action (Hull, Que.)†
0706-3369	Alberta. Horticultural Research Center. Annual Report†
0706-3504	Australian Veterinary Association. Year Book
0706-3547	Canadian Jewish Historical Society Journal
0706-3601	B. C. Economic Development†
0706-3679	Canada. Statistics Canada. Education in Canada/Education au Canada
0706-3792	Manitoba. Municipal Employees Benefits Board. Annual Report
0706-3857	Fireweed
0706-3962	Transpo
0706-4063	Monthly Record, Meteorological Observations in Eastern Canada/Resume Mensuel des Donnees Meteorologiques pour le Canada Oriental changed to Monthly Record, Meteorological Observations in Canada
0706-4071	Monthly Record, Meteorological Observations in Western Canada/Resume Mensuel des Donnees Meteorologiques pour le Canada Occidental changed to Monthly Record, Meteorological Observations in Canada
0706-408X	Monthly Record, Meteorological Observation in Northern Canada/Resume Mensuel des Donnees Meteorologiques pour le Canada Septentrional changed to Monthly Record, Meteorological Observations in Canada
0706-4152	C C I Technical Bulletins
0706-4284	Physio-Quebec
0706-4306	Ministry of Agriculture. Berry Production Guide changed to British Columbia. Ministry of Agriculture and Food. Berry Production Guide
0706-4403	Prince Edward Island. Department of Municipal Affairs. Annual Report†
0706-4551	Ontario. Geological Survey. Mineral Deposits Circular
0706-4810	British Columbia. Ministry of Health. Annual Report
0706-4845	Canadian Journal of Anthropology†
0706-4926	Saskatchewan. Department of Labour. Wages and Working Conditions by Occupation
0706-5000	College Media Director Newsletter
0706-5019	Occupational Health and Safety Law
0706-5043	Occupational Health and Safety Topics
0706-506X	Automotive Review
0706-5086	N F A Journal
0706-5132	Diver Magazine
0706-5159	British Columbia Housing Quarterly†
0706-5213	Highlights of Agricultural Research in Ontario
0706-5264	Producteur Agricole
0706-5302	Vancouver Gastronomic
0706-5310	Calgary Gastronomic†
0706-5337	Chaos
0706-5388	Carswell's Practice Cases
0706-5426	British Columbia. Human Rights Commission. Annual Report changed to Human Rights Act of British Columbia
0706-5469	E C S Newsletter†
0706-5531	Nicola Valley Archives Association Newsletter changed to Nicola Valley Archives Association. Historical Quarterly
0706-5582	Canadian Journal of Life Insurance
0706-5590	Mission Magazine changed to Mandate "Special"
0706-5604	Thalia
0706-5639	Debacle†
0706-5655	Estates & Trusts Reports
0706-568X	National Research Council, Canada. Division of Electrical Engineering. Bulletin
0706-585X	Ravings†
0706-5965	University of Western Ontario. Computing Centre Newsletter†
0706-6007	Canada. Treasury Board Secretariat. Federal Expenditure Plan changed to Canada. Treasury Board Secretariat. Estimates. Part I: Government Expenditures Plan
0706-6031	Law and Accounting Practice Management Manual†
0706-6449	Journal of Studies in the Bhagavadgita
0706-6457	Canadian Technical Report of Fisheries and Aquatic Sciences
0706-6473	Canadian Manuscript Report of Fisheries and Aquatic Sciences
0706-6481	Canadian Special Publication of Fisheries and Aquatic Sciences
0706-6503	Canadian Bulletin of Fisheries and Aquatic Sciences
0706-652X	Canadian Journal of Fisheries and Aquatic Sciences
0706-666X	Directory of the Australian Gas Industry see 0727-3541
0706-6678	Australian Music Directory
0706-6902	Australian Video and Communications changed to What's on Video and Cinema
0706-6910	Atlantic Provinces Linguistic Association Journal
0706-7054	Earthcare Information Centre. Newsletter
0706-7372	En Avant†
0706-7402	Echo des Cantons
0706-7410	SonEcran
0706-7437	Canadian Journal of Psychiatry
0706-7534	Footwear Forum
0706-7623	Canadian Bluegrass Review
0706-7658	Transit Fact Book & Membership Directory see 0821-2996
0706-7666	Family Law Reports
0706-7682	Great Expeditions
0706-7747	Forest Times
0706-7798	Manitoba. Public Library Services. Newsletter
0706-7852	Benefits for Saskatchewan Industry from Resource Development
0706-7860	Direction (Regina)†
0706-7909	Canada & Arab World
0706-7917	Arab Directory
0706-795X	Livres et des Jeunes
0706-8018	Contact (Willowdale, Ont.)
0706-8042	Animals Canada
0706-8069	Canadian Churchman and Crosstalk changed to Crosstalk
0706-8085	Reaching the Manitoba Market
0706-8093	From an Island see 0826-5909
0706-8204	Canadian Women's Studies see 0713-3235
0706-8328	Annuaire de l'Eglise du Quebec
0706-8441	Labour History†
0706-8662	What's New in Publications
0706-8913	Council for Exceptional Children, Manitoba Branch. Magazine
0706-8921	NorAct
0706-8956	Dunhill Insurance Law Report changed to Dunhill Personal Injury Awards Annotator
0706-8964	Dunhill Liability Loss Report
0706-9006	Stoney Monday
0706-9014	Borealis†
0706-9278	Canadian Emergency Services News
0706-9391	Saskatchewan Research Council. Physics Division. Annual Climatic Summary changed to Saskatchewan Research Council. Climatological Reference Station. Annual Summary
0706-9758	Canadian Student Traveller
0706-9820	Unican†
0706-9839	Alberta Teachers' Association. Members' Handbook
0706-9847	University of Manitoba Alumni Journal
0706-9928	Apostolat
0707-0047	Directory of Lifestyle Change Services†
0707-0152	Saskatchewan. Prescription Drug Plan. Annual Report
0707-0195	Provincial Council of Women of British Columbia. Newsletter†
0707-0349	National P C President
0707-0365	Saskatchewan Motor Transport Guide changed to Saskatchewan Trucking-Ship by Truck Directory
0707-0462	British Columbia. Medical Services Plan. Physician's Newsletter changed to British Columbia. Medical Services Plan. Practitioners' Newsletter
0707-0780	Heritage Seekers
0707-090X	Copper Toadstool
0707-0926	Open Interest†
0707-0934	M S Ontario
0707-0942	Directory of Co-Operative Naturalists' Projects in Ontario.
0707-1000	Energy and Natural Resources Library Journals†
0707-1027	Of Steam and Stone changed to Steam and Stone
0707-1434	Alberta. Health and Social Services Disciplines Committee. Annual Report
0707-1442	Ontario Tourism News
0707-1868	Pentecostal Assemblies of Canada. Cell Pak see 0832-9354
0707-1922	Probe Post
0707-1949	Business & Government News†
0707-1965	Maintenance Management see 0710-362X
0707-2031	Videorecordings Available in the Public Libraries of Metropolitan Toronto†
0707-2279	Worldwind
0707-2287	Eidos
0707-2392	Common Cents Magazine†
0707-2422	Geosciences in Canada
0707-2430	Aspects of the Geosciences in Canada see 0707-2422
0707-2511	Vie Pedagogique
0707-2554	Highland Heritage
0707-2562	Saskatchewan Mineral Resources. Petroleum and Natural Gas Reservoir Annual changed to Saskatchewan Energy & Mines. Petroleum and Natural Gas Reservoir Annual
0707-2570	Saskatchewan. Department of Mineral Resources. Statistical Yearbook changed to Saskatchewan Energy and Mines. Mineral Statistics Yearbook
0707-2783	Alberta. Fish and Wildlife Division. Fisheries Pollution Report
0707-2791	Alberta. Fish and Wildlife Division. Pollution Report see 0707-2783
0707-2899	Economics in Canadian Schools
0707-2937	Monthly Collector
0707-2945	Canadian Muslim
0707-2996	Canada. Geological Survey. Index of Publications of the Geological Survey of Canada
0707-3062	C E C Newsletter
0707-3135	Microlog Index
0707-3143	Ontario Indian
0707-3151	Algoma Outdoors
0707-3178	Ontario Out of Doors
0707-3186	Runner
0707-3232	Canadian Genealogist
0707-3240	B.C. Runner
0707-3291	B C I T: The Career Campus changed to B C I T Annual Report
0707-3356	Bottin des Organismes Franco-Ontariens see 0706-1021
0707-3364	Northland Today
0707-3372	Arab News of Toronto
0707-3380	Asian Tribune
0707-3542	Rollcall
0707-3739	British Columbia. Ministry of the Environment. Northeast Coal Study Preliminary Environmental Report
0707-3747	C O N S E R Microfiche
0707-3836	Hilborn Family Journal
0707-3844	Canadian Association of Geographers. Directory
0707-3887	Natural History Contributions
0707-4409	Calgary Magazine
0707-4611	Chickadee
0707-4808	Canadian Agricultural Economics Society. Proceedings of the Workshop changed to Canadian Agricultural Economics and Farm Management Society. Proceedings of the Workshop
0707-4875	Current Law Notes see 0707-4883
0707-4883	Current Law Newsletter†
0707-4891	Aikamme
0707-5006	Log Home Guide for Builders and Buyers
0707-5014	British Columbia Motor Transport Directory
0707-5065	Socialist Albania
0707-5103	Con Brio
0707-5324	Lusitano
0707-5332	International History Review
0707-5405	Newfoundland and Labrador Recreation Advisory Council for Special Groups. Newsletter†
0707-5456	Directory of Canadian Plays and Playwrights changed to Playwrights Union of Canada Catalogue of Canadian Plays
0707-5553	Canadian Distributor & Retailer†
0707-5588	Ascent (Toronto)†
0707-5723	Analysis
0707-5766	Current Economic and Industrial Relations Indicators
0707-5987	Cancer Comment see 0707-5995
0707-5995	Canadian Cancer Society, Manitoba Division. Communique
0707-6894	Southeast Regional Library (Sask.) Library Directory
0707-7106	Swamp Gas Journal
0707-7114	B.C. Agent
0707-7130	Connections (Pointe Claire)
0707-7165	Envol
0707-7300	CanAsian Multicultural Scene
0707-7327	Alberta Council of College Librarians. Newsletter see 0829-4321
0707-7351	Management Consulting Institute. Bulletin†
0707-7459	Igalaaq
0707-7629	Canadian Locations of Journals Indexed for Medicine
0707-7718	Canada. Parks Canada. (Western Region). Library Information Bulletin
0707-7793	Agricultural Science Bulletin
0707-7807	Journal of Practical Approaches to Developmental Handicap
0707-7904	Dairy Industry Research Report
0707-7920	Confluent Education Newsletter changed to M A C E Newsletter
0707-7955	Canadian Association of University Research Administrators. Research Bulletin
0707-8013	Ingot
0707-8021	Point de Mire
0707-803X	Outwest Magazine
0707-8048	Canadian Federation for the Humanities. Bulletin
0707-8056	Warrior
0707-8064	Calgary Commerce
0707-820X	Blackwell Newsletter
0707-8412	Resources for Feminist Research
0707-8552	Studies in Political Economy. Socialist Review.
0707-8897	Kaleidoscope Canada
0707-9087	Teaching of Adults Series†

ISSN INDEX 1589

ISSN	Title
0707-9184	Snowmobile Accidents, Manitoba
0707-9559	Canada. Statistics Canada. Private and Public Investment in Canada, Mid-Year Review/Investissements Prives et Publics au Canada. Revue de la Mi-Annee *see* 0823-0668
0707-9664	Astro-Directory News
0707-9680	Canadian Library Handbook *see* 0827-3715
0707-9699	Revue Internationale d'Action Communautaire
0707-9753	Canada. Statistics Canada. Telephone Statistics
0707-9788	Monthly Summary Report of Saskatchewan Minerals†
0707-9834	Nova Scotia. Commission on Drug Dependency. Annual Report
0707-9850	Canada. Environment Canada. Land
0707-994X	Alberta Authors Bulletin *changed to* Alberta Film & Literary Arts Bulletin
0708-0131	Conseil de Presse du Quebec. Rapport Annuel
0708-0263	At a Glance
0708-028X	Saskatchewan Rail Committee. News Bulletin *changed to* Transport 2000 Canada. News Bulletin
0708-0719	B.C. Technologist†
0708-0727	Canadian Shipping Project Newsletter *changed to* Maritime History Group Newsletter
0708-0743	Recreation Saskatchewan *see* 0821-0160
0708-076X	International Sivananda Yoga Life and Yoga Vacations *changed to* Yoga Life
0708-0840	B.C. News *see* 0708-0859
0708-0859	B.C. Peace News
0708-1006	Physioquebec
0708-1073	Construction Sightlines
0708-1332	Export Canada
0708-1375	New Brunswick Construction Products Directory *changed to* New Brunswick Construction Directory
0708-1936	Bio-Joule Newsletter *changed to* Bio-Joule Magazine
0708-1987	Etape
0708-2061	Ontario. Geological Survey. Aggregate Resources Inventory Paper
0708-2169	Hiballer Forest Magazine
0708-2177	Restoration
0708-2193	Directory of University Correspondence Courses *changed to* Canadian University Distance Education Directory
0708-2398	Etudes Creoles
0708-2495	36 Manieres†
0708-2533	Devindex†
0708-2673	Alberta Health Education Programs†
0708-2762	Canada. Statistics Canada. Radio Broadcasting†
0708-2770	S A A Bulletin
0708-2800	S A A Newsletter *see* 0708-2770
0708-3017	Alberta. Agricultural Processing Branch. Processing & Manufacturing Guide
0708-3025	Agricultural Processing and Manufacturing Guide *see* 0708-3017
0708-3041	Small Business News
0708-3106	Alberta. Department of Education. Early Childhood Services Program Highlights
0708-3165	Canadian Criminology Forum
0708-319X	Etienne Gilson Series
0708-3629	Nova Scotia Fisherman†
0708-3637	New Brunswick. Department of Social Services. Quarterly Statistical Bulletin†
0708-3793	Spectrum†
0708-3882	Saskatchewan. Department of Social Welfare. Annual Report *changed to* Saskatchewan. Department of Social Services. Annual Report
0708-3963	Consumer Bulletin/Bulletin aux Consommateurs *see* 0821-3747
0708-4226	Canada's Atlantic Folklore and Folklife Series
0708-4331	High Flight
0708-4366	E P & T
0708-448X	Datum†
0708-4625	Free! the Newsletter of Free Materials and Services
0708-4924	Flare
0708-501X	Pulp & Paper Canada Directory
0708-5052	Baha'i Studies
0708-5206	Agricultural Development Corporation of Saskatchewan. Annual Report
0708-5397	C I P Forum†
0708-5435	Photo Communique
0708-5591	Canadian Psychology
0708-6024	Sales & Marketing Management in Canada
0708-6113	Directory of Sports, Recreation and Physical Education
0708-6164	Dairy Goat Gazette
0708-6172	Forintek Canada Corp., Western Laboratory. Technical Reports†
0708-6180	About Women (Winnipeg)
0708-6431	Les Cahiers Nicoletains
0708-6474	C O N A Journal
0708-6954	British Columbia. Provincial Archaeologist's Office. Annual Report *changed to* British Columbia. Heritage Conservation Branch. Annual Research Report
0708-7012	Canada. Statistics Canada. Estimates of Population for Canada and the Provinces/Estimations de la Population du Canada et des Provinces†
0708-7632	Temps de Vivre
0708-8302	Alberta English Language Arts Council Newsletter *see* 0832-8315
0708-9031	Canada. Department of National Revenue. Excise News/Nouvelles de l'Accise
0708-9066	Ex Libris†
0708-918X	Planetary Association for Clean Energy. Newsletter
0708-9422	Connexions
0708-949X	Indo Canadian Times
0708-9511	Federation of Canadian Municipalities. Annual Conference Proceedings†
0708-9619	Intercultural Education Council. Newsletter *see* 0829-9137
0708-9635	Canadian Musician
0709-003X	Business Journal *changed to* Metropolitan Toronto Business Journal
0709-0412	Government of Canada Publications Quarterly Catalogue
0709-0471	Copie Zero
0709-0528	Alberta Teachers' Association. Industrial Education Council. News & Notes
0709-0536	Serials Holdings in Newfoundland Libraries
0709-0579	Money Reporter
0709-0706	Children's Aid Society of Ottawa. Information Bulletin *see* 0705-1123
0709-082X	Nuclear Free Press†
0709-1141	Background
0709-1370	National
0709-1532	Western Sportsman
0709-2016	Le Temps
0709-2334	Dimensions (Montreal)
0709-2431	Alberta Construction
0709-2563	Pulp & Paper Canada's Annual & Directory
0709-2652	Arctic Seas†
0709-2679	Coup d'Oeil sur le Saguenay-Lac-Saint-Jean
0709-325X	Saskatchewan FarmStart Corporation. Annual Report *changed to* Agricultural Credit Corporation of Saskatchewan. Annual Report
0709-3373	Poetry Canada Review
0709-3519	Journal of Comparative Sociology & Religion
0709-3756	Bibliographical Society of Canada. Bulletin
0709-3845	Le Communiste
0709-4035	Wot
0709-4272	Pyramid
0709-4434	A-V Canada
0709-4515	Survey of Wage Rates from Collective Agreement Settlements in Nova Scotia†
0709-4671	Ontario. Geological Survey. Northern Ontario Engineering Geology Terrain Study
0709-4698	Victorian Periodicals Review
0709-4779	Canada. Statistics Canada. International Vessel Statistics *see* 0714-1955
0709-5112	Eclipse†
0709-5341	Motor Vehicle Reports
0709-5368	Transpotech†
0709-549X	Ultimate Reality and Meaning
0709-5562	Historic Guelph
0709-5600	Supreme Court of Canada Decisions. Civil and Criminal
0709-616X	Salt
0709-6941	Participation
0709-7115	Select Home Designs: Cottage Country†
0709-7123	Select Home Designs: Home Design and Decor *see* 0713-8075
0709-7727	Creative Source
0709-7751	Language and Society
0709-776X	B.C. Sea Angling Guide†
0709-7778	B.C. Fresh Water Fishing Guide†
0709-8006	F A P U Q Nouvelles Universitaires
0709-8383	British Columbia. Ministry of Education. Annual Report
0709-8413	Art Gallery of Ontario. The Gallery *see* 0829-4437
0709-8502	Annales de Biochimie Clinique du Quebec
0709-8987	University of Toronto. Library Automation Systems. New Publications Awareness List†
0709-9010	Indian Book Review Digest
0709-9177	Hibou
0709-9762	Canada: Travel Information
0709-9797	Broadcast Technology
0709-9959	Canada. Northern Forestry Centre. Forestry Report
0710-0167	Revue Quebecoise de Linguistique
0710-0353	Canadian University Music Review
0710-0469	Pappus
0710-0477	C G S News *changed to* Geotechnical News
0710-068X	Cross-Cultural Psychology Bulletin
0710-0841	Windsor Yearbook of Access to Justice
0710-0868	Universite de Sherbrooke. Department de Geographie. Bulletin de Recherche
0710-1023	Canada. Statistics Canada. Provincial Government Finance: Assets, Liabilities, Source and Application of Funds
0710-1244	Hands Magazine
0710-1457	Phoenix Rising
0710-1481	Canadian Journal of Native Education
0710-1511	Personal Financial Planning Letter
0710-1678	Time Out†
0710-2259	C C T A Communique
0710-2852	M.G.S. News *see* 0226-6105
0710-300X	Magazine C E Q *see* 0823-5651
0710-3360	Northwest Travel Guide - Northwest Territories†
0710-3441	Commodity and Currency Reporter *changed to* Personal Wealth Reporter
0710-362X	P E M: Plant Engineering & Maintenance
0710-362X	P E M: Plant Engineering and Maintenance Sourcebook
0710-3697	Glenbow
0710-4251	Canada. Petawawa National Forestry Institute. Program Review
0710-4340	Canadian Journal of Educational Communication
0710-5118	Communiqu'elles
0710-538X	Ombudsman Journal
0710-6076	Rock Express
0710-622X	Canadian Oil & Gas Handbook
0710-6629	Who's Who in Canadian Law
0710-6874	Alberta Energy Resource Industries. Monthly Statistics
0710-8575	Canadian Recycling Market†
0710-8702	Great Lakes Science Advisory Board. Annual Report
0710-8974	Resource Technology *see* 0824-4952
0710-9326	Canadian R V Dealer
0710-9628	Key to Kingston
0710-9911	Equinox
0711-0049	Quarterly Report on Transportation *changed to* Transportation Business
0711-026X	Revue Jonathan
0711-0782	Canada. Department of Fisheries and Oceans. Annual Report
0711-0855	Focus on Great Lakes Water Quality *changed to* Focus on International Joint Commission Activities
0711-1150	Maritime Sediments and Atlantic Geology
0711-1215	Yukon Water Studies†
0711-124X	Badminton Canada
0711-2521	Alberta Teachers' Association. Math Monograph
0711-2866	Canada. National Museums of Canada. Annual Bulletin
0711-3048	Choosing Life†
0711-3226	Score
0711-3277	Mining Review
0711-3560	Ordre des Comptables Agrees du Quebec. Journal *see* 0828-6833
0711-3765	Dismantler
0711-382X	Algonquian and Iroquoian Linguistics
0711-4370	Cannon
0711-4818	Cahiers des Arts Visuels au Quebec
0711-5210	Moving to Los Angeles & Orange Counties†
0711-5229	Moving to Greater San Diego†
0711-5342	Nexus
0711-5377	Canadian Leader
0711-5539	Oldtimers' Sports News *changed to* Oldtimers' Hockey News
0711-5601	Corpus Agribusiness Report†
0711-561X	Corpus Plastics Report†
0711-5652	Highlights *changed to* Hospital Highlights (Year)
0711-5784	Energy Pricing News
0711-642X	Radio Guide
0711-6454	Snow Goer
0711-6659	Canadian Acoustics
0711-6683	S I M Now
0711-6780	Environments
0711-6829	Alliance
0711-7051	Academic and Administrative Officers at Canadian Universities
0711-7108	Globehopper Magazine
0711-7388	Human: Life Issues for Canadians†
0711-7485	Herizons
0711-7914	Videomania
0711-818X	Canada. Livestock Feed Board of Canada. Annual Report†
0711-8244	British Columbia Export/Import Opportunities
0711-8309	Ministry of Agriculture. Greenhouse-Cucumber and Tomato Production Guide *changed to* British Columbia. Ministry of Agriculture and Food. Greenhouse-Cucumber and Tomato Production Guide
0711-8422	Manitoba. Environmental Council. Topics
0711-849X	Canada. Labour Relations Board. Annual Report
0711-8635	Canadian Directory of Awards for Graduate Study
0712-1318	Pundit
0712-1326	Now
0712-1539	Strike!
0712-2349	Export U.S.A.
0712-3094	Tallyboard
0712-3183	N A C Memo *see* 0831-3377
0712-435X	Science Express X
0712-4384	Literary Markets
0712-4481	R R S P *changed to* Retirement Security Reporter
0712-4635	E D U Q
0712-4767	Renaissance Universal Journal
0712-4813	Spectroscopy: an International Journal
0712-6115	LibSat
0712-6506	Health Management Forum
0712-6662	Canada Tax Letter
0712-7243	Resource-Mag
0712-7456	Training Resources Tourism/Hospitality/Recreation
0712-7561	Etudes Strategiques et Militaires (Collection)

0712-7685 Integrity International
0712-8231 Quebec (Province). Regie des Rentes du Quebec. Statistical Outlook
0712-8487 Videotex Canada *see* 0823-8294
0712-8657 Teoros
0712-8762 Canada. Statistics Canada. System of National Accounts, Provincial Gross Domestic Product by Industry†
0712-9343 Alberta Insurance Directory
0712-9467 Technology Today
0712-9939 Technical University of Nova Scotia. Newsletter†
0713-0376 Canadian Export Association. Export Digest Bulletin
0713-0406 Conference Board of Canada. Quarterly Canadian Forecast *see* 0829-8416
0713-3235 Canadian Woman Studies
0713-3286 Canadian Money Saver
0713-3545 Gamut
0713-357X Canadian Institute of Chartered Accountants. Uniform Final Examination Report
0713-4118 Jeux et Jouets
0713-4517 Canadian Police Chief Newsletter
0713-4819 Moving to Denver
0713-5424 Graphics Interface. Proceedings/ Comptes Rendus
0713-5807 Pulp & Paper Journal
0713-6315 Antique Showcase
0713-7907 Weekly Digest of Family Law
0713-7931 Bank of Canada. Technical Reports
0713-7958 Revue de l'Histoire du Quebec et du Canada Francais
0713-8075 Select Homes
0713-8369 Moving to & Around Alberta
0713-8377 Moving to and Around Toronto & Area
0713-8776 Manitoba Ship by Truck Directory
0713-8865 British Columbia Weekly Law Digest
0713-892X Alberta Weekly Law Digest
0714-0339 Ethos
0714-0983 Canada. National Museums, Ottawa: Publications in Natural Science
0714-1181 Canada. Northern Forestry Centre. Forest Management Note
0714-1734 Forest Pest Management Institute Newsletter
0714-1955 Canada. Statistics Canada. International Seaborne Shipping Statistics†
0714-2870 Inkstone
0714-3508 Toronto South Asian Review
0714-3672 Nova Scotia Genealogist
0714-4210 Small Business
0714-4369 Reggae
0714-5896 Living Safety
0714-5918 Resources
0714-6116 Sel & Poivre
0714-6140 Revue Canadienne de Biologie et Biologie Experimentale *changed to* Experimental Biologie
0714-7023 Directory of Museums, Art Galleries and Archives of British Columbia
0714-7074 C N S Bulletin
0714-7295 Moving to San Fransisco and the Bay Area *changed to* Moving to the San Francisco Bay and Greater Sacramento
0714-7503 Work Abroad
0714-7511 Canadian Journal of Biochemistry and Cell Biology/Revue Canadien de Biochimie et Biologie Cellulaire *see* 0829-8211
0714-7724 Canadian Catholic Review
0714-816X Explore
0714-8305 P H S C Journal
0714-8550 Connections Journal (Edmonton)
0714-8992 Insight on Collectables
0714-900X Infoage†
0714-9670 C E C M Bulletin d'Information
0714-9808 Canadian Journal on Aging
0715-1489 Landmarks
0715-3155 Alberta, Saskatchewan, Manitoba - Criminal Conviction Cases
0715-3759 Briefly Speaking
0715-4623 Teaching Electronics and Computing *see* 0823-9940
0715-4798 British Columbia Decisions - Statute Citator
0715-5689 City & Country Home
0715-5808 British Columbia Decisions - Labour Relations Board Decisions
0715-5948 Hi-Rise
0715-6626 Studio Magazine
0715-7045 Currents
0715-7053 Moving to & Around Winnipeg & Manitoba
0715-7320 Thought for Food Newsletter†
0715-755X Touring Artists' Directory of the Performing Arts in Canada (Year)
0715-7657 Statistics on Alcohol and Drug Use in Canada and Other Countries
0715-7983 Northern Decisions
0715-8114 Moving to & Around Southwestern Ontario
0715-8602 Journal: News of the Blood Programme in Canada
0715-8610 Rubicon
0715-8726 Vox Benedictina
0715-8947 Pets Magazine
0715-9684 Psychotropes
0716-0003 C E N I D Notas Informativas†
0716-0046 Cuadernos de Economia
0716-0062 Mensaje
0716-0151 Resumenes Analiticos en Educacion
0716-0194 Carta Geologica de Chile
0716-0208 Revista Geologica de Chile
0716-0224 Museo Nacional de Historia Natural. Publicacion Ocasional
0716-0240 Estudios Internacionales
0716-0321 Estudios Sociales
0716-0348 Apuntes de Ingenieria
0716-0356 Trilogia
0716-0364 Informaciones Geograficas
0716-0496 Cuadernos de Educacion
0716-050X Estudios Pedagogicos
0716-0526 Academia (Santiago)
0716-0631 C I E P L A N Coleccion Estudios
0716-0720 Parasitologia al Dia
0716-0909 Acta Literaria
0716-1042 Mineria Chilena
0716-1069 Revista Investigaciones Marinas
0716-1115 Estudios Publicos
0716-1123 Centro de Estudios Publicos. Documento de Trabajo
0716-1468 Estudios Norteamericanos
0716-1484 Dimension Historica de Chile
0716-176X Chile. Direccion de Bibliotecas Archivos y Museos. Bibliografia Chilena
0716-1832 Cuadernos de Historia
0716-1840 Atenea (1984)
0716-2405 Indicadores de Comercio Exterior
0716-2448 Banco Central de Chile, Santiago. Memoria Anual
0716-2642 Revista Trabajo Social
0716-3460 Hoy
0720-0056 Bruckmanns Pantheon
0720-0218 Stadtansichten
0720-0447 Forum Kritische Psychologie
0720-0463 Rind und Schlegel
0720-048X European Journal of Radiology
0720-0501 Computertomographie Sonographie und Andere Neue Bilddiagnostische Methoden *see* 0724-7591
0720-0730 Herz und Gefaesse
0720-0773 Seawater and Desalting
0720-0986 Sugia
0720-0994 Balkan-Archiv Neue Folge Beiheft
0720-101X Elektronik-Applikation†
0720-1028 Apotheker Journal
0720-1168 Hispanorama
0720-1214 Qualitaet und Zuverlaessigkeit *changed to* Q Z Qualitaet und Zuverlaessigkeit
0720-1249 Dragoco Report: Flavoring Information Service
0720-1281 Schwaedds
0720-1605 Strafenverteidiger
0720-1842 Zoophysiology
0720-213X Zoomorphology
0720-2245 Phila-Report
0720-2520 Gauke's Jahrbuch
0720-2849 Alles fuer die Katz
0720-3098 Allmende
0720-3322 Radiologie
0720-3373 Krankenhaus-Hygiene & Infektionsverhuetung
0720-3438 Waermetechnik
0720-3489 Aerzteblatt Baden-Wuerttemberg
0720-3551 Aktion Jugendschutz. Informationen
0720-3683 Welthandel
0720-3705 Naturwissenschaftlicher Verein fuer Schwaben. Berichte
0720-3896 Ballett-Journal/das Tanzarchiv
0720-390X Rheuma
0720-3926 Wind-Energie
0720-3977 Krankenhaus Technik
0720-4280 Pharmacopsychiatria *see* 0176-3679
0720-4299 Fortschritte der Neurologie - Psychiatrie *changed to* Fortschritte der Neurologie, Psychiatrie
0720-4442 M C
0720-4507 Busverkehr
0720-4523 Jaeger
0720-454X Geooekodynamik
0720-4612 V D I Informationsdienst. Drahtherstellung u. Drahterzeugnisse
0720-4868 Ostseejahrbuch
0720-5104 Reiten und Fahren
0720-5775 Rhetoric†
0720-5953 Konstruktion
0720-597X Made in Europe - Medical Equipment and Supply Guide
0720-5988 Mexicon
0720-6259 Pastoraltheologie - Monatsschrift fuer Wissenschaft und Praxis in Kirche und Gesellschaft
0720-6542 Niespulver
0720-6593 T Z Tapetenzeitung
0720-6615 Journal of the Nepal Research Centre
0720-6666 Jidische Schtudies
0720-6763 A B I Technik
0720-678X Springer Series in Information Sciences
0720-728X Mathematische Semesterberichte
0720-7301 Hochzeit
0720-8243 Disaster Medicine†
0720-8642 Log In
0720-8782 Ibykus
0720-8863 Geology of Petroleum
0720-9061 Aegypten und Altes Testament
0720-9118 Arbeitshilfen fuer die Erwachsenenbildung
0720-9258 Impressum
0720-9282 Karpatenland
0720-9355 Haemostaseologie
0720-941X Henkel Referate
0720-9738 Bremer Beitraege zur Geographie und Raumplanung
0720-9746 Universitaet Bremen - Schwerpunkt Geographie. Materialien und Manuskripte
0720-9835 Denkmalpflege in Niedersachsen. Berichte
0720-9878 V D I Informationsdienst. Neue Fertigungsverfahren
0720-9886 V D I Informationsdienst. Mechanische Verbindungstechnik
0720-9916 Dienst am Wort - Gedanken zur Sonntagspredigt
0720-9983 Kreolische Bibliothek
0721-0035 Cibedo - Dokumentationen und Texte
0721-0086 Studien zur Bevoelkerungsoekonomie
0721-0167 Globus
0721-0442 Archivum Calderonianum
0721-0477 Handelspartner
0721-0981 Journal of Veterinary Medicine. Series A
0721-1295 Informationsdienst zur Auslaenderarbeit
0721-1392 American University Studies. Series 1. Germanic Languages and Literature
0721-1856 Journal of Veterinary Medicine. Series B
0721-1872 Zeitschriftenbibliographie Gerontologie
0721-1902 D B - Deutsche Bauzeitung
0721-1937 Anzeiger fuer die Seelsorge
0721-2089 Scandica Magazin
0721-2097 Im Gespraech
0721-2178 Entwicklung und Zusammenarbeit
0721-2585 Holz- und Kunststoffverarbeitung
0721-2631 Statistics and Decisions
0721-2720 A U M A Kalender Ausland
0721-2747 A U M A Kalender Regional
0721-3115 Propellants, Explosives, Pyrotechnics
0721-3220 Shipping Statistics Yearbook
0721-3719 Japanese Studies in German Language and Literature
0721-3751 Institut fuer Seeverkehrswirtschaft Bremen *changed to* Shipping Statistics
0721-3808 Zeitschrift fuer Wirtschaftspolitik
0721-4235 Daidalos
0721-4340 Kuschitische Sprachstudien Cushitic Language Studies
0721-4383 Bayreuther Beitraege zur Sprachwissenschaft
0721-4405 Innovations-Berater
0721-4553 Chemical Plants and Processing *see* 0009-2800
0721-4561 Internationale Germanistische Bibliographie†
0721-4588 Reno
0721-4626 Zusammen
0721-5088 Informationsdienst Suedliches Afrika
0721-5096 Die Kontaktlinse
0721-5118 Ernaehrungsrundbrief
0721-5169 Arabische Pferde
0721-5231 Asien
0721-5665 Pharma-Marketing Journal
0721-5681 Siemens Power Engineering Product News *changed to* Siemens Energy and Automation with Product News
0721-5894 Fluessiggas
0721-6076 Medizin in Berlin (West)
0721-6203 Quellen und Untersuchungen zur Lateinischen Philologie des Mittelalters
0721-6513 Andrias
0721-6742 Exil
0721-6831 Signal
0721-6890 Wistra
0721-6971 Frau in der Offenen Gesellschaft *changed to* Frau in Unserer Zeit
0721-7072 Etage
0721-7242 V D I Informationsdienst. Strangpressen von Metallen
0721-7250 Applied Physics. A: Solids and Surfaces
0721-7269 Applied Physics. B: Photophysics and Laser Chemistry
0721-7587 Koelner Arbeiten zum Bibliotheks- und Dokumentationswesen
0721-7595 Journal of Plant Growth Regulation
0721-7714 Plant Cell Reports
0721-7854 Baustoff-Technik
0721-8206 D B B Nachrichten fuer den Oeffentlichen Dienst
0721-832X Graefe's Archive for Clinical and Experimental Ophthalmology
0721-8400 Praxis Deutsch
0721-8486 Kinder Jugend Film Korrespondenz
0721-8516 Z U M A - Nachrichten
0721-8761 "Meteor" Forschungsergebnisse. Reihe A/B: Allgemeines, Physik und Chemie des Meeres Maritime Meteorologie†
0721-8923 Bayreuther Beitraege zur Sprachwissenschaft. Dialektologie
0721-9067 Zeitschrift fuer Sprachwissenschaft
0721-9075 Human Neurobiology
0721-9105 Arbeitsgemeinschaft der Bibliotheken und Dokumentationsstellen der Osteuropa-, Suedosteuropa- und DDR-Forschung. Mitteilungen
0721-9121 Fruehfoerderung Interdisziplinaer
0721-9156 Progress in Sensory Physiology
0721-9431 Russia Mediaevalis
0721-9539 Schachmagazin 64
0721-9679 Giesserei-Literaturschau
0721-9903 Hobby
0721-9954 Informationen zur Deutschdidaktik
0722-0057 Referateorgan: Messen Mechanischer Groessen
0722-0111 Entwicklungslaender-Studien
0722-0170 D G E G-Nachrichten
0722-0227 Konjunkturindikatoren
0722-0456 K F A Intern
0722-060X Literaturinformationdienst Schrifttum Bauwesen: Gesamtausgabe
0722-0987 Computer Persoenlich
0722-1258 Deutsches Textilforum

ISSN INDEX 1591

0722-1541 Nervenheilkunde
0722-1819 Handchirurgie - Mikrochirurgie - Plastische Chirurgie
0722-1843 Lernen Konkret
0722-2181 Afrikanisches Recht. Jahrbuch
0722-219X Tumordiagnostik & Therapie
0722-2416 German Yearbook on Business History
0722-2912 D I N Mitteilungen *see* 0011-4952
0722-3056 Zentralblatt Rechtsmedizin
0722-3064 Zentralblatt Neurologie-Psychiatrie
0722-3072 Zentralblatt Radiologie
0722-3218 Packaging Science and Technology Abstracts
0722-3226 Military Technology *changed to* Military Technology and Economics: Miltech
0722-3234 Zuversicht und Staerke
0722-3269 Advances in Physical Geochemistry
0722-3277 Zeitschrift fuer Physik. Section B: Condensed Matter
0722-3676 Quantitative Structure-Activity Relationships
0722-3773 Neue Entomologische Nachrichten
0722-4028 International Society for Reef Studies. Journal *changed to* Coral Reefs
0722-4060 Polar Biology
0722-4303 Arab Tech
0722-4400 Z Kg-International
0722-477X P M D - Praxis Medizinischer Dokumentation
0722-480X Suedost-Europa. Zeitschrift fuer Gegenwartsforschung
0722-494X Tuexenia
0722-5091 Clinical Neuropathology
0722-5407 Zentralblatt fuer Bakteriologie, Mikrobiologie und Hygiene. Abstracts
0722-5474 Alternative Kommunalpolitik
0722-5679 Archiv fuer Rechts und Sozialphilosophy. Supplementa
0722-5733 Z F L - Internationale Zeitschrift fuer Lebensmittel-Technologie und - Verfahrenstechnik
0722-6012 Industrie Elektrik und Elektronik Productronic. Elektronik Fertigung und Test *changed to* Industrie Elektrik und Elektronik
0722-6179 I E E - Industrie, Elektrik und Elecktronik
0722-6268 Ballett International
0722-6349 Research
0722-6675 German Mining
0722-6691 Messenger
0722-6713 Portugal - Nachrichten *changed to* Portugal - Magazin
0722-6934 B R A K - Mitteilungen
0722-6950 Dynamik im Handel
0722-6985 Zentralorgan Chirurgie
0722-706X Fischwaid
0722-7159 Braunschweiger Veroeffentlichungen zur Geschichte der Pharmazie und Naturwissenschaften
0722-7337 D I N - Handbook
0722-7531 Rottenbuerger Jahrbuch fuer Kirchengeschichte
0722-7647 Forum
0722-7833 Spiel
0722-7841 K F Z-Betrieb
0722-8058 Blues Forum†
0722-8120 Frau und Mutter
0722-8147 Quellen und Forschungen zur Geschichte des Ersten Weltkriees *changed to* Quellen und Studien zu den Friedensversuchen des Ersten Weltkrieges
0722-821X Die Asphaltstrasse
0722-8244 Mikrowellen and Military Electronics
0722-8252 Himmel & Erde
0722-8481 Universitaet-Gesamthochschule Duisburg. Universitaets-Report
0722-8589 Drachenflieger
0722-8600 Lehrer Journal *changed to* Lehererjournal Grundschulmagazin
0722-8600 Lehrer Journal *changed to* Lehrerjournal Hauptschulmagazin
0722-8821 Suedostasien Aktuell
0722-8910 Zeitschrift fuer Wasserrecht
0722-8953 Zentralblatt Kinderheilkunde
0722-8988 Schwarzer Faden
0722-9151 Zeitschrift fuer Religionspaedagogik *changed to* Religion Heute
0722-9313 Katalog fuer Technische Regeln *changed to* D I N - Katalog fuer Technische Regeln
0722-9399 Berliner Verkehrsblaetter
0722-964X Argument-Beiheft
0722-9852 Berichte Gynaekologie und Geburtshilfe Sowie Deren Grenzgebiete *changed to* Berichte Gynaekologie - Geburtshilfe
0722-9860 Zentralblatt Praktische Innere Medizin und Grenzgebiete *changed to* Zentralblatt Innere Medizin
0722-9917 Kuechenplaner
0722-9933 Zentralblatt Ophthalmologie
0723-0095 R W P
0723-0192 Kunststoffe - German Plastics
0723-0338 Real
0723-0788 Schriftenreihe der Hochschule der Kuenste Berlin
0723-0834 Geowissenschaften in Unserer Zeit
0723-0877 Einhorn-Jahrbuch
0723-0931 Neuropsychiatria Clinica†
0723-1237 Zeitschrift fuer Personenzentrierte Psychologie und Psychotherapie
0723-1350 Weinwirtschaft-Markt
0723-1369 Weinwirtschaft Technik
0723-1393 Medicine and Law
0723-1407 Beitraege zur Theorie und Praxis des Tennisunterrichts und -trainings
0723-1520 Brauwissenschaft *changed to* Monatsschrift fuer Brauwissenschaft
0723-1679 Geographische Hochschulmanuskripte. Diskussionspapiere
0723-175X Geographische Hochschulmanuskripte
0723-2020 Systematic and Applied Microbiology
0723-2632 Rock Mechanics and Rock Engineering
0723-2977 Arbitrium
0723-3078 M & A Infodienst
0723-3264 Historische und Paedagogische Studien
0723-3280 Neue Didaktische Modelle
0723-3299 Beitraege zur Zeitgeschichte
0723-3353 International Journal of Mycology and Lichenology
0723-3361 M & A Report
0723-4007 Ostsprachige Fachliteratur: Ausgabe Japan Technik†
0723-4015 Ostsprachige Fachliteratur: Ausgabe Japan Naturwissenschaften†
0723-4066 D A T Z
0723-4384 Europaeische Integration - Dokumentation
0723-4864 Experiments in Fluids
0723-5003 Medizinische Klinik
0723-5038 Natur
0723-5062 Baumarkt Tip
0723-5070 Paraplegiker
0723-5100 Arab Medico
0723-5208 Handbuch der Modernen Datenverarbeitung
0723-5259 Vorschau-Monats-Tabelle
0723-5321 Bundesforschungsanstalt fuer Landwirtschaft. Mitteilungen und Informationen
0723-5453 Beitraege zur Wirtschafts und Sozialgeschichte
0723-5607 Z A Information
0723-5658 Bau Trichter. Ausgabe B
0723-6050 Latein und Griechisch in Berlin
0723-6174 Souvenir & Geschenk
0723-6506 Bau Trichter. Ausgabe A/B
0723-6638 Kurt-Schwitters-Almanach
0723-6689 Verkehrswirtschaft
0723-6913 Arzneimitteltherapie
0723-6980 Development and Cooperation
0723-7006 Desarrollo y Cooperacion
0723-7022 Bayerische Buergermeister
0723-712X C S Q - Computational Statistics Quarterly
0723-7367 S T Saegewerkstechnik
0723-7553 Wartturm
0723-7561 Die B G
0723-7669 Kommune
0723-7685 D I N. Catalog of Technical Rules
0723-7928 Lehrer im Berufsfeld Koerperpflege
0723-8045 Fortschritte der Ophthalmologie
0723-8061 WerWasWos? im Taschenbuch
0723-8630 Funde und Ausgrabungen im Bezirk Trier
0723-8673 Hermetika
0723-8886 Medizinrecht
0723-9297 Budo und transkulturelle Bewegungsforschung
0723-9416 Zeitschrift fuer Wirtschaftsrecht
0723-9432 Europaeische Wehrkunde/ Wehrwissenschaftliche Rundschau
0723-9653 Ostsprachige Fachliteratur: Ausgabe Osteuropa Bauwesen†
0723-9688 Ostsprachige Fachliteratur: Ausgabe Osteuropa, Chemie, Chemische Technik, Kunststoffe†
0723-970X Ostsprachige Fachliteratur: Ausgabe Osteuropa Elektrotechnik, Energietechnik†
0723-9726 Ostsprachige Fachliteratur: Ausgabe Osteuropa Geowissenschaften, Bergbau†
0723-9734 Ostsprachige Fachliteratur: Ausgabe Osteuropa Huettenwesen, Werkstoffkunde†
0723-9793 Ostsprachige Fachliteratur: Ausgabe Osteuropa Mathematik, Physik†
0723-9815 Ostsprachige Fachliteratur: Ausgabe Osteuropa Umweltprobleme†
0723-9874 Universitaet Kiel. Geographisches Institut. Schriften
0724-0031 Computer Operations in the Laboratory *changed to* I & C Intelligent Instruments and Computers Applications in the Laboratory
0724-0279 Horizont
0724-0457 A U M A Zahlenspiegel Regional
0724-0554 A U M A Zahlenspiegel Messeplatz Deutschland
0724-1070 Kontrolle
0724-1348 Heterocera Sumatrana
0724-1445 American University Studies. Series 3. Comparative Literature
0724-1453 American University Studies. Series 5. Anglo-Saxon Language and Literature *see* 0741-0700
0724-1569 Teppe und Gelaender
0724-1712 Roboter
0724-1720 Process Engineering Magazine
0724-1976 Verein Deutscher Ingenieure. Informationsdienst. Instandhaltung
0724-2034 Arcus
0724-2247 Recht & Psychiatrie
0724-2263 Islamic Book Review Index
0724-2557 Schriften des Werksarchivs
0724-2573 Diabetes Mellitus
0724-2603 Horvath Blaetter†
0724-2689 Delfin
0724-2778 Una Voce Korrespondenz
0724-3111 Berliner Botanischer Verein. Verhandlung
0724-343X Kulturchronik
0724-3464 Sozialwissenschaften und Berufsverband
0724-3472 Tribologie und Schmierungstechnik
0724-3499 Grundschulmagazin *changed to* Lehererjournal Grundschulmagazin
0724-3618 Kindergesundheit
0724-3766 Zwischenschritte
0724-3820 Leben und Weg
0724-4177 Agrargeographie
0724-4223 Bombus
0724-4266 Deutsche Getraenke Wirtschaft
0724-4320 Dokumentation Sprachwissenschaftliche Forschungsvorhaben
0724-4339 G M D-Spiegel
0724-4371 Datenschutz und Datensicherung - Informationsrecht - Kommunikationssysteme
0724-438X International Journal of Biological Research in Pregnancy and Perinatology *changed to* Biological Research in Pregnancy and Perinatology
0724-4681 I C-Wissen Buerokommunikation
0724-469X P C Personal Computer
0724-4703 Freiburger Fernoestliche Forchungen
0724-472X Wolfenbuettler Arbeiten zur Barockforschung
0724-4983 World Journal of Urology
0724-4991 Oralprophylaxe
0724-5092 Zelte Planen Markisen
0724-553X Deutsche Steuer-Zeitung. Eildienst
0724-5637 Deutsche Steuer-Zeitung
0724-567X Neue Arzneimittel
0724-5890 Lecture Notes on Coastal and Estuarine Studies
0724-6226 Contactologia-Bucherei
0724-6358 Gemeinsame Koerperschaftsdatei
0724-6706 Einstein Quarterly Journal of Biology and Medicine
0724-6722 Abacus
0724-6803 J M C I: Journal of Molecular and Cellular Immunology
0724-6811 M.D. Computing (New York)
0724-696X Brauwelt
0724-6994 Arbeitsgestaltung fuer Behinderte
0724-7001 Buchwissenschaftliche Beitraege aus dem Deutschen Bucharchiv Muenchen
0724-7206 Moto Cross & Enduro
0724-7265 Thyssen Edelstahl Technische Berichte
0724-7281 GaFa - Garten - Fachhandel Saatgutwirtschaft
0724-7435 D C G Informationen
0724-7567 Mediteranean Language Review
0724-7591 Digitale Bilddiagnostik
0724-7613 Kaufmaennische Schule
0724-7931 Baupraxis Zeitung
0724-8016 I L C O Praxis
0724-8156 Jahrbuch fuer Opernforschung
0724-8172 Medical Focus
0724-8199 Speedway International†
0724-8415 Bibliography of Chinese Studies
0724-844X Forensia
0724-8482 Jahrbuch Stahl
0724-8555 Erdoel-Erdgas *see* 0179-3187
0724-8741 Pharmaceutical Research
0724-8822 Archivum Eurasiae Medii Aevi
0724-8849 Altenhilfe
0724-8857 Bayerisches Bienen-Blatt
0724-9179 Gastro-Entero-Hepatologie
0724-9519 Z Das Neue Zeitalter
0724-956X Wolfenbuettler Abhandlungen zur Renaissanceforschung
0724-9578 Repertorien zur Erforschung der Freuhen Neuzeit
0724-9586 Wolfenbuettler Schriften zur Geschichte des Buchwesens
0724-9594 Wolfenbuettler Forschungen
0724-9624 Das Abendland
0724-9713 Linguistik und Didaktik *changed to* Sprache und Literatur in Wissenschaft und Unterricht
0724-9780 Forum Loccum
0725-0037 Aquisition, Bibliography, Cataloguing News
0725-0045 Trees and Victoria's Resources *see* 0814-4680
0725-0096 Scripsi
0725-0142 Commonwealth Scientific and Industrial Research Organization of Energy and Earth Resources. Division of Mineral Physics. Biennial Report *changed to* Commonwealth Scientific and Industrial Research Organization. Institute of Energy and Earth Resources. Division of Mineral Physics & Mineralogy. Biennial Report
0725-0150 Australian Weeds *see* 0815-2195
0725-0207 S L A N T News
0725-0290 Labor Resourcer
0725-0320 Reserve Bank of Australia. Bulletin
0725-0371 Commonwealth Taxation Board of Review Decisions†
0725-055X Watchmakers of Australia
0725-0665 Australian Credit Unions Magazine
0725-086X Australasian Textiles
0725-1122 Health in Schools†
0725-1394 Australian Sound & Broadcast
0725-1424 Herpetofauna

0725-1688 Healthright
0725-2285 I A S AAustralian Branch Newsletter *see* 0818-5646
0725-2293 Australia. Australian Water Resources Council. Occasional Papers Series
0725-2323 Philas News
0725-2803 Social Sciences Bibliography Series†
0725-2919 Technical Aid to the Disabled Journal
0725-2986 Journal of Electrical and Electronics Engineering, Australia
0725-3141 Communicable Diseases Intelligence
0725-3338 Farm
0725-3575 C.S.I.R.O. Division of Materials Science. Research Report
0725-3850 Investment Projects in the Hunter Region
0725-4598 Commonwealth Scientific and Industrial Research Organization. Marine Laboratories. Report
0725-4644 Insurance Record of Australia & New Zealand
0725-5039 New South Wales in Brief
0725-5136 Thesis Eleven
0725-5454 Agricultural Trends
0725-5462 Australian Serials in Print
0725-556X Clinical Reproduction and Fertility
0725-6361 New South Wales. Department of Agriculture. Plant Disease Survey
0725-6639 Tension
0725-6701 Horticultural Trends
0725-6809 Hunter Region Quarterly Economic Indicators
0725-7090 International Clinical Nutrition Review
0725-8186 Parents & Children Magazine
0725-8526 Commonwealth Scientific and Industrial Research Organization. Division of Soils. Divisional Report
0725-8968 Hostelling
0725-900X Scitech
0725-9131 Mining Monthly *changed to* Australia's Mining Monthly
0725-9565 Fibre Forum *changed to* Textile-Fibre Forum
0725-9573 Child Accident Prevention Foundation of Australia. Quarterly Journal *changed to* Safeguard
0726-0458 Nelen Yubu
0726-0644 A B N News
0726-0717 University of Wollongong. Undergraduate Handbook
0726-0725 Western Australia. Department of Fisheries and Wildlife. Wildlife Research Bulletin
0726-0733 Western Australia. Department of Fisheries and Wildlife. Report
0726-0741 F.I.N.S.
0726-0822 Australian Society of Sugar Cane Technologists. Proceedings.
0726-1276 A B N Authorities
0726-1527 South Australia. Department of Mines and Energy. Special Publications
0726-1586 University of Wollongong. Faculties Sector Postgraduate Handbook *changed to* University of Wollongong. Postgraduate Handbook
0726-1772 Commonwealth Scientific and Industrial Research Organization. Institute of Energy and Earth Resources. Technical Communication.
0726-1780 Commonwealth Scientific and Industrial Research Organization. Institute of Energy and Earth Resources. Investigation Report.
0726-1926 South Australia. Department of Environment and Planning. Land Monitoring Report. Adelaide Statistical Division.
0726-2469 Western Australian Nature Reserve Management Plan†
0726-2655 Education and Society Journal
0726-3589 Creative Source Australia
0726-3724 Asia/Pacific Work and Patrol Boat *see* 0812-1648
0726-3864 Australia and New Zealand Journal of Developmental Disabilities
0726-4097 Victorian Baptist Witness
0726-4143 Editor's Clip Sheets
0726-416X Curriculum and Teaching
0726-4240 Australian Journal on Ageing
0726-4275 Commonwealth Scientific and Industrial Research Organization. Marine Laboratories. Circular†
0726-4283 Commonwealth Scientific and Industrial Research Organization. Marine Laboratories. Microfiche Report
0726-4291 Commonwealth Scientific and Industrial Research Organization. Marine Laboratories. Research Report
0726-4305 Lutheran Church of Australia. Yearbook
0726-4399 Primitiae
0726-4550 Australian Alcohol - Drug Review *changed to* Australian Drug and Alcohol Review
0726-4690 This is Newcastle and the Hunter Region
0726-4844 University of Wollongong. Legislation
0726-4941 Australian Folk Directory
0726-5816 Administrative Law Decisions
0726-6065 Australian Company Law & Practice
0726-6286 Discovery
0726-6510 Commonwealth Scientific and Industrial Research Organization. Division of Geomechanics. Geomechanics of Coal Mining Report
0726-657X C S I R O Net News
0726-6715 Historic Environment
0726-6782 Creation - Ex Nihilo
0726-6987 Australian Waste Disposal Catalogue
0726-7002 Victoria, Australia. Department of Education. Education Nationally and Internationally†
0726-7215 Flinders Journal of History and Politics
0726-7819 Australian Coal Miner
0726-7827 Australian Electrical World (1980)
0726-9072 Mask
0726-9366 Western Australia. Department of Agriculture. Annual Report
0726-9501 Western Australia. Department of Industrial Development. Building Investment
0726-951X Western Australia Products Directory†
0726-9587 Joint Serials Catalogue of Western Australian Academic Libraries
0726-9609 Western Australian Naturalist Scientific Journal
0727-0003 A.A.P.A. Asphalt Review
0727-0119 Green Pages: Directory of Non-Government Environmental Groups in Australia
0727-1182 Art & Text
0727-1239 Artlink
0727-1255 Classroom
0727-1689 Australia. Bureau of Statistics. Monthly Summary of Statistics
0727-2367 Australia. Bureau of Statistics. Western Australian Office. Monthly Summary of Statistics
0727-2596 Australian Energy Statistics
0727-260X Major Energy Statistics
0727-2723 Australia. Air Transport Statistics. International Air Transport
0727-2731 Australia. Air Transport Statistics. Airline Aircraft Utilisation
0727-274X Australia. Air Transport Statistics. Commuter Air Transport
0727-2758 Australia. Air Transport Statistics. Aerial Agriculture Operations
0727-2766 Australia. Air Transport Statistics. Survey of Hours Flown
0727-2774 Australia. Air Transport Statistics. Flight Crew Licences
0727-2782 Australia. Air Transport Statistics. Provisional Statistics of Domestic Scheduled Airline Performance
0727-2790 Australia. Air Transport Statistics. Monthly Provisional Statistics of International Scheduled Air Transport
0727-2804 Australia. Land Transport Statistics. Non-Government Railways *changed to* Australia. Non-Government Railways Statistics
0727-324X A.C.S. Newsletter
0727-338X Air Pilot
0727-3541 Australian Gas Industry Directory
0727-3606 Australian Grapegrower & Winemaker
0727-3959 Photoworld
0727-3967 Photoworld Annual
0727-3983 Photoworld Buyer's Guide. Photoguide†
0727-419X Australian Journal of Coal Mining Technology and Research
0727-4211 Collection of Australian Stamps
0727-4327 Sydney for Kids
0727-4459 Stereo Buyer's Guide. Amplifiers, FM Tuners and Receivers *see* 0819-0194
0727-5447 C A R T *changed to* Truck Australia
0727-5803 Victorian Consultative Committee on Social Development. Annual Review
0727-6125 Australia. Sea Transport Statistics. Stevedoring Industrial Disputes. Nature of Issue and Extent
0727-6672 Australia. Air Transport Statistics. Australian Air Distances
0727-6753 Directory of C S I R O Research Programs
0727-6982 Review of Australia's Demographic Trends
0727-7121 Photoworld Buyer's Guide. Lenses†
0727-7369 Mechanical Engineering Transactions
0727-7687 Australasian Office News *changed to* Office News & Automation
0727-8926 A P A I S: Australian Public Affairs Information Service
0727-9256 New South Wales. Department of Mineral Resources. Annual Report
0727-9264 New South Wales. Department of Mineral Resources. Annual Report. Statistical Supplement†
0727-9418 New South Wales. Geological Survey. Mine Data Sheets and Metallogenic Study
0727-9620 Cunninghamia
0728-0734 Trends in Animal Industries†
0728-0912 Vox Reformata
0728-1307 Neville Coleman's Underwater
0728-3210 Paul's Police Offences
0728-3636 P A C E
0728-3873 What's New in Electronics
0728-4276 Australia. Northern Territory Information Service. Territory Digest
0728-4330 Indian Ocean Newsletter
0728-4713 Journal of Food and Nutrition
0728-490X Australian Rehabilitation Digest
0728-5531 Australian Children's Folklore Newsletter
0728-5582 Council and Community
0728-5639 Lighting in Australia
0728-5671 Aboriginal Law Bulletin *see* 0817-3516
0728-5701 Image
0728-5914 Meridian
0728-5965 Animal Production in Australia
0728-6414 A N A R E News
0728-6503 In Unity
0728-6856 Australia. Department of Industry, Technology and Commerce. Annual Report
0728-6864 Australia. Office of the Life Insurance Commissioner. Half Yearly Financial & Statistical Bulletin
0728-6910 National Health and Medical Research Council. Report
0728-6929 Australia. Department of Primary Industry. Poultry Industry Assistance. Annual Report
0728-7275 Owner Builder Magazine
0728-7429 Libraries and Resources Centres in the Northern Territory. List
0728-7569 Contact (Goodna, Qld.)
0728-7615 Commonwealth Scientific and Industrial Research Organization. Division of Fossil Fuels. Report of Research
0728-8387 Australian Teacher
0728-8425 Australian Advances in Veterinary Science
0728-8433 Australian Cultural History
0728-8948 Muse News
0728-9006 Secondary Journal (Sydney)
0728-9359 Majalah Ikawiria
0728-9383 Mingay's Retailer & Merchandiser
0728-9413 Factory Equipment News
0728-9502 Australia. Australian Water Resources Council. Water Management Series
0729-0012 Western Australia. Department of Agriculture. Bulletin
0729-0403 Ebb and Flow
0729-0446 Social Accounting Monitor
0729-056X Commonwealth Scientific and Industrial Research Organization. Institute of Energy and Earth Resources. Annual Report
0729-0691 Australia. Department of Foreign Affairs. Development Assistance Bureau. Annual Review
0729-1167 Video Week
0729-1957 Videoworld
0729-1965 Videoworld Buyer's Guide Annual
0729-2368 New Zealand and Dependencies Stamp Catalogue†
0729-2384 Auditopics
0729-2473 War and Society
0729-2716 Human Rights: Newsletter of the Human Rights Commission
0729-2759 Breastfeeding Review
0729-2775 Company and Securities Law Journal
0729-3356 Australian Journal of Law and Society
0729-3445 Western Australian Egg Marketing Board. Newsletter
0729-3542 Presbyterian Banner
0729-3828 Superfunds
0729-4115 Creve Salope
0729-4336 Commonwealth Scientific and Industrial Research Organization. Division of Soils. Research Report
0729-4352 Australian Aboriginal Studies
0729-4360 Higher Education Research and Development. Research Papers
0729-5030 Hunter Valley Research Foundation. Working Papers
0729-5154 Southern Courier
0729-5529 Scuba Diver
0729-5588 Rural Merchant Magazine
0729-5936 Domestic Travel in Queensland†
0729-5944 International Travel in Queensland†
0729-5995 Institute of Art Education. Journal
0729-6096 Australia. Air Transport Statistics. Airport Traffic Data
0729-6274 Journal of the Australian War Memorial
0729-6509 State Trends†
0729-6533 A N A R E Research Notes
0729-6924 Australian Science Magazine
0729-8463 A C R O D Newsletter
0729-8528 Education Guidelines
0729-8579 International Journal of Eclectic Psychotherapy *changed to* Journal of Integrative and Eclectic Psychotherapy
0729-8595 Australian Society
0729-8714 Architecture Bulletin
0729-8773 Ringing Towers
0729-9389 Sonics
0729-9745 Medical Practice
0730-0069 Center Journal (Notre Dame)†
0730-0077 Clinical and Experimental Hypertension. Part A: Theory and Practice
0730-0085 Clinical and Experimental Hypertension. Part B: Hypertension in Pregnancy
0730-0107 Occasional Papers/Reprint Series in Contemporary Asian Studies
0730-0131 Industrial Real Estate Market Survey
0730-0158 Keyboard
0730-0212 Mortgage Banking
0730-0220 Literatura Chilena Creacion Y Critica
0730-0263 TeleServices Report
0730-028X Swedish-American Historical Quarterly
0730-0301 A C M Transactions on Graphics
0730-0808 Mirrow
0730-0832 Neonatal Network
0730-0913 American College of Toxicology. Journal
0730-0980 Peterson's Guide to Engineering, Science and Computer Jobs (Year)
0730-1014 Semiconductor Industry & Business Survey
0730-1022 Scott Report *changed to* International Computer Law Advisor

ISSN INDEX 1593

0730-1049 T'ai Chi
0730-1162 Sports and Athletes†
0730-1189 Electronics Retailing†
0730-1219 G-Gram: Newsletter for Nurse Managers and Educators†
0730-1251 Coalition Close-Up *changed to* Close-Up (Washington)
0730-1316 Biography and Genealogy Master Index
0730-1367 California Periodicals Index
0730-1383 Teaching History: a Journal of Methods
0730-1502 Offshoots of Orgonomy
0730-1618 News & Clues
0730-1677 Foundation Center National Data Book
0730-1723 National Symposium Electromagnetic Compatibility. Symposium Digest *changed to* I E E E International Symposium on Electromagnetic Compatibility. (Record)
0730-174X Frontiers of Science *changed to* International U F O Reporter
0730-1766 Alternative Media Magazine
0730-1790 International Congress on Instrumentation in Aerospace Simulation Facilities. Proceedings *see* 0730-2010
0730-1928 Psycscan: Learning Disabilities/Mental Retardation *changed to* Psycscan: Learning and Communication Disorders and Mental Retardation
0730-1936 Shepard's Bankruptcy Citations
0730-2010 International Congress on Instrumentation in Aerospace Simulation Facilities. Record
0730-2134 Discount America Guide†
0730-2150 Skiers Directory
0730-2177 Southeastern Political Review
0730-2185 Restoration
0730-2207 Planting Breeding Reviews
0730-2223 S P E X
0730-2290 Discontinued I C's D.A.T.A. Book *changed to* Digital & Audio-Video Discontinued Devices D.A.T.A. Book
0730-2304 Critical Texts: A Review of Theory and Criticism
0730-2312 Journal of Cellular Biochemistry
0730-2347 Texas Heart Institute Journal
0730-2355 Intellectual Activist
0730-2363 Religion and Life Letters
0730-2371 S S C Booknews
0730-2487 Kitchen & Bath Business
0730-2533 Directory of Auto Supply Chains *see* 0736-0452
0730-2568 Drinking/Driving Law Letter
0730-2584 Mexican Forum/El Foro Mexicano†
0730-2606 Annual Editions: Marketing
0730-2614 Journal of Halacha and Contemporary Society
0730-2703 Directory of Drug Store and H B A Chains
0730-272X Michigan Economy
0730-2894 Money Fund Safety Ratings *changed to* Income & Safety
0730-2908 Insiders
0730-2916 Comic Book Price Guide *changed to* Official Overstreet Comic Book Price Guide
0730-2967 Dallas Review
0730-305X Sulfur
0730-3084 Journal of Physical Education, Recreation and Dance
0730-3114 Advocate (Athens)†
0730-3130 50,000 Leading U S Corporations *changed to* Ward's Directory of Largest U S Companies
0730-3157 C O M P S A C
0730-3173 Hemisphere Engineering Paperback
0730-3262 Media Monitor
0730-3300 Textures and Microstructures
0730-3319 Fact (New York)
0730-3327 Translator Referral and Translation Services Directory†
0730-3335 Reference Sources for the Social Sciences and Humanities
0730-3416 Bibliognost *changed to* Book Collector's Market
0730-3475 Oro Madre
0730-3491 Practical Diabetology
0730-3564 A A S History Series
0730-3785 Library Compensation Review†
0730-4625 Dimensions of Critical Care Nursing
0730-4633 Shepard's Federal Citations
0730-465X Shepard's Code of Federal Regulations Citations
0730-4684 Shepard's Federal Labor Law Citations
0730-479X Tocqueville Review
0730-4838 Discontinued Thyristors D.A.T.A. Book *changed to* Thyristor Discontinued Devices D.A.T.A. Book
0730-4846 Transistor Discontinued Devices D.A.T.A. Book
0730-4862 Computerized Radiology
0730-4889 Tennessee Valley Authority. Power Program Summary
0730-4919 California Trial Lawyers Association. Journal *see* 0889-7751
0730-4943 Discontinued Type Locator D.A.T.A. Book *changed to* International Directory of Discontinued I Cs & Semiconductors D.A.T.A. Book
0730-4978 Burnett Family Newsletter
0730-4986 Scott Scanner
0730-5001 Carillon News *see* 0827-5955
0730-5028 Federal Financial Regulatory Digest
0730-5036 Gilcrease Magazine of American History and Art
0730-5087 Justice Reporter†
0730-5125 O C L C Annual Report
0730-5141 Minority/Ethnic Media Guide†
0730-515X New Southern Literary Messenger
0730-5168 Rota Gene
0730-5176 Western Wood Products Association. Export Report
0730-5214 Mennonite Family History
0730-5303 High Speed Diesel Report
0730-532X National Lawyers Guild Practitioner
0730-5419 Food Microstructure
0730-5435 Perceptions (Indianapolis)
0730-5796 Security Industry Yearbook *changed to* Securities Industry Yearbook
0730-613X Islamic Revolution
0730-6148 Journal of American Indian Family Research
0730-6156 Telemarketing
0730-6172 Plains Poetry Journal
0730-6199 Compumath Citation Index
0730-6202 Cable T V Tax Letter
0730-6229 Shepard's Professional and Judicial Conduct Citations
0730-6237 Taft Foundation Reporter
0730-630X Northeastern Environmental Science
0730-6466 Handicraft/Hobby Index
0730-6474 Minerals Exploration Alert
0730-6482 Ultrastructural Pathology Publication
0730-6490 Sugar Processing Research Conference. Proceedings
0730-6636 Informed
0730-6679 Advances in Polymer Technology
0730-6687 Electronic Games *changed to* Computer Entertainment
0730-675X Sculptors International *changed to* International Sculpture
0730-6776 Master Type Locator D.A.T.A. Book *changed to* International Directory I Cs & Semiconductors D.A.T.A. Book
0730-6784 Air Force Magazine
0730-6792 Animal Rights Law Reporter†
0730-6857 Stanford Italian Review
0730-689X Banking Expansion Reporter
0730-692X Get Rich Investment Guide-Money Maker *changed to* Money Maker
0730-6962 Annual Editions: Social Psychology†
0730-7004 American Health
0730-7039 Shepard's Federal Circuit Table
0730-7071 Datapro Directory of On-Line Services
0730-711X Catalyst (Des Moines)
0730-7128 American Association on Mental Deficiency. Monographs
0730-7187 Art Documentation
0730-725X Magnetic Resonance Imaging
0730-7268 Environmental Toxicology and Chemistry
0730-7322 Progress (Muscle Shoals)
0730-7594 American Politics Yearbook†
0730-7608 Pest Control Technology
0730-7616 Radio Electronics Special Projects *changed to* Hands-On Electronics
0730-7659 Birth
0730-7764 Nickel Topics†
0730-7780 American Journal of Pharmacy (1981)
0730-7799 Communication Briefings
0730-7802 Llama Newsletter *changed to* Llama World Magazine
0730-7810 Medical Abstracts Newsletter
0730-7829 Music Perception
0730-7845 Arab School on Science and Technology. Proceedings
0730-7853 Sharing Barbara's Mail *see* 0741-5729
0730-8000 Journal of Shellfish Research
0730-8124 Hydrolysis and Wood Chemistry U.S.S.R.
0730-8213 Structural Engineering Practice: Analysis, Design, Mangement
0730-823X Journal of Bioelectricity
0730-8396 Journal of Cardiovascular Ultrasonography
0730-8418 Respiratory Care (1980)
0730-8450 Executive Skills
0730-8485 Journal of Experimental Pathology
0730-8604 Tax Notes Microfiche Data Base
0730-8612 Bibliophilos
0730-8639 Mathematics and Computer Education
0730-8647 Runzheimer on Cars & Living Costs
0730-8655 Runzheimer Reports on Transportation
0730-8663 Runzheimer Reports on Travel Management
0730-868X Thoreau Quarterly
0730-8736 World of Banking
0730-8876 Transafrica Forum
0730-8884 Work and Occupations
0730-8930 Readings in Health *see* 0278-4653
0730-9023 ArtSearch
0730-904X Explorations in Ethnic Studies
0730-9058 C W/P S Special Studies
0730-9066 World University. International Newsletter *changed to* Liftoff
0730-9082 Georgetowner
0730-9112 Global Report
0730-9139 Studies in Latin American Popular Culture
0730-9147 Seminars in Urology
0730-9163 Molysulfide Newsletter
0730-918X Food Products Formulary Series†
0730-9198 I F T Basic Symposium Series
0730-9244 I E E E International Conference on Plasma Science. I E E E Conference Record-Abstracts
0730-9287 Tax Notes Index-Digest Bulletin
0730-9295 Information Technology and Libraries
0730-9384 Politics and the Life Sciences
0730-9503 Cultural Democracy
0730-9511 Guide to Federal Budget†
0730-952X Legal Briefs for the Construction Industry†
0730-9538 Control and Computers
0730-9791 Jazz Educators Journal
0730-9813 Impact of Travel on State Economies
0730-9872 Telecommunications Sourcebook
0730-9937 Catalog Marketer
0731-0056 Marketing Letter (English Edition)†
0731-0064 Marketing Letter (Spanish Edition)†
0731-0234 Social Questions Bulletin
0731-0250 Cable T V Investor
0731-0269 Cable T V Franchising
0731-0277 Assessment Digest
0731-0285 Property Tax Journal
0731-0307 Union Labor Report's on the Line
0731-0315 Physician Characteristics & Distribution in the U S
0731-0323 Malcriado
0731-0331 Directory of Religious Broadcasting
0731-034X New Socialist†
0731-0358 International Symposium on Quantum Biology and Quantum Pharmacology. Proceedings
0731-0366 Purrrrr!
0731-0382 Embers
0731-0455 Places (Cambridge)
0731-0641 Annual Review of Jazz Studies
0731-0668 Ground Water Energy Newsletter†
0731-0714 Pre/Text
0731-0862 CraftsWoman†
0731-0897 Xin Tang
0731-0935 Savings and Loan Sourcebook
0731-1125 Global Church Growth
0731-1133 Racial Ethnic Brotherhood *see* 0736-6086
0731-1214 Sociological Perspectives
0731-1222 Telltale Compass†
0731-1230 Photonics Spectra
0731-1265 International Journal of Legal Information
0731-1273 Journal of Group Psychotherapy, Psychodrama & Sociometry
0731-1281 Journal of Cash Management
0731-129X Criminal Justice Ethics
0731-1303 Retail Technology†
0731-1362 Digest of Emergency Medical Care *see* 0884-4712
0731-163X Michigan Occasional Papers in Women's Studies†
0731-1745 Educational Measurement: Issues and Practice
0731-1850 Educational Computer Magazine†
0731-1966 State of Michigan's Annual Highway Safety Plan.
0731-1974 Creditweek
0731-2148 Journal of Religion & Psychical Research
0731-2180 Sextant
0731-2199 Advances in Health Economics and Health Services Research
0731-2342 A M S Studies in the Seventeenth Century
0731-2350 Ask!
0731-2369 Worldwide Synthetic Fuels and Alternate Energy Directory
0731-2377 C M P Bulletin
0731-2385 Notes (New York)
0731-2474 Colorado Historical Society. Monograph Series *changed to* Essays and Monographs in Colorado History
0731-2504 Kinesiology for Dance Newsletter *changed to* Kinesiology for Dance
0731-2547 Orthodox Observer
0731-2652 International Life
0731-2784 Kentucky Geological Survey. Annual Report *changed to* Kentucky Geological Survey. Series 11. Annual Report
0731-2911 Inter-Society Color Council News
0731-2946 Missouri Folklore Society. Journal
0731-2970 Solar Engineering and Contracting *see* 0148-382X
0731-2989 Art and Crafts Catalyst
0731-3071 International Symposium on Fault-Tolerant Computing. Digest of Papers
0731-3233 Index: Foreign Broadcast Information Service Daily Reports: South Asia
0731-3276 Index: Foreign Broadcast Information Service Daily Reports: Soviet Union
0731-3284 Ohio Arts Council. Biennial Report
0731-3292 Geographical Bulletin
0731-3381 Health Care Supervisor†
0731-339X Annual Guide to Public Policy Experts
0731-3403 Medieval and Renaissance Drama in England
0731-3411 C A B Air Carrier Traffic Statistics
0731-356X Electric Machines and Power Systems
0731-3616 Desktop Computing†
0731-3632 Magnetic Separation News
0731-3667 Journal of Developmental Reading *see* 0022-4103
0731-3675 Media Spectrum
0731-3764 Journal of Undergraduate Research in Physics
0731-3810 Journal of Toxicology: Clinical Toxicology
0731-3829 Journal of Toxicology: Cutaneous and Ocular Toxicology
0731-3837 Journal of Toxicology: Toxin Reviews
0731-3896 Delaware Genealogical Society. Journal
0731-4019 Virrasztó†

0731-4027 D J M Enzyme Report
0731-4094 Granite and Marble Directory *changed to* A M A Product Directory
0731-4116 Index: Foreign Broadcast Information Service Daily Reports: Eastern Europe
0731-4213 Collegiate Microcomputer
0731-4221 Mississippi. Department of Wildlife Conservation. Annual Report to the Regular Session of the Mississippi Legislature *see* 0733-2017
0731-4361 Journal of Obesity and Weight Regulation
0731-437X Aviation Accident Investigator†
0731-4388 Book Report
0731-4442 Frommer's Dollarwise Guide to Germany
0731-4523 New Plays U S A
0731-4531 International Society of Certified Employee Benefit Specialists. Newsbriefs
0731-454X Business and Technology Videolog†
0731-4639 International Property Investment Journal
0731-4655 Mideast Press Report
0731-4663 Passaic Review
0731-4728 World Affairs Journal
0731-4817 Rackham Journal of the Arts and Humanities
0731-5082 Stanford Journal of International Law
0731-5090 Journal of Guidance, Control and Dynamics
0731-5112 Southeastern Campbook
0731-5163 Drug Newsletter
0731-5171 Ferroelectrics Letters
0731-518X I D Handbook of Foodservice Distribution
0731-5198 Independent (New York)
0731-5236 Poetics Journal
0731-5244 Contemporary Education Review (Washington)†
0731-5414 International Demographics
0731-5465 Occasional Papers on Religion in Eastern Europe
0731-5589 Trends Update
0731-5600 Better Homes and Gardens Kitchen & Bath Ideas
0731-5627 Weather Almanac
0731-566X People with Special Needs/Down Syndrome Report
0731-5708 Progressive Media *changed to* C M J New Music Report
0731-5724 American College of Nutrition. Journal
0731-5732 Environmental Forum
0731-5759 Tax Sheltered Investments Law Report
0731-5767 Immigration Law Report
0731-5775 Bulletins on Science and Technology for the Handicapped
0731-5783 Licensing Law Handbook
0731-5821 Tax Sheltered Investments Handbook
0731-5945 Health Sciences Videolog†
0731-602X American Association of Colleges for Teacher Education. Briefs
0731-6143 Gallup Report
0731-6291 Energygrams
0731-6305 Middle East Business Intelligence
0731-6321 University of California, Berkeley. Institute of International Studies. Policy Papers in International Affairs
0731-633X Directory of Special Libraries and Information Centers in the U S and Canada *changed to* Directory of Special Libraries and Information Centers
0731-6399 Book Production Magazine *see* 0273-8724
0731-6445 Hydro-Abstracts
0731-6526 Woodall's Retirement Directory
0731-6704 MacRae's Arizona State Industrial Directory *see* 0739-8476
0731-6720 MacRae's Nebraska State Industrial Directory *see* 0740-428X
0731-6739 MacRae's Maine State Industrial Directory *see* 0740-2945
0731-6763 American Arab Affairs
0731-6844 Journal of Reinforced Plastics & Composites
0731-6925 Directory of General Merchandise, Variety Chains and Specialty Stores
0731-6933 Slick
0731-6941 Economic Development and Law Center Report
0731-6984 Critical Reviews in Bioengineering *see* 0278-940X
0731-7085 Journal of Pharmaceutical and Biomedical Analysis
0731-7107 Child & Family Behavior Therapy
0731-7115 Clinical Gerontologist
0731-7123 Residential Group Care and Treatment *changed to* Residential Treatment for Children & Youth
0731-7131 Technical Services Quarterly
0731-714X Topics in Strategic Planning for Health Care *see* 0735-9683
0731-7158 Psychotherapy in Private Practice
0731-7174 Texas Vision
0731-7239 Systems Research
0731-7247 Journal of African Earth Sciences
0731-7441 Better Homes and Gardens Decorating Ideas
0731-7700 China Business and Trade
0731-7824 Herbarium News
0731-7875 Carnahan Conference on Security Technology. Proceedings *changed to* Carnahan Conference on Security Technology. Proceedings
0731-7883 S U N Y L A Newsletter
0731-7891 Worldwide Videotex Update
0731-7956 Ringling Museums
0731-7980 Cumberland Poetry Review
0731-7999 Research in Real Estate
0731-8006 Photoplay Magazine *see* 0031-885X
0731-8014 Heisey News
0731-8081 Directory of Unpublished Experimental Mental Measures
0731-8103 Southwestern Campbook
0731-8111 Boletin Anglohispano†
0731-812X Batter Performance Handbook
0731-8138 Pitcher Performance Handbook
0731-8146 Insiders Baseball Fact-Book Extra
0731-8162 Insiders Baseball Fact-Book
0731-8189 Current Treaty Index
0731-8235 Clinical Reviews in Allergy
0731-8332 Journal of Prison and Jail Health
0731-8367 On-Line (Durham)
0731-843X Disc Collector
0731-8464 Statistics of Virginia Public Libraries and Institutional Libraries
0731-8499 Snow Surveys and Water Supply Outlook for Alaska *changed to* Alaska Snow Surveys
0731-8510 Directory of Multihospital Systems
0731-8529 Dallas Opera Magazine
0731-860X Progress in Solar Energy *changed to* American Solar Energy Society. Annual Meeting
0731-8618 Advances in Solar Energy. An Annual Review of Research and Development
0731-8626 Progress in Passive Solar Energy Systems *changed to* American Solar Energy Society. Passive Conference. Annual Meeting
0731-8650 Occupational Programs in California Public Community Colleges
0731-8774 Chemical Business
0731-8863 Statistics of Paper, Paperboard and Wood Pulp
0731-8898 Journal of Environmental Pathology, Toxicology and Oncology
0731-8987 Atavist
0731-9053 Advances in Econometrics
0731-9096 Oregon International Trade Directory
0731-9126 Michigan Audubon
0731-9150 Runzheimer Reports on Relocation
0731-9169 International Journal for Biosocial Research
0731-9177 Financial Planning Strategist
0731-9185 National Five Digit Zip Code and Post Office Directory
0731-9207 S. Klein Newsletter on Computer Graphics
0731-9258 Journal of Computers in Mathematics and Science Teaching
0731-9290 Wordwatching
0731-938X Veridian
0731-9398 Classroom Computer News *see* 0746-4223
0731-9541 Soccer Rulebook
0731-9622 Fleet Owner *changed to* Fleet Owner: Big Fleet Edition
0731-9649 Research: Virginia Tech
0731-9711 L R E Report
0731-9770 Sports Medicine Digest
0731-9991 Teen Bag
0732-0051 Public Press Newsletter†
0732-006X Collectibles Illustrated†
0732-0078 Center for Peace and Conflict Studies. Occasional Papers
0732-0124 International Talent and Touring Directory†
0732-0159 Exporters' Encyclopaedia
0732-0167 Nutrition & the M.D.
0732-037X Developing Human Resources *changed to* University Associates, Inc. Annual
0732-0469 Bond Buyer
0732-0485 Everybody's Money Complaint Directory for Consumers
0732-0515 Asian and Pacific Census Forum *see* 0891-2823
0732-0523 Table Rock Sentinel
0732-0531 East-West Population Institute. Working Papers *changed to* East-West Population Institute. Papers
0732-0582 Annual Review of Immunology
0732-0590 Canadian County Connections
0732-0671 Advances in Library Administration and Organization
0732-071X Colorado City Retail Sales by Standard Industrial Classification
0732-0760 Drug and Cosmetic Catalog
0732-085X Contributions to the Study of Aging
0732-0868 Psychiatric Medicine
0732-0876 Orion Nature Quarterly
0732-0914 Heritage (Waltham)
0732-0922 Lawyer's Microcomputer *see* 0740-0942
0732-0965 Probation and Parole Directory
0732-0973 Design for Arts in Education
0732-0981 Origin to Destination
0732-099X Salaries (Year)†
0732-1007 Eaglet
0732-1031 American Judicature Society. Annual Report
0732-1112 MacRae's Massachusetts State Industrial Directory *see* 0740-4689
0732-1139 Topics in Geriatrics
0732-118X New Ideas in Psychology
0732-1228 Political Anthropology
0732-1295 Cognitive Science Series (Cambridge)
0732-1317 Research in Public Policy Analysis and Management
0732-1341 Directory of Agencies Serving the Visually Handicapped in the U.S.
0732-1511 Picture†
0732-1562 Women's Studies Quarterly
0732-1597 Numbers News
0732-1813 Federal Reserve Bank of Atlanta. Economic Review
0732-183X Journal of Clinical Oncology
0732-1856 National Cooperative Transit Research and Development Program Synthesis of Transit Practice
0732-1864 Nineteenth-Century Literary Criticism
0732-1872 Homily Service
0732-1902 Sporting News Pro Football Guide
0732-1910 American Bar Association. Forum Committee on Franchising. Journal *changed to* Franchise Law Journal
0732-1929 Literature and Belief
0732-2224 Beckett Circle
0732-2283 Kagan Census of Cable and Pay TV
0732-2305 Electric Power Monthly
0732-233X Facts About Store Development
0732-2364 Workers Under Communism
0732-2399 Marketing Science
0732-2402 Impulse
0732-2569 Country Living (New York)
0732-2607 International Symposium on Urban Hydrology, Hydraulic Infrastructures and Water Quality Control. Proceedings†
0732-2631 Supply and Demand for Scientists and Engineers *changed to* Technological Marketplace: Supply and Demand for Scientists and Engineers
0732-2666 California Risk Management Report: For the Female Executive *changed to* Risk Management for Executive Women
0732-2674 Working Papers in Irish Studies
0732-2755 Directory of Graduate Programs in the Communication Arts and Sciences
0732-2844 Softball Rule Book
0732-2852 Art Com: Contemporary Art Communications
0732-2895 M F A Bulletin *see* 0739-5736
0732-2941 Co-Op Development Report†
0732-295X Electrical Engineering Problems in the Rubber and Plastics Industry Technical Conference. Record *see* 0272-4685
0732-2968 Memphis State Review
0732-300X Theatre Times
0732-3085 Asia Foundation. President's Review and Annual Report *changed to* Asia Foundation. Annual Report
0732-3093 Official New Mexico Blue Book
0732-3123 Journal of Mathematical Behavior
0732-3336 Pyramid Guide†
0732-3395 Meyer's Directory of Genealogical Societies in the U S A & Canada
0732-3565 Advances in Law and Child Development
0732-3581 Your Public Lands†
0732-3867 South Asia Bulletin
0732-4073 Memo
0732-4170 MacRae's Iowa State Industrial Directory *see* 0740-428X
0732-4189 MacRae's Montana State Industrial Directory *see* 0740-6088
0732-4197 MacRae's Colorado State Industrial Directory *see* 0740-6126
0732-4200 MacRae's Idaho State Industrial Directory *see* 0740-6088
0732-4235 Discontinued Optoelectronics D.A.T.A. Book *changed to* Optoelectronics Discontinued Devices D.A.T.A. Book
0732-4375 Photovoltaics
0732-4383 Current Topics in Chinese Science
0732-4405 Current Topics in Chinese Science. Section C: Mathematics
0732-4421 Current Topics in Chinese Science. Section E: Astronomy
0732-4456 Contributions to the Study of Mass Media and Communications
0732-4464 Contributions to Criminology and Penology
0732-4499 A L P S Newsletter *see* 0740-235X
0732-4642 Entrepreneurial Woman Newsletter†
0732-4650 A: a Journal of Contemporary Literature
0732-4766 Research Perspectives
0732-4839 National Cooperative Transit Research and Development Program Report
0732-4928 Society of Christian Ethics. Annual
0732-4944 Contemporary Philosophy
0732-5223 Clinical Supervisor
0732-524X Office Systems Ergonomics Report
0732-5258 P I P College "H E L P S" Newsletter
0732-5282 Compensation (Washington)
0732-5371 A C E I Exchange
0732-538X Photoplay (1916) *see* 0031-885X
0732-5452 Kentucky Libraries
0732-5509 Noncovalent Interactions in Macromolecules†
0732-5517 From the Dragon's Den
0732-5533 Technology Update
0732-5541 Planning Update†
0732-555X Marketing Update
0732-5568 Chemical Industry Update (North American Report)

ISSN INDEX 1595

0732-5576 Chemical Industry Update (Overseas Report)
0732-5584 Facility Capacities Update†
0732-5592 Process Engineering Update†
0732-5800 Review of Books and Religion *see* 0890-0841
0732-5819 E F L Gazette
0732-5894 Application Notes Reference D.A.T.A. Book
0732-5983 Directory of Major Malls
0732-6092 Thyristor D.A.T.A. Book
0732-6203 Transistor D.A.T.A. Book
0732-6416 Afroasiatic Dialects
0732-6424 Sources from the Ancient Near East
0732-6432 American Research Center in Egypt. Reports
0732-6440 Bibliotheca Mesopotamica
0732-6467 Bibliotheca Aegyptia
0732-6475 Occasional Papers on the Near East
0732-6483 Syro-Mesopotamian Studies
0732-6491 Monographs on the Ancient Near East
0732-6505 Aids and Research Tools in Ancient Near Eastern Studies
0732-6572 Directory of Incentive Travel International
0732-6580 Journal of Biological Response Modifiers
0732-6599 Buy Books Where, Sell Books Where
0732-6602 Ms Outdoors
0732-6610 Freedom in the World
0732-6629 Natural Gas Production and Consumption *changed to* Natural Gas Annual
0732-6637 Literary Magazine Review
0732-6653 Producer's MasterGuide
0732-667X Glitches
0732-6718 Machine-Mediated Learning
0732-6726 Inversion and Imaging†
0732-6734 Commonwealth Novel in English
0732-6750 Inti
0732-6882 Sea Letter
0732-6920 Intake (New Hyde Park) *changed to* Nutrition Action Healthletter
0732-6971 Statistical Services Directory
0732-703X American Academy of Osteopathy Yearbook
0732-7196 Broadcasting/Cablecasting Yearbook
0732-7218 Modern Methods in Pharmacology
0732-7269 Black Caucus Journal
0732-7277 Urban Research Review
0732-7315 Northeastern Campbook
0732-7366 Guide to the Energy Industry†
0732-7382 Technology N.Y. Newsletter
0732-7471 Flexible Automation
0732-7501 Portable Companion
0732-7536 Legal Times of Washington *changed to* Legal Times
0732-7595 Logsdon Connections
0732-7668 Satellite Orbit
0732-7714 Shepard's Federal Tax Citations
0732-7722 Shepard's Federal Occupational Safety and Health Citations
0732-7773 Dynamath
0732-7781 Gist
0732-7919 Hughes Report *changed to* Management Report
0732-7927 Environmental Analyst†
0732-8001 Lector
0732-8117 Ice Hockey Rule Book
0732-815X Means Square Foot Costs
0732-8265 Urban Outlook
0732-8303 Journal of Carbohydrate Chemistry
0732-8311 Nucleosides & Nucleotides
0732-8346 Computer Business
0732-8508 Shasta Abbey. Journal *see* 0891-1177
0732-8516 Financial Review
0732-8648 Television and Cable Factbook
0732-8699 Crystal Lattice Defects and Amorphous Materials
0732-8818 Experimental Techniques
0732-8869 New Directions in Funding†
0732-8877 American Export Marketer
0732-8893 Diagnostic Microbiology and Infectious Disease
0732-8923 Bifrost†
0732-894X Hennepin County Library Cataloging Bulletin
0732-8958 Taft Corporate Giving Directory
0732-9059 N C A A Lacrosse Guide *see* 0736-7775
0732-9113 Journal of Legal Pluralism and Unofficial Law
0732-9121 New York State Dairy Statistics
0732-913X Mid-American Review of Sociology
0732-9199 S. Klein Directory of Computer Graphics Suppliers
0732-9210 Living Bird Quarterly
0732-9407 Fiber Optics and Communications Weekly News Service
0732-9415 Telehints†
0732-9466 Johnson Survey *changed to* America's Fastest Growing Companies
0732-9482 Cancer Drug Delivery
0732-9512 Micro Discovery†
0732-9539 Masson Monographs in Diagnostic Cytopathology
0732-9598 Advances in Infancy Research
0732-9636 Medical Liability Monitor
0732-9695 MacRae's Maryland State Industrial Directory *changed to* MacRae's Maryland/D.C./Delaware State Industrial Directory
0732-9709 Brooklyn College Alumni Literary Review
0732-9792 Fatal Accident Reporting System
0732-9814 Rutgers University Studies in Classical Humanities
0732-9881 Disciplìana
0732-989X Geophysics: The Leading Edge of Exploration
0732-992X Women Organizing†
0732-9962 Family Life Educator
0733-0073 Black Willow Poetry†
0733-0103 Buying Strategy Forecast
0733-0138 Early Warning Forecast
0733-0154 Advanced Solar Energy Technology Newsletter†
0733-0219 Oliphant Washington Service. Energy Summary
0733-026X O T C Handbook
0733-0308 Bamboo Ridge, The Hawaii Writers' Quarterly
0733-0324 Fordyce Letter
0733-0332 H R Planning Newsletter
0733-0405 B N A's Weekly Tax Report *see* 0884-6057
0733-0448 A C C Basketball Handbook
0733-0456 Eugene O'Neill Newsletter
0733-0464 Seafood Business Report *see* 0889-3217
0733-0529 Golden Years
0733-0553 Petroleum Supply Monthly
0733-0677 Waterfront World
0733-0707 Restoration and Management Notes
0733-0928 Offshore Rig Location Report *changed to* Offshore Rig Location Report
0733-0960 Museum Studies Journal
0733-1142 Research Materials in Microform Available in the Harvard University Library
0733-1169 Northeast Conference on the Teaching of Foreign Languages. Northeast Conference Reports
0733-1177 N E C Reports *see* 0733-1169
0733-1274 Software Protection
0733-1290 American Journal of Forensic Psychology
0733-1320 Personal Wealth Digest
0733-1355 College Catalog Collection
0733-1428 Journal of Existential Psychiatry *see* 0014-4673
0733-1533 Africus†
0733-1606 Dramatists Sourcebook
0733-1614 Electronics Insight†
0733-172X Noise Pollution Publications Abstracts†
0733-1738 PrintNews†
0733-1746 Public Law Reporter†
0733-1924 Soviet Journal of Friction and Wear
0733-2017 Mississippi. Department of Wildlife Conservation. Annual Report
0733-2033 Theatre History Studies
0733-2076 Aquariculture and Aquatic Sciences. Journal
0733-2130 Collector Editions
0733-2165 L C R *changed to* Literary Criticism Register
0733-2173 Softalk for the I B M Personal Computer†
0733-222X Bio/Technology
0733-2238 Dolls
0733-2327 Clinical Nutrition
0733-2378 World Food Trade and U.S. Agriculture
0733-2408 Business Forum (Los Angeles)
0733-2459 Journal of Clinical Apheresis
0733-2467 Neurourology and Urodynamics
0733-2491 Journal of Law & Commerce
0733-2599 Abstracts of Research in Pastoral Care and Counseling
0733-2629 Nuclear Magnetic Resonance Literature-Abstracts & Index†
0733-2637 Options Handbook
0733-2823 College Football Yearbook
0733-2831 Soviet Journal of Chemical Physics
0733-2947 MacRae's Delaware State Industrial Directory *changed to* MacRae's Maryland/D.C./Delaware State Industrial Directory
0733-2998 Left Index
0733-3005 Book Alert (Somerville)
0733-3013 Mothering
0733-3021 Journal of Climate and Applied Meteorology
0733-303X Lasers & Applications
0733-3048 American Society of Indexers. Newsletter
0733-3056 Equipment Management
0733-3129 Classroom Computer News Directory of Educational Computing Resources *changed to* Classroom Computer Learning Directory of Educational Computing Resources
0733-3188 Zoo Biology
0733-3196 Footloose Librarian
0733-3234 MacRae's Louisiana State Industrial Directory
0733-3242 Postcard Dealer and Collector†
0733-3315 Popular Communications
0733-3323 Explorations in Sights and Sounds
0733-3382 Research Review of Equal Education†
0733-3390 Irish Literary Supplement
0733-3552 Greater New York Industrial Directory *see* 0740-2953
0733-3684 MacRae's New Jersey State Industrial Directory
0733-3692 MacRae's West Virginia State Industrial Directory *see* 0740-4328
0733-401X U C L A Journal of Environmental Law and Policy
0733-4176 MacRae's Ohio State Industrial Directory
0733-4265 Masson Monographs in Diagnostic Pathology
0733-4281 Linxletter†
0733-4346 American Journal of Videology†
0733-4443 Current Awareness in Biological Sciences
0733-4451 MacRae's Rhode Island State Industrial Directory *see* 0740-4689
0733-4540 Comparative Civilizations Review
0733-4559 Our Heritage
0733-4567 AirCal Magazine *changed to* AirCal
0733-4575 Nutrition and Behavior
0733-4605 Sound Advice *changed to* Wes English's Sound Advice
0733-463X Traveling Exhibition Information Service. Newsletter
0733-4648 Journal of Applied Gerontology
0733-4664 Harris Ohio Marketers Industrial Directory *changed to* Harris Ohio Industrial Directory
0733-4680 Journal of Trace and Microprobe Techniques
0733-4923 Garden Design
0733-4931 MacRae's South Carolina State Industrial Directory†
0733-4958 MacRae's Michigan State Industrial Directory
0733-4974 MacRae's New Hampshire State Industrial Directory *see* 0740-2945
0733-4982 MacRae's Georgia State Industrial Directory
0733-5016 MacRae's Alabama State Industrial Directory
0733-5113 Journal of Arts Management and Law
0733-5121 Advances in World Archaeology
0733-5172 Pension Planning Strategist†
0733-5180 Retirement Planning Strategist
0733-5210 Journal of Cereal Science
0733-5237 Pennsylvania Directory of Manufacturers
0733-5253 Musician
0733-5350 Middle East Annual
0733-5369 Divine Slave Gita
0733-5385 Arab Perspectives
0733-558X Research in the Sociology of Organizations
0733-5644 Journal of V L S I and Computer Systems *see* 0888-224X
0733-5660 Showforth†
0733-5695 Playguy
0733-5709 Biotechnology Research Abstracts
0733-5768 Marketing Science Institute. Newsletter
0733-5776 Studies in Mayan Linguistics
0733-5881 Songsmith Journal†
0733-5946 David McCalden Revisionist Newsletter
0733-6020 Independent Study Catalog: N U C E A's Guide to Independent Study Through Correspondence Instruction
0733-6047 Sporting News Pro-College Basketball Yearbook
0733-6098 Eastern Mineral Law Foundation. Annual Institute. Proceedings
0733-6136 Teacher Brothers Modern-Day Almanac†
0733-6314 Abrams Planetarium Sky Calendar
0733-6349 Phila City Paper
0733-6357 Faulkner Newsletter & Yoknapatawpha Review
0733-6373 Interscience Conference on Antimicrobial Agents and Chemotherapy. Program and Abstracts
0733-6403 Residential /Light Commercial Cost Data
0733-642X Economic Review of Travel in America
0733-6446 Reclamation Era (Denver)†
0733-6519 Romanticism Past and Present
0733-6527 W A R M Journal
0733-6535 Journal of Volunteer Administration
0733-6551 Today's Delinquent
0733-6608 Grassroots Development
0733-6683 Clearwater Journal
0733-6764 Borgo Family Histories
0733-8058 Catastrophism and Ancient History
0733-8074 Access (Research Triangle Park)
0733-8112 Basin Bulletin
0733-8252 New Product Development
0733-8309 Rand McNally Campground and Trailer Park Guide. Eastern.
0733-8317 Practicing Midwife *changed to* Birth Gazette
0733-835X North Central Tour Book *changed to* TourBook: North Central
0733-8627 Emergency Medicine Clinics of North America
0733-8635 Dermatologic Clinics
0733-8651 Cardiology Clinics
0733-8678 Space Press
0733-8716 I E E E Journal on Selected Areas in Communications
0733-8724 Journal of Lightwave Technology
0733-8759 Country Heritage
0733-8813 SurView
0733-8902 C L A O Journal
0733-8910 I E C A Report
0733-8929 I W I Monthly
0733-8937 Kindex
0733-8961 Washington Researchers Information Report
0733-9003 Progress and Topics in Cytogenetics
0733-9011 Composites Technology Review *changed to* Journal of Composites Technology and Research

0733-9097 Calli's Tales
0733-9178 Masson Monographs in Dermatopathology
0733-9305 Infoperspectives
0733-9364 Journal of Construction Engineering and Management
0733-9372 Journal of Environmental Engineering
0733-9380 Journal of Professional Issues in Engineering
0733-9399 Journal of Engineering Mechanics
0733-9402 Journal of Energy Engineering
0733-9410 Journal of Geotechnical Engineering
0733-9429 Journal of Hydraulic Engineering
0733-9437 Journal of Irrigation and Drainage
0733-9445 Journal of Structural Engineering
0733-9453 Journal of Surveying Engineering
0733-9461 Journal of Technical Topics in Civil Engineering†
0733-947X Journal of Transportation Engineering
0733-9488 Journal of Urban Planning and Development
0733-9496 Journal of Water Resources Planning and Management
0733-950X Journal of Waterway, Port, Coastal and Ocean Engineering
0733-9542 New Vico Studies
0733-9739 D B S News
0733-9836 Dental Asepsis Review
0734-0133 S Q†
0734-0141 On Campus with Women
0734-015X MacRae's Nevada State Industrial Directory *see* 0740-6126
0734-0168 Criminal Justice Review
0734-0222 New Criterion
0734-0265 New York Alive
0734-0281 On Key
0734-0311 Soviet Progress in Virology
0734-032X Missouri Population Estimates
0734-0451 Seminars in Hearing *see* 0734-0478
0734-0478 Seminars in Speech and Language
0734-0486 C M R E Monographs
0734-0508 N C A A Men's Water Polo Rules
0734-0575 Japan Economic Daily
0734-0605 Directory of American Poets and Fiction Writers
0734-0648 Urban Transportation Abstracts
0734-0664 Gerodontology
0734-0788 Notes on Translation
0734-0842 From the State Capitals. Alcoholic Beverage Control
0734-0869 From the State Capitals. Disaster and Emergency Planning *see* 0749-2782
0734-0877 From the State Capitals. Drug Abuse Control
0734-0885 From the State Capitals. Prison Administration *see* 0749-2790
0734-0907 From the State Capitals. School Financing
0734-0990 L R E Project Exchange
0734-1024 Soviet Energy Technology
0734-1032 Journal of the Conductors' Guild
0734-1059 From the State Capitals. Fire Administration *see* 0749-2782
0734-1067 From the State Capitals. Fish and Game Regulations *see* 0734-113X
0734-1105 From the State Capitals. Labor Relations *changed to* Labor Relations
0734-1113 From the State Capitals. Milk Control†
0734-1121 From the State Capitals. Taxes--Property
0734-113X From the State Capitals. Parks and Recreation Trends
0734-1148 From the State Capitals. Police Administration *see* 0749-2782
0734-1156 From the State Capitals. Public Health
0734-1164 From the State Capitals. School Construction *see* 0749-2766
0734-1199 From the State Capitals. Tourist Business Promotion
0734-1202 From the State Capitals. Federal Action Affecting the States
0734-1229 From the State Capitals. Wage Hour Regulations *changed to* Labor Relations
0734-1237 From the State Capitals. Water Supply
0734-1245 From the State Capitals. Workers Compensation and Unemployment Compensation *changed to* Labor Relations
0734-1423 Chilton's Commercial Carrier Journal
0734-1482 Prototype Modeler
0734-1490 Northern Illinois University Law Review
0734-1504 Scientific and Applied Photography and Cinematography
0734-1512 History and Technology
0734-1520 Physics, Chemistry and Mechanics of Surfaces
0734-1601 From the State Capitals. Public Assistance and Welfare Trends
0734-1628 From the State Capitals. Industrial Development
0734-1636 From the State Capitals. Airport Construction and Financing *see* 0749-2766
0734-1679 Soviet Journal of Water Chemistry and Technology
0734-1717 National Logo Exchange *see* 0888-6970
0734-175X E E's Electronics Distributor
0734-1784 Plastics Business News
0734-1865 Bibliotheca Americana
0734-189X Computer Vision, Graphics, and Image Processing
0734-1962 A S C E Publications Information
0734-1970 Medical Utilization Review
0734-1997 Annals of Sports Medicine
0734-2047 Transactions on Office Information Systems
0734-2055 Rainey Times
0734-2071 Transactions on Computer Systems
0734-2101 Journal of Vacuum Science and Technology. Part A. Vacuum, Surfaces and Films
0734-211X Journal of Vacuum Science and Technology. Part B. Microelectronics Processing and Phenomena
0734-2128 Ear
0734-2306 Boston Review
0734-2705 Mideastern Campbook
0734-2799 Partnership Strategist *changed to* Tax Shelter Insider
0734-2802 New Canaan Historical Society Annual
0734-2829 Journal of Psychoeducational Assessment
0734-2837 Alliance
0734-2845 Dun's Business Rankings
0734-2861 Dun and Bradstreet Million Dollar Directory *changed to* Million Dollar Directory
0734-2926 Family Studies Review Yearbook
0734-2934 Bellingham Review
0734-3027 Prophetic Voices
0734-3051 Computer Enhanced Spectroscopy
0734-306X Journal of Labor Economics
0734-3078 Shelter Sense
0734-3086 American Library Association. Memorandum *changed to* O I F Memorandum
0734-3116 W U U A Newsletter
0734-3299 Year Book of Critical Care Medicine
0734-3302 Today's Supervisor
0734-3310 Research Strategies
0734-3329 Goethe Yearbook
0734-3469 Congress and the Presidency
0734-3671 Confederate Historical Institute Journal
0734-371X Review of Public Personnel Administration
0734-3795 Nibble
0734-3825 Idaho. Geological Survey. Bulletin
0734-4031 Henry George Newsletter
0734-4066 Original New England Guide
0734-4082 Technology & Responsibility
0734-4171 Clearinghouse Report on Science and Human Rights
0734-4325 Packaging and Manufacturing Electronics Data Service†
0734-4392 American Music
0734-4473 Totline
0734-452X Midwest Arts & Literature†
0734-4589 Jeffries Report
0734-4651 Federal/State Executive Directory
0734-4856 C O R D Newsletter
0734-4937 Studies of Israeli Society
0734-4961 Lawrence Review of Natural Products. Monograph System
0734-497X River City Review
0734-5054 U S A 23 Milliones
0734-5089 Virginia Historical Abstracts†
0734-5097 Online Micro-Software Guide & Directory (Year)†
0734-5119 C B A S S E Newsletter
0734-5151 Biotechnology Chemonomics
0734-5399 S M A T V News
0734-5402 Computers for Design & Construction
0734-5410 Journal of Craniomandibular Practice
0734-5437 Circle Track
0734-5453 California Homes and Lifestyles
0734-5496 Grand Street
0734-5542 E A R for Children
0734-5569 Areco's Quarterly Index to Periodical Literature on Aging *see* 0882-3405
0734-578X Southeastern Archaeology
0734-5801 American Single Shot Rifle News
0734-5836 Nuclear Times
0734-5844 Quality Assurance News for the Clinical Laboratory†
0734-5860 Investing in Real Estate
0734-5895 Speleonews
0734-5917 Bus Facts *see* 0278-1565
0734-600X Neurochemical Pathology
0734-6018 Representations
0734-6166 Drug Law Report
0734-6506 Mid-Week Report
0734-6514 F-D-C Reports: The Pink Sheet *changed to* Prescription and O T C Pharmaceuticals: The Pink Sheet
0734-6603 Virginia Country
0734-6735 Independent Higher Education
0734-6786 Directory of U.S. Labor Organizations
0734-6794 Openers
0734-6816 Cable T V Finance
0734-6891 Baseball Research Journal
0734-6905 National Pastime
0734-6980 Flexo
0734-7138 Inkling (Alexandria) *changed to* Writers' Journal
0734-7146 Advanced Materials
0734-7219 N E A Today
0734-7324 Alcoholism Treatment Quarterly
0734-7332 Journal of Psychosocial Oncology
0734-7367 Music Therapy
0734-743X International Journal of Impact Engineering
0734-7537 Minnesota Tax Journal
0734-7545 American Language Journal
0734-757X Contributions to the Study of Computer Science
0734-7618 A M S Studies in Ars Poetica *changed to* A M S Ars Poetica
0734-7642 National Union Catalog. U.S. Books†
0734-7650 National Union Catalog. Books
0734-8169 Children's Media Market Place
0734-8401 U Turn†
0734-841X Specialized Subject Bibliographies Series†
0734-8428 Cache Review
0734-8479 Means Site Work Cost Data
0734-8495 Topeka Genealogical Society Quarterly
0734-8541 Harris Pennsylvania Marketing Directory *changed to* Harris Pennsylvania Industrial Directory
0734-8584 Rhetorica
0734-8630 Reproductive Endocrinology *changed to* Seminars in Reproductive Endrocrinology
0734-8665 Brecht Yearbook
0734-9033 Whole Again Resource Guide
0734-9041 Journal of Fire Sciences
0734-905X Maneapa
0734-9068 Encyclopedia of Information Systems and Services
0734-9149 Public Administration Quarterly†
0734-9165 I A I A Bulletin *changed to* Impact Assessment Bulletin
0734-9343 Coal Preparation
0734-9513 Federal Court Procurement Decisions
0734-9556 Maine Agricultural Experiment Station. Technical Bulletin
0734-9564 Maine Agricultural Experiment Station. Miscellaneous Report.
0734-9637 Information Sources
0734-970X Beer Marketing Management
0734-9742 Chemical Engineer Diary & Institution News
0734-9750 Biotechnology Advances
0734-9831 History of Psychoanalysis
0734-9874 Entomography
0734-9890 Emotions and Behavior. Monograph
0734-9963 Cutbank
0734-9998 Mutual Aid
0735-0015 Journal of Business and Economic Statistics
0735-0082 Superintendent's Digest
0735-0287 Genealogical Computer Pioneer
0735-0295 Bookmark (Moscow)
0735-0317 Photron
0735-0368 N C A A Men's Soccer Rules
0735-0414 Alcohol & Alcoholism
0735-0651 Gene Analysis Techniques
0735-066X Lumber Price Index (PNW Coast Index)
0735-0686 Symposium on Surface Mining, Hydrology, Sedimentology and Reclamation. Proceedings
0735-0732 Healthcare Financial Management
0735-0791 Reliability Physics
0735-0864 Anselm Studies
0735-1097 American College of Cardiology. Journal
0735-1232 Journal of Pascal and Ada *changed to* Journal of Pascal, Ada, & Modula-2
0735-1283 American Review of Diagnostics
0735-1313 Molecular Biology and Medicine
0735-1321 Satsang
0735-1364 Tibet Society. Journal
0735-1399 Society for Commercial Archaeology. News Journal
0735-1402 Non-Profit Executive *see* 0882-5521
0735-1623 Lone Star *changed to* Lone Star Humor
0735-1631 American Journal of Perinatology
0735-1755 Horizons (Washington, 1981)†
0735-1844 Integrated Service Digital Networks
0735-1895 Theaterwork
0735-1909 Vitae Scholasticae
0735-1917 Water Supply
0735-1925 Microcomputer Market Place
0735-1933 International Communications in Heat and Mass Transfer
0735-1968 Journal of Park & Recreation Administration
0735-2417 Indiana Manufacturers Directory
0735-2476 Alabama Business and Economic Reports *changed to* Southern Business & Economic Journal
0735-2484 Direct Energy Conversion (Oak Ridge, 1982)
0735-2492 Nuclear Reactor Safety
0735-2506 Nuclear Fuel Cycle
0735-2522 Foundation Grants Index Bimonthly
0735-2689 C R C Critical Reviews in Plant Sciences
0735-2700 Soviet Agricultural Sciences
0735-2719 Soviet Journal of Contemporary Mathematical Analysis
0735-2840 Erde International
0735-3081 Resource Recovery Report
0735-309X Pioneer Wagon
0735-3103 J D: Journalism Directory *changed to* Journalism and Mass Communication Directory
0735-3170 Journal of Childhood Communication Disorders
0735-3707 Directory of Outplacement Firms
0735-3723 E T C†
0735-3847 Integrative Psychiatry
0735-3863 Data Processing Auditing Report
0735-388X Telecommunications Counselor
0735-3928 Crime and Justice†
0735-3936 Behavioral Sciences and the Law Journal
0735-3995 World S F Newsletter
0735-4355 Dirt Rider Magazine
0735-4398 Celibate Woman
0735-4576 Hyst'ry Myst'ry Magazine†
0735-4592 Guthrie Bulletin *see* 0882-696X

0735-4665 Sagetrieb
0735-469X Home Video and Cable Yearbook†
0735-4738 Employee Relations Report
0735-4754 Mason Memories
0735-4797 American Federation of Astrologers Bulletin
0735-5467 Missouri Archaeological Society. Special Publications
0735-5475 N C A A Football
0735-5513 Official International Business Directory of the Spanish Speaking World *changed to* Official International Business Directory of the Latin American World
0735-5688 Sightsaving
0735-5920 Quarterly Review of Doublespeak
0735-6161 Wood and Fiber Science
0735-6250 International Journal of Entomology†
0735-6315 Perspectives (Washington)
0735-6323 National Centurion
0735-6331 Journal of Educational Computing Research
0735-6358 Choices: a Core Collection for Young Reluctant Readers
0735-6471 Ethnic Racial Review
0735-648X Journal of Crime & Justice
0735-6501 Critique (Santa Rosa)
0735-6544 Street Pharmacologist
0735-6552 Language Planning Newsletter†
0735-665X Publishers' Catalogs Annual
0735-6722 Journal of Health Administration Education
0735-6757 American Journal of Emergency Medicine
0735-6846 Journal of Humanistic Education and Development
0735-6870 Southern Echoes
0735-7028 Professional Psychology: Research and Practice
0735-7036 Journal of Comparative Psychology
0735-7044 Behavioral Neuroscience
0735-7877 ImportCar (Akron, 1984?)
0735-7885 Kalliope
0735-7907 Cancer Investigation
0735-7915 Clinical Research Practices and Drug Regulatory Affairs
0735-7923 Journal of Industrial Irradiation Technology
0735-7931 Polymer Process Engineering
0735-8202 Another Season
0735-8253 Steam Coal Watch
0735-8296 S C O P E
0735-8318 U S Catholic Historian
0735-8393 Performing Arts Journal
0735-8423 Electronic Office
0735-8490 Editors Only
0735-8547 American Journal of Police
0735-8571 New Library Scene
0735-8644 Southern Neighborhoods
0735-8652 Agave
0735-8660 Keraulophon
0735-8776 Daily Guide to Richer Living†
0735-8938 Rutgers Computer & Technology Law Journal
0735-9055 Swallow's Tale Magazine†
0735-9144 Taylor Quarterly
0735-9195 N C A A Men's Ice Hockey Rules and Interpretations
0735-9225 Investing & Trading with Spanish Speaking Countries†
0735-9276 Simulation Series
0735-9314 Commercial Space Report
0735-9330 Code News (Cleveland)
0735-9349 Polish Genealogical Society Newsletter
0735-9381 Processed World
0735-939X Journal of Agricultural Entomology
0735-9543 U C L A Symposium Series on Molecular and Cellular Biology
0735-9551 Ob/Gyn Litigation Reporter
0735-9683 Health Marketing Quarterly
0735-9713 Painting and Wallcovering Contractor
0735-9780 Coming Revolution
0735-9799 King Saud University. College of Science. Journal
0735-9950 Private Placements *changed to* Private Placement Letter
0735-9969 School Microcomputing Bulletin
0735-9977 Auerbach Data Base Management
0735-9985 Auerbach Systems Development Management
0735-9993 Auerbach Data Processing Management
0736-0002 Auerbach Data Communications Management
0736-0010 Foodlines
0736-0037 Nutrition Research Newsletter
0736-0053 Opera Quarterly
0736-007X Al Hanson's Economic Newsletter
0736-0096 Nutrition Week
0736-0118 Medical Oncology & Tumor Pharmacotherapy
0736-0142 C L S Quarterly
0736-0258 Journal of Clinical Neurophysiology
0736-0266 Journal of Othopaedic Research
0736-0274 Catalyst Media Review†
0736-038X Oilfield Service, Supply, and Manufacturers Worldwide Directory *changed to* U S A Oilfield Service, Supply, and Manufacturers Directory
0736-0401 Security Letter Source Book
0736-0452 Auto Aftermarket Suppliers
0736-0460 Indo-Pacific Fishes
0736-0509 Contributions from the New York Botanical Garden
0736-055X Scholastic News: News Ranger
0736-0576 Scholastic News: News Trails
0736-0592 Scholastic News: News Explorer
0736-0622 Scholastic News: Newstime
0736-0673 Notes on Linguistics
0736-0703 Cost of Doing Business for Retail Sporting Goods Stores
0736-0711 Plays in Process
0736-0770 Visual Arts Research
0736-0789 Space Journal *changed to* Space R & D Alert
0736-0886 Kershner Kinfolk
0736-0894 P C Retailing
0736-0983 Planning for Higher Education
0736-0991 Solar Utilization News (Estes Park)†
0736-1122 Barnhart Dictionary Companion
0736-1688 Refunding Update
0736-1696 Continuing Education Alternatives Update
0736-170X Almost Free Cookbooks & Recipes Update
0736-1718 Family Systems Medicine
0736-1823 International C A D/C A M Industry Directory
0736-1831 International Industrial Sensor Directory
0736-1858 Family Records Today
0736-1874 A P Roach *see* 8750-6106
0736-1890 Recycling Update
0736-1904 Barter Update
0736-2048 E L T Documents
0736-2056 Avicultura Profesional
0736-2102 Crawford Families Exchange
0736-217X Reporting from the Russell Sage Foundation
0736-2188 Group Members Only
0736-2196 Family Practice Survey†
0736-220X Beverage Alcohol Market Report
0736-2277 Wisconsin Natural Resources
0736-2498 Mar-Marr-Marrs-Mars Exchange
0736-2501 Noise Control Engineering Journal
0736-2536 Aerospace Engineering Magazine
0736-2544 Patients' Rights in California
0736-2579 New England Review and Bread Loaf Quarterly
0736-265X Indian-Artifact Magazine
0736-2676 Wildlife Publications Review
0736-2684 Answer Man Newsletter
0736-2692 Book of Apple Software
0736-2706 Book of Atari Software†
0736-2714 Contributions in Psychology
0736-2773 Intelligence Report (Washington)
0736-2803 Clinical Rheumatology in Practice
0736-2862 Oracle Science Fiction and Fantasy Anthology Magazine *changed to* Oracle Science Fiction and Fantasy Magazine
0736-2870 Michigan Purchasing Directory†
0736-2889 Michigan Manufacturers Directory
0736-2900 Coastal Plains Farmer
0736-2951 Bits'n Bytes Gazette†
0736-2994 Stochastic Analysis and Applications
0736-3001 Journal of Environmental Science and Health. Part C: Environmental Carcinogenesis Reviews
0736-3427 Index: Foreign Broadcast Information Service Daily Reports: Middle East and North Africa *changed to* Index: Foreign Broadcast Information Service Daily Reports: Middle East and Africa
0736-3559 Almanac of Seapower
0736-3583 Bulletin of Clinical Neurosciences
0736-3605 Focus on Critical Care
0736-3621 Auerbach Computer Programming Management
0736-3648 Auerbach Data Center Operations Management
0736-3680 Planetary Report
0736-3761 Journal of Consumer Marketing
0736-3877 ComputerTalk Directory of Pharmacy Systems *changed to* ComputerTalk Pharmacy Systems Buyers Guide
0736-3885 ComputerTalk for the Physician†
0736-3893 ComputerTalk for the Pharmacist
0736-3907 Mosasaur
0736-3966 Poetry Index Annual
0736-3974 Text (New York)
0736-3982 C U N Y English Forum
0736-4083 Unique
0736-4121 Strategic Moves
0736-4148 Latin America and Caribbean Contemporary Record
0736-4156 Telecommunications Product Review
0736-4202 Stimuli for Writers†
0736-4261 Fort Smith Historical Society. Journal
0736-427X High Tech Investor
0736-4377 Chiropractic History
0736-4393 Journal of Clinical Immunoassay
0736-4547 Protein Abnormalities
0736-458X Physical Bioinorganic Chemistry Series†
0736-4660 N A F S A Directory
0736-4679 Journal of Emergency Medicine
0736-4733 Creative Woman
0736-4822 Metropolitan Life Foundation. Statistical Bulletin *see* 0741-9767
0736-489X Cable T V Law & Finance
0736-4903 L C Folk Archive Finding Aid
0736-4962 Dairy World
0736-4970 Adrift
0736-5020 Personal Computer News *changed to* Computer Trader
0736-5039 Isotope Effects in Chemical Reactions†
0736-5047 T & D Health and Safety Report *see* 0737-5743
0736-5071 A I Trends
0736-511X National Collegiate Athletic Association Wrestling Rules
0736-5128 N C A A Men's & Women's Swimming and Diving Rules
0736-5152 Chinese Journal of Acoustics
0736-5160 National Collegiate Athletic Association Football Rules & Interpretations
0736-5179 N C A A Illustrated Men's Rules *changed to* N C A A Men's Illustrated Basketball Rules
0736-5209 N C A A Baseball Rules
0736-5225 Management Technology†
0736-5268 Models of Scientific Thought
0736-5314 Seybold Report on Professonal Computing *changed to* Seybold Outlook on Professional Computing
0736-5527 Journal of Buyouts & Acquisitions
0736-5659 Banking Literature Index
0736-5705 Electronic Business Forecast
0736-5713 Guide to United States Treaties in Force
0736-5721 International Gas Research Conference. Proceedings
0736-573X Environmental Statutes
0736-5748 International Journal of Developmental Neuroscience
0736-5810 Journal of Defense & Diplomacy
0736-5829 Adapted Physical Activity Quarterly
0736-5845 Robotics and Computer-Integrated Manufacturing
0736-5853 Telematics and Informatics
0736-6086 Ethnic Racial Brotherhood
0736-6094 Wildlife Disease Review
0736-6108 Clinical Progress in Pacing and Electrophysiology *changed to* Clinical Progress in Electrophysiology and Pacing
0736-6132 Come-All-Ye
0736-6205 BioTechniques
0736-6213 Bioengineering Abstracts
0736-6256 No Load Fund Investor
0736-6264 Handbook for No-Load Fund Investors
0736-6272 Urban Insights Monograph Series
0736-6299 Solvent Extraction and Ion Exchange
0736-6396 I L R Report
0736-6477 Wilderness
0736-6531 Strategy and Tactics
0736-6574 Journal of Macromolecular Science. Part C. Reviews in Macromolecular Chemistry and Physics
0736-6620 Geothermal Energy Technology
0736-6825 Facial Plastic Surgery
0736-6884 Smithsonian Institution. Astrophysical Observatory. Minor Planet Circulars/Minor Planets and Comets
0736-6892 S I G U C C S Newsletter
0736-6906 S I G C H I Bulletin
0736-6922 International Comet Quarterly
0736-6957 Small Business Computer News
0736-6981 E D P A C S
0736-7023 Cryptozoology
0736-7163 Georgetown University Center for Strategic and International Studies. Significant Issues Series
0736-718X Minerva: Quarterly Report on Women and the Military
0736-721X A C M Ada Letters
0736-7236 Journal of Social and Clinical Psychology
0736-7244 Somatosensory Research
0736-7252 A P P A Newsletter
0736-7260 Seybold Report on Publishing Systems
0736-7392 Method: Journal of Lonergan Studies
0736-7430 Independence (Baltimore)†
0736-7457 Professional Publishing *see* 0884-951X
0736-7511 State Education Leader
0736-7635 Employee Communication *changed to* Communication Illustrated
0736-7643 Astute Investor
0736-7716 Population Trends and Public Policy
0736-7740 Music Reference Collection
0736-7759 Directory of Free Programs, Performing Talent and Attractions
0736-7775 N C A A Men's Lacrosse Rules
0736-7783 N C A A Men's & Women's Cross Country and Track & Field Rules
0736-7929 Healthline†
0736-8003 Ohio State University. Agricultural Research and Development Center. Special Circular
0736-8038 Zero to Three
0736-8046 Pediatric Dermatology
0736-8054 International Society for British Genealogy and Family History. Newsletter
0736-8089 Telephone Cost and Call Management
0736-8143 Cable T V Financial Databook
0736-8194 Two/Sixteen Magazine *see* 0743-4278
0736-8232 P T C Newsletter
0736-8259 Master Production Scheduling
0736-8305 Execution and Control Systems
0736-8313 Manufacturing Resource Planning
0736-8321 Material Requirements Planning
0736-8348 Smarts Insurance Bulletin
0736-8496 Oregon Wine Review
0736-8534 Development News for Libraries†
0736-8593 Computers in Nursing
0736-8607 CoED Journal
0736-8879 Footnotes
0736-9069 Broadcast Investor Charts
0736-9077 Health Professions Report
0736-9123 Papers in Comparative Studies
0736-9166 Work Times
0736-9182 Free Inquiry in Creative Sociology
0736-9212 Yellow Silk

1598 ISSN INDEX

0736-9239 Exporter (New York)
0736-928X Trivia
0736-931X Directory of Discount Department Stores *changed to* Directory of Discount Stores
0736-9417 Laser Medicine & Surgery News
0736-9492 Color Computer Magazine†
0736-9522 Conservation (Year)†
0736-9549 Reed Organ Society. Bulletin
0736-9573 Directory of Hardware Distributors *see* 0882-536X
0736-9603 Environmental Opportunities
0736-9689 Pest Alerts
0736-9719 Nursing Report
0736-9735 Psychoanalytic Psychology
0736-9743 Better Beagling
0736-9921 Supreme Court Economic Review
0736-9999 Index to USA Today
0737-0008 Cognition and Instruction
0737-0016 Journal of Community Health Nursing
0737-0024 Human-Computer Interaction
0737-0032 Musical Woman
0737-0083 Research Publications. Report
0737-0318 Growing Child Research Review
0737-0334 Computer Book Review
0737-0342 Western Humor and Irony Membership Serial Yearbook *changed to* World Humor and Irony Membership Serial Yearbook
0737-0393 Mississippi Kite
0737-0407 Aristos
0737-0415 Industrial Communications
0737-0423 Real Estate Tax Planning Newsletter
0737-0466 Coyote†
0737-0482 Monthly Rent†
0737-0555 Langston Hughes Review
0737-0652 Journal of Energetic Materials
0737-0660 N F A I S Trainers' Circuit Newsletter†
0737-0679 Walt Whitman Quarterly Review
0737-0881 Timex Sinclair User†
0737-089X Law & Inequality
0737-0903 Distribution Management
0737-0911 Sporting News Draft Guide†
0737-0938 Psychotherapy Newsletter
0737-0946 Business Computer Digest
0737-0954 Oxcart
0737-0989 North Jersey Regional Industrial Purchasing Guide
0737-0997 Dance Notation Journal
0737-1020 High Volume Printing
0737-1055 I C P Data Processing Management
0737-1160 Conference on Crime Countermeasures and Security. Proceedings *changed to* Carnahan Conference on Security Technology. Proceedings
0737-1187 Personal Computer Buyers Guide†
0737-1195 Journal of Polymorphous Perversity
0737-1292 E R I C-A A H E Research Reports *see* 0884-0040
0737-1306 Starmont Studies in Literary Criticism
0737-139X Cuyahoga Review
0737-1411 Ethnic American Voluntary Organizations
0737-1454 International Journal of Cell Cloning
0737-1667 Beatniks from Space
0737-1888 Today's Education Annual
0737-1888 Today's Education: Educational Support Edition†
0737-2094 Chapter I Handbook: Understanding and Implementing the Program
0737-2108 Science Citation Index. Abridged Edition†
0737-2124 Personal Communications *see* 0885-6710
0737-2140 Computer Classified Bluebook†
0737-2159 Banking Law Anthology
0737-2175 Biology (Year)†
0737-2191 Japan, Inc.
0737-2620 National Travel Survey
0737-268X Alaska Quarterly Review
0737-2817 Insulation Guide
0737-285X N Y C
0737-2884 International Journal of Satellite Communications
0737-2906 Personal Computer Age†
0737-2914 Perspectives in Clinical Pharmacology
0737-3082 Hypnotica†
0737-3112 Probate Law Journal
0737-3139 Medicom Drug Information Newsletter
0737-3147 Washington Business Journal
0737-3163 Guide to Four-Year Colleges (Year)
0737-3171 Peterson's Guide to Two-Year Colleges (Year)
0737-318X Calligraphy Idea Exchange
0737-3252 Journal of Health Care Marketing
0737-3368 Wharton Annual†
0737-3457 Abridged Catholic Periodical and Literature Index
0737-3481 Fiscal Policy Forum
0737-3635 American Poetry
0737-3716 Compute! Gazette
0737-3724 New International
0737-3732 Outlook (Seattle)
0737-3740 Country Home
0737-3813 NewsBank (New Canaan)
0737-3929 International Television†
0737-3937 Drying Technology
0737-3945 Pediatric and Adolescent Gynecology†
0737-3988 NewsBank Review of the Arts: Film and Television
0737-3996 NewsBank Review of the Arts: Performing Arts
0737-4003 NewsBank Review of the Arts: Fine Arts and Architecture
0737-4038 Molecular Biology and Evolution
0737-4135 Standard & Poor's Stock Guide
0737-4143 Southwest Journal of Linguistics
0737-4313 Computers (Year)†
0737-4445 Ward's Directory of 49,000 Private U.S. Companies
0737-4453 Source: Notes in the History of Art
0737-4461 Index to International Statistics
0737-4720 Linguistic Notes from La Jolla
0737-4747 Poetry Flash
0737-4844 Telephone Equipment Selection Guide
0737-4984 L H R T Newsletter
0737-500X Computers, Reading and Language Arts
0737-5077 Mobile Phone News
0737-5123 Parenting Studies
0737-5131 Paedovita
0737-514X Paedoperisse
0737-5158 Paedonoson
0737-5166 Acta Paedologica
0737-5174 Trisomy 21
0737-5182 Chiaroscuro†
0737-5255 Government Programs and Projects Directory
0737-5298 Luna Tack
0737-5328 Teacher Education Quarterly
0737-5336 E P B: Electronic Publishing and Bookselling *see* 0888-0948
0737-5344 Design Book Review
0737-5379 New York Spectator
0737-545X Surveys, Polls, Censuses and Forecasts Directory
0737-5506 Salthouse
0737-5700 Robotics Update
0737-5743 Transmission/Distribution Health & Safety Report
0737-5840 Mystics Quarterly
0737-5875 Washington Tax Review *see* 0887-2562
0737-5883 Creative
0737-5905 American Prometheus
0737-5999 Central Nervous System Trauma
0737-6006 A I D S Research
0737-6146 Advances in Anesthesia
0737-6227 Hunter Safety Instructor
0737-6413 Banking World
0737-6553 Electronic Imaging†
0737-660X C A D/C A M Technology *changed to* C I M Technology
0737-6650 American Asian Review
0737-6707 Notes on Literacy
0737-6782 Journal of Product Innovation Management
0737-6812 A N S News
0737-6839 Personal Property Section News
0737-6855 Muppet Magazine
0737-6871 Social Process in Hawaii
0737-688X Engel-Poh Family History Newsletter
0737-7037 Folklore Research Journal
0737-7169 Hemlocks and Balsams
0737-7266 Liquid Fuels Technology *see* 0884-3759
0737-7363 Journal of Continuing Higher Education
0737-7371 Ohio C P A *changed to* Ohio C P A Journal
0737-738X Patristic and Byzantine Review
0737-7495 Ohio Manufacturers Directory
0737-7576 Light Impressions Review
0737-7592 O A/F A Update†
0737-772X Recent Transportation Literature for Planning and Engineering Librarians
0737-7746 Aviation Litigation Reporter
0737-7762 Social Concept
0737-7770 Information Intelligence Online Libraries and Microcomputers
0737-7797 Resource Sharing & Information Networks
0737-7843 Periodical Title Abbreviations
0737-7851 Current Issues in Psychoanalytic Practice
0737-7908 Robotics World
0737-7932 Itawamba Settlers
0737-7940 Iowa Manufacturers Register
0737-8076 Hot Off the Computer
0737-8092 Center for Holocaust Studies Newsletter
0737-8122 Officemation Reports *changed to* Officemation Product Reports
0737-8173 Lighted Pathway
0737-8181 International Dredging Review
0737-8246 Quaker Yeomen
0737-8262 Current Psychological Research and Reviews
0737-8289 Living Abroad *changed to* International American
0737-8505 Personal Robotics News†
0737-8513 Toxic Chemicals Litigation Reporter
0737-8548 World Spaceflight News
0737-8742 Discurso Literario
0737-8831 Library Hi Tech
0737-8939 P C World
0737-8947 Boston University International Law Journal
0737-8998 Office Systems Research Journal
0737-9021 E M I E Bulletin
0737-903X Hospital Management Review
0737-9080 Film Review Annual
0737-9269 Blind Alleys
0737-9285 National Center for the Study of Collective Bargaining in Higher Education and the Professions. Newsletter
0737-948X Federal Reserve Bank of Minneapolis. Agricultural Credit Conditions Survey
0737-9501 Software Publishing Report†
0737-951X Data Base Alert *see* 0749-6680
0737-9587 C R C Critical Reviews in Oncology-Hematology
0738-0070 Wisconsin Manufacturers Register
0738-0089 International Hazardous Materials Transport *changed to* International Hazardous Materials Transport Manual
0738-0097 Biography Almanac
0738-0127 Starmont Reference Guides
0738-0143 Winning Sweepstakes Newsletter
0738-0186 Leader's Legal Tech Newsletter
0738-0194 P C Tech Journal
0738-0208 Jobless Newsletter
0738-0232 Hazardous Waste Consultant
0738-0453 MicroWorld
0738-050X Southeast Asia Chronicle†
0738-0518 Consumer Sourcebook
0738-0569 Computers in the Schools
0738-0577 Occupational Therapy in Health Care
0738-0585 Forest Planning
0738-0593 International Journal of Educational Development
0738-0623 Police Misconduct and Civil Rights Law Report
0738-064X A M S Studies in Anthropology
0738-0658 Puerto Rico Health Sciences Journal
0738-0666 Journal of Mechanisms, Transmissions and Automation in Design
0738-0674 New Relationships
0738-0690 Preview
0738-0739 Holocaust Studies Annual
0738-0755 Studies in Black American Literature
0738-0763 Essays in Graham Greene: An Annual Review
0738-0771 Smart Machines†
0738-081X Clinics in Dermatology
0738-0895 Journal of Architectural and Planning Research†
0738-0925 Recent Publications in Natural History
0738-0968 Space Age Times
0738-1026 Malpractice Reporter
0738-1093 Overland Journal
0738-1131 Architecture California
0738-114X Planning & Zoning News
0738-1360 Journal of Marine Resource Economics *changed to* Marine Resource Economics
0738-1379 Latin American Jewish Studies Newsletter
0738-1387 Robot - X News
0738-1395 C O A Review
0738-1409 C S S E D C Quarterly
0738-1425 International Development Resource Books
0738-1433 Women's Review of Books
0738-1441 Lens Research
0738-1514 Minnesota Manufacturers Register
0738-1522 Information America
0738-1719 Ethnic Information Sources of the U.S.
0738-1727 Journal of Modern Greek Studies
0738-1751 Antimicrobic Newsletter
0738-1859 Small Farm Advocate
0738-1891 Oregon Genealogical Society Quarterly
0738-1913 Collective Bargaining in Higher Education and the Professions. Annual Bibliography
0738-2022 Journal of Forth Application and Research
0738-2170 B O M A Experience Exchange Report
0738-2227 New Products Marketplace
0738-2278 Advances in Orthopaedic Surgery
0738-2294 Gesar
0738-2324 Guide to the High Technology and Industries†
0738-2421 Holly Society Journal
0738-2472 Coastal Ocean Pollution Assessment News†
0738-2480 Law and History Review
0738-2502 Precious Metals Performance Digest
0738-2588 S C A: Radio Subcarrier Report
0738-260X National Fact Book of Savings Banking *see* 8756-9043
0738-2685 American Bus Association. Annual Report *see* 0278-1565
0738-2766 Consumer Health Reporter†
0738-2898 Journal of Environmental Horticulture
0738-2928 Journal of Hospital Supply, Processing and Distribution *changed to* Journal of Healthcare Materiel Management
0738-3045 Telecommunications Systems and Services Directory
0738-3169 American Foreign Policy Newsletter
0738-3223 Central America Bulletin
0738-3231 Instrumentation Symposium for the Process Industries
0738-3312 Government Union Critique
0738-3355 Technical Analysis of Stocks and Commodities
0738-3371 NEWRADIO Cable Audio & Pay Radio Report
0738-3398 I B C D: International Business Conditions Digest
0738-3401 Administration and Policy Journal
0738-341X Inter-Connection
0738-3568 Database Update *see* 0737-0946
0738-3576 Digit Magazine
0738-3614 Computers in Psychiatry/Psychology
0738-3789 Food Service Marketing for Independent Operators *see* 0746-1887
0738-3843 Online Data Access *changed to* Access (Year)
0738-386X Indiana Review
0738-3991 Patient Education and Counseling
0738-4173 Sylvia Porter's Personal Finance Magazine

ISSN INDEX 1599

0738-4203 For Your Eyes Only
0738-4211 Selling Direct
0738-4254 Food Service Marketing for Independent Restaurants *see* 0746-1887
0738-4262 COM-S A C
0738-4270 COM - A N D
0738-4300 Government Computer News
0738-4351 Securities Traders' Monthly
0738-4548 Indochina Issues
0738-4556 M D S News
0738-4599 MacRae's Directory of Manufacturers' Representatives *changed to* MacRae's Verified Directory of Manufacturers' Representatives
0738-467X Caring (Washington)
0738-4718 Make it with Leather *changed to* Leather Craftsman
0738-4912 T A I C H Directory†
0738-4920 Smoking and Health and Reporter
0738-4947 Alabama Medicine
0738-517X Puerto del Sol
0738-5390 Saint Louis University Public Law Forum *changed to* Saint Louis University Public Law Review
0738-5560 Chismearte Magazine
0738-5579 Bond Fund Survey
0738-565X Wheels of Time
0738-5676 Power Line
0738-5692 C A D/C A M Alert
0738-5714 F.C.C. Week
0738-5919 Antitrust Law Handbook
0738-5927 Public Citizen
0738-5943 Rice World & Soybean News
0738-6001 Creation/Evolution
0738-601X Latin America Update
0738-6044 Workplace Democracy *changed to* New Workplace
0738-6079 Family Computing
0738-6168 Hazardous Waste
0738-6176 Psychotherapy Patient
0738-6184 Journal of Religion & Aging
0738-6206 Pace Environmental Law Review
0738-6354 Micro Software Marketing
0738-6370 Hospital Capital Formation & Reorganization Report
0738-6494 Just Compensation
0738-6508 International Policy Report
0738-6532 Renewable Resources Journal
0738-6583 Executive Housekeeping Today
0738-6613 Printout *see* 0887-7556
0738-6648 Jacksoniana
0738-6729 Behavior Analyst
0738-6753 Midwest Agricultural Law Journal *changed to* Rural Practice Law Journal
0738-6761 Midwest Labor & Employment Law Journal†
0738-677X Illinois Journal of Family Law†
0738-6869 Business News (San Diego)
0738-6931 D.C. Real Estate Reporter
0738-6958 Private Security Case Law Reporter
0738-7008 Crab Creek Review
0738-7016 Portable 100/200/600
0738-7105 Institute of Modern Russian Culture Newsletter
0738-7113 Latin America in Books
0738-713X Microcontamination
0738-7148 Boy Meets Girl
0738-7156 Microbanker
0738-7172 Book of IBM Software
0738-7237 Mirror
0738-7245 Nautical Research Journal
0738-7326 Investor's Guide to High Technology Corporations†
0738-7334 New Issues in High Technology *changed to* Directory of High Technology Corporations. Supplement
0738-7342 High Technology Outlook†
0738-7369 Directory of Public High Technology Corporations
0738-7393 High Technology Overviews†
0738-7512 High Technology Growth Trends†
0738-7555 G P Newsletter
0738-7644 Texas Optometry
0738-7687 Living Off the Land
0738-7776 ChemEcology
0738-7806 Generations (San Francisco)
0738-7911 Talkin' Union
0738-7954 Augsburg Media Messenger
0738-7962 Parish Teacher
0738-7989 Journal of Materials Education
0738-7997 Journal of Northeast Asian Studies
0738-8012 Word from Washington
0738-8020 Pottery Southwest
0738-8063 W.A.S. Newsletter
0738-811X Health Facts
0738-825X Reynolds Family Newsletter†
0738-8268 Goodlet Family Newsletter†
0738-8357 Folk Art Finder
0738-8381 Rocky Mountain Quarter Horse Magazine
0738-839X Directory of Computer & Software Retailers
0738-8446 Exchange (Washington)†
0738-8489 Evangelist
0738-8497 Roundup (Washington)†
0738-8535 Washington State Genealogical and Historical Review *changed to* Washington Heritage
0738-8543 List†
0738-8551 C R C Critical Reviews in Biotechnology
0738-8586 Victor Valley Magazine
0738-8640 Knowledge
0738-8675 American Radio
0738-8705 Panhandler
0738-8748 C I R R
0738-8756 Penny Stock Performance Digest
0738-8772 Laboratory Computer Letter
0738-8845 C M C News
0738-8853 Beverage Digest
0738-8861 Progressive Platter Music Review
0738-8888 International Currency Report
0738-8896 Communications International *see* 0748-8920
0738-8993 Spoon River Quarterly
0738-9000 Creative Black Book
0738-9035 Pacific Rim Intelligence Report
0738-9124 Land Mobile Product News
0738-9191 International Terrorism Newsletter
0738-9264 Futurific
0738-9299 Frank
0738-9302 Ligature
0738-9310 Science of Food and Agriculture
0738-9345 Contributions to the Study of World Literature
0738-9361 Arts & Sciences (Evanston)
0738-9396 Mid-Atlantic Archivist
0738-9477 N E C N P Newsletter†
0738-9515 Travel Industry World Yearbook
0738-9604 Carefree Enterprise *changed to* Carefree Enterprise Magazine
0738-9671 New Mexico Humanities Review
0738-968X I P M Practitioner
0738-9701 Journal of Developmental Education
0738-9728 International Lawyers' Newsletter
0738-9744 Dental Computer Newsletter
0738-9760 Journal of Applied Rabbit Research
0738-9779 Tribune
0738-985X Natchez Trace Traveler
0738-9981 Collectrix
0738-999X Florida Field Naturalist
0739-0025 Luren
0739-0033 Fillers for Publications
0739-0041 Florida Geographer
0739-0068 Near East Archaeological Society Bulletin
0739-0203 Pontiac-Oakland and County Legal News
0739-0289 Morticians of the Southwest
0739-0408 Tennessee Education
0739-0416 Global Electronics Information Newsletter *changed to* Global Electronics
0739-0491 Textile Business Outlook
0739-0572 Journal of Atmospheric and Oceanic Technology
0739-0653 Peek 65
0739-0718 Hue Points
0739-0750 Fielding's Economy Caribbean
0739-0769 Fielding's Bermuda and the Bahamas
0739-0785 Fielding's Economy Europe
0739-0793 Fielding's Mexico
0739-084X Grand River Valley Review
0739-0874 Computer Economics Report
0739-0939 Airpost Journal
0739-0971 TraNet
0739-0998 Jail and Prisoner Law Bulletin
0739-1048 Star Tech Journal
0739-1056 College Media Review
0739-1064 3 L Llama Magazine *changed to* Llamas Magazine
0739-1137 I A S S I S T Quarterly
0739-1161 Performing Arts Forum
0739-1188 New England Classical Newsletter
0739-1218 Philosophy and the Arts
0739-1242 Noninvasive Medical Imaging†
0739-1277 Willow Springs
0739-134X Landers Landing
0739-1390 International Council for Traditional Music. Bulletin
0739-1544 N C E C A Journal
0739-1552 N C E C A Newsletter *changed to* N C E C A News
0739-1609 U S 1 Worksheets
0739-1692 Cancer Update
0739-1706 Lawyer Hiring & Training Report
0739-1749 Daughters of Sarah
0739-1781 Journal of Weather Modification
0739-1803 Lesbian News
0739-1854 Harvard International Review
0739-1862 Company Thesaurus
0739-1897 Entertainment, Publishing and the Arts Handbook
0739-1935 Satellite Audio Report
0739-1943 Journal of Southwest Georgia History
0739-1951 National Legal Bibliography
0739-2044 Medicine & Computer†
0739-2184 Smith Funding Report
0739-2214 N P T A Management News
0739-2265 Computer Executive Letter
0739-2281 Searching Together
0739-229X Sonus
0739-2311 Utah Holiday
0739-2354 Crosscurrents
0739-2451 Annual Review of Banking Law
0739-2486 Genealogy Today *see* 8755-7584
0739-2494 Barrister (Philadelphia)
0739-2907 Electronic Publishing Abstracts
0739-2931 Association of Part-Time Professionals. National Newsletter
0739-2958 All About Mail Order
0739-2966 Teleconferencing Resources Directory
0739-2974 Northern Lights Studies in Creativity
0739-2990 Managing International Development†
0739-3016 B N A's Employee Relations Weekly
0739-3024 Association of American University Presses Directory
0739-3067 Sporting News Official N B A Register
0739-3075 Energy Statistics
0739-3156 Office Professional
0739-3164 University R & D
0739-3253 High-Tech New Issues Advisory†
0739-344X Tradeswomen
0739-3474 Carrier Pidgin
0739-3482 Virginia Appalachian Notes
0739-3490 National Association of Railroad Passengers News
0739-3520 Commodity Trading Digest
0739-3563 Reality Theory Newsletter
0739-3571 Line of March
0739-3601 Paralegal
0739-361X National Association of Academies of Science. Directory and Proceedings
0739-3717 Journal of Vibration, Acoustics, Stress and Reliability in Design
0739-3733 Atterbury Letter - Wine, Dining & Travel
0739-3784 Road Race Management Newsletter
0739-3938 Southern Political Report
0739-3946 Design Cost & Data for Management of Building Design
0739-4098 Mediation Quarterly
0739-4144 Textile Pricing Outlook
0739-4268 I M C Newsletter
0739-4314 Digital Review
0739-4322 Counterspy *changed to* National Reporter
0739-4330 County Agents Directory
0739-439X University of California, Los Angeles. Institute of Industrial Relations. Monograph and Research Series
0739-4462 Archives of Insect Biochemistry and Physiology
0739-4497 Walking! Journal
0739-456X Journal of Planning Education and Research
0739-4586 V A H P E R D Journal
0739-4640 Global Risk Assessments
0739-4667 Book on Starting Pitchers
0739-4683 D.I.N. Newservice
0739-4691 Texas Blue Book of Life Insurance Statistics
0739-4713 Freshman English News
0739-4853 Against the Current (Detroit)
0739-4942 Warren Family Historian
0739-4969 Outerbridge
0739-5043 Career Opportunities News
0739-5086 Judaica Librarianship
0739-5132 L.O.G.I.C.
0739-5175 I E E E Engineering in Medicine and Biology Magazine
0739-5272 Motheroot Journal
0739-5299 Federal Reserve Bank of Kansas City. Financial Letter
0739-5418 Friendly Letter
0739-5515 Advantage
0739-5531 Television Index
0739-5574 T V Pro-Log
0739-5612 Archaeological Society of Connecticut. Bulletin
0739-5663 Field Notes (Concord) *changed to* Fish & Game Highlights of New Hampshire
0739-5728 Helicopter Annual
0739-5736 Museum of Fine Arts, Boston. Bulletin†
0739-5795 Goucher *changed to* Goucher Quarterly
0739-5876 Radioactive Waste Management and the Nuclear Fuel Cycle
0739-5914 Mind: The Meetings Index
0739-6074 Nationwide Directory of Sporting Goods Buyers
0739-618X Business Publications Index and Abstracts†
0739-6198 Philateli-Graphics
0739-6201 ComputerTalk Directory of Medical Computer Systems
0739-621X Rain
0739-6244 Asia/Pacific Currency Report
0739-6260 Micron and Microscopica Acta
0739-6325 Annual Report on Research and Development
0739-6422 Christian Life Communities Harvest
0739-6449 Investment Column Quarterly
0739-6562 Drug Abuse Update
0739-6686 Annual Review of Nursing Research
0739-6694 Beginning (Iowa City)
0739-6732 Quality Control Scanner
0739-6767 N C T V News
0739-6813 Americans for Legal Reform
0739-6821 Exhibitor Magazine
0739-6821 Illustrated Buyers Guide to Exhibits
0739-7089 Videodisc Monitor
0739-7100 U M T R I Research Review
0739-7240 Domestic Animal Endocrinology
0739-7348 Infectious Disease Alert
0739-747X Nor'westing
0739-7704 E E R C News
0739-7712 School Library Media Annual
0739-7828 Currents
0739-7895 Book Arts Review
0739-8042 California Today
0739-8093 Fayette Connection
0739-8123 Personal Electronics†
0739-814X A S F A Aquaculture Abstracts
0739-8158 Fram: The Journal of Polar Studies
0739-8182 Impact: Office Automation†
0739-828X Emotional First Aid
0739-8298 Concrete and Masonry Cost Data *changed to* Means Concrete Cost Data
0739-8328 Problems in General Surgery

1600 ISSN INDEX

0739-8417 Cybernetics and Computing Technology
0739-8425 Soviet Journal of Superhard Materials
0739-8433 Soviet Immunology
0739-845X MacRae's North Carolina State Industrial Directory *changed to* MacRae's North Carolina/South Carolina/Virginia
0739-8468 MacRae's North Dakota/South Dakota State Industrial Directory
0739-8476 MacRae's Arizona/New Mexico State Industrial Directory
0739-8484 MacRae's Texas State Industrial Directory
0739-862X N A R F Legal Review
0739-8689 Securities & Syndication Review
0739-8743 Automated Office Systems
0739-876X Satellite Dealer *changed to* Satellite Direct
0739-8999 Soviet Machine Science
0739-9006 Peterson's Annual Guides: Summer Opportunities for Kids and Teenagers *changed to* Peterson's Summer Opportunities for Kids and Teenagers
0739-9014 Journal of Information Systems Management (Pennsauken)
0739-9022 Automated Materials Handling and Storage
0739-9049 Information Management (New York)
0739-9065 Equine Veterinary Data
0739-9227 Community Services Catalyst
0739-9294 Public Employee (Boston)
0739-9405 Programmer's Market†
0739-9413 Business and Health
0739-9502 Gallup Monthly Report on Eating Out
0739-9529 Seminars in Interventional Radiology
0739-9537 Northwest Edition *changed to* Northwest Living
0739-9553 Computer-Using Educators Newsletter *changed to* C U E Newsletter
0739-9561 Hospital Pharmacy Service Instant Up-Date
0739-957X Hospital Pharmacy Director's Monthly Management Series
0739-9588 Vital Signs Pharmacy Services Newsletter
0739-9723 Merchant
0739-9820 Special Services in the Schools
0739-9847 Medical Month†
0739-9863 Hispanic Journal of Behavioral Sciences
0739-988X Link-Up
0739-9928 Computer Negotiations Report
0739-9936 Bank Acquisition Report†
0740-0004 Central America and the Caribbean: Development Assistance Abroad
0740-0020 Food Microbiology
0740-0101 In Cider
0740-0179 T A C D A Alert
0740-0187 Construction Bargaineer
0740-0195 Focus (Washington, 1970)
0740-0403 Museum Year
0740-0411 Supervisor's Newsletter
0740-0438 Personal Software Magazine *changed to* Personal Computing
0740-0446 American University Studies. Series 7. Theology and Religion
0740-0454 American University Studies. Series 8. Psychology
0740-0462 American University Studies. Series 9. History
0740-0470 American University Studies. Series 10. Political Science
0740-0489 American University Studies. Series 11. Anthropology and Sociology
0740-0497 American University Studies. Series 12. Slavic Languages and Literature
0740-0527 California Cable Letter
0740-0578 Lifelong Learning
0740-0640 Radiation Protection Management
0740-0659 Faith and Mission
0740-0675 History of Philosophy Quarterly
0740-0780 Carrousel Art
0740-0942 Lawyer's P C
0740-1388 Excess Express
0740-1434 Ag-Pilot International
0740-1469 Computer Industry Litigation Reporter
0740-1558 Yearbook for Traditional Music
0740-1590 A Plus *changed to* A Plus: The Number One Apple II Magazine
0740-1604 P C Week
0740-1825 Faxon News†
0740-1892 Media Profiles: Health Sciences Edition
0740-1906 Media Profiles: Career Development Edition
0740-1957 Madness Network News†
0740-1965 Schatzkammer
0740-2007 Ancient Philosophy
0740-2074 Draft Review and Preview†
0740-2082 International Journal of Sport Biomechanics
0740-2155 Software Supermarket†
0740-2252 Acid Precipitation Digest
0740-235X A L P S Monthly†
0740-2368 Mole†
0740-2376 B M E Tax Newsletter
0740-2384 New York Sports†
0740-2392 Agada
0740-2430 Quarterly Index: Information Access for the Small Animal Practitioner
0740-2511 Laser Focus Including Electro-Optics Magazine *see* 8755-1853
0740-252X Technology Network†
0740-2546 Corporate Finance Bluebook
0740-2570 Seminars in Diagnostic Pathology
0740-2732 Great Plains National Instructional Television Library. Recorded Visual Instruction *changed to* G P N Educational Media. Elementary-Secondary
0740-2732 Great Plains National Instructional Television Library. Recorded Visual Instruction *changed to* G P N Educational Media. College-Adult
0740-2732 Great Plains National Instructional Television Library. Recorded Visual Instruction *changed to* G P N Educational Media. Crossover
0740-2740 Sellers Letters†
0740-2775 World Policy Journal
0740-283X Creative Black Book. Portfolio Edition
0740-2856 Boca Raton Magazine
0740-2937 MacRae's Connecticut State Industrial Directory
0740-2945 MacRae's Maine/New Hampshire/Vermont State Industrial Directory
0740-2953 MacRae's New York State Industrial Directory
0740-2961 A S T M Standards Infobriefs
0740-3119 Catalog Age
0740-3194 Magnetic Resonance in Medicine
0740-3224 Optical Society of America. Journal Part B
0740-3232 Optical Society of America. Journal Part A
0740-3291 Cultural Survival Quarterly
0740-3313 DNotes†
0740-3534 Automation in Housing and Manufactured Home Dealer
0740-3550 New from Japan
0740-3569 New from Europe
0740-3577 New from U S
0740-3585 World Electronic Developments
0740-3666 Investing in Crisis
0740-3739 Fine Chemicals Directory
0740-3763 Popular Magazine Review
0740-3968 Computer User (Cerritos)†
0740-3984 D.C. Directory
0740-4018 America's Corporate Families and International Affiliates
0740-4050 A B A/B N A Lawyers' Manual on Professional Conduct
0740-4085 Computer Publishers & Publications
0740-4093 Quilt Digest
0740-4182 Credences: A Journal of Twentieth Century Poets and Poetics
0740-4247 Video Marketing Survey and Forecasts
0740-4271 Secondary Mortgage Markets
0740-428X MacRae's Iowa/Nebraska State Industrial Directory
0740-4298 MacRae's Pennsylvania State Industrial Directory
0740-431X Alabama State Industrial Directory *see* 0733-5016
0740-4328 MacRae's Kentucky/West Virginia State Industrial Directory
0740-4336 MacRae's Illinois State Industrial Directory
0740-4409 Under Construction
0740-445X Computers in Human Services
0740-4549 Source Book: Social and Health Services in the Greater New York Area
0740-4557 American University Studies. Series 13. Linguistics
0740-4565 American University Studies. Series 14. Education
0740-4638 MacRae's California State Industrial Directory
0740-4646 MacRae's Tennessee State Industrial Directory
0740-4654 MacRae's Mississippi State Industrial Directory
0740-4662 MacRae's Oklahoma State Industrial Directory
0740-4670 MacRae's Arkansas State Industrial Directory
0740-4689 MacRae's Massachusetts/Rhode Island State Industrial Directory
0740-4697 MacRae's Florida State Industrial Directory
0740-4824 Brooklyn Journal of International Law
0740-4832 Grassroots Fundraising Journal
0740-4859 Hyatt's P C News Report
0740-4921 Details
0740-4956 Focus: Library Service to Older Adults, People with Disabilities
0740-4999 Trail Tracer
0740-5006 Iredell County Tracks (N C)
0740-5022 Software Publishers' Catalogs Annual
0740-5103 Investment Decisions
0740-5111 American University Studies. Series 15. Communications
0740-5138 International Journal of Reviews in Library and Information Science
0740-5162 International Coal Testing Conference
0740-5200 Data Based Advisor
0740-5294 Rehabfilm Newsletter
0740-5324 Perspective on A T & T and Boc Products and Marketing
0740-5375 International Journal of Islamic of Arabic Studies
0740-5383 Grant Advisor
0740-5405 Cyrano's Journal
0740-5464 Bottomline
0740-5472 Journal of Substance Abuse Treatment
0740-5502 Information and Behavior
0740-5537 Journal of Civil Defense
0740-5901 Jews for Jesus Newsletter
0740-5960 Academic Journal
0740-6045 MacRae's Indiana State Industrial Directory
0740-6053 MacRae's Wisconsin State Industrial Directory
0740-6061 MacRae's Minnesota State Industrial Directory
0740-607X MacRae's Missouri State Industrial Directory
0740-6088 MacRae's Idaho/Montana/Wyoming State Industrial Directory
0740-610X MacRae's Oregon State Industrial Directory
0740-6118 MacRae's Kansas State Industrial Directory
0740-6126 MacRae's Colorado/Utah/Nevada State Industrial Directory
0740-6134 MacRae's Washington State Industrial Directory
0740-6169 Society for Historians of American Foreign Relations. Newsletter
0740-6215 Yankee Magazine's Travel Guide to New England
0740-6231 Computer Publishing and Advertising Report
0740-624X Government Information Quarterly
0740-669X International Report (Irvine)
0740-672X Mutual Beneficial Association of Rail Transportation Employees. Mutual Magazine
0740-6738 Astro Talk
0740-6797 Society for Computer Simulation. Transactions
0740-6800 Data Base Product Reports
0740-6819 Automated Law Office Consultant†
0740-6851 Long-Distance Letter
0740-6932 LocalNetter Designer's Handbook
0740-6967 Cataract/International Journal of Cataract Surgery
0740-6983 Practice Marketing & Management
0740-722X Aerospace America
0740-7289 Career Guide: Dun's Employment Opportunities Directory
0740-7459 I E E E Software
0740-7467 I E E E/A S S P
0740-7475 I E E E Design & Test of Computers
0740-7513 International Publishing Newsletter
0740-7548 Self-Help Group Directory
0740-7556 Artificial Intelligence Report *see* 0885-9957
0740-7610 Zoos and Aquariums in the Americas *changed to* Zoological Parks & Aquariums in the Americas
0740-7629 Parapsychology Abstracts International
0740-7769 Journal of In Vitro Fertilization and Embryo Transfer
0740-7785 Exhibit Reporter†
0740-7793 Washington Report on Health Legislation and Regulation *changed to* Health Legislation
0740-7815 Exquisite Corpse
0740-7998 Biblical Evangelist
0740-8013 Oak Leaves
0740-8188 Library & Information Science Research
0740-820X M.D. Anderson Hospital and Tumor Institute at Houston. Cancer Bulletin
0740-8293 Buried Treasure from Aceto Genealogical Files†
0740-8307 Eidos
0740-834X Eagle (Naugatuck)
0740-8439 Book
0740-8498 Wellness Newsletter
0740-8528 American Council for Judaism. Special Interest Report
0740-8625 Studies in Contemporary Jewry
0740-8668 Midwest Technology *changed to* New & Emerging Technology
0740-8684 Nutrition Report
0740-8714 Nelson's Directory of Wall Street Research *see* 0886-0521
0740-8765 P M T
0740-8870 Stephen Wright's Mystery Notebook
0740-8943 Communications from the International Brecht Society
0740-896X Tri-State Packet
0740-8978 American Public Opinion Index
0740-9087 Employers' Health Costs Savings Letter
0740-9125 Plough (Rifton)
0740-9133 Northeast African Studies
0740-9214 Arts Quarterly
0740-9257 American University Studies. Series 2. Romance Languages and Literature
0740-9303 Ophthalmic Plastic and Reconstructive Surgery
0740-9311 Clockwatch Review
0740-946X Siglo XX-20th Century
0740-9567 Africa Research and Publications Project. Working Papers Series†
0740-9680 Times of Restoration
0740-9699 Mohawk
0740-9702 Saratoga
0740-9710 Food and Foodways
0740-9737 Genewatch
0740-9745 Benchmark Sites News†
0740-9893 Excellence in Teaching
0740-9982 Hospital Manager†
0741-0042 C A D/C A M: Management Strategies
0741-0050 Executive Computing
0741-0069 Communications Concepts
0741-0204 Global Perspectives
0741-0271 Sunrust
0741-0298 Brasilians
0741-0395 Genetic Epidemiology
0741-0522 Chronicle (Austin)

ISSN INDEX 1601

0741-0700 American University Studies. Series 4. English Language and Literature
0741-0786 Fiction Monthly *changed to* Short Story Review
0741-0794 Ceilidh
0741-0808 High-Tech Materials Alert
0741-0883 Written Communication
0741-1111 American Politics
0741-1235 Sociology of Sport Journal
0741-1308 Urban Resources
0741-1316 Nebo
0741-1413 International Electrochemical Progress
0741-160X Radiology and Imaging Letter
0741-1618 Current Advances in Biochemistry
0741-1626 Current Advances in Cell and Developmental Biology
0741-1634 Current Advances in Endocrinology
0741-1642 Current Advances in Genetics and Molecular Biology
0741-1650 Current Advances in Immunology
0741-1669 Current Advances in Microbiology
0741-1677 Current Advances in Neuroscience
0741-1685 Current Advances in Pharmacology and Toxicology
0741-1693 Current Advances in Physiology
0741-1707 Gold Skills†
0741-1715 S & V C
0741-1731 Space Calendar
0741-1790 Avalon to Camelot
0741-1995 Concerned Investors Guide
0741-2029 S A E Technical Literature Abstracts
0741-2037 Crossroads (DeKalb)
0741-2088 Belli Law Journal†
0741-2150 American University Studies. Series 16. Economics
0741-2223 Journal of Robotic Systems
0741-2347 Apple Index
0741-2355 I B M - P C Index
0741-2363 Business Computer Index
0741-2460 Wavelength
0741-2851 Open Systems Communication
0741-286X Open Systems Data Transfer
0741-2878 C I S Federal Register Index
0741-2940 I S C A Quarterly
0741-3017 Health Letter (New York)†
0741-3106 I E E E Electron Device Letters
0741-3149 Midway Review
0741-3157 Party Mail†
0741-3173 Local/State Funding Report
0741-3335 Plasma Physics and Controlled Fusion
0741-3351 Artist's Magazine
0741-336X Standard for Auditing Computer Applications
0741-3432 San Antonio Living
0741-3440 South Florida Living (North Edition)
0741-3467 From the State Capitals. Consumer Protection†
0741-3475 From the State Capitals. General Trends
0741-3483 From the State Capitals. Urban Development
0741-3491 From the State Capitals. Construction: Institutional *see* 0749-2766
0741-3505 From the State Capitals. Family Relations
0741-3513 From the State Capitals. Parking Regulations *see* 0749-2774
0741-3521 From the State Capitals. Public Employee Policy
0741-353X From the State Capitals. Civil Rights
0741-3548 From the State Capitals. Banking *see* 0749-2812
0741-3556 From the State Capitals. Taxation and Revenue
0741-3564 From the State Capitals. Urban Transit *see* 0749-2774
0741-3572 From the State Capitals. Women and the Law
0741-3599 Minnesota Genealogical Journal
0741-3610 C P A Digest
0741-3629 Energy Design Update
0741-3653 Journal of Educational Public Relations
0741-3696 Sports-Nutrition News
0741-3750 Opportunity Magazine
0741-4218 Clinical Cardiology Alert
0741-4234 Neurology Alert
0741-4242 Long Story
0741-4269 International Tax and Business Law
0741-4285 Run
0741-4501 Software Maintenance News
0741-4579 Arts Review
0741-4609 International Association of Assessing Officers. News Bulletin *changed to* I A A O Update
0741-4617 Contractor Profit News
0741-4641 Business Computing†
0741-465X American Council for Judaism. Issues
0741-482X Security and Special Police Legal Update
0741-501X Assessor's Data Exchange
0741-5028 Bluefish
0741-5044 Agenda (Westport) *changed to* Animals' Agenda
0741-5095 Hospitality Education and Research Journal†
0741-5141 Mental Health Law Reporter
0741-5192 K Power†
0741-5214 Journal of Vascular Surgery
0741-5222 Laser Research
0741-5230 Acid Precipitation
0741-5249 Solar Thermal Energy Technology
0741-5257 Coal Preparation and Pollution Control
0741-5281 Index to the Boston Globe
0741-5362 I S C Newsletter
0741-5397 Journal of Medical Technology
0741-5400 Journal of Leukocyte Biology
0741-5478 Austin Living
0741-5486 Denver Living
0741-5494 Dallas/Fort Worth Living
0741-5516 Phoenix Living
0741-5672 Society for American Archaeology. Bulletin
0741-5702 Formations
0741-5729 National Home Business Report
0741-5737 American Salon Eighty-Five *changed to* American Salon
0741-5745 Human Intelligence International Newsletter
0741-5753 Society for German-American Studies. Newsletter
0741-5796 W O H R C News
0741-580X Modem Notes
0741-5818 Travel Smart for Business
0741-5826 Travel Smart
0741-5834 Lightwave
0741-5842 Shaw Annual
0741-5869 Optical Memory News
0741-5877 International Series in Heat and Mass Transfer
0741-5931 S P I E Optical Engineering Reports *changed to* Optical Engineering Reports
0741-6016 Microcomputer Industry Update
0741-6024 Fiction Network Magazine
0741-6091 Kovels on Antiques and Collectibles
0741-6105 Texarkana U S A Quarterly
0741-6148 Book Research Quarterly
0741-6156 Theory and Practice
0741-6202 Kafka Society of America. Newsletter *changed to* Kafka Society of America. Journal
0741-6210 Croton Review
0741-6229 Zetetic Scholar
0741-6245 Mayo Clinic Health Letter
0741-6261 Rand Journal of Economics
0741-6423 Case Study
0741-644X Productivity Brief
0741-6458 Productivity Perspectives
0741-6466 Productivity Digest
0741-6474 Productivity Letter
0741-6512 D R G Monitor
0741-6555 Feminist Bookstore News
0741-6601 Sales & Marketing Digest (Boca Raton)
0741-6776 Entrepreneurial Economy
0741-6857 American Homeopathy/Consumer Edition *see* 0747-606X
0741-6865 American Homeopathy/Professional Edition *see* 0747-606X
0741-6873 American Homeopathy/Affiliate Edition *see* 0747-606X
0741-6997 H R Reporter
0741-7004 Foundation Giving Watch
0741-7160 Export Graficas U S A
0741-7284 Knox County Illinois Genealogical Society. Quarterly
0741-739X C S C Reports
0741-7403 Familia Latina
0741-7497 Northern California Review of Business and Economics
0741-7527 Annali d'Italianistica
0741-756X Poetry North Review†
0741-7586 Pacific Maritime Magazine
0741-7713 Coal-Based Synfuels
0741-7721 Unconventional Petroleum
0741-7748 Consuming Passions
0741-7772 Legal Assistant Today, Inc.
0741-7780 Sheet Music Exchange
0741-8132 Business Book Review
0741-8264 Circuit Rider (Springfield)
0741-8280 Advances in Economic Botany
0741-8329 Alcohol
0741-8337 Blue Chip Economic Worldscan
0741-8345 Blue Chip Financial Forecasts
0741-8361 Report on A T & T
0741-837X School Finance News†
0741-8388 State Telephone Regulation Report
0741-8477 Boston University Journal of Tax Law
0741-8485 Urban Institute. Policy and Research Report
0741-8531 Wrap Up on Latin American Agriculture, Food, Fishing & Livestock†
0741-854X Wrap Up on Latin American Banking & Finance†
0741-8558 Wrap Up on Latin American Chemicals, Cosmetics, Pharmaceuticals & Medical Equipment†
0741-8566 Wrap Up on Latin American Construction, Housing & Real Estate†
0741-8574 Wrap Up on Latin American Mining & Forestry†
0741-8582 Wrap Up on Latin American Textile & Leather, Rubber & Plastic Industries†
0741-8590 Wrap Up on Latin American Machinery, Electronics & Communications†
0741-8604 Wrap Up on Latin American Energy†
0741-8620 Journal of Dental Practice Administration
0741-8639 Sage: A Scholarly Journal on Black Women
0741-8647 Macworld
0741-8736 G M U Law Review
0741-8760 Locomotive
0741-8787 Journal of the Senses
0741-8795 Esoteric Review
0741-8825 Justice Quarterly
0741-8841 Packaging Patents Newsletter
0741-885X Plastics Processing Patents Newsletter
0741-8868 Plastics Materials Patents Newsletter
0741-9031 Kentucky Manufacturers Register
0741-9058 Library Hi Tech News
0741-9066 Compleat Lawyer
0741-9147 National Women's Health Report
0741-918X Keystone
0741-9309 American University Studies. Series 17. Classical Language and Literature
0741-9325 R A S E
0741-9333 Cogitations on Law and Government
0741-9384 Hora
0741-9422 N Y P C Newsletter
0741-9430 Electric Utility Instrumentation†
0741-9449 Minnesota Journal
0741-9457 Yale Journal on Regulation
0741-9767 Metropolitan Life Insurance Company. Statistical Bulletin S B
0741-9791 SoftNews†
0741-9821 Writers West
0741-983X Solar and Wind Technology
0741-9872 Concord
0741-9945 Polish Music History Series
0741-9953 International Book Collectors Almanac/Newsletter†
0742-0005 I B M P C Update
0742-0013 Prism
0742-0021 Real Estate Finance Today
0742-0250 Education Computer News
0742-0269 International Journal of Applied Engineering Education
0742-0293 Word Processing News (Burbank)†
0742-0374 A B M S Directory of Certified Urologists
0742-0463 Volcanology & Seismology
0742-0498 State Budget and Tax News
0742-0501 Publishers Directory
0742-051X Teaching and Teacher Education
0742-0528 Chronobiology International
0742-0552 Blueprints
0742-0587 Sports Afield Fishing Annual *changed to* Sports Afield Fishing
0742-0595 Sports Afield Fishing Secrets
0742-0609 Sports Afield Bass
0742-0668 Clinics in Podiatry *changed to* Clinics in Podiatric Medicine & Surgery
0742-0676 Software Digest Ratings Newsletter
0742-0714 Journal of Gambling Behavior
0742-0935 Mature Outlook
0742-096X Allegheny Review
0742-1036 Professional Computing
0742-1044 Aletheia
0742-1095 Want's Federal-State Court Directory
0742-1117 Bibliotheca Afroasiatica
0742-1125 Islamic Art and Architecture
0742-1133 Invited Lectures on the Middle East at the University of Texas at Austin
0742-1141 Byzantina Kai Metabyzantina
0742-115X Humana Civilitas
0742-1168 Studies in Near Eastern Culture and Society
0742-1184 Other Realities
0742-1206 U-News†
0742-1222 Journal of Management Information Systems
0742-1427 Data Sets: Cuneiform Texts
0742-1478 Health Care Strategic Management
0742-1494 Vintage '45
0742-1648 Interior Landscape Industry Magazine
0742-1656 Art Therapy
0742-1702 County Executive Directory
0742-1710 Municipal Executive Directory
0742-1737 Small Group Letter
0742-1877 Grito del Sol *changed to* Grito del Sol Collection
0742-1923 American University Studies. Series 18. African Literature
0742-1931 International Journal of Adult Orthodontics and Orthognathic Surgery
0742-2008 Washington Credit Letter *changed to* Consumer Credit Letter
0742-2016 Federal Reserve Week *changed to* Financial Services Week
0742-2024 Industry News *changed to* Sports Industry News
0742-2075 Hudson Valley Regional Review
0742-2091 Cell Biology and Toxicology
0742-2113 Stories
0742-2334 Computer Aided Research in Near Eastern Studies
0742-2393 Trinity University Monograph Series in Religion
0742-2644 Real Estate Quarterly
0742-2733 Philosophy in Context
0742-2741 Telecommunications Patents Newsletter
0742-2768 Rag Mag
0742-2792 Trumpeter Swan Society Newsletter
0742-2822 Echocardiography†
0742-3071 Diabetic Medicine
0742-3098 Journal of Pineal Research
0742-3101 Engineering Geology Abstracts
0742-3225 Family Medicine
0742-3438 Aging Network News
0742-3446 Merritt Risk Management Review
0742-3470 Afro-American Journal of Philosophy
0742-3578 Techniques
0742-3632 C I N C O M: Courses in Communications
0742-3640 International Journal on World Peace
0742-3667 National Center for the Study of Collective Bargaining in Higher Education and the Professions. Annual Conference Proceedings
0742-3713 Economic Development Review

0742-3772 Sourceview *changed to* Sourceview Journal of Software Evaluations, Reviews & Ratings
0742-3780 Michie's Texas Tort Reporter†
0742-3918 Track Technique: Official Technical Publication
0742-3977 Woodall's Tenting Directory
0742-3985 International Periodicals and Reference Works
0742-406X Gates Researcher†
0742-4221 Diabetes-Metabolism Reviews
0742-4299 U S F L Guide and Register†
0742-4337 Energy Meetings & Trade Shows Directory†
0742-4434 Raw
0742-4469 Compute's PC & PC jr.†
0742-4515 Good Money
0742-454X Red Fox Review at Mohegan Community College
0742-4612 Mississippi Rag
0742-4647 Mealey's Litigation Report: Asbestos
0742-4655 Mealey's Litigation Report: Iranian Claims
0742-4671 Journal of Film and Video
0742-4779 Warren County Genealogical Society Quarterly *changed to* Heir Lines
0742-4787 Journal of Tribology
0742-4795 Journal of Engineering for Gas Turbines and Power *changed to* Journal of Turbomachinery
0742-4868 Nuclear Plant Safety
0742-4876 Interpreter (Sacramento)
0742-4914 B C T V: Bibliography on Cable Television
0742-5244 Insight (Boston)
0742-5260 Scientists Center for Animal Welfare. Newsletter
0742-5279 Election Politics
0742-5341 Report on I B M (Alexandria)
0742-535X World Right-to-Die Newsletter
0742-5376 Hemlock Quarterly
0742-5414 Plant Shutdowns Monitor
0742-5457 Asian Theatre Journal
0742-5473 Dickens Quarterly
0742-5538 Historical Guides to the World's Periodicals and Newspapers
0742-5562 Midwest Modern Language Association. Journal
0742-5627 Innovative Higher Education
0742-5635 Wild and Free
0742-5686 Comput-A-Cal
0742-5708 Hospital Capital Finance†
0742-5732 Videodisc and Optical Disk Update *see* 0887-5162
0742-5740 Videodisc and Optical Disk *changed to* Optical Information Systems Magazine
0742-5759 Library Software Review
0742-5783 Radio P C Report
0742-5821 International Directory of Nuclear Utilities
0742-5902 Computer User (Minneapolis)
0742-597X Journal of Management in Engineering
0742-5996 Ring Systems Handbook
0742-6011 MicroSoftware Today *changed to* Personal Computers Today
0742-6089 Used Computer Guide
0742-6348 Northern Journal of Applied Forestry
0742-6429 Shortwave Guide *changed to* World Radio Report
0742-6445 Telecom Insider
0742-6453 Office Automation Reporting Service
0742-647X Computer Industry Report
0742-6496 Computers in Banking
0742-6534 Catalyst (Worcester)
0742-6542 Administrator's Update
0742-6569 News Basket
0742-6704 P C Accounting Trends *changed to* C P A Micro Report
0742-6747 Hi-Res
0742-6763 American Journal of Islamic Social Sciences
0742-6801 Bibliographies and Indexes in World Literature
0742-681X Bibliographies and Indexes in Psychology
0742-6828 Bibliographies and Indexes in American History
0742-6836 Bibliographies and Indexes in Religious Studies
0742-6844 Bibliographies and Indexes in Anthropology
0742-6852 Bibliographies and Indexes in World History
0742-6860 Bibliographies and Indexes in American Literature
0742-6879 Bibliographies and Indexes in Library and Information Science
0742-6887 Bibliographies and Indexes in Philosophy
0742-6895 Bibliographies and Indexes in Sociology
0742-6909 Bibliographies and Indexes in Law and Political Science
0742-6917 Bibliographies and Indexes in Education
0742-6925 Bibliographies and Indexes in Afro-American and African Studies
0742-6933 Bibliographies and Indexes in the Performing Arts
0742-6941 Bibliographies and Indexes in Women's Studies
0742-695X Bio-Bibliographies in American Literature
0742-6968 Bio-Bibliographies in Music
0742-6984 Religion & Society Report
0742-7018 W I T S
0742-7123 New Books on Women & Feminism
0742-7425 Virginia Polytechnic Institute and State University. College of Agriculture and Life Sciences. Information Series
0742-7778 C A L I C O Journal
0742-7840 Update: Mideast
0742-8014 Rahavard
0742-8111 Video Movies *changed to* Video Times
0742-812X Collectible Automobile
0742-8219 Hortideas
0742-8472 Overholser Family Association. Bulletin
0742-8820 White Light
0742-8839 Motion Picture Investor
0742-8936 South Dakota Authors' Catalog
0742-8944 Matrimonial, Overseas Jobs and Real Estate International Newsletter
0742-8987 Campbell's List
0742-9096 Strategic Banking *changed to* Financial Services Week
0742-9290 A S A Newsletter
0742-9312 Tom Mann's Outdoors†
0742-938X V D T News
0742-9517 American Society of C L U. Journal†
0742-955X Digital Bypass Report
0742-9568 Entertainment Magazine
0742-9576 Arab American Almanac
0742-9614 Micro Communications†
0742-9630 Black Sheep Review†
0742-9665 Lebanon News (English Edition)
0742-9681 Reader (Houghton)
0742-969X Hospice Journal
0742-9703 Journal of Psychotherapy & the Family
0742-9711 Physical Therapy in Health Care
0742-9770 Pryor Report
0742-9789 Using Personal Computers in Nonprofit Agencies
0742-9797 Mexican Studies
0742-9800 Coding Clinic for ICD-9-CM
0742-9916 Outlook on I B M
0742-9940 Practice (New York)
0743-0159 Financial Computing†
0743-0167 Journal of Rural Studies
0743-0175 Defense Analysis
0743-0183 A I Ch E Applications Software Survey of Personal Computers
0743-0221 Hands On!
0743-0272 Corporate Control Alert
0743-0302 Microcomputers for Libraries
0743-0310 Benchmark (Cumberland)
0743-0361 Satellite Business
0743-0388 Current Issues (Arlington)
0743-0671 Communications Product Report
0743-0701 Robot Insider†
0743-0744 Florida Tourism Hotline
0743-0809 Prudent Speculator
0743-0841 Animal Welfare Institute. Quarterly
0743-085X Muslin Scientist *changed to* International Journal of Science and Technology
0743-0884 American International Journal of Arts, Sciences, Engineering and Medicine
0743-0957 Bonnet-t-e's and Kin
0743-1066 Journal of Logic Programming
0743-1120 Writer's Journal
0743-1163 Texas Manufacturers Register
0743-1759 North Carolina Journal of International Law and Commercial Regulation
0743-1848 La Voix des Prairies
0743-1872 Crime Laboratory Digest
0743-216X Day Researcher
0743-2208 Bowker's Electronic News†
0743-2240 Eye
0743-2283 TeleSpan Newsletter
0743-2356 Woman of Power
0743-2445 Logo and Education Computing Journal
0743-2461 Best-Selling Home Plans
0743-2534 P C Abstracts
0743-2542 Strategy and Executive Action
0743-2550 Journal of Christian Nursing
0743-2755 Amelia
0743-2836 Computer Graphics Directory
0743-2860 Dorm Magazine
0743-2909 Limberlost Review
0743-2941 Washington
0743-3069 Space Enterprise Today†
0743-3204 Bomb
0743-3263 Western Electronics†
0743-3271 Industrial West
0743-3301 Kerista
0743-3387 Manager's Notebook
0743-345X P R N Forum *see* 0885-3924
0743-3492 Index to Electric Utility Week
0743-3522 Art Deco News
0743-3808 Behavior Research Methods, Instruments, and Computers
0743-3832 Meeting Planners Alert
0743-412X Trial Advocate Quarterly
0743-4170 International Directory of Special Events and Festivals *changed to* Official Directory of Festivals, Sports & Special Events
0743-4200 Dvorak Developments
0743-4235 Butson Family Newsletter
0743-4251 Abstracts in Maryland Archeology
0743-4278 Advanced Computing Magazine
0743-4324 Survey of Press Freedom in Latin America
0743-4456 Prostaglandins Bibliography
0743-4618 A A C: Augmentative and Alternative Communication
0743-4634 Annual Review of Cell Biology
0743-4642 Christian Computing *changed to* Christian Computing and Communications
0743-4685 Semiconductors/ICs Patents Newsletter
0743-4758 A T C C Quarterly Newsletter
0743-4839 Library Times International
0743-5223 Itinerary
0743-524X Eucharistic Minister
0743-5258 Mass Market Retailers
0743-5266 Art and the Law *see* 0888-4226
0743-5363 World Currency Yearbook
0743-5398 International Business Monthly
0743-5436 A.I.D. Highlights
0743-5495 Bicycle Sport†
0743-5606 Great Activities Newspaper
0743-5657 Arizona Labor Market Newsletter *changed to* Arizona Labor Market Information Newsletter
0743-5738 Vista Magazine Miami Metro Guide
0743-5797 Analytical Instrumentation
0743-5800 Endocrine Research
0743-5878 Access: Apple
0743-5886 Access: I B M
0743-5983 Office Guide to Miami
0743-619X Digital Audio Magazine
0743-6238 Anabiosis: The Journal for Near-Death Studies *see* 0891-4494
0743-6351 Federal Reserve Bank of Kansas City. Banking Studies
0743-636X Mississippi Arts and Letters†
0743-6408 Daily Planetary Guide
0743-6629 Travel South†
0743-6750 Petroleum Software Directory
0743-684X Journal of Reconstructive Microsurgery
0743-6882 Newsletter Inago
0743-7188 Mignot-Luccote Historical Review
0743-7250 Goldthwait Polar Library Accessions List
0743-7277 Buildings Design Journal
0743-7315 Journal of Parallel and Distributed Computing
0743-7439 Southern Friend
0743-7463 Langmuir
0743-7471 Graywolf Annual
0743-751X Ophthalmology Annual†
0743-7528 Material Culture Directories
0743-7560 Bibliographies and Indexes in Gerontology
0743-7633 M300 and P C Report
0743-7641 Missouri Archaeological Society. Quarterly
0743-7757 Echad
0743-779X Alabama Business and Economic Journal *changed to* Southern Business & Economic Journal
0743-7803 Archer Quarterly
0743-7951 Wisconsin International Law Journal
0743-8036 Current Literature in Nephrology
0743-8079 Medical Benefits
0743-8095 Magazine of Virginia Genealogy
0743-8125 Eastern Boating
0743-8176 Primary Care & Cancer
0743-8346 Journal of Perinatology
0743-8354 O B/G Y N Clinical Report
0743-8400 Agrichemical Briefing
0743-8494 C S P A Stateside
0743-8591 Edwards Journal
0743-8613 Information Strategy: The Executive's Journal
0743-863X South Florida Home & Garden
0743-8907 Prairie Wool Companion
0743-8915 University of Kentucky Libraries. Occasional Papers
0743-8958 Bridge Builder
0743-8974 Social Science News Letter *changed to* Social Science (Chapel Hill)
0743-913X Light Year
0743-9156 Journal of Marketing and Public Policy *changed to* Journal of Public Policy & Marketing
0743-9180 United Nations Issues Conference. Report
0743-9229 Medical Heritage
0743-9245 State, Culture and Society
0743-9288 Videosat News†
0743-9296 Journal of Management Case Studies
0743-9466 I B M Compatibles Plus
0743-9474 Burroughs World
0743-9482 N C R Monthly
0743-9490 Honeywell Monthly
0743-9504 Business MicroWorld
0743-9512 T I Professional Computing
0743-9539 Annual Review of Chronopharmacology
0743-9547 Journal of South-East Asian Earth Sciences
0743-9628 Borgo Bioviews
0743-9636 International Journal of Micrographics and Video Technology
0743-9644 U F S I Reports
0743-9679 Home and Educational Computing *see* 0194-357X
0743-9873 Children's Magazine Guide
0743-9989 Small Farmer's Journal
0744-0049 National Strength & Conditioning Association Journal
0744-0073 Diesel Progress North American
0744-0081 Computer Industry Update
0744-0154 N E A Now
0744-0219 Daylily Journal
0744-0359 American Sunbeam†
0744-0405 Fast Service/Family Restaurants†
0744-060X New York Native
0744-074X MotorHome
0744-0820 Woodstove, Wood, Coal and Solar Equipment Directory *changed to* Woodheat
0744-0901 Doll Reader
0744-0987 Texas Gardener

ISSN INDEX 1603

0744-1088 Associations Report
0744-1193 Builder (Washington)
0744-1223 I I A Today
0744-1339 Radio Free Europe Research Reports *changed to* Radio Free Europe Research Reports on Eastern Europe
0744-1355 Speech Technology
0744-138X Upholstering Today
0744-1444 Herzl Institute Bulletin
0744-1584 Computer/Electronic Service News
0744-1657 Test & Measurement World
0744-1673 Data Sources
0744-1738 Hobby Merchandiser
0744-1908 Hairstylist *changed to* Salon Talk
0744-1916 Foodservice Technology Int'l. (Kitchen Planning)†
0744-1932 Earth Shelter Living *changed to* Earth Shelter Living. Newsletter
0744-2149 Construction Times
0744-2319 Craft and Needlework Age/World of Miniatures *changed to* Craft and Needlework Age
0744-2386 Commline
0744-2416 National Masters News
0744-2475 Peelings II†
0744-2602 I C P Business Software Review
0744-267X Catholic Sun
0744-2688 Bankers News Weekly *changed to* A B A Bankers Weekly
0744-2750 Corporate Design *changed to* Corporate Design
0744-2785 Predicasts F & S Index of Corporate Change
0744-2815 Today's Office
0744-2823 Drugs & Drug Abuse Education. Newsletter
0744-2890 U.S. Department of Agriculture. Cotton and Wool Outlook and Situation
0744-3056 Side-Saddle News
0744-3064 Shreveport†
0744-3102 Magazine & Bookseller
0744-3420 Chart Your Course *changed to* Creative Kids
0744-3501 Electric Utility Fleet Management *changed to* Utility Fleet Management
0744-351X Drives and Controls International *see* 0885-0259
0744-3633 Performance Horseman
0744-3676 Employee Services Management
0744-3692 Louisiana Game and Fish
0744-3749 Antique Angler
0744-3854 Instant Printer *changed to* Instant & Small Commercial Printer
0744-3897 Hotels and Restaurants International
0744-396X Kentucky Dental Association. Journal
0744-4052 Christian Missions in Many Lands
0744-415X Victorian Homes
0744-4168 Hazardous Waste Training Bulletin for Supervisors *changed to* Hazardous Materials Training Bulletin for Supervisors
0744-4230 Pennsylvania Magazine
0744-4249 Byline
0744-4389 American National CattleWomen Newsletter
0744-446X Computer Update
0744-4567 Microcomputing†
0744-4664 Seafood Leader
0744-4680 Northwest Arts
0744-4710 Resource Recycling
0744-4788 Rowing U S A *changed to* American Rowing
0744-4923 Home Healthcare Business†
0744-5105 Muscle & Fitness
0744-5121 Shape
0744-5326 International Railway Journal and Rapid Transit Review
0744-5474 Arizona Land and People
0744-561X Long Island Life†
0744-5709 National Leader†
0744-5733 Verdicts and Settlements
0744-5881 Oil and Gas Investor
0744-5989 Collectors' Showcase
0744-6063 Forum (Tallahassee)
0744-6179 Blade Magazine
0744-6241 Defense Science & Electronics
0744-625X Alimentos Procesados
0744-6349 First Hand
0744-6403 Apparel News South
0744-6470 Hospital Employee Health
0744-6594 Nasinec
0744-6608 Sheltie Pacesetter
0744-6616 American Printer (Chicago, 1982)
0744-6640 Home Shop Machinist
0744-6667 Computer Gaming World
0744-6713 Journal of State Taxation
0744-673X Computer Retail News *changed to* Computer Reseller News
0744-6853 Plywood & Panel World
0744-6861 New England Bride
0744-7078 Administrator (Madison)
0744-7108 Interface. Administrative & Accounting
0744-7140 National Ad Search
0744-7167 Construction Supervision & Safety Letter
0744-7175 Utility Supervision
0744-7418 River Cities
0744-7590 Long Island's Nightlife *changed to* New York's Nightlife
0744-7671 Bankruptcy Law Letter
0744-7698 Interface. Manufacturing and Engineering
0744-7701 Fur Rancher
0744-7779 Employee Relations and Human Resources Bulletin
0744-7868 80 Micro
0744-7884 Voice of Universarius
0744-7892 National O T C Stock Exchange *see* 0745-7049
0744-7981 Texas Public Utility News
0744-8120 Camperways
0744-8279 Pastoral Renewal
0744-8376 Ohio State Bar Association Report
0744-8481 Journal of American College Health
0744-8619 Neurologic Clinics
0744-8635 Interiorscape
0744-8686 California Tomorrow
0744-8732 Nursing and Allied Health Index *see* 0146-5554
0744-8899 Ohio State Alumni Magazine
0744-8988 Greenhouse Manager
0744-9062 Financial Managers' Statement
0744-9070 Gulf Coast Oil Reporter *changed to* Gulf Coast Oil World
0744-9143 Apartment Management Newsletter
0744-916X Scholastic News: News Pilot
0744-9194 Lakeland Boating
0744-9216 D E C Professional
0744-933X Pilot
0744-9372 3rd Coast
0744-9488 Champion
0744-9585 Catholic Voice
0744-9704 Defense Science 2000-Plus *changed to* Defense Science 2004-Plus
0744-9836 Working Papers Magazine *changed to* Modern Times
0744-9860 Sproutletter
0744-9879 Collectors Mart
0744-9917 A.N.A.L.O.G. Computing
0744-9984 Journal of Chiropractic
0745-0214 Aviation Equipment Maintenance
0745-0257 Southern Cross
0745-0265 Current Consumer and Lifestudies
0745-0311 Electronic Media
0745-0419 Interface. Insurance Industry
0745-0516 A.H.A. Perspectives *changed to* Perspectives (Washington)
0745-0745 Business Computer Systems†
0745-0753 Multi Level Marketing News
0745-080X 73: Amateur Radio's Technical Journal *see* 0883-234X
0745-0877 C P A Personnel Report
0745-0893 N.Y. Habitat
0745-0990 Pharmaceutical Manufacturing *changed to* Pharmaceutical and Cosmetic Equipment
0745-1032 Candy Industry
0745-1075 Computers in Healthcare
0745-113X Electronics West†
0745-1172 Between Times
0745-1199 Communications Industry Report
0745-1237 Missouri Schools
0745-1253 Brookings Review
0745-1342 C P A Computer Report
0745-1369 Attorneys Marketing Report
0745-1385 Black Powder Times *see* 8750-5886
0745-1458 Computers & Electronics†
0745-1474 Tennessee Business
0745-1490 Stamp Review
0745-1636 Corporate Meetings & Incentives
0745-1784 Grower
0745-1962 Circle K
0745-2152 Remodeling World *see* 0885-8039
0745-2209 G F W C Clubwoman
0745-225X Pennsylvania Outdoors
0745-2292 Jorgensen Report
0745-2349 Action Films†
0745-2357 Scholastic Editor's Trends in Publications
0745-2500 P C: The Independent Guide to I B M Personal Computers *changed to* P C Magazine: The Independent Guide to I B M-Standard Personal Computing
0745-2527 Antic: The Atari Resource
0745-2578 I S O World *see* 0746-6765
0745-2594 Record (New York)
0745-2616 Human Services (Woodhaven)
0745-2802 Cable Television Business
0745-2810 Collage
0745-2896 Makai
0745-3043 Automotive Products Report
0745-3116 Country Handcrafts
0745-3167 Adopted Child
0745-3256 Alliance Witness
0745-3299 Roze Maryi
0745-3345 Kansas Alumni Magazine
0745-3469 Nut Grower
0745-368X Agenda for Citizen Involvement
0745-3787 Pork (Year)
0745-3981 Stanford Magazine
0745-4058 Journal of Educational Communication *see* 0741-3653
0745-4171 Lifelines: The Software Magazine†
0745-421X Attorneys Computer Report
0745-4295 Visual Merchandising & Store Design
0745-4309 Electri-Onics
0745-4309 Electri-Onics Desk Manual
0745-4325 Office Administration and Automation *see* 0884-5905
0745-449X Die Casting Management
0745-4503 Food Institute Report
0745-452X Agri-Practice
0745-4570 Comics Buyers Guide
0745-4678 Health Industry Today
0745-4791 User's Guide to C P-M Systems and Software *see* 0747-8534
0745-4929 Restaurant and Hotel Design
0745-5070 Geriatric Guide to Pertinent Publications
0745-5100 Air Cargo World
0745-5720 Art Now/U S A-National Art Museum and Gallery Guide
0745-5925 Shepard's Uniform Commercial Code Citations
0745-5933 Business Marketing
0745-5941 High-Performance Pontiac
0745-6050 Catholic Times
0745-6077 Hot Boat
0745-6921 Management of World Wastes
0745-7049 National O T C Stock Journal
0745-7189 Teddy Bear and Friends
0745-7243 Screen Actor News *see* 0036-956X
0745-7324 Greenhouse Grower
0745-7790 Employment Relations Today
0745-7839 American Rhododendron Society. Quarterly Journal
0745-7847 Islands
0745-8088 Industrial News
0745-8304 Senior High Class
0745-841X F P G Weekly News Update
0745-8509 Star
0745-8738 Midwest Poetry Review
0745-8746 Psychic Guide
0745-8754 Drafting and Repro Digest *changed to* Design Graphics World
0745-8851 Alaska Native Magazine
0745-9009 Georgetown Magazine
0745-9033 Dairymen's Digest: North Central Region Edition
0745-9130 Whiskers' Summer Weekly Reader
0745-9416 Eastern Horse World
0745-9726 C I M E
0745-9807 Houston Magazine†
0745-9874 N T S B Reporter
0745-9971 Amerikan Uutiset
0746-0023 Business Facilities
0746-004X Canal Zone Philatelist
0746-0066 Contemporary Christian *changed to* Contemporary Christian Music
0746-0252 L C/Liquid Chromatography and H P L C Magazine *changed to* L C/G C
0746-0554 Architecture: The A I A Journal
0746-1070 Ophthalmology Management
0746-1321 Savings Institutions
0746-133X A H E P A N
0746-147X Software Merchandising *changed to* Home Computer & Software Merchandising
0746-1887 Independent Restaurants
0746-1984 Institute of Certified Financial Planners. Journal
0746-2344 Remodeling Contractor (Chicago)
0746-2360 Business Systems Product Update
0746-2379 Business Systems Update
0746-2395 Chilton's I & C S
0746-2441 Fastener Technology International
0746-2468 Futures (Chicago)
0746-2468 Futures Magazine Reference Guide to Futures Markets
0746-2603 Campaign California Report
0746-2743 I C A S News *changed to* World Air Show News
0746-2964 Denver Business
0746-312X Shepard's Federal Energy Law Citations
0746-3138 Shepard's Immigration and Naturalization Citations
0746-3286 Videopro
0746-3405 Computerized Manufacturing
0746-3472 Queen City Heritage
0746-3545 Student Activities
0746-3618 New Age *changed to* New Age Journal
0746-3677 G S D News
0746-3766 Jojoba Happenings
0746-3820 Packaging
0746-3928 Portuguese Times
0746-4118 Antiqueweek/Tri-State Trader *see* 0888-5451
0746-4134 Gas Turbine World
0746-4185 El Heraldo Catolico
0746-4215 Orange County Magazine
0746-4223 Classroom Computer Learning
0746-4541 Recreational Skier
0746-469X Clinical Laser Monthly
0746-4703 Prospective Payment Survival
0746-4797 Rainbow (Prospect)
0746-4851 World Farming Agrimanagement *changed to* Agribusiness Worldwide
0746-5335 Changes *see* 0739-4853
0746-5505 C D Rateline
0746-5963 Georgia Journal
0746-6072 Telecommunication Products Plus Technology
0746-6102 Postcard Collector
0746-6110 D & B Reports
0746-6129 Library Administrator's Digest
0746-6498 Innkeeping World (Seattle)
0746-6765 Micro Marketworld
0746-7141 Converting Magazine
0746-7265 E D P Auditing
0746-7281 Auerbach Data Security Management
0746-7400 W E S: Voice of the Window Treatment Industry *changed to* Window Fashions Magazine
0746-7656 MusicLine†
0746-7672 Rubberstampmadness
0746-7680 Videolog
0746-7761 Chief: Civil Service Leader
0746-7915 Financial Planning (Atlanta)
0746-7966 Baseball Card News
0746-813X C E R L Forum†
0746-8288 Indiana Medicine
0746-8342 College Mathematics Journal
0746-8652 Corporate Board

0746-8687 Collectors Motor News *changed to* Collectors Car News
0746-8911 Business Radio
0746-8989 Audio Visual Directions *see* 0747-1335
0746-9012 C P I Purchasing Chemicals Directory
0746-9039 TeenAge
0746-9152 Lawn Servicing
0746-9179 Research & Development
0746-9306 Sports Medicine Bulletin
0746-9438 Nemo: The Classic Comics Library
0746-9462 Sensors
0746-9489 Back Pain Monitor
0746-9586 Fire Command
0746-9683 Employment Relations Bulletin
0746-9888 Baker Valley News
0747-0088 A B A Journal
0747-0398 Chemical Product News
0747-0460 P C M
0747-055X Home Computer Magazine
0747-0711 Empire State Report
0747-0843 American Traveler†
0747-1335 A V Video
0747-1599 Hybrid Circuit Technology
0747-1637 Milton Caniff's Steve Canyon Magazine
0747-167X Memphis Business Journal
0747-1971 Pickups & Mini-Trucks†
0747-217X Magazine of Positive Thinking *changed to* Plus: Magazine of Positive Thinking
0747-234X Fantasy Review
0747-2528 Oil & Gas Producing Industry in Your State
0747-2536 Prepared Foods
0747-315X Athletic Business
0747-3168 Advertising & Graphic Arts Techniques
0747-3192 Spirits, Wine & Beer Marketing in Missouri
0747-3206 Spirits, Wine & Beer Marketing in Minnesota, North & South Dakota
0747-3214 Spirits, Wine & Beer Marketing in Iowa
0747-3583 Journal of Imaging Technology
0747-3680 Law Enforcement Technology
0747-3818 Contact (Berkeley)†
0747-4032 Radioactive
0747-444X Greater Phoenix Jewish News
0747-4482 Silver
0747-4857 Data Book of Social Studies Materials and Resources
0747-489X Imagine (Boston)
0747-4938 Econometric Reviews
0747-4946 Sequential Analysis
0747-5411 Serials Perspective
0747-5438 B N A Online
0747-5446 Early Childhood Music
0747-5500 A W E A Wind Energy Weekly
0747-5527 National Stampagraphic
0747-5535 Quarterly Journal of Business and Economics
0747-5543 Cross Sections
0747-5632 Computers in Human Behavior
0747-5667 Missouri State Genealogical Association Journal
0747-5675 Hughes Family Letter
0747-606X American Homeopathy
0747-6078 Shells and Sea Life
0747-6086 Community Service Business
0747-6213 Inside Drug Law
0747-6353 Advances in Forensic Psychology and Psychiatry
0747-6388 F M R
0747-640X Expanding Horizons†
0747-6558 Die Pommerschen Leute
0747-6663 Latah County Genealogical Society. Quarterly
0747-6817 Center for Sports Sponsorship's Sponsor Quest
0747-7171 Journal of Symbolic Computation
0747-7368 Journal of Gastronomy
0747-7449 Air and Space Lawyer
0747-7503 Community Development Executive
0747-7805 Western Maryland Genealogy
0747-8003 Corporate Giving Watch
0747-8127 Washington Weekly
0747-8216 Microcosm/Lyrical Ways
0747-8291 Ultrapure Water
0747-847X BookNotes: Information for the Small and Self-Publisher
0747-8534 User's Guide
0747-8607 Tax Management. Compensation Planning Journal
0747-8739 News from the Northwest
0747-8887 Hot Wire
0747-8895 Mid-American Review
0747-8917 Bankruptcy Strategist
0747-8933 Computer Law Strategist
0747-900X American Buddhist
0747-9026 Knitters
0747-9131 Benefits Today
0747-9182 Minerals and Metallurgical Processing
0747-9190 Partnership
0747-9255 Colorado Monthly Magazine
0747-9298 Legal Information Management Index
0747-9301 American Society for Armenian Studies. Journal
0747-931X Unveiling
0747-9360 Design Issues
0747-9395 Fordham International Law Journal
0747-9409 Sites
0747-9549 Data Entry Awareness Report
0747-9573 Packaged Software Reports
0747-9670 Computer Graphics Today
0747-9697 Prickly Pear Tucson
0747-9700 Federal Contract Disputes
0747-9727 Thirteen (Portlandville)
0747-9735 Waterworld News
0747-9891 N E H G S Nexus
0748-0008 Texas Economic Forecast
0748-0024 Tribal Arts Review *see* 0893-0120
0748-0059 Image Understanding
0748-0067 Advances in Teacher Education
0748-0164 Cross Currents
0748-0172 International Trade Reporter
0748-0466 Carolina ChemTips
0748-0571 Report of a Vantage Conference
0748-061X Compensation & Benefits Management
0748-0636 Contemporary Authors Autobiography Series
0748-0725 Peacework
0748-075X Journal of Health Care Technology†
0748-0784 San Bernardino County Studies
0748-0792 Cable Advertising, Merchandising & Programming Report
0748-0822 Home Video Publisher
0748-0903 Turbomachinery International Handbook
0748-1071 Lancaster County Connections
0748-1187 Death Studies
0748-1195 December Rose
0748-1691 Lawson Letters
0748-1756 Measurement and Evaluation in Counseling and Development
0748-1780 Image Magazine
0748-1853 Brickman Letter
0748-1896 Fusion Technology
0748-1942 Surgery Alert
0748-1977 Journal of Clinical Monitoring
0748-1985 Journal of Rational-Emotive Therapy
0748-223X Worldwide Directory of East Indians
0748-2272 I S K C O N Report†
0748-2280 I S K C O N World Review
0748-2302 Minorities in America. Annual Bibliography
0748-237X Clipper Studies in the American Theater
0748-2396 Camp Resort Law Report
0748-2418 Fabbro *changed to* Limestone
0748-2469 Official Directory of New Jersey Libraries Media Centers Including Buyers' Guide
0748-2485 Roots & Leaves
0748-2531 Aqualine Abstracts
0748-2558 Shakespeare Bulletin
0748-2604 American Arts Project
0748-2655 National Prison Project Journal
0748-2698 Mechanical Cost Data
0748-2809 U S - Japan Relations
0748-2906 Bet-Nahrain
0748-2914 Horror Show
0748-2922 Economic Trends
0748-3007 Cladistics: The International Journal of the Willi Hennig Society
0748-3015 Hibiscus
0748-3058 Esto America
0748-3066 East Village Eye *changed to* International Eye
0748-3155 Exercise Physiology
0748-321X Journal of Veterinary Medical Education
0748-3252 Electronics Week *see* 0883-4989
0748-3392 Q 38 Technical Journal
0748-3406 Venture Inward
0748-4054 Preschool Perspectives
0748-4089 Asia-Pacific/Africa-Middle East Petroleum
0748-4321 Legacy
0748-433X United Nations of the Next Decade Conference. Report
0748-4356 Africa Insider
0748-4364 Higher Education Abstracts
0748-450X Journal of Clinical Hypertension
0748-4518 Journal of Quantitative Criminology
0748-4526 Negotiation Journal
0748-4623 Journal of Professional Services Marketing
0748-4631 Interflo
0748-4658 Journal of Propulsion and Power
0748-4739 Runzheimer International Letter
0748-4755 Pricing Advisor
0748-4895 Strategic Planning Management
0748-5190 Annotated Bibliographies of Serials: A Subject Approach
0748-5247 Freedonia Gazette
0748-5328 Journal of Nephrology Nursing
0748-5476 A M S Asian Studies
0748-5484 Research in Word Processing Newsletter
0748-5492 Issues in Science and Technology
0748-5514 Journal of Free Radicals in Biology
0748-5557 A M A Directory of Officials and Staff
0748-5743 Interactive Learning International
0748-5786 Journal of Education for Library and Information Science
0748-5786 Association for Library and Information Science Education. Directory
0748-6022 Farmer's Market
0748-6464 Center Magazine
0748-6472 Manhattan, Inc.
0748-6480 Seminars in Adolescent Medicine
0748-6510 Pomono
0748-6618 Today's Man
0748-6901 Quality of Life and Cardiovascular Care
0748-7002 Means Electrical Cost Data
0748-7347 TransitPulse
0748-7630 Journal of Reading, Writing, and Learning Disabilities International
0748-7649 Culture Sculpture†
0748-7789 Texas Facts
0748-7878 Worker's Compensation Law Bulletin
0748-7975 Accountants' Index
0748-7991 Journal of Molecular Electronics
0748-8009 Medicine and War
0748-8017 Quality and Reliability Engineering International
0748-8025 Communications in Applied Numerical Methods
0748-8149 Illinois Historical Journal
0748-8157 Frontiers of Health Services Management
0748-8165 Nutrition Forum
0748-822X Agricultural Biotechnology News
0748-8386 Stress Medicine
0748-8394 Outpost Exchange
0748-8408 Inn Review Newsletter
0748-8475 Thought & Action
0748-8513 Key (Lansdale)†
0748-8548 Chicago Geographic Directory
0748-8572 Advances in Applied Developmental Psychology
0748-8580 Current Research in Film
0748-8599 Annual Review of Political Science
0748-8602 Advances in Human/Computer Interaction
0748-8785 Parnassus Literary Journal
0748-8793 Journal of Child and Adolescent Psychotherapy
0748-8807 Macintosh Connection†
0748-8815 Kettering Review
0748-8831 One-Person Library
0748-8920 International Communications News
0748-8939 Telecom Trade Reporter
0748-8947 Audio-Digest Emergency Medicine
0748-9056 West's International Law Bulletin
0748-9188 Canine Collectors Companion
0748-9196 I E E E ElectroTechnology Review
0748-9234 University of California, Berkeley Wellness Letter
0748-9250 C I M Strategies
0748-9269 Computers and the Social Sciences
0748-9528 Second Opinion (San Francisco)
0748-9536 L'An ha-Erev
0748-9579 Timeline
0748-9633 Journal of Counseling and Development
0748-9641 Strategy for Peace U.S. Foreign Policy Conference. Report
0748-9668 International University Collegiate Sports Report
0748-9676 International University Poetry Quarterly
0749-0003 Employee Assistance Quarterly
0749-0151 Stereo T V Report
0749-0194 Change (Swarthmore)†
0749-0208 Journal of Coastal Research
0749-0291 James Dickey Newsletter
0749-0372 Biotechnology Software Report
0749-064X Contemporary Theatre, Film & Television
0749-0674 N A T O - Warsaw and Strategies
0749-0690 Clinics in Geriatric Medicine
0749-0704 Critical Care Clinics
0749-0712 Hand Clinics
0749-0720 Veterinary Clinics of North America: Food Animal Practice
0749-0739 Veterinary Clinics of North America: Equine Practice
0749-0755 Sound Post
0749-0771 Slipstream
0749-078X Tenant Communications
0749-1069 World Environment Handbook
0749-1093 MacRae's Directory of Firms Marketing through Manufacturers' Representatives
0749-1204 Business-to-Business Catalog Marketer
0749-1301 Behavioral Counseling and Community Interventions†
0749-1352 Trail Walker
0749-1387 Faces
0749-1395 Scientific Sleuthing Newsletter
0749-1409 Women's Studies in Communication
0749-1484 Data Processing & Communications Security
0749-1565 American Journal of Hospice Care
0749-1573 Impact (Year)
0749-1581 Magnetic Resonance in Chemistry
0749-159X Numerical Methods for Partial Differential Equations
0749-1670 S R R T Newsletter
0749-1786 Bibliographies and Indexes in Economics and Economic History
0749-1948 Coal Mining
0749-1980 U S Water News
0749-2014 Writers Connection
0749-2022 Top Shelf
0749-2081 Seminars in Oncology Nursing
0749-2227 Journal of Law and Politics
0749-2308 African Special Bibliographic Series
0749-2448 Population Today
0749-2510 Christian Retailing
0749-260X Dog River Review
0749-2766 Construction Policies
0749-2774 Transportation Policies
0749-2782 Public Safety
0749-2790 Justice Policies
0749-2812 Banking Policies
0749-2871 Crescent Review
0749-2898 Psi Research *changed to* Psi
0749-3509 Vibrant Life (Hagerstown)
0749-3517 Islander
0749-3584 Bible of Weather Forecasting
0749-3797 American Journal of Preventive Medicine
0749-3851 2600
0749-3908 Acts (San Francisco)
0749-3967 Marble & Ivy Review
0749-4025 Journal of Classroom Interaction
0749-4122 Multihulls
0749-470X Bibliographies of Modern Authors
0749-4823 General Physics Advance Abstracts

0749-4831 Documents in Imperial History
0749-5021 Peterson's Guide to Business and Management Jobs (Year)
0749-503X Yeast
0749-5056 Whole Earth Review
0749-5161 Pediatric Emergency Care
0749-517X Around the Bend
0749-5307 National Legal Bibliography. Subject Lists
0749-5579 Chilton's Labor Guide and Parts Manual. Motor Age Professional Mechanics Edition
0749-5900 Peace & Democracy News
0749-5927 Ancestry Newsletter
0749-5951 Immigrant Communities & Ethnic Minorities in the United States & Canada
0749-596X Journal of Memory and Language
0749-5978 Organizational Behavior and Human Decision Processes
0749-5986 MacRae's Industrial Directory *changed to* MacRae s Blue Book
0749-6001 Censorship News
0749-6036 Superlattices and Microstructures
0749-6214 Central America Writers Bulletin
0749-6419 International Journal of Plasticity
0749-6532 Working Smart *changed to* Executive Strategies
0749-6664 Vealer
0749-6680 Data Base Directory
0749-6737 Insecta Mundi
0749-6753 International Journal of Health Planning and Management
0749-6818 Wisconsin Counties
0749-6931 A S A Footnotes
0749-7644 Gestus
0749-7946 Impact Yearbook
0749-7989 Alcohol in History: A Multidisciplinary Newsletter *see* 0887-2783
0749-8004 Journal of Entomological Science
0749-8020 Endocrinology Abstracts
0749-8047 Clinical Journal of Pain
0749-8055 Convulsive Therapy
0749-8063 Arthroscopy
0749-839X A B M S Directory of Certified Plastic Surgeons
0749-856X Vital Signs (Farmington)
0749-8578 P C Netline
0749-8586 Disability Rag
0749-8659 Children's Album
0749-8667 Insurance Review (New York)
0749-9213 Carpatho-Rusyn American
0749-9361 Showboat Centennials Newsletter
0749-9418 Business First
0749-9779 Stockowners' News
0750-0750 Reunion. Institut National de la Statistique et des Etudes Economiques. Indicateurs Conjoncturels
0750-0769 Economie de la Reunion
0750-1331 Commission Departementale des Monuments Historiques du Pas-de-Calais. Bulletin *see* 0758-2722
0750-1455 Le Supplement
0750-2036 Langues et Cultures du Pacifique
0750-3695 Letter from Taize
0750-3725 Vogue Hommes
0750-4764 Filiere Maille
0750-6244 Archives of Otolaryngology
0750-6252 American Journal of Diseases of Children
0750-7186 Revue Francaise des Sciences de l'Eau *changed to* Sciences de l'Eau
0750-7321 Biologia Gallo-Hellenica
0750-7569 S N E C M A Informations
0750-7658 Annales Francaises d'Anesthesie et de Reanimation
0750-7674 B.O.P.I. Brevets d'Invention - Abreges et Listes
0750-7933 Societe Sciences Nat. Miscellanea Entomologia
0750-8123 Casse-Tete de Poche
0750-8158 Enfants S'amusent
0750-8743 I S T P M Rapports Techniques†
0751-4239 Universite de Provence. Centre d'Aix. Cahiers d'Etudes Germaniques
0751-4875 Lacito Documents Asie-Austronesie
0751-4883 Lacito Documents Eurasie
0751-5464 Publi 10
0751-5766 Hospitalisation Nouvelle
0751-5839 Universite Syndicaliste
0751-5871 Activite Economique†
0751-588X Entreprises Rhone Alpes
0751-5944 Travaux Publics et Batiment du Midi
0751-5987 Pour la Verite
0751-6037 Circuits Culture
0751-6614 O F C E Observations et Diagnostics Economiques. Revue
0751-7599 Institut National de la Statistique et des Etudes Economiques. Service Departemental de la Guyane. Bulletin Trimestriel de Statistiques
0751-7718 Consultation
0751-8145 F E N-Hebdo
0751-9907 Sauvagine et Sa Chasse
0752-4072 T S I
0752-4676 I C A Executive Search Newsletter
0752-4978 Robots
0752-5222 L'Ecrit-Voir
0752-5702 Histoire Economie et Societe
0753-1621 Software in Healthcare
0753-311X France. Direction du Tourisme. Economie du Tourisme†
0753-3322 Biomedecine and Pharmacotherapy
0753-3454 Relais
0753-3969 Annales de Paleontologie (Vert.Invert)
0753-4590 Cahiers Henri Bosco
0753-4655 Societe d'Histoire Naturelle du Doubs. Bulletin
0753-9053 Annales de Chirurgie de la Main
0754-0264 Genetique, Selection, Evolution
0754-054X Ouvertures
0754-1996 Industrie de l'Information
0754-2143 P C M L-Flash *changed to* Flash Alternative
0754-2445 Lacito Documents Afrique
0754-2623 Ondes Courtes Informations
0754-281X Travailleurs (Paris)
0754-3786 Nouvelles du Vietnam
0754-927X Luvah
0754-9725 Ge Magazine
0755-0251 Gai Pied Hebdo
0755-0960 Fabula
0755-1088 Chronique du Transporteur
0755-1150 Thesindex Pharmaceutique†
0755-1959 Classiques Francais du Moyen Age
0755-2025 Chambre Syndicale de la Siderugie Francaise. Bulletin Statistique. Serie Rouge. Production.
0755-2807 Recherches Iberiques Strasbourg II *changed to* Recherches Iberiques et Cinematographiques
0755-3218 France. Ministere de l'Agriculture. Series "S". Production Vegetale et Forestieres
0755-5016 Eau et l'Industrie *changed to* L'Eau, l'Industrie, les Nuisances
0755-5202 Energie Magazine
0755-5350 Energie Nucleaire Magazine *see* 0755-5202
0755-7469 Nord Genealogie
0755-7647 Comite Francais de Cartographie. Bulletin
0755-9291 Applications et Transferts
0755-9305 Langues et Cultures Africaines
0755-9313 Europe de Tradition Orale
0756-3205 Cite
0756-4392 I C C Business World
0756-4481 European Paper & Board Film Converter Letter
0756-5860 Les Dossiers de l'Art Public
0756-7138 Universite de Lille III. Lexique
0756-8037 Lettre Confidentielle des Transports
0756-8630 France. Ministere du Travail. Dossiers Statistiques du Travail et de l'Emploi
0756-967X References
0757-0090 Vogue Sport
0757-0139 Harmonie - Panorama Musique
0757-2271 Beaux Arts Magazine
0757-6714 Etat du Monde
0757-7699 Etudes Ethno-Linguistiques Maghreb-Sahara
0758-1874 Machine-Outil Produire
0758-1998 France. Ministere des Affaires Sociales et de la Solidarite Nationale. Secretariat d'Etat Charge de la Sante. Bulletin Officiel
0758-2714 Cahiers d'Anthropologie et Biometrie Humaine
0758-2722 Commission Departementale d'Histoire et d'Archeologie. Bulletin
0758-413X Arts et Metiers du Livre
0758-4164 Boulangerie Francaise
0758-4431 Monde Alpin et Rhodanien
0758-5055 Toute l'Alimentation
0758-573X Point Economique
0758-5756 Inform'optique
0758-6639 Annuaire Nautisme
0758-6922 S T P Pharma
0758-6957 Automobile Magazine
0758-7244 Reunion. Service de Statistique Agricole. Bulletin de Statistique Agricole
0758-7686 Proxima
0758-7724 I N S E E Premiers Resultats
0758-802X Praxis Juridique et Religion
0759-0083 France. Ministere des Affaires Sociales et de la Solidarite Nationale. Ministere Charge de l'Emploi. Conventions Collectives
0759-3686 Dictionnaire-Annuaire de l'Agriculture
0759-6774 Tahiti Sun
0759-9161 Bulletin on Applied Research for the Protection of Man at Work
0760-1263 Africasia (Year)
0760-1999 Boissons de France - Jean Primus
0760-4211 Lettre du Groupement National de la Cooperation
0760-5641 Valenciennes
0760-629X Consequences
0760-9620 Philosophie Imaginaire
0761-0076 Revue de l'Artisan Electricien Electronicien
0761-2095 Petrole et Gaz
0761-2397 Mondes Hispanophone et Lusophone
0761-3067 Gaussenia
0761-3652 Agro Industrie
0761-392X Comites Francais de Geodesie et Geophysique. Annales
0761-3938 France. I.F.Re.Mer. Centre de Brest. Publications. Serie: Rapports Economiques et Juridiques
0761-3962 France. I.F.Re.Mer. Centre de Brest. Colloques. Actes
0761-3970 France. I.F.Re.Mer. Centre de Brest. Publications. Serie: Rapports Scientifiques et Techniques
0761-3989 France. I.F.Re.Mer. Centre de Brest. Publications. Serie: Resultats des Campagnes a la Mer
0761-7143 Territoires
0761-7267 Dossiers de la Bible
0761-7593 Actu'A G F
0761-8417 Revue de Pneumologie Clinique
0761-9553 Clarinette Magazine
0762-6819 Nouvelle Revue d'Ethnopsychiatrie
0762-7203 Temps Micro
0762-7378 Neptune Nautisme
0763-062X Club des Hebraisants
0763-1529 Cahiers Raymond Abellio
0763-5184 Equipes St Vincent
0763-7098 France. Institut National de la Sante et de la Recherche Medicale. Colloques
0764-0382 Degres
0765-0019 Traitement du Signal
0765-1376 Kouakou
0765-1597 Science et Sports
0765-1937 C R E D I F Bulletin Bibliographique
0765-3204 Flexo-Europe
0765-4847 Facultes de Droit et de la Science Juridique. Revue d'Histoire
0765-5762 Entreprises Formation
0766-4214 Cahiers de Semiotique Textuelle
0766-4516 Bulletin d'Histoire de la Revolution Francaise
0766-5105 Geodynamique
0766-5598 Revue des Etudes Byzantines
0766-5725 Technique & Biologie
0766-6330 Etudiant
0766-916X Lettre du Musicien
0767-2640 Documentation Touristique: Bibliographie Analytique Internationale
0767-2659 Touristic Analysis Review
0767-3981 Fundamental and Clinical Pharmacology
0767-6891 Sciences Orgonomiques
0767-709X Revue Archeologique de l'Ouest
0768-9454 Technologie
0768-9829 Cahiers des Sciences Humaines
0769-0878 Observations et Travaux
0769-1033 Satellites Galileens de Jupiter
0769-2609 Institut Pasteur. Annales. Microbiologie
0769-2617 Institut Pasteur. Annales. Virologie
0769-2625 Institut Pasteur. Annales. Immunologie
0769-3206 Materiaux pour l'Histoire de notre Temps
0769-3478 Dossiers de l'Outre-Mer
0770-0075 Critique Regionale
0770-0717 Revue Belge de Geographie
0770-0911 Travaux Geographiques de Liege
0770-0962 Universite de Bruxelles. Revue
0770-1055 Universite Libre de Bruxelles. Institut de Sociologie. Revue
0770-1640 Cinemaniac *see* 0773-2279
0770-1683 O I E C Bulletin
0770-1713 Cerevisia
0770-1748 Natuurwetenschappelijk Tijdschrift
0770-2477 Lumen Vitae
0770-2515 Lait et Nous
0770-3244 N A T O Scientific Publications. Newsletter
0770-4372 Bibliotheque Royal Albert 1er. Bulletin Trimestriel d'Information
0770-4526 Bibliotheque Royale Albert 1er. Rapport Annuel
0770-4720 Interface
0770-7436 Presence de l'Histoire
0770-7576 Societe Geographique de Liege. Bulletin
0770-7762 Koninklijke Academie voor Nederlandse Taal- en Letterkunde. Jaarboek
0770-8378 Degres
0770-8602 Revue Generale
0770-9412 Tractionel News *changed to* Tractebel News
0770-9595 Tractionel. Annual Report *changed to* Tractebel. Annual Report
0771-0410 Nationaal Instituut voor de Statistiek. Weekbericht
0771-1107 Journal "A"
0771-2022 I U S S P Newsletter
0771-2588 Operatie Veiligheid
0771-2782 Promosafe
0771-2987 F E B Bulletin
0771-3371 Zakenidee†
0771-4025 Technivisie
0771-4890 Institut de Linguistique de Louvain. Cahiers
0771-4963 Universite Libre de Bruxelles. Institut de Philosophie. Annales
0771-517X Nationale Maatschappij van Belgische Spoorwegen. Documentatiebulletin
0771-5323 Universite Libre de Bruxelles. Institut de Sociologie. Annales†
0771-5692 Cercle Royal d'Histoire et d'Archeologie d'Ath et de la Region et Musees Athois. Etudes et Documents
0771-6303 Soundtrack! The Collector's Quarterly
0771-6435 Cahiers d'Histoire de Seconde Guerre Mondiale
0771-677X Recherches Sociologiques
0771-6826 Technologia
0771-6842 Vie Consacree
0771-713X Genealogie and Computer
0771-7415 Technologia Bruxellensis *see* 0771-6826
0771-7520 Fiskoloog International
0771-7873 Societe Belge de Photogrammetrie-Teledetection et de Cartographie. Bulletin Trimestriel
0771-7911 European Communities and Other European Organizations Who's Who
0772-1099 Ami des Fleurs
0772-3776 Bibliotheque Royale Albert 1er. Publications Annoncees
0772-4802 Social Trends *changed to* Personeel

1606 ISSN INDEX

0772-4837 Fiskoloog
0772-4853 Balans
0772-4942 Industrie Magazine
0772-6112 Enquetes et Documents d'Histoire Africaine
0772-7054 Boer en de Tuinder
0772-7151 Gentse Bijdragen tot de Kunstgeschiedenis
0772-7402 Zonnekind
0772-7488 Archaelogia Belgica
0772-9898 Zonnestraal
0773-0004 Vie Professionnelle
0773-0179 Doremi
0773-0292 Dauphin
0773-0306 Bonjour!
0773-0543 Gestion 2000
0773-1027 Vlaamse Filmpjes
0773-1051 Top
0773-2279 Cine-Fiches de Grand Angle
0773-7777 Reseau Automatique Belge de la Pollution Atmospherique
0774-1847 Tijdschrift voor de Studie van de Verlichting en van het Vrije Denken
0774-4056 Technisch Management
0774-8396 Commission Royale de Toponymie et de Dialectologie. Bulletin
0774-9937 Algebras, Groups and Geometries
0780-1335 Finland. Kehittaemis ja Koerakentamistiedotek *changed to* Finland. Rakennushallitus. Tutkimus-ja Kehitystoiminnan. Tiedote
0780-4199 Visio
0780-4288 Rotary Norden
0780-6884 Finnview
0780-7295 Meteorological Yearbook of Finland. Part 3. Statistics of Radiosonde Observations 1961-1980
0780-8399 Surveying Science in Finland
0780-9352 Finland. Tilastokeskus. Tulo- ja Varallisuustilasto
0781-2078 MikroBitti
0781-2442 Yhdistyneiden Kansakuntien Yleiskokous (Year)
0781-2477 P E P S Y
0781-4437 Suomen Joukkovelkakirjalainat
0781-5611 Finland. Tilastokeskus. Tyovoimatutkimus
0781-6758 Metsaeteollissus†
0781-7177 J P
0781-7347 Assa
0781-8602 I.D.E.A.
0782-0496 Riskienhallinta
0782-2952 Energy
0782-2987 Scanp
0782-3789 Terveys 2000
0782-4386 Journal of Agricultural Science in Finland
0782-8454 Suomi-Finland USA
0790-0260 Geological Survey of Ireland. Guide Series
0790-0279 Geological Survey of Ireland. Report Series
0790-0864 Micro News and Market *changed to* Micro News
0790-1186 Irish Journal of Psychiatry
0790-1267 New Democrat *changed to* Fine Gael News
0790-150X Software Abstracts for Engineers
0790-1712 Labour Comment (Cork)
0790-178X Irish Arts Review
0790-2360 R I A I Bulletin
0790-2743 Irish Council for Civil Liberties. Rights
0790-388X Trinity College. Friends of the Library. Newsletter
0790-3979 Central Bank of Ireland. Statistical Supplement
0790-4568 Irish Cooperative Organization Society. Annual Report
0790-4940 Focus (Dublin)
0790-5068 Liberty News
0790-5750 International Structural Engineering Abstracts
0790-5769 International Building Science & Construction Abstracts
0790-5866 Ireland. Central Statistics Office. Labour Force Survey. First Results
0790-6080 Ireland. Central Statistics Office. Census of Industrial Production
0790-6277 Postal and Telecommunications Journal
0790-6862 In Dublin
0790-7184 Irish Political Studies
0790-732X Dairy Executive
0794-2877 Nigeria Business Guide Annual
0794-3415 Heritage
0794-3733 Medipharm Medical Journal
0800-000X N U P I Rapport
0800-0018 N U P I Notat
0800-0093 Seilas og Baatliv
0800-0484 Kriminal Journalen
0800-0549 R - O - C - K
0800-0638 Europe's 15000 Largest Companies
0800-0646 Speideren
0800-0816 A M S - Skrifter
0800-0824 Invandrerinformasjon
0800-0999 Valdres Historielag. Aarbok
0800-1200 Where to Build - Where to Repair
0800-1235 Skandinaviske Skipsrederier
0800-1936 Bonytt
0800-2169 Norway. Statistisk Sentralbyraa. Utdanningsstatistikk: Educational Statistics
0800-2177 Norway. Televerket. Statistikk
0800-2509 Gerontologisk Magasin
0800-2606 Norwegica Pharmaceutica Acta
0800-2789 European Paediatric Haematology & Oncology
0800-403X Norway. Statistisk Sentralbyraa. Helsepersonellstatistikk
0800-4129 Norway. Riksbibliotektjenesten. Skrifter/Papers
0800-4153 Norway. Riksbibliotektjenesten. Aarsmelding
0800-4412 N D R E Publications
0800-532X Teknisk Ukeblad Data *see* 0332-8171
0800-580X Norway. Statistisk Sentralbyraa. Industristatistikk/Industrial Statistics. Vol.1
0800-5818 Norway. Statistisk Sentralbyraa. Industristatistikk/Industrial Statistics. Vol.2
0800-6016 Vaapenjournalen
0800-6032 4H - Klubben
0800-6113 Universitet i Oslo. Pedagogisk Forskningsinstitutt. Rapport
0800-658X Stafo-Nytt
0800-7896 Norsk Energi
0800-8159 Praktisk Oekonomi
0801-0986 Paa Hjul
0801-1087 Norwegian Music Information Center. Bulletin
0801-1400 Norsk Maskin-Tidende Styrmansblad
0801-1745 Norsk Statsvitenskapelig Tidsskrift
0801-2067 Araby. Nordic Studies on the Arab and Islamic World
0801-2334 Norges Landbrukshoegskole. Institutt for Jordskifte og Arealplanlegging. Melding
0801-3799 Astma Allergi
0810-0055 Australia New Zealand Foundation. Annual Report (Year)
0810-1442 Confederation of Western Australian Industry. Confederation Report
0810-1868 Australian Journal of Historical Archaeology.
0810-2201 Australian & New Zealand Booksellers
0810-2236 See Australia
0810-2740 Matilda Literary and Art Magazine *changed to* Matilda Magazine: Literary and Art Magazine
0810-2872 Bike Australia
0810-4115 Dairy Industry Leader
0810-4123 Australasian Drama Studies
0810-4387 Commonwealth Scientific and Industrial Research Organization. Division of Water and Land Resources
0810-4395 University of Tasmania. Environmental Studies. Occasional Paper
0810-4468 Australian Short Stories
0810-4476 Victoria. State Film Centre. New Films and Videotapes
0810-4972 Victoria. Ministry of Housing. Annual Report
0810-5030 Western Australian Institute of Technology. Library. Western Library Studies
0810-5200 Sinatra International
0810-5294 University of Wollongong. Institute Sector Handbook *see* 0726-0717
0810-5391 Accounting and Finance
0810-5928 Australian Shooters Journal
0810-6029 Design World
0810-6142 Mathematics Students' Gazette
0810-6150 Mathmag
0810-6797 Australia. Bureau of Agricultural Economics. Situation and Outlook (Year). Farm Inputs†
0810-6800 Australia. Bureau of Agricultural Economics. Situation and Outlook (Year). Fish Products†
0810-6959 Victoria, Australia. Geological Survey. Reports
0810-736X Water Research in Australia *changed to* Water Research in Australia: Current Projects
0810-7440 Australian Dental Association. News Bulletin
0810-7483 Ad Art
0810-8285 Road Patrol
0810-8889 Association of Australasian Palaeontologists. Memoirs
0810-9028 Prometheus
0810-9176 Australia. Bureau of Statistics. Tasmanian Office. Fruit
0811-0174 Bibliography of Education Theses in Australia
0811-0670 Building Construction Materials & Equipment
0811-0875 V A T Journal (Year)
0811-0905 Insurance in Australia and New Zealand
0811-0964 National Trust of Australia (New South Wales) National Trust Magazine
0811-112X Australasian College Libraries (South Australia)
0811-1154 Western Australia. Education Department. Schools & Staffing
0811-1197 Maffra & District Historical Society. Bulletin
0811-1863 Australia. Department of Employment and Industrial Relations. Employee Participation News
0811-191X Storylines
0811-2169 Outrage
0811-2274 Jewellery World
0811-2762 What's New in Computing
0811-3149 A M C News
0811-3394 Queensland Family Historian
0811-3513 Market Facts (Adelaide)
0811-353X Market Facts (Perth) *see* 0818-1152
0811-3548 Market Facts (Sydney)
0811-3556 Market Facts (Melbourne) *see* 0818-1152
0811-3564 Market Facts (Brisbane)
0811-3688 Australian Transport Information Directory
0811-3696 Australasian Arachnology
0811-3742 Talking Electronics
0811-4188 Insight
0811-4269 Peace Studies *see* 0817-895X
0811-4684 Tactual Mapping Newsletter
0811-4692 A.C.F.O.A News
0811-5400 Liane Newsletter
0811-5680 Small Business Review
0811-6148 Market Facts (Gold Coast)
0811-6199 National Health and Medical Council. Medical Research
0811-6202 Australian Journal of Communication
0811-6407 Defender
0811-6504 South Australian Geographical Papers
0811-7497 N M A
0811-8698 Hoofbeats
0811-8892 Media Ownership in Australia
0811-9066 Eyespy
0811-9929 Scan
0812-0099 Australian Journal of Earth Sciences
0812-0811 Australian Lectionary (Year)
0812-1648 Work and Patrol Boat World
0812-1729 Australia. Department of Primary Industry. Rural Industry Directory
0812-2024 Intellectual Property Reports
0812-2040 What's On in Victoria
0812-2237 Commonwealth Scientific and Industrial Research Organization. Division of Wildlife and Rangelands Research. Technical Paper
0812-2288 Tenders Australia
0812-230X Melbourne College of Advanced Education. Handbook
0812-3314 Institution of Engineers, Australia. Transactions. Multi-Disciplinary Engineering
0812-3330 Open Door Poetry Journal
0812-3470 Westpac Banking Corporation. Review
0812-3594 Australian Electrical Contractor
0812-3705 National Thomson's Liquor Guide *changed to* National Liquor News
0812-3896 Australasian Health & Healing
0812-3985 Exploration Geophysics
0812-4663 Disability Aids Directory
0812-5074 Consumer Views
0812-5864 Blackall Leader
0812-6267 A A C O B S Annual Report
0812-6453 Mingay's Product Service - Appliances
0812-6461 Mingay's Product Service - Home Entertainment
0812-6585 Australian Stationers & Office Suppliers Reference Book
0812-6763 Tasmania. Major Economic Indicators
0812-695X Australian Tax Forum
0812-7131 J A I A
0812-7336 Commonwealth Scientific and Industrial Research Organization. Division of Animal Health. Research Report
0812-7352 Riverina Library Review
0812-7387 Australian Museum, Sydney. Supplements
0812-7417 Threshold†
0812-7735 Australia. Department of Resources and Energy. Streamline Update
0812-7883 Museums Australia
0812-8014 R.A.O.U. Newsletter
0812-8227 Australian Wellbeing
0812-8685 C C J P Issues
0812-9428 Australasian and Pacific Society for Eighteenth-Century Studies. Newsletter
0812-955X Australian Small Farms Directory
0813-0051 Aust-Asian Robotics Journal
0813-006X Badminton Sidelines
0813-0426 Rock Art Research
0813-0493 Commonwealth Scientific and Industrial Research Organization. Division of Wildlife and Rangelands Research. Technical Memorandum
0813-0531 Australian Journal of Advanced Nursing
0813-1295 Royal Historical Society of Victoria. Journal *changed to* Victorian Historical Journal
0813-1600 Cinedossier
0813-1694 National Safety Council of Australia. Annual Report
0813-1724 New South Wales Association For Mental Health. Newsletter
0813-1759 V I S E. Occasional Papers†
0813-1988 S P U M S Journal
0813-2194 Australian Intitute of Psychic Research Bulletin
0813-2283 A C H P E R National Journal
0813-2402 Special Education Journal
0813-2844 Asia Today
0813-4537 Australian Disability Review
0813-4626 My Baby
0813-4650 Solo
0813-4804 Building Management & Maintenance
0813-5150 Viewprints†
0813-5231 Australian Seed Industry Magazine
0813-5436 C C J P Occasional Papers
0813-6394 A M A Victoria Branch News
0813-6580 Tasmanian Teacher *changed to* Teacher
0813-6645 Albury & District Historical Society. Bulletin
0813-7455 Jobson's Quarterly
0813-7471 Hospital and Healthcare Australia

ISSN INDEX 1607

0813-7544 Australian Hotelier
0813-782X Motor Vehicle Reports
0813-7951 Word of Salvation
0813-796X Trowel and Sword
0813-815X Royal Australian Historical Society. Newsletter
0813-9091 Women Australia
0813-9474 Australia. National Institute of Economic & Industry Research. National Economic Review
0813-9806 Nowa Epoka
0814-0049 University of Tasmania. Center for Environmental Studies. Project Report
0814-0545 New South Wales. Department of Agriculture. Fisheries Bulletin
0814-1266 Australian National University. Development Studies Centre. Working Papers
0814-1819 Museum of Victoria. Occasional Papers
0814-2610 A A M R Journal *changed to* Interaction (Canberra)
0814-2769 Video & Audio Marketing
0814-3668 Australian Table Tennis
0814-401X Community Quarterly
0814-4125 Youth Affairs in Australia
0814-4273 Business Council of Australia Bulletin
0814-4680 Trees and Natural Resources
0814-480X Postmark News
0814-4990 Rutherglen Research Institute. Research Report
0814-5296 Mansfield Historical Society's Magazine
0814-5504 Economic Growth of the Australian States†
0814-6802 Education Links
0814-6942 Ad News
0814-7078 V/Line News
0814-771X P L News
0814-7833 Gallery
0814-8074 Chartac Accounting Report
0814-8112 Chartac Computer Report†
0814-8120 Chartac Taxation Report
0814-8589 Australian Bar Review
0814-8805 Metaphysical Review
0814-883X Artswest
0814-9267 Wheat Australia International
0814-9321 C I S Policy Report
0814-9593 Australia. Bureau of Statistics. Tasmanian Office. Labour Force Statistics
0814-9933 S.A. Crafts News
0815-0249 Nuclear Spectrum
0815-0303 A B N Catalogue
0815-1458 Australia. Bureau of Agricultural Economics. Occasional Papers
0815-1881 Australia. Department of the Treasury. Round-Up of Economic Statistics *changed to* Australia. Department of the Treasury. Round-up
0815-2195 Plant Protection Quarterly
0815-2292 Inventors
0815-3205 Electrical and Computer Engineering in Australia†
0815-3396 Star Observer *changed to* Sydney Star Observer
0815-3701 Australian T A F E Teacher
0815-3752 Technology in Education
0815-3809 Northern Territory at a Glance
0815-452X Carrionflower Writ
0815-5046 Australian Electronics Monthly
0815-5232 Directory of Australian Composers
0815-5992 Adelaide Review
0815-6344 Asia Pacific Context
0815-6816 Pelang
0815-7138 Macquarie University French Monographs
0815-9297 Australian Poultry Digest
0815-9424 Development Dossier
0815-9769 Dairy Goat Society of Australia. Victorian Branch Newsletter
0815-9777 British Alpine Breeders Group of Australia. Newsletter
0815-9904 Herald
0816-0031 Salt
0816-0627 Asutralia. Bureau of Statistics. Digest of Current Economic Statistics
0816-1070 C R R E R I S Renewable Energy Index
0816-1089 Australian Journal of Experimental Agriculture
0816-1909 Photo Retailer
0816-2271 Western Australian Resource Developement Services Directory
0816-2425 Rock
0816-2484 Management Reports on the Australian Economy
0816-2905 Truck & Bus Road Tests†
0816-3456 Economic Advice to Business
0816-3588 Textile and Apparel Manufacturer
0816-3596 Australian Paint and Panel
0816-3634 Food Manufacturing News
0816-4290 Melbourne's Star Observer
0816-486X Animal Liberation
0816-5416 T N C Workers Research Brief
0816-6013 Commonwealth Scientific and Industrial Research Organization. Division of Geomechanics. Geomechanics Computer Programs
0816-6668 Organic Growing (Ulverstone)
0816-6773 Education Department of Victoria. Textbooks†
0816-7656 D O G S Newsletter
0817-2285 Sydney Organ Journal
0817-2668 A I M M Bulletin and Proceedings
0817-3052 Drugs: Australia
0817-3516 Legal Service Bulletin
0817-3524 Social Security Reporter *see* 0817-3516
0817-3532 Freedom of Information Review
0817-4075 Tasmanian Numismatist
0817-623X Australian Journal of Family Law
0817-6337 Australian Plumbing Industry
0817-6353 Who's Pegging
0817-6825 Australia. Department of Primary Industry. Domestic and Overseas Fish Market Notes
0817-8771 University of Sydney. Department of Agricultural Economics. Research Report.
0817-895X Peace Magazine Australia
0817-9263 Australia. Bureau of Mineral Resources. Geology and Geophysics. Australian Petroleum Accumulations Report
0818-0229 Australian Institute of Family Studies. Newsletter
0818-1152 Market Facts
0818-1233 R A I A Memo
0818-2019 A.C.T. Science Teacher
0818-4127 National Trotguide
0818-4380 Queensland Hosteller
0818-4445 Prescription Products Guide
0818-4453 Non-Prescription Products Guide
0818-4674 South Australia in Business
0818-5093 Dun's Gazette
0818-5204 Transit Australia
0818-545X Queensland Researcher
0818-5646 Australasian Sound Archive
0818-7169 South Australian Dairyfarmer's Journal
0819-0194 Stereo Buyer's Guide. Loudspeakers, Amplifiers and Tuners
0819-0208 Stereo Buyer's Guide. C D Players, Cassettes Decks and Turntables
0819-0216 Stereo Buyer's Guide. Audio Yearbook
0820-005X Perspectives Universitaires
0820-0165 Muse (Ottawa)
0820-0416 Music Directory Canada
0820-0467 Lottery and Gaming *see* 8750-801X
0820-0521 Library and Information Science Update
0820-0750 Microcomputer Applications
0820-0858 Offshore Resources
0820-6686 Worldlit
0820-6848 Prairie Landscape Magazine
0820-7356 C L E M
0820-7364 N A P O News
0820-7941 Alberta Teachers' Association. Science Council. Bulletin
0820-8093 National Library of Canada. Technical News *see* 0825-9658
0820-8204 Atlantic Provinces Linguistic Association. Annual Meeting. Papers
0820-9006 Arthritis News
0820-9111 Goodwin's†
0820-9189 Phenomenology & Pedagogy
0820-957X Journal of Small Business - Canada
0820-988X Boreal Institute for Northern Studies. Report of Activities
0821-0020 B.C. Economic Bulletin
0821-0160 Take Five
0821-0306 Investment in Canadian High Technology Companies *changed to* Canadian Technology Investment Letter
0821-0705 Education Express
0821-1108 Chorus
0821-1124 Prairie Fire
0821-1272 C U S O Journal
0821-1450 C M : Canadian Materials for Schools and Libraries *changed to* C M: A Reviewing Journal of Canadian Materials for Young People
0821-1809 Torpet
0821-1841 Forintek Review
0821-2015 HospitAlta
0821-2996 Urban Transit Facts in Canada. Membership Directory
0821-3275 Markwick Midden
0821-3747 Lemon Aid Bulletin
0821-3925 Health News (Toronto)
0821-4425 Essays in Theatre
0821-5073 Horse Sense
0821-5308 Videocom
0821-5359 Generations (Fredericton)
0821-5774 Canada Century Home
0821-5839 Briercrest Echo
0821-5855 Gardening and Leisure Living†
0821-5871 V C C Voice *see* 0822-7896
0821-6371 Truth on Fire
0821-6452 McGill Studies in International Development
0821-6827 Vice Versa Magazine
0821-6916 Pensions and Benefits†
0821-719X Canadian Charter of Rights Decisions
0822-0603 C A D/C A M & Robotics
0822-207X C I J Bulletin
0822-2509 A O S T R A Journal of Research
0822-2517 Yorkview
0822-4277 Mental Retardation and Learning Disability Bulletin
0822-4749 Choirs Ontario
0822-4838 Operational Geographer
0822-5672 En Passant
0822-5745 Ontario Lawyers Weekly *changed to* Lawyers Weekly
0822-5931 Museum Quarterly (Toronto)
0822-6377 Our Times Magazine
0822-6830 Canadian Banker
0822-7098 Coulicou
0822-7217 Inuit Arts and Craft†
0822-7896 Voice
0822-8426 C H A C Info
0822-8515 M B A Magazine
0822-8523 Trouvez un Nom *see* 0822-8531
0822-8531 En Tete
0822-8981 Edmonton Metropolitan Regional Planning Commission. Regional Update *see* 0829-9153
0822-9058 Physiology Canada
0823-0269 Sciences et Techniques de l'Eau
0823-0498 Monde du Rock
0823-0552 Fungi Canadenses
0823-065X Canada. Statistics Canada. Private and Public Investment in Canada. Intentions/Investissements Prives et Publics au Canada. Perspectives
0823-0668 Canada. Statistics Canada. Private and Public Investment in Canada. Revised Intentions/Investissements Prives et Publics au Canada. Perspective Revisee
0823-1117 Alberta Teachers' Association. Mathematics Council. Newsletter
0823-1346 Jewellery World
0823-1745 P E G G
0823-1931 International Skyline
0823-2539 Alumeto
0823-2601 International Education Forum/Forum de l'Education International *see* 0827-0678
0823-4604 Maine-Anjou International
0823-4744 Current Canadian Ophthalmic Practice
0823-5228 Canadian Chemical News/Actualite Chimique Canadienne
0823-5651 Mouvements
0823-5740 C U S O Forum
0823-6283 Multicultural Education Journal
0823-6437 Computing Now!
0823-6526 Kick it Over
0823-6720 Alberta Farmagazine
0823-8294 Videotex World†
0823-9266 Great Expectations
0823-9436 Justice Report
0823-9452 T.O.: The Magazine of Toronto
0823-9940 Computers in Education
0824-0469 Marine Mammal Science
0824-0868 2 x 4
0824-1333 Allergy Alert
0824-2062 Catalyst
0824-2119 Forintek Canada Corp., Western Laboratory. Special Publications
0824-2992 Green's Magazine
0824-3336 Risk Abstracts
0824-3441 Optical Prism
0824-3492 Zest
0824-4790 Computer Law
0824-4855 A T A C C Journal
0824-4863 Health & Physical Education Newsletter
0824-4936 L'Estuaire Genealogique
0824-4952 Oil & Gas Report
0824-5134 University of Alberta. Centre for Criminological Research. Discussion Papers
0824-5487 World of Wheels
0824-6017 Tsu Chi *changed to* Footprint
0824-7064 Intellectual Property Journal
0824-717X British Columbia Decisions - Civil Cases
0824-7188 British Columbia Decisions - Municipal Law Cases
0824-7196 British Columbia Decisions - Family Law Cases
0824-720X British Columbia Decisions - Insurance Law Cases
0824-7226 Freewheeler
0824-7242 British Columbia Decisions - Criminal Cases
0824-7269 Ontario Decisions - Criminal Cases
0824-7277 Alberta Decisions. Rules and Statute Citator
0824-7285 Saskatchewan Decisions - Rules and Statute Citator
0824-7293 Manitoba Decisions - Rules and Statute Citator
0824-734X Marine Engineering Digest
0824-7528 Eco/Log Canadian Pollution Legislation
0824-7749 Special Libraries Association. Eastern Canada Chapter/Section de l'Est du Canada. Bulletin
0824-7870 Der Shmaiser
0824-7935 Computational Intelligence
0824-8001 C.D. Howe Institute Commentary
0824-801X Inflation Monitor
0824-8028 Perspective (Toronto)†
0824-8192 B I N S Bibliographic Series
0824-8206 Ministry of Agriculture. Greenhouse-Ornamental Production Guide *changed to* British Columbia. Ministry of Agriculture and Food. Greenhouse-Ornamental Production Guide
0824-8672 Salus
0824-8818 Realisations Recents a Petawawa
0824-8907 Canadian Jewish Congress. National Archives Newsletter
0825-0170 Canada. National Energy Board. Information Bulletins
0825-0367 T P U G Magazine
0825-1746 L'Incunable
0825-2777 Cultures du Canada Francais
0825-3021 Canadian Communications Network Letter
0825-3706 International Business Perspectives
0825-3854 Canadian Art
0825-432X Canada. Statistics Canada. Homicide in Canada: a Statistical Perspective/L'Homicide au Canada: Perspective Statistique
0825-4729 Classroom
0825-4982 Business & the Law

ISSN INDEX

ISSN	Title
0825-5318	Heartwood
0825-592X	Policy Commentary†
0825-7531	Empathic Parenting
0825-754X	Canadian Vet Supplies
0825-799X	Spring Wind
0825-8422	Big Time Music Magazine†
0825-8597	Journal of Palliative Care
0825-9224	Canada. Statistics Canada. Provincial and Territorial Government Employment
0825-9658	Bibliotech
0826-0265	Ottawa Newcomer
0826-0532	Forest Pest Management Institute. Technical Note Series
0826-2713	Aeroscope
0826-3515	Magazine Ressources Humaines
0826-3663	Canadian Journal of Latin American and Caribbean Studies
0826-4716	Canadian Journal for Exceptional Children
0826-4805	Interchange
0826-5003	Windsport
0826-581X	Environmental Law Centre Newsletter†
0826-5909	Raddle Moon
0826-595X	Building Renovation
0826-6778	Canadian Critical Care Nursing Journal
0826-6972	Last Issue
0826-7731	En Ville
0826-791X	Ontario. Geological Survey. Exploration Technology Development Fund Grants
0826-8185	Robotics and Automation
0826-8193	Transportation Forum
0826-8371	Maritime Industries
0826-8983	Research and Development in the Canadian Corporate Section
0826-9343	C S N D T Journal
0826-9521	Peace Magazine
0826-9874	Quebec Pharmacie
0826-9939	C.D. Howe Institute. Policy Review and Outlook
0826-9947	Observation
0827-0678	International Education Magazine
0827-1038	Clinical Biofeedback and Health
0827-1364	Cercles des Jeunes Naturalistes. Bulletin de Nouvelles
0827-1550	Intercultural Horizons
0827-1755	Maple Orchard
0827-1844	Apprentissage et Socialisation en Piste
0827-2042	B.C. Sport Fishing Magazine
0827-2115	Marketing & Advertising Law Reporter
0827-2123	Pollution Law Reporting Service
0827-2557	Free Flight
0827-262X	Computek
0827-2638	Bowbender
0827-2824	Island Grower
0827-2921	Prairie Journal
0827-3049	Teaching Today
0827-3669	Carleton-Ottawa Mathematical Lecture Note Series
0827-3677	Tax Profile
0827-3715	Canadian Library Yearbook
0827-4061	Renewable Energy Alerting Database Service
0827-4576	O H & S Canada
0827-4789	Initiative
0827-4916	Shalom Magazine
0827-5564	A L A I. Servicio Mensual de Informacion y Documentacion
0827-570X	Okay Anglers Fishing Directory & Atlas
0827-5785	Provincial Outlook
0827-5831	Conference Board of Canada. Consumer Attitudes and Buying Intentions
0827-5955	Guild of Carillonneurs in North America. Bulletin
0827-6277	Conference Board of Canada. Business Attitudes and Investment Spending Intentions
0827-6374	Formula 2000
0827-7230	Greater Vancouver Japanese Canadian Citizens Association Bulletin
0828-0851	Canada. Statistics Canada. Current Economic Indicators/Indicateurs Conjoncturels
0828-086X	Canada. Statistics Canada. Quarterly Economic Summary/Apercu Economique Trimestriel
0828-0878	Canada. Statistics Canada. Quarterly Economic Summary. Statistical Supplement/Apercu Economique Trimestriel. Supplement Statistique
0828-1890	10
0828-282X	Canadian Journal of Cardiology
0828-2897	Canada. Statistics Canada. Surface and Marine Transport. Service Bulletin/Bulletin de Service Transports Terrestre et Maritimes
0828-4083	Grail
0828-4253	Up Here
0828-4466	Hilborn's Family Newsletter Directory
0828-4474	Canada Tomorrow
0828-4539	Table Tennis Technical
0828-5748	Catholic Health Association of Canada. Directory
0828-6833	Ordre des Comptables Agrees du Quebec. Bilans
0828-6949	A T A C C Newsletter
0828-7198	Indicator
0828-797X	Interculture
0828-8089	Magazine P M E
0828-8259	Canadian Historical Horticulture
0828-864X	Equinews
0828-8755	Calgary Stampede
0828-9522	Resource: The Canadian Journal of Real Estate†
0828-9824	Canada. Statistics Canada. Communications and Other Electronic Industries/Industries de l'Equipement et d'Autre Materiel Electronique
0828-9832	Canada. Statistics Canada. Jewellery and Precious Metal Industries/Industries de la Bijouterie et de L'Orfevrerie
0828-9867	Canada. Statistics Canada. Sawmill, Planing Mill and Shingle Mill Products Industries/Industries des Produits de Scieries et d'Ataliers de Rabotage
0828-9913	Canada. Statistics Canada. Wire and Wire Products Industries/Industries du Fil Metallique et de ses Produits
0828-9921	Canada. Statistics Canada. Ornamental and Architectural Metal Products Industry/Industrie des Produits Metalliques d'Ornement et d'Architecture
0829-0032	Humus
0829-0547	Western Canadian Anthropologist
0829-1756	Canada. Statistics Canada. Passenger Bus and Urban Transit/Statistique du Transport des Voyageurs par Autobus et du Transport Urbain
0829-2132	Canadian Aviation News
0829-2906	C Magazine
0829-3163	Canada. Statistics Canada. Honey Production and Value, Production Forecast/Production et Valeur du Miel, Provision de la Production
0829-3201	Canadian Journal of Law and Society
0829-3279	Sea Kayaker
0829-352X	Wastewater Technology Centre Newsletter
0829-3716	Sports Business
0829-4321	Alberta Association of College Librarians. Newsletter
0829-4437	A G O News
0829-4666	Gospel Herald
0829-4836	Canadian Journal of Marketing Research
0829-4909	University of Toronto. Institute for Policy Analysis. Working Paper Series
0829-4976	From My Bookshelf
0829-5026	Canadian West
0829-5425	University Computing and Information Services Newsletter
0829-559X	B.S.D.A. News
0829-5654	Wedding Bells Magazine
0829-7010	Tyro Magazine
0829-7274	Canadian Video Marketing changed to Video Marketing
0829-7762	Verve
0829-8157	Trade Asia Magazine
0829-8203	Ontario. Geological Survey. Summary of Field Work
0829-8211	Biochemistry and Cell Biology
0829-8416	Canadian Outlook
0829-8564	Compleat Mother
0829-8629	Canadian Government Buyer
0829-8777	Canadian Magazine Index
0829-9137	Multicultural Education
0829-9153	Edmonton Metropolitan Regional Planning Commission. Metro Planning Review
0829-9552	Canadian Women's Periodicals
0829-9889	Housewares Canada
0830-0348	World Review of Doulton
0830-0445	Journal of Distance Education
0830-0593	Canadian Thoroughbred
0830-0739	Okanagan Business
0830-0763	Non-Wage Provisions in Saskatchewan Collective Agreements
0830-8284	Wilderness Alberta
0830-8721	Guitar Canada
0830-8810	Industrial Maintenance Repair and Overhaul News
0830-9000	Canadian Journal of Veterinary Research
0830-9434	Epson Today
0831-0041	Telecom Bulletin
0831-0114	Quebec ce Mois-ci
0831-0254	Network
0831-067X	En Voyage
0831-0998	Practical Allergy & Immunology
0831-2338	Prairie Farmers Catalogue
0831-2559	Border Crossings
0831-2796	Genome
0831-2893	Canadian Academy of Sport Medicine Review
0831-3040	M S O S Journal
0831-3377	Feminist Action
0831-3881	C M A
0831-4020	Canadian Environmental Mediation Newsletter
0831-4160	Toronto Business Magazine
0831-4306	Environmental Notes from the National Capital
0831-4446	Eastern Synod Lutheran
0831-5000	Geotechnical Science Laboratories. Publications, Reports, and Theses
0831-5671	Algonquian Conference Papers
0831-5698	Canadian Social Trends
0831-5825	Echange
0831-6708	Inuit Art
0831-7496	City of Ottawa. Corporate Financial and Statistical Information
0831-8093	Saint Mary's University. Atlantic Region Geographical Studies
0831-8107	Saint Mary's University. Occasional Papers in Geography
0831-8603	Machinery & Equipment M R O
0832-1191	Faith Today
0832-1418	Action Bulletin see 0831-3377
0832-6096	Manitoba Medicine
0832-6266	Saint Mary's University. Studies in Marine and Coastal Geography
0832-655X	Canadian Statistics Index
0832-6614	New Biotech
0832-705X	Farm Business
0832-7912	Policy Study
0832-8196	Performance
0832-8315	Voices
0832-865X	Directory of the Arts
0832-8781	Canadian Journal of Women and the Law
0832-9354	Resource
0832-9966	Le Beffroi
0833-0026	M T L Montreal
0833-0530	L'Orientation
0833-062X	Business Report
0833-0689	Timberlines
0833-093X	Native Press
0833-2002	Canada. Statistics Canada. Communications and Energy Wire and Cable Industry/Industrie des Fils et Cables Electriques et de Communications
0833-823X	Earthkeeping
0833-8264	Canadian Dental Assistants Association. Journal
0833-8388	Association de la Construction de Montreal et du Quebec. Bulletin
0833-9406	Contract Magazine
0833-9570	Stereo/Video Guide
0834-0242	Outlook
0834-0471	Agent Canada
0834-406X	Canada. Canadian Forestry Service-Maritimes, Fredericton, New Brunswick. Information Report M-X
0835-0310	Paddler
0850-010X	Senegal. Archives du Senegal. Rapport Annuel
0850-1602	Senegal. Centre de Recherche Oceanographique. Document Scientifique
0850-3907	Africa Development
0850-4008	Register Development Research Projects Africa
0850-430X	West African Archivist
0856-0005	Educational Abstracts for Tanzania
0856-003X	Tanzania National Bibliography
0856-0048	Africa Theological Journal
0856-0056	African Review
0856-0080	T P R I Bulletin
0856-0129	Mulika
0856-0161	Tanzania. Ministry of Trade. Foreign Trade News Bulletin
0856-017X	Tanzania News Review
0856-0323	Gazette of the United Republic of Tanzania
0856-0366	Home Builders Journal
0856-0374	Tanzania. Bureau of Standards. Director's Annual Report
0856-0382	Rasilimali
0856-0455	East Africana Accessions Bulletin
0856-0498	Mapinduzi Katika Uandishi
0856-0560	Studies in Adult Education
0856-065X	Tanzanian Mathematical Bulletin
0856-1109	Journal of Adult Education
0856-1222	Ngao
0856-1621	Tanzania Library Service. Occasional Paper
0857-0361	S E A M E O Quarterly
0857-2410	Monthly Agrometeorological Report
0857-2984	Thailand Industrial Buyer's Guide
0860-0260	Akademia Gorniczo-Hutnicza im. Stanislawa Staszica. Zeszyty Naukowe. Fizyka
0860-0783	Politechnika Krakowska. Zeszyty Naukowe. Transport
0860-1100	Akademia Gorniczo-Hutnicza im. Stanislawa Staszica. Zeszyty Naukowe. Chemia
0860-1194	Politechnika Wroclawska. Instytut Historii Architektury, Sztuki i Techniki. Prace Naukowe. Konferencje
0860-1615	Politechnika Wroclawska. Centrum Obliczeniowe. Prace Naukowe. Konferencje
0860-1623	Politechnika Wroclawska. Centrum Obliczeniowe. Prace Naukowe. Studia i Materialy
0860-2441	Acta Biologica Silesiana
0860-2603	Acta Academiae Agriculturae ac Technicae Olstenensis. Zootechnica
0860-2611	Acta Academiae Agriculturae ac Technicae Olstenensis. Protectio Aquarum et Piscatoria
0860-262X	Acta Academiae Agriculturae ac Technicae Olstenensis. Geodaesia et Ruris Regulatio
0860-2727	Akademia Gorniczo-Hutnicza im. Stanislawa Staszica. Zeszyty Naukowe. Opuscula Mathematica
0860-2832	Acta Academiae Agriculturae ac Technicae Olstenensis. Agricultura/Agriculture
0860-2840	Acta Academiae Agriculturae ac Technicae Olstenensis. Veterynaria
0860-2859	Acta Academiae Agriculturae ac Technicae Olstenensis. Technologia Alimentorum
0860-2948	Acta Academiae Agriculturae ac Technicae Olstenensis. Oekonomika
0860-2956	Acta Academiae Agriculturae ac Technicae Olstenensis. Aedificatio et Mechanica

0860-3200 Politechnika Wroclawska. Instytut Nauk Ekonomiczno-Spolecznych. Prace Naukowe. Konferencje
0860-4045 Polski Klub Ekologiczney Okregu Malopolska. Prace Naukowe
0860-410X Kalendarz Slowa Bozego
0870-0001 Garcia de Orta: Serie de Zoologia
0870-001X Estudos Ensaios e Documentos
0870-0028 Instituto de Investigacao Cientifica Tropical. Centro de Estudos de Historia e Cartografia Antiga. Studia
0870-0036 Instituto de Investigacao Cientifica Tropical. Memorias
0870-0133 Evphrosyne
0870-0141 Classica
0870-015X Instituto de Investigacao Cientifica Tropical. Centro de Estudos de Historia e Cartografia Antiga. Serie de Memorias
0870-0168 Garcia de Orta: Serie de Antropobiologia
0870-0974 Bibliotecas, Arquivos e Museus
0870-0990 Antropologia Portuguesa
0870-1245 Portugal. Instituto Nacional de Investigacao das Pescas. Boletim
0870-2594 Estado das Culturas e Previsao de Colheitas
0870-2950 Anuario Climatologico
0870-3205 Portugal. Instituto Nacional de Estatistica. Servicos Centrais. Estatisticas das Sociedades. Continente e Ilhas Adjacentes *changed to* Portugal. Instituto Nacional de Estatistica. Servicos Centrais. Estatisticas das Sociedades: Continente, Acores e Madeira
0870-3701 Cruz Vermelha Portugesa. Boletim de Informacao
0870-3841 Coloquio/Artes
0870-3876 Museu Municipal do Funchal. Boletim
0870-4104 Clio (Lisbon)
0870-4546 Cultura, Historia y Filosofia
0870-4686 Boletim Meteorologico
0870-4694 Boletim Meteorologico para a Agricultura
0870-4716 Centro de Fisica da Atmosfera de Lisboa. Gago Coutinho. Boletim
0870-4724 Projecto I2 do PIDDAC. Boletim
0870-4732 Resumos Meteorologicos para a Aeronautica
0870-4740 Boletim Actinometrico de Portugal
0870-4759 Portugal. Instituto Nacional de Meteorologia e Geofisica. Revista
0870-4783 Jornal de Psicologia
0870-5283 Revista Portuguesa de Filosofia
0870-5364 Electricidade
0870-6506 Portugal. Instituto Nacional de Estatistica. Estatisticas de Seguranca Social, Associacoes Sindicais e Patronais. Continente, Acores e Madeira
0870-6891 Estudos de Antropologia Cultural
0882-0082 Bowker's Complete Sourcebook of Personal Computing†
0882-0104 Data General Micro World
0882-0139 Immunological Investigations
0882-0147 Fertilizer Technology†
0882-0163 C A E Electronics Alert
0882-018X Rundy's Journal and Confederation Courier
0882-0228 Selections (Los Angeles)
0882-0236 D O S S U Journal
0882-0287 Communications in Statistics: Stochastic Models
0882-0317 Utopian Classroom
0882-0384 Texas League Savings Account
0882-0422 Genealogical Clearinghouse Quarterly†
0882-0481 Fitness Management
0882-0511 Seminars in Veterinary Medicine and Surgery: Small Animal
0882-052X Seminars in Orthopaedics
0882-0538 Seminars in Ophthalmology
0882-0554 New England Sampler
0882-0627 Journal of Nursing Staff Development
0882-0635 Tennessee Ancestors
0882-066X Widener Review
0882-0775 Unlisted Market Guide
0882-0813 Vajradhatu Sun
0882-0929 California Chamber of Commerce Alert
0882-0953 Radiological Respiratory Protection Newsletter
0882-1100 S P E Monograph Series
0882-1135 Women's Quarterly Review
0882-116X L F L Reports
0882-1232 Journal of Curriculum and Supervision
0882-1240 Dimensions: A Journal of Holocaust Studies
0882-1305 L B L Research Review
0882-133X Physician's Legal Alert†
0882-1348 Scifant
0882-1402 Acid Rain Abstracts
0882-1410 Artificial Intelligence Abstracts
0882-1429 Telecommunications Abstract
0882-1437 C A D/C A M Abstracts
0882-1445 Public Technology
0882-147X Morning Coffee Chapbook Series
0882-1496 Market Moves
0882-1577 Health Progress
0882-1593 Black Elected Officials
0882-1666 Systems and Computers in Japan
0882-178X Option Magazine
0882-1852 Biological Therapies in Dentistry Newsletter
0882-1879 Island Properties Report
0882-1933 Olschwanger Journal
0882-195X Annual Index to Poetry in Periodicals
0882-200X Computer & Electronics Graduate
0882-2042 Chicora Foundation Research Series
0882-2123 Ambassador Report
0882-2131 Executive Health Report
0882-2190 Schabacker Investment Management. Weekly Advisory Bulletin
0882-2212 Catgut Acoustical Society. Journal
0882-2271 I N T V Journal
0882-231X Faxletter
0882-2522 American Native Press
0882-2549 Duplex Planet
0882-2557 Texas Instruments Technical Journal
0882-2573 Kane's Beverage Week
0882-2743 Contents of Periodicals on Latin America
0882-276X D A R Systems International's White Paper Series in Computer Programming†
0882-2808 Node
0882-2832 A B M S Directory of Certified Neurological Surgeons
0882-2840 A L A N Review
0882-2867 Nontoxic & Natural News *see* 0889-8421
0882-3030 Folio (Brockport)
0882-3189 Pitts Choice
0882-326X Database End-User *changed to* Database Searcher
0882-3316 Emerging Patterns of Work and Communications in an Information Age
0882-3332 Pipe & Quill
0882-3391 Lifestyles
0882-3405 Index to Periodical Literature on Aging
0882-3472 Attitude
0882-3499 Soft-Letter
0882-3537 Energy Policy Studies
0882-3588 Arc - The Rural Arts Newsletter
0882-3723 Fourth World Journal
0882-3758 Thermology
0882-3804 Letter Exchange
0882-3944 Monitor (Arlington)
0882-410X Federal Reserve Bank of Minneapolis. District Economic Conditions
0882-4150 Hamersky & Allied Families Newsletter
0882-4347 Applied Orgonometry
0882-438X A M S Studies in Education
0882-4401 Nautical Brass
0882-4681 Corporate Times
0882-4738 Utah. Office of Administrative Rules. Utah State Bulletin.
0882-4746 Good Stuff
0882-4754 Marketing Trends
0882-4843 Feminist Teacher
0882-4959 I E E E Translation Journal on Magnetics in Japan
0882-4967 I E E E Journal of Robotics and Automation
0882-4983 Geotechnical Fabrics Report
0882-5181 Caquelin Chronicle†
0882-5297 Afro-American Culture and Society Monograph Series
0882-5300 C A A S Special Publication Series
0882-5351 American Magazine and Historical Chronicle
0882-536X Directory of Hardware and Housewares Distributors
0882-5394 Hadronic Journal. Supplement
0882-5424 Tapori
0882-5475 Humanities Education
0882-5491 Arkansas Archeological Survey. Publications on Archeology. Research Series
0882-5521 Taft Nonprofit Executive
0882-553X SportSearch
0882-5572 Arizona Wildlife Views
0882-5637 Federal Career Insights
0882-5645 Topics in Pain Management Newsletter
0882-5696 Hazardous Waste & Hazardous Materials
0882-570X Soviet Journal of Automation & Information Sciences
0882-5734 Flavour & Fragrance Journal
0882-5793 Federation Review†
0882-584X Urban Wildlife Manager's Notebook
0882-5858 Urban Wildlife News
0882-5874 Durch die Fensterscheibe
0882-5882 Heller Helper
0882-5890 Schartzer - Schertzer Connection
0882-5904 Schneider Connections
0882-5955 Constitution
0882-5963 Journal of Pediatric Nursing
0882-6072 Hypnosis Reports
0882-617X Independent Report on Martin Marietta *see* 0884-3260
0882-6188 Ground Water Monitor
0882-6277 Impact (New York, 1983)
0882-6366 Workers' Advocate Supplement
0882-648X Bogg
0882-6501 Avotaynu
0882-6528 St. Clair County Genealogical Society Quarterly
0882-6587 Government Microcomputer Letter
0882-6803 Latin Travel Review
0882-6846 C R I A R L Newsletter
0882-696X Guthrie Journal
0882-6994 Soviet Economy
0882-701X Direct Response Marketing to Schools Newsletter
0882-7036 Preaching
0882-7052 Bio-Bibliographies in Law and Political Science
0882-7133 Annual DeGarmo Lectures
0882-7141 Society of Professors of Education. Occasional Papers
0882-7206 Wine Spectator Wine Maps
0882-7214 United Church News
0882-7400 Published
0882-7508 Mineral Processing and Extractive Metallurgy
0882-7737 European Travel & Life
0882-7907 Hurricane Alice
0882-7958 Advanced Materials & Processes
0882-7974 Psychology and Aging
0882-7982 Yarn Market News
0882-7990 Ward's Business Directory of Largest U S Companies
0882-8008 Ward's Business Directory of Major U S Private Companies
0882-8016 Ward's Business Directory of Major International Companies
0882-8032 Applied Industrial Hygiene
0882-8083 Hematology Reviews and Communications
0882-8091 Speedx
0882-8202 Barron Family Newsletter
0882-8377 G.A.S. Lites
0882-8415 Software Developer's Monthly
0882-8431 A R P E News
0882-8458 Women's Travel Connections
0882-8466 Lacan Study Notes
0882-8512 Freethought Today
0882-8555 Medical Malpractice Litigation Reporter
0882-8644 Philippine Report
0882-8679 Quarterly Report
0882-8695 Athens News
0882-8709 Corporate Travel
0882-9047 National Forum of Educational Administration and Supervision *see* 0888-8132
0882-908X F L I C C Newsletter
0882-9233 Surgical Research Communications
0882-9284 Agricultural Computing
0882-9403 Senior Citizens Advocate
0882-9691 Wheat Grower
0882-990X Bulletin Board Systems
0883-0061 Keeper's Log
0883-0126 Red Bass
0883-0185 International Reviews in Immunology
0883-0231 Europe for Travelers!
0883-0258 Dimensional Stone Magazine
0883-0347 U S Swimming News
0883-0452 HealthSpan
0883-0487 Letter of Credit Update
0883-0738 Journal of Child Neurology
0883-0754 Experimental Musical Instruments
0883-0762 Health Care Instrumentation
0883-0940 Cloud Family Journal
0883-1130 Creative Crafters Journal
0883-119X Wise Woman
0883-1203 A B M S Directory of Certified Pathologists
0883-1211 A B M S Directory of Certified Orthopaedic Surgeons
0883-122X A B M S Directory of Certified Anesthesiologists
0883-1238 A B M S Directory of Certified Radiologists
0883-1297 Legal Information Alert
0883-1300 S C P Journal
0883-1319 S C P Newsletter
0883-1351 Palaios
0883-1394 Journal of Inferential and Deductive Biology
0883-1416 Changing Work
0883-1424 Computer Aided Publishing Report
0883-1440 Current Christian Abstracts
0883-1483 Government Accountant's Journal
0883-1505 International Logo Exchange *see* 0888-6970
0883-1580 Sports Periodicals Index
0883-1599 Temblor
0883-1688 S H H H
0883-1718 Character II (Chicago)
0883-1963 Consumer Health and Nutrition Index
0883-2102 A P I Account
0883-2234 Retail Security Management Letter
0883-2293 Person-Centered Review
0883-2323 Journal of Education for Business
0883-234X 73 for Radio Amateurs
0883-2382 Pleasure Hunt Magazine
0883-2390 AmigaWorld
0883-282X Spectrum
0883-2986 A B M S Directory of Certified Physical Medicine & Rehabilitation Physicians
0883-2994 A B M S Directory of Certified Allergy-Immunology Physicians
0883-3001 A B M S Directory of Certified Otolaryngologists
0883-3095 Pre- and Peri-Natal Psychology Journal
0883-3559 Historians of Early Modern Europe
0883-4202 Cybernetic
0883-4296 Microeconomics
0883-4326 Clothed with the Sun
0883-4687 Foreign Trade Fairs New Products Newsletter
0883-4725 Current Titles in Ocean, Coastal, Lake & Waterway Sciences
0883-4989 Electronics
0883-5365 Oral Tradition
0883-5403 Journal of Arthroplasty
0883-5470 Poet's Market
0883-5527 World Biolicensing Report
0883-556X Madden Family Newsletter
0883-5594 Recognition Technologies Today *changed to* Remittance and Document Processing

0883-5683 Computer Pictures
0883-5705 Kit Car
0883-5713 Attorneys Office Management Report
0883-573X Voice (East Lansing)
0883-5799 Washington Trooper
0883-5810 A T H A Newsletter†
0883-5853 New Resources for State Government & Agencies
0883-587X Chesapeake and Ohio Historical Newsletter *see* 0886-6287
0883-5926 Allees All Around
0883-5977 Computer Industry Digest†
0883-6027 Urban Analysis and Public Management *changed to* Journal of Urban Analysis and Public Management
0883-6159 California Broker
0883-6264 California Facts
0883-6337 Notebook: A Little Magazine
0883-6493 TechNotes
0883-6590 Pulteney St. Survey
0883-6612 Annals of Behavioral Medicine
0883-6671 Health Insurance Medical Records Risk Management Report
0883-6728 Colorado Episcopalian
0883-6884 Contributions in Military Studies
0883-6949 Mannlicher Collector
0883-6973 In House Graphics
0883-7066 System Dynamics Review
0883-721X India-West
0883-7287 Nelson's Official Research Guide
0883-7392 A R E A Magazine
0883-7481 F E: The Magazine for Financial Executives *changed to* Financial Executives
0883-7554 I E E E Electrical Insulation Magazine
0883-7562 Journal of Independent Social Work
0883-7570 Journal of Hospital Marketing
0883-7589 Journal of Marketing for Mental Health
0883-7597 Journal of Pharmaceutical Marketing and Management
0883-7635 Orim: A Jewish Journal at Yale
0883-7708 Lamb's Pastures
0883-7732 Tibet Society Bulletin
0883-7805 Manley Family Newsletter
0883-7902 Mental and Physical Disability Law Reporter
0883-8038 Thoroughbred Business
0883-8100 World Resources Institute. Journal†
0883-8127 Open Shop Building Construction Cost Data (Year)
0883-8135 World Today Series: Canada
0883-8151 Journal of Broadcasting and Electronic Media
0883-8216 Health Science
0883-8305 Paleoceanography
0883-8364 In Vitro Cellular & Developmental Biology
0883-8518 Oink! *changed to* New American Writing
0883-8526 Alaska Native Language Center Research Papers
0883-8534 Journal of Multicultural Counseling and Development
0883-8550 Daugherty Family Newsletter
0883-8577 Palestine Focus
0883-8690 Government Assistance Almanac
0883-8712 Urgent Care Business Report
0883-8992 Western Art Digest
0883-9026 Journal of Business Venturing
0883-9115 Journal of Bioactive & Compatible Polymers
0883-9131 Beloit Fiction Journal
0883-9174 Celebration
0883-9182 Annual Review of Biophysics and Biophysical Chemistry
0883-9212 Journal of Cardiopulmonary Rehabilitation
0883-9301 Computer Industry Forecast *see* 0883-931X
0883-931X Computer Industry Abstracts
0883-9417 Archives of Psychiatric Nursing
0883-9425 Informatics in Pathology
0883-9433 Journal of Post Anesthesia Nursing
0883-9441 Journal of Critical Care
0883-9492 Molecular Biology and Toxicology
0883-9514 Applied Artificial Intelligence
0883-9549 American Association for the Advancement of Slavic Studies. Newsletter
0883-9697 Journal of Middle Atlantic Archaeology
0883-9778 Burrelle's New Jersey Media Directory
0883-9808 Micrographics Newsletter
0883-9824 Argonaut
0883-9875 Nuclear Resister
0883-9891 Willett House Quarterly
0883-993X Resources (Washington, 1980)
0883-9956 In Dance
0883-9999 Burrelle's New England Media Directory
0884-0024 Military Police Journal
0884-0040 A S H E-E R I C Higher Education Report Series
0884-0075 California Prisoner
0884-0318 Journal of Wind Energy Technology
0884-0504 Group's Jr. High Ministry Magazine
0884-0709 Computers and Translation
0884-0822 Forth Dimensions
0884-0830 Capital P C Monitor
0884-0873 Desktop Publishing *changed to* Publish!
0884-0989 Choices†
0884-0997 MacUser
0884-1020 She-Ra Princess of Power Magazine
0884-1055 Early Cello Series. Modern Edition
0884-1233 Journal of Teaching in Social Work
0884-1357 V M E Bus Systems
0884-1403 Alcoholism & Addiction
0884-1454 A B M S Directory of Certified Nuclear Medicine Specialists
0884-1462 A B M S Directory of Certified Thoracic Surgeons
0884-1470 A B M S Directory of Certified Colon & Rectal Surgeons
0884-1489 A B M S Directory of Certified Dermatologists
0884-1497 A B M S Directory of Certified Pediatricians
0884-1500 A B M S Directory of Certified Neurologists
0884-1519 A B M S Directory of Certified Psychiatrists
0884-1527 A B M S Directory of Certified Surgeons
0884-1535 A B M S Directory of Certified Obstetricians & Gynecologists
0884-1543 A B M S Compendium of Certified Medical Specialists
0884-1829 Minority Engineer
0884-2175 J O G N N
0884-2205 Mo Info
0884-2558 Advanced Manufacturing Processes
0884-2884 Drug Design and Delivery
0884-2957 Belles Lettres
0884-2973 Marketing & Sales Promotion Update *changed to* Hotel Marketing and Sales Promotion Update
0884-2981 Euthanasia Review
0884-3244 Immigration Journal
0884-3252 Rodale's Organic Gardening
0884-3260 Star Wars Intelligence Report
0884-3279 Western New York Index
0884-3635 Brilliant Star
0884-3740 R A L Report
0884-3759 Fuel Science and Technology International
0884-3929 Nibble Mac
0884-3988 Holistic Medicine
0884-3996 Journal of Bioluminescence and Chemiluminescence
0884-4089 Greener Pastures Gazette
0884-4097 Monosson on D E C
0884-4194 Current Concepts of Cerebrovascular Disease: Stroke
0884-4240 Irish America Magazine
0884-4356 American Voice
0884-450X Rare Books and Manuscripts Librarianship
0884-4674 Competitive Edge (Tempe)†
0884-4712 Emergency Medical Care Digest
0884-4720 Electronic Musician
0884-4739 Bassin'
0884-4755 Aviation Digest
0884-495X World Trade Report
0884-4992 T V Game Show Magazine
0884-5506 Christian Education Today
0884-5816 Age of Johnson
0884-5905 Administrative Management
0884-593X Wired Librarian's Newsletter
0884-6057 Tax Management Weekly Report
0884-6146 Photocopy Authorizations Report
0884-6421 Utah State Digest
0884-643X A B M S Directory of Certified Family Practitioners
0884-6448 A B M S Directory of Certified Internists
0884-6510 Bennett Exchange
0884-6596 Health Care Marketer-Target Market
0884-660X Leather Today
0884-6677 Y E S Quarterly
0884-6685 Voice Processing
0884-6952 Studies in Judaica & the Holocaust
0884-7355 Women's Health Magazine
0884-7622 Andrew Harper's Hideaway Report
0884-7649 Quarterly Byte
0884-7827 Texas Real Estate
0884-8106 N A T S Journal
0884-8181 Toxicity Assessment
0884-8297 International Journal of Psychosomatics
0884-8319 Scientific Serials Review: Biomedicine
0884-8335 Economics & Business
0884-8424 Association of Children's Prosthetic-Orthotic Clinics. Journal
0884-8521 Hospital Home Health
0884-8548 Florida Shipper
0884-8688 Journal of Aging and Judaism
0884-8696 Georgia State Literary Studies
0884-870X Stress in Modern Society
0884-8726 Information Marketing Newsletter
0884-8815 Brookgreen Journal
0884-8823 Popular Woodworking
0884-8858 Sinsemilla Tips
0884-8998 Drug Utilization Review
0884-9064 Washington's Almanac
0884-9498 Public Computing†
0884-9501 Baseball History
0884-951X Personal Publishing
0884-9536 National Directory of Bulletin Board Systems
0884-9749 T V - T S Tapestry
0884-9757 Electronic Chemicals & Materials News†
0885-0003 Waste Treatment Technology News
0885-0259 Powerconversion & Intelligent Motion
0885-0429 Ch L A Quarterly
0885-064X Journal of Complexity
0885-0666 Journal of Intensive Care Medicine
0885-0690 Good Food
0885-0704 Food & Justice
0885-0763 Sports Fitness
0885-1158 Medical Problems of Performing Artists
0885-1174 Human Stress Current Advances in Research
0885-1522 Tanning Trends
0885-1603 Private Schools of the United States
0885-2006 Early Childhood Research Quarterly
0885-2014 Cognitive Development
0885-2030 Outlaw Biker
0885-2138 High Spots
0885-2308 Computer Speech & Language
0885-2332 Maat†
0885-2510 Micro Ticker Report
0885-2715 High Technology Law Journal
0885-3010 I E E E Transactions on Ultrasonics, Ferroelectrics and Frequency Control
0885-307X Maine Seine
0885-3177 Pancreas
0885-3282 Journal of Biomaterials Applications
0885-3290 Washington Book Review (Washington, 1985)
0885-3312 Marketing Research Review
0885-3363 International Advertiser
0885-3460 Council for Exceptional Children. Division for Early Childhood. Journal
0885-3886 Phenomenological Inquiry
0885-3894 Public Garden
0885-3924 Journal of Pain and Symptom Management
0885-4017 Open-Apple
0885-4122 Journal of Planning Literature
0885-4262 Photomarket
0885-4270 Photobulletin
0885-4300 Socialism and Democracy
0885-4327 Mineral News
0885-4483 Comments on Condensed Matter Physics
0885-4505 Biochemical Medicine and Metabolic Biology
0885-4513 Biotechnology and Applied Biochemistry
0885-4572 Adult Day Care Letter
0885-470X M/r Magazine
0885-4726 Journal of Health Care Chaplaincy
0885-4734 Journal of Chemical Dependency Treatment
0885-4750 Fabulous Mustangs and Exotic Fords
0885-4777 100 Highest Yields
0885-4823 Haynes Family Association. Chronicle
0885-4831 Connecticut Historical Society. Bulletin
0885-4858 Optimal Health
0885-4890 Brilliant Ideas For Publishers
0885-4947 Pilgrim Journal
0885-5765 Physiological and Molecular Plant Pathology
0885-579X Journal of Personality Disorders
0885-5943 Florida State Collection of Arthropods. Occasional Papers
0885-6087 Hydrological Processes
0885-6095 Western Journal of Applied Forestry
0885-6206 Nielsen Researcher
0885-6222 Human Psychopharmacology: Clinical and Experimental
0885-6230 International Journal of Geriatric Psychiatry
0885-6249 Social Behaviour
0885-6257 European Journal of Special Needs Education
0885-6273 Current Maryland Archeology
0885-6583 Ohio Chess Bulletin
0885-6710 Personal Communications Technology†
0885-6729 S I N E T
0885-6788 I C A's Newsletter
0885-6877 Food-Service East
0885-7156 Powder Diffraction
0885-7237 Econews
0885-7423 Psychology and Sociology of Sport
0885-7474 Journal of Scientific Computing
0885-7482 Journal of Family Violence
0885-7490 Metabolic Brain Disease
0885-7555 Reference Guides to Archives and Manuscript Collections on Immigrant Culture
0885-7741 Recorder
0885-7776 General Council of the Assemblies of God. Memos
0885-7962 C O D A Newsletter
0885-8039 Remodeling
0885-8411 Fence Industry/Access Control
0885-8500 Common Boundary
0885-856X Tort & Insurance Law Journal
0885-8616 Merger Management Report
0885-8624 Journal of Business & Industrial Marketing
0885-8950 I E E E Transactions on Power Systems
0885-8969 I E E E Transactions on Energy Conversion
0885-8977 I E E E Transactions on Power Delivery
0885-8985 I E E E Aerospace and Electronic Systems Magazine
0885-8993 I E E E Transactions on Power Electronics
0885-9000 I E E E Expert
0885-9124 Faxnet
0885-9159 Contribution to the Study of World History
0885-9205 Manhattan Poetry Review
0885-9221 S P E Production Engineering
0885-923X S P E Formation Evaluation
0885-9248 S P E Reservoir Engineering
0885-9256 P S (Wynantskil)
0885-9361 Art Today
0885-968X Emblematica
0885-9744 S P E Drilling Engineering
0885-9841 Shopping Centers Today
0885-9914 Indian Health Trends and Services

0885-9922 Lutheran Partners
0885-9930 Building Economic Alternatives
0885-9949 Marine Textiles
0885-9957 Spang Robinson Report
0885-9973 Maine Bar Journal
0886-0009 Biotech Update†
0886-0114 International Arbitration Report
0886-0122 Mealey's Litigation Report: Tobacco
0886-0149 Ocean Navigator
0886-0165 Non-Credit Learning News
0886-019X Optical Information Systems Update: Library & Information Center Applications
0886-022X Renal Failure
0886-0238 Hematologic Pathology
0886-0262 Heritage Quest
0886-0408 Law Books in Review
0886-0440 Journal of Cardiac Surgery
0886-0467 Lasers in the Life Sciences
0886-0475 B N A's Corporate Counsel Weekly
0886-0483 How
0886-0505 Children's Environments Quarterly
0886-0521 Directory of Wall Street Research
0886-053X Revenue Enhancement Reporter
0886-0653 Medical Ethics Advisor
0886-0807 Washington Summary
0886-0912 Pay Dirt. Rocky Mountain Edition
0886-0920 Pay Dirt. Southwestern Edition
0886-103X Technology Management Action
0886-1099 Affilia
0886-1196 U S O: America's Spirit
0886-1285 Seeker Magazine *changed to* Emerging
0886-1293 Company
0886-1714 News in Physiological Sciences
0886-1862 Hogaku
0886-1935 Closing the Gap
0886-1943 Iowa Journal of Speech Communication
0886-2109 Historic New Orleans Collection Newsletter
0886-2249 Rolling Stock
0886-2362 Token Perspectives Newsletter
0886-2397 LocalNetter Newsletter
0886-2400 Datacom Reader Service
0886-2419 Linkup (Minneapolis)
0886-2605 Journal of Interpersonal Violence
0886-2729 Florida Market Update
0886-2796 Dorot
0886-3156 Spiritual Mothering Journal
0886-3474 Underwater Medicine: Abstracts from the Literature
0886-3490 Arms Control Reporter
0886-3601 Hooks Family Chronicles
0886-3741 Candy Marketer (Cleveland)
0886-3768 Western Investor Newsletter
0886-3806 Cypris
0886-3954 Dance Research Annual†
0886-4047 Abacus (Elmwood)
0886-4128 Cost Cutting Digest (Arlington) *see* 0892-3612
0886-4187 Blue Pitcher
0886-4217 U S Aviation Reports
0886-4268 Precious Fibers
0886-4616 New Frontier
0886-4780 Washington - Oregon Potato Country
0886-4802 Young Viewers
0886-5051 Cotton Ball
0886-5140 Comments on Toxicology
0886-5159 American Presbyterians: Journal of Presbyterian History
0886-537X Telephone Bypass News
0886-5388 Shared Tenant Service News
0886-5396 Pay Phone News
0886-5477 Journal of Pastoral Psychotherapy
0886-5647 Nationwide Overnight Stabling Directory
0886-5949 Exteriors
0886-6015 Civilian-Based Defense: News and Opinion
0886-6104 Pro Motion
0886-6163 What to Buy for Business (U S Edition)
0886-618X Surface Mount Technology Today
0886-6236 Global Biogeochemical Cycles
0886-6287 Chesapeake and Ohio Historical Magazine
0886-6511 News About the A - V Scene
0886-6570 Cinematograph
0886-666X Stanford Literature Review
0886-6678 Legal Plan Letter
0886-6694 Preventing Sexual Abuse
0886-6910 Iskcon Review
0886-7097 Studies in American Drama, 1945-Present
0886-7186 Clinical Oncology Alert
0886-7194 Computer Marketing Newsletter
0886-7402 Handbook of Living Will Laws
0886-7976 Midland Review
0886-8026 Key Ophthalmology
0886-8093 Q E X A R R L Experimenters' Exchange and A M S A T Satellite Journal
0886-8204 Commercial Lending Review
0886-8573 Candle (Naselle)†
0886-8611 Rural Development News
0886-8743 2 A M Magazine
0886-876X Minute-a-Day Health Newsletter
0886-8832 Military Club & Hospitality
0886-9375 Regulated Rivers: Research and Management
0886-9448 Sea Frontiers *changed to* Sea Frontiers/Sea Secrets
0886-9723 Journal of Ambulatory Care Marketing
0886-9901 Cleaning and Restoration
0887-0004 N D Banner
0887-011X Wellsprings
0887-0144 Convenience Care Update
0887-0241 Johns Hopkins University. Population Information Program. Population Reports. English Edition.
0887-025X Johns Hopkins University. Population Information Program. Population Reports. French Edition
0887-0268 Johns Hopkins University. Population Information Program. Population Reports. Spanish Edition
0887-0276 Johns Hopkins University. Population Information Program. Population Reports. Portuguese Edition
0887-0292 A I D S Alert
0887-0373 Public Affairs Quarterly
0887-0535 Food & Nutrition Quarterly Index
0887-056X Accomplishments in Oncology
0887-0594 Central America News Pak
0887-0624 Energy & Fuels
0887-0950 M D N Motorcycle Dealer News *see* 0888-4234
0887-1027 Gym Dandies
0887-106X National Legal Bibliography. Part 2. Government Documents from Official and Commercial Sources
0887-1132 Charter Connections
0887-1167 Single Adult Ministry Information
0887-137X E B R I Issue Brief
0887-1388 Employee Benefit Notes
0887-1493 A I D S Policy and Law
0887-1612 Conditioned Response
0887-1639 C M J S Centerpieces
0887-1655 Van Wert County Genealogical Quarterly
0887-1701 T V Technology
0887-1930 Corporate Technology Directory
0887-2074 South Coast Poetry Journal
0887-2082 Journal of Biochemical Toxicology
0887-2120 Woman Engineer
0887-2139 Frederick Forerunners
0887-2147 Au Courant Newsmagazine
0887-2198 Ad Nurse
0887-2201 Private Funding Advisor
0887-221X Expert Systems Strategies
0887-2236 Biological and Cultural Tests for Control of Plant Diseases
0887-2279 Alaska Business Newsletter
0887-2309 Westchester Business Journal
0887-2406 Curly Cues
0887-252X Journal of Theoretical Psychology
0887-2562 Tax Management Washington Tax Review
0887-2783 Social History of Alcohol Review
0887-2856 Lest-We-Forget
0887-3208 Florida Real Estate and Development Update
0887-3267 Humanistic Psychologist
0887-3569 Contemporary Social Issues: A Bibliographic Series
0887-3763 Reference and Research Book News
0887-3771 Utah Centennial Series
0887-3852 A I D S & Public Policy
0887-3887 Mobile Graduate News and Notes
0887-4115 Bellowing Ark
0887-428X Washington Spectator
0887-4301 Northrop University Law Journal of Aerospace, Business and Taxation
0887-4468 Public Innovation Abroad
0887-5057 Erotic Fiction Quarterly
0887-5162 Optical Information Systems Update: Hardware & Software Developments
0887-5170 Hayden's Ferry Review
0887-5480 Relationship Ideal and Family Forever
0887-5812 Journal of Real Estate Development
0887-5901 Who's Who in Technology
0887-6312 Frary Family Newsletter
0887-6320 Frary Family Journal
0887-6827 Offshore Service Vessels
0887-6835 Offshore Tugs
0887-6851 Video Librarian
0887-686X Hydrological Science and Technology: Short Papers
0887-7394 Toxics Law Reporter
0887-7505 Bed & Breakfast Update
0887-7556 Datek Printer Report
0887-7629 Political Risk Letter
0887-7637 Political Climate for International Business
0887-7793 Corporate Officers and Directors Liability Litigation Reporter
0887-7807 Failed Bank and Thrift Litigation Reporter
0887-7815 Pharmaceutical Litigation Reporter
0887-7831 Tobacco Industry Litigation Reporter
0887-784X Commodities Litigation Reporter
0887-7858 Insurance Industry Litigation Reporter
0887-7866 Andrews School Asbestos Alert
0887-7874 Racketeering Litigation Reporter
0887-7963 Transfusion Medicine Reviews
0887-7971 American Journal of Cardiac Imaging
0887-8013 Journal of Clinical Laboratory Analysis
0887-8048 New Jersey Folklife
0887-8218 Forum for Applied Research and Public Policy
0887-8447 National Gardening Magazine
0887-8625 International Journal of Childbirth Education
0887-8722 Journal of Thermophysics and Heat Transfer
0887-8935 Station Relay
0887-896X A B A Juvenile and Child Welfare Law Reporter
0887-8986 Applied Artificial Intelligence Reporter
0887-9087 G H A A News
0887-9109 Family Therapy Today
0887-9117 Yearbook on Socialist Legal Systems
0887-9206 Notes on Computing
0887-9249 South Carolina Out-of-Doors
0887-9273 Menses†
0887-9338 Scope/36
0887-9354 Lybarger Linkages
0887-9486 Teaching and Learning: the Journal of Natural Inquiry
0887-9672 P C I Journal *see* 0032-793X
0887-9753 Environmental Manager's Compliance Advisor
0887-9982 Tikkun Magazine
0888-000X Zone 3
0888-0328 Middle East Report
0888-0387 Interior Construction
0888-0786 Serodiagnosis and Immunotherapy
0888-0794 Postal Employees' Newsletter
0888-0832 Windham Phoenix
0888-0948 Electronic Publishing Business
0888-1065 Carib-Basin Trade Update
0888-1081 Avalon Hill General
0888-1391 National Alliance
0888-1472 Farm Woman
0888-188X Ball State University Forum
0888-191X Na'Amat Woman
0888-1928 Gambit
0888-2061 Whole Life
0888-2088 Computer Software Engineering Series
0888-2096 Principles of Computer Science Series
0888-2118 Digital System Design Series
0888-2134 Electrical Engineering Communications and Signal Processing *changed to* Electrical Engineering, Telecommunications and Signal Processing
0888-2177 Computers in Education Series
0888-2193 Computers and Math Series
0888-2207 Advances in Satellite Communications Series
0888-2215 Advances in Biomedical Computing Series
0888-2223 Advances in Telecommunications Networks Series
0888-2231 Applications of Computer Science Series
0888-224X Advances in V L S I and Computer Systems
0888-2274 Augustinian Heritage
0888-2460 Mideast Monitor
0888-2673 Length of Stay by Operation, United States, Northeastern Region
0888-2746 Housing and Society
0888-3033 T C Interface
0888-3114 Mealey's Litigation Report: National Tort Reform
0888-3254 Eastern European Politics & Societies
0888-3262 Personal Computing Series
0888-3270 Mechanical Systems & Signal Processing
0888-3327 Marketers Forum Magazine
0888-3440 Ultimate Issues
0888-3459 Westchester Commerce
0888-3475 Aboriginal S F
0888-3483 Nutrition Clinics
0888-4080 Applied Cognitive Psychology
0888-4153 High Plains Literary Review
0888-4226 Columbia-V L A Journal of Law & the Arts
0888-4234 Motorcycle DealerNews
0888-4250 G H A A Journal
0888-4285 New York Facts
0888-4463 Library Administration and Management
0888-4498 Audio Publishing Report
0888-4552 Practicing Anthropology
0888-4641 M and M Rapper
0888-4722 Expo Info
0888-4773 Journal of Sport Management
0888-4781 Sport Psychologist
0888-5109 Consultant Pharmacist
0888-5257 Vstrechi
0888-5427 Realtors Land Institute
0888-5451 Antiqueweek
0888-5613 Latin American Indian Literatures Journal
0888-5680 Photo/Design
0888-5729 Nucleus (Cambridge)
0888-5753 Studies in Popular Culture
0888-580X East Asian Business Intelligence
0888-5842 Y M
0888-5869 Asian Religious Studies Information
0888-5931 Who's Who in Electronics & Computer Science
0888-594X Who's Who in Mechanical Engineering & Materials Science
0888-5958 Who's Who in Chemistry & Plastics
0888-5966 Who's Who in Civil Engineering, Earth Sciences & Energy
0888-5974 Who's Who in Physics & Optics
0888-5982 Who's Who in Biotechnology
0888-6288 Jona's Nursing Scan in Administration
0888-6296 Journal of Cardiothoracic Anesthesia
0888-658X Medical Malpractice Verdicts, Settlements & Experts
0888-661X Hudson Valley G R E E N Times
0888-6814 Appalachian Roots
0888-6970 Logo Exchange
0888-6989 M A P Netter
0888-7039 Health Facilities in Southern New York: A Guide to Inpatient, Outpatient, and Long-Term Care
0888-7233 Comparative Economic Studies
0888-7314 Journal of Decorative and Propaganda Arts
0888-7411 Stall

1612 ISSN INDEX

0888-7446 Privatization
0888-7543 Genomics
0888-7586 Contraband (Lake Charles)
0888-7926 U S Statistics
0888-7950 Clinical Laboratory Management Review
0888-8027 Linguistics and Language Behavior Abstracts
0888-8132 N F E A S Journal
0888-8191 Circulation Management
0888-9007 Jusur
0888-904X Japan Electronics
0888-9511 Hi-Tech Alert for the Professional Communicator
0888-9538 Video Monitor
0888-9724 In the Mainstream
0888-983X Harvard Review
0889-0153 Drew
0889-0196 Electronics Purchasing
0889-0293 International Journal of Social Education
0889-0331 Health and Health Care in New York City: Local, State, and National Perspectives
0889-0404 Defense Daily
0889-0749 National School Bus Report
0889-0803 Notus New Writing
0889-0889 Transportation in America
0889-0897 Professional Investor
0889-0935 Valley Forge
0889-1575 Journal of Food Composition and Analysis
0889-1583 Journal of the Japanese and International Economics
0889-1591 Brain, Behavior, and Immunity
0889-1605 Journal of Ultrastructure and Molecular Structure Research
0889-1893 American Journal of Alternative Agriculture
0889-2148 Afghanistan Forum
0889-2288 Carlsonreport for Shopping Center Management
0889-2423 Independent Florida Alligator
0889-2474 M E A Advocate
0889-2644 Broadcast Banker/Broker
0889-2725 Political Risk Yearbook
0889-2857 Ketch Pen
0889-2865 Voices of Youth
0889-2997 Sabermetric Review
0889-3217 Seafood Business
0889-3241 A C I Structural Journal
0889-325X A C I Materials Journal
0889-3268 Journal of Business and Psychology
0889-3454 Hazardous Materials Newsletter
0889-3594 N D G S Newsletter
0889-3640 Miami Meanderings
0889-3667 International Journal of Comparative Psychology
0889-3675 Journal of Poetry Therapy
0889-3764 A P I S
0889-3918 Automotive Week
0889-3985 More Light Update
0889-4019 Career Development Quarterly
0889-4302 Apple Assembly Line
0889-4396 Quarterly Pension Investment Report
0889-4469 Liability & Insurance Bulletin
0889-4523 Corporate Television
0889-4663 Environmental Management Report
0889-468X Continuing the Conversation
0889-4698 Problems in Anesthesia
0889-4701 Problems in Critical Care
0889-471X Problems in Urology
0889-4752 Popular Lures
0889-485X Jonesreport for Shopping Center Marketing
0889-5007 Country Facts
0889-5201 Bebop and Beyond
0889-5643 Montessori Observer
0889-5694 Computer Crime Digest
0889-5716 Organized Crime Digest
0889-5724 Criminal Justice Digest
0889-5732 Training Aids Digest
0889-6089 Amateur Satellite Report
0889-6119 Online Hotline News Service
0889-6216 Start (San Francisco)
0889-6313 Psychobiology
0889-6321 Maeventec Software Review
0889-6348 Proteus
0889-6410 Lake Street Review
0889-6720 Montessori News
0889-6984 Del-gen-data Bank
0889-7042 Michaels on Etiquette
0889-7085 Specialty Travel Index
0889-7182 Scholarly Inquiry for Nursing Practice
0889-7190 A S A I O Transactions
0889-7204 Progress in Cardiovascular Nursing
0889-7352 Alaska Oil and Industry News
0889-759X Jean Rhys Review
0889-7751 C T L A Forum
0889-8022 E R I C/C U E Trends and Issues
0889-8030 E R I C/C U E Urban Diversity Series
0889-8049 E R I C Clearinghouse on Urban Education. Digest
0889-8391 Journal of Cognitive Psychotherapy
0889-8421 Everything Natural
0889-8464 N T I S Tech Notes
0889-8529 Endocrinology and Metabolism Clinics
0889-8537 Anaesthesiology Clinics
0889-8545 Obstetrics and Gynaecology Clinics
0889-8553 Gastroenterology Clinics
0889-8561 Immunology and Allergy Clinics
0889-857X Rheumatic Diseases Clinics
0889-8588 Haematology-Oncology Clinics
0889-8685 Creative Loafing
0889-8731 Al-Arabiyya
0889-9118 Silver Wings
0889-9185 Latter-Day Woman
0889-9479 Blois Voice
0889-9487 A A A S Directory of Programs
0889-9495 Radiance
0889-9657 Education and Self Management of the Psychiatric Patient
0889-9746 Journal of Fluids and Structures
0890-0159 Advances in Behavioral Economics
0890-0299 Wine & Spirits
0890-0396 Air & Water Pollution Control
0890-0477 Louisiana Literature
0890-0582 A I Ch E M I Modular Instruction. Series G: Design of Equipment
0890-068X National Tombstone Epitaph
0890-0841 Books and Religion
0890-099X Orthodox America
0890-1171 American Journal of Health Promotion
0890-118X Across Frontiers
0890-1406 Japan Computer Technology and Applications Abstracts
0890-1570 Second Opinion
0890-1619 New Options
0890-2070 European Journal of Personality
0890-2097 Rapa Nui Notes
0890-2194 Recreation Executive Report
0890-2364 Oswald Outlines
0890-2755 Advances in Sensor Technology
0890-2763 Advances in R & D
0890-2771 Advances in High-Tech Materials
0890-278X A G H E Exchange
0890-2941 New Law Books Reviewer
0890-2968 Redwood Researcher
0890-3050 Lake Superior Magazine
0890-3263 Food Industry Skirmisher
0890-3344 Journal of Human Lactation
0890-3360 Gossage Regan Manager's Memo
0890-3670 Scientist
0890-3743 Glass News
0890-3816 A P G Quarterly
0890-3921 Garden State Home & Garden
0890-4073 Advances in Health Education
0890-4081 International Christian Digest
0890-4197 Nathaniel Hawthorne Review
0890-4251 International Trade and Investment Letter
0890-426X Eximbank Letter
0890-4448 Cherokee One Feather
0890-4928 Political Risk Database
0890-4952 Country Database
0890-5010 Sub Rosa
0890-5339 Journal of Orthopaedic Trauma
0890-5401 Information and Computation
0890-5436 Food Biotechnology
0890-5444 Membrane Separation Engineering
0890-5452 Mechanics of Structures and Machines
0890-5460 Ocean Physics and Engineering
0890-5509 Waste Minimization & Recycling Report
0890-5533 Biomaterials, Artificial Cells and Artificial Organs
0890-5568 Living Prayer
0890-5592 Catastrophism and Ancient History. Proceedings
0890-6130 Nature, Society, and Thought
0890-6408 Apalachee Quarterly
0890-6599 Journal of Neurological and Orthopaedic Medicine & Surgery
0890-6866 Universe in a Classroom
0890-7005 Le Mercenaire Newsletter
0890-7129 Towpaths
0890-7137 Canal Society of Ohio. Newsletter
0890-7366 Minute-a-Day Drug Letter
0890-7471 A A A Today Magazine
0890-7587 M D R Watch
0890-7722 Magill Book Reviews
0890-782X Official Video Directory & Buyer's Guide
0890-8044 I E E E Network
0890-815X Privatization Report
0890-8192 Man from Mainz and His Descendants
0890-8265 Access to Energy
0890-8508 Molecular and Cellular Probes
0890-8583 Reformed Worship
0890-8621 Laboratory Decisions Online
0890-8648 U S A
0890-8885 Cross Timbers Review
0890-9059 Technology for Nursing
0890-9083 I S I Atlas of Science: Pharmacology
0890-9369 Genes & Development
0890-9512 Morgan Report on Directory Publishing
0890-9539 Chartering
0890-9695 Women Wise
0890-9792 Perspectives (Columbus)
0890-9911 Exchange Book
0891-0634 B N A's Banking Report
0891-0758 Carto-Philatelist
0891-1029 Center City Report
0891-1150 Cleveland Clinic Journal of Medicine
0891-1177 Order of Buddhist Contemplatives. Journal
0891-1223 Pediatric Length of Stay by Diagnosis and Operation, United States
0891-124X Grenade
0891-1622 Sales Promotion Monitor
0891-1800 Surgical Rounds for Orthopaedics
0891-1851 Kitplanes
0891-1886 C P I Digest
0891-1916 International Journal of Political Economy
0891-1924 Health Technology
0891-2114 Length of Stay by Diagnosis, Canada
0891-2122 Length of Stay by Diagnosis, United States, Northeastern Region
0891-2130 Length of Stay by Diagnosis, United States, Southern Region
0891-2149 Length of Stay by Diagnosis, United States
0891-2157 Length of Stay by Diagnosis, United States, Western Region
0891-2165 Length of Stay by Diagnosis, United States, North Central Region
0891-2173 Geriatric Length of Stay by Diagnosis and Operation, United States
0891-2181 Length of Stay by Operation, Canada
0891-219X Length of Stay by Operation, United States, Southern Region
0891-2203 Length of Stay by Operation, United States
0891-2211 Length of Stay by Operation, United States, Western Region
0891-222X Length of Stay by Operation, United States, North Central Region
0891-2521 Journal of Educational Techniques and Technologies
0891-2548 Crystal Gazing
0891-2823 Asian and Pacific Population Forum
0891-3188 C D - R O M Review
0891-4028 International Obesity Newsletter
0891-4036 Metalworking News
0891-4052 Fundamentals of Test Measurement
0891-4141 Labor Relations Week
0891-4478 International Journal of Technology & Aging
0891-4486 International Journal of Politics, Culture, and Society
0891-4494 Journal of Near-Death Studies (Anabiosis)
0891-5202 Careers & the Handicapped
0891-5326 Re: View
0891-5709 National Report on Substance Abuse
0891-5857 Selling Space
0891-5865 Journal of Documentation Project Management
0891-6055 Index Chemicus
0891-6136 Poets & Writers Magazine
0891-6144 Himalayan Institute Quarterly Guide
0891-639X Wind Energy and Diesel Installations International (Year)
0891-6403 California Wind Farm Project Report
0891-6624 H M O Practice
0891-6632 Journal of Diabetic Complications
0891-6640 Journal of Veterinary Internal Medicine
0891-6780 East-West Film Journal
0891-6985 Chicano Periodical Index
0891-7213 Aegean Review: Contemporary Greek Arts and Letters
0891-7698 Mercer County Board of Realtors. Newsline
0891-7701 Midwifery Today
0891-771X Bird Talk
0891-8287 A B C Forum
0891-8791 Positive Approach
0891-9194 Maine Organic Farmer and Gardener
0892-0869 Futures Factors - The Futures Portfolio Advisor
0892-0966 Naseeha
0892-1008 R P C Voice
0892-130X Darshan
0892-1733 North American Serials Interest Group. Newsletter
0892-2632 O T C Growth Stock Watch
0892-2683 Cellular Sales & Marketing
0892-3345 Atlanta Jewish Times
0892-3566 Freight Marketing Report
0892-3612 Survival News for Cities and Towns
0892-371X Psychedelic Monographs and Essays
0892-4201 A M S Studies in the Emblem
0892-4945 Noah's Ark
0892-5100 Slowo i Liturgia
0892-5429 Mutable Dilemna
0892-6514 Cat Fancy
0892-6522 Dog Fancy
0892-6638 F A S E B Journal. Federation Proceedings
0892-6735 Five Owls
0892-7138 Stanford Environmental Law Journal
0892-757X Food Service Forum
0893-0120 EthnoArts Index
0893-0139 Index to Reproductions in Art Periodicals
0893-0872 Messenger (Worcester)
0893-0880 Signal
0893-1925 Imaging on Campus
0893-2115 Libertarian E-Mail Directory
0894-184X Food Marketers' Handbook
0900-002X Folk og Minder fra Koebenhavn
0900-0119 Teaterbladet
0900-0178 Skat
0900-0186 Vegetarisk Koekkenkalender
0900-0267 N H P Rapport
0900-0275 Normtalsundersoegelsen for Isenkrambranchen
0900-0283 Normtalsundersoegelse for Sportsbranchen
0900-0380 Landsforeningen af Kronisk Syge. Medlemsblad
0900-050X Limousine Nyt
0900-0526 University of Copenhagen. Statistical Research Unit. Research Report
0900-0542 Danmarks Biblioteksskole. Bibliotek. Biblioteks Tilvaeksliste *see* 0900-0550
0900-0550 Danmarks Biblioteksskole. Nye Boeger, Nye Blade, Nye Baand
0900-064X Jazz Festivals and Related Major Jazz Events. Directory
0900-078X Globalia Nyt
0900-081X Magistrenes Universitetslaererforeningen. Beskrivelse *changed to* Universitetslaereren. Beskrivelse

ISSN INDEX 1613

0900-1131 Foeroyar
0900-114X Gerontologi og Samfund
0900-1174 Logos†
0900-1204 Musik Nyt
0900-1301 Herning Kunstmuseums Bulletin
0900-1395 Ungdomsuddannelser
0900-1409 Moentsamleren
0900-1484 Kommunal Aarbog
0900-1565 Aarbog for Kvindeforskning
0900-1573 Almanak for Teologi og Litteratur
0900-1581 Dagdryp
0900-162X Om Forsoegsarbejdet
0900-1646 Kemikaliekontrollen Aarsberetning
0900-1808 Copenhagen School of Economics and Business Administration. Research Paper
0900-1972 Tique
0900-1980 Social Administration
0900-1999 Danmarks Transport. Tidendes Destinationregister
0900-2006 Skole og Edb
0900-2030 Social Sikring
0900-2049 Familien Danmarks Forbruger. Haandbog
0900-2103 Sydthy Aarbog
0900-2219 Dansk Selskab for Mykopatologi. Meddeleser
0900-2278 Theses and Other Publications of the University of Copenhagen
0900-2367 Botanisk Centralbibliotek. Fortegnelse over Loebende Periodica
0900-2472 Handelshoejskolen i Koebenhavn. Center for Uddannelses Forskning. Arbejdsnote
0900-2499 Levevilkaar i Danmark
0900-2510 Denmark. Ministeriet for Groenland. Statistike Meddelelser
0900-2596 Hoeje-Tastrup Kommunes. Lokalhistoriske Arkiv. Aarskrift
0900-2650 Amatoerfiskeren
0900-2685 Nyhedsbrev for Social og Sundhedssektor
0900-2731 Erhvervs og Samfundsbeskrivelse. Noter og Opgaver
0900-274X Koebenhavns Universitet. Institut for Samfundsfag og Forvaltning. Forskningsrapport
0900-2758 Denmark. Lovinformation fra Miljoestyrelsen
0900-2855 Konkylien
0900-2863 Vanfoeres Jul
0900-2871 Danske Selskab. Nyt
0900-288X Faellesudvalget til Kaninavlens Fremme Beretning
0900-2995 Frankrig Information. Nyhedsbrev
0900-3002 Tidsskrift for Sygeplejeforskning
0900-3037 Folkesagn i Tekst og Billed fra Noerreherred
0900-3045 Dansk Ingenioerforening. Medlemsfortegnelse
0900-3053 Faglig Solidaritet
0900-3096 Amtskommunale Enkeltfagskurser
0900-3126 Lokalhistorisk Arkiv for Fredericia og Omegn. Aarsskrift
0900-3134 Bag Kulisserne
0900-3142 Afhaenging
0900-3339 Retorik
0900-3347 Tools
0900-3355 Paa Vej
0900-338X Argos
0900-3452 Musikbladet†
0900-3460 Skalmejen
0900-3479 Uddannelse og Erhverv Katalog
0900-3517 Design Denmark *changed to* D D Bulletin
0900-372X Dansk Curling
0900-3738 Denmark. Betaenkning fra Miljoestyrelsen
0900-3746 Miljoepolitik
0900-3754 Break 19
0900-3762 Technical Product Update
0900-4041 Dansk Kirurgisk Selskab. Nyhedsbrev
0900-419X Energylab Newsletter
0900-4262 Astma Allergi Bladet
0900-4645 Danmarks Tekniske Bibliotek. Katalog
0900-470X Sidesporet
0900-4858 Medicintakst
0900-5072 M S Biblioteksnyt
0900-5129 R U N Commodore - Magasin
0900-5269 Mikro-Bladet
0900-5285 Agro-Kemi
0900-5323 Europeisk Nyhedsbrev
0900-5579 D A N T E C Information
0900-5587 Polio-Nyt
0900-5781 Danmarks Laererhoejskole. Institut for Informatik. Arbejdspapir
0900-579X Tidsskrift for Miljoeteknik
0900-5846 Stambog over Shetland Ponyer
0900-6230 Mikronyt i Specialundervisningen
0900-6559 Dats
0900-6664 Foreningen af Filmlaerere i Gymnasiet. Meddelelser
0900-6788 Denmark. Redegoerelse fra Miljoestyrelsen
0900-6885 Denmark. Direktoratet for Arbejdstilsynet. Arbejdstilsynets Aarsberetning
0900-7008 Idraettens Forskningsraad. Forskningsoversigt
0900-7105 Tennis Avisen
0900-7350 Dramapaedagogik i Nordisk Perspektiv
0900-7679 Emigranten
0900-8012 Handbog for Kaveghold
0900-8047 Laegaest: Arkeologi i Nordlesvig
0900-8187 Om Statsregnskabet
0900-8373 D E H Bladet
0900-8632 Idraetshistorisk Aarbog
0900-8659 Bil Testen
0900-8675 North Western European Language Evolution
0900-8691 Guide Nyt
0900-8764 Molsbibliotekets Lokalhistorisk Arkiv
0900-8772 Nordisk Psykologisk Litteratur
0900-8829 Antal Modtagere, Adresseloese Postforsendelser
0900-9507 Prepublications
0900-9787 Fiskeriaarbogen
0900-9825 Fredningsstyrelsen Rapport
0900-9876 Kobenhavns Universitet. Sociologisk Institut. Arbejdspapir
0900-9922 Kobenhavns Universitet. Sociologisk Institut. Afhandling
0901-0025 Micro Publications. Social Science Series
0901-0106 Teater for Boern og Unge
0901-0114 Sko og Laedervarer
0901-036X Gacela/Gazela. Tidsskrift for Latinamerikastudier
0901-0602 Handbog i Sociallovgivning
0901-0637 Blaavand Fuglestation. Rapport
0901-067X C A S Nyt
0901-0815 Arkeologiske Udgravninger i Danmark
0901-0963 Statens Vejlaboratorium. Nye Publikationer
0901-1056 Ulricks Strikkeideer
0901-1374 Arabiske Verden. Nyhedsbrev
0901-1595 Fodbold Poster Bladet
0901-1811 Spotlight
0901-1919 Koebenhavns-Nyt
0901-1943 Goedskingrapport
0901-201X Para - nyt
0901-2273 Actualitates de Interlingua
0901-2281 Kollegie Nyt
0901-2737 Frisoerfagene *changed to* Frisoerfaget
0901-2982 Monthly Journal of Scientology
0901-3067 Hobby Bladet
0901-3229 Bilruten
0901-3741 D J I F Fritid
0901-3768 Energy in Denmark
0901-4233 Info-Tex
0901-4306 Blindes Jul
0901-4497 Aarhus Universitet. Teologiske Fakultet. Bibliografi
0901-4500 Cystisk Fibrose
0901-5027 International Journal of Oral and Maxillofacial Surgery
0901-5213 Aarhus Universitet. Institut for Statskundskab. Arbejdspapir
0901-5469 Punkt 95
0901-6120 Bilismen i Danmark
0901-6139 Statistik over Registrering Af Nye Automobiler i Danmark
0901-6171 I F U Annual Report
0901-7496 Kongelige Bibliotek og Universitetsbiblioteket. Magasin
0901-800X Setting up in Denmark
0901-8735 Firmengruendung in Daenemark
0901-9928 Pharmacology and Toxicology
0901-9936 Pharmacology and Toxicology. Supplementum
0902-1612 S F. Status
0910-0377 Hirosaki Daigaku Igakubu Eiseigaku Kyoshitsu Gyosekishu
0910-0717 Nagoya University. Cosmic-Ray Research Laboratory. Proceedings
0910-075X Quarterly Forecast of Japan's Economy by the S.A. Method
0910-1780 Diamond's Japan Business Directory
0910-2078 Tansuigyo
0910-4208 Yobo Jiho
0910-4496 Marine Parks Journal
0910-4534 Japan Insurance News
0910-4607 P H P Intersect
0910-5050 Gann-Japanese Journal of Cancer Research
0910-5719 Statistics of Life Insurance Business in Japan
0910-5727 Statistics of Japanese Non-Life Insurance Business
0910-6340 Analytical Sciences
0910-6510 Abstracts on Science and Technology in Japan: Electronics and Communication
0910-6529 Japanese Journal of Behavior Therapy
0910-7800 Wing Weekly
0910-7908 Japan English Publications in Print
0910-8327 Heart and Vessels
0910-9684 Jidousha Hoyu Sharyosu
0911-0119 Graphs and Combinatorics
0911-0305 Kyoto Institute of Technology. Faculty of Engineering and Design. Memoirs
0911-0704 Control
0911-0755 J O I C F P News
0911-0844 Japanese Nursing Association Research Report
0911-1018 Nikkei New Materials
0911-4041 Token Bijutsu
0911-5625 Cross and Talk
0911-6052 Japan Society of Plant Taxonomists. Proceedings
0911-6567 New Cicada
0911-6923 Research Institute of Industrial Safety. Research Report
0911-8004 Japanese Annual Bibliography of Economics†
0911-8012 Science Council of Japan. Annual Report on the Progress of Agriculture†
0911-8063 Research Institute of Industrial Safety. Technical Recommendation
0912-1420 Nara Women's University. Health Administration Center. News
0912-1722 Environmental Pollution, City Development and Regional Development Index
0912-2826 Yokohama City Institute of Health. Annual Report
0912-3075 Dream International Quarterly
0912-7437 Umi to Anzen
0913-025X Materials on Asia-Accession List and Review
0913-6681 Hospice Letter
0915-2210 Passenger & In-Flight Service
0920-1211 Epilepsy Research
0920-1319 Nieuws Berichten Informatie
0920-1580 Netherlands Journal of Housing and Environmental Research
0920-1610 Maritime Information Review
0920-1637 Clinical Neuropsychologist
0920-203X China Information
0920-2307 Materials Science Reports
0920-3745 Informatierecht
0920-3958 Terugblik
0920-4741 Water Resources Management
0920-4849 S E R Bulletin
0920-5489 Computer Standards and Interfaces
0920-6299 International Journal of Flexible Manufacturing Systems
0920-9786 Catalogus van Nederlandse Zeekaarten en Andere Hydrografische Publikaties/ Catalog of Charts and Other Hydrographic Publications
0930-0775 Kinderschutz Aktuell
0930-0791 Deutscher Tischtennis Sport
0930-1127 Muenchener Beitraege zur Mediaevistik und Renaissance-Forschung
0930-1208 Heidelberger Althistorische Beitraege und Epigraphische Studien
0930-2794 Surgical Endoscopy, Ultrasound and Interventional Techniques
0930-2980 Blatt fuer Patent, Muster- und Zeichenwesen
0930-312X Surgical and Radiologic Anatomy
0930-3839 Bundesforschungsanstalt fuer Landeskunde und Raumordnung. Seminare - Symposien - Arbeitspapiere
0930-3847 European Coatings Journal
0930-4282 Spektrum der Augenheilkunde
0930-4584 Polen und Wir
0930-5157 P I K
0930-6404 Historische Grundwissenschaften in Einzeldarstellungen
0930-6749 Der Garten
0930-7133 Profitips fuer Selbermacher
0930-7370 Zeitschrift fuer Binnenschiffahrt und Wasserstrassen
0930-7834 Logistik im Unternehmen
0930-7923 Reports in Applied Measurement
0930-830X Friedensforschung Aktuell
0930-8458 Einkaufer im Markt
0930-8490 P P S Report
0930-858X S D/Sammlerdienst
0930-8679 Catholic Media Council. Information Bulletin
0930-8792 Estonia
0930-8873 Der Evangelische Buchberater
0930-8954 Musik - Almanach
0930-9225 Zeitschrift fuer Herz, Thorax- und Gefaesschirurgie
0931-427X Zav
0931-7775 S H - Technik
0931-8623 Wuerzburger Geographische Manuskript
0950-0014 Ceram Research Progress
0950-0170 Work, Employment & Society
0950-0197 Bathrooms
0950-0502 Adrenergic Receptors
0950-0561 Oncogenes
0950-1533 Artificial Intelligence Abstracts
0950-1584 Leadscan
0950-1592 Zincscan
0950-1711 Natural Product Updates
0950-1991 Development
0950-2092 Micronutrient Analysis
0950-2114 Image Technology Journal of the B K S T S
0950-2262 World Copper Databook
0950-2548 Iron Ore Databook
0950-3153 Practice
0950-317X Which P C?
0950-3188 Putting Your Amstrad to Work
0950-3285 Texas Oil and Gas Law Journal
0950-3471 Historical Research
0950-3668 Insurance Statistics (1981-1985)
0950-4109 International Journal of Law and the Family
0950-4125 Reference Reviews
0950-4214 Gas Separation and Purification
0950-4222 Industry and Higher Education
0950-4303 New Dance
0950-4753 Key Abstracts - Advanced Materials
0950-4761 Key Abstracts - Antennas & Propagation
0950-477X Key Abstracts - Artificial Intelligence
0950-4788 Key Abstracts - Computer Communications and Storage
0950-4796 Key Abstracts - Computing in Electronics & Power
0950-480X Key Abstracts - Electronic Instrumentation
0950-4818 Key Abstracts - Measurements in Physics
0950-4826 Key Abstracts - Optoelectronics
0950-4834 Key Abstracts - Power Systems & Applications
0950-4842 Key Abstracts - Robotics & Control

0950-4850 Key Abstracts - Semiconductor Devices
0950-4869 Key Abstracts - Software Engineering
0950-4877 Key Abstracts - Telecommunications
0950-5024 The Stocklists
0950-5113 Manufacturing Automation News
0950-5121 Princess Grace Irish Library Lectures
0950-5199 Surface Treatment Technology Abstracts
0950-5202 Surface Treatment
0950-5431 Science as Culture
0950-5458 Adviser
0950-575X British Journal of Russian Philately
0950-5849 Information and Software Technology
0950-6195 Investment International
0950-6608 International Materials Review
0950-7051 Knowledge-Based Systems
0950-7116 Welding International
0950-7140 Separation
0950-7191 Come Learn Beginners
0950-7205 Come Learn Primaries
0950-7213 Come Learn Juniors
0950-7221 Go Teach Beginners
0950-7248 Go Teach Juniors
0950-7256 Go Teach Young Teens
0950-8163 Noise & Vibration in Industry
0950-8171 Acoustical Summaries for Architects
0950-8376 Orthodox Outlook
0950-8732 Cirplan
0950-9038 Industrial Marketing Digest
0950-9550 Hockey Digest
0950-9593 Great Britain. Overseas Development Administration. Report on Research and Development
0951-0346 Construction Repair
0951-0869 Metallurgical Journal
0951-1326 Folk Roots
0951-1865 Agricultural Administration Research Extension Network. Newsletter
0951-3051 International Analyst
0951-5224 Higher Education Quarterly
0951-7391 Latin and Greek Texts
0960-2992 Writers Forum
0969-8027 Pakistan Management Review
0970-0048 International Library Movement
0970-0137 Journal of Structural Engineering
0970-0153 Annals of Biology
0970-0188 N I S S A T Newsletter
0970-0277 Osmania Papers in Linguistics
0970-0285 Shipping and Marine Industries Journal
0970-0293 Social Scientist
0970-0307 Ganita Bharati
0970-034X Dataquest
0970-0358 Indian Journal of Plastic Surgery
0970-0366 Aquaworld
0970-0374 Journal of Optics
0970-0420 Environment and Ecology
0970-0447 Management Professionals Association. Events Diary
0970-0447 Management Professionals Association. Journal
0970-0560 Economic and Commercial News
0970-0595 Himachal Journal of Agricultural Research
0970-0765 Bulletin of Pure & Applied Sciences. Section A: Animal Science
0970-0838 Journal of Polymer Materials
0970-0846 Journal of Aquaculture in the Tropics
0970-0870 Indian Textile Bulletin
0970-0897 Indian Journal of Behaviour
0970-0919 Madhuprapancha
0970-0927 Indian Anthropologist
0970-0935 Indian Journal of Colo-Proctology
0970-096X Akavita
0970-0978 Yuva Kavi
0970-0986 Samkaleen Kala Aur Kavita
0970-1001 Art and Poetry Today
0970-1060 Administrative Tribunals Cases
0970-1117 Jeevadhara
0970-1222 Vidyajyoti
0970-1257 Tibetan Medicine
0970-1370 Journal of Soil Biology and Ecology
0970-1397 Vayu Mandal
0970-1400 Indian Journal of Acarology
0970-1427 Glory of India
0970-1435 M L B D Newsletter
0970-163X Non-Ferrous Report
0970-1648 Metal Scrap Report
0970-1761 Inside/Outside
0970-177X Minerals Market Reporter
0970-1788 Iron & Steel Newsletter
0970-1850 International Information, Communication and Education
0970-1923 Purabhilekh - Puratatva
0970-2059 International Journal of Microbiology
0980-3637 Institut d'Etudes Slaves Informations
0986-4415 P C Publishing
1010-0709 Arab Journal of Administration
1010-576X Kenya Medical Research Institute. Proceedings of the Annual Medical Research Conferences
1080-8000 Christian Example
1508-1788 Prakriti *changed to* Prakriti Vani
1661-2434 Teamwork†
2209-7007 Communisme
2306-2525 Family Planning International Assistance Newsletter†
6377-9137 Enhanced Recovery Week
8750-0183 Earthwatch
8750-0256 Utne Reader
8750-0477 Art & Style International
8750-0507 Contemporary Pediatrics
8750-1090 Herb Basket
8750-1104 Shepard's Corporation Law Citations
8750-1112 Shepard's Partnership Law Citations
8750-1139 Shepard's Products Liability Citations
8750-1147 Metropolitan Detroit
8750-1244 D I T N: Diabetes in the News
8750-1643 Vegetarian Health Science *see* 0883-8216
8750-1880 Purebred Picture
8750-2011 Leaven
8750-216X New England Monthly
8750-2224 Prepress Bulletin
8750-2321 M D A Newsmagazine
8750-2348 Sandara
8750-2356 S R C Blue Book of 5-Trend Cycli-Graphs
8750-2461 S R C Red Book of 5-Trend Security Charts
8750-2577 Goldmine
8750-2798 Accountants I B Micro Report
8750-2836 Hospital Practice
8750-331X International Journal of Chinese Medicine†
8750-3603 Bowling Digest
8750-3697 Culpepper Letter
8750-4170 Spokane, A Great Place, The Magazine†
8750-4294 Southwest Journal of Business and Economics *see* 8750-6033
8750-4634 Southwest Hotel-Motel Review
8750-488X Opus
8750-5347 Sinfonian Magazine
8750-5622 Focus Magazine (Hartford)
8750-5851 Baseball Cards
8750-5886 Then and Now
8750-6033 El Paso Economic Review
8750-6106 Progressive Rentals
8750-653X Women's Sports and Fitness
8750-6637 State Policy Reports
8750-6718 Pacific Banker
8750-6807 Florida Hotel & Motel Journal
8750-7218 Meeting Manager
8750-7242 Bop
8750-7595 Countryside and Small Stock Journal
8750-7838 Modern Percussionist
8750-7927 U S C Trojan Family
8750-7935 Microwave Systems News and Communications Technology *changed to* Microwave Systems News & Technology
8750-801X Lottery & Gaming Review
8750-8133 W & J Magazine
8750-8613 Church Life
8750-8672 O A G Travel Planner & Hotel/Motel Guide. Pacific Area Edition
8750-8877 Crochet Fantasy
8750-8915 Flex Magazine
8750-8990 Veterinary Technician
8750-9210 Stone Review
8750-9261 Coach's Legal Report *changed to* Athletic Director & Coach
8750-9482 Micro/Systems Journal
8750-9563 Welcome Home
8750-9628 V A X Professional
8750-9989 Red and Black (Middletown)
8755-0024 Applied Stochastic Models and Data Analysis
8755-0032 Advances in Neural and Behavioral Development
8755-0040 Current Topics in Human Intelligence
8755-0059 Kansas Medicine
8755-0229 Medical Practice Management
8755-0237 Buildings Energy Conservation
8755-0245 Energy from Biomass
8755-0253 Professional Document Retrieval
8755-027X Africa Commentary
8755-0423 Home Mechanix
8755-0474 Oceans Policy Study Series
8755-0547 Sherbondy Beacon
8755-0628 Tax Management Real Estate Journal
8755-0725 Chamber Music Magazine
8755-0970 Topics in Ocular Pharmacology and Toxicology†
8755-1020 National Association of Document Examiners. Journal
8755-1039 Diagnostic Cytopathology
8755-1209 Reviews of Geophysics
8755-1225 Journal of Pharmacy Technology
8755-1616 Laser Focus/Electro Optics Buyers' Guide
8755-1675 American Computer Law Digest
8755-1721 Johnson Journal
8755-1748 Southern Genealogical Index
8755-1853 Laser Focus
8755-1985 Journal of Protective Coatings and Linings
8755-2035 Porticus
8755-2094 Educational Media and Technology Yearbook
8755-2108 Library Science Annual
8755-2167 Waconda Roots and Branches
8755-2353 Dorchester County Genealogical Magazine
8755-2523 Chilton's Industrial Maintenance & Plant Operation
8755-254X Chilton's Hardware Age
8755-2566 Chilton's Industrial Safety & Hygiene News
8755-2582 Corporate Artnews
8755-2914 Columbia
8755-2922 Learning Resources Directory for Healthcare Executives
8755-2930 Earthquake Spectra
8755-3023 Golden Roots of the Mother Lode
8755-3031 Social Science Microcomputer Review
8755-3112 Nautica
8755-3139 Stamp Dealer Forum†
8755-321X Successful Marketing to Senior Citizens
8755-3228 Llewellyn's Astrological Guide to California†
8755-3406 Volume Reversal Survey
8755-3651 El Gato Tuerto
8755-3732 C A A S News
8755-3759 Words on Tape
8755-3767 Wrestling Masters
8755-3996 I E E E Circuits and Devices Magazine
8755-4151 Mutual Fund Source Book
8755-416X Legal Newsletters in Print
8755-4305 International Journal of Personal Property Appraising
8755-4348 Appraisers' Information Exchange
8755-4364 Freemen Digest *see* 0882-5955
8755-4615 Computers and Composition
8755-464X Profiles (Solana Beach)
8755-4682 Seiche
8755-4747 Pathways
8755-4755 Weekly Takeover Target Forecast
8755-4909 Call-A.P.P.L.E.
8755-5034 Africa International†
8755-5107 Educational Software Selector
8755-5123 Northeast Journal of Business & Economics
8755-514X Nebraska Review
8755-5271 Heartline
8755-5298 I Know You Know
8755-5301 Lanthanide and Actinide Research†
8755-5360 Studies in Social Welfare Policies and Programs
8755-5379 E R I S A Newsletter
8755-5689 Draw Magazine†
8755-5727 C D Data Report
8755-5751 Printout
8755-5786 Micro Software Report (Library Edition) †
8755-5794 Micro Software Evaluations
8755-5824 Electrum
8755-5832 Boombah Herald
8755-5913 Phillips County Historical Quarterly
8755-6073 Hardin County Historical Quarterly
8755-612X Interbehaviorist
8755-6154 Record Collector's Monthly
8755-6286 Information Today
8755-6340 Legerete
8755-6863 Pediatric Pulmonology
8755-6898 Mammoth Trumpet
8755-6901 Christopher News Notes
8755-7169 Software Reviews on File
8755-7215 Military Electronics *changed to* Advanced Military Computing
8755-7223 Journal of Professional Nursing
8755-724X National Geographic Research
8755-7339 Data Sources' Guide to V A Rs and Distributors
8755-741X Spitball
8755-7452 Weirdbook
8755-7460 Soft Sector
8755-7479 Fantasy Mongers
8755-7509 Reporter on the Legal Profession
8755-7525 Microcomputer Review
8755-7541 Interior Cost Data (Year)
8755-7584 Genealogy Tomorrow†
8755-7606 Creative Person†
8755-7614 Nonprofit World Report *changed to* Nonprofit World
8755-7878 Human Ecologist
8755-8270 Industrial Accident Law Bulletin
8755-8289 Narcotics Law Bulletin
8755-8297 School Law Bulletin (Boston)
8755-8300 Arrest Law Bulletin
8755-8343 Roots Digest
8755-8378 C P C National Directory
8755-8564 Journal of Fluid Control
8755-8734 Hot Buttoneer
8755-8769 Teach
8755-8785 Magazine of Speculative Poetry
8755-8831 Third World Resources
8755-8912 Islam International
8755-898X Current Research in the Pleistocene
8755-9005 Mealey's Litigation Report: Insurance
8755-9013 Ecological Illness Law Report
8755-9129 Food Reviews International
8755-9137 Fast Folk Musical
8755-9218 Collegiate Career Woman Magazine
8755-9404 Interfaith Action
8755-9412 Policy Notes
8755-9560 Show Music
8755-9633 Best Books By Consensus (Year)
8755-965X Discovery Y M C A
8755-9668 Advances in Free Radical Biology and Medicine
8755-9854 Tippah County Historical and Genealogical Society. News and Journal
8755-9889 Mutual Fund Forecaster
8755-9978 Annual Report on High-Tech Materials
8756-0208 Guide to the American Left
8756-0216 Guide to the American Right
8756-0291 Creeping Bent
8756-0313 Flat Earth News
8756-0364 Stroking Times
8756-0380 SingleLife Magazine
8756-0402 Ophthalmic Laser Therapy
8756-0410 Current Problems in Obstetrics and Gynecology and Fertility
8756-0550 C E P A Newsletter
8756-0569 Southern Feminist
8756-0577 A D A Data
8756-0615 Michigan Yearbook of International Legal Studies
8756-0666 Black Bear Review
8756-0674 C I M Magazine
8756-0801 Journal of Urban & Contemporary Law

ISSN INDEX

ISSN	Title
8756-0844	China Rights Annals
8756-0879	Journal of Plastic Film and Sheeting
8756-0909	Youth Policy
8756-0941	New Information Times *changed to* Information Times
8756-1247	Crucible and Scientific Atheist
8756-1263	Benefits Quarterly
8756-1271	Advances in Writing Research
8756-1360	Tax Management Financial Planning Journal
8756-1387	Apartment & Condominium News
8756-1409	Hospital Outsidecare Advisory†
8756-1417	Journal of Ship Production
8756-1492	Trade Secret Law Reporter
8756-1530	Insecticide Product Guide
8756-1697	Turn-of-the-Century Women
8756-1727	O C A W Reporter
8756-1964	Heavy-Ion Reactions
8756-1972	Association for Business Communication. Bulletin
8756-1980	Prophet Newsline
8756-2049	Fiber Optics News
8756-2057	Reporter on Human Reproduction & the Law
8756-2154	California Technology Stock Letter
8756-2316	Florida Parishes Genealogical Newsletter
8756-2332	Jumbo Rate News
8756-2367	Islamic Horizons
8756-2855	Marketing Technology†
8756-2898	Gelosophist
8756-3002	Regeneration Newsletter
8756-3010	Afterwords
8756-3053	American Business Trend Synopsis
8756-3061	Accounting Practices & Regulation
8756-310X	Helping Out in the Outdoors
8756-3142	Iron Mountain†
8756-3185	Mongy Oak
8756-3320	Ocular Pharmacology
8756-3479	Brookfield Zoo Bison
8756-3487	Rock and Soul
8756-3592	Naturalist
8756-372X	Cogeneration Report
8756-3754	Doctor's Office Lab News
8756-3789	American Hockey Magazine
8756-3894	TechTrends: For Leaders in Education and Training
8756-4017	Sensor Technology
8756-4076	Connection Technology
8756-4173	Alki
8756-4467	Center for Migration Studies Newsletter
8756-4572	Drexel Polymer Notes
8756-4610	Loss Grief & Care
8756-4629	Journal of Geriatric Drug Therapy
8756-4696	Other Voices
8756-4718	Nash Notations
8756-4726	Hayes Maze
8756-4793	Journal of Diagnostic Medical Sonography
8756-4807	Computer Smyth
8756-4815	Underwater Equipment & Technology Review†
8756-4963	Type Reporter
8756-5099	Long Pond Review
8756-5196	O C L C Micro
8756-5277	Worcester Review
8756-5285	International Water Color Guild Newsletter
8756-5293	Cornell East Asia Papers
8756-5315	Tempo Magazine
8756-5323	Western Publisher
8756-5331	L 5 News
8756-534X	Green Book: International Directory of Marketing Research Houses *changed to* Green Book: International Directory of Marketing Research Houses and Services
8756-5366	National Safety and Health News *changed to* Safety & Health
8756-5382	Sun Dance Reprints
8756-5633	Zyzzyva
8756-5641	Developmental Neuropsychology
8756-5668	Pennsylvania Review
8756-5900	Communicator (Reno)
8756-5919	Nutrition News (Pomona)
8756-5935	Drugs and Device Recall Bulletin
8756-5978	Portable Lower East Side
8756-6060	Nutrition Legislation News
8756-6109	Artificial Intelligence Markets
8756-6176	Sound Choice
8756-6206	Journal of Pediatric & Perinatal Nutrition
8756-6354	Calypso Log
8756-6362	Dolphin Log
8756-6508	Consultation
8756-6559	Adult Foster Care Journal
8756-6605	Garden State Report
8756-6648	Soviet Journal of Communications Technology and Electronics
8756-6931	Will - Grundy Counties Genealogical Society Quarterly
8756-7016	Annual Review of Computer Science
8756-7067	Lapeer Legacy
8756-7075	Trails to Churchill County
8756-7172	I F A R Reports
8756-7180	Electro-Optics Report
8756-7202	Small Press Book Review
8756-7245	Gypsy Lore Society. North American Chapter. Publications
8756-7296	American Heritage of Invention & Technology
8756-7334	Lotus
8756-7474	Diagnostic Testing Alert
8756-7482	Catholic Challenge
8756-7547	Genetic, Social, and General Psychology Monographs
8756-7555	College Teaching
8756-7652	Old Toy Soldier Newsletter
8756-7717	1/1 Quarterly
8756-7741	Roberts Register
8756-7822	P C Letter
8756-7881	Common Sense Pest Control Quarterly
8756-7903	Revenews
8756-7938	Biotechnology Progress
8756-8187	Ceramic Source
8756-8217	Breathless Magazine
8756-8225	Journal of College Student Psychotherapy
8756-8233	Drugs & Society
8756-8357	American Brahms Society. Newsletter
8756-8446	Fremont County Nostalgia News
8756-8519	Hospital Ethics
8756-8535	Espionage Magazine
8756-8578	Technology for Anesthesia
8756-8586	Technology for Cardiology
8756-8594	Technology for Emergency Medicine
8756-8608	Technology for Materials Management
8756-8616	Technology for Respiratory Therapy
8756-8624	Technology for Surgery
8756-8667	Flutist Quarterly
8756-890X	Movements in the Arts
8756-9043	National Fact Book of Savings Institutions
8756-9116	Business Week Guide to Careers
8756-9175	A B M S Directory of Certified Ophthalmologists
8756-9639	Business Media Week *changed to* Business Publisher
8756-9647	LitAlert
8756-9736	C Journal
8756-9965	M O T C's Notebook
8756-9981	New Beginnings (Franklin Park)
9066-1605	International Directory of Published Market Research *changed to* Marketsearch

Title Index

Page numbers in italics refer to location of main entries, those in roman type refer to location of subject cross references.

A A A Annual Report (American Arbitration Association) (US) *649*
A A A Campbooks (American Automobile Association) (US) *1043*, 1105
A A A S Miscellaneous Publication *see* A A A S Publication *986*
A A A S Publication (American Association for the Advancement of Science) (US ISSN 0271-2229) *986*
A A A S S Directory of Programs (American Association for the Advancement of Slavic Studies) (US ISSN 0889-9487) *501*
A A C C Newsletter (American Automatic Control Council) (US) *484*
A A C O B S Annual Report (Australian Advisory Council on Bibliographical Services) (AT ISSN 0812-6267) *672*
A A E C Nuclear News (AT ISSN 0157-6224) *463*, 862, 986
A A F M Proceedings of Annual Meeting (American Association of Feed Microscopists) (US ISSN 0569-2628) 169, *795*
A A G Bijdragen (Afdeling Agrarische Geschiedenis) (NE ISSN 0511-0726) 22, *573*
A A L L Publications Series (American Association of Law Libraries) (US ISSN 0065-7255) 649, *672*
A A M C Curriculum Directory (Association of American Medical Colleges) (US ISSN 0092-0371) *446*, 756
A A M C Directory of American Medical Education (Association of American Medical Colleges) (US ISSN 0360-7437) 431, *442*, 756
A A P G Studies in Geology Series (American Association of Petroleum Geologists) (US ISSN 0271-8510) *382*, 862
A A R Academy Series (American Academy of Religion) (US ISSN 0277-1071) *966*
A A R Dissertation Series *see* A A R Academy Series *966*
A A R Studies in Religion (American Academy of Religion) (US ISSN 0084-6287) *966*
A A S C U Studies (American Association of State Colleges and Universities) (US ISSN 0065-7344) *431*

A.A.'s Far East Businessman's Directory (Artists Associates) (HK ISSN 0532-9175) *301*
A A S Goddard Memorial Symposium. Proceedings. (American Astronautical Society, Inc.) (US) *17*
A A S History Series (American Astronautical Society) (US ISSN 0730-3564) *17*
A A S Microfiche Series (American Astronautical Society, Inc.) (US ISSN 0065-7417) *17*
A.A.T.E. Guide to English Books (Australian Association for the Teaching of English) (AT ISSN 0084-7216) 422, *738*
A A U Code *see* Amateur Athletic Union of the United States. Official Handbook of the A A U Code *1032*
A A U Junior Olympic Handbook (Amateur Athletic Union of the United States) (US ISSN 0361-4654) 335, *1032*
A A U Official Handbook: Baton Twirling *see* Baton Twirling Handbook *1033*
A A V S O Bulletin *see* A A V S O Bulletin--Predicted Dates of Maxima and Minima of Long Period Variable Stars *114*
A A V S O Bulletin--Predicted Dates of Maxima and Minima of Long Period Variable Stars (American Association of Variable Star Observers) (US) *114*
A A V S O Report (US) *114*
A B A F A News *see* B A A F News *1015*
A B A Lawyers' Title Guaranty Funds Newsletter (American Bar Association) (US ISSN 0361-3763) *649*
A B Bookman's Yearbook (US ISSN 0065-0005) *959*
A B C (Annuaire Belge de Chauffage et Climatisation) (BE) *553*
A B C: Anuario Brasileiro da Construcao (BL) *181*
A B C - Arab Trade Reference: Arab & Middle East Countries (UA) *252*
A B C British Columbia Lumber Trade Directory and Year Book (CN ISSN 0065-0013) *529*
A B C der Deutschen Wirtschaft (GW) *301*
A B C Europe Production (GW ISSN 0065-003X) *252*
A B C Freight Guide (UK ISSN 0308-9304) *1104*

A B C Guide to Party Booking *see* Guide to Party Booking *1111*
A B C of Book Trade (US ISSN 0065-0048) *959*
A B C Pol Sci (US ISSN 0001-0456) 1, 668, *911*, 947
A B C Privrede Jugoslavije (YU) *301*
A B F Research Reporter *see* American Bar Foundation Research Reporter *1146*
A B H B *see* Annual Bibliography of the History of the Printed Book and Library *931*
A B M S Compendium of Certified Medical Specialists (American Board of Medical Specialties) (US ISSN 0884-1543) *756*
A B M S Directory of Certified Allergy-Immunology Physicians (American Board of Medical Specialties) (US ISSN 0883-2994) *773*
A B M S Directory of Certified Anesthesiologists (American Board of Medical Specialties) (US ISSN 0883-122X) *774*
A B M S Directory of Certified Colon & Rectal Surgeons (American Board of Medical Specialties) (US ISSN 0884-1470) *782*
A B M S Directory of Certified Dermatologists (American Board of Medical Specialties) (US ISSN 0884-1489) *780*
A B M S Directory of Certified Emergency Physicians (American Board of Medical Specialties) (US) *756*
A B M S Directory of Certified Family Practitioners (American Board of Medical Specialties) (US ISSN 0884-643X) *756*
A B M S Directory of Certified Internists (American Board of Medical Specialties) (US ISSN 0884-6448) *756*
A B M S Directory of Certified Neurological Surgeons (American Board of Medical Specialties) (US ISSN 0882-2832) *788*, 793
A B M S Directory of Certified Neurologists (American Board of Medical Specialties) (US ISSN 0884-1500) *788*
A B M S Directory of Certified Nuclear Medicine Specialists (American Board of Medical Specialties) (US ISSN 0884-1454) *792*

A B M S Directory of Certified Obstetricians & Gynecologists (American Board of Medical Specialties) (US ISSN 0884-1535) *784*
A B M S Directory of Certified Ophthalmologists (American Board of Medical Specialties) (US ISSN 8756-9175) *785*
A B M S Directory of Certified Orthopaedic Surgeons (American Board of Medical Specialties) (US ISSN 0883-1211) *786*
A B M S Directory of Certified Otolaryngologists (American Board of Medical Specialties) (US ISSN 0883-3001) *786*
A B M S Directory of Certified Pathologists (American Board of Medical Specialties) (US ISSN 0883-1203) *782*
A B M S Directory of Certified Pediatricians (American Board of Medical Specialties) (US ISSN 0884-1497) *787*
A B M S Directory of Certified Physical Medicine & Rehabilitation Physicians (American Board of Medical Specialties) (US ISSN 0883-2986) *777*
A B M S Directory of Certified Plastic Surgeons (American Board of Medical Specialties) (US ISSN 0749-839X) *787*
A B M S Directory of Certified Preventive Medicine Physicians (American Board of Medical Specialties) (US) *756*
A B M S Directory of Certified Psychiatrists (American Board of Medical Specialties) (US ISSN 0884-1519) *788*
A B M S Directory of Certified Radiologists (American Board of Medical Specialties) (US ISSN 0883-1238) *792*
A B M S Directory of Certified Surgeons (American Board of Medical Specialties) (US ISSN 0884-1527) *794*
A B M S Directory of Certified Thoracic Surgeons (American Board of Medical Specialties) (US ISSN 0884-1462) *756*, 794
A B M S Directory of Certified Urologists (American Board of Medical Specialties) (US ISSN 0742-0374) *795*

A B O I Catalogue (Association of British Oceanic Industries) (UK) *1098*

A B P A Directory of Members (Australian Book Publishers Association) (AT) *959*

A B's Guide to Souvenirs and Novelties *see* Buyers' Guide for the Mass Entertainment Industry *1044*

A C A Bulletin (Association for Communication Administration) (US ISSN 0360-0939) *278, 342*

A C A Index (Americans for Constitutional Action) (US ISSN 0066-1228) *901*

A.C.A. Review (Anglers Cooperative Association) (UK ISSN 0044-8257) *363, 507*

A C C Basketball Handbook (Atlantic Coast Conference) (US ISSN 0733-0448) *1037*

A C I Bibliography (American Concrete Institute) (US ISSN 0084-6325) *121*

A C I L *see* Amsterdam Studies in the Theory and History of Linguistic Science. Series 1: Amsterdam Classics in Linguistics, 1800-1925 *690*

A C I Manual of Concrete Practice (American Concrete Institute) (US ISSN 0065-7875) *181*

A C I Year Book (Australian Cat Federation, Inc.) (AT) *868*

A C M Administrative Directory of College and University Computer Science/Data Processing Programs and Computer Facilities (Association for Computing Machinery, Inc.) (US) *351, 360*

A C M E Newsletter (Academy of Country Music Entertainment) (CN ISSN 0704-6138) *832*

A C M Guide to Computing Literature (US ISSN 0149-1199) *353*

A C M/I E E E Design Automation Conference. Proceedings (US) *356*

A C M Monograph Series (Association for Computing Machinery) (US) *351*

A C M Symposium on the Theory of Computing (Association for Computing Machinery) (US) *363*

A C O L A M Newsletter (Advisory Committee on Latin American Materials) (UK ISSN 0263-6832) *672*

A C S A Faculty Directory *see* Architecture Schools in North America *97*

A C S Monographs (American Chemical Society) (US ISSN 0065-7719) *321*

A C S Research Report (Agricultural Cooperative Service) (US) *44*

A C S S O Policy (Year) (Australian Council of State School Organisations) (AT) *409*

A C S Symposium Series (American Chemical Society) (US ISSN 0097-6156) *321*

A C T F L Foreign Language Education Series (American Council on the Teaching of Foreign Languages) (US ISSN 0147-1236) *446*

A C T F L Review of Foreign Languages Education *see* A C T F L Foreign Language Education Series *446*

A C T Handbook for Financial Aid Administrators *see* American College Testing Program. Handbook for Financial Aid Administrators *442*

A C T Monograph Series (American College Testing Program) (US ISSN 0065-7832) *431*

A C T Research Report (American College Testing Program) (US ISSN 0569-3993) *431*

A C T Research Service Report *see* A C T Research Report *431*

A C T Special Report Series (US) *431*

A C T U National Youth Brochure (Australian Council of Trade Unions) (AT) *647*

A D A C - Campingfuehrer. Band 1: Suedeuropa (GW) *1043*, 1105

A D A C - Campingfuehrer. Band 2: Deutschland, Mittel- und Nordeuropa *see* A D A C - Campingfuehrer. Band 2: Deutschland, Mitteleuropa, Nordeuropa *1043*

A D A C - Campingfuehrer. Band 2: Deutschland, Mitteleuropa, Nordeuropa (GW) *1043*, 1105

A.D.A. News Information (Alberta Dental Association) (CN ISSN 0383-6355) *778*

A D A P S O Membership *see* A D A P S O Membership Directory *360*

A D A P S O Membership Directory (Association of Data Processing Service Organizations (ADAPSO)) (US) *360*

A D B S Annuaire (Association Francaise des Documentalistes et des Bibliothecaires Specialises) (FR ISSN 0066-9210) *1145*

A D C A: American Directory of Collection Agencies and Attorneys (US ISSN 0084-5833) *222*

A D F A Audio Visual Catalogue (Alcohol and Drug Foundation, Australia) (AT) *687, 886*

A.D.F.& G. Technical Data Report (Department of Fish and Game) (US ISSN 0095-4632) *507*

A.D.K. Booklet: Facts and Figures/A.D.K. Schriftenreihe: Daten und Fakten (Afrikaans Duitse Kultuurunie (S W A)) (SX) *564*

A.D.K. Schriftenreihe: Daten und Fakten *see* A.D.K. Booklet: Facts and Figures *564*

A D L Law Report (Anti Defamation League of B'nai B'rith) (US) *649*

A D T V - Nachrichten (Allgemeiner Deutscher Tanzlehrer Verband) (GW ISSN 0001-0979) *374*

A D U K (Adresar Ukraintsiv u Vilnomu Sviti) (FR) *914*

A E (SW) *463, 469, 895*

A E C/A N S Monographs *see* Nuclear Science Technology Monograph Series *898*

A E C L Report Series (Atomic Energy of Canada Ltd.) (CN ISSN 0067-0367) *463, 895*

A E E Directory of Energy Professionals (Association of Energy Engineers) (US ISSN 0164-0917) *469*

A E M S Seminar (Papers) (American Engineering Model Society) (US) *181, 469*

A.E.T.F.A.T. Index (Association pour l'Etude Taxonomique de la Flore d'Afrique Tropicale) (BE ISSN 0066-9784) *1, 149*

A F A D D Audio Visual Acquisitions List *see* A D F A Audio Visual Catalogue *687*

A F A D D Audio Visual Catalogue *see* A D F A Audio Visual Catalogue *687*

A F A D D Library Periodicals Holdings List (Australian Foundation on Alcoholism and Drug Dependence) (AT) *1145*

A F A Danmark Fireblokke (DK) *874*

A F A Danmark Frimaerkekatalog (DK) *874*

A F A Europa Frimaerkekatalog *see* A F A Vesteuropa Frimaerkekatalog *874*

A F A Europe Frimaerkekatolog *see* A F A Oesteuropa Frimaerkekatalog *874*

A F A Oesteuropa Frimaerkekatalog (Aarhus Frimaerkehandel) (DK) *874*

A F A Skandinavien Frimaerkekatalog (DK) *874*

A F A Vesteuropa Frimaerkekatalog (Aarhus Frimaerkehandel) (DK) *874*

A F L - C I O Convention Proceedings(US) *647*

A F R A Member Directory and Ancestral Surname Registry (American Family Records Association) (US) *534*

A F R C Food Research Institute. Biennial Report (Agricultural & Food Research Council) (UK) *1145*

A F R C Institute of Engineering Research. Divisional Notes (Agricultural & Food Research Council) (UK) *51*

A F R C Institute of Engineering Research. Reports (Agricultural & Food Research Council) (UK) *51*

A F R C Institute of Engineering Research. Translations (Agricultural & Food Research Council) (UK) *51*

A F R C Institute of Food Research Technical Bulletins (Agriculture and Food Research Council) (UK) *61*

A F R O Technical Papers (Regional Office for Africa) (UN) *952*

A F R O Technical Report Series. Reports of Meetings of Expert Committees (Regional Office for Africa) (UN) *952*

A F T Issues Bulletin (American Federation of Teachers) (US) *409, 647*

A Fin L A Yearbook (Association Finlandaise de Linguistique Appliquee) (FI ISSN 0356-8156) *689*

A G M Reporter (CN ISSN 0703-766X) *442*

A G S Dairy Goat Yearbook *see* American Goat Society. Year Book *64*

A.G.S. Guides (Alpine Garden Society) (UK) *531*

A G V A News *see* A G V A Newsletter *648*

A G V A Newsletter (American Guild of Variety Artists) (US) *648*

A Guide to National Associations, Service Organizations and Unions Operating in the Arts *see* Directory of the Arts *104*

A H A Health Services Monographs (Australian Hospital Association) (AT) *616*

A H R C Chronicle (Association for the Help of Retarded Children) (US ISSN 0001-1436) *788*

A I A A/A S M E/S A E Structures, Structural Dynamics, and Materials Conference. Proceedings (US) *17*

A I A A Atmospheric Flight Mechanics Conference Proceedings (American Institute of Aeronautics and Astronautics) (US) *17*

A I A A Communications Satellite Systems Conference. Technical Papers (American Institute of Aeronautics and Astronautics) (US) *17, 342*

A I A A/I E E E Digital Avionics Systems Conference. Proceedings *see* I E E E/A I A A Digital Avionics Systems Conference. Proceedings *19*

A I A A/I E E E Digital Avionics Systems Conference. Technical Papers *see* I E E E/A I A A Digital Avionics Systems Conference. Proceedings *19*

A I A A Roster (American Institute of Aeronautics and Astronautics) (US ISSN 0065-8693) *17*

A I C P A Professional Standards (American Institute of Certified Public Accountants) (US) *220*

A I Ch E Applications Software Survey of Personal Computers (American Institute of Chemical Engineers) (US ISSN 0743-0183) *362, 362*

A I Ch E Equipment Testing Procedures (American Institute of Chemical Engineers) (US ISSN 0569-5473) *477, 781*

A I Ch E M I Modular Instruction. Series A: Process Control (American Institute of Chemical Engineers) (US ISSN 0270-6229) *1145*

A I Ch E M I Modular Instruction. Series B: Stagewise and Mass Transfer Operations (American Institute of Chemical Engineers) (US ISSN 0270-7624) *1145*

A I Ch E M I Modular Instruction. Series C: Transport (American Institute of Chemical Engineers) (US ISSN 0270-7632) *477*

A I Ch E M I Modular Instruction. Series D: Thermodynamics (American Institute of Chemical Engineers) (US ISSN 0270-7640) *1145*

A I Ch E M I Modular Instruction. Series E: Kinetics (American Institute of Chemical Engineers) (US ISSN 0270-7659) *1145*

A I Ch E M I Modular Instruction. Series F: Material and Energy Balances (American Institute of Chemical Engineers) (US ISSN 0270-7667) *1145*

A I Ch E M I Modular Instruction. Series G: Design of Equipment (American Institute of Chemical Engineers) (US ISSN 0890-0582) *477*

A I Ch E Monograph Series (American Institute of Chemical Engineers) (US ISSN 0065-8804) *477*

A I Ch E Symposium Series (American Institute of Chemical Engineers) (US ISSN 0065-8812) *477*

A I Ch E Workshop Series (American Institute of Chemical Engineers) (US ISSN 0569-5457) *477*

A I G A Best Books Show *see* A I G A Graphic Design U S A *930*

A I G A Graphic Design U S A (American Institute of Graphic Arts) (US ISSN 0275-9470) *930*

A I I S Annual Report *see* American Institute of Indian Studies. Biennial Report *568*

A.I.J. Manual of Australasian Life Assurance (Australasian Insurance Journal) (AT ISSN 0084-697X) *637*

A I M M Symposia Series (Australasian Institute of Mining and Metallurgy) (AT) *796, 813*

A I M S Bulletin (American Institute of Musical Studies) (US) *832*

A I M S Monograph Series (Australian Institute of Marine Science) (AT) *404*

A I P Conference Proceedings (American Institute of Physics) (US ISSN 0094-243X) *886*

A I Recommends (Associated Industries of New York State, Inc.) (US) *901*

A I S E Yearbook (Association of Iron and Steel Engineers) (US) *796*

A I T Reports and Publications on Renewable Energy Resources. Abstracts (Asian Institute of Technology) (TH) *468*

A.I. Voeikov Main Geophysical Observatory, Leningrad. Data of Measurements of Electric Field Strength of the Atmosphere at Various Altitudes by the Results of Soundings (UR ISSN 0065-0080) *398*

A.I. Voeikov Main Geophysical Observatory, Leningrad. Results of Ground Observations of Atmospheric Electricity. Additional Issue (UR ISSN 0065-0099) *398*

A Is A (US) *709*

A Is A Newsletter *see* A Is A *709*

A J M E News (Americans for Justice in the Middle East) (LE) *611, 914*

A Kemia Ujabb Eredmenyei (HU ISSN 0075-5397) *321*

A L A Handbook of Organization (American Library Association) (US ISSN 0084-6406) *672*

A L A Handbook of Organization and Membership Directory *see* A L A Handbook of Organization *672*

A L A Sights to See Book (Automobile Legal Association) (US ISSN 0090-8614) *1105*

A L A Studies in Librarianship (American Library Association) (US ISSN 0065-907X) *672*

A L A Worldwide Directory and Fact Book (American Logistics Association) (US) *282, 340, 522, 810*

A L A Yearbook (American Library Association) (US ISSN 0364-1597) *672*

A L P R News (Association for Arid Lands Studies) (US) *22, 153, 540*

A L R C Report Series (Australia Law Reform Commission) (AT) *649*

A L Z A Conference Series (US) *1145*
A La Carte (US) *619*
A la Premiere Personne (FR) *133*
A M A Directory of Officials and Staff (American Medical Association) (US ISSN 0748-5557) *756*
A M A Management Briefings (American Management Associations) (US) *278*
A M A Product Directory (American Monument Association) (US) 531, *813*
A M A Survey Reports (American Management Associations) (US) *278*
A M C H A M Morocco (MR ISSN 0065-7689) *234*
A M D E L Bulletin (Australia Mineral Development Laboratories) (AT ISSN 0045-0707) 382, *813*
A M P L A Yearbook (Australian Mining and Petroleum Law Association Ltd.) (AT ISSN 0157-2083) 813, *862*
A M S Ars Poetica (US) *739*
A M S Asian Studies (US ISSN 0748-5476) *568*
A M S Data Processing Salaries Report (Association for Management Success) (US) 269, *278*
A M S Directory of Office Salaries *see* A M S Office Salaries Report *269*
A M S Guide to Management Compensation (Association for Management Success) (US ISSN 0278-1506) 269, *278*
A M S Office Salaries Report (Association for Management Success) (US) 269, *278*
A M S - Skrifter (Arkeologisk Museum i Stavanger) (NO ISSN 0800-0816) *79*
A M S - Smaatrykk (Arkeologisk Museum i Stavanger) (NO ISSN 0332-6411) *79*
A M S Studies in Anthropology (US ISSN 0738-064X) *69*
A M S Studies in Ars Poetica *see* A M S Ars Poetica *739*
A M S Studies in Criminal Justice (US ISSN 0270-2991) 369, *649*
A M S Studies in Education (US ISSN 0882-438X) *409*
A M S Studies in Modern Literature (US ISSN 0270-2983) *713*
A M S Studies in Modern Society (US ISSN 0275-8407) *713*
A M S Studies in Social History (US ISSN 0270-6253) *554*
A M S Studies in the Eighteenth Century (US ISSN 0196-6561) *713*
A M S Studies in the Emblem (Abrahams Magazine Service) (US ISSN 0892-4201) 534, *810*
A M S Studies in the Middle Ages (US ISSN 0270-6261) 554, *713*
A M S Studies in the Nineteenth Century (US ISSN 0196-657X) *713*
A M S Studies in the Renaissance (US ISSN 0195-8011) 713, *1076*
A M S Studies in the Seventeenth Century (Abrahams Magazine Service) (US ISSN 0731-2342) *713*
A M S Systems and Processing Salaries Report *see* A M S Data Processing Salaries Report *269*
A M S - Varia (Arkeologisk Museum i Stavanger) (NO ISSN 0332-6306) *79*
A M T I D: Application of Modern Technology to International Development (US) 121, 911, *1072*
A M U (Annuario Italiano Macchine Utensili e Complementari) (IT ISSN 0393-0483) *745*
A M U Press Alaskana Series (Alaska Methodist University) *see* A P U Press Alaskana Book Series *602*
A N A R E Report (Australian National Antarctic Research Expeditions) (AT) 378, *986*
A N A R E Research Notes (Australian National Antarctic Research Expeditions) (AT ISSN 0729-6533) *986*
A N A R E Scientific Report *see* A N A R E Report *986*
A N E C (Asociacion Nacional de Enfermeras de Colombia) (CK ISSN 0044-930X) *783*

A N E P *see* European Petroleum Yearbook *864*
A N Z A A S Congress Papers (Australian and New Zealand Association for the Advancement of Science) (AT ISSN 0312-8059) *986*
A O A Yearbook and Directory of Osteopathic Physicians (American Osteopathic Association) (US) *777*
A O P A's Airports U.S.A. (Aircraft Owners and Pilots Association) (US ISSN 0271-065X) *1087*
A P A I S: Australian Public Affairs Information Service (AT ISSN 0727-8926) 1, *948*
A P A Newspaper Directory *see* Alabama Press Association. Rate and Data Guide *673*
A.P.C.A. Directory and Resource Book *see* A P C A Government Agencies Directory *493*
A P C A Government Agencies Directory (US) *493*
A P D U Membership Directory (Association of Public Data Users) (US) *301*
A.P.E.A. Journal (Australian Petroleum Exploration Association) (AT ISSN 0084-7534) 382, *862*
A P E C *see* I E E E Applied Power Electronics Conference and Exposition. Conference Proceedings *454*
A P G A Annual/A P K V Jaarblad (Apricot, Peach and Pear Growers' Association) (SA) *531*
A P I Abstracts/Literature (American Petroleum Institute) (US) 1, *867*
A P I Abstracts/Oilfield Chemicals (American Petroleum Institute) (US) 1, *867*
A P I Abstracts/Patents (American Petroleum Institute) (US) 1, *867*
A P I C E Journal *see* Revista A P I C E *1161*
A P I C Studies in Data Processing Series (US) *357*
A P I Patent Alert *see* A P I Abstracts/Patents *867*
A P I Research Project 44. Selected Values of Properties of Hydrocarbons and Related Compounds. Category A: Tables of Selected Values of Physical and Thermodynamic Properties of Hydrocarbons *see* Thermodynamics Research Center. Hydrocarbon Project. Selected Values of Properties of Hydrocarbons and Related Compounds. Category A: Tables of Selected Values of Physical and Thermodynamic Properties of Hydrocarbons *333*
A P I Research Project 44. Selected Values of Properties of Hydrocarbons and Related Compounds. Category B: Selected Infrared Spectral Data *see* Thermodynamics Research Center. Hydrocarbon Project. Selected Values of Properties of Hydrocarbons and Related Compounds. Category B: Selected Infrared Spectral Data *327*
A P I Research Project 44. Selected Values of Properties of Hydrocarbons and Related Compounds. Category C: Selected Ultraviolet Spectral Data *see* Thermodynamics Research Center. Hydrocarbon Project. Selected Values of Properties of Hydrocarbons and Related Compounds. Category C: Selected Ultraviolet Spectral Data *327*
A P I Research Project 44. Selected Values of Properties of Hydrocarbons and Related Compounds. Category D: Selected Raman Spectral Data *see* Thermodynamics Research Center. Hydrocarbon Project. Selected Values of Properties of Hydrocarbons and Related Compounds. Category D: Selected Raman Spectral Data *327*

A P I Research Project 44. Selected Values of Properties of Hydrocarbons and Related Compounds. Category E: Selected Mass Spectral Data *see* Thermodynamics Research Center. Hydrocarbon Project. Selected Values of Properties of Hydrocarbons and Related Compounds. Category E: Selected Mass Spectral Data *327*
A P I Research Project 44. Selected Values of Properties of Hydrocarbons and Related Compounds. Category F: Selected Nuclear Magnetic Resonance Data *see* Thermodynamics Research Center. Hydrocarbon Project. Selected Values of Properties of Hydrocarbons and Related Compounds. Category F: Selected Nuclear Magnetic Resonance Data *327*
A P I Research Project 44. Selected Values of Properties of Hydrocarbons and Related Compounds. Category G: Selected 13 C Nuclear Magnetic Resonance Spectral Data *see* Thermodynamics Research Center. Hydrocarbon Project. Selected Values of Properties of Hydrocarbons and Related Compounds. Category G: Selected 13-C Nuclear Magnetic Resonance Spectral Data *327*
A P K V Jaarblad *see* A P G A Annual *531*
A P O Annual Report (Asian Productivity Organization) (UN ISSN 0066-846X) 261, *287*
A P R *see* Algemene Practische Rechtverzameling *650*
A P R E S Proceedings (American Peanut Research and Education Society) (US ISSN 0197-8748) *51*
A P S A Departmental Services Program Survey of Departments (American Political Science Association) (US ISSN 0094-7954) *901*
A P S A Directory of Department Chairmen *see* A P S A Directory of Department Chairpersons *901*
A P S A Directory of Department Chairpersons (American Political Science Association) (US) *901*
A P S Directory (Alternative Press Syndicate) (US) *645*
A P U Press Alaskana Book Series (Alaska Pacific University Press) (US) 69, 409, 602, *713*
A P U Press Alaskana Series *see* A P U Press Alaskana Book Series *602*
A-Plus Buyer's Guide (US) *1145*
A Q (GW ISSN 0173-0851) *1145*
A R D - Jahrbuch (GW ISSN 0066-5746) *347*
A R D U Publication (Arussi Rural Development Unit) (ET) *22*
A R E L S Brochure *see* A R E L S - F E L C O Brochure *409*
A R E L S - F E L C O Brochure (Association of Recognised English Language Schools, Federation of English Language Course Organisations) (UK) *409*
A R E L S Handbook *see* A R E L S - F E L C O Brochure *409*
A R I S (Art Research in Scandinavia) (SW ISSN 0044-5711) 96, *100*
A R K (DK ISSN 0106-441X) *689*
A R L Annual Salary Survey (Association of Research Libraries) (US ISSN 0361-5669) *672*
A R L Statistics (Association of Research Libraries) (US ISSN 0147-2135) *687*
A R R L Repeater Directory (American Radio Relay League, Inc.) (US ISSN 0190-3632) *347*
A R S Legislative Service *see* Arizona Legislative Service *651*
A.R.S. N.C. Agricultural Research Service. North Central Region *see* U.S. Agricultural Research Service. A R S - N C *35*
A.R.S.S. Agricultural Research Service. Southern Region *see* U.S. Agricultural Research Service. A R S-S *1164*
A R T A N E S *see* Aids and Research Tools in Ancient Near Eastern Studies *611*

A R T B A Officials and Engineers Directory, Transportation Agency Personnel (American Road and Transportation Builders Association) (US ISSN 0360-6996) 181, 480, *1095*
A R T I Reports (Aeronautical Research and Test Institute) (CS) *17*
A R T M E S *see* Aids and Research Tools in Middle Eastern Studies *611*
A Report on the Work and Programs of Scripps Institution of Oceanography *see* Scripps Institution of Oceanography. Annual Report *407*
A S A E Monograph Series (American Society of Agricultural Engineers) (US) *469*
A S A E Standards (American Society of Agricultural Engineers) (US) *51*
A S A I H L. Seminar Reports (Association of Southeast Asian Institutions of Higher Learning) (TH ISSN 0066-9695) 431, *568*
A S A Monograph (American Society of Appraisers) (US ISSN 0569-7840) 637, *964*
A S A Monographs *see* A S A Research Methods in Social Anthropology *69*
A S A Papers (African Studies Association) (US) *501*
A S A Refresher Courses in Anesthesiology (American Society of Anesthesiologists) (US ISSN 0363-471X) *774*
A S A Research Methods in Social Anthropology (Association of Social Anthropologists of the Commonwealth) (US) *69*
A S A Special Publication (American Society of Agronomy, Inc.) (US ISSN 0066-0566) *22*
A S C A P Biographical Dictionary (American Society of Composers, Authors and Publishers) (US) 133, 713, *832*
A S C Cybernetics Forum *see* Cybernetic *359*
A S C E Annual Combined Index (American Society of Civil Engineers) (US) *480*
A S C Mini-File (UK) 96, *181*
A S C U S Annual - A Job Search Handbook for Educators (Association for School, College and University Staffing) (US) *442*
A S C U S Annual - Teaching Opportunities for You *see* A S C U S Annual - A Job Search Handbook for Educators *442*
A S C U S Directory of Membership and Subject Field Index (Association for School, College and University Staffing) (US ISSN 0066-9164) *442*
A S D A Handbook (American Student Dental Association) (US ISSN 0277-3619) *778*
A S H A Directory (American Speech and Hearing Association) *see* American Speech - Language - Hearing Association. Directory *787*
A S H A Reports (American Speech-Language-Hearing Association) (US ISSN 0569-8553) 375, 444, *786*
A S H R A E Handbook (American Society of Heating, Refrigerating and Air-Conditioning Engineers Inc.) (US) *553*
A S H R A E Handbook & Product Specification File *see* A S H R A E Handbook *553*
A S I L S International Law Journal (Association of Student International Law Societies) (US ISSN 0161-1402) 431, *649*
A S I S Handbook and Directory *see* American Society for Information Science. Handbook and Directory *673*
A S L A Members Handbook (American Society of Landscape Architects) (US ISSN 0192-5067) *96*
A S L S Newsletter (Association for Scottish Literary Studies) (UK) *713*
A S M Bibliography Series (American Society for Metals) (US ISSN 0001-2556) 1, *801*

A S M Translations Index *see* Translations Index *802*
A S N E 19 (American Society of Newspaper Editors) (US) *645*
A S P A C Seminar on Audio-Visual Education. Proceedings (Asian and Pacific Council) (KO ISSN 0066-8311) *1145*
A S P E C T (Anti-Static Proposals & Electro-Conductive Technologies) (UK) *450*
A S R A Journal (Association for the Study of Reptilia and Amphibia) (UK ISSN 0142-5145) *172*
A S S A Proceedings (Association for Sociology in Southern Africa) (SA) *1023*
A S T D Buyers Guide and Consultants Directory (US) *269, 286*
A S T I S Bibliography (Arctic Science & Technology Information System) (CN ISSN 0226-1685) *1*
A S T I S Occasional Publications (Arctic Science & Technology Information System) (CN ISSN 0225-5170) *121*
A S T M Proceedings (American Society for Testing and Materials) (US ISSN 0066-0515) *485*
A S U C Journal of Music Scores (American Society of University Composers) (US) *832*
A T A Professional Services Directory *see* Translation Services Directory *706*
A T A V E Boletin Informativo (Asociacion de Tecnicos Azucareros de Venezuela) (VE ISSN 0084-683X) *517*
A T F Annual Report (Australian Teachers' Federation) (AT) *409, 648*
A T F Monthly Report *see* A T F Annual Report *409*
A T F Newsletter (US) *930*
A T L A Bibliography Series (American Theological Library Association) (US) *967*
A T L A Monograph Series (American Theological Library Association) (US) *967*
A T M Directory (Automated Teller Machines) (US) *222, 745*
A T M Occasional Papers (Association of Teachers of Management) (UK ISSN 0066-9709) *278, 431*
A T S S Bulletin (Association of Teachers of Social Studies in the City of New York) (US ISSN 0044-9687) *446, 1005*
A U B E R Bibliography *see* University Research in Business and Economics: a Bibliography of (Year) Publications *220*
A U D - Nyt (Aalborg Universitetsdatacenter) (DK ISSN 0109-4157) *351*
A U M A Kalender Ausland (GW ISSN 0721-2720) *282, 795*
A U M A Kalender Regional (GW ISSN 0721-2747) *282, 795*
A U M A Zahlenspiegel Messeplatz Deutschland (Ausstellungs- und Messe-Ausschuss der Deutschen Wirtschaft E.V.) (GW ISSN 0724-0554) *282*
A U M A Zahlenspiegel Regional (GW ISSN 0724-0457) *282, 795*
A V - Branche (Year) (GW) *342, 347*
A V C A Directory *see* Serving Australian Agriculture *1162*
A V D Auto Bordbuch (GW) *1090, 1105*
A V E in Japan (Japan Audio-Visual Education Association) (JA ISSN 0065-0102) *446*
A V M A R C *see* British Catalogue of Audio-Visual Materials *1032*
A V S Biomedical Bulletin *see* Biomedical Bulletin *179*
A.V.S. Journal *see* Pegasus *1122*
A. W. Mellon Lectures in the Fine Arts(US ISSN 0065-0129) *100*
A Y H Handbook (American Youth Hostels, Inc.) (US) *1105*
A Y R S Airs (Amateur Yacht Research Society) (UK ISSN 0144-1396) *1041*

A - Z de la Construccion y la Decoracion (VE) *181*
A - Z of U.K. Marketing Data (UK ISSN 0260-6488) *282*
Aabenraa Proevecenter for Ny Informationsteknologi Rapport *see* I N F A A Rapport *679*
Aabo Akademi. Aarsskrift (FI ISSN 0355-5798) *431*
Aabo Akademi. Statsvetenskapliga Fakulteten. Meddelanden (FI) *1005*
Aabo Akademi. Statsvetenskapliga Fakulteten. Meddelanden. Serie A *see* Aabo Akademi. Statsvetenskapliga Fakulteten. Meddelanden *1005*
Aabo Akademi. Statsvetenskapliga Fakulteten. Meddelanden. Serie B *see* Aabo Akademi. Statsvetenskapliga Fakulteten. Meddelanden *1005*
Aachener Beitraege zur Komparatistik (GW) *713*
Aachener Geschichtsverein. Zeitschrift (GW ISSN 0065-0137) *573*
Aalandsk Odling (FI) *573*
Aalborg Stiftsbog (DK ISSN 0107-5055) *573*
Aalborg Universitetscenter. Institut for Elektroniske Systemer. Rapport (DK) *450*
Aalborg Universitetscenter. Instituttet for Bygningsteknik. Note (DK ISSN 0105-8185) *181*
Aalborg Universitetscenter. Instituttet for Bygningsteknik. Rapport (DK ISSN 0105-7421) *181*
Aalborg Universitetscenter Kvindestudier ved A U C. Aarbog *see* Kvindestudier ved A U C. Aarbog *1129*
Aalborg Universitetsdatacenter. Publikation (DK ISSN 0109-3770) *351*
Aalborg Universitetsdatacenter Nyt *see* A U D - Nyt *351*
Aarbog for Arbejderbevaegelsens Historie (DK ISSN 0106-5912) *269, 573*
Aarbog for Folkeskolen (DK ISSN 0106-0465) *442*
Aarbog for Kvindeforskning (DK ISSN 0900-1565) *1128*
Aarbog for Svendborg e Omegns Museum (DK ISSN 0106-2220) *573*
Aarbok for den Norske Kirke (NO ISSN 0400-227X) *967*
Aarbok for Hadeland (NO ISSN 0572-4562) *573*
Aarbok for Telemark (NO ISSN 0587-4076) *573*
Aaret Rundt (DK) *469*
Aaret som Gaatt (Tjaenstemaennens Central Organisation) (SW) *269*
Aarets Bandy (SW) *1032*
Aarets Fotboll (SW ISSN 0567-4565) *1037*
Aarets Idrott (SW ISSN 0567-4573) *1032*
Aarets Ishockey (SW) *1032*
Aarets Pressefoto (DK ISSN 0109-4440) *645, 884*
Aarhus Frimaerkehandel Oesteuropa Frimaerkekatalog *see* A F A Oesteuropa Frimaerkekatalog *874*
Aarhus Frimaerkehandel Vesteuropa Frimaerkekatalog *see* A F A Vesteuropa Frimaerkekatalog *874*
Aarhus Kommunes Statistiske Kontor. Information (DK ISSN 0107-7120) *1048*
Aarhus Universitet. Geografisk Institut. Notat (DK ISSN 0106-9047) *540*
Aarhus Universitet. Geologisk Institut. Geokompendier (DK ISSN 0105-8258) *382*
Aarhus Universitet. Geologisk Institut. Georapporter (DK ISSN 0105-8266) *382*
Aarhus Universitet. Geologisk Institut. Geoskrifter (DK ISSN 0105-824X) *382, 540*
Aarhus Universitet. Institut for Statskundskab. Arbejdspapir (DK ISSN 0901-5213) *901*
Aarhus Universitet. Matematisk Institut. Datalogisk Afdeling. DAIMI FN (DK ISSN 0105-8533) *746*

Aarhus Universitet. Matematisk Institut. Datalogisk Afdeling. DAIMI IR (DK ISSN 0106-9969) *746*
Aarhus Universitet. Matematisk Institut. Datalogisk Afdeling. DAIMI MD (DK ISSN 0105-8525) *746*
Aarhus Universitet. Matematisk Institut. Datalogisk Afdeling. DAIMI PB (DK ISSN 0105-8517) *746*
Aarhus Universitet. Matematisk Institut. Elementaerafdeling (DK ISSN 0106-8997) *746*
Aarhus Universitet. Matematisk Institut. Lecture Notes Series (DK ISSN 0065-017X) *746*
Aarhus Universitet. Matematisk Institut. Memoirs (DK) *746*
Aarhus Universitet. Matematisk Institut. Various Publications Series (DK ISSN 0065-0188) *746*
Aarhus Universitet. Psykologisk Skriftseri (DK ISSN 0105-2861) *932*
Aarhus Universitet. Romansk Institut. Spansk Afdelingen. Information (DK ISSN 0107-6531) *689*
Aarhus Universitet. Slavisk Institut. Arbejdspapirer (DK ISSN 0105-4112) *573*
Aarhus Universitet. Socialmedicinsk Institut. Rapport (DK ISSN 0109-9973) *756*
Aarhus Universitet. Teologiske Fakultet. Bibliografi (DK ISSN 0901-4497) *967*
Aarhus University. Botanical Institute. Reports (DK ISSN 0105-4236) *153*
Aarni (FI ISSN 0355-1644) *574*
Aarsberetning Vedkommende Norges Fiskerier (NO) *507*
Aarsbok foer Skolan (SW ISSN 0065-0196) *409*
Aarsbok foer Sveriges Kummuner (SW ISSN 0065-020X) *948*
Aarsskrift for Sottrup Sogn (DK ISSN 0108-2787) *574*
Aarsskrift for Toender Landbrugsskole (DK ISSN 0107-0304) *22*
Abacus (NR ISSN 0001-3099) *747*
Abe Bailey Institute of Inter-Racial Studies. Annual Report *see* Centre for Intergroup Studies. Annual Report *1025*
Das Abendland (GW ISSN 0724-9624) *628*
Aberdeen - Angus Herd Book (UK) *64*
Aberdeen - Angus Review (UK ISSN 0001-317X) *64*
Aberdeen Port Handbook (UK ISSN 0267-7377) *301, 862, 1098*
Aberlour Child Care Trust. Newsletter (UK) *1145*
Abertay Historical Society. Series of Monographs (UK) *574*
Abhandlungen aus dem Gebiet der Auslandskunde. Series B & C (GW ISSN 0343-7051) *986*
Abhandlungen aus dem Gesamten Buergerlichen Recht, Handelsrecht und Wirtschaftsrecht (GW ISSN 0065-0307) *649*
Abhandlungen des Deutschen Palaestinavereins (GW ISSN 0173-1904) *849*
Abhandlungen fuer die Kunde des Morgenlandes (GW ISSN 0567-4980) *849*
Abhandlungen und Materialen zur Publizistik (GW ISSN 0065-0323) *645*
Abhandlungen zu den Wirtschaftlichen Staatswissenschaften (GW) *250*
Abhandlungen zur Handels- und Sozialgeschichte (GE ISSN 0065-0358) *574*
Abhandlungen zur Kunst-, Musik- und Literaturwissenschaft (GW ISSN 0567-4999) *100, 709, 832*
Abhandlungen zur Philosophie, Psychologie und Paedagogik (GW ISSN 0065-0366) *409, 875*
Abingdon Clergy Income Tax Guide (US ISSN 0163-1241) *292, 967*
Ablex Series in Artificial Intelligence (US) *354*
Ablex Series in Software Engineering (US) *356*
Abordage (CN) *269*

Aboriginal History (AT ISSN 0314-8769) *69, 572*
Abortion Bibliography (US ISSN 0092-9522) *121, 179*
Abr-Nahrain (NE ISSN 0065-0382) *849*
Abr-Nahrain. Supplements (NE ISSN 0065-0390) *849*
Abraham Lincoln Association. Papers (US ISSN 0195-914X) *901*
Abrahams Magazine Service Studies in the Emblem *see* A M S Studies in the Emblem *534*
Abrahams Magazine Service Studies in the Seventeenth Century *see* A M S Studies in the Seventeenth Century *713*
Abrasive Engineering Society. Abrasive Usage Conference. Proceedings (US ISSN 0363-8065) *469*
Abraxas (US ISSN 0361-1663) *713*
Abridged Readers' Guide to Periodical Literature (US ISSN 0001-334X) *1*
Absorption Spectra in the Ultraviolet and Visible Region (HU ISSN 0065-0412) *331, 899*
Abstract Journal in Earthquake Engineering (US ISSN 0363-5732) *1, 475*
Abstract Newsletter: Administration and Management (US) *1, 948*
Abstract Newsletter: Agriculture & Food (US ISSN 0364-7994) *1, 38, 521*
Abstract Newsletter: Civil Engineering (US ISSN 0163-1454) *1, 476*
Abstract Newsletter: Computers, Control & Information Theory (US) *1, 353*
Abstract Newsletter: Electrotechnology (US ISSN 0163-1462) *1, 461*
Abstract Newsletter: Energy (US ISSN 0148-446X) *1, 468*
Abstract Newsletter: Government Inventions for Licensing (US) *1, 1072*
Abstract Newsletter: Health Planning & Health Services Research (US) *1, 886*
Abstract Newsletter: Manufacturing Technology (US) *1, 355, 1072*
Abstract Newsletter: Materials Sciences(US) *1, 476*
Abstract Newsletter: N A S A Earth Resources Survey Program (US) *1145*
Abstract Newsletter: Natural Resources & Earth Sciences (US ISSN 0163-1438) *1, 368, 381*
Abstract Newsletter: Ocean Technology & Engineering (US) *1, 381, 476*
Abstract Newsletter: Physics (US ISSN 0163-1446) *1, 892*
Abstract Newsletter: Problem-Solving Information for State and Local Governments (US) *1, 948*
Abstract Newsletter: Urban and Regional Technology and Development (US ISSN 0163-1535) *1, 627, 1072*
Abstracta Iranica (NE ISSN 0240-8910) *611*
Abstracting and Indexing Bulletin for Agricultural and Animal Husbandry *see* Agricultural Abstracts for Tanzania *38*
Abstracting and Indexing Services Directory (US) *1*
Abstracts and Abridgements of Patent Specifications (UK) *860, 861*
Abstracts for Social Workers *see* Social Work Research and Abstracts *1023*
Abstracts from Current Scientific and Technical Literature (UK ISSN 0001-3439) *1, 521, 847*
Abstracts in Anthropology (US ISSN 0001-3455) *1, 78*
Abstracts in German Anthropology (GW ISSN 0173-2986) *78*
Abstracts in Maryland Archeology (US ISSN 0743-4251) *1, 96*
Abstracts of Bulgarian Scientific Literature. Agriculture and Forestry. Veterinary Medicine (BU ISSN 0001-3463) *1, 38, 529*
Abstracts of Bulgarian Scientific Literature. Economics and Law (BU ISSN 0204-6032) *1, 202, 668*

ACADEMY OF   1621

Abstracts of Bulgarian Scientific Literature. Geology and Geography see Abstracts of Bulgarian Scientific Literature. Nauki za Zemiata 381
Abstracts of Bulgarian Scientific Literature. Industry, Building and Transport (BU ISSN 0204-5265) 2, 188, 202
Abstracts of Bulgarian Scientific Literature. Mathematical and Physical Sciences (BU ISSN 0204-9449) 2, 755, 892
Abstracts of Bulgarian Scientific Literature. Mathematics, Physics, Astronomy, Geophysics, Geodesy see Abstracts of Bulgarian Scientific Literature. Mathematical and Physical Sciences 755
Abstracts of Bulgarian Scientific Literature. Nauki za Zemiata (BU ISSN 0204-9406) 2, 381, 551
Abstracts of Bulgarian Scientific Literature. Philosophy, Psychology and Pedagogics see Abstracts of Bulgarian Scientific Literature. Philosophy, Sociology, Science of Sciences, Psychology and Pedagogics 422
Abstracts of Bulgarian Scientific Literature. Philosophy, Sociology, Science of Sciences, Psychology and Pedagogics (BU) 2, 422, 883
Abstracts of Bulgarian Scientific Medical Literature (BU ISSN 0001-3536) 2, 768
Abstracts of Current Technical Literature see Irrigation and Power Abstracts 1128
Abstracts of Efficiency Studies in the National Health Service see Great Britain. Department of Health and Social Security. Notes on Good Practices 617
Abstracts of Geochronology and Isotope Geology (BE ISSN 0304-5935) 1145
Abstracts of Health Care Management Studies (US ISSN 0194-4908) 2, 618
Abstracts of Hospital Management Studies see Abstracts of Health Care Management Studies 618
Abstracts of Military Bibliography (AG) 2, 813
Abstracts of Refining Literature see A P I Abstracts/Literature 867
Abstracts of Research in Pastoral Care and Counseling (US ISSN 0733-2599) 2, 974
Abstracts of Supreme Court Decisions Interpreting the Interstate Commerce Act (US ISSN 0571-6373) 649, 1104
Abstracts of the Intermag Conference see International Magnetics Conference. Digests of the Intermag Conference 889
Abstracts of Uppsala Dissertations in Science (SW ISSN 0001-3676) 2, 1003
Abstracts on Cassava (CK ISSN 0120-2898) 2, 38
Abstracts on Crime and Juvenile Delinquency see Criminal Justice Abstracts 373
Abstracts on Criminology and Penology see Criminology & Penology Abstracts 373
Abstracts on Field Beans (CK ISSN 0120-2928) 2, 38
Abstracts on Hygiene see Abstracts on Hygiene and Communicable Diseases 756
Abstracts on Hygiene and Communicable Diseases (UK ISSN 0260-5511) 756, 768
Abstracts on Police Science see Police Science Abstracts 374
Abstracts on Productivity, Technology and Training see Productivity Insights 1073
Abstracts on Science and Technology in Japan: Electronics and Communication (JA ISSN 0910-6510) 345, 461
Abstracts on Science and Technology in Japan: Renewable Energy (JA ISSN 0287-5012) 468

Abstracts on Tropical Agriculture (NE ISSN 0304-5951) 2, 38, 521
Abstracts Strengthening Research Library Resources Program (US) 672
Abu Dhabi. Department of Planning. Statistical Abstract and Yearbook (TS) 938
Abu Dhabi Offical Gazette (TS) 938
Academia Alfonso X el Sabio. Cuadernos Bibliograficos (SP) 121
Academia Boliviana de Ciencias Economicas. Revista (BO) 240
Academia Boliviana de la Lengua. Anales (BO) 689
Academia Brasileira de Literatura. Revista (BL) 713
Academia Campinense de Letras. Publicacoes (BL ISSN 0065-0447) 713
Academia Chilena de Medicina. Boletin Anual (CL) 756
Academia de Ciencias. Anual de Literatura y Linguistica (US) 689, 713
Academia de Ciencias de Cuba. Centro para el Estudio de las Neurosis. Boletin (CU) 1145
Academia de Ciencias de Cuba. Instituto de Geologia. Resumenes, Communicaciones y Notas del Consejo Cientifico (CU) 382
Academia de Ciencias de Cuba. Instituto de Geologia. Resumenes del Consejo Cientifico see Academia de Ciencias de Cuba. Instituto de Geologia. Resumenes, Communicaciones y Notas del Consejo Cientifico 382
Academia de Ciencias de Cuba. Instituto de Geologia. Serie Geologica (CU) 382
Academia de Ciencias de Cuba. Instituto de Oceanologia. Informes Cientificos Tecnicos see Academia de Ciencias de Cuba. Instituto de Oceanologia. Reporte de Investigacion 404
Academia de Ciencias de Cuba. Instituto de Oceanologia. Reporte de Investigacion (CU) 404
Academia de Ciencias de Cuba. Instituto de Oceanologia. Serie Oceanologica (CU ISSN 0567-5782) 1145
Academia de Ciencias de Cuba. Instituto de Oceanologia. Tablas de Mareas (CU) 404
Academia de Ciencias de Cuba. Instituto de Zoologia. Informe Cientifico-Tecnico (CU) 172
Academia de Ciencias de Cuba. Instituto de Zoologia. Miscelanea Zoologica (CU) 172
Academia de Ciencias de la Republica Dominicana. Anuario (DR) 986
Academia de Ciencias Politicas y Sociales. Boletin. (VE) 901, 1005
Academia de Geografia e Historia de Guatemala. Anales (GT ISSN 0252-337X) 540, 602
Academia de Medicina. Boletin see Academia Chilena de Medicina. Boletin Anual 756
Academia de Stiinte Agricole si Silvice. Bulletin (RM) 22, 523
Academia Dominicana de la Historia. Publicaciones (DR ISSN 0567-5871) 602
Academia Espanola, Madrid. Anejos del Boletin (SP ISSN 0065-0455) 713
Academia Guatemalteca de Estudios Genealogicos, Heraldicos e Historicos. Revista (GT ISSN 0065-0463) 534
Academia Hondurena de la Lengua. Boletin (HO ISSN 0065-0471) 689
Academia Mexicana de la Historia. Memorias (MX) 602
Academia Nacional de Bellas Artes. Anuario (AG) 100
Academia Nacional de Ciencias Morales y Politicas. Anales (AG) 901
Academia Nacional de la Historia. Boletin (AG ISSN 0001-382X) 554
Academia Nacional de la Historia. Investigaciones y Ensayos (AG ISSN 0539-242X) 602

Academia Norteamericana de la Lengua Espanola. Boletin (US) 713
Academia Paulista de Letras. Revista (BL ISSN 0001-3846) 689, 713
Academia Pernambucana de Letras. Revista (BL) 713
Academia Portuguesa da Historia. Anais (PO) 574
Academia Provincial de la Historia. Boletin (AG ISSN 0567-6029) 602
Academia Republicii Socialiste Rumania. Institutul de Speologie Emil Racovitza. Travaux see Institut de Speologie Emil Racovitza. Travaux 399
Academia Scientiarum Fennica. Proceedings/Sitzungsberichte see Academia Scientiarum Fennica. Yearbook 986
Academia Scientiarum Fennica. Yearbook/Suomalainen Tiedeakatemia. Vuosikirja (FI ISSN 0356-6927) 986
Academia Scientiarum Hungarica. Acta Chimica see Acta Chimica Hungarica 321
Academia Scientiarum Hungarica. Acta Physica see Acta Physica Hungarica 887
Academia Sinica. Institute of Chemistry. Bulletin (CH ISSN 0001-3927) 321
Academia Sinica. Institute of Modern History. Bulletin/Chung Yang Yen Chiu Yuan. Chiu Tai Shih Yen Chiu So Chi K'an (CH) 554
Academia Sinica. Institute of Physics. Annual Report (CH ISSN 0304-5293) 886
Academiae Analecta. Mededelingen van de Koninklijke Academie voor Wetenschappen, Letteren en Schone Kunsten van Belgie. Series 1: Klasse der Wetenschappen (BE) 986
Academiae Analecta. Mededelingen van de Koninklijke Academie voor Wetenschappen, Letteren en Schone Kunsten van Belgie. Series 2. Klasse der Letteren (BE) 628
Academiae Analecta. Mededelingen van de Koninklijke Academie voor Wetenschappen, Letteren en Schone Kunsten van Belgie. Series 3: Klasse der Schone Kunsten (BE) 100
Academiae Medicae Gedanensis. Annales (PL ISSN 0303-4135) 756
Academic and Administrative Officers at Canadian Universities/Dirigeants et Administrateurs des Universites Canadiennes (CN ISSN 0711-7051) 431
Academic Collective Bargaining Information Service. Monographs (US) 442
Academic Collective Bargaining Information Service. Research Summary (US) 442
Academic Collective Bargaining Information Service. Special Reports (US) 442
Academic Library Statistics see A R L Statistics 687
Academic Life see Akademiska Dzive 501
Academic Press Geology Series (US) 382
Academic Press Series in Cognition and Perception (US) 932
Academic Year Abroad (US) 441
Academica Helvetica (SZ) 431
Academie d'Architecture (FR ISSN 0001-3994) 96
Academie d'Architecture, Paris. Annuaire (FR ISSN 0084-5876) 96
Academie de France a Rome. Correspondance des Directeurs. Nouvelle Serie (IT) 574
Academie de Marine. Communications/Marine Academie. Mededelingen (BE) 1098
Academie des Inscriptions et Belles-Lettres. Etudes et Commentaires (FR ISSN 0065-0544) 80, 554, 689
Academie des Sciences. Annuaire (FR ISSN 0065-0552) 986
Academie des Sciences. Index Biographique des Membres et Correspondants (FR ISSN 0065-0560) 986

Academie des Sports, Paris. Annuaire (FR ISSN 0065-0579) 1032
Academie Francaise. Annuaire (FR ISSN 0065-0587) 713
Academie Internationale d'Histoire des Sciences. Collection des Travaux (GW ISSN 0366-8258) 554, 986
Academie Polonaise des Sciences. Centre d'Archeologie Mediterraneenne. Etudes et Travaux (PL ISSN 0079-3566) 80
Academie Polonaise des Sciences. Centre Scientifique, Paris. Conferences (PL ISSN 0079-3159) 986
Academie Royale de Langue et de Litterature Francaises. Annuaires (BE ISSN 0567-6584) 689, 709
Academie Royale des Sciences, des Lettres et des Beaux-Arts de Belgique. Annuaire (BE) 628, 986
Academie Royale des Sciences, des Lettres et des Beaux-Arts de Belgique. Classe des Beaux-Arts. Memoires (BE) 100
Academie Royale des Sciences, des Lettres et des Beaux-Arts de Belgique. Classe des Lettres et des Science Morales et Politiques. Memoires (BE) 628
Academie Royale des Sciences, des Lettres et des Beaux Arts de Belgique. Classe des Sciences. Memoires (BE) 986
Academie Royale des Sciences, des Lettres et des Beaux Arts de Belgique. Index Biographique des Membres, Correspondants et Associes (BE ISSN 0065-0609) 121
Academie Serbe des Sciences et des Arts. Classe des Sciences Mathematiques et Naturelles. Bulletin. Nouvelle Serie see Academie Serbe des Sciences et des Arts. Classe des Sciences Mathematiques et Naturelles. Bulletin. Sciences Mathematiques 747
Academie Serbe des Sciences et des Arts. Classe des Sciences Mathematiques et Naturelles. Bulletin. Sciences Mathematiques (YU) 114, 747, 986
Academy of American Franciscan History. Bibliographical Series (US ISSN 0567-6630) 980
Academy of American Franciscan History. Documentary Series (US ISSN 0065-0633) 980
Academy of American Franciscan History. Monograph Series (US ISSN 0065-0641) 980
Academy of American Franciscan History. Propaganda Fide Series (US ISSN 0065-065X) 980
Academy of American Poets. Lamont Poetry Selection and Walt Whitman Selection (US) 739
Academy of American Poets. Lamont Poetry Selections see Academy of American Poets. Lamont Poetry Selection and Walt Whitman Selection 739
Academy of Country Music Entertainment Newsletter see A C M E Newsletter 832
Academy of Management. Proceedings (US ISSN 0065-0668) 278
Academy of Natural Sciences of Philadelphia. Monographs (US ISSN 0096-7750) 986
Academy of Natural Sciences of Philadelphia. Proceedings (US ISSN 0097-3157) 986
Academy of Natural Sciences of Philadelphia. Special Publications (US ISSN 0097-3254) 986
Academy of Political Science. Proceedings (US ISSN 0065-0684) 901
Academy of Sciences of the U S S R. Crimean Astrophysical Observatory. Bulletin (US ISSN 0190-2717) 114
Academy of Sciences of the U S S R. Special Astrophysical Observatory-North Caucasus. Bulletin (US ISSN 0190-2709) 114

Academy of the Hebrew Language. Linguistic Studies see Academy of the Hebrew Language. Texts & Studies 689
Academy of the Hebrew Language. Specialized Dictionaries (IS ISSN 0065-0692) 689
Academy of the Hebrew Language. Texts & Studies (IS) 689
Academy of the Social Sciences in Australia. Annual Report (AT) 1005
Acarologie (GW ISSN 0567-672X) 172
Accademia dei Concordi Rovigo. Collana di Musiche (IT) 832
Accademia dei Fisiocritici, Siena. Sezione Medico-Fisica see Accademia delle Scienze di Siena Detta de Fisiocritici. Atti 756
Accademia delle Scienze di Siena Detta de Fisiocritici. Atti (IT ISSN 0390-7783) 22, 756
Accademia delle Scienze di Torino. Memorie. Part 1. Classe di Scienze Fisiche, Matematiche e Naturali (IT ISSN 0373-3033) 747, 986
Accademia Etrusca di Cortona. Annuario (IT ISSN 0065-0730) 574
Accademia Italiana di Scienze Forestali. Annali (IT ISSN 0515-2178) 523
Accademia Ligure di Scienze e Lettere. Atti (IT ISSN 0392-2219) 628, 986
Accademia Medica Lombarda. Atti (IT ISSN 0001-4427) 756
Accademia Medica Pistoiese "Filippo Pacini". Bolletino (IT) 756
Accademia Musicale Chigiana. Quaderni see Chigiana 834
Accademia Nazionale di San Luca. Annuario (IT) 431
Accademia Nazionale Italiana di Entomologia. Rendiconti (IT ISSN 0065-0757) 163
Accademia Patavina di Scienze Lettere ed Arti. Collana Accademica (IT ISSN 0065-0765) 986
Accademia Toscana di Scienze e Lettere La Colombaria. Studi (IT ISSN 0065-0781) 986
Accent on Living Buyer's Guide (US) 1023
Accepted Dental Remedies see Accepted Dental Therapeutics 778
Accepted Dental Therapeutics (US ISSN 0065-079X) 778
Access (Washington) (US) 1145
Access: The Supplementary Index to Periodicals (US ISSN 0095-5698) 2
Accessoirex (FR) 756, 869
Accessories Directory (US) 339
Accident Facts (US ISSN 0148-6039) 952
Accident/Incident Bulletin see U.S. Federal Railroad Administration. Office of Safety. Accident/Incident Bulletin 1095
Accidents in American Mountaineering see Accidents in North American Mountaineering 1044
Accidents in North American Mountaineering (US ISSN 0065-082X) 1044
Accidents to Aircraft on the British Register (UK ISSN 0306-3550) 1087
Accord (US) 278
Accountancy Research Foundation, Melbourne. Accounting and Auditing Research Committee. Research Studies see Australian Accounting Research Foundation. Research Studies 221
Accountants' & Administrators' Handbook (UK ISSN 0263-0974) 220
Accountants' Index (US ISSN 0748-7975) 2, 202
Accounting and Auditing Update Service (US) 220
Accounting & Data Processing Abstracts (UK ISSN 0001-4796) 2, 202, 353
Accounting/Financial Report see Compensation in the Accounting/Financial Field 270
Accounting Journal (MY ISSN 0126-625X) 220

Accredited Colleges of Pharmacy see Accredited Professional Programs of Colleges and Schools of Pharmacy 869
Accredited Institutions of Postsecondary Education (US ISSN 0270-1715) 428
Accredited Institutions of Postsecondary Education and Programs see Accredited Institutions of Postsecondary Education 428
Accredited Journalism and Mass Communication Education (US) 428, 645
Accredited Journalism Education see Accredited Journalism and Mass Communication Education 645
Accredited Professional Programs of Colleges and Schools of Pharmacy (US) 869
Accredited Programs in Architecture (US) 96
Accredited Schools of Architecture see Accredited Programs in Architecture 96
Achsav (IS ISSN 0568-7306) 713
Acid Rain Annual Index (US) 493
Ackerman's Surgical Pathology (US ISSN 0081-9646) 794
Acoplasticos (CK) 900
Acoustical Holography see Acoustical Imaging: Recent Advances in Visualization and Characterization 899
Acoustical Imaging: Recent Advances in Visualization and Characterization (US ISSN 0270-5117) 884, 899
Acoustics Abstracts (UK ISSN 0001-4974) 2, 892
Acrobatics Magazine (UK) 1145
Acronyms and Initialisms Dictionary see Acronyms, Initialisms and Abbreviations Dictionary 689
Acronyms, Initialisms and Abbreviations Dictionary (US ISSN 0270-4404) 689
Acta (Albany) (US ISSN 0361-7491) 554
Acta (Binghamton) (US ISSN 0361-7491) 554
Acta Academiae Aboensis. Series A: Humaniora (FI ISSN 0355-578X) 1145
Acta Academiae Aboensis, Series B: Mathematica et Physica (FI ISSN 0001-5105) 747, 986
Acta Academiae Agriculturae ac Technicae Olstenensis. Aedificatio et Mechanica/Mechanics and Building Engineering (PL ISSN 0860-2956) 181, 491
Acta Academiae Agriculturae ac Technicae Olstenensis. Agricultura/Agriculture (PL ISSN 0860-2832) 22
Acta Academiae Agriculturae ac Technicae Olstenensis. Geodaesia et Ruris Regulatio/Geodesy and Agricultural Arrangement (PL ISSN 0860-262X) 22
Acta Academiae Agriculturae ac Technicae Olstenensis. Oekonomika/Economics (PL ISSN 0860-2948) 190
Acta Academiae Agriculturae ac Technicae Olstenensis. Protectio Aquarum et Piscatoria/Water Conservation and Inland Fisheries (PL ISSN 0860-2611) 507, 1123
Acta Academiae Agriculturae ac Technicae Olstenensis. Technologia Alimentorum/Food Technology (PL ISSN 0860-2859) 517
Acta Academiae Agriculturae ac Technicae Olstenensis. Veterynaria/Veterinary Medicine (PL ISSN 0860-2840) 1120
Acta Academiae Agriculturae ac Technicae Olstenensis. Zootechnica/Zootechnics (PL ISSN 0860-2603) 172
Acta Academiae Regiae Gustavi Adolphi (SW ISSN 0065-0897) 514
Acta Ad Archaeologiam et Artium Historiam Pertinentia (Miscellaneous) (IT ISSN 0333-1512) 80
Acta Ad Archaeologiam et Artium Historiam Pertinentia (Monograph) (IT ISSN 0065-0900) 80

Acta Adriatica (YU ISSN 0001-5113) 404, 507
Acta Agraria et Silvestris. Series Agraria (PL ISSN 0065-0919) 51
Acta Agraria et Silvestris. Series Silvestris (PL ISSN 0065-0927) 523
Acta Agraria et Silvestris. Series Zootechnica (PL ISSN 0065-0935) 64
Acta Agrobotanica (PL ISSN 0065-0951) 22, 404
Acta Albertina Ratisbonensia (GW ISSN 0515-2712) 137, 378
Acta Allergologica. Supplementum see Allergy. Supplementum 773
Acta Anaesthesiologica Scandinavica. Supplementum (DK ISSN 0515-2720) 774
Acta Archaelogica Lundensia: Monographs of Lunds Universitets Historiska Museum. Series in 4 (SW ISSN 0065-1001) 80
Acta Archaelogica Lundensia: Monographs of Lunds Universitets Historiska Museum. Series in 8 (SW ISSN 0065-0994) 80
Acta Archaeologica (DK ISSN 0065-101X) 80
Acta Archaeologica see Arheoloski Vestnik 82
Acta Archaeologica Carpathica (PL ISSN 0001-5229) 80
Acta Archaeologica Lodziensia (PL ISSN 0065-0986) 80
Acta Archaeologica Lovaniensia (BE) 80
Acta Arctica (DK ISSN 0065-1028) 986
Acta Arithmetica (PL ISSN 0065-1036) 747
Acta Baltica (GW ISSN 0567-7289) 574
Acta Baltico - Slavica (PL ISSN 0065-1044) 574
Acta Bernensia: Beitraege zur Praehistorischen, Klassischen und Juengeren Archaeologie (SZ ISSN 0065-1052) 80
Acta Bibliothecae Gothoburgensis see Acta Bibliothecae Universitatis Gothoburgensis 673
Acta Bibliothecae Regiae Stockholmiensis (SW ISSN 0065-1060) 673
Acta Bibliothecae Universitatis Gothoburgensis (SW ISSN 0065-1079) 673
Acta Biologica see Acta Biologica Silesiana 137
Acta Biologica Debrecina (HU ISSN 0567-7327) 137
Acta Biologica Iugoslavica. Serija E: Ichthyologia (YU ISSN 0579-7152) 172
Acta Biologica Paranaense (BL ISSN 0301-2123) 153
Acta Biologica Silesiana (PL ISSN 0860-2441) 137
Acta Botanica see Acta Botanica Slovaca 153
Acta Botanica Barcinonensia (SP ISSN 0210-7597) 153
Acta Botanica Cuba see Acta Botanica Cubana 153
Acta Botanica Cubana (CU) 153
Acta Botanica Horti Bucuriestiensis (RM ISSN 0068-3329) 153, 531
Acta Botanica Islandica/Timarit Um Islenzka Grasafraedi (IC) 153
Acta Botanica Slovaca (CS) 153
Acta Botanica Taiwanica see Taiwania 161
Acta Botanica Venezuelica (VE ISSN 0084-5906) 153
Acta Carsologica/Krasoslovni Zbornik (YU) 378
Acta Chimica Hungarica (HU ISSN 0231-3146) 321
Acta Classica (SA ISSN 0065-1141) 689
Acta Colloquii Didactici Classici (BE) 409, 689
Acta Comeniana. Archiv pro Badani o Zivote a Dile Jana Amose Komenskeho (CS ISSN 0231-5955) 574
Acta Concilium Ophthalmicum (NE ISSN 0065-115X) 785

Acta Dendrobiologica (CS ISSN 0231-5335) 523
Acta Electronica (FR ISSN 0001-558X) 450
Acta Endocrinologica. Supplementum (DK) 780
Acta Endocrinologica Congress. Advance Abstracts (DK ISSN 0300-9750) 768, 780
Acta Endocrinologica Panamericana (AG ISSN 0065-1192) 780
Acta Entomologica (CS) 163
Acta Entomologica Fennica (FI ISSN 0001-561X) 163
Acta Ethnologica Slovaca (CS) 69, 514
Acta Facultatis Forestalis, Zvolen/Vysoka Skola Lesnicka a Drevarska vo Zvolene. Lesnicka Fakulta. Zbornik Vedeckych Prac (CS) 523
Acta Facultatis Medicae Universitatis Brunensis (CS) 137, 756
Acta Facultatis Pharmaceuticae Bohemoslovenicae see Universitas Comeniana. Acta Pharmaceuticae 873
Acta Facultatis Politico-Juridicae Universitatis Scientiarum Budapestiensis de Rolando Eotvos Nominatae (HU ISSN 0524-904X) 650, 901
Acta Faunistica Entomologica (CS ISSN 0554-9264) 163
Acta Forestalia Fennica (FI ISSN 0001-5636) 523
Acta Geobotanica Barcinonensia see Acta Botanica Barcinonensis 153
Acta Geographica Dedrecina (HU ISSN 0567-7475) 382, 540, 802
Acta Geographica Lodziensia (PL ISSN 0065-1249) 540
Acta Geographica Lovaniensia (BE ISSN 0065-1257) 540
Acta Geologica Lilloana (AG ISSN 0567-7513) 383
Acta Geologica Taiwanica (CH ISSN 0065-1265) 383
Acta Germanica (SA) 689
Acta Gerontologica Japonica see Yokufukai Geriatric Journal 552
Acta Herediana (PE ISSN 0567-753X) 539
Acta Histochemica (GE ISSN 0065-1281) 756
Acta Historiae Rerum Naturalium nec non Technicarum (CS ISSN 0231-6005) 378, 574
Acta Historica (IT ISSN 0065-1303) 574
Acta Historica et Archaeologica Mediaevalia (SP) 80
Acta Historica Leopoldina (GE ISSN 0001-5857) 756, 987
Acta Historica Nova (YU) 574
Acta Historica Scientiarum Naturalium et Medicinalium (DK ISSN 0065-1311) 987
Acta Historico-Oeconomica Iugoslaviae (YU) 250
Acta Horticulturae (NE ISSN 0567-7572) 531
Acta Humboldtiana. (GW ISSN 0400-4043) 69, 540
Acta Humboldtiana. Series Geologica, Palaeontologica et Biologica (GW ISSN 0375-5452) 137, 383
Acta Humboldtiana. Series Historica (GW ISSN 0567-7599) 554
Acta Hydrobiologica (PL ISSN 0065-132X) 137
Acta Ichthyologica et Piscatoria (PL) 172
Acta Iranica (NE) 611
Acta Juridica (SA ISSN 0065-1346) 650
Acta Jutlandica (DK ISSN 0065-1354) 967
Acta Linguistica see Acta Linguistica Hafniensia 689
Acta Linguistica Hafniensia (DK ISSN 0374-0463) 689
Acta Linguistica Hafniensia (BE) 409, 689
Acta Literaria (CL ISSN 0716-0909) 713
Acta Manilana (PH ISSN 0065-1370) 153, 167, 329, 774
Acta Marxistica Leninistica. Filozofiai Tanulmanyok (HU ISSN 0324-6302) 875

Acta Marxistica Leninistica. Politikai Gazdasagtan Tanulmanyok (HU ISSN 0324-6256) *190*
Acta Marxistica Leninistica. Tudomanyos Szocializmus Tanulmanyok (HU ISSN 0324-6353) *875*
Acta Mediaevalia (PL) *574, 980*
Acta Medica et Sociologica (BU ISSN 0515-2925) *885, 1023*
Acta Medicae Historiae Patavina (IT ISSN 0065-1389) *756*
Acta Mexicana de Ciencia y Tecnologia(MX ISSN 0567-7785) *987*
Acta Musei Apulensis see Apulum *575*
Acta Musei Moraviae. Scientia Naturales 3: Folia Mendeliana (CS) *166*
Acta Museorum Agriculturae (CS) *22*
Acta Mycologica (PL ISSN 0001-625X) *153*
Acta Naturalia Islandica (IC ISSN 0365-4850) *153, 172, 383*
Acta Neophilologica (YU ISSN 0567-784X) *713*
Acta Neurochirurgica. Supplement see Acta Neurochirurgica. Supplementa *788*
Acta Neurochirurgica. Supplementa (US ISSN 0001-6268) *788, 794*
Acta Neurologica Scandinavica. Supplementum (DK ISSN 0065-1427) *788*
Acta Neuropathologica. Supplement (US ISSN 0065-1435) *788*
Acta Neurovegetativa. Supplement see Journal of Neural Transmission. Supplement *790*
Acta Nuntiaturae Gallicae (VC ISSN 0065-1443) *980*
Acta Oceanographica Taiwanica (CH) *404*
Acta Ophthalmologica. Supplementum (DK ISSN 0065-1451) *785*
Acta Ordinis Sancti Augustini (IT ISSN 0001-642X) *980*
Acta Organologica (GW ISSN 0567-7874) *832*
Acta Orientalia (DK ISSN 0001-6438) *849*
Acta Ornithologica (PL ISSN 0001-6454) *170*
Acta Orthopaedica Scandinavica. Supplementum (DK ISSN 0300-8827) *786*
Acta Oto-Laryngologica. Supplement (DK ISSN 0365-5237) *786*
Acta Oto-Rhino-Laryngologica Belgica (BE ISSN 0001-6497) *786*
Acta Pacis Westphalicae (GW ISSN 0065-146X) *574*
Acta Paedagogica Debrecina (HU ISSN 0567-7912) *409*
Acta Palaeobotanica (PL ISSN 0001-6594) *153, 856*
Acta Pathologica et Microbiologica Scandinavica. Section A: Pathology. Supplementum see Acta Pathologica, Microbiologica et Immunologica Scandinavica. Section A: Pathology. Supplementum *137*
Acta Pathologica et Microbiologica Scandinavica. Section B: Microbiology. Supplementum see Acta Pathologica, Microbiologica et Immunologica Scandinavica. Section B: Microbiology. Supplementum *137*
Acta Pathologica et Microbiologica Scandinavica. Section C: Immunology. Supplementum see Acta Pathologica, Microbiologica et Immunologica Scandinavica. Section C: Immunology. Supplementum *773*
Acta Pathologica, Microbiologica et Immunologica Scandinavica. Section A: Pathology. Supplementum (DK ISSN 0108-0172) *137, 756*
Acta Pathologica, Microbiologica et Immunologica Scandinavica. Section B: Microbiology. Supplementum (DK ISSN 0108-0199) *137, 167*
Acta Pathologica, Microbiologica et Immunologica Scandinavica. Section C: Immunology. Supplementum (DK ISSN 0108-0210) *773*
Acta Pharmacologica et Toxicologica. Supplementum see Pharmacology and Toxicology. Supplementum *872*

Acta Philologica (IT ISSN 0065-1516) *689*
Acta Philologica (PL ISSN 0065-1524) *689*
Acta Philologica Aenipontana (AU ISSN 0065-1532) *689*
Acta Philologica Scandinavica (DK ISSN 0001-6691) *689*
Acta Philosophica et Theologica (IT ISSN 0065-1540) *876, 967*
Acta Philosophica Gothoburgensia (SW ISSN 0283-2380) *876*
Acta Physica Austriaca. Supplement (US ISSN 0065-1559) *887*
Acta Physica et Chimica Debrecina (HU ISSN 0567-7947) *321, 887*
Acta Physica Hungarica (HU ISSN 0231-4428) *887*
Acta Phytogeographica Suecica (SW ISSN 0084-5914) *153, 540*
Acta Phytomedica (GW ISSN 0065-1567) *153*
Acta Poetica (MX ISSN 0185-3082) *739*
Acta Polytechnica Scandinavica. Applied Physics Series (FI ISSN 0355-2721) *895*
Acta Polytechnica Scandinavica. Chemical Technology and Metallurgy(FI ISSN 0001-6853) *321, 796*
Acta Polytechnica Scandinavica. Civil Engineering and Building Construction Series (FI ISSN 0355-2705) *181, 480*
Acta Polytechnica Scandinavica. Electrical Engineering Series (FI ISSN 0001-6845) *450*
Acta Polytechnica Scandinavica. Mathematics and Computer Science Series (FI ISSN 0355-2713) *351, 755*
Acta Polytechnica Scandinavica. Mathematics and Computing Machinery Series see Acta Polytechnica Scandinavica. Mathematics and Computer Science Series *351*
Acta Polytechnica Scandinavica. Mechanical Engineering Series (FI ISSN 0001-687X) *491*
Acta Polytechnica Scandinavica. Physics Including Nucleonics Series see Acta Polytechnica Scandinavica. Applied Physics Series *895*
Acta Praehistorica et Archaeologica (GW ISSN 0341-1184) *80, 574*
Acta Psychiatrica Scandinavica. Supplementum (DK ISSN 0065-1591) *788*
Acta Psychologica - Gothoburgensia (SW ISSN 0065-1605) *932*
Acta Psychologica Taiwanica see Chinese Journal of Psychology *933*
Acta Radiobotanika et Genetika/ Hoshasen Ikushujo Kenkyu Hokoku (JA ISSN 0065-1621) *137, 166*
Acta Regiae Societatis Scientiarum et Litterarum Gothoburgensis. Botanica (SW ISSN 0347-4917) *153*
Acta Regiae Societatis Scientiarum et Litterarum Gothoburgensis. Geophysica (SW ISSN 0072-4815) *398*
Acta Regiae Societatis Scientiarum et Litterarum Gothoburgensis. Humaniora (SW ISSN 0072-4823) *628*
Acta Regiae Societatis Scientiarum et Litterarum Gothoburgensis. Interdisciplinaria (SW ISSN 0347-4925) *628, 987*
Acta Regiae Societatis Scientiarum et Litterarum Gothoburgensis. Zoologica (SW ISSN 0072-4807) *172*
Acta Regiae Societatitis Humaniorum Litteratum Lundensis (SW) *80, 554, 689*
Acta Rei Cretariae Romanae Fautorum. Supplementa (GW) *80*
Acta Sagittariana (GW ISSN 0001-6942) *832*
Acta Scientiarum Socialium (IT ISSN 0065-1656) *1023*
Acta Seminarii Neotestamentici Upsaliensis see Coniectanea Biblica. New Testament Series *969*

Acta Sociologica. Serie Promocion Social (MX) *1023*
Acta Theologica Danica (NE ISSN 0065-1672) *967*
Acta Theriologica (PL ISSN 0001-7051) *172*
Acta Universitatis Carolinae: Biologica (CS ISSN 0001-7124) *137*
Acta Universitatis de Attila Jozsef Nominatae. Acta Antiqua et Archaeologica (HU ISSN 0567-7246) *80, 336*
Acta Universitatis de Attila Jozsef Nominatae. Acta Biologica (HU ISSN 0563-0592) *137*
Acta Universitatis de Attila Jozsef Nominatae. Acta Climatologica (HU ISSN 0563-0614) *802*
Acta Universitatis de Attila Jozsef Nominatae. Acta Historiae Litterarum Hungaricarum (HU ISSN 0586-3708) *713*
Acta Universitatis de Attila Jozsef Nominatae. Acta Historica (HU ISSN 0324-6965) *574, 602*
Acta Universitatis de Attila Jozsef Nominatae. Acta Iuridica et Politica (HU ISSN 0563-0606) *650, 901*
Acta Universitatis de Attila Jozsef Nominatae. Acta Mineralogica - Petrographica (HU ISSN 0365-8066) *813, 862*
Acta Universitatis de Attila Jozsef Nominatae. Acta Romanica (HU ISSN 0567-8099) *689, 713*
Acta Universitatis de Attila Jozsef Nominatae. Papers in English and American Studies (HU ISSN 0230-2780) *689, 713*
Acta Universitatis Debreceniensis de Ludovico Kossuth Nominatea. Series Historica. Egyetemes Torteneti Tanulmanyok (HU ISSN 0418-4556) *574*
Acta Universitatis Debreceniensis de Ludovico Kossuth Nominatea. Series Historica. Magyar Torteneti Tanulmanyok (HU ISSN 0324-5454) *574*
Acta Universitatis Lodziensis: Folia Archaeologica (PL) *80, 409*
Acta Universitatis Lodziensis: Folia Biochimica et Biophysica (PL ISSN 0208-614X) *150, 152, 409*
Acta Universitatis Lodziensis: Folia Botanica (PL) *153, 409*
Acta Universitatis Lodziensis: Folia Chimica (PL) *321, 409*
Acta Universitatis Lodziensis: Folia Ethnographica (PL) *69, 409*
Acta Universitatis Lodziensis: Folia Geographica (PL ISSN 0208-6123) *409, 540*
Acta Universitatis Lodziensis: Folia Historica (PL) *409, 554*
Acta Universitatis Lodziensis: Folia Iuridica (PL) *409, 650*
Acta Universitatis Lodziensis: Folia Limnologica (PL) *402, 409*
Acta Universitatis Lodziensis: Folia Linguistica (PL ISSN 0208-6077) *409, 689*
Acta Universitatis Lodziensis: Folia Litteraria (PL) *409, 713*
Acta Universitatis Lodziensis: Folia Mathematica (PL ISSN 0208-6204) *409, 747*
Acta Universitatis Lodziensis: Folia Oeconomica (PL) *190, 409*
Acta Universitatis Lodziensis: Folia Paedagogica et Psychologica (PL ISSN 0208-6093) *409, 932*
Acta Universitatis Lodziensis: Folia Philosophica (PL ISSN 0208-6107) *409, 876*
Acta Universitatis Lodziensis: Folia Physica (PL ISSN 0208-6190) *409, 887*
Acta Universitatis Lodziensis: Folia Scientiarum Artium et Librorum Politologia (PL) *409, 628*
Acta Universitatis Lodziensis: Folia Sociologica (PL) *409, 1023*
Acta Universitatis Lodziensis: Folia Zoologica et Anthropologica (PL) *69, 172, 409*
Acta Universitatis Nicolai Copernici. Archeologia (PL ISSN 0137-6616) *80*

Acta Universitatis Nicolai Copernici. Biologia (PL ISSN 0208-4449) *137*
Acta Universitatis Nicolai Copernici. Ekonomia (PL ISSN 0208-5305) *190*
Acta Universitatis Nicolai Copernici. Filologia Germanska (PL ISSN 0208-5259) *689*
Acta Universitatis Nicolai Copernici. Filologia Polska (PL ISSN 0208-5321) *689*
Acta Universitatis Nicolai Copernici. Filozofia (PL ISSN 0208-564X) *876*
Acta Universitatis Nicolai Copernici. Geografia (PL ISSN 0208-5291) *541*
Acta Universitatis Nicolai Copernici. Historia (PL ISSN 0137-5830) *574*
Acta Universitatis Nicolai Copernici. Nauki Polityczne (PL ISSN 0137-6667) *901*
Acta Universitatis Nicolai Copernici. Prace Limnologiczne (PL ISSN 0208-5348) *404*
Acta Universitatis Nicolai Copernici. Prawo (PL ISSN 0208-5283) *650*
Acta Universitatis Nicolai Copernici. Socjologia Wychowania (PL ISSN 0208-5267) *409*
Acta Universitatis Nicolai Copernici. Zabytkoznawstwo i Konserwatorstwo(PL ISSN 0208-533X) *363*
Acta Universitatis Ouluensis. Series D. Medica (FI ISSN 0355-3221) *167*
Acta Universitatis Szegediensis. Sectio Philosophica see Acta Universitatis Szegediensis de Attila Jozsef Nominatae. Section Philosophica - Filozofia *876*
Acta Universitatis Szegediensis de Attila Jozsef Nominatae. Acta Bibliothecaria (HU ISSN 0001-7175) *409, 673*
Acta Universitatis Szegediensis de Attila Jozsef Nominatae. Acta Scientiarum Mathematicarum (HU ISSN 0001-6969) *747*
Acta Universitatis Szegediensis de Attila Jozsef Nominatae. Dissertationes Slavicae see Acta Universitatis Szegediensis de Attila Jozsef Nominatae. Dissertationes Slavicae. Sectio Linguistica *689*
Acta Universitatis Szegediensis de Attila Jozsef Nominatae. Dissertationes Slavicae see Acta Universitatis Szegediensis de Attila Jozsef Nominatae. Sectio Historiae Litterarum *690*
Acta Universitatis Szegediensis de Attila Jozsef Nominatae. Dissertationes Slavicae. Sectio Linguistica (HU) *689, 713*
Acta Universitatis Szegediensis de Attila Jozsef Nominatae. Sectio Ethnographica et Linguistica (HU ISSN 0209-9543) *689*
Acta Universitatis Szegediensis de Attila Jozsef Nominatae. Sectio Historiae Litterarum (HU) *690, 713*
Acta Universitatis Szegediensis de Attila Jozsef Nominatae. Sectio Oeconomico-Politica. Politikai Gazdasagtan (HU ISSN 0563-0622) *190*
Acta Universitatis Szegediensis de Attila Jozsef Nominatae. Sectio Paedagogica et Psychologica (HU ISSN 0324-7260) *409, 932*
Acta Universitatis Szegediensis de Attila Jozsef Nominatae. Section Philosophica - Filozofia (HU ISSN 0231-2670) *876*
Acta Universitatis Szegediensis de Attila Jozsef Nominatae. Sectio Scientiae Socialismi. Tudomanyos Szocializmus (HU ISSN 0563-0657) *902*
Acta Universitatis Upsaliensis (SW) *987*
Acta Universitatis Upsaliensis. Historia Litterarum (SW ISSN 0440-9078) *713*
Acta Universitatis Upsaliensis. Studia Germanistisca Upsaliensis (SW) *713*

Acta Universitatis Wratislaviensis. Prace Pedagogiczne (PL ISSN 0137-1096) *409*
Acta Veterinaria Scandinavica. Supplementum (DK ISSN 0065-1699) *1120*
Acta Visbyensia (SW ISSN 0065-1702) *574*
Acta Wasaensia (FI ISSN 0355-2667) *250*
Acta Wexionensia. Serie 1: History & Geography (SW ISSN 0349-0564) *541, 574*
Acta Zoologica Bulgarica (BU ISSN 0324-0770) *172*
Acta Zoologica Cracoviensia (PL ISSN 0065-1710) *172*
Acta Zoologica et Pathologica Antverpiensia (BE ISSN 0001-7280) *172, 1120*
Acta Zoologica Fennica (FI ISSN 0001-7299) *173*
Acta Zoologica Lilloana (AG ISSN 0065-1729) *173*
Actas del Cabildo Colonial de Guayaquil (EC) *602*
Action Committee Against Narcotics. Annual Report see Hong Kong Narcotics Report *376*
Action Report (AT ISSN 0311-2527) *902*
Active Parenting (US) *333*
Activite Economique de la Haute-Normandie see Regards sur l'Economie de la Haute-Normandie *237*
Activites Mineres au Cameroun (CM ISSN 0575-7258) *813*
Activities of O E C D: Report by the Secretary General see Organization for Economic Cooperation and Development. Activities of O.E.C.D.: Report by the Secretary General *263*
Activity Holidays in Britain (UK ISSN 0261-5924) *1105*
The Acts the Shelflife (US) *709*
Actualidad Cultural (CU) *538*
Actualidades (VE) *709*
Actualidades de la Ingenieria Agronomica (CU) *51*
Actualite Rhumatologique Presentee au Praticien (FR ISSN 0065-1818) *793*
Actualites Bibliographiques en Medecine, Pharmacie et Sciences Biomedicales (FR) *1145*
Actualites Nephrologiques (FR ISSN 0073-3326) *795*
Actualites Protozoologiques (US) *162, 173*
Ad Guide: an Advertiser's Guide to Scholarly Periodicals (US ISSN 0065-3586) *14*
Adan E. Treganza Anthropology Museum. Papers (US ISSN 0065-1850) *69*
Adaptations Series (US ISSN 0065-1877) *713*
Addab Journal (SJ ISSN 0302-8844) *628*
Addiction Research Foundation of Ontario. Annual Report (CN) *376*
Addiction Research Foundation of Ontario. Bibliographic Series (CN ISSN 0065-1885) *378*
Addis Ababa Chamber of Commerce. Chamber News (ET) *234*
Addis Ababa University. Library. Annual Report (ET) *673*
Addis Ababa University. University Testing Center. Technical Report (ET ISSN 0072-9388) *409*
Additives for Plastics D.A.T.A. Book (US) *477*
Adelaar (NE ISSN 0001-8139) *341*
Adelaide. Institute of Medical and Veterinary Science. Annual Report of the Council (AT ISSN 0065-1907) *756, 1120*
Adelaide Botanic Gardens. Journal (AT ISSN 0313-4083) *153, 531*
Adelaide City Council Municipal Reference Book (AT) *950*
Adelaide City Council Municipal Yearbook see Adelaide City Council Municipal Reference Book *950*
Adelphia see Adelphia Law Journal *340*
Adelphia Law Journal (US) *340, 650*

Adhesion Society of Japan. Journal/Nihon Setchaku Kyokaishi (JA ISSN 0001-8201) *900*
Adhesives Age (US ISSN 0001-821X) *477*
Adhesives Age Directory (US) *477*
Adhesives D.A.T.A. Book (US) *887*
Adhesives Directory (UK ISSN 0305-3199) *1067*
Adhesives Euro-Guide (UK) *301, 321*
Adhesives Red Book see Adhesives Age Directory *477*
Adiestramento para el Desarrollo Agropecuario y Rural see Training for Agriculture and Rural Development *427*
Administracao-Geral do Porto de Lisboa. Relatorio (PO) *1098*
Administratief en Gerechtelijk Jaarboek voor Belgie see Annuaire Administratif et Judiciaire de Belgique *939*
Administration in Kenya see Kenya Institute of Administration. Journal *943*
Administration of Justice Memoranda (US) *650*
Administration of Juvenile Justice in California (US) *369, 650*
Administration of the Employee Retirement Income Security Act see U.S. Department of Labor. Employee Retirement Income Security Act. Report to Congress *276*
Administration of the Marine Mammal Protection Act of 1972 see Marine Mammal Protection Act of 1972 Annual Report *366*
Administrative Affairs in Bangladesh (BG) *938*
Administrative Digest Business Directory see Office Product News Directory *281*
Administrative Directory of College and University Computer Science Departments and Computer Centers see A C M Administrative Directory of College and University Computer Science/Data Processing Programs and Computer Facilities *351*
Administrative Law Decisions (AT ISSN 0726-5816) *650*
Administrative Law Reports (CN) *650*
Administrative Officials Classified by Functions see State Administrative Officials (Classified by Functions) *946*
Administrative Sciences Association of Canada. Proceedings, Annual Conference (CN) *278*
Admission Requirements of American Dental Schools see Admission Requirements of U S and Canadian Dental Schools *778*
Admission Requirements of American Medical Colleges, Including Canada see Medical School Admission Requirements, United States and Canada *437*
Admission Requirements of U S and Canadian Dental Schools (US ISSN 0091-729X) *428, 778*
Adolescent Psychiatry (US ISSN 0065-2008) *788*
Adresar Ukraintsiv u Vilnomu Sviti see A D U K *914*
Adressbuch fuer den Deutschsprachigen Buchhandel (GW ISSN 0065-2032) *959*
Adresseloese Postforsendelser (DK ISSN 0107-4350) *346*
Adresserede Brevforsendelser (DK ISSN 0107-4369) *346*
Adrichalut (IS ISSN 0334-794X) *96*
Adult & Community Education Organizations & Leaders Directory (US) *426*
Adult Planbook (US ISSN 0149-998X) *978*
Advance see Aberlour Child Care Trust. Newsletter *1145*
Advance Locator for Capitol Hill (US) *902, 938*
Advanced Manufacturing Technology (UK) *282, 491*
Advanced Series in Agricultural Sciences (US ISSN 0172-4207) *22*
Advanced Textbooks in Economics (NE) *190*

Advanced Water Conference. Proceedings. (US) *1123*
Advancement in Test Measurement. Proceedings (US ISSN 0568-0204) *485*
Advancement 2: Literature, Media Arts, Opera-Musical Theatre, Visual Arts (US) *100, 713, 1076*
Advances and Technical Standards in Neurosurgery (US ISSN 0095-4829) *788, 794*
Advances in Accounting (US) *220*
Advances in Activation Analysis (US ISSN 0065-2091) *1145*
Advances in Aerosol Physics (US) *887*
Advances in Agronomy (US ISSN 0065-2113) *22*
Advances in Agronomy and Crop Science/Fortschritte im Acker- und Pflanzenbau (GW ISSN 0301-2735) *51*
Advances in Alcohol & Substance Abuse (US ISSN 0270-3106) *376*
Advances in Alicyclic Chemistry (US ISSN 0065-2121) *329*
Advances in Anatomy, Embryology and Cell Biology (US ISSN 0301-5556) *137, 162*
Advances in Anesthesia (US ISSN 0737-6146) *774*
Advances in Animal Breeding and Genetics/Fortschritte der Tierzuetung und Zuechtungsbiologie (GW ISSN 0344-208X) *166*
Advances in Animal Physiology and Animal Nutrition see Fortschritte in der Tierphysiologie und Tierernaehrung *66*
Advances in Applied Business Strategy (US) *278*
Advances in Applied Developmental Psychology (US ISSN 0748-8572) *932*
Advances in Applied Mechanics (US ISSN 0065-2156) *485, 894*
Advances in Applied Microbiology (US ISSN 0065-2164) *167*
Advances in Applied Microeconomics (US ISSN 0278-0984) *250*
Advances in Applied Social Psychology(US) *932, 1023*
Advances in Aquatic Microbiology (US ISSN 0161-8954) *167*
Advances in Archaeological Method and Theory (US ISSN 0162-8003) *80*
Advances in Artificial Intelligence see Ablex Series in Artificial Intelligence *354*
Advances in Atomic and Molecular Physics (US ISSN 0065-2199) *895*
Advances in Audiology (SZ ISSN 0254-8747) *787*
Advances in Automation and Robotics (US) *354, 355*
Advances in Behavioral Biology (US) *932*
Advances in Behavioral Economics (US ISSN 0890-0159) *241, 932*
Advances in Behavioral Pediatrics see Advances in Developmental and Behavioral Pediatrics *787*
Advances in Behavioral Pharmacology (US ISSN 0147-071X) *869*
Advances in Biochemical Engineering (US ISSN 0065-2210) *150, 469*
Advances in Biochemical Psychopharmacology (US ISSN 0065-2229) *788, 869*
Advances in Bioengineering (US ISSN 0360-9960) *137, 469*
Advances in Biological and Medical Physics (US ISSN 0065-2245) *152, 756*
Advances in Biological Psychiatry (SZ ISSN 0378-7354) *788*
Advances in Biomedical Computing Series (US ISSN 0888-2215) *484, 778*
Advances in Botanical Research (US ISSN 0065-2296) *154*
Advances in Cancer Chemotherapy (US ISSN 0190-4817) *869*
Advances in Cancer Research (US ISSN 0065-230X) *774*
Advances in Carbohydrate Chemistry see Advances in Carbohydrate Chemistry and Biochemistry *329*

Advances in Carbohydrate Chemistry and Biochemistry (US ISSN 0065-2318) *150, 329*
Advances in Cardiology (SZ ISSN 0065-2326) *776*
Advances in Cardiovascular Physics (SZ ISSN 0378-6900) *776*
Advances in Catalysis (US ISSN 0360-0564) *331*
Advances in Cell Culture (US ISSN 0275-6358) *162*
Advances in Cellular Neurobiology (US ISSN 0270-0794) *173*
Advances in Chemical Engineering (US ISSN 0065-2377) *477*
Advances in Chemical Physics (US ISSN 0065-2385) *331, 887*
Advances in Chemistry Series (US ISSN 0065-2393) *321*
Advances in Child Development and Behavior (US ISSN 0065-2407) *787, 932*
Advances in Chromatography (US ISSN 0065-2415) *326*
Advances in Clinical Chemistry (US ISSN 0065-2423) *150, 869*
Advances in Clinical Enzymology (SZ ISSN 0250-4197) *150*
Advances in Comparative Physiology and Biochemistry (US ISSN 0065-244X) *150, 171*
Advances in Computer Programming Management (US ISSN 0196-870X) *357, 360*
Advances in Computer Security Management (US ISSN 0197-1514) *358, 374*
Advances in Computers (US ISSN 0065-2458) *351*
Advances in Computing Research (US) *351*
Advances in Consumer Research (US ISSN 0098-9258) *282, 368*
Advances in Control Systems see Control and Dynamic Systems: Advances in Theory and Applications *18*
Advances in Corrosion Science and Technology (US ISSN 0065-2474) *485*
Advances in Cryogenic Engineering (US ISSN 0065-2482) *469, 894*
Advances in Cyclic Nucleotide Research see Advances in Cyclic Nucleotide Research and Protein Phosphorylation Research *150*
Advances in Cyclic Nucleotide Research and Protein Phosphorylation Research (US) *150*
Advances in Cytopharmacology (US ISSN 0084-5949) *162, 869*
Advances in Data Base Management (US ISSN 0196-8718) *360*
Advances in Data Communications Management (US ISSN 0197-1476) *360*
Advances in Data Processing Management (US ISSN 0196-8696) *360*
Advances in Dermatology (US) *780*
Advances in Descriptive Psychology (US ISSN 0276-9913) *932*
Advances in Developmental and Behavioral Pediatrics (US) *787*
Advances in Developmental Psychology(US ISSN 0275-3049) *932*
Advances in Discourse Processes (US) *690*
Advances in Distributed Processing Management (US ISSN 0197-1433) *360*
Advances in Drug Research (US ISSN 0065-2490) *869*
Advances in Drying (US ISSN 0272-4790) *477, 491, 858*
Advances in Dynamic Stereochemistry (UK) *321*
Advances in Early Education and Day Care (US ISSN 0270-4021) *409*
Advances in Earth and Planetary Sciences (NE) *383*
Advances in Ecological Research (US ISSN 0065-2504) *493*
Advances in Econometrics (US ISSN 0731-9053) *190*
Advances in Economic Botany (US ISSN 0741-8280) *154*

Advances in Electrochemistry and Electrochemical Engineering (US ISSN 0567-9907) 328, 477
Advances in Electronics and Electron Physics (US ISSN 0065-2539) 450, 887
Advances in Engineering (US ISSN 0065-2555) 1090
Advances in Environmental Psychology(US) 493, 932
Advances in Environmental Science and Engineering (US ISSN 0141-8106) 493, 1067
Advances in Environmental Science and Technology (US ISSN 0065-2563) 493
Advances in Enzyme Regulation (US ISSN 0065-2571) 171, 756
Advances in Enzymology and Related Areas of Molecular Biology (US ISSN 0065-258X) 150
Advances in Enzymology and Related Subjects of Biochemistry see Advances in Enzymology and Related Areas of Molecular Biology 150
Advances in Ethology/Fortschritte der Verhaltensforschung (GW ISSN 0301-2808) 173
Advances in Experimental Medicine and Biology (US ISSN 0065-2598) 137, 756
Advances in Experimental Social Psychology (US ISSN 0065-2601) 932, 1023
Advances in Family Intervention, Assessment and Theory (US ISSN 0270-9228) 932, 1023
Advances in Financial Planning and Forecasting (US) 222
Advances in Fisheries Oceanography (JA) 173, 404
Advances in Food Research (US ISSN 0065-2628) 517
Advances in Forensic Psychology and Psychiatry (US ISSN 0747-6353) 788, 932
Advances in General and Cellular Pharmacology (US ISSN 0146-3810) 1145
Advances in Genetics (US ISSN 0065-2660) 166
Advances in Geophysical Data Processing (US) 351, 383
Advances in Geophysics (US ISSN 0065-2687) 398
Advances in Gerontological Research (US ISSN 0065-2709) 551
Advances in Group Processes (US) 1023
Advances in Health Economics and Health Services Research (US ISSN 0731-2199) 885
Advances in Health Education (US ISSN 0890-4073) 446, 885, 932
Advances in Heat Transfer (US ISSN 0065-2717) 894
Advances in Heterocyclic Chemistry (US ISSN 0065-2725) 329
Advances in High-Tech Materials (US ISSN 0890-2771) 1067
Advances in High Temperature Chemistry (US ISSN 0065-2741) 331
Advances in Human/Computer Interaction (US ISSN 0748-8602) 355
Advances in Human Fertility & Reproductive Endocrinology (US) 780, 784
Advances in Human Genetics (US ISSN 0065-275X) 166
Advances in Human Psychopharmacology (US ISSN 0272-068X) 788, 869
Advances in Hydroscience (US ISSN 0065-2768) 402
Advances in Image Pickup and Display (US ISSN 0094-7032) 450
Advances in Immunity and Cancer Therapy (US) 774
Advances in Immunology (US ISSN 0065-2776) 173
Advances in Inclusion Science (NE) 329
Advances in Industrial and Labor Relations (US) 269
Advances in Infancy Research (US ISSN 0732-9598) 787, 932

Advances in Inflammation Research (US ISSN 0197-8322) 756
Advances in Information Processing in Organizations (US) 361
Advances in Information Systems Science (US ISSN 0065-2784) 1145
Advances in Inorganic and Bioinorganic Mechanisms (US) 328
Advances in Inorganic Chemistry and Radiochemistry (US ISSN 0065-2792) 321, 328
Advances in Insect Physiology (US ISSN 0065-2806) 163
Advances in Instructional Psychology (US ISSN 0163-5379) 932
Advances in Instrumentation (US ISSN 0065-2814) 636
Advances in Internal Medicine (US ISSN 0065-2822) 756
Advances in Internal Medicine and Pediatrics see Ergebnisse der Inneren Medizin und Kinderheilkunde. New Series 760
Advances in International Comparative Management (US) 253, 278
Advances in International Maternal and Child Health (UK) 787
Advances in Irrigation (US ISSN 0275-7915) 52
Advances in Large Scale Systems (US) 358
Advances in Law and Child Development (US ISSN 0732-3565) 333, 650
Advances in Learning and Behavioral Disabilities (US) 333, 444, 932
Advances in Librarianship (US ISSN 0065-2830) 673
Advances in Library Administration and Organization (US ISSN 0732-0671) 673
Advances in Limnology see Ergebnisse der Limnologie 402
Advances in Lipid Research (US ISSN 0065-2849) 150
Advances in Liquid Crystals (US) 327
Advances in Magnetic Resonance (US ISSN 0065-2873) 450, 887
Advances in Man-Machine Systems Research (US) 358
Advances in Marine Biology (US ISSN 0065-2881) 137, 404
Advances in Meat Research Series (US) 64
Advances in Medical Social Science: Health and Illness as Viewed by Anthropology, Geography, History, Psychology and Sociology (US ISSN 0275-5742) 756, 1005
Advances in Metabolic Disorders (US ISSN 0065-2903) 780
Advances in Metabolic Disorders. Supplements see Advances in Metabolic Disorders 780
Advances in Microbial Physiology (US ISSN 0065-2911) 167
Advances in Microbioal Ecology (US) 167
Advances in Microbiology of the Sea see Advances in Aquatic Microbiology 167
Advances in Microcirculation (SZ ISSN 0065-2938) 776
Advances in Microwaves (US ISSN 0065-2946) 450, 887
Advances in Molten Salt Chemistry (US ISSN 0065-2954) 328
Advances in Motivation and Achievement (US) 932
Advances in Motor Development Research (US) 333, 551, 885
Advances in Nephrology (US) 795
Advances in Nephrology from the Necker Hospital see Advances in Nephrology 795
Advances in Neural and Behavioral Development (US ISSN 8755-0032) 932
Advances in Neurochemistry (US ISSN 0098-6089) 151, 788
Advances in Neurogerontology (US) 551, 788
Advances in Neurology (US ISSN 0091-3952) 788
Advances in Neurosurgery (US ISSN 0302-2366) 788, 794
Advances in Nonprofit Marketing (US) 282

Advances in Nuclear Physics (US ISSN 0065-2970) 895
Advances in Nuclear Science and Technology (US ISSN 0065-2989) 469, 895
Advances in Nutritional Research (US ISSN 0149-9483) 845
Advances in Obstetrics and Gynaecology see Contributions to Gynecology and Obstetrics 785
Advances in Ophthalmic Plastic & Reconstructive Surgery (US ISSN 0276-3508) 785
Advances in Ophthalmology see Developments in Ophthalmology 785
Advances in Optical and Electron Microscopy (UK ISSN 0065-3012) 169, 899
Advances in Oral Biology (US ISSN 0065-3020) 778
Advances in Organic Coatings Science and Technology (US) 329, 855
Advances in Organometallic Chemistry (US ISSN 0065-3055) 329
Advances in Oto-Rhino-Laryngology (SZ ISSN 0065-3071) 787
Advances in Pain Research and Therapy (US ISSN 0146-0722) 788
Advances in Parapsychological Research (US) 1145
Advances in Parasitology (US ISSN 0065-308X) 173
Advances in Parenteral Sciences (US) 756
Advances in Pediatrics (US ISSN 0065-3101) 787
Advances in Personality Assessment (US ISSN 0278-2367) 788, 932
Advances in Pharmaceutical Sciences (US ISSN 0065-3136) 869
Advances in Pharmacology and Chemotherapy (US ISSN 0065-3144) 869
Advances in Pharmacotherapy (SZ ISSN 0253-2093) 869
Advances in Photochemistry (US ISSN 0065-3152) 331
Advances in Physical Geochemistry (US ISSN 0722-3269) 383
Advances in Physical Organic Chemistry (US ISSN 0065-3160) 331
Advances in Plant Breeding/Fortschritte der Pflanzenzeuchtung (GW ISSN 0301-2727) 52
Advances in Plant Pathology (US) 154
Advances in Plastic and Reconstructive Surgery (US) 794
Advances in Political Science (US) 902
Advances in Pollen Spore Research (II ISSN 0376-480X) 154
Advances in Polyamine Research (US ISSN 0160-2179) 151, 756
Advances in Polymer Science/ Fortschritte der Hochpolymeren-Forschung (US ISSN 0065-3195) 329, 477
Advances in Probability see Advances in Probability and Related Topics 747
Advances in Probability and Related Topics (US) 747
Advances in Prostaglandin and Thromboxane Research (US ISSN 0361-5952) 780
Advances in Protein Chemistry (US ISSN 0065-3233) 151
Advances in Psychological Assessment (US ISSN 0065-325X) 1145
Advances in Psychosomatic Medicine (SZ ISSN 0065-3268) 788
Advances in Quantum Chemistry (US ISSN 0065-3276) 321
Advances in R & D (US ISSN 0890-2763) 1067
Advances in Radiation Biology (US ISSN 0065-3292) 152
Advances in Reading/Language Research (US) 410
Advances in Research and Technology of Seeds (NE ISSN 0376-7329) 154
Advances in Risk Analysis (US) 493, 952, 1048
Advances in Satellite Communications Series (US ISSN 0888-2207) 346, 484
Advances in School Psychology (US ISSN 0270-3920) 932

Advances in Sensor Technology (US ISSN 0890-2755) 354, 1067
Advances in Shock Research (US ISSN 0195-878X) 756
Advances in Social Psychology (US) 1145
Advances in Software Engineering (US) 362
Advances in Soil Sciences (US) 378
Advances in Solar Energy. An Annual Review of Research and Development (US ISSN 0731-8618) 463
Advances in Solid State Technology (NE) 331, 887
Advances in Space Science and Technology (US ISSN 0065-3373) 17
Advances in Space Science and Technology. Supplement see Advances in Space Science and Technology 17
Advances in Special Education (US ISSN 0270-4013) 444
Advances in Statistical Analysis and Statistical Computing (US) 351, 1048
Advances in Stereoencephalotomy (SZ ISSN 0065-3381) 788
Advances in Steroid Biochemistry see Advances in Steroid Biochemistry and Pharmacology (Year) 151
Advances in Steroid Biochemistry and Pharmacology (Year) (US) 151, 869
Advances in Strategic Management (US) 278
Advances in Substance Abuse: Behavioral and Biological Research (US ISSN 0272-1740) 376
Advances in Surgery (US ISSN 0065-3411) 794
Advances in Teacher Education (US ISSN 0748-0067) 446
Advances in Test Anxiety Research (US) 410, 932
Advances in the Astronautical Sciences (US ISSN 0065-3438) 17
Advances in the Astronautical Sciences. Supplement see Science and Technology Series 21
Advances in the Economics of Energy and Resources (US ISSN 0192-558X) 463
Advances in the Psychology of Human Intelligence (US ISSN 0278-2359) 446, 932
Advances in the Study of Behavior (US ISSN 0065-3454) 932
Advances in the Study of Communication and Affect. (US) 932, 1023
Advances in Transport Processes (US ISSN 0271-2334) 477
Advances in Trauma (US) 786
Advances in Urethane Science and Technology (US ISSN 0044-6378) 329, 477, 900
Advances in V L S I and Computer Systems (US ISSN 0888-224X) 361
Advances in Vegetation Science (NE) 154
Advances in Verterinary Medicine/ Fortschritte der Veterinaermedizin (GW ISSN 0301-2794) 1120
Advances in Veterinary Science and Comparative Medicine (US ISSN 0065-3519) 1120
Advances in Virus Research (US ISSN 0065-3527) 167, 777
Advances in World Archaeology (US ISSN 0733-5121) 80
Advances in Writing Research (US ISSN 8756-1271) 713
Advances in X-Ray Analysis (US ISSN 0069-8490) 485, 792, 796, 987, 1067
Adventure Book see Sobek's Adventure Vacation 1116
Adventure Holidays (UK) 1105
Adventure Travel (New York) see Adventure Travel North America 1105
Adventure Travel North America (US) 1105
Adventures in Western New York History (US ISSN 0001-883X) 410, 602
Advertiser's Annual (UK ISSN 0065-3578) 14

Advertising Age Yearbook (US ISSN 0276-9751) *14*
Advertising and Press Annual of Southern Africa *see* Promadata *647*
Advertising Directions *see* Creativity *15*
Advertising Law Anthology (US) *14, 650*
Advertising Specialty Register: Product Research and Source Data (US) *14*
Advertising Standards Authority, London. Annual Report (UK ISSN 0065-3659) *14*
Advocacy Institute. Proceedings (US ISSN 0462-3134) *650*
Advocate (CN ISSN 0382-456X) *650*
Adyar Library Bulletin *see* Brahmavidya *850*
AEB *see* Annual Egyptological Bibliography *562*
Aegypten und Altes Testament (GW ISSN 0720-9061) *849*
Aegyptica Helvetica (SZ) *80*
Aegyptologische Abhandlungen (GW ISSN 0568-0476) *850*
Aegyptologische Forschungen (US) *80, 100, 611*
Aeldre Danske Tingboeger (DK ISSN 0065-3667) *574*
Aequatoria *see* Annales Aequatoria *69*
Aerial Archaeology (UK ISSN 0140-9220) *80, 884*
Aero (BL) *17*
Aeromedical Reviews *see* U.S. Air Force. School of Aerospace Medicine. Standard Technical Report Series *767*
Aeronautica Meridiana (SA ISSN 0257-8573) *17*
Aeronautical Research and Test Institute Reports *see* A R T I Reports *17*
Aeronautical Society of South Africa. Journal *see* Aeronautica Meridiana *17*
Aeronavegacion Comercial Argentina (AG ISSN 0325-9293) *17*
Aeronomica Acta (BE ISSN 0065-3713) *17*
Aeroports de Paris. Rapport du Conseil d'Administration (FR ISSN 0065-3721) *1087*
Aeroports de Paris. Service Statistique. Statistique de Trafic (FR ISSN 0078-947X) *1087*
Aeroports de Paris. Trafic des Principaux Aeroports Mondiaux (FR) *1087*
Aerosol Review (UK ISSN 0568-062X) *301*
Aerospace Defense Markets and Technology (US) *2, 813*
Aerospace Facts and Figures (US) *22*
Aerospace Industries Annual Report (US) *17*
Aerospace Industry Yearbook (JA) *17*
Aerospace Medicine & Biology (NASA) (US) *137, 756*
Aerospace References in Medicine and Biology *see* Aerospace Medicine & Biology (NASA) *756*
Aerospace Testing Seminar. Proceedings (US) *17, 493, 1067*
Aerospaco (BL) *17*
Aestetik (DK ISSN 0106-9918) *118, 118*
Aesthetics in Music Series (US) *832*
Aesthetics Magazine *see* Revista de Estetica *109*
Aethiopistische Forschungen (GW ISSN 0170-3196) *850*
Affaires et Gens d'Affaires (FR ISSN 0065-3799) *222, 574*
Affiliates & Offices of Japanese Firms in the U.S.A. Directory (US) *301*
Affirmation (CN ISSN 0441-4128) *912*
Affirmative Action Compliance Manual for Federal Contractors (US ISSN 0148-8147) *269*
Afghan Studies *see* South Asian Studies *613*
Afghanistan. Ministry of Justice. Official Gazette/Rasmi Jaridah (AF) *650*
Afghanistan Republic Annual (AF ISSN 0304-6133) *568*
AFinLA Yearbook *see* A Fin L A Yearbook *689*

Africa (BL ISSN 0100-8153) *564*
Africa Bibliography (UK ISSN 0266-6731) *121*
Africa Contemporary Record. Annual Survey and Documents (US ISSN 0065-3845) *564*
Africa Cooperative Savings and Credit Association. Annual Report *see* African Confederation of Savings and Credit Cooperatives. Annual Report *222*
Africa Development Research Annual/ Annuaire des Recherches Africaines sur les Problemes de Developpement *see* Register Development Research Projects Africa *264*
Africa Guide *see* Africa Review *241*
Africa in the Modern World (US) *564, 1005*
Africa Index *see* Africa Index to Continental Periodical Literature *2*
Africa Index to Continental Periodical Literature (UK) *2*
Africa Institute. Occasional Publications(SA) *241, 564*
Africa Institute. Special Publications *see* Africa Institute. Occasional Publications *564*
Africa Institute of South Africa. Occasional Papers *see* Africa Institute. Occasional Publications *564*
Africa International (KE) *564*
Africa Review (UK) *241, 902*
Africa Seminar: Collected Papers (SA ISSN 0250-0116) *250, 564*
Africa Since Independence Stamp Catalogue (UK ISSN 0142-9868) *874*
Africa South of the Sahara (UK ISSN 0065-3896) *241, 541, 564*
Africa South of the Sahara: Index to Periodical Literature. Supplements (US) *562*
African Adult Education Association. Journal (KE) *426*
African - American Heritage Series (US) *501, 602*
African - American Issues Center Discussion Papers (US) *1005*
African American Museums Association. Annual Meeting Report (US) *826*
African Archaeological Review (UK ISSN 0263-0338) *80, 564*
African Bibliographic Center, Washington D.C. Special Bibliographic Series *see* African Special Bibliographic Series *562*
African Bibliography Series (US) *121, 562*
African Book World and Press: A Directory (UK) *959*
African Books in Print (UK ISSN 0306-9516) *121*
African Confederation of Savings and Credit Cooperatives. Annual Report (KE) *222*
African Development Bank. Annual Report *see* African Development Bank. Report by the Board of Directors *261*
African Development Bank. Report by the Board of Directors/Banque Africaine de Developpement. Rapport du Conseil d'Administration(IV ISSN 0568-1308) *261*
African Development Fund. Annual Report/Fonds Africain de Developpement. Rapport Annuel (IV) *261*
African Documents Series (US) *565*
African Economic History (US ISSN 0145-2258) *250*
African Economic History Review *see* African Economic History *250*
African Environment (SG) *493*
African Environment. Occasional Papers/Etudes et Recherches (SG) *493*
African Environment Special Reports (UK ISSN 0309-345X) *493*
African Historian (NR ISSN 0568-1332) *565*
African Historical Dictionaries (US) *565*

African Institute for Economic Development and Planning. Programme (SG) *261*
African Institute for Economic Development and Planning. Series in Economic and Social Development/ Institut Africain de Developpement Economique et de Planification. Collection d'Etudes sur le Developpement Economique et Social (SG) *261*
African Law Studies *see* Journal of Legal Pluralism and Unofficial Law *658*
African Literature Today (US ISSN 0065-4000) *1146*
African Music (SA ISSN 0065-4019) *832*
African Music Society. Newsletter *see* African Music *832*
African Musicology (KE) *832*
African News Sheet (SZ ISSN 0379-7074) *637*
African Philosophical Journal *see* Cahiers Philosophiques Africains *877*
African Regional Trade Union Conference. Report (BE ISSN 0065-4027) *648*
African Research Studies (US) *565, 1005*
African Social Security Series *see* African News Sheet *637*
African Special Bibliographic Series (US ISSN 0749-2308) *121, 562*
African Studies (US) *501*
African Studies (CH) *565*
African Studies Association Papers *see* A S A Papers *501*
African Studies Series (UK ISSN 0065-406X) *565*
African Study Monographs (JA ISSN 0285-1601) *22, 69*
African Study Monographs. Supplementary Issue (JA ISSN 0286-9667) *22, 69*
African Trade/Commerce Africain (UN) *239, 253*
African Trader/Commercant Africain *see* African Trade *253*
Africana Gandensia (BE) *69*
Africana Journal (US ISSN 0095-1080) *121, 673*
Africana Library Journal *see* Africana Journal *121*
Africana Society of Pretoria. Journal (SA) *565*
Africana Society of Pretoria. Yearbook/ Africana Vereniging van Pretoria. Jaarboek (SA) *565*
Africana Vereniging van Pretoria. Jaarboek *see* Africana Society of Pretoria. Yearbook *565*
Africanus (SA ISSN 0304-615X) *902, 938*
Afrika Studiecentrum. Documentatieblad *see* Documentatieblad: The Abstracts Journal of the African Studies Centre Leiden *563*
Afrika Studien (GW) *190*
Afrikaans Duitse Kultuurunie (S W A) Booklet: Facts and Figures *see* A.D.K. Booklet: Facts and Figures *564*
Afrikanisches Recht. Jahrbuch (GW ISSN 0722-2181) *650*
Afrique et Philosophie (ZA) *876*
Afro-American Affairs (US) *501*
Afro-American Culture and Society Monograph Series (US ISSN 0882-5297) *501, 1005*
Afro-American Music Opportunities Association. Resource Papers (US) *832*
Afro-Asia (BL ISSN 0002-0591) *554, 690, 850*
Afro-Asian Peoples' Conference. Proceedings (UA ISSN 0065-4191) *565, 568*
Afro-Asian Peoples' Solidarity Organization. Council. Documents of the Session (UA ISSN 0078-6233) *565, 568*
Afro-Asian Publications (UA ISSN 0515-6327) *568*
Afro Technical Papers *see* A F R O Technical Papers *952*

Afroasiatic Dialects (US ISSN 0732-6416) *690*
Afroasiatic Linguistics (US ISSN 0362-3637) *690*
Afskrivning m.v. *see* Skatten. Erhverv *299*
After School (UK) *428*
Aftermarket Business A P A A Show Daily (US) *190*
Aftermarket Business Big "I" Show Daily (US) *190*
Aftermarket Business Buyer's Guide (US) *282, 1090*
Afurika Kenkyu *see* Journal of African Studies *566*
Ag'Chem Business (FR) *52*
Age of Johnson (US ISSN 0884-5816) *554, 713*
Agence pour la Securite de la Navigation Aerienne en Afrique et a Madagascar. Direction de l'Exploitation Meteorologique. Publications. Serie 1 (SG ISSN 0065-4248) *802*
Agence pour la Securite de la Navigation Aerienne en Afrique et a Madagascar. Direction de l'Exploitation Meteorologique. Publications. Serie 2 (SG ISSN 0084-6015) *802*
Agenda American Almanac (Year) (CN) *1042*
Agenda de la Quincaillerie (FR ISSN 0065-4256) *796*
Agenda del Dirigente di Azienda (IT ISSN 0065-4264) *190*
Agenda dello Sport (IT) *1037*
Agenda des Armees (FR) *810*
Agenda dos Criadores e Agricultores (BL) *22*
Agenda Edizione Guida Monaci. S.p.A.(IT) *278*
Agenda Estadistica (MX) *1048*
Agenda/Guida dell'Ospitalita (IT) *619*
Agenda Nautica (IT) *1098*
Agent (UK) *709*
Agent's and Buyer's Guide (US ISSN 0065-4272) *637*
Agent's Hotel Gazetteer: America (UK) *619, 1105*
Agent's Hotel Gazetteer: Cities of Europe (UK) *619*
Agent's Hotel Gazetteer: Resorts *see* Agent's Hotel Gazetteer: Resorts of Europe *619*
Agent's Hotel Gazetteer: Resorts of Europe (UK) *619, 1106*
Agent's Hotel Gazetteer: Tourist Cities *see* Agent's Hotel Gazetteer: Cities of Europe *619*
Agevolazioni e Vantaggi per i Pescatori Federati (IT) *1044*
Aging (New York) (US ISSN 0361-0179) *551*
AgLink Index *see* AgLink Index and Catalogue *38*
AgLink Index and Catalogue (NZ ISSN 0112-2320) *22, 38*
AgLink Leaflets (NZ) *22, 154*
Agora (Ravenna) (IT) *876, 1023*
Agrarian Development Studies (UK ISSN 0065-4337) *44*
Agrarirodalmi Szemle (HU ISSN 0002-1067) *2, 38*
Agrarmarkt-Studien (GW ISSN 0065-4345) *44*
Agrarsoziale Gesellschaft. Arbeitsbericht *see* Agrarsoziale Gesellschaft. Geschaefts- und Arbeitsbericht *1023*
Agrarsoziale Gesellschaft. Geschaefts- und Arbeitsbericht (GW ISSN 0065-437X) *22, 1023*
Agrarsoziale Gesellschaft. Kleine Reihe (GW ISSN 0170-7671) *22, 1023*
Agrarsoziale Gesellschaft. Materialsammlung (GW ISSN 0344-5712) *23, 1024*
Agri-Book Magazine. Corn in Canada (CN) *23*
Agri-book Magazine. Elevator Manager, Farm Chemical & Fertilizer Dealer (CN) *52*
Agri-Book Magazine. Potatoes in Canada (CN) *23*
Agri-Book Magazine. Seed in Canada (CN) *23*
Agri Hortique Genetica (SW ISSN 0002-1172) *52, 154*

Agricoltore Veronese (IT) *23*
Agricultura e Industrias Agropecuarias y Pesca *see* Agricultura y Pesca *514*
Agricultura Espanola *see* Agricultura Espanola en (Year) *23*
Agricultura Espanola en (Year) (SP) *23*
Agricultura, la Pesca y la Alimentacion Espanolas (SP) *23, 507, 845*
Agricultura y la Pesca Espanolas (SP) *23, 507*
Agricultura y Pesca (CL) *514*
Agricultural Abstracts for Tanzania (TZ ISSN 0251-2440) *2, 38*
Agricultural & Food Research Council Food Research Institute. Biennial Report *see* A F R C Food Research Institute. Biennial Report *1145*
Agricultural & Food Research Council Institute of Engineering Research. Divisional Notes *see* A F R C Institute of Engineering Research. Divisional Notes *51*
Agricultural & Food Research Council Institute of Engineering Research. Reports *see* A F R C Institute of Engineering Research. Reports *51*
Agricultural & Food Research Council Institute of Engineering Research. Translations *see* A F R C Institute of Engineering Research. Translations *51*
Agricultural and Veterinary Chemicals Association of Australia Ltd. Serving Australian Agriculture *see* Serving Australian Agriculture *1162*
Agricultural Co-Operation in the United Kingdom: Summary of Statistics *see* Agricultural Co-Operatives in the United Kingdom. Statistics *44*
Agricultural Co-Operatives in the United Kingdom. Statistics (UK) *44*
Agricultural Cooperative Service Research Report *see* A C S Research Report *44*
Agricultural Credit Corporation of Saskatchewan. Annual Report (CN) *44*
Agricultural Development and Marketing Corporation. Annual Report *see* Agricultural Development and Marketing Corporation. Annual Report and Statement of Accounts *44*
Agricultural Development and Marketing Corporation. Annual Report and Statement of Accounts (MW) *44*
Agricultural Development Bank of Pakistan. Annual Report and Statement of Accounts (PK ISSN 0065-4426) *44, 222*
Agricultural Development Corporation. Annual Report (KE) *23*
Agricultural Development Corporation. Balance Sheet and Accounts *see* Agricultural Development and Marketing Corporation. Annual Report and Statement of Accounts *44*
Agricultural Development Corporation of Saskatchewan. Annual Report (CN ISSN 0708-5206) *44*
Agricultural Development in Pakistan (PK) *23*
Agricultural Directory of Malaysia (MY) *23*
Agricultural Engineering. Scientific Activities (IS) *52*
Agricultural Engineering Abstracts (UK ISSN 0308-8863) *2, 38, 476*
Agricultural Engineering in South Africa (SA) *51, 52*
Agricultural Engineers Yearbook of Standards *see* A S A E Standards *51*
Agricultural Enterprise Studies in England and Wales (UK) *44*
Agricultural Experiment Station Suriname. Annual Report *see* Landbouwproefstation Suriname. Jaarverslag *31*
Agricultural Finance Outlook *see* Agricultural Finance Outlook and Situation *44*
Agricultural Finance Outlook and Situation (US) *44*
Agricultural Finance Review (US ISSN 0002-1466) *44*
Agricultural Land Bulletin (AT) *23*

Agricultural Market Review *see* Agricultural Review for Europe *44*
Agricultural Pesticide Society. Annual Meeting. Proceedings *see* Canadian Pest Management Society Proceedings *53*
Agricultural Prices in India (II) *23*
Agricultural Processing and Manufacturing Guide *see* Alberta. Agricultural Processing Branch. Processing & Manufacturing Guide *45*
Agricultural Production Levels in Bangladesh (BG) *44*
Agricultural Progress (UK ISSN 0065-4493) *44*
Agricultural Regions of Cyprus (CY) *23*
Agricultural Research Center. Proceedings of the Annual Meeting (US) *23*
Agricultural Research Centres (UK) *23*
Agricultural Research Council of Malawi. Annual Report *see* Malawi. Department of Agricultural Research. Annual Report *31*
Agricultural Research Guyana (GY ISSN 0065-4523) *23*
Agricultural Research Index *see* Agricultural Research Centres *23*
Agricultural Research Organization. Special Publications (IS) *23*
Agricultural Review for Europe (UN) *44, 241*
Agricultural Science *see* Agricultural Science Bulletin *23*
Agricultural Science and Technology *see* AgLink Leaflets *22*
Agricultural Science Bulletin (CN ISSN 0707-7793) *23*
Agricultural Science in the Netherlands (NE ISSN 0169-4901) *23*
Agricultural Shows Annual (AT) *23*
Agricultural Situation in Eastern Europe *see* World Agriculture Regional Supplement: Eastern Europe *50*
Agricultural Situation in the People's Republic of China *see* World Agriculture Regional Supplement: China *50*
Agricultural Situation in Western Europe *see* World Agriculture Regional Supplement: Western Europe *50*
Agricultural Society of Nigeria. Proceedings (NR ISSN 0065-454X) *23*
Agricultural Statistics, England (UK ISSN 0262-2394) *23*
Agricultural Statistics, England and Wales *see* Agricultural Statistics, England *23*
Agricultural Statistics, Madhya Pradesh *see* Madhya Pradesh. Directorate of Agriculture. Agricultural Statistics *42*
Agricultural Statistics, Massachusetts *see* Massachusetts Agricultural Statistics *42*
Agricultural Statistics of Bangladesh *see* Yearbook of Agricultural Statistics of Bangladesh *37*
Agricultural Statistics of Greece (GR ISSN 0065-4574) *38, 1048*
Agricultural Statistics of Sabah (MY) *38*
Agricultural Statistics of Sarawak (MY) *38*
Agricultural Statistics, Scotland *see* Economic Report on Scottish Agriculture *46*
Agricultural Statistics, United Kingdom (UK ISSN 0065-4590) *23*
Agricultural Trade in Europe (UN) *45, 241*
Agricultural University of Norway. Department of Land Use Planning. Serie *see* Norges Landbrukshoegskole. Institutt for Jordskifte og Arealplanlegging. Melding *48*
Agricultural Wages in India (II ISSN 0084-6066) *45, 269*
Agricultural Zoology Reviews (UK ISSN 0269-0543) *173*
Agriculture Africaine (FR) *45*

Agriculture and Food Research Council Institute of Food Research Technical Bulletins *see* A F R C Institute of Food Research Technical Bulletins *61*
Agriculture Asia/Ajia Nogyo (JA ISSN 0515-8672) *23*
Agriculture at Los Banos *see* Research at Los Banos *33*
Agriculture in Scotland (UK) *23*
Agrikultura (CS) *23, 574*
Agro Chemie-Koerier (NE) *52*
Agro-Kemi (DK ISSN 0900-5285) *52*
Agro-Nouvelles (CN ISSN 0065-4655) *23*
Agroborealis (US ISSN 0002-1822) *23*
Agrochemicals Handbook (UK) *23, 321*
Agroindustry: Latin American Industrial Report (US) *45*
Agronomia Mocambicana (MZ ISSN 0044-6858) *23, 154*
Agronomy: a Series of Monographs (US ISSN 0065-4663) *23*
Agronomy Abstracts (US ISSN 0065-4671) *2, 38*
Agronomy Institute. Annual Report (RH) *23*
Agronomy Society of New Zealand. Proceedings (NZ ISSN 0110-6589) *52*
Agropecuaria *see* Retrospectiva da Agropecuaria *49*
Agroselekt. Reihe 1: Landtechnik (GE ISSN 0233-2655) *2, 38*
Agroselekt. Reihe 2: Pflanzenproduktion (GE ISSN 0233-2701) *2, 38*
Agroselekt. Reihe 3: Tierproduktion (GE ISSN 0233-2752) *2, 38*
Agrupacion Astronomica de Sabadell. Circular Informativa (SP) *114*
Agrupacion Astronomica de Sabadell. Circular Mensual *see* Agrupacion Astronomica de Sabadell. Circular Informativa *114*
Agrupacion Sindical Nacional de Empresas de Financiacion. Censo (SP) *222*
Ahmadu Bello University. Centre for the Study of Nigerian Languages. Harsunan Nijeriya *see* Harsunan Nijeriya *695*
Ahmadu Bello University. Centre of Islamic Legal Studies. Journal (NR ISSN 0065-468X) *975*
Ahmadu Bello University. Department of Geography. Occasional Paper (NR ISSN 0065-4698) *541*
Ahmadu Bello University. Institute for Agricultural Research. Annual Report (NR ISSN 0065-471X) *23*
Ahmadu Bello University. Institute for Agricultural Research. Soil Survey Bulletin (NR ISSN 0065-4728) *52*
Ahmadu Bello University. Institute of Education. Paper (NR ISSN 0065-4752) *410*
Ahmadu Bello University. Northern History Research Scheme. Interim Report (NR) *565*
Ahmadu Bello University. Northern History Research Scheme. Papers *see* Ahmadu Bello University. Northern History Research Scheme. Interim Report *565*
Ahmedabad Textile Industry's Research Association. Joint Technological Conferences. Proceedings (II ISSN 0075-4005) *1073*
Ahnenlisten Kartei (GW ISSN 0170-2653) *534*
Ahram Index (UA ISSN 0303-2728) *2*
Aichi Cancer Center Research Institute. Annual Report (JA ISSN 0374-5295) *774*
Aichi-ken Kyodo Shiryo Sogo Mokuroku (JA) *121*
Aichi Kyoiku Daigaku Kenkyu Hokoku (JA ISSN 0388-7367) *100, 614*
Aid Memo (US) *914*
Aide Juridique Nouveau Brunswick Rapport Annuel *see* Legal Aid New Brunswick Annual Report *659*
Aids and Research Tools in Ancient Near Eastern Studies (US ISSN 0732-6505) *611*

Aids and Research Tools in Middle Eastern Studies (US) *611*
Aids for Industry - North West England (UK) *1146*
Aids Index to How to do It Information *see* Index to How to Do It Information *7*
Aileron (US) *100, 713, 884*
Ailleurs et Demain; Classiques (FR ISSN 0065-4787) *713*
Aiolika Grammata (GR) *713*
Air Canada. Annual Report (CN ISSN 0568-3424) *17*
Air Conditioning, Ventilating and Heating Equipment *see* H V A C Red Book of Heating, Ventilating and Air Conditioning Equipment *553*
Air Force List (UK) *810*
Air Forces of the World (SZ) *810*
Air New Zealand. Annual Report (NZ ISSN 0065-4817) *1087*
Air Pollution Effects Surveillance Network Data Report *see* Air Quality Data for Arizona *493*
Air Quality Data for Arizona. (US) *493*
Air Rhodesia Annual Report *see* Air Zimbabwe Annual Report *1087*
Air Traffic Control Association. Fall Conference Proceedings (US ISSN 0192-8740) *17*
Air Transport (US) *1087*
Air Transport Association of Canada. Annual Report (CN ISSN 0065-485X) *1087*
Air Transportation Annual (Bombay) (II) *1087*
Air University Library Index to Military Periodicals (US ISSN 0002-2586) *2, 813*
Air Zimbabwe Annual Report (RH) *1087*
Aircraft Accident Digest (UN ISSN 0065-4876) *17*
Aircraft Armament (SZ) *810*
Aircraft Illustrated Annual (UK) *17*
Aircraft Industry Record (UK ISSN 0002-2683) *17*
Aircraft Owners and Pilots Association. A O P A Airport Directory *see* A O P A's Airports U.S.A *1087*
Aircraft Owners and Pilots Association Airports U.S.A. *see* A O P A's Airports U.S.A *1087*
Airfinance Annual (UK ISSN 0266-2132) *265*
Airline Guide to Flight Attendant Career (US) *847, 1087*
Airline Guide to Stewardess & Stewards Career *see* Airline Guide to Flight Attendant Career *847*
Airline Handbook (US ISSN 0095-4683) *1087*
Airman's Information Manual (US) *17, 1087*
Aisthesis (CL ISSN 0568-3939) *100, 410, 876*
Ajia Nogyo *see* Agriculture Asia *23*
Ajuris (BL) *650*
Akademia Athenon. Kentron Ereunes tes Hellenikes Laographias. Epeteris (GR) *514, 574*
Akademia Athenon. Pragmateiai (GR) *574*
Akademia Athenon. Praktika (GR) *574*
Akademia Ekonomiczna, Krakow. Zeszyty Naukowe (PL ISSN 0208-7944) *190*
Akademia Ekonomiczna, Krakow. Zeszyty Naukowe. Seria Specjalna: Monografie (PL ISSN 0209-1674) *190*
Akademia Ekonomiczna, Poznan. Zeszyty Naukowe. Seria 1 (PL ISSN 0079-4546) *190*
Akademia Ekonomiczna, Poznan. Zeszyty Naukowe. Seria 2. Prace Habilitacyjne i Doktorskie (PL ISSN 0079-4554) *190*
Akademia Ekonomiczna we Wroclawiu. Prace Naukowe (PL) *190*
Akademia Gorniczo-Hutnicza im. Stanislawa Staszica. Instytut Ceramiki Specjalnej i Ogniotrwalej. Prace Naukowe *see* Akademia Gorniczo-Hutnicza im. Stanislawa Staszica. Zeszyty Naukowe. Ceramika *319*

Akademia Gorniczo-Hutnicza im. Stanislawa Staszica. Instytut Gornictwa Podziemnego. Prace (PL ISSN 0372-9400) 814
Akademia Gorniczo-Hutnicza im. Stanislawa Staszica. Zeszyty Naukowe. Automatyka (PL ISSN 0454-4773) 450
Akademia Gorniczo-Hutnicza im. Stanislawa Staszica. Zeszyty Naukowe. Drilling Oil Gas (PL) 862
Akademia Gorniczo-Hutnicza im. Stanislawa Staszica. Zeszyty Naukowe. Elektrotechnika (PL ISSN 0239-5312) 450
Akademia Gorniczo-Hutnicza im. Stanislawa Staszica. Zeszyty Naukowe. Ceramika (PL) 319
Akademia Gorniczo-Hutnicza im. Stanislawa Staszica. Zeszyty Naukowe. Chemia (PL ISSN 0860-1100) 321
Akademia Gorniczo-Hutnicza im. Stanislawa Staszica. Zeszyty Naukowe. Fizyka (PL ISSN 0860-0260) 887
Akademia Gorniczo-Hutnicza im. Stanislawa Staszica. Zeszyty Naukowe. Geodezja (PL ISSN 0452-6457) 814
Akademia Gorniczo-Hutnicza im. Stanislawa Staszica. Zeszyty Naukowe. Gornictwo (PL) 814
Akademia Gorniczo-Hutnicza im. Stanislawa Staszica. Zeszyty Naukowe. Hutnictwo (PL ISSN 0075-7004) 796
Akademia Gorniczo-Hutnicza im. Stanislawa Staszica. Zeszyty Naukowe. Mechanika (PL ISSN 0239-5320) 491
Akademia Gorniczo-Hutnicza im. Stanislawa Staszica. Zeszyty Naukowe. Opuscula Mathematica (PL ISSN 0860-2727) 747
Akademia Gorniczo-Hutnicza im. Stanislawa Staszica. Zeszyty Nukowe. Metalurgia i Odlewnictwo (PL ISSN 0137-6535) 796
Akademia Gorniczo-Hutnicza im. Stanislawa Staszica. Zeszyty Naukowe. Geologia (PL) 383
Akademia Medyczna im. J. Marchlewskiego w Bialymstoku. Roczniki/Annales Academiae Medicae Bialostocensis (PL ISSN 0067-6489) 757
Akademia Medyczna we Wroclawiu. Prace Naukowe (PL ISSN 0084-277X) 757
Akademia Muzyczna. Prace Specjalne (PL) 832
Akademia Muzyczna. Skrypty (PL) 832
Akademia Muzyczna. Sprawozdania (PL) 832
Akademia Muzyczna. Wydawnictwa Okolicznosciowe (PL) 832
Akademia Rolnicza, Krakow. Rolnictwo(PL) 23
Akademia Rolnicza, Poznan. Rocznik. Melioracje Wodne see Akademia Rolnicza, Poznan. Roczniki. Melioracje 52
Akademia Rolnicza, Poznan. Rocznik. Technologia Drewna see Akademia Rolnicza, Poznan. Roczniki. Chemiczna Technologia Drewna 529
Akademia Rolnicza, Poznan. Rocznik. Technologia Rolno-Spozywcza see Akademia Rolnicza, Poznan. Roczniki. Technologia Zywnosci 517
Akademia Rolnicza, Poznan. Roczniki. Algorytmy Biometryczne i Statystyczne (PL ISSN 0137-169X) 747
Akademia Rolnicza, Poznan. Roczniki. Archeozoologia (PL ISSN 0137-1703) 173
Akademia Rolnicza, Poznan. Roczniki. Chemiczna Technologia Drewna (PL) 529
Akademia Rolnicza, Poznan. Roczniki. Ekonomika i Organizacja Rolnictwa (PL ISSN 0137-1711) 45
Akademia Rolnicza, Poznan. Roczniki. Fizyka, Chemia (PL ISSN 0208-8940) 321, 887

Akademia Rolnicza, Poznan. Roczniki. Lesnictwo (PL ISSN 0137-172X) 523
Akademia Rolnicza, Poznan. Roczniki. Mechaniczna Technologia Drewna (PL ISSN 0137-1800) 491
Akademia Rolnicza, Poznan. Roczniki. Melioracje (PL) 52
Akademia Rolnicza, Poznan. Roczniki. Ogrodnictwo (PL ISSN 0137-1738) 531
Akademia Rolnicza, Poznan. Roczniki. Ornitologia Stosowana (PL ISSN 0137-1746) 170
Akademia Rolnicza, Poznan. Roczniki. Rolnictwo (PL ISSN 0137-1754) 23
Akademia Rolnicza, Poznan. Roczniki. Rozprawy Naukowe (PL ISSN 0208-8436) 23
Akademia Rolnicza, Poznan. Roczniki. Technologia Zywnosci (PL) 517
Akademia Rolnicza, Poznan. Roczniki. Zootechnika (PL ISSN 0137-1770) 64, 173
Akademia Rolnicza w Szczecinie. Informatory (PL) 23
Akademia Rolnicza w Szczecinie. Rozprawy (PL) 23
Akademia Rolnicza w Szczecinie. Zeszyty Naukowe. Ekonomika, Organizacja i Kierowanie (PL) 190
Akademia Rolnicza w Szczecinie. Zeszyty Naukowe. Nauk Spolecznych i Ekonomicznych (PL) 250, 1006
Akademia Rolnicza w Szczecinie. Zeszyty Naukowe. Rolnictwo. (PL) 24
Akademia Rolnicza w Szczecinie. Zeszyty Naukowe. Rolnictwo. Seria Agrotechniczna (PL) 52
Akademia Rolnicza w Szczecinie. Zeszyty Naukowe. Rolnictwo. Seria Przyrodnicza (PL) 24, 154
Akademia Rolnicza w Szczecinie. Zeszyty Naukowe. Rolnictwo. Seria Techniczna (PL) 52
Akademia Rolnicza w Szczecinie. Zeszyty Naukowe. Rybactwo Morskie i Technologia Zywnosci (PL) 507, 517
Akademia Rolnicza w Szczecinie. Zeszyty Naukowe. Zootechnika (PL) 64
Akademia Rolnicza w Szczecinie. Zeszyty Naukowe. Zootechnika. Teratologica Scripta (PL) 64
Akademia Rolnicza, Warsaw. Zeszyty Naukowe. Ogrodnictwo see Warsaw Agricultural University. S G G W-A R. Annals. Horticulture 534
Akademia Rolnicza, Warsaw. Zeszyty Naukowe. Zootechnika see Warsaw Agricultural University. S G G W A R. Annals. Animal Science 68
Akademia Rolnicza, Wroclaw. Rolnictwo (PL) 24
Akademia Rolniczo-Techniczna. Agriculture see Acta Academiae Agriculturae ac Technicae Olstenensis. Agricultura/Agriculture 22
Akademie der Wissenschaften. Berlin. Jahrbuch see Akademie der Wissenschaften der DDR. Jahrbuch 987
Akademie der Wissenschaften, Berlin. Sektion fuer Vor- und Fruehgeschichte. Schriften see Schriften zur Ur- und Fruehgeschichte 560
Akademie der Wissenschaften, Berlin. Volkskundliche Veroeffentlichungen see Veroeffentlichungen zur Volkskunde und Kulturgeschichte 517
Akademie der Wissenschaften, Berlin. Zentralinstitut fuer Sprachwissenschaft. Schriften see Sprache und Gesellschaft 704
Akademie der Wissenschaften der D.D.R. Zentralinstitut fuer Wirtschaftswissenschaften. Schriften (GE ISSN 0138-3469) 191
Akademie der Wissenschaften der DDR. Abhandlungen. Abteilung Mathematik, Naturwissenschaften, Technik (GE ISSN 0138-1059) 1006

Akademie der Wissenschaften der DDR. Geodaetisches Institut. Veroeffentlichungen see Akademie der Wissenschaften der DDR. Zentralinstitut fuer Physik der Erde. Veroeffentlichungen 541
Akademie der Wissenschaften der DDR. Institut fuer Geographie und Geooekologie. Wissenschaftliche Veroeffentlichungen see Beitraege zur Geographie 541
Akademie der Wissenschaften der DDR. Jahrbuch (GE ISSN 0304-2154) 987
Akademie der Wissenschaften der DDR. Studien der Geschichte (GE ISSN 0138-4112) 987
Akademie der Wissenschaften der DDR. Zentralinstitut fuer Geschichte. Schriften (GE ISSN 0138-3566) 574
Akademie der Wissenschaften der DDR. Zentralinstitut fuer Physik der Erde. Veroeffentlichungen (GE) 541
Akademie der Wissenschaften, Goettingen. Jahrbuch (GW ISSN 0084-6082) 987
Akademie der Wissenschaften, Goettingen. Nachrichten 1. Philologisch-Historische Klasse (GW ISSN 0065-5287) 554, 690
Akademie der Wissenschaften, Goettingen. Nachrichten 2. Mathematisch-Physikalische Klasse (GW ISSN 0065-5295) 747, 887
Akademie der Wissenschaften in Goettingen. Abhandlungen. Mathematisch-Physikalische Klasse. Dritte Folge (GW) 747, 887
Akademie der Wissenschaften in Goettingen. Abhandlungen. Mathematisch-Physikalische Klasse. Dritte Sonderhefte (GW) 747
Akademie der Wissenschaften und der Literatur. Geistes- und Sozialwissenschaftliche Klasse. Abhandlungen (GW ISSN 0002-2977) 628
Akademie der Wissenschaften und der Literatur, Mainz. Jahrbuch (GW ISSN 0084-6104) 628, 987
Akademie der Wissenschaften und der Literatur, Mainz. Klasse der Literatur. Abhandlungen (GW ISSN 0002-2985) 713
Akademie der Wissenschaften und der Literatur, Mainz. Mathematisch-Naturwissenschaftliche Klasse. Abhandlungen (GW ISSN 0002-2993) 987
Akademie der Wissenschaften und der Literatur, Mainz. Orientalische Kommission. Veroeffentlichungen (GW ISSN 0568-4447) 850
Akademie fuer Fuehrungskraefte der Wirtschaft. Taschenbuecher zur Betriebspraxis (GW ISSN 0065-5384) 278
Akademie fuer Oeffentliches Gesundheitswesen. Schriftenreihe (GW ISSN 0172-2131) 952
Akademie fuer Staatsmedizin, Duesseldorf. Jahrbuch see Akademie fuer Oeffentliches Gesundheitswesen. Schriftenreihe 952
Akademiet for de Tekniske Videnskaber. Lydteknisk Institut. Rapport (DK ISSN 0105-614X) 899
Akademija Nauka i Umjetnosti Bosne i Hercegovine. Centar za Balkanoloska Ispitivanja. Godisnjak (YU ISSN 0350-0020) 574
Akademija Nauka i Umjetnosti Bosne i Hercegovine. Odeljenje Drustvenih Nauka. Radovi (YU ISSN 0350-0039) 1006
Akademija Nauka i Umjetnosti Bosne i Hercegovine. Odeljenje Istorijsko Filoloskih Nauk. Djela (YU) 574, 690
Akademische Vortraege und Abhandlungen (GW ISSN 0065-5538) 987
Akademska Dzive/Academic Life (US ISSN 0516-3145) 501, 574
Akademiya Nauk Azerbaidzhanskoi S.S.R. Muzei Istorii. Trudy (UR) 832

Akademiya Nauk Belorusskoi S.S.R. Belorusskii Etnograficheskii Sbornik. Seriya Fol'klora i Etnografii (UR) 1146
Akademiya Nauk C.S.S.R. Vostochno-Sibirskii Filial, Irkutsk. Institut Geokhimii. Geokhimya Endogennykh Protsessov (UR) 378
Akademiya Nauk C.S.S.R. Vostochno-Sibirskii Filial, Irkutsk. Institut Geokhimii. Geokhimicheskie Metody Poiskov, Metody Analiza (UR) 378
Akademiya Nauk Kazakhskoi S.S.R. Astrofizicheskii Institut. Trudy (UR) 114
Akademiya Nauk Kazakhskoi S.S.R. Institut Khimicheskikh Nauk. Trudy (UR) 329
Akademiya Nauk Kazakhskoi S.S.R. Institut Metallurgii i Obogashcheniya. Trudy (UR) 796
Akademiya Nauk Kazakhskoi S.S.R. Institut Organicheskogo Kataliza i Elektrokhimii. Trudy (UR) 328
Akademiya Nauk Litovskoi S.S.R. Silumine Fizika/Thermophysics/Teplofizika (UR ISSN 0082-4089) 894
Akademiya Nauk S.S.S.R. Institut Arkheologii. Kratkie Soobshcheniya (UR) 80
Akademiya Nauk S.S.S.R. Institut Etnografii. Polevye Issledovaniya (UR) 69
Akademiya Nauk S.S.S.R. Sibirskoe Otdelenie. Ural'skii Nauchnyi Tsentr. Institut Elektrokhimii. Trudy (UR ISSN 0568-6776) 1146
Akademiya Nauk S.S.S.R. Sibirskoe Otdelenie. Vostochno-Sibirskii Filial. Institut Geokhimii. Ezhegodnik (UR) 383
Akal Bolsillo (SP) 740
Akal Universitaria. Serie: Arqueologia (SP) 80
Akal Universitaria. Serie Historia Contemporanea (SP) 574
Akim Review (IS) 444
Akita Journal of Rural Medicine/Akita-ken Noson Igakkai Zasshi (JA ISSN 0002-368X) 757
Akita-ken Noson Igakkai Zasshi see Akita Journal of Rural Medicine 757
Akita Prefectural College of Agriculture. Bulletin (JA) 154, 402
Akiyoshi-dai Museum of Natural History. Bulletin (JA) 826
Akiyoshi-dai Science Museum. Bulletin see Akiyoshi-dai Museum of Natural History. Bulletin 826
Akkerbouw (NE) 45
Aksel (DK ISSN 0109-3762) 410
Die Aktion (GW) 709
Aktiviteten i Sygehusvaesenet (DK ISSN 0107-7619) 952
Aktual'nye Problemy Leksikologii i Slovoobrazovaniya (UR) 690
Aktuell Internationell Statistik i SCBs Bibliotek see Sweden. Statistika Centralbyraan Bibliotek. Statistik fraan Internationella Organ 1163
Aktuelle Literaturinformationen aus dem Obstbau (GW ISSN 0302-4601) 52, 534
Aktuelle Probleme in Chirurgie und Orthopadie (SZ) 786
Aktuelle Probleme in der Chirurgie see Aktuelle Probleme in Chirurgie und Orthopadie 786
Aktuelle Probleme in der Klinischen Biochemie see Current Problems in Clinical Biochemistry 151
Aktuelle Probleme in der Psychiatrie, Neurologie, Neurochirurgie (SZ ISSN 0065-5600) 788
Aktuelle Steuer-Informationen see Steuer-Telex 299
Aktuellt och Historiskt see Militaerhistorisk Tidskrift 590
Akustyka (PL ISSN 0554-8039) 899
Alabama. Commission on Higher Education. Annual Report (US) 431
Alabama. Department of Industrial Relations. Annual Manpower Planning Report see Alabama. Department of Industrial Relations. Annual Planning Information 269

Alabama. Department of Industrial Relations. Annual Planning Information (US) *269*
Alabama. Public Library Service. Annual Report (US) *673*
Alabama. Public Library Service. Basic State Plan and Annual Program *see* Alabama. Public Library Service. Annual Report *673*
Alabama Agricultural Experiment Station. Research Report Series (US) *24, 523, 531*
Alabama Archaeological Society. Special Publication (US) *80*
Alabama Contractor (US ISSN 0002-418X) *553*
Alabama County Data Book (US) *938*
Alabama Department of Education. Library Media Output (US) *673*
Alabama Directory of Mining and Manufacturing (US ISSN 0145-4048) *234*
Alabama Economic Outlook (US) *241*
Alabama Geological Society. Guidebook for the Annual Field Trip (US ISSN 0065-5635) *383*
Alabama International Trade Directory (US) *1146*
Alabama, Louisiana, Mississippi TourBook *see* Tourbook: Alabama, Louisiana, Mississippi *1117*
Alabama Marine Resources Bulletin (US ISSN 0090-8843) *137, 507*
Alabama Planning Resource Checklist (US) *621*
Alabama Press Association. Rate and Data Guide (US) *673*
Alabama State Industrial Directory *see* MacRae's Alabama State Industrial Directory *312*
Alabama World Trade Directory *see* Alabama International Trade Directory *1146*
Alabama's Vital Events (US ISSN 0095-3431) *948, 1048*
Al-Abhath (LE ISSN 0002-3973) *850*
Alahli Bank of Kuwait K.S.C. Annual Report and Balance Sheet (KU) *222*
Alai Siach (IS ISSN 0334-4827) *713*
Alan Rogers' Good Camps Guide for France (UK) *1044, 1106*
Alan Rogers' Selected Sites for Caravanning and Camping in Europe(UK ISSN 0065-5686) *1044, 1106*
Alaska. Department of Fish and Game. Annual Report (US ISSN 0065-5708) *363*
Alaska. Department of Fish and Game. Commercial Operators (US) *507*
Alaska. Department of Fish and Game. Informational Leaflet (US ISSN 0516-4303) *363*
Alaska. Department of Fish and Game. Wildlife Booklet Series (US ISSN 0084-0130) *363*
Alaska. Department of Revenue. State Investment Portfolio (US ISSN 0092-6736) *265, 292*
Alaska. Department of Revenue. Treasury Division. Annual Financial Report *see* Treasury Alaska *1066*
Alaska. Division of Game. Annual Report of Survey - Inventory Activities (US ISSN 0362-6962) *1044*
Alaska. Division of Geological and Geophysical Surveys. Geologic/ Professional Report (US) *383, 398*
Alaska. Division of Geological and Geophysical Surveys. Information Circular (US ISSN 0065-5759) *383, 398*
Alaska. Division of Geological and Geophysical Surveys. Laboratory Report *see* Alaska. Division of Geological and Geophysical Surveys. Geologic/Professional Report *383*
Alaska. Division of Geological and Geophysical Surveys. Open-File Report *see* Alaska. Division of Geological and Geophysical Surveys. Report of Investigations *383*
Alaska. Division of Geological and Geophysical Surveys. Report of Investigations (US) *383, 398*
Alaska. Division of Geological and Geophysical Surveys. Special Report (US ISSN 0360-3881) *383, 398*

Alaska. Division of Medical Assistance. Medicaid Annual Status Report *see* Alaska Medicaid Status Report *1146*
Alaska. Division of Oil and Gas Conservation. Statistical Report *see* Alaska. Oil and Gas Conservation Commission. Statistical Report *867*
Alaska. Legislature. Budget and Audit Committee. Annual Report. (US ISSN 0095-3865) *938*
Alaska. Office of Alcoholism. Report (US ISSN 0095-3318) *376*
Alaska. Office of Ombudsman. Report of the Ombudsman (US ISSN 0363-5376) *938*
Alaska. Oil and Gas Conservation Commission. Statistical Report (US ISSN 0273-1916) *867*
Alaska. State Housing Authority. Annual Report (US) *621*
Alaska. State Library, Juneau. Historical Monographs (US ISSN 0084-6139) *603*
Alaska. State Library, Juneau. State and Local Publications Received-Alaska (US ISSN 0568-8442) *948*
Alaska. Violent Crimes Compensation Board. Annual Report (US ISSN 0095-3415) *369*
Alaska Adult Education (US) *426*
Alaska Agricultural Statistics (US ISSN 0065-5694) *38*
Alaska Almanac: Facts About Alaska (US ISSN 0270-5370) *1106*
Alaska Blue Book (US ISSN 0092-1858) *939*
Alaska Economy; Year-End Performance Report *see* Performance Report of the Alaska Economy *248*
Alaska Fisheries Commercial Operators. *see* Alaska. Department of Fish and Game. Commercial Operators *507*
Alaska Index *see* Alaska Summary Report/Index *862*
Alaska Libraries and Library Personnel Directory *see* Alaska Library *673*
Alaska Library (US) *673*
Alaska Medicaid Status Report (US ISSN 0095-4667) *1146*
Alaska Municipal Officials Directory (US) *950*
Alaska Native Language Center Research Papers (US ISSN 0883-8526) *69, 690*
Alaska Pacific University Press Press Alaskana Book Series *see* A P U Press Alaskana Book Series *602*
Alaska Petroleum and Industrial Directory (US ISSN 0065-5813) *862*
Alaska Petroleum Directory *see* Alaska Petroleum and Industrial Directory *862*
Alaska Planning Information (US) *1146*
Alaska Review of Business and Economic Conditions *see* Alaska Review of Social and Economic Conditions *241*
Alaska Review of Social and Economic Conditions (US ISSN 0162-5403) *241*
Alaska Science Conference. Proceedings *see* Arctic Science Conference. Proceedings *987*
Alaska Shippers Guide (US ISSN 0271-8987) *1098*
Alaska Statewide Annual Planning Information *see* Alaska Planning Information *1146*
Alaska Summary Report/Index (US) *862*
Alaska Today (US ISSN 0191-328X) *540*
Alaska Travel Guide (US ISSN 0065-5848) *1106*
Alba Regia (HU ISSN 0324-542X) *826*
Albania Report (US ISSN 0002-4651) *241, 902*
Albanian Catholic Bulletin/Buletini Katolik Shqiptar (US ISSN 0272-7250) *967*
Albanian Resistance (FR) *902*
Albarregas (VE) *410, 628*
Alberta. Agricultural Processing Branch. Processing & Manufacturing Guide (CN ISSN 0708-3017) *45*

Alberta. Alberta Culture. Annual Report (CN ISSN 0702-9659) *1006*
Alberta. Alcohol and Drug Abuse Commission. Annual Report (CN) *376*
Alberta. Alcoholism and Drug Abuse Commission. Annual Report *see* Alberta. Alcohol and Drug Abuse Commission. Annual Report *376*
Alberta. Department of Agriculture. Annual Report *see* Alberta Agriculture. Annual Report *24*
Alberta. Department of Agriculture. Production Economics Branch. Economics of Milk Production in Alberta (CN) *62*
Alberta. Department of Energy and Natural Resources. Annual Report (CN ISSN 0700-2645) *1146*
Alberta. Department of Health and Social Development. Annual Report *see* Alberta. Department of Social Services and Community Health. Annual Report *1015*
Alberta. Department of Industry and Commerce. Economic Research Branch. Executive Report *see* Alberta. Department of Industry and Commerce. Executive Report *241*
Alberta. Department of Industry and Commerce. Executive Report (CN) *241*
Alberta. Department of Social Services and Community Health. Annual Report (CN ISSN 0381-4327) *952, 1015*
Alberta. Department of the Environment. Annual Report (CN ISSN 0383-3739) *493*
Alberta. Department of Transportation. Annual Report *see* Alberta Transportation. Annual Report *1080*
Alberta. Department of Utilities and Telecommunications. Annual Report *see* Alberta. Department of Utilities. Annual Report *939*
Alberta. Department of Utilities. Annual Report (CN) *939*
Alberta. Fish and Wildlife Division. Fisheries Pollution Report (CN ISSN 0707-2783) *494, 507*
Alberta. Fish and Wildlife Division. Pollution Report *see* Alberta. Fish and Wildlife Division. Fisheries Pollution Report *494*
Alberta. Health and Social Services Disciplines Committee. Annual Report (CN ISSN 0707-1434) *952, 1015*
Alberta. Health Care Insurance Commission. Annual Report *see* Alberta. Health Care Insurance Plan. Annual Report *637*
Alberta. Health Care Insurance Plan. Annual Report (CN) *616, 637*
Alberta. Horticultural Research Center. Annual Report (CN ISSN 0706-3369) *1146*
Alberta. Legislature Library. Annual Report (CN ISSN 0383-3712) *673*
Alberta. Office of the Superintendent of Insurance and Real Estate. Annual Report *see* Alberta Insurance Report *637*
Alberta Agriculture. Annual Report (CN) *24*
Alberta Art Foundation. Annual Report(CN ISSN 0704-9056) *100*
Alberta Catholic Directory (CN ISSN 0316-473X) *980*
Alberta Chamber of Commerce. Legislative Report (CN) *234*
Alberta Coal Industry, Annual Statistics(CN ISSN 0380-4321) *814*
Alberta Dental Association News Information *see* A.D.A. News Information *778*
Alberta Economic Accounts (CN ISSN 0319-4264) *202, 1048*
Alberta Electric Industry, Annual Statistics (CN ISSN 0706-1420) *450, 463*
Alberta Electric Industry, Cumulative Annual Statistics *see* Alberta Electric Industry, Annual Statistics *463*
Alberta Fishing Guide (CN ISSN 0318-4943) *1044*
Alberta Genealogical Society. Ancestor Index (CN) *534*

Alberta Golf Guide (CN) *1037*
Alberta Hail and Crop Insurance Corporation. Annual Report (CN ISSN 0319-3535) *52, 637*
Alberta Hospitals and Medical Care. Annual Report (CN ISSN 0227-7883) *616, 757*
Alberta Insurance Directory (CN ISSN 0712-9343) *637*
Alberta Insurance Report (CN ISSN 0229-7108) *637, 965*
Alberta Landrace Association. Newsletter (CN ISSN 0044-7145) *64*
Alberta Learning Resources Journal (CN ISSN 0380-1306) *446*
Alberta Library Board. Annual Report (CN) *673*
Alberta Motor Transport Directory (CN ISSN 0084-6171) *1104*
Alberta Opportunity Company. Annual Report (CN ISSN 0318-3971) *222*
Alberta Reports (CN) *650*
Alberta Research. Highways and River Engineering Reports *see* Alberta Research Council. River Engineering and Surface Hydrology Reports *480*
Alberta Research Council. Annual Report (CN ISSN 0080-1526) *987, 1067*
Alberta Research Council. Atmospheric Sciences Reports (CN) *987, 1067*
Alberta Research Council. Bulletins (CN ISSN 0034-5172) *383*
Alberta Research Council. Contribution Series (CN ISSN 0080-1534) *241*
Alberta Research Council. Earth Science Reports (CN) *378*
Alberta Research Council. Hail Studies Reports *see* Alberta Research Council. Atmospheric Sciences Reports *987*
Alberta Research Council. Information Series (CN ISSN 0034-5180) *862*
Alberta Research Council. List of Publications (CN ISSN 0080-1569) *687*
Alberta Research Council. Reports (CN) *987, 1067*
Alberta Research Council. River Engineering and Surface Hydrology Reports (CN) *402, 480*
Alberta Science Education Journal (CN ISSN 0701-1024) *446, 987*
Alberta Shippers Guide *see* Alberta Motor Transport Directory *1104*
Alberta Statutes and Rules of Court - Judicially Considered (CN) *650*
Alberta Teachers' Association. Math Monograph (CN ISSN 0711-2521) *446, 747*
Alberta Teachers' Association. Members' Handbook (CN ISSN 0706-9839) *410*
Alberta Teachers' Association. Special Education Council. Newsletter (CN ISSN 0315-3509) *444*
Alberta Teachers' Association Communicator *see* I N D E C Communicator *426*
Alberta Transportation. Annual Report (CN ISSN 0702-7702) *1080*
Albertan Geographer (CN ISSN 0065-6097) *541*
Alberta's Reserve of Gas: Complete Listing (CN ISSN 0229-8546) *463, 862*
Album de Recuerdos (PR) *347*
Album of Concert Pieces (UR) *832*
Album Slavnych Sportovcov (CS) *1032*
Alcan Facts - Australia (Year) (AT) *278, 554*
Alcatraz (US) *713*
Alchemist (CN ISSN 0384-8523) *713, 740*
Alcohol Abuse and Alcoholism: A Directory of Community Services in California *see* Alcohol Recovery Services: Directory of Community Resources in California *376*
Alcohol and Drug Foundation, Australia Audio Visual Catalogue *see* A D F A Audio Visual Catalogue *687*
Alcohol, Drugs and Driving: Abstracts and Reviews (US) *376, 782*
Alcohol Recovery Services: Directory of Community Resources in California (US) *376*

ALCOHOL STATISTICS

Alcohol Statistics *see* Sweden. Socialstyrelsen. Alkoholstatistik *121*
Alcoholism and Drug Addiction Research Foundation. Annual Report *see* Addiction Research Foundation of Ontario. Annual Report *376*
Alcuin (UK) *967*
Aldrich Entomology Club. Newsletter (US ISSN 0065-6143) *163*
Alea (FR ISSN 0249-3446) *100, 713, 876*
Alemannisches Jahrbuch (GW ISSN 0516-5644) *1146*
Alembic (UK ISSN 0140-5136) *740*
Alessandria, Italy. Centro Documentazione e Richerche Economico-Sociali. Quaderni CeDRES (IT ISSN 0065-6151) *241*
Aletheia (LH ISSN 0149-2004) *876*
Aletheia (US ISSN 0742-1044) *912*
Alexander Lectures (CN ISSN 0065-616X) *713*
Alexander von Humboldt Foundation. Annual Report (GW ISSN 0342-6785) *628*
Alexander von Humboldt-Stiftung. Jahresbericht *see* Alexander von Humboldt Foundation. Annual Report *628*
Alfa (BL ISSN 0002-5216) *690, 714*
Alfred Benzon Symposium. Proceedings(DK ISSN 0065-6186) *171, 757*
Alfred P. Sloan Foundation. Report (US ISSN 0065-6216) *628*
Algebraic Conference. Proceedings (YU) *747*
Algemeen Arbeidsongeschiktheidsfonds. Jaarverslag *see* Arbeidsongeschiktheidsfonds en Algemeen Arbeidsongeschiktheidsfonds. Jaarverslag *637*
Algemeen Jaarboek der Schone Kunsten *see* Jaarboek der Schone Kunsten *106*
Algemeen Werkloosheidsfonds. Jaarverslag/Annual Report (NE ISSN 0401-331X) *637*
Algemene Practische Rechtverzameling (BE) *650*
Algeria. Institut National Algerien du Commerce Exterieur. Annuaire des Exportateurs (AE) *253*
Algodon Hace Sus Cuentas (SP) *1073*
ALGOL Bulletin (UK ISSN 0084-6198) *357*
Algological Studies (GW ISSN 0342-1120) *137, 154, 402*
Algoma Outdoors (CN ISSN 0707-3151) *1106*
Algonquian Conference Papers (CN ISSN 0831-5671) *69, 80, 690*
Algorithms and Combinatorics (US) *747*
Alif (UA) *714, 740*
Aligarh Journal of Statistics (CN) *1048*
Aligarh Muslim University, Aligarh, India. Department of History. Publication (II ISSN 0065-6259) *568*
Alim (IS ISSN 0334-5084) *410*
Alimentaria (MX) *517*
Alkaloids (US) *329, 869*
Alkmaarse Historische Reeks (NE) *574*
All About Arizona, the Healthful State (US) *1106*
All About Hawaii *see* Thrum's All About Hawaii *1117*
All About Mail Order (US ISSN 0739-2958) *282*
All Africa Conference of Churches. Refugee Department. Progress Report (KE) *967*
All Africa Conference of Churches. Refugee Department. Project List (KE) *967*
All-Asia Guide (HK ISSN 0072-4939) *541*
All England Law Reports. Annual Review (UK ISSN 0265-766X) *650*
All India Architects Directory *see* Indian Architects Directory *98*
All-India Conference of Linguists. Proceedings (II) *690*
All-India Conference of Linguists. Souvenir (II) *690*

All India Crime Prevention Society. Annual Report and Audited Statement of Accounts (II ISSN 0065-6283) *369*
All India Handloom Exporters Guide (II) *1073*
All India Ophthalmological Society. Proceedings (II) *785*
All-India Oriental Conference. Summaries of Papers (II) *850*
All India Report on Agricultural Census *see* Agricultural Prices in India *23*
All India Textiles Directory (II) *301, 1073*
All of Mexico at Low Cost (US ISSN 0533-0653) *1106*
All Pakistan Textile Mills Association. Annual Report *see* All Pakistan Textile Mills Association. Chairman's Review *287*
All Pakistan Textile Mills Association. Chairman's Review (PK) *287, 1073*
All Pakistan Women's Association. Triennial Conference Report (PK) *1128*
All States Tourist Park Guide (AT) *1106*
Allan Hancock Monographs in Marine Biology (US ISSN 0065-6364) *1146*
Alle Boerns Jul (DK) *335, 967*
Alle Tiders Odsherreds (DK ISSN 0108-9846) *80, 574*
Allegheny Review (US ISSN 0742-096X) *714*
Allensbacher Almanach (GW) *574*
Allensbacher Berichte (GW) *1006*
Allensbacher Jahrbuch der Demoskopie(GW) *1024*
Allergologicum; Transactions of the Collegium Internationale (SZ ISSN 0065-6372) *773*
Allergy. Supplementum (FI) *773*
Allertonia (US) *154, 531*
Allesoe, Broby, Naesby Lokalarkiv (DK ISSN 0108-7142) *574*
Allgaeuer Geschichtsfreund (GW) *574*
Allgemeine Gastarife in der Bundesrepublik Deutschland (GW) *862*
Allgemeiner Caecilien-Verband. Schriftenreihe (GW) *832, 980*
Allgemeiner Deutscher Tanzlehrer Verband Nachrichten *see* A D T V - Nachrichten *374*
Alliance (Charleston) (US) *341, 757*
Alliance Atlantique. Structure, Faits et Chiffres *see* North Atlantic Treaty Organization. Facts and Figures *917*
Alliance for Engineering in Medicine and Biology. Proceedings of the Annual Conference (US ISSN 0589-1019) *137, 469, 757*
Alliance of Information and Referral Systems Directory of Information and Referral Agencies in the United States and Canada *see* Directory of Information and Referral Agencies in the United States and Canada *369*
Alliance Review (US ISSN 0002-6093) *410, 967*
Allied Artists of America. Annual Exhibition (Bulletin) (US) *826*
Allied Artists of America. Exhibition Catalog (US ISSN 0065-6410) *826*
Allied Dunbar Tax Guide (UK) *292*
Allied Health Education Directory (US ISSN 0194-3766) *428, 757*
Allied Landscape Industry Member Directory *see* American Association of Nurserymen Directory for the Nursery Industry and Related Associations *24*
Allied Medical Education Directory *see* Allied Health Education Directory *428*
Allionia (IT ISSN 0065-6429) *154*
Allmende (GW ISSN 0720-3098) *709, 740*
Alloys Index (US ISSN 0094-8233) *2, 801*
Almanac for Computers (US ISSN 0191-3867) *114, 351*
Almanac for Geodetic Engineers (PH ISSN 0569-0838) *114*
Almanac of Business and Industrial Financial Ratios (US) *222, 265*
Almanac of China's Foreign Relations and Trade (HK) *250, 265*

Almanac of Seapower (US ISSN 0736-3559) *810*
Almanac of the Pacific *see* Thrum's All About Hawaii *1117*
Almanacco Calcistico Svizzero (SZ) *1037*
Almanacco la Moto (IT) *1041*
Almanacco Repubblicano (IT) *462*
Almanacco Roulotte (IT) *1044*
Almanach der Oesterreichischen Forschung (AU) *1146*
Almanach du Peuple (CN ISSN 0065-650X) *133, 462*
Almanach du Vieux Geneve *see* Revue du Vieux Geneve *594*
Almanach Moderne (CN) *301*
Almanach Sceny Polskiej (PL ISSN 0065-6526) *1076*
Almanahul Cinema (RM) *822*
Almanak for Teologi og Litteratur (DK ISSN 0900-1573) *714, 967*
Almanak NUBIKA *see* Almanak Nuklir Biologi dan Kimia *895*
Almanak Nuklir Biologi dan Kimia (IO) *137, 321, 895*
Almanakh Gomonu Ukrainy (CN ISSN 0441-1196) *462, 501*
Almanaque (UY) *404*
Almanaque Abril (BL) *538*
Almanaque Brazil (BL) *538*
Almanaque del Peru (PE) *603*
Almanaque Misal (SP) *967*
Almanaque Nautico (SP ISSN 0210-735X) *114*
Almanaque Nautico Reducido para Uso con Maquinas de Calcular (SP ISSN 0210-8046) *114, 462*
Almanaque Puertorriqueno (Year) (PR) *462*
Almanaque Salvadoreno (ES ISSN 0084-6236) *803*
Almennyttige Boligselskabers Regnskaber (DK ISSN 0107-1572) *621*
Almindelige Danske Laegeforening *see* Laegeforeningens Vejviser *763*
Almogaren *see* Institutum Canarium Yearbook. Almogaren *87*
Alon Lamorah Lesifrut (IS ISSN 0334-5076) *410*
Alon le-Tekhnologyah be-Khinukh *see* Israel. Ministry of Education and Culture. Department of Educational Technology. Bulletin *448*
Alpeninstitut. Schriftenreihe (GW) *987*
Alpha (CN) *100, 714, 1076*
Alpha Psi Omega: Playbill (US) *341, 1076*
Alphabetisation *see* Literacy *416*
Alpine Garden Society Guides *see* A.G.S. Guides *531*
Alpine Journal (UK ISSN 0065-6569) *541*
Alsterverein Jahrbuch (GW) *574*
Alt-Katholisches Jahrbuch (GW) *983*
Alt-Thueringen (GE ISSN 0065-6585) *69, 574*
Alt- und Neu-Indische Studien (GW ISSN 0170-3242) *568*
Alta Direccion. Monografias (SP) *278*
Altadena Review (US ISSN 0162-8208) *740*
Altamura (IT ISSN 0569-1346) *826*
Altbabylonische Briefe im Umschrift und Uebersetzung (NE ISSN 0065-6593) *850*
Altdeutsche Textbibliothek. Ergaenzungsreihe (GW ISSN 0065-6607) *714*
Alte Abenteuerliche Reiseberichte (GW) *714*
Altech (II ISSN 0065-6623) *1067*
Altenburger Naturwissenschaftliche Forschungen (GE ISSN 0232-5381) *137, 383*
Alternate Celebrations Catalogue (US) *301, 514*
Alternate Christmas Catalogue *see* Alternate Celebrations Catalogue *301*
Alternate Routes (CN ISSN 0702-8865) *69, 1006*
Alternative America (US) *540*
Alternative Communities Magazine (UK) *1024*
Alternative England and Wales (UK) *462*
Alternative London *see* Alternative England and Wales *462*

Alternative Press Annual (US) *709*
Alternative Press Index (US ISSN 0002-662X) *2, 712, 911*
Alternative Press Syndicate Directory *see* A P S Directory *645*
Alternative Trading News (US) *238, 253, 261, 914*
Alternatives Economiques (FR) *191*
Alternatives to "A" Level (UK) *431*
Altes Handwerk (GW) *514*
Altfraenkische Bilder *see* Altfraenkische Bilder und Wappenkalender *575*
Altfraenkische Bilder und Wappenkalender (GW ISSN 0342-8699) *575*
Althochdeutsches Woerterbuch (GE) *690*
Altrive Chapbooks (UK ISSN 0266-8521) *714, 740*
Aluminium Development Council of Australia. Technical Papers (AT ISSN 0084-6279) *796*
Aluminium Industry in the Soviet Union (UK) *796*
Aluminium Intern: Aluminium und Automobil (GW) *796*
Aluminum Smelters (GW) *814*
Aluminum Standards and Data (US ISSN 0065-6658) *796*
Aluminum Standards and Data-Metric (US) *796*
Aluminum Statistical Review (US ISSN 0065-6666) *796*
Alumni Publications: a Catalogue (II) *121*
Am I Eligible? The Easy Way to Calculate the B E O G Index *see* College Grants from Uncle Sam *433*
AMACADMY (US) *96, 100, 714*
Amakusa Marine Biological Laboratory. Contributions (JA ISSN 0065-6674) *137*
Amakusa Marine Biological Laboratory. Publications (JA ISSN 0065-6682) *137*
Amateur Athletic Association. Handbook (UK ISSN 0065-6690) *1032*
Amateur Athletic Union of the United States. Official Handbook of the A A U Code (US ISSN 0091-3405) *1032*
Amateur Athletic Union of the United States Junior Olympic Handbook *see* A A U Junior Olympic Handbook *1032*
Amateur Chamber Music Players. Directory (US ISSN 0065-6704) *832*
Amateur Hockey Association of the United States. Official Guide (US ISSN 0516-8635) *1032*
Amateur Hockey Association of the United States. Rule Book (US) *1032*
Amateur Musician/Musicien Amateur (CN) *832*
Amateur Skating Union of the United States. Offical Handbook (US ISSN 0516-866X) *1032*
Amateur Softball Association of America. Official Guide and Rule Book (US ISSN 0065-6739) *1037*
Amateur Swimming Association Handbook (UK) *1032*
Amateur Trapshooting Association. Official Trapshooting Rules (US ISSN 0065-6747) *1044*
Amateur Yacht Research Society Airs *see* A Y R S Airs *1041*
Amateurfilm Journal (SZ) *822*
Amazonia - Bibliografia (BL ISSN 0100-0977) *121*
Amazoniana; Limnologia et Oecologia Regionalis Systemae Fluminis Amazonas (GW ISSN 0065-6755) *137*
Ambient Assessment Air Portion *see* National Air Quality and Emissions Trends Report *498*
Ambulatory Care Statistics *see* Profiles and Trends *1161*
America by Car (US ISSN 0569-1966) *1106*
America: History and Life. Part A: Article Abstracts and Citation (US ISSN 0002-7065) *2, 562*
America: History and Life. Part B: Index to Book Reviews (US ISSN 0097-6172) *2, 562*

America: History and Life. Part C: American History Bibliography (US ISSN 0363-1249) *562*
America: History and Life. Part D: Annual Index (US) 2, *562*
America Latina. Boletin (PE) *980*
America Meridional (UY) *603*
America - Problema (PE ISSN 0065-6763) *1024*
America Votes (US ISSN 0065-678X) *902*
American Academy and Institute of Arts and Letters. Proceedings (US ISSN 0145-8493) *628*
American Academy for Jewish Research. Proceedings of the A A J R (US ISSN 0065-6798) *976*
American Academy in Rome. Memoirs (IT ISSN 0065-6801) *96, 100*
American Academy in Rome. Papers and Monographs (IT ISSN 0065-681X) *336*
American Academy of Allergy. Pollen and Mold Committee. Statistical Report (US) *773*
American Academy of Arts and Letters. Proceedings *see* American Academy and Institute of Arts and Letters. Proceedings *628*
American Academy of Environmental Engineers. Consultant Directory (US) *469, 494*
American Academy of Environmental Engineers. Roster (US ISSN 0065-6860) *469, 494*
American Academy of Orthopaedic Surgeons. Committee on Instructional Courses. Instructional Course Lectures (US ISSN 0065-6895) *786*
American Academy of Orthopaedic Surgeons. Directory (US ISSN 0516-8856) *786*
American Academy of Osteopathy Yearbook (US ISSN 0732-703X) *777*
American Academy of Pediatrics. Committee on Infectious Diseases. Report (US ISSN 0065-6909) *787*
American Academy of Religion. Annual Meeting (US) *967*
American Academy of Religion Academy Series *see* A A R Academy Series *966*
American Academy of Religion Studies in Religion *see* A A R Studies in Religion *966*
American Accounting Association. Southeast Regional Group. Collected Papers of the Annual Meeting (US ISSN 0360-8840) *220*
American Agricultural Economics Association. Handbook *see* American Agricultural Economics Association. Handbook-Directory *45*
American Agricultural Economics Association. Handbook-Directory (US) *45*
American Alpine Journal (US ISSN 0065-6925) *1044*
American Animal Hospital Association. Annual Meeting Scientific Proceedings (US) *616, 1120*
American Anthropological Association. Abstracts of Meetings (US) *69*
American Arbitration Association Annual Report *see* A A A Annual Report *649*
American Art Directory (US ISSN 0065-6968) *100*
American Artist Art School Directory *see* American Artist Directory of Art Schools & Workshops *101*
American Artist Directory of Art Schools & Workshops (US ISSN 0146-9606) *101, 410*
American Arts Pamphlet Series *see* Exeter's Studies in American & Commonwealth Arts *722*
American Assembly of Collegiate Schools of Business. Accredited Schools, Officers, Committees *see* American Assembly of Collegiate Schools of Business. Membership Directory *191*
American Assembly of Collegiate Schools of Business. Membership Directory. (US) *191, 431*

American Association for Automotive Medicine. Proceedings (US ISSN 0401-6351) *757, 1090*
American Association for the Advancement of Science. Committee on Desert and Arid Zone Research. Contributions (US ISSN 0569-2393) *378*
American Association for the Advancement of Science. Handbook; Officers, Organization, Activities (US ISSN 0361-7874) *987*
American Association for the Advancement of Science. Meeting Program. (US ISSN 0361-1833) *987*
American Association for the Advancement of Science Publication *see* A A A S Publication *986*
American Association for the Advancement of Slavic Studies Directory of Programs *see* A A A S S Directory of Programs *501*
American Association of Cereal Chemists. Monograph Series (US ISSN 0065-7107) *517*
American Association of Colleges for Teacher Education. Directory (US ISSN 0516-9313) *428, 431*
American Association of Colleges of Pharmacy. Annual Survey of Faculty Salaries (US) *869*
American Association of Cost Engineers. Transactions of the Annual Meeting (US ISSN 0065-7158) *469*
American Association of Engineering Societies. Engineering Manpower Commission. Engineering and Technology Degrees (US ISSN 0071-0393) *469*
American Association of Engineering Societies. Engineering Manpower Commission. Engineering and Technology Enrollments (US ISSN 0071-0407) *269, 469*
American Association of Engineering Societies. Engineering Manpower Commission. Engineers' Salaries: Special Industry Report. (US ISSN 0071-0415) *269, 469*
American Association of Engineering Societies. Engineering Manpower Commission. Professional Income of Engineers. (US ISSN 0071-0423) *269, 469*
American Association of Engineering Societies. Engineering Manpower Commission. Salaries of Engineers in Education. (US) *431, 469*
American Association of Equine Practitioners. Proceedings of the Annual Convention (US ISSN 0065-7182) *1120*
American Association of Feed Microscopists Proceedings of Annual Meeting *see* A A F M Proceedings of Annual Meeting *795*
American Association of Foot Specialists. Program Journal *see* American College of Foot Specialists. Annual Yearbook *794*
American Association of Genito-Urinary Surgeons. Transactions (US ISSN 0065-7204) *782, 784*
American Association of Law Libraries Publications Series *see* A A L L Publications Series *672*
American Association of Medical Clinics. Directory *see* American Group Practice Association Directory *616*
American Association of Medical Milk Commissions. Methods and Standards for the Production of Certified Milk (US ISSN 0065-7263) *62*
American Association of Motor Vehicle Administrators. Annual Conference. Proceedings (US ISSN 0065-7271) *1104*
American Association of Nurserymen Directory for the Nursery Industry and Related Associations (US) *24, 531*

American Association of Nurserymen Membership Directory *see* American Association of Nurserymen Directory for the Nursery Industry and Related Associations *24*
American Association of Obstetricians and Gynecologists. Transactions (US ISSN 0065-728X) *784*
American Association of Pathologists and Bacteriologists. Symposium. Monographs (US ISSN 0065-7298) *137, 167, 757*
American Association of Petroleum Geologists. Memoir (US ISSN 0065-731X) *383, 862*
American Association of Petroleum Geologists Studies in Geology Series *see* A A P G Studies in Geology Series *382*
American Association of Petroleum Landmen. Membership Directory (US ISSN 0272-8370) *862*
American Association of State Colleges and Universities. Proceedings (US) *431*
American Association of State Colleges and Universities Studies *see* A A S C U Studies *431*
American Association of State Highway and Transportation Officals. Reference Book *see* Reference Book of Highway Personnel *1083*
American Association of State Highway and Transportation Officials. Proceedings (US) *1095*
American Association of State Highway and Transportation Officials. Sub-Committee on Computer Technology. National Conference. Proceedings (US ISSN 0091-5122) *1093*
American Association of Stratigraphic Palynologists. Abstracts of Papers Presented at the Annual Meetings. (US ISSN 0192-7272) *2, 381, 858*
American Association of Stratigraphic Palynologists. Contributions Series (US ISSN 0160-8843) *383, 856*
American Association of Stratigraphic Palynologists Foundation. Field Trip Guide (US ISSN 0192-737X) *856*
American Association of Suicidology. Proceedings of the Annual Meeting (US) *932*
American Association of Teachers of Italian. Directory *see* Italica *415*
American Association of Textile Chemists and Colorists. Buyer's Guide (US ISSN 0040-490X) *1073*
American Association of Textile Chemists and Colorists. National Technical Conference. Book of Papers (US ISSN 0192-4699) *1073*
American Association of Textile Chemists and Colorists. Products Buyer's Guide *see* American Association of Textile Chemists and Colorists. Buyer's Guide *1073*
American Association of Textile Chemists and Colorists. Technical Manual (US) *1073*
American Association of Theological Schools in the United States and Canada. Bulletin *see* Association of Theological Schools in the United States and Canada. Bulletin *967*
American Association of Theological Schools in the United States and Canada. Directory *see* Association of Theological Schools in the United States and Canada. Directory *967*
American Association of Variable Star Observers Bulletin--Predicted Dates of Maxima and Minima of Long Period Variable Stars *see* A A V S O Bulletin--Predicted Dates of Maxima and Minima of Long Period Variable Stars *114*
American Association of Veterinary Laboratory Diagnosticians. Proceedings of Annual Meeting (US ISSN 0098-3543) *1120*
American Association of Zoological Parks and Aquariums. Proceedings. Annual A A Z P A Conference (US ISSN 0090-4473) *173*
American Association on Mental Deficiency. Monographs (US ISSN 0730-7128) *932*

American Astronautical Society. Proceedings of the Annual Meeting (US ISSN 0516-9593) *17*
American Astronautical Society History Series *see* A A S History Series *17*
American Astronautical Society, Inc. Goddard Memorial Symposium. Proceedings. *see* A A S Goddard Memorial Symposium. Proceedings *17*
American Astronautical Society, Inc. Microfiche Series *see* A A S Microfiche Series *17*
American Automatic Control Council Newsletter *see* A A C C Newsletter *484*
American Automobile Association. Digest of Motor Laws (US ISSN 0093-4062) *650, 1090*
American Automobile Association Campbooks *see* A A A Campbooks *1043*
American Bankers Association. Committee on Uniform Security Identification Procedures. C U S I P Directory *see* C U S I P Master Directory *265*
American Bankers Association. Committee on Uniform Security Identification Procedures. C U S I P Directory: Corporate Directory *see* C U S I P Corporate Directory *265*
American Bankers Association. National Automation Conference. Proceedings *see* American Bankers Association. National Operations & Automation Conference. Proceedings *234*
American Bankers Association. National Operations & Automation Conference. Proceedings (US ISSN 0095-5396) *234, 360*
American Bankers Association. Operations and Automation Division. Results of the National Automation Survey *see* American Bankers Association. Operations and Automation Division. Results of the National Operations & Automation Survey *234*
American Bankers Association. Operations and Automation Division. Results of the National Operations & Automation Survey (US ISSN 0363-2539) *234, 360*
American Bankers Association Key to Routing Numbers (US) *222*
American Bankers Association Master Directory *see* C U S I P Master Directory *265*
American Bantam Association. Yearbook (US ISSN 0065-745X) *64*
American Baptist Churches in the U.S.A. Directory (US ISSN 0091-9381) *978*
American Baptist Churches in the U.S.A. Yearbook (US ISSN 0092-3478) *978*
American Bar Association Lawyers' Title Guaranty Funds Newsletter *see* A B A Lawyers' Title Guaranty Funds Newsletter *649*
American Bar Foundation. Research Contributions (US ISSN 0065-7549) *1146*
American Bar Foundation Research Reporter (US) *1146*
American Bar Reference Handbook *see* American Bar - The Canadian Bar - The International Bar *650*
American Bar - The Canadian Bar - The International Bar (US ISSN 0094-3584) *650*
American Bell Association. Directory (US ISSN 0093-1330) *832*
American Bench (US) *650*
American Bibliography of Russian and East European Studies *see* American Bibliography of Slavic and East European Studies *562*
American Bibliography of Slavic and East European Studies (US ISSN 0094-3770) *562*
American Blue Book of Funeral Directors (US ISSN 0065-7565) *531*

American Board of Medical Specialties. Annual Report see American Board of Medical Specialties. Annual Report & Reference Handbook 757
American Board of Medical Specialties. Annual Report & Reference Handbook (US ISSN 0272-9741) 757
American Board of Medical Specialties Compendium of Certified Medical Specialists see A B M S Compendium of Certified Medical Specialists 756
American Board of Medical Specialties Directory of Certified Allergy-Immunology Physicians see A B M S Directory of Certified Allergy-Immunology Physicians 773
American Board of Medical Specialties Directory of Certified Anesthesiologists see A B M S Directory of Certified Anesthesiologists 774
American Board of Medical Specialties Directory of Certified Colon & Rectal Surgeons see A B M S Directory of Certified Colon & Rectal Surgeons 782
American Board of Medical Specialties Directory of Certified Dermatologists see A B M S Directory of Certified Dermatologists 780
American Board of Medical Specialties Directory of Certified Emergency Physicians see A B M S Directory of Certified Emergency Physicians 756
American Board of Medical Specialties Directory of Certified Family Practitioners see A B M S Directory of Certified Family Practitioners 756
American Board of Medical Specialties Directory of Certified Internists see A B M S Directory of Certified Internists 756
American Board of Medical Specialties Directory of Certified Neurologists see A B M S Directory of Certified Neurologists 788
American Board of Medical Specialties Directory of Certified Neurological Surgeons see A B M S Directory of Certified Neurological Surgeons 788
American Board of Medical Specialties Directory of Certified Nuclear Medicine Specialists see A B M S Directory of Certified Nuclear Medicine Specialists 792
American Board of Medical Specialties Directory of Certified Obstetricians & Gynecologists see A B M S Directory of Certified Obstetricians & Gynecologists 784
American Board of Medical Specialties Directory of Certified Ophthalmologists see A B M S Directory of Certified Ophthalmologists 785
American Board of Medical Specialties Directory of Certified Orthopaedic Surgeons see A B M S Directory of Certified Orthopaedic Surgeons 786
American Board of Medical Specialties Directory of Certified Otolaryngologists see A B M S Directory of Certified Otolaryngologists 786
American Board of Medical Specialties Directory of Certified Pathologists see A B M S Directory of Certified Pathologists 782
American Board of Medical Specialties Directory of Certified Pediatricians see A B M S Directory of Certified Pediatricians 787
American Board of Medical Specialties Directory of Certified Physical Medicine & Rehabilitation Physicians see A B M S Directory of Certified Physical Medicine & Rehabilitation Physicians 777
American Board of Medical Specialties Directory of Certified Plastic Surgeons see A B M S Directory of Certified Plastic Surgeons 794
American Board of Medical Specialties Directory of Certified Preventive Medicine Physicians see A B M S Directory of Certified Preventive Medicine Physicians 756

American Board of Medical Specialties Directory of Certified Psychiatrists see A B M S Directory of Certified Psychiatrists 788
American Board of Medical Specialties Directory of Certified Radiologists see A B M S Directory of Certified Radiologists 792
American Board of Medical Specialties Directory of Certified Surgeons see A B M S Directory of Certified Surgeons 794
American Board of Medical Specialties Directory of Certified Thoracic Surgeons see A B M S Directory of Certified Thoracic Surgeons 756
American Board of Medical Specialties Directory of Certified Urologists see A B M S Directory of Certified Urologists 795
American Book Prices Current (US ISSN 0091-9357) 963
American Book Prices Current. Five Year Index see American Book Prices Current. Four Year Index 963
American Book Prices Current. Four Year Index (US) 963
American Book Publishing Record/B P R (US ISSN 0002-7707) 963
American Book Trade Directory (US ISSN 0065-759X) 959
American Broncho-Esophagological Association. Transactions (US ISSN 0065-7603) 787
American Bureau of Metal Statistics. Year Book see Non-Ferrous Metal Data 799
American Bureau of Shipping. Record (US) 1098
American Bus Association. Annual Report see American Bus Association. Report 1080
American Bus Association. Report (US ISSN 0278-1565) 1080
American Business in Argentina (AG) 302
American Camellia Yearbook (US ISSN 0065-762X) 531
American Car Prices see Car Prices 1091
American Catholic Philosophical Association. Proceedings (US ISSN 0065-7638) 876, 980
American Cement Directory (US ISSN 0065-7646) 181
American Cemetery Association. Membership Directory (US) 531
American Chamber of Commerce for Brazil. Annual Directory (BL ISSN 0065-7662) 234
American Chamber of Commerce in France. Directory (FR ISSN 0065-7670) 234
American Chamber of Commerce in Italy. Directory (IT ISSN 0569-3667) 234
American Chamber of Commerce in Morocco. Annual Review see A M C H A M Morocco 234
American Chamber of Commerce in Thailand. Handbook Directory (TH) 234
American Chamber of Commerce of Venezuela. Yearbook and Membership Directory see Venezuelan - American Chamber of Commerce and Industry. Yearbook and Membership Directory 237
American Chemical Society. Abstracts of Papers (at the National Meeting) (US ISSN 0065-7727) 321
American Chemical Society. Abstracts of Papers (at the Regional Meetings) (US ISSN 0065-7735) 321
American Chemical Society. Directory of Graduate Research (US ISSN 0193-5011) 321, 428
American Chemical Society. Reports of Research Supported By The Petroleum Research Fund see Reports on Research Assisted by the Petroleum Research Fund 866
American Chemical Society Laboratory Guide to Instruments, Equipment and Chemicals. Lab Guide see Laboratory Guide to Instruments, Equipment and Chemicals. Lab Guide 323

American Chemical Society Monographs see A C S Monographs 321
American Chemical Society Symposium on Analytical Calorimetry see Analytical Calorimetry 894
American Chemical Society Symposium Series see A C S Symposium Series 321
American Classical Studies (US ISSN 0278-5943) 690
American Clinical and Climatological Association. Transactions (US ISSN 0065-7778) 757
American College of Cardiology. Symposia (US) 776
American College of Foot Specialists. Annual Yearbook (US) 786, 794
American College of Healthcare Executives. Directory (US) 616
American College of Hospital Administrators. Directory see American College of Healthcare Executives. Directory 616
American College of Neuropsychiatrists. Bulletin (US ISSN 0002-7995) 789
American College Public Relations Association. Directory see Council for Advancement and Support of Education. Membership Directory 433
American College Testing Program. Annual Report (US ISSN 0517-0680) 431
American College Testing Program. Handbook for Financial Aid Administrators (US ISSN 0094-2227) 442
American College Testing Program Monograph Series see A C T Monograph Series 431
American College Testing Program Research Report see A C T Research Report 431
American Companesation Association. Conference Highlights (US) 269
American Compensation Association. Conference. Proceedings (US) 269
American Compensation Association. National Conference. Proceedings see American Compensation Association. Conference. Proceedings 269
American Concrete Institute. Compilation (US ISSN 0517-0745) 181
American Concrete Institute. Proceedings (US ISSN 0097-4145) 181
American Concrete Institute. Special Publication (US ISSN 0065-7891) 181
American Concrete Institute Bibliography see A C I Bibliography 121
American Concrete Institute Manual of Concrete Practice see A C I Manual of Concrete Practice 181
American Conference of Academic Deans. Proceedings (US ISSN 0065-7905) 431
American Conference of Governmental Industrial Hygienists. Transactions of the Annual Meeting (US) 635
American Congress on Surveying and Mapping. Papers from the Annual Meetings see American Congress on Surveying and Mapping. Technical Papers 541
American Congress on Surveying and Mapping. Proceedings of Annual Meeting see American Congress on Surveying and Mapping. Technical Papers 541
American Congress on Surveying and Mapping. Technical Papers (US ISSN 0277-2876) 541
American Control Conference. Conference Proceedings (US) 450
American Control Conference. Conference Records see American Control Conference. Conference Proceedings 450
American Cooperation Yearbook (US ISSN 0065-793X) 238
American Correctional Association. Annual Congress of Correction. Proceedings (US ISSN 0065-7948) 369

American Council of Independent Laboratories. Directory (US ISSN 0065-7964) 987, 1067
American Council on Consumer Interests. Proceedings of the Annual Conference (US ISSN 0275-1356) 368
American Council on Industrial Arts Teacher Education. Yearbook (US ISSN 0084-6333) 410
American Council on the Teaching of Foreign Languages Foreign Language Education Series see A C T F L Foreign Language Education Series 446
American Crystallographic Association. Monographs (US ISSN 0514-8863) 327
American Crystallographic Association. Program & Abstracts (US ISSN 0569-4221) 327, 887
American Crystallographic Association. Transactions (US ISSN 0065-8006) 327
American Cultural Heritage Series (US) 1024
American Dental Association. Annual Reports and Resolutions see American Dental Association. Transaction Series: Annual Reports and Resolutions, Supplements One and Two, Transactions 779
American Dental Association. Transaction Series: Annual Reports and Resolutions, Supplements One and Two, Transactions (US) 779
American Dental Directory (US ISSN 0065-8073) 779
American Dexter Cattle Association. Herd Book (US ISSN 0065-8081) 64
American Dialect Society. Publications (US ISSN 0002-8207) 690
American Dissertations on Foreign Education (US) 121, 422
American Doctoral Dissertations (US ISSN 0065-809X) 432
American Druggist Blue Book (US ISSN 0364-7471) 869
American Druggist Blue Price Book see American Druggist Blue Book 869
American Electronics Association Directory (US) 450
American Engineering Model Society Seminar (Papers) see A E M S Seminar (Papers) 469
American Entomological Institute. Contributions (US ISSN 0569-4450) 163
American Entomological Institute. Memoirs (US ISSN 0065-8162) 163
American Entomological Society. Memoirs (US ISSN 0065-8170) 163
American Ephemeris and Nautical Almanac see Astronomical Almanac 115
American Ethnological Society. Monographs (US ISSN 0065-8197) 1024
American Ethnological Society. Proceedings of Spring Meeting (US ISSN 0065-8200) 69
American Exploration and Travel (US ISSN 0065-8219) 603
American Export Register (US ISSN 0272-1163) 253
American Family Records Association Member Directory and Ancestral Surname Registry see A F R A Member Directory and Ancestral Surname Registry 534
American Federation of Teachers. Convention Proceedings (Abridged) (US) 410, 648
American Federation of Teachers Issues Bulletin see A F T Issues Bulletin 647
American Feed Industry Association. Annual Meeting of the Nutrition Council. Proceedings (US) 64
American Feed Manufacturers Association. Annual Meeting of the Nutrition Council. Proceedings see American Feed Industry Association. Annual Meeting of the Nutrition Council. Proceedings 64
American Fertilizer Handbook see Farm Chemicals Handbook 55

American Film and Video Festival Guide (US) 822
American Film & Video Review (US) 822
American Film Festival Guide see American Film and Video Festival Guide 822
American Film Review see American Film & Video Review 822
American Fisheries Society. Special Publication (US ISSN 0097-0638) 507
American Fisheries Society Monograph (US ISSN 0362-1715) 507
American Folk Music Occasional (US ISSN 0065-8316) 832
American Forage and Grassland Council. Proceedings of the Research Industry Conference (US) 63
American Foreign Policy Library (US) 603
American Foundation for the Blind. Annual Report (US ISSN 0065-8359) 1015
American Foundation for the Study of Man. Publications (US ISSN 0569-4833) 69
American Foundations and their Fields see Foundation Directory 1022
American Foundrymen's Society. Transactions (US ISSN 0065-8375) 796
American Friends Service Committee. Annual Report (US ISSN 0071-9617) 1015
American Frozen Food Institute. Membership Directory see American Frozen Food Institute. Membership Directory and Buyers' Guide 518
American Frozen Food Institute. Membership Directory and Buyers' Guide (US ISSN 0361-0888) 518
American Fulbright Scholars see Directory of American Fulbright Scholars 441
American Gas Association. Operating Section. Proceedings (US ISSN 0362-4994) 862
American Gas Association Rate Service(US) 862
American Geophysical Union. Geophysical Monograph see American Geophysical Union. Geophysical Monograph Book Series 398
American Geophysical Union. Geophysical Monograph Book Series (US) 398
American-German Studies/Deutsch-Amerikanische Studien (GW) 914
American Goat Society. Year Book (US ISSN 0065-8456) 64
American Group Practice Association Directory (US ISSN 0098-2377) 616
American Group Psychotherapy Monograph Series (US) 932
American Guild of Variety Artists Newsletter see A G V A Newsletter 648
American Gynecological and Obstetrical Society. Transactions of the A G O S (US) 784
American Gynecological Society. Transactions of the A G S see American Gynecological and Obstetrical Society. Transactions of the A G O S 784
American Heart Association. Monographs (US ISSN 0065-8499) 776
American Helicopter Society. Annual Forum. Proceedings (US) 17
American Helicopter Society. National Forum. Proceedings see American Helicopter Society. Annual Forum. Proceedings 17
American-Hellenic Chamber of Commerce. Business Directory see American-Hellenic Chamber of Commerce. Business Directory. Special Issue 302
American-Hellenic Chamber of Commerce. Business Directory. Special Issue (GR ISSN 0065-8537) 302
American Heritage Cumulative Index (US) 2, 562

American Heritage Index see American Heritage Cumulative Index 562
American Historical Association. Annual Report (US ISSN 0065-8561) 554
American History (US) 121, 562
American Home Economics Association. Textiles and Clothing Section. Textile Handbook (US ISSN 0065-8588) 1146
American Hospital Association. Guide to the Health Care Field (US ISSN 0094-8969) 618, 952
American Hospital Formulary Service see American Hospital Formulary Service Drug Information 869
American Hospital Formulary Service Drug Information (US) 869
American Hotel and Motel Association. Buyers Guide for Hotels & Motels. (US) 619
American Hotel and Motel Association. Product News. see American Hotel and Motel Association. Buyers Guide for Hotels & Motels 619
American Humane Association. National Humane Report see American Humane Association Annual Report 1015
American Humane Association Annual Report (US) 1015
American Humanities Index (US ISSN 0361-0144) 2, 634, 738
American Indian Archaeological Institute. Occasional Paper (US) 80
American Indian Bibliographic Series (US) 506
American Indian Libraries Newsletter (US ISSN 0193-8207) 501, 673
American Indian Treaties Publications Series (US) 501, 603, 650
American Industrial Arts Association. Yearbook see American Council on Industrial Arts Teacher Education. Yearbook 410
American Industrial Hygiene Association. Conference Proceedings (US) 635
American Institute for Conservation of Historic and Artistic Works. Book & Paper Group Annual (US) 959
American Institute for Conservation of Historic and Artistic Works. Postprints see American Institute for Conservation of Historic and Artistic Works. Book & Paper Group Annual 959
American Institute for Conservation of Historic and Artistic Works. Preprints of Papers Presented at the Annual Meeting (US ISSN 0272-3727) 101
American Institute for Decision Sciences. Annual Meeting Proceedings (US) 278
American Institute for Decision Sciences. National Conference Proceedings see American Institute for Decision Sciences. Annual Meeting Proceedings 278
American Institute for Decision Sciences. Southeast Section. Proceedings (US ISSN 0360-7100) 278
American Institute for Marxist Studies. Bibliographic Series (US ISSN 0065-8650) 911
American Institute for Marxist Studies. Occasional Papers (US ISSN 0084-6368) 902
American Institute of Aeronautics and Astronautics Atmospheric Flight Mechanics Conference Proceedings see A I A A Atmospheric Flight Mechanics Conference Proceedings 17
American Institute of Aeronautics and Astronautics Communications Satellite Systems Conference. Technical Papers see A I A A Communications Satellite Systems Conference. Technical Papers 17
American Institute of Aeronautics and Astronautics Roster see A I A A Roster 17
American Institute of Architects. International Directory (US ISSN 0272-0906) 96

American Institute of Certified Public Accountants. Division of Federal Taxation. Statements on Responsibilities in Tax Practice (US ISSN 0065-874X) 221, 292
American Institute of Certified Public Accountants. Public Oversight Board. Annual Report (US) 221
American Institute of Certified Public Accountants Professional Standards see A I C P A Professional Standards 220
American Institute of Chemical Engineers Ch E Applications Software Survey of Personal Computers see A I Ch E Applications Software Survey of Personal Computers 362
American Institute of Chemical Engineers Ch E Equipment Testing Procedures see A I Ch E Equipment Testing Procedures 477
American Institute of Chemical Engineers Ch E M I Modular Instruction. Series A: Process Control see A I Ch E M I Modular Instruction. Series A: Process Control 1145
American Institute of Chemical Engineers Ch E M I Modular Instruction. Series B: Stagewise and Mass Transfer Operations see A I Ch E M I Modular Instruction. Series B: Stagewise and Mass Transfer Operations 1145
American Institute of Chemical Engineers Ch E M I Modular Instruction. Series C: Transport see A I Ch E M I Modular Instruction. Series C: Transport 477
American Institute of Chemical Engineers Ch E M I Modular Instruction. Series D: Thermodynamics see A I Ch E M I Modular Instruction. Series D: Thermodynamics 1145
American Institute of Chemical Engineers Ch E M I Modular Instruction. Series E: Kinetics see A I Ch E M I Modular Instruction. Series E: Kinetics 1145
American Institute of Chemical Engineers Ch E M I Modular Instruction. Series F: Material and Energy Balances see A I Ch E M I Modular Instruction. Series F: Material and Energy Balances 1145
American Institute of Chemical Engineers Ch E M I Modular Instruction. Series G: Design of Equipment see A I Ch E M I Modular Instruction. Series G: Design of Equipment 477
American Institute of Chemical Engineers Ch E Monograph Series see A I Ch E Monograph Series 477
American Institute of Chemical Engineers Ch E Symposium Series see A I Ch E Symposium Series 477
American Institute of Chemical Engineers Ch E Workshop Series see A I Ch E Workshop Series 477
American Institute of Chemists. Membership Directory see American Institute of Chemists. Professional Directory 321
American Institute of Chemists. Professional Directory (US) 321
American Institute of Graphic Arts Graphic Design U S A see A I G A Graphic Design U S A 930
American Institute of Indian Studies. Biennial Report (US) 568
American Institute of Industrial Engineers. Health Services Division. Annual Conference Proceedings see Institute of Industrial Engineers. Health Services Division. Annual Conference Proceedings 617
American Institute of Mining, Metallurgical and Petroleum Engineers. National Open Hearth and Basic Oxygen Steel Division. Proceedings of the Conference see Steelmaking Conference: Proceedings 820
American Institute of Musical Studies Bulletin see A I M S Bulletin 832

American Institute of Musicology. Miscellanea (GW ISSN 0065-8855) 832
American Institute of Physics. Symposium on Temperature. Proceedings see Temperature: Its Measurement and Control in Science and Industry 894
American Institute of Physics Conference Proceedings see A I P Conference Proceedings 886
American Institute of Ultrasound in Medicine. Annual Scientific Conference. Proceedings (US) 757, 900
American Institute of Ultrasound in Medicine. Annual Scientific Conference. Program see American Institute of Ultrasound in Medicine. Annual Scientific Conference. Proceedings 757
American Insurance Services Group. Engineering and Safety Service. Special Interest Bulletin (US) 637
American Iron and Steel Institute. Annual Statistical Report (US) 188, 476
American Italian Historical Association. Proceedings (US) 501
American Jewish Alternatives to Zionism. Report (US) 501, 914
American Jewish Committee. Domestic Affairs Department. Pertinent Papers(US) 902
American Jewish Communal History (US ISSN 0065-8936) 603
American Jewish Historical Society. News see Heritage (Waltham) 976
American Jewish Historical Society. Report see Heritage (Waltham) 976
American Jewish Year Book (US ISSN 0065-8987) 976
American Journal of Jurisprudence (US ISSN 0065-8995) 650
American Judicature Society. Annual Report (US ISSN 0732-1031) 650
American Language Journal (US ISSN 0734-7545) 446, 690
American Laryngological, Rhinological and Otological Society. Transactions (US ISSN 0065-9037) 787
American Law Institute. Annual Meeting. Proceedings (US ISSN 0065-9045) 650
American Lawyer Guide to Law Firms see American Lawyer Guide to Leading Law Firms 1146
American Lawyer Guide to Leading Law Firms (US) 1146
American Library Association. Annual Conference Program (US) 673, 795
American Library Association Handbook of Organization see A L A Handbook of Organization 672
American Library Association Studies in Librarianship see A L A Studies in Librarianship 672
American Library Association Yearbook see A L A Yearbook 672
American Library Directory (US ISSN 0065-910X) 673
American Library Laws (US) 650, 673
American Literary Scholarship (US ISSN 0065-9142) 714
American Littoral Society. Special Publications (US ISSN 0065-9150) 364
American Logistics Association Worldwide Directory and Fact Book see A L A Worldwide Directory and Fact Book 810
American Lutheran Church. Yearbook see Lutheran Church in America. Yearbook 979
American Man (US ISSN 0271-9487) 1146
American Management Association. Research Studies (US ISSN 0065-9185) 278
American Management Association. Seminar Program (US ISSN 0065-9193) 278
American Management Associations Management Briefings see A M A Management Briefings 278
American Management Associations Survey Reports see A M A Survey Reports 278

American Marketing Association. Annual Marketing Educators' Conference. Proceedings (US) *282*
American Marketing Association. International Membership Directory and Marketing Services Guide (US) *282, 302*
American Marketing Association. Membership Roster and Directory of International Marketing Service Organizations *see* American Marketing Association. International Membership Directory and Marketing Services Guide *282*
American Marketing Association. Proceedings *see* American Marketing Association. Annual Marketing Educators' Conference. Proceedings *282*
American Material Culture and Folklife(US) *514*
American Mathematical Society. Colloquium Publications (US ISSN 0065-9258) *747*
American Mathematical Society. New Publications *see* Current Mathematical Publications *755*
American Mathematical Society. Proceedings of Symposia in Applied Mathematics *see* S I A M - A M S Proceedings *752*
American Mathematical Society. Translations. Series 2 (US ISSN 0065-9290) *747*
American Meat Science Association. Reciprocal Meat Conference. Proceedings (US) *64, 518*
American Medical Association. Council on Ethical and Judicial Affairs. Current Opinions (US) *757*
American Medical Association. Directory of Officials and Staff *see* A M A Directory of Officials and Staff *756*
American Medical Association. Directory of Residency Training Programs *see* Directory of Residency Training Accredited by the Accreditation Council for Graduate Medical Education *434*
American Medical Association. Judicial Council. Current Opinions *see* American Medical Association. Council on Ethical and Judicial Affairs. Current Opinions *757*
American Medical Association Directory of Officials and Staff *see* A M A Directory of Officials and Staff *756*
American Medical Directory (US) *757*
American Medical Directory of Physicians *see* American Medical Directory *757*
American Men and Women of Science. Physical and Biological Sciences (US ISSN 0065-9347) *133, 987*
American Merchant Marine Conference. Proceedings (US) *1098*
American Merchant Marine Library Association. Report (US ISSN 0065-938X) *673*
American Meteorological Society. Meteorological Monographs (US ISSN 0065-9401) *803*
American Midland Naturalist Monograph Series (US ISSN 0065-9436) *137*
American Monument Association. Retailer's Guide *see* A M A Product Directory *813*
American Monument Association Product Directory *see* A M A Product Directory *813*
American Museum Novitates (US ISSN 0003-0082) *987*
American Museum of Natural History. Annual Report (US) *826, 987*
American Museum of Natural History. Anthropological Papers (US ISSN 0065-9452) *69*
American Museum of Natural History. Bulletin (US ISSN 0003-0090) *826, 987*
American Musical Instrument Society. Journal (US ISSN 0362-3300) *832*
American Musicological Society. Studies and Documents (US) *832*

American National Red Cross. Annual Report *see* American Red Cross. Annual Report *1015*
American Newspaper Markets Circulation (US) *645*
American Nuclear Society. Proceedings of the Executive Conference (US) *895*
American Nuclear Society. Proceedings of the National Topical Meeting (US) *895*
American Nuclear Society. Proceedings of the Pacific Basin Conference on Nuclear Power Development (US) *895*
American Numismatic Society. Annual Report (US ISSN 0569-6720) *844*
American O R T Federation. Yearbook (US) *501*
American Ophthalmological Society. Transactions (US ISSN 0065-9533) *785*
American Oriental Series (US ISSN 0065-9541) *850*
American Orthopsychiatric Association. Papers Presented at the Annual Convention (US) *789*
American Orthoptic Journal (US ISSN 0065-955X) *785*
American Osteopathic Association Yearbook and Directory of Osteopathic Physicians *see* A O A Yearbook and Directory of Osteopathic Physicians *777*
American Otological Society. Transactions (US) *787*
American Peanut Research and Education Society Proceedings *see* A P R E S Proceedings *51*
American Petroleum Institute. Abstracts of Refining Patents *see* A P I Abstracts/Patents *867*
American Petroleum Institute. Central Abstracting and Indexing Service. Thesaurus (US ISSN 0193-5151) *673, 862*
American Petroleum Institute. Division of Refining. Proceedings. *see* American Petroleum Institute. Refining Department. Proceedings *862*
American Petroleum Institute. Health and Environmental Sciences Department. Research Reports (US) *862, 952, 1067*
American Petroleum Institute. Information Retrieval System, Subject Authority List. *see* American Petroleum Institute. Central Abstracting and Indexing Service. Thesaurus *862*
American Petroleum Institute. Medicine and Biological Science Department. Medical Research Reports *see* American Petroleum Institute. Health and Environmental Sciences Department. Research Reports *952*
American Petroleum Institute. Refining Department. Proceedings (US ISSN 0163-495X) *862*
American Petroleum Institute Abstracts Literature *see* A P I Abstracts/Literature *867*
American Petroleum Institute Abstracts Oilfield Chemicals *see* A P I Abstracts/Oilfield Chemicals *867*
American Petroleum Institute Abstracts Patents *see* A P I Abstracts/Patents *867*
American Philatelic Congress. Congress Book (US) *874*
American Philological Association. Directory of Members (US ISSN 0044-779X) *336, 690, 714*
American Philological Association. Special Publications (US ISSN 0065-9703) *336, 690, 714*
American Philological Association. Transactions (US ISSN 0360-5949) *690*
American Philological Association. Transactions and Proceedings *see* American Philological Association. Transactions *690*
American Philosophical Society. Memoirs (US ISSN 0065-9738) *554, 876, 987*

American Philosophical Society. Transactions (US ISSN 0065-9746) *554, 876, 987*
American Philosophical Society. Yearbook (US ISSN 0065-9762) *876*
American Phytopathological Society. Monographs (US ISSN 0569-6992) *154*
American Podiatric Medical Association. Desk Reference and Directory (US) *786, 794*
American Podiatry Association. Desk Reference and Directory *see* American Podiatric Medical Association. Desk Reference and Directory *794*
American Poetry Anthology (US) *740*
American Poetry Index (US) *738, 740*
American Poetry Series (US) *740*
American Political Science Association Departmental Services Program Survey of Departments *see* A P S A Departmental Services Program Survey of Departments *901*
American Political Science Association Directory of Department Chairpersons *see* A P S A Directory of Department Chairpersons *901*
American Popular Culture (US ISSN 0193-6859) *603*
American Power Boat Association. A P B A Rule Book (US ISSN 0065-9797) *1041*
American Power Conference. Proceedings. (US ISSN 0097-2126) *463, 1067*
American Printing House for the Blind, Louisville, Kentucky. Department of Educational Research. Annual Report *see* American Printing House for the Blind, Louisville, Kentucky. Department of Educational Research. Report of Research and Development Activities *444*
American Printing House for the Blind, Louisville, Kentucky. Department of Educational Research. Report of Research and Development Activities(US) *444*
American Problems Studies (US) *603*
American Production and Inventory Control Society. Annual Conference Proceedings *see* American Production and Inventory Control Society. Annual International Conference Proceedings *278*
American Production and Inventory Control Society. Annual International Conference Proceedings (US) *278*
American Psychiatric Association. Scientific Proceedings in Summary Form (US ISSN 0090-1881) *789*
American Psychiatric Association. Task Force Reports (US) *789*
American Psychoanalytic Association. Journal. Monograph (US ISSN 0065-9843) *932*
American Psychoanalytic Association. Workshop Series (US) *932*
American Psychological Association. Biographical Directory *see* American Psychological Association. Directory *133*
American Psychological Association. Directory (US ISSN 0196-6545) *133, 932*
American Psychological Association. Membership Register (US ISSN 0569-714X) *133, 932*
American Psychopathological Association. Proceedings of the Annual Meeting (US ISSN 0091-7389) *789*
American Psychopathological Association. Publications (US ISSN 0065-9886) *1146*
American Public Opinion Data (US) *540*
American Public Opinion Index (US ISSN 0740-8978) *2, 1031*
American Public Welfare Association. W - Memo (US ISSN 0163-8300) *1015*
American Public Works Association. Directory (US ISSN 0360-6899) *939, 1067*

American Public Works Association. Research Foundation. Special Reports (US ISSN 0065-9932) *480*
American Racehorse Owners & Breeders Almanac *see* Agenda American Almanac (Year) *1042*
American Radio Relay League, Inc. Repeater Directory *see* A R R L Repeater Directory *347*
American Railway Bridge and Building Association. Proceedings (US ISSN 0065-9940) *181*
American Railway Engineering Association. Proceedings (US) *1094*
American Railway Engineering Association. Proceedings of the Annual Convention *see* American Railway Engineering Association. Proceedings *1094*
American Railway Engineering Association. Proceedings, Technical Conference *see* American Railway Engineering Association. Proceedings *1094*
American Red Cross. Annual Report (US) *1015*
American Reference Books Annual (US ISSN 0065-9959) *121, 687*
American Register of Exporters and Importers *see* American Export Register *253*
American Register of Printing and Graphic Arts Services (US ISSN 0276-5519) *930*
American Research Center in Egypt. Journal (US ISSN 0065-9991) *80, 101*
American Research Center in Egypt. Reports (US ISSN 0732-6432) *101*
American Review (JA ISSN 0387-2815) *914*
American Rheumatism Association. Directory (US) *793*
American Road and Transportation Builders Association Officials and Engineers Directory, Transportation Agency Personnel *see* A R T B A Officials and Engineers Directory, Transportation Agency Personnel *1095*
American Romanian Academy of Arts and Sciences. Publications (US) *501*
American Rose Annual (US ISSN 0066-0000) *531*
American Samoa Bar Association. Newsletter *see* Samoan Pacific Law Journal *663*
American Savings Directory (US) *222*
American School of Prehistoric Research. Bulletins (US ISSN 0066-0027) *80*
American Schools of Oriental Research. Annual (US ISSN 0066-0035) *80, 612*
American Series of Foreign Penal Codes (US ISSN 0066-0051) *369*
American Shoemaking Directory (US) *302, 1005*
American Society for Abrasive Methods. Technical Conference. Proceedings *see* Abrasive Engineering Society. Abrasive Usage Conference. Proceedings *469*
American Society for Adolescent Psychiatry. Annals. *see* Adolescent Psychiatry *788*
American Society for Armenian Studies. Journal (US ISSN 0747-9301) *101, 501, 714*
American Society for Conservation Archaeology. Proceedings (US) *80*
American Society for Cybernetics. Proceedings of the Annual Symposium (US ISSN 0066-0086) *359*
American Society for Engineering Education. Annual Conference Proceedings (US ISSN 0190-1052) *469*
American Society for Horticultural Science. Caribbean Region. Proceedings of the Annual Meeting *see* American Society for Horticultural Science. Tropical Region. Proceedings of the Annual Meeting *531*

American Society for Horticultural Science. Tropical Region. Proceedings of the Annual Meeting (MX ISSN 0066-0116) *531*
American Society for Information Science. Handbook and Directory (US) *302, 673*
American Society for Information Science, Western Canada Chapter. Annual Meeting Proceedings (CN ISSN 0318-9937) *673*
American Society for Metals Bibliography Series *see* A S M Bibliography Series *801*
American Society for Metals Metallurgy - Materials Education Yearbook *see* Metallurgy - Materials Education Yearbook *799*
American Society for Metals Metals Abstracts *see* Metals Abstracts *801*
American Society for Metals Metals Abstracts Index *see* Metals Abstracts Index *801*
American Society for Metals Translations Index *see* Translations Index *802*
American Society for Microbiology. Abstracts of the Annual Meeting (US ISSN 0094-8519) *167*
American Society for Microbiology. Eastern Pennsylvania Branch. Symposia (US) *167*
American Society for Neurochemistry. Transactions (US ISSN 0066-0132) *789*
American Society for Photogrammetry and Remote Sensing. Technical Papers from the Annual Meeting (US) *469, 541*
American Society for Photogrammetry and Remote Sensing Fall Convention. Technical Papers (US) *114, 541*
American Society for Public Administration. Section on International and Comparative Administration. Occasional Papers (US) *939*
American Society for Quality Control. Annual Technical Conference Transactions (US ISSN 0360-6929) *808*
American Society for Quality Control. Transactions of Annual Technical Conferences *see* American Society for Quality Control. Annual Technical Conference Transactions *808*
American Society for Reformation Research. Newsletter *see* Historians of Early Modern Europe *585*
American Society for Testing and Materials. Compilation of A S T M Standards in Building Codes (US ISSN 0066-0523) *181, 485*
American Society for Testing and Materials. Data Series Publications (US ISSN 0066-0531) *485*
American Society for Testing and Materials. Five-Year Index to A S T M Technical Papers and Reports (US ISSN 0066-054X) *485*
American Society for Testing and Materials. Special Technical Publications (US ISSN 0066-0558) *485*
American Society for Testing and Materials Annual Book of A S T M 1.1 *see* Annual Book of A S T M Standards. Volume 01.01. Steel-Piping, Tubing, Fittings *485*
American Society for Testing and Materials Proceedings *see* A S T M Proceedings *485*
American Society for Training and Development. Membership Directory *see* Who's Who in Training and Development *282*
American Society of Agricultural Engineers Monograph Series *see* A S A E Monograph Series *469*
American Society of Agricultural Engineers Standards *see* A S A E Standards *51*
American Society of Agronomy, Inc. Special Publication *see* A S A Special Publication *22*

American Society of Anesthesiologists Refresher Courses in Anesthesiology *see* A S A Refresher Courses in Anesthesiology *774*
American Society of Animal Science. Western Section Proceedings (US ISSN 0569-7832) *1120*
American Society of Appraisers Monograph *see* A S A Monograph *964*
American Society of Bakery Engineers. Proceedings of the Annual Meeting (US ISSN 0066-0582) *522*
American Society of Bookplate Collectors and Designers. Year Book (US ISSN 0275-1569) *101, 614, 959*
American Society of Civil Engineers. Official Register (US) *480*
American Society of Civil Engineers. Transactions (US ISSN 0066-0604) *476*
American Society of Civil Engineers Annual Combined Index *see* A S C E Annual Combined Index *480*
American Society of Composers, Authors and Publishers Biographical Dictionary *see* A S C A P Biographical Dictionary *832*
American Society of Heating, Refrigerating and Air-Conditioning Engineers Inc. Handbook *see* A S H R A E Handbook *553*
American Society of International Law. Occasional Papers *see* Studies in Transnational Legal Policy *665*
American Society of International Law. Proceedings of the Annual Meeting (US ISSN 0272-5045) *669*
American Society of Landscape Architects Members Handbook *see* A S L A Members Handbook *96*
American Society of Mammalogists. Special Publications (US ISSN 0569-8219) *173*
American Society of Newspaper Editors 19 *see* A S N E 19 *645*
American Society of Photogrammetry. Technical Papers from the Annual Meeting *see* American Society for Photogrammetry and Remote Sensing. Technical Papers from the Annual Meeting *541*
American Society of Photogrammetry Fall Convention. Technical Papers *see* American Society for Photogrammetry and Remote Sensing Fall Convention. Technical Papers *541*
American Society of Plant Physiologists. Proceedings of Annual Meeting *see* Plant Physiology. Supplement Abstracts of Annual Meeting *160*
American Society of Plastic and Reconstructive Surgeons. Symposia (US) *794*
American Society of Safety Engineers. Proceedings. Professional Conference(US) *469*
American Society of Sanitary Engineering. Year Book (US ISSN 0066-068X) *952*
American Society of Sephardic Studies Series *see* Sephardic Scholar *505*
American Society of University Composers Journal of Music Scores *see* A S U C Journal of Music Scores *832*
American Sociological Association. Proceedings of Annual Meeting (US) *1024*
American Solar Energy Society. Annual Meeting (US) *463*
American Solar Energy Society. Passive Conference. Annual Meeting (US) *463*
American Solar Energy Society. Research Reports (US) *463*
American Speech - Language - Hearing Association. Directory (US) *375, 444, 787*
American Speech-Language-Hearing Association Reports *see* A S H A Reports *786*
American Statistical Association. Business and Economic Statistics Section. Proceedings (US ISSN 0066-0736) *202*

American Statistical Association. Section on Statistical Education. Proceedings. (US) *410, 1048*
American Statistical Association. Social Statistics Section. Proceedings (US ISSN 0066-0752) *925*
American Statistical Association. Statistical Computing Section. Proceedings (of the Annual Meeting) (US ISSN 0149-9963) *353, 1048*
American Statistical Association. Survey Research Methods. Proceedings (US) *1048*
American Statistics Index (US ISSN 0091-1658) *1048*
American Stock Exchange. AMEX Databook *see* American Stock Exchange. AMEX Fact Book *265*
American Stock Exchange. AMEX Fact Book (US) *265*
American Stock Exchange. Annual Report (US ISSN 0066-0779) *265*
American Stock Exchange Directory (US) *265*
American Student Dental Association Handbook *see* A S D A Handbook *778*
American Studies Research Centre. Newsletter (II ISSN 0066-0795) *603*
American Subsidiaries of German Firms(US) *234*
American Surgical Association. Transactions (US ISSN 0066-0833) *794*
American Theological Library Association. Conference. Summary of Proceedings (US ISSN 0066-0868) *673*
American Theological Library Association Bibliography Series *see* A T L A Bibliography Series *967*
American Theological Library Association Monograph Series *see* A T L A Monograph Series *967*
American Trail Series (US ISSN 0066-0884) *603*
American Translators Association Translation Services Directory *see* Translation Services Directory *706*
American Trucking Trends. Statistical Report *see* American Trucking Trends - (Year) *1104*
American Trucking Trends - (Year) (US) *1104*
American Type Culture Collection. Catalogue of Animal and Plant Viruses, Chlamydiae, Rickettsiae and Virus Antisera (US) *167*
American Type Culture Collection. Catalogue of Bacteria, Phages, and rD N A Vectors *see* American Type Culture Collection. Catalogue of Recombinant D N A Collections *168*
American Type Culture Collection. Catalogue of Cell Lines and Hybridomas (US) *168*
American Type Culture Collection. Catalogue of Fungi/Yeasts (US) *168*
American Type Culture Collection. Catalogue of Protists. Algae/Protozoa (US) *168*
American Type Culture Collection. Catalogue of Recombinant D N A Collections (US) *168*
American Type Culture Collection. Catalogue of Strains II, Animal Cell Lines, Animal Viruses, Bacterial Viruses, Mycoviruses, Plant Viruses, Rickettsiae, Chlamydiae *see* American Type Culture Collection. Catalogue of Animal and Plant Viruses, Chlamydiae, Rickettsiae and Virus Antisera *167*
American Type Culture Collection. Catalogue of Strains 1: Algae, Bacteria, Bacteriophages, Plasmids, Fungi, Plant Viruses and Antisera and Protozoa *see* American Type Culture Collection. Catalogue of Fungi/Yeasts *168*
American Type Culture Collection. Catalogue of Strains 1: Algae, Bacteria, Bacteriophages, Plasmids, Fungi, Plant Viruses and Antisera and Protozoa *see* American Type Culture Collection. Catalogue of Protists. Algae/Protozoa *168*

American Type Culture Collection. Catalogue of Strains 2: Animal Cell Lines, Animal Viruses, Bacterial Viruses, Mycoviruses, Plant Viruses, Rickettsiae, Chlamydiae *see* American Type Culture Collection. Catalogue of Cell Lines and Hybridomas *168*
American Universities and Colleges (US ISSN 0066-0922) *428*
American University Studies. Series 1. Germanic Languages and Literature (US ISSN 0721-1392) *690*
American University Studies. Series 2. Romance Languages and Literature (US ISSN 0740-9257) *714*
American University Studies. Series 3. Comparative Literature (US ISSN 0724-1445) *714*
American University Studies. Series 4. English Language and Literature (US ISSN 0741-0700) *714*
American University Studies. Series 5. Anglo-Saxon Language and Literature *see* American University Studies. Series 4. English Language and Literature *714*
American University Studies. Series 5. Philosophy (US) *876*
American University Studies. Series 6. Foreign Language Instruction (US) *690*
American University Studies. Series 7. Theology and Religion (US ISSN 0740-0446) *554, 967*
American University Studies. Series 8. Psychology (US ISSN 0740-0454) *932*
American University Studies. Series 9. History (US ISSN 0740-0462) *554*
American University Studies. Series 10. Political Science (US ISSN 0740-0470) *650*
American University Studies. Series 11. Anthropology and Sociology (US ISSN 0740-0489) *1006*
American University Studies. Series 12. Slavic Languages and Literature (US ISSN 0740-0497) *690*
American University Studies. Series 13. Linguistics (US ISSN 0740-4557) *690*
American University Studies. Series 14. Education (US ISSN 0740-4565) *442*
American University Studies. Series 15. Communications (US ISSN 0740-5111) *14*
American University Studies. Series 16. Economics (US ISSN 0741-2150) *920, 1024*
American University Studies. Series 17. Classical Language and Literature (US ISSN 0741-9309) *714*
American University Studies. Series 18. African Literature (US ISSN 0742-1923) *714*
American University Studies. Series 19. General Literature (US) *714*
American Veterinary Medical Association. Directory (US ISSN 0066-1147) *1121*
American Vocational Association. Yearbook (US) *1146*
American Water Resources Conferences. Annual Proceedings *see* American Water Resources Symposia. Annual Proceedings *1123*
American Water Resources Symposia. Annual Proceedings (US) *1123*
American Water Works Association. Proceedings, A W W A Annual Conference (US ISSN 0360-814X) *1123*
American Welding Society Annual Meeting. Abstracts of Papers (US) *802*
American Wine Society. Bulletin (US ISSN 0149-6778) *119, 614*
American Wine Society Manual (US ISSN 0149-676X) *119*
American Wood Preservers' Association. Proceedings. (US) *529*
American Youth Hostels Guide and Handbook *see* A Y H Handbook *1105*
American Youth Hostels, Inc. Handbook *see* A Y H Handbook *1105*

Americana Annual (US ISSN 0196-0180) 462
Americans for Constitutional Action. Report (US ISSN 0066-1236) 902
Americans for Constitutional Action Index see A C A Index 901
Americans for Justice in the Middle East News see A J M E News 611
America's Corporate Families and International Affiliates (US ISSN 0740-4018) 302
America's Cup Challenge and Guide to Australia (US) 1032, 1106
America's Favorite National Parks (US) 1106
Amerindia (UY) 69
Amex Fact Book see American Stock Exchange. AMEX Fact Book 265
Amino-Acids, Peptides, and Proteins (UK ISSN 0306-0004) 151
Amis de l'E.N.S.B.A.N.A. see Ecole Nationale Superieure de Biologie Appliquee a la Nutrition et a l'Alimentation. Cahiers 846
Amis de l'Histoire de la Perade. Collection "Nos Vieilles Familles" (CN) 534
Amis de Ramuz. Bulletin (FR ISSN 0293-0773) 133, 714
Amitie Henri Bosco. Cahiers see Cahiers Henri Bosco 718
Amli Studies in Music Bibliography (IS ISSN 0066-1260) 1146
Ammonia Plant Safety and Related Facilities (US ISSN 0149-3701) 477
Amnesty International Annual Report see Amnesty International Report 914
Amnesty International Report (UK) 912, 914
Amptelike Suid-Afrikaanse Munisipale Jaarboek see Official South African Municipal Yearbook 951
Ampurias (SP) 80
Amsterdam-Rotterdam Bank. Annual Report (NE ISSN 0066-1309) 222
Amsterdam Stock Exchange (NE) 265
Amsterdam Studies in the Theory and History of Linguistic Science. Series 1: Amsterdam Classics in Linguistics, 1800-1925 (US ISSN 0304-0712) 690
Amsterdam Studies in the Theory and History of Linguistic Science. Series 2: Classics in Psycholinguistics (US ISSN 0165-716X) 690, 933
Amsterdam Studies in the Theory and History of Linguistic Science. Series 3: Studies in the History of the Language Sciences (US) 690
Amsterdam Studies in the Theory and History of Linguistic Science. Series 4: Current Issues in Linguistic Theory (US ISSN 0304-0763) 690
Amsterdam Studies in the Theory and History of Linguistic Science. Series 5: Library and Information Sources in Linguistics (US ISSN 0165-7267) 709
Amsterdam Studies In The Theory and History of the Linguistic Science. Series 3: Studies In the History of Linguistics see Amsterdam Studies in the Theory and History of Linguistic Science. Series 3: Studies in the History of the Language Sciences 690
Amsterdam Studies in Theology (NE ISSN 0169-0272) 967
Amsterdamer Beitraege zur Neueren Germanistik (NE ISSN 0304-6257) 575, 714
Amsterdamer Publikationen zur Sprache und Literatur (NE ISSN 0169-0221) 690, 714
Amstkommunernes Oekonomi (DK ISSN 0105-8509) 950
Amternes Oekonomi (DK ISSN 0109-7822) 191
Amtrak Annual Report (US ISSN 0097-7039) 1094
Amtskommunale Enkeltfagskurser (DK ISSN 0900-3096) 410
Amtskommunernes Oekonomi see Amternes Oekonomi 191
Amusement Business's AudArena Stadium Guide see Audarena Stadium Guide and International Directory 14

Amusement Business's Directory North American Fairs see Directory of North American Fairs and Expositions 15
Amusement Business's Funparks Directory see Funparks Directory 1110
Amusement Equipment Buyers Guide see Buyers' Guide for the Mass Entertainment Industry 1044
Amusement Rides & Games Buyers' Guide (US) 1032
Anadolu Sanati Arastirmalari/ Researches on Anatolian Art (TU ISSN 0066-1333) 101
Anaesthesia Essays and Researches (JO ISSN 0259-1162) 774
Anaesthesiologie und Intensivmedizin/ Anaesthesiology and Intensive Care Medicine (US ISSN 0171-1814) 774
Anaesthesiology and Intensive Care Medicine see Anaesthesiologie und Intensivmedizin 774
Anaesthesiology and Resuscitation see Anaesthesiologie und Intensivmedizin 774
Anagnostika Hetaireia Kerkyras. Deltion (GR) 575
Anais: An International Journal (US) 714
Anais de Historia see Historia 557
Anais Hidrograficos (BL) 1123
Analecta Biblica (IT ISSN 0066-135X) 980
Analecta Boerhaaviana (NE ISSN 0066-1368) 757
Analecta Cartesiana (NE) 876
Analecta Cartusiana (AU) 575, 714, 967
Analecta Gregoriana (VC ISSN 0066-1376) 980
Analecta Husserliana (NE) 876
Analecta Musicologia (GW ISSN 0569-9827) 832
Analecta Orientalia (VC) 850
Analecta Praehistorica Leidensia (NE ISSN 0569-9843) 80
Analecta Romana Instituti Danici (IT ISSN 0066-1392) 575
Analecta Romana Instituti Danici. Supplementum (IT ISSN 0066-1406) 575
Analecta Romanica (GW ISSN 0569-986X) 690, 714
Analecta Vaticano-Belgica. Deuxieme Serie. Section A: Nonciature de Flandre (BE ISSN 0066-1414) 980
Analecta Vaticano-Belgica. Deuxieme Serie. Section B: Nonciature de Cologne (BE ISSN 0066-1422) 980
Analecta Vaticano-Belgica. Deuxieme Serie. Section C: Nonciature de Bruxelles (BE ISSN 0066-1430) 980
Analecta Vaticano-Belgica. Premiere Serie: Documents Relatifs aux Anciens Dioceses de Cambrai, Liege, Therouanne et Tournai (BE ISSN 0066-1449) 980
Analecta Vlatadon (GR) 983
Anales de Arqueologia y Etnologia (AG ISSN 0325-0288) 69, 80
Anales de Cirugia (AG ISSN 0066-1465) 794
Anales de Geografia (MX) 541
Anales de la Comunidad Israelita de Buenos Aires (AG) 501
Anales de la Universidad Hispalense. Serie: Arquitectura (SP) 96
Anales de la Universidad Hispalense. Serie: Ciencias (SP ISSN 0374-5880) 987
Anales de la Universidad Hispalense. Serie: Derecho (SP ISSN 0210-7686) 650
Anales de la Universidad Hispalense. Serie: Economicas y Empresariales see Anales de la Universidad Hispalense. Serie: Empresariales 191
Anales de la Universidad Hispalense. Serie: Empresariales (SP) 191
Anales de la Universidad Hispalense. Serie: Filosofia y Letras (SP ISSN 0210-7678) 628, 987
Anales de la Universidad Hispalense. Serie: Ingenieria (SP) 469

Anales de la Universidad Hispalense. Serie: Medicinas (SP ISSN 0586-9919) 757
Anales de la Universidad Hispalense. Serie: Veterinaria (SP) 1121
Anales de Literatura Hispanoamericana (SP ISSN 0210-4547) 714
Anales de Moral Social y Economica (SP ISSN 0066-1473) 1024
Anales del Instituto de Etnologia Americana see Anales de Arqueologia y Etnologia 80
Anales Galdosianos (US) 714
Anali za Sumarstvo see Annales Forestales 523
Analise Jurisprudencal (BL) 650
Analizy i Proby Technik Badawczych w Socjologii (PL) 1024
Analog Dialogue (US ISSN 0161-3626) 355, 356, 358
Analogo-Diskretnye Preobrazovaniya Signalov (UR ISSN 0135-1281) 361
Analysen (GW ISSN 0072-9426) 902
Analyses of Natural Gases of the United States (US ISSN 0066-149X) 862
Analyses of New Jersey Public Library Statistics for (Year) (US) 673
Analysis (CN ISSN 0707-5723) 494
Analysis of Official Pesticide Samples see Louisiana. Department of Agriculture. Analysis of Official Pesticide Samples; Annual Report 57
Analysis of Oregon Personal Income (US) 292
Analysis of Oregon's Personal Income Tax Returns see Analysis of Oregon Personal Income 292
Analysis of Organic Materials: an International Series of Monographs (US) 329
Analysis of Public Utility Financing (US ISSN 0421-9910) 222
Analysis of School Finances, New York State School Districts (US ISSN 0077-9342) 442
Analysis of Workers' Compensation Laws (US ISSN 0191-118X) 637, 650, 1015
Analysis of Workmen's Compensation Laws see Analysis of Workers' Compensation Laws 1015
Analysis: Quaderni di Anglistica (IT) 714
Analysts Handbook (US) 265
Analytical Calorimetry (US ISSN 0066-1538) 469, 894
Analytical Chemistry (US ISSN 0003-2700) 326
Analytical Chemistry of the Elements Series (US) 326
Analytical Chemistry Symposia Series (NE) 326
Analytical Profiles of Drug Substances (US) 869
Analytical Sciences Monographs (UK ISSN 0583-8894) 326
Analytical Trilogy see Revista de Psicanalise Integral 936
Ananda Acharya Universal Series (II) 714, 876
Anatolian Studies (UK ISSN 0066-1546) 80
Anatolica (NE ISSN 0066-1554) 80, 568
Anatomische Gesellschaft. Verhandlungen (GE ISSN 0066-1562) 757
Anatomischer Anzeiger (GE ISSN 0003-2786) 137, 757
Anbar Management Publications Bibliography (UK ISSN 0261-0108) 202
Anbar Management Services Abstracts see Personnel & Training Abstracts 216
Anbar Management Services Abstracts see Top Management Abstracts 219
Anbar Management Services Abstracts see Work Study & O and M Abstracts 220
Anbar Management Services Abstracts see Accounting & Data Processing Abstracts 353
Anbar Management Services Bibliography see Anbar Management Publications Bibliography 202

Anbar Yearbook (UK ISSN 0307-0409) 278
Anciens Pays et Assemblees d'Etats (BE ISSN 0066-1589) 902
Ancient Ceylon (CE) 80
Ancient Coins in North American Collections (US) 844
Ancient Greek Cities Report (GR) 554, 621, 1024
Ancient Iranian Cultural Society. Publication/Anjoman-e Farhang-e Iran-e Bastan. Nashriyeh (IR ISSN 0517-8045) 714
Ancient Monuments Board for England. Annual Report (UK ISSN 0072-5625) 575
Ancient Monuments Society Transactions (UK) 80, 96, 181
Ancient Near Eastern Society. Journal (US) 850
Ancient Near Eastern Texts and Studies (US) 612
Ancient Society (BE ISSN 0066-1619) 555
Ancient States in the Territory of the U.S.S.R. see Drevneishie Gosudarstva na Territorii S.S.S.R 85
Anda (IO) 933
Andalucia Islamica. Textos y Estudios (SP ISSN 0212-159X) 612
Andar per Ceramiche (IT ISSN 0003-2891) 319
Anderseniana (DK ISSN 0084-6465) 714
Andhra Historical Research Society. Journal (II) 568
Andhra Pradesh, India. Department of Archaeology and Museums. Annual Report (II) 81
Andhra Pradesh, India. Department of Archaeology and Museums. Archaeological Series. (II) 81, 101
Andhra Pradesh, India. Department of Archaeology and Museums. Archaeological Series: A.P. Journal of Archaeolgy (II) 81
Andhra Pradesh, India. Department of Archaeology and Museums. Art and Architectural Series see Andhra Pradesh, India. Department of Archaeology and Museums. Archaeological Series 101
Andhra Pradesh, India. Department of Archaeology and Museums. Epigraphy Series (II) 81, 568
Andhra Pradesh, India. Department of Archaeology and Museums. Museum Series (II) 568, 844
Andhra Pradesh, India. Department of Archaeology and Museums. Museum Objects and Numismatics Series see Andhra Pradesh, India. Department of Archaeology and Museums. Museum Series 844
Andhra Pradesh, India. Department of Archaeology. Epigraphy Series see Andhra Pradesh, India. Department of Archaeology and Museums. Epigraphy Series 81
Andhra Pradesh State Financial Corporation. Report see Andhra Pradesh State Financial Corporation. Report and Accounts 292
Andhra Pradesh State Financial Corporation. Report and Accounts (II) 292
Andhra Pradesh State Trading Corporation Limited. Annual Report (II ISSN 0376-5512) 282
Andhra University Memoirs in Oceanography (II ISSN 0066-1686) 404
Andre Gide (FR ISSN 0180-9350) 714
Andrew W. Mellon Foundation. Report(US ISSN 0066-1694) 628
Andrews University. Monographs (US ISSN 0066-1708) 978
Andrias (GW ISSN 0721-6513) 154, 383
Androgyne (US) 740
Andvari (IC) 575
Andy Awards (US ISSN 0270-2525) 14
Anejos de Archivo Espanol de Arqueologia (SP ISSN 0561-3663) 81
Angela Thirkell Society. Journal (IE) 714

Angel's National Directory of Personnel Managers see Multinational Marketing & Employment Directory 314
Angelstone (US) 740, 1128
Angeltread (US) 101, 714
Angewandte Ornithologie/Applied Ornithology (GW ISSN 0003-3154) 170
Angewandte Statistik und Oekonometrie (GW) 250
Anglers Cooperative Association Review see A.C.A. Review 507
Anglers Mail Annual (UK) 1044
Anglesey Antiquarian Society Transactions (UK ISSN 0306-5790) 81
Anglica et Americana (DK ISSN 0105-9963) 690
Anglica Germanica: Series 2 (UK) 690, 1076
Anglican Chiurch of Canada. General Synod. Journal of Proceedings see Anglican Church of Canada. General Synod. Journal 978
Anglican Church of Canada. General Synod. Journal (CN) 978
Anglican Year Book (CN ISSN 0317-8765) 978
Angling Guide (UK) 1044
Angling Holidays in Ireland (UK) 1106
Anglistica (DK ISSN 0066-1805) 714
Anglistische Forschungen (GW) 714
Anglo-American Forum (GW) 555, 690, 714
Anglo-Catalan Society. Occasional Publications (UK ISSN 0144-5863) 575
Anglo-Norman Studies (US) 575
Anglo-Saxon England (UK ISSN 0263-6751) 628
Angol Filologiai Tanulmanyok/Hungarian Studies in English (HU ISSN 0570-0973) 690, 714
Angola. Direccao dos Servicos de Estatistica. Anuario Estatistico (AO ISSN 0066-5193) 948, 1048
Angola. Direccao dos Servicos de Estatistica. Estatistica dos Veiculos Motorisados (AO) 1084
Angola. Direccao dos Servicos de Estatistica. Estatisticas do Comercio Externo (AO ISSN 0066-1848) 202
Angola. Direccao dos Servicos de Estatistica. Informacoes Estatisticas (AO) 948, 1048
Angola. Direccao Provincial dos Servicos de Geologia e Minas. Boletim (AO ISSN 0003-3456) 383, 814
Angola. Secretaria Provincial de Saude, Trabalho. Previdencia e Assistencia. Sintese da Actividade dos Servicos e Organismos (AO) 885, 939
Angus District Council. Housing Plans and Programmes (UK ISSN 0261-5932) 621
Animal and Grassland Research Institute, Hurley, England (Berkshire) Technical Reports (UK) 52
Animal Anti-Cruelty League. Chairman's Report (SA ISSN 0379-654X) 868
Animal Breeding Abstracts (UK ISSN 0003-3499) 2, 149
Animal Health see Animal Health Trust. Annual Report 1121
Animal Health International Directory (UK) 1121
Animal Health Research Centre. Annual Report (UG) 1121
Animal Health Trust. Annual Report (UK ISSN 0142-6591) 1121
Animal Production and Health Newsletter (UN) 792
Animal Production in Australia (AT ISSN 0728-5965) 64
Animal Quarantine (AT) 1121
Animal Resources (US) 768, 781
Animals for Research see Animals for Research - A Directory of Sources 173
Animals for Research - A Directory of Sources (US) 173, 757
Anjoman-e Dabiran-e Zabanha-Ye Khareji. Nashriyeh see English Language Teachers Association. Review 447

Anjoman-e Farhang-e Iran-e Bastan. Nashriyeh see Ancient Iranian Cultural Society. Publication 714
Ankenaevnet for Arbejdsloeshedsforsikringen. Beretning (DK ISSN 0109-1107) 269, 637
Anklagemyndighedens Aarsberetning (DK ISSN 0108-7169) 650
Anlaegsgartneren see Groent Miljoe 532
Anleitung fuer die Chemische Laboratoriumspraxis see Anleitung fuer die Chemische Laboratoriumspraxis/Chemical Laboratory Practice 321
Anleitung fuer die Chemische Laboratoriumspraxis/Chemical Laboratory Practice (US) 321, 781
Anmeldelser i Paedagogiske Tidsskrifter(DK ISSN 0106-8172) 422
Annale van die Natalse Museum see Natal Museum. Annals 176
Annalen der Meteorologie. Neue Folge (GW ISSN 0072-4122) 803
Annalen der Mijnen van Belgie see Annales des Mines de Belgique 814
Annales Academiae Medicae Bialostocensis see Akademia Medyczna im. J. Marchlewskiego w Bialymstoku. Roczniki 757
Annales Academiae Medicae Cracoviensis. Index Dissertationum Editarum (PL ISSN 0066-1937) 768
Annales Academiae Medicae Stetinensis/Roczniki Pomorskiej Akademii Medycznej w Szczecinie (PL ISSN 0066-1945) 757
Annales Academiae Scientiarum Fennicae. Dissertationes Humanarum Litterarum (FI ISSN 0355-113X) 628
Annales Academiae Scientiarum Fennicae. Series A, I: Mathematica (FI ISSN 0066-1953) 747
Annales Academiae Scientiarum Fennicae. Series A, I: Mathematica Dissertationes (FI ISSN 0355-0087) 747
Annales Academiae Scientiarum Fennicae. Series A, II: Chemica (FI ISSN 0066-1961) 321
Annales Academiae Scientiarum Fennicae. Series A, III: Geologica-Geographica (FI ISSN 0066-197X) 383
Annales Academiae Scientiarum Fennicae. Series A, V: Medica (FI ISSN 0066-1996) 757
Annales Academiae Scientiarum Fennicae. Series A, VI: Physica (FI ISSN 0066-2003) 887
Annales Academiae Scientiarum Fennicae. Series B (FI ISSN 0066-2011) 1006
Annales Aequatoria (ZR ISSN 0254-4296) 69, 690
Annales Benjamin Constant (UK ISSN 0263-7383) 628
Annales Bogorienses (IO ISSN 0517-8452) 154
Annales d'Esthetique/Chronika Aisthetikes (GR ISSN 0066-2119) 101, 876
Annales d'Etudes Internationales (BE ISSN 0066-2135) 914
Annales d'Histoire Sociale et Economiques see Roczniki Dziejow Spolecznych i Gospodarczych 595
Annales de Demographie Historique (FR ISSN 0066-2062) 920
Annales de Droit Aerien et Spatial see Annals of Air and Space Law 17
Annales de l'Institut Fourier see Universite Scientifique et Medicale de Grenoble. Institut Fourier. Annales 754
Annales des Mines de Belgique/Annalen der Mijnen van Belgie (BE ISSN 0003-4290) 814
Annales du Tabac (FR) 1079
Annales Economiques de Clermont-Ferrand (FR) 191
Annales Forestales/Anali za Sumarstvo (YU ISSN 0351-2045) 523
Annales Hindemith see Hindemith-Jahrbuch 836

Annales Hydrographiques (FR ISSN 0373-3629) 402
Annales Islamologiques (UA ISSN 0570-1716) 850, 975
Annales Medicinae Internae see Annals of Clinical Research. Supplementum 781
Annales Moreau de Tours (FR ISSN 0066-2186) 869
Annales Musei Archaeologici Posnaniensis see Fontes Archaeologici Posnanienses 86
Annales Musei Goulandris (GR) 826
Annales Paderewski (SZ) 832
Annales Paediatriae Fenniae. Supplementum see Annals of Clinical Research. Supplementum 781
Annales Polonici Mathematici (PL ISSN 0066-2216) 747
Annales Silesiae (PL ISSN 0066-2224) 575
Annales Societatis Mathematicae Polonae. Seria 3: Matematyka Stosowana (PL) 747
Annales Universitatis Mariae Curie-Sklodowska. Sectio A. Mathematica (PL ISSN 0365-1029) 747
Annales Universitatis Mariae Curie-Sklodowska. Sectio AA. Chemia (PL ISSN 0137-6853) 321
Annales Universitatis Mariae Curie-Sklodowska. Sectio AA. Physica et Chemica see Annales Universitatis Mariae Curie-Sklodowska. Sectio AAA. Physica 887
Annales Universitatis Mariae Curie-Sklodowska. Sectio AAA. Physica (PL ISSN 0137-6861) 887
Annales Universitatis Mariae Curie-Sklodowska. Sectio B. Geographia, Geologia, Mineralogia et Petrographia (PL ISSN 0137-1983) 383, 541
Annales Universitatis Mariae Curie-Sklodowska. Sectio C. Biologia (PL ISSN 0066-2232) 137
Annales Universitatis Mariae Curie-Sklodowska. Sectio D. Medicina (PL ISSN 0066-2240) 757
Annales Universitatis Mariae Curie-Sklodowska. Sectio DD. Medicina Veterinaria (PL ISSN 0301-7737) 1121
Annales Universitatis Mariae Curie-Sklodowska. Sectio E. Agricultura (PL ISSN 0365-1118) 24
Annales Universitatis Mariae Curie-Sklodowska. Sectio EE. Zootechnika (PL ISSN 0239-4243) 1121
Annales Universitatis Mariae Curie-Sklodowska. Sectio F. Historia (PL) 555
Annales Universitatis Mariae Curie-Sklodowska. Sectio F. Humaniora see Annales Universitatis Mariae Curie-Sklodowska. Sectio F. Historia 555
Annales Universitatis Mariae Curie-Sklodowska. Sectio FF. Philologiae (PL) 690
Annales Universitatis Mariae Curie-Sklodowska. Sectio G. Ius (PL ISSN 0458-4317) 650
Annales Universitatis Mariae Curie-Sklodowska. Sectio H. Oeconomia (PL ISSN 0459-9586) 191
Annales Universitatis Mariae Curie-Sklodowska. Sectio I. Philosophia-Sociologia (PL ISSN 0137-2025) 876, 1024
Annales Universitatis Saraviensis. Rechtswissenschaftliche Abteilung. Schriftenreihe (GW) 650
Annales Universitatis Saraviensis. Reihe: Mathematisch-Naturwissenschaftliche Fakultaet (GW ISSN 0080-5165) 1146
Annales Universitatis Saraviensis. Wirtschaftswissenschaftliche Abteilung. Schriftenreihe (GW) 191
Annales Zoologici (PL ISSN 0003-4541) 173
Annali Alfieriani (IT) 714
Annali d'Italianistica (US ISSN 0741-7527) 714
Annali dell'Architettura Italiana Contemporanea (IT) 96
Annali di Botanica (IT) 154
Annali di Matematica (IT ISSN 0003-4622) 747

Annali di Microbiologia ed Enzimologia(IT ISSN 0003-4649) 151, 168
Annali di Radioprotezione (IT) 792
Annali di Storia Economica e Sociale see Quaderni Internazionali di Storia Economica e Sociale 594
Annali di Studi Giuridici e Socio-Economici sui Servizii Sanitari Nazionale e Regionale (IT) 952
Annali Lateranensi (1937-1962) see Pontifico Museo Missionario Etnologico. Annali 75
Annals of Air and Space Law/Annales de Droit Aerien et Spatial (CN ISSN 0701-158X) 17, 650
Annals of Child Development (US) 335, 933
Annals of Clinical Research. Supplementum (FI ISSN 0066-2291) 757, 781
Annals of Dyslexia (US ISSN 0474-7534) 444
Annals of Glaciology (UK ISSN 0260-3055) 383
Annals of International Studies see Annales d'Etudes Internationales 914
Annals of Mathematics Studies (US) 747
Annals of Phenomenological Sociology see Phenomenology and the Human Sciences 1028
Annals of Public Administration (US ISSN 0278-4289) 939
Annals of the Carnegie Museum see Carnegie Museum of Natural History. Annals of (the) Carnegie Museum 989
Annals of Theoretical Psychology (US) 933
Annee Africaine (FR) 669, 912
Annee Automobile see Automobile Year 1090
Annee Balzacienne (FR ISSN 0084-6473) 714
Annee du Cinema (FR) 822
Annee du Cyclisme (FR) 1041
Annee du Football (FR) 1037
Annee du Rugby (FR) 1037
Annee du Tennis (FR) 1037
Annee Epigraphique; Revue des Publications Epigraphiques Relatives a l'Antiquite Romaine (FR ISSN 0066-2348) 690
Annee Philologique (FR) 339
Annee Politique (FR ISSN 0066-2356) 902
Annee Politique Africaine (SG ISSN 0066-2364) 902
Annee Politique Africaine see Annee Politique Africaine 902
Annee Politique Suisse/Schweizerische Politik im Jahre (SZ ISSN 0066-2372) 902
Annee Sociologique (FR ISSN 0066-2399) 1024
Annee Sportive U.S.M.T. (Union Sportive Metropolitaine des Transports) (FR) 341, 1032
Annee Therapeutique en Ophtalmologie see Annee Therapeutique et Clinique en Ophtalmologie 785
Annee Therapeutique et Clinique en Ophtalmologie (FR ISSN 0301-4495) 785
Annotated Accessions List of Studies and Reports in the Field of Science Statistics (UN) 121
Annotated Bibliographies of Serials: A Subject Approach (US ISSN 0748-5190) 121, 673
Annotated Bibliography and Index of the Geology of Zambia (ZA ISSN 0066-2410) 383
Annotated Catalogue of Books Published in Japan see Contemporary Japanese Books 125
Annotated Guide to Taiwan Periodical Literature (CH ISSN 0066-2445) 121
Annotated Secondary Bibliography Series on English Literature in Transition, 1880-1920 (US) 738
Annuaire Administratif de la Republique du Mali (ML ISSN 0066-2453) 939

1638 ANNUAIRE ADMINISTRATIF

Annuaire Administratif et Judiciaire de Belgique/Administratief en Gerechtelijk Jaarboek voor Belgie (BE ISSN 0066-2461) *939*

Annuaire Batiment et Travaux Publics (FR) *181, 480*

Annuaire Belge de Chauffage et Climatisation *see* A B C *553*

Annuaire Bilingue de l'Industrie Nucleaire Francaise *see* Annuaire de l'Activite Nucleaire Francaise *895*

Annuaire Biographique du Cinema et de la Television en France et en Belgique (FR ISSN 0066-247X) *347, 822*

Annuaire Canadien de Droit International *see* Canadian Yearbook of International Law *669*

Annuaire Canadien des Orchestres et Orchestres. des Jeunes *see* Directory of Canadian Orchestras and Youth Orchestras *835*

Annuaire Catholique de France (FR ISSN 0066-2488) *980*

Annuaire Chatfield European de Peintures et Produits Assimiles *see* Chatfield's European Directory of Paints and Allied Products *855*

Annuaire d'Etudes en Education au Canada *see* Directory of Education Studies in Canada *412*

Annuaire d'Exportation de l'Autriche *see* Herold Export-Adressbuch von Oesterreich *309*

Annuaire de l'Activite Nucleaire Francaise (FR ISSN 0066-2593) *469, 895*

Annuaire de l'Administration des Mines(FR) *814*

Annuaire de l'Administration et du Corps des Mines *see* Annuaire de l'Administration des Mines *814*

Annuaire de l'Afrique du Nord (FR ISSN 0066-2607) *1006*

Annuaire de l'Ameublement (FR) *643*

Annuaire de l'Ameublement et des Industries s'y Rattachant *see* Annuaire de l'Ameublement *643*

Annuaire de l'Armement a la Peche (FR ISSN 0066-2623) *507*

Annuaire de l'Art International (FR) *101*

Annuaire de l'Eclairage (FR ISSN 0066-264X) *450*

Annuaire de l'Eglise Catholique a Madagascar *see* Eglise Catholique a Madagascar *982*

Annuaire de l'Eglise Catholique au Zaire (ZR) *980*

Annuaire de l'Exportation du Danemark *see* Udenrigs Handelskalenderen for Danmark *318*

Annuaire de l'U.R.S.S. *see* Annuaire de l'U R S S et des Pays Socialistes Europeens *1006*

Annuaire de l'U R S S et des Pays Socialistes Europeens (FR ISSN 0397-8249) *1006*

Annuaire de la Chaussure et des Cuirs (FR ISSN 0066-2526) *672*

Annuaire de la Cooperation F.N.C.C. (Federation Nationale des Cooperatives de Consommateurs) (FR ISSN 0071-4356) *238*

Annuaire de la France Rurale dans le Marche Commun (FR ISSN 0066-2534) *24*

Annuaire de la Maree (FR ISSN 0066-2542) *507*

Annuaire de la Marine Marchande (FR ISSN 0066-2550) *1098*

Annuaire de la Mecanique (FR) *745*

Annuaire de la Mecanographie, Materiel de Bureau, Informatique (FR) *286*

Annuaire de la Mercerie, Nouveautes, Bonneterie, Lingerie, Confections (FR) *339*

Annuaire de la Noblesse de France et d'Europe (FR ISSN 0066-2569) *534*

Annuaire de la Photographie Professionnelle (FR ISSN 0084-6481) *884*

Annuaire de la Presse et de la Publicite (FR ISSN 0066-2585) *645*

Annuaire de la Presse Francaise et Etrangere *see* Annuaire de la Presse et de la Publicite *645*

Annuaire de Legislation Francaise et Etrangere (FR ISSN 0066-2658) *650*

Annuaire de Statistique Agricole du Departement de la Reunion (RE ISSN 0336-5697) *38*

Annuaire Dentaire (FR ISSN 0066-2712) *779*

Annuaire des Abonnes Telex du Danemark *see* Telex Danmark *351*

Annuaire des Administrateurs et des Societes (FR) *191*

Annuaire des Agents Commerciaux Courtiers et Representants de Commerce-France et Marche Commun (FR) *253*

Annuaire des Annuaires *see* Repertoire des Annuaires *130*

Annuaire des Arachnologistes Mondiaux (FR ISSN 0066-2739) *163*

Annuaire des Architectes (FR ISSN 0066-2747) *1146*

Annuaire des Assurances et l'Assureur-Conseil (FR) *637*

Annuaire des Boissons et des Liquides Alimentaires/Jahrbuch der Getraenke und Fluessigen Nahrmittel (FR ISSN 0066-2763) *119*

Annuaire des Caisses d'Epargne; France et Outre-Mer *see* Annuaire du Reseau Ecureuil *222*

Annuaire des Centrales et Groupements d'Achats (FR) *302*

Annuaire des Centres de Recherche Demographique/Directory of Demographic Research Centers (FR) *920*

Annuaire des Chambres de Commerce et d'Industrie (FR ISSN 0066-2798) *234*

Annuaire des Chercheurs Francais du Fonds de Bourses de Recherche Scientifique et Technique de l'Organisation du Traite de l'Atlantique Nord (FR ISSN 0066-2771) *432*

Annuaire des Communautes d'Enfants (FR ISSN 0069-7761) *333, 410*

Annuaire des Departements de Sociologie, d'Anthropologie et d'Archeologie des Universites et des Musees du Canada *see* Guide to Departments of Sociology, Anthropology and Archaeology in Universities and Museums in Canada *435*

Annuaire des Docteurs (Lettres) de l'Universite de Paris et Autres Universites Francaises (FR ISSN 0066-281X) *432*

Annuaire des Employeurs des Nouveaux Diplomes de College *see* Employers of New University Graduates: Directory *848*

Annuaire des Entreprises d'Afrique Noire, des Organismes Officiels et Professionels d'Outre-Mer, des Organismes de Cooperation Francais, Etrangers et Internationaux *see* Annuaire des Entreprises et Organismes d'Outre-Mer *253*

Annuaire des Entreprises du Mali (ML ISSN 0080-0988) *234*

Annuaire des Entreprises du Zaire (ZR) *234*

Annuaire des Entreprises et Organismes d'Outre-Mer (FR) *253*

Annuaire des Exportateurs Francais Commercant avec l'U.R.S.S. (FR) *302*

Annuaire des Femmes de Montreal (CN) *1128*

Annuaire des Fournisseurs de Laboratoires de Recherches (FR) *987*

Annuaire des Fournisseurs de Laboratoires Pharmaceutiques *see* Annuaire des Fournisseurs de Laboratoires Pharmaceutiques et Cosmetiques *869*

Annuaire des Fournisseurs de Laboratoires Pharmaceutiques et Cosmetiques (FR ISSN 0396-0625) *869*

Annuaire des Geographes de la France et de l'Afrique Francophone *see* Repertoire des Geographes Francais *547*

Annuaire des Hopitaux du Canada *see* Canadian Hospital Directory *616*

Annuaire des Hypermarches (FR) *302*

Annuaire des Institutions d'Enseignement Secondaire *see* Association des Institutions d'Enseignement Secondaire. Annuaire *410*

Annuaire des Instituts de Religieuses en France (FR ISSN 0066-2860) *967*

Annuaire des Laboratoires d'Analyses de Biologie Medicale de France (FR) *781*

Annuaire des Laboratoires d'Analyses de France *see* Annuaire des Laboratoires d'Analyses de Biologie Medicale de France *781*

Annuaire des Marees pour l'An. Tome 1. Ports de France (FR ISSN 0180-989X) *404*

Annuaire des Marees pour l'An. Tome 2. Ports d'Outre Mer (FR ISSN 0180-9962) *404*

Annuaire des Mineraux du Canada *see* Canadian Minerals Yearbook *815*

Annuaire des Notables Regionaux (FR) *541*

Annuaire des Organisations Internationales *see* Yearbook of International Organizations *920*

Annuaire des Pays de l'Ocean Indien (FR ISSN 0247-400X) *541, 1006*

Annuaire des Professeurs de Droit *see* Directory of Law Teachers *655*

Annuaire des Professions au Liban *see* Lebanese Industrial and Commercial Directory *312*

Annuaire des Societes Libanaises a Responsibilite Limitee *see* Year-Book of the Lebanese Limited Liability Companies *269*

Annuaire des Societes Libanaises Par Action *see* Year-Book of the Lebanese Joint-Stock Companies *269*

Annuaire des Statistiques du Commerce Exterieur du Togo (TG) *1048*

Annuaire Desechaliers (FR) *302*

Annuaire Desfosses *see* Annuaire des Administrateurs et des Societes *191*

Annuaire Diplomatique et Consulaire de la Republique Francaise (FR ISSN 0066-295X) *914*

Annuaire du Cinema et Television *see* Annuaire du Cinema et Television-Video *822*

Annuaire du Cinema et Television-Video (FR) *822*

Annuaire du Commerce du Norvege *see* Norges Handels-Kalender *315*

Annuaire du Commerce Exterieur d'Haiti: Importations, Exportations (HT) *253*

Annuaire du Diocese de Lyon (FR) *980*

Annuaire du Madagascar (MG) *1146*

Annuaire du Marketing (FR ISSN 0066-300X) *282*

Annuaire du Quebec (CN ISSN 0066-3018) *1048*

Annuaire du Reseau Ecureuil (FR) *222*

Annuaire du Spectacle (FR ISSN 0066-3026) *1076*

Annuaire du Tiers Monde (FR ISSN 0396-2156) *261*

Annuaire Economique (FR) *191*

Annuaire Economique de la Tunisie (TI ISSN 0066-3042) *241*

Annuaire Economique des Pays Membres de l'Organisation de l'Unite Africaine/Economic Yearbook of Member States of the Organization of African Unity (ET) *241*

Annuaire Europeen des Directeurs Commerciaux et de Marketing (FR ISSN 0066-3077) *282*

Annuaire Europeen du Petrole *see* European Petroleum Yearbook *864*

Annuaire Federal de l'Horticulture et des Pepinieres (FR) *531*

Annuaire Francais d'Australie (AT) *302*

Annuaire Francais de Droit International (FR ISSN 0066-3085) *669*

Annuaire Franco-Italien (FR ISSN 0066-3115) *234*

Annuaire Franco-Ontarien (CN ISSN 0706-1021) *902*

Annuaire Fructidor (FR ISSN 0066-3131) *52*

Annuaire General de la Publicite (FR) *14*

Annuaire General des Cooperatives Francaises et de Leurs Fournisseurs; France, Afrique et Marche Commun (FR ISSN 0066-3182) *239*

Annuaire General des Publicitaires de France *see* Annuaire General de la Publicite *14*

Annuaire-Guide du Chauffage et du Conditionnement d'Air. *see* Catalogue National du Genie Climatique-Chauffage et Conditionnement d'Air *553*

Annuaire H L M (Habitations a Loyer Modere) (FR) *621, 1015*

Annuaire Industriel. Repertoire General de la Production Francaise *see* La France de l'Industrie et ses Services *308*

Annuaire International des Collectionneurs (FR) *614*

Annuaire International des Jus de Fruits(FR ISSN 0066-3255) *119*

Annuaire International des Ventes (FR ISSN 0066-3263) *101*

Annuaire Interprofessionnel de la Surgelation et de la Congelation (FR) *518*

Annuaire Magnetique *see* Rocznik Magnetyczny *401*

Annuaire Maritime *see* Antwerp Port Annual *302*

Annuaire Medical de l'Hospitalisation Francaise. (FR ISSN 0066-3298) *616, 757*

Annuaire Medical du Dr. Porcheron et Prof. G. Beltrami (FR) *757*

Annuaire Mondial des Corses (FR) *133*

Annuaire National de l'Aviculture (FR ISSN 0066-3328) *64*

Annuaire National de la Conserve (FR ISSN 0245-1301) *518*

Annuaire National des Beaux-Arts (FR ISSN 0066-3352) *101*

Annuaire National des Fournisseurs des Administrations Francaises (FR ISSN 0066-3379) *287*

Annuaire National des Industries de la Conserve *see* Annuaire National de la Conserve *518*

Annuaire National des Lettres (FR ISSN 0066-3387) *714*

Annuaire National des Masseurs Kinesitherapeutes (FR ISSN 0337-5935) *757, 777, 793*

Annuaire National des Matieres Premieres de Recuperation et du Materiel d'Occasion (FR) *745*

Annuaire National des Specialistes Qualifies Exclusifs en Pediatrie (FR ISSN 0066-3514) *787*

Annuaire National des Transports (FR ISSN 0066-3549) *1080*

Annuaire National du Lait (FR ISSN 0084-6538) *62*

Annuaire National M.K.D.E. France *see* Annuaire National des Masseurs Kinesitherapeutes *757*

Annuaire National Officiel de la Republique Gabonaise (GO) *939*

Annuaire Nautisme (FR ISSN 0758-6639) *1041*

Annuaire O.G.M. (Office General de la Musique) (FR ISSN 0066-3565) *347*

Annuaire Officiel de la Charcuterie (FR ISSN 0293-9967) *64*

Annuaire Paris: Bijoux (FR ISSN 0066-3581) *644*

Annuaire Pluviometrique (BD) *803*

Annuaire Polonais de Droit International *see* Polish Yearbook of International Law *671*

Annuaire Professionnel de l'Horticulture et des Pepinieres *see* Annuaire Federal de l'Horticulture et des Pepinieres *531*

Annuaire Protestant; la France Protestante et les Eglises de Langue Francaise (FR ISSN 0066-362X) *978*

Annuaire Repertoire de la Motoculture de Plaisance Jardinage (FR ISSN 0224-2478) *531, 745*

Annuaire Roumain d'Anthropologie (RM) *69*
Annuaire Souvenir Normand (DK) *1106*
Annuaire Statistique de Benin (DM) *1048*
Annuaire Statistique de la Belgique (BE ISSN 0066-3646) *1048*
Annuaire Statistique de la Belgique et du Congo Belge *see* Annuaire Statistique de la Belgique *1048*
Annuaire Statistique de la France (FR ISSN 0066-3654) *1048*
Annuaire Statistique de la Sante Publique/Statistisch Jaarboek van Volksgezondheid (BE ISSN 0522-7690) *958*
Annuaire Statistique de la Suisse *see* Statistisches Jahrbuch der Schweiz *1065*
Annuaire Statistique de la Tunisie (TI ISSN 0066-3689) *1048*
Annuaire Statistique des Telecommunications du Secteur Public *see* Yearbook of Common Carrier Telecommunication Statistics *345*
Annuaire Statistique du Dahomey *see* Annuaire Statistique de Benin *1048*
Annuaire Statistique du Maroc (MR ISSN 0066-3719) *1048*
Annuaire Statistique du Togo (TG) *1048*
Annuaire Statistique pour l'Asie et le Pacifique *see* Statistical Yearbook for Asia and the Pacific *1064*
Annuaire Sucrier (FR) *522*
Annuaire Suisse de Science Politique/Schweizerisches Jahrbuch fuer Politische Wissenschaft/Swiss Political Science Yearbook (SZ ISSN 0066-3727) *902*
Annuaire Suisse du Monde et des Affaires *see* Swiss Biographical Index of Prominent Persons *135*
Annuaire Technique de la Sous-Traitance Mecanique (FR) *745*
Annuaires Francais et Listes d'Adresses Susceptibles d'Interesser le Commerce et l'Industrie (FR ISSN 0066-3743) *234*
Annual Abstract of Statistics (UK) *1048*
Annual Agricultural Outlook Conference. Proceedings *see* Outlook (Year) Proceedings *48*
Annual Aid Review (CN) *261*
Annual Aid Review, Memorandum of New Zealand *see* Annual Development Assistance Review, Memorandum of New Zealand *261*
Annual Allerton Conference on Circuit and System Theory *see* Annual Allerton Conference on Communication, Control and Computing *450*
Annual Allerton Conference on Communication, Control and Computing (US) *450*
Annual Almanac of Records and Results (AT) *1044*
Annual Art Sales Index: Oil Paintings, Drawings, Water Colours and Sculptures *see* Art Sales Index: Oil Paintings, Drawings, Water Colours and Sculpture *102*
Annual Automation Report to the Arizona Legislature (US) *355*
Annual Basic Hobby Industry Trade Directory *see* Hobby Publications Annual Trade Directory *614*
Annual Bibliography of Computer-Oriented Books (US) *121, 353*
Annual Bibliography of English Language and Literature (UK ISSN 0066-3786) *738*
Annual Bibliography of Scottish Literature (UK ISSN 0307-9864) *738*
Annual Bibliography of the History of Natural History (DK) *562*
Annual Bibliography of the History of the Printed Book and Library (NE) *931*
Annual Bibliography of Victorian Studies (CN ISSN 0227-1400) *121, 738*

Annual Book of A S T M Standards. Part 2. Ferrous Castings, Ferro Alloys *see* Annual Book of A S T M Standards. Volume 01.02. Ferrous Castings, Ferro Alloys; Shipbuilding *485*
Annual Book of A S T M Standards. Part 3. Steel Plate, Sheet, Strip and Wire; Metallic Coated Products; Fences *see* Annual Book of A S T M Standards. Volume 01.03. Steel Plate, Sheet, Strip Wire *485*
Annual Book of A S T M Standards. Part 3. Steel Plate, Sheet, Strip and Wire; Metallic Coated Products; Fences *see* Annual Book of A S T M Standards. Volume 01.06. Coated Steel Products *485*
Annual Book of A S T M Standards. Part 4. Structural Steel; Concrete Reinforcing Steel; Pressure Vessel Plate and Forgings; Steel Rails, Wheels, and Tires; Steel Fasteners *see* Annual Book of A S T M Standards. Volume 01.04. Steel-Structural, Reinforcing, Pressure Vessel; Railway *485*
Annual Book of A S T M Standards. Part 4. Structural Steel; Concrete Reinforcing Steel; Pressure Vessel Plate and Forgings; Steel Rails, Wheels and Tires; Steel Fasteners *see* Annual Book of A S T M Standards. Volume 15.08. Fasteners *488*
Annual Book of A S T M Standards. Part 5. Steel Bars, Chain, and Springs; Bearing Steel; Steel Forgings *see* Annual Book of A S T M Standards. Volume 01.05. Steel-Bars, Bearings, Forgings, Chain, Springs *485*
Annual Book of A S T M Standards. Part 6. Copper and Copper Alloys (Including Electrical Conductors) *see* Annual Book of A S T M Standards. Volume 02.01. Copper and Copper Alloys *485*
Annual Book of A S T M Standards. Part 6. Copper and Copper Alloys (Including Electrical Conductors) *see* Annual Book of A S T M Standards. Volume 02.03. Electrical Conductors *485*
Annual Book of A S T M Standards. Part 7. Die-Cast Metals; Light Metals and Alloys (Including Electrical Conductors) *see* Annual Book of A S T M Standards. Volume 02.02. Die-Cast Metals; Aluminum and Magnesium Alloys *485*
Annual Book of A S T M Standards. Part 7. Die-Cast Metals; Light Metals and Alloys (Including Electrical Conductors) *see* Annual Book of A S T M Standards. Volume 02.03. Electrical Conductors *485*
Annual Book of A S T M Standards. Part 10. Metals--Mechanical, Fracture and Corrosion Testing; Fatigue; Erosion; Effect of Temperature *see* Annual Book of A S T M Standards. Volume 03.02. Wear and Erosion; Metal Corrosion *486*
Annual Book of A S T M Standards. Part 15. Road and Paving Materials; Bituminous Materials for Highway Construction, Waterproofing and Roofing, and Pipe; Traveled Surface Characteristics *see* Annual Book of A S T M Standards. Volume 04.03. Road and Paving Materials; Traveled Surface Characteristics *486*
Annual Book of A S T M Standards. Part 15. Road and Paving Materials; Bituminous Materials for Highway Construction, Waterproofing and Roofing, and Pipe; Traveled Survace Characteristics *see* Annual Book of A S T M Standards. Volume 04.04. Roofing, Waterproofing, and Bituminous Materials *486*

Annual Book of A S T M Standards. Part 17. Refractories, Glass and Other Ceramic Materials; Manufactured Carbon and Graphite Products *see* Annual Book of A S T M Standards. Volume 15.01. Refractories, Manufactured Carbon and Graphite Products; Activated Carbon *488*
Annual Book of A S T M Standards. Part 17. Refractories, Glass and Other Ceramic Materials; Manufactured Carbon and Graphite Products *see* Annual Book of A S T M Standards. Volume 15.02. Glass; Ceramic Whitewares *488*
Annual Book of A S T M Standards. Part 18. Thermal Insulation; Building Seals and Sealants; Fire Tests; Building Construction; Environmental Acoustics *see* Annual Book of A S T M Standards. Volume 04.06. Thermal Insulation; Environmental Acoustics *486*
Annual Book of A S T M Standards. Part 18. Thermal Insulation; Building Seals and Sealants; Fire Tests; Building Constructions; Environmental Acoustics *see* Annual Book of A S T M Standards. Volume 04.07. Building Seals and Sealants; Fire Standards; Building Constructions *486*
Annual Book of A S T M Standards. Part 19. Natural Building Stones; Soil and Rock *see* Annual Book of A S T M Standards. Volume 04.08. Soil and Rock; Building Stones *486*
Annual Book of A S T M Standards. Part 20. Paint, Varnish, Lacquer, and Related Products - Materials Specifications and Tests; Naval Stores; Industrial Aromatic Hydrocarbons and Related Chemicals *see* Annual Book of A S T M Standards. Volume 06.03. Paint - Fatty Oils and Acids, Solvents, Miscellaneous; Aromatic Hydrocarbons *487*
Annual Book of A S T M Standards. Part 20. Paper; Packaging; Business Copy Products *see* Annual Book of A S T M Standards. Volume 15.09. Paper; Packaging; Flexible Barrier Materials; Business Copy Products *488*
Annual Book of A S T M Standards. Part 21. Cellulose; Leather; Flexible Barrier Materials *see* Annual Book of A S T M Standards. Volume 15.04. Soaps; Polishes; Cellulose; Leather; Resilient Floor Covering *488*
Annual Book of A S T M Standards. Part 22. Wood; Adhesives *see* Annual Book of A S T M Standards. Volume 04.09. Wood *486*
Annual Book of A S T M Standards. Part 22. Wood; Adhesives *see* Annual Book of A S T M Standards. Volume 15.06. Adhesives *488*
Annual Book of A S T M Standards. Part 26. Gaseous Fuels; Coal and Coke; Atmospheric Analysis *see* Annual Book of A S T M Standards. Volume 05.05. Gaseous Fuels; Coal and Coke *487*
Annual Book of A S T M Standards. Part 26. Gaseous Fuels; Coal and Coke; Atmospheric Analysis *see* Annual Book of A S T M Standards. Volume 11.03. Atmospheric Analysis; Occupational Health and Safety *487*
Annual Book of A S T M Standards. Part 30. Soap; Engine Collants; Polishes; Halogenated Organic Solvents; Activated Carbon *see* Annual Book of A S T M Standards. Volume 15.04. Soaps; Polishes; Cellulose; Leather; Resilient Floor Covering *488*
Annual Book of A S T M Standards. Part 30. Soap; Engine Coolants; Polishes; Halogenated Organic Solvents; Activated Carbon *see* Annual Book of A S T M Standards. Volume 15.05. Engine Coolants; Halogenated Organic Solvents; Industrial Chemicals *488*

Annual Book of A S T M Standards. Part 31. Water *see* Annual Book of A S T M Standards. Volume 11.01. Water (1) *487*
Annual Book of A S T M Standards. Part 34. Plastic Pipe *see* Annual Book of A S T M Standards. Volume 08.04. Plastic Pipe and Building Products *487*
Annual Book of A S T M Standards. Part 35. Plastics--General Test Methods; Nomenclature *see* Annual Book of A S T M Standards. Volume 08.01. Plastics (1): C 177 to D 1600 *487*
Annual Book of A S T M Standards. Part 36. Plastics--Materials, Film, Reinforced and Cellular Plastics; High Modulus Fibers and Their Composites *see* Annual Book of A S T M Standards. Volume 08.02. Plastics (2): D 1601 to D 3099 *487*
Annual Book of A S T M Standards. Part 39. Electrical Insulation--Test Methods; Solids and Solidifying Fluids *see* Annual Book of A S T M Standards. Volume 10.02. Electrical Insulation; Wire and Cable, Heatings and Electrical Tests--Solids (2) *487*
Annual Book of A S T M Standards. Part 40. Electrical Insulation--Specifications: Solids, Liquids, and Gases; Test Methods: Liquids and Gases; Protective Equipment *see* Annual Book of A S T M Standards. Volume 10.03. Electrical Insulating Liquids and Gases; Electrical Proective Equipment *487*
Annual Book of A S T M Standards. Part 41. General Test Methods, Nonmetal; Statistical Methods; Space Simulation; Particle Size Measurement; Laboratory Apparatus; Durability of Nonmetallic Materials; Metric Practice; Solar Energy Conversion *see* Annual Book of A S T M Standards. Volume 14.02. General Test Methods, Nonmetal; Laboratory Apparatus; Statistical Methods; Appearance of Materials; Durability of Nonmetallic Materials *488*
Annual Book of A S T M Standards. Part 41. General Test Methods, Nonmetal; Statistical Methods; Space Simulation; Particle Size Measurement; Laboratory Apparatus; Durability of Nonmetallic Materials; Metric Practice; Solar Energy Conversion *see* Annual Book of A S T M Standards. Volume 15.03. Space Simulation; Aerospace Materials; High Modulus Fibers and Their Composites *488*
Annual Book of A S T M Standards. Part 42. Emission, Molecular, and Mass Spectroscopy; Chromatography; Resinography; Microscopy; Computerized Systems *see* Annual Book of A S T M Standards. Volume 03.06. Emission Spectroscopy; Surface Analysis *486*
Annual Book of A S T M Standards. Part 43. Electronics *see* Annual Book of A S T M Standards. Volume 10.05. Electronics (2) *487*
Annual Book of A S T M Standards. Part 45. Nuclear Standards *see* Annual Book of A S T M Standards. Volume 12.01. Nuclear Energy (1) *488*
Annual Book of A S T M Standards. Part 45. Nuclear Standards *see* Annual Book of A S T M Standards. Volume 12.02. Nuclear (2), Solar, and Geothermal Energy *488*
Annual Book of A S T M Standards. Part 46. End Use and Consumer Products *see* Annual Book of A S T M Standards. Volume 15.07. End Use Products *488*
Annual Book of A S T M Standards. Volume 03.03. Metallography; Nondestructive Testing *see* Annual Book of A S T M Standards. Volume 03.03. Nondestructive Tests *486*

Annual Book of A S T M Standards. Volume 03.05. Chemical Analysis of Metals; Sampling and Analysis of Metal Bearing Ores *see* Annual Book of A S T M Standards. Volume 03.05. Chemical Analysis of Metals; Metal Bearing Ores *486*

Annual Book of A S T M Standards. Volume 04.05. Chemical-Resistant Nonmetallic Materials; Vitrified Clay, Concrete Pipe and Tile; Masonary Mortars and Units; Fiber-Cement Products, Precast Concrete Products *see* Annual Book of A S T M Standards. Volume 04.05. Chemical-Resistant Materials; Vitrified Clay, Concrete; Masonry; Mortars; Fiber-Cement Products *486*

Annual Book of A S T M Standards. Volume 05.01. Petroleum Products and Lubricants (1); D 56 to D 1947 *see* Annual Book of A S T M Standards. Volume 05.01. Petroleum Products and Lubricants (1) *486*

Annual Book of A S T M Standards. Volume 05.02. Petroleum Products and Lubricants (2); D 1949 to D 3601 *see* Annual Book of A S T M Standards. Volume 05.02. Petroleum Products and Lubricants (2) *486*

Annual Book of A S T M Standards. Volume 05.03. Petroleum Products and Lubricants (3); D 3602 to Latest; Catalysts *see* Annual Book of A S T M Standards. Volume 05.03. Petroleum Products and Lubricants (3); Catalysts *487*

Annual Book of A S T M Standards. Volume 06.03. Paint - Fatty Oils and Acids, Solvents, Miscellaneous; Aromatic Hydrocarbons (Includes Naval Stores) *see* Annual Book of A S T M Standards. Volume 06.03. Paint - Fatty Oils and Acids, Solvents, Miscellaneous; Aromatic Hydrocarbons *487*

Annual Book of A S T M Standards. Volume 10.01. Electrical Insulation-- Soils (1) *see* Annual Book of A S T M Standards. Volume 10.01. Electrical Insulation, Composites, and Coatings--Solids *487*

Annual Book of A S T M Standards. Volume 10.02. Electrical Insulation-- Solids (2) *see* Annual Book of A S T M Standards. Volume 10.02. Electrical Insulation; Wire and Cable, Heatings and Electrical Tests--Solids (2) *487*

Annual Book of A S T M Standards. Volume 14.01. Molecular Mass Spectroscopy; Chromatography; Resinography; Temperature Measurement; Microscopy; Computerized Systems *see* Annual Book of A S T M Standards. Volume 14.01. Analytical Methods - Spectroscopy; Chromatography; Temperature Measurement; Computerized Systems *488*

Annual Book of A S T M Standards. Volume 00.01. Index (US ISSN 0066-0493) *485*

Annual Book of A S T M Standards. Volume 01.01. Steel-Piping, Tubing, Fittings (American Society for Testing and Materials) (US ISSN 0066-0183) *485, 796*

Annual Book of A S T M Standards. Volume 01.02. Ferrous Castings, Ferro Alloys; Shipbuilding (US) *485, 796*

Annual Book of A S T M Standards. Volume 01.03. Steel Plate, Sheet, Strip Wire (US) *485, 796*

Annual Book of A S T M Standards. Volume 01.04. Steel-Structural, Reinforcing, Pressure Vessel; Railway(US) *485, 796*

Annual Book of A S T M Standards. Volume 01.05. Steel-Bars, Bearings, Forgings, Chain, Springs (US) *485, 796*

Annual Book of A S T M Standards. Volume 01.06. Coated Steel Products(US) *485, 797*

Annual Book of A S T M Standards. Volume 02.01. Copper and Copper Alloys (US) *485, 797*

Annual Book of A S T M Standards. Volume 02.02. Die-Cast Metals; Aluminum and Magnesium Alloys (US) *485, 797*

Annual Book of A S T M Standards. Volume 02.03. Electrical Conductors (US) *450, 485*

Annual Book of A S T M Standards. Volume 02.04. Nonferrous Metals-Nickel, Lead, Tin Alloys, Precious, Primary, Reactive Metals (US) *485, 797*

Annual Book of A S T M Standards. Volume 02.05. Metallic and Inorganic Coatings; Metal Powders, Sintered P/M Structural Parts (US) *485, 797*

Annual Book of A S T M Standards. Volume 03.01. Metals-Mechanical Testing; Elevated and Low-Temperature Tests Metallography (US) *486, 797*

Annual Book of A S T M Standards. Volume 03.02. Wear and Erosion; Metal Corrosion (US) *486, 797*

Annual Book of A S T M Standards. Volume 03.03. Nondestructive Tests (US) *486, 797*

Annual Book of A S T M Standards. Volume 03.04. Magnetic Properties; Metallic Materials for Thermostats, Electrical Resistance, Heating, Contacts (US) *486*

Annual Book of A S T M Standards. Volume 03.05. Chemical Analysis of Metals; Metal Bearing Ores (US ISSN 0066-0485) *326, 486, 797*

Annual Book of A S T M Standards. Volume 03.06. Emission Spectroscopy; Surface Analysis (US) *486*

Annual Book of A S T M Standards. Volume 04.01. Cement; Lime; Gypsum (US) *181, 486*

Annual Book of A S T M Standards. Volume 04.02. Concrete and Mineral Aggregates (Including Manual of Aggregate and Concrete Testing) (US) *181, 486*

Annual Book of A S T M Standards. Volume 04.03. Road and Paving Materials; Traveled Surface Characteristics (US) *486*

Annual Book of A S T M Standards. Volume 04.04. Roofing, Waterproofing, and Bituminous Materials (US) *486*

Annual Book of A S T M Standards. Volume 04.05. Chemical-Resistant Materials; Vitrified Clay, Concrete; Masonry; Mortars; Fiber-Cement Products (US) *181, 486*

Annual Book of A S T M Standards. Volume 04.06. Thermal Insulation; Environmental Acoustics (US) *181, 486*

Annual Book of A S T M Standards. Volume 04.07. Building Seals and Sealants; Fire Standards; Building Constructions (US) *486*

Annual Book of A S T M Standards. Volume 04.08. Soil and Rock; Building Stones (US) *52, 181, 486*

Annual Book of A S T M Standards. Volume 04.09. Wood (US) *486, 529, 900*

Annual Book of A S T M Standards. Volume 05.01. Petroleum Products and Lubricants (1) (US) *486, 862*

Annual Book of A S T M Standards. Volume 05.02. Petroleum Products and Lubricants (2) (US) *486, 862*

Annual Book of A S T M Standards. Volume 05.03. Petroleum Products and Lubricants (3); Catalysts (US) *487, 862*

Annual Book of A S T M Standards. Volume 05.04. Test Methods for Rating Motor, Diesel, and Aviation Fuels (US) *487*

Annual Book of A S T M Standards. Volume 05.05. Gaseous Fuels; Coal and Coke (US) *487, 814, 862*

Annual Book of A S T M Standards. Volume 06.01. Paint - Tests for Formulated Products and Applied Coatings (US ISSN 0066-037X) *487, 855*

Annual Book of A S T M Standards. Volume 06.02. Paint - Pigments, Resins and Polymers (US) *487, 855*

Annual Book of A S T M Standards. Volume 06.03. Paint - Fatty Oils and Acids, Solvents, Miscellaneous; Aromatic Hydrocarbons (US) *478, 487, 855*

Annual Book of A S T M Standards. Volume 07.01. Textiles--Yarn, Fabrics, and General Test Methods (US ISSN 0066-040X) *487, 1073*

Annual Book of A S T M Standards. Volume 07.02. Textiles--Fibers, Zippers (US) *487, 1073*

Annual Book of A S T M Standards. Volume 08.01. Plastics (1): C 177 to D 1600 (US) *487, 900*

Annual Book of A S T M Standards. Volume 08.02. Plastics (2): D 1601 to D 3099 (US) *487, 900*

Annual Book of A S T M Standards. Volume 08.03. Plastics (3): D 3100 to Latest (US) *487*

Annual Book of A S T M Standards. Volume 08.04. Plastic Pipe and Building Products (US) *181, 487, 900*

Annual Book of A S T M Standards. Volume 09.01. Rubber, Natural and Synthetic--General Test Methods; Carbon Black (US) *487, 985*

Annual Book of A S T M Standards. Volume 09.02. Rubber Products, Industrial--Specifications and Related Test Methods; Gaskets; Tires (US) *487, 985*

Annual Book of A S T M Standards. Volume 10.01. Electrical Insulation, Composites, and Coatings--Solids (US) *450, 487*

Annual Book of A S T M Standards. Volume 10.02. Electrical Insulation; Wire and Cable, Heatings and Electrical Tests--Solids (2) (US) *487*

Annual Book of A S T M Standards. Volume 10.03. Electrical Insulating Liquids and Gases; Electrical Proective Equipment (US) *450, 487*

Annual Book of A S T M Standards. Volume 10.04. Electronics (1) (US) *450, 487*

Annual Book of A S T M Standards. Volume 10.05. Electronics (2) (US) *450, 487*

Annual Book of A S T M Standards. Volume 11.01. Water (1) (US) *487, 494*

Annual Book of A S T M Standards. Volume 11.02. Water (2) (US) *487*

Annual Book of A S T M Standards. Volume 11.03. Atmospheric Analysis; Occupational Health and Safety (US) *487*

Annual Book of A S T M Standards. Volume 11.04. Pesticides; Resource Recovery; Hazardous Substances and Oil Spill Response; Waste Disposal; Biological Effects (US) *487*

Annual Book of A S T M Standards. Volume 12.01. Nuclear Energy (1) (US) *469, 488*

Annual Book of A S T M Standards. Volume 12.02. Nuclear (2), Solar, and Geothermal Energy (US) *463, 488*

Annual Book of A S T M Standards. Volume 13.01. Medical Devices (US) *488, 757*

Annual Book of A S T M Standards. Volume 14.01. Analytical Methods - Spectroscopy; Chromatography; Temperature Measurement; Computerized Systems (US) *326, 488*

Annual Book of A S T M Standards. Volume 14.02. General Test Methods, Nonmetal; Laboratory Apparatus; Statistical Methods; Appearance of Materials; Durability of Nonmetallic Materials (US) *488*

Annual Book of A S T M Standards. Volume 15.01. Refractories, Manufactured Carbon and Graphite Products; Activated Carbon (US) *319, 488*

Annual Book of A S T M Standards. Volume 15.02. Glass; Ceramic Whitewares (US) *488*

Annual Book of A S T M Standards. Volume 15.03. Space Simulation; Aerospace Materials; High Modulus Fibers and Their Composites (US) *488*

Annual Book of A S T M Standards. Volume 15.04. Soaps; Polishes; Cellulose; Leather; Resilient Floor Covering (US) *488*

Annual Book of A S T M Standards. Volume 15.05. Engine Coolants; Halogenated Organic Solvents; Industrial Chemicals (US) *478, 488*

Annual Book of A S T M Standards. Volume 15.06. Adhesives (US) *488*

Annual Book of A S T M Standards. Volume 15.07. End Use Products (US) *488*

Annual Book of A S T M Standards. Volume 15.08. Fasteners (US) *488*

Annual Book of A S T M Standards. Volume 15.09. Paper; Packaging; Flexible Barrier Materials; Business Copy Products (US) *488, 854, 858*

Annual Bulletin of Coal Statistics for Europe (UN ISSN 0066-3808) *814*

Annual Bulletin of Electric Energy Statistics for Europe (UN ISSN 0066-3816) *461, 468, 1048*

Annual Bulletin of Gas Statistics for Europe/Bulletin Annuel de Statistiques de Gaz pour l'Europe (UN ISSN 0066-3824) *468*

Annual Bulletin of General Energy Statistics for Europe (UN) *468*

Annual Bulletin of Historical Literature (UK ISSN 0066-3832) *714*

Annual Bulletin of Housing and Building Statistics for Europe (UN) *181*

Annual Bulletin of Steel Statistics for Europe (UN) *801, 1048*

Annual Bulletin of Trade in Chemical Products (UN ISSN 0251-0081) *287, 321*

Annual Bulletin of Transport Statistics for Europe (UN ISSN 0066-3859) *1080*

Annual Canadian-American Seminar. Proceedings (CN ISSN 0384-1103) *914*

Annual Catalogue of Government Publications (UK) *939*

Annual Causes and Conditions of Poverty in South Dakota *see* Poverty in South Dakota *1020*

Annual Chart Summaries (UK) *832*

Annual Coal Production Report *see* Coal Production (Year) *815*

Annual Conference on Activated Sludge Process Control. Proceedings (US) *469, 952*

Annual Conference on Applications of X-Ray Analysis. Proceedings *see* Advances in X-Ray Analysis *1067*

Annual Conference on Fire Research (US) *506*

Annual DeGarmo Lectures (US ISSN 0882-7133) *432*

Annual Descriptive Report of Program Activities for Vocational Education *see* Idaho. State Board for Vocational Education. Annual Descriptive Report of Program Activities for Vocational Education *426*

Annual Development Assistance Review, Memorandum of New Zealand (NZ) *261*

Annual Directory of Booksellers in the British Isles Specialising in Antiquarian and Out-Of-Print Books (UK ISSN 0066-3913) *959*

Annual Directory of Oklahoma Libraries (US) *673*

Annual Directory through Press and Advertising *see* Stamm Leitfaden Durch Presse und Werbung *131*

Annual Dog Watch *see* Dog Watch *1100*

Annual Economic Review (RH) *241*

Annual Editions. Focus: Aging *see* Annual Editions: Aging *551*

Annual Editions: Aging (US ISSN 0272-3808) *551*

Annual Editions: American Government (US) *902*

Annual Editions: American History (US) *603*

Annual Editions: Anthropology (US) 69
Annual Editions: Biology (US) 137
Annual Editions: Business/Management(US ISSN 0090-4309) 191
Annual Editions: Comparative Politics (US) 902
Annual Editions: Criminal Justice (US ISSN 0272-3816) 369
Annual Editions: Early Childhood Education (US) 410
Annual Editions: Economics (US) 191
Annual Editions: Educating Exceptional Children (US ISSN 0198-7518) 444
Annual Editions: Education (US) 410
Annual Editions: Educational Psychology (US) 410, 933
Annual Editions: Environment (US ISSN 0272-9008) 494
Annual Editions: Global Issues (US) 541
Annual Editions: Health (US ISSN 0278-4653) 885
Annual Editions: Human Development see Annual Editions: Readings in Human Development 171
Annual Editions: Human Sexuality (US) 137, 933, 1024
Annual Editions: Macroeconomics (US) 277
Annual Editions: Marketing (US ISSN 0730-2606) 283
Annual Editions: Marriage and Family (US ISSN 0272-7897) 1024
Annual Editions: Personal Growth and Adjustment see Annual Editions: Personal Growth and Behavior 933
Annual Editions: Personal Growth and Behavior (US ISSN 0198-912X) 933
Annual Editions: Psychology (US ISSN 0272-3794) 933
Annual Editions: Readings in American Government see Annual Editions: American Government 902
Annual Editions: Readings in American History (US ISSN 0090-4511) 603
Annual Editions: Readings in Anthropology see Annual Editions: Anthropology 69
Annual Editions: Readings in Biology see Annual Editions: Biology 137
Annual Editions: Readings in Criminal Justice see Annual Editions: Criminal Justice 369
Annual Editions: Readings in Economics see Annual Editions: Economics 191
Annual Editions: Readings in Education(US ISSN 0095-5787) 410
Annual Editions: Readings in Human Development (US ISSN 0090-5348) 171, 757, 933
Annual Editions: Readings in Human Sexuality see Annual Editions: Human Sexuality 137
Annual Editions: Readings in Marriage and Family see Annual Editions: Marriage and Family 1024
Annual Editions: Readings in Personality and Adjustment see Annual Editions: Personal Growth and Behavior 933
Annual Editions: Readings in Psychology see Annual Editions: Psychology 933
Annual Editions: Readings in Social Problems see Annual Editions: Social Problems 1015
Annual Editions: Readings in Sociology see Annual Editions: Sociology 1024
Annual Editions: Social Problems (US ISSN 0272-4464) 1015
Annual Editions: Sociology (US ISSN 0277-9315) 1024
Annual Editions: State & Local Government (US) 939
Annual Editions: Urban Society (US ISSN 0160-9815) 1024
Annual Editions: Western Civilization (US) 555
Annual Educational Summary, New York State (US ISSN 0085-4077) 410

Annual Egyptological Bibliography/Bibliographie Egyptologique Annuelle/Jaehrliche Aegyptologische Bibliographie (NE) 562
Annual Electric Power Survey see Electric Power Annual Report 452
Annual Energy Litigation Institute. Effective Strategies and Techniques (US ISSN 0273-7000) 464, 650
Annual Epidemiological and Vital Statistics see World Health Statistics Annual 959
Annual Estimates of the Population of Scotland (UK ISSN 0066-3964) 920
Annual Evaluation Report - North Dakota State Advisory Council for Vocational Education see North Dakota. State Advisory Council for Vocational Education. Annual Evaluation Report 448
Annual Executive Compensation Report(US) 286
Annual Executive Compensation Study see Annual Executive Compensation Report 286
Annual Fertilizer Review see F A O Fertilizer Yearbook 55
Annual Foreign Trade Statistics of Bangladesh see Foreign Trade Statistics of Bangladesh 208
Annual Franchise Handbook Directory (US) 302
Annual Frequency Control Symposium see Frequency Control Symposium 453
Annual General Meeting of the Asiatic Society of Bangladesh; Report of the General Secretary (BG) 850
Annual Geomagnetic Bulletin of Pakistan (PK) 803
Annual Guide to Careers for Young People see N U T Guide to Careers Work 848
Annual Guide to Public Policy Experts (US ISSN 0731-339X) 939
Annual Guide to Ribbons and Toner (US) 930
Annual Guide to Stewardess Career see Airline Guide to Flight Attendant Career 847
Annual Handbook for Group Facilitators see University Associates, Inc. Annual 1030
Annual Hospital Directory see Nursingworld Journal Nursing Job Guide 784
Annual Index of Rheumatology (US ISSN 0097-921X) 1146
Annual Index to Poetry in Periodicals (US ISSN 0882-195X) 738
Annual Institute on Securities Regulation (US) 222, 650
Annual International Congress Calendar(BE) 795
Annual International Technical Conference and Exhibit see Abrasive Engineering Society. Abrasive Usage Conference. Proceedings 469
Annual Local Government Financial Report, State of Florida see Florida. Bureau of Local Government Finance. Annual Local Government Financial Report 295
Annual Madison Conference of Applied Research and Practice on Municipal and Industrial Waste see Madison Waste Conference. Annual Proceedings 497
Annual Meeting - American Association for the Advancement of Science see American Association for the Advancement of Science. Meeting Program 987
Annual Microprogramming Workshop. Proceedings see Microprogramming Workshop. Proceedings 362
Annual Mosquito Review see New Jersey Mosquito Control Association. Proceedings 165
Annual National Conference on Labor at New York University. Proceedings(US ISSN 0193-3418) 269
Annual New Mexico Water Conference. Proceedings (US ISSN 0161-4924) 1123

Annual of Advertising Art in Japan/Nenkan Kokoku Bijutsu (JA ISSN 0548-1643) 14
Annual of Advertising, Editorial and Television Art and Design with the Annual Copy Awards see Art Directors Annual 101
Annual of Armenian Linguistics (US ISSN 0271-9800) 690
Annual of Czechoslovak Medical Literature (CS) 768
Annual of Indian Photography (II) 884
Annual of Psychoanalysis (US ISSN 0092-5055) 933
Annual of Urdu Studies (US) 691, 850
Annual Organ Handbook (US) 832
Annual Performance Report and Continuation of the State Plan for Drug Abuse Prevention see Louisiana. Division of Mental Health. Annual Performance Report and Continuation of the State Plan for Drug Abuse Prevention 377
Annual Phoenix Conference on Computers and Communications. Proceedings see Phoenix Conference on Computers and Communications. Conference Proceedings 346
Annual Plan of Work - Department of Human Resources see North Carolina. Department of Human Resources. Annual Plan of Work 1019
Annual Planning Information Bridgeport-Norwalk-Stamford-Valley Service Delivery Area (US) 269
Annual Planning Information for Stamford Labor Market Area see Annual Planning Information Bridgeport-Norwalk-Stamford-Valley Service Delivery Area 269
Annual Planning Information: Sacramento Metropolitan Statistical Area (US) 269
Annual Planning Information: Sacramento Standard Metropolitan Statistical Area see Annual Planning Information: Sacramento Metropolitan Statistical Area 269
Annual Practice see Supreme Court Practice 665
Annual Progress in Child Psychiatry and Child Development (US ISSN 0066-4030) 789
Annual Progress Report - U.S. Army Medical Research Institute of Infectious Diseases see U.S. Army Medical Research Institute of Infectious Diseases. Annual Progress Report 778
Annual Register (US) 555, 914
Annual Register of Grant Support: a Directory of Funding Soures (US ISSN 0066-4049) 432
Annual Register of Pharmaceutical Chemists (UK ISSN 0260-955X) 869
Annual Register World Events (UK ISSN 0066-4057) 902
Annual Report see Algemeen Werkloosheidsfonds. Jaarverslag 637
Annual Report and Accounts-Cameroon Development Corporation see Cameroon Development Corporation. Annual Report and Accounts/Rapport Annuel et Compte-Rendu Financier 287
Annual Report-Andhra Pradesh State Trading Corporation Limited see Andhra Pradesh State Trading Corporation Limited. Annual Report 282
Annual Report - Asia Society see Asia Society. Annual Report 568
Annual Report-Association of American Publishers see Association of American Publishers. Annual Report 960
Annual Report - Central Sericultural Research and Training Institute see Central Sericultural Research and Training Institute. Annual Report 25
Annual Report - Citizens Advisory Council (Harrisburg) see Pennsylvania. Citizens Advisory Council to the Department of Environmental Resources. Annual Report 498

ANNUAL REPORT 1641

Annual Report--Cotton Corporation of India see Cotton Corporation of India. Annual Report 46
Annual Report - Criminal Injuries Compensation Commission see Hawaii. Criminal Injuries Compensation Commission. Annual Report 370
Annual Report - Damon Runyon-Walter Winchell Cancer Fund see Damon Runyon-Walter Winchell Cancer Fund. Annual Report 775
Annual Report - Department of Environmental Protection (Trenton) see New Jersey. Department of Environmental Protection. Annual Report 498
Annual Report - Department of Health and Social Services see Delaware. Department of Health and Social Service. Annual Report 953
Annual Report - Department of Safety see Tennessee. Department of Safety. Annual Report 1097
Annual Report - Educational Testing Service see Educational Testing Service Annual Report 413
Annual Report - Engineering Experiment Station (Madison) see University of Wisconsin, Madison. Engineering Experiment Station. Annual Report 807
Annual Report - Family Planning Association of Kenya see Family Planning Association of Kenya. Annual Report 179
Annual Report - Federal Home Loan Bank of San Francisco see Federal Home Loan Bank of San Francisco. Annual Report 228
Annual Report for the Department of Industrial Relations see California. Department of Industrial Relations. Annual Report 270
Annual Report - Indian Council of Historical Research see Indian Council of Historical Research. Annual Report 569
Annual Report - Indian School of Mines see Indian School of Mines. Annual Report 817
Annual Report - Institute of Secretariat Training and Management see Institute of Secretariat Training and Management. Annual Report 286
Annual Report - Jammu & Kashmir Minerals Limited see Jammu & Kashmir Minerals Limited. Annual Report 817
Annual Report - Madhya Pradesh State Agro-Industries Development Corporation Ltd. see Madhya Pradesh State Agro-Industries Development Corporation Ltd. Annual Report 48
Annual Report - Meghalaya Industrial Development Corporation see Meghalaya Industrial Development Corporation. Annual Report 197
Annual Report - Mississippi Marine Resources Council see Mississippi Marine Resources Council. Annual Report 407
Annual Report - National Arthritis Advisory Board see U.S. National Arthritis Advisory Board. Annual Report 793
Annual Report - National Association of Independent Schools see National Association of Independent Schools. Annual Report 417
Annual Report - Nebraska State Patrol see Nebraska. State Patrol. Annual Report 371
Annual Report - New York State Medical Care Facilities Finance Agency see New York State Medical Care Facilities Finance Agency. Annual Report 955
Annual Report of Advocacy for Nursing Home Reform (US) 551, 616

Annual Report of Births, Deaths, Marriages and Divorces as Reported to the Bureau of Vital Statistics (Little Rock) *see* Arkansas. Bureau of Vital Statistics. Annual Report of Births, Deaths, Marriages and Divorces as Reported to the Bureau of Vital Statistics 926

Annual Report of Community Services Administration *see* U.S. Community Services Administration. Annual Report of Community Services Administration 1021

Annual Report of Educational Psychology in Japan/Kyoiku Shinrigaku Nempo (JA ISSN 0452-9650) 410, 933

Annual Report of Fire and Disaster Prevention *see* Saigai No Jittai To Shobo No Genkyo 507

Annual Report of Life Insurance, Republic of China *see* Life Insurance Business in Taiwan (Year) 640

Annual Report of Oklahoma Libraries (US) 673

Annual Report of Public Health, Saitama Prefecture *see* Saitama-Ken Eisei Tokei Nenpo 956

Annual Report of Survey - Inventory Activities *see* Alaska. Division of Game. Annual Report of Survey - Inventory Activities 1044

Annual Report of the Arizona Department of Health Services *see* Arizona. Department of Health Services. Annual Report 952

Annual Report of the Arts Activities in Alabama (US ISSN 0096-1388) 101

Annual Report of the Department of Business Regulation (Helena) *see* Montana. Department of Business Regulation. Annual Report 944

Annual Report of the Department of Environmental Quality *see* Wyoming. Department of Environmental Quality. Annual Report 500

Annual Report of the Department of Revenue and Taxation of the State of Wyoming *see* Wyoming. Department of Revenue and Taxation. Annual Report 300

Annual Report of the Division of Police (Cincinnati) *see* Cincinnati. Division of Police. Annual Report 370

Annual Report of the Federal Trade Commission *see* U.S. Federal Trade Commission. Annual Report 240

Annual Report of the Health and Social Services *see* Wyoming. Department of Health and Social Services. Annual Report 1022

Annual Report of the Idaho Department of Labor and Industrial Services *see* Idaho. Department of Labor and Industrial Services. Annual Report 272

Annual Report of the Michigan State Advisory Council for Vocational Education *see* Michigan. Advisory Council for Vocational Education. Annual Report 445

Annual Report of the Oklahoma Water Resources Research Institute *see* Oklahoma Water Resources Research Institute. Annual Report 1125

Annual Report of the Register of Copyrights *see* U.S. Copyright Office. Annual Report of the Register of Copyrights 861

Annual Report of the State Superintendent of Public Instruction Utah Public School System *see* Utah. State Office of Education. Annual Report of the State Superintendent of Public Instruction 444

Annual Report of the Superintendent of Public Instruction *see* Arizona. Department of Education. Annual Report of the Superintendent of Public Instruction 410

Annual Report of the Treasurer, State of Connecticut *see* Connecticut. Treasury Department. Annual Report 294

Annual Report of the U.S. Department of Health and Human Services to the Congress of the United States on Services Provided to Handicapped Children in Project Head Start *see* U.S. Department of Health and Human Services. Annual Report to the Congress of the United States on Services Provided to Handicapped Children in Project Head Start 445

Annual Report of the Virginia State Water Control Board *see* Virginia. State Water Control Board. Annual Report 1127

Annual Report of the Working and Affairs of Mysore Minerals Limited (II) 814

Annual Report - Ombudsman for Corrections (St. Paul) *see* Minnesota. Office of Ombudsman for Corrections. Annual Report 371

Annual Report on Advanced Dental Education (US) 446, 779

Annual Report on Dental Auxiliary Education (US ISSN 0084-6554) 422, 768

Annual Report on Dental Education (US ISSN 0065-8030) 422, 768

Annual Report on Development Assistance to Mauritius (UN) 261

Annual Report on Development Assistance to the Seychelles (UN) 261

Annual Report on High-Tech Materials (US ISSN 8755-9978) 1067

Annual Report on Highway Safety Improvement Programs *see* U.S. Department of Transportation. Highway Safety Stewardship Report 1098

Annual Report on National Account (JA) 241

Annual Report on Research and Development (US ISSN 0739-6325) 1067

Annual Report on Results of Treatment in Gynecological Cancer (SW ISSN 0348-8799) 774

Annual Report on the Administration of Prisons in Kenya (KE) 369

Annual Report on the Results of Treatment in Carcinoma of the Uterus, Vagina, and Ovary *see* Annual Report on Results of Treatment in Gynecological Cancer 774

Annual Report on the Working and Affairs of Mysore Sales International Limited (II) 239

Annual Report on Tourism Statistics, Republic of China (CH) 1106

Annual Report on Unemployment *see* Labour Statistics Report 212

Annual Report on Work of Fabian Society *see* Fabian Society. Annual Report 904

Annual Report - Overseas Development Council *see* Overseas Development Council. Annual Report 263

Annual Report - Overseas Private Investment Corporation *see* Overseas Private Investment Corporation. Annual Report 267

Annual Report - Petroleum Division *see* Minnesota. Department of Revenue. Petroleum Division. Annual Report 865

Annual Report - Punjab National Bank *see* Punjab National Bank. Annual Report 231

Annual Report - Rajasthan State Tanneries Limited *see* Rajasthan State Tanneries Limited. Annual Report 672

Annual Report - Regional Institute of Social Welfare Research *see* Regional Institute of Social Welfare Research. Annual Report 1020

Annual Report - Republic Forge Company *see* Republic Forge Company. Annual Report 291

Annual Report - Robert Wood Johnson Foundation *see* Robert Wood Johnson Foundation. Annual Report 766

Annual Report - San Francisco Bay Area Rapid Transit District *see* San Francisco Bay Area Rapid Transit District. Annual Report 1083

Annual Report - Securities Investor Protection Corporation *see* Securities Investor Protection Corporation. Annual Report 268

Annual Report - Southeast Michigan Council of Governments *see* Southeast Michigan Council of Governments. Annual Report 946

Annual Report - Southern California Rapid Transit District. *see* Southern California Rapid Transit District. Annual Report 1083

Annual Report - State Consumer Protection Board *see* New York (State) Consumer Protection Board. Annual Report 369

Annual Report - State of Alaska. Violent Crimes Compensation Board *see* Alaska. Violent Crimes Compensation Board. Annual Report 369

Annual Report - State of Alaska, Legislative Budget and Audit Committee *see* Alaska. Legislature. Budget and Audit Committee. Annual Report 938

Annual Report - State of Connecticut, Council on Environmental Quality *see* Connecticut. Council on Environmental Quality. Annual Report 494

Annual Report - State of Florida, Department of Transportation *see* Florida. Department of Transportation. Annual Report 1153

Annual Report - State of Hawaii. State Commission on the Status of Women *see* Hawaii. State Commission on the Status of Women. Annual Report 1129

Annual Report: State of Idaho Johnson-O'Malley Program *see* Idaho. State Superintendent of Public Instruction. Annual Report. State of Idaho Johnson-O'Malley Program 414

Annual Report - State of New York, Division of Criminal Justice Services *see* New York (State). Division of Criminal Justice Service. Annual Report 372

Annual Report - Susquehanna River Basin Commission *see* Susquehanna River Basin Commission. Annual Report 1126

Annual Report - the Institute for Certification of Computer Professionals *see* Institute for the Certification of Computer Professionals. Annual Report 352

Annual Report to Congress on the Automotive Technology Development Program *see* U.S. Department of Energy. Annual Report to Congress on the Automotive Technology Program 1093

Annual Report to Congress - Urban Initiatives Anti-Crime Program *see* U.S. Urban Initiatives Anti-Crime Program. Annual Report to Congress 373

Annual Report to the Congress by the Office of Technology Assessment *see* U.S. Office of Technology Assessment Annual Report to the Congress 947

Annual Report to the Governor and Legislature - Teacher's Retirement Board *see* California. Teachers Retirement Board. State Teacher's Retirement System; Annual Report to the Governor and the Legislature 442

Annual Report to the President and the Congress on the State Energy Conservation Program *see* U.S. Department of Energy. Office of State and Local Programs. Annual Report to the President and the Congress on the State Energy Conservation Program 467

Annual Report to the Supreme Court of Illinois *see* Illinois. Administrative Office of Illinois Courts. Annual Report to the Supreme Court of Illinois 657

Annual Report - University of Georgia, Institute of Ecology *see* University of Georgia. Institute of Ecology. Annual Report 500

Annual Report - Vermont Industrial Development Authority *see* Vermont Industrial Development Authority. Annual Report 292

Annual Report - Western Society of Malacologists *see* Western Society of Malacologists. Annual Report 178

Annual Report - Woodrow Wilson International Center for Scholars *see* Woodrow Wilson International Center for Scholars. Annual Report 442

Annual Reports in Inorganic and General Syntheses (US ISSN 0092-1335) 328, 331

Annual Reports in Medicinal Chemistry(US ISSN 0065-7743) 869

Annual Reports in Organic Synthesis (US ISSN 0066-409X) 331

Annual Reports on Analytical Atomic Spectroscopy (UK ISSN 0306-1353) 899

Annual Reports on competition in O E C D Member Countries *see* Competition Policy in O E C D Countries 288

Annual Reports on Fermentation Processes (US ISSN 0140-9115) 321

Annual Reports on N M R Spectroscopy (US ISSN 0066-4103) 899

Annual Returns of Production from Quarries and Mineral Production Statistics (NZ ISSN 0112-2584) 821, 1048

Annual Review and Planning Framework for Telecommunication in the Government of Canada (CN) 350

Annual Review and Planning Framework in the Government of Canada *see* Annual Review and Planning Framework for Telecommunication in the Government of Canada 350

Annual Review in Automatic Programming (US ISSN 0066-4138) 358

Annual Review of Agriculture, Kinkei District/Kinki Nogyo Josei Hokoku (JA) 24

Annual Review of Allergy *see* Bi-Annual Review of Allergy 773

Annual Review of Anthropology (US ISSN 0084-6570) 69

Annual Review of Applied Linguistics (UK) 691

Annual Review of Astronomy and Astrophysics (US ISSN 0066-4146) 114, 887

Annual Review of Banking Law (US ISSN 0739-2451) 222, 650

Annual Review of Behavior Therapy: Theory & Practice *see* Review of Behavior Therapy: Theory & Practice 936

Annual Review of Biochemistry (US ISSN 0066-4154) 151

Annual Review of Biophysics and Bioengineering *see* Annual Review of Biophysics and Biophysical Chemistry 152

Annual Review of Biophysics and Biophysical Chemistry (US ISSN 0883-9182) 152, 469

Annual Review of California-Alaska Oil and Gas Exploration (US) 863

Annual Review of California Oil and Gas Exploration *see* Annual Review of California-Alaska Oil and Gas Exploration 863

Annual Review of Cell Biology (US ISSN 0743-4634) 162

Annual Review of Chronopharmacology(US ISSN 0743-9539) 869

Annual Review of Clinical Biochemistry(US) 151

Annual Review of Computer Science (US ISSN 8756-7016) 351

Annual Review of Criminal Law (Year) (CN) 650

Annual Review of Earth and Planetary Sciences (US ISSN 0084-6597) 114, 378
Annual Review of Ecology and Systematics (US ISSN 0066-4162) 494
Annual Review of Energy (US ISSN 0362-1626) 464
Annual Review of Engineering Industries and Automation (UN ISSN 0255-9293) 488
Annual Review of Entomology (US ISSN 0066-4170) 163
Annual Review of Fluid Mechanics (US ISSN 0066-4189) 894
Annual Review of Genetics (US ISSN 0066-4197) 166
Annual Review of Gerontology & Geriatrics (US ISSN 0198-8794) 551
Annual Review of Immunology (US ISSN 0732-0582) 773
Annual Review of Information Science and Technology (NE ISSN 0066-4200) 673
Annual Review of Jazz Studies (US ISSN 0731-0641) 832
Annual Review of Materials Science (US ISSN 0084-6600) 987
Annual Review of Medicine see Annual Review of Medicine: Selected Topics in the Clinical Sciences 757
Annual Review of Medicine: Selected Topics in the Clinical Sciences (US) 757
Annual Review of Microbiology (US ISSN 0066-4227) 168
Annual Review of N M R Spectroscopy see Annual Reports on N M R Spectroscopy 899
Annual Review of Neuroscience (US ISSN 0147-006X) 789
Annual Review of Nuclear and Particle Science (US ISSN 0163-8998) 896
Annual Review of Nuclear Science see Annual Review of Nuclear and Particle Science 896
Annual Review of Nursing Research (US ISSN 0739-6686) 783
Annual Review of Nutrition (US ISSN 0199-9885) 846
Annual Review of Pharmacology see Annual Review of Pharmacology and Toxicology 869
Annual Review of Pharmacology and Toxicology (US ISSN 0362-1642) 869
Annual Review of Physical Chemistry (US ISSN 0066-426X) 331
Annual Review of Physiology (US ISSN 0066-4278) 171
Annual Review of Phytopathology (US ISSN 0066-4286) 154
Annual Review of Plant Physiology (US ISSN 0066-4294) 154
Annual Review of Political Science (US ISSN 0748-8599) 902
Annual Review of Psychology (US ISSN 0066-4308) 933
Annual Review of Public Health (US ISSN 0163-7525) 952
Annual Review of Rehabilitation (US ISSN 0197-2251) 1015
Annual Review of Sociology (US ISSN 0360-0572) 1024
Annual Review of the Chemical Industry (UN ISSN 0255-4291) 287, 321
Annual Review of the Residential Property Market (AT ISSN 0155-9508) 627
Annual Review of United Nations Affairs (US ISSN 0066-4340) 914
Annual Simulation Symposium. Proceedings see Simulation Symposium. Record of Proceedings 358
Annual Solar Heating and Cooling Research and Development Branch Contractors' Meeting. Proceedings (US) 464
Annual Statement of the Overseas Trade of the United Kingdom (UK ISSN 0072-5846) 253
Annual Statistical Bulletin Sarawak (MY ISSN 0080-6439) 1048
Annual Statistical Report of the Colorado Judiciary (US ISSN 0094-7504) 668

Annual Statistical Review: The Distilled Spirits Industry (US ISSN 0066-4367) 1146
Annual Statistical Survey of Cancer see Etesia Statistike. Erevna tou Karkinou 775
Annual Statistics of Actual Production of Railway Cars/Tetsudo Sharyoto Seisan Dotai Tokei Nenpo (JA) 1084
Annual Statistics of Maritime Safety (JA ISSN 0448-3294) 1098
Annual Statistics of Water Works see Suido Jigyo Nenpo 1128
Annual Student Symposium on Marine Affairs. Proceedings (US ISSN 0270-1480) 137, 410
Annual Summary of Australian Notices to Mariners (AT) 1098
Annual Summary of Business Statistics, New York State (US ISSN 0066-4375) 202
Annual Summary of Merchant Ships Completed in the World (UK ISSN 0261-2720) 1098
Annual Summary of Merchant Ships Launched/Completed in the World see Annual Summary of Merchant Ships Completed in the World 1098
Annual Summary of Progress in Gravitation Sciences (US) 887
Annual Summary of Vital Statistics (Boise) see Idaho. Department of Health and Welfare. Annual Summary of Vital Statistics 958
Annual Survey of African Law (UK ISSN 0066-4405) 650
Annual Survey of Bankruptcy Law (US) 650
Annual Survey of Clerical Employees (CN) 234
Annual Survey of Computer Users (JA) 351
Annual Survey of Illinois Law see DePaul Law Review: Illinois Law Issue 654
Annual Survey of Indian Law (II ISSN 0570-2666) 650
Annual Survey of Massachusetts Law (US ISSN 0570-2674) 651
Annual Symposium on Engineering Geology and Soils Engineering. Proceedings see Engineering Geology and Soils Engineering Symposium. Proceedings 481
Annual T N G Convention Officers' Report see Newspaper Guild. Annual T.N.G. Convention Officers' Report 646
Annual Task Summary, Contract Research Program see U.S. Office of Naval Research. Annual Task Summary: Contract Research Program 813
Annual Textile Industry Technical Conference (Publication) see Textile Industry Technical Conference (Publication) 1075
Annual Trade Report of Tanzania, Uganda and Kenya see Kenya. Commissioner of Customs and Excise. Annual Trade Report 257
Annual Water Quality Report to Congress see Wisconsin. Department of Natural Resources. Annual Water Quality Report to Congress 500
Annual Work Plan - North Cal-Neva Resource Conservation and Development Project see North Cal-Neva Resource Conservation and Development Project. Annual Work Plan 366
Annual World's Best S F (US) 13, 714
Annual Worldwide T V Survey (JA) 347
Annuale Mediaevale (US ISSN 0066-4456) 714
Annuario Amministrativo Italiano/Italian Administrative Directory (IT ISSN 0084-6619) 939
Annuario Articoli Casalinghi e Articoli Regalo (IT) 319, 643
Annuario Audio & Video (IT) 347
Annuario Brasileiro de Ceramica (BL ISSN 0100-8633) 319
Annuario Cattolico d'Italia (IT ISSN 0066-4464) 980
Annuario Ceramica (IT ISSN 0066-4472) 319

Annuario dei Fornitori (IT ISSN 0392-5978) 302, 319
Annuario dell'Agricoltura Italiana (IT ISSN 0066-4502) 24
Annuario dell'Industria Italiana della Gomma/Yearbook of the Italian Rubber Industry (IT ISSN 0066-4499) 985
Annuario dell'Industria Italiana della Maglieria e della Calzetteria (IT) 1073
Annuario della Nautica (IT) 1041
Annuario delle Ceramiche Italiane per l'Edilizia (IT) 302, 319
Annuario di Contabilita Nazionale Tomo 1 (IT ISSN 0390-654X) 948
Annuario di Contabilita Nazionale Tomo 2 (IT ISSN 0390-6531) 948
Annuario di Diritto Comparato e di Studi Legislativi (IT ISSN 0003-5149) 651
Annuario di Elettronica (IT) 450
Annuario di Statistiche del Lavoro e dell'Emigrazione see Italy. Istituto Centrale di Statistica. Annuario di Statistiche del Lavoro 927
Annuario di Statistiche Giudiziarie - Tomo 2 (IT) 651
Annuario Diplomatico del Regno d'Italia see Annuario Diplomatico della Repubblica Italiana 914
Annuario Diplomatico della Repubblica Italiana (IT) 914
Annuario Europeo dell'Ambiente (IT) 494, 621, 651
Annuario Filosofico (Year) (IT) 876
Annuario Fotografico (IT) 884
Annuario Generale delle Imprese di Viaggio e Turismo (IT) 1106
Annuario Generale Italiano (IT ISSN 0084-6627) 239
Annuario Illustrato del Tennis (IT) 1037
Annuario Italiano delle Imprese Assicuratrici (IT ISSN 0084-6635) 637
Annuario Italiano Macchine Utensili e Complementari see A M U 745
Annuario Italiano Pubblicita Marketing Relazioni Pubbliche (IT) 14
Annuario Musical (SP) 832
Annuario Musicale Italiano (IT) 832
Annuario Ottico Italiano (IT) 287
Annuario Sanitario (IT) 952
Annuario Sanitario Italiano/Italian Sanitary Directory (IT) 757
Annuario Statistico dell'Attivita Edilizia e delle Opere Pubbliche (IT ISSN 0075-1804) 188
Annuario Statistico dell'Istruzione-Tomo 1 (IT ISSN 0390-6582) 422
Annuario Statistico dell'Istruzione-Tomo 2 (IT ISSN 0390-6590) 422
Annuario Statistico Italiano (IT ISSN 0066-4545) 1048
Annuarium Statisticum Ecclesiae/Statistique de l'Eglise/Statistical Yearbook of the Church. (VC) 974, 1048
Ano del Transporte (SP) 1080
Anon Nine (US) 714
Anorganische und Allgemeine Chemie in Einzeldarstellungen see Inorganic Chemistry Concepts 328
Another Season (US ISSN 0735-8202) 709, 714
Anschlaege (GW ISSN 0344-2667) 832
Anschriften Deutscher Verlage und Auslaendischer Verlage mit Deutschen Auslieferungen (GW ISSN 0066-4596) 959
Anschriften Deutschsprachiger Zeitschriften see Deutschsprachige Zeitschriften Deutschland - Oesterreich - Schweiz 125
Anselm Studies (US ISSN 0735-0864) 967
Anson G. Phelps Lectureship on Early American History (US ISSN 0066-4618) 603
Antaeus (HU ISSN 0133-6924) 81
Antarctic Bibliography (US ISSN 0066-4626) 541
Antarctic Meteorite Newsletter (US) 114
Antarctic Research Book Series (US) 541

Antarctic Research Series see Antarctic Research Book Series 541
Antartida (AG ISSN 0302-5691) 541
Antemurale (IT ISSN 0066-4642) 575
Antennas and Propagation (US) 450
Antepasados (US ISSN 0044-8362) 603
Anthologia Medica Santoriana (IT) 757
Anthology of Magazine Verse see Anthology of Magazine Verse and Yearbook of American Poetry 740
Anthology of Magazine Verse and Yearbook of American Poetry (US ISSN 0196-2221) 740
Anthony and Berryman's Magistrates' Court Guide (UK ISSN 0262-3234) 651
Anthropologica (Lima) (PE ISSN 0254-9212) 69
Anthropological Analyses (DK ISSN 0106-0880) 69, 81
Anthropological Forum (AT ISSN 0066-4677) 69
Anthropological Index to Current Periodicals in the Library of the Museum of Mankind (UK) 2, 78
Anthropological Literature (US ISSN 0190-3373) 69, 78
Anthropologie (GW ISSN 0066-4685) 69
Anthropologische Gesellschaft, Vienna. Mitteilungen (AU ISSN 0066-4693) 69
Anthropologischer Anzeiger (GW ISSN 0003-5548) 2, 78
Anthropologist (II ISSN 0003-5556) 69
Anthropology U C L A (US ISSN 0003-5564) 69
Anthropos (GW ISSN 0066-4723) 69, 856
Anthropos (IT ISSN 0391-3163) 69
Anthropos: Yearbook in Anthropology (GR) 69
Anti-Apartheid Movement. Annual Report of Activities and Developments (UK) 912
Anti Defamation League of B'nai B'rith Law Report see A D L Law Report 649
Anti-Quarium see A Q 1145
Anti-Slavery Reporter (UK) 912
Anti-Static Proposals & Electro-Conductive Technologies see A S P E C T 450
Antibiotics and Chemotherapy (SZ ISSN 0066-4758) 869
Antichita, Archeologia, Storia dell'Arte (IT) 81, 101
Antichita Classica e Cristiana (IT ISSN 0066-4766) 555, 691, 876
Antichita Pisane (IT) 81
Antichthon (AT ISSN 0066-4774) 336
Antigua Commercial Bank. Annual Report (AQ) 222
Antike Kunst. Beihefte (SZ ISSN 0066-4782) 79, 81, 101
Antikvitetsudstilling, Odd-Fellow Palaeet (DK ISSN 0109-2499) 79
Antiquarian (US) 79, 101
Antiquarian Trade List Annual (US ISSN 0197-0364) 959
Antiques Directory (US) 79
Antiques Folio (UK) 79, 101
Antiques in Britain see Antiques Folio 79
Antiquitas. Reihe 1. Abhandlungen zur Alten Geschichte (GW ISSN 0066-4839) 555
Antiquitas. Reihe 2. Abhandlungen aus dem Gebiete der Vor- und Fruehgeschichte (GW ISSN 0066-4847) 555
Antiquitas. Reihe 3. Abhandlungen zur Vor- und Fruehgeschichte, zur Klassischen und Provinzial-Roemischen Archaeologie und zur Geschichte des Altertums (GW ISSN 0066-4855) 81, 555
Antiquitas. Reihe 4. Beitraege zur Historia-Augusta-Forschung (GW ISSN 0066-4863) 555
Antiquites Africaines (FR ISSN 0066-4871) 81, 565
Antiquittaeten und Kunst Adressen Lexikon (GW) 79
Antitrust (US ISSN 0162-7996) 651
Antitrust Law Handbook (US ISSN 0738-5919) 651

Antologia Poetica de Esteban Echevarria see Antologia Poetica del Partido de Esteban Echeverria 740
Antologia Poetica del Partido de Esteban Echeverria (AG) 740
Antropologia (PL ISSN 0137-1460) 69
Antropologia Andina (PE) 69
Antropologia Ecuatoriana (EC) 69
Antropologia Fisica (PE) 69
Antropologia Portuguesa (PO ISSN 0870-0990) 69
Antwerp Handbook 1984 (UK ISSN 0264-1259) 302, 1098
Antwerp Port Annual (BE) 302, 1098
Antwerpens Oudheidkundige Kring. Jaarboek see Koninklijke Oudheidkundige Kring van Antwerpen. Jaarboek 89
Anuario A B D I B (Associacao Brasileira para o Desenvolvimento das Industrias de Base) (BL) 287
Anuario Agricola e Avicola (BL) 64
Anuario Antropologico (BL) 70
Anuario Avicola (BL) 64
Anuario Baja California y sus Hombres (MX) 541
Anuario Bibliografico Colombiano (CK ISSN 0570-393X) 121
Anuario Bibliografico Costarricense (CR ISSN 0066-5010) 121
Anuario Bibliografico Dominicano (DR) 121
Anuario Bibliografico Ecuatoriano (EC) 121
Anuario Bibliografico Uruguayo (UY) 121
Anuario Brasileiro de Media (BL) 342
Anuario Brasileiro de Propaganda (BL ISSN 0570-3956) 14
Anuario - C B A - Yearbook (UY) 121
Anuario Climatologico (PO ISSN 0870-2950) 803
Anuario Colombiano de Historia Social y de la Cultura (CK ISSN 0066-5045) 1006
Anuario Cultural del Peru (PE ISSN 0570-4006) 709
Anuario da Provincia de Mocambique see Anuario do Estado de Mocambique 565
Anuario das Industrias do Estado do Rio Grande do Sul (BL) 287
Anuario de Arquitectura Mexicana (MX) 96
Anuario de Bibliotecologia, Archivologia e Informatica see Centro de Bibliotecologia, Archivologia e Informacion. Anuario 675
Anuario de Comercio Exterior de Mexico (MX) 1146
Anuario de Derecho Civil Uruguayo (UY) 651
Anuario de Derecho Internacional (SP) 669
Anuario de Empresas Exportadoras (SP) 302
Anuario de Estadisticas Estatales (MX) 541, 1048
Anuario de Estudios Americanos (SP ISSN 0210-5810) 70
Anuario de Estudios Medievales (SP ISSN 0066-5061) 575
Anuario de Eusko-Folklore (SP ISSN 0210-7732) 70, 514
Anuario de Exportacion de Austria see Herold Export-Adressbuch von Oesterreich 309
Anuario de Filologia (VE ISSN 0066-507X) 691
Anuario de Filologia (SP ISSN 0210-1343) 691, 714
Anuario de Filosofia del Derecho (SP) 651
Anuario de Geomagnetismo - Observatorios de San Pablo (Toledo) y Almeria see Anuarios de Geomagnetismo (Year) 398
Anuario de Historia del Derecho Espanol (SP ISSN 0304-4319) 575, 669
Anuario de Historia Moderna y Contemporanea (SP ISSN 0210-9603) 555
Anuario de Importacion - Exportacion del Uruguay (UY) 253
Anuario de Jurisprudencia Argentina see Jurisprudencia Argentina 658

Anuario de la Economica Mexicana/ Mexican Economy Annual (MX) 241
Anuario de la Exportacion de Dinamarca see Udenrigs Handelskalenderen for Danmark 318
Anuario de la Mineria de Chile (CL ISSN 0066-5096) 383, 814
Anuario de la Prensa Chilena see Chile. Direccion de Bibliotecas Archivos y Museos. Bibliografia Chilena 125
Anuario de la Relojeria en Espana see Anuario de Relojeria y Arte en Metal para Espana e Hispanoamerica 644
Anuario de Legislacion Argentina see Revista de Legislacion Argentina 663
Anuario de Letras (MX ISSN 0543-758X) 715
Anuario de los Paises de A L A L C see Anuario del Comercio Exterior Latino-Americano 253
Anuario de Poetas Contemporaneos (AG) 1146
Anuario de Portos e Navios (BL) 1098
Anuario de Relojeria y Arte en Metal para Espana e Hispanoamerica (SP ISSN 0066-510X) 644
Anuario de Sociologia y Psicologia Juridicas (SP ISSN 0210-1785) 651, 933, 1024
Anuario del Arte Espanol (SP ISSN 0302-6965) 101
Anuario del Comercio Exterior Latino-Americano (AG ISSN 0066-5118) 253
Anuario del Cuento Costarricense (CR ISSN 0587-5196) 715
Anuario Delta Larousse (BL) 462
Anuario do Estado de Mocambique (MZ) 565
Anuario dos Criadores (BL ISSN 0518-0937) 24
Anuario Ecuatoriano de Derecho Internacional (EC ISSN 0570-4251) 669
Anuario Empresarial de Colombia (CK) 302
Anuario Enfermedades de Notificacion Obligatoria (CL) 757
Anuario Espanol de Seguros (SP) 637
Anuario Estadistico Centroamericano de Comercio Exterior (GT ISSN 0570-426X) 202
Anuario Estadistico de America Latina see Statistical Yearbook for Latin America 1064
Anuario Estadistico de Cuba (CU ISSN 0574-6132) 1048
Anuario Estadistico de Espana (SP ISSN 0066-5177) 1048
Anuario Estadistico de los Andes; Venezuela (VE ISSN 0066-5185) 203
Anuario Estadistico del Paraguay (PY) 1048
Anuario Estadistico das Ferrovias do Brasil (BL) 1094
Anuario Estadistico de Energia Electrica(BL) 468, 1048
Anuario Estadistico do Brasil/Statistical Yearbook of Brazil (BL ISSN 0100-1299) 1048
Anuario Estadistico do Estado de Sao Paulo (BL ISSN 0100-8730) 1048
Anuario Estadistico do Rio Grande de Sul (BL) 1048
Anuario Estadistico dos Transportes (BL) 1080
Anuario F.H.I. Argentina: Frutas y Hortalizas Industriarizadas y Frescas/F.H.I. Annual: Fresh and Industrialized Fruits and Vegetables (AG ISSN 0066-5207) 52
Anuario Financiero y de Sociedades Anonimas de Espana (SP ISSN 0301-7443) 222, 287
Anuario Geografico del Peru (PE ISSN 0066-5223) 541, 692
Anuario Hidrologico del Istmo Centroamericano (UN) 402
Anuario Hortofruticola Espanol (SP ISSN 0210-637X) 45
Anuario Iberoamericano (SP ISSN 0570-4324) 1006
Anuario Indigenista/Indianist Yearbook(MX) 70

Anuario Industrial de Minas Gerais see Guia Economico e Industrial do Estado de Minas Gerais 816
Anuario Interamericano de Archivos (AG ISSN 0325-3899) 603, 673
Anuario Interamericano de Derechos Humanos/Inter-American Yearbook on Human Rights (US) 669
Anuario Juridico (MX ISSN 0185-3295) 651
Anuario Latinoamericano de los Plasticos (MX) 900
Anuario Martiano see Centro de Estudios Martianos. Anuario 604
Anuario Mineral Brasileiro (BL) 814
Anuario Politico de America Latina (MX) 902
Anuarios de Geomagnetismo (Year) (SP) 383, 398
Anuarul de Folclor (RM) 514
Anul Cinematografic (RM) 822
Anzeiger des Germanischen Nationalmuseums (GW ISSN 0341-8383) 101, 575
Anzeiger fuer Slavische Philologie (AU ISSN 0066-5282) 691
Apartment Gazetteer (Europe) (UK) 1106
Apercu de la Statistique Federale Allemande see Survey of German Federal Statistics 1065
Apicultural Abstracts (UK ISSN 0003-648X) 2, 38
Apocalypso (US) 709
Apotheker - Jahrbuch (GW ISSN 0066-5347) 869
Appalachian Financial Review. see Financial Review 228
Appalachian Nature and Culture see Now and Then 729
Appalachian Regional Commission. Annual Report (US ISSN 0503-5422) 1012
Appaloosa Horse; Stud Book and Registry (US) 1042
Apparat Upravleniya Sotsialisticheskogo Gosudarstva (UR) 715
Apparel Buyers Guide Year Book (NZ) 302, 1073
Apparel: Latin American Industrial Report (US) 339
Apparel Plant Wages and Personnel Policies see Personnel Policies and Benefits for the Apparel Industry 287
Apparel Plant Wages and Personnel Policies see Apparel Plant Wages Survey 1073
Apparel Plant Wages Survey (US ISSN 0275-8873) 339, 1073
Appel Service; Repertoire d'Adresses Utiles pour le Commerce et l'Industrie (FR ISSN 0066-5398) 302
Appelles: The Georgia Arts Journal (US) 1146
Appeltjes van het Meetjesland (BE) 515, 575
Appendix see Maritime Guide 1102
Appliance Manufacturer Buyers Guide (US) 302
Appliances: Latin American Industrial Report (US) 643
Application of Modern Technology to International Development see A M T I D: Application of Modern Technology to International Development 1072
Applications et Transferts (Societe d'Etudes Linguistiques et Anthropologiques de France (SELAF)) (FR ISSN 0755-9291) 70, 691
Applications of Computer Science Series (US ISSN 0888-2231) 1005
Applications of Cryogenic Technology (US) 1146
Applications of Management Science (US ISSN 0276-8976) 278
Applications of Mathematics (US ISSN 0172-4568) 747
Applied Chemical News (AT) 478
Applied Ecology Abstracts see Ecology Abstracts 1128
Applied Geography Conferences (US ISSN 0192-8996) 541
Applied Health Physics Abstracts and Notes (UK ISSN 0305-7615) 2, 892, 958

Applied Language Studies (US) 691
Applied Linguistics see Jezykoznawstwo Stosowane 697
Applied Linguistics. Annual Review (US) 691
Applied Mathematical Sciences (US ISSN 0066-5452) 747
Applied Mathematics and Mechanics (US ISSN 0066-5479) 747, 894
Applied Mathematics Notes/Notes de Mathematiques Appliquees (CN ISSN 0700-9224) 747
Applied Mechanisms Conference Proceedings (US) 491
Applied Mineralogy. Technische Mineralogie (US ISSN 0066-5487) 814
Applied Optics. Supplement (US ISSN 0066-5495) 899
Applied Ornithology see Angewandte Ornithologie 170
Applied Physics and Engineering (US ISSN 0066-5509) 469, 887
Applied Polymer Symposia see Journal of Applied Polymer Science. Symposia 478
Applied Polymer Symposium. Papers (US ISSN 0066-5517) 478
Applied Radiology Buyer's Guide (US) 792
Applied Research Summary of Awards (US ISSN 0275-939X) 469
Applied Science and Technology Index (US ISSN 0003-6986) 2, 476, 1003
Applied Social Psychology Annual (US ISSN 0196-4151) 933, 1024
Applied Solid State Science (US ISSN 0066-5533) 450
Applied Virology Research (US) 168
Appraisal Institute Digest (CN ISSN 0003-7079) 965
Appraisal Manual see Means Square Foot Costs 965
Approaches to Semiotics (GW ISSN 0066-5576) 691
Approches (IS) 715
Approved Courses for Accountancy Education (UK ISSN 0263-1768) 221, 432
Apricot, Peach and Pear Growers' Association Annual see A P G A Annual 531
Apulum (RM) 575
Aqua (AT ISSN 0003-7206) 1123
Aquarian Arrow (UK ISSN 0141-0121) 860
Aquarian Lights (US) 1146
Aquariculture and Aquatic Sciences. Journal (US ISSN 0733-2076) 138, 1123
Aquarimantima (CK) 740
Aquario (AG) 740
Aquatic Biology Abstracts see Aquatic Sciences & Fisheries Abstracts. Part 2: Ocean Technology, Policy and Non-Living Resources 1127
Aquatic Sciences and Fisheries Abstracts see Aquatic Sciences & Fisheries Abstracts. Part 1: Biological Sciences & Living Resources 1127
Aquatic Sciences and Fisheries Abstracts see Aquatic Sciences & Fisheries Abstracts. Part 2: Ocean Technology, Policy and Non-Living Resources 1127
Aquatic Sciences & Fisheries Abstracts. Part 1: Biological Sciences & Living Resources (US ISSN 0140-5373) 2, 364, 514, 1127
Aquatic Sciences & Fisheries Abstracts. Part 2: Ocean Technology, Policy and Non-Living Resources (US ISSN 0140-5381) 2, 514, 1127
Aquatic Toxicology (US) 138
Aqui (UY ISSN 0066-5606) 715
Aquiculture (CH ISSN 0254-6493) 507
Aquileia Nostra (IT) 81
Aquilo. Ser. Zoologica (FI ISSN 0570-5177) 170, 173
Aquinas Law Journal (CE) 651
Aquinas Lecture Series (US ISSN 0066-5614) 876
Arab American Almanac (US ISSN 0742-9576) 501
Arab Bank for Economic Development in Africa. Annual Report (SJ) 222, 261

Arab Banking and Finance Handbook (BA) 222
Arab Book Annual/Al-Kitab Al-Arabi Fi Aam (AE ISSN 0066-5630) 963
Arab Business Yearbook (UK ISSN 0140-1874) 253
Arab Buyers' Guide to British Industry (UK) 302
Arab Fund for Economic and Social Development. Annual Report (KU ISSN 0304-6729) 261
Arab Horse Stud Book (UK) 1042
Arab Industry Review (BA) 287
Arab Medicare (UK ISSN 0268-4861) 757
Arab Oil & Gas Directory (FR) 863
Arab School on Science and Technology. Proceedings (US ISSN 0730-7845) 464, 469
Arab Shipping (UK) 1098
Arab Trade Directory (UK) 302
Arabia Past & Present Series (UK) 612
Arabian Computer Guide (UK) 357
Arabian Construction (UK) 181
Arabian Government and Public Services (UK ISSN 0261-6793) 939
Arabian Hotel & Travel Guide (UK) 619, 1106
Arabian Insurance Guide (UK) 637
Arabian Studies (UK ISSN 0305-036X) 612, 902
Arabian Studs and Stallions Magazine (AT) 1042
Arabian Trade Digest see Arabian Year Book 241
Arabian Transport Guide (UK) 1080
Arabian Year Book (KU) 241
Arabian Yearbook (UK) 302
Al-Arabiyya (US ISSN 0889-8731) 691, 715
Araisa (VE) 710
Araneta Research Journal (PH ISSN 0115-0820) 24, 523, 1121
Arastirma Eserleri Serisi (TU) 163, 168, 173
Arbeidsongeschiktheidsfonds en Algemeen Arbeidsongeschiktheidsfonds. Jaarverslag (NE) 637
Arbeiten aus dem Paul-Ehrlich-Institut, dem Georg-Speyer-Haus und dem Ferdinand-Blum-Institut (GW ISSN 0066-5665) 138, 757
Arbeiten und Text zur Slavistik (GW ISSN 0173-2307) 715
Arbeiten zur Angewandten Statistik (GW ISSN 0066-5673) 1048
Arbeiten zur Deutschen Philologie see Nemet Filologiai Tanulmanyok 699
Arbeiten zur Geschichte des Antiken Judentums und des Urchristentums (NE ISSN 0066-5681) 976
Arbeiten zur Geschichte des Pietismus (GW) 967
Arbeiten zur Kirchlichen Zeitgeschichte. Reihe B (GW) 967
Arbeiten zur Literatur und Geschichte des Hellenistischen Judentums (NE) 976
Arbeiten zur Paedagogik (GW ISSN 0066-569X) 410
Arbeiten zur Pastoraltheologie (GW) 967
Arbeiten zur Rechtsvergleichung (GW ISSN 0066-5703) 651
Arbeiten zur Rheinischen Landeskunde (GW ISSN 0373-7187) 541
Arbeiten zur Theologie. Reihe 1 (GW ISSN 0066-5711) 967
Arbeits und Forschungsberichte zur Saechsischen Bodendenkmalpflege (GE ISSN 0402-7817) 826
Das Arbeitsgebiet der Bundesstatistik (GW ISSN 0072-162X) 1048
Arbeitsgemeinschaft der Parlaments- und Behoerdenbibliotheken. Arbeitshefte (GW ISSN 0518-2220) 673
Arbeitsgemeinschaft der Sektion Geschichte der Akademie der Wissenschaften Geschichte der Buergerlichen Parteien in Deutschland. Mitteilungsblatt see Jenaer Beitraege zur Parteiegeschichte 587
Arbeitsgemeinschaft fuer Klinische Nephrologie. Mitteilungen (GW ISSN 0172-7311) 789

Arbeitsgemeinschaft fuer Lebensniveauvergleiche. Schriftenreihe (AU) 241, 1006
Arbeitsgemeinschaft Katholisch-Theologischer Bibliotheken. Mitteilungsblatt (GW ISSN 0177-8358) 673
Arbeitsgemeinschaft Saechsischer Botaniker. Berichte (GE) 154
Arbeitsinformationen ueber Studienprojekte auf dem Gebiet der Geschichte des Deutschen Judentums und des Antisemitismus (GW ISSN 0341-8340) 575, 976
Arbeitskosten in der Industrie Oesterreichs (AU) 269
Arbeitskreis Zweiter Weltkrieg. Bulletin(GE ISSN 0302-6329) 575
Arbeitsmarkt Politik (AU ISSN 0587-1689) 269
Arbeitsmethoden der Medizinischen und Naturwissenschaftlichen Kriminalistik (GW ISSN 0570-5886) 782
Arbeitsrecht der Gegenwart (GW ISSN 0066-586X) 269, 651
Arbeitsrecht und Arbeitslosenversicherung (SZ ISSN 0003-777X) 269
Arbeitstechnische Merkhefte der Waldarbeit (GW ISSN 0003-7796) 523
Arbejderbevaegelsens Bibliotek og Arkiv/Labour Movement Library and Archive, Denmark (DK ISSN 0107-9018) 203, 269
Arbejderbevaegelsens Bibliotek og Arkiv. Bibliografiske Serie (DK ISSN 0107-4628) 269
Arbejderbevaegelsens Erhvervsraad. Beretning (DK ISSN 0108-9625) 269
Arbejderhistorie (DK) 269
Arbejdermuseet. Aarbog (DK ISSN 0109-1158) 269
Arbejdsbetingede Lidelser. Yearbook (DK) 635
Arbejdsdirektoratet Beretning om Arbejdsformidligen og Arbejdsloeshedsforsikringen (DK ISSN 0109-1514) 269
Arbejdsformidlingsstatistik for Erhvervshaemmede (DK ISSN 0107-444X) 203
Arbejdsmarkedet og Arbejdsmarkedspolotik/Labor Market and Labor Market Policy (DK ISSN 0107-9735) 270
Arbejdsmarkedets Regelsamling (DK ISSN 0107-9743) 1146
Arbejdsmarkedsoversigt (DK ISSN 0106-7826) 270
Arbejdsretlige Domme see Arbejdsretligt Tidsskrift 270
Arbejdsretlige Kendelser see Arbejdsretligt Tidsskrift 270
Arbejdsretligt Tidsskrift (DK ISSN 0108-7150) 270, 651
Arbejdsulykker. Aarsstatistik (DK ISSN 0106-9683) 636
Arbetarnas Kulturhistoriskap. Notiser see Arbetaroerelsens Aarsbok 270
Arbetaroerelsens Aarsbok (SW) 270, 575
Arbetsskador (SW ISSN 0562-861X) 638
Arbitration & the Law (US) 270, 651
Arbo Jaarboek (NE) 635
Arbogen for Skjern (DK) 575
Arbok Visindafelags Islendinga (IC) 987
Arboretum Kornickie (PL ISSN 0066-5878) 154
Arc (IS) 715, 740
ARCA (UK ISSN 0309-5541) 336
Arcadia Bibliographica Virorum Eruditorum (US ISSN 0195-7163) 121
Arch (CN) 341
Archaelogia Belgica (BE ISSN 0772-7488) 81
Archaelogische Forschungen (GW) 81
Archao-Physika (GW ISSN 0066-5886) 81
Archaeoastronomy (UK ISSN 0142-7253) 114
Archaeologia (UK ISSN 0261-3409) 79, 81, 101, 534

Archaeologia Austriaca (AU ISSN 0003-8008) 70, 81
Archaeologia Cantiana (UK ISSN 0066-5894) 81
Archaeologia Historica (CS ISSN 0231-5823) 81
Archaeologia Japonica (JA ISSN 0402-852X) 81
Archaeologia Polona (PL ISSN 0066-5924) 81
Archaeologia Transatlantica (BE) 81
Archaeologia Zambiana (ZA ISSN 0570-6068) 81
Archaeologica Slovaca. Catalogi (GW ISSN 0066-5932) 81
Archaeologica Slovaca. Fontes (GW ISSN 0066-5940) 81
Archaeological Bibliography for Great Britain and Ireland (UK ISSN 0066-5967) 1146
Archaeological Completion Report Series (US) 81, 603
Archaeological Excavation Reports see Israel. Ministry of Education and Culture. Department of Antiquities and Museums. Atiqot (English Series) 88
Archaeological Excavations (UK) 81
Archaeological Excavations (IS) 81
Archaeological Exploration of Sardis. Monographs (US ISSN 0066-5975) 81
Archaeological Institute of America. Abstracts of the General Meeting (US) 96, 101
Archaeological Journal (UK ISSN 0066-5983) 81
Archaeological Reports (UK ISSN 0141-8971) 81
Archaeological Research Tools (US) 81
Archaeological Society of Connecticut. Bulletin (US ISSN 0739-5612) 81
Archaeological Society of Delaware. Bulletin (US ISSN 0003-8067) 81
Archaeological Society of Delaware. Monograph (US) 81
Archaeological Society of New Mexico. Papers (US) 81
Archaeological Society of North Carolina. Newsletter (US) 81
Archaeologicum Belgii Speculum (BE) 81
Archaeologische Ausgrabungen (GW ISSN 0341-1222) 575
Archaeologische Bibliographie (GW) 96
Archaeologische Funde und Denkmaeler des Rheinlandes (GW ISSN 0066-6009) 81
Archaeologische Informationen. Mitteilungen zur Ur- und Fruehgeschichte (GW) 82
Archaeologische Mitteilungen aus Iran. Neue Folge (GW ISSN 0066-6033) 82
Archaeology in Britain (Year) (UK ISSN 0308-8456) 82
Archaeology in Korea (KO) 82
Archaeology of Eastern North America(US ISSN 0360-1021) 82
Archaeonautica (FR) 82, 404
Archailogike Hetaireia en Athenais. Praktika (GR) 82
Archaiologike Ephemeris (GR) 82
Archdiocese of Baltimore. Directory see Catholic Directory of the Archdiocese of Baltimore 981
Archdiocese of Cincinnati Directory and Buyer's Guide (US) 980
Archeia tes Pharmakeutikes (Athens) (GR ISSN 0003-8148) 321, 869
Archeion (PL ISSN 0066-6041) 575
Archeion Euvoikon Meleton (GR) 82, 575
Archeion Pontou (GR) 82, 575
Archeion Thessalikon Meleton (GR) 82, 575
Archenhold-Sternwarte. Vortraege und Schriften (GE ISSN 0570-6262) 114
Archeografo Triestino (IT ISSN 0392-0038) 82
Archeologia (Poznan) (PL ISSN 0554-8195) 82
Archeologia (Wroclaw) (PL ISSN 0066-605X) 82
Archeologia Classica (IT ISSN 0003-8172) 82, 336

Archeological Society of South Carolina. Occasional Papers (US) 82
Archeologicke Vyskumy a Nalezy na Slovensku (CS) 82, 575
Archeologie de la Moldavie see Arheologia Moldovei 576
Archeologie en Bretagne (FR ISSN 0335-5233) 82
Archeologie Mediterraneenne (FR ISSN 0066-6084) 82
Archeologische Kaarten van Belgie (BE ISSN 0066-6025) 82
Archief- en Bibliotheekwezen in Belgie see Archives et Bibliotheques de Belgique 575
Archigram (UK ISSN 0066-6092) 96
Architectonika Themata see Architecture in Greece 97
Architects (UK) 96
Architects, Contractors & Engineers Guide to Construction Costs (US ISSN 0066-6157) 181
Architects Directory (SA) 96
Architects' Guide to Glass, Metal & Glazing (US) 96, 319
Architect's Handbook of Professional Practice (US ISSN 0066-6173) 96
Architects Standard Catalogues see A S C Mini-File 96
Architects' Year Book (UK ISSN 0066-619X) 1146
Architectura (HU ISSN 0066-6270) 97
Architectura (DK ISSN 0106-3030) 97
Architectural and Archaeological Society of Durham and Northumberland. Transactions. New Series see Durham Archaeological Journal 86
Architectural & Building Directory of India (II) 97, 181, 302
Architectural Annual Review (UK) 97
Architectural Association Annual Review see Architectural Annual Review 97
Architectural Handbook (US) 1146
Architectural Heritage Society of Scotland. Journal and Annual Report(UK) 97
Architectural History (UK ISSN 0066-622X) 97
Architectural Index (US ISSN 0570-6483) 97
Architectural Monographs (UK) 97
Architectural Services Books of Plans (UK) 97
Architecture and Urban Design (US) 97
Architecture in Greece/Architectonika Themata (GR ISSN 0066-6262) 97
Architecture Schools in North America (US ISSN 0092-7856) 97
Architecture Series: Bibliography (US ISSN 0194-1356) 100, 1215
Architektenhandbuch Schleswig-Holstein (GW) 97
Architektenkammer Niedersachsen (GW) 97
Architettura Urbanistica: Metodi di Programmazione e Progetti (IT) 97
Archiv (AU ISSN 0003-8849) 270
Archiv der Deutschen Jugendbewegung. Jahrbuch (GW ISSN 0587-5277) 575
Archiv fuer Diplomatik, Schriftgeschichte, Siegel- und Wappenkunde (GW ISSN 0066-6297) 575
Archiv fuer Eisenbahntechnik (GW ISSN 0341-0463) 1094
Archiv fuer Fischereiwissenschaft (GW ISSN 0003-9063) 507
Archiv fuer Frankfurts Geschichte und Kunst (GW ISSN 0341-8324) 575
Archiv fuer Geschichte von Oberfranken (GW ISSN 0066-6335) 575
Archiv fuer Hessische Geschichte und Altertumskunde (GW ISSN 0066-636X) 575
Archiv fuer Indische Philosophie see Wiener Zeitschrift fuer die Kunde Suedasiens und Archiv fuer Indische Philosphie 883
Archiv fuer Kinderheilkunde. Beihefte see Buecherei des Paediaters 787
Archiv fuer Liturgiewissenschaft (GW ISSN 0066-6386) 967

Archiv fuer Mittelrheinische Kirchengeschichte (GW ISSN 0066-6432) *967*
Archiv fuer Musikwissenschaft. Beihefte(GW ISSN 0570-6769) *833*
Archiv fuer Oeffentliche und Freigemeinnuetzige Unternehmen (GW ISSN 0003-9314) *287*
Archiv fuer Orientforschung (AU ISSN 0066-6440) *612*
Archiv fuer Papyrusforschung und Verwandte Gebiete (GE ISSN 0066-6459) *82, 555*
Archiv fuer Physikalische Therapie, Balneologie und Klimatologie *see* Zeitschrift fuer Physiotherapie *768*
Archiv fuer Protistenkunde (GE ISSN 0003-9365) *138*
Archiv fuer Rechts- und Sozialphilosophie. Beihefte (GW ISSN 0341-079X) *651, 876*
Archiv fuer Rechts und Sozialphilosophy. Supplementa (GW ISSN 0722-5679) *876*
Archiv fuer Reformationsgeschichte *see* Archive for Reformation History *575*
Archiv fuer Reformationsgeschichte. Literaturbericht *see* Archive for Reformation History. Literature Review *967*
Archiv fuer Religionspsychologie (GW ISSN 0084-6724) *933, 967*
Archiv fuer Schlesische Kirchengeschichte (GW ISSN 0066-6491) *555, 967*
Archiv fuer Sozialgeschichte (GW ISSN 0066-6505) *575*
Archiv fuer Vaterlaendische Geschichte und Topographie (AU ISSN 0003-9462) *575*
Archiv fuer Voelkerkunde (AU ISSN 0066-6513) *70, 515*
Archiv pro Badani o Zivote a Dile Jana Amose Komenskeho *see* Acta Comeniana. Archiv pro Badani o Zivote a Dile Jana Amose Komenskeho *574*
Archivalische Zeitschrift (GW ISSN 0003-9497) *555*
Archivas de Farmacologia y Toxicologia(SP) *869*
Archive (Tucson) (US) *884*
Archive for New Poetry Newsletter (US) *740*
Archive for Reformation History/ Archiv fuer Reformationsgeschichte (US) *575*
Archive for Reformation History. Literature Review/Archiv fuer Reformationsgeschichte. Literaturbericht (US) *715, 967*
Archives and the User (UK ISSN 0066-653X) *673*
Archives Bakounine/Bakunin-Archiv (NE ISSN 0066-6548) *575*
Archives, Bibliotheques et Musees de Belgique *see* Archives et Bibliotheques de Belgique *575*
Archives Claudeliennes (FR ISSN 0066-6556) *715*
Archives d'Anatomie, d'Histologie et d'Embryologie (FR ISSN 0003-9586) *138, 162, 757*
Archives d'Anthropologie *see* Musee Royal de l'Afrique Centrale. Archives d'Anthropologie *74*
Archives d'Ethnographie *see* Musee Royal de l'Afrique Centrale. Archives d'Anthropologie *74*
Archives d'Histoire Doctrinale et Litteraire du Moyen Age (FR ISSN 0373-5478) *876*
Archives de Philosophie du Droit (FR ISSN 0066-6564) *651*
Archives des Lettres Canadiennes (CN ISSN 0066-6572) *715*
Archives des Lettres Modernes (FR ISSN 0003-9675) *715*
Archives et Bibliotheques de Belgique/ Archief- en Bibliotheekwezen in Belgie (BE ISSN 0003-9748) *575, 673, 826*
Archives for Scandinavian Philology *see* Arkiv for Nordisk Filologi *691*
Archives Internationales d'Histoire des Idees/International Archives of the History of Ideas (NE ISSN 0066-6610) *876*

Archives of Asian Art (US ISSN 0066-6637) *101*
Archives of Labor and Urban Affairs Newsletter (US) *270*
Archives of Labor History and Urban Affairs Newsletter *see* Archives of Labor and Urban Affairs Newsletter *270*
Archives of Medical Hydrology (IT ISSN 0003-9934) *758*
Archives of Toxicology. Supplement (US ISSN 0171-9750) *869*
Archiviniana (PH) *673*
Archivio di Vecchi (IT ISSN 0004-0061) *758*
Archivio del Teatro Italiano (IT ISSN 0066-6661) *1076*
Archivio Italiano per la Storia della Pieta (IT ISSN 0066-6688) *967*
Archivio Linguistico Veneto. Quaderni. (IT ISSN 0066-6696) *691*
Archivio per l'Alto Adige (IT) *101, 515, 691*
Archivio per l'Antropologia e la Etnologia (IT) *70*
Archivio Putti di Chirurgia degli Organi di Movimento (IT ISSN 0066-670X) *794*
Archivio Storico Italiano. Biblioteca (IT ISSN 0066-6718) *575*
Archivio Storico Lodigiano (IT ISSN 0004-0347) *575*
Archivio Storico per le Province Parmensi (IT) *539*
Archivio Storico Sardo (IT) *575*
Archivium Hibernicum (IE ISSN 0044-8745) *575*
Archivo di Oceanografia e Limnologia (IT ISSN 0066-667X) *402, 404*
Archivo Epistolar Colombiano (CK ISSN 0066-6734) *715*
Archivo General de la Nacion. Revista (AG ISSN 0325-2868) *673*
Archivo Historico del Guayas. Coleccion Monografica (EC) *603*
Archivo Historico Diocesano de San Cristobal de las Casas. Boletin (MX) *70*
Archivos de Biologia y Medicina Experimentales (CL ISSN 0004-0533) *138, 781*
Archivos de Botanica do Estado de Sao Paulo *see* Rickia *161*
Archivos de Farmacologia y Toxicologia (SP ISSN 0304-8616) *869*
Archivos de Historia Andina (PE) *515, 603*
Archivs (AT) *501*
Archivum (GW ISSN 0066-6793) *673*
Archivum (Oviedo) (SP) *876*
Archivum Bibliographicum Carmelitanum (VC ISSN 0570-7242) *974*
Archivum Calderonianum (GW ISSN 0721-0442) *691*
Archivum Eurasiae Medii Aevi (GW ISSN 0724-8822) *850*
Archivum Fratrum Praedicatorum (IT) *576*
Archivum Historiae Pontificae (VC ISSN 0066-6785) *980*
Archivum Iuridicum Cracoviense (PL ISSN 0066-6882) *651*
Archivum Musicum (IT) *833*
Archivum Ottomanicum (GW ISSN 0378-2808) *612*
Archivum Romanicum. Biblioteca. Serie 1: Storia Letteraria-Paleografia (IT ISSN 0066-6807) *715*
Archivum Romanicum. Biblioteca. Serie 2: Linguistica (IT ISSN 0066-6815) *691*
Archiwum Trebonense (CS) *191, 576*
Archiwum Dziejow Oswiaty (PL ISSN 0066-6831) *410*
Archiwum Filologiczne (PL ISSN 0066-6866) *336, 691*
Archiwum Historii Filozofii i Mysli Spolecznej (PL ISSN 0066-6874) *876, 1006*
Archiwum Kryminologii (PL ISSN 0066-6890) *369*
Archiwum Literackie (PL ISSN 0066-6904) *715*
Archiwum Tlumaczen z Teorii Literatury i Metodologii Badan Literackich (PL ISSN 0208-7596) *691, 715*

Archiwum Veterinarium Polonicum *see* Polskie Archiwum Weterynaryjne *1122*
Arctic Science & Technology Information System Bibliography *see* A S T I S Bibliography *1*
Arctic Science & Technology Information System Occasional Publications *see* A S T I S Occasional Publications *121*
Arctic Science Conference. Proceedings(US) *987*
Arctic Summary Report *see* Alaska Summary Report/Index *862*
Arctos; Acta Philologica Fennica (FI ISSN 0570-734X) *336, 691*
Area and Production of Principal Crops in India. Summary Tables (II) *52*
Area Development Industrial Development Directory of Canada (US) *191*
Area Metalurgia (CL) *797*
Areco's Index to Periodical Literature on Aging *see* Index to Periodical Literature on Aging *552*
Areco's Quarterly Index to Periodical Literature on Aging *see* Index to Periodical Literature on Aging *552*
Arena *see* Stadion *1036*
Arena, Auditorium, Stadium Guide *see* Audarena Stadium Guide and International Directory *14*
Arenaturist (YU) *1106*
Areopag (GW ISSN 0570-751X) *342*
Arerugia (JA ISSN 0287-0185) *773, 792*
Aret Fortalt i Billeder (DK) *101, 576*
Argamon (IS ISSN 0334-326X) *173*
Argentina. Biblioteca del Congreso. Boletin *see* Argentina. Biblioteca del Congreso de la Nacion. Boletin *121*
Argentina. Biblioteca del Congreso. Boletin Legislativo (AG ISSN 0301-7818) *939*
Argentina. Biblioteca del Congreso de la Nacion. Boletin (AG) *121*
Argentina. Caja Federal de Ahorro y Prestamo para la Vivienda. Memoria y Balance (AG) *621*
Argentina. Central de Estadisticas Nacionales. Informe (AG) *1048*
Argentina. Comision Nacional de Valores. Informacion Estadistica (AG) *1048*
Argentina. Congreso. Biblioteca. Serie Bibliografica (AG ISSN 0325-3147) *911*
Argentina. Departamento de Estadistica Educativa. Boletin Informativo. (AG ISSN 0066-7021) *410*
Argentina. Departamento de Estudios Historicos Navales. Serie A: Cultura Nautica (AG ISSN 0066-703X) *810*
Argentina. Departamento de Estudios Historicos Navales. Serie B: Historia Naval Argentina (AG ISSN 0066-7048) *810*
Argentina. Departamento de Estudios Historicos Navales. Serie C: Biografias Navales Argentinas (AG ISSN 0066-7056) *133, 810*
Argentina. Departamento de Estudios Historicos Navales. Serie E: Documentos (AG) *603, 810*
Argentina. Departamento de Estudios Historicos Navales. Serie J: Libros y Impresos Raros (AG ISSN 0066-7080) *813*
Argentina. Direccion General de Coordinacion e Informacion Energetica. Anuario de Combustibles. *see* Argentina. Direccion General de Evaluacion Energetica. Anuario de Combustibles *450*
Argentina. Direccion General de Coordinacion e Informacion Energetica. Anuario Energia Electrica. *see* Argentina. Direccion General de Evaluacion Energetica. Anuario Energia Electrica *450*
Argentina. Direccion General de Evaluacion Energetica. Anuario de Combustibles. (AG) *450*
Argentina. Direccion General de Evaluacion Energetica. Anuario Energia Electrica. (AG) *450*

Argentina. Direccion General de Parques Nacionales. Anales de Parques Nacionales *see* Argentina. Servicio Nacional de Parques Nacional. Anales *939*
Argentina. Direccion General de Planificacion y Control Energetico. Anuario Estadistico. Combustibles. *see* Argentina. Direccion General de Evaluacion Energetica. Anuario de Combustibles *450*
Argentina. Estacion Experimental Agropecuaria Manfredi. Serie Informacion Tecnica (AG ISSN 0066-7242) *1146*
Argentina. Instituto de Asuntos Tecnicos. Estadisticas (AG) *1072*
Argentina. Instituto Forestal Nacional. Anuario de Estadistica Forestal (AG ISSN 0570-8834) *523*
Argentina. Instituto Nacional de Estadistica y Censos. Anuario Estadistico (AG) *926, 1048*
Argentina. Instituto Nacional de Estadistica y Censos. Indicadores Industriales. Serie I (AG) *1146*
Argentina. Instituto Nacional de Estadistica y Censos. Informe Serie E: Edificacion (AG ISSN 0066-7196) *1146*
Argentina. Instituto Nacional de Estadistica y Censos. Serie Informacion Demografica (AG) *1146*
Argentina. Instituto Nacional de Geologia y Mineria. Revista *see* Argentina. Servicio Nacional Minero Geologico. Revista *383*
Argentina. Instituto Nacional de Tecnologia Agropecuaria. Suelos (AG) *1146*
Argentina. Instituto Nacional de Tecnologia Industria. Boletin Tecnico(AG ISSN 0325-6278) *1067*
Argentina. Junta Nacional de Carnes. Sintesis Estadistica (AG ISSN 0066-7269) *38*
Argentina. Mercado Nacional de Hacienda. Anuario (AG) *64*
Argentina. Ministerio de Cultura y Educacion. Estadisticas de la Educacion (AG) *422*
Argentina. Museo Provincial de Ciencias Naturales. Comunicaciones *see* Argentina. Museo Provincial de Ciencias Naturales. Comunicaciones. Nueva Serie *138*
Argentina. Museo Provincial de Ciencias Naturales. Comunicaciones. Nueva Serie (AG ISSN 0325-3856) *138, 856*
Argentina. Oficina Sectorial de Desarrollo de Energia. Anuarios Estadisticos. Energia Electrica *see* Argentina. Direccion General de Evaluacion Energetica. Anuario Energia Electrica *450*
Argentina. Secretaria de Estado de Agricultura y Ganaderia. Area de Trabajo de Lecheria. Resena Estadistica (AG) *38*
Argentina. Secretaria de Estado de Agricultura y Ganaderia. Comunicado de Prensa (AG) *24*
Argentina. Secretaria de Estado de Hacienda. Memoria (AG) *292*
Argentina. Secretaria de Estado de Salud Publica. Programa Nacional de Estadisticas de Salud (AG) *958*
Argentina. Secretaria de Guerra. Direccion de Estudios Historicos. Boletin Bibliografico (AG ISSN 0066-7293) *603, 810*
Argentina. Servicio de Hidrografia Naval. Boletin (AG ISSN 0004-1076) *404*
Argentina. Servicio de Inteligencia Naval. Bibliotecas de la Armada. Boletin Bibliografico. (AG ISSN 0066-7331) *813*
Argentina. Servicio Nacional de Economia y Sociologia Rural. Publicacion E S R (AG) *24*
Argentina. Servicio Nacional de Parques Nacional. Anales (AG ISSN 0302-5705) *939*
Argentina. Servicio Nacional Minero Geologico. Anales (AG ISSN 0066-7145) *383, 814*

Argentina. Servicio Nacional Minero Geologico. Boletin (AG ISSN 0066-7153) *383*, 814
Argentina. Servicio Nacional Minero Geologico. Estadistica Minera (AG ISSN 0066-7161) *814*
Argentina. Servicio Nacional Minero Geologico. Informes Tecnicos (AG) *383*
Argentina. Servicio Nacional Minero Geologico. Revista (AG ISSN 0066-717X) *383*
Argentine-American Business Review Directory (US) *253*
Argentine Economic Development (AG) *241*
Argentine Republic. Direccion Nacional de Geologia y Mineria. Anales *see* Argentina. Servicio Nacional Minero Geologico. Anales *383*
Argentine Republic. Direccion Nacional de Geologia y Mineria. Boletin *see* Argentina. Servicio Nacional Minero Geologico. Boletin *383*
Argentine Republic. Direccion Nacional de Geologia y Mineria. Estadistica Minera *see* Argentina. Servicio Nacional Minero Geologico. Estadistica Minera *814*
Argentine Republic. Junta Nacional de Carnes. Resena *see* Argentina. Junta Nacional de Carnes. Sintesis Estadistica *38*
Argentine Republic. Mercado Nacional de Hacienda. Memoria *see* Argentina. Mercado Nacional de Hacienda. Anuario *64*
Argo *see* Probe (Santa Barbara) *914*
Argonaut (US ISSN 0883-9824) *710*
Argos (AG ISSN 0325-4194) *336*
Argument-Beiheft (GW ISSN 0722-964X) *710*
Arguments of the Philosophers (UK) *876*
Argus de la Poesie Francaise (FR ISSN 0066-734X) *740*
Argus du Livre Ancien et Moderne *see* Argus du Livre de Collection et de l'Autographe *738*
Argus du Livre de Collection et de l'Autographe (FR) *738*
Argus F C & S Chart (Fire Casualty & Surety) (US ISSN 0360-8921) *638*
Argus Insurance Chart *see* Argus F C & S Chart *638*
Arheologia Moldovei/Archeologie de la Moldavie (RM ISSN 0066-7358) *82*, *576*
Arheoloski Muzej u Zagrebu. Vjesnik (YU ISSN 0350-7165) *82*
Arheoloski Vestnik/Acta Archaeologica(YU ISSN 0570-8966) *82*
Arhivski Vjesnik (YU) *576*
Arhus Stifts Arboeger (DK) *576*
Ariane (PO) *715*
Ariel (PK ISSN 0254-3028) *715*
Aristotelion Panepistemion Thessalonikes. Philosophike Schole. Epistemonike Epeteris (GR) *576*
Aristotelion Panepistemion Thessalonikes. Theologike Schole. Epistemonike Epeteris (GR) *576*, *967*
Arizona. Commission on the Arizona Environment. Annual Report (US) *494*
Arizona. Department of Economic Security. Annual Report *see* D E S Activities Report *940*
Arizona. Department of Education. Annual Report of the Superintendent of Public Instruction (US ISSN 0095-5310) *410*
Arizona. Department of Health Services. Annual Report (US ISSN 0362-1421) *952*
Arizona. Department of Water Resources. Bulletin *see* Arizona. Department of Water Resources. Report *1123*
Arizona. Department of Water Resources. Report (US) *1123*
Arizona. Governor's Commission on Arizona Environment. Biennial Report *see* Arizona. Commission on the Arizona Environment. Annual Report *494*

Arizona. Oil and Gas Conservation Commission. Report of Investigation (US) *383*, *863*
Arizona. State Advisory Council for Vocational Education. Annual Report *see* Arizona. State Advisory Council for Vocational Technical Education. Annual Report *446*
Arizona. State Advisory Council for Vocational Technical Education. Annual Report (US) *446*
Arizona Archaeologist (US) *82*
Arizona Commission on the Arts. Report to the Governor (US ISSN 0098-7387) *101*
Arizona Commission on the Arts and Humanities. Report to the Governor *see* Arizona Commission on the Arts. Report to the Governor *101*
Arizona Directory of Exports (US) *253*, *302*
Arizona Forestry Notes (US ISSN 0066-7404) *523*
Arizona Geological Society Digest (US ISSN 0066-7412) *383*
Arizona Historical Society. Historical Monographs (US) *603*
Arizona Historical Society. Museum Monograph Series (US) *603*
Arizona Legislative Service (US ISSN 0094-4246) *651*
Arizona, New Mexico TourBook *see* Tourbook: Arizona, New Mexico *1117*
Arizona Radiation Regulatory Agency. Annual Report (US) *952*
Arizona Radiation Review (US) *494*, *896*
Arizona Reports (US) *651*
Arizona-Sonora Desert Museum. Annual Report *see* Sonorensis. Annual Report *830*
Arizona State Plan for the Education of Migratory Children (US) *410*
Arizona State University. Center for Asian Studies. Monograph Series (US) *568*, *715*
Arizona State University. Center for Asian Studies. Occasional Papers *see* Arizona State University. Center for Asian Studies. Monograph Series *715*
Arizona State University. Governmental Finance Institute. Proceedings *see* Papers in Public Administration *945*
Arizona State University Anthropological Research Papers (US ISSN 0271-0641) *70*
Arizona State University Directory of A S U Latin Americanists *see* Directory of A S U Latin Americanists *605*
Arizona Statistical Review (US ISSN 0518-6242) *203*, *1048*
Arizona U S A International Trade Directory *see* Arizona Directory of Exports *302*
Arkansas. Bureau of Vital Statistics. Annual Report of Births, Deaths, Marriages and Divorces as Reported to the Bureau of Vital Statistics (US ISSN 0094-3576) *920*, *926*
Arkansas. Division of Rehabilitation Services. Annual Report (US *758*, *1015*
Arkansas. Geological Commission. Information Circulars (US) *383*
Arkansas. Geological Commission. Miscellaneous Publications (US) *383*
Arkansas. Geological Commission. Water Resources Circulars (US ISSN 0571-0278) *1123*
Arkansas Agricultural Experiment Station. Mimeograph Series *see* Arkansas Agricultural Experiment Station. Research Series *38*
Arkansas Agricultural Experiment Station. Research Series (US ISSN 0099-5010) *38*, *52*
Arkansas Archeological Survey. Publications on Archeology. Popular Series (US ISSN 0587-3533) *82*
Arkansas Archeological Survey. Publications on Archeology. Research Reports (US ISSN 0277-6308) *82*
Arkansas Archeological Survey. Publications on Archeology. Research Series (US ISSN 0882-5491) *82*

Arkansas Archeological Survey. Publications on Archeology. Technical Papers (US) *82*
Arkansas Archeologist (US ISSN 0004-1718) *82*
Arkansas Average Covered Employment and Earnings by County and Industry *see* Arkansas Covered Employment and Earnings *270*
Arkansas Covered Employment and Earnings (US) *270*
Arkansas, Kansas, Missouri, Oklahoma TourBook *see* Tourbook: Arkansas, Kansas, Missouri, Oklahoma *1117*
Arkansas State Directory (US) *939*
Arkansas State Industrial Directory *see* MacRae's Arkansas State Industrial Directory *312*
Arkansas Tech University. Department of History. Occasional Papers (US) *603*
Arkansas Travel and Tourism Report (US) *1106*
Arkansas Vital Statistics (US ISSN 0364-0728) *920*, *926*
Arkansas Vital Statistics Report *see* Arkansas. Bureau of Vital Statistics. Annual Report of Births, Deaths, Marriages and Divorces as Reported to the Bureau of Vital Statistics *926*
Arken-Tryk (DK ISSN 0107-4520) *967*
Arkeologisk Museum i Stavanger. Skrifter *see* A M S - Skrifter *79*
Arkeologisk Museum i Stavanger Skrifter *see* A M S - Skrifter *79*
Arkeologisk Museum i Stavanger Smaatrykk *see* A M S - Smaatrykk *79*
Arkeologisk Museum i Stavanger Varia *see* A M S - Varia *79*
Arkeologiske Udgravninger i Danmark (DK ISSN 0901-0815) *82*
Arkheograficheskii Ezhegodnik (UR) *82*, *555*
Arkheologicheskie Raboty v Tadzhikistane (UR) *82*
Arkheologiya i Etnografiya Udmurtii (UR) *82*
Arkhiyon ha-Merkazi le-Toldot ha-Am ha-Yehudi. Yediot *see* Central Archives for the History of the Jewish People Newsletter *612*
Arkib Negara Malaysia. Laporan Tahunan *see* National Archives of Malaysia. Annual Report *570*
Arkiv for Det Fysiske Seminar i Trondheim (NO ISSN 0365-2459) *887*
Arkiv for Nordisk Filologi/Archives for Scandinavian Philology (SW ISSN 0066-7668) *691*
Arkiv for Sjoerett/Scandinavian Journal of Maritime Law (NO ISSN 0004-2102) *651*
Arkiv, Samhaelle och Forskning (SW ISSN 0349-0505) *555*, *673*
Arkiver: Folkemindesamlinger og Museer i Faaborg Kommune *see* Faaborg-Aarbogen *581*
Arlington Historical Magazine (US ISSN 0066-7684) *603*
Armamentaria (NE) *576*, *810*
Armarium Codicum Insignium (BE) *576*, *967*
Armas e Trofeus (PO) *101*, *534*, *576*
Armazenagem (BL) *52*
Armenian Texts and Studies (US) *576*
Armidale and District Historical Society. Journal and Proceedings (AT ISSN 0084-6732) *572*
Armstrong Oil Directories: Louisiana, Texas Gulf Coast, East Texas, Arkansas and Mississippi *see* Armstrong Oil Directory: Louisiana, Mississippi, Arkansas, Texas Gulf Coast and East Texas *863*
Armstrong Oil Directories: Rocky Mountain and Central United States (US ISSN 0273-5229) *863*
Armstrong Oil Directory: Central United States *see* Armstrong Oil Directories: Rocky Mountain and Central United States *863*
Armstrong Oil Directory: Louisiana, Mississippi, Arkansas, Texas Gulf Coast and East Texas (US ISSN 0273-4931) *863*

Armstrong Oil Directory: Texas Including Southeast New Mexico (US) *863*
Army List (UK) *810*
Army Museum (UK) *810*, *826*
Army Museum Newsletter (US ISSN 0004-2536) *1146*
Army Ski Association. Year Book (UK) *1044*
Arnamagnaean Institute. Bulletin *see* Arnamagnaean Institute and Dictionary. Bulletin *715*
Arnamagnaean Institute and Dictionary. Bulletin (DK ISSN 0107-1475) *691*, *715*
Arnoldia Zimbabwe (RH ISSN 0250-6386) *378*
Arnoldia Zimbabwe Rhodesia *see* Arnoldia Zimbabwe *378*
Arqueologicas (PE ISSN 0066-7803) *82*
Arquivo de Anatomia e Antropologia (PO ISSN 0066-7811) *171*
Arquivos de Botanica do Estado de Sao Paulo *see* Hoehnea *157*
Arquivos de Cirurgia Clinica e Experimental (BL ISSN 0066-7846) *781*, *794*
Arquivos de Patologia Geral e Anatomia Patologica (PO ISSN 0066-7854) *758*
Arquivos de Zoologia (BL ISSN 0066-7870) *173*
Arrowsmith's Bristol Channel Tide Table (UK) *1098*
Ars Decorativa (HU ISSN 0133-6673) *826*
Ars Islamica *see* Ars Orientalis *850*
Ars Nova (SA ISSN 0379-6485) *833*
Ars Orientalis (US ISSN 0571-1371) *101*, *850*
Ars Quatuor Coronatorum (UK ISSN 0066-7900) *341*
Ars, Revista de Arte (AG) *101*
Ars Suecica (SW ISSN 0066-7919) *101*, *576*
Arsenal (US) *101*, *740*
Arstryck (SW ISSN 0432-1251) *82*, *515*
Art (UN ISSN 0004-5535) *101*
Art/Kunst (SZ) *113*
Art Actuel *see* World Art Trends *112*
Art and Archaeology Technical Abstracts (US ISSN 0004-2994) *2*, *96*, *113*
Art and Architecture Bibliographies (US) *100*, *113*
Art and Architecture Book Guide *see* Bibliographic Guide to Art and Architecture *100*
Art and Architecture Information Guide Series (US) *100*, *113*
Art and Crafts Market *see* Artist's Market *102*
Art and Design in the Region (UK) *101*, *432*
Art and Life (II ISSN 0004-3044) *101*
Art and Philosophy (US) *101*
Art and the Artist (II) *101*
Art at Auction; the Year at Sotheby's and Parke-Bernet (US ISSN 0084-6783) *79*
Art Bulletin of Victoria (AT ISSN 0066-7935) *826*
Art, Crafts & Related Fields (US) *614*
Art Directors Annual (US) *101*
Art et les Grandes Civilisations (FR ISSN 0066-7951) *101*
Art Gallery News (AT) *101*
Art Gallery of Ontario. Annual Report (CN ISSN 0082-5018) *826*
Art History Series (US) *101*
Art - Language (UK ISSN 0587-3584) *691*
Art Material Directory and Product Information Guide *see* Art Material Trade News Directory *101*
Art Material Trade News Directory (US) *101*
Art News Directory of Corporate Art Collections (US) *101*, *826*
Art of the Orient *see* Kunst des Orients *106*
Art on the Line (US ISSN 0277-7053) *715*
Art-Price Annual *see* Kunstpreis-Jahrbuch *106*
Art Reference Collection (US ISSN 0193-6867) *101*

Art Research in Scandinavia see A R I S 100
Art Romanic (SP) 82, 101
Art Sales Index: Oil Paintings, Drawings, Water Colours and Sculpture (US) 102
Art Workers Guild. Annual Report (UK) 102
ARTANES see Aids and Research Tools in Ancient Near Eastern Studies 611
Artbibliographies Current Titles (UK ISSN 0095-1420) 2, 113
Artbibliographies Modern (UK ISSN 0300-466X) 2, 113
De Arte (SA ISSN 0004-3389) 102
Arte e Archeologia (IT) 82, 102
Arte Orientale in Italia (IT) 850
Arte Veneta (IT) 102
Arte y Arqueologia (BO ISSN 0587-5447) 82, 102
Arte y Vida (VE) 710
Artefact (AT ISSN 0044-9075) 82
Artes Populares (HU ISSN 0139-4649) 515
Artes Textiles: Bijragen tot de Geschiedenis van de Tapijt (BE ISSN 0571-1924) 1073
Artful Dodge (US ISSN 0196-691X) 715
Artha Vijnana Reprint Series (II) 191
Arthika Vivaranaya see Central Bank of Ceylon. Review of the Economy 242
Arthritis Foundation Annual Report (US ISSN 0191-2836) 793
Arthrology (US) 792, 794
Arthropods of Florida and Neighboring Land Areas (US ISSN 0066-8036) 163
Arthur Frommer's Dollarwise Guide to Germany see Frommer's Dollarwise Guide to Germany 1110
Arthur Holmes Society. Journal (UK ISSN 0066-8044) 378
Arthur Rimbaud (FR ISSN 0180-9385) 715
Arthurian Literature (US) 715
Arti Musices/Musicological Yearbook (YU ISSN 0587-5455) 833
Artibus Asiae Supplementa (SZ) 82, 102, 850
Articulata (GW ISSN 0171-4090) 138
Articulos en Linguistica y Campos Afines (CK) 691
Artikkel-Indeks for Skip see Ship Abstracts 1086
Artikler i Boeger/Danish National Bibliography. Articles in Books (DK ISSN 0108-0261) 121
Artillery Journal (II ISSN 0004-3826) 810
Artistas Ecuatorianos (EC) 102
Artistes and Their Agents (UK ISSN 0143-8131) 1076
Artistes du Canada. Liste Collective des Dossiers d'Artistes see Artists in Canada: Union List of Artists Files 102
Artist's and Photographer's Market see Artist's Market 102
Artists Associates Far East Businessman's Directory see A.A.'s Far East Businessman's Directory 301
Artists in Canada see Artists in Canada: Union List of Artists Files 102
Artists in Canada: Union List of Artists Files/Artistes du Canada. Liste Collective des Dossiers d'Artistes (CN) 102, 826
Artist's Market (US ISSN 0161-0546) 102
Artpark (US ISSN 0164-1298) 102
Arts (AT ISSN 0004-8095) 102
Arts Address Book (UK) 102
Arts & Business Council. Annual Report (US) 102
Arts Asiatiques (FR ISSN 0004-3958) 97, 102, 850
Arts Council of Australia. Annual Report (AT) 102
Arts Council of Great Britain. Annual Report and Accounts (UK ISSN 0066-8133) 102
Arts et Objets du Maroc (FR) 102
Arts in Alabama see Annual Report of the Arts Activities in Alabama 101
Arts of Himachal (II) 102

Arts Patronage Series (US ISSN 0066-8168) 102
Arts Review Yearbook (UK) 102
Arts Support by Private Foundations see National Directory of Arts Support by Private Foundations 108
Arts Support by Private Foundations and Business Corporations see National Directory of Arts and Education Support by Business Corporations 108
Arts Support by Private Foundations and Business Corporations see National Directory of Arts Support by Private Foundations 108
Artviews (AT ISSN 0311-0095) 102
Arusia. Historiske Skrifter (DK ISSN 0108-0075) 576
Arussi Rural Development Unit Publication see A R D U Publication 22
Arv/Journal of Scandinavian Folklore (SW ISSN 0066-8176) 515
Arv og Eje (DK ISSN 0105-0192) 576
Arvernia Biologica: Botanique (FR ISSN 0066-8184) 154
Arx Tavastica (FI ISSN 0358-3414) 576
Arzobispado de Santiago. Vicaria de la Solidaridad. Estudios (CL) 980
A's and B's of Academic Scholarships see A's & B's: Your Guide to Academic Scholarship 432
A's & B's: Your Guide to Academic Scholarship (US) 432
Asbestos Producer/Producteur d'Amiante (CN ISSN 0478-4049) 181, 814
Asclepio (SP ISSN 0210-4466) 70, 758
Asepelt Series (NE) 191
Asfar (NE) 975
Ashleys Addenda Annual (US) 535
Ashleys of America see Ashleys Addenda Annual 535
Asia - Africa World Trade Register (II ISSN 0066-8230) 253
Asia and Pacific see Asia & Pacific Review 241
Asia & Pacific Review (UK) 241, 902
Asia and the Far East Commision on Agricultural Statistics. Periodic Report see Food and Agriculture Organization of the United Nations. Asia and the Pacific Commission on Agricultural Statistics. Periodic Report 40
Asia Corporate Profile and National Finance (HK) 241
Asia Foundation. Annual Report (US) 568
Asia Foundation. President's Review and Annual Report see Asia Foundation. Annual Report 568
Asia-Pacific/Africa-Middle East Petroleum (US ISSN 0748-4089) 863
Asia-Pacific Petroleum Directory see Asia-Pacific/Africa-Middle East Petroleum 863
Asia Society. Annual Report (US ISSN 0098-1214) 568
Asia Travel Trade Directory see Travel Directory 1118
Asia Yearbook (HK) 191
Asiabanking Almanac (HK) 222
Asian Agribusiness Buyers Guide (UK) 24
Asian Agriculture Buyers Guide see Asian Agribusiness Buyers Guide 24
Asian American Trade Directory (US) 234, 302
Asian and African Studies (CS ISSN 0571-2742) 565, 568, 850
Asian and Pacific Archaeology Series (US ISSN 0066-829X) 82
Asian and Pacific Council. Cultural and Social Centre. Annual Report (KO ISSN 0066-8303) 1146
Asian and Pacific Council. Museum Conference. Proceedings (KO) 1146
Asian and Pacific Council Seminar on Audio-Visual Education. Proceedings see A S P A C Seminar on Audio-Visual Education. Proceedings 1145
Asian Banking Directory see Asiabanking Almanac 222

Asian Banking Guide see Banking Guides - Asia, Australia, New Zealand with Principal Hotels and Bank Holidays 224
Asian Book Trade Directory (II ISSN 0066-8362) 960
Asian Computer Directory (HK) 351
Asian Computer Yearbook see Asian Computer Directory 351
Asian Cultural Centre for Unesco. Organization and Activities (UN) 850
Asian Cultural Studies (JA ISSN 0454-2150) 568, 850
Asian Development Bank. Annual Report (PH ISSN 0066-8370) 222, 261
Asian Development Bank. Board of Governors. Summary of Proceedings (of the) Annual Meeting (PH ISSN 0066-8389) 222, 261
Asian Development Bank. Key Indicators of Developing Member Countries of A D B (PH) 222, 261
Asian Development Bank. Occasional Papers (PH ISSN 0066-8397) 222, 261
Asian Electricity Catalogue (UK) 450
Asian Geotechnical Engineering Abstracts (TH ISSN 0301-4169) 2, 381, 476
Asian Institute of Technology. Research Summary (TH ISSN 0572-4198) 1067
Asian Institute of Technology Reports and Publications on Renewable Energy Resources. Abstracts see A I T Reports and Publications on Renewable Energy Resources. Abstracts 468
Asian Law Series (US) 651
Asian Living Costs (UK ISSN 0268-2257) 253
Asian Music Publications. Series A: Bibliographic and Research Aids (US ISSN 0081-1319) 833
Asian Music Publications. Series B. Translations (US ISSN 0081-1327) 833
Asian Music Publications. Series C: Reprints (US ISSN 0081-1335) 833
Asian Music Publications. Series D: Monographs (US ISSN 0081-1343) 833
Asian Pacific Congress of Cardiology. Symposia (IO ISSN 0587-5471) 776
Asian Parliamentarians' Union. Central Secretariat. Report on Meeting of APU Secretaries-General in Tokyo (JA) 914
Asian Peoples' Anti-Communist League. Charts About Chinese Communists on the Mainland (CH ISSN 0571-2939) 568
Asian Population Studies Series (UN ISSN 0066-8451) 920
Asian Press (KO) 645
Asian Press and Media Directory (HK) 14
Asian Productivity Organization Annual Report see A P O Annual Report 287
Asian Regional Conference on Industrial Relations. Proceedings (JA) 270
Asian Studies (PH ISSN 0004-4679) 850
Asian Studies (BG) 1146
Asian Studies Association of Australia. Conference Papers (AT ISSN 0156-0182) 568, 850
Asian Studies at Hawaii Monograph Series (US ISSN 0066-8486) 568
Asian Studies Center Backgrounder (US) 501
Asian Studies Monographs Series (CN) 568, 850
Asian Studies Series (SZ) 568, 850
Asia's 7500 Largest Companies (UK) 223
Asiatic Society. Annual Report (II ISSN 0403-4457) 501, 539
Asiatic Society, Bombay. Journal (II ISSN 0004-4709) 850
Asiatic Society, Calcutta. Journal (II ISSN 0571-3161) 850
Asiatic Society, Calcutta. Monograph Series (II) 850

Asiatic Society, Calcutta. Seminar Series (II) 850
Asiatische Forschungen (GW ISSN 0571-320X) 850
Asie du Sud-Est et Monde Insulindien (FR ISSN 0224-2680) 70, 691
Asien - Afrika - Lateinamerika. Jahrbuch (GE ISSN 0232-8410) 565, 568, 603
Asien-Studier i Skandinavien see C I N A - Nytt 851
Asilomar Conference on Circuits and Systems. Conference Record see Asilomar Conference on Circuits, Systems and Computers. Conference Record 355
Asilomar Conference on Circuits, Systems and Computers. Conference Record (US) 351, 355, 358
Asimptoticheskie Metody v Teorii Sistem (UR) 747
Askov Laerlinge (DK ISSN 0106-7478) 410
Aslib Annual Report (UK) 673
Aslib Directory of Information Sources in the United Kingdom. Volume 1: Science, Technology and Commerce (UK) 987, 1067
Aslib Directory of Information Sources in the United Kingdom. Volume 2: Social Sciences, Medicine and the Humanities (UK) 628, 758, 1006
Aslib Occasional Publications (UK ISSN 0066-8532) 673
Asociacao Medica Brasileira. Boletim (BL) 758
Asociacion Argentina de Actores. Memoria y Balance (AG) 648, 1076
Asociacion Costarricense de Bibliotecarios. Boletin (CR ISSN 0004-4784) 673
Asociacion Cultural Humboldt. Boletin (VE ISSN 0004-4792) 514
Asociacion de Academias de la Lengua Espanola. Comision Permanente. Boletin (SP) 1147
Asociacion de Bibliotecarios de Instituciones de Ensenanza Superior e Investigacion. Archivos (MX) 674
Asociacion de Economistas Argentinos. Coleccion Instituto Superior (AG) 191
Asociacion de Escribanos del Uruguay. Revista (UY ISSN 0376-5024) 651
Asociacion de Investigacion Textil Algodonera. Coleccion de Manuales Tecnicos (SP ISSN 0571-3609) 1073
Asociacion de Investigacion Textil Algodonera. Estudios y Documentos (SP) 1073
Asociacion de Tecnicos Azucareros de Venezuela Boletin Informativo see A T A V E Boletin Informativo 517
Asociacion Espanola Contra el Cancer. Memoria de la Assemblea General see Asociacion Espanola Contra el Cancer. Memoria Tecnico-Administrativa 774
Asociacion Espanola Contra el Cancer. Memoria Tecnico-Administrativa (SP) 774
Asociacion Espanola de Orientalistas. Boletin (SP ISSN 0571-3692) 850
Asociacion Espanola de Prensa Tecnica. Catalogo de Publicaciones Asociadas (SP) 1072
Asociacion Espanola de Tecnicos de Maquinaria para la Construccion y Obras Publicas Revista A T E M C O P. Especial Alquiladores see Revista A T E M C O P. Especial Alquiladores 483
Asociacion Interamericana de Bibliotecarios y Documentalistas Agricolas. Boletin Especial (CR ISSN 0074-0748) 24, 674
Asociacion Latinoamericana de Libre Comercio. Comercio Exterior. Argentina. Exportacion see Asociacion Latinoamericana de Libre Comercio. Estadisticas de Comercio Exterior - Serie A: Exportaciones 1147

Asociacion Latinoamericana de Libre Comercio. Comercio Exterior Argentina. Importacion see Asociacion Latinoamericana de Libre Comercio. Estadisticas de Comercio Exterior-Serie B-Importaciones *1147*

Asociacion Latinoamericana de Libre Comercio. Comercio Exterior Brasil. Importacion see Asociacion Latinoamericana de Libre Comercio. Estadisticas de Comercio Exterior-Serie C-Importaciones Zonales *1147*

Asociacion Latinoamericana de Libre Comercio. Estadisticas de Comercio Exterior - Serie A: Exportaciones (UY) *1147*

Asociacion Latinoamericana de Libre Comercio. Estadisticas de Comercio Exterior-Serie B-Importaciones (UY) *1147*

Asociacion Latinoamericana de Libre Comercio. Estadisticas de Comercio Exterior-Serie C-Importaciones Zonales (UY) *1147*

Asociacion Latinoamericana de Produccion Animal. Memoria (VE) *64*

Asociacion Mexicana de Facultades y Escuelas de Medicina. Boletin (MX ISSN 0004-4857) *758*

Asociacion Nacional de Enfermeras de Colombia see A N E C *783*

Asociacion Nacional de Enfermeras de Colombia. A N E C. Revista see A N E C *783*

Asociacion Nacional de Instituciones Financieras. Simposio sobre Mercado de Capitales (CK) *223*

Asociacion Nacional del Cafe. Departamento de Asuntos Agricolas. Annual Memory see Asociacion Nacional del Cafe. Departamento de Asuntos Agricolas. Informe Anual *119*

Asociacion Nacional del Cafe. Departamento de Asuntos Agricolas. Informe Anual (GT ISSN 0066-8567) *119*

Asociacion Panamericana de Instituciones de Credito Educativo Revista A P I C E see Revista A P I C E *1161*

Asociacion Salvadorena de Industriales Directorio de Asociados (ES) *302*

Asociacion Venezolana de Archiveros. Coleccion Doctrina (VE ISSN 0066-8591) *674*

Asociacion Venezolana de Enfermeras Profesionales. Boletin (VE ISSN 0066-8613) *783*

Asociacion Venezolano Britanica de Comercio e Industria. Anuario see Camara Venezolano Britanica de Comercio e Industria. Anuario *235*

Aspectos Gerais e Principais Tendencias da Agropecuaria Paraibana (BL) *45*

Aspects of Edenbridge (UK ISSN 0261-8850) *535*

Aspects of Education (UK ISSN 0066-8672) *410*

Aspects of Educational Technology (UK ISSN 0141-5956) *446*

Aspects of France (AT) *501*, *1024*

Aspects of Greek and Roman Life (US) *336*, *1006*

Aspects of Homogeneous Catalysis: a Series of Advances (NE) *329*

Aspects of Plant Science see Current Trends in Life Sciences *140*

Aspects of Plant Science (II) *154*

Aspects of the Geosciences in Canada see Geosciences in Canada *388*

Asphalt Paving Technology see Association of Asphalt Paving Technologists. Proceedings *480*

Aspis (UK ISSN 0260-2474) *253*, *302*

Assam Directory & Tea Areas Handbook (II) *119*, *302*

Assam Directory of Tea Areas see Assam Directory & Tea Areas Handbook *302*

Assam Economic Journal (II) *251*

Assaph. Section C. Studies in the Theatre (IS ISSN 0334-5963) *1076*

Assays (US) *715*

Assemblees de Dieu de France. Annuaire (FR ISSN 0083-6184) *983*

Assembling see Assembling Annual *960*

Assembling Annual (US) *645*, *960*

Assembly Directory and Handbook see Assembly Technology Buyer's Guide *469*

Assembly Engineering Master Catalog see Assembly Technology Buyer's Guide *469*

Assembly Technology Buyer's Guide (US) *469*

Assia (IS ISSN 0334-3871) *758*

Associacao Brasileira da Industria Farmaceutica. Pesquisa (BL) *1147*

Associacao Brasileira para o Desenvolvimento das Industrias de Base Anuario A B D I B see Anuario A B D I B *287*

Associacao Promotora de Estudos de Economia Diagnosticos A P E C see Diagnosticos A P E C *243*

Associacao Promotora de Estudos de Economia Economia Brasileira e suas Perspectivas - A P E C A O see Economia Brasileira e suas Perspectivas - A P E C A O *243*

Associate Committee on the National Building Code News see N B C/N F C News *186*

Associate Degree Education for Nursing (US) *432*, *783*

Associated British Ports Handbook (UK ISSN 0262-1630) *302*, *1098*

Associated British Ports Holdings PlC. Annual Report and Accounts (UK) *1098*

Associated Church Press. Directory (US ISSN 0066-8710) *974*

Associated Equipment Distributors. Rental Rates Compilation (US ISSN 0164-0593) *181*, *745*

Associated Industries of New York State. Bulletin (US) *287*

Associated Industries of New York State, Inc. Recommends see A I Recommends *901*

Associated Public Schools Systems. Yearbook (US ISSN 0066-8753) *442*

Associated Scientific and Technical Societies of South Africa. Annual Proceedings (SA ISSN 0373-4250) *987*, *1067*

Associated Society of Locomotive Engineers and Firemen. Annual Report and Balance Sheet (UK) *506*

Associated Western Universities. Biennial Report see Associated Western Universities. Program Report *432*

Associated Western Universities. Program Report (US) *432*

Association Aeronautique et Astronautique de France. Annuaire (FR) *18*

Association Belge pour l'Etude, l'Essai et l'Emploi des Materiaux. Publication A.B.E.M (BE ISSN 0066-8796) *488*

Association Belge pour l'Etude, l'Essai et l'Emploi des Materiaux. Proces Verbal de l'Assemblee Generale Ordinaire (BE ISSN 0066-8818) *488*

Association Canadienne des Bibliothecaires de Langue Francaise. Rapport see Association pour l'Avancement des Sciences et des Techniques de la Documentation. Rapport *674*

Association Canadienne-Francaise pour l'Avancement des Sciences. Annales (CN ISSN 0066-8842) *987*

Association Canadienne pour la Sante Mentale. Rapport Annuel see Canadian Mental Health Association. Annual Report *933*

Association de l'Ecole Nationale Superieure des Bibliothecaires. Annuaire (FR ISSN 0066-8877) *674*

Association des Amis d'Alfred de Vigny. Bulletin (FR ISSN 0066-8893) *715*

Association des Amis de Pierre Teilhard de Chardin. Bulletin (FR ISSN 0066-8907) *967*

Association des Banques du Liban. Bilans des Banques (LE) *223*

Association des Banques du Liban. Rapport Annuel see Association des Banques du Liban. Rapport du Conseil *241*

Association des Banques du Liban. Rapport du Conseil (LE) *241*

Association des Bibliothecaires Francais. Annuaire (FR ISSN 0066-8931) *674*

Association des Colleges du Quebec Annuaire (CN ISSN 0228-7730) *410*

Association des Ingenieurs et Techniciens Africains de Cote d'Ivoire. Annuaire (IV) *470*

Association des Institutions d'Enseignement Secondaire. Annuaire (CN ISSN 0066-8990) *410*

Association des Journalistes Agricoles. Annuaire (FR) *24*, *645*

Association des Naturalistes du Mali. Bulletin (ML) *987*

Association des Societes et Fonds Francais d'Investissement. Annuaire (FR ISSN 0066-9008) *265*

Association des Traducteurs et Interpretes de l'Ontario. Repertoire/Association of Translators and Interpreters of Ontario. Directory (CN ISSN 0066-9016) *691*

Association Euratom-Ital. Annual Report (NE ISSN 0066-9040) *24*, *518*

Association Finlandaise de Linguistique Appliquee Fin L A Yearbook see A Fin L A Yearbook *689*

Association for African Literature in English. Bulletin see African Literature Today *1146*

Association for Arid Lands Studies News see A L P R News *22*

Association for Asian Studies. Enduring Scholarship. Reference Series see Association for Asian Studies. Monographs, Occasional Papers and Reference Series *568*

Association for Asian Studies. Monographs, Occasional Papers and Reference Series (US) *568*

Association for Asian Studies. Southeast Conference. Annals (US) *568*

Association for Communication Administration Bulletin see A C A Bulletin *278*

Association for Computing Machinery. Proceedings of National Conference (US ISSN 0066-9091) *351*

Association for Computing Machinery, Inc. Administrative Directory of College and University Computer Science Data Processing Programs and Computer Facilities see A C M Administrative Directory of College and University Computer Science/Data Processing Programs and Computer Facilities *351*

Association for Computing Machinery Monograph Series see A C M Monograph Series *351*

Association for Computing Machinery Symposium on the Theory of Computing see A C M Symposium on the Theory of Computing *363*

Association for Continuing Higher Education. Proceedings (US) *432*

Association for Education and Rehabilitation of the Blind and Visually Impaired. Yearbook (US ISSN 0067-9186) *1015*

Association for Educational Communications and Technology. Directory of Human Resources see Association for Educational Communications and Technology. Membership Directory and Human Resources *446*

Association for Educational Communications and Technology. Membership Directory and Data Book see Association for Educational Communications and Technology. Membership Directory and Human Resources *446*

Association for Educational Communications and Technology. Membership Directory and Human Resources (US) *446*

Association for Educational Data Systems. Annual Convention Proceedings (US ISSN 0147-9296) *356*, *427*

Association for Integrated Manufacturing Technology. Proceedings (US) *470*, *1067*

Association for Library and Information Science Education. Directory (US ISSN 0748-5786) *674*

Association for Management Success Data Processing Salaries Report see A M S Data Processing Salaries Report *269*

Association for Management Success Guide to Management Compensation see A M S Guide to Management Compensation *269*

Association for Management Success Office Salaries Report see A M S Office Salaries Report *269*

Association for Professional Education for Ministry. Report of the Biennial Meeting (US) *432*, *967*

Association for Research in Nervous and Mental Disease. Research Publications (US ISSN 0091-7443) *789*

Association for Rural Advancement. Reports (SA) *902*

Association for School, College and University Staffing Annual - A Job Search Handbook for Educators see A S C U S Annual - A Job Search Handbook for Educators *442*

Association for School, College and University Staffing Directory of Membership and Subject Field Index see A S C U S Directory of Membership and Subject Field Index *442*

Association for Scottish Literary Studies Newsletter see A S L S Newsletter *713*

Association for Social Anthropology in Oceania. Monograph Series (US ISSN 0066-9172) *70*

Association for Sociology in Southern Africa Proceedings see A S S A Proceedings *1023*

Association for Supervision and Curriculum Development. Curriculum Materials see Association for Supervision and Curriculum Development. Curriculum Materials Digest *446*

Association for Supervision and Curriculum Development. Curriculum Materials Digest (US) *446*

Association for the Advancement of Polish Studies. Bulletin (US) *576*

Association for the Help of Retarded Children Chronicle see A H R C Chronicle *788*

Association for the Study of Reptilia and Amphibia Journal see A S R A Journal *172*

Association for Voluntary Surgical Contraception, Inc. Biomedical Bulletin see Biomedical Bulletin *179*

Association Francaise d'Informatique et de Recherche Operationnelle. Annuaire see Association Francaise pour la Cybernetique Economique et Technique. Annuaire *359*

Association Francaise de Calcul et de Traitement d'Information. Annuaire see Association Francaise pour la Cybernetique Economique et Technique. Annuaire *359*

Association Francaise des Documentalistes et des Bibliothecaires Specialises Annuaire see A D B S Annuaire *1145*

Association Francaise des Experts de la Cooperation Technique Internationale. Annuaire (FR ISSN 0066-9288) *1067*

Association Francaise des Ingenieurs du Caoutchouc et des Plastiques. Annuaire (FR ISSN 0066-9229) *900*, *985*

Association Francaise des Ingenieurs et Chefs d'Entretien. Annuaire (FR ISSN 0066-9237) *470*

1650 ASSOCIATION FRANCAISE

Association Francaise des Ingenieurs et Techniciens de l'Aeronautique et de l'Espace. Annuaire *see* Association Aeronautique et Astronautique de France. Annuaire 18

Association Francaise des Techniciens et Ingenieurs de Securite et des Medecins du Travail. Annuaire (FR ISSN 0066-927X) 635

Association Francaise pour la Cybernetique Economique et Technique. Annuaire (FR) 359

Association Internationale d'Etudes Patristiques. Bulletin d'Information et de Liaison (IT) 967

Association Internationale du Droit Commercial. Et du Droit Affaires. Groupe Francais. Travaux *see* International Law Association. Reports of Conferences 671

Association Internationale pour l'Histoire du Verre. Bulletin (BE ISSN 0447-9823) 319

Association Nationale d'Etude et de Lutte Contre les Fleaux Atmospheriques. Rapport de Campagne (FR ISSN 0242-4002) 803

Association Nationale de Lutte Contre les Fleaux Atmospheriques. Rapport de Campagne *see* Association Nationale d'Etude et de Lutte Contre les Fleaux Atmospheriques. Rapport de Campagne 803

Association of Academies of Science. Directory and Proceedings *see* National Association of Academies of Science. Directory and Proceedings 995

Association of African Universities. New Acquisitions List (GH) 432, 674

Association of African Universities. Report of the General Conference (GH) 432

Association of American Feed Control Officials. Official Publication (US) 63

Association of American Geographers. Directory (US) 541

Association of American Geographers. Handbook-Directory *see* Association of American Geographers. Directory 541

Association of American Law Schools. Proceedings (US ISSN 0066-9407) 651

Association of American Library Schools Directory *see* Association for Library and Information Science Education. Directory 674

Association of American Medical Colleges Curriculum Directory *see* A A M C Curriculum Directory 446

Association of American Medical Colleges Directory of American Medical Education *see* A A M C Directory of American Medical Education 442

Association of American Pesticide Control Officials. Official Publication(US ISSN 0066-9431) 52

Association of American Physicians. Transactions (US ISSN 0066-9458) 758

Association of American Plant Food Control Officials. Official Publication(US ISSN 0094-8764) 52

Association of American Publishers. Annual Report (US ISSN 0276-5349) 960

Association of American Publishers. Exhibits Directory (US ISSN 0147-0310) 960

Association of American Railroads. Data Systems Division. Papers (US) 1093

Association of American University Presses Directory (US ISSN 0739-3024) 960

Association of Animal Allergic Veterinary Association. Newsletter (US) 1147

Association of Asphalt Paving Technologists. Proceedings (US ISSN 0066-9466) 480

Association of Attenders and Alumni of the Hague Academy of International Law. Yearbook (NE ISSN 0066-8923) 669

Association of Australasian Palaeontologists. Memoirs (AT ISSN 0810-8889) 856

Association of British Oceanic Industries Catalogue *see* A B O I Catalogue 1098

Association of College Admissions Counselors. Membership Directory *see* National Association of College Admissions Counselors. Membership Directory 437

Association of College Honor Societies, Booklet of Information (US) 341

Association of College Unions-International. Directory (US) 432

Association of College Unions-International. Proceedings of the Annual Conference (US ISSN 0147-1120) 432

Association of Colleges for Further and Higher Education. Handbook (UK) 432

Association of Collegiate Schools of Architecture. Proceedings of the Annual Meeting (US ISSN 0194-410X) 97

Association of Commonwealth Universities. Annual Report of the Council Together with the Accounts of the Association (UK ISSN 0307-2274) 432

Association of Commonwealth Universities. Report of the Council Together with the Accounts of the Association *see* Association of Commonwealth Universities. Annual Report of the Council Together with the Accounts of the Association 432

Association of Consulting Engineers of Canada. Specialization Typical Projects *see* Consulting Engineers-Canada-Ingenieurs-Conseils 470

Association of Contemporary Historians. Bulletin (UK) 555

Association of County Councils. Yearbook (UK ISSN 0305-2044) 939

Association of Data Processing Service Organizations (ADAPSO) Membership Directory *see* A D A P S O Membership Directory 360

Association of Departments and Administrators in Speech Communication. Bulletin *see* A C A Bulletin 278

Association of Energy Engineers Directory of Energy Professionals *see* A E E Directory of Energy Professionals 469

Association of Engineering Geologists. Special Publications (US) 383

Association of Exploration Geochemists. Special Publications (CN) 378

Association of Faculties of Pharmacy of Canada. Proceedings (CN ISSN 0066-9555) 869

Association of Football Statisticians. Annual (UK ISSN 0263-0354) 1037

Association of Graduate Dance Ethnologists U.C.L.A. Journal *see* U.C.L.A. Journal of Dance Ethnology 375

Association of History Teachers in Nigeria (NR) 446, 565

Association of Independent Camps. Buyers Guide and Camp Directory (US) 1044

Association of Independent Television Stations, Inc. Census *see* I N T V Census 348

Association of Indian Engineering Industry. Handbook of Statistics (II) 470

Association of Institutes for European Studies. Annuaire (SZ ISSN 0571-6322) 576

Association of Institutes for European Studies. Year-Book (SZ ISSN 0571-6330) 576

Association of Iron and Steel Engineers. A I S E Proceedings *see* A I S E Yearbook 796

Association of Iron and Steel Engineers Yearbook *see* A I S E Yearbook 796

Association of Island Marine Laboratories of the Caribbean. Proceedings (PR ISSN 0066-9571) 138, 321, 383

Association of Japanese Geographers. Special Publication (JA ISSN 0066-958X) 541

Association of Jewish Sponsored Camps. Camp Directory (US) 501, 1044

Association of Life Insurance Medical Directors of America. Transactions (US ISSN 0066-9598) 638, 758

Association of Marshall Scholars and Alumni. Newsletter *see* Marshall News 341

Association of Midwest Fish and Wildlife Agencies. Proceedings (US) 364

Association of Midwest Fish and Wildlife Commissioners. Proceedings *see* Association of Midwest Fish and Wildlife Agencies. Proceedings 364

Association of Municipal Electricity Undertakings of South Africa. Proceedings of Convention (SA) 450

Association of National Health Service Supplies Officers. Reference Book & Buyer's Guide (UK ISSN 0140-4563) 952

Association of New Brunswick Land Surveyors. Annual Report (CN ISSN 0318-2126) 965

Association of Official Analytical Chemists. Official Methods of Analysis (US ISSN 0066-961X) 326

Association of Official Seed Certifying Agencies. Production Publication (US) 52

Association of Ontario Land Surveyors. Annual Report (CN ISSN 0700-5989) 480

Association of Pacific Coast Geographers. Yearbook (US ISSN 0066-9628) 541

Association of Private Camps. Buyers Guide and Camp Directory *see* Association of Independent Camps. Buyers Guide and Camp Directory 1044

Association of Professional Genealogists. List of Professional Genealogists and Related Services (US) 535

Association of Professional Recording Studios Guide to A P R S Member Studios *see* Guide to A P R S Member Studios 1031

Association of Public Data Users Membership Directory *see* A P D U Membership Directory 301

Association of Recognised English Language Schools Brochure *see* A R E L S - F E L C O Brochure 409

Association of Research Libraries. Office of Management Studies. Occasional Paper (US) 674

Association of Research Libraries. University Library Management Studies Office. Occasional Paper *see* Association of Research Libraries. Office of Management Studies. Occasional Paper 674

Association of Research Libraries Annual Salary Survey *see* A R L Annual Salary Survey 672

Association of Research Libraries Statistics *see* A R L Statistics 687

Association of Social Anthropologists of the Commonwealth Research Methods in Social Anthropology *see* A S A Research Methods in Social Anthropology 69

Association of Southeast Asian Institutions of Higher Learning. Handbook: Southeast Asian Institutions of Higher Learning (TH ISSN 0066-9687) 432

Association of Southeast Asian Institutions of Higher Learning Seminar Reports *see* A S A I H L. Seminar Reports 431

Association of Student International Law Societies International Law Journal *see* A S I L S International Law Journal 649

Association of Summer Session Deans and Directors. Summary of Reports *see* Association of University Summer Sessions. Summary Report 432

Association of Surgeons of East Africa. Proceedings (ZA) 410, 794

Association of Teachers of Management Occasional Papers *see* A T M Occasional Papers 278

Association of Teachers of Social Studies in the City of New York Bulletin *see* A T S S Bulletin 1005

Association of the Concrete Industry of Finland. Publication *see* Suomen Betoniteollisuuden Keskusjarjesto. Julkaisu 187

Association of Theological Schools in the United States and Canada. Bulletin (US ISSN 0362-1472) 967

Association of Theological Schools in the United States and Canada. Directory (US) 428, 967

Association of Translators and Interpreters of Ontario. Directory *see* Association des Traducteurs et Interpretes de l'Ontario. Repertoire 691

Association of University Evening Colleges. Proceedings *see* Association for Continuing Higher Education. Proceedings 432

Association of University Summer Sessions. Summary Report (US ISSN 0066-975X) 432

Association of Urban Authorities. Annual Bulletin (MF ISSN 0304-6451) 950

Association pour l'Avancement des Sciences et des Techniques de la Documentation. Rapport (CN ISSN 0316-0955) 674

Association pour l'Etude Taxonomique de la Flore d'Afrique Tropicale Index *see* A.E.T.F.A.T. Index 114

Association pour le Developpement International de l'Observatoire de Nice. Bulletin (FR ISSN 0249-7522) 114

Association pour le Developpement International de l'Observatoire de Nice. Bulletin d'Information *see* Association pour le Developpement International de l'Observatoire de Nice. Bulletin 114

Association Scientifique de la Precontrainte. Sessions d'Etudes (FR ISSN 0066-9792) 488

Association Technique de Fonderie. Annuaire (FR) 797

Association Technique Maritime et Aeronautique, Paris. Bulletin (FR ISSN 0066-9814) 18, 1099

Associazione Elettrotecnica Ed Elettronica Italiana. Rendiconti della Riunione Annuale (IT ISSN 0066-9822) 450

Associazione Genetica Italiana. Atti (IT ISSN 0066-9830) 166

Associazione Italiana Biblioteche. Quaderni del Bollettino d'Informazioni (IT ISSN 0519-2048) 674

Associazione Italiana Laringectomizzati. Atti (Del) Convegno Nazionale (IT ISSN 0066-9865) 787

Associazione Nazionale per la Tutela del Patrimonio Storico Artistico e Naturale della Nazione. Atti di Convegni (IT) 576

Associazione Nazionale per la Tutela del Patrimonio Storico Artistico e Naturale della Nazione. Documenti (IT) 576

Associazione Nazionale per la Tutela del Patrimonio Storico Artistico e Naturale della Nazione. Quaderni (IT) 576

Associazione Nazionale per la Tutela del Patrimonio Storico Artistico e Naturale della Nazione. Studi (IT) 576

Associazione per l'Archeologia industriale. Bolletino (IT) 97

Assur (US ISSN 0145-6334) 612

Assurance-Chomage Canada. Rapport Annuel *see* Unemployment Insurance Canada. Annual Report 642

Assyriological Studies (US ISSN 0066-9903) *691*
Asta-Press (GW ISSN 0076-1745) *442*
Astro Annual *see* New Age Astrology Guide (Year) *114*
Astrodynamics (US) *18*
Astrofizicheskie Issledovaniia (BU ISSN 0324-1459) *114*
Astrolabe (CN) *114*
Astrolettre (FR) *114*
Astrology (Year) (US) *114*
Astrology Annual Reference Book *see* Astrology Reference Book *114*
Astrology Reference Book (US) *114*
Astronomia (PL ISSN 0554-8233) *114*
Astronomical Almanac (UK) *115*
Astronomical Ephemeris *see* Astronomical Almanac *115*
Astronomical Ephemeris of Geocentric Places of Planets (II ISSN 0066-9970) *115*
Astronomical Phenomena (US ISSN 0083-2421) *115*
Astronomical Society of Victoria. Astronomical Yearbook (AT ISSN 0067-0006) *115*
Astronomicheski Kalendar na Observatoriiata v Sofia (BU ISSN 0068-3639) *115*
Astronomische Grundlagen fuer den Kalender (GW ISSN 0067-0014) *115*
Astronomischer Jaresbericht *see* Astronomy and Astrophysics Abstracts *118*
Astronomy and Astrophysics Abstracts (US ISSN 0067-0022) *2, 118, 892*
Astronomy Through Practical Investigation (US) *115*
Astrophysics and Space Science Library(NE ISSN 0067-0057) *115, 887*
Asturiensia Medievalia (SP) *555*
Asunto (VE) *342*
At the Polls Series (US) *902*
Atalanta (IT) *715*
Ateneo Parmense. Collana di Monografie (IT ISSN 0365-5377) *758*
Atheist (US ISSN 0304-1409) *876, 967*
Athena (GR) *576*
Athenisin Ethnikon kai Kapodistrakion Panepistemion. Theologike Schole. Epistemonike Epeteris (GR) *983*
Athens. Ethnikon kai Kapodistriakon Panepistemion. Philosophike Schole. Epistemonike Epeteris (GR) *576*
Athens Center of Ekistics. Research Report (GR ISSN 0067-0073) *621*
Atherosclerosis (US) *776*
Atherosclerosis Reviews (US ISSN 0362-1650) *776*
Athlerama (Today) (FR) *1032*
Athletisme Francais *see* Athlerama (Today) *1032*
Atlanta Constitution: a Georgia Index (US ISSN 0093-1179) *647*
Atlantic Canada Economics Association. Annual Conference: A C E A Papers (CN ISSN 0319-003X) *191*
Atlantic Canada Shipping Project. Annual Conference. Proceedings (CN) *1099*
Atlantic City Action (US) *265, 619, 1032*
Atlantic Coast Conference Basketball Handbook *see* A C C Basketball Handbook *1037*
Atlantic Mail (FR ISSN 0519-3125) *669*
Atlantic Provinces and Quebec; New Brunswick Newfoundland, Nova Scotia, Prince Edward Island, Quebec TourBook *see* Tourbook: Atlantic Provinces and Quebec *1117*
Atlantic Provinces Economic Council. Annual Report (CN ISSN 0067-0162) *241*
Atlantic Provinces Linguistic Association. Annual Meeting. Papers (CN ISSN 0820-8204) *691*
Atlantic Provinces Linguistic Association Journal (CN ISSN 0706-6910) *691*
Atlantic Provinces Reporters (CN) *651*
Atlantic Salmon Federation. Special Publication Series (CN) *364, 507*

Atlantic Salmon References (CN) *149*
Atlantic Summary Report/Index (US) *383, 863*
Atlantida (VE) *1006*
Atlantide Report. Scientific Results of the Danish Expedition to the Coasts of Tropical West Africa (DK ISSN 0067-0227) *987*
Atlas der Verbreitung Palaearktischer Voegel (GE) *170*
Atlas Florae Europaeae (FI) *154*
Atlas Flory Polskiej i Ziem Osciennych/Florae Polonicae Terraruniqe Adiacentium Sconographia (PL ISSN 0067-0294) *154*
Atlas Polskich Strojow Ludowych (PL ISSN 0067-0316) *70, 82, 515*
Atlas Rozmieszczenia Drzew i Krzewow w Polsce (PL ISSN 0067-0324) *154*
Atma Jaya Research Centre. Annual Report (IO) *446*
Atma Jaya Research Centre. Education Development Research Report/Pusat Penelitian Atma Jaya. Studi Tentang Pengembangan Pendidikan (IO) *410*
Atma Jaya Research Centre. International Contract Labour (IO) *270, 669*
Atma Jaya Research Centre. Socio-Medical Research Report/Pusat Penelitian Atma Jaya. Penelitian Tentang Kebutuhan Kesehatan Masyarakat dan Sistem Peleyanan Kesehatan di Kecamatan Penjaringan(IO) *758, 1024*
Atma Jaya Research Centre. Socio-Religious Research Report/Pusat Penelitian Atma Jaya. Laporan Penelitian Keagamaan (IO) *977, 1024*
Atmosferos Fizika/Atmospheric Physics(UR ISSN 0135-1419) *803*
Atmospheric Optics (US) *1147*
Atmospheric Physics *see* Atmosferos Fizika *803*
Atmospheric Science Paper *see* Colorado State University. Atmospheric Science Paper *803*
Atmospheric Science Research Report *see* Colorado State University. Atmospheric Science Paper *803*
Atmospheric Science Technical Paper *see* Colorado State University. Atmospheric Science Paper *803*
Atmospheric Sciences Library (NE) *378*
Atoll Research Bulletin (US ISSN 0077-5630) *987*
Atomedia (PH ISSN 0115-3757) *896*
Atomic Absorption & Emission Spectrometry Abstracts (UK ISSN 0309-1813) *2, 892*
Atomic Absorption and Flame Emission Spectroscopy Abstracts *see* Atomic Absorption & Emission Spectrometry Abstracts *892*
Atomic Energy Levels and Grotrian Diagrams (NE) *887*
Atomic Energy of Canada. Annual Report (CN ISSN 0067-0383) *464, 896*
Atomic Energy of Canada. List of Publications (CN ISSN 0067-0405) *468, 892*
Atomic Energy of Canada Ltd. Report Series *see* A E C L Report Series *895*
Atomic Energy Pocketbook (JA) *464, 896*
Atomic Physics (US ISSN 0090-6360) *896*
Atraves (BL) *715*
Atti dello Psicodramma (IT) *933, 1076*
Atti e Memorie della Deputazione di Storia Patria per le Antiche Provincie(IT) *576*
Attila Jozsef University. Acta Geographica (HU ISSN 0324-5268) *541*
Attorneys and Agents Registered to Practice Before the U.S. Patent and Trademark Office (US ISSN 0361-3844) *860*

Attorneys and Agents Registered to Practice Before the U.S. Patent Office *see* Attorneys and Agents Registered to Practice Before the U.S. Patent and Trademark Office *860*
Attorney's Directory of Forensic Psychiatrists in the United States and Canada (US ISSN 0278-0879) *651, 782, 789*
Attrezzatura Alberghiera in Italia (IT) *621*
Attualita Cinematografiche (IT) *822*
Attualita di Laboratorio (IT ISSN 0004-7309) *1147*
Auburn University. Water Resources Research Institute. Annual Report (US ISSN 0067-043X) *1123*
Auchmuty Library Publication (AT ISSN 0158-6610) *121, 674*
Auckland Institute and Museum. Bulletin (NZ ISSN 0067-0456) *826*
Auckland Institute and Museum. Records (NZ ISSN 0067-0464) *826*
Auckland University Law Review (NZ ISSN 0067-0510) *651*
Auction Prices of American Artists-Volume 5 (US) *102, 191*
Audarena Stadium Guide and International Directory (US ISSN 0067-0537) *14*
Audi/Daily Mail Skier's Holiday Guide(UK) *1044*
Audio-Cassette Directory *see* Directory of Spoken-Word Audio-Cassettes *1032*
Audio-Technik (GW ISSN 0571-8678) *375*
Audio-Video I Cs D.A.T.A. Book (US) *351, 892*
Audio Video Market Place (US) *446*
Audio/Video/Tape Directory *see* Billboard's Audio/Video/Tape Sourcebook *1031*
Audio Visual and Micro-Computer Handbook (UK) *361*
Audio Visual Directory (UK) *342*
Audio-Visual Equipment Directory *see* Equipment Directory of Audio-Visual, Computer and Video Products *308*
Audio Visual Handbook *see* Audio Visual and Micro-Computer Handbook *361*
Audio-Visuelle Materialer: Skolebiblioteket (DK ISSN 0107-9654) *674*
Audiocassette Finder (National Information Center for Educational Media) (US) *2, 422*
Audiotecnica News *see* Noise and Smog News *498*
Audiovisual Market Place *see* Audio Video Market Place *446*
Audiovisual Materials: A Listing of Criminal Justice Films and Videotapes (US) *369*
Audiozine (US) *102*
Auditing Research Monographs (US ISSN 0146-9819) *221*
Augsburger Schriften zum Staats- und Voelkerrecht (GW) *669*
August Derleth Society. Newsletter (US) *715*
Augustan Society Newsletter (US) *535*
Augustana College Library Publications *see* Augustana Library Publications *628*
Augustana Historical Society, Rock Island, Illinois. Publications (US ISSN 0067-0588) *555*
Augustana Library Publications (US ISSN 0067-057X) *628*
Augustinian Studies (US ISSN 0094-5323) *981*
Aula Abierta (PE) *410*
Aurifex (BE) *644*
Aurora (GW ISSN 0341-1230) *102, 715*
Aurora (Madison) (US ISSN 0275-3715) *14, 1128*
Aurora (Richmond) (US) *715*
Aurora A F X Road Racing Handbook (US ISSN 0092-6256) *1032*
Aurora-Buchreihe (GW ISSN 0171-6530) *102, 715*
Aurora S F *see* Aurora (Madison) *14*

Auroral Observatory. Magnetic Observations (NO ISSN 0373-4854) *115, 887*
Aus dem Schweizerischen Landesmuseum (SZ ISSN 0067-0618) *826*
Aus der Schatzkammer der Buecher *see* Buecher (Year) *963*
Aus Forschung und Kunst (GW ISSN 0067-0642) *102*
Aus Oesterreichs Wissenschaft (AU) *1147*
Ausgabe (GW) *102, 715*
Auslaendische Aktiengesetze (GW ISSN 0067-0669) *651*
Ausruestung in Luft- und Raumfahrt (GW ISSN 0067-0685) *1147*
Ausstellungs- und Messe-Ausschuss der Deutschen Wirtschaft E.V. Zahlenspiegel Messeplatz Deutschland *see* A U M A Zahlenspiegel Messeplatz Deutschland *282*
Austin Healey Year Book (UK ISSN 0260-664X) *1090*
Australasian and Pacific Parliamentary Seminar. Summary Report of Proceedings (AT) *651*
Australasian and Pacific Society for Eighteenth-Century Studies. Newsletter (AT ISSN 0812-9428) *576*
Australasian Commercial Teachers' Association. Journal (AT ISSN 0084-6961) *446*
Australasian Conference on Hydraulics and Fluid Mechanics. Proceedings (NZ ISSN 0571-9291) *490*
Australasian Corrosion Association. Annual Conference Proceedings (AT ISSN 0155-6002) *328*
Australasian Country Music Annual (AT) *833*
Australasian Institute of Metals. Proceedings of the Annual Conference (AT) *797*
Australasian Institute of Mining and Metallurgy Symposia Series *see* A I M M Symposia Series *813*
Australasian Insurance Journal Manual of Australasian Life Assurance *see* A.I.J. Manual of Australasian Life Assurance *637*
Australasian Journal of Philosophy. Monograph Series (AT) *876*
Australasian Society of Engineers. Engineers Handbook (AT ISSN 0084-6996) *470*
Australasian Solar Index and Buyers Guide (AT) *302, 464*
Australasian Stamp Catalogue (AT ISSN 0155-8498) *874*
Australasian Stud and Stable *see* Stud and Stable *1043*
Australasian Studies in History and Philosophy *see* Australasian Studies in History and Philosophy of Science *1006*
Australasian Studies in History and Philosophy of Science (NE) *876, 1006*
Australia. Advisory Committee on Research and Development in Education. Annual Report *see* Australia. Education Research and Development Committee. Annual Report *410*
Australia. Air Transport Statistics. Airport Traffic Data (AT ISSN 0729-6096) *1048, 1084*
Australia. Air Transport Statistics. Australian Air Distances (AT ISSN 0727-6672) *1048, 1084*
Australia. Air Transport Statistics. Flight Crew Licences (AT ISSN 0727-2774) *1048, 1084*
Australia. Atomic Energy Commission. Research Establishment. A A E C/E(AT ISSN 0067-1657) *470, 896*
Australia. Atomic Energy Commission. Research Establishment. A A E C/IP(AT) *896*
Australia. Atomic Energy Commission. Research Establishment. A A E C/M(AT ISSN 0067-1665) *470, 896*
Australia. Atomic Energy Commission. Research Establishment. List of Report Publications (AT) *892*

Australia. Australian Bureau of Statistics. Tasmanian Office. Mining Tasmania (AT ISSN 0314-1888) *821*, *1048*
Australia. Australian Water Resources Council. Conference Series (AT) *402*
Australia. Australian Water Resources Council. Hydrological Series (AT ISSN 0067-219X) *402*
Australia. Australian Water Resources Council. Occasional Papers Series (AT ISSN 0725-2293) *402*
Australia. Australian Water Resources Council. Technical Paper (AT) *402*
Australia. Australian Water Resources Council. Water Management Series (AT ISSN 0728-9502) *402*
Australia. Bureau of Agricultural Economics. Coarse Grains and Oilseeds Situation *see* Australia. Bureau of Agricultural Economics. Coarse Grains: Situation and Outlook *1147*
Australia. Bureau of Agricultural Economics. Coarse Grains and Oilseeds Situation *see* Australia. Bureau of Agricultural Economics. Oilseeds: Situation and Outlook *1147*
Australia. Bureau of Agricultural Economics. Coarse Grains: Situation and Outlook (AT ISSN 0311-0788) *1147*
Australia. Bureau of Agricultural Economics. Dairy Products: Situation and Outlook (AT ISSN 0311-8843) *1147*
Australia. Bureau of Agricultural Economics. Dairy Situation *see* Australia. Bureau of Agricultural Economics. Dairy Products: Situation and Outlook *1147*
Australia. Bureau of Agricultural Economics. Egg Situation *see* Australia. Bureau of Agricultural Economics. Eggs: Situation and Outlook *1147*
Australia. Bureau of Agricultural Economics. Eggs: Situation and Outlook (AT) *1147*
Australia. Bureau of Agricultural Economics. Fibre Review (AT ISSN 0311-2950) *1147*
Australia. Bureau of Agricultural Economics. Fibres Other Than Wool *see* Australia. Bureau of Agricultural Economics. Fibre Review *1147*
Australia. Bureau of Agricultural Economics. Meat Situation *see* Australia. Bureau of Agricultural Economics. Meat: Situation and Outlook *1147*
Australia. Bureau of Agricultural Economics. Meat: Situation and Outlook (AT ISSN 0311-0885) *1147*
Australia. Bureau of Agricultural Economics. Occasional Papers (AT ISSN 0815-1458) *45*
Australia. Bureau of Agricultural Economics. Oilseeds: Situation and Outlook (AT ISSN 0311-8789) *1147*
Australia. Bureau of Agricultural Economics. Situation and Outlook (Year). Cotton (AT ISSN 0311-8835) *1147*
Australia. Bureau of Agricultural Economics. Situation and Outlook (Year). Farm Inputs (AT ISSN 0810-6797) *1147*
Australia. Bureau of Agricultural Economics. Situation and Outlook (Year). Fish Products (AT ISSN 0810-6800) *1147*
Australia. Bureau of Agricultural Economics. Wheat: Situation and Outlook (AT ISSN 0310-9917) *1147*
Australia. Bureau of Industry Economics. Research Report (AT ISSN 0156-3394) *191*
Australia. Bureau of Meteorology. Bulletin (AT ISSN 0067-1312) *803*
Australia. Bureau of Meteorology. Meteorological Study (AT ISSN 0067-1320) *803*

Australia. Bureau of Mineral Resources. Geology and Geophysics. Australian Petroleum Accumulations Report (AT ISSN 0817-9263) *378*, *863*
Australia. Bureau of Mineral Resources, Geology and Geophysics. Bulletin (AT ISSN 0084-7089) *378*
Australia. Bureau of Mineral Resources, Geology, and Geophysics. Publications (AT) *121*, *541*
Australia. Bureau of Mineral Resources, Geology and Geophysics. Reports (AT ISSN 0084-7100) *378*
Australia. Bureau of Mineral Resources. Geology and Geophysics. Resource Report (AT) *378*, *814*
Australia. Bureau of Mineral Resources. Geology and Geophysics. Yearbook (AT ISSN 0158-7285) *378*
Australia. Bureau of Mineral Resources, Geology, and Geophysics. 1: 250000 Geological Maps and Explanatory Notes Series (AT) *378*, *383*
Australia. Bureau of Statistics. Adoptions (AT) *948*, *1048*
Australia. Bureau of Statistics. Apparent Consumption of Foodstuffs and Nutrients (AT) *948*, *1049*
Australia. Bureau of Statistics. Apparent Consumption of Selected Foodstuffs, Preliminary (AT) *948*, *1049*
Australia. Bureau of Statistics. Australian Capital Territory. Statistical Summary (AT ISSN 0067-1754) *1049*
Australia. Bureau of Statistics. Australian Exports Bulletin *see* Australia. Bureau of Statistics. Australian Exports, Country by Commodity *203*
Australia. Bureau of Statistics. Australian Exports, Country by Commodity (AT ISSN 0705-0534) *203*
Australia. Bureau of Statistics. Australian Imports Bulletin *see* Australia. Bureau of Statistics. Australian Imports, Country by Commodity *1147*
Australia. Bureau of Statistics. Australian Imports, Country by Commodity (AT ISSN 0705-0542) *1147*
Australia. Bureau of Statistics. Australian Municipal Information System (AT) *1147*
Australia. Bureau of Statistics. Australian National Accounts: Gross Product by Industry (AT) *203*
Australia. Bureau of Statistics. Australian National Accounts - National Income and Expenditure (AT ISSN 0312-6250) *203*
Australia. Bureau of Statistics. Balance of Payments, Australia (AT ISSN 0045-0111) *203*
Australia. Bureau of Statistics. Births (AT) *948*, *1049*
Australia. Bureau of Statistics. Catalogue of Publications (AT) *948*, *1049*
Australia. Bureau of Statistics. Causes of Death, Australia (AT ISSN 0067-0766) *926*
Australia. Bureau of Statistics. Child Care Arrangements (AT) *1147*
Australia. Bureau of Statistics. Child Care Arrangements. Preliminary (AT) *1147*
Australia. Bureau of Statistics. Child in Care (AT) *948*, *1049*
Australia. Bureau of Statistics. Commonwealth Government Finance(AT ISSN 0705-0550) *939*
Australia. Bureau of Statistics. Deaths (AT) *948*, *1049*
Australia. Bureau of Statistics. Directory of A B S Energy Statistics (AT) *1147*
Australia. Bureau of Statistics. Distribution and Composition of Employee Earnings & Hours (AT) *203*
Australia. Bureau of Statistics. Divorces(AT) *948*, *1049*

Australia. Bureau of Statistics. Earnings and Hours of Employment *see* Australia. Bureau of Statistics. Distribution and Composition of Employee Earnings & Hours *203*
Australia. Bureau of Statistics. Estimated Resident Population Sex and Age: States and Territories of Australia (AT) *948*, *1049*
Australia. Bureau of Statistics. Estimates of Gross Product by Industry at Current and Constant Prices *see* Australia. Bureau of Statistics. Australian National Accounts: Gross Product by Industry *203*
Australia. Bureau of Statistics. Ex-Service Personnel (AT) *1147*
Australia. Bureau of Statistics. Expenditure on Education, Australia (AT) *422*
Australia. Bureau of Statistics. Foreign Trade, Australia, Part 1: Exports and Imports (AT) *203*
Australia. Bureau of Statistics. Foreign Trade, Australia. Part 2: Comparative and Summary Tables (AT ISSN 0705-0526) *203*
Australia. Bureau of Statistics. Government Financial Estimates, Australia (AT) *203*, *1049*
Australia. Bureau of Statistics. Labour Report *see* Australia. Bureau of Statistics. Labour Statistics, Australia *203*
Australia. Bureau of Statistics. Labour Statistics, Australia (AT) *203*
Australia. Bureau of Statistics. List of Publications to be Released (AT) *1049*
Australia. Bureau of Statistics. Livestock and Livestock Products, Australia (AT) *38*
Australia. Bureau of Statistics. Manufacturing Commodities: Principal Articles Produced, Australia(AT) *1147*
Australia. Bureau of Statistics. Manufacturing Establishments: Summary of Operations by Industry Class, Australia (AT) *1147*
Australia. Bureau of Statistics. Marriages (AT) *948*, *1049*
Australia. Bureau of Statistics. Mineral Exploration, Australia (AT) *821*
Australia. Bureau of Statistics. Mineral Production, Australia (AT ISSN 0311-8975) *814*
Australia. Bureau of Statistics. National Schools Statistics Collection (AT) *948*, *1049*
Australia. Bureau of Statistics. National Schools Statistics Collection. Preliminary (AT) *948*, *1049*
Australia. Bureau of Statistics. New South Wales Office. Tertiary Education, New South Wales (AT) *422*
Australia. Bureau of Statistics. Northern Territory Statistical Summary (AT ISSN 0067-0855) *1049*
Australia. Bureau of Statistics. Overseas Trade, Australia, Part 1: Exports and Imports *see* Australia. Bureau of Statistics. Foreign Trade, Australia, Part 1: Exports and Imports *203*
Australia. Bureau of Statistics. Overseas Trade, Australia. Part 2: Comparative and Summary Tables *see* Australia. Bureau of Statistics. Foreign Trade, Australia. Part 2: Comparative and Summary Tables *203*
Australia. Bureau of Statistics. Perinatal Deaths (AT) *948*, *1049*
Australia. Bureau of Statistics. Pocket Compendium of Australian Statistics *see* Australia. Bureau of Statistics. Pocket Year Book, Australia *1049*
Australia. Bureau of Statistics. Pocket Year Book, Australia (AT ISSN 0705-0488) *1049*
Australia. Bureau of Statistics. Projections of the Population (AT) *948*, *1049*
Australia. Bureau of Statistics. Public Authority Finance. Public Authority Estimates *see* Australia. Bureau of Statistics. Government Financial Estimates, Australia *203*

Australia. Bureau of Statistics. Public Authority Finance. State and Local Authorities *see* Australia. Bureau of Statistics. State and Local Government Finance, Australia *203*
Australia. Bureau of Statistics. Queensland Office. Estimated Resident Population and Areas for each Local Authority Area, Queensland (AT) *926*, *1049*
Australia. Bureau of Statistics. Queensland Office. Government Finance, Queensland (AT) *203*
Australia. Bureau of Statistics. Queensland Office. Law and Order, Queensland (AT) *373*
Australia. Bureau of Statistics. Queensland Office. Population Estimates and Areas for Local Authority Areas *see* Australia. Bureau of Statistics. Queensland Office. Estimated Resident Population and Areas for each Local Authority Area, Queensland *926*
Australia. Bureau of Statistics. Queensland Office. Public Finance: Government Authorities *see* Australia. Bureau of Statistics. Queensland Office. Government Finance, Queensland *203*
Australia. Bureau of Statistics. Seasonally Adjusted Indicators (AT ISSN 0571-964X) *948*, *1049*
Australia. Bureau of Statistics. Social Indicators (AT ISSN 0705-0496) *948*, *1049*
Australia. Bureau of Statistics. South Australian Office. Births, South Australia (AT ISSN 0067-088X) *920*, *926*
Australia. Bureau of Statistics. South Australian Office. Deaths, South Australia (AT ISSN 0067-0898) *920*, *926*
Australia. Bureau of Statistics. South Australian Office. Divorces, South Australia (AT ISSN 0067-0901) *920*, *926*
Australia. Bureau of Statistics. South Australian Office. Manufacturing Establishments *see* Australia. Bureau of Statistics. South Australian Office. Manufacturing Establishments, Details of Operations by Industry *203*
Australia. Bureau of Statistics. South Australian Office. Manufacturing Establishments, Details of Operations by Industry (AT) *203*
Australia. Bureau of Statistics. State and Local Government Finance, Australia(AT) *203*, *1049*
Australia. Bureau of Statistics. Tasmanian Office. Divorces Tasmania (AT ISSN 0705-5773) *920*, *926*
Australia. Bureau of Statistics. Tasmanian Office. Finance *see* Australia. Bureau of Statistics. Tasmanian Office. Local Government Finance *203*
Australia. Bureau of Statistics. Tasmanian Office. Fruit (AT ISSN 0810-9176) *39*
Australia. Bureau of Statistics. Tasmanian Office. Fruit Production *see* Australia. Bureau of Statistics. Tasmanian Office. Fruit *39*
Australia. Bureau of Statistics. Tasmanian Office. Labour Force Statistics (AT ISSN 0814-9593) *203*
Australia. Bureau of Statistics. Tasmanian Office. Labour, Wages and Prices *see* Australia. Bureau of Statistics. Tasmanian Office. Labour Force Statistics *203*
Australia. Bureau of Statistics. Tasmanian Office. Local Government Finance (AT ISSN 0312-7850) *203*
Australia. Bureau of Statistics. Tasmanian Office. Pocket Year Book of Tasmania (AT ISSN 0314-1640) *1049*
Australia. Bureau of Statistics. Tasmanian Office. Tasmanian Year Book (AT ISSN 0082-2116) *572*
Australia. Bureau of Statistics. Technical Papers (AT) *948*, *1049*

Australia. Bureau of Statistics. Tertiary Education (AT) *948,* 1049
Australia. Bureau of Statistics. Trade Union Statistics, Australia (AT ISSN 0312-1437) *203*
Australia. Bureau of Statistics. Value of Agricultural Commodities Produced, Australia (AT) *39*
Australia. Bureau of Statistics. Value of Primary Production, Excluding Mining, and Indexes of Quantum and Unit Gross Value of Agricultural Production *see* Australia. Bureau of Statistics. Value of Agricultural Commodities Produced, Australia *39*
Australia. Bureau of Statistics. Victorian Office. Demography Summary Statement, Victoria (AT) *1147*
Australia. Bureau of Statistics. Victorian Office. Demography, Victoria *see* Australia. Bureau of Statistics. Victorian Office. Demography Summary Statement, Victoria *1147*
Australia. Bureau of Statistics. Victorian Office. Estimated Population in Local Government Areas, Victoria *see* Australia. Bureau of Statistics. Victorian Office. Estimated Resident Population In Local Government Areas, Victoria *926*
Australia. Bureau of Statistics. Victorian Office. Estimated Resident Population In Local Government Areas, Victoria (AT) *926*
Australia. Bureau of Statistics. Victorian Office. Government Finance *see* Australia. Bureau of Statistics. Victorian Office. Local Government Finance, Victoria *292*
Australia. Bureau of Statistics. Victorian Office. Local Government Finance, Victoria (AT) *292*
Australia. Bureau of Statistics. Victorian Office. National Schools Statistics, Victoria (AT) *410,* 572
Australia. Bureau of Statistics. Victorian Office. Primary and Secondary Education, Victoria *see* Australia. Bureau of Statistics. Victorian Office. National Schools Statistics, Victoria *410*
Australia. Bureau of Statistics. Victorian Office. Value of Agricultural Commodities Produced. (AT) *39*
Australia. Bureau of Statistics. Victorian Office. Value of Primary Commodities Produced (Excluding Mining) *see* Australia. Bureau of Statistics. Victorian Office. Value of Agricultural Commodities Produced *39*
Australia. Bureau of Statistics. Victorian Office. Victorian Pocket Yearbook (AT ISSN 0067-1207) *1049*
Australia. Bureau of Statistics. Victorian Office. Victorian Yearbook (AT ISSN 0067-1223) *1049*
Australia. Bureau of Statistics. Western Australian Office. Abstract of Statistics of Local Government Areas. *see* Australia. Bureau of Statistics. Western Australian Office. Local Government, Western Australia *948*
Australia. Bureau of Statistics. Western Australian Office. Census of Manufacturing Establishments. Summary of Operations by Industry Class (AT) *203*
Australia. Bureau of Statistics. Western Australian Office. Economic Censuses: Manufacturing Establishments: Summary of Operations by Industry Class *see* Australia. Bureau of Statistics. Western Australian Office. Census of Manufacturing Establishments. Summary of Operations by Industry Class *203*
Australia. Bureau of Statistics. Western Australian Office. Fisheries (AT ISSN 0705-2146) *507*
Australia. Bureau of Statistics. Western Australian Office. Industrial Accidents (AT) *203,* 636

Australia. Bureau of Statistics. Western Australian Office. Industrial Accidents *see* Australia. Bureau of Statistics. Western Australian Office. Industrial Accidents *203*
Australia. Bureau of Statistics. Western Australian Office. Local Government, Western Australia (AT) *948*
Australia. Bureau of Statistics. Year Book Australia (AT) *1049*
Australia. Commonwealth Grants Commission. Grants Commission Report on Financial Assistance for Local Government (AT) *293*
Australia. Department of Aboriginal Affairs. Report (AT) *501*
Australia. Department of Civil Aviation. Civil Aviation Report *see* Australian Transport *1080*
Australia. Department of Foreign Affairs. Development Assistance Bureau. Annual Review (AT ISSN 0729-0691) *261*
Australia. Department of Foreign Affairs. International Treaties and Conventions *see* Australia. Department of Foreign Affairs. Select Documents on International Affairs *914*
Australia. Department of Foreign Affairs. Select Documents on International Affairs (AT ISSN 0519-5950) *914*
Australia. Department of Health. Annual Report (AT) *952*
Australia. Department of Home Affairs. Norfolk Island Annual Report (AT) *572*
Australia. Department of Industry, Technology and Commerce. Annual Report (AT ISSN 0728-6856) *293*
Australia. Department of Police and Customs. Review of Activities *see* Australia. Department of Industry, Technology and Commerce. Annual Report *293*
Australia. Department of Primary Industry. Annual Report (AT ISSN 0158-1309) *241*
Australia. Department of Primary Industry. Australian Fishing Industry Directory (AT ISSN 0157-9630) *507*
Australia. Department of Primary Industry. Australian Plague and Locust Commission. Annual Report (AT ISSN 0313-2781) *45*
Australia. Department of Primary Industry. Conditions for Export of Experimental Shipments (AT) *253*
Australia. Department of Primary Industry. Conditions for Export of Grapes (AT) *253*
Australia. Department of Primary Industry. Conditions for Export of Pears *see* Australia. Department of Primary Industry. Conditions for Export of Primary Products *253*
Australia. Department of Primary Industry. Conditions for Export of Primary Products (AT) *253*
Australia. Department of Primary Industry. Fishing Industry Research Committee. Annual Report (AT ISSN 0311-8959) *507*
Australia. Department of Primary Industry. Industry Price Indexes (AT) *1147*
Australia. Department of Primary Industry. Operation of the Fishing Industry, A.C.T. Annual Report (AT ISSN 0067-1436) *507*
Australia. Department of Primary Industry. Poultry Industry Assistance. Annual Report (AT ISSN 0728-6929) *64*
Australia. Department of Primary Industry. Raw Cotton Marketing Advisory Committee. Annual Report(AT) *52*
Australia. Department of Primary Industry. Rural Industry Directory (AT ISSN 0812-1729) *24*
Australia. Department of Primary Industry. Tobacco Industry Trust. Account Annual Report (AT ISSN 0404-181X) *1079*

Australia. Department of Primary Industry. Wheat Industry Research, A.C.T. Annual Report (AT ISSN 0572-0451) *52*
Australia. Department of Resources and Energy. Streamline Update (AT ISSN 0812-7735) *1123*
Australia. Department of Social Security. Annual Report of the Director-General (AT) *638*
Australia. Department of Territory of Norfolk Island. Report *see* Australia. Department of Home Affairs. Norfolk Island Annual Report *572*
Australia. Department of the Treasury. Income Tax Statistics (AT ISSN 0067-1444) *203*
Australia. Department of the Treasury. Round-up (AT) *203*
Australia. Department of the Treasury. Round-Up of Economic Statistics *see* Australia. Department of the Treasury. Round-up *203*
Australia. Department of the Treasury. Taxation Branch. Taxation Statistics (AT ISSN 0519-6035) *203*
Australia. Department of the Treasury. Treasury Economic Paper (AT) *293*
Australia. Designs Office. Annual Record of Designs Office Proceedings (AT) *860*
Australia. Designs Office. Registered Owners of Designs *see* Australia. Designs Office. Annual Record of Designs Office Proceedings *860*
Australia. Designs Office. Registered Owners of Designs and Articles in Respect of Which Designs Have Been Registered *see* Australia. Designs Office. Annual Record of Designs Office Proceedings *860*
Australia. Designs Office. Registered Owners of Designs and Articles in Respect of Which Designs Have Been Registered Under the Designs Act *see* Australia. Designs Office. Annual Record of Designs Office Proceedings *860*
Australia. Education Research and Development Committee. Annual Report (AT) *410*
Australia. Environmental Studies Working Papers (AT ISSN 0313-5780) *364, 464, 494*
Australia. Fishing Industry Research Committee. Annual Report (AT) *507, 651*
Australia. Foreign Investment Review Board. Report (AT) *265*
Australia. Grants Commission. Grants Commission Report on Financial Assistance for Local Government *see* Australia. Commonwealth Grants Commission. Grants Commission Report on Financial Assistance for Local Government *293*
Australia. Industries Assistance Commission. Annual Report (AT) *287*
Australia. Insurance Commissioner. Annual Report (AT) *638*
Australia. Land Transport Statistics. Non-Government Railways *see* Australia. Non-Government Railways Statistics *1084*
Australia. Law Reform Commission. Annual Report (AT ISSN 0312-6994) *651*
Australia. National Capital Development Commission. Annual Report (AT ISSN 0067-1517) *621*
Australia. National Capital Development Commission. Technical Papers (AT ISSN 0313-9948) *470, 494, 621*
Australia. National Drug Information Service. Technical Information Bulletin *see* Australia. National Information Service on Drug Abuse. Technical Information Bulletin *376*
Australia. National Information Service on Drug Abuse. Technical Information Bulletin (AT ISSN 0157-8200) *376*
Australia. National Library. Annual Report (AT ISSN 0313-1971) *674*

Australia. National Library. Annual Report of the Council *see* Australia. National Library. Annual Report *674*
Australia. National Women's Advisory Council. Annual Report (AT) *1128*
Australia. Non-Government Railways Statistics (AT) *1049, 1084*
Australia. Patent Office. Annual Report of Activities (AT ISSN 0311-2152) *860*
Australia. Patent Office. Report *see* Australia. Patent Office. Annual Report of Activities *860*
Australia. ProfessionaL Fisherman's Fishing Vessel Yearbook (AT) *508*
Australia. Public Service Board. Annual Report (AT) *939*
Australia at a Glance (AT) *1049*
Australia Handbook (AT ISSN 0067-1495) *573*
Australia Law Reform Commission Report Series *see* A L R C Report Series *649*
Australia Mineral Development Laboratories Bulletin *see* A M D E L Bulletin *382*
Australia Mineral Industry Review *see* Australian Mineral Industry. Annual Review *814*
Australia New Zealand Foundation. Annual Report (Year) (AT ISSN 0810-0055) *914,* 1015
Australia Parliamentary Seminar. Summary Report of Proceedings *see* Australasian and Pacific Parliamentary Seminar. Summary Report of Proceedings *651*
Australia Party. Victorian Branch. Report *see* Action Report *902*
Australian Academy of Science. National Committee for Antarctic Research. Australian Antarctic and Sub-Antarctic Research Programmes (AT) *398*
Australian Academy of Science. Records *see* Historical Records of Australian Science *992*
Australian Academy of Science. Reports (AT ISSN 0067-1568) *988*
Australian Academy of Science. Year Book (AT ISSN 0067-1584) *988*
Australian Academy of the Humanities. Proceedings (AT ISSN 0067-1592) *628*
Australian Accommodation Guide (AT) *619*
Australian Accounting Research Foundation. Research Studies (AT) *221*
Australian Advances in Veterinary Science (AT ISSN 0728-8425) *1121*
Australian Advisory Council on Bibliographical Services. Library Services for Australia *see* A A C O B S Annual Report *672*
Australian Advisory Council on Bibliographical Services Annual Report *see* A A C O B S Annual Report *672*
Australian Agriculture, Fisheries and Forestry Directory *see* Rural Industry Directory *33*
Australian-American Business Review (US) *253*
Australian-American News N.S.W. Annual Edition (AT) *914,* 1106
Australian and New Zealand Association for the Advancement of Science Congress Papers *see* A N Z A A S Congress Papers *986*
Australian and New Zealand Hospitals and Health Services Yearbook *see* Australian Hospitals and Health Services Yearbook *616*
Australian and New Zealand Studies in German Language and Literature (SZ) *715*
Australian Association for Adolescent Health. Newsletter (AT) *335, 758*
Australian Association for the Teaching of English Guide to English Books *see* A.A.T.E. Guide to English Books *738*
Australian Association of Neurologists Proceedings *see* Clinical and Experimental Neurology *789*

AUSTRALIAN BIBLICAL

Australian Biblical Review (AT ISSN 0045-0308) 967
Australian Biochemical Society. Proceedings (AT ISSN 0067-1703) 151
Australian Biochemical Society. Programme and Abstracts see Australian Biochemical Society. Proceedings 151
Australian Book Publishers Association Directory of Members see A B P A Directory of Members 959
Australian Books (AT ISSN 0067-1738) 121
Australian Booksellers (AT) 960
Australian Capital Territory at a Glance(AT) 1049
Australian Cat Federation, Inc. Year Book see A C I Year Book 868
Australian Catholic Historical Society. Journal (AT ISSN 0084-7259) 573
Australian Centre for Maritime Studies. Occasional Papers in Maritime Affairs (AT) 1147
Australian Chess Lore (AT) 1032
Australian Coal Industry Research Laboratories. Annual Report (AT ISSN 0067-1762) 814
Australian Company Law Reports (AT ISSN 0313-8445) 651
Australian Composer (AT ISSN 0311-2764) 833
Australian Conference on Chemical Engineering. Proceedings (AT) 478, 863
Australian Congress of Trade Unions. Decisions (AT) 648
Australian Conservation Foundation. Annual Report (AT ISSN 0587-5846) 364
Australian Conservation Foundation. Conservation Directory see Green Pages: Directory of Non-Government Environmental Groups in Australia 365
Australian Contract Furnishing Cyclopaedia (AT) 302, 643
Australian Contract Yearbook (AT) 643
Australian Council for Educational Research. Annual Report (AT) 410
Australian Council for Educational Research. Occasional Papers (AT ISSN 0067-1835) 410
Australian Council for Educational Research. Research Series (AT) 410
Australian Council of State School Organisations Policy (Year) see A C S S O Policy (Year) 409
Australian Council of Trade Unions. Bulletin (AT ISSN 0314-2868) 648
Australian Council of Trade Unions National Youth Brochure see A C T U National Youth Brochure 647
Australian Cricket Yearbook (AT ISSN 0084-7291) 1037
Australian Crime Prevention Council. National Conference. Proceedings. (AT) 369
Australian Crime Prevention Council. National Newsletter (AT) 370
Australian Cultural History (AT ISSN 0728-8433) 573
Australian Defence Equipment Catalogue (AT) 810
Australian Digest (AT ISSN 0067-1843) 651
Australian Directory of Exports see Australian Exports 253
Australian Directory of Services for Alcoholism and Drug Dependence (AT ISSN 0311-9629) 1147
Australian Early Childhood Association. Victorian Branch. Newsletter (AT) 333, 410
Australian Economy; Business Forecast see Management Reports on the Australian Economy 246
Australian Electronics Directory (AT ISSN 0159-2947) 450
Australian Energy Statistics (AT ISSN 0727-2596) 468, 1049
Australian Engineering Case Studies (AT) 488
Australian Engineering Directory (AT ISSN 0159-2955) 470
Australian Entomological Society. Miscellaneous Publications (AT) 163
Australian Exports (AT) 253

Australian Family Law Cases (AT) 651
Australian Film and Television School. Annual Report see Australian Film, Television and Radio School. Annual Report 342
Australian Film and Television School Handbook see Australian Film, Television and Radio School Handbook 347
Australian Film, Television and Radio School. Annual Report (AT) 342, 347
Australian Film, Television and Radio School Handbook (AT ISSN 0313-8461) 347
Australian Films (AT ISSN 0045-0448) 82, 121, 822
Australian Fire Protection Association. Conference Papers (AT) 506
Australian Folk Directory (AT ISSN 0726-4941) 833
Australian Forest Industries Directory (AT) 529
Australian Forest Resources (AT ISSN 0314-1438) 523
Australian Foundation on Alcoholism and Drug Dependence Library Periodicals Holdings List see A F A D D Library Periodicals Holdings List 1145
Australian Gas Industry Directory (AT ISSN 0727-3541) 491, 863
Australian Gliding Yearbook (AT ISSN 0084-7364) 18
Australian Government Directory see Commonwealth Government Directory 940
Australian Hi-Fi Annual (AT ISSN 0310-8902) 1031
Australian Honey Board. Annual Report (AT ISSN 0067-1894) 518
Australian Horse Racing Annual (AT ISSN 0084-7402) 1042
Australian Hospital Association Health Services Monographs see A H A Health Services Monographs 616
Australian Hospitals and Health Services Yearbook (AT ISSN 0312-5599) 616
Australian Imports (AT ISSN 0155-7009) 253, 302
Australian Imports of Dairy Produce (AT) 1147
Australian Income Tax Assessment Act see Australian Income Tax Assessment Act and Regulations 293
Australian Income Tax Assessment Act and Regulations (AT) 293
Australian Institute of Family Studies. Annual Report (AT) 920
Australian Institute of Marine Science. Yearly Report (AT) 404
Australian Institute of Marine Science Monograph Series see A I M S Monograph Series 404
Australian Institute of Metals. Proceedings of the Annual Conference see Australasian Institute of Metals. Proceedings of the Annual Conference 797
Australian Institute of Petroleum. Annual Report (AT ISSN 0314-3171) 384, 863
Australian Jaycees National Directory (AT) 341
Australian Journal of Historical Archaeology. (AT ISSN 0810-1868) 82
Australian Journal of Law and Society (AT ISSN 0729-3356) 651
Australian Key Business Directory (AT ISSN 0311-2667) 302
Australian Ladies Golf Union. Official Yearbook (AT) 1044
Australian Lectionary (Year) (AT ISSN 0812-0811) 967, 978
Australian Legal Aid Review Committee. Report (AT) 651
Australian Legal Directory (AT ISSN 0155-297X) 302, 651
Australian Liberal (AT ISSN 0004-9654) 902
Australian Lutheran Almanac see Lutheran Church of Australia. Yearbook 979
Australian Mammalogy (AT ISSN 0310-0049) 173

Australian Maps (AT ISSN 0045-0677) 121, 541
Australian Market Guide (US ISSN 0067-1959) 265, 302
Australian Marxist Review (AT ISSN 0310-8252) 902
Australian Master Tax Guide (AT) 293
Australian Meat Research Committee. Annual Report. (AT) 64, 518
Australian Metal Trades Export Group's Export Note Pad see M T I A N E G's Export Note Pad 799
Australian Mineral Industries Research Association. Bulletin (AT) 1148
Australian Mineral Industries Research Association. Non-Confidential Research Information (AT) 1148
Australian Mineral Industry. Annual Review (AT ISSN 0084-7488) 814
Australian Mining and Petroleum Law Association Ltd. Yearbook see A M P L A Yearbook 813
Australian Mining and Petroleum Law Journal see A M P L A Yearbook 813
Australian Mining Industry Council. Directory (AT) 814
Australian Mining Year Book (AT ISSN 0314-7762) 814
Australian Mission to the United Nations. United Nations General Assembly. Australian Delegation. Report see United Nations General Assembly: Report of the Australian Delegation 919
Australian Motion Picture Yearbook see Cinema Papers Yearbook 823
Australian Museum Memoirs see Australian Museum, Sydney. Supplements 826
Australian Museum, Sydney. Supplements (AT ISSN 0812-7387) 826
Australian Music Directory (AT ISSN 0706-6678) 833
Australian National Antarctic Research Expeditions Report see A N A R E Report 986
Australian National Antarctic Research Expeditions Research Notes see A N A R E Research Notes 986
Australian National Parks and Wildlife Service. Report (AT) 364
Australian National University. Canberra. Department of Demography. Family and Fertility Change (AT) 920, 1024
Australian National University. Centre for Resource and Environmental Studies. Working Papers (AT ISSN 0313-7414) 364
Australian National University. Development Studies Centre. Demography Teaching Notes (AT ISSN 0157-6232) 1006
Australian National University. Development Studies Centre. Monograph (AT ISSN 0157-5767) 1006
Australian National University. Development Studies Centre. Pacific Research Monograph (AT ISSN 0155-9060) 1006
Australian National University. Development Studies Centre. Working Papers (AT ISSN 0814-1266) 1006
Australian National University. Research School of Physical Sciences. Annual Report (AT ISSN 0155-624X) 887
Australian National University, Canberra. Department of Demography. Studies in Migration and Urbanization (AT) 920
Australian National University, Canberra. Department of Engineering Physics. Publication Ep-Rr (AT ISSN 0084-7496) 484
Australian National University, Canberra. Department of Political Science. Occasional Paper. see Australian National University, Canberra. Research School of Social Sciences. Department of Political Science. Occasional Papers 902

Australian National University, Canberra. Geology Department. Publication (AT ISSN 0084-750X) 384
Australian National University, Canberra. Research School of Physical Sciences. Research Paper (AT ISSN 0084-7518) 887
Australian National University, Canberra. Research School of Social Sciences. Department of Political Science. Occasional Papers (AT) 902
Australian Numismatic Journal (AT ISSN 0004-9875) 844
Australian Oilseeds Industry Statistics (AT) 52
Australian Parliamentary Handbook see Parliamentary Handbook of the Commonwealth of Australia 907
Australian Petroleum Exploration Association Journal see A.P.E.A. Journal 862
Australian Photography Directory see Australian Photography Photo-Directory 884
Australian Photography Photo-Directory (AT) 884
Australian Photography Professional and Industrial Catalogue see Professional and Industrial Photographic Equipment 885
Australian Pre-School Association. Victoria Branch. Newsletter see Australian Early Childhood Association. Victorian Branch. Newsletter 410
Australian Public Affairs Information Service see A P A I S: Australian Public Affairs Information Service 948
Australian Renewable Energy Resources Index see C R R E R I S Renewable Energy Index 468
Australian Research Grants Committee. Report see Australian Research Grants Scheme. Report on Grants Approved 411
Australian Research Grants Scheme. Report on Grants Approved (AT) 411
Australian Road Index (AT ISSN 0312-2115) 2, 476, 1084
Australian Road Research Board. Proceedings (AT ISSN 0572-1431) 480, 1095
Australian Road Research Board. Research Report (AT) 1080, 1090
Australian Road Research Board. Special Report (AT ISSN 0572-144X) 1080, 1090
Australian Road Research Board. Technical Manual (AT ISSN 0313-895X) 1080, 1090
Australian Road Research in Progress (AT ISSN 0705-9213) 2, 476, 1084
Australian Sales Tax Guide (AT) 293
Australian School Leavers Yearbook (AT) 847
Australian Science Education Research Association. Research in Science Education (AT ISSN 0157-244X) 446
Australian Shipping and Shipbuilding (AT) 1099
Australian Ski Yearbook (AT ISSN 0084-7593) 1044
Australian Slavonic and East European Studies (AT) 691, 715
Australian Small Farms Directory (AT ISSN 0812-955X) 51, 64
Australian Society for Education in Film and Television. President's Newsletter (AT) 446
Australian Society for Historical Archeology. (Annual Publication) see Australian Journal of Historical Archaeology 82
Australian Society of Animal Production. Proceedings see Animal Production in Australia 64
Australian Society of Sugar Cane Technologists. Proceedings. (AT ISSN 0726-0822) 518
Australian Speleo Abstracts (AT) 384
Australian Stamp Bulletin (AT) 874
Australian Stud Pig Herd Book (AT) 64

Australian Studies in Health Service Administration (AT ISSN 0067-2165) *952*
Australian Sugar Year Book (AT ISSN 0067-2173) *518*
Australian Superannuation and Employee Benefits Guide (AT) *638, 1015*
Australian Superannuation and Employee Benefits Planning in Action *see* Australian Superannuation and Employee Benefits Guide *1015*
Australian Tax Cases (AT) *293, 651*
Australian Taxpayer's Association. Annual Taxation Summary (AT) *293*
Australian Teacher *see* Teachers Guild of New South Wales. Proceedings *420*
Australian Teacher of the Deaf (AT ISSN 0005-0334) *375, 411*
Australian Teachers' Federation Annual Report *see* A T F Annual Report *409*
Australian Telecommunication Monographs (AT ISSN 0067-2181) *350*
Australian Tourist Commission. Annual Report (AT) *1106*
Australian Transport (AT ISSN 0311-628X) *1080*
Australian Transport Information Directory (AT ISSN 0811-3688) *1049, 1080*
Australian Treaty List *see* Australian Treaty Series *669*
Australian Treaty Series (AT) *669*
Australian Veterinary Association. Year Book (AT ISSN 0706-3504) *1121*
Australian Waste Disposal Catalogue (AT ISSN 0726-6987) *494*
Australian Water Resources Council. Water Resources Series (AT) *1123*
Australian Weed Control Handbook (AT ISSN 0310-0405) *52*
Australian Wool *see* Australian Wool Sale Statistics. Statistical Analysis. Part A & B *1075*
Australian Wool Sale Statistics. Statistical Analysis. Part A & B (AT ISSN 0311-9882) *1075*
Australian Workers' Union. Official Report of the Annual Convention (AT) *648*
Australian Yearbook of International Law (AT ISSN 0084-7658) *669*
Australian Youth Hostels Handbook (AT ISSN 0156-0107) *1106*
Australia's External Aid *see* Australia's Overseas Development Assistance. Budget Paper *914*
Australia's Overseas Development Assistance *see* Australia's Overseas Development Assistance. Budget Paper *914*
Australia's Overseas Development Assistance. Budget Paper (AT) *914*
Australia's Top 500 Companies (AT) *283*
Austria. Bundesamt fuer Eich- und Vermessungswesen. Amtsblatt fuer das Eichwesen (AU) *808*
Austria. Bundesministerium fuer Bauten und Technik. Abteilung Baukoordinierung. Vorschau (AU) *181*
Austria. Bundesministerium fuer Land- und Forstwirtschaft. Taetigkeitsbericht (AU ISSN 0067-2262) *24*
Austria. Bundesministerium fuer Unterricht und Kunst. Schriftenreihe (AU) *102, 446*
Austria. Bundesministerium fuer Wissenschaft und Forschung. Bericht der Bundesregierung an den Nationalrat (AU ISSN 0300-2772) *988*
Austria. Bundesministerium fuer Wissenschaft und Forschung. Hochschulbericht (AU) *432*
Austria. Oberlandesgericht Wien im Leistungsstreitverfahren Zweiter Instanz der Sozialversicherung (SSV). Entscheidungen (AU) *651*
Austria. Statistisches Zentralamt. Baustatistik (AU) *188*

Austria. Statistisches Zentralamt. Demographisches Jahrbuch Oesterreichs (AU) *926*
Austria. Statistisches Zentralamt. Die Natuerliche Bevoelkerungsbewegung (AU ISSN 0067-2335) *920, 926*
Austria. Statistisches Zentralamt. Die Wohnbautaetigkeit (AU ISSN 0067-2300) *188*
Austria. Statistisches Zentralamt. Ergebnisse der Landwirtschaftlichen Maschinenzaehlung (AU) *39*
Austria. Statistisches Zentralamt. Ergebnisse der Landwirtschaftlichen Statistik (AU ISSN 0067-2327) *39*
Austria. Statistisches Zentralamt. Erhebung der Land und Forstwirtschaftlichen Arbeitskraefte (AU) *203*
Austria. Statistisches Zentralamt. Gewerbestatistik Part 2 (AU) *203*
Austria. Statistisches Zentralamt. Industrie Statistik *see* Austria. Statistisches Zentralamt. Industrie und Gewerbestatistik Part 1 *203*
Austria. Statistisches Zentralamt. Industrie Statistik und Gewerb *see* Austria. Statistisches Zentralamt. Industrie und Gewerbestatistik Part 1 *203*
Austria. Statistisches Zentralamt. Industrie und Gewerbestatistik Part 1(AU) *203, 1049*
Austria. Statistisches Zentralamt. Jugendwohlfahrtspflege (AU) *1015*
Austria. Statistisches Zentralamt. Kindergaerten (Kindertagsheime) (AU) *422*
Austria. Statistisches Zentralamt. Mikrozensus; Jahresergebnisse (AU) *1049*
Austria. Statistisches Zentralamt. Oeffentliche Fuersorge. (AU) *1022*
Austria. Statistisches Zentralamt. Statistik der Aktiengesellschaften in Oesterreich (AU ISSN 0081-5233) *203*
Austria. Statistisches Zentralamt. Statistik der Rechtspflege (AU) *668*
Austria. Statistisches Zentralamt. Statistische Nachrichten (AU) *1049*
Austria. Zentralanstalt fuer Meteorologie und Geodynamik. Jahrbuch (AU ISSN 0067-2351) *398, 803*
Austria & Hungary Stamp Catalogue (UK ISSN 0142-9760) *874*
Austrian Export Directory *see* Herold Export-Adressbuch von Oesterreich *309*
Austrian History Newsletter *see* Austrian History Yearbook *576*
Austrian History Yearbook (US ISSN 0067-2378) *576*
Ausztraliai Magyar Ujsaf. Hungarian Weekly (AT) *501*
Author Biographics Master Index (US) *133*
Author's and Writer's Who's Who *see* International Authors and Writers Who's Who *134*
Authors in the News (US ISSN 0145-1499) *133, 715*
Auto Aftermarket Suppliers (US ISSN 0736-0452) *189, 302*
Auto Data Digest (SA) *1090*
Das Auto-International-in Zahlen/ International Auto Statistics (GW ISSN 0175-9531) *1090*
Auto-Jahr *see* Automobile Year *1090*
Auto-Katalog (GW) *1090*
Auto-Modelle *see* Auto-Katalog *1090*
Auto Nyts Leverandoerregister (DK ISSN 0106-0473) *51, 1090*
Autocatalogue (FR ISSN 0067-2424) *1090*
Autolla Ulkomaille (FI ISSN 0355-2896) *1106*
Automated Manufacturing Directory (UK ISSN 0268-1188) *355*
Automated Materials Handling and Storage (US ISSN 0739-9022) *355, 1080*
Automated Teller Machines Directory *see* A T M Directory *222*
Automatic Data Processing Information Bulletin (SZ ISSN 0379-0258) *360*

Automatic Programming Information Centre. Studies in Data Processing Series *see* A P I C Studies in Data Processing Series *357*
Automatic Support Systems Symposium for Advanced Maintainability. Proceedings *see* Autotestcon *451*
Automation Directory *see* Automated Manufacturing Directory *355*
Automation in Housing & Manufactured Home Dealer Annual Buyers' Guide (US) *622*
Automation in Housing/Systems Building News Annual Buyers' Guide *see* Automation in Housing & Manufactured Home Dealer Annual Buyers' Guide *622*
Automobile Association. Budget Guide *see* Guesthouses, Farmhouses and Inns in Britain *1110*
Automobile Association of Zimbabwe. Members' Handbook (RH) *1090*
Automobile Facts and Figures *see* M V M A Motor Vehicle Facts and Figures *1092*
Automobile in Cifre (IT) *1084*
Automobile Industry - Japan and Toyota (JA) *1090*
Automobile Legal Association Sights to See Book *see* A L A Sights to See Book *1105*
Automobile News Annual (II ISSN 0067-2548) *1090*
Automobile Year/Annee Automobile/ Auto-Jahr (SZ ISSN 0084-7674) *1090*
Automobiles: Latin American Industrial Report (US) *1090*
Automotive Age Buyer's Guide (US) *1090*
Automotive and Ancillary Industry *see* Automotive Industry of India - Facts & Figures *1090*
Automotive Applications on Microprocessors *see* I E E E Workshop on Automotive Applications of Electronics (Publication) *1093*
Automotive Body Repair News (Year) Buyers Guide and Fact Book (US) *1090*
Automotive Contact Automotive Directory. Indiana (US) *1090*
Automotive Dismantlers and Recyclers Buyers Guide/Membership Roster (US) *302*
Automotive Encyclopedia (US) *1090*
Automotive Fuel Economy Program. Annual Report to the Congress (US) *863*
Automotive Herald. Facts & Info (JA) *1090*
Automotive Industry Directory (SA) *1090*
Automotive Industry of India - Facts & Figures (II) *1090*
Automotive Literature Index (US) *1084*
Automotive News Almanac *see* Automotive News Market Data Book *1090*
Automotive News Market Data Book (US) *1090*
Automotive Products Directory *see* Automotive Industry Directory *1090*
Automotive Service Data Book (CN ISSN 0068-9629) *1090*
Automotriz (MX) *1090*
Autores Africanos (BL) *715*
Autoridades e Executivos (BL) *302, 342*
Autorisationsregister *see* Register over Autoriserede Laboratorier *782*
Autoriserede Laeger, Tandlaeger, Dyrlaeger i Danmark (DK ISSN 0108-4739) *758*
Autosprint Anno (IT) *1090*
Autotestcon/I E E E International Automatic Testing Conference (US) *451*
Autoveicoli Circolanti in Italia (IT) *1084*
Autumn School of Studies on Alcohol & Drugs. Proceedings of Seminars (AT) *335, 376*
Available from Wales *see* Wales Business Directory *237*
Avalon Dispatch (US) *740*

Avalon Foundation. Report *see* Andrew W. Mellon Foundation. Report *628*
Avances en Obstetricia y Ginecologia (SP ISSN 0210-7171) *784*
Avances en Psicologia Clinica Latinoamericana (CK ISSN 0120-3797) *933*
Avances en Terapeutica (SP ISSN 0210-3397) *869*
Avant-Siecle (FR ISSN 0067-2610) *715*
Avante (CU) *810*
Average Wage Rates of Farm Workers in the Philippines (PH) *45, 270*
Avery Index to Architectural Periodicals (US) *2, 100*
Aves del Arca (UY ISSN 0067-2637) *715*
Aviation Annual of Japan (JA) *18*
Aviation Cases in the Courts (US) *1087*
Aviation Directory of Asia (II ISSN 0067-2645) *1087*
Aviation Europe (UK ISSN 0143-1145) *18*
Aviation Focus *see* International Air Show Guide *1088*
Aviation Medical Education Series (US ISSN 0067-2661) *18, 758*
Aviation/Space Writers Association. Yearbook and Directory (US) *18*
Aviation/Space Writers Association Manual *see* Aviation/Space Writers Association. Yearbook and Directory *18*
Aviation Week & Space Technology. Marketing Directory. (US) *18*
Avionics Data Sheets *see* Directed Energy and Avionics Data Sheets *18*
Aviron (FR) *1044*
Avis-Kronik-Index *see* Dansk Artikelindeks: Aviser og Tidsskrifter *647*
Avtomatizirovannye Sistemy Upravleniya (UR) *355*
Avvenire Medico (IT) *758*
Awakener (US ISSN 0005-2388) *983*
Awards for Commonwealth University Academic Staff (UK ISSN 0144-4611) *432*
Awards for Commonwealth University Staff *see* Awards for Commonwealth University Academic Staff *432*
Awards, Honors and Prizes (US ISSN 0196-6316) *462*
Awards in the Visual Arts (US) *102, 826*
Awards to Academic Institutions by the Department of Transportation *see* U.S. Department of Transportation. Office of University Research. Awards to Academic Institutions by the Department of Transportation *1084*
Awrag *see* Awraq Yadida *576*
Awraq Yadida (SP) *576, 715*
Axbridge Archaeological and Local History Society. Journal (UK) *576*
Axe Factory Review (US) *710, 715, 822*
Ayer Directory of Publications *see* Gale Directory of Publications *126*
Azania (KE ISSN 0067-270X) *82, 565*
B A A *see* Uebersee-Museum, Bremen. Veroeffentlichungen. Reihe F: Bremer Afrika-Archiv *567*
B A A F Discussion Series (British Agencies for Adoption & Fostering) (UK ISSN 0260-082X) *1015*
B A A F News (British Agencies for Adoption & Fostering) (UK ISSN 0260-3888) *1015*
B A A F Practice Series (British Agencies for Adoption and Fostering) (UK) *1015*
B A A F Research Series (British Agencies for Adoption & Fostering) (UK) *1015*
B.A.C.A. Calendar of Cultural Events (Brooklyn Arts and Culture Association, Inc.- Brooklyn Arts Council) (US ISSN 0045-3242) *826*
B.A.I.E. Membership Directory (British Association of Industrial Editors) (UK) *302*
B A Magazine (Brooklyn Academy of Music) (US) *833*

1656 B A

B A R - B R I Bar Review. Civil Procedure (US ISSN 0099-1244) 651
B A R - B R I Bar Review. Community Property (US) 651
B A R - B R I Bar Review. Constitutional Law (US ISSN 0098-7638) 651
B A R - B R I Bar Review. Contracts (US ISSN 0098-762X) 651
B A R - B R I Bar Review. Corporations (US ISSN 0099-1236) 651
B A R-B R I Bar Review. Criminal Law(US ISSN 0098-8049) 370
B A R - B R I Bar Review. Evidence (US) 651
B A R - B R I Bar Review. Professional Responsibility (US) 652
B A R - B R I Bar Review. Real Property (US) 652
B A R - B R I Bar Review. Remedies (US ISSN 0098-7999) 652
B A R-B R I Bar Review. Torts (US ISSN 0098-7611) 370
B A R - B R I Bar Review. Trusts (US) 287
B A R - B R I Bar Review. Wills (US) 652
B A R G Bulletin see Bristol and Avon Archaeology 83
B A R G Review see Bristol and Avon Archaeology 83
B A S A see Bangladesh Agricultural Sciences Abstracts 39
B A S S Fishing Guide (Bass Anglers Sportsman Society) (US) 1044
B A S S Master Fishing Annual (Bass Anglers Sportsman Society) (US) 1044
B A T: Taschenbuch fuer den Oeffentlichen Dienst (GW ISSN 0082-1888) 939
B and C Tests see Biological and Cultural Tests for Control of Plant Diseases 155
B B C Annual Report and Handbook (British Broadcasting Corp.) (UK ISSN 0068-1377) 347
B B C Music Guides (British Broadcasting Corp. Music Guide) (US ISSN 0084-8018) 833
B.C. Association of Teachers of Classics. Newsletter see Vexillum 339
B C I R A Abstracts of International Foundry Literature see B C I R A Abstracts of International Literature on Metal Castings Production 801
B C I R A Abstracts of International Literature on Metal Castings Production (British Cast Iron Research Association (BCIRA)) (UK ISSN 0268-3393) 2, 801
B C I T Annual Report (British Columbia Institute of Technology) (CN) 1067
B C I T: The Career Campus see B C I T Annual Report 1067
B C Journal of Special Education (CN) 444
B.C. News see B.C. Peace News 914
B.C. Peace News (CN ISSN 0708-0859) 914
B.C. Research. Annual Report (CN) 988
B C S T A Convention Reporter see A G M Reporter 442
B.C. Science Teacher (CN ISSN 0381-6036) 446, 988
B C T V: Bibliography on Cable Television (US ISSN 0742-4914) 121, 347
B D E F - Jahrbuch (Bund Deutscher Eisenbahn-Freunde) (GW) 1094
B D I Alemania Suministra see B D I Deutschland Liefert 253
B D I Deutschland Liefert/B D I Germany Supplies/B D I l'Allemagne Fournit/B D I Alemania Suministra (Bundesverband der Deutschen Industrie) (GW ISSN 0415-7508) 253
B D I Germany Supplies see B D I Deutschland Liefert 253
B D I l'Allemagne Fournit see B D I Deutschland Liefert 253

B E F A R. Publication (Bibliotheque des Ecoles Francaises d'Athenes et de Rome) (FR) 83, 336
B E M A Engineering Directory (Bristol and West of England Engineering Manufacturers Association Ltd.) (UK ISSN 0067-5709) 470
B E N E L U X Economic Union. Conseil Central de l'Economie. Rapport du Secretaire sur l'Activite du Conseil (BE) 287
B F L Information see S L F Information 419
B F S S Reference Book (British Field Sports Society) (UK) 1044
B G L see Bibliothek der Griechischen Literatur 337
B.G. Rudolph Lectures in Judaic Studies (US ISSN 0067-2742) 976
B H F Directory (British Hardware Federation) (UK) 189
B.H.R.A. Fluid Engineering Series (UK) 490
B H R C A Guide to Hotels and Restaurants see Official Guide to Hotels & Restaurants in Great Britain, Ireland and Overseas 620
B I A Certification Handbook see N M M A Certification Handbook 1042
B I B E Annual Summary (International Bulletin of Bibliography on Education) (UN ISSN 0211-8335) 422
B I C-Code (Bureau International des Containers-Code) (FR) 854, 1081
B I C E R I Abstracts from Technical and Patent Publications. (British Internal Combustion Engine Research Institute Ltd.) (UK ISSN 0001-3447) 2, 476
B I G Book see Big Book 182
B I H E P (Bibliographic Index of Health Education Periodicals) (US ISSN 0278-2340) 2, 886, 952
B.I.M. Boletin del Instituto de Maternidad "Alberto Peralta Ramos" (AG) 784
B I/Memo see Saudi Arabia Market Conditions 259
B I Middle East Marketing Conditions: Egypt (Business International Corporation) (US) 253
B I Middle East Marketing Conditions: Saudi Arabia see Saudi Arabia Market Conditions 259
B I N D E Annual Report see Revista do B I N D E 232
B I/P E R S Annual Compensation Survey see B I/P E R S Executive Compensation Report 278
B I/P E R S Executive Compensation Report (Business International S A) (SZ) 278
B L A C (Black Literature and Arts Congress) (SA) 102, 501, 715
B L S-Bulletin of Literary Semiotics see Semiotic Scene 1162
B L V S see Literarischer Verein in Stuttgart. Bibliothek 726
B M C I S Building Maintenance Price Book (Building Maintenance Cost Information Service) (UK ISSN 0261-2933) 181
B M F T Risiko- und Sicherheitsforschung (Bundesministerium fuer Forschung und Technologie) (US) 952
B N A's Law Reprints: Criminal Law Series see Law Reprints: Criminal Law Series 371
B N A's Law Reprints: Labor Law Series see Law Reprints: Labor Law Series 273
B N A's Law Reprints: Patent, Trademark and Copyright Series see Law Reprints: Patent, Trademark & Copyright Series 861
B N A's Law Reprints: Securities Regulation Series see Law Reprints: Securities Regulation Series 659
B N A's Law Reprints: Trade Regulation Series see Law Reprints: Trade Regulation Series 258
B N H Relatorio de Atividades (Banco Nacional da Habitacao) (BL) 223
B.O.C.A. Basic Fire Prevention Code see B O C A Basic-National Fire Prevention Code 506

B O C A Basic Housing-Property Maintenance Code see B O C A Basic-National Existing Structures Code 181
B O C A Basic Mechanical Code see B O C A Basic-National Mechanical Code 181
B O C A Basic National Building Code (Building Officials and Code Administrators International) (US) 181, 652
B O C A Basic-National Existing Structures Code (Building Officials and Code Administrators International) (US) 181, 652
B O C A Basic-National Fire Prevention Code (Building Officials and Code Administrators International) (US) 506
B O C A Basic-National Mechanical Code (Building Officials and Code Administrators International) (US) 181, 652
B O C A Basic-National Plumbing Code (Building Officials and Code Administrators International) (US) 553, 652
B O C A Basic Plumbing Code see B O C A Basic-National Plumbing Code 553
B O M A Experience Exchange Report (Building Owners and Managers Association International) (US ISSN 0738-2170) 278, 965
B O M A International Convention Directory (Building Owners and Managers Association International) (US) 795
B.O.P.I. Statistiques (Bulletin Officiel de la Propriete Industrielle) (FR) 860
B/P A A Membership Directory and Yellow Pages (Business Professional Advertising Association) (US) 15, 343
B P C (Building Products Catalog) see Hutton's Building Products Catalog 184
B P R see American Book Publishing Record 963
B P Statistical Review of World Energy (British Petroleum Co. p.l.c.) (UK) 863
B R A D S (Bollettino del Repertorio e dell'Atlante Demologico Sardo) (IT ISSN 0067-9860) 515
B R I Research Papers/Kenchiku Kenkyusho Chosa Shiken Kenkyu Gaiyo Hokoku (Building Research Institute) (JA ISSN 0453-4972) 181
B.R.M.A. Directory Rubber and Polyurethane (British Rubber Manufacturers' Association Ltd.) (UK ISSN 0266-397X) 985
B S Handbook 3. Summaries of British Standards for Building (UK) 181, 480
B S I Catalogue (UK) 808
B S R I A Application Guides (Building Services Research and Information Association) (UK ISSN 0305-5973) 553
B S R I A Technical Notes (Building Services Research and Information Association) (UK ISSN 0309-0248) 553
B T A Studycards (British Trade Alphabet) (UK) 15
B T B (Branchevejviser for Traelast og Byggemarkeder) (DK ISSN 0107-6779) 181
B T H A Buyers Guide (British Toy & Hobby Manufacturers Association) (UK) 283, 552, 614
B W P A Magazine (British Women Pilots Association) (UK) 18, 1128
Baad Jul (DK) 1148
Baad - Revyen (DK) 1041
Baas Becking Geobiological Laboratory. Annual Report (AT ISSN 0572-5860) 168, 384
Babesch see Bulletin Antieke Beschaving 555
Baby Book (UK) 333
Baccalaureate Education in Nursing: Key to a Professional Career in Nursing (US ISSN 0069-5602) 432, 783

Bach-Jahrbuch (GE ISSN 0084-7682) 833
Background Notes on the Countries of the World (US ISSN 0501-9966) 541
Backgrounder see Asian Studies Center Backgrounder 501
Backgrounder Updates (US) 939
Backstage T V Film/Tape & Syndication Directory (US ISSN 0098-5481) 347, 822
Baconiana (UK) 710
Bacon's International Publicity Checker(US ISSN 0161-4363) 15
Bacon's Publicity Checker (US ISSN 0162-3125) 16
Bacteriological Proceedings see American Society for Microbiology. Abstracts of the Annual Meeting 167
Bad Breath see So and So Magazine 744
Badania Fizjograficzne nad Polska Zachodnia. Seria A. Geografia Fizyczna (PL ISSN 0067-2807) 541
Badania Fizjograficzne nad Polska Zachodnia. Seria B. Biologia see Badania Fizjograficzne nad Polska Zachodnia. Seria B. Botanika 154
Badania Fizjograficzne nad Polska Zachodnia. Seria B. Botanika (PL) 154
Badania Fizjograficzne nad Polska Zachodnia. Seria C. Zoologia (PL ISSN 0137-6683) 173
Badania z Dziejow Spolecznych i Gospodarczych (PL ISSN 0067-2793) 576
Die Badeplaetze in Daenemark (GW) 1106
Die Badeplaetze in Jugoslawien (GW) 1106
Badische Biographien Neue Folge (GW) 576
Badischer Landesverein fuer Naturkunde und Naturschutz, Freiburg. Mitteilungen. Neue Folge (GW ISSN 0067-2858) 138, 384
Badminton (GW) 1037
Badminton Association of England. Annual Handbook (UK ISSN 0262-1940) 1032
Badminton Association of England. Official Handbook see Badminton Association of England. Annual Handbook 1032
Badminton Ireland (IE) 1032
Badminton Jul see Badminton Revy 1033
Badminton Revy (DK ISSN 0107-766X) 1033
Badminton Sporting Diary (UK) 1033
Der Baer von Berlin (GW ISSN 0522-0033) 576
Baetica (SP) 102, 541, 576
Baghdader Mitteilungen (GW ISSN 0418-9698) 83
Bagnoguida (IT) 643
Baha'i Studies (CN ISSN 0708-5052) 967
Baha'i World (IS ISSN 0045-1320) 968
Bahamas. Chamber of Commerce. Annual Directory (BF) 234
Bahamas. Department of Statistics. Annual Review of Prices: Report (BF) 203
Bahamas. Department of Statistics. External Trade (BF) 203
Bahamas. Department of Statistics. Household Income Report (BF) 203
Bahamas. Department of Statistics. Labour Force and Income Distribution see Bahamas. Department of Statistics. Household Income Report 203
Bahamas. Department of Statistics. Statistical Abstract (BF) 1049
Bahamas. Ministry of Education and Culture. Annual Report (BF) 411
Bahamas. Ministry of Works and Utilities. Annual Report (BF) 480
Bahamas. Ministry of Works. Annual Report see Bahamas. Ministry of Works and Utilities. Annual Report 480
Bahamas. Port and Marine Department. Ministry of Transport. Annual Report (BF) 1099

Bahamas Family Islands Travel Guide (BF) 1106
Bahamas Handbook (BF) 241
Bahamas Handbook and Businessman's Annual see Bahamas Handbook 241
Bahamas Out Islands Travel Guide see Bahamas Family Islands Travel Guide 1106
Bahia, Brazil (State). Centro de Estatistica e Informacoes. Anuario Estatistico (BL) 1049
Bahrain. Monetary Agency. Annual Report (BA) 293
Bahrain Trade Directory (BA ISSN 0408-215X) 302
Bahubacana (BG) 1076
Baileya (US ISSN 0005-4003) 154, 531
Bailliere's Handbook of First Aid (UK) 758
Bailliere's Midwives' Dictionary (UK) 784
Bailliere's Nurses' Dictionary (UK) 783
Bailliere's Pocket Book of Ward Information (UK) 783
Bailrigg Papers on International Security (UK) 374, 669, 914
Baily's Hunting Directory (UK ISSN 0067-2947) 1044
Baja California Travels Series (US ISSN 0067-2955) 603, 1106
Baker Series in Chemistry (US) 321
Bakery Production and Marketing Red Book (US) 522
Baking Directory/Buyers Guide (US) 63, 302
Bakunin-Archiv see Archives Bakounine 575
Balai Pendidikan Dan Latihan Tenaga Social. Laporan (IO) 446, 1015
Balai Penelitian Perkebunan, Bogor. Statistik Coklat see Research Institute for Estate Crops, Bogor. Cocoa Statistics 59
Balai Penelitian Perkebunan, Bogor. Statistik Karet see Research Institute for Estate Crops, Bogor. Rubber Statistics 59
Balai Penelitian Perkebunan, Bogor. Statistik Kopi see Research Institute for Estate Crops, Bogor. Coffee Statistics 59
Balance of Payments of Barbados see Central Bank of Barbados. Balance of Payments 206
Balance of Payments of Jamaica (JM) 253
Balance of Payments of Sierra Leone (SL ISSN 0067-2998) 253, 293
Balance of Payments of Trinidad and Tobago (TR ISSN 0067-3005) 253, 293
Balance of Payments Yearbook see International Monetary Fund. Balance of Payments Statistics 277
Balance Suisse des Paiements see Zahlungsbilanz der Schweiz 300
Balance Wheel for Accreditation (US) 432
Balanco Energetico Nacional (BL ISSN 0101-6636) 464
Balanza de Pagos de Espana (SP ISSN 0067-3021) 253, 293
Balcanica (YU) 576
Baldwin Lectures (US) 411
Baldwin Lectures in Teacher Education see Baldwin Lectures 411
Baldwin's Ohio Legislative Service (US ISSN 0092-0959) 939
Bale Catalogue of Israel Postage Stamps(UK) 874
Bale Catalogue of Palestine and Israel Stamps see Bale Catalogue of Israel Postage Stamps 874
Balkan-Archiv Neue Folge (GW ISSN 0170-8007) 691
Balkan-Archiv Neue Folge Beiheft (GW ISSN 0720-0994) 691
Balkanika Symmeikta (GR) 576
Balkanistica (US ISSN 0360-2206) 1148
Balkanologische Veroeffentlichungen see Freie Universitaet Berlin. Osteuropa-Institut. Balkanologische Veroeffentlichungen 695
Balkans Stamp Catalogue (UK ISSN 0142-9779) 874
Balkanskie Issledovaniya (UR) 576

Ball State Monographs (US ISSN 0073-6821) 628
Ballena Press Anthropological Papers (US) 70
Ballon Kurier (GW ISSN 0005-4364) 874
Ballroom Dancing Year Book see Dancing Year Book 375
Balskrishnan - Neustadt Series (US) 747, 1067
Baltic Philology see Filologia Baltycka 694
Baltica (UR ISSN 0067-3064) 384
Baltimore/Annapolis (Year) (US) 603
Baltische Hefte (GW ISSN 0005-4534) 576
Baltische Studien (GW ISSN 0067-3099) 576
Bamah (IS) 774
Bamladesa Arthanaitika Jaripa (BG) 191
Bampton Lectures in America (US ISSN 0067-3129) 102, 603, 968
Banana Rag (US) 1148
Banaras Metallurgist (II) 797
Banas (BL ISSN 0005-4585) 223
Banas-Classificado Industrial Brasileiro see Banas 223
Banas Informa see Banas 223
Banbury Reports (US ISSN 0198-0068) 138
Banbury Reports Series see Banbury Reports 138
Banca d'Italia. Assemblea Generale Ordinaria dei Partecipanti. (IT ISSN 0067-3161) 223
Banca d'Italia. Contributi alla Analisi Economica (IT) 241, 251
Banca d'Italia. Contributi alla Ricerca Economica see Banca d'Italia. Contributi alla Analisi Economica 241
Banca d'Italia. Servizio Studi. Temi di Discussione (IT) 223
Banca Nazionale del Lavoro. Condensed Statement of Condition (IT) 241
Banca Romana de Comert Exterior. Annual Bulletin (RM) 223, 253
Banco Agrario del Peru. Memoria (PE) 45
Banco Agricola y Pecuario. Informe see Instituto de Credito Agricola y Pecuario. Informe Annual 245
Banco Central de Chile, Santiago. Memoria Anual (CL ISSN 0716-2448) 223, 241
Banco Central de Costa Rica. Balanza de Pagos (CR) 241
Banco Central de Costa Rica. Estadisticas Economicas (CR ISSN 0522-098X) 203
Banco Central de Costa Rica. Informacion Economica Semanal (CR ISSN 0408-3172) 241
Banco Central de Costa Rica. Memoria Anual (CR ISSN 0067-320X) 223
Banco Central de Costa Rica. Serie "Comentarios sobre Asuntos Economicos" (CR) 241
Banco Central de Ecuador. Memoria Anual de Actividades see Banco Central del Ecuador. Boletin-Anuario 241
Banco Central de Honduras. Informe Economico (HO) 241
Banco Central de Honduras. Memoria (HO ISSN 0067-3218) 241
Banco Central de Honduras. Seccion de Seguros. Boletin de Estadisticas de Seguros (HO) 203, 642
Banco Central de la Republica Argentina. Centro de Estudios Monetarios y Bancarios. Discussion Paper (AG) 223
Banco Central de la Republica Argentina. Centro de Estudios Monetarios y Bancarios. Serie de Computacion (AG) 223
Banco Central de la Republica Argentina. Centro de Estudios Monetarios y Bancarios. Serie de Estudios Tecnicos (AG) 223
Banco Central de la Republica Argentina. Centro de Estudios Monetarios y Bancarios. Serie de Informacion Publica (AG) 223
Banco Central de la Republica Dominicana. Memoria (DR) 223

Banco Central de Nicaragua. Biblioteca y Servicios de Informacion. Barricada Indice Tematico y Onomastico (NQ) 223
Banco Central de Nicaragua. Boletin Anual (NQ) 223
Banco Central de Nicaragua. Boletin Semestral see Banco Central de Nicaragua. Boletin Anual 223
Banco Central de Nicaragua. Boletin Trimestral see Banco Central de Nicaragua. Boletin Anual 223
Banco Central de Nicaragua. Comercio Exterior de Nicaragua Por Productos y Paises (NQ) 253
Banco Central de Nicaragua. Departmento de Estudios Economicos. Indicadores Economicos(NQ) 241
Banco Central de Nicaragua. Informe Anual (NQ ISSN 0067-3226) 223
Banco Central de Reserva de el Salvador. Memoria (ES) 223
Banco Central de Reserva del Peru. Memoria (PE) 223
Banco Central de Venezuela. Anuario de Cuentas Nacionales (VE) 223
Banco Central de Venezuela. Informe Economico (VE ISSN 0067-3250) 241
Banco Central de Venezuela. Memoria (VE ISSN 0067-3269) 223
Banco Central de Venezuela. Seccion A.L.A.L.C. Algunas Estadisticas de los Paises de A.L.A.L.C. (Seccion Asociacion Latinoamericana de Libre Comercio) (VE ISSN 0522-1153) 203
Banco Central del Ecuador. Acuerdos Internacionales de Comercio y Pagos(EC) 253
Banco Central del Ecuador. Balanza de Pagos (EC) 204, 223
Banco Central del Ecuador. Boletin-Anuario (EC) 241
Banco Central del Ecuador. Division Tecnica. Cuentas Nacionales del Ecuador (EC) 241
Banco Central del Ecuador. Memoria del Gerente General (EC ISSN 0067-3277) 223
Banco Central del Paraguay. Memoria (PY ISSN 0067-3285) 223
Banco Central del Uruguay. Departamento de Estadisticas Economicas. Producto e Ingreso Nacionales (UY) 277
Banco Central del Uruguay. Division Asesoria Economica y Estudios. Producto e Ingreso Nacionales. Actualizacion de las Principales Variables see Banco Central del Uruguay. Departamento de Estadisticas Economicas. Producto e Ingreso Nacionales 277
Banco Central del Uruguay. Indicadores de la Actividad Economico-Financiera (UY) 241
Banco Central del Uruguay. Resena de la Actividad Economico-Financiera (UY) 223
Banco da Amazonia. Centro de Documentacao e Biblioteca. Contexto Boletim (BL) 1148
Banco de Bibliografias (BL ISSN 0101-0697) 24
Banco de Bilbao. Agenda Financiera (SP) 223
Banco de Bilbao. Economic Report (SP) 241
Banco de Bilbao. Informe Economico (SP ISSN 0522-1315) 241
Banco de Bilbao. Informe - Memoria (SP) 223
Banco de Bilbao. Memoria see Banco de Bilbao. Informe - Memoria 223
Banco de Desenvolvimento do Parana. Information on Parana see Information on Parana 245
Banco de Espana. Estudios de Historia Economia (SP) 251
Banco de Espana. Informe Anual (SP ISSN 0522-3315) 223
Banco de Financiacion Industrial. Banca Privada (SP) 1148
Banco de Guatemala. Estadisticas del Sector Externo (GT) 241

Banco de Guatemala. Estudio Economico y Memoria de Labores (GT) 223
Banco de la Republica. Biblioteca Luis Angel Arango. Boletin Cultural y Bibliografico (CK ISSN 0006-6184) 121, 628
Banco de la Republica. Bogota. Registros de Importaciones see Banco de la Republica. Registros de Exportacion e Importacion 1148
Banco de la Republica. Registros de Exportacion e Importacion (CK ISSN 0302-9611) 1148
Banco de Mexico. Informe Anual (MX ISSN 0067-3374) 223, 241
Banco do Brasil. Annual Report (BL ISSN 0101-0646) 223
Banco do Estado de Pernambuco. BANDEPE Relatorio (BL) 223
Banco do Nordeste do Brasil. Serie Estudos Economicos e Sociais (BL) 241
Banco Minero de Bolivia. Memoria (BO) 223
Banco Nacional da Habitacao. Assessoria Tecnica de Documentacao. Boletim Bibliografico(BL) 627
Banco Nacional da Habitacao. Relatorio de Atividades (BL) 622
Banco Nacional da Habitacao Linhas de Financiamento do B N H see Linhas de Financiamento do B N H 230
Banco Nacional da Habitacao Relatorio de Atividades see B N H Relatorio de Atividades 223
Banco Nacional de Comercio Exterior, Mexico. Annual Report (MX) 223
Banco Nacional de Desarrollo Agricola. Memoria Anual (HO) 223
Banco Nacional de Fomento. Informe de Labores (EC) 241
Banco Nacional de Fomento, Tegucigalpa. Memoria Anual see Banco Nacional de Desarrollo Agricola. Memoria Anual 223
Banco Nacional de Panama. Asesoria Economica. Memoria Anual (PN) 223
Banco Nacional de Panama. Asesoria Economica y Planificacion. Carta Economica (PN) 242
Banco Nacional de Panama. Informacion Economica y Financiera de la Republica de Panama (PN) 293
Banco Nacional de Panama. Informe del Gerente General (PN) 223
Banco Nacional do Desenvolvimento Economico. Annual Report (BL) 223
Banco Nacional do Desenvolvimento Economico. Plan of Action see Banco Nacional do Desenvolvimento Economico. Plano de Acao 287
Banco Nacional do Desenvolvimento Economico. Plano de Acao/Banco Nacional do Desenvolvimento Economico. Plan of Action (BL) 287
Banco Nacional do Desenvolvimento Economico. Relatorio Anual see Revista do B I N D E 232
Banco Nacional do Desenvolvimento Economico. Relatorio das Atividades(BL) 242
Banco Nacional do Desenvolvimento Economico Revista do B I N D E see Revista do B I N D E 232
Banco Paraguayo de Datos Cuadernos B P D. Serie: Economia see Cuadernos B P D. Serie: Economia 193
Banco Paraguayo de Datos Cuadernos B P D. Serie: Social see Cuadernos B P D. Serie: Social 1025
Banco Regional de Desenvolvimento do Extremo Sul. Annual Report (BL) 242
Banco Regional de Desenvolvimento do Extremo Sul. Relatorio Annal see Banco Regional de Desenvolvimento do Extremo Sul. Annual Report 242
Banco Regional de Desenvolvimento do Extremo Sul. Relatorio da Directoria see Banco Regional de Desenvolvimento do Extremo Sul. Annual Report 242

Banco Sindical. Memoria y Balance General (AG) 223
Bancoseguros see Seguros 641
Bancroftiana (US ISSN 0067-3412) 674
Band Music Guide (US ISSN 0084-7704) 833
Bandersnatch (UK ISSN 0306-8404) 715
Bangiya Sahityakosha (II) 121
Bangkok, Thailand. College of Education. Thesis Abstract Series (TH ISSN 0067-3498) 422
Bangladesh. Directorate of Agricultural Marketing. Agricultural Marketing Series (BG ISSN 0070-8143) 45
Bangladesh. Directorate of Agriculture. Season and Crop Report (BG ISSN 0070-8151) 52
Bangladesh. Education Directorate. Report on Pilot Project on Adult Education (BG ISSN 0070-8135) 426
Bangladesh. Ministry of Foreign Affairs. List of the Diplomatic Corps and Other Foreign Representatives (BG) 939
Bangladesh. Planning Commission. Annual Development Programme (BG) 242
Bangladesh Agricultural Sciences Abstracts (BG) 2, 39
Bangladesh Association for Voluntary Sterilization. Annual Report (BG) 179
Bangladesh Bank. Annual Report (BG) 223
Bangladesh Bank. Statistics Department. Annual Balance of Payments (BG) 204, 253, 293, 1049
Bangladesh Bank. Statistics Department. Annual Import Payments. (BG) 204
Bangladesh Directory and Year Book (II) 302
Bangladesh Economic Survey see Bamladesa Arthanaitika Jaripa 191
Bangladesh Forest Industries Development Corporation. Annual Report (BG) 529
Bangladesh Itihas Samiti. Journal/ Itihasa Samiti Patrika (BG) 568
Bangladesh Jatiya Ainjibi Samity. Annual Law Journal see Bangladesh Jatiya Ainjibi Samity Souvenir 652
Bangladesh Jatiya Ainjibi Samity Souvenir (BG) 652
Bangladesh National Bibliography (BG) 122
Bangladesh Political Studies (BG) 902
Bangladesh Research and Evaluation Centre. Report (BG ISSN 0070-8178) 1024
Bangladesh Rice Research Institute. Annual Report (BG) 52
Bangladesh Science Conference. Proceedings (BG) 988
Bangladesh Sugar Mills Corporation. Annual Report (BG) 518
Bangladesh Tea Research Institute. Annual Report (BG) 24
Bangladesh University of Engineering and Technology, Dacca. Technical Journal (BG ISSN 0070-8186) 470
Bangor Occasional Papers in Economics(UK ISSN 0306-9338) 191
Bangsbomuseet. Aarbog (DK ISSN 0109-8489) 826
Banicke Listy/Folia Montana (CS) 814
Bank (DK ISSN 0108-7177) 223
Bank al-Inma al-Sinai. Annual Report and Balance Sheet see Industrial Development Bank. Annual Report and Balance Sheet 229
Bank Al-Markazi Al-Urduni. Annual Report see Central Bank of Jordan. Annual Report 226
Bank Brussel Lambert. Annual Reports see Banque de Bruxelles Lambert. Rapports de l'Exercice 225
Bank Directory of Canada (CN ISSN 0045-1436) 223
Bank Directory of New England (US) 224
Bank Directory of the Ninth Federal Reserve District (US) 224
Bank Ekspor Impor Indonesia. Annual Report/Laporan Tahunan (IO ISSN 0302-6795) 224

Bank Facts: Chartered Banks of Canada(CN) 224
Bank for International Settlements. Annual Report (SZ ISSN 0067-3560) 224
Bank Guide (PK) 224
Bank Ha-Sapanut le-Yisrael. Annual Report. see Maritime Bank of Israel. Annual Report 230
Bank Holding Company Facts (US ISSN 0519-1572) 224
Bank Income Tax Return Manual (US) 224, 293, 652
Bank Leumi Economic Review see Leumi Review 246
Bank Leumi Israel Macroperspectives see Leumi Review 246
Bank Microcomputer Directory (US) 1148
Bank of Canada. Annual Report (CN ISSN 0067-3587) 224
Bank of Canada. Staff Research Studies see Bank of Canada. Technical Reports 224
Bank of Canada. Technical Reports (CN ISSN 0713-7931) 224
Bank of Ceylon. Annual Report see Bank of Ceylon. Annual Report and Accounts 224
Bank of Ceylon. Annual Report and Accounts (CE) 224
Bank of England. Report see Bank of England. Report and Accounts 224
Bank of England. Report and Accounts (UK ISSN 0308-5279) 224
Bank of Finland. Annual Statement (FI ISSN 0081-945X) 224
Bank of Finland. Publications. Series A see Suomen Pankki. Julkaisuja. Sarja A 200
Bank of Finland. Publications. Series B see Suomen Pankki. Julkaisuja. Sarja B 200
Bank of Finland. Publications. Series C see Suomen Pankki. Julkaisuja. Sarja C 200
Bank of Finland. Publications. Series D see Suomen Pankki. Julkaisuja. Sarja D 200
Bank of Finland. Publications. Studies on Finland's Economic Growth see Suomen Pankki. Julkaisuja. Kasvututkimuksia 292
Bank of Finland. Yearbook (FI ISSN 0081-9468) 224
Bank of Israel. Annual Report (IS ISSN 0067-365X) 224
Bank of Israel. Annual Statistics of Israel's Banking System (IS ISSN 0334-4541) 204, 224
Bank of Israel. Bulletin see Bank of Israel. Economic Review 242
Bank of Israel. Economic Review (IS) 224, 242
Bank of Israel. Israel's Banking System (IS ISSN 0334-2093) 224
Bank of Israel. Main Points of the Annual Report (IS ISSN 0067-3641) 224
Bank of Jamaica. Report and Statement of Accounts (JM ISSN 0067-3668) 224
Bank of Japan. Annual Report (JA) 224
Bank of Japan. Annual Report of the Policy Board see Bank of Japan. Annual Report 224
Bank of Japan. Economic Statistics Annual (JA ISSN 0070-8666) 204
Bank of Japan. Export and Import Price Indexes Annual see Bank of Japan. Price Indexes Annual 253
Bank of Japan. Price Indexes Annual (JA) 253
Bank of Japan. Special Paper (JA ISSN 0067-3692) 242
Bank of Korea. Annual Report (KO ISSN 0067-3706) 224
Bank of Libya. Annual Report of the Board of Directors (LY ISSN 0067-3714) 242
Bank of Libya. Balance of Payments (LY ISSN 0075-921X) 253, 293
Bank of Mauritius. Annual Report (MF ISSN 0067-3722) 224
Bank of Papua New Guinea. Report and Financial Statements (PP) 224
Bank of Seoul and Trust Company. Economic Review (KO) 224

Bank of Sierra Leone. Annual Report see Bank of Sierra Leone. Annual Report and Statement of Accounts 224
Bank of Sierra Leone. Annual Report and Statement of Accounts (SL) 224
Bank of Sudan. Foreign Trade Statistical Digest (SJ ISSN 0522-246X) 204
Bank of Sudan. Report (SJ ISSN 0067-3749) 224
Bank of Tanzania. Economic and Operations Report (TZ ISSN 0067-3757) 224, 242
Bank of Tanzania. Economic Report see Bank of Tanzania. Economic and Operations Report 242
Bank of Thailand. Annual Economic Report (TH ISSN 0067-3773) 242
Bank of Thailand. Paper (TH) 242
Bank of Tokyo Annual Report (JA) 224
Bank of Tokyo Semiannual Report see Bank of Tokyo Annual Report 224
Bank of Tonga. Annual Report (TO) 224
Bank of Zambia. Report and Statement of Accounts (ZA) 224
Bank Pembangunan Indonesia. Annual Report (IO ISSN 0408-4632) 224
Bank Sorting Code Numbers (UK) 224
Bankangestellte see Deutsches Banken-Handbuch (Year) 227
Banker og Sparekasser (DK ISSN 0108-9129) 224
Bankers Almanac and Year Book (UK ISSN 0067-379X) 224
Bankers' Almanac World Ranking (UK) 224
Bankers Diary and Guide (US) 224
Bankers Handbook for Asia (HK) 224
Bankers' Who's Who (II ISSN 0067-3803) 224
Banking Guides - Asia, Australia, New Zealand with Principal Hotels and Bank Holidays (US) 224
Banking in the E E C (UK) 224
Banking: Latin American Industrial Report (US) 224
Banking Law Anthology (US ISSN 0737-2159) 224, 652
Banking Law Journal Digest (Supplement) (US) 224, 652
Banking Statistics of Pakistan (PK ISSN 0067-3811) 225
Banking Structures and Sources of Finance in the European Community see Banking in the E E C 224
Banking Structures and Sources of Finance in the Far East (UK) 225
Bankin'Ny Indostria. Rapport Annuel (MG) 225
Banks and Financial Institutions in Singapore (SI) 225
Bankwirtschaftliche Forschungen (SZ ISSN 0067-382X) 225
Banque Africaine de Developpement. Rapport Annuel see African Development Bank. Report by the Board of Directors 261
Banque Africaine de Developpement. Rapport du Conseil d'Administration see African Development Bank. Report by the Board of Directors 261
Banque Centrale de Tunisie. Bulletin (TI ISSN 0067-3854) 225
Banque Centrale de Tunisie. Rapport d'Activite (TI ISSN 0067-3862) 225
Banque Centrale des Etats de l'Afrique de l'Ouest. Rapport Annuel (SG ISSN 0067-3889) 225
Banque Centrale des Etats de l'Afrique de l'Ouest. Rapport d'Activite. (SG ISSN 0067-3897) 225
Banque Commerciale Zairoise. Reports and Balance Sheets (ZR) 225
Banque de Bruxelles. Rapport Annuel see Banque de Bruxelles Lambert. Rapports de l'Exercice 225
Banque de Bruxelles Lambert. Rapports de l'Exercice/Bank Brussel Lambert. Annual Reports (BE) 225
Banque de Credit de Bujumbura. Rapports et Bilan (BD) 225

Banque de France. Comite Monetaire de la Zone Franc. Secretariat. Rapport see Banque de France. La Zone Franc en (Year) 242
Banque de France. Compte-Rendu (FR ISSN 0067-3927) 225
Banque de France. Direction de la Conjoncture. Situation Financiere des Regions En (Year) (FR) 242
Banque de France. Direction de la Conjoncture. Structure et Evolution Financiere des Regions de Province see Banque de France. Direction de la Conjoncture. Situation Financiere des Regions En (Year) 242
Banque de France. La Zone Franc en (Year) (FR) 242
Banque de la Republique du Burundi. Rapport Annuel (BD ISSN 0067-3935) 225
Banque des Etats de l'Afrique Centrale. Rapport d'Activite (CM ISSN 0067-3900) 225
Banque du Maroc. Rapport Annuel (MR ISSN 0067-396X) 225
Banque du Zaire. Rapport Annuel (ZR ISSN 0300-1172) 225
Banque Internationale a Luxembourg. Cahiers Economiques (LU) 242
Banque Internationale pour l'Afrique Occidentale. Conseil d'Administration. Rapport et Resolutions, Rapport des Commissaires aux Comptes (FR) 242
Banque Marocaine du Commerce Exterieur. Annual Report (MR) 225
Banque Nationale de Belgique. Rapport sur les Operations (BE ISSN 0067-3978) 225
Banque Nationale de Developpement Economique du Burundi. Rapport Annuel (BD) 225
Banque Nationale du Congo. Rapport Annuel see Banque du Zaire. Rapport Annuel 225
Banque Nationale du Rwanda. Rapport Annuel see Banque Nationale du Rwanda. Rapport d'Activites 225
Banque Nationale du Rwanda. Rapport d'Activites (RW) 225
Banque Nationale Malagasy de Developpement. Rapport d'Activite see Bankin'Ny Indostria. Rapport Annuel 225
Banque Nationale pour le Developpement Economique. Rapport Annuel (MR) 287
Banque Nationale pour le Developpement Rural. Rapport Annuel (MG) 225
Banque Rwandaise de Developpement. Rapport Annuel (RW) 225
Banque Togolaise de Developpement. Rapport Annuel see Banque Togolaise de Developpement. Rapport d'Activites 225
Banque Togolaise de Developpement. Rapport d'Activites (TG) 225
Bantu Treasury (SA ISSN 0067-4044) 715
Banyaszati Szakirodalmi Tajekoztato/ Mining Abstracts (HU ISSN 0231-0651) 2, 814, 821
Baor Hatorah (IS) 976
Baptist Missionary Association of America. Directory and Handbook (US ISSN 0091-2743) 978
Baptist Missionary Society, London. Annual Report (UK ISSN 0067-4060) 978
Baptist Missionary Society, London. Official Report and Directory of Missionaries (UK ISSN 0067-4079) 978
Baptist Union Directory (UK ISSN 0302-3184) 978
Baptist Union of Western Canada. Yearbook (CN ISSN 0067-4087) 978
Baptist World Alliance. Congress Reports (US ISSN 0067-4095) 978
Baptist Yearbook (CN) 978, 1049
Bar-Ilan: Annual of Bar-Ilan University (IS ISSN 0067-4109) 976, 1006
Bar Ilan Law Studies (IS) 652
Bar-Ilan University. Studies in Judaica and the Humanities see Bar-Ilan: Annual of Bar-Ilan University 976

Barbacane (FR) 102, *715*
Barbados. Export Directory (BB) *302*
Barbados. Ministry of Finance and Planning. Economic Report (BB) *242*
Barbados. Ministry of Health and Community Services. Chief Medical Officer. Annual Report (BB) *952*
Barbados. Ministry of Health and Welfare. Chief Medical Officer. Annual Report *see* Barbados. Ministry of Health and Community Services. Chief Medical Officer. Annual Report *952*
Barbados. Parks and Beaches Commission. Annual Report (BB) *1106*
Barbados. Registration Office. Report on Vital Statistics & Registrations (BB) *926, 948*
Barbados. Statistical Service. Digest of Tourism Statistics. (BB) *1119*
Barbados. Statistical Service. Overseas Trade Report (BB ISSN 0067-4125) *2, 204*
Barbados Museum and Historical Society. Journal (BB ISSN 0005-5891) *102, 603*
Barbados National Bank. Annual Report & Statement of Accounts (BB) *225*
Barbados Nursing Journal (BB ISSN 0572-6042) *783*
Barbados Tourist Board. Annual Report(BB) *1106*
Barbara Woodhouse Animal Annual (UK) *868*
Barbour Compendium Building Products (UK ISSN 0260-9169) *181, 643*
Barcelona Port (SP) *1099*
Barclays Country Reports (UK ISSN 0307-4552) *242*
Bardsey Observatory Report (UK ISSN 0408-5655) *138, 170*
Bargain Paradises of the World *see* Retirement Paradises of the World *1116*
Bargain Shopper's Guide to Melbourne (AT) *239, 368*
Bargain Shoppers Guide to Sydney (AT) *239, 368*
Barkai (IS ISSN 0334-1380) *976*
Die Barke (AU ISSN 0067-4206) *335, 715*
Barker-Joslyn Family Tree Climber (US) *535*
Barley Genetics Newsletter (US) *154*
Barne og Ungdomslitteratur. Utvalg av Boker Utkommeti (NO) *335*
Barnwood (US) *710*
Baroda Reporter (II) *920*
Baroque (FR ISSN 0067-4222) *716*
Barque's Pakistan Trade Directory and Who's Who (PK ISSN 0067-4230) *302*
Barrett Branches (US) *535*
Barrister (NR ISSN 0331-0086) *652*
Barron's Guide to Graduate Business Schools (US) *191, 432*
Barron's Guide to Graduate Business Schools: Eastern Edition *see* Barron's Guide to Graduate Business Schools *432*
Barron's Index (US) *2, 204*
Barron's Profiles of American Colleges. Vol. 1: Descriptions of the Colleges (US) *428*
Barron's Profiles of American Colleges. Vol. 2: Index to Major Areas of Study (US ISSN 0533-1072) *428*
Barrow Docks and Silloth Dock Tidal Predictions (UK) *1099*
Barry Fain's Private Blue Book of Gun Values *see* Blue Book of Gun Values *1033*
Barshika Bibarani Bayaska Siksha Parikshya Prakalpa Bangladesh *see* Bangladesh. Education Directorate. Report on Pilot Project on Adult Education *426*
Barshika Unnayana Karmasuci *see* Bangladesh. Planning Commission. Annual Development Programme *242*
Bartonia (US ISSN 0198-7356) *154*
Baseball Case Book (US ISSN 0270-4218) *1037*
Baseball Forecast (Year) (US) *1037*

Baseball Guide (US ISSN 0067-4273) *1037*
Baseball Historical Review (US) *1037*
Baseball Illustrated (Year) (US) *1037*
Baseball Preview (Year) (US) *1037*
Baseball Register *see* Official Baseball Register *1039*
Baseball Research Journal (US ISSN 0734-6891) *1037*
Baseball Rulebook (US) *1037*
Baseball Umpires Manual (US) *1037*
Basebook (US ISSN 0093-8025) *287*
Basel Africa Bibliography. Communications *see* Basler Afrika Bibliographien. Mitteilungen *565*
Basel Institute for Immunology. Annual Report (SZ ISSN 0301-3782) *773*
Bashavil Harefuah (IS) *758, 976*
Basic & Clinical Endocrinology (US) *781*
Basic and Clinical Nutrition (US) *846*
Basic Auto Repair Manual (US ISSN 0067-4338) *1148*
Basic Bodywork and Painting (US ISSN 0067-4362) *1148*
Basic Cams, Valves and Exhaust Systems (US ISSN 0067-4370) *1148*
Basic Chassis, Suspension and Brakes (US ISSN 0067-4397) *1148*
Basic Clutches and Transmissions (US ISSN 0067-4400) *1148*
Basic Collection of Science and Technology Books *see* Science and Technology (Pittsburgh) *683*
Basic Concepts in Educational Psychology Series (US) *411, 933*
Basic Concepts in Psychology Series (US) *411, 933*
Basic Economic Data for Idaho (US ISSN 0094-1115) *242*
Basic Facts about the United Nations (UN ISSN 0067-4419) *914*
Basic Ignition and Electrical Systems (US ISSN 0067-4427) *1148*
Basic Life Sciences (US ISSN 0090-5542) *138*
Basic Port Statistics of India (II) *1099*
Basic Road Statistics of India (II ISSN 0067-6462) *1084*
Basic Software (SZ) *362*
Basistexte Personalwesen (GW ISSN 0174-6200) *286*
Basketball Annual (Year) (US) *1037*
Basketball Case Book (US ISSN 0525-4663) *1037*
Basketball Forecast (Year) (US) *1037*
Basketball Guide, with Official Rules and Standards *see* N A G W S Guide. Basketball *1158*
Basketball Handbook (US) *1037*
Basketball Officials Manual (US ISSN 0270-4226) *1037*
Basketball Rulebook *see* Basketball - Simplified & Illustrated Rules *1037*
Basketball - Simplified & Illustrated Rules (US) *1037*
Basketball Statisticians' Manual (US) *1037*
Basler Afrika Bibliographien. Mitteilungen/Basel Africa Bibliography. Communications (SZ ISSN 0170-5091) *565*
Basler Beitraege zur Geographie (SZ ISSN 0067-4486) *541*
Basler Beitraege zur Geschichtswissenschaft (SZ) *555*
Basler Effektenboerse. Jahresbericht/ Rapport Annuel/Annual Report (SZ) *265*
Basler Geometodisches Colloquium. Veroeffentlichungen/Basel Geomethodological Meeting. Proceedings *see* Geomethodica *379*
Basler Studien zur Deutschen Sprache und Literatur (SZ ISSN 0067-4508) *716*
Basler Studien zur Rechtswissenschaft (SZ) *652*
Basler Veroeffentlichungen zur Geschichte der Medizin und der Biologie (SZ ISSN 0067-4524) *138, 758*
Basler Zeitschrift fuer Geschichte und Altertumskunde (SZ ISSN 0067-4540) *576*
Basrah Natural History Museum. Bulletin (IQ) *988*

Basrah Natural History Museum. Publication (IQ) *988*
Bass and Freshwater Fishing (US) *1044*
Bass Anglers Sportsman Society Fishing Guide *see* B A S S Fishing Guide *1044*
Bass Anglers Sportsman Society Master Fishing Annual *see* B A S S Master Fishing Annual *1044*
Bass Fishing Guide *see* Field & Stream Bass Fishing Annual *1045*
Bass Fishing Guide *see* B A S S Fishing Guide *1044*
Bassmaster *see* B A S S Master Fishing Annual *1044*
Bateman Datum (US) *535*
Bath and West Show Catalogue *see* Royal Bath & West Show Catalogue *33*
Baton Twirling Handbook (US) *1033*
Baton Twirling Rules and Regulations *see* Baton Twirling Handbook *1033*
Battelle Institute Materials Science Colloquia (US) *1148*
Battelle Memorial Institute. Published Papers and Articles (US ISSN 0084-7712) *1003*
Batter Performance Handbook (US ISSN 0731-812X) *1037*
Battered Women's Directory (US) *912, 1128*
Battery Council International. Convention Minutes (US) *1081*
Battery Replacement Data Book (US) *451*
Battle Conference on Anglo-Norman Studies III *see* Anglo-Norman Studies *575*
Baubeschlag-Taschenbuch (GW ISSN 0067-4583) *189*
Bauen mit Aluminium (GW) *181*
Bauernhaeuser aus Mitteleuropa (GW) *70, 97, 555*
Bauernhaeuser der Schweiz (GW ISSN 0067-4591) *515*
Bauhinia (SZ ISSN 0067-4605) *154*
Baustatistisches Jahrbuch (GW ISSN 0084-7739) *188*
Bausteine zur Geschichte des Neuhochdeutschen *see* Bausteine zur Sprachgeschichte des Neuhochdeutschen *691*
Bausteine zur Sprachgeschichte des Neuhochdeutschen (GE) *691*
Bauwelt Katalog (GW ISSN 0067-4664) *181*
Bavaria (GW) *576*
Bawl Street Journal (US) *225, 710*
Bay Area Review Course. Legal Ethics *see* B A R - B R I Bar Review. Professional Responsibility *652*
Bayavaya Uskalos (CN ISSN 0005-6952) *502, 716*
Bayer Agrochem Courier (GW) *52*
Bayer-Mitteilungen fuer die Gummi-Industrie (GW ISSN 0005-6987) *1148*
Bayer-Symposien (US ISSN 0067-4672) *758*
Bayerische Akademie der Wissenschaften. Historische Kommission. Schriftenreihe (GW) *555*
Bayerische Akademie der Wissenschaften. Jahrbuch (GW ISSN 0084-6090) *988*
Bayerische Akademie der Wissenschaften. Mathematisch-Naturwissenschaftliche Klasse. Abhandlungen (GW ISSN 0005-6995) *988*
Bayerische Akademie der Wissenschaften. Mathematisch-Naturwissenschaftliche Klasse. Sitzungsberichte (GW ISSN 0340-7586) *747, 988*
Bayerische Akademie der Wissenschaften. Philosophisch-Historische Klasse. Abhandlungen (GW ISSN 0005-710X) *628, 988*
Bayerische Akademie der Wissenschaften. Philosophisch-Historische Klasse. Sitzungsberichte (GW ISSN 0342-5991) *628, 988*
Bayerische Botanische Gesellschaft. Berichte (GW ISSN 0373-7640) *154*

Bayerische Denkmalpflege. Jahrbuch (GW ISSN 0341-9150) *102*
Bayerische Kommission fuer die Internationale Erdmessung. Veroeffentlichungen (GW ISSN 0340-7691) *115*
Bayerische Staatsbibliothek, Munich. Jahresbericht (GW ISSN 0342-0221) *674*
Bayerische Staatsgemaeldesammlungen. Jahresbericht (GW) *102*
Bayerische Staatssammlung fuer Palaeontologie und Historische Geologie. Mitteilungen (GW ISSN 0077-2070) *384, 856*
Bayerische Vorgeschichtsblaetter (GW ISSN 0341-3918) *577*
Bayerisches Beamten-Jahrbuch (Year) (GW ISSN 0067-4702) *939*
Bayerisches Forstdienst-Taschenbuch (GW ISSN 0067-4710) *523*
Bayerisches Jahrbuch fuer Volkskunde (GW ISSN 0067-4729) *502, 515*
Bayerisches Staatsministerium fuer Unterricht und Kultus. Amtsblatt (GW ISSN 0005-7207) *411*
Baylor Dental Journal (US ISSN 0005-7258) *779*
Bayreuther Beitraege zur Sprachwissenschaft (GW ISSN 0721-4383) *691*
Bayreuther Beitraege zur Sprachwissenschaft. Dialektologie (GW ISSN 0721-8923) *691*
Bazak Guide to Spain (IS) *1106*
Be-Ne-Lux Genealogist (US) *535*
Be Safe at Home/Wees Veilig Tuis (SA) *952*
Bean Improvement Cooperative. Annual Report (US ISSN 0084-7747) *52*
Beans *see* International Center for Tropical Agriculture. Bean Program Annual Report *29*
Beau (IE) *716*
Beau Fleuve Series (US) *716*
Beaufortia (NE ISSN 0067-4745) *173*
Beauty & Barber Dealers World (US ISSN 0405-1157) *118*
Beaux-Arts (CN ISSN 0315-2359) *102*
Bebop Drawing Club Book (US) *102, 502, 716*
Bed and Breakfast in Britain (UK ISSN 0267-3436) *1106*
Bed and Breakfast in South and Southwest England *see* Bed and Breakfast in Britain *1106*
Bed and Breakfast in Wales, Northern England and Scotland *see* Bed and Breakfast in Britain *1106*
Bed & Breakfast Stops (UK ISSN 0267-3363) *1106*
Bed and Breakfast U S A (US) *1106*
Bed, Breakfast & Evening Meal (UK) *1106*
Bedford Institute of Oceanography. Biennial Review *see* Bedford Institute of Oceanography Review *404*
Bedford Institute of Oceanography Review (CN ISSN 0229-8910) *404*
Bedfordshire County Bowling Association. Handbook (UK) *1037*
Bedfordshire Historical Record Society. Publications (UK ISSN 0067-4826) *577*
Bedi Kartlisa (BE ISSN 0373-1537) *577*
Bedrijfschap voor de Lederwarenindustrie. Jaarverslag (NE ISSN 0067-4834) *672*
Bedrijfsuitkomsten in de Nederlandse Particuliere Bosbouw (NE) *523*
Bedrijfsuitkomsten tot Financiele Positie(NE) *24, 45*
Beduin (II ISSN 0005-769X) *716*
Beef Roundup (US) *64*
Beehive History (US) *603*
Beer-Sheva. (IS) *612, 976*
Beethoven-Jahrbuch (GW ISSN 0522-5949) *833*
Befolkningen i Januar *see* Befolkningen i Koebenhavn i Januar *1049*
Befolkningen i Koebenhavn i Januar (DK ISSN 0107-5071) *1049*
Befolkningen i Kommunerne / Populations of Municipalities (DK ISSN 0108-8076) *906*
Befolkningens Energisparebestraebelser (DK ISSN 0109-4149) *464*

Befolkningens Forbrug af Psykiatriske Sengepladser (DK ISSN 0107-4156) 768
Before You Build (SA) 97, 181
Beginners Please see Investing for Beginners 266
Behaviormetrika (JA) 938
Behaviour. Supplements (NE) 173
Behind the Scenes (CN) 1076
Behind the Scenes see Tours and Visits Directory 1117
Behindertenhilfe Durch Erziehung, Unterricht und Therapie (GW ISSN 0171-9718) 444
Behoerden und Organisationen der Land- Forst- und Ernaehrungswirtschaft (GW ISSN 0522-604X) 24
Behring Institute Mitteilungen (GW ISSN 0301-0457) 321
Beihefte der Bonner Jahrbuecher (GW ISSN 0067-4893) 102
Beihefte zur Internationalen Wissenschaftlichen Korrespondenz zur Geschichte der Deutschen Arbeiterbewegung (GW ISSN 0342-3875) 270
Beihefte zur Theologischen Zeitschrift see Sonderbaende zur Theologischen Zeitschrift 972
Beihefte zur Wiener Zeitschrift fuer die Kunde des Morgenlandes (AU ISSN 0259-0654) 568, 850
Beilsteins Handbuch der Organischen Chemie. Fourth Supplement (US ISSN 0067-4915) 329
Beiruter Texte und Studien (GW ISSN 0067-4931) 612
Beitraege Archaeologie des Romischen Rheinlands (GW ISSN 0341-910X) 83
Beitraege zu Infusionstherapie und Klin. Ernaehrung (SZ ISSN 0378-8679) 758
Beitraege Zum Auslaendischen Oeffentlichen Recht und Voelkerrecht (US ISSN 0172-4770) 669
Beitraege zum Buch- und Bibliothekswesen (GW ISSN 0408-8107) 674
Beitraege zum Deutschstudium see Faustchen 694
Beitraege zum Rundfunkrecht (GW ISSN 0067-4966) 347, 652
Beitraege zum Universitaetsrecht (AU) 652
Beitraege zur Aegyptischen Bauforschung und Altertumskunde (GW ISSN 0170-3218) 565
Beitraege zur Afrikakunde (SZ ISSN 0171-1660) 70, 565
Beitraege zur Alexander-von Humboldt-Forschung (GE ISSN 0232-1556) 988
Beitraege zur Algebra und Geometrie (GE ISSN 0138-4821) 748
Beitraege zur Archaeologie see Technische Beitraege zur Archaeologie 94
Beitraege zur Archaeologie des Mittelalters (GW ISSN 0341-9185) 83
Beitraege zur Deutschen Philologie (GW) 691, 716
Beitraege zur Erforschung der Deutschen Sprache (GE ISSN 0232-2714) 691
Beitraege zur Forschungstechnologie (GE ISSN 0323-5130) 887
Beitraege zur Geographie (GE ISSN 0138-4422) 494, 541
Beitraege zur Gerichtlichen Medizin (AU ISSN 0067-5016) 782
Beitraege zur Geschichte der Philosophie und Theologie des Mittelalters Neue Folge (GW ISSN 0067-5024) 876, 968
Beitraege zur Geschichte der Reichskirche in der Neuzeit (GW ISSN 0408-8344) 577
Beitraege zur Geschichte der Universitaet Erfurt (1392-1816) (GE ISSN 0522-6562) 577
Beitraege zur Geschichte der Universitaet Mainz (GW ISSN 0408-8379) 577
Beitraege zur Geschichte der Wissenschaft und der Technik (GW ISSN 0522-6570) 988
Beitraege zur Geschichte des Alten Moenchtums und des Benediktinerordens (GW ISSN 0342-1341) 968
Beitraege zur Geschichte des Niederheins. Jahrbuch des Duesseldorfer Geschichtsvereins see Duesseldorfer Jahrbuch 581
Beitraege zur Geschichte des Parlementarismus und der Politischen Parteien (GW ISSN 0522-6643) 902
Beitraege zur Geschichte Thueringens (GE) 1006
Beitraege zur Geschichte und Kultur der Stadt Nuernberg (GW ISSN 0078-2785) 577
Beitraege zur Harmonikalen Grundlagenforschung (AU ISSN 0067-5067) 833
Beitraege zur Heimatkunde der Stadt Schwelm und ihrer Umgebung (GW) 577
Beitraege zur Hygiene und Epidemiologie (GE ISSN 0067-5083) 952
Beitraege zur Individualpsychologie (GW) 933
Beitraege zur Inkunabelkunde. Dritte Folge (GE ISSN 0067-5091) 674, 960
Beitraege zur Intensiv- und Notfallmedizin (SZ ISSN 0254-8275) 758
Beitraege zur Japanologie (AU ISSN 0522-6759) 568, 850
Beitraege zur Jazzforschung/Studies in Jazz Research (AU) 833
Beitraege zur Kinderpsychotherapie (GW ISSN 0067-5105) 787
Beitraege zur Klassischen Philologie (GW) 691
Beitraege zur Kolonial und Ueberseegeschichte (GW ISSN 0522-6848) 577
Beitraege zur Kommunikationswissenschaft und Medienforschung (GW) 343, 645
Beitraege zur Kritik der Buergerlichen Ideologie und des Revisionismus (GE ISSN 0232-2803) 876, 902
Beitraege zur Kryptogamenflora der Schweiz see Cryptogamica Helvetica 156
Beitraege zur Kunst des Christlichen Ostens (GW ISSN 0067-5121) 102
Beitraege zur Kunstgeschichte (GW) 102
Beitraege zur Landesentwicklung (GW ISSN 0525-4736) 364
Beitraege zur Literatur des 15.-18. Jahrhunderts (GW ISSN 0170-3315) 716
Beitraege zur Luxemburgischen Sprach- und Volkskunde (LU) 691
Beitraege zur Meereskunde (GE ISSN 0067-5148) 404
Beitraege zur Mittelamerikanischen Voelkerkunde (GW ISSN 0408-8514) 70
Beitraege zur Mittelstandsforschung (GW) 1024
Beitraege zur Naturkunde in Osthessen (GW) 138, 384
Beitraege zur Oberpfalzforschung (GW ISSN 0067-5164) 577
Beitraege zur oekonomischen Forschung(GW) 191
Beitraege zur Oekumenischen Theologie(GW ISSN 0067-5172) 968
Beitraege zur Oesterreichischen Statistik(AU ISSN 0067-2319) 1049
Beitraege zur Onkologie see Contributions to Oncology 759
Beitraege zur Palaeontologie von Oesterreich (AU) 856
Beitraege zur Phonetik und Linguistik (GW ISSN 0178-1723) 691
Beitraege zur Psychodiagnostik des Kindes (GW ISSN 0340-0123) 933
Beitraege zur Psychologie und Soziologie des Kranken Menschen (GW ISSN 0173-0967) 758, 933, 1024
Beitraege zur Psychopathologie (US) 933
Beitraege zur Rheumatologie (GE ISSN 0067-5199) 793
Beitraege zur Romanischen Philologie des Mittelalters (GW ISSN 0067-5202) 691, 716
Beitraege zur Schwabischen Literatur- und Geistesgeschichte und Mitteilungen des Justinius Kerner-Vereins und Frauenvereins (GW) 716
Beitraege zur Sexualforschung (GW ISSN 0067-5210) 933
Beitraege zur Sozial- und Wirtschaftsgeschichte (GW) 555
Beitraege zur Sprachinselforschung (AU ISSN 0259-0662) 691
Beitraege zur Strafvollzugswissenschaft (GW ISSN 0067-5237) 370
Beitraege zur Suedasienforschung (GW ISSN 0170-3137) 568
Beitraege zur Suedosteuropa-Forschung (GW) 577
Beitraege zur Tabakforschung see Beitraege zur Tabakforschung International 1079
Beitraege zur Tabakforschung International (GW ISSN 0173-783X) 1079
Beitraege zur Theorie und Praxis des Tennisunterrichts und -trainings (GW ISSN 0723-1407) 1037
Beitraege zur Umweltgestaltung. Reihe A (GW ISSN 0340-9716) 494
Beitraege zur Umweltgestaltung. Reihe B. (GW ISSN 0340-949X) 494
Beitraege zur Ur- und Fruehgeschichte der Bezirke Rostock, Schwerin und Neubrandenburg (GE ISSN 0138-4279) 826
Beitraege zur Ur- und Fruehgeschichtlichen Archaeologie des Mittelmeerkulturraumes (GW ISSN 0067-5245) 83
Beitraege zur Urgeschichte des Rheinlandes (GW ISSN 0341-9193) 83
Beitraege zur Urologie (SZ ISSN 0250-3212) 795
Beitraege zur Wehrforschung (GW ISSN 0067-5253) 1148
Beitraege zur Westfaelischen Familienforschung (GW ISSN 0067-5261) 535
Beitraege zur Wirtschafts- und Sozialgeschichte (GW ISSN 0723-5453) 577
Beitraege zur Wirtschaftspolitik (SZ ISSN 0522-7216) 251
Beitraege zur Zeitgeschichte (GW ISSN 0723-3299) 555, 902
Bekaempelsesmidler see Denmark. Miljoestyrelsen. Oversigt over Godkendte Bekaempelsesmidler 26
Bekleidungs-Industrie. Jahrbuch (GW) 339
Beknopte Feitebron see South Africa Foundation. Information Digest (Year) 249
Belaruski Instytut Navuki Mactatstva. Zapisy/Byelorussian Institute of Arts and Sciences. Annals (US ISSN 0510-3746) 502, 577
Belastingdruk in Nederland/Burden of Taxes in the Netherlands (NE ISSN 0077-670X) 293
Belfast and Northern Ireland Directory (UK ISSN 0067-5342) 1106
Belgian American Chamber of Commerce in the United States. Directory (US ISSN 0196-7622) 287
Belgian American Trade Directory (US) 234
Belgian Environmental Research Index (BE ISSN 0379-1815) 2, 500
Belgian Patents Abstracts (UK) 2, 862
Belgian Patents Report see Belgian Patents Abstracts 862
Belgisch Centrum voor Landelijke Geschiedenis. Publikaties see Centre Belge d'Histoire Rurale. Publications 579
Belgisch Tijdschrift voor Muziekwetenschap see Revue Belge de Musicologie 841
Belgische Cementnijverheid see Industrie Cimentiere Belge 184
Belgische Economie in (Year) see Economie Belge en (Year) 244
Belgium. Administration de la Marine et de la Navigation Interieure. Rapport Annuel sur l'Evolution de la Flotte de Peche (BE) 1099
Belgium. Administration de la Marine. Rapport Annuel sur l'Evolution de la Flotte de Peche see Belgium. Administration de la Marine et de la Navigation Interieure. Rapport Annuel sur l'Evolution de la Flotte de Peche 1099
Belgium. Administration des Eaux et Forets. Station de Recherche des Eaux et Forets. Travaux. Serie D. Hydrobiologie see Belgium. Station de Recherches Forestieres et Hydrobiologiques. Travaux. Serie D. Hydrobiologie 138
Belgium. Administration des Mines. Service: Statistiques. Siderurgie, Houille, Agglomeres, Cokes see Belgium. Administration des Mines. Statistiques: Houille, Cokes, Agglomeres Metallurgie, Carrieres/Statistieken: Steenkolen, Cokes, Agglomeraten, Metaalnijverheid, Groeven 814
Belgium. Administration des Mines. Statistiques: Houille, Cokes, Agglomeres Metallurgie, Carrieres/Statistieken: Steenkolen, Cokes, Agglomeraten, Metaalnijverheid, Groeven (BE) 814
Belgium. Centre d'Etude de la Population et de la Famille. Annual Report (BE) 920
Belgium. Centre d'Etude de la Population et de la Famille. Dossiers (BE) 920
Belgium. Commission Royale des Monuments et des Sites. Bulletin (BE ISSN 0522-7496) 83, 97
Belgium. Conseil Superieur des Classes Moyennes. Rapport Annuel du Secretaire General (BE ISSN 0067-5393) 301
Belgium. Fonds National de la Recherche Scientifique. Bibliographie see Belgium. Nationaal Fonds voor Wetenschappelijk Onderzoek. Bibliografie 1148
Belgium. Fonds National de la Recherche Scientifique. Listes des Beneficiaires d'une Subvention see Belgium. Nationaal Fonds voor Wetenschappelijk Onderzoek. Lijst der Kredietgenieters 988
Belgium. Fonds National de la Recherche Scientifique. Rapport Annuel see Belgium. Nationaal Fonds voor Wetenschappelijk Onderzoek. Jaarverslag 988
Belgium. Hoge Raad voor de Middenstand. Jaarverslag van de Secretaris Generaal see Belgium. Conseil Superieur des Classes Moyennes. Rapport Annuel du Secretaire General 301
Belgium. Institut National d'Assurances Sociales pour Travailleurs Independants. Rapport Annuel (BE) 638
Belgium. Institut National d'Assurances Sociales pour Travailleurs Independants. Statistiques des Beneficiaires de Prestations de Retraite et de Survie/Belgium. Rijkinstituut voor de Social Verzekeringen der Zelfstandigen. Statistiek van de Personen die een Rust- en Overlevingsprestatie Genieten (BE) 638
Belgium. Institut National d'Assurances Sociales pour Travailleurs Independants. Statistique des Enfants Beneficiaires d'Allocations Familiales/Belgium. Rijkinstituut voor de Sociale Verzekeringen der Zelfstandigen. Statistiek van de Kinderen die Recht Geven Op Kinderbijslag (BE) 642

Belgium. Institut National d'Assurances Sociales pour Travailleurs Independants. Statistiques des Personnes Assujetties au Statut Social des Travailleurs Independants/ Belgium. Rijksinstituut voor de Sociale Verzekeringen der Zelfstandigen. Statistiek van de Personen die Onder de Toepassing Vallen van het Sociaal Statuut van de Zelfstandigen (BE) *638*

Belgium. Institut National de Statistique. Annuaire de Statistiques Regionales (BE) *1049*

Belgium. Institut National de Statistique. Annuaire Statistique de Poche (BE ISSN 0067-5431) *1049*

Belgium. Institut National de Statistique. Annuaire Statistique de l'Enseignement *see* Belgium. Ministere de l'Education Nationale et de la Culture Francaise. Annuaire Statistique de l'Enseignement *422*

Belgium. Institut National de Statistique. Batiments et Logements *see* Belgium. Institut National de Statistique. Statistiques de la Construction et du Logement *188*

Belgium. Institut National de Statistique. Bevolkingsstatistieken (BE) *926*

Belgium. Institut National de Statistique. Etudes Statistiques (BE) *1049*

Belgium. Institut National de Statistique. Statistique de la Navigation du Rhin *see* Belgium. Institut National de Statistique. Statistique de la Navigation Interieure *1084*

Belgium. Institut National de Statistique. Statistique de la Navigation Interieure (BE ISSN 0067-5539) *1049, 1084*

Belgium. Institut National de Statistique. Statistique des Accidents de la Circulation sur la Voie Publique(BE ISSN 0067-5504) *958, 1049*

Belgium. Institut National de Statistique. Statistique des Accidents de Roulage *see* Belgium. Institut National de Statistique. Statistique des Accidents de la Circulation sur la Voie Publique *958*

Belgium. Institut National de Statistique. Statistique des Vehicules a Moteur Neufs Mis en Circulation (BE ISSN 0067-5555) *1049, 1085*

Belgium. Institut National de Statistique. Statistique du Tourisme et de l'Hotellerie (BE ISSN 0067-5547) *1049, 1119*

Belgium. Institut National de Statistique. Statistiques de la Construction et du Logement (BE) *188, 1050*

Belgium. Institut National de Statistique. Statistiques des Causes de Deces (BE) *926*

Belgium. Institut National de Statistique. Statistiques Judiciaires (BE) *668*

Belgium. Institut National de Statistique. Statistiques Sociales (BE ISSN 0067-5563) *1014*

Belgium. Institut Royal Meteorologique. Annuaire: Magnetisme Terrestre/ Jaarboek: Aardmagnetisme (BE ISSN 0524-7764) *384*

Belgium. Institut Royal Meteorologique. Annuaire: Rayonnement Solaire/ Jaarboek: Zonnestraling (BE ISSN 0524-7780) *803*

Belgium. Institut Royal Meteorologique. Publications (BE ISSN 0020-255X) *398, 803*

Belgium. Ministere de l'Education Nationale et de la Culture Francaise. Annuaire Statistique de l'Enseignement (BE) *422, 1050*

Belgium. Ministere de l'Education Nationale et de la Culture Francaise. Rapport Annuel (BE ISSN 0067-5598) *411*

Belgium. Ministere de la Prevoyance Sociale. Rapport General sur la Securite Sociale/Algemeen Verslag over de Sociale Zekerheid (BE ISSN 0067-558X) *638*

Belgium. Ministere de la Sante Publique et de la Famille. Premiers et Principaux Resultats Statistiques de l'Enquete dans les Etablissements de Soins/Eerste en Voornaamste Statistische Uitkomsten van de Enquete in de Verzorgingsinstellingen(BE) *958, 1050*

Belgium. Ministere de la Sante Publique et de la Famille. Rapport Annuel (BE) *952, 1015*

Belgium. Ministere des Affaires Economiques. Rapport Annuel sur les Investissements Etrangers en Belique/Jaarlijks Rapport over de Buitenlandse Investeringen (BE) *265*

Belgium. Ministere des Affaires Etrangeres. Repertoire des Theses de Doctorat/Belgium. Ministerie van Buitenlandse Zaken. Repertorium van de Doctorale Proefschriften (BE) *432*

Belgium. Ministerie van Buitenlandse Zaken. Repertorium van de Doctorale Proefschriften *see* Belgium. Ministere des Affaires Etrangeres. Repertoire des Theses de Doctorat *432*

Belgium. Ministerie van Volksgezondheid en van het Gezin. Centrum voor Bevolkings- en Gezinsstudies. Technisch Rapport (BE) *952, 1015*

Belgium. Nationaal Fonds voor Wetenschappelijk Onderzoek. Bibliografie/Belgium. Fonds National de la Recherche Scientifique. Bibliographie (BE) *1148*

Belgium. Nationaal Fonds voor Wetenschappelijk Onderzoek. Bibliografische Lijst van de Werken/ Liste Bibliographique des Travaux *see* Belgium. Nationaal Fonds voor Wetenschappelijk Onderzoek. Bibliografie *1148*

Belgium. Nationaal Fonds voor Wetenschappelijk Onderzoek. Jaarverslag/Belgium. Fonds National de la Recherche Scientifique. Rapport Annuel (BE ISSN 0067-5407) *988*

Belgium. Nationaal Fonds voor Wetenschappelijk Onderzoek. Lijst der Kredietgenieters/Belgium. Fonds National de la Recherche Scientifique. Listes des Beneficiaires d'une Subvention (BE) *988*

Belgium. Office Belge du Commerce Exterieur. Bijvoegsel B B H. Reeks B(BE ISSN 0067-561X) *253*

Belgium. Office National de l'Emploi. Etudes Economiques et Sociales (BE) *270*

Belgium. Office National de l'Emploi. Liste des Informations Statistiques et des Publications de l'O N E M (BE) *204*

Belgium. Office National de l'Emploi. Rapport Annuel *see* Belgium. Office National de l'Emploi. Etudes Economiques et Sociales *270*

Belgium. Regie des Postes. Rapport d'Activite (BE) *346*

Belgium. Rijkinstituut voor de Social Verzekeringen der Zelfstandigen. Statistiek van de Personen die een Rust- en Overlevingsprestatie Genieten *see* Belgium. Institut National d'Assurances Sociales pour Travailleurs Independants. Statistiques des Beneficiaires de Prestations de Retraite et de Survie *638*

Belgium. Rijkinstituut voor de Sociale Verzekeringen der Zelfstandigen. Jaarverslag *see* Belgium. Institut National d'Assurances Sociales pour Travailleurs Independants. Rapport Annuel *638*

Belgium. Rijksinstituut voor de Sociale Verzekeringen der Zelfstandigen. Statistiek van de Kinderen die Recht Geven Op Kinderbijslag *see* Belgium. Institut National d'Assurances Sociales pour Travailleurs Independants. Statistique des Enfants Beneficiaires d'Allocations Familiales *642*

Belgium. Rijksinstituut voor de Sociale Verzekeringen der Zelfstandigen. Statistiek van de Personen die Onder de Toepassing Vallen van het Sociaal Statuut van de Zelfstandigen *see* Belgium. Institut National d'Assurances Sociales pour Travailleurs Independants. Statistiques des Personnes Assujetties au Statut Social des Travailleurs Independants *638*

Belgium. Rijksstation voor Landbouwtechniek. Mededelingen (BE ISSN 0303-9056) *24*

Belgium. Rijksstation voor Sierplantenteelt. Mededelingen (BE ISSN 0303-903X) *531*

Belgium. Rijksstation voor Zeevisserij. Mededelingen (BE ISSN 0303-9072) *508*

Belgium. Station de Recherches Forestieres et Hydrobiologiques. Travaux. Serie D. Hydrobiologie (BE) *138*

Belgrade. Univerzitet. Elektrotehnicki Fakultet. Publikacije. Serija: Telekomunikacije i Elektronika *see* Beogradski Univerzitet. Elektrotehnicki Fakultet. Publikacije. Serija: Elektronika, Telekomunikacije, Automatika *451*

Belisane (FR ISSN 0339-8498) *876*

Belize. Department of Agriculture. Annual Report and Summmary of Statistics (BH) *24*

Bell and Howell Transdex *see* Transdex Index *647*

Bell & Howell's Newspaper Index to the Detroit Area *see* Index to the Detroit News *647*

Bellona (UK ISSN 0005-8645) *1148*

Belmontia (NE) *155*

Beloit Poetry Journal. Chapbook (US ISSN 0067-5695) *740*

Bemfam (BL) *1015*

Ben-Gurion University of the Negev. Research and Development Authority. Applied Research Institute. Scientific Activities *see* Ben-Gurion University of the Negev. The Institutes for Applied Research. Scientific Activities *988*

Ben-Gurion University of the Negev. The Institutes for Applied Research. Scientific Activities. (IS) *988*

Benchmark Papers in Acoustics (US) *900*

Benchmark Papers in Analytical Chemistry (US ISSN 0145-5338) *326*

Benchmark Papers in Animal Behavior *see* Benchmark Papers in Behavior *173*

Benchmark Papers in Behavior (US) *173, 938*

Benchmark Papers in Biochemistry (US) *151*

Benchmark Papers in Biological Concepts (US) *138*

Benchmark Papers in Ecology (US ISSN 0095-4640) *138*

Benchmark Papers in Electrical Engineering & Computer Science (US) *351, 484*

Benchmark Papers in Genetics (US) *166*

Benchmark Papers in Geology (US) *384*

Benchmark Papers in Human Physiology (US ISSN 0093-5557) *171, 758*

Benchmark Papers in Inorganic Chemistry (US) *328*

Benchmark Papers in Microbiology (US) *168*

Benchmark Papers in Nuclear Physics (US) *896*

Benchmark Papers in Optics (US) *899*

Benchmark Papers in Organic Chemistry (US) *329*

Benchmark Papers in Physical Chemistry and Chemical Physics (US) *331*

Benchmark Papers in Polymer Chemistry (US) *321, 900*

Benchmark Papers in Soil Science (US) *384*

Benchmark Papers in Systematic and Evolutionary Biology (US) *138, 166*

Benchmark Papers on Energy (US) *464*

Benchmark Soils Project. Technical Report Series (US) *52*

Bendel State. Ministry of Home Affairs and Information. Mid-Western State Estimates *see* Bendel State. Ministry of Information, Social Development and Sports. Estimate *939*

Bendel State. Ministry of Information, Social Development and Sports. Estimate (NR) *939*

Bender's Dictionary of 1040 Deductions(US ISSN 0270-5206) *652*

Benedictine Almanac *see* Benedictine Yearbook *981*

Benedictine Yearbook (UK ISSN 0522-8883) *981*

Benefits for Saskatchewan Industry from Resource Development (CN ISSN 0706-7852) *191*

Benelux.Genealogist *see* Be-Ne-Lux Genealogist *535*

Benelux Economic Union. Conseil Consultatif Economique et Social Rapport du Secretaire Concernant les Activites du Conseil *see* B E N E L U X Economic Union. Conseil Central de l'Economie. Rapport du Secretaire sur l'Activite du Conseil *287*

Benelux Publikatieblad/Bulletin Benelux(BE ISSN 0005-8777) *939*

Benelux Rail (SW) *1094*

Benelux Stamp Catalogue (UK ISSN 0142-9787) *874*

Bengal Motion Picture Diary and General Information *see* Indian Motion Picture Almanac *824*

Benibana (JA) *52, 858*

Benjamin F. Fairless Lectures (US ISSN 0067-5717) *902*

Benki ya Nyumba Tanzania. Ripoti ya Mwaka *see* Tanzania Housing Bank. Annual Report and Statement of Accounts *233*

Benn Electronics Executive (UK ISSN 0265-0959) *451*

Bennington Review (US) *1148*

Benn's Direct Marketing Service (UK) *283*

Benn's Hardware Directory *see* Benn's Hardware Directory & D-I-Y Buyers Guide *189*

Benn's Hardware Directory & D-I-Y Buyers Guide (UK ISSN 0261-1465) *189*

Benn's International Hardware Exporter(UK) *189*

Benn's Media Directory (UK ISSN 0269-8358) *645*

Benn's Press Directory *see* Benn's Media Directory *645*

Benson and Hedges Cricket Year (UK) *1037*

Bent (CN ISSN 0067-5733) *716*

Bentham Newsletter (UK) *341*

Bentley Historical Library Annual Report (US ISSN 0362-6881) *674*

Benzene-Toluene-Xylenes and Derivatives *see* World Aromatics and Derivatives *325*

Beogradski Univerzitet. Elektrotehnicki Fakultet. Publikacije. Serija: Elektronika, Telekomunikacije, Automatika (YU ISSN 0351-2177) *451*

Berckers Katolischer Taschenkalender (GW) *968*

Berckers Taschenkalender *see* Berckers Katolischer Taschenkalender *968*

Beretning for Psykiatriske Institutioner i Danmark (DK ISSN 0108-7819) *789*

Beretning om Atomenergikommissionens Virksomhed *see* Forskningscenter Risoe. Aarsberetning *465*

Beretning om de Almennyttige Boligselskabers Regnskaber see Almennyttige Boligselskabers Regnskaber 621
Beretning over Arbejdsmiljoefondets Virksomhed (DK ISSN 0106-7052) 270
Berg (Year) (GW ISSN 0179-1419) 1044
Bergakademie Freiberg. Wissenschaftliches Informationszentrum. Veroeffentlichungen (GE) 674
Bergbau-Berufsgenossenschaft. Geschaeftsbericht see Bergbau-Berufsgenossenschaft. Jahresbericht 648
Bergbau-Berufsgenossenschaft. Jahresbericht (GW) 648, 814
Berger Building & Design Cost File. Unit Prices. Vol. 1: General Construction Trades (US) 182
Berger Building & Design Cost File. Unit Prices. Vol. 2: Mechanical and Electrical Trades (US) 182, 451
Berger Building Cost File see Berger Building & Design Cost File. Unit Prices. Vol. 1: General Construction Trades 182
Berger Building Cost File see Berger Building & Design Cost File. Unit Prices. Vol. 2: Mechanical and Electrical Trades 182
Berger Design Cost File see Berger Building & Design Cost File. Unit Prices. Vol. 1: General Construction Trades 182
Berger Design Cost File see Berger Building & Design Cost File. Unit Prices. Vol. 2: Mechanical and Electrical Trades 182
Bergey's Manual of Determinative Bacteriology (US) 168
Bergischer Geschichtsverein. Zeitschrift (GW ISSN 0067-5792) 577
Bericht der Bundesregierung an den Nationalrat see Austria. Bundesministerium fuer Wissenschaft und Forschung. Bericht der Bundesregierung an den Nationalrat 988
Bericht ueber die Lage der oesterreichischen Landwirtschaft (AU) 45
Berichte des Vereins Natur und Heimat und des Naturhistorischen Museums zu Luebeck (GW ISSN 0067-5806) 988
Berichte Naturwissenschaftlich-Medizinischen Vereins in Innsbruck (AU) 138, 758
Berichte ueber Landwirtschaft. Sonderhefte (GW ISSN 0301-2689) 24
Berichte zur Orts-, Regional- und Landesplanung (SZ) 622
Berichten van de Afdeling Volkskredietwezen (NE ISSN 0005-9110) 225
Bering Sea Summary Report see Alaska Summary Report/Index 862
Berita Prasejarah see Bulletin of Prehistory 1149
Berkeley Journal of Sociology (US ISSN 0067-5830) 1024
Berkeley Papers in History of Science (US ISSN 0145-0379) 988
Berkeley Symposia on Mathematical Statistics and Probability (US) 748
Berkeley Works (US) 1148
Berkshire Archaeological Committee. Publication (UK) 83
Berkshire Archaeological Journal (UK ISSN 0309-3093) 83
Berkshire Review (US ISSN 0005-920X) 710
Berlin (GW ISSN 0344-4910) 577
Berlin. Freie Universitaet. Institut fuer Statistik und Versicherungsmathematik. Berichte see Arbeiten zur Angewandten Statistik 1048
Berlin in Zahlen see Statistisches Jahrbuch Berlin 1064
Berliner Beitraege zur Archaeometrie (GW ISSN 0344-5089) 83
Berliner Botanischer Verein. Verhandlung (GW ISSN 0724-3111) 138, 155

Berliner Byzantinistische Arbeiten (GE ISSN 0067-6055) 336, 577
Berliner Handelsregister Verzeichnis (GW ISSN 0067-6063) 303
Berliner Historische Kommission. Veroeffentlichungen (GW) 577
Berliner Islamstudien (GW ISSN 0174-2477) 968
Berliner Tierpark-Buch (GE ISSN 0067-6098) 173
Berliner Turfantexte (GE ISSN 0138-4228) 850
Berliner Wirtschaftsdaten (GW) 242
Berliner Wissenschaftlicher Gesellschaft. Jahrbuch (GW ISSN 0171-3302) 988
Berlinische Reminiszenzen (GW ISSN 0067-611X) 577
Bermuda. Biological Station for Research. Special Publications (BM) 405, 494
Bermuda. Department of Agriculture and Fisheries. Report for the Year (BM) 24, 508
Bermuda Historical Society. Occasional Publications (BM ISSN 0409-2163) 603
Bern. Universitaet. Archaeologisches Seminar. Hefte (SZ) 83
Bernard Shaw Series (UK) 716
Bernard Shaw Society Journal (UK) 716, 1076
Bernard und Graefe Aktuell (GW) 810
Bernards and Babani Press Radio & Electronics & Computer Books (UK) 347, 352, 451
Bernards and Babani Press Radio and Electronics Books see Bernards and Babani Press Radio & Electronics & Computer Books 347
Berner Beitraege zur Nationaloekonomie (SZ ISSN 0067-6128) 191
Berner Beitraege zur Soziologie (SZ ISSN 0067-6136) 1024
Berner Boersenverein. Jahresbericht (SZ) 265
Berner Kriminologische Untersuchungen(SZ ISSN 0067-6144) 370
Berner Studien zum Fremdenverkehr (SZ ISSN 0067-6152) 191, 1106
Bernice P. Bishop Museum Bulletin (US ISSN 0005-9439) 988
Bernice Pauahi Bishop Museum, Honolulu. Occasional Papers (US ISSN 0067-6160) 70, 988
Bernice Pauahi Bishop Museum, Honolulu. Special Publications (US ISSN 0067-6179) 70, 988
Bertine Koperberg Conference (Proceedings) (SW) 793
Bertrand Russell Today see Philosophy and the Arts 880
Beruf und Gesundheit/Occupational Health (GW) 2, 636
Berytus Archeological Studies (LE ISSN 0067-6195) 83
Beschreibende Bibliographien (NE ISSN 0169-0477) 122
Beschrijvende Rassenlijst voor Landbouwgewassen (NE) 53
Best American Short Stories (US ISSN 0067-6233) 716
Best & Most in Cigarettes, Cigars and Pipe Tobaccos see Duty & Tax-Free Shop World Guide Series. Vol. 3: Best "N" Most in Cigarettes, Cigars and Tobacco 255
Best & Most in Liquors see Duty & Tax-Free Shop World Guide Series. Vol. 1: Best "N" Most in Wines & Spirits 255
Best & Most Special Edition see Duty & Tax-Free Shop World Guide Series. Vol. 4: Best "N" Most in D F S 255
Best Books By Consensus (Year) (US ISSN 8755-9633) 963
Best Canadian Stories (CN ISSN 0703-9476) 716
Best Editorial Cartoons of the Year (US ISSN 0091-2220) 102, 710
Best in Advertising (US) 15
Best in Advertising Campaigns see Best in Advertising 15
Best in Annual Reports (US ISSN 0308-8743) 278
Best in Covers see Best in Covers and Posters 960

Best in Covers and Posters (US) 102, 960
Best in Environmental Graphics (US ISSN 0360-8271) 102
Best in Packaging (US ISSN 0360-8689) 854
Best in Posters see Best in Covers and Posters 960
Best "N" Most in Cigarettes, Cigars and Pipe Tobaccos see Duty & Tax-Free Shop World Guide Series. Vol. 3: Best "N" Most in Cigarettes, Cigars and Tobacco 255
Best 'N' Most in Liquors see Duty & Tax-Free Shop World Guide Series. Vol. 1: Best "N" Most in Wines & Spirits 255
Best "N" Most Special Edition see Duty & Tax-Free Shop World Guide Series. Vol. 4: Best "N" Most in D F S 255
Best Newspaper Writing (US ISSN 0195-895X) 645
Best of E R I C (Educational Management) (US) 442
Best of Micro (US ISSN 0271-8189) 1148
Best of Photojournalism (US) 884
Best Plays of ... (Year) (US) 1076
Best Science Fiction of the Year (US ISSN 0095-7119) 14, 716
Best Sellers and Best Choices (Year) see Best Books By Consensus (Year) 963
Best Short Plays (US ISSN 0067-6284) 716
Best Sports Stories (US ISSN 0067-6292) 1033
Best's Agents Guide to Life Insurance Companies (US ISSN 0094-9973) 638
Best's Directory of Recommended Independent Insurance Adjusters see Best's Directory of Recommended Insurance Adjusters 638
Best's Directory of Recommended Insurance Adjusters (US) 638
Best's Directory of Recommended Insurance Attorneys (US ISSN 0277-1551) 638
Best's Insurance Report: Life-Health (US) 638
Best's Insurance Report: Property-Casualty (US ISSN 0148-3218) 638
Best's Insurance Report: Property-Liability see Best's Insurance Report: Property-Casualty 638
Best's Insurance Securities Research Service (US ISSN 0362-8701) 265
Best's Recommended Insurance Attorneys see Best's Directory of Recommended Insurance Attorneys 638
Best's Safety Directory (US ISSN 0090-7480) 635
Bestseller Almanach (GW) 716
Bestuurlike Informasie/Managerial Information (SA ISSN 0067-6349) 221
Beta Phi Mu Chapbook (US ISSN 0067-6357) 674
Beton-Kalender (GW) 182
Beton- og Konstruktionsinstituttet. Rapport (DK ISSN 0109-291X) 182
Beton- und Fertigteil-Jahrbuch (GW ISSN 0067-6365) 480
Betonstein-Jahrbuch see Beton- und Fertigteil-Jahrbuch 480
Betontechnische Berichte (GW ISSN 0409-2740) 182
Betriebs- und Arbeitswirtschaft in der Praxis (GW ISSN 0405-6485) 24
Betriebs- und Marktwirtschaft im Gartenbau (GW ISSN 0303-1241) 531
Betriebs- und Wirtschaftsinformatik (US) 238
Betriebswirtschaftliche Mitteilungen see Management Praxis 280
Better Homes & Dykes (US) 615, 1128
Better Homes and Gardens Christmas Ideas (US ISSN 0405-6590) 614, 614
Better Homes and Gardens Holiday Crafts (US) 614
Better Homes and Gardens Home Plan Ideas (US) 531, 614

Better Homes and Gardens Low-Calorie Recipes (US) 885
Better Homes and Gardens Window & Wall Ideas (US ISSN 0277-836X) 643
Between Two Rivers (US) 716
Beverage and Food World (II) 119, 518
Beverage Industry Annual Manual (US) 119
Beverage World's Daily Desk Reference Living Directory see Beverage World's Databank 119
Beverage World's Databank (US) 119
Beverage World's Living Directory see Beverage World's Databank 119
Beverages: Latin American Industrial Report (US) 119
Bevoelkerungsstruktur und Wirtschaftskraft der Bundeslaender (GW ISSN 0072-1867) 921
Beyond S F Anthology (GW) 14
Beyond Science Fiction (US) 716
Bezirkshauptmannschaft Amstetten. Heimatkundliche Beilage zum Amstblatt (AU) 555
Bezirkshauptmannschaft Melk. Heimatkundliche Beilage zum Amtsblatt (AU) 555
Bezirkshauptmannschaft Tulln. Heimatkundliches Beiblatt zum Amtsblatt (AU) 555
Bhabha Atomic Research Centre. Nuclear Physics Division. Annual Report (II) 896
Bhagyavati Panchanga (II) 115
Bhandarkar Oriental Research Institute. Annals (II) 850
Bharat Krishak Samaj. Year Book (II ISSN 0067-6454) 24
Bharatiya Purabhilekha Patrika see Studies in Indian Epigraphy 705
Bharatiya Sthalanama Patrika see Studies in Indian Place Names 705
Bhugola Samayiki (BG) 542
Bi-Annual Review of Allergy (US ISSN 0278-9566) 773
Bialostockie Towarzystwo Naukowe. Prace (PL ISSN 0067-6470) 577
Biannual of Electronics Research see Texas Annual of Electronics Research 460
La Bibbia nella Storia (IT) 981
Bibel im Jahr(Year) (GW) 968
Biblica et Orientalia (VC) 850, 981
Biblical Research (US ISSN 0067-6535) 968
Biblical Scholarship in North America (US ISSN 0277-0474) 968
Bibliografi Negara Malaysia see Malaysian National Bibliography 564
Bibliografi over Danmarks Offentlige Publikationer (DK ISSN 0067-6543) 122
Bibliografi over Dansk Kunst (DK) 113
Bibliografi over Europaeiske Kunstneres Ex Libris/Europaeische Ex Libris/European Book Plates/Ex Libris d'Europe (DK) 113
Bibliografia Agricola Chilena (CL) 39
Bibliografia Agrometeorologii/Bibliography of Agrometeorology (PL ISSN 0239-958X) 39, 808
Bibliografia Argentina de Psicologia (AG ISSN 0523-1698) 938
Bibliografia Bibliografii i Nauki o Ksiazce/Bibliography of Bibliographies and Library Science (PL ISSN 0509-6413) 122, 687
Bibliografia Bibliotecologica Argentina (AG ISSN 0067-656X) 687
Bibliografia Boliviana see Bio-Bibliografia Boliviana 123
Bibliografia Brasileira de Agricultura (year) (BL) 24
Bibliografia Brasileira de Botanica (BL ISSN 0067-6586) 1148
Bibliografia Brasileira de Ciencias Agricolas see Bibliografia Brasileira de Agricultura (year) 24
Bibliografia Brasileira de Ciencias Sociais (BL ISSN 0067-6608) 122, 1022
Bibliografia Brasileira de Direito (BL ISSN 0067-6616) 122, 668
Bibliografia Brasileira de Documentacao(BL ISSN 0067-6624) 361, 688

Bibliografia Brasileira de Energia Nuclear (BL) *468*
Bibliografia Brasileira de Engenharia (BL ISSN 0100-0705) *122, 476*
Bibliografia Brasileira de Fisica (BL ISSN 0067-6640) *122, 892*
Bibliografia Brasileira de Matematica (BL ISSN 0067-6667) *122, 755*
Bibliografia Brasileira de Matematica e Fisica *see* Bibliografia Brasileira de Matematica *755*
Bibliografia Brasileira de Matematica e Fisica *see* Bibliografia Brasileira de Fisica *892*
Bibliografia Brasileira de Medicina (BL ISSN 0067-6675) *122, 768*
Bibliografia Brasileira de Odontologia (BL ISSN 0100-6266) *768*
Bibliografia Brasileira de Quimica *see* Bibliografia Brasileira de Quimica e Quimica Tecnologica *204*
Bibliografia Brasileira de Quimica e Quimica Tecnologica (BL ISSN 0100-0756) *122, 204*
Bibliografia Brasileira de Quimica Tecnologia *see* Bibliografia Brasileira de Quimica e Quimica Tecnologica *204*
Bibliografia Brasileira de Zoologia (BL ISSN 0067-6691) *122, 149*
Bibliografia de la Literatura Hispanica (SP) *122, 738*
Bibliografia de Publicacoes Oficiais Brasileiras (BL ISSN 0100-722X) *122*
Bibliografia Dobrogei (RM) *122*
Bibliografia e Storia della Critica (IT) *738*
Bibliografia Economica de Mexico *see* Bibliografia Economica de Mexico. Libros *204*
Bibliografia Economica de Mexico. Libros (MX) *204*
Bibliografia Economico-Social *see* Bibliografia Brasileira de Ciencias Sociais *1022*
Bibliografia Eritysiryhmien Liikunnan Tutkimuksesta/Bibliography on Research in Physical Education and Sport for the Handicapped (FI ISSN 0357-2498) *422, 444*
Bibliografia Espanola (Annual) (SP ISSN 0523-1760) *122*
Bibliografia Espanola. Suplemento de Publicaciones Periodicas (SP ISSN 0210-8372) *122*
Bibliografia Geologiczna Polski (PL ISSN 0373-1987) *381, 384*
Bibliografia Gospodarki i Inzynierii Wodnej/Bibliography of Water Management and Engineering (PL ISSN 0239-622X) *122, 402*
Bibliografia Historica Mexicana (MX ISSN 0185-1578) *562*
Bibliografia Historii Polskiej (PL ISSN 0067-6721) *563*
Bibliografia Hydrologii i Oceanologii/ Bibliography of Hydrology and Oceanology (PL ISSN 0239-6246) *122, 381*
Bibliografia Internationala Cinema/ Bibliographie Internationale Cinema (RM ISSN 0084-7828) *1148*
Bibliografia Jugoslovenske Periodike *see* Bibliografija Jugoslavije. Serijske Publikacije *122*
Bibliografia Meteorologii/Bibliography of Meteorology (PL ISSN 0239-6270) *122, 803*
Bibliografia Missionaria (IT) *974*
Bibliografia na Bulgarskata Bibliografiia/ Bibliography of Bulgarian Bibliographies (BU ISSN 0204-7373) *122*
Bibliografia Pomorza Zachodniego (PL ISSN 0409-3453) *563*
Bibliografia Portuguesa de Construcao Civil *see* Bibliografia Portuguesa de Engenharia Civil *476*
Bibliografia Portuguesa de Engenharia Civil (PO) *476*
Bibliografia Prac Magisterkich, Doktoskich i Habilitacyjnych Przyjetych w S G G W - A R w Warszawie (Szkola Glowna Gospodarstwa Wiejskiego-Akademia Rolnicza) (PL ISSN 0208-4252) *39*

Bibliografia Publikacji Pracownikow S G G W - A R w Warszawie (Szkola Glowna Gospodarstwa Wiejskiego-Akademia Rolnicza) (PL ISSN 0208-4260) *39*
Bibliografia Teologica Comentada del Area Iberoamericana (AG ISSN 0326-6680) *122, 968*
Bibliografia Ticinese (SZ ISSN 0067-6772) *577*
Bibliografia Venezolana (VE ISSN 0006-1085) *674*
Bibliografia Venezuela Anuario *see* Bibliografia Venezolana *674*
Bibliografia Wydawnictw Ciaglych/ Bibliography of Polish Serials (PL ISSN 0239-4421) *122, 687*
Bibliografia z Zakresu Meteorologii Rolniczej i Lesnej *see* Bibliografia Agrometeorologii *808*
Bibliografica Folclorica (BL) *70, 515*
Bibliograficheskie Posobiya Belorusskoi S.S.R. (UR) *122*
Bibliograficky Katalog C S S R. Ceske Knihy. Zvlastni Sesit. Bibliografie a V T I *see* Bibliografie Ceskeho Knihovnictvi. Bibliografie a V T I *674*
Bibliograficky Katalog C S S R. Ceske Knihy. Zvlastni Sesit. Ceska Grafika a Mapy v Roce (CS ISSN 0323-1712) *122*
Bibliograficky Katalog C S S R. Ceske Knihy. Zvlastni Sesit. Soupis Ceskych Bibliografii (CS ISSN 0323-1860) *122*
Bibliograficky Katalog C S S R: Ceske Knihy. Zvlastni Sesit. Ceske Disertace (CS ISSN 0232-041X) *122*
Bibliograficky Katalog C S S R: Ceske Knihy. Zvlastni Sesit. Ceskoslovenske Disertace *see* Bibliograficky Katalog C S S R: Ceske Knihy. Zvlastni Sesit. Ceske Disertace *122*
Bibliograficky Zbornik (CS ISSN 0067-6780) *122*
Bibliografie Ceskeho Knihovnictvi. Bibliografie a V T I (CS ISSN 0139-8539) *674*
Bibliografie Nederlandse Sociologie (NE) *1031*
Bibliografie van in Nederland verschenen demografische Studies *see* Selected Annotated Bibliography of Population Studies in the Netherlands *929*
Bibliografie van Nederlandse Proefschriften/Dutch Theses (NE ISSN 0166-9966) *122*
Bibliografija Jugoslavije. Serijske Publikacije (YU ISSN 0350-0349) *122*
Bibliografija Medicinske Periodike Jugoslavije/Index Medicus Iugoslavicus (YU ISSN 0067-6799) *768*
Bibliografija Prevoda U S F R J (YU ISSN 0350-9974) *122*
Bibliografija Zvanicnih Publikacija S F R J (YU ISSN 0350-2562) *122*
Bibliographia Brasiliana (BL) *963*
Bibliographia Cartographica (GW ISSN 0340-0409) *122, 551*
Bibliographia Franciscana (IT) *136, 975*
Bibliographia Humboldtiana (GW) *628*
Bibliographia Internationalis Spiritualitatis (VC ISSN 0084-7836) *883*
Bibliographia Musicologica (NE ISSN 0084-7844) *843*
Bibliographia Phytosociologica Syntaxonomica (GW) *155*
Bibliographia Scientiae Naturalis Helvetica (SZ ISSN 0067-6829) *1003*
Bibliographic Guide to Art and Architecture (US ISSN 0360-2699) *100, 122*
Bibliographic Guide to Black Studies (US ISSN 0360-2710) *122, 506*
Bibliographic Guide to Conference Publications (US ISSN 0360-2729) *122*
Bibliographic Guide to Dance (US ISSN 0360-2737) *122, 375*
Bibliographic Guide to Education (US) *122, 422*

Bibliographic Guide to Government Publications (US ISSN 0360-2796) *122*
Bibliographic Guide to Government Publications-Foreign (US ISSN 0360-280X) *122*
Bibliographic Guide to Law (US ISSN 0360-2745) *122, 668*
Bibliographic Guide to Maps and Atlases (US) *122, 551*
Bibliographic Guide to Music (US ISSN 0360-2753) *122, 843*
Bibliographic Guide to North American History (US ISSN 0147-6491) *122, 563*
Bibliographic Guide to Psychology (US ISSN 0360-277X) *122, 938*
Bibliographic Guide to Soviet and European Studies (US ISSN 0162-5322) *577*
Bibliographic Guide to Technology (US ISSN 0360-2761) *122, 1067*
Bibliographic Guide to Theatre Arts (US ISSN 0360-2788) *1076*
Bibliographic Index of Health Education Periodicals *see* B I H E P *886*
Bibliographica Judaica (US ISSN 0067-6853) *975*
Bibliographical Bulletin *see* Bibliographische Berichte *123*
Bibliographical Selection of Museological Literature *see* Selected Bibliography of Museological Literature *832*
Bibliographical Series on Coconut (CE ISSN 0379-1564) *53*
Bibliographical Services Throughout the World (UN) *122*
Bibliographical Society of Canada. Facsimile Series (CN ISSN 0067-687X) *122*
Bibliographical Society of Canada. Monographs (CN ISSN 0067-6888) *122*
Bibliographical Society of Canada. Newsletter *see* Bibliographical Society of Canada. Papers *123*
Bibliographical Society of Canada. Papers (CN ISSN 0067-6896) *123*
Bibliographie Analytique de l'Afrique Antique (FR) *563*
Bibliographie Annuelle de l'Histoire de France (FR ISSN 0067-6918) *563*
Bibliographie Annuelle de Madagascar (MG ISSN 0067-6926) *123*
Bibliographie Bildende Kunst (GE ISSN 0232-5810) *113*
Bibliographie Courante d'Articles de Periodiques Posterieurs a 1944 sur les Problemes Politiques, Economiques et Sociaux/Index to Post-1944 Periodical Articles on Political, Economic and Social Problems (US) *123, 1014*
Bibliographie d'Histoire Luxembourgeoise (LU ISSN 0067-7043) *563*
Bibliographie de l'Histoire Bernoise *see* Bibliographie der Berner Geschichte *563*
Bibliographie de la France. Supplement 4: Atlas, Cartes et Plans (FR ISSN 0150-5998) *551*
Bibliographie der Antiquariats-, Auktions- und Kunstkataloge (GE) *113*
Bibliographie der Berner Geschichte/ Bibliographie de l'Histoire Bernoise (SZ ISSN 0250-5673) *123, 563*
Bibliographie der Deutschen Literaturwissenschaft *see* Bibliographie der Deutschen Sprach- und Literaturwissenschaft *738*
Bibliographie der Deutschen Sprach- und Literaturwissenschaft (GE ISSN 0341-9363) *738*
Bibliographie der Deutschsprachigen Psychologischen Literatur (GW ISSN 0303-5999) *938*
Bibliographie der Deutschsprachigen Schweizerliteratur (SZ) *738*
Bibliographie der Franzoesischen Literaturwissenschaft (GW ISSN 0523-2465) *738*
Bibliographie der Paedagogischen Veroeffentlichungen in der Deutschen Demokratischen Republik (GE ISSN 0067-6969) *422*

Bibliographie des Schweizerischen Rechts (SZ) *668*
Bibliographie des Travaux en Langue Francaise sur l'Afrique au Sud du Sahara, Sciences Humaines et Sociales (FR) *537, 1014*
Bibliographie Egyptologique Annuelle *see* Annual Egyptological Bibliography *562*
Bibliographie en la Langue Francaise d'Histoire du Droit de 987 a 1875 *see* Bibliographie en Langue Francaise d'Histoire du Droit de 987 a 1914 *668*
Bibliographie en Langue Francaise d'Histoire du Droit de 987 a 1914 (FR) *668*
Bibliographie Ethnographique de l'Afrique Sud-Saharienne (BE) *1014*
Bibliographie Ethnographique du Congo Belge et des Regions Avoisinantes *see* Bibliographie Ethnographique de l'Afrique Sud-Saharienne *1014*
Bibliographie Europeene des Travaux sur l'URSS et l'Europe de l'Est *see* European Bibliography of Soviet, East European and Slavonic Studies *563*
Bibliographie Geschichte der Technik (GE ISSN 0323-4355) *563, 1072*
Bibliographie International de l'Histoire des Religions *see* International Bibliography of the History of Religions *975*
Bibliographie Internationale Cinema *see* Bibliografia Internationala Cinema *1148*
Bibliographie Internationale D'Ethnologie *see* Internationale Volkskundliche Bibliographie *517*
Bibliographie Internationale de l'Humanisme et de la Renaissance (SZ ISSN 0067-7000) *634*
Bibliographie Internationale de la Demographie Historique *see* International Bibliography of Historical Demography *922*
Bibliographie Juridique *see* Rechtsbibliographie *669*
Bibliographie Linguistischer Literatur (GW ISSN 0172-3960) *709, 738*
Bibliographie Luxembourgeoise (LU) *123, 577*
Bibliographie Musik (GE ISSN 0232-7678) *843*
Bibliographie Paedagogik/Educational Bibliography (GW ISSN 0523-2678) *123, 411*
Bibliographie Papyrologique sur Fiches (BE) *336*
Bibliographie Programmierter Unterricht *see* Bibliographie Paedagogik *123*
Bibliographie Relative aux Irrigations, au Drainage, a la Regularisation des Cours d'Eau et la Matrise des Crues *see* Bibliography on Irrigation, Drainage, River Training and Flood Control *1127*
Bibliographie Romane *see* Romanische Bibliographie *709*
Bibliographie Suisse de Statistique et d'Economie Politique *see* Schweizerische Bibliographie fuer Statistik und Volkswirtschaft *1162*
Bibliographie Universelle de Securite Sociale *see* World Bibliography of Social Security *220*
Bibliographie Unselbstaendiger Literatur-Linguistik *see* Bibliographie Linguistischer Literatur *738*
Bibliographie zur Archaeo-Zoologie und Geschichte der Haustiere (GE ISSN 0232-4865) *83, 123*
Bibliographie zur Kunstgeschichtlichen Literatur in Ost- und Suedosteuropaeischen Zeitschriften (GW ISSN 0173-1637) *100, 113*
Bibliographie zur Symbolik, Ikonographie und Mythologie (GW ISSN 0067-706X) *78, 517*
Bibliographien zur Deutschen Literatur des Mittelalters (GW ISSN 0523-2767) *716, 738*
Bibliographien zur Philosophie (GW ISSN 0173-1831) *123, 876*
Bibliographien zur Romanistik (GW ISSN 0171-0125) *739*
Bibliographies Analytiques sur l'Afrique Centrale (BE) *123, 563*

1664 BIBLIOGRAPHIES AND

Bibliographies and Indexes in Afro-American and African Studies (US ISSN 0742-6925) *563*

Bibliographies and Indexes in American History (US ISSN 0742-6828) *563*

Bibliographies and Indexes in American Literature (US ISSN 0742-6860) *739*

Bibliographies and Indexes in Anthropology (US ISSN 0742-6844) *79*

Bibliographies and Indexes in Economics and Economic History (US ISSN 0749-1786) 123, *204*

Bibliographies and Indexes in Education(US ISSN 0742-6917) *422*

Bibliographies and Indexes in Gerontology (US ISSN 0743-7560) *552*

Bibliographies and Indexes in Law and Political Science (US ISSN 0742-6909) *668*, 911

Bibliographies and Indexes in Library and Information Science (US ISSN 0742-6879) *687*

Bibliographies and Indexes in Philosophy (US ISSN 0742-6887) *884*

Bibliographies and Indexes in Psychology (US ISSN 0742-681X) *938*

Bibliographies and Indexes in Religious Studies (US ISSN 0742-6836) *975*

Bibliographies and Indexes in Sociology(US ISSN 0742-6895) *1031*

Bibliographies and Indexes in the Performing Arts (US ISSN 0742-6933) *375, 1079*

Bibliographies and Indexes in Women's Studies (US ISSN 0742-6941) *1130*

Bibliographies and Indexes in World History (US ISSN 0742-6852) *563*

Bibliographies and Indexes in World Literature (US ISSN 0742-6801) *739*

Bibliographies and Literature of Agriculture (US) 24, *39*

Bibliographies in American Music (US) *843*

Bibliographies in the History of Psychology and Psychiatry (US) 768, 933, *938*

Bibliographies of Modern Authors (US ISSN 0749-470X) *123*, 716

Bibliographies of the History of Science and Technology (US) *1003*, 1072

Bibliographische Berichte/Bibliographical Bulletin (GW ISSN 0006-1506) *123*

Bibliographischer Informationsdienst der Deutschen Buecherei (GE ISSN 0070-3931) *123*

Bibliography and Index of Geology (US ISSN 0098-2784) 3, *381*

Bibliography and Subject Index of Current Computing Literature *see* A C M Guide to Computing Literature *353*

Bibliography and Subject Index of South African Geology (SA ISSN 0584-2360) 123, *382*

Bibliography Newsletter (US ISSN 0145-3084) *687*, 963

Bibliography of Agriculture (US ISSN 0006-1530) 24, *39*, 123

Bibliography of Agrometeorology *see* Bibliografia Agrometeorologii *808*

Bibliography of Appraisal Literature (US) 102, 265, 638, *966*

Bibliography of Asian Studies (US ISSN 0067-7159) *563*

Bibliography of Bibliographies and Library Science *see* Bibliografia Bibliografii i Nauki o Ksiazce *687*

Bibliography of Bioethics (US ISSN 0363-0161) *768*

Bibliography of Books for Children (US ISSN 0147-250X) *963*

Bibliography of Bulgarian Bibliographies *see* Bibliografia na Bulgarskata Bibliografiia *122*

Bibliography of Canadian Bibliographies(CN ISSN 0067-7175) *123*

Bibliography of Chinese Studies (GW ISSN 0724-8415) *123*

Bibliography of Developmental Medicine and Child Neurology. Books and Articles Received (UK ISSN 0067-7183) *768*

Bibliography of Doctoral Dissertations; Natural and Applied Sciences (II) 123, *1003*

Bibliography of Doctoral Dissertations: Social Sciences and Humanities (II) 123, *1014*

Bibliography of Economic and Statistical Publications on Tanzania (TZ) 123, *204*, 1050

Bibliography of Education Theses in Australia (AT ISSN 0811-0174) *422*, 674, 933, 1006

Bibliography of Fossil Vertebrates (US ISSN 0272-8869) *856*

Bibliography of French 17th Century Studies *see* French 17 *563*

Bibliography of Germfree Research (US) *149*

Bibliography of Hotel and Restaurant Administration (US) 123, *621*

Bibliography of Hotel and Restaurant Administration and Related Subjects *see* Bibliography of Hotel and Restaurant Administration *621*

Bibliography of Hydrology and Oceanology *see* Bibliografia Hydrologii i Oceanologii *381*

Bibliography of Indian Fisheries *see* Indian Fisheries Abstracts *514*

Bibliography of Italian Publications Published or Distributed in Great Britain (UK) *123*

Bibliography of Maritime and Naval History Periodical Articles (US) 563, *1085*

Bibliography of Meteorology *see* Bibliografia Meteorologii *803*

Bibliography of Old Norse-Icelandic Studies (DK ISSN 0067-7213) *563*

Bibliography of Periodical Articles Relating to the South Pacific *see* South Pacific Periodicals Index *131*

Bibliography of Polish Serials *see* Bibliografia Wydawnictw Ciaglych *687*

Bibliography of Publications from Economic Research Centres in India (II) *204*

Bibliography of Publications of University Bureaus of Business and Economic Research *see* University Research in Business and Economics: a Bibliography of (Year) Publications *220*

Bibliography of Skiing Studies (US) 123, *1036*

Bibliography of South African Government Publications (SA ISSN 0067-7256) *123*

Bibliography of Surgery of the Hand (US ISSN 0067-7264) *769*

Bibliography of the Geology of Fiji (FJ ISSN 0252-8398) *382*, 384

Bibliography of the Geology of Missouri (US ISSN 0067-7272) *382*

Bibliography of the History of Medicine(US ISSN 0067-7280) *769*

Bibliography of the Middle East (SY ISSN 0067-7302) *123*

Bibliography of Tourism and Travel Research Studies, Reports and Articles (US) *123*

Bibliography of Water Management and Engineering *see* Bibliografia Gospodarki i Inzynierii Wodnej *402*

Bibliography of Works by Polish Scholars and Scientists Published outside Poland in Languages Other Than Polish (UK ISSN 0067-7310) *123*

Bibliography on Cold Regions Science & Technology (US) 123, 378, *476*

Bibliography on Economics of Containerization *see* Containerization: A Bibliography *1085*

Bibliography on Foreign and Comparative Law: Books and Articles in English. (US ISSN 0067-7329) *668*

Bibliography on Irrigation, Drainage, River Training and Flood Control/Bibliographie Relative aux Irrigations, au Drainage, a la Regularisation des Cours d'Eau et la Matrise des Crues (II ISSN 0523-302X) *1127*

Bibliography on Philippine Geology, Mining and Mineral Resources (PH) *814*

Bibliography on Research in Physical Education and Sport for the Handicapped *see* Bibliografia Erityshyhmien Liikunnan Tutkimuksesta *422*

Bibliography on Satellite Geodesy and Related Subjects *see* International Association of Geodesy. Central Bureau for Satellite Geodesy. Bibliography *551*

Bibliography on Smoking and Health (US ISSN 0067-7361) *886*

Bibliologia (BE) 577, 716, *960*

Biblioteca Alfa-Omega de Poesia Brasileira: Serie 1 (BL) *740*

Biblioteca Apostolica Vaticana. Cataloghi di Manoscritti (VC) *981*

Biblioteca Apostolica Vaticana. Cataloghi di Mostre (VC) *981*

Biblioteca Apostolica Vaticana. Illustrazioni di Codici. Codici Vaticani. Series Major (VC) *981*

Biblioteca Apostolica Vaticana. Illustrazioni di Codici. Codici Vaticani. Series Minor (VC) *981*

Biblioteca Apostolica Vaticana. Studi e Testi (VC) *981*

Biblioteca Azuaya (EC) *603*

Biblioteca Clasica Gredos (SP) *336*

Biblioteca Clasicos Colorados (PY) *1006*

Biblioteca Colombiana (CK) *716*

Biblioteca Cultura Popular (AG) *537*

Biblioteca de Arheologie (RM ISSN 0067-7388) *83*

Biblioteca de Autores Espanoles. Publicacion (SP) *716*

Biblioteca de Ciencias Sociales (AG) *1006*

Biblioteca de Cultura Andina. Ediciones. (PE) *70*

Biblioteca de Economia, Politica, Sociedad. Serie Mayor (AG) *1006*

Biblioteca de Economia, Politica, Sociedad. Serie Menor (AG) *1006*

Biblioteca de Educacao (BL) *411*

Biblioteca de Estudios Paraguayos (PY) 603, 652, *876*

Biblioteca de Filologia Hispanica Onomastica y Toponimia (SP) *692*

Biblioteca de Filosofia (PO) *876*

Biblioteca de la Cultura Panamena (PN) *603*

Biblioteca de Linguistica (SP) *692*

Biblioteca de Menendez Pelayo. Boletin(SP ISSN 0006-1646) 555, *674*, 716

Biblioteca de Temas y Autores de Anzoategui (VE) *603*

Biblioteca de Teologia (SP ISSN 0067-740X) *968*

Biblioteca degli Studi Classici e Orientali (IT) 336, *850*

Biblioteca di Bibliografia Italiana (IT ISSN 0067-7418) *123*

Biblioteca di Labeo (IT ISSN 0067-7434) *628*

Biblioteca di Letteratura e Arte (IT) *716*

Biblioteca di Storia Toscana Moderna e Contemporanea Studi e Documenti (IT ISSN 0067-7442) *577*

Biblioteca di Studi Etruschi (IT ISSN 0067-7450) *692*

Biblioteca do Educador Profissional (PO ISSN 0067-7469) *628*

Biblioteca Filologica. Ensayos (SP) *692*

Biblioteca Filologica. Manuales (SP) *692*

Biblioteca Historica Lundensis (SW) *555*

Biblioteca Istorica (RM ISSN 0067-7493) *577*

Biblioteca Jose Jeronimo Triana (Serial) (CK) *988*

Biblioteca Marsilio: Architettura e Urbanistica (IT) 97, *622*

Biblioteca N T (SP) *628*

Biblioteca Nacional. Boletin *see* Universidad Nacional Autonoma de Mexico. Instituto de Investigaciones Bibliograficas. Boletin *132*

Biblioteca Napoletana di Storia e Arte (IT) 102, *577*

Biblioteca Paraguaya de Antropologia (PY) *70*

Biblioteca Praehistorica Hispana (SP ISSN 0067-7507) *83*

Biblioteca Promocion del Pueblo (SP ISSN 0405-9212) *577*

Biblioteca Romanica Hispanica (SP) *716*

Biblioteca Romanica Hispanica. Estudios y Ensayos *see* Biblioteca Romanica Hispanica *716*

Biblioteca Statale e Libreria Civica di Cremona. Annali (IT ISSN 0392-0550) *577*

Biblioteca Statale e Libreria Civica di Cremona. Mostre (IT) *123*

Biblioteca Storica Toscana *see* Biblioteca Storica Toscana. Serie I *577*

Biblioteca Storica Toscana. Serie I (IT) *577*

Biblioteca Storica Toscana. Serie II (IT) *577*

Biblioteca Theologiae Practicae (SW) *968*

Biblioteca Universitaria y Provincial, Barcelona. Boletin de Noticias (SP) *123*

Bibliotecas e Arquivos de Portugal *see* Patrimonio Cultural *1160*

Bibliotecas Universitarias (NQ) *674*

Bibliotecas y Archivos (MX) *674*

Bibliotecologia y Documentacion Paraguaya (PY) *674*

Biblioteconomia e Bibliografia. Saggi e Studi (IT ISSN 0067-7531) *123*

Biblioteka Archeologiczna (PL ISSN 0067-7639) *83*

Biblioteka Chopinowska (PL) *833*

Biblioteka Etnografii Polskiej (PL ISSN 0067-7655) *1024*

Biblioteka Fizyki (PL ISSN 0137-5059) *887*

Biblioteka Kornicka. Pamietnik (PL ISSN 0551-3790) *674*

Biblioteka Krakowska (PL ISSN 0067-7698) *103*, 577

Biblioteka Matematyczna (PL ISSN 0519-8356) *748*

Biblioteka Mechaniki Stosowanej (PL ISSN 0067-7701) *488*

Biblioteka Narodowa. Rocznik/National Library Year-Book (PL ISSN 0083-7261) *674*

Biblioteka Pediatry (PL) *787*

Biblioteka Pisarzow Polskich *see* Biblioteka Pisarzow Polskich. Seria A *716*

Biblioteka Pisarzow Polskich. Seria A (PL ISSN 0519-8631) *716*

Biblioteka Pisarzy Reformacyjnych (PL ISSN 0519-8658) *968*

Biblioteka Polonijna/Polonia Library (PL) 555, *902*

Biblioteka Res Facta (PL ISSN 0208-9963) *833*

Biblioteka Slaska. Biuletyn Informacyjny *see* Biblioteka Slaska. Ksiaznica Slaska *674*

Biblioteka Slaska. Ksiaznica Slaska (PL) *674*

Biblioteka Sluchacza Koncertowego. Seria Wprowadzajaca (PL ISSN 0067-7779) *833*

Biblioteka Wiadomosci Statystycznych (PL ISSN 0067-7795) *926*

Bibliotekarstvo/Librarianship (YU ISSN 0006-1832) *674*

Bibliotekovedenie, Bibliografiya i Informatika (UR) *674*

Bibliotekoznanie, Bibliografiia, Knigoznanie, Nauchna Informatsiia (BU ISSN 0324-1858) *674*

Biblioteksaarbog (DK ISSN 0084-957X) *674*

Bibliotekshistorie (DK ISSN 0109-923X) *674*

Biblioteksvejviser/Guide to Danish Libraries (DK) *674*

Bibliotheca Aegyptia (US ISSN 0732-6467) *83*, 692

Bibliotheca Aegyptiaca (BE ISSN 0067-7817) *83*

BIOLOGISCHE BUNDESANSTALT 1665

Bibliotheca Afroasiatica (US ISSN 0742-1117) *692*
Bibliotheca Anatomica (SZ ISSN 0067-7833) *138*, *758*
Bibliotheca Archaeologica (SP ISSN 0519-9603) *83*
Bibliotheca Arnamagnaeana (DK ISSN 0067-7841) *716*
Bibliotheca Arnamagnaeana. Supplementum (DK ISSN 0067-785X) *716*
Bibliotheca Athena (IT ISSN 0067-7868) *692*
Bibliotheca Australiana (NE ISSN 0067-7876) *573*
Bibliotheca Bibliographica Aureliana (GW ISSN 0067-7884) *123*
Bibliotheca Bibliographica Neerlandica (NE) *123*
Bibliotheca Botanica (GW ISSN 0067-7892) *155*
Bibliotheca Cardiologica (SZ ISSN 0067-7906) *776*
Bibliotheca Cartographica *see* Bibliographia Cartographica *551*
Bibliotheca Celtica (UK ISSN 0067-7914) *123*
Bibliotheca del Planeamiento Educativo(AG ISSN 0067-7922) *442*
Bibliotheca Dissidentium (GW) *123*, *968*
Bibliotheca Ephemeridum Theologicarum Lovaniensium (BE) *968*
Bibliotheca Gastroenterologica *see* Frontiers of Gastrointestinal Research *782*
Bibliotheca Germanica. Handbuecher, Texte und Monographien aus dem Gebiete der Germanischen Philologie(SZ ISSN 0067-7477) *692*
Bibliotheca Heamatologica *see* Current Studies in Hematology and Blood Transfusion *783*
Bibliotheca Helvetica Romana (SZ ISSN 0067-7965) *336*
Bibliotheca Historica Romaniae. Monographies (RM ISSN 0067-799X) *577*
Bibliotheca Historica Romaniae. Studies(RM ISSN 0067-7981) *577*
Bibliotheca Historico Militaris (UK) *810*
Bibliotheca Humanistica & Reformatorica (NE) *968*
Bibliotheca Hungarica Antiqua (HU ISSN 0067-8007) *930*, *960*
Bibliotheca Ibero-Americana (GW ISSN 0067-8015) *911*
Bibliotheca Indonesica (NE ISSN 0067-8023) *70*
Bibliotheca Instituti Historici Societatis Iesu (IT) *981*
Bibliotheca Islamica (GW ISSN 0170-3102) *850*, *975*
Bibliotheca Latina Medii et Recentiori Aevi (PL ISSN 0067-8031) *83*, *577*
Bibliotheca Lichenologica (GW) *155*
Bibliotheca Mesopotamica (US ISSN 0732-6440) *612*
Bibliotheca Microbiologia *see* Contributions to Microbiology and Immunology *773*
Bibliotheca Mycologica (GW ISSN 0067-8066) *155*
Bibliotheca Nostratica (US ISSN 0342-4871) *123*
Bibliotheca Nutritio et Dieta (SZ ISSN 0067-8198) *846*
Bibliotheca Oeconomica (RM ISSN 0067-8082) *191*
Bibliotheca Ophthalmologica *see* Developments in Ophthalmology *785*
Bibliotheca Orientalis Hungarica (HU ISSN 0067-8104) *850*
Bibliotheca Paediatrica *see* Monographs in Paediatrics *788*
Bibliotheca Phycologica (GW ISSN 0067-8112) *155*
Bibliotheca Primatologica *see* Contributions to Primatology *174*
Bibliotheca Psychiatrica (SZ ISSN 0067-8147) *789*
Bibliotheca Romanica (SZ ISSN 0067-7515) *692*

Bibliotheca Russica (GW ISSN 0341-3217) *692*, *716*
Bibliotheca Seraphico-Capuccina (IT ISSN 0067-8163) *981*
Bibliotheca Unitariorum (NE) *978*
Bibliotheca Vita Humana *see* Contributions to Human Development *759*
Biblioteck (UK ISSN 0006-193X) *960*
Bibliothek der Griechischen Literatur (GW ISSN 0340-7853) *337*
Bibliothek der Klassischen Altertumswissenschaften. Neue Folge(GW ISSN 0067-8201) *555*
Bibliothek des Buchwesens (B B) (GW ISSN 0340-8051) *674*
Bibliothek fuer Zeitgeschichte, Stuttgart. Jahresbibliographie (GW ISSN 0081-8992) *563*
Bibliothek fuer Zeitgeschichte, Stuttgart. Schriften (GW ISSN 0081-900X) *555*
Bibliothek und Wissenschaft (GW ISSN 0067-8236) *674*
Bibliothekar-Lehrinstitut des Landes Nordrhein-Westfalen. Arbeiten aus dem B L I *see* Koelner Arbeiten zum Bibliotheks- und Dokumentationswesen *680*
Bibliothekar-Lehrinstitut des Landes Nordrhein-Westfalen. Bibliographische Hefte *see* Koelner Arbeiten zum Bibliotheks- und Dokumentationswesen *680*
Bibliotheken der Bundesrepublik Deutschland. Datierte Handschriften (GW ISSN 0175-6796) *675*
Bibliotheks Taschenbuch (GW) *675*
Bibliothekspraxis (GW ISSN 0300-287X) *675*
Bibliotheksstudien (GW) *675*
Bibliotheque Africaine. Catalogue des Acquisitions. Catologus van de Aanwinsten (BE ISSN 0067-5601) *123*, *563*
Bibliotheque d'Etudes Balkaniques (FR ISSN 0067-8325) *692*, *716*
Bibliotheque d'Histoire Antillaise (GP) *603*
Bibliotheque de la Mer (FR ISSN 0067-8260) *1036*
Bibliotheque de la Revue d'Histoire Ecclesiastique (BE ISSN 0067-8279) *981*
Bibliotheque des Cahiers Archeologiques (FR ISSN 0067-8309) *83*
Bibliotheque des Ecoles Francaises d'Athenes et de Rome Publication *see* B E F A R. Publication *83*
Bibliotheque des Lettres Quebecoises (CN) *628*
Bibliotheque du Museon *see* Universite Catholique de Louvain. Institut Orientaliste. Publications *572*
Bibliotheque Francaise et Romane. Serie A: Manuels et Etudes Linguistiques (FR ISSN 0067-8341) *692*
Bibliotheque Francaise et Romane. Serie B: Editions Critiques de Textes (FR ISSN 0067-835X) *716*
Bibliotheque Francaise et Romane. Serie C: Etudes Litteraires (FR ISSN 0067-8368) *716*
Bibliotheque Francaise et Romane. Serie D: Initiation, Textes et Documents (FR ISSN 0067-8376) *716*
Bibliotheque Francaise et Romane. Serie E: Langue et Litterature Francaises au Canada (FR ISSN 0067-8384) *692*, *716*
Bibliotheque Historique (FR) *555*
Bibliotheque Historique Vaudoise (SZ ISSN 0067-8406) *577*
Bibliotheque Introuvable (FR ISSN 0067-8422) *716*
Bibliotheque Philosophique de Louvain (BE ISSN 0067-8430) *876*
Bibliotheque Royale Albert 1er. Rapport Annuel (BE ISSN 0770-4526) *675*
Bibliotheque Royale de Belgique. Rapport Annuel *see* Bibliotheque Royale Albert 1er. Rapport Annuel *675*

Bibliotheque Universitaire, Grenoble. Publications (FR ISSN 0072-7520) *988*
Bibliotheques et Musees (SZ) *577*, *826*
Biblische Beitraege (SZ ISSN 0582-1673) *968*
Biblische Untersuchungen (GW ISSN 0523-5154) *968*
Biblisches Seminar (GW) *968*
Biblos (PO) *716*
Bicycle Dealer Showcase Buyers Guide (US) *1041*
Bidrag til H. C. Andersens Bibliografi (DK ISSN 0067-8473) *739*
Bidrag till Kaennedom av Finlands Natur och Folk (FI ISSN 0067-8481) *629*, *1006*
Biennale Internationale de la Tapisserie *see* Catalogue Biennale Internationale de Lausanne *103*
Biennial Report-Educational Communications Board *see* Wisconsin. Educational Communications Board. Biennial Report *421*
Biennial Report of the Arts Activities in Alabama *see* Annual Report of the Arts Activities in Alabama *101*
Biennial Report - State of Minnesota, Department of Revenue *see* Minnesota. Department of Revenue. Biennial Report *297*
Biennial Report - Texas Department of Health Resources *see* Texas. Department of Health Resources. Biennial Report *956*
Biennial Survey of Advertising Expenditures Around the World *see* World Advertising Expenditures *16*
Bifidobacteria and Microflora (JA) *138*, *155*
Big Apple Dyke News (US) *615*, *1128*
Big Book (US) *182*
Big Enid Blyton Story Annual (UK) *335*
Big Scream (US) *710*
Big Ten Football Yearbook (US) *341*, *1037*
Biggest Greatest Cracked Annual (US) *710*
Bihar Research Society. Journal (II) *612*, *1024*
Bijdrage tot de Geschiedenis van het Zeewezen (NE ISSN 0523-5774) *577*, *810*
Bijdragen tot de Bibliotheekwetenschap/Contributions to Library Science (BE ISSN 0067-8538) *675*
Bijdragen tot de Geschiedenis der Stad Deinze en van Het Land aan Leie en Schelde (BE) *555*
Bijdragen tot de Geschiedenis van Arnhem (NE ISSN 0067-8554) *577*
Bijdragen tot de Geschiedenis van de Tweede Wereldoorlog (BE) *577*
Bikini Girl (US) *710*
Bil Jul (DK) *1148*
Bil-Revyen (DK) *1090*
Bil Testen (DK ISSN 0900-8659) *491*
Bildung im Geschichtsmuseum (GE) *578*, *826*
Bildung im Zahlenspiegel (GW) *423*, *1050*
Bilens Aarsrevy (DK ISSN 0108-5018) *1090*
Bilismen i Danmark (DK ISSN 0901-6120) *1090*
Bilismen i Sverige *see* Motor Traffic in Sweden *1092*
Bill of Rights Journal (US) *912*
Billboard. International Buyer's Guide of the Music-Record Industry *see* Billboard's International Buyer's Guide of the Music-Record-Tape Industry *833*
Billboard International Directory of Recording Studios *see* Billboard's International Recording Equipment & Studio Directory *1031*
Billboard International Tape Directory *see* Billboard's Audio/Video/Tape Sourcebook *1031*
Billboard's Audio/Video/Tape Sourcebook (US) *1031*
Billboard's Country Music Sourcebook *see* Country Music Sourcebook *835*

Billboard's International Buyer's Guide of the Music-Record-Tape Industry (US ISSN 0067-8600) *833*
Billboard's International Recording Equipment & Studio Directory (US ISSN 0160-7790) *1031*
Billboard's International Recording Studio and Equipment Directory (US) *1031*
Billboard's Talent in Action *see* Billboard's Year-End Issue Talent in Action *833*
Billboard's Year-End Awards/Talent in Action *see* Billboard's Year-End Issue Talent in Action *833*
Billboard's Year-End Issue Talent in Action (US) *833*
Bilten za Hematologiju i Transfuziju (YU ISSN 0523-6150) *783*
BiN *see* Bibliography Newsletter *687*
Binghamton Public Library. Annual Report (US) *675*
Die Binnengewaesser (GW ISSN 0067-8643) *138*, *402*
Binsted's Directory of Food Trade Marks and Brand Names (UK ISSN 0067-8651) *518*
Ha-Binui Be-Yisrael *see* Israel. Central Bureau of Statistics. Construction in Israel *185*
Bio-Bibliografia Boliviana (BO) *123*
Bio-Bibliographies in American Literature (US ISSN 0742-695X) *739*
Bio-Bibliographies in Law and Political Science (US ISSN 0882-7052) *668*
Bio-Bibliographies in Music (US ISSN 0742-6968) *843*
Biochemical Pathology *see* Biochemistry of Disease *151*
Biochemical Reviews (II ISSN 0365-9429) *151*
Biochemical Society Symposia (US) *151*
Biochemistry of Disease (US ISSN 0067-8678) *151*, *758*
Biochemistry: Series of Monographs (US ISSN 0194-0538) *151*
Bioengineering Abstracts (US ISSN 0736-6213) *3*, *476*
Biofeedback Society of America. Proceedings of the Annual Meeting (US ISSN 0094-0895) *789*, *933*
Biofizika Zhivoi Kletki (UR ISSN 0301-2425) *163*
Bioraficke Studie (CS ISSN 0067-8724) *133*
Biographical Dictionaries and Related Works (US) *123*, *133*
Biographical Dictionaries and Related Works. Supplement (US) *136*
Biographical Dictionaries Master Index *see* Biography and Genealogy Master Index *136*
Biography Almanac (US ISSN 0738-0097) *133*
Biography and Genealogy Master Index(US ISSN 0730-1316) *3*, *136*
Biography Index (US ISSN 0006-3053) *3*, *136*
BioIndonesia (IO ISSN 0126-0758) *138*
Biokhimiya Zhivotnykh i Cheloveka (UR ISSN 0136-9377) *151*
Biologi (DK ISSN 0108-1942) *138*
Biologia (PL ISSN 0554-811X) *138*
Biological and Agricultural Index (US ISSN 0006-3177) *3*, *39*, *149*
Biological and Cultural Tests for Control of Plant Diseases (US ISSN 0887-2236) *155*
Biological Research Reports from the University of Jyvaskyla (FI ISSN 0356-1062) *138*
Biological Structure and Function (UK ISSN 0308-5384) *171*
Biological Substances (UN) *138*
Biologicheskie Nauki (UR) *138*
Biologie du Sol *see* Pedofauna *58*
Biologische Abhandlungen (GW ISSN 0006-3282) *138*
Biologische Bundesanstalt fuer Land- und Forstwirtschaft, Berlin-Dahlem. Mitteilungen (Biologische Bundesanstalt fuer Land- und Forstwirtschaft in Berlin-Dahlem) (GW ISSN 0067-5849) *24*, *523*

BIOLOGISCHE BUNDESANSTALT

Biologische Bundesanstalt fuer Land- und Forstwirtschaft in Berlin-Dahlem
Biologische Bundesanstalt fuer Land- und Forstwirtschaft, Berlin-Dahlem. Mitteilungen *see* Biologische Bundesanstalt fuer Land- und Forstwirtschaft, Berlin-Dahlem. Mitteilungen *24*
Biologiya Laboratornykh Zhivotnykh (UR) *781*
Biology Series (Seattle) (US) *138*
Biomassa (BL) *331*
Biomathematics (US ISSN 0067-8821) *138, 748*
Biomechanics *see* Biomekhanika *894*
Biomedical Bulletin (Association for Voluntary Surgical Contraception, Inc.) (US) *179*
Biomedical Engineering and Health Systems: A Wiley-Interscience Series(US) *758, 952*
Biomedical Engineering and Instrumentation Series (US) *470*
Biomedical Engineering Series of Monographs *see* Biomedical Engineering and Health Systems: A Wiley-Interscience Series *758*
Biomedical Research Technology Program (US) *138, 149*
Biomedical Sciences Instrumentation (US ISSN 0067-8856) *636, 758*
Biomekhanika/Biomechanics (BU ISSN 0204-7594) *152, 894*
Biomembranes (US ISSN 0067-8864) *163*
Biometeorology; Proceedings (NE ISSN 0067-8902) *803*
Bionika (UR ISSN 0374-6569) *153*
Biophysical Society. Abstracts (US ISSN 0067-8910) *153*
Biophysical Society. Symposium Proceedings *see* Biophysical Society. Abstracts *153*
Biopsy Interpretation Series (US) *781*
BIOSIS/CAS Selects: Biochemistry of Fermented Foods (US ISSN 0276-3109) *3, 521*
Biosis: List of Serials *see* Serial Sources for the Biosis Data Base *150*
BIOSIS Search Guide (US) *3, 149*
Biotechnology Abstracts *see* Biotechnology Research Abstracts *149*
Biotechnology and Genetic Engineering Reviews (UK ISSN 0264-8725) *24, 138, 478, 758*
Biotechnology Directory (US) *303*
Biotechnology in Agricuiulture and Forestry (US) *24, 523, 1067*
Biotechnology Research Abstracts (US ISSN 0733-5709) *149*
Biotechnology Resources *see* Biomedical Research Technology Program *149*
Biotronics (JA ISSN 0289-0011) *138, 494*
Birbal (II ISSN 0006-3614) *335*
Bird Control Seminar. Proceedings (US ISSN 0067-8945) *1148*
Bird Effort (US) *710*
Bird Research (UK) *170*
Bird Watch (US) *170, 1044*
Birdwatcher's Yearbook *see* Birdwatcher's Yearbook and Diary *170*
Birdwatcher's Yearbook and Diary (UK) *170, 364*
Birkbeck College Discussion Papers in Economics (UK) *191*
Birkner Eurolignum (GW) *189*
Birmingham & Warwickshire Archaeological Society. Transactions (UK ISSN 0140-4202) *83*
Birmingham & West Midlands Chambers of Commerce Directory (UK ISSN 0307-0158) *234*
Birmingham Historical Society. Journal (US) *603*
Birmingham International Trade Directory (US) *253, 303*
Birmingham Post & Mail Year Book and Who's Who (UK) *133*
Birmingham Post Year Book and Who's Who *see* Birmingham Post & Mail Year Book and Who's Who *133*
Birth Defects Institute. Symposia (US) *758*
Birth Defects Original Article Series (US ISSN 0547-6844) *758*
Birthstone (US) *103, 740*
Bistandshaandbogen (DK ISSN 0108-8351) *1015*
Bit International (YU) *347*
Bithell Series of Dissertations *see* University of London. Institute of Germanic Studies. Bithell Series of Dissertations *736*
Bituminous Coal Data *see* Coal Data *815*
Bituminous Coal Facts *see* Coal Facts *815*
Biuletyn Geologiczny (PL ISSN 0067-9003) *384*
Biuletyn Meteorologiczny (PL) *803*
Biuletyn Peryglacjalny (PL ISSN 0067-9038) *398*
Biuletyn Slawistyczny (PL ISSN 0137-5431) *692*
Biuletyn Warzywniczy (PL ISSN 0509-6839) *531*
Bizantion Nea Hellas (CL) *629, 692*
Bjerg-Posten. Medlemsblad (DK ISSN 0107-072X) *578*
B'kitzur/Briefs (US) *976*
Blaavand Fuglestation. Rapport (DK ISSN 0901-0637) *170*
Black & Decker Build It (US) *614, 614*
Black Bag (UK ISSN 0045-2084) *758*
Black Bart (US) *710*
Black Bart Brigade *see* Black Bart *710*
Black Caucus Journal (US ISSN 0732-7269) *502*
Black Coal in Australia (AT) *814*
Black Country Bugle Annual (UK) *538*
Black Country Geologist (UK ISSN 0260-714X) *384*
Black Elected Officials (US ISSN 0882-1593) *502, 939*
Black Experience in Children's Books (US ISSN 0067-9070) *334*
Black Jack (US) *502, 716*
Black Lechwe (ZA ISSN 0045-219X) *364*
Black Literature and Arts Congress *see* B L A C *501*
Black Maria (US ISSN 0045-222X) *716, 1128*
Black Messiah (US) *502*
Black Ministries (US) *502, 978*
Black Oracle *see* Cinemacabre *823*
Black Pages Pamphlet Series (US) *502*
Black Papers (US) *1015*
Black Political Studies (US) *902*
Black Position (US ISSN 0084-7909) *740, 912*
Black Resource Guide (US) *502*
Black Review (SA) *502*
Black River Review (US) *740*
Black Studies Series (US) *1033*
Black Who's Who of Southern Africa (SA) *133, 191*
Blackberry (US) *740*
Blackface Sheep Breeders' Association Journal (UK) *64*
Black's Guide to the Office Space Market. Connecticut/New York Suburbs (US) *965*
Black's Guide to the Office Space Market. Northern New Jersey (US) *965*
Black's Guide to the Office Space Market. Philadelphia and Suburbs (US) *965*
Black's Guide to the Office Space Market. Washington/Baltimore (US) *965*
Blacks in the New World (US) *502*
Black's Medical Dictionary (UK) *758*
Black's Veterinary Dictionary (UK) *1121*
Blackwell Newsletter (CN ISSN 0707-820X) *535*
Blaetter der Rilke-Gesellschaft (SZ) *716*
Blaetter fuer deutsche Landesgeschichte(GW ISSN 0006-4408) *578*
Blaetter fuer Pfaelzische Kirchengeschichte und Religioese Volkskunde (GW ISSN 0341-9452) *978*
Blaetter fuer Technikgeschichte (US ISSN 0067-9127) *1067*
Blaetter fuer Wuerttembergische Kirchengeschichte (GW ISSN 0067-9461) *578, 968*
Blakes Boating Holiday Books (UK) *1041*
Blakes Boating Holidays (UK) *1041, 1106*
Blakes Boating in Britain *see* Blakes Boating Holidays *1106*
Blakes Boating in Europe *see* Blakes Boating Holidays *1106*
Blank Tape *see* Bikini Girl *710*
Blantyre Water Board. Annual Report and Statement of Accounts (MW ISSN 0084-7925) *1123*
Blastpipe (UK ISSN 0263-0125) *1094*
Blaue Datei der Krankenhauslieferanten(GW) *616*
Blaue Datei der Krankenhauslieferanten mit Krankenhausverzeichnis *see* Blaue Datei der Krankenhauslieferanten *616*
Blicheregnens Museumsforening. Aarsskrift (DK ISSN 0107-6094) *578*
Blick hinter die Fassade (GW ISSN 0067-9178) *1015*
Blind Donkey (US) *977*
Blindes Jul (DK ISSN 0901-4306) *179*
Blindness *see* Association for Education and Rehabilitation of the Blind and Visually Impaired. Yearbook *1015*
Blindness, Visual Impairment, Deaf-Blindness *see* Association for Education and Rehabilitation of the Blind and Visually Impaired. Yearbook *1015*
Bliss Classification Bulletin (UK ISSN 0520-2795) *675*
Blixeniana (DK ISSN 0105-2071) *1148*
Bloemfontein Agricultural Show Catalogue (SA) *25*
Bloodroot (Grand Forks) (US ISSN 0161-2506) *716*
Bloodstock Breeders' Review (UK ISSN 0067-9224) *64*
Bloodstock Sales Review and Stud Register (UK) *1042*
Bloomsbury Geographer (UK ISSN 0067-9232) *542*
Blue Book, Inboard/Outdrive Boat Trade-in Guide (US ISSN 0520-2949) *1041*
Blue Book: Leaders of the English-Speaking World (US ISSN 0067-9240) *133*
Blue Book of British Broadcasting (UK) *347*
Blue Book of College Athletics (US) *1033*
Blue Book of Food Store Operators & Wholesalers (CN ISSN 0316-9537) *521, 1050*
Blue Book of Fur Farming (US) *672*
Blue Book of Gun Values (US) *1033*
Blue Book of Junior & Community College Athletics (US) *1033*
Blue Book of Junior College Athletics *see* Blue Book of Junior & Community College Athletics *1033*
Blue Book of Major Home Builders (US ISSN 0195-8461) *182*
Blue Book of Materials, Compounding Ingredients and Machinery for Rubber (US) *985*
Blue Book of Occupational Education *see* Occupational Education *437*
Blue Book of Optometrists (US ISSN 0067-9283) *785*
Blue Book of S.A. Business *see* Business Blue Book of S.A *192*
Blue Buildings (US) *740*
Blue Chart Report (CN) *638*
Blue Chip Stocks (US) *265*
Blue Guitar (IT) *716*
Blue Horse (US) *716*
Blue Pig (US) *740*
Blue Sky News (US) *939*
Bluegrass Directory (US) *636, 833*
Blueline (US ISSN 0198-9901) *716*
Blues Research (US) *833*
Board of Celtic Studies. Bulletin (UK ISSN 0142-3363) *578, 692, 717*
Boat & Motor Dealer (US ISSN 0006-5366) *303, 1041*
Boat & Motor Dealer's Market (US) *1041*
Boat Owners Buyers Guide *see* Yachting's Boat Buyers Guide *1042*
Boat World (UK ISSN 0067-933X) *1041*
Boatbuilder's International Directory (US) *1099*
Boating Almanac - Florida (US) *1148*
Boating Almanac, Vol. 1 - Rhode Island, Massachusetts, Maine, New Hampshire (US) *1041*
Boating Almanac, Vol. 2 - Long Island, Connecticut, Rhode Island, Southern Massachusetts (US) *1041*
Boating Almanac, Vol. 3 - New Jersey, Delaware Bay, Hudson River, Lake Champlain, Erie Canal (US) *1041*
Boating Almanac, Vol. 4 - Chesapeake Bay, Delaware, Maryland, District of Columbia, Virginia (US) *1041*
Boating Almanac, Vol. 5-North Carolina, South Carolina, Georgia (US) *1148*
Boating Industry Marine Buyers Guide (US) *303, 1099*
Boating Registration Statistics (US ISSN 0163-7207) *1036*
Boating Statistics (US) *1036*
Bob Wilson's T V Sports Annual (UK) *1033*
Bob Zwirz' Fishing Annual *see* Fishing and Boating Illustrated *1045*
Bocagiana (PO) *155, 173*
Bochum Studies in English *see* Bochumer Anglistische Studien *717*
Bochumer Anglistische Studien/Bochum Studies in English (NE ISSN 0169-6165) *717*
Bochumer Materialen zur Entwicklungsforschung und Entwicklungspolitik (GW ISSN 0170-1916) *261, 914*
Bochumer Schriften zur Entwicklungsforschung und Entwicklungspolitik (GW ISSN 0572-6654) *261, 914*
Bodendenkmalpflege in Mecklenburg (GE ISSN 0067-9461) *827*
Body Fashions Directory and Source of Supply *see* Body Fashions/Intimate Apparel Directory *340*
Body Fashions/Intimate Apparel Directory (US ISSN 0362-2452) *340*
Boernebibliotekskatalog. Boeger z Tidsskrifter Emnekatalog (DK ISSN 0106-9713) *123*
Boernebibliotekskatalog. Boeger z Tidsskrifter Forfatterkatalog (DK ISSN 0106-9691) *123*
Boernebibliotekskatalog. Boeger z Tidsskrifter Titelkatalog (DK ISSN 0106-9705) *123*
Boernebibliotekskatalog. Dias, Film *see* Boernebibliotekskatalog. Dias, Film, Video *334*
Boernebibliotekskatalog. Dias, Film, Video (DK ISSN 0109-2030) *334, 825*
Boernebibliotekskatalog. Grammofonplader Kassetteband (DK ISSN 0106-729X) *843*
Boernebibliotekskatalog. Lydboeger *see* Boernebibliotekskatalog. Lydboeger, Bog & Baand *334*
Boernebibliotekskatalog. Lydboeger, Bog & Baand (DK ISSN 0109-193X) *334*
Boernebladets Jul *see* Alle Boerns Jul *335*
Boernebogsserier *see* Boernebogsserier Tegneserier *335*
Boernebogsserier Tegneserier (DK ISSN 0106-8199) *335*
Boernefilmkataloget (DK ISSN 0105-1377) *335, 822*
Boernefilmkataloget. Supplement (DK ISSN 0106-7990) *335, 825*
Boerneplader Boernekassetter *see* Boernebibliotekskatalog. Grammofonplader Kassetteband *843*
Boernetandplejen i Danmark (DK ISSN 0108-6618) *333, 779*
Boerse (AU) *225, 265*
Boethius (GW ISSN 0523-8226) *988*
Bog og Baand (DK ISSN 0107-5187) *960*
Bogazici Universitesi Dergisi: Ey Oneticilik, Ekonomi, ve Sosyal Bilimler *see* Bogazici University Journal: Management, Economic and Social Sciences *1006*
Bogazici University Journal: Engineering (TU) *470*

BOSTON SEA 1667

Bogazici University Journal: Management, Economic and Social Sciences/Bogazici Universitesi Dergisi: Ey Oneticilik, Ekonomi, ve Sosyal Bilimler (TU) *1006*
Bogazici University Journal: Sciences (TU) *988*
Bogazici University Journal: Social Sciences see Bogazici University Journal: Management, Economic and Social Sciences *1006*
Bogg (US ISSN 0882-648X) *717*
Boghvedegryn (DK ISSN 0108-2019) *717*
Bogvennen (DK ISSN 0006-5749) *930, 960*
Bohemia: Zeitschrift fuer Geschichte und Kultur der Bohemischen Laender(GW ISSN 0523-8587) *578*
Bol og by see Landbohistorisk Tidsskrift *589*
Boletim Alagoano de Folclore (BL) *515*
Boletim Climatologico (BL ISSN 0067-9585) *803*
Boletim de Analise e Logica Matematica (BL) *748*
Boletim de Bibliografia Portuguesa see Boletim de Bibliografia Portuguesa. Publicacoes em Serie *687*
Boletim de Bibliografia Portuguesa see Boletim de Bibliografia Portuguesa. Documentos nao Textuais *687*
Boletim de Bibliografia Portuguesa. Documentos nao Textuais (PO ISSN 0253-343X) *687*
Boletim de Bibliografia Portuguesa. Publicacoes em Serie (PO ISSN 0253-3421) *687*
Boletim de Ciencias do Mar (BL ISSN 0067-9593) *138*
Boletim de Engenharia de Producao (BL ISSN 0067-9607) *470*
Boletim de Indicadores Energeticos (BL) *464*
Boletim de Pesquisa (BL ISSN 0101-5117) *25*
Boletim de Zoologia (BL ISSN 0101-3580) *139*
Boletim de Zoologia e Biologia Marinha. Nova Serie see Boletim de Zoologia *139*
Boletim Microssismico (PO) *1148*
Boletim Paulista de Geografia (BL ISSN 0006-6079) *542*
Boletim Sismico (PO ISSN 0006-6109) *1148*
Boletin de Filologia (CL ISSN 0067-9674) *692*
Boletin de Informacion Comercial (UY) *1148*
Boletin de la Sociedad Cientifica del Paraguay y del Museo Etnografico (PY ISSN 0560-4168) *70*
Boletin de Medicinica Tradicional Grupo "Juan Tomas Roig" (CU) *758*
Boletin de Pequena Jurisprudencia (SP) *652*
Boletin de Salud Publica (VE) *952*
Boletin del Archivo de la Paz (BO) *603*
Boletin Epidemiologico (MX) *952*
Boletin Epidemiologico Anual see Boletin Epidemiologico *952*
Boletin Genetico (AG ISSN 0067-9720) *166*
Boletin Geologico (CK ISSN 0120-1425) *384*
Boletin Hemerografico see Sintesis Bibliografica *217*
Boletin Hidrologico (CR ISSN 0067-9747) *402*
Boletin Historico see Boletin Historico del Ejercito *555*
Boletin Historico del Ejercito (UY) *555*
Boletin Informativo S A E (CU) *652*
Boletin Ingenieria Comercial (CL) *470*
Boletin Interamericano de Archivos see Anuario Interamericano de Archivos *603*
Boletin Interamericano de Contabilidad (AG) *221*
Boletin Trimestral de Informacion Economica (EC) *191*
Bolivia. Instituto Nacional de Estadistica. Anuario de Comercio Exterior (BO) *204, 1050*
Bolivia. Instituto Nacional de Estadistica. Anuario de Estadisticas Industriales (BO) *204, 1050*
Bolivia. Instituto Nacional de Estadistica. Estadisticas Regionales Departamentales (BO) *948, 1050*
Bolivia. Instituto Nacional de Estadistica. Indice de Precios al Consumidor (BO) *204*
Bolivia. Servicio Geologico. Boletin (BO ISSN 0067-9828) *378*
Bolivia. Servicio Geologico. Circulare (BO ISSN 0067-9836) *378*
Bolivia. Servicio Geologico. Informe (BO ISSN 0067-9844) *378*
Bolivia. Servicio Geologico. Serie Mineralogica. Contribucione (BO ISSN 0067-9852) *378, 814*
Bolivia. Superintendencia Nacional de Seguros y Reaseguros. Coleccion Estudios (BO) *638*
Bolivia en Cifras (BO) *1050*
Bolivia: Guia Eclesiastica (BO) *981*
Bollettino del Repertorio e dell'Atlante Demologico Sardo see B R A D S *515*
Bollettino dell'Atlante Linguistico Italiano (IT) *502, 692*
Bollettino dell'Attivita di Inanellamento/Bulletin of Bird Ringing Activity (IT) *170*
Bollettino di Zoologia Agraria e di Bachicoltura (IT ISSN 0366-2403) *164*
Bolsa (AG) *234*
Bolsa de Barcelona. Memoria (SP) *265*
Bolsa de Cereales. Revista Institucional. Numero Estadistico (AG ISSN 0084-7968) *25*
Bolsa de Comercio de Buenos Aires. Boletin see Bolsa *234*
Bolsa de Comercio de Rosario. Revista (AG ISSN 0006-6931) *234*
Bolsa de Valores de Lima. Memoria (PE) *265*
Bolsa de Valores de Quito. Informes y Memoria Anual (EC) *265*
Bolsa de Valores de Sao Paulo. Relatorio (BL) *265*
Bolsa de Valores do Rio de Janeiro. Resumo Anual (BL ISSN 0557-0506) *265*
Bolsilibros (UY ISSN 0067-9909) *603, 717*
Bolton Landing Conference. Proceedings (US) *470*
Bomb Summary see U.S. Federal Bureau of Investigation. Bomb Summary *373*
Bombay Labour Journal (II ISSN 0067-9917) *270*
Bombay Technologist (II ISSN 0067-9925) *321, 1067*
Bond Market: Analysis and Outlook (US) *265*
Bond Market in Luxemburg Francs and in Ecu (LU) *204, 265*
Bonner Akademische Reden (GW ISSN 0344-1857) *876*
Bonner Arbeiten zur Deutschen Literatur (GW ISSN 0068-001X) *717*
Bonner Beitraege zur Bibliotheks- und Buecherkunde (GW ISSN 0068-0028) *675*
Bonner Beitraege zur Kunstwissenschaft(GW ISSN 0068-0036) *103*
Bonner Beitraege zur Soziologie (GW ISSN 0068-0044) *1024*
Bonner Geographische Abhandlungen (GW ISSN 0373-0468) *542*
Bonner Geschichtsblaetter (GW ISSN 0068-0052) *578*
Bonner Meteorologische Abhandlungen (GW ISSN 0006-7156) *803*
Bonner Romanistische Arbeiten (GW) *692*
Bonner Zoologische Monographien (GW ISSN 0302-671X) *173*
Bonny Moor Hen (UK ISSN 0142-7660) *170*
Bonplandia (AG ISSN 0524-0476) *155*
Bontebok (SA) *494*
Book Auction Records (UK ISSN 0068-0125) *960*
Book Collectors' Handbook of Values (US) *960*

Book Dealers' and Collectors' Year-Book and Diary (UK ISSN 0142-9523) *1148*
Book Forum (US ISSN 0094-9426) *629, 717, 960*
Book Industry Study Group. Research Report see Book Industry Trends *960*
Book Industry Trends (US ISSN 0160-970X) *960*
Book Markets in the Americas, Africa, Asia and Australasia (UK) *960*
Book Markets in Western and Eastern Europe (UK) *283, 960*
Book of Apple Software (US ISSN 0736-2692) *361, 362, 362*
Book of Bantams (US ISSN 0068-0117) *64*
Book of Baseball Records (US) *1037*
Book of IBM Software (US ISSN 0738-7172) *361, 362, 362*
Book of Junior Authors and Illustrators see Junior Authors and Illustrators Series *646*
Book of Papers, National Technical Conference see American Association of Textile Chemists and Colorists. National Technical Conference. Book of Papers *1073*
Book of the States (US ISSN 0068-0125) *939, 1050*
Book on Starting Pitchers (US ISSN 0739-4667) *1037*
Book Publishers (UK) *283, 960*
Book Publishers in Canada see Book Trade in Canada *960*
Book Publishing Annual (US) *1148*
Book Report (UK ISSN 0142-7628) *960, 963*
Book Review Digest (US ISSN 0006-7326) *3, 963*
Book Review Index: Annual Clothbound Cumulations (US ISSN 0524-0581) *3, 739*
Book Talk (US ISSN 0145-627X) *960*
Book Trade in Canada/Industrie du Livre au Canada (CN ISSN 0700-5296) *960*
Bookdealers in India, Pakistan and Sri Lanka (US ISSN 0143-0270) *960*
Bookdealers in North America see Sheppard's Bookdealers in North America *963*
Bookman's Guide to Americana (US ISSN 0068-0133) *960*
Bookman's Price Index (US ISSN 0068-0141) *960*
Bookmark (AT ISSN 0310-0391) *675, 960*
Bookmark (UK ISSN 0260-0315) *717*
Bookmark (Albany) (US ISSN 0006-7407) *675*
Bookmark (Chapel Hill) (US ISSN 0006-7393) *675*
Books About Malaysia see Books about Singapore *1119*
Books About Negro Life for Children see Black Experience in Children's Books *334*
Books about Singapore (SI ISSN 0068-0176) *563, 1119*
Books and Articles on Oriental Subjects Published in Japan (JA ISSN 0524-0654) *103, 568, 717, 977*
Books and Libraries at the University of Kansas (US ISSN 0006-7458) *675, 960*
Books at Brown (US ISSN 0147-0787) *717*
Books for Everybody (CN) *960*
Books for Secondary School Libraries (US ISSN 0068-0184) *411, 675*
Books for the Teen Age (US ISSN 0068-0192) *675*
Books from Israel (IS ISSN 0333-6166) *1148*
Books from Pakistan (PK ISSN 0068-0206) *124*
Books in Arabic (CN ISSN 0705-7172) *124, 717*
Books in Armenian (CN ISSN 0705-8209) *124, 717*
Books in Bengali (CN ISSN 0316-7437) *124, 717*
Books in Chinese (CN) *124, 717*
Books in Danish (CN ISSN 0705-2332) *124, 717*
Books in Dutch (CN ISSN 0705-2294) *124, 717*

Books in Finnish (CN ISSN 0705-1883) *124, 717*
Books in Hindi (CN ISSN 0705-8373) *124, 717*
Books in Hungarian (CN ISSN 0705-6494) *124, 717*
Books in Library and Information Science Series (US) *675*
Books in Print (US ISSN 0068-0214) *124*
Books in Print Supplement (US ISSN 0000-0310) *124*
Books in Series (US ISSN 0000-0906) *124*
Books in Series in the United States see Books in Series *124*
Books in Soils and the Environment Series (US ISSN 0081-1890) *53*
Books in Spanish (CN ISSN 0705-7156) *124, 717*
Books in Urdu (CN ISSN 0705-825X) *124, 717*
Books of Oral Tradition (US) *860*
Books Out of Print (US ISSN 0000-0736) *124*
Booksellers Association of Great Britain and Ireland. Charter Group. Economic Survey (UK ISSN 0141-917X) *283, 960*
Booksellers Association of Great Britain and Ireland. Directory of Members (UK) *960*
Booksellers Association of Great Britain and Ireland. List of Members see Booksellers Association of Great Britain and Ireland. Directory of Members *960*
Booksellers Association of Great Britain and Ireland. Trade Reference Book (UK ISSN 0068-0257) *960*
Bor'ba s Gazom v Ugol'nykh Shakhtakh(UR) *814*
Bord Iascaigh Mhara. Tuarascail Agus Cuntaisi/Irish Sea Fisheries Board. Annual Report (IE ISSN 0068-0265) *508*
Border Agricultural Show Prize List (SA) *64*
Border Issues and Public Policy. Research Papers (US) *603, 902*
Border Leicester Flock Book (UK) *64*
Border Perspectives. Research Papers (US) *603, 902*
Border States (US ISSN 0092-4571) *603*
Bordtennis Aarbogen (DK ISSN 0109-6761) *1037*
Boreal Institute, Edmonton. Miscellaneous Publications (CN ISSN 0068-029X) *629*
Boreal Institute, Edmonton. Occasional Publications (CN ISSN 0068-0303) *603*
Boreal Institute, Edmonton. Report of Activities see Boreal Institute for Northern Studies. Report of Activities *603*
Boreal Institute for Northern Studies. Report of Activities (CN ISSN 0820-988X) *603*
Boreas (GW) *83*
Borgo Bioviews (US ISSN 0743-9628) *133, 717*
Borgo Family Histories (US ISSN 0733-6764) *535*
Borgo Political Scenarios (US ISSN 0278-9752) *717, 902*
Borgo Reference Library (US ISSN 0270-3653) *124, 555, 717, 902*
Bornholmske Samlinger (DK ISSN 0084-7976) *578*
Borough of Twickenham Local History Society. Papers (UK ISSN 0084-7984) *578*
Borthwick Institute Bulletin (UK ISSN 0305-9898) *578*
Boss (US ISSN 0006-792X) *103, 717, 740*
Boston College Studies in Philosophy (NE ISSN 0524-112X) *876*
Boston Marathon (US) *1033*
Boston Museum of Fine Arts. Museum Year. Annual Report see Museum Year *829*
Boston Organ Club Newsletter (US) *833*
Boston Sea and Air Port Handbook (UK ISSN 0267-2243) *303, 1087, 1099*

Boston Studies in the Philosophy of Science (NE ISSN 0068-0346) *877*, 988
Boston University Journal of Tax Law (US ISSN 0741-8477) *293*, 652
Boston University Papers on Africa (US) 565, *1006*
Boston University Studies in Philosophy and Religion (US) 877, *968*
Bostonian Society. Proceedings. (US ISSN 0190-3586) *603*
Bostwick Paper (US ISSN 0068-0354) *191*
Botanica Gothoburgensia (SW ISSN 0068-0370) *155*
Botanical Monographs (US) *155*
Botanical Museum Leaflets (US ISSN 0006-8098) *155*
Botanical Society of America. Directory(US) *155*
Botanical Society of America. Miscellaneous Publications *see* Careers in Botany *155*
Botanical Society of America. Yearbook *see* Botanical Society of America. Directory *155*
Botanical Society of Edinburgh. Transactions and Proceedings *see* Botanical Society of Edinburgh Transactions *155*
Botanical Society of Edinburgh Transactions (UK ISSN 0374-6607) *155*
Botanical Survey of India. Occasional Publications (II) *155*
Botanical Survey of South Africa. Memoirs (SA) *155*
Botanische Staatssammlung Muenchen. Mitteilungen (GW ISSN 0006-8179) *155*
Botanisk Centralbibliotek. Fortegnelse over Loebende Periodica (DK ISSN 0900-2367) *149*
Botaniste *see* Revue de Cytologie et de Biologie Vegetales-la Botaniste *161*
Botany as a Profession *see* Careers in Botany *155*
Bothalia (SA ISSN 0006-8241) *155*
Bothnia (FI) *578*
Botschaft des Alten Testaments (GW ISSN 0068-0443) *968*
Botswana. Annual Statements of Accounts (BS ISSN 0068-0451) *293*
Botswana. Central Statistics Office. Employment Survey (BS) *204*
Botswana. Central Statistics Office. Tourist Statistics (BS) *1119*
Botswana. Commissioner of the Police. Annual Report (BS ISSN 0068-046X) *370*
Botswana. Department of Health. Report *see* Botswana. Ministry of Health. Report *952*
Botswana. Department of Income Tax. Annual Report (BS) *293*
Botswana. Department of Mines. Air Pollution Control. Annual Report (BS) *494*
Botswana. Estimates of Revenue and Expenditure (BS ISSN 0524-1448) *293*
Botswana. Geological Survey and Mines Department. Annual Reports *see* Botswana. Geological Survey Department. Annual Reports *384*
Botswana. Geological Survey Department. Annual Reports (BS) *384*
Botswana. Ministry of Agriculture. Annual Report (BS ISSN 0068-0478) *25*
Botswana. Ministry of Agriculture. Division of Arable Crops Research. Annual Report (BS) 51, *53*
Botswana. Ministry of Agriculture. Division of Co-Operative Development. Annual Report (BS) *238*
Botswana. Ministry of Agriculture. Farm Management Survey Results (BS) *45*, 53
Botswana. Ministry of Agriculture. Livestock Management Survey Results (BS) *65*

Botswana. Ministry of Commerce and Industry. Farm Management Survey Results *see* Botswana. Ministry of Agriculture. Farm Management Survey Results *45*
Botswana. Ministry of Health. Report (BS) *952*
Botswana. National Archives. Report on the National Archives (BS) *675*
Botswana. National Library Service. Report (BS) *675*
Botswana Development Corporation. Annual Report (BS) *287*
Botswana Notes and Records (BS ISSN 0525-5090) *565*
Bottin Administratif (FR) *939*
Bottin Auto-Cycle-Moto (FR) 303, 1041, *1091*
Bottin Communes (FR) *950*
Bottin de l'Auto et du Cycle *see* Bottin Auto-Cycle-Moto *1091*
Bottin des Organismes Franco-Ontariens *see* Annuaire Franco-Ontarien *902*
Bottin International (FR ISSN 0068-0494) *1148*
Bottin Mondain (FR) *133*
Bottin Professions (FR) *303*
Bottomfish (US) *717*
Boundary Historical Society. Report (CN ISSN 0068-0524) *603*
Bounty Baby Book (UK) *333*
Bourne Society Local History Records (UK ISSN 0520-6790) *578*
Boussole des Chiffres *see* Germany (Federal Republic, 1949-) Statistisches Bundesamt. Zahlenkompass *1056*
Bouteille a la Mer (FR) *717*
Bow & Arrow Magazine's Bowhunter's Annual (US) *1044*
Bowdoin College. Museum of Art. Occasional Papers (US ISSN 0084-7992) *827*
Bowhunter's Annual *see* Bow & Arrow Magazine's Bowhunter's Annual *1044*
Bowker Annual (US ISSN 0068-0540) *675*, 960
Bowker/Bantam Complete Sourcebook of Personal Computing *see* Bowker's Complete Sourcebook of Personal Computing *1148*
Bowker's Complete Sourcebook of Personal Computing (US ISSN 0882-0082) *1148*
Bowker's Law Books and Serials in Print (US ISSN 0000-0752) 124, *668*
Bowling and Billiard Buyers Guide (US ISSN 0068-0559) *1037*
Bowling Buyers Guide *see* Bowling and Billiard Buyers Guide *1037*
Bowling-Fencing Guide *see* N A G W S Guide. Bowling - Golf *1158*
Bowling Green Studies in Applied Philosophy (US) *877*
Box 749 (US ISSN 0364-3344) *710*
Boxing News Annual (UK) *1033*
Boy Scouts of America. Annual Report to Congress (US) 333, *341*
Boy Scouts World Bureau *see* World Scout Bureau Report *334*
Boyce Thompson Institute for Plant Research. Annual Report (US) *139*
Boyce's Service Station Manual (AT) *491*
Boys Baseball. Blue Book *see* Pony Baseball. Blue Book *1040*
Boys' Brigade, London. Annual Report (UK ISSN 0068-0605) *335*
Boys Gymnastics Rulebook (US ISSN 0160-3280) *1033*
Braby's Bloemfontein Directory (SA ISSN 0520-7010) *303*
Braby's Business Directory of Johannesburg (SA) *303*
Braby's Cape Province Directory (SA ISSN 0378-9179) *303*
Braby's Commercial Directory of South, East & Central Africa (SA) *303*
Braby's Commercial Directory of Southern Africa (SA) *303*
Braby's East London Directory (SA ISSN 0378-9217) *303*
Braby's Natal Directory (SA) *303*
Braby's Orange Free State Directory (SA ISSN 0378-9292) *303*

Braby's Pietermaritzburg Directory (SA ISSN 0520-7037) *303*
Braby's Transvaal Directory (SA ISSN 0068-0621) *303*
Bracara Augusta (PO ISSN 0006-8640) 83, *578*
Brad Directories and Annuals (UK ISSN 0263-1040) *124*
Braddock's Federal-State-Local Government Directory (US ISSN 0363-6275) *939*
Bradea (BL ISSN 0084-800X) *155*
Bradford Center Occasional Papers (UK ISSN 0260-8952) *555*, 717
Bradford Occasional Papers (UK ISSN 0261-0353) *717*
Bradford's Directory of Marketing Research Agencies and Management Consultants in the United States and the World (US ISSN 0068-063X) *283*
Bragantia (BL ISSN 0006-8705) *25*, 139, 321, 384
Brahmavidya (II ISSN 0001-902X) *850*, 977
Brahms-Gesellschaft Hamburg. Jahresgabe *see* Brahms Studien *833*
Brahms Studien (GW) *833*
Braille Books (Large Print Edition) (US ISSN 0277-5247) 124, *180*, 423
Braille Scores Catalog - Choral *see* Music & Musicians: Braille Scores Catalog - Choral (Large Print Edition) *180*
Braille Scores Catalog - Organ *see* Music & Musicians: Braille Scores Catalog - Organ (Large Print Edition) *180*
Braille Scores Catalog - Piano *see* Music & Musicians: Braille Scores Catalog - Piano (Large Print Edition) *180*
Braille Scores Catalog - Voice *see* Music & Musicians: Braille Scores Catalog - Vocal (Large Print Edition) *180*
Braives (BE) *83*
Branchevejviser for Traelast og Byggemarkeder *see* B T B *181*
Brand Book (US) *603*
Brandenburg-Berlinisches Woerterbuch (GE) *692*
Brasil Financeiro e Grandes Companhias *see* Banas *223*
Brasil Industrial *see* Banas *223*
Brasilia. Departamento de Estradas de Rodagem do Distrito Federal. Diretoria Geral. Relatorio Anual. *see* Brasilia. Departamento de Estradas de Rodagem do Distrito Federal. Diretoria Geral. Relatorio de Atividades *1095*
Brasilia. Departamento de Estradas de Rodagem do Distrito Federal. Diretoria Geral. Relatorio de Atividades (BL) *1095*
Brasilia. Fundacao do Servico Social do Distrito Federal. Relatorio Anual das Atividades (BL) *1015*
Brass Players' Guide (US) *833*
Brass Research Series (US ISSN 0363-454X) *833*
Bratislava. Rocenka (CS) *578*
Bratislava-Studia (CS) *83*
Brauereien und Maelzereien in Europa (GW ISSN 0068-0710) *119*
Braunschweiger Geographische Studien (GW ISSN 0524-2444) *542*
Braunschweiger Naturkundliche Schriften (GW ISSN 0174-3384) *173*
Braunschweiger Veroeffentlichungen zur Geschichte der Pharmazie (GW) 578, *869*
Braunschweiger Veroeffentlichungen zur Geschichte der Pharmazie und Naturwissenschaften (GW ISSN 0722-7159) *870*
Braunschweigische Wissenschaftliche Gesellschaft. Abhandlungen (GW) *988*
Braunschweigisches Jahrbuch (GW ISSN 0068-0745) *578*
Braunviehzuchter (GW) *25*, 65
Brauwissenschaft *see* Monatsschrift fuer Brauwissenschaft *120*
Bravo (US ISSN 0275-6080) 502, *740*

Bravura Studies in Music (UK) 833, *843*
Brazil. Arquivo Nacional. Serie de Publicacoes (BL) *603*
Brazil. Biblioteca Nacional. Anais (BL ISSN 0100-1922) *675*
Brazil. Camara dos Deputados. Almanaque dos Funcionarios de Secretaria (BL) *939*
Brazil. Centro Nacional de Pesquisa de Mandioca e Fruticultura. Circular Tecnica (BL ISSN 0100-8064) *25*
Brazil. Centro Nacional de Pesquisa de Mandioca e Fruticultura. Comunicado Tecnico (BL ISSN 0100-8854) *25*
Brazil. Comissao de Financiamento da Producao. Anuario Estatistico (BL) *204*, 1050
Brazil. Companhia de Financiamento da Producao. Relatorio anual da C F P (Comissao de Financiamento da Producao) (BL) *45*
Brazil. Conselho Federal de Farmacia. Relatorio (BL) *870*
Brazil. Conselho Nacional de Desenvolvimento Cientifico e Tecnologico. Boletim (BL) *988*, 1067
Brazil. Conselho Nacional de Desenvolvimento Cientifico e Tecnologico. Programa do Tropica Semi-Arido (Publicacion) (BL) *988*
Brazil. Conselho Nacional de Desenvolvimento Cientifico e Tecnologico. Relatorio de Atividades(BL) *988*
Brazil. Conselho Nacional de Desenvolvimento de Pecuaria. Mercado Atacadista de Gado e Carne: Analise da Variacao dos Precos (BL) *1148*
Brazil. Coordenacao de Assistencia Medica e Hospitalar. Cadastro de Estabelecimentos de Saude (BL) *616*
Brazil. Coordencacao de Assistencia Medica e Hospitalar. Cadastro Hospitalar Brasileiro *see* Brazil. Coordenacao de Assistencia Medica e Hospitalar. Cadastro de Estabelecimentos de Saude *616*
Brazil. Departamento de Assuntos Universitarios. Coordenacao de Avaliacao e Controle. Atividades das Instituicoes Federais de Ensino Superior (BL) *432*
Brazil. Departamento de Assuntos Universitarios. Coordenacao de Availiacao e Controle. Catalogo Geral das Instituicoes de Ensino Superior (BL) *432*
Brazil. Departamento Nacional da Producao Mineral. Avulso (BL) *814*
Brazil. Departamento Nacional da Producao Mineral. Boletim (BL) *814*
Brazil. Departamento Nacional da Producao Mineral. Programacao (BL) *814*
Brazil. Departamento Nacional de Obras Contra as Secas. Relatorio (BL ISSN 0101-5680) *939*
Brazil. Departamento Nacional de Pesquisa Agropecuaria. Divisao de Pesquisa Pedologica. Boletim Tecnico *see* Brazil. Servico Nacional de Levantamento e Conservacao de Solos. Boletim Tecnico *53*
Brazil. Departamento Nacional de Servico Social do Comercio. Centro de Estudos e Informacao. Boletin Bibliografico (BL) *261*
Brazil. Inspetoria-Geral de Financas. Balancos Gerais da Uniao (BL) *939*
Brazil. Instituto do Acucar e do Alcool. Conselho Deliberativo. Coletanea de Resolucoes *see* Brazil. Instituto do Acucar e do Alcool. Conselho Deliberativo. Coletanea de Resolucoes (e) Presidencia. Coletanea de Atos *53*
Brazil. Instituto do Acucar e do Alcool. Conselho Deliberativo. Coletanea de Resolucoes (e) Presidencia. Coletanea de Atos (BL) *53*, 119, 652

Brazil. Instituto do Acucar e do Alcool. Presidencia. Coletanea de Actas *see* Brazil. Instituto do Acucar e do Alcool. Conselho Deliberativo. Coletanea de Resolucoes (e) Presidencia. Coletanea de Atos *53*
Brazil. Instituto Nacional de Colonizacao e Reforma Agraria. Acao Associativista (BL) *1148*
Brazil. Instituto Nacional de Estudos e Pesquisas Educacionais. Conferencia Nacional de Educacao. Anais (BL ISSN 0068-080X) *1148*
Brazil. Instituto Nacional de Previdencia Social. Balanco Geral (BL) *638*
Brazil. Instituto Nacional do Livro. Relatorio de Atividades (BL) *675*
Brazil. Ministerio da Agricultura. Commissao de Financiamento da Producao. Relatorio Anual da C F P *see* Brazil. Companhia de Financiamento da Producao. Relatorio anual da C F P *45*
Brazil. Ministerio da Agricultura. Departamento de Assistencia ao Cooperativismo. Serie Contabilidade (BL) *1148*
Brazil. Ministerio da Agricultura Departamento de Assistenica ao Cooperativismo. Serie Integracao (BL) *1148*
Brazil. Ministerio da Agricultura. Escritorio de Estatistica. Cadastro das Empresas Produtoras de Oleos, Gorduras Vegetais e Sabprodutos (BL) *39*
Brazil. Ministerio da Agricultura. Escritorio de Estatistica. Oleos e Gorduras Vegetais. (BL) *25*
Brazil. Ministerio da Agricultura. Escritorio de Estatistica. Pecuaria, Avicultura, Apicultura, Sericicultura (BL) *39*
Brazil. Ministerio da Agricultura. Subsecretaria de Planejamento e Orcamento. Producao e Abastecimento, Perspectivas e Proposicoes: Sintese (BL) *25*
Brazil. Ministerio da Educacao e Cultura. Servico de Estatistica da Educacao e Cultura. Sinopse Estatistica da Educacao Basica (BL) *411, 423*
Brazil. Ministerio da Educacao e Cultura. Servico de Estatistica da Educacao e Cultura. Sinopse Estatistica do Ensino Superior (BL) *423*
Brazil. Ministerio da Educacao. Sercico de Estatistica da Educacao e Cultura. SInopse Estatistica do Ensino Superior-Pos-Graduacao *see* Brazil. Ministerio da Educacao e Cultura. Servico de Estatistica da Educacao e Cultura. Sinopse Estatistica do Ensino Superior *423*
Brazil. Ministerio da Educacao. Servico de Estatistica da Educacao e Cultura. Sinopse Estatistica da Educacao Pre-Escolar (BL) *423*
Brazil. Ministerio do Trabalho e Previdencia Social. Centro de Documentacao e Informatica. Mercado de Trabalho: Flutuacao (BL) *270*
Brazil. Museu do Indio. Boletim. Antropologia (BL) *70*
Brazil. Museu do Indio. Boletim. Documentacao (BL ISSN 0101-0484) *604, 827*
Brazil. Museu do Indio. Boletim. Etno-Historia (BL ISSN 0100-7475) *604*
Brazil. Museu do Indio. Boletim. Linguistica (BL ISSN 0101-0530) *692*
Brazil. Servico de Estatistica da Educacao e Cultura. Sinopse Estatistica do Ensino Primario. *see* Brazil. Ministerio da Educacao. Servico de Estatistica da Educacao e Cultura. Sinopse Estatistica da Educacao Pre-Escolar *423*
Brazil. Servico Nacional de Levantamento e Conservacao de Solos. Boletim Tecnico (BL ISSN 0100-123X) *53*

Brazil. Servico Social do Comercio. Administracao Regional do Estado de Sao Paulo. Relatoria Annual (BL) *1015*
Brazil. Servico Social do Comercio. Anuario Estatistico (BL) *948, 1050*
Brazil. Servico Social do Comercio. Colecao Bibliografica (BL) *124*
Brazil. Superintendencia da Borracha. Annuario Estatistico. Mercado Estrangeiro (BL ISSN 0572-5534) *986*
Brazil. Superintendencia do Desenvolvimento da Amazonia. S U D A M Documenta (BL ISSN 0045-2742) *287*
Brazil. Superintendencia do Desenvolvimento do Nordeste. Departamento de Agricultura e Abastecimento. Programa de Trabalho para a Agricultura Nordestina (BL) *45*
Brazil. Superintendencia do Desenvolvimento do Nordeste. Nordeste, Oportunidades de Investimentos (BL) *265*
Brazil. Superintendencia do Desenvolvimento do Nordeste. Relatorio Anual (BL) *242*
Brazil. Superintendencia do Desenvolvimento do Nordeste. Relatorio Sintetico, Andamento do Programa de Irrigacao do Nordeste (BL) *1123*
Brazil. Superintendencia do Desenvolvimento do Nordeste. SU D E N E Plano de Acao (BL) *622*
Brazil. Supremo Tribunal Federal. Indices de Legislacao Federal (BL) *652*
Brazil. Supremo Tribunal Federal. Juriscivel do S.T.F. (BL) *652*
Brazil. Supremo Tribunal Federal. Relatorio dos Trabalhos Realizados (BL) *652*
Brazil Development Series/Series Desenvolvimento Brasileiro (BL) *287*
Brazil - U.S. Business Listing (US) *303*
Brazilian Economic Studies (BL ISSN 0100-2910) *191*
Brazilian Energy Statistics *see* Estatistica Brasileira de Energia *468*
Brazilian Index Yearbook *see* Indice do Brasil *245*
Bread Caterers' Directory *see* Pan Directorio de Proveedores *522*
Breast Feeding (UK) *787*
Breastfeeding Abstracts (US) *3, 334*
Breathless Magazine (US ISSN 8756-8217) *103, 717*
Brecht Yearbook (US ISSN 0734-8665) *717*
Breifne (IE ISSN 0068-0877) *83, 578*
Bremer Afrika-Archiv *see* Uebersee-Museum, Bremen. Veroeffentlichungen. Reihe F: Bremer Afrika-Archiv *567*
Bremer Archaeologische Blaetter (GW ISSN 0068-0907) *83*
Bremer Beitraege zur Geographie und Raumplanung (GW ISSN 0720-9738) *542*
Bremer Schulblatt (GW ISSN 0006-9582) *442*
Bremer Suedpazifik-Archiv *see* Uebersee-Museum Bremen. Veroeffentlichungen. Reihe G: Bremer Suedpazifik-Archiv *573*
Bremisches Jahrbuch (GW ISSN 0341-9622) *578*
Brenesia (CR ISSN 0304-3711) *988*
Brennessel (GW) *877*
Brennstoffstatistik der Waermekraftwerke fuer die Oeffentliche Elektrizitaetsversorgung in Oesterreich (AU ISSN 0520-9048) *451, 939*
Brentford and Chiswick Local History Society. Journal (UK ISSN 0144-672X) *578*
Breviora (US ISSN 0006-9698) *173*
Brewer/Distiller and Bottler and Beverage and Food World *119*
Brewers Digest Annual Buyers Guide and Brewery Directory (US ISSN 0006-971X) *119, 303*

Brewing and Malting Barley Research Institute. Annual Report (CN ISSN 0068-094X) *119*
Brewing Industry Research Foundation. Bulletin of Current Literature *see* Brewing Research Foundation. Bulletin of Current Literature *120*
Brewing Research Foundation. Bulletin of Current Literature (UK) *120*
Bricker's International Directory of University Executive Development Programs *see* Bricker's International Directory of University Executive Programs *278*
Bricker's International Directory of University Executive Programs (US ISSN 0361-1108) *278, 428*
Bridges in Japan *see* Hashi *481*
Bridging the Gap: What's Happening Now (US) *335*
Briefing Paper on Southern Africa (UK ISSN 0262-3781) *912*
Briefs *see* B'kitzur *976*
Brigham Young University. Center for Thermochemical Studies. Contributions (US ISSN 0572-6921) *331*
Brigham Young University. College of Engineering Sciences and Technology. Annual Engineering Symposium. Abstracts (US ISSN 0068-1008) *470*
Brightonian (UK ISSN 0007-0157) *341*
Bringin' Home the Bacon (US) *535*
Bristol and Avon Archaeology (UK ISSN 0263-1091) *83*
Bristol and Gloucestershire Archaeological Society, Bristol, England. Transactions (UK ISSN 0068-1032) *83, 578*
Bristol and West of England Engineering Manufacturers Association Ltd. Engineering Directory *see* B E M A Engineering Directory *470*
Bristol Chamber of Commerce and Industry Directory (UK) *234*
Bristol-Meyers Cancer Symposia. Proceedings (US) *774*
Bristol Naturalists' Society. Proceedings(UK ISSN 0068-1040) *988*
Bristow's Book of Motor Cruisers *see* Bristow's Book of Yachts *1041*
Bristow's Book of Sailing Cruisers *see* Bristow's Book of Yachts *1041*
Bristow's Book of Yachts (UK ISSN 0309-1252) *1041*
Britain: An Official Handbook (UK ISSN 0068-1075) *578*
Britain and the Netherlands (NE) *578*
Britain: Hotels & Restaurants (UK) *1106*
Britain in Brief (UK) *578*
Britain in the World Today (US ISSN 0068-1105) *1148*
Britain Welcomes Coaches (UK) *1106*
Britain's Best Holidays - A Quick Reference Guide (UK ISSN 0267-1468) *1106*
Britain's D I Y Industry (UK) *283, 361*
Britain's Data Communications Equipment Suppliers (UK) *283, 286*
Britain's Defence Service Industry (UK) *810*
Britain's Fire Protection Industry (UK) *283, 506*
Britain's Freight-Forwarding Industry (UK) *283, 1081*
Britain's Grocery Retailers (UK) *522*
Britain's Heritage *see* Stately Homes, Museums, Castles and Gardens in Britain *1116*
Britain's Privately Owned Companies: The Second 2000 (UK) *303*
Britain's Privately Owned Companies: The Top 2000 (UK) *303*
Britain's Top Private Companies. The First and Second Thousand *see* Britain's Privately Owned Companies: The Second 2000 *303*
Britain's Top 1000 Foreign-Owned Companies (UK ISSN 0263-242X) *303*
Britain's Top 500 Electronic Companies(UK ISSN 0263-2446) *303, 451*

Britain's Wine Industry (UK) *119, 283*
Britannia (UK ISSN 0068-113X) *578*
Britannia Monograph Series (UK) *337*
Britannica Atlas (US ISSN 0068-1148) *542*
Britannica Book of the Year (US ISSN 0068-1156) *462*
Britannica Yearbook of Science and the Future *see* Yearbook of Science and the Future *1003*
Britaiin's Top Private Companies. The First and Second Thousand *see* Britain's Privately Owned Companies: The Top 2000 *303*
Britischer Export *see* British Exports *253*
British Academy. Proceedings (UK) *578*
British Agencies for Adoption & Fostering Discussion Series *see* B A A F Discussion Series *1015*
British Agencies for Adoption & Fostering News *see* B A A F News *1015*
British Agencies for Adoption and Fostering Practice Series *see* B A A F Practice Series *1015*
British Agencies for Adoption & Fostering Research Series *see* B A A F Research Series *1015*
British Aid Statistics; Statistics of U.K. Economic Aid to Developing Countries (UK ISSN 0068-1210) *204*
British Alternative Theatre Directory (UK ISSN 0142-5218) *303, 1076*
British Amateur Journalist (UK ISSN 0007-0238) *645*
British Antarctic Survey. Annual Report (UK ISSN 0141-3325) *988*
British Antarctic Survey. Scientific Reports (UK ISSN 0068-1261) *1148*
British Antique Dealers' Association Handbook (UK) *79*
British Archaeological Association. Conference Transactions (UK) *83, 97, 103*
British Archaeological Association. Journal (UK ISSN 0068-1288) *83*
British Art & Antiques Directory (UK) *79*
British Art and Antiques Yearbook *see* British Art & Antiques Directory *79*
British Association of Industrial Editors. B A I E Directory of Members *see* B.A.I.E. Membership Directory *302*
British Association of Industrial Editors Membership Directory *see* B.A.I.E. Membership Directory *302*
British Association of Social Workers. Annual Report (UK) *1015*
British Astronomical Association. Handbook (UK ISSN 0068-130X) *115*
British Authors Series (UK ISSN 0068-1334) *717*
British Baker Directory and Buyers Guide (UK) *522*
British Baking Industries Research Association. Abstracts *see* Flour Milling and Baking Research Association Abstracts *521*
British Baking Industries Research Association. Annual Report *see* Flour Milling and Baking Research Association. Annual Report and Accounts *518*
British Book Design & Production (UK ISSN 0302-2846) *960*
British Book Production *see* British Book Design & Production *960*
British Books in Print (UK ISSN 0068-1350) *124*
British Broadcasting Corp. Annual Report and Handbook *see* B B C Annual Report and Handbook *347*
British Broadcasting Corp. Music Guide Music Guides *see* B B C Music Guides *833*
British Building Products Catalogue (UK ISSN 0084-8026) *182*
British Cast Iron Research Association (BCIRA) Abstracts of International Literature on Metal Castings Production *see* B C I R A Abstracts of International Literature on Metal Castings Production *801*

British Catalogue of Audio-Visual Materials (UK) 423, 885, *1032*
British Catalogue of Music (UK ISSN 0068-1407) *833*
British Cave Research Association. Transactions *see* Cave Science: Transactions of the British Cave Research Association *385*
British Ceramic Abstracts (UK ISSN 0300-4570) 3, *320*
British Ceramic Research. Special Publications (UK ISSN 0144-2147) *319*
British Ceramic Research Association. Technical Notes (UK ISSN 0144-3631) *319*
British Ceramic Society. Proceedings (UK ISSN 0524-5141) *319*
British Chamber of Commerce in France. Year Book *see* Franco-British Chamber of Commerce and Industry. Year Book *236*
British Chemical Industry (UK ISSN 0263-2438) *303*, *321*
British Chemicals and Their Manufacturers *see* Chemicals *322*
British Clothing Industry Yearbook (UK) *340*
British Columbia. Cancer Foundation. Annual Report *see* British Columbia Cancer Research Centre. Annual Report *774*
British Columbia. Department of Health. Annual Report *see* British Columbia. Ministry of Health. Annual Report *953*
British Columbia. Department of Labour. Annual Report *see* British Columbia. Ministry of Labour. Annual Report *270*
British Columbia. Energy Commission. Annual Report *see* British Columbia. Utilities Commission. Annual Report *464*
British Columbia. Forest Service. Annual Report *see* British Columbia. Ministry of Forests and Lands. Annual Report *523*
British Columbia. Forest Service. Research Review *see* British Columbia. Ministry of Forests and lands. Research Review *523*
British Columbia. Housing Management Commission. Annual Report (CN ISSN 0225-509X) *622*
British Columbia. Human Rights Commission. Annual Report *see* Human Rights Act of British Columbia *913*
British Columbia. Labour Relations Board. Annual Report (CN ISSN 0319-0404) *270*
British Columbia. Law Reform Commission. Annual Report (CN ISSN 0381-2510) *652*
British Columbia. Library Development Commission. Public Libraries, Statistics *see* British Columbia Public Libraries, Statistics *687*
British Columbia. Medical Services Plan. Physician's Newsletter *see* British Columbia. Medical Services Plan. Practitioners' Newsletter *758*
British Columbia. Medical Services Plan. Practitioners' Newsletter (CN) *758*, *952*
British Columbia. Ministry of Agriculture and Food. Agricultural Aid to Developing Countries (CN ISSN 0227-3802) *25*, *261*
British Columbia. Ministry of Agriculture and Food. Berry Production Guide (CN) *1149*
British Columbia. Ministry of Agriculture and Food D.A.T.E. Program Report (CN) *25*
British Columbia. Ministry of Agriculture and Food. Field Crop Production Guide (CN) *53*
British Columbia. Ministry of Agriculture and Food. Grape Production Guide (CN) *53*
British Columbia. Ministry of Agriculture and Food. Greenhouse-Cucumber and Tomato Production Guide (CN) *53*

British Columbia. Ministry of Agriculture and Food. Greenhouse-Ornamental Production Guide (CN) *53*
British Columbia. Ministry of Agriculture and Food. Nursery Production Guide (CN) *53*
British Columbia. Ministry of Agriculture and Food. Tree Fruit (CN) *53*
British Columbia. Ministry of Agriculture and Food. Vegetable Production Guide (CN) *53*
British Columbia. Ministry of Agriculture D.A.T.E. Program Report *see* British Columbia. Ministry of Agriculture and Food D.A.T.E. Program Report *25*
British Columbia. Ministry of Education. Annual Report (CN ISSN 0709-8383) *411*
British Columbia. Ministry of Energy, Mines and Petroleum Resources. Annual Report (CN ISSN 0365-9356) *814*, *863*
British Columbia. Ministry of Energy, Mines and Petroleum Resources. Bulletin (CN ISSN 0068-144X) *384*, *863*
British Columbia. Ministry of Environment and Parks. Annual Report (CN) *364*, *1123*
British Columbia. Ministry of Environment. Annual Report *see* British Columbia. Ministry of Environment and Parks. Annual Report *364*
British Columbia. Ministry of Forests and Lands. Annual Report (CN) *523*
British Columbia. Ministry of Forests and Lands. Research Notes (CN ISSN 0226-9368) *523*
British Columbia. Ministry of Forests and lands. Research Review (CN) *523*
British Columbia. Ministry of Forests. Research Notes *see* British Columbia. Ministry of Forests and Lands. Research Notes *523*
British Columbia. Ministry of Health. Annual Report (CN ISSN 0706-4810) *953*
British Columbia. Ministry of Human Resources. Services for People *see* British Columbia. Ministry of Social Services and Housing. Services for People. Annual Report (Year) *1015*
British Columbia. Ministry of Labour. Annual Report (CN ISSN 0705-9698) *270*
British Columbia. Ministry of Labour. Negotiated Working Conditions (CN ISSN 0703-0665) *270*, *635*
British Columbia. Ministry of Municipal Affairs. Municipal Statistics, Including Regional Districts (CN ISSN 0702-6641) *622*
British Columbia. Ministry of Social Services and Housing. Services for People. Annual Report (Year) (CN) *1015*
British Columbia. Ministry of the Environment. Northeast Coal Study Preliminary Environmental Report (CN ISSN 0707-3739) *494*, *814*
British Columbia. Utilities Commission. Annual Report (CN) *464*
British Columbia. Workers' Compensation Board. Workers' Compensation Reporter (CN) *638*
British Columbia Art Teachers' Association. Journal (CN ISSN 0316-1544) *103*, *446*
British Columbia Art Teachers' Association. Newsletter *see* British Columbia Art Teachers' Association. Journal *446*
British Columbia Association of Mathematics Teachers. Newsletter *see* Vector *755*
British Columbia Cancer Research Centre. Annual Report (CN) *774*
British Columbia Counsellors' Association. Newsletter *see* British Columbia School Counsellors' Association. Newsletter *411*
British Columbia Court Forms (CN) *652*

British Columbia Economic Activity *see* Economic Review and Outlook *301*
British Columbia Energy Board. Annual Report *see* British Columbia. Utilities Commission. Annual Report *464*
British Columbia English Teacher *see* British Columbia English Teachers' Association. Journal *446*
British Columbia English Teachers' Association. Journal (CN ISSN 0316-0173) *446*, *692*
British Columbia Fruit Growers Association. Horticultural Forum Proceedings (CN) *531*
British Columbia Fruit Growers Association. Minutes of the Proceedings of the Annual Convention (CN ISSN 0068-1563) *531*
British Columbia Geographical Series: Occasional Papers in Geography (CN ISSN 0068-1571) *542*
British Columbia Government News (CN ISSN 0007-0513) *939*
British Columbia Guide (CN) *1037*
British Columbia Historical Documents Series *see* Recollections of the Pioneers of British Columbia *609*
British Columbia Institute of Technology Annual Report *see* B C I T Annual Report *1067*
British Columbia Insurance Directory. Insurance Companies, Agents and Adjusters (CN ISSN 0068-1598) *638*
British Columbia List (CN) *950*, *1050*
British Columbia Monthly (CN ISSN 0382-5272) *740*
British Columbia Motor Transport Directory (CN ISSN 0707-5014) *1091*
British Columbia Mountaineer (CN ISSN 0045-2998) *1044*
British Columbia Municipal Yearbook (CN ISSN 0068-161X) *265*
British Columbia Music Educator (CN ISSN 0007-0564) *833*
British Columbia Ports Handbook 1984 (UK ISSN 0265-8178) *303*, *1099*
British Columbia Practice (CN) *652*
British Columbia Public Libraries, Statistics (CN) *687*
British Columbia Research Council. Annual Report *see* B.C. Research. Annual Report *988*
British Columbia School Counsellors' Association. Newsletter (CN ISSN 0705-8802) *411*
British Columbia School Trustees Association. Newsletter (CN ISSN 0381-5978) *442*
British Columbia Social Studies Teachers' Association. Newsletter *see* Horizon *447*
British Columbia Teachers' Federation. Newsletter (CN ISSN 0005-2965) *411*
British Columbia Water and Waste Association. Proceedings of the Annual Conference (CN) *1123*
British Commonwealth Stamp Catalogue (UK ISSN 0142-9752) *874*
British Computer Society. Microform Specialist Group. Annual Proceedings(UK) *352*
British Construction Equipment and Cranes. Directory (UK) *303*
British Cycling Federation. Handbook (UK ISSN 0068-1938) *1033*
British Cycling Federation. Racing Handbook *see* British Cycling Federation. Handbook *1033*
British Decorators Association. Members Reference Handbook (UK) *855*
British Design & Art Direction Annual (UK) *15*
British Distilling Industry (UK ISSN 0263-3698) *1149*
British Education Index (UK ISSN 0007-0637) 3, *423*
British Electrotechnical Approvals Board. Annual List of Approved Electrotechnical Equipment (UK ISSN 0140-766X) *1067*
British Equestrian Directory (UK ISSN 0144-7203) *1042*

British Exporters *see* Sell's British Exporters *259*
British Exports/Exportations Britanniques/Britischer Export/ Exportaciones Britanicas (UK) *253*
British Exports. Export Services. *see* British Exports *253*
British Federation of Music Festivals. Yearbook (UK ISSN 0309-8044) *833*
British Fern Gazette *see* Fern Gazette *156*
British Field Sports Society. Annual Journal *see* B F S S Reference Book *1044*
British Field Sports Society Reference Book *see* B F S S Reference Book *1044*
British Film Fund Agency. Annual Report (UK ISSN 0068-2004) *822*
British Friesian Herd Book (UK ISSN 0068-2012) *65*
British Frozen Food Federation. Year Book (UK) *518*
British Gas Corporation. Monitor *see* British Gas Plc. Monitor *464*
British Gas Corporation. Report and Accounts (UK ISSN 0072-0216) *863*
British Gas Plc. Monitor (UK) *451*, *464*
British Geomorphological Research Group. Technical Bulletin (UK ISSN 0306-3380) *384*
British Glass Industry Research Association. Annual Report (UK ISSN 0068-2020) *319*
British Goat Society. Herd Book (UK ISSN 0068-2039) *65*
British Goat Society. Year Book (UK ISSN 0068-2047) *65*
British Hardware Federation Directory *see* B H F Directory *189*
British Helicopter Advisory Board Handbook (UK) *1087*
British Horse Society Diary (UK) *1042*
British Horse Society Year Book & Event Guide (UK) *1042*
British Hospitals Contributory Schemes Association. Directory of Convalescent Homes Serving the Provinces. (UK ISSN 0068-208X) *616*
British Hospitals Contributory Schemes Association. Directory of Hospitals Contributory Scheme Benefits (UK ISSN 0068-2098) *616*
British Hospitals Contributory Schemes Association. Report (UK ISSN 0068-2101) *616*
British Hotel Industry (UK ISSN 0263-368X) *303*, *619*
British Hotels, Restaurants & Caterers Association Diary (UK) *619*
British Hotels, Restaurants and Caterers Association Official Guide to Hotels & Restaurants in Great Britain, Ireland and Overseas *see* Official Guide to Hotels & Restaurants in Great Britain, Ireland and Overseas *620*
British Humanities Index (UK ISSN 0007-0815) 3, *634*
British Hydromechanics Research Association. Proceedings of Hydrotransport (UK ISSN 0306-6916) *490*
British Hydromechanics Research Association. Proceedings of Pneumotransport (UK ISSN 0140-1785) *490*
British Imperial Calendar and Civil Service List *see* Civil Service Year Book *940*
British Independent Steel Companies and Their Products (UK) *797*
British Institute in Eastern Africa. Annual Report (KE ISSN 0068-2152) *565*
British Institute in Eastern Africa. Memoirs (KE) *565*
British Institute of History and Archaeology in East Africa. Report *see* British Institute in Eastern Africa. Annual Report *565*
British Institute of Interior Design Members' Reference Book (UK ISSN 0263-2047) *643*

British Internal Combustion Engine Research Institute Ltd. Abstracts from Technical and Patent Publications. see B I C E R I Abstracts from Technical and Patent Publications 476
British International Law Cases (US ISSN 0068-2195) 669
British Invisible Exports Council. Annual Report (UK) 253
British Isles and Ireland Travel Guide see Travel Guide to Europe 1118
British Jeweller. Buyer's Guide (UK) 644
British Jewellers Association. Buyer's Guide (UK) 283, 644
British Journal of Dermatology. Supplement (UK ISSN 0366-077X) 780
British Journal of Photography Annual (UK ISSN 0068-2217) 884
British Journal of Russian Philately (UK ISSN 0950-575X) 874
British Librarianship & Information Science see British Librarianship & Information Work 675
British Librarianship & Information Work (UK) 675
British Library. Annual Report (UK ISSN 0305-7887) 675
British Library. Bibliographic Services Division. Cataloguing Practice Notes for UKMARC Records (UK ISSN 0262-0278) 675
British Library. Document Supply Centre. Index of Conference Proceedings Received (UK) 3, 796
British Library. Document Supply Centre. Science Reference and Information Service. Current Serials Received (UK) 124
British Library. Lending Division. Current Serials Received see British Library. Document Supply Centre. Science Reference and Information Service. Current Serials Received 124
British Library. Lending Division. Index of Conference Proceedings Recieved see British Library. Document Supply Centre. Index of Conference Proceedings Received 796
British Library. Precis Vocabulary Fiche(UK) 3, 687
British Library. Subject Authority Fiche(UK) 3, 687
British Library Research Reviews (UK ISSN 0261-2178) 675
British Marine Industries Federation Handbook (UK) 1099
British Middle Market Directory see Guide to Key British Enterprises I and II 309
British Museum (Natural History) Bulletin see British Museum (Natural History) Report 139
British Museum (Natural History) Bulletin. Botany (UK ISSN 0068-2292) 155
British Museum (Natural History). Bulletin. Entomology (UK ISSN 0524-6431) 164
British Museum (Natural History) Bulletin. Geology (UK ISSN 0007-1471) 384
British Museum (Natural History) Bulletin. Historical (UK ISSN 0068-2306) 139, 378
British Museum (Natural History) Bulletin. Mineralogy see British Museum (Natural History) Bulletin. Geology 384
British Museum (Natural History) Bulletin. Zoology (UK ISSN 0007-1498) 173
British Museum (Natural History) Report (UK) 139
British Music Education Yearbook (UK ISSN 0266-2329) 833
British Music Yearbook (UK ISSN 0306-5928) 833
British National Association for Soviet and East European Studies. Information Bulletin (UK ISSN 0307-2061) 914
British National Film Catalogue (UK ISSN 0007-1552) 825
British Newspaper Industry (UK ISSN 0263-2462) 1149

British-North American Committee Publications (UK) 191
British-North American Research Association. Committee Publications see British-North American Committee Publications 191
British-North American Research Association. Occasional Papers (UK) 191
British Numismatic Journal (UK) 844
British Nutrition Foundation Briefing Papers (UK) 846
British Nutrition Foundation Monograph (UK) 846
British Nutrition Foundation Newsletter see British Nutrition Foundation Monograph 846
British Nutrition Foundation Task Force Reports (UK) 846
British Olympic Association Year Book and Diary (UK) 1033
British Orthoptic Journal (UK ISSN 0068-2314) 785
British Paper and Board Industry Federation. Technical Association. Fundamental Research International Symposia see Paper Industry Technical Association. Fundamental Research International Symposia 858
British Paper and Board Industry Federation. Technical Association. Technical Papers (UK ISSN 0068-2330) 858
British Paperbacks in Print (UK ISSN 0262-9763) 1149
British Patents Abstracts (UK ISSN 0007-1609) 3, 862
British Petroleum Co. p.l.c. Statistical Review of World Energy see B P Statistical Review of World Energy 863
British Pharmacological Society. Symposia (UK) 870
British Pharmacopoeia (Veterinary) (UK) 870, 1121
British Philatelic Federation. Congress Handbook (UK) 874
British Pirandello Society. Yearbook (UK ISSN 0260-9215) 717
British Policy in Asia: India Office Memoranda (UK) 1149
British Political Sociology Yearbook (US) 1024
British Practice in International Law (UK ISSN 0007-1676) 1149
British Psychological Society. Annual Report (UK ISSN 0309-7773) 933
British Psychological Society. Division of Criminological & Legal Psychology. Occasional Papers (UK) 933
British Pteridological Society. Bulletin (UK ISSN 0301-9195) 155
British Pteridological Society. Newsletter see British Pteridological Society. Bulletin 155
British Pump Manufacturers Association. Technical Conference Proceedings (UK ISSN 0140-2145) 490, 491
British Pump Market (UK) 863
British Qualifications (UK ISSN 0141-5972) 411
British Rabbit Council Year Book (UK) 65
British Railways Board. Report and Statement of Accounts (UK ISSN 0068-242X) 1094
British Rate & Data Directories and Annuals (UK) 124
British Regional Geology (UK) 384
British Relais Routiers Guide see Good Value Guide 1110
British Rowing Almanack (UK ISSN 0068-2446) 1041
British Rubber Industry Directory see B.R.M.A. Directory Rubber and Polyurethane 985
British Rubber Manufacturers' Association Ltd. Directory Rubber and Polyurethane see B.R.M.A. Directory Rubber and Polyurethane 985
British School at Athens. Annual (UK ISSN 0068-2454) 83
British School at Rome. Papers. Archaeology (UK ISSN 0068-2462) 83, 578

British Security Companies (UK ISSN 0263-3655) 265, 303
British Security Industry Buyer's Guide (Year) (UK ISSN 0268-568X) 374, 506
British Ship Research Association. B.S.R.A. Bibliographies (UK) 1085
British Society for Cell Biology. Symposia (UK) 163
British Society for Developmental Biology. Symposia (UK) 171
British Society for the History of Pharmacy. Transactions (UK ISSN 0068-2519) 870
British Society of Master Glass Painters Journal see Journal of Stained Glass 113
British Stamp Values (UK) 874
British Standards Year Book see B S I Catalogue 808
British Steel Corporation. Annual Report and Accounts (UK ISSN 0068-2586) 797
British Technology Index see Current Technology Index 1072
British Theatre Directory (UK ISSN 0306-4107) 303, 1076
British Toy & Hobby Manufacturers Association Buyers Guide see B T H A Buyers Guide 552
British Trade Alphabet Studycards see B T A Studycards 15
British Transport Docks Board. Annual Report and Accounts see Associated British Ports Holdings PlC. Annual Report and Accounts 1098
British Trust for Ornithology. Annual Report (UK ISSN 0068-2675) 170
British Universities' Guide to Graduate Studies (UK) 428
British Virgin Islands. Statistics Office. Balance of Payments (VB) 204, 1050
British Virgin Islands. Statistics Office. National Income and Expenditure (VB) 204, 1050
British Waterways Board. Annual Report and Accounts (UK ISSN 0068-2683) 1099
British Women Pilots Association Magazine see B W P A Magazine 18
British Year Book of International Law (UK ISSN 0068-2691) 669
Britoil. Annual Report (UK) 863
Broadcast Engineering Notes (UK ISSN 0141-9471) 343
Broadcast Engineering Spec Book (US) 347
Broadcast Yearbook and Diary (UK) 347
Broadcasting Cable Sourcebook see Broadcasting/Cablecasting Yearbook 347
Broadcasting/Cable Yearbook see Broadcasting/Cablecasting Yearbook 347
Broadcasting/Cablecasting Yearbook (US ISSN 0732-7196) 347
Broadcasting Yearbook see Broadcasting/Cablecasting Yearbook 347
Broadman Comments; International Sunday School Lessons (US ISSN 0068-2721) 968
Broadside Critics Series (US) 1149
Brome County Historical Society. Publication (CN ISSN 0381-6206) 604
Bronte Newsletter (US) 717
Bronte Society Transactions (UK ISSN 0309-7765) 717
Bronze Swagman Book of Bush Verse (AT ISSN 0310-2467) 740
Brookfield Bandarlog (US ISSN 0068-2780) 173
Brookhaven Highlights (US ISSN 0092-1548) 896
Brookhaven Lecture Series (US) 896
Brookhaven Symposia in Biology (US ISSN 0068-2799) 139
Brookings Dialogues in Public Policy see Dialogues in Public Policy 941
Brookings Pamphlet Series see Brookings Reprint Series 1006
Brookings Reprint Series (US) 1006
Brooklyn Academy of Music Magazine see B A Magazine 833

Brooklyn Arts and Culture Association, Inc.- Brooklyn Arts Council Calendar of Cultural Events see B.A.C.A. Calendar of Cultural Events 826
Brooklyn Review (US) 717
Brookside Columns (US) 604
Brorfelde, Magnetic Results (DK ISSN 0109-2170) 398
Brots de Collcerola (SP) 341
Brown Boveri Symposia. Proceedings (US) 451
Brown Thumber's Handbook of House Plants (US) 532
Brown University. Program in Judaic Studies. Annual Report (US) 502
Browning Institute Studies (US ISSN 0092-4725) 717
Browning Newsletter see Studies in Browning and His Circle 734
Brown's Directory of North American and International Gas Companies (US ISSN 0197-8098) 863
Brown's Directory of North American Gas Companies see Brown's Directory of North American and International Gas Companies 863
Browns Mills Review (US) 717
Brown's Nautical Almanac (UK ISSN 0068-290X) 1041
Bruce County Historical Society. Year Book (CN ISSN 0084-8115) 604
Brucellosis Surveillance; Annual Summary see U.S. Center for Disease Control. Brucellosis Surveillance: Annual Summary 956
Bruckmanns Pantheon (GW ISSN 0720-0056) 103
Bruecke-Archiv (GW ISSN 0572-7146) 103
Bruges Quarterly see Cahiers de Bruges 903
Brujula (AG) 638
Brujula see Universidad de San Carlos. Facultad de Ingenieria. Escuela Regional de Ingenieria Sanitaria. Carta Periodica 957
Brunei Museum. Special Publication/ Muzium Brunei. Penerbitan Khas (BX ISSN 0084-8131) 827
Brunei Museum Journal (BX ISSN 0068-2918) 827
Brunswick. Technische Universitaet Carolo-Wilhelmina. Pharmaziegeschichtliches Seminar. Veroeffentlichung see Braunschweiger Veroeffentlichungen zur Geschichte der Pharmazie 578
Brussels Museum of Musical Instruments. Bulletin (NE) 833
Bryozoa (US ISSN 0108-0326) 173
Das Buch der Jugend (GW ISSN 0068-3043) 124
Buch und Buchhandel in Zahlen (GW ISSN 0068-3051) 960
Buchhandelsgeschichte. Zweite Folge (GW ISSN 0170-5105) 960
Buchwissenschaftliche Beitraege see Buchwissenschaftliche Beitraege aus dem Deutschen Bucharchiv Muenchen 960
Buchwissenschaftliche Beitraege aus dem Deutschen Bucharchiv Muenchen (GW ISSN 0724-7001) 960
Budapest Statisztikai Evkonyve (HU ISSN 0521-4882) 1050
Budapest Statisztikai Zsebkonyve (HU ISSN 0438-2242) 1050
Buddhist Studies (II) 977
Budget in Brief - Department of Transportation (Washington) see U.S. Department of Transportation. Fiscal Year Budget in Brief 1084
Budget in Brief - State of Florida see Florida. Office of the Governor. Budget in Brief 941
Budget of the Government of Liberia (LB) 939
Budget of the Government of Pakistan. Demands for Grants and Appropriations (PK) 293
Budget Representations to the Chancellor (UK ISSN 0268-2265) 293
Le Budget Tunisien (TI) 1149
Budkavlen (FI ISSN 0302-2447) 578
Budo und transkulturelle Bewegungsforschung (GW ISSN 0723-9297) 1033

Budowa Geologiczna Polski (PL) *384*, 856
Buecher (Year) (AU) *963*
Buecher fuer Alle *see* Buecher (Year) *963*
Buecherei des Augenarztes (GW ISSN 0068-3361) *785*
Buecherei des Frauenarztes (GW ISSN 0068-337X) *785*
Buecherei des Orthopaeden (GW ISSN 0068-3388) *786*
Buecherei des Paediaters (GW ISSN 0373-3165) *787*
Ein Buechertagebuch (GW ISSN 0068-3396) *739*
Buenos Aires. Centro de Investigacion de Biologia Marina. Contribucion Cientifica (AG ISSN 0068-340X) *139*
Buenos Aires. Instituto de Fitotecnia. Boletin Informativo (AG ISSN 0068-3418) *53*
Buenos Aires. Museo Argentino de Ciencias Naturales Bernardino Rivadavia. Instituto Nacional de Investigacion de las Ciencias Naturales. Revista. Ciencias Botanicas *see* Museo Argentino de Ciencias Naturales "Bernardino Rivadavia." Instituto Nacional de Investigacion de las Ciencias Naturales. Revista. Botanica *159*
Buenos Aires. Museo Argentino de Ciencias Naturales Bernardino Rivadavia. Instituto Nacional de Investigacion de las Ciencias Naturales. Revista. Ciencias Geologicas. *see* Museo Argentino de Ciencias Naturales "Bernardino Rivadavia." Instituto Nacional de Investigacion de las Ciencias Naturales. Revista. Geologia *392*
Buenos Aires (Province). Archivo Historico. Publicaciones. Sexta Serie (AG ISSN 0524-9864) *604*
Buffalo (CN ISSN 0045-334X) *333, 341*
Buffalo Area Chamber of Commerce Directory-Metroplitan Buffalo *see* Greater Buffalo Business Directory *309*
Buffalo Society of Natural Sciences. Bulletin (US) *378*
Buildcore Index (CN ISSN 0227-0595) *182, 189*
Builders of Indian Anthropology (II) *133, 1006*
Building Abstracts Service C I B (CS ISSN 0007-3326) *3, 188*
Building and Engineering Review (UK ISSN 0084-814X) *182*
Building Board Directory (UK ISSN 0068-3523) *182*
Building Construction Cost Data (US ISSN 0068-3531) *182*
Building Index (SA) *1149*
Building Maintenance Cost Information Service Building Maintenance Price Book *see* B M C I S Building Maintenance Price Book *181*
Building Officials and Code Administrators International Basic National Building Code *see* B O C A Basic National Building Code *181*
Building Officials and Code Administrators International Basic-National Existing Structures Code *see* B O C A Basic-National Existing Structures Code *181*
Building Officials and Code Administrators International Basic-National Fire Prevention Code *see* B O C A Basic-National Fire Prevention Code *506*
Building Officials and Code Administrators International Basic-National Mechanical Code *see* B O C A Basic-National Mechanical Code *181*
Building Officials and Code Administrators International Basic-National Plumbing Code *see* B O C A Basic-National Plumbing Code *553*
Building Owners and Managers Association International Experience Exchange Report *see* B O M A Experience Exchange Report *965*

Building Owners and Managers Association International International Convention Directory *see* B O M A International Convention Directory *795*
Building Research Institute Research Papers *see* B R I Research Papers *181*
Building Services Research and Information Association Application Guides *see* B S R I A Application Guides *553*
Building Services Research and Information Association Technical Notes *see* B S R I A Technical Notes *553*
Building Societies. Year Book (UK ISSN 0068-3566) *225*
Building Societies Association. Report of the Council (UK ISSN 0262-8155) *182, 965*
Building Societies Association of Jamaica Factbook (JM) *182*
Building Societies in (Year) *see* Building Society Factbook (Year) *965*
Building Societies Who's Who (UK) *303, 480*
Building Society Factbook (Year) (UK ISSN 0266-4828) *204, 225, 965*
Buitenlandse Handel van de B.L.E.U. met de Industrielanden (Niet E.E.G.-en E.V.A.-Lidstaten Bruxelles) *see* Commerce Exterieur de l'U.E.B.L. avec les Pays Industrialises (Autre Que les Pays de la C.E.E. et l'A.E.L.E.) *254*
Buitenlandse Handel van de B.L.E.U. Met de Landen van Azie Bruxelles *see* Commerce Exterieur de l'U.E.B.L. Avec les Pays d'Asie *254*
Buitenlandse Handel van de B.L.E.U. Met de Landen van Latijns Amerika Bruxelles *see* Commerce Exterieur de l'U.E.B.L. Avec les Pays d'Amerique Latine *254*
Buitenlandse Handel van de B.L.E.U. Met de Oostlanden Bruxelles *see* Commerce Exterieur de l'U.E.B.L. Avec les Pays de l'Est *254*
Buitlandse Handel van de B.L.E.U. Met de E.E.G.-Lidstaten Bruxelles *see* Commerce Exterieur de l'U.E.B.L. Avec les Pays de la C.E.E *254*
Buku Saku Statistik Indonesia *see* Statistical Pocketbook of Indonesia *1064*
Buletin de Informare Pedagogica *see* Probleme de Pedagogie Contemporana *418*
Buletini Katolik Shqiptar *see* Albanian Catholic Bulletin *967*
Bulgaria in Foreign Literature *see* Bulgaria v Chuzhdata Literatura *124*
Bulgaria v Chuzhdata Literatura/Bulgaria in Foreign Literature (BU ISSN 0323-9969) *124*
Bulgarian Academic Books (BU) *124*
Bulgarian Chamber of Commerce and Industry. Statistical Reference Book (BU) *234*
Bulgarian Periodicals *see* Bulgarski Periodichen Pechat *124*
Bulgarian Review (BL ISSN 0007-3946) *578*
Bulgarska Akademiia na Naukite. Arkheologicheski Institut Izvestiia (BU ISSN 0068-3620) *83*
Bulgarska Akademiia na Naukite. Geologicheski Institut. Izvestiia *see* Paleontologiia, Stratigrafiia i Litologiia *857*
Bulgarska Akademiia na Naukite. Geologicheski Institut. Izvestiia. Seriie Neftena i Vuglishtna Geologiia *see* Neftena i Vuglistna Geologiia *392*
Bulgarska Akademiia na Naukite. Institut po Khidrologiia i Meteorologiia. Izvestiia *see* Hydrology and Meteorology *804*
Bulgarska Akademiia na Naukite. Institut po Vodni Problemi. Izvestiia *see* Vodni Problemi *1127*
Bulgarska Akademiia na Naukite. Institut za Bulgarski Ezik. Izvestiia (BU ISSN 0068-3787) *692*
Bulgarska Akademiia na Naukite. Institut za Istoriia. Izvestiia (BU ISSN 0323-9985) *578*

Bulgarska Akademiia na Naukite, Sofia. Zoologicheski Institut S Muzei. Izvestiia *see* Acta Zoologica Bulgarica *172*
Bulgarski Disertacii (BU ISSN 0323-9411) *124*
Bulgarski Gramofonni Plochi (BU ISSN 0323-9365) *843*
Bulgarski Periodichen Pechat/Bulgarian Periodicals (BU ISSN 0323-9764) *124*
Bulk Carrier Register (UK ISSN 0305-0122) *863*
Bulk Handling & Transport (UK) *1081, 1099*
Bulk Wheat (AT) *63*
Bull Sheet (US) *868*
Bulletin A B Q *see* Q L A Bulletin *683*
Bulletin Annuel de Statistiques de Gaz pour l'Europe *see* Annual Bulletin of Gas Statistics for Europe *862*
Bulletin Antieke Beschaving (NE ISSN 0165-9367) *555*
Bulletin Benelux *see* Benelux Publikatieblad *939*
Bulletin Bibliographique de la Prevention *see* C I S Abstracts *636*
Bulletin Bibliographique International du Machinisme Agricole/International Farm Machinery Abstracts (FR ISSN 0007-4160) *3, 39*
Bulletin Bibliographique Speleologique *see* Speleological Abstracts *382*
Bulletin Bibliographique Thematique (FR ISSN 0076-0137) *124*
Bulletin C I S *see* C I S Abstracts *636*
Bulletin Critique des Annales Islamologiques (UA ISSN 0259-7373) *850, 975*
Bulletin d'Archeologie et d'Histoire Dalmates *see* Vjesnik za Arheologiju i Historiju Dalmatinsku *95*
Bulletin d'Archeologie Marocaine (MR ISSN 0068-4015) *83*
Bulletin d'Archeologie Sud-Est Europeenne. (RM) *83*
Bulletin d'Histoire de la Revolution Francaise (FR ISSN 0766-4516) *578*
Bulletin d'Histoire Economique et Sociale de la Revolution Francaise *see* Bulletin d'Histoire de la Revolution Francaise *578*
Bulletin d'Information Statistique pour l'Afrique *see* Statistical Information Bulletin for Africa *218*
Bulletin d'Informations Proustiennes (FR ISSN 0338-0548) *717*
Bulletin de Correspondance Hellenique (FR ISSN 0007-4217) *83, 337*
Bulletin de la Murithienne (SZ) *378*
Bulletin de la Protection Civile de la Prefecture de Police *see* France. Service Interdepartemental de la Protection Civile. Bulletin *336*
Bulletin de Philosophie Medievale (BE ISSN 0068-4023) *877*
Bulletin de Societe Royale Belge de Geographie *see* Revue Belge de Geographie *547*
Bulletin du Cange (NE) *337*
Bulletin Economique et Social du Maroc (MR ISSN 0007-4586) *191, 1006*
Bulletin International des Douanes *see* International Customs Journal *296*
Bulletin Linguistique et Ethnologique (LU ISSN 0068-4066) *692*
Bulletin - Museum of Natural History, University of Oregon *see* University of Oregon. Museum of Natural History. Bulletin *1165*
Bulletin - Norges Geologiske Undersokelse *see* N G U Bulletin *392*
Bulletin of Abstracts: Welding and Allied Processes *see* Referate Organ: Schweissen und Verwandte Verfahren *802*
Bulletin of Agri-Horticulture (SI) *25, 532*
Bulletin of Agricultural Statistics of the Sudan *see* Sudan Yearbook of Agricultural Statistics *49*
Bulletin of Bingham Oceanographic Collection *see* Peabody Museum of Natural History. Bulletin *998*

Bulletin of Bird Ringing Activity *see* Bollettino dell'Attivita di Inanellamento *170*
Bulletin of Chemical Thermodynamics (1977) (US ISSN 0149-2268) *3, 325*
Bulletin of Comparative Labour Relations (NE) *270*
Bulletin of Earth Sciences (II) *378*
Bulletin of Ethiopian Manuscripts (ET) *960*
Bulletin of Experimental Archaeology (UK) *83*
Bulletin of Informatics and Cybernetics (JA ISSN 0286-522X) *748*
Bulletin of Iranian Studies *see* University of Teheran. Faculty of Letters and Humanities. Bulletin of Iranian Studies *613*
Bulletin of Mathematical Statistics *see* Bulletin of Informatics and Cybernetics *748*
Bulletin of Medieval Canon Law. New Series (US ISSN 0146-2989) *555, 652*
Bulletin of New Zealand Art History (NZ) *103*
Bulletin of Prehistory/Berita Prasejarah (IO) *1149*
Bulletin of Research in Music Education (US) *833*
Bulletin of Sugar Beet Research. Supplement/Tensai Kenkyu Hokoku Hokan (JA ISSN 0068-4090) *53*
Bulletin of Sung and Yuan Studies (US ISSN 0049-254X) *850*
Bulletin of the European Communities. Supplement (EI ISSN 0068-4120) *242*
Bulletin of the Middle Eastern Culture (GW ISSN 0177-1647) *850*
Bulletin of the National Museums of Sri Lanka *see* Spolia Zeylanica *1000*
Bulletin of the Seismological Laboratory (Reno) *see* University of Nevada. Seismological Laboratory. Bulletin *402*
Bulletin of Thermodynamics and Thermochemistry *see* Bulletin of Chemical Thermodynamics (1977) *325*
Bulletin of Tibetology (SK ISSN 0007-5159) *70, 568, 1024*
Bulletin of Volcanic Eruptions (JA ISSN 0525-1524) *398*
Bulletin of Zoo Management (AT ISSN 0084-8182) *173*
Bulletin Officiel de la Marine Marchande (FR) *1099*
Bulletin Officiel de la Propriete Industrielle Statistiques *see* B.O.P.I. Statistiques *860*
Bulletin Officiel du Ministere de l'Environnement et du Cadre de Vie et du Ministere des Transports (FR ISSN 0154-0033) *939*
Bulletin on Scale Insects *see* Studies on the Morphology and Systematics of Scale Insects *166*
Bulletin - Peabody Museum of Natural History *see* Peabody Museum of Natural History. Bulletin *998*
Bulletin - S V P *see* Environnement *496*
Bulletin Scientifique. Section B: Sciences Humanies (YU ISSN 0350-1604) *629, 634*
Bulletin Scientifique de Bourgogne (FR ISSN 0373-2061) *856, 988*
Bulletin Signaletique. Part 120: Astronomie - Physique Spatiale - Geophysique *see* P A S C A L Explore. Part 49: Meteorologie *808*
Bulletin Signaletique. Part 130: Physique Mathematique, Optique, Acoustique, Mechanique, Chaleur *see* P A S C A L Explore. Part 32: Metrologie et Appareillage en Physique et Physicochimie *810*
Bulletin Signaletique. Part 130: Physique Mathematique, Optique, Acoustique, Mechanique, Chaleur *see* P A S C A L Explore. Part 27: Methodes de Formation et Traitement des Images *893*
Bulletin Signaletique. Part 140: Electrotechnique (1983) *see* P A S C A L Folio. Part 21: Electrotechnique *462*

Bulletin Signaletique. Part 145: Electronique see P A S C A L Explore. Part 20: Electronique et Telecommunications 461
Bulletin Signaletique. Part 160: Physique de l'Etat Condense see P A S C A L Explore. Part 12: Etat Condense 893
Bulletin Signaletique. Part 160: Structure de la Matiere 1 see P A S C A L Explore. Part 11: Physique Atomique et Moleculaire. Plasmas 893
Bulletin Signaletique. Part 165: Atomes et Molecules. Plasmas see P A S C A L Explore. Part 11: Physique Atomique et Moleculaire. Plasmas 893
Bulletin Signaletique. Part 215: Biotechnologies (French Edition) see P A S C A L Thema. Part 215: Biotechnologies (Edition Francaise) 772
Bulletin Signaletique. Part 215: Biotechnology (English Edition) see P A S C A L Thema. Part 216: Biotechnology (English Edition) 772
Bulletin Signaletique. Part 233: Medicine Tropicale see P A S C A L Thema. Part 235: Medecine Tropicale 772
Bulletin Signaletique. Part 310: Genie Biomedical. Informatique Biomedicale. Physique Biomedicale see P A S C A L Explore. Part 84: Genie Biomedical. Informatique Biomedicale 772
Bulletin Signaletique. Part 346: Ophtalmologie see P A S C A L Explore. Part 71: Ophtalmologie 772
Bulletin Signaletique. Part 347: Oto-Rhino-Laryngologie, Stomatologie, Pathologie Cervicofaciale see P A S C A L Explore. Part 72: Otorhinolaryngologie. Stomatologie. Pathologie Cervicofaciale 772
Bulletin Signaletique. Part 348: Dermatologie - Venereologie see P A S C A L Explore. Part 73: Dermatologie. Maladies Sexuellement Transmissibles 772
Bulletin Signaletique. Part 349: Anesthesie. Reanimation see P A S C A L Explore. Part 83: Anesthesie et Reanimation 772
Bulletin Signaletique. Part 351: Revue Bibliographique Cancer see P A S C A L Thema. Part 251: Cancerologie (Cancernet) 773
Bulletin Signaletique. Part 352: Maladies de l'Appareil Respiratoire, du Coeur et des Vaisseaux. Chirurgie Thoracique et Vasculaire see P A S C A L Explore. Part 75: Cardiologie et Appareil Circulatoire 772
Bulletin Signaletique. Part 354: Maladies de l'Appareil Digestif. Chirurgie Abdominale see P A S C A L Explore. Part 76: Gastroenterologie, Foie, Pancreas, Abdomen 772
Bulletin Signaletique. Part 355: Maladies des Reins et des Voies Urinaires. Chirurgie see P A S C A L Explore. Part 77: Nephrologie. Voies Urinaires 772
Bulletin Signaletique. Part 356: Maladies du Systeme Nerveux Myopathies-Neurochirurgie see P A S C A L Explore. Part 78: Neurologie 772
Bulletin Signaletique. Part 357: Maladies des Os et des Articulations. Chirurgie Orthopedique. Traumatologie see P A S C A L Explore. Part 79: Pathologie et Physiologie Osteoarticulaires 772
Bulletin Signaletique. Part 359: Maladies du Sang see P A S C A L Explore. Part 80: Hematologie 772
Bulletin Signaletique. Part 361: Reproduction. Gynecologie. Obstetrique. Embryologie. Endocrinologie see P A S C A L Folio. Part 54: Reproduction des Vertebres. Embryologie des Vertebres et des Invertebres 772

Bulletin Signaletique. Part 361: Reproduction. Gynecologie. Obstetrique. Embryologie. Endocrinologie see P A S C A L Explore. Part 64: Endocrinologie Humaine et Experimentale. Endocrinopathies 772
Bulletin Signaletique. Part 361: Reproduction. Gynecologie. Obstetrique. Embryologie. Endocrinologie see P A S C A L Explore. Part 82: Gynecologie. Obstetrique. Andrologie 772
Bulletin Signaletique. Part 362: Diabete. Maladies Metaboliques see P A S C A L Explore. Part 81: Maladies Metaboliques 772
Bulletin Signaletique. Part 362: Maladies de l'Appareil Respiratoire du Coeur et des Vaisseaux. Chirurgie Thoracique et Vasculaire see P A S C A L Explore. Part 74: Pneumologie 772
Bulletin Signaletique. Part 390: Psychologie. Psychopathologie. Psychiatrie see P A S C A L Explore. Part 65: Psychologie. Psychopathologie. Psychiatrie 772
Bulletin Signaletique. Part 521: Sociologie - Ethnologie (FR ISSN 0007-5566) 3, 79, 96, 1031
Bulletin Signaletique. Part 524: Sciences du Langage (FR ISSN 0007-5590) 3, 709
Bulletin Signaletique. Part 730: Combustibles. Energie see P A S C A L Thema. Part 230: Energie 893
Bulletin Signaletique. Part 740: Metaux. Metallurgie see P A S C A L Thema. Part 240: Metaux. Metallurgie 802
Bulletin Signaletique. Part 745: Soudage, Brasage et Techniques Connexes see P A S C A L Thema. Part 245: Soudage, Brasage et Techniques Connexes 802
Bulletin Signaletique: Bibliographie des Sciences de la Terre. Section 221. Gisements Metalliques et Non Metalliques. Economie Miniere see P A S C A L Folio. Part 41: Gisements Metalliques et Non-Metalliques. Economie Miniere 822
Bulletin Signaletique d'Information Administrative (FR ISSN 0293-9614) 948
Bulletin Socialiste see Le Poing et la Rose 908
Bulletin Thomiste see Rassegna di Letteratura Tomistica 881
Bulletin Usuel des Lois et Arretes (BE) 652
Bulletin - Utah Geological and Mineral Survey see Utah Geological and Mineral Survey. Bulletin 397
Bulletin - Yale University Art Gallery see Yale University Art Gallery. Bulletin 831
Bulletins of Marine Ecology (UK ISSN 0068-4198) 1149
Bullinger's Postal and Shippers Guide for the United States and Canada (US ISSN 0068-4201) 346, 1099
Bulwer Lytton Circle Chronicle (UK) 717
Bunadarrit (IC ISSN 0251-2661) 25, 65
Bund Deutscher Eisenbahn-Freunde Jahrbuch see B D E F - Jahrbuch 1094
Bund Deutscher Kriegsopfer. Jahrbuch (GW) 341
Bunda College of Agriculture. Research Bulletin (MW) 25
Bundesanstalt fuer Alpine Landwirtschaft. Versuchsergebnisse see Bundesversuchsanstalt fuer Alpenlaendische Landwirtschaft Gumpenstein. Versuchsergebnisse 25
Bundesanstalt fuer Pflanzenbau und Samenpruefung, Vienna. Jahrbuch see Bundesanstalt fuer Pflanzenbau, Vienna. Jahrbuch
Bundesanstalt fuer Pflanzenbau, Vienna. Jahrbuch (AU) 53, 155
Bundesarbeitsgemeinschaft Hilfe fuer Behinderte. Jahresspiegel (GW) 444, 758

Bundesforschungsanstalt fuer Forst- und Holzwirtschaft, Hamburg. Mitteilungen (GW ISSN 0007-5892) 523, 529
Bundesforschungsanstalt fuer Landeskunde und Raumordnung. Seminare - Symposien - Arbeitspapiere (GW ISSN 0930-3839) 622
Bundesinstitut fuer Ostwissenschaftliche und Internationale Studien. Berichte (GW ISSN 0435-7183) 914
Bundesinstitut fuer Sportwissenschaft. Berichte und Aspekte (Year) (GW) 1033
Bundesministerium fuer Forschung und Technologie Risiko- und Sicherheitsforschung see B M F T Risiko- und Sicherheitsforschung 952
Bundesverband der Deutschen Industrie Deutschland Liefert see B D I Deutschland Liefert 253
Bundesversuchsanstalt fuer Alpenlaendische Landwirtschaft Gumpenstein. Versuchsergebnisse (AU) 25
Bunka Kagaku Kiyo see Journal of Cultural Sciences 630
Burajiru Nikkei Kigyo Nenkan see Empresas Japonesas No Brasil. Annuario 308
Burden of Taxes in the Netherlands see Belastingdruk in Nederland 293
Bureau Eurisotop. Cahiers d'Information (EI) 896
Bureau Eurisotop. Informations Technico-Economiques. (EI) 896
Bureau International de l'Heure. Rapport Annuel (FR ISSN 0068-4236) 115
Bureau International des Containers-Code Code see B I C-Code 854
Bureau International des Societes Gerant les Droits d'Enregistrement et de Reproduction Mecanique. Bulletin(FR ISSN 0572-7529) 930, 960
Bureau Maritieme Historie van de Marinestaf. Mededelingenblad see Bijdrage tot de Geschiedenis van het Zeewezen 810
Bureau National d'Ethnologie. Publication (HT) 1149
Bureau Universitaire de Recherche Operationnelle. Cahiers (FR ISSN 0078-950X) 279
Burgan Bank. Annual Report (KU) 225
Burgen und Schloesser in Oesterreich (AU) 555
Burgenlaendische Forschungen (AU ISSN 0007-621X) 578
Burke's Family Index (UK) 535
Burke's Guide to Country Houses (UK) 1106
Burke's Introduction to Irish Ancestry (UK) 1106
Burke's Irish Family Records (UK) 535
Burke's Royal Families of the World. Vol. 1; Europe and Latin America (UK) 535
Burke's Royal Families of the World. Vol. 2: Africa & the Middle East (UK) 535
Burkina Faso. Direction de l'Hydraulique et de l'Equipement Rural. Service I.R.H. Rapport d'Activites (UV) 53, 1123
Burkina Faso. Direction des Eaux et Forets et de la Conservation des Sols. Rapport Annuel (UV) 508, 523
Burkina Faso. Institut National de la Statistique et de la Demographie. Bulletin Annuaire d'Information Statistique et Economique (UV) 204
Burkina Faso. Service des Statistiques Agricoles. Annuaire (UV) 25
Burns Chronicle Club Directory (UK) 717
Burrelle's Black Media Directory (US) 1149
Burrelle's Hispanic Media Directory (US) 1149
Burrelle's New England Media Directory (US ISSN 0883-9999) 15
Burrelle's New Jersey Media Directory (US ISSN 0883-9778) 15

BUSINESS LAWS 1673

Burrelle's New York State Media Directory (US) 15
Burrelle's Pennsylvania Media Directory (US ISSN 0276-7872) 15
Burrelle's Special Groups Media Directory (US) 1149
Burrelle's Women's Media Directory (US) 1149
Burroughs Bulletin (US ISSN 0007-6333) 717
Burt Franklin American Classics in History and Social Sciences (US ISSN 0068-4287) 604, 1006
Burt Franklin Art History and Art Reference Series (US ISSN 0068-4295) 103, 555
Burt Franklin Bibliography and Reference Series (US ISSN 0068-4309) 124
Burt Franklin Essays in History, Economics, and Social Sciences (US ISSN 0068-4317) 191, 555, 1006
Burt Franklin Essays in Literature and Criticism (US ISSN 0068-4325) 717
Burt Franklin Ethnic Bibliographical Guides (US) 506
Burt Franklin Philosophy Monograph Series see Monographs in Philosophy and Religious History 879
Burt Franklin Research and Source Works Series (US ISSN 0068-4341) 555
Burundi. Departement des Etudes et Statistiques. Bulletin Annuaire (BD) 1050
Bus Facts see American Bus Association. Report 1080
Bus Garage Index (US) 1081
Bus Industry Directory see Bus Ride: Bus Industry Directory 1081
Bus Ride: Bus Industry Directory (US ISSN 0363-3764) 1081
Buses Annual (UK ISSN 0068-4376) 1104
Busi Business Services Index (UK) 191
Business and Economic History (US) 191
Business Archives (UK ISSN 0007-6538) 191
Business Assistance Monograph Series (US ISSN 0146-4744) 191
Business Blue Book of S.A. (SA) 192
Business Blue-Book of Southern Africa see Business Blue Book of S.A 192
Business Contacts in Finland (FI ISSN 0355-0346) 303
Business Data Processing: a Wiley Series (US) 360
Business Directory of Hong Kong (HK) 303
Business Economics and Finance Series(US) 192
Business Education Films Catalog (US) 192, 411, 822
Business Education Index (US ISSN 0068-4414) 423
Business Franchise Guide (US) 301, 652
Business Graduates Association Address Book (UK ISSN 0308-0455) 279
Business Guide Book to Jakarta (IO) 303
Business Information for Dallas (US) 192
Business Information Sourcebook (UK) 192, 675
Business International Corporation Middle East Marketing Conditions: Egypt see B I Middle East Marketing Conditions: Egypt 253
Business International S A Executive Compensation Report see B I/P E R S Executive Compensation Report 278
Business Law Reports (CN ISSN 0703-5551) 192, 652
Business Laws of Arab Emirates (UK) 239, 652
Business Laws of Egypt (UK) 239, 652
Business Laws of Iraq (UK) 239, 652
Business Laws of Kuwait (UK) 239, 652
Business Laws of Oman (UK) 239, 652
Business Laws of Saudi Arabia (UK) 239, 652

1674 BUSINESS LOCATION

Business Location Handbook (UK ISSN 0261-796X) *239*
Business Management *see* Annual Editions: Business/Management *191*
Business Monitor (UK) *192*
Business Monitor: Miscellaneous Series. M2 Cinemas (UK ISSN 0068-4449) *823*
Business Monitor: Miscellaneous Series. M3 Company Finance (UK ISSN 0068-4457) *225*
Business Monitor: Miscellaneous Series. M4 Overseas Transactions (UK ISSN 0068-4465) *254*
Business Opportunities in Spain (SP) *242*
Business Organizations, Agencies, and Publications Directory (US) *303*
Business Organizations and Agencies Directory *see* Business Organizations, Agencies, and Publications Directory *303*
Business Periodicals Index (US ISSN 0007-6961) *3, 204*
Business Professional Advertising Association Membership Directory and Yellow Pages *see* B/P A A Membership Directory and Yellow Pages *15*
Business Radio Buyers Guide (US) *347*
Business Report (abridged version) (GW) *192*
Business Report (unabridged version) (GW) *192*
Business Resources Tourism/Hospitality/Recreation (CN) *432, 847*
Business Studies Series (IE) *192*
Business Traveler's City Guide (US) *192, 1106*
Business Trends: Argentine Economic Legislation *see* Tendencias Economicas: Legislacion Economicas Argentina *200*
Business Trends Asia Report: Indonesia(MY) *242*
Business Who's Who Australian Buying Reference (AT ISSN 0311-5070) *283*
Business Who's Who of Australia (AT ISSN 0068-4503) *303*
Business Who's Who of Australia and Australian Purchasing Yearbook *see* Business Who's Who of Australia *303*
Businessday's Corporate Profiles (PH) *303*
Businessman's Directory, The Republic of China (CH) *303*
Butson Family Newsletter (US ISSN 0743-4235) *535*
Butterworths Budget Tax Tables (UK ISSN 0525-3063) *293*
Butterworths International Medical Reviews: Neurology (UK ISSN 0260-0137) *789*
Butterworths South African Law Review *see* Acta Juridica *650*
Buy Books Where, Sell Books Where (US ISSN 0732-6599) *675, 960*
Buy from India (II ISSN 0304-968X) *303*
Buyer Study (US) *638*
Buyers Guide: Footnotes (US) *374, 833*
Buyers Guide for Fresh Produce (US) *522*
Buyers' Guide for the Mass Entertainment Industry (US ISSN 0362-6180) *1044*
Buyers' Guide: Nuclear Industry in Japan (JA) *896*
Buyers' Guide to the Automotive Industry of Great Britain for International Buyers (UK) *1091*
Buyers' Guide to the Motor Industry of Great Britain *see* Buyers' Guide to the Automotive Industry of Great Britain for International Buyers *1091*
Buyer's Guide to the New York Market(US) *303*
Buyers' Guide: Watch Industry, Jewellery and Allied Trades *see* Guide des Acheteurs: Horlogerie, Bijouterie et Branches Annexes *644*
Buzetski Zbornik (YU) *83, 578*
By og Bygd (NO ISSN 0084-8212) *70, 578*

Bydgoskie Towarzystwo Naukowe. Wydzial Nauk Humanistycznych. Prace. Seria B (Jezyk i Literatura) (PL ISSN 0068-4570) *692, 717*
Bydgoskie Towarzystwo Naukowe. Wydzial Nauk Humanistycznych. Prace. Seria C (Historia i Archeologia) (PL ISSN 0068-4589) *578*
Bydgoskie Towarzystwo Naukowe. Wydzial Nauk Humanistycznych. Prace. Seria D: (Sztuka) (PL ISSN 0067-947X) *103*
Bydgoskie Towarzystwo Naukowe. Wydzial Nauk Technicznych. Prace. Seria Z: (Prace Zbiorowe) (PL ISSN 0068-4597) *1067*
Byelorussian Institute of Arts and Sciences. Annals *see* Belaruski Instytut Navuki Mactatstva. Zapisy *577*
Bygdeserien (FI) *97*
Bygge Nyts Leverandoerregister (DK) *182*
Bygge- og Boligpolitiske Oversigt (DK ISSN 0107-119X) *182*
Bygge- og Boligpolitiske Udvikling *see* Bygge- og Boligpolitiske Oversigt *182*
Bygningsstatiske Meddelelser (DK ISSN 0106-3715) *182*
Byhornet (DK ISSN 0105-6433) *83, 578*
Byoin Yoran *see* Japanese Hospital Directory *617*
Byron Journal (UK ISSN 0301-7257) *740*
Byron Society Newsletter (US ISSN 0196-8998) *717*
Byzantina (GR) *337*
Byzantina Kai Metabyzantina (US ISSN 0742-1141) *612*
Byzantina Neerlandica (NE ISSN 0525-4507) *578*
Byzantine and Modern Greek Studies (UK ISSN 0307-0131) *692, 717*
Byzantinobulgarica (BU ISSN 0068-4686) *578*
C A A P Directory: Wholesalers of Organic Produce & Products (California Agrarian Action Project) (US) *25, 303*
C A A Research Series *see* K A C Research Series *88*
C A A S Monograph Series *see* Afro-American Culture and Society Monograph Series *1005*
C A A S Special Publication Series (Center for Afro-American Studies) (US ISSN 0882-5300) *502, 1006*
C.A.B. International Bureau of Agricultural Economics. Annotated Bibliographies Series A (UK) *39*
C.A.B. International Bureau of Agricultural Economics. Annotated Bibliographies. Series B: Agricultural Policy and Rural Development in Africa (UK) *39*
C.A.B. International Bureau of Nutrition. Annotated Bibliographies (UK) *847*
C.A.B. International Bureau of Soils. Annotated Bibliographies (UK) *39*
C.A.B. International. Forestry Bureau. Annotated Bibliographies (UK) *124, 529*
C.A.B. International. Mycological Institute. Phytopathological Papers (UK) *155*
C A D/C A M Industry Directory *see* International C A D/C A M Industry Directory *356*
C A D/C A M: Management Strategies(US ISSN 0741-0042) *355*
C A D Systems Update *see* Low Cost C A D/C A M Systems *356*
C A D U Publications *see* A R D U Publication *22*
C A L I C O. Monograph Series (Computer Assisted Language & Instruction Consortium) (US) *356, 432, 446*
C A L L S *see* California Academic Libraries List of Serials *963*
C A L U S Research Reports (Centre for Advanced Land Use Studies) (UK) *182, 965*

C A M S Manual of Motor Sport (Confederation of Australian Motor Sport) (AT) *1033*
C A N M E T Report (Canada Centre for Mineral and Energy Technology) (CN ISSN 0705-5196) *814*
C A N M E T Review *see* C A N M E T Report *814*
C A O Times (US ISSN 0146-3365) *114*
C A P A I D M *see* I E E E Computer Society Workshop on Computer Architecture for Pattern Analysis and Image Database Management. Proceedings *356*
C A R D Report (Center for Agricultural and Rural Development) (US ISSN 0271-7190) *25*
C A R N E S *see* Computer Aided Research in Near Eastern Studies *612*
C A S Newsletter (Catholic Archives Society) (UK ISSN 0262-6896) *981*
C A S S I *see* Chemical Abstracts Service Source Index *325*
C A T M O G (Concepts and Techniques in Modern Geography) (UK ISSN 0306-6142) *542*
C A.T.S. Reports (Centre for Advanced T V Studies) (UK) *347*
C A T V and Station Coverage Atlas and 35-Mile Zone Maps *see* Cable and Station Coverage Atlas and 35-Mile Zone Maps *347*
C & C A Technical Report (Cement and Concrete Association) (UK) *182*
C B A Annual Report (Council for British Archaeology) (UK ISSN 0589-9028) *83*
C B A Boletin Informativo *see* Hispanic American Arts *105*
C B A Media Guide/Yearbook (Continential Basketball Association) (US) *1037*
C B C Classical Record Reference Book (Canadian Broadcasting Corporation) (CN) *834*
C B C Features (Children's Book Council, Inc.) (US) *333, 960*
C B I Aarsberaettelse/Report of Activities (Cement- och Betonginstitutet) (SW) *1149*
C B I Annual Report (Confederation of British Industry) (UK ISSN 0268-2273) *192*
C B I Forskning/Research (Cement- och Betonginstitutet) (SW ISSN 0346-6906) *182*
C B I Rapporter/Reports (Cement- och Betonginstitutet) (SW ISSN 0346-8240) *182*
C B S *see* Cardinal Bea Studies *981*
C C/A & H *see* Current Contents/Arts & Humanities *634*
C-B S E/Current Contents, Behavioral, Social and Educational Sciences *see* Current Contents/Social & Behavioral Sciences *1031*
C C/C M *see* Current Contents/Clinical Medicine *769*
C C C Yellow Pages *see* Christian Chamber of Commerce. Classified Membership Directory *15*
C C E T S W Reporting (Central Council for Education and Training in Social Work) (UK) *426, 1024*
C C H/O S H A Compliance Guide (US) *635*
C C H R Newsletter (Citizens Committee on Human Rights) (AT) *376, 789*
C C I A Background Information (World Council of Churches, Commission on International Affairs) (SZ) *903, 968*
C C I Technical Bulletins (Canadian Conservation Institute) (CN ISSN 0706-4152) *364*
C C I Year Book & Directory (Cape Chamber of Industries) (SA) *235*
C C R *see* Current Chemical Reactions *325*
C C R S Newsletter (Los Angeles Community Church of Religious Science) (US) *1149*
C C/S & B S *see* Current Contents/Social & Behavioral Sciences *1031*
C.D. Howe Institute Commentary (CN ISSN 0824-8001) *192*

C.D. Howe Institute. Policy Review and Outlook (CN ISSN 0826-9939) *192*
C. D. Howe Research Institute. Policy Review and Outlook *see* C.D. Howe Institute. Policy Review and Outlook *192*
C D R Project Paper (Centre for Development Research) (DK ISSN 0106-0805) *45*
C D R Research Reports (Centre for Development Research) (DK ISSN 0108-6596) *45*
C E A Handbook/Ki-es-Ki (Canadian Education Association) (CN ISSN 0068-8657) *411*
C E B V (Communaute Economique du Betail et de la Viande) (UV) *65*
C E C O N *see* Cleveland Electrical/Electronics Conference and Exposition. Conference Record *451*
C E C T A L Conference Papers Series (Centre for English Cultural Tradition and Language) (UK ISSN 0261-314X) *692, 717*
C.E.D.E. Coleccion-Debates (Centro de Estudios sobre Desarrollo Economico) (CK) *242*
C.E.D.E. Documentos de Trabajo (Centro de Estudios sobre Desarrollo Economico) (CK) *242*
C E D Newsletter (Committee for Economic Development) (US ISSN 0069-682X) *261, 287*
C E E International. Droit et Affaires (Communaute Economique Europeenne) (BE) *669*
C E G B Abstracts (Central Electricity Generating Board) (UK ISSN 0267-0372) *461, 896*
C E G B Digest *see* C E G B Abstracts *461*
C E G B Research (Central Electricity Generating Board) (UK ISSN 0305-7194) *451*
C E M A G R E F Bulletin d'Information (Centre National du Machinisme Agricole du Genie Rural, des Eaux et des Forets) (FR ISSN 0249-4779) *1149*
C E M A G R E F Etudes (Centre National du Machinisme Agricole du Genie Rural, des Eaux et des Forets) (FR ISSN 0249-4787) *1149*
C E M A M Reports (Center for the Study of the Modern Arab World) (LE) *850*
C E P A L Studies and Reports *see* Estudios e Informes de la C E P A L *262*
C E P Reports and C E P Studies (Council on Economic Priorities) (US) *251*
C E P S Papers (Centre for European Policy Studies) (BE) *192, 251*
C E P S Working Documents (Economic) (Centre for European Policy Studies) (BE) *192, 251*
C E P S Working Documents (Political) (Centre for European Policy Studies) (BE) *903, 915*
C E R N Annual Report (SZ ISSN 0304-2901) *887, 896*
C E R N-H E R A Reports (SZ ISSN 0366-5690) *887, 896*
C E R N Rapport Annuel *see* C E R N Annual Report *887*
C E R N Reports (SZ ISSN 0007-8328) *887, 896*
C E R N School of Computing. Proceedings (SZ ISSN 0304-2898) *1005*
C E R N School of Physics. Proceedings (SZ ISSN 0531-4283) *887, 896*
C E T A Bulletin (Chinese-English Translation Assistance Group) (US) *692*
C F D C Annual Report *see* Telefilm Canada Annual Report *825*
C F F S Index of Feature Films *see* Index of 16 mm & 35 mm Feature Length Films Available in Canada *1155*
C F I Occasional Papers *see* O F I Occasional Papers *526*
C G O U Technical Report (U.S. Coast Guard, Oceanographic Unit) (US) *405*

C G R B Bulletin (Citizens' Governmental Research Bureau) (US) 411, *950*
C H A C Directory *see* Catholic Health Association of Canada. Directory *759*
C H I N O P E R L News *see* C H I N O P E R L Papers *717*
C H I N O P E R L Papers (Conference on Chinese Oral and Performing Literature) (US ISSN 0193-7774) *717*
C I A C (CU) *903*
C.I.A. Revue (Confederation Internationale des Accordeonistes) (AU ISSN 0574-9468) *834*
C I A T Report (Centro Internacional de Agricultura Tropical) (CK ISSN 0120-3169) *25*
C I B Directory of Building Research Information and Development Organizations *see* International Directory of Building Research, Information and Development Organizations *185*
C.I.C.A.E. Bulletin d'Information (Confederation Internationale des Cinemas d'Art et d'Essai) (FR ISSN 0526-6513) *823*
C I C A Handbook (Canadian Institute of Chartered Accountants) (CN ISSN 0068-8983) *221*
C I C R I S Directory (Cooperative Industrial and Commercial Reference and Information Service) (UK) *675*
C I C R I S Directory and Guide to Resources *see* C I C R I S Directory *675*
C I C's State School Directories (Curriculum Information Center) (US ISSN 0162-9646) *428*
C I D A (Centro de Investigacion y Difusion Aeronautico Espacial) (UY) *18*
C.I.D.A. Annual Review *see* Canadians in the Third World *261*
C I E News *see* C I T E News *182*
C.I.E. Newsletter (Central Institute of Education) (II ISSN 0007-8425) *411*
C I F A Technical Papers (Food and Agriculture Organization of the United Nations, Committee for Inland Fisheries of Africa) (UN) *508*
C I I L Adult Literacy Series (Central Institute of Indian Languages) (II) *426*
C I I L Bilingual Hindi Series (Central Institute of Indian Languages) (II) *692*
C I I L Folklore Series (Central Institute of Indian Languages) (II) *515*
C I I L Grammar Series (Central Institute of Indian Languages) (II) *692*
C I I L Occasional Monograph Series (Central Institute of Indian Languages) (II) *692*
C I L T *see* Amsterdam Studies in the Theory and History of Linguistic Science. Series 4: Current Issues in Linguistic Theory *690*
C.I.M. Directory (Canadian Institute of Mining and Metallurgy) (CN ISSN 0068-9009) 797, *815*
C I N A H L'S List of Subject Headings *see* Cumulative Index to Nursing & Allied Health Literature (C I N A H L) *769*
C I N A - Nytt (Centralinstitut foer Nordisk Asienforskning) (DK ISSN 0109-4203) *851*
C I N C O M: Courses in Communications (Communications Institute) (US ISSN 0742-3632) 347, *428*
C I N D A (UN) 3, *892*
C I N T E R F O R Estudios y Monografias (Centro Interamericano de Investigacion y Documentacion Sobre Formacion Profesional) (UY ISSN 0577-2931) *411*
C I P L *see* Amsterdam Studies in the Theory and History of Linguistic Science. Series 2: Classics in Psycholinguistics *690*
C I R I A. Bulletin *see* C I R I A Annual Report *480*

C I R I A Annual Report (Construction Industry Research and Information Association) (UK ISSN 0305-4047) 182, *480*
C I R I A Report (Construction Industry Research and Information Association) (UK ISSN 0305-408X) 182, *480*
C I R I A Technical Note (Construction Industry Research and Information Association) (UK ISSN 0305-1781) 182, *480*
C.I.R.M. (Centro Internazionale Radio-Medico) (IT) 347, *758*
C I S (Chromosome Information Service) (JA ISSN 0574-9549) *166*
C I S Abstracts (International Labour Office) (UN ISSN 0302-7651) 3, *636*
C I S Federal Register Index (Congressional Information Service, Inc.) (US ISSN 0741-2878) 3, *939*
C I S Index (Congressional Information Service, Inc.) (US ISSN 0007-8514) 3, *948*
C I T E News (Construction Information-Training Education Project) (UK) *182*
C J A and H S A Newsletter (Council of Justice to Animals and Humane Slaughter Association) (UK ISSN 0263-1407) *868*
C L A C S O Boletin *see* David y Goliath *1007*
C L A Directory (Canadian Library Association) (CN) *675*
C L A I M Report to the British Library and Development Department (Centre for Library and Information Management) (UK) *1149*
C L A Organization Handbook and Membership List *see* C L A Directory *675*
C L E M (Contact List of Electronic Music) (CN ISSN 0820-7356) *834*
C L E O *see* Conference on Lasers and Electro-Optics (Publications) *451*
C L R *see* Clinical Laboratory Reference *781*
C L R Recent Developments (Council on Library Resources, Inc.) (US ISSN 0034-1169) *1149*
C M C I *see* Compumath Citation Index *755*
C M E Annual Report (Center for Music Experiment) (US) 357, *834*
C M G Conference Proceedings (Computer Measurement Group) (US) *352*
C M I T *see* Current Medical Information and Terminology *760*
C M I Year Book (SW) *1099*
C M R E Monetary Tracts *see* C M R E Monographs *225*
C M R E Monographs (Committee for Monetary Research and Education, Inc.) (US ISSN 0734-0486) *225*
C N C Statistiques (Centre National de la Cinematographie) (FR) *825*
C N E E M A Bulletin d'Information *see* C E M A G R E F Bulletin d'Information *1149*
C N E E M A Etudes *see* C E M A G R E F Etudes *1149*
C O F I E C. Informe Anual (Compania Financiera Ecuatoriana de Desarrollo) (EC) *225*
C O M A R *see* Code of Maryland Regulations *940*
C O M E C O N Data (Council for Mutual Economic Assistance) (US ISSN 0263-3701) *254*
C O M E C O N Foreign Trade Data (Council for Mutual Economic Assistance) (US) *254*
C O M P M E D *see* Frontiers of Engineering and Computing in Health Care *778*
C O M P S A C/I E E E Computer Society's. International Computer Software & Applications Conference. Proceedings (US ISSN 0730-3157) *362*
C O N S E R Microfiche (Conversion of Serials) (CN ISSN 0707-3747) *124*
C O R D Research Annual *see* Dance Research Annual *1151*

C O R E J *see* Contents of Recent Economics Journals *206*
C O R S I Bulletin (Operational Research Society of India, Calcutta Branch) (II ISSN 0078-5261) *279*
C P C Annual (College Placement Council, Inc.) (US) *847*
C P C National Directory (US ISSN 8755-8378) *847*
C P C U Public Affairs Forum (Society of Chartered Property & Casualty Underwriters) (US) *638*
C P E M Digest *see* Conference on Precision Electromagnetic Measurements. Digest *451*
C P I Product Profiles (CN) 303, *321*
C P I Purchasing Chemicals Directory (US ISSN 0746-9012) 303, *478*
C P S A *see* Copenhagen Political Studies Abstracts *911*
C P T (Physicians' Current Procedural Terminology) (US ISSN 0276-8283) *758*
C R C Critical Reviews in Biotechnology (US ISSN 0738-8551) 139, *1067*
C R C Critical Reviews in Oncology-Hematology (C R C Press, Inc.) (US ISSN 0737-9587) 774, *783*
C R C Critical Reviews in Plant Sciences (C R C Press, Inc.) (US ISSN 0735-2689) *53*
C R C Press, Inc. Critical Reviews in Oncology-Hematology *see* C R C Critical Reviews in Oncology-Hematology *774*
C R C Press, Inc. Critical Reviews in Plant Sciences *see* C R C Critical Reviews in Plant Sciences *53*
C R I C Rapport de Recherche (Centre National de Recherches Scientifiques et Techniques pour l'Industrie Cimentiere) (BE ISSN 0069-2026) 989, *1067*
C R R E R I S Renewable Energy Index (AT ISSN 0816-1070) 3, *468*
C R R I Road Abstracts (Central Road Research Institute) (II ISSN 0045-6055) 3, *476*
C R S Perspectives (Centre for Resource Studies) (CN ISSN 0228-1821) 192, *815*
C S A S Occasional Papers (Centre for Southern African Studies) (UK) *565*
C.S.D. Advance Locator *see* Advance Locator for Capitol Hill *902*
C S E Monograph Series in Evaluation (Center for the Study of Evaluation) (US) *446*
C S I Congressional Record Abstracts: Energy Edition (US) 3, 464, *948*
C S I R Annual Report (Council for Scientific and Industrial Research) (SA ISSN 0370-8454) 989, *1067*
C S I R Handbook (Council for Scientific and Industrial Research) (GH) *989*
C S I R O Directory (Commonwealth for Scientific and Industrial Research Organisation) (AT ISSN 0157-7204) 989, *1068*
C.S.I.R.O. Division of Materials Science. Research Report (AT ISSN 0725-3575) 328, *887*
C S I R O Film Catalogue (Commonwealth for Scientific and Industrial Research Organisation) (AT ISSN 0069-7192) 989, *1068*
C S I R O Organisation and Activities (Council for Scientific and Industrial Research Organisation) (SA ISSN 0081-9700) 989, *1068*
C S I R Research Reports *see* National Institute for Transport and Road Research. Bulletins *1096*
C S I R Special Reports *see* National Institute for Transport and Road Research. P A D Series *1096*
C.S.O. Statistical Bulletins (Central Statistical Office) (TR) *1050*
C S R Yearbook *see* Country Song Roundup Yearbook *835*
C S S R. Kronika Vnitropolitickych Udalosti (CS ISSN 0303-2221) *578*
C T A A. Boletim de Pesquisa (Centro Nacional de Pesquisa de Tecnologia Agroindustrial de Alimentos) (BL ISSN 0101-630X) *518*

C.T. Directory of South Africa (Cape Town) (SA) *303*
C T O (Call to Order) (UK ISSN 0260-5821) *103*
C.T.T.S. Annual (College of Textile Technology, Serampore) (II ISSN 0084-8859) *1073*
C T V D: Cinema - TV - Digest (US ISSN 0097-9219) 347, *823*
C U Directory (Chicago Unlimited, Inc.) (US ISSN 0363-745X) *823*
C U I S Credit Union Directory and Buyers' Guide *see* Credit Union Directory and Buyers' Guide *227*
C U N Y English Forum (US ISSN 0736-3982) *717*
C U N Y Forum (US) *692*
C U S Bulletin (Centre for Urban Studies) (BG) *622*
C U S I P Corporate Directory (Committee on Uniform Security Identification Procedures) (US) *265*
C U S I P Master Directory (American Bankers Association, Committee on Uniform Security Identification Procedures) (US) *265*
C U S O Journal (CN ISSN 0821-1272) *441*
C V P R *see* I E E E Computer Society Conference on Computer Vision and Pattern Recognition. Proceedings *356*
C V R Hotel Guide to Southern Africa (Chris van /Rensburg Publications (Pty) Ltd.) (SA) *619*
C V R Travel and Hotel Guide to Southern Africa *see* C V R Hotel Guide to Southern Africa *619*
C W I Tracts (NE) *748*
C W M Report (Council for World Mission) (UK) *978*
C W/P S Special Studies (Center for War-Peace Studies) (US ISSN 0730-9058) *915*
C W/P S Study *see* C W/P S Special Studies *915*
Cabbages and Kings (AT ISSN 0310-1584) *573*
Cable and Station Coverage Atlas and 35-Mile Zone Maps (US ISSN 0193-3639) *347*
Cable T V Financial Databook (US ISSN 0736-8143) *347*
CableFile (US ISSN 0363-1915) *347*
Cadastro Brasileiro de Materias-Primas Farmaceuticas, Por Produto, Por Fabricante (BL ISSN 0068-4775) *1149*
Cadastro Delta (BL) *192*
Cadastro Industrial do Para (BL) *287*
Cadeau et l'Entreprise (FR) 15, *283*
Caderno de Direito Economico (BL) *652*
Caderno de Pesquisas Tributarias (BL) *652*
Cadernos Condicao Feminina (PO) *1128*
Cadernos de Estudos Brasileiros. (BL) *629*
Cadernos de Estudos Linguisticos/Cadernos de Estvdos Lingvisti (BL) *692*
Cadernos de Estudos Rurais e Urbanos (BL) *1024*
Cadernos de Estvdos Lingvisti *see* Cadernos de Estudos Linguisticos *692*
Cadernos de Folclore (BL ISSN 0575-0075) *515*
Cadernos Politicos de Educacao Popular (PO) *903*
Cadmium Abstracts *see* Cadscan *801*
Cadscan (UK) *801*
Caesaraugusta (SP ISSN 0007-9502) 70, *84*
Cafeteria (US) *740*
Cahiers Alsaciens d'Archeologie d'Art et d'Histoire (FR) *84*
Cahiers Amitie Franco-Vietnamienne (FR ISSN 0084-8220) *915*
Cahiers Binchois (BE) *84*
Cahiers Canadiens Claudel (CN ISSN 0068-4961) *1149*
Cahiers Charles du Bos (FR ISSN 0575-0415) *717*
Cahiers Congolais de la Recherche et du Developpement *see* Cahiers Zairois de la Recherche et du Developpement *539*

Cahiers d'Analyse Textuelle (FR ISSN 0575-0466) 717
Cahiers d'Economie Politique (FR) 251
Cahiers d'Etudes Mongoles et Siberiennes (FR) 70, 692
Cahiers d'Histoire see Universite Laval. Les Cahiers d'Histoire 562
Cahiers d'Histoire de Seconde Guerre Mondiale (BE ISSN 0771-6435) 578
Cahiers de Bruges/Bruges Quarterly (BE ISSN 0575-0571) 903, 915
Cahiers de Droit Fiscal International (NE) 669
Cahiers de Jules Romains (FR) 717
Cahiers de l'Avenir de la Bretagne (FR ISSN 0182-2705) 555, 912
Cahiers de l'U E R Froissart see Valenciennes 737
Cahiers de la Renaissance Vaudoise (SZ ISSN 0007-9847) 717
Cahiers de Linguistique Hispanique Medievale (FR) 692
Cahiers de Linguistique Structurale see Cahiers de Psychomecanique de Langage 692
Cahiers de Mariemont (BE) 827
Cahiers de Micropaleontologie (FR ISSN 0068-5054) 856
Cahiers de Philologie (FR ISSN 0153-5048) 692
Cahiers de Psychomecanique de Langage (CN ISSN 0068-5070) 692
Cahiers de Recherche Ethique (CN) 968
Cahiers de Recherches en Sciences de la Religion (CN ISSN 0704-7924) 1149
Cahiers de Saint-Michel de Cuxa (FR ISSN 0068-5089) 717
Cahiers de Sante Publique see Public Health Papers 955
Cahiers de Sciences Sociales (CN ISSN 0068-5097) 1149
Cahiers de Traductologie (CN) 692
Cahiers Debussy (FR) 834
Cahiers des Etudes Anciennes (CN ISSN 0317-5065) 84
Cahiers des Explorateurs (FR ISSN 0526-8133) 70, 542
Cahiers du C R S R see Cahiers de Recherches en Sciences de la Religion 1149
Cahiers du Memontois (FR ISSN 0180-9261) 84
Cahiers du Sart Tilman (BE ISSN 0575-0970) 622
Cahiers du Tourisme (FR ISSN 0068-5151) 1106
Cahiers Economiques et Monetaires (FR) 192, 225
Cahiers Ferdinand de Saussure (SZ ISSN 0068-516X) 692
Cahiers Geologiques (FR ISSN 0008-0241) 384
Cahiers Henri Bosco (FR ISSN 0753-4590) 718
Cahiers Internationaux d'Histoire Economique et Sociale see Quaderni Internazionali di Storia Economica e Sociale 594
Cahiers Internationaux de Symbolisme (BE ISSN 0008-0284) 877
Cahiers Ligures de Prehistoire et d'Archeologie see Cahiers Ligures de Prehistoire et de Protohistoire 84
Cahiers Ligures de Prehistoire et de Protohistoire (IT) 84
Cahiers Naturalistes (FR ISSN 0008-0365) 718
Cahiers Nepalais (FR ISSN 0068-5194) 903
Cahiers Nivellois (BE) 740
Cahiers Philosophiques Africains/African Philosophical Journal (ZR) 877
Cahiers Raymond Abellio (FR ISSN 0763-1529) 877
Cahiers Saint-Exupery (FR) 718
Cahiers Saint-John Perse (FR) 740
Cahiers Sociale Geschiedenis (NE) 578
Cahiers Suisses Romain Rolland (SZ) 718
Cahiers Tristan l'Hermit (FR) 740
Cahiers Vilfredo Pareto (SZ ISSN 0008-0497) 1007
Cahiers Zairois de la Recherche et du Developpement (ZR) 539
Cain (VE ISSN 0068-5259) 604

Cain Connections (US) 535
Cairngorm Club Journal (UK ISSN 0068-5267) 1033
Caisse Centrale de Cooperation Economique. Rapport Annuel (FR) 238
Caisse Centrale de Cooperation Economique. Rapport d'Activite see Caisse Centrale de Cooperation Economique. Rapport Annuel 238
Caisse d'Epargne de l'Etat du Grand-Duche de Luxembourg. Rapports et Bilans (LU) 225
Caisse Nationale des Autoroutes. Rapport Annuel (FR) 1096
Caisses Centrales de Mutualite Sociale Agricole. Statistiques. (FR) 652, 1024
Caja de Ahorros y Monte de Piedad de las Baleares. Memoria (SP ISSN 0409-9192) 225
Caja de Credito Agrario, Industrial y Minero. Financiamento de la Pequena y Mediana Industria (CK) 301
Cal-Vet Insurance Plans. Annual Report(US) 638, 810
Calcified Tissue Abstracts (US ISSN 0008-0586) 3, 149
Calcutta Management Association. Annual Report (II ISSN 0068-5356) 279
Calcutta Market see Thapar's Indian Industrial Directory and Import and Export Directory of the World 317
Caledonian (CN ISSN 0381-856X) 710
Calendar see C B C Features 960
Calendar of Congresses of Medical Sciences (SZ ISSN 0301-2891) 758, 795
Calendar of International Congresses of Medical Sciences see Calendar of Congresses of Medical Sciences 795
Calendar of Regional Congresses of Medical Sciences see Calendar of Congresses of Medical Sciences 795
Calendario Agricola (VE) 45
Calendario Cultural do Brasil (BL) 1107
Calendario Escolar (AG) 411
Calendario Meteoro-Fenologico see Calendario Meteorologico 803
Calendario Meteorologico (SP) 803
Calendars and Indexes to the Letters and Papers of the Archbishops of Canterbury in Lambeth Palace Library (UK) 1149
Calgary Airport Business Directory (CN) 1087
Calgary Archaeologist (CN ISSN 0384-191X) 70, 84
Calgary in Fact (CN) 242
Caliban (FR ISSN 0575-2124) 718
California. Administrative Office of the Courts. Annual Report (US ISSN 0068-5488) 652
California. Air Resources Board. Annual Report (US ISSN 0068-5496) 494
California. Air Resources Board. Fact Sheets (US) 494
California. Bureau of Criminal Statistics and Special Services. Criminal Justice Profile; Statewide (US) 373
California. Bureau of Criminal Statistics. Crime and Delinquency see Crime and Delinquency in California 370
California. Bureau of Criminal Statistics. Criminal Justice Profile; Statewide see California. Bureau of Criminal Statistics and Special Services. Criminal Justice Profile; Statewide 373
California. Bureau of Entomology. Occasional Papers see Occasional Papers in Entomology 165
California. Department of Consumer Affairs. Annual Report (US) 283
California. Department of Education. Annual Report on Publicly Subsidized Child Care Services (US ISSN 0197-744X) 333
California. Department of Fish and Game. Fish and Game Code (US) 364
California. Department of Fish and Game. Fish and Game Code. Supplement (US) 364

California. Department of Forestry. State Forest Notes see California Forestry Note 523
California. Department of Industrial Relations. Annual Report (US ISSN 0362-4129) 270, 635
California. Department of Parks and Recreation. Archaeological Report see California Archeological Reports 84
California. Department of Water Resources. Bulletin (US ISSN 0084-8263) 1123
California. Department of Water Resources. California State Water Project see California State Water Project 1123
California. Department of Water Resources. Inventory of Waste Water Production and Waste Water Reclamation Practices in California (US ISSN 0092-9158) 1123
California. Division of Mines and Geology. Bulletin (US ISSN 0008-1000) 384, 815
California. Division of Mines and Geology. Special Publication (US) 384, 815
California. Division of Mines and Geology. Special Report (US ISSN 0527-0014) 384, 815
California. Division of Oil and Gas. Annual Report of the State Oil and Gas Supervisor (US ISSN 0362-1243) 863
California. Law Revision Commission. Reports, Recommendations and Studies (US) 652
California. Office of Administrative Law. Anniversary Report (US) 652, 940
California. Secretary of State. Roster see Roster-California State, County, City and Township Officials State Officials of the United States 945
California. State Board of Cosmetology. Rules and Regulations. (US ISSN 0094-4327) 118, 652
California. State Board of Equalization. Annual Report (US ISSN 0068-5801) 293
California. State College, San Francisco. Department of Anthropology. Occasional Papers in Anthropology see Adan E. Treganza Anthropology Museum. Papers 69
California. State Energy Commission. Biennial Report (US) 464
California. Teachers Retirement Board. State Teacher's Retirement System; Annual Report to the Governor and the Legislature (US ISSN 0090-5593) 442
California Academic Libraries List of Serials (US ISSN 0198-8433) 963
California Academy of Sciences. Memoirs (US) 139
California Academy of Sciences. Occasional Papers (US ISSN 0068-5461) 989
California Academy of Sciences. Proceedings (US ISSN 0068-547X) 989
California Agrarian Action Project Directory: Wholesalers of Organic Produce & Products see C A A P Directory: Wholesalers of Organic Produce & Products 25
California Agricultural Export Directory(US) 45
California Air Basins (US) 494
California Alcohol Program Plan see California Alcohol Program: Report to the Legislature (Year) 376
California Alcohol Program: Report to the Legislature (Year) 376
California and Nevada Legal Services Programs Directory (US) 653
California Archeological Reports (US) 84
California Architecture and Architects (US) 97
California Community Colleges. Master Plan and Inventory of Programs (US) 432
California Condor see Raptor Report 170

California Cooperative Oceanic Fisheries Investigations Reports (US) 173
California County Fact Book (US) 1050
California County Law Library Basic List (US ISSN 0068-5879) 653
California Data Brief (US) 1149
California Directory of Water Resources Expertise (US) 1123
California Enviromental Yearbook and Directory see California Environmental Directory 494
California Environmental Directory (US ISSN 0148-0324) 494
California Facts (US ISSN 0883-6264) 542
California Farmlands Project. Working Papers (US) 1149
California Fish and Game Code see California. Department of Fish and Game. Fish and Game Code 364
California Forestry and Forest Products(US ISSN 0008-1094) 529
California Forestry Note (US) 523
California Fruit and Nut Acreage (US ISSN 0527-2181) 39
California Government & Politics Annual (US ISSN 0084-8271) 903
California Handbook (US ISSN 0068-5615) 462, 940, 1007
California Health Facilities Commission. Annual Report to the Governor and Legislature of the State of California (US) 616, 759
California Industrial Relations Reports (US ISSN 0008-1191) 270
California Insect Survey. Bulletin (US ISSN 0068-5631) 164
California Institute of Technology. Division of Engineering and Applied Science. Annual Report see California Institute of Technology. Division of Engineering and Applied Science. Research Report 470
California Institute of Technology. Division of Engineering and Applied Science. Research Report (US) 470
California Institute of Technology. Division of Geological and Planetary Sciences. Report on Geological and Planetary Sciences for the Year (US ISSN 0045-3943) 115, 384
California Journal Almanac of State Government and Politics (US) 940
California Livestock Statistics (US ISSN 0361-9095) 39
California Lodging Industry (US) 619
California Macadamia Society. Yearbook (US ISSN 0068-5720) 53
California Manufacturers Register (US ISSN 0068-5739) 303
California Natural History Guides (US ISSN 0068-5755) 139
California - Nevada Campbook (US) 1044, 1107
California-Nevada Camping see California - Nevada Campbook 1107
California, Nevada TourBook see Tourbook: California, Nevada 1117
California Newspaper Publishers Association. Directory and Rate Book (US) 645
California Newspaper Publishers' Association. Newspaper Directory see California Newspaper Publishers Association. Directory and Rate Book 645
California Notary Law Primer (US) 653
California Periodicals Index (US ISSN 0730-1367) 3
California Periodicals on Microfilm (US) 124
California Personnel & Guidance Association. Monographs (US) 847
California Private School Directory (US ISSN 0098-5147) 428
California Public School Directory (US ISSN 0068-5771) 428
California Restaurant Operations (US) 619
California Roster see Roster-California State, County, City and Township Officials State Officials of the United States 945
California Roster (US) 950
California Services Register (US ISSN 0271-6615) 192

California State Health Plan (US) 616
California State Industrial Directory see MacRae's California State Industrial Directory 312
California State Plan for Rehabilitation Facilities (US) 1015
California State University, Los Angeles. Center for the Study of Armament and Disarmament. Occasional Papers Series (US) 915
California State Water Project (US ISSN 0090-5968) 1123
California Street (US) 645, 710
California Studies in Classical Antiquity see Classical Antiquity 337
California Studies in the History of Art (US ISSN 0068-5909) 103
California Water Resources Center. Annual Report see California Water Resources Center. Report 402
California Water Resources Center. Contribution (US ISSN 0575-4941) 1123
California Water Resources Center. Report (US) 402
California Work Injuries see California Work Injuries and Illnesses 636
California Work Injuries and Illnesses (US ISSN 0164-1530) 270, 636, 1050
California Youth Authority's Status of Female Employees. Report (US) 270, 1128
Californians in Congress (US ISSN 0068-6530) 133, 940
Call to Order see C T O 103
Callisto (UK) 675, 688
Calwer Theologische Monographien. Reihe A: Bibelwissenschaft (GW) 968
Calwer Theologische Monographien. Reihe B: Systematische Theologie und Kirchengeschichte (GW) 968
Calwer Theologische Monographien. Reihe C: Praktische Theologie und Missionswissenschaft (GW) 968
Camara Brasileira do Livro. Centro de Catalogaco na Fonte. Oficina de Livros: Novidades Catalogadas na Fonte (BL ISSN 0101-6903) 675
Camara Colombiana de la Construccion. Asamblea Nacional. Documento (CK) 182
Camara de Comerciantes en Artefactos para el Hogar. Revista (AG) 239, 643
Camara de Comercio de la Guaira. Boletin Estadistico. (VE ISSN 0008-1876) 235
Camara de Estudos e Debates Economicos e Sociais Colecao C E D E S. Grandes Temas see Colecao C E D E S. Grandes Temas 26
Camara Nacional de la Industria del Hierro y del Acero. Informe del Presidente (MX) 797
Camara Venezolano Britanica de Comercio e Industria. Anuario (VE) 235
Cambrian Law Review (UK ISSN 0084-8328) 653
Cambric Poetry Project see Poetry Project 1160
Cambridge Air Surveys (UK ISSN 0068-659X) 84
Cambridge Antiquarian Society. Proceedings (UK) 84, 578
Cambridge Authors' and Printers' Guides see Cambridge Authors' and Publishers' Guides 961
Cambridge Authors' and Publishers' Guides (UK) 930, 961
Cambridge Bibliographical Society. Transactions (UK ISSN 0068-6611) 124
Cambridge Bibliographical Society. Transactions. Monograph Supplements (UK ISSN 0068-662X) 124
Cambridge Chemistry Texts see Cambridge Texts in Chemistry and Biochemistry 321
Cambridge Classical Studies (UK) 337
Cambridge Classical Texts and Commentaries (UK ISSN 0068-6638) 337
Cambridge Commonwealth Series (UK) 555, 629, 1007

Cambridge Computer Science Texts (UK) 352
Cambridge Earth Science Series (UK) 378
Cambridge Economic Handbooks. New Series (UK) 192
Cambridge Geographical Studies (UK ISSN 0068-6654) 542
Cambridge Greek and Latin Classics (UK) 718
Cambridge Latin American Studies (UK ISSN 0068-6689) 604
Cambridge Latin Texts (UK) 692, 718
Cambridge Monographs in Experimental Biology (UK ISSN 0068-6697) 139
Cambridge Monographs on Mathematical Physics (UK) 748, 887
Cambridge Monographs on Mechanics and Applied Mathematics (UK) 748, 894
Cambridge Monographs on Physics (UK) 887
Cambridge Papers in Social Anthropology (UK ISSN 0068-6719) 70
Cambridge Papers in Sociology (UK ISSN 0068-6727) 1024
Cambridge Philological Society. Proceedings (UK ISSN 0068-6735) 337, 692
Cambridge Philological Society. Proceedings. Supplement (UK ISSN 0068-6743) 337, 692
Cambridge Planetary Science Series (UK) 384
Cambridge Solid State Science Series (UK) 887
Cambridge South Asian Studies (UK ISSN 0575-6863) 568
Cambridge Studies in Chinese History, Literature and Institutions (UK) 568
Cambridge Studies in Cultural Systems (UK) 70
Cambridge Studies in Early Modern History (UK ISSN 0084-8336) 556
Cambridge Studies in Economic History(UK) 251
Cambridge Studies in English Legal History (UK) 653
Cambridge Studies in Historical Geography (UK) 542
Cambridge Studies in International and Comparative Law (UK ISSN 0068-6751) 653
Cambridge Studies in Linguistics (UK ISSN 0068-676X) 692
Cambridge Studies in Mathematical Biology (UK) 139
Cambridge Studies in Medieval Life and Thought. Fourth Series (UK) 579
Cambridge Studies in Medieval Life and Thought. Third Series see Cambridge Studies in Medieval Life and Thought. Fourth Series 579
Cambridge Studies in Oral and Literate Culture (UK) 70
Cambridge Studies in Social Anthropology (UK ISSN 0068-6794) 70
Cambridge Studies in Sociology (UK ISSN 0068-6808) 1024
Cambridge Studies in the History and Theory of Politics (UK ISSN 0575-6871) 903
Cambridge Texts and Studies in the History of Education (UK ISSN 0068-6816) 411
Cambridge Texts in Chemistry and Biochemistry (UK) 321
Cambridge Texts in the Physiological Sciences (UK) 171
Cambridge Town, Gown & County Series (UK) 538
Cambridge Tracts in Mathematics (UK) 748
Cambridge Tracts in Mathematics and Mathematical Physics see Cambridge Tracts in Mathematics 748
Cambridge University. Department of Applied Economics. Monographs (UK ISSN 0068-6832) 192
Cambridge University. Department of Applied Economics. Occasional Papers (UK ISSN 0068-6840) 192

Cambridge University. Department of Applied Economics. Papers in Industrial Relations and Labour (UK) 270
Cambridge University. Institute of Criminology. Bibliographical Series (UK ISSN 0068-6883) 373
Cambridge University. Institute of Criminology. Occasional Papers (UK) 370
Cambridge University. Library Management Research Unit. Report to the Office for Scientific and Technical Information see C L A I M Report to the British Library and Development Department 1149
Cambridge University. Oriental Publications (UK ISSN 0068-6891) 568
Cambridge University Handbook (UK) 432
Cambridge University Library. Genizah Series (UK) 124
Cambridge University Library. Historical Bibliography Series (UK) 124, 556
Cambridge University Library. Librarianship Series (UK) 675
Cambridge University Reporter (UK) 432
Cambridge Urban and Architectural Studies (UK) 97, 622
Camden Fourth Series (UK ISSN 0068-6905) 579
Camden History Review (UK ISSN 0305-4756) 579
Camellia Journal (US ISSN 0008-204X) 532
Camels Coming Newsletter (US) 718
Camera dei Deputati. Bollettino di Informazioni Costituzionali e Parlamentari (IT) 653, 940
Camera dei Deputati. Bollettino di Legislazione e Documentazione Regionale (IT) 653
Camera dei Deputati. Notiziario di Statistiche (IT) 668
Camera di Commercio, Industria Artigianato e Agricoltura di Milano. Scambi Commerciali Con l'Estero (IT) 235
Camera di Commercio, Industria, Artigianato e Agricoltura di Padova. Notiziario Estero (IT) 235
Camera Test (UK) 884
CamerArt Photo Trade Directory (JA) 303, 884
Cameroon. Provincial Statistical Service of the South West. Annual Statistical Report, South West Province (CM) 1050
Cameroon Development Corporation. Annual Report and Accounts/Rapport Annuel et Compte-Rendu Financier (CM) 287
Cameroon Year Book (CM ISSN 0301-7753) 542
Cameroonian Culture see Culture Camerounaise 565
Cameroun. Direction de la Statistique et de la Comptabilite Nationale. Comptes Nationaux du Cameroun see Comptes Nationaux du Cameroun 294
Cameroun. Direction de la Statistique et de la Comptabilite Nationale. Note Annuelle de Statistique (CM) 204, 1050
Cameroun. Regie Nationale des Chemins de Fer. Compte Rendu de Gestion (CM) 1094
Cameroun. Regie Nationale des Chemins de Fer. Statistiques (CM) 1094
Cameroun. Service d'Hydrometeorologie. Pluviometrie Mensuelle et Annuelle (CM) 803
Camp Directors Purchasing Guide (US) 303, 1044
Campaign Against U.S. Intervention (US) 915
Campaign Guide for Congressional Candidate and Committees (US) 940
Campaign Guide for Corporations and Labor Organizations (US) 903
Campaign Guide for Non-connected Committees (US) 903

Campaign Guide for Party Committees (US) 940
Campbell Paterson's Loose-Leaf Colour Catalogue of New Zealand Stamps (Specialised) (NZ) 874
Campbell's List (US ISSN 0742-8987) 653
CampBook. Western Canada and Alaska. see Western Canada Alaska Campbook 1119
Camping and Caravanning in Britain (UK) 1044
Camping and Caravanning U.K. see Camping and Caravanning in Britain 1044
Camping and Sports Equipment Trades Directory see Camping Caravanning and Sports Equipment Trades Directory 303
Camping Benelux see Holland Camping 1045
Camping, Caravaning in France (FR ISSN 0076-7735) 1107
Camping Caravanning and Sports Equipment Trades Directory (UK ISSN 0068-6948) 303, 1044
Camping Club Handbook and Sites List(UK) 1044
Camping Club of Great Britain and Ireland. Year Book with List of Camp Sites see Camping Club Handbook and Sites List 1044
Camping Guide see Explore Minnesota Campgrounds 1108
Camping Sites in Britain and France see Practical Camper's Sites Guide 1046
Campitur: Camping, Caravaning, Villaggi Turistici (IT) 1044, 1107
Can Manufacturers Institute. Annual Cans Shipment Report (US) 855
Can Manufacturers Institute. Annual Metal Cans Shipment Report see Can Manufacturers Institute. Annual Cans Shipment Report 855
Canada. Advisory Council on the Status of Women. Annual Report (CN ISSN 0705-6028) 1128
Canada. Agriculture Canada. Animal Research Centre. Research Report (CN) 65
Canada. Agriculture Canada. Animal Research Institute. Research Report see Canada. Agriculture Canada. Animal Research Centre. Research Report 65
Canada. Agriculture Canada. Annual Report of Prairie Farm Rehabilitation Administration/Rapport Annual: Retablissement Agricole des Prairies (CN) 53, 494, 1123
Canada. Agriculture Canada. Annual Report on Prairie Farm Rehabilitation and Related Activities/Rapport Annual: Retablissement Agricole des Prairies et Travaux Connexes see Canada. Agriculture Canada. Annual Report of Prairie Farm Rehabilitation Administration/Rapport Annual: Retablissement Agricole des Prairies 53
Canada. Agriculture Canada. Economics Branch. Trade in Agricultural Products (CN ISSN 0068-7286) 45
Canada. Agriculture Canada. Engineering & Statistical Research Institute, Ottawa. Research Report (CN) 53
Canada. Agriculture Canada. Food Research Institute, Ottawa. Research Report (CN ISSN 0068-7308) 518
Canada. Agriculture Canada. Livestock Market Review (CN ISSN 0068-7324) 65
Canada. Agriculture Canada. Research Station, Melfort, Saskatchewan. Research Highlights. Annual Publications see Canada. Agriculture Canada. Research Station, Melfort, Saskatchewan. Research Station Report 25
Canada. Agriculture Canada. Research Station, Melfort, Saskatchewan. Research Station Report (CN) 25
Canada. Anti-Dumping Tribunal. Annual Report see Canada. Canadian Import Tribunal. Annual Report 254

Canada. Atmospheric Environment Service. Climatological Studies (CN ISSN 0068-7715) *803*

Canada. Atmospheric Environment Service. Meteorological Translations (CN ISSN 0068-7782) *803*

Canada. Atmospheric Environment Service. Snow Cover Data/Donnees d'Enneigement (CN ISSN 0068-7790) *803*

Canada. Atmospheric Environment Service. Technical Memoranda (CN ISSN 0068-7804) *803*

Canada. Board of Grain Commissioners. Canadian Grain Exports. see Canada. Grain Commission. Economics and Statistics Division. Canadian Grain Exports *63*

Canada. Canadian Forestry Service. Insect and Disease Conditions in Canada (CN) *523*

Canada. Canadian Forestry Service-Maritimes, Fredericton, New Brunswick. Information Report M-X (CN ISSN 0834-406X) *523*

Canada. Canadian Import Tribunal. Annual Report (CN) *254*

Canada. Canadian Radio-Television and Telecommunications Commission. Annual Report (CN) *347*

Canada. Canadian Wildlife Federation. Publication List (CN) *364*

Canada. Commissioner of Official Languages. Annual Report (CN ISSN 0382-1161) *940*

Canada. Conseil du Tresor. Budget des Depenses. Partie I: Plan de Depenses du Gouvernement see Canada. Treasury Board Secretariat. Estimates. Part I: Government Expenditures Plan *940*

Canada. Conseil du Tresor. Budget des Depenses. Partie II: Budget des Depenses see Canada. Treasury Board Secretariat. Estimates. Part II: Estimates *940*

Canada. Conseil National de Recherches. Publications see Canada. National Research Council. Publications *1068*

Canada. Correctional Investigator. Annual Report (CN ISSN 0383-4379) *370*

Canada. Department of Agriculture. Engineering Research Service, Ottawa. Research Report see Canada. Agriculture Canada. Engineering & Statistical Research Institute, Ottawa. Research Report *53*

Canada. Department of Consumer & Corporate Affairs. Annual Report (CN) *940*

Canada. Department of Consumer and Corporate Affairs. Director of Investigations and Research. Report (CN) *242*

Canada. Department of External Affairs. Reference Papers (CN) *915*

Canada. Department of External Affairs. Statements and Speeches (CN) *915*

Canada. Department of Finance. Small Business Loans Act. Annual Report see Canada. Department of Industry, Trade and Commerce. Small Business Loans Act. Annual Report *301*

Canada. Department of Fisheries and Oceans. Annual Report (CN ISSN 0711-0782) *508*

Canada. Department of Indian Affairs and Northern Development. Mines and Minerals, Activities see Canada. Indian and Northern Affairs Canada. Mines and Mineral Activities (Year) *815*

Canada. Department of Indian and Northern Affairs. Oil and Gas Land and Exploration Section. Oil and Gas Activities. North of 60 see Canada. Energy, Mines and Resources Canada. Indian and Northern Affairs. Canada Oil and Gas Lands Administration Annual Report (Year) *863*

Canada. Department of Indian and Northern Affairs. Schedule of Wells, Oil and Gas North of 60. see Canada. Indian and Northern Affairs Canada. Schedule of Wells *384*

Canada. Department of Industry, Trade and Commerce. Small Business Loans Act. Annual Report (CN) *301*

Canada. Department of Insurance. List of Securities (CN ISSN 0380-1020) *638*

Canada. Department of Insurance. Report. Co-Operative Credit Associations (CN ISSN 0068-7383) *225*, *638*

Canada. Department of Insurance. Report of the Superintendent of Insurance (CN ISSN 0068-7405) *638*

Canada. Department of Insurance. Report. Small Loans Companies and Money-Lenders (CN ISSN 0068-7413) *225*, *638*

Canada. Department of Insurance. Report. Trust and Loan Companies (CN ISSN 0068-7391) *225*, *638*

Canada. Department of Labor. Labour and Industrial Relations Research in Canada. Progress Report see Industrial Relations Research in Canada *272*

Canada. Department of National Defence. Defence (Year) (CN ISSN 0383-4638) *810*

Canada. Department of National Defence. Directorate of History. Monograph Series (CN) *810*

Canada. Department of National Defence. Directorate of History. Occasional Paper see Canada. Department of National Defence. Directorate of History. Monograph Series *810*

Canada. Department of National Health and Welfare. Annual Report (CN ISSN 0068-7456) *953*, *1015*

Canada. Department of National Health and Welfare. Library. Acquisitions (CN) *958*, *1022*

Canada. Department of National Revenue. Report: Customs, Excise and Taxation (CN) *293*

Canada. Department of the Environment. Forest Insect and Disease Survey. Annual Report see Canada. Canadian Forestry Service. Insect and Disease Conditions in Canada *523*

Canada. Earth Physics Branch. Geodynamic Series (CN) *398*

Canada. Earth Physics Branch. Geomagnetic Series (CN ISSN 0704-3015) *398*

Canada. Earth Physics Branch. Geothermal Series (CN) *398*

Canada. Earth Physics Branch. Gravity Map Series (CN) *398*

Canada. Earth Physics Branch. Seismological Series (CN ISSN 0084-8387) *398*

Canada. Energy, Mines and Resources Canada. Indian and Northern Affairs. Canada Oil and Gas Lands Administration Annual Report (Year) (CN) *863*

Canada. Energy, Mines and Resources Canada. Indian and Northern Affairs. Canada Oil and Gas Lands Administration Released Geophysical/Geological Data (CN ISSN 0317-4085) *863*

Canada. Environment Canada. Conservation and Protection Service. Annual Summary: National Air Pollution Surveillance (CN) *494*

Canada. Environment Canada. Environment Protection Service. Annual Summary: National Air Pollution Surveillance see Canada. Environment Canada. Conservation and Protection Service. Annual Summary: National Air Pollution Surveillance *494*

Canada. Environment Canada. Insect and Disease Conditions in Canada see Canada. Canadian Forestry Service. Insect and Disease Conditions in Canada *523*

Canada. Epidemiology Division. Venereal Disease in Canada see Venereal Diseases in Canada *780*

Canada. Federal-Provincial Wildlife Conference. Wildlife Management Papers see Canada. Canadian Wildlife Federation. Publication List *364*

Canada. Fisheries and Environment Canada. Annual Report see Canada. Department of Fisheries and Oceans. Annual Report *508*

Canada. Fisheries and Environment Canada. Occasional Paper (CN) *494*

Canada. Fisheries and Environment Canada. Report of Operations Under the Canada Water Act (CN) *364*

Canada. Fisheries and Marine Service. Recreational Fisheries Branch. Statistics on Sales of Sport Fishing Licences in Canada see Canada. Fisheries and Oceans. Communications Directorate. Statistics on Sales of Sport Fishing Licences in Canada *514*

Canada. Fisheries and Marine Service. Technical Report Series see Canadian Technical Report of Fisheries and Aquatic Sciences *508*

Canada. Fisheries and Oceans. Communications Directorate. Statistics on Sales of Sport Fishing Licences in Canada (CN) *514*

Canada. Fisheries and Oceans. Pacific Region. Annual Summary of British Columbia Catch Statistics (CN) *508*

Canada. Fisheries Research Board. Bulletin see Canadian Bulletin of Fisheries and Aquatic Sciences *508*

Canada. Fisheries Research Board. Miscellaneous Special Publication Series see Canadian Special Publication of Fisheries and Aquatic Sciences *508*

Canada. Foreign Investment Review Agency. Annual Report see Canada. Investment Canada. Annual Report *265*

Canada. Forest Management Institute. Program Review see Canada. Petawawa National Forestry Institute. Program Review *524*

Canada. Geological Survey. Bulletin (CN ISSN 0068-7626) *384*

Canada. Geological Survey. Economic Geology Report (CN) *384*

Canada. Geological Survey. Index of Publications of the Geological Survey of Canada (CN ISSN 0707-2996) *3*, *382*

Canada. Geological Survey. Memoir (CN ISSN 0068-7634) *384*

Canada. Geological Survey. Miscellaneous Report (CN ISSN 0068-7642) *384*

Canada. Geological Survey. Paper (CN ISSN 0068-7650) *384*

Canada. Grain Commission. Economics and Statistics Division. Canadian Grain Exports (CN) *63*, *254*

Canada. Grain Commission. Economics and Statistics Division. Visible Grain Supplies and Disposition (CN ISSN 0380-8718) *45*, *63*

Canada. Grain Commission. Marketings, Distribution and Visible Carry-over of Canadian Grain in and Through Licensed Elevators see Canada. Grain Commission. Economics and Statistics Division. Visible Grain Supplies and Disposition *63*

Canada. Grains Council. Annual Report(CN ISSN 0700-2866) *63*

Canada. Grains Council. Statistical Handbook (CN) *63*

Canada. Hydrographic Service. Activity Report/Canada. Service Hydrographique. Rapport des Activites (CN ISSN 0701-6786) *1123*

Canada. Hydrographic Service. Annual Report see Canada. Hydrographic Service. Activity Report *1123*

Canada. Hydrographic Service. Water Levels see Canada. Hydrographic Service. Water Levels. Vol. 1: Daily Means *378*

Canada. Hydrographic Service. Water Levels see Canada. Hydrographic Service. Water Levels. Vol. 2: Tidal Highs and Lows *378*

Canada. Hydrographic Service. Water Levels. Vol. 1: Daily Means (CN ISSN 0706-2354) *378*, *405*

Canada. Hydrographic Service. Water Levels. Vol. 2: Tidal Highs and Lows(CN ISSN 0706-2346) *378*, *405*

Canada. Immigration and Demographic Policy Group. Immigration Statistics (CN) *921*, *926*

Canada. Immigration Division. Immigration Statistics see Canada. Immigration and Demographic Policy Group. Immigration Statistics *926*

Canada. Indian and Northern Affairs Canada. Mines and Mineral Activities (Year) (CN) *815*

Canada. Indian and Northern Affairs Canada. Schedule of Wells (CN) *384*

Canada. Information Commissioner. Annual Report (CN) *669*, *913*

Canada. Inland Waters Directorate. Water Resources Research Support Program /Programme de Subvention a la Recherche sur les Resources en Eau (CN) *402*

Canada. Institut Forestier National de Petawawa. Rapport d'Information see Canada. Petawawa National Forestry Institute. Information Report *524*

Canada. Investment Canada. Annual Report (CN) *265*

Canada. Labour Canada. Annual Review (CN) *270*

Canada. Labour Canada. Wage Rates, Salaries and Hours of Labour (CN ISSN 0068-743X) *270*

Canada. Labour Relations Board. Annual Report (CN ISSN 0711-849X) *270*

Canada. Law Reform Commission. Administrative Law Series. Study Papers (CN) *653*

Canada. Law Reform Commission. Annual Report (CN ISSN 0382-1463) *653*, *940*

Canada. Law Reform Commission. Criminal Law Series. Study Papers (CN) *653*

Canada. Law Reform Commission. Modernization of Statutes. Study Papers (CN) *653*

Canada. Law Reform Commission. Protection of Life Series. Study Papers (CN) *653*

Canada. Law Reform Commission. Report to Parliament (CN) *653*

Canada. Law Reform Commission. Working Paper (CN) *653*

Canada. Marine Environmental Data Service. Manuscript Report Series see Canadian Manuscript Report of Fisheries and Aquatic Sciences *494*

Canada. Maritimes Forest Research Centre, Fredericton, New Brunswick. Information Report M-X see Canada. Canadian Forestry Service-Maritimes, Fredericton, New Brunswick. Information Report M-X *523*

Canada. Marketing and Trade Division. Animal and Animal Products: Outlook (CN) *45*, *65*

Canada. Mineral Development Center. Mineral Survey see Canada. Mineral Policy Sector. Mineral Survey *1149*

Canada. Mineral Policy Sector. Mineral Bulletins (CN) *815*

Canada. Mineral Policy Sector. Mineral Information Bulletin see Canada. Mineral Policy Sector. Mineral Bulletins *815*

Canada. Mineral Policy Sector. Mineral Survey (CN ISSN 0229-8325) *1149*

Canada. Ministry of State for Science and Technology. Annual Report/ Rapport Annuel (CN) *989*, *1068*

Canada. Musee National de l'Homme. Collection Mercure. Centre Canadien d'Etudes sur la Culture Traditionnelle. Dossiers see Canada. National Museum of Man. Mercury Series. Canadian Centre for Folk Culture Studies. Papers *70*

CANADA. STATISTICS 1679

Canada. Musee National de l'Homme. Collection Mercure. Commission Archaeologique du Canada. Dossiers. see Canada. National Museum of Man. Mercury Series. Archaeological Survey of Canada. Papers *84*
Canada. Musee National de l'Homme. Collection Mercure. Division de l'Histoire. Dossiers see Canada. National Museum of Man. Mercury Series. History Division. Papers *556*
Canada. Musee National de l'Homme. Collection Mercure. Musee Canadien de la Guerre. Dossiers see Canada. National Museum of Man. Mercury Series. Canadian War Museum. Papers *810*
Canada. Musee National de l'Homme. Collection Mercure. Service Canadien d'Ethnologie. Dossiers see Canada. National Museum of Man. Mercury Series. Canadian Ethnology Service. Papers *70*
Canada. Musees Nationaux du Canada. Bulletin Annuel see Canada. National Museums of Canada. Annual Bulletin *827*
Canada. National Energy Board. Annual Report (CN ISSN 0068-7901) *464*
Canada. National Energy Board. Information Bulletins (CN ISSN 0825-0170) *940*
Canada. National Energy Board. Reasons for Decision (CN) *464*
Canada. National Energy Board. Reports to the Governor in Council (CN) *940*
Canada. National Energy Board. Staff Papers see Canada. National Energy Board. Information Bulletins *940*
Canada. National Farm Products Marketing Council. Annual Report (CN ISSN 0383-414X) *45*
Canada. National Museum of Man. Mercury Series. Archaeological Survey of Canada. Papers/Canada. Musee National de l'Homme. Collection Mercure. Commission Archaeologique du Canada. Dossiers.(CN ISSN 0317-2244) *84*
Canada. National Museum of Man. Mercury Series. Canadian Centre for Folk Culture Studies. Papers/Canada. Musee National de l'Homme. Collection Mercure. Centre Canadien d'Etudes sur la Culture Traditionnelle. Dossiers (CN ISSN 0316-1897) *70*
Canada. National Museum of Man. Mercury Series. Canadian Ethnology Service. Papers/Canada. Musee National de l'Homme. Collection Mercure. Service Canadien d'Ethnologie. Dossiers (CN ISSN 0316-1862) *70*
Canada. National Museum of Man. Mercury Series. Canadian War Museum. Papers/Canada. Musee National de l'Homme. Collection Mercure. Musee Canadien de la Guerre. Dossiers (CN ISSN 0316-1919) *810*
Canada. National Museum of Man. Mercury Series. History Division. Papers/Canada. Musee National de l'Homme. Collection Mercure. Division de l'Histoire. Dossiers (CN ISSN 0316-1900) *556*
Canada. National Museums of Canada. Annual Bulletin/Canada. Musees Nationaux du Canada. Bulletin Annuel (CN ISSN 0711-2866) *827*
Canada. National Museums, Ottawa: Publications in Natural Science/ Publications de Sciences Naturelles (CN ISSN 0714-0983) 155, 170, *173*
Canada. National Research Council. Publications/Canada. Conseil National de Recherches. Publications(CN) *1068*

Canada. Northern Economic Development Branch. Oil and Gas Technical Reports- North of 60. see Canada. Energy, Mines and Resources Canada. Indian and Northern Affairs. Canada Oil and Gas Lands Administration Released Geophysical/Geological Data *863*
Canada. Northern Forestry Centre. Forest Management Note (CN ISSN 0714-1181) *523*
Canada. Northern Forestry Centre. Forestry Report (CN ISSN 0709-9959) *524*
Canada. Northern Forestry Centre. Information Report (CN ISSN 0704-7673) *524*
Canada. Northern Natural Resources and Environment Branch. Mining Section. North of 60: Mines and Mineral Activities see Canada. Indian and Northern Affairs Canada. Mines and Mineral Activities (Year) *815*
Canada. Northern Natural Resources and Environment Branch. Oil and Mineral Division. North of 60: Oil and Gas Technical Reports see Canada. Energy, Mines and Resources Canada. Indian and Northern Affairs. Canada Oil and Gas Lands Administration Released Geophysical/Geological Data *863*
Canada. Pacific Forest Research Centre. Information Report (CN) *524*
Canada. Pension Review Board. Reports/Recueil des Arrets du Conseil de Revision des Pensions (CN ISSN 0382-1587) 270, *810*
Canada. Petawawa National Forestry Institute. Information Report/ Canada. Institut Forestier National de Petawawa. Rapport d'Information (CN ISSN 0228-0736) *524*
Canada. Petawawa National Forestry Institute. Program Review (CN ISSN 0710-4251) *524*
Canada. Privacy Commissioner. Annual Report (CN) 358, 669, 903
Canada. Public Archives. Register of Post Graduate Dissertations in Progress in History and Related Subjects see Canada. Register of Post Graduate Dissertations in Progress in History and Related Subjects *556*
Canada. Radio-Television Commission. Annual Report see Canada. Canadian Radio-Television and Telecommunications Commission. Annual Report *347*
Canada. Register of Post Graduate Dissertations in Progress in History and Related Subjects (CN) *556*
Canada. Service Hydrographique. Rapport Annuel see Canada. Hydrographic Service. Activity Report *1123*
Canada. Service Hydrographique. Rapport des Activites see Canada. Hydrographic Service. Activity Report *1123*
Canada. Statistics Canada. Aggregate Productivity Measures/Mesures Globales de Productivite (CN ISSN 0317-7882) 204, *1050*
Canada. Statistics Canada. Aggregate Productivity Trends/Tendances de la Productivite des Agregats see Canada. Statistics Canada. Aggregate Productivity Measures/Mesures Globales de Productivite *204*
Canada. Statistics Canada. Air Passenger Origin and Destination. Canada-United States Report/Origine et Destination des Passagers Aeriens. Rapport sur le Trafic Canada-Etat Unis (CN ISSN 0705-4343) 1050, *1085*
Canada. Statistics Canada. Annual Report/Rapport Annuel (CN ISSN 0703-2633) *1050*
Canada. Statistics Canada. Aviation Statistics Centre. Service Bulletin/ Bulletin de Service du Centre des Statistiques de l'Aviation (CN ISSN 0068-7057) 1050, *1085*

Canada. Statistics Canada. Building Permits. Annual Summary/Permis de Batir (CN ISSN 0575-7975) *188*, 1050
Canada. Statistics Canada. Cable Television/Telediffusion (CN ISSN 0703-7244) 345, 1050
Canada. Statistics Canada. Canada's Mineral Production: Preliminary Estimate/Production Minerale du Canada, Calcul Preliminaire (CN ISSN 0380-7797) 821, 1050
Canada. Statistics Canada. Cane and Beet Sugar Processors/Traitement du Sucre de Canne et de Betteraves (CN ISSN 0384-2843) *521*, 1050
Canada. Statistics Canada. Carpet, Mat and Rug Industry/Industrie des Tapis, des Carpettes et de la Moquette (CN ISSN 0527-4893) 1050, *1075*
Canada. Statistics Canada. Causes of Death, Provinces by Sex and Canada by Sex and Age/Causes de Deces, Par Provinces Selon le Sexe et le Canada Selon le Sexe et l'Age (CN ISSN 0380-7533) *926*, 1050
Canada. Statistics Canada. Coal Mines/ Mines de Charbon (CN ISSN 0705-436X) *821*, 1050
Canada. Statistics Canada. Coastwise Shipping Statistics (CN ISSN 0225-1507) 1050, *1085*
Canada. Statistics Canada. Communications and Energy Wire and Cable Industry/Industrie des Fils et Cables Electriques et de Communications (CN ISSN 0833-2002) *451*, 461, 797, 801, 1050
Canada. Statistics Canada. Communications and Other Electronic Industries/Industries de l'Equipement et d'Autre Materiel Electronique (CN ISSN 0828-9824) 345, 1050
Canada. Statistics Canada. Communications Equipment Meanufacturers/Fabricants d'Equipement de Telecommunication see Canada. Statistics Canada. Communications and Other Electronic Industries/Industries de l'Equipement et d'Autre Materiel Electronique *345*
Canada. Statistics Canada. Communications Service Bulletin/ Communications-Bulletin de Service (CN ISSN 0380-0334) 345, 1050
Canada. Statistics Canada. Community Antenna Television/Services de Television a Antenne Collective see Canada. Statistics Canada. Cable Television/Telediffusion *345*
Canada. Statistics Canada. Consolidated Government Finance: Fiscal Year Ended Nearest to December 31/ Finances Publiques Consolidees: Annee Financiere Terminee le Plus Pres de 31 Decembre (CN ISSN 0575-8254) 204, 1050
Canada. Statistics Canada. Construction in Canada/Construction au Canada (CN ISSN 0527-4974) *188*, 1050
Canada. Statistics Canada. Control and Sale of Alcoholic Beverages in Canada/Controle et la Vente des Boissons Alcooliques au Canada/ Controle et la Vente des Boissons Alcooliques au Canada (CN ISSN 0705-4319) *120*, 1050
Canada. Statistics Canada. Corporation Financial Statistics (CN ISSN 0575-8262) *204*, 1050
Canada. Statistics Canada. Corporation Taxation Statistics (CN ISSN 0576-0119) *204*, 1050
Canada. Statistics Canada. Credit Unions (CN ISSN 0576-0100) *204*, 1050
Canada. Statistics Canada. Crude Petroleum and Natural Gas Industry/ Industrie du Petrole Brut et du Gaz Naturel (CN ISSN 0068-7103) *867*, 1050
Canada. Statistics Canada. Direct Selling in Canada/Vente Directe au Canada (CN ISSN 0590-5702) *204*, 1050

Canada. Statistics Canada. Education in Canada/Education au Canada (CN ISSN 0706-3679) *423*, 1050
Canada. Statistics Canada. Electric Power Statistics Volume 1: Annual Electric Power Survey of Capability and Load/Statistique de l'Energie Electrique. Volume 1: Enquete Annuelle sur la Puissance Maximale et sur la Charge des Reseaux (CN ISSN 0380-951X) 461, 468, *1051*
Canada. Statistics Canada. Electrical Contracting Industry/Entrepreneurs d'Installations Electriques (CN ISSN 0702-8083) 188, *461*, 1051
Canada. Statistics Canada. Elementary-Secondary School Enrollment/ Effectifs des Ecoles Primaires et Secondaires (CN ISSN 0704-6596) *423*, 1051
Canada. Statistics Canada. Enrollment in Community Colleges/Effectifs des Colleges Communautaires (CN ISSN 0382-0920) *423*, 1051
Canada. Statistics Canada. Exports-Merchandise Trade/Exportations-Commerce de Merchandises (CN ISSN 0317-5375) *205*, 1051
Canada. Statistics Canada. Family Incomes (Census Families) /Revenus des Famille (Familles de Recensement) (CN ISSN 0703-7368) 205, 926, 1051
Canada. Statistics Canada. Farm Net Income/Revenu Net Agricole (CN ISSN 0068-712X) *39*, 1051
Canada. Statistics Canada. Federal Government Employment in Metropolitan Areas/Emploi dans l'Administration Federale Regions Metropolitaines (CN ISSN 0527-5148) 205, *948*, 1051
Canada. Statistics Canada. Federal Government Finance: Revenue and Expenditure, Assets and Liabilities/ Finances Publiques Federales: Recettes and Depenses, Actif et Passif (CN ISSN 0575-8521) *205*, 1051
Canada. Statistics Canada. Financial Statistics of Education/Statistiques Financieres de l'Education (CN ISSN 0703-9328) *423*, 1051
Canada. Statistics Canada. Fish Products Industry/Industrie de la Transformation du Poisson (CN ISSN 0527-5172) 514, 521, 1051
Canada. Statistics Canada. Flour and Breakfast Cereal Products Industry/ Meunerie et Fabrication de Cereales de Table (CN ISSN 0700-0324) *521*, 1051
Canada. Statistics Canada. For-Hire Trucking Survey/Enquete sur le Transport Routier de Marchandises pour Compte d'Autrui (CN ISSN 0382-0939) *1149*
Canada. Statistics Canada. Fruit and Vegetable Processing Industries/ Preparation de Fruits et de Legumes (CN ISSN 0384-4420) *521*, 1051
Canada. Statistics Canada. Fruit and Vegetable Production/Production de Fruits et de Legumes (CN ISSN 0383-008X) *39*, 1051
Canada. Statistics Canada. Gas Utilities (Transport and Distribution Systems) /Services de Gaz (Reseaux de Transport et de Distribution) (CN ISSN 0527-5318) *867*, 1051
Canada. Statistics Canada. General Review of the Mineral Industries/ Revue Generale sur les Industries Minerales (CN ISSN 0575-8645) *822*, 1051
Canada. Statistics Canada. Glass and Glass Products Industries/Industries du Verre et d'Articles en Verre (CN) *320*, 1051
Canada. Statistics Canada. Glass and Glass Products Manufacturers/ Fabricants de Verre et d'Articles en Verre see Canada. Statistics Canada. Glass and Glass Products Industries/ Industries du Verre et d'Articles en Verre *320*

CANADA. STATISTICS

Canada. Statistics Canada. Highway, Road, Street and Bridge Contracting Industry/Entrepreneurs de Grande Route, Chemin, rue et Pont (CN ISSN 0706-2451) *476,* 1051

Canada. Statistics Canada. Historical Labour Force Statistics, Actual Data, Seasonal Factors, Seasonally Adjusted Data/Statistiques Chronologiques sur la Population Active, Chiffres Reels, Facteurs Saisonniers et Donnees Desaisonnalisees (CN ISSN 0703-2684) *205,* 1051

Canada. Statistics Canada. Homicide in Canada: a Statistical Perspective/ L'Homicide au Canada: Perspective Statistique (CN ISSN 0825-432X) *373,* 1051

Canada. Statistics Canada. Homicide Statistics/Statistique de l'Homicide *see* Canada. Statistics Canada. Homicide in Canada: a Statistical Perspective/L'Homicide au Canada: Perspective Statistique *373*

Canada. Statistics Canada. Honey Production and Value, Production Forecast/Production et Valeur du Miel, Provision de la Production (CN ISSN 0829-3163) *39,* 1051

Canada. Statistics Canada. Honey Production/Production de Miel *see* Canada. Statistics Canada. Honey Production and Value, Production Forecast/Production et Valeur du Miel, Provision de la Production *39*

Canada. Statistics Canada. Hospitals Section. List of Canadian Hospitals and Related Institutions and Facilities/Liste des Hopitaux Canadiens et des Etablissements et Installations Connexes *see* Canada. Statistics Canada. List of Canadian Hospitals and Special Care Facilities/ Liste des Hopitaux Canadiens et des Etablissements de Soins Speciaux *618*

Canada. Statistics Canada. Household Facilities and Equipment/ L'Equipment Menager (CN ISSN 0318-5273) *615,* 1051

Canada. Statistics Canada. Imports-Merchandise Trade/Importations-Commerce de Marchandises (CN ISSN 0380-1349) *205,* 1051

Canada. Statistics Canada. Index of Farm Production/Indice de la Production Agricole (CN ISSN 0068-7146) *39,* 1051

Canada. Statistics Canada. Jewellery and Precious Metal Industries/ Industries de la Bijouterie et de L'Orfevrerie (CN ISSN 0828-9832) *645,* 1051

Canada. Statistics Canada. Jewellery and Silverware Manufacturers *see* Canada. Statistics Canada. Jewellery and Precious Metal Industries/ Industries de la Bijouterie et de L'Orfevrerie *645*

Canada. Statistics Canada. List of Canadian Hospitals and Special Care Facilities/Liste des Hopitaux Canadiens et des Etablissements de Soins Speciaux (CN ISSN 0225-5642) *618, 1022,* 1051

Canada. Statistics Canada. Listing of Supplementary Documents (CN ISSN 0228-5134) *1051*

Canada. Statistics Canada. Livestock and Animal Products Statistics/ Statistique du Betail et des Produits Animaux (CN ISSN 0068-7154) *39,* 1051

Canada. Statistics Canada. Local Government Finance: Revenue and Expenditure, Assets and Liabilities, Actual/Finances Publiques Locales: Revenus et Depenses, Actif et Passif, Chiffres Reels (CN ISSN 0703-2749) *948,* 1051

Canada. Statistics Canada. Manufacturers of Electric Wire and Cable/Fabricants de Fils et de Cables Electriques *see* Canada. Statistics Canada. Communications and Energy Wire and Cable Industry/ Industrie des Fils et Cables Electriques et de Communications *451*

Canada. Statistics Canada. Manufacturing Industries of Canada: Sub-Provincial Areas/Industries Manufactures du Canada: Niveau Infraprovincial/Industries Manufacturieres du Canada: Niveau Infraprovincial (CN ISSN 0382-4012) *205,* 1051

Canada. Statistics Canada. Market Research Handbook (CN ISSN 0590-9325) *205,* 1051

Canada. Statistics Canada. Mechanical Contracting Industry/Les Entrepreneurs d'Installations Mecaniques (CN ISSN 0576-0097) *188, 476,* 1051

Canada. Statistics Canada. Men's Clothing Industries/Industrie des Vetements pour Hommes (CN ISSN 0527-5679) *340,* 1051

Canada. Statistics Canada. Miscellaneous Clothing Industries/ Industries Diverses de l'Habillement (CN ISSN 0384-3769) *340,* 1051

Canada. Statistics Canada. Miscellaneous Food Processors/ Traitment des Produits Alimentaires Divers (CN ISSN 0384-3696) *521,* 1051

Canada. Statistics Canada. Miscellaneous Manufacturing Industries/Industries Manufacturieres Diverses (CN ISSN 0575-9021) *205,* 1051

Canada. Statistics Canada. Motion Picture Theatres and Film Distributors/Cinemas et Distributeurs de Films (CN ISSN 0380-6294) *825,* 1051

Canada. Statistics Canada. Motor Vehicle. Part 2. Motive Fuel Sales/ Vehicules a Moteur. Partie 2. Ventes des Carburants *see* Canada. Statistics Canada. Road Motor Vehicles-Fuel Sales/Vehicules Automobiles-Ventes de Carburants *1085*

Canada. Statistics Canada. Murder Statistics/Statistique de l'Homicide *see* Canada. Statistics Canada. Homicide in Canada: a Statistical Perspective/L'Homicide au Canada: Perspective Statistique *373*

Canada. Statistics Canada. Non-Residential General Building Contracting Industry/Industrie des Entreprises Generales en Construction Non Domiciliaire (CN ISSN 0703-7295) *188,* 1051

Canada. Statistics Canada. Ornamental and Architectural Metal Industry/ Industrie des Produits Metalliques d'Architecture et d'Ornement *see* Canada. Statistics Canada. Ornamental and Architectural Metal Products Industry/Industrie des Produits Metalliques d'Ornement et d'Architecture *801*

Canada. Statistics Canada. Ornamental and Architectural Metal Products Industry/Industrie des Produits Metalliques d'Ornement et d'Architecture (CN ISSN 0828-9921) *801,* 1051

Canada. Statistics Canada. Passenger Bus and Urban Transit Statistics/ Statistique du Transport des Voyageurs Par Autobus et du Transport Urbain (CN ISSN 0383-5766) *1051, 1085*

Canada. Statistics Canada. Pension Plans in Canada/Regimes de Pensions au Canada (CN ISSN 0701-5488) *642,* 1051

Canada. Statistics Canada. Printing, Publishing and Allied Industries (CN ISSN 0575-9412) *931, 963,* 1052

Canada. Statistics Canada. Private and Public Investment in Canada. Intentions/Investissements Prives et Publics au Canada. Perspectives (CN ISSN 0823-065X) *205,* 1052

Canada. Statistics Canada. Private and Public Investment in Canada, Mid-Year Review/Investissements Prives et Publics au Canada. Revue de la Mi-Annee *see* Canada. Statistics Canada. Private and Public Investment in Canada. Revised Intentions/Investissements Prives et Publics au Canada. Perspective Revisee *205*

Canada. Statistics Canada. Private and Public Investment in Canada. Outlook/Investissements Prives et Publics au Canada. Perspectives *see* Canada. Statistics Canada. Private and Public Investment in Canada. Intentions/Investissements Prives et Publics au Canada. Perspectives *205*

Canada. Statistics Canada. Private and Public Investment in Canada. Revised Intentions/Investissements Prives et Publics au Canada. Perspective Revisee (CN ISSN 0823-0668) *205,* 1052

Canada. Statistics Canada. Production and Value of Maple Products/ Production et Valeur des Produits de l'Erable (CN ISSN 0317-9672) *40,* 1052

Canada. Statistics Canada. Production of Poultry and Eggs/Production de Volaille et Oeufs (CN ISSN 0068-7189) *40,* 1052

Canada. Statistics Canada. Products Shipped by Canadian Manufacturers/ Produits Livres Par les Fabricants Canadiens (CN ISSN 0575-9455) *205,* 1052

Canada. Statistics Canada. Provincial Government Enterprise Finance: Income and Expenditure, Assets, Liabilities and Net Worth/Revenus et Depenses, Actif, Passif et Valeur Nette (CN ISSN 0575-9463) *205,* 1052

Canada. Statistics Canada. Provincial Government Finance: Assets, Liabilities, Source and Application of Funds (CN ISSN 0710-1023) *205,* 1052

Canada. Statistics Canada. Provincial Government Finance: Assets, Liabilities, Sources and Uses of Funds *see* Canada. Statistics Canada. Provincial Government Finance: Assets, Liabilities, Source and Application of Funds *205*

Canada. Statistics Canada. Pulp and Paper Mills/Usines de Pates et Papiers (CN ISSN 0384-4633) *529,* 1052

Canada. Statistics Canada. Radio and Television Broadcasting/ Radiodiffusion et Television (CN ISSN 0575-9560) *345,* 1052

Canada. Statistics Canada. Railway Transport. Service Bulletin *see* Canada. Statistics Canada. Surface and Marine Transport. Service Bulletin/Bulletin de Service Transports Terrestre et Maritimes *1085*

Canada. Statistics Canada. Report on Fur Farms/Rapport sur les Fermes a Fourrure (CN ISSN 0318-7888) *672,* 1052

Canada. Statistics Canada. Retail Chain and Department Stores (CN ISSN 0227-017X) *205,* 1052

Canada. Statistics Canada. Retail Chain Stores/Magasins de Detail a Succursales *see* Canada. Statistics Canada. Retail Chain and Department Stores *205*

Canada. Statistics Canada. Road Motor Vehicles-Fuel Sales/Vehicules Automobiles-Ventes de Carburants (CN ISSN 0703-654X) *1052, 1085*

Canada. Statistics Canada. Road Motor Vehicles-Registrations/Vehicules Automobiles-Immatriculations (CN ISSN 0706-067X) *1052, 1085*

Canada. Statistics Canada. Rubber Products Industries (CN ISSN 0300-0214) *986,* 1052

Canada. Statistics Canada. Salaries and Qualifications of Teachers in Public, Elementary and Secondary Schools/ Traitements et Qualifications des Enseignants des Ecoles Publiques, Primaires et Secondaires (CN ISSN 0318-3874) *423,* 1052

Canada. Statistics Canada. Sawmill, Planing Mill and Shingle Mill Products Industries/Industries des Produits de Scieries et d'Ateliers de Rabotage (CN ISSN 0828-9867) *529,* 1052

Canada. Statistics Canada. Sawmills and Planing Mills and Shingle Mills/ Scieries et Ateliers de Rabotage et Usines de Bardeaux *see* Canada. Statistics Canada. Sawmill, Planing Mill and Shingle Mill Products Industries/Industries des Produits de Scieries et d'Ateliers de Rabotage *529*

Canada. Statistics Canada. Scientific and Professional Equipment Industries/Fabrication de Materiel Scientifique et Professionnel (CN ISSN 0384-4242) *637,* 1052

Canada. Statistics Canada. Shorn Wool Production/Production de Laine Tondue (CN ISSN 0527-6179) *40,* 1052

Canada. Statistics Canada. Smelting and Refining/Fonte et Affinage (CN ISSN 0384-4935) *797*

Canada. Statistics Canada. Sporting Goods and Toy Industries/ Fabrication d'Articles de Sport et de Jouets (CN ISSN 0575-979X) *1036,* 1052

Canada. Statistics Canada. Surface and Marine Transport. Service Bulletin/ Bulletin de Service Transports Terrestre et Maritimes (CN ISSN 0828-2897) *1052, 1085*

Canada. Statistics Canada. Surgical Procedures and Treatments/ Interventions Chirurgicales et Traitements (CN ISSN 0317-3720) *769,* 1052

Canada. Statistics Canada. Survey of Canadian Nursery Trades Industry/ Enquete sur l'Industrie des Pepinieres Canadiennes (CN ISSN 0318-5184) *534,* 1052

Canada. Statistics Canada. System of National Accounts, Canada's International Investment Position/ Systeme de Comptabilite Nationale Bilan Canadien des Investissements Internationaux (CN) *205,* 1052

Canada. Statistics Canada. System of National Accounts, Domestic Product by Industry/Systeme de Comptabilite Nationale. Produit Interieur par Industrie: Releve de la Production *see* Canada. Statistics Canada. System of National Accounts, Provincial Gross Domestic Product by Industry *1149*

Canada. Statistics Canada. System of National Accounts, Provincial Gross Domestic Product by Industry (CN ISSN 0712-8762) *1149*

Canada. Statistics Canada. Telecommunications Statistics/ Statistique des Telecommunications (CN ISSN 0703-7252) *345,* 1052

Canada. Statistics Canada. Therapeutic Abortions/Avortements Therapeutiques (CN ISSN 0700-138X) *1149*

Canada. Statistics Canada. Tobacco Products Industries/Industrie du Tabac (CN ISSN 0300-0249) *1052, 1080*

Canada. Statistics Canada. Travel Between Canada and Other Countries/Voyages Entre le Canada et les Autres Pays (CN ISSN 0317-6738) *1052, 1119*

Canada. Statistics Canada. Trusteed Pension Plans-Financial Statistics/ Regimes de Pensions en Fiducie Statistique Financiere (CN ISSN 0575-9978) *205,* 1052

CANADIAN FOREIGN 1681

Canada. Statistics Canada. Vegetable Oil Mills/Moulins a Huile Vegetale (CN ISSN 0527-6403) *521,* 1052
Canada. Statistics Canada. Vending Machine Operators/Exploitants de Distributeurs Automatiques (CN ISSN 0527-6411) *205,* 1052
Canada. Statistics Canada. Water Transportation/Transport Par Eau (CN ISSN 0380-0342) 1052, *1085*
Canada. Statistics Canada. Wire and Wire Products Industries/Industries du Fil Metallique et de ses Produits (CN ISSN 0828-9913) *801,* 1052
Canada. Statistics Canada. Wire and Wire Products Manufacturers see Canada. Statistics Canada. Wire and Wire Products Industries/Industries du Fil Metallique et de ses Produits *801*
Canada. Statistics Canada. Women's and Children's Clothing Industries/Industries des Vetements pour Dames et pour Enfants (CN ISSN 0384-4498) *340,* 1052
Canada. Statistics Canada. Wool Production and Supply/Production et Stocks de Laine (CN ISSN 0300-0265) 1052, *1075*
Canada. Transport Commission. Annual Report (CN ISSN 0068-9912) *1081*
Canada. Treasury Board. Access Register (CN) 225
Canada. Treasury Board. Index of Federal Information Banks see Canada. Treasury Board. Index to Personal Information 225
Canada. Treasury Board. Index of Federal Information Banks see Canada. Treasury Board. Access Register 225
Canada. Treasury Board. Index to Personal Information (CN) 225
Canada. Treasury Board Secretariat. Estimates. Part I: Government Expenditures Plan/Canada. Conseil du Tresor. Budget des Depenses. Partie I: Plan de Depenses du Gouvernement (CN) 940
Canada. Treasury Board Secretariat. Estimates. Part II: Estimates/Canada. Conseil du Tresor. Budget des Depenses. Partie II: Budget des Depenses (CN) 940
Canada. Treasury Board Secretariat. Federal Expenditure Plan see Canada. Treasury Board Secretariat. Estimates. Part I: Government Expenditures Plan 940
Canada. Women's Bureau. Women in the Labour Force (CN) *270,* 653, 1128
Canada. Women's Bureau. Women in the Labour Force: Facts and Figures see Canada. Women's Bureau. Women in the Labour Force 270
Canada (Year) (US) *1107*
Canada Addictions Foundation. Directory/Fondation Canadienne des Toxicomanies. Repertoire (CN ISSN 0705-5587) 376
Canada Business Corporations Act with Regulations (CN ISSN 0317-6649) 653
Canada Centre for Mineral and Energy Technology Report see C A N M E T Report 814
Canada Council Annual Report and Supplement/Rapport Annuel du Conseil des Arts du Canada et son Supplement (CN ISSN 0576-4300) *103,* 823, 1076
Canada Health Manpower Inventory (CN ISSN 0381-2561) 759
Canada in World Affairs (CN ISSN 0068-7685) *915*
Canada Institute for Scientific and Technical Information. Annual Report/Institut Canadien de l'Information Scientifique et Technique. Rapport Annuel (CN ISSN 0703-0320) *989*
Canada-Japan, the Export-Import Picture (CN ISSN 0702-0333) *254*
Canada Land Inventory. Report (CN ISSN 0068-7693) *364*
Canada Legal Directory (CN) *653*

Canada Mortgage and Housing Corporation. Annual Report (CN ISSN 0226-0336) *622*
Canada on Stage: Canadian Theatre Review Yearbook see Canada on Stage: The National Theatre Yearbook 1076
Canada on Stage: The National Theatre Yearbook (CN) *1076*
Canada Pension Plan and Old Age Security Legislation (CN) *653*
Canada Postal Guide Part 1: Postal Law and Regulations (CN) *346*
Canada Postal Guide Part 2: International Mails, Rates and Conditions (CN) *346*
Canada Statute Citator (CN) *653*
Canada Today/d'Aujourd'hui (Washington) (US ISSN 0045-4257) *903*
Canada: Travel Information (CN ISSN 0709-9762) *1107*
Canada-U.K. Year Book (UK ISSN 0309-0329) *235*
Canada-United States Law Journal (US ISSN 0163-6391) *669*
Canada Who's Who of the Poultry Industry (CN ISSN 0068-8134) *65*
Canada's Atlantic Folklore and Folklife Series (CN ISSN 0708-4226) *515,* 834
Canada's International Investment Position/Bilan Canadien des Investissements Internationaux see Canada. Statistics Canada. System of National Accounts, Canada's International Investment Position/Systeme de Comptabilite Nationale Bilan Canadien des Investissements Internationaux 205
Canadian Agricultural Economics and Farm Management Society. Proceedings of the Workshop (CN) *45*
Canadian Agricultural Economics Society. Proceedings of the Workshop see Canadian Agricultural Economics and Farm Management Society. Proceedings of the Workshop 45
Canadian Agricultural Insect Pest Review (CN ISSN 0068-8185) *53*
Canadian Almanac and Directory (CN ISSN 0068-8193) *604*
Canadian Alpine Journal (CN ISSN 0068-8207) *1044*
Canadian Amateur Advanced Study Guide (CN) *347*
Canadian Amateur Certificate Study Guide (CN) *347*
Canadian Amateur Radio Regulations Handbook (CN) *347*
Canadian and Provincial Golf Records (CN ISSN 0316-8131) *1038*
Canadian Annual Review see Canadian Annual Review of Politics and Public Affairs 604
Canadian Annual Review of Politics and Public Affairs (CN ISSN 0315-1433) *604*
Canadian Archaeological Association. Bulletin see Canadian Journal of Archaeology 84
Canadian Architect's Yardsticks for Costing see Yardsticks for Costing 100
Canadian Art Sales Index (CN) *103,* 113
Canadian Artists Series/Collection: Artistes Canadiens (CN ISSN 0383-5405) *103*
Canadian Association of Administrative Sciences. Proceedings, Annual Conference see Administrative Sciences Association of Canada. Proceedings, Annual Conference 278
Canadian Association of Geographers. Directory (CN ISSN 0707-3844) *542*
Canadian Association of Geographers. Newsletter see Canadian Association of Geographers. Directory 542
Canadian Association of Management Consultants. Annual Report (CN ISSN 0068-8320) *279*

Canadian Association of University Schools of Music. Journal. see Canadian University Music Review 834
Canadian Automobile Association. Public Policy Booklet (CN) *1091*
Canadian Automotive Aftermarket Directory/Marketing Guide (CN) *304,* 1091
Canadian Bar Association. Annual Report of Proceedings (CN) *653*
Canadian Bar Association. British Columbia Branch. Program Report (CN ISSN 0384-5753) *653*
Canadian Books for Young People/Livres Canadiens pour la Jeunesse (CN) *124,* 334
Canadian Books in Print (CN ISSN 0068-8398) *124*
Canadian Broadcasting Corporation Classical Record Reference Book see C B C Classical Record Reference Book 834
Canadian Building Abstracts (CN ISSN 0008-3089) 3, *188*
Canadian Bulletin of Fisheries and Aquatic Sciences (CN ISSN 0706-6503) 139, *508*
Canadian Bureau for International Education. Annual Report. (CN) *441*
Canadian Business Index (CN ISSN 0227-8669) 3, *205*
Canadian Business Periodicals Index see Canadian Business Index 205
Canadian Campus see Canadian Campus Career Directory 1149
Canadian Campus Career Directory (CN ISSN 0383-2406) *1149*
Canadian Cases on Employment Law Reports (CN) *286,* 653
Canadian Cases on the Law of Insurance (CN) *638,* 653
Canadian Cases on the Law of Torts (CN ISSN 0701-1733) *653*
Canadian Catholic Historical Association. Annual Report (CN) *1149*
Canadian Ceramic Society. Journal (CN ISSN 0068-8444) *319*
Canadian Certified General Accountants' Research Foundation. Study Papers (CN) *221,* 254
Canadian Chemical Directory see Canadian Chemical, Pharmaceutical and Product Directory 304
Canadian Chemical Industry: A Corpus Survey (CN) *322*
Canadian Chemical, Pharmaceutical and Product Directory (CN ISSN 0068-8452) *304*
Canadian Children's Annual (CN ISSN 0316-8484) *335*
Canadian Clinical Engineering Conference. Proceedings (CN) *759,* 781
Canadian Co-operative Wool Growers Magazine (CN ISSN 0319-7387) *65*
Canadian Commission for Unesco. Annual Report (CN ISSN 0317-5693) *915*
Canadian Communications and Energy Conference (Proceedings) / Conference Canadienne sur les Communications et l'Energie (Proceedings) see International Communications and Energy Conference (Proceedings) 343
Canadian Community Law Journal/Revue Canadienne de Droit Communautaire (CN ISSN 0704-0857) *653*
Canadian Composer/Compositeur Canadien (CN ISSN 0008-3259) *834*
Canadian Composers Series (CN) *834*
Canadian Conference of the Arts. Miscellaneous Reports (CN ISSN 0068-8487) *103*
Canadian Conference on Earthquake Engineering. Proceedings (CN) *480*
Canadian Conservation Directory (CN ISSN 0318-2789) *364*
Canadian Conservation Institute Technical Bulletins see C C I Technical Bulletins 364

Canadian Construction Association. Documentation de Reference (CN ISSN 0316-9375) *182*
Canadian Corn (CN) *1149*
Canadian Correspondence Courses for University Credit see Canadian University Distance Education Directory 426
Canadian Council of Churches. Record of Proceedings (CN ISSN 0701-4309) *968*
Canadian Council on Social Development. Annual Report/Rapport Annuel (CN ISSN 0068-8584) *1015*
Canadian Directory of Awards for Graduate Study/Repertoire Canadien des Bourses d'Études Superieures (CN ISSN 0711-8635) *432*
Canadian Directory of Professional Photography (CN) *884*
Canadian Directory of Shopping Centres (CN) *283*
Canadian Earthquakes/Tremblements de Terre Canadiens (CN ISSN 0225-6002) *398*
Canadian Education Association Handbook see C E A Handbook 411
Canadian Education Index/Repertoire Canadien sur l'Education (CN ISSN 0008-3453) *3,* 423
Canadian Electrical Association. Engineering and Operating Division. Transactions (CN ISSN 0576-5161) *451*
Canadian Electronics Engineering Annual Buyers' Guide and Catalog Directory see Canadian Electronics Engineering Components and Equipment Directory 451
Canadian Electronics Engineering Components and Equipment Directory (CN) *451*
Canadian Engineering & Industrial Year Book (CN ISSN 0068-8665) *287,* 470
Canadian Engineering and Machinery Year Book see Canadian Engineering & Industrial Year Book 470
Canadian Environmental Advisory Council. Annual Review (CN) *494*
Canadian Environmental Advisory Council. Reports (CN) *494*
Canadian Environmental Law (CN) *494,* 653
Canadian Fact Book on Poverty/Donnees de Base sur la Pauvrete au Canada (CN) *1015*
Canadian Federation for the Humanities. Annual Report (CN ISSN 0225-6932) *629*
Canadian Federation of Biological Societies. Newsletter (CN ISSN 0068-8681) *139*
Canadian Federation of Biological Societies. Proceedings see Canadian Federation of Biological Societies. Programme and Proceedings of the Annual Meeting 139
Canadian Federation of Biological Societies. Programme and Proceedings of the Annual Meeting (CN) *139*
Canadian Federation of Biological Societies. Programme of the Annual Meeting see Canadian Federation of Biological Societies. Programme and Proceedings of the Annual Meeting *139*
Canadian Federation of Film Societies Index of 16 mm & 35 mm Feature Length Films Available in Canada see Index of 16 mm & 35 mm Feature Length Films Available in Canada *1155*
Canadian Film Series (CN ISSN 0705-548X) *823*
Canadian Fisheries. Statistical Highlights (CN) *514*
Canadian Folk Music Journal (CN ISSN 0068-8746) *834*
Canadian Food and Packaging Directory (CN ISSN 0068-8754) *304,* 518
Canadian Footwear & Leather Directory (CN ISSN 0068-8762) *304,* 672, 1005
Canadian Foreign Relations. (CN) *915*

Canadian Forest Fire Weather Index (CN) 524
Canadian Forestry Service. Department of Fisheries & Forestry. Prairies Region. Information Report see Canada. Northern Forestry Centre. Information Report 524
Canadian Forestry Service. Prairies Region. Forestry Report see Canada. Northern Forestry Centre. Forestry Report 524
Canadian Fruit Wholesalers' Association. Yearbook (CN ISSN 0068-8770) 518
Canadian Furniture & Furnishings Directory (CN ISSN 0068-8789) 304, 644
Canadian Gas Association. Membership Directory (CN ISSN 0315-8233) 464
Canadian Gas Association. Statistical Summary of the Canadian Gas Industry (CN ISSN 0068-8800) 464, 863
Canadian Gas Association Directory (CN) 464, 863
Canadian Gas Facts (CN ISSN 0316-3547) 464, 863
Canadian Gas Utilities Directory see Canadian Gas Association Directory 464
Canadian Gladiolus Society. Annual (CN ISSN 0319-1915) 532
Canadian Government Buyer (CN ISSN 0829-8629) 3, 283
Canadian Government Series (CN ISSN 0068-8835) 903
Canadian Grain Commission Grain Research Laboratory. Annual Report (CN ISSN 0317-1892) 63
Canadian Grain Exports see Canada. Grain Commission. Economics and Statistics Division. Canadian Grain Exports 63
Canadian Gunner (CN ISSN 0068-8843) 810
Canadian Hackney Stud Book (CN ISSN 0382-5795) 1042
Canadian Hardware, Electrical & Building Supply Directory (CN ISSN 0456-3867) 304, 451
Canadian Health Insurance Facts see Canadian Life and Health Insurance Facts 638
Canadian Heart Foundation. Annual Report (CN ISSN 0068-8851) 776
Canadian Historical Association. Historical Booklets. Brochures Historiques (CN ISSN 0068-886X) 604
Canadian Historical Association. Historical Papers (CN ISSN 0068-8878) 556
Canadian Historical Horticulture/Histoire de l'Horticulture au Canada (CN ISSN 0828-8259) 532
Canadian Horticultural Council. Annual Meeting Reports (CN ISSN 0068-8908) 532
Canadian Horticultural Council. Committee on Horticultural Research. Annual Reports (CN ISSN 0068-8916) 532
Canadian Hospital Directory/Annuaire des Hopitaux du Canada (CN ISSN 0068-8932) 616
Canadian Hotel & Restaurant (CN) 619
Canadian Hotel and Restaurant's Product Hot Lines/Produits Vedettes see Canadian Hotel & Restaurant 619
Canadian Hotel, Restaurant, Institution & Store Equipment Directory (CN ISSN 0381-5765) 304, 619
Canadian Housing Statistics (CN ISSN 0068-8940) 627
Canadian Income Tax for Businessmen and Accountants (CN) 293
Canadian Industry Report of Fisheries and Aquatic Sciences (CN ISSN 0704-3694) 405, 508
Canadian Industry Shows and Exhibitions (CN ISSN 0068-8967) 795
Canadian Information Processing Society. Computer Census (CN ISSN 0316-8956) 360

Canadian Insect Pest Review see Canadian Agricultural Insect Pest Review 53
Canadian Institute of Chartered Accountants. Uniform Final Examination Handbook see Canadian Institute of Chartered Accountants. Uniform Final Examination Report 221
Canadian Institute of Chartered Accountants. Uniform Final Examination Report (CN ISSN 0713-357X) 221
Canadian Institute of Chartered Accountants Handbook see C I C A Handbook 221
Canadian Institute of Forestry. Annual Report (CN ISSN 0068-8991) 524
Canadian Institute of Mining and Metallurgy Directory see C.I.M. Directory 815
Canadian Insurance. Annual Statistical Issue (CN ISSN 0068-9025) 638
Canadian International Development Agency Canadians in the Third World see Canadians in the Third World 261
Canadian Jersey Cattle Club. Record see Canadian Jersey Herd Record 65
Canadian Jersey Herd Record (CN ISSN 0382-6406) 65
Canadian Jewellery & Giftware Directory (CN ISSN 0068-9041) 304, 552, 644
Canadian Jewish Archives (New Series) (CN ISSN 0576-5528) 502, 976
Canadian Jewish Congress. National Archives Newsletter (CN ISSN 0824-8907) 3, 502
Canadian Journal of Archaeology (CN ISSN 0705-2006) 84
Canadian Journal of Law and Society (CN ISSN 0829-3201) 653, 1024
Canadian Journal of Marketing Research (CN ISSN 0829-4836) 283
Canadian Journal of Political & Social Theory/Revue Canadienne de Theorie Politique et Sociale (CN ISSN 0380-9420) 903, 1024
Canadian Journal of Social Work Education see Canadian Social Work Review 1016
Canadian Key Business Directory (CN ISSN 0315-0879) 304
Canadian Labour Terms (CN ISSN 0068-905X) 270
Canadian Lacombe Breeders Association. Newsletter (CN ISSN 0008-4344) 65
Canadian Ladies' Golf Association. Year Book (CN ISSN 0084-8565) 1038
Canadian Law List (CN ISSN 0084-8573) 653
Canadian Library Association. Occasional Papers (CN ISSN 0068-9092) 675
Canadian Library Association Directory see C L A Directory 675
Canadian Library Handbook see Canadian Library Yearbook 675
Canadian Library Yearbook (CN ISSN 0827-3715) 675
Canadian Life and Health Insurance Facts (CN ISSN 0068-9157) 638
Canadian Life Insurance Facts see Canadian Life and Health Insurance Facts 638
Canadian Local Histories to 1950. A Bibliography. Histoires Locales et Regionales Canadiennes des Origines A 1950 (CN ISSN 0068-9165) 604
Canadian Locations of Journals Indexed for Medicine/Depots Canadiens des Revues Indexees pour Medecine (CN ISSN 0707-7629) 3, 769
Canadian Locations of Journals Indexed in Index Medicus see Canadian Locations of Journals Indexed for Medicine 769
Canadian Magazine Index (CN ISSN 0829-8777) 3, 538
Canadian Manuscript Report of Fisheries and Aquatic Sciences (CN ISSN 0706-6473) 405, 494
Canadian Master Tax Guide (CN) 293

Canadian Mathematical Congress. Notes, News and Comments see Canadian Mathematical Society. Notes, News and Comments 748
Canadian Mathematical Society. Notes, News and Comments (CN) 748
Canadian Medical and Biological Engineering Conference. Digest of Papers (CN) 759, 781
Canadian Medical Directory (CN ISSN 0068-9203) 759
Canadian Mental Health Association. Annual Report/Association Canadienne pour la Sante Mentale. Rapport Annuel (CN ISSN 0068-9211) 933, 953
Canadian Meteorological and Oceanographic Society. Annual Congress (CN) 803
Canadian Meteorological Memoirs (CN ISSN 0068-9246) 803
Canadian Meteorological Research Reports (CN) 803
Canadian Meteorological Society. Annual Congress see Canadian Meteorological and Oceanographic Society. Annual Congress 803
Canadian Minerals Yearbook/Annuaire des Mineraux du Canada (CN ISSN 0068-9270) 815
Canadian Mines Handbook (CN ISSN 0068-9289) 815
Canadian Mines Register of Dormant and Defunct Companies (CN ISSN 0068-9297) 815
Canadian Mines Register of Dormant and Defunct Companies. Supplement(CN ISSN 0068-9300) 815
Canadian Mining Journal's Reference Manual & Buyers' Guide (CN ISSN 0315-9140) 815
Canadian Mining Manual see Canadian Mining Journal's Reference Manual & Buyers' Guide 815
Canadian Music Directory (CN ISSN 0381-5730) 304, 834
Canadian National Annual Report (CN) 350, 1081
Canadian National Energy Forum Proceedings (CN) 451, 464, 863
Canadian National Institute for the Blind. National Annual Report (CN ISSN 0068-9378) 179, 1015
Canadian News Index (CN ISSN 0225-7459) 3, 647
Canadian Newspaper Index see Canadian News Index 647
Canadian Nuclear Association. Annual International Conference Proceedings(CN) 896
Canadian Nuclear Association. Annual International Conference. Summaries see Canadian Nuclear Association. Annual International Conference Proceedings 896
Canadian Nuclear Society. Annual Conference Proceedings (CN ISSN 0227-1907) 896
Canadian Nuclear Society. Annual Conference Summaries (CN ISSN 0227-0129) 896
Canadian Nuclear Society. Transactions see Canadian Nuclear Society. Annual Conference Summaries 896
Canadian Numismatic Research Society. Transactions (CN ISSN 0045-5202) 844
Canadian Nurses Association. Entrance Requirements for Diploma Schools of Nursing and Schools of Practical Nursing. (CN ISSN 0319-4787) 411, 783
Canadian Nurses Association. Nursing Programs and Entrance Requirements at Canadian Universities. (CN ISSN 0229-7345) 411, 783
Canadian Office Redbook (CN) 1149
Canadian Oil & Gas Handbook (CN ISSN 0710-622X) 815, 863
Canadian Oral History Association. Journal (CN ISSN 0383-6894) 604
Canadian Papers in Rural History (CN) 25, 579, 604
Canadian Paraplegic Association. Annual Report (CN ISSN 0068-9424) 1016

Canadian Parliamentary Guide (CN ISSN 0315-6168) 903
Canadian Periodical Index (CN ISSN 0008-4719) 3
Canadian Perspective (CN ISSN 0705-6680) 270, 1016
Canadian Pest Management Society Proceedings (CN ISSN 0227-7980) 53
Canadian Plastics Directory and Buyer's Guide (CN ISSN 0068-9459) 900
Canadian Political Science Association. Updating Theses in Canadian Political Science, Completed and in Progress (CN) 903
Canadian Pro Football (CN) 1038
Canadian Public Health Association. Proceedings of the Annual Meeting (CN ISSN 0319-2644) 1149
Canadian Pulp and Paper Association. Annual Newsprint Supplement (CN ISSN 0316-4241) 859
Canadian Pulp and Paper Association. Pulp and Paper Report (CN ISSN 0068-9505) 858
Canadian Pulp and Paper Association. Technical Section. Proceedings (CN) 858
Canadian Pulp and Paper Association. Woodlands Section. Publications (CN) 858
Canadian Quaker History Newsletter (CN) 984
Canadian Real Estate Annual see Real Estate Development Annual 966
Canadian Red Cross Blood Transfusion Service. Annual Report (CN) 783
Canadian Red Cross Society. Annual Report (CN ISSN 0068-9572) 1016
Canadian Rehabilitation Council for the Disabled. Annual Report (CN ISSN 0068-9580) 759
Canadian Review of Art Education Research (CN ISSN 0384-1839) 103, 411
Canadian Review of Physical Anthropology/Review Canadienne d'Anthropologie Physique (CN ISSN 0225-9958) 70
Canadian Rock Mechanics Symposium. Proceedings (CN ISSN 0375-605X) 1149
Canadian Seed Growers Association. Annual Report (CN ISSN 0068-9610) 53
Canadian Self-Medication (CN) 870
Canadian Serials Directory/Repertoire des Publications Seriees Canadiennes(CN ISSN 0000-0345) 687
Canadian Shipping Project Newsletter see Maritime History Group Newsletter 1102
Canadian Short Story Library (CN) 718
Canadian Social Work Review (CN) 1016
Canadian Society for Education Through Art. Annual Journal (CN ISSN 0068-9645) 103, 411
Canadian Society for Horticultural Science. Newsletter (CN) 532
Canadian Society for Horticultutral Science. Journal see Canadian Society for Horticultural Science. Newsletter 532
Canadian Society for Immunology. Bulletin (CN ISSN 0068-9653) 773
Canadian Society of Biblical Studies. Bulletin/Societe Canadienne des Etudes Bibliques. Bulletin (CN ISSN 0068-970X) 968
Canadian Special Publication of Fisheries and Aquatic Sciences (CN ISSN 0706-6481) 139, 508
Canadian Sporting Goods & Playthings. Directory (CN ISSN 0316-7771) 304, 1033
Canadian Standards Association. Annual Report (CN) 808
Canadian Standards Association. Catalogue (CN) 808
Canadian Standards Association. List of Publications see Canadian Standards Association. Catalogue 808
Canadian Standards Association. Standards Catalogue see Canadian Standards Association. Catalogue 808

Canadian Statistics Index (CN ISSN 0832-655X) *1052*
Canadian Structural Engineering Conference. Proceedings (CN ISSN 0318-0522) *480*
Canadian Studies in Criminology (CN ISSN 0068-9777) *370*
Canadian Tax Foundation. Provincial and Municipal Finances (CN ISSN 0317-946X) *293*
Canadian Tax Foundation. Provincial Finances *see* Canadian Tax Foundation. Provincial and Municipal Finances *293*
Canadian Tax Foundation. Tax Conference. Report of Proceedings (CN ISSN 0316-3571) *293*
Canadian Tax Papers (CN ISSN 0008-512X) *293*
Canadian Taxation of Mining Income (CN) *293*
Canadian Teachers' Federation. Bibliographies in Education (CN) *423*
Canadian Technical Asphalt Association. Proceedings of the Annual Conference (CN ISSN 0068-984X) *182*
Canadian Technical Report of Fisheries and Aquatic Sciences (CN ISSN 0706-6457) *139*, *508*
Canadian Textile Directory (CN ISSN 0068-9858) *304*, *1073*
Canadian Theatre Checklist (CN ISSN 0226-5125) *1149*
Canadian Theatre Review (CN) *1076*
Canadian Theatre Review Yearbook *see* Canadian Theatre Review *1076*
Canadian Theses/Theses Canadiennes (CN ISSN 0068-9874) *124*
Canadian Tide and Current Tables (CN ISSN 0068-9882) *405*
Canadian Toy Fair. Trade Show Directory *see* Toy and Decoration Fair Directory *553*
Canadian Toy, Notion and Stationery Directory *see* Canadian Variety Merchandise Directory *304*
Canadian Trade Index (CN ISSN 0068-9904) *304*
Canadian Truckers' Guide (CN) *1104*
Canadian Unemployment Insurance Legislation (CN) *653*
Canadian University Distance Education Directory (CN) *426*
Canadian University Music Review/Revue de Musique des Universites Canadiennes (CN ISSN 0710-0353) *446*, *834*
Canadian Urban Sources *see* Microlog Index *9*
Canadian Variety Merchandise Directory (CN ISSN 0068-9955) *304*
Canadian Volleyball Annual and Rule Book (CN) *1038*
Canadian War Museum. Historical Publications (CN) *556*
Canadian Who's Who (CN ISSN 0068-9963) *133*
Canadian Wildlife Service. Monograph Series (CN ISSN 0069-0015) *170*, *173*, *364*
Canadian Wildlife Service. Occasional Papers (CN ISSN 0576-6370) *364*
Canadian Wildlife Service. Progress Notes/Service Canadien de la Faune. Cahiers de Biologie (CN ISSN 0069-0023) *364*
Canadian Wildlife Service. Report Series (CN ISSN 0069-0031) *139*, *364*
Canadian Wool Grower *see* Canadian Co-operative Wool Growers Magazine *65*
Canadian Yearbook of International Law/Annuaire Canadien de Droit International (CN ISSN 0069-0058) *669*
Canadians in the Third World (Canadian International Development Agency) (CN) *261*
Canadiens dans le Tiers Monde *see* Canadians in the Third World *261*
Canado-Americain (US) *502*, *915*
Canary Islands Shipping Handbook 1983/4 (UK ISSN 0263-7073) *304*, *1099*

Canberra Mathematical Association. Newsletter (AT) *748*
Canberra Papers in Continuing Education (AT ISSN 0310-1649) *426*
Cancer Biochemistry - Biophysics (UK ISSN 0305-7232) *151*, *153*, *774*
Cancer Biology Reviews (US ISSN 0198-6473) *774*
Cancer Campaign (GW ISSN 0342-8893) *774*
Cancer Data: Deaths and Cases Reported *see* Cancer Data: New Registrations and Deaths *769*
Cancer Data: New Registrations and Deaths (NZ) *769*
Cancer Detection and Prevention (US ISSN 0361-090X) *774*
Cancer Facts and Figures (US ISSN 0069-0147) *774*
Cancer in Ontario (CN ISSN 0315-9884) *774*
Cancer in Puerto Rico (PR) *774*
Cancer Incidence in Slovenia *see* Incidenca Raka v Sloveniji *775*
Cancer Incidence in Sweden (SW ISSN 0069-0155) *774*
Cancer Institute Scientific Report (JA) *774*
Cancer News Journal (US ISSN 0099-2372) *774*
Cancer Research Campaign. Annual Report (UK ISSN 0365-9623) *774*
Cancer Seminar Proceedings (US ISSN 0069-0171) *775*
Candelabrum (UK) *740*
Candian Theses on Microfiche (Supplement) *see* Canadian Theses *124*
Candlelighters Childhood Cancer Foundation/Annotated Bibliography and Resource Guide (US) *125*, *334*, *769*
Candlelighters Foundation Bibliography and Resource Guide *see* Candlelighters Childhood Cancer Foundation/Annotated Bibliography and Resource Guide *125*
Candy Buyers Directory (US) *304*, *522*
Candy Family History Newsletter (AT ISSN 0314-7894) *1149*
Candy Industry Buying Guide (US) *522*
Canterbury Archaeological Society. Occasional Papers (UK ISSN 0069-0198) *84*
Canterbury Botanical Society. Journal (NZ ISSN 0110-5892) *155*
Canterbury Engineering Journal (NZ ISSN 0069-0201) *1149*
Canu Gwerin/Folk Song (UK) *515*, *834*
Capacitors D.A.T.A. Book (US) *451*
Cape Chamber of Industries Year Book & Directory *see* C C I Year Book & Directory *235*
Cape Cod and Islands Atlas and Guide Book (US) *1107*
Cape Cod Resort Directory (US) *1107*
Cape of Good Hope. Department of Nature Conservation and Museum Services. Annual Report (SA) *364*, *494*
Cape of Good Hope. Department of Nature Conservation. Annual Report *see* Cape of Good Hope. Department of Nature Conservation and Museum Services. Annual Report *364*
Cape of Good Hope Imvo/News (US) *341*, *432*
Cape Show Programme & Catalogue (SA) *25*
Cape Times Peninsula Directory (SA) *304*
Cape Town Directory of South Africa *see* C.T. Directory of South Africa *303*
Capital Expenditure and Debt Financing Statistics (UK ISSN 0263-2985) *205*, *1052*
Capital Goods Review (US ISSN 0008-588X) *277*, *287*
Capital Investments of the World Petroleum Industry (US ISSN 0577-571X) *265*
Capital Punishment (US) *370*
Capitalismo e Socialismo (IT ISSN 0391-1934) *251*, *903*

Capitulo Criminologico (VE) *370*, *653*
Captain Lillie's Coast Guide and Radiotelephone Directory (CN ISSN 0318-3742) *304*, *1099*
Car and Driver Buyers Guide (US) *1091*
Car and Driver Yearbook *see* Car and Driver Buyers Guide *1091*
Car and Locomotive Cyclopedia (US) *1094*
Car Prices (US) *1091*
Caracas (VE) *540*
Caraher Family History Society. Journal (UK ISSN 0260-8391) *535*
Caravan *see* Coe Review *718*
Caravan & Chalet Sites Guide (UK ISSN 0069-0317) *1107*
Caravan Buyers Manual (AT) *1107*
Caravan Camping Directory (AT) *1044*
Caravan Factfinder (UK) *1091*, *1107*
Caravan Industry Directory (UK) *1107*
Caravan Industry Supplies & Services Directory (UK) *622*
Caravan Park, Camping & Backpacking Guide to Southern African/Woonwapark, Kamper and Voetslaangids vir Suider-Afrika (SA) *1044*
Caravan Sites (UK) *1107*
Caravan Sites and Mobile Home Parks *see* Caravan Sites *1107*
Caravan Yearbook *see* Caravan Factfinder *1107*
Carbet (MQ) *1007*
Carbohydrate Chemistry *see* Carbohydrate Chemistry. Part 1: Mono-, Di-, & Tri-saccharides & Their Derivatives *329*
Carbohydrate Chemistry *see* Carbohydrate Chemistry. Part 2: Macromolecules *329*
Carbohydrate Chemistry. Part 1: Mono-, Di-, & Tri-saccharides & Their Derivatives (UK) *329*
Carbohydrate Chemistry. Part 2: Macromolecules (UK) *329*
Carbon & High Performance Fibres Directory (UK ISSN 0268-0491) *900*, *1073*
Carbon Dioxide Review (US) *322*
Carcinogenesis (US ISSN 0147-4006) *775*
Carcinogenesis Abstracts (US ISSN 0008-6258) *3*, *769*
Cardamom Statistics (II) *40*
Cardiff Working Papers in Welsh Linguistics/Papuran Gwaith Ieithyddol Cymraeg Caerdydd (UK ISSN 0263-0362) *693*
Cardinal Bea Studies (PH) *981*
Cardiology Update (US ISSN 0163-1675) *776*
Cardiovascular Diseases; Current Status and Advances *see* Clinical Cardiology Monographs *776*
Cardiovascular Review (US ISSN 0271-4779) *776*
Cardiovascular Surgery (US ISSN 0069-0406) *776*, *794*
Care Magazine (UK) *789*
Care News (UK) *789*
Career Guide: Dun's Employment Opportunities Directory (US ISSN 0740-7289) *847*
Career Index *see* Chronicle Career Index *847*
Career Resource Directory (US) *1149*
Careering (SA) *847*
Careers (AT) *847*
Careers Encyclopedia (UK) *847*
Careers for Geologists *see* Opportunities for Geologists and Geophysicists *848*
Careers for Graduates/Carrieres pour Diplomes (CN ISSN 0318-6229) *847*
Careers Guide (AT) *847*
Careers in Botany (US) *155*
Careers in Depth (US ISSN 0069-0449) *847*
Careers in Hospitals and Health Services in Victoria (AT) *616*, *847*
Careers Information Series (II) *847*
Carfax News (UK) *961*
Cargo Tank Hazardous Material Regulations (US) *1105*
Caribbean/American Directory (US ISSN 0275-2883) *304*
Caribbean-American Studies (US) *903*

Caribbean, Bermuda, and the Bahamas (Year) (US) *1107*
Caribbean Congress of Labour. Report (BB ISSN 0576-7547) *648*
Caribbean Directory (XK) *304*
Caribbean Economic Almanac (TR ISSN 0069-0481) *242*
Caribbean Geography (JM ISSN 0252-9939) *542*
Caribbean Handbook (AQ) *192*
Caribbean Islands Research Institute. Annual Report *see* Caribbean Research Institute. Report *604*
Caribbean Monograph Series (PR ISSN 0069-0511) *604*
Caribbean Newsletter (BB) *368*
Caribbean Ports Handbook (JM) *1099*
Caribbean Research Institute. Report (VI) *139*, *364*, *604*
Caribbean Tourism Statistical Report (BB) *1107*
Caribbean Tourism Statistics *see* Caribbean Tourism Statistical Report *1107*
Carillon News *see* Guild of Carillonneurs in North America. Bulletin *836*
Caritas Internationalis. International Yearbooks (IT ISSN 0069-0554) *1150*
Caritas; Jahrbuch des Deutschen Caritasverbandes (GW ISSN 0069-0570) *1016*
Caritas-Kalender (GW) *462*, *968*
Carl Newell Jackson Lectures (US ISSN 0528-1458) *515*, *968*
Carleton Germanic Papers (CN ISSN 0317-7254) *718*
Carleton Lecture Note Series *see* Carleton-Ottawa Mathematical Lecture Note Series *748*
Carleton Mathematical Series (CN ISSN 0069-0600) *748*
Carleton-Ottawa Mathematical Lecture Note Series (CN ISSN 0827-3669) *748*
Carleton University, Ottawa. Department of Geology. Geological Papers (CN ISSN 0069-0619) *1150*
Carleton University, Ottawa. Norman Paterson School of International Affairs. Bibliography Series (CN ISSN 0383-2848) *915*
Carlton Newsletter (AT) *622*
Carlyle Newsletter (UK) *133*, *718*
Carmarthen Museum. Publication (UK) *827*
Carnahan Conference on Security Technology. Proceedings (US) *374*
Carnegie Corporation of New York. Annual Report (US ISSN 0069-0635) *629*
Carnegie Corporation of New York. Reports of the Officers *see* Carnegie Corporation of New York. Annual Report *629*
Carnegie Endowment for International Peace. Financial Report (US ISSN 0094-3029) *915*
Carnegie Endowment for International Peace in the 1970's (US) *915*
Carnegie Endowment for International Peace Report *see* Carnegie Endowment for International Peace in the 1970's *915*
Carnegie Foundation for the Advancement of Teaching. Annual Report (US ISSN 0069-0651) *411*
Carnegie Institute. Annual Report (US) *827*
Carnegie Institution of Washington. Year Book (US ISSN 0069-066X) *989*
Carnegie International (US) *827*
Carnegie-Mellon Symposia on Cognition (US) *333*, *933*
Carnegie Museum of Natural History. Annals of (the) Carnegie Museum (US ISSN 0097-4463) *70*, *139*, *856*, *989*
Carnegie Museum of Natural History. Bulletin (US ISSN 0145-9058) *70*, *139*, *856*, *989*
Carnegie Museum of Natural History. Special Publication (US ISSN 0145-9031) *989*
Carnegie Symposium on Cognition *see* Carnegie-Mellon Symposia on Cognition *933*

CARNES see Computer Aided Research in Near Eastern Studies 612
Carnival & Circus Booking Guide (US ISSN 0090-2985) 1076
Carnuntum Jahrbuch (AU ISSN 0411-129X) 84
Carolinea (GW ISSN 0176-3997) 155, 173, 378
Carotenoids Other Than Vitamin A (UK ISSN 0069-0732) 151
Carpenter and Joiner (AT) 182
Carpet and Rug Industry Review (US) 643
Carpet and Rug Institute. Directory (US) 1073
Carpet and Rug Institute. Directory and Report see Carpet and Rug Institute. Directory 1073
Carpet and Rug Institute. Review-State of the Industry see Carpet and Rug Industry Review 643
Carpet Annual (UK ISSN 0069-0767) 1073
Carpet Specifier's Handbook (US ISSN 0095-6457) 1073
Carrell (US ISSN 0008-6894) 675
Carribean Occasional Series (PR) 604
Carrieres pour Diplomes see Careers for Graduates 847
Carrionflower Writ (AT ISSN 0815-452X) 718, 740
Carroll Alumni Journal (US) 341
Carroll Studies see Lewis Carroll Society of North America. Chapbook 128
Cars in Australia. Annual (AT) 1091
Carson-Newman College, Jefferson City, Tennessee. Faculty Studies (US ISSN 0069-0783) 432
Carswell's Practice Cases (CN ISSN 0706-5388) 653
Carta Geologica de Chile (CL ISSN 0716-0194) 384
Carta Geologica do Brasil Ao Milionesimo (BL) 384
Carta Metalurgica (CK) 815
Carte d'Identite du Senegal (SG) 940
Cartes de Peches de Chalutiers Quebecois. Cahier Special d'Information (CN) 508
Cartes Synoptiques de la Chromosphere Solaire see Cartes Synoptiques de la Chromosphere Solaire et Catalogues des Filaments et des Centres d'Activite 115
Cartes Synoptiques de la Chromosphere Solaire et Catalogues des Filaments et des Centres d'Activite (FR) 115
Cartha (DK) 827
Cartoonists' Market see Artist's Market 102
Casa de Velasquez, Madrid. Melanges/Casa de Velasquez, Madrid. Miscellanies (FR ISSN 0076-230X) 84, 103
Casa de Velasquez, Madrid. Miscellanies see Casa de Velasquez, Madrid. Melanges 103
Case Analysis in Social Science and Social Therapy (US ISSN 0149-6948) 933, 1007, 1025
Case Studies in Cultural Anthropology (US) 70
Case Studies in Education and Culture (US) 411
Case Studies on Broadcasting Systems (UK) 347
Case Western Reserve University. Warner Swasey Observatory. Publications (US ISSN 0160-2500) 115
Casebook Series on European Politics and Society (UK) 903
Casebooks in Earth Sciences (US) 384
Cases and Materials on Constitutional Law (US) 653
Cases and Materials on Trade Regulation (US) 653
Cases in Public Policy and Management(US) 205, 949
Casesamling (DK ISSN 0107-5586) 192
Cass Library of African Studies. Africana Modern Library (UK ISSN 0069-0880) 70
Cass Library of African Studies. General Studies (UK ISSN 0069-0899) 565

Cass Library of African Studies. Researches and Travels (UK ISSN 0069-0902) 565
Cass Library of African Studies. South African Studies (UK ISSN 0069-0910) 565
Cass Library of African Studies. Travels and Narratives (UK ISSN 0069-0929) 565
Cass Library of Industrial Classics (UK ISSN 0069-0937) 192
Cass Library of Science Classics (UK ISSN 0069-0945) 989
Cassal Bequest Lectures (UK ISSN 0069-0961) 718
Cassell and Publishers Association Directory of Publishing in Great Britain, the Commonwealth, Ireland, South Africa and Pakistan (UK) 961
Cassell's Directory of Publishing in Great Britain, The Commonwealth, Ireland, South Africa and Pakistan see Cassell and Publishers Association Directory of Publishing in Great Britain, the Commonwealth, Ireland, South Africa and Pakistan 961
Cassette Books (US ISSN 0363-9029) 180, 675
Casualty Actuarial Society. Proceedings(US) 638
Casualty Return (UK ISSN 0268-0815) 1099
Casualty Return Statistical Summary see Casualty Return 1099
Casualty Return Statistical Summary of Merchant Ships Totally Lost, Broken Up, Etc see Casualty Return 1099
Cat Fanciers' Association. Annual Yearbook (US) 868
Cat Fanciers' Magazine (AT) 868
Catalog of Captioned Films for the Deaf (US) 375, 823
Catalog of Dealers' Prices for Marine Shells (US ISSN 0084-862X) 174
Catalog of Mailing Lists see United States & Canadian Mailing Lists 16
Catalog of Model Services and Supplies(US) 182, 470
Catalog of Museum Publications and Media (US) 3, 831
Catalog of World Bank Publications (UN ISSN 0095-5434) 261
Catalogo Bolaffi dei Vini Rossi d'Italia see Catalogo dei Vini d'Italia 119
Catalogo Brasileiro de Engenharia Sanitaria e Ambiental (BL) 480
Catalogo Colectivo de Publicaciones Periodicas (EC) 1150
Catalogo Colectivo de Publicaciones Periodicas Existentes en Bibliotecas Cientificas y Tecnicas Argentina (AG) 963
Catalogo Colectivo de Publicaciones Periodicas Existentes en las Bibliotecas de la Universidad (MX) 125
Catalogo Coletivo de Publicacoes Periodicas (in Microfiches) see Catalogo Coletivo Nacional de Publicacoes Periodicas (in Microfiches) 125
Catalogo Coletivo Nacional de Publicacoes Periodicas (in Microfiches) (BL) 125
Catalogo de Exportadores (SP) 235
Catalogo de Importadores (SP) 235
Catalogo de Manuales Latinoamericanos see Catalogo de Publicaciones Didacticas Latinoamericanas de Formacion Profesional 426
Catalogo de Pesquisas Concluidas e Em Desenvolvimento (BL) 433
Catalogo de Publicaciones Didacticas Latinoamericanas de Formacion Profesional (UY) 426
Catalogo de Publicaciones Latinoamericanas Sobre Formacion Profesional (UY ISSN 0069-1046) 125, 411, 849
Catalogo dei Libri in Commercio/Italian Books in Print (IT) 964
Catalogo dei Libri Italiani in Commercio see Catalogo dei Libri in Commercio 964
Catalogo dei Periodici Italiani (IT) 125
Catalogo dei Vini d'Italia (IT) 119

Catalogo dell'Arte Italiana dell'Ottocento (IT) 103
Catalogo dell'Arte Moderna Italiana (IT) 103
Catalogo della Grafica Italiana (IT) 103, 930
Catalogo della Pittura Italiana dell'Ottocento see Catalogo dell'Arte Italiana dell'Ottocento 103
Catalogo della Scultura Italiana (IT) 103
Catalogo dos Cursos de Pos-Graduacao No Brasil (BL) 433
Catalogo Ilustrado de las Plantas de Cundinamarca (CK) 155
Catalogo Motoristico (IT) 1091
Catalogo Nazionale Bolaffi d'Arte Moderna see Catalogo dell'Arte Moderna Italiana 103
Catalogo Nazionale Bolaffi della Grafica see Catalogo della Grafica Italiana 103
Catalogo Productos y Servicios del Estado de Mexico (MX) 304
Catalogue Afnor (Normes Francaises) (FR) 808
Catalogue Biennale Internationale de Lausanne (SZ) 103, 1073
Catalogue Collectif des Publications Scientifiques dans les Bibliotheques Canadiennes see Union List of Scientific Serials in Canadian Libraries 1005
Catalogue de l'Edition Francaise see Livres Disponibles 128
Catalogue des Catalogues Automobile (FR ISSN 0069-1097) 1091
Catalogue des Coleopteres de Belgique (BE) 164
Catalogue des Constructeurs Francais d'Equipements pour les Industries Alimentaires (FR) 745
Catalogue des Normes Francaises see Catalogue Afnor (Normes Francaises) 808
Catalogue des Produits Agrees Par Qualite-France (FR ISSN 0069-1100) 239
Catalogue General de l'Industrie et du Commerce Automobile de Belgique (BE) 1091
Catalogue National du Chauffage et du Conditionnement d'Air see Catalogue National du Genie Climatique-Chauffage et Conditionnement d'Air 553
Catalogue National du Genie Climatique-Chauffage et Conditionnement d'Air/National Catalogue of Heating and Air Conditioning/Nazionaler Katalog der Heizung und Klimatisierung (FR ISSN 0153-999X) 553
Catalogue National du Traitement des Surfaces et de l'Anticorrosion et des Traitements Thermiques (FR ISSN 0396-1214) 855
Catalogue of American Amphibians and Reptiles (US) 174
Catalogue of Arabic Manuscripts in Salar Jung Museum see Concise Descriptive Catalogue of Arabic Manuscripts in the Salar Jung Museum and Library 831
Catalogue of Australian Brass and Concert Band Music (AT) 834
Catalogue of Australian Choral Music (AT) 834
Catalogue of Books Recommended for Libraries/Sentei Tosho Somokuroku (JA) 125
Catalogue of Canadian Recreation and Leisure Research (CN) 1044, 1107
Catalogue of Contemporary Welsh Music (UK) 834
Catalogue of Indian Chemical Plants see Guide to Indian Chemical Plants and Equipment 478
Catalogue of N A L Technical Translations (National Aeronautical Laboratory) (II ISSN 0077-2968) 18
Catalogue of Persian Manuscripts in Salar Jung Museum see Concise Descriptive Catalogue of the Persian Manuscripts in the Salar Jung Museum and Library 831
Catalogue of Polish Feature Films (PL) 823

Catalogue of Reproductions of Paintings Prior to 1860 (UN ISSN 0069-1135) 103
Catalogue of Reproductions of Paintings, 1860-1973 (UN ISSN 0069-1143) 103
Catalogue of Statistical Materials of Developing Countries (JA) 1052
Catalogue of Urdu Manuscripts in Salar Jung Museum see Concise Descriptive Catalogue of the Urdu Manuscripts in the Salar Jung Museum and Library 831
Catalogus Bouwwereld (NE) 182
Catalogus Faunae Austria (AU) 139
Catalogus Musicus (GW ISSN 0069-116X) 834
Catalogus Scheepvaart (NE) 1099
Catalogus Translationem et Commentatorium (US ISSN 0528-2594) 739
Catalogus van Academische Geschriften in Nederland Verschenen see Bibliografie van Nederlandse Proefschriften 122
Catalogus van Nederlandse Zeekaarten en Andere Hydrografische Publikaties/Catalog of Charts and Other Hydrographic Publications (NE ISSN 0920-9786) 1123
Cataluna Exporta (SP ISSN 0069-1178) 235
Catalysis by Metal Complexes (NE) 329
Catalysis in Organic Syntheses (US ISSN 0197-534X) 1150
Catalysis: Science and Technology (US) 322
Catalyst (UK ISSN 0144-9931) 675
Catalyst (Peterborough) (US ISSN 0008-7661) 1007
Catalyst for Environment/Energy (US ISSN 0194-1445) 464, 494
Catalyst for Environmental Quality see Catalyst for Environment/Energy 494
Catastrophism and Ancient History. Procceedings (US ISSN 0890-5592) 84
Catering (London, 1984) (UK) 283, 619
Catering Manager's Buyer's Guide (Year) (UK ISSN 0268-5663) 518
Cathair na Mart (IE ISSN 0332-4117) 579
Cathartic (US ISSN 0145-8310) 718
Cathedra (IS ISSN 0334-4657) 612
Cathedrals & Monastic Buildings in the British Isles see Courtauld Institute Illustration Archives. Archive 1 104
Catholic Almanac (US ISSN 0069-1208) 981
Catholic Archives (UK ISSN 0261-4316) 981
Catholic Archives Society Newsletter see C A S Newsletter 981
Catholic Bible Quarterly Monograph Series (US) 968
Catholic Book Notes see Catholic Truth 981
Catholic Central Union of America. Proceedings (US ISSN 0069-1216) 981
Catholic Directory (UK ISSN 0069-1224) 981
Catholic Directory (San Diego) (US) 981
Catholic Directory (San Francisco) (US) 462, 981
Catholic Directory for Scotland (UK ISSN 0306-5677) 981
Catholic Directory for the Clergy and Laity in Scotland see Catholic Directory for Scotland 981
Catholic Directory of England and Wales (UK) 981
Catholic Directory of Southern Africa (SA) 981
Catholic Directory of the Archdiocese of Baltimore (US) 981
Catholic Education (UK) 411, 981
Catholic Health Association of Canada. Directory (CN ISSN 0828-5748) 759, 981
Catholic Health Association of the United States. Guidebook (US) 616, 968

Catholic Hospital Association of Canada. Directory see Catholic Health Association of Canada. Directory 759
Catholic Housing Aid Society. Annual Report (UK) 622
Catholic Periodical and Literature Index(US ISSN 0008-8285) 3, 975
Catholic Periodical Index see Catholic Periodical and Literature Index 975
Catholic Press Directory (US ISSN 0008-8307) 125
Catholic Relief Services. Annual Report(US) 1016
Catholic Telephone Guide (US) 981
Catholic Theological Society of America. Proceedings (US ISSN 0069-1267) 981
Catholic Truth (UK ISSN 0411-275X) 961, 981
Catholic University of America. School of Law. Center for National Policy Review. Annual Report. see Center for National Policy Review. Annual Report 1150
Catholicisme Hier, Aujourd'hui, Demain (FR) 981
Causes of Death in Denmark see Doedsaarsagerne 953
Cavalcade and Directory of Acts and Attractions see Cavalcade of Acts & Attractions 1076
Cavalcade and Directory of Fairs see Directory of North American Fairs and Expositions 15
Cavalcade of Acts & Attractions (US) 1076
Cave Science: Transactions of the British Cave Research Association (UK ISSN 0263-760X) 385
Cayman Islands. Currency Board. Report (CJ) 293
Cayman Islands. Department of Finance and Development. Estimates of Gross Domestic Product and Related Aggregates (CJ) 1150
Cayman Islands. Education Department. Report of the Chief Education Officer (CJ) 411
Cayman Islands. Legislative Assembly. Minutes (CJ ISSN 0300-4740) 940
Cayman Islands Handbook and Businessman's Guide (CJ) 304
Cayman Islands Holiday Guide (CJ) 1107
Cayman Islands Real Estate Review (CJ) 965
Cebal (DK) 693
Celebrate; the Annual for Cake Decorators see Wilton Yearbook of Baking and Cake Decorating 615
Celebration (US ISSN 0883-9174) 740
Celebrity Directory (US) 823, 834, 1033
Celebrity Service International Contact Book (US ISSN 0069-1372) 823, 1076
Celibate Woman (US ISSN 0735-4398) 1128
Cell and Developmental Biology of the Eye (US) 785
Cell Biology Monographs (US ISSN 0172-4665) 163
Cell Membranes, Methods and Reviews(US) 139
Cell Surface Reviews (NE) 151
Celtica (IE ISSN 0069-1399) 433
Cement (YU ISSN 0008-882X) 182
Cement & Concrete Association. Development Report (UK ISSN 0143-1560) 182
Cement and Concrete Association Technical Report see C & C A Technical Report 182
Cement Association of Japan. Review of the General Meeting (JA) 182
Cement Association of Japan. Review of the General Meeting. Technical Session (JA) 182
Cement Industry Technical Conference. Record see I E E E Cement Industry Technical Conference. Record 184
Cement: Latin American Industrial Report (US) 182
Cement Market and Outlook see European Cement Association. European Annual Review 188

Cement- och Betonginstitutet Aarsberaettelse Report of Activities see C B I Aarsberaettelse/Report of Activities 1149
Cement- och Betonginstitutet Forskning Research see C B I Forskning/ Research 182
Cement- och Betonginstitutet Rapporter Reports see C B I Rapporter/Reports 182
Cement Research Institute of India. Annual Report see National Council for Cement and Building Materials. Annual Report 186
Cement Standards of the World (FR) 182
Cemento Portland (AG ISSN 0008-8927) 182
Cements Research Progress (US ISSN 0363-8642) 320
Cenacolo (IT ISSN 0008-8935) 103, 718
Censo de Poblacion y Viviendas (CU) 926, 1052
Censored see Spectrum 684
Census Bureau Methodological Research see U.S. Bureau of the Census. Census Bureau Methodological Research 1014
Census of Distribution see Census of Wholesale and Retail Trade 205
Census of Industrial Production in Zambia (ZA ISSN 0069-1429) 205
Census of Inland Shipping in the Netherlands at Locks and Bridges see Statistiek van de Scheepvaartbeweging in Nederland 1104
Census of Maine Manufactures (US ISSN 0090-7111) 288
Census of Manufacturing Industries of Puerto Rico (PR ISSN 0552-5276) 288
Census of Motor Traffic on Main International Traffic Arteries (UN) 1096
Census of Private Non-Profit Making Institutions in Fiji. A Report (FJ) 205, 1052
Census of Traffic on Main International Traffic Arteries see Census of Motor Traffic on Main International Traffic Arteries 1096
Census of U.S. Civil Aircraft (US ISSN 0069-1437) 1087
Census of Wholesale and Retail Trade (CY) 205
Centar za Drustvena Istrazivanija Slavonije i Baranje. Zbornik see Slavonski Povijesni Zbornik 632
Centar za Proucananje i Suzbijanje Alkoholizma i Drugih Ovisnosti. Radovi (YU ISSN 0033-8567) 376
Centaur (UY) 1107
Centauros (AG ISSN 0008-8986) 1033
Center for Adult Diseases, Osaka. Annual Report (JA ISSN 0078-6632) 759
Center for Agricultural Economic Research, Rehovot. Working Papers (IS) 45
Center for Anthropological Studies. Ethnohistorical Report Series (US) 70
Center for Chinese Research Materials. Bibliographical Series (US ISSN 0084-6902) 687
Center for Creative Leadership. Technical Report (US) 279
Center for Hermeneutical Studies in Hellenistic and Modern Culture. Protocol Series of the Colloquies (US ISSN 0098-0900) 629
Center for High Energy Forming. International Conference. Proceedings (US) 470
Center for Holocaust Studies Newsletter (US ISSN 0737-8092) 502, 579
Center for Law and Education. Newsnotes (US ISSN 0276-203X) 411, 653
Center for Music Experiment Annual Report see C M E Annual Report 834
Center for National Policy Review. Annual Report. (US) 1150

Center for Peace and Conflict Studies. Occasional Papers (US ISSN 0732-0078) 915
Center for Philosophic Exchange. Annual Proceedings (US) 877
Center for Pre-Columbian Studies. Conference Proceedings see Dumbarton Oaks Conference Proceedings 85
Center for Research in Water Resources Newsletter see Watermarks 1127
Center for Research Libraries. Handbook (US) 675
Center for the Study of Early Man. Current Research see Current Research in the Pleistocene 85
Center for the Study of the Presidency. Proceedings (US) 903
Center for War-Peace Studies Special Studies see C W/P S Special Studies 915
Centering (US) 740
Centers of Civilization Series (US ISSN 0069-1461) 556
Centra Bulteno see Semajna Bulteno 703
Centraal Bureau voor Genealogie. Jaarboek (NE) 535
Central Africa Historical Association. Local Series Pamphlets see Historical Association of Zimbabwe. Local Series Pamphlets 566
Central African Power Corporation. Annual Report and Accounts (RH ISSN 0069-147X) 451
Central America and the Caribbean: Development Assistance Abroad (US ISSN 0740-0004) 915
Central America Stamp Catalogue (UK ISSN 0142-9876) 874
Central Archives for the History of the Jewish People Newsletter/Arkhiyon ha-Merkazi le-Toldot ha-Am ha-Yehudi. Yediot (IS) 612
Central Asia Book Series (US) 568
Central Asia Stamp Catalogue (UK ISSN 0142-9884) 874
Central Asian Collectanea (US) 125, 915
Central Atlantic States Manufacturers Directory see Directory of Central Atlantic States Manufacturers. Maryland, Delaware, Virginia, West Virginia, North Carolina, South Carolina 305
Central Bank of Barbados. Annual Report (BB ISSN 0304-6796) 242
Central Bank of Barbados. Annual Statistical Digest (BB ISSN 0255-8440) 225
Central Bank of Barbados. Balance of Payments (BB ISSN 0255-8432) 206
Central Bank of Ceylon. Annual Report(CE ISSN 0069-1496) 226
Central Bank of Ceylon. Report and Accounts see Bank of Ceylon. Annual Report and Accounts 224
Central Bank of Ceylon. Review of the Economy/Arthika Vivaranaya (CE) 242
Central Bank of China. Annual Report (CH ISSN 0069-150X) 226
Central Bank of Cyprus. Annual Report(CY ISSN 0069-1518) 226
Central Bank of Egypt. Annual Report (UA) 226
Central Bank of Egypt. Board of Directors. Report see Central Bank of Egypt. Annual Report 226
Central Bank of Iraq, Baghdad. Report (IQ ISSN 0069-1534) 226
Central Bank of Ireland. Annual Report(IE ISSN 0069-1542) 226
Central Bank of Ireland. Irish Economic Statistics (IE ISSN 0332-2696) 206, 226
Central Bank of Jordan. Annual Report/Bank Al-Markazi Al-Urduni. Annual Report (JO ISSN 0069-1550) 226
Central Bank of Kenya. Annual Report (KE ISSN 0069-1569) 226
Central Bank of Kuwait. Annual Report(KU) 226
Central Bank of Kuwait. Economic Chart Book (KU) 242
Central Bank of Kuwait. Economic Report (KU) 242

Central Bank of Malta. Annual Report (MM ISSN 0577-0653) 226
Central Bank of Nigeria. Annual Report and Statement of Accounts (NR ISSN 0069-1577) 226
Central Bank of Nigeria. Economic and Financial Review (NR ISSN 0008-9281) 242
Central Bank of Somali. Annual Report and Statement of Accounts (SO) 226
Central Bank of Swaziland. Annual Report (SQ) 226
Central Bank of Sweden. Annual Report see Sveriges Riksbank. Foervaltningsberaettelse 233
Central Bank of Sweden. Statistical Yearbook see Sveriges Riksbank. Statistisk Aarsbok 233
Central Bank of the Bahamas. Annual Report and Statement of Accounts. (BF) 226
Central Bank of the Gambia. Annual Report (GM) 226
Central Bank of the Philippines. Annual Report (PH ISSN 0069-1585) 226
Central Bank of the Republic of Turkey. Annual Report (TU) 226
Central Bank of Trinidad and Tobago. Report (TR ISSN 0069-1593) 226
Central Bank of Yemen. Annual Report(YE ISSN 0301-6625) 226
Central Building Research Institute. Building Research Note (II) 182
Central Building Research Institute. List of Publications (II ISSN 0557-322X) 182
Central Conference of American Rabbis. Yearbook (US ISSN 0069-1607) 976
Central Conference of Teamsters. Chairman's Report see Central Conference of Teamsters. Officers' Report 648
Central Conference of Teamsters. Officers' Report (US ISSN 0069-1615) 648
Central Council for Education and Training in Social Work Reporting see C C E T S W Reporting 1024
Central Electric Railfans' Association. Bulletin (US ISSN 0069-1623) 1094
Central Electricity Generating Board Abstracts see C E G B Abstracts 461
Central Electricity Generating Board Research see C E G B Research 451
Central Europe and Scandinavia Travel Guide see Travel Guide to Europe 1118
Central Inland Fisheries Research Institute. Annual Report (II) 508
Central Inland Fisheries Research Institute. Bulletin (II ISSN 0008-9427) 508
Central Inland Fisheries Research Institute. Technical Progress Report see Central Inland Fisheries Research Institute. Annual Report 508
Central Institute of Education Newsletter see C.I.E. Newsletter 411
Central Institute of Indian Languages Adult Literacy Series see C I I L Adult Literacy Series 426
Central Institute of Indian Languages Bilingual Hindi Series see C I I L Bilingual Hindi Series 692
Central Institute of Indian Languages Folklore Series see C I I L Folklore Series 515
Central Institute of Indian Languages Grammar Series see C I I L Grammar Series 692
Central Institute of Indian Languages Occasional Monograph Series see C I I L Occasional Monograph Series 692
Central Library of Agricultural Sciences. Acquistion List (IS) 40
Central Literary Magazine (UK ISSN 0069-164X) 718
Central Marine Fisheries Research Institute. Bulletin (II ISSN 0577-084X) 405, 508
Central Mine Planning & Design Institute. Manuals (II) 815
Central Mining Research Station, Dhanbad. Annual Report (II) 815

Central Mining Research Station, Dhanbad. Progress Research see Central Mining Research Station, Dhanbad. Annual Report 815
Central Mississippi Planning and Development District. Annual Report(US) 622
Central Mortgage and Housing Corporation. Annual Report see Canada Mortgage and Housing Corporation. Annual Report 622
Central Nacional de Pesquisa de Mandioca e Fruticultura. Relatorio Tecnico Anual (BL) 25
Central Naugatuck Valley Regional Planning Agency. Annual Report (US ISSN 0069-1674) 288
Central Plantation Crops Research Institute. Annual Report (II ISSN 0374-7115) 25, 45, 155
Central Road Research Institute, New Delhi. Road Research Paper (II ISSN 0069-1690) 1081
Central Road Research Institute Road Abstracts see C R R I Road Abstracts 476
Central Scientific-Ethical Committee of Denmark. Report see Centrale Videnskabsetiske Komite. Beretning 989
Central Serials Record (US ISSN 0193-7405) 675
Central Sericultural Research and Training Institute. Annual Report (II ISSN 0304-6818) 25
Central States Conference on the Teaching of Foreign Languages. Education Series (US) 446, 693
Central Statistical Office Statistical Bulletins see C.S.O. Statistical Bulletins 1050
Central Tobacco Research Institute and its Regional Research Stations. Annual Report (II) 1079
Centrale Videnskabsetiske Komite. Beretning/Central Scientific-Ethical Committee of Denmark. Report (DK ISSN 0107-9786) 989
Centralinstitut foer Nordisk Asienforskning Nytt see C I N A - Nytt 851
Centralite (PH) 341
Centralny Katalog Biezacych Czasopism Zagranicznych w Bibliotakach Polskich see Centralny Katalog Zagranicznych Wydawnictw Ciaglych w Bibliotekach Polskich. Alfabetyczny Wykaz Tytulow 687
Centralny Katalog Zagranicznych Wydawnictw Ciaglych w Bibliotekach Polskich. Alfabetyczny Wykaz Tytulow (PL ISSN 0239-8931) 125, 687
Centralny Osrodek Badan i Rozwoju Techniki Kolejnictwa. Prace COBiRTK (PL) 1094
Centre (BE) 634, 968
Centre Belge d'Histoire Rurale. Publications/Belgisch Centrum voor Landelijke Geschiedenis. Publikaties (BE ISSN 0076-1192) 579
Centre Culturel Francais, Alger. Rencontres Culturelles (AE ISSN 0069-1720) 718
Centre Culturel Francais de Yaounde. Programme Saison (CM) 103, 834, 1076
Centre d'Ecologie Forestiere. Notes Techniques see Centre d'Ecologie Forestiere et Rurale. Notes Techniques. B: Herbageres 524
Centre d'Ecologie Forestiere. Notes Techniques see Centre d'Ecologie Forestiere et Rurale. Notes Techniques. A: Forestieres 524
Centre d'Ecologie Forestiere et Rurale. Communications (BE) 139, 524
Centre d'Ecologie Forestiere et Rurale. Notes Techniques. A: Forestieres (BE) 524
Centre d'Ecologie Forestiere et Rurale. Notes Techniques. B: Herbageres (BE) 524
Centre d'Enquetes Statistiques de Caen. Enquete Annuelle d'Entreprise: Industries Diverses (FR) 206, 1052
Centre d'Enseignement Superieur de Brazzaville. Annales (CF) 433

Centre d'Etudes Ethnologiques. Publications see Centre d'Etudes Ethnologiques Bandundu. Publications 70
Centre d'Etudes Ethnologiques. Publications. Serie 2: Memoires et Monographies (ZR) 70, 565, 1025
Centre d'Etudes Ethnologiques. Publications. Serie 3: Travaux Linguistiques (ZR) 693
Centre d'Etudes Ethnologiques Bandundu. Publications (ZR) 70, 565, 1025
Centre d'Histoire et d'Art de la Thudinie. Publications (BE) 103, 579
Centre de Cartographie Phytosociologique. Communications see Centre d'Ecologie Forestiere et Rurale. Communications 524
Centre de Commerce Mondial de Montreal. Repertoire des Associations (CN) 235
Centre de Documentation et de Recherche sur l'Asie. Etudes et Documents see Asian Studies Series 568
Centre de Geomorphologie, Caen. Bulletin (FR ISSN 0068-4791) 385
Centre de l'Astronomie et des Sciences Spatiales. Observations Solaires (RM) 115
Centre de Recherche d'Histoire et Civilisation de Byzance. Travaux et Memoires (FR) 579, 612
Centre de Recherche en Civilisation Canadienne-Francaise. Bulletin see Cultures du Canada Francais 605
Centre de Recherche en Civilisation Canadienne-Francaise. Cahiers see French-Canadian Civilization Research Center. Cahiers 605
Centre de Recherche en Litterature Canadienne-Francaise. Cahiers see French-Canadian Civilization Research Center. Cahiers 605
Centre de Recherche Industrielles en Afrique Centrale. Bulletin d'Information see Sciences, Techniques, Informations C R I A C 291
Centre de Recherches Archeologiques. Cahier (FR) 84
Centre de Recherches en Mathematiques Pures. Publications. Serie 1. Courtes Publications (SZ) 748
Centre de Recherches en Mathematiques Pures. Publications. Serie 2. Monographies (SZ) 748
Centre de Recherches en Mathematiques Pures. Publications. Serie 3. Oeuvres (SZ) 748
Centre de Recherches en Mathematiques Pures. Publications. Serie 4. Conferences Communications (SZ) 748
Centre de Recherches et d'Etudes Historiques de la Seconde Guerre Mondiale. Bulletin (BE) 579
Centre de Recherches Industrielles en Afrique Centrale Sciences, Techniques, Informations C R I A C see Sciences, Techniques, Informations C R I A C 291
Centre de Recherches pour le Developpement International. Rapport Annuel see International Development Research Centre. Annual Report 196
Centre Europeen d'Etudes Burgondo-Medianes. Publication (SZ ISSN 0069-1895) 542, 579
Centre for Advanced Land Use Studies Research Reports see C A L U S Research Reports 965
Centre for Advanced T V Studies Reports see C.A.T.S. Reports 347
Centre for Development Research Project Paper see C D R Project Paper 45
Centre for Development Research Research Reports see C D R Research Reports 45
Centre for English Cultural Tradition and Language Conference Papers Series see C E C T A L Conference Papers Series 692

Centre for European Policy Studies Papers see C E P S Papers 192
Centre for European Policy Studies Working Documents (Economic) see C E P S Working Documents (Economic) 192
Centre for European Policy Studies Working Documents (Political) see C E P S Working Documents (Political) 903
Centre for Intergroup Studies. Annual Report (SA) 1025
Centre for Library and Information Management Report to the British Library and Development Department see C L A I M Report to the British Library and Development Department 1149
Centre for Resource Studies. Annual Report (CN) 815
Centre for Resource Studies. Proceedings (CN) 815
Centre for Resource Studies. Technical Papers (CN) 815
Centre for Resource Studies Perspectives see C R S Perspectives 815
Centre for Resources Studies. Working Papers (CN ISSN 0226-7616) 815
Centre for South-East Asian Studies. Bibliography and Literature Series (UK ISSN 0269-1760) 568
Centre for South-East Asian Studies. Occasional Papers (UK ISSN 0269-1779) 568
Centre for Urban and Community Studies. Bibliographic Series (CN ISSN 0316-4691) 542, 622, 1025
Centre for Urban and Community Studies. Major Report Series (CN ISSN 0319-4620) 622, 921, 1025
Centre for Urban and Community Studies. Research Papers (CN ISSN 0316-0068) 622, 921, 1025
Centre for Urban Studies Bulletin see C U S Bulletin 622
Centre International de Documentation Arachnologiques. Liste des Travaux Arachnologiques (FR ISSN 0085-2783) 3, 149
Centre International de Documentation Occitane. Bibliotheque. Catalogue (FR) 693
Centre International de Documentation Occitane. Serie Bibliographique (FR) 125, 579
Centre International de Documentation Occitane. Serie Etudes (FR ISSN 0398-3765) 579
Centre International de Liaison des Ecoles de Cinema et de Television. Bulletin d'Informations (BE ISSN 0528-4759) 347, 823
Centre Interuniversitaire d'Histoire Contemporaine. Cahiers/ Interuniversitair Centrum voor Hedendaagse Geschiedenis. Mededelingen (BE ISSN 0577-179X) 579
Centre National d'Art et de Culture Georges Pompidou. Annuaire des Concepteurs (FR) 103, 1068
Centre National d'Etudes Spatiales. Rapport d'Activite (FR ISSN 0069-2034) 18
Centre National de Documentation Scientifique et Technique. Rapport d'Activite (BE ISSN 0069-1968) 989, 1068
Centre National de la Cinematographie Statistiques see C N C Statistiques 825
Centre National de la Recherche Scientifique. Annuaire Europeen d'Administration Publique (FR) 940
Centre National de la Recherche Scientifique. Colloques Internationaux. Sciences Humaines (FR ISSN 0069-1976) 629
Centre National de la Recherche Scientifique. Colloques Internationaux. Sciences Mathematiques, Physiques, Chimiques, Biologiques et Medicales (FR) 989

Centre National de la Recherche Scientifique. Colloques Internationaux. Sciences Mathematiques, Physico-Chimiques, Biologiques et Naturelles see Centre National de la Recherche Scientifique. Colloques Internationaux. Sciences Mathematiques, Physiques, Chimiques, Biologiques et Medicales 989
Centre National de la Recherche Scientifique. Rapport d'Activite (FR ISSN 0071-8327) 989
Centre National de la Recherche Scientifique. Seminaire d'Econometrie. Cahiers (FR ISSN 0071-8343) 192
Centre National de la Recherche Scientifique. Seminaire d'Econometrie. Monographies (FR ISSN 0071-8270) 192
Centre National de la Recherche Scientifique Courrier du C N R S Supplement see Courrier du C N R S Supplement 990
Centre National de Recherches Appliques au Developpement Rural. Departement de Recherches Agronomiques. Rapport Annuel (MG) 25
Centre National de Recherches Appliques au Developpement Rural. Departement de Recherches Agronomiques. Rapport d'Activite (MG) 25
Centre National de Recherches Archeologiques en Belgique. Repertoires Archeologiques. Serie A: Repertoires Bibliographiques/ Nationaal Centrum voor Oudheidkundige Navorsingen in Belgie. Oudheidkundige Repertoria. Reeks A: Bibliografische Repertoria (BE ISSN 0069-1992) 84
Centre National de Recherches Archeologiques en Belgique. Repertoires Archeologiques. Serie B: Repertoires des Collections (BE ISSN 0069-200X) 84
Centre National de Recherches Archeologiques en Belgique. Repertoires Archeologiques. Serie C: Repertoires Divers (BE ISSN 0069-2018) 84
Centre National de Recherches Scientifiques et Techniques pour l'Industrie Cimentiere Rapport de Recherche see C R I C Rapport de Recherche 989
Centre National du Commerce Exterieur. Annuaire (FR ISSN 0071-836X) 1150
Centre National du Machinisme Agricole du Genie Rural, des Eaux et des Forets Bulletin d'Information see C E M A G R E F Bulletin d'Information 1149
Centre National du Machinisme Agricole du Genie Rural, des Eaux et des Forets Etudes see C E M A G R E F Etudes 1149
Centre Regional de Documentation Pedagogique de Toulouse. Annales (FR ISSN 0069-2069) 411
Centre Regional de Recherche et de Documentation Pedagogiques de Lyon. Annales (FR ISSN 0069-2050) 446
Centre Technique du Bois et de l'Ameublement. Cahiers (FR ISSN 0008-9885) 529
Centre Technique Forestiere Tropical du Cameroun. Rapport Annuel (CM) 524
Centre Universitaire de la Reunion. Cahier see Universite de la Reunion. Cahier 706
Centrifugal Pump Spec Book (US) 745
Centrifugal Pump Specifications (US) 328
Centro Camuno di Studi Preistorici. Archivi (IT) 84, 103
Centro Camuno di Studi Preistorici. Bollettino (IT ISSN 0577-2168) 84, 103, 968
Centro Camuno di Studi Preistorici. Studi Camuni (IT) 84, 103

Centro Camuno di Studi Preistorici. Symposia (IT) 84, *103*, 968
Centro Cultural Portugues. Arquivos (FR) *739*
Centro de Bibliotecologia, Archivologia e Informacion. Anuario (MX) *675*
Centro de Desarrollo Industrial del Ecuador. Noticias Tecnicas (EC) *288*
Centro De Edafologia y Biologia Aplicada. Anuario (SP ISSN 0210-8623) *45*, 331, 385, 1121
Centro de Estudios de la Realidad Economica y Social. Serie Cochabamba (BO) 242, *1025*
Centro de Estudios de la Realidad Economica y Social. Serie Estudios Regionales (BO) *242*, 1025
Centro de Estudios de la Realidad Economica y Social. Serie Estudios Urbanos (BO) 242, *1025*
Centro de Estudios de la Realidad Economica y Social. Serie Movimientos Sociales (BO) 242, *1025*
Centro de Estudios de la Realidad Puertorriquena. Cuadernos (PR) *903*
Centro de Estudios Genealogicos de Cordoba. Boletin (AG) *535*
Centro de Estudios Martianos. Anuario (CU) *604*
Centro de Estudios Monetarios Latinoamericanos. Ensayos (MX ISSN 0577-2451) *226*
Centro de Estudios Orientales. Anuario (MX ISSN 0066-8249) *568*
Centro de Estudios Publicos. Documento de Trabajo (CL ISSN 0716-1123) *242*, 653, 903
Centro de Estudios Urbanos y Regionales. Cuadernos (AG ISSN 0326-1417) *1025*
Centro de Estudios Urbanos y Regionales. Informes de Investigacion(AG) *1025*
Centro de Estudos de Cabo Verde. Revista: Serie de Ciencias Humanas (CV) *1007*
Centro de Estudos Regionais. Boletim Cultural (PO) *71*, 84
Centro de Historia del Tachira. Boletin (VE ISSN 0411-5023) *604*
Centro de Informacion y Divulgacion Agropecuario. Boletin de Resenas. Serie: Forestales *see* Cuba. Centro de Informacion y Documentacion Agropecuario. Boletin de Resenas. Serie: Forestales *524*
Centro de Informaciones y Estudios del Uruguay. Cuadernos (UY) *1007*
Centro de Investigacion y Promocion del Campesinado. Cuadernos de Investigacion (BO) *242*
Centro de Investigacion y Promocion del Campesinado Cuadernos C I P C A (Serie Popular) *see* Cuadernos C I P C A (Serie Popular) *426*
Centro de Investigaciones Agricolas de Tamaulipas. Informe Anual de Labores (MX ISSN 0084-8697) *25*
Centro de Investigaciones Agricolas de Tamaulipas Circular C I A T *see* Circular C I A T *26*
Centro de Investigaciones Pesqueras. Revista de Investigaciones *see* Revista Cubana de Investigaciones Pesqueras. Boletines Bibliograficos *512*
Centro de Navegacion Transatlantica. C.N.T. Handbook. River Plate Handbook for Shipowners and Agents (AG) *1099*
Centro de Navegacion Transatlantica. C.N.T. Year Book; Ship Owners' and Agents' Handbook, River Plate Ports *see* Centro de Navegacion Transatlantica. C.N.T. Handbook. River Plate Handbook for Shipowners and Agents *1099*
Centro de Pesquisa Agropecuaria do Tropico Umido. Boletim de Pesquisa (BL ISSN 0100-8102) *25*
Centro de Pesquisas do Cacau. Boletin Tecnico (BL ISSN 0100-0845) *25*
Centro de Pesquisas do Cacau. Informe Tecnico (BL ISSN 0100-5065) *25*, 508

Centro de Salud "Max Arias Schreiber", Lima. Congreso Nacional de Tuberculosis y Enfermedades Respiratorias (PE ISSN 0069-2166) *792*
Centro di Documentazione Sul Movimento dei Disciplinati. Quaderni *see* Centro di Ricerca e di Studio Sul Movimento dei Disciplinati. Quaderni *556*
Centro di Ricerca e di Studio Sul Movimento dei Disciplinati. Quaderni (IT) *556*
Centro di Ricerche Storiche, Rovigno. Atti (YU ISSN 0352-1427) *579*
Centro di Ricerche Storiche, Rovigno. Quaderni (YU ISSN 0350-6746) *579*
Centro di Riferimento Italiano Diane. Notiziario (IT ISSN 0392-0143) *352*
Centro di Studi Vichiani. Bollettino (IT ISSN 0392-7334) *877*
Centro Interamericano de Fotointerpretacion. Revista (CK ISSN 0120-2499) *542*
Centro Interamericano de Investigacion y Documentacion Sobre Formacion Profesional. Cuadro Comparativo y Fichas Descriptivas (UY) *1150*
Centro Interamericano de Investigacion y Documentacion Sobre Formacion Profesional. Informes (UY) *426*
Centro Interamericano de Investigacion y Documentacion Sobre Formacion Profesional. Serie Bibliografica (UY) *411*
Centro Interamericano de Investigacion y Documentacion Sobre Formacion Profesional Colecciones Basicas C I N T E R F O R *see* Colecciones Basicas C I N T E R F O R *426*
Centro Interamericano de Investigacion y Documentacion Sobre Formacion Profesional Estudios y Monografias *see* C I N T E R F O R Estudios y Monografias *411*
Centro Internacional de Agricultura Tropical. Annual Report *see* C I A T Report *25*
Centro Internacional de Agricultura Tropical Report *see* C I A T Report *25*
Centro Internazionale di Studi di Architettura Andrea Palladio (IT) *97*
Centro Internazionale Radio-Medico *see* C.I.R.M *758*
Centro Latinoamericano de Demografia. Serie A: Informes sobre Investigaciones Realizadas *see* United Nations. Regional Centre for Demographic Training and Research in Latin America. Serie A *924*
Centro Latinoamericano de Demografia. Serie C: Informes sobre Investigaciones Realizadas Por los Alumnos del Centro *see* United Nations. Regional Centre for Demographic Training and Research in Latin America. Serie C *924*
Centro Latinoamericano de Demografia. Serie D: Traducciones, Estudios, Conferencias y Otros Trabajos Preparados por Profesores y Expertos Visitantes *see* United Nations. Regional Centre for Demographic Training and Research in Latin America. Serie D *924*
Centro Latinoamericano de Demografia. Serie E: Libros *see* United Nations. Regional Centre for Demographic Training and Research in Latin America. Serie E *925*
Centro Latinoamericano de Demografia. Serie OI: Publicaciones Conjuntas con Instituciones Nacionales de Paises de America Latina (UN) *921*
Centro Micologico Friulano. Bolletino (IT) *155*
Centro Nacional de Pesquisa de Tecnologia Agroindustrial de Alimentos Boletim de Pesquisa *see* C T A A. Boletim de Pesquisa *518*
Centro Panamericano de Zoonosis. Boletin Informativo *see* Centro Panamericano de Zoonosis. Boletin Informativo. Brucellosis en las Americas *174*

Centro Panamericano de Zoonosis. Boletin Informativo *see* Centro Panamericano de Zoonosis. Boletin Informativo. Tuberculosis en las Americas *1150*
Centro Panamericano de Zoonosis. Boletin Informativo *see* Centro Panamericano de Zoonosis. Boletin Informativo. Leptospirosis en las Americas *1150*
Centro Panamericano de Zoonosis. Boletin Informativo *see* Centro Panamericano de Zoonosis. Boletin Informativo. Hidatidosis en las Americas *1150*
Centro Panamericano de Zoonosis. Boletin Informativo *see* Centro Panamericano de Zoonosis. Boletin Informativo. Enfermedades Transmitidas por Alimentos en las Americas *1150*
Centro Panamericano de Zoonosis. Boletin Informativo. Brucellosis en las Americas (AG) *174*
Centro Panamericano de Zoonosis. Boletin Informativo. Enfermedades Transmitidas por Alimentos en las Americas (AG) *1150*
Centro Panamericano de Zoonosis. Boletin Informativo. Hidatidosis en las Americas (AG) *1150*
Centro Panamericano de Zoonosis. Boletin Informativo. Leptospirosis en las Americas (AG) *1150*
Centro Panamericano de Zoonosis. Boletin Informativo. Tuberculosis en las Americas (AG) *1150*
Centro Regional de Educacion de Adultos y Alfabetizacion Funcional para America Latina Cuadernos del C R E F A L *see* Cuadernos del C R E F A L *426*
Centro Studi per la Magna Grecia, Naples. Pubblicazioni Proprie (IT ISSN 0069-2204) *84*
Centro Superiore di Logica e Scienze Comparate. Quaderni (IT) *877*
Centrul de Astronomie si Stiinte Spatiale. Anuarul Astronomic (RM) *115*
Centrum voor Onderzoek en Voorlichting voor de Pluimveehouderij. Het Spelderholt. Jaarverlag (NE) *65*
Centur (UY) *1091*, 1107
Ceol (IE ISSN 0009-0174) *834*
Ceramic Abstracts (US ISSN 0095-9960) *3*, 320
Ceramic Data Book (US) *320*
Ceramic Source (US ISSN 8756-8187) *320*
Ceramica de Cultura Maya (US ISSN 0577-3334) *71*, 84
Ceramics and Glass: Science and Technology Series (US) *1150*
Ceramics and Glass Series *see* Ceramics and Glass: Science and Technology Series *1150*
Ceramics: Latin American Industrial Report (US) *320*
Cerberus Security (SZ) *374*
Cercle Belge de la Librairie. Annuaire (BE) *675*, 961
Cercle d'Etudes Numismatiques. Travaux (BE ISSN 0069-2247) *844*
Cercle d'Histoire et d'Archeologie de Saint-Ghislain et de la Region. Anales (BE) *84*, 579
Cercle d'Histoire et d'Archeologie de Saint-Ghislain et de la Region. Miettes d'Histoire *see* Cercle d'Histoire et d'Archeologie de Saint-Ghislain et de la Region. Anales *579*
Cercle Historique et Archeologique de Renaux et du Tenement d'Inde. Annales *see* Geschied- en Oudheidkundige Kring van Ronse en het Tenement van Inde. Annalen *583*
Cercle Historique et Folklorique de Braine-le-Chateau de Tubize et des Regions Voisines. Annales (BE) *84*, 579
Cercle Hutois des Sciences et Beaux-Arts. Annales (BE) *97*, 579
Cercle Royal d'Histoire et d'Archeologie d'Ath et de la Region et Musees Athois. Annales (BE) *84*

Cercle Royal d'Histoire et d'Archeologie d'Ath et de la Region et Musees Athois. Etudes et Documents (BE ISSN 0771-5692) *84*
Cercle Royal Historique et Archeologique de Courtrai. Memoires *see* Koninklijke Geschied- en Oudheidkundige Kring van Kortrijk. Handelingen *588*
Cereal Rust Bulletin (US) *53*
Cerebral Function Symposium. Proceedings (US) *789*
Cerebrovascular Diseases *see* Princeton Research Conferences on Cerebrovascular Diseases *777*
Ceredigion (UK ISSN 0069-2263) *556*
Cerrahpasa Medical Review (TU) *759*
Certification Reciprocity Policies in the U.S. *see* Teacher Certification Reciprocity Policies in the U.S *1164*
Certificats de Vaccination Exiges et Conseils d'Hygiene pour les Voyages Internationaux *see* Vaccination Certificate Requirements and Health Advice for International Travel *957*
Ceska Bibliografie (CS ISSN 0577-3490) *125*
Ceskoslovenska Akademie Ved. Archivni Zpravy (CS ISSN 0323-1313) *579*
Ceskoslovenska Akademie Ved. Rozpravy. M P V: Rada Matematickych a Prirodnich Ved (CS ISSN 0069-228X) *989*
Ceskoslovenska Akademie Ved. Rozpravy. S V: Rada Spolecenskych Ved (CS ISSN 0069-2298) *1007*
Ceskoslovenska Akademie Ved. Rozpravy. T V: Rada Technickych Ved (CS ISSN 0069-2301) *1068*
Ceskoslovenska Akademie Ved. Ustredni Archiv. Archivni Zpravy (CS) *675*
Ceskoslovenska Akademie Ved Archeologicky Ustav. Zachranne Oddeleni. Bulletin *see* Vyzkumy v Cechach *95*
Ceskoslovenske Akademie Zemedlskych Ved z Dejin Zemedlstvi a Lesnictve *see* Zemedelske Muzeum. Vedecke Prace *38*
Ceskoslovensko (CS) *874*
Ceskoslovensko-Sovetske Vztahy (CS) *579*
Ceskoslovensky Kolorista (CS ISSN 0009-0727) *339*
Ceskoslovensky Kras (CS) *542*
Ceux Qui Font l'Edition (FR) *961*
Ceux Qui Font la Presse (FR) *645*
Ceylon Chamber of Commerce. Annual Review of Business and Trade (CE) *235*
Ceylon Chamber of Commerce. Directory of Importers (CE) *235*
Ceylon Chamber of Commerce. Register of Members (CE) *235*
Ceylon Coconut Quarterly *see* Cocos *26*
Ceylon Historical Journal (CE ISSN 0577-4691) *568*
Ceylon Institute of Scientific & Industrial Research. Annual Report (CE) *989*, 1068
Ceylon Periodical Index *see* Sri Lanka Periodicals Index *12*
Ceylon Rationalist Ambassador (CE ISSN 0577-4772) *877*
Ceylon Shipping Corporation. Annual Report & Statement of Accounts (CE) *1099*
Ceylon Tourist Board. Annual Statistical Report (CE) *1119*
Ceylon Yearbook *see* Sri Lanka Yearbook *218*
Chadarim (IS) *740*
Chain Shoe Stores and Leased Shoe Department Operators (US ISSN 0069-2387) *1005*
Chain Store Age Supermarket Sales Manual (US ISSN 0069-2395) *1150*
Chain Store Guide Directory: Food Service Distributors *see* Directory of Food Service Distributors *522*
Challenge (Petersham North) (AT ISSN 0159-8872) *538*, 903
Challenges in the New Caribbean (BB) *540*

1688 CHALMERS TEKNISKA

Chalmers Tekniska Hoegskola. Institutionen foer Skeppshydromekanik. Rapport/Chalmers University of Technology. Department of Ship Hydromechanics. Report (SW ISSN 0009-112X) *1099*

Chalmers University of Technology. Department of Sanitary Engineering (SW ISSN 0280-4026) *494, 1124*

Chalmers University of Technology. Department of Ship Hydromechanics. Report see Chalmers Tekniska Hoegskola. Institutionen foer Skeppshydromekanik. Rapport *1099*

Chamber of Commerce and Industry in West Java. Member List/Kamar Dagang dan Industri di Jawa Barat. Daftar Anggota (IO) *235*

Chamber of Commerce and Industry of Malawi. Industrial and Trade Directory (MW) *304*

Chamber of Commerce of Sierra Leone. Journal (SL ISSN 0080-9527) *235*

Chamber of Commerce of the Philippines. Trade Directory (PH) *235*

Chamber's Trade Directory (PK) *304*

Chambre de Commerce, d'Artisanat et d'Industrie de Haute-Volta. Annuaire see Chambre de Commerce, d'Industrie et d'Artisanat du Burkina Faso. Annuaire *235*

Chambre de Commerce, d'Industrie et d'Artisanat du Burkina Faso. Annuaire (UV) *235*

Chambre de Commerce, d'Industrie et des Mines du Cameroun. Compte-Rendu d'Activites (CM) *235*

Chambre de Commerce, d'Industrie et des Mines du Cameroun. Rapport Annuel (CM ISSN 0069-2530) *815*

Chambre de Commerce et d'Industrie de Paris. Contribution des Employeurs a l'Effort de Construction (FR) *622*

Chambre de Commerce et d'Industrie du Mali. Precis Fiscal, Commercial, des Changes et des Echanges (ML ISSN 0067-3110) *235*

Chambre de Commerce Franco-Asiatique. Annuaire des Membres (FR ISSN 0069-2557) *235*

Chambre de Commerce Japonaise en France. Annuaire (FR ISSN 0069-2565) *235*

Chambre Officielle Franco Allemande de Commerce et d'Industrie. Liste des Membres/Offizielle Deutsch-Franzoesische Industrie- und Handelskammer. Mitgliederliste (FR ISSN 0069-2581) *235*

Chambre Regionale de Commerce et d'Industrie d'Alsace. Rapport sur les Activites (FR) *235*

Chambre Syndicale de la Siderugie Francaise. Bulletin Statistique. Serie Bleue. Commerce Exterieur. (FR) *797, 815*

Chambre Syndicale de la Siderugie Francaise. Bulletin Statistique. Serie Rouge. Production. (FR ISSN 0755-2025) *797, 815*

Chambre Syndicale des Mines de Fer de France. Rapport d'Activite (FR ISSN 0069-259X) *815*

Chambre Syndicale Nationale des Electriciens et Specialistes de l'Automobile. Annuaire (FR) *451, 1091*

Chambre Syndicale Nationale des Entreprises et Industries de l'Hygiene Publique. Annuaire (FR ISSN 0069-2603) *953*

Champaign County Historical Archives Historical Publications Series (US) *604, 884*

Champlain Society. Ontario Series (CN ISSN 0078-5091) *604*

Champlain Society, Toronto. Report (CN ISSN 0069-2646) *556*

Chanakya Defence Annual (II ISSN 0069-2654) *810*

Chancellor College. Department of Religious Studies. Staff Seminar Paper (MW) *968*

Chancellor College. Journal of Social Science see Malawi Journal of Social Science *1009*

Chaney Chronical (US) *718*

Change and Continuity in Africa (GW) *565*

Changing Japan (JA) *539*

Changing Public Attitudes on Governments and Taxes (US ISSN 0272-6017) *293*

Channel Islands Specialised Catalogue (UK ISSN 0142-5625) *874*

Channel Islands Stamps and Postal History (UK) *874*

Chantiers de Pedagogie Mathematique (FR ISSN 0395-7837) *446, 748*

Chants des Peuples (FR ISSN 0395-7845) *718, 740*

Charbonnages de France. Publications Techniques (FR ISSN 0009-1685) *815*

Charge Fiscale en Suisse see Steuerbelastung in der Schweiz *299*

Charioteer (US ISSN 0577-5574) *502, 710, 740*

Charite Annalen. Neue Folge (GE) *759*

Charities Digest (UK ISSN 0590-9783) *1016*

Charity Statistics (UK) *1022, 1052*

Charles C. Moskowitz Lectures see Joseph I. Lubin Memorial Lectures *196*

Charles Eliot Norton Lectures (US) *629*

Charles F. Kettering Foundation. Annual Report see Kettering Report *906*

Charles Redd Monographs in Western History (US ISSN 0162-217X) *556*

Charles S. Peirce Newsletter (US) *1150*

Charlottenborg Foraarsudstillingen (DK ISSN 0109-3479) *103*

Charlottes (CN ISSN 0316-6724) *604*

Charter (US ISSN 0069-2786) *629*

Chartered Institute of Building. Year Book (UK ISSN 0260-7727) *182*

Chartered Institute of Building. Year Book and Directory of Members see Chartered Institute of Building. Year Book *182*

Chartered Institute of Building Diary (UK) *480*

Chartered Institute of Patents Agents. Register of Patent Agents (UK) *860*

Chartered Institute of Public Finance and Accountancy. Administration of Justice. Estimates (UK ISSN 0264-6552) *370, 373*

Chartered Institute of Public Finance and Accountancy. Block Grant Statistics (UK ISSN 0266-9013) *950*

Chartered Institute of Public Finance and Accountancy. Cemeteries & Crematoria Statistics. Actuals (UK ISSN 0263-2969) *958, 1052*

Chartered Institute of Public Finance and Accountancy. Cemeteries Statistics. Actuals see Chartered Institute of Public Finance and Accountancy. Cemeteries & Crematoria Statistics. Actuals *958*

Chartered Institute of Public Finance and Accountancy. Charges for Leisure Services (UK ISSN 0142-1484) *1036, 1052*

Chartered Institute of Public Finance and Accountancy. Conference Handbook (UK) *221*

Chartered Institute of Public Finance and Accountancy. Crematoria Statistics. Actuals see Chartered Institute of Public Finance and Accountancy. Cemeteries & Crematoria Statistics. Actuals *958*

Chartered Institute of Public Finance and Accountancy. Direct Labour Statistics. Actuals (UK ISSN 0263-2977) *182, 188*

Chartered Institute of Public Finance and Accountancy. Education Estimates Statistics (UK ISSN 0307-0514) *423, 1052*

Chartered Institute of Public Finance and Accountancy. Education Statistics. Actuals (UK ISSN 0309-5614) *423, 1052*

Chartered Institute of Public Finance and Accountancy. Education Statistics. Unit Costs (UK ISSN 0264-7125) *423, 1033*

Chartered Institute of Public Finance and Accountancy. Environmental Health Statistics. Actuals (UK ISSN 0266-9552) *953*

Chartered Institute of Public Finance and Accountancy. Financial General & Rating Statistics (UK ISSN 0263-2276) *206, 1052*

Chartered Institute of Public Finance and Accountancy. Fire Service Statistics. Actuals (UK ISSN 0309-622X) *507, 1053*

Chartered Institute of Public Finance and Accountancy. Fire Service Statistics. Estimates (UK ISSN 0307-0573) *507, 1053*

Chartered Institute of Public Finance and Accountancy. Highways and Transportation. Actuals (UK ISSN 0260-9886) *1053, 1085*

Chartered Institute of Public Finance and Accountancy. Highways and Transportation Statistics. Estimates (UK ISSN 0260-9894) *1053, 1085*

Chartered Institute of Public Finance and Accountancy. Homelessness Statistics (UK ISSN 0144-4514) *627, 1053*

Chartered Institute of Public Finance and Accountancy. Housing Estimate Statistics see Chartered Institute of Public Finance and Accountancy. Housing Revenue Account Estimate Statistics *627*

Chartered Institute of Public Finance and Accountancy. Housing Maintenance & Management. Actuals Statistics (UK ISSN 0307-0468) *627, 1053*

Chartered Institute of Public Finance and Accountancy. Housing Part 1: Rents. Actuals Statistics see Chartered Institute of Public Finance and Accountancy. Housing Rents. Statistics *627*

Chartered Institute of Public Finance and Accountancy. Housing Part 2: Revenue Accounts. Actuals Statistics see Chartered Institute of Public Finance and Accountancy. Housing Revenue Accounts. Actuals Statistics *627*

Chartered Institute of Public Finance and Accountancy. Housing Revenue Accounts. Actuals Statistics (UK ISSN 0260-4078) *627, 1053*

Chartered Institute of Public Finance and Accountancy. Housing Revenue Account Estimate Statistics (UK) *627, 1053*

Chartered Institute of Public Finance and Accountancy. Housing Rents. Statistics (UK ISSN 0260-406X) *627, 1053*

Chartered Institute of Public Finance and Accountancy. Leisure and Recreation Statistics. Estimates (UK ISSN 0141-187X) *1036, 1053*

Chartered Institute of Public Finance and Accountancy. Leisure Estimate Statistics see Chartered Institute of Public Finance and Accountancy. Leisure and Recreation Statistics. Estimates *1036*

Chartered Institute of Public Finance and Accountancy. Leisure Usage. Actuals (UK ISSN 0266-9560) *1036, 1053*

Chartered Institute of Public Finance and Accountancy. Local Authority Airports. Accounts and Statistics see Chartered Institute of Public Finance and Accountancy. Local Authority Airports. Accounts and Statistics. Actuals Statistics *1085*

Chartered Institute of Public Finance and Accountancy. Local Authority Airports. Accounts and Statistics. Actuals Statistics (UK) *1053, 1085*

Chartered Institute of Public Finance and Accountancy. Local Government Comparative Statistics (UK ISSN 0260-9762) *949, 1053*

Chartered Institute of Public Finance and Accountancy. Local Health and Social Services Statistics see Chartered Institute of Public Finance and Accountancy. Personal Social Services Statistics. Actuals *1022*

Chartered Institute of Public Finance and Accountancy. Non-Teaching Hospital Costs. Statistics (UK ISSN 0267-1182) *618*

Chartered Institute of Public Finance and Accountancy. Personal Social Services Estimate Statistics (UK ISSN 0144-610X) *1022, 1053*

Chartered Institute of Public Finance and Accountancy. Personal Social Services Statistics. Actuals (UK ISSN 0309-653X) *1022, 1053*

Chartered Institute of Public Finance and Accountancy. Planning and Development Statistics. Actuals (UK ISSN 0260-8642) *949, 1053*

Chartered Institute of Public Finance and Accountancy. Planning and Development Statistics. Estimates (UK) *949, 1053*

Chartered Institute of Public Finance and Accountancy. Planning Estimates Statistics. Actuals see Chartered Institute of Public Finance and Accountancy. Planning and Development Statistics. Estimates *949*

Chartered Institute of Public Finance and Accountancy. Planning Estimates Statistics. Actuals see Chartered Institute of Public Finance and Accountancy. Planning and Development Statistics. Actuals *949*

Chartered Institute of Public Finance and Accountancy. Police Statistics. Actuals (UK ISSN 0144-9915) *373, 1053*

Chartered Institute of Public Finance and Accountancy. Police Statistics. Estimates (UK ISSN 0144-9885) *373, 1053*

Chartered Institute of Public Finance and Accountancy. Probation. Estimates (UK ISSN 0264-6544) *1016, 1022*

Chartered Institute of Public Finance and Accountancy. Probation Statistics. Actuals (UK ISSN 0140-8291) *1016*

Chartered Institute of Public Finance and Accountancy. Public Library Statistics. Actuals (UK ISSN 0309-6629) *687, 1053*

Chartered Institute of Public Finance and Accountancy. Public Library Statistics. Estimates (UK ISSN 0307-0522) *687, 1053*

Chartered Institute of Public Finance and Accountancy. Rate Collection Statistics. Actuals (UK ISSN 0260-5546) *206, 1053*

Chartered Institute of Public Finance and Accountancy. Return of Rates see Chartered Institute of Public Finance and Accountancy. Financial General & Rating Statistics *206*

Chartered Institute of Public Finance and Accountancy. School Meals Statistics (UK ISSN 0266-2949) *423, 1053*

Chartered Institute of Public Finance and Accountancy. Teaching Hospital Statistics. Actuals (UK ISSN 0267-1174) *619*

Chartered Institute of Public Finance and Accountancy. Waste Collection Statistics. Actuals (UK ISSN 0260-7603) *949, 1053*

Chartered Institute of Public Finance and Accountancy. Waste Disposal Statistics. Actuals (UK ISSN 0140-0150) *949, 958, 1053*

Chartered Institute of Public Finance and Accountancy. Waste Disposal Statistics. Estimates (UK ISSN 0140-0142) *949, 958, 1053*

Chartered Institute of Public Finance and Accountancy. Water Services Charges Statistics (UK ISSN 0141-7835) *1053, 1128*

Chartered Institute of Transport. Annual (NR) *1081*

Chartered Institute of Transport.
  Handbook (UK ISSN 0306-9559)
  1081
Chartering Annual (US) *1099*
Chase World Guide for Exporters (US)
  254
Chaseform Jumping Annual (UK) *1033*
Chasers and Hurdlers (UK) *1042*
Chases' Calendar of Annual Events (US
  ISSN 0577-5728) *462*
Chateauguay Valley Historical Society
  Annual Journal/Journal Annuel de la
  Societe Historique de la Vallee de la
  Chateauguay (CN) *604*
Chatfields Europaeisches Adressbuch
  fuer Anstrichmittel-und Verwandte
  Produkte *see* Chatfield's European
  Directory of Paints and Allied
  Products *855*
Chatfield's European Directory of
  Paints and Allied Products/Annuaire
  Chatfield European de Peintures et
  Produits Assimiles/Chatfields
  Europaeisches Adressbuch fuer
  Anstrichmittel-und Verwandte
  Produkte (UK) *855*
Chaucer Library (US) *718*
Chaukhambha Oriental Research
  Studies (II) *851*
Cheap Eats in Sydney (AT) *239*
Check Your Tax (UK) *293*
Checklist of Available Vermont State
  Publications *see* Checklist of
  Vermont State Publications *949*
Checklist of Basic American Legal
  Publications *see* Pimsleur's Checklist
  of Basic American Legal Publications
  669
Checklist of British Official Serial
  Publications (UK ISSN 0084-8085)
  687
Checklist of Canadian Theatres *see*
  Canadian Theatre Checklist *1149*
Checklist of Kentucky State
  Publications (US) *1150*
Checklist of Vermont State
  Publications(US) *949*
Checklists in the Humanities and
  Education (US ISSN 0069-2824)
  634
Checkpoint (Washington) (US) *989*,
  1068
Chefs-d'Oeuvre de la Galerie Nationale
  du Canada *see* Masterpieces in the
  National Gallery of Canada *107*
Chelmer Working Papers in
  Environmental Planning (UK ISSN
  0144-9877) *494*, *1007*
Chelsea (US ISSN 0009-2185) *718*
Chelsea Spelaeological Society.
  Records(UK ISSN 0309-409X) *385*
Cheltenham Ladies College Magazine
  (UK) *433*
Chem Sources - U.S.A. (US) *304*, *322*
Chemcyclopedia (US) *322*
Chemfacts: Belgium (UK) *322*
Chemfacts: Canada (UK) *322*
Chemfacts: Federal Republic of
  Germany (UK) *322*
Chemfacts: France (UK) *322*
Chemfacts: Italy (UK) *322*
Chemfacts: Japan (UK) *322*
Chemfacts: Netherlands (UK) *322*
Chemfacts: Scandinavia (UK) *1150*
Chemfacts: Spain (UK) *322*
Chemfacts: United Kingdom (UK) *322*
Chemia (PL ISSN 0554-8241) *322*
Chemical Abstracts Service Source
  Index (US ISSN 0001-0634) *3*,
  325
Chemical Analysis (US ISSN 0069-
  2883) *326*
Chemical Buyers Directory *see* O P D
  Chemical Buyers Directory *315*
Chemical Buyers Guide (CN ISSN
  0069-2891) *304*
Chemical Company Profiles: The
  Americas (UK) *322*
Chemical Engineering. Equipment
  Buyer's Guide Issue *see* Chemical
  Engineering Equipment Buyer's
  Guide *478*
Chemical Engineering Abstracts *see*
  Vegyipari Szakirodalmi Tajekoztato
  326
Chemical Engineering Abstracts (UK
  ISSN 0262-6438) *476*
Chemical Engineering Catalog (US
  ISSN 0276-8429) *478*

Chemical Engineering Equipment
  Buyer's Guide (US ISSN 0272-
  4057) *478*
Chemical Engineering Faculties (US)
  433, *478*
Chemical Engineering Faculties of
  Canada and the United States *see*
  Chemical Engineering Faculties *478*
Chemical Engineering Index *see*
  Process Engineering Index *477*
Chemical Engineering Monographs
  (NE) *478*
Chemical Engineering Progress. Safety
  in Air and Ammonia Plants *see*
  Ammonia Plant Safety and Related
  Facilities *477*
Chemical Engineering Progress
  Symposium Series *see* A I Ch E
  Symposium Series *477*
Chemical India Annual (II ISSN 0304-
  1166) *478*
Chemical Industries Series (US) *478*
Chemical Industry Directory (UK
  ISSN 0069-2980) *478*
Chemical Industry Institute of
  Toxicology Series (US ISSN 0278-
  6265) *494*, *635*, *953*
Chemical Industry of Americas *see*
  Chemical Company Profiles: The
  Americas *322*
Chemical Industry Year Book (UK)
  1150
Chemical Market Abstracts *see*
  Predicasts Overview of Markets and
  Technologies *477*
Chemical Plant Contractor Profiles
  (UK) *478*
Chemical Processing & Engineering: An
  International Series (US) *1150*
Chemical Reference Manual (US ISSN
  0094-6249) *322*
Chemical Regulation Reporter (US
  ISSN 0148-7973) *322*, *494*
Chemical Society. Annual Reports on
  the Progress of Chemistry. Section
  A: Physical and Inorganic Chemistry
  see Royal Society of Chemistry.
  Annual Reports on the Progress of
  Chemistry. Section A: Inorganic
  Chemistry *329*
Chemical Society, London. Annual
  Reports on the Progress of
  Chemistry. Section A: General,
  Physical and Inorganic Chemistry *see*
  Royal Society of Chemistry. Annual
  Reports on the Progress of
  Chemistry. Section A: Inorganic
  Chemistry *329*
Chemicals (UK) *322*
Chemicals and Allied Products Export
  Promotion Council. Exporters
  Directory (II ISSN 0531-5980) *254*,
  322
Chemicals: Latin American Industrial
  Report (US) *322*
Chemie der Erde/Geochemistry;
  Journal for Chemical Problems of the
  Geo-sciences and Extraterrestrial
  Mineralogy (GE ISSN 0009-2819)
  385
Chemie der Pflanzenschutz- und
  Schaedlingsbekaempfungsmittel (US)
  155
Chemie Mikrobiologie Technologie der
  Lebensmittel (GW ISSN 0366-7154)
  151, *168*
Chemie, Physik und Technologie der
  Kunststoffe in Einzeldarstellungen
  see Polymers-Properties and
  Applications *901*
Chemiekaarten (NE) *635*
ChemInform *see* Chemischer
  Informationsdienst *325*
Chemischer Informationsdienst (GW
  ISSN 0009-2975) *3*, *325*
Chemisches Zentralblatt *see*
  Chemischer Informationsdienst *325*
Chemist & Druggist Directory (UK
  ISSN 0262-5881) *870*
Chemist Catalogue (AT) *322*
Chemistry and Biochemistry of Amino
  Acids, Peptides, and Proteins (US
  ISSN 0069-3111) *151*
Chemistry and Pharmacology of Drugs
  (US) *322*, *870*
Chemistry and Physics of Carbon: A
  Series of Advances (US ISSN 0069-
  3138) *329*

Chemistry and Soil Research Institute.
  Annual Report (RH) *53*
Chemistry of Functional Groups (US
  ISSN 0069-3146) *322*
Chemistry of Heterocyclic Compounds
  (US ISSN 0069-3154) *329*
Chemistry of Natural Products (UK
  ISSN 0069-3162) *329*
Chemistry of Plant Protection (US)
  155, *322*
Chemists and Chemistry (NE) *133*,
  322
Chemists' Quarterly *see* Kimika *323*
Chemoreception Abstracts (US ISSN
  0300-1261) *3*, *325*
Chemsphere Americas (US) *1150*
Cherbourg Port Handbook (UK ISSN
  0268-649X) *304*, *1099*
Cherwell Guide to Oxford (UK) *1107*
Chesapeake Bay Foundation. Annual
  Report (US) *494*
Chesapeake Bay Journal *see*
  Chesapeake Bay Foundation. Annual
  Report *494*
Cheshire Archaeological Bulletin (UK
  ISSN 0307-6628) *84*
Cheshire Ornithological Association.
  Bird Report (UK ISSN 0262-7655)
  170
Chetham Society Publications-Remains,
  Historical and Literary, Connected
  with the Palatine Countries of
  Lancaster and Chester (UK ISSN
  0080-0880) *579*
Chewton Glen Hotel Magazine (UK)
  619
Chhandita (II ISSN 0009-3432) *718*
Chi e' Chi del Giornalismo dell'Auto
  (IT) *645*
Chi e Chi in Svizzera? *see* Swiss
  Biographical Index of Prominent
  Persons *135*
Chi e Dove (IT) *834*
Chiaka Chronika (GR) *84*, *515*, *579*,
  693
Chiao T'ung Yin Hang. Annual Report
  (CH) *226*
Chiaroscuro (US ISSN 0737-5182)
  1150
Chiasma (AT ISSN 0084-8735) *25*
Chiba Daigaku Engeigakubu Gakujutsu
  Hokoku *see* Chiba University.
  Faculty of Horticulture. Technical
  Bulletin *532*
Chiba University. Faculty of
  Horticulture. Technical Bulletin/
  Chiba Daigaku Engeigakubu
  Gakujutsu Hokoku (JA ISSN 0069-
  3227) *532*
Chicago Academy of Sciences. Bulletin
  (US ISSN 0009-3491) *989*
Chicago Architectural Journal (US) *97*
Chicago Area Transportation Study.
  Annual Report (US) *1081*
Chicago, Cook County and Illinois
  Industrial Directory (US ISSN 0069-
  3251) *304*
Chicago Geographic Directory (US
  ISSN 0748-8548) *304*
Chicago Geographic Edition *see*
  Chicago Geographic Directory *304*
Chicago History of American
  Civilization (US ISSN 0069-3278)
  604
Chicago History of American Religion
  (US) *968*
Chicago History of Science and
  Medicine (US ISSN 0073-2745)
  556, *759*
Chicago Lectures in Mathematics (US
  ISSN 0069-3286) *748*
Chicago Lectures in Physics (US ISSN
  0069-3294) *887*
Chicago Linguistic Society. Papers from
  the Regional Meetings (US ISSN
  0577-7240) *693*
Chicago M B A (US ISSN 0196-7525)
  192
Chicago Media Directory (US) *645*
Chicago Mercantile Exchange
  Yearbook(US ISSN 0577-7259) *254*
Chicago Renaissance (US) *718*, *884*
Chicago Unlimited, Inc. Directory *see*
  C U Directory *823*
Chicagoland Wedding Guide (US)
  1128
Chicano Law Review (US) *502*, *653*
Chicano Periodical Index (US ISSN
  0891-6985) *502*

Chicora Foundation Research Series
  (US ISSN 0882-2042) *84*
Chicorel Index Series (US) *125*
Chien d'Or/Golden Dog (CN ISSN
  0315-467X) *718*
Chigiana (IT ISSN 0069-3391) *834*
Chikusan Shikenjo, Ibaraki, Japan.
  Chikusan Shikenjo Kenkyu Hokoku.
  see National Institute of Animal
  Industry, Ibaraki, Japan. Bulletin *67*
Child and Family Policy (US) *411*
Child Behavior and Development (US
  ISSN 0193-7421) *787*, *789*, *933*
Child Care Handbook (US) *333*
Child Development Abstracts and
  Bibliography (US ISSN 0009-3939)
  3, *334*
Child Health and Development (SZ
  ISSN 0251-2467) *933*
Child in His Family *see* International
  Association for Child Psychiatry and
  Allied Professions. Yearbook *790*
Child Study Journal Monograph (US)
  333, *411*, *933*
Child Welfare League of America.
  Directory of Member And Associate
  Agencies Listing *see* Child Welfare
  League of America. Directory of
  Member And Associate Agencies
  1016
Child Welfare League of America.
  Directory of Member And Associate
  Agencies (US) *1016*
Childbirth (Year) (US) *785*
Childhood in Poetry (US) *333*, *334*,
  740
Children in Custody (US) *333*
Children Welcome! (UK ISSN 0069-
  3456) *1107*
Children's Authors and Illustrators (US)
  136, *739*
Children's Book Council, Inc. Features
  see C B C Features *960*
Children's Book International.
  Proceedings and Book Catalog *see*
  Children's Books International.
  Proceedings *335*
Children's Book Review Index (US) *3*,
  334
Children's Books and Recordings:
  Suggested as Holiday Gifts *see*
  Children's Books: One Hundred
  Titles for Reading and Sharing *961*
Children's Books: Awards and Prizes
  (US ISSN 0069-3472) *961*
Children's Books for Schools and
  Libraries *see* Children's Books in
  Print *739*
Children's Books in Print (UK ISSN
  0577-781X) *125*
Children's Books in Print (US ISSN
  0069-3480) *739*
Children's Books International.
  Proceedings (US ISSN 0163-1756)
  335
Children's Books of the Year (UK
  ISSN 0266-4232) *335*, *961*
Children's Books of the Year (Year)
  (US) *335*, *411*, *961*
Children's Books: One Hundred Titles
  for Reading and Sharing (US) *961*
Children's Catalog (US) *334*
Children's Language (US ISSN 0163-
  2809) *693*
Children's Literary Almanac *see*
  International Directory of Children's
  Literature *964*
Children's Literature (New Haven) (US
  ISSN 0092-8208) *718*
Children's Literature Abstracts (UK
  ISSN 0306-2015) *3*, *334*, *964*
Children's Literature Review (US ISSN
  0362-4145) *335*
Children's Literature Series (II) *335*,
  718
Children's Media Market Place (US
  ISSN 0734-8169) *283*
Chile. Centro de Documentacion
  Pedagogica. Bibliografia de la
  Educacion Chilena (CL) *423*
Chile. Direccion de Agricultura y
  Pesquera. Departamento Estadistica.
  Anuario Estadistico de Pesca. *see*
  Chile. Servicio Nacional de Pesca.
  Anuario Estadistico de Pesca *508*
Chile. Direccion de Bibliotecas
  Archivos y Museos. Bibliografia
  Chilena (CL ISSN 0716-176X) *125*

Chile. Direccion de Presupuestos. Calculo de Entradas de la Nacion (CL) *293*
Chile. Direccion de Presupuestos. Departamento de Estudios Financieros. Finanzas Publicas (CL) *293*
Chile. Direccion de Presupuestos. Exposicion sobre el Estado de la Hacienda Publica (CL) *293*
Chile. Direccion de Presupuestos. Instrucciones para la Ejecucion de la Ley de Presupuestos (CL) *293*
Chile. Direccion de Presupuestos. Ley de Presupuestos (CL) *293*
Chile. Instituto de Investigaciones Agropecuarias. Memoria Anual (CL) *25*
Chile. Instituto Nacional de Estadisticas. Anuario Estadistico see Chile. Instituto Nacional de Estadisticas. Series Estadisticas *1053*
Chile. Instituto Nacional de Estadisticas. Comercio Exterior (CL) *206, 254*
Chile. Instituto Nacional de Estadisticas. Compendio Estadistico (CL) *1053*
Chile. Instituto Nacional de Estadisticas. Estadisticas de Salud (CL) *958*
Chile. Instituto Nacional de Estadisticas. Indice de Precios al Consumidor (CL) *206*
Chile. Instituto Nacional de Estadisticas. Series Estadisticas (CL) *1053*
Chile. Oficina de Planificacion Nacional. Informe Economico Anual (CL) *1150*
Chile. Servicio Agricola y Ganadero. Division Proteccion Pesquera. Anuario Estadistico see Chile. Servicio Nacional de Pesca. Anuario Estadistico de Pesca *508*
Chile. Servicio Nacional de Geologia y Mineria. Boletin (CL ISSN 0020-3939) *385*
Chile. Servicio Nacional de Pesca. Anuario Estadistico de Pesca (CL) *508*
Chile. Superintendencia de Seguridad Social. Boletin de Estadisticas de Seguridad see Chile. Superintendencia de Seguridad Social. Seguridad Social: Estadisticas *638*
Chile. Superintendencia de Seguridad Social. Seguridad Social: Estadisticas (CL) *638*
Chilton's Auto Repair Manual (US ISSN 0069-3634) *1091*
Chilton's Import Automotive Repair Manual see Chilton's Import Car Repair Manual *1091*
Chilton's Import Car Repair Manual (US) *1091*
Chilton's Labor Guide and Parts Manual. Motor Age Professional Mechanics Edition (US ISSN 0749-5579) *1091*
Chilton's Motor Age Labor Guide and Parts Manual see Chilton's Labor Guide and Parts Manual. Motor Age Professional Mechanics Edition *1091*
Chilton's Motor-Age Professional Automotive Service Manual (US ISSN 0363-2393) *1091*
Chilton's Motor-Age Professional Labor Guide and Parts Manual see Chilton's Labor Guide and Parts Manual. Motor Age Professional Mechanics Edition *1091*
Chilton's Motorcycle Repair Manual (US) *1041*
Chilton's Truck and Van Repair Manual(US) *1091*
Chilton's Truck Repair Manual see Chilton's Truck and Van Repair Manual *1091*
Chimes (US ISSN 0009-4285) *341, 718*
Chimes (HK ISSN 0069-3642) *718*
Chin-Tan Society. Chin-Tan Hak-po (KO) *1007*
China Coal Industry Yearbook (HK ISSN 0258-3062) *815*

China Development Corporation. Annual Report (CH) *288*
China Directory (JA) *133, 940*
China Facts and Figures Annual (US ISSN 0190-602X) *568, 903, 1053*
China Glass and Tableware Red Book Directory (US ISSN 0069-3677) *320*
China Medical Board of New York. Annual Report (US ISSN 0069-3685) *759*
China Report: Economic Affairs (US) *192*
China Report: Political, Sociological, and Military Affairs (US) *810, 903, 1025*
China Report: Science and Technology (US) *989, 1068*
China, Republic. Central Geological Survey. Bulletin (CH) *385*
China, Republic. Directorate-General of Budget, Accounting and Statistics. Report on the Survey of Personal Income Distribution in Taiwan Area (CH) *277*
China, Republic. Export Processing Zone Administration. Exports of E P Z (CH) *254*
China, Republic. Geological Survey of Taiwan. Bulletin see China, Republic. Central Geological Survey. Bulletin *385*
China, Republic. Machinery and Electrical Apparatus Industry Yearbook/Chung-Hua Min Kuo Chi Chi Yu Tien Kung Chi Tsai Nien Chien (CH) *451, 745*
China, Republic. Mining Research and Service Organisation. M R S O Special Report (CH) *815*
China Rights Annals (US ISSN 8756-0844) *903, 913*
China Science & Technology Abstracts. Series 1: Mathematics, Astronomy, Physics (HK) *755*
China Stamp Catalogue (UK ISSN 0142-9892) *874*
China's Exports (HK) *254*
Chinese Art Society of America. Archives see Archives of Asian Art *101*
Chinese Culture Association, Magazine (US) *502*
Chinese-English Translation Assistance Group Bulletin see C E T A Bulletin *692*
Chinese Historical Society of America. Anniversary Bulletin (US) *502, 568*
Chinese Journal of Physiology (CH) *171, 759*
Chinese Journal of Psychology (CH) *933*
Chinese Science (US ISSN 0361-9001) *568, 851, 989*
Chinese Science Abstracts (CC) *3, 1003*
Chinese University of Hong Kong. Chung Chi College. Music Department. Holdings of the Chinese Music Archives (HK) *834*
Chinese University of Hong Kong. Institute of Chinese Studies. Journal (HK) *851*
Chiricu (US ISSN 0277-7223) *718*
Chiron (GW ISSN 0069-3715) *84*
Chiropractic History (US ISSN 0736-4377) *133, 556, 777*
Chishitsugaku Ronshu/Geological Society of Japan. Memoirs (JA ISSN 0385-8545) *385*
Chislennye Metody v Dinamike Razrezhennykh Gazov (UR) *894*
Chittagong Port Authority. Yearbook (BG) *1099*
Chittagong Port Trust. Yearbook of Information see Chittagong Port Authority. Yearbook *1099*
Chitty's Ontario Annual Practice see Ontario Annual Practice *661*
Choi Nenpo/Yearbook of Tidal Records(JA) *405*
Choice (Binghamton) (US) *103, 740*
Choices: a Core Collection for Young Reluctant Readers (US ISSN 0735-6358) *335*
Choir Director's Library (UR) *834*
Choix Jeunesse: Jeux et Jouets see Jeux et Jouets *553*

Chonguk Kiopche Chongnam/Directory of Korean Business (KO) *304*
Choosing Life (CN ISSN 0711-3048) *1150*
Chord and Discord (US ISSN 0069-3758) *433*
Der Chordirigent (GW ISSN 0009-5036) *834*
Chorherrenstift Klosterneuburg. Jahrbuch (AU) *579*
Chris van /Rensburg Publications (Pty) Ltd. Hotel Guide to Southern Africa see C V R Hotel Guide to Southern Africa *619*
Christian Brethren Review (UK ISSN 0263-466X) *981*
Christian Chamber of Commerce. Classified Membership Directory (US) *15, 235, 968*
Christian Chamber of Commerce. Membership Directory and Buyers Guide see Christian Chamber of Commerce. Classified Membership Directory *15*
Christian Democratic Study and Documentation Center. Cahiers d'Etudes (BE) *903*
Christian Directory (TH) *984*
Christian Endeavour Programme Book (UK) *984*
Christian Endeavour Topic Book see Christian Endeavour Programme Book *984*
Christian Family Chronicles (US ISSN 0197-0798) *535*
Christian Institute for Ethnic Studies in Asia. Bulletin (PH ISSN 0045-6810) *851, 968*
Christian Librarian (UK ISSN 0309-4170) *676, 961, 978*
Christian Literature (GR) *984*
Christian Periodical Index (US ISSN 0069-3871) *3, 975*
Christian Prisoners in the U.S.S.R. (US) *903, 968*
Christian Referdex (AT) *304*
Christian Research Institute. Newsletter see Christian Research Journal *968*
Christian Research Journal (US) *968*
Christian Science Monitor. Cumulated Index see Index to the Christian Science Monitor *647*
Christian Service Committee of the Churches in Malawi. Annual Report (MW) *969*
Christian Year (UK) *978*
Christmas: An American Annual of Christmas Literature and Art (US ISSN 0069-3928) *718*
Christ's College Magazine (UK) *433*
Chromatographic Science Series (US ISSN 0069-3936) *326*
Chromatography Symposia Series see Analytical Chemistry Symposia Series *326*
Chromosome Information Service see C I S *166*
Chronica Nova (SP) *579*
Chronicle Annual Vocational School Manual see Chronicle Vocational School Manual *428*
Chronicle Career Index (US ISSN 0276-0355) *847*
Chronicle Career Index Annual see Chronicle Career Index *847*
Chronicle College Chart see Chronicle Four-Year College Databook *428*
Chronicle College Charts see Chronicle Two-Year College Databook *428*
Chronicle College Counseling for Transfers see Chronicle Guide for Transfers *1150*
Chronicle Four-Year College Databook (US ISSN 0191-3670) *428*
Chronicle Guide for Transfers (US ISSN 0276-0363) *1150*
Chronicle Guide to Two-Year College Majors and Careers see Chronicle Two-Year College Databook *428*
Chronicle of International Events see Hronika Medjunarodnih Dogadjaja *916*
Chronicle of Parliamentary Elections see Chronicle of Parliamentary Elections and Developments *903*
Chronicle of Parliamentary Elections and Developments (SZ) *653, 903*

Chronicle of the Catholic Church in Lithuania (US ISSN 0197-0348) *502, 981*
Chronicle Student Aid Annual (US ISSN 0190-339X) *433*
Chronicle Two-Year College Databook (US ISSN 0191-3662) *428*
Chronicle Vocational School Manual (US ISSN 0276-0371) *428*
Chronico (GR) *710*
Chronika (IS) *502*
Chronika Aisthetikes see Annales d'Esthetique *101*
Chubu Institute of Technology. Bulletin see Chubu Institute of Technology. Memoirs *470*
Chubu Institute of Technology. Memoirs/Chubu Kogyo Daigaku. Kiyo (JA ISSN 0009-6202) *470, 1068*
Chubu Kogyo Daigaku. Kiyo see Chubu Institute of Technology. Memoirs *470*
Chuchoteries (CN ISSN 0316-599X) *446, 693*
Chung Chi Bulletin (HK ISSN 0009-6261) *341*
Chung Chi College Bulletin see Chung Chi Bulletin *341*
Chung-Hua Min Kuo Chi Chi Yu Tien Kung Chi Tsai Nien Chien see China, Republic. Machinery and Electrical Apparatus Industry Yearbook *451*
Chung-Hua Min Kuo Tai-Wan Sheng She Hui Shih Yeh Tung Chi see Social Affairs Statistics of Taiwan *1023*
Chung-Kuo Yin Hang. Annual Report see International Commercial Bank of China. Annual Report *229*
Chung Yang Yen Chiu Yuan. Chiu Tai Shih Yen Chiu So Chi K'an see Academia Sinica. Institute of Modern History. Bulletin *554*
Chuo Daigaku Rikogakubu Kiyo see Chuo University. Faculty of Science and Engineering. Bulletin *989*
Chuo University. Faculty of Science and Engineering. Bulletin/Chuo Daigaku Rikogakubu Kiyo (JA ISSN 0578-2228) *989, 1068*
Church Army. Front Line (UK) *978*
Church Monuments (UK ISSN 0268-7518) *97*
Church of England Yearbook (UK ISSN 0069-3987) *978*
Church of Scotland. Yearbook (UK ISSN 0069-3995) *978*
Church Pocket Book and Diary (UK) *969*
Churchman's Pocket Book and Diary see Church Pocket Book and Diary *969*
Churchscape (UK ISSN 0262-4966) *97, 103*
Ciba Collection of Medical Illustrations (US ISSN 0084-8786) *103, 759*
Ciceroniana (IT ISSN 0009-6687) *718*
Ciclo Vida y Obra (SP) *834*
Ciencia (BL ISSN 0084-8794) *989*
Ciencia Agropecuaria (PN) *25*
Ciencia Biologica: Biologia Molecular e Celular (PO) *174*
Ciencia Medica (SP ISSN 0212-6052) *759*
Ciencia y Tecnica en la Agricultura. Serie: Apicultura (CU) *26*
Ciencia y Tecnologia del Mar (CL) *405*
Ciencias Economicas (BL) *192*
Ciencias Socias Hoje (Year) (BL) *1007*
Ciencias Tecnicas Fisicas y Matematicas (CU ISSN 0253-7397) *989, 1068*
Cifras de Cuentas Nacionales (CR) *1053*
Cifras sobre Produccion Agropecuaria (CR) *45*
Cifras sobre Produccion Industrial (CR) *288*
Cimbebasia (SX) *71, 84*
Cimbebasia. Series A: Natural History (SX ISSN 0590-6342) *192*
Cimbebasia. Series B: Cultural History (SX) *1007*
Cimbebasia Memoirs (SX) *1007*
Cina (IT ISSN 0529-7451) *569*

Cincinnati. Division of Police. Annual Report (US ISSN 0091-8806) *370*
Cincinnati Art Museum. Bulletin (US ISSN 0069-4061) *827*
Cincinnati Classical Studies. New Series(NE) *337*
Cincinnati Journal of Ceremonial Magic *see* Cincinnati Journal of Magic *877*
Cincinnati Journal of Magic (US) 860, *877*
Cine Club del Uruguay. Cuadernos (UY ISSN 0069-4118) *823*
CineFan (US ISSN 0277-5891) *823*
Cineguia (SP ISSN 0069-4134) 347, *823*, *1076*
Cinema (SZ) *823*
Cinema and Society (UK) *823*, *1076*
Cinema e Societa (IT ISSN 0009-7152) *823*
Cinema Francais Production (FR ISSN 0292-7292) *823*
Cinema Papers Yearbook (AT ISSN 0158-698X) *823*
Cinema Preview (UK) *823*
Cinemacabre (US ISSN 0198-1064) *823*
Cinematograph (US ISSN 0886-6570) *823*
Cinematograph (US ISSN 0886-6570) *823*
Cinemonkey (US ISSN 0162-0126) *823*
Cinmay Smrti Pathagara (II) 103, *718*
Circe (FR ISSN 0069-4177) *718*
Circle (US) *740*
Circles of Friends (US) *1150*
Circlets (US) *740*
Circolo Culturale B.G. Duns Scoto di Roccarainola. Atti (IT ISSN 0392-9884) 84, *539*
Circular C I A T (Centro de Investigaciones Agricolas de Tamaulipas) (MX ISSN 0084-8689) *26*
Circulation *see* American Newspaper Markets Circulation *645*
Circulation Auditing Around the World(US) *221*
Circulation Data and Marketing Data *see* Oplagstal og Markedstal *16*
Circulo (IT ISSN 0009-7349) *629*
Circulo Poetico (US) *740*
Cirencester Excavations (UK) 84, *579*
Ciret Studien (GW ISSN 0170-5679) *192*
Citizens' Business (US ISSN 0009-756X) *950*
Citizens Committee on Human Rights Newsletter *see* C C H R Newsletter *789*
Citizens' Governmental Research Bureau Bulletin *see* C G R B Bulletin *950*
Citizen's Guide to Local Government (US) *940*
Citizen's Guide to School District Budgeting (US) *442*
Citizens Union Foundation. Occasional Paper Series (US) *950*
Citizens Union Research Foundation. Occasional Paper Studies *see* Citizens Union Foundation. Occasional Paper Series *950*
Citrus Engineering Conference. Transactions (US ISSN 0412-6300) *53*
City and Society (US) *1025*
City College Papers (US ISSN 0077-894X) *1150*
City Directory (UK ISSN 0308-9088) *265*
City Employment *see* Current Governments Reports: City Employment *206*
City Handbook (UK ISSN 0260-9290) 304, *1099*
City Lights Anthology (US) *718*
City Lights Journal (US) *718*
City Manager Yearbook *see* Municipal Year Book *951*
City of Birmingham Directory of Industry & Commerce (UK ISSN 0266-9064) *304*
City of Birmingham Symphony Orchestra. Annual Prospectus (UK) *834*
City of Birmingham Symphony Orchestra. Prom Prospectus (UK) *834*

City of London Directory & Livery Companies Guide (UK ISSN 0142-5072) *304*
City of London School Chronicle (UK) *411*
City of Ottawa. Corporate Financial and Statistical Information (CN ISSN 0831-7496) *293*
City of Ottawa. Financial and Other Statistics *see* City of Ottawa. Corporate Financial and Statistical Information *293*
City of Perth. Annual Report *see* City of Perth. Lord Mayor's Report *950*
City of Perth. Lord Mayor's Report (AT) *950*
City of Westminster Chamber of Commerce Directory *see* Westminster Chamber of Commerce Directory *237*
City Sparrows (UK) *333*
Cityguide - The San Francisco Bay Area and Northern California (US ISSN 0277-0342) *1107*
Civetta (IT) *103*
Civic Trust Awards (UK) 97, 182, *494*
Civica Stazione Idrobiologica di Milano. Quaderni (IT) *139*
Civil Engineering Advisory Council. Annual Report/Siviele Ingenieurswese-Adviesraad. Jaarverslag (SA) *480*
Civil Engineering Hydraulics Abstracts (UK ISSN 0305-9456) 3, *476*
Civil Engineering in Japan (JA ISSN 0578-3747) *480*
Civil Engineering Report Series *see* Water Resources Report Series *1127*
Civil Engineering Series (US) *480*
Civil Engineering Working Papers (AT ISSN 0578-2126) *480*
Civil Procedure *see* B A R - B R I Bar Review. Civil Procedure *651*
Civil Rights in Michigan *see* Michigan. Civil Rights Commission. Annual Report *913*
Civil Service Digest *see* Public Employees Journal *945*
Civil Service News (US) *940*
Civil Service News Releases *see* Civil Service News *940*
Civil Service Year Book (UK ISSN 0302-329X) *940*
Civil War Collectors' Dealer Directory (US ISSN 0094-1182) 79, *810*
Civilian Congress (US) 653, 810, 903, *1025*
Civilisation Malgache (FR ISSN 0578-3917) *71*
Civilisations et Societes (GW ISSN 0069-4290) *1007*
Civilization and Society: Studies in Social, Economic and Cultural History (US) 556, *1007*
Civilization of the American Indian (US ISSN 0069-4304) *604*
Civilta Asiatiche (IT ISSN 0069-4312) *569*
Civilta Veneziana. Dizionari Dialettali e Studi Linguistici (IT ISSN 0069-4339) *693*
Civilta Veneziana. Fonti e Testi. Serie Prima: Fonti e Testi per la Storia dell'Arte Veneta (IT ISSN 0069-4355) 103, *579*
Civilta Veneziana. Fonti e Testi. Serie Terza (IT ISSN 0069-4347) *579*
Civilta Veneziana. Saggi (IT ISSN 0069-4371) *579*
Civilta Veneziana. Studi (IT ISSN 0069-438X) *579*
Clairlieu: Tijdschrift gewijd aan de Geschiedenis der Kruisheren (BE) 556, *969*
Clan MacDonald Annual (CN) *433*
Claremont Reading Conference. Yearbook (US) *446*
Claretianum (VC ISSN 0578-4182) *981*
Clark County History (US ISSN 0090-449X) *604*
Clark University (Worcester, Mass.) Dissertations and Theses *see* Clark University Bulletin (Worcester, Mass.) *423*
Clark University Bulletin (Worcester, Mass.) (US) *423*

Clarke Institute of Psychiatry. Monograph Series (CN ISSN 0069-441X) *789*
Clark's Directory of Southern Hospitals(US) *616*
Clark's Directory of Southern Textile Mills (US) *1073*
Clasicos Colombianos (CK ISSN 0069-4444) *717*
Class, State and Development (US) *903*
Classic (SA) 710, *718*
Classica (PO ISSN 0870-0141) *337*
Classica et Mediaevalia (DK ISSN 0106-5815) *337*
Classical Antiquity (US ISSN 0278-6656) *337*
Classical Association. Proceedings (UK ISSN 0069-4460) 556, *718*
Classical Association of New England. Annual Bulletin (US) *337*
Classici Italiani Minori (IT) *718*
Classics in Anthropology (US ISSN 0069-4487) *71*
Classics in Psychoanalysis (US) *933*
Classics of British Historical Literature (US ISSN 0069-4509) 579, *718*
Classification Management (US ISSN 0009-8434) *279*
Classified Directory of Dahlias and Guide to Judging (UK) *532*
Classified Directory of Wisconsin Manufacturers (US ISSN 0069-4525) *304*
Classified International Business Directory for China (HK) *304*
Classified Roll of the State School Teachers in the Secondary Schools Division *see* Victoria. Classified Roll of Postprimary State School Teachers *421*
Classiques de la Pensee Politique (SZ ISSN 0069-4533) *903*
Clavis Kleine Kunsthistorische Monografieen (NE) *103*
Clavis Kunsthistorische Monografieen (NE) *103*
Clay Resources Bulletin (US ISSN 0069-4592) *815*
Clean Air Conference (Gt. Brit.) (UK ISSN 0301-9039) *494*
Clematis (AT) *989*
Clements' Encyclopedia of World Governments (US ISSN 0145-9686) *915*
Clemson University. College of Architecture. Semester Review (US ISSN 0009-871X) 97, *103*
Clemson University. Department of Forestry. Forest Research Series (US) *524*
Clemson University. Department of Forestry. Forestry Bulletin (US ISSN 0093-0083) *524*
Clemson University. Department of Forestry. Technical Paper (US) *524*
Clemson University. Water Resources Research Institute. Report (US ISSN 0069-4657) *1124*
Clergy's Federal Income Tax Guide *see* Abingdon Clergy Income Tax Guide *292*
Cleveland Electrical/Electronics Conference and Exposition. Conference Record (US ISSN 0278-7024) *451*
Cleveland Foundation Perspective *see* Perspective. Cleveland Foundation Occasional Paper *1020*
Cleveland Public Library Staff Association. News and Views (US ISSN 0009-885X) *676*
Client Counseling Update (US ISSN 0276-752X) *653*
Climatological Data for Jakarta Observatory (IO ISSN 0009-8957) *803*
Clin-Alert (US ISSN 0069-4770) 3, *873*
Clinica Neuropsichiatrica (IT) *789*
Clinical and Biochemical Analysis (US ISSN 0095-4861) 151, 326, *579*
Clinical and Experimental Hypertension *see* Clinical and Experimental Hypertension. Part A: Theory and Practice *759*
Clinical and Experimental Hypertension. Part A: Theory and Practice (US ISSN 0730-0077) *759*

Clinical and Experimental Neurology (AT ISSN 0158-1597) *789*
Clinical Biochemistry (US) *151*
Clinical Biochemistry Reviews *see* Annual Review of Clinical Biochemistry *151*
Clinical Biomechanics (US ISSN 0191-7870) *759*
Clinical Cardiology Monographs (US) *776*
Clinical Engineering Series (US) *759*
Clinical Immunobiology (US) 139, *773*
Clinical Infant Reports. Monograph (US) *789*
Clinical Laboratory Reference (US ISSN 0093-8076) 636, *781*
Clinical Monographs in Obstetrics and Gynecology (US) *785*
Clinical Neuropharmacology (US ISSN 0362-5664) *870*
Clinical Neurosurgery; Proceedings (US ISSN 0069-4827) 789, *794*
Clinical Perspectives in Obstetrics and Gynecology (US) *785*
Clinical Practice in Urology (US) *795*
Clinical Sociology Review (US) *1025*
Clinical Topics in Infectious Disease (US) 759, *777*
Clinics in Developmental Medicine (UK ISSN 0069-4835) 787, *789*
Clinton Historical Society. Newsletter (US) *604*
Clio (GW) 759, *1128*
Clio (Lisbon) (PO ISSN 0870-4104) *579*
Clio Bibliography Series (US) 563, *634*
Clio Historical Periodicals Directory (US) *556*
Clio Periodicals Directory *see* Clio Historical Periodicals Directory *556*
Clipper Studies in the American Theater (US ISSN 0748-237X) 718, *1076*
Clivages (FR) *740*
Clothing and Footwear Institute Year Book and Membership Register (UK) 340, *1005*
Clothing Institute Year Book and Membership Register *see* Clothing and Footwear Institute Year Book and Membership Register *340*
Club Cricket Conference Official Handbook (UK) *1038*
Clydesdale Bank Scottish Football League Review (UK ISSN 0260-8804) *1038*
Clydesdale Stud Book (UK) *1042*
Coach Tours in Britain and Ireland *see* Luxury Coach Tours in Britain & Europe *1112*
Coaches & Parties Welcome (UK) *1107*
Coal Abstracts (UK ISSN 0309-4979) 815, *822*
Coal Data (US ISSN 0145-417X) *815*
Coal Facts (US) *815*
Coal in Canada, Supply and Demand *see* Statistical Review of Coal in Canada *820*
Coal-Pennsylvania Anthracite *see* Coal Production (Year) *815*
Coal Production (Year) (US) *815*
Coal Production Annual *see* Coal Production (Year) *815*
Coal Research Projects (UK) *815*
Coal Research Projects. Coal Research Database *see* Coal Research Projects *815*
Coal Traffic Annual (US ISSN 0069-4916) *815*
Coast Marine and Transportation Directory (US) *1099*
Coastal Engineering in Japan (JA ISSN 0578-5634) *480*
Coastal Engineering Research Council. Proceedings (US) 405, *480*
Coastal Society. Annual Conference. Proceedings (US) *139*
Coates's Herd Book (Beef) (UK ISSN 0069-4924) *65*
Coates's Herd Book (Dairy) (UK ISSN 0069-4932) *62*
Coburger Landesstiftung. Jahrbuch (GW ISSN 0084-8808) *579*
Cockpit *see* New Jersey Instructional Series *1159*
Cocoa Research Institute. Annual Report (GH ISSN 0300-1385) *518*

COCOS

Cocos (CE) 26
Code Name Directory (US) 676
Code of Maryland Regulations (US) 653, 940
Codes Larcier (BE ISSN 0010-0188) 653
Codex Bandito (UK) 1150
Codex Committee on Pesticide Residues. Report on the Meeting see Pesticide Residues in Food 955
Codice del Vaticano II (IT) 981
Codices Arabici Antiqui (GW ISSN 0340-6393) 851
Codices Manuscripti, Bibliotheca Universitatis Leidensis (NE) 718
Coe Review (US) 718
Coffee Annual (US) 119
Coffee Board of Kenya. Annual Report, Balance Sheet and Accounts (KE) 518
Coffee International Directory (UK ISSN 0264-5378) 518
Cognition and Computing (US) 356
Cognition and Literacy (US) 411, 933
Cognitive Science Series (Cambridge) (US ISSN 0732-1295) 933
Cognitive Science Series (Hillsdale) (US) 933
Coin Hoards (UK ISSN 0140-1149) 844
COIN: Indexed Checklist to Colorado State Publications see Index to Colorado State Publications 127
Coin World Almanac (US ISSN 0361-0845) 844
Coin Yearbook (UK ISSN 0307-6571) 844
Coins Market Values (UK ISSN 0069-4983) 844
Coke Oven Managers' Association. Year Book (UK ISSN 0069-4991) 797, 815
Cold-Drill (US ISSN 0084-8816) 718
Cold Spring Harbor Laboratory. Abstracts of Papers Presented at Meetings (US ISSN 0084-8824) 139
Cold Spring Harbor Laboratory. Annual Report (US ISSN 0069-5009) 139
Cold Spring Harbor Laboratory. Symposia on Quantitative Biology (US ISSN 0091-7451) 139
Cold Spring Harbor Monograph Series (US ISSN 0270-1847) 139
Cold Spring Harbor Reports in the Neurosciences (US ISSN 0276-4695) 1150
Colecao Arquivos de Folclore (BL) 515
Colecao C E D E S. Grandes Temas (Camara de Estudos e Debates Economicos e Sociais) (BL) 26
Colecao Caminhos Brasileiros (BL) 903
Colecao Cinema (BL) 823
Colecao Cultura Brasileira (BL) 515
Colecao de Estudos Bibliograficos (BL) 125
Colecao de Estudos Filologicos (BL ISSN 0587-6435) 693
Colecao de Estudos Historicos (BL) 604
Colecao de Estudos Juridicos (BL ISSN 0530-0657) 654
Colecao Economia (BL) 242
Colecao Ecumenismo e Humanismo (BL) 877
Colecao em Cima do Fato (BL) 242
Colecao Encanto Radical (BL) 710
Colecao Escritores Brasileiros (BL) 718
Colecao Fe e Realidade (BL) 981
Colecao Jornalismo Catarinense (BL) 645
Colecao Polemicas do Nosso Tiempo (BL) 710
Colecao Primeiros Passos (BL) 710
Colecao Teatro (BL) 1076
Colecao Temas Brasileiros (BL) 604
Colecao Tendencias (BL) 903
Colecao Tirando de Letra (BL) 718
Coleccao Arquivos (PO) 579
Coleccao Ensaio (PO) 718
Coleccao Forma (PO) 740
Coleccao Horizonte Universitario (PO) 192, 903
Coleccao Literatura (PO) 718
Coleccao N'gola (AO) 565, 710
Coleccao: Poesia (Lisbon) (PO) 740
Coleccao Poesia (Porto) (PO) 740
Coleccion Amanece (AG) 969
Coleccion "Aniversarios Culturales" (VE ISSN 0069-5033) 133
Coleccion Antropologia e Historia (ES) 71
Coleccion Aragon (SP) 579
Coleccion Arquitectura/Perspectivas (SP) 97
Coleccion Arquitectura y Critica (SP) 97
Coleccion "Bahia" (SP) 740
Coleccion Canonica (SP ISSN 0069-505X) 981
Coleccion Cien Temas Basicos (UY) 903
Coleccion Ciencia Urbanistica (SP ISSN 0069-5068) 97, 622
Coleccion Ciencias Biologicas (SP) 139
Coleccion Ciencias, Humanidades e Ingenieria (SP) 989
Coleccion Ciencias Medicas de Bolsillo (SP) 759
Coleccion Comunicacion (CK) 969
Coleccion Comunicacion Visual (SP) 343
Coleccion Correspondencia Diplomatica de los Nuncios en Espana (SP) 579
Coleccion Cuadernos CEDAL (CR) 903
Coleccion Cuadernos de Trabajo Social (SP) 1016
Coleccion de Economia (SP) 251
Coleccion Debate (ES) 903
Coleccion Direccion de Empresas y Organizaciones (SP) 279
Coleccion: Documentos e Historia de la Ciencia en Colombia (SP) 989
Coleccion Editorial Universitaria (GT) 378
Coleccion Ensayos (AG) 710
Coleccion Estructuras y Formas (SP ISSN 0071-1632) 97
Coleccion Estudios Latinoamericanos (AG) 604, 718
Coleccion Estudios Politicos (DR) 903
Coleccion Ethos-Arte (SP) 103, 834
Coleccion Fe e Historia (CL) 1007
Coleccion Filosofica (SP ISSN 0069-5076) 877
Coleccion "Foros y Seminarios." Serie Foros (VE ISSN 0069-5084) 604
Coleccion "Foros y Seminarios." Serie Seminarios (VE ISSN 0069-5092) 604
Coleccion Fundacion F O E S S A. Serie Estudios (Fundacion Fomento de Estudios Sociales y Sociologia Aplicada) (SP) 1025
Coleccion Historia (PY) 604
Coleccion Historia de la Iglesia (SP) 981
Coleccion Historica (SP ISSN 0069-5106) 579
Coleccion "Humanism y Ciencia" (VE ISSN 0069-5114) 629
Coleccion Iberica (SP) 903
Coleccion Ingenieria (SP) 470
Coleccion Juridica (SP ISSN 0069-5122) 654
Coleccion Jurisprudencia y Textos Legales (SP) 654
Coleccion la Alquitrana (VE) 863
Coleccion la Empresa y Su Entorno. Serie A C (SP) 279
Coleccion la Empresa y su Entorno. Serie L (SP) 279
Coleccion Libro de Bolsillo. Serie Ensayo (MX) 710
Coleccion Libros de Enfermeria (SP) 783
Coleccion Libros de Medicina (SP) 759
Coleccion Linguistica Indigena (MX) 693
Coleccion Literatura (PY) 719
Coleccion Manuales de Finanzas Publicas (DR) 293
Coleccion Medicina see Coleccion Libros de Medicina 759
Coleccion Miguel Salguero (CR) 502, 719
Coleccion Monografias Politicas (VE) 903
Coleccion Mundo Antiguo (SP ISSN 0077-2054) 556
Coleccion Oriente-Occidente (AG) 851
Coleccion Pentesilea (SP) 741
Coleccion Poesia del Nuevo Tiempo (AG) 741
Coleccion Popular de Literatura Nicaraguense. Documentos (NQ) 719
Coleccion Primero de Mayo (SP) 648
Coleccion Senda Abierta. Serie 2 (Azul): Judaismo (SP) 976
Coleccion Signo y Sociedad (MX) 741
Coleccion Tablero (SP) 192
Coleccion Tecnologia y Sociedad (SP) 1068
Coleccion Temas Basicos de Ingenieria (SP) 470
Coleccion Temas de Ahorro y Credito (SP) 1150
Coleccion Temas de Arquitectura Actual (SP ISSN 0082-2701) 97
Coleccion Teologica (SP) 981
Coleccion Textos Legislativos (VE) 654
Coleccion Viera y Clavijo (SP) 903
Coleccindina Mica y Siembra (VE) 133
Colecciones Basicas C I N T E R F O R (Centro Interamericano de Investigacion y Documentacion Sobre Formacion Profesional) (UY) 426
Colectanea de Jurisprudencia Canonica (SP ISSN 0210-0711) 969
Colega Agropecuario (CK) 65
Colegio de Ingenieros de Venezuela. Directorio (VE) 470
Colegio Mayor P. Felipe Scio. Publicaciones (SP) 981
Colegio Militar do Rio de Janeiro. Revista Didactica (BL ISSN 0080-3103) 411
Colfeian (UK ISSN 0010-0676) 341
Colimpex Agricultural Execupad (SA) 26
Colimpex Architect's Execupad (SA) 97
Colimpex Electrical Execupad (SA) 451
Colimpex Insurance Brokers Execupad (SA) 638
Colimpex Medical Execupad (SA) 759
Colimpex Mining Execupad (SA) 815
Colimpex Paediatric Execuped (SA) 783
Collana Corpus Antiquitatum Americanensium Italia (IT) 84
Collana Corpus Vasorum Antiquorum Italia (IT) 85
Collana del Teatro di Roma (IT) 1076
Collana di Cultura (IT ISSN 0069-5165) 719
Collana di Documenti in Memoria del Conte Giuseppe Matarazzo di Licosa(IT) 579
Collana di Poesia (IT) 741
Collana di Storia Moderna e Contemporanea (IT ISSN 0391-3279) 579
Collana di Studi e Documentazione (IT) 304
Collana di Studi e Saggi (IT ISSN 0069-5203) 719
Collana di Studi in Memoria del Conte Giuseppe Matarazzo di Licosa (IT) 579
Collana di Studi Paletnologici (IT) 71, 85
Collana di Studi Su Problemi Urbanistici Fiorentino (IT) 622
Collana di Testi e di Critica (IT) 719
Collana Ricciana. Fonti (IT ISSN 0069-5254) 981
Collation see Annual Report of Advocacy for Nursing Home Reform 616
Colleccio de Materials (SP) 103
Collecion Poliedro (SP) 719
Colleccion Vortex (US ISSN 0277-6782) 741
Collect Birds on Stamps (UK) 874
Collect Channel Islands and Isle of Man Stamps (UK) 874
Collect Channel Islands Stamps see Collect Channel Islands and Isle of Man Stamps 874
Collectanea Botanica (SP ISSN 0010-0730) 155
Collectanea Cartesiana see Analecta Cartesiana 876
Collectanea Historiae Musicae (IT ISSN 0069-5270) 834
Collectanea Instituti Anthropos (GW) 71
Collected Papers from the Journal of the Royal Society of New Zealand (NZ ISSN 0112-2479) 989
Collected Papers of the Annual Meeting, Southeast Regional Group, American Accounting Association see American Accounting Association. Southeast Regional Group. Collected Papers of the Annual Meeting 220
Collected Papers on Sciences of Atmosphere and Hydrosphere (JA ISSN 0547-1435) 379
Collected Papers on South Asia (UK ISSN 0141-0156) 851
Collected Works of Erasmus (CN) 629, 877
Collected Works on Cardio-Pulmonary Disease (US ISSN 0069-5319) 776
Collection: Artistes Canadiens see Canadian Artists Series 103
Collection Ca-Cinema (FR) 823
Collection "Chants des Peuples" (FR) 719
Collection d'Etudes Musicologiques see Sammlung Musikwissenschaftlicher Abhandlungen 841
Collection d'Histoire Contemporaine (FR ISSN 0069-5343) 556
Collection E F G (Economie-Formation-Gestion) (FR) 279
Collection Formation des Enseignants see Collection Formation des Enseignants et Formation Continue 748
Collection Formation des Enseignants et Formation Continue (FR) 748
Collection Franco-Judaica (FR) 502, 976
Collection Knowledge & Technique: Youth (FR) 335
Collection l'Etat et le Citoyen see Repertoire Administratif 908
Collection Lignes Quebecoises (CN) 710
Collection Lignes Quebecoises. Textuelles see Collection Lignes Quebecoises 710
Collection of Australian Stamps (AT ISSN 0727-4211) 573, 874
Collection of Documents for the Study of International Non-Governmental Relations (BE ISSN 0503-2407) 670
Collection of Works and Documents Illustrating the History of Paper see Monumenta Chartae Papyraceae Historiam Illustrantia 858
Collection Oralites-Documents (FR ISSN 0220-746X) 693
Collection Philosophica (CN) 877
Collection Psychologie et Pedagogie de la Musique (FR) 834, 933
Collection Radiographie du Capital - les Liaisons Financieres (FR) 226
Collection Vietnamienne (BE) 719
Collective Agreement Expiration in Nova Scotia (CN ISSN 0229-4958) 1150
Collective Bargaining in Higher Education and the Professions. Annual Bibliography (US ISSN 0738-1913) 433, 648
Collectors' Auction (Baltimore) see Harris Auction Galleries. Collectors' Auction 827
College Admissions Data see College Admissions Data Handbook 433
College Admissions Data Handbook (US) 433
College Admissions Data Service see College Admissions Data Handbook 433
College Alumni Publications (US) 125, 342
College and Adult Reading (US) 426
College and Pro Football Guide see Football Guide 1038
College and University Administrators Directory (US ISSN 0195-3990) 433
College and University Admissions and Enrollment, New York State (US ISSN 0147-5894) 433
College and University Computer Directory: Facilities and Personnel (US) 427

College and University Degrees Conferred, New York State (US ISSN 0077-9172) 433
College and University Employees, New York State (US ISSN 0093-3414) 433
College and University Enrollment in New York State see College and University Admissions and Enrollment, New York State 433
College Art Association Monographs see Monographs on the Fine Arts 107
College Blue Book (US ISSN 0069-5572) 428
College de France. Annuaire (FR ISSN 0069-5580) 433
College de France. Institut des Hautes Etudes Chinoises. Memoirs (FR) 851
College des Medecins et Chirurgiens de la Province de Quebec. Bulletin see Corporation Professionnelle des Medecins du Quebec. Bulletin 759
College Facts Chart (US ISSN 0069-5688) 428
College Football Yearbook (US ISSN 0733-2823) 1038
College Grants from Uncle Sam (US) 433
College - Industry Education Conference. Proceedings (US) 433, 470
College Loans from Uncle Sam (US) 433
College Media Director Newsletter (CN ISSN 0706-5000) 411, 446
College Music Symposium (US ISSN 0069-5696) 834
College of Dairy Agriculture, Hokkaido. Journal see College of Dairying. Journal; Cultural and Social Sciences 26
College of Dairy Agriculture, Hokkaido. Journal see College of Dairying. Journal; Natural Science 62
College of Dairying. Journal; Cultural and Social Sciences/Rakuno Gakuen Daigaku Kiyo, Jinbun Shakaikagaku Hen (JA ISSN 0388-0028) 26, 45, 719
College of Dairying. Journal; Natural Science/Rakuno Gakuen Daigaku Kiyo, Shizen Kagaku Hen (JA ISSN 0388-001X) 62
College of Engineering, Trivandrum. Magazine (II) 470
College of Insurance. General Bulletin (US ISSN 0069-5718) 639
College of Librarianship Wales Serials in C L W Library see Serials in C L W Library 131
College of Physicians and Surgeons of British Columbia. Annual Report (CN) 759
College of Physicians and Surgeons of British Columbia. Medical Directory (CN ISSN 0069-5726) 759
College of Textile Technology, Serampore Annual see C.T.T.S. Annual 1073
College Placement Annual see C P C Annual 847
College Placement Council, Inc. Annual see C P C Annual 847
College Planning/Search Book (US) 847
College Reading Association. Monographs (US) 687
College Recruiting Report (US ISSN 0361-5057) 270
College Student Personnel Abstracts see Higher Education Abstracts 435
College Transfer Guide (US) 428
Colleges and Universities Granting Degrees in Microbiology (US) 168, 428
Colleges and Universities with Accredited Undergraduate Social Work Programs (US) 433, 1016
Collegium Carolinum. Bohemia-Jahrbuch see Bohemia: Zeitschrift fuer Geschichte und Kultur der Boehmischen Laender 578
Collegium Carolinum. Veroeffentlichungen (GW ISSN 0530-9794) 579
Collegium Musicum: Yale University (US ISSN 0147-0108) 834

Collegium Philosophicum Jenense (GE) 877
Collezioni e Musei Archeologici del Veneto (IT ISSN 0392-0879) 85
Collier's Yearbook (US ISSN 0069-5793) 462
Colloid Science (UK ISSN 0305-9723) 331
Colloque de Metallurgie (FR ISSN 0069-5807) 797
Colloques Economiques (SZ) 192
Colloques Internationaux d'Histoire Maritime. Travaux (FR ISSN 0069-5815) 1099
Colloques Phytosociologiques (GW) 155
Colloquia in Anthropology (US ISSN 0146-4167) 71
Colloquim Series on Transportation. Proceedings see University of Manitoba. Center for Transportation Studies. Seminar Series on Transportation. Proceedings 1084
Colloquium Geographicum (GW ISSN 0588-3253) 542
Colloquium Mathematicum (PL ISSN 0010-1354) 748
Colloquium Mosbach (US ISSN 0366-5887) 151
Colloquium on Hispanic Linguistics. Proceedings (US) 693
Colloquium on Scottish Studies. Proceedings see Scottish Tradition 596
Colloquium on the History of Landscape Architecture. Papers (US) 97
Colloquium on the Law of Outer Space. Proceedings (US ISSN 0069-5831) 18, 670
Colombia. Corporacion Nacional de Turismo. Boletin de Estadistica Turistica. (Year) (CK) 1119
Colombia. Corporacion Nacional de Turismo. Boletin de Investigaciones e Informacion Turistica see Colombia. Corporacion Nacional de Turismo. Boletin de Estadistica Turistica. (Year) 1119
Colombia. Departamento Administrativo Nacional de Estadistica. Anuario Demografico (CK) 921, 926
Colombia. Departamento Administrativo Nacional de Estadistica. Anuario de Comercio Exterior (CK) 254
Colombia. Departamento Administrativo Nacional de Estadistica. Anuario de Estadisticas Fiscales y Financieras (CK) 206
Colombia. Departamento Administrativo Nacional de Estadistica. Anuario de Estadisticas Industriales (CK) 288
Colombia. Departamento Administrativo Nacional de Estadistica. Anuario de Justicia (CK) 1053
Colombia. Departamento Administrativo Nacional de Estadistica. Anuario General de Estadistica - Justicia see Colombia. Departamento Administrativo Nacional de Estadistica. Anuario de Justicia 1053
Colombia. Departamento Administrativo Nacional de Estadistica. Division Politico-Administrativa (CK) 940
Colombia. Departamento Administrativo Nacional de Estadistica. Estadisticas Historicas (CK) 1053
Colombia. Departamento Administrativo Nacional de Estadistica. Industria Manufacturera Nacional see Colombia. Departamento Administrativo Nacional de Estadistica. Anuario de Estadisticas Industriales 288
Colombia. Direccion General del Presupuesto. Proyecto de Presupuesto(CK) 294
Colombia. Ministerio de Educacion Nacional. Educacion para Desarrollo (CK) 411

Colombia. Ministerio de Minas y Energia. Memoria al Congreso de la Republica (CK) 385
Colombia. Ministerio de Minas y Petroleos. Informe see Colombia. Ministerio de Minas y Energia. Memoria al Congreso de la Republica 385
Colombia. Ministerio de Trabajo, Higiene y Prevision Social. Memoria see Colombia. Ministerio de Trabajo y Seguridad Social. Memoria 270
Colombia. Ministerio de Trabajo y Seguridad Social. Memoria (CK) 270, 639
Colombia. Observatorio Astronomico Nacional. Anuario (CK ISSN 0120-2758) 115
Colombia. Observatorio Astronomico Nacional. Publicaciones (CK ISSN 0067-9518) 115
Colombia. Superintendencia Bancaria. Informe de Labores (CK) 226
Colombia. Superintendencia Bancaria. Seguros y Capitalizacion (CK) 192, 639
Colombian Economy (CK) 277
Colombo Law Review (CE ISSN 0069-5939) 654
Colombo Observatory. Report (CE) 115
Colombo Plan Bureau. Technical Cooperation Under the Colombo Plan. Report see Colombo Plan Bureau. The Colombo Plan Council Report 261
Colombo Plan Bureau. The Colombo Plan Council Report (CE) 261
Colombo Plan for Co-operative Economic and Social Development in Asia and the Pacific. Consultative Committee. Proceedings and Conclusions (CE) 261
Colombo Plan for Co-operative Economic and Social Development in Asia and the Pacific. Consultative Committee. Report see Colombo Plan for Co-operative Economic and Social Development in Asia and the Pacific. Consultative Committee. Proceedings and Conclusions 261
Colombo Plan for Co-operative Economic and Social Development in Asia and the Pacific. Development Perspectives. Country Issues Papers by Member Governments to the Consultative Committee (CE) 261
Colombo Plan for Co-operative Economic Development in South and South East Asia. Country Issues Papers see Colombo Plan for Co-operative Economic and Social Development in Asia and the Pacific. Development Perspectives. Country Issues Papers by Member Governments to the Consultative Committee 261
Colon Free Zone Directory see F O B Colon Free Zone 239
Colonial Society of Massachusetts. Publications (US) 604
Colonial Williamsburg Archaeological Series (US ISSN 0069-5971) 85, 604
Colonial Williamsburg Occasional Papers in Archaeology (US) 85
Colonnades (US) 710
Coloquio de Estudos Luso Brasileiros. Anais (JA ISSN 0069-598X) 693, 1007
Color y Decoracion en el Hogar (SP) 643
Colorado. Department of Highways. Traffic Volume Study see Colorado State Highway Condition and Volume Report 1096
Colorado. Division of Wildlife. Special Report (US ISSN 0084-8875) 364
Colorado. Division of Wildlife. Technical Publication (US ISSN 0084-8883) 364
Colorado Fisheries Research Review (US ISSN 0588-4462) 1150
Colorado Rail Annual (US ISSN 0069-6048) 1094
Colorado School of Mines. Professional Contributions (US ISSN 0069-6056) 379, 815, 856

Colorado Shakespeare Festival Annual see On-Stage Studies 1077
Colorado Ski and Winter Recreation Statistics (US ISSN 0084-8891) 1033
Colorado State Highway Condition and Volume Report (US) 1096
Colorado State University. Atmospheric Science Paper (US ISSN 0067-0340) 803
Colorado State University Libraries. Publication (US ISSN 0084-8905) 676
Colorado, Utah TourBook see Tourbook: Colorado, Utah 1117
Colorado-Wyoming Academy of Sciences Journal (US ISSN 0096-2279) 989
Colston Research Papers see Colston Research Society, Bristol, England. Proceedings of the Symposium. Colston Research Papers 989
Colston Research Society, Bristol, England. Proceedings of the Symposium. Colston Research Papers(UK ISSN 0069-6277) 989
Colstonian (UK ISSN 0010-1842) 411
Columbia. Departamento Administrativo Nacional de Estadistica. Anuario General de Estadistica - Transportes y Comunicaciones (CK) 345, 1053, 1085
Columbia: A Magazine of Poetry and Prose (US ISSN 0161-486X) 719
Columbia Biological Series (US ISSN 0069-6285) 139
Columbia Essays on the Great Economists (US ISSN 0069-6323) 251
Columbia Review (US ISSN 0010-1982) 710, 719
Columbia River Water Management Report (US ISSN 0360-6864) 1124
Columbia Series in Molecular Biology (US) 163
Columbia Studies in Economics (US ISSN 0069-6331) 192
Columbia Studies in the Classical Tradition (NE) 337
Columbia University. American Language Program. Bulletin (US) 693
Columbia University. Ancient Near Eastern Society. Journal see Ancient Near Eastern Society. Journal 850
Columbia University. East Asian Institute. Studies (US) 569, 851
Columbia University. Institute on East Central Europe. East Central European Studies (US) 579
Columbia University. Russian Institute. Studies (US ISSN 0588-5477) 580
Columbia University Graduate School of Business. Dissertations Series (US) 192
Combat Culturel (FR) 903
Combat Fleets of the World (US ISSN 0364-3263) 811
Combined Cumulative Index to Pediatrics (US ISSN 0190-4981) 3, 769, 787
Combined Heat and Power Association. Handbook (UK) 553
Combined Jersey Herd Book, Directory and Elite Register of the U.K. see Jersey Herd Book and Members Directory 67
Combined Simulation (DK ISSN 0106-357X) 358
Combustion (US) 894
Comecon Data (Year) (UK) 261
Comecon Merchant Ships (UK) 1099
Comentario Sociologico (SP ISSN 0210-1432) 243
Comentarios Bibliograficos Americanos. Anuario see Anuario - C B A - Yearbook 121
Comercial and Industrial Directory of Panama see Directorio Comercial e Industrial de Panama 305
Comercio Exterior de Mexico see Anuario de Comercio Exterior de Mexico 1146
Comercio Exterior do Brasil (BL) 1150
Comic Book Price Guide see Official Overstreet Comic Book Price Guide 614
Comicos (CU) 538

Comision de Integracion Electrica Regional. Directorio del Sector Electrico (UY) *451*
Comision de Integracion Electrica Regional. Recursos Energeticos de los Paises de la C I E R (UY) *863, 1124*
Comision Economica para America Latina (CEPAL) Cuadernos de la C E P A L *see* Cuadernos de la C E P A L *238*
Comision Economica para America Latina (CEPAL) Estudios e Informes de la C E P A L *see* Estudios e Informes de la C E P A L *262*
Comision Inter-Americana del Atun Tropical *see* Inter-American Tropical Tuna Commission. Annual Report *510*
Comision Interamericana de Mujeres. Asamblea Extraordinaria. Acta Final *see* Inter-American Commission of Women. Special Assembly. Final Act *913*
Comision Interamericana del Atun Tropical. Boletin *see* Inter-American Tropical Tuna Commission. Bulletin *510*
Comision Mixta de Coordinacion Estadistica de Barcelona. Estadisticas de Ensenanza de la Provincia de Barcelona (SP) *411*
Comitatus; a Journal of Medieval and Renaissance Studies (US ISSN 0069-6412) *104, 556, 719*
Comite Consultatif pour la Masse et les Grandeurs Apparentees (FR) *808*
Comite de Accion Interamericana de Colombia. Boletin (CK) *904*
Comite de Controle de l'Electricite et du Gaz. Rapport Annuel (BE) *451, 863*
Comite de Iglesias. Cuadernos de Investigacion (PY) *243*
Comite de Investigaciones Tecnologicas de Chile (CL) *1068*
Comite des Travaux Historiques et Scientifiques. Section de Geographie. Actes du Congres National des Societes Savantes (FR ISSN 0071-8424) *542*
Comite des Travaux Historiques et Scientifiques. Section de Philologie et Histoire. Actes Du Congres National des Societes Savantes (FR) *580*
Comite des Travaux Historiques et Scientifiques. Section des Sciences. Bulletin (FR) *989*
Comite des Travaux Historiques et Scientifiques. Section des Sciences. Comptes Rendus du Congres National des Societes Savantes (FR) *989*
Comite International de Cooperation dans les Recherches Nationales en Demographie. Actes des Seminaires (FR) *921*
Comite International des Poids et Mesures. Comite Consultatif d'Electricite. (Rapport et Annexes) (FR) *451, 808*
Comite International des Poids et Mesures. Comite Consultatif de Photometrie et Radiometrie.(Rapport et Annexes) (FR ISSN 0588-621X) *808, 899*
Comite International des Poids et Mesures. Comite Consultatif de Thermometrie. Rapports et Annexes (FR) *808, 894*
Comite International des Poids et Mesures. Comite Consultatif des Unites (Rapport et Annexes) (FR) *808*
Comite International des Poids et Mesures. Comite Consultatif pour la Definition de la Seconde. (Rapport et Annexes) (FR ISSN 0588-6228) *808*
Comite International des Poids et Mesures. Comite Consultatif pour la Definition du Metre (Rapport et Annexes) (FR ISSN 0588-6236) *808*

Comite International des Poids et Mesures. Comite Consultatif pour les Etalons des Mesure des Radiations Ionisantes(Rapport et Annexes) *see* Comite International des Poids et Mesures. Comite Consultatif pour les Etalons des Mesure des Rayonnements Ionisants (Rapport et Annexes) *808*
Comite International des Poids et Mesures. Comite Consultatif pour les Etalons des Mesure des Rayonnements Ionisants (Rapport et Annexes) (FR) *808*
Comite International des Poids et Mesures. Proces-Verbaux des Seances(FR) *808*
Comite International des Poids et Mesures. Systeme International d'Unites (FR) *808*
Comite National de l'Organisation Francaise. Annuaire (FR ISSN 0069-651X) *279*
Comites Francais de Geodesie et Geophysique. Annales (FR ISSN 0761-392X) *405*
Comment Evaluer la Part du Trafic Maritime de Notre Commerce Exterieur qui Echappe aux Ports Francais (FR) *1085*
Commentaires des Principales Decisions du Tribunal Administratif de la Reunion (RE) *940*
Commentaries on Research in Breast Disease (US ISSN 0194-1666) *1150*
Commentationes Balticae (GW ISSN 0588-6414) *580, 719*
Commentationes Humanarum Litterarum (FI ISSN 0069-6587) *629*
Commentationes Physico-Mathematicae(FI ISSN 0069-6609) *748, 887*
Commentationes Scientiarum Socialium(FI ISSN 0355-256X) *1007*
Comments & Criticisms (US ISSN 0267-9469) *877, 933*
Comments from C A S T (Council for Agricultural Sciences and Technology) (US ISSN 0194-4096) *26, 518, 532, 846*
Comments on Astrophysics (US ISSN 0146-2970) *115, 887*
Comments on Astrophysics and Space Physics *see* Comments on Astrophysics *115*
Commerce. Le Point (CN) *239*
Commerce Africain *see* African Trade *253*
Commerce Exterieur de l'U.E.B.L. Avec les Pays d'Afrique (BE) *254*
Commerce Exterieur de l'U.E.B.L. Avec les Pays d'Amerique Latine/Buitenlandse Handel van de B.L.E.U. Met de Landen van Latijns Amerika Bruxelles (BE) *254*
Commerce Exterieur de l'U.E.B.L. Avec les Pays d'Asie/Buitenlandse Handel van de B.L.E.U. Met de Landen van Azie Bruxelles (BE) *254*
Commerce Exterieur de l'U.E.B.L. Avec les Pays de l'Est/Buitenlandse Handel van de B.L.E.U. Met de Oostlanden Bruxelles (BE) *254*
Commerce Exterieur de l'U.E.B.L. Avec les Pays de la C.E.E/Buitlandse Handel van de B.L.E.U. Met de E.E.G.-Lidstaten Bruxelles (BE) *254*
Commerce Exterieur de l'U.E.B.L. avec les Pays Industrialises (Autre Que les Pays de la C.E.E. et l'A.E.L.E.)/Buitenlandse Handel van de B.L.E.U. met de Industrielanden (Niet E.E.G.-en E.V.A.-Lidstaten Bruxelles) (BE) *254*
Commerce Exterieur de la Cote d'Ivorie: Resultats et Evolution (IV) *254*
Commerce Exterieur de la Grece (GR) *206*
Commerce Exterieur des Regions Provence, Cote d'Azur et Corse (FR) *235*
Commerce Exterieur du Senegal *see* Senegal. Ministere de l'Economie et des Finances. Analyse du Commerce Exterieur *259*

Commerce in Nigeria *see* Nigerian Business Journal *237*
Commerce Yearbook of Ports, Shipping and Shipbuilding (II) *1099*
Commerce Yearbook of Public Sector (II ISSN 0591-1710) *239*
Commerce Yearbook of Road Transport(II) *1096*
Commerce Yearbook of Shipping and Shipbuilding *see* Commerce Yearbook of Ports, Shipping and Shipbuilding *1099*
Commercial Agriculture in Zimbabwe (RH ISSN 0259-3238) *26*
Commercial Air Transport Industry (SZ) *18, 811*
Commercial and Industrial Floorspace Statistics (UK ISSN 0262-5334) *188*
Commercial Bank of Ethiopia. Annual Report (ET ISSN 0588-6694) *226*
Commercial Bank of Ethiopia. Trade Directory (ET) *304*
Commercial Bank of Greece. Report (GR) *226*
Commercial Bank of Greece. Report of the Chairman of the Board of Directors (GR ISSN 0424-9402) *226*
Commercial Bank of Kuwait. Annual Report of the Board of Directors and Accounts (KU) *226*
Commercial Directory of South Africa *see* Braby's Commercial Directory of Southern Africa *303*
Commercial Interiors International (UK) *643*
Commercial News U S A. New Products Annual Directory (US ISSN 0270-2460) *304*
Commercial Transport Handbook and Buyer's Guide for S.A. *see* Transport Manager's Handbook *1105*
Commercial Vehicle & Buyer's Guide (UK) *1081*
Commercial Vehicle and P S V Buyer's Guide *see* Commercial Vehicle & Buyer's Guide *1081*
Commercial Vehicle Data Digest (SA) *1105*
Commercial West Bank Directory (US) *226*
Commission Bancaire. Rapport Annuel (FR) *226*
Commission Belge de Bibliographie, Repertoire des Comptes-Rendus de Congres Scientifiques (BE ISSN 0080-0937) *125*
Commission d'Energie du Nord Canadien. Revue Annuelle *see* Northern Canada Power Commission. Annual Report *466*
Commission d'Energie du Nord Canadien. Revue de l'Exploitation *see* Northern Canada Power Commission. Annual Report *466*
Commission de Controle des Banques. Rapport Annuel *see* Commission Bancaire. Rapport Annuel *226*
Commission Departementale d'Histoire et d'Archeologie. Bulletin (FR ISSN 0758-2722) *85, 97*
Commission Departementale des Monuments Historiques du Pas-de-Calais. Bulletin *see* Commission Departementale d'Histoire et d'Archeologie. Bulletin *85*
Commission des Anciennes Lois et Ordonnances de Belgique. Proces-Verbaux *see* Commission Royale des Anciennes Lois et Ordonnances de Belgique. Bulletin *556*
Commission des Communautes Europeennes. Rapports Annuels sur l'Etat des Travaux de Recherches Encouragees par la CECA *see* Commission of the European Communities. Annual Reports on the Progress of Research Work Promoted by the ECSC *953*
Commission for the Geological Map of the World. Bulletin (FR ISSN 0074-9427) *379*
Commission Nationale Belge de Folklore. Annuaire *see* Commission Royale de Toponymie et de Dialectologie. Bulletin *556*

Commission of the European Communities. Annual Reports on the Progress of Research Work Promoted by the ECSC (EI) *953*
Commission of the European Communities. Centre for Information and Documentation. Annual Report: Program Biology-Health Protection *see* Commission of the European Communities. Joint Research Centre, Ispra. Annual Report: Program Biology-Health Protection *139*
Commission of the European Communities. Collection of Agreements (EI) *254, 670*
Commission of the European Communities. Community Law (EI ISSN 0590-6563) *670*
Commission of the European Communities. Conjoncture Energetique dans la Communaute *see* Commission of the European Communities. Energy Situation in the Community *1150*
Commission of the European Communities. Directorate of Taxation. Inventory of Taxes (EI) *294*
Commission of the European Communities. Directory (EI ISSN 0591-1745) *670*
Commission of the European Communities. Energy Situation in the Community (EI) *1150*
Commission of the European Communities. Etudes: Serie Aide au Developpement *see* Commission of the European Communities. Studies: Development Series *1150*
Commission of the European Communities. Etudes: Serie Concurrence-Rapprochement des Legislations *see* Commission of the European Communities. Studies: Competition-Approximation of Legislation *1150*
Commission of the European Communities. Etudes: Serie Energie *see* Commission of the European Communities. Studies: Energy Series *1150*
Commission of the European Communities. Etudes: Serie Industrie *see* Commission of the European Communities. Studies: Industry Series *1151*
Commission of the European Communities. Etudes: Serie Politique Sociale *see* Commission of the European Communities. Studies: Social Policy Series *904*
Commission of the European Communities. Europa Transport. Annual Report (EI) *1081*
Commission of the European Communities. European Regional Development Fund. Annual Report (EI) *261*
Commission of the European Communities. Expose sur l'Evolution Sociale dans la Communaute *see* Commission of the European Communities. Report on the Social Situation *1007*
Commission of the European Communities. Financial Report (EI ISSN 0590-6571) *294*
Commission of the European Communities. Investments in the Community Coal Mining and Iron and Steel Industries. Report on the Survey (EI ISSN 0069-6757) *815*
Commission of the European Communities. Joint Research Centre, Ispra. Annual Report: Program Biology-Health Protection (EI) *139*
Commission of the European Communities. Marches Agricoles: Serie "Prix". Notes Explicatif (EI) *45*
Commission of the European Communities. Marches Agricoles: Serie "Prix". Produits Animaux (EI) *45, 65*
Commission of the European Communities. Marches Agricoles: Serie "Prix". Produits Vegetaux (EI) *46, 53*

Commission of the European Communities. Operation of Nuclear Power Stations (EI) *896*
Commission of the European Communities. Report on Competition Policy/Rapport sur la Politique de Concurrence (EI) *254, 288*
Commission of the European Communities. Report on the Social Situation (EI) *1007*
Commission of the European Communities. Specialized Department Terminology and Computer Applications. Bulletin de Terminologie et de Traduction (EI) *693*
Commission of the European Communities. Studies: Agricultural Series (EI ISSN 0069-6765) *1150*
Commission of the European Communities. Studies: Competition-Approximation of Legislation (EI) *1150*
Commission of the European Communities. Studies: Development Aid Series see Commission of the European Communities. Studies: Development Series *1150*
Commission of the European Communities. Studies: Development Series (EI) *1150*
Commission of the European Communities. Studies: Economic and Financial Series (EI ISSN 0069-6773) *1150*
Commission of the European Communities. Studies: Energy Series (EI) *1150*
Commission of the European Communities. Studies: Industry Series (EI) *1151*
Commission of the European Communities. Studies: Social Policy Series (EI) *904*
Commission of the European Communities. Studies: Transport Series (EI ISSN 0069-679X) *1151*
Commission of the European Communities. Terminology Bureau. Terminology Bulletin/Bulletin de Terminologie see Commission of the European Communities. Specialized Department Terminology and Computer Applications. Bulletin de Terminologie et de Traduction *693*
Commission Royale de Toponymie et de Dialectologie. Bulletin/Koninklijke Commissie voor Toponymie en Dialectologie. Handelingen (BE ISSN 0774-8396) *556*
Commission Royale des Anciennes Lois et Ordonnances de Belgique. Bulletin/Koninklijke Commissie voor de Uitgave der Oude Wetten en Verordeningen van Belgie. Handelingen (BE) *556, 654*
Commissione Archeologica Comunale di Roma. Bullettino (IT) *85*
Commissions Royales d'Art et d'Archeologie. Bulletin see Belgium. Commission Royale des Monuments et des Sites. Bulletin *97*
Committee for Aerospace Structures. Research Report (JA) *18*
Committee for Economic Development Newsletter see C E D Newsletter *261*
Committee for Economic Development of Australia. C E D A Information Papers (IP Series) (AT) *288*
Committee for Economic Development of Australia. C E D A "M" Series (AT) *288*
Committee for Economic Development of Australia. C E D A "P" Series (AT) *288*
Committee for Monetary Research and Education, Inc. Monographs see C M R E Monographs *225*
Committee of the Professional Photographers of Europe. General Assembly. Report of Proceedings (SZ ISSN 0573-0473) *884*
Committee on Institutional Cooperation. Annual Report see Committee on Institutional Cooperation. Biennial Report *433*

Committee on Institutional Cooperation. Biennial Report (US) *433*
Committee on Invisible Exports. Annual Report see British Invisible Exports Council. Annual Report *253*
Committee on Uniform Security Procedures Digest of Changes in C U S I P see Digest of Changes in C U S I P *227*
Committee to Combat Huntingtons Disease Newsletter see Maker *790*
Commodities Magazine Reference Guide to Futures Markets see Futures Magazine Reference Guide to Futures Markets *266*
Commodity Classification for Foreign Trade Statistics: Japan see Export Statistical Schedule of Japan (Year) *255*
Commodity Classification for Foreign Trade Statistics: Japan see Import Statistical Schedule of Japan (Year) *256*
Commodity Drain Report of Florida's Primary Forest Industries (US ISSN 0362-191X) *524*
Commodity Prices (US) *265*
Commodity Year Book (US ISSN 0069-6862) *266*
Commodity Yearbook Statistical Abstract Service (US ISSN 0010-3241) *3, 40*
Common Focus (US) *333*
Common Name - Kartei Pflanzenschutz- und Schaedlingsbekaempfungsmittel (GE ISSN 0138-4074) *322*
Common Sense Economics (CN ISSN 0319-7549) *251*
Commonsense (US ISSN 0163-3023) *1151*
Commonwealth Bibliographies (UK ISSN 0306-1124) *125*
Commonwealth Broadcasting Association. Handbook (UK) *347*
Commonwealth Bureau of Agricultural Economics. Annotated Bibliographies Series A see C.A.B. International Bureau of Agricultural Economics. Annotated Bibliographies Series A *39*
Commonwealth Bureau of Agricultural Economics. Annotated Bibliographies. Series B: Agricultural Policy and Rural Development in Africa see C.A.B. International Bureau of Agricultural Economics. Annotated Bibliographies. Series B: Agricultural Policy and Rural Development in Africa *39*
Commonwealth Bureau of Nutrition. Annotated Bibliographies see C.A.B. International Bureau of Nutrition. Annotated Bibliographies *847*
Commonwealth Bureau of Soils. Annotated Bibliographies see C.A.B. International Bureau of Soils. Annotated Bibliographies *39*
Commonwealth Catalogue of Queen Elizabeth Stamps (UK ISSN 0142-7830) *1151*
Commonwealth Fact Sheets (UK) *1151*
Commonwealth for Scientific and Industrial Research Organisation Directory see C S I R O Directory *989*
Commonwealth for Scientific and Industrial Research Organisation Film Catalogue see C S I R O Film Catalogue *989*
Commonwealth Forestry Bureau Annotated Bibliographies see C.A.B. International. Forestry Bureau. Annotated Bibliographies *529*
Commonwealth Government Directory (AT) *940*
Commonwealth Grants to Tasmania see Tasmania. Department of the Treasury. Commonwealth Grants to Tasmania *299*
Commonwealth Income Tax Statistics see Australia. Department of the Treasury. Income Tax Statistics *203*
Commonwealth Institute, London. Annual Report (UK ISSN 0069-7109) *542, 915*
Commonwealth Law Reports (AT ISSN 0069-7133) *654*

Commonwealth Magistrates' Conference. Report (UK ISSN 0307-6539) *654*
Commonwealth Mycological Institute. Phytopathological Papers see C.A.B. International. Mycological Institute. Phytopathological Papers *155*
Commonwealth of Australia Gazette: Periodic (AT) *940*
Commonwealth of Australia Gazette: Special (AT) *940*
Commonwealth of Kentucky. Annual Economic Report (Year) (US) *192*
Commonwealth of Pennsylvania. Airport Directory (US) *18*
Commonwealth of Pennsylvania. Executive Budget see Pennsylvania. Office of the Budget. Program Budget *418*
Commonwealth of Pennsylvania Aeronautical Chart (US) *18*
Commonwealth Parliamentary Association. Malawi Branch. Conference. Report of Proceedings (MW) *940*
Commonwealth Parliamentary Association. Malawi Branch. Executive Committee. Annual Report(MW) *940*
Commonwealth Regional Renewable Energy Resources Index see C R R E R I S Renewable Energy Index *468*
Commonwealth Scientific and Industrial Research Organisation. Division of Horticultural Research. Report (AT ISSN 0069-7435) *532*
Commonwealth Scientific and Industrial Research Organisation. Wheat Research Unit. Report (AT ISSN 0069-7680) *63*
Commonwealth Scientific and Industrial Research Organization. Annual Report (AT ISSN 0069-7184) *1068*
Commonwealth Scientific and Industrial Research Organization. C S I R O Textile News (AT ISSN 0312-5211) *1073*
Commonwealth Scientific and Industrial Research Organization. Division of Animal Health. Annual Report see Commonwealth Scientific and Industrial Research Organization. Division of Animal Health. Research Report *1121*
Commonwealth Scientific and Industrial Research Organization. Division of Animal Health. Research Report (AT ISSN 0812-7336) *1121*
Commonwealth Scientific and Industrial Research Organization. Division of Atmospheric Physics. Annual Report see Commonwealth Scientific and Industrial Research Organization. Division of Atmospheric Research. Research Report *803*
Commonwealth Scientific and Industrial Research Organization. Division of Applied Physics. Biennial Report (AT) *808*
Commonwealth Scientific and Industrial Research Organization. Division of Animal Production Report (AT ISSN 0155-7742) *171, 174*
Commonwealth Scientific and Industrial Research Organization. Division of Animal Physiology. Report. see Commonwealth Scientific and Industrial Research Organization. Division of Animal Production Report *171*
Commonwealth Scientific and Industrial Research Organization. Division of Atmospheric Physics. Technical Paper see Commonwealth Scientific and Industrial Research Organization. Division of Atmospheric Research. Technical Paper *803*
Commonwealth Scientific and Industrial Research Organization. Division of Animal Production Technical Report (AT) *65, 171*

Commonwealth Scientific and Industrial Research Organization. Division of Animal Physiology. Technical Report see Commonwealth Scientific and Industrial Research Organization. Division of Animal Production Technical Report *171*
Commonwealth Scientific and Industrial Research Organization. Division of Atmospheric Research. Research Report (AT ISSN 0159-0219) *803*
Commonwealth Scientific and Industrial Research Organization. Division of Atmospheric Research. Technical Paper (AT) *803*
Commonwealth Scientific and Industrial Research Organization. Division of Building Research. Technical Paper (AT) *183*
Commonwealth Scientific and Industrial Research Organization. Division of Entomology. Report (AT ISSN 0069-732X) *164*
Commonwealth Scientific and Industrial Research Organization. Division of Entomology. Technical Paper (AT ISSN 0069-7338) *164*
Commonwealth Scientific and Industrial Research Organization. Division of Fisheries and Oceanography. Annual Report see Commonwealth Scientific and Industrial Research Organization. Marine Laboratories. Report *508*
Commonwealth Scientific and Industrial Research Organization. Division of Fossil Fuels. Report of Research (AT ISSN 0728-7615) *816*
Commonwealth Scientific and Industrial Research Organization. Division of Food Research. Report of Research (AT ISSN 0069-7419) *518*
Commonwealth Scientific and Industrial Research Organization. Division of Food Research. Technical Paper (AT ISSN 0069-7427) *518*
Commonwealth Scientific and Industrial Research Organization. Division of Geomechanics. Geomechanics Computer Programs (AT ISSN 0816-6013) *1005*
Commonwealth Scientific and Industrial Research Organization. Division of Geomechanics. Geomechanics of Coal Mining Report (AT ISSN 0726-6510) *816*
Commonwealth Scientific and Industrial Research Organization. Division of Geomechanics. Technical Report (AT ISSN 0069-7249) *379, 480, 816*
Commonwealth Scientific and Industrial Research Organization. Division of Land Use Research. Technical Paper see Commonwealth Scientific and Industrial Research Organization. Division of Water and Land Resources *46*
Commonwealth Scientific and Industrial Research Organization. Division of Protein Chemistry. Annual Report (AT ISSN 0314-254X) *151*
Commonwealth Scientific and Industrial Research Organization. Division of Plant Industry. Annual Report see Commonwealth Scientific and Industrial Research Organization. Division of Plant Industry. Report *53*
Commonwealth Scientific and Industrial Research Organization. Division of Plant Industry. Report (AT) *53*
Commonwealth Scientific and Industrial Research Organization. Division of Soils. Biennial Report see Commonwealth Scientific and Industrial Research Organization. Division of Soils. Research Report *54*
Commonwealth Scientific and Industrial Research Organization. Division of Soils. Divisional Report (AT ISSN 0725-8526) *53*

Commonwealth Scientific and Industrial Research Organization. Division of Soil Mechanics. Technical Report *see* Commonwealth Scientific and Industrial Research Organization. Division of Geomechanics. Technical Report *816*
Commonwealth Scientific and Industrial Research Organization. Division of Soils. Research Report (AT ISSN 0729-4336) *54*
Commonwealth Scientific and Industrial Research Organization. Division of Soils. Technical Papers (AT ISSN 0365-723X) *54*
Commonwealth Scientific and Industrial Research Organization. Division of Tropical Crops and Pastures. Annual Report (AT ISSN 0158-538X) *54, 155*
Commonwealth Scientific and Industrial Research Organization. Division of Tropical Crops and Pastures. Genetic Resources Communication (AT ISSN 0159-6071) *54, 65*
Commonwealth Scientific and Industrial Research Organization. Division of Tropical Crops and Pastures. Research Report (AT ISSN 0156-2444) *26*
Commonwealth Scientific and Industrial Research Organization. Division of Tropical Crops and Pastures. Tropical Agronomy Technical Memorandum (AT ISSN 0157-9711) *26*
Commonwealth Scientific and Industrial Research Organization. Division of Tropical Crops and Pastures. Technical Paper (AT) *54, 155*
Commonwealth Scientific and Industrial Research Organization. Division of Textile Physics. Annual Report (AT) *888, 1073*
Commonwealth Scientific and Industrial Research Organization. Division of Tropical Pastures. Technical Paper *see* Commonwealth Scientific and Industrial Research Organization. Division of Tropical Crops and Pastures. Technical Paper *54*
Commonwealth Scientific and Industrial Research Organization. Division of Water and Land Resources (AT ISSN 0810-4387) *46, 288*
Commonwealth Scientific and Industrial Research Organization. Division of Wildlife and Rangelands Research. Technical Memorandum (AT ISSN 0813-0493) *364*
Commonwealth Scientific and Industrial Research Organization. Division of Wildlife and Rangelands Research. Technical Paper (AT ISSN 0812-2237) *364*
Commonwealth Scientific and Industrial Research Organization. Division of Wildlife Research. Technical Memorandum *see* Commonwealth Scientific and Industrial Research Organization. Division of Wildlife and Rangelands Research. Technical Memorandum *364*
Commonwealth Scientific and Industrial Research Organization. Institute of Animal and Food Sciences. Annual Report (AT ISSN 0158-7390) *26*
Commonwealth Scientific and Industrial Research Organization. Institute of Energy and Earth Resources. Annual Report (AT ISSN 0729-056X) *816*
Commonwealth Scientific and Industrial Research Organization. Institute of Energy and Earth Resources. Division of Mineral Physics & Mineralogy. Biennial Report (AT) *816*
Commonwealth Scientific and Industrial Research Organization. Institute of Energy and Earth Resources. Investigation Report. (AT ISSN 0726-1780) *816*
Commonwealth Scientific and Industrial Research Organization. Institute of Energy and Earth Resources. Technical Communication. (AT ISSN 0726-1772) *816*

Commonwealth Scientific and Industrial Research Organization. Institute of Earth Resources. Annual Report. *see* Commonwealth Scientific and Industrial Research Organization. Institute of Energy and Earth Resources. Annual Report *816*
Commonwealth Scientific and Industrial Research Organization. Institute of Earth Resources. Investigation Report. *see* Commonwealth Scientific and Industrial Research Organization. Institute of Energy and Earth Resources. Investigation Report *816*
Commonwealth Scientific and Industrial Research Organization. Institute of Earth Resources. Technical Communication. *see* Commonwealth Scientific and Industrial Research Organization. Institute of Energy and Earth Resources. Technical Communication *816*
Commonwealth Scientific and Industrial Research Organization. Marine Laboratories. Fishery Situation Report (AT ISSN 0157-8081) *508*
Commonwealth Scientific and Industrial Research Organization. Marine Laboratories. Microfiche Report (AT ISSN 0726-4283) *508*
Commonwealth Scientific and Industrial Research Organization. Marine Laboratories. Report (AT ISSN 0725-4598) *405, 508*
Commonwealth Scientific and Industrial Research Organization. Marine Laboratories. Research Report (AT ISSN 0726-4291) *405, 508*
Commonwealth Scientific and Industrial Research Organization. National Measurement Laboratory. Biennial Report *see* Commonwealth Scientific and Industrial Research Organization. Division of Applied Physics. Biennial Report *808*
Commonwealth Scientific and Industrial Research Organization. Wool Research Laboratories. C S I R O Wool Textile News *see* Commonwealth Scientific and Industrial Research Organization. C S I R O Textile News *1073*
Commonwealth Scientific and Industrial Research Organization of Energy and Earth Resources. Division of Mineral Physics. Biennial Report *see* Commonwealth Scientific and Industrial Research Organization. Institute of Energy and Earth Resources. Division of Mineral Physics & Mineralogy. Biennial Report *816*
Commonwealth Scientific Industrial Research Organization. Division of Fisheries and Oceanography. Report *see* Commonwealth Scientific and Industrial Research Organization. Marine Laboratories. Research Report *508*
Commonwealth Teaching Service. Annual Report (AT) *412*
Commonwealth Universities Yearbook (UK ISSN 0069-7745) *433*
Communaute Economique du Betail et de la Viande *see* C E B V *65*
Communaute Economique Europeenne International. Droit et Affaires *see* C E E International. Droit et Affaires *669*
Communaute Europeenne du Charbon et de l'Acier. Comite Consultatif. Annuaire *see* European Coal and Steel Community. Consultative Committee. Yearbook *262*
Communaute Europeenne du Charbon et de l'Acier. Commission des Communautes Europeennes. Comite Consultatif. Manuel *see* European Coal and Steel Community. Consultative Committee. Handbook *262*
Communautes Francophones: Bibliographie, Chroniques *see* Etudes Strategiques et Militaires (Collection) *709*
Communicatio Publica (SZ) *343*
Communication Abstracts (US ISSN 0162-2811) *3, 345*

Communication & Broadcasting (UK ISSN 0305-3601) *348*
Communication and Cybernetics (US ISSN 0340-0034) *359*
Communication and the Human Condition (US ISSN 0275-2069) *719*
Communication Graphics *see* A I G A Graphic Design U S A *930*
Communication Research and Broadcasting (GW) *348*
Communication Research Reports (US) *343*
Communication Statistics (IO) *1053*
Communication Theory in the Cause of Humanity (US) *346, 634*
Communication Theory in the Cause of Man *see* Communication Theory in the Cause of Humanity *634*
Communication Theory in the Cause of Mankind *see* Communication Theory in the Cause of Humanity *634*
Communication Yearbook (US ISSN 0147-4642) *1007*
Communications and Control Engineering Series (US) *470*
Communications de Demographie Historique *see* Historisch-Demographische Mitteilungen *922*
Communications Handbook (US ISSN 0069-777X) *343*
Communications Institute Courses in Communications *see* C I N C O M: Courses in Communications *428*
Communications: Latin American Industrial Report (US) *343*
Communicator (Indianapolis) (US) *348, 451*
Communique (Nashville) (US) *834*
Communist (US ISSN 0193-3469) *1151*
Communist Program (FR) *904*
Communistes Francais et l'Europe (FR) *904*
Community and Junior College Directory *see* Community, Technical, and Junior College Directory: a Statistical Analysis *428*
Community Computer Centers. Newsletter (US) *1151*
Community Improvement Corporation. Annual Report/Societe d'Amenagement Regional. Rapport Annuel (CN ISSN 0069-7842) *243*
Community Leaders and Noteworthy Americans *see* Community Leaders of America *134*
Community Leaders of America (US) *134*
Community Memory News (US) *357*
Community Resources Directory (US) *1016*
Community Service Statistics: Scotland (UK ISSN 0144-5081) *1022, 1053*
Community Studies Series (UK ISSN 0143-7704) *693, 1007*
Community, Technical, and Junior College Directory *see* Community, Technical, and Junior College Directory: a Statistical Analysis *428*
Community, Technical, and Junior College Directory: a Statistical Analysis (US) *428*
Community Work (UK ISSN 0307-6067) *1016*
Compagnie Europeenne et d'Outre-Mer. Rapports *see* Compagnie Financiere Europeenne et d'Outre-Mer. Finoutremer. Rapport Annuel *254*
Compagnie Financiere Europeenne et d'Outre-Mer. Finoutremer. Rapport Annuel (BE) *254*
Companhia de Eletricidade de Brasilia. Relatorio de Administracao (BL) *451*
Companhia de Eletricidade de Brasilia. Relatorio de Atividades *see* Companhia de Eletricidade de Brasilia. Relatorio de Administracao *451*
Companhia Estadual de Tecnologia de Saneamento Basico e de Defesa do Meio Ambiente. Directoria Relatoria Anual (BL) *494, 953*
Companhia Paranaense de Energia. Informe Estatistico Anual (BL) *468, 1053*
Companhia Paulista de Forca e Luz. Boletim Estatistico (BL) *451*

Compania Argentina de Seguros. Memoria y Balance General *see* Brujula *638*
Compania Financiera Ecuatoriana de Desarrollo Informe Anual *see* C O F I E C. Informe Anual *225*
Company Information Sourcebook (UK) *192, 676*
Company Thesaurus (US ISSN 0739-1862) *192*
Comparatist (US ISSN 0195-7678) *719*
Comparative Animal Nutrition (SZ ISSN 0304-5374) *174, 1121*
Comparative Criticism (UK ISSN 0144-7564) *719*
Comparative Digest of Credit Union Acts (US) *226*
Comparative Education Society in Europe. Proceedings of the General Meeting (BE ISSN 0588-9049) *412*
Comparative Frontier Studies (US) *1151*
Comparative Guide to American Colleges (US) *428*
Comparative Juridical Review (US ISSN 0069-7893) *654*
Comparative Social Research (US ISSN 0195-6310) *1025*
Comparative Studies in Overseas History (NE) *580*
Comparative Studies in Sociology *see* Comparative Social Research *1025*
Comparison of (Years) Production Expenses for Selected Steam Electric Plants (US) *451*
Compas d'Or *see* Gulden Passer *961*
Compas de Cifras *see* Germany (Federal Republic, 1949-) Statistisches Bundesamt. Zahlenkompass *1056*
Compendia (UK) *709*
Compendia Rerum Iudaicarum Ad Novum Testamentum (NE) *976*
Compendio Dati (IT) *950*
Compendio Estadistico Centroamericano (GT ISSN 0588-912X) *206, 1053*
Compendio Statistico *see* Compendio Statistico Italiano *1053*
Compendio Statistico Italiano (IT ISSN 0069-7958) *1053*
Compendium des Produits et Specialites Pharmaceutiques *see* Compendium of Pharmaceuticals and Specialties *870*
Compendium Gezondheidsstatistiek Nederland/Compendium Health Statistics of the Netherlands (NE) *958*
Compendium Health Statistics of the Netherlands *see* Compendium Gezondheidsstatistiek Nederland *958*
Compendium of Advanced Courses in Colleges of Further & Higher Education (UK) *428, 433*
Compendium of Drug Therapy *see* Internist's Compendium of Drug Therapy *871*
Compendium of New Zealand Farm Production Statistics (NZ) *40, 1053*
Compendium of Pharmaceuticals and Specialties (CN ISSN 0069-7966) *870*
Compendium of Texas Colleges & Financial Aid Calendar for High School Seniors (US) *428*
Compendium of University Entrance Requirements for First Degree Courses in the United Kingdom (UK ISSN 0571-625X) *433*
Compendium on Development Assistance to Kenya (UN) *261*
Compensation (Washington) (US ISSN 0732-5282) *286, 950*
Compensation in Human Resources Development *see* Compensation in Training & Development *271*
Compensation in Manufacturing - Engineers and Managers (US ISSN 0278-0992) *270*
Compensation in the Accounting/Financial Field (US) *270*
Compensation in the M I S/D P Field (US) *270*
Compensation in the Security/Loss Prevention Field (US) *270, 374*
Compensation in Training & Development (US) *271*

Compensation of Attorneys (Non-Law Firms) (US) 271, 654
Compensation of Industrial Engineers (US) 271
Competition Policy in O E C D Countries (FR) 288
Compilation of State and Federal Privacy Laws (US) 654
Complete Baseball Record Book (US) 1038
Complete Catalogue of Plays (year) (US) 1076
Complete Commodity Futures Directory (US) 304
Complete Guide to Gospel Music see Gospel Music Offical Directory 836
Complete Handbook of Pro Football (US ISSN 0361-2988) 1038
Complete Internal Revenue Code see Internal Revenue Code 296
Complete Sports see Complete Sports Baseball Special 1033
Complete Sports Baseball Special (US) 1033
Complete Sports Pro Football Special (US) 1038
Composers of the Americas/ Compositores de America (US ISSN 0069-8016) 134, 834
Composers of Wales Series (UK) 834
Composite Catalog of Oil Field Equipment & Services (US) 304, 863
Compositeur Canadien see Canadian Composer 834
Compositores de America see Composers of the Americas 834
Comprehensive Annual Services Program Plan for Social Services Under Title 20 see Louisiana. Health and Human Resources Administration Comprehensive Annual Services Program Plan for Social Services Under Title 20 1018
Comprehensive Biochemistry see New Comprehensive Biochemistry 152
Comprehensive Chemical Kinetics (NE ISSN 0069-8040) 331
Comprehensive Endocrinology (US ISSN 0160-242X) 781
Comprehensive Gerontology. Serie C: Interdisciplinary Topics (DK) 552
Comprehensive Manuals in Pediatrics (US) 787
Comprehensive Manuals in Radiology (US ISSN 0172-4843) 792
Comprehensive Manuals of Surgical Specialities (US ISSN 0172-4827) 794
Comptes Economiques de la Guadeloupe (GP) 206
Comptes Economiques de la Martinique(MQ) 206
Comptes Economiques du Territoire Francais des Afars et des Issas (FR) 206
Comptes Economiques Nationaux du Rwanda (RW) 206
Comptes Nationaux de la Belgique (BE ISSN 0069-8075) 206
Comptes Nationaux du Cameroun (CM) 294
Compton Yearbook see Compton's Yearbook 462
Compton's Yearbook (US) 462
Compu-Data (GR) 357
CompuBibs (US) 563
Compumath Citation Index (US ISSN 0730-6199) 3, 353, 755
Computational Mathematics and Applications (US) 359
Computational Microelectronics (US) 888
Computer Abstracts (UI ISSN 0010-4469) 3, 353
Computer Aided Design i Danmark (DK ISSN 0573-9985) 356
Computer Aided Design Low Cost C A D/C A M Systems see Low Cost C A D/C A M Systems 356
Computer-Aided Design of Electronic Circuits (NE) 484
Computer Aided Research in Ancient Near Eastern Studies see Computer Aided Research in Near Eastern Studies 612
Computer Aided Research in Near Eastern Studies (US ISSN 0742-2334) 612

Computer & Control Abstracts (UK ISSN 0036-8113) 4, 352, 354
Computer and Information Systems see Computer and Information Systems Abstract Journal 354
Computer and Information Systems Abstract Journal (US ISSN 0191-9776) 4, 354
Computer Applications in Archaeology (UK) 96
Computer Applications in Shipping and Shipbuilding (NE) 1093
Computer Applications in Social Work and Allied Professions (UK ISSN 0267-1980) 357
Computer Assisted Language & Instruction Consortium Monograph Series see C A L I C O. Monograph Series 356
Computer-Based Systems in Information Management (US) 360
Computer Bookbase (US) 361, 362, 961
Computer Books and Serials in Print (US ISSN 0000-0779) 1151
Computer Contents (US) 4, 352, 354, 361
Computer Design and Architecture Series (US) 356
Computer Directory and Buyer's Guide(US) 357
Computer for Architects and Engineers see Guide to Computer Software for Architects and Engineers 1154
Computer Graphics Directory (US ISSN 0743-2836) 356
Computer Graphics Marketplace (US ISSN 0278-2774) 356
Computer Industry Abstracts (US ISSN 0883-931X) 354
Computer Industry Forecast see Computer Industry Abstracts 354
Computer Industry Update (US ISSN 0744-0081) 4, 354
Computer Katalog (GW) 362
Computer Literature Index (US ISSN 0270-4846) 4, 354
Computer Measurement Group Conference Proceedings see C M G Conference Proceedings 352
Computer Methods in the Geosciences (US) 1005
Computer Networking Symposium. Proceedings (US) 357
Computer Publishers & Publications (US ISSN 0740-4085) 964
Computer Readable Bibliographic Data Bases see Computer Readable Databases 354
Computer Readable Databases (US) 354, 357
Computer Science and Applied Mathematics (US) 352, 755
Computer Science Technical Report Anthology (US) 352
Computer Security Buyers Guide (US) 304, 358
Computer Services. Software (UK) 283, 286
Computer Software & Applications Conference (Proceedings) see C O M P S A C 362
Computer Software Engineering Series (US ISSN 0888-2088) 484
Computer Studies: Computers in Education (US) 427
Computer Systems Engineering (UK) 358
Computer Users Handbook (SA) 286, 361, 362
Computer Users' Year Book (UK) 358
Computers (CN ISSN 0382-1005) 352
Computers and Math Series (US ISSN 0888-2193) 427, 755
Computers & Office Equipment: Latin American Industrial Report (US) 286, 352
Computers and People Series (US) 352, 634
Computers in Cardiology (US ISSN 0276-6574) 778
Computers in Chemical and Biochemical Research (US) 1005
Computers in Education Series (US ISSN 0888-2177) 427
ComputerTalk Directory of Pharmacy Systems see ComputerTalk Pharmacy Systems Buyers Guide 778

ComputerTalk Pharmacy Systems Buyers Guide (US) 361, 778, 870
Computing Decisions (UK) 352
Computing Journal Abstracts (UK ISSN 0309-8885) 4, 354
Computing Reviews (US ISSN 0010-4884) 354
Computing Supplementa (US ISSN 0344-8029) 352
Compuviews (CN) 352
Comsearch: Broad Topics (US) 1022
Comsearch: Geographics (US) 1022
Comsearch Printouts see Comsearch: Subjects 1022
Comsearch Printouts: Subjects see Comsearch: Subjects 1022
Comsearch: Subjects (US) 1022
Comune di Roma. Ufficio di Statistica e Censimento. Bollettino Statistico (IT ISSN 0010-4957) 926
Comunicacion (VE) 343
Comunidades y Culturas Peruanas (PE) 71, 515
Concentus Musicus (GW) 834
Concepts and Techniques in Modern Geography see C A T M O G 542
Concepts in Chemistry (US) 322
Concepts in Immunopathology (SZ ISSN 0255-7983) 781
Concepts in Pediatric Neurosurgery (SZ ISSN 0251-2068) 787, 789
Concepts in Toxicology (SZ ISSN 0254-8739) 759, 870
Conceptus-Studien (AU ISSN 0259-0670) 877
Concerned Investors Guide (US ISSN 0741-1995) 266
Concerning Poetry (US ISSN 0010-5201) 741
Conchological Society Special Publication (UK ISSN 0144-9826) 174
Concise Descriptive Catalogue of Arabic Manuscripts in the Salar Jung Museum and Library (II) 831
Concise Descriptive Catalogue of the Persian Manuscripts in the Salar Jung Museum and Library (II) 831
Concise Descriptive Catalogue of the Urdu Manuscripts in the Salar Jung Museum and Library (II) 831
Concise Statistical Yearbook of Greece (GR ISSN 0069-8245) 1053
Concord Inflight Entertainment Guide (UK) 1088
Concrete Abstracts (US ISSN 0045-8007) 4, 188
Concrete and Masonry Cost Data see Means Concrete Cost Data 185
Concrete Pipe Industry Statistics (US ISSN 0360-2877) 488
Concrete Society. Technical Report (UK) 183
The Concrete Year Book (UK ISSN 0069-8288) 183
Condenser (SA) 192
Condition of Education (US ISSN 0098-4752) 423
Conditions (US ISSN 0147-8311) 615, 719, 1128
Conditions de Travail dans l'Industrie Canadienne. see Working Conditions in Canadian Industry 277
Condominium Development Guide (US) 622
Confectionery Buyer's Guide (UK) 522
Confederacao Brasileira de Desportos. Relatorio see Confederacao Brasileira de Futebol. Relatorio 1033
Confederacao Brasileira de Futebol. Relatorio (BL) 1033
Confederacao Nacional dos Trabalhadores Em Comunicacoes e Publicidade. Relatorio Anual (BL) 343, 648
Confederacion Colombiana de Camaras de Comercio. Asamblea General. Informe Final (CK) 235
Confederacion Espanola de Cajas de Ahorros. Fondo para Investigacion Economica y Social. Coleccion Temas de Ahorro y Credito see Coleccion Temas de Ahorro y Credito 1150
Confederacion Latinoamericana de Asociaciones Cristianas de Jovenes. Carta (UY) 969
Confederate Calendar (US) 604, 811

Confederate Regimental Histories (US) 1151
Confederation des Industries Ceramiques de France. Annuaire (FR ISSN 0069-830X) 320
Confederation Europeenne pour la Therapie Physique. Congress Reports(FR ISSN 0071-2817) 759
Confederation Internationale des Accordeonistes Revue see C.I.A. Revue 834
Confederation Internationale des Cinemas d'Art et d'Essai Bulletin d'Information see C.I.C.A.E. Bulletin d'Information 823
Confederation Nationale de la Construction. Annuaire (BE ISSN 0045-8023) 183
Confederation of Australian Motor Sport Manual of Motor Sport see C A M S Manual of Motor Sport 1033
Confederation of British Industry Annual Report see C B I Annual Report 192
Confederazione Italiana dei Servizi Pubblici degli Enti Locali. Annuario (IT) 950
The Conference Blue Book (UK ISSN 0260-2431) 795
Conference Board. Annual Survey of Corporate Contributions (US ISSN 0146-0986) 192
Conference Board. Report on Company Contributions see Conference Board. Annual Survey of Corporate Contributions 192
Conference Board Cumulative Index (US ISSN 0069-8350) 192
Conference Board of the Mathematical Sciences. Regional Conference Series in Applied Mathematics (US ISSN 0097-4455) 755
Conference Generale des Poids et Mesures. Comptes Rendus des Seances (FR) 808
The Conference Green Book (UK ISSN 0260-2199) 795
Conference International de l'Education. Rapport Final see International Conference on Education. Final Report 415
Conference Internationale sur les Communications et l'Energie (Proceedings) see International Communications and Energy Conference (Proceedings) 343
Conference Internationale sur les Phenomenes d'Ionisation dans les Gaz. Comptes Rendus (UR ISSN 0573-3022) 331
Conference of Electrical Engineering Problems in the Rubber and Plastics Industries. I E E E Conference Record (US ISSN 0272-4685) 900, 985
Conference of Presidents of Major American Jewish Organizations. Annual Report (US ISSN 0160-7057) 502, 976
Conference of Presidents of Major American Jewish Organizations. Report see Conference of Presidents of Major American Jewish Organizations. Annual Report 502
Conference of South African Surveyors. Proceedings/Konferensie van Suid-Afrikaanse Opmeters. Verrigtinge (SA) 480, 542
Conference of Southeast Asian Librarians. Proceedings (SI) 676
Conference of State Sanitary Engineers. Report of Proceedings (US ISSN 0069-8474) 953
Conference of Vice-Chancellors. Proceedings (II) 433
Conference of Vice-Chancellors. Report(II) 433
Conference on Aerospace and Aeronautical Meteorology. Preprints see Conference on Atmospheric Environment of Aerospace Systems and Applied Meteorology. Preprints 803
Conference on Agriculture & Forest Meteorology. Publication (US) 803
Conference on American Economic Enterprise. Papers (US) 243

Conference on Artifical Insemination of Beef Cattle. Proceedings *see* Conference on Artificial Insemination and Embryo Transfer of Beef Cattle. Proceedings *1151*
Conference on Artificial Insemination and Embryo Transfer of Beef Cattle. Proceedings. (US) *1151*
Conference on Artificial Intelligence Applications. Proceedings (US) *354*
Conference on Atmospheric Environment of Aerospace Systems and Applied Meteorology. Preprints (US) *803*
Conference on Atmospheric Radiation. Abstracts (US) *808*
Conference on Bank Structure and Competition. Proceedings (US ISSN 0084-9154) *226*
Conference on Chinese Oral and Performing Literature Papers *see* C H I N O P E R L Papers *717*
Conference on Coastal Meteorology. (Preprints) (US) *804*
Conference on Contingency Planning for Plastics. Proceedings (US) *900*
Conference on Coordination Chemistry Proceedings (CS) *322*
Conference on Crime Countermeasures and Security. Proceedings *see* Carnahan Conference on Security Technology. Proceedings *374*
Conference on Data Systems Languages. Data Base Task Group. Report (US ISSN 0090-7383) *358*
Conference on Editorial Problems: University of Toronto (US) *104*, *580*, *719*, *877*
Conference on Electric Process Heating in Industry. Conference Record *see* Electrical Process Heating in Industry. Technical Conference. Record *452*
Conference on Electrical Insulation and Dielectric Phenomena. Annual Report (US ISSN 0084-9162) *451*
Conference on Engineering in Medicine and Biology. Record (US) *759*
Conference on Frontiers in Education. Digest *see* Frontiers in Education Conference. Proceedings *454*
Conference on Ground Water. Proceedings (US ISSN 0094-9671) *402*
Conference on Human Relations in Industry. Proceedings (II ISSN 0069-8555) *271*
Conference on Hydrometeorology. Preprint (US) *804*
Conference on Labor, New York University. Proceedings *see* Annual National Conference on Labor at New York University. Proceedings *269*
Conference on Laser and Electro-Optical Systems (CLEOS) *see* Conference on Lasers and Electro-Optics (Publications) *451*
Conference on Laser Engineering and Applications *see* Conference on Lasers and Electro-Optics (Publications) *451*
Conference on Lasers and Electro-Optics (Publications) (US) *451*
Conference on Local Computer Networks (Proceedings) (US) *357*
Conference on Modern Jewish Studies Annual *see* Modern Jewish Studies Annual *727*
Conference on Mountain Meteorology (Publication) (US) *804*
Conference on Numerical Weather Prediction. (Publication) (US) *804*
Conference on Planned and Inadvertent Weather Modification. Preprints (US) *804*
Conference on Precision Electromagnetic Measurements. Digest (US) *451*, *636*
Conference on Probability and Statistics in Atmospheric Sciences. Preprints (US) *748*, *804*
Conference on Radar Meteorology. Preprints (US ISSN 0069-8636) *804*
Conference on Remote Systems Technology. Proceedings (US ISSN 0069-8644) *470*, *896*
Conference on Research in Income and Wealth *see* Studies in Income and Wealth *278*
Conference on Scottish Studies. Proceedings *see* Scotia *505*
Conference on Severe Local Storms. Preprints (US ISSN 0069-8679) *804*
Conference on Software Maintenance. Proceedings (US) *362*
Conference on Space Simulation. Proceedings (US) *18*, *494*, *1068*
Conference on Taxation. Proceedings *see* National Tax Association - Tax Institute of America. Proceedings of the Annual Conference *297*
Conference on Teacher Education in the Eastern Caribbean. Report *see* Eastern Caribbean Standing Conference on Teacher Education. Report *447*
Conference on Trace Substances in Environmental Health. Proceedings *see* Trace Substances in Environmental Health *499*
Conference on U S Technological Policy. Proceedings *see* Conference on U S Technology Policy. Proceedings *1068*
Conference on U S Technology Policy. Proceedings (US) *1068*
Conference on United Nations Procedures. Report *see* United Nations Issues Conference. Report *919*
Conference on Weather Forecasting and Analysis. (Publication) (US) *804*
Conference on Weather Forecasting and Analysis and Aviation Meteorology. Preprints *see* Conference on Weather Forecasting and Analysis. (Publication) *804*
Conference on Weather Modification. Preprints *see* Conference on Planned and Inadvertent Weather Modification. Preprints *804*
Conference Papers Annual Index (US ISSN 0194-0546) *4*, *795*
Conference Publications Guide *see* Bibliographic Guide to Conference Publications *122*
Conference Record, Industry Applications Society, I E E E - I A S Annual Meeting *see* Industry Applications Society. I E E E - I A S Annual Meeting. Conference Record *455*
Conference Universitaire Suisse. Rapport Annuel (SZ) *433*
Conferences & Exhibitions International Worldwide Convention Centres Yearbook (UK) *795*
Conferences Meetings & Exhibitions Welcome (UK ISSN 0260-776X) *795*, *1107*
Conferencia de Facultades Latinoamericanas de Derecho. (Documentos Oficiales) (PE ISSN 0573-4347) *654*
Conferencias de Bioquimica (CL ISSN 0069-8784) *139*, *151*
Conferenze (PL ISSN 0079-3167) *629*
Confins (BE ISSN 0010-5694) *719*, *741*
Confluents (FR) *556*
Confluents Psychanalytiques (FR) *933*
Congregational Church in England and Wales. Congregational Year book *see* United Reformed Church in the United Kingdom. United Reformed Church Year Book *980*
Congregational Council for World Mission. Annual Report *see* C W M Report *978*
Congres Archeologique de France (Publication.) (FR ISSN 0069-8881) *85*
Congres International d'Histoire des Sciences. Actes (CN ISSN 0074-9540) *645*, *990*
Congres International de la Population. Proceedings *see* International Population Conference. Proceedings *922*
Congres International des Etudes Byzantines. Actes *see* International Congress for Byzantine Studies. Acts *586*

Congres Portuaire International. Compte-Rendu *see* International Harbour Congress. Proceedings *1101*
Congreso Internacional de Americanistas. Actas (PE) *71*
Congreso Internacional de Vivienda Popular (CK) *1007*
Congreso Latinamericano de Siderurgia. Memoria Tecnica (CL ISSN 0589-2813) *797*
Congreso Mexicano de Control de Calidad. Annual Proceedings (MX) *808*
Congreso Nacional de Arqueologia. Actas (UY) *85*
Congreso Nacional de Bibliotecas. Ponencias, Comunicaciones y Cronica (SP) *676*
Congreso Nacional de Profesionales en Ciencias Economicas. Memoria (ES) *192*
Congresos Indigenistas Interamericanos. Actas (MX ISSN 0074-0810) *71*
Congress and the Nation (US) *904*, *940*
Congress F A T I P E C (Federation d'Associations de Techniciens des Industries des Peintures, Vernis, Emaux et Encres d'Imprimerie de l'Europe Continentale) (FR ISSN 0430-2222) *478*
Congress in Park and Recreation Administration. Programme (UK) *795*
Congress in Park and Recreation Administration. Reports (UK) *1044*
Congress International Medical de Pays de Langue Francaise de l'Hemisphere Americain. Rapports et Communications (MQ ISSN 0414-4406) *759*
Congress Marches Ahead (II ISSN 0376-5776) *904*
Congress of International Congress Organizers and Technicians. Proceeding (BE ISSN 0573-5661) *795*
Congress of Micronesia. Joint Committee on Program and Budget Planning. Public Hearings on High Commissioner's Preliminary Budget (TT) *294*, *940*
Congress of Micronesia. Senate. Journal(TT) *654*, *940*
Congressi C C S S. Bollettino (PH) *783*, *796*
Congressional Directory *see* U.S. Congress. Congressional Directory *910*
Congressional Index (US) *654*
Congressional Information Service, Inc. Federal Register Index *see* C I S Federal Register Index *3*
Congressional Information Service, Inc. Index *see* C I S Index *948*
Congressional Presentation, Fiscal Year *see* U.S. International Development Cooperation Agency. Congressional Presentation, Fiscal Year *264*
Congressional Record Digest and Tally of Roll Call Votes (US ISSN 0069-892X) *940*
Congressional Roll Call (Year) (US) *904*
Congressional Staff Directory (US ISSN 0069-8938) *904*, *940*
Congressional Summary *see* Summary of Congress *910*
Congresso Brasileiro de Economia e Sociologia Rural. Anais (BL ISSN 0102-2253) *46*
Congresso Europeo di Storia Ospitaliera. Atti (IT ISSN 0589-3267) *616*
Congresso Latinoamericano de Hidraulica (Papers) (BL ISSN 0589-3305) *1124*
Congressus Numerantium (CN ISSN 0384-9864) *748*
Coniectanea Biblica. New Testament Series (SW ISSN 0069-8946) *969*
Coniectanea Biblica. Old Testament Series (SW ISSN 0069-8954) *969*
Coniectanea Neotestamentica *see* Coniectanea Biblica. New Testament Series *969*
Conimbriga (PO ISSN 0084-9189) *85*

Conjoncture Suisse et Perspectives *see* Schweizerische Konjunktur und Vorausschau *249*
Connaissance de l'Orient. Collection Unesco d'Oeuvres Representatives (FR ISSN 0589-3496) *719*
Connaissance de l'Ouest (FR ISSN 0396-2024) *288*, *542*
Connaissance des Temps (FR ISSN 0181-3048) *115*
Connaitre la Wallonie/To Know Wallony (BE ISSN 0010-602X) *580*
Connecticut. Advisory Council on Vocational and Career Education. Vocational Education Evaluation Report (US ISSN 0363-650X) *412*
Connecticut. Agricultural Experiment Station, New Haven. Bulletin (US ISSN 0097-0905) *164*
Connecticut. Commission on the Deaf and Hearing-Impaired. Annual Report (US) *375*
Connecticut. Commission to Study and Investigate the Problems of Deaf and Hearing-Impaired Persons. Annual Report *see* Connecticut. Commission on the Deaf and Hearing-Impaired. Annual Report *375*
Connecticut. Council on Environmental Quality. Annual Report (US ISSN 0095-4624) *494*
Connecticut. Department of Community Affairs Division of Research and Program Evaluation. Construction Activity Authorized by Building Permits. Summary *see* Connecticut Housing Production and Permit Authorized Construction *183*
Connecticut. Department of Correction. Publications (US ISSN 0090-2756) *370*
Connecticut. Department on Aging. Report to the Governor and General Assembly (US ISSN 0090-6077) *552*
Connecticut. Judicial Department. Report (US ISSN 0098-8138) *654*
Connecticut. Law Revision Commission. Annual Report (US) *654*
Connecticut. Treasury Department. Annual Report (US ISSN 0099-0108) *294*
Connecticut Academy of Arts and Sciences. Memoirs (US ISSN 0069-8970) *629*, *990*
Connecticut Academy of Arts and Sciences. Transactions (US ISSN 0069-8989) *629*, *990*
Connecticut and Rhode Island Directory of Manufacturers (US) *304*
Connecticut Education Association. Legislative Bulletin (US) *412*, *654*
Connecticut Hospice Newsletter (US) *933*
Connecticut Housing Market. Annual Report (US) *622*
Connecticut Housing Production and Permit Authorized Construction (US) *183*
Connecticut Market Data (US ISSN 0573-665X) *283*
Connecticut, Massachusetts, Rhode Island TourBook *see* Tourbook: Connecticut, Massachusetts, Rhode Island *1117*
Connecticut Master Transportation Plan(US ISSN 0069-9039) *1081*
Connecticut News Handbook (US ISSN 0277-5956) *645*
Connecticut Poetry Review (US ISSN 0277-7770) *741*, *1076*
Connecticut State Industrial Directory *see* MacRae's Connecticut State Industrial Directory *312*
Connecticut Urban Research Report (US ISSN 0069-9055) *1025*
Connecticut Vacation Guide (US) *1107*
Connecticut Walk Book (US ISSN 0092-5764) *1044*
Connecticut Water Resources Bulletin. (US ISSN 0589-400X) *402*
Connecticut West (US) *1107*
Connecticut Writer (US) *719*
Connections (US) *741*
Connexions (GW) *710*, *1025*, *1107*
Conscientia (GW ISSN 0589-4069) *877*

Consciousness and Self-Regulation: Advances in Research (US) 877
Conseil de Presse du Quebec. Rapport Annuel (CN ISSN 0708-0131) 348
Conseil de Recherches en Sciences Naturelles et en Genie du Canada. Liste des Bourses et Subventions de Recherche see Natural Sciences and Engineering Research Council of Canada. List of Scholarships and Grants in Aid of Research 437
Conseil de Recherches en Sciences Naturelles et en Genie du Canada. Rapport du President see Natural Sciences and Engineering Research Council of Canada. Report of the President 437
Conseil National de la Recherche Scientifique. Rapport Annuel see National Council for Scientific Research. Annual Report 437
Conseil National de Recherches, Canada. Comite Associe sur les Criteres Scientifiques. Rapport d'Activite see National Research Council, Canada. Associate Committee on Scientific Criteria for Environmental Quality. Status Report 498
Conseil National de Recherches du Canada. Division de Genie Electrique. Bulletin see National Research Council, Canada. Division of Electrical Engineering. Bulletin 473
Conseil National du Patronat Francais. Annuaire (FR) 279
Conseil Suisse de la Science. Rapport Annuel see Schweizerischer Wissenschaftsrat. Jahresbericht 999
Conseil Superieur du Livre. Annuaire see Societe de Developpement du Livre et du Periodique. Annuaire 684
Consejo Central Ejecutivo del Partido Liberal de Honduras. Memoria (HO) 904
Consejo Latinoamericano de Ciencias Sociales. Serie Poblacion. Informe de Investigacion (AG) 921
Consejo Nacional de Investigaciones Cientificas y Tecnicas. Informe Sobre Un Ano de Labor (AG) 990
Consejo Nacional de Investigaciones Cientificas y Tecnologicas. Departamento de Educacion. Directorio Nacional de Cursos de Postgrado (VE) 433
Consejo Nacional de Investigaciones Cientificas y Tecnologicas, Costa Rica. Informe Anual (CR ISSN 0253-2492) 1068
Conservation Council of Ontario. Conference Proceedings (CN) 364
Conservation Council of Ontario. Reports (CN) 364
Conservation Directory (US ISSN 0069-911X) 364
Conservation in Kansas (US ISSN 0094-1670) 364
Conservation of Cultural Property in India (II ISSN 0376-7965) 85
Conservation of Library Materials (US ISSN 0069-9136) 676
Conservation of Nature and Natural Resources see Nature and Environment Series 366
Conservator (UK ISSN 0140-0096) 364
Consolidated Federal Funds Report (US) 940
Consolidated Report on Elementary and Secondary Education in Colorado (US ISSN 0095-5329) 412
Consolidated Tax Return (Supplement) (US) 294
Consort (UK) 834
Consortium for Comparative Legislative Studies. Publications (US) 654
Consorzio Universitario. Pubblicazioni. Sezione Miscellanea (IT) 433
Conspectus Florae Orientalis (IS) 156
Conspectus For...Of Further Education in the Inner and Outer London Region (UK ISSN 0260-3853) 1151
Constitutional Law see B A R - B R I Bar Review. Constitutional Law 651

Construction and Industry Bulletin see Informador de la Construccion y de la Industria 184
Construction Annual (GW) 183
Construction Computer Applications Directory (US) 183, 363
Construction Costs: U S Steam Electrical Plants, 1970-1985 (US) 451, 464
Construction Directory see Construction Industries of Massachusetts Directory 305
Construction Engineering Research Institute Foundation Report see Kensetsu Kogaku KenKyushyo Hokoku 489
Construction Equipment Buyers Guide (US) 183, 524, 816
Construction History (UK) 97, 183
Construction in Hawaii (US ISSN 0069-9187) 183
Construction Industries and Trade Annual (II) 183
Construction Industries and Trade Journal see Construction Industries and Trade Annual 183
Construction Industries of Massachusetts Directory (US) 183, 305, 1096
Construction Industry Europe (UK) 183, 622
Construction Industry Research and Information Association Annual Report see C I R I A Annual Report 480
Construction Industry Research and Information Association Report see C I R I A Report 480
Construction Industry Research and Information Association Technical Note see C I R I A Technical Note 480
Construction Industry U.K. see House's Guide to the Construction Industry 184
Construction: Latin American Industrial Report (US) 183
Construction Law Reports (CN) 183, 654
Construction Navale (FR) 1099
Construction Surveyors Institute Diary (UK) 183
Construction Writers Association. Newsletter (US ISSN 0069-9217) 183
Consultants and Consulting Organizations see Consultants and Consulting Organizations Directory 279
Consultants and Consulting Organizations Directory (US ISSN 0196-1292) 279, 305
Consultation on Church Union. Digest (US) 969
Consulting Engineers-Canada-Ingenieurs-Conseils (CN ISSN 0317-6525) 470
Consulting Rates and Business Practices. Annual Survey (US) 193, 847
Consumer Affairs Council. Annual Report (AT) 368
Consumer Complaint Contact System, Annual Report (US ISSN 0193-9297) 368
Consumer Credit Association of the United Kingdom. Membership Directory (UK) 226, 283
Consumer Credit Control (UK) 193, 654
Consumer Europe (UK ISSN 0308-4353) 283
Consumer-Farmer Cooperator (US) 614, 622
Consumer Guide Magazine (US ISSN 0097-8337) 1091
Consumer Health and Nutrition Index (US ISSN 0883-1963) 847
Consumer I C's D.A.T.A. Book see Audio-Video I Cs D.A.T.A. Book 360
Consumer Protection Directory (US) 1151
Consumer Sourcebook (US ISSN 0738-0518) 368
Consumers Affairs Council of Tasmania. Annual Report (AT) 368, 1016

Consumers Directory (NE ISSN 0069-9284) 368
Consumers Index (US ISSN 0094-0534) 4, 369
Consumers Protection Council of Tasmania. Annual Report see Consumers Affairs Council of Tasmania. Annual Report 368
Consumer's Resource Handbook (US) 368
Consumo Industrial de Energia Eletrica do Estado da Bahia (BL) 452
Contabilidad Nacional de Espana (SP ISSN 0069-9292) 294
Contact see Prairie Wind 498
Contact. The UK News Contact Directory see Hollis Press and Public Relations Annual 15
Contact avec le Danemark see Contact with Denmark 580
Contact List of Electronic Music see C L E M 834
Contact with Denmark (DK ISSN 0105-7669) 580
Contact with the Martinus Institute of Spiritual Science see Kosmos 971
Contactologia-Bucherei (GW ISSN 0724-6226) 785
Contacts (SA ISSN 0250-2003) 961, 1076
Contacts & Facilities (AT) 374, 834, 1076
Container Contacts (GW) 305, 1081
Container News Worldwide Intermodal Directory (US) 1151
Containerisation International Yearbook(UK ISSN 0305-7402) 1081
Containerization: A Bibliography (US ISSN 0069-9314) 1085
Contamination Control Abstracts (UK) 476, 873
Contatti con la Danimarca see Contact with Denmark 580
Contatto (IT) 1091
Contemporanea (IT) 556, 719
Contemporary African Monographs (KE ISSN 0069-9330) 565
Contemporary American Art Critics (US) 104
Contemporary American History Series (US ISSN 0069-9357) 604
Contemporary Architects (US) 97
Contemporary Artists (US) 104
Contemporary Authors (US ISSN 0010-7468) 134
Contemporary Authors Autobiography Series (US ISSN 0748-0636) 134
Contemporary Authors News see Authors in the News 715
Contemporary Biology (UK) 139
Contemporary China Papers (AT) 569, 904
Contemporary Community Health Series (US) 953
Contemporary Concepts in Physics (US ISSN 0272-2488) 888
Contemporary Drama Series (US ISSN 0069-9381) 719
Contemporary Evaluation Research (US) 1007, 1016
Contemporary Geriatric Medicine (US) 552
Contemporary German Philosophy (US) 877
Contemporary Glass see New Glass Review 113
Contemporary Glass Microfiche Program see New Glass Review 113
Contemporary Government Series (US) 940
Contemporary Hematology/Oncology (US ISSN 0197-3649) 783
Contemporary Issues Criticism (US) 710
Contemporary Issues Series (UK ISSN 0069-942X) 1025
Contemporary Japanese Books (JA) 125, 961
Contemporary Jewry (US ISSN 0147-1694) 502, 976
Contemporary Literary Criticism Series (US ISSN 0091-3421) 719
Contemporary Mathematics (US ISSN 0271-4132) 748
Contemporary Nephrology (US) 795
Contemporary Neurology Series (US ISSN 0069-9446) 789
Contemporary Nursing Series (US) 783

Contemporary Perspectives in Rehabilitation (US) 444
Contemporary Philosophy Series (US ISSN 0414-7790) 877
Contemporary Photographers (US) 884
Contemporary Physics (US) 888
Contemporary Practice of the United Kingdom in the Field of International Law see British Practice in International Law 1149
Contemporary Problems of Childhood (US ISSN 0147-1082) 333
Contemporary Quarterly (US ISSN 0162-7201) 741
Contemporary Studies in Applied Behavioral Science (US) 1025
Contemporary Studies in Economic and Financial Analysis (US) 193, 226
Contemporary Studies in Sociology (US) 1025
Contemporary Theatre, Film & Television (US ISSN 0749-064X) 134, 1076
Contemporary Topics in Immunobiology (US ISSN 0093-4054) 139, 773
Contemporary Topics in Molecular Immunology (US ISSN 0090-8800) 773
Contents of Contemporary Mathematical Journals see Current Mathematical Publications 755
Contents of Recent Economics Journals(UK ISSN 0045-8368) 4, 206
Contents Pages in Education (UK ISSN 0265-9220) 423
Contents Pages in Management (UK ISSN 0306-3224) 206
Context (Leeds) (UK ISSN 0144-3399) 719
Conti degli Italiani (IT ISSN 0390-6574) 949
Continent (FR) 710
Continental Motoring Holidays (UK) 1091, 1107
Continental Research Series (HK ISSN 0069-9535) 569
Continential Basketball Association Media Guide Yearbook see C B A Media Guide/Yearbook 1037
Continuing Engineering Studies Series see College - Industry Education Conference. Proceedings 470
Continuum (US) 719
Contraband (Falmouth) (US) 719
Contract Interior's Catalogue (UK) 643, 644
Contractors Plant and Equipment (Hong Kong Catalogue) (HK) 183
Contracts see B A R - B R I Bar Review. Contracts 651
Contrary Opinion Library (US) 266
Contrast (IS ISSN 0010-7948) 719, 741
Contrebis (UK ISSN 0307-5087) 85
Contribuicoes em Ciencias Sociais (BL) 1007
Contribuicoes em Desenvolvimento Urbano (BL) 622
Contribuicoes em Economia (BL) 193
Contribuicoes em Psicologia, Psiquiatria e Psicanalise (BL) 789, 933
Contributi di Sociologia (IT ISSN 0391-1926) 1025
Contributi di Sociologia. Readings (IT ISSN 0391-3171) 1025
Contributii Botanice (RM ISSN 0069-9616) 156
Contribution to Precambrian Geology (US) 385
Contribution to the Study of World History (US ISSN 0885-9159) 502, 556
Contributions a la Connaissance des Elites Africaines (FR) 134, 565
Contributions from the New York Botanical Garden (US ISSN 0736-0509) 156
Contributions in Afro-American and African Studies (US ISSN 0069-9624) 565, 604
Contributions in American History (US ISSN 0084-9219) 604
Contributions in American Studies (US ISSN 0084-9227) 604
Contributions in Biology and Geology (US) 139, 385, 856

Contributions in Comparative Colonial Studies (US ISSN 0163-3813) *604*
Contributions in Drama and Theatre Studies (US ISSN 0163-3821) *1076*
Contributions in Economics and Economic History (US ISSN 0084-9235) *251*
Contributions in Ethnic Studies (US ISSN 0196-7088) *502*
Contributions in Family Studies (US ISSN 0147-1023) *1025*
Contributions in Intercultural and Comparative Studies (US ISSN 0147-1031) *1025*
Contributions in Labor History (US ISSN 0146-3608) *271*
Contributions in Legal Studies (US ISSN 0147-1074) *654*
Contributions in Librarianship and Information Science (US ISSN 0084-9243) *676*
Contributions in Marine Science (US) *139*
Contributions in Medical History (US ISSN 0147-1058) *759*
Contributions in Military History *see* Contributions in Military Studies *811*
Contributions in Military Studies (US ISSN 0883-6884) *811*
Contributions in Oceanography *see* Texas A & M University. College of Geosciences. Contributions in Oceanography *408*
Contributions in Philosophy (US ISSN 0084-926X) *877*
Contributions in Political Science (US ISSN 0147-1066) *904*
Contributions in Psychology (US ISSN 0736-2714) *933*
Contributions in Science (US ISSN 0459-8113) *990*
Contributions in Sociology (US ISSN 0084-9278) *1025*
Contributions in Women's Studies (US ISSN 0147-104X) *1128*
Contributions of the Astronomical Observatory on Skalnate Pleso *see* Prace Astronomickeho Observatoria na Skalnatom Plese *117*
Contributions to Criminology and Penology (US ISSN 0732-4464) *370*
Contributions to Current Research in Geophysics (SZ) *398*
Contributions to Economic Analysis (NE ISSN 0573-8555) *251*
Contributions to Epidemiology and Biostatistics (SZ ISSN 0377-3574) *953*
Contributions to Gynecology and Obstetrics (SZ ISSN 0304-4246) *785*
Contributions to Himalayan Geology (II) *385*
Contributions to Human Development (SZ ISSN 0301-4193) *171, 759*
Contributions to Library Science *see* Bijdragen tot de Bibliotheekwetenschap *675*
Contributions to Marine Science (UK ISSN 0069-9691) *405*
Contributions to Microbiology and Immunology (SZ ISSN 0301-3081) *168, 773*
Contributions to Music Education (US ISSN 0190-4922) *834*
Contributions to Oncology/Beitraege zur Onkologie (SZ ISSN 0250-3220) *759*
Contributions to Political Economy (UK) *243, 904*
Contributions to Primatology (SZ ISSN 0301-4231) *174*
Contributions to Residential Treatment (US) *333, 444, 934*
Contributions to Sedimentology (GW ISSN 0343-4125) *385*
Contributions to Sensory Physiology (US ISSN 0069-9705) *171, 759*
Contributions to Southeast Asian Ethnography (SI ISSN 0217-2992) *71*
Contributions to the History of Natural Sciences and Technology in the Baltic/Iz Istorii Estestvoznaniya i Tekhniki Pribaltiki (UR ISSN 0130-3252) *990, 1068*
Contributions to the History of Science and Technology in Baltics. *see* Contributions to the History of Natural Sciences and Technology in the Baltic *990*
Contributions to the Sociology of Language (GW) *693, 1025*
Contributions to the Study of Aging (US ISSN 0732-085X) *552*
Contributions to the Study of Childhood and Youth (US ISSN 0273-124X) *333*
Contributions to the Study of Computer Science (US ISSN 0734-757X) *352*
Contributions to the Study of Education(US ISSN 0196-707X) *412*
Contributions to the Study of Mass Media and Communications (US ISSN 0732-4456) *345*
Contributions to the Study of Music and Dance (US ISSN 0193-9041) *374, 834*
Contributions to the Study of Popular Culture (US ISSN 0198-9871) *71, 1025*
Contributions to the Study of Religion (US ISSN 0196-7053) *969*
Contributions to the Study of Science Fiction and Fantasy (US ISSN 0193-6875) *14, 719*
Contributions to the Study of World Literature (US ISSN 0738-9345) *719*
Contributions to Vertebrate Evolution (SZ ISSN 0376-4230) *166*
Control and Dynamic Systems *see* Control and Dynamic Systems: Advances in Theory and Applications *18*
Control and Dynamic Systems: Advances in Theory and Applications (US ISSN 0090-5267) *18*
Control Magazine (UK ISSN 0069-973X) *104*
Controle et la Vente des Boissons Alcooliques au Canada *see* Canada. Statistics Canada. Control and Sale of Alcoholic Beverages in Canada/Controle et la Vente des Boissons Alcooliques au Canada *120*
Controversia (CK ISSN 0120-4165) *904*
Convegno Nazionale dei Commercianti de Mobili. Atti e Relazioni (IT ISSN 0069-9764) *1151*
Convenience Store Industry Report (US ISSN 0084-9294) *522*
Convenios Centroamericanos de Integration Economica. (GT ISSN 0553-6863) *261*
Convention London (UK) *1107*
Convention of Electrical and Electronics Engineers in Israel. Proceedings (US) *452*
Convention of the International Association of Fish and Wildlife Agencies *see* International Association of Fish and Wildlife Agencies. Proceedings of the Convention *365*
Conventions & Meetings-Canada (CN ISSN 0226-8922) *796*
Convergence: International Colloquium on Automotive Electronic Technology. Proceedings (US) *452, 1091*
Conversations With (US) *540*
Conversion of Serials Microfiche *see* C O N S E R Microfiche *124*
Converter Directory (UK ISSN 0309-2143) *305*
Cookeia (RH ISSN 0250-2992) *565*
Cooper Monographs on English and American Language and Literature (SZ ISSN 0069-9780) *693*
Cooperador Dental (AG ISSN 0069-9799) *779*
Co-operative Bank of Kenya. Annual Report & Accounts (KE) *226*
Co-operative Bank of Kenya. Annual Report and Statement of Accounts *see* Co-operative Bank of Kenya. Annual Report & Accounts *226*
Cooperative Bank of Taiwan. Annual Report/Tai-Wan Shena Ho Tso Chin Ku. Annual Report. (CH) *226*

Co-Operative Communications (UK) *46, 238, 283*
Cooperative Education Association Membership Directory (US ISSN 0069-9810) *412*
Cooperative Housing Journal (US ISSN 0589-6355) *622*
Cooperative Industrial and Commercial Reference and Information Service Directory *see* C I C R I S Directory *675*
Cooperative Press in South-East Asia (II) *645*
Co-operative Statistics (UK) *238*
Cooperative Trade Directory for Southeast Asia (II ISSN 0069-9837) *238, 305*
Cooperatives & the Law (US) *1151*
Cooperatives in Campus Areas of North America *see* N A S C O Campus Co-Op Directory *314*
Coordenacao do Sistema de Tributacao, Brazil. Pareceres Normativos (BL) *294*
Coordination Chemistry (UK ISSN 0069-9845) *322*
Coordination Directory of State and Federal Water Resource Officials in the Missouri River Basin (US) *364, 1124*
Copenhagen Handelsbank. Annual Report *see* Copenhagen Handelsbank. Report and Accounts *226*
Copenhagen Handelsbank. Report and Accounts (DK) *226*
Copenhagen Political Studies Abstracts (DK ISSN 0107-0452) *911*
Copenhagen School of Economics and Business Administration. Marketing Institute. Working Papers (DK ISSN 0109-3401) *283*
Copenhagen School of Economics and Business Administration. Research Paper (DK ISSN 0900-1808) *193, 283*
Copenhagen Stock Exchange. Annual Report *see* Koebenhavns Fondsboers. Aarsrapport *267*
Coping Catalog (US) *376*
Copper Abstracts *see* International Copper Information Bulletin *801*
Copper in Agriculture (UK ISSN 0261-5436) *4, 40*
Copper Survey *see* World Copper Survey *821*
Copperbelt Education (ZA) *412*
Copperbelt of Zambia Mining Industry Year Book *see* Zambia Mining Yearbook *821*
Coptic Studies (NE) *969*
Copyright Law Symposium (US ISSN 0069-9950) *860*
Copyright Laws and Treaties of the World. Supplements (UN ISSN 0069-9969) *860*
Corax (GW ISSN 0589-686X) *170*
Cord Sportfacts Guns Guide (US ISSN 0590-6776) *614, 1033*
Cord Sportfacts: Hunting (US ISSN 0092-8216) *1044*
Cordell's Who's Who in Building: Housing (AT) *183*
Cordell's Who's Who in Building: Non-Housing (AT) *183*
Cordell's Who's Who in Design Specifying (AT) *97, 183*
Cork Historical and Archaeological Society. Journal (IE ISSN 0010-8731) *85, 580*
Corn Annual (US ISSN 0069-9993) *54*
Cornell Agricultural Waste Management Conference. Proceedings (US ISSN 0065-4604) *1151*
Cornell Biennial Electrical Engineering Conference (US ISSN 0070-0002) *452*
Cornell East Asia Papers (US ISSN 8756-5293) *851*
Cornell International Agricultural Development Mimeographs *see* Cornell International Agriculture Mimeographs *26*
Cornell International Agriculture Mimeographs (US) *26*

Cornell International Industrial and Labor Relations Reports (US ISSN 0070-0029) *271*
Cornell Linguistic Contributions (NE) *693*
Cornell Recommendations for Commercial Tree-Fruit Production (US) *532*
Cornell Recommendations for Commercial Vegetable Production (US) *54*
Cornell Report on Productivity in Grocery Distribution Centers (US) *522*
Cornell Studies in Industrial and Labor Relations (US ISSN 0070-0053) *271*
Cornell University. City and Regional Planning Publications. Occasional Papers (US) *622*
Cornell University. City and Regional Planning Publications. Research Reports (US) *622*
Cornell University. Modern Indonesia Project. Interim Reports (US) *851*
Cornell University. Modern Indonesia Project. Monographs *see* Cornell University. Modern Indonesia Project Publications. Monographs, Translations, Bibliographies *851*
Cornell University. Modern Indonesia Project Publications. Monographs, Translations, Bibliographies (US ISSN 0589-7300) *125, 851*
Cornell University. New York State College of Agriculture and Life Sciences. Biometrics Unit. Annual Report (US) *149*
Cornell University. Program in Urban and Regional Studies. Occasional Papers *see* Cornell University. City and Regional Planning Publications. Occasional Papers *622*
Cornell University. Program in Urban and Regional Studies. Research Reports *see* Cornell University. City and Regional Planning Publications. Research Reports *622*
Cornell University. Southeast Asia Program. Data Papers (US ISSN 0070-0215) *1151*
Cornell University Conference on Agricultural Waste Management *see* Cornell Agricultural Waste Management Conference. Proceedings *1151*
Corner (DK ISSN 0107-9794) *104*
Cornfield Review (US ISSN 0363-4574) *104*
Cornish Archaeology (UK ISSN 0070-024X) *85*
Cornish Biological Records (UK) *139, 502*
Cornish Play Series (UK) *1076*
Cornwall Blue Book Guide and County Handbook (UK) *1107*
Corona (US ISSN 0270-6687) *719, 877*
Corporacion Costarricense de Financiamiento Industrial. Memoria Anual (CR) *288*
Corporacion Financiera Colombiana. Ejercicio (CK) *193*
Corporate Diagrams and Administrative Personnel of the Chemical Industry (US ISSN 0574-1181) *305*
Corporate Finance Bluebook (US ISSN 0740-2546) *226, 305*
Corporate Finance Sourcebook (US ISSN 0163-3031) *193*
Corporate Fitness and Recreation Buyer's Guide *see* Corporate Fitness Buyer's Guide *885*
Corporate Fitness Buyer's Guide (US) *885*
Corporate Fund Raising Directory *see* Corporate Fund Raising Directory (Year) *226*
Corporate Fund Raising Directory (Year) (US) *226*
Corporate Management Tax Conference(CN ISSN 0070-0282) *294*
Corporate Profiles for Executives & Investors (US ISSN 0145-692X) *193, 266*
Corporate Report Fact Book (US ISSN 0589-7920) *305*

Corporate Report Fact Book Wisconsin (US) 305
Corporate Report Who's Who in Upper Midwest Business see Corporate Report Fact Book 305
Corporate Technology Directory (US ISSN 0887-1930) 1068
Corporate Thesaurus see Company Thesaurus 192
Corporate 1000 (US) 279
Corporate 500: the Directory of Corporate Philanthropy (US ISSN 0197-937X) 305, 1016
Corporation des Ingenieurs Forestiers du Quebec. Congres Annuel. Texte des Conferences see Ordre des Ingenieurs Forestiers du Quebec. Congres Annuel. Texte des Conferences 526
Corporation Professionnelle des Medecins du Quebec. Annuaire Medical (CN ISSN 0315-226X) 759
Corporation Professionnelle des Medecins du Quebec. Bulletin (CN ISSN 0315-2979) 759
Corporations see B A R - B R I Bar Review. Corporations 651
Corps Diplomatique et Representants Consulaires et Autres au Canada see Diplomatic Corps and Consular and Other Representatives in Canada 915
Corpus Almanac & Canadian Sourcebook (CN ISSN 0315-7083) 462
Corpus Catholicorum (GW ISSN 0070-0320) 981
Corpus Christianorum. Continuatio Mediaevalis (BE) 981
Corpus Christianorum. Series Apocryphorum (BE) 981
Corpus Christianorum. Series Graeca (BE) 982
Corpus Christianorum. Series Latina (BE) 982
Corpus de Mosaicos Romanos de Espana (SP) 85
Corpus der Byzantinischen Miniaturenhandschriften (C B M) (GW) 337
Corpus Hispanorum de Pace (SP ISSN 0589-8056) 654
Corpus Medicorum Graecorum (GE ISSN 0070-0347) 759
Corpus Mensurabilis Musicae (GW ISSN 0070-0363) 834
Corpus Musicae Popularis Hungaricae see Regi Magyar Dallamok Tara 841
Corpus Occupational Health and Safety Management Handbook (CN) 635
Corpus of Early Keyboard Music (GW) 834
Corpus Palladianum (US ISSN 0070-038X) 98
Corpus Philosophorum Medii Aevi. Serie I. Catalogo di Manoscritti Filosofici Nelle Biblioteche Italiane (IT) 877
Corpus Philosophorum Medii Aevi. Serie II. Studi e Testi (IT) 877
Corpus Sacrae Scripturae Neerlandicae Medii Aevii see Verzameling van Middelnederlandse Bijbelteksten 737
Corpus Scriptorum Christianorum Orientalium: Aethiopica (BE ISSN 0070-0398) 984
Corpus Scriptorum Christianorum Orientalium: Arabica (BE ISSN 0070-0401) 984
Corpus Scriptorum Christianorum Orientalium: Armeniaca (BE ISSN 0070-041X) 984
Corpus Scriptorum Christianorum Orientalium: Coptica (BE ISSN 0070-0428) 984
Corpus Scriptorum Christianorum Orientalium: Iberica (BE ISSN 0070-0436) 984
Corpus Scriptorum Christianorum Orientalium: Subsidia (BE ISSN 0070-0444) 984
Corpus Scriptorum Christianorum Orientalium: Syriaca (BE ISSN 0070-0452) 984
Corpus Scriptorum de Musica (GW ISSN 0070-0460) 835
Corpus Vasorum Antiquorum. Italia (IT ISSN 0070-0479) 827

Corpus Vitrearum Medii Aevi (GE ISSN 0232-1459) 104, 556, 580
Correio Agricola (Portugal) (PO) 54
Correios e Telecomunicacoes de Portugal. Anuario Estatistico (PO) 343, 346
Correspondence Educational Directory (US) 412
Corrosion Abstracts (US ISSN 0010-9339) 4, 801
Corrosion Control Abstracts (English translation of: Referativnyi Zhurnal. Korroziya i Zashchita ot Korrozii) (UK ISSN 0010-9347) 4, 801
Corrosion Database (US) 478
Corrosion Monograph Series (US) 797
Corsi Internazionali di Cultura sull'Arte Ravennate e Bizantina. Atti (IT) 85, 104
Coscienza del Tempo (IT) 629
Cosmetic Science and Technology Series (US) 118, 759
Cosmetics: Latin American Industrial Report (US) 118
Cosmic Circus see Beyond Science Fiction 716
Cosmopolitan Contact (US ISSN 0010-955X) 915
Cost and Production Survey Report (US ISSN 0196-2434) 759, 1053
Cost Data for Landscape Construction (US ISSN 0271-2067) 480
Cost Engineers' Notebook (US) 221, 470
Cost of Doing Business for Retail Sporting Goods Stores (US ISSN 0736-0703) 1033
Cost of Health Care in the Netherlands see Kosten en Financiering van de Gezondheidzorg in Nederland 954
Cost of Personal Borrowing in the United States. (US ISSN 0091-3855) 226
Cost of Picking and Hauling Florida Citrus Fruits (US ISSN 0093-6553) 46, 518
Cost of Social Security (UN ISSN 0538-8295) 1016
Costa Rica. Archivo Nacional. Revista (CR ISSN 0034-9003) 542, 556
Costa Rica. Direccion General de Estadistica y Censos. Encuesta de Hogares, Empleo y Desempleo: Area Metropolitana de San Jose (CR) 206
Costa Rica. Direccion General de Estadistica y Censos. Inventario de las Estadisticas Nacionales (CR ISSN 0589-8544) 1053
Costa Rica. Direccion General de la Tributacion Directa. Estadistica Demografia Fiscal del Impuesto Sobre la Renta. Periodos (CR) 294
Costa Rica. Ministerio de Hacienda Oficina del Presupuesto. Informe (CR ISSN 0070-0576) 294
Costa Rica. Ministerio de Obras Publicas y Transportes. Memorias (CR) 1096
Costa Rica. Ministerio de Transportes. Memoria see Costa Rica. Ministerio de Obras Publicas y Transportes. Memorias 1096
Costa Rica. Revista de Estudios y Estadisticas. Serie Demografica (CR) 1151
Costerus (US) 693, 719
Costs at U S Educational Institutions (US) 442
Costume (UK ISSN 0590-8876) 340, 580
Cote d'Ivoire en Chiffres (SG) 565
Cotton and Allied Textile Industries see International Textile Manufacturing 1074
Cotton and Tropical Fibres Abstracts (UK ISSN 0308-6577) 4, 40
Cotton Corporation of India. Annual Report (II ISSN 0304-6907) 46
Cotton International (US ISSN 0070-0673) 1073
Cotton Lint and Seed Marketing Board. Annual Report and Accounts (KE) 54
Cotton Trade Journal International see Cotton International 1073

Council for Advancement and Support of Education. Directory see Council for Advancement and Support of Education. Membership Directory 433
Council for Advancement and Support of Education. Membership Directory (US) 433
Council for Agricultural Sciences and Technology Comments from C A S T see Comments from C A S T 26
Council for Basic Education. Occasional Papers (US ISSN 0070-069X) 412
Council for British Archaeology Annual Report see C B A Annual Report 83
Council for Mineral Technology (MINTEK). Special Publication see Mintek. Special Publications 818
Council for Mutual Economic Assistance Data see C O M E C O N Data 254
Council for Mutual Economic Assistance Foreign Trade Data see C O M E C O N Foreign Trade Data 254
Council for Old World Archaeology: C O W A Surveys and Bibliographies. Area 5: Central Europe (US ISSN 0070-0770) 1151
Council for Scientific and Industrial Research Annual Report see C S I R Annual Report 989
Council for Scientific and Industrial Research, Ghana. Forest Product Research Institute. Annual Report see Forest Products Research Institute. Annual Report 530
Council for Scientific and Industrial Research Handbook see C S I R Handbook 989
Council for Scientific and Industrial Research Organisation Organisation and Activities see C S I R O Organisation and Activities 989
Council for the Social Sciences in East Africa. Social Science Conference. Proceedings (TZ) 1007
Council for Tobacco Research--U.S.A. Report (US ISSN 0361-1612) 376, 760, 1079
Council for World Mission Report see C W M Report 978
Council of American Building Officials. One and Two Family Dwelling Code(US) 183
Council of Better Business Bureaus. Annual Report (US ISSN 0094-8853) 369
Council of Engineering Institutions Diary (UK) 470
Council of Europe. Committee of Independent Experts on the European Social Charter. Conclusions. (FR) 915, 1016
Council of Europe. Committee on Cooperation in Municipal and Regional Matters. Study Series: Local and Regional Authorities in Europe see Council of Europe. Steering Committee on Regional and Municipal Matters. Study Series: Local and Regional Authorities in Europe 950
Council of Europe. Consultative Assembly. Documents; Working Papers/Documents de Seance see Council of Europe. Parliamentary Assembly. Documents; Working Papers/Documents de Seance 670
Council of Europe. Consultative Assembly. Texts Adopted by the Assembly/Textes Adoptes Par l'Assemblee see Council of Europe. Parliamentary Assembly. Texts Adopted by the Assembly/Textes Adoptes Par l'Assemblee 670
Council of Europe. European Information Centre for Nature Conservation. Documentation Series (FR) 364
Council of Europe. European Treaty Series (FR ISSN 0070-105X) 670
Council of Europe. Parliamentary Assembly. Documents; Working Papers/Documents de Seance (FR ISSN 0252-0656) 670
Council of Europe. Parliamentary Assembly. Official Report of Debates. (FR ISSN 0252-0664) 670

Council of Europe. Parliamentary Assembly. Texts Adopted by the Assembly/Textes Adoptes Par l'Assemblee (FR ISSN 0377-6093) 670
Council of Europe. Standing Committee on the European Convention on Establishment (Individuals). Periodical Report. (FR) 913
Council of Europe. Steering Committee on Regional and Municipal Matters. Study Series: Local and Regional Authorities in Europe (FR) 950
Council of Europe. Symposium on Legal Processing. Proceedings (FR) 669
Council of Graduate Schools in the United States. Proceedings of the Annual Meeting (US ISSN 0070-1076) 433
Council of Justice to Animals and Humane Slaughter Association Newsletter see C J A and H S A Newsletter 868
Council of Legal Education. Calendar (UK ISSN 0305-411X) 654, 796
Council of Ontario Universities. Research Division. Application Statistics (CN ISSN 0382-912X) 423
Council of Ontario Universities Quadrennial Review (CN) 433
Council of Ontario Universities Triennial Review see Council of Ontario Universities Quadrennial Review 433
Council of State Governments. Southern Legislative Conference. Summary, Annual Meeting (US ISSN 0099-006X) 1151
Council of State Governments. Suggested State Legislation see Suggested State Legislation 946
Council of the European Communities. Review of the Council's Work (EI) 243
Council on Consumer Information. Proceedings of Annual Conference see American Council on Consumer Interests. Proceedings of the Annual Conference 368
Council on Economic Priorities Reports and C E P Studies see C E P Reports and C E P Studies 251
Council on Foreign Relations. Annual Report (US ISSN 0192-236X) 915
Council on Foreign Relations. President's Report see Council on Foreign Relations. Annual Report 915
Council on International Nontheatrical Events. Yearbook (US) 823
Council on Library Resources Annual Report (US) 676
Council on Library Resources, Inc. Recent Developments see C L R Recent Developments 1149
Council on Library Resources Report see Council on Library Resources Annual Report 676
Council on Municipal Performance. Annual Report (US) 1151
Councils, Committees and Boards (UK ISSN 0070-1211) 940
Counselor Education Directory: Personnel and Programs see Counselor Preparation (Year) 412
Counselor Preparation (Year) (US ISSN 0271-5368) 412
Countries of the World see Countries of the World and Their Leaders Yearbook 904
Countries of the World and Their Leaders Yearbook (US ISSN 0196-2809) 904
Country Dance and Song (US ISSN 0070-1262) 375, 515, 835
Country Dancer see Country Dance and Song 375
Country Music Sourcebook (US ISSN 0273-1428) 835
Country Shows Annual see Agricultural Shows Annual 23
Country Song Roundup Yearbook (US ISSN 0277-1292) 835
Country Vacations U.S.A. see Farm, Ranch and Country Vacations 1108

Countryside Planning Yearbook see International Yearbook of Rural Planning 623
County Agents Directory (US ISSN 0739-4330) 26
County and Municipal Year Book for Scotland see Scotlands Regions 946
County Court Practice (UK ISSN 0269-3291) 654
County Economic Indicators (US) 243
County Kildare Archaeological Society. Journal (IE) 85
County Louth Archaeological and Historical Journal (IE ISSN 0070-1327) 85
County Louth Archaeological Journal see County Louth Archaeological and Historical Journal 85
Cour Europeenne des Droits de l'Homme. Publications. Serie A: Arrets et Decisions see European Court of Human Rights. Publications. Series A: Judgments and Decisions 913
Cour Europeenne des Droits de l'Homme. Publications. Serie B: Memoires, Plaidoiries et Documents see European Court of Human Rights. Publications. Series B: Pleadings, Oral Arguments and Documents 913
Courrier du C N R S Supplement (Centre National de la Recherche Scientifique) (FR) 990
Courrier Technique Arts Graphiques (FR) 930
Court Cases of Interest to the Ombudsman Institution (CN ISSN 0227-6178) 654
Court of Justice of the European Communities. Recueil de la Jurisprudence see Court of Justice of the European Communities. Report of Cases of the Court 670
Court of Justice of the European Communities. Report of Cases of the Court (EI) 670
Courtauld Institute Illustration Archives. Archive 1 (UK ISSN 0307-8051) 98, 104
Courtauld Institute Illustration Archives. Archive 2 (UK ISSN 0307-806X) 104
Courtauld Institute Illustration Archives. Archive 3 (UK ISSN 0307-8078) 104
Courtauld Institute Illustration Archives. Archive 4 (UK ISSN 0307-8086) 104
Courtenay Facsimiles see Courtenay Reformation Facsimiles 580
Courtenay Library of Reformation Classics (UK ISSN 0070-1394) 580, 969
Courtenay Reformation Facsimiles (UK) 580, 969
Courtenay Studies in Reformation Theology (UK ISSN 0070-1408) 580, 969
Coventry Evening Telegraph Year Book & Who's Who (UK) 580
Covered Employment Trends in New Jersey (US) 271
Covered Employment Trends in New Jersey by Geographical Areas of the State see Covered Employment Trends in New Jersey 271
Covered Wagon (US ISSN 0574-3680) 604
Covered Wagon Women (US) 605, 1128
Covers see A I G A Graphic Design U S A 930
Cow Neck Peninsula Historical Journal (US) 515, 605
Cowles Foundation for Research in Economics at Yale University. Monographs see Cowles Foundation Monographs 193
Cowles Foundation Monographs (US) 193
Craft and Needlework Age/World of Miniatures Annual Trade Directory see Hobby Publications Annual Trade Directory 614
Craft Buyer's Guide see E.I.D.C.T.-C.D.T. Year Book 447

Craft, Model and Hobby Industry Annual Trade Directory see Hobby Publications Annual Trade Directory 614
Craftsman's Directory (UK ISSN 0261-2135) 113
Crain's Detroit Business (US) 193
Cranbrook Institute of Science, Bloomfield Hills, Michigan. Bulletin (US ISSN 0070-1416) 990
Cranes Today Handbook (UK ISSN 0260-745X) 183
Crawford's Directory of City Connections (UK) 226, 305
Crawl Out Your Window (US) 719
Creation/Evolution (US ISSN 0738-6001) 989
Creative Arts & Crafts Handbook (UK) 446
Creative Black Book (US ISSN 0738-9000) 15
Creative Black Book. Portfolio Edition (US ISSN 0740-283X) 15, 884
Creative Canada (CN ISSN 0315-3290) 134, 1077
Creative Handbook (UK) 104, 113
Creative Handbook Diary (UK) 104, 113
Creative Homes (SI ISSN 0217-7706) 98
Creative Source Australia (AT ISSN 0726-3589) 104, 113, 884
Creativity (US ISSN 0097-6075) 15, 104
Credit Agricole Annual Report see France. Caisse Nationale de Credit Agricole. Rapport sur le Credit Agricole Mutuel 229
Credit Communal de Belgique. Actes des Colloques Internationaux. Collection Histoire. Series in 8 (BE) 580
Credit Manual of Commercial Laws (US ISSN 0070-1467) 226, 283
Credit Union Directory and Buyers' Guide (US ISSN 0092-4954) 227, 238
Credit Union National Association. Credit Union Report (US) 227, 238
Credit Union Yearbook (US ISSN 0074-4468) 227, 238
Creditanstalt-Bankverein. Annual Report (AU) 227
Creditanstalt-Bankverein. Report see Creditanstalt-Bankverein. Annual Report 227
Cresterea Patrimoniului Muzeal (RM) 827
Cricket Quadrant (AT ISSN 0310-9356) 1038
Crime and Delinquency in California (US) 370, 373
Crime and Justice (US ISSN 0735-3928) 1151
Crime in Nebraska see State of Nebraska Uniform Crime Report 372
Crime in the United States see Uniform Crime Reports for the United States 373
Crime in Virginia (US ISSN 0146-5759) 370
Crime, Law, and Deviance Series (US) 370, 1007
Criminal Injuries Compensation (CN) 654, 1016
Criminal Injury Compensation see Criminal Injuries Compensation 654
Criminal Justice Abstracts (US ISSN 0146-9177) 4, 373
Criminal Justice History (US ISSN 0194-0953) 370
Criminal Justice Information Exchange Directory (US) 370
Criminal Justice Periodical Index (US ISSN 0145-5818) 4, 373
Criminal Justice Plan for New Jersey (US ISSN 0092-4652) 370
Criminal Law see B A R-B R I Bar Review. Criminal Law 370
Criminal Law in New South Wales. Volume 2: Summary Offences (AT ISSN 0705-7385) 654
Criminal Law Outline (US ISSN 0145-7322) 654
Criminal Law Review (US ISSN 0192-3323) 370
Criminal Lawyers Commonplace Book (CN) 654

Criminal Practices see Gilbert Law Summaries. Criminal Procedure 656
Criminal Procedure (CN) 370, 654
Criminal Victimization in the United States (US ISSN 0095-5833) 370
Criminalidad (1963-1973) see Estadistica de Criminalidad 374
Criminalist's Source Book (US) 373, 782
Criminology & Penology Abstracts (NE ISSN 0166-6231) 4, 373
Criminology Review Yearbook (US ISSN 0163-9056) 370
Crisi e Letteratura (IT ISSN 0011-1406) 629, 719, 741
Criss-Cross Art Communications (US) 104
Criterio Universitario (MX) 629
Criterios (CU) 904
Critica (UY) 540
Critica Andina (PE) 1007
Critica Social (BL) 1016
Critica y Utopia (AG ISSN 0325-9676) 1007
Critical Bibliography of French Literature (US) 719
Critical Communications Review (US) 343
Critical Essays in Modern Literature (US ISSN 0070-153X) 719
Critical Heritage Series (UK) 719
Critical Issues (US) 495, 654
Critical Reports on Applied Chemistry (UK ISSN 0263-5917) 26, 322, 870
Critical Review (AT) 556, 719, 877
Critical Review Melbourne see Critical Review 719
Critical Studies on Black Life and Culture (US) 502, 515
Criticism and Interpretation (IS ISSN 0084-9456) 629, 719
Criticism Monographs (US) 719
Critiques de Notre Temps Et... (FR ISSN 0070-1556) 719
Croissance Urbaine et Progres des Nations (FR ISSN 0070-1572) 251
Cromwelliana (UK ISSN 0307-5583) 580
Cronache Ercolanesi (IT ISSN 0391-1535) 693
Cronache Pompeiane (IT ISSN 0391-1527) 85
Crop Breeding Institute. Annual Report(RH) 54
Crop Physiology Abstracts (UK ISSN 0306-7556) 4, 40
Crop Production see U.S. Crop Reporting Board. Crop Production 60
Crop Protection Monographs (US) 139
Crops Guide (CN) 54
Cropwood Round-Table Conference Papers (UK) 370
Cross and Talk (JA ISSN 0911-5625) 15, 283
Cross-country Ski X-C see Ski X-C 1046
Cross Cultural Research and Methodology Series see Sage Series in Cross Cultural Research and Methodology 937
Cross Currents (US ISSN 0748-0164) 719
Cross-Reference (US) 629
Cross River State. Ministry of Economic Development and Reconstruction. State Development Plan (NR) 294
Croton Review (US ISSN 0741-6210) 104, 719
Croydon Bibliographies for Regional Survey (UK ISSN 0309-8591) 1003
Croydon Chamber of Commerce and Industry Directory see Southern Home Counties Chamber of Commerce Directory 237
Croydon Natural History & Scientific Society. Proceedings and Transactions (UK ISSN 0309-8656) 990
Crucible see Crucible and Scientific Atheist 877
Crucible and Scientific Atheist (US ISSN 8756-1247) 877
Cruciferae Newsletter (UK ISSN 0263-9459) 26, 532
Cruising Association Yearbook (UK) 1041

Crustaceana. Supplements (NE) 174
Crustal and Upper Mantle Structure in Europe. Monographs (US) 398
Cruz Ansata (PR) 629
Cryogenic Engineering Conference Proceedings see Advances in Cryogenic Engineering 894
Cryptogamica Helvetica (SZ) 156
Cryptozoology (US ISSN 0736-7023) 174
Crystal Mirror (US ISSN 0097-7209) 977
Crystals: Growth, Properties and Applications (US ISSN 0172-5076) 327
Cuadernas Simancas de Investigaciones Historicas. Monografias see Investigaciones Historicas 586
Cuadernos B P D. Serie: Economia (Banco Paraguayo de Datos) (PY) 193
Cuadernos B P D. Serie: Social (Banco Paraguayo de Datos) (PY) 1025
Cuadernos Bibliograficos (SP ISSN 0590-1545) 709
Cuadernos C I P C A (Serie Popular) (Centro de Investigacion y Promocion del Campesinado) (BO) 426, 1025
Cuadernos Canarios de Ciencias Sociales (SP) 1151
Cuadernos D E I (Departamento Ecumenico de Investigaciones) (CR) 969
Cuadernos de Capacitacion (PE) 426
Cuadernos de Critica (Mexico) (MX ISSN 0185-2604) 710, 877
Cuadernos de Derecho Internacional Privado (UY) 670
Cuadernos de Estudio (PE) 982
Cuadernos de Estudios Judios (AG) 502
Cuadernos de Estudios Latinoamericanos (AG) 904
Cuadernos de Estudios Medievales (SP) 580
Cuadernos de Filosofia (AG) 877
Cuadernos de Filosofia (CL) 877
Cuadernos de Historia (CL ISSN 0716-1832) 605
Cuadernos de Historia de la Farmacia (SP ISSN 0210-6566) 870
Cuadernos de Historia del Arte (AG ISSN 0070-1688) 104
Cuadernos de Historia del Islam (SP) 612
Cuadernos de Historia del Islam. Serie Monografica Islamica Occidentalia see Cuadernos de Historia del Islam 612
Cuadernos de la C E P A L (Comision Economica para America Latina (CEPAL)) (UN) 238
Cuadernos de Linguistica (MX) 693
Cuadernos de los Institutos (AG) 654
Cuadernos de Maipu (AG) 537
Cuadernos de Orientacion (VE ISSN 0070-170X) 433
Cuadernos de Pedagogia (VE ISSN 0070-1718) 412
Cuadernos de Prehistoria (SP) 85
Cuadernos de Psicologia (CL) 934
Cuadernos de Realidades Sociales (SP ISSN 0302-7724) 1025
Cuadernos de Salud Publica see Public Health Papers 955
Cuadernos de Seccion. Cinencias Sociales y Economicas (SP) 193
Cuadernos de Semiotica (UY) 693
Cuadernos de Session. Cinematografia (SP) 823
Cuadernos de Sociedad y Politica (PE) 1007
Cuadernos de Teologia Actual, Ciencias Sociales y Realidad Nacional (PE) 969
Cuadernos de Teologia y Pastoral (CK) 982
Cuadernos de Trabajo de Historia (SP) 580
Cuadernos del C R E F A L (Centro Regional de Educacon de Adultos y Alfabetizacion Funcional para America Latina) (MX) 426
Cuadernos del Taller de Folklore (PE) 515
Cuadernos Geograficos (SP ISSN 0210-5462) 542
Cuadernos N T (SP) 629

Cuadernos para el Debate Regional (PE) *622*
Cuadernos para el Estudio de la Estetica y la Literatura (AG) *719*
Cuadernos Populares (PE) *426*
Cuadernos Salmantinos de Filosofia (SP ISSN 0210-4857) *877*
Cuadernos Simancas de Investigaciones Historicas: Monografias (SP) *580*
Cuadernos Valencianos de Historia de la Medicina y de la Ciencia (SP ISSN 0011-2577) *760, 990*
Cuba. Centro de Informacion y Divulgacion Agropecuario. Boletin de Resenas. Serie: Arroz see Cuba. Centro de Informacion y Documentacion Agropecuario. Boletin de Resenas. Serie: Arroz *26*
Cuba. Centro de Informacion y Divulgacion Agropecuario. Boletin de Resenas. Serie: Avicultura (CU) *65*
Cuba. Centro de Informacion y Divulgacion Agropecuario. Boletin de Resenas. Serie: Citricos (CU ISSN 0138-8339) *54*
Cuba. Centro de Informacion y Divulgacion Agropecuario. Boletin de Resenas. Serie: Cafe y Cacao see Cuba. Centro de Informacion y Documentacion Agropecuario. Boletin de Resenas. Serie: Cafe y Cacao *54*
Cuba. Centro de Informacion y Divulgacion Agropecuario. Boletin de Resenas. Serie: Ganado Porcino see Cuba. Centro de Informacion y Documentacion Agropecuario. Boletin de Resenas. Serie: Ganado Porcino *65*
Cuba. Centro de Informacion y Divulgacion Agropecuario. Boletin de Resenas. Serie: Genetica y Reproduccion see Cuba. Centro de Informacion y Documentacion Agropecuario. Boletin de Resenas. Serie: Mejoramiento Animal *174*
Cuba. Centro de Informacion y Divulgacion Agropecuario. Boletin de Resenas. Serie: Mecanizacion see Cuba. Centro de Informacion y Documentacion Agropecuario. Boletin de Resenas. Serie: Mecanizacion de la Agricultura *51*
Cuba. Centro de Informacion y Divulgacion Agropecuario. Boletin de Resenas. Serie: Pastos see Cuba. Centro de Informacion y Documentacion Agropecuario. Boletin de Resenas. Serie: Pastos y Forrajes *63*
Cuba. Centro de Informacion y Divulgacion Agropecuario. Boletin de Resenas. Serie: Proteccion de Plantas see Cuba. Centro de Informacion y Documentacion Agropecuario. Boletin de Resenas. Serie: Proteccion de Plantas *54*
Cuba. Centro de Informacion y Divulgacion Agropecuario. Boletin de Resenas. Serie: Plantas Medicinales see Cuba. Centro de Informacion y Documentacion Agropecuario. Boletin de Resenas. Serie: Plantas Medicinales *156*
Cuba. Centro de Informacion y Divulgacion Agropecuario. Boletin de Resenas. Serie: Riego y Drenaje see Cuba. Centro de Informacion y Documentacion Agropecuario. Boletin de Resenas. Serie: Riego y Drenaje *54*
Cuba. Centro de Informacion y Divulgacion Agropecuario. Boletin de Resenas. Serie: Suelos y Agroquimica see Cuba. Centro de Informacion y Documentacion Agropecuario. Boletin de Resenas. Serie: Suelos y Agroquimica *54*
Cuba. Centro de Informacion y Divulgacion Agropecuario. Boletin de Resenas. Serie: Veterinaria see Cuba. Centro de Informacion y Documentacion Agropecuario. Boletin de Resenas. Serie: Veterinaria *1121*

Cuba. Centro de Informacion y Divulgacion Agropecuario. Boletin de Resenas. Serie: Viandas, Hortalizas y Granos see Cuba. Centro de Informacion y Documentacion Agropecuario. Boletin de Resenas. Serie: Viandas Tropicales *54*
Cuba. Centro de Informacion y Divulgacion Agropecuario. Boletin de Resenas. Serie: Viandas, Hortalizas y Granos see Cuba. Centro de Informacion y Documentacion Agropecuario. Boletin de Resenas. Serie: Hortalizas, Papas, Granos y Fibras *54*
Cuba. Centro de Informacion y Documentacion Agropecuario. Boletin de Resenas. Serie: Arroz (CU ISSN 0138-838X) *26*
Cuba. Centro de Informacion y Documentacion Agropecuario. Boletin de Resenas. Serie: Avicultura see Cuba. Centro de Informacion y Divulgacion Agropecuario. Boletin de Resenas. Serie: Avicultura *65*
Cuba. Centro de Informacion y Documentacion Agropecuario. Boletin de Resenas. Serie: Cafe y Cacao (CU ISSN 0138-8436) *54*
Cuba. Centro de Informacion y Documentacion Agropecuario. Boletin de Resenas. Serie: Citricos y Otras Frutales see Cuba. Centro de Informacion y Divulgacion Agropecuario. Boletin de Resenas. Serie: Citricos *54*
Cuba. Centro de Informacion y Documentacion Agropecuario. Boletin de Resenas. Serie: Economia Agropecuaria (CU) *46*
Cuba. Centro de Informacion y Documentacion Agropecuario. Boletin de Resenas. Serie: Forestales (CU ISSN 0138-7782) *524*
Cuba. Centro de Informacion y Documentacion Agropecuario. Boletin de Resenas. Serie: Ganado Porcino (CU) *65*
Cuba. Centro de Informacion y Documentacion Agropecuario. Boletin de Resenas. Serie: Hortalizas, Papas, Granos y Fibras (CU ISSN 0138-8231) *54*
Cuba. Centro de Informacion y Documentacion Agropecuario. Boletin de Resenas. Serie: Mejoramiento Animal (CU) *26, 174*
Cuba. Centro de Informacion y Documentacion Agropecuario. Boletin de Resenas. Serie: Mecanizacion de la Agricultura (CU) *51*
Cuba. Centro de Informacion y Documentacion Agropecuario. Boletin de Resenas. Serie: Proteccion de Plantas (CU ISSN 0138-8088) *54*
Cuba. Centro de Informacion y Documentacion Agropecuario. Boletin de Resenas. Serie: Plantas Medicinales (CU ISSN 0138-8037) *156, 870*
Cuba. Centro de Informacion y Documentacion Agropecuario. Boletin de Resenas. Serie: Pastos y Forrajes (CU ISSN 0138-7839) *63*
Cuba. Centro de Informacion y Documentacion Agropecuario. Boletin de Resenas. Serie: Riego y Drenaje (CU ISSN 0138-788X) *54*
Cuba. Centro de Informacion y Documentacion Agropecuario. Boletin de Resenas. Serie: Suelos y Agroquimica (CU ISSN 0138-7936) *54*
Cuba. Centro de Informacion y Documentacion Agropecuario. Boletin de Resenas. Serie: Veterinaria(CU ISSN 0138-8134) *1121*
Cuba. Centro de Informacion y Documentacion Agropecuario. Boletin de Resenas. Serie: Viandas Tropicales (CU) *54*
Cuba en Cifras (CU) *206, 1053*
Cuban American National Foundation. Publication (US) *913*
Cuban Economy see Economia Cubana *243*

Cuban Studies/Estudios Cubanos (US ISSN 0361-4441) *911*
Cuban Studies Newsletter/Boletin de Estudios Cubanos see Cuban Studies *911*
Cuban Update (US) *913*
Cuisine Chez Sol (FR ISSN 0339-7963) *614*
Cultura (IT ISSN 0391-8505) *629*
Cultura e Mass Media (IT ISSN 0392-2111) *1025*
Cultura, Historia y Filosofia (PO ISSN 0870-4546) *580, 877*
Cultura Sarda (IT) *580*
Cultural Context of Infancy (US) *934*
Culture & Tradition (CN ISSN 0701-0184) *515*
Culture Camerounaise/Cameroonian Culture (CM) *565*
Culture et Societe (BD) *710*
Culture, Illness and Healing (NE) *71*
Cultures du Canada Francais (CN ISSN 0825-2777) *502, 605, 1007*
Cumberland and Westmorland Antiquarian and Archaeological Society. Research Series (UK) *85*
Cumberland and Westmorland Antiquarian and Archaeological Society. Transactions (UK ISSN 0309-7986) *85*
Cumbria and North Lancashire Catering and Hotel Year Book (UK) *619*
Cumbria and North Lancashire Farming Year Book (UK) *26*
Cumbria & North Lancashire Industry and Building Industry Year Book (UK) *193, 1081*
Cumbria and North Lancashire Industry and Transport Year Book see Cumbria & North Lancashire Industry and Building Industry Year Book *193*
Cumbria and North Lancashire Industry Year Book see Cumbria & North Lancashire Industry and Building Industry Year Book *193*
Cumitechs (Cumulative Techniques and Procedures in Clinical Microbiology) (US) *760*
Cumulated Abridged Index Medicus (US ISSN 0090-1377) *4, 769*
Cumulated Index Medicus (US ISSN 0090-1423) *4, 769*
Cumulative Annual Statistics, Alberta Coal Industry see Alberta Coal Industry, Annual Statistics *814*
Cumulative Bibliography of Literature Examined by the Radiation Shielding Information Center (US) *125, 892, 896*
Cumulative Book Index (US ISSN 0011-300X) *125, 961*
Cumulative Index to Nursing & Allied Health Literature (C I N A H L) (US ISSN 0146-5554) *4, 769*
Cumulative Index to Nursing Literature see Cumulative Index to Nursing & Allied Health Literature (C I N A H L) *769*
Cumulative Index to Nursing Literature, Nursing Subject Headings see Cumulative Index to Nursing & Allied Health Literature (C I N A H L) *769*
Cumulative Techniques and Procedures in Clinical Microbiology Cumitechs see Cumitechs *760*
Cunninghamia (AT ISSN 0727-9620) *156*
CUNYForum see C U N Y Forum *692*
Curacao Trade and Industry Directory. (NA) *305*
Curiopress International (FR) *125*
Curley's Streets & Trades Directories of Wembley, Middlesex & Selby, Yorkshire (UK) *305, 580*
Current Abstracts of Chemistry and Index Chemicus see Index Chemicus *325*
Current Abstracts of the Soviet Press see Current Digest of the Soviet Press *911*
Current Advances in Plant Science (US ISSN 0306-4484) *149*
Current African Issues (SW ISSN 0280-2171) *565*

Current Agro-Technology for Potato Production (PK) *26, 54*
Current Aircraft Prices (SZ) *18, 811*
Current Asian & Australasian Directories (UK) *206*
Current Audiovisuals for Mental Health Education (US) *1151*
Current Australian and New Zealand Legal Literature Index (AT ISSN 0310-5415) *4, 668*
Current Awareness in Biological Sciences (US ISSN 0733-4443) *4, 150*
Current Bibliographic Directory of the Arts and Sciences see Current Contents Address Directory-Science & Technology *990*
Current Bibliographic Directory of the Arts and Sciencies see Current Contents Address Directory-Social Sciences/Arts & Humanities *1007*
Current Bibliographies on Science & Technology: Biology, Pharmacy & Food Science (KO) *4, 40, 150, 873*
Current Bibliographies on Science and Technology: Mechanical Engineering & Construction Engineering (KO) *4, 801, 1072*
Current Bibliographies on Science and Technology: Metallurgy, Natural Resources & Energy (KO) *468, 797, 801*
Current Bibliography for Aquatic Sciences and Fisheries see Aquatic Sciences & Fisheries Abstracts. Part 2: Ocean Technology, Policy and Non-Living Resources *1127*
Current Bibliography on Science and Technology see Current Bibliographies on Science and Technology: Mechanical Engineering & Construction Engineering *801*
Current Biographies of Leading Archaeologists (US ISSN 0361-4735) *134*
Current Biography Yearbook (US ISSN 0084-9499) *134*
Current Biotechnology Abstracts (UK) *150, 1003*
Current British Directories (UK ISSN 0070-1858) *206*
Current Business Reports (US) *243*
Current Cardiology (US ISSN 0163-9501) *776*
Current Career and Occupational Literature (US ISSN 0161-0562) *4, 849*
Current Chemical Concepts (US) *322*
Current Chemical Reactions (US ISSN 0163-6278) *4, 325*
Current Christian Abstracts (US ISSN 0883-1440) *975*
Current Christian Books (US ISSN 0270-2347) *125, 975*
Current Christian Books. Authors and Titles see Current Christian Books *975*
Current Christian Books. Titles, Authors, and Publishers see Current Christian Books *975*
Current Clinical Topics in Infectious Diseases (US ISSN 0195-3842) *777*
Current Concepts in Nutrition (US ISSN 0090-0443) *846*
Current Construction Costs (US ISSN 0161-7257) *183*
Current Construction Reports (US) *183*
Current Construction Reports: Housing Units Authorized by Building Permits(US) *183, 622*
Current Construction Reports: Housing Units Authorized by Building Permits and Public Contracts see Current Construction Reports: Housing Units Authorized by Building Permits *622*
Current Construction Reports: New One Family Homes Sold and for Sale(US ISSN 0363-8537) *622*
Current Contents Address Directory-Science & Technology (US) *990*
Current Contents Address Directory-Social Sciences/Arts & Humanities (US) *629, 1007*
Current Contents/Arts & Humanities (US ISSN 0163-3155) *125, 634*
Current Contents/Clinical Medicine (US) *4, 769*

Current Contents/Clinical Pratice see
  Current Contents/Clinical Medicine
  769
Current Contents in Management see
  Contents Pages in Management 206
Current Contents of Academic Journals
  in Japan (JA ISSN 0386-7293) 125
Current Contents/Social & Behavioral
  Sciences (US ISSN 0092-6361) 4,
  423, 1031
Current Diagnostic Pediatrics (US
  ISSN 0172-1232) 787
Current Digest of the Soviet Press (US
  ISSN 0011-3425) 4, 911, 1014
Current Digest of the Soviet Press.
  Annual Index. (US) 904
Current European Directories (UK
  ISSN 0070-1955) 206
Current Events (Fredericton) see N.B.
  Power News 457
Current Gastroenterology (US ISSN
  0198-8085) 782
Current Genealogical Publications (US)
  535
Current Geological and Geophysical
  Studies in Montana (US ISSN 0092-
  9565) 385, 398
Current Governments Reports (US)
  940
Current Governments Reports: Chart
  Book on Government Data.
  Organization, Finances and
  Employment (US ISSN 0360-2508)
  294
Current Governments Reports: City
  Employment (US ISSN 0091-9209)
  206
Current Governments Reports: City
  Government Finances (US ISSN
  0082-9439) 294
Current Governments Reports: County
  Employment (US) 271, 940
Current Governments Reports: County
  Government Finances (US ISSN
  0098-678X) 294
Current Governments Reports:
  Finances of Employee Retirement
  Systems of State and Local
  Governments (US ISSN 0096-3224)
  271, 294, 940
Current Governments Reports:
  Governmental Finances (US ISSN
  0095-3741) 294
Current Governments Reports: Local
  Government Finances in Selected
  Metropolitan Areas and Large
  Counties (US) 294
Current Governments Reports: Public
  Employment (US) 271
Current Governments Reports:
  Quarterly Summary of State and
  Local Tax Revenue (US ISSN 0501-
  7718) 294
Current Governments Reports: State
  and Local Government Special
  Studies (US) 294
Current Governments Reports: State
  Government Finances (US ISSN
  0090-5895) 206
Current Governments Reports: State
  Government Tax Collections (US
  ISSN 0270-0808) 294
Current Hematology and Oncology
  (US) 775, 783
Current Housing Reports (US) 622
Current Housing Reports: American
  Housing Survey: Metropolitan
  Areas.(US) 622
Current Housing Reports: American
  Housing Survey: United States and
  Regions (US) 622
Current Housing Reports: Annual
  Housing Survey: Metropolitan Areas
  see Current Housing Reports:
  American Housing Survey:
  Metropolitan Areas 622
Current Housing Reports: Annual
  Housing Survey: United States and
  Regions see Current Housing
  Reports: American Housing Survey:
  United States and Regions 622
Current Housing Reports: Housing
  Characteristics (US ISSN 0498-
  8450) 622
Current Housing Reports: Housing
  Vacancies (US ISSN 0498-8469)
  623

Current Housing Reports: Market
  Absorption of Apartments (US ISSN
  0363-8286) 623
Current Index to Journals in Education
  (US ISSN 0011-3565) 4, 423
Current Index to Journals in Science
  and Technology: Biology,
  Agriculture, Pharmacy see Current
  Bibliographies on Science &
  Technology: Biology, Pharmacy &
  Food Science 150
Current Index to Journals in Science
  and Technology: Mechanical,
  Metallurgical, Natural Resources and
  Construction Engineering see
  Current Bibliographies on Science
  and Technology: Mechanical
  Engineering & Construction
  Engineering 801
Current Index to Statistics (US ISSN
  0364-1228) 4, 1053
Current Industrial Relations Scene in
  Canada (CN ISSN 0318-952X) 271
Current Industrial Reports (US ISSN
  0498-8477) 288
Current Industrial Reports: Fats and
  Oils. Oilseed Crushings (US ISSN
  0145-5168) 521, 1053
Current Industrial Reports: Fats and
  Oils. Production, Consumption, and
  Factory and Warehouse Stocks (US
  ISSN 0145-5176) 521, 1053
Current Industrial Reports: Finished
  Fabrics. Production, Inventories, and
  Unfilled Orders (US) 1054, 1075
Current Industrial Reports: Woven
  Fabrics. Production, Inventories, and
  Unfilled Orders see Current
  Industrial Reports: Finished Fabrics.
  Production, Inventories, and Unfilled
  Orders 1075
Current Issues (Arlington) (US ISSN
  0743-0388) 915
Current Issues and Research in
  Advertising (US ISSN 0163-3392)
  15
Current Issues in Banking see Current
  Issues in Banks & Thrift Institutions
  227
Current Issues in Banks & Thrift
  Institutions (US) 227
Current Issues in Higher Education (US
  ISSN 0070-1971) 433
Current Issues in Music Education (US
  ISSN 0070-198X) 446, 835
Current Issues in Savings Institutions
  see Current Issues in Banks & Thrift
  Institutions 227
Current Issues in Toxicology (US) 870
Current Labour Force Statistics for
  Nova Scotia (CN ISSN 0382-1102)
  1151
Current Law Index (US ISSN 0196-
  1780) 4, 668
Current Leather Literature (II ISSN
  0011-3638) 4, 672
Current Legal Problems (UK ISSN
  0070-1998) 654
Current Literature in Family Planning
  (US ISSN 0092-6000) 179
Current Literature on Aging (US ISSN
  0011-3662) 552
Current Literature on General Medical
  Practice see Health Service Abstracts
  1023
Current Literature on Health Services
  see Health Service Abstracts 1023
Current Literature on Venereal Disease
  see Sexually Transmitted Diseases.
  Abstracts & Bibliography 773
Current Malaysian Serials (Non-
  Government)/Terbitan Bersiri Kini
  Malaysia (Bukan Kerajaan) (MY
  ISSN 0127-1555) 125
Current Malaysian Serials/Terbitan
  Bersiri Kini Malaysia see Current
  Malaysian Serials (Non-Government)
  125
Current Mammology (US) 174
Current Mathematical Publications (US
  ISSN 0361-4794) 755
Current Medical Information and
  Terminology (US ISSN 0070-2005)
  760
Current Medical Research and Opinion
  (UK ISSN 0300-7995) 760
Current Medical Terminology see
  Current Medical Information and
  Terminology 760

Current Municipal Problems (US ISSN
  0011-3727) 654, 950
Current Nephrology (US ISSN 0148-
  4265) 795
Current Neurology (US ISSN 0161-
  780X) 789
Current Ornithology (US) 170
Current Packaging Abstracts (US ISSN
  0091-0120) 4, 855
Current Papers in Physics (UK ISSN
  0011-3786) 4, 115, 892
Current Perspectives in Social Theory
  (US ISSN 0278-1204) 1025
Current Physics Index (US ISSN 0098-
  9819) 4, 892
Current Population Reports (US ISSN
  0082-9471) 921
Current Population Reports: Consumer
  Income (US) 277, 921
Current Population Reports: Consumer
  Income. Money Income in (Year) of
  Families and Persons in the United
  States see Current Population
  Reports: Consumer Income. Money
  Income of Households, Families and
  Persons in the United States (Year)
  277
Current Population Reports: Consumer
  Income. Money Income of
  Households, Families and Persons in
  the United States (Year) (US) 277
Current Population Reports: Farm
  Population (US) 921
Current Population Reports: Federal-
  State Cooperative Program for
  Population Estimates see Current
  Population Reports: Local Population
  Estimates 921
Current Population Reports:
  International Population Data see
  International Population Data 922
Current Population Reports: Local
  Population Estimates (US) 921
Current Population Reports, P-25:
  Population Estimates and Projections.
  Estimates of the Population of the
  United States by Age, Color, and Sex
  see Current Population Reports:
  Population Estimates and Projections.
  Estimates of the Population of the
  United States by Age, Race and Sex
  921
Current Population Reports: Population
  Characteristics (US ISSN 0363-
  6836) 921
Current Population Reports: Population
  Characteristics. Geographic Mobility
  (US) 921
Current Population Reports: Population
  Characteristics. Household and
  Family Characteristics (US) 921
Current Population Reports: Population
  Characteristics. Marital Status and
  Family Status see Current Population
  Reports: Population Characteristics.
  Marital Status and Living
  Arrangements 921
Current Population Reports: Population
  Characteristics. Marital Status and
  Living Arrangements (US) 921
Current Population Reports: Population
  Characteristics. Mobility of the
  Population of the United States see
  Current Population Reports:
  Population Characteristics.
  Geographic Mobility 921
Current Population Reports: Population
  Characteristics. School Enrollment:
  Social and Economic Characteristics
  of Students (US) 921
Current Population Reports: Population
  Characteristics. Social and Economic
  Characteristics of the Black
  Population (US) 921
Current Population Reports: Population
  Estimates and Projections (US) 921
Current Population Reports: Population
  Estimates and Projections. Estimates
  of the Population of the United
  States and Components of Population
  Change (US ISSN 0071-1616) 921
Current Population Reports: Population
  Estimates and Projections. Estimates
  of the Population of the United
  States by Age, Race and Sex (US)
  921
Current Population Reports: Special
  Censuses (US) 921

Current Population Reports: Special
  Studies (US ISSN 0498-8485) 921
Current Practices in Dryland Resources
  and Technology (II) 1124
Current Practices in Environmental
  Engineering see Current Practices in
  Environmental Science and
  Engineering 495
Current Practices in Environmental
  Science and Engineering (II) 495,
  1124
Current Practices in Geotechnical
  Engineering (II ISSN 0253-5122)
  385, 398, 480
Current Problems in Clinical
  Biochemistry (SZ ISSN 0300-1725)
  151, 760
Current Problems in Dermatology (SZ
  ISSN 0070-2064) 780
Current Problems in Pulmonology (US)
  776
Current Procedural Terminology see C
  P T 758
Current Programs Annual Index see
  Conference Papers Annual Index 4
Current Publications in Legal and
  Related Fields (US ISSN 0011-
  3859) 668
Current Radiology (US ISSN 0161-
  7818) 792
Current Research and Development
  Projects in Israel: Natural Sciences
  and Technology (IS ISSN 0301-
  4657) 1151
Current Research in Britain. Biological
  Sciences (UK ISSN 0267-1956) 4,
  150, 687
Current Research in Britain.
  Humanities(UK ISSN 0267-1972)
  629
Current Research in Britain. Physical
  Sciences (UK ISSN 0267-1948) 4,
  687, 1003
Current Research in Britain. Social
  Sciences (UK ISSN 0267-1964) 4,
  687, 1014
Current Research in British Studies by
  American and Canadian Scholars
  (US ISSN 0590-417X) 629, 1007
Current Research in Film (US ISSN
  0748-8580) 823
Current Research in French Studies at
  Universities and Polytechnics in the
  United Kingdom (UK) 125, 709,
  739
Current Research in French Studies at
  Universities and University Colleges
  in the United Kingdom see Current
  Research in French Studies at
  Universities and Polytechnics in the
  United Kingdom 709
Current Research in the Pleistocene
  (US ISSN 8755-898X) 85, 856
Current Science and Technology
  Research in Japan (JA) 990
Current Soviet Policies (US) 904
Current Studies in Hematology and
  Blood Transfusion (SZ ISSN 783
Current Studies in Librarianship (US)
  676
Current Sweden (SW) 540
Current Swedish Periodicals see Svensk
  Tidskriftsfoerteckning 131
Current Technology Index (UK ISSN
  0260-6593) 4, 1072
Current Titles in Electrochemistry (II
  ISSN 0037-9689) 4, 325
Current Titles in Ocean, Coastal, Lake
  & Waterway Sciences (US ISSN
  0883-4725) 4, 382, 1128
Current Topics in Anaesthesia (UK
  ISSN 0144-8684) 774
Current Topics in Bioenergetics (US
  ISSN 0070-2129) 153, 885
Current Topics in Cardiovascular
  Medicine (UK) 776
Current Topics in Cellular Regulation
  (US ISSN 0070-2137) 140
Current Topics in Chinese Science (US
  ISSN 0732-4383) 990
Current Topics in Chinese Science.
  Section C: Mathematics (US ISSN
  0732-4405) 748
Current Topics in Chinese Science.
  Section E: Astronomy (US ISSN
  0732-4421) 115
Current Topics in Clinical and
  Community Psychology (US ISSN
  0070-2145) 934

Current Topics in Comparative Pathobiology (US ISSN 0090-8584) 140, 760
Current Topics in Developmental Biology (US ISSN 0070-2153) 140
Current Topics in Early Childhood Education (US ISSN 0363-8332) 412
Current Topics in Environmental and Toxicological Chemistry (US ISSN 0275-2581) 322, 495, 870
Current Topics in Experimental Endocrinology (US ISSN 0091-7397) 781
Current Topics in Eye Research (US ISSN 0190-2970) 785
Current Topics in Hematology (US ISSN 0190-1486) 1151
Current Topics in Human Intelligence (US ISSN 8755-0040) 934
Current Topics in Immunology (UK) 773
Current Topics in Infection (UK ISSN 0260-1664) 760
Current Topics in Learning Disabilities (US) 934
Current Topics in Materials Science (NE ISSN 0165-1854) 888
Current Topics in Membranes and Transport (US ISSN 0070-2161) 140, 174
Current Topics in Microbiology and Immunology (US ISSN 0070-217X) 168
Current Topics in Molecular Endocrinology (US ISSN 0094-6761) 1151
Current Topics in Neuroendocrinology (US) 781, 789
Current Topics in Nutrition and Disease (US ISSN 0191-2453) 846
Current Topics in Pathology (US ISSN 0070-2188) 140, 760
Current Topics in Surgical Research (US ISSN 0070-2196) 794
Current Topics of Contemporary Thought (US ISSN 0275-9098) 990
Current Treatment of Cancer (US) 775
Current Treaty Index (US ISSN 0731-8189) 670
Current Trends in Life Sciences (II ISSN 0378-7540) 140
Current Trends in Programming Methodology (US) 358
Current U.S. Government Periodicals on Microfiche see Index to U.S. Government Periodicals 7
Current Work in the History of Medicine (UK ISSN 0011-3999) 769
Curricula in the Atmospheric and Oceanographic Sciences see Curricula in the Atmospheric, Oceanic and Related Sciences 804
Curricula in the Atmospheric, Oceanic and Related Sciences (US) 433, 804
Curricula in the Atmospheric Sciences see Curricula in the Atmospheric, Oceanic and Related Sciences 804
Curriculum Improvement (US ISSN 0094-1050) 412
Curriculum Information Center State School Directories see C I C's State School Directories 428
Curriculum Plans see United Methodist Church. Curriculum Plans 980
Curtain, Drapery and Bedspread National Buyers Guide see Interior Textiles National Buyers Guide 1074
Curtis Legacy (US) 535
Cusanus-Gesellschaft. Buchreihe (GW ISSN 0070-2234) 969
Cushman Foundation for Foraminiferal Research. Special Publication (US ISSN 0070-2242) 856
Custom Chemical Synthesis Services in France (UK) 305, 322
Custom Chemical Synthesis Services in the U.K. (UK) 305, 322
Custom Chemical Synthesis Services in West Germany (UK) 305, 322
Custom House Guide (US ISSN 0070-2250) 254
Custom Integrated Circuits Conference. Proceedings. see I E E E Custom Integrated Circuits Conference. Proceedings 454

Customs and Practices of Notaries Public and Digest of Notary Laws in the U.S. see Journal of Notarial Acts and Recordkeeping Practices 658
Customs and Practices of Notaries Public and Digest of Notary Laws in the U.S. see Notary Public Practices & Glossary 661
Customs Officer's Association of Australia. Fourth Division. Fourth Division Customs Officer (AT) 254
Cut Your Own Taxes and Save (Year) (US) 294
Cybernetic (US ISSN 0883-4202) 359
Cybernetics Abstracts (English translation of: Referativnyi Zhurnal-Kibernetika) (UK ISSN 0011-4243) 4, 354
Cybernetics: Documents de Travail see Cybernetics: Works in Progress 359
Cybernetics: Works in Progress/Cybernetics: Documents de Travail (BE) 359
Cycle Buyers Guide (US ISSN 0070-2277) 1039
Cycle Street and Touring Guide (US ISSN 0272-8923) 1041
Cycle World Buyer's Guide (US) 1041
Cycle World Road Test Annual see Cycle World Test Annual and Buyers Guide 1041
Cycle World Test Annual and Buyers Guide (US ISSN 0270-2746) 1041
Cyclen see Cykle-Jul 1041
Cyclists Touring Club Handbook (UK) 1151
Cyclopedia (CN) 412
Cyfres Barddoniaeth Pwyllgor Cyfieithiadau Yr Academi (UK) 741
Cyfres Clasuron Yr Academi (UK) 719
Cyfres Llygad y Ffynnon (UK) 556
Cykle-Jul (DK ISSN 0107-7805) 1041
Cypher (UK) 14, 719
Cypris (US ISSN 0886-3806) 174, 856
Cyprus. Agricultural Research Institute. Agricultural Economics Report (CY ISSN 0379-0827) 46
Cyprus. Agricultural Research Institute. Annual Report (CY ISSN 0070-2307) 26
Cyprus. Agricultural Research Institute. Miscellaneous Reports (CY ISSN 0253-6749) 26
Cyprus. Agricultural Research Institute. Technical Bulletin (CY ISSN 0070-2315) 26
Cyprus. Budget: Estimates of Revenue and Expenditure (CY ISSN 0070-2323) 294
Cyprus. Chief Veterinary Officer. Annual Report (CY) 1121
Cyprus. Department of Agriculture. Annual Report (CY) 26
Cyprus. Department of Agriculture. Soils and Plant Nutrition Section. Report (CY ISSN 0070-234X) 54
Cyprus. Department of Antiquities. Annual Report (CY ISSN 0070-2374) 85
Cyprus. Department of Antiquities. Monographs (CY ISSN 0070-2366) 85
Cyprus. Department of Customs and Excise. Annual Report (CY) 254
Cyprus. Department of Fisheries. Annual Report of the Cyprus Fisheries see Cyprus. Department of Fisheries. Annual Report on the Department of Fisheries and the Cyprus Fisheries 508
Cyprus. Department of Fisheries. Annual Report on the Department of Fisheries and the Cyprus Fisheries (CY) 508
Cyprus. Department of Social Welfare Services. Annual Report (CY ISSN 0070-2404) 1016
Cyprus. Department of Statistics and Research. Agricultural Statistics (CY ISSN 0379-0924) 26
Cyprus. Department of Statistics and Research. Agricultural Survey. see Cyprus. Department of Statistics and Research. Agricultural Statistics 26

Cyprus. Department of Statistics and Research. Annual Industrial Production Survey see Cyprus. Department of Statistics and Research. Industrial Production Survey 1151
Cyprus. Department of Statistics and Research. Census of Cottage Industry(CY) 1054
Cyprus. Department of Statistics and Research. Census of Industrial Production. (CY) 206, 1054
Cyprus. Department of Statistics and Research. Census of Poultry. (CY) 40, 1054
Cyprus. Department of Statistics and Research. Construction and Housing Report (CY ISSN 0253-8725) 183
Cyprus. Department of Statistics and Research. Criminal Statistics (CY ISSN 0253-8695) 373, 1054
Cyprus. Department of Statistics and Research. Demographic Report (CY ISSN 0590-4846) 926
Cyprus. Department of Statistics and Research. Demographic Survey. (Year) (CY) 926, 1054
Cyprus. Department of Statistics and Research. Economic Report (CY ISSN 0070-2412) 206
Cyprus. Department of Statistics and Research. Functions and Services (CY) 1054
Cyprus. Department of Statistics and Research. Household Expenditure Survey (CY) 206, 1054
Cyprus. Department of Statistics and Research. Industrial Production Survey (CY) 1151
Cyprus. Department of Statistics and Research. Motor Vehicles and Road Accidents (CY ISSN 0574-8399) 1151
Cyprus. Department of Statistics and Research. Multi-Round Demographic Survey. Migration in Cyprus (CY) 926, 1054
Cyprus. Department of Statistics and Research. Multi-Round Demographic Survey. Summary of Main Demographic Characteristics (CY) 926, 1054
Cyprus. Department of Statistics and Research. Multi-Round Demographic Survey. Main Report see Cyprus. Department of Statistics and Research. Demographic Survey. (Year) 926
Cyprus. Department of Statistics and Research. Questionnaires for Censuses and Surveys (CY) 1054
Cyprus. Department of Statistics and Research. Services Survey (CY ISSN 0253-8598) 288
Cyprus. Department of Statistics and Research. Shipping and Aviation Statistics see Cyprus. Department of Statistics and Research. Shipping Statistics 1151
Cyprus. Department of Statistics and Research. Shipping Statistics (CY ISSN 0070-2439) 1151
Cyprus. Department of Statistics and Research. Statistical Abstract (CY ISSN 0253-875X) 1054
Cyprus. Department of Statistics and Research. Statistical Pocket Book (CY) 1054
Cyprus. Department of Statistics and Research. Statistics of Imports and Exports (CY ISSN 0070-2420) 254
Cyprus. Department of Statistics and Research. Statistics of Imports, Exports and Shipping see Cyprus. Department of Statistics and Research. Shipping Statistics 1151
Cyprus. Department of Statistics and Research. Tourism, Migration and Travel Statistics (CY ISSN 0253-8709) 926, 1119
Cyprus. Department of Statistics and Research. Wages, Salaries and Hours of Work (CY ISSN 0253-8660) 1151
Cyprus. Development Estimates (CY ISSN 0084-9510) 294
Cyprus. Five Year Plans (CY) 243

Cyprus. Geological Survey Department. Annual Report (CY ISSN 0574-8267) 379
Cyprus. Geological Survey Department. Bulletin (CY) 379
Cyprus. Geological Survey Department. Memoirs (CY ISSN 0574-8259) 379
Cyprus. Loan Commissioners. Accounts and Statistics for the Year (CY ISSN 0574-8305) 294
Cyprus. Meteorological Service. Summary of the Weather in Cyprus (CY ISSN 0379-0916) 804
Cyprus. Mines Department. Annual Report of the Senior Mines Officer for the Year see Cyprus. Mines Service. Annual Report 816
Cyprus. Mines Service. Annual Report (CY) 816
Cyprus. Ministry of Health. Department of Medical & Public Health Services. Annual Report (CY) 619
Cyprus. Ministry of Labour and Social Insurance. Annual Report (CY ISSN 0070-2390) 271, 639
Cyprus. Tourism Organisation. Annual Report (CY) 254, 1107
Cyprus Chamber of Commerce and Industry Directory (CY ISSN 0070-2331) 305
Cyprus Development Bank. Annual Report (CY) 227
Cyprus Research Center. Annual see Kentron Epistemonikon Ereunon. Epeteris 697
Cystic Fibrosis Club Abstracts (US ISSN 0070-2455) 4, 354
Cystic Fibrosis G A P Conference Reports (US ISSN 0196-2418) 793
Cystisk Fibrose (DK ISSN 0901-4500) 760
Czasopismo Prawno-Historyczne (PL ISSN 0070-2471) 580
Czechoslovak Academy of Sciences. Institute of Landscape Ecology. Section of Hydrobiology. Annual Report (CS) 140
Czechoslovak Cooperative Movement in Figures (CS) 238
Czechoslovak Economic Papers (CS ISSN 0590-5001) 193
Czechoslovakia. Academy of Sciences. Hydrobiological Laboratory. Annual Report see Czechoslovak Academy of Sciences. Institute of Landscape Ecology. Section of Hydrobiology. Annual Report 140
Czechoslovakia. Federalni Statisticky Urad. Statisticka Rocenka (CS ISSN 0070-248X) 1054
Czechoslovakia & Poland Stamp Catalogue (UK ISSN 0142-9795) 874

C4 Hydrocarbons and Derivatives see World C4 Hydrocarbons and Derivatives 325
D A F i Tal (Dansk Athletik Forbund) (DK ISSN 0107-4547) 1036
D A N T E C Information (US ISSN 0900-5579) 452, 808
D.A.T.A. Book of Discontinued Transistors see Transistor Discontinued Devices D.A.T.A. Book 460
D'Art (SP ISSN 0211-0768) 104
D B Report (Deutsche Bundesbahn) (GW ISSN 0072-1549) 1094
D C A M M Report (Danish Center for Applied Mathematics and Mechanics) (DK ISSN 0106-6366) 748, 894
D C & see Dewey Decimal Classification Additions, Notes and Decisions 676
D C C - Camping Fuehrer Europa (Deutscher Camping Club e.V.) (GW ISSN 0078-3943) 1107
D C C - Caravan Modellfuehrer (Deutscher Camping Club e.V.) (GW) 1045, 1091
D C C - Touristik Service (Deutscher Camping Club e.V.) (GW) 1045, 1107
D.C. Directory (US ISSN 0740-3984) 502
D C S Manila Teachers of Secondary English English Quarterly see M S T English Quarterly 448

1706 D D

D D R Film Information (GE) *823*
D D V - Analysen (Danske Vedligeholdelsesforening) (DK ISSN 0107-5403) *1068*
D E G *see* Organisationer og Tal i Gartneriet *533*
D E I Cuadernos (Departamento Ecumenico de Investigaciones) (CR) *982*
D E K Haandbog (Dansk Elektroteknisk Komite) (DK ISSN 0107-4466) *452*
D E S Activities Report (Department of Economic Security) (US) *940*
D F V L R-Forschungsberichte und D F V L R-Mitteilungen (Deutsche Forschungs- und Versuchsanstalt fuer Luft- und Raumfahrt e.V.) (GW) *18*
D F V L R Jahresbericht (Deutsche Forschungs- und Versuchsanstalt fuer Luft- und Raumfahrt e.V.) (GW ISSN 0070-3966) *18*
D G D Schriftenreihe (Deutsche Gesellschaft fuer Dokumentation e.V.) (GW ISSN 0344-5372) *676*
D.G.L.R. Jahrbuecher (Deutsche Gesellschaft fuer Luft und Raumfahrt e.V.) (GW ISSN 0070-4083) *18*
D H Driftsoekonomi *see* Driftsoekonomi *193*
D.H.E. Data Briefs (Department of Higher Education) (US) *433*
D.H.E. Research Note (Department of Higher Education) (US) *433*
D.H. Hill Library Focus (US) *676*
D I A Yearbook - Design Action (UK ISSN 0306-6185) *495*
D I D S Doings (Decision Information Display System) (US) *360*
D I F Flyaarbog (Dansk Ingenioerforening) (DK ISSN 0107-0886) *18*
D I N. Catalog of Technical Rules (Deutsches Institut fuer Normung (DIN)) (GW ISSN 0723-7685) *654, 1068*
D I N - Handbook (Deutsches Institut fuer Normung e.V. (D I N)) (GW ISSN 0722-7337) *808*
D I N - Katalog fuer Technische Regeln (Deutsches Institut fuer Normung e.V.) (GW) *808*
D I N - Taschenbuecher (Deutsches Institut fuer Normung e.V. (D I N)) (GW ISSN 0342-801X) *809*
D I S A Information. Measurement and Analysis *see* D A N T E C Information *808*
D I S C U S Facts Book (Distilled Spirits Council of the United States, Inc.) (US ISSN 0160-1504) *1151*
D J H *see* Danmarks Journalisthoejskoles Aarskrift *434*
D J OE F - Haandbogen (Danmarks Juris- og Oekonomforbund) (DK ISSN 0108-3627) *193, 654*
D K (DK ISSN 0109-3371) *874*
D L A Bulletin (Division of Library Automation) (US ISSN 0272-037X) *355, 688*
D M C Information (Dansk Management Center) (DK ISSN 0107-8216) *279*
D M D (US) *341, 779*
D M V Nyt (Dansk Miljoevaern) (DK ISSN 0109-4033) *495*
D N O C S - Fins e Atividades (Departamento Nacional de Obras Contra as Secas) (BL) *54, 490*
D N P A (Departamento Nacional de Producao Animal) (BL) *65*
D O G Career Guides Series (UK) *847*
D P E D Newsletter (Department of Planning and Economic Development) (US) *623*
D P I Yellow Pages *see* Directory of Nebraska Services *941*
D P Index and Software Register (AT ISSN 0314-1578) *360, 363*
D R C Book & Monograph Series (US ISSN 0164-1875) *1025*
D R C Historical and Comparative Disasters Series (US ISSN 0164-1867) *1025*
D S I Notat (Dansk Sygehus Institut) (DK ISSN 0106-6706) *616*
D S I R Discussion Paper (Department of Scientific and Industrial Research) (NZ ISSN 0110-5221) *26, 193, 990*
D S I R Industrial Information Series (NZ ISSN 0111-8587) *279, 288, 470*
D S L Praesentationshaefte (Danske Sprog og Litteraturselskab) (DK ISSN 0105-208X) *693, 720*
D S S -Nyt (Danish Speleological Society) (DK ISSN 0109-1085) *399*
D V Bogen (Danske Vognmaend Hovedorganisationen) (DK) *1081*
D.V.R.P.C. Annual Report *see* Delaware Valley Regional Planning Commission. Annual Report *288*
D W *see* Dialectes de Wallonie *693*
Dacca Visva Vidyalaya Patrika *see* Dhaka Bisvabidyalaya Patrika *538*
Dacoromania (GW) *693, 720*
Dada/Surrealism (US ISSN 0084-9537) *104, 720*
Dados Estatisticos da Movimentacao de Carga e Passageiros (BL) *1099*
Dados Estatisticos da Navegacao *see* Dados Estatisticos da Movimentacao de Carga e Passageiros *1099*
Dados Sobre a Situacao da Agropecuaria Municipal no Estado do Parana (BL) *46*
Daedalus (SW ISSN 0070-2528) *827, 990, 1068*
Daenische Revue *see* Denmark Review *243*
Daenische Rundschau *see* Danish Journal *538*
Daenische Themen *see* Factsheet Denmark *503*
Daenischer Handelskalender *see* Udenrigs Handelskalenderen for Danmark *318*
Daffodil Society. Journal (UK) *532*
Daffodils (UK ISSN 0070-2544) *532*
Daftar Pengadaan Bahan Indonesia *see* Indonesian Acquisitions List *127*
Dagdryp (DK ISSN 0900-1581) *969*
Dagestanskii Etnograficheskii Sbornik (UR) *71, 1025*
Daguerreotypes (US) *1036*
Dahlem Workshop Reports. Life Sciences Research Report (US) *140*
Dahlem Workshop Reports. Physical and Chemical Sciences Research Report (US) *322, 888*
Daily Bread (US ISSN 0092-7147) *984*
Daily Express Guide to World Cars (UK) *1091*
Daily Mail Book of Home Plans (UK) *98*
Daily Mail Income Tax Guide (UK) *294*
Daily Mail Motor Review (UK) *1091*
Daily Mail Skier's Holiday Guide *see* Audi/Daily Mail Skier's Holiday Guide *1044*
Daily Mail Year Book (UK ISSN 0301-7761) *462*
Daily Planet Almanac (US) *114, 532*
Daily Planetary Guide (US ISSN 0743-6408) *114*
Daily Watchwords (UK) *978*
Dainichi-Nippon Cables Review *see* Mitsubishi Cable Industries Review *457*
Dairy Executive. Directory and Diary (IE) *62*
Dairy Facts and Figures at a Glance (CN ISSN 0317-6207) *193*
Dairy Industry Research Report (CN ISSN 0707-7904) *62*
Dairy: Latin American Industrial Report (US) *62*
Dairy Policy (CN ISSN 0318-2967) *193*
Dairy Producer Highlights (US) *62*
Dairy Roundup (US) *62*
Dairyfarming Annual (NZ) *62*
Dairyman Buyers Guide & Directory (US) *62*
Dairyman's Yearbook (UK ISSN 0144-5251) *1151*
Daito Hogaku *see* Journal of Law and Politics *658*
Dalhousie Dental Journal (CN) *779*
Dalhousie University. Computer Centre. Newsletter *see* University Computing and Information Services Newsletter *353*
Dalhousie University. Institute of Public Affairs. Occasional Papers (CN ISSN 0381-7024) *243*
Dalhousie University. School of Library Service. Newsletter (CN ISSN 0315-0054) *676*
Dalhousie University. School of Library Service. Occasional Papers *see* Dalhousie University. University Libraries and School of Library Service. Occasional Papers *688*
Dalhousie University. School of Library Service. Y-A Hotline (CN ISSN 0701-8894) *676*
Dalhousie University. University Libraries and School of Library Service. Occasional Papers (CN) *688*
Dallas Civic Opera Magazine *see* Dallas Opera Magazine *835*
Dallas Cowboys Outlook (US) *1038*
Dallas Institute of Humanities and Culture. Institute Newsletter (US) *629, 877, 950*
Dallas Museum of Art. Annual Report (US) *827*
Dallas Opera Magazine (US ISSN 0731-8529) *835*
Dalton's New York Metropolitan Directory: Business/Industry (US) *305*
Dalton's Philadelphia Metropolitan Directory: Business/Industry (US) *305*
Dalyaglyady Litaraturny Zbornik (UR) *720*
Damascus Road (US) *720*
Damilica (II ISSN 0376-8090) *337*
Damon Runyon Memorial Fund for Cancer Research. Report *see* Damon Runyon-Walter Winchell Cancer Fund. Annual Report *775*
Damon Runyon-Walter Winchell Cancer Fund. Annual Report (US ISSN 0095-6775) *775*
Dan River Anthology (Year) (US) *720*
Dana (DK ISSN 0106-553X) *508*
Dana-Report (DK ISSN 0070-2668) *140, 405*
Dance: Current Selected Research (US) *375, 556*
Dance Directory (US ISSN 0070-2676) *375*
Dance Magazine Annual *see* Performing Arts Directory *375*
Dance Magazine Annual Performing Arts Directory *see* Performing Arts Directory *375*
Dance Magazine College Guide (US ISSN 0193-1202) *375, 428*
Dance Magazine Directory of College and University Dance *see* Dance Magazine College Guide *375*
Dance Notation Bureau Newsletter (US) *375, 693*
Dance Research Annual (US ISSN 0886-3954) *1151*
Dance World (US ISSN 0070-2692) *375*
Dancing Year Book (UK) *375*
Dandelion (US) *877, 904*
Daneshgah-e Tehran. Daneshkade-Ye Adabiyat va 'olum-e Ensani. Majalle-Ye Iranshenasi *see* University of Teheran. Faculty of Letters and Humanities. Bulletin of Iranian Studies *613*
Daneshgah-e Tehran. Ketabkhane-Ye Markazi. Nashriye-Ye Ketabkhaneh *see* University of Teheran. Central Library. Library Bulletin *686*
Danforth Foundation. Annual Report (US) *433*
Dangermouse Annual (UK) *1151*
Dania Polyglotta (DK ISSN 0070-2714) *125, 739*
Danish Contract (DK ISSN 0108-982X) *643*
Danish Dairy Industry (DK ISSN 0024-9645) *62*
Danish Films (DK ISSN 0418-3304) *823*
Danish Folk High School Today (DK) *426*
Danish Foreign Office Journal *see* Danish Journal *538*
Danish Index of Articles: Newspapers and Periodicals *see* Dansk Artikelindeks: Aviser og Tidsskrifter *647*
Danish Journal (DK ISSN 0011-6084) *538*
Danish Journal of Plant and Soil Science *see* Tidsskrift for Planteavl *162*
Danish Medical Bulletin (DK ISSN 0011-6092) *760*
Danish Medical Research Council. Statistical Research Unit. Research Report *see* University of Copenhagen. Statistical Research Unit. Research Report *1066*
Danish National Bibliography. Articles in Books *see* Artikler i Boeger *121*
Danish National Bibliography: Music *see* Dansk Musikfortegnelse *835*
Danish Offshore Guide *see* Danish Offshore Guide and Yearbook *863*
Danish Offshore Guide and Yearbook (DK) *863*
Danish Ophthalmological Society. Transactions (DK) *785*
Danish Photography (Year) (DK) *884*
Danish Plant Protection Service. Annual Report (DK ISSN 0415-3944) *524*
Danish Review of Game Biology (DK ISSN 0374-7344) *174*
Danish Ships and Shipping *see* Danmarks Skibe og Skibsfart *1085*
Danish Speleological Society Nyt *see* D S S -Nyt *399*
Danish Textile Export Guide *see* Dansk Textil Exportguide *1073*
Danish Yearbook of Philosophy (DK ISSN 0070-2749) *877*
Danmark Export: Food & Beverages/ Produits Alimentaires & Boissons/ Lebensmittel & Getraenke (DK ISSN 0108-3910) *254*
Danmark i Tal (DK ISSN 0107-7139) *1054*
Danmarks Biblioteksskole. Skrifter (DK ISSN 0069-9861) *676*
Danmarks Biblioteksskole. Studier (DK) *676*
Danmarks Deltagelse i det Internationale Udvikligssamarbejde (DK) *261*
Danmarks Fiskeri og Havundersoegelser. Rapport (DK ISSN 0109-4432) *508*
Danmarks Fiskeri- og Havunersoegelser. Ferskvandsfiskerilaboratoriet. Meddelelser. *see* Meddelelser fra Ferskvandsfiskerilaboratoriet *511*
Danmarks Folkehoejskoler (DK ISSN 0108-3082) *428*
Danmarks Geologiske Undersoegelse/ Geological Survey of Denmark (DK ISSN 0011-6114) *385*
Danmarks Geologiske Undersoegelse. Aarbog/Geological Survey of Denmark. Yearbook (DK ISSN 0105-063X) *385*
Danmarks Geologiske Undersoegelse. Serie A/Geological Survey of Denmark. Series A (DK) *385*
Danmarks Hoejskoler *see* Danmarks Folkehoejskoler *428*
Danmarks Ingenioerakademi. Bygningsafdelningen. Dialog (DK ISSN 0105-7871) *183*
Danmarks Jordbrugsvidenskabelige Kandidatforbund. Medlemsfortegnelse *see* Haandbog for D J V K: Agronomer, Forstkandidater, Hortonomer, Licentiater *28*
Danmarks Journalisthoejskoles Aarskrift(DK ISSN 0108-285X) *434, 645*
Danmarks Juris- og Oekonomforbund OE F - Haandbogen *see* D J OE F - Haandbogen *654*
Danmarks Laererhoejskole. Geografisk Institut. Skrifter (DK ISSN 0105-4856) *542*
Danmarks Laererhoejskole. Institut for Informatik. Arbejdspapir (DK ISSN 0900-5781) *412*

Danmarks Laererhoeskole. Institut for Paedagogik og Psykologi. Testsamling(DK ISSN 0107-1637) *412*, *934*
Danmarks Nationalbank. Beretning og Regnskab (Dansk Udgave) (DK ISSN 0108-6979) *227*
Danmarks Nationalbank. Report and Accounts for the Year (Year) (DK ISSN 0108-6995) *227*
Danmarks Riges Breve see Diplomatarium Danicum *580*
Danmarks Skibe og Skibsfart/Danish Ships and Shipping (DK ISSN 0070-3486) *1085*
Danmarks Tekniske Bibliotek. Katalog (DK ISSN 0900-4645) *676*
Danmarks Tekniske Bibliotek. Uddrag (DK) *1151*
Danmarks Tekniske Hoejskole. Afdelingen B (DK ISSN 0108-0571) *183*
Danmarks Tekniske Hoejskole. Afdelingen for Baerende Konstruktioner. Serie I (DK ISSN 0108-058X) *183*
Danmarks Tekniske Hoejskole. Afdelingen for Baerende Konstruktioner. Serie R. (DK ISSN 0108-0768) *488*
Danmarks Tekniske Hoejskole. Fysisk Laboratorium 1. Report (DK ISSN 0105-0907) *888*
Danmarks Tekniske Hoejskole. Institutet for Veje, Trafik og Byplan. Notat/Technical University of Denmark. Institute of Roads, Transport and Town Planning. Paper (DK ISSN 0107-0134) *623*, *1096*
Danmarks Tekniske Hoejskole. Institutet for Landmaaling og Fotogrammetri. Meddelelse (DK ISSN 0105-5194) *542*
Danmarks Tekniske Hoejskole. Institutet for Teleteknik. Rapport I T (DK ISSN 0105-8541) *343*
Danmarks Tekniske Hoejskole. Laboratoriet for Akustik. Publikation (DK ISSN 0105-2853) *900*
Danmarks Tekniske Hoejskole. Matematisk Institut. Mat - P R (DK ISSN 0106-9306) *748*
Danmarks Transport. Tidendes Destinationregister (DK ISSN 0900-1999) *1081*
Danmarks Turist Vejviser (DK ISSN 0109-6125) *1107*
Danmarks Vareindfoersel og-Udfoersel/External Trade of Denmark (DK ISSN 0070-2781) *206*
Danmarks 1000 Stoerste Virkomheder see Danmarks 2000 Stoerste Virksomheder *288*
Danmarks 200 Stoerste Virksomheder (DK ISSN 0106-9977) *288*
Danmarks 2000 Stoerste Virksomheder/2000 Largest Companies in Denmark(DK ISSN 0106-9985) *288*
Dansk Artikelindeks: Aviser og Tidsskrifter/Danish Index of Articles: Newspapers and Periodicals (DK ISSN 0106-147X) *4*, *647*
Dansk Artist Forbund. Show Guide (DK ISSN 0109-8411) *104*
Dansk Athletik Forbund. Statistik see D A F i Tal *1036*
Dansk Athletik Forbund Tal see D A F i Tal *1036*
Dansk Botanisk Arkiv see Opera Botanica *160*
Dansk Dendrologisk Arsskrift (DK ISSN 0416-6906) *156*
Dansk Digtkatalog see Dansk Digtregister *741*
Dansk Digtregister (DK ISSN 0107-4431) *741*
Dansk Elektroteknisk Komite Haandbog see D E K Haandbog *452*
Dansk Elforsyning (DK ISSN 0106-4711) *452*
Dansk Elvaerksstatistik see Dansk Elforsyning *452*
Dansk Fagpresseforenings Medlemsliste see Fagpressenoeglen *645*
Dansk Fagpresskatalog (DK ISSN 0109-0968) *647*

Dansk Forsikrings Aarbog (DK ISSN 0106-2735) *639*
Dansk Geologisk Forening. Aarsskrift (DK ISSN 0420-1132) *385*
Dansk Golfhaandbog (DK ISSN 0109-5994) *1038*
Dansk Golfkalender see Dansk Golfhaandbog *1038*
Dansk Historisk Aarsbibliografi (DK ISSN 0107-0436) *563*
Dansk Idraets-Forbund. Aarbog (DK) *1033*
Dansk Illustreret Skibsliste (DK ISSN 0107-8011) *1099*
Dansk Ingenioerforening. Flyveteknisk Sektion. Aarbog see D I F Flyaarbog *18*
Dansk Ingenioerforening. Medlemsfortegnelse (DK ISSN 0900-3045) *470*
Dansk Ingenioerforening Flyaarbog see D I F Flyaarbog *18*
Dansk Kunst (DK ISSN 0109-4165) *1151*
Dansk Kunstnerraad (DK ISSN 0108-8572) *104*
Dansk Management Center Information see D M C Information *279*
Dansk Maskinhandlerforening. Handbog(DK ISSN 0302-5349) *51*
Dansk Media Index (DK) *343*, *345*
Dansk Medicinhistorisk Aarbog/Yearbook of Danish Medical History(DK ISSN 0084-9588) *760*
Dansk Miljoevaern Nyt see D M V Nyt *495*
Dansk Museer see Arv og Eje *576*
Dansk Musikfortegnelse/Danish National Bibliography: Music (DK ISSN 0105-8045) *835*
Dansk Natur-Dansk Skole (DK ISSN 0106-5726) *538*
Dansk Naturhistorisk Forening. Videnskabelige Meddelelser (DK ISSN 0373-3874) *990*
Dansk Naturhistorisk Forening i Koebenhavn. Videnskabelige Meddelelser see Dansk Naturhistorisk Forening. Videnskabelige Meddelelser *990*
Dansk Ornithologisk Forenings Tidsskrift (DK ISSN 0011-6394) *170*
Dansk Paediatrisk Selskab. Aarbog (DK ISSN 0105-9289) *787*
Dansk Rumforskninginstitut. Publikationer (DK ISSN 0109-6605) *18*
Dansk Sangindeks (DK ISSN 0108-2272) *843*
Dansk Skolehistorie. Aarbog see Uddannelshistorie. Selskabet for Dansk Skolehistorie. Aarbog *420*
Dansk Sportsheste Avlsforbunds Stambog see Stambog *1043*
Dansk Sygehus Institut Notat see D S I Notat *616*
Dansk Teknisk Litteraturselskab. Skriftserie (DK ISSN 0416-6981) *720*
Dansk Textil Exportguide/Danish Textile Export Guide (DK ISSN 0109-8586) *254*, *1073*
Dansk Tidsskrift Index see Dansk Artikelindeks: Aviser og Tidsskrifter *647*
Danske Bank af 1871. Annual Report (DK) *227*
Danske Bibelselskabs Aarbog (DK ISSN 0109-5846) *969*
Danske Bibelselskabs Aarsberetning see Danske Bibelselskabs Aarbog *969*
Danske Byggemarkeder (DK ISSN 0106-1941) *183*, *283*
Danske Hedeselskab. Forsoegsvirksomheden. Beretning (DK ISSN 0106-0031) *495*, *524*, *1124*
Danske Illustratorer (DK ISSN 0109-3339) *104*
Danske Laegemiddelstandarder (DK ISSN 0105-7480) *870*
Danske Landmandsbank. Annual Report see Danske Bank af 1871. Annual Report *227*
Danske Magazin (DK ISSN 0070-2846) *580*
Danske Plantevaernskonference (DK ISSN 0109-3142) *156*

Danske Reklamefotografer (DK ISSN 0108-0814) *15*, *884*
Danske Selskab. Nyt (DK ISSN 0900-2871) *915*
Danske Sprog og Litteraturselskab Praesentationshaefte see D S L Praesentationshaefte *720*
Danske Statslaan (DK ISSN 0105-4554) *940*
Danske Statsskoves Udbytte af Ved og Penge (DK ISSN 0109-5234) *524*
Danske Studier (DK) *580*
Danske Vedligeholdelsesforening Analysen see D D V - Analysen *1068*
Danske Vognmaend Hovedorganisationen Bogen see D V Bogen *1081*
Danskerne (DK ISSN 0107-4393) *538*
Dante Society of America. Report with Accompanying Papers see Dante Studies *720*
Dante Studies (US ISSN 0070-2862) *720*
Dantec see D A N T E C Information *808*
Dapai Tamar (IS) *539*
Dapim Licheker Tikufat Hashoah (IS ISSN 0333-5151) *556*
Dar es Salaam University Law Journal (TZ ISSN 0418-3770) *654*
Dark Winds (US) *720*
Darlington Astronomical Society. Newsletter (UK ISSN 0260-7794) *115*
Darmstaedter Archivschriften (GW) *580*
Darwin Port Handbook (UK ISSN 0268-6503) *305*, *1099*
Dat Was de Toestand in de Wereld (NE) *556*
Data (Athens) see Compu-Data *357*
Data and Documents About Environment Protection see Daten und Dokumente Zum Umweltschutz *1151*
Data Base Monograph Series (US) *360*
Data Book of Social Studies Materials and Resources (US ISSN 0747-4857) *446*, *1007*
Data Book on Illinois Higher Education(US ISSN 0098-5279) *434*
Data Center - Nyt see A U D - Nyt *351*
Data Communications Product Directory (US) *346*, *361*, *363*
Data-Data Iklim di Indonesia (IO ISSN 0303-1969) *804*
Data of Glaciological Studies see Materialy Glyatsiologicheskikh Issledovanii *400*
Data om Markedet/Data on the Market(DK ISSN 0109-5013) *283*
Data on Denmark see Danmark i Tal *1054*
Data on Iowa's Area Schools (US ISSN 0092-3761) *434*
Data on Iowa's Area Schools and Public Junior College see Data on Iowa's Area Schools *434*
Data on the Market see Data om Markedet *283*
Data on the Medicaid Program: Eligibility/Service/Expenditures see Medicare and Medicaid Data Book *640*
Data Processing Digest (US ISSN 0011-6858) *360*
Data Resources Transportation Review (US) *1081*
Data Sets: Cuneiform Sources see Data Sets: Cuneiform Texts *612*
Data Sets: Cuneiform Texts (US ISSN 0742-1427) *612*
Datalogi O (DK ISSN 0108-3708) *352*, *360*
Datalogiske Skrifter (DK ISSN 0109-9779) *352*
Datapro Reports on Banking Automation (US) *234*, *360*
Datapro Who's Who in Microcomputing (US) *357*
Daten und Dokumente Zum Umweltschutz/Data and Documents About Environment Protection (GW ISSN 0170-608X) *1151*
Datos Etno-Linguisticos (PE) *71*, *515*, *693*

Datos Socio-Economicos de Costa Rica(CR) *243*
Datos y Cifras de la Ensenanza en Espana (SP ISSN 0070-2897) *412*
David Davies Memorial Institute of International Studies, London. Annual Memorial Lecture (UK ISSN 0070-2900) *915*
David y Goliath (AG) *1007*
Davis Medieval Texts and Studies (NE) *580*
Davison's Knit Goods Trade (US ISSN 0070-2943) *1152*
Davison's Salesman's Book (US ISSN 0363-5252) *1073*
Davison's Textile Blue Book (US ISSN 0070-2951) *1073*
Davison's Textile Buyer's Guide (US) *1073*
Davy's Devon Herd Book (UK ISSN 0070-2986) *65*
Dawn Song see Dawn Song and All Day *365*
Dawn Song and All Day (UK ISSN 0070-3001) *365*
Day Tonight/Night Today (US ISSN 0275-3073) *741*
Dayan Center for Middle Eastern and African Studies. Bulletin (IS) *539*, *904*
Dayig Be-Yisrael Be-Misparim see Israel. Ministry of Agriculture. Department of Fisheries. Israel Fisheries in Figures *511*
Dayton Art Institute. Annual Report see Dayton Art Institute. Annual Report and Bulletin *827*
Dayton Art Institute. Annual Report and Bulletin (US) *827*
De Proprietatibus Litterarum. Series Didactica (GW) *720*
De Proprietatibus Litterarum. Series Major (GW ISSN 0070-3060) *720*
De Proprietatibus Litterarum. Series Minor (GW ISSN 0070-3079) *720*
De Proprietatibus Litterarum. Series Practica (GW ISSN 0070-3087) *720*
De Textos (BO) *870*, *1025*, *1128*
Dead Sea Works, Beersheba, Israel. Report of the Directors (IS ISSN 0070-3095) *405*
Deakin University. Guide to Off Campus Studies (AT) *341*
Death and Dying A to Z (US) *934*, *1025*
Debate (BL) *243*
Debate Socialista (PE) *904*
Debates/Cenpes see Debate *243*
Debates en Antropologia see Anthropologica (Lima) *69*
Debates en Sociologia (PE) *1025*
Debates of the European Parliament (EI ISSN 0071-3015) *670*
Debreceni Orvostudomanyi Egyetem Evkonyve (HU ISSN 0133-9060) *760*
Debrett's Handbook (UK) *134*, *535*
Debrett's Handbook of Australia and New Zealand see Debrett's Handbook *535*
Debrett's Peerage & Baronetage (UK) *535*
Debrett's Register of Yachts (UK) *1041*
Deccan College. Postgraduate & Research Institute. Bulletin (II ISSN 0045-9801) *569*, *693*, *1007*
December (US ISSN 0070-3141) *720*
Dechema Monographien (GW ISSN 0070-315X) *326*, *781*
Decheniana-Beihefte (Bonn) (GW ISSN 0416-833X) *140*, *379*
Decision Information Display System Doings see D I D S Doings *360*
Decision Research (US) *279*
Decisions of the United States Courts Involving Copyrights (US ISSN 0070-3176) *860*
Deck Plan Guide see Ford's Deck Plan Guide *1110*
Deco (GW) *643*
Decorating Contractor Annual Directory (UK ISSN 0070-3192) *643*
Deer and Big Game (US) *1045*
Deer Hunting see Field and Stream
Deer Hunter's Guide Annual *1045*

Deer Hunting (Los Angeles) (US ISSN 0270-0069) *1045*
Defects in Crystalline Solids *see* Defects in Solids *888*
Defects in Solids (NE) *327, 888*
Defense Electronics. Marketing Directory and Buyers Guide (US) *305, 452, 811*
Defense Foreign Affairs Handbook (US) *811, 915*
Defense Markets and Technology *see* Aerospace Defense Markets and Technology *813*
Defense Reference (US ISSN 0099-166X) *811*
DeGarmo Lectures *see* Annual DeGarmo Lectures *432*
Degre Second: Studies in French Literature (US ISSN 0148-561X) *720*
Degre Second: Studies in French Literature from the Renaissance to the Present *see* Degre Second: Studies in French Literature *720*
Degree Course Offers (UK) *434*
Degree Studies and the Accountancy Profession *see* Approved Courses for Accountancy Education *221*
Dehio: Handbuch der deutschen Kunstdenkmaeler (GE) *98, 104*
Deine Stadt (GW) *104, 720, 827, 835*
Z Dejin Hutnictvi (CS) *580, 797*
Z Dejin Vied a Techniky na Slovensku (CS) *580*
Dejiny Socialistickeho Ceskoslovenska (CS ISSN 0232-0150) *580*
Dejiny Vyrobnich Sil (CS) *1072*
Delaware. Court of Chancery. Delaware Chancery Reports *see* Delaware Reporter *654*
Delaware. Department of Health and Social Service. Annual Report (US ISSN 0095-6422) *953, 1016*
Delaware. Department of Highways and Transportation. Traffic Summary (US ISSN 0070-329X) *1096*
Delaware. Department of Natural Resources and Environmental Control. Annual Report (US ISSN 0084-9642) *365, 495*
Delaware. Department of Public Instruction. Educational Personnel Directory (US ISSN 0091-6188) *412*
Delaware. Department of Public Instruction. Teacher Supply and Demand *see* Supply and Demand: Educational Personnel in Delaware *420*
Delaware. State Board of Education. Report of Educational Statistics (US ISSN 0362-8787) *412*
Delaware. State Highway Department. Traffic Summary *see* Delaware. Department of Highways and Transportation. Traffic Summary *1096*
Delaware. State Treasurer. Annual Report (US ISSN 0084-9685) *294*
Delaware Art Museum. Annual Report (US) *104*
Delaware Directory of Commerce and Industry (US ISSN 0272-8117) *305*
Delaware Geological Survey Bulletins (US ISSN 0070-3273) *385*
Delaware Geological Survey Reports of Investigations (US ISSN 0011-7749) *385*
Delaware Museum of Natural History. Monograph Series (US ISSN 0084-9650) *990*
Delaware Museum of Natural History. Reproduction Series (US ISSN 0084-9669) *990*
Delaware Reporter (US ISSN 0091-5564) *654*
Delaware River Basin Biennial Water Resources Conference. Proceedings (US) *1124*
Delaware River Basin Water Resources Conference. Proceedings *see* Delaware River Basin Biennial Water Resources Conference. Proceedings *1124*
Delaware Symposia on Language Studies Series (US) *693*

Delaware Symposia Series *see* Delaware Symposia on Language Studies Series *693*
Delaware Valley Regional Planning Commission. Annual Report (US) *288*
Delaware Valley Regional Planning Commission. Biennial Report *see* Delaware Valley Regional Planning Commission. Annual Report *288*
Delegation Archeologique Francaise en Iran. Cahiers (FR) *85*
Delek. Annual Report (IS) *863*
Delft Soil (NE) *480*
Delhi Law Review (II) *654*
Delirante (FR ISSN 0011-7889) *741*
Delirium (US) *1152*
Delitti e delle Pene (IT) *370*
Dellplain Latin American Studies (US) *605*
Delphinium Society Yearbook (UK) *532*
Delpinoa (IT ISSN 0416-928X) *140*
Delta Pi Epsilon. Research Bulletin (US ISSN 0416-9336) *447*
Deltion Pneumatikes kai Kallitechnikes Drasteriotetos see Anagnostika Hetaireia Kerkyras. Deltion *575*
Demag Kurier (GW ISSN 0011-815X) *491*
Democratic Republic of the Sudan Gazette. Legislative Supplement (SJ) *654, 941*
Democratic Republic of the Sudan Gazette. Special Legislative Supplement *see* Democratic Republic of the Sudan Gazette. Legislative Supplement *941*
Demografie *see* I P D Working Papers *927*
Demografska Statistika (YU ISSN 0084-4357) *921, 926*
Demographic Guide to Arizona (Year) (US) *921*
Demographic Handbook for Africa/Guide Demographie de l'Afrique (UN) *921*
Demographic Monographs (US ISSN 0275-9594) *921*
Demographic Training and Research Centre. Annual Report *see* International Institute for Population Sciences. Director's Report *922*
Demographic Yearbook (UN ISSN 0082-8041) *921*
Demographie Africaine: Bulletin de Liaison (CM ISSN 0151-1408) *921*
Demographie en Afrique d'Expression Francaise: Bulletin de Liaison *see* Demographie Africaine: Bulletin de Liaison *921*
Demographie et Sciences Humaines (FR ISSN 0070-3354) *921*
Demographie et Societes (FR ISSN 0070-3362) *921*
Demokratie- und Arbeitergeschichte (GW) *495, 502, 580, 648*
Denken, Schauen, Sinnen (GW ISSN 0070-3419) *877*
Denki Seirigaku *see* Electrophysiology *153*
Denki Tsushin Daigaku Denki Tsushin Kenkyu Shisetsu Nenpo *see* University of Electrocommunications. Research Institute for Communication Sciences. Annual Report *345*
Denkmaeler der Buchkunst (GW ISSN 0341-2474) *104*
Denmark. Arbejdstilsynet. Rapport (DK ISSN 0106-6838) *271*
Denmark. Atomenergikomissionens Forsoegsanlaeg, Risoe. Risoe Report *see* Denmark. Forsoegsanlaeg Risoe. Risoe-R *896*
Denmark. Betaenkning fra Miljoestyrelsen (DK ISSN 0900-3738) *495*
Denmark. Boligministeriet. Building Regulations (DK ISSN 0108-9803) *183*
Denmark. Danmarks Fiskeri- og Havundersoegelser. Meddelelser fra *see* Dana *508*
Denmark. Danmarks Fiskeri- og Havundersoegelser. Skrifter fra *see* Fisk og Hav *509*

Denmark. Danmarks Statistik. Arbejdsloesheden/Unemployment (DK ISSN 0070-346X) *206*
Denmark. Danmarks Statistik. Befolkningen i de Enkelte Kommuner *see* Befolkningen i Kommunerne /Populations of Municipalities *926*
Denmark. Danmarks Statistik. Befolkningens Bevaegelser/Vital Statistics (DK ISSN 0070-3478) *921, 926*
Denmark. Danmarks Statistik. Bygningsopgoerelsen /Stock of Building (DK ISSN 0108-7568) *188*
Denmark. Danmarks Statistik. Driftsregnskabsstatistik for Industrien *see* Denmark. Danmarks Statistik. Regnskabsstatistik for Industrien / Industrial Accounts Statistics *206*
Denmark. Danmarks Statistik. Ejendomssalg/Sales of Real Property (DK ISSN 0070-3508) *966*
Denmark. Danmarks Statistik. Faerdselsuheld/Road Traffic Accidents (DK ISSN 0070-3516) *921, 926, 953*
Denmark. Danmarks Statistik. Folke- og Boligtaellingen *see* Denmark. Danmarks Statistik. Bygningsopgoerelsen /Stock of Building *188*
Denmark. Danmarks Statistik. Handelsstatistiske Meddelelser. Maanedsstatistik over Udenrigshandelen-Monthly Bulletin of External Trade *see* Denmark. Danmarks Statistik. Udenrigshandel/External Trade *206*
Denmark. Danmarks Statistik. Indkomster og Formuer /Income and Property Assessments (DK ISSN 0107-105X) *206*
Denmark. Danmarks Statistik. Indkomster og Formuer Ved Slutligningen *see* Denmark. Danmarks Statistik. Indkomster og Formuer /Income and Property Assessments *206*
Denmark. Danmarks Statistik. Industristatistik/Industrial Statistics (DK ISSN 0070-3532) *206*
Denmark. Danmarks Statistik. Kommunale Finanser for Regnskabsaaret *see* Denmark. Danmarks Statistik. Kommunale Finanser /Local Government Finance *949*
Denmark. Danmarks Statistik. Kommunale Finanser /Local Government Finance (DK ISSN 0106-9802) *949*
Denmark. Danmarks Statistik. Kreditmarkedsstatistik *see* Denmark. Danmarks Statistik. Penge og Kapitalmarked *206*
Denmark. Danmarks Statistik. Kriminalstatistik /Crime Statistics (DK ISSN 0070-3540) *373*
Denmark. Danmarks Statistik. Kvartalsstatistik for Industrien. Varestatistik, 4. Kvartal og Aaret *see* Denmark. Danmarks Statistik. Varestatistik for Industri *207*
Denmark. Danmarks Statistik. Landbrugsstatistik/Agricultural Statistics (DK) *40*
Denmark. Danmarks Statistik. Landbrugsstatistik Herunder Gartneri og Skovbrug *see* Denmark. Danmarks Statistik. Landbrugsstatistik/Agricultural Statistics *40*
Denmark. Danmarks Statistik. Loen- og Indkomststatistik (DK ISSN 0107-8771) *206*
Denmark. Danmarks Statistik. Nationalregnskabsstatistik /National Accounts Statistics (DK ISSN 0108-8173) *949*
Denmark. Danmarks Statistik. Penge og Kapitalmarked. (DK ISSN 0108-5476) *206*
Denmark. Danmarks Statistik. Regnskabsstatistik for Industrien / Industrial Accounts Statistics (DK ISSN 0108-738X) *206*

Denmark. Danmarks Statistik. Skatter og Afgifter/Taxes and Duties. Oversigt (DK ISSN 0105-1164) *206*
Denmark. Danmarks Statistik. Statistisk Aarbog/Statistical Yearbook (DK ISSN 0070-3567) *1054*
Denmark. Danmarks Statistik. Statistisk Tiars-Oversigt/Statistical Ten-Year Review (DK ISSN 0070-3583) *1054*
Denmark. Danmarks Statistik. Statistiske Undersogelser (DK ISSN 0039-0682) *1054*
Denmark. Danmarks Statistik. Udenrigshandel/External Trade (DK ISSN 0108-5506) *206*
Denmark. Danmarks Statistik. Valgene til de Kommunale og Amtskommunale Raad (DK ISSN 0107-0371) *949*
Denmark. Danmarks Statistik. Valgene til de Kommunale Raad *see* Denmark. Danmarks Statistik. Valgene til de Kommunale og Amtskommunale Raad *949*
Denmark. Danmarks Statistik. Varestatistik for Industri/ Manufacturers' Sales of Commodities(DK ISSN 0107-7031) *207*
Denmark. Danmarks Statistik. Vejviser i Statistiken (DK ISSN 0109-8314) *1054*
Denmark. Dantest-Nyt. Aarsberetning (DK) *809*
Denmark. Direktoratet for Arbejdstilsynet. Arbejdstilsynets Aarsberetning (DK ISSN 0900-6885) *271*
Denmark. Direktoratet for Kriminalforsorgen. *see* Kriminalforsorgens Aarsberetning *371*
Denmark. Direktoratet for Kriminalforsorgen. Kriminalpolitisk Forskningsgruppe. Forskningsrapport (DK) *370*
Denmark. Direktoratet for Patent- og Varemaerkevaesenet. Aarsberetning *see* Direktorat under Forandring *860*
Denmark. Direktoratet for Toldvaesenet. Toldvaesenet *see* Denmark. Direktoratet for Toldvaesenet. Toldvaesenets Aarsberetning *294*
Denmark. Direktoratet for Toldvaesenet. Toldvaesenet Aktiviteter *see* Denmark. Direktoratet for Toldvaesenet. Toldvaesenets Aarsberetning *294*
Denmark. Direktoratet for Toldvaesenet. Toldvaesenets Aarsberetning (DK ISSN 0109-6672) *294*
Denmark. Egnsudviklingsraadet. Beretning *see* Investering i Produktion *290*
Denmark. Energiministeriet. Energiforskningsprogram (DK ISSN 0108-4011) *464*
Denmark. Finansministeriet. Budgetdepartementet. Budgetredegoerelse (DK ISSN 0106-3006) *294*
Denmark. Fiskeriministeriet. Forsoegslaboratorium. Aarsberetning/ Annual Report (DK ISSN 0070-3605) *140, 508*
Denmark. Forsoegsanlaeg Risoe. Fysikafdelingen. Annual Progress Report (DK ISSN 0107-8348) *888*
Denmark. Forsoegsanlaeg Risoe. Risoe-R (DK ISSN 0106-2840) *464, 470, 896*
Denmark. Forsoegslaboratoriet. Beretning *see* Denmark. Statens Husdyrbrugsforsog. Beretning *65*
Denmark. Forsvarsministeriet. Forsvarsministerens Aarlige Redegoerelse (DK ISSN 0108-7193) *336*
Denmark. Geografisk Magasin (DK ISSN 0108-0504) *1152*

Denmark. Handelsministeriet. Oversigt over Erhvervfremmende og Forbruger Politiske Foranstaltninger see Erhvervfremmende og Forbrugerpolitiske Foranstaltninger *369*
Denmark. Indenrigsministeriet. Indenrigsministeriets Afgoerelser og Udtalelser om Kommunale Forhold (DK ISSN 0108-979X) *941*
Denmark. Jordbrugsoekonomisk Institut. Aarsberetning (DK ISSN 0106-4967) *193*
Denmark. Jordbrugsoekonomisk Institut. Landbrugets Oekonomi (DK ISSN 0106-1291) *193*
Denmark. Jordbrugsoekonomisk Institut. Rapport (DK ISSN 0107-5357) *46*
Denmark. Jordbrugsoekonomisk Institut. Serie A: Landbrugets Regnskabsstatistik (DK ISSN 0107-5675) *46*
Denmark. Jordbrugsoekonomisk Institut. Serie B: Oekonomien i Landbrugets Driftsgrene/Economics of Agricultural Enterprises (DK ISSN 0107-5683) *46*
Denmark. Jordbrugsoekonomisk Institut. Serie C: Landbrugets Prisforhold (DK ISSN 0107-5691) *46*
Denmark. Jordbrugsoekonomisk Institut. Serie D: Gartneri-Regnskabsstatistik (DK ISSN 0107-5705) *46*
Denmark. Justervaesenet. Aarsberetning. see Denmark. Dantest-Nyt. Aarsberetning *809*
Denmark. Kongelige Bibliotek. Fund og Forskning (DK ISSN 0069-9896) *676*
Denmark. Kungl Veterinaer og Landbohoejskole. Meddelelser (DK ISSN 0105-2543) *1121*
Denmark. Lovinformation fra Miljoestyrelsen (DK ISSN 0900-2758) *495, 654*
Denmark. Miljoekreditraadet. Beretning(DK ISSN 0108-7487) *495*
Denmark. Miljoeministeriet. Miljoeministerens Redegoerelse om Landsplanlaegning (DK ISSN 0108-6901) *623*
Denmark. Miljoeministeriet. Miljoeministeriet Publikationsregister.(DK ISSN 0109-7695) *501*
Denmark. Miljoeministeriet. Redegoerelse fra Miljoeministeren om Landsplanlaegning see Denmark. Miljoeministeriet. Miljoeministerens Redegoerelse om Landsplanlaegning *623*
Denmark. Miljoestyrelsen. Havforureningslaboratorium. Report of the Marine Pollution Laboratory (DK ISSN 0107-7430) *495,* 1099
Denmark. Miljoestyrelsen Kemikaliekontrol. Aarsberetning (DK) *495*
Denmark. Miljoestyrelsen. Oversigt over Godkendte Bekaempelsesmidler (DK ISSN 0107-1815) *26*
Denmark. Ministeriet for Groenland. Statistike Meddelelser (DK ISSN 0900-2510) *921*
Denmark. Ministeriet for Groenland. Statistisk Kontor. Meddelelser see Denmark. Ministeriet for Groenland. Statistike Meddelelser *921*
Denmark. Nationalmuseet. Arbejdsmarkt (DK ISSN 0084-9308) *827*
Denmark. Nationalmuseet. Publications: Archaeological Historical Series (DK) *85*
Denmark. Nationalmuseet. Publications: Ethnographical Series (DK) *71*
Denmark. Nationalmuseet. Working Papers (DK) *827*
Denmark. Nordisk Statistisk Sekretariat. Tekniske Rapporter (DK ISSN 0106-9039) *1054*
Denmark. Nyt fra Miljoestyrelsen (DK ISSN 0105-5836) *495*

Denmark. Orientering fra Miljoestyrelsen (DK ISSN 0107-2722) *495*
Denmark. Planlaegningsraadet for Forskingen-Statens 6 Forskningsraed. Beretning see Denmark. Planlaegningsraadet for Forskningen Dandok-Statens 6 Forskningsraed. Beretning *990*
Denmark. Planlaegningsraadet for Forskningen Dandok-Statens 6 Forskningsraed. Beretning (DK) *990*
Denmark. Planstyrelsen. Regionplanorientering (DK ISSN 0105-9602) *623*
Denmark. Redegoerelse fra Miljoestyrelsen (DK ISSN 0900-6788) *495*
Denmark. Rigsbibliotekarembedet. Accessionskatalog (DK ISSN 0084-9715) *125*
Denmark. Socialforskningsinstitutt. Publikation (DK ISSN 0583-712X) *1016*
Denmark. Socialforskningsinstituttet. Beretning om Socialforskningsinstituttets Virksomhed (DK ISSN 0081-0584) *1016*
Denmark. Socialforskningsinstituttet. Meddelelser (DK) *1016,* 1025
Denmark. Socialforskningsinstituttet. Pjecer (DK) *1016,* 1025
Denmark. Socialforskningsinstituttet. Publikationer (DK) *1016,* 1025
Denmark. Socialforskningsinstituttet. Smaatryk (DK) *1016,* 1025
Denmark. Socialforskningsinstituttet. Socialforskningsinstituttets Virksomhed see Denmark. Socialforskningsinstituttet. Beretning om Socialforskningsinstituttets Virksomhed *1016*
Denmark. Socialforskningsinstituttet. Studier (DK) *1016,* 1025
Denmark. Statens Byggeforskningsinstitut. Aarsberetning see S B I Aarsberetning *187*
Denmark. Statens Byggeforskningsinstitut. Landbrugsbyggeri (DK ISSN 0589-6665) *26*
Denmark. Statens Byggeforskningsinstitut. Program Resumeer (DK ISSN 0109-0321) *183*
Denmark. Statens Filmcentral. Information og Beretning (DK ISSN 0109-4076) *823*
Denmark. Statens Filmcentral. Katalog over 16mm Film see Denmark. Statens Filmcentral. S F C, 16mm Film *823*
Denmark. Statens Filmcentral. S F C Catalogue (DK) *823*
Denmark. Statens Filmcentral. S F C Film see Denmark. Statens Filmcentral. S F C Catalogue *823*
Denmark. Statens Filmcentral. S F C, 16mm Film (DK ISSN 0105-5526) *823*
Denmark. Statens Filmcentral. Statistik over Udlejning af 16mm Film i Finansaaret (DK ISSN 0105-5070) *823*
Denmark. Statens Husdyrbrugsforsoeg. Aarsrapport (DK) *868*
Denmark. Statens Husdyrbrugsforsoeg. Indeks (DK ISSN 0105-9807) *65*
Denmark. Statens Husdyrbrugsforsog. Beretning (DK ISSN 0105-6883) *65, 168,* 171
Denmark. Statens Kunstfond. Beretning(DK ISSN 0107-2951) *104*
Denmark. Statens Levnedsmiddelinstitut. Publikation (DK ISSN 0107-0517) *518*
Denmark. Statens Ligningsdirektorat og Ligningsraadet. Indkomst- og Formueskat see Denmark. Statsskattedirektoratet og Ligningsraadet. Meddelelser 1. Haefte: Indkomst- og Formueansaettelser *294*
Denmark. Statens Mejerifrosoeg. Beretning (DK ISSN 0366-3221) *62*

Denmark. Statens Paedagogiske Forsoegscenter. Arbejdsbeskrivelse (DK ISSN 0107-4652) *412*
Denmark. Statens Paedagogiske Forsoegscenter. Projektbeskrivelser see Denmark. Statens Paedagogiske Forsoegscenter. Arbejdsbeskrivelse *412*
Denmark. Statens Uddannelsesstoette. Regelsamling for Stoetteaaret (DK ISSN 0107-5152) *412*
Denmark. Statens Vejlaboratorium. Laboratorierapport (DK ISSN 0106-312X) *1096*
Denmark. Statens Vejlaboratorium. Notat (DK) *1096*
Denmark. Statsskatedirektoratet og Ligningsraadet. Vurdering af Fast Ejendom see Denmark. Statsskattedirektoratet og Ligningsraadet. Meddelelser 2. Haefte: Vurdering af Fast Ejendom *294*
Denmark. Statsskattedirektoratet og Ligningsraadet. Meddelelser 1. Haefte: Indkomst- og Formueansaettelser (DK ISSN 0106-4908) *294*
Denmark. Statsskattedirektoratet og Ligningsraadet. Meddelelser 2. Haefte: Vurdering af Fast Ejendom (DK) *294*
Denmark. Sundhedsstyrelsen. Kursusoversigt (DK ISSN 0108-9781) *760*
Denmark. Undervisningsministeriet. Oekonomisk-Statistiske Konsulent. Statistik de Videregaaende Uddannelser (DK) *423*
Denmark. Vejdirektoratet. Aarsberetning (DK ISSN 0109-2405) *1096*
Denmark. Vejdirektoratet. Aarsrapport see Denmark. Vejdirektoratet. Aarsberetning *1096*
Denmark. Vejdirektoratet. Black-Spotundersoegelse paa Hovedlandeveje og Sikkerhedsmaessig Vurdering og Prioritering af Mindre Anlaegsarbejder paa Hovedlandeveje *1097*
Denmark. Vejdirektoratet. Oekonomisk-Statistisk Afdeling. Trafikrapport (DK) *1096*
Denmark. Vejdirektoratet. Trafikrapport see Denmark. Vejdirektoratet. Oekonomisk-Statistisk Afdeling. Trafikrapport *1096*
Denmark. Vejledning fra Mijoestyrelsen(DK) *495*
Denmark Bibliotekstilsynet. Beretning (DK ISSN 0107-8003) *676*
Denmark Review (DK ISSN 0418-6745) *243*
Denmark's Development Assistance. Annual Report (DK) *261*
Denmarks Nationalbank. Reports and Accounts see Danmarks Nationalbank. Beretning og Regnskab (Dansk Udgave) *227*
Denning Law Society. Journal see Dar es Salaam University Law Journal *654*
Denominations in America (US ISSN 0193-6883) *969*
Densanki Riyo Ni Kansuru Shinpojumu Koengaiyo/Proceedings of the Symposium of Computer Research (JA) *352,* 481
Dental Abstracts (US ISSN 0011-8486) *4, 769*
Dental Admission Testing Program (US) *779*
Dental Annual (UK ISSN 0266-6073) *779*
Dental Guide (CN ISSN 0070-3656) *779*
Dental Laboratory Buyer's Guide see Dental Laboratory Review Buyer's Guide *781*
Dental Laboratory Review Buyer's Guide (US) *779, 781*
Dental Register of Ireland (IE ISSN 0084-9723) *779*
Dental Statistics Handbook (US) *769*
Dental Students' Register see Annual Report on Dental Education *768*

Dental Technician Yearbook & Directory (UK) *779*
Dentistry in Japan (JA ISSN 0070-3737) *779*
Dentist's Desk Reference (US) *779*
Departamento Ecumenico de Investigaciones Cuadernos see D E I Cuadernos *982*
Departamento Ecumenico de Investigaciones Cuadernos D E I see Cuadernos D E I *969*
Departamento Nacional de Obras Contra as Secas Fins e Atividades see D N O C S - Fins e Atividades *54*
Department of Agriculture and Fisheries for Scotland. Freshwater Fisheries Laboratory. Triennial Review of Research (UK) *508*
Department of Economic Security Activities Report see D E S Activities Report *940*
Department of Energy. Publications in Print (UK ISSN 0141-5689) *464, 476*
Department of Fish and Game Technical Data Report see A.D.F.& G. Technical Data Report *507*
Department of Higher Education Data Briefs see D.H.E. Data Briefs *433*
Department of Higher Education Research Note see D.H.E. Research Note *433*
Department of Planning and Economic Development Newsletter see D P E D Newsletter *623*
Department of Scientific and Industrial Research Discussion Paper see D S I R Discussion Paper *990*
DePaul Law Review: Illinois Law Issue (US) *654*
Deposit Insurance Corporation. Annual Report: Directors' Report, Balance Sheet and Accounts (II ISSN 0304-6966) *639*
Depots Canadiens des Revues Indexees pour Medecine see Canadian Locations of Journals Indexed for Medicine *769*
Deputazione di Storia Patria per l'Umbria. Bollettino (IT ISSN 0300-4422) *580*
Derby Area Trades Union Council Directory (UK) *305*
Derbyshire Archaeological Journal (UK ISSN 0070-3788) *85*
Derecho (PE) *654*
Dermatology Series (US) *780*
Dermatology Update (US ISSN 0163-1691) *780*
Derriere le Miroir see Reperes *109*
Desalination Abstracts (IS ISSN 0011-9172) *1152*
Desarrollo (MX ISSN 0011-9199) *1152*
Desarrollo Industrial y Mercantil en la Provincia de Zaragoza see Provincia de Zaragoza. Informe Economico *237*
Descendants of James Bingham of County Down, Northern Ireland. Newsletter (US) *535*
Description and Analysis of Contemporary Standard Russian (GW ISSN 0070-3826) *693*
Descriptions of Plant Viruses (UK ISSN 0305-2680) *54*
Descriptive and Applied Linguistics. Annual Reports (JA ISSN 0385-8960) *693*
Desenvolvimento Brasileiro see Brazil Development Series *287*
Deseret News Church Almanac (US ISSN 0093-786X) *984*
Desert Bighorn Council. Transactions (US ISSN 0418-7598) *365*
Desert Locust Control Organization for Eastern Africa. Annual Report (ET ISSN 0418-761X) *54*
Desert Research Institute Publications in the Social Sciences (US ISSN 0077-7951) *71*
Desert Tortoise Council. Proceedings of Symposium (US ISSN 0191-3875) *140, 379*
Design and Art Direction Annual see British Design & Art Direction Annual *15*

Design and Art in Greece/Themata Chorou & Technon (GR) 98, 104
Design and Industries Association. Year Book and Membership List see D I A Yearbook - Design Action 495
Design Automation Conference. Proceedings see A C M/I E E E Design Automation Conference. Proceedings 356
Design Automation Workshop. Proceedings see A C M/I E E E Design Automation Conference. Proceedings 356
Design Compudata (Year) (US) 352
Design Directory (US ISSN 0195-4326) 305, 643
Design Engineers Master (BE) 452
Design from Denmark see Design from Scandinavia 644
Design from Scandinavia (DK ISSN 0108-0695) 643, 644, 1073
Design in Finland (FI) 643
Design in Greece see Design and Art in Greece 98
Design International (UK ISSN 0265-1092) 340
Design News Electrical/Electronic Directory (US) 745
Design News Electrical/Electronic Reference Edition see Design News Electrical/Electronic Directory 745
Design News Fastening Directory (US) 745
Design News Fastening Reference Edition see Design News Fastening Directory 745
Design News Fluid Power Directory (US) 745
Design News Fluid Power Reference Edition see Design News Fluid Power Directory 745
Design News Materials Directory (US) 745
Design News Materials Reference Edition see Design News Materials Directory 745
Design News Power Transmission Directory (US) 745
Design News Power Transmission Reference Edition see Design News Power Transmission Directory 745
Designed in Finland see Design in Finland 643
Designers West Resource Directory (US) 98, 643
Desktop Bank Directory (US) 227
Dessinateurs, Peintres et Sculpteurs de Belgique see Jaarboek der Schone Kunsten 106
Destabanda (UY) 710
Destaques (BL ISSN 0101-658X) 1152
Detailforskrifter for Koeretoejer (DK ISSN 0108-1306) 1096
Detroit Monographs in Musicology (US) 835
Detroit News. Newspaper Index see Index to the Detroit News 647
Detroit News Travel Directory (US) 1088, 1099, 1107
Detroit Studies in Music Bibliography (US ISSN 0070-3885) 843
Deutsch-Amerikanische Studien see American-German Studies 914
Deutsch-Auslaendische Beziehungen. Schriftenreihe (GW ISSN 0080-7125) 915
Deutsch-Slawische Forschungen zur Namenkunde und Siedlungsgeschichte (GE ISSN 0070-3893) 580, 693
Deutsche Akademie fuer Sprache und Dichtung. Jahrbuch (GW ISSN 0070-3923) 693, 720
Deutsche Akademie fuer Sprache und Dichtung. Preisschriften (GW) 720
Deutsche Akademie fuer Sprache und Dichtung. Schriftenreihe (GW) 720
Deutsche Annalen (GW) 580
Deutsche Bibliographie. Fuenfjahres-Verzeichnis (GW) 964
Deutsche Bibliothek (GE ISSN 0420-0152) 720, 741
Deutsche Branchen-Fernsprechbuch (GW ISSN 0170-284X) 305
Deutsche Buecherei. Jahrbuch (GE ISSN 0459-004X) 961
Deutsche Bundesbahn Report see D B Report 1094

Deutsche Bundesbank. Geschaeftsbericht (GW ISSN 0070-394X) 227
Deutsche Bundesbank. Report see Deutsche Bundesbank. Geschaeftsbericht 227
Deutsche Demokratische Republik. Gesetzblatt (GE ISSN 0138-1644) 654
Deutsche Dendrologische Gesellschaft. Mitteilungen (GW ISSN 0070-3958) 156, 524
Deutsche Dialektgeographie (GW) 693
Das Deutsche Firmen-Alphabet (GW ISSN 0418-8381) 305
Deutsche Forschungs- und Versuchsanstalt fuer Luft- und Raumfahrt e.V. Forschungsberichte und D F V L R-Mitteilungen see D F V L R-Forschungsberichte und D F V L R-Mitteilungen 18
Deutsche Forschungs- und Versuchsanstalt fuer Luft- und Raumfahrt e.V. Jahresbericht see D F V L R Jahresbericht 18
Deutsche Forschungsgemeinschaft. Denkschriften zur Lage der Deutschen Wissenschaft (GW ISSN 0070-3974) 990
Deutsche Forschungsgemeinschaft. Forschungsberichte (GW ISSN 0070-3982) 990
Deutsche Forschungsgemeinschaft. Kommissionenmitteilungen (GW ISSN 0070-3990) 990
Deutsche Forschungsgemeinschaft. Mexiko-Projekt (GW ISSN 0418-842X) 990
Deutsche Gaue (GW ISSN 0070-4016) 580
Deutsche Genossenschaftsbank. Bericht see DG Bank Deutsche Genossenschaftsbank. Bericht ueber das Geschaeftsjahr 227
Deutsche Geodaetische Kommission. Veroeffentlichungen: Reihe A. Theoretische Geodaesie (GW ISSN 0065-5309) 542
Deutsche Geodaetische Kommission. Veroeffentlichungen: Reihe B. Angewandte Geodaesie (GW ISSN 0065-5317) 542
Deutsche Geodaetische Kommission. Veroeffentlichungen: Reihe C. Dissertationen (GW ISSN 0065-5325) 542
Deutsche Geodaetische Kommission. Veroeffentlichungen: Reihe D. Tafelwerke (GW ISSN 0065-5333) 542
Deutsche Geodaetische Kommission. Veroeffentlichungen: Reihe E. Geschichte und Entwicklung der Geodaesie (GW ISSN 0065-5341) 542
Deutsche Geographische Blaetter see Uebersee-Museum, Bremen. Veroeffentlichungen. Reihe C: Geographie 549
Deutsche Geschichte. Jahresberichte (GE ISSN 0075-286X) 580
Deutsche Gesellschaft fuer Chronometrie. Jahrbuch (GW ISSN 0070-4040) 644
Deutsche Gesellschaft fuer Dokumentation e.V. Schriftenreihe see D G D Schriftenreihe 676
Deutsche Gesellschaft fuer Innere Medizin. Verhandlungen (US ISSN 0070-4067) 760
Deutsche Gesellschaft fuer Luft und Raumfahrt e.V. Jahrbuecher see D.G.L.R. Jahrbuecher 18
Deutsche Gesellschaft fuer Musik des Orients. Mitteilungen (GW ISSN 0417-2051) 835
Deutsche Gesellschaft fuer Pathologie. Verhandlungen (GW ISSN 0070-4113) 140, 760
Deutsche Gesellschaft fuer Urologie. Verhandlungen (US) 795
Deutsche Gesellschaft fuer Urologie. Verhandlungsbericht see Deutsche Gesellschaft fuer Urologie. Verhandlungen 795
Deutsche Gesellschaft fuer Volkskunde. D G V Informationen (GW) 515

Deutsche Handelsakten des Mittelalters und der Neuzeit (GW ISSN 0170-3080) 580
Deutsche Hochschule fuer Koerperkultur. Wissenschaftliche Zeitschrift (GE ISSN 0457-3919) 1033
Deutsche Hydrographische Zeitschrift. Ergaenzungsheft. Reihe A (GW ISSN 0070-4164) 405
Deutsche Hydrographische Zeitschrift. Ergaenzungsheft. Reihe B (GW ISSN 0070-4172) 405
Deutsche Keramik (GW) 320
Deutsche Keramische Gesellschaft. Fachausschussberichte (GW) 320
Deutsche Kraftfahrtforschung und Strassenverkehrstechnik (GW ISSN 0070-4210) 1081
Deutsche Krankenhausgesellschaft. Jahresbericht (GW) 616
Die Deutsche Lebensversicherung. Jahrbuch (GW ISSN 0070-4237) 639
Deutsche Luft-und Raumfahrt Forschungsberichte und D F V L R-Forschungsberichte und D F V L R-Mitteilungen 18
Deutsche Messen und Ausstellungen - Ein Zahlenspiegel see A U M A Zahlenspiegel Messeplatz Deutschland 282
Deutsche Morgenlaendische Gesellschaft. Zeitschrift. Supplementa (GW ISSN 0341-0803) 851
Deutsche Orient-Gesellschaft. Abhandlung (GW) 85
Deutsche Orient-Gesellschaft. Mitteilungen (GW ISSN 0342-118X) 612
Deutsche Physikalische Gesellschaft. Verhandlungen (GW ISSN 0420-0195) 888
Deutsche Rheologische Gesellschaft. Berichte see Dokumentation Rheologie 892
Deutsche Schiller-Gesellschaft. Jahrbuch (GW ISSN 0070-4318) 720
Deutsche Shakespeare-Gesellschaft West. Jahrbuch (GW ISSN 0070-4326) 720
Deutsche Sprache in Europa und Uebersee (GW ISSN 0170-3153) 693
Deutsche Texte des Mittelalters (GE ISSN 0070-4334) 720
Deutsche Verkehrswissenschaftliche Gesellschaft. Schriftenreihe. Reihe A. Dokumentation (GW) 1081
Deutsche Wissenschaftliche Kommission fuer Meeresforschung. Berichte see Meeresforschung 407
Deutsche Zoologische Gesellschaft. Verhandlungen (GW ISSN 0070-4342) 174
Deutschen Braumeister- und Malzmeister-Bundes (GW) 119
Deutscher Arbeitskreis Wasser. Schriftenreihe see Dokumentationszentrale Wasser Schriftenreihe 1124
Deutscher Camping Club e.V. Camping Fuehrer Europa see D C C - Camping Fuehrer Europa 1107
Deutscher Camping Club e.V. Caravan Modellfuehrer see D C C - Caravan Modellfuehrer 1091
Deutscher Camping Club e.V. Touristik Service see D C C - Touristik Service 1107
Deutscher Fachhochschulfuehrer (GW) 426
Deutscher Fischerei-Almanach see Deutscher Kuesten-Almanach 1099
Deutscher Forstverein. Jahresbericht (GW) 780
Deutscher Glaserkalender (GW) 320
Deutscher Hochschulfuehrer (GW) 428
Deutscher Hugenotten-Verein E.V. Geschichtsblaetter (GW ISSN 0344-2934) 580, 978
Deutscher Kuesten-Almanach (GW ISSN 0070-4377) 1099
Deutscher Schiffbau (GW) 1100
Deutscher Turner-Bund. Jahrbuch der Turnkunst (GW ISSN 0075-2401) 1033

Deutscher Volkskalender Nordschleswig(DK ISSN 0107-8720) 1107
Deutscher Werbekalender (GW) 15
Deutscher Wetterdienst. Berichte (GW ISSN 0072-4130) 804
Deutscher Wetterdienst. Bibliographien (GW ISSN 0072-4149) 125, 808
Deutscher Wetterdienst. Seewetteramt. Einzelveroeffentlichungen (GW ISSN 0072-1603) 804
Deutscher Zahnaerztekalender (GW) 779
Deutsches Banken-Handbuch (Year) (GW) 227, 648
Deutsches Beamten-Jahrbuch; Bundesausgabe (GW ISSN 0070-4423) 941
Deutsches Buecherverzeichnis (GE ISSN 0323-374X) 676, 961
Deutsches Buehnen-Jahrbuch (GW ISSN 0070-4431) 1077
Deutsches Bundes-Adressbuch der Firmen aus Industrie, Handel und Verkehr see Deutsches Bundes-Adressbuch: Industrie, Gross- und Aussenhandel, Dienstleistungen, Organisationen 305
Deutsches Bundes-Adressbuch: Industrie, Gross- und Aussenhandel, Dienstleistungen, Organisationen (GW ISSN 0343-589X) 305
Deutsches Gewaesserkundliches Jahrbuch. Donaugebiet (GW ISSN 0340-5176) 402, 1124
Deutsches Gewaesserkundliches Jahrbuch. Kuestengebiet der Nord- und Ostsee (GW ISSN 0340-5184) 402, 1124
Deutsches Gewaesserkundliches Jahrbuch. Rheingebiet Teil 2: Main (GW ISSN 0173-7260) 402, 1124
Deutsches Hydrographisches Institut. Jahresbericht (GW ISSN 0070-4458) 405
Deutsches Institut fuer Normung (DIN) Catalog of Technical Rules see D I N. Catalog of Technical Rules 1068
Deutsches Institut fuer Normung e.V. (D I N) Handbook see D I N - Handbook 808
Deutsches Institut fuer Normung e.V. (D I N) Taschenbuecher see D I N - Taschenbuecher 809
Deutsches Institut fuer Normung e.V. Katalog fuer Technische Regeln see D I N - Katalog fuer Technische Regeln 808
Deutsches Institut fuer Puppenspiel. Forschung und Lehre (GW ISSN 0070-4490) 1152
Deutsches Jahrbuch der Musikwissenschaft see Jahrbuch Peters 837
Deutsches Krebsforschungszentrum. Veroeffentlichungen (GW ISSN 0070-4229) 775
Deutsches Mittelalter, Kritische Studientexte der Monumenta Germaniae Historica (GW ISSN 0340-8396) 580
Deutsches Mozartfest (GW) 835
Deutsches Museum. Abhandlungen und Berichte (GW ISSN 0012-1339) 827
Deutsches Musikleben (Year) (GW) 835
Deutsches Soldatenjahrbuch (GW ISSN 0417-3635) 811
Deutsches Verlagsregister (GW) 961
Deutsches Wollforschungsinstitut. Vortraege (GW) 1074
Deutschkanadisches Jahrbuch see German-Canadian Yearbook 503
Deutschkurse/German Language Courses (AU ISSN 0012-1398) 447
Deutschland Liefert see B D I Deutschland Liefert 253
Deutschlandfunk. Jahrbuch (GW ISSN 0084-9790) 348
Deutschsprachige Zeitschriften Deutschland - Oesterreich - Schweiz (GW ISSN 0419-005X) 125
Developing Education (AT ISSN 0310-5709) 444
Developing Horizons in Special Education Series (UK) 447
Developing Railways (UK ISSN 0309-1465) 1094

Developing World Communications (UK) *350*
Developing World Health (UK) *262*
Developing World Water (UK) *1124*
Development Academy of the Philippines. Annual Report *see* Development Academy of the Philippines. President's Report to the Board of Trustees *288*
Development Academy of the Philippines. President's Report to the Board of Trustees (PH) *288*
Development Administration Journal (PH ISSN 0115-7000) *941*
Development Assistance to Malawi; Annual Report (UN) *262*
Development Assistance to the Democratic Republic of the Sudan *see* Report on Development Cooperation to the Democratic Republic of the Sudan *264*
Development Bank of Mauritius. Report and Accounts (MF) *227*
Development Bank of Solomon Islands. Annual Report (BP) *227, 262*
Development Bank of Zambia. Annual Report (ZA) *227*
Development Finance Company of Kenya. Annual Report and Statement of Accounts (KE) *227*
Development in Mammals (NE) *174*
Development Information Abstracts (UN ISSN 0254-2412) *4, 207*
Development of Education in Pakistan (PK ISSN 0080-1321) *412*
Developmental & Behavioral Pediatrics: Selected Topics (US) *787, 934*
Developmental and Cell Biology Monographs (UK) *140*
Developments in Agricultural and Managed Forest Ecology (NE) *26, 524*
Developments in Animal and Veterinary Sciences (NE) *1121*
Developments in Aquaculture and Fisheries Science (NE) *174, 508*
Developments in Atmospheric Science (NE) *804*
Developments in Biochemistry (NE) *151*
Developments in Bioenergetics and Biomembranes (NE) *140*
Developments in Cell Biology (NE) *140*
Developments in Clinical Psychology (US) *934*
Developments in Crop Science (NE) *54*
Developments in Earth and Planetary Sciences (NE) *385*
Developments in Economic Geology (NE) *385*
Developments in Endocrinology (NE) *781*
Developments in Food Science (NE) *329*
Developments in Geochemistry (NE) *385*
Developments in Geomathematics (NE) *399, 748*
Developments in Geotechnical Engineering (NE) *481*
Developments in Geotectonics (NE ISSN 0419-0254) *385*
Developments in Hydrobiology (NE) *140, 402*
Developments in Immunology (NE) *140*
Developments in Landscape Management and Urban Planning (NE) *623*
Developments in Marketing Science (US ISSN 0149-7421) *283*
Developments in Mineral Processing (NE) *385*
Developments in Molecular and Cellular Biochemistry *see* Molecular and Cellular Biochemistry *152*
Developments in Neurology (NE ISSN 0166-5960) *789*
Developments in Neuroscience (NE) *789*
Developments in Oncology (NE) *775*
Developments in Ophthalmology (SZ ISSN 0250-3751) *785*
Developments in Palaeontology and Stratigraphy (NE) *856*
Developments in Petroleum Science (NE) *863*
Developments in Petrology (NE) *385*
Developments in Plant and Soil Sciences (NE) *54*
Developments in Precambrian Geology (NE) *385*
Developments in Psychiatry (NE ISSN 0166-2481) *789*
Developments in Sedimentology (NE ISSN 0070-4571) *385*
Developments in Soil Science (NE) *54*
Developments in Solar System and Space Science (NE) *18, 115*
Developments in Solid Earth Geophysics (NE ISSN 0070-458X) *399*
Developments in the European Communities. Report (IE) *243*
Developments in Toxicology and Environmental Science (NE) *140*
Developments in Transport Studies (NE) *1081*
Developments in Water Science (NE) *402*
Devindex (CN ISSN 0708-2533) *1152*
Devindex Canada *see* Devindex *1152*
Devon. Property Department. Tourism and Recreation. Annual Report *see* Devon Tourism Review *1107*
Devon Archaeological Society. Proceedings (UK ISSN 0305-5795) *85*
Devon Archaeology (UK ISSN 0264-7540) *85*
Devon County Planning Department. Tourism and Recreation. Annual Report *see* Devon Tourism Review *1107*
Devon Tourism Review (UK) *1107*
Devonshire Association for the Advancement of Science, Literature and Art. Report and Transactions (UK ISSN 0309-7994) *104, 720, 990*
Dewey Decimal Classification Additions, Notes and Decisions (US ISSN 0083-1573) *676*
DG Bank Deutsche Genossenschaftsbank. Bericht ueber das Geschaeftsjahr (GW) *227*
Dhaka Bisvabidyalaya Patrika (BG) *538*
Dhaka Law Reports: Civil Digest (BG) *654*
Dhaniram Bhalla Granthamala (II) *569, 851*
Diabetes Annual (NE) *781*
Diagnostic Radiology Series (US) *792*
Diagnosticos A P E C (Associacao Promotora de Estudos de Economia) (BL) *243*
Dial Industry *see* Telekompass *317*
Dialectes de Wallonie (BE) *693*
Dialectic (AT ISSN 0084-9804) *877*
Dialectics and Revolution (NE) *877*
Dialettica (IT) *877*
Dialog der Gesellschaft (GW ISSN 0419-0637) *15*
Dialogo (AU) *915*
Dialogos Hispanicos de Amsterdam (NE) *693, 720*
Dialogues *see* Dialogues et Cultures *693*
Dialogues d'Histoire Ancienne (FR) *556*
Dialogues et Cultures (FR ISSN 0226-6881) *447, 693*
Dialogues in Public Policy (US) *941*
Diamond's Japan Business Directory (JA ISSN 0910-1780) *305*
Diana's Almanac (US) *720*
Dianoia (MX ISSN 0419-0890) *877*
Diario de Centro America (GT) *941*
Diario de Congresos Medicos (SP ISSN 0210-5578) *760, 796*
Diatomeenschalen im Elektronenmikroskopischen Bild *see* Micromorphology of Diatom Valves *169*
Dibrugarh University. Centre for Sociological Study of the Frontier Region. North Eastern Research Bulletin (II) *1025*
DIC-AGRI *see* Dictionnaire-Annuaire de l'Agriculture *26*
Diccionario Agroquimico (MX) *26, 322*
Diccionario de Especialidades Bioquimicas (MX) *151*
Diccionario de Especialidades Farmaceuticas (MX) *870*
Dichter und Zeichner (GW ISSN 0070-4695) *104, 741*
Dicionario de Especialidades Farmaceuticas (BL) *870*
Dickens Studies Annual (US ISSN 0084-9812) *720*
Dictionaries, Encyclopedias, and Other Word-Related Books (US) *709*
Dictionary of Canadian Biography (CN ISSN 0070-4717) *134*
Dictionary of Contemporary American Artists (US) *104, 134*
Dictionary of Contemporary Quotations (US ISSN 0360-215X) *694, 720*
Dictionary of Latin American and Caribbean Biography (UK ISSN 0070-4733) *134*
Dictionary of Literary Biography (US) *136, 720*
Dictionary of Literary Biography Yearbook (US) *134, 720*
Dictionary of Mauritian Biography *see* Dictionnaire de Biographie Mauricienne *134*
Dictionary of New Information Technology Acronyms (US) *343*
Dictionary of Scandinavian Biography (UK) *134*
Dictionnaire-Annuaire de l'Agriculture (FR ISSN 0759-3686) *26*
Dictionnaire de Biographie Mauricienne/Dictionary of Mauritian Biography (MF) *134, 565*
Dictionnaire de l'Industrie Francaise (FR) *288, 305*
Dictionnaire de Specialites Pharmaceutiques *see* Dictionnaire Vidal *870*
Dictionnaire des Communes (Lavauzelle et Cie) (FR) *462, 941*
Dictionnaire des Valeurs des Meubles et Objets d'Art (FR ISSN 0070-4776) *104*
Dictionnaire Vidal (FR ISSN 0419-1153) *870*
Dictionnaires du Savoir Moderne (FR ISSN 0073-4640) *462*
Didactica Classica Gandensia (BE ISSN 0070-4792) *337*
Didatica (BL ISSN 0101-059X) *412*
Diderot Studies (SZ ISSN 0070-4806) *877*
Diebeners Goldschmiede- und Uhrmacher-Jahrbuch *see* Goldschmiede- und Uhrmacher-Jahrbuch *644*
Die Dienststellen des Freistaates Bayern in den Kreisfreien Staedten und Landkreisen (GW) *1054*
Diesel and Gas Turbine World Wide Catalog (US ISSN 0070-4822) *491*
Diesel Electric Locomotive Examination Book *see* Diesel Locomotive Question & Answer Manual *1094*
Diesel Locomotive Question & Answer Manual (US ISSN 0070-4830) *1094*
Diet and Exercise *see* Better Homes and Gardens Low-Calorie Recipes *885*
Digest of Agricultural Economics and Marketing *see* World Agricultural Economics and Rural Sociology Abstracts *44*
Digest of Changes in C U S I P (Committee on Uniform Security Procedures) (US) *227*
Digest of Commercial Laws of the World (US ISSN 0419-1285) *254, 670*
Digest of English-Language Textile Literature *see* Textile Digest *1076*
Digest of Health Statistics for England and Wales *see* Health and Personal Social Services Statistics *953*
Digest of Indological Studies (II) *569*
Digest of Legal Activities of International Organizations and Other Institutions (US ISSN 0070-4857) *655*
Digest of Motor Laws *see* American Automobile Association. Digest of Motor Laws *1090*
Digest of Neurology & Psychiatry (US ISSN 0012-2769) *4, 769*
Digest of Technical Papers *see* S I D International Symposium. Digest of Technical Papers *474*
Digest of the United States Practice in International Law (US ISSN 0095-3369) *670*
Digest of United Kingdom Energy Statistics (UK ISSN 0307-0603) *464*
Digest of Welsh Statistics (UK ISSN 0262-8295) *1054*
Digest of World Events (PK ISSN 0070-4873) *556, 915*
Digital & Audio-Video Discontinued Devices D.A.T.A. Book (US) *356*
Digital System Design Series (US ISSN 0888-2118) *484*
Dillingham Family Genealogy Exchange Bulletin (US) *535*
Dime Bag: Fiction Issue (CN ISSN 0702-8520) *1152*
Dimension Historica de Chile (CL ISSN 0716-1484) *605*
Dimension: Languages (US ISSN 0070-4881) *447, 694*
Dimensions (Waterbury) (US) *720*
Dimensions of Philippine Exports (PH) *254*
Dinamika Izluchayuschego Gaza (UR) *863*
Dine Israel (IS ISSN 0070-4903) *655*
Diocese de Saint-Jean-Longueuil. Annuaire (CN) *982*
Diode D.A.T.A. Book (US ISSN 0271-0803) *452*
Diode Discontinued Devices D.A.T.A. Book (US) *452*
Dioezese Linz. Jahrbuch (AU) *982*
Diotima (GR) *877*
Diozese Gurk. Jahrbuch/Krske Skofije. Zbornik (AU) *502, 982*
Dipavali (II) *741*
Diplomatarium Danicum (DK ISSN 0070-4938) *580*
Diplomatic & Consular Year Book (UK) *915*
Diplomatic Corps and Consular and Other Representatives in Canada/Corps Diplomatique et Representants Consulaires et Autres au Canada (CN ISSN 0486-4514) *915*
Diplomatic List and List of Representatives of United Nations and Its Specialized Agencies and Other Missions (NP) *915*
Diplomatic Service List (UK) *915*
Diputacio Provincial. Biblioteca Catalunya Cataleg la Produccion Editorial Barcelonesa (SP ISSN 0210-6833) *964*
Direct Mail Databook (UK) *15, 283*
Direct Marketing Market Place (US ISSN 0192-3137) *15, 283*
Directed Energy and Avionics Data Sheets. (UK) *18*
Directie Kinderbescherming (NE) *333*
Directoire Enterprises Textiles de Processus Cotonnier *see* Directory of the Spanish Cotton-System Textile Enterprises *1074*
Directori Empreses Textils de Proces Cotoner *see* Directory of the Spanish Cotton-System Textile Enterprises *1074*
Directories of Hawaii (US ISSN 0094-209X) *305*
Directorio Agropecuario de Colombia (CK) *26*
Directorio Colombiano de Unidades de Informacion (CK) *676*
Directorio Comercial e Industrial (ES) *235*
Directorio Comercial e Industrial de Panama/Comercial and Industrial Directory of Panama (PN) *305*
Directorio de Instituciones Financieras (CK) *227*
Directorio de la Educacion Superior en Colombia (CL ISSN 0120-5056) *428*
Directorio de la Exportacion *see* Export Directory Chile *308*
Directorio de Servicios para Familias Migrantes *see* Directory of Services for Migrant Families *1017*
Directorio Empresas Textiles de Proceso Algodonero *see* Directory of the Spanish Cotton-System Textile Enterprises *1074*

Directorio Industrial Azucarero (VE) 54
Directorio Nacional de Entidades Cooperativos (CK) 238
Directorio Nacional de la Industria de los Plasticos y Proveedores (Year) see Anuario Latinoamericano de los Plasticos 900
Directorio Nacional de Profesionales (CK) 847
Directors Guild of America. Directory of Members (US ISSN 0419-2052) 648
Directory. Diocesan Agencies of Catholic Charities and Catholic Charities U S A Member Institutions. United States, Puerto Rico and Canada (US) 1016
Directory. Diocesan Agencies of Catholic Charities and NCCC Member Institutions. United States, Puerto Rico and Canada see Directory. Diocesan Agencies of Catholic Charities and Catholic Charities U S A Member Institutions. United States, Puerto Rico and Canada 1016
Directory: a Guide to Colleges, Vocational-Technical and Diploma Schools of Nursing see Directory: A Guide to Colleges, Vocational-Technical Schools & Special Purpose Institutions 428
Directory: A Guide to Colleges, Vocational-Technical Schools & Special Purpose Institutions (US) 428
Directory - American Bell Association see American Bell Association. Directory 832
Directory and Handbook - Baptist Missionary Association of America see Baptist Missionary Association of America. Directory and Handbook 978
Directory and Statistics of Oregon Libraries (US ISSN 0162-0290) 676
Directory and Who's Who in Liberia (LB) 305
Directory for a New World see Unity-and-Diversity World Directory 882
Directory for Disabled People (UK ISSN 0309-4413) 1016
Directory for Exceptional Children (US ISSN 0070-5012) 444, 934
Directory for the Nonwoven Fabrics and Disposable Soft Goods Industries see International Directory of the Nonwoven Fabrics Industry 1074
Directory: Graduate Programs in Public Affairs and Public Administrator see Graduate Programs in Public Affairs and Public Administration 942
Directory: Home Centers and Hardware Chains, Auto Supply Chains see Home Center Operators & Hardware Chains (Year) 309
Directory Information Service (US ISSN 0146-7085) 125
Directory Iron and Steel Plants (US ISSN 0070-5039) 797
Directory Listing Curriculums Offered in the Community Colleges of Pennsylvania (US ISSN 0092-8526) 1152
Directory: North Dakota City Officials (US ISSN 0090-1989) 950
Directory of A S U Latin Americanists (Arizona State University) (US) 605
Directory of Accredited Camps (CN ISSN 0316-1226) 1045
Directory of Accredited Home Study Schools (US) 428
Directory of Accredited Institutions see Directory of Educational Institutions 193
Directory of Accredited Private Home Study Schools see Directory of Accredited Home Study Schools 428
Directory of Administrative and Supervisory Personnel of California Public Schools see California Public School Directory 428
Directory of Administrative Officials in Public Education - Canada see C E A Handbook 411

Directory of Advertising and Marketing Services see Handbook of Advertising and Marketing Services 15
Directory of Aerospace Education see Directory of Aviation and Space Education 18
Directory of African Universities (GH) 434
Directory of Afrikanamerican Research Centers (US) 502
Directory of Agencies Serving the Visually Handicapped in the U.S. (US ISSN 0732-1341) 180
Directory of Agricultural Co-Operatives in the United Kingdom (UK ISSN 0307-689X) 46
Directory of Aids for Disabled and Elderly People (UK) 1016
Directory of Alberta's Agricultural Processing Industry see Alberta. Agricultural Processing Branch. Processing & Manufacturing Guide 45
Directory of Alcohol and Drug Treatment Resources in Ontario (CN ISSN 0228-863X) 376
Directory of American Business in Argentina see American Business in Argentina 302
Directory of American Fiction Writers see Directory of American Poets and Fiction Writers 741
Directory of American Firms Operating in Foreign Countries (US ISSN 0070-5071) 254, 305
Directory of American Fulbright Scholars (US) 441
Directory of American Horticulture see North American Horticulture: A Reference Guide 533
Directory of American Jewish Institutions see Who's Who in American Jewry (Los Angeles) 135
Directory of American Medical Education see A A M C Directory of American Medical Education 442
Directory of American Philosophers (US ISSN 0070-508X) 878
Directory of American Poets see Directory of American Poets and Fiction Writers 741
Directory of American Poets and Fiction Writers (US ISSN 0734-0605) 741
Directory of American Research and Technology (US) 1068
Directory of American Savings and Loan Associations (US ISSN 0070-5098) 227
Directory of American Scholars (US ISSN 0070-5101) 134
Directory of Apparel Specialty Stores. Women's and Children's see Directory of Women's & Children's Wear Specialty Stores 340
Directory of Architects for Health Facilities (US ISSN 0192-2297) 98, 616
Directory of Arkansas Manufacturers (US) 305
Directory of Arts Centres (UK ISSN 0144-7459) 104, 305
Directory of Asian Book Trade see Asian Book Trade Directory 960
Directory of Asian Forest Products see White Paper on Japan's Forest Industries 531
Directory of Associations in Canada (CN ISSN 0316-0734) 462
Directory of Australian Associations (AT ISSN 0110-666X) 4, 125
Directory of Australian Composers (AT ISSN 0815-5232) 835
Directory of Australian Music Organisations (AT ISSN 0157-6402) 835
Directory of Auto Supply Chains see Auto Aftermarket Suppliers 302
Directory of Automated Criminal Justice Information Systems see Directory of Criminal Justice Information Sources 669
Directory of Aviation and Space Education (US) 18, 428
Directory of Bankers Schools (US ISSN 0084-9855) 227, 428
Directory of Behavioral Graduate Study(US) 429, 789, 934

Directory of Bond Agents see Standard and Poor's Directory of Bond Agents 268
Directory of Book Publishers and Wholesalers (UK) 961
Directory of Book Publishers, Wholesalers and Their Terms see Directory of Book Publishers and Wholesalers 961
Directory of British Associations (UK ISSN 0070-5152) 462
Directory of British Biotechnology (UK ISSN 0265-8275) 26, 140
Directory of British Brass Bands (UK) 835
Directory of Brush and Allied Trades (UK ISSN 0070-5179) 190
Directory of Business Schools see Directory of Educational Institutions 193
Directory of Buying Offices and Accounts (US ISSN 0070-5195) 340
Directory of C E, Photography & Major Appliance Retailers & Distributors (US) 884
Directory of C S I R O Research Programs (AT ISSN 0727-6753) 990
Directory of Canadian Chartered Accountants (CN ISSN 0527-9275) 221
Directory of Canadian Community Funds and Councils see United Way of Canada. Directory of Members 1021
Directory of Canadian Map Collections(CN ISSN 0070-5217) 542, 676
Directory of Canadian Orchestras and Youth Orchestras/Annuaire Canadien des Orchestres et Orchestres. des Jeunes (CN ISSN 0705-6249) 835
Directory of Canadian Plays and Playwrights see Playwrights Union of Canada Catalogue of Canadian Plays 1079
Directory of Canadian Scientific and Technical Databases see Repertoire des Bases de Donnees Scientifiques et Techniques au Canada 1070
Directory of Canadian Trust Companies(CN ISSN 0070-5225) 227
Directory of Canadian Universities/ Repertoire des Universites Canadiennes (CN ISSN 0706-2338) 434
Directory of Canadian Universities and Colleges see Directory of Canadian Universities 434
Directory of Candy Brokers see Candy Buyers Directory 304
Directory of Cardamom Planters (II) 54, 305
Directory of Career Resources for Minorities (US) 271
Directory of Central America Organizations (US) 305
Directory of Central Atlantic States (US) 305
Directory of Central Atlantic States Manufacturers. Maryland, Delaware, Virginia, West Virginia, North Carolina, South Carolina (US ISSN 0070-5241) 305
Directory of Certified Appliances and Accessories (CN) 464, 863
Directory of Certified Products in Singapore (SI ISSN 0217-8311) 288
Directory of Chain Restaurant Operators (US ISSN 0411-7085) 305, 619
Directory of Chemical Engineering Consultants (US) 478
Directory of Chemical Engineering Research in Canadian Universities (CN ISSN 0070-525X) 478
Directory of Chemical Producers-U.S.A.(US ISSN 0012-3277) 322
Directory of Chemical Producers-Western Europe (US) 322
Directory of Chinese American Librarians (US) 676
Directory of Chinese External Economic Organizations & Industrial/Commercial Enterprises (HK ISSN 0259-1146) 305

Directory of Church of England Moral and Social Welfare Work see Directory of Church of England Social Services 1016
Directory of Church of England Social Services (UK ISSN 0070-5268) 1016
Directory of Churches and Synagogues (US) 969
Directory of Co-Operative Naturalists' Projects in Ontario. (CN ISSN 0707-0942) 170, 365
Directory of College and University Libraries in New York State (US ISSN 0070-5276) 676
Directory of College Facilities and Services for the Disabled (US) 429, 444
Directory of College Stores (US ISSN 0084-988X) 434
Directory of Colorado Libraries (US ISSN 0094-8403) 676
Directory of Colorado Manufacturers (US ISSN 0084-9898) 305
Directory of Commerce & Industry (SY) 306
Directory of Community, Junior, and Technical Colleges (US) 429
Directory of Community Resources and Services (US) 1016
Directory of Community Services for Drug Abuse in California see Drug Abuse: Directory of Community Services in California 376
Directory of Community Services in Metropolitan Toronto (CN ISSN 0315-0631) 1016
Directory of Community Services of Greater Montreal (CN ISSN 0319-258X) 1016
Directory of Companies Filing Annual Reports with the Securities and Exchange Commission Under the Securities Exchange Act of 1934 see Directory of Companies Required to File Annual Reports with the Securities and Exchange Commission Under the Securities Exchange Act of 1934 266
Directory of Companies Required to File Annual Reports with the Securities and Exchange Commission Under the Securities Exchange Act of 1934 (US ISSN 0149-6581) 266
Directory of Company Secretaries (II ISSN 0070-5322) 279
Directory of Computer & Software Retailers (US ISSN 0738-839X) 352, 357, 358, 363
Directory of Computer Installations: Mid-Atlantic State (US) 357, 358, 361, 362, 363
Directory of Computer Software (US) 363
Directory of Computer Training see Directory of Training 360
Directory of Computerized Data Files (US) 125, 357, 676
Directory of Connecticut Libraries and Media Centers and Buyers' Guide see Directory of Connecticut Libraries and Media Centers Including Buyers' Guide 676
Directory of Connecticut Libraries and Media Centers Including Buyers' Guide (US) 676
Directory of Connecticut Manufacturers(US) 306
Directory of Consulting Engineering Services in North Carolina (US) 306, 470
Directory of Consumer Protection and Environmental Agencies see Consumer Protection Directory 1151
Directory of Contract Wallcoverings and Specifications (US) 306, 643
Directory of Contractors and Construction Industries Buyers Guide see Directory of Contractors and Public Works Annual & Construction Industries Buyers Guide 183
Directory of Contractors and Public Works Annual & Construction Industries Buyers Guide (UK) 183
Directory of Convenience Store Companies see Directory of Convenience Stores 518

DIRECTORY OF 1713

Directory of Convenience Store Companies and Profile of the Industry see Directory of Convenience Stores 518
Directory of Convenience Stores (US) 518
Directory of Conventions (US ISSN 0417-5751) 796
Directory of Cooperatives, Voluntaries and Wholesale Grocers (US ISSN 0277-1969) 239
Directory of Corporate Affiliations (US ISSN 0070-5365) 15
Directory of Corporate Art Collections see Art News Directory of Corporate Art Collections 101
Directory of Correctional Services in Canada /Repertoire des Services de Correction du Canada see Justice - Directory of Services 1018
Directory of Country Clubs (US) 1107
Directory of Courses/Tourism/ Hospitality/Recreation (CN ISSN 0705-8160) 434, 847
Directory of Craft Info (AT) 113
Directory of Crematoria (UK ISSN 0143-3164) 531
Directory of Criminal Justice Information Sources (US) 358, 669
Directory of Current Research in Israel: Physical and Life Sciences see Current Research and Development Projects in Israel: Natural Sciences and Technology 1151
Directory of Dance Companies (US ISSN 0363-972X) 375
Directory of Day Schools in the United States and Canada (US) 429, 502
Directory of Day Schools in the United States, Canada and Latin America see Directory of Day Schools in the United States and Canada 429
Directory of Dealers in Secondhand and Antiquarian Books in the British Isles see Sheppard's Book Dealers in British Isles 963
Directory of Defense Electronic Products and Services: United States Suppliers (US) 452
Directory of Delaware Schools (US ISSN 0362-5710) 412
Directory of Demographic Research Centers see Annuaire des Centres de Recherche Demographique 920
Directory of Dental and Allied Dental Educators see Directory of Dental Educators 434
Directory of Dental Educators (US) 434, 779
Directory of Department Stores (US ISSN 0419-2508) 306
Directory of Departments and Programs of Religious Studies in North America (US) 969
Directory of Development and Training Institutes in Africa (SG) 262, 306, 412
Directory of Directories (UK ISSN 0275-5580) 125
Directory of Directors (II ISSN 0070-542X) 134, 279
Directory of Directors (UK ISSN 0070-5438) 279
Directory of Discount Department Stores see Directory of Discount Stores 306
Directory of Discount Stores (US) 306
Directory of Distinguished Americans (US) 125
Directory of Drug Store and H B A Chains (US ISSN 0730-2703) 306
Directory of Drug Store Chains see Directory of Drug Store and H B A Chains 306
Directory of East Asian Collections in North American Libraries (US ISSN 0148-0065) 569, 676
Directory of Economic Research Centres in India (II) 193
Directory of Editorial Resources (US) 961
Directory of Education Studies in Canada/Annuaire d'Etudes en Education au Canada (CN ISSN 0070-5454) 412
Directory of Educational Facilities for the Learning Disabled see Directory of Services and Facilities for the Learning Disabled 444

Directory of Educational Institutions (US) 193, 429
Directory of Educational Institutions in New Mexico (US ISSN 0084-991X) 412
Directory of Educational Opportunities in Georgia see Directory: A Guide to Colleges, Vocational-Technical Schools & Special Purpose Institutions 428
Directory of Electric Light and Power Companies (US ISSN 0092-4970) 306, 452, 863
Directory of Electrical Wholesale Distributors (US) 306
Directory of Electronics & Instrumentation (NZ) 452
Directory of Electronics, Instruments & Computers (UK ISSN 0267-1441) 357, 358
Directory of Employers Associations, Trade Unions, Joint Organizations Etc. (UK) 271
Directory of Employers Offering Employment to New University Graduates see Employers of New University Graduates: Directory 848
Directory of Engineering/Architectural Minority and Women Owned Firms (US) 306, 470
Directory of Engineering Capacity (UK) 306
Directory of Engineering College Research and Graduate Study see Engineering College Research and Graduate Study 471
Directory of Engineering Societies and Related Organizations (US ISSN 0070-5470) 306, 470
Directory of Engineers see Institution of Engineers of Ireland. Register of Chartered Engineers and Members 472
Directory of Engineers and Land Surveyors Registered in South Carolina (US ISSN 0420-2155) 306, 470
Directory of Environmental Organizations (US) 365, 495
Directory of European Associations. Part 1: National Industrial Trade and Professional Associations see Directory of European Industrial & Trade Associations 306
Directory of European Associations. Part 2: National Learned, Scientific & Technical Societies (UK ISSN 0309-5339) 990
Directory of European Industrial & Trade Associations (UK) 306
Directory of European Retailers & International Buying Agents (UK) 283, 306
Directory of Executive Recruiters (US ISSN 0090-6484) 279
Directory of Exhibit Opportunities see Association of American Publishers. Exhibits Directory 960
Directory of Export Buyers in the U.K. (UK ISSN 0142-4769) 254, 306
Directory of Exporters (CE) 235
Directory of Exporters and Manufacturers see Pakistan Trade Directory - Exporters and Manufacturers 259
Directory of Faculty Contracts and Bargaining Agents in Institutions of Higher Education (US ISSN 0276-7805) 434, 648
Directory of Family 'One-Name' Periodicals (US) 535
Directory of Federal Aid for Health and Allied Fields (US) 1016
Directory of Federal Aid for the Aging (US) 552, 1016
Directory of Federal Aid for the Handicapped (US) 180, 375, 444, 1016
Directory of Federal Laboratories (US) 306, 1068
Directory of Federally Supported Research in Universities/Repertoire de la Recherche dans les Universites Subventionnee Par le Gouvernement Federal (CN ISSN 0316-0297) 990
Directory of Fee-Based Information Services (US ISSN 0147-1678) 676

Directory of First Degree and Diploma of Higher Education Courses (UK ISSN 0266-8467) 434
Directory of Florida Industries (US) 306
Directory of Florida Writers (US) 15, 645, 961
Directory of Food Service Distributors (US ISSN 0271-7662) 522
Directory of Franchising Organizations (US ISSN 0070-556X) 283
Directory of Free Programs, Performing Talent and Attractions (US ISSN 0736-7759) 348
Directory of Free Vacation & Travel Information (US) 1107
Directory of Fulbright Alumni (II ISSN 0084-9936) 434
Directory of Further Education (UK) 434
Directory of Garment Manufacturers (CE) 235, 306
Directory of Gas Utility Companies (US) 306, 863
Directory of Genealogical Periodicals (US) 535
Directory of Genealogical Societies in the U S A & Canada see Meyer's Directory of Genealogical Societies in the U S A & Canada 536
Directory of General Merchandise, Variety Chains and Specialty Stores (US ISSN 0731-6925) 306
Directory of Geoscience Departments, United States and Canada (US ISSN 0364-7811) 379, 429
Directory of Government Document Collections and Librarians (US ISSN 0276-959X) 676
Directory of Government Production Primecontractors (US ISSN 0070-5594) 306
Directory of Governmental Air Pollution Agencies see A P C A Government Agencies Directory 493
Directory of Graduate Programs in the Communication Arts and Sciences (US ISSN 0732-2755) 429, 434
Directory of Graduate Programs in the Speech Communication Arts and Sciences see Directory of Graduate Programs in the Communication Arts and Sciences 434
Directory of Grant-Making Trusts (UK ISSN 0070-5624) 1016
Directory of Hardlines Distributors (US) 239
Directory of Hardware and Housewares Distributors (US ISSN 0882-536X) 190, 306
Directory of Hardware Distributors see Directory of Hardware and Housewares Distributors 306
Directory of Hazardous Waste Services (CN) 306, 495
Directory of Health, Welfare and Recreation Services of Greater Montreal see Directory of Community Services of Greater Montreal 1016
Directory of High-Volume Independent Restaurants (US) 619
Directory of Higher Education see Illinois. Board of Higher Education. Directory of Higher Education 436
Directory of Historians of Latin American Art (US) 85, 104
Directory of Historical Societies and Agencies in the United States and Canada (US ISSN 0070-5659) 605
Directory of Home Care Services in New York see Home Care Services in New York State 1018
Directory of Home Furnishings Retailers (US) 644
Directory of Homosexual Organizations and Publications (US) 615
Directory of Hong Kong Industries (HK) 306
Directory of Hotel and Motel Systems (US) 619
Directory of Hotels in Kenya (KE) 619
Directory of Incentive Travel International (US ISSN 0732-6572) 1107
Directory of Independent IBM Personal Computer Hardware and Software see Infopro: The Directory 361

Directory of Indian Engineering Exporters (II ISSN 0417-5964) 306, 470
Directory of Indian Exporters (II) 254
Directory of Industrial Establishments in Punjab (PK) 306
Directory of Industrial Laboratories in Israel (IS) 306, 471
Directory of Industry Data Sources, U.S. and Canada (US ISSN 0278-0119) 193
Directory of Information and Referral Agencies in the United States and Canada (Alliance of Information and Referral Systems) (US) 369
Directory of Information on Medical Practitioners in Malaysia (MY) 760
Directory of Information Resources for the Handicapped (US) 180, 375, 444
Directory of Institutions Offering of Planning Programs for the Training of Library Technical Assistants see Directory of Institutions Offering or Planning Programs for the Training of Library Technical Media Assistants 676
Directory of Institutions Offering or Planning Programs for the Training of Library Technical Media Assistants (US) 676
Directory of Instruments, Electronics, Automation see Directory of Electronics, Instruments & Computers 357
Directory of Insurance Companies Licensed in New York State (US ISSN 0070-5691) 639
Directory of Interior Designers (II ISSN 0256-4025) 643
Directory of International Broadcasting (UK ISSN 0262-9771) 348
Directory of International Mail (US) 346
Directory of International Personnel in Tanzania see Directory: Organizations of the United Nations System in the United Republic of Tanzania 262
Directory of International Trade (US) 54, 254
Directory of Internships, Residencies and Registrarships Available in Victorian Hospitals (AT ISSN 0157-2784) 616, 847
Directory of Investor-Owned Hospitals and Hospital Management Companies see Directory of Investor-Owned Hospitals, Hospital Management Companies and Health Systems 616
Directory of Investor-Owned Hospitals, Hospital Management Companies and Health Systems (US ISSN 0095-5191) 616
Directory of Iowa Manufacturers (US ISSN 0075-0379) 306
Directory of Iranian Periodicals (IR ISSN 0084-9960) 125
Directory of Iron and Steel Works of the United States and Canada (US) 306
Directory of Israel (IS) 306
Directory of Israeli Merchants and Manufacturers see Directory of Israel 306
Directory of Japanese Firms, Offices and Other Organizations in the United States (US) 193
Directory of Japanese Firms, Offices and Subsidiaries in the United States see Directory of Japanese Firms, Offices and Other Organizations in the United States 193
Directory of Japanese Scientific Periodicals (JA) 1003
Directory of Jewish Community Centers (US) 502
Directory of Jewish Federations, Welfare Funds and Community Councils (US ISSN 0161-2638) 1017
Directory of Jewish Resident Summer Camps (US) 502, 1045
Directory of Kansas Manufacturers and Products (US ISSN 0070-5721) 306
Directory of Key Bulgarian Government and Party Officials (BU) 904

Directory of Korean Business *see* Chonguk Kiopche Chongnam 304
Directory of Labor Unions and Employee Organizations in New York State (US) 648
Directory of Labour Organizations in Canada/Repertoire des Organisations de Travailleurs au Canada (CN ISSN 0075-7578) 648
Directory of Labour Unions in Nova Scotia *see* Labour Organizations in Nova Scotia 648
Directory of Land and Hydrographic Survey Services in the United Kingdom (UK ISSN 0260-5007) 481
Directory of Latin Americanists *see* Directory of A S U Latin Americanists 605
Directory of Law Libraries (US) 655, 676
Directory of Law Teachers (US ISSN 0070-573X) 655
Directory of Law Teachers/Annuaire des Professeurs de Droit (CN ISSN 0383-8358) 655
Directory of Lawyer Referral Services (US) 655
Directory of Leading Chain Stores (US) 306
Directory of Legal Aid and Defender Offices in the United States (US ISSN 0276-5365) 655
Directory of Libraries and Library Resources in the South Central Research Library Council Region (US) 676
Directory of Libraries in Manitoba (CN ISSN 0317-8536) 676
Directory of Libraries in Southeast Saskatchewan *see* Southeast Regional Library (Sask.) Library Directory 684
Directory of Library Reprographic Services (US ISSN 0160-6077) 676, 884
Directory of Library Resources for the Blind and Physically Handicapped *see* Library Resources for the Blind and Physically Handicapped (Large Print Edition) 681
Directory of Library Systems in New York State (US) 676
Directory of Licensed Products (US) 183
Directory of Lifestyle Change Services (CN ISSN 0707-0047) 1152
Directory of Literary Magazines (US) 741
Directory of Little Magazines, Small Presses and Underground Newspapers *see* International Directory of Little Magazines and Small Presses 964
Directory of Long Island Libraries and Media Centers and Buyers' Guide *see* Directory of Long Island Libraries and Media Centers Including Buyers' Guide 687
Directory of Long Island Libraries and Media Centers Including Buyers' Guide (US) 687
Directory of Long-Term Care Centres in Canada/Repertoire des Centres de Soins de Longue Duree au Canada (CN ISSN 0226-5419) 783
Directory of Louisiana Cities, Towns and Villages (US ISSN 0092-0614) 950
Directory of Louisiana Manufacturers (US ISSN 0275-1089) 306
Directory of Low Cost Vacations with a Difference (US) 1107
Directory of Machine Tools and Related Products *see* U S Machine Tool Directory 493
Directory of Mail Drops in the United States and Canada (US) 346
Directory of Mailing List Houses (US ISSN 0419-2923) 15, 306
Directory of Mailing List Houses (New York) (US) 15, 306
Directory of Maine Labor Organizations (US) 648
Directory of Major Malls (US ISSN 0732-5983) 283, 965
Directory of Management Consultants (US) 279

Directory of Management Consultants in the UK (UK) 279
Directory of Management Training *see* Directory of Training 360
Directory of Manufacturers in Arkansas *see* Directory of Arkansas Manufacturers 305
Directory of Manufacturers - Minnesota(US) 306
Directory of Manufacturers of Lumber, Plywood, and Building Materials Made in B.C. (CN) 1152
Directory of Manufacturers, State of Delaware *see* Delaware Directory of Commerce and Industry 305
Directory of Maryland Manufacturers (US ISSN 0070-5802) 306
Directory of Massachusettes Libraries and Media Centers and Buyers' Guide *see* Directory of Massachusettes Libraries and Media Centers Including Buyer's Guide 676
Directory of Massachusettes Libraries and Media Centers Including Buyer's Guide (US) 676
Directory of Massachusetts Manufacturers (US) 306
Directory of Medical Libraries in New York State (US ISSN 0070-5810) 677
Directory of Medical Practitioners Malaysia *see* Directory of Information on Medical Practitioners in Malaysia 760
Directory of Medical Schools Worldwide (Year) (US) 429, 760
Directory of Medical Specialists (US ISSN 0070-5829) 134, 760
Directory of Men's and Boy's Specialty Stores *see* Directory of Men's and Boys' Wear Specialty Stores 340
Directory of Men's and Boys' Wear Specialty Stores (US ISSN 0277-9625) 340
Directory of Michigan Institutions of Higher Education (US) 434
Directory of Michigan Manufacturers *see* Michigan Manufacturers Directory 284
Directory of Michigan Mineral Operators *see* Michigan Mineral Producers Annual Directory 1158
Directory of Middle East Importers (US) 255
Directory of Middle East Imports *see* Directory of Middle East Importers 255
Directory of Minnesota City Officials (US) 950
Directory of Minnesota Municipal Officials *see* Directory of Minnesota City Officials 950
Directory of Minority Four Year Teacher Preparatory Institutions (US) 429
Directory of Missouri Libraries (US ISSN 0092-4067) 677
Directory of Missouri's Regional Planning Commissions (US) 288
Directory of Missouri's Regional Planning System *see* Directory of Missouri's Regional Planning Commissions 288
Directory of Model-Talent Agencies and Schools USA and International (US) 429, 848
Directory of Montana Manufacturers *see* Montana Manufacturers & Products Directory 314
Directory of Montana Schools (US) 442
Directory of Multihospital Systems (US ISSN 0731-8510) 616
Directory of Municipal Natural Gas Systems (US) 864
Directory of Municipal Officials of New Mexico *see* Directory of New Mexico Municipal Officials 941
Directory of Museums & Living Displays (UK ISSN 0267-9698) 827
Directory of Museums, Art Galleries and Archives of British Columbia (CN ISSN 0714-7023) 827
Directory of Music Faculties in American Colleges and Universities *see* Directory of Music Faculties in Colleges & Universities U S and Canada 835

Directory of Music Faculties in Colleges & Universities U S and Canada (US ISSN 0098-664X) 412, 835
Directory of National Environmental Organizations (US) 495
Directory of Nebraska Manufacturers (US ISSN 0070-5926) 306
Directory of Nebraska Services (US) 941, 1017
Directory of New England Manufacturers (US) 306
Directory of New Mexico Municipal Officials (US) 941
Directory of New York Manufacturers (US) 306
Directory of New York State Public Schools and Administrators *see* Directory of Public Schools and Administrators, New York State 442
Directory of Nonprofit Immigration Counseling Agencies (US ISSN 0277-724X) 922
Directory of Nonpublic Schools and Administrators, New York State (US) 442
Directory of North American Computer Companies *see* Worldwide Directory of Computer Companies 1166
Directory of North American Fairs and Expositions (US ISSN 0361-4255) 15
Directory of North Carolina Municipal Officials (US) 950
Directory of North Dakota Lawyers *see* North Dakota Directory of Lawyers and Judges 661
Directory of North Dakota Manufacturers (US ISSN 0090-5577) 306
Directory of Nurses with Doctoral Degrees (US) 783
Directory of Nursing Home Facilities (US) 1017
Directory of Nursing Homes in the United States, U.S. Possessions and Canada *see* Modern Nursing Home Directory of Nursing Homes in the United States, U.S. Possessions and Canada 1158
Directory of Obsolete Securities *see* Financial Stock Guide Service. Directory of Obsolete Securities 266
Directory of Official Architects and Planners *see* Directory of Official Architecture and Planning 98
Directory of Official Architecture and Planning (UK) 98, 495
Directory of Oil Marketing and Wholesale Distributors (US ISSN 0070-5993) 864
Directory of Oil Well Drilling Contractors (US ISSN 0415-9764) 306, 864
Directory of Oil Well Supply Companies (US ISSN 0415-9772) 288, 306, 864
Directory of Oklahoma (US) 941
Directory of On-Going Research in Cancer Epidemiology (FR) 775
Directory of On-Going Research in Smoking and Health (US ISSN 0070-6000) 376
Directory of Opportunities for Graduates (UK ISSN 0070-6019) 848
Directory of Oregon Libraries *see* Directory and Statistics of Oregon Libraries 676
Directory of Oregon Manufacturers (US) 307
Directory of Organizations and Personnel in Educational Management *see* Directory of Organizations and Researchers in Educational Management 442
Directory of Organizations and Researchers in Educational Management (US) 442
Directory of Organizations Concerned with Scientific Research and Technical Services in Rhodesia *see* Directory of Organizations Concerned with Scientific Research and Technical Services in Zimbabwe 990

Directory of Organizations Concerned with Scientific Research and Technical Services in Zimbabwe (RH) 990
Directory of Outplacement Firms (US ISSN 0735-3707) 271
Directory of Overseas Summer Jobs (UK ISSN 0070-6051) 848
Directory of Pakistan Exporters *see* Pakistan Trade Directory - Exporters and Manufacturers 259
Directory of Pakistani Scholars Abroad (PK ISSN 0070-606X) 441
Directory of Pathology Training Programs (US ISSN 0070-6086) 140, 760
Directory of Periodicals Online. Vol. 1: News, Law & Business (US) 677, 689
Directory of Periodicals Publishing Articles on English and American Literature and Language (US ISSN 0070-6094) 694, 720
Directory of Personal Image Consultants (US ISSN 0163-6537) 15
Directory of Philippine Exporters and Importers (PH) 307
Directory of Philippine Manufacturers and Producers (PH) 307
Directory of Physics and Astronomy Facilities in North American Colleges and Universities *see* Directory of Physics & Astronomy Staff (Year) 434
Directory of Physics & Astronomy Staff (Year) (US) 115, 434, 888
Directory of Physics & Astronomy Staff Members *see* Directory of Physics & Astronomy Staff (Year) 434
Directory of Plans, Executives, Policies for PCs, Office Automation, Datacom, Electronic Mail (US) 279, 343, 677
Directory of Poetry Publishers (US) 741, 961
Directory of Polish Officials (US ISSN 0090-9955) 134
Directory of Post Offices *see* National Five Digit Zip Code and Post Office Directory 346
Directory of Postgraduate and Post-Experience Courses (UK ISSN 0266-8459) 434
Directory of Postgraduate and Post-Graduate Experience Courses *see* Directory of Postgraduate and Post-Experience Courses 434
Directory of Premium and Incentive Buyers *see* Directory of Premium, Incentive and Travel Buyers 283
Directory of Premium, Incentive and Travel Buyers (US ISSN 0196-8262) 283, 307
Directory of Primes (US) 307
Directory of Private Elementary Schools and High Schools in California *see* California Private School Directory 428
Directory of Private Hospitals and Health Services (UK ISSN 0260-8820) 617, 760
Directory of Producers and Drilling Contractors: California (US) 307, 864
Directory of Producers and Drilling Contractors: Kansas (US) 307, 864
Directory of Producers and Drilling Contractors: Louisiana, Arkansas, Florida, Georgia (US) 307, 864
Directory of Producers and Drilling Contractors: Michigan, Indiana, Illinois, Kentucky (US) 307, 864
Directory of Producers and Drilling Contractors: Oklahoma (US) 307, 864
Directory of Producers and Drilling Contractors: Rocky Mountain Region, Williston Basin, Four Corners New Mexico (US) 307, 864
Directory of Producers and Drilling Contractors: Texas (US) 307, 864
Directory of Professional Electrologists (US ISSN 0417-6383) 118

Directory of Professional Genealogists and Related Services *see* Association of Professional Genealogists. List of Professional Genealogists and Related Services 535
Directory of Professional Personnel: State Higher Education Agencies and Boards (US) 434
Directory of Professional Photography (US ISSN 0070-6140) 884
Directory of Professional Puppeteers (UK) 1077
Directory of Programs in Linguistics (US) 694
Directory of Property Investors and Developers (AT) 266, 965
Directory of Public Enterprises in India(II ISSN 0376-8546) 288
Directory of Public High Technology Corporations (US ISSN 0738-7369) 266, 307, 1068
Directory of Public Refrigerated Warehouses (US ISSN 0070-6167) 553
Directory of Public Schools and Administrators, New York State (US) 442
Directory of Public Schools in the U S (US) 429
Directory of Public Service Internships (US) 1152
Directory of Public Vocational Technical Schools and Institutes (US) 429, 848
Directory of Publishing Opportunities *see* Directory of Publishing Opportunities in Journals and Periodicals 1152
Directory of Publishing Opportunities in Journals and Periodicals (US ISSN 0275-3820) 1152
Directory of Real Estate Investors (US ISSN 0277-9986) 965
Directory of Regional Councils (US) 941
Directory of Registered Federal and State Lobbyists *see* Directory of Registered Lobbyists and Lobbyist Legislation 1152
Directory of Registered Lobbyists and Lobbyist Legislation (US ISSN 0146-0323) 1152
Directory of Religious Broadcasting (US ISSN 0731-0331) 348, 429
Directory of Research & Development Contractors (US) 950, 990
Directory of Research and Developmental Projects (AT) 333, 412, 444, 447
Directory of Research and Special Libraries in Ghana (GH) 677
Directory of Research, Development and Demonstration Projects (US ISSN 0270-8264) 1081
Directory of Research, Development, and Demonstrations *see* Directory of Research, Development and Demonstration Projects 1081
Directory of Research Grants (US ISSN 0146-7336) 434
Directory of Research Institutes and Industrial Laboratories in Israel (IS ISSN 0334-3197) 1152
Directory of Research Institutes and Industrial Research Units in Israel *see* Directory of Research Institutes and Industrial Laboratories in Israel 1152
Directory of Research Institutes in Israel (IS) 677, 990
Directory of Residency Training Accredited by the Accreditation Council for Graduate Medical Education (US) 434, 760
Directory of Resources for Alcoholics *see* Coping Catalog 376
Directory of Restaurant & Fast Food Chains in Canada (CN) 307, 518
Directory of Retail Chains in Canada (CN) 307
Directory of Retailer Owned Cooperative Chains, Wholesaler Sponsored Voluntary Chains, Wholesale Grocers *see* Directory of Cooperatives, Voluntaries and Wholesale Grocers 239
Directory of San Francisco Attorneys (US ISSN 0092-9174) 655

Directory of Science Resources for Maryland (US ISSN 0070-6256) 990
Directory of Scientific and Technical Associations and Institutes in Israel *see* Directory of Scientific and Technical Associations in Israel 990
Directory of Scientific and Technical Associations in Israel (IS ISSN 0334-2824) 990, 1068
Directory of Scientific Directories (UK ISSN 0070-6272) 990
Directory of Scientific Periodicals of Pakistan (PK) 4, 1003
Directory of Scientific Research in Indian Universities (II ISSN 0376-8554) 1003
Directory of Scientific Research in Nigeria (NR ISSN 0070-6280) 990
Directory of Services and Facilities for the Learning Disabled (US) 429, 444
Directory of Services Available to Visually Handicapped South Africans *see* Directory of Services for Visually Handicapped South Africans 180
Directory of Services for Migrant Families/Directorio de Servicios para Familias Migrantes (US ISSN 0362-7179) 1017
Directory of Services for Visually Handicapped South Africans (SA) 180
Directory of Sheltered Workshops, Activity Centres and Other Vocational Rehabilitation Facilities in N.S.W and A.C.T. (AT) 1017
Directory of Shipowners, Shipbuilders and Marine Engineers (UK ISSN 0070-6310) 1100
Directory of Shop-by-Mail Bargain Sources (US) 283
Directory of Shopping Centers in the United States (US) 307
Directory of Small Magazine/Press Editors and Publishers (US ISSN 0095-6414) 125, 964
Directory of Social and Health Agencies of New York City (US ISSN 0085-0012) 953, 1017
Directory of South Dakota Manufacturers and Processors *see* South Dakota Manufacturers & Processors Directory 317
Directory of Speakers (US) 343
Directory of Special Databases in Israel(IS) 357, 360
Directory of Special Education and Guidance Services in New Zealand (NZ) 444
Directory of Special Libraries and Information Centers (US) 677
Directory of Special Libraries and Information Centers in the U S and Canada *see* Directory of Special Libraries and Information Centers 677
Directory of Special Libraries and Information Sources (IO) 677
Directory of Special Libraries in Ghana *see* Directory of Research and Special Libraries in Ghana 677
Directory of Special Libraries in Indonesia *see* Directory of Special Libraries and Information Sources 677
Directory of Special Libraries in Israel (IS) 677
Directory of Special Libraries in Montreal *see* Directory of Special Libraries in the Montreal Area 677
Directory of Special Libraries in the Montreal Area/Repertoire des Bibliotheques Specialisees de la Region de Montreal (CN) 677
Directory of Special Opportunities for Women (US ISSN 0273-2157) 848, 1128
Directory of Special Programs for Minority Group Members; Career Information Services, Employment Skills, Banks, Financial Aid Sources (US ISSN 0093-9501) 429, 502, 848
Directory of Specialist Bookdealers *see* Directory of Specialist Bookdealers in the UK Handling Mainly New Books 961

Directory of Specialist Bookdealers in the UK Handling Mainly New Books(UK) 961
Directory of Spoken-Word Audio-Cassettes (US) 1032
Directory of State and Federal Funds Available for Business Development (US ISSN 0070-640X) 193
Directory of State Corporations (CE) 307
Directory of State, County, and Federal Officials (US ISSN 0440-4947) 941
Directory of State Environment Agencies (US) 365, 495, 941
Directory of Statisticians (US ISSN 0278-405X) 1054
Directory of Steel Foundries in the United States, Canada and Mexico (US ISSN 0070-6426) 307, 797
Directory of Summer Jobs Abroad (UK ISSN 0308-7123) 848
Directory of Summer Jobs in Britain (UK ISSN 0143-3490) 848
Directory of Summer Law Programs *see* Student Guide to Summer Law Study Programs 665
Directory of Supermarket, Grocery & Convenience Store Chains (US ISSN 0196-1845) 307, 522
Directory of Technical and Further Education (UK ISSN 0309-5290) 848
Directory of Tennessee Municipal Officials (US) 941
Directory of Texas Manufacturers (US ISSN 0070-6450) 307
Directory of the American Left *see* Guide to the American Left 905
Directory of the American Right *see* Guide to the American Right 905
Directory of the Arts (CN ISSN 0832-865X) 104, 1077
Directory of the Australian Gas Industry *see* Australian Gas Industry Directory 863
Directory of the Canning, Freezing, Preserving Industries (US) 307, 518
Directory of the College Student Press in America (US ISSN 0085-0020) 125
Directory of the Cultural Organizations of the Republic of China (CH ISSN 0419-3733) 4, 423
Directory of the Forest Products Industry (US ISSN 0070-6477) 307, 529
Directory of the Mutual Savings Banks of the United States *see* National Council of Savings Institutions Directory 231
Directory of the National Productivity Organizations in A P O Member Countries (UN) 262, 288
Directory of the Scientists, Technologists, and Engineers of the P C S I R (Pakistan Council of Scientific and Industrial Research) (PK) 307, 471, 991, 1068
Directory of the Solar Industry (US) 307, 888
Directory of the Spanish Cotton-System Textile Enterprises/Directorio Empresas Textiles de Proceso Algodonero/Directori Empreses Textils de Proces Cotoner/Directoire Enterprises Textiles de Processus Cotonnier (SP) 307, 1074
Directory of the Stainless Steel Industry *see* Stainless Steel Directory 800
Directory of the Turf (UK ISSN 0419-3806) 1043
Directory of Trainer Support Services (UK) 412
Directory of Training (UK) 360, 361
Directory of Trust Institutions (US ISSN 0093-951X) 227
Directory of Trust Institutions of United States and Canada *see* Directory of Trust Institutions 227
Directory of U.S. Institutions of Higher Education *see* Education Directory. (School Year): Colleges and Universities 429
Directory of U.S. Labor Organizations (US ISSN 0734-6786) 648
Directory of U K Fluid Power Distributors (UK) 307, 402
Directory of Unit Trusts *see* Unit Trust Yearbook 233

Directory of United States Importers (US ISSN 0070-6531) 255, 307
Directory of United States Standardization Activities (US ISSN 0070-6558) 809
Directory of University Correspondence Courses *see* Canadian University Distance Education Directory 426
Directory of University Professors and Researchers in Japan (JA) 429
Directory of Unpublished Experimental Mental Measures (US ISSN 0731-8081) 934, 1025
Directory of Utah Manufacturers *see* Utah Directory of Business and Industry 318
Directory of V A Rs (US) 193
Directory of Veterans Organizations (US) 811
Directory of Virginia Manufacturing and Mining *see* Virginia Industrial Directory 318
Directory of Visiting Fulbright Scholars and Occasional Lecturer Program *see* Directory of Visiting Fulbright Scholars and Occasional Lecturers 441
Directory of Visiting Fulbright Scholars and Occasional Lecturers (US) 441
Directory of Wall Street Research (US ISSN 0886-0521) 266
Directory of Washington Manufacturers *see* Washington Manufacturers Register 319
Directory of Washington Representatives of American Associations and Industry *see* Washington Representatives 947
Directory of Water Resources Expertise *see* California Directory of Water Resources Expertise 1123
Directory of Westchester Libraries and Media Centers and Buyers' Guide *see* Directory of Westchester Libraries and Media Centers Including Buyers' Guide 677
Directory of Westchester Libraries and Media Centers Including Buyers' Guide (US) 677
Directory of Wire Companies of North America (US) 307
Directory of Women Attorneys in the United States *see* Directory of Women Law Graduates and Attorneys in the U.S.A 1152
Directory of Women Law Graduates and Attorneys in the U.S.A. (US) 1152
Directory of Women's & Children's Wear Specialty Stores (US ISSN 0277-9617) 340
Directory of Wool, Hosiery and Fabrics(II) 307, 1074
Directory of World Chemical Producers(US ISSN 0196-0555) 307, 322
Directory: Organizations of the United Nations System in the United Republic of Tanzania (UN) 262
Directory: Research in Housing - Australia and New Zealand (AT) 623
Directory - Technical Association of the Pulp and Paper Industry *see* Technical Association of the Pulp and Paper Industry. Directory 859
Directory to the Furnishing Trade (UK ISSN 0070-6604) 644
Direktorat under Forandring (DK) 860
Direktorium fuer das Bistum Muenster (GW) 969
Diretorio Brasileiro da Industria Farmaceutica (BL ISSN 0070-6612) 870
Dirigeants et Administrateurs des Universites Canadiennes *see* Academic and Administrative Officers at Canadian Universities 431
Dirigo: Me *see* Me 107
Diritto e Societa (Naples) (IT ISSN 0390-8542) 655
Disability Aids Directory (AT ISSN 0812-4663) 1017
Disarmament (UN) 811
Discharges and Electrical Insulation in Vacuum *see* International Symposium on Discharges and Electrical Insulation 456

Disclosure (US ISSN 0196-8203) *369*
Disco 80 Annual (UK) *835*
Discographies (US ISSN 0192-334X) *1031*
Discography Series (US ISSN 0095-8115) *835*
Discontinued Diodes D.A.T.A. Book *see* Diode Discontinued Devices D.A.T.A. Book *452*
Discontinued I C's D.A.T.A. Book *see* Digital & Audio-Video Discontinued Devices D.A.T.A. Book *356*
Discontinued Optoelectronics D.A.T.A. Book *see* Optoelectronics Discontinued Devices D.A.T.A. Book *458*
Discontinued Transistors D.A.T.A. Book *see* Transistor Discontinued Devices D.A.T.A. Book *460*
Discontinued Type Locator D.A.T.A. Book *see* International Directory of Discontinued I Cs & Semiconductors D.A.T.A. Book *361*
Discountbutikker (Year) (DK ISSN 0108-5255) *301*
Discourse Analysis Monographs (UK ISSN 0307-1006) *694*
Discourse Units in Human Communication for Librarians (US ISSN 0070-6663) *677*
Discover North America (UK) *1107*
Discover the Far East (UK) *1107*
Discoveramericard Directory of Cities and Hotels *see* Discovericard Directory of Cities and Hotels *1107*
Discovericard Directory of Cities and Hotels (US ISSN 0277-8416) *1107*
Discoveries in the Judaean Desert of Jordan (US ISSN 0070-668X) *85*
Discovery (Richmond) (US ISSN 0300-7316) *98, 365, 556*
Discovery Reports (UK ISSN 0070-6698) *405*
Discretio (IT ISSN 0012-3668) *629, 710*
Disc'ribe (US) *835*
Discussions in Environmental Health Planning (US) *495, 623*
Discussions on Teaching (US ISSN 0277-2736) *412*
Diskurs (GW ISSN 0173-007X) *1152*
Dislocations in Solids (NE) *888*
Disney Magazine Annual (UK) *823*
Disneyland (Year) (US) *1107*
Disneyland Annual (UK) *1107*
Disoo (SG) *1152*
Disorders of Human Communication (US ISSN 0173-170X) *343*
Dispersion y Unidad (IS ISSN 0334-8903) *612, 976*
Disquisitiones Mathematicae Hungaricae (HU ISSN 0070-671X) *748*
Dissertation Abstracts *see* Dissertation Abstracts International. Section A: Humanities and Social Sciences *634*
Dissertation Abstracts *see* Dissertation Abstracts International. Section B: Physical Sciences and Engineering *1072*
Dissertation Abstracts International. Section A: Humanities and Social Sciences (US ISSN 0419-4209) *634, 1014*
Dissertation Abstracts International. Section B: Physical Sciences and Engineering (US ISSN 0419-4217) *4, 1072*
Dissertation Abstracts International. Section C: European Abstracts (US ISSN 0307-6075) *126*
Dissertationes Archaeologicae Gandenses (BE ISSN 0419-4241) *85*
Dissertationes Botanicae (GW ISSN 0070-6728) *156*
Dissertationes Mathematicae/Rozprawy Matematyczne (PL ISSN 0012-3862) *748*
Dissertationes Orientales (CS) *851*
Distilled Spirits Council of the United States, Inc. Facts Book *see* D I S C U S Facts Book *1151*
Distillers Feed Conference. Proceedings(US) *63*
Distribution Management (US ISSN 0737-0903) *283*
Distribution of Dentists in the U S (US) *779*
Distribution of High School Graduates and College Going Rate, New York State (US ISSN 0077-9210) *412*
Distributor Manufacturer News B B S I Convention Daily (US) *193*
District Heating Association. Handbook *see* Combined Heat and Power Association. Handbook *553*
District Memoir (MY ISSN 0126-9046) *322, 385, 856*
District of Columbia. Air Monitoring Division. Annual Report on the Quality of the Air in Washington, D.C. *see* District of Columbia. Air Monitoring Section. Annual Report on the Quality of the Air in Washington, D.C *495*
District of Columbia. Air Monitoring Section. Annual Report on the Quality of the Air in Washington, D.C. (US) *495*
Division Interdisciplinar para la Familia(SP) *655*
Division of Forestry Research. Leaflet (IS) *1152*
Divitiae Musicae Artis. Series A (NE) *835*
Divorce Chats (US ISSN 0012-4230) *655, 1025*
Divrei ha-Akademia ha-Leumit ha-Yisraelit Lemadaim (IS ISSN 0334-2816) *556, 720, 878*
Divrei ha-Akademia ha-Leumit ha-Yisraelit Lemadaim-ha-Hativa le-Madaei ha-Teva (IS) *174, 385, 748, 888*
Divulgacao (AO) *288*
Dix-Huitieme Siecle (FR ISSN 0070-6760) *629*
Dizionario Bibliografico delle Riviste Giuridiche Italiane (IT ISSN 0419-4632) *668*
Dizionario Enciclopedico d'Informazioni (IT) *462*
Djakarta Business Guide Book *see* Business Guide Book to Jakarta *303*
Do-It-Yourself Report (UK ISSN 0263-5437) *183, 283*
Doboku Gakkai Nenji Koenkai Koen Gaiyoshu/Japan Society of Civil Engineers. Proceedings of the Annual Conference. (JA) *481*
Doboku Keikakugaku Shinpojumu/ Symposium on Civil Engineering Planning. Proceedings (JA) *481*
Doc; Documentazione *see* Doc Italia *434*
Doc Italia (IT) *434*
Doctoral Dissertations on Transportation (US ISSN 0070-6809) *126, 1085*
Doctoral Scientists and Engineers in the United States. Profile *see* Science, Engineering, and Humanities Doctorates in the United States: Profile *849*
Doctor's Manual (IS) *760*
Documenta (SW ISSN 0347-5719) *991*
Documenta et Monumenta Orientis Antiqui (NE) *612*
Documenta Homoeopathica (GW) *760*
Documenta Musicae Novae (BE) *835*
Documenta Ophthalmologica Proceedings Series (NE) *785*
Documenta Romaniae Historica. Serie A: La Moldavie (RM ISSN 0070-6825) *580*
Documenta Romaniae Historica. Serie B: La Valachie (RM ISSN 0070-6833) *581*
Documentacao Amazonica (BL ISSN 0101-4854) *126*
Documentacion Bibliotecologica (AG ISSN 0070-6841) *677*
Documentacion Cervantina (US) *720*
Documentacion Internacional (UY) *915*
Documentary Reference Collections (US) *556*
Documentary Studies in Modern Russian Poetry (US) *720*
Documentatieblad: The Abstracts Journal of the African Studies Centre Leiden (NE ISSN 0166-2694) *563, 739, 911*
Documentatio Didactica Classica (BE ISSN 0070-685X) *337*
Documentation Danoise *see* Factsheet Denmark *503*
Documentation de Reference - Association Canadienne de la Construction *see* Canadian Construction Association. Documentation de Reference *182*
Documentation Europeenne - Serie Agricole (EI ISSN 0537-6297) *26*
Documentation Europeenne - Serie Syndicale et Ouvriere (EI) *271*
Documentation, Libraries and Archives: Bibliographies and Reference Works (UN) *687*
Documentation, Libraries and Archives: Studies and Research (UN) *677*
Documentation List: Africa (II ISSN 0418-582X) *4, 563*
Documentation on Asia (II ISSN 0419-5345) *911*
Documentation Politique Internationale *see* International Political Science Abstracts *912*
Documentation Rheology *see* Dokumentation Rheologie *892*
Documentation Theatrale (FR) *1077*
Documentation Tribology *see* Dokumentation Tribologie *476*
Documentazione Europea - Serie Agricola *see* Documentation Europeenne - Serie Agricole *26*
Documenti di Vita Comunale (IT ISSN 0012-4737) *950*
Documenti e Testimonianze di Storia Contemporanea (IT) *556*
Documenti Sulle Arti del Libro (IT ISSN 0070-6906) *126*
Documentos de Geohistoria Regional (AG ISSN 0325-9404) *542, 605*
Documentos Institucionales Oficiales (BO) *1025*
Documentos Oficiales de la Organizacion de los Estados Americanos: Lista General Indice Analitico *see* Organization of American States. Official Records. Indice y Lista General *608*
Documentos Taller Multidisciplinario del Medio Ambiente (CL) *495*
Documents d'Etudes (FR) *655*
Documents d'Histoire de l'Art Canadien *see* Documents in the History of Canadian Art *104*
Documents d'Histoire Maghrebine (FR) *851*
Documents de Cartographie Ecologique(FR ISSN 0335-5330) *140, 542*
Documents de Linguistique Quantitative(FR ISSN 0085-4786) *709*
Documents et Debats (FR ISSN 0012-477X) *934*
Documents for New Poetry (US) *741*
Documents Historiques des Sciences (BE) *581, 991*
Documents in Imperial History (US ISSN 0749-4831) *556*
Documents in Socialist History (UK) *904*
Documents in the History of Canadian Art/Documents d'Histoire de l'Art Canadien (CN ISSN 0383-4514) *104*
Documents of Medieval History (UK) *581*
Documents of Modern Art (US) *1152*
Documents of Modern History (US) *556*
Documents of Revolution (US) *556, 904*
Documents of Ukrainian Samvydav (US) *502, 913*
Documents Pedozoologiques (FR ISSN 0180-9555) *54*
Documents pour la Carte de la Vegetation des Alpes *see* Documents de Cartographie Ecologique *140*
Documents sur l'Esperanto. Nouvelle Serie *see* Esperanto-Dokumentoj. Nova Serio *694*
Dodge Assemblies Cost Data (US) *183*
Dodge Construction Systems Costs *see* Dodge Assemblies Cost Data *183*
Dodge Digest of Building Costs and Specifications *see* Dodge Square Foot Cost Data *183*
Dodge Guide to Public Works and Heavy Construction Costs *see* Dodge Heavy Construction Cost Data *183*
Dodge Heavy Construction Cost Data (US) *183, 481*
Dodge Manual for Building Construction Pricing and Scheduling *see* Dodge Unit Cost Data *183*
Dodge Remodelling & Retrofit Cost Data (US) *183*
Dodge Square Foot Cost Data (US) *183*
Dodge Unit Cost Data (US) *183*
Dod's Parliamentary Companion (UK ISSN 0070-7007) *904*
Doeblinger Heimatmuseum *see* Doeblinger Museumsblaetter *581*
Doeblinger Museumsblaetter (AU) *581*
Doedsaarsagerne/Causes of Death in Denmark (DK ISSN 0108-5646) *953*
Doedsaarsagerne i Kongeriget Danmark *see* Doedsaarsagerne *953*
Doeves Jul (DK ISSN 0105-7723) *375*
Dog Volume 3. Administration, Management, Marketing and Sales (UK) *283, 848*
Dog Watch (AT) *1100*
Dog World Annual (UK ISSN 0070-7015) *868*
Dogs in Canada Annual (CN) *868*
Doing Business with the Federal Government: A Procurement Guide (US) *904, 941*
Dokumentation Arbeitsmedizin/ Documentation Occupational Health *see* Beruf und Gesundheit *636*
Dokumentation Neusprachlicher Unterricht (GW ISSN 0343-3420) *694*
Dokumentation Rheologie/ Documentation Rheology (GW ISSN 0340-8388) *4, 892*
Dokumentation Sprachwissenschaftliche Forschungsvorhaben (GW ISSN 0724-4320) *434, 677, 694*
Dokumentation Tribologie/ Documentation Tribology (GW ISSN 0340-3475) *4, 476*
Dokumentation Verschleiss, Reibung und Schmierung *see* Dokumentation Tribologie *476*
Dokumentationszentrale Wasser Schriftenreihe (GW ISSN 0012-0030) *1124*
Dokumente zum Hochschulsport (GW ISSN 0173-0843) *434, 1033*
Dokumente zur Deutschlandpolitik (GW ISSN 0070-7031) *581, 904*
Dokumente zur Deutschlandpolitik. Beihefte (GW ISSN 0341-3276) *581, 904*
Doland's Medical Directory. New York Metropolitan Area Edition (US) *760*
Dollars and Cents of Shopping Centers (US ISSN 0070-704X) *965*
Domestic and International Commercial Loan Charge-Offs *see* Report on Domestic and International Commercial Loan Charge-Offs *231*
Domestic Cars. Tune-up, Mechanical Transmission Service & Repair *see* Domestic Cars, Imported Cars and Trucks, Domestic Light Trucks. Mechanical, Air Conditioning and Transmission Service and Repair *1091*
Domestic Cars, Imported Cars and Trucks, Domestic Light Trucks. Mechanical, Air Conditioning and Transmission Service and Repair (US) *1091*
Domestic Mail Manual (US) *346*
Domestic Oceanborne and Great Lakes Commerce of the United States *see* Domestic Waterborne Trade of the United States *1100*
Domestic Tourism Statistics (SP) *1152*
Domestic Travel in Queensland (AT ISSN 0729-5936) *1152*
Domestic Waterborne Trade of the United States (US) *239, 1100*
Dominica. Ministry of Finance and Development. Annual Overseas Trade Report (DQ ISSN 0417-9382) *255*

Dominica. Ministry of Finance and Development. Statistical Digest *see* Dominica. Ministry of Finance and Development. Statistical Division. Digest *243*
Dominica. Ministry of Finance and Development. Statistical Division. Digest (DQ) *243*
Dominica. Ministry of Finance and Development. Vital Statistics Report (DQ) *243*
Dominica. Registrar of Co-Operative Societies. Report (DQ) *26*
Dominica Agricultural and Industrial Development Bank. Annual Report and Financial Statements *see* National Commercial & Development Bank. Annual Report and Financial Statements *230*
Dominican Republic. Centro Dominicano de Promocion de Exportaciones. Boletin Estadistico (DR) *255*
Dominican Republic. Centro Dominicano de Promocion de Exportaciones. Informe de Labores *see* Dominican Republic. Centro Dominicano de Promocion de Exportaciones. Boletin Estadistico *255*
Dominican Republic. Centro Dominicano de Promocion de Exportaciones. Memoria Anual *see* Dominican Republic. Centro Dominicano de Promocion de Exportaciones. Boletin Estadistico *255*
Dominican Republic. Centro Nacional de Investigaciones Agropecuarias. Laboratorio de Sanidad Vegetal. Sanidad Vegetal (DR) *140*
Dominican Republic. Direccion General de Bellas Artes. Catalogo de la Bienal de Artes Plasticas (DR) *104*
Dominican Republic. Oficina Nacional de Presupuesto. Ejecucion del Presupuesto *see* Dominican Republic. Oficina Nacional de Presupuesto. Ejecucion Presupuestaria. Informe *941*
Dominican Republic. Oficina Nacional de Presupuesto. Ejecucion Presupuestaria. Informe (DR) *941*
Dominican Republic. Secretaria de Obras Publicas y Comunicaciones. Estadistica *see* Dominican Republic Secretaria de Estado de Obras Publicas y Comunicaciones. OPC *941*
Dominican Republic. Secretaria de Sanidad y Asistencia Publica. Cuadros Estadisticos (DR) *1022*
Dominican Republic. Superintendencia de Bancos. Anuario Estadistico (DR) *227*
Dominican Republic Secretaria de Estado de Obras Publicas y Comunicaciones. OPC (DR) *941*
Dominion Museum Records *see* National Museum of New Zealand Records *829*
Domova Pokladnica (CS) *720, 796, 904, 1107*
Donaldson's Port Elizabeth Directory *see* Donaldson's Port Elizabeth , Uitenhage and Despatch Directory *307*
Donaldson's Port Elizabeth , Uitenhage and Despatch Directory (SA ISSN 0416-2706) *307*
Donan Igakukai (JA ISSN 0288-1829) *760*
Donauschwaebisches Schrifttum (GW ISSN 0070-7074) *581*
Donnees de Base sur la Pauvrete au Canada *see* Canadian Fact Book on Poverty *1015*
Donnees Mondiales sur l'Ozone *see* Ozone Data for the World *806*
Donnelley-Directory Record (US) *961*
Don't Miss Out (US ISSN 0277-6987) *434*
Donum Dei (CN ISSN 0318-0123) *969*
Doopsgezinde Bijdragen (NE) *581, 978*
Door County Almanak (US) *540*
Doorways to the Mind (US) *1152*
Doriana (IT ISSN 0417-9927) *991*

Dorland's Medical Directory. Delaware Valley Edition (US) *760*
Dorland's Medical Directory. Philadelphia Metropolitan Area *see* Dorland's Medical Directory. Delaware Valley Edition *760*
Dorland's Medical Directory. Western Philadelphia Tri-State Area Edition (US) *760*
Dorset Down Flock Book (UK) *65*
Dorset Natural History & Archaeological Society. Monograph Series (UK) *85*
Dorset Natural History and Archaeological Society. Proceedings (UK ISSN 0070-7112) *85, 991*
Dorset Worthies (UK ISSN 0070-7120) *134*
Dortmunder Beitraege zur Landeskunde(GW) *140, 379, 856*
Dortmunder Beitraege zur Zeitungsforschung (GW ISSN 0417-9994) *645*
Doshisha American Studies (JA ISSN 0420-0918) *605*
Doshisha Bungaku *see* Doshisha Literature *720*
Doshisha Literature (JA ISSN 0046-063X) *694, 720*
Doshisha Studies in Foreign Literature (JA) *720*
Dossier de l'Industrie Africaine (FR) *193*
Dossier Sahel (FR) *243*
Dossiers Antilles Guyane. Etudes Diverses (FR ISSN 0291-8706) *243*
Dossiers Beaux-Jeux (CN) *1152*
Dossiers de Demographie de la Belgique (BE) *922*
Dostignuca (YU ISSN 0012-5636) *412*
Dostoevsky Studies (US) *710, 720*
Douai Magazine (UK ISSN 0012-5695) *341, 969*
Dover Port Handbook (UK ISSN 0265-1165) *307, 1100*
Dow Jones Investor's Handbook (US) *266*
Dow Jones-Irwin Business Almanac *see* Dow Jones-Irwin Business and Investment Almanac *193*
Dow Jones-Irwin Business and Investment Almanac (US) *193*
Down Home Music Newsletter (US) *835, 1031*
Downdraft (US ISSN 0070-7171) *412, 502*
Downhill Only Journal (UK ISSN 0070-718X) *1045*
Dozenal Journal (UK ISSN 0260-4884) *748*
Dozenal Review *see* Dozenal Journal *748*
Dragon (UK ISSN 0012-589X) *104, 720, 823, 835*
Dramapaedagogik i Nordisk Perspektiv (DK ISSN 0900-7350) *720*
Dramascripts Series (UK ISSN 0070-7198) *720*
Dramatists Sourcebook (US ISSN 0733-1606) *1077*
Dramau'r Byd (UK ISSN 0141-1179) *1077*
Draper Fund Report (US ISSN 0191-3905) *922*
Draper World Population Fund Report *see* Draper Fund Report *922*
Dredging Seminar. Proceedings (US) *1124*
Dress (US ISSN 0361-2112) *340, 556*
Drevneishie Gosudarstva na Territorii S.S.S.R / Ancient States in the Territory of the U.S.S.R. (UR) *85, 581*
Drexel Faculty Publication (US) *991*
Drexel Research Conference. Summary Report *see* Drexel Faculty Publication *991*
Driftsoekonomi (DK ISSN 0106-9535) *193*
Driftsteknikerbogen (DK ISSN 0108-6707) *1068*
Driftsteknikerdag *see* Driftsteknikerbogen *1068*
Drivers License Guide *see* I D Checking Guide (Year) *370*
Drop Shipping Source Directory of Major Consumer Product Lines (US) *283, 307*

Drosophila Information Service (US ISSN 0070-7333) *164*
Druck-Sachen (GW) *930*
Drug Abuse and Alcoholism Review *see* Advances in Alcohol & Substance Abuse *376*
Drug Abuse Bibliography (US ISSN 0093-2515) *126, 378*
Drug Abuse: Directory of Community Services in California (US) *376*
Drug and Chemical Toxicology Series (US) *870*
Drug and Cosmetic Catalog (US ISSN 0732-0760) *118, 870*
Drug Approval and Licensing Procedures in Japan (JA ISSN 0289-9922) *870*
Drug Design and Delivery (US ISSN 0884-2884) *870*
Drug Development and Evolution (GW ISSN 0343-4842) *870*
Drug Facts and Comparisons *see* Facts and Comparisons *870*
Drug Store Market Guide (US ISSN 0277-3716) *283, 307, 870*
Drug Store News Reference for Pharmacy Practice (US) *870*
Drug Topics Redbook (US ISSN 0070-7376) *870*
Drug Trade Name Cross Reference List(US) *870, 873*
Drugs and the Pharmaceutical Sciences (US) *870*
Drugs in Current Use and New Drugs (US ISSN 0070-7392) *870*
Drugs of Choice (US ISSN 0070-7406) *870*
Drum (Amherst) (US) *720*
Drumlin (UK) *542*
Drustveni Proizvod i Narodni Dohodak(YU ISSN 0300-2527) *207*
Dryland Resources and Technology *see* Current Practices in Dryland Resources and Technology *1124*
Dublin. National Library of Ireland. Council of Trustees Report (IE ISSN 0332-0006) *677*
Dublin Institute for Advanced Studies. Communications. Series A (IE ISSN 0070-7414) *888*
Dublin Institute for Advanced Studies. Communications. Series D *see* Dublin Institute for Advanced Studies. School of Cosmic Physics. Geophysical Bulletin *399*
Dublin Institute for Advanced Studies. School of Cosmic Physics. Geophysical Bulletin (IE ISSN 0070-7422) *399*
Dublin Seminar for New England Folklife. Annual Proceedings (US) *1026*
Dubrovacki Horizonti (YU ISSN 0419-7925) *581*
Duck Soup (US) *710*
Duck Stamp Data (US) *874, 1045*
Duckburg Times (US) *614, 823*
Dude Ranch Magazine/Directory (US) *1107*
Dude Rancher (US) *1108*
Duengungsratschlaege fuer den Bauernhof (GW) *55*
Duesseldorf. Statistisches Jahrbuch (GW) *1054*
Duesseldorf in Zahlen (GW ISSN 0418-1263) *1054*
Duesseldorfer Jahrbuch (GW ISSN 0342-0078) *581*
Duke Endowment. Annual Report (US ISSN 0419-8050) *629*
Duke Monographs in Medieval and Renaissance Studies (US) *581*
Duke Press Global Issues Series (US) *495, 904*
Duke Press Policy Studies (US) *904*
Duke University. Center for International Studies. Publications (US) *915*
Duke University. Commonwealth-Studies Center. Publications *see* Duke University. Center for International Studies. Publications *915*
Duke University Library Newsletter (US ISSN 0012-7108) *677*
Dukhovna Akademiya SV. Kliment Okhridski. Godishnik (BU ISSN 0323-9578) *581, 969*

DUTY & 1717

Dumbarton Oaks Bibliographies (UK) *1152*
Dumbarton Oaks Conference Proceedings (US) *85, 104*
Dumbarton Oaks Papers (US ISSN 0070-7546) *85*
Dumbarton Oaks Studies (US ISSN 0070-7554) *86*
Dumbarton Oaks Texts (US ISSN 0070-7562) *556*
Dun and Bradstreet Exporters' Encyclopaedia - World Marketing Guide *see* Exporters' Encyclopaedia *255*
Dun and Bradstreet Metalworking Directory *see* Dun's Industrial Guide/Metalworking Directory *797*
Dun and Bradstreet Middle Market Directory *see* Million Dollar Directory *285*
Dun and Bradstreet Million Dollar Directory *see* Million Dollar Directory *285*
Dun and Bradstreet Reference Book of Corporate Managements *see* Reference Book of Corporate Managements *281*
Dun and Bradstreet Register *see* Dun & Bradstreet Standard Register *307*
Dun and Bradstreet/Seyd's Register *see* Dun & Bradstreet Standard Register *307*
Dun & Bradstreet Standard Register (US) *307*
Dun & Bradstreet's Guide to Your Investments (US ISSN 0098-2466) *266*
Dun's Business Rankings (US ISSN 0734-2845) *307*
Dun's Employment Opportunities Directory *see* Career Guide: Dun's Employment Opportunities Directory *847*
Dun's Industrial Guide/Metalworking Directory (US ISSN 0278-8799) *307, 797*
Duncan's Radio Market Guide (US) *307, 348*
Dundee and Tayside Chamber of Commerce and Industry. Buyer's Guide and Trade Directory (UK) *235, 307*
Dundee Chamber of Commerce. Buyer's Guide and Trade Directory *see* Dundee and Tayside Chamber of Commerce and Industry. Buyer's Guide and Trade Directory *235*
Dunsink Observatory. Publications (IE ISSN 0070-7643) *115*
Duquesne Studies. Language and Literature Series (US) *694, 720*
Duquesne Studies. Philological Series *see* Duquesne Studies. Language and Literature Series *694*
Durban Corporation Directory (SA) *307*
Durban Metropolitan Economy Project (SA) *193*
Durban Municipal Library. Annual Report (SA) *677*
Durch Stipendien Studieren (GW ISSN 0070-7767) *412*
Durham Archaeological Journal (UK) *86, 581*
Durham Archaeological Record *see* Durham Archaeological Journal *86*
Durham Classified Business Directory & Consumers' Guide (CN) *307*
Durham University Geological Society. Journal *see* Arthur Holmes Society. Journal *378*
Durham Yellow Directory *see* Durham Classified Business Directory & Consumers' Guide *307*
Dutch Archaeological and Historical Society. Studies (NE ISSN 0420-1078) *86, 581*
Dutch Film (NE) *823*
Dutch Theses *see* Bibliografie van Nederlandse Proefschriften *122*
Dutchess County Historical Society. Yearbook (US) *605*
Duty & Tax-Free Shop World Guide Series. Vol. 1: Best "N" Most in Wines & Spirits (SW ISSN 0349-2737) *119, 255*

Duty & Tax-Free Shop World Guide Series. Vol. 3: Best "N" Most in Cigarettes, Cigars and Tobacco (SW ISSN 0349-2737) 255, 1079

Duty & Tax-Free Shop World Guide Series. Vol. 4: Best "N" Most in D F S (SW) 255, 1108

Duty and Tax-Free Shop World Review. Vol. 1: Best "N" Most in Liquors see Duty & Tax-Free Shop World Guide Series. Vol. 1: Best "N" Most in Wines & Spirits 255

Duty and Tax-Free Shop World Review. Vol. 3. Best "N" Most in Cigarettes, Cigars and Pipe Tobaccos see Duty & Tax-Free Shop World Guide Series. Vol. 3: Best "N" Most in Cigarettes, Cigars and Tobacco 255

Duty and Tax-Free Shop World Review. Vol. 4: Best "N" Most Special Edition see Duty & Tax-Free Shop World Guide Series. Vol. 4: Best "N" Most in D F S 255

Dwarf Iris Society Portfolio (US ISSN 0418-2057) 532

Dwight's Special Truck Equipment Manual see Dwight's Truck Equipment Manual 1081

Dwight's Truck Equipment Manual (US) 1081

Dychova Hudba (CS) 835

Dyke Diannic Wicca Separatist Amazon Magick (US) 615, 1128

Dyn (UK) 71

Dynamic Economics Series see Dynamic Economics: Theory and Applications (Series) 193

Dynamic Economics: Theory and Applications (Series) (NE) 193

Dynamica (SA ISSN 0250-0027) 193

Dynamis (SP ISSN 0211-9536) 760

Dzieje Lublina (PL ISSN 0419-8816) 581

Dzieje Polskiej Granicy Zachodniej (PL ISSN 0070-7791) 581

E A A Review (Edinburgh Architectural Association) (UK ISSN 0307-1634) 98

E A A S Newsletter (European Association for American Studies) (NE ISSN 0423-6645) 915

E A C R O T A N A L Information (Eastern African Centre for Research on Oral Traditions and African National Languages) (TZ) 694, 721

E A C R O T A N A L Studies & Documents (Eastern African Centre for Research on Oral Traditions and African National Languages) (TZ) 694, 721

E A G Publicaciones (Secretaria de Estado de Agricultura y Ganaderia) (AG) 26

E A P R Abstracts of Conference Papers (European Association for Potato Research) (NE) 55

E A R (Edinburgh Architecture Research) (UK ISSN 0140-5039) 98

E A S C O N. Annual Electronics and Aerospace Systems Conference. (Record) see I E E E/E A S C O N. Electronics and Aerospace Conference. (Record) 454

E A S C O N. Electronics and Aerospace Conference and Exposition. (Record) see I E E E/E A S C O N. Electronics and Aerospace Conference. (Record) 454

E A S C O N. Electronics and Aerospace Systems Convention. Record see I E E E/E A S C O N. Electronics and Aerospace Conference. (Record) 454

E A T C Monographs in Theoretical Computer Science (US) 352

E B G (Electronics Buyers Guide) (JA) 307, 452

E B I C Banks. Annual Review (European Banks International) (BE) 1152

E B U Monographs, Legal and Administrative Series (European Broadcasting Union) (SZ) 348

E B U Seminars for Producers and Directors of Educational Television for Schools and Adults (European Broadcasting Union) (SZ) 348

E B U Workshops for Producers and Directors of Television Programmes for Children and Young People (European Broadcasting Union) (SZ) 348

E C A Year Book Desk Diary (Electrical Contractors' Association) (UK) 307, 452

E C & M's Electrical Products Yearbook (Electrical Construction and Maintenance) (US ISSN 0093-3236) 452

E C Index (NE ISSN 0255-9900) 4, 207

E C Update (European Community) (US) 1152

E D A P see European Directory of Agrochemical Products 27

E D B - Kursuskatalog (DK ISSN 0108-9900) 941

E D P Buyer's Guide (CN) 360

E D R A. Annual Conference Proceedings see Environmental Design Research Association. Annual Conference Proceedings 98

E E C Dairy Facts and Figures (UK) 62

E E C - Tin in Tinplate (UK) 797

E E G Vademecum/Selected Agri-Figures of the E.E.C (NE) 40

E E M (Electronic Engineers Master) (US ISSN 0423-9938) 307, 452

E E O C Compliance Manual (US) 271

E E R C Reports (Earthquake Engineering Research Center) (US ISSN 0271-0323) 481

E F I L Documentation (European Federation for Intercultural Learning) (BE) 441

E F I News see E F I Nytt 207

E F I Nytt/E F I News (Ekonomiska Forskningsinstitutet) (SW) 4, 207

E F T A Trade (European Free Trade Association) (SZ ISSN 0531-4119) 255

E G V Information (Ensomme Gamles Vaern) (DK ISSN 0107-8275) 1017

E I (Excerpta Indonesica) (NE ISSN 0046-0885) 79, 563, 709, 739

E I A Guide (US ISSN 0070-7821) 283

E I C see Electrical/Electronics Insulation Conference. Proceedings 452

E.I.D.C.T.- C.D.T. Year Book (Educational Institute of Design Craft & Technology) (UK ISSN 0266-9544) 447

E I S C A T Technical Note (European Incoherent Scatter Scientific Association) (SW ISSN 0349-2710) 900

E I S Cumulative (Environmental Impact Statement) (US ISSN 0190-0250) 501

E I S S Annuaire see E I S S Yearbook 1017

E I S S Yearbook/E I S S Annuaire (European Institute for Social Security) (NE) 1017

E I U World Outlook (Economist Intelligence Unit) (UK ISSN 0424-3331) 243

E L T S A Newsletter (End Loans to Southern Africa) (UK) 915

E M Complaint Directory for Consumers see Everybody's Money Complaint Directory for Consumers 369

E/M J International Directory of Mining (US) 797, 816

E/M J International Directory of Mining and Mineral Processing Operations see E/M J International Directory of Mining 797

E N I Annual Report (Ente Nazionale Idrocarburi) (IT) 464, 471, 816, 1074

E N R Directory of Contractors (US ISSN 0098-6453) 184

E N R Directory of Design Firms (US ISSN 0098-6305) 184, 307, 471

E N S B A N A Cahiers see Ecole Nationale Superieure de Biologie Appliquee a la Nutrition et a l'Alimentation. Cahiers 846

E O C Research Bulletin (Equal Opportunities Commission) (UK ISSN 0142-4866) 271

E P & T's Electrosource Product Reference Guide & Telephone Directory (CN) 452

E P I A see Electric Power Industry Abstracts 461

E P News (EI ISSN 0250-5754) 670

E P O: Catalogo de Equipos para Oficina (VE) 286

E R B see Ethnic Racial Brotherhood 503

E R B Occasional Paper Series see University of Dar es Salaam. Economic Research Bureau. Occasional Paper 201

E R B Papers see University of Dar es Salaam. Economic Research Bureau. Papers 201

E-R-C Directory (Employee Relocation Council) (US ISSN 0160-9629) 965

E R D A Energy Research Abstracts see Energy Research Abstracts 468

E R E A C Directory see E-R-C Directory 965

E R I C/C U E Trends and Issues (US ISSN 0889-8022) 333, 412, 502

E R I C/C U E Urban Diversity Series (E R I C Clearinghouse on Urban Education) (US ISSN 0889-8030) 412

E R I C Clearinghouse for Junior Colleges. Horizons Issues. Monograph Series (US) 434

E R I C Clearinghouse for Junior Colleges. Topical Paper Series (US ISSN 0531-9315) 434

E R I C Clearinghouse on Teacher Education. Bulletin (US) 1152

E R I C Clearinghouse on Teacher Education. Current Issues Publications (US) 412

E R I C Clearinghouse on Teacher Education. Quarterly Information Bulletin see E R I C Clearinghouse on Teacher Education. Bulletin 1152

E R I C Clearinghouse on Teacher Education. Special Current Issues Publications see E R I C Clearinghouse on Teacher Education. Current Issues Publications 412

E R I C Clearinghouse on Tests, Measurement, and Evaluation. T M E Report Series (US) 413, 934

E R I C Clearinghouse on Urban Education. Digest (US ISSN 0889-8049) 333, 413, 502

E R I C Clearinghouse on Urban Education Urban Diversity Series see E R I C/C U E Urban Diversity Series 412

E R R see Ethnic Racial Review 503

E S A Foelgeforskning (European Space Agency) (DK ISSN 0109-1115) 18

E S A Scientific-Technical Reports, Notes and Memoranda (European Space Agency) (FR) 18

E S G - Nachrichten (Evangelische Studentengemeinde in der Bundesrepublik Deutschland und Berlin (West)) (GW ISSN 0012-7981) 969

E S I G see Expert Systems in Government Symposium 354

E S O Foelgeforskning (European Southern Observatory) (DK ISSN 0108-9358) 115

E S O P see Epigraphic Society. Occasional Publications 86

E S R C Studentship Handbook (Economic and Social Research Council) (UK) 429, 1007

E S R O Scientific-Technical Reports, Notes and Memoranda see E S A Scientific-Technical Reports, Notes and Memoranda 18

E.S. Woodward Lectures in Economics (CN) 193

E.T.A. Hoffmann-Gesellschaft. Mitteilungen (GW ISSN 0073-2885) 721

E T B A Investment Guide see Hellenic Industrial Development Bank. Investment Guide 266

E T C H (Ethical Tablet and Capsule Handbook) (AT ISSN 0157-9509) 870

E U R O N O R M (EI) 809

E U T Reports see Eindhoven University of Technology. Research Reports 1068

E W R (GW) 119

E W Special (NE) 1081

Ealing Miscellany (UK) 581, 677

Early Cello Series. Facsimile Reprint Edition (US) 835

Early Cello Series. Modern Edition (US ISSN 0884-1055) 835

Early China (US ISSN 0362-5028) 569

Early Days (AT ISSN 0080-4738) 573

Early Diagnosis Papers (UK) 760

Early Music History (UK ISSN 0261-1279) 835

Earn & Learn: Cooperative Education Opportunities Offered by the Federal Government (US ISSN 0277-7002) 434

Earth and Extraterrestrial Sciences see Comments on Astrophysics 115

Earth Circles (US) 26, 615, 1128

Earth Sciences Series (UN ISSN 0070-7910) 379

Earthmind Newsletter (US) 464

Earthquake History of the United States(US) 399

East Africa Directory (KE) 307

East Africa High Commissions Desert Locust Survey. Report see Desert Locust Control Organization for Eastern Africa. Annual Report 54

East Africa Report on Trade and Industry (KE) 243

East African Academy. Foundation Lectures see Kenya National Academy for Advancement of Arts and Sciences. Foundation Lectures 630

East African Academy. Proceedings see Kenya National Academy for Advancement of Arts and Sciences. Proceedings 630

East African Community. East African Meteorological Department. Annual Report see Kenya Meteorological Department. Annual Report 805

East African Development Bank. Annual Report (UG) 227

East African Freshwater Fisheries Research Organization. Annual Report see Uganda Freshwater Fisheries Research Organization. Annual Report 513

East African Geographical Review (UG ISSN 0070-7961) 542

East African Institute of Malaria and Vectorborne Diseases. Annual Report(TZ) 777

East African Research Information Centre. E A R I C Information Circular see Kenya National Academy for Advancement of Arts and Sciences. Research Information Circulars 566

East African Studies (KE ISSN 0424-0928) 1007

East and Maghreb (IS) 502, 629

East Anglia Guide (UK) 1108

East Anglian Archaeology. Report (UK ISSN 0307-2460) 86

East Asia Bibliography (UK) 126, 207

East Asia Library Series (US) 126

East Asian Cultural Studies (JA ISSN 0012-8414) 851

East Asian Genealogist (US) 535

East Asian Historical Monographs (US) 569, 851

East Asian Social Science Monographs (US) 569, 1007

East Carolina College Publications in History see East Carolina University Publications in History 605

East Carolina University Publications in History (US ISSN 0070-8089) 605

East Europe in German Books (US ISSN 0070-8097) 563, 1119

East Europe Monographs (US ISSN 0070-8100) 915

East Europe Report (US) 904, 1026

East Lakes Geographer (US ISSN 0070-8127) 542

East Malling Research Station. Annual Report (UK ISSN 0306-6398) 55, 532

East Midland Archaeological Bulletin see East Midlands Archaeology 86

East Midlands Archaeology (UK) 86

East Midlands Chambers of Commerce Regional Directory (UK ISSN 0263-404X) 235
East of England Show Catalogue (UK) 26
East Pakistan. Education Directorate. Adult Education Branch. Report on Pilot Project on Adult Education see Bangladesh. Education Directorate. Report on Pilot Project on Adult Education 426
East Riding Archaeologist (UK ISSN 0012-852X) 86
East Tennessee Historical Society's Publications (US ISSN 0361-6193) 605
East-West Center. Papers see East-West Population Institute. Papers 922
East West European Economic Interaction (US) 193
East-West Perspectives (NE) 915
East-West Population Institute. Papers (US) 922
East-West Trade Yearbook (BE) 1152
East Yorkshire Local History Series (UK ISSN 0070-8208) 581
Eastbournian (UK ISSN 0012-8643) 341
Eastern African Centre for Research on Oral Traditions and African National Languages Information see E A C R O T A N A L Information 694
Eastern African Centre for Research on Oral Traditions and African National Languages Studies & Documents see E A C R O T A N A L Studies & Documents 694
Eastern Canada Campbook (US ISSN 0363-2091) 1045, 1108
Eastern Canada Camping see Eastern Canada Campbook 1108
Eastern Canada Tour Book see Tourbook: Atlantic Provinces and Quebec 1117
Eastern Caribbean Standing Conference on Teacher Education. Report (BB) 447
Eastern Europe Travel Guide see Travel Guide to Europe 1118
Eastern European Genealogist (US) 535, 581
Eastern Hemisphere Petroleum Directory see European Petroleum Directory 864
Eastern Mineral Law Foundation. Annual Institute. Proceedings (US ISSN 0733-6098) 655
Eastern New Mexico University. Contributions in Anthropology (US ISSN 0070-8232) 71, 86
Eastern States Archeological Federation. Bulletin (US) 86
Eastern Transportation Law Seminar Papers and Proceedings (US ISSN 0271-437X) 655, 1105
Eastern Utilization Research and Development Division. Publications and Patents see U.S. Department of Agriculture. Eastern Regional Research Center. Publications and Patents 1164
Eats & Treats see Gut Essen 620
Ebb and Flow (AT ISSN 0729-0403) 405
Echad (US ISSN 0743-7757) 502
Echange (CN ISSN 0831-5825) 447, 694
Echange d'Informations sur les Recherches en Droit Europeen see Exchange of Information on Research in European Law 668
Eck Mata Journal (US) 984
Eck News see Eck Mata Journal 984
Ecletica Quimica (BL ISSN 0100-4670) 322, 888
Eco-Humane Letter (US) 365
Eco-Letter see Eco-Humane Letter 365
Ecole d'Ete de Physique Theorique. Les Houches see Les Houches Summer School Proceedings 888
Ecole de Medecine Veterinaire, Saint-Hyacinthe, Quebec. Annuaire see Universite de Montreal. Faculte de Medecine Veterinaire. Annuaire 1122
Ecole Francaise d'Extreme-Orient. Bulletin (FR) 851
Ecole Francaise de Rome. Collection (FR) 86

Ecole Francaise de Rome. Melanges: Antiquite (FR) 86
Ecole Francaise de Rome. Melanges: Moyen Ages, Temps Moderne (FR) 581
Ecole Francaise de Rome. Melanges: Supplement see Ecole Francaise de Rome. Collection 86
Ecole Francaise des Attaches de Presse. Association des Anciens Eleves. Annuaire (FR ISSN 0070-8321) 645
Ecole Nationale Superieure d'Agronomie et des Industries Alimentaires. Bulletin (FR ISSN 0374-6003) 46, 55
Ecole Nationale Superieure de Biologie Appliquee a la Nutrition et a l'Alimentation. Cahiers (FR) 846
Ecole Nationale Superieure de Techniques Avancees Centre d'Edition et de Documentation. Rapport d'Activite sur les Recherches (FR) 1068
Ecole Polytechnique Federale de Lausanne. Publication (SZ) 991
Ecole Pratique des Hautes Etudes. Centre de Recherches sur le Portugal de la Renaissance. Series Textes (FR) 581, 721
Ecole Pratique des Hautes Etudes. Quatrieme Section. Historiques et Philologiques. Annuaire see Linet de la Quatrieme Section, Ecole Pratique Hautes Etudes 559
Ecological Life Style. Newsletter see Practical Alternatives 498
Ecological Society of Australia. Proceedings (AT ISSN 0070-8348) 140
Ecological Studies; Analysis and Synthesis (US ISSN 0070-8356) 140
Ecology see University of Georgia. Institute of Ecology. Annual Report 500
Ecology Abstracts (US ISSN 0143-3296) 4, 501, 1128
Econometrics and Operations Research see Oekonometrie und Unternehmensforschung 198
Economia (CK) 193
Economia see Revista de Economia 199
Economia Alavesa (SP ISSN 0568-8876) 235
Economia Brasileira e suas Perspectivas - A P E C A O (Associacao Promotora de Estudos de Economia) (BL) 243
Economia Cubana (CU) 243
Economia e Storia (IT ISSN 0070-8402) 251
Economia Mexicana (MX) 193
Economia Politica (HO ISSN 0424-2483) 193
Economia Salvadorena (ES ISSN 0012-9860) 243
Economia Salvadorena see El Salvador, Informe Economico y Social 244
Economic Abstracts see Key to Economic Science 212
Economic Analysis of North American Ski Areas (US ISSN 0147-4243) 193, 1045
Economic and Scientific Research Foundation. Annual Report (II ISSN 0070-8437) 193
Economic and Social History Surveys (UK ISSN 0140-0061) 193
Economic and Social Progress in Latin America see Economic and Social Progress in Latin America; Annual Report 243
Economic and Social Progress in Latin America; Annual Report (US ISSN 0095-2850) 243
Economic and Social Research Council Studentship Handbook see E S R C Studentship Handbook 429
Economic and Social Research Institute. Policy Series (IE) 193
Economic and Social Research Institute. Publications Series. Paper (IE ISSN 0070-8755) 193
Economic and Social Survey of Asia and the Pacific (UN ISSN 0252-5704) 243
Economic Anthropology (US) 71

Economic Conditions In/And Outlook for Thailand (TH) 243
Economic Council of Canada. Annual Report (CN ISSN 0070-847X) 243
Economic Council of Canada. Annual Review (CN ISSN 0070-8488) 243
Economic Council of Canada. Discussion Papers (CN ISSN 0225-8013) 194
Economic Development Programme for the Republic of South Africa (SA ISSN 0070-8518) 288
Economic Fact Book on Metropolitan Milwaukee see Metropolitan Milwaukee Economic Fact Book 246
Economic Growth of the Australian States (AT ISSN 0814-5504) 1152
Economic Handbook of the Machine Tool Industry (US ISSN 0070-8550) 745
Economic Impact of the Negro Traveler(US) 502, 1108
Economic Indicators (Charleston) (US) 941
Economic Indicators of Turkey (TU) 277
Economic Microbiology (US) 168
Economic Outlook for New Jersey (US) 194
Economic Poisons see Pesticides (Sacramento) 58
Economic Priorities Report see C E P Reports and C E P Studies 251
Economic Questions for Illinois Agriculture (US ISSN 0070-8615) 1152
Economic Reflections see Journal of Economic Reflections 196
Economic Report of the President (US) 243
Economic Report on Scottish Agriculture (UK) 46
Economic Review (BG ISSN 0070-8631) 194
Economic Review (Year) (JM ISSN 0259-9171) 243
Economic Review and Outlook (CN) 301
Economic Review of New Zealand Agriculture (NZ ISSN 0111-1108) 1152
Economic Review of Travel in America(US ISSN 0733-642X) 1108
Economic Review of World Tourism (SP ISSN 0070-864X) 1108
Economic Road Maps (US) 194
Economic Situation in the Year (Year) (PO) 243
Economic Statistics of Japan see Bank of Japan. Economic Statistics Annual 204
Economic Survey of Asia and the Far East see Economic and Social Survey of Asia and the Pacific 243
Economic Survey of Europe (UN ISSN 0070-8712) 243
Economic Survey of India see Economic Survey of Maharashtra 244
Economic Survey of Indian Agriculture see India. Ministry of Agriculture. Bulletin on Commercial Crops Statistics 47
Economic Survey of Japan (English edition of: Annual Economic White Paper of Economic Planning Agency, Japan) (JA ISSN 0021-4833) 243
Economic Survey of Latin America see Economic Survey of Latin America and the Caribbean 243
Economic Survey of Latin America and the Caribbean (UN) 243
Economic Survey of Liberia (LB ISSN 0303-853X) 243
Economic Survey of Maharashtra (II) 244
Economic Survey of Rhodesia see Annual Economic Review 241
Economic Survey of Singapore (SI ISSN 0376-8791) 244
Economic Titles see Economic Titles/Abstracts 207
Economic Titles/Abstracts (NE ISSN 0303-4879) 4, 207

Economic Trends and Their Implications for the United States see Foreign Economic Trends and Their Implications for the United States 245
Economic Yearbook of Member States of the Organization of African Unity see Annuaire Economique des Pays Membres de l'Organisation de l'Unite Africaine 241
Economic Yearbook of Tunisia (TI ISSN 0070-8747) 244
Economics see Acta Academiae Agriculturae ac Technicae Olstenensis. Oekonomika 190
Economics: Encyclopedia see Encyclopedia of Economics 279
Economics, Management and Marketing see Electricity Council Abstracts Bulletin 468
Economics of Agricultural Enterprises see Denmark. Jordbrugsoekonomisk Institut. Serie B: Oekonomien i Landbrugets Driftsgrene 46
Economics of Fruit Farming (UK ISSN 0070-8763) 46, 55
Economicus (BG) 251
Economie Africaine see Annee Politique Africaine 902
Economie Algerienne (FR) 244
Economie Belge en (Year)/Belgische Economie in (Year) (BE) 244
Economie Camerounaise (FR) 244
Economie de la Tunisie en Chiffres (TI ISSN 0070-878X) 244
Economie des Pays d'Afrique Noire (FR) 244
Economie et Societe (FR ISSN 0070-8801) 194
Economie-Formation-Gestion Collection E F G see Collection E F G 279
Economie Francaise en (Year) (FR) 244
Economie Francaise en Donnees d'Encadrement (FR) 244
Economie Francaise en Perspectives Sectorielles: Filiere Batiment, Genie Civil, Materiaux de Construction (FR) 184, 194, 244, 481
Economie Francaise en Perspectives Sectorielles: Industries de Biens de Consommation (FR) 244, 288
Economie Francaise en Perspectives Sectorielles: Industries de Biens d'Equipement (FR) 244, 288
Economie Francaise en Perspectives Sectorielles: Industries de Biens Intermediaries (FR) 244, 288
Economie Gabonaise (FR) 244
Economie Ivoirienne (FR) 244
Economie Sucriere see Zuckerwirtschaftliches Taschenbuch 521
Economies et Societes. Serie A B. Economie du Travail (FR ISSN 0068-4821) 194, 271
Economies et Societes. Serie AF. Histoire Quantitative de l'Economie Francaise (FR ISSN 0068-4864) 251
Economies et Societes. Serie AG. Progres et Agriculture (FR ISSN 0068-4899) 46
Economies et Societes. Serie EM. Economie Mathematique et Econometrie (FR ISSN 0013-0567) 251
Economies et Societes. Serie F. Developpement, Croissance, Progres des Pays en Voie de Developpement (FR ISSN 0068-4813) 262
Economies et Societes. Serie G. Economie Planifiee (FR ISSN 0068-483X) 194
Economies et Societes. Serie M. Philosophie - Sciences Sociales Economie (FR ISSN 0068-4880) 251
Economies et Societes. Serie MO. Economie Monetaire (FR) 227
Economies et Societes. Serie P. Relations Economiques Internationales (FR ISSN 0068-4902) 288
Economies et Societes. Serie S. Etudes de Marxologie (FR ISSN 0068-4856) 251

Economies et Societes. Serie S G. Science de Gestion (FR) *279*
Economies et Societies. Serie T. Information - Recherche Innovation (FR ISSN 0068-4872) *194*
Economisch- en Sociaal-Historisch Jaarboek (NE) *251*, *581*
Economisch-Historisch Jaarboek *see* Economisch- en Sociaal-Historisch Jaarboek *251*
Economisch Instituut voor Het Midden-en Kleinbedrijf. Year Report (NE ISSN 0070-8836) *301*
Economist Intelligence Unit World Outlook *see* E I U World Outlook *243*
Economy of Hawaii *see* Hawaii Annual Economic Review *245*
Economy of the Principality of Liechtenstein (LH) *244*
Ecrits Libres (FR ISSN 0070-8860) *969*
Ecriture (SZ ISSN 0070-8879) *721*
Ecuador. Centro de Desarrollo Industrial. Informe de Labores (EC ISSN 0070-8887) *288*
Ecuador. Comision de Valores. Corporacion Financiera Nacional. Memoria *see* Ecuador. Corporacion Financiera Nacional. Memoria *294*
Ecuador. Corporacion Financiera Nacional. Boletin Estadistico (EC) *244*
Ecuador. Corporacion Financiera Nacional. Memoria (EC) *294*
Ecuador. Departamento de Estadisticas Fiscales. Estadisticas Fiscales (EC) *207*
Ecuador. Direccion General de Recaudaciones. Boletin (EC) *294*
Ecuador. Instituto Nacional de Investigaciones Agropecuarias. Informe Tecnico (EC) *55*
Ecuador. Instituto Nacional de Meteorologia e Hidrologia. Anuario Hidrologico (EC) *402*
Ecuador. Instituto Nacional de Meteorologia e Hidrologia. Anuario Meteorologico (EC) *804*
Ecuador. Ministerio de Industrias, Comercio e Integracion. Boletin de Informacion de las Empresas Acogidas a la Ley de Fomento Industrial (EC) *288*
Ecuador. Ministerio de Industrias, Comercio e Integracion. Documento (EC) *239*
Ecuador. Ministerio de Industrias, Comercio e Integracion. Empresas Acogidas a la Ley de Fomento Industrial. Directorio Industrial (EC) *307*
Ecuador. Ministerio de Industrias, Comercio e Integracion. Informe a la Nacion (EC) *239*
Ecuador. Ministerio de Recursos Naturales y Energeticos. Informe de Labores (EC) *365*
Ecuador. Servicio Nacional de Meteorologia e Hidrologia. Anuario Hidrologico *see* Ecuador. Instituto Nacional de Meteorologia e Hidrologia. Anuario Hidrologico *402*
Ecuador. Servicio Nacional de Meteorologia e Hidrologia. Anuario Meteorologico *see* Ecuador. Instituto Nacional de Meteorologia e Hidrologia. Anuario Meteorologico *804*
Ecuador. Superintendencia de Bancos. Boletin (EC) *227*
Ecuador. Superintendencia de Bancos. Documentos (EC) *227*
Ecuador. Superintendencia de Bancos. Inversiones Extranjeras en el Ecuador (EC) *227*
Ecuador. Superintendencia de Bancos. Memoria (EC) *227*
Ecuador Economico (EC ISSN 0070-8925) *194*
Ecuatorial (UK ISSN 0260-2113) *741*
Edgar Brookes Academic and Human Freedom Lecture (SA ISSN 0070-8976) *434*, *534*
Ediafric - la Documentation Africaine. Plans de Developpement (FR) *244*
Ediciones del Pueblo (PE) *515*, *721*
Ediciones Peninsula. Serie Universitaria. Historia, Ciencia, Sociedad (SP) *1007*
Edicoes Cadernos Culturais (BL) *710*
Edinburgh Architectural Association E A A Yearbook *see* E A A Review *98*
Edinburgh Architectural Association Review *see* E A A Review *98*
Edinburgh Architecture Research *see* E A R *98*
Edinburgh Chamber of Commerce and Manufactures Directory (UK) *235*
Edinburgh Studies in Sociology (UK) *1026*
Edisi Chusus Bulletin Koperasi (IO) *244*
Edison Electric Institute. Statistical Yearbook of the Electric Utility Industry. (US) *452*
Editeurs Belges de Langue Francaise et Leurs Livres (BE) *126*
Editiones Arnamagnaeanae. Series A (DK ISSN 0070-9069) *694*, *721*
Editiones Arnamagnaeanae. Series B (DK ISSN 0070-9077) *694*, *721*
Editiones Arnamagnaeanae. Supplementum (DK ISSN 0070-9085) *721*
Editions d' /Organisation Serie E O/ International *see* Serie E O/ International *249*
Editions Organisation. Fiches E O-Formation Permanente *see* Fiches E O - Formation Permanente *279*
Editor & Publisher International Year Book (US ISSN 0424-4923) *343*, *645*
Editor & Publisher Market Guide (US) *283*
Editor's Choice (US) *104*, *721*
Edmonton Area Series Report (CN ISSN 0703-8763) *922*
Edmonton Revival Centre. News *see* End-Time News *978*
Edmund's Auto-Pedia *see* Edmund's Car Savvy *1091*
Edmund's Car Prices (US) *1091*
Edmund's Car Savvy (US) *1091*
Edmund's Economy Car Buying Guide (US) *1091*
Edmunds Prescription Drug Prices (US) *870*
Edubba (AT ISSN 0085-0187) *556*
Educacion (PE) *413*
Educacion en Iberoamerica: Sistema de Indicadores Socio Economicos y Educativos *see* Sistema de Indicadores Socio-Economicos y Educativos de la O E I *1011*
Educacion Sanitaria (SP) *953*
Educacion y Planeamiento (GT) *413*
Educating Exceptional Children *see* Annual Editions: Educating Exceptional Children *444*
Educating the Disadvantaged *see* Readings on Equal Education *445*
Education Advisory (CN) *413*
Education & Careers in South Africa (SA) *413*, *848*
Education and Culture. Section 1: Cultural Development (FR) *413*
Education and Culture. Section 2: Higher Education and Research (FR) *413*
Education and Culture. Section 3: Out-of-School Education (FR) *1152*
Education and Science *see* Great Britain. Department of Education and Science. Annual Report *414*
Education and Training in Indexing and Abstracting (US) *413*, *677*
Education Around the World (US) *413*
Education Authorities' Directory and Annual (UK ISSN 0070-9131) *413*
Education Commission of the States. National Assessment of Educational Progress. Assessment Reports *see* National Assessment of Educational Progress. Assessment Reports *448*
Education Committees Year Book *see* Education Year Book *413*
Education Department of Victoria. Textbooks (AT ISSN 0816-6773) *1152*
Education des Adultes *see* I.C.E.A. Cahiers *1154*
Education Development Center. Annual Report (US ISSN 0424-5407) *413*
Education Directory. Local Education Agencies (US ISSN 0273-4346) *413*
Education Directory. Public Schools Systems *see* Education Directory. Local Education Agencies *413*
Education Directory. (School Year): Colleges and Universities (US) *429*
Education Exchange *see* Educational International *1152*
Education for Business and Management in the Region (UK) *429*, *434*
Education for Health: the Selective Guide (US) *1152*
Education for Migrant Children; Arizona State Plan *see* Arizona State Plan for the Education of Migratory Children *410*
Education for Nursing: The Diploma Way (US ISSN 0070-9166) *434*, *784*
Education for the Construction Industry in the Region (UK) *184*, *434*
Education Guidelines (AT ISSN 0729-8528) *4*, *413*
Education in Asia and Oceania: Reviews, Reports and Notes *see* Education in Asia and the Pacific: Reviews, Reports and Notes *413*
Education in Asia and the Pacific: Reviews, Reports and Notes (UN) *413*
Education in Europe. Cultural Development (FR) *413*
Education in Europe. Section 1: Higher Education and Research (FR ISSN 0070-9182) *434*
Education in Europe. Section 3: Out-of-School Education *see* Education and Culture. Section 3: Out-of-School Education *1152*
Education in India (II) *413*
Education in Japan; A Graphic Presentation (JA ISSN 0070-9220) *413*
Education in Kenya (KE) *423*, *434*
Education in Korea (KO) *441*
Education in the North (UK ISSN 0424-5512) *413*
Education in the Royal County of Berkshire (UK ISSN 0261-8966) *413*
Education Index (US ISSN 0013-1385) *4*, *423*
Education Information Guide Series (US) *1152*
Education Law Bulletin (US ISSN 0276-718X) *413*, *655*
Education Libraries Bulletin Supplements (UK ISSN 0076-079X) *677*
Education News from Metrologic (US ISSN 0046-144X) *413*, *636*
Education Statistics for the United Kingdom (UK) *413*
Education Statistics, New York State (US) *423*, *1054*
Education Year Book (UK ISSN 0143-5469) *413*
Educational Abstracts for Tanzania (TZ ISSN 0856-0005) *423*
Educational Administration Abstracts (US ISSN 0013-1601) *4*, *423*
Educational Administration and History Monographs (UK ISSN 0140-0428) *442*, *556*
Educational and Psychological Interactions (SW ISSN 0070-9263) *413*, *934*
Educational Assessment Program State Report *see* New Jersey. Department of Education. Educational Assessment Program State Report *417*
Educational Bibliography *see* Bibliographie Paedagogik *123*
Educational Building Digest (UN) *184*, *442*
Educational Commission for Foreign Medical Graduates. Annual Report (US ISSN 0145-2037) *760*
Educational Council for Foreign Medical Graduates. Annual Report *see* Educational Commission for Foreign Medical Graduates. Annual Report *760*
Educational Development *see* Studies of Higher Education and Research *439*
Educational Directory of Mississippi Schools *see* Mississippi Educational Directory *430*
Educational Drama Association. Newsletter (UK ISSN 0260-311X) *375*, *413*, *1077*
Educational Film and Video (Year) (US) *423*, *825*
Educational Film Locator *see* Educational Film/Video Locator *825*
Educational Film/Video Locator (US) *447*, *825*
Educational Films *see* Educational Film and Video (Year) *423*
Educational Front *see* Zambia Educational Journal *422*
Educational Institute of Design Craft & Technology Year Book *see* E.I.D.C.T.- C.D.T. Year Book *447*
Educational International (UK) *1152*
Educational Law Review *see* Nihon Kyoikuho Gakkai Nempo *661*
Educational Leaflet *see* New York State Museum. Leaflet *996*
Educational Media and Technology Yearbook (US ISSN 8755-2094) *447*
Educational Media Catalogs on Microfiche (US) *447*
Educational Media Yearbook *see* Educational Media and Technology Yearbook *447*
Educational Microcomputing Annual (US) *361*
Educational Opportunities of Greater Boston (US) *429*
Educational Personnel in Delaware *see* Supply and Demand: Educational Personnel in Delaware *420*
Educational Resources Information Center Thesaurus of E R I C Descriptors *see* Thesaurus of E R I C Descriptors *420*
Educational Series - North Dakota Geological Survey *see* North Dakota. Geological Survey. Educational Series *393*
Educational Software Selector (US ISSN 8755-5107) *363*, *427*
Educational Standards in Japan (JA) *413*
Educational Statistics in O E C D Countries (Organisation for Economic Cooperation and Development) (FR) *413*
Educational Statistics of Punjab (PK) *413*
Educational Statistics Yearbook *see* Educational Statistics in O E C D Countries *413*
Educational Studies and Documents (UN ISSN 0070-9344) *413*
Educational Technology Abstracts (UK ISSN 0266-3368) *4*, *424*
Educational Testing Service Annual Report (US ISSN 0091-8989) *413*
Educators Grade Guide to Free Teaching Aids (US ISSN 0070-9387) *447*
Educators Guide to Free Audio and Video Materials (US ISSN 0160-1296) *447*
Educators Guide to Free Films (US ISSN 0070-9395) *447*
Educators Guide to Free Filmstrips (US ISSN 0070-9409) *447*
Educators Guide to Free Guidance Materials (US ISSN 0070-9417) *447*
Educators Guide to Free Health, Physical Education & Recreation Materials (US ISSN 0424-6241) *447*
Educators Guide to Free Home Economics Materials (US) *614*
Educators Guide to Free Science Materials (US ISSN 0070-9425) *447*
Educators Guide to Free Social Studies Materials (US ISSN 0070-9433) *447*
Educators Guide to Free Tapes, Scripts, and Transcriptions *see* Educators Guide to Free Audio and Video Materials *447*
Educators Index of Free Materials (US) *447*

Edward H. Tarr Series (US ISSN 0363-4558) *835*
Edward Sapir Monograph Series in Language, Culture, and Cognition (US ISSN 0163-3848) *694*
Edwardian Studies (UK) *721, 1077*
Eesti Filatelist/Estonian Philatelist (SW) *874*
Efrydiau Athronyddol (UK ISSN 0142-3371) *878*
Efterskoler. Fortegnelse (DK ISSN 0108-8262) *413*
Eftersyn (DK ISSN 0109-3304) *104*
Egeszsegneveles Szakkonyvtara (HU ISSN 0073-4012) *953*
Egg Production Tests: United States and Canada (US) *65*
Eglise Catholique a Madagascar (MG) *982*
Egnshistorisk Forening i Grundsoe. Aarsskrift (DK ISSN 0109-0194) *581*
Ego *see* The Egoist *904*
The Egoist (UK) *904*
Egon Ronay's Bulmer Pub Guide to Food and Accommodation *see* Egon Ronay's Guinness Pub Guide to Food and Accommodation *619*
Egon Ronay's Dunlop Guide to Hotels and Restaurants in the British Isles *see* Egon Ronay's Lucas Guide to Hotels, Restaurants and Inns in Great Britain and Ireland *619*
Egon Ronay's Guide to 500 Good Restaurants in Major Cities of Europe (UK) *619, 1108*
Egon Ronay's Guinness Pub Guide to Food and Accommodation (UK) *619*
Egon Ronay's Lucas Guide to Hotels, Restaurants and Inns in Great Britain and Ireland (UK) *619*
Egon Ronay's TWA Guide: 500 Good Restaurants in Major Cities, Europe and United States *see* Egon Ronay's Guide to 500 Good Restaurants in Major Cities of Europe *619*
Egypt. Central Agency for Public Mobilisation and Statistics. Statistical Yearbook (UA) *1054*
Egypt. Meteorological Authority. Annual Meteorological Report (UA) *804*
Egypt. Service des Antiquites. Annales (UA ISSN 0082-7835) *86*
Egyptian Museum. Library. Catalogue (UA) *96, 126*
Egyptian National Museum. Library. Catalogue *see* Egyptian Museum. Library. Catalogue *96*
Egyptian Review of International Law/Revue Egyptienne de Droit International (UA ISSN 0080-259X) *670*
Egyptian Society of Endocrinology and Metabolism. Journal (UA ISSN 0070-9506) *781*
Egyptologische Uitgaven (NE) *612*
Ehe- und Familienrechtliche Entscheidungen (AU ISSN 0531-674X) *655*
Ehime University. Memoirs. Serie: Natural Science (JA ISSN 0422-7727) *385, 856*
Ehrenpreis Deutsche Keramik (GW) *320*
Ei-Beibungaku *see* Studies in British & American Literature *734*
Eidgenoessische Anstalt fuer das Forstliche Versuchswesen. Berichte (SZ) *524*
Eidgenoessische Anstalt fuer das Forstliche Versuchswesen. Jahresbericht (SZ) *524*
Eidgenoessische Technische Hochschule Zuerich. Bibliothek. Schriftenreihe (SZ ISSN 0514-0668) *677*
Eidgenoessische Technische Hochschule Zuerich. Institut fuer Baustatik und Konstruktion. Allgemeine Berichte (SZ) *488*
Eidgenoessische Technische Hochschule Zuerich. Institut fuer Baustatik und Konstruktion. Versuchsberichte (SZ) *489*

Eidgenoessische Technische Hochschule Zuerich. Mitteilungen. Aerodynamik (SZ ISSN 0084-5744) *894*
Eidgenoessische Technische Hochschule Zuerich. Mitteilungen. Photoelastizitaet (SZ ISSN 0084-5752) *899*
Eidgenoessische Technische Hochschule Zuerich. Versuchsanstalt fuer Wasserbau, Hydrologie und Glaziologie. Jahresbericht (SZ) *402, 490*
Eidgenoessische Technische Hochschule Zuerich. Versuchsanstalt fuer Wasserbau, Hydrologie und Glaziologie. Mitteilungen (SZ) *402, 490*
Eidgenoessische Zukunft: Bausteine fuer Die Kommende Schweiz (SZ ISSN 0070-9514) *277*
Eight Ball (US) *645*
Eight Peak Index of Mass Spectra (UK) *4, 325*
Eighteen Nineties Society. Journal (UK) *721*
Eighteenth Century: A Current Bibliography (US ISSN 0161-0996) *721*
Eighties (US) *710, 741*
Eigo Kyoiku Jaanaru *see* Modern English Journal *699*
Eigse (IE ISSN 0013-2608) *694*
Eindhoven University of Technology. Research Reports (NE ISSN 0167-9708) *1068*
Einhorn-Jahrbuch (GW ISSN 0723-0877) *581*
Einkaufs 1x1 der Deutschen Industrie (GW ISSN 0343-5881) *307*
Einkaufsfuehrer durch die Pelz- und Ledermode (GW ISSN 0070-9530) *672*
Einst und Jetzt (GW ISSN 0420-8870) *581*
Einunim Bibikoret Hamedina (IS) *904*
Eirene (CS ISSN 0046-1628) *86, 581*
Eirene (NE) *337, 721*
Eisei Shikenjo Hokoku *see* National Institute of Hygienic Sciences. Bulletin *955*
Eisei Tokei Kara Mita Aichi-Ken No Sugata (JA) *958*
Eisenbahngeschichte der Vereinigten Staaten von Amerika (SZ) *1094*
Eiszeitalter und Gegenwart (GW ISSN 0424-7116) *856*
Ejendomsinformation (DK ISSN 0108-2698) *965*
Ek Bacharer Srestha Kabita (II) *741*
Ekarai Israel (IS) *27*
Ekistic Index (GR ISSN 0013-2934) *5, 627, 1031*
Ekologiia (BU ISSN 0204-7675) *140*
Ekologiya Ptits Litovskoi S.S.R. (UR) *140*
Ekonomika *see* Acta Academiae Agriculturae ac Technicae Olstenensis. Oekonomika *190*
Ekonomika Promyslovosti (UR) *288*
Ekonomika Ugol'noi Promyshlennosti (UR) *822*
Ekonomiko-Matematicheskie Metody Planirovaniya i Upravleniya (UR) *279*
Ekonomiko-Matematicheskie Metody v Planirovanii Narodnogo Khozyaistva (UR) *251*
Ekonomisk-Historiska Studier *see* Uppsala Studies in Economic History *252*
Eksperimental'naya i Prikladnaya Psikhologiya (UR) *934*
Eksperimental'noe Issledovanie Lichnosti i Temperamenta (UR) *934*
Eksportfremmeraadet. Beretning *see* Eksportkredit, Eksportfremme: Aarsberetninger *255*
Eksportkredit, Eksportfremme: Aarsberetninger (DK ISSN 0108-7509) *255*
Eksportkreditraadet. Beretning *see* Eksportkredit, Eksportfremme: Aarsberetninger *255*
El Hi Textbooks and Serials in Print (US ISSN 0000-0825) *424*
El Hi Textbooks in Print *see* El Hi Textbooks and Serials in Print *424*
El Paso Archaeological Society. Special Reports (US ISSN 0070-9573) *86*

El Salvador. Direccion General de Economia Agropcuaria. Anuario de Estadisticas Agropcuarias (ES) *27*
El Salvador. Direccion General de Economia Agropecuaria. Prognostico de Algodon (ES) *40*
El Salvador. Direccion General de Economia Agropecuaria. Prognostico de Zafra (ES) *40*
El Salvador. Direccion General de Estadistica y Censos. Anuario Estadistico (ES ISSN 0080-5661) *1054*
El Salvador. Ministerio de Agricultura y Ganaderia. Direccion General de Recursos Naturales Renovables. Plan Anual Operativo (ES) *365*
El Salvador. Ministerio de Planificacion y Coordinacion del Desarrollo Economico y Social. Memoria de Labores (ES) *244*
El Salvador. Superintendencia de Bancos y Otras Instituciones Financieras. Estadistica: Seguros, Finanzas, Bancos (ES) *227, 639*
El Salvador. Superintendencia de Bancos y Otras Instituciones Financieras. Estadistica: Seguros, Finanzas, Capitalizacion *see* El Salvador. Superintendencia de Bancos y Otras Instituciones Financieras. Estadistica: Seguros, Finanzas, Bancos *639*
El Salvador en Cifras (ES) *1054*
El Salvador, Informe Economico y Social (ES) *244*
El Salvador Nyt *see* Mellemamerika Nyt *607*
Eldridge Reeves Johnson Foundation for Medical Physics. Colloquium. Proceedings (US ISSN 0070-959X) *760*
Elected and Appointed Black Judges in the United States (US) *655*
Election Laws of Hawaii *see* Election Laws of Hawaii Handbook *655*
Election Laws of Hawaii Handbook (US) *655*
Electri-Onics Desk Manual (US ISSN 0745-4309) *452*
Electric Power Annual Report (US) *452*
Electric Power in Asia and the Pacific (UN ISSN 0252-4406) *452*
Electric Power in Canada (CN ISSN 0070-962X) *452, 464*
Electric Power Industry Abstracts (US) *452, 461*
Electric Rate Book (US) *464*
Electric Utility Generation Planbook (US) *452*
Electrical and Electronic Trader Year Book (UK ISSN 0070-9638) *452*
Electrical & Electronics Abstracts (UK ISSN 0036-8105) *5, 346, 461*
Electrical Blue Book (CN) *452*
Electrical Construction and Maintenance Electrical Products Yearbook *see* E C & M's Electrical Products Yearbook *452*
Electrical Contacts (US) *1152*
Electrical Contractors' Association Year Book Desk Diary *see* E C A Year Book Desk Diary *452*
Electrical Contractors' Year Book *see* E C A Year Book Desk Diary *452*
Electrical/Electronics Insulation Conference. Proceedings (US) *452*
Electrical/Electronics Insulation Conference. Record (US ISSN 0070-9697) *452*
Electrical Engineering Abstracts *see* Elektrotechnikai Szakirodalmi Tajekoztato *461*
Electrical Engineering Communications and Signal Processing *see* Electrical Engineering, Telecommunications and Signal Processing *484*
Electrical Engineering Problems in the Rubber and Plastics Industry Technical Conference. Record *see* Conference of Electrical Engineering Problems in the Rubber and Plastics Industries. I E E E Conference Record *985*
Electrical Engineering, Telecommunications and Signal Processing (US) *346, 484*

Electrical Equipment Representatives Association. Directory (US ISSN 0070-9689) *452*
Electrical Insulation Conference. Proceedings *see* Electrical/Electronics Insulation Conference. Proceedings *452*
Electrical Insulation Technical Conference. Record *see* Electrical/Electronics Insulation Conference. Record *452*
Electrical Machinery: Latin American Industrial Report (US) *239, 452*
Electrical Process Heating in Industry. Technical Conference. Record (US ISSN 0070-9719) *452*
Electrical Products Yearbook *see* E C & M's Electrical Products Yearbook *452*
Electrical World Directory of Electric Utilities (US) *452*
Electrical Yearbook/Unki Yonkam (KO) *452*
Electricite de France. Rapport d'Activite (FR ISSN 0070-9735) *452*
Electricite de France. Statistiques de la Production et de la Consommation (FR ISSN 0070-9751) *452*
Electricity and Industry in Hokuriki *see* Hokuriku no Denki to kogyo *468*
Electricity Consumers Council. Annual Report (UK ISSN 0261-2127) *452*
Electricity Council Abstracts Bulletin (UK ISSN 0269-7513) *453, 468*
Electricity Supply Handbook (UK ISSN 0070-976X) *453, 489*
Electrification and Mechanization in Mining and Metallurgy *see* Elektryfikacja i Mechanizacja Gornictwa i Hutnictwa *816*
Electro (SI) *453*
Electro. Annuaire (FR) *453*
Electro Medical Trade Association. Products Directory (UK) *760*
Electroanalytical Chemistry: A Series of Advances (US ISSN 0070-9778) *326*
Electrochemical News *see* Current Titles in Electrochemistry *325*
Electrochemical Society Series (US) *328*
Electrochemistry (UK ISSN 0305-9979) *328*
Electrolux. Annual Report (SW) *644*
Electromechanical Bench Reference (US) *453*
Electromedical & Electrosurgical Equipment Spec Book (US) *636, 794*
Electron, Ion and Laser Beam Technology Conference. Record *see* Conference on Lasers and Electro-Optics (Publications) *451*
Electron Microscopy of Proteins (UK) *163, 169*
Electron Microscopy Society of America. Proceedings (US ISSN 0424-8201) *169*
Electron Microscopy Society of Southern Africa. Proceedings/Elektronmikroskopievereniging van Suidelike Afrika. Verrigtings (SA ISSN 0250-0418) *169, 899*
Electron Spin Resonance (UK ISSN 0305-9758) *331*
Electron Spin Resonance Spectroscopy Abstracts (UK ISSN 0301-7575) *5, 892*
Electronic and Atomic Collisions *see* International Conference on the Physics of Electronic and Atomic Collisions. Abstracts of Contributed Papers and Invited Papers *897*
Electronic Components Conference. Proceedings (US ISSN 0569-5503) *453*
Electronic Components Symposium. Proceedings *see* Electronic Components Conference. Proceedings *453*
Electronic Connector Study Group. Annual Connector Symposium. Proceedings (US ISSN 0145-0085) *453*
Electronic Design's Gold Book (US) *307, 453*

ELECTRONIC ENGINEERING

Electronic Engineering Association. Annual Report (UK ISSN 0070-9859) *453*
Electronic Engineering Index (UK ISSN 0308-8375) *453, 461*
Electronic Engineers Master *see* E E M *307*
Electronic Industries Association. Membership List *see* Electronic Industries Association. Trade Directory and Membership List *308*
Electronic Industries Association. Trade Directory and Membership List (US ISSN 0091-9519) *308, 453*
Electronic Industries Review *see* Electronic Market Data Book *453*
Electronic Industries Yearbook *see* Electronic Market Data Book *453*
Electronic Industry Telephone Directory (US ISSN 0422-9053) *308, 453*
Electronic Mail Executives Directory *see* Directory of Plans, Executives, Policies for PCs, Office Automation, Datacom, Electronic Mail *343*
Electronic Market Data Book (US ISSN 0070-9867) *283, 453*
Electronic News Financial Fact Book and Directory (US ISSN 0070-9875) *453*
Electronic Printing Systems: Directions in Digital Imaging. Conference Proceedings (US) *930, 961*
Electronic Product Data *see* Electronic Engineering Index *461*
Electronic Publishing Abstracts (US ISSN 0739-2907) *5, 354, 964*
Electronic Representatives Directory (US) *308, 453*
Electronic Warfare (SZ) *811*
Electronicom. Conference Proceedings (US) *308, 453*
Electronics Abstracts Journal *see* Electronics and Communications Abstracts Journal *345*
Electronics and Communications Abstracts (UK ISSN 0013-5119) *5, 345, 461*
Electronics and Communications Abstracts Journal (US ISSN 0361-3313) *5, 345, 461*
Electronics Buyers' Guide (US ISSN 0090-5291) *308, 453*
Electronics Buyers Guide *see* E B G *452*
Electronics: Latin American Industrial Report (US) *453*
Electronique Francaise *see* Groupement des Industries Electroniques. Rapport d'Activites *454*
Electrons in Semiconductors *see* Elektrony v Poluprovodnikakh *453*
Electrophysiology/Denki Seirigaku (JA) *153*
Electrosonic World (UK ISSN 0261-2666) *343, 453*
Elektro-Industrie (GW) *453*
Elektro-Jahr (GW ISSN 0070-9956) *453*
Elektroenergetika i Avtomatizatsiya Energoustanovok (UR) *471*
Elektronik Indkoebsbogen (DK ISSN 0108-8149) *453*
Elektronik Nyts Leverandoerregister (DK) *453*
Elektronikindustriens Indkoebsbog (DK) *308, 453*
Elektronmikroskopievereniging van Suidelike Afrika. Verrigtings *see* Electron Microscopy Society of Southern Africa. Proceedings *169*
Elektrony v Poluprovodnikakh/ Electrons in Semiconductors (UR) *453*
Elektrotechnika ir Mechanika (UR) *453, 491*
Elektrotechnikai Szakirodalmi Tajekoztato/Electrical Engineering Abstracts (HU ISSN 0231-0783) *5, 461*
Elektrovymiriuvalna Tekhnika (UR) *453*
Elektryfikacja i Mechanizacja Gornictwa i Hutnictwa/ Electrification and Mechanization in Mining and Metallurgy (PL ISSN 0070-9964) *797, 816*
Elementa Ad Fontium Editiones (IT ISSN 0070-9972) *581*

Elementary School Library Collection (US) *413, 677*
Elementary Teachers Guide to Free Curriculum Materials (US ISSN 0070-9980) *447*
Elements du Bilan Economique (ML ISSN 0071-0008) *235*
Elements Fondamentaux de l'Impot *see* Tax Principles to Remember *299*
Elenchus Bibliographicus Biblicus (VC ISSN 0392-7423) *975*
Elettronica *see* Annuario di Elettronica *450*
Eliot Janeway Lectures on Historical Economics (US) *194*
Elixir (CN) *721*
Elizabethan and Renaissance Studies (AU) *721*
Elizabethan Catalogue of Modern Commonwealth Stamps (UK) *874*
Elizabethan Club Series (US ISSN 0085-0225) *581*
Elizabethan Stamp Catalogue *see* Elizabethan Catalogue of Modern Commonwealth Stamps *874*
Elkab (BE) *86*
Ellis Island Series: Immigration & the Pluralist Society (US) *605*
Elsevier Oceanography Series (NE ISSN 0078-3326) *405*
Elsner; Handbuch fuer Strassenbau und Strassenverkehrstechnik *see* Elsners Handbuch fuer Strassenwesen *481*
Elsners Handbuch fuer Staedtischen Ingenieurbau *see* Elsners Handbuch fuer Staedtisches Ingenieurwesen *471*
Elsners Handbuch fuer Staedtisches Ingenieurwesen (GW) *471*
Elsners Handbuch fuer Strassenwesen (GW) *481*
Elsners Taschenbuch der Eisenbahntechnik (GW ISSN 0071-0075) *1094*
Elvis Special (UK) *835*
Emballageinstituttets Leverandoerhaandbog *see* Leverandoerhaandbogen (Skovlunde) *855*
Embroidery Directory (US ISSN 0080-6811) *308, 1074*
Embroidery News (US) *1074*
Eme Eme (DR) *982*
Emerald Seas (US) *1152*
Emergency Economic Action Plans *see* Cyprus. Five Year Plans *243*
Emergency Response Guidebook (US) *953, 1091*
Emerging Patterns of Work and Communications in an Information Age (US ISSN 0882-3316) *343, 848*
Emerging Technologies (US) *1068*
Emigranten (DK ISSN 0900-7679) *922*
Emneregister, Selskabs- og Hovedaktionaerforhold m.v. (DK ISSN 0109-0305) *221*
Emotion (US) *934*
Emotions and Behavior. Monograph (US ISSN 0734-9890) *789*
Empirica (GW ISSN 0340-8744) *244*
Empirical Research in Accounting, Selected Studies *see* Journal of Accounting Research. Supplement *221*
Empirical Research in Theatre *see* Empirical Research in Theatre Annual *1077*
Empirical Research in Theatre Annual (US) *1077*
Empirical Studies of Psychoanalytic Theories, 1 & 2 (US) *934*
Empleo y Desempleo en Puerto Rico/ Employment and Unemployment in Puerto Rico: Calendar Years (PR ISSN 0555-6635) *271*
Emplois d'Ete en France (FR) *441, 848*
Employee Benefit Costs in Canada (CN ISSN 0701-1539) *271*
Employee Relocation Council Directory *see* E-R-C Directory *965*
Employee Retirement Income Security Act. Report to Congress *see* U.S. Department of Labor. Employee Retirement Income Security Act. Report to Congress *276*

Employers Guide to A B A Approved N A L P Member Law Schools *see* Employers Guide to Law Schools *655*
Employers Guide to Law Schools (US) *655*
Employers of New Community College Graduates: Directory (CN ISSN 0381-3711) *848*
Employers of New University Graduates: Directory (CN ISSN 0381-372X) *848*
Employment and Earnings Statistics for the United States *see* Employment and Earnings: United States *207*
Employment and Earnings: United States (US ISSN 0271-4787) *207*
Employment and Unemployment in Puerto Rico: Calendar Years *see* Empleo y Desempleo en Puerto Rico *271*
Employment Law Reports *see* Canadian Cases on Employment Law Reports *653*
Employment, Output and Capital Formation in the Industrial Sector (CY) *1152*
Employment Relations Abstracts *see* Work Related Abstracts *220*
Employment Relations Abstracts: Subject Heading List *see* Work Related Abstracts Subject Heading List *686*
Employment Safety and Health Guide (US ISSN 0093-1535) *635, 655*
Empresa Brasileira de Telecommunicacoes. Relatorio Anual(BL) *343*
Empresa Brasileira de Turismo. Anuario Estatistico (BL) *1108*
Empresa Brasileira de Turismo. Calendario Turistico (BL) *1108*
Empresa Brasileira de Turismo. Tourist Calendar *see* Empresa Brasileira de Turismo. Calendario Turistico *1108*
Empresa de Navegacao da Amazonia. Estatistica da Navegacao (BL) *1100*
Empresa Nacional de Electricidad. Memoria (CL) *453*
Empresa Nacional de Energia Electrica. Datos Estadisticos (HO) *453*
Empresa Nacional de Telecommunicaciones del Peru. Memoria Anual (PE) *348*
Empresas Japonesas No Brasil. Annuario/Burajiru Nikkei Kigyo Nenkan (BL) *308*
En Bref du Danemark *see* Feature fra Danmark *538*
En Passant/Poetry (US ISSN 0271-5023) *741*
En Passant Poetry Quarterly *see* En Passant/Poetry *741*
Encanto Radical *see* Colecao Encanto Radical *710*
Enchoria (GW ISSN 0340-627X) *694*
Enciclopedia Nacional del Petroleo Petrolquimica y Gas (SP) *864*
Encomia (US ISSN 0363-4841) *721*
Encore (US ISSN 0071-0164) *721, 1077*
Encounterer (US) *789, 934*
Encuentro Nacional de Investigadores en Administracion. Memorias (CK) *941*
Encuesta Agropecuaria (VE) *46*
Encuesta Avicola (ES) *65*
Encuesta Industrial *see* Guatemala. Direccion General de Estadistica. Encuesta de la Industria Manufacturera Fabril *1056*
Encuesta Industrial: Resultados Nacionales (VE) *207*
Encyclia (US ISSN 0196-9110) *104, 991*
Encyclopaedia Africana. Information Report (GH ISSN 0013-712X) *565, 1007*
Encyclopaedia Judaica Year Book (IS ISSN 0303-7819) *976*
Encyclopedia of Associations (US ISSN 0071-0202) *462*
Encyclopedia of Business Information Sources (US ISSN 0071-0210) *279*
Encyclopedia of Earth Sciences Series (US) *379*
Encyclopedia of Economics (US) *279, 462*

Encyclopedia of Geographic Information Sources (US) *542*
Encyclopedia of Governmental Advisory Organizations (US ISSN 0092-8380) *941*
Encyclopedia of Information Systems and Services (US ISSN 0734-9068) *352, 357*
Encyclopedia of Occultism and Parapsychology (US) *860*
Encyclopedia of Plant Physiology. New Series (US) *156*
Encyclopedia of Social Work (US ISSN 0071-0237) *1017*
Encyclopedia Year Book (US ISSN 0196-0172) *462*
End Loans to Southern Africa Newsletter *see* E L T S A Newsletter *915*
End-Time News (CN ISSN 0702-844X) *978*
Endicott Report *see* Northwestern Endicott Report *848*
Endocrine Society of Australia. Proceedings (AT ISSN 0312-4738) *781*
Endocrinology Abstracts (US ISSN 0749-8020) *5, 769*
Energi Nyt (DK) *464*
Energia ed Idrocarburi/Energy and Hydrocarbons (IT) *816*
Energia ed Idrocarburi. Sommario Statistico *see* Energia ed Idrocarburi *816*
Energie Electrique de la Cote d'Ivoire. Compte Rendu de Gestion *see* Energie Electrique de la Cote d'Ivoire. Rapport Annuel *453*
Energie Electrique de la Cote d'Ivoire. Rapport Annuel (IV) *453*
Energieonderzoek Centrum Nederland. Jaarverslag (NE) *464*
Energy (FI ISSN 0782-2952) *453, 464*
Energy *see* Journal of Energy Engineering *482*
Energy Abstracts (US ISSN 0093-8408) *5, 468, 476*
Energy Abstracts for Policy Analysis (US ISSN 0098-5104) *5, 468*
Energy and Hydrocarbons *see* Energia ed Idrocarburi *816*
Energy Balances of O.E.C.D. Countries (Organization for Economic Cooperation and Development) (US) *464*
Energy Conversion Abstracts *see* Energy Abstracts *468*
Energy Developments (GW ISSN 0342-5665) *464*
Energy Directory (US) *1152*
Energy, Environment and Development in Africa (SW ISSN 0281-8515) *464*
Energy from the Wind - Annotated Bibliography (US) *1152*
Energy in Denmark (DK ISSN 0901-3768) *464*
Energy Index (US ISSN 0094-6281) *5, 468, 501*
Energy Industries Council Catalogue (UK) *464*
Energy Information Abstracts (US ISSN 0147-6521) *5, 468*
Energy Information Abstracts Annual *see* Energy Information Index/ Abstracts Annual *468*
Energy Information Index/Abstracts Annual (US) *5, 468*
Energy: Latin American Industrial Report (US) *464*
Energy Policy Studies (US ISSN 0882-3537) *464*
Energy Report from Chase *see* Petroleum Situation *466*
Energy Research (NE) *464*
Energy Research Abstracts (US ISSN 0160-3604) *5, 468*
Energy Statistics Yearbook (UN) *465*
Energy Technology *see* Energy Technology Conference. Proceedings *465*
Energy Technology Conference. Proceedings (US ISSN 0161-6048) *465*
Energylab Newsletter (DK ISSN 0900-419X) *465*
Enfo (US ISSN 0276-9956) *495*

EQUIPMENT DIRECTORY 1723

Engineer Buyers Guide (UK ISSN 0071-0288) 308, *471*
Engineered Materials Abstracts (US) 5, *476*
Engineering Application Software D.A.T.A. Book (US) 471, *485*
Engineering College Research and Graduate Study (US) 434, *471*
Engineering Committee on Oceanic Resources. Proceedings of the General Assembly (US) 471, *1124*
Engineering Education in the Region (UK) *434*, 471
Engineering Employers' Federation Directory (UK ISSN 0141-7592) *471*
Engineering Enrollment Data *see* American Association of Engineering Societies. Engineering Manpower Commission. Engineering and Technology Enrollments *469*
Engineering Experiment Station University of Arizona. College of Engineering. E E S Series Report *see* University of Arizona. College of Engineering. E E S Series Report *475*
Engineering Foundation Annual Report(US) *471*
Engineering Geology and Soils Engineering Symposium. Proceedings(US ISSN 0071-0318) *481*
Engineering Geology Case Histories (US ISSN 0071-0326) *481*
Engineering Geology Symposium. Proceedings *see* Engineering Geology and Soils Engineering Symposium. Proceedings *481*
Engineering in Medicine and Biology Conference. Record *see* Conference on Engineering in Medicine and Biology. Record *759*
Engineering Index *see* Engineering Index Monthly and Author Index *476*
Engineering Index Annual (US ISSN 0360-8557) *476*
Engineering Index Cumulative Index (US) 5, *476*
Engineering Index Monthly and Author Index (US ISSN 0162-3036) 5, *476*
Engineering Industries Association. Classified Directory and Buyers Guide (UK ISSN 0071-0342) 308, *471*
Engineering Industries Association. Diary (UK) *471*
Engineering Industries in O E C D Member Countries: New Basic Statistics (FR) *288*
Engineering Industries in OECD Member Countries *see* Engineering Industries in O E C D Member Countries: New Basic Statistics *288*
Engineering Journal of Singapore (SI ISSN 0129-6531) *471*
Engineering Know-How in Engine Design (US ISSN 0489-5606) *1091*
Engineering Manpower Bulletin (US ISSN 0013-8037) *471*
Engineering Now (US) *471*
Engineering Research Centres (US) *471*
Engineering Science Library *see* Ingenieurwissenschaftliche Bibliothek *472*
Engineering Sciences Data Index *see* Engineering Sciences Data Unit Index *476*
Engineering Sciences Data Unit Index (UK) 5, *476*
Engineering Times Annual Directory (II) *471*
Engineers of Distinction *see* Who's Who in Engineering *475*
England. Economic and Social Research Council. Research Programme Bulletin (UK ISSN 0267-8128) *244*
England and Scotland on Twenty Dollars a Day *see* England and Scotland on Twenty-Five Dollars a Day *1108*
England and Scotland on Twenty-Five Dollars a Day (US) *1108*
England and Wales National Health Service. Health Services Costing Returns (UK) *617*

England's Best Holidays (UK ISSN 0267-3398) *1108*
Englera (GW ISSN 0170-4818) *156*
English and American Studies in German (GW ISSN 0071-0490) *694*
English and Germanic Studies *see* English Philological Studies *694*
English Benedictine Congregation. Ordo. (UK) *982*
English Ceramic Circle. Transactions (UK ISSN 0071-0547) *320*
English Church Music *see* World of Church Music *1166*
English Folk Dance and Song Society. Journal *see* Folk Music Journal *835*
English Goethe Society. Publications (UK) *721*, 741
English Guernsey Herd Book (UK ISSN 0071-0571) *65*
English Historical Documents (US ISSN 0071-058X) *581*
English Institute. Selected Essays (US ISSN 0071-0598) *721*
English Language and Orientation Programs in the United States (US ISSN 0071-0601) *447*
English Language Publications from Pakistan *see* Books from Pakistan *124*
English Language Research Journal (UK) *694*
English Language Teachers Association. Review/Anjoman-e Dabiran-e Zabanha-Ye Khareji. Nashriyeh (IR) *447*
English Legal Manuscripts (SZ) *655*
English Literary Renaissance Monographs *see* English Literary Renaissance Supplements *721*
English Literary Renaissance Supplements (US ISSN 0013-8312) *721*
English Little Magazines (UK ISSN 0071-061X) *721*
English Miscellany (IT ISSN 0425-0575) *721*
English Monarch Series (US ISSN 0071-0628) *581*
English Philological Studies (UK ISSN 0308-0129) *694*
English Place-Name Society (UK ISSN 0071-0636) *694*
English Translations of German Standards *see* English Translations of German Standards. Catalogue *809*
English Translations of German Standards. Catalogue (GW ISSN 0174-3805) *809*
Enjoy Scotland *see* Scotland's for Me *1116*
Enjoying the Arts (US) *375, 835, 1077*
Enlightenment and Dissent (UK ISSN 0262-7612) *557*, 904
Ennemi (FR) *104*, 721
Enquete Permanente sur l'Utilisation des Vehicules de Transport en Commun de Personnes en (year) (FR) *1081*
Enquete sur les Enterprises Industrielles et Commerciales du Togo (TG) *239, 288*
Enquetes et Documents d'Histoire Africaine (BE ISSN 0772-6112) *565*
Enrico Fermi International Summer School of Physics (NE) *888*
Ensaios Linguisticos (BL) *694*
Ensayistas (US ISSN 0148-8627) *710*
Ensayo y Testimonio (UY ISSN 0071-0679) *721*
Ensayos E C I E L (Programa de Estudios Conjuntos para la Integracion Economica Latinoamericano) (BL) *244*
Ensayos - Planeta de Economia y Ciencias Sociales (SP) *1007*
Enseignement et la Pedagogie en Roumanie (RM) *413*
Enseignement Superieur en Cote-d'Ivoire (IV) *413*
Ensenanza de la Religion (SP) *969*
Ensomme Gamles Vaern Information *see* E G V Information *1017*
Ente Nazionale Idrocarburi. Report and Statement of Accounts (IT ISSN 0071-0687) *864*

Ente Nazionale Idrocarburi Annual Report *see* E N I Annual Report *464*
Enterprise (AT ISSN 0085-0268) *239*
Entertainment Industry Series (US ISSN 0071-0695) *283*
Entertainment, Publishing and the Arts Handbook (US ISSN 0739-1897) *348*, 961, 1077
Entomography (US ISSN 0734-9874) *164*
Entomological Society of Alberta. Proceedings (CN ISSN 0071-0709) *164*
Entomological Society of America. Miscellaneous Publications (US ISSN 0071-0717) *164*
Entomological Society of Australia (N.S.W.) Journal *see* General and Applied Entomology *164*
Entomological Society of British Columbia. Journal (CN ISSN 0071-0733) *164*
Entomological Society of Canada. Memoirs (CN ISSN 0071-075X) *164*
Entomological Society of Egypt. Bulletin *see* Societe Entomologique d'Egypte. Bulletin *166*
Entomological Society of Manitoba. Proceedings (CN ISSN 0315-2146) *164*
Entomological Society of New Zealand. Bulletin (NZ ISSN 0110-4527) *164*
Entomological Society of Ontario. Proceedings (CN ISSN 0071-0768) *164*
Entomological Society of Pennsylvania. Newsletter (US ISSN 0071-0776) *164*
Entomological Society of Southern Africa. Memoirs (SA) *164*
Entomological Society of Southern Africa. Proceedings of the Congress (SA) *164*
Entomologicke Problemy (CS ISSN 0071-0792) *164*
Entomology Abstracts (US ISSN 0013-8924) 5, *150*
Entomology Memoirs *see* South Africa. Department of Agriculture. Entomology Memoirs *166*
Entomology Newsletter (BL) *164*
Entomology of the California Channel Islands (US) *991*
Entrance *see* Exit *722*
Entreprise Europeenne (FR ISSN 0014-9373) *184*, 481
L'Entreprise Ivoirienne (IV) *235*
Entretien et Travaux Neufs (FR) *481*
Entretiens sur l'Antiquite Classique (SZ ISSN 0071-0822) *337*
Entwicklungslaender-Studien (GW ISSN 0722-0111) *262, 385, 760*
Envase y Embalaje (MX) *855*
Envio (NQ) *605*, 904
Enviroline User's Manual (US ISSN 0270-0751) *495*
Environ (TR) *495*
Environment in Africa *see* African Environment *493*
Environment Index (US ISSN 0090-791X) *501*
Environment Law Review *see* Land Use & Environment Law Review *497*
Environment Planning and Conservation in Sweden *see* Current Sweden *540*
Environmental Assessment of the Alaskan Continental Shelf. Annual Reports Summary (US) *495, 543*
Environmental Biology (US) *140, 465, 495*
Environmental Biology of Fishes (NE ISSN 0378-1909) *174*
Environmental Building Developments Ltd. News *see* Practical Alternatives *498*
Environmental Chemistry (UK ISSN 0305-7712) *322, 495*
Environmental Coalition on Nuclear Power Newsletter (US) *465, 896*
Environmental Defense Fund. Annual Report (US ISSN 0091-9837) *495*
Environmental Design Perspectives (US) *1153*
Environmental Design Research Association. Annual Conference Proceedings (US) *98, 623*

Environmental Design Series (US) *495*
Environmental Directory (UK) *495*
Environmental Fluid Mechanics (NE) *379*
Environmental Hotline (US) *365, 495*
Environmental Impact Statement Cumulative *see* E I S Cumulative *501*
Environmental Law Reform Group. Publication (AT) *495*
Environmental Medicine *see* Nagoya University. Research Institute of Environmental Medicine. Annual Report *764*
Environmental Pollution, City Development and Regional Development Index (JA ISSN 0912-1722) *365, 495*
Environmental Pollution in Meguro Ward *see* Meguro-ku No Kogai *497*
Environmental Pollution in Niigata City *see* Niigata-Shi Ni Okeru Kogai *498*
Environmental Radiation Surveillance in Washington State. Annual Report (US ISSN 0509-769X) *495, 953*
Environmental Radioactivity at Risoe *see* Environmental Radioactivity in Denmark *888*
Environmental Radioactivity in Denmark (DK ISSN 0106-407X) *888*
Environmental Radioactivity in Greenland (DK ISSN 0108-0962) *888*
Environmental Radioactivity in the Faroes (DK ISSN 0107-9069) *888*
Environmental Research in Japan (JA) *495*
Environmental Science and Technology: a Wiley-Interscience Series of Texts and Monographs (US ISSN 0194-0287) *495, 1068*
Environmental Statutes (US ISSN 0736-573X) *495, 655*
Environnement (CN) *496*
Envol/Flight (CN ISSN 0707-7165) *170*
Enzyme Engineering (US ISSN 0094-8500) *151*
Enzymology Series (US) *1153*
Eotvos Lorand Geophysical Institute of Hungary. Annual Report/Magyar Allami Eotvos Lorand Geofizikai Intezet evi Jelentese (HU ISSN 0524-8655) *399*
Ephemerides *see* France. Bureau des Longitudes. Annuaire: Ephemerides *116*
Ephemerides Astronomiques *see* France. Bureau des Longitudes. Annuaire: Ephemerides *116*
Ephemeris of the Sun, Polaris and Other Selected Stars with Companion Data and Tables (US ISSN 0071-0962) *115*
Epidecides Lunaires/Lunar Epidecis (FR ISSN 0240-8376) *115*
Epidemiologia Cientifica: Teoria y Practica (EC) *760, 787*
Epidemiologic Reviews (US ISSN 0193-936X) *760, 953*
Epigraphia Indica (II ISSN 0013-9564) *86*
Epigraphic Society. Occasional Publications (US ISSN 0192-5148) *86*, 694
Epigraphische Studien (GW ISSN 0071-0989) *557*
Epimenides/Epimenis (FR ISSN 0240-8368) *115*, 405
Epimenis *see* Epimenides *115*
Episcopal Clerical Directory (US) *978*
Episteme (NE) *991*
Epistimoniki Epiteris Kteniatrikis Scholis (GR) *1121*
Epoche (US) *557, 969*
Equal Employment Opportunity. Annual Program (US) *913*
Equal Employment Opportunity Report *see* U.S. Equal Employment Opportunity Commission. Annual Report *276*
Equal Opportunities Commission Research Bulletin *see* E O C Research Bulletin *271*
Equipment Directory of Audio-Visual, Computer and Video Products (US) *308, 348*

1724 EQUIPMENT MARKET

Equipment Market Abstracts *see* Predicasts Overview of Markets and Technologies 477
Equipment Show Daily (US) 471
Equipo (MX) 745
Era *see* Philomel 730
Erasmus in English (CN ISSN 0071-1063) 629
Erasmus Studies (CN ISSN 0318-3319) 629
Erasmus Universiteit, Rotterdam. Centrum voor Maatschappijgeschiedenis. Mededelingen/Information Bulletin (NE) 1026
Erdkundliches Wissen (GW ISSN 0425-1741) 543
Erdstall (GW) 86
Erdwissenschaftliche Forschung (GW ISSN 0170-3188) 379
Eretz-Israel. Archaeological, Historical and Geographical Studies (IS ISSN 0071-108X) 86, 543, 569
Erfdeel van de Klassieke Romeinse Juristen (NE) 557, 655
Ergebnisse der Allgemeinen Pathologie und Pathologischen Anatomie *see* Current Topics in Pathology 760
Ergebnisse der Angewandten Mathematik *see* Springer Tracts in Natural Philosophy 1001
Ergebnisse der Exacten Naturwissenschaften *see* Springer Tracts in Modern Physics 891
Ergebnisse der Inneren Medizin und Kinderheilkunde. New Series/Advances in Internal Medicine and Pediatrics (US ISSN 0071-111X) 760, 787
Ergebnisse der Limnologie/Advances in Limnology (GW ISSN 0071-1128) 140, 402
Ergebnisse der Mathematik und Ihrer Grenzgebiete. Neue Folge (US ISSN 0071-1136) 748
Ergebnisse der Mikrobiologie und Immunitaetsforschung *see* Current Topics in Microbiology and Immunology 168
Ergebnisse der Physiologie, Biologischen Chemie und Experimentellen Pharmakologie *see* Reviews of Physiology, Biochemistry and Experimental Pharmacology 172
Ergebnisse der Plasmaphysik und der Gaselektronik. Schriftenreihe (GE) 888
Ergebnisse und Fortschritte der Zoologie *see* Fortschritte der Zoologie 174
Ergonomics Abstracts (UK ISSN 0046-2446) 5, 476
Erhvervfremmende og Forbrugerpolitiske Foranstaltninger (DK ISSN 0105-5992) 369
Erhvervs og Samfundsbeskrivelse. Noter og Opgaver (DK ISSN 0900-2731) 721
Erhvervshistorisk Arbog (DK) 581
Erhvervsnoeglen (DK ISSN 0105-6662) 194
Erhvervssituationen (DK) 1153
Eriu (IE) 721
Erkrankungen der Zootiere (GE ISSN 0138-5003) 1121
Erlanger Bausteine zur Fraenkischen Heimatforschung (GW) 126, 156, 385, 557
Ernest Bloch Lectures (US ISSN 0071-1187) 434
Ernest Bloch Society. Bulletin (US) 835
Ernest Bloch Society. Newsletter *see* Ernest Bloch Society. Bulletin 835
Ernst-Mach-Institut, Freiburg. Bericht (GW ISSN 0340-8833) 991
Ernst-Mach-Institut, Freiburg. Wissenschaftlicher Bericht *see* Ernst-Mach-Institut, Freiburg. Bericht 991
Ernstia (VE ISSN 0252-8274) 156
Erotic Fiction Quarterly (US ISSN 0887-5057) 721
Ertekezesek a Torteneti Tudomanyok Korebol (HU ISSN 0071-1233) 557
Ertragsbilanz der Schweiz *see* Zahlungsbilanz der Schweiz 300
Erziehung und Unterricht (SZ ISSN 0071-125X) 413

Erziehungs- und Schulgeschichte Jahrbuch (GE ISSN 0075-2622) 413
Esakia (JA ISSN 0071-1268) 164
Escola Superior de Agricultura "Luiz de Queiroz". Anais (BL ISSN 0071-1276) 27
Escola Superior de Agricultura "Luiz de Queiroz". Boletim de Divulgacao (BL ISSN 0071-1292) 27
Escribano (US) 605
Escritos (CK ISSN 0120-1263) 721, 878
Escuela de Gerentes de Cooperativas. Cartillas de Cooperacion (SP ISSN 0084-5132) 289
Escuela de Gerentes de Cooperativas. Coleccion Textos (SP ISSN 0084-5159) 289
Escuela de Gerentes de Cooperativas. Cuadernos de Practicas (SP ISSN 0084-5167) 289
Escuela de Gerentes de Cooperativas. Serie Especial (SP ISSN 0084-5175) 289
Escuela Diplomatica. Cuadernos (SP ISSN 0464-3755) 1153
Escuela Interamericana de Bibliotecologia. Estadisticas (CK ISSN 0071-1314) 677
Eso Monographs (US) 761
Esoterik Almanach (GW) 721
Espana - sus Monumentos y Artes; Su Naturaleza e Historia (SP) 581
Espasa Universitaria. Filosofia y Pensamiento (SP) 878
Esperanto Documents. New Series *see* Esperanto-Dokumentoj. Nova Serio 694
Esperanto-Dokumentoj. Nova Serio (NE ISSN 0165-2524) 694
Esprit et Liberte (FR ISSN 0071-1330) 978
Essais de Dialectologie Interlinguale (NE) 694
Essais Philosophiques (BE ISSN 0071-1349) 878
Essay and General Literature Index (US ISSN 0014-083X) 5
Essays and Studies (US ISSN 0071-1357) 721
Essays by Divers Hands (US) 721
Essays for the Third Century (US) 605, 904
Essays in Biochemistry (US ISSN 0071-1365) 151
Essays in Chemistry (US ISSN 0071-1373) 322
Essays in Economic and Business History (US) 251
Essays in Foreign Languages and Literatures/Gaikokugo Gaikoku Bungaku Kenkyu (JA) 694, 721
Essays in Graham Greene: An Annual Review (US ISSN 0738-0763) 721
Essays in History (US ISSN 0071-1411) 557
Essays in International Finance (US ISSN 0071-142X) 227
Essays in Physics (US ISSN 0071-1438) 888
Essays in Public Works History (US) 557, 941
Essays in Toxicology (US ISSN 0071-1446) 870
Essays on Asian Theater, Music and Dance (US) 375, 835, 1077
Essays on Modern Music (US) 835
Essays on the Economy and Society of the Sudan (SJ) 244, 1007
Essence (Wayne) (US) 710
Essener Bibliographie (GW ISSN 0071-1462) 126
Essential Articles (US ISSN 0071-1470) 721
Essex Education (UK) 413
Essex Naturalist (UK ISSN 0071-1489) 140
Essor (FR) 255
Establecimientos Manufactureras en Puerto Rico (PR) 207, 1054
Estacion Experimental Agropecuaria Pergamino. Informe Tecnico *see* Estacion Experimental Region Agropecuaria Pergamino. Informe Tecnico 27
Estacion Experimental de Aula Dei. Anales (SP ISSN 0365-1800) 55, 156

Estacion Experimental Region Agropecuaria Pergamino. Informe Tecnico (AG ISSN 0325-1799) 27, 65
Estadistica Basica del Sistema Educativo Nacional (MX) 424
Estadistica de Criminalidad (CK) 374
Estadistica del Comercio Exterior de Espana (SP ISSN 0071-1527) 207
Estadistica Educativa *see* Argentina. Ministerio de Cultura y Educacion. Estadisticas de la Educacion 422
Estadistica Panamena. Boletin (PN) 1054
Estadistica Panamena. Estadistica Electoral *see* Estadistica Panamena. Situacion Politica, Administrativa y Justicia. Seccion 611. Estadistica Electoral 904
Estadistica Panamena. Inversiones Directas Extranjeras en Panama (PN) 207
Estadistica Panamena. Situacion Cultural. Seccion 511. Educacion (PN ISSN 0378-4967) 424, 1054
Estadistica Panamena. Situacion Demografica. Seccion 221. Estadisticas Vitales (PN ISSN 0379-4237) 926, 1054
Estadistica Panamena. Situacion Demografica. Seccion 231. Migracion Internacional (PN ISSN 0378-4975) 926
Estadistica Panamena. Situacion Economica. Indice de Volumen Fisico de la Produccion Industrial *see* Estadistica Panamena. Situacion Economica. Seccion 323. Indice de Volumen Fisico de la Produccion Industrial 207
Estadistica Panamena. Situacion Economica. Seccion 312. Produccion Pecuaria (PN ISSN 0378-2581) 40, 1054
Estadistica Panamena. Situacion Economica. Seccion 312. Siembra y Cosecha de Hortilizas (PN ISSN 0250-4324) 46
Estadistica Panamena. Situacion Economica. Seccion 312. Superficie Sembrada y Cosecha de Arroz, Maiz y Frijol de Bejuco (PN ISSN 0378-2565) 40, 1054
Estadistica Panamena. Situacion Economica. Seccion 312. Superficie Sembrada y Cosecha de Arroz y Maiz *see* Estadistica Panamena. Situacion Economica. Seccion 312. Superficie Sembrada y Cosecha de Arroz, Maiz y Frijol de Bejuco 40
Estadistica Panamena. Situacion Economica. Seccion 312. Superficie Sembrada y Cosecha de Cafe, Tabaco y Cana de Azucar (PN ISSN 0378-2573) 40, 1054
Estadistica Panamena. Situacion Economica. Seccion 321 y 325. Industria Encuesta (PN ISSN 0379-4245) 207
Estadistica Panamena. Situacion Economica. Seccion 323. Indice de Volumen Fisico de la Produccion Industrial (PN) 207, 1054
Estadistica Panamena. Situacion Economica. Seccion 331-Comercio. Anuario de Comercio Exterior (PN) 207, 1054
Estadistica Panamena. Situacion Economica. Seccion 331-Comercio. Comercio Exterior (Annual) *see* Estadistica Panamena. Situacion Economica. Seccion 331-Comercio. Anuario de Comercio Exterior 207
Estadistica Panamena. Situacion Economica. Seccion 331. Comercio Exterior (Preliminary Report) (PN ISSN 0378-4983) 207, 1054
Estadistica Panamena. Situacion Economica. Seccion 333 y 334. Transporte y Comunicaciones (PN ISSN 0378-7389) 343, 1081
Estadistica Panamena. Situacion Economica. Seccion 341. Balanza de Pagos (PN ISSN 0378-7397) 255, 294
Estadistica Panamena. Situacion Economica. Seccion 342. Cuentas Nacionales (PN ISSN 0378-2603) 941

Estadistica Panamena. Situacion Economica. Seccion 343-344. Hacienda Publica y Finanzas (PN ISSN 0378-6730) 207, 1054
Estadistica Panamena. Situacion Economica. Seccion 351. Precios Pagados por el Productor Agropecuario (PN ISSN 0378-2530) 40, 1054
Estadistica Panamena. Situacion Economica. Seccion 352. Hoja de Balance de Alimentos (PN ISSN 0378-4991) 207, 1054
Estadistica Panamena. Situacion Fisica. Seccion 121-Clima. Meteorologia *see* Estadistica Panamena. Situacion Fisica. Seccion 121. Meteorologia 804
Estadistica Panamena. Situacion Fisica. Seccion 121. Meteorologia (PN) 804
Estadistica Panamena. Situacion Politica, Administrativa y Justicia. Seccion 611. Estadistica Electoral (PN ISSN 0250-4316) 904
Estadistica Panamena. Situacion Politica, Administrativa y Justicia. Seccion 631. Justicia (PN ISSN 0378-259X) 668, 1054
Estadistica Panamena. Situacion Social. Seccion 431. Asistencia Social (PN ISSN 0378-262X) 1022, 1054
Estadistica Panamena. Situacion Social. Seccion 441. Estadisticas del Trabajo(PN ISSN 0379-072X) 207
Estadistica Panamena. Situacion Social. Seccion 441-Trabajo y Salarios. Estadisticas del Trabajo *see* Estadistica Panamena. Situacion Social. Seccion 441. Estadisticas del Trabajo 207
Estadistica Panamena. Situacion Social. Seccion 451. Accidentes de Transito (PN ISSN 0378-6765) 1031, 1054
Estadisticas de la Aviacion Civil en Espana (SP ISSN 0421-4986) 1088
Estadisticas de Produccion Industrial (SP) 207
Estadisticas de Vehiculos en Circulacion en Guatemala (GT) 1153
Estadisticas del Comercio Exterior de Venezuela. Boletin *see* Estadisticas del Comercio Exterior de Venezuela. Periodicidad Anual 207
Estadisticas del Comercio Exterior de Venezuela. Periodicidad Anual (VE) 207
Estadisticas Minera y Metalurgica de Espana (SP ISSN 0071-1563) 816
Estadisticas Relativas a la Ciencia y a la Tecnologia *see* Unesco. Statistics on Science and Technology 1004
Estadisticas, Seguros, Fianzas, Bancos *see* El Salvador. Superintendencia de Bancos y Otras Instituciones Financieras. Estadisticas: Seguros, Finanzas, Bancos 639
Estatistica Brasileira de Energia/Brazilian Energy Statistics (BL ISSN 0512-350X) 468
Estatisticas da Energia: Continente e Ilhas Adjacentes *see* Portugal. Estatisticas da Energia: Continente, Acores e Madeira 466
Estimated World Requirements of Narcotic Drugs (UN ISSN 0082-8335) 376, 870, 953
Estimates of Area and Production of Principal Crops in India. Summary Tables *see* Area and Production of Principal Crops in India. Summary Tables 52
Estimates of Consolidated Fund Expenditure *see* Ghana 245
Estimates of the Population of the United States and Components of Population Change *see* Current Population Reports: Population Estimates and Projections. Estimates of the Population of the United States and Components of Population Change 921
Estimates of the Population of the United States by Age, Sex, and Race *see* Current Population Reports: Population Estimates and Projections. Estimates of the Population of the United States by Age, Race and Sex 921

Estimates of the Revenue and Expenditure of the Kingdom of Lesotho (LO) 295
Estonian Panorama (UR) 540
Estonian Philatelist see Eesti Filatelist 874
Estructuras y Formas see Coleccion Estructuras y Formas 97
Estuaries and Coastal Waters of the British Isles (UK ISSN 0261-0663) 126, 150
Estuaries of the British Isles see Estuaries and Coastal Waters of the British Isles 150
Estudio Atacamenos (CL) 86
Estudios Cubanos see Cuban Studies 911
Estudios de Arte y Estetica (MX ISSN 0071-1659) 104
Estudios de Ciencias y Letras (UY ISSN 0256-3061) 629
Estudios de Cultura Maya (MX ISSN 0071-1667) 605
Estudios de Cultura Nahuatl (MX) 605
Estudios de Folklore (MX ISSN 0071-1683) 515
Estudios de Historia Moderna y Contemporanea de Mexico (MX ISSN 0014-147X) 605
Estudios de Historia Novohispana (MX ISSN 0185-2523) 605
Estudios de Literatura (MX ISSN 0071-1691) 721
Estudios de Literatura Contemporanea (SP ISSN 0071-1705) 721
Estudios de Poblacion y Desarrollo (BO) 1026
Estudios de Promocion Femenina (BO) 1128
Estudios de Recursos Humanos (BO) 1026
Estudios de Sociologia Familiar (BO) 1026
Estudios e Informes de la C E P A L/C E P A L Studies and Reports (Comision Economica para America Latina (CEPAL)) (UN) 262
Estudios Economicos (SP ISSN 0213-2699) 244
Estudios en Educacion Matematica see Studies in Mathematics Education 442
Estudios en el Extranjero see Study Abroad 442
Estudios Etnohistoricos del Ecuador (EC) 71, 605
Estudios Filologicos (CL ISSN 0071-1713) 694
Estudios Filosoficos (VE) 878
Estudios Folkloricos Paraguayos (PY) 515
Estudios Fronterizos Mexico - Estados Unidos (MX) 1026
Estudios Historicos (PE) 605
Estudios Historicos y Documentos de los Archivos de Protocolos (SP) 581
Estudios Latinoamericanos (PL ISSN 0137-3080) 605
Estudios Oceanologicos (CL ISSN 0071-173X) 405
Estudios Pedagogicos (CL ISSN 0716-050X) 434
Estudios Urbanos (BO) 1026
Estudios y Fuentes del Arte en Mexico (MX ISSN 0071-1748) 104
Estudos Baianos (BL) 721
Estudos de Antropologia Cultural (PO ISSN 0870-6891) 71
Estudos de Cartografia Antiga see Instituto de Investigacao Cientifica Tropical. Centro de Estudos de Historia e Cartografia Antiga. Serie de Memorias 545
Estudos Ensaios e Documentos (PO ISSN 0870-001X) 379
Estudos Filosoficos (PO) 1153
Estudos Germanicos (BL) 721
Estudos Historicos see Historia 557
Estudos Italianos em Portugal (PO) 104, 557, 721
Estudos Para o Planeamento Regional e Urbano (PO) 543
Estudos sobre o Nordeste (BL) 244
Estudos Universitarios (BL) 629
Etat du Monde (FR ISSN 0757-6714) 194
Etc (PO) 721

Etesia Statistike. Erevna tou Karkinou/ Annual Statistical Survey of Cancer (GR ISSN 0302-9697) 775, 1054
Etgar (Tel Aviv) (IS) 1017
Ethical Tablet and Capsule Handbook see E T C H 870
Ethics and International Affairs (US) 878, 915
Ethics and Public Policy Center. Newsletter (US) 502, 941
Ethics and Public Policy Essays (US) 1153
Ethics and Public Policy Reprints see Ethics and Public Policy Essays 1153
Ethiope Law Series (NR) 655
Ethiopia. Customs Head Office. External Trade Statistics (ET ISSN 0425-4309) 207
Ethiopian Chamber of Commerce. Statistical Digest (ET) 235
Ethiopian Monograph Series see Northeast African Monograph Series 504
Ethiopian Publications: Books, Pamphlets, Annuals and Periodical Articles (ET ISSN 0071-1772) 126
Ethnic American Voluntary Organizations (US ISSN 0737-1411) 502, 1017
Ethnic Directory of Canada (CN) 503
Ethnic Information Sources of the U.S. (US ISSN 0738-1719) 503
Ethnic Racial Brotherhood (US ISSN 0736-6086) 503
Ethnic Racial Review (US ISSN 0735-6471) 503
Ethnic Review (US) 503
Ethnic Studies Information Guide Series (US) 1153
Ethnike Trapeza tes Hellados. Apologismos see National Bank of Greece. Annual Report 230
Ethnodisc Journal of Recorded Sound (US ISSN 0364-9210) 835
Ethnodisc Recordings see Ethnodisc Journal of Recorded Sound 835
Ethnographic Review see Neprajzi Ertesito 74
Ethnographica (GW ISSN 0071-1837) 71
Ethnographical Museum of Sweden. Monograph Series (SW ISSN 0081-5632) 71
Ethnologia Europaea (DK ISSN 0425-4597) 71
Ethnologia Polona (PL ISSN 0137-4079) 503
Ethnologia Scandinavica (SW ISSN 0348-9698) 71
Ethnologia Slavica (CS) 581
Ethnologica Scandinavica (SW) 71
Ethos (AG ISSN 0325-5387) 878
Ethos see Ethos Annual 1007
Ethos Annual (AT) 1007
Ethylene and Derivatives see World Ethylene and Derivatives 325
Etienne Gilson Series (CN ISSN 0708-319X) 878
Etnografia (PL ISSN 0209-2077) 515
Etnografski Muzej na Cetinju. Glasnik (YU) 71
Etnografski Muzej u Beogradu. Glasnik (YU) 71
Etnologia see Studi Etno-Antropologici 76
Etnologia-Antropologia Culturale (IT) 71
Etnologie et Traditions Populaires de l'Iran/Mardom Sensai Va Farhange-e Amme-e Iran (IR) 503, 515
Etnologiska Studier (SW) 71
Ettela'at Va Tazeha-Ye Fanni see Informations et Nouveautes Techniques 992
Ettore Majorana International Science Series. Life Sciences (US) 140
Etude des Conditions Economiques et Sociales en Afrique see Survey of Economic and Social Conditions in Africa 264
Etude sur la Situation Financiere des Regions see Situation Financiere des Regions de Province en (Year) 249
Etudes a l'Etranger see Study Abroad 442
Etudes Aequatoria (ZR) 71, 694
Etudes Baudelairiennes (SZ ISSN 0531-9455) 721, 741

Etudes Celtiques (FR) 694
Etudes Cinematographiques (FR ISSN 0014-1992) 823, 1077
Etudes d'Histoire Africaine/Studies in African History (ZR ISSN 0071-1993) 566
Etudes d'Histoire de l'Art (BE ISSN 0071-1969) 104
Etudes d'Histoire Economique et Sociale (BE ISSN 0071-1977) 251
Etudes de Droit Libanais see Proche-Orient Etudes Juridiques 662
Etudes de Logique Juridique (BE) 655
Etudes de Philologie, d'Archeologie et d'Histoire Ancienne (BE ISSN 0071-1926) 694
Etudes de Philologie et d'Histoire (SZ ISSN 0071-1934) 581, 721
Etudes de Pollution Atmospherique a Paris et dans les Departments Peripheriques (FR ISSN 0071-1942) 496
Etudes Eburneennes (IV ISSN 0423-5673) 71
Etudes et Documentation de la R.T.A. (FR) 1091
Etudes et Documents Missionnaires see Missionswissenschaftliche Abhandlungen und Texte 971
Etudes et Travaux d'Archeologie Marocaine (MR ISSN 0071-2027) 86
Etudes Ethno-Linguistiques Maghreb-Sahara (FR ISSN 0757-7699) 71, 694
Etudes Finno-Ougriennes (FR ISSN 0071-2051) 694, 721
Etudes Gregoriennes (FR ISSN 0071-2086) 835, 969
Etudes Historiques (HU ISSN 0071-2108) 557
Etudes Historiques (BU ISSN 0525-0846) 581
Etudes Linguistiques (FR ISSN 0071-2124) 694
Etudes Mongoles see Cahiers d'Etudes Mongoles et Siberiennes 70
Etudes Nervaliennes et Romantiques (BE) 694
Etudes Nigeriennes (NG) 71
Etudes Orientales (BE ISSN 0531-1926) 851
Etudes Picardes (FR ISSN 0071-2140) 1153
Etudes Prehistoriques (FR) 86
Etudes Preliminaires aux Religions Orientales dans l'Empire Romain (NE ISSN 0531-1950) 851, 969
Etudes Rabelaisiennes (SZ) 721
Etudes Romanes de Lund (SW) 694
Etudes Savoisiennes (FR) 581
Etudes Senegalaises (SG) 566, 1026
Etudes Strategiques et Militaires (Collection) (CN ISSN 0712-7561) 126, 709
Etudes sur l'Egypte et le Soudan Anciens see Habitats et Societes Urbaines en Egypte et au Soudan 566
Etudes sur l'Enseignement des Mathematiques see Studies in Mathematics Education 442
Etudes sur le Judaisme Medieval (NE) 976
Etudes Teilhardiennes/Teilhardian Studies (FR ISSN 0082-2612) 969
Etudes Universitaires sur l'Integration Europeenne/University Studies on European Integration (EI ISSN 0071-2213) 915
Etudiants des Hautes Ecoles Suisses see Studenten an der Schwiez. Hochschulen 438
Etudos Anglo-Hispanico see Mimesis 727
Etyka (PL ISSN 0014-2263) 878
Eucarpia (NE ISSN 0071-2221) 156
Eulenspiegel-Jahrbuch (GW ISSN 0531-2159) 515, 722
Eurail Guide (US ISSN 0085-0330) 1094, 1108
EURATOM Information see Euro Abstracts Section I. Euratom and EEC Research 892
Eureka: the Archimedean's Journal (UK ISSN 0071-2248) 748
Euro Abstracts see Euro Abstracts Section I. Euratom and EEC Research 892

Euro Abstracts Section I. Euratom and EEC Research (EI) 5, 892
Euro Abstracts Section II. Coal and Steel (EI ISSN 0378-3472) 5, 801, 822
Euro Cooperation; Economic Studies on Europe (FR ISSN 0302-0622) 194
Euro Kompass Denmark. Chemicals see Kompass Select Export. Chemical Industry 257
Euro Kompass Denmark. Construction see Kompass Select Export. Building Construction, Contractors 257
Euro Kompass Denmark. Electrical and Electronic Equipment see Kompass Select Export. Electrical and Electronic Equipment 257
Euro Kompass Denmark. Foods and Beverages see Kompass Select Export. Food Industry 257
Euro Kompass Denmark. Furniture see Kompass Select Export. Furniture 257
Euro Kompass Denmark. Machinery see Kompass Select Export. Machine Industry 257
Euro Kompass Denmark. Metal see Kompass Select Export. Metal Products 257
Euro Kompass Denmark. Paper and Graphic Arts see Kompass Select Export. Paper Industry, Graphic Arts 257
Euro Kompass Denmark. Plastics and Rubber see Kompass Select Export. Rubber Industry, Plastics Industry 257
Euro Kompass Denmark. Scientific and Industrial Instruments see Kompass Select Export. Scientific and Industrial Instruments, Watch Industry 257
Euro Kompass Denmark. Services see Kompass Select Export. Business Services 257
Euro Kompass Denmark. Textiles, Clothing and Footwear see Kompass Select Export. Textiles, Clothing and Footwear 258
Euro Kompass Denmark. Transport Equipment see Kompass Select Export. Transport Equipment 258
Euro Kompass Denmark. Wood Industry see Kompass Select Export. Wood Industry 258
Euro Kompass U K Industrial Sections (UK) 194
Euro Property see Villa Guide 621
Euro Reports and Studies (UN ISSN 0250-8710) 953
Euroasiatica (IT) 694
EUROFIMA Annual Report see European Company for the Financing of Railway Rolling Stock. Annual Report 1094
Eurofinas. Annual Report see European Federation of Finance House Associations. Annual Report 227
Eurofinas. Conference Proceedings see European Federation of Finance House Associations. Conference Proceedings 227
Eurographic Seminars (US) 352
Euromonitor Reports on D I Y and Home Improvement Markets see Do-It-Yourself Report 183
Europa. Revue de Presse Europeenne (FR ISSN 0071-2299) 645
Europa Camping und Caravaning. Internationaler Fuehrer (GW ISSN 0071-2272) 1045, 1108
Europa Facile (IT) 1108
Europa Handbuch der Werbegesellschaften (GW ISSN 0085-0349) 15
Europa Year Book (UK ISSN 0071-2302) 462
Europaeische Dokumentation - Schriftenreihe Landwirtschaft see Documentation Europeenne - Serie Agricole 26
Europaeische Ex Libris see Bibliografi over Europaeiske Kunstneres Ex Libris 113
Europaeische Gemeinschaft fuer Kohle und Stahl. Beratender Ausschuss. Jahrbuch see European Coal and Steel Community. Consultative Committee. Yearbook 262

Europaeische Integration -
 Dokumentation (GW ISSN 0723-
 4384) 677
Europaeische Schriften (GW ISSN
 0071-2329) 916
Europaeische Volksmusikinstrumente.
 Handbuch (GE ISSN 0073-0025)
 515, 835
Europaische Bibliographie der Sowjet-
 und Oesteuropastudien see European
 Bibliography of Soviet, East
 European and Slavonic Studies 563
Europe (Year) (US) 1108
Europe de Tradition Orale (FR ISSN
 0755-9313) 71, 694
Europe for Business Travelers (US)
 194, 1108
Europe in the Middle Ages (NE) 581
Europe Laitiere (FR) 62
Europe-Latin America Report: Science
 and Technology (US) 991, 1068
Europe on Twenty-Five Dollars a Day
 (US) 1108
Europe Review (UK) 244
European Academy of Allergy.
 Proceedings (NE ISSN 0531-2612)
 773
European and Mediterranean Plant
 Protection Organization. Publications.
 Series B: Plant Health Newsletter
 (FR ISSN 0071-2396) 55
European and North American Scrap
 Directory (UK ISSN 0261-426X)
 797
European Art Exhibitions. Catalog (FR
 ISSN 0071-2426) 105
European Aspects, Law Series (FR
 ISSN 0531-2671) 655
European Aspects, Social Studies
 Series(FR ISSN 0531-2663) 1026
European Association for American
 Studies Newsletter see E A A S
 Newsletter 915
European Association for Animal
 Production. Publications (IT ISSN
 0071-2477) 65
European Association for Animal
 Production. Symposia on Energy
 Metabolism (IT ISSN 0071-2485)
 65
European Association for Personnel
 Management. Congress Reports (FR
 ISSN 0071-2493) 286
European Association for Potato
 Research. Proceedings of the
 Triennial Conference see E A P R
 Abstracts of Conference Papers 55
European Association for Potato
 Research Abstracts of Conference
 Papers see E A P R Abstracts of
 Conference Papers 55
European Association for Research on
 Plant Breeding. Report of the
 Congress see Eucarpia 156
European Association of Exploration
 Geophysicists. Constitution and By-
 Laws, Membership List. (UK ISSN
 0531-2728) 399
European Atomic Energy Community.
 Contamination Radioactive des
 Denrees Alimentaires dans les Pays
 de la Communaute (EI) 953
European Atomic Energy Community.
 Resultats des Mesures de la
 Radioactivite Ambiante dans les Pays
 de la Communaute: Air-Retombee-
 Eaux (EI) 953
European Banks International Banks.
 Annual Review see E B I C Banks.
 Annual Review 1152
European Bibliography of Soviet, East
 European and Slavonic Studies/
 Bibliographie Europeene des Travaux
 sur l'URSS et l'Europe de l'Est/
 Europaische Bibliographie der
 Sowjet- und Oesteuropastudien (FR
 ISSN 0140-492X) 126, 563
European Book Plates see Bibliografi
 over Europaeiske Kunstneres Ex
 Libris 113
European Bookdealers (UK ISSN
 0071-2523) 961
European Brewery Convention.
 Proceedings of the International
 Congress (NE ISSN 0071-2531)
 119

European Broadcasting Union
 Monographs, Legal and
 Administrative Series see E B U
 Monographs, Legal and
 Administrative Series 348
European Broadcasting Union Seminars
 for Producers and Directors of
 Educational Television for Schools
 and Adults see E B U Seminars for
 Producers and Directors of
 Educational Television for Schools
 and Adults 348
European Broadcasting Union
 Workshops for Producers and
 Directors of Television Programmes
 for Children and Young People see E
 B U Workshops for Producers and
 Directors of Television Programmes
 for Children and Young People 348
European Cement Association.
 European Annual Review (FR) 188
European Cement Association.
 Statistical Review see European
 Cement Association. World
 Statistical Review 189
European Cement Association. World
 Statistical Review (FR) 189
European Chemical Buyer's Guide
 (UK) 1153
European Civil Aviation Conference
 (Report of Session) (UN ISSN
 0071-2558) 1088
European Co-Operation (FR ISSN
 0589-9575) 670
European Coal and Steel Community.
 Consultative Committee. Handbook
 (EI) 262
European Coal and Steel Community.
 Consultative Committee. Yearbook
 (EI ISSN 0423-6831) 262
European Coal and Steel Community.
 Organe Permanent pour la Securite
 dans les Mines de Houille. Rapport
 see Mines Safety and Health
 Commission. Report 818
European Colloquium on Renal
 Physiology (Proceedings) (SW) 795
European Communities and Other
 European Organizations Who's Who
 (BE ISSN 0771-7911) 134, 308
European Communities Index see E C
 Index 207
European Community Update see E C
 Update 1152
European Companies (UK ISSN 0071-
 2582) 207
European Company for the Financing
 of Railway Rolling Stock. Annual
 Report (SZ ISSN 0071-2264) 1094
European Conference of Local and
 Regional Authorities. Official Reports
 of Debates (FR) 941
European Conference of Local and
 Regional Authorities. Texts Adopted
 (FR) 941
European Conference of Local
 Authorities. Official Reports of
 Debates see European Conference of
 Local and Regional Authorities.
 Official Reports of Debates 941
European Conference of Local
 Authorities. Texts Adopted see
 European Conference of Local and
 Regional Authorities. Texts Adopted
 941
European Conference on
 Microcirculation. Proceedings see
 Bibliotheca Anatomica 758
European Conference on Mixing and
 Centrifugal Separation. Proceedings
 (UK ISSN 0140-2129) 478
European Congress of Anaesthesiology.
 Proceedings (SP ISSN 0071-2671)
 774
European Congress of Cardiology.
 Abstracts of Papers (NE ISSN
 0421-7527) 776
European Congress of Cardiology.
 (Proceedings) (NE ISSN 0423-7242)
 776
European Congress on Electron
 Microscopy (IS ISSN 0071-2647)
 169
European Congress on Sleep Research.
 Proceedings see Sleep 1162
European Convention on Human
 Rights. Yearbook (NE ISSN 0071-
 2701) 913

European Coordination Centre for
 Research and Documentation in
 Social Sciences. Publications (GW
 ISSN 0071-271X) 1008
European Cotton Industry Statistics (IT
 ISSN 0423-7269) 1075
European Court of Human Rights.
 Publications. Series A: Judgments
 and Decisions/Cour Europeenne des
 Droits de l'Homme. Publications.
 Serie A: Arrets et Decisions (GW
 ISSN 0073-3903) 913
European Court of Human Rights.
 Publications. Series B: Pleadings,
 Oral Arguments and Documents/
 Cour Europeenne des Droits de
 l'Homme. Publications. Serie B:
 Memoires, Plaidoiries et Documents
 (GW ISSN 0073-3911) 913
European Directory of Agrochemical
 Products (UK) 27, 322
European Directory of Paints and
 Allied Products see Chatfield's
 European Directory of Paints and
 Allied Products 855
European Economic Community
 Savings Bank Group. Report (EI)
 227
European Electrical & Electronic
 Engineering (GW) 453
European Environmental Yearbook see
 Annuario Europeo dell'Ambiente
 494
European Federation for Intercultural
 Learning Documentation see E F I L
 Documentation 441
European Federation of Finance House
 Associations. Annual Report (BE
 ISSN 0071-2787) 227
European Federation of Finance House
 Associations. Conference
 Proceedings(BE ISSN 0071-2795)
 227
European Free Trade Association.
 Annual Report (SZ ISSN 0531-
 4127) 255
European Free Trade Association Trade
 see E F T A Trade 255
European Glass Directory and Buyer's
 Guide (UK ISSN 0306-204X) 320
European Grassland Federation.
 Proceedings of the General Meeting
 (BE ISSN 0071-2825) 55
European Illustration (UK) 105
European Incoherent Scatter Scientific
 Association. Annual Report (SW)
 900
European Incoherent Scatter Scientific
 Association Technical Note see E I S
 C A T Technical Note 900
European Institute for Social Security
 Yearbook see E I S S Yearbook
 1017
European Institute on the Prevention
 and Treatment of Alcoholism.
 Selected Papers see International
 Institute on the Prevention and
 Treatment of Alcoholism. Selected
 Papers 377
European Investment Bank. Annual
 Report (EI ISSN 0071-2868) 227
European Journal of Respiratory
 Diseases. Supplementum (DK ISSN
 0106-4347) 793
European League for Economic
 Cooperation. Publications (BE ISSN
 0071-2884) 262
European League for Economic
 Cooperation. Report of the Secretary
 General on the Activities of
 E.L.E.C.(BE ISSN 0531-7436) 262
European League for Economic
 Cooperation. Reports of the
 International Congress (BE ISSN
 0071-2892) 262
European Leather Guide see Leather
 Guide 672
European Literary Market Place see
 International Literary Market Place
 962
European Marketing Data and
 Statistics(UK ISSN 0071-2930) 283
European Markets: a Guide to
 Company and Industry Information
 Sources (US) 255, 308
European Microwave Conference
 Proceedings (UK) 453

European Monographs in Health
 Education Research (UK ISSN
 0143-5094) 885
European Monographs in Social
 Psychology (US) 934
European Ophtalmological Society.
 Congress Acta (NE ISSN 0301-
 326X) 785
European Organisation for Civil
 Aviation Electronics. General
 Assembly. Annual Report (FR ISSN
 0531-7444) 18, 453
European Organization for Nuclear
 Research. Liste des Publications
 Scientifiques/List of Scientific
 Publications (SZ ISSN 0304-2871)
 126, 892
European Organization for Nuclear
 Research. Repertoire des
 Communications Scientifiques. Index
 of Scientific Publications see
 European Organization for Nuclear
 Research. Liste des Publications
 Scientifiques/List of Scientific
 Publications 892
European Organization for Quality
 Control. Conference Proceedings (SZ
 ISSN 0071-2981) 809
European Organization for Research on
 Treatment of Cancer. Monograph
 Series (US) 775
European Parliament. Committee
 Report (EI) 796
European Parliament. Documents de
 Seance see European Parliament.
 Working Documents 670
European Parliament. Selected
 Documents see European Parliament.
 Committee Report 796
European Parliament. Working
 Documents (EI) 670
European Parliament News see E P
 News 670
European Passenger Train Timetable
 Conference Minutes (SZ ISSN
 0071-3120) 1081
European Patent Office. Annual
 Report(GW ISSN 0170-9291) 861
European Patents Handbook (UK) 861
European Petroleum Directory (US
 ISSN 0275-3871) 864
European Petroleum Yearbook/
 Jahrbuch der Europaeischen
 Erdoelindustrie/Annuaire Europeen
 du Petrole (GW ISSN 0342-6947)
 864
European Photography (UK) 884
European Plastics Buyers Guide (UK
 ISSN 0306-5502) 1153
European Racing Manual (IT) 1153
European Regional Incentives (UK)
 244
European Research Centres (UK) 308,
 991, 1068
European Rig- and Supply Ship
 Owners(NO) 308, 1100
European Scrap Directory see European
 and North American Scrap Directory
 797
European Social Fund. Annual Report
 on the Activities of the New
 European Social Fund (EI) 444
European Socialist Thought Series (UK)
 904
European Solid State Device Research
 Conference. Solid State Devices
 (UK) 900
European Sources of Scientific and
 Technical Information (UK) 991,
 1068
European Southern Observatory.
 Annual Report (GW ISSN 0531-
 4496) 115
European Southern Observatory
 Foelgeforskning see E S O
 Foelgeforskning 115
European Space Agency
 Foelgeforskning see E S A
 Foelgeforskning 18
European Space Agency Scientific-
 Technical Reports, Notes and
 Memoranda see E S A Scientific-
 Technical Reports, Notes and
 Memoranda 18
European Studies in Law (NE) 655

European Symposium on Chemical Reaction Engineering. Proceedings *see* International Symposium on Chemical Reaction Engineering. Proceedings *478*
European Symposium on Concrete Pavements. Reports (FR) *481*
European Tableware Buyers Guide (UK) *113*
European Travel Guide for Jews *see* Guide Touristique Europeen pour Israelites *503*
European Yearbook (NE ISSN 0071-3139) *126*
Europe's 10000 Largest Companies *see* Europe's 15000 Largest Companies *289*
Europe's 15000 Largest Companies (UK ISSN 0800-0638) *289*
Europhysics Conference Abstracts (SZ) *888*
Europlastics Year Book *see* European Plastics Buyers Guide *1153*
Euroski (IT) *1033*
Evaluation Comment (US) *413*, *1026*
Evaluation Methods Series *see* U.S. Civil Service Commission. Bureau of Personnel Management Evaluation. Evaluation Methods Series *287*
Evaluation Studies Review Annual (US ISSN 0364-7390) *1008*
Evangelical Baptist Churches in Canada. Fellowship Yearbook (CN ISSN 0317-266X) *978*
Evangelisch-Lutherisch Missionswerk in Niedersachsen. Jahrbuch (Year) (GW) *978*
Evangelische Mission Jahrbuch *see* Jahrbuch Mission *970*
Evangelische Studentengemeinde in der Bundesrepublik Deutschland und Berlin (West) Nachrichten *see* E S G - Nachrichten *969*
Evening Times Wee Red Book (UK) *1038*
Evensongs/Yeh Ko (CH) *710*
Eventi e Interventi (IT) *105*, *722*
Evento Teatrale. Sezione: Autori Italiani del Novecento (IT) *1077*
Everybody's Money Complaint Directory for Consumers (US ISSN 0732-0485) *369*
Everymans Own Lawyer (UK) *655*
Everyman's United Nations *see* Everyone's United Nations *916*
Everyone's United Nations (UN) *916*
Evolutionary Biology (US ISSN 0071-3260) *167*
Evolutionary Monographs (US) *71*, *140*
Evolutionary Theory (US ISSN 0093-4755) *71*, *140*
Evphrosyne (PO ISSN 0870-0133) *337*
Ex Libris d'Europe *see* Bibliografi over Europaeiske Kunstneres Ex Libris *113*
Exact Science and Technology. Life Sciences. Lexicon *see* Science Exactes et Technologie. Sciences de la Vie. Lexique *146*
Excavaciones Arqueologicas en Espana (SP ISSN 0071-3279) *86*
Excavation of the Roman Forts of the Classis Britannica at Dover 1970-1977 (UK ISSN 0141-2264) *86*
Excavations at Dura-Europos (US ISSN 0071-3287) *86*
Exceptional Child (AT ISSN 0156-6555) *444*
Excerpta Botanica. Sectio A: Taxonomica et Chorologica (GW ISSN 0014-4037) *156*
Excerpta Botanica. Sectio B: Sociologica (GW ISSN 0014-4045) *156*
Excerpta Indonesica *see* E I *79*
Excerpta Medica. Section 1: Anatomy, Anthropology, Embryology & Histology (NE ISSN 0014-4053) *5*, *79*, *150*, *769*
Excerpta Medica. Section 2: Physiology(NE ISSN 0014-4061) *5*, *150*, *769*
Excerpta Medica. Section 3: Endocrinology (NE ISSN 0014-407X) *5*, *769*

Excerpta Medica. Section 4: Microbiology: Bacteriology, Mycology and Parasitology (NE) *5*, *150*, *769*
Excerpta Medica. Section 4: Microbiology-Bacteriology, Virology, Mycology and Parasitology *see* Excerpta Medica. Section 4: Microbiology: Bacteriology, Mycology and Parasitology *769*
Excerpta Medica. Section 5: General Pathology and Pathological Anatomy(NE ISSN 0014-4096) *5*, *150*, *769*
Excerpta Medica. Section 6: Internal Medicine (NE ISSN 0014-410X) *5*, *769*
Excerpta Medica. Section 7: Pediatrics *see* Excerpta Medica. Section 7: Pediatrics and Pediatric Surgery *769*
Excerpta Medica. Section 7: Pediatrics and Pediatric Surgery (NE) *5*, *769*
Excerpta Medica. Section 8: Neurology and Neurosurgery (NE ISSN 0014-4126) *5*, *769*
Excerpta Medica. Section 9: Surgery (NE ISSN 0014-4134) *5*, *769*
Excerpta Medica. Section 10: Obstetrics and Gynecology (NE ISSN 0014-4142) *5*, *769*
Excerpta Medica. Section 11: Otorhinolaryngology (NE ISSN 0014-4150) *5*, *769*
Excerpta Medica. Section 12: Ophthalmology (NE ISSN 0014-4169) *5*, *770*
Excerpta Medica. Section 13: Dermatology and Venereology (NE ISSN 0014-4177) *5*, *770*
Excerpta Medica. Section 14: Radiology(NE ISSN 0014-4185) *5*, *770*
Excerpta Medica. Section 15: Chest Diseases, Thoracic Surgery and Tuberculosis (NE ISSN 0014-4193) *5*, *770*
Excerpta Medica. Section 16: Cancer (NE ISSN 0014-4207) *5*, *770*
Excerpta Medica. Section 17: Public Health, Social Medicine & Hygiene (NE ISSN 0014-4215) *5*, *770*, *958*
Excerpta Medica. Section 19: Rehabilitation and Physical Medicine(NE ISSN 0014-4231) *5*, *770*
Excerpta Medica. Section 20: Gerontology and Geriatrics (NE ISSN 0014-424X) *5*, *552*, *770*
Excerpta Medica. Section 23: Nuclear Medicine (NE ISSN 0014-4274) *5*, *770*
Excerpta Medica. Section 24: Anesthesiology (NE ISSN 0014-4282) *5*, *770*
Excerpta Medica. Section 25: Hematology (NE ISSN 0014-4290) *5*, *770*
Excerpta Medica. Section 26: Immunology, Serology and Transplantation (NE ISSN 0014-4304) *5*, *770*
Excerpta Medica. Section 27: Biophysics, Bio-Engineering and Medical Instrumentation (NE ISSN 0014-4312) *5*, *150*, *770*
Excerpta Medica. Section 28: Urology and Nephrology (NE ISSN 0014-4320) *5*, *770*
Excerpta Medica. Section 29: Biochemistry *see* Excerpta Medica. Section 29: Clinical Biochemistry *770*
Excerpta Medica. Section 29: Clinical Biochemistry (NE ISSN 0300-5372) *5*, *150*, *770*
Excerpta Medica. Section 31: Arthritis and Rheumatism (NE ISSN 0014-4355) *5*, *770*
Excerpta Medica. Section 32: Psychiatry (NE ISSN 0014-4363) *5*, *770*
Excerpta Medica. Section 33: Orthopedic Surgery (NE ISSN 0014-4371) *5*, *770*
Excerpta Medica. Section 34: Plastic Surgery (NE ISSN 0014-438X) *5*, *770*

Excerpta Medica. Section 35: Occupational Health and Industrial Medicine (NE ISSN 0014-4398) *5*, *770*, *958*
Excerpta Medica. Section 36: Health Economics and Hospital Management (NE ISSN 0300-5321) *5*, *619*, *770*
Excerpta Medica. Section 38: Adverse Reactions Titles (NE ISSN 0001-8848) *5*, *770*
Excerpta Medica. Section 46: Environmental Health *see* Excerpta Medica. Section 46: Environmental Health and Pollution Control *501*
Excerpta Medica. Section 46: Environmental Health and Pollution Control (NE ISSN 0300-5194) *5*, *501*, *770*, *958*
Excerpta Medica. Section 47: Virology (NE ISSN 0304-4084) *5*, *150*, *770*
Excerpta Medica. Section 48: Gastroenterology (NE ISSN 0031-3580) *5*, *770*
Excerpta Medica. Section 49: Forensic Science (NE ISSN 0031-0743) *5*, *770*
Excerpta Medica. Section 50: Epilepsy (NE ISSN 0303-8459) *5*, *770*
Excerpta Medica. Section 51: Leprosy and Related Subjects (NE ISSN 0165-2222) *5*, *770*
Exchange of Information on Research in European Law/Echange d'Informations sur les Recherches en Droit Europeen (FR ISSN 0252-0648) *668*
Exchange Rate Movements Year Book (UK ISSN 0262-7663) *1153*
Excited States (US ISSN 0093-1713) *322*
Execution and Control Systems (US ISSN 0736-8305) *356*, *358*
Executive (PK) *279*
Executive Bio-Pictorial Directory (US) *605*, *904*
Executive Compensation Service. Reports on International Compensation. Argentina (US ISSN 0095-4144) *279*
Executive Compensation Service. Reports on International Compensation. Brazil (US) *271*, *279*
Executive Compensation Service. Reports on International Compensation. Puerto Rico (US ISSN 0090-9971) *279*
Executive Compensation Service. Technician Report (US ISSN 0093-8750) *271*, *279*
Executive Grapevine (UK) *279*
Executive Memorandum (US) *916*
Executive Pensions (UK) *639*
Executives Guide to Information Sources *see* Encyclopedia of Business Information Sources *279*
Exercise and Sport Sciences Reviews (US ISSN 0091-6331) *793*
Exercise Physiology (US ISSN 0748-3155) *846*, *886*
Exeter's Studies in American & Commonwealth Arts (UK) *105*, *722*, *835*
Exile (US ISSN 0421-9090) *722*
Exit (US ISSN 0195-3516) *722*
Exit *see* V E S Newsletter *1030*
Exlibriskunst und Graphik *see* Exlibriskunst und Graphik. Jahrbuch *105*
Exlibriskunst und Graphik. Jahrbuch (GW ISSN 0172-2859) *105*
Expatriate Survival Kit (UK) *227*
Expatriate's Guide to Retiring Abroad (UK) *227*
Expatriate's Guide to Savings and Investment (UK ISSN 0263-1229) *266*
Expectations (US) *180*, *335*
Expense Analysis: Condominiums, Cooperatives and Planned Unit Developments (US ISSN 0191-2208) *965*
Experientia. Supplementum (SZ ISSN 0071-335X) *991*, *1068*
Experiment (US ISSN 0014-4770) *741*
Experiment in International Living. Annual Report (US) *441*

Experiment in International Living. President's Report *see* Experiment in International Living. Annual Report *441*
Experiment Theatre (US) *1077*
Experimental and Clinical Psychiatry (US) *789*
Experimental Biology and Medicine (SZ ISSN 0071-3384) *140*, *761*
Experimental Botany; An International Series of Monographs (US ISSN 0071-3392) *156*
Experimental Brain Research. Supplementa (US ISSN 0172-9039) *789*
Experimental Virology (US) *168*
Expert Systems in Government Symposium (US) *354*
Explor (US ISSN 0362-0867) *969*
Exploration (US) *722*, *1108*
Exploration Geophysics (US ISSN 0071-3473) *1153*
Exploration in British Columbia (CN) *385*, *816*
Exploration of the Deep Continental Crust (US) *385*
Explorations in Education (US ISSN 0071-3481) *413*
Explorations in Feminism (UK) *1128*
Explorations in Language Study (UK) *694*
Explorations in Renaissance Culture (US ISSN 0098-2474) *105*, *581*, *722*
Explorations in Sights and Sounds (US ISSN 0733-3323) *503*
Explorations in the World Economy (US) *244*
Explorations in Urban Analysis (UK) *1008*, *1026*
Explore Canada *see* Guide to Canada *1111*
Explore Minnesota Arts and Attractions(US) *1108*
Explore Minnesota Bed and Breakfast/Historic Inns (US) *1108*
Explore Minnesota Biking (US) *1041*, *1108*
Explore Minnesota Campgrounds (US) *1045*, *1108*
Explore Minnesota Canoeing, Backpacking & Hiking (US) *1045*, *1108*
Explore Minnesota Minnetours (US) *543*, *1108*
Explore Minnesota on Skis (US) *1045*, *1108*
Exploring France (UK) *1108*
Export-Adressbuch von Oesterreich *see* Herold Export-Adressbuch von Oesterreich *309*
Export Canada (CN ISSN 0708-1332) *255*, *308*
Export Data (UK) *255*
Export Data Exporters Year Book *see* Export Data *255*
Export Directory Chile/Directorio de la Exportacion (CL) *308*
Export Directory of Brazil/Guia Brasileiro de Exportacao (BL) *308*
Export Directory of Denmark (DK) *255*
Export Directory/U.S. Buying Guide *see* Exporters Directory/U.S. Buying Guide *255*
Export Documentation Handbook (US ISSN 0276-556X) *1153*
Export Graficas U S A (US ISSN 0741-7160) *855*, *930*
Export Guide to Europe (Year) (UK) *255*
Export-Import Bank of Japan. Annual Report (JA ISSN 0071-3503) *227*, *255*
Export-Import Bank of Korea. Annual Report (KO) *255*
Export-Import Bank of the United States. Annual Report (US ISSN 0270-5109) *227*
Export-Import Bank of the United States. Report to Congress on Export Credit Competition and the Export-Import Bank of the United States (US) *228*

1728 EXPORT-IMPORT BANK

Export-Import Bank of the United States. Semiannual Report to Congress on Export Credit Competition and the Export-Import Bank of the United States *see* Export-Import Bank of the United States. Report to Congress on Export Credit Competition and the Export-Import Bank of the United States *228*

Export-Import Bank of the United States. Statement of Conditions *see* Export-Import Bank of the United States. Annual Report *227*

Export-Import Markets (PR ISSN 0270-5184) *255*

Export Services (UK) *255*

Export Statistical Schedule of Japan (Year) (JA) *255*

Export Statistics of Afghanistan/Ihsa'iyah-i Amual-i Sadirati-i Afghanistan (AF) *207*, *1054*

Exportaciones Britanicas *see* British Exports *253*

Exportadores de Sud Africa *see* South African Exporters *259*

Exportateurs Sud-Africains *see* South African Exporters *259*

Exportations Britanniques *see* British Exports *253*

Exporter Guide - Caribbean and Latin America *see* Export-Import Markets *255*

Exporters Directory/U.S. Buying Guide(US) *255*

Exporters' Encyclopaedia (US ISSN 0732-0159) *255*

Exports by Pennsylvania Manufacturers(US ISSN 0556-3585) *255*

Exports of the Republic of China (CH ISSN 0301-9217) *255*

Expo's Baseball Magazine *see* Expo's Baseball Yearbook *1038*

Expo's Baseball Yearbook (CN) *1038*

Exposition World (US) *284*

Expression (FR ISSN 0014-5327) *105*, *1128*

Expression (AT ISSN 0085-039X) *722*

Extel Issuing House Year Book (UK ISSN 0308-8499) *228*

Extension Bibliografica (BO) *126*, *1014*

Extensions and Corrections to the U D C (NE ISSN 0014-5424) *677*

External Trade of Denmark *see* Danmarks Vareindfoersel og-Udfoersel *206*

External Trade of Liberia: Import and Export (LB) *255*

External Trade Statistics of Gambia (GM) *207*, *1054*

Extra Cover (AT) *1045*

Extra Special Cracked (US) *710*

Extraordinary Contractual Relief Reporter (US) *244*

Exxon Background Series (US) *465*

Eye Care (II ISSN 0255-4062) *785*

F A C E N A (Facultad de Ciencias Exactas y Naturales y Agrimensura) (AG ISSN 0325-4216) *134*, *322*, *856*

F A C: Revista Practica de Medicina (SP ISSN 0210-8852) *761*

F A C: Revista Practica del Estudiante de Medicina *see* F A C: Revista Practica de Medicina *761*

F.A.I. Abstract Service (Fertiliser Association of India) (II ISSN 0014-5564) *5*, *40*

F A M L I (Family Medicine Literature Index) (AT ISSN 0227-2393) *770*

F A O Agricultural Development Paper(UN ISSN 0071-6960) *27*

F A O Agricultural Services Bulletin (Food and Agriculture Organization of the United Nations (FAO)) (UN) *46*

F A O Agricultural Studies *see* F A O Animal Production and Health Series *65*

F A O Animal Production and Health Series (Food and Agriculture Organization of the United Nations) (UN) *65*

F A O Commodity Review and Outlook (UN ISSN 0071-7002) *46*

F A O Economic and Social Development Paper (Food and Agriculture Organization of the United Nations) (UN) *194*, *1026*

F A O Fertilizer and Plant Nutrition Bulletin (Food and Agriculture Organization of the United Nations) (UN) *46*

F A O Fertilizer Yearbook (Food and Agriculture Organization of the United Nations) (UN) *55*

F A O Fisheries Circulars (UN ISSN 0429-9329) *508*

F A O Fisheries Reports (UN ISSN 0429-9337) *508*

F A O Fisheries Series (UN) *509*

F A O Fisheries Studies *see* F A O Fisheries Series *509*

F A O Fisheries Synopsis (Food and Agriculture Organization of the United Nations) (UN) *509*

F A O Fisheries Technical Paper (UN ISSN 0429-9345) *509*

F A O Food and Nutrition Series (UN) *846*

F A O Forestry and Forest Products Studies *see* F A O Forestry Studies *524*

F A O Forestry Studies (Food and Agriculture Organization of the United Nations) (UN) *524*, *529*

F A O Irrigation and Drainage Papers (Food and Agriculture Organization of the United Nations) (UN) *1124*

F A O Legislative Series (UN ISSN 0071-7045) *27*

F A O Manuals in Fisheries Science (UN ISSN 0071-7061) *509*

F A O Nutritional Study *see* F A O Food and Nutrition Series *846*

F A O Regional Conference for Africa (UN ISSN 0429-9353) *27*

F A O Regional Conference for Asia and the Far East. Report *see* F A O Regional Conference for Asia and the Pacific. Report *27*

F A O Regional Conference for Asia and the Pacific. Report (UN) *27*

F A O Regional Conference for Europe. Report of the Conference (UN) *27*

F A O Regional Conference for Latin America. Report *see* F A O Regional Conference for Latin America and the Caribbean. Report *27*

F A O Regional Conference for Latin America and the Caribbean. Report (UN) *27*

F A O Regional Conference for the Near East. Report (UN ISSN 0427-8089) *27*

F A O Terminology Bulletin (UN ISSN 0532-0313) *27*

F A S Handbook (Federation of Astronomical Societies) (UK) *115*

F A T - Bladet (Foreningen af Teleteknikere) (DK ISSN 0108-9048) *1068*

F & O S Executive and Ownership Report (Financial and Operating Statistics) (US) *1105*

F & O S Motor Carrier Annual Report (Financial and Operating Statistics) (US ISSN 0160-4570) *1105*

F and S Europe *see* Predicasts F & S Index Europe *216*

F and S Index Europe *see* Predicasts F & S Index Europe *216*

F and S Index of Corporations and Industries *see* Predicasts F & S Index United States *216*

F and S International *see* Predicasts F & S Index International *216*

F & J Japanese Industry Letter (US) *194*

F & S Reports (US) *194*

F C L Action (Friends Committee on Legislation of California) (US ISSN 0071-9560) *370*, *904*, *1017*

F D A Clinical Experience Abstracts (U.S. Food and Drug Administration) (US ISSN 0429-9442) *518*, *870*

F D A Compliance Policy Guide *see* F D A Compliance Policy Guides. Manual *518*

F D A Compliance Policy Guides. Manual (U.S. Food and Drug Administration) (US) *518*, *870*

F D A Drug Bulletin (US ISSN 0361-4344) *376*

F E & Z N (UK ISSN 0014-5785) *797*

F F Communications (Folklore Fellows) (FI ISSN 0014-5815) *515*

F.H.A. Homes *see* U.S. Federal Housing Administration. F H A Homes *626*

F.H.I. Annual: Fresh and Industrialized Fruits and Vegetables *see* Anuario F.H.I. Argentina: Frutas y Hortalizas Industriarizadas y Frescas *52*

F I A Year Book of Automobile Sport (FR) *1091*

F.I.D./C.R. Report Series (International Federation for Documentation) (GW ISSN 0074-5804) *689*

F I D Directory (International Federation for Documentation) (NE ISSN 0379-3680) *677*

F I D I C International Directory of Consulting Engineers (UK) *308*, *471*

F I D/R I Meetings Reports (International Federation for Documentation, Committee on Research on the Theoretical Basis of Information) (NE) *677*

F I D/R I Series of Collected Articles *see* F I D/R I Series on Problems of Information Science *677*

F I D/R I Series on Problems of Information Science (International Federation for Documentation, Committee on Research on the Theoretical Basis of Information) (NE ISSN 0203-6495) *677*

F I D Yearbook *see* F I D Directory *677*

F I S Frettabref (Felag Islenzkra Storkaupmanna) (IC) *308*

F I W - Schriftenreihe (Forschunginstitut fuer Wirtschaftsverfassung und Wettbewerb e.V.) (GW ISSN 0071-769X) *194*

F J C C *see* Fall Joint Computer Conference. Proceedings *355*

F L C Newsletter *see* F L I C C Newsletter *677*

F L I C C Newsletter (Federal Library and Information Center Committee) (US ISSN 0882-908X) *677*

F L I R T Newsletter *see* Federal Librarian *677*

F M Compilation of the Statutes of Canada (CN ISSN 0380-2639) *655*

F M I Annual Financial Review (US) *522*

F M I Monthly Index Service *see* Reference Point: Food Industry Abstracts *522*

F M U Occasional Lectures (Financial Management Unit) (II ISSN 0085-1795) *941*

F.N.P.P. Annuaire *see* Federation Nationale de la Photographie Profesionelle. Annuaire *884*

F O B Colon Free Zone (PN) *239*

F P A P Biennial Report (Family Planning Association of Pakistan) (PK) *179*

F R A M (Fra Ringkoebing Amts Museer) (DK ISSN 0108-3643) *827*

F R V Kapala Cruise Report (Fisheries Research Vessel) (AT) *509*

F S U Faculty Publications *see* Florida State University. Publications of the Faculty *435*

F T A Yearbook (Freight Transport Association Ltd.) (UK) *1081*

F T C S *see* International Symposium on Fault-Tolerant Computing. Digest of Papers *352*

F W S Series (US) *524*

Faaborg-Aarbogen (DK ISSN 0106-8822) *581*

Faaborg-Bogen *see* Faaborg-Aarbogen *581*

Faaglar i Kvismaren (SW ISSN 0283-2852) *170*

Faba Bean Abstracts (UK ISSN 0260-8456) *6*, *40*

Fabian Research Series (UK ISSN 0305-3555) *904*

Fabian Society. Annual Report (UK ISSN 0071-3570) *904*

Fabula Press Award Reader (GW) *710*

Fabulous Mexico (US ISSN 0429-9639) *1108*

Face to Face with Talent (CN) *348*, *835*, *1077*

Facena *see* F A C E N A *134*

Facetten (AU) *722*

Fachberichte Messen - Steuern - Regeln(US ISSN 0172-5203) *1068*

Fachberichte Simulation (US) *352*

Fachliteratur zum Buch- und Bibliothekswesen/International Bibliography of the Book Trade and Librarianship (GW ISSN 0071-3627) *677*, *961*

Fachschwester - Fachpfleger (US ISSN 0172-5238) *784*

Facilities Directory/Repertoire des Salles de Spectacle (CN) *375*, *835*, *1077*

Facility Manager's Buyer's Guide *see* Buyers' Guide for the Mass Entertainment Industry *1044*

Facolta di Scienze Nautiche. Annali (IT) *1041*, *1100*

Fact Book (US) *413*

Fact Book. Alabama Institutions of Higher Education, Universities and Colleges *see* Fact Book. Higher Education in Alabama *434*

Fact Book. Higher Education in Alabama (US) *434*

Fact Book for Academic Administrators *see* Fact Book for Higher Education *435*

Fact Book for Higher Education (US) *435*

Fact Book on Higher Education in the South (US ISSN 0191-1643) *435*

Fact Book on Theological Education (US) *969*

Fact Paper on Southern Africa (UK) *904*

Fact Sheet on the Netherlands (NE) *1017*

Fact Sheets on Institutional Racism (US) *913*, *1026*

Fact Sheets on Institutional Sexism (US) *913*

Factbook: Chartered Banks of Canada *see* Bank Facts: Chartered Banks of Canada *224*

Factbook on the Philippine Financial System (PH) *228*

Factory Outlet Shopping Guide for New England (US) *369*

Factotum (UK ISSN 0141-3635) *677*, *930*

Facts About Alaska *see* Alaska Almanac: Facts About Alaska *1106*

Facts About Blacks (US) *503*

Facts About Haryana (II) *1055*

Facts about Lewisham (UK ISSN 0261-9911) *1153*

Facts About Maryland Public Education *see* Fact Book *413*

Facts About Maryland Schools *see* Fact Book *413*

Facts About New Supermarkets *see* Facts About Store Development *522*

Facts About States for the Dentist Seeking a Location (US ISSN 0517-1024) *779*

Facts About Store Development (US ISSN 0732-233X) *522*

Facts and Advice for Airline Passengers(US) *953*, *1088*, *1108*

Facts and Comparisons (US) *870*

Facts & Figures (AU) *262*, *465*, *864*

Facts and Figures on Footwear *see* Footwear Manual *1005*

Facts and Figures on Government Finance (US ISSN 0071-3678) *295*

Facts & Views *see* Yugoslav Facts and Views *920*

Facts, Medicine and Health Care, Denmark *see* Tal og Data, Medicin og Sundhedsvaesen *873*

Facts om Danmark (DK ISSN 0108-996X) *543*

Facts on File. Yearbook (US ISSN 0196-0040) *563*, *904*

Facts on Women at Work in Australia (AT) *271*, *1128*

Factsheet Denmark (DK ISSN 0107-6183) *503*

Factuelles (FR) *934*

Faculdade de Ciencias Farmaceuticas de Araraquara. Revista *see* Revista de Ciencias Farmaceuticas *872*

Faculdade de Filosofia, Ciencias e Letras de Araraquara. Cadeira de Sociologia e Fundamentos Sociologicos da Educao. Boletim (BL) *1153*
Facultad de Ciencias Exactas y Naturales y Agrimensura *see* F A C E N A *134*
Facultad Nacional de Agronomia Medellin (CK ISSN 0304-2847) *27, 140, 524, 745*
Faculte de Droit de Namur. Travaux (BE) *655*
Faculty of Actuaries in Scotland. Transactions (UK ISSN 0071-3686) *639*
Faculty of Architects & Surveyors Diary (UK) *98*
Faculty of Building. Register of Members. (UK) *184*
Faellesraadet Vedroerende Mineraliske Raastoffer i Groenland. Beretning (DK ISSN 0107-3117) *816*
Faellesudvalget for Statens Mejeri- og Husdyrbrugsforsog. Beretning (DK) *62*
Faellesudvalget til Kaninavlens Fremme Beretning (DK ISSN 0900-288X) *65*
Faeroesk Lovregister (DK ISSN 0108-142X) *655*
Fag Rag (US ISSN 0046-3167) *615*
Fagpressenoeglen (DK ISSN 0108-2027) *645*
Fair Credit Reporting Manual (US) *228*
Fairchild's Financial Manual of Retail Stores (US ISSN 0071-3716) *284*
Fairchild's Textile & Apparel Financial Directory (US) *340, 1074*
Fairfield Experimental Horticulture Station. Summary Annual Review (UK ISSN 0260-8081) *532*
Fairplay Marine Computing Guide (UK ISSN 0267-0879) *357, 1100*
Fairplay World Ports Directory (UK ISSN 0261-2356) *1100*
Fairplay World Shipping Year Book (UK ISSN 0140-5047) *1100*
Faith and Order Papers (SZ ISSN 0512-2589) *969*
Fajabefa Nyt (DK ISSN 0105-5933) *835*
Falconer's Current Drug Handbook (US ISSN 0272-197X) *870*
Falkland Islands Journal (FK ISSN 0256-1824) *1108*
Fall Joint Computer Conference. Proceedings (US) *355*
Falmouth Port and Industry Handbook 1984 (UK ISSN 0260-9282) *308, 1100*
Familien Danmarks Forbruger. Haandbog (DK ISSN 0900-2049) *369*
Familien-Kalender (GW) *376*
Familiengeschichtliche Blaetter (GW ISSN 0427-9522) *535*
Familienkundliches Jahrbuch Schleswig-Holstein (GW ISSN 0430-0440) *535*
Familienverband Avenarius. Familienzeitschrift (GW ISSN 0014-7176) *535*
Family Associations, Societies & Reunions (US) *535*
Family Expenditure Survey (IS) *1055*
Family Genealogies (CN ISSN 0227-0994) *535*
Family Guide on Where to Go (UK) *1108*
Family Holiday Guide (UK ISSN 0071-3740) *1108*
Family Law Reports (AT ISSN 0706-7666) *655*
Family Medicine Literature Index *see* F A M L I *770*
Family Newsletter Directory *see* Hilborn's Family Newsletter Directory *536*
Family Notes *see* Family Notes: a Journal of the Hueck Families *535*
Family Notes: a Journal of the Hueck Families (GW) *535*
Family Physician's Compendium of Drug Therapy (US ISSN 0276-4318) *870*
Family Planning Association of India. Report (II ISSN 0377-7774) *179*

Family Planning Association of Kenya. Annual Report (KE) *179*
Family Planning Association of Pakistan. Annual Report *see* F P A P Biennial Report *179*
Family Planning Association of Pakistan Biennial Report *see* F P A P Biennial Report *179*
Family Planning Programs in Oklahoma(US ISSN 0095-3121) *179*
Family Planning Services; Annual Survey *see* U.S. Centers for Disease Control. Family Planning Services: Annual Summary *179*
Family Studies Review Yearbook (US ISSN 0734-2926) *1026*
Fanatic (UK) *710*
Fanatic Reader (US) *6, 540*
Fanfare (UK) *835*
Fantasy Tales (UK) *14*
Fantasy Voices (US ISSN 0271-7808) *722*
Far da Se Almanacco (IT) *614*
Far East and Australasia (UK ISSN 0071-3791) *244, 543, 573*
Far East Businessman's Directory *see* A.A.'s Far East Businessman's Directory *301*
Far East Shipping (UK ISSN 0144-8781) *1100*
Far Eastern Economic Review. Yearbook *see* Asia Yearbook *191*
Far Eastern Series *see* U.S. Department of State. East Asian and Pacific Series *919*
Far Seas Fisheries Research Laboratory. Bulletin (JA ISSN 0386-7285) *174, 365, 509*
Far Seas Fisheries Research Laboratory. Series (JA) *174, 365, 509*
Faraday Symposia (UK ISSN 0301-5696) *331*
Faravid (FI ISSN 0356-5629) *581*
Fardase Almanacco *see* Far da Se Almanacco *614*
Farm & Country Holidays (UK) *1108*
Farm and Garden Index (US ISSN 0193-8487) *6, 40*
Farm and Garden Periodicals on Microfilm (US) *126, 534*
Farm Animal Welfare Co-ordinating Executive. Newsletter (UK ISSN 0144-6169) *65*
Farm Business Management (US) *46*
Farm Business Statistics for South East England (UK) *40, 1055*
Farm Chemicals Handbook (US ISSN 0430-0750) *55*
Farm Classification in England and Wales (UK ISSN 0071-3848) *46*
Farm Credit Administration. Annual Report (US) *46, 238*
Farm Credit Corporation Canada. Annual Report (CN ISSN 0071-3864) *228*
Farm Credit Corporation Canada. Federal Farm Credit Statistics/Statistiques du Credit Agricole Federal (CN ISSN 0071-3872) *228*
Farm Credit in the Canadian Financial System/Financement de l'Agriculture Canadienne (CN) *228*
Farm Economist *see* Oxford Agrarian Studies *48*
Farm Facts *see* Kansas. State Board of Agriculture. Annual Report with Farm Facts *30*
Farm Holiday Guide (England Edition) *see* Farm Holiday Guide (England, Wales & Ireland) *1108*
Farm Holiday Guide (England, Wales & Ireland) (UK) *1108*
Farm Holiday Guide (Scotland Edition) (UK ISSN 0267-288X) *1108*
Farm Holiday Guide (Wales Edition) *see* Farm Holiday Guide (England, Wales & Ireland) *1108*
Farm Holidays in Ireland (IE) *1108*
Farm Income (US) *46*
Farm Incomes in England (UK) *27*
Farm Incomes in England and Wales *see* Farm Incomes in England *27*
Farm Letter/Lettre au Cultivateur (CN ISSN 0014-8024) *27*
Farm Machinery Yearbook/Nogyo Kikai Nenkan (JA ISSN 0071-3937) *51*

Farm Management Notes *see* Farming in the East Midlands *55*
Farm Management Notes for Asia and the Far East (UN ISSN 0430-084X) *46*
Farm Management Pocketbook (UK) *46*
Farm Production and Practice *see* AgLink Leaflets *22*
Farm, Ranch and Country Vacations (US ISSN 0195-8437) *1108*
Farmers Handbook & Budgeting Guide (AT) *27*
Farming in the East Midlands (UK ISSN 0071-3961) *55*
Farming in the East Midlands. Financial Results (UK) *46*
Farming Statistics (NZ ISSN 0110-084X) *40*
Farming Uncle (US ISSN 0272-3417) *27, 532*
Farnborough Air Show (Public Programme) (UK ISSN 0071-402X) *18*
Faroerne og Groenland (DK ISSN 0108-5557) *922*
Farvandvaesenets Trafikanalyse (DK ISSN 0109-5811) *1100*
Fasciculi Historici (PL ISSN 0071-4038) *581*
Fasciculi Mathematici (PL ISSN 0044-4413) *748*
Fashion Index (UK ISSN 0142-2081) *340*
Fastener Standards (US ISSN 0071-4046) *489*
Fastener Technology Buyers' Guide (US) *190, 308*
Fastfacts European Hotel Locator (US ISSN 0192-1347) *1108*
Fastfacts U S A Hotel Motel Locator (US ISSN 0197-9477) *1108*
Fat Tuesday (US ISSN 0276-2072) *722*
Fataburen (SW ISSN 0348-971X) *71*
Fatal Accident Reporting System (US ISSN 0732-9792) *1096*
Fatal Accident Reporting System. Annual Report *see* Fatal Accident Reporting System *1096*
Fates Hippiques Belges (BE) *1043*
Fathers of the Church (US ISSN 0014-8814) *982*
Fats and Oils. Oilseed Crushings *see* Current Industrial Reports: Fats and Oils. Oilseed Crushings *521*
Fats and Oils. Production, Consumption, and Factory and Warehouse Stocks *see* Current Industrial Reports: Fats and Oils. Production, Consumption, and Factory and Warehouse Stocks *521*
Fauna & Flora (SA ISSN 0250-7013) *156, 174, 365*
Fauna Entomologica Scandinavica (DK ISSN 0106-8377) *140, 164*
Fauna Fennica *see* Acta Zoologica Fennica *174*
Fauna Hungariae *see* Magyarorszag Allatvilaga *176*
Fauna Norrlandica (SW ISSN 0349-0823) *543*
Fauna Norvegica Series A. Norwegian Fauna except Entomology and Ornithology (NO ISSN 0332-768X) *174*
Fauna of New Zealand (NZ ISSN 0111-5383) *140, 164, 174*
Fauna of Russia and Adjacent Countries (IS) *174*
Fauna of the U.S.S.R. (IS) *174*
Fauna Palaestina (IS) *174*
Fauna Slodkowodna Polski (PL ISSN 0071-4089) *174*
Faustchen (AU) *694*
Fawley Foundation Lectures (UK ISSN 0071-4097) *1068*
Faxon Librarians' Guide *see* Faxon Librarians' Guide to Serials *126*
Faxon Librarians' Guide to Serials (US ISSN 0275-8466) *126*
Fearnleys Review (NO) *1100*
Fearnly and Egers Chartering Co. Review *see* Fearnleys Review *1100*
Feature Films Available for Rental, Sale and Lease *see* Feature Films on 8mm, 16mm and Videotape *447*

Feature Films on 8mm and 16mm *see* Feature Films on 8mm, 16mm and Videotape *447*
Feature Films on 8mm, 16mm and Videotape (US) *447*
Feature fra Danmark (DK ISSN 0109-6702) *538*
Fed in Print (US) *207*
Federacao dos Trabalhadores na Agricultura do Estado do Parana. Relatorio (BL) *648*
Federacion Argentina de Periodistas. Gaceta (AG) *961*
Federacion Nacional de Cafeteros de Colombia. Boletin de Informacion Estadistica Sobre Cafe (CK ISSN 0084-7941). *119*
Federacion Nacional de Cafeteros de Colombia. Informe de Labores de los Comites Departamentales de Cafeteros (CK) *55, 518*
Federacion Sudamericana de Asociaciones Cristianas de Jovenes. Noticias *see* Confederacion Latinoamericana de Asociaciones Cristianas de Jovenes. Carta *969*
Federal Art Patronage Notes (US) *1153*
Federal Audit Guides (US) *221*
Federal Aviation Administration: High Altitude Pollution Program (US) *1088*
Federal Aviation Regulations for Pilots (US ISSN 0533-0963) *18*
Federal Benefits for Veterans and Dependents, IS-1 Fact Sheet (US) *639, 811*
Federal Business Development Bank. Annual Report (CN) *228*
Federal Civilian Work Force Statistics. Affirmative Employment Statistics (US) *271*
Federal Civilian Work Force Statistics. Equal Employment Opportunity Statistics *see* Federal Civilian Work Force Statistics. Affirmative Employment Statistics *271*
Federal Civilian Work Force Statistics. Occupations of Federal White-Collar and Blue-Collar Workers (US) *271*
Federal Civilian Work Force Statistics. Occupations of Federal White-Collar Workers *see* Federal Civilian Work Force Statistics. Occupations of Federal White-Collar and Blue-Collar Workers *271*
Federal Civilian Work Force Statistics. Pay Structure of the Federal Civil Service (US) *271*
Federal Civilian Work Force Statistics. Work Years and Personnel Costs. Executive Branch, United States Government (US ISSN 0277-3325) *271*
Federal Coal Management Report (US) *864*
Federal Data Base Finder (US) *357*
Federal Employees Almanac (US ISSN 0071-4127) *941*
Federal Estate and Gift Taxation (Supplement) (US) *295*
Federal Estate and Gift Taxes Explained *see* Federal Estate and Gift Taxes Explained, Including Estate Planning *295*
Federal Estate and Gift Taxes Explained, Including Estate Planning (US ISSN 0092-6531) *295*
Federal Funding Guide (US ISSN 0273-4435) *623, 950, 953, 1017*
Federal Funding Guide for Education *see* Guide to Federal Funding for Education *443*
Federal Funding Guide for Local Governments *see* Federal Funding Guide *950*
Federal Government and Cooperative Education *see* Earn & Learn: Cooperative Education Opportunities Offered by the Federal Government *434*
Federal Government Legal Career Opportunities *see* Now Hiring *848*
Federal Graduated Withholding Tax Tables (US ISSN 0071-4135) *295*
Federal Grant-in-Aid Activity in Florida: a Summary Report (US ISSN 0361-1582) *295*

Federal Home Loan Bank of Atlanta. Annual Report (US) *228*
Federal Home Loan Bank of Chicago. Annual Report (US) *228*
Federal Home Loan Bank of Dallas. Annual Report (US) *228*
Federal Home Loan Bank of Des Moines. Annual Report (US) *228*
Federal Home Loan Bank of Indianapolis. Annual Report (US) *228*
Federal Home Loan Bank of Little Rock. Annual Report (US) *228*
Federal Home Loan Bank of San Francisco. Annual Report. (US ISSN 0098-2830) *228*
Federal Home Loan Bank of San Francisco. Proceedings of the Annual Conference (US) *228*
Federal Home Loan Bank of Seattle. Annual Report (US) *228*
Federal Home Loan Bank of Topeka. Annual Report (US) *228*
Federal Home Loan Bank System. List of Member Institutions (US) *639*
Federal Home Loan Mortgage Corporation. Report (US ISSN 0094-7156) *228*
Federal Income Tax Guide (US ISSN 0196-1349) *295*
Federal Income Tax Law (US) *295*
Federal Income Tax Law (Supplement) *see* Federal Income Tax Law *295*
Federal Income Taxation of Banks and Financial Institutions (Supplement) (US) *228, 295*
Federal Law Reports (AT ISSN 0085-0462) *655*
Federal Librarian (US ISSN 0273-1061) *677*
Federal Library Resources (US) *677*
Federal Maritime Commission Service (US) *655, 1100*
Federal Outlays in Summary *see* U.S. Community Services Administration. Federal Outlays in Summary *300*
Federal Personnel Guide (US ISSN 0163-7665) *286*
Federal-Provincial Wildlife Conference. Transactions (CN ISSN 0069-0007) *140, 496*
Federal Regulatory Directory (US ISSN 0195-749X) *904, 941*
Federal Reserve Bank of Atlanta. Research Paper Series (US) *244*
Federal Reserve Bank of Atlanta. Working Paper Series (US) *194*
Federal Reserve Bank of Boston. Conference Series (US ISSN 0361-8714) *244*
Federal Reserve Bank of Cleveland. Working Paper (US) *228, 639*
Federal Reserve Bank of Kansas City. Banking Studies (US ISSN 0743-6351) *228*
Federal Reserve Bank of Minneapolis. Annual Report (US ISSN 0361-8013) *228*
Federal Reserve Bank of New York. Annual Report (US) *228*
Federal Savings and Loan Insurance Corporation. List of Member Institutions *see* Federal Home Loan Bank System. List of Member Institutions *639*
Federal Staff Directory (US) *904, 941*
Federal/State Executive Directory (US ISSN 0734-4651) *941*
Federal Tax Compliance Reports *see* Federal Tax Manual with Monthly Reports *295*
Federal Tax Litigation *see* Federal Tax Litigation (Supplement) *295*
Federal Tax Litigation (Supplement) (US) *295*
Federal Tax Manual with Monthly Reports (US) *295*
Federally Coordinated Program of Highway Research and Development *see* U.S. Federal Highway Administration. Federally Coordinated Program of Highway Research and Development *1098*
Federalni Ministerstvo Financi. Vestnik *see* Financni Zpravodaj *228*

Federated Taxpayer's Association of Australia. Annual Taxation Summary *see* Australian Taxpayer's Association. Annual Taxation Summary *293*
Federatie van Bedrijfsverenigingen. Jaarverslag (NE ISSN 0071-4151) *639*
Federatie van Nederlandstalige Verenidenis voor Oudheidkunde en Geschiedenis van Belgische. Jaarboeken *see* Federation Archeologique et Historique de Belgique. Annales *581*
Federation Archeologique et Historique de Belgique. Annales/Federatie van Nederlandstalige Verenidenis voor Oudheidkunde en Geschiedenis van Belgische. Jaarboeken (BE) *86, 515, 581*
Federation d'Associations de Techniciens des Industries des Peintures, Vernis, Emaux et Encres d'Imprimerie de l'Europe Continentale. Congress Proceedings *see* Congress F A T I P E C *478*
Federation d'Associations de Techniciens des Industries des Peintures, Vernis, Emaux et Encres d'Imprimerie de l'Europe Continentale Congress F A T I P E C *see* Congress F A T I P E C *478*
Federation d'Associations de Techniciens des Industries des Peintures, Vernis, Emaux et Encres d'Imprimerie de l'Europe Continentale. Annuaire Officiel. Official Yearbook. Amtliches Jahrbuch (FR ISSN 0071-416X) *855*
Federation de l'Industrie Horlogere Suisse. Annual Report (SZ) *644*
Federation des Debitants de Tabac de l'Ile-de-France. Annuaire Officiel (FR) *1079*
Federation des Entrepreneurs de Nettoyage de France. Annuaire Officiel (FR) *339*
Federation des Entreprises de Belgique. Rapport Annuel/Verbond van Belgische Ondernemingen. Jaarlyks Verslag (BE) *289, 369*
Federation des Entreprises de l'Industrie des Fabrications Metalliques, Mecaniques, Electriques et de la Transformation des Matieres Plastiques. Centre de Recherches Scientifiques et Techniques. Section: Fonderie (FD). Research Reports (BE) *797*
Federation des Industries Belges. Rapport Annuel *see* Federation des Entreprises de Belgique. Rapport Annuel *289*
Federation des Industries Chimiques de Belgique. Annuaire (BE ISSN 0425-9076) *308, 478*
Federation des Industries Chimiques de Belgique. Rapport Annuel (BE ISSN 0085-0489) *244, 478*
Federation des Societes d'Histoire Naturelle de Franche-Comte. Bulletin *see* Societe d'Histoire Naturelle du Doubs. Bulletin *1000*
Federation Equestre Francaise. Guide Officiel du Cavalier (FR) *1033, 1043*
Federation Exchange (US) *761*
Federation Francaise de Natation. Annuaire (FR ISSN 0071-4194) *1041*
Federation Francaise des Sports Equestres. Annuaire Officiel *see* Federation Equestre Francaise. Guide Officiel du Cavalier *1043*
Federation Horlogere Suisse. Annual Report *see* Federation de l'Industrie Horlogere Suisse. Annual Report *644*
Federation Internationale de Laiterie. Bulletin Annuel *see* International Dairy Federation. Annual Bulletin *62*
Federation Internationale de Laiterie. Memento Annuel *see* International Dairy Federation. Annual Memento *62*

Federation Internationale de Laiterie. Norme Internationale *see* International Dairy Federation. International Standard *62*
Federation Internationale de Rugby Amateur. Annuaire (FR ISSN 0071-4267) *1038*
Federation Internationale des Professeurs de Francais. Bulletin *see* Dialogues et Cultures *693*
Federation Internationale du Batiment et des Trauvaux Publics. Revue *see* Entreprise Europeenne *184*
Federation Internationale Motocycliste. Annuaire (SZ ISSN 0071-4283) *1041*
Federation Interprofessionnelle de la Congelation Ultra-Rapide. Rapport Statistique Annuel (FR) *518*
Federation Nationale de la Photographie Profesionelle. Annuaire(BE) *884*
Federation Nationale des Cooperatives de Consommateurs Annuaire de la Cooperation F.N.C.C. *see* Annuaire de la Cooperation F.N.C.C *238*
Federation Nationale des Enseignants et des Enseignantes du Quebec Women's Network *see* Women's Network *422*
Federation Nationale des Societes d'Economie Mixte de Construction, d'Amenagement et de Renovation. Annuaire (FR ISSN 0081-1262) *623*
Federation Nationale du Credit Agricole. Annuaire du Credit Agricole Mutuel (FR ISSN 0071-4380) *228*
Federation News (UK ISSN 0014-9411) *648*
Federation of Astronomical Societies Handbook *see* F A S Handbook *115*
Federation of Canadian Archers. Rules Book (CN ISSN 0226-773X) *1033*
Federation of Egyptian Industries. Yearbook *see* Ittihad al-Sinaat al-Misriyah. Yearbook *310*
Federation of European Biochemical Societies. (Proceedings of Meeting) (UK ISSN 0071-4402) *151*
Federation of Finnish Industries. List of Members *see* Suomen Teollisuusliitto. Jasenluettelo *317*
Federation of Migros Cooperatives. Annual Report (SZ ISSN 0071-4410) *238*
Federation of Pakistan Chambers of Commerce and Industry. Directory of Exporters (PK) *308*
Federation of Pakistan Chambers of Commerce Industry. Brief Report of Activities (PK ISSN 0071-4429) *235*
Federation of Societies for Coatings Technology. Yearbook and Annual Membership Directory (US) *855*
Federation of Societies for Paint Technology. Yearbook *see* Federation of Societies for Coatings Technology. Yearbook and Annual Membership Directory *855*
Federation of Swedish Co-Operative Banks. Annual Report (SW) *228, 238*
Federation Professionnelle des Producteurs et Distributeure d'Electricite de Belgique. Repertoire des Enterprises de Production d'Electricite/Repertorium des Ondernemingen van Electriciteitscoorbrenging *see* Federation Professionnelle des Producteurs et Distributeurs d'Electricite de Belgique. Repertoire des Centrales Electriques/ Repertorium van de Elektrische Centrales *453*
Federation Professionnelle des Producteurs et Distributeurs d'Electricite de Belgique. Repertoire des Centrales Electriques/ Repertorium van de Elektrische Centrales (BE) *453*
Federation Professionnelle des Producteurs et Distributeurs d'Electricite de Belgique. Secteurs de Distribution (BE ISSN 0071-4488) *453*

Federation Protestante de France. Annuaire (FR) *978*
Fed's Fiscale Brochures (NE) *295*
Feed Additive Compendium (US ISSN 0071-450X) *63*
Feed Bag Red Book *see* Feed Industry Red Book *63*
Feed Industry Red Book (US ISSN 0071-4518) *63, 308*
Feinkost-Revue (GW ISSN 0014-9691) *518*
Felag Islenzkra Storkaupmanna Frettabref *see* F I S Frettabref *308*
Felix Ravenna; Rivista di Antichita Ravennati, Cristiane e Bizantine (IT ISSN 0085-0500) *86, 105*
Felixstowe Dock & Railway Company Diary (UK) *1094*
Felixstowe Shipping Diary (UK) *1100*
Fellows of the Royal Society. Biographical Memoirs (UK) *134*
Fellowship of Australian Composers. Newsletter *see* Australian Composer *833*
Fellowship Yearbook *see* Evangelical Baptist Churches in Canada. Fellowship Yearbook *978*
Felsmechanik und Ingenieurgeologie. Rock Mechanics and Engineering Geology. Supplement *see* Rock Mechanics/Felsmechanik/ Mechanique des Roches. Supplement *820*
Felt and Damaging Earthquakes (UK ISSN 0144-2376) *399*
Feltornithologen *see* Fugle *170*
Feltundersoegelse (DK ISSN 0109-856X) *140*
Female Impersonator News (US) *615, 1077*
Femmes en Litterature (FR) *722, 1128*
Fence Industry/Access Control Directory (US) *184, 308*
Fence Industry Directory *see* Fence Industry/Access Control Directory *308*
Fencing Rules for Competitions *see* U S F A Rule Book: U S & International Rules *1036*
Fenix (PE ISSN 0015-0002) *677*
Fenno-Ugrica (GW ISSN 0341-311X) *694*
Fenomenos Astronomicos (SP ISSN 0210-8127) *115*
Fer-Blanc en France et dans le Monde (FR ISSN 0085-0519) *797*
Ferguson's Ceylon Directory *see* Ferguson's Sri Lanka Directory *308*
Ferguson's Sri Lanka Directory (CE) *308*
Fern Gazette (UK ISSN 0308-0838) *156*
Fernerkundung in Raumordung und Stadtebau (GW ISSN 0176-1633) *543*
Ferro Alloy Directory (UK ISSN 0266-3198) *797*
Der Fertighaus-Katalog (GW ISSN 0071-4585) *184*
Fertigung und Betrieb (US ISSN 0171-5062) *289*
Fertiliser Association of India. Fertiliser Statistics (II ISSN 0430-327X) *40, 1055*
Fertiliser Association of India Abstract Service *see* F.A.I. Abstract Service *40*
Fertilizer Industry Round Table. Proceedings (US) *27*
Fertilizer Industry Series (UN ISSN 0071-4615) *1153*
Fertilizer Science and Technology Series (US ISSN 0071-4623) *55*
Fertilizer Trends (US ISSN 0071-4631) *55*
Festival Film Guide *see* American Film and Video Festival Guide *822*
Festivals Sourcebook (US) *1108*
Festschrift Series (US) *835*
Fettesian (UK ISSN 0046-3701) *341*
Feuerwehr-Jahrbuch (GW ISSN 0071-4674) *506*
Feux et Signaux de Brume (FR ISSN 0223-5358) *1100*
Fiber Optics Technical Directory (US) *1068*
Fiber Science Series (US ISSN 0071-4682) *1074*

Fiches Analytiques de la Presse Technique Francaise (FR ISSN 0071-4704) *1153*
Fiches d'Identification des Maladies et Parasites des Poissons, Crustaces et Mollusques/Identification Leaflets for Diseases and Parasites of Fish and Shellfish (DK ISSN 0109-2510) *174*
Fiches d'Identification du Plancton (DK ISSN 0109-2529) *140*
Fiches d'Identification du Zooplancton *see* Fiches d'Identification du Plancton *140*
Fiches E O - Formation Permanente (FR) *279*
Fiches Techniques R.T.A. (FR) *1091*
Fiches Techniques R.T.C. (FR) *1091*
Fiches Techniques R.T.D. (FR) *1091*
Fiches Techniques R.T.D. Applications Agricoles (FR) *51*
Fiction Catalog (US ISSN 0160-4880) *739*
Fiction International (US ISSN 0092-1912) *722*
Fiction Writer's Market (US ISSN 0275-2123) *722*
Fidia Research Series (US) *761*
Field & Stream Bass Fishing Annual (US ISSN 0163-5468) *1045*
Field and Stream Deer Hunter's Guide Annual (US) *1045*
Field and Stream Deer Hunting Annual *see* Field and Stream Deer Hunter's Guide Annual *1045*
Field & Stream Fishing Annual (US ISSN 0362-6385) *1045*
Field & Stream Hunting Annual (US ISSN 0361-3011) *1045*
Field Crop Abstracts (UK ISSN 0015-069X) *6, 40*
Field Hockey-Lacrosse Guide *see* N A G W S Guide. Field Hockey *1039*
Field Hockey-Lacrosse Guide *see* N A G W S Guide. Lacrosse *1159*
Field Hockey Rulebook (US) *1033*
Field of Vision (US) *823, 884*
Field Studies (UK ISSN 0428-304X) *496*
Field Studies Council. Occasional Publications (UK) *496*
Fieldiana: Anthropology (US ISSN 0071-4739) *71*
Fieldiana: Botany (US ISSN 0015-0746) *156*
Fieldiana: Geology (US ISSN 0096-2651) *385*
Fieldiana: Zoology (US ISSN 0015-0754) *174*
Fielding's Bermuda and the Bahamas (US ISSN 0739-0769) *1108*
Fielding's Caribbean (US) *1108*
Fielding's Economy Caribbean (US ISSN 0739-0750) *1108*
Fielding's Economy Europe (US ISSN 0739-0785) *1108*
Fielding's Europe (US ISSN 0192-5326) *1109*
Fielding's Low-Cost Europe *see* Fielding's Economy Europe *1108*
Fielding's Mexico (US ISSN 0739-0793) *1109*
Fielding's Selective Shopping Guide to Europe (US ISSN 0071-478X) *1109*
Fielding's Travel Guide to Europe *see* Fielding's Europe *1109*
Fiera di Milano (IT) *284*
Fiere nel Mondo (IT) *284*
Fifth Sun (US) *722*
Fight the Right (US) *913*
Figura. Nova Series (SW ISSN 0071-481X) *105, 581*
Figures de Wallonie (BE ISSN 0069-5386) *134, 581*
Fihrist (LE) *6, 126, 612*
Fiji. Bureau of Statistics. Aircraft Statistics (FJ) *22*
Fiji. Bureau of Statistics. Annual Statistical Abstract (FJ ISSN 0071-4828) *1153*
Fiji. Bureau of Statistics. Census of Building and Construction (FJ) *189*
Fiji. Bureau of Statistics. Census of Distribution and Services (FJ) *207, 1055*
Fiji. Bureau of Statistics. Census of Industrial Production (FJ) *207*

Fiji. Bureau of Statistics. Economic and Functional Classification of Government Accounts (FJ) *207, 295*
Fiji. Bureau of Statistics. Employment Survey of Fiji (FJ) *207*
Fiji. Bureau of Statistics. Fiji Fertility Survey (FJ) *922, 926*
Fiji. Bureau of Statistics. Fiji Household Income and Expenditure Survey (FJ) *207*
Fiji. Bureau of Statistics. Nationwide Unemployment Survey (FJ) *271*
Fiji. Bureau of Statistics. Population of Fiji (FJ) *922, 926*
Fiji. Bureau of Statistics. Shipping Statistics (FJ) *1085*
Fiji. Bureau of Statistics. Survey of Distributive Trade (FJ) *207*
Fiji. Bureau of Statistics. Trade Report (FJ) *207*
Fiji. Bureau of Statistics. Vital Statistics (FJ) *244*
Fiji. Central Monetary Authority. Annual Report (FJ) *295*
Fiji. Department of Agriculture. Annual Report *see* Fiji. Ministry of Agriculture & Fisheries. Annual Report *27*
Fiji. Department of Agriculture. Bulletin *see* Fiji. Ministry of Agriculture & Fisheries. Bulletin *1153*
Fiji. Geological Survey. Economic Investigation *see* Fiji. Mineral Resources Department. Economic Investigation *816*
Fiji. Housing Authority. Report (FJ) *623*
Fiji. Mineral Resources Department. Annual Report (FJ ISSN 0252-2462) *816*
Fiji. Mineral Resources Department. Bulletin (FJ ISSN 0379-1580) *385*
Fiji. Mineral Resources Department. Economic Investigation (FJ) *816*
Fiji. Mineral Resources Department. Geothermal Report (FJ ISSN 0250-7277) *386*
Fiji. Mineral Resources Department. Memoir (FJ ISSN 0252-2497) *386*
Fiji. Mineral Resources Division. Annual Report *see* Fiji. Mineral Resources Department. Annual Report *816*
Fiji. Mineral Resources Division. Bulletin *see* Fiji. Mineral Resources Department. Bulletin *385*
Fiji. Mineral Resources Division. Economic Investigation *see* Fiji. Mineral Resources Department. Economic Investigation *816*
Fiji. Ministry of Agriculture & Fisheries. Annual Report (FJ ISSN 0071-4844) *27*
Fiji. Ministry of Agriculture & Fisheries. Annual Research Report (FJ) *27*
Fiji. Ministry of Agriculture & Fisheries. Bulletin (FJ) *1153*
Fiji. Ministry of Education. Report (FJ) *414*
Fiji. Ministry of Education, Youth and Sport. Report *see* Fiji. Ministry of Education. Report *414*
Fiji. Office of the Ombudsman. Annual Report of the Ombudsman (FJ) *655*
Fiji. Printing Department Report (FJ) *645*
Fiji Classification & Dictionary of Occupations (FJ) *271, 308*
Fiji Department of Agriculture. Annual Research Report *see* Fiji. Ministry of Agriculture & Fisheries. Annual Research Report *27*
Fiji Facts and Figures (FJ) *207*
Fiji Information *see* Fiji Today *941*
Fiji Library Directory (FJ) *677*
Fiji Mineral Resources Division. Memoir *see* Fiji. Mineral Resources Department. Memoir *386*
Fiji National Bibliography (FJ) *126*
Fiji Register of Research and Investigations *see* South Pacific Research Register *131*
Fiji Sugar Year Book (FJ) *55, 518*
Fiji Today (FJ) *941*
Filament (US) *823*
Filatelija (YU ISSN 0015-0967) *874*

Filatelistisk Katalog-Noegle/Philatelistic Catalogue Key/Philatelistischer Katalog-Schluessel (DK ISSN 0108-0296) *874*
File (CN ISSN 0315-2456) *105*
Filipinas *see* Pilipinas *571*
Film Aarbogen (DK ISSN 0109-2774) *823*
Film & Video Finder (US) *6, 424*
Film and Video Makers Directory (US) *823*
Film Angels (US) *348*
Film Australia Catalogue (AT) *71, 105, 335, 414, 823*
Film Dope (UK ISSN 0305-1706) *823*
Film-Echo Filmwoche. Verleih-Katalog (GW ISSN 0071-4879) *823*
Film Edmonton (CN ISSN 0704-9536) *823*
Film Literature Index (US ISSN 0093-6758) *6, 826*
Film Music Buyer's Guide (US) *824, 835*
Film Premierer (DK ISSN 0109-1174) *1153*
Film Programmer's Guide to 16mm Rentals (US) *363, 832*
Film Reader (US ISSN 0361-722X) *824*
Film Review (UK ISSN 0071-4917) *824*
Film Review Annual (US ISSN 0737-9080) *824*
Film und Fernsehen in Forschung und Lehre (GW ISSN 0173-4970) *824, 826*
Filmarsboken/Swedish Film Annual (SW ISSN 0071-4925) *824*
Filmatiserede Boeger (DK ISSN 0107-0940) *126, 824*
Filmliste *see* Spielfilmliste *825*
Filmmakers and Film Production Services of Israel *see* Israel Film Industry Directory *824*
Filmore Bungle (US) *134*
Filmoteca Ultramarina Portuguesa. Boletim (PO ISSN 0430-4497) *557, 916*
Filmregistret (DK ISSN 0106-8180) *826*
Films on Video (UK) *348, 824*
Films: the Visualization of Anthropology (US) *79, 826*
Filmsaesonen: Dansk Filmfortegnelse (DK ISSN 0107-1033) *824*
Filmstatistisches Taschenbuch (GW ISSN 0071-4941) *824*
Filmvidenskabeligt Arbog (DK) *824*
Filologia (AG ISSN 0071-495X) *694*
Filologia Angielska (PL ISSN 0554-8144) *694*
Filologia Baltycka/Baltic Philology (PL) *694, 722*
Filologia Klasyczna (PL ISSN 0554-8160) *337, 695*
Filologos Colombianos (CK ISSN 0071-4976) *695*
Filoloski Fakultet. Katedra za Istocnoslovenski i Zapadnoslovenski Jazici i Knizeunosti. Slavisticki Studii(YU ISSN 0352-3055) *695*
Filosofi og Videnskabsteori paa Roskilde Universitetscenter (DK ISSN 0106-6668) *878, 991*
Filosofia della Religione. Testi e Studi (IT) *969*
Filosofiske Studier (DK ISSN 0106-0449) *878*
Filosofskie Nauki (UR) *878*
Filozofia-Logika (PL) *878*
Filozofiai Tanulmanyok (HU ISSN 0071-4992) *878*
Filter: a Paper for Secondary Science Teachers (AT ISSN 0310-6020) *447*
Finance Facts Yearbook (US) *228*
Finance for New Projects in UK (UK) *244*
Finance: Latin American Industrial Report (US) *228*
Financement de l'Agriculture Canadienne *see* Farm Credit in the Canadian Financial System *228*
Finances of the Public School Systems (US) *1055*
Finances Publiques en Suisse *see* Offentliche Finanzen der Schweiz *298*

Financial Aid for First Degree Study at Commonwealth Universities (UK ISSN 0260-0749) *435*
Financial Aids to Illinois Students (US ISSN 0085-0543) *435*
Financial Analysis of a Group of Petroleum Companies (US) *266*
Financial Analysis of the Motor Carrier Industry (US ISSN 0099-2445) *1105*
Financial and Monetary Policy Studies (NE) *228*
Financial and Monetary Studies *see* Financial and Monetary Policy Studies *228*
Financial and Operating Results of Department and Specialty Stores (US ISSN 0547-8804) *239*
Financial and Operating Statistics Executive and Ownership Report *see* F & O S Executive and Ownership Report *1105*
Financial and Operating Statistics Motor Carrier Annual Report *see* F & O S Motor Carrier Annual Report *1105*
Financial Assistance for Library Education (US ISSN 0569-6275) *435, 677*
Financial Corporate Bond Transfer Service *see* Financial Corporate Municipal Bond Transfer Service *266*
Financial Corporate Municipal Bond Transfer Service (US) *266*
Financial Directories of the World (UK) *228*
Financial Industry Number Standard Directory (US ISSN 0362-1405) *228*
Financial Institutions Retirement Fund. Annual Report (US) *286, 295*
Financial Outlook (UK) *228*
Financial Post Canadian Markets (CN ISSN 0227-6038) *284*
Financial Post Corporation Service. Eight Year Price Range *see* Financial Post Eight Year Price Range *228*
Financial Post Directory of Directors (CN ISSN 0071-5042) *279*
Financial Post Eight Year Price Range (CN) *228, 266*
Financial Post Report on the Nation (CN) *194*
Financial Post Survey of Industrials (CN ISSN 0071-5050) *266*
Financial Post Survey of Markets *see* Financial Post Canadian Markets *284*
Financial Post Survey of Mines *see* Financial Post Survey of Mines and Energy Resources *816*
Financial Post Survey of Mines and Energy Resources (CN ISSN 0227-1656) *465, 816*
Financial Post Survey of Predecessor and Defunct Companies (CN) *194*
Financial Report - Carnegie Endowment for International Peace *see* Carnegie Endowment for International Peace. Financial Report *915*
Financial Reporting in Canada (CN ISSN 0071-5115) *221*
Financial Results of Horticultural Holdings (UK) *532*
Financial Review (US ISSN 0066-5363) *228*
Financial Statements and Operating Ratios for the Mortgage Banking Industry (US ISSN 0278-6567) *228*
Financial Statistics of Japan (JA ISSN 0289-1522) *228*
Financial Statistics of Selected Electric Utilities (US) *461, 468, 1055*
Financial Stock Guide Service. Directory of Active Stocks (US ISSN 0364-0752) *266*
Financial Stock Guide Service. Directory of Obsolete Securities (US ISSN 0085-0551) *266*
Financial Studies of the Small Business (US ISSN 0363-8987) *228*
Financial Times International Year Books: Mining (UK ISSN 0141-3244) *816*
Financial Times International Year Books: Oil and Gas (UK ISSN 0141-3228) *864*

1732 FINANCIAL TIMES

Financial Times International Year Books: Who's Who in World Oil and Gas (UK ISSN 0141-3236) *864*
Financial Times International Year Books: World Hotel Directory (UK ISSN 0308-8464) *620, 1109*
Financial Times International Year Books: World Insurance (UK ISSN 0309-751X) *639*
Financial Times of Canada. Guide to R R S Ps (CN) *639*
Financial Times World Shipping Yearbook (UK) *1100*
Financiele Positie van de Landbouw (NE) *27, 46*
Financing and Insuring Exports: A User's Guide to Eximbank and F.C.I.A. Programs (US) *228*
Financing Higher Education (US) *435*
Financni Zpravodaj (CS ISSN 0322-9653) *228*
Finanzwissenschaftliche Schriften (GW) *251*
Findex (US ISSN 0273-4125) *284*
Fine (CN ISSN 0318-7489) *105, 414*
Fine Arts Work Center in Provincetown. Newsletter *see* Fine Arts Work Center in Provincetown. Visual Catalogue *105*
Fine Arts Work Center in Provincetown. Visual Catalogue (US) *105*
Fine Chemicals Directory (US ISSN 0740-3739) *328*
Finger Lakes Travel Guide *see* I Love New York: The Finger Lakes Travel Guide *1111*
Finishing Diary (UK) *855*
Finishing Handbook and Directory (UK ISSN 0071-5182) *797*
Fink-S (FI ISSN 0356-178X) *126*
Finland (FI ISSN 0356-827X) *582, 904*
Finland. Central Statistical Office. Banks *see* Finland. Tilastokeskus. Pankit *208*
Finland. Central Statistical Office. Building Construction Statistics *see* Finland. Tilastokeskus. Talonrakennustilasto *627*
Finland. Central Statistical Office. Causes of Death in Finland *see* Finland. Tilastokeskus. Kuolemansyyt *208*
Finland. Central Statistical Office. Construction of Dwellings *see* Finland. Tilastokeskus. Asuntotuotanto *627*
Finland. Central Statistical Office. Criminality. Criminal Cases Tried by the Courts *see* Finland. Tilastokeskus. Rikollisuus. Tuomioistuinten Tutkimat Rikokset *374*
Finland. Central Statistical Office. Criminality. Criminality Known to the Police *see* Finland. Tilastokeskus. Rikollisuus. Poliisin Tietoon Tullut Rikollisuus *374*
Finland. Central Statistical Office. Farm Economy *see* Finland. Tilastokeskus. Maatilatalous *40*
Finland. Central Statistical Office. Function of Courts *see* Finland. Tilastokeskus. Tuomioistuinten Toiminta *374*
Finland. Central Statistical Office. General Education *see* Finland. Tilastokeskus. Yleissivistavat Oppilaitokset *424*
Finland. Central Statistical Office. Government Statistics *see* Finland. Tilastokeskus. Valtion Tilastojulkaisut *1055*
Finland. Central Statistical Office. Handbooks *see* Finland. Tilastokeskus. Kasikirjoja *1055*
Finland. Central Statistical Office. Higher Education *see* Finland. Tilastokeskus. Korkeakoulut *424*
Finland. Central Statistical Office. Income Distribution Statistics *see* Finland. Tilastokeskus. Tulonjakotilasto *208*
Finland. Central Statistical Office. Industrial Statistics *see* Finland. Tilastokeskus. Teollisuustilasto *208*

Finland. Central Statistical Office. Labour Force Survey *see* Finland. Tilastokeskus. Tyovoimatutkimus *208*
Finland. Central Statistical Office. Living Conditions in Finland *see* Finland. Statistikcentralen. Statistiska Meddelanden. Levnadsfoerhaalanden i Finland *1026*
Finland. Central Statistical Office. Mortality. Life Tables *see* Finland. Tilastokeskus. Kuolleisuus. Kuolleisuus- Ja Eloonjaamistauluja *927*
Finland. Central Statistical Office. Municipal Elections *see* Finland. Tilastokeskus. Kunnallisvaalit *949*
Finland. Central Statistical Office. Municipal Finances *see* Finland. Tilastokeskus. Kuntien Talous *208*
Finland. Central Statistical Office. National Elections. Parliamentary Elections *see* Finland. Tilastokeskus. Valtiolliset Vaalit. Kansanedustajain Vaalit *911*
Finland. Central Statistical Office. Population *see* Finland. Tilastokeskus. Vaesto *927*
Finland. Central Statistical Office. Population and Housing Census *see* Finland. Tilastokeskus. Vaesto- ja Asuntolaskenta *927*
Finland. Central Statistical Office. Research Activity *see* Finland. Tilastokeskus. Tutkimustoiminta *1003*
Finland. Central Statistical Office. Road Traffic Accidents *see* Finland. Tilastokeskus. Tieliikenneonnettomuudet *1085*
Finland. Central Statistical Office. Statistical Surveys. Cultural Statistics *see* Finland. Tilastokeskus. Tilastollisia Tiedonantoja. Kulttuuritilasto *1014*
Finland. Central Statistical Office. Statistical Surveys. Environmental Statistics *see* Finland. Tilastokeskus. Tilastollisia Tiedonantoja. Ymparistotilasto *501*
Finland. Central Statistical Office. Statistical Surveys. Household Survey *see* Finland. Tilastokeskus. Tilastollisia Tiedonantoja. Kotitaloustiedustelu *208*
Finland. Central Statistical Office. Statistical Surveys. Position of Women *see* Finland. Tilastokeskus. Tilastollisia Tiedonantoja. Naisten Asema *1026*
Finland. Central Statistical Office. Statistics of Income and Property *see* Finland. Tilastokeskus. Tulo- ja Varallisuustilasto *208*
Finland. Central Statistical Office. Studies *see* Finland. Tilastokeskus. Tutkimuksia *208*
Finland. Central Statistical Office. Vocational Education *see* Finland. Tilastokeskus. Ammatilliset Oppilaitokset *207*
Finland. Central Statistical Office. Yearbook of Transport Statistics *see* Finland. Tilastokeskus. Liikennetilastollinen Vuosikirja *1085*
Finland. Folkpensionsanstalt. Statistisk Aarsbok *see* Finland. Kansanelakelaitos. Tilastollinen Vuosikirja *642*
Finland. Folkpensionsanstalten. Beraettelse *see* Finland Kansanelakelaitos. Toimintakertomus *639*
Finland. Kansanelakelaitos. Julkaisuja. Sarja A (FI ISSN 0430-5205) *1008*
Finland. Kansanelakelaitos. Julkaisuja. Sarja AL (FI ISSN 0355-4813) *761*
Finland. Kansanelakelaitos. Julkaisuja. Sarja E (FI ISSN 0355-4848) *1008*
Finland. Kansanelakelaitos. Julkaisuja. Sarja EL (FI ISSN 0355-4856) *761, 846*
Finland. Kansanelakelaitos. Julkaisuja. Sarja M (FI ISSN 0355-4821) *1008*
Finland. Kansanelakelaitos. Julkaisuja. Sarja ML (FI ISSN 0355-483X) *761, 846*

Finland. Kansanelakelaitos. Tilastollinen Vuosikirja/Finland. Folkpensionsanstalt. Statistisk Aarsbok/Finland. Social Insurance Institution. Statistical Yearbook (FI ISSN 0075-5247) *642*
Finland. Kansantalousosasto. Kansantalouden Kehitysarvio. Summary: National Budget for Finland (FI ISSN 0071-5255) *295*
Finland. Kansantalousosasto. Taloudellinen Katsaus. Economic Survey (FI ISSN 0071-5271) *244*
Finland. Laakintohallitus. Laakarit, Hammaslaakarit/Lakare, Tandlaekare(FI) *761, 779*
Finland. Laakintohallitus. Laakarit, Hammaslaakarit, Sairaalat *see* Finland. Laakintohallitus. Laakarit, Hammaslaakarit/Lakare, Tandlaekare *761*
Finland. Merentutkimuslaitoksen. Julkaisu *see* Finnish Marine Research *405*
Finland. Ministry of Labour. Labour Reports *see* Finland. Tyovoimaministerio. Tyovoimakatsaus *271*
Finland. Ministry of Social Affairs and Health. Research Department. Special Social Studies *see* Finland. Sosiaali- ja Terveysministerio. Tukimusosasto. Sosiaalisia Erikoistutkimuksia *1017*
Finland. National Board of Social Welfare. Homehelp. *see* Finland. Sosiaalihallitus. Huoltoapu *1017*
Finland. National Board of Social Welfare. Social Assistance *see* Finland. Sosiaalihallitus. Kodinhoitoapu *1017*
Finland. National Board of Social Welfare. Yearbook of Social Welfare Statistics *see* Finland. Sosiaalihallitus. Sosiaalihuoltotilaston Vuosikirja *1017*
Finland. Posti-ja Lennatinlaitos. Kotimaisten Sanomalehtien Hinnasto. Inhemsk Tidningstaxa (FI ISSN 0071-5298) *126*
Finland. Posti-ja Lennatinlaitos. Ulkomaisten Sanomalehtien Hinnasto. Utlandsk Tidningstaxa (FI ISSN 0071-5301) *645*
Finland. Social Insurance Institution. Annual Report *see* Finland Kansanelakelaitos. Toimintakertomus *639*
Finland. Social Insurance Institution. Statistical Yearbook *see* Finland. Kansanelakelaitos. Tilastollinen Vuosikirja *642*
Finland. Socialstyrelsen. Hemvaardshjaelp *see* Finland. Sosiaalihallitus. Kodinhoitoapu *1017*
Finland. Socialstyrelsen. Socialhjaelp *see* Finland. Sosiaalihallitus. Huoltoapu *1017*
Finland. Socialstyrelsen. Socialvaardsstatistik Aarsbok *see* Finland. Sosiaalihallitus. Sosiaalihuoltotilaston Vuosikirja *1017*
Finland. Sosiaali- ja Terveysministerio. Tukimusosasto. Sosiaalisia Erikoistutkimuksia/Finland. Ministry of Social Affairs and Health. Research Department. Special Social Studies (FI ISSN 0071-5336) *1017*
Finland. Sosiaalihallitus. Huoltoapu/ Finland. National Board of Social Welfare. Homehelp/Finland. Socialstyrelsen. Socialhjaelp (FI ISSN 0355-4759) *1017*
Finland. Sosiaalihallitus. Kodinhoitoapu/Finland. National Board of Social Welfare. Social Assistance/Finland. Socialstyrelsen. Hemvaardshjaelp (FI ISSN 0355-4767) *1017*
Finland. Sosiaalihallitus. Sosiaalihuoltotilaston Vuosikirja/ Finland. National Board of Social Welfare. Yearbook of Social Welfare Statistics/Finland. Socialstyrelsen. Socialvaardsstatistik Aarsbok (FI ISSN 0071-5328) *1017*

Finland. Statistikcentraleen. Statistiska Meddelanden. Kvinnornas Staellning *see* Finland. Tilastokeskus. Tilastollisia Tiedonantoja. Naisten Asema *1026*
Finland. Statistikcentralen. Allmaenbildande Laeroanstalter *see* Finland. Tilastokeskus. Yleissivistavat Oppilaitokset *424*
Finland. Statistikcentralen. Arbetskraftsundersokningen *see* Finland. Tilastokeskus. Tyovoimatutkimus *208*
Finland. Statistikcentralen. Bankerna *see* Finland. Tilastokeskus. Pankit *208*
Finland. Statistikcentralen. Befolkning *see* Finland. Tilastokeskus. Vaesto *927*
Finland. Statistikcentralen. Bostadsproduktionen *see* Finland. Tilastokeskus. Asuntotuotanto *627*
Finland. Statistikcentralen. Brottslighet. Brottsligheten Som Kommit till Polishens Kaennedom *see* Finland. Tilastokeskus. Rikollisuus. Poliisin Tietoon Tullut Rikollisuus *374*
Finland. Statistikcentralen. Brottslighet. Vid Domstolar Rannsakade Brott *see* Finland. Tilastokeskus. Rikollisuus. Tuomioistuinten Tutkimat Rikokset *374*
Finland. Statistikcentralen. Doedlighet. Doedlighets- och Livslaengdstabeller *see* Finland. Tilastokeskus. Kuolleisuus. Kuolleisuus- Ja Eloonjaamistauluja *927*
Finland. Statistikcentralen. Doedsorsaker *see* Finland. Tilastokeskus. Kuolemansyyt *208*
Finland. Statistikcentralen. Domstolarnas Verksamhet *see* Finland. Tilastokeskus. Tuomioistuinten Toiminta *374*
Finland. Statistikcentralen. Energistatistik *see* Finland. Tilastokeskus. Energiatilastot *465*
Finland. Statistikcentralen. Folk- och Bostadsraekningen *see* Finland. Tilastokeskus. Vaesto- ja Asuntolaskenta *927*
Finland. Statistikcentralen. Forskningsverksamheten *see* Finland. Tilastokeskus. Tutkimustoiminta *1003*
Finland. Statistikcentralen. Gaardsbruk *see* Finland. Tilastokeskus. Maatilatalous *40*
Finland. Statistikcentralen. Handboecker *see* Finland. Tilastokeskus. Kasikirjoja *1055*
Finland. Statistikcentralen. Hoegskolora *see* Finland. Tilastokeskus. Korkeakoulut *424*
Finland. Statistikcentralen. Husbyggnadsstatistik *see* Finland. Tilastkekus. Talonrakennustilasto *627*
Finland. Statistikcentralen. Inkomst- och Foermoegenhetstatistik *see* Finland. Tilastokeskus. Tulo- ja Varallisuustilasto *208*
Finland. Statistikcentralen. Inkomstfoerdelningsstatistik *see* Finland. Tilastokeskus. Tulonjakotilasto *208*
Finland. Statistikcentralen. Kommunalvalen *see* Finland. Tilastokeskus. Kunnallisvaalit *949*
Finland. Statistikcentralen. Kommunernas Ekonomi *see* Finland. Tilastokeskus. Kuntien Talous *208*
Finland. Statistikcentralen. Samfaerdselstatistiskaarsbok *see* Finland. Tilastokeskus. Liikennetilastollinen Vuosikirja *1085*
Finland. Statistikcentralen. Statens Statistiska Publikationer *see* Finland. Tilastokeskus. Valtion Tilastojulkaisut *1055*
Finland. Statistikcentralen. Statistika Meddelanden. Miljoestatistik *see* Finland. Tilastokeskus. Tilastollisia Tiedonantoja. Ymparistotilasto *501*

Finland. Statistikcentralen. Statistiska Meddelanden. Hushaallsbudgetundersoekningen see Finland. Tilastokeskus. Tilastollisia Tiedonantoja. Kotitaloustiedustelu 208
Finland. Statistikcentralen. Statistiska Meddelanden Kulturstatistik see Finland. Tilastokeskus. Tilastollisia Tiedonantoja. Kulttuuritilasto 1014
Finland. Statistikcentralen. Statistiska Meddelanden. Levnadsfoerhaalanden i Finland/Finland. Central Statistical Office. Living Conditions in Finland (FI) 1026, 1055
Finland. Statistikcentralen. Statliga Val. Ridsdagsmannavalen see Finland. Tilastokeskus. Valtiolliset Vaalit. Kansanedustajain Vaalit 911
Finland. Statistikcentralen. Undersoekningar see Finland. Tilastokeskus. Tutkimuksia 208
Finland. Statistikcentralen. Yrkesutbildningsanstalterna see Finland. Tilastokeskus. Ammatilliset Oppilaitokset 207
Finland. Statistikcentralen. Vaegtrafikolyckor see Finland. Tilastokeskus. Tieliikenneonnettomuudet 1085
Finland. Tilastokeskus. Ammatilliset Oppilaitokset/Finland. Statistikcentralen. Yrkesutbildningsanstalterna/Finland. Central Statistical Office. Vocational Education (FI ISSN 0357-2625) 207, 414
Finland. Tilastokeskus. Asuntotuotanto/ Finland. Statistikcentralen. Bostadsproduktionen/Finland. Central Statistical Office. Construction of Dwellings (FI ISSN 0355-2152) 627
Finland. Tilastokeskus. Energiatilastot/ Finland. Statistikcentralen. Energistatistik (FI ISSN 0358-2019) 465, 468
Finland. Tilastokeskus. Kansanedustajain Vaalit see Finland. Tilastokeskus. Valtiolliset Vaalit. Kansanedustajain Vaalit 911
Finland. Tilastokeskus. Kansanopetus see Finland. Tilastokeskus. Yleissivistavat Oppilaitokset 424
Finland. Tilastokeskus. Kasikirjoja/ Finland. Statistikcentralen. Handboecker/Finland. Central Statistical Office. Handbooks (FI ISSN 0355-2063) 1055
Finland. Tilastokeskus. Korkeakoulut/ Finland. Statistikcentralen. Hoegskolora/Finland. Central Statistical Office. Higher Education (FI ISSN 0355-2225) 424
Finland. Tilastokeskus. Kunnallisvaalit/ Finland. Statistikcentralen. Kommunalvalen/Finland. Central Statistical Office. Municipal Elections(FI ISSN 0355-2217) 949
Finland. Tilastokeskus. Kuntien Finanssitilasto see Finland. Tilastokeskus. Kuntien Talous 208
Finland. Tilastokeskus. Kuntien Talous/ Finland. Statistikcentralen. Kommunernas Ekonomi/Finland. Central Statistical Office. Municipal Finances (FI ISSN 0359-081X) 208
Finland. Tilastokeskus. Kuolemansyyt/ Finland. Statistikcentralen. Doedsorsaker/Finland. Central Statistical Office. Causes of Death in Finland (FI ISSN 0355-2144) 208, 761
Finland. Tilastokeskus. Kuolleisuus- Ja Eloonjaamistauluja see Finland. Tilastokeskus. Kuolleisuus. Kuolleisuus- Ja Eloonjaamistauluja 927
Finland. Tilastokeskus. Kuolleisuus. Kuolleisuus- Ja Eloonjaamistauluja/ Finland. Statistikcentralen. Doedlighet. Doedlighets- och Livslaengdstabeller/Finland. Central Statistical Office. Mortality. Life Tables (FI) 927

Finland. Tilastokeskus. Liikennetilastollinen Vuosikirja/ Finland. Statistikcentralen. Samfaerdselstatistikaarsbok/Finland. Central Statistical Office. Yearbook of Transport Statistics (FI ISSN 0430-5272) 1085
Finland. Tilastokeskus. Liikepankit ja Kiinnitys Luottolaitokset see Finland. Tilastokeskus. Pankit 208
Finland. Tilastokeskus. Maatilatalous/ Finland. Statistikcentralen. Gaardsbruk/Finland. Central Statistical Office. Farm Economy (FI ISSN 0356-2913) 40
Finland. Tilastokeskus. Oppikoulut see Finland. Tilastokeskus. Yleissivistavat Oppilaitokset 424
Finland. Tilastokeskus. Osuuspankkitilasto see Finland. Tilastokeskus. Pankit 208
Finland. Tilastokeskus. Pankit/Finland. Statistikcentralen. Bankerna/Finland. Central Statistical Office. Banks (FI ISSN 0355-2454) 208
Finland. Tilastokeskus. Rikollisuus. Poliisin Tietoon Tullut Rikollisuus/ Finland. Statistikcentralen. Brottslighet. Brottslighet Som Kommit till Polishens Kaennedom/ Finland. Central Statistical Office. Criminality. Criminality Known to the Police (FI ISSN 0355-2160) 374
Finland. Tilastokeskus. Rikollisuus. Tuomioistuinten Tutkimat Rikokset/ Finland. Statistikcentralen. Brottslighet. Vid Domstolar Rannsakade Brott/Finland. Central Statistical Office. Criminality. Criminal Cases Tried by the Courts (FI ISSN 0355-2179) 374
Finland. Tilastokeskus. Saastopankkitilasto see Finland. Tilastokeskus. Pankit 208
Finland. Tilastokeskus. Talonrakennustilasto/Finland. Statistikcentralen. Husbyggnadsstatistik/Finland. Central Statistical Office. Building Construction Statistics (FI ISSN 0430-5604) 627
Finland. Tilastokeskus. Teollisuustilasto/Finland. Central Statistical Office. Industrial Statistics (FI ISSN 0071-5344) 208
Finland. Tilastokeskus. Tieliikenneonnettomuudet/Finland. Statistikcentralen. Vaegtrafikolyckor/Finland. Central Statistical Office. Road Traffic Accidents (FI ISSN 0355-2284) 1085
Finland. Tilastokeskus. Tilastollisia Tiedonantoja see Finland. Tilastokeskus. Tilastollisia Tiedonantoja. Kotitaloustiedustelu 208
Finland. Tilastokeskus. Tilastollisia Tiedonantoja. Kotitaloustiedustelu/ Finland. Statistikcentralen. Statistiska Meddelanden. Hushaallsbudgetundersoekningen/ Finland. Central Statistical Office. Statistical Surveys. Household Survey(FI) 208
Finland. Tilastokeskus. Tilastollisia Tiedonantoja. Kulttuuritilasto/ Finland. Statistikcentralen. Statistiska Meddelanden Kulturstatistik/Finland. Central Statistical Office. Statistical Surveys. Cultural Statistics (FI) 1014
Finland. Tilastokeskus. Tilastollisia Tiedonantoja. Naisten Asema/ Finland. Statistikcentraleen. Statistiska Meddelanden. Kvinnornas Staellning/Finland. Central Statistical Office. Statistical Surveys. Position of Women (FI) 1026, 1055
Finland. Tilastokeskus. Tilastollisia Tiedonantoja. Ymparistotilasto/ Finland. Statistikcentralen. Statistiska Meddelanden. Miljoestatistik/ Finland. Central Statistical Office. Statistical Surveys. Environmental Statistics (FI) 501

Finland. Tilastokeskus. Tilastotiedotus KT. Kansantalouden Tilinpito/ National Raekenskaper/National Accounts (FI ISSN 0355-2276) 208
Finland. Tilastokeskus. Tulo- ja Omaisuustilasto see Finland. Tilastokeskus. Tulo- ja Varallisuustilasto 208
Finland. Tilastokeskus. Tulo- ja Varallisuustilasto/Finland. Statistikcentralen. Inkomst- och Foermoegenhetstatistik/Finland. Central Statistical Office. Statistics of Income and Property (FI ISSN 0780-9352) 208
Finland. Tilastokeskus. Tulonjakotilasto/Finland. Statistikcentralen. Inkomstfoerdelningsstatistik/Finland. Central Statistical Office. Income Distribution Statistics (FI ISSN 0358-2825) 208
Finland. Tilastokeskus. Tuomioistuinten Toiminta/Finland. Statistikcentralen. Domstolarnas Verksamhet/Finland. Central Statistical Office. Function of Courts (FI ISSN 0355-2187) 374
Finland. Tilastokeskus. Tutkimuksia/ Finland. Statistikcentralen. Undersoekningar/Finland. Central Statistical Office. Studies (FI ISSN 0355-2071) 208
Finland. Tilastokeskus. Tutkimustoiminta/Finland. Statistikcentralen. Forskningsverksamheten/Finland. Central Statistical Office. Research Activity (FI ISSN 0355-2233) 1003
Finland. Tilastokeskus. Tyovoimatiedustelu see Finland. Tilastokeskus. Tyovoimatutkimus 208
Finland. Tilastokeskus. Tyovoimatutkimus/Finland. Statistikcentralen. Arbetskraftsundersokningen/Finland. Central Statistical Office. Labour Force Survey (FI ISSN 0781-5611) 208
Finland. Tilastokeskus. Vaesto/Finland. Statistikcentralen. Befolkning/ Finland. Central Statistical Office. Population (FI) 927
Finland. Tilastokeskus. Vaesto- ja Asuntolaskenta/Finland. Statistikcentralen. Folk- och Bostadsraekningen/Finland. Central Statistical Office. Population and Housing Census (FI) 927
Finland. Tilastokeskus. Vaestolaskenta see Finland. Tilastokeskus. Vaesto- ja Asuntolaskenta 927
Finland. Tilastokeskus. Vaestonmuutokset see Finland. Tilastokeskus. Vaesto 927
Finland. Tilastokeskus. Valtiolliset Vaalit. Kansanedustajain Vaalit/ Finland. Statistikcentralen. Statliga Val. Ridsdagsmannavalen/Finland. Central Statistical Office. National Elections. Parliamentary Elections (FI) 911
Finland. Tilastokeskus. Valtiolliset Vaalit. Tasavallan Presidentin Vaalit Valisijamiesten (FI ISSN 0355-2195) 905, 911
Finland. Tilastokeskus. Valtion Tilastojulkaisut/Finland. Statistikcentralen. Statens Statistiska Publikationer/Finland. Central Statistical Office. Government Statistics (FI ISSN 0357-0614) 1055
Finland. Tilastokeskus. Yleissivistavat Oppilaitokset/Finland. Statistikcentralen. Allmaenbildande Laeroanstalter/Finland. Central Statistical Office. General Education (FI ISSN 0355-2446) 424
Finland. Tyovoimaministerio. Tyovoimakatsaus/Finland. Ministry of Labour. Labour Reports (FI ISSN 0430-5280) 271
Finland. Valtakunnansuunnittelutoimisto. Julkaisuja. Sarja A see Finland. Valtioneuvoston Kanslian. Julkaisuja 289

Finland. Valtioneuvoston Kanslian. Julkaisuja (FI ISSN 0355-8878) 289
Finland. Vestientutkimuslaitos. Julkaisuja/Finland. Water Research Institute. Publications (FI ISSN 0355-0982) 1124
Finland. Water Research Institute. Publications see Finland. Vestientutkimuslaitos. Julkaisuja 1124
Finland Kansanelakelaitos. Toimintakertomus (FI ISSN 0355-5003) 639
Finlands Bank. Aarsbok see Bank of Finland. Yearbook 224
Finlands Bank. Publikationer. Serie A see Suomen Pankki. Julkaisuja. Sarja A 200
Finlands Bank. Publikationer. Serie B see Suomen Pankki. Julkaisuja. Sarja B 200
Finlands Bank. Publikationer. Serie C see Suomen Pankki. Julkaisuja. Sarja C 200
Finlands Bank. Publikationer. Serie D see Suomen Pankki. Julkaisuja. Sarja D 200
Finlands Industrifoerbund. Medlemsfoerteckning see Suomen Teollisuusliitto. Jasenluettelo 317
Finlandska Masskuldevrevslan see Suomen Joukkovelkakirjalainat 268
Finnisch-Ugrische Forschungen (FI ISSN 0355-1253) 582, 695
Finnische Geodaetische Institut. Veroeffentlichungen see Suomen Geodeettisen Laitoksen. Julkaisuja 401
Finnish Boatbuilding Industry (FI ISSN 0356-7753) 1041
Finnish Bond Issues see Suomen Joukkovelkakirjalainat 268
Finnish Broadcasting Company. Planning and Research Department. Research Reports (FI) 348
Finnish Broadcasting Company. Section for Long-Range Planning. Research Reports see Finnish Broadcasting Company. Planning and Research Department. Research Reports 348
Finnish Buyer's Guide (UK) 255
Finnish Dental Society. Proceedings. Supplement see Suomen Hammaslaakariseura. Toimituksia. Supplementa 780
Finnish Fisheries Research (FI ISSN 0301-908X) 509
Finnish Game Research/ Riistatieteellisia Julkaisuja (FI ISSN 0015-2447) 141, 365
Finnish Geodetic Institute. Publications see Suomen Geodeettisen Laitoksen. Julkaisuja 401
Finnish Geodetic Institute. Reports see Suomen Geodeettisen Laitoksen. Tiedonantoja 401
Finnish Insurance Yearbook see Suomen Vakuutusvuosikirja 641
Finnish Journal of Dairy Science see Meijeritieteellinen Aikakauskirja 62
Finnish Marine Research (FI ISSN 0357-1076) 405
Finnish Meteorological Institute. Contributions (FI ISSN 0071-5190) 804
Finnish Photographic Yearbook see Valokuvauksen Vuosikirja 885
Finsk Fotografisk Arsbok see Valokuvauksen Vuosikirja 885
Finskt Museum (FI ISSN 0355-1814) 71, 86
Fire Casualty & Surety Argus F C & S Chart see Argus F C & S Chart 638
Fire Prevention News (CN ISSN 0071-5395) 506
Fire Protection Directory (UK ISSN 0071-5409) 506
Fire Protection Handbook (US ISSN 0071-5417) 506
Fire Protection Handbook Study Guide (US ISSN 0071-5425) 1153
Fire Protection Reference Directory (US ISSN 0361-8382) 506
Fire Research Publications (US) 507
Fire Statistics United Kingdom (UK ISSN 0260-3098) 770
Fire Yearbook (US ISSN 0071-5468) 506

Firearms, State Laws and Published Ordinances *see* State Laws and Published Ordinances, Firearms 664
Firehouse Magazine Buyers Guide (US) 506
Firmengruendung in Daenemark (DK ISSN 0901-8735) 244
First Catholic Slovak Union of America. Minutes of Annual Meeting(US ISSN 0275-6145) 982
First Empire State Corporation. Interim Report (US) 228
First Hand Information (GE) 582, 916
First National City Bank, Liberia. Annual Report (LB) 229
First to Final (US ISSN 0015-2803) 930
First Year of Life (US) 333, 785, 886
Fiscalite Europeenne (FR) 295
Fish and Wildlife Gazette (AT) 509
Fish Disease Leaflets (US ISSN 0071-5492) 509
Fish Stock Record *see* Great Britain. Ministry of Agriculture, Fisheries and Food. Directorate of Fisheries Research. Fishing Prospects 509
Fishdex (NZ) 509
Fisheries and Wildlife Research (US) 509, 1045
Fisheries Bulletin (IE ISSN 0332-4338) 174, 509
Fisheries Bulletin *see* Malawi. Fisheries Department. Fisheries Bulletin 511
Fisheries of Scotland Report (UK ISSN 0080-1283) 509
Fisheries of the United States (US) 509
Fisheries Research Bulletin of Zambia (ZA ISSN 0084-4713) 509
Fisheries Research Review *see* Colorado Fisheries Research Review 1150
Fisheries Statistics of Japan (JA ISSN 0071-5581) 509
Fisherman Union of Indonesia. Central Governing Board. Annual Report/ Himpunan Nelayan Selurah Indonesia. Dewan Pimpanan Pusat. Laporan Kegiatan (IO) 509
Fishery Statistics *see* Norway. Statistisk Sentralbyraa. Fiskeristatistikk 514
Fishery Statistics of the United States *see* Fisheries of the United States 509
Fishing *see* Field & Stream Fishing Annual 1045
Fishing and Boating Illustrated (US) 1045
Fishing Handbook (UK ISSN 0261-7943) 1045
Fishing in Maryland (US ISSN 0164-0941) 1045
Fishing in New Jersey (US) 1045
Fishing in the Mid-Atlantic *see* Fishing in Maryland 1045
Fishing in the Mid-Atlantic *see* Fishing in New Jersey 1045
Fishing: Latin American Industrial Report (US) 509
Fisk og Hav (DK ISSN 0105-9211) 509
Fisken og Havet (NO ISSN 0071-5638) 509
Fiskeri og Fiskeriundersoegelser ved Groenland *see* Fiskeriet ved Groenland & Groenlands Fiskeriundersoegelsers Aktivitet 509
Fiskeriaarbogen (DK ISSN 0900-9787) 509
Fiskeriet ved Groenland & Groenlands Fiskeriundersoegelsers Aktivitet (DK ISSN 0108-8629) 509
Fitech (UK ISSN 0307-2118) 507
Fitologija (BU ISSN 0324-0975) 156
Fitossanidade (BL ISSN 0100-4204) 156
Fitzgerald/Hemingway Annual (US ISSN 0071-5654) 722
FitzHardinge's Nobiliary (AT ISSN 0157-8804) 535
Five Year Economic Forecast/Gokanen Keizai Yosoku (JA) 244
Five Years Work in Librarianship *see* British Librarianship & Information Work 675
Fizicheskaya Mekhanika (UR) 894
Fizika Aerodispersnykh Sistem (UR) 804
Fizika Nizhnei Atmosfery (UR) 804

Fiziko-Khimicheska Mekhanika/ Physico-Chemical Mechanics (BU ISSN 0204-5958) 331, 894
Fiziko-Khimicheskaya Mekhanika i Liofilnost' Dispersnykh Sistem (UR ISSN 0367-2409) 331
Fiziologicheski Aktivnye Veshchestva (UR ISSN 0533-1153) 171
Fizyka (PL ISSN 0554-825X) 888
Fizyka i Chemia Metali (PL ISSN 0208-578X) 797
Flamenco (SP) 515, 543
Flannery O'Connor Bulletin (US ISSN 0091-4924) 722
Flea Market Almanac (US) 79
Flea Market Quarterly *see* Flea Market Almanac 79
Flea Market Trader (US ISSN 0364-023X) 79
Fleischleistungspruefung fuer Rinder, Legeleistungspruefung fuer Huehner, Fleischleistungspruefung fuer Schafe (GW) 62, 65
Flensburger Statistische Blaetter (GW) 1055
Flensburger Zahlenspiegel (Year) (GW) 1055
Flexographic Technical Association. Report of the Proceedings: Annual Meeting and Technical Forum (US ISSN 0428-5670) 930
Fliegerkalender (GW) 18
Flies of the Nearctic Region (GW) 164
Flight *see* Envol 170
Flight Directory of British Aviation (UK) 1088
Flinders Asian Studies Lecture (AT ISSN 0085-0586) 851
Flinders Asian Studies Monograph (AT) 851
Flinders Institute for Atmospheric and Marine Sciences. Computing Reports(AT) 405, 804
Flinders Institute for Atmospheric and Marine Sciences. Cruise Reports (AT) 405
Flinders Institute for Atmospheric and Marine Sciences. Research Reports (AT) 405, 804
Flinders Institute for Atmospheric and Marine Sciences. Technical Reports (AT) 405, 804
Flinders Journal of History and Politics (AT ISSN 0726-7215) 573, 905
Flintshire Historical Society. Publications, Journal and Record Series (UK ISSN 0140-8429) 582
Floating Island (US ISSN 0147-1686) 722
Flock Book of Devon Cornwall Longwool Sheep (UK) 66
Flock Book of Oxford Down Sheep (UK) 66
Floodlight (UK) 429
Flora *see* Acta Botanica Islandica 153
Flora (EC ISSN 0015-380X) 156
Flora (GE ISSN 0367-2530) 156
Flora de Colombia (CK ISSN 0120-4351) 156
Flora Ecologica de Restingas do Sudeste do Brasil (BL ISSN 0071-5751) 156
Flora et Vegetatio Mundi (GW ISSN 0071-576X) 156
Flora Malesiana. Series 2: Pteridophyta (NE ISSN 0071-5786) 156
Flora Neotropica (US ISSN 0071-5794) 156
Flora of Ecuador (SW) 156
Flora of Southern Africa (SA) 156
Flora of the U.S.S.R. (IS) 156
Flora Palaestina (IS) 156
Flora Polska; Rosliny Naczyniowe Polski i Ziem Osciennych (PL ISSN 0071-5816) 156
Flora Polska: Rosliny Zarodnikowe Polski i Ziem Osciennych (PL ISSN 0071-5824) 156
Flora Slodkowodna Polski (PL ISSN 0071-5840) 157
Florae Polonicae Terrarunique Adiacentium Sconographia *see* Atlas Flory Polskiej i Ziem Osciennych 154
Floral Marketing Directory and Buyer's Guide (US) 534
Flore d'Afrique Centrale (Zaire - Rwanda - Burundi) (BE) 157

Flore de la Nouvelle Caledonie et Dependances (FR ISSN 0430-666X) 157
Flore de Madagascar et des Comores (FR) 157
Flore du Cambodge, du Laos et du Vietnam (FR ISSN 0071-5867) 157
Flore du Cameroun (CM ISSN 0071-5875) 157
Flore du Congo, du Rwanda et du Burundi *see* Flore d'Afrique Centrale (Zaire - Rwanda - Burundi) 157
Flore du Gabon (FR ISSN 0071-5883) 157
Florida. Bureau of Geology. Geological Bulletins (US ISSN 0085-0608) 386
Florida. Bureau of Geology. Information Circulars (US ISSN 0085-0616) 386
Florida. Bureau of Geology. Map Series(US ISSN 0085-0624) 386
Florida. Bureau of Geology. Report of Investigations (US ISSN 0096-0489) 386
Florida. Bureau of Geology. Special Publications (US ISSN 0085-0640) 386
Florida. Bureau of Local Government Finance. Annual Local Government Financial Report (US ISSN 0094-8551) 295
Florida. Department of Corrections. Annual Report (US) 1017
Florida. Department of Education. Professional Practices Council. Report (US) 414
Florida. Department of Health and Rehabilitative Services. Annual Statistical Report (US) 1022
Florida. Department of Transportation. Annual Report (US ISSN 0095-2060) 1153
Florida. Division of Corrections. Financial Report *see* Florida. Department of Corrections. Annual Report 1017
Florida. Division of Family Services. Annual Statistical Report *see* Florida. Department of Health and Rehabilitative Services. Annual Statistical Report 1022
Florida. Division of Motor Vehicles. Tags and Revenue (US ISSN 0092-0177) 1081
Florida. Division of Plant Industry. Biennial Report (US ISSN 0071-5948) 27, 157
Florida. Division of State Planning. Annual Report on State and Regional Planning (US) 623
Florida. Legislature. Joint Legislative Management Committee. Summary of General Legislation (US ISSN 0090-1520) 655
Florida. Mental Health Program Office. Statistical Report of Hospitals (US ISSN 0094-2294) 619
Florida. Office of the Governor. Budget in Brief (US ISSN 0095-5175) 941
Florida and the Other Forty-Nine (US) 235
Florida Builders and Contractors Directory (US ISSN 0276-8208) 184, 308
Florida Community-County Comparison *see* Florida County Profiles 235
Florida County Comparisons (US) 235
Florida County Profiles (US) 235
Florida Economy (US) 236
Florida Education Directory (US) 429
Florida Festival Arts Directory *see* Florida Folklife Resource Directory 105
Florida Folklife Resource Directory (US) 105, 835
Florida Geographer (US ISSN 0739-0041) 543
Florida International University. Latin American and Caribbean Center. Occasional Papers Series (US) 605
Florida Lodging Industry (US) 620
Florida Manufacturers Register (US) 308
Florida Marine Research Publications (US ISSN 0095-0157) 141
Florida Notary Law Primer (US) 655
Florida Requirements for Teacher Certification (US ISSN 0071-5999) 435

Florida Senate (US ISSN 0093-4089) 655
Florida State Collection of Arthropods. Occasional Papers (US ISSN 0885-5943) 164
Florida State Industrial Directory *see* MacRae's Florida State Industrial Directory 312
Florida State Museum. Bulletin. Biological Sciences (US) 557
Florida State Museum. Bulletin. Biological Series *see* Florida State Museum. Bulletin. Biological Sciences 557
Florida State Museum. Contributions. Anthropology and History (US) 71
Florida State Museum. Contributions. Social Sciences *see* Florida State Museum. Contributions. Anthropology and History 71
Florida State Poetry Society. Selected Poems (US) 741
Florida State University. Center for Yugoslav-American Studies, Research, and Exchanges. Proceedings and Reports of Seminars and Research (US) 582, 1008
Florida State University. Instructional Support Center. Film *see* Florida State University. Instructional Support Center. Film and Video 826
Florida State University. Instructional Support Center. Film and Video (US) 826
Florida State University. Publications of the Faculty (US ISSN 0428-6766) 435
Florida State University. Publications of the Faculty and Theses Directed *see* Florida State University. Publications of the Faculty 435
Florida State University. Robert Manning Strozier Library. Collection Series (US) 722
Florida State University. Slavic Papers *see* Florida State University. Center for Yugoslav-American Studies, Research, and Exchanges. Proceedings and Reports of Seminars and Research 582
Florida Statistical Abstract (US ISSN 0071-6022) 1055
Florida Statistical Abstracts Annual *see* Florida Statistical Abstract 1055
Florida Tour Book *see* Tourbook: Florida 1117
Florida Tourist Study *see* Florida's Visitors 1109
Florida Vital Statistics (US) 927, 1055
Florida's Economy *see* Florida Economy 236
Florida's Visitors (US) 1109
Florilegium (CN) 337, 722
Floristisch-Soziologische Arbeitsgemeinschaft. Mitteilungen *see* Tuexenia 1066
Flour Milling and Baking Research Association. Annual Report and Accounts (UK ISSN 0071-6243) 518
Flour Milling and Baking Research Association Abstracts (UK ISSN 0430-7941) 6, 40, 521
Flow of Funds in Taiwan District, Republic of China (CH) 229
Flower Essence Society Members' Newsletter *see* Flower Essence Society Newsletter 157
Flower Essence Society Newsletter (US) 157, 886
Flower of the Forest Black Genealogical Journal (US) 503, 535
Flowering Plants of Africa (SA ISSN 0015-4504) 157
Flowering Plants of South Africa *see* Flowering Plants of Africa 157
Fluid Dynamics Transactions (PL ISSN 0137-6462) 895
Fluid Flow Measurement Abstracts (UK ISSN 0305-9235) 6, 476
Fluid Power Abstracts (UK ISSN 0015-4644) 6, 476
Fluid Power and Control Series (US) 490
Fluid Power Handbook & Directory (US ISSN 0428-7738) 308, 489
Fluid Power Standards (US) 490
Fluid Power Symposium. Proceedings (UK ISSN 0140-2099) 490

Fluid Sealing Abstracts (UK ISSN 0015-4660) 6, *476*, 1072
Fluoridation Census (US) *779*
Flygtekniska Foersoeksanstalten. Meddelande/Report (SW ISSN 0081-5640) *18*
Flying Annual & Buyers' Guide (US ISSN 0163-1144) *18*
Flying Buyers Guide *see* Flying Annual & Buyers' Guide *18*
Flying Doctor Yearbook (AT) *617*, 1088
Flying Yearbook (US ISSN 0190-6526) *1153*
Flytninger (DK) *623*
Focal Points (US ISSN 0278-1808) *953*
Focus (JM) *722*
Focus (Dublin) (IE ISSN 0790-4940) *884*
Focus (Moscow) (US) *365*, 524
Focus, an Economic Profile of the Apparel Industry (US) *340*
Focus: Biology *see* Annual Editions: Biology *137*
Focus on Dance (US ISSN 0071-6294) *375*
Focus on Issues (US) *1153*
Focus on Nature Conservation (UK) *365*
Focus on Nebraska Highways *see* Nebraska. Department of Roads. Challenge of the 80's *483*
Focus on Politics (SA) *557*, 905
Focus on Renewable Natural Resources(US) *174*, *509*, 524
Focus on Sci-Tech (US) *991*, 1068
Focus paa Undervisning (DK ISSN 0108-7746) *414*
Focus: Urban Society *see* Annual Editions: Urban Society *1024*
Focuses (US) *722*
Fodbold Jul (DK) *1038*
Fodbold Poster Bladet (DK ISSN 0901-1595) *1038*
Fodboldens Aarsrevy (DK ISSN 0108-5077) *1038*
Fodor's Alaska (US ISSN 0271-2776) *1109*
Fodor's American Cities on a Budget (US) *1109*
Fodor's Australia, New Zealand and the South Pacific (US ISSN 0191-2321) *1109*
Fodor's Austria (US ISSN 0071-6340) *1109*
Fodor's Bahamas (US) *1109*
Fodor's Beijing, Guangzhou and Shanghai (US) *1109*
Fodor's Belgium and Luxembourg (US ISSN 0071-6359) *1109*
Fodor's Bermuda (US) *1109*
Fodor's Boston (US) *1109*
Fodor's Brazil (US ISSN 0163-0628) *1109*
Fodor's Budget Britain *see* Fodor's Budget Travel Britain *1109*
Fodor's Budget Canada *see* Fodor's Budget Travel Canada *1109*
Fodor's Budget Caribbean *see* Fodor's Budget Travel Caribbean *1109*
Fodor's Budget Europe (US ISSN 0197-4998) *1109*
Fodor's Budget France *see* Fodor's Budget Travel France *1109*
Fodor's Budget Germany *see* Fodor's Budget Travel Germany *1109*
Fodor's Budget Italy *see* Fodor's Budget Travel Italy *1109*
Fodor's Budget Japan *see* Fodor's Budget Travel Japan *1109*
Fodor's Budget Mexico *see* Fodor's Budget Travel Mexico *1109*
Fodor's Budget Spain *see* Fodor's Budget Travel Spain *1109*
Fodor's Budget Travel Britain (US) *1109*
Fodor's Budget Travel Canada (US) *1109*
Fodor's Budget Travel Caribbean (US) *1109*
Fodor's Budget Travel France (US) *1109*
Fodor's Budget Travel Germany (US) *1109*
Fodor's Budget Travel in America *see* Fodor's American Cities on a Budget *1109*
Fodor's Budget Travel Italy (US) *1109*

Fodor's Budget Travel Japan (US) *1109*
Fodor's Budget Travel Mexico (US) *1109*
Fodor's Budget Travel Spain (US) *1109*
Fodor's California (US ISSN 0192-9925) *1109*
Fodor's Canada (US ISSN 0160-3906) *1109*
Fodor's Cape Cod (US) *1109*
Fodor's Caribbean (US) *1109*
Fodor's Caribbean and Bahamas *see* Fodor's Caribbean *1109*
Fodor's Caribbean and Bahamas *see* Fodor's Bahamas *1109*
Fodor's Central America (US ISSN 0270-8183) *1109*
Fodor's Chicago (US) *1109*
Fodor's Chicago and the Great Lakes *see* Fodor's Chicago *1109*
Fodor's Colorado (US ISSN 0276-9018) *1109*
Fodor's Eastern Europe (US) *1109*
Fodor's Egypt (US ISSN 0147-8176) *1109*
Fodor's Europe on a Budget *see* Fodor's Budget Europe *1109*
Fodor's Far West (US ISSN 0192-3730) *1109*
Fodor's Florida (US ISSN 0193-9556) *1109*
Fodor's France (US ISSN 0071-6383) *1109*
Fodor's Germany (US) *1109*
Fodor's Germany: West and East *see* Fodor's Germany *1109*
Fodor's Great Britain (US ISSN 0071-6405) *1109*
Fodor's Greece (US ISSN 0071-6413) *1109*
Fodor's Guide to India *see* Fodor's India & Nepal *1109*
Fodor's Hawaii (US ISSN 0071-6421) *1109*
Fodor's Holland (US ISSN 0071-643X) *1109*
Fodor's Hong Kong and Macau (US) *1109*
Fodor's India *see* Fodor's India & Nepal *1109*
Fodor's India & Nepal (US ISSN 0276-5500) *1109*
Fodor's Ireland (US ISSN 0071-6464) *1109*
Fodor's Israel (US ISSN 0071-6588) *1109*
Fodor's Italy (US ISSN 0071-6472) *1109*
Fodor's Japan (US) *1109*
Fodor's Japan and East Asia *see* Fodor's Southeast Asia *1110*
Fodor's Japan and Korea *see* Fodor's Japan *1109*
Fodor's Japan and Korea *see* Fodor's Korea *1109*
Fodor's Korea (US) *1109*
Fodor's Lisbon (US) *1109*
Fodor's London (US ISSN 0071-6596) *1109*
Fodor's Madrid (US) *1109*
Fodor's Mexico (US ISSN 0071-6499) *1110*
Fodor's Munich (US) *1110*
Fodor's New England (US ISSN 0192-3412) *1110*
Fodor's New York *see* Fodor's New York City *1110*
Fodor's New York City (US) *1110*
Fodor's North Africa (US) *1110*
Fodor's Pacific North Coast (US) *1110*
Fodor's Paris (US ISSN 0149-1288) *1110*
Fodor's People's Republic of China (US ISSN 0192-2378) *1110*
Fodor's Portugal (US ISSN 0071-6510) *1110*
Fodor's Rome (US ISSN 0276-2560) *1110*
Fodor's San Diego (US) *1110*
Fodor's San Francisco (US) *1110*
Fodor's Scandinavia (US ISSN 0071-6529) *1110*
Fodor's Scotland (US) *1110*
Fodor's South (US ISSN 0147-8680) *1110*
Fodor's South America (US ISSN 0071-6537) *1110*
Fodor's Southeast Asia (US ISSN 0160-8991) *1110*

Fodor's Soviet Union (US ISSN 0095-1358) *1110*
Fodor's Spain (US ISSN 0071-6545) *1110*
Fodor's Stockholm, Copenhagen, Oslo, Helsinki & Reykjavik (US) *1110*
Fodor's Switzerland (US ISSN 0071-6553) *1110*
Fodor's Turkey (US ISSN 0071-6618) *1110*
Fodor's U S A (US ISSN 0147-8745) *1110*
Fodor's Vienna (US) *1110*
Fodor's Yugoslavia (US ISSN 0071-657X) *1110*
Foederalismus-Studien (AU) *905*
Foerdermittelkatalog (SZ) *745*
Foeredrag vid Pyroteknikdagen (SW ISSN 0348-6613) *478*
Foereningen Armemusei Vaenner. Meddelande: Kungliga Armemuseum *see* Meddelande Armemuseum. Yearbook *828*
Foeroyar (DK ISSN 0900-1131) *71*
Foersaekringsaarsbok foer Finland *see* Suomen Vakuutusvuosikirja *641*
Foerteckning Oever Advokater och Advokatbyraaer (SW) *655*
Fogra-Literatur-Profil (GW) *930*
Foldrajzi Monografiak (HU ISSN 0428-819X) *543*
Foldrajzi Tanulmanyok (HU ISSN 0071-6650) *543*
Folger Shakespeare Library Annual Report (US ISSN 0428-8211) *678*, 722
Folia Anatomica Iugoslavica (YU ISSN 0350-0233) *761*
Folia Anatomica Universitatis Conimbricensis (PO) *781*
Folia Antropologica (VE ISSN 0428-8254) *71*
Folia Biochimica et Biologica Graeca (GR ISSN 0015-5489) *141*, 151
Folia Dendrologica (CS) *141*, *524*, 532
Folia Facultatis Scientiarum Naturalium Universitatis Purkynianae Brunensis: Biologia (CS) *141*
Folia Facultatis Scientiarum Naturalium Universitatis Purkynianae Brunensis: Chemia (CS) *322*
Folia Facultatis Scientiarum Naturalium Universitatis Purkynianae Brunensis: Geologia (CS) *386*
Folia Facultatis Scientiarum Naturalium Universitatis Purkynianae Brunensis: Geographia (CS) *991*
Folia Facultatis Scientiarum Naturalium Universitatis Purkynianae Brunensis: Physica (CS ISSN 0323-0287) *888*
Folia Forestalia Polonica. Series A. Lesnictwo (PL ISSN 0071-6677) *524*
Folia Forestalia Polonica. Series B. Drzewnictwo (PL ISSN 0071-6685) *529*
Folia Geographica. Geographica-Oeconomica (PL ISSN 0071-6707) *543*
Folia Geographica. Geographica-Physica (PL ISSN 0071-6715) *386*, *543*
Folia Geographica Danica (DK ISSN 0071-6693) *543*
Folia Historiae Artium (PL ISSN 0071-6723) *105*
Folia Historica (HU ISSN 0133-6622) *582*
Folia Historica Bohemica (CS ISSN 0231-7494) *582*
Folia Historica del Nordeste (AG ISSN 0325-8238) *605*
Folia Limnologica Scandinavica (SW ISSN 0367-2476) *141*
Folia Mendeliana *see* Acta Musei Moraviae. Scientia Naturales 3: Folia Mendeliana *166*
Folia Montana *see* Banicke Listy *814*
Folia Numismatica (CS) *844*
Folia Oeconomica Cracoviensia (PL ISSN 0071-674X) *194*
Folia Orientalia (PL ISSN 0015-5675) *851*
Folia Quaternaria (PL ISSN 0015-573X) *856*
Folia Slavica (US ISSN 0160-9394) *695*
Folia Venatoria (CS) *524*, 1121

Folio (Brockport) (US ISSN 0882-3030) *629*, 722
Folio Limnologica Scandinavica (DK) *402*
Folio: The Adguide (US) *1153*
Folio: 400 (US) *1153*
Folk Dance Directory (US ISSN 0163-528X) *375*
Folk; Dansk Etnografisk Tidsskrift (DK ISSN 0085-0756) *72*
Folk Directory (UK) *375*
Folk Fortaeller (DK ISSN 0109-8365) *582*
Folk Life (UK ISSN 0430-8778) *72*
Folk Music Journal (UK ISSN 0531-9684) *375*, *835*
Folk og Liv paa Roendeegnen-. Dengang (DK ISSN 0109-2766) *582*
Folk og Minder fra Koebenhavn (DK ISSN 0900-002X) *582*
Folk og Minder fra Nordsjaelland (DK) *582*
Folk Song *see* Canu Gwerin *834*
Folkebibliotekernes Udenlanske Boernebogssamling. Katalog (DK ISSN 0109-8853) *334*
Folkebiblioteksstatistik, Budgetter, Virksomhed (DK ISSN 0105-6077) *678*
Folkehoejskoler (DK ISSN 0107-4504) *429*
Folkemusikhusringen (DK ISSN 0107-7074) *835*
Folkesagn i Tekst og Billed fra Noerreherred (DK ISSN 0900-3037) *582*
Folkeskolen i de Enkelte Kommuner (DK ISSN 0106-2530) *429*
Folketingets Haandbog (DK ISSN 0107-9670) *941*
Folkl-Liv *see* Ethnologia Scandinavica *71*
Folklife Annual (US) *515*
Folklivsskildringar och Bygdesstudier (SW ISSN 0071-6766) *515*
Folklivsstudier (FI ISSN 0085-0764) *72*
Fol'klor Urala (UR) *515*
Folklore and Mythology Studies (US ISSN 0162-6280) *515*
Folklore Annual *see* University Folklore Association. Folklore Papers *517*
Folklore du Monde (BE) *515*
Folklore Fellows Communications *see* F F Communications *515*
Folklorica Publications in Folksong and Balladry (US) *835*
Folkskolans Aarsbok *see* Aarsbok foer Skolan *409*
Folktales of the World (US ISSN 0071-6804) *515*
Fondation Canadienne des Toxicomanies. Repertoire *see* Canada Addictions Foundation. Directory *376*
Fondation Maurice Careme (BE) *722*, 741
Fondation pour la Recherche et le Developpement dans l'Ocean Indien. Documents et Recherches (RE) *566*
Fondazione Giangiacomo Feltrinelli. Annali (IT ISSN 0544-1374) *1008*
Fondazione Giovanni Agnelli. Progetto Politica Industriale. Quaderno di Ricerca (IT) *194*
Fondazione Luigi Einaudi, Annali (IT) *539*
Fondo de Cultura. Serie de Lecturas (MX) *194*
Fondo de Promocion de Exportaciones. Directorio de Exportadores/Export Directory (CK) *255*
Fonds Africain de Developpement. Rapport Annuel *see* African Development Fund. Annual Report *261*
Fonds de Developpment Economique et Social. Conseil de Direction. Rapport(FR ISSN 0071-6847) *289*
Fontes *see* Slovenskeho Narodneho Muzea. Fontes Etnografickeho *75*
Fontes *see* Slovenskeho Narodneho Muzea. Fontes Historickeho *560*
Fontes Archaeologici Posnanienses/ Annales Musei Archaeologici Posnaniensis (PL ISSN 0071-6863) *86*, *582*

Fontes Archaeologici Pragenses (CS ISSN 0015-6183) 86
Fontes Iuris Gentium see Fontes Iuris Gentium. Section 2 670
Fontes Iuris Gentium. Section 2 (US ISSN 0426-7230) 670
Fontes Rerum Austriacarum. Reihe 1. Scriptores (AU) 582
Fontes Rerum Austriacarum. Reihe 2. Diplomataria et Acta (AU) 582
Fontes Rerum Austriacarum. Reihe 3. Fontes Juris (AU ISSN 0071-6898) 582, 655
Fonti e Studi per la Storia del Santo a Padova (IT) 982
Fonti e Studi per la Storia di Bologna e delle Province Emiliane e Romagnole(IT) 105, 582
Fonti Sui Comuni Rurali Toscani (IT ISSN 0071-6901) 582
Food Additives - Descriptions, Functions and U.K. Legislations (UK) 518, 655
Food and Agriculture Organization of the United Nations. Plant Protection Committee for Southeast Asia and Pacific Region. Technical Document see Food and Agriculture Organization of the United Nations. Asia and Pacific Plant Protection Commission. Technical Document 55
Food and Agriculture Organization of the United Nations. Agricultural Planning Studies (UN ISSN 0532-0194) 47
Food and Agriculture Organization of the United Nations. Asia and Pacific Plant Protection Commission. Information Letter (UN) 55
Food and Agriculture Organization of the United Nations. Asia and Pacific Plant Protection Commission. Technical Document (UN) 55
Food and Agriculture Organization of the United Nations. Asia and the Pacific Commission on Agricultural Statistics. Periodic Report (UN) 40
Food and Agriculture Organization of the United Nations. Basic Texts (UN ISSN 0532-0208) 27
Food and Agriculture Organization of the United Nations. European Inland Fisheries Advisory Commission. Occasional Papers (UN) 509
Food and Agriculture Organization of the United Nations. European Inland Fisheries Advisory Commission. Technical Papers (UN) 509
Food and Agriculture Organization of the United Nations (FAO) Agricultural Services Bulletin see F A O Agricultural Services Bulletin 46
Food and Agriculture Organization of the United Nations. Plant Protection Committee for Southeast Asia and Pacific Region. Information Letter see Food and Agriculture Organization of the United Nations. Asia and Pacific Plant Protection Commission. Information Letter 55
Food and Agriculture Organization of the United Nations. Production Yearbook (UN ISSN 0071-7118) 47
Food and Agriculture Organization of the United Nations. Soils Bulletins (UN ISSN 0532-0437) 55
Food and Agriculture Organization of the United Nations. Trade Yearbook (UN ISSN 0071-7126) 47, 255
Food and Agriculture Organization of the United Nations. World Soil Resources Reports (UN ISSN 0532-0488) 55
Food and Agriculture Organization of the United Nations Animal Production and Health Series see F A O Animal Production and Health Series 65
Food and Agriculture Organization of the United Nations Conference. Report (UN ISSN 0071-6944) 27
Food and Agriculture Organization of the United Nations Economic and Social Development Paper see F A O Economic and Social Development Paper 194

Food and Agriculture Organization of the United Nations Fertilizer and Plant Nutrition Bulletin see F A O Fertilizer and Plant Nutrition Bulletin 46
Food and Agriculture Organization of the United Nations Fertilizer Yearbook see F A O Fertilizer Yearbook 55
Food and Agriculture Organization of the United Nations Fisheries Synopsis see F A O Fisheries Synopsis 509
Food and Agriculture Organization of the United Nations Forestry Studies see F A O Forestry Studies 524
Food and Agriculture Organization of the United Nations Irrigation and Drainage Papers see F A O Irrigation and Drainage Papers 1124
Food and Agriculture Organization of the United Nations Technical Papers see C I F A Technical Papers 508
Food and Drink Trade Handbook (UK) 119, 518
Food and Nutrition Programs see U.S. Food and Nutrition Service. Food and Nutrition Programs 1023
Food Consumption in the O.E.C.D. see Food Consumption Statistics in the O.E.C.D. Countries 521
Food Consumption Statistics in the O.E.C.D. Countries (FR) 521
Food Economics Yearbook/Shokuryo Keizai Nenkan (JA) 308
Food Industries Manual (UK ISSN 0071-7177) 518
Food Industries Yearbook and Buyers' Directory see Food Industries Yearbook and Buyers' Guide 518
Food Industries Yearbook and Buyers' Guide (SA) 518
Food Industry Directory (US) 308, 519
Food Industry Directory (UK ISSN 0264-4037) 518
Food Irradiation Newsletter (UN) 519
Food: Latin American Industrial Report(US) 519
Food Legislation Surveys (UK) 519, 655
Food Manufacture Ingredient and Machinery Survey (UK) 519, 745
Food Marketers' Handbook (US ISSN 0894-184X) 522
Food Marketing Industry Speaks (US ISSN 0190-3349) 522
Food Policy Notes see Policy Notes 263
Food Processing (UK) 284, 519
Food Processing Industry Directory see Food Industry Directory 518
Food Research Institute Bristol. Biennial Report see Institute of Food Research - Bristol. Laboratory Biennial Report 519
Food Research Institute Studies (US ISSN 0193-9025) 47, 519
Food Research Institute Studies in Agricultural Economics, Trade, and Development see Food Research Institute Studies 47
Food Science and Technology Abstracts(UK ISSN 0015-6574) 6, 521
Food Science Series (US ISSN 0071-7223) 519
Food Service Directory and Buyers Guide for Fresh Produce see Buyers Guide for Fresh Produce 522
Food Service Research Abstracts (US) 519
Food Technology see Acta Academiae Agriculturae ac Technicae Olstenensis. Technologia Alimentorum 517
Food Technology and Catering in the Region (UK) 435
Food Trades Directory & Food Buyer's Yearbook (UK ISSN 0309-0264) 519
Foodborne and Waterborne Disease in Canada (CN) 519
Foodborne & Waterborne Disease Outbreaks. Annual Summary see U.S. Center for Disease Control. Foodborne & Waterborne Disease Outbreaks. Annual Summary 956

Foodnews Dairy Products Review (UK) 1153
Foodservice Information Abstracts (US) 519, 521
Football Association Year Book (UK ISSN 0071-724X) 1038
Football Case Book (US ISSN 0163-6200) 1038
Football Champions (UK) 1038
Football Forecast (Year) (US) 1038
Football Guide (US ISSN 0069-5548) 1038
Football Handbook (US) 1038
Football Officials Handbook see Football Officials Manual 1038
Football Officials Manual (US) 1038
Football Register (US ISSN 0071-7258) 1038
Football Roundup (US) 1038
Football Rulebook (US) 1038
Football Rules - Simplified and Illustrated (US) 1038
Football Statistician's Manual (US) 1038
Footwear Industry Statistical Review (UK ISSN 0308-9398) 1005
Footwear Manual (US ISSN 0095-1048) 1005
Footwear News Fact Book (US ISSN 0429-0208) 1005
For Christ and Peace (UK) 969
For Graduates Only (US) 435
For Younger Readers, Braille and Talking Books (Large Print Edition) (US ISSN 0093-2825) 126, 180, 424
Forage (AT) 27
Forbes Handbook of Home Economics & Consumer Education (UK) 369
Forbruger. Haandbog see Familien Danmarks Forbruger. Haandbog 369
Forbrugerindeks (DK ISSN 0105-9122) 369
Forbrugerklagenaevnet. Aarsberetning (DK ISSN 0106-4932) 369
Forbruget af Somatiske Sengepladser (DK ISSN 0107-7627) 617
Ford Almanac (US) 27, 462
Ford Foundation Annual Report (US ISSN 0071-7274) 414, 503, 629, 1008, 1128
Ford's Deck Plan Guide (US ISSN 0096-1353) 1100, 1110
Forebyggende (DK ISSN 0107-7503) 335
Forecast (US ISSN 0071-7282) 245
Forecast of Shop Rents (UK ISSN 0260-8812) 266, 965
Foreign Aero-Space Literature/Gaikoku Koku Uchu Bunken Mokuroku (JA ISSN 0454-191X) 22
Foreign Buyers of Philippine Cottage Industry Products (PH) 308
Foreign Callbook (US) 348
Foreign Consular Offices in the United States (US ISSN 0071-7320) 916
Foreign Economic Trends and Their Implications for the United States (US ISSN 0090-9467) 245
Foreign Investment Opportunities in the Philippines (PH ISSN 0085-0802) 289
Foreign Investments in Brazil see Foreign Investments in Brazil. Legislation 255
Foreign Investments in Brazil. Legislation (BL) 255, 655
Foreign Market Airgrams see International Trade Administration Reports 257
Foreign Market Reports see International Trade Administration Reports 257
Foreign Policy Research Institute. Annual Report (US) 916
Foreign Policy Research Institute. Monograph Series see Philadelphia Policy Papers 917
Foreign Radio Amateur Callbook Magazine see Foreign Callbook 348
Foreign Relations of the United States (US ISSN 0071-7355) 916
Foreign Trade Marketplace (US) 255
Foreign Trade of Greece see Commerce Exterieur de la Grece 206
Foreign Trade Reports. Bunker Fuels (US ISSN 0363-6798) 255, 864

Foreign Trade Reports. Summary of U.S. Export and Import Merchandise Trade (US ISSN 0361-0047) 255
Foreign Trade Reports. U.S. Airborne Exports and General Imports (US ISSN 0095-7771) 255
Foreign Trade Reports. U.S. Imports for Consumption and General Imports; Tariff Schedules Annotated by Country see Foreign Trade Reports. U.S. Imports for Consumption and General Imports-T S U S A Commodity by Country of Origin: Annual (Year) 255
Foreign Trade Reports. U.S. Imports for Consumption and General Imports-T S U S A Commodity by Country of Origin: Annual (Year) (US) 255
Foreign Trade Reports. U.S. Trade with Puerto Rico and U.S. Possessions (US ISSN 0565-1204) 256
Foreign Trade Reports. U.S. Waterborne Exports and General Imports (US ISSN 0095-0890) 256
Foreign Trade Reports. Vessel Entrances and Clearances (US) 256
Foreign Trade Statistics of Africa. Series A: Direction of Trade (UN ISSN 0071-7398) 208
Foreign Trade Statistics of Africa. Series B: Trade by Commodity (UN ISSN 0071-7401) 208
Foreign Trade Statistics of Africa. Series C: Summary Tables/Statistiques Africaines du Commerce Exterieur. Serie C: Tableaux Recapitulatifs (UN) 208
Foreign Trade Statistics of Asia and the Pacific. Series A (UN ISSN 0252-4538) 208
Foreign Trade Statistics of Asia and the Pacific. Series B (UN ISSN 0252-4546) 208
Foreign Trade Statistics of Bangladesh (BG) 208
Foreign Trade Statistics of Iran. Yearbook (IR ISSN 0075-0492) 208
Foreign Trade Statistics of the Philippines (PH) 208
Foreign Trade Statistics of Yemen Arab Republic (YE) 208
Foreningen af Filmlaerere i Gymnasiet. Meddelelser (DK ISSN 0900-6664) 414, 824
Foreningen af Teleteknikere see F A T - Bladet 1068
Foreningen af Teleteknikere Bladet see F A T - Bladet 1068
Foreningen til Norske Fortidsminnesmerkers Bevaring. Aarbok (NO ISSN 0071-7436) 582
Forensic Science Progress (US) 782
Forensic Services Directory (US ISSN 0192-3145) 655
Forest and Timber (AT ISSN 0015-7392) 524, 529
Forest Farmer. Manual Edition (US ISSN 0071-7452) 524
Forest Log (US ISSN 0015-7449) 525
Forest Pest Management Institute. Information Report Series (CN ISSN 0704-772X) 164, 525
Forest Pest Management Institute. Technical Note Series (CN ISSN 0826-0532) 164, 525
Forest Pest Management Institute Program Review (CN) 141, 322, 496, 525
Forest Products Abstracts (UK ISSN 0140-4784) 6, 529
Forest Products Research Institute. Annual Report (GH ISSN 0586-8440) 530
Forest Products Trade Statistics of Indonesia see Indonesian Statistics on Trade of Forest Products 525
Forest Research Bulletin (IO) 525
Forest Research Institute. Report see Forest Research Bulletin 525
Forest Research Institute New Zealand. F R I Bulletin see New Zealand. F R I Bulletin 526
Forest Research Institute: Research Pamphlet (MY ISSN 0126-8198) 525
Forest Resources see Australian Forest Resources 523

Forest Science Monographs (US ISSN 0071-7568) 525
Forest Tree Improvement (DK ISSN 0105-4120) 525
Forest World (US) 525
Forestry Abstracts (UK ISSN 0015-7538) 6, 529
Forestry Abstracts. Leading Article Reprint Series (UK ISSN 0071-7584) 6, 529
Forestry Facts see Yankee Woodlot 529
Forestry: Latin American Industrial Report (US) 525
Forestry Log (AT) 525
Forestry Newsletter of the Asia-Pacific Region (UN ISSN 0532-0747) 525
Forestry Research Institute of Malawi. Research Record (MW) 525
Forintek Canada Corp., Western Laboratory. Special Publications (CN ISSN 0824-2119) 530
Forlagsseriekatalog see Forlagsseriekatalog for Boerne- og Skolebiblioteker 424
Forlagsseriekatalog for Boerne- og Skolebiblioteker (DK ISSN 0107-1491) 424
Forlagsvejviser (DK ISSN 0109-405X) 961
Forma Abierta (SP) 710
Forma Italiae. Serie I (IT) 86
Forma Italiae. Serie II. Documenti (IT) 86
Format (UK ISSN 0015-7740) 741
Formation pour l'Agriculture et le Developpement Rural see Training for Agriculture and Rural Development 427
Formator Symposium on Mathematical Methods for the Analysis of Large-Scale Systems (CS) 748
Forme del Significato (IT ISSN 0390-2153) 722
Forretnings- og Bedriftslederen (NO ISSN 0071-7630) 279
Forschung im Strassenwesen (GW ISSN 0340-3998) 481
Forschungen aus Staat und Recht (US ISSN 0071-7657) 655
Forschungen und Beitraege zur Wiener Stadtgeschichte (AU) 557
Forschungen zur Aelteren Musikgeschichte (AU) 835
Forschungen zur Aeltesten Entwicklung Dresdens (GE) 1153
Forschungen zur Antiken Sklaverei (GW ISSN 0071-7665) 557
Forschungen zur Europaeischen und Vergleichenden Rechtsgeschichte (AU) 655
Forschungen zur Geschichte Oberoesterreichs (AU) 582
Forschungen zur Innsbrucker Universitaetsgeschichte (AU ISSN 0429-1573) 435
Forschungen zur Kirchen- und Dogmengeschichte (GW) 969
Forschungen zur Kunstgeschichte und Christlichen Archaeologie (GW ISSN 0532-2189) 86, 105
Forschungen zur Mittelalterlichen Geschichte (GE ISSN 0071-7673) 582
Forschungen zur Osteuropaeischen Geschichte see Freie Universitaet Berlin. Osteuropa-Institut. Historische Veroeffentlichungen 583
Forschungen zur Raumentwicklung (GW ISSN 0341-244X) 623
Forschungen zur Rechtsarchaeologie und Rechtlichen Volkskunde (SZ) 86, 515, 655
Forschungen zur Religion und Literatur des Alten und Neuen Testaments (GW) 969
Forschungen zur Volkskunde (GW) 72
Forschungen zur Wirtschaftsgeschichte (GE ISSN 0138-5100) 251
Forschunginstitut fuer Wirtschaftsverfassung und Wettbewerb e.V. Schriftenreihe see F I W - Schriftenreihe 194
Forschungsarbeiten aus dem Strassenwesen. Schriftenreihe (GW ISSN 0341-5872) 481

Forschungsbereichs fuer Geo- und Kosmoswissenschaften. Veroeffentlichen (GE ISSN 0138-4600) 399
Forschungsberichte des Landes Nordrhein-Westfalen (GW) 538
Forschungsberichte zur D D R-Literatur (NE ISSN 0168-9770) 722
Forschungsdokumentation zur Arbeitsmarkt- und Berufsforschung (GW ISSN 0340-8973) 208, 271, 426
Forschungsgesellschaft fuer das Strassenwesen. Arbeitsgruppe Asphalt- und Teerstrassen. Schriftenreihe see Forschungsgesellschaft fuer Strassen- und Verkehrswesen. Arbeitsgruppe Asphalt- und Teerstrassen. Schriftenreihe 481
Forschungsgesellschaft fuer das Strassenwesen. Arbeitsgruppe Betonstrassen. Schriftenreihe see Forschungsgesellschaft fuer Strassen- und Verkehrswesen. Arbeitsgruppe Betonstrassen. Schriftenreihe 481
Forschungsgesellschaft fuer Strassen- und Verkehrswesen. Arbeitsgruppe Asphalt- und Teerstrassen. Schriftenreihe (GW) 481
Forschungsgesellschaft fuer Strassen- und Verkehrswesen. Arbeitsgruppe Betonstrassen. Schriftenreihe (GW) 481
Forschungsgesellschaft fuer Strassen- und Verkehrswesen. Arbeitsgruppe Mineralstoffe im Strassenbau (GW) 1096
Forschungsinstitut der Eidgenoessischen Turn- und Sportschule Magglingen. Wissenschaftliche Schriftenreihe (SZ) 886
Forschungsprobleme der Vergleichenden Literaturgeschichte (GW ISSN 0071-7703) 722
Forschungsstelle fuer Jagdkunde und Wildschadenverhuetung. Schriftenreihe (GW ISSN 0071-7711) 525, 1045
Forschungsstelle fuer Voelkerrecht und Auslaendisches Oeffentliches Recht. Werkhefte see Universitaet Hamburg. Institut fuer Internationale Angelegenheiten. Werkhefte 672
Forsikringsraadet. Beretning om Raadets Virksomhed see Forsikringstilsynet. Beretning om Tilsynets Virksomhed 639
Forsikringstilsynet. Beretning om Tilsynets Virksomhed (DK ISSN 0108-7304) 639
Forskning i Groenland-Tusaat (DK ISSN 0105-7502) 379, 761
Forskningscenter Risoe. Aarsberetning/Risoe Annual Report (DK) 465
Forskningscenter Risoe. Energi Systems Gruppen. Annual Progress Report (DK) 465
Forskningslaboratoriet for Frugt og Groentindustri. Aarsberetning (DK ISSN 0106-2573) 532
Forsoegsanlaeg Risoe. see Forskningscenter Risoe. Energi Systems Gruppen. Annual Progress Report 465
Forsoegsanlaeg Risoe. Aarsberetning see Forskningscenter Risoe. Aarsberetning 465
Forstlige Forsoegsvaesen i Danmark (DK ISSN 0367-2174) 525
Forstschritte der Tierzuetung und Zuechtungsbiologie see Advances in Animal Breeding and Genetics 166
Forststatistisches Jahrbuch (GW ISSN 0084-7690) 529
Forstwissenschaftliche Forschungen (GW ISSN 0071-7972) 525
Fort (UK ISSN 0261-586X) 557, 582
Fort Belknap Genealogical Association. Bulletin (US ISSN 0071-7738) 535
Fort Burgwin Research Center. Publications (US ISSN 0071-7754) 605
Fort Hare Papers (SA ISSN 0015-8054) 341
Fort Point Salvo (US) 605, 811
Fortbildung und Praxis (GW ISSN 0071-7835) 1017

Fortbildungskurse fuer Rheumatologie (SZ ISSN 0071-7851) 793
Fortegnelse over Anerkendte Avlscentre, Aspirantbesaetninger, Opformeringsbesaetninger (DK ISSN 0107-6922) 66
Fortegnelse over Anerkendte Avlscentre, Fremavlssteder, Aspirantbesaetninger, Opformeringsbesaetninger see Fortegnelse over Anerkendte Avlscentre, Aspirantbesaetninger, Opformeringsbesaetninger 66
Fortegnelse over Autoriserede Laeger, Tandlaeger, Dyrlaeger i Danmark see Autoriserede Laeger, Tandlaeger, Dyrlaeger i Danmark 758
Fortegnelse over Dansk Udviklingsforskning (DK ISSN 0109-4955) 194
Fortegnelse over Fabrikanter og Importoerer af Goedninger og Grundforbedringsmidler (DK ISSN 0109-5498) 55
Fortegnelse over Fabrikanter og Importoerer af Goedningsstoffer og Grundforbedringsmidler see Fortegnelse over Fabrikanter og Importoerer af Goedninger og Grundforbedringsmidler 55
Forth Naturalist and Historian (UK ISSN 0309-7560) 365, 496, 991
Forth Ports Handbook 1984 (UK ISSN 0262-8880) 308, 1100
Fortschritte der Arzneimittelforschung/Progress in Drug Research/Progres des Recherches Pharmaceutiques (SZ ISSN 0071-786X) 871
Fortschritte der Botanik see Progress in Botany 160
Fortschritte der Chemie Organischer Naturstoffe/Progress in the Chemistry of Organic Natural Products (US ISSN 0071-7886) 329
Fortschritte der Chemischen Forschung see Topics in Current Chemistry 325
Fortschritte der Hochpolymeren-Forschung see Advances in Polymer Science 329
Fortschritte der Krebsforschung see Recent Results in Cancer Research 776
Fortschritte der Medizinischen Mikrobiologie/Progress in Medical Microbiology (GW) 168
Fortschritte der Onkologie (GE ISSN 0323-5084) 701
Fortschritte der Praktischen Dermatologie und Venerologie (US ISSN 0071-7932) 780
Fortschritte der Urologie und Nephrologie (GW ISSN 0071-7975) 795
Fortschritte der Verhaltensforschung see Advances in Ethology 173
Fortschritte der Veterinaermedizin see Advances in Veterinary Medicine 1120
Fortschritte der Zoologie/Progress in Zoology (GW ISSN 0071-7991) 174
Fortschritte im Acker- und Pflanzenbau see Advances in Agronomy and Crop Science 51
Fortschritte in der Geologie von Rheinland und Westfalen (GW ISSN 0071-8009) 386
Fortschritte in der Tierphysiologie und Tierernaehrung/Advances in Animal Physiology and Animal Nutrition (GW ISSN 0301-2743) 66, 174
Fortschritte der Pflanzenzeuchtung see Advances in Plant Breeding 52
Fortune Directory (US) 289
Fortune Directory see Fortune World Business Directory 308
Fortune Double 500 see Fortune Directory 289
Fortune World Business Directory (US ISSN 0197-7792) 308
Fortvivl (DK ISSN 0109-1425) 414
Forum (DK ISSN 0108-3279) 905
Forum der Psychiatrie (GW ISSN 0071-8025) 789
Forum Law Journal see Law Forum 659
Forum Linguisticum (GW) 695

Forum on Fundamental Surgical Problems (US ISSN 0071-8041) 794
Forum Phoneticum (GW ISSN 0341-3144) 695
Forvm (AU) 557, 905
Forward (Oakland) (US) 905
Forward (San Juan Capistrano) see Christian Research Journal 968
Forward and Back (US) 375
Fossils and Strata (NO) 856
Foto Cine Guia (AG) 824
Foto Galaxis (SP) 884
Foto-Revyen (DK ISSN 0108-0016) 884
Fotogrametria, Fotointerpretacion y Geodesia (MX) 884
Fotogrammetriska Meddelanden/Photogrammetric Notes (SW ISSN 0071-8068) 543
Fotointerpretacja w Geografii (PL ISSN 0071-8076) 543
Fouilles de Delphes: Collection (FR) 86
Fouling Prevention Research Digest (UK ISSN 0143-3598) 894
Foulsham's Original Old Moore's Almanack (UK ISSN 0071-8084) 462
Foundation Center. Annual Report (US ISSN 0190-3357) 1022
Foundation Center. Report see Foundation Center. Annual Report 1022
Foundation Center National Data Book (US ISSN 0730-1677) 1022
Foundation Directory (US ISSN 0071-8092) 1022
Foundation Directory Supplement (US) 1022
Foundation Facts (US ISSN 0015-8933) 481
Foundation for Business Responsibilities. Dialogues (UK) 194
Foundation for Business Responsibilities. Discussion Paper (UK ISSN 0073-7410) 194
Foundation for Business Responsibilities. Occasional Papers (UK ISSN 0073-7429) 194
Foundation for Business Responsibilities. Research Paper (UK ISSN 0073-7437) 194
Foundation for Reformation Research. Bulletin of the Library see Sixteenth Century Bibliography 564
Foundation for the Study of Cycles. Research Bulletin (US ISSN 0071-8106) 251
Foundation Grants Index (US) 1022
Foundation Grants to Individuals (US) 1022
Foundation of Thanatology Series (US) 934
Foundation 500 (US) 1055
Foundations in Library and Information Science (US) 678
Foundations of Medieval History (UK) 582, 612
Foundations of Modern History (UK) 582
Foundations Today: Current Facts and Figures on Private Foundations (US) 1022
Foundry Catalog File see Foundry Databook & Catalog File 797
Foundry Databook & Catalog File (US) 797
Foundry Directory and Register of Forges (UK ISSN 0071-8130) 798
Foundry Yearbook (UK ISSN 0306-4212) 798
Fountain see Mabua 727
Four Zoas (US ISSN 0362-0247) 722
Fourth Quadrant (US) 114
Fra Als og Sundeved (DK ISSN 0085-0845) 582
Fra Bjerringbro Kommune (DK ISSN 0107-2757) 582
Fra Bornholms Museum (DK ISSN 0107-4849) 827
Fra Bov Museum (DK ISSN 0106-8229) 582, 827
Fra Bov Sogns Museum see Fra Bov Museum 827
Fra Esbjerg Museums Virke see Mark og Montre 590
Fra Frederiksborg Amt. Aarbog (DK) 582

Fra Himmerland og Kjaer Herred (DK) 582
Fra Holback Amt: Historiske Aarboeger(DK) 582
Fra Koebenhavns Amt (DK) 582
Fra Kvangaard til Humlekule (DK ISSN 0107-895X) 582
Fra Nationalmuseets Arbejdsmark see Nationalmuseets Arbejdsmark 591
Fra Ribe Amt (DK ISSN 0046-4864) 582
Fra Ringkoebing Amts Museer see F R A M 827
Fra Viborg Amt. Aarbog (DK ISSN 0085-0853) 582
Fracht-Schiffahrts-Konferenzen see Guetertransport in Seeverkehr 1100
Fraenkische Geographische Gesellschaft. Mitteilungen (GW ISSN 0071-8173) 543
Fraenkische Studien see Wuerzburger Geographische Arbeiten 551
Fraenkischer Hauskalender und Caritaskalender (GW ISSN 0173-5543) 134, 741, 982, 1017
Fragen des Sozialistischen Weltsystems (GE) 277
Fragmenta Balcanica Musei Macedonici Scientiarum Naturalium (YU ISSN 0015-9298) 169
Fragmenta Coleopterologica (JA ISSN 0429-2871) 164
Fragmenta Entomologica (IT ISSN 0429-288X) 164
Fragmenta Faunistica (PL ISSN 0015-9301) 174
Frame/Work (US) 884, 1026
France. Activites Internationales. Rapport Annuel d'Activite-Electricite de France (FR) 453
France. Bureau Centrale de Statistique Industrielle. Annuaire de Statistique Industrielle see France. Service d'Etude des Strategies et des Statistiques Industrielles. Annuaire de Statistique Industrielle 209
France. Bureau de Recherches Geologiques et Minieres. Documents (FR ISSN 0221-2536) 386
France. Bureau de Recherches Geologiques et Minieres. Manuels et Methodes (FR ISSN 0245-9345) 386, 816
France. Bureau de Recherches Geologiques et Minieres. Memoires (FR ISSN 0071-8246) 386, 816
France. Bureau de Recherches Geologiques et Minieres. Resume des Principaux Resultats Scientifiques et Techniques (FR) 386
France. Bureau des Longitudes. Annuaire: Ephemerides (FR) 116
France. Caisse Nationale de Credit Agricole. Rapport sur le Credit Agricole Mutuel (FR ISSN 0071-8254) 47, 229
France. Caisse Nationale de l'Assurance Maladie des Travailleurs Salaries. Statistiques de l'Annee (FR) 642
France. Caisse Nationale des Allocations Familiales. Action Sociale see France. Caisse Nationale des Allocations Familiales. Statistiques Action Sociale 1022
France. Caisse Nationale des Allocations Familiales. Prestations Familiales. Resultats Generaux: Recettes, Depenses, Beneficiaires see France. Caisse Nationale des Allocations Familiales. Statistiques Prestations Familiales. Resultats Generaux: Recettes, Depenses, Beneficiaires 1022
France. Caisse Nationale des Allocations Familiales. Statistiques Action Sociale (FR ISSN 0181-0804) 1022
France. Caisse Nationale des Allocations Familiales. Statistiques Prestations de Logement (FR ISSN 0184-6469) 1017
France. Caisse Nationale des Allocations Familiales. Statistiques Prestations Familiales. Resultats Generaux: Recettes, Depenses, Beneficiaires (FR ISSN 0182-1598) 1022
France. Centre d'Dtudes de l'Emploi. Cahiers (FR) 272
France. Centre d'Etudes de l'Emploi. Dossiers de Recherche (FR) 272
France. Centre de Recherche Zoologique. Departement de Genetique Animale. Bulletin Technique see France. Centre de Recherche Zootechnique. Departement de Genetique Animale. Bulletin Technique 1121
France. Centre de Recherche Zootechnique. Departement de Genetique Animale. Bulletin Technique (FR ISSN 0249-5740) 1121
France. Centre National de la Recherche Scientifique. Colloques Nationaux (FR ISSN 0071-8319) 991
France. Centre National pour l'Exploitation des Oceans. Centre Oceanologique de Bretagne. Recueil des Travaux see France. I.F.Re.Mer. Centre de Brest. Recueil des Travaux 1153
France. Centre National pour l'Exploitation des Oceans. Colloques. Actes see France. I.F.Re.Mer. Centre de Brest. Colloques. Actes 405
France. Centre National pour l'Exploitation des Oceans. Publications. Serie: Resultats des Campagnes a la Mer see France. I.F.Re.Mer. Centre de Brest. Publications. Serie: Resultats des Campagnes a la Mer 405
France. Centre National pour l'Exploitation des Oceans. Publications. Serie: Rapports Economiques et Juridiques see France. I.F.Re.Mer. Centre de Brest. Publications. Serie: Rapports Economiques et Juridiques 405
France. Centre National pour l'Exploitation des Oceans. Publications. Serie: Rapports Scientifiques et Techniques see France. I.F.Re.Mer. Centre de Brest. Publications. Serie: Rapports Scientifiques et Techniques 405
France. Comite des Travaux Historiques et Scientifiques. Bulletin Archeologique. (FR ISSN 0071-8394) 86
France. Comite des Travaux Historiques et Scientifiques. Section d'Archeologie. Actes du Congres National des Societes Savantes (FR ISSN 0071-8416) 86
France. Comite des Travaux Historiques et Scientifiques. Section de Geographie. Bulletin (FR ISSN 0071-8432) 543
France. Comite des Travaux Historiques et Scientifiques. Section d'Histoire Moderne et Contemporaine. Actes du Congres National des Societes Savantes (FR ISSN 0071-8440) 582
France. Comite des Travaux Historiques et Scientifiques. Section d'Histoire Moderne et Contemporaine. Bulletin (FR ISSN 0071-8459) 582
France. Comite des Travaux Historiques et Scientifiques. Section d'Histoire Moderne et Contemporaine (Depuis 1610). Bulletin see France. Comite des Travaux Historiques et Scientifiques. Section d'Histoire Moderne et Contemporaine. Bulletin 582
France. Commissariat a l'Energie Atomique. Annual Report (FR ISSN 0071-8467) 465, 471, 896
France. Commission Centrale des Marches. Guide du Fournisseur de l'Etat see France. Commission Centrale des Marches. Guide du Fournisseur de l'Etat et des Collectivites Locales 239
France. Commission Centrale des Marches. Guide du Fournisseur de l'Etat et des Collectivites Locales (FR ISSN 0071-8483) 239
France. Commission Centrale pour la Navigation du Rhin. Rapport Annuel(FR) 1100
France. Commission de la Concurrence. Rapports Economiques (FR ISSN 0071-8505) 245
France. Commission Departementale d'Histoire et d'Archeologie. Memoires. (FR) 582
France. Commission Departementale des Monuments Historiques du Pas-de-Calais. Memoires. see France. Commission Departementale d'Histoire et d'Archeologie. Memoires 582
France. Commission des Operations de Bourse. Rapport au President de la Republique (FR) 266
France. Commission Nationale de l'Amenagement du Territoire. Rapport (FR ISSN 0071-8491) 941
France. Conseil des Impots. Rapport au President de la Republique (FR) 295
France. Conseil National de la Comptabilite. Rapport d'Activite (FR ISSN 0071-8513) 941
France. Conseil National du Credit. Rapport Annuel (FR) 229
France. Delegation Generale a la Recherche Scientifique et Technique. Repertoire National des Laboratoires; la Recherche Universitaire; Sciences Exactes et Naturelles. Tome 2: Biologie see France. Ministere de l'Industrie et de la Recherche. Repertoire National des Laboratoires; la Recherche Universitaire. Tome 2: Sciences de la Vie 141
France. Delegation Generale a la Recherche Scientifique et Technique. Repertoire National des Laboratoires; la Recherche Universitaire; Sciences Exactes et Naturelles. Tome 4: Mathematiques, Sciences de l'Espace et de la terre see France. Ministere de la Recherche et de l'Industrie. Repertoire National des Laboratoires; la Recherche Universitaire; Sciences Exactes et Naturelles. Tome 4: Mathematiques, Sciences de l'Espace et de la Terre 749
France. Delegation Generale a la Recherche Scientifique et Technique. Repertoire National des Laboratoires; la Recherche Universitaire; Sciences Exactes et Naturelles. Tome 1: Physique see France. Ministere de l'Industrie et de la Recherche. Repertoire National des Laboratoires; la Recherche Universitaire; Tome 1: Sciences de la Matiere 888
France. Delegation Generale a la Recherche Scientifique et Technique. Repertoire National des Laboratoires; la Recherche Universitaire; Sciences Exactes et Naturelles. Tome 3: Chimie see France. Ministere de l'Industrie et de la Recherche. Repertoire National des Laboratoires; la Recherche Universitaire. Tome 3: Sciences Humaines et Sociales 1008
France. Delegation Generale a la Recherche Scientifique et Technique. Repertoire Permanent de l'Administration Publique see Repertoire Permanent de l'Administration Francaise 945
France. Departement des Statistiques de Transport. Annuaire Statistique des Transports (FR) 1085
France. Departement des Statistiques de Transport. Memento de Statistiques des Transports (FR) 1085
France. Departement des Statistiques Transports. Resultats Generaux - Trafic Interieur et International see S.I.T.R.A.M. Resultats Generaux: Trafic Interieur - Trafic International 1086
France. Direction des Affaires Economiques et Internationales. Informations Rapides (FR ISSN 0291-8897) 184
France. Direction des Affaires Exterieures et de la Cooperation. Rapport d'Activite-Electricite de France see France. Activites Internationales. Rapport Annuel d'Activite-Electricite de France 453
France. Direction des Forets. Production de la Branche Exploitation Forestiere et Production des Branches Science et Carbonisation en Foret (FR) 525
France. Direction des Forets. Rapport sur le Fonds Forestier National (FR) 525
France. Direction du Gaz et de l'Electricite. Statistiques Officielles de l'Industrie Gaziere en France see Statistiques de l'Industrie Gaziere en France 867
France. Direction Generale de l'Aviation Civile. Bulletin Statistique (FR) 22
France. Direction Generale de la Concurrence et des Prix. Bulletin Officiel des Services des Prix (FR ISSN 0071-870X) 289
France. Direction Generale des Douanes et Droits Indirects. Annuaire Abrege de Statistiques (FR ISSN 0071-8637) 295
France. Direction Generale des Douanes et Droits Indirects. Commentaires Annuels des Statistiques du Commerce Exterieur (FR ISSN 0071-8645) 256
France. Direction Generale des Douanes et Droits Indirects. Statistiques du Commerce Exterieur: Importations- Exportations. Nomenclature: N.G.P. (Nomenclature Generale des Produits) (FR ISSN 0071-8688) 208
France. Direction Generale des Impots. Precis de Fiscalite (FR) 295, 656
France. Direction Nationale des Douanes et Droits Indirects. Tableau General des Transports (FR ISSN 0071-8726) 256
France. Direction Nationale des Douanes et Droits Indirects. Transport du Commerce Exterieur (FR ISSN 0071-8718) 256
France. I.F.Re.Mer. Centre de Brest. Colloques. Actes (Institut Francais de Recherche pour l'Exploitation de la Mer (IFREMER)) (FR ISSN 0761-3962) 405
France. I.F.Re.Mer. Centre de Brest. Publications. Serie: Rapports Economiques et Juridiques (Institut Francais de Recherche pour l'Exploitation de la Mer (IFREMER)) (FR ISSN 0761-3938) 405, 656
France. I.F.Re.Mer. Centre de Brest. Publications. Serie: Rapports Scientifiques et Techniques (FR ISSN 0761-3970) 405
France. I.F.Re.Mer. Centre de Brest. Publications. Serie: Resultats des Campagnes a la Mer (Institut Francais de Recherche pour l'Exploitation de la Mer (IFREMER)) (FR ISSN 0761-3989) 405
France. I.F.Re.Mer. Centre de Brest. Recueil des Travaux (Institut Francais de Recherche pour l'Exploitation de la Mer (IFREMER) -Centre de Brest) (FR) 1153
France. Imprimerie Nationale. Annuaire. (FR ISSN 0078-9666) 961
France. Inspection Generale des Finances. Annuaire (FR ISSN 0071-8742) 295
France. Institut National d'Etudes Demographiques. Cahiers de Travaux et Documents (FR ISSN 0071-8823) 922
France. Institut National de la Sante et de la Recherche Medicale. Colloques(FR ISSN 0763-7098) 761, 796
France. Institut National de la Statistique et des Etudes Economiques. Collections. Serie C, Comptes et Planification (FR ISSN 0533-0793) 208
France. Institut National de la Statistique et des Etudes Economiques. Collections. Serie D, Demographie et Emploi (FR ISSN 0533-0807) 272, 922, 927
France. Institut National de la Statistique et des Etudes Economiques. Collections. Serie E, Enterprises (FR ISSN 0533-0815) 208

France. Institut National de la Statistique et des Etudes Economiques. Collections. Serie M, Menages (FR ISSN 0533-0823) *208*
France. Institut National de la Statistique et des Etudes Economiques. Collections. Serie R, Regions (FR ISSN 0533-0831) *208, 1055*
France. Institut National de la Statistique et des Etudes Economiques. Documents Divers (FR ISSN 0336-6979) *208*
France. Institut National de la Statistique et des Etudes Economiques. L'Enseignement dans les Departments d'Outre-Mer (FR) *424*
France. Institut National de la Statistique et des Etudes Economiques. Serie C: Comptes et Planification (FR) *221, 245*
France. Institut National de la Statistique et des Etudes Economiques. Serie E: Entreprises (FR) *251*
France. Institut National de la Statistique et des Etudes Economiques. Serie M: Menages (FR) *1031*
France. Institut National de la Statistique et des Etudes Economiques. Serie R: Regions (FR) *245*
France. Institut National de Recherche en Informatique et en Automatique. Rapports de Recherche (FR) *352*
France. Institut National de Recherche et de Documentation Pedagogiques. Cahiers de Documentation (FR) *1153*
France. Institut National de Recherche et de Documentation Pedagogiques. Repertoire d'Etablissements Publics d'Enseignement et de Services (FR ISSN 0071-8963) *1153*
France. Laboratoire Central des Ponts et Chaussees. Rapport de Recherche (FR ISSN 0222-8394) *481, 1096*
France. Laboratoires des Ponts et Chausees. Rapport de Recherche (FR ISSN 0085-2643) *481*
France. Mediateur. Rapport Annuel du Mediateur (FR) *916*
France. Ministere de l'Agriculture. Informations Rapides Agro-Alimentaires *see* France. Ministere de l'Agriculture. Informations Rapides. Statistiques des Entreprises *40*
France. Ministere de l'Agriculture. Informations Rapides. Fruits (FR ISSN 0243-6108) *47*
France. Ministere de l'Agriculture. Informations Rapides. Legumes (FR ISSN 0243-6140) *47*
France. Ministere de l'Agriculture. Informations Rapides. Statistiques des Entreprises (FR ISSN 0243-6167) *40, 47*
France. Ministere de l'Agriculture. Informations Rapides. Viticulture (FR) *47*
France. Ministere de l'Agriculture. Series "S". Departements d'Outre-Mer (FR ISSN 0243-6574) *47*
France. Ministere de l'Agriculture. Series "S". Industries Agricoles et Alimentaires (FR ISSN 0243-6647) *47*
France. Ministere de l'Agriculture. Series "S". Methodes et Applications Scientifiques (FR ISSN 0243-8585) *47*
France. Ministere de l'Agriculture. Series "S". Production Animale (FR ISSN 0243-6566) *47*
France. Ministere de l'Agriculture. Series "S". Production Vegetale *see* France. Ministere de l'Agriculture. Series "S". Production Vegetale et Forestieres *47*
France. Ministere de l'Agriculture. Series "S". Production Vegetale et Forestieres (FR ISSN 0755-3218) *47*

France. Ministere de l'Agriculture. Series "S". Reseau d'Information Comptable Agricole (FR ISSN 0291-8102) *47*
France. Ministere de l'Agriculture. Series "S". Statistique Forestiere *see* France. Ministere de l'Agriculture. Series "S". Production Vegetale et Forestieres *47*
France. Ministere de l'Agriculture. Series "S". Structures et Environnement des Exploitations (FR ISSN 0243-6639) *47*
France. Ministere de l'Agriculture. Series "S". Synthese Statistique Comptes et Revenus (FR ISSN 0244-5271) *40, 47*
France. Ministere de l'Economie, des Finances et du Budget. Rapport du Conseil de Direction du Fond de Developpement Economique et Social (FR) *289*
France. Ministere de l'Economie et des Finances. Balance des Paiements Entre la France et l'Exterieur (FR ISSN 0071-8890) *256, 295*
France. Ministere de l'Economie et des Finances. Budget *see* France. Ministere du Budget. Budget *295*
France. Ministere de l'Economie et des Finances. Caisses d'Epargne Ordinaire (FR) *229*
France. Ministere de l'Economie et des Finances. Statistiques et Etudes Financieres. Finances Publiques. Serie Rouge (FR) *194*
France. Ministere de l'Economie. Rapport du Conseil de Direction du Fonds de Developpement Economique et Social *see* France. Ministere de l'Economie, des Finances et du Budget. Rapport du Conseil de Direction du Fond de Developpement Economique et Social *289*
France. Ministere de l'Environment et du Cadre de Vie. Inspection Generale de l'Equipement (FR) *941*
France. Ministere de l'Industrie, des P & T et du Tourisme. Enquete Annuelle d'Entreprise (FR) *209, 1055*
France. Ministere de l'Industrie et de la Recherche. Repertoire National des Laboratoires; la Recherche Universitaire; Tome 1: Sciences de la Matiere (FR) *888*
France. Ministere de l'Industrie et de la Recherche. Repertoire National des Laboratoires; la Recherche Universitaire. Tome 2: Sciences de la Vie (FR) *141*
France. Ministere de l'Industrie et de la Recherche. Repertoire National des Laboratoires; la Recherche Universitaire. Tome 3: Sciences Humaines et Sociales (FR) *1008*
France. Ministere de la Cooperation. Sous-Direction des Etudes de Developpement. Etudes et Documents *see* France. Ministere des Relations Exterieures. Sous-Directions des Etudes et Developpement. Etudes et Documents *916*
France. Ministere de la Culture et de l'Environnement. Bilan d'Activite des Agences Financieres de Bassin (FR) *496*
France. Ministere de la Recherche et de l'Industrie. Repertoire National de Laboratoires; la Recherche Universitaire; Sciences Exactes et Naturelles. Tome 4: Mathematiques, Sciences de l'Espace et de la Terre (FR) *749*
France. Ministere de la Sante et de la Securite Sociale. Annuaire des Statistiques Sanitaires et Sociales (FR) *953*
France. Ministere de la Sante et de la Securite Sociale. Notes d'Information(FR) *953*

France. Ministere de la Sante et de la Securite Sociale. Tableaux Statistiques "Sante et Securite Sociale" *see* France. Ministere de la Sante et de la Securite Sociale. Annuaire des Statistiques Sanitaires et Sociales *953*
France. Ministere de la Sante. Note d'Information *see* France. Ministere de la Sante et de la Securite Sociale. Notes d'Information *953*
France. Ministere de Redeploiement Industriel et du Commerce Exterieur. Enquete Annuelle *see* France. Ministere de l'Industrie, des P & T et du Tourisme. Enquete Annuelle d'Entreprise *209*
France. Ministere des Affaires Etrangeres. Recueil des Traites et Accords de la France (FR ISSN 0071-8971) *670*
France. Ministere des Affaires Sociales et de la Solidarite Nationale. Bulletin Mensuel de Statistiques du Travail. Supplement (FR) *209*
France. Ministere des Affaires Sociales. Information Actualites *see* France. Ministere de la Sante et de la Securite Sociale. Notes d'Information *953*
France. Ministere des Relations Exterieures. Sous-Directions des Etudes et Developpement. Etudes et Documents (FR) *916*
France. Ministere du Budget. Budget (FR ISSN 0071-8904) *295*
France. Office National d'Etudes et de Recherches Aerospatiales. Activities (FR ISSN 0078-3773) *18*
France. Office National d'Etudes et de Recherches Aerospatiales. Notes Techniques (FR ISSN 0078-3781) *19*
France. Office National d'Etudes et de Recherches Aerospatiales. Publications (FR ISSN 0078-379X) *19*
France. Office National d'Etudes et de Recherches Aerospatiales. Recueil de Notes sur l'Activite de ONERA *see* France. Office National d'Etudes et de Recherches Aerospatiales. Activities *18*
France. Office National d'Immigration. Statistiques de l'Immigration (FR ISSN 0071-903X) *927*
France. Secretariat d'Etat aux Affaires Etrangeres Charge de la Cooperation. Direction de l'Aide au Developpement. Cote d'Ivoire. Dossier d'Information Economique (FR) *262*
France. Secretariat d'Etat aux Affaires Etrangeres Charge de la Cooperation. Direction de l'Aide au Developpement. Mali. Dossier d'Information Economique (FR) *262*
France. Secretariat d'Etat aux Affaires Etrangeres Charge de la Cooperation. Direction de l'Aide au Developpement. Niger. Dossier d'Information Economique (FR) *262*
France. Service d'Etude des Strategies et des Statistiques Industrielles. Annuaire de Statistique Industrielle (FR) *209*
France. Service d'Etude des Strategies et des Statistiques Industrielles. Collections: Traits Fondamentaux du Systeme Industriel Francais (FR ISSN 0244-7118) *209*
France. Service d'Etude des Strategies et des Statistiques Industrielles. Recueil Statistiques *see* France. Service d'Etude des Strategies et des Statistiques Industrielles. Collections: Traits Fondamentaux du Systeme Industriel Francais *209*
France. Service d'Etude des Strategies et des Statistiques Industrielles. Societes d'Etudes et de Conseils, Ingenieurs-Conseils (FR) *194, 471*
France. Service de Documentation et de Cartographie Geographiques. Memoires et Documents. (FR ISSN 0071-8262) *543*

France. Service du Traitement de l'Information et des Statistiques Industrielles. Annuaire de Statistique Industrielle *see* France. Service d'Etude des Strategies et des Statistiques Industrielles. Annuaire de Statistique Industrielle *209*
France. Service du Traitement de l'Information et des Statistiques Industrielles. Societe d'Etudes et de Conseils, Ingenieurs-Conseils *see* France. Service d'Etude des Strategies et des Statistiques Industrielles. Societes d'Etudes et de Conseils, Ingenieurs-Conseils *194*
France. Service Interdepartemental de la Protection Civile. Bulletin (FR) *336*
France (Year) (US) *1110*
France-Allemagne (FR ISSN 0071-8181) *916*
France-Collectivites: Guide National des Chefs des Services d'Achats et des Fournisseurs de Collectivites (FR ISSN 0071-8386) *239*
La France de l'Industrie et ses Services (FR) *308, 861*
France des Points Chauds (FR) *905*
France en Poche. Total Guide (FR ISSN 0071-8734) *1110*
France-Iberie Recherche. Etudes et Documents (FR ISSN 0082-5409) *905*
France-Iberie Recherche. These et Documents *see* France-Iberie Recherche. Theses et Recherches *582*
France-Iberie Recherche. Theses et Recherches (FR) *582*
France Ministere du Travail. Bulletin de Statistiques du Travail. Supplement *see* France. Ministere des Affaires Sociales et de la Solidarite Nationale. Bulletin Mensuel de Statistiques du Travail. Supplement *209*
France-Peinture (FR ISSN 0071-9048) *855*
France Plastiques (FR ISSN 0071-9056) *900*
France Prostestante *see* Federation Protestante de France. Annuaire *978*
France-Sports (FR ISSN 0071-9102) *1033, 1045*
France Stamp Catalogue (UK ISSN 0142-9809) *874*
Francexport (FR ISSN 0244-710X) *6, 308*
Franchise Annual (US ISSN 0318-8752) *308*
Franchise Law Review (US) *194, 656*
Franchising in the Economy (US) *301*
Franchising Opportunities Handbook (US) *284*
Francis Thompson Society. Journal *see* Eighteen Nineties Society. Journal *721*
Franciscan Studies (US ISSN 0080-5459) *878, 982*
Franco-British Chamber of Commerce and Industry. Year Book (FR) *236*
Franco British Trade Directory (UK ISSN 0071-917X) *236, 256*
Frankfurt am Main. Statistisches Amt und Wahlamt. Statistisches Jahrbuch (GW ISSN 0071-9218) *1055*
Frankfurt am Main. Universitaet. Institut fuer Wissenschaftliche Irenik. Schriften *see* Studia Irenica *973*
Frankfurter Abhandlungen zur Slavistik (GW ISSN 0473-5277) *695*
Frankfurter Althistorische Studien (GW) *583*
Frankfurter Beitraege zur Germanistik (GW ISSN 0071-9226) *695, 722*
Frankfurter Historische Abhandlungen (GW ISSN 0170-3226) *583*
Frankfurter Historische Vortraege (GW ISSN 0170-3293) *583*
Frankfurter Judaistische Beitraege (GW ISSN 0342-0078) *503, 722, 976*
Frankfurter Kirchliches Jahrbuch (GW) *583, 969*
Franklin Foundation Lecture Series (US) *286*
De Franse Nederlanden/Pays-Bas Francais (BE ISSN 0251-2408) *503, 991*
Franz Delitzsch-Vorlesungen. Neue Folge (GW) *557, 722*

Frary Family Journal (US ISSN 0887-6320) *535*
Fraser's Canadian Trade Directory (CN ISSN 0071-9277) 284, *308*
Die Frauenfrage in Deutschland. Bibliographie (GW ISSN 0344-1415) 126, *1130*
Fraunhofer-Institute fuer Produktionstechnik und Automatisierung Forschung und Praxis *see* I P A - Forschung und Praxis *471*
Fravaer ved Anmeldte Arbejdsulykker (DK ISSN 0109-5129) *635*
Frederiksberg Gennem Tiderne (DK ISSN 0108-8777) *583*
Frederiksborgmuseet. Aarsskrift (DK ISSN 0105-9858) *827*
Frederiksvaerkegnens Museumsforening. Aarbog *see* Frederiksvaerkegnens Museumsforening. Aarsskrift *583*
Frederiksvaerkegnens Museumsforening. Aarsskrift (DK ISSN 0107-9476) *583*
Fredningsstyrelsen Rapport (DK ISSN 0900-9825) *365*
Free Albanian/Shqiptari i Lire (US ISSN 0488-728X) *905*
Freedom in the World (US ISSN 0732-6610) *913*
Freedom of Information Fact Sheets (US) 496, *656*, *953*
Freedom of Speech Yearbook *see* S C A Free Speech Yearbook *909*
Freelance Editors' Association of Canada. Directory of Members (CN ISSN 0226-9031) *308*, *961*
Freelancers of North America (US) 15, 284, 848, *961*
Freeland and Allied Families (US) *536*
Freeman (UK) *583*
Freeman and Freeman's Tax Practice Deskbook (Supplement) *see* Tax Practice Deskbook (Supplement) *299*
Freeman Footnotes (US) *536*
Freer Gallery of Art, Washington, D.C. Occasional Papers (US ISSN 0071-9382) *105*
Freiberger Forschungshefte. Montanwissenschaften. Reihe A. Bergbau und Geotechnik, Arbeitsschutz und Sicherheitstechnik, Grundstoff-Verfahrenstechnik, Maschinen- und Energietechnik (GE ISSN 0071-9390) *465*
Freiberger Forschungshefte. Montanwissenschaften: Reihe B. Metallurgie *see* Freiberger Forschungshefte. Montanwissenschaften: Reihe B. Metallurgie und Werstofftechnik *798*
Freiberger Forschungshefte. Montanwissenschaften: Reihe B. Metallurgie und Werstofftechnik (GE) *798*
Freiberger Forschungshefte. Montanwissenschaften: Reihe C. Geowissenschaften (GE ISSN 0071-9404) *379*, *856*
Freiberger Forschungshefte. Montanwissenschaften. Reihe D: Economic Sciences. (GE ISSN 0071-9412) *245*
Freiburger Altorientalische Studien (GW ISSN 0170-3307) *851*
Freiburger Beitraege zur Indologie (GW ISSN 0340-6261) *851*
Freiburger Fernoestliche Forchungen (GW ISSN 0724-4703) *851*
Freiburger Geographische Hefte (GW ISSN 0071-9447) *543*
Freiburger Islamstudien (GW ISSN 0170-3285) *851*, *975*
Freie Universitaet Berlin. John F. Kennedy-Institut fuer Nordamerika Studien. Materialien (GW) *605*
Freie Universitaet Berlin. Osteuropa-Institut. Balkanologische Veroeffentlichungen (GW ISSN 0170-1533) *695*
Freie Universitaet Berlin. Osteuropa-Institut. Berichte (GW ISSN 0409-1477) *583*, *629*, *905*
Freie Universitaet Berlin. Osteuropa-Institut. Bibliographische Mitteilungen (GW ISSN 0067-5881) *563*
Freie Universitaet Berlin. Osteuropa-Institut. Erziehungswissenschaftliche Veroeffentlichungen (GW ISSN 0067-589X) *414*, *905*
Freie Universitaet Berlin. Osteuropa-Institut. Historische Veroeffentlichungen (GW ISSN 0067-5903) *583*
Freie Universitaet Berlin. Osteuropa-Institut. Philosophische und Soziologische Veroeffentlichungen (GW ISSN 0067-5911) *878*, *905*, *1026*
Freie Universitaet Berlin. Osteuropa-Institut. Rechtswissenschaftliche Veroeffentlichungen (GW ISSN 0343-835X) *656*
Freie Universitaet Berlin. Osteuropa-Institut. Slavistische Veroeffentlichungen (GW ISSN 0067-592X) *695*, *722*
Freie Universitaet Berlin. Osteuropa-Institut. Wirtschaftswissenschaftliche Veroeffentlichungen (GW ISSN 0067-5938) *194*
Freies Deutsches Hochstift, Frankfurt am Main. Jahrbuch (GW ISSN 0071-9463) *722*
Freight Industry Yearbook (UK ISSN 0071-9471) *1081*
Freight Transport Association Ltd. Yearbook *see* F T A Yearbook *1081*
Freiwilliger Feuerwehren *see* Feuerwehr-Jahrbuch *506*
Fremdenverkehr in Oesterreich (AU ISSN 0071-948X) *1110*
Fremont Schools (US ISSN 0016-1004) *414*
French-Canadian Civilization Research Center. Cahiers/Centre de Recherche en Civilisation Canadienne-Francaise. Cahiers (CN ISSN 0069-1771) *605*
French Colonial Historical Society. Proceedings of the Meeting (US) *583*
French Company Handbook (FR) *308*
French Edition *see* Electric Power in Canada *464*
French Engineering Catalog (FR ISSN 0245-0283) *471*
French Farm and Village Holiday Guide (UK) *1110*
French Foreign Trade Directory *see* Repertoire Francais du Commerce Exterieur *259*
French Genealogist (US) *536*
French Literature Series (US ISSN 0271-6607) *739*
French Patents Abstracts (UK ISSN 0016-1098) 6, *862*, *1072*
French Periodical Index/Repertoriex (US ISSN 0362-5044) *126*
French XX Bibliography (US) *583*, *964*
French 7 Bibliography, Critical and Biographical References for the Study of Contemporary French Literature *see* French 20 Bibliography; Critical and Biographical References for the Study of French Literature since 1885 *126*
French 17 (US ISSN 0191-9199) 126, *563*, *713*
French 20 Bibliography; Critical and Biographical References for the Study of French Literature since 1885 (US ISSN 0085-0888) *126*
Frente Nacional pro-Defensa del Petroleo Venezolano. Actuaciones (VE) *864*
Frequency Control Symposium (US) *453*, *900*
Frequency Symposium *see* Frequency Control Symposium *453*
Fresh Produce Foodservice Directory (US) *519*, *522*
Freshwater Biological Association. Annual Report (UK ISSN 0374-7646) *141*
Freshwater Biological Association. Occasional Publications (UK ISSN 0308-6739) *141*
Freshwater Biological Association. Scientific Publications (UK ISSN 0367-1887) *141*
Fresno County Medical Society. Bulletin *see* Vital Signs (Fresno) *768*
Freude mit Buechern (GW) *964*
Freunde der Bayerischen Vor- und Fruehgeschichte. Mitteilungen (GW) *557*
Frieden (GW) *905*
Friends Committee on Legislation of California Action *see* F C L Action *904*
Friends Historical Society. Journal (UK ISSN 0071-9587) *984*
Friends in Action *see* Alternative Trading News *261*
Friends of the National Libraries. Annual Report (UK) 678, *961*
Friends Service Council. Annual Report *see* Quaker Peace & Service. Annual Report *1020*
Fringe Benefit Costs in Canada *see* Employee Benefit Costs in Canada *271*
Friskoler og Private Grundskoler (DK ISSN 0108-4259) *414*
Fritts/Fritz Family Newsletter (US) *536*
Frodskaparrit; Annales Societatis Scientiarum Faeroensis (FA ISSN 0085-0896) *991*
Frodskaparrit; Annales Societatis Scientiarum Faeronsis. Supplementa (FA ISSN 0429-7539) *991*
From the Ground Up (US ISSN 0317-056X) *19*
Frommer's Dollarwise Guide to Egypt (US) *1110*
Frommer's Dollarwise Guide to Germany (US ISSN 0731-4442) *1110*
Frommer's Dollarwise Guide to Italy (US) *1110*
Frommer's Dollarwise Guide to New England (US) *1110*
Frontier Military Series (US ISSN 0071-9641) *605*, *811*
Frontier News (AT ISSN 0016-2108) *978*
Frontiers in Aging Series (US ISSN 0271-955X) *552*
Frontiers in Diabetes (SZ ISSN 0251-5342) *781*
Frontiers in Education Conference. Proceedings (US ISSN 0190-5848) *454*
Frontiers in European Radiology (US) *792*
Frontiers in Neuroendocrinology (US ISSN 0532-7466) *781*
Frontiers in Physics (US ISSN 0429-7725) *888*
Frontiers of Engineering and Computing in Health Care (US) *778*
Frontiers of Gastrointestinal Research (SZ) *782*
Frontiers of Hormone Research (SZ ISSN 0301-3073) *781*
Frontiers of Matrix Biology (SZ ISSN 0301-0155) *141*
Frontiers of Oral Physiology (SZ ISSN 0301-536X) *779*
Frontiers of Power Technology Conference. Proceedings (US ISSN 0161-5319) *1068*
Frontiers of Radiation Therapy and Oncology (SZ ISSN 0071-9676) *775*, *792*
Frozen and Chilled Foods Year Book (UK) *519*
Frozen Fishery Products. Annual Summary (US ISSN 0162-6108) 514, *1055*
Frozen Food Factbook and Directory *see* National Frozen Food Association Directory *520*
Frozen Foods in Denmark (DK) *519*
Frozen Foods Year Book *see* Frozen and Chilled Foods Year Book *519*
Frozen Waffles (US) *710*
Fructidor International (FR) *55*
Fruehmittelalterliche Studien (GW) *583*
Fruit and Vegetable Truck Rate and Cost Summary (US) 27, *194*
Fryske Nammen (NE) *536*
Fu Jen Studies (CH) *695*, *722*, *851*
Fuchsia Annual (UK ISSN 0071-9730) *532*
Fuehrer durch die technische Literatur (GW ISSN 0071-9749) *1068*
Fuehrer zu Archaeologischen Denkmaelern in Deutschland (GW ISSN 0071-9757) 86, *105*
Fuehrung und Organisation der Unternehmung (SZ ISSN 0071-9765) *279*
Fuel Abstracts and Current Titles *see* Fuel and Energy Abstracts *868*
Fuel and Energy Abstracts (UK ISSN 0140-6701) 6, 476, *868*
Fuentes Cartograficas Espanolas (SP) *543*
Fuentes e Investigaciones para la Historia del Peru (PE) *605*
Fuentes Indigenas de la Cultura Nahuatl (MX ISSN 0071-9773) *605*
Fuentes para el Estudio de la Cultura Maya (MX) *72*
Fuentes Primarias (BL) *72*
Fuentes y Usos de Fondos (DR) 229, *277*
Fuer die Sicherheit im Bergland (AU) *1045*
Fuera de Coleccion (SP) *629*
Fugle (DK ISSN 0107-3729) *170*
Fugle i Nordjylland (DK ISSN 0108-7282) *170*
Fuglelivet ved Roskilde Fjord (DK ISSN 0109-9078) *170*
Fuglevaern *see* Fugle *170*
Fujikura Technical Review (JA ISSN 0429-8357) *454*
Fukui University. Faculty of Education. Memoirs. Series 2: Natural Science (JA ISSN 0071-9781) *991*
Fukui University. Faculty of Education. Memoirs. Series 3: Applied Science and Agricultural Science (JA) *27*
Fukui University. Faculty of Education. Memoirs. Series 4: Applied Science and Home Economics (JA) *614*
Fukui University. Faculty of Education. Memoirs. Series 5: Applied Science and Technology (JA) *1068*
Fukui University. Faculty of Education. Memoirs. Series 6: Physical Education (JA) *447*
Fukuoka Environmental Research Center. Annual Report *see* Fukuoka-Ken Eisei Kogai Senta Nenpo *953*
Fukuoka-Ken Eisei Kogai Senta Nenpo/Fukuoka Environmental Research Center. Annual Report (JA ISSN 0287-1254) 496, *953*
Fulbright Scholar Program: Faculty Grants, Research and Lecturing Awards (US) *441*
Fulbright Scholar Program: Research Awards and Lectureships *see* Fulbright Scholar Program: Faculty Grants, Research and Lecturing Awards *441*
Fulcrum (SA ISSN 0071-979X) *471*
Fulda. Statistischer Bericht (GW) *1055*
Fuldaer Geschichtsblaetter (GW ISSN 0016-2612) *583*
Funboard (GW) *1033*
Functional Neuroscience (US) *789*
Functiones et Approximatio Commentarii Mathematici (PL ISSN 0208-6573) *749*
Fundacao Centro de Pesquisas Economicas e Sociais do Piaui. Atividades C E P R O *see* Fundacao Centro de Pesquisas Economicas e Sociais do Piaui. Relatorio de Atividades *1026*
Fundacao Centro de Pesquisas Economicas e Sociais do Piaui. Relatorio de Atividades (BL) 194, *1026*
Fundacao Cultural de Curitiba. Relatorio (BL) *605*
Fundacao de Assistencia Aos Municipios do Estado do Parana. Boletim dos Municipios (BL) *1017*
Fundacao de Assistencia Aos Municipios do Estado do Parana. Boletim Informativo (BL) *950*
Fundacao Joaquim Nabuco. Serie Cursos e Conferencias (BL) *1026*
Fundacao Joaquim Nabuco. Serie Documentos (BL) *1026*
Fundacao Joaquim Nabuco. Serie Estudos e Pesquisas (BL) *1026*
Fundacao Joaquim Nabuco. Serie Monografias (BL) *1008*

Fundacion Bariloche. Departamento de Recursos Naturales y Energia. Publicaciones *see* Fundacion Bariloche. Instituto de Economia de la Energia. Publicaciones *465*
Fundacion Bariloche. Departamento de Recursos Naturales y Energia. Publicaciones *see* Fundacion Bariloche. Grupo de Analisis de Sistemas Ecologicos. Publicaciones *496*
Fundacion Bariloche. Departamento de Sociologia. Documentos de Trabajo *see* Fundacion Bariloche. Desarrollos Sinergicos. Publicaciones *1026*
Fundacion Bariloche. Departamento de Sociologia. Publicaciones *see* Fundacion Bariloche. Desarrollos Sinergicos. Publicaciones *1026*
Fundacion Bariloche. Desarrollos Sinergicos. Publicaciones (AG) *1026*
Fundacion Bariloche. Grupo de Analisis de Sistemas Ecologicos. Publicaciones (AG) *496*
Fundacion Bariloche. Instituto de Economia de la Energia. Publicaciones (AG) *465*, 816
Fundacion Bariloche. Memoria Anual (AG) *991*
Fundacion Bariloche. Programa de Recursos Naturales y Energia. Publicaciones *see* Fundacion Bariloche. Instituto de Economia de la Energia. Publicaciones *465*
Fundacion Dominicana de Desarrollo. Informe Anual (DR) *245*
Fundacion Fomento de Estudios Sociales y Sociologia Aplicada Coleccion Fundacion F O E S S A. Serie Estudios *see* Coleccion Fundacion F O E S S A. Serie Estudios *1025*
Fundacion Miguel Lillo. Miscelanea (AG ISSN 0074-025X) *157*, 164, 386
Fundacion Miguel Lillo. Serie Conservacion de la Naturaleza (AG) *157*, 365
Fundacion Rodriguez Demorizi. Boletin(DR) *878*
Fundacion Roux-Ocefa. Archivos (AG ISSN 0016-271X) *1153*
Fundamenta Mathematicae (PL ISSN 0016-2736) *749*
Fundamental Aspects of Pollution Control and Environmental Science (NE) *496*
Fundamental Studies in Computer Science (NE) *352*
Fundamental Studies in Engineering (NE) *471*
Fundamental Theories of Physics (NE) *888*
Fundamentals of Aerospace Instrumentation. (US ISSN 0094-3975) *19*
Fundamentals of Educational Planning (UN ISSN 0071-9862) *441*
Fundamentals of Educational Planning. Lecture-Discussion Series (UN ISSN 0071-9870) *1153*
Fundamentals of Test Measurement (US ISSN 0891-4052) *489*
Fundberichte aus Baden-Wuerttemberg (GW) *86*
Fundberichte aus Hessen (GW ISSN 0071-9889) *86*
Fundberichte aus Oesterreich (AU) *98*
Fundberichte aus Schwaben, Neue Folge *see* Fundberichte aus Baden-Wuerttemberg *86*
Funde und Ausgrabungen im Bezirk Trier (GW ISSN 0723-8630) *86*, 105
Fundheft fuer Arbeits- und Sozialrecht (GW ISSN 0173-1688) *126*, 649, *668*
Fundheft fuer Arbeitsrecht *see* Fundheft fuer Arbeits- und Sozialrecht *668*
Fundheft fuer Oeffentliches Recht (GW ISSN 0071-9919) *656*
Fundheft fuer Zivilrecht (GW ISSN 0071-9927) *656*
Funeral Service Abstracts *see* Thanatology Abstracts *938*
Fungal Genetics Newsletter (US) *141*
Fungi Canadenses (CN ISSN 0823-0552) *55*, 157

Fungicide and Nematicide Tests (US ISSN 0148-9038) *55*
Fungus *see* Kavaka *158*
Funktionsanalyse Biologischer Systeme (GW ISSN 0340-0840) *141*, 171
Funparks Directory (US) *1110*
Funspots Directory *see* Funparks Directory *1110*
Furdek (US) *503*
Furman Studies (US ISSN 0190-4701) *710*, 722
Furman University Bulletin. Furman Studies Issue *see* Furman Studies *722*
Furnished Holiday Homes and Caravans *see* Self-Catering Holiday Homes, Caravans & Boats *1116*
Furnished Holidays in Britain *see* Self-Catering and Furnished Holidays *1116*
Furniture: Latin American Industrial Report (US) *643*
Furukawa Review (JA ISSN 0429-9159) *454*
Fusion-Fission Energy Systems Review Meeting. Proceedings (US) *465*
Future - Abstracts (US) *6*, *1014*
Future Journalists of America. Newsletter (US) *645*
Future Survey (US ISSN 0190-3241) *6*, *1004*
Futures Magazine Reference Guide to Futures Markets (US ISSN 0746-2468) *266*
Fyens Stiftsbog (DK ISSN 0107-8399) *583*
Fynboer og Arkaeologi (DK ISSN 0109-1441) *86*
Fynske Aarboeger (DK ISSN 0085-0918) *583*
Fynske Minder (DK ISSN 0427-7945) *86*, 105, *583*
Fysiktips (DK ISSN 0109-6664) *888*
G A Document (Global Architecture) (JA) *98*
G A/Global Architecture (JA) *98*
G A Houses (Global Architecture) (JA) *98*, 623
G.A.P.E (Guyana Association of Professional Engineers) (GY) *471*
G A T F Technical Services Report (Graphic Arts Technical Foundation) (US) *1068*
G A T T Studies in International Trade (General Agreement on Tariffs and Trade) (UN) *256*
G B E: Export Directory of Brazil *see* Export Directory of Brazil/Guia Brasileiro de Exportacao *308*
G C S A A Membership Directory *see* Golf Course Superintendents Association of America. Membership Directory *1038*
G; Documentation Technique et Commerciale des Vendeurs de Gaz (FR ISSN 0072-0046) *194*
G E C-A E I Telecommunications *see* G E C Telecommunications Journal *1153*
G E C Telecommunications Journal (General Electric Co. p.l.c. of England) (UK ISSN 0046-5593) *1153*
G.E.P.L *see* Guide Europeen des Progiciels *238*
G F A/Gallup National Gardening Survey (Year) *see* National Gardening Survey (Year) *533*
G I P (Germansk Institut Publikationer) (DK ISSN 0106-0872) *695*
G L V Mitteilungen (Graphische Lehr- und Versuchsanstalt) (AU ISSN 0016-3562) *414*, 930
G P Guide to Emergency & Medical Services (UK ISSN 0262-1010) *617*, 761
G P N Educational Media. College-Adult (Great Plains National Instructional Television Library) (US) *435*
G P N Educational Media. Crossover (Great Plains National Instructional Television Library) (US) *414*
G P N Educational Media. Elementary-Secondary (US) *447*
G R I Newsletter (Gravure Research Institute) (US ISSN 0534-0489) *930*
G U A Papers of Geology (NE) *386*

G.W. Leibniz: Saemliche Schriften und Briefe (GE) *583*, 878
G W U M C. Department of Biochemistry. Annual Spring Symposia Series (US) *151*
Ga As I C Symposium (US) *454*
Gabinetto Disegni e Stampe degli Uffizi. Cataloghi. (IT ISSN 0072-0070) *827*
Gabon. Direction Generale des Finances et du Budget. Projet du Budget General (GO) *295*
Gabon. Ministere de l'Education Nationale. Annuaire Statistique de l'Enseignement (GO) *424*
Gabriel's Home Improvement Annual (AT) *184*, 643, 644
Gabriel's Kitchens and Bathrooms Annual (AT) *184*, 643, 644
Gaceta Bibliotecaria del Peru (PE ISSN 0433-0730) *678*
Gadney's Guide to International Contests, Festivals & Grants in Film & Video, Photography, TV-Radio Broadcasting, Writing, Poetry, Playwriting & Journalism (US) *348*, 645, *824*, 884
Gadney's Guide to 1800 International Contests, Festivals and Grants in Film and Video, Photography, TV-Radio Broadcasting, Writing, Poetry, Playwriting and Journalism *see* Gadney's Guide to International Contests, Festivals & Grants in Film & Video, Photography, TV-Radio Broadcasting, Writing, Poetry, Playwriting & Journalism *824*
Gaelic Society of Inverness. Transactions (UK) *695*
Gaertnerische Berufspraxis (GW ISSN 0301-2719) *53*
Gaesdoncker Blatter (GW) *341*
Gaia's Guide (UK) *615*, *1110*, 1128
Gaikoku Bungaku Kenkyu *see* Studies in British & American Literature *734*
Gaikoku Koku Uchu Bunken Mokuroku *see* Foreign Aero-Space Literature *22*
Gaikokugo Gaikoku Bungaku Kenkyu *see* Essays in Foreign Languages and Literatures *694*
Gal-ed (IS ISSN 0334-4258) *503*
Gale Directory of Publications (US) *126*
Galerie Nierendorf, Berlin. Kunstblaetter (GW ISSN 0072-0089) *827*
Galerie Sanct Lucas. Gemaelde Alter Meister (AU) *827*
Galicia y Rio de la Plata. Compania de Seguros. Memoria y Balance General(AG) *639*
Galleria del Cavallino. Mostre (IT) *827*
Gallery (AT) *105*
Gallery (UK ISSN 0306-1256) *741*
Gallery Works (US) *741*
Gallia. Supplement (FR ISSN 0072-0119) *86*
Gallia Prehistoire. Supplement (FR ISSN 0072-0100) *87*, 543
Galloway Herd Book (UK) *66*
Galloway Journal (UK ISSN 0430-9928) *66*
Galpin Society Journal (UK ISSN 0072-0127) *836*
Galten Egnsarkiv. Annales (DK ISSN 0108-0032) *583*
Gambia. Central Statistics Department. Annual Report of External Trade Statistics *see* External Trade Statistics of Gambia *207*
Gambia. Central Statistics Department. Directory of Establishments (GM) *308*
Gambia. Central Statistics Department. Education Statistics (GM) *424*, 1055
Gambia. Central Statistics Department. Tourist Statistics (GM) *1055*, *1119*
Gambia. Education Department. Education Statistics *see* Gambia. Central Statistics Department. Education Statistics *424*
Gambia. Oilseeds Marketing Board. Report *see* Gambia. Produce Marketing Board. Annual Report *47*
Gambia. Produce Marketing Board. Annual Report (GM ISSN 0301-8423) *47*

Gambit (UK ISSN 0016-4283) *1077*
Game Conservancy Annual Review (UK) *170*, 365
Games and Toys Yearbook *see* Toys & Games Trader Yearbook *553*
Gamle Loejt (DK ISSN 0108-3791) *583*
Gamma Field Symposia (JA ISSN 0435-1096) *27*, 167
Ganban Rikigaku Ni Kansuri Shinpojumu Ronbunshu/Proceedings of the Symposium on Rock Mechanics (JA) *386*, 481
Gandhi Peace Foundation Lectures (II) *916*
Ganglia *see* Gronk *711*
Ganley's Catholic Schools in America - Elementary/Secondary *see* N C E A Ganley's Catholic Schools in America *430*
Gap Conference Reports (US) *761*
Garden Fax (CN) *532*
Garden History (UK ISSN 0307-1243) *532*
Garden Supply Retailer Green Book (US ISSN 0195-1386) *532*
Gardening (US ISSN 0270-3041) *532*
Gardening Handbook (UK ISSN 0261-7951) *532*
Gardens in England and Wales (UK) *532*
Gardens Open to the Public in England and Wales *see* Gardens in England and Wales *532*
Garland English Texts (US) *722*
Garland Folklore Casebooks (US) *515*
Garment Manufacturer's Index (US) *340*
Garston Docks Tide Table (UK) *1100*
Gartneriregnskabsstatistik *see* Denmark. Jordbrugsoekonomisk Institut. Serie D: Gartneri-Regnskabsstatistik *46*
Gas Abstracts (US ISSN 0016-4844) *6*, *868*
Gas and Fuel Corporation of Victoria. Annual Report (AT ISSN 0072-0208) *864*
Gas Calorimeter Workshop. Proceedings (US) *465*
Gas Council (Great Britain) Report and Accounts *see* British Gas Corporation. Report and Accounts *863*
Gas Directory and Undertakings of the World *see* Gas Directory and Who's Who *864*
Gas Directory and Who's Who (UK ISSN 0307-3084) *864*
Gas Facts (US) *864*
Gas Marketing Pocket Book and Diary (UK ISSN 0072-0259) *864*
Gas Processors Association. Annual Convention. Proceedings (US ISSN 0096-8870) *864*
Gas Scope (US ISSN 0016-4976) *864*
Gas Services Pocket Book *see* Gas Marketing Pocket Book and Diary *864*
Gasolin 23 (GW) *722*
Gastroenterology Annual (US) *782*
Gastroenterology Series (US) *782*
Gauhati University. Department of Anthropology. Bulletin. (II) *1153*
Gauke's Jahrbuch (GW ISSN 0720-2520) *722*
Gauldalsminne (NO) *583*
Gaussenia (FR ISSN 0761-3067) *525*
Gavi (AG) *352*
Gay Bibliography (US) *616*
Gay Counselling (AT ISSN 0705-5935) *615*, 934, 1017, 1026
Gay Information (AT) *615*, 710, *913*, 1026
Gaya (PO) *87*, *583*
Gayana: Botanica (CL ISSN 0016-5301) *157*
Gayana: Miscelanea (CL ISSN 0374-7999) *141*
Gayana: Zoologica (CL ISSN 0016-531X) *174*
Gayellow Pages (US ISSN 0363-826X) *308*, *615*
Gaz de France. Secretariat General. Schema d'Organisation Profor (FR ISSN 0072-0321) *864*
Gaz et L'Industrie *see* G; Documentation Technique et Commerciale des Vendeurs de Gaz *194*

Gazdasagtorteneti Ertekezesek (HU ISSN 0072-033X) 251
Gazella. Annual Report and Scientific Articles (CS) 174
Gazelle Review of Literature on the Middle East (UK ISSN 0308-7999) 722, 741
Gazeteer of India (II ISSN 0072-0348) 569
Gazetteer of Canada (CN ISSN 0576-1999) 543
Gazi Husrevbegova Biblioteka. Anali (YU ISSN 0350-1418) 569, 851
Gdanski Rocznik Kulturalny see Rocznik Kulturalny Ziemi Gdanskiej 595
Gdanskie Towarzystwo Naukowe. Wydzial 1. Nauk Spolecznych i Humanistycznych. Komisja Archeologiczna. Prace (PL ISSN 0072-0410) 87, 583
Gdanskie Towarzystwo Naukowe. Wydzial 1. Nauk Spolecznych i Humanistycznych. Seria Monografii (PL ISSN 0433-230X) 583
Gdanskie Towarzystwo Naukowe. Wydzial 1. Nauk Spolecznych i Humanistycznych. Seria Popularnonaukowa "Pomorze Gdanskie" (PL ISSN 0072-0429) 583
Gdanskie Towarzystwo Naukowe. Wydzial 1. Nauk Spolecznych i Humanistycznych. Seria Zrodel (PL ISSN 0072-0437) 583
Gdanskie Towarzystwo Naukowe. Wydzial 3. Nauk Matematyczno-Przyrodniczych. Rozprawy (PL ISSN 0072-0445) 749, 991
Gebbie House Magazine Directory see Internal Publications Directory 962
Gebbie Press All-In-One Directory see Gebbie Press All-in-One Media Directory 343
Gebbie Press All-in-One Media Directory (US) 343
GECAMINES Annual Report/ GECAMINES Rapport Annuel (Generale des Carrieres et des Mines) (ZR) 816
GECAMINES Rapport Annuel see GECAMINES Annual Report 816
Gefahrgut Kontakte see Hazardous Cargo Contacts 1100
Gegenschein (AT ISSN 0310-9968) 711
Geiriadur Prifysgol Cymru (UK ISSN 0072-0542) 695
Geirui Kenkyusho Eibun Hokoku see Whales Research Institute, Tokyo, Japan. Scientific Reports 178
Geistige Begegnung (GW ISSN 0072-0550) 722
Gelderse Historische Reeks (NE) 583
Gelosophist (US ISSN 8756-2898) 711
Geltende Seekriegsrecht in Einzeldarstellungen see Das Geltende Seevoelkerrecht in Einzeldarstellungen 670
Das Geltende Seevoelkerrecht in Einzeldarstellungen (GW) 670, 811
Gem & Jewellery Yearbook (II) 644
Gemeindebote (AU ISSN 0016-609X) 950
Gemeinsame Koerperschaftsdatei (GW ISSN 0724-6358) 678
Gemeinsames Amtsblatt des Landes Baden-Wuerttemberg (GW ISSN 0016-6200) 950
Gemeinschaft der Selbst-Verwirklichung. Jahresheft see Selbst-Verwirklichung: Jahresheft 881
Genava (SZ ISSN 0072-0585) 87, 105
Genealogical Abstracter see Genealogical Abstracts 537
Genealogical Abstracts (US) 537
Genealogical Periodical Annual Index (US) 537
Genealogical Research Directory (AT) 536
Genealogisches Handbuch des Bayerischen Adels (GW ISSN 0085-0934) 536
Genealogisches Jahrbuch (GW ISSN 0514-3292) 536
Genealogysk Jierboekje (NE) 536
Geneeskundig Adresboek (NE) 761

Geneeskundig Adresboek voor Nederland see Geneeskundig Adresboek 761
Geneeskundig Jaarboek Medicijnen (NE) 761
Geneeskundig Jaarboekje see Geneeskundig Adresboek 761
Geneeskundig Jaarboekje see Geneeskundig Jaarboek Medicijnen 761
Genera (UK) 741
General Agreement on Tariffs and Trade. Basic Instruments and Selected Documents Series. Supplement (UN ISSN 0072-0623) 256
General Agreement on Tariffs and Trade. G A T T Activities in (Year) (UN ISSN 0072-615X) 256
General Agreement on Tariffs and Trade. International Trade (UN ISSN 0072-064X) 256
General Agreement on Tariffs and Trade Studies in International Trade see G A T T Studies in International Trade 256
General and Applied Entomology (AT ISSN 0158-0760) 164
General and Synthetic Methods (UK ISSN 0141-2140) 329
General Aviation Statistical Databook (US) 1088
General Catalogue of Unesco and Unesco-Sponsored Publications (UN ISSN 0072-0658) 912
General Clinical Research Centers (US) 770, 781
General Commission on Safety and Health in the Iron and Steel Industry. Report (EI) 635, 798
General Conference of the New Church. Yearbook (UK ISSN 0072-0666) 984
General Convention of the New Jerusalem. Journal (US) 969
General Dental Council. Dentists Register (UK ISSN 0072-0674) 779
General Dental Council. Minutes of the Proceedings (UK ISSN 0072-0682) 779
General Directory of the Perfume and Cosmetic Industry see Guide de la Parfumerie 309
General Directory of the Press and Periodicals in Jordan and Kuwait (SY ISSN 0072-0690) 645, 961
General Directory of the Press and Periodicals in Syria (SY ISSN 0072-0704) 645, 961
General Education Reading Material Series (II ISSN 0072-0720) 414
General Electric Co. p.l.c. of England Telecommunications Journal see G E C Telecommunications Journal 1153
General Fisheries Council for the Mediterranean. Proceedings and Technical Papers. Debats et Documents Techniques (UN ISSN 0072-0747) 509
General Fisheries Council for the Mediterranean. Reports of the Sessions (UN ISSN 0072-0755) 509
General Fisheries Council for the Mediterranean. Studies and Reviews (UN ISSN 0433-3519) 509
General Information Concerning Trademarks (US ISSN 0083-3029) 861
General Medical Council. Medical Register (UK ISSN 0072-0763) 761
General Medical Council. Minutes (UK) 761
General Minutes of the Annual Conferences of the United Methodist Church see United Methodist Church. General Minutes of the Annual Conferences 980
General Motors Public Interest Report (US) 289, 1091
General Motors Symposia Series (US) 1091
General Pathology, Pathological Anatomy see Zentralblatt fuer Allgemeine Pathologie und Pathologische Anatomie 768
General Physics Advance Abstracts (US ISSN 0749-4823) 892

General Report on the Activities of the European Communities (EI ISSN 0069-6749) 245
General Science Index (US ISSN 0162-1963) 6, 1004
General Semantics Bulletin (US ISSN 0072-0771) 695
General Social Surveys (US ISSN 0161-3340) 905, 1008, 1026
General Systems Yearbook (US ISSN 0072-0798) 991
General Teaching Council for Scotland. Bulletin (UK ISSN 0142-2154) 414
General Technical Report P S W see U.S. Forest Service. Pacific Southwest Forest and Range Experiment Station. General Technical Report P S W 528
General Treaty for Central American Economic Integration. Permanent Secretariat. Newsletter (GT ISSN 0553-6898) 262
Generale des Carrieres et des Mines. Monographie (ZR) 816
Generale des Carrieres et des Mines GECAMINES Annual Report see GECAMINES Annual Report 816
Generale des Carrieres et Mines du Zaire. Monographie see Generale des Carrieres et des Mines. Monographie 816
Generations (US) 789
Genesis (US) 341
Genesis of Behavior (US) 789, 934
Genetic Engineering (US ISSN 0196-3716) 167, 168
Genetics Abstracts (US ISSN 0016-674X) 6, 150
Genetics and Cellular Technology Series (US) 1153
Genetik (GE) 167
Genie Industriel; Catalogue de l'Ingenierie (FR ISSN 0072-0844) 471
Genoa Port and Shipping Handbook (UK) 308, 1100
Genootschap Amstelodamum. Jaarboek (NE) 583
Die Genossenschaften in der Bundesrepublik Deutschland (GW) 238
Genshiryoku Hatsudensyo see Nuclear Power Plants in the World 898
Genshiryoku Nenkan see Nuclear Almanac 897
Genshiryoku Nenpo see Japan Atomic Energy Commission. Annual Report 897
Gentes Herbarum (US ISSN 0072-0879) 157
Gentle Folk and Other Creatures (AT ISSN 0310-639X) 741
Gentofte-Bogen (DK) 583
Gentse Bijdragen tot de Kunstgeschiedenis (BE ISSN 0772-7151) 98, 105
Genuine Irish Old Moore's Almanac (IE ISSN 0072-0887) 462
Geo Abstracts A (Landforms and the Quaternary) see Geographical Abstracts A (Landforms and the Quaternary) 551
Geo Abstracts B (Climatology and Hydrology) see Geographical Abstracts B (Climatology and Hydrology) 551
Geo Abstracts C (Economic Geography) see Geographical Abstracts C (Economic Geography) 551
Geo Abstracts D (Social and Historical Geography) see Geographical Abstracts D (Social & Historical Geography) 551
Geo Abstracts E (Sedimentology) see Geographical Abstracts E (Sedimentology) 382
Geo Abstracts F (Regional and Community Planning) see Geographical Abstracts F (Regional and Community Planning) 627
Geo Abstracts G (Remote Sensing Photogrammetry and Cartogrpaphy) see Geographical Abstracts G (Remote Sensing Photogrammetry and Cartography) 551

Geo Katalog. Band 1. Touristische Veroeffentlichungen see Geo Katalog (Year). Volume 1. Touristische Veroeffentlichungen 543
Geo Katalog. Band 2. Geowissenschaften (GW) 386
Geo Katalog. Band 2. International see Geo Katalog. Band 2. Geowissenschaften 386
Geo Katalog (Year). Volume 1. Touristische Veroeffentlichungen (GW) 543, 1119
Geobios New Reports (II ISSN 0253-3340) 141, 379
Geobotanisches Institut ETH, Stiftung Ruebel, Zurich. Berichte (SZ ISSN 0373-7896) 157
Geobotanisches Institut ETH, Stiftung Ruebel, Zurich. Veroeffentlichungen (SZ ISSN 0254-9433) 157
Geochemical Society of India. Journal (II ISSN 0368-2323) 386
Geochemistry; Journal for Chemical Problems of the Geo-sciences and Extraterrestrial Mineralogy see Chemie der Erde 385
GeoChile (CL ISSN 0431-1930) 1110
Geociencias (BL ISSN 0101-9082) 379
Geodaetisk Institut. Meddelelse (DK ISSN 0105-9696) 399
Geodesy and Agricultural Arrangement see Acta Academiae Agriculturae ac Technicae Olstenensis. Geodaesia et Ruris Regulatio 22
Geodezja i Urzadzenia Rolne see Acta Academiae Agriculturae ac Technicae Olstenensis. Geodaesia et Ruris Regulatio 22
Geoecological Research (GW ISSN 0170-3250) 379, 496
Geofizika (YU ISSN 0352-3659) 399
Geografi (DK ISSN 0108-7657) 543
Geografia (PL ISSN 0554-8128) 543
Geografia Urbana (BL ISSN 0533-9286) 543, 1026
Geografica (AG) 543
Geografie see Universitatea "Al. I. Cuza" din Iasi. Analele Stiintifice. Geologie-Geografie 396
Geografija ir Geologija (UR ISSN 0202-327X) 386, 543
Geografinis Metrastis/Geographical Annual (UR ISSN 0072-0917) 543
Geographers (UK ISSN 0308-6992) 543
Geographia (PL ISSN 0208-5054) 543
Geographia Medica (HU ISSN 0300-807X) 543, 761
Geographia Medica Hungarica see Geographia Medica 543
Geographia Polonica (PL ISSN 0016-7282) 543
Geographica (MY) 543
Geographical Abstracts A (Landforms and the Quaternary) (UK ISSN 0268-7879) 6, 551
Geographical Abstracts B (Climatology and Hydrology) (UK ISSN 0268-7887) 6, 551
Geographical Abstracts C (Economic Geography) (UK ISSN 0268-7895) 6, 551
Geographical Abstracts D (Social & Historical Geography) (UK ISSN 0268-7909) 6, 551
Geographical Abstracts E (Sedimentology) (UK ISSN 0268-7917) 6, 382
Geographical Abstracts F (Regional and Community Planning) (UK ISSN 0268-7925) 6, 627
Geographical Abstracts G (Remote Sensing Photogrammetry and Cartography) (UK ISSN 0268-7933) 6, 551
Geographical Annual see Geografinis Metrastis 543
Geographical Chronicles see Geographika Chronika 544
Geographical Distribution of Financial Flows to Developing Countries. (Disbursement) (FR) 262
Geographical Distribution of Financial Flows to Less Developed Countries. (Disbursements) see Geographical Distribution of Financial Flows to Developing Countries. (Disbursement) 262

Geographical Education (AT ISSN 0085-0969) 447, 543
Geographical Field Group (Nottingham). Regional Studies (UK ISSN 0078-2084) 543
Geographical Journal of Nepal (NP) 544
Geographical Observer (II ISSN 0072-0925) 544
Geographical Papers (UK ISSN 0305-5914) 544
Geographical Research Forum see Geography Research Forum 544
Geographical Society of China. Bulletin(CH) 352, 544, 629, 796
Geographika Chronika/Geographical Chronicles (CY) 544
Geographische Gesellschaft in Hamburg. Mitteilungen (GW ISSN 0374-9061) 544
Geographische Gesellschaft, Munich. Mitteilungen (GW ISSN 0072-0941) 544
Geographische Gesellschaft von Bern. Jahrbuch (SZ) 544
Geographische Hochschulmanuskripte (GW ISSN 0723-175X) 544
Geographische Hochschulmanuskripte. Diskussionspapiere (GW ISSN 0723-1679) 544
Geographisches Jahrbuch (GE ISSN 0072-095X) 544
Geographisches Taschenbuch (GW ISSN 0072-0968) 544
Geography of the British Isles Series (UK) 544
Geography of World Agriculture (HU ISSN 0303-6634) 544
Geography Research Forum (US) 544
Geokhimiya i Rudoobrazovanie (UR ISSN 0130-1128) 386
Geolgical Survey of Queensland Publications (AT ISSN 0079-8800) 386
Geologia Applicata e Idrogeologia (IT ISSN 0435-3870) 386, 402, 481
Geologia Colombiana (CK ISSN 0072-0992) 386
Geologica Bavarica (GW ISSN 0016-755X) 386
Geologica et Palaeontologica (GW ISSN 0072-1018) 386, 856
Geologica Ultraiectina (NE ISSN 0072-1026) 386
Geological Abstracts: Economic Geology (UK ISSN 0268-800X) 6, 382
Geological Abstracts: Geophysics and Tectonics (UK ISSN 0268-7941) 6, 382
Geological Abstracts: Palaeontology and Stratigraphy (UK ISSN 0268-8018) 6, 382
Geological Abstracts: Sedimentary Geology (UK) 6, 382
Geological Abstracts: Sedimentology see Geological Abstracts: Sedimentary Geology 382
Geological Association of Canada. Special Paper (CN ISSN 0072-1042) 386
Geological Correlation (UN ISSN 0302-069X) 386
Geological Journal - Special Issues (UK ISSN 0435-3951) 386
Geological Map Series (US) 386
Geological, Mining and Metallurgical Society of India. Bulletin (II ISSN 0016-7576) 386, 798, 816
Geological Society of America. Abstracts with Programs (US ISSN 0016-7592) 6, 382
Geological Society of America. Membership Directory (US ISSN 0277-5816) 386
Geological Society of America. Memoirs (US ISSN 0072-1069) 386
Geological Society of America. Memorials (US ISSN 0091-5041) 386
Geological Society of America. Special Papers (US ISSN 0072-1077) 386
Geological Society of America. Yearbook see Geological Society of America. Membership Directory 386
Geological Society of Australia. Abstracts Series. (AT) 379, 387

Geological Society of Australia. Special Publication (AT ISSN 0072-1085) 387
Geological Society of China. Memoirs (CH) 387
Geological Society of China. Proceedings (CH) 379, 387, 399
Geological Society of Egypt. Annual Meeting. Abstracts of Papers (UA ISSN 0446-4648) 387
Geological Society of Iraq. Journal (IQ ISSN 0533-8301) 387
Geological Society of Jamaica Journal (JM ISSN 0435-401X) 387
Geological Society of Japan. Memoirs see Chishitsugaku Ronshu 385
Geological Society of Malaysia. Bulletin(MY ISSN 0126-6187) 387
Geological Society of South Africa. Special Publication (SA) 387
Geological Survey Circular (US ISSN 0364-6017) 387
Geological Survey of Denmark see Danmarks Geologiske Undersoegelse 385
Geological Survey of Denmark. Series A see Danmarks Geologiske Undersoegelse. Serie A 385
Geological Survey of Denmark. Yearbook see Danmarks Geologiske Undersoegelse. Aarbog 385
Geological Survey of Greenland. Bulletin see Groenlands Geologiske Undersoegelse. Bulletin 388
Geological Survey of Greenland. Report see Groenlands Geologiske Undersoegelse. Rapport 388
Geological Survey of Hokkaido. Report (JA ISSN 0441-0785) 379, 387
Geological Survey of Ireland. Bulletin (IE ISSN 0085-0985) 387
Geological Survey of Ireland. Guide Series (IE ISSN 0790-0260) 387
Geological Survey of Ireland. Information Circulars (IE ISSN 0085-0993) 387
Geological Survey of Ireland. Report Series (IE ISSN 0790-0279) 387
Geological Survey of Ireland. Special Papers (IE ISSN 0085-1019) 387
Geological Survey of N.S.W. Mineral Resources see New South Wales. Geological Survey. Mineral Resources Series 818
Geological Survey of South Australia. Bulletin (AT) 387
Geological Survey of South Australia. Explanatory Notes (AT ISSN 0572-0125) 387
Geological Survey of South Australia. Report of Investigations (AT ISSN 0016-7681) 387
Geological Survey of South West Africa/Namibia. Memoirs (SX) 387
Geologija (YU ISSN 0016-7789) 387
Geologische Abhandlungen Hessen (GW ISSN 0341-4043) 387, 399, 856
Geologische Bundesanstalt, Vienna. Abhandlungen (AU ISSN 0378-0864) 387
Geologische Bundesanstalt, Vienna. Jahrbuch (AU ISSN 0016-7800) 387, 856
Geologische Gesellschaft, Vienna. Mitteilungen see Oesterreichische Geologische Gesellschaft. Mitteilungen 393
Geologisches Jahrbuch. Reihe A: Allgemeine und Regionale Geologie B.R. Deutschland und Nachbargebiete, Tektonik, Stratigraphie, Palaeontologie (GW ISSN 0341-6399) 387, 856
Geologisches Jahrbuch. Reihe B: Regionale Geologie Ausland (GW ISSN 0341-6402) 387
Geologisches Jahrbuch. Reihe C: Hydrogeologie. Ingenieurgeologie (GW ISSN 0341-6410) 387, 402
Geologisches Jahrbuch. Reihe D: Mineralogie. Petrographie, Geochemie, Lagerstaettenkunde (GW ISSN 0341-6429) 387, 816
Geologisches Jahrbuch. Reihe E: Geophysik (GW ISSN 0341-6437) 387

Geologisches Jahrbuch. Reihe F: Bodenkunde (GW ISSN 0341-6445) 387
Geologisches Jahrbuch Hessen (GW ISSN 0341-4027) 387, 399, 856
Geologist's Directory (UK ISSN 0260-0463) 387
Geologists' Year Book (UK) 387
Geology, Exploration, and Mining in British Columbia see Exploration in British Columbia 385
Geology of Petroleum (GW ISSN 0720-8863) 387
Geoloski Vjesnik (YU ISSN 0016-7924) 387
Geomedical Monograph Series see Medizinische Laenderkunde. Geomedical Monograph Series 764
Geomethodica (SZ ISSN 0171-1687) 379
Geonews (PK ISSN 0435-4311) 388
Geooekodynamik (GW ISSN 0720-454X) 388, 402, 544
Geophysica Norvegica (NO ISSN 0072-1174) 399
Geophysical Directory (US) 399
Geophysics and Astrophysics Monographs (NE) 116, 399
Geophysics and Tectonics Abstracts see Geological Abstracts: Geophysics and Tectonics 382
Geophysik und Geologie (GE ISSN 0138-2357) 399
Georg Forster: Saemliche Schriften, Tagebuecher, Briefe (GE) 722, 741
George D. Hall's New York Manufacturers Directory (US ISSN 0272-1074) 308
George Eliot Fellowship Review (UK) 722
George Ernest Morrison Lectures in Ethnology (AT ISSN 0072-1190) 72
George Washington University. Population Information Program. Population Reports see Johns Hopkins University. Population Information Program. Population Reports. Arabic Edition 923
Georgetown University Center for Strategic and International Studies. Significant Issues Series (US ISSN 0736-7163) 905
Georgetown University Round Table on Languages and Linguistics (US ISSN 0196-7207) 695
Georgia. Department of Education. Statistical Report (US ISSN 0094-1557) 424
Georgia. Geologic Survey. Bulletin (US) 388
Georgia. Geologic Survey. Circular 1. List of Publications (US) 382
Georgia. Geologic Survey. Circular 3. The Mineral Industry of Georgia (US) 816
Georgia. Geologic Survey. Circular 4. Water Use in Georgia (US) 1124
Georgia. Geologic Survey. Circular 5. Monitoring Well Construction for Hazardous-Waste Sites in Georgia (US) 496
Georgia. Geologic Survey. Geologic Guide (US) 388
Georgia. Geologic Survey. Geologic Report (US) 388
Georgia. Geologic Survey. Guidebook (US) 388
Georgia. Geologic Survey. Open File Report (US) 388
Georgia. Geologic Survey. Special Publication (US) 388
Georgia. Geological Survey. Circular 1. List of Publications see Georgia. Geologic Survey. Circular 1. List of Publications 382
Georgia. Geological Survey. Circular 2. Mining Directory of Georgia (US) 816
Georgia. Geological Survey. Information Circular (US ISSN 0433-5473) 816
Georgia. Office of Planning and Budget. State Investment Plan (US ISSN 0196-1098) 194
Georgia. State Data Center. City Population Estimates see Georgia Descriptions in Data 927

Georgia Congress of Parents and Teachers. Annual Leadership Training Conference. Workshop for P T A Leaders (US) 442
Georgia Congress of Parents and Teachers. Annual Summer Institute. Handbook for P T A Leaders see Georgia Congress of Parents and Teachers. Annual Leadership Training Conference. Workshop for P T A Leaders 442
Georgia Descriptions in Data (US) 927, 1055
Georgia Journal of Accounting (US ISSN 0275-8911) 221
Georgia Legislative Review (US ISSN 0362-5931) 656
Georgia Manufacturing Directory (US ISSN 0435-5482) 308
Georgia, North Carolina, South Carolina TourBook see Tourbook: Georgia, North Carolina, South Carolina 1117
Georgia State Industrial Directory see MacRae's Georgia State Industrial Directory 312
Georgia State Literary Studies (US ISSN 0884-8696) 722
Georgia Statistical Abstract (US ISSN 0085-1043) 209, 1055
Georgia Vital and Health Statistics see Georgia Vital Statistics Data Book 927
Georgia Vital Statistics Data Book (US) 922, 927
Georgian Bay Regional Library System. Directory-Member Libraries (CN ISSN 0380-8068) 678
Geos (VE ISSN 0435-5601) 388
Geoscience and Man see Palynology 393
Geoscience Documentation (UK ISSN 0016-8483) 6, 382
Geoscience Information Society. Proceedings (US ISSN 0072-1409) 379
Geoscience Wisconsin (US ISSN 0164-2049) 388
Geosciences in Canada (CN ISSN 0707-2422) 388
Geoserials see Geosources 379
Geosources (UK) 379
Geotechnical Abstracts (GW ISSN 0016-8491) 6, 476
Geotechnical Science Laboratories. Publications, Reports, and Theses (CN ISSN 0831-5000) 382, 496
Geotehnika (YU) 388
Geoteknisk Institut, Copenhagen. Bulletin (DK ISSN 0069-987X) 399
Geothermal Resources Council. Special Report (US ISSN 0149-8991) 399
Geothermal Resources Council. Transactions (US ISSN 0193-5933) 399
Geothermal World Directory (US ISSN 0094-9779) 388, 465
Geotimes (US ISSN 0016-8556) 379
Geriatric Guide to Pertinent Publications (US ISSN 0745-5070) 1017
Geriatric Length of Stay by Diagnosis and Operation, United States (US ISSN 0891-2173) 617, 1055
Geriatrika (SP ISSN 0212-9744) 552
German-American Studies see Yearbook of German-American Studies 738
German Arab Trade (UA ISSN 0072-1433) 236
German Books in Print see Verzeichnis Lieferbarer Buecher
German-Canadian Yearbook/Deutschkanadisches Jahrbuch (CN ISSN 0316-8603) 503, 605
German Democratic Republic. Consumer Co-operative Societies. Magazine (GE ISSN 0138-5410) 238, 239, 289, 620
German Exporter see Technic International 1164
German Journal of Psychology (CN ISSN 0705-5870) 6, 938
German Language Courses see Deutschkurse 447
German Merchant Fleet (GW ISSN 0070-4148) 1100
German Motor Tribune (GW ISSN 0072-145X) 1091

German Patents Abstracts (UK ISSN 0016-8807) 6, *862*, 1072
German Texts (UK) *695*
German-Thai Chamber of Commerce Handbook (TH) *236*
German Yearbook of International Law(GW ISSN 0344-3094) *670*
German Yearbook on Business History (US ISSN 0722-2416) *194*
Germania (GW ISSN 0016-8874) 72, *87*
Germania Slavica (GW) *583*
Germanische Denkmaeler der Voelkerwanderungszeit (GW ISSN 0418-9779) *87*
Germanistische Linguistik (GW ISSN 0072-1492) *695*
Germansk Institut Publikationer *see* G I P *695*
Germany (Democratic Republic, 1949-). Meteorologischer Dienst. Abhandlungen (GE ISSN 0138-5658) *804*
Germany (Democratic Republic, 1949-). Ministerium fuer Hoch- und Fachschulwesen. Verfuegungen und Mitteilungen (GE) *435*
Germany (Federal Republic). Bundesministerium fuer das Post- und Fernmeldewesen. Jahresnachweisung ueber die Einnahmen und Ausgaben der Deutschen Bundespost *see* Germany (Federal Republic, 1949-). Bundesministerium fuer das Post- und Fernmeldewesen. Jahresrechnung, Nachweisung ueber die Einnahmen und Ausgaben der Deutschen Bundespost *346*
Germany (Federal Republic). Bundesministerium fuer Verkehr. Strassenbaubericht (GW) *1096*
Germany (Federal Republic, 1949-). Bundesanstalt fuer Arbeit. Berufsberatung. Ergebnisse der Berufsberatungsstatistik (GW) *209*, 1055
Germany (Federal Republic, 1949-). Bundesanstalt fuer Arbeit. Foerderung der Beruflichen Bildung; Ergebnisse der Teilnehmerstatistik. (GW) *447*
Germany (Federal Republic, 1949-). Bundesanstalt fuer Gewaesserkunde. Jahresbericht (GW) *1124*
Germany (Federal Republic, 1949-). Bundesanstalt fuer Materialpruefung. Jahresbericht (GW ISSN 0341-0528) *489*
Germany (Federal Republic, 1949-). Bundesanstalt fuer Strassenwesen, Erfahrungsaustausch ueber Erdarbeiten im Strassenbau (GW) *481*
Germany (Federal Republic, 1949-). Bundesaufsichtsamt fuer das Versicherungswesen. Geschaeftsbericht (GW ISSN 0302-5608) *639*
Germany (Federal Republic, 1949-). Bundesminister des Innern. Schutzkommission. Berichte der Fachausschuesse *see* Germany (Federal Republic, 1949-). Bundesminister des Innern. Schutzkommission. Taetigkeitsbericht *336*
Germany (Federal Republic, 1949-). Bundesminister des Innern. Schutzkommission. Taetigkeitsbericht(GW) *336*
Germany (Federal Republic, 1949-). Bundesministerium fuer Arbeit und Sozialordnung. Hauptergebnisse der Arbeits- und Sozialstatistik (GW ISSN 0341-7840) *209*
Germany (Federal Republic, 1949-). Bundesministerium fuer Bildung und Wissenschaft. Forschungsbericht der Bundesregierung *see* Germany (Federal Republic, 1949-). Bundesministerium fuer Forschung und Technologie, Bundesbericht Forschung *941*

Germany (Federal Republic, 1949-). Bundesministerium fuer das Post- und Fernmeldewesen. Jahresrechnung, Nachweisung ueber die Einnahmen und Ausgaben der Deutschen Bundespost (GW ISSN 0435-7329) *346*
Germany (Federal Republic, 1949-). Bundesministerium fuer Ernaehrung, Landwirtschaft und Forsten. Agrarbericht der Bundesregierung (GW) *1153*
Germany (Federal Republic, 1949-). Bundesministerium fuer Ernaehrung, Landwirtschaft und Forsten. Jahresbericht. Forschung im Bereich des Bundesministers. *see* Germany (Federal Republic, 1949-). Bundesministerium Fuer Ernaehrung, Landwirtschaft und Forsten. Jahresbericht. Forschung im Geschaeftsbereich des Bundesministers fuer Ernaerungland, Wirtschaft und Forsten *27*
Germany (Federal Republic, 1949-). Bundesministerium Fuer Ernaehrung, Landwirtschaft und Forsten. Jahresbericht. Forschung im Geschaeftsbereich des Bundesministers fuer Ernaerungland, Wirtschaft und Forsten (GW ISSN 0343-7477) *27*
Germany (Federal Republic, 1949-). Bundesministerium fuer Forschung und Technologie, Bundesbericht Forschung (GW) *941*
Germany (Federal Republic, 1949-). Bundesministerium fuer Forschung und Technologie. B M F T Foerderungskatalog (GW) *991*, 1069
Germany (Federal Republic, 1949-). Deutscher Bundestag. Wissenschaftliche Dienste. Bibliographien (GW) *126*
Germany (Federal Republic, 1949-). Deutscher Bundestag. Wissenschaftliche Dienste. Materialien (GW ISSN 0344-9130) *126*, 916
Germany (Federal Republic, 1949-). Presse- und Informationsamt Bulletin Archive Supplement (GW) *941*
Germany (Federal Republic, 1949-). Sachverstaendigenrat zur Begutachtung der Gesamtwirtschaftlichen Entwicklung. Jahresgutachten (GW ISSN 0072-159X) *289*
Germany (Federal Republic, 1949-). Statistisches Bundesamt. Alphabetisches Laenderverzeichnis fuer die Aussenhandelsstatistik (GW ISSN 0072-1638) *209*
Germany (Federal Republic, 1949-). Statistisches Bundesamt Arbeiten *see* Survey of German Federal Statistics *1065*
Germany (Federal Republic, 1949-). Statistisches Bundesamt. Fachserie 7, Aussenhandel, Reihe 2: Aussenhandel nach Waren und Laendern (Spezialhandel) (GW ISSN 0072-1654) *209*, 1055
Germany (Federal Republic, 1949-). Statistisches Bundesamt. Fachserie 7, Aussenhandel, Reihe 4. Aussenhandel mit Ausgewaehlten Waren (GW) *209*
Germany (Federal Republic, 1949-). Statistisches Bundesamt. Fachserie 7, Aussenhandel, Reihe 6: Durchfuhr im Seeverkehr und Seeumschlag (GW ISSN 0072-1697) *209*
Germany (Federal Republic, 1949-). Statistisches Bundesamt. Fachserie 7, Aussenhandel, Reihe 7: Sonderbeitraege. (GW ISSN 0072-1700) *209*, 1055
Germany (Federal Republic, 1949-). Statistisches Bundesamt. Fachserie 1, Bevoelkerung und Erwerbstaetigkeit, Reihe 1: Gebiet und Bevoelkerung (GW ISSN 0072-1794) *927*
Germany (Federal Republic, 1949-). Statistisches Bundesamt. Fachserie 1, Bevoelkerung und Erwerbstaetigkeit, Reihe 3: Haushaelte und Familien (GW) *927*

Germany (Federal Republic, 1949-). Statistisches Bundesamt. Fachserie 1, Bevoelkerung und Erwerbstaetigkeit, Reihe 4: Erwerbetaetigkeit (GW ISSN 0072-1832) *209*
Germany (Federal Republic, 1949-). Statistisches Bundesamt. Fachserie 5, Bautaetigkeit und Wohnungen, Reihe 1: Bautaetigkeit (GW ISSN 0072-1735) *189*, 1055
Germany (Federal Republic, 1949-). Statistisches Bundesamt. Fachserie 5, Bautaetigkeit und Wohnungen, Reihe 2: Bewilligungen im Sozialen Wohnungsbau (GW ISSN 0072-1743) *189*, 1055
Germany (Federal Republic, 1949-). Statistisches Bundesamt. Fachserie 5, Bautaetigkeit und Wohnungen, Reihe 3: Bestand an Wohnungen (GW ISSN 0072-1751) *189*
Germany (Federal Republic, 1949-). Statistisches Bundesamt. Fachserie 6, Handel, Gastgewerbe, Reiseverkehr; Reihe 1: Grosshandel (GW ISSN 0072-1964) *209*
Germany (Federal Republic, 1949-). Statistisches Bundesamt. Fachserie 6, Handel, Gastgewerbe, Reiseverkehr; Reihe 3: Einzelhandel (GW ISSN 0072-1972) *209*, 1055
Germany (Federal Republic, 1949-). Statistisches Bundesamt. Fachserie 6, Handel, Gastgewerbe, Reiseverkehr; Reihe 5: Wahrenverkehr mit Berlin (West) (GW) *209*, 1055
Germany (Federal Republic, 1949-). Statistisches Bundesamt. Fachserie 6, Handel, Gastgewerbe, Reiseverkehr; Reihe 7: Reiseverkehr (GW ISSN 0072-1999) *1119*
Germany (Federal Republic, 1949-). Statistisches Bundesamt. Fachserie 3, Land- und Fortswirtschaft, Fischerei; Reihe 2: Betriebs-, Arbeits- und Einkommensverhaeltnisse (GW ISSN 0072-3681) *41*, 1055
Germany (Federal Republic, 1949-). Statistisches Bundesamt. Fachserie 3, Land- und Fortwirtschaft, Fischerei; Reihe 3: Bodennutzueung und Pflanzliche Erzeugung (GW) *41*, 534
Germany (Federal Republic, 1949-). Statistisches Bundesamt. Fachserie 3, Land- und Fortwirtschaft, Fischerei; Reihe 4: Viehbestand und Tierische Erzeugung (GW) *41*
Germany (Federal Republic, 1949-). Statistisches Bundesamt. Fachserie 3, Land- und Fortwirtschaft, Fischerei; Reihe 4.5: Fischerei (GW ISSN 0072-3673) *514*
Germany (Federal Republic, 1949-). Statistisches Bundesamt. Fachserie 4, Produzierendes Gewerbe, Reihe 3.1: Produktion Gewerbe des In- und Auslandes (GW) *209*, 1055
Germany (Federal Republic, 1949-). Statistisches Bundesamt. Fachserie 4, Produzierendes Gewerbe, Reihe 5 (GW) *189*
Germany (Federal Republic, 1949-). Statistisches Bundesamt. Fachserie 4, Produzierendes Gewerbe, Reihe 5: Sonderbeitraege (GW ISSN 0072-2073) *209*
Germany (Federal Republic, 1949-). Statistisches Bundesamt. Fachserie 4, Produzierende Gastgewerbe, Reihe 7: Handwerk. Beschaeftigte um Umsatz im Handwerk (GW ISSN 0072-2103) *209*
Germany (Federal Republic, 1949-). Statistisches Bundesamt. Fachserie 2, Unternehmen und Arbeitsstatten, Reihe 2.1: Abschluesse der Kapitalgesellschaften (GW) *209*
Germany (Federal Republic, 1949-). Statistisches Bundesamt. Fachserie 2, Unternehmen und Arbeitsstatten, Reihe 3: Abschluesse der Oeffentlichen Versorgungs- und Verkehrsunternehmen (GW) *209*
Germany (Federal Republic, 1949-). Statistisches Bundesamt. Fachserie 8, Verkehr, Reihe 3: Strassenverkehr (GW ISSN 0072-405X) *1085*

Germany (Federal Republic, 1949-). Statistisches Bundesamt. Fachserie 8, Verkehr, Reihe 3.3: Haushaelte und Familien (GW ISSN 0072-4068) *1055*, 1085
Germany (Federal Republic, 1949-) Statistisches Bundesamt. Fachserie 3, Reihe 3: Pflanzliche Erzeugung *see* Germany (Federal Republic, 1949-). Statistisches Bundesamt. Fachserie 3, Land- und Fortwirtschaft, Fischerei; Reihe 3: Bodennutzueng und Pflanzliche Erzeugung *41*
Germany (Federal Republic, 1949-). Statistisches Bundesamt. Fachserie 3, Reihe 4: Tierische Erzeugung *see* Germany (Federal Republic, 1949-). Statistisches Bundesamt. Fachserie 3, Land- und Fortwirtschaft, Fischerei; Reihe 4: Viehbestand und Tierische Erzeugung *41*
Germany (Federal Republic, 1949-). Statistisches Bundesamt. Fachserie 4, Reihe 5: Beschaeftigung, Umsatz, Investitionen und Kosten Struktur im Baugewerbe *see* Germany (Federal Republic, 1949-). Statistisches Bundesamt. Fachserie 4, Produzierendes Gewerbe, Reihe 5 *189*
Germany (Federal Republic, 1949-). Statistisches Bundesamt. Fachserie 11: Bildung und Kultur (GW ISSN 0072-1778) *424*, 1055
Germany (Federal Republic, 1949-). Statistisches Bundesamt. Fachserie 14: Finanzen und Steuern (GW) *209*
Germany (Federal Republic, 1949-). Statistisches Bundesamt. Fachserie 12, Gesundheitswesen, Reihe 1: Ausgewaehlte Zahlen fuer das Gesundheitswesen (GW ISSN 0072-1840) *958*, 1055
Germany (Federal Republic, 1949-). Statistisches Bundesamt. Fachserie 16, Loehne und Gehaelter, Reihe 5.2: Tarifloehne und Gehaelter des Auslandes (GW) *209*, 1055
Germany (Federal Republic, 1949-). Statistisches Bundesamt. Fachserie 17, Preise, Reihe 1: Preise und Preisindizes fuer die Land- und Forstwirtschaft (GW ISSN 0072-3894) *41*, 1055
Germany (Federal Republic, 1949-). Statistisches Bundesamt. Fachserie 17, Preise, Reihe 9: Preise fuer Verkehrsleistungen (GW ISSN 0072-3924) *1055*, 1085
Germany (Federal Republic, 1949-). Statistisches Bundesamt. Fachserie 10. Rechtspflege (GW ISSN 0072-1859) *668*, 1055
Germany (Federal Republic, 1949-). Statistisches Bundesamt. Fachserie 16, Reihe 1: Arbeiterverdienste in der Landwirtschaft (GW) *41*, 209
Germany (Federal Republic, 1949-). Statistisches Bundesamt. Fachserie 13, Sozialhilfe, Reihe 3: Kriegsopferfuersorge (GW ISSN 0072-3754) *1022*
Germany (Federal Republic, 1949-). Statistisches Bundesamt. Fachserie 13, Sozialleistungen, Reihe 6: Jugendhilfe (GW ISSN 0072-3762) *334*, 1023
Germany (Federal Republic, 1949-). Statistisches Bundesamt. Fachserie 19, Umweltschutz, Reihe 2: Wasserversorgung und Abwasserbeseitigung (GW) *468*, 1128
Germany (Federal Republic, 1949-). Statistisches Bundesamt. Fachserie 18, Volkswirtschaftliche Gesamtrechnungen, Reihe 1: Konten und Standardtabellen (GW ISSN 0072-4009) *209*
Germany (Federal Republic, 1949-). Statistisches Bundesamt. Fremdsprachige Veroeffentlichungen Nr. 6370010: Foreign Trade According to the Standard International Trade Classification (SITC) - Special Trade (GW) *210*
Germany (Federal Republic, 1949-). Statistisches Bundesamt. Laenderberichte (GW) *1055*

Germany (Federal Republic, 1949-). Statistisches Bundesamt. Loehne und Gehaelter. Reihe 1: Arbeiterverdienste in der Landwirtschaft *see* Germany (Federal Republic, 1949-). Statistisches Bundesamt. Fachserie 16, Reihe 1: Arbeiterverdienste in der Landwirtschaft *209*
Germany (Federal Republic, 1949-) Statistisches Bundesamt. Warenverzeichnis fuer die Aussenhandelsstatistik (GW ISSN 0072-4106) *210, 1055*
Germany (Federal Republic, 1949-) Statistisches Bundesamt. Zahlenkompass/Statistical Compass/ Boussole des Chiffres/Compas de Cifras (GW ISSN 0072-4114) *1056*
Germany Stamp Catalogue (UK ISSN 0142-9817) *874*
Geroldsecker Land (GW) *538*
Gerontological Abstracts (US) *6, 552*
Gerontological Society. Monographs (US) *552*
Gesamthochschule Wuppertalerschriftenreihe Literaturwissenschaft *see* Wuppertaler Schriftenreihe Literatur *737*
Gesamtregister mit den Rechtssaetzen und Fundstellen der Entscheidungen der Zeitschrift fuer Verkehrsrecht (AU) *656*
Gesamtstatistik der Kraftfahrtversicherung (GW ISSN 0435-7442) *642*
Gesamtverzeichnis Oesterreichischer Dissertationen (AU ISSN 0072-4165) *126*
Geschichte der Naturwissenschaften, Technik und Medizin. Schriftenreihe *see* N T M Geschichte der Naturwissenschaften, Technik und Medizin. Schriftenreihe *995*
Geschichte der Sozialistischen Laender Europas. Jahrbuch (GE ISSN 0075-2665) *583*
Geschichte der Stadt Leipzig. Jahrbuch *see* Leipzig aus Vergangenheit und Gegenwart *589*
Geschichte des Arabischen Schrifttums (NE) *612*
Geschichte des Buchwesens. Beitraege (GE ISSN 0067-5040) *961*
Geschichtliche Landeskunde (GW ISSN 0072-4203) *583*
Geschichtliches Eupen (BE) *583*
Geschichtsblaetter fuer Waldeck (GW ISSN 0342-0965) *515, 583*
Geschied- en Oudheidkundige Kring van Ronse en het Tenement van Inde. Annalen/Cercle Historique et Archeologique de Renaux et du Tenement d'Inde. Annales (BE ISSN 0591-1133) *583*
Geschied- en Oudheidkundige Kring voor Leuven en Omgeving. Jaarboek (BE ISSN 0433-8456) *583*
Geselecteerde Agrarische Cijfers van de E E C *see* E E G Vademecum *40*
Gesellschaft der Geologie- und Bergbaustudenten. Mitteilungen (AU) *388, 402, 856*
Gesellschaft fuer Bibliothekswesen und Dokumentation des Landbaues. Mitteilungen (GW ISSN 0433-860X) *6, 41*
Gesellschaft fuer Biologische Chemie, Mosbach. Colloquium *see* Colloquium Mosbach *151*
Gesellschaft fuer die Geschichte des Protestantismus in Oesterreich. Jahrbuch (AU) *583, 978*
Gesellschaft fuer die Geschichte und Bibliographie des Brauwesens. Jahrbuch (GW ISSN 0072-422X) *119*
Gesellschaft fuer Griechische und Hellenistische Rechtsgeschichte. Akten (AU) *656*
Gesellschaft fuer Kernforschung. Bericht ueber Forschungs- und Entwicklungsarbeiten *see* Kernforschungszentrum Karlsruhe. Ergebnisbericht ueber Forschung und Entwicklung *897*

Gesellschaft fuer Naturkunde in Wuerttemberg. Jahreshefte (GW ISSN 0368-2307) *141*
Gesellschaft fuer Niedersaechsische Kirchengeschichte. Jahrbuch (GW ISSN 0072-4238) *583, 978*
Gesellschaft fuer Physiologische Chemie, Mosbach. Colloquium *see* Colloquium Mosbach *151*
Gesellschaft fuer Reaktorsicherheit. Jahresbericht (GW) *471*
Gesellschaft fuer Salzburger Landeskunde. Mitteilungen (AU) *583*
Gesellschaft Naturforschender Freunde zu Berlin. Sitzungsberichte. Neue Folge (GW ISSN 0037-5942) *991*
Gesellschaft pro Vindonissa. Jahresbericht (SZ ISSN 0072-4270) *87*
Gesellschaft pro Vindonissa. Veroeffentlichungen (SZ ISSN 0072-4289) *87*
Gesellschaft, Recht, Wirtschaft (GW) *1008*
Gesetz- und Verordnungsblatt fuer Berlin (GW) *656*
Gesetz und Verordnungsblatt fuer das Land Hessen (GW ISSN 0342-3557) *950*
Gesher (US ISSN 0016-9145) *711, 878, 976*
Gest-Guest Quarterly (US) *536*
Gestione Informata (IT) *279*
Geyer's Who Makes It Directory (US ISSN 0072-4327) *286*
Gezeitentafeln (GW ISSN 0084-9774) *405*
Gezinssociologische Documentatie *see* Gezinswetenschappelijke Documentatie *927*
Gezinswetenschappelijke Documentatie (BE) *6, 927*
Ghana (GH ISSN 0304-1190) *245*
Ghana. Central Bureau of Statistics. Economic Survey (GH ISSN 0072-4335) *210, 1056*
Ghana. Meteorological Department. Climatological Notes (GH) *804*
Ghana. Meteorological Department. Professional Notes (GH) *804*
Ghana. Meteorological Department. Sun and Moon Tables for Ghana (GH) *804*
Ghana. Ministry of Education. Educational Statistics (GH) *414*
Ghana. National Council for Higher Education. Annual Report (GH) *435*
Ghana. National Council on Women and Development. Annual Report (GH) *1128*
Ghana. Supreme Military Council. Budget Proposals (GH) *295*
Ghana Commercial Bank. Annual Report (GH ISSN 0435-9348) *245*
Ghana Economic Review (GH) *194*
Ghana Geographical Association. Bulletin (GH ISSN 0016-9536) *544*
Ghana Law Reports (GH ISSN 0072-436X) *656*
Ghana Library Journal (GH ISSN 0016-9552) *678*
Ghana National Bibliography (GH ISSN 0072-4378) *126*
Ghana Population Studies (GH) *922*
Ghana Science Abstracts (GH) *6, 1004*
Ghost Dance (US ISSN 0016-9633) *741*
Giannini Foundation of Agricultural Economics. Information Series (US) *47*
Giannini Foundation of Agricultural Economics. Monograph (US ISSN 0575-4208) *47*
Giannini Foundation of Agricultural Economics. Research Report (US ISSN 0072-4459) *47*
Giappone (IT) *569*
Gibraltar Point Observatory Report *see* Lincolnshire Bird Report *170*
Gibridnye Vychislitel'nye Mashiny i Kompleksy (UR ISSN 0207-0111) *359*
Gids bij de Prijscourant (NE ISSN 0072-4467) *266*
Giessener Schriftenreihe Tierzucht und Haustiergenetik (GW ISSN 0434-0035) *66*

Giesserei-Kalender (GW ISSN 0340-8175) *798*
Gift and Decorative Accessories Buyers Directory (US ISSN 0072-4505) *320, 552*
Gift and Tableware Reporter. Gift Guide (US ISSN 0148-9437) *309, 552*
Gifu Daigaku Nogakubu Kenkyu Hokoku *see* Gifu University. Faculty of Agriculture. Research Bulletin *28*
Gifu Pharmaceutical University. Annual Proceedings (JA ISSN 0434-0094) *871*
Gifu University. Faculty of Agriculture. Research Bulletin/Gifu Daigaku Nogakubu Kenkyu Hokoku (JA ISSN 0072-4513) *28*
Gilbert Law Summaries. Criminal Procedure (US ISSN 0193-8010) *656*
Gilberto Amado Memorial Lecture (UN) *670*
Gilleleje Museum (DK ISSN 0109-6656) *583*
Giorgio Levi della Vida Conferences. Reports of the Conference. (US ISSN 0340-6369) *612*
Giornale di Fisica. Quaderni (IT ISSN 0391-5905) *1153*
Giornale Italiano di Entomologia (IT ISSN 0392-7296) *164*
Giornale Italiano di Psicologia. Quaderni (IT) *934*
Giornale Storico della Lunigiana e del Territorio Lucense (IT ISSN 0017-050X) *584*
Giovane Critica (IT ISSN 0017-0526) *711*
Gioventu Passionista/Passionist Youth (IT ISSN 0072-4548) *970*
Girl Annual (UK ISSN 0262-9208) *341*
Girls Gymnastics Manual *see* Girls Gymnastics Rules and Manual *1033*
Girls Gymnastics Rules *see* Girls Gymnastics Rules and Manual *1033*
Girls Gymnastics Rules and Manual (US) *1033*
Girls School Year Book *see* Independent Schools Yearbook: Girls Schools *443*
Gitarre (GW) *836*
Giurisprudenza Annotata di Diritto Industriale (IT) *656*
Giustizia Civile. Repertorio Generale Annuale (IT) *656*
Giving U.S.A. Annual Report (US) *1017*
Glaciological Data (US ISSN 0149-1776) *388*
Glaciological Notes *see* Glaciological Data *388*
Glaciology and Quaternary Geology (NE) *388, 544*
Gladiolus Annual (UK) *534*
Gladius (SP ISSN 0436-029X) *79, 811*
Glanures (MF) *1056*
Glasenapp-Stiftung (GW ISSN 0170-3455) *851*
Glasgow & West of Scotland Family History Society. Newsletter (UK ISSN 0141-8009) *536*
Glasgow Archaeological Journal (UK ISSN 0305-8980) *87*
Glasgow Chamber of Commerce. Annual Report (UK) *236*
Glasgow Chamber of Commerce. Industrial Index to Glasgow & West of Scotland *see* Scotland Chambers of Commerce. Directory *237*
Glasgow Chamber of Commerce. Regional Directory *see* Scotland Chambers of Commerce. Directory *237*
Glasgow Chamber of Commerce and Manufactures Regional Directory *see* Scottish Chambers of Commerce National Directory *237*
Glasgow Directory of Voluntary Organizations (UK ISSN 0143-7429) *1017*
Glasgow Naturalist (UK ISSN 0373-241X) *141, 991*
Glasnik Arhiva i Drustava Arhivskih Radnika Bosne i Hercegovine (YU) *584*

Glasnik Hemicara i Tehnologa Bosne i Hercegovine (YU ISSN 0367-4444) *323, 478*
Glasnik Zemaljskog Muzeja u Sarajevu *see* Zemaljski Muzej Bosne i Hercegovine. Glasnik. Arheologija *96*
Glasnik Zemaljskog Muzeja u Sarajevu *see* Zemaljski Muzej Bosne i Hercegovine. Glasnik. Prirodne Nauke *1003*
Glasra (IE ISSN 0332-0235) *157*
Glass and Glazing News (UK ISSN 0260-6321) *320*
Glass Containers *see* Glass Packaging Institute. Annual Report *855*
Glass Directory and Buyer's Guide *see* European Glass Directory and Buyer's Guide *320*
Glass: Latin American Industrial Report(US) *320*
Glass/Metal Catalog *see* International Glass/Metal Catalog *320*
Glass Packaging Institute. Annual Report (US) *855*
Glass, Potteries and Ceramic Annual (II) *113*
Glass, Potteries and Ceramic Journal *see* Glass, Potteries and Ceramic Annual *113*
Glass Science and Technology (NE ISSN 0271-2938) *320*
Glasshouse Crops Research Institute. Annual Report (UK ISSN 0436-0524) *532*
Glass's Car Check Book (UK) *1091*
Glass's Commercial Vehicle Check Book (UK) *1081*
Glass's Index of Registration Marks (UK) *1091*
Glass's Motor Cycle Check Book (UK) *1041*
Glaube und Lernen (GW ISSN 0179-3551) *970*
Gleanings (Cambridge) (US ISSN 0160-2373) *1153*
Glenbow-Alberta Institute. Occasional Paper (CN ISSN 0072-467X) *503, 605*
Glenbow Foundation. Archives Series *see* Glenbow Museum. Archives Series *605*
Glenbow Foundation. Occasional Paper *see* Glenbow-Alberta Institute. Occasional Paper *605*
Glenbow Museum. Archives Series (CN) *605*
Glens Falls Review (US) *722*
Glimpse of London with American Express (UK) *1110*
Glimpses in Plant Research (II) *157*
Glitches (US ISSN 0732-667X) *356*
Global Architecture Document *see* G A Document *98*
Global Architecture Houses *see* G A Houses *98*
Global Focus Series (US ISSN 0072-4742) *1153*
Global Market Surveys (US) *256*
Global Report (US ISSN 0730-9112) *916*
Global Risk Assessments (US ISSN 0739-4640) *256, 916*
Global Tectonics and Metallogeny (GW ISSN 0163-3171) *388*
Globe (AT ISSN 0311-3930) *544*
GLOBECOM *see* I E E E Global Telecommunications Conference. Conference Record *343*
Globusfreund (AU ISSN 0436-0664) *544*
Glottodidactica; an International Journal of Applied Linguistics (PL ISSN 0072-4769) *695*
Glyndebourne Festival Programme Book (UK ISSN 0434-1066) *836*
Goa, Daman, and Diu. Directorate of Economics, Statistics, and Evaluation. Evaluation Report (II) *245*
Gode Gamle Fysiktips *see* Fysiktips *888*
Gode Lydboeger (DK ISSN 0107-5209) *126*
Godesberger Heimatblaetter (GW ISSN 0436-1024) *584*
Godhavn Geophysical Observatory. Magnetic Results *see* Godhavn Magnetic Results *399*

Godhavn Magnetic Results (DK ISSN 0109-4300) *399*
Godishnik na Muzeite ot Severna Bulgariia (BU ISSN 0204-4048) *584*
Goedskingrapport (DK ISSN 0901-1943) *55*
Goeje-Stichting. Uitgaven (NE) *851*
Goer det Selv Indeks (DK ISSN 0105-8134) *614*
Goeteborg Studies in Educational Sciences (SW ISSN 0436-1121) *414*
Goteborg Studies in Politics (SW) *905*
Goeteborg Women's Studies (SW ISSN 0283-2399) *1128*
Goeteborger Germanistische Forschungen (SW ISSN 0072-4793) *695, 722*
Goeteborgs Etnografiska Museum. Aarstryck (SW ISSN 0436-2020) *72*
Goeteborgs Kungliga Vetenskaps- och Vitterhets-Samhaelle. Aarsbok (SW ISSN 0436-113X) *629*
Goeteborgs Kungliga Vetenskaps- och Vitterhets- Samhaelle. Handlingar *see* Acta Regiae Societatis Scientiarum et Litterarum Gothoburgensis. Botanica *153*
Goeteborgs Kungliga Vetenskaps- och Vitterhets-Samhaelle. Handlingar *see* Acta Regiae Societatis Scientiarum et Litterarum Gothoburgensis. Zoologica *172*
Goeteborgs Kungliga Vetenskaps- och Vitterhets-Samhaelle. Handlingar *see* Acta Regiae Societatis Scientiarum et Litterarum Gothoburgensis. Geophysica *398*
Goeteborgs Kungliga Vetenskaps- och Vitterhets- Samhaelle. Handlingar *see* Acta Regiae Societatis Scientiarum et Litterarum Gothoburgensis. Humaniora *628*
Goeteborgs Kungliga Vetenskaps- och Vitterhets-Samhaelle. Handlingar Bihang *see* Goeteborgs Kungliga Vetenskaps- och Vitterhets-Samhaelle. Aarsbok *629*
Goeteborgs Universitet. Demographic Research Institute. Reports (SW) *922*
Goeteborgs Universitet. Ekonomisk-Historiska Institutionen. Meddelanden (SW ISSN 0072-5080) *251*
Goeteborgs Universitet. Institutionen foer Praktisk Pedagogik. Rapport (SW ISSN 0348-2219) *447*
Goeteborgs Universitet. Nationalekonomiska Institutionen. Ekonomiska Studier (SW ISSN 0434-2410) *251*
Goeteborgs Universitet. Oceanografiska Institutionen. Reports (SW) *405*
Goeteborgs Universitet. Sociologiska Institutionen. Forsknings-Rapport (SW ISSN 0072-5099) *1008*
Goeteborgs Universitet. Sociologiska Institutionen. Monografier (SW ISSN 0072-5102) *1026*
Goeteborgs Universitet. Statistiska Institutionen. Skriftserie. Publications(SW ISSN 0072-5110) *1056*
Goeteborgs Universitet. Universitetsbibliotek. Aarsberaettelse (SW ISSN 0347-884X) *678*
Goethe-Gesellschaft. Jahrbuch *see* Goethe-Jahrbuch *723*
Goethe-Institut zur Pflege der Deutschen Sprache im Auslad und zur Foerderung der Internationalen Kulturellen Zusammenarbeit. Jahrbuch (GW) *695*
Goethe-Institut zur Pflege Deutscher Sprache und Kultur im Ausland. Jahrbuch *see* Goethe-Institut zur Pflege der Deutschen Sprache im Ausland und zur Foerderung der Internationalen Kulturellen Zusammenarbeit. Jahrbuch *695*
Goethe-Jahrbuch (GE ISSN 0323-4207) *723*
Goethe Woerterbuch (GW) *723*
Goethe Yearbook (US ISSN 0734-3329) *723*
Goettinger Floristische Rundbriefe (GW ISSN 0340-4145) *157*
Goettinger Jahrbuch (GW ISSN 0072-4882) *584*
Goettinger Orientforschungen. Reihe I: Syriaca (GW ISSN 0340-6326) *569, 851*
Goettinger Orientforschungen. Reihe II: Studien zur Spaetantiken und Fruehchristlichen Kunst (GW ISSN 0173-2358) *851*
Goettinger Orientforschungen. Reihe IV: Aegypten (GW ISSN 0340-6342) *569, 851*
Goettinger Studien zur Rechtsgeschichte (GW) *656*
Goettinger Universitaetsreden (GW ISSN 0085-1108) *435*
Goffs Travellers Guide (UK) *1153*
Goias, Brazil. Secretaria do Planejamento e Coordenacao. Boletim Estadistico (BL) *1056*
Going-To-College Handbook (US ISSN 0072-4904) *435*
Gokanen Keizai Yosoku *see* Five Year Economic Forecast *244*
Gokhale Institute Mimeograph Series (II ISSN 0436-1326) *194, 905*
Gokhale Institute of Politics and Economics. Studies (II ISSN 0072-4912) *194, 905*
Gokuldas Sanskrit Series (II) *878*
Gold Book of MultiHousing (US ISSN 0195-847X) *184, 623*
Gold Book of Snowmobile Data and Used Prices (CN ISSN 0318-9422) *1045*
Golda Meir Library Newsletter (US) *678*
Golden Dog *see* Chien d'Or *718*
Golden Guide to South and East Asia *see* All-Asia Guide *541*
Golden List of Beaches (UK) *496, 1045*
Goldschmiede- und Uhrmacher-Jahrbuch (GW) *644*
Golf (GW ISSN 0017-1735) *1038*
Golf and Country Club Guest Policy Directory *see* Private Country Club Guest Policy Directory *1040*
Golf Course Builders of America Directory (US) *184, 309, 1038*
Golf Course Superintendents Association of America. Membership Directory (US ISSN 0436-1474) *1038*
Golf Course Superintendents Association of America. Proceedings of the International Conference and Show (US ISSN 0072-4947) *1038*
Golf Courses of Alberta *see* Alberta Golf Guide *1037*
Golf en France (FR) *1038*
Golf Guide (US ISSN 0072-4955) *1033*
Golf Rules Illustrated (UK ISSN 0072-4963) *1038*
Golf - Where to Play and Where to Stay (UK ISSN 0263-4066) *1038*
Golfer's Handbook (UK ISSN 0072-498X) *1038*
Golfing Year (UK) *1038*
Gondwana Newsletter (BL ISSN 0072-4998) *379*
Good Beer Guide (UK ISSN 0265-0681) *119*
The Good Book Guide to Children's Books (UK) *335, 961*
Good Camps Guide (UK ISSN 0142-5978) *1045, 1110*
Good Food Guide (UK ISSN 0072-5005) *620*
Good Hotel Guide (UK) *620*
Good News *see* New York Good News *540*
Good Pub Guide (UK) *119*
Good Sam Club's Recreational Vehicle Owners Directory *see* Trailer Life's Recreational Vehicle Campground and Services Directory *1047*
Good Value Guide (UK) *1110*
Goodfellow Catalog of Wonderful Things (US) *614*
Goodhear-Willcox Automotive Encyclopedia *see* Automotive Encyclopedia *1090*
Goods Vehicle Costing and Pricing Handbook (UK) *1091*
Goods Vehicle Year Book *see* Freight Industry Yearbook *1081*
Goodwin Series. Occasional Papers (SA ISSN 0304-3460) *87*
Goole Port Handbook (UK ISSN 0262-1622) *309, 1100*
Gordon's Print Price Annual (Year) (US) *105*
Goriski Letnik (YU ISSN 0350-2929) *827*
Gornoslaskie Studia Socjologiczne (PL ISSN 0072-5013) *1026*
Gortania (IT ISSN 0391-5859) *87, 141, 379*
Goryo Daehakgyo Nonmunjip Science *see* Science and Technology *999*
Gospel Informatie-Handboek (NE) *836*
Gospel Music Offical Directory (US) *836*
Gosudarstvennyi Muzei Izobrazitel'nykh Iskusstv im. Pushkina. Soobshcheniya (UR ISSN 0077-1562) *827*
Gothenburg and Western Sweden Chamber of Commerce. Membership Directory (SW) *236*
Gothenburg Studies in Art and Architecture (SW ISSN 0348-4114) *98, 105*
Gothenburg Studies in English (SW ISSN 0072-503X) *695, 723*
Gothenburg Studies in Social Anthropology (SW ISSN 0348-4076) *72*
Gothenburg Studies in the History of Science and Ideas (SW ISSN 0348-6788) *991*
Gothic (US) *14, 723*
Gothic Chapbook Series *see* Gothic *723*
Gourmetour (SP) *620, 1110*
GOURS (SP) *1153*
Governance of England (UK) *584*
Governance of Metropolitan Regions. Series (US) *1154*
Government and Municipal Contractors(UK ISSN 0140-5764) *942*
Government and Public Administration Society. Journal (SI) *942*
Government Assistance Almanac (US ISSN 0883-8690) *950*
Government Business Worldwide Reports (US ISSN 0017-2588) *256*
Government Contracts Directory (US ISSN 0072-5137) *289*
Government Contracts Monographs (US ISSN 0072-5153) *942*
Government Documents and Information Conference. Proceedings(US) *678*
Government Employees *see* Sweden. Statistiska Centralbyraan. Statsanstaellda *1163*
Government Finance Brief. New Series (US ISSN 0072-5161) *295*
Government Gazette of Mauritius (MF) *942*
Government Gazette of Mauritius. Legal Supplement. Act (MF) *942*
Government Gazette of Mauritius. Legal Supplement. Government Notice (MF) *942*
Government Gazette of Mauritius. Legal Supplement. Proclamation (MF) *942*
Government Gazette of Mauritius. Special Legal Supplement. A Bill (MF) *942*
Government in Hawaii (US ISSN 0072-517X) *942*
Government Life Insurance Programs for Veterans and Members of the Services. Annual Report (US) *639, 811*
Government of Andhra Pradesh. Audit Report *see* Government of Andhra Pradesh. Report *942*
Government of Andhra Pradesh. Report(II) *942*
Government Oriental Manuscripts Library. Bulletin. (II) *678, 851*
Government Programs and Projects Directory (US ISSN 0737-5255) *942*
Government Publications Guide *see* Bibliographic Guide to Government Publications *122*
Government Reference Books (US ISSN 0072-5188) *126*
Government Research Centers Directory *see* Government Research Directory *1069*
Government Research Directory (US) *1069*
Government Support for British Business (UK) *245*
Governmental Finances (Washington) *see* Current Governments Reports: Governmental Finances *294*
Governmental Research Association Directory (US ISSN 0072-520X) *942*
Governors of Oklahoma (US) *942*
Grace, Kennedy Foundation. Annual Report (JM) *1017*
Gradiva (US ISSN 0363-8057) *723*
Gradjevinski Fakultet. Institut za Materijale i Konstrukcije. Zbornik Istrazivackih Radova (YU ISSN 0350-1701) *184*
Graduate Assistantship Directory in Computer Sciences (US) *357*
Graduate Careers in Sales and Marketing for Graduates and Postgraduates *see* Dog Volume 3. Administration, Management, Marketing and Sales *848*
Graduate Fellowship Awards Announced by National Science Foundation (US ISSN 0072-5250) *435*
Graduate Management Admission Test Official Guide for G M A T Review *see* Official Guide for G M A T Review *281*
Graduate Outlook (AT) *848*
Graduate Professional Schools of Social Work in Canada and the U.S.A. *see* Schools of Social Work with Accredited Master's Degree Programs *438*
Graduate Programs in Public Affairs and Public Administration (US) *942*
Graduate Programs: Physics, Astronomy, and Related Fields (US ISSN 0147-1821) *116, 435, 888*
Graduate School Guide (US) *429, 982*
Graduate School Journal (PH ISSN 0115-3110) *435, 443, 942, 1026*
Graduate School Programs in Public Affairs and Public Administration *see* Graduate Programs in Public Affairs and Public Administration *942*
Graduate Science Education Student Support and Postdoctorals *see* U.S. National Science Foundation. Graduate Science Education Student Support and Postdoctorals *439*
Graduate Studies (UK) *435*
Graduate Study in Psychology *see* Graduate Study in Psychology and Associated Fields *934*
Graduate Study in Psychology and Associated Fields (US) *429, 934*
Graduate Texts in Contemporary Physics (US) *888*
Graduate Texts in Mathematics (US ISSN 0072-5285) *749*
Graezer Beitraege (AU) *584*
Grafiske Funktionaerer (DK ISSN 0109-0879) *930*
Grafiske Funktionaerers Landsforening. Orientering *see* Grafiske Funktionaerer *930*
Graham's Town Series (SA) *134*
Grain Directory/Buyers's Guide *see* Grain Guide/North American Grain Yearbook *309*
Grain Guide/North American Grain Yearbook (US) *63, 309*
Grainlist (Year) (CN) *28, 309*
Gramophone Spoken Word & Miscellaneous Catalogue (UK ISSN 0262-0812) *1031*
Grand Manan Historian (CN ISSN 0316-2702) *606*
Grandes Figures de la Charite (FR ISSN 0072-5404) *584*
Grandes Temas do Jornalismo (BL) *1154*
Grandes Todos (UY ISSN 0072-5439) *723*
Grandes Vultos da Engenharia Brasileira (BL) *471*
Granite and Marble Directory *see* A M A Product Directory *813*
Granny Square & Craft Ideas (US) *844*

GREAT BRITAIN. 1747

Grant Data Quarterly see Annual Register of Grant Support: a Directory of Funding Soures 432
Grant Funding and Small Business Aid Programs Federal and Provincial (CN) 961
Grants and Aid to Individuals in the Arts see National Directory of Grants and Aid to Individuals in the Arts, International 108
Grants and Awards Available to American Writers (US ISSN 0092-5268) 723
Grants for Study Visits by University Administrators and Librarians (UK ISSN 0144-462X) 435
Grants Register (US) 441
Grants Register (UK) (UK) 435
Graph-Agri (FR ISSN 0242-2085) 47
Graphic Arts Abstracts (US ISSN 0017-3282) 6, 931
Graphic Arts Green Book (US ISSN 0147-1651) 930
Graphic Arts Japan (JA ISSN 0072-548X) 105
Graphic Arts Technical Foundation. Research Progress Report see Graphic Arts Technical Foundation. Research Project Report 931
Graphic Arts Technical Foundation. Research Project Report (US ISSN 0096-1159) 931
Graphic Arts Technical Foundation Technical Services Report see G A T F Technical Services Report 1068
Graphic Arts Trade Directory and Register see Graphic Arts Green Book 930
Graphic Interface Conference. Proceedings see Graphics Interface. Proceedings/Comptes Rendus 357
Graphical Survey of the Economy of Taiwan District, Republic of China (CH) 245
Graphics Interface. Proceedings/Comptes Rendus (CN ISSN 0713-5424) 357
Graphiq'emballage see J'emballe 855
Graphis Annual (SZ ISSN 0072-5528) 15, 105, 931
Graphis Posters (SZ) 105, 884
Graphische Lehr- und Versuchsanstalt Mitteilungen see G L V Mitteilungen 930
Graphische Unternehmungen Oesterreichs. Jahrbuch (AU ISSN 0075-2266) 931
Grass Roots Perspectives on American History (US ISSN 0148-771X) 606
Grassland Society of Southern Africa. Journal (SA ISSN 0256-6702) 55
Grassland Society of Southern Africa. Proceedings of the Annual Congresses see Grassland Society of Southern Africa. Journal 55
Gravure Research Institute Newsletter see G R I Newsletter 930
Gray Herbarium. Contributions (US) 157
Graywolf Annual (US ISSN 0743-7471) 723
Great Barrier Reef Marine Park Authority Bulletin (AT ISSN 0705-8764) 405
Great Barrier Reef Marine Park Authority Workshop Series (AT ISSN 0156-5842) 405
Great Basin Naturalist Memoirs (US) 157, 174
Great Britain. Advisory Council for Adult and Continuing Education. Annual Report (UK ISSN 0260-3306) 426
Great Britain. Aeronautical Research Council. Current Paper Series (UK ISSN 0072-5595) 19
Great Britain. Aeronautical Research Council. Reports and Memoranda Series (UK ISSN 0072-5609) 19
Great Britain. Agricultural Science Service. Research and Development Reports: Animal Science (UK ISSN 0261-698X) 66
Great Britain. Agricultural Science Service. Research and Development Reports: Crop and Pest Diseases (UK ISSN 0261-6963) 55
Great Britain. Agricultural Science Service. Research and Development Reports: Crop Nutrition and Soil Science (UK ISSN 0261-717X) 55
Great Britain. Agricultural Science Service. Research and Development Reports: Mammal and Bird Pests (UK ISSN 0261-7161) 55
Great Britain. Agricultural Science Service. Research and Development Reports: Pesticide Science (UK) 55
Great Britain. Agricultural Science Service. Research and Development Reports: Storage Pest (UK) 55
Great Britain. Air Transport Licensing Board. Report see Great Britain. Civil Aviation Authority. Annual Report and Accounts 1088
Great Britain. Air Transport Users Committee Annual Report (UK) 1088
Great Britain. Board of Inland Revenue. The Survey of Personal Incomes (UK) 277, 295
Great Britain. Board of Trade. Insurance Business: Annual Report see Great Britain. Department of Trade. Insurance Business: Annual Report 639
Great Britain. British Airports Authority. Annual Report and Accounts (UK ISSN 0068-1229) 1088
Great Britain. British Geological Survey. Annual Report (UK) 388
Great Britain. British Geological Survey. Classical Areas of British Geology (UK) 388
Great Britain. British Geological Survey. Geomagnetic Bulletin (UK) 399
Great Britain. British Geological Survey. Memoirs (UK) 388
Great Britain. British Geological Survey. Metric Well Inventory (UK) 1154
Great Britain. British Geological Survey. Mineral Assessment Report (UK) 388, 816
Great Britain. British Geological Survey. Overseas Geology and Mineral Resources (UK) 388, 816
Great Britain. British Geological Survey. Overseas Memoirs (UK) 388
Great Britain. British Geological Survey. Report (UK) 388
Great Britain. British Geological Survey. Seismological Bulletins (UK) 399
Great Britain. Building Research Establishment. Annual Report (UK ISSN 0068-354X) 184
Great Britain. Building Research Establishment. Reports (UK) 184, 507, 530
Great Britain. Central Office of Information. Overseas Publications Division. Reference Pamphlets Series(UK ISSN 0072-5722) 584
Great Britain. Central Statistical Office. Annual Abstract of Statistics (UK ISSN 0072-5730) 1056
Great Britain. Central Statistical Office. Guide to Official Statistics (UK ISSN 0261-1791) 1056
Great Britain. Central Statistical Office. Regional Statistics see Great Britain. Central Statistical Office. Regional Trends 1056
Great Britain. Central Statistical Office. Regional Trends (UK ISSN 0261-1783) 1056
Great Britain. Central Statistical Office. Research Series (UK ISSN 0072-5757) 1056
Great Britain. Central Statistical Office. Social Trends (UK ISSN 0072-5765) 1026
Great Britain. Central Statistical Office. Studies in Official Statistics (UK ISSN 0081-8313) 1056
Great Britain. Cinematograph Films Council. Annual Report (UK ISSN 0072-5773) 824
Great Britain. Civil Aviation Authority. Air Transport Users Committee Annual Report see Great Britain. Air Transport Users Committee Annual Report 1088
Great Britain. Civil Aviation Authority. Annual Report and Accounts (UK ISSN 0306-3569) 1088
Great Britain. Civil Aviation Authority. Annual Statistics see Great Britain. Civil Aviation Authority. U.K. Airlines Annual Operating, Traffic & Financial Statistics 1088
Great Britain. Civil Aviation Authority. Annual Statistics see Great Britain. Civil Aviation Authority. U.K. Airports Annual Statements of Movements, Passengers and Cargo 1088
Great Britain. Civil Aviation Authority. Civil Aviation Publications (UK ISSN 0072-5641) 1088
Great Britain. Civil Aviation Authority. General Aviation Airmiss Bulletin (UK) 1088
Great Britain. Civil Aviation Authority. General Aviation Airmisses see Great Britain. Civil Aviation Authority. General Aviation Airmiss Bulletin 1088
Great Britain. Civil Aviation Authority. International Register of Civil Aircraft (UK) 1088
Great Britain. Civil Aviation Authority. U.K. Airlines Annual Operating, Traffic & Financial Statistics (UK) 1088
Great Britain. Civil Aviation Authority. U.K. Airports Annual Statements of Movements, Passengers and Cargo (UK) 1088
Great Britain. Civil Service Department. Report (UK ISSN 0307-9589) 942
Great Britain. Commonwealth Office. Yearbook see Yearbook of the Commonwealth 602
Great Britain. Department of Education and Science. Annual Report (UK) 414
Great Britain. Department of Education and Science. Architects and Building Branch. Broadsheets (UK ISSN 0260-0471) 443
Great Britain. Department of Education and Science. Assessment of Performance Units. Summaries of Reports (UK ISSN 0144-8048) 443
Great Britain. Department of Education and Science. Building Bulletins (UK ISSN 0072-5870) 443
Great Britain. Department of Education and Science. Computer Board for Universities and Research Councils. Report (UK ISSN 0072-582X) 352
Great Britain. Department of Education and Science. Education Surveys (UK ISSN 0072-5897) 414
Great Britain. Department of Education and Science. Science Policy Studies (UK ISSN 0072-5919) 991
Great Britain. Department of Education and Science. Statistics of Education (UK ISSN 0072-5900) 414
Great Britain. Department of Employment. Changes in Rates of Wages and Hours of Work see Great Britain. Department of Employment. Statistics Division. Time Rates of Wages and Hours of Work 210
Great Britain. Department of Employment. Family Expenditure Survey (UK ISSN 0072-5927) 277
Great Britain. Department of Employment. New Earnings Survey (UK ISSN 0308-1419) 272
Great Britain. Department of Employment. Research (UK) 272
Great Britain. Department of Employment. Statistics Division. Time Rates of Wages and Hours of Work (UK) 210
Great Britain. Department of Energy. Development of the Oil and Gas Resources of the United Kingdom (UK) 465, 864
Great Britain. Department of Health and Social Security. Health Building Notes (UK) 617, 1017
Great Britain. Department of Health and Social Security. Health Equipment Notes (UK ISSN 0141-1403) 617, 1017
Great Britain. Department of Health and Social Security. Hospital Building Notes see Great Britain. Department of Health and Social Security. Health Building Notes 617
Great Britain. Department of Health and Social Security. Hospital Equipment Notes see Great Britain. Department of Health and Social Security. Health Equipment Notes 617
Great Britain. Department of Health and Social Security. Hospital In-Patient Inquiry (UK ISSN 0072-6036) 953, 1017
Great Britain. Department of Health and Social Security. Notes on Good Practices (UK) 617
Great Britain. Department of Health and Social Security. On the State of the Public Health (UK ISSN 0072-6087) 953
Great Britain. Department of Health and Social Security. Social Security Statistics (UK) 1017
Great Britain. Department of Health and Social Security. Statistical and Research Report Series (UK) 617, 1017
Great Britain. Department of Health and Social Security. Statistical Report Series see Great Britain. Department of Health and Social Security. Statistical and Research Report Series 617
Great Britain. Department of Industry. Business Statistics Office Report on the Census of Production see Great Britain. Department of Trade and Industry. Business Statistics Office Report on the Census of Production 210
Great Britain. Department of the Environment. Archaeological Reports(UK ISSN 0072-6842) 87, 584
Great Britain. Department of the Environment. Engineering Specifications (UK ISSN 0072-6850) 481
Great Britain. Department of the Environment. Fire Research Station. Fire Notes see Great Britain. Building Research Establishment. Reports 507
Great Britain. Department of the Environment. Fire Research Station. Technical Papers see Great Britain. Building Research Establishment. Reports 507
Great Britain. Department of the Environment. Highway Statistics see Transport Statistics Great Britain 1097
Great Britain. Department of the Environment. Library Services. D.O.E. Annual List of Publications see Great Britain. Departments of the Environment and Transport. Library Services. Annual List of Publications 501
Great Britain. Department of the Environment. Local Government Financial Statistics: England and Wales (UK ISSN 0308-1745) 295, 951
Great Britain. Department of the Environment. Metrication in the Construction Industry (UK ISSN 0072-6869) 184, 809
Great Britain. Department of the Environment. Rate Rebates in England and Wales (UK) 295
Great Britain. Department of the Environment. Rates and Rateable Values in England and Wales (UK) 295
Great Britain. Department of the Environment. Report on Research and Development (UK) 496, 1026
Great Britain. Department of the Environment. Statistics for Town and Country Planning. Series 1 (UK ISSN 0072-6818) 623, 942

Great Britain. Department of the Environment. Statistics for Town and Country Planning. Series 2 (UK ISSN 0072-6826) *623*, 942
Great Britain. Department of Trade and Industry. Business Statistics Office Report on the Census of Production (UK) *210*
Great Britain. Department of Trade and Industry. Digest of Energy Statistics see Digest of United Kingdom Energy Statistics *464*
Great Britain. Department of Trade. Bankruptcy: General Annual Report (UK ISSN 0072-5633) *229*
Great Britain. Department of Trade. Companies: General Annual Report (UK ISSN 0072-565X) *289*
Great Britain. Department of Trade. Export of Works of Art (UK ISSN 0072-5668) *105*, 256
Great Britain. Department of Trade. Import Duties Act 1958. Annual Report (UK ISSN 0072-5676) *256*
Great Britain. Department of Trade. Insurance Business: Annual Report (UK ISSN 0308-499X) *639*
Great Britain. Department of Trade. Particulars of Dealers in Securities and of Trust Units (UK ISSN 0072-5692) *266*
Great Britain. Department of Trade. Patents, Design and Trade Marks (Annual Report) (UK ISSN 0072-5706) *861*
Great Britain. Department of Transport. Policy for Roads: England (UK) *1096*
Great Britain. Department of Transport. Roads in England see Great Britain. Department of Transport. Policy for Roads: England *1096*
Great Britain. Departments of the Environment and Transport. Library Services. Annual List of Publications (UK ISSN 0141-2604) *501*
Great Britain. Economic & Social Research Council. Bursary Handbook(UK) *435*, *1008*
Great Britain. Economic and Social Research Council. Report (UK ISSN 0266-2043) *1008*
Great Britain. Economic and Social Research Council. Research Supported by the Economic and Social Research Council (UK ISSN 0266-2159) *1008*
Great Britain. Economic & Social Research Council. Studentship Handbook (UK) *435*, *1008*
Great Britain. Electricity Council. Annual Report and Accounts (UK ISSN 0307-1146) *454*
Great Britain. Foreign and Commonwealth Office. Treaty Series (UK ISSN 0072-6397) *916*
Great Britain. General Register Office. Studies on Medical and Population Subjects (UK ISSN 0072-6400) *761*, *922*
Great Britain. Government Actuary. Occupational Pension Board. Annual Report (UK) *1008*
Great Britain. H.M.S.O. Government Publications Sectional Lists (UK) *184*
Great Britain. Health and Safety Executive. Health and Safety: Coal Mines (UK) *816*
Great Britain. Health and Safety Executive. Health and Safety: Mines (UK) *816*
Great Britain. Health and Safety Executive. Health and Safety: Quarries (UK) *816*
Great Britain. Home Office. Research Studies (UK ISSN 0072-6435) *370*
Great Britain. Home Office. Statistics of the Misuse of Drugs in the United Kingdom, Supplementary Tables (UK) *770*, 1056
Great Britain. Home Office. Studies in the Causes of Delinquency and the Treatment of Offenders (UK ISSN 0072-6443) *333*, 370
Great Britain. Institute of Animal Physiology. Report (UK ISSN 0065-4507) *175*

Great Britain. Institute of Geological Sciences. Annual Report see Great Britain. British Geological Survey. Annual Report *388*
Great Britain. Institute of Geological Sciences. Classical Areas of British Geology see Great Britain. British Geological Survey. Classical Areas of British Geology *388*
Great Britain. Institute of Geological Sciences. Geomagnetic Bulletin see Great Britain. British Geological Survey. Geomagnetic Bulletin *399*
Great Britain. Institute of Geological Sciences. Memoirs of the Geological Survey of Great Britain see Great Britain. British Geological Survey. Memoirs *388*
Great Britain. Institute of Geological Sciences. Metric Well Inventory see Great Britain. British Geological Survey. Metric Well Inventory *1154*
Great Britain. Institute of Geological Sciences. Mineral Assessment Report see Great Britain. British Geological Survey. Mineral Assessment Report *388*
Great Britain. Institute of Geological Sciences. Overseas Geology and Mineral Resources see Great Britain. British Geological Survey. Overseas Geology and Mineral Resources *388*
Great Britain. Institute of Geological Sciences. Overseas Memoirs see Great Britain. British Geological Survey. Overseas Memoirs *388*
Great Britain. Institute of Geological Sciences. Report see Great Britain. British Geological Survey. Report *388*
Great Britain. Institute of Geological Sciences. Seismological Bulletins see Great Britain. British Geological Survey. Seismological Bulletins *399*
Great Britain. Institute of Terrestrial Ecology. Bangor Occasional Paper (UK ISSN 0260-6925) *365*, 379
Great Britain. Institute of Terrestrial Ecology. Merlewood Research and Development Paper (UK ISSN 0308-3675) *365*, 379
Great Britain. Institute of Terrestrial Ecology. Report (UK ISSN 0308-1125) *141*
Great Britain. Institute of Terrestrial Ecology. Statistical Checklist (UK ISSN 0141-6464) *365*, 379
Great Britain. Institute of Terrestrial Ecology. Symposia (UK ISSN 0263-8614) *365*
Great Britain. Keeper of Public Records. Annual Report of the Keeper of Public Records on the Work of the Public Record Office and the Report of the Advisory Council on Public Records (UK ISSN 0072-6516) *584*, 678
Great Britain. Laboratory of the Government Chemist. Annual Report of the Government Chemist (UK ISSN 0072-6524) *323*
Great Britain. Land Resources Development Centre. Progress Report (UK ISSN 0309-1082) *262*
Great Britain. Land Resources Division. Progress Report see Great Britain. Land Resources Development Centre. Progress Report *262*
Great Britain. Manpower Research Unit. Manpower Studies (UK ISSN 0072-6532) *272*
Great Britain. Medical Research Council. Annual Report (UK ISSN 0141-2256) *761*
Great Britain. Medical Research Council. Handbook (UK ISSN 0309-0132) *761*
Great Britain. Medical Research Council. Report see Great Britain. Medical Research Council. Annual Report *761*
Great Britain. Mercantile Navy List (UK ISSN 0072-6591) *1100*
Great Britain. Meteorological Office. Annual Report (UK ISSN 0072-6605) *804*
Great Britain. Meteorological Office. Geophysical Memoirs (UK ISSN 0072-6613) *399*

Great Britain. Meteorological Office. Scientific Paper (UK ISSN 0072-6621) *804*
Great Britain. Ministry of Agriculture, Fisheries and Food. Directorate of Fisheries Research. Fishing Prospects(UK ISSN 0308-0935) *509*
Great Britain. Ministry of Agriculture, Fisheries and Food. Directorate of Fisheries Research. Fisheries Research Technical Report (UK ISSN 0308-5589) *496*, 509
Great Britain. Ministry of Agriculture, Fisheries and Food. Directorate of Fisheries Research. Laboratory Leaflet (UK ISSN 0143-8018) *509*
Great Britain. Ministry of Agriculture, Fisheries and Food. Directorate of Fisheries Research. Report of the Director of Fisheries Research (UK ISSN 0308-5570) *496*, 509
Great Britain. Ministry of Agriculture, Fisheries and Food. Technical Bulletin (UK ISSN 0072-6729) *28*
Great Britain. Monks Wood Experimental Station. Symposia see Great Britain. Institute of Terrestrial Ecology. Symposia *365*
Great Britain. National Film Finance Corporation. Annual Report (UK ISSN 0072-6958) *824*
Great Britain. National Health Service. Health Services Costing Returns see England and Wales National Health Service. Health Services Costing Returns *617*
Great Britain. Natural Environment Research Council. Report (UK ISSN 0072-7008) *496*
Great Britain. Office of Fair Trading. Report (UK) *656*
Great Britain. Office of Population Censuses and Surveys. Population Estimates: England and Wales (UK) *922*
Great Britain. Overseas Development Administration. Report on Research and Development (UK ISSN 0950-9593) *262*
Great Britain. Pest Infestation Control Laboratory. Report see Great Britain. Agricultural Science Service. Research and Development Reports: Crop Nutrition and Soil Science *55*
Great Britain. Pest Infestation Control Laboratory. Report see Great Britain. Agricultural Science Service. Research and Development Reports: Crop and Pest Diseases *55*
Great Britain. Pest Infestation Control Laboratory. Report see Great Britain. Agricultural Science Service. Research and Development Reports: Mammal and Bird Pests *55*
Great Britain. Pest Infestation Control Laboratory. Report see Great Britain. Agricultural Science Service. Research and Development Reports: Pesticide Science *55*
Great Britain. Pest Infestation Control Laboratory. Report see Great Britain. Agricultural Science Service. Research and Development Reports: Storage Pest *55*
Great Britain. Pest Infestation Control Laboratory. Report see Great Britain. Agricultural Science Service. Research and Development Reports: Animal Science *66*
Great Britain. Public Record Office. Handbooks (UK ISSN 0072-7016) *678*
Great Britain. Public Works Loan Board. Report (UK ISSN 0072-7032) *942*
Great Britain. Royal Commission on Ancient and Historical Monuments in Wales. Interim Report (UK) *87*, 584
Great Britain. Royal Commission on Historical Manuscripts. Accessions to Repositories and Reports Added to the National Register of Archives (UK) *126*, 563

Great Britain. Royal Commission on Historical Manuscripts. Commissioners' Reports to the Crown (UK ISSN 0072-7083) *126*, 563
Great Britain. Royal Commission on Historical Manuscripts. Joint Publication (UK ISSN 0072-7091) *126*, 563
Great Britain. Royal Commission on Historical Manuscripts. Secretary's Report to the Commissioners (UK ISSN 0533-9685) *557*
Great Britain. Royal Commission on the Ancient and Historical Monuments and Constructions in Wales and Monmouthshire. Interim Report see Great Britain. Royal Commission on Ancient and Historical Monuments in Wales. Interim Report *584*
Great Britain. Royal Commission on the Ancient and Historical Monuments and Constructions of England. Interim Report see Great Britain. Royal Commission on the Historical Monuments of England. Interim Report *584*
Great Britain. Royal Commission on the Historical Monuments of England. Interim Report (UK) *87*, 584
Great Britain. Royal Greeenwich Observatory. Bulletin (UK ISSN 0308-5074) *116*
Great Britain. Royal Greenwich Observatory. Annual Report (UK ISSN 0308-3322) *116*
Great Britain. Schools Council Publications. Curriculum Bulletins (UK ISSN 0072-7113) *447*
Great Britain. Schools Council Publications. Examinations Bulletins (UK ISSN 0072-7121) *414*
Great Britain. Schools Council Publications. Working Papers (UK ISSN 0072-713X) *414*
Great Britain. Science Research Council. Report see Science and Engineering Research Council. Report *999*
Great Britain. Scottish Health Services Planning Council. Annual Report (UK ISSN 0080-7877) *953*
Great Britain. Scottish Law Commission. Annual Report (UK ISSN 0080-7915) *656*
Great Britain. Sea Fish Industry Authority. Annual Report and Accounts (UK) *510*
Great Britain. Social Science Research Council. Bursary Scheme see Great Britain. Economic & Social Research Council. Bursary Handbook *1008*
Great Britain. Social Science Research Council. Report see Great Britain. Economic and Social Research Council. Report *1008*
Great Britain. Social Science Research Council. Research Supported by the Social Science Research Council see Great Britain. Economic and Social Research Council. Research Supported by the Economic and Social Research Council *1008*
Great Britain. Social Science Research Council. Studentship Handbook see Great Britain. Economic & Social Research Council. Studentship Handbook *1008*
Great Britain. Soil Survey of England and Wales. Records (UK ISSN 0072-7180) *55*
Great Britain. Soil Survey of England and Wales. Report (UK ISSN 0072-7199) *55*
Great Britain. Soil Survey of England and Wales. Special Surveys (UK ISSN 0072-7202) *56*
Great Britain. Soil Survey of England and Wales. Technical Monographs (UK ISSN 0072-7210) *56*
Great Britain. Treasury. Supply Estimates (UK) *295*
Great Britain. University Grants Committee. Annual Survey (UK ISSN 0072-7237) *435*

Great Britain. Victoria and Albert Museum. Illustrated Booklets see Great Britain. Victoria and Albert Museum. Illustrated Books 827
Great Britain. Victoria and Albert Museum. Illustrated Books (UK) 827
Great Britain. Victoria and Albert Museum. Monographs (UK ISSN 0083-5919) 827
Great Britain. Warren Spring Laboratory. Annual Review (UK ISSN 0141-3279) 496
Great Britain. Warren Spring Laboratory. Investigation of Air Pollution: National Survey, Smoke and Sulphur Dioxide see Great Britain. Warren Spring Laboratory. U K Smoke and Sulphur Dioxide Monitoring Networks 496
Great Britain. Warren Spring Laboratory. U K Smoke and Sulphur Dioxide Monitoring Networks (UK) 496
Great Britain. Water Resources Board. Publication (UK ISSN 0072-7245) 1124
Great Britain. Water Resources Board. Report (UK ISSN 0072-7253) 1124
Great Britain and Ireland (Year) (US) 1110
Great Britain Specialised Stamp Catalogue (UK ISSN 0072-7229) 874
Great Decisions (US ISSN 0072-727X) 916
Great Ideas Today (US ISSN 0072-7288) 557
Great Issues of the Day (US ISSN 0270-7497) 723, 905, 1026
Great Lakes Campbook (US) 1045
Great Lakes Camping see Great Lakes Campbook 1045
Great Lakes Fishery Commission (United States and Canada) Annual Report (US ISSN 0072-7296) 510
Great Lakes Fishery Commission (United States and Canada) Technical Report Series (US ISSN 0072-730X) 510
Great Lakes Red Book (US ISSN 0072-7318) 1100
Great Lakes Research Advisory Board. Annual Report see Great Lakes Science Advisory Board. Annual Report 1124
Great Lakes Science Advisory Board. Annual Report (CN ISSN 0710-8702) 1124
Great Outdoors Almanac (US) 1154
Great Plains Journal (US ISSN 0017-3673) 540
Great Plains Libraries (US) 678
Great Plains National Instructional Television Library. Recorded Visual Instruction see G P N Educational Media. Crossover 414
Great Plains National Instructional Television Library. Recorded Visual Instruction see G P N Educational Media. College-Adult 435
Great Plains National Instructional Television Library. Recorded Visual Instruction see G P N Educational Media. Elementary-Secondary 447
Great Plains National Instructional Television Library Educational Media. Crossover see G P N Educational Media. Crossover 414
Great Plains National Instructional Television Library Educational Media. College-Adult see G P N Educational Media. College-Adult 435
Great Wall (AT) 874
Great West and Indian Series (US ISSN 0072-7342) 606
Great Yarmouth Port and Industry Handbook (UK ISSN 0260-9517) 309, 1100
Greater Boston Media Directory (US) 1154
Greater Buffalo Business Directory (US) 309
Greater London Papers (UK ISSN 0072-7350) 942
Greater Manchester Archaeological Journal (UK) 87

Greater New York Industrial Directory see MacRae's New York State Industrial Directory 313
Greece (GR ISSN 0432-6105) 1110
Greece. National Statistical Service. Annual Industrial Survey (GR ISSN 0072-7393) 210
Greece. National Statistical Service. Annual Statistical Survey of Mines, Quarries and Salterns (GR ISSN 0072-7415) 822, 1056
Greece. National Statistical Service. Employment Survey Conducted in Urban and Semi-Urban Areas see Greece. National Statistical Service. Labour Force Survey 210
Greece. National Statistical Service. Labour Force Survey (GR ISSN 0256-3576) 210, 1056
Greece. National Statistical Service. Public Finance Statistics (GR) 210
Greece. National Statistical Service. Results of Sea Fishery Survey by Motor Vessels (GR ISSN 0256-3584) 514, 1056
Greece. National Statistical Service. Results of the Annual Industrial Survey see Greece. National Statistical Service. Annual Industrial Survey 210
Greece. National Statistical Service. Shipping Statistics (GR ISSN 0072-7423) 1056, 1085
Greece. National Statistical Service. Social Welfare and Health Statistics (GR ISSN 0253-9454) 958, 1023, 1056
Greece. National Statistical Service. Statistical Yearbook of Public Finance see Greece. National Statistical Service. Public Finance Statistics 210
Greece. National Statistical Service. Statistics on Civil, Criminal and Reformatory Justice (GR ISSN 0256-3665) 374, 1056
Greece. National Statistical Service. Statistics on the Declared Income of Legal Entities and Its Taxation (GR ISSN 0302-1416) 210, 1056
Greece. National Statistical Service. Statistics on the Declared Income of Physical Persons and Its Taxation (GR ISSN 0302-1114) 210, 1056
Greece. National Statistical Service. Transport and Communication Statistics (GR) 345, 1056, 1085
Greek Coins in North American Collections see Ancient Coins in North American Collections 844
Greek Export Directory (GR) 236
Greek Golden Guide (AT) 309, 951
Greek Mathematical Society. Bulletin/ Hellenike Mathematike Hetaireia. Deltion (GR ISSN 0072-7466) 749
Greek National Committee for Astronomy. Annual Reports of the Astronomical Institutes of Greece (GR ISSN 0072-7385) 116
Greek Orthodox Calendar (UK ISSN 0265-6922) 503, 984
Greek, Roman and Byzantine Monographs (US ISSN 0072-7474) 337
Greek, Roman, and Byzantine Studies. Scholarly Aids (US ISSN 0072-7482) 337
Green Book (UK ISSN 0017-3932) 51
Green Book: International Directory of Marketing Research Houses see Green Book: International Directory of Marketing Research Houses and Services 284
Green Book: International Directory of Marketing Research Houses and Services (US) 284
Green Feather (US ISSN 0190-3314) 14, 723
Green Pages (IS) 532
Green Pages: Directory of Non-Government Environmental Groups in Australia (AT ISSN 0727-0119) 365, 496
Green Sheet (US ISSN 0046-6409) 1154
Greenbrier Historical Society. Journal (US) 536, 606
Greener Pastures Gazette (US ISSN 0884-4089) 544, 965

Greenfield Review Chapbook (US) 741
Greenland Biosciences see Meddelelser om Groenland, Bioscience 143
Greenland Biosciences see Meddelelser om Groenland, Geoscience 391
Greenland in Figures (DK ISSN 0106-2875) 1056
Greenland, Man and Society see Meddelelser om Groenland, Man & Society 73
Greenland Newsletter (GL ISSN 0107-9948) 538
Greens (DK) 309
Greensboro Substitute (US) 1154
Greensward (UK ISSN 0017-4092) 28
Greenwood Encyclopedia of American Institutions (US ISSN 0271-9509) 414
Greenwood Encyclopedia of Black Music (US ISSN 0272-0264) 503, 836
Greenwood Encyclopedia of the World's Political Parties see Greenwood Historical Encyclopedia of the World's Political Parties 905
Greenwood Historical Encyclopedia of the World's Political Parties (US) 905
Greenwood's Guide to Great Lakes Shipping (US ISSN 0072-7490) 1100
Gregory Awards (UK ISSN 0261-5576) 741
Greinar (IC) 991
Grenaa og Noerre Djurs Foer og Nu (DK ISSN 0107-8372) 584
Grenaa og Omegn Foer og Nu see Grenaa og Noerre Djurs Foer og Nu 584
Grenzfragen (GW) 991
Grenzland (DK ISSN 0107-9840) 538
Greves et Lock-out au Canada see Strikes and Lockouts in Canada 275
Grey Bibliographies (SA) 687
Greyfriar/Siena Studies in Literature (US ISSN 0533-2869) 711
Griechischen Christlichen Schriftsteller der ersten Jahrhunderte (GE ISSN 0232-2900) 695, 970
Grist (US) 741
Griswold Family of England & America(US) 536
Grocer Directory see Grocer Marketing Directory 522
Grocer Marketing Directory (UK) 522
Groenland i Tal (DK ISSN 0106-0899) 1056
Groenlands Befolkning/Kalatdlit Nunane Inuit (DK ISSN 0105-0885) 922
Groenlands Geologiske Undersoegelse. Bulletin/Geological Survey of Greenland. Bulletin (DK ISSN 0105-3507) 388
Groenlands Geologiske Undersoegelse. Gletscher-hydrologiske Meddelelser (DK ISSN 0109-2073) 402
Groenlands Geologiske Undersoegelse. Rapport/Geological Survey of Greenland. Report (DK ISSN 0418-6559) 388
Groent Miljoe (DK ISSN 0108-4755) 532
Groniek (NE ISSN 0169-2801) 584
Groniek. Onafhankelijk Gronings Historisch Studentenblad see Groniek 584
Gronk (CN ISSN 0017-453X) 711
Gross Island Product of Guam (GU) 289
Gross Product by Industry at Current and Constant Prices see Australia. Bureau of Statistics. Australian National Accounts: Gross Product by Industry 203
Der Grosse Gartenkatalog (GW ISSN 0072-7717) 532
Grosse Heimatbuecher (SZ ISSN 0072-7725) 584
Grosse Naturforscher (GW ISSN 0072-7741) 134
Grotte d'Italia (IT) 388, 403, 544
Groundwater Bulletin (US ISSN 0468-5067) 403
Group for the Advancement of Psychiatry. Publication (US) 790

Group for the Advancement of Psychiatry. Report see Group for the Advancement of Psychiatry. Publication 790
Group for the Advancement of Psychiatry. Symposium see Group for the Advancement of Psychiatry. Publication 790
Groupe Bruxelles Lambert. Annual Reports (BE) 266
Groupe International d'Etude de la Ceramique Egyptienne. Bulletin de Liaison (UA ISSN 0255-0903) 113
Groupe Linguistique d'Etudes Chamito-Semitiques. Comptes Rendus (FR) 695
Groupement des Entreprises Francaises dans la Lutte Contre le Cancer. Bulletin National de Liaison (FR ISSN 0072-7806) 775
Groupement des Industries Electroniques. Rapport d'Activites (FR) 454
Groupement des Industries Electroniques. Statistiques Annuelles (FR) 454
Groupement des Societes Immobilieres d'Investissement. Annuaire (FR ISSN 0066-2933) 229
Groups: a Journal of Group Dynamics and Psychotherapy (US ISSN 0093-4763) 934
Grovvarelederen (DK) 47
Grow Dahlias with Us (UK) 532
Growing Native Plants (AT) 157
Growth (AT ISSN 0085-1280) 289
Growth of World Industry see Industrial Statistics Yearbook 211
Grundbegriffe der Modernen Biologie. (GW ISSN 0085-1299) 141
Grundlagen der Exakten Naturwissenschaften (GW) 991
Grundlagen der Germanistik (GW) 695
Grundlagen und Fortschritte der Lebensmitteluntersuchung see Grundlagen und Fortschritte der Lebensmitteluntersuchung und Lebensmitteltechnologie 519
Grundlagen und Fortschritte der Lebensmitteluntersuchung und Lebensmitteltechnologie (GW ISSN 0341-0498) 519
Grundlagen und Praxis des Bank- und Boersenwesens (GW) 229, 266
Grundlehren der Mathematischen Wissenschaften (US) 749
Grundlehren der Mathematischen Wissenschaften in Einzeldarstellungen see Grundlehren der Mathematischen Wissenschaften 749
Grundriss der Sozialwissenschaft (GW) 1008
Grundtvig Studier (DK) 348
Grupo de Investigacao Arqueologica do Norte. Trabalhos (PO) 87
Grupo I N I (Resumen de Actividades) (Instituto Nacional de Industria) (SP) 289
Gruppenpsychotherapie und Gruppendynamik (GW ISSN 0017-4947) 790
Gruppenpsychotherapie und Gruppendynamik. Beihefte (GW ISSN 0085-1302) 934
Guacharo (VE ISSN 0583-774X) 388
Guam. Department of Commerce. Occasional Paper (GU) 239
Guam. Department of Commerce. Statistical Abstract see Guam Annual Economic Review 245
Guam. Department of Revenue and Taxation. Report (GU ISSN 0072-7873) 295
Guam Annual Economic Review (GU) 245
Guam Business Directory (GU ISSN 0072-7865) 309
Guam Economic Annual Review see Guam Annual Economic Review 245
Guam Trade with the United States and Foreign Countries. (GU) 309
Guanabara: O Balanco Economico (BL) 245
Guatemala. Banco Nacional de Desarrollo Agricola. Memoria (GT) 47, 245

Guatemala. Direccion General de Estadistica. Departamento de Estudios Especiales y Estadisticas Continuas. Produccion, Venta y Otros Ingresos de la Encuesta Anual de la Industria Manufacturera Fabril see Guatemala. Direccion General de Estadistica. Encuesta de la Industria Manufacturera Fabril 1056
Guatemala. Direccion General de Estadistica. Encuesta de la Industria Manufacturera Fabril (GT) 1056
Guatemala. Instituto Nacional de Estadistica. Anuario Estadistico (GT) 1056
Guatemala. Instituto Nacional de Estadistica. Boletin Estadistico (GT ISSN 0017-5048) 1056
Guatemala. Instituto Nacional de Estadistica. Directorio Nacional de Establecimientos Industriales (GT) 210
Guatemala. Instituto Nacional de Estadistica. Encuesta Pecuaria. (GT) 1154
Guatemala. Instituto Nacional de Estadistica. Informador Estadistico (GT) 1056
Guatemala en Cifras see Guatemala. Instituto Nacional de Estadistica. Anuario Estadistico 1056
Guatemala Filatelica (GT ISSN 0046-6549) 874
Guatemalteco see Diario de Centro America 941
Guest Author (US ISSN 0160-6565) 723
Guesthouses, Farmhouses and Inns in Britain (UK) 1092, 1110
Guetertransport in Seeverkehr (GW) 1100
Guia Automotriz de Venezuela/Venezuelan Automotive Guide (VE) 1092
Guia Bolivia (BO) 245
Guia das Editoras Brasileiras (BL) 309, 961
Guia das Livrarias e Pontos de Venda de Livros No Brasil (BL) 961
Guia de Audio (AG) 1031
Guia de Centros Docentes de la Iglesia see Guia de Centros Educativos Catolicos 429
Guia de Centros Educativos Catolicos (SP ISSN 0211-4410) 429
Guia de Editores y de Libreros de Espana (SP ISSN 0072-7903) 961
Guia de Hoteles: Espana (SP) 1110
Guia de la Iglesia see Bolivia: Guia Eclesiastica 981
Guia de la Industria: Alimentaria (MX) 519
Guia de la Industria: Automotriz/Guide to Industry: Automotive (MX) 1092
Guia de la Industria del Caucho (AG ISSN 0533-4500) 985
Guia de la Industria: Equipo y Materiales (MX) 745
Guia de la Industria: Hulera (MX) 985
Guia de la Industria: Laboratorios de Especialades y Control (MX) 636
Guia de la Industria Quimica (MX) 478
Guia de la Industria: Republica del Paraguay (PY) 309
Guia de los Caballos Verificados en Espana (SP ISSN 0085-1337) 1043
Guia de Reuniones Cientificas y Tecnicas en la Argentina (AG ISSN 0301-7567) 796
Guia de Valencia: Turistica, Urbana, Comercial (SP) 1110
Guia del Comercio Exterior Mexicano (MX) 256
Guia del Comercio y de la Industria (Year) (SP) 236
Guia del Comercio y de la Industria de Madrid see Guia del Comercio y de la Industria (Year) 236
Guia del Equipo Petrolero see Guia Petrolera de Equipos Servicios 864
Guia Economico e Industrial do Estado de Minas Gerais (BL) 816
Guia General de las Industrias Azulejeras y Auxiliares de Espana (SP) 309, 320
Guia Industrial de Venezuela (VE) 195
Guia Oficial de Centro-America (HO) 1110

Guia para Inversiones en el Uruguay (UY) 245
Guia Petrolera de Equipos Servicios (US) 864
Guia Quatro Rodas. Brazil (BL) 1110
Guia Quatro Rodas. Camping (BL) 1045, 1110
Guia Quatro Rodas. Rio de Janeiro (BL) 1110
Guia Quatro Rodas. Rodoviario (BL) 1110
Guia Quatro Rodas. Sao Paulo (BL) 1111
Guia Quatro Rodas. Sul (BL) 1111
Guia Turistica de Caracas, Litoral y Venezuela (VE) 1111
Guia Turistica de Rosario y Sante Fe (AG) 1111
Guia Venezolana de Publicidad y Mercadeo (VE) 15, 284
Guias Bibliograficas (PE) 563
Guida All'abbigliamento Italiano (IT) 340
Guida Camping d'Italia (IT ISSN 0072-792X) 1045
Guida del Mercato Ristretto (IT) 266
Guida della Stampa Periodica Italiana (IT) 126
Guida delle Regioni d'Italia (IT) 309
Guida Dello Sciatore (IT) 1033, 1111
Guida di Veterinaria e Zootecnia (IT) 1121
Guida Monaci. Annuario Sanitario see Annuario Sanitario Italiano 757
Guida Pollini: Industria Elettrotecnica ed Elettronica (IT) 454
Guida Sardegna d'Oggi (IT ISSN 0487-3750) 1111
Guidance and Control (US) 19
Guide a l'Usage des Amateurs de Livres(FR) 961
Guide Ai Musei e Agli Scavi Archeologici della Calabria (IT) 87
Guide & Directory of Port of Yokohama (JA) 1100
Guide-Annuaire de l'Equipement Agricole (FR) 51
Guide Annuaire des H.L.M. see Annuaire H L M 621
Guide Annuaire du Commerce Franco-Allemand/Jahrbuch fuer den Deutsch-Franzoesischen Handel (FR ISSN 0072-7962) 236
Guide-Annuaire Officiel de l'Artisanat et de Metiers see Repertoire des Entreprises Artisanales 1161
Guide Annuaire Officiel du Complexe de Rungis GUIDOR see GUIDOR 522
Guide Astrologique (FR) 114
Guide Camping see Guide du Camping 1045
Guide d'Achat de la Photographie (FR) 884
Guide d'Achat de la Photographie: 20 Objectifs pour Appareils Reflex 24 x 36 see Guide d'Achat de la Photographie 884
Guide d'Une Carriere a Succes see Guide de Reussite dans la Carriere d'Assureur-Vie 639
Guide de l'Habitat et de l'Amenagement Rural (FR) 623
Guide de l'Habitat Rural see Guide de l'Habitat et de l'Amenagement Rural 623
Guide de l'Investisseur Industriel au Senegal (SG) 289
Guide de la Chimie International (FR) 323
Guide de la Jeune Maman (FR) 333
Guide de la Parfumerie/General Directory of the Perfume and Cosmetic Industry (FR ISSN 0072-7989) 118, 309
Guide de Reussite dans la Carriere d'Assureur-Vie (CN ISSN 0317-2678) 639
Guide Demographie de l'Afrique see Demographic Handbook for Africa 921
Guide des Acheteurs: Horlogerie, Bijouterie et Branches Annexes/Buyers' Guide: Watch Industry, Jewellery and Allied Trades (SZ) 644

Guide des Acheteurs pour l'Horlogerie et les Branches Annexes see Guide des Acheteurs: Horlogerie, Bijouterie et Branches Annexes 644
Guide des Relais Routiers see Routiers Guide to France 1116
Guide du Camping (CN ISSN 0705-8314) 1045
Guide du Commanditaire pour les Annees 80 see Sponsors' Handbook for The 80's 1078
Guide du Contribuable Canadien (CN) 295
Guide du Directeur de Tournees de Spectacles see Tour Organizers' Handbook 1079
Guide du Feu (FR ISSN 0337-5781) 507
Guide du Feu et de la Protection Civile see Guide du Feu 507
Guide du Livre Ancien et du Livre d'Occasion see Guide a l'Usage des Amateurs de Livres 961
Guide du Show-Business; Guide Professionnel du Spectacle (FR ISSN 0072-8063) 1077
Guide du Tourisme Nigerien see Nigeria Tourist Guide 1114
Guide Economique de la Tunisie (TI ISSN 0330-9290) 309
Guide Emer see Guide Europeen de l'Amateur d'Art, de l'Antiquaire et du Bibliophile 105
Guide Europeen de l'Amateur d'Art, de l'Antiquaire et du Bibliophile (FR ISSN 0066-3069) 105
Guide Europeen des Produits Logiciels see Guide Europeen des Progiciels 238
Guide Europeen des Progiciels (FR ISSN 0294-0701) 238
Guide for Buyers of Quality Hardwoods(US) 309
Guide for Laboratory Animal Facilities and Care see Guide for the Care and Use of Laboratory Animals 781
Guide for Planning Educational Facilities (US ISSN 0072-8101) 443
Guide for Planning School Plants see Guide for Planning Educational Facilities 443
Guide for the Care and Use of Laboratory Animals (US) 781
Guide i Jylland (DK ISSN 0106-3022) 1111
Guide Medical et Hospitalier (FR ISSN 0072-8144) 617, 761
Guide Naturiste Internationale see International Naturist Guide 1045
Guide Officiel Camping - Caravaning (FR) 1045
Guide Pratique des Aeroports et de l'Aviation Commerciale (FR) 1088
Guide Rosenwald: Annuaire Medical et Pharmaceutique (FR ISSN 0072-8209) 761
Guide Routier et Touristique: Madagascar, Reunion, Maurice, Comores et Seychelles (MG) 1092
Guide to A P R S Member Studios (Association of Professional Recording Studios) (UK) 836, 1031
Guide to a Successful Life Insurance Career (CN ISSN 0381-6532) 639
Guide to Afro-American Resources (US) 503
Guide to Agricultural Production in Malawi (MW) 28
Guide to Alternative Periodicals (US) 713, 1014
Guide to American Directories (US ISSN 0533-5248) 126
Guide to American Educational Directories (US) 424
Guide to American Scientific and Technical Directories (US ISSN 0094-4505) 126, 1004, 1072
Guide to Available Technologies (US) 861, 1069
Guide to Biomedical Standards (US ISSN 0085-1353) 141, 761
Guide to Britain's Best Holidays see Britain's Best Holidays - A Quick Reference Guide 1106
Guide to C O P A Recognized Accrediting Bodies (US) 429
Guide to Cairo (UK) 1111
Guide to Canada (US) 1111

Guide to Caravan and Camping Holidays (UK ISSN 0267-3355) 1045, 1111
Guide to Christian Camps see Guide to Christian Camps & Conference Centers 970
Guide to Christian Camps & Conference Centers (US) 970
Guide to Collections of Manuscripts Relating to Australia (AT) 126, 563
Guide to College Courses in Film and Television (US ISSN 0072-8284) 426, 824
Guide to Communication Services see Planning Guide X-1 350
Guide to Computer Software for Architects and Engineers (US) 1154
Guide to Correspondence Studies in Colleges and Universities see Independent Study Catalog: N U C E A's Guide to Independent Study Through Correspondence Instruction 430
Guide to Cruising the Chesapeake Bay (US) 1111
Guide to Danish Libraries see Biblioteksvejviser 674
Guide to Dental Materials and Devices see Dentist's Desk Reference 779
Guide to Departments of Anthropology (Year) (US) 72
Guide to Departments of Geography in the United States and Canada (US) 429, 544
Guide to Departments of History (Year) (US) 429, 606
Guide to Departments of Sociology and Anthropology in Canadian Universities see Guide to Departments of Sociology, Anthropology and Archaeology in Universities and Museums in Canada 435
Guide to Departments of Sociology, Anthropology and Archaeology in Universities and Museums in Canada/Annuaire des Departementes de Sociologie, d'Anthropologie et d'Archeologie des Universities et des Musees du Canada (CN ISSN 0316-1854) 435
Guide to Design Criteria for Metal Structures see Guide to Stability Design Criteria for Metal Structures 184
Guide to East Africa (UK) 1111
Guide to Egypt (UK) 1111
Guide to Electronics Industry in India (II) 454
Guide to Engineered Materials (US) 489
Guide to Federal Funding for Education (US) 295, 443
Guide to Federal Income Taxes for Savings Institutions (US) 229
Guide to Federal Procurement see Doing Business with the Federal Government: A Procurement Guide 904
Guide to Fluorescence Literature (US ISSN 0072-8403) 323, 888
Guide to Four-Year College Databook see Chronicle Four-Year College Databook 428
Guide to Four-Year Colleges (Year) (US ISSN 0737-3163) 429
Guide to Free Computer Materials (US) 352
Guide to Gas Chromatography Literature (US ISSN 0072-8446) 325
Guide to Government in Hawaii (US ISSN 0072-8454) 942
Guide to Government-Loan Films (US) 811, 824
Guide to Government-Loan Films Volume 1: the Civilian Agencies (US ISSN 0072-8462) 826
Guide to Graduate Departments of Geography in the United States and Canada see Guide to Departments of Geography in the United States and Canada 544
Guide to Graduate Departments of Sociology (US ISSN 0091-7052) 435, 1026
Guide to Graduate Education in Speech-Language Pathology and Audiology (US) 375, 429

Guide to Graduate Study in Botany for the United States and Canada (US ISSN 0072-8500) 157, 429
Guide to Graduate Study in Political Science. (US ISSN 0091-9632) 429
Guide to Grants and Fellowships in Linguistics (US) 695
Guide to Greece (UK) 1111
Guide to Hotels in South Africa see C V R Hotel Guide to Southern Africa 619
Guide to Hunting in Florida (US) 1045
Guide to Independent Study Through Correspondence Instruction see Independent Study Catalog: N U C E A's Guide to Independent Study Through Correspondence Instruction 430
Guide to Independent Television and Independent Local Radio see Television & Radio 349
Guide to Indian Chemical Plants and Equipment (II) 478
Guide to Indian Periodical Literature (II ISSN 0017-5285) 126
Guide to Industry: Automotive see Guia de la Industria: Automotriz 1092
Guide to International Periodicals see International Periodicals and Reference Works 647
Guide to Intra L A T A Communications Services see Planning Guide 2. Intra-L A T A Telecommunications Rates and Services 350
Guide to Japanese Taxes (JA ISSN 0072-8551) 295
Guide to Key British Enterprises I and II (US) 309
Guide to Manufactured Homes (US ISSN 0160-7340) 1154
Guide to Manuscripts Relating to Australia see Guide to Collections of Manuscripts Relating to Australia 563
Guide to Microforms in Print see Guide to Microforms in Print. Author, Title 127
Guide to Microforms in Print. Author, Title (US ISSN 0164-0747) 127, 678, 961
Guide to Microforms in Print. Subject (US ISSN 0163-8386) 127
Guide to Microforms in Print. Supplement (US) 127
Guide to Military-Loan Films see Guide to Government-Loan Films 824
Guide to Minority Business Directories see Guide to Obtaining Minority Business Directories 309
Guide to Minority Resources see Guide to Afro-American Resources 503
Guide to National Bibliographical Information Centres (UN ISSN 0072-8608) 678
Guide to National Endowment for the Arts (US) 105
Guide to Nebraska State Agencies (US ISSN 0091-0716) 942
Guide to New Zealand Income Tax Practice see Staples' Guide to New Zealand Income Tax Practice 299
Guide to Obtaining Minority Business Directories (US) 309
Guide to Party Booking (UK) 1111
Guide to Periodicals and Newspapers in the Public Libraries of Metropolitan Toronto (CN ISSN 0315-7288) 127
Guide to Petroleum Statistical Information (US) 868
Guide to Port Entry (UK) 1100
Guide to Postgraduate Degrees, Diplomas and Courses in Medicine (UK ISSN 0265-2730) 435
Guide to Premium Users (UK) 15
Guide to Private English Language Schools in the U.K. for Overseas Students (UK) 429, 695
Guide to Professional Bodies in Malawi(MW) 462
Guide to Programs in Linguistics see Directory of Programs in Linguistics 694
Guide to Publishers and Related Industries in Japan (JA) 15, 961

Guide to Radio Electronics & Components Trade and Industry in India see Guide to Electronics Industry in India 454
Guide to Recognized Accrediting Agencies see Guide to C O P A Recognized Accrediting Bodies 429
Guide to Reference Books (US ISSN 0072-8624) 127
Guide to Reference Books for School Media Centers (US) 127, 678
Guide to Reference Material (UK ISSN 0072-8640) 127
Guide to Religious Careers for Catholic Men and Women see Guide to Religious Ministries for Catholic Men and Women 982
Guide to Religious Ministries for Catholic Men and Women (US) 982
Guide to Reprints (US ISSN 0072-8667) 127
Guide to Restoration Experts (UK) 184, 644
Guide to Scientific Instruments (US ISSN 0533-5426) 636
Guide to Sources of International Population Assistance (UN) 922
Guide to Special Issues and Indexes of Periodicals (US) 6
Guide to Stability Design Criteria for Metal Structures (US) 184
Guide to Steam Trains in the British Isles (UK ISSN 0262-3943) 1094
Guide to Summer Camps and Summer Schools (US ISSN 0072-8705) 429
Guide to the American Left (US ISSN 8756-0208) 905
Guide to the American Right (US ISSN 8756-0216) 905
Guide to the Antique Shops of Britain (UK) 79
Guide to the Coalfields (UK ISSN 0072-8713) 817
Guide to the Evaluation of Educational Experiences in the Armed Services (US) 443
Guide to the Food Regulations in the U.K. (UK) 519, 656
Guide to the Port of Yokohama (JA) 1100
Guide to the Press of the World see Little Red Book 128
Guide to the Recommended Country Inns of New England (US ISSN 0093-4585) 620
Guide to the Social Services (UK ISSN 0072-8756) 1017
Guide to the Sources of the History of the Nations. B: Africa (SZ) 563
Guide to the Use of Insecticides and Fungicides in South Africa see Guide to the Use of Pesticides and Fungicides in the Republic of South Africa 56
Guide to the Use of Pesticides and Fungicides in the Republic of South Africa (SA) 56
Guide to Tourist Homes and Guest Houses see Bed and Breakfast U S A 1106
Guide to Translation of Danish Legislation with an Alphabetic Index see Oversaettelser af Dansk Lovgivning med Alfabetisk Register. Fortegnelse 662
Guide to U.S. Government Directories (US) 905
Guide to U S G S Geologic and Hydrologic Maps (US) 379, 465, 864
Guide to U S Government Publications (US) 6, 127
Guide to U S Government Statistics (US) 1056
Guide to Venture Capital Sources see Pratt's Guide to Venture Capital Sources 267
Guide to World Commodity Markets (US) 256
Guide Touristique Europeen pour Israelites/European Travel Guide for Jews (BE) 503
Guidebook of Catholic Hospitals see Catholic Health Association of the United States. Guidebook 616
Guidebook of United States Coins (US ISSN 0072-8829) 844

Guidebook - State of Ohio, Department of Natural Resources, Division of Geological Survey see Ohio. Division of Geological Survey. Guidebook 393
Guidebook to California Taxes (US ISSN 0072-8837) 295
Guidebook to Fair Employment Practices (US ISSN 0196-7975) 656
Guidebook to Florida Taxes (US ISSN 0093-8637) 295
Guidebook to Illinois Taxes (US ISSN 0072-8845) 295
Guidebook to Labor Relations (US ISSN 0072-8853) 272, 656
Guidebook to Massachusetts Taxes (US ISSN 0072-8861) 295
Guidebook to Michigan Taxes (US ISSN 0072-887X) 295
Guidebook to New Jersey Taxes (US ISSN 0072-8888) 295
Guidebook to New York Taxes (US ISSN 0072-8896) 296
Guidebook to North Carolina Taxes (US ISSN 0091-1186) 296
Guidebook to Ohio Taxes (US ISSN 0091-4010) 296
Guidebook to Pennsylvania Taxes (US ISSN 0072-890X) 296
Guidebook to Wisconsin Taxes (US ISSN 0093-8645) 296
Guidelines (AT ISSN 0156-6717) 6, 687
Guidelines for Industrial Investors in Kenya see Kenya: The Gateway to Africa 311
Guidelines for Teachers (UK ISSN 0072-8918) 447
Guides to Practice in Corrosion Control(UK ISSN 0143-6082) 798
GUIDOR (Guide Annuaire Officiel du Complexe de Rungis) (FR) 309, 522
Guild of Agricultural Journalists Year Book (UK) 28, 645
Guild of Carillonneurs in North America. Bulletin (US ISSN 0827-5955) 836
Guild of Master Craftsmen Directory of Members (UK) 79, 184
Guild of Prescription Opticians of America. Reference List (US ISSN 0072-8977) 786
Guildhall Poets (UK) 741
Guild's Engineer see Spanner (London) 1163
Guimaraes. Arquivo Municipal "Alfredo Pimenta." Boletim de Trabalhos Historicos (PO) 606
Guinness Book of Records see Guinness Book of World Records 463
Guinness Book of World Records (US) 463
Gujarat Industrial Development Corporation. Annual Report (II) 289
Gujarat State Financial Corporation. Annual Report (II ISSN 0533-649X) 296
Gulden Passer/Compas d'Or (BE) 961
Gule Oversigt see Plantevaern i Landbruget 59
Gulf and Caribbean Fisheries Institute. Annual Proceedings (US ISSN 0072-9019) 510
Gulf Coast Conference Proceedings (US) 606
Gulf Directory (BA) 350
Gulf Guide & Diary (UK) 1111
Gulf Handbook (US) 612
Gulf of Mexico Index see Gulf of Mexico Sumary Report/Index 864
Gulf of Mexico Sumary Report/Index (US) 864
Gulf of Mexico Summary Report see Gulf of Mexico Sumary Report/Index 864
Gulf Research Reports (US ISSN 0072-9027) 1154
Gulf Telephone Directory see Gulf Directory 350
Gumma Symposia on Endocrinology (JA ISSN 0533-6724) 781
Gun Traders Guide (US) 614
Gun World Annual (US) 1045
Gun World Hunting Guide see Gun World Annual 1045
Gunma Journal of Liberal Arts and Sciences (JA ISSN 0367-4061) 630

Gunma University. Faculty of Education. Annual Report: Cultural Science Series (JA ISSN 0386-4294) 630
Gunma University. Faculty of Education. Science Reports (JA ISSN 0017-5668) 991
Gunma University. Faculty of Education. Annual Report: Art, Technology, Health & Physical Education, and Science of Human Living Series (JA ISSN 0533-6627) 105, 1069
Gunneria (NO ISSN 0332-8554) 87, 141, 157
Guns and Ammo Annual (US ISSN 0072-906X) 1154
Guns Guide see Cord Sportfacts Guns Guide 614
Guru Nanak Commemorative Lectures (II) 977
Guss Produkte (GW) 745
Gustav-Adolf-Blatt (GW ISSN 0017-5730) 970
Gustav Stern Symposia on Perspectives in Virology see Perspectives in Virology 1160
Gut Essen/Eats & Treats (GW) 620, 1111
Gutenberg (FR) 931
Gutenberg-Jahrbuch (GW ISSN 0072-9094) 931
Guyana. Geological Survey Department. Annual Reports see Guyana. Geology & Mines Commission. Annual Report 388
Guyana. Geological Survey Department. Mineral Resources Pamphlet see Guyana. Geology & Mines Commission. Mineral Resources Pamphlet 388
Guyana. Geology & Mines Commission. Annual Report (GY) 388
Guyana. Geology & Mines Commission. Mineral Resources Pamphlet (GY) 388
Guyana. Hydrometeorological Service. Annual Climatological Data Summary (GY) 804
Guyana. National Insurance Board. Annual Report (GY) 639
Guyana. Statistical Bureau. Annual Account Relating to External Trade (GY ISSN 0533-991X) 256
Guyana Association of Professional Engineers see G.A.P.E 471
Guyana Sugar Corporation. Annual Reports and Accounts (GY) 56
Guyana Trade Directory (UK) 309
Gwechall (FR ISSN 0220-276X) 87, 584
Gwent Family History Society. Journal (UK ISSN 0262-4672) 536
Gwynedd Archives Service. Bulletin (UK ISSN 0306-3151) 1154
Gymnasieingenjoeren see T L I - Ingenjoeren 474
Gymnastics Guide see N A G W S Guide. Gymnastics 1034
Gyoko Kensetsu Gijutsu Kenkyu Happyokai Koenshu/Proceedings of Fishing Port Engineering (JA) 481
Gypsy Lore Society. North American Chapter. Publications (US ISSN 8756-7245) 72, 515, 557, 695
H B S Case Bibliography (Harvard University, Graduate School of Business Administration) (US) 210
H E C A B see Higher Education Current Awareness Bulletin 1154
H G V Driver's Handbook see Truck Driver's Handbook 1093
H K I Report (Helen Keller International) (US) 180
H L A Journal (Hawaii Library Association) (US) 678
H M Customs and Excise Official V A T Guides (UK) 296
H M T: the Science and Application of Heat Mass Transfer (UK) 553, 894
H R I S Abstracts (Highway Research Information Service) (US ISSN 0017-6222) 6, 476, 1085
H.R. Macmillan Lectureship in Forestry(CN ISSN 0072-9140) 525
H S G's Aarbog (Hvad Skovsoeen / Gemte) (DK ISSN 0108-0830) 14, 723

1752 H S

H S G's Science Fiction & Fantasy Aarbog see H S G's Aarbog 14
H.S.M.A. Hotel Facilities Digest (Hotel Sales & Marketing Association International) (US) 1154
H.S.M.A. Hotel-Motel Directory and Facilities Guide see H.S.M.A. Hotel Facilities Digest 1154
H T T P O see Healthcare Technology Transfer and Product Opportunities 761
H U D Statistical Yearbook see U.S. Department of Housing and Urban Development. Statistical Yearbook 628
H V A C Red Book of Heating, Ventilating and Air Conditioning Equipment (UK) 553
Haanbog for Boerne- og Ungdominstitutioner. Doegninstitutioner (DK) 333, 1017
Haandarbejdets Fremme. Aarets Korssting (DK ISSN 0107-9611) 105
Haandarbejdets Fremme. Kalender see Haandarbejdets Fremme. Aarets Korssting 105
Haandbog for Boerne- og Ungdominstitutioner see Haanbog for Boerne- og Ungdominstitutioner. Doegninstitutioner 1017
Haandbog for Bygningsindustrien (DK) 184
Haandbog for D J V K: Agronomer, Forstkandidater, Hortonomer, Licentiater (DK ISSN 0107-122X) 28
Haandbog for Studerende ved H D Studiet i Organisation see Handelshoejskolen i Koebenhavn. Institut for Organisation og Arbejdssociologi. H D Studiet i Organisation 272
Haandbog for Studerende ved Landbohoejskolen see Kongelige Veterinaer og Landbohoejskole. Haandbog 30
Haandbog i Dansk Politik (DK ISSN 0106-0392) 1154
Habelts Dissertationsdrucke. Reihe Aegyptologie (GW) 612
Habelts Dissertationsdrucke. Reihe Alte Geschichte (GW ISSN 0072-9175) 557
Habelts Dissertationsdrucke. Reihe Germanistik (GW) 723
Habelts Dissertationsdrucke. Reihe Klassische Archaeologie (GW ISSN 0072-9183) 87
Habelts Dissertationsdrucke. Reihe Klassische Philologie (GW ISSN 0072-9191) 695
Habelts Dissertationsdrucke. Reihe Kunstgeschichte (GW ISSN 0072-9205) 105
Habelts Dissertationsdrucke. Reihe Mittelalterliche Geschichte (GW ISSN 0072-9213) 557
Habinyan (SA ISSN 0017-6354) 905
Habis (SP ISSN 0210-7694) 337
Habitat Philippines (PH ISSN 0115-4990) 1154
Habitat Ufficio see Office Furniture 643
Habitations a Loyer Modere Annuaire H L M see Annuaire H L M 621
Habitats et Societes Urbaines en Egypte et au Soudan (FR) 566
Hacettepe Fen ve Muhendislik Bilimleri Dergisi (TU ISSN 0072-9221) 471, 991
Hacheinuch ve Sivevo (IS) 414
Hackney Horse Society Year Book (UK) 1043
Hackney Stud Book (UK) 1043
Hadassah Medical Organization. Report(IS ISSN 0072-923X) 761
Hadassah Vocational Guidance Institute. Annual Report for the Year(IS) 848
Hadassah Vocational Guidance Institute. Report see Hadassah Vocational Guidance Institute. Annual Report for the Year 848
Haderslav Stifts Arbog see Haderslev Stiftsbog 584
Haderslev Stiftsbog (DK) 584
Hadorom (US ISSN 0017-6532) 976

Haematologie und Bluttransfusion (US ISSN 0440-0607) 783
Hafenbautechnische Gesellschaft. Jahrbuch (US ISSN 0340-4838) 481
Hafnia; Copenhagen Papers in the History of Art (DK ISSN 0085-1361) 105
Hague Conference on Private International Law. Actes et Documents (NE ISSN 0072-9272) 670
Haifa University. Institute for Study and Research of the Kibbutz and the Cooperative Idea. Discussion Papers (IS) 238
Haiku Review (US) 678, 741, 961
Haiteny, Haisorata, Hairaha (MG) 711
Haiti. Conseil National de Developpement et de Planification. Plan Annuel et Budget de Developpement see Haiti. Secretaire d'Etat du Plan. Plan Annuel et Budget de Developpement 251
Haiti. Institut Haitien de Statistique. Bulletin Trimestriel de Statistique (HT ISSN 0017-6788) 1056
Haiti. Secretaire d'Etat du Plan. Plan Annuel et Budget de Developpement(HT) 251
Hakko Kenkyusho Hokoku see Institute for Fermentation, Osaka. Research Communications 168
Hakodate Kogyo Koto Senmon Gakko Kiyo see Hakodate Technical College. Research Reports 1069
Hakodate Technical College. Research Reports/Hakodate Kogyo Koto Senmon Gakko Kiyo (JA) 1069
Halle Prospectus see Halle Year Book 836
Halle Year Book (UK) 836
Hallesche Studien zur Geschichte der Sozialdemokratie (GE) 584
Halloween (CN) 1077
Halsbury's Laws of England Annual Abridgment (UK ISSN 0308-4388) 656
Hambro Euromoney Directory (UK ISSN 0306-3933) 229
Hamburg the Quick Port (GW) 1100
Hamburger Abhandlungen (GW ISSN 0072-9507) 656
Hamburger Beitraege fuer Russischlehrer (GW ISSN 0072-9515) 695
Hamburger Beitraege zur Archaeologie (GW ISSN 0341-3152) 87
Hamburger Beitraege zur Numismatik (GW ISSN 0072-9523) 844
Hamburger Historische Studien (GW ISSN 0072-9558) 557
Hamburger Jahrbuch fuer Musikwissenschaft (GW) 836
Hamburger Jahrbuch fuer Wirtschafts- und Gesellschaftspolitik (GW ISSN 0072-9566) 195
Hamburger Juristische Studien (GW ISSN 0341-3179) 656
Hamburger Oeffentlich-Rechtliche Nebenstunden (GW ISSN 0072-9574) 656, 670
Hamburger Philologische Studien (GW ISSN 0072-9582) 695
Hamburger Phonetische Beitraege see Beitraege zur Phonetik und Linguistik 691
Hamburger Studien zur Philosophie (GW ISSN 0072-9604) 878
Hamburgisches Museum fuer Voelkerkunde. Mitteilungen (GW ISSN 0072-9469) 172
Hamburgisches Zoologisches Museum und Institut. Mitteilungen (GW ISSN 0072-9612) 175
Hamdard Foundation. Report (PK) 975
Hameenlinna see Hameenlinna-Wanaja 584
Hameenlinna-Wanaja (FI) 584
Hameenmaa (FI) 584
Ha-Mesivta (US ISSN 0094-9701) 656, 976
Hampshire Field. Proceedings see Hampshire Field Club and Archaeological Society Proceedings 87
Hampshire Field Club and Archaeological Society Proceedings (UK ISSN 0142-8950) 87, 584

Handakten fuer die Standesamtliche Arbeit (GW ISSN 0438-5004) 656, 942
Handball und Faustball in Oesterreich (AU ISSN 0072-9690) 1033
Handboek voor Parfumerie en Schoonheidssalon (NE) 118
Handbog for Kavegkold (DK ISSN 0900-8012) 66
Handbog i Sociallovgivning (DK ISSN 0901-0602) 656
Handbook and Directory of Crematoria see Directory of Crematoria 531
Handbook for Accountants' & Administrators see Accountants' & Administrators' Handbook 220
Handbook for Christian Writers see Successful Writers and Editors Guidebook 973
Handbook for Libraries & Other Organizational Users Which Copy From Serials & Separates (US) 678, 861, 961
Handbook for Metric Usage (US) 809
Handbook for No-Load Fund Investors (US ISSN 0736-6264) 266
Handbook for Recruiting at Minority Colleges see Handbook for Recruiting Minority College Students 435
Handbook for Recruiting Minority College Students (US) 435
Handbook of Adult Education in Scotland see Scottish Handbook of Adult and Continuing Education 427
Handbook of Advertising and Marketing Services (US) 15, 284
Handbook of Air Transport Legislation (CN) 1088
Handbook of Aroma Research (NE) 519
Handbook of Basic Statistics of Maharashtra State (II ISSN 0072-9728) 1056
Handbook of Business Finance and Capital Sources (US ISSN 0163-4615) 296
Handbook of Canadian Consumer Markets (CN ISSN 0225-4190) 284, 369
Handbook of Community Nursing (UK) 784
Handbook of Contract Floor Covering see Specifier's Guide to Contract Floor Coverings 644
Handbook of Degree and Advanced Courses in Institutes/Colleges of Higher Education, Colleges of Education, Polytechnics, University Departments of Education (UK) 429, 435
Handbook of Denominations in the U.S. (US ISSN 0072-9787) 970
Handbook of Electronic Materials (US ISSN 0072-9795) 454, 489
Handbook of Environmental Chemistry (US) 323, 496
Handbook of Experimental Pharmacology (US ISSN 0171-2004) 871
Handbook of Exploration Geochemistry(NE) 388
Handbook of Food Preparation (US ISSN 0278-906X) 519, 614
Handbook of Industrial Safety and Health (UK) 635
Handbook of Inflammation (NE ISSN 0167-5567) 761
Handbook of International Documentaion and Information see Handbuch der Internationalen Dokumentation und Information 678
Handbook of Korea (KO) 1111
Handbook of Labor Force Data for Selected Areas of Oklahoma (US) 272
Handbook of Latin American Studies: A Selected and Annotated Guide to Recent Publications (US ISSN 0072-9833) 606
Handbook of Living Will Laws (US ISSN 0886-7402) 656
Handbook of Medical Treatment (US ISSN 0072-9841) 761
Handbook of Medicinal Feed Additives(UK) 1121
Handbook of National Development Plans (UK) 262

Handbook of Natural Toxins (US) 761, 871
Handbook of Noise and Vibration Control (UK) 900
Handbook of Nuclear Safeguards (JA) 896
Handbook of Ocular Therapeutics and Pharmacology see Ocular Therapeutics and Pharmacology 786
Handbook of Oklahoma Employment Statistics (US) 210
Handbook of Paper Science (NE) 858
Handbook of Papua and New Guinea see Papua New Guinea Handbook 1115
Handbook of Physiology (US ISSN 0072-9876) 171
Handbook of Powder Technology (NE) 481
Handbook of Power Drives (UK) 465
Handbook of Private Schools (US ISSN 0072-9884) 429
Handbook of Psychology and Health (US) 886, 934
Handbook of Science and Technology see Kwahak Kisul Yoram 1069
Handbook of Securities of the United States Government and Federal Agencies and Related Money Market Instruments (US ISSN 0072-9892) 266
Handbook of Self-Employed Pensions see Self-Employed Pensions 641
Handbook of Sensory Physiology (US ISSN 0072-9906) 761
Handbook of Service Members' and Veterans' Benefits (US) 811
Handbook of Servicemen's and Veterans' Benefits see Handbook of Service Members' and Veterans' Benefits 811
Handbook of the Indian Cotton Textile Industry (II ISSN 0436-7316) 1074
Handbook of the Japan Drug Industry see Japan Drug Industry Review 871
Handbook of the Nations (US ISSN 0194-3790) 916
Handbook of the Northern Wood Industries (SW ISSN 0072-9922) 530
Handbook of the Spinal Cord (US) 761
Handbook of Trade and Technical Careers and Training (US ISSN 0278-4920) 426, 429
Handbook of United States Coins (US ISSN 0072-9949) 844
Handbook of Women Workers see Time of Change: Handbook on Women Workers 276
Handbook on Hospital-Associated Infections (US) 168, 617
Handbook on the U.S. - German Tax Convention (NE) 296
Handbook on U.S. Luminescent Stamps(US ISSN 0072-9981) 874
Handbooks in Maritime Archaeology (UK ISSN 0260-5570) 827
Handbuch der Allgemeinbildenden Hoeheren Schulen Oesterreichs (AU) 435
Handbuch der Grossunternehmen (GW ISSN 0073-0068) 289
Handbuch der Internationalen Dokumentation und Information/ Handbook of International Documentaion and Information (GW ISSN 0340-1332) 678
Handbuch der Internationalen Kautschukindustrie/International Rubber Directory/Manuel International de Caoutchouc (SZ ISSN 0073-0076) 985
Handbuch der Internationalen Kunstoffindustrie/International Plastics Directory/Manuel International des Plastiques (SZ ISSN 0073-0084) 900
Handbuch der Justiz (GW ISSN 0073-0092) 571
Handbuch der Oeffentlichen Bibliotheken (GW ISSN 0301-9225) 678
Handbuch der Oesterreichischen Sozialversicherung (AU) 642, 1056
Handbuch der Oologie (GE) 170
Handbuch der Rationalisierung (GW ISSN 0073-0122) 280

Handbuch der Steuerveranlagungen: Einkommensteuer, Koerperschaftsteuer, Gewerbesteuer, Umsatzsteuer (GW) 296
Handbuch der Stratigraphischen Geologie (GW ISSN 0073-0130) 388
Handbuch der Sudetendeutschen Kulturgeschichte (GW ISSN 0073-0149) 557
Handbuch der Technischen Dokumentation und Bibliographie see Handbuch der Internationalen Dokumentation und Information 678
Handbuch der Virusforschung see Virology Monographs 169
Handbuch des Bauherrn (GW ISSN 0017-7202) 184
Handbuch des Grundstuecks- und Baurechts (GW) 184, 656
Handbuch fuer den Werbenden Buch- und Zeitschriftenhandel (GW ISSN 0073-0165) 962
Handbuch fuer die Druckindustrie Berlin (GW ISSN 0073-0173) 931
Handbuch fuer die Sanitaetsberufe Oesterreich (AU ISSN 0073-0181) 784
Handbuch Holz (GW ISSN 0518-0147) 530
Handbuch Oeffentlicher Verkehrsbetriebe (GW ISSN 0073-019X) 1081
Handbuch zur Deutschen Militaergeschichte (GW) 811
Handels- og Soefartsmuseet paa Kronborg. Aarbog (DK ISSN 0085-1418) 1100
Handelshoejskolen i Aarhus. Institut for Finansiering og Kreditvaesen. Kompendium D (DK ISSN 0105-4058) 229
Handelshoejskolen i Aarhus. Institut for Markedsoekonomi. Skriftserie E (DK ISSN 0105-533X) 195
Handelshoejskolen i Aarhus. Skriftserie (DK ISSN 0106-8490) 1056
Handelshoejskolen i Koebenhavn. Center for Uddannelses Forskning. Arbejdsnote (DK ISSN 0900-2472) 195, 414
Handelshoejskolen i Koebenhavn. H A-Center. Rapport (DK ISSN 0109-5587) 195, 435
Handelshoejskolen i Koebenhavn. Institut for Organisation og Arbejdssociologi. H D Studiet i Organisation (DK ISSN 0107-4458) 272
Handelshoejskolen i Koebenhavn. Institut for Trafik-, Turist- og Regionaloekonomi. Publikation (DK) 195
Handelshoeskolen i Aarhus. Institute for Erhvervs- og Samfundsbeskrivelse. Skriftserie C (DK ISSN 0106-4363) 195
Handelsministeriets Energiforskningsprogram (DK) 465
Handelsrechtliche Entscheidungen (AU ISSN 0567-1469) 656
Handelsregister Oesterreich (AU) 309
Handicapped Funding Directory (US) 444, 1017
Handicapped Requirements Handbook (US ISSN 0194-7818) 272
Handling and Shipping. Presidential Issue see Handling & Shipping Managements Presidential Issue 1081
Handling & Shipping Managements Presidential Issue (US) 1081
Handling Chemicals Safely (NE) 635
Hands On! (US ISSN 0743-0221) 427, 435
Handsatzletter (GW) 931, 962
Hanguk Sinmun Pangsong Yongam see Korean Press Annual 646
Hanguk Tonggye Yongam see Korea Statistical Yearbook 1058
Hank Seale Oil Directory: Louisiana, Mississippi, Arkansas, Texas Gulf Coast and East Texas see Armstrong Oil Directory: Louisiana, Mississippi, Arkansas, Texas Gulf Coast and East Texas 863

Hank Seale Oil Directory: Texas Including Southeast New Mexico see Armstrong Oil Directory: Texas Including Southeast New Mexico 863
Hankuk Baksa Mit Seuksa Hak Wee Lonmun Chong Mokrok see List of Theses for the Doctor's and Master's Degree in Korea 424
Hannah Research (UK ISSN 0266-9021) 62
Hannah Research Institute. Report see Hannah Research 62
Hannover Extra see Niespulver 711
Han'quk Ch'ulp an Yon'gam. see Korean Publications Yearbook 962
Hans Kelsen-Institut. Schriftenreihe (AU) 656
Hansische Geschichtsblaetter (GW ISSN 0073-0327) 584
Hapdong Yongam see Korea Annual 311
Happiness Holding Tank (US ISSN 0046-6832) 741
Happy Day Diary (UK) 970
Harbinger File (US) 465, 496
Hardsyssels Aarbog (DK ISSN 0046-6840) 584
Hardware Age "Who Makes It" Buyers' Guide (US) 190, 309
Hardware Age "Who Makes It" Directory see Hardware Age "Who Makes It" Buyers' Guide 309
Hardware Retailer News (AT) 190
Hardy Plant Directory (UK) 534
Harian Creative Press see What's Cooking in Congress 737
Harja (DK ISSN 0105-1660) 87
Harmon Memorial Lectures in Military History (US ISSN 0073-0394) 811
Harold C. Mack Symposium. Proceedings (US) 171, 785
Harold L. Lyon Arboretum Lecture (US) 157
Harpers Directory of the Wine and Spirit Trade see Harpers Wine and Spirit Annual 119
Harpers Guide to Sports Trade (UK ISSN 0073-0416) 309, 1033
Harpers Wine and Spirit Annual (UK) 119
Harris Auction Galleries. Collectors' Auction (US ISSN 0093-1047) 827
Harris Indiana Industrial Directory (Year) (US) 309
Harris Indiana Marketers Industrial Directory see Harris Indiana Industrial Directory (Year) 309
Harris Michigan Industrial Directory (US) 309
Harris Michigan Marketers Industrial Directory see Harris Michigan Industrial Directory 309
Harris Ohio Industrial Directory (US) 309
Harris Ohio Marketers Industrial Directory see Harris Ohio Industrial Directory 309
Harris Pennsylvania Industrial Directory (US) 309
Harris Pennsylvania Marketing Directory see Harris Pennsylvania Industrial Directory 309
Harris Postage Stamp Price Index (US ISSN 0273-0200) 1154
Harrison's Inland Revenue Index to Tax Cases (UK) 296
Harry Browne's Special Reports (US) 245, 496
Harry G. Johnson Memorial Lectures (UK) 256
Harry S. Truman Research Institute for the Advancement of Peace. Reprint Series (IS) 127, 1008
Harry S. Truman Research Institute, Jerusalem. Occasional Papers see Harry S. Truman Research Institute for the Advancement of Peace. Reprint Series 127
Harsunan Nijeriya (NR) 695
Harvard Architecture Review (US ISSN 0194-3650) 98
Harvard Armenian Texts and Studies (US ISSN 0073-0459) 584
Harvard Books in Biology (US ISSN 0073-0467) 1154
Harvard Books in Biophysics (US ISSN 0073-0475) 153

Harvard Business School. Annual Report (US) 195
Harvard Business School. Baker Library. Core Collection, An Author and Subject Guide (US) 210
Harvard Business School. Baker Library. Current Periodical Publications in Baker Library (US) 210
Harvard Business School. Baker Library. Kress Library of Business and Economics. Publications (US) 195
Harvard Celtic Colloquium. Proceedings(US) 584, 695, 723
Harvard Contemporary China Series (US) 569
Harvard Directory of Computer Graphics Suppliers see S. Klein Directory of Computer Graphics Suppliers 357
Harvard East Asian Monographs (US ISSN 0073-0483) 569
Harvard East Asian Series (US ISSN 0073-0491) 569
Harvard Economic Studies (US ISSN 0073-0505) 195
Harvard English Studies (US ISSN 0073-0513) 695, 723
Harvard Historical Monographs (US ISSN 0073-0521) 557
Harvard Historical Studies (US ISSN 0073-053X) 557
Harvard Iranian Series (US) 612
Harvard Judaic Monographs (US) 503, 976
Harvard Librarian (US ISSN 0073-0564) 678
Harvard Middle Eastern Monographs (US ISSN 0073-0572) 1154
Harvard Middle Eastern Studies (US ISSN 0073-0580) 612
Harvard Monographs in the History of Science (US) 1154
Harvard Oriental Series (US ISSN 0073-0599) 1154
Harvard Papers in Theoretical Geography (US ISSN 0073-0610) 544
Harvard Political Studies (US) 1154
Harvard Publications in Music (US ISSN 0073-0629) 836
Harvard Semitic Monographs (US ISSN 0073-0637) 695, 970
Harvard Semitic Series (US ISSN 0073-0645) 612
Harvard Slavic Monographs (US) 1154
Harvard Studies in American-East Asian Relations (US) 569
Harvard Studies in Business History (US ISSN 0073-067X) 251
Harvard Studies in Classical Philology (US ISSN 0073-0688) 337, 695
Harvard Studies in Comparative Literature (US ISSN 0073-0696) 723
Harvard Studies in Romance Languages(US ISSN 0073-0718) 723
Harvard Studies in Urban History (US) 623
Harvard Theological Studies (US ISSN 0073-0726) 970
Harvard Ukrainian Research Institute. Minutes of the Seminar in Ukrainian Studies (US ISSN 0362-8078) 503
Harvard University. Center for International Affairs. Annual Report (US ISSN 0073-0734) 916
Harvard University. Computation Laboratory. Mathematical Linguistics and Automatic Translation; Report to National Science Foundation (US ISSN 0073-0769) 678
Harvard University. Graduate School of Business Administration. Baker Library. Core Collection, An Author and Subject Guide see Harvard Business School. Baker Library. Core Collection, An Author and Subject Guide 210
Harvard University. Graduate School of Business Administration. Baker Library. Current Periodical Publications in Baker Library see Harvard Business School. Baker Library. Current Periodical Publications in Baker Library 210

Harvard University. Graduate School of Business Administration. Baker Library. Kress Library of Business and Economics. Publications see Harvard Business School. Baker Library. Kress Library of Business and Economics. Publications 195
Harvard University. Graduate School of Business Administration. Program for Management Development. Publication (US ISSN 0073-0785) 280
Harvard University. Museum of Comparative Zoology. Bulletin see Museum of Comparative Zoology. Bulletin 176
Harvard University. Museum of Comparative Zoology. Department of Mollusks. Occasional Papers on Mollusks (US ISSN 0073-0807) 175
Harvard University. Russian Research Center. Russian Research Center Studies (US ISSN 0073-0831) 584
Harvard University Case Bibliography see H B S Case Bibliography 210
Harvard Women's Law Journal (US ISSN 0270-1456) 656, 1128
Harvard-Yenching Institute. Monograph Series (US ISSN 0073-084X) 569, 695, 723
Harvard-Yenching Institute. Studies (US ISSN 0073-0858) 569
Harvard-Yenching Library Bibliographical Series (US) 127, 539
Harvest see Connecticut Writer 719
Harvest (UK ISSN 0266-4771) 934
Harvest Book Series (US ISSN 0146-5414) 195, 515, 557, 1026
Harvester (US) 105, 723
Harvey Lectures (US ISSN 0073-0874) 761
Harz-Zeitschrift (GW ISSN 0073-0882) 584
Hasapanut Hayisraelit (IS) 1100
Hashi/Bridges in Japan (JA) 481
Hat Life Yearbook & Directory (US) 340
Hatcheries and Dealers Participating in the National Poultry Improvement Plan (US ISSN 0082-9722) 66
Haulage Manual (UK) 1105
Hauptverband der Oesterreichischen Sparkassen. Jahresbericht (AU) 229
Hautes Etudes du Monde Greco-Romain (SZ ISSN 0073-0939) 337, 695
Hautes Etudes Islamiques et Orientales d'Histoire Comparee (SZ ISSN 0073-0947) 612
Hautes Etudes Medievales et Modernes(SZ ISSN 0073-0955) 584
Hautes Etudes Numismatiques (SZ ISSN 0073-0963) 844
Hautes Etudes Orientales (SZ ISSN 0073-0971) 851
Havsfiskelaboratoriet. Meddelande (SW ISSN 0374-8030) 510
Hawaii. Children's Health Services Division. Crippled Children Branch Report see Hawaii. Family Health Services Division. Crippled Children Services Branch. Report 1017
Hawaii. Commission on Judicial Discipline. Annual Report (US) 656
Hawaii. Criminal Injuries Compensation Commission. Annual Report. (US ISSN 0098-5708) 370
Hawaii. Department of Education. Educational Directory: State & District Office (US ISSN 0092-1777) 414
Hawaii. Department of Education. Office of Business Services. Public and Private School Enrollment (US) 414
Hawaii. Department of Education. Office of Library Services. Annual Report (US) 678
Hawaii. Department of Education. Office of Research and Planning. Information Systems Branch. Public and Private School Enrollment see Hawaii. Department of Education. Office of Business Services. Public and Private School Enrollment 414

1754   HAWAII. DEPARTMENT

Hawaii. Department of Health. Division of Mental Health. Children's Health Services see Hawaii. Department of Health. Waimano Training School and Hospital Division (Report) 617
Hawaii. Department of Health. Mental Health Services for Children and Youth (US ISSN 0362-6296) 333, 953, 1017
Hawaii. Department of Health. Research and Statistics Office. R & S Report (US ISSN 0093-3481) 886, 922, 927
Hawaii. Department of Health. Waimano Training School and Hospital Division (Report) (US) 617, 1017
Hawaii. Department of Planning and Economic Development. Annual Report (US ISSN 0073-1072) 289
Hawaii. Family Health Services Division. Crippled Children Services Branch. Report (US) 787, 1017
Hawaii. Insurance Division. Report of the Insurance Commissioner of Hawaii (US ISSN 0073-1110) 639
Hawaii. Judiciary Department. Annual Report see Hawaii. State Judiciary. Annual Report 656
Hawaii. Legislative Auditor. Special Reports (US) 296, 942
Hawaii. Legislative Reference Bureau. Report (US ISSN 0073-1277) 942
Hawaii. Office of the Ombudsman. Report (US ISSN 0073-1137) 951
Hawaii. State Commission on the Status of Women. Annual Report (US ISSN 0092-9190) 656, 1129
Hawaii. State Judiciary. Annual Report (US) 656
Hawaii (Year) (US) 1111
Hawaii Annual Economic Review (US ISSN 0067-3633) 245
Hawaii Conference on High Energy Physics (US) 896
Hawaii Dental Association. Transactions (US ISSN 0073-1021) 779
Hawaii Institute of Geophysics. Contributions see Hawaii Institute of Geophysics. Yearbook 399
Hawaii Institute of Geophysics. Technical Reports and Special Publications (US) 399
Hawaii Institute of Geophysics. Technical Reports, Data Reports and Special Publications see Hawaii Institute of Geophysics. Technical Reports and Special Publications 399
Hawaii Institute of Geophysics. Yearbook (US) 399
Hawaii Institute of Marine Biology. Technical Reports (US ISSN 0073-1331) 141
Hawaii International Conference on System Sciences. Proceedings (US ISSN 0073-1129) 358
Hawaii Library Association Journal see H L A Journal 678
Hawaii on 25 Dollars a Day see Hawaii on 35 Dollars a Day 1111
Hawaii on 35 Dollars a Day (US) 1111
Hawaii Series (US ISSN 0073-1145) 606
Hawaii Topical Conference in Particle Physics. Proceedings see Hawaii Conference on High Energy Physics 896
Hawaii TourBook see TourBook: Hawaii 1117
Hawaii Visitors Bureau. Annual Research Report (US ISSN 0066-412X) 1111
Hawaiian Entomological Society. Proceedings (US) 164
Hawaiian Historical Society. Annual Report (US) 573
Hawaiian Journal of History (US ISSN 0440-5145) 573
Hawaiian Philatelist (US) 875
Hawaiian Planters' Record (US ISSN 0073-1358) 56
Hawaiian Sugar Planters' Association Experiment Station. Annual Report (US ISSN 0073-1366) 56
Hayden's Ferry Review (US ISSN 0887-5170) 741

Haydn-Studien (GW ISSN 0440-5323) 134, 836
Hayes & Becker Information Sciences Series see Information Sciences Series 679
Hayes Directory of Dental Supply Houses (US ISSN 0073-1404) 779
Hayes Directory of Medical Supply Houses (US) 617
Hayes Directory of Physician and Hospital Supply Houses see Hayes Directory of Medical Supply Houses 617
Hayes Druggist Directory (US ISSN 0073-1420) 871
Hayling Island Magazine see Holiday Islander 1111
Hayling Islander see Holiday Islander 1111
Hazardous Cargo Contacts (GW) 309, 1100
Hazardous Waste Management Handbook (CN) 496
Hazell's Guide to the Judiciary & the Courts with the Holborn Law Society's Bar List by Chambers (UK) 656
Hazell's Guide to the Judiciary and the Courts with the Holborn Law Society's List of Barristers by Chambers see Hazell's Guide to the Judiciary & the Courts with the Holborn Law Society's Bar List by Chambers 656
Head Start Services to Handicapped Children see U.S. Department of Health and Human Services. Annual Report to the Congress of the United States on Services Provided to Handicapped Children in Project Head Start 445
Health and Beauty News (UK) 886
Health and Health Care in New York City: Local, State, and National Perspectives (US ISSN 0889-0331) 617
Health & Medical Horizons (US) 761, 886
Health and Personal Social Services Statistics (UK) 953
Health and Safety Officer's Handbook (UK ISSN 0267-2014) 635
Health and Safety: Quarries (UK ISSN 0263-3094) 635, 817
Health and Social Service Manpower in Alberta (CN) 953, 1017
Health and Welfare Directory see Human Services Directory 1018
Health Care Instrumentation (US ISSN 0883-0762) 491, 636, 781, 1069
Health Care Viewpoint (US) 639
Health Commision of Victoria. Annual Report see Health Department Victoria. Annual Report 617
Health Consequences of Smoking (US ISSN 0098-311X) 376, 761
Health Department Victoria. Annual Report (AT) 617
Health Devices Alerts (US ISSN 0163-0458) 770
Health Devices Sourcebook (US ISSN 0278-3452) 617, 761
Health Education Focal Points see Focal Points 953
Health Education Index (UK ISSN 0140-3273) 6, 886
Health Facilities in Southern New York: A Guide to Inpatient, Outpatient, and Long-Term Care (US ISSN 0888-7039) 617
Health for Children see Shoni No Hoken 334
Health Industry Buyers Guide (US) 761
Health Insurance Viewpoints see Health Care Viewpoint 639
Health Law Bulletin (US) 656, 761, 953
Health of Kansas Chart Book (US ISSN 0276-606X) 886
Health Organizations of the U.S., Canada and the World (US ISSN 0440-5609) 761, 953
Health, Physical Education and Recreation Microform Publications Bulletin (US ISSN 0090-5119) 886, 1036
Health Physics Research Abstracts (UN ISSN 0085-1450) 6, 958

Health Policy Series (US) 886
Health Sciences Information in Canada: Associations/Information en Sciences de la Sante au Canada: Associations (CN) 761
Health Sciences Information in Canada: Libraries/Information en Sciences de la Sante au Canada: Bibliotheques (CN) 761
Health Service Abstracts (UK) 958, 1023
Health Service Buyers Guide (UK ISSN 0140-5748) 617
Health Services (UK) 954
Health Services Law Victoria (AT) 656, 954
Health Statistics (CY ISSN 0253-8601) 1154
Health Systems Management (US ISSN 0361-0195) 617, 954
Health, United States (US ISSN 0361-4468) 1018
Healthcare Marketing Abstracts (US) 15, 617
Healthcare Technology Transfer and Product Opportunities (US) 761
Heat Pump Technology Conference Proceedings (US) 491
Heathen (UK) 984
Heather Society. Yearbook (UK ISSN 0440-5757) 532
Heating and Ventilating Research Association. Laboratory Reports see B S R I A Application Guides 553
Heating and Ventilating Research Association. Technical Notes see B S R I A Technical Notes 553
Heating and Ventilating Year Book see Heating, Ventilating and Air Conditioning Year Book 553
Heating, Plumbing, Air Conditioning Buyers' Guide (CN ISSN 0382-6996) 553
Heating, Ventilating and Air Conditioning Year Book (UK ISSN 0306-3585) 553
Hebbel-Jahrbuecher (GW ISSN 0073-1560) 723
Hebrew Annual Review (US) 630, 723
Hebrew Computational Linguistics (IS) 695
Hebrew Union College Annual (US ISSN 0360-9049) 503, 976
Hebrew Union College Annual Supplements (US ISSN 0275-9993) 503, 976
Hebrew University of Jerusalem. Authority for Research and Development. Current Research (IS ISSN 0333-6964) 1008
Hebrew University of Jerusalem. Authority for Research and Development. Research Report: Humanities, Social Sciences, Law, Education, Social Work, Library see Hebrew University of Jerusalem. Authority for Research and Development. Current Research 1008
Hebrew University of Jerusalem. Authority for Research and Development. Research Report: Science and Agriculture see Hebrew University of Jerusalem. Authority for Research and Development. Current Research 1008
Hebrew University of Jerusalem. Authority for Research and Development. Research Report. Medicine, Pharmacy, Dental Medicine see Hebrew University of Jerusalem. Authority for Research and Development. Current Research 1008
Hebrew University of Jerusalem. Department of Atmospheric Sciences. List of Contributions (IS) 804
Hebrew University of Jerusalem. Folklore Research Center. Studies (IS ISSN 0075-3661) 515
Hebrew University of Jerusalem. Lionel Cohen Lectures (IS ISSN 0075-9740) 656
Hednos Daneses (DK ISSN 0108-8653) 538
Heemkring Okegem. Annalen (BE) 584
Heere International (GW) 811

Hefte zur Unfallheilkunde (US ISSN 0085-1469) 786
Hegel Society of America. Proceedings (US) 878
Hegel-Studien (GW ISSN 0073-1587) 878
Hegel-Studien Beihefte (GW ISSN 0440-5927) 878
Heidelberg Science Library (US ISSN 0073-1595) 991
Heidelberger Akademie der Wissenschaften. Mathematisch-Naturwissenschaftliche Klasse. Sitzungsberichte (US ISSN 0371-0165) 991
Heidelberger Althistorische Beitraege und Epigraphische Studien (GW ISSN 0930-1208) 557
Heidelberger Arbeitsbuecher (US ISSN 0073-1633) 992, 1069
Heidelberger Jahrbuecher (US ISSN 0073-1641) 992, 1069
Heidelberger Rechtsvergleichende und Wirtschaftsrechliche Studien (GW) 656
Heidelberger Rechtswissenschaftliche Abhandlungen. Neue Folge (GW ISSN 0073-165X) 656
Heidelberger Sociologica (GW ISSN 0073-1676) 1026
Heidelberger Taschenbuecher (US ISSN 0073-1684) 992, 1069
Heimat am Inn (GW) 584
Heimat im Weinland (AU) 584
Heimatbrief der Stadt Germersheim (GW) 515, 584
Heimatbuch des Kreises Viersen (GW) 557
Heimatgruss (GW ISSN 0440-6230) 584
Heimatkunde, Kulturpflege, Stadtgeschichte (AU) 584
Heimatkundliche Nachrichten (AU) 584
Heimatkundliches Beiblatt see Heimat im Weinland 584
Heimatkundliches Jahrbuch fuer den Kreis Segeberg (GW) 584
Heine-Jahrbuch (GW ISSN 0073-1692) 723
Heine Saekularausgabe: Werke-Briefwechsel-Lebenszeugnisse (GE) 723, 741
Hej see Cystisk Fibrose 760
Helen Keller International Report see H K I Report 180
Helicopter Annual (US ISSN 0739-5728) 1088
Helikon (IT ISSN 0017-9981) 337
Hellenic Industrial Development Bank. Investment Guide (GR) 266
Hellenika (GW ISSN 0018-0084) 630, 723
Hellenike Mathematike Hetaireia. Deltion see Greek Mathematical Society. Bulletin 749
Hello Delhi (II) 1111
Helminthological Abstracts. Series A: Animal and Human Helminthology (UK ISSN 0300-8339) 6, 41, 150
Helminthological Abstracts. Series B: Plant Nematology (UK ISSN 0300-8320) 6, 41, 150
Helps for Students of History (UK ISSN 0073-1714) 447
Helsingfors Universitets Biblioteks Skrifter see Helsingin Yliopiston Kirjaston. Julkaisuja 678
Helsingin Kauppakorkeakoulu. F-Sarja. Tyoepaperejta- Working Papers (FI) 195
Helsingin Kauppakorkeakoulu. Julkaisusarja A. Vaeitoeskirjoja (FI) 435
Helsingin Kauppakorkeakoulu. Julkaisusarja B. Tutkimuksia (FI) 195
Helsingin Kauppakorkeakoulu. Julkaisusarja C. Oppikirjoja. (FI) 195
Helsingin Kauppakorkeakoulu. Julkaisusarja D. Laitosjulkaisuja (FI ISSN 0356-8164) 210
Helsingin Kauppakorkeakoulu. Julkaisusarja E. Selvityksiae (FI) 195
Helsingin Kauppakorkeakoulu. Julkaisusarja F. Tyopapereita (FI ISSN 0358-2973) 195

Helsingin Kauppakorkeakoulu. Kirjasto. Julkaisusarja see Helsingin Kauppakorkeakoulu. Julkaisusarja D. Laitosjulkaisuja 210
Helsingin Kaupungin Tilastollinen Vuosikirja (FI ISSN 0356-9489) 1056
Helsingin Yliopiston Kirjaston. Julkaisuja/Helsingfors Universitets Biblioteks Skrifter/Helsinki University Library. Publications (FI ISSN 0355-1350) 678
Helsingoer Bymuseum. Aarbog see Helsingoer Kommunes Museer. Aarbog 827
Helsingoer Kommunes Museer. Aarbog (DK ISSN 0108-0393) 827
Helsingoer som Fotografen saa det (DK ISSN 0106-5440) 827
Helsinki University Library. Publications see Helsingin Yliopiston Kirjaston. Julkaisuja 678
Helvetia Politica (SZ ISSN 0073-182X) 905
Helvetica Paediatrica Acta. Supplementum (SZ ISSN 0073-1811) 787
Hematology Series (US) 783
Hemisphere Engineering Paperback (US ISSN 0730-3173) 491
Hemlocks and Balsams (US ISSN 0737-7169) 711
Hemming's Vintage Auto Almanac (US ISSN 0363-4639) 79
Hempstead County Historical Society. Journal (US) 606
Hempstead County Historical Society (Publication) see Hempstead County Historical Society. Journal 606
Henkel Referate (GW ISSN 0720-941X) 323
Henkel Referate see Henkel Referate 323
Her World Annual (SI ISSN 0217-1058) 1129
Herald Caravanning Guide (AT ISSN 0085-1477) 1045, 1111
Herald Motel Guide (AT ISSN 0085-1485) 620
Herald of Library Science (II ISSN 0018-0521) 678
Heraldisch-Genealogische Gesellschaft Adler. Jahrbuch (AU ISSN 0073-1897) 536
Heraldiske Studier (DK ISSN 0109-3061) 536
Herb Collector's Manual & Marketing Guide (US) 1154
Herbage Abstracts (UK ISSN 0018-0602) 6, 41
Herbarist (US) 532
Herbergen der Christenheit (GE ISSN 0437-3014) 584
Herbert Read Series (UK ISSN 0073-1927) 723
Herbertia (US) 157
Herd Book (UK) 66
Herd Book for Angora Goats in Australia (AT ISSN 0310-2971) 66
Herd Book of Hereford Cattle (UK ISSN 0073-1943) 66
Here and Now (CN ISSN 0085-1493) 934
Here Is Your Indiana Government (US) 236
Hereford Breed Journal (UK ISSN 0073-1951) 66
Herforder Jahrbuch; Beitraege zur Geschichte der Stadt des Kreises und des Stiftes Herford (GW) 584
Herforder Jahrbuch; Beitraege zur Geschichte der Stadt und des Stiftes Herford see Herforder Jahrbuch; Beitraege zur Geschichte der Stadt des Kreises und des Stiftes Herford 584
Heritage (RH) 566
Heritage (Waltham) (US ISSN 0732-0914) 976
Heritage Britain. Where to Visit: Where to Stay (UK ISSN 0267-3371) 1111
Heritage Foundation. Issue Bulletins (US) 657
Heritage Lectures (US ISSN 0272-1155) 942
Heritage of Sociology (US ISSN 0073-1986) 1026
Herkimer County Historical Society (US) 606

Hermaea (GW) 723
Hermeneutics: Studies in the History of Religion (US) 970
Hermeneutische Untersuchungen zur Theologie (GW ISSN 0440-7180) 970
Hermes-Einzelschriften (GW ISSN 0341-0064) 337, 695
Herne in Zahlen. Jahresveroeffentlichungen (GW) 210, 245, 951
Herning-Bogen (DK ISSN 0108-8017) 585
Herold Export-Adressbuch von Oesterreich/Austrian Export Directory/Annuaire d'Exportation de l'Autriche/Anuario de Exportacion de Austria (AU ISSN 0531-5824) 309
Heron (JA ISSN 0387-9348) 695, 723
Herpetological Association of South Africa. Journal (SA ISSN 0441-6651) 175
Hesse. Minister fuer Landesentwicklung, Umwelt, Landwirtschaft und Forsten. Ernten, Maerkte, Preise see Hesse. Minister fuer Landwirtschaft, Forsten. Ernten, Maerkte, Preisen 522
Hesse. Minister fuer Landesentwicklung, Umwelt, Landwirtschaft und Forsten. Mitteilungen. Land und Umwelt (GW) 28, 496, 522, 525
Hesse. Minister fuer Landwirtschaft, Forsten. Ernten, Maerkte, Preisen (GW) 522
Hessische Beitraege zur Geschichte der Arbeiterbewegung (GW) 585, 648
Hessische Bibliographie (US) 127
Hessische Staatsarchiv Darmstadt. Repertorien (GW) 585
Hessischer Kulturminister. Bildungspolitische Informationen (GW) 443
Hessisches Jahrbuch fuer Landesgeschichte (GW ISSN 0073-2001) 585
Hestia (GW) 878
Het Jaar in Woord en Beeld see Winkler Prins Encyclopedisch Jaarboek 601
Heterocera Sumatrana (GW ISSN 0724-1348) 164
Heterocyclic Chemistry (UK ISSN 0144-8773) 329
Heutiges Deutsch. Reihe I: Linguistische Grundlagen (GW ISSN 0073-201X) 696
Hevra u-Revaha see Society and Welfare 1020
Hi Fi Aarbogen (DK ISSN 0441-5833) 836
Hi-Fi and Video Revyen (DK ISSN 0108-4658) 1032
Hi-Fi Annual and Test see Which Hi-Fi 1032
Hi-Fi Revyen see Hi-Fi and Video Revyen 1032
Hi-Fi Sound Annual see Which Hi-Fi 1032
Hickenia (AG ISSN 0325-3732) 157
Hickman's International Air Traveller (UK) 1088
Hidrologija i Meteorologija see Hydrology and Meteorology 804
Hierro (VE) 822
Hiersemanns Bibliographische Handbuecher (GW ISSN 0170-2408) 127
High Energy Particle Physics see Physics and Applications 890
High Energy Physics Index/ Hochenergiephysik-Index (GW ISSN 0018-1447) 6, 893
High-Performance Liquid Chromatography (US ISSN 0270-8531) 326
High Points (US ISSN 0018-148X) 414
High Schools Statistics in Punjab (PK) 414
High Solids Coatings (US ISSN 0146-4752) 323
High Tech & Manufacturing Directory of Idaho (US) 309
Higher Education see Higher Education Current Awareness Bulletin 1154

Higher Education Abstracts (US ISSN 0748-4364) 6, 127, 435, 1056
Higher Education Current Awareness Bulletin (UK ISSN 0309-9113) 1154
Higher Education Exchange see Educational International 1152
Higher Education in the United Kingdom (UK ISSN 0306-1744) 435
Higher Education Opportunities for Minorities and Women: Annotated Selections (US) 435, 1129
Highland Heritage (CN ISSN 0707-2554) 536
Highlands Field Station Report (KE) 623
Highlights of Persian Art (US) 105
Highlights of V A Medical Research see Medical Research in the V.A 763
Highway Code (UK) 657, 1096
Highway Planning Notes (US ISSN 0073-2176) 481
Highway Research Board Special Publication see Transportation Research Board Special Report 1098
Highway Research Information Service Abstracts see H R I S Abstracts 1085
Highway Research Record (II) 481, 1096
Highway Research Record see Transportation Research Record 1098
Highway Safety Improvement Programs see U.S. Department of Transportation. Highway Safety Stewardship Report 1098
Higiene y Sanidad Animal see Spain. Instituto Nacional de Investigaciones Agrarias. Comunicaciones. Serie: Higiene y Sanidad 68
Hikobia (JA ISSN 0046-7413) 157
Hikuin (DK ISSN 0105-8118) 87, 585
Hilberg-Easley Report (US) 19
Hilborn's Family Newsletter Directory (CN ISSN 0828-4466) 536
Hildy's Ford Blue Book (US) 1092
Hilgardia (US ISSN 0073-2230) 28
Hill and Holler (US) 723
Hilprecht: Sammlung (GE ISSN 0232-3001) 851
Himalaya see Journal of Himalayan Studies and Regional Development 73
Himalayan Geology (II ISSN 0379-5101) 388
Himalayan International Institute/ Eleanor N. Dana Laboratory. Research Bulletin (US ISSN 0276-4148) 886, 970
Himalayan Journal (II) 1045
Himalayan Review (NP) 544
Himmel & Erde (GW ISSN 0722-8252) 905
Das Himmelsjahr (GW ISSN 0439-1551) 116
Himpunan Nelayan Seluruh Indonesia. Dewan Pimpanan Pusat. Laporan Kegiatan see Fisherman Union of Indonesia. Central Governing Board. Annual Report 509
Hind Mazdoor Sabha. Report of the Annual Convention (II ISSN 0073-2273) 648
Hindemith-Jahrbuch/Annales Hindemith (GW) 836
Hindi Kahani (II) 723
Hindu Astronomical and Mathematical Text Series (II ISSN 0073-2281) 749
Hindustan Latex. Annual Reports see Hindustan Latex. Varshika Riporta 900
Hindustan Latex. Varshika Riporta/ Hindustan Latex. Annual Reports (II) 323, 900
Hine's Directory of Insurance Adjusters(US) 639
Hine's Insurance Counsel (US) 639, 657
Hinnat ja Kilpailu/Priser och Konkurrens (FI ISSN 0356-5092) 239
Hints to Exporters (UK) 256
Hints to Potato Growers (US ISSN 0018-1986) 56
Hip (US ISSN 0095-7216) 786

Hirosaki Daigaku Igakubu Eiseigaku Kyoshitsu Gyosekishu (JA ISSN 0910-0377) 761, 776
Hiroshima Daigaku Genbaku Hoshano Igaku Kenkyusho Nenpo see Hiroshima University. Research Institute for Nuclear Medicine and Biology. Proceedings 792
Hiroshima Daigaku Rika Kiyo, Dobutsugaku see Hiroshima University. Journal of Science. Series B. Division 1: Zoology 175
Hiroshima University. Department of Geology. Geological Report (JA ISSN 0073-2303) 388
Hiroshima University. Faculty of Engineering. Memoirs (JA ISSN 0073-2311) 471
Hiroshima University. Journal of Science. Series B. Division 1: Zoology/Hiroshima Daigaku Rika Kiyo, Dobutsugaku (JA) 175
Hiroshima University. Journal of Science. Series C. Geology and Mineralogy (JA ISSN 0075-4374) 388, 817
Hiroshima University. Laboratory for Amphibian Biology. Scientific Report(JA) 141, 175
Hiroshima University. Research Institute for Nuclear Medicine and Biology. Proceedings/Hiroshima Daigaku Genbaku Hoshano Igaku Kenkyusho Nenpo (JA ISSN 0073-232X) 792
Hirschmannbrief (GW) 1045
Hispanic American Arts (UY) 105, 836, 1077
Hispanic American Periodicals Index (US ISSN 0361-5502) 563
Hispanic Focus (US) 506
Histadrut Nachrichten see Labour in Israel 648
Histoire de l'Horticulture au Canada see Canadian Historical Horticulture 532
Histoire de la Pensee (FR ISSN 0073-2362) 992
Histoire des Idees et Critique Litteraire (SZ ISSN 0073-2397) 723
Histoire et Civilisation Arabe (FR ISSN 0073-2400) 612
Histoire et Civilisation du Livre (SZ ISSN 0073-2419) 557
Histoire et Theorie (FR) 585
Historia (BL ISSN 0101-9074) 557
Historia (CL ISSN 0073-2435) 606
Historia. Einzelschriften (GW ISSN 0341-0056) 557
Historia Archaeologica (YU) 87, 585
Historia de Espana en el Mundo Moderno. Estudios (SP) 585
Historia Grafica de Catalunya Dia a Dia (SP) 585
Historia Hospitalium (GW) 557, 617, 761
Historia i Wspolczesnosc (PL ISSN 0137-3277) 557
Historia Militar del Paraguay (US) 606, 811
Historia Moderna e Contemporanea see Universidade do Parana. Departamento de Historia. Boletim 561
Historia Natural de Costa Rica (CR) 606
Historia Scientiarum (JA) 992
Historia Sztuki (PL ISSN 0083-4270) 105
Historia Universal (SP) 557
Historia y Cultura (PE ISSN 0073-2486) 606
Historia y Filosofia de la Ciencia. Serie Mayor. Encuadernada (SP ISSN 0073-2494) 992
Historia y Filosofia de la Ciencia. Serie Menor. Rustica (SP ISSN 0073-2508) 992
Historiae Musicae Cultores Biblioteca (IT ISSN 0073-2516) 836
Historiae Scientiarum Elementa (GW ISSN 0073-2532) 992
Historiallinen Arkisto (FI ISSN 0073-2540) 585
Historiallinen Kirjasto (FI ISSN 0359-3223) 557
Historiallisia Tutkimuksia (FI ISSN 0073-2559) 585

Historian Aitta (FI ISSN 0439-2183) 557
Historian Opettajien Vuosikirja (FI) 585
Historians of Early Modern Europe (US ISSN 0883-3559) 585, 970
Historic Bethlehem. Newsletter (US) 606
Historic Documents (US) 606, 905
Historic Guelph (CN ISSN 0709-5562) 98, 134, 606
Historic Houses, Castles and Gardens see Historic Houses, Castles and Gardens in Great Britain and Ireland 585
Historic Houses, Castles and Gardens in Great Britain and Ireland (UK) 585
Historic Madison. Journal (US ISSN 0361-574X) 606
Historic Michigan Travel Guide (US) 1154
Historic Society of Lancashire and Cheshire. Transactions (UK ISSN 0140-332X) 585
Historic Textiles of India (II) 1074
Historica (CS) 585
Historical Abstracts. Part A: Modern History Abstracts, 1450-1914 (US ISSN 0363-2717) 6, 563, 912
Historical Abstracts. Part B: Twentieth Century Abstracts, 1914 to the Present (US ISSN 0363-2725) 6, 563, 912
Historical Arms Series (CN ISSN 0440-9221) 79
Historical Association, London. General Series (UK) 557
Historical Association of Kenya. Pamphlet (KE) 566
Historical Association of Tanzania. Papers (KE ISSN 0440-9264) 566
Historical Association of Zimbabwe. Local Series Pamphlets (RH) 566
Historical Aviation Album (US ISSN 0018-2443) 19
Historical Blue Book of New Mexico see Official New Mexico Blue Book 608
Historical Breechloading Smallarms Association. Journal (UK ISSN 0305-0440) 811
Historical Chart Book (US) 229
Historical Geography Research Series (UK ISSN 0143-683X) 544
Historical Guides to the World's Periodicals and Newspapers (US ISSN 0742-5538) 645
Historical Harpsichord Series (US) 836
Historical Intelligencer (US ISSN 0270-4919) 557, 978
Historical Journal (AT ISSN 0311-8924) 573
Historical Miscellany (SI) 557
Historical Museums in Michigan see Historic Michigan Travel Guide 1154
Historical Plant Cost and Annual Production Expenses for Selected Electric Plants (US) 184
Historical Problems: Studies and Documents (UK ISSN 0073-2621) 557
Historical Records of Australian Science (AT) 992
Historical Reprint Series see Champaign County Historical Archives Historical Publications Series 604
Historical Research. Special Supplement(UK) 585
Historical Research for Higher Degrees in the United Kingdom. Part 1: Theses Completed (UK ISSN 0268-6716) 557
Historical Research for Higher Degrees in the United Kingdom. Part 2: Theses in Progress (UK ISSN 0268-6724) 558
Historical Research for University Degrees in the United Kingdom. Part 1: Theses Completed see Historical Research for Higher Degrees in the United Kingdom. Part 1: Theses Completed 557
Historical Research for University Degrees in the United Kingdom. Part 2: Theses in Progress see Historical Research for Higher Degrees in the United Kingdom. Part 2: Theses in Progress 558
Historical Society of South Australia. Guidesheet (AT) 127
Historical Society of the Church in Wales. Journal (UK) 585, 978
Historical Society of the Presbyterian Church of Wales. Journal (UK) 585, 978
Historical Statistics of the Gas Industry(US ISSN 0073-2656) 864
Historical Statistics of the United States(US ISSN 0073-2664) 1056
Historical Studies (UK ISSN 0075-0743) 585
Historical Studies (Pakistan) Series (PK) 569
Historical Studies in the Life Sciences (US) 1154
Historical Studies in the Physical Sciences (US) 992
Historiches Jahrbuck der Stadt Graz (AU ISSN 0440-9728) 585
Historicka Demografie (CS ISSN 0323-0937) 585
Historicka Geografie (CS ISSN 0323-0988) 585
Historicke Studie (CS ISSN 0440-9515) 585
Historie (Ballerup) (DK ISSN 0108-1934) 558
Historie og Samtidsorientering (DK) 447, 558
Historisch-Demographische Mitteilungen/Communications de Demographie Historique (HU ISSN 0134-0050) 922
Historisch Jaarboek Vlaardingen (NE) 585
Historisch Sozialwissenschaftliche Forschungen (GW ISSN 0173-2153) 1154
Historische Documenten van de Wetenschappen (BE) 992
Historische Forschungen (GW ISSN 0440-9558) 558
Historische Grundwissenschaften in Einzeldarstellungen (GW ISSN 0930-6404) 558
Historische Kommission zu Berlin. Einzelveroeffentlichungen (GW ISSN 0067-5857) 558
Historische Studien (GW) 585
Historische und Paedagogische Studien (GW ISSN 0723-3264) 414, 558
Historische Vereniging Vlaardingen. Tijdschrift see Historisch Jaarboek Vlaardingen 585
Historischer Verein der Pfalz. Mitteilungen (GW ISSN 0073-2680) 585
Historischer Verein des Kantons Bern. Archiv (SZ) 536, 585
Historischer Verein des Kantons St. Gallen. Neujahrsblatt (SZ) 585
Historischer Verein Dillingen an der Donau. Jahrbuch (GW ISSN 0073-2699) 585
Historischer Verein fuer das Fuerstentum Liechtenstein. Jahrbuch (LH) 87, 585
Historischer Verein fuer Steiermark. Zeitschrift (AU) 585
Historisches Jahrbuch der Stadt Linz (AU ISSN 0440-9736) 585
Historisk Aarbog for Felsted Sogn (DK ISSN 0109-2138) 585
Historisk Aarbog for Roedding Kommune (DK ISSN 0107-783X) 585
Historisk Aarbog for Skive og Omegn (DK ISSN 0107-721X) 585
Historisk Aarbog fra Randers Amt (DK ISSN 0108-4100) 585
Historisk Arbog for Thisted Amt see Historisk Arbog for Thy, Mors og Vester Hanherred 585
Historisk Arbog for Thy, Mors og Vester Hanherred (DK) 585
Historisk Arbog for Thy og Mors see Historisk Arbog for Thy, Mors og Vester Hanherred 585
Historisk Arbog fra Roskilde Amt (DK) 585
Historisk Arkiv for Broerup og Omegn. Aarsskrift (DK ISSN 0109-0674) 586
Historisk Forening for Vaerloese Kommune. Arsskrift (DK ISSN 0108-6804) 586
Historisk Samfund for Arhus Stift. Arboger (DK) 586
Historisk Samfund for Praesto Amt. Aarbog (DK ISSN 0107-6868) 586
Historisk Samfund for Soenderjylland. Skrifter (DK ISSN 0109-9264) 586
Historisk Samfund for Soro Amt. Arbog(DK) 586
Historisk-Topografisk Selskab for Gjentofte Kommune. Meddelelser see Gentofte-Bogen 583
Historiska och Litteraturhistoriska Studier (FI ISSN 0073-2702) 630
Historiska Samfundet i Abo. Skrifter Utgivna (FI ISSN 0356-1496) 586
Historiske Meddelelser om Koebenhavn(DK) 586
History. Annual Supplement see U.S. Army Infantry School. History; Annual Supplement 813
History and Structure of Languages (US ISSN 0073-2710) 696
History in Africa (US ISSN 0361-5413) 566
History in Malawi (MW) 566
History in Zambia (ZA) 563
History Journal (UK ISSN 0144-2791) 558
History of Anthropology (US) 72
History of Art Research Reports see Sponsored Research in the History of Art 110
History of Higher Education Annual (US) 435
History of Psychoanalysis (US ISSN 0734-9831) 934
History of Technology (UK ISSN 0307-5451) 1069
History of the Aztec Club of 1847 (US) 606
History of Universities (UK ISSN 0144-5138) 435, 586
History of World Architecture (US) 98
History Teaching Review (UK) 558
Historygram (US) 606
Historyka; Studia Metodologiczne (PL ISSN 0073-277X) 586
Hito to Kokudo. see People and National Land Policy 291
Hitotsubashi Journal of Arts and Sciences (JA ISSN 0073-2788) 630, 992
Hitotsubashi Journal of Economics (JA ISSN 0018-280X) 195
Hitotsubashi Journal of Law and Politics (JA ISSN 0073-2796) 657, 905
Hitotsubashi Journal of Social Studies (JA ISSN 0073-280X) 1008
Hjerteforeningen (DK ISSN 0105-9785) 776
Hjertenyt (DK ISSN 0108-8904) 776
Hobart Paperbacks (UK ISSN 0309-1783) 251
Hobart Papers (UK ISSN 0073-2818) 195
Hobby Publications Annual Trade Directory (US) 614, 844
Hobbyindeks for Boernebiblioteker (DK) 6, 614
Hobson's Engineering Casebook (UK) 454, 481, 491
Hochenergiephysik-Index see High Energy Physics Index 893
Hochschulbuecher fuer Mathematik (GE ISSN 0073-2842) 749
Hochschulbuecher fuer Physik (GE ISSN 0073-2850) 888
Hochschule fuer Bodenkultur in Wien. Dissertationen see Universitaet fuer Bodenkultur in Wien. Dissertationen 36
Hochschule fuer Maschinenbau Karl-Marx-Stadt. Wissenschaftliche Zeitschrift see Technische Hochschule Karl-Marx-Stadt. Wissenschaftliche Zeitschrift 474
Hochschule fuer Welthandel in Wien. Dissertationen see Wirtschaftsuniversitaet Wien. Dissertationen 202
Hochschule fuer Welthandel, Wien. Institut fuer Organisation und Revisionswesen. Veroeffentlichungen (AU) 221
Hochschule fuer Welthandel, Wien. Institut fuer Organisation und Revisionswesen. Verhandlungen see Hochschule fuer Welthandel, Wien. Institut fuer Organisation und Revisionswesen. Veroeffentlichungen 221
Hochschule St. Gallen fuer Wirtschafts- und Sozialwissenschaften. Forschungsinstitut fuer Absatz und Handel. Schriftenreihe (SZ ISSN 0080-603X) 239
Hochschule St. Gallen fuer Wirtschafts- und Sozialwissenschaften. Veroeffentlichungen. Schriftenreihe Betriebswirtschaft (SZ) 280
Hocken Lecture (NZ) 72, 573
Hockey Association. Official Handbook(UK ISSN 0085-1566) 1038
Hockey Guide (US ISSN 0278-4955) 1033
Hockey Register (US ISSN 0090-2292) 1038
Hoehnea (BL ISSN 0073-2877) 157
Hoeje-Tastrup Kommunes. Lokalhistoriske Arkiv. Aarskrift (DK ISSN 0900-2596) 586
Hoerbuchverzeichnis (GE) 180
Hofstra University Cultural and Intercultural Studies (US ISSN 0195-802X) 1154
Hofstra University Yearbook of Business (US ISSN 0073-2907) 195
Hoge Raad voor de Middenstand. Jaarverslag (BE) 272, 942
Hohenheimer Arbeiten (GW ISSN 0340-9783) 28
Hojas de Poesia (AG) 741
Hojin Kigyo No Jittai see Zeimu Tokei Kara Mita Hojin Kigyo No Jittai 300
Hok see Jescheidenis van Wortel 587
Hokkaido Daigaku Rigakubu Kaiso Kenkyusho Obun Hokoku see Hokkaido University. Institute of Algological Research. Scientific Papers 406
Hokkaido Dental Association. Journal/Hokkaido Shika Ishikaishi, Doshikai Tsushin (JA ISSN 0073-2915) 779
Hokkaido Economic Papers see Hokudai Economic Papers 195
Hokkaido Eiyo Syokuryo Gakkaishi/Hokkaido Society of Food and Nutrition. Journal (JA ISSN 0285-1806) 62, 519
Hokkaido Fisheries Experimental Station. Scientific Reports (JA ISSN 0441-084X) 151, 157
Hokkaido Kogai Boshi Kenkyujo Ho. see Hokkaido Research Institute for Environmental Pollution. Report 496
Hokkaido Kogyo Kaihatsu Shikenjo Gijutsu see Japan. Government Industrial Development Laboratory, Hokkaido. Technical Data 1069
Hokkaido Kogyo Kaihatsu Shikenjo Hokoku see Japan. Government Industrial Development Laboratory, Hokkaido. Reports 1069
Hokkaido Kogyo Kaihatsu Shikenjo Nempo see Japan. Government Industrial Development Laboratory, Hokkaido. Annual Report 290
Hokkaido Librarians Study Circle. Bulletin/Hokkaido Toshokan Kenkyukai. Kaiho (JA ISSN 0018-3431) 678
Hokkaido National Agricultural Experiment Station. Soil Survey Report/Hokkaido Nogyo Shikenjo Dojo Chosa Hokoku (JA ISSN 0073-2923) 56
Hokkaido Nogyo Shikenjo Dojo Chosa Hokoku see Hokkaido National Agricultural Experiment Station. Soil Survey Report 56
Hokkaido Rehabilitation/Hokkaido Rihabirteshon Gakkai Zasshi (JA) 1154

Hokkaido Research Institute for Environmental Pollution. Report/Hokkaido Kogai Boshi Kenkyujo Ho.(JA) *496*
Hokkaido Rihabirteshon Gakkai Zasshi see Hokkaido Rehabilitation *1154*
Hokkaido Shika Ishikaishi, Doshikai Tsushin see Hokkaido Dental Association. Journal *779*
Hokkaido Society of Food and Nutrition. Journal see Hokkaido Eiyo Syokuryo Gakkaishi *62*
Hokkaido Toshokan Kenkyukai. Kaiho see Hokkaido Librarians Study Circle. Bulletin *678*
Hokkaido University. Faculty of Agriculture. Journal (JA ISSN 0018-344X) *28*
Hokkaido University. Faculty of Engineering. Memoirs (JA) *471*
Hokkaido University. Faculty of Fisheries. Data Record of Oceanographic Observations and Exploratory Fishing/Kaiyo Chosa Gyogyo Shiken Yoho (JA ISSN 0439-3511) *406, 510*
Hokkaido University. Faculty of Science. Journal. Series 5: Botany (JA ISSN 0368-2145) *157*
Hokkaido University. Faculty of Science. Journal. Series 6: Zoology (JA ISSN 0368-2188) *175*
Hokkaido University. Faculty of Science. Journal. Series 7: Geophysics (JA ISSN 0441-067X) *399*
Hokkaido University. Institute of Algological Research. Scientific Papers/Hokkaido Daigaku Rigakubu Kaiso Kenkyusho Obun Hokoku (JA) *157, 406*
Hokkaido University. Institute of Immunological Science. Bulletin (JA) *773, 793*
Hokkaido University. Institute of Low Temperature Science. Series A. Physical Science see Low Temperature Science. Series A. Physical Science *894*
Hokkaido University. Institute of Low Temperature Science. Series B. Biological Science see Low Temperature Science. Series B. Biological Science *143*
Hokkaido University. Research Institute of Applied Electricity. Monograph Series (JA ISSN 0439-3465) *454*
Hokke Bunka Kenkyu see Institute for the Comprehensive Study of Lotus Sutra. Journal *977*
Hokudai Economic Papers (JA ISSN 0441-7410) *195*
Hokuriku no Denki to kogyo/Electricity and Industry in Hokuriku (JA) *468*
Holiday Haunts in Great Britain (UK) *1111*
Holiday Hints Handbook (UK) *1111*
Holiday Homes, Cottages & Apartments in Britain (UK) *1111*
Holiday Islander (UK) *1111*
Holiday News Series (UK) *1111*
Holiday Parks (UK ISSN 0266-4429) *1111*
Holiday U.S.A. and Canada Magazine see Discover North America *1107*
Holidays in Britain (UK ISSN 0073-3024) *1111*
Holidays in Wales see Wales Best Holidays *1118*
Holland Camping (NE) *1045*
Holland Exports (NE ISSN 0073-3032) *256*
Hollis Press and Public Relations Annual (UK ISSN 0073-3059) *15*
Hollywood Reporter Studio Blu-Book Directory (US ISSN 0278-419X) *348, 824*
Holm Conference on Electrical Contacts (Proceedings) (US) *454*
Holocaust Studies Annual (US ISSN 0738-0739) *503, 586, 913*
Holography Directory (US) *899*
Holstebro Museum. Aarsskrift (DK ISSN 0107-6752) *586*
Holy Places of Palestine (IS) *612, 970, 1111*
Die Holzschwelle (GW ISSN 0018-3865) *530*

Home & Auto A P A A Show Daily see Aftermarket Business A P A A Show Daily *190*
Home & Auto Big "I" Show Daily see Aftermarket Business Big "I" Show Daily *190*
Home & Auto Buyer's Guide see Aftermarket Business Buyer's Guide *282*
Home & Garden Supply Merchandiser Green Book see Garden Supply Retailer Green Book *532*
Home Care Services, Day Care Establishments, Day Services - Scotland (UK ISSN 0260-5295) *1018*
Home Care Services in New York State(US) *784, 1018*
Home Center Operators & Hardware Chains (Year) (US ISSN 0272-0167) *309, 644*
Home Decorating Ideas see Woman's Day Home Decorating Ideas *643*
Home Ec News (CN ISSN 0018-4004) *615*
Home Economics in Institutions Granting Bachelors or Higher Degrees (US ISSN 0073-3105) *435, 615*
Home Economics Yearbook (UK) *615*
Home Energy see WoodHeat *467*
Home Entertainment see Television: the New Era *350*
Home Furnishings Survey (UK) *644*
Home Health Care Products Directory & Resource Guide (US) *637*
Home Sewing Industry Resource Directory (US) *309, 615*
Homebringing Mission of Jesus Christ see Universal Life - The Inner Religion *974*
Homemaker's Guide (US) *615*
Homemaker's Handbook see Homemaker's Guide *615*
Homeservice Stations Outside the Tropical Bands (DK ISSN 0109-9140) *348*
Homesewing Resource Directory of Branded Line Merchandise in the Homesewing Industry (US) *340*
Homicide in California (US ISSN 0098-8537) *370, 374*
Homine (IT ISSN 0018-4292) *878*
Homing World Stud Book (UK ISSN 0073-3164) *1033*
Hominids, Oh! see New Toy *711*
Hommes et la Terre (FR ISSN 0073-3202) *558*
Hommes et les Lettres (FR) *723*
Homo (FR ISSN 0563-9743) *1026*
Homo Sociologicus (SP) *1026*
Homogeneous Catalysis in Organic and Inorganic Chemistry see Catalysis by Metal Complexes *329*
Homosexual Information Center. Newsletter (US) *616, 913*
Hon: a Book-Bin for Scholars (JA ISSN 0046-7839) *1154*
Honduras. Congreso Nacional. Boletin (HO) *942*
Honduras. Consejo Superior de Planificacion Economica. Plan Operativo Anual. Sector Industrial (HO) *195*
Honduras. Consejo Superior de Planificacion Economica. Plan Operativo Anual. Sector Turismo (HO) *195, 1111*
Honduras. Secretaria de Trabajo y Prevision Social. Boletin de Estadisticas Laborales (HO) *1018*
Honduras. Universidad Nacional Autonoma. Revista de la Universidad(HO) *414*
Honduras al Dia (HO) *538*
Honduras en Cifras (HO) *1056*
Hong Kong. Annual Digest of Statistics(HK) *1056*
Hong Kong. Estimates of Gross Domestic Product (HK) *210, 1056*
Hong Kong. Royal Observatory. Climatological Note see Hong Kong. Royal Observatory. Technical Note *804*
Hong Kong. Royal Observatory. Occasional Paper (HK) *804*
Hong Kong. Royal Observatory. Technical Note (HK) *804*
Hong Kong Annual Report (HK) *245*

Hong Kong Architects & Designers Catalogue (HK) *98, 184*
Hong Kong Bargain Guide to Factory Outlets (US) *284*
Hong Kong Builder Directory (HK) *184*
Hong Kong Catholic Church Directory/Hsiang-Kang T'ien Chu Chiao Shou T'se (HK ISSN 0073-3210) *982*
Hong Kong Economic Papers (HK ISSN 0018-4578) *195*
Hong Kong Economic Yearbook (HK) *195*
Hong Kong Export Credit Insurance Corporation. Annual Report (HK) *229*
Hong Kong Handbook (UK ISSN 0260-7786) *1100*
Hong Kong in Figures (HK) *1056*
Hong Kong Industrial Investment (HK) *266*
Hong Kong Industrial Products Directory/Hsiang-Kang Kung Yeh Chih Pin Nien Chien (HK) *1069*
Hong Kong Interbank Directory (HK) *229*
Hong Kong Jewellery & Watches (HK) *644*
Hong Kong Junior Chamber. Annual Review (HK) *236*
Hong Kong Library Association. Journal (HK ISSN 0073-3237) *678*
Hong Kong Manufacturers and Exporters Register (HK ISSN 0073-3245) *309*
Hong Kong Medical Association. Bulletin see Hong Kong Medical Association. Journal *761*
Hong Kong Medical Association. Journal (HK) *761*
Hong Kong Narcotics Report (HK) *376*
Hong Kong Productivity Council & Centre Annual Report (HK) *289*
Hong Kong Review of Overseas Trade (HK) *256*
Hong Kong Social and Economic Trends (HK) *245, 1026*
Hong Kong Streets and Places (HK) *1111*
Hong Kong Tourist Association. Digest of Annual Statistics see Statistical Review of Tourism in Hong Kong *1120*
Hong Kong Toys (HK) *553*
HongKongiana (HK ISSN 0379-5853) *6*
Hongrie see Magyarorszag *1059*
Hontanar (AG ISSN 0073-327X) *127*
Hoogstratens Oudheidkundige Kring Jescheidenis van Wortel see Jescheidenis van Wortel *587*
Hooker's Icones Planetarium (UK) *157*
Hoppenstedt Vademecum der Investmentfonds (GW ISSN 0073-3342) *266*
Hoppenstedt Versicherungs-Jahrbuch (GW ISSN 0073-3350) *639*
Hor-Tasy (US) *723*
Hor Yezh (FR) *711*
Horace M. Albright Conservation Lectureship (US ISSN 0073-3369) *365, 525*
Horizon (CN ISSN 0315-8527) *447*
Horizons (IS ISSN 0334-3774) *544*
Horizons in Biblical Theology (US ISSN 0195-9085) *970*
Horizons in Biochemistry and Biophysics (US ISSN 0096-2708) *151, 153*
Horna Nitra (CS) *586*
Hornero/Oven Bird (AG ISSN 0073-3407) *170*
Hornsey Historical Society. Bulletin (UK ISSN 0268-7836) *586*
Hornsey Historical Society. Occasional Papers (UK) *586*
Horse Action (US) *1043*
Horse & Rider All-Western Yearbook (US) *1043*
Horse Care (US) *1043*
Horse Holidays in W. Europe (DK ISSN 0109-4777) *1043*
Horse Industry Directory (US) *1043*
Horse Lover's (US) *1043*
Horse Owners and Breeders Tax Manual (US) *221, 266, 296, 1043*
Horse Racing Quiz Book (UK) *1043*
Horse Women (US) *1043*

Horticultural Abstracts (UK ISSN 0018-5280) *6, 534*
Horticultural Guide to Australian Plants(AT) *532*
Horticultural Produce and Practice see AgLink Leaflets *22*
Horticultural Research International (NE ISSN 0441-7461) *532*
Horticultural Reviews (US ISSN 0163-7851) *533*
Horticultural Society of Ethiopia. Bulletin (ET) *533*
Horticultural Trades Association Members' Reference Book (UK ISSN 0264-1291) *256, 533*
Horticulture and Coffee Research Institute. Annual Report. Part 1. Horticultural Research Centre (RH) *56*
Horticulture and Coffee Research Institute. Annual Report. Part 2. Coffee Research Station (RH) *56*
Horticulture and Coffee Research Institute. Annual Report. Part 3. Rhodes Experimental Station (RH) *56*
Horvath Blaetter (GW ISSN 0724-2603) *1154*
Hoseasons Boating Holidays (UK) *1111*
Hoseasons Holiday Boats and Bungalows Hire see Hoseasons Boating Holidays *1111*
Hoseasons Holiday-Homes see Hoseasons Holiday-Homes in U.K *1111*
Hoseasons Holiday-Homes in U.K. (UK) *1111*
Hoshasen Ikushujo Kenkyu Hokoku see Acta Radiobotanika et Genetika *137*
Hosiery Statistics (US) *340*
Hospital Abstracts see Health Service Abstracts *1023*
Hospital & Health Services Yearbook Australia (AT) *617*
Hospital and Nursing Yearbook of Southern Africa (SA ISSN 0441-2613) *617, 784*
Hospital and Selected Morbidity Data (NZ ISSN 0548-9938) *619*
Hospital Consultants and Specialists Association Year Book (UK) *617*
Hospital Contracts Manual (US) *617*
Hospital-Escola Sao Camilo e Sao Luis. Boletim (BL) *617*
Hospital for Sick Children, Toronto. Research Institute. Annual Report (CN ISSN 0082-5034) *761, 787*
Hospital Literature Index (US ISSN 0018-5736) *6, 619*
Hospital Management Systems Society. Annual Conference Proceedings (US ISSN 0193-0486) *617*
Hospital Rate Directory of Southern New York (US) *1154*
Hospital Statistics see Hospital Statistics (Year) *619*
Hospital Statistics (CY ISSN 0253-8628) *1154*
Hospital Statistics (Year) (US) *619, 1056*
Hospital Statistics of New Zealand see New Zealand. Department of Health. Hospital Management Data *619*
Hospitality Buyers Guide (AT ISSN 0156-3688) *620*
Hospitality Buyers Guide and Diary see Hospitality Buyers Guide *620*
Hosteling Holidays (US) *1045, 1111*
Hosteling U.S.A (US) *1154*
Hot Chocolate Fairy Tale Series (US) *723*
Hot Logarithm (US) *711*
Hot Water Review (US ISSN 0278-4173) *741*
Hotel & Motel Management Show Daily (US) *195, 620*
Hotel and Motel Red Book (US ISSN 0073-3490) *620*
Hotel Guide to Turkey see Turkey: Hotels-Camping *620*
Hotel, Motel and Travel Directory see Hotel, Motel Index *620*
Hotel, Motel Index (AT ISSN 0156-3661) *620*
Hotel, Restaurant and Catering Supplies(UK ISSN 0142-1824) *519*

HOTEL SALES

Hotel Sales & Marketing Association International Hotel Facilities Digest see H.S.M.A. Hotel Facilities Digest 1154
Hoteles de Spana; Guia Oficial Abreviada. see Guia de Hoteles: Espana 1110
Hotelier and Caterer see Hotelier & Caterer Buyer's Guide 620
Hotelier & Caterer Buyer's Guide (SA) 620
Hotels & Tourism: Latin American Industrial Report (US) 1111
Hotels de la France (FR) 620
Hotels de la France et d'Outre-Mer see Hotels de la France 620
Hotels, Motels and Guest Houses in New Providence and Paradise Island (BF) 1111
Hotelsko-Turisticki Adresar see Yugoslavia; Hotel and Tourist Directory 621
Les Houches Summer School Proceedings (NE) 888
House and Garden. Real-Life Kitchen Guide (UK) 538
House and Garden Gardening Guide see Gardening 532
House Beautiful's Houses and Plans (US ISSN 0073-3571) 98
House Ear Institute. Progress Report (US ISSN 0197-3657) 787
Household Chemical Market see Household Cleaning Report 323
Household Cleaning Report (UK) 323
Houser Hunters: Family of Charles Franklin Houser (US) 536
House's Guide to the Construction Industry (UK) 184
Housing Activity in Hawaii see Construction in Hawaii 183
Housing and Planning Year Book (UK ISSN 0073-3644) 623
Housing and Urban Development Digest (KE) 623
Housing and Urban Planning in Sweden. Annual Report/Svenska Bostaeder. Aarsredovisning (SW) 623
Housing Construction Catalogue (UK) 184
Housing Finance Company of Kenya. Annual Report and Accounts (KE) 229, 623
Housing in Canada see Canadian Housing Statistics 627
Housing Units in Connecticut. Annual Summary see Connecticut Housing Production and Permit Authorized Construction 183
Housing Vacancies see Current Housing Reports: Housing Vacancies 623
Housing Year Book (UK ISSN 0264-5181) 623
Housman Society Journal (UK ISSN 0305-926X) 723
Houston Building and Construction Directory (US) 1154
Houston Post. Newspaper Index see Index to the Houston Post 647
Houtadresboek (NE) 530
Houtland (BE) 515, 586
How to Avoid Financial Tangles (US ISSN 0424-2769) 229
How to Avoid Financial Tangles: Section B. Wills and Trusts, Taxes, and Help for the Widow see How to Avoid Financial Tangles 229
How to Buy and Sell Business Opportunities (US) 266, 965
How to Find Company Intelligence in State Documents (US) 195, 309
How to Find Information About Companies (US) 195, 309
How to Find Information About Japanese Companies and Industries (US) 195, 309
How to Find Out About Further Education and Training see After School 428
How to Get Help for Kids (US ISSN 0275-4819) 444
How to Invest in Brazil (BL) 266
How to Live in Britain (UK) 1018
Howard Florey Institute of Experimental Physiology & Medicine. Annual Report and Notice of Meeting (AT ISSN 0314-6162) 762

Hronika Medjunarodnih Dogadjaja/Chronicle of International Events (YU) 916
Hsiang-Kang Kung Yeh Chih Pin Nien Chien see Hong Kong Industrial Products Directory 1069
Hsiang-Kang T'ien Chu Chiao Shou T'se see Hong Kong Catholic Church Directory 982
Hudobny Archiv (CS) 836
Hudson Institute. Report to the Members (US ISSN 0073-3776) 916
Hudson's Directory (US) 645
Hudson's Washington News Media Contacts Directory (US ISSN 0441-389X) 645
Hue Points (US ISSN 0739-0718) 105, 1129
Hueber Hochschulreihe (GW ISSN 0073-3792) 414, 696
Huebner Foundation Monograph (US) 639
Der Huettenmann (GW) 369
Hughes on Copyright and Industrial Design (CN) 861
Hugin (DK) 586
Huguenot Society of London. Proceedings (UK ISSN 0309-8346) 536, 586
Huguenot Society of London. Quarto Series (UK ISSN 0309-8354) 536, 586
Hukerikar Memorial Lecture Series (II ISSN 0419-0432) 195
Hulera (MX) 985
Hull Monographs on South-East Asia (SZ) 569
Hull Papers in Politics (UK ISSN 0142-7377) 905
Human Behavior and Environment (US) 934
Human Communication and Its Disorders (US) 444, 696
Human/Computer Interaction (US) 356
Human Development (Norwood) (US) 934
Human Ecology. Annual Report (US) 886
Human Factors Society. Proceedings of the Annual Meeting see Human Factors Society Annual Meeting. Proceedings 934
Human Factors Society Annual Meeting. Proceedings (US ISSN 0163-5182) 471, 934
Human Gene Mapping (SZ ISSN 0378-9861) 167, 781
Human Genetics. Supplement (US ISSN 0172-7699) 167
Human Genetics, Informational and Educational Materials. Supplement (US ISSN 0197-8160) 777
Human Industrial Design (AU ISSN 0018-7224) 1069
Human Life Matters (UK) 615, 922
Human-Oekologie see Uebersee-Museum, Bremen. Veroeffentlichungen. Reihe E: Human-Oekologie 1030
Human Relations see Affirmation 912
Human Resources Abstracts (US ISSN 0099-2453) 6, 905, 1026
Human Resources Information Network Update (US) 964
Human Resources Research Organization. Professional Papers (US ISSN 0073-3873) 942
Human Rights Act of British Columbia (CN) 913
Human Rights Directory see North American Human Rights Directory 913
Human Rights Organizations & Periodicals Directory (US ISSN 0098-0579) 912, 913
Human Sciences Research Council. Annual Report (SA) 630, 1008
Human Services Directory (CN) 1018
Human Settlement Issues (CN) 623, 1008
Human Settlements Situation and Related Trends and Policies (DK ISSN 0108-562X) 623
Human Stress Current Advances in Research (US ISSN 0885-1174) 333, 934, 1026

Humana Civilitas (US ISSN 0742-115X) 586
Humanidad (PR ISSN 0441-4144) 1018
Humanidades (GT ISSN 0018-7356) 630
Humanidades (PO) 630
Humaniora (DK ISSN 0105-5216) 1154
Humanist (DK ISSN 0107-9573) 630
Humanistic Studies in the Communications Arts (US) 1154
Humanistica Lovaniensia (BE) 337
Humanistica Lovaniensia. Supplementa (BE) 337
Humanities, Christianity and Culture (JA ISSN 0073-3938) 970
Humanities in Review (UK) 630
Humanities Index (US ISSN 0095-5981) 7, 634
Humanities Research Council of Canada. Report see Canadian Federation for the Humanities. Annual Report 629
Humboldt-Universitaet zu Berlin. Universitaetsbibliothek. Schriftenreihe(GE ISSN 0522-9898) 678
Humboldtiana see Bibliographia Humboldtiana 628
Humphreys County Historical Society. Publication (US) 606
Hungarian Academy of Sciences. Research Institute for Agricultural Economics. Bulletin see Research Institute for Agricultural Economics. Bulletin 49
Hungarian Academy of Sciences. Research Institute for Microbiology. Proceedings see Magyar Tudomanyos Akademia. Mikrobiologiai Kutato Intezet. Proceedings 168
Hungarian Building Bulletin (HU ISSN 0018-7720) 28, 184
Hungarian Economic Literature see Magyar Kozgazdasagi Irodalom 212
Hungarian Law Review (HU ISSN 0441-4411) 657
Hungarian P.E.N./P.E.N. Hongrois (HU ISSN 0439-9080) 723
Hungarian R and D Abstracts. Science and Technology (HU ISSN 0237-0808) 7, 1004, 1072
Hungarian Studies in English see Angol Filologiai Tanulmanyok 690
Hungarian Technical Abstracts see Hungarian R and D Abstracts. Science and Technology 1004
Hungary see Magyarorszag 1059
Hungary. Kozponti Statisztikai Hivatal. Agazati Kapcsolatok Merlege (HU ISSN 0209-6919) 210
Hungary. Kozponti Statisztikai Hivatal. Belkereskedelmi Evkonyv (HU ISSN 0134-1138) 211
Hungary. Kozponti Statisztikai Hivatal. Beruhazasi, Epitoipari, Lakasepitesi Zsebkonyv (HU ISSN 0139-3510) 189
Hungary. Kozponti Statisztikai Hivatal. Demografiai Evkonyv (HU ISSN 0073-4020) 922, 927
Hungary. Kozponti Statisztikai Hivatal. Epitoipari Arak Alakulasa (HU ISSN 0237-0298) 189
Hungary. Kozponti Statisztikai Hivatal. Foglalkoztatottsag es Kereseti Aranyok (HU ISSN 0133-543X) 210, 272
Hungary. Kozponti Statisztikai Hivatal. Haztartasstatisztika (HU ISSN 0439-9285) 615
Hungary. Kozponti Statisztikai Hivatal. Idegenforgalmi Evkonyv (HU ISSN 0230-4414) 1119
Hungary. Kozponti Statisztikai Hivatal. Ipari Zsebkonyv (HU ISSN 0133-8684) 210
Hungary. Kozponti Statisztikai Hivatal. Iparstatisztikai Evkonyv (HU ISSN 0209-4002) 210, 289
Hungary. Kozponti Statisztikai Hivatal. Kozlekedesi es Hirkozlesi Evkonyv see Hungary. Kozponti Statisztikai Hivatal. Kozlekedesi Posta es Tavkozlesi 345
Hungary. Kozponti Statisztikai Hivatal. Kozlekedesi Posta es Tavkozlesi (HU) 345

Hungary. Kozponti Statisztikai Hivatal. Kulkereskedelmi Statisztikai Evkonyv(HU ISSN 0139-3634) 210
Hungary. Kozponti Statisztikai Hivatal. Lakasepites es Megszunes see Hungary. Kozponti Statisztikai Hivatal. Lakasstatisztikai Evkonyu 189
Hungary. Kozponti Statisztikai Hivatal. Lakasstatisztikai Evkonyu (HU ISSN 0236-9524) 189
Hungary. Kozponti Statisztikai Hivatal. Mezogazdasagi Statisztikai Zsebkonyu (HU ISSN 0441-4683) 41
Hungary. Kozponti Statisztikai Hivatal. Mezogazdasagi Statisztikai Evkonyv/Yearbook of Agricultural Statistics (HU ISSN 0230-4066) 41
Hungary. Kozponti Statisztikai Hivatal. Nemzetkozi Statisztikai Evkonyv (HU ISSN 0441-4713) 1056
Hungary. Kozponti Statisztikai Hivatal. Statisztikai Evkonyv (HU ISSN 0073-4039) 1057
Hungary. Kozponti Statisztikai Hivatal. Szamitastechnikai Statisztikai Evkonyv (HU ISSN 0139-3286) 354
Hungary. Kozponti Statisztikai Hivatal. Teruleti Statisztikai Evkonyv (HU ISSN 0303-5344) 1057
Hungary. Kozponti Statisztikai Hivatal. Tudomanyos Kutatas es Feolesztes (HU ISSN 0302-2226) 1004
Hungary. Kozponti Statisztikai Hivatal. Vizgazdalkodasi Statisztikai Zsebkonyv (HU ISSN 0209-7915) 1128
Hunter Valley Poets see Nimrod's Quarry 742
Hunter Valley Research Foundation. Monographs (AT ISSN 0085-1663) 365
Hunter Valley Research Foundation. Working Papers (AT ISSN 0729-5030) 245, 1057, 1124
Hunter's Hill Trust Journal (AT ISSN 0310-0111) 365
Huntia (US ISSN 0073-4071) 157
Hunting Annual see Field & Stream Hunting Annual 1045
Hunting Annual (US) 1045
Hunting Guns by Outdoor Life & Jim Carmichel (US) 1045
Husholdningsarbejdet (DK ISSN 0108-786X) 615
Husitsky Tabor (CS) 586
Husserliana (NE ISSN 0439-9714) 878
Hutton's Building Products Catalog (US) 184
Hutton's Building Systems and Controls Catalog (US) 343, 374, 465
Hutton's Mechanical Products Catalog (US) 184
Hutton's Plumbing-Heating-Cooling Catalog (US) 553
Hvad Skovsoeen /Gemte Aarbog see H S G's Aarbog 14
Hvad Skovsoeen Gemte's Science Fiction-Aarbog see H S G's Aarbog 14
Hvalraadets Skrifter/Scientific Results of Marine Biological Research (NO ISSN 0073-4128) 141
Hvar Observatory Bulletin (YU) 116, 399
Hvem, Hvad, Hvor (DK ISSN 0106-4177) 905
Hybrid Microelectronics Symposium. (Papers) (UK ISSN 0073-4136) 454
Hydraulic Handbook (UK) 490
Hydro-Abstracts (US ISSN 0731-6445) 7, 1128
Hydrobiology (BU ISSN 0324-0924) 141
Hydrocarbon Processing Catalog see Hydrocarbon Processing Catalog and Directory 864
Hydrocarbon Processing Catalog and Directory (US) 864
Hydrological Yearbook of Israel/Shenaton Hidrologi Le-Yisrael (IS ISSN 0073-4217) 403
Hydrology and Meteorology/Hidrologija i Meteorologija (BU ISSN 0018-1331) 804

Hydrometeorologicky Ustav. Vyrocni Zprava (CS) *804*
Hydrometeorologicky Ustav, Bratislava. Zbornik Prac (CS) *804*
Hydronymia Germaniae (GW ISSN 0441-5302) *544*
Hydrotechnical Transactions *see* Rozprawy Hydrotechniczne *1125*
Hyman Blumberg Symposium Series (US) *414, 934*
Hyperguide des Hypermarches *see* Annuaire des Hypermarches *302*
Hypomnemata (GW ISSN 0085-1671) *337, 878*
I A (Industrial Archeology) (US ISSN 0160-1040) *87*
I A A E E (International Association for the Advancement of Ethnology and Eugenics). Monographs *see* I C H E International Commission on Human Ecology *72*
I A A E E (International Association for the Advancement of Ethnology and Eugenics). Reprint *see* White Paper on Human Ecology *78*
I A B S E Congress Report (International Association for Bridge and Structural Engineering) (SZ) *481*
I A B S E Report (International Association for Bridge and Structural Engineering) (SZ) *481*
I A E A Film Catalog *see* I A E A Library Film Catalog *893*
I A E A Library Film Catalog (International Atomic Energy Agency) (UN ISSN 0534-7319) *893*
I.A.E.A. Occasional Papers (Institute of Asian Economic Affairs) *see* I.D.E. Occasional Papers Series *195*
I A E A Technical Documents Series (International Atomic Energy Agency) (UN) *896*
I A E S T E Annual Report *see* International Association for the Exchange of Students for Technical Experience. Annual Report *441*
I A G A News (International Association of Geomagnetism and Aeronomy) (UK ISSN 0536-1095) *399*
I A M P News Bulletin (International Association of Meteorology and Atmospheric Physics) (US) *805*
I.A.M.R. Reports (Institute of Applied Manpower Research) (II ISSN 0418-5633) *272*
I A M S Newsletter (Institute of Archaeo-Metallurgical Studies) (UK ISSN 0261-068X) *87*
I A P A Bulletin (International Association of Physicians in Audiology) (UK ISSN 0262-6853) *787*
I A R C Monographs on the Evaluation of the Carcinogenic Risk of Chemicals to Humans (International Agency for Research on Cancer) (UN ISSN 0250-9555) *775*
I A R C Scientific Publications (International Agency for Research on Cancer) (UN ISSN 0300-5038) *775*
I A S Annual Meeting. Conference Record *see* Industry Applications Society. I E E E - I A S Annual Meeting. Conference Record *455*
I A S Bulletin (Iowa Academy of Science) (US ISSN 0075-0344) *992*
I A S E R Discussion Papers (Institute of Applied Social & Economic Research) (PP) *1008*
I A S E R Monographs (Institute of Applied Social & Economic Research) (PP) *1008*
I A S E R Special Publications (Institute of Applied Social and Economic Research of Papua New Guinea) (PP) *1008*
I A S L Conference Proceedings (International Association of School Librarianship) (US ISSN 0257-3229) *414, 678*
I A S L I C Special Publication (Indian Association of Special Libraries and Information Centres) (II ISSN 0073-6279) *678*

I A S L I C Technical Pamphlets (Indian Association of Special Libraries and Information Centres) (II ISSN 0073-6260) *678*
I A S P Newsletter (International Association of Scholarly Publishers) (NO ISSN 0333-3620) *436*
I A S S W Directory *see* I A S S W Directory; Member Schools and Associations *1018*
I A S S W Directory; Member Schools and Associations (International Association of Schools of Social Work) (AU ISSN 0098-8278) *1018*
I A T A Annual Report (International Air Transport Association) (CN) *1088*
I A T A Dangerous Goods Regulations (International Air Transport Association) (CN) *1088*
I A T A Live Animals Regulations (International Air Transport Association) (CN) *1088*
I A T U L Proceedings *see* I A T U L Quarterly *678*
I A T U L Quarterly (International Association of Technological Universities Libraries) (SW) *471, 678, 992*
I & C S Buyers' Guide (US) *471, 637*
I B A Technical Review (Independent Broadcasting Authority) (UK ISSN 0308-423X) *348*
I B M - P C Index (US ISSN 0741-2355) *7, 354*
I B M Research Symposia Series (US ISSN 0085-2082) *749, 888*
I B Nachrichten (Oesterreichisches Institut fuer Bauforschung) (AU ISSN 0018-8697) *184*
I B R O Neuroscience Calendar (International Brain Research Organization) (US ISSN 0271-521X) *790*
I B Z (International Bibliography of Periodical Literature from all Fields of Knowledge) (GW ISSN 0020-9201) *127*
I Byen's Spiseguide (DK ISSN 0107-8313) *620*
I C *see* Index Chemicus *325*
I C A A C Program and Abstracts *see* Interscience Conference on Antimicrobial Agents and Chemotherapy. Program and Abstracts *168*
I C A M Annuaire (Institut Catholique d'Arts et Metiers de Lille) (FR ISSN 0066-8982) *471*
I C A O Circulars (International Civil Aviation Organization) (UN ISSN 0074-2481) *1088*
I C A P Lista de Nuevas Adquisiciones (Instituto Centroamericano de Administracion Publica) (CR ISSN 0487-1596) *687*
I C A S A L S Annual Report (International Center for Arid and Semi-Arid Land Studies) (US) *365, 544*
I C B O Plumbing Code (International Conference of Building Officials) (US) *553*
I C B P Parrot Working Group Meeting. Proceedings (International Council for Bird Preservation) (UK ISSN 0277-1330) *170*
I C C A Congress Series (NE) *657*
I C C A D *see* I E E E International Conference on Computer-Aided Design. Proceedings *356*
I C C Annual Review (International Chamber of Commerce) (FR) *236, 251*
I C C D *see* I E E E International Conference on Computer Design. V L S I in Computers. Proceedings *356*
I C C E *see* I E E E International Conference on Consumer Electronics. Digest of Technical Papers *454*
I C C E T Annual Report (Imperial College of Science and Technology) (UK) *496*
I C D L *see* International Conference on Conduction and Breakdown in Dielectric Liquids. Conference Record *455*

I.C.E.A. Cahiers (Institut Canadien d'Education des Adultes) (CN ISSN 0018-8891) *1154*
I C E I Industrial and Control Applications of Microprocessors. Proceedings. *see* I E C O N: International Conference on Industrial Electronics, Control and Instrumentation. Proceedings *637*
I C E L References (International Council on Environmental Law) (GW) *501, 668*
I C E List of Members (Institution of Civil Engineers) (UK) *481*
I C E S Oceanographic Data Lists *see* I C E S Oceanographic Data Lists and Inventories *406*
I C E S Oceanographic Data Lists and Inventories (DK ISSN 0106-6935) *406*
I C E Supplement. Serie C (BE ISSN 0067-5628) *256*
I C E V H Educator (International Council for Education of the Visually Handicapped) (GW) *444*
I C E Yearbook *see* I C E List of Members *481*
I C H E International Commission on Human Ecology (US) *72, 167*
I C H P E R Congress Proceedings (International Council on Health, Physical Education and Recreation) (US) *762, 886*
I C H P E R Congress Reports *see* I C H P E R Congress Proceedings *762*
I C I A Membership Directory (International Communications Industries Association, Inc.) (US) *447*
I C I A S F Record *see* International Congress on Instrumentation in Aerospace Simulation Facilities. Record *20*
I C J C Newsletter (International Council of Jews from Czechoslovakia) (UK) *503*
I C L A R M Bibliographies (International Center for Living Aquatic Resources Management) (PH ISSN 0115-5997) *514*
I C L A R M Conference Proceedings. (International Center for Living Aquatic Resources Management) (PH ISSN 0115-4435) *175, 510*
I C L A R M Studies and Reviews (International Center for Living Aquatic Resources Management) (PH ISSN 0115-4389) *510*
I C L A R M Technical Reports (International Center for Living Aquatic Resources Management) (PH ISSN 0115-5547) *510*
I C L A R M Translations (International Center for Living Aquatic Resources Management) (PH ISSN 0115-4141) *510*
I C M E News (International Committee for Museums of Ethnography) (UK ISSN 0253-4894) *544, 916*
I C Master (US) *454*
I C N-U C L A Symposium on Molecular Biology Proceedings *see* U C L A Symposium on Molecular Biology Proceedings *163*
I.C.R. Scientific Report (US) *167, 775*
I C R W Occasional Paper Series (International Center for Research on Women) (US) *1129*
I C S D *see* International Conference on Conduction and Breakdown in Solid Dielectrics. Proceedings *455*
I C S S R Journal of Abstracts and Reviews *see* I C S S R Journal of Abstracts and Reviews: Sociology & Social Anthropology *79*
I C S S R Journal of Abstracts and Reviews: Geography (Indian Council of Social Science Research) (II ISSN 0250-9687) *551*
I C S S R Journal of Abstracts and Reviews: Sociology & Social Anthropology (Indian Council of Social Science Research) (II) *7, 79, 1031*
I C S S R Union Catalogue of Social Science Periodicals/Serials *see* Union Catalogue of Social Science Periodicals/Serials *1014*

I C T A Directory (Institute of Certified Travel Agents) (US) *1111*
I C T A Roster *see* I C T A Directory *1111*
I C T C Review (International Co-operative Training Centre) (UK) *238, 436*
I C U I S Abstract Service *see* I C U I S Justice Ministries *975*
I C U I S Justice Ministries (Institute on the Church in Urban Industrial Society) (US ISSN 0161-6072) *7, 912, 975*
I C Update Master *see* I C Master *454*
I C Y R A/N A Directory (Intercollegiate Yacht Racing Association of North America) (US) *1042*
I D Checking Guide (Year) (US) *370*
I D E A Industry Directory (International Dance-Exercise Association) (US) *309, 886*
I D E A Monographs (Institute for Development of Educational Activities, Inc.) (US ISSN 0073-8697) *414*
I D E A Occasional Papers (Institute for Development of Educational Activities, Inc.) (US ISSN 0073-8700) *414*
I D E E S (Innovations, Demarches, Experiences dans l'Enseignement Superieur) (CN ISSN 0382-0769) *436*
I.D.E. Occasional Papers Series (Institute of Developing Economies) (JA ISSN 0537-9202) *195, 289*
I D E S T *see* Index Documentation-Economie-Science-Technique *210*
I.D.E. Symposium Proceedings (JA) *262*
I D G-Bulletin (Information and Documentation Centre for the Geography of the Netherlands) (NE) *544*
I D Handbook of Foodservice Distribution (Institutional Distribution) (US ISSN 0731-518X) *309, 519*
I D - Informationsdienst fuer die Personalabteilung (GW ISSN 0173-0665) *280*
I D Mini-File *see* Contract Interior's Catalogue *643*
I E C Catalogue of Publications (International Electrotechnical Commission) (SZ) *461*
I E C E C *see* Intersociety Energy Conversion Conference. Proceedings *897*
I E C O N: International Conference on Industrial Electronics, Control and Instrumentation. Proceedings (US) *637*
I E E Conference Publication Series (Institution of Electrical Engineers) (UK ISSN 0537-9989) *454*
I E E E/A E S S Dayton Chapter Symposium (US) *19*
I E E E/A E S-S Seminar *see* I E E E/A E S S Dayton Chapter Symposium *19*
I E E E/A E S S Symposium (Proceedings) *see* I E E E/A E S S Dayton Chapter Symposium *19*
I E E E/A I A A Digital Avionics Systems Conference. Proceedings (US) *19*
I E E E Aerospace Applications Conference. Digest (US) *19*
I E E E Antennas and Propagation Society. International Symposium Digest *see* Antennas and Propagation *450*
I E E E Applied Power Electronics Conference and Exposition. Conference Proceedings. (US) *454*
I E E E/C H M T International Electronic Manufacturing Technology Symposium *see* I E E E International Electronic Manufacturing Technology Symposium *454*
I E E E Cement Industry Technical Conference. Record (US) *184*
I E E E Computer Society Conference on Ada Applications and Environments (US) *358*

I E E E Computer Society Conference on Computer Vision and Pattern Recognition. Proceedings (Institute of Electrical and Electronics Engineers, Inc.) (US) 356

I E E E Computer Society Conference on Pattern Recognition and Image Processing. P R I P. Proceedings see I E E E Computer Society Conference on Computer Vision and Pattern Recognition. Proceedings 356

I E E E Computer Society Workshop on Computer Architecture for Pattern Analysis and Image Database Management. Proceedings (US) 356

I E E E Computer Society Workshop on Visual Languages (US) 709

I E E E Computer Society's. International Computer Software & Applications Conference. Proceedings see C O M P S A C 362

I E E E Conference on Decision and Control. Proceedings (US) 1069

I E E E Conference on Decision and Control, Including the Symposium on Adaptive Processes. Proceedings see I E E E Conference on Decision and Control. Proceedings 1069

I E E E Conference on Human Factors and Nuclear Safety. Conference Record. (US) 454, 896, 954

I E E E Conference on Human Factors and Power Plants see I E E E Conference on Human Factors and Nuclear Safety. Conference Record 896

I E E E Conference on U S Technology Policy. Proceedings see Conference on U S Technology Policy. Proceedings 1068

I E E E Custom Integrated Circuits Conference. Proceedings (US) 454

I E E E/E A S C O N. Electronics and Aerospace Conference. (Record) (US) 19, 454

I E E E ElectroTechnology Review (US ISSN 0748-9196) 454

I E E E Engineering in Medicine and Biology Society. Annual Conference. Proceedings see Frontiers of Engineering and Computing in Health Care 778

I E E E Frontiers of Computers in Medicine see Frontiers of Engineering and Computing in Health Care 778

I E E E Frontiers of Engineering in Health Care see Frontiers of Engineering and Computing in Health Care 778

I E E E Global Telecommunications Conference. Conference Record (US) 343

I E E E Holm Conference on Electric Contact Phenomena. Proceedings see Electrical Contacts 1152

I E E E Holm Conference on Electrical Contacts. Proceedings. see Electrical Contacts 1152

I E E E/I E C O N. Proceedings. see I E C O N: International Conference on Industrial Electronics, Control and Instrumentation. Proceedings 637

I E E E Industrial Electronics Society Conference see I E C O N: International Conference on Industrial Electronics, Control and Instrumentation. Proceedings 637

I E E E Infocom. Proceedings (US) 346

I E E E Instrumentation and Measurement Technology Conference. Proceedings. (US) 637, 809

I E E E International Automatic Testing Conference see Autotestcon 451

I E E E International Conference on Acoustics, Speech and Signal Processing. Proceedings (US) 454

I E E E International Conference on Acoustics, Speech and Signal Processing. Record see I E E E International Conference on Acoustics, Speech and Signal Processing. Proceedings 454

I E E E International Conference on Circuits and Computers. I C C C Proceedings see I E E E International Conference on Computer-Aided Design. Proceedings 356

I E E E International Conference on Circuits and Computers. I C C C Proceedings see I E E E International Conference on Computer Design. V L S I in Computers. Proceedings 356

I E E E International Conference on Communications. Conference Record(US ISSN 0536-1486) 343

I E E E International Conference on Computer-Aided Design. Proceedings(US) 356

I E E E International Conference on Computer Design. V L S I in Computers. Proceedings (US) 356

I E E E International Conference on Consumer Electronics. Digest of Technical Papers (US) 454

I E E E International Conference on Engineering in the Ocean Environment. Record see Oceans. Conference Record 473

I E E E International Conference on Plasma Science. I E E E Conference Record-Abstracts (US ISSN 0730-9244) 454

I E E E International Conference on Robotics and Automation. Proceedings (US) 355, 355

I E E E International Conference on Systems, Man, and Cybernetics. Proceedings (US) 359

I E E E International Electronic Manufacturing Technology Symposium (US) 454, 489

I E E E International Pulsed Power Conference. Digest of Technical Papers see I E E E Pulsed Power Conference. Digest of Technical Papers 471

I E E E International Pulsed Power Conference. Proceedings see I E E E Pulsed Power Conference. Digest of Technical Papers 471

I E E E International Solid State Circuits Conference. Digest of Technical Papers (US ISSN 0193-6530) 454

I E E E International Symposium on Circuit Theory. Symposium Digest. Summaries of Papers see I E E E International Symposium on Circuits and Systems. Proceedings 454

I E E E International Symposium on Circuits and Systems. Proceedings (US ISSN 0277-674X) 454

I E E E International Symposium on Electrical Insulation. I E E E Conference Record (US) 454

I E E E International Symposium on Electromagnetic Compatibility. (Record) (US) 454

I E E E International Symposium on Information Theory. Abstracts of Papers (US ISSN 0271-4655) 361

I E E E/M T T - S International Microwave Symposium. Digest (US ISSN 0149-645X) 454

I E E E/M T T - S International Microwave Symposium. Digest of Technical Papers see I E E E/M T T - S International Microwave Symposium. Digest 454

I E E E Microwave and Millimeter-Wave Monolithic Circuits Symposium. Digest of Papers (US) 455

I E E E Military Communications Conference. Conference Record (US) 455

I E E E Military Communications Conference. Proceedings see I E E E Military Communications Conference. Conference Record 455

I E E E National Aerospace and Electronics Conference. Proceedings (US ISSN 0547-3578) 19

I E E E National Radar Conference. Proceedings (US) 455

I E E E/O S A Conference on Laser Engineering and Applications. Digest of Technical Papers see Conference on Lasers and Electro-Optics (Publications) 451

I E E E Photovoltaic Specialists Conference. Conference Record (US ISSN 0160-8371) 455

I E E E Position Location and Navigation Symposium. Record (US) 343, 455

I E E E Power Electronics Specialists Conference. Record (US ISSN 0275-9306) 19

I E E E Power Engineering Society. Summer Meeting. Preprints (US) 455

I E E E Power Engineering Society. Winter Meeting. Preprints (US) 455

I E E E Power Processing and Electronics Specialists Conference. Record see I E E E Power Electronics Specialists Conference. Record 19

I E E E Professional Communication Society Conference. Record see International Professional Communication Conference. Conference Record 343

I E E E Pulsed Power Conference. Digest of Technical Papers. (US) 471

I E E E Region 5 Conference. Record (US ISSN 0073-9197) 455

I E E E Southeastcon (Region 3 Conference) Record (Institute of Electrical and Electronics Engineers, Inc.) (US) 455

I E E E Student Papers (Institute of Electrical and Electronics Engineers, Inc.) (US ISSN 0362-4536) 455

I E E E Symposium on Mass Storage Systems. Digest of Papers (US) 238, 286, 352

I E E E Symposium on Security and Privacy. Proceedings (US ISSN 0278-7032) 358, 374

I E E E Trends in Electronics Conference. Proceedings see T E N C O N (I E E E Region 10 Conference). Proceedings 353

I E E E Vehicular Technology Conference. Record (Institute of Electrical and Electronics Engineers, Inc.) (US ISSN 0098-3551) 1092

I E E E Working Conference on Current Measurement. Proceedings (US) 403, 455

I E E E Workshop on Automotive Applications of Electronics (Publication) (US) 1093

I E E E Workshop on Languages for Automation (Proceedings) (US) 355

I E F Information (Institut for Europaeisk Folkelivsforskning) (DK ISSN 0105-0532) 1026

I E M T see I E E E International Electronic Manufacturing Technology Symposium 454

I.E.N.S. Press Handbook see Indian & Eastern Newspaper Society Press Handbook 645

I E S A Information (International Society for Electrosleep and Electroanaesthesia) (AU ISSN 0539-0230) 790

I E S Lighting Handbook (Illuminating Engineering Society) (US ISSN 0073-5469) 455

I E S Proceedings (Institution of Environmental Sciences) (UK ISSN 0260-4833) 496

I F A C Symposium on Multivariable Technical Control Systems. Proceedings (International Federation of Automatic Control) (US) 491

I F A Congress Seminar Series (NE) 296

I F A Seminar Series (International Fiscal Association) (NE) 670

I F C A T I Directory see I T M F Directory 1074

I.F.H.P.M. News see I.F.P.S.M. News 954

I F I Bulletin: Textile Notes (International Fabricare Institute) (US) 1154

I F I P Information Bulletin (International Federation for Information Processing) (SZ) 678

I F L A Annual (International Federation of Library Associations and Institutions) (GW ISSN 0074-5987) 678

I F L A Communications (DK ISSN 0109-5366) 687

I F L A Directory (International Federation of Library Associations and Institutions) (NE ISSN 0074-6002) 678

I F L A Publications (International Federation of Library Associations and Institutions) (GW) 679

I F M R Publications (Institute for Financial Management and Research) (II) 280

I F O Forschungsberichte der Abteilung Entwicklungslaender (GW) 195

I F O Institut fuer Wirtschaftsforschung. Studien zu Handels- und Dienstleistungsfragen (GW ISSN 0170-5695) 195

I F O Institut fuer Wirtschaftsforschung. Studien zu Handelsfragen see I F O Institut fuer Wirtschaftsforschung. Studien zu Handels- und Dienstleistungsfragen 195

I F O Mitteilungen der Abteilung Entwicklungslaender (GW) 262

I F O Mitteilungen: Entwicklungslaender - Afrika Studienstelle see I F O Mitteilungen der Abteilung Entwicklungslaender 262

I F O S A. Minutes of the General Meeting (International Federation of Stationers' Associations) (SZ) 286

I F O Spiegel der Wirtschaft (GW ISSN 0170-3617) 245

I F O Studien zur Entwicklungsforschung (GW) 195

I F P R I Research Report (International Food Policy Research Institute) (US) 47

I.F.P.S.M. News (International Federation for Preventive and Social Medicine) (IT) 954

I F T Basic Symposium Series (Institute of Food Technologists) (US ISSN 0730-9198) 519, 846

I F T World Directory and Buyers' Guide (Institute of Food Technologists) (US ISSN 0073-9286) 1154

I F U (Institut fuer Umformtechnik) (US) 1069

I F U Annual Report (Industrialiserings Fonden for Udviklingslandene) (DK ISSN 0901-6171) 262

I F U's Participation in Joint Ventures see I F U Annual Report 262

I G A R S S see International Geoscience and Remote Sensing Symposium Digest 456

I G E News (International Guiding Eyes) (US) 180, 868

I.G.I. see Indian Geological Index 382

I I A S A Annual Report (International Institute for Applied Systems Analysis) (AU) 358

I I A S Occasional Papers (Indian Institute of Advanced Study) (II) 436, 630

I I C Abstracts see Art and Archaeology Technical Abstracts 113

I I E P Occasional Papers (International Institute for Educational Planning) (UN ISSN 0074-6401) 441

I I E P Research Reports (International Institute for Educational Planning) (UN) 441

I I E P Seminar Papers (International Institute for Educational Planning) (UN) 262, 441

I I M C Bulletin (Indian Institute of Mass Communication) (II) 343

I I R B Winter Congress Proceedings see International Institute for Sugar Beet Research. Reports of the Winter Congress 57

I I R S Occasional Report Series (Institute for Industrial Research and Standards) (IE) 1069

I I T C Directory (Indian International Trade Center) (II ISSN 0073-6546) 256
I J A. Research Reports (Institute of Jewish Affairs) (UK ISSN 0257-6406) 503, 913
I K O Newsletter see Nikhef K Bulletin 889
I L C A Annual Report (International Livestock Centre for Africa) (UN ISSN 0255-0040) 66
I L C A Proceedings (International Livestock Centre for Africa) (UN) 66
I L C A Programme and Budget (International Livestock Centre for Africa) (UN) 66
I L C A Research Report (International Livestock Centre for Africa) (UN) 66
I L P E S Cuadernos (Instituto Latinamericano de Planificacion Economica y Social) (UN) 277, 1026
I L R Paperbacks (New York State School of Industrial and Labor Relations) (US ISSN 0070-0177) 272
I L S I Human Nutrition Reviews (US) 846
I L T A M Technical Reports (IS) 352
I L Z R O Annual Research Review see I L Z R O Annual Review 798
I L Z R O Annual Review (International Lead Zinc Research Organization, Inc.) (US) 323, 328, 496, 798
I L Z R O Environmental Health Research Digest (International Lead Zinc Research Organization, Inc.) (US) 496
I L Z R O Lead Research Digest (International Lead Zinc Research Organization, Inc.) (US ISSN 0146-7980) 323, 328, 798
I L Z R O Zinc/Cadium Research Digest (International Lead Zinc Research Organization, Inc.) (US) 323, 328, 798
I L Z R O Zinc Research Digest see I L Z R O Zinc/Cadium Research Digest 798
I Love New York: The Finger Lakes Travel Guide (US) 1111
I M A C A Directory (US) 553
I M A Volumes in Mathematics and its Applications (US) 749
I M B I S (GW ISSN 0303-4577) 150, 770
I M G-T N O Research Institute for Environmental Hygiene. Annual Report (NE) 496
I M M Abstracts (Institution of Mining and Metallurgy) (UK ISSN 0019-0020) 7, 382, 801, 822
I M S Directory of Publications see Gale Directory of Publications 126
I M S Lecture Notes. Monograph Series (Institute of Mathematical Statistics) (US) 749
I M T C see I E E E Instrumentation and Measurement Technology Conference. Proceedings 637
I N D A Association of the Nonwoven Fabrics Industry. Technical Symposium Papers (US) 1074
I N D E C Communicator (Alberta Teachers' Association, Industrial Education Council) (CN ISSN 0705-1166) 426
I N E S Informations see Institut d'Etudes Slaves Informations 630
I N E T Up-Date (US) 414
I N F A A Rapport (Aabenraa Proevecenter for Ny Informationsteknologi) (DK) 679
I N F A Press and Advertisers Year Book (India News and Feature Alliance) (II ISSN 0073-4284) 463
I N F O C O M Proceedings see I E E E Infocom. Proceedings 346
I N I R E B Informa (Instituto Nacional de Investigaciones sobre Recursos Bioticos) (MX ISSN 0185-0369) 141
I N I S Atomindex (UN ISSN 0004-7139) 7, 893
I N I S Reference Series (UN) 679, 896

I N R S Lettre d'Information sur la Recherche (Institut National de Recherche et de Securite pour la Prevention des Accidents du Travail et des Maladies Professionnelles) (FR) 635
I N S D O C Union Catalogue Series (Indian National Scientific Documentation Centre) (II ISSN 0073-6627) 127
I N T E L E C see International Telecommunications Energy Conference. Proceedings 348
I N T V Census (Association of Independent Television Stations, Inc.) (US) 348
I N U F A: Internationaler Nutzfahrzeug-Katalog/International Catalogue for Commercial Vehicles see I N U F A Katalog 1105
I N U F A Katalog (SZ) 1105
I O C C/I S C M A see International Office of Cocoa and Chocolate and the International Sugar Confectionary Manufacturers' Association. Annual Statistical Bulletin 522
I.O. Evans Studies in the Philosophy & Criticism of Literature (US ISSN 0271-9061) 723
I O I Occasional Papers see International Ocean Institute. Occasional Papers 406
I O L R Collected Reports (Israel Oceanographic and Limnological Research Ltd.) (IS ISSN 0333-5194) 1124
I P A Conference Report (UK ISSN 0074-7416) 333
I P A - Forschung und Praxis (Fraunhofer-Institute fuer Produktionstechnik und Automatisierung) (US) 471
I P C C see International Professional Communication Conference. Conference Record 343
I P C Monographs (Institute of Philippine Culture) (PH ISSN 0073-9537) 1026
I P C Papers (Institute of Philippine Culture) (PH ISSN 0073-9545) 1026
I P C Poverty Research Series (Institute of Philippine Culture) (PH) 1018, 1027
I P C R Accelerator Progress Report see Riken. Accelerator Progress Report 898
I P C R Cyclotron Report see Riken. Cyclotron Report 898
I P D Working Papers (Interuniversity Programme in Demography) (BE) 927
I P E A Estudos para o Planejamento (Instituto de Planejamento Economico e Social) (BL) 289
I P E A Relatorios de Pesquisa (Instituto de Planejamento Economico e Social) (BL) 1027
I P E A Serie Monografica (Instituto de Planejamento Economico e Social) (BL) 289
I P E A Serie P N P E (Instituto de Planejamento Economico e Social, Programa Nacional de Pequisa Economico) (BL) 195
I P E A Serie Pensamento Economico Brasileiro (Instituto de Planejamento Economico e Social) (BL) 195
I P F C Proceedings (Indo-Pacific Fishery Commission) (UN) 510
I P I Bulletin (International Potash Institute) (SZ) 56
I P I Research Topics (International Potash Institute) (SZ) 56
I P M Catalogue of Picture Postcards & Year Book (UK) 614
I P P F Annual Report (International Planned Parenthood Federation) (UK) 179
I P P F in Action see I P P F Annual Report 179
I P R A Studies in Peace Research (International Peace Research Association) (GW ISSN 0074-7289) 1154
I P Z Information. Reihe S: Subversion (Institut fuer Politologische Zeitfragen) (SZ) 905
I-Punkt (GW) 272

I.Q.S. (Instituto Quimico de Sarria) (SP ISSN 0210-508X) 323
I.R.C.A. Foreign Log (International Radio Club of America) (US ISSN 0093-1926) 348
I R C Special Publication (Indian Roads Congress) (II) 1096
I R R I. Research Highlights (International Rice Research Institute) (PH ISSN 0115-1142) 63
I R R I Annual Report (International Rice Research Institute) (PH ISSN 0074-7793) 63
I R R I Research Paper Series (International Rice Research Institute) (PH ISSN 0115-3862) 63
I R S A Items (International Rural Sociology Association) (AT) 1027
I R T S Gold Medal Annual (International Radio and Television Society, Inc.) (US ISSN 0074-7564) 348
I R T S Gold Medal Journal see I R T S Gold Medal Annual 348
I S A A Architect Directory see Building Index 1149
I S A Aerospace Instrumentation Symposium. Proceedings see Instrumentation in the Aerospace Industry 19
I S A Aerospace Instrumentation Symposium. Proceedings see Advancement in Test Measurement. Proceedings 485
I S A Directory of Instrumentation (US ISSN 0272-8141) 637
I S A Mining and Metallurgy Instrumentation Symposium. Proceedings see Instrumentation in the Mining and Metallurgy Industries 798
I S A Transducer Compendium see I S A Directory of Instrumentation 637
I S Annual (Inter-School Christian Fellowship) (UK ISSN 0261-1325) 978
I S B N Review (International Standard Book Number) (GW ISSN 0342-4634) 679, 962
I S E C Monograph (Institute for Social and Economic Change) (II) 245
I S E G R Occasional Papers see I S E R Occasional Papers 1008
I S E G R Research Notes see I S E R Research Notes 195
I S E R Occasional Papers (Institute of Social and Economic Research) (US) 245, 1008
I S E R Research Notes (Institute of Social and Economic Research) (US) 195, 1008
I S H I Occasional Papers in Social Change (Institute for the Study of Human Issues) (US) 905, 1027
I S I Atlas of Science see I S I Atlas of Science: Vol. 1: Biochemistry and Molecular Biology 1154
I S I Atlas of Science see I S I Atlas of Science: Vol. 2: Biotechnology and Molecular Genetics 1154
I S I Atlas of Science: Vol. 1: Biochemistry and Molecular Biology (Institute for Scientific Information) (US) 1154
I S I Atlas of Science: Vol. 2: Biotechnology and Molecular Genetics (Institute for Scientific Information) (US) 1154
I S I Journal Citation Reports see Science Citation Index Journal Citation Report 999
I S I Journal Citation Reports see Social Sciences Citation Index Journal Citation Reports 1014
I S I R I Yearbook (Institute of Standards and Industrial Research of Iran) (IR) 809
I S I's Who Is Publishing in Science see Current Contents Address Directory-Science & Technology 990
I S M A Occasional Papers (Institute for the Study of Man in Africa) (SA ISSN 0073-893X) 72
I S M A Papers (Institute for the Study of Man in Africa) (SA ISSN 0073-8921) 72

I S M A Technical Conference. Proceedings (International Superphosphate Manufacturers Association, Ltd.) (FR) 56
I S O Catalogue (International Organization for Standardization) (SZ ISSN 0303-3309) 809
I S O Information see Organ Building Periodical 840
I S O International Standards (International Organization for Standardization) (SZ) 809
I S O Memento (International Organization for Standardization) (SZ ISSN 0536-2067) 809
I S R see Index to Scientific Reviews 1004
I S S L S see International Symposium on Subscriber Loop and Services. Proceedings 456
I S T P M Rapports Techniques (Institut Scientifique et Technique des Peches Maritimes) (FR ISSN 0750-8743) 1154
I S U Constitution (International Skating Union) (SZ) 1033
I S U Regulations (International Skating Union) (SZ) 1034
I T C C Review (International Technical Cooperation Centre) (IS ISSN 0047-1216) 262
I T C-U N E S C O International Seminar. Proceedings (NE) 1154
I T E M (Interference Technology Engineers Master) (US ISSN 0190-0943) 455
I T M F Directory (International Textile Manufacturers Federation) (SZ) 1074
I T M Yearbook (Institute of Travel Managers) (UK) 1111
I U A E S Commission on Urgent Anthropological Research. Newsletter (AU) 72
I U C N Annual Report (International Union for Conservation of Nature and Natural Resources) (SZ) 365
I U C N Yearbook see I U C N Annual Report 365
I U I Yearbook (Industriens Utredningsinstitut) (FI) 195
I U P Stress and Health Series (International Universities Press, Inc.) (US) 790
I U S S P Papers/U I E S P Documents de l'Union (International Union for the Scientific Study of Population) (BE) 179, 922
I U S Y Bulletin (International Union of Socialist Youth) (AU) 905
I U S Y Survey see I U S Y Bulletin 905
I W F A Yearbook (International Women's Fishing Association) (US) 1045, 1129
I W G I A Boletin (International Work Group for Indigenous Affairs) (DK ISSN 0107-556X) 72
I W G I A Documento see I W G I A Documents 72
I W G I A Documents (International Work Group for Indigenous Affairs) (DK ISSN 0105-4503) 72, 503, 913
I W G I A Newsletter (International Work Group for Indigenous Affairs) (DK ISSN 0105-6387) 72, 503, 913
I W S A Year Book (International Water Supply Association) (UK) 309
I'anson Times (UK) 536
Ibadan Social Sciences Series (NR) 1008
Ibaraki University. Faculty of Science. Bulletin. Series A: Mathematics (JA) 749
Ibero-American Bureau of Education. Information and Publications Department Series V: Technical Seminars and Meetings (SP ISSN 0536-2512) 414
Iberoamericana Pragensia (CS) 606
Ibidem: Glendon College Student Handbook (CN) 195
Ibsen Aarboken/Ibsen Yearbook (NO ISSN 0073-4365) 586, 723
Ibsen Yearbook see Ibsen Aarboken 723
ICarbS (US ISSN 0360-8409) 679

Ice Hockey Rule Book (US ISSN 0732-8117) *1034*
Iceland. Landsbokasafn Islands. Arbok *see* Iceland. Landsbokasafn Islands. Arbok. Nyr Flokkur *679*
Iceland. Landsbokasafn Islands. Arbok *see* Islensk Bokaskra *688*
Iceland. Landsbokasafn Islands. Arbok. Nyr Flokkur (IC) *679*
Icelandic National Bibliography *see* Islensk Bokaskra *688*
Ichthyologia *see* Acta Biologica Iugoslavica. Serija E: Ichthyologia *172*
Icon. Cahier (BE) *723*
Icon Newsletter (US) *358, 363*
Icon-Werkgroep Jean Ray. Cahier *see* Icon. Cahier *723*
Icones Plantarum Africanarum (SG ISSN 0073-4403) *157*
Iconographia Ecclesiae Orientalis (GW ISSN 0341-8448) *1154*
Iconography of Religions (NE) *970*
Idaho. Bureau of Mines and Geology. Bulletin *see* Idaho. Geological Survey. Bulletin *817*
Idaho. Bureau of Mines and Geology. Information Circular *see* Idaho. Geological Survey. Information Circular *817*
Idaho. Department of Employment. Annual Planning Report (US) *272*
Idaho. Department of Employment. Annual Rural Employment Report (US) *1155*
Idaho. Department of Employment. Annual Rural Manpower Report *see* Idaho. Department of Employment. Annual Rural Employment Report *1155*
Idaho. Department of Fish and Game. Federal Aid Investigation Projects. Progress Reports and Publications (US ISSN 0073-4527) *365, 510*
Idaho. Department of Health and Welfare. Annual Summary of Vital Statistics (US ISSN 0362-9279) *958, 1023, 1057*
Idaho. Department of Labor and Industrial Services. Annual Report (US ISSN 0362-3912) *272*
Idaho. Geological Survey. Bulletin (US ISSN 0734-3825) *389, 817*
Idaho. Geological Survey. Information Circular (US) *389, 817*
Idaho. Geological Survey. Open-File Report *see* Idaho. Geological Survey. Technical Report *389*
Idaho. Geological Survey. Technical Report (US) *389*
Idaho (Moscow) (US ISSN 0160-5305) *105, 723*
Idaho. State Board for Vocational Education. Annual Descriptive Report of Program Activities for Vocational Education (US ISSN 0091-5882) *426*
Idaho. State Superintendent of Public Instruction. Annual Report. State of Idaho Johnson-O'Malley Program (US ISSN 0093-7223) *414, 503*
Idaho Agricultural Statistics. (US ISSN 0094-1271) *41*
Idaho Education Association. Proceedings (US ISSN 0073-4497) *414*
Idaho Educational Directory (US) *429*
Idaho, Montana, Wyoming TourBook *see* Tourbook: Idaho, Montana, Wyoming *1117*
Idaho Museum of Natural History. Occasional Papers (US ISSN 0196-7703) *992*
Idaho Museum of Natural History. Special Publication (US) *827*
Idaho Occupation Wage Survey (US) *245*
Idaho State University Museum. Occasional Papers *see* Idaho Museum of Natural History. Occasional Papers *992*
Ideas (II ISSN 0301-9101) *606*
Ideas and Ideologies (UK) *878*
Ideas y Valores (CK ISSN 0019-140X) *878*
Ideasworth (US) *15*
Idegenforgalmi Statisztika *see* Hungary. Kozponti Statisztikai Hivatal. Idegenforgalmi Evkonyv *1119*

Identification Leaflets for Diseases and Parasites of Fish and Shellfish *see* Fiches d'Identification des Maladies et Parasites des Poissons, Crustaces et Mollusques *174*
Identified Sources of Supply (US) *809*
Ideologia y Politica (PE) *905*
Idesia (CL ISSN 0073-4675) *28*
Idioms and Phrases Index (US) *696*
Idraetshistorisk Aarbog (DK ISSN 0900-8632) *1034*
Idraettens Forskningsraad. Forskningsoversigt (DK ISSN 0900-7008) *1034*
Idrijski Razgledi (YU ISSN 0019-1523) *540*
Idryma Meleton Chersonesou Aimou. Ekthoseis *see* Institute for Balkan Studies. Publications *586*
Ife Journal of Agriculture (NR) *28*
IG-TNO Research Institute for Environmental Hygiene. Annual Report *see* I M G-T N O Research Institute for Environmental Hygiene. Annual Report *496*
Igakushi Kenkyu *see* Studies on History of Medicine *767*
Igbo Philosophy (NR) *72*
Igra (IS) *723*
Iheringia. Serie Antropologia (BL ISSN 0073-4691) *72*
Iheringia. Serie Botanica (BL ISSN 0073-4705) *158*
Iheringia. Serie Geologia (BL ISSN 0073-4713) *389*
Iheringia. Serie Miscelanea (BL) *158, 175*
Iheringia. Serie Zoologia (BL ISSN 0073-4721) *175*
Ihsa'iyah-i Amual-i Sadirati-i Afghanistan *see* Export Statistics of Afghanistan *207*
Ihsa'iyah-i Amual-i Varidati-i Afghanistan *see* Imports Statistics of Afghanistan *210*
Ijo Tenko Hokoku (JA) *805*
Ikonenkalender (GW) *105*
Illinois. Administrative Office of Illinois Courts. Annual Report to the Supreme Court of Illinois (US ISSN 0536-3713) *657*
Illinois. Board of Higher Education. Directory of Higher Education (US ISSN 0094-8322) *436*
Illinois. Board of Higher Education. Statewide Space Survey (US ISSN 0362-5524) *436*
Illinois. Department of Mental Health. Administrator's Data Manual *see* Mental Health Statistics for Illinois *1019*
Illinois. Department of Public Instruction. Annual State of Education Message *see* Illinois. State Board of Education. Annual Report *414*
Illinois. Division of Air Pollution Control. Annual Air Quality Report (US) *496*
Illinois. Housing Development Authority. Annual Report (US ISSN 0090-3248) *623*
Illinois. Junior College Board. Annual Report *see* Illinois Community College Board. Biennial Report *436*
Illinois. Natural History Survey. Biological Notes (US ISSN 0073-490X) *141*
Illinois. Natural History Survey. Bulletin (US ISSN 0073-4918) *992*
Illinois. Natural History Survey. Circular (US ISSN 0073-4926) *992*
Illinois. State Board of Education. Annual Report (US ISSN 0147-2860) *414*
Illinois. State Geological Survey. Bulletins (US ISSN 0073-5051) *389*
Illinois. State Geological Survey. Circulars (US ISSN 0073-506X) *389*
Illinois. State Geological Survey. Educational Series (US ISSN 0073-5078) *389*
Illinois. State Geological Survey. Environmental Geology Notes (US ISSN 0073-5086) *389*
Illinois. State Geological Survey. Guidebook Series (US ISSN 0073-5094) *389*

Illinois. State Geological Survey. Industrial Mineral Notes *see* Illinois Minerals Notes *817*
Illinois. State Geological Survey. Mineral Economic Briefs *see* Illinois Minerals Notes *817*
Illinois. State Museum. Guidebooklet Series (US ISSN 0162-1939) *992*
Illinois. State Museum. Handbook of Collections (US ISSN 0445-3387) *106*
Illinois. State Museum. Inventory of the Collections (US ISSN 0095-2893) *992*
Illinois. State Museum. Popular Science Series (US ISSN 0360-0297) *992*
Illinois. State Museum. Reports of Investigations (US ISSN 0360-0270) *87*
Illinois. State Museum. Research Series. Papers in Anthropology (US ISSN 0095-2915) *72*
Illinois. State Museum. Scientific Papers Series (US ISSN 0445-3395) *87, 141, 606, 992*
Illinois. State Museum. Story of Illinois Series (US ISSN 0360-0289) *606*
Illinois Air Quality Report *see* Illinois. Division of Air Pollution Control. Annual Air Quality Report *496*
Illinois Air Sampling Network Report *see* Illinois. Division of Air Pollution Control. Annual Air Quality Report *496*
Illinois Attorney General's Report and Opinions (US) *657*
Illinois Biological Monographs (US ISSN 0073-4748) *141*
Illinois Classical Studies (US ISSN 0363-1923) *337*
Illinois Community College Board. Biennial Report (US) *436*
Illinois Dealer Directory and Buyer's Guide (US) *184*
Illinois Directory and Suppliers Listing *see* Illinois Dealer Directory and Buyer's Guide *184*
Illinois Government. *see* Illinois Government Research *942*
Illinois Government Research (US ISSN 0195-7783) *905, 942*
Illinois Health Sciences Libraries Serials Holdings List (US ISSN 0148-0650) *1155*
Illinois, Indiana, Ohio, TourBook *see* Tourbook: Illinois, Indiana, Ohio *1117*
Illinois Labor History Society Reporter (US ISSN 0085-1728) *848*
Illinois Manufacturers Directory (US ISSN 0160-3302) *309*
Illinois Minerals Notes (US ISSN 0094-9442) *389, 817*
Illinois Mining Institute. Proceedings (US) *817*
Illinois Petroleum (US) *389, 864*
Illinois Property Tax Statistics (US) *296*
Illinois Services Directory (US ISSN 0092-3818) *309*
Illinois Speech and Theatre Association. Journal (US) *447, 1077*
Illinois State and Regional Economic Data Book (US ISSN 0093-9552) *245*
Illinois State Bar Association. Legislative Bulletin (US) *657*
Illinois State Industrial Directory *see* MacRae's Illinois State Industrial Directory *312*
Illinois Studies in Anthropology (US ISSN 0073-5167) *72*
Illinois Travel and Recreation Guide (US) *1111*
Illuminating Engineering Society Lighting Handbook *see* I E S Lighting Handbook *455*
Illustrated Buyers Guide to Exhibits (US ISSN 0739-6821) *15, 284, 301*
Illustrated Guide to the Protozoa (US) *175*
Illustration in Japan (JA) *106*
Illustrators: The Annual of American Illustration (US ISSN 0073-5477) *1155*
Illustrierte Historische Hefte (GE) *558*
Ilmi A'ino (PK) *964*

Ilmu Alam (MY ISSN 0126-7000) *544*
Ilocos Review (PH ISSN 0019-2538) *573, 723*
Image Magazine (US ISSN 0748-1780) *723*
Image of Woman (US) *1129*
Image Understanding (US ISSN 0748-0059) *355*
Imagem do Brasil e da America Latina *see* Banas *223*
Imagen U.C.V. (Universidad Catolica de Valparaiso) (CL) *1155*
Images de la Chimie (FR) *323*
Imago Mvndi (UK ISSN 0308-5694) *544*
Imago Musicae (US) *606, 836*
Immenstaader Heimatblaetter (GW) *515, 586*
Immer Gruen (GW) *979*
Immigrant Communities & Ethnic Minorities in the United States & Canada (US ISSN 0749-5951) *503, 922*
Immigration and Nationality Law Review (US ISSN 0149-9807) *657, 922*
Immigration Law Reporter (CN) *657, 922*
Immunology Abstracts (US ISSN 0307-112X) *7, 770*
Immunology: An International Series of Monographs and Treatises (US ISSN 0092-6019) *168*
Impact (New York, 1983) (US ISSN 0882-6277) *119*
Impact (Year) (US ISSN 0749-1573) *28*
Impact American Beer Market Review and Forecast (US ISSN 0198-9952) *119*
Impact American Distilled Spirits Market Review and Forecast (US ISSN 0163-9536) *119*
Impact of the Negro Traveler *see* Economic Impact of the Negro Traveler *1108*
Impact of Travel on State Economies (US ISSN 0730-9813) *1111*
Impact the American Wine Market Review and Forecast (US ISSN 0163-9544) *119*
Impact Yearbook (US ISSN 0749-7946) *119, 309*
Imperial Cancer Research Fund. Scientific Report (UK) *775*
Imperial College of Science and Technology Annual Report *see* I C C E T Annual Report *496*
Imperialism: Events, Facts, Documents (UR) *711*
Import/Export Wood Purchasing Guide *see* Importing Wood Purchasing Guide *530*
Import Statistical Schedule of Japan (Year) (JA) *256*
Import Trade Control: Handbook of Rules and Procedures (II ISSN 0536-9983) *256*
Import Trade Control Policy (II ISSN 0536-9061) *256*
Importers and Exporters Trade Promotion Guide (US ISSN 0073-5604) *256*
Importfile (CN ISSN 0383-6304) *256*
Importing Wood Purchasing Guide (US) *256, 530*
Imports of the Republic of China (CH) *256*
Imports Statistics of Afghanistan/ Ihsa'iyah-i Amual-i Varidati-i Afghanistan (AF) *210, 1057*
Imprimatur. Neue Folge (GW) *931*
Imprimatur; Jahrbuch fuer Buecherfreunde. Neue Folge *see* Imprimatur. Neue Folge *931*
Imprints on the Sands of Marquette County (US) *606*
Improving Urban Mobility *see* Directory of Research, Development and Demonstration Projects *1081*
Impulse aus Wissenschaft und Forschung (AU) *992*
Impulstechniken (GW) *1155*
In Common (US ISSN 0363-5058) *970*
In Defense of the Alien (US ISSN 0275-634X) *922*

In Gang Fun Arbet: Yidish Un Mizrakh Eyropeishe Yidishe Shtudies *see* Working Papers in Yiddish and East European Jewish Studies 506
In Search of the Guibord-Chopp Family(US) 536
In Terris (PE ISSN 0300-4031) 741
In the Life (US) 616, 1129
In the Making (UK ISSN 0309-3298) 238, 1027
In Theory Only (US ISSN 0360-4365) 836
Incentive Travel International *see* Directory of Incentive Travel International 1107
Incentives for Better Books in Pakistan *see* Literary Prizes in Pakistan 726
Incidenca Raka v Sloveniji/Cancer Incidence in Slovenia (YU ISSN 0079-9580) 775
Income, Employment, Estate and Gift Tax Provisions: Internal Revenue Code (US) 296
Income, Estate and Gift Tax Provisions: Internal Revenue Code *see* Income, Employment, Estate and Gift Tax Provisions: Internal Revenue Code 296
Income-Expense Analysis. Apartments, Condominiums and Cooperatives *see* Expense Analysis: Condominiums, Cooperatives and Planned Unit Developments 965
Income-Expense Analysis: Apartments *see* Income-Expense Analysis: Conventional Apartments 965
Income-Expense Analysis: Conventional Apartments (US ISSN 0194-1941) 184, 965
Income-Expense Analysis: Office Buildings, Downtown and Suburban (US) 965
Income-Expense Analysis: Suburban Office Buildings *see* Income-Expense Analysis: Office Buildings, Downtown and Suburban 965
Income in Sales/Marketing Management (US) 272, 284
Income Stocks (US) 266
Incompatex (FR) 871
Inconscio e Cultura (IT) 934
Incontri Linguistici (IT) 696
Incorporated Brewers Guild Directory (UK) 119
Incorporated Law Society of Sri Lanka. Annual Report (CE ISSN 0073-5728) 657
Incorporated Law Society of Sri Lanka. Journal (CE ISSN 0073-5736) 657
Incorporated Society of Musicians Handbook *see* Incorporated Society of Musicians Yearbook 836
Incorporated Society of Musicians Yearbook (UK) 836
Incorporated Society of Organ Builders. Journal (UK ISSN 0073-5744) 836
Incunabula Graeca (IT ISSN 0073-5752) 337
Indagini e Prospettive (IT) 723, 905, 1027
Indeks Madjalah Ilmiah *see* Index of Indonesian Learned Periodicals 127
Indeks Majalah Malaysia *see* Malaysian Periodicals Index 9
Indeks Persidangan Malaysia *see* Index to Malaysian Conferences 7
Indeks Suratkhabar Malaysia/Malaysian Newspaper Index (MY ISSN 0126-9062) 7
Independent (Washington) (US) 522
Independent Bakers Association Newsletter (US) 522
Independent Broadcasting Authority. Annual Report and Accounts (UK ISSN 0309-0175) 348
Independent Broadcasting Authority Technical Review *see* I B A Technical Review 348
Independent Higher Education (US ISSN 0734-6735) 436
Independent Journal of Philosophy/Revue Independante de Philosophie (FR ISSN 0378-4789) 878
Independent Phonefacts *see* Phonefacts 350
Independent Schools Association of the Southwest. Membership List (US ISSN 0073-5779) 430

Independent Schools Yearbook: Boys Schools (UK) 443
Independent Schools Yearbook: Girls Schools (UK) 443
Independent Study Catalog: N U C E A's Guide to Independent Study Through Correspondence Instruction (US ISSN 0733-6020) 430
Index *see* Index Chemicus 325
Index (US) 354
Index and Directory of U.S. Industry Standards (US ISSN 0197-3401) 471, 809
Index Asia Series in Humanities (II) 7, 634
Index Chemicus (US ISSN 0891-6055) 7, 325
Index de References: Inventaire des Stations Hydrometriques (CN) 403, 1124
Index der Rechtsmittelentscheidungen und des Schrifttums (AU) 657
Index des Projects en Developpment sur l'Ecologie des Zones Arides *see* Indice de Proyectos en Desarrollo en Ecologia de Zonas Aridas 1155
Index/Directory of Women's Media (US ISSN 0197-3401) 1129, 1130
Index Documentation-Economie-Science-Technique (MR) 7, 210, 1004, 1072
Index Filicum (UK) 141
Index: Foreign Broadcast Information Service Daily Reports: Asia and Pacific (US ISSN 0272-3875) 912, 916
Index: Foreign Broadcast Information Service Daily Reports: China (US ISSN 0271-1761) 912, 916
Index: Foreign Broadcast Information Service Daily Reports: Eastern Europe (US ISSN 0731-4116) 912, 916
Index: Foreign Broadcast Information Service Daily Reports: Latin America(US ISSN 0278-1360) 912, 916
Index: Foreign Broadcast Information Service Daily Reports: Middle East and Africa (US) 912, 916
Index: Foreign Broadcast Information Service Daily Reports: Middle East and North Africa *see* Index: Foreign Broadcast Information Service Daily Reports: Middle East and Africa 912
Index: Foreign Broadcast Information Service Daily Reports: People's Republic of China *see* Index: Foreign Broadcast Information Service Daily Reports: China 912
Index: Foreign Broadcast Information Service Daily Reports: South Asia (US ISSN 0731-3233) 912, 916
Index: Foreign Broadcast Information Service Daily Reports: Soviet Union (US ISSN 0731-3276) 912, 916
Index: Foreign Broadcast Information Service Daily Reports: Sub-Saharan Africa *see* Index: Foreign Broadcast Information Service Daily Reports: South Asia 912
Index: Foreign Broadcast Information Service Daily Reports: Western Europe (US) 912, 916
Index Hepaticarum (GW ISSN 0073-5787) 158
Index India (II ISSN 0019-3844) 7
Index Internationalis Indicus (II) 975, 977
Index Islamicus (UK ISSN 0306-9524) 127
Index Kewensis (UK) 141
Index Medicus (US ISSN 0019-3879) 7, 771
Index Medicus Iugoslavicus *see* Bibliografija Medicinske Periodike Jugoslavije 768
Index Medicus Latinoamericano (BL ISSN 0100-4743) 7, 771
Index Nominum (SZ) 871
Index of American Periodical Verse (US ISSN 0090-9130) 7, 739
Index of Art in the Pacific Northwest (US ISSN 0085-1760) 106
Index of Articles on Jewish Studies/Reshimat Ma'amarim Be-Mada'e Ha-Yahadut (IS ISSN 0073-5817) 7, 975

Index of Current Research in Arid Zones Ecology *see* Indice de Proyectos en Ecologia de Zonas Aridas 1155
Index of Current Research on Pigs (UK ISSN 0568-2800) 7, 41
Index of Current Tropical Ecology Research *see* Indice de Proyectos en Desarrollo en Ecologia Tropical 1155
Index of Economic Articles in Journals and Collective Volumes (US) 7, 210
Index of English Literary Manuscripts (UK) 739
Index of Feature Length Films *see* Index of 16 mm & 35 mm Feature Length Films Available in Canada 1155
Index of Indonesian Learned Periodicals/Indeks Madjalah Ilmiah (IO ISSN 0216-6216) 127
Index of Industrial Relations Literature (CN ISSN 0226-1537) 7, 210
Index of Insurance and Employee Benefits Proceedings (US) 639
Index of Mathematical Papers (US ISSN 0019-3917) 7, 755
Index of N L M Serial Titles (National Library of Medicine) (US ISSN 0162-6639) 1155
Index of Patents Issued from the United States Patent and Trademark Office (US ISSN 0362-0719) 861
Index of Pig Research *see* Meat and Livestock Commission, Bucks., England. Index of Research 67
Index of Psychoanalytic Writings (US ISSN 0073-5884) 938
Index of Publications of the Geological Survey of Canada *see* Canada. Geological Survey. Index of Publications of the Geological Survey of Canada 382
Index of Reviews in Organic Chemistry(UK ISSN 0536-6518) 7, 325
Index of Trademarks Issued from the U.S. Patent and Trademark Office (US ISSN 0099-0809) 861
Index of Trademarks Issued from the United States Patent Office *see* Index of Trademarks Issued from the U.S. Patent and Trademark Office 861
Index of 16 mm & 35 mm Feature Length Films Available in Canada (Canadian Federation of Film Societies) (CN ISSN 0316-5019) 1155
Index Seminum (IS) 158
Index to All Books *see* Index to Who's Who Books 962
Index to Book Reviews in the Humanities (US ISSN 0073-5892) 634
Index to Business Reports (UK ISSN 0266-0180) 210, 256
Index to Chinese Legal Periodicals (CH) 7, 668
Index to Chinese Periodicals (CH ISSN 0378-0112) 7
Index to Chinese Periodicals-Humanities and Social Sciences *see* Index to Chinese Periodicals 7
Index to Chinese Periodicals-Science and Technology *see* Index to Chinese Periodicals 7
Index to Colorado State Publications (US) 127, 942
Index to Current Urban Documents (US ISSN 0046-8908) 7, 627, 949
Index to Dental Literature (US ISSN 0019-3992) 7, 771
Index to Ecology *see* Science and Computer Literacy Audiovisuals 361
Index to Foreign Legal Periodicals (US ISSN 0019-400X) 7, 668
Index to Free Periodicals (US ISSN 0147-5630) 7
Index to How to Do It Information (US ISSN 0073-5930) 7
Index to Indian Medical Periodicals (II ISSN 0019-4042) 7, 771
Index to International Public Opinion (US ISSN 0193-905X) 916, 1008
Index to International Statistics (US ISSN 0737-4461) 1057
Index to Legal Essays (UK) 1155
Index to Legal Periodicals (US ISSN 0019-4077) 7, 668

Index to Legal Studies *see* Index to Legal Essays 1155
Index to Malaysian Conferences/Indeks Persidangan Malaysia (MY ISSN 0127-4880) 7
Index to New England Periodicals (US ISSN 0163-0466) 7
Index to New Zealand Periodicals (NZ ISSN 0073-5957) 1155
Index to Periodical Articles by and About Blacks (US ISSN 0161-8245) 7, 506
Index to Periodical Articles by and About Negroes *see* Index to Periodical Articles by and About Blacks 506
Index to Periodical Articles Related to Law (US ISSN 0019-4093) 7, 668
Index to Periodical Literature on Aging(US ISSN 0882-3405) 552
Index to Periodicals of the Church of Jesus Christ of Latter-Day Saints. Cumulative Edition (US ISSN 0073-5981) 975
Index to Philippine Periodicals (PH ISSN 0073-599X) 127
Index to Plant Chromosome Numbers (NE ISSN 0073-6007) 158
Index to Post-1944 Periodical Articles on Political, Economic and Social Problems *see* Bibliographie Courante d'Articles de Periodiques Posterieurs a 1944 sur les Problemes Politiques, Economiques et Sociaux 1014
Index to Proceedings of the General Assembly of the United Nations (UN ISSN 0082-8157) 912
Index to Religious Periodical Literature *see* Religion Index One: Periodicals 975
Index to Reproductions in Art Periodicals (US ISSN 0893-0139) 7, 106, 320, 503
Index to Reviews of Bibliographical Publications (US ISSN 0161-4029) 127
Index to Scientific Reviews (US ISSN 0360-0661) 7, 1004
Index to Selected Periodicals *see* Index to Periodical Articles by and About Blacks 506
Index to South African Periodicals/Repertorium van Suid-Afrikaanse Tydskrifartikels (SA ISSN 0379-0584) 7, 964
Index to Spanish Science and Technology (SP) 1004, 1072
Index to Textile Auxiliaries (UK ISSN 0073-604X) 1074
Index to Thai Newspapers (TH) 1155
Index to Thai Periodical Literature (TH ISSN 0125-5827) 7, 1014
Index to the Boston Globe (US ISSN 0741-5281) 7, 647
Index to the Christian Science Monitor (US ISSN 0098-1184) 647
Index to the Code of Federal Regulations (US ISSN 0198-9014) 7, 942
Index to the Denver Post (US ISSN 0195-6434) 647
Index to the Detroit News (US) 647
Index to the Houston Post (US) 647
Index to the Los Angeles Times (US ISSN 0195-6418) 647
Index to the National Assembly Records/Kuk Hoe Hoe Eu Rok Saegin (KO) 7, 687
Index to the National Observer (US) 7, 647
Index to the New Orleans Times-Picayune (US ISSN 0195-640X) 647
Index to the St. Louis Post-Dispatch (Wooster) (US ISSN 0275-858X) 7, 647
Index to the St. Paul Pioneer Press and Dispatch (US) 7, 647
Index to the San Francisco Chronicle (US ISSN 0195-6396) 7, 647
Index to the Science Fiction Magazines *see* N.E.S.F.A. Index: Science Fiction Magazines and Anthologies 14
Index to the U.S. Patent Classification (US) 861
Index to U.S. Government Periodicals (US ISSN 0098-4604) 7

Index to USA Today (US ISSN 0736-9999) 7, *647*
Index to Who's Who Books (US) *962*
Index Translationum (UN ISSN 0073-6074) *679*
Index Veterinarius (UK ISSN 0019-4123) 7, *1123*
India. Cardamom Board. Annual Report(II) *56*
India. Central Board of Revenue. Central Excise Manual (II ISSN 0073-6120) *296*
India. Central Statistical Organisation. National Accounts Statistics: Sources and Methods (II) *277*
India. Central Statistical Organization. Annual Report (II) *1057*
India. Central Statistical Organization. Annual Survey of Industries/Udyogen Ka Varshika Sarvekshana (II ISSN 0073-6139) *210*
India. Central Statistical Organization. Estimates of National Income *see* India. Central Statistical Organization. National Accounts Statistics *277*
India. Central Statistical Organization. Monthly Abstract of Statistics (II ISSN 0019-4174) *1057*
India. Central Statistical Organization. National Accounts Statistics (II) *277*
India. Central Statistical Organization. Sample Surveys of Current Interest in India. Report *see* India. Central Statistical Organization. Annual Report *1057*
India. Central Statistical Organization. Statistical Abstract (II ISSN 0073-6155) *1057*
India. Central Vigilance Commission. Report (II ISSN 0073-6171) *942*
India. Committe on Science and Technology. Annual Report *see* India. Department of Science & Technology. Annual Report *992*
India. Department of Atomic Energy. Annual Report (II ISSN 0073-618X) *896*
India. Department of Culture. Demands for Grants/Samskriti Vibhaga Ki Anudanom Ki Mangem (II) *443*
India. Department of Economic Affairs. Budget Division. Key to the Budget Documents (II) *942*
India. Department of Labour and Employment. Annual Report *see* India. Ministry of Labour. Annual Report *272*
India. Department of Power. Report (II) *465, 942*
India. Department of Rural Development. Administrative Intelligence Division. Progress Report on Small Farmers Development Agency Programme (II) *47, 1057*
India. Department of Rural Development. Administrative Intelligence Division. Some Special Programmes of Rural Development; Statistics (II) *47*, 1057
India. Department of Science & Technology. Annual Report (II ISSN 0085-1779) *992*, 1069
India. Department of Science and Technology. Report. (II) *1069*
India. Department of Science and Technology. Research and Development Statistics (II) *1004, 1072*
India. Department of Space. Annual Report (II ISSN 0376-5466) *19*
India. Finance Department. Budget of the Central Government (II) *296*
India. Labour Bureau. Pocket Book of Labour Statistics (II) *210*
India. Meteorological Department. Memoirs (II) *805*
India. Ministry of Agriculture. Bulletin on Commercial Crops Statistics (II) *47*
India. Ministry of Agriculture. Bulletin on Food Statistics (II) *47, 66*
India. Ministry of Education and Social Welfare. Department of Education. Report (II) *415*

India. Ministry of Education and Social Welfare. Department of Education. Report *see* India. Ministry of Education and Social Welfare. Department of Education. Report *415*
India. Ministry of Education and Social Welfare. Department of Social Welfare. Documentation Service Bulletin (II) 7, *1014*
India. Ministry of Education and Social Welfare. Provisional Statistics of Education in the States (II ISSN 0579-6105) *415*
India. Ministry of Finance. Budget *see* India. Finance Department. Budget of the Central Government *296*
India. Ministry of Heavy Industry. Report (II) *195*
India. Ministry of Home Affairs. Vital Statistics Division. Causes of Death; a Survey (II) *922, 927*
India. Ministry of Home Affairs. Vital Statistics Division. Sample Registration Bulletin (II) *922, 927*
India. Ministry of Labour. Annual Report (II) *272*
India. Office of the Comptroller and Auditor-General. Report: Union Government (Posts and Telegraphs) (II ISSN 0536-7506) *343*
India. Office of the Registrar General. Newsletter *see* India. Ministry of Home Affairs. Vital Statistics Division. Sample Registration Bulletin *927*
India. Parliament. Public Accounts Committee. Report on the Accounts (II ISSN 0445-6831) *942*
India (Republic). Meteorological Department Report on Seismology *see* National Report for India: Seismology and Physics of the Earth's Interior *806*
India (Republic) Ministry of Shipping and Transport. Statistics of Water Transport Industries *see* Water Transport Statistics of India *1087*
India. Textiles Committee. Consumer Purchases of Textiles (II) *1074*
India. Tobacco Board. Annual Report (II) *1079*
India. Union Public Service Commission Report (II ISSN 0073-6236) *942*
India. Zoological Survey. Annual Report (II ISSN 0537-0744) *175*
India. Zoological Survey. Newsletter (II) *175*
India: a Reference Annual (II ISSN 0073-6090) *127*
India and Pakistan Wool, Hosiery and Fabrics *see* Directory of Wool, Hosiery and Fabrics *1074*
India and World Affairs: an Annual Bibliography (II) *564*, 912
India News and Feature Alliance Press and Advertisers Year Book *see* I N F A Press and Advertisers Year Book *463*
India Transport Statistics *see* Pocket Book of Transport Statistics of India *1082*
India Who's Who (II ISSN 0073-6244) *134*
Indian Academy of Geoscience. Journal(II) *379*
Indian Agriculture in Brief (II ISSN 0084-781X) *28*
Indian & Eastern Newspaper Society Press Handbook (II) *645*, 931
Indian Architects Directory (II ISSN 0256-4017) *98, 134*
Indian Association of American Studies. Papers (II) *606*
Indian Association of Physiotherapists. Journal (II) *762*
Indian Association of Special Libraries and Information Centres Special Publication *see* I A S L I C Special Publication *678*
Indian Association of Special Libraries and Information Centres Technical Pamphlets *see* I A S L I C Technical Pamphlets *678*
Indian Astronomical Ephemeris (II) *116*
Indian Biography (II) *134*

Indian Biophysical Society. Proceedings(II) *153*
Indian Book Review Digest (CN ISSN 0709-9010) *503, 962*
Indian Books in Print (II) *127*
Indian Chemical Directory (II ISSN 0073-6295) *323, 478*
Indian Chemicals and Pharmaceuticals Statistics (II) *873*
Indian Congress of American History. Papers *see* Indian Association of American Studies. Papers *606*
Indian Cotton Textile Industry; Annual Statistical Bulletin (II) *1075*
Indian Council for Child Welfare. Annual Report (II) *335, 1018*
Indian Council of Historical Research. Annual Report (II ISSN 0304-7032) *569*
Indian Council of Social Research. Annual Report (II) *1008*
Indian Council of Social Science Research Journal of Abstracts and Reviews: Geography *see* I C S S R Journal of Abstracts and Reviews: Geography *551*
Indian Council of Social Science Research Journal of Abstracts and Reviews: Sociology & Social Anthropology *see* I C S S R Journal of Abstracts and Reviews: Sociology & Social Anthropology *79*
Indian Education Abstracts (II ISSN 0019-4697) 7, *424*
Indian Education Annual Report *see* Idaho. State Superintendent of Public Instruction. Annual Report. State of Idaho Johnson-O'Malley Program *414*
Indian Electronics Directory (II ISSN 0377-7340) *455*
Indian Engineering & Industries Register *see* Engineering Times Annual Directory *471*
Indian Ephemeris and Nautical Almanac *see* Indian Astronomical Ephemeris *116*
Indian Export Year Book (II) *256*
Indian Fertilizer Statistics (II) *41*
Indian Films (II ISSN 0377-7359) *824*
Indian Fisheries Abstracts (II) *514*
Indian Foreign Policy Annual Survey (II) *916*
Indian Forest Bulletin (New Series) (II ISSN 0073-635X) *525*
Indian Forest Leaflets (New Series) (II ISSN 0073-6368) *525*
Indian Forest Records (New Series) Botany (II ISSN 0073-6376) *158*
Indian Forest Records (New Series) Composite Wood (II ISSN 0073-6384) *530*
Indian Forest Records (New Series) Entomology (II ISSN 0073-6392) *164*
Indian Forest Records (New Series) Forest Management and Mensuration(II) *525*
Indian Forest Records (New Series) Forest Pathology (II ISSN 0073-6406) *525*
Indian Forest Records (New Series) Logging (II ISSN 0073-6414) *530*
Indian Forest Records (New Series) Mycology *see* Indian Forest Records (New Series) Forest Pathology *525*
Indian Forest Records (New Series) Silviculture (II ISSN 0073-6422) *525*
Indian Forest Records (New Series) Statistical (II ISSN 0073-6430) *525*
Indian Forest Records (New Series) Timber Mechanics (II ISSN 0073-6449) *530*
Indian Forest Records Wood Anatomy (II ISSN 0442-6827) *530*
Indian Forest Records Wood Technology *see* Indian Forest Records Wood Anatomy *530*
Indian Geological Index (II ISSN 0379-511X) 7, *382*
Indian Geophysical Union Bulletin (II) *399*
Indian Geoscience Association. Journal *see* Indian Academy of Geoscience. Journal *379*
Indian Health Trends and Services (US ISSN 0885-9914) *922, 954*

Indian History and Culture. Series (II) *503, 569*
Indian Hosiery Directory (II) *309, 340*
Indian Institute of Advanced Study. Transactions and Monographs (II ISSN 0073-6465) *630*
Indian Institute of Advanced Study Occasional Papers *see* I I A S Occasional Papers *436*
Indian Institute of Foreign Trade. Report (II ISSN 0073-6473) *256*
Indian Institute of Mass Communication. Annual Report (II) *343*
Indian Institute of Mass Communication Bulletin *see* I I M C Bulletin *343*
Indian Institute of Metals. Proceedings (II) *798*
Indian Institute of Sugarcane Research, Lucknow. Annual Report (II ISSN 0073-649X) *56*
Indian Institute of Technology, Bombay. Series (II ISSN 0073-6503) *1069*
Indian Institute of Technology, Madras. Annual Report (II ISSN 0073-6511) *1069*
Indian Institute of Technology, Madras. Ph.D. Dissertation Abstracts (II) 7, *1072*
Indian Institute of Tropical Meteorology. Annual Report (II ISSN 0250-6017) *805*
Indian Institute of Tropical Meteorology. Contributions (II ISSN 0252-1075) *805*
Indian Institute of Tropical Meteorology. Research Report *see* Indian Institute of Tropical Meteorology. Contributions *805*
Indian Institute of World Culture. Annual Report (II) *630*
Indian International Trade Center Directory *see* I I T C Directory *256*
Indian Jewry (IS) *503*
Indian Journal of Engineers. Annual Foundry Number (II ISSN 0073-6554) *471*
Indian Journal of Fisheries (II ISSN 0537-2003) *175, 510*
Indian Journal of Heredity (II ISSN 0374-826X) *28, 167, 329*
Indian Journal of Medical Research. Supplement (II ISSN 0367-9012) *762*
Indian Journal of Mushrooms (II) *533*
Indian Jute Mills Association. Annual Summary of Jute and Gunny Statistics (II ISSN 0073-6562) *1074*
Indian Jute Mills Association. Loom and Spindle Statistics (II ISSN 0073-6570) *1074*
Indian Library and Information Science Indexes Series (II) *688*
Indian Library Science Abstracts (II ISSN 0019-5790) 8, *688*
Indian Linguistics Monograph Series (II ISSN 0073-6589) *696*
Indian Literature in Environmental Engineering (II) *477, 501*
Indian Mathematical Society. Journal (II ISSN 0019-5839) *749*
Indian Minerals Year Book (II ISSN 0445-7897) *817*
Indian Motion Picture Almanac (II) *824*
Indian Museum Bulletin (II ISSN 0019-5987) *827*
Indian Music Journal (II ISSN 0019-5995) *415, 836*
Indian National Bibliography (II ISSN 0019-6002) *127*
Indian National Science Academy. Biographical Memoirs of Fellows (II) *134, 992*
Indian National Science Academy. Bulletin (II ISSN 0378-6242) *992*
Indian National Science Academy. Mathematical Tables (II) *749*
Indian National Science Academy. Monographs (II) *992*
Indian National Science Academy. Proceedings (II ISSN 0073-6600) *992*
Indian National Science Academy. Transactions (II) *992*

INDUSTRIAL &   1765

Indian National Science Academy. Year Book (II ISSN 0073-6619) *992*
Indian National Scientific Documentation Centre Union Catalogue Series *see* I N S D O C Union Catalogue Series *127*
Indian Ocean Fishery Commission. Report of the Session *see* F A O Fisheries Reports *508*
Indian Petroleum and Chemicals Statistics *see* Indian Petroleum and Petrochemicals Statistics *868*
Indian Petroleum and Petrochemicals Statistics (II) *868, 1057*
Indian Pharmaceutical Guide (II ISSN 0073-6635) *871*
Indian Philosophical Annual. (II ISSN 0376-4109) *878*
Indian Phytopathological Society. Bulletin (II ISSN 0537-2410) *158*
Indian Poultry Industry Yearbook (II) *66, 1121*
Indian Psychological Abstracts (II ISSN 0250-9679) *8, 938*
Indian Railways Yearbook (II ISSN 0376-9909) *1086*
Indian Records (II ISSN 0302-6744) *836, 1032*
Indian Review of Life Sciences (II ISSN 0252-9920) *28, 72*
Indian Roads Congress. Journal (II ISSN 0046-905X) *1096*
Indian Roads Congress Special Publication *see* I R C Special Publication *1096*
Indian Rubber Statistics (II ISSN 0073-6651) *985*
Indian School of Mines. Annual Report(II ISSN 0304-1158) *817*
Indian Science Abstracts (II ISSN 0019-6339) *8, 1004*
Indian Science Congress Association. Proceedings (II ISSN 0085-1817) *992*
Indian Society of Gastroenterology. Proceedings of the Annual Conference (II) *783*
Indian Society of Statistics and Operations Research. Journal (II ISSN 0250-9636) *355, 1057*
Indian Statistical Institute. Annual Report (II ISSN 0073-6686) *1057*
Indian Statistical Institute. Documentation Research and Training Centre. D R T C Annual Seminar (II ISSN 0067-3439) *679*
Indian Statistical Institute. Documentation Research and Training Centre. D R T C Refresher Seminar (II) *679*
Indian Statistical Institute. Econometric and Social Sciences Series. Research Monographs (II ISSN 0073-6694) *1008*
Indian Statistical Institute. Lecture Notes (II) *1057*
Indian Statistical Institute. Library. Bibliographic Series (II ISSN 0073-6708) *127*
Indian Statistical Institute. Research and Training School. Publications *see* Indian Statistical Institute. Lecture Notes *1057*
Indian Statistical Institute. Statistics and Probability Series. Research Monographs (II ISSN 0073-6716) *1057*
Indian Statistical Series (II ISSN 0073-6724) *1057*
Indian Stratigraphy (II) *389*
Indian Textile Annual & Directory (II ISSN 0537-2666) *1074*
Indian Veterinary Research Institute. Annual Report (II ISSN 0304-7067) *1121*
Indian Yearbook of International Affairs (II ISSN 0537-2704) *569, 916*
Indiana (GW ISSN 0341-8642) *72, 87, 606*
Indiana. Agricultural Experiment Station. Inspection Report (US ISSN 0073-6783) *28*
Indiana. Agricultural Experiment Station. Research Bulletin (US ISSN 0073-6791) *28*
Indiana. Council on Vocational Education. Annual Report (US) *447*

Indiana. Environmental Management Board. Annual Report (US ISSN 0094-5749) *496*
Indiana. Geological Survey. Annual Report of the State Geologist (US ISSN 0362-3513) *389*
Indiana. State University Council for Vocational Technical Education. Annual Report *see* Indiana. Council on Vocational Education. Annual Report *447*
Indiana Academy of Science. Monograph (US ISSN 0073-6759) *992*
Indiana Academy of Science. Proceedings (US ISSN 0073-6767) *992*
Indiana Automotive Directory *see* Automotive Contact Automotive Directory. Indiana *1090*
Indiana Ball State Teachers College *see* Ball State Monographs *628*
Indiana Directory of Music Teachers (US) *415, 836*
Indiana Historical Collections (US ISSN 0073-6880) *606*
Indiana Historical Society. Prehistory Research Series (US ISSN 0073-6899) *72*
Indiana Historical Society. Publications (US ISSN 0073-6902) *606*
Indiana Historical Society News (US) *606*
Indiana Historical Society Newsletter *see* Indiana Historical Society News *606*
Indiana History Resource Series (US) *606*
Indiana Industrial Directory *see* Harris Indiana Industrial Directory (Year) *309*
Indiana International Trade Directory (US) *256*
Indiana Libraries (US ISSN 0275-777X) *679*
Indiana Manufacturers Directory (US ISSN 0735-2417) *310*
Indiana School Directory (US) *430*
Indiana State Industrial Directory *see* MacRae's Indiana State Industrial Directory *312*
Indiana State Plan for Vocation-Technical Education. (Fiscal Year) (US) *444*
Indiana State Plan for Vocational Education. *see* Indiana State Plan for Vocation-Technical Education. (Fiscal Year) *444*
Indiana State University. Department of Geography and Geology. Professional Paper (US ISSN 0073-6937) *544*
Indiana Studies in Higher Education (US) *448*
Indiana Studies in Prediction *see* Indiana Studies in Higher Education *448*
Indiana University. Department of Geography. Geographic Monograph Series (US ISSN 0073-6953) *544*
Indiana University. Department of Geography. Occasional Publication. (US ISSN 0073-6961) *544*
Indiana University. Folklore Institute. Monograph Series (US ISSN 0073-6996) *1155*
Indiana University. Research Institute for Inner Asian Studies. Uralic and Altaic Series. (US ISSN 0073-7097) *696*
Indiana University. School of Public and Environmental Affairs. Occasional Papers (US) *1155*
Indiana University Art Museum Bulletin (US) *827*
Indiana University Bookman (US ISSN 0019-6800) *962*
Indiana University Museum. Occasional Papers and Monographs *see* William Hammond Mathers Museum. Occasional Papers and Monographs *831*
Indiana University Publications. African Series (US) *566*
Indianist Yearbook *see* Anuario Indigenista *70*
India's Production, Exports, and Internal Consumption of Coir (II) *256*

Indicators for the Telegram Retransmission System (TRS) - Telex Identification Codes (UN) *350*
Indice Agricola Colombiano (CK ISSN 0073-7151) *41*
Indice-Catalogo Medico Brasileiro *see* Bibliografia Brasileira de Medicina *768*
Indice de Actualidad Farmacologica (SP) *871*
Indice de la Literatura Dental en Castellano *see* Indice de la Literatura Dental Periodica en Castellano *127*
Indice de la Literatura Dental Periodica en Castellano (AG ISSN 0325-0679) *127, 779*
Indice de la Literatura Dental Periodica en Castellano y Portugues *see* Indice de la Literatura Dental Periodica en Castellano *127*
Indice de Proyectos en Desarrollo en Ecologia de Zonas Aridas/Index of Current Research in Arid Zones Ecology/Index des Projects en Developpment sur l'Ecologie des Zones Arides (MX) *1155*
Indice de Proyectos en Desarrollo en Ecologia Tropical/Index of Current Tropical Ecology Research (MX) *1155*
Indice do Brasil/Brazilian Index Yearbook (BL) *245, 1057*
Indice Espanol de Sciencia y Tecnologia *see* Index to Spanish Science and Technology *1004*
Indice General de la Revista Hoy (CL) *1155*
Indice General de Publicaciones Periodicas Cubanas (CU) *8*
Indice Medico Espanol (SP ISSN 0019-7068) *8, 771*
Indices Naturwissenschaftlich-Medizinischer Periodica bis 1850 (GW ISSN 0340-8094) *771*
Indices Verborum Linguae Mongoliae Monumentis Traditorum (HU ISSN 0073-7194) *696, 851*
Indices Zum Altdeutschen Schrifttum (NE ISSN 0169-037X) *723*
Indices zur Deutschen Literatur (GW ISSN 0073-7208) *1155*
Individually Paced or Self Teaching Instruction Source Book (US) *127*
Indo-Burma Petroleum Company. Annual Report (II) *864*
Indo-Pacific Fisheries Council. Regional Studies (UN ISSN 0537-3654) *510*
Indo-Pacific Fishery Commission Proceedings *see* I P F C Proceedings *510*
Indo-Pacific Fishes (US ISSN 0736-0460) *175*
Indo-Pacific Mollusca (US ISSN 0073-7240) *175*
Indologica Taurinensia (FR) *851*
Indonesia. Departemen Pekerjaan Umum dan Tenaga Listrik. Biro Umum. Laporan Tahunan *see* Indonesia. Department of Public Works and Electric Power. Administration Bureau. Annual Report *455*
Indonesia. Departemen Penerangan. Siaran Umum (IO) *942*
Indonesia. Department of Public Works and Electric Power. Administration Bureau. Annual Report/Indonesia. Departemen Pekerjaan Umum dan Tenaga Listrik. Biro Umum. Laporan Tahunan (IO) *455*
Indonesia. Directorate General of Higher Education. Annual Report/Indonesia. Direktorat Jenderal Pendidikan Tinggi. Laporan Tahunan(IO) *436*
Indonesia. Directorate General of Protestant Affairs. Annual Report/Indonesia. Direktorat Jenderal Bimbingan Masyarakat Kristen/Protestan Laporan Tahunan (IO) *979*
Indonesia. Direktorat Jenderal Bimbingan Masyarakat Kristen/Protestan Laporan Tahunan *see* Indonesia. Directorate General of Protestant Affairs. Annual Report *979*

Indonesia. Direktorat Jenderal Pendidikan Tinggi. Laporan Tahunan *see* Indonesia. Directorate General of Higher Education. Annual Report *436*
Indonesia. Direktorat Perumahan Rakjat. Laporan Kerdja (IO) *623*
Indonesia. Export by Commodity, Country of Destination and Port of Export (IO ISSN 0126-3714) *256*
Indonesia. Import by Commodity and Country of Origin (IO ISSN 0126-4419) *256*
Indonesia. National Scientific Documentation Center. Annual Report/Indonesia. Pusat Dokumentasi Ilmiah Nasional. Laporan Tahunan (IO ISSN 0126-0812) *992*
Indonesia. Pusat Dokumentasi Ilmiah Nasional. Laporan Tahunan *see* Indonesia. National Scientific Documentation Center. Annual Report *992*
Indonesia. Social Welfare Indicators (IO) *1057*
Indonesia Oil Statistics/Statistik Perminyakan Indonesia (IO) *868, 1057*
Indonesia Statistics (IO ISSN 0376-9984) *210, 1057*
Indonesia Tourist Statistics (IO) *1057, 1119*
Indonesian Acquisitions List/Daftar Pengadaan Bahan Indonesia (AT ISSN 0310-6659) *127*
Indonesian Importers (IO ISSN 0216-1052) *256, 310*
Indonesian Statistics on Trade of Forest Products (IO) *525*
Indonesian Women's Congress. Bulletin/Kongres Wanita Indonesia. Berita (IO) *1129*
Indretningshaandbogen (DK) *455*
Indsatsen mod Ungdomsarbejdsloesheden (DK ISSN 0109-4319) *272*
Induced Abortion: A World Review (US) *922*
Industria Aseguradora Colombiana. Estadisticas Anuales (CK) *639*
Industria del Petrolio in Italia (IT ISSN 0073-7275) *864*
Industria Italiana del Ciclo e del Motociclo. Annuario (IT ISSN 0073-7291) *1092*
Industria Petrolera en Mexico (MX) *864, 868*
Industria Quimica en Mexico (MX) *478*
Industria Siderurgica en Mexico (MX) *798*
Industrial Abstracts for Tanzania (TZ ISSN 0251-2459) *8, 1072*
Industrial Accident Prevention Association. Annual Report (CN ISSN 0073-7305) *635*
Industrial Accident Prevention Association. Guide to Safety (CN ISSN 0073-7313) *272*
Industrial Aerodynamics Abstracts (UK ISSN 0019-7823) *8, 477*
Industrial Aids in the UK - A Businessman's Guide *see* Government Support for British Business *245*
Industrial Alabama *see* Alabama Directory of Mining and Manufacturing *234*
Industrial and Business Directory Kerala (Year) (II) *310*
Industrial and Commercial Development Corporation. Annual Report and Accounts (KE) *239*
Industrial and Commercial Power Systems and Electrical Space Heating and Air Conditioning Joint Technical Conference. Record *see* Industrial and Commercial Power Systems Technical Conference *455*
Industrial and Commercial Power Systems Technical Conference (US) *455*
Industrial and Labor Relations Bibliography Series (US ISSN 0070-0142) *210*
Industrial & Trade Directory (KE) *195, 310*

INDUSTRIAL ARBITRATION

Industrial Arbitration Reports, New South Wales (AT ISSN 0155-2589) 272
Industrial Arbitration Service (AT ISSN 0312-4029) 657
Industrial Archeology see I A 87
Industrial Arts Index see Business Periodicals Index 204
Industrial Bank of Kuwait. Annual Report (KU) 229
Industrial Bank of Sudan. Board of Directors. Annual Report (SJ ISSN 0073-7356) 229
Industrial/Commercial Real Estate Managers' Directory see U S Real Estate Register 16
Industrial Development Abstracts (United Nations Industrial Development Organization) (UN ISSN 0378-2654) 8, 211
Industrial Development and the Social Fabric (US) 195
Industrial Development Bank. Annual Report and Balance Sheet/Bank al-Inma al-Sinai. Annual Report and Balance Sheet (JO) 229
Industrial Development Bank Limited. Annual Report and Accounts (KE) 229
Industrial Development Bank of India. Annual Report (II ISSN 0073-7372) 229
Industrial Development Bank of Israel Limited. Report (IS ISSN 0073-7380) 229
Industrial Development Bank of Pakistan. Report (PK ISSN 0073-7399) 229
Industrial Development Bank of Turkey. Annual Statement (TU ISSN 0073-7402) 229
Industrial Development in the T.V.A. Area (Tennessee Valley Authority) (US ISSN 0495-145X) 289
Industrial Development News - Asia and the Pacific see Industy and Technology Development News - Asia and the Pacific 262
Industrial Directory and Brand Names Index of Malawi see Chamber of Commerce and Industry of Malawi. Industrial and Trade Directory 304
Industrial Directory of the Commonwealth of Pennsylvania see Harris Pennsylvania Industrial Directory 309
Industrial Directory of Wales (UK) 310
Industrial Educational and Research Foundation. Dialogues see Foundation for Business Responsibilities. Dialogues 194
Industrial Entreprises Incorporated. Annual Report see Prince Edward Island Development Agency. Annual Report 291
Industrial Fabric Products Review Buyer's Guide (US ISSN 0019-8307) 1074
Industrial Fasteners Handbook (UK) 471
Industrial Finishing Buyer's Guide (US) 855
Industrial Fire Protection & Security Handbook (UK) 374, 635
Industrial Growth in Tennessee, Annual Report (US ISSN 0099-1872) 289
Industrial Health Foundation. Chemical-Toxicological Series. Bulletin (US ISSN 0073-7488) 635
Industrial Health Foundation. Engineering Series. Bulletin (US ISSN 0073-7496) 635
Industrial Health Foundation. Legal Series Bulletin. (US ISSN 0073-750X) 635, 657
Industrial Health Foundation. Medical Series. Bulletin (US ISSN 0073-7518) 635, 762
Industrial Health Foundation. Nursing Series. Bulletins (US) 635, 784
Industrial Health Foundation. Technical Bulletin. Management Series (US) 635
Industrial Hygiene Foundation. Chemical-Toxicological Series. Bulletin see Industrial Health Foundation. Chemical-Toxicological Series. Bulletin 635

Industrial Hygiene Foundation. Nursing Series. Bulletins see Industrial Health Foundation. Nursing Series. Bulletins 635
Industrial Hygiene Foundation of America. Legal Series Bulletin. see Industrial Health Foundation. Legal Series Bulletin 635
Industrial Institute for Economic and Social Research. Current Research Projects (SW) 251
Industrial Location Handbook/Kogyo Ritchi Handobukku (JA) 289
Industrial Locations in Canada (CN ISSN 0073-7569) 289
Industrial Machinery: Latin American Industrial Report (US) 745
Industrial Minerals Directory see Industrial Minerals Directory - World Guide to Producers and Processors 817
Industrial Minerals Directory - World Guide to Producers and Processors (UK ISSN 0269-1701) 817
Industrial Property Law. Annual (UK) 657, 861
Industrial Property, Statistics B/ Propriete Industrielle, Statistiques B (UN ISSN 0377-0044) 862
Industrial Real Estate Market Survey (US ISSN 0730-0131) 965
Industrial Relations Research Association. Annual Research Volume (US) 272
Industrial Relations Research Association. Proceedings of Annual Winter Meeting see Industrial Relations Research Association. Proceedings of the Annual Meeting 272
Industrial Relations Research Association. Proceedings of the Annual Meeting (US) 272
Industrial Relations Research Association. Proceedings of the Annual Spring Meeting (US) 272
Industrial Relations Research Association. Proceedings of the Annual Winter Meeting see Industrial Relations Research Association. Proceedings of the Annual Meeting 272
Industrial Relations Research in Canada/Recherche sur les Relations Industrielles au Canada (CN ISSN 0073-7593) 272
Industrial Relations Service Bureau's Wisconsin Employment Relations Commission, Reporter see Wisconsin. Employment Relations Commission. Reporter 277
Industrial Research in United Kingdom (UK ISSN 0263-7952) 289
Industrial Research Laboratories of the United States see Directory of American Research and Technology 1068
Industrial Review (RH) 196
Industrial Review of Japan see Japan Economic Almanac 290
Industrial Sabotage (CN) 106, 723, 741
Industrial Sensor Directory see International Industrial Sensor Directory 472
Industrial Society. Handbook and Diary(UK) 289
Industrial Statistics Yearbook (UN) 211
Industrial Structure of Rajasthan (II ISSN 0073-7666) 289
Industrial Ventilation; a Manual of Recommended Practice (US ISSN 0569-4043) 553, 635
Industrial Waste Conference, Purdue University, Lafayette, Indiana. Proceedings (US ISSN 0073-7682) 496
Industrialiserings Fonden for Udviklingslandene Annual Report see I F U Annual Report 262
Industrias do Arroz no Rio Grande do Sul (BL) 47
Industrie Camerounaise (CM) 289
Industrie Cimentiere Belge/Belgische Cementnijverheid (BE) 184
Industrie Compass Oesterreich (AU ISSN 0073-7712) 310

Industrie de la Manutention dans les Ports Francais (FR ISSN 0073-7720) 1100
Industrie du Livre au Canada see Book Trade in Canada 960
Industrie Electronique Francaise see Groupement des Industries Electroniques. Statistiques Annuelles 454
Industrie et Artisanat (GW ISSN 0073-7739) 1069
Industrie Francaise des Moteurs a Combustion Interne (FR ISSN 0073-7747) 1092
Industrie- und Handelskammer Hannover-Hildesheim. Information-Kommentare see Industrie- und Handelskammer Hannover-Hildesheim. Yearbook - Information Kommentare 236
Industrie- und Handelskammer Hannover-Hildesheim. Yearbook - Information Kommentare (GW) 236
Industrieabwaesser (GW ISSN 0073-7755) 490
Industriegesellschaft und Recht (GW) 657
Industriegewerkschaft Druck und Papier. Schriftenreihe fuer Betriebsrate (GW ISSN 0170-3463) 858, 931
Industriens Hovedtal see Key Figures on Danish Industry 1157
Industriens Utredningsinstitut Yearbook see I U I Yearbook 195
Industries Directory, Capitals (II ISSN 0073-7763) 310
Industries Directory, Delhi (II ISSN 0073-7771) 310
Industries Directory, Northern India (II ISSN 0073-7798) 310
Industries Manufacturieres du Canada: Niveau Infraprovincial see Canada. Statistics Canada. Manufacturing Industries of Canada: Sub-Provincial Areas/Industries Manufactures du Canada: Niveau Infraprovincial 205
Industries of Japan (JA ISSN 0446-1266) 289
Industrijski Proizvodi (YU) 211
Industry Analysis in the Federal Government see Who Knows About Industries and Markets 202
Industry Applications Society. I E E E - I A S Annual Meeting. Conference Record (US ISSN 0197-2618) 455
Industry - Engineering Education Series see College - Industry Education Conference. Proceedings 470
Industry Guide to Private Pay Telephones (US) 350
Industry in East Africa (KE ISSN 0073-781X) 290
Industry Norms and Key Business Ratios. Library Edition (US) 245
Industy and Technology Development News - Asia and the Pacific (UN ISSN 0252-4481) 262
Inedita (PE) 606
Infektionskrankheiten und ihre Erreger (GE) 168
Inflation Monitor (CN ISSN 0824-801X) 196
Info see Infodont 779
Info-F N E E Q see Women's Network 422
Info Guide (Year) (CN) 352, 358
Info-Nature (RE) 365
Infodont (DK ISSN 0107-8097) 779
Infopro: The Directory (US) 361, 362, 363
Informacao Cultural (PO) 711
Informacije Rade Koncar see Koncar Strucne Informacije 456
Informacion Express. Serie: Ganado Equino (CU ISSN 0138-7537) 66
Informacion Express. Serie: Plantas Medicinales y Flores (CU) 158
Informacion Juridica (CU) 657
Informaciones Bayer para la Industria del Caucho (GW) 1155
Informaciones Danesas see Danish Journal 538
Informacoes sobre a Industria Cinematografica Brasileira. Anuario (BL) 824
Informador de la Construccion y de la Industria/Construction and Industry Bulletin (VE) 184

Informat (SA ISSN 0256-4106) 679
Informatheque (FR ISSN 0073-7836) 905
Informatik (GW) 352
Informatik-Fachberichte (US ISSN 0343-3005) 352
Informatik - Kybernetic - Rechentechnik. Schriftenreihe (GE ISSN 0232-1351) 359
Information and Behavior (US ISSN 0740-5502) 343
Information and Documentation Centre for the Geography of the Netherlands Bulletin see I D G-Bulletin 544
Information Bulletin on Variable Stars (HU ISSN 0374-0676) 116
Information Chicago (US ISSN 0196-3643) 257
Information Circular on Radiation Techniques and Their Applications to Insect Pests (UN) 792
Information Circular - State of Washington, Department of Natural Resources, Division of Geology and Earth Resources see Washington (State). Division of Geology and Earth Resources. Information Circular 821
Information en Sciences de la Sante au Canada: Associations see Health Sciences Information in Canada: Associations 761
Information en Sciences de la Sante au Canada: Bibliotheques see Health Sciences Information in Canada: Libraries 761
Information for Foreign Students Intending to Study at an Austrian Institution of Higher Learning see Information fuer auslaendische Studienbewerber an oesterreichischen Hochschulen 436
Information from the Volunteer Centre Media Project (UK ISSN 0266-1233) 348
Information fuer auslaendische Studienbewerber an oesterreichischen Hochschulen/Information for Foreign Students Intending to Study at an Austrian Institution of Higher Learning (AU ISSN 0020-0077) 436
Information Industry Market Place see North American Online Directory 344
Information Malaysia (MY) 569
Information Management Source Book (US) 679
Information Media & Technology (UK ISSN 0266-6960) 884
Information Moscow see Information Moscow, Western Edition 1111
Information Moscow, Western Edition (US) 310, 1111
Information nicht nuer fuer Studieanfaenger see Wo Geht's Lang 441
Information on Education (US) 415
Information on Environmental Pollution in Foreign Countries (AT) 496
Information on Parana (BL) 245
Information Pamphlet - Department of Employment and Social Services (Baltimore) see Maryland. Department of Human Resources. Information Pamphlet 1019
Information Processing Association of Israel. National Conference on Data Processing. Proceedings (IS ISSN 0073-7879) 361, 689
Information Resources Annual (BE ISSN 0252-1105) 8
Information Science Abstracts (US ISSN 0020-0239) 8, 688
Information Sciences Series (US) 679
Information Series in Agricultural Economics (US) 48
Information Series on Agricultural Economics see Giannini Foundation of Agricultural Economics. Information Series 47
Information Series - Tennessee State Board of Vocational Education see Tennessee. State Board for Vocational Education. Information Series 445

Information Service of the European Communities. Documentation Europeenne - Serie Agricole *see* Documentation Europeenne - Serie Agricole 26
Information Service of the European Communities. Documentation Europeenne - Serie Syndical et Ouvriere *see* Documentation Europeenne - Serie Syndicale et Ouvriere 271
Information Service of the European Communities. Newsletter on the Common Agricultural Policy (EI ISSN 0073-7895) 48
Information Service of the European Communities. Trade Union News (EI ISSN 0073-7909) 648
Information Sharing Index (US) 335
Information Sources (US ISSN 0734-9637) 343, 352, 861, 962
Information Technology Series (US) 361
Information Veterinaire (CN ISSN 0581-3263) 1121
Informational Report- United States Department of the Interior, Mining Enforcement and Safety Administration *see* U.S. Mining Enforcement and Safety Administration. Informational Report 821
Informationen aus dem Philosophischen Leben in der D.D.R. *see* Informationsbulletin 878
Informationen zu Aktuellen Fragen der Sozial- und Wirtschaftpolitik (AU ISSN 0083-6125) 905
Informations Annuelles de Caryosystematique et Cytogenetique (FR ISSN 0073-7917) 158, 167
Informations Bayer pour l'Industrie du Caoutchouc (GW) 1155
Informations et Etudes Socialistes (FR ISSN 0073-7925) 905
Informations et Nouveautes Techniques/Ettela'at Va Tazeha-Ye Fanni (IR) 992
Informations Recentes sur les Comptes Nationaux des Pays en Developpment/Latest Information on National Accounts of Developing Countries (FR ISSN 0252-2683) 211, 1057
Informationsaufnahme und Informationsverarbeitung im Lebenden Organismus (GW ISSN 0344-4430) 141
Informationsblaetter zu Nachbarwissenschaften der Ur- und Fruehgeschichte (GW) 87
Informationsbulletin (GE ISSN 0138-242X) 878
Informationsdienst Uebersetzungen (GE) 679
Informatique dans les Administrations et les Entreprises Publiques (FR) 361
Informatique dans les Administrations Francaises *see* Informatique dans les Administrations et les Entreprises Publiques 361
Informativni Bilten Urbanisticnega Instituta SR Slovenije. Sporocila (YU ISSN 0351-0174) 623
Informator Archeologiczny (PL ISSN 0085-1876) 87
Informator dla Kandydaton na Studia Podyplomowe i Doktoranckie (PL ISSN 0239-9253) 436
Informator Nauki Polskiej (PL ISSN 0537-667X) 992
Informator Robotniczy (PL) 463
Informatore Farmaceutico (IT ISSN 0073-7984) 871
Informatory Regionalne (PL) 537
Informe Anual de las Actividades de las Unidades Operativas de Salud en el Programa de Planificacion Familiar del Ministerio de Salud (EC) 179
Informe Anual del Programa de Pastos Tropicales (CK ISSN 0120-2391) 28
Informe de Operacion de las Principales Empresas Productoras y Distribuidoras de Energia Electrica de Costa Rica (CR ISSN 0074-0047) 455

Informe Demografico (BL ISSN 0100-7173) 544, 922
Informe Economico Regional (SP ISSN 0211-8734) 236
Informes (PE) 905
Informes J.E.N. (SP ISSN 0081-3397) 896
Inforum: Energy-Environment Information System *see* Electric Power Industry Abstracts 461
Infoterm Series (International Information Centre for Terminology, Vienna) (GW) 679, 696
Infoterra International (KE) 262, 496
Infrared Society of Japan. Proceeding (JA ISSN 0386-8044) 894, 899, 1069
Infrared Spectroscopy Abstracts *see* Laser Raman & Infrared Spectroscopy Abstracts 893
Ingenieurbauten (US ISSN 0172-8008) 482
Ingenieurwissenschaftliche Bibliothek/ Engineering Science Library (US ISSN 0173-0274) 472
Ingenioer (DK ISSN 0109-9639) 472
Ingenioeren Indkoebsbog (DK ISSN 0446-2491) 290, 310
Inglis Lecture (US ISSN 0073-800X) 415
Initiation. Serie Textes, Bibliographies (FR ISSN 0073-8034) 127
Initiation a la Linguistique. Serie A. Lectures (FR ISSN 0073-8018) 696
Initiation a la Linguistique. Serie B. Problemes et Methodes (FR ISSN 0073-8026) 696
Initiations et Etudes Africaines *see* Institut Fondamental d'Afrique Noire. Initiations et Etudes Africaines 566
Initiative (AU) 335
Initiative (CN ISSN 0827-4789) 1018
Inklings (US ISSN 0190-0234) 723
Inky Trails (US) 741
Inland Revenue Clearances (UK) 296
Inland Revenue Official Tax Guides (UK) 296
Inland Revenue Practices and Concessions (UK) 296
Inland River Guide (US) 1100
Inland River Record (US) 1100
Inland Waterways Guide (UK) 1100
Inlet (US ISSN 0085-1884) 724
Innovations, Demarches, Experiences dans l'Enseignement Superieur *see* I D E E S 436
Innovative Graduate Programs Directory (US ISSN 0363-2601) 436
Innsbruck. Statistisches Jahrbuch (AU) 1057
Innsbrucker Beitraege zur Musikwissenschaft (AU) 836
Innsbrucker Universitaetsreden (AU) 436
Inorganic Chemistry Concepts (US ISSN 0172-7966) 328
Inorganic Syntheses Series (US ISSN 0073-8077) 331
Inpharma (NZ ISSN 0156-2703) 871
Inprint (AT ISSN 0314-285X) 724
Inquiry into the Future (KO) 569
Ins and Outs (NE ISSN 0167-3696) 711
Inscape (Pasadena) (US ISSN 0094-2715) 742
Inschriften Griechischer Staedte aus Kleinasien (GW) 87
INSEAD Address Book (UK ISSN 0304-4270) 280
Insect Chemoreception *see* Khemoretseptsiya Nasekomykh 479
Insecta Matsumurana (JA ISSN 0020-1804) 165
Insecticide and Acaricide Tests (US ISSN 0276-3656) 165
Insecticide Product Guide (US ISSN 8756-1530) 478
Insects of Micronesia (US ISSN 0073-8115) 165
Insects of Virginia (US ISSN 0098-1222) 165
Insel-Almanach (GW ISSN 0443-2460) 724
Inseminacao Artificial (BL) 66
Inside F M S (US) 745
Inside Outside Bankstreet (US) 1155

Inside the Leading Mail Order Houses (US) 284, 310
Insiders Baseball Fact-Book (US ISSN 0731-8162) 1038
Insiders Baseball Fact-Book Extra (US ISSN 0731-8146) 1038
Insider's Guide to Prep Schools (US ISSN 0271-535X) 1155
Insides *see* A I G A Graphic Design U S A 930
Insights (CN ISSN 0073-8123) 415
Insite (Year) (US) 519
INSPEC. Section A *see* Physics Abstracts 893
Inspec Matters (UK ISSN 0266-1616) 455, 1005
INSPEC, Section B. *see* Electrical & Electronics Abstracts 461
INSPEC, Section C. *see* Computer & Control Abstracts 354
INSPEC Thesaurus (UK) 455, 1005
Installations Nyts Leverandoerregister (DK) 455
Instead (AT ISSN 0313-3249) 436, 443
Institucion Principe de Viana. Coleccion Historia (SP) 586
Institut Africain de Developpement Economique et de Planification. Collection d'Etudes sur le Developpement Economique et Social *see* African Institute for Economic Development and Planning. Series in Economic and Social Development 261
Institut Archeologique du Luxembourg. Annales (BE) 87
Institut Archeologique Liegeois. Bulletin(BE) 87
Institut Canadien d'Education des Adultes Cahiers *see* I.C.E.A. Cahiers 1154
Institut Canadien de l'Information Scientifique et Technique. Rapport Annuel *see* Canada Institute for Scientific and Technical Information. Annual Report 989
Institut Catholique d'Arts et Metiers de Lille Annuaire *see* I C A M Annuaire 471
Institut Catholique de Paris. Annuaire (FR) 982
Institut Collegial Europeen. Actes des Colloques de Loches (FR) 415
Institut d'Economie Regionale Bourgogne-Franche-Comte. Cahiers (FR) 245
Institut d'Elevage et de Medecine Veterinaire des Pays Tropicaux. Rapport d'Activite (FR ISSN 0246-2303) 1121
Institut d'Emission d'Outre Mer, Paris. Rapport d'Activite (FR ISSN 0073-8247) 262
Institut d'Ethnologie. Archives et Documents, Micro Edition. Sciences Humaines (FR) 72
Institut d'Etudes du Developpement. Cahiers (FR) 262
Institut d'Etudes Politiques de Paris. Livret (FR ISSN 0078-995X) 1155
Institut d'Etudes Slaves. Lexiques (FR ISSN 0154-0157) 696
Institut d'Etudes Slaves Informations (FR ISSN 0980-3637) 630
Institut d'Etudes Slaves, Paris. Bibliotheque Russe (FR ISSN 0078-9976) 724
Institut d'Etudes Slaves, Paris. Collection de Grammaires (FR ISSN 0078-9984) 696
Institut d'Etudes Slaves, Paris. Collection de Manuels (FR ISSN 0078-9992) 696
Institut d'Etudes Slaves, Paris. Collection Historique (FR ISSN 0079-0001) 586
Institut d'Etudes Slaves, Paris. Documents Pedagogiques (FR ISSN 0300-2594) 696
Institut d'Etudes Slaves, Paris. Textes (FR ISSN 0079-001X) 724
Institut d'Etudes Slaves, Paris. Travaux (FR ISSN 0079-0028) 586, 696, 724
Institut de France. Annuaire (FR ISSN 0073-8190) 630, 992

Institut de la Communaute Europeenne pour les Etudes Universitaires. Recherche. Research (EI) 436
Institut de Linguistique de Louvain. Bibliotheque de la C I L L (BE) 696
Institut de Linguistique de Lund. Travaux (SW) 696
Institut de Medecine Legale et de Medecine Sociale. Archives (FR ISSN 0075-9473) 782
Institut de Recherche et d'Histoire des Textes, Paris. Documents, Etudes et Repertoires (FR ISSN 0073-8212) 724
Institut de Speologie Emil Racovitza. Travaux (RM ISSN 0065-0498) 399
Institut des Etudes Occitanes. Publications (FR ISSN 0073-8263) 724
Institut des Hautes Etudes de l'Amerique Latine. Collection des Travaux et Memoires (FR) 606, 905
Institut des Hautes Etudes de l'Amerique Latine. Travaux et Memoires *see* Institut des Hautes Etudes de l'Amerique Latine. Collection des Travaux et Memoires 606
Institut des Peches Maritimes. Bulletin (MR ISSN 0069-0821) 510
Institut des Sciences Agronomiques du Rwanda. Departement des Productions Animales. Compte Rendu des Travaux (RW) 66
Institut des Sciences Agronomiques du Rwanda. Departement des Productions Vegetales. Compte Rendu des Travaux (RW) 28
Institut des Sciences Nucleaires Grenoble. Rapport (FR) 896
Institut Economique Agricole. Cahiers/ L.E.I. Schriften (BE ISSN 0303-8971) 1155
Institut Economique Agricole. Courrier (BE) 1155
Institut Eksperimental'noi Meteorologii. Trudy (UR) 805
Institut "Finanzen und Steuern." Gruene Briefe (GW ISSN 0067-9941) 229, 296
Institut "Finanzen und Steuern." Schriftenreihe (GW ISSN 0067-995X) 229, 296
Institut Fondamental d'Afrique Noire. Catalogues et Documents (SG ISSN 0070-2617) 566
Institut Fondamental d'Afrique Noire. Initiations et Etudes Africaines (SG ISSN 0070-2625) 566
Institut Fondamental d'Afrique Noire. Memoires (SG ISSN 0070-2633) 566
Institut Fondamental d'Afrique Noire. Rapport Annuel (SG) 1018
Institut for Afsaetningsoekonomi. Nyt (DK ISSN 0108-1489) 284
Institut for Finansiering og Kreditvaesen. Kompendium (DK) 229
Institut for Graenseregionsforskning. Arbejdspapir (DK ISSN 0106-8628) 245
Institut Forestier National de Petawawa. Revue de Programme *see* Canada. Petawawa National Forestry Institute. Program Review 524
Institut Francais d'Archeologie Orientale du Caire. Bulletin (UA ISSN 0255-0962) 87
Institut Francais d'Etudes Andines. Travaux (PE) 72, 389, 606
Institut Francais d'Indologie. Publications (II ISSN 0073-8352) 569, 724
Institut Francais de Pondichery. Section Scientifique et Technique. Travaux (II ISSN 0073-8336) 992
Institut Francais de Pondichery. Section Scientifique et Technique. Travaux. Hors Serie (II ISSN 0073-8344) 993
Institut Francais de Recherche pour l'Exploitation de la Mer (IFREMER) -Centre de Brest France. I.F.Re.Mer. Centre de Brest. Recueil des Travaux *see* France. I.F.Re.Mer. Centre de Brest. Recueil des Travaux 1153

INSTITUT FRANCAIS

Institut Francais de Recherche pour l'Exploitation de la Mer (IFREMER) France. I.F.Re.Mer. Centre de Brest. Colloques. Actes see France. I.F.Re.Mer. Centre de Brest. Colloques. Actes 405

Institut Francais de Recherche pour l'Exploitation de la Mer (IFREMER) France. I.F.Re.Mer. Centre de Brest. Publications. Serie: Resultats des Campagnes a la Mer see France. I.F.Re.Mer. Centre de Brest. Publications. Serie: Resultats des Campagnes a la Mer 405

Institut Francais de Recherche pour l'Exploitation de la Mer (IFREMER) France. I.F.Re.Mer. Centre de Brest. Publications. Serie: Rapports Economiques et Juridiques see France. I.F.Re.Mer. Centre de Brest. Publications. Serie: Rapports Economiques et Juridiques 405

Institut Francais des Experts Comptables. Cahiers (FR) 221

Institut Francais des Sciences Administratives. (Publications) (FR) 280

Institut Francais du Petrole. Collection Colloques et Seminaires (FR ISSN 0073-8360) 864

Institut Francais du Petrole. Rapport Annuel (FR ISSN 0073-8379) 864

Institut fuer Allgemeine Botanik und Botanischer Garten. Mitteilungen (GW) 158

Institut fuer Angewandte Geodaesie. Mitteilungen (GW ISSN 0071-9196) 544

Institut fuer Asienkunde. Schriften (GW ISSN 0073-8387) 851

Institut fuer den Wissenschaftlichen Film. Publikationen zu Wissenschaftlichen Filmen. Sektion Biologie (GW ISSN 0073-8417) 141, 824

Institut fuer den Wissenschaftlichen Film. Publikationen zu Wissenschaftlichen Filmen. Sektion Ethnologie (GW ISSN 0341-5910) 72, 824

Institut fuer den Wissenschaftlichen Film. Publikationen zu Wissenschaftlichen Filmen. Sektion Geschichte, Publizistik (GW ISSN 0341-5937) 415, 558, 824

Institut fuer den Wissenschaftlichen Film. Publikationen zu Wissenschaftlichen Filmen. Sektion Medizin (GW ISSN 0341-5929) 762, 824

Institut fuer den Wissenschaftlichen Film. Publikationen zu Wissenschaftlichen Filmen. Sektion Technische Wissenschaften, Naturwissenschaften (GW ISSN 0073-8433) 824, 1069

Institut fuer den Wissenschaftlichen Film. Publikationen zu Wissenschaftlichen Filmen. Sektion Voelkerkunde see Institut fuer den Wissenschaftlichen Film. Publikationen zu Wissenschaftlichen Filmen. Sektion Ethnologie 824

Institut fuer Europaeische Geschichte, Mainz. Veroeffentlichungen. Abteilung Universalgeschichte. Beihefte (GW ISSN 0170-365X) 558

Institut fuer Europaeische Geschichte, Mainz. Veroeffentlichungen. Abteilung Universalgeschichte und Abteilung fuer Abendlaendische Religionsgeschichte (GW) 970

Institut fuer Europaeische Geschichte, Mainz. Veroeffentlichungen. Abteilung Universitaetsgeschichte und Abteilung fuer Abendlaendische Religionsphilosophie see Institut fuer Europaeische Geschichte, Mainz. Veroeffentlichungen. Abteilung Universalgeschichte und Abteilung fuer Abendlaendische Religionsgeschichte 970

Institut fuer Europaeische Geschichte, Mainz. Vortraege. Abteilung Universalgeschichte und Abteilung fuer Abendlaendische Religionsgeschichte (GW) 970

Institut fuer Europaeische Geschichte, Mainz. Vortraege. Abteilung Universalgeschichte und Abteilung fuer Abendlaendische Religionsphilosophie see Institut fuer Europaeische Geschichte, Mainz. Vortraege. Abteilung Universalgeschichte und Abteilung fuer Abendlaendische Religionsgeschichte 970

Institut fuer Gegenwartsvolkskunde. Mitteilungen (AU) 515

Institut fuer Gesellschaftspolitik. Mitteilungen (AU ISSN 0046-9696) 1008

Institut fuer Iberoamerika-Kunde. Schriftenreihe (GW ISSN 0073-8948) 263, 916

Institut fuer Internationales Recht und Internationale Beziehungen. Schriftenreihe (SZ) 670

Institut fuer Meeresforschung, Bremerhaven. Veroeffentlichungen (GW ISSN 0068-0915) 1155

Institut fuer Ostrecht. Studien (GW ISSN 0073-8492) 657

Institut fuer Politologische Zeitfragen Information. Reihe S: Subversion see I P Z Information. Reihe S: Subversion 905

Institut fuer Raumordnung. Mitteilungen. see Forschungen zur Raumentwicklung 623

Institut fuer Reaktorsicherheit der Technischen Ueberwachungs-Vereine. Taetigkeitsbericht see Gesellschaft fuer Reaktorsicherheit. Jahresbericht 471

Institut fuer Wasserwirtschaft, Hydrologie und landwirtschaftlichen Wasserbau (GW) 403, 1124

Institut Geographique du Congo. Rapport see Institut Geographique du Zaire. Rapport Annuel 544

Institut Geographique du Zaire. Rapport Annuel (ZR ISSN 0443-3173) 544

Institut Henri Poincare. Groupe d'Etude d'Analyse Ultrametrique. Exposes (FR) 749

Institut Historique Belge de Rome. Bibliotheque (BE ISSN 0073-8522) 586

Institut Historique Belge de Rome. Bulletin (BE ISSN 0073-8530) 586

Institut Historique et Archeologique Neerlandais de Istamboul. Publications (NE ISSN 0073-8549) 87, 569

Institut Hodowli i Aklmatyzacji Roslin. Biuletyn/Institute of Plant Breeding and Acclimatization Bulletin (PL ISSN 0373-7837) 56

Institut Jules Destree. Collection: Connaitre la Wallonie see Connaitre la Wallonie 580

Institut Jules Destree. Collection: Etudes et Documents see Institut Jules Destree. Etudes et Documents 586

Institut Jules Destree. Collection: Figures de Wallonie see Figures de Wallonie 581

Institut Jules Destree. Etudes et Documents (BE ISSN 0073-8557) 586

Institut Mediterraneen des Transports Maritimes (FR) 1081, 1100

Institut Michel Pacha. Annales (FR ISSN 0073-8565) 172

Institut National de la Recherche Agronomique de Tunisie. Documents Techniques (TI ISSN 0020-238X) 28

Institut National de Preparation Professionnelle. Cahier (ZR) 272

Institut National de Recherche et de Securite pour la Prevention des Accidents du Travail et des Maladies Professionnelles Lettre d'Information sur la Recherche see I N R S Lettre d'Information sur la Recherche 635

Institut National de Recherche Scientifique. Rapport pour l'Annee (RW) 993

Institut National des Industries Extractives. Rapport Annuel (BE) 817

Institut National des Langues et Civilisations Orientales. Livret de l'Etudiant (FR) 569

Institut National Genevois. Acts (SZ) 630

Institut National pour l'Etude et la Recherche Agronomique. Rapport Annuel (ZR) 28

Institut Oceanographique. Bulletin (MC ISSN 0304-5722) 406

Institut Oceanographique. Memoires (MC ISSN 0304-5714) 406

Institut Panafricain pour le Developpement. Centre d'Etudes et de Recherches Appliquees. Evaluation du Seminaire sur la Methodologie du Management des Projets (CM) 263, 280

Institut Panafricain pour le Developpement. Centre de Formation au Management des Projets. Bilan des Activites (CM) 263, 280

Institut Panafricain pour le Developpement. Travaux Manuscrits (CM) 48, 263

Institut Pasteur d'Algerie. Archives (AE ISSN 0020-2460) 168, 777

Institut Pasteur de Bangui. Rapport Annuel see Institut Pasteur de Bangui. Rapport Bisannuel 762

Institut Pasteur de Bangui. Rapport Bisannuel (CX) 762

Institut Pasteur de Dakar. Rapport sur le Fonctionnement Technique (SG) 168

Institut Pasteur Hellenique. Archives (GR ISSN 0004-6620) 168, 777

Institut Phytopathologique Benaki. Annales (GR ISSN 0365-5814) 28, 56

Institut Provincial d'Etudes et Recherches Bibliotheconomiques. Memoires (BE) 127, 679, 724

Institut Royal de Patrimoine Artistique. Bulletin/Koninklijk Instituut voor het Kunstpatrimonium. Bulletin (BE ISSN 0085-1892) 106

Institut Royal des Sciences Naturelles de Belgique. Bulletin. Serie Biologie (BE) 141, 496

Institut Royal de Sciences Naturelles de Belgique. Bulletin. Serie Entomologie(BE ISSN 0374-6232) 141

Institut Royal des Sciences Naturelles de Belgique. Bulletin. Serie Sciences de la Terre (BE ISSN 0374-6291) 389

Institut Royal des Sciences Naturelles de Belgique. Documents de Travail see Koninklijk Belgisch Instituut voor Natuurwetenschappen. Studiedocumenten 142

Institut Royal des Sciences Naturelles de Belgique. Memoires see Koninklijk Belgisch Instituut voor Natuurwetenschappen. Verhandelingen 1157

Institut Scientifique et Technique des Peches Maritimes Rapports Techniques see I S T P M Rapports Techniques 1154

Institut Teknologi Mara. Laporan Tahunan see Mara Institute of Technology. Annual Report 436

Institut Vodnogo Transporta, Leningrad. Gidrotekhnicheskaya Laboratoriya. Materialy (UR) 490

Institut za Arhitekturu i Urbanizam Srbije. Zbornik Radova (YU) 98, 623

Institut za Kriminoloska i Socioloska Istrazivanja. Zbornik (YU) 370, 1027

Institut za Medjunarodnu Politiku i Privredu. Godisnijak (YU) 905, 916

Instituta et Monumenta. Series 1: Monumenta (IT ISSN 0073-8611) 836

Instituta et Monumenta. Series 2. Instituta (IT ISSN 0392-629X) 836

Institute Collegial Europeen. Bulletin see Institut Collegial Europeen. Actes des Colloques de Loches 415

Institute for Balkan Studies. Publications/Idryma Meleton Chersonesou Aimou. Ekthoseis (GR ISSN 0073-862X) 586

Institute for Canadian-American Relations (Papers) see Annual Canadian-American Seminar. Proceedings 914

Institute for Clinical Science. Proficiency Test Service. Report (US ISSN 0073-8638) 762

Institute for Comparative Studies of Culture. Annals (JA ISSN 0563-8186) 1008

Institute for Comparative Studies of Culture. Publications see Institute for Comparative Studies of Culture. Annals 1008

Institute for Defense Analyses. Studies (US ISSN 0073-8670) 811

Institute for Development of Educational Activities, Inc. Monographs see I D E A Monographs 414

Institute for Development of Educational Activities, Inc. Occasional Papers see I D E A Occasional Papers 414

Institute for Fermentation, Osaka. Annual Report see Institute for Fermentation, Osaka. Research Communications 168

Institute for Fermentation, Osaka. Research Communications/Hakko Kenkyusho Hokoku (JA ISSN 0073-8751) 168

Institute for Financial Management and Research Publications see I F M R Publications 280

Institute for Human Evolution. Monographs see I C H E International Commission on Human Ecology 72

Institute for Human Evolution. Reprint see White Paper on Human Ecology 78

Institute for Industrial Research and Standards Occasional Report Series see I I R S Occasional Report Series 1069

Institute for Management Education and Development. Report (IO) 280

Institute for Migration, Turku. Migration Studies see Migration Institute. Migration Studies 923

Institute for Monetary Research. Monographs (US ISSN 0073-8778) 1155

Institute for Orgonomic Science. Annals(US) 172

Institute for Palestine Studies. Arabic Annual Documentary Series (LE) 569

Institute for Palestine Studies. Arabs Under Israeli Occupation Series (LE) 612

Institute for Palestine Studies. Basic Documents Series see Institute for Palestine Studies. United Nations Resolutions on Palestine and the Arab-Israeli Conflict Series 1155

Institute for Palestine Studies. I.P.S. Papers Series (LE) 612

Institute for Palestine Studies. International Annual Documentary Series (LE ISSN 0073-8808) 569

Institute for Palestine Studies. Israeli Knesset Series (LE) 612

Institute for Palestine Studies. Monograph Series (LE ISSN 0073-8816) 569

Institute for Palestine Studies. United Nations Resolutions on Palestine and the Arab-Israeli Conflict Series (LE) 1155

Institute for Palestine Studies. Zionist Congress Series (LE) 612

Institute for Petroleum Research and Geophysics, Holon, Israel. Report (IS ISSN 0073-8832) 399, 864

Institute for Rewriting Indian History. Annual Report and General Meeting Invitation (II) 569

Institute for Scientific Information Atlas of Science: Vol. 1: Biochemistry and Molecular Biology see I S I Atlas of Science: Vol. 1: Biochemistry and Molecular Biology 1154

Institute for Scientific Information Atlas of Science: Vol. 2: Biotechnology and Molecular Genetics see I S I Atlas of Science: Vol. 2: Biotechnology and Molecular Genetics 1154

INSTITUTE OF   1769

Institute for Scientific Information Science Citation Index Journal Citation Report *see* Science Citation Index Journal Citation Report   *999*
Institute for Sea Training. Journal (JA ISSN 0386-1198)   *406*
Institute for Social and Economic Change Monograph *see* I S E C Monograph   *245*
Institute for Studies in American Music. Monographs (US)   *836*
Institute for the Certification of Computer Professionals. Annual Report (US ISSN 0098-2431)   *352, 357*
Institute for the Comprehensive Study of Lotus Sutra. Journal/Hokke Bunka Kenkyu (JA)   *977*
Institute for the Study of Human Issues Occasional Papers in Social Change *see* I S H I Occasional Papers in Social Change   *1027*
Institute for the Study of Man in Africa Occasional Papers *see* I S M A Occasional Papers   *72*
Institute for the Study of Man in Africa Papers *see* I S M A Papers   *72*
Institute of Actuaries. Year Book (UK ISSN 0073-8980)   *1155*
Institute of Actuaries Students' Society. Journal (UK ISSN 0020-269X)   *639*
Institute of Agricultural Engineering, Bet Dagan. Scientific Activities (IS)   *51*
Institute of Applied Manpower Research Reports *see* I.A.M.R. Reports   *272*
Institute of Applied Social & Economic Research Discussion Papers *see* I A S E R Discussion Papers   *1008*
Institute of Applied Social & Economic Research Monographs *see* I A S E R Monographs   *1008*
Institute of Applied Social and Economic Research of Papua New Guinea Special Publications *see* I A S E R Special Publications   *1008*
Institute of Archaeo-Metallurgical Studies Newsletter *see* I A M S Newsletter   *87*
Institute of Certified Travel Agents Directory *see* I C T A Directory   *1111*
Institute of Chartered Accountants in Australia. Annual Report and Accounts (AT)   *221*
Institute of Chartered Accountants in England and Wales. Exposure Drafts and Statements of Standard Accounting Practice (UK)   *221*
Institute of Chartered Accountants in England and Wales. Management Information Series (UK ISSN 0073-9030)   *221*
Institute of Chartered Accountants in England and Wales. Practice Administration Series, Exposure Drafts and Statements of Standard Accounting Practice *see* Institute of Chartered Accountants in England and Wales. Exposure Drafts and Statements of Standard Accounting Practice   *221*
Institute of Chartered Accountants in England and Wales. Tax Digest (UK ISSN 0260-6496)   *296*
Institute of Chartered Accountants of Guyana. Newsletter (GY ISSN 0380-4011)   *221*
Institute of Chartered Accountants of Scotland. Official Directory (UK ISSN 0073-9057)   *221*
Institute of Chartered Shipbrokers. Reference Book and List of Members (Year) (UK ISSN 0267-2006)   *1100*
Institute of Clerk of Works of Great Britain Incorporated. Year Book (UK ISSN 0073-9073)   *185*
Institute of Cornish Studies. Special Bibliography (UK)   *503*
Institute of Cost and Management Accountants. Framework Series in Accounting (UK)   *221*
Institute of Cost and Management Accountants. Occasional Papers Series (UK)   *221*
Institute of Developing Economies. Annual Report (JA)   *263*

Institute of Developing Economies Occasional Papers Series *see* I.D.E. Occasional Papers Series   *195*
Institute of Development Management. Report of the Activities of the Institute (TZ)   *280*
Institute of Development Studies. Annual Report (UK)   *263, 1027*
Institute of Early American History and Culture. News Letter (US ISSN 0020-2843)   *606*
Institute of Economic Affairs. Occasional Papers (UK ISSN 0073-909X)   *196*
Institute of Economic Affairs. Research Monographs (UK ISSN 0073-9103)   *196*
Institute of Economic Growth, Delhi. Census Studies (II ISSN 0070-3311)   *922*
Institute of Economic Research. Publications on Demography (II)   *922*
Institute of Economic Research. Publications on Economics (II)   *196*
Institute of Economic Research. Publications on Family Planning (II)   *179*
Institute of Electrical and Electronics Engineers, Inc. Computer Society Conference on Computer Vision and Pattern Recognition. Proceedings *see* I E E E Computer Society Conference on Computer Vision and Pattern Recognition. Proceedings   *356*
Institute of Electrical and Electronics Engineers, Inc. Southeastcon (Region 3 Conference) Record *see* I E E E Southeastcon (Region 3 Conference) Record   *455*
Institute of Electrical and Electronics Engineers, Inc. Student Papers *see* I E E E Student Papers   *455*
Institute of Electrical and Electronics Engineers, Inc. Vehicular Technology Conference. Record *see* I E E E Vehicular Technology Conference. Record   *1092*
Institute of Electrolysis. List of Qualified Operators (UK)   *118*
Institute of Energy. Northern Ireland Section. Year Book (UK)   *865*
Institute of Energy. Papers of the National Convention (UK)   *865*
Institute of Energy. Report and Accounts (UK)   *465, 865*
Institute of Energy. Symposium Series. (UK)   *478*
Institute of Environmental Sciences. Annual Meeting. Proceedings (US ISSN 0073-9227)   *142, 472, 496*
Institute of Environmental Sciences. Tutorial Series (US ISSN 0073-9251)   *142, 472, 496*
Institute of European Studies. Annali I S E (IT)   *586, 657, 905*
Institute of European Studies. Announcements (US ISSN 0073-926X)   *441*
Institute of European Studies. Papers and Addresses of the Annual Conference and Academic Council (US ISSN 0073-9278)   *441*
Institute of Field and Garden Crops. Scientific Activities (IS)   *56*
Institute of Finance Management. Prospectus (TZ)   *229*
Institute of Food Research - Bristol. Laboratory Biennial Report (UK)   *519*
Institute of Food Technologists Basic Symposium Series *see* I F T Basic Symposium Series   *846*
Institute of Food Technologists World Directory and Buyers' Guide *see* I F T World Directory and Buyers' Guide   *1154*
Institute of Forest Genetics, Suwon, Korea. Research Report (KO ISSN 0073-9294)   *525*
Institute of Freshwater Research, Drottningholm. Report (SW ISSN 0082-0032)   *403*
Institute of Fuel. Northern Ireland Section. Year Book *see* Institute of Energy. Northern Ireland Section. Year Book   *865*

Institute of Fuel. Papers of the National Convention *see* Institute of Energy. Papers of the National Convention   *865*
Institute of Fuel. Symposium Series *see* Institute of Energy. Symposium Series   *478*
Institute of Gas Technology. Annual Report (US)   *865*
Institute of Gas Technology. Director's Report *see* Institute of Gas Technology. Annual Report   *865*
Institute of Geological Sciences, London. Statistical Summary of the Mineral Industry *see* World Mineral Statistics   *822*
Institute of Geoscience. Annual Report (JA)   *399*
Institute of Human Biology, Papua New Guinea. Monograph Series *see* Papua New Guinea Institute of Medical Research. Monograph Series   *765*
Institute of Industrial Engineers. Health Services Division. Annual Conference Proceedings (US)   *617*
Institute of Insurance Consultants. Reference Book and List of Members (Year) (UK ISSN 0267-3673)   *639*
Institute of Jewish Affairs Research Reports *see* I J A. Research Reports   *503*
Institute of Labor and Industrial Relations. Policy Papers in Human Resources and Industrial Relations (US ISSN 0073-9421)   *272*
Institute of Maintenance and Building Management. Reference Book and List of Members (UK ISSN 0267-2030)   *185*
Institute of Management Consultants. Yearbook (UK ISSN 0260-373X)   *280*
Institute of Marine Engineers. Transactions *see* Institute of Marine Engineers Technical Reports   *1086*
Institute of Marine Engineers Technical Reports (UK ISSN 0309-3948)   *8, 1086*
Institute of Mathematical Sciences, Madras, India. Proceedigs of Symposia and Summer Schools *see* Symposia on Theoretical Physics and Mathematics   *753*
Institute of Mathematical Statistics Lecture Notes. Monograph Series *see* I M S Lecture Notes. Monograph Series   *749*
Institute of Mathematics and Its Applications. Proceedings (UK)   *749*
Institute of Medical Laboratory Sciences. London, Annual Report (UK)   *781*
Institute of Medical Laboratory Technology. London. Annual Report *see* Institute of Medical Laboratory Sciences. London, Annual Report   *781*
Institute of Mennonite Studies Series (US ISSN 0073-9456)   *984*
Institute of Mining and Metallurgy. Transactions: Metallurgical Series *see* Vysoka Skola Banska. Sbornik Vedeckych Praci: Rada Hutnicka   *800*
Institute of Nature Education in Shiga Heights. Bulletin/Shiga Shizen Kyoiku Kenkyu Shisetsu Kenkyu Gyoseki (JA ISSN 0389-9128)   *379*
Institute of Navigation. National Technical Meeting Proceedings (US)   *19*
Institute of Navigation. Proceedings of the Annual Meeting (US)   *1100*
Institute of Nuclear Agriculture. Annual Report (BG)   *28*
Institute of Nuclear Materials Management. Proceedings of Annual Meeting (US ISSN 0073-9472)   *472, 897*
Institute of Oceanographic Sciences. Annual Report (UK ISSN 0309-4472)   *406*
Institute of Oceanographic Sciences. Collected Reprints (UK ISSN 0309-7463)   *406*
Institute of Paper Chemistry. Abstract Bulletin (US ISSN 0020-3033)   *8, 859*

Institute of Paper Chemistry. Bibliographic Series (US ISSN 0073-9480)   *859*
Institute of Patent Attorneys of Australia. Annual Proceedings (AT)   *657, 861*
Institute of Physical and Chemical Research Riken. Accelerator Progress Report *see* Riken. Accelerator Progress Report   *898*
Institute of Physics, London. Conference Series. Proceedings (UK ISSN 0305-2346)   *888*
Institute of Phytopathological Research. Annual Report *see* Instituut voor Plantenziektenkundig Onderzoek. Jaarverslag   *56*
Institute of Phytopathological Research. Communications *see* Instituut voor Plantenziektenkundig Onderzoek. Mededeling   *57*
Institute of Plant Breeding and Acclimatization Bulletin *see* Institut Hodowli i Aklmatyzacji Roslin. Biuletyn   *56*
Institute of Plant Protection. Scientific Activities (IS)   *56*
Institute of Primate Research. Annual Report (KE)   *167, 175*
Institute of Psychophysical Research. Proceedings (UK ISSN 0073-9561)   *934*
Institute of Public Administration, Dublin. Administration Yearbook and Diary (IE ISSN 0073-9596)   *942*
Institute of Public Administration, Dublin. Annual Report (IE ISSN 0073-9588)   *942*
Institute of Public Administration, Khartoum. Occasional Papers (SJ ISSN 0073-9618)   *942*
Institute of Public Administration, Khartoum. Proceedings of the Annual Round Table Conference (SJ ISSN 0073-9626)   *942*
Institute of Public Health. Annual Report/Kokuritsu Koshu Eisei-in Nenpo (JA)   *954*
Institute of Race Relations. Annual Report (UK)   *1027*
Institute of Refrigeration. Proceedings (UK)   *554*
Institute of Secretariat Training and Management. Annual Report (II ISSN 0304-7083)   *286*
Institute of Social and Economic Research. Reports (US)   *196, 1008*
Institute of Social, Economic and Government Research. Reports *see* Institute of Social and Economic Research. Reports   *196*
Institute of Social Studies, The Hague. Research Report Series (NE)   *1027*
Institute of Soils & Water. Scientific Activities (IS)   *56*
Institute of Southeast Asian Studies. Annual Report (SI)   *569*
Institute of Southeast Asian Studies. Annual Review (SI ISSN 0377-5437)   *905*
Institute of Southeast Asian Studies. Current Issues Seminar Series (SI)   *569*
Institute of Southeast Asian Studies. Field Reports Series (SI)   *1008*
Institute of Southeast Asian Studies. Library Bulletin (SI ISSN 0073-9723)   *679*
Institute of Southeast Asian Studies. Local History and Memoirs (SI)   *569*
Institute of Southeast Asian Studies. Monographs Series (SI)   *905*
Institute of Southeast Asian Studies. Occasional Paper (SI ISSN 0073-9731)   *569*
Institute of Southeast Asian Studies. Oral History Programmes *see* Institute of Southeast Asian Studies. Local History and Memoirs   *569*
Institute of Southeast Asian Studies. Proceedings of International Conferences (SI)   *245*
Institute of Southeast Asian Studies. Research Notes and Discussion Series (SI ISSN 0129-8828)   *570*
Institute of Standards and Industrial Research of Iran Yearbook *see* I S I R I Yearbook   *809*

1770 INSTITUTE OF

Institute of Statistical Mathematics. Annual Report/Tokei Suri Kenkyusho Nenpo (JA) *1155*

Institute of Swimming Teachers & Coaches Directory of Membership (UK) *1034*

Institute of the Black World. Black Paper (US) *503*

Institute of the Black World. Occasional Paper Series (US) *503*

Institute of Travel Managers Yearbook *see* I T M Yearbook *1111*

Institute of Water Pollution Control Handbook (UK) *1155*

Institute on Pluralism and Group Identity. Working Paper Series (US) *503, 1027*

Institute on the Church in Urban Industrial Society Justice Ministries *see* I C U I S Justice Ministries *975*

Institute Orientaliste de Louvain. Publications *see* Universite Catholique de Louvain. Institut Orientaliste. Publications *572*

Institute T N O for Building Materials and Building Structures. Annual Report (NE) *185*

Institutet foer Metallforskning. Forskningsverksamheten (SW ISSN 0015-7953) *798*

Institution Analysis (US) *1018*

Institution of Civil Engineers List of Members *see* I C E List of Members *481*

Institution of Electrical Engineers Conference Publication Series *see* I E E Conference Publication Series *454*

Institution of Engineering Designers Official Reference Book and Buyers Guide (UK ISSN 0261-7641) *472*

Institution of Engineers. Year Book (BG ISSN 0073-9219) *472*

Institution of Engineers, Australia. General Engineering Transactions *see* Institution of Engineers, Australia. Transactions. Multi-Disciplinary Engineering *472*

Institution of Engineers, Australia. Transactions. Multi-Disciplinary Engineering (AT ISSN 0812-3314) *472*

Institution of Engineers of Ireland. Register of Chartered Engineers and Members (IE) *472*

Institution of Engineers of Ireland. Transactions (IE ISSN 0073-9790) *472*

Institution of Engineers, Sri Lanka. Transactions (CE) *472*

Institution of Engineers, Sri Lanka. Year Book (CE) *472*

Institution of Environmental Sciences Proceedings *see* I E S Proceedings *496*

Institution of Mining and Metallurgy Abstracts *see* I M M Abstracts *822*

Institution of Public Health Engineers Data Book *see* Institution of Public Health Engineers Yearbook *954*

Institution of Public Health Engineers Yearbook (UK) *954*

Institution of Railway Signal Engineers. Proceedings (UK ISSN 0073-9839) *1094*

Institution of Structural Engineers. Sessional Yearbook and Directory of Members (UK) *482*

Institution of Structural Engineers. Yearbook *see* Institution of Structural Engineers. Sessional Yearbook and Directory of Members *482*

Institution of Water Engineers & Scientists Handbook (UK) *1155*

Institutional Distribution Handbook of Foodservice Distribution *see* I D Handbook of Foodservice Distribution *309*

Instituto Antartico Chileno. Contribution. Serie Cientifica (CL ISSN 0073-9871) *573*

Instituto Antartico Chileno. Publicacion *see* Instituto Antartico Chileno. Contribution. Serie Cientifica *573*

Instituto Bahiano do Fumo. Boletim Informativo: Comercio Exterior - Esportacao de Fumo Em Folhas (BL) *1080*

Instituto Biologico da Bahia. Boletim (BL ISSN 0020-3661) *142*

Instituto Brasileiro de Economia. Centro de Estudos Agricolas. Agropecuaria (BL) *28*

Instituto Brasileiro do Cafe. Departamento Economico. Anuario Estatistico do Cafe (BL) *119*

Instituto Brasileiro do Cafe. Departamento Economico. Anuario Estatistico do Cafe. *see* Instituto Brasileiro do Cafe. Departamento Economico. Anuario Estatistico do Cafe *119*

Instituto Brasileiro do Cafe. Grupo Executivo de Racionalizacao de Cafeicultura. Relatorio do Gerca (BL) *120*

Instituto Butantan. Coletanea de Trabalhos (BL) *762*

Instituto Butantan. Memorias (BL ISSN 0073-9901) *175*

Instituto Caro y Cuervo. Publicaciones (CK) *630*

Instituto Caro y Cuervo. Seminario Andres Bello. Cuadernos (CK) *696*

Instituto Caro y Cuervo. Serie Bibliografica (CK ISSN 0073-991X) *127*

Instituto Caro y Cuervo. Serie Granada Entreabierta (CK) *724*

Instituto Caro y Cuervo. Serie Minor (CK ISSN 0073-9928) *696, 724*

Instituto Centro Americano de Investigacion y Tecnologia Industrial. Publicaciones Geologicas (GT ISSN 0073-9936) *389*

Instituto Centroamericano de Administracion Publica. Serie 100. Aspectos Humanos de la Administracion (CR ISSN 0073-9944) *942*

Instituto Centroamericano de Administracion Publica. Serie 200. Ciencia de la Administracion (CR ISSN 0073-9952) *943*

Instituto Centroamericano de Administracion Publica. Serie 300: Investigacion (CR ISSN 0073-9960) *943*

Instituto Centroamericano de Administracion Publica. Serie 400: Economia y Finanzas (CR ISSN 0073-9979) *943*

Instituto Centroamericano de Administracion Publica. Serie 600: Informes de Seminarios (CR ISSN 0073-9995) *943*

Instituto Centroamericano de Administracion Publica. Serie 700: Materiales de Informacion (CR ISSN 0074-0004) *943*

Instituto Centroamericano de Administracion Publica. Serie 800: Metodologia de la Administracion (CR ISSN 0074-0012) *943*

Instituto Centroamericano de Administracion Publica. Serie 900: Miscelaneas (CR ISSN 0074-0020) *943*

Instituto Centroamericano de Administracion Publica Lista de Nuevas Adquisiciones *see* I C A P Lista de Nuevas Adquisiciones *687*

Instituto Colombiano Agropecuario. Boletin Tecnico (CK ISSN 0538-0391) *28*

Instituto Colombiano Agropecuario. Catalogo de Publicaciones Periodicas (CK) *41*

Instituto Colombiano de Cultura. Gaceta (CK) *1009*

Instituto Costarricense de Turismo. Memoria Anual (CR) *1111*

Instituto Cultural Italo-Brasileiro. Caderno (BL) *916*

Instituto de Antropologia e Historia. Anuario (VE) *1155*

Instituto de Biologia Marina. Serie Contribuciones *see* Instituto Nacional de Investigacion y Desarrollo Pesquero. Serie Contribuciones *406*

Instituto de Biologia Marinha e Oceanografia. Trabalhos *see* Universidade Federal de Pernambuco. Departamento de Oceanografia. Centro de Tecnologia. Trabalhos Oceanograficos *148*

Instituto de Ciencia Politica Rafael Bielsa. Anuario (AG ISSN 0074-0063) *905*

Instituto de Credito Agricola y Pecuario. Informe Annual (VE) *245*

Instituto de Desarrollo de los Recursos Naturales Renovables. Oficina de Planeacion. Estadisticas Pesqueras (CK) *514*

Instituto de Desarrollo Urbano Noticiero I.D.U.N. *see* Noticiero I.D.U.N *624*

Instituto de Economia y Producciones Ganaderas del Ebro. Comunicaciones(SP ISSN 0374-8189) *28*

Instituto de Economia y Producciones Ganaderas del Ebro. Trabajos (SP ISSN 0375-3417) *28*

Instituto de Estudios Andinos. Cuadernos (PE) *1027*

Instituto de Estudios Andinos. Trabajo de Campo (PE) *72*

Instituto de Estudios de Administracion Local. Catedra Calvo Sotelo. Conferencias (SP) *951*

Instituto de Estudios Gerundenses. Anales (SP ISSN 0211-2329) *503*

Instituto de Estudios Gerundenses. Serie Monografica (SP ISSN 0211-2477) *503*

Instituto de Estudios Madrilenos. Anales (SP ISSN 0584-6374) *630*

Instituto de Estudios Peruanos. Analisis Economico (PE) *245*

Instituto de Estudios Peruanos. Coleccion Minima (PE) *1027*

Instituto de Estudios Peruanos. Estudios de la Sociedad Rural (PE) *1027*

Instituto de Estudios Peruanos. Historia Andina (PE) *606*

Instituto de Estudios Peruanos. Proyecto de Estudios Etnologicos del Valle de Chancay. Monografia (PE) *72*

Instituto de Estudios Tarraconenses Ramon Berenguer IV. Publicacion (SP ISSN 0534-3364) *586*

Instituto de Estudios Tarraconenses Ramon Berenguer IV. Seccion de Estudios Juridicos. Publicacion (SP) *657*

Instituto de Filosofia, Ciencias y Letras. Cuadernos (UY) *630*

Instituto de Filosofia del Derecho. Boletin Informativo (VE) *657*

Instituto de Fomento Pesquero. Boletin Cientifico *see* Serie Investigacion Pesquera *513*

Instituto de Geografia. Annales *see* Anales de Geografia *541*

Instituto de Higiene e Medicina Tropical. Anais (PO ISSN 0303-7762) *777, 954*

Instituto de Investigacao Agronomica de Angola. Divisao de Meteorologia Agricola. Anuario (AO) *28, 805*

Instituto de Investigacao Agronomica de Angola. Relatorio (AO ISSN 0078-2254) *28*

Instituto de Investigacao Agronomica de Angola. Serie Cientifica (AO ISSN 0078-2262) *28*

Instituto de Investigacao Agronomica de Angola. Serie Tecnica (AO ISSN 0078-2270) *28*

Instituto de Investigacao Agronomica de Mocambique. Centro de Documentacas Agraria. Memorias (MZ ISSN 0077-1791) *28*

Instituto de Investigacao Agronomica de Mocambique. Comunicacoes *see* Agronomia Mocambicana *23*

Instituto de Investigacao Cientifica de Angola. Bibliograficas Tematicas (AO ISSN 0074-008X) *1004*

Instituto de Investigacao Cientifica de Angola. Memorias e Trabalhos (AO ISSN 0074-0098) *993*

Instituto de Investigacao Cientifica de Angola. Relatorios e Communicacoes(AO ISSN 0003-343X) *993*

Instituto de Investigacao Cientifica Tropical. Bibliografia Cientifica (PO) *1155*

Instituto de Investigacao Cientifica Tropical. Centro de Estudos de Historia e Cartografia Antiga. Serie de Memorias (PO ISSN 0870-015X) *545*

Instituto de Investigacao Cientifica Tropical. Centro de Estudos de Historia e Cartografia Antiga. Serie Separatas (PO) *545, 558*

Instituto de Investigacao Cientifica Tropical. Memorias (PO ISSN 0870-0036) *379*

Instituto de Investigaciones Economicas. Revista (BO) *251*

Instituto de Investigaciones Electricas. Informe Anual (MX) *455*

Instituto de Investigaciones Geologicas. Boletin *see* Chile. Servicio Nacional de Geologia y Mineria. Boletin *385*

Instituto de Investigaciones Veterinarias. Boletin *see* Veterinaria Tropical *1122*

Instituto de la Patagonia. Anales *see* Instituto de la Patagonia. Anales. Social Sciencies *606*

Instituto de la Patagonia. Anales. Social Sciencies (CL) *142, 606*

Instituto de Matematica Beppo Levi. Cuadernos (AG ISSN 0326-0690) *749*

Instituto de Nutricion de Centro America y Panama. Informe Anual (UN ISSN 0533-4179) *846*

Instituto de Pesca, Sao Paulo. Boletim (BL ISSN 0046-9939) *510*

Instituto de Pesca, Sao Paulo. Boletim. Serie de Divulgacao (BL) *510*

Instituto de Pesquisa Agropecuaria do Norte. Boletim Tecnico *see* Centro de Pesquisa Agropecuaria do Tropico Umido. Boletim de Pesquisa *25*

Instituto de Pesquisas Rodoviarias. Relatorio das Atividades (BL) *1096*

Instituto de Pesquisas Veterinarias Desiderio Finamor. Boletim (BL) *1121*

Instituto de Pesquisas Zootecnicas "Francisco Osorio". Anuario Tecnico (BL) *63, 66*

Instituto de Planejamento Economico e Social Estudos para o Planejamento *see* I P E A Estudos para o Planejamento *289*

Instituto de Planejamento Economico e Social Relatorios de Pesquisa *see* I P E A Relatorios de Pesquisa *1027*

Instituto de Planejamento Economico e Social Serie Monografica *see* I P E A Serie Monografica *289*

Instituto de Planejamento Economico e Social Serie P N P E *see* I P E A Serie P N P E *195*

Instituto de Planejamento Economico e Social Serie Pensamento Economico Brasileiro *see* I P E A Serie Pensamento Economico Brasileiro *195*

Instituto de Tecnologia de Alimentos. Coletanea (BL ISSN 0100-350X) *519, 846*

Instituto de Tecnologia de Alimentos. Estudos Economicos. Alimentos Processados (BL ISSN 0100-4964) *519, 522*

Instituto de Tecnologia de Alimentos. Instrucoes Praticas (BL ISSN 0074-0144) *846*

Instituto de Tecnologia de Alimentos. Instrucoes Tecnicas (BL ISSN 0074-0152) *846*

Instituto de Vivienda y Urbanismo. Memoria Presentada por el Director General *see* Panama. Ministerio de Vivienda. Memoria *625*

Instituto de Zoologia "Dr. Augusto Nobre". Publicacoes (PO ISSN 0020-4021) *175*

Instituto de Zootecnia. Facultad de Veterinaria. Catalogo de Publicaciones (SP) *66*

Instituto del Mar del Peru. Boletin (PE ISSN 0378-7699) *510*

Instituto del Mar del Peru. Informe. (PE ISSN 0378-7702) *510*

Instituto do Patrimonio Historico e Artistico Nacional. Publicacoes (BL) *630*

Instituto Espanol de Oceanografia. Boletin (SP ISSN 0074-0195) *406*

Instituto Espanol de Oceanografia. Trabajos (SP ISSN 0074-0209) *406*

Instituto Florestal. Boletim Tecnico (BL ISSN 0100-3151) *525*

Instituto Geografico Agustin Codazzi. Informe de Labores (CK) *545*
Instituto Historico e Geografico do Espirito Santo. Revista (BL) 545, *558*
Instituto Hondureno de Seguridad Social. Departamento de Estadistica y Procesamiento de Datos. Anuario Estadistico (HO ISSN 0074-0233) *639*
Instituto Indigenista Interamericano Serie de Ediciones Especiales (MX) *72*
Instituto Interamericano de Ciencias Agricolas de la O E A. Documentos Oficiales see Instituto Interamericano de Cooperacion para la Agricultura - O E A. Documentos Oficiales *28*
Instituto Interamericano de Cooperacion para la Agricultura - O E A. Documentos Oficiales (CR) *28*
Instituto Interamericano de Etnomusicologia y Folklore. Revista (VE) 516, *836*
Instituto Interamericano del Nino. Educacion Especial. Informes Tecnicos (UY) 444, *1018*
Instituto Interamericano del Nino. Estadistica e Informatica. Informes Tecnicos (UY) *1018*, 1057
Instituto Interamericano del Nino. Juridico Social. Informes Tecnicos (UY) 657, *1027*
Instituto Interamericano del Nino. Publicaciones sobre Servicio Social see Instituto Interamericano del Nino. Servicio Social. Informes Tecnicos *1018*
Instituto Interamericano del Nino. Registro Civil. Informes Tecnicos (UY) *1018*
Instituto Interamericano del Nino. Servicio Social. Informes Tecnicos (UY) *1018*
Instituto Internacional de Historia del Derecho Indiano. Actas y Estudios (SP) *668*
Instituto Joaquim Nabuco de Pesquisas Sociais. Serie Cursos e Conferencias see Fundacao Joaquim Nabuco. Serie Cursos e Conferencias *1026*
Instituto Joaquim Nabuco de Pesquisas Sociais. Serie Documentos see Fundacao Joaquim Nabuco. Serie Documentos *1026*
Instituto Joaquim Nabuco de Pesquisas Sociais. Serie Estudos e Pesquisas see Fundacao Joaquim Nabuco. Serie Estudos e Pesquisas *1026*
Instituto Joaquim Nabuco de Pesquisas Sociais. Serie Monografias see Fundacao Joaquim Nabuco. Serie Monografias *1008*
Instituto Latinamericano de Planificacion Economica y Social Cuadernos see I L P E S Cuadernos *277*
Instituto Linguistico de Verano. Documentos de Trabajo (PE) *696*
Instituto Linguistico de Verano. Serie Sintactica (CK) *696*
Instituto Linguistico de Verano en Colombia. Bibliografia (CK) *709*
Instituto Mexicano del Seguro Social. Boletin Estadistico (MX) *954*
Instituto Mexicano del Seguro Social. Boletin sobre Morbilidad Hospitalaria(MX) *954*
Instituto Mexicano del Seguro Social. Boletin sobre Mortalidad (MX) *954*
Instituto Mexicano del Seguro Social. Boletin sobre Motivos de Consulta (MX) *954*
Instituto Nacional de Antropologia e Historia. Coleccion Cientifica (MX ISSN 0076-7611) *72*
Instituto Nacional de Antropologia e Historia. Series Cientifica see Instituto Nacional de Antropologia e Historia. Coleccion Cientifica *72*
Instituto Nacional de Astrofisica, Optica y Electronica. Boletin (MX) *116, 455*
Instituto Nacional de Colonizacao e Reforma Agraria. Coordenadoria Regional do Parana. Sinopse do Cooperativismo No Parana (BL) *238*
Instituto Nacional de Estadistica. Boletin Anual (PE) *277*

Instituto Nacional de Industria Grupo I N I (Resumen de Actividades) see Grupo I N I (Resumen de Actividades) *289*
Instituto Nacional de Investigacao Cientifica. Textos Classicos (PO) *878*
Instituto Nacional de Investigacao Cientifica. Textos de Linguistica (PO) *696*
Instituto Nacional de Investigacao Cientifica. Textos Humanisticos Portugueses (PO) *630*
Instituto Nacional de Investigacion y Desarrollo Pesquero. Memoria (AG ISSN 0325-6987) *510*
Instituto Nacional de Investigacion y Desarrollo Pesquero. Serie Contribuciones (AG ISSN 0325-6790) *406*
Instituto Nacional de Investigaciones Folkloricas. Cuadernos (AG) *516*
Instituto Nacional de Investigaciones Forestales. Boletin Divulgativo (MX ISSN 0185-2361) *165, 525*
Instituto Nacional de Investigaciones Forestales. Boletin Tecnico (MX ISSN 0185-2310) *165, 525*
Instituto Nacional de Investigaciones Forestales. Catalogo (MX) *525*
Instituto Nacional de Investigaciones Forestales. Publicacion Especial (MX ISSN 0185-2566) *165, 525*
Instituto Nacional de Investigaciones Geologico Mineras. Informe Anual de Actividades (CK) *389*
Instituto Nacional de Investigaciones Geologico Mineras. Publicaciones Geologicas Especiales del Ingeominas(CK) *389*
Instituto Nacional de Investigaciones sobre Recursos Bioticos. Nota Tecnica (MX) *530*
Instituto Nacional de Investigaciones sobre Recursos Bioticos Informa see I N I R E B Informa *141*
Instituto Nacional de Seguros. Informe Anual see Instituto Nacional de Seguros Memoria Anual *639*
Instituto Nacional de Seguros. Memoria Anual I.N.S. see Instituto Nacional de Seguros Memoria Anual *639*
Instituto Nacional de Seguros Memoria Anual (CR) *639*
Instituto Nacional de Tecnologia Agropecuaria. Estacion Experimental Regional Agropecuaria. Boletin de Divulgacion Tecnica (AG ISSN 0325-1772) *29*
Instituto Nacional de Tecnologia Agropecuaria. Estacion Experimental Regional Agropecuaria. Publicacion Tecnica see Instituto Nacional de Tecnologia Agropecuaria. Estacion Experimental Regional Agropecuaria. Boletin de Divulgacion Tecnica *29*
Instituto Peruano de Derecho Agrario. Cuadernos Agrarios (PE) *29, 657*
Instituto Politecnico Nacional. Escuela National de Ciencias Biologicas. Anales (MX ISSN 0026-1777) *175*
Instituto Provincial de Investigaciones y Estudios Toledanos. Publicaciones (SP) *586*
Instituto Quimico de Sarria see I.Q.S *323*
Instituto Sperimentale Talassografico, Trieste. Pubblicazione (IT ISSN 0082-6456) *406*
Instituto Superior de Agronomia. Anais (PO) *29, 586*
Instituto Superior de Estudios Eclesiasticos. Libro Anual (MX) *970*
Instituto Tecnologico de Santo Domingo. Documentos (DR ISSN 0378-956X) *993*
Instituto Teologico del Uruguay. Cuadernos (UY) *970*
Instituto Torcuato di Tella. Centro de Estudios Urbanos Regionales. Documentos de Trabajo (AG ISSN 0074-0330) *1155*
Instituto Torcuato di Tella. Centro de Investigaciones Economicas. Documentos de Trabajo (AG ISSN 0074-0349) *1155*

Instituto Torcuato di Tella. Centro de Investigaciones Sociales. Documentos de Trabajo (AG ISSN 0074-0357) *1155*
Instituto y Observatorio de Marina. Efemerides Astronomicas (SP ISSN 0080-5971) *116*
Instituto y Observatorio de Marina. Observaciones Meteorologicas, Magneticas y Sismicas. Anales (SP ISSN 0080-5955) *399*
Instituttet for Matematisk Statistik og Operationsanalyse. Working Paper (DK ISSN 0107-5233) *749*
Institutul Agronomic Cluj-Napoca. Buletinul see Institutul Agronomic Cluj-Napoca. Buletinul. Seria Agricultura *29*
Institutul Agronomic Cluj-Napoca. Buletinul. Seria Agricultura (RM ISSN 0557-465X) *29, 533*
Institutul Agronomic Cluj-Napoca. Buletinul. Seria Agricultura se Horticultura see Institutul Agronomic Cluj-Napoca. Buletinul. Seria Agricultura *29*
Institutul Agronomic Cluj-Napoca. Buletinul. Seria Zootehnie si Medicina Veterinara (RM ISSN 0557-4668) *66, 1121*
Institutul Agronomic Ion Ionescu de la Brad. Lucrari Stiintifice. Seria Agronomie (RM ISSN 0379-8364) *29*
Institutul Agronomic Ion Ionescu de la Brad. Lucrari Stiintifice. Seria Agronomie-Horticultura see Institutul Agronomic Ion Ionescu de la Brad. Lucrari Stiintifice. Seria Agronomie *29*
Institutul Agronomic Ion Ionescu de la Brad. Lucrari Stiintifice. Seria Agronomie-Horticultura see Institutul Agronomic Ion Ionescu de la Brad. Lucrari Stiintifice. Seria Horticultura *533*
Institutul Agronomic Ion Ionescu de la Brad. Lucrari Stiintifice. Seria Horticultura (RM ISSN 0379-8372) *533*
Institutul Agronomic Ion Ionescu de la Brad. Lucrari Stiintifice, Seria Zootehnie - Medicina Veterinaria (RM ISSN 0075-3513) *66, 1121*
Institutul de Cercetari Pentru Cereale si Plante Tehnice. Laborator Sfecla de Zahar. Anale. Lucrari Stiintifice (RM) *56*
Institutul de Cercetari Pentru Cultura Cartofului si Sfeclei de Zahar, Brasov. Anale. Cartoful see Institutul de Cercetari si Productie a Cartofului, Brasov. Anale. Lucrari Stiintifice *56*
Institutul de Cercetari Pentru Cultura Cartofului si Sfeclei de Zahar, Brasov. Anale. Sflecla de Zahar see Institutul de Cercetari Pentru Cereale si Plante Tehnice. Laborator Sfecla de Zahar. Anale. Lucrari Stiintifice *56*
Institutul de Cercetari pentru Protectia Plantelor. Analele/Research Institute for Plant Protection. Annals (RM) *29, 165, 168, 175*
Institutul de Cercetari si Productie a Cartofului, Brasov. Anale. Lucrari Stiintifice (RM) *56*
Institutul de Fizica Atomica. Sesiunea Stiintifica Anuala de Comunicari; Program si Rezumate (RM) *897*
Institutul de Geologie si Geofizica. Anuarul (RM) *389*
Institutul de Geologie si Geofizica. Studii Tehnice si Economice (RM) *389*
Institutul de Istorie si Arheologie "A.D. Xenopol" - Iasi. Anuarul (RM ISSN 0074-039X) *87, 586*
Institutul de Istorie si Arheologie - Cluj-Napoca. Anuarul (RM ISSN 0065-048X) *87, 586*
Institutul de Studii Cercetari si Proiectari Pentru Gospodarirea Apelor. Studii de Economia Apelor. (RM) *1124*
Institutul Geologie si Geofizica. Memoire (RM ISSN 0020-4234) *379*

INSTITUUT VOOR   1771

Institutul Pedagogic Oradea. Lucrari Stiintifice Seria Biologic (RM) *142*
Institutul Pedagogic Oradea. Lucrari Stiintifice Seria Chimie (RM) *323*
Institutul Pedagogic Oradea. Lucrari Stiintifice Seria Educatie Fizica si Sport (RM) *1034*
Institutul Pedagogic Oradea. Lucrari Stiintifice: Seria Fizica (RM) *888*
Institutul Pedagogic Oradea. Lucrari Stiintifice: Seria Geografie (RM) *545*
Institutul Pedagogic Oradea. Lucrari Stiintifice: Seria Istorie (RM) *558*
Institutul Pedagogic Oradea. Lucrari Stiintifice: Seria Lingvistica (RM) *696*
Institutul Pedagogic Oradea. Lucrari Stiintifice: Seria Literatura (RM) *724*
Institutul Pedagogic Oradea. Lucrari Stiintifice: Seria Matematica (RM) *749*
Institutul Pedagogic Oradea. Lucrari Stiintifice: Seria Pedagogie, Psihologie, Metodica (RM) *415, 934*
Institutul Pedagogic Oradea. Lucrari Stiintifice: Seria Stiinte Sociale (RM) *1009*
Institutum Canarium Yearbook. Almogaren (AU) *72, 87*
Instituut voor Bodemvruchtbaarheid. Jaarverslag (NE ISSN 0434-6785) *56*
Instituut voor Cultuurtechniek en Waterhuishouding. Jaarverslag (NE ISSN 0165-0610) *56, 497, 1124*
Instituut voor Cultuurtechniek en Waterhuishouding. Mededeling see Instituut voor Cultuurtechniek en Waterhuishouding. Mededeling. Nieuwe Serie *56*
Instituut voor Cultuurtechniek en Waterhuishouding. Mededeling. Nieuwe Serie (NE) *56, 497, 1124*
Instituut voor Cultuurtechniek en Waterhuishouding. Miscellaneous Reprints see Instituut voor Cultuurtechniek en Waterhuishouding. Technical Bulletins. New Series *56*
Instituut voor Cultuurtechniek en Waterhuishouding. Rapporten. Nieuwe Serie (NE) *56, 1124*
Instituut voor Cultuurtechniek en Waterhuishouding. Reports (NE) *56, 1124*
Instituut voor Cultuurtechniek en Waterhuishouding. Technical Bulletin see Instituut voor Cultuurtechniek en Waterhuishouding. Technical Bulletins. New Series *56*
Instituut voor Cultuurtechniek en Waterhuishouding. Technical Bulletins. New Series (NE) *56, 497, 1124*
Instituut voor Cultuurtechniek en Waterhuishouding. Verspreide Overdrukken see Instituut voor Cultuurtechniek en Waterhuishouding. Mededeling. Nieuwe Serie *56*
Instituut voor Hygiene en Epidemiologie. Reseau Soufre-Fumee/Zwavel-Rook Meetnet (BE ISSN 0378-892X) *954*
Instituut voor Plantenziektenkundig Onderzoek. Jaarverslag (NE ISSN 0074-0446) *56*
Instituut voor Plantenziektenkundig Onderzoek. Mededeling/Institute of Phytopathological Research. Communications (NE ISSN 0019-0349) *57*
Instituut voor Pluimveeonderzoek Het Spelderholt. Jaarverslag see Centrum voor Onderzoek en Voorlichting voor de Pluimveehouderij. Het Spelderholt. Jaarverlag *65*
Instituut voor Rassenonderzoek van Landbouwgewassen. Jaarverslag see Rijksinstituut voor het Rassenonderzoek van Cultuurgewassen. Jaarverslag *59*
Instituut voor Rassenonderzoek van Landbouwgewassen. Mededelingen see Rijksinstituut voor het Rassenonderzoek van Cultuurgewassen. Mededelingen *59*

1772 INSTITUUT VOOR

Instituut voor Veevoedingsonderzoek. Jaarverslag (NE) 66
Instituut voor Veevoedingsonderzoek "Hoorn". Jaarverslag see Instituut voor Veevoedingsonderzoek. Jaarverslag 66
Instituut voor Veevoedingsonderzoek "Hoorn." Report see Rapport I V V O 67
Instructional Cassette Recordings Catalog see Music & Musicians: Instructional Cassette Recordings Catalog (Large Print Edition) 180
Instructions Nautiques (FR ISSN 0223-534X) 1100
Instructor Computer Directory for Schools (US) 1155
Instrument Society of America. International I S A Aerospace Instrumentation Symposium. Tutorial Proceedings see Fundamentals of Aerospace Instrumentation 19
Instrument Society of America Instrumentation in the Mining and Metallurgy Industries see Instrumentation in the Mining and Metallurgy Industries 798
Instrumenta Lexicologia Latina. Series A & B (BE) 337, 970
Instrumentation in the Aerospace Industry. (US ISSN 0096-7238) 19
Instrumentation in the Chemical and Petroleum Industries (US ISSN 0074-0551) 478, 637
Instrumentation in the Food Industry (US ISSN 0095-0777) 519, 637
Instrumentation in the Mining and Metallurgy Industries (Instrument Society of America) (US ISSN 0361-3070) 798
Instrumentation in the Power Industry (US ISSN 0074-056X) 637
Instrumentation in the Pulp and Paper Industry (US ISSN 0361-4719) 858
Instrumentation Symposium for the Process Industries (US ISSN 0738-3231) 637
Instruments and Control Systems Buyers' Guide see I & C S Buyers' Guide 471
Instruments and Instrumentation Handbook (UK) 637
Instruments, Electronics and Automation Purchasing Directory see Directory of Electronics, Instruments & Computers 357
Instytut Automatyki Systemow Energetycznych. Prace (PL ISSN 0084-2788) 472
Instytut Badan Jadrowych. Zaklad Radiobiologii i Ochrony Zdrowia. Prace Doswiadczaine (PL ISSN 0074-0640) 153, 792, 954
Instytut Elektrotechniki. Prace (PL ISSN 0032-6216) 455
Instytut Geologiczny. Biuletyn. Geology of Poland (PL ISSN 0138-0389) 389
Instytut Geologiczny. Prace (PL ISSN 0208-645X) 389, 856
Instytut Gospodarki Wodnej. Prace (PL ISSN 0074-0586) 1124
Instytut Lacznosci. Prace (PL ISSN 0020-451X) 343
Instytut Naftowy. Prace (PL ISSN 0032-6232) 865
Instytut Obrobki Skrawaniem. Zeszyty Naukowe (PL ISSN 0020-4528) 489, 745
Instytut Sadownictwa i Kwiaciarstwa w Skierniewicach. Prace. Seria B: Rosliny Ozdobne (PL ISSN 0208-5925) 533
Instytut Sadownictwa i Kwiaciarstwa w Skierniewicach. Seria A: Prace Doswiadczalne z Zakresu Sadownictwa (PL ISSN 0208-5933) 29, 142
Instytut Slaski. Kommunikaty. Seria Niemcoznawcza (PL ISSN 0074-0616) 1155
Instytut Slaski. Wydawnictwa (PL ISSN 0074-0632) 1155
Instytut Transportu Samochodowego. Zeszyty Naukowe (PL) 1081
Instytutu Ochrony Roslin. Biuletyn (PL ISSN 0020-448X) 29
Insulation/Circuits Desk Manual see Electri-Onics Desk Manual 452

Insulation Handbook (UK) 185, 507
Insurance Almanac; Who, What, When and Where in Insurance (US ISSN 0074-0675) 639
Insurance Company Profile (PH) 640
Insurance Directory and Year Book (UK ISSN 0074-0691) 640
Insurance Directory of New Zealand (NZ) 640
Insurance Facts (US ISSN 0074-0713) 642
Insurance Facts and Figures see Insurance Statistics (1981-1985) 640
Insurance in Australia and New Zealand (AT ISSN 0811-0905) 640
Insurance Index (UK ISSN 0144-6304) 8, 642
Insurance Law Anthology (US) 640, 657
Insurance Marketplace (US ISSN 0538-2629) 640
Insurance Periodicals Index (US ISSN 0074-073X) 8, 642
Insurance Statistics (1981-1985) (UK ISSN 0950-3668) 640
Insurance Statistics of Fiji (FJ) 642
Insurance Statistics Yearbook (KO) 1155
Integracion Financiera (CK) 245
Integrated Rural Development. Publications (IS ISSN 0333-9874) 922
Integrated Voice/Data P B X's (US) 361
Intel Yellow Pages (US) 357, 361, 362
Intellectual Activist (US ISSN 0730-2355) 245, 906
Intellectual Property Law Review (US ISSN 0193-4864) 861
Inter (IS) 906
Inter American Press Association. Minutes of the Annual Meeting (US) 646
Inter-African Conference of the Mechanisation of Agriculture Meeting (NG ISSN 0534-4794) 51
Inter-African Conference on Co-Operative Societies Meeting. Reunion (NG ISSN 0534-4697) 238
Inter-African Conference on Food and Nutrition. Programa e Informacoes (NG ISSN 0534-4700) 846
Inter-African Conference on Food and Nutrition. Report (NG ISSN 0538-2785) 846
Inter-African Conference on Industrial Commercial and Agricultural Education Meeting (NG ISSN 0534-4727) 441
Inter-African Conference on Medical Co-Operation. Meeting (NG ISSN 0534-4735) 762
Inter-African Conference on Social Science Meeting (NG ISSN 0534-4751) 1009
Inter-African Conference on the Treatment of Offenders. Meetings. Reunion (NG ISSN 0534-4816) 370
Inter-African Forestry Conference. Conference Forestiere Interafricaine (Communications) (NG ISSN 0534-4824) 525
Inter-African Labour Conference Reports, Recommendations and Conclusions (NG ISSN 0538-2807) 272
Inter-American Bar Association. Conference Proceedings (US) 657
Inter-American Centre for Agricultural Documentation and Information. Documentacion e Informacion Agricola (CR ISSN 0301-438X) 41
Interamerican Children's Institute. Report of the General Director (UY) 335, 1018
Inter-American Commission of Women. News Bulletin (US ISSN 0538-2912) 1129
Inter-American Commission of Women. Noticiero (US ISSN 0538-2920) 1129
Inter-American Commission of Women. Special Assembly. Final Act/Comision Interamericana de Mujeres. Asamblea Extraordinaria. Acta Final (US ISSN 0074-0764) 913

Inter-American Conference on Indian Life. Acta/Congresos Indigenistas Interamericanos. Acta see Congresos Indigenistas Interamericanos. Actas 71
Inter-American Council for Education, Science, and Culture. Final Report (US ISSN 0074-0829) 415, 993
Inter-American Council of Commerce and Production. Uruguayan Section. Publicaciones (UY ISSN 0538-3048) 263
Inter-American Development Bank. Annual Report (US) 229, 263
Inter-American Development Bank. Board of Governors. Anales (de la) Reunion see Inter-American Development Bank. Board of Governors. Proceedings of the Meeting 229
Inter-American Development Bank. Board of Governors. Proceedings of the Meeting (US ISSN 0074-0861) 229, 263
Inter-American Development Bank. Informe Anual see Inter-American Development Bank. Annual Report 229
Inter-American Development Bank. Institute for Latin American Integration. Annual Report (AG ISSN 0538-3110) 263
Inter-American Development Bank. Statement of Loans see Inter-American Development Bank. Annual Report 229
Inter-American Economic and Social Council. Final Report of the Annual Meeting at the Ministerial Level (US ISSN 0074-0918) 606, 1009
Inter-American Foundation Annual Report (US) 263
Inter-American Institute for Cooperation on Agriculture. Executive Committee. Yearly Meeting Report (CR) 29
Inter-American Institute for Cooperation on Agriculture. Informe Anual (CR) 29
Inter-American Institute of Agricultural Sciences. Bibliografias see Inter-American Centre for Agricultural Documentation and Information. Documentacion e Informacion Agricola 41
Inter-American Institute of Agricultural Sciences. Center for Training and Research. Bibliotecologia y Documentacion see Inter-American Centre for Agricultural Documentation and Information. Documentacion e Informacion Agricola 41
Inter-American Institute of Agricultural Sciences. Informe Anual see Inter-American Institute for Cooperation on Agriculture. Informe Anual 29
Inter-American Institute of Agricultural Sciences. Technical Advisory Council. Junta Directiva. Reunion Anual. Resoluciones y Documentos see Inter-American Institute for Cooperation on Agriculture. Executive Committee. Yearly Meeting Report 29
Inter-American Tropical Tuna Commission. Annual Report/Comision Inter-Americana del Atun Tropical (US ISSN 0074-1000) 510
Inter-American Tropical Tuna Commission. Bulletin/Comision Interamericana del Atun Tropical. Boletin (US ISSN 0074-0993) 510
Inter-American Tropical Tuna Commission. Data Report (US ISSN 0538-3609) 510
Inter-American Tropical Tuna Commission. Special Report (US) 510
Inter-American Yearbook on Human Rights see Anuario Interamericano de Derechos Humanos 669
Interavia A B C (SZ ISSN 0074-1116) 19
Inter-City Wage & Salary Differentials (US) 272
Intercollegiate Bibliography. New Cases in Administration. see H B S Case Bibliography 210

Intercollegiate Yacht Racing Association of North America Directory see I C Y R A/N A Directory 1042
Intercom (CN ISSN 0383-6061) 979
Intercom (New York) (US ISSN 0020-5273) 415
Intercon (Spanish translation of: Vademecum) (SP) 762
Intercultural Education Council. Newsletter see Multicultural Education 416
Interdisciplinary Topics in Gerontology (SZ ISSN 0074-1132) 552
Interdom Christian Referdex see Christian Referdex 304
Interface & Memory Discontinued Devices D.A.T.A. Book (US) 455
Interference Technology Engineers Master see I T E M 455
Interferences, Arts, Lettres (FR ISSN 0074-1140) 106, 724
Interferon (US ISSN 0276-1076) 168
Intergovermental Council for Automatic Data Processing. Proceedings of Conference see International Council for Automatic Data Processing in Government Administration. Proceedings of Conference 360
Intergovernmental Committee for European Migration. Review of Achievements see Intergovernmental Committee for Migration. Review of Achievements 922
Intergovernmental Committee for Migration. Review of Achievements (SZ) 922
Intergovernmental Council of Copper Exporting Countries. Statistical Bulletin (FR) 822
Intergovernmental Oceanographic Commission. Technical Series (UN ISSN 0074-1175) 406
Interior Cost Data (Year) (US ISSN 8755-7541) 185
Interior Design Buyers Guide (US) 310, 643
Interior Design Catalogues see Contract Interior's Catalogue 643
Interior Design Directory see Interior Design Buyers Guide 310
Interior Designer's Handbook (UK) 643
Interior Textiles National Buyers Guide(US) 1074
Internal Publications Directory (US) 962
Internal Revenue Code (US) 296
Internal Trade of Iran (IR ISSN 0074-1213) 239
Internationaal Havenkongres. Verslagboek see International Harbour Congress. Proceedings 1101
International Abstracts in Operations Research (NE ISSN 0020-580X) 8, 354
International Abstracts of Biological Sciences see Current Awareness in Biological Sciences 150
International Academy of Indian Culture. Report see International Academy of Indian Culture. Satapitaka Series 570
International Academy of Indian Culture. Satapitaka Series (II ISSN 0074-123X) 570
International Academy of Legal Medicine and Social Medicine. (Congress Reports) (IT ISSN 0074-1248) 782
International Actuarial Congress. Transactions (SZ ISSN 0074-1264) 640
International Advances in Surgical Oncology (US ISSN 0190-1575) 1155
International Advertising Association. United Kingdom Chapter. Concise Guide to International Markets (UK ISSN 0538-4168) 15
International Aeronautic Federation. Annual Information Bulletin (FR) 19
International Aeronautic Federation. General Conference Minutes (of the) Business Meetings see International Aeronautic Federation. Annual Information Bulletin 19

INTERNATIONAL BACCALAUREATE 1773

International Aeronautic Federation. Latest World Records see World Aeronautical Records 22
International Aerospace Abstracts (US ISSN 0020-5842) 8, 22
International African Bibliography Cumulation (UK) 1155
International African Library (UK) 679
International Agency for Research on Cancer. I A R C Technical Publications see I A R C Scientific Publications 775
International Agency for Research on Cancer Monographs on the Evaluation of the Carcinogenic Risk of Chemicals to Humans see I A R C Monographs on the Evaluation of the Carcinogenic Risk of Chemicals to Humans 775
International Agency for Research on Cancer Scientific Publications see I A R C Scientific Publications 775
International Air Safety and Corporate Aviation Safety Seminar Proceedings (US) 19
International Air Safety Seminar Proceedings see International Air Safety and Corporate Aviation Safety Seminar Proceedings 19
International Air Show Guide (NE) 1088
International Air Transport Association. Annual General Meeting. Reports and Proceedings (CN) 1088
International Air Transport Association. Annual Report see International Air Transport Association. Annual General Meeting. Reports and Proceedings 1088
International Air Transport Association. Economics and Industry Finance Department. Bulletin see International Air Transport Association. Industry Automation and Finance Services Department. Publications 1088
International Air Transport Association. Industry Automation and Finance Services Department. Publications (SZ) 1088
International Air Transport Association Annual Report see I A T A Annual Report 1088
International Air Transport Association Dangerous Goods Regulations see I A T A Dangerous Goods Regulations 1088
International Air Transport Association Live Animals Regulations see I A T A Live Animals Regulations 1088
International Alban Berg Society Newsletter (US) 836
International Amateur Basketball Federation. Official Report of the World Congress see International Basketball Federation. Official Report of the World Congress 1039
International Anatomical Congress. Proceedings (UR ISSN 0074-1353) 142, 762
International and Comparative Broadcasting (US) 348
International and Intercultural Communication Annual (US) 343
International Animated Film Association. Bulletin (RM ISSN 0538-4281) 824
International Archery Federation. Bulletin Officiel (UK ISSN 0074-137X) 1034
International Archives of the History of Ideas see Archives Internationales d'Histoire des Idees 876
International Art Material Directory and Buyers Guide (US) 106
International Arthurian Society. Bibliographical Bulletin/Societe Internationale Arthurienne. Bulletin Bibliographique (CN ISSN 0074-1388) 517, 739
International Arthurian Society. Report on Congress see International Arthurian Society. Bibliographical Bulletin 739
International Assembly on Emergency Medical Services. Proceedings (US) 1092

International Association for Bridge and Structural Engineering. Final Report (of Congress) see I A B S E Congress Report 481
International Association for Bridge and Structural Engineering. Reports of the Working Commissions see I A B S E Report 481
International Association for Bridge and Structural Engineering Congress Report see I A B S E Congress Report 481
International Association for Bridge and Structural Engineering Report see I A B S E Report 481
International Association for Byzantine Studies. Bulletin d'Information et de Coordination (GR ISSN 0571-5857) 586, 612
International Association for Cereal Chemistry. Working and Discussion Meetings Reports (AU ISSN 0074-1450) 519
International Association for Child Psychiatry and Allied Professions. Yearbook (US ISSN 0074-963X) 790
International Association for Classical Archaeology. Proceedings of Congress (IT ISSN 0074-1469) 87, 337
International Association for Cross-Cultural Psychology. International Conference. Selected Papers (NE) 934
International Association for Dental Research. Abstracts of the General Meeting (US ISSN 0534-669X) 779
International Association for Educational and Vocational Information. Studies and Reports (FR) 415, 848
International Association for Hydraulic Research. Congress Proceedings (NE ISSN 0074-1477) 490
International Association for Mass Communications Research. Letter from the President (UK ISSN 0579-3742) 343
International Association for Mass Communications Research. Monographs (UK) 343
International Association for Religion & Parapsychology Journal see Research for Religion & Parapsychology 860
International Association for Scientific Study of Mental Deficiency. Proceedings of International Congress (IE ISSN 0085-2007) 790
International Association for the Advancement of Educational Research. Congress Reports see World Association for Educational Research. Congress Reports 422
International Association for the Exchange of Students for Technical Experience. Annual Report (GR ISSN 0538-4427) 441
International Association for the Physical Science of the Ocean. Proces-Verbaux see Comites Francais de Geodesie et Geophysique. Annales 405
International Association of Applied Psychology. Proceedings of Congress (BE ISSN 0074-1574) 935
International Association of Chain Stores. Report of Plenary Session (FR ISSN 0074-1582) 284
International Association of Coroners and Medical Examiners. Proceedings (US) 1155
International Association of Democratic Lawyers. Congress Report (BE ISSN 0074-1604) 657
International Association of Fish and Wildlife Agencies. Proceedings of the Convention (US ISSN 0161-3332) 365
International Association of French Studies. Cahiers (FR ISSN 0571-5865) 724
International Association of Geodesy. Central Bureau for Satellite Geodesy. Bibliography (GR) 551
International Association of Geodesy. Central Bureau for Satellite Geodesy. Information Bulletin (GR ISSN 0081-0312) 545

International Association of Geodesy. Commission Permanente des Marees Terrestres. Marees Terrestres Bulletin d'Information (BE ISSN 0542-6766) 399, 545
International Association of Geomagnetism and Aeronomy News see I A G A News 399
International Association of Gerontology. European Clinical Section Proceedings (IT ISSN 0074-1620) 552
International Association of Hydrogeologists. Memoires (FR ISSN 0579-6733) 403
International Association of Jewish Lawyers and Jurists. Bulletin (IS) 657
International Association of Law Libraries. Directory (US) 679
International Association of Liberal Religious Women. Newsletter (US) 970
International Association of Logopedics and Phoniatrics. Reports of Congress (SZ ISSN 0074-1655) 790
International Association of Meteorology and Atmospheric Physics. Report of Proceedings of General Assembly (US ISSN 0074-1663) 805
International Association of Meteorology and Atmospheric Physics News Bulletin see I A M P News Bulletin 805
International Association of Milk Control Agencies. Proceedings of Annual Meetings (US ISSN 0074-1671) 62
International Association of Museums of Arms and Military History. Congress Reports (GW ISSN 0074-168X) 811, 828
International Association of Performing Arts Libraries and Museums. Congress Proceedings (FR) 106, 679
International Association of Physical Education and Sports for Girls and Women. Proceedings of the International Congress (JA ISSN 0074-1728) 1034
International Association of Physicians in Audiology Bulletin see I A P A Bulletin 787
International Association of Scholarly Publishers Newsletter see I A S P Newsletter 436
International Association of School Librarianship Conference Proceedings see I A S L Conference Proceedings 678
International Association of Schools of Social Work. Directory of Members and Constitution see I A S S W Directory; Member Schools and Associations 1018
International Association of Schools of Social Work Directory; Member Schools and Associations see I A S S W Directory; Member Schools and Associations 1018
International Association of Seed Crushers. Proceedings of the Annual Congress (UK ISSN 0074-1736) 29
International Association of Sound Archives. Directory of Member Archives (UK) 679
International Association of State Lotteries. (Reports of Congress) (SZ ISSN 0074-1744) 296
International Association of Students in Economics and Management. International Compendium. Annual Report (BE ISSN 0074-1752) 196
International Association of Technological Universities Libraries Quarterly see I A T U L Quarterly 678
International Association of Thalassotherapy. Congress Reports (FR ISSN 0074-1760) 762
International Association of Theoretical and Applied Limnology. Communications (GW ISSN 0538-4680) 142, 403

International Association of Theoretical and Applied Limnology. Proceedings/Internationale Vereinigung fuer Theoretische und Angewandte Limnologie. Verhandlungen (GW ISSN 0368-0770) 142, 403, 406
International Association of Universities. Papers & Reports (UK) 436
International Association of Workers for Maladjusted Children. Congress Reports (FR ISSN 0074-1787) 444
International Astronautical Federation (I A F). International Congress. Invited Papers (US) 19
International Astronomical Union. Central Bureau for Astronomical Telegrams. Circular (US ISSN 0081-0304) 116
International Astronomical Union. General Assembly. Highlights (NE) 116
International Astronomical Union. General Assembly. Proceedings see International Astronomical Union. General Assembly. Highlights 116
International Astronomical Union. Proceedings of Symposia (NE ISSN 0074-1809) 116
International Astronomical Union. Transactions (NE ISSN 0080-1372) 116
International Astronomical Union. Transactions and Highlights see International Astronomical Union. Transactions 116
International Athletics Guide (UK) 1034, 1045
International Atlantic Salmon Foundation. Special Publication Series see Atlantic Salmon Federation. Special Publication Series 507
International Atomic Energy Agency. Annual Report (UN ISSN 0085-2023) 472, 897
International Atomic Energy Agency. Legal Series (UN ISSN 0074-1868) 657, 897
International Atomic Energy Agency. Nuclear Power Reactors in the World (UN) 472, 897
International Atomic Energy Agency. Panel Proceedings Series (UN ISSN 0074-1876) 472, 897
International Atomic Energy Agency. Power Reactors in Member States see International Atomic Energy Agency. Nuclear Power Reactors in the World 897
International Atomic Energy Agency. Proceedings Series (UN ISSN 0074-1884) 472, 897
International Atomic Energy Agency. Radiation Data for Medical Use; Catalogue see Radiation Dosimetry Data; Catalogue 792
International Atomic Energy Agency. Safety Series (UN ISSN 0074-1892) 954
International Atomic Energy Agency. Technical Directories (UN ISSN 0074-1906) 472, 897
International Atomic Energy Agency. Technical Report Series (UN ISSN 0074-1914) 472, 897
International Atomic Energy Agency Library Film Catalog see I A E A Library Film Catalog 893
International Atomic Energy Agency Technical Documents Series see I A E A Technical Documents Series 896
International Auction Records (US ISSN 0074-1922) 106
International Auction Records (US) 106, 257
International Authors and Writers Who's Who (UK ISSN 0143-8263) 134, 724
International Auto Statistics see Das Auto-International-in Zahlen 1090
International Baccalaureate Office. Annual Bulletin (SZ ISSN 0074-1973) 415

International Baccalaureate Office. Semi-Annual Bulletin see International Baccalaureate Office. Annual Bulletin 415
International Badminton Federation. Annual Handbook see International Badminton Federation. Annual Statute Book 1034
International Badminton Federation. Annual Statute Book (UK ISSN 0255-4437) 1034
International Basketball Federation. Official Report of the World Congress (GW) 1039
International Beekeeping Congress. Reports (RM ISSN 0074-2007) 29
International Bibliographical and Library Series (US) 679
International Bibliography of Cropping Systems (PH) 41
International Bibliography of Economics see International Bibliography of the Social Sciences. Economics 211
International Bibliography of Historical Demography/Bibliographie Internationale de la Demographie Historique (BE ISSN 0255-0849) 922
International Bibliography of Historical Sciences (US ISSN 0074-2015) 564
International Bibliography of Periodical Literature from all Fields of Knowledge see I B Z 127
International Bibliography of Political Science see International Bibliography of the Social Sciences. Political Science 912
International Bibliography of Research in Marriage and the Family see Inventory of Marriage and Family Literature 1031
International Bibliography of Rice Research (PH ISSN 0074-2031) 41
International Bibliography of Selected Police Literature (UK) 374
International Bibliography of Social and Cultural Anthropology see International Bibliography of the Social Sciences. Social and Cultural Anthropology 79
International Bibliography of Sociology see International Bibliography of the Social Sciences. Sociology 1031
International Bibliography of Special Directories see Internationale Bibliographie der Fachadressbuecher 127
International Bibliography of Structural Engineering (IE) 477
International Bibliography of Studies on Alcohol (US ISSN 0074-204X) 378
International Bibliography of the Book Trade and Librarianship see Fachliteratur zum Buch- und Bibliothekswesen 677
International Bibliography of the Forensic Sciences (US ISSN 0098-2393) 771
International Bibliography of the History of Religions/Bibliographie International de l'Histoire des Religions (NE) 975
International Bibliography of the Social Sciences. Economics (US ISSN 0085-204X) 211
International Bibliography of the Social Sciences. Political Science (US ISSN 0085-2058) 912
International Bibliography of the Social Sciences. Social and Cultural Anthropology (US ISSN 0085-2074) 79
International Bibliography of the Social Sciences. Sociology (US ISSN 0085-2066) 1031
International Bibliography on Burns (US ISSN 0090-0575) 771
International Bio-Sciences Monographs (II ISSN 0253-7206) 142
International Biodeterioration Symposium. Proceedings. Biodeterioration of Materials (US) 168
International Biological Program Synthesis Series see U S-I B P Synthesis Series 147
International Biological Programme Series (UK) 142

International Biometeorological Congress. Proceedings see Biometeorology; Proceedings 803
International Biometeorological Congress. Summaries and Reports Presented to the Congress (NE ISSN 0074-2082) 142
International Biophysics Congress. Abstracts (US) 8, 150
International Bioscience Series (II) 158
International Biotechnology Directory see Biotechnology Directory 303
International Boehringer Mannheim. Symposia (US ISSN 0173-0282) 776
International Books in Print (GW) 127, 964
International Botanical Congress. Abstracts of Papers (AT ISSN 0074-2090) 158
International Botanical Congress. Proceedings (AT) 158
International Boundary Study (US ISSN 0502-0034) 545, 670
International Brain Research Organization Monograph Series (US ISSN 0361-0462) 790
International Brain Research Organization Neuroscience Calendar see I B R O Neuroscience Calendar 790
International Brewer's Directory (SZ ISSN 0074-9796) 120
International Bridge Conference. Proceedings (US) 482
International Bridge, Tunnel and Turnpike Association. Report of the Annual Meeting (US) 1096
International Building Services Abstracts (UK ISSN 0140-4237) 8, 554
International Bulletin of Bibliography on Education Annual Summary see B I B E Annual Summary 422
International Bureau of Fiscal Documentation. Annual Report (NE ISSN 0074-2104) 296
International Bureau of Fiscal Documentation. Publication (NE ISSN 0074-2112) 296
International Business Equipment (US ISSN 0020-6288) 286
International Business Opportunities. Egypt (UK) 257
International Business Opportunities. Iraq (UK) 257
International Business Opportunities. Oil & Gas in Africa (UK) 465, 865
International Business Opportunities. Oil & Gas in the Middle East (UK) 465, 865
International Business Opportunities. Saudi Arabia (UK) 257
International Business Opportunities. Top African Banks (UK) 229
International Business Opportunities. Top 200 Arab Banks (UK) 229
International Businessmen's Who's Who(UK) 310
International Buyer's Guide of Mobile Air Conditioning see I M A C A Directory 553
International Buyers Guide of the Music, Record and Tape Industry see Billboard's International Buyer's Guide of the Music-Record-Tape Industry 833
International C A D/C A M Industry Directory (US ISSN 0736-1823) 310, 356, 485
International Cargo Handling Coordination Association. Buyers' Guide to Manufacturers (UK ISSN 0266-3996) 1101
International Catalogue of Films, Filmstrips and Slides on Public Education About Cancer (SZ) 775
International Catalogue of Films for Public Education About Cancer see International Catalogue of Films, Filmstrips and Slides on Public Education About Cancer 775
International Catalogue of Occupational Safety and Health Films (UN ISSN 0074-2147) 636
International Catholic Movement for Intellectual Cultural Affairs. Proceedings of the Plenary Assembly see Pax Romana 983

International Cellular Plastics Conference. Proceedings (US ISSN 0579-5400) 900
International Cemetery Directory see American Cemetery Association. Membership Directory 531
International Center for Arid and Semi-Arid Land Studies Annual Report see I C A S A L S Annual Report 365
International Center for Living Aquatic Resources Management Bibliographies see I C L A R M Bibliographies 514
International Center for Living Aquatic Resources Management Conference Proceedings. see I C L A R M Conference Proceedings 510
International Center for Living Aquatic Resources Management Studies and Reviews see I C L A R M Studies and Reviews 510
International Center for Living Aquatic Resources Management Technical Reports see I C L A R M Technical Reports 510
International Center for Living Aquatic Resources Management Translations see I C L A R M Translations 510
International Center for Research on Women Occasional Paper Series see I C R W Occasional Paper Series 1129
International Center for Tropical Agriculture. Bean Program Annual Report (CK ISSN 0120-2235) 29
International Centre for Heat and Mass Transfer. Proceedings (US ISSN 0272-880X) 472
International Centre for Mechanical Sciences (CISM). Courses and Lectures (US) 491
International Centre for Settlement of Investment Disputes. Annual Report (US ISSN 0074-2163) 266, 670
International Centre for Theoretical Physics. Annual Report (UN ISSN 0304-7091) 888
International Centre for Theoretical Physics. Report see International Centre for Theoretical Physics. Annual Report 888
International Centre of Insect Physiology and Ecology. Annual Report (KE) 167, 365
International Ceramic Congress. Proceedings (FR ISSN 0074-218X) 320
International Ceramic Directory (UK) 320
International Chamber of Commerce. Handbook (FR) 236
International Chamber of Commerce Annual Review see I C C Annual Review 236
International Children's Centre. Paris. Report of the Director-General to the Executive Board (FR ISSN 0538-5490) 333, 1027
International Children's Centre. Paris. Travaux et Documents (FR ISSN 0534-8021) 333, 1027
International Christian Democratic Study and Documentation Center. Cahiers d'Etudes see Christian Democratic Study and Documentation Center. Cahiers d'Etudes 903
International Christian Democratic Study and Documentation Center. Informations see Panorama Democrate Chretien 907
International Christian University. Institute for Educational Research and Service. Educational Studies/Kokusai Kirisutokyo Daigaku, Kyoiku Kenkyu (JA) 415
International Christian University. Publications IV-B. Christianity and Culture see Humanities, Christianity and Culture 970
International Civil Airports Association. Statistiques de Traffic. Resultats Generaux (FR) 1088
International Civil Aviation Association. Aeronautical Agreements and Arrangements. Annual Supplement (UN ISSN 0074-221X) 1088

International Civil Aviation Organization. Air Navigation Plan. Africa-Indian Ocean Region (UN ISSN 0074-2287) 1088
International Civil Aviation Organization. Air Navigation Plan. Caribbean Region (UN) 1088
International Civil Aviation Organization. Air Navigation Plan. Middle East and Asia Regions (UN) 1088
International Civil Aviation Organization. Air Navigation Plan. Middle East and South East Asia Regions see International Civil Aviation Organization. Air Navigation Plan. Middle East and Asia Regions 1088
International Civil Aviation Organization. Air Navigation Plan. North Atlantic, North American and Pacific Regions (UN ISSN 0074-2325) 1088
International Civil Aviation Organization. Airworthiness Committee. Report of Meeting (UN ISSN 0074-2244) 19
International Civil Aviation Organization. All-Weather Operations Panel. Report of Meeting (UN ISSN 0074-2333) 19
International Civil Aviation Organization. Assembly. Report and Minutes of the Legal Commission (UN ISSN 0074-2368) 1089
International Civil Aviation Organization. Assembly. Report of the Economic Commission (UN ISSN 0074-2376) 1089
International Civil Aviation Organization. Assembly. Report of the Technical Commission (UN ISSN 0074-2384) 19
International Civil Aviation Organization. Assembly. Resolutions (UN ISSN 0074-235X) 1089
International Civil Aviation Organization. Automated Data Interchange Systems Panel. Report of Meeting (UN ISSN 0074-2252) 19
International Civil Aviation Organization. Council. Annual Report (UN) 1089
International Civil Aviation Organization. Digests of Statistics. Series AT. Airport Traffic (UN ISSN 0074-2422) 1089
International Civil Aviation Organization. Digests of Statistics. Series F. Financial Data (UN ISSN 0074-2430) 1089
International Civil Aviation Organization. Digests of Statistics. Series FP. Fleet, Personnel (UN ISSN 0074-2449) 1089
International Civil Aviation Organization. Digests of Statistics. Series R. Civil Aircraft on Register (UN ISSN 0074-2457) 1089
International Civil Aviation Organization. Digests of Statistics. Series T. Traffic (UN ISSN 0074-2465) 1089
International Civil Aviation Organization. Digests of Statistics. Series TF. Traffic Flow (UN ISSN 0074-2473) 1089
International Civil Aviation Organization. Indexes to I C A O Publications. Annual Cumulation (UN ISSN 0074-249X) 22, 1086
International Civil Aviation Organization. Legal Committee. Minutes and Documents (of Sessions) (UN ISSN 0074-2503) 1089
International Civil Aviation Organization. Obstacle Clearance Panel. Report of Meeting (UN ISSN 0074-252X) 19
International Civil Aviation Organization. (Panel On) Application of Space Techniques Relating to Aviation. Report of Meeting (UN ISSN 0074-2228) 19
International Civil Aviation Organization. Sonic Boom Panel. Report of the Meeting (UN ISSN 0074-2562) 19

International Civil Aviation Organization. Technical Panel on Supersonic Transport. Report of Meeting (UN ISSN 0074-2570) *20*

International Civil Aviation Organization. Visual Aids Panel. Report of Meeting (UN ISSN 0074-2589) *20*

International Civil Aviation Organization Circulars *see* I C A O Circulars *1088*

International Civil Engineering Abstracts (IE ISSN 0332-4095) *8, 477*

International Claim Association Proceedings (US) *640*

International Clean Air Congress. Proceedings (US ISSN 0085-2090) *497*

International Co-operative Training Centre Review *see* I C T C Review *238*

International Coal (US) *257, 817*

International Coal Exploration Symposium. Proceedings (US) *1155*

International Coal Testing Conference (US ISSN 0740-5162) *389*

International CODEN Directory (US ISSN 0364-3670) *679*

The International Collection of Interior Design (UK) *643*

International College of Dentists. European Section. Newsletter (UK) *779*

International College of Psychosomatic Medicine. Proceedings of the Congress (SZ) *790*

International Colloquium on Prospective Biology (Proceedings) (SZ ISSN 0251-6810) *1156*

International Commercial Bank of China. Annual Report (CH) *229*

International Commission for the Conservation of Atlantic Tunas. Collective Volume of Scientific Papers (SP) *510*

International Commission for the Conservation of Atlantic Tunas. Newsletter (SP) *510*

International Commission for the Conservation of Atlantic Tunas. Report (SP ISSN 0377-368X) *175, 365*

International Commission for the Conservation of Atlantic Tunas. Statistical Bulletin (SP) *514, 1057*

International Commission for the Northwest Atlantic Fisheries. Annual Report *see* N A F O Annual Report *511*

International Commission for Uniform Methods of Sugar Analysis. Report of the Proceedings of the Session (UK) *519*

International Commission of Agricultural Engineering. Reports of Congress (FR ISSN 0074-2694) *57*

International Commission of Maritime History. Colloques. Actes (FR) *1101*

International Commission of Sugar Technology. Proceedings of the General Assembly (BE ISSN 0074-2708) *519*

International Commission on Illumination. Proceedings (HU ISSN 0074-2724) *455*

International Commission on Irrigation and Drainage. Congress Reports (II ISSN 0074-2732) *490*

International Commission on Irrigation and Drainage. Report (II ISSN 0538-5768) *29, 1124*

International Commission on Large Dams. Bulletin (FR ISSN 0534-8293) *482*

International Commission on Large Dams. Transactions (US ISSN 0074-4115) *482*

International Commission on Radiological Protection. Report (UK ISSN 0074-2759) *792*

International Commission on Trichinellosis. Proceedings (PL ISSN 0074-3356) *777*

International Committee for Historical Science. Bulletin d'Information (FR ISSN 0074-2783) *558*

International Committee for Museums of Ethnography News *see* I C M E News *544*

International Committee for Standardization in Hematology. Symposia (GW) *783*

International Committee of Onomastic Sciences. Congress Proceedings (BE ISSN 0074-2791) *696*

International Committee of the Red Cross. Annual Report/Rapport d'Activite/Informe de Actividad/Taetigkeitsbericht (SZ) *1018*

International Committee on Laboratory Animals. Proceedings of Symposium *see* International Council for Laboratory Animal Science. Proceedings of the Symposium *762*

International Committee on Urgent Anthropological and Ethnological Research. Bulletin (AU ISSN 0538-5865) *72*

International Communications and Energy Conference (Proceedings)/Conference Internationale sur les Communications et l'Energie (Proceedings) (US) *343, 455, 465*

International Communications Industries Association, Inc. Membership Directory *see* I C I A Membership Directory *447*

International Comparative Literature Association. Proceedings of the Congress (GW ISSN 0074-2813) *724*

International Computer Graphics Directory (US) *356*

International Computer Vision Directory (US) *355*

International Confederation for Agricultural Credit. Assembly and Congress Reports (SZ ISSN 0074-2856) *48*

International Confederation of Free Trade Unions. World Congress Reports (BE ISSN 0074-2872) *648*

International Confederation of Societies of Authors and Composers (FR ISSN 0074-2899) *861*

International Conference for the Sociology of Religion (CH ISSN 0074-297X) *970, 1027*

International Conference of Agricultural Economists. Proceedings (UK ISSN 0074-2902) *48*

International Conference of Building Officials. Accumulative Supplement to the Uniform Codes (US) *185*

International Conference of Building Officials. Accumulative Supplements to the Codes *see* International Conference of Building Officals. Accumulative Supplement to the Uniform Codes *185*

International Conference of Building Officials. Analysis of Revisions to the Uniform Building Code (US) *185*

International Conference of Building Officials. Building Department Administration (US) *185*

International Conference of Building Officials. Code Changes Committee. Annual Report (US ISSN 0579-3769) *185*

International Conference of Building Officials. Dwelling Construction Under the Uniform Building Code (US) *185*

International Conference of Building Officials. One and Two Family Dwelling Code *see* Council of American Building Officials. One and Two Family Dwelling Code *183*

International Conference of Building Officials. Uniform Building Code (US ISSN 0082-7584) *185*

International Conference of Building Officials. Uniform Code for the Abatement of Dangerous Buildings (US) *185*

International Conference of Building Officials. Uniform Fire Code (US) *185*

International Conference of Building Officials. Uniform Housing Code (US ISSN 0501-1213) *185*

International Conference of Building Officials. Uniform Mechanical Code (US) *185*

International Conference of Building Officials Plumbing Code *see* I C B O Plumbing Code *553*

International Conference of Educators of Blind Youth. Proceedings *see* I C E V H Educator *444*

International Conference of Ethiopian Studies. Proceedings (ET ISSN 0074-2945) *566*

International Conference of Lasers. Proceedings (US ISSN 0190-4132) *899*

International Conference of Orientalists in Japan. Transactions (JA ISSN 0538-6012) *558, 630, 1009*

International Conference of Social Work. Conference Proceedings (US ISSN 0074-2961) *1018*

International Conference of Social Work. Japanese National Committee. Progress Report *see* Japanese Report to the International Council on Social Welfare *1018*

International Conference on Acoustics. Reports (CN ISSN 0074-400X) *900*

International Conference on Aerospace Computers in Rockets and Spacecraft. Proceedings (FR) *20, 22*

International Conference on Atmospheric Electricity. Publication (US) *805, 894*

International Conference on Atomic Physics. Proceedings *see* Atomic Physics *896*

International Conference on Cloud Physics. Proceedings (CN ISSN 0074-3011) *805*

International Conference on Communications. Conference Record *see* I E E E International Conference on Communications. Conference Record *343*

International Conference on Computational Linguistics. Proceedings (GW) *709*

International Conference on Computer Communications. (Proceedings) (US) *360*

International Conference on Computer Workstations. Proceedings (US) *361*

International Conference on Computing Fixed Points with Applications. Proceedings (US) *749*

International Conference on Conduction and Breakdown in Dielectric Liquids. Conference Record (US) *455*

International Conference on Conduction and Breakdown in Solid Dielectrics. Proceedings (US) *455*

International Conference on Cosmic Rays. (Proceedings) (II ISSN 0074-3046) *897*

International Conference on Cybernetics and Society. Proceedings *see* I E E E International Conference on Systems, Man, and Cybernetics. Proceedings *359*

International Conference on Data Engineering (Proceedings) (US) *356*

International Conference on Distributed Computing Systems. Proceedings (US) *358*

International Conference on Education. Final Report/Conference International de l'Education. Rapport Final (UN) *415*

International Conference on Education. Proceedings *see* International Conference on Education. Final Report *415*

International Conference on Electron and Ion Beam Science and Technology. Abstracts (US ISSN 0534-8676) *888*

International Conference on Fertilizers. Proceedings (UK) *57*

International Conference on Fluid Sealing. Proceedings (UK ISSN 0074-3089) *491*

International Conference on Global Impacts of Applied Microbiology. Proceedings (US ISSN 0074-3097) *168*

International Conference on Information Processing. Proceedings *see* World Congresses on Information Processing. Proceedings *686*

International Conference on Infrared and Millimeter Waves. Conference Digest (US) *455*

International Conference on Large High Tension Electric Systems. Proceedings *see* International Conference on Large High Voltage Electric Systems. Proceedings *455*

International Conference on Large High Voltage Electric Systems. Proceedings (FR ISSN 0074-3151) *455*

International Conference on Lead. Proceedings (UK ISSN 0074-316X) *798*

International Conference on Lighthouses and Other Aids to Navigation. (Reports) (FR ISSN 0538-6128) *1101*

International Conference on Liquefied Natural Gas. Papers (US) *865*

International Conference on Liquefied Natural Gas. Proceedings *see* International Conference on Liquefied Natural Gas. Papers *865*

International Conference on Live-Line Maintenance. Conference Papers. *see* International Conference on Transmission and Distribution Construction and Live-Line Maintenance. Conference Papers *456*

International Conference on Livestock and Poultry in the Tropics (Proceedings) (US) *66*

International Conference on Low Temperature Physics. Reports (JA ISSN 0074-3178) *894*

International Conference on Oral Biology. Proceedings (US ISSN 0074-3216) *779*

International Conference on Parallel Processing. Proceedings (US ISSN 0190-3918) *360*

International Conference on Pattern Recognition. Proceedings (US) *356*

International Conference on Physics of Semiconductors. Proceedings *see* Physics of Semiconductors *1160*

International Conference on Piagetian Theory and the Helping Professions. Proceedings (US) *415, 444*

International Conference on Plasma Science. Conference Record Abstracts *see* I E E E International Conference on Plasma Science. I E E E Conference Record-Abstracts *454*

International Conference on Pressure Surges. Proceedings (UK ISSN 0140-2080) *491*

International Conference on Radar (Publication) *see* International Radar Conference. Record *344*

International Conference on Robotics. Proceedings *see* I E E E International Conference on Robotics and Automation. Proceedings *355*

International Conference on Science and World Affairs. Proceedings (US ISSN 0534-8803) *993*

International Conference on Software Engineering. Proceedings (US ISSN 0270-5257) *363*

International Conference on Structural Mechanics in Reactor Technology. Proceedings (NE) *888*

International Conference on Supercomputing Systems. Proceedings (US) *358*

International Conference on Synthetic Fibrinolytic--Thrombolytic Agents. Proceedings *see* Progress in Chemical Fibrinolysis and Thrombolysis *777*

International Conference on the Environmental Impact of Aerospace Operations in the High Atmosphere. (Proceedings) (US) *20, 497*

International Conference on the Physics of Electronic and Atomic Collisions. Abstracts of Contributed Papers and Invited Papers (US) *897*

International Conference on the Physics of Electronic and Atomic Collisions. Papers *see* International Conference on the Physics of Electronic and Atomic Collisions. Abstracts of Contributed Papers and Invited Papers *897*

International Conference on the Protection of Pipes. Proceedings (UK) 472

International Conference on the Structural Design of Asphalt Pavements. Proceedings (US ISSN 0074-3348) 1096

International Conference on Thermoelectric Energy Conversion. Proceedings (US) 455

International Conference on Transmission and Distribution Construction and Live-Line Maintenance. Conference Papers (US) 456

International Conference on Trends in Industrial and Labour Relations (CN) 272

International Conference on Vehicle Structural Mechanics. Proceedings (US) 1092

International Conference on Very Large Data Bases. Proceedings (US) 360

International Conference on World Politics. Conference Papers (NE ISSN 0579-8108) 916

International Congress for Byzantine Studies. Acts/Congres International des Etudes Byzantines. Actes (GR ISSN 0074-3542) 586, 612

International Congress for Cybernetics. Proceedings. Actes (BE ISSN 0074-3380) 359

International Congress for Logic, Methodology and Philosophy of Science. Proceedings (NE ISSN 0074-3402) 993

International Congress for Papyrology. Proceedings (UK ISSN 0074-3429) 87

International Congress for Stereology. Proceedings (US ISSN 0074-3437) 489

International Congress for the Study of Pre-Columbian Cultures of the Lesser Antilles. Proceedings (CN ISSN 0538-6381) 73

International Congress of Angiology. Proceedings (IT ISSN 0074-347X) 776

International Congress of Anthropological and Ethnological Sciences. Proceedings (UK ISSN 0074-3496) 73

International Congress of Automatic Control. Proceedings (UK ISSN 0074-3526) 355

International Congress of Biochemistry. Proceedings (JA ISSN 0074-3534) 151

International Congress of Compartative Law. Israel Reports (IS) 657

International Congress of Entomology (UK ISSN 0074-364X) 165

International Congress of Food Science and Technology. Proceedings (US ISSN 0074-3666) 519

International Congress of Graphoanalysts. Proceedings (US ISSN 0534-9044) 935

International Congress of Hematology. Proceedings (AG ISSN 0074-3682) 783

International Congress of Histochemistry and Cytochemistry. Proceedings (FI ISSN 0074-3690) 151, 163

International Congress of Historical Sciences. Proceedings see Etudes Historiques 557

International Congress of History of Medicine. Proceedings (FR ISSN 0074-3704) 762

International Congress of Home Economics. Report (FR ISSN 0074-3712) 615

International Congress of Life Assurance Medicine. Proceedings (SZ ISSN 0074-3747) 640, 762

International Congress of Linguists. Proceedings (NE ISSN 0074-3755) 696

International Congress of Nephrology. Abstracts of Reports and Communications (GR ISSN 0074-3771) 795

International Congress of Nephrology. Proceedings (SZ ISSN 0074-378X) 1156

International Congress of Occupational Therapy. Proceedings (AT ISSN 0074-3828) 762

International Congress of Ophthalmology see Acta Concilium Ophthalmologicum 785

International Congress of Orthoptists. Transactions (NE ISSN 0074-3844) 786

International Congress of Parasitology. Proceedings (IT ISSN 0074-3860) 175

International Congress of Primatology. Proceedings (US ISSN 0074-3895) 73, 175

International Congress of Psychology. Proceedings (NE ISSN 0085-2112) 935

International Congress of Psychopathological Art. Program. Programme (FR ISSN 0534-9168) 860

International Congress of Pure and Applied Chemistry. (Lectures) (UK ISSN 0074-3925) 323, 478

International Congress of Radiology. (Reports) (SZ ISSN 0074-3933) 792

International Congress of Sugarcane Technologists. Proceedings (IO ISSN 0074-3968) 519

International Congress of the Transplantation Society. Proceedings see Transplantation Today 794

International Congress of Verdi Studies. Proceedings. (IT) 836

International Congress on Alcoholism and Drug Dependence. Proceedings (SZ) 377

International Congress on Animal Reproduction and Artificial Insemination. Proceedings (SW ISSN 0074-4026) 1121

International Congress on Clinical Chemistry. Abstracts (AU ISSN 0074-4042) 152, 871

International Congress on Clinical Chemistry. Papers (AU ISSN 0074-4069) 152, 871

International Congress on Combustion Engines. Proceedings (FR ISSN 0074-4077) 491

International Congress on Experimental Mechanics. Proceedings (US ISSN 0071-3422) 489

International Congress on Hygiene and Preventive Medicine. Proceedings (IT) 886, 954

International Congress on Instrumentation in Aerospace Simulation Facilities. Proceedings see International Congress on Instrumentation in Aerospace Simulation Facilities. Record 20

International Congress on Instrumentation in Aerospace Simulation Facilities. Record (US ISSN 0730-2010) 20

International Congress on Metallic Corrosion. (Proceedings) (GW ISSN 0074-4123) 798

International Congress on Mushroom Science. Proceedings see Mushroom Science 159

International Congress on Photobiology. Proceedings (US) 1156

International Congress on the History of Art. Proceedings (FR ISSN 0074-4190) 106

International Congress Science Series (BE ISSN 0538-6772) 796

International Congresses on Tropical Medicine and Malaria. (Proceedings) (GR ISSN 0074-4212) 777

International Container Directory (US) 855

International Convention Facilities Directory see Successful Meetings Facilities Directory 796

International Convocation on Immunology. Papers (SZ ISSN 0074-4220) 773

International Cooperative Alliance. Congress Report (SZ ISSN 0074-4247) 238

International Cooperative Alliance. Cooperative Series (II ISSN 0074-4255) 238

International Copper Information Bulletin (UK ISSN 0309-2216) 801

International Cotton Advisory Committee. Country Statements Presented in Connection with the Plenary Meetings (US) 57

International Cotton Industry Statistics (SZ ISSN 0538-6829) 1057, 1075

International Cotton Industry Statistics. Supplement see International Textile Machinery Shipment Statistics 1076

International Cotton-System Fibre Consumption Statistics (SZ) 1057, 1076

International Council for Automatic Data Processing in Government Administration. Proceedings of Conference (SP) 360

International Council for Bird Preservation. British Section. Report (UK ISSN 0074-4263) 170

International Council for Bird Preservation. Proceedings of Conferences (UK ISSN 0074-4271) 170

International Council for Bird Preservation Parrot Working Group Meeting. Proceedings see I C B P Parrot Working Group Meeting. Proceedings 170

International Council for Building Research, Studies and Documentation. Congress Reports (FR ISSN 0074-428X) 1156

International Council for Education of the Visually Handicapped Educator see I C E V H Educator 444

International Council for Laboratory Animal Science. Proceedings of the Symposium (NO) 762, 781

International Council for Philosophy and Humanistic Studies. Bulletin (UN) 630, 878

International Council for Philosophy and Humanistic Studies. General Assembly. Compte Rendu see International Council for Philosophy and Humanistic Studies. Bulletin 630

International Council for Research in Agroforestry. Annual Report (KE) 525

International Council for Scientific Management. Proceedings of World Congress (JA ISSN 0085-2120) 280

International Council for the Exploration of the Sea. Annales Biologiques (DK ISSN 0106-1003) 142, 510

International Council for the Exploration of the Sea. Bulletin Hydrographique see I C E S Oceanographic Data Lists and Inventories 406

International Council for the Exploration of the Sea. Bulletin Statistique (DK ISSN 0373-2045) 406, 510

International Council for the Exploration of the Sea. Cooperative Research Reports (DK ISSN 0105-3213) 406, 510

International Council for the Exploration of the Sea. Journal du Conseil (DK ISSN 0020-6466) 406, 510

International Council for the Exploration of the Sea. Rapports et Proces-Verbaux des Reunions (DK ISSN 0074-4336) 406, 510

International Council of Jews from Czechoslovakia Newsletter see I C J C Newsletter 503

International Council of Scientific Unions. Year Book (FR ISSN 0074-4387) 993

International Council on Archives. Committee on Conservation and Restauration. Committee on Archival Reprography (Bulletin) (SP ISSN 0255-3139) 679

International Council on Archives. East and Central Africa Regional Branch. General Conference Proceedings (LO) 679

International Council on Archives. Microfilm Committee. Bulletin see International Council on Archives. Committee on Conservation and Restauration. Committee on Archival Reprography (Bulletin) 679

International Council on Environmental Law References see I C E L References 501

International Council on Health, Physical Education and Recreation Congress Proceedings see I C H P E R Congress Proceedings 762

International Countermeasures Handbook (US ISSN 0145-2584) 811

International Court of Justice. Yearbook/Annuaire (UN ISSN 0074-445X) 670

International Credit Union Yearbook see Credit Union Yearbook 227

International Crop Improvement Association. Production Publication see Association of Official Seed Certifying Agencies. Production Publication 52

International Cryogenic Materials Conferences see Advances in Cryogenic Engineering 894

International Cryogenics Monograph Series (US ISSN 0538-7051) 894

International Customs Journal/Bulletin International des Douanes (BE ISSN 0074-4476) 257, 296

International Cycling Guide (UK) 1156

International Dairy Federation. Annual Bulletin/Federation Internationale de Laiterie. Bulletin Annuel (BE ISSN 0074-4484) 62

International Dairy Federation. Annual Memento/Federation Internationale de Laiterie. Memento Annuel (BE ISSN 0538-7078) 62

International Dairy Federation. Catalogue of I D F Publications. Catalogue des Publications de la F I L (BE ISSN 0538-7086) 41

International Dairy Federation. International Standard/Federation Internationale de Laiterie. Norme Internationale (BE ISSN 0538-7094) 62

International Dairy Products Review see Foodnews Dairy Products Review 1153

International Dance-Exercise Association Industry Directory see I D E A Industry Directory 309

International Data Processing Conference. Proceedings (US) 1156

International Defense Directory (SZ ISSN 0256-7822) 811

International Design Conference in Aspen. Report (US ISSN 0534-9710) 643

International Development Abstracts (UK ISSN 0262-0855) 8, 551

International Development Research Centre. Annual Report/Centre de Recherches pour le Developpement International. Rapport Annuel (CN ISSN 0704-7584) 196

International Development Resource Books (US ISSN 0738-1425) 245

International Directory of Antiquarian Booksellers/Repertoire International de la Librairie Ancienne (DK ISSN 0538-7159) 962

International Directory of Arts (GW ISSN 0074-4565) 106

International Directory of Arts (Year) (US) 106, 310

International Directory of Building Research, Information and Development Organizations (UK) 185

International Directory of Centers for Asian Studies (HK) 430, 851

International Directory of Children's Literature (US) 335, 964

International Directory of Conchologists (US) 614

International Directory of Corporate Affiliations (US) 310

International Directory of Current Research in the History of Cartography and in Carto-Bibliography (UK ISSN 0307-6113) 545

International Directory of Discontinued I Cs & Semiconductors D.A.T.A. Book (US) 361
International Directory of Eighteenth-Century Studies/Repertoire International des Dix-Huitiemistes (UK) 630
International Directory of Executive Recruiters (US ISSN 0092-4989) 286
International Directory of Importers: Africa (US) 257, 310
International Directory of Importers: South/Central America (US) 257, 310
International Directory of Investigators in Psychopharmacology (US) 871
International Directory of Little Magazines and Small Presses (US ISSN 0092-3974) 127, 964
International Directory of Marine Scientists (UN) 142, 406
International Directory of Marketing Research Houses and Services (US ISSN 0074-459X) 284, 310
International Directory of New and Renewable Energy (UN) 465
International Directory of News Libraries and Buyers' Guide (Year) see International Directory of News Libraries Including Buyer's Guide (Year) 679
International Directory of News Libraries Including Buyer's Guide (Year) (US) 679
International Directory of Nuclear Utilities (US ISSN 0742-5821) 465, 897
International Directory of Occupational Safety and Health Services and Institutions (UN ISSN 0579-8140) 635
International Directory of Philosophy and Philosophers (US ISSN 0074-4603) 878
International Directory of Prisoners' Aid Agencies (US ISSN 0538-7191) 370, 1018
International Directory of Private Presses (US) 310, 931
International Directory of Programs in Business and Commerce (US ISSN 0074-4611) 1156
International Directory of Published Market Research see Marketsearch 284
International Directory of Special Events and Festivals see Official Directory of Festivals, Sports & Special Events 285
International Directory of Specialized Cancer Research and Treatment Establishments (SZ) 775
International Directory of the Nonwoven Fabrics Industry (US ISSN 0095-683X) 1074
International Directory of 16MM Film Collectors (US ISSN 0074-462X) 824
International Display Research Conference. Conference Record (US) 456
International District Heating Association. Proceedings (US ISSN 0074-4638) 554
International Documentation on Macedonia (SZ) 586, 913
International Documents on Palestine see Institute for Palestine Studies. International Annual Documentary Series 569
International Dostoevsky Society Bulletin see Dostoevsky Studies 720
International Dredging Abstracts see World Ports and Harbours Abstracts 1087
International Economic Association. Proceedings of the Conferences and Congresses (UK ISSN 0074-4646) 196
International Economic Indicators see Internationale Wirtschaftszahlen 1057
International Economic Studies Institute. Contemporary Issues (US) 196
International Economics see Surrey Papers in Economics 200

International Egg Marketing Conference. Proceedings (AT ISSN 0534-9869) 66
International Electrical, Electronics Conference and Exposition. Conference Digest see Electronicom. Conference Proceedings 453
International Electrical, Electronics Donference and Exposition. Proceedings see Electronicom. Conference Proceedings 453
International Electron Devices Meeting. Abstracts see International Electron Devices Meeting. I E D M Technical Digest 456
International Electron Devices Meeting. I E D M Technical Digest (US ISSN 0163-1918) 456
International Electronics Packaging Society. (Publication) (US) 456
International Electrotechnical Commission. Central Office Report see International Electrotechnical Commission. Yearbook/Annuaire 456
International Electrotechnical Commission. Directory see International Electrotechnical Commission. Repertoire 456
International Electrotechnical Commission. Repertoire/ International Electrotechnical Commission. Directory (SZ) 456
International Electrotechnical Commission. Yearbook/Annuaire (SZ ISSN 0074-4697) 456
International Electrotechnical Commission Catalogue of Publications see I E C Catalogue of Publications 461
International Energy Annual (US) 465
International Engineering Directory (US ISSN 0074-5774) 472
International Engineering/Scientific Software Directory (US) 363
International Engineering Software Directory see International Engineering/Scientific Software Directory 363
International Eucharist Congress. Proceedings (IT ISSN 0074-5782) 982
International Exchange of Information on Current Criminological Research Projects in Member States (FR ISSN 0252-063X) 370
International Executive Transfers (UK ISSN 0267-7717) 280
International Fabricare Institute Bulletin: Textile Notes see I F I Bulletin: Textile Notes 1154
International Falcon Movement. Conference Reports (BE ISSN 0074-5790) 335
International Farm Machinery Abstracts see Bulletin Bibliographique International du Machinisme Agricole 39
International Federation for Documentation. P-Notes (NE ISSN 0378-7656) 679
International Federation for Documentation. Proceedings of Congress (NE ISSN 0074-5812) 679
International Federation for Documentation Directory see F I D Directory 677
International Federation for Documentation Meetings Reports see F I D/R I Meetings Reports 677
International Federation for Documentation Report Series see F.I.D./C.R. Report Series 689
International Federation for Documentation Series on Problems of Information Science see F I D/R I Series on Problems of Information Science 677
International Federation for Housing and Planning. Directory (NE) 623
International Federation for Housing and Planning. Yearbook see International Federation for Housing and Planning. Directory 623
International Federation for Information Processing Information Bulletin see I F I P Information Bulletin 678

International Federation for Medical Psychotherapy. Congress Reports (SZ ISSN 0074-5847) 790
International Federation for Preventive and Social Medicine News see I.F.P.S.M. News 954
International Federation of Agricultural Producers. General Conference Proceedings (FR ISSN 0074-5863) 29
International Federation of Asian and Western Pacific Contractors' Associations. Proceedings of the Annual Convention (PH ISSN 0074-588X) 796
International Federation of Associations of Textile Chemists and Colorists. Reports of Congress (IT ISSN 0074-5898) 339, 1074
International Federation of Automatic Control Symposium on Multivariable Technical Control Systems. Proceedings see I F A C Symposium on Multivariable Technical Control Systems. Proceedings 491
International Federation of Catholic Universities. General Assembly. (Report) (FR ISSN 0579-3866) 436
International Federation of European Contractors of Building and Public Works Review see Entreprise Europeenne 184
International Federation of Fruit Juice Producers. Proceedings. Berichte. Rapports see International Federation of Fruit Juice Producers. Rapport Annuel d'Activite 519
International Federation of Fruit Juice Producers. Proceedings of Congress. Compte-Rendu du Congres (FR ISSN 0074-5952) 120
International Federation of Fruit Juice Producers. Rapport Annuel d'Activite (FR) 519
International Federation of Library Associations and Institutions Annual see I F L A Annual 678
International Federation of Library Associations and Institutions Directory see I F L A Directory 678
International Federation of Library Associations and Institutions Publications see I F L A Publications 679
International Federation of Medical Students' Associations. Minutes and Reports of the General Assembly (AU ISSN 0074-6037) 762
International Federation of Operational Research Societies. Airline Group (A G I F O R S) Proceedings (US ISSN 0538-7442) 1089
International Federation of Plantation, Agricultural and Allied Workers. Report of the Secretariat to the I F P A A W World Congress (SZ ISSN 0538-7477) 48, 648
International Federation of Prestressing. Congress Proceedings (UK ISSN 0074-6045) 482
International Federation of Stationers' Associations Minutes of the General Meeting see I F O S A. Minutes of the General Meeting 286
International Field Hockey Rules (US) 1034
International Film and T.V. Yearbook see Screen International Film and T.V. Yearbook 825
International Film Guide (UK ISSN 0074-6053) 824
International Finance Corporation. Report (UN ISSN 0074-6061) 229
International Financial Statistics (UN ISSN 0020-6725) 211
International Financial Statistics Yearbook (UN ISSN 0250-7463) 245
International Finishing Industries Manual see Finishing Diary 855
International Fiscal Association. Yearbook (NE) 670
International Fiscal Association Seminar Series see I F A Seminar Series 670
International Fiscal Harmonization Series (NE) 296
International Flight Information Manual(US) 20

International Foamed Plastic Markets and Directory see U S Foamed Plastics Markets and Directory 901
International Folk Music Council. Internationale Arbeitstagung der Study Group on Folk Musical Instruments (SW) 836
International Folk Music Council. Yearbook see Yearbook for Traditional Music 843
International Folklore Bibliography see Internationale Volkskundliche Bibliographie 517
International Food Directory (US) 310, 519
International Food Policy Research Institute Research Report see I F P R I Research Report 47
International Football Book (UK ISSN 0074-610X) 1039
International Forum of Light Music in Radio (SZ) 348
International Foundation Directory (US) 441
International Foundry Congress. Papers and Communications (US ISSN 0074-6118) 798
International Gas Bearing Symposium. Proceedings (UK) 491
International Gas Research Conference. Proceedings (US ISSN 0736-5721) 465, 865
International Gas Union. Proceedings of Conferences see International Gas Union. Proceedings of World Gas Conferences 865
International Gas Union. Proceedings of World Gas Conferences (FR) 865
International Gemological Symposium Proceedings (US) 379
International Geographical Union. Papers (UR ISSN 0074-6134) 545
International Geophysics Series (US ISSN 0074-6142) 399
International Geoscience and Remote Sensing Symposium Digest (US) 343, 456
International Glass/Metal Catalog (US ISSN 0147-300X) 320
International Gondwana Symposium. Papers (AT) 1156
International Graphical Federation. Report of Activities (SZ ISSN 0074-6177) 648
International Grassland Congress. Proceedings (UR ISSN 0074-6185) 57
International Green Book (US ISSN 0074-6193) 310
International Guide (CN) 620, 1111
International Guide to Psi-Periodicals see Whole Again Resource Guide 1015
International Guide to Scientific Instruments & Chemicals (UK) 323, 637
International Guiding Eyes. Newsletter see I G E News 868
International Guiding Eyes News see I G E News 868
International Handbook of Resources for the Educators of Adults see Resources for Educators of Adults 427
International Handbook of Universities see International Handbook of Universities and Other Institutions of Higher Education 436
International Handbook of Universities and Other Institutions of Higher Education (UK ISSN 0074-6215) 436
International Harbour Congress. Proceedings/Internationaal Havenkongres. Verslagboek/Congres Portuaire International. Compte-Rendu/Internationale Hafentagung. Berichte (BE) 1101
International Health Care Construction & Equipment (UK) 185
International Heat Transfer Conference (US) 472
International Histological Classification of Tumours (UN ISSN 0538-7736) 1156
International Hop Growers Convention. Report of Congress (YU ISSN 0074-6223) 63

International Horticultural Congress. Proceedings (NE ISSN 0074-6231) 533
International Hotel Guide (FR ISSN 0074-624X) 620
International Humanist and Ethical Union. Proceedings of the Congress (NE ISSN 0074-6258) 878
International Hydrographic Bureau. Yearbook see International Hydrographic Organization. Yearbook 406
International Hydrographic Conference. Reports of Proceedings (MC ISSN 0074-6274) 403, 406
International Hydrographic Organization. Yearbook (MC) 403, 406
International Hydrological Programme: Operational Hydrological Programme: Yearbook Federal Republic of Germany and Berlin (West) see Internationale Hydrologisches Programm: Operationelles Hydrologisches Programm: Jahrbuch Bundesrepublik Deutschland und Berlin (West) 403
International I E E E V L S I Mutilevel Interconnection Conference. Proceedings (US) 456
International I S A Pulp and Paper Instrumentation Symposium Proceedings see Instrumentation in the Pulp and Paper Industry 858
International I S B N Publishers' Directory (US) 962
International Index to Film Periodicals (UK ISSN 0000-0388) 8, 826
International Index to Television Periodicals (UK ISSN 0143-5663) 345, 348
International Industrial Sensor Directory (US ISSN 0736-1831) 310, 472
International Information Centre for Terminology, Vienna Infoterm Series see Infoterm Series 696
International Information Flows (US) 1156
International Institute for Applied Systems Analysis Annual Report see I I A S A Annual Report 358
International Institute for Educational Planning Occasional Papers see I I E P Occasional Papers 441
International Institute for Educational Planning Research Reports see I I E P Research Reports 441
International Institute for Educational Planning Seminar Papers see I I E P Seminar Papers 441
International Institute for Labour Studies. Public Lecture Series (UN) 272
International Institute for Labour Studies. Publications (UK ISSN 0074-6509) 272
International Institute for Labour Studies. Research Series (UN) 272
International Institute for Land Reclamation and Improvement. Annual Report (NE ISSN 0074-6428) 57
International Institute for Land Reclamation and Improvement. Bibliography (NE ISSN 0074-6436) 41
International Institute for Land Reclamation and Improvement. Publication (NE ISSN 0074-6452) 57
International Institute for Population Sciences. Director's Report (II) 922
International Institute for Population Studies. Annual Report see International Institute for Population Sciences. Director's Report 922
International Institute for Population Studies. Director's Report see International Institute for Population Sciences. Director's Report 922
International Institute for Sugar Beet Research. Reports of the Winter Congress (BE ISSN 0074-6460) 57
International Institute of Administrative Sciences. Reports of the International Congress (BE ISSN 0074-6479) 943

International Institute of Ibero-American Literature. Congress Proceedings. Memoria (US ISSN 0074-6495) 724
International Institute of Philosophy. Actes (FR ISSN 0074-6525) 878
International Institute of Public Finance. Papers and Proceedings (US ISSN 0074-6533) 296
International Institute of Refrigeration. Proceedings of Commission Meetings(FR ISSN 0074-6541) 554
International Institute of Seismology and Earthquake Engineering. Bulletin(JA ISSN 0074-655X) 399, 482
International Institute of Seismology and Earthquake Engineering. Individual Studies by Participants at I I S E E (JA) 400, 482
International Institute of Seismology and Earthquake Engineering. Report of Individual Study by Participants to I S E E see International Institute of Seismology and Earthquake Engineering. Individual Studies by Participants at I I S E E 400
International Institute of Seismology and Earthquake Engineering. Year Book (JA ISSN 0074-6614) 400, 482
International Institute of Space Law. Colloquium. Proceedings (US) 657
International Institute of Synthetic Rubber Producers. Annual Meeting Proceedings (US ISSN 0146-3977) 985
International Institute of Tropical Agriculture. Annual Report (NR) 29
International Institute of Tropical Agriculture. Report see International Institute of Tropical Agriculture. Annual Report 29
International Institute of Tropical Agriculture. Research Highlights (NR ISSN 0331-4340) 29
International Institute on the Prevention and Treatment of Alcoholism. Selected Papers (SZ ISSN 0074-6622) 377
International Institute on the Prevention and Treatment of Drug Dependence. Selected Papers (SZ) 377
International Interdisciplinary Seminar on Piagetian Theory and Its Implications for the Helping Professions. Proceedings (US) 445
International Iron and Steel Institute. Report of Conference Proceedings (BE ISSN 0074-6630) 798
International Joint Conference on Pattern Recognition. Proceedings see International Conference on Pattern Recognition. Proceedings 356
International Journal of Abstracts see Statistical Theory and Method Abstracts 12
International Journal of Alternative Communities see Alternative Communities Magazine 1024
International Journal of Andrology. Supplement (DK ISSN 0106-1607) 795
International Journal of Chemical Kinetics. Symposium (US) 331
International Journal of Economic and Social History see Quaderni Internazionali di Storia Economica e Sociale 594
International Journal of Educational Sciences (II) 415
International Journal of Group Tensions(US ISSN 0047-0732) 906, 935, 1027
International Journal of Mycology and Lichenology (GW ISSN 0723-3353) 158
International Journal of Psychiatry see International Journal of Psychoanalytic Psychotherapy 1156
International Journal of Psychoanalytic Psychotherapy (US ISSN 0091-0600) 1156

International Journal of Quantum Chemistry. Symposium see International Symposium on Atomic, Molecular and Solid-State Theory, Collision Phenomena and Computational Methods. Proceedings 323
International Journal of Rock Mechanics and Mining Sciences see International Journal of Rock Mechanics and Mining Sciences & Geomechanics Abstracts 822
International Journal of Rock Mechanics and Mining Sciences & Geomechanics Abstracts (US ISSN 0148-9062) 8, 822
International Journal of Turkish Studies(US ISSN 0272-7919) 545, 612
International Kierkegaard Newsletter (DK ISSN 0108-3104) 878
International Labor Studies (US ISSN 0074-6657) 1156
International Labour Conference. Reports to the Conference and Record of Proceedings (UN ISSN 0074-6673) 272
International Labour Law Reports (NE) 272, 657
International Labour Office. Official Bulletin see International Labour Office. Official Bulletin. Series A 273
International Labour Office. Official Bulletin see International Labour Office. Official Bulletin. Series B 273
International Labour Office. Official Bulletin. Series A (UN ISSN 0378-5882) 273
International Labour Office. Official Bulletin. Series B (UN ISSN 0378-5890) 273
International Labour Office. P R E A L C. Investigaciones sobre Empleo (Programa Regional del Empleo para America Latina y el Caribe) (UN) 245, 251
International Labour Office. Special Report of the Director-General on the Application of the Declaration Concerning the Policy of Apartheid of the Republic of South Africa (UN ISSN 0538-8333) 913
International Labour Office Abstracts see C I S Abstracts 636
International Law Association. American Branch. Proceedings (US) 670
International Law Association. Reports of Conferences (UK ISSN 0074-6738) 671
International Law Commission Yearbook (UN) 671
International Lead Zinc Research Organization, Inc. Annual Review see I L Z R O Annual Review 798
International Lead Zinc Research Organization, Inc. Environmental Health Research Digest see I L Z R O Environmental Health Research Digest 496
International Lead Zinc Research Organization, Inc. Lead Research Digest see I L Z R O Lead Research Digest 798
International Lead Zinc Research Organization, Inc. Zinc Cadium Research Digest see I L Z R O Zinc/Cadium Research Digest 798
International Leadership (US) 916
International League for Human Rights. Annual Report (US ISSN 0363-9347) 913
International League for the Rights of Man. Annual Report see International League for Human Rights. Annual Report 913
International League of Societies for Persons With Mental Handicap. World Congress Proceedings. (BE) 790, 935
International League of Societies for the Mentally Handicapped. World Congress Proceedings see International League of Societies for Persons With Mental Handicap. World Congress Proceedings 935

International Lecture Series in Computer Science (US) 352
International Lesson Annual (US) 970
International Linguistic Association. Monograph (US ISSN 0074-6797) 696
International Linguistic Association. Special Publications (US ISSN 0074-6800) 696
International Literary and Artistic Association. Proceedings and Reports of Congress (FR ISSN 0074-6819) 630
International Literary Market Place (US ISSN 0074-6827) 962
International Livestock Centre for Africa Annual Report see I L C A Annual Report 66
International Livestock Centre for Africa Proceedings see I L C A Proceedings 66
International Livestock Centre for Africa Programme and Budget see I L C A Programme and Budget 66
International Livestock Centre for Africa Research Report see I L C A Research Report 66
International Logistics Symposium Proceedings see Society of Logistics Engineers. Proceedings 1071
International Machine Tool Design and Research Conference. Proceedings (UK ISSN 0074-6835) 745
International Magnetics Conference. Digest see International Magnetics Conference. Digests of the Intermag Conference 889
International Magnetics Conference. Digests of the Intermag Conference (US) 889
International Manufacturing Software Directory (US) 363
International Marine Safety Directory (UK) 1101
International Maritime Committee. Documentation see C M I Year Book 1099
International Maritime Law Seminar. Publication (CN) 657, 671
International Market Guide - Continental Europe see Market Guide Continental Europe 267
International Marketing Data and Statistics (UK ISSN 0308-2938) 211
International Markets for Meat (UN) 66
International Media Guide. Consumer Magazines Edition see International Media Guide. Consumer Magazines Worldwide 17
International Media Guide. Consumer Magazines Worldwide (US) 17, 1086
International Media Guide. Newspapers: Worldwide (US ISSN 0093-9447) 17
International Media Guides. Business/Professional Publications Edition (US) 17
International Medical Who's Who (UK) 134, 762
International Meeting of Animal Nutrition Experts. Proceedings (SP ISSN 0074-6959) 66
International Meeting on Cattle Diseases. Reports (GW ISSN 0074-6975) 66, 1121
International Meeting Place (UK ISSN 0268-5671) 1111
International Metalworkers' Congress. Reports (SZ ISSN 0074-6983) 798
International Meteorological Institute in Stockholm. Annual Report (SW ISSN 0349-0068) 805
International Microfilm Source Book see International Micrographics Source Book 688
International Microforms in Print see Guide to Microforms in Print. Subject 127
International Micrographics Source Book (US ISSN 0272-0310) 688
International Microwave Symposium Digest see I E E E/M T T - S International Microwave Symposium. Digest 454

INTERNATIONAL RELATIONS

International Migration Newsletter *see* International Newsletter on Migration 922
International Mineralogical Association. Proceedings of Meetings (GW ISSN 0074-7017) 817
International Monetary Fund. Annual Report of the Executive Board (UN ISSN 0250-7498) 229
International Monetary Fund. Annual Report of the Executive Directors *see* International Monetary Fund. Annual Report of the Executive Board 229
International Monetary Fund. Annual Report on Exchange Arrangements and Exchange Restrictions (UN ISSN 0250-7366) 229
International Monetary Fund. Annual Report on Exchange Restrictions *see* International Monetary Fund. Annual Report on Exchange Arrangements and Exchange Restrictions 229
International Monetary Fund. Balance of Payments Statistics (UN ISSN 0252-3051) 257, 277
International Monetary Fund. Government Finance Statistics Yearbook (UN ISSN 0250-7374) 211, 1057
International Monetary Fund. Occasional Papers (UN ISSN 0251-6365) 229
International Monetary Fund. Pamphlet Series (UN ISSN 0538-8759) 230
International Monetary Fund. Selected Decisions of the Executive Directors and Selected Documents *see* International Monetary Fund. Selected Decisions of the International Monetary Fund and Selected Documents 230
International Monetary Fund. Selected Decisions of the International Monetary Fund and Selected Documents (UN ISSN 0094-1735) 230
International Monetary Fund. Summary Proceedings of the Annual Meeting of the Board of Governors (UN ISSN 0074-7025) 230
International Monetary Market Yearbook *see* Chicago Mercantile Exchange Yearbook 254
International Monographs on Advanced Biology and Biophysics (II ISSN 0074-7033) 142, 153
International Monographs on Advanced Chemistry (II ISSN 0074-7041) 323
International Monographs on Advanced Mathematics and Physics (II ISSN 0074-705X) 749, 889
International Monographs on Studies in Indian Economics (II ISSN 0074-7068) 196
International Motion Picture Almanac (US ISSN 0074-7084) 824
International Museum of Cultures. Publication (US ISSN 0197-3746) 73
International Music and Opera Guide (UK) 836
International Music Guide *see* International Music and Opera Guide 836
International Musicological Society and the American Musicological Society. Report (US) 836
International Narcotic Enforcement Officers Association. Annual Conference Report (US ISSN 0538-8821) 370
International Narcotics Control Board. Comparative Statement of Estimates and Statistics on Narcotic Drugs Furnished by Governments in Accordance with the International Treaties *see* International Narcotics Control Board. Comparative Statement of Estimates and Statistics on Narcotic Drugs for (Year) 871
International Narcotics Control Board. Comparative Statement of Estimates and Statistics on Narcotic Drugs for (Year) (UN) 377, 871, 954

International Narcotics Control Board. Report for (Year) (UN ISSN 0257-3717) 377, 871, 954
International Narcotics Control Board. Statistics on Narcotic Drugs for (Year) (UN) 377, 871, 954
International Narcotics Control Board. Statistics on Psychotropic Substances for (Year) (UN) 377, 871, 954
International Naturist Guide/Internationaler FKK-Reisefuehrer/Guide Naturiste Internationale (GW ISSN 0074-7122) 1045
International Navigation Congress. Papers (BE) 1101
International Navigation Congress. Proceedings (BE) 1101
International Newsletter on Migration (CN ISSN 0383-2767) 922
International North Pacific Fisheries Commission. Annual Report (CN ISSN 0074-7165) 1156
International North Pacific Fisheries Commission. Bulletin (CN ISSN 0074-7157) 1156
International North Pacific Fisheries Commission. Statistical Yearbook (CN ISSN 0535-1588) 1156
International Nursing Index *see* International Nursing Index Including Nursing Citation Index 771
International Nursing Index Including Nursing Citation Index (US) 8, 771
International Ocean Institute. Occasional Papers (MM) 406
International Ocean Institute. Pacem in Maribus. Proceedings (MM) 406
International Oceanographic Tables (UN ISSN 0538-8880) 406
International Office Automation Guide *see* Wharton's Complete Office Automation Guide 353
International Office of Cocoa and Chocolate and the International Sugar Confectionary Manufacturers' Association. Annual Statistical Bulletin (BE) 522
International Office of Cocoa and Chocolate and the International Sugar Confectionary Manufacturers' Association. Periodic Bulletin *see* International Office of Cocoa and Chocolate and the International Sugar Confectionary Manufacturers' Association. Annual Statistical Bulletin 522
International Office of Cocoa and Chocolate and the International Sugar Confectionary Manufacturers' Association. Report of the General Assembly (BE ISSN 0535-1626) 522
International Offshore Craft Conference. Proceedings (UK) 1101
International Offshore Exploration Conference (US) 406
International Oil and Gas Development Yearbook (US) 389, 865
International Oil Scouts Association Directory (US) 310, 389, 865
International Olympic Academy. Report of the Sessions (GR ISSN 0074-7181) 1034
International Ombudsman Institute Bibliography (CN) 127, 668
International Online Information Meeting (Proceedings) (UK) 357
International Optical Year Book (UK) 786
International Organization for Cooperation in Health Care. General Assembly. Report (NE) 762
International Organization for Medical Cooperation. General Assembly. Report *see* International Organization for Cooperation in Health Care. General Assembly. Report 762
International Organization for Standardization Catalogue *see* I S O Catalogue 809
International Organization for Standardization International Standards *see* I S O International Standards 809
International Organization for Standardization Memento *see* I S O Memento 809

International Organization of Consumers Unions. Proceedings (NE ISSN 0538-8988) 369
International Organizing Committee of World Mining Congresses. Report *see* World Mining Congress. Report 821
International P.E.N. Congress. Report (UK ISSN 0074-722X) 724
International Pacific Halibut Commission. Report *see* International Pacific Halibut Commission (U.S. and Canada). Technical Reports 510
International Pacific Halibut Commission (U.S. and Canada). Annual Report (US ISSN 0074-7238) 510
International Pacific Halibut Commission (U.S. and Canada). Scientific Reports (US ISSN 0074-7246) 510
International Pacific Halibut Commission (U.S. and Canada). Technical Reports (US ISSN 0579-3920) 510
International Pacific Salmon Fisheries Commission. Annual Report (CN ISSN 0074-7254) 1156
International Pacific Salmon Fisheries Commission. Bulletin (CN ISSN 0074-7262) 1156
International Pacific Salmon Fisheries Commission. Progress Report (CN ISSN 0074-7270) 1156
International Packaging Abstracts (US ISSN 0260-7409) 8, 855
International Peace Research Association. Proceedings of the Conference (GW ISSN 0074-7297) 1156
International Peace Research Association Studies in Peace Research *see* I P R A Studies in Peace Research 1154
International Peace Research Institute. Basic Social Science Monographs (NO ISSN 0522-4497) 1156
International Pediatric Association. Proceedings of Congress (AU ISSN 0074-7300) 787
International Periodicals and Reference Works (US ISSN 0742-3985) 127, 647
International Petroleum Abstracts (UK ISSN 0309-4944) 8, 868
International Petroleum Encyclopedia (US ISSN 0148-0375) 865
International Pharmaceutical Abstracts (US ISSN 0020-8264) 8, 873
International Pharmaceutical Technology & Product Manufacture Abstracts (UK ISSN 0264-2247) 873
International Philanthropy *see* Comsearch: Broad Topics 1022
International Philatelic Federation. General Assembly. Proces-Verbal (SZ ISSN 0074-7343) 875
International Photobiological Congress. Proceedings (US ISSN 0074-7351) 1156
International Planned Parenthood Federation Annual Report *see* I P P F Annual Report 179
International Plant Propagators' Society. Combined Proceedings of Annual Meetings (US) 533
International Plant Protection Center. Infoletter (US ISSN 0145-6288) 57
International Plastics Directory *see* Handbuch der Internationalen Kunststoffindustrie 900
International Poetry (US) 742
International Polar Motion Service. Annual Report/Kokusai Kyoku-Undo Kansoku Jigyo Nenpo (JA ISSN 0074-7432) 116
International Police Association. Meeting of the International Executive Council (UK ISSN 0579-5567) 370
International Police Association. Travel Scholarships (UK ISSN 0579-6881) 371
International Political Science Abstracts/Documentation Politique Internationale (FR ISSN 0020-8345) 8, 912

International Political Science Association. World Conference. Proceedings *see* International Political Science Association. World Congress 906
International Political Science Association. World Congress (CN) 906
International Polymer Science and Technology (UK ISSN 0307-174X) 323, 900
International Population Conference. Proceedings (BE ISSN 0074-9338) 179, 922
International Population Data (US) 922
International Potash Institute. Colloquium. Proceedings (SZ ISSN 0074-7491) 57
International Potash Institute. Congress Proceedings (SZ) 57
International Potash Institute. Congress Report *see* International Potash Institute. Congress Proceedings 57
International Potash Institute Bulletin *see* I P I Bulletin 56
International Potash Institute Research Topics *see* I P I Research Topics 56
International Powder & Bulk Solids Abstracts (UK ISSN 0266-2922) 477, 478
International Powder Metallurgy Conference. Proceedings-Modern Developments in Powder Metallurgy (US ISSN 0074-7513) 798
International Power Systems (US) 465
International Process Technology Abstracts (UK ISSN 0266-2930) 477, 478
International Production Cost Comparison (SZ) 1074
International Professional Communication Conference. Conference Record. (US) 343
International Programmable Controllers Directory (US) 355
International Progress in Urethanes (US) 329, 900
International Psycho-Analytical Association. Monograph (US) 790
International Publishers Association. Proceedings of Congress (SZ ISSN 0074-7556) 962
International Pulp & Paper Directory (US ISSN 0097-2509) 310, 858
International Quantum Electronics Conference. Digest of Technical Papers (US ISSN 0538-9275) 456
International Radar Conference. Record(US) 20, 344, 456
International Radio and Television Society, Inc. Gold Medal Annual *see* I R T S Gold Medal Annual 348
International Radio Club of America Foreign Log *see* I.R.C.A. Foreign Log 348
International Railway Progress *see* Developing Railways 1094
International Railway Statistics. Statistics of Individual Railways (FR ISSN 0074-7580) 1094
International Rayon and Synthetic Fibres Committee. Statistical Yearbook (FR ISSN 0074-7599) 8, 1076
International Recording Studio and Equipment Directory *see* Billboard's International Recording Studio and Equipment Directory 1031
International Reference Annual for Building and Equipment of Sports, Tourism, Recreation Installations (FR ISSN 0074-7645) 1034
International Refractories Handbook & Directory (UK) 310, 320
International Register of Telegraphic and Trade Addresses *see* Marconi's International Register 313
International Rehabilitation Review (US ISSN 0020-8477) 762
International Reinforced Plastics Conference. Papers and Proceedings. *see* Reinforced Plastics Congress 901
International Relations Association. Journal *see* Journal of International Relations 917

International Relations Committee. New Energy Foundation. Annual Report on International Relations (JA) *916*
International Reliability Physics Symposium. Proceedings *see* Reliability Physics *893*
International Repertory of Music Literature Abstracts of Music Literature *see* R I L M Abstracts of Music Literature *844*
International Rescue Committee Annual Report (US ISSN 0538-9461) *1018*
International Research Centers Directory (US ISSN 0278-2731) *415*
International Research Seminar on Vocational Rehabilitation of the Mentally Retarded. Special Publications Series (US) *1156*
International Review of Connective Tissue Research (US ISSN 0074-767X) *163*
International Review of Criminal Policy(UN ISSN 0074-7688) *371*
International Review of Cytology (US ISSN 0074-7696) *163*
International Review of Experimental Pathology (US ISSN 0074-7718) *762*
International Review of General and Experimental Zoology (US ISSN 0074-7734) *175*
International Review of Neurobiology (US ISSN 0074-7742) *790*
International Review of Research in Mental Retardation (US ISSN 0074-7750) *445, 790*
International Review of Tropical Medicine (US ISSN 0074-7777) *777*
International Reviews in Immunology (US ISSN 0883-0185) *993*
International Rice Research Institute Annual Report *see* I R R I Annual Report *63*
International Rice Research Institute Research Highlights *see* I R R I. Research Highlights *63*
International Rice Research Institute Research Paper Series *see* I R R I Research Paper Series *63*
International Road Congresses. Proceedings (FR ISSN 0074-7815) *482, 1096*
International Road Haulage by United Kingdom Registered Vehicles (UK ISSN 0262-6195) *1105*
International Robotics Industry Directory (US) *355*
International Robotics Yearbook *see* World Yearbook of Robotics Research and Development *355*
International Rubber Directory *see* Handbuch der Internationalen Kautschukindustrie *985*
International Rubber Forum (UK) *985*
International Rubber Study Group. Summary of Proceedings of the Group Meetings and Assemblies (UK ISSN 0074-7823) *985*
International Running Guide *see* International Athletics Guide *1034*
International Rural Housing Journal *see* Revista Internacional de Vivienda Rural *625*
International Rural Sociology Association Items *see* I R S A Items *1027*
International S A M P E Technical Conference Series. N S T C Preprint Series (Society for the Advancement of Material and Process Engineering) (US) *489*
International Savings Banks Institute. Report (SZ) *230*
International Scholars Directory (US) *1156*
International School of Physics "Enrico Fermi". Italian Physical Society. Proceedings (US) *889*
International School of Physics "Enrico Fermi." Proceedings *see* International School of Physics "Enrico Fermi". Italian Physical Society. Proceedings *889*
International School of Physics "Ettore Majorana." Proceedings *see* International School of Physics "Enrico Fermi". Italian Physical Society. Proceedings *889*
International Scientific Council for Trypanosomiasis Research and Control (KE) *1121*
International Scientific Radio Union. Proceedings of General Assemblies *see* International Union of Radio Science. Proceedings of General Assemblies *348*
International Scientific Software Directory (US) *363, 1005*
International Seaweed Symposium. Proceedings (NO ISSN 0074-7874) *158, 406*
International Security Directory (UK ISSN 0074-7890) *374, 943, 954*
International Sedimentary Petrographical Series (NE ISSN 0538-9771) *400*
International Sedimentological Congress. Guidebook (GW ISSN 0074-7904) *389*
International Seminar on Digital Processing of Analog Signals (Proceedings) *see* International Zurich Seminar on Digital Communications. (Proceedings) *361*
International Seminar on Integrated Surveys. Proceedings *see* I T C-U N E S C O International Seminar. Proceedings *1154*
International Series in Experimental Psychology (UK ISSN 0074-8137) *935*
International Series in Heat and Mass Transfer (US ISSN 0741-5877) *472, 894*
International Series in Nonlinear Mathematics (UK) *749*
International Series in Pure and Applied Mathematics (UK ISSN 0539-0125) *749*
International Series in Solid State Physics (UK ISSN 0539-0133) *889*
International Series of Monographs in Electrical Engineering (UK ISSN 0074-803X) *456*
International Series of Monographs in Pure and Applied Mathematics *see* International Series in Pure and Applied Mathematics *749*
International Series of Monographs on Chemistry (US) *323*
International Series of Monographs on Earth Sciences *see* International Series on Earth Sciences *379*
International Series of Monographs on Heating, Ventilation and Refrigeration *see* International Series on Heating, Ventilation and Refrigeration *554*
International Series of Monographs on Physics (US) *889*
International Series of Monographs on Solid State Physics *see* International Series in Solid State Physics *889*
International Series on Earth Sciences (UK ISSN 0538-9984) *379*
International Series on Heating, Ventilation and Refrigeration (UK ISSN 0538-9895) *554*
International Series on the Quality of Working Life (US) *273*
International Shipping and Shipbuilding Directory (UK ISSN 0074-8358) *1101*
International Sivananda Yoga Life and Yoga Vacations *see* Yoga Life *886*
International Skating Union. Ice Dancing Regulations (SZ ISSN 0539-0168) *1034*
International Skating Union. Minutes of Congress (SZ ISSN 0535-2479) *1034*
International Skating Union Constitution *see* I S U Constitution *1033*
International Skating Union Regulations *see* I S U Regulations *1034*
International Social Science Council. Publications (GW ISSN 0074-8404) *1009*
International Social Security Association. Etudes et Recherches/Studies and Research (SZ) *640*
International Social Security Association. Reports of the General Assemblies of the ISSA (SZ ISSN 0251-1339) *640*
International Social Security Association. Technical Reports of Assemblies *see* International Social Security Association. Reports of the General Assemblies of the ISSA *640*
International Society for Electrosleep and Electroanaesthesia Information *see* I E S A Information *790*
International Society for Performing Arts Libraries and Museums. Congress Proceedings *see* International Association of Performing Arts Libraries and Museums. Congress Proceedings *106*
International Society for Rock Mechanics. Congress. Proceedings (PO ISSN 0074-848X) *389, 482*
International Society for Soil Mechanics and Foundation Engineering. Proceedings (MX ISSN 0074-3313) *482*
International Society for Terrain-Vehicle Systems. Proceedings of International Conference (US ISSN 0074-8498) *482*
International Society for the Study of Church Monuments. Bulletin *see* Church Monuments *97*
International Society for the Study of Time. Proceedings *see* Study of Time *117*
International Society of Blood Transfusion. Proceedings of the Congress (FR ISSN 0074-8528) *777, 783*
International Society of Citriculture. Proceedings (US) *29, 796*
International Society of Criminology. Bulletin (FR ISSN 0539-032X) *371*
International Society of Criminology. Rapports Quinquennaux (FR) *371*
International Society of Internal Medicine. Congress Proceedings (SZ ISSN 0074-8544) *762*
International Society of Organbuilders Organ Building Periodical *see* Organ Building Periodical *840*
International Society of Plant Morphologists. Yearbook (II ISSN 0539-0346) *158*
International Society of Urology. Reports of Congress (FR ISSN 0074-8579) *795*
International Softball Congress (Year) Official Yearbook and Guide (US) *1039*
International Solar Energy Society. American Section. Annual Meeting. Proceedings *see* American Solar Energy Society. Annual Meeting *463*
International Solid State Circuits Conference. Digest *see* I E E E International Solid State Circuits Conference. Digest of Technical Papers *454*
International Standard Book Number Review *see* I S B N Review *962*
International Statistical Handbook of Urban Public Transport/Recueil International de Statistiques des Transports Publics Urbains/Internationales Statistik-Handbuch fuer den Oeffentlichen Stadtverkehr (BE ISSN 0378-1968) *1081*
International Statistical Institute. Bulletin (NE) *1057*
International Statistical Institute. Bulletin. Proceedings of the Biennial Sessions (NE ISSN 0074-8609) *1057*
International Statistical Institute. Comparative Studies. Cross-National Summaries *see* International Statistical Institute. Comparative Studies. Cross-National Summaries and E C E Reports *1057*
International Statistical Institute. Comparative Studies. Cross-National Summaries and E C E Reports (NE) *1057*
International Statistical Institute. Proceedings of Specialized Meetings (NE) *1057*
International Steel Statistics - Complete Series (UK) *801*
International Steel Statistics - Summary Tables (UK) *801*
International Straits of the World (NE) *545, 916*
International Structural Engineering Abstracts (IE ISSN 0790-5750) *477*
International Studies in Education (UN) *415*
International Studies in Planning (US) *623*
International Studies in Sociology and Social Anthropology (NE ISSN 0074-8684) *1009, 1027*
International Sugar Organization. Annual Report (UK ISSN 0074-8706) *57, 519*
International Sugar Organization. Sugar Year Book (UK) *519*
International Superphosphate and Compound Manufacturers Association Limited. Technical Meeting. Proceedings (UK ISSN 0074-8714) *57*
International Superphosphate Manufacturers Association. Technical Meeting. Proceedings *see* International Superphosphate and Compound Manufacturers Association Limited. Technical Meeting. Proceedings *57*
International Superphosphate Manufacturers Association, Ltd. Technical Conference. Proceedings *see* I S M A Technical Conference. Proceedings *56*
International Survey of Roman Law. Index *see* Quaderni Camerti di Studi Romanistici. Index *662*
International Symposium of the Technical Committee on Photon-Detectors (HU ISSN 0237-2215) *899*
International Symposium on Acoustical Imaging. Proceedings *see* Acoustical Imaging: Recent Advances in Visualization and Characterization *899*
International Symposium on Atherosclerosis. Proceedings (US ISSN 0074-8765) *777*
International Symposium on Atomic, Molecular and Solid-State Theory and Quantum Statistics. Proceedings *see* International Symposium on Atomic, Molecular and Solid-State Theory, Collision Phenomena and Computational Methods. Proceedings *323*
International Symposium on Atomic, Molecular and Solid-State Theory, Collision Phenomena and Computational Methods. Proceedings(US) *323*
International Symposium on Canine Heartworm Disease. Proceedings (US) *1121*
International Symposium on Cartography and Computing. Proceedings *see* International Symposium on Computer-Assisted Cartography. Proceedings *545*
International Symposium on Cell Biology and Cytopharmacology. Proceedings *see* Advances in Cytopharmacology *162*
International Symposium on Chemical Reaction Engineering. Proceedings (US ISSN 0071-3112) *478*
International Symposium on Circuits and Systems *see* I E E E International Symposium on Circuits and Systems. Proceedings *454*
International Symposium on Combustion. Proceedings *see* Symposium (International) on Combustion *332*
International Symposium on Computer-Assisted Cartography. Proceedings (US) *545*
International Symposium on Computer Hardware Description Languages. Proceedings (US) *361*
International Symposium on Crop Protection. Communications *see* International Symposium on Crop Protection. Proceedings *57*

International Symposium on Crop Protection. Proceedings (BE ISSN 0368-9697) 57
International Symposium on Discharges and Electrical Insulation (US) 456
International Symposium on Dredging Technology. Proceedings (UK ISSN 0140-1769) 490
International Symposium on Fault-Tolerant Computing. Digest see International Symposium on Fault-Tolerant Computing. Digest of Papers 352
International Symposium on Fault-Tolerant Computing. Digest of Papers (US ISSN 0731-3071) 352
International Symposium on Fault-Tolerant Computing. Proceedings see International Symposium on Fault-Tolerant Computing. Digest of Papers 352
International Symposium on Insulation of High Voltages in Vacuum. see International Symposium on Discharges and Electrical Insulation 456
International Symposium on Jet Cutting Technology. Proceedings (UK ISSN 0306-2732) 490, 491
International Symposium on Laboratory Animals see International Council for Laboratory Animal Science. Proceedings of the Symposium 762
International Symposium on Logic Programming. Proceedings. see Symposium on Logic Programming Proceedings 358
International Symposium on Mini and Microcomputers. Proceedings (CN) 361, 362
International Symposium on Molecular Biology. Proceedings (US) 1156
International Symposium on Molecular Biology Publications. see Miles International Symposium 163
International Symposium on Multiple-Valued Logic. Proceedings (US ISSN 0195-623X) 356
International Symposium on Quantum Biology and Quantum Pharmacology. Proceedings (US ISSN 0731-0358) 142, 871
International Symposium on Regional Development. Papers and Proceedings (JA ISSN 0074-8897) 623
International Symposium on Silicon Materials Science and Technology. Proceedings (CI ISSN 0091-391X) 328
International Symposium on Subscriber Loop and Services. Proceedings (US) 456
International Symposium on Surface Physics. Solid-Vacuum Interface. Proceedings (NE) 889
International Symposium on Surgical Heart Disease. Proceedings (UK) 777, 794
International Symposium on Switching Arc Phenomena. Proceedings (PL) 472
International Symposium on the Aerodynamics and Ventilation of Vehicle Tunnels. Proceedings (UK) 482, 1081
International Symposium on the Chemistry of Cement. Proceedings (JA) 323
International Symposium on the Pharmacology of Thermoregulation (SZ ISSN 0301-3154) 331, 871
International Symposium on Urban Hydrology, Hydraulic Infrastructures and Water Quality Control. Proceedings (US ISSN 0732-2607) 1156
International Symposium on Urban Hydrology, Hydraulics and Sediment Control. Proceedings see International Symposium on Urban Hydrology, Hydraulic Infrastructures and Water Quality Control. Proceedings 1156

International Symposium on Urban Storm Water Management. Proceedings. see International Symposium on Urban Hydrology, Hydraulic Infrastructures and Water Quality Control. Proceedings 1156
International Symposium on Wave and Tidal Energy. Proceedings (UK) 465, 1124
International Symposium on Wind Energy Systems. Proceedings (UK) 456, 465
International Symposium on Wound Ballistics. Proceedings (SW) 371
International T V & Video Guide (UK) 348
International Tax-Free Trade Buyers Guide & Directory (UK ISSN 0263-5488) 257
International Tax Systems and Planning Techniques (UK) 296
International Technical Communication Conference Proceedings (US) 344
International Technical Cooperation Centre Review see I T C C Review 262
International Telcom Directory (US) 350
International Telecommunication Union. Central Library. Liste des Periodiques. List of Periodicals. Lista de Revistas (UN) 345
International Telecommunication Union. Central Library. Listes des Publications Annuelles. List of Annuals. Lista de Publicaciones Anuales (UN) 345
International Telecommunication Union. List of Telegraph Offices Open for International Service (UN ISSN 0074-9044) 350
International Telecommunication Union. Report on the Activities (UN ISSN 0085-2201) 350
International Telecommunications Energy Conference. Proceedings (US ISSN 0275-0473) 348
International Teleconferencing Symposium (Proceedings) (US) 344
International Telephone Directory of T D D Users (US) 350, 375
International Telephone Directory of the Deaf see International Telephone Directory of T D D Users 375
International Telephone Energy Conference. Proceedings see International Telecommunications Energy Conference. Proceedings 348
International Television Almanac see International Television & Video Almanac 348
International Television & Video Almanac (US) 348
International Television Symposium and Technical Exhibition, Montreux. (Papers) (SZ ISSN 0082-0776) 348
International Telex Directory. International Service (AT ISSN 0310-8031) 350
International Test Conference. Digest of Papers see International Test Conference. Proceedings 361
International Test Conference. Proceedings (US) 352, 361
International Textile Machinery (UK ISSN 0074-9087) 745, 1074
International Textile Machinery Shipment Statistics (SZ) 1057, 1076
International Textile Manufacturers Federation Directory see I T M F Directory 1074
International Textile Manufacturing (SZ) 1074
International Thermal Spraying Conference. Preprint of Papers (US) 802
International Tin Council. Statistical Yearbook see Tin Statistics 802
International Tin Research Council. Annual Report see International Tin Research Institute. Annual Report 798
International Tin Research Institute. Annual Report (UK) 798
International Touring Alliance. Minutes of the General Assembly (SZ ISSN 0074-9133) 1112

International Tourism Policy in OECD Member Countries see Organization for Economic Cooperation and Development. Tourism Committee. Tourism Policy and International Tourism in O E C D Member Countries 1115
International Tracts in Computer Studies (UI) 352
International Trade Administration Reports (US) 257
International Trade and Development Statistics. Handbook/Statistiques du Commerce International et du Development. Manuel (SZ ISSN 0251-9461) 257, 263
International Trade Conference of Workers of the Building, Wood and Building Materials Industries. (Brochure) (FI) 185
International Trade Statistics Yearbook (UN ISSN 0084-3822) 211
International Trade Union Conference for Action Against Apartheid. Resolution (CS) 648, 913
International Transport Workers' Federation Report on Activities (UK ISSN 0539-0915) 648, 1082
International Travel in Queensland (AT ISSN 0729-5944) 1156
International Trends in Manufacturing Technology (US) 290, 745, 1069
International Trombone Association Series (US ISSN 0363-5708) 836
International Tug Convention Proceedings (UK) 1101
International Understanding at School (UN ISSN 0047-1240) 415
International Union against Cancer. Manual/Union Internationale Contre le Cancer. Manuel (SZ ISSN 0074-9192) 775
International Union Against Cancer Technical Report Series see U I C C Technical Report Series 776
International Union for Conservation of Nature and Natural Resources. Proceedings and Papers of the Technical Meeting (SZ ISSN 0074-9281) 365
International Union for Conservation of Nature and Natural Resources. Proceedings of the General Assembly (SZ ISSN 0074-929X) 365
International Union for Conservation of Nature and Natural Resources Annual Report see I U C N Annual Report 365
International Union for Inland Navigation. Annual Report (BE ISSN 0074-9311) 1082
International Union for Quaternary Research. Congress Proceedings (SZ ISSN 0074-932X) 389
International Union for the Scientific Study of Population Papers see I U S S P Papers 922
International Union of Biological Sciences. General Assemblies. Proceedings (FR) 142
International Union of Biological Sciences. Reports of General Assemblies see International Union of Biological Sciences. General Assemblies. Proceedings 142
International Union of Building Societies and Savings Associations. Congress Proceedings (US ISSN 0074-9370) 230
International Union of Crystallography. Abstracts of the Triennial Congress (DK ISSN 0074-9389) 327
International Union of Food and Allied Workers' Associations. Meeting of the Executive Committee. I. Documents of the Secretariat. II. Summary Report (SZ ISSN 0579-8299) 519, 648
International Union of Food and Allied Workers' Associations. Tobacco Workers' Trade Group Board. Meeting (SZ ISSN 0579-8302) 1156
International Union of Forestry Research Organizations. Congress Proceedings/Rapports du Congres/Kongressberichte (AU ISSN 0074-9400) 525

International Union of Geodesy and Geophysics. Monograph (CN ISSN 0539-1016) 400, 545
International Union of Geodesy and Geophysics. Proceedings of the General Assembly (FR ISSN 0074-9419) 400, 545
International Union of Latin Notaries. Proceedings of Congress (IT ISSN 0074-9435) 943
International Union of Liberal Christian Women. Newsletter see International Association of Liberal Religious Women. Newsletter 970
International Union of Physiological Sciences. Newsletter (HU ISSN 0539-1113) 172
International Union of Physiological Sciences. Proceedings of Congress (FR ISSN 0074-946X) 172
International Union of Producers and Distributors of Electrical Energy. (Congress Proceedings) (FR ISSN 0074-9486) 456
International Union of Public Transport. Proceedings of the International Congress (BE) 1082
International Union of Public Transport. Reports and Proceedings of the International Congress see International Union of Public Transport. Proceedings of the International Congress 1082
International Union of Public Transport. Technical Reports of the Congresses (BE) 1082
International Union of Public Transport. Transports Publics dans les Principales Villes du Monde see International Statistical Handbook of Urban Public Transport 1081
International Union of Radio Science. Proceedings of General Assemblies (BE ISSN 0074-9516) 348
International Union of Railways. Tableaux et Graphiques (FR) 1086
International Union of School and University Health and Medicine. Congress Reports (BE ISSN 0074-9524) 415, 762, 954
International Union of Socialist Youth Bulletin see I U S Y Bulletin 905
International Union of Students. Congress and Executive Committee Meetings Resolutions (CS) 436
International Union of Students. Congress Resolutions see International Union of Students. Congress and Executive Committee Meetings Resolutions 436
International Union of Theoretical and Applied Mechanics. Symposia (US) 472
International Universities Press, Inc. Stress and Health Series see I U P Stress and Health Series 790
International Vegetarian Handbook (UK) 846, 1112
International Vending Buyer's Guide and Directory (US) 284
International Video Exchange Directory(CN) 348
International Video Yearbook see Professional Video International Yearbook 349
International Violin and Guitar Makers Association. Journal (US) 836
International Water Conference. Proceedings (US ISSN 0074-9575) 490, 1124
International Water Supply Association Year Book see I W S A Year Book 309
International Whaling Commission. Report (UK ISSN 0074-9591) 175, 365, 510
International Whaling Commission. Special Issues (UK ISSN 0255-2760) 142, 365
International Wheat Council. Annual Report (UK) 29
International Wheat Council. Record of Operations of Member Countries (UK ISSN 0539-130X) 29
International Wheat Council. Report for Crop Year see International Wheat Council. Annual Report 29

International Wheat Council. Review of the World Grains Situation *see* Review of the World Wheat Situation 33
International Wheat Council. Secretariat Papers (UK ISSN 0539-1326) 29
International Who's Who (UK ISSN 0074-9613) 134
International Who's Who in Art and Antiques (UK) 79, 106, 134
International Who's Who in Community Service (UK) 1018
International Who's Who in Education (UK) 134, 415
International Who's Who in Energy and Nuclear Sciences (UK) 465
International Who's Who in Engineering (UK) 134
International Who's Who in Medicine (UK) 134
International Who's Who in Music and Musicians' Directory (UK ISSN 0307-2894) 836
International Who's Who in Poetry (UK ISSN 0539-1342) 1156
International Who's Who in the Arab World (UK ISSN 0261-0310) 134
International Who's Who in Water Supply *see* I W S A Year Book 309
International Wine and Food Society Journal *see* World Gastronomy 120
International Women's Fishing Association Yearbook *see* I W F A Yearbook 1045
International Women's Writing Guild. Symposium Monograph (US) 724, 1129
International Work Group for Indigenous Affairs Boletin *see* I W G I A Boletin 72
International Work Group for Indigenous Affairs Documents *see* I W G I A Documents 72
International Work Group for Indigenous Affairs Newsletter *see* I W G I A Newsletter 72
International Workshop on Models and Languages for Software Specification and Design (Proceedings) *see* International Workshop on Software Specification and Design (Proceedings) 363
International Workshop on Nude Mice. Proceedings (NO) 781
International Workshop on Software Specification and Design (Proceedings) (US) 363
International Year Book and Statesmen's Who's Who (UK ISSN 0074-9621) 906, 1009
International Yearbook for Child Psychiatry and Allied Disciplines *see* International Association for Child Psychiatry and Allied Professions. Yearbook 790
International Yearbook for Studies of Leaders and Leadership 906
International Yearbook of Educational & Instructional Technology (UK ISSN 0307-9732) 448
International Yearbook of Organization Studies (UK) 1009
International Yearbook of Organizational Democracy (US) 648, 906
International Yearbook of Rural Planning (UK) 623
International Youth in Achievement (UK) 134
International Zoo Yearbook (UK ISSN 0074-9664) 175
International Zurich Seminar on Digital Communications. (Proceedings) (US) 361
International Zurich Seminar on Integrated Systems for Speech, Video and Data Communications. Proceedings *see* International Zurich Seminar on Digital Communications. (Proceedings) 361
Internationale Beitraege zur Markt-, Meinungs- und Zukunftsforschung (GW) 284
Internationale Bibliographie der Fachadressbuecher/International Bibliography of Special Directories (GW ISSN 0074-9672) 127

Internationale Bibliographie zur Deutschen Klassik 1750-1850 (GE) 128
Internationale Gesellschaft fuer Geschichte der Pharmazie. Veroeffentlichungen. Neue Folge (GW ISSN 0074-9729) 871
Internationale Gesellschaft fuer Urheberrecht. Schriftenreihe (AU) 657
Internationale Gesellschaft fuer Urheberrecht. Yearbook (AU ISSN 0539-1512) 861
Internationale Hafentagung. Berichte *see* International Harbour Congress. Proceedings 1101
Internationale Hydrologische Dekade: Yearbook of the Federal Republic of Germany *see* Internationale Hydrologisches Programm: Operationelles Hydrologisches Programm: Jahrbuch Bundesrepublik Deutschland und Berlin (West) 403
Internationale Hydrologisches Programm: Operationelles Hydrologisches Programm: Jahrbuch Bundesrepublik Deutschland und Berlin (West)/International Hydrological Programme: Operational Hydrological Programme: Yearbook Federal Republic of Germany and Berlin (West) (GW ISSN 0344-5259) 403
Internationale Politik und Wirtschaft (GW) 916
Internationale Vereinigung fuer Theoretische und Angewandte Limnologie. Verhandlungen *see* International Association of Theoretical and Applied Limnology. Proceedings 403
Internationale Vereinigung zur Foerderung des Studiums der Hegelschen Philosophie. Veroeffentlichung *see* Hegel-Studien Beihefte 878
Internationale Volkskundliche Bibliographie/International Folklore Bibliography/Bibliographie Internationale D'Ethnologie (GW ISSN 0074-9737) 517
Internationale Wirtschaftszahlen/International Economic Indicators (GW) 1057
Internationaler Campingfuehrer *see* A D A C - Campingfuehrer. Band 1: Suedeuropa 1043
Internationaler FKK-Reisefuehrer *see* International Naturist Guide 1045
Internationaler Spitalbedarf (SZ ISSN 0074-977X) 617
Internationaler Verband fuer Oeffentliches Verkehrswesen. Technische Berichte zu den Internationalen Kongressen *see* International Union of Public Transport. Technical Reports of the Congresses 1082
Internationaler Weltkongress der U F O-Forscher. Dokumentarbericht (GW ISSN 0579-6938) 20
Internationales Archiv fuer Sozialgeschichte der Deutschen Literatur (GW ISSN 0340-4528) 724
Internationales Bibliotheks-Handbuch/World Guide to Libraries (GW ISSN 0000-0221) 679
Internationales Bodensee-Jahrbuch der Sportschiffahrt (GW) 1042
Internationales Bodensee Regatta Programm (GW) 1042
Internationales Firmenregister der Brauindustrie, Malzerien, Brennereien, Mineralwasser und Erfrischungsgetranke *see* International Brewer's Directory 120
Internationales Handbuch fuer Rundfunk und Fernsehen (GW ISSN 0535-4358) 349
Internationales Jahrbuch fuer Kartographie (GW ISSN 0341-0986) 545
Internationales Recht und Diplomatie (GW ISSN 0020-9503) 671, 916
Internationales Statistik-Handbuch fuer den Oeffentlichen Stadtverkehr *see* International Statistical Handbook of Urban Public Transport 1081

Internationales Verlagsadressbuch/Publishers' International Directory (GW ISSN 0074-9877) 964
Internationales Verzeichnis der Wirtschaftsverbaende/World Guide to Trade Associations (GW ISSN 0302-2196) 310
Internist's Compendium of Drug Therapy (US ISSN 0276-4342) 871
Internships (US ISSN 0272-5460) 286, 848
Inter-Parliamentary Union. Conference Proceedings/Union Interparlementaire. Comptes Rendus des Conferences (SZ ISSN 0074-1051) 916
Inter-Parliamentary Union. Series: "Reports and Documents" (SZ ISSN 0579-8337) 906
Interplay (Malibu) (US) 106, 724
Interplay of Phonology, Morphology & Syntax *see* Chicago Linguistic Society. Papers from the Regional Meetings 693
Interpretazioni (IT) 878
Interprete (IT) 724
Inter-School Christian Fellowship Annual *see* I S Annual 978
Interscience Conference on Antimicrobial Agents and Chemotherapy. Program and Abstracts (US ISSN 0733-6373) 168
Interscience Tracts in Pure and Applied Mathematics *see* Pure and Applied Mathematics: A Wiley Interscience Series of Texts, Monographs and Tracts 752
Intersociety Energy Conversion Conference. Proceedings (US) 465, 897
Interstate (US ISSN 0363-9991) 724
Interstate Commission on the Potomac River Basin. Proceedings (US ISSN 0535-4676) 497, 1124
Interstate Commission on the Potomac River Basin. Technical Bulletin *see* Interstate Commission on the Potomac River Basin. Technical Reports 497
Interstate Commission on the Potomac River Basin. Technical Reports (US) 497
Interstate Manufacturers and Industrial Directory Buyers Guide (US) 310
Interstate Oil Compact Commission Annual Report (US) 865
Interstellar Bulletins (IC) 860, 878
Interstellar Communication *see* Interstellar Bulletins 878
Interuniversitair Centrum voor Hedendaagse Geschiedenis. Mededelingen *see* Centre Interuniversitaire d'Histoire Contemporaine. Cahiers 579
Inter-University Case Program. Case Study (US ISSN 0074-106X) 943
Interuniversity Centre for European Studies. International Colloquium Proceedings (CN) 586
Interuniversity Centre for European Studies. Research Report (CN) 586
Inter-University Consortium for Political and Social Research. Annual Report (US ISSN 0074-1078) 906
Inter-University Consortium for Political and Social Research. Guide to Resources and Services. (US ISSN 0362-8736) 1009
Interval (US ISSN 0276-3052) 836, 900
Interventi Classensi (IT) 106, 558, 724, 878
Intimate Fashion News Directory (US) 340
Intisari (MY) 1156
Introduction to the Korean Securities Market (KO) 266
Invalid Children's Aid Association Year Book *see* Invalid Children's Aid Nationwide Year Book 1018
Invalid Children's Aid Nationwide Year Book (UK) 333, 1018
Invandrarfraagor. Aarsbok (SW ISSN 0280-8773) 504, 540
Inventaire des Archives Historiques/Inventaris van het Historisch Archief(BE) 566

Inventaire General des Monuments et des Richesses Artistiques de la France (FR ISSN 0075-0018) 98, 106, 828
Inventaires Economiques et Industriels Regionaux *see* Kompass Regionaux 196
Inventare Nichtstaatlicher Archive (GW ISSN 0535-5079) 128
Inventari dei Manoscritti delle Biblioteche d'Italia (IT ISSN 0075-0026) 688
Inventaria Archaeologica (GE) 87
Inventaria Archaeologica Belgique (GW ISSN 0075-0034) 88
Inventaria Archaeologica Ceskoslovensko (GW ISSN 0075-0042) 88
Inventaria Archaeologica Denmark (GW ISSN 0075-0050) 88
Inventaria Archaeologica Deutschland (GW ISSN 0075-0069) 88
Inventaria Archaeologica Espana (GW ISSN 0075-0077) 88
Inventaria Archaeologica France (GW ISSN 0075-0085) 88
Inventaria Archaeologica Great Britain (GW ISSN 0075-0093) 88
Inventaria Archaeologica Italia (GW ISSN 0075-0107) 88
Inventaria Archaeologica Jugoslavija (GW ISSN 0075-0115) 88
Inventaria Archaeologica Norway (GW ISSN 0075-0123) 88
Inventaria Archaeologica Oesterreich (GW ISSN 0075-0131) 88
Inventaria Archaeologica Pologne (GW ISSN 0075-014X) 88
Inventaria Archaeologica The Netherlands (GW) 88
Inventaria Archaeologica Ungarn (GW ISSN 0075-0158) 88
Inventaris van het Historisch Archief *see* Inventaire des Archives Historiques 566
Inventaris van Het Kunstpatrimonium van Oost-Vlaanderen (BE ISSN 0075-0166) 586
Inventory of Industrial Parks in Quebec(CN) 196
Inventory of Marriage and Family Literature (US ISSN 0094-7814) 1031
Inventory of Population Projects in Developing Countries Around the World (US ISSN 0363-5155) 922
Inventory of Waste Water Production and Waste Water Reclamation Practices in California *see* California. Department of Water Resources. Inventory of Waste Water Production and Waste Water Reclamation Practices in California 1123
Inventory of Water Resources Research in Australia (AT) 403
Invest in Ecuador (EC) 266
Invest in Panama (PN) 266
Invest Yourself (US ISSN 0148-6802) 1018
Investbanka. Annual Report (YU) 230
Investering i Produktion (DK ISSN 0108-2329) 266, 290
Investeringsforeninger Tilsynet (DK ISSN 0109-9426) 266
Investicije (YU) 211
Investigacion y Educacion en Enfermeria (CK) 784
Investigaciones de Campo (PE) 73
Investigaciones Historicas (SP) 586
Investigations in Fish Control *see* U.S. Fish and Wildlife Service. Investigations in Fish Control 513
Investigative Reports (US) 646
Investing for Beginners (UK) 266
Investing, Licensing & Trading Conditions Abroad (US ISSN 0021-003X) 257
Investing, Licensing and Trading Conditions in 5 Countries *see* Investing, Licensing & Trading Conditions Abroad 257
Investissements Etrangers en Belgique *see* Belgium. Ministere des Affaires Economiques. Rapport Annuel sur les Investissements Etrangers en Belique 265
Investment Africa (UN) 263

IRON ORE   1783

Investment and Development Bank of Malawi. Annual Report and Accounts (MW) 230
Investment Companies (US ISSN 0075-0271) 266
Investment Decisions Directory of Wall Street Research see Directory of Wall Street Research 266
Investment Promotion Newsletter see Investment Africa 263
Investment Sources and Ideas see S I E Guide to Investment Services 268
Investments and Credit Corporation of Oyo State. Industrial Directory (NR) 310
Investor Responsibility Research Center. Annual Report (US) 267
Investors' Guide to Nepal (NP) 267
Investors Guide to the Stockmarket (UK) 267
Invisible City (US ISSN 0147-4936) 711, 742
Invited Lectures on the Middle East at the University of Texas at Austin (US ISSN 0742-1133) 612
Io (US ISSN 0021-0331) 73, 724, 860, 1039
Ion Exchange; a Series of Advances see Ion Exchange and Solvent Extraction 331
Ion Exchange and Solvent Extraction (US ISSN 0092-0193) 331
Ionnye Rasplavy i Tverdye Electrolity (UR ISSN 0234-4483) 328
Ios (GR ISSN 0021-0404) 711
Iowa. Bureau of Labor. Biennial Report (US) 211
Iowa. Bureau of Labor. Occupational Injuries and Illnesses Survey (US ISSN 0092-6299) 635
Iowa. College Aid Commission. Biennium Report (US) 443
Iowa. Crop and Livestock Reporting Service. Planting to Harvest. Weather and Field Crops see Iowa Agricultural Statistics 41
Iowa. Department of Job Service. Annual Report (US ISSN 0149-449X) 273
Iowa. Department of Public Instruction. Summary of Federal Programs (US ISSN 0091-8962) 415
Iowa. Employment Security Commission. Annual Report see Iowa. Department of Job Service. Annual Report 273
Iowa. Geological Survey. Annual Report of the State Geologist to the Governor (US) 1156
Iowa. Geological Survey. Annual Report of the State Geologist to the Geological Board see Iowa. Geological Survey. Annual Report of the State Geologist to the Governor 1156
Iowa. Higher Education Facilities Commission. Biennium Report see Iowa. College Aid Commission. Biennium Report 443
Iowa Academy of Science Bulletin see I A S Bulletin 992
Iowa Agricultural Statistics (US) 41
Iowa Agriculture and Home Economics Experiment Station. Research Bulletin (US ISSN 0097-3416) 29, 615, 889
Iowa Agriculture and Home Economics Experiment Station. Special Report (US ISSN 0097-5125) 29
Iowa Archeological Society. Journal (US ISSN 0535-5729) 88
Iowa Civil Rights Commission. Annual Report (US) 913
Iowa Civil Rights Commission. Case Reports (US) 913
Iowa Comprehensive State Plan for Substance Abuse (Year) (US) 377
Iowa Comprehensive State Plan for Substance Abuse Prevention: Annual Performance Report see Iowa Comprehensive State Plan for Substance Abuse (Year) 377
Iowa County Engineers Annual Highway Reports. Summary (US) 1096
Iowa Detailed Report of Vital Statistics see Vital Statistics of Iowa 930
Iowa English Bulletin (US) 448

Iowa English Bulletin--Yearbook see Iowa English Bulletin 448
Iowa Genealogical Society. Surname Index (US ISSN 0090-905X) 536
Iowa Geological Survey. Reports of Investigations see Iowa Geological Survey Bureau. Reports of Investigations 389
Iowa Geological Survey Bureau. Reports of Investigations (US) 389
Iowa International Directory (US) 310
Iowa Manufacturer's Export Directory see Iowa International Directory 310
Iowa Manufacturers Register (US ISSN 0737-7940) 310
Iowa Middle Level Educators Bulletin (US) 448
Iowa Nurses' Association. Bulletin (US ISSN 0075-0387) 784
Iowa Official Register (US) 906, 951, 1057
Iowa State Archaeologist. Report (US ISSN 0085-2252) 88
Iowa State Nurses' Association. Bulletin see Iowa Nurses' Association. Bulletin 784
Iowa State University. Engineering Research Institute. Engineering Research Report (US ISSN 0075-0433) 472
Iowa State University. Library. Series in Bibliography (US) 1156
Iowa State University. Statistical Laboratory. Annual Report (US) 749, 755, 1057
Iowa Summary of Vital Statistics see Vital Statistics of Iowa 930
Iparmuveszeti Muzeum. Evkonyv see Ars Decorativa 826
Ipswich & Suffolk Directory of Industry & Commerce (UK ISSN 0269-2716) 310
Ipswich Port Handbook 1984 (UK) 310, 1101
Iran (UK ISSN 0578-6967) 630
Iran. Geological Survey. Report (IR ISSN 0075-0484) 389
Iran. Ministry of Economy. Bureau of Statistics. Series (IR) 211
Iran. Ministry of Economy. Internal Wholesale Trade Statistics (IR) 211
Iran. Ministry of Economy. International Trade Statistics (IR) 211
Iran Almanac and Book of Facts (IR ISSN 0075-0476) 566
Iran Chamber of Commerce, Industries and Mines. Directory (IR) 236
Iran Trade & Industry Annual Review (IR) 246
Iran Yearbook (IR) 613, 1057
Iranian Industrial Statistics (IR ISSN 0075-0506) 211
Iranian Mineral Statistics (IR ISSN 0075-0514) 817
Iranian National Bibliography (IR ISSN 0075-0522) 128
Iranica Antiqua (NE ISSN 0021-0870) 88, 852
Iraq (UK ISSN 0021-0889) 88, 852
Iraq. Central Statistical Organization. Annual Abstract of Statistics (IQ) 1057
Iraq. Central Statistical Organization. Results of the Industrial Survey of Large Establishments in Iraq (IQ) 211
Iraq. Central Statistical Organization. Statistical Pocket Book (IQ) 1057
Iraq. Central Statistical Organization. Summary of Foreign Trade Statistics (IQ ISSN 0021-0900) 211
Iraq. Ministry of Information. Information Series (IQ) 943
Iraq Government Gazette (IQ) 943
Iraq Natural History Museum. Bulletin (IQ) 993
Iraq Natural History Museum. Publication (IQ) 142, 993
Iraq Natural History Research Center and Museum. Bulletin see Iraq Natural History Museum. Bulletin 993
Iraq Natural History Research Centre and Museum. Publications see Iraq Natural History Museum. Publication 993

Ireland. Central Statistics Office. Analysis of External Trade by Ports (IE) 211
Ireland. Central Statistics Office. Balance of International Payments (IE) 211
Ireland. Central Statistics Office. Building and Construction: Average Earnings and Hours Worked (IE) 189, 211
Ireland. Central Statistics Office. Building and Construction Planning Permissions (IE) 189, 211
Ireland. Central Statistics Office. Census of Building and Construction (IE) 189, 211
Ireland. Central Statistics Office. Census of Industrial Production (IE ISSN 0790-6080) 196, 211
Ireland. Central Statistics Office. Distribution of Cattle and Pigs by Size of Herd (IE) 41
Ireland. Central Statistics Office. Estimated Area, Yield and Produce of Crops (IE) 41
Ireland. Central Statistics Office. Estimated Numbers and Expenditure of Visitors to Ireland and Irish Visitors Abroad (IE) 211
Ireland. Central Statistics Office. Labour Force Survey. First Results (IE ISSN 0790-5866) 211
Ireland. Central Statistics Office. Particulars of Vehicles Registered and Licensed for the First Time (IE) 1086
Ireland. Central Statistics Office. Pig Enumeration (IE) 41
Ireland. Central Statistics Office. Road Freight Transport Survey (IE) 211
Ireland. Central Statistics Office. Statistics of Port Traffic (IE) 1086
Ireland. Department of Agriculture and Fisheries. Annual Report see Ireland. Department of Agriculture. Annual Report 29
Ireland. Department of Agriculture. Annual Report (IE) 29
Ireland. Department of Social Welfare. Statistical Information on Social Welfare (IE) 1018
Ireland (Eire) Central Statistics Office. Agricultural Output see Ireland (Eire) Central Statistics Office. Estimated Output, Input and Income Arising in Agriculture 29
Ireland (Eire) Central Statistics Office. Business of Advertising Agencies (IE) 17
Ireland (Eire) Central Statistics Office. Crops and Livestock Enumeration (IE) 41, 66
Ireland (Eire) Central Statistics Office. Crops and Pasture and Numbers of Livestock see Ireland (Eire) Central Statistics Office. Crops and Livestock Enumeration 41
Ireland (Eire) Central Statistics Office. Estimated Output, Input and Income Arising in Agriculture (IE) 29
Ireland (Eire) Central Statistics Office. Hire-Purchase and Credit Sales (IE ISSN 0075-0573) 230, 284
Ireland (Eire) Central Statistics Office. Inquiry into Advertising Agencies Activities. see Ireland (Eire) Central Statistics Office. Business of Advertising Agencies 17
Ireland (Eire) Central Statistics Office. Livestock Enumeration (IE) 66
Ireland (Eire) Central Statistics Office. Livestock Numbers see Ireland (Eire) Central Statistics Office. Livestock Enumeration 66
Ireland (Eire) Central Statistics Office. National Income and Expenditure (IE ISSN 0075-0603) 277, 296
Ireland (Eire) Central Statistics Office. Tuarascail Ar Staidreamh Beatha. Report on Vital Statistics (IE ISSN 0075-062X) 1057
Ireland (Eire) Department of Finance. Financial Statement of the Minister for Finance (IE ISSN 0075-0670) 296
Ireland. Public Service Advisory Council. Report (IE) 943

Ireland Department of Education. Liosta de Iar-Bhunscoileanna Aitheanta. List of Recognised Post-Primary Schools (IE ISSN 0075-0662) 430
Ireland Ports & Shipping Handbook (UK ISSN 0260-924X) 310, 1101
Iris Year Book (UK ISSN 0075-0700) 533
Irish Agricultural Organization Society. Annual Report see Irish Cooperative Organization Society. Annual Report 29
Irish-American Genealogist (US ISSN 0272-1015) 536
Irish Archives Bulletin (IE) 679
Irish Badminton Handbook see Badminton Ireland 1032
Irish Baptist Historical Society. Journal (UK ISSN 0075-0727) 979
Irish Biblical Association. Proceedings (IE ISSN 0332-4427) 970
Irish Bird Report see Irish Birds 170
Irish Birds (IE ISSN 0332-0111) 170
Irish Catholic Directory (UK ISSN 0075-0735) 982
Irish Cooperative Organization Society. Annual Report (IE ISSN 0790-4568) 29
Irish Countrywomen's Association: an Grianan Programme (IE) 415
Irish Creamery Managers' Association. Creamery Directory and Diary see Dairy Executive. Directory and Diary 62
Irish Drama Selections (UK ISSN 0260-7964) 724, 1077
Irish Economic and Social History (IE ISSN 0332-4893) 586, 1009
Irish Fisheries Investigations. Series A: Freshwater (IE) 142, 510
Irish Fisheries Investigations. Series B: Marine (IE) 142, 510
Irish Folk Music Studies (IE) 837
Irish Genealogical Helper see Irish-American Genealogist 536
Irish Georgian Society. Bulletin (IE ISSN 0021-1206) 98
Irish History Workshop/Saotharlann Staire Eireann (IE ISSN 0332-3633) 587
Irish in Britain Directory (UK ISSN 0260-650X) 504
Irish Journal of Agricultural Economics and Rural Sociology (IE ISSN 0021-1249) 48, 1027
Irish Literary Studies (UK ISSN 0140-895X) 724
Irish Motorsport Yearbook (IE) 1034
Irish Play Series (US ISSN 0075-0816) 724
Irish Political Studies (IE ISSN 0790-7184) 906
Irish Sea Fisheries Board. Annual Report see Bord Iascaigh Mhara. Tuarascail Agus Cuntaisi 508
Irish Showjumping Annual (IE) 1043
Irish Slavonic Studies (UK ISSN 0260-2067) 587, 724
Irish Statistical Survey see Ireland (Eire) Central Statistics Office. National Income and Expenditure 296
Irish Studies (UK ISSN 0260-8480) 1156
Irish Studies in International Affairs (IE ISSN 0332-1460) 263, 916
Irish Studies Series (US) 724
Irodalom - Szocializmus (HU ISSN 0075-0824) 724, 906
Irodalomelmelet Klasszikusai (HU ISSN 0075-0832) 724
Irodalomtorteneti Fuzetek (HU ISSN 0075-0840) 724
Irodalomtorteneti Konyvtar (HU ISSN 0075-0859) 724
Iron & Manganese Ores Survey (UK ISSN 0140-8402) 798
Iron and Steel. Annual Statistics for the United Kingdom (UK ISSN 0075-0867) 801
Iron & Steel Industry in China (UK) 798
Iron & Steel Industry Profiles (UK) 1156
Iron and Steel Works of the World (UK ISSN 0075-0875) 798
Iron Ore Databook (UK ISSN 0950-2548) 798

Irregular Serials and Annuals (US ISSN 0000-0043) *128*
Irrigation and Power Abstracts (II ISSN 0021-1672) 8, 41, *1128*
Irrigation Association. Technical Conference Proceedings (US ISSN 0160-7499) *57*
Irrigation Research Institute, Lahore. Report (PK) *1124*
Is *see* Transient *735*
Iseljenicki Kalendar (YU ISSN 0543-1077) *539*
Isis Cumulative Bibliography (UK) *1156*
Isizwe (SA) *545*
Iskcon Review (US ISSN 0886-6910) *984*
Iske Ha-Bituah Be-Yisrael *see* Israel. Central Bureau of Statistics. Insurance in Israel *642*
Iskos (FI ISSN 0355-3108) *88*
Islamic Art and Architecture (US ISSN 0742-1125) 98, *106*, 613
Islamic Book Review Index (GW ISSN 0724-2263) *975*
Islamic Development Bank. Annual Report (SU) *230*
Islamic Surveys (UK ISSN 0075-093X) *570*
Islamiyat (MY) *852*
Isle of Man Natural History and Antiquarian Society. Proceedings (UK) *558*, 993
Islensk Bokaskra/Icelandic National Bibliography (IC) *688*
Islensk Hljodritaskra (IC) *128*, 837
Islenzk Sagnabloed *see* Skirnir *596*
Islenzka Fornleifafelags. Arbok (IC) 88, *587*
Isotope and Radiation Research (UA ISSN 0021-1907) *792*
Isotopes in Organic Chemistry (NE) *330*
Isotype Titles *see* Zidis *220*
Isozymes: Current Topics in Biological and Medicine Research (US ISSN 0160-3787) *142*
Ispat (BG) *798*
Israel. Atomic Energy Commission. Annual Report (IS ISSN 0333-5771) *897*
Israel. Atomic Energy Commission. IA-Reports (IS ISSN 0075-0980) *897*
Israel. Central Bureau of Statistics. Annual Foreign Trade Statistics (IS) *211*
Israel. Central Bureau of Statistics. Causes of Death (IS ISSN 0075-0999) 923, *927*
Israel. Central Bureau of Statistics. Construction in Israel/Ha-Binui Be-Yisrael (IS ISSN 0069-9195) *185*
Israel. Central Bureau of Statistics. Criminal Statistics (IS ISSN 0075-1006) *371*
Israel. Central Bureau of Statistics. Diagnostic Statistics of Hospitalized Patients (IS ISSN 0075-1014) 617, *1018*
Israel. Central Bureau of Statistics. Foreign Trade Statistics Quarterly *see* Israel. Central Bureau of Statistics. Annual Foreign Trade Statistics *211*
Israel. Central Bureau of Statistics. Inputs in Research and Development in Academic Institutions (IS) *424*
Israel. Central Bureau of Statistics. Insurance in Israel/Iske Ha-Bituah Be-Yisrael (IS ISSN 0074-0705) *642*
Israel. Central Bureau of Statistics. Judicial Statistics (IS ISSN 0075-1030) *657*
Israel. Central Bureau of Statistics. Labour Force Surveys (IS ISSN 0075-1049) *211*
Israel. Central Bureau of Statistics. Motor Vehicles (IS ISSN 0075-1057) *1105*
Israel. Central Bureau of Statistics. Road Accidents with Casualties (IS) *1086*
Israel. Central Bureau of Statistics. Schools and Kindergartens (IS ISSN 0075-1065) *424*
Israel. Central Bureau of Statistics. Staff in Universities (IS ISSN 0333-600X) *424*, 1057

Israel. Central Bureau of Statistics. Statistical Abstract of Israel/Shenaton Statisti le-Yisrael (IS ISSN 0081-4679) *1057*
Israel. Central Bureau of Statistics. Students in Academic Institutions *see* Israel. Central Bureau of Statistics. Students in Universities *415*
Israel. Central Bureau of Statistics. Students in Universities (IS) *415*
Israel. Central Bureau of Statistics. Suicides and Attempted Suicides (IS) 923, *927*
Israel. Central Bureau of Statistics. Survey of Housing Conditions (IS ISSN 0075-109X) *623*
Israel. Central Bureau of Statistics. Vital Statistics (IS ISSN 0075-1111) *927*, 1057
Israel. Commissioner for Complaints from the Public (Ombudsman) Annual Report (IS) *943*
Israel. Department of Customs and Excise. Yalkut *see* Israel. Department of Customs and V A T. Yalkut *296*
Israel. Department of Customs and V A T. Yalkut (IS) *296*
Israel. Department of Surveys. Cartographic Papers (IS) *545*
Israel. Department of Surveys. Geodetic Papers (IS ISSN 0075-1138) *545*
Israel. Department of Surveys. Photogrammetric Papers (IS) *545*
Israel. Environment Protection Agency. Ekhut ha-Svivah be-Yisrael. Luakh Shnati *see* Israel. Environmental Protection Service. Ekhut ha-Svivah be-Yisrael. Luakh Shnati *497*
Israel. Environmental Protection Service. Ekhut ha-Svivah be-Yisrael. Luakh Shnati (IS ISSN 0334-3162) *497*
Israel. Geological Survey. Bulletin (IS ISSN 0075-1200) *389*
Israel. Geological Survey. Current Research (IS ISSN 0333-6425) *389*
Israel. Institute for Technology and Storage of Agricultural Products. Scientific Activities (IS) 29, *1069*
Israel. Knesset. Finance Committee. Data on Activities *see* Israel. Knesset. Va'adat Ha-Kesafim Misparim al Va'adat Ha-Kesafim *296*
Israel. Knesset. Ha-Va'ada le-Inyanei Bikoret ha-Medina. Sikumeha ve-Hatsa 'oteha shel ha-Va'ada le-Inyanei Bikoret ha-Medina le-Din ve-Kheshbon shel Mevaker ha-Medina (IS) *951*
Israel. Knesset. Va'adat Ha-Kesafim Misparim al Va'adat Ha-Kesafim/Israel. Knesset. Finance Committee. Data on Activities (IS) *296*
Israel. Meteorological Service. Rainfall Season (IS) *805*, 1125
Israel. Meteorological Service. Series B: Observational Data. Annual Rainfall Summary (IS ISSN 0075-126X) *805*
Israel. Meteorological Service. Series B: Observational Data. Annual Weather Report (IS ISSN 0075-1286) *805*
Israel. Meteorological Society. Meteorologia Be-Israel (IS) *805*
Israel. Ministry of Agriculture. Department of Fisheries. Israel Fisheries in Figures/Dayig Be-Yisrael Be-Misparim (IS ISSN 0075-1189) *511*
Israel. Ministry of Commerce and Industry. Surveys and Development Plans of Industry in Israel/Ta'asiyah Ha-Yisra'elit (IS ISSN 0081-9743) *290*
Israel. Ministry of Communications. Statistics/Israel. Misrad Ha-Tikshoret. Statistikah (IS ISSN 0075-1308) *346*
Israel. Ministry of Education and Culture. Department of Antiquities and Museums. Atiqot (English Series) (IS ISSN 0066-488X) *88*
Israel. Ministry of Education and Culture. Department of Antiquities and Museums. Atiqot (Hebrew Series) (IS ISSN 0067-0138) *88*

Israel. Ministry of Education and Culture. Department of Educational Technology. Bulletin/Alon le-Tekhnologyah be-Khinukh (IS) *448*
Israel. Ministry of Labour. Registrar of Cooperative Societies. Report on the Cooperative Movement in Israel (IS ISSN 0080-1313) *238*
Israel. Misrad Ha-Tikshoret. Statistikah *see* Israel. Ministry of Communications. Statistics *346*
Israel. National Council for Research and Development. Scientific Research in Israel (IS ISSN 0080-7753) *993*
Israel. Rural Planning and Development Authority. Agricultural and Rural Development Report *see* Israel. Rural Planning and Development Authority. Agricultural and Rural Economic Report *30*
Israel. Rural Planning and Development Authority. Agricultural and Rural Economic Report (IS) *30*
Israel Academy of Sciences and Humanities. Section of Humanities. Proceedings (IS ISSN 0578-9230) *993*, 1069
Israel Academy of Sciences and Humanities. Section of Sciences. Proceedings (IS ISSN 0333-6190) *993*
Israel Annual Conference on Aviation and Astronautics. Proceedings (IS ISSN 0075-0972) *20*
Israel au Travail *see* Labour in Israel *648*
Israel Book Trade Directory (IS ISSN 0333-6018) 931, *962*
Israel Book Trades Directory: a Select List *see* Israel Book Trade Directory *962*
Israel C P A (IS) *221*
Israel Dance (IS ISSN 0334-2301) *375*
Israel Discount Bank. Report (IS ISSN 0075-1146) *230*
Israel Export Directory (IS ISSN 0075-1154) *257*
Israel Film Centre. Information Bulletin(IS) *257*
Israel Film Industry Directory (IS) *824*
Israel Industry/Commerce and Export News (IS) *257*
Israel Institute for Biological Research. Scientific Activities (IS) *142*
Israel Institute of Animal Science. Scientific Activities (IS) *782*, 1121
Israel Institute of Horticulture. Scientific Activities (IS) *533*
Israel Institute of Packaging. Packaging Directory (IS) 310, *855*
Israel Institute of Technology. President's Report and Reports of Other Officers *see* Technion - Israel Institute of Technology. President's Report *1071*
Israel Institute of Technology-Technion. Abstracts of Research Theses (IS) *436*
Israel Institute of Technology-Technion. Research Reports (IS) *185*
Israel Journal of Entomology (IS ISSN 0075-1243) *165*
Israel Journal of Physiotherapy (IS ISSN 0021-2199) *762*
Israel Museum Journal (IS ISSN 0333-7499) *828*
Israel Museum News *see* Israel Museum Journal *828*
Israel Oceanographic and Limnological Research. Biennial Report (IS ISSN 0304-7423) *406*
Israel Oceanographic and Limnological Research. Triennial Report *see* Israel Oceanographic and Limnological Research. Biennial Report *406*
Israel Oceanographic and Limnological Research Ltd. Collected Reports *see* I O L R Collected Reports *1124*
Israel Oriental Studies (IS ISSN 0334-4401) *852*
Israel Physical Society. Annals (IS ISSN 0309-8710) *889*
Israel Plastics *see* Plastika Be-Israel *901*
Israel Ports Authority. Annual Report (IS) *1101*

Israel Society for Rehabilitation of the Disabled. Annual (IS ISSN 0075-1383) *445*, 1018
Israel Studies in Criminology (IS ISSN 0075-1391) *371*
Israel Studies in Musicology (IS ISSN 0334-2026) *837*
Israel Tax Law Letter (IS) *296*
Israel Tourist Statistics/Tayarut Be-Yisrael (IS ISSN 0075-1405) *1119*
Israel Yearbook (IS ISSN 0075-1413) *570*
Israel Yearbook on Human Rights (IS ISSN 0333-5925) 657, *913*
Israeli Family Planning Association. Bulletin (IS) *179*
Israeli Life Table (IS ISSN 0077-5037) *640*
Israeli Publishers and Authors and Their Books on the World Publishing Scene (IS) *1156*
Israelitische Kultusgemeinde Fuerth (GW) *504*
Israelske Ambassade. Information (DK ISSN 0108-3783) *916*
Issledovania po Teorii Algorifmov i Matematicheskoi Logike (UR ISSN 0302-9085) 749, *878*
Issledovanie, Konstruirovanie i Raschet Rezbovykh Soedinenii (UR) *472*
Issledovaniya v Oblasti Khimii Redkozemel'nykh Elementov (UR) 328, *379*
Issue (US ISSN 0047-1607) *711*
Issue (CN) *984*
Issues, Events & Ideas (CN ISSN 0704-6936) *415*
Issues in Canadian Social Policy/Politique Sociale au Canada (CN) *1018*
Issues in Higher Education (US) *436*
Issues in Southeast Asian Security (SI) *916*
Issues in the New Caribbean *see* Challenges in the New Caribbean *540*
Istanbuler Mitteilungen (GW ISSN 0341-9142) *88*, 852
Istituto Campano per la Storia della Resistenza. Bollettino (IT) 448, *558*
Istituto Centrale per la Patologia del Libro "Alfonso Gallo." Bollettino (IT ISSN 0391-5972) 128, *964*
Istituto Comeliana di Lugano. Collectio Monographica Minor (IT) *993*
Istituto della Enciclopedia Italiana. Annuario (IT) *463*
Istituto della Enciclopedia Italiana. Bibliotheca Biographica (IT) *463*
Istituto di Diritto Romano. Bollettino (IT) *657*
Istituto di Filologia Greca. Bollettino (IT) *696*
Istituto di Fisica dell'Atmosfera, Rome. Bibliografia Generale. (IT ISSN 0075-1901) *808*
Istituto di Fisica dell'Atmosfera, Rome. Contributi Scientifici: Pubblicazioni di Fisica dell'Atmosfera e di Meteorologia. (IT ISSN 0075-191X) *805*
Istituto di Fisica dell'Atmosfera, Rome. Pubblicazioni Didattiche (IT ISSN 0075-1928) *805*
Istituto di Fisica dell'Atmosfera, Rome. Pubblicazioni Scientifiche (IT ISSN 0075-1936) *805*
Istituto di Fisica dell'Atmosfera, Rome. Pubblicazioni Varie. (IT ISSN 0075-1944) *805*
Istituto di Fisica dell'Atmosfera, Rome. Rapporti Interni Provvisori Adiffusione Limitata (IT ISSN 0075-1952) *805*
Istituto di Fisica dell'Atmosfera, Rome. Rapporti Scientifici (IT ISSN 0075-1960) *805*
Istituto di Fisica dell'Atmosfera, Rome. Rapporti Tecnici (IT ISSN 0075-1979) *805*
Istituto di Patologia del Libro "Alfonso Gallo." Bollettino *see* Istituto Centrale per la Patologia del Libro "Alfonso Gallo." Bollettino *964*
Istituto di Scienze Religiose in Trento. Pubblicazioni (IT) *982*
Istituto di Storia dell'Architettura. Quaderni (IT) *98*

Istituto di Studi e Documentazioni sull'Est Europeo. Serie Giuridica (IT) *671*

Istituto e Museo di Storia della Scienza. Biblioteca (IT ISSN 0075-1499) *993*

Istituto Ellenico di Studi Bizantini e Postbizantini, Venice. Biblioteca (IT ISSN 0075-1502) *587*, 613

Istituto Giapponese di Cultura, Rome. Annuario. (IT ISSN 0080-391X) *587*, 630, 1009

Istituto Giapponese di Cultura, Rome. Notiziario. (IT ISSN 0080-3928) *570*

Istituto Gramsci Piemontese. Materiali (IT) *906*

Istituto Internazionale di Studi Liguri. Collezione di Monografie Preistoriche Ed Archeologiche (IT ISSN 0530-9867) *88*

Istituto Italiano di Idrobiologia. Memorie (IT ISSN 0374-9118) *142*

Istituto Italiano di Numismatica. Annali(IT ISSN 0578-9923) *844*

Istituto Lombardo Accademia di Scienze e Lettere. Rendiconti. A (IT ISSN 0021-2504) *993*

Istituto Mobiliare Italiano. Annual Report (IT ISSN 0075-1529) *196*

Istituto Nazionale di Archeologia e Storia dell'Arte. Rivista (IT) *88*, 106

Istituto per la Documentazione Giuridica. Bibliografia. Diritto Civile (IT ISSN 0392-7571) *668*

Istituto per la Documentazione Giuridica. Bibliografia. Diritto Internazionale (IT) *668*

Istituto Ricerche Pesca Marittima. Quaderni (IT ISSN 0393-3571) *406, 511*

Istituto Siciliano di Studi Bizantini e Neoellenici. Quaderni (IT ISSN 0075-1545) *587*

Istituto Siciliano di Studi Bizantini e Neoellenici. Testi e Monumenti. Testi (IT ISSN 0075-1553) *587*

Istituto Sperimentale per il Tabacco. Annali (IT) *1080*

Istituto Sperimentale per l'Enologia Asti. Annali (IT ISSN 0374-5791) *120*

Istituto Sperimentale per la Cerealicoltura. Annali (IT) *63*

Istituto Sperimentale per la Floricoltura. Annali (IT ISSN 0304-0550) *57*

Istituto Sperimentale per la Selvicoltura. Annali (IT) *526*

Istituto Sperimentale Talassografico, Trieste. Annuario. (IT ISSN 0082-6448) *805*

Istituto Storico Artistico Orvietano. Bollettino (IT ISSN 0391-8211) *587*

Istituto Storico Italo-Germanico in Trento. Annali/Italienisch-Deutschen Historischen Instituts. Jahrbuch (IT) *587*

Istituto Universitario di Bergamo. Studi Archeologici (IT) *88*

Istituto Universitario Navale, Naples. Annali (IT ISSN 0075-1588) *811*

Istituto Universitario Orientale. Annali (IT) *504*, 696

Istituto Universitario Orientale. Annali (IT) *852*

Istituto Universitario Orientale di Napoli. Seminario di Studi del Mondo Classico. Annali. Sezione Linguistica (IT) *337, 852*

Istituto Universitario Orientale di Napoli. Seminario di Studi del Mondo Classico. Sezione Archeologia e Storia Antica. Annali. (IT) *88*

Istituzioni Culturali (IT ISSN 0391-321X) *1156*

Istituzioni Culturali Piemontesi. Pubblicazioni (IT) *1077*

Istochnikovedenie Otechestvennoi Istorii (UR) *587*

Istoricheskie Zapiski (UR) *558*

Istorie si Civilizatie (RM ISSN 0075-1626) *558*

Istoriko-Matematicheskie Issledovaniya (UR) *749*

Istoriya i Istoriki (UR) *587*

Istorychni Doslidzhennya. Istoriya Zarubizhnykh Krayin (UR ISSN 0135-2202) *558*

Istorychni Doslidzhennya. Vitchyznyana Istoriya (UR ISSN 0135-2210) *558*

It (AT) *1046*

It Goes on the Shelf (US) *14*

Italia Dialettale (IT ISSN 0085-2295) *696*

Italian Administrative Directory see Annuario Amministrativo Italiano *939*

Italian Books in Print see Catalogo dei Libri in Commercio *964*

Italian Culture (US ISSN 0161-4622) *724*

Italian Genealogist (US) *536*, 587

Italian Golden Guide (AT) *310, 951*

Italian Journal of Zoology. Monographs see Monitore Zoologico Italiano. Monografie *176*

Italian Journal of Zoology. Supplement see Monitore Zoologico Italiano. Supplemento *176*

Italian Private English Language Schools & Italian Language Schools for Overseas & Italy (UK) *430*, 696, 724

Italian Sanitary Directory see Annuario Sanitario Italiano *757*

Italian Studies (UK ISSN 0075-1634) *724*

Italian Texts (UK) *696*

Italian Trade-Marks see Siglario Italiano *861*

Italian Yearbook of International Law (IT) *671*

Italianist (UK ISSN 0261-4340) *587*, 724

Italica (US) *415*, 696

Italienisch-Deutschen Historischen Instituts. Jahrbuch see Istituto Storico Italo-Germanico in Trento. Annali *587*

Italy. Direzione Generale delle Fonti di Energia e delle Industrie di Base. Bilanci Energetici (IT ISSN 0075-1650) *465*

Italy. Istituto Centrale di Statistica. Annuario delle Statistiche Culturali (IT ISSN 0075-1677) *962*

Italy. Istituto Centrale di Statistica. Annuario di Statistica Agraria (IT ISSN 0075-1669) *30*

Italy. Istituto Centrale di Statistica. Annuario di Statistica Forestale (IT ISSN 0075-1707) *526*

Italy. Istituto Centrale di Statistica. Annuario di Statistiche del Lavoro (IT ISSN 0390-6450) *927*

Italy. Istituto Centrale di Statistica. Annuario di Statistiche Demografiche(IT ISSN 0075-1685) *923, 927*

Italy. Istituto Centrale di Statistica. Annuario di Statistiche Giudiziarie-Tomo 1 (IT ISSN 0075-1715) *657*

Italy. Istituto Centrale di Statistica. Annuario di Statistiche Industriali (IT ISSN 0075-1723) *211, 1057*

Italy. Istituto Centrale di Statistica. Annuario di Statistiche Meteorologiche (IT ISSN 0075-1731) *805*

Italy. Istituto Centrale di Statistica. Annuario di Statistiche Sanitarie (IT ISSN 0075-1758) *958*

Italy. Istituto Centrale di Statistica. Annuario Statistiche Zootecniche see Italy. Istituto Centrale di Statistica. Annuario Statistico della Zootecnia, della Pesca e della Caccia *41*

Italy. Istituto Centrale di Statistica. Annuario Statistico del Commercio Interno see Italy. Istituto Centrale di Statistica. Annuario Statistico del Commercio Interno e del Turismo *211*

Italy. Istituto Centrale di Statistica. Annuario Statistico del Commercio Interno e del Turismo (IT) *211*, 257, 1058

Italy. Istituto Centrale di Statistica. Annuario Statistico dell'Assistenza e della Previdenza Sociale (IT ISSN 0075-1790) *642*

Italy. Istituto Centrale di Statistica. Annuario Statistico della Navigazione Marittima (IT ISSN 0075-1898) *1058, 1086*, 1101

Italy. Istituto Centrale di Statistica. Annuario Statistico della Zootecnia, della Pesca e della Caccia (IT ISSN 0390-6426) *41*

Italy. Istituto Centrale di Statistica. Bolletino Mensile di Statistica. Supplementi (IT ISSN 0390-6434) *1058*

Italy. Istituto Centrale di Statistica. Statistica Annuale del Commercio con l'Estero see Italy. Istituto Centrale di Statistica. Statistica Annuale del Commercio con l'Estero. Tomo 1 *211*

Italy. Istituto Centrale di Statistica. Statistica Annuale del Commercio con l'Estero see Italy. Istituto Centrale di Statistica. Statistica Annuale del Commercio con l'Estero. Tomo 2 *211*

Italy. Istituto Centrale di Statistica. Statistica Annuale del Commercio con l'Estero. Tomo 1 (IT ISSN 0390-6558) *211*, 257, 1058

Italy. Istituto Centrale di Statistica. Statistica Annuale del Commercio con l'Estero. Tomo 2 (IT ISSN 0390-6566) *211*, 257, 1058

Italy. Istituto di Studi sulla Ricerca e Documentazione Scientifica. Note di Bibliografia e Documentazione Scientifica (IT) *679*

Italy. Istituto Nazionale per lo Studio della Congiuntura. Quaderni Analitici(IT ISSN 0075-1987) *290*

Italy. Ministero del Bilancio e della Programmazione Economica. Relazione Generale Sulla Situazione Economica del Paese (IT ISSN 0075-1995) *246*

Italy & Switzerland Stamp Catalogue (UK ISSN 0142-9825) *875*

Itaviitta (FI) *587*

Itihasa Samiti Patrika see Bangladesh Itihas Samiti. Journal *568*

Itogi Nauki i Tekhniki: Algebra - Topologiya - Geometriya (UR ISSN 0202-7445) *749*

Itogi Nauki i Tekhniki: Astronomiya (UR ISSN 0202-0742) *116*

Itogi Nauki i Tekhniki: Avtomobil'nyi i Gorodskoi Transport (UR ISSN 0202-7844) *482*, 1096

Itogi Nauki i Tekhniki: Biofizika see Itogi Nauki i Tekhniki: Biofizika Membran *153*

Itogi Nauki i Tekhniki: Biofizika Membran (UR ISSN 0234-2979) *153*

Itogi Nauki i Tekhniki: Biologicheskaya Khimiya (UR ISSN 0202-795X) *152*

Itogi Nauki i Tekhniki: Dvigateli Vnutrennogo Sgoraniya (UR ISSN 0202-7542) *491*

Itogi Nauki i Tekhniki: Elektricheskie Apparaty (UR ISSN 0202-8301) *456*

Itogi Nauki i Tekhniki: Elektricheskie Stantsii i Seti (UR) *456*

Itogi Nauki i Tekhniki: Elektricheskie Stantsii, Seti i Sistemy see Itogi Nauki i Tekhniki: Elektricheskie Stantsii i Seti *456*

Itogi Nauki i Tekhniki: Elektrokhimiya (UR ISSN 0202-8093) *328*

Itogi Nauki i Tekhniki: Elektronika (UR) *456*

Itogi Nauki i Tekhniki: Elektrosvyaz' (UR ISSN 0130-6804) *344*

Itogi Nauki i Tekhniki: Fiziologiya Cheloveka i Zhivotnykh (UR ISSN 0134-2673) *172*

Itogi Nauki i Tekhniki: Genetika Cheloveka (UR ISSN 0301-391X) *167*

Itogi Nauki i Tekhniki: Geodeziya i Aeros'emka (UR ISSN 0202-0726) *545*

Itogi Nauki i Tekhniki: Geografiya Zarubezhnykh Stran (UR ISSN 0202-7208) *545*

Itogi Nauki i Tekhniki: Geokhimiya - Mineralogiya - Petrografiya (UR ISSN 0202-7348) *389*, 817

ITOGI NAUKI 1785

Itogi Nauki i Tekhniki: Geomagnetizm i Vysokie Sloi Atmosfery (UR ISSN 0202-7275) *400*

Itogi Nauki i Tekhniki: Gidrogeologiya. Inzhenernaya Geologiya (UR ISSN 0202-7356) *403*

Itogi Nauki i Tekhniki: Issledovanie Kosmicheskogo Prostranstva (UR ISSN 0202-0734) *116*

Itogi Nauki i Tekhniki: Kartografiya (UR ISSN 0202-7240) *545*

Itogi Nauki i Tekhniki: Khimiya i Tekhnologiya Vysokomolekulyarnykh Soedinenii (UR ISSN 0202-8069) *478*

Itogi Nauki i Tekhniki: Kinetika. Kataliz (UR ISSN 0202-7968) *331*

Itogi Nauki i Tekhniki: Korroziya i Zashchita ot Korrozii (UR ISSN 0202-7976) *798*

Itogi Nauki i Tekhniki: Kristallokhimiya(UR ISSN 0202-7984) *327*

Itogi Nauki i Tekhniki: Matematicheskii Analiz (UR ISSN 0202-7453) *749*

Itogi Nauki i Tekhniki: Mekhanika Zhidkosti i Gaza (UR ISSN 0202-781X) *491*

Itogi Nauki i Tekhniki: Mestorozhdeniya Goryuchikh Poleznykh Iskopaemykh (UR ISSN 0302-542X) *389*

Itogi Nauki i Tekhniki: Metallovedenie i Termicheskaya Obrabotka (UR ISSN 0202-7739) *798*

Itogi Nauki i Tekhniki: Metallurgicheskaya Teplotekhnika (UR ISSN 0202-7755) *798*

Itogi Nauki i Tekhniki: Metallurgiya Tsvetnykh Metallov (UR ISSN 0202-7747) *798*

Itogi Nauki i Tekhniki: Molekulyarnaya Biologiya (UR ISSN 0202-7070) *142*

Itogi Nauki i Tekhniki: Obogashchenie Poleznykh Iskopaemykh (UR ISSN 0202-7437) *817*

Itogi Nauki i Tekhniki: Obshchaya Geologiya (UR ISSN 0202-7372) *389*

Itogi Nauki i Tekhniki: Obshchie Problemy Biologii (UR ISSN 0203-5405) *142*

Itogi Nauki i Tekhniki: Okhrana Prirody i Vosproizvodstvo Prirodnykh Resursov (UR ISSN 0202-7321) *497*

Itogi Nauki i Tekhniki: Onkologiya (UR ISSN 0202-7127) *142*, 775

Itogi Nauki i Tekhniki: Organicheskaya Khimiya (UR ISSN 0137-0251) *330*

Itogi Nauki i Tekhniki: Organizatsiya Upravleniya Transportom (VINITI) (UR ISSN 0134-7799) *1082*

Itogi Nauki i Tekhniki: Problemy Geometrii (UR ISSN 0202-7461) *749*

Itogi Nauki i Tekhniki: Promyshlennyi Transport (UR ISSN 0202-7909) *1082*

Itogi Nauki i Tekhniki: Protsessy i Apparaty Khimicheskoi Tekhnologii (UR ISSN 0202-8018) *478*

Itogi Nauki i Tekhniki: Radiotekhnika (UR ISSN 0202-0769) *349*

Itogi Nauki i Tekhniki: Rastenievodstvo(UR ISSN 0202-716X) *158*

Itogi Nauki i Tekhniki: Razrabotka Mestorozhdenii Tverdykh Poleznykh Iskopaemykh (UR ISSN 0202-7410) *817*

Itogi Nauki i Tekhniki: Razrabotka Neftyanykh i Gazovykh Mestorozhdenii (UR ISSN 0202-7429) *865*

Itogi Nauki i Tekhniki: Rudnye Mestorozhdeniya (UR ISSN 0202-7380) *817*

Itogi Nauki i Tekhniki: Svarka (UR ISSN 0202-778X) *802*

Itogi Nauki i Tekhniki: Tekhnicheskaya Kibernetika (UR ISSN 0130-6774) *359*

Itogi Nauki i Tekhniki: Teoriya Veroyatnostej - Matematicheskaya Statistika-Teoreticheskaya Kibernetika (UR ISSN 0202-7488) *359*, 749

Itogi Nauki i Tekhniki: Truboprovodnyi Transport (UR ISSN 0202-7917) 491

Itogi Nauki i Tekhniki: Vodnyi Transport (UR ISSN 0202-7879) 1101

Itogi Nauki i Tekhniki: Vozdushnyi Transport (UR ISSN 0202-7887) 1089

Itogi Nauki i Tekhniki: Zoologiya Pozvonochnykh (UR ISSN 0202-702X) 175

It's Happening (US ISSN 0098-7549) 415

Itsuu Kenkyusho Nenpo see Itsuu Laboratory, Tokyo. Annual Report 330

Itsuu Laboratory, Tokyo. Annual Report/Itsuu Kenkyusho Nenpo (JA ISSN 0075-2010) 330

Ittihad (US ISSN 0579-2290) 504

Ittihad al-Sinaat al-Misriyah. Yearbook (UA) 310

Ittihad al-Sinaat Bi-al-Jumhuriyah al-Arabiyah al-Muttahidah. Yearbook see Ittihad al-Sinaat al-Misriyah. Yearbook 310

Iura (IT ISSN 0021-3241) 657

Ius Romanum Medii Aevi (IT ISSN 0075-2037) 657

Ivory Coast. Direction des Investissements. Budget Special d'Investissement et d'Equipement. Rapport de Presentation (IV) 267

Ivory Coast. Direction des Mines et de la Geologie. Rapport Provisoire sur les Activities du Secteur (IV) 389, 817

Ivory Coast. Direction du Budget Special d'Investissement et d'Equipment. Rapport de Presentation du Budget Special d'Investissement et d'Equipment (IV) 943

Ivory Coast. Ministere de l'Agriculture. Statistiques Agricoles (IV) 41

Ivory Coast. Ministere de l'Economie, des Finances et du Plan. Comptes de la Nation (IV) 296

Ivory Coast. Ministere du Plan. Comptes de la Nation see Ivory Coast. Ministere de l'Economie, des Finances et du Plan. Comptes de la Nation 296

L'Ivre de Pierres (FR ISSN 0183-5742) 98, 106

Iwate Daigaku Kogakubu Kenkyu Hokoku see Iwate University. Faculty of Engineering. Technology Reports 472

Iwate Medical University School of Liberal Arts & Sciences. Annual Report (JA ISSN 0385-4132) 630, 1009

Iwate University. Faculty of Education. Annual Report (JA ISSN 0367-7370) 448, 724, 993, 1009

Iwate University. Faculty of Engineering. Technology Reports/Iwate Daigaku Kogakubu Kenkyu Hokoku (JA ISSN 0085-2325) 472

Iwate University. Mountains Land Use Research Laboratory. Bulletin (JA) 48

Iyo Kizai Kenkyusho Hokoku see Tokyo Medical and Dental University. Institute for Medical and Dental Engineering. Reports 767

Iz Istorii Estestvoznaniya i Tekhniki Pribaltiki see Contributions to the History of Natural Sciences and Technology in the Baltic 990

Iz Starog i Novog Zagreba (YU) 98, 106

Izsledovaniia po Bulgarska Istoriia (BU) 587

Izsledovaniya za Istoriiata na Bulgarskiya Narod (BU) 587

Izvestiya na Muzeite ot Iugoiztochna Bulgariya (BU ISSN 0204-403X) 88, 587

Izvestiya na Muzeite ot Iuzhna Bulgariya (BU ISSN 0204-4072) 88, 587

Izvestiya na Muzeite v Severozapadna Bulgariya (BU ISSN 0204-4013) 88, 587

Izvestiya na Narodnata Biblioteka Kiril i Metodii i na Bibliockata na Sofiiskiya Universitet Kliment Okhridski see Narodna Biblioteka Kiril i Metodii. Izvestiya 591

Izvori Srpskog Prava/Sources de Droit Serbe/Serbische Rechtsquellen (YU) 657

J A E R I Report (Japan Atomic Energy Research Institute) (JA) 893

J A E R I Reports. List (Japan Atomic Energy Research Institute) (JA) 897

J A G Journal see Naval Law Review 660

J A N E S see Ancient Near Eastern Society. Journal 850

J. B. Speed Art Museum Bulletin (US ISSN 0021-356X) 828

J C A T S see C.A.T.S. Reports 347

J C I World see Leader (Coral Gables) 341

J.C. Poggendorff: Biographisch-Literarisches Handwoerterbuch der Exakten Naturwissenschaften (GE) 993

J D: Journalism Directory see Journalism and Mass Communication Directory 646

J E B Theatre (BE) 1077

J. Gruber's Hagers-Town Town and Country Almanack (US) 114, 463

J I L A Data Center. Report (Joint Institute for Laboratory Astrophysics) (US) 897

J I L A Information Center. Report see J I L A Data Center. Report 897

J.K. Lasser's Your Income Tax (US ISSN 0084-4314) 296

J.K. Lasser's Your Income Tax, Professional Ed (US ISSN 0075-2061) 296

J L B Smith Institute of Ichthyology. Ichthyological Bulletin (SA ISSN 0073-4381) 175

J L B Smith Institute of Ichthyology. Special Publication (SA ISSN 0075-2088) 175

J N F Illustrated (Jewish National Fund) (IS ISSN 0021-3705) 943

J N R Bulletin (Japanese National Railways) (JA ISSN 0047-1925) 1094

J P S Bookmark see Bookmark (Albany) 675

J. Paul Getty Museum Journal (US ISSN 0362-1979) 106

J S A S see American Society for Armenian Studies. Journal 501

J S P S Annual Report/Nippon Gakujutsu Shinkokai (Japan Society for the Promotion of Science) (JA) 993

Jaarbericht "Ex Oriente Lux" see Vooraziatisch-Egyptisch Genootschap "Ex Oriente Lux". Jaarbericht 572

Jaarboek Achterhoek en Liemers (NE) 587

Jaarboek der Schone Kunsten/Algemeen Jaarboek der Schone Kunsten (BE ISSN 0066-3174) 106

Jaarboek Eindhoven (NE) 1058

Jaarboek/Vademecum voor het Verzekeringswezen (NE) 640

Jaarboek van de Christelijke Gereformeerde Kerken in Nederland (NE) 984

Jaarboek van de Openbare Gasvoorziening (NE) 465, 865

Jaarboek voor Munt en Penningkunde (NE) 844

Jaarlijks Rapport over de Buitenlandse Investeringen see Belgium. Ministere des Affaires Economiques. Rapport Annuel sur les Investissements Etrangers en Belique 265

Jackson Laboratory Annual Report see Jackson Laboratory Scientific Report 167

Jackson Laboratory Scientific Report (US) 167, 762

Jacob Blaustein Lectures in International Affairs (US ISSN 0075-2142) 916

Jacob Marschak Interdisciplinary Colloquium on Mathematics in the Behavioral Sciences (US ISSN 0160-7146) 280

Jacobean Drama Studies (AU) 724, 1077

Jadavpur Journal of Comparative Literature (II ISSN 0448-1143) 724

Jaeger and Waldmann International Telefax Directory see Telefax International. International Telefax Directory 351

Jaeger and Waldmann International Telex and Teletex Directory see Telex & Teletex International. Telex and Teletex Directory 351

Jaeger's Intertravel (GW ISSN 0075-2150) 1112

Jaehrliche Aegyptologische Bibliographie see Annual Egyptological Bibliography 562

Jag (US ISSN 0021-390X) 879, 906

Jagger Journal (SA ISSN 0256-0070) 679

Jahangirnagar University. Department of English. Bulletin (BG) 724

Jahrbuch der Auktionspreise see Jahrbuch der Auktionspreise fuer Buecher, Handschriften und Autographen 828

Jahrbuch der Auktionspreise fuer Buecher, Handschriften und Autographen (GW) 679, 828, 962

Jahrbuch der Berliner Museen (GW ISSN 0075-2207) 828

Jahrbuch der Bibliotheken, Archive und Informationstellen der Deutschen Demokratischen Republik (GE ISSN 0075-2215) 679

Jahrbuch der Bibliotheken, Informationsstellen und Archive der D D R see Jahrbuch der Bibliotheken, Archive und Informationstellen der Deutschen Demokratischen Republik 679

Jahrbuch der Deutschen Bibliotheken (GW ISSN 0075-2223) 679

Jahrbuch der Erzdioese von Wien (AU) 982

Jahrbuch der Europaeischen Erdoelindustrie see European Petroleum Yearbook 864

Jahrbuch der Export- und Versandtleiter (GW ISSN 0075-224X) 257

Jahrbuch der Fachanwaelte fuer Steuerrecht (GW) 1094

Jahrbuch der Getraenke und Fluessigen Nahrmittel see Annuaire des Boissons et des Liquides Alimentaires 119

Jahrbuch der Historischen Forschung in der Bundesrepublik Deutschland (GW ISSN 0341-9177) 587

Jahrbuch der Luftfahrt und Raumfahrt see Reuss Jahrbuch der Luft- und Raumfahrt 21

Jahrbuch der Oeffentlichen Meinung see Allensbacher Jahrbuch der Demoskopie 1024

Jahrbuch der Oesterreichischen Sozialversicherung see Handbuch der Oesterreichischen Sozialversicherung 642

Jahrbuch der Oesterreichischen Wirtschaft (AU) 246

Jahrbuch der Psychoanalyse (GW ISSN 0075-2363) 935

Jahrbuch der Schleiff-, Hon-, Laepp- und Poliertechnik see Jahrbuch Schleiffen, Honen, Laeppen und Polieren, Verfahren und Maschinen 492

Jahrbuch der Wehrtechnik (GW ISSN 0075-2428) 811

Jahrbuch der Werbung (GW ISSN 0344-712X) 828

Jahrbuch der Wirtschaft Osteuropas/Yearbook of East-European Economics (GW ISSN 0449-5225) 246

Jahrbuch des Baltischen Deutschtums (GW ISSN 0075-2436) 587

Jahrbuch des Deutschen Bergbaus see Jahrbuch fuer Bergbau, Energie, Mineraloel und Chemie 817

Jahrbuch des Eisenbahnwesens (GW ISSN 0075-2479) 1094

Jahrbuch des Instituts fuer Christliche Sozialwissenschaften see Jahrbuch fuer Christliche Sozialwissenschaften 1027

Jahrbuch des Kameramanns (GW ISSN 0075-2509) 824

Jahrbuch des Oeffentlichen Rechts der Gegenwart (GW ISSN 0075-2517) 657

Jahrbuch des Schwalm-Eder-Kreises (GW) 587

Jahrbuch des Vereins fuer Niederdeutsche Sprachforschung (GW ISSN 0083-5617) 696

Jahrbuch Deutsch Als Fremdsprache (GW ISSN 0342-6300) 436, 696

Jahrbuch Deutscher Dichtung (GW) 742

Jahrbuch Elektrotechnik (GW) 456

Jahrbuch fuer Antike und Christentum (GW ISSN 0075-2541) 970

Jahrbuch fuer Bergbau, Energie, Mineraloel und Chemie (GW) 817

Jahrbuch fuer Berlin-Brandenburgische Kirchengeschichte (GW ISSN 0075-2568) 970

Jahrbuch fuer Betriebswirte (GW) 221, 280, 284

Jahrbuch fuer Biotechnologie (GW) 142, 153, 169, 993

Jahrbuch fuer Blindenfreunde (GW) 180, 445, 786

Jahrbuch fuer Brandenburgische Kirchengeschichte see Jahrbuch fuer Berlin-Brandenburgische Kirchengeschichte 970

Jahrbuch fuer Bundesbahnbeamte (GW ISSN 0075-2576) 1094

Jahrbuch fuer Christliche Sozialwissenschaften (GW ISSN 0075-2584) 970, 1027

Jahrbuch fuer das Elektrohandwerk (GW ISSN 0344-6581) 456

Jahrbuch fuer den Deutsch-Franzoesischen Handel see Guide Annuaire du Commerce Franco-Allemand 236

Jahrbuch fuer den Kreis Pinneberg (GW ISSN 0448-150X) 587

Jahrbuch fuer den Oesterreichischen Tierarzt (AU ISSN 0075-2606) 1122

Jahrbuch fuer die Gefluegelwirtschaft (GW ISSN 0447-2713) 66

Jahrbuch fuer die Kirche von Wien see Jahrbuch der Erzdioese von Wien 982

Jahrbuch fuer Eisenbahnliteratur (GW) 1094

Jahrbuch fuer Elektromaschinenbau und Elektronik (GW) 456

Jahrbuch fuer Fraenkische Landesforschung (GW ISSN 0446-3943) 587, 923

Jahrbuch fuer Fremdenverkehr (GW ISSN 0075-2649) 1112

Jahrbuch fuer Geologie (GE ISSN 0448-1518) 389

Jahrbuch fuer Geschichte (GE ISSN 0448-1526) 587

Jahrbuch fuer Geschichte der USSR und der Volksdemokratischen Laender Europas see Geschichte der Sozialistischen Laender Europas. Jahrbuch 583

Jahrbuch fuer Geschichte des Feudalismus (GE) 587

Jahrbuch fuer Geschichte von Staat, Wirtschaft und Gesellschaft Lateinamerikas. (GW ISSN 0075-2673) 606

Jahrbuch fuer Internationales Recht see German Yearbook of International Law 670

Jahrbuch fuer Liturgik und Hymnologie(GW ISSN 0075-2681) 837, 970

Jahrbuch fuer Musikalische Volks- und Voelkerkunde (GW ISSN 0075-2703) 516, 837

Jahrbuch fuer Numismatik und Geldgeschichte (GW ISSN 0075-2711) 844

Jahrbuch fuer Opernforschung (GW ISSN 0724-8156) 837

Jahrbuch fuer Optik und Feinmechanik (GW ISSN 0075-272X) 899

Jahrbuch fuer Ostdeutsche Volkskunde (GW ISSN 0075-2738) 73, 516

Jahrbuch fuer Ostrecht (GW ISSN 0075-2746) 657

Jahrbuch fuer Praktiker des Rechnungswesens (GW) 221

Jahrbuch fuer Regionalgeschichte (GE ISSN 0085-2341) 587

Jahrbuch fuer Regionalwissenschaft (GW ISSN 0173-7600) *993*
Jahrbuch fuer Salesianische Studien (GW ISSN 0075-2754) *587*
Jahrbuch fuer Schlesische Kirchengeschichte (GW ISSN 0075-2762) *970*
Jahrbuch fuer Soziologie und Sozialpolitik (GE ISSN 0138-435X) *1009, 1027*
Jahrbuch fuer Volkskunde und Kulturgeschichte. Neue Folge (GE ISSN 0138-4503) *516*
Jahrbuch fuer Volksliedforschung (GW ISSN 0075-2789) *837*
Jahrbuch fuer Westdeutsche Landesgeschichte (GW ISSN 0170-2025) *587*
Jahrbuch fuer Wirtschaftsgeschichte (GE ISSN 0075-2800) *251*
Jahrbuch fuer Zeitgeschichte (AU) *587*
Jahrbuch Kreis Euskirchen (GW) *630*
Jahrbuch Landkreis Kassel (GW) *587, 630*
Jahrbuch Mission (GW) *970*
Jahrbuch Oberflaechentechnik (Year) (GW ISSN 0075-2819) *798*
Jahrbuch Peters (GW) *837*
Jahrbuch Schleiffen, Honen, Laeppen und Polieren, Verfahren und Maschinen (GW) *492*
Jahrbuch Stahl (GW ISSN 0724-8482) *798*
Jahrbuch Ueberblicke Mathematik (GW ISSN 0172-8512) *749*
Jahrbuch zur Alkohol- und Tabakfrage see Jahrbuch zur Frage der Suchtgefahren *377*
Jahrbuch zur Frage der Suchtgefahren (GW ISSN 0170-7337) *377*
Jahrbuch zur Geschichte Dresdens (GE) *587*
Jahrbuecher fuer Nationaloekonomie und Statistik (GW ISSN 0021-4027) *211*
Jahresbericht see European Free Trade Association. Annual Report *255*
Jahresbericht der Bayerischen Bodendenkmalpflege (GW ISSN 0075-2835) *558*
Jahresbericht des Deutschen Wetterdienstes (GW ISSN 0433-8251) *805*
Jahresbericht ueber die Deutsche Fischwirtschaft (GW ISSN 0075-2851) *511*
Jahresbibliographie Massenkommunikation (GW) *128, 346*
Jahresfachkatalog Recht-Wirtschaft-Steuern (GW ISSN 0075-2886) *196, 296, 657*
Jahreskatalog Philosophie see Katalog Philosophie *879*
Jahreskatalog Psychologie (GW ISSN 0075-2924) *935*
Jahresring (GW) *538*
Jahresschrift fuer Mitteldeutsche Vorgeschichte (GE ISSN 0075-2932) *587*
Jahresverzeichnis der Deutschen Hochschulschriften see Jahresverzeichnis der Hochschulschriften der DDR, der BRD und Westberlins *424*
Jahresverzeichnis der Hochschulschriften der DDR, der BRD und Westberlins (GE ISSN 0323-455X) *8, 424*
Jahresverzeichnis der Musikalien und Musikschriften (GE ISSN 0075-2959) *843*
Jahresverzeichnis der Verlagsschriften und Einer Auswahl der Ausserhalb des Buchhandels Erschienenen Veroeffentlichungen der D.D.R., der B.R.D. und Westberlins Sowie der Deutschsprachigen Werke Anderer Laender (GE ISSN 0300-8436) *1156*
Jahresverzeichnis des Deutschen Schrifttums see Jahresverzeichnis der Verlagsschriften und Einer Auswahl der Ausserhalb des Buchhandels Erschienenen Veroeffentlichungen der D.D.R., der B.R.D. und Westberlins Sowie der Deutschsprachigen Werke Anderer Laender *1156*

Jakarta Business Directory (IO) *310*
Jakarta Metropolitan Buyers' Guide (IO) *310*
Jam to-Day (US ISSN 0362-8302) *724*
Jamaica. Department of Statistics. Annual Abstract of Statistics see Statistical Institute of Jamaica. Statistical Abstract *1064*
Jamaica. Department of Statistics. Demographic Statistics see Statistical Institute of Jamaica. Demographic Statistics *929*
Jamaica. Department of Statistics. External Trade Annual Review see Statistical Institute of Jamaica. External Trade Annual Review *218*
Jamaica. Department of Statistics. Monetary Statistics see Statistical Institute of Jamaica. Monetary Statistics Report *218*
Jamaica. Department of Statistics. National Income and Product see Statistical Institute of Jamaica. National Income and Product *218*
Jamaica. Department of Statistics. Pocketbook of Statistics see Statistical Institute of Jamaica. Pocketbook of Statistics *1063*
Jamaica. Department of Statistics. Statistical Abstract see Statistical Institute of Jamaica. Statistical Abstract *1064*
Jamaica. Ministry of Pensions and Social Security. Report see Jamaica. Ministry of Social Security. Report *640*
Jamaica. Ministry of Social Security. Report (JM) *640*
Jamaica. National Insurance Scheme. Annual Reports see Jamaica. Ministry of Social Security. Report *640*
Jamaica Chamber of Commerce Journal(JM ISSN 0021-4094) *236*
Jamaica Dental Association. Newsletter(JM) *779*
Jamaica Geographical Society Proceedings see Jamaican Geographical Society Newsletter *545*
Jamaica Library Association. Annual Bulletin see Jamaica Library Association. Bulletin *679*
Jamaica Library Association. Bulletin (JM) *679*
Jamaican Association of Sugar Technologists. Proceedings (JM) *57*
Jamaican Bar Association. Annual Report (JM) *657*
Jamaican Exporter (JM) *257*
Jamaican Geographical Society Newsletter (JM) *545*
Jamaican Historical Review (JM) *606*
Jamaican Packaging Directory (JM) *855*
James Arthur Lecture on the Evolution of the Human Brain (US) *167, 790*
James Cook University of North Queensland. Department of Geography. Monograph Series (AT) *545*
James Hogg Society. Newsletter (UK ISSN 0263-7022) *134*
James K. Whittemore Lectures in Mathematics Given at Yale University (US) *1156*
Jaminraitu (II) *742*
Jammu and Kashmir. Legislative Council. Committee on Privileges. Report (II ISSN 0448-2433) *906*
Jammu & Kashmir Minerals Limited. Annual Report (II ISSN 0304-7164) *817*
Jane's Airport Equipment (UK) *20, 1089*
Jane's All the World Aircraft (UK ISSN 0075-3017) *20*
Jane's Armour and Artillery (UK) *811*
Jane's Aviation Annual see Jane's Aviation Review *20*
Jane's Aviation Review (UK) *20*
Jane's Avionics (UK) *20*
Jane's Combat Support Equipment see Jane's Military Vehicles and Ground Support Equipment *811*
Jane's Fighting Ships (UK ISSN 0075-3025) *811, 1101*

Jane's Freight Containers (UK ISSN 0075-3033) *1094*
Jane's High-Speed Marine Craft and Air Cushion Vehicles (UK) *1101*
Jane's Infantry Weapons (UK ISSN 0306-3410) *811*
Jane's Military Communications (UK ISSN 0144-0004) *811*
Jane's Military Review (UK) *811*
Jane's Military Vehicles and Ground Support Equipment (UK) *811*
Jane's Naval Annual see Jane's Naval Review *1101*
Jane's Naval Review (UK) *1101*
Jane's Spaceflight Directory (UK) *20*
Jane's Surface Skimmers see Jane's High-Speed Marine Craft and Air Cushion Vehicles *1101*
Jane's Urban Transport Systems (UK) *1082*
Jane's Weapon Systems (UK ISSN 0075-3068) *811*
Jane's World Railways (UK ISSN 0075-3084) *1094*
Janmabhoomi Panchang (II) *114*
Janua Linguarum. Series Anastatica (GW) *696*
Janua Linguarum. Series Critica (GW ISSN 0075-3092) *696*
Janua Linguarum. Series Didactica (GW ISSN 0075-3106) *696*
Janua Linguarum. Series Major (GW ISSN 0075-3114) *696*
Janua Linguarum. Series Minor (GW ISSN 0075-3122) *697*
Janua Linguarum. Series Practica (GW ISSN 0075-3130) *697*
January Bulletin (UK) *533*
Janus see Aurora (Madison) *14*
Japan. Annual Report on National Life (JA) *246*
Japan. Finance Department. Bulletin of Financial Statistics. see Financial Statistics of Japan *228*
Japan. Forestry and Forest Products Research Institute. Annual Report/Norinsho Ringyo Shikenjo Nenpo (JA) *526*
Japan. Forestry and Forest Products Research Institute. Bulletin (JA) *526*
Japan. Government Forest Experiment Station. Kyushu Branch. Annual Report/Ringyo Shikenjo Kyushu Shijo Nenpo (JA ISSN 0557-0395) *526*
Japan. Government Forest Experiment Station, Tokyo. Annual Report see Japan. Forestry and Forest Products Research Institute. Annual Report *526*
Japan. Government Industrial Development Laboratory, Hokkaido. Annual Report/Hokkaido Kogyo Kaihatsu Shikenjo Nempo (JA) *290*
Japan. Government Industrial Development Laboratory, Hokkaido. Reports/Hokkaido Kogyo Kaihatsu Shikenjo Hokoku (JA ISSN 0441-0734) *1069*
Japan. Government Industrial Development Laboratory, Hokkaido. Technical Data/Hokkaido Kogyo Kaihatsu Shikenjo Gijutsu (JA) *1069*
Japan. Government Industrial Research Institute, Kyushu Annual Report/Kyushu Kogyo Gijutsu Shikenjo Nempo (JA) *290*
Japan. Institute of Population Problems. Annual Report (JA) *923*
Japan. Maritime Safety Agency. Hydrographic Department. Hydrographic Bulletin/Suiro Yoho (JA ISSN 0021-4485) *403*
Japan. Maritime Safety Agency. Hydrographic Department. Report of Hydrographic Research (JA) *403*
Japan. Meteorological Agency. Annual Report/Kisho-cho Nenpo Zenkoku Kishohyo (JA ISSN 0448-3758) *805*
Japan. Ministry of Agriculture and Forestry. Annual Report/Norin-sho Nenpo (JA ISSN 0446-5458) *30, 526*

JAPAN. STATISTICS   1787

Japan. Ministry of Health and Welfare. Statistics and Information Department. Report on Basic Survey of Health and Welfare Administration (JA) *958, 1023, 1058*
Japan. Ministry of Health and Welfare. Statistics and Information Department. Report on Occupational Statistics on Vital Events (JA) *849, 1058*
Japan. Ministry of Health and Welfare. Statistics and Information Department. Report on Survey of Livelihood Aid Services (JA) *1023, 1058*
Japan. Ministry of Health and Welfare. Statistics and Information Department. Report on Survey of National Medical Care Insurance Services (JA) *642, 1058*
Japan. Ministry of Health and Welfare. Statistics and Information Department. Report on Survey of Socio-Economic Aspects on Vital Events (JA) *211, 1014, 1058*
Japan. Ministry of Health and Welfare. Statistics and Information Department. Report on Survey of Social Welfare Facilities (JA) *1023, 1058*
Japan. Ministry of Health and Welfare. Statistics and Information Department. Statistical Handbook on Health and Social Welfare (JA) *958, 1023, 1058*
Japan. Ministry of Health and Welfare. Statistics and Information Department. Statistics on Activities of Health Centers (JA) *771, 1058*
Japan. Ministry of Health and Welfare. Statistics and Information Department. Statistical Report on Communicable Diseases (JA) *771, 1058*
Japan. Ministry of Health and Welfare. Statistics and Information Department. Statistical Report on Communicable Diseases and Food Poisonings see Japan. Ministry of Health and Welfare. Statistics and Information Department. Statistical Report on Communicable Diseases *771*
Japan. Ministry of Health and Welfare. Statistics and Information Department. Statistical Report on Communicable Diseases and Food Poisonings see Japan. Ministry of Health and Welfare. Statistics and Information Department. Statistical Report on Food Poisonings *771*
Japan. Ministry of Health and Welfare. Statistics and Information Department. Statistical Report on Food Poisonings (JA) *771, 1058*
Japan. Ministry of Health and Welfare. Statistics and Information Department. Statistical Report on Public Health Services (JA) *958, 1058*
Japan. Ministry of Health and Welfare. Statistics and Information Department. Statistical Report on Social Welfare Services (JA) *1023, 1058*
Japan. Ministry of Health and Welfare. Statistics and Information Department. Vital Statistics (JA ISSN 0075-3270) *1058*
Japan. Ministry of Labour. Yearbook of Labour Statistics (JA) *211*
Japan. National Diet Library. Annual Report/Kokuritsu Kokkai Toshokan Nenpo (JA ISSN 0385-325X) *680*
Japan. National Veterinary Assay Laboratory. Annual Report (JA ISSN 0388-7421) *1122*
Japan. Ship Research Institute. Papers/Senpaku Gijutsu Kenkyusho Obun Hokoku (JA) *1156*
Japan. Statistics Bureau. Annual Report on Family Income and Expenditures see Japan. Statistics Bureau. Annual Report on Family Income and Expenditure Survey *615*
Japan. Statistics Bureau. Annual Report on Family Income and Expenditure Survey (JA) *615, 1058*

1788　JAPAN. STATISTICS

Japan. Statistics Bureau. Employment Status Survey (JA) 211, 1058
Japan Almanach see Mainichi Daily News 463
Japan & Korea Stamp Catalogue (UK ISSN 0142-9906) 875
Japan Annual of Law and Politics (JA ISSN 0075-3157) 1156
Japan Annual Reviews in Electronics, Computers & Telecommunications. Amorphous Semiconductor Technologies & Devices (JA ISSN 0167-5036) 346, 456
Japan Anti-Tuberculosis Association. Reports on Medical Research Problems/Kekkaku Yobokai Kenkyu Gyoseki (JA ISSN 0075-3165) 793
Japan Association for Philosophy of Science. Annals (JA ISSN 0453-0691) 879, 993
Japan Atomic Energy Commission. Annual Report/Genshiryoku Nenpo (JA ISSN 0449-4830) 472, 897
Japan Atomic Energy Research Institute Report see J A E R I Report 893
Japan Atomic Energy Research Institute Reports. List see J A E R I Reports. List 897
Japan Audio-Visual Education Association Japan see A V E in Japan 446
Japan Aviation Directory (JA ISSN 0286-0635) 20, 310
Japan Business Directory. see Diamond's Japan Business Directory 305
Japan Chemical Annual (JA ISSN 0075-319X) 478
Japan Chemical Directory (JA ISSN 0075-3203) 478
Japan Comparative Education Society. Bulletin (JA ISSN 0289-405X) 415
Japan Computer Technology and Applications Abstracts (US ISSN 0890-1406) 354
Japan Congress on Materials Research. Proceedings/Zairyo Kenkyu Rengo Koenkai Ronbunshu (JA ISSN 0368-3141) 489
Japan Cotton Statistics and Related Data (JA ISSN 0447-5321) 1076
Japan Directory (JA ISSN 0075-322X) 310
Japan Directory of Professional Associations (JA ISSN 0287-9530) 962
Japan Drug Industry Review (JA) 871
Japan Economic Almanac (JA) 246, 290
Japan Economic Research Center. Center Paper Series (JA ISSN 0075-3238) 246
Japan Electronic Materials Society. Bulletin (JA ISSN 0285-3833) 472, 489
Japan Electronics Almanac (US) 456
Japan Electronics Buyers' Guide (US) 310, 456
Japan English Books in Print see Japan English Publications in Print 128
Japan English Magazine Directory see Japan English Publications in Print 128
Japan English Publications in Print (JA ISSN 0910-7908) 128
Japan Fact Book see Japan Electronics Almanac 456
Japan Federation of Composers. Catalogue of Publications (JA) 843
Japan Foundation Annual Report (JA) 630
Japan Hotel Guide (JA ISSN 0446-6217) 620
Japan Industrial Safety and Health Association. Research and Survey Division. Barometer of Occupational Safety (JA) 635
Japan Industrial Safety and Health Association. Research and Survey Division. Guidebook on Occupational Health (JA) 635
Japan Industrial Safety and Health Association. Research and Survey Division. Yearbook of Industrial Safety (JA) 635

Japan Institute of Labour. Proceedings see Asian Regional Conference on Industrial Relations. Proceedings 270
Japan International Cooperation Agency. Organization and Functions (JA) 263
Japan Marine Science and Technology Center. Annual Report (JA) 380
Japan Meteorological Agency. Agricultural Meteorology. Annual Report (JA) 30, 805
Japan Meteorological Agency. Report of Geomagnetic and Geoelectric Observations (JA) 400
Japan Meteorological Agency. Report of Magnetic Pulsations (JA) 400
Japan P.E.N. News see Japanese Literature Today 724
Japan Petroleum Industry Yearbook (JA) 865
Japan Port Information (JA) 1101
Japan Printing Art Annual/Nihon Insatsu Nenkan (JA ISSN 0546-0719) 931
Japan Register of Merchants, Manufacturers and Shippers see Standard Trade Index of Japan 237
Japan Report: Science and Technology (US) 993, 1069
Japan Science Review: Economic Sciences (JA ISSN 0448-8709) 212
Japan Society for Cancer Therapy. Proceedings of the Congress (JA ISSN 0075-3327) 775
Japan Society for the Promotion of Science Annual Report see J S P S Annual Report 993
Japan Society of Civil Engineers. Proceedings of the Annual Conference. see Doboku Gakkai Nenji Koenkai Koen Gaiyoshu 481
Japan Society of Lubrication Engineers. Journal. International Edition (JA ISSN 0389-5483) 472, 745
Japan Society of Plant Taxonomist. News see Syokubutsu Bunrui Gakkai Nyusu 161
Japan Statistical Association. Annual Report on the Internal Migration in Japan Derived from the Basic Resident Registers (JA) 273
Japan Statistical Association. Annual Report on the Labour Force Survey (JA) 273
Japan Statistical Association. Annual Report on the Retail Price Survey (JA) 273
Japan Statistical Association. Annual Report on the Unincorporated Enterprise Survey (JA) 273
Japan Statistical Yearbook (JA ISSN 0389-9004) 1058
Japan Steel Works Technical News (JA) 798
Japan Sugar Yearbook. (JA) 519
Japan: the Official Guide see New Official Guide: Japan 1114
Japan Times Directory (JA) 310
Japan - Tin in Tinplate (UK) 798
Japan Trade Directory/Nihon Boeki Shinkokai (JA) 310
Japan Typography Annual/Nihon Taipogurafi Nenkan (JA) 931
Japanese Annual Bibliography of Economics (JA ISSN 0911-8004) 1157
Japanese Antarctic Research Expedition Data Reports. (JA ISSN 0075-3343) 380
Japanese Antarctic Research Expedition, 1956-1962. Scientific Reports. Series B: Meteorology see National Institute of Polar Research. Memoirs. Series B: Meteorology 806
Japanese Antarctic Research Expedition, 1956-1962. Scientific Reports. Series C: Earth Sciences. see National Institute of Polar Research. Memoirs. Series C: Earth Sciences 380
Japanese Antarctic Research Expedition, 1956-1962. Scientific Reports. Series D: Oceanography see National Institute of Polar Research. Memoirs. Series D: Oceanography 407

Japanese Antarctic Research Expedition, 1956-1962. Scientific Reports. Series E. Biology see National Institute of Polar Research. Memoirs. Series E: Biology and Medical Science 144
Japanese Antarctic Research Expedition, 1956-1962. Scientific Reports. Series F: Logistic see National Institute of Polar Research. Memoirs. Series F: Logistics 995
Japanese Antarctic Research Expedition, 1956-1962. Scientific Reports. Special Issue see National Institute of Polar Research. Memoirs. Special 380
Japanese Books in Print (Year) (JA) 128
Japanese Bulletin of Art Therapy (JA) 106, 935
Japanese Circulation Journal Supplement (JA) 777
Japanese Collagen Club. Proceedings of the Annual Meeting (JA) 142, 762
Japanese Communist Party. Central Committee. Bulletin: Information for Abroad (JA ISSN 0007-4683) 906
Japanese Economic Statistics see Economic Survey of Japan 243
Japanese Hospital Directory/Byoin Yoran (JA ISSN 0408-0904) 617
Japanese Insurance Business Statistics: Life see Statistics of Life Insurance Business in Japan 641
Japanese Insurance Business Statistics: Non-Life see Statistics of Japanese Non-Life Insurance Business 641
Japanese Literature Today (JA) 724
Japanese Medical Researchers Directory (JA) 762
Japanese National Bibliography/Zen Nihon Shuppanbutsu Somokuroku (JA ISSN 0385-3284) 128
Japanese National Railways. Facts and Figures (JA ISSN 0546-093X) 1094
Japanese National Railways Bulletin see J N R Bulletin 1094
Japanese Neurochemical Society. Bulletin/Shinkei Kagaku (JA) 790
Japanese Nursing Association Research Report (JA ISSN 0911-0844) 784, 848
Japanese Periodicals Index. Humanities and Social Science Section/Zasshi Kiji Sakuin. Jimbun Shakai-hen (JA ISSN 0021-5341) 8, 634, 1014
Japanese Periodicals Index. Science and Technology/Zasshi Kiji Sakuin. Kagaku Gijutsu-hen (JA) 1004
Japanese Phonograph Records of Folk Songs, Classical and Popular Music (JA ISSN 0075-3459) 837
Japanese Report to the International Council on Social Welfare (JA) 1018
Japanese Society for Public Administration. Annals/Nippon Gyosei Kenkyu Nenpo (JA) 943
Japanese Studies in German Language and Literature/Japanische Studien zur deutschen Sprache und Literatur (SZ ISSN 0721-3719) 697, 725
Japanese Studies in the History of Science see Historia Scientiarum 992
Japanese Sword Society of the U.S. Bulletin (US) 79, 106
Japanische Studien zur deutschen Sprache und Literatur see Japanese Studies in German Language and Literature 725
Japan's Bicycle Guide (JA ISSN 0446-6667) 1041
Japan's Economy and Japan-U S Trade (JA) 257
Japan's Economy and Trade see Japan's Economy and Japan-U S Trade 257
Japan's Electronics Almanac and Leading Firms see Japan Electronics Almanac 456
Japan's Iron and Steel Industry (JA ISSN 0075-3475) 798
Jardim Botanico do Rio de Janeiro. Arquivos (BL) 158, 526, 533
Jardin Botanique de Montreal. Annuelle see Jardin Botanique de Montreal. Annuelles et Legumes: Resultats des Cultures d'Essai 533

Jardin Botanique de Montreal. Annuelles et Legumes: Resultats des Cultures d'Essai (CN ISSN 0319-3098) 533
Jarlibro (NE ISSN 0075-3491) 697
Jatuli (FI) 587
Jaune et la Rouge (FR ISSN 0021-5554) 482
Jazykovedne Studie (CS ISSN 0448-9241) 697
Jazz Festivals and Related Major Jazz Events. Directory (DK ISSN 0900-064X) 837
Jazz Index (GW ISSN 0344-5399) 128, 843
Jazz Research see Jazzforschung 837
Jazzforschung/Jazz Research (AU ISSN 0075-3572) 837
Jazzmen's Reference Book (US) 837
Jazzologist (US) 837
Jean-Paul-Gesellschaft. Jahrbuch (GW ISSN 0075-3580) 725
Jebat (MY) 570
Jednota Kalendar see Kalendar Jednota 982
Jefferson Memorial Lecture Series (US ISSN 0075-3599) 607
Jeg Arbejder Med (DK ISSN 0105-8347) 536
Jehovah's Witnesses Yearbook (US ISSN 0075-3602) 984
J'emballe (FR) 855
Jenaer Beitraege zur Parteiegeschichte (GE ISSN 0138-3604) 587
Jeong-Gi Kanhaengmul Kisa Saegin see Korean Periodicals Index 8
Jeopardy (US ISSN 0021-5880) 106, 725, 742
Jernal Antropoloji dan Sosioloji (MY) 73, 1027
Jernal Sains Malaysia see Malaysian Journal of Science 994
Jerome Lectures (US ISSN 0075-3610) 558
Jersey at Home (UI ISSN 0446-7310) 62
Jersey Herd Book and Members Directory (UK) 67
Jerusalem Cathedra see Cathedra 612
Jerusalem Chamber of Commerce. Bulletin (IS ISSN 0447-6719) 1157
Jerusalem Conference on Accountancy (IS) 221
Jerusalem Historical Medical Publications see Koroth 771
Jerusalem Institute for Israel Studies. Discussion Papers (IS ISSN 0333-9831) 630, 906, 1009
Jerusalem Letter (IS ISSN 0334-4096) 504
Jerusalem Papers on Peace Problems (IS ISSN 0334-2786) 906, 917
Jerusalem Symposia on Quantum Chemistry and Biochemistry (NE ISSN 0075-3696) 332
Jerusalem Urban Studies (IS) 623, 1027
Jescheidenis van Wortel (Hoogstratens Oudheidkundige Kring) (BE) 88, 587
Jeunesse du Vietnam see Vietnam Youth 540
Jeux et Jouets (CN ISSN 0713-4118) 553
Jewellers' Reference Book (UK) 644
Jewelry Fashion Guide (US) 644
Jewish Book Annual (US ISSN 0075-3726) 976
Jewish Boston (US ISSN 0085-2368) 504
Jewish Boston and New England Jewry see Jewish Boston 504
Jewish Braille Institute of America. Directory of Services (US) 180
Jewish Civilization: Essays and Studies (US ISSN 0191-3034) 504
Jewish Community Handbook (US) 504
Jewish Federations, Welfare Funds and Community Councils Directory see Directory of Jewish Federations, Welfare Funds and Community Councils 1017
Jewish Heritage Libraries. Ethnic Studies Institute. Year End Report (US) 504
Jewish Historical Society of England. Annual Report and Accounts for the Session (UK ISSN 0306-7998) 976

Jewish Historical Society of England.
Report and Balance Sheet see Jewish
Historical Society of England.
Annual Report and Accounts for the
Session 976
Jewish Historical Society of England.
Transactions (UK) 976
Jewish Historical Society of New York.
Publications (US) 504
Jewish Historical Society of Western
Canada. Annual Publication (CN
ISSN 0317-1655) 504
Jewish Language Review (IS ISSN
0333-8347) 504, 697, 725, 976
Jewish Law Annual (NE) 657, 976
Jewish Law Annual Supplements (NE)
504, 658
Jewish National Fund Illustrated see J
N F Illustrated 943
Jewish Proclaimer (US) 504, 976
Jewish Social Service Yearbook (US
ISSN 0075-3742) 1157
Jewish Social Work Forum (US ISSN
0021-6712) 1018
Jewish Studies (US) 504
Jewish Travel Guide (UK ISSN 0075-
3750) 1112
Jewish Year Book (UK ISSN 0075-
3769) 976
Jews and the Jewish People (IS ISSN
0021-6895) 906
Jews of the Soviet Union (IS ISSN
0334-0953) 913, 976
Jezykoznawstwo Stosowane/Applied
Linguistics (PL ISSN 0137-1444)
697
Jiddah Chamber of Commerce &
Industry Annual Trade Directory
(US) 1157
Jidische Schtudies (GW ISSN 0720-
6666) 697, 725
Jimbun (JA ISSN 0084-5515) 630
Jimbun Gakuho see Journal of Social
Sciences and Humanities 1009
Jisunu (BO) 73
Jizni Morava (CS ISSN 0449-0436)
587
Joachim-Junglus-Gesellschaft der
Wissenschaften, Hamburg.
Veroeffentlichungen (GW) 993
Joanneum. Museum fuer Bergbau,
Geologie und Technik. Mitteilungen
see Landesmuseum Joanneum.
Abteilung fuer Geologie,
Palaeontologie und Bergbau.
Mitteilungen 856
Job Catalog (US ISSN 0278-5706)
848
Job Market (US) 848
Job Service North Dakota. Annual
Report (US) 273
Job Service North Dakota. Biennial
Report to the Governor (US) 273
Jobs in the 'Gap' Year (UK) 848
Jobson's Investment Digest of Australia
and New Zealand see Jobson's Year
Book of Public Companies 267
Jobson's Liquor Handbook (US) 120
Jobson's Mining Year Book (AT ISSN
0075-3777) 817
Jobson's Wine Marketing Handbook
(US) 120
Jobson's Year Book of Public
Companies (AT ISSN 0075-3785)
267
Jodhpur Management Journal (II) 280
Jodrell Laboratory. Notes (UK) 158
Joedisk Plevy (DK ISSN 0107-7333)
504
Johannes-Kepler-Hochschule Linz.
Dissertationen see Johannes-Kepler-
Universitaet Linz. Dissertationen
993
Johannes-Kepler-Universitaet Linz.
Dissertationen (AU ISSN 0259-
0689) 993
Johannesburg Public Library. Annual
Report (SA) 680
Johari za Kiswahili (KE ISSN 0449-
0738) 742
John Alexander Monograph Series on
Various Phases of Thoracic Surgery
(US ISSN 0075-3815) 794
John Clare Society Journal (UK) 725,
742
John Jay College of Criminal Justice.
Criminal Justice Center.
Monographs(US) 371

John Marshall Journal of Practice and
Procedure see John Marshall Law
Review 658
John Marshall Law Review (US ISSN
0270-854X) 658
John Wilcock's Secret Diary see Other
Scenes 712
Johns Hopkins Oceanographic Studies
(US ISSN 0075-3858) 406
Johns Hopkins Series in Integration and
Community Building in Eastern
Europe (US ISSN 0075-3866) 1157
Johns Hopkins Studies in Atlantic
History and Culture (US) 607
Johns Hopkins Studies in the History of
Technology (US) 1069
Johns Hopkins Symposia in
Comparative History (US ISSN
0075-3874) 558
Johns Hopkins University. Population
Information Program. Population
Reports. Arabic Edition (US) 923
Johns Hopkins University Studies in
Geology (US ISSN 0075-3890) 390
Johns Hopkins University Studies in
Historical and Political Science (US
ISSN 0075-3904) 558, 906
Johnsonia (US ISSN 0075-3920) 175
Joint A S M E/I E E E/A A R
Railroad Conference. I E E E
Technical Papers see Joint A S M E/
I E E E Railroad Conference. I E E
E Technical Papers 1094
Joint A S M E/I E E E Railroad
Conference. I E E E Technical
Papers (US) 1094
Joint A S M E/I E E E Railroad
Technical Conference. I E E E
Papers see Joint A S M E/I E E E
Railroad Conference. I E E E
Technical Papers 1094
Joint Automatic Control Conference.
Record see American Control
Conference. Conference Proceedings
450
Joint Center for Urban Studies.
Publications (US ISSN 0075-3947)
624
Joint Conference of the I E E E
Computer and Communications
Societies see I E E E Infocom.
Proceedings 346
Joint Conference on Applications of Air
Pollution Meteorology (Publication)
(US) 805
Joint Conference on Fire and Forest
Meteorology. (Publication) (US) 805
Joint F A O/W H O Codex
Alimentarius Commission. Report of
the Session (UN ISSN 0449-122X)
519, 954
Joint Financial Management
Improvement Program. Annual
Report (US) 280
Joint Governmental Salary Survey:
Arizona (US) 273
Joint I E E E/A S M E Railroad
Conference see Joint A S M E/I E E
E Railroad Conference. I E E E
Technical Papers 1094
Joint Institute for Laboratory
Astrophysics Data Center. Report
see J I L A Data Center. Report
897
Joint Nuclear Research Center, Ispra,
Italy. Annual Report (EI) 897
Joint Railroad Conference. I E E E
Papers see Joint A S M E/I E E E
Railroad Conference. I E E E
Technical Papers 1094
Joint Railroad Technical Conference.
Preprint see Joint A S M E/I E E E
Railroad Conference. I E E E
Technical Papers 1094
Joint Serials Catalogue of Western
Australian Academic Libraries (AT
ISSN 0726-9587) 680
Jokull (IC ISSN 0449-0576) 390,
400, 403
Jordan. Department of Statistics.
Agricultural Statistical Yearbook and
Agricultural Sample Survey (JO) 30
Jordan. Department of Statistics.
Annual Statistical Yearbook (JO
ISSN 0075-4013) 1058
Jordan. Department of Statistics.
External Trade Statistics (JO ISSN
0075-4021) 212

Jordan. Department of Statistics.
National Accounts (JO ISSN 0449-
1513) 277
Jordan. Ministry of Tourism and
Antiquities. Tourism Annual Report
(JO) 1157
Jordan. Ministry of Tourism and
Antiquities. Tourist Arrivals in
Numbers (JO) 1112
Jordan. Ministry of Tourism and
Antiquities. Travel Statistics see
Jordan. Ministry of Tourism and
Antiquities. Tourist Arrivals in
Numbers 1112
Jordanian National Bibliography (JO)
128, 613
Jordbrug (DK ISSN 0108-884X) 30
Jornadas Nacionales de Derecho
Aeronautico y Espacial. Trabajos
(AG) 20, 658, 1089
Joseph Haas Gesellschaft.
Mitteilungensblatt (GW ISSN 0446-
9577) 837
Joseph I. Lubin Memorial Lectures
(US) 196
Jouets et Jeux (FR ISSN 0075-4056)
553
Jouko (FI) 587
Journal Annuel de la Societe Historique
de la Vallee de la Chateauguay see
Chateauguay Valley Historical
Society Annual Journal 604
Journal Contents in Quantitative
Methods (UK ISSN 0142-5951)
212, 230, 284
Journal de l'Annee (FR ISSN 0449-
4733) 463
Journal des Employes Publics see Public
Employees Journal 945
Journal for Photogrammetrists &
Surveyors (GE) 482
Journal for the Protection of All
Beings(US ISSN 0075-4099) 1157
Journal for the Study of the New
Testament. Supplement Series (UK
ISSN 0143-5108) 970
Journal for the Study of the Old
Testament. Supplement Series (UK
ISSN 0309-0787) 970
Journal Francais d'Orthoptique (FR
ISSN 0240-7914) 786
Journal Holdings in the Washington-
Baltimore Area (US ISSN 0362-
4544) 680
Journal McIlvanea see McIlvainea 159
Journal of Abstracts in International
Education (US ISSN 0094-2383) 8,
424
Journal of Accounting Research.
Supplement (US) 221
Journal of Adult Education (TZ ISSN
0856-1109) 427
Journal of African Studies/Afurika
Kenkyu (JA ISSN 0065-4140) 566
Journal of Aging and Judaism (US
ISSN 0884-8688) 552
Journal of Agricultural Science in
Finland (FI ISSN 0782-4386) 30
Journal of Agronomic Education (US
ISSN 0094-2391) 57, 448
Journal of Ancient and Medieval
Studies (US) 536
Journal of Ancient Indian History (II
ISSN 0075-4110) 570
Journal of Animal Science. Supplement
(US ISSN 0075-4129) 67, 1122
Journal of Anthropology at McMaster
see Nexus 74
Journal of Applied Polymer Science.
Symposia (US ISSN 0570-4898)
478
Journal of Applied Systems Analysis
(UK ISSN 0308-9541) 238, 359
Journal of Aquariculture see
Aquariculture and Aquatic Sciences.
Journal 138
Journal of Arabic Literature (NE ISSN
0085-2376) 725, 852
Journal of Archaeology in Andhra
Pradesh (II) 88
Journal of Asian Culture (US ISSN
0162-6795) 852
Journal of Astrological Studies (US
ISSN 0085-2384) 114
Journal of Australian Political
Economy(AT) 246, 252
Journal of Ballistics (US ISSN 0146-
4140) 323, 492

Journal of Beckett Studies (UK ISSN
0309-5207) 725, 1077
Journal of Biodynamic Psychology (UK
ISSN 0143-1218) 935
Journal of Byelorussian Studies (UK
ISSN 0075-4161) 587
Journal of Canadian Poetry (CN ISSN
0705-1328) 742
Journal of Cardiovascular Surgery.
Congress Proceedings (IT) 794
Journal of Chemical Industry and
Engineering China (CC) 479
Journal of Chinese Art History see
Soochow University Journal of
Chinese Art History 110
Journal of Chinese Religions (US) 852,
977
Journal of Chromatography Library
(NE) 326
Journal of Civil Procedure/Minji Sosho
Zasshi (JA ISSN 0075-4188) 658
Journal of Classical Studies/Seiyo
Kotengaku Kenkyu (JA ISSN 0582-
4524) 337
Journal of Clinical Reading: Research
and Programs (US) 448
Journal of Commerce Transportation
Telephone Tickler see Transportation
Telephone Tickler 318
Journal of Comparative Sociology &
Religion (CN ISSN 0709-3519)
970, 1027
Journal of Crime & Justice (US ISSN
0735-648X) 371, 658
Journal of Croatian Studies (US ISSN
0075-4218) 587, 711
Journal of Cultural Sciences/Bunka
Kagaku Kiyo (JA ISSN 0521-7903)
630
Journal of Cultural Sciences see
Tokushima University. Journal of
Gakugei 632
Journal of Current Laser Abstracts (US
ISSN 0022-0264) 8, 389
Journal of Cytology and Genetics (II
ISSN 0253-7605) 167, 762
Journal of Danish Archaeology (DK
ISSN 0108-464X) 88
Journal of Development Planning (UN
ISSN 0085-2392) 263
Journal of Digital Systems see
Advances in V L S I and Computer
Systems 361
Journal of Documentation (UK ISSN
0022-0418) 680
Journal of Drug Research see Journal of
Drug Research of Egypt 871
Journal of Drug Research of Egypt (UA
ISSN 0085-2406) 871
Journal of Earth Sciences (JA ISSN
0022-0442) 380
Journal of Economic and Taxonomic
Botany see Journal of Plant Anatomy
and Morphology 158
Journal of Economic Reflections (TZ)
196
Journal of Economics (Vermillion) (US
ISSN 0361-6576) 196
Journal of Education in Museums (UK
ISSN 0260-9126) 828
Journal of Educational Research/Jurnal
Pendidikan (MY) 415
Journal of Egyptian Archaeology (UK
ISSN 0307-5133) 88
Journal of Electroanalytical Chemistry
see Journal of Electroanalytical
Chemistry and Interfacial
Electrochemistry 326
Journal of Electroanalytical Chemistry
and Interfacial Electrochemistry (SZ
ISSN 0022-0728) 326
Journal of Energy Engineering (US
ISSN 0733-9402) 482
Journal of Experimental Animal Science
see Zeitschrift fuer Versuchstierkunde
782
Journal of Ferrocement (TH ISSN
0125-1759) 185
Journal of Financial Education (US
ISSN 0093-3961) 230, 436
Journal of Freshwater Ecology (US
ISSN 0270-5060) 403, 497
Journal of Geological Sciences:
Anthropozoic see Sbornik
Geologickych Ved: Antropozoikum
394

Journal of Geological Sciences: Applied Geophysics see Sbornik Geologickych Ved: Uzita Geofyzika 401
Journal of Geological Sciences: Economic Geology, Mineralogy see Sbornik Geologickych Ved: Loziskova Geologie, Mineralogie 394
Journal of Geological Sciences: Geology see Sbornik Geologickych Ved: Geologie 394
Journal of Geological Sciences: Hydrogeology, Engineering Geology see Sbornik Geologickych Ved: Hydrogeologie, Inzenyrska Geologie 404
Journal of Geological Sciences: Paleontology see Sbornik Geologickych Ved: Paleontologie 857
Journal of Geological Sciences: Technology, Geochemistry see Sbornik Geologickych Ved: Technologie, Geochemie 394
Journal of Geosciences/Osaka-shiritsu Daigaku Rigakubu Chigaku Kiyo (JA ISSN 0449-2560) 380
Journal of German-American Studies see Yearbook of German-American Studies 738
Journal of Glass Studies (US ISSN 0075-4250) 113
Journal of Hellenic Studies (UK ISSN 0075-4269) 337, 697
Journal of Himalayan Studies and Regional Development (II ISSN 0250-8346) 73, 263, 497
Journal of Historic Madison, Inc. of Wisconsin see Historic Madison. Journal 606
Journal of History and Political Science see Journal of Political Science 906
Journal of Human Communications Research (US) 346, 634
Journal of Indian Museums (II) 828
Journal of Indo-European Studies Monograph Series (US) 1009
Journal of Industry and Management/ Sangyo Keiei Kenkyushoho (JA) 280
Journal of Inferential and Deductive Biology (US ISSN 0883-1394) 142
Journal of Intercultural Studies (JA ISSN 0388-0508) 1009
Journal of International Relations (TZ) 917
Journal of Jazz Studies see Annual Review of Jazz Studies 832
Journal of Jewish Art (NE ISSN 0160-208X) 106, 976
Journal of Jewish Lore and Philosophy see Hebrew Union College Annual 503
Journal of Jewish Music and Liturgy (US ISSN 0197-0100) 837, 976
Journal of Juristic Papyrology (PL ISSN 0075-4277) 88, 658
Journal of Karyopathology/Saibokaku Byorigaku Zasshi (JA ISSN 0022-2119) 775
Journal of Law and Politics/Daito Hogaku (JA) 658
Journal of Legal Pluralism and Unofficial Law (US ISSN 0732-9113) 658
Journal of Magic History (US ISSN 0192-9917) 614, 1034, 1077
Journal of Maltese Studies (MM ISSN 0075-4285) 588
Journal of Marketing and Public Policy see Journal of Public Policy & Marketing 284
Journal of Marketing for Higher Education (US) 284, 436
Journal of Mathematics (JA ISSN 0075-4293) 749
Journal of Medical Entomology. Supplement (US ISSN 0146-6631) 165
Journal of Methods-Time Measurement see M T M 280
Journal of Middle Atlantic Archaeology(US ISSN 0883-9697) 88
Journal of Mormon History (US ISSN 0094-7342) 984
Journal of Muscle Shoals History (US ISSN 0094-8039) 607

Journal of Music Scores see A S U C Journal of Music Scores 832
Journal of Natural Science (JA ISSN 0075-4307) 993
Journal of Neural Transmission. Supplement (US ISSN 0303-6995) 790
Journal of Neuro-Visceral Relations. Supplement see Journal of Neural Transmission. Supplement 790
Journal of New Jersey Poets (US ISSN 0363-4205) 742
Journal of New World Archaeology (US ISSN 0147-9024) 88
Journal of Notarial Acts and Recordkeeping Practices (US) 658
Journal of Occult Studies see Metascience Annual 860
Journal of Oriental Research (II ISSN 0022-3301) 852
Journal of Our Time (CN ISSN 0381-6524) 725, 879
Journal of Outdoor Education (US ISSN 0022-3336) 415
Journal of Pastoral Psychotherapy (US ISSN 0886-5477) 935, 970
Journal of Pediatric Endocrinology (IS) 781, 787
Journal of Periodontal Research. Supplementum (DK ISSN 0075-4331) 779
Journal of Plant Anatomy and Morphology (II ISSN 0256-436X) 158
Journal of Plant Physiology (GW) 158
Journal of Political Science (PK) 570, 906
Journal of Polymer Science. Part C Polymer Symposia see Journal of Polymer Science. Polymer Symposia Edition 330
Journal of Polymer Science. Polymer Symposia Edition (US ISSN 0360-8905) 330
Journal of Probation and Parole (US ISSN 0278-1042) 371
Journal of Psychoanalysis in Groups see Groups: a Journal of Group Dynamics and Psychotherapy 934
Journal of Public Communication see Journal of Public Communication and Membership Directory 646
Journal of Public Communication and Membership Directory (US) 646
Journal of Public Policy & Marketing (US) 284
Journal of Pure and Applied Sciences/ Temel ve Uygulamali Bilmler Dergisi(TU ISSN 0022-4057) 993, 1069
Journal of Roman Studies (UK ISSN 0075-4358) 338
Journal of Scandinavian Folklore see Arv 515
Journal of Seed Technology (US ISSN 0146-3071) 30
Journal of Separation Process Technology (UK ISSN 0260-6275) 479
Journal of Shellfish Research (US ISSN 0730-8000) 175
Journal of Social and Political Studies Monograph Series (US) 906
Journal of Social Sciences (JA) 1009
Journal of Social Sciences and Humanities/Jimbun Gakuho (JA) 1009
Journal of Soil and Water Conservation in India (II ISSN 0022-457X) 30, 365, 1125
Journal of Southwest Georgia History (US ISSN 0739-1943) 607
Journal of Stained Glass (UK) 113
Journal of Studies in the Bhagavadgita (AT ISSN 0706-6449) 977
Journal of Studies on Alcohol. Supplement (US ISSN 0363-468X) 377
Journal of Supervision and Training in Ministry (US ISSN 0160-7774) 970
Journal of Surveying and Mapping see Journal of Surveying Engineering 482
Journal of Surveying Engineering (US ISSN 0733-9453) 482
Journal of Teaching in Social Work (US ISSN 0884-1233) 448, 1018
Journal of the Alleghenies (US ISSN 0276-7449) 607

Journal of the American Musical Instrument Society see American Musical Instrument Society. Journal 832
Journal of the Graduate Music Students at the Ohio State University (US ISSN 0364-2216) 837
Journal of the Legal Profession (US) 658
Journal of the Midwest History of Education Society see Midwest History of Education Society. Journal 416
Journal of the Nepal Research Centre (GW ISSN 0720-6615) 852
Journal of the Philosophy of Sport (US ISSN 0094-8705) 879, 1034
Journal of the St. Clair County Historical Society see St. Clair County Historical Society. Journal 609
Journal of the Short Story in English (FR) 725
Journal of the Theory and Criticism of the Visual Arts (US) 106
Journal of the Warburg and Courtauld Institutes (UK ISSN 0075-4390) 630
Journal of Turkish Studies (US) 613
Journal of Turkish Studies (Duxbury)/ Turkluk Bilgisi Arastirmalari (US) 613
Journal of U F O Studies (US) 20
Journal of Ultrastructure Research. Supplement (US ISSN 0075-4404) 142
Journal of Urban Affairs (US) 624
Journal of Urban Planning and Development (US ISSN 0733-9488) 482, 624
Journal of V L S I and Computer Systems see Advances in V L S I and Computer Systems 361
Journal of Weather Modification (US ISSN 0739-1781) 805
Journal Officiel de la Republique de Djibouti (FT) 943
Journal Subcelluar Biochemistry see Sub Cellular Biochemistry 152
Journalism Abstracts (US ISSN 0075-4412) 646
Journalism and Mass Communication Directory (US) 430, 646
Journalism Career and Scholarship Guide (US) 430, 646
Journalism Career Guide for Minorities (US) 646, 848
Journalism Scholarship Guide see Journalism Career and Scholarship Guide 646
Journalism Yearbook (IS ISSN 0334-2948) 646
Journalist (NE ISSN 0022-555X) 646
Journalisten - Handbuch (GW) 646
Journalisten Jahrbuch (GW ISSN 0176-9707) 344, 646
Journalistenhandbuch Entwicklungspolitik (GW) 263
Journals of Dissent and Social Change (US) 912, 1031
Journee de Reeducation (FR ISSN 0075-4420) 445
Journees Annuelles de Diabetologie de l'Hotel Dieu (FR ISSN 0075-4439) 781
Journees Biochimiques Latines. Rapports (IT ISSN 0075-4447) 152
Journees de Physiologie Appliquee au Travail Humain (FR ISSN 0075-4455) 172
Journees de Strasbourg (FR) 116
Journees Internationales d'Etude du Baroque. Actes see Baroque 716
Journees Internationales d'Etudes du Baroque see Baroque 716
Journees Parisiennes de Pediatrie (FR ISSN 0075-4471) 787
Judaica Iberoamericana (CL) 73, 504
Judean Desert Studies (IS ISSN 0075-4501) 88
Judicial Staff Directory (US) 658, 943
Judicial Statistics see Michigan. State Court Administrator. Annual Report 669
Jugendherbergs-Verzeichnis (GW ISSN 0075-4528) 545
Jugopetrol, Trgovinsko Preduzece za Promet Nafte i Naftinih Derivata. Bilten (YU) 865

Jugoslavenska Akademija Znanosti i Umjetnosti. Historijski Institut, Dubrovnik. Anali. (YU ISSN 0449-3648) 588
Jugoslavenske Akademije Znanosti i Umjetnosti. Razred za Prirodne Znanosti. Rad (YU ISSN 0351-3297) 142, 390
Juifs Celebres see Sir Moses Montefiore Collections des Juifs Celebres 972
Jul i Frederikssund (DK ISSN 0107-5446) 588
Jul i Lejre (DK ISSN 0108-2965) 588
Jul i Nordsjaelland see Folk og Minder fra Nordsjaelland 582
Jul i Skive see Skive-egnens Jul 596
Julehilsen (DK ISSN 0107-8887) 415
Jules Verne Voyages (UK) 14
Julian Block's Guide to Year-Round Tax Savings (US) 1157
Julius C. Stevens Annual Lectures in Education (LB) 415
Jump Cut (US ISSN 0146-5546) 824
Junction (US) 742
Junction Magazine see Brooklyn Review 717
Junior Authors and Illustrators Series (US) 106, 333, 646
Junior College Research Review see Junior College Resource Review 436
Junior College Resource Review (US) 436
Junior High School Library Catalog (US) 680
Junta de Estudios Historicos de Mendoza. Revista (AG ISSN 0076-6380) 607
Junta de Investigacoes Cientifica do Ultramar. Memorias see Instituto de Investigacao Cientifica Tropical. Memorias 379
Junta de Investigacoes Cientificas do Ultramar. Bibliografia Cientifica see Instituto de Investigacao Cientifica Tropical. Bibliografia Cientifica 1155
Junta del Acuerdo de Cartagena. Publicaciones (PE) 246
Junta Nacional dos Produtos Pecuarios. Publicacoes (PO) 30
Juntendo University, Tokyo. Medical Ultrasonics Research Center. Annual Report (JA ISSN 0075-4579) 762
Juridica (MX) 658
Jurisprudencia Aragonesa. (SP) 658
Jurisprudencia Argentina (AG) 658
Juristische Abhandlungen (GW ISSN 0449-4342) 658
Jurnal Pendidikan see Journal of Educational Research 415
Just a Bite (UK) 620
Just B'twx Us: An Interlibrary Loan Information Bulletin (US) 680
Just B'twx Us: An Interlibrary Loan Newsletter see Just B'twx Us: An Interlibrary Loan Information Bulletin 680
Justice - Directory of Services/Justice - Repertoire des Services (CN ISSN 0225-4115) 1018
Justice Expenditure and Employment Data in the U.S. see Justice Expenditure and Employment in the U.S 371
Justice Expenditure and Employment in the U.S. (US) 371
Justice in America Series (US) 371, 658
Justice in Urban America Series see Justice in America Series 658
Justice Institute of British Columbia. Annual Report (CN) 436, 658
Justice - Repertoire des Services see Justice - Directory of Services 1018
Justiz in Zahlen (GW) 1058
Jusur (US ISSN 0888-9007) 613, 975
Jutaku Sangyo Handbook (JA) 624
Jutaku Sangyo Handobukku see Jutaku Sangyo Handbook 624
Jutland Archaeological Society. Publications see Jysk Arkaeologisk Selskabs. Skrifter 588
Juvenile and Adult Correctional Departments, Institutions, Agencies, and Paroling Authorities of the United States and Canada (US ISSN 0190-2555) 371

Jysk Arkaeologisk Selskabs. Skrifter/ Jutland Archaeological Society. Publications (DK ISSN 0107-2854) 88, *588*

Jyvaskyla Studies in Computer Science, Economics and Statistics (FI ISSN 0357-9921) 238, *352*

Jyvaskyla Studies in Education, Psychology and Social Research (FI ISSN 0075-4625) 415, *935*

Jyvaskyla Studies in the Arts (FI ISSN 0075-4633) *106*, 725

Jyvaskylan Yliopisto. Department of Physics. Research Report (FI ISSN 0075-465X) *889*

Jyvaskylan Yliopisto. Matematiikan Laitos. Report (FI ISSN 0075-4641) *749*

K A C Research Series (Kampsville Archaeological Center) (US) *88*

K B D see Australian Key Business Directory *302*

K B S Anvisningar/K B S Directions see K B S Tekniska Foereskrifter *624*

K B S-Rapporter (SW ISSN 0022-7293) 482, *624*

K B S Technical Regulations see K B S Tekniska Foereskrifter *624*

K B S Tekniska Foereskrifter/K B S Technical Regulations (SW) 185, 482, *624*

K G I Preprint see Kiruna Geophysical Institute. Preprint *400*

K G I Scientific Report see Kiruna Geophysical Institute. Scientific Report *400*

K G I Software Report see Kiruna Geophysical Institute. Software Report *400*

K G I Technical Report see Kiruna Geophysical Institute. Technical Report *400*

K G S - N C I C Newsletter (Kentucky Geological Survey) (U.S. National Cartographic Information Center) (US) *545*

K I A Occasional Papers (Kenya Institute of Administration) (KE ISSN 0075-5761) *943*

K I R D I Annual Report and Statement of Accounts (Kenya Industrial Research and Development Institute) (KE) *239*

K J E S see Kakatiya Journal of English Studies *725*

K K C Brief (JA) 196, *246*

K L M News (NE ISSN 0022-7374) *1089*

K N A A S News see Kenya National Academy for Advancement of Arts and Sciences. Newsletter *993*

K S M Review (Kerjasama Serbaguna Malaysia) (MY) *30*

K T (DK ISSN 0109-890X) *906*

K T B L - Schriften (Kuratorium fuer Technik und Bauwesen in der Landwirtschaft e.V.) (GW) *30*

K V I C Annual Report (Khadi and Village Industries Commission) (II) *301*

Kacic (YU ISSN 0453-0578) *588*, 970

Kaduna State. Ministry of Works. Report (NR) *943*

Kaduna State Statistical Yearbook (NR) *1058*

Kaerntner Gemeindeblatt (AU ISSN 0022-7552) *951*

Kaerntner Heimatleben (AU ISSN 0022-7560) *516*

Kaerntner Museumsschriften (AU ISSN 0022-7587) *106*, 558, 828

Kaerntner Naturschutzblaetter (AU ISSN 0022-7595) *365*

Kagai Keizai Kyoryoku Kikin Nenpo see Overseas Economic Cooperation Fund. Annual Report *263*

Kagaku Keisatsu Kenkyusho Nenpo see National Research Institute of Police Science. Annual Report *371*

Kagawa Prefective Agricultural Experiment Station. Bulletin (JA ISSN 0374-8804) 30, *142*

Kaigai Kogyo Jijo Chosa Hokokusho: Indo, Pakisutan, Bangurasisshu see Report of Overseas Mining Investigation: India, Pakistan, Bangladesh *820*

Kaigai Kogyo Jijo Chosa Hokokusho: Madagasukaru, Suwajirando see Report of Overseas Mining Investigation: Madagascar, Swaziland *820*

Kaigaki Kagaku Gijutsu Joho Shiryo see Scientific and Technical Information in Foreign Countries *1000*

Kaigan Kogaku Koenkai Ronbunshu/ Proceedings of the Japanese Conference on Coastal Engineering (JA) *482*

Kaikuja Hameesta (FI) *588*

Kairi (TR) *711*

Kaiser Foundation Medical Care Program. Annual Report (US ISSN 0075-4668) *954*

Kaiyo Chosa Gyogyo Shiken Yoho see Hokkaido University. Faculty of Fisheries. Data Record of Oceanographic Observations and Exploratory Fishing *406*

Kaiyo Kaihatsu Ronbunshu/Proceedings of the Ocean Development Symposium (JA) *482*

Kakatiya Journal of English Studies (II) *725*

Kaktusbluete (GW) 333, *1112*

Kalaallit Nunaata Imartaant Aalisarneq Aalisarnikkullu Mississuisut. Suliarisimasaat see Fiskeriet ved Groenland & Groenlands Fiskeriundersoegelsers Aktivitet *509*

Kalamanakaranaya (CE) *280*

Kalastuspaikkaopas (FI ISSN 0075-4684) *1034*

Kalatdlit Nunane Inuit see Groenlands Befolkning *922*

Kalatdlitnunane Augtitagssanik Atortugssiagssiat Pivdlugit. Faellesraadet Naluaeruit see Faellesraadet Vedroerende Mineraliske Raastoffer i Groenland. Beretning *816*

Kalava Ha Sahityaya (CE) *106*, 725

Kaldron (US) *106*, 742

Kale Memorial Lectures see R.B.R.R. Kale Memorial Lectures *908*

Kalendar-Al'manakh Novoho Shliakhu/ New Pathway Almanac (CN) *504*

Kalendar Jednota (US) *982*

Kalendar Odborara (CS) *648*, 796

Kalendarz Robotniczy see Informator Robotniczy *642*

Kalendarz Slowa Bozego (PL ISSN 0860-410X) *982*

Kalevalaseuran Vuosikirja (FI ISSN 0355-0311) *725*

Al-Kalima (YE) *711*

Kalininskii Nauchno-issledovatel'skii Institut Tekstil'noi Promyshlennosti. Nauchno-issledovatel'skie Trudy (UR) *1074*

Kalki (US ISSN 0022-7994) *725*

Kalmia (US ISSN 0453-1388) *158*

Kalnirnay (II) *114*, 615

Kalulu (MW) 73, *725*

Kalyani (CE) *630*, 1009

Kamar Dagang dan Industri di Jawa Barat. Daftar Anggota see Chamber of Commerce and Industry in West Java. Member List *235*

Kamer van Koophandel en Fabrieken voor Amsterdam. Jaarrede (NE) *236*

Kampsville Seminars in Archeology (US) *88*

Kanagawa Association of Psychiatry. Journal see Kanagawa-ken Seishin Igakkaishi *790*

Kanagawa Dental College. Bulletin (JA ISSN 0385-1443) *779*

Kanagawa Horticultural Experiment Station. Bulletin (JA ISSN 0374-8731) *533*

Kanagawa-ken Seishin Igakkaishi/ Kanagawa Association of Psychiatry. Journal (JA ISSN 0288-9617) *790*

Kanagawa University. Institute of Humanities. Bulletin (JA) *630*

Kanan (PE) *725*

Kanazawa Daigaku Kyoikugakubu Kiyo, Shizenkagaku- Hen see Kanazawa University. Faculty of Education. Bulletin: Natural Science *993*

Kanazawa Daigaku Kyoyobu Ronshu, Shizenkagaku- Hen see Kanazawa University. College of Liberal Arts. Annals of Science *993*

Kanazawa University. College of Liberal Arts. Annals of Science/Kanazawa Daigaku Kyoyobu Ronshu, Shizenkagaku- Hen (JA ISSN 0302-0479) *993*

Kanazawa University. Faculty of Education. Bulletin: Humanities, Social and Educational Sciences (JA) *415*

Kanazawa University. Faculty of Education. Bulletin: Natural Science/ Kanazawa Daigaku Kyoikugakubu Kiyo, Shizenkagaku- Hen (JA) *993*

Kanazawa University. Faculty of Law and Literature. Studies and Essays (JA ISSN 0453-1981) 658, *725*

Kankyo Mondai Shinpojumu Koen Ronbunshu/Proceedings of the Symposium on Environmental Problems (JA) *482*, 497

Kano State of Nigeria Gazette (NR) 658, *943*

Kano State Statistical Year Book (NR) *1058*

Kano Studies (NR) *1027*

Kanon (AU ISSN 0259-0727) *658*, 970

Kansai Daigaku Kogaku Kenkyu Hokoku see Kansai University Technology Reports *1069*

Kansai University Technology Reports/ Kansai Daigaku Kogaku Kenkyu Hokoku (JA ISSN 0453-2198) *1069*

Kansainvalinen Automatkailu see Autolla Ulkomaille *1106*

Kansas. Department of Health and Environment. Annual Summary of Vital Statistics (US) *923*

Kansas. Juvenile Justice Information Center. Annual Report (US) *371*

Kansas. State Board of Agriculture. Annual Report with Farm Facts (US) *30*

Kansas. State Board of Agriculture. Report see Kansas. State Board of Agriculture. Annual Report with Farm Facts *30*

Kansas. State Conservation Commission. Conservation in Kansas see Conservation in Kansas *364*

Kansas Agriculture Report see Kansas. State Board of Agriculture. Annual Report with Farm Facts *30*

Kansas City Grocer Annual Food Industry Directory (US) *522*

Kansas Corn Performance Tests (US) *63*

Kansas Geological Survey. Basic Data Series. Ground-Water Releases (US) *403*

Kansas Geological Survey. Bulletin (US) *390*

Kansas Geological Survey. Chemical Quality Series (US) *390*

Kansas Geological Survey. Educational Series (US) *390*

Kansas Geological Survey. Energy Resources Series (US) 380, *465*

Kansas Geological Survey. Geology Series (US) *390*

Kansas Geological Survey. Ground Water Series (US) *403*

Kansas Geological Survey. Short Papers in Research (US ISSN 0075-4935) *390*

Kansas Geological Survey. Subsurface Geology Series (US) *390*

Kansas Grain Sorghum Performance Tests see Kansas Sorghum Performance Tests. Grain & Forage *63*

Kansas Justice Information System. Resource Directory (Year) (US) *658*

Kansas Sorghum Performance Tests. Grain & Forage (US) *63*

Kansas State Industrial Directory see MacRae's Kansas State Industrial Directory *312*

Kansas State University. Center for Energy Studies. Report (US ISSN 0145-0093) *1157*

Kansas State University. Food and Feed Grain Institute. Technical Assistance in Food Grain Drying, Storage, Handling and Transportation see Kansas State University. Food and Feed Grain Institute. Technical Assistance in Grain Storage, Processing and Marketing, and Agribusiness Development *63*

Kansas State University. Food and Feed Grain Institute. Technical Assistance in Grain Storage, Processing and Marketing, and Agribusiness Development (US) *63*

Kansas State University. Library Bibliography Series (US ISSN 0075-4951) *128*

Kansas Water Resources Research Institute. Annual Report (US ISSN 0160-2659) *1125*

Kansatieteellinen Arkisto (FI ISSN 0355-1830) *73*

Kansokujo Kisho Nenpo (JA) *805*

Kappa Pi International Honorary Art Fraternity. Sketch Book see Sketch Book *110*

Kappa Tau Alpha. Newsletter (US) *646*

Karachi. Chamber of Commerce and Industry. Annual Report (PK ISSN 0075-5079) *236*

Karachi. Chamber of Commerce and Industry. Guide for Industrial Investment in Pakistan (PK) *267*

Karachi. Chamber of Commerce and Industry. Pattern of Foreign Trade of Pakistan (PK) *257*

Karachi. Chamber of Commerce and Industry. Report see Karachi. Chamber of Commerce and Industry. Annual Report *236*

Karachi Port Trust. Year Book of Information, Port of Karachi, Pakistan (PK ISSN 0075-5109) *1082*

Karakul (SX) *67*

Karamu (US ISSN 0022-8990) *711*

Karate International Annual (MY ISSN 0085-2481) *1034*

Karger Continuing Education Series (SZ ISSN 0254-1270) *416*

Karjala (FI) *588*

Karl-August-Forster-Lectures (GW ISSN 0340-5419) *142*

Karl-May-Gesellschaft. Jahrbuch (GW) *725*

Karlebynejden (FI) *588*

Karnatak University, Dharwad, India. Journal. Humanities (II ISSN 0075-515X) *630*

Karnatak University, Dharwad, India. Journal. Science (II ISSN 0075-5168) *993*

Karnatak University, Dharwad, India. Journal. Social Sciences (II ISSN 0075-5176) *1009*

Karnataka. Department of Tourism. Annual Report (II) *943*, 1112

Karnataka. Finance Department. Annual Report (II) *296*

Karpaten Jahrbuch (GW) *588*

Karthago (FR ISSN 0453-3429) *89*

Karthago. Collection Epigraphique (FR ISSN 0075-5184) *89*

Kartoffel-Nyt (DK ISSN 0106-9276) *57*

Kartograficheskaya Letopis' (UR) *545*

Kasetsart Journal (TH ISSN 0075-5192) *30*

Kasetsart University, Bangkok, Thailand. Faculty of Fisheries. Notes(TH ISSN 0125-7978) *511*

Kasmera (VE ISSN 0075-5222) *762*

Kataliz i Katalizatory (UR ISSN 0453-3585) *323*

Katallagete (US ISSN 0022-9288) 913, *971*

Katalog Ceskoslovenskych Znamek see Ceskoslovensko *874*

Katalog Fauny Pasozytniczej Polski (PL ISSN 0075-5230) *175*

Katalog Fauny Polski (PL ISSN 0453-3623) *175*

Katalog for Boerne- og Skolebiblioteker see Boernebibliotekskatalog. Boeger z Tidsskrifter Emnekatalog *123*

Katalog for Boerne- og Skolebiblioteker see Boernebibliotekskatalog. Boeger z Tidsskrifter Forfatterkatalog *123*

Katalog for Boerne- og Skolebiblioteker see Boernebibliotekskatalog. Boeger z Tidsskrifter Titelkatalog *123*
Katalog for Boerne- og Skolebiblioteker see Katalog for Skolebiblioteker. Emnekatalog *128*
Katalog for Boerne- og Skolebiblioteker see Katalog for Skolebiblioteker. Titelkatalog *128*
Katalog for Skolebiblioteker. Emnekatalog (DK ISSN 0106-7591) *128*, 416
Katalog for Skolebiblioteker. Forfatterkatalog see Katalog for Skolebiblioteker. Emnekatalog *128*
Katalog for Skolebiblioteker. Titelkatalog (DK ISSN 0106-7583) *128*, 416
Katalog fuer Technische Regeln see D I N - Katalog fuer Technische Regeln *808*
Katalog Philosophie (GW) *879*
Katalog Sefarim Kelali (IS) *962*
Katalog Slovenskych Plagatov (CS) *106*
Katalog Stranih Serijskih Publikacija u Bibliotekama Jugoslavije (YU ISSN 0350-0411) *128*
Katalog Zabytkow Sztuki w Polsce (PL ISSN 0075-5257) *106*
Katherine Asher Engel Lectures (US ISSN 0075-5265) *630*
Katholiek Documentatie Centrum. Archieven (NE) *982*
Katholiek Documentatie Centrum. Bibliografieen (NE) *975*
Katholiek Documentatie Centrum. Jaarboek (NE) *982*
Katholiek Documentatie Centrum. Publicaties (NE) *982*
Katholisches Leben und Kirchenreform im Zeitalter der Glaubensspaltung (GW ISSN 0170-7302) *982*
Katib al-Filastini (LE) *613*, 917
Katolicki Uniwersytet Lubelski. Wydzial Filozoficzny. Rozprawy (PL) *879*
Katolicki Uniwersytet Lubelski. Wydzial Nauk Spolecznych. Rozprawy (PL) *1009*
Katolicki Uniwersytet Lubelski. Wydzial Teologiczno-Kanoniczny. Rozprawy (PL) *982*
Katolicki Uniwersytet Lubelski Wydzial Historyczno-Filologiczny. Rozprawy (PL) *558*, 697
Kattegat-Skagerrak-Projectet. Meddelelser (DK ISSN 0280-8463) *588*
Katunob: Occasional Publications in Mesoamerican Anthropology (US) *73*
Kaukomieli (FI) *588*
Kauperts Deutschland Staedte-, Hotel- und Reisefuehrer (GW) *1112*
Kavaka/Fungus (II ISSN 0379-5179) *158*
Kawa to Hakimono see Leather & Footwears *672*
Kazakhskii Nauchno-Issledovatel'skii Institut Onkologii i Radiologii. Trudy(UR ISSN 0075-529X) *775*, 792
Kazanskii Gosudarstvennyi Pedagogicheskii Institut. Voprosy Istorii, Teorii Muzyki i Muzykal'nogo Vospitaniya. Sbornik (UR) *837*
Kazanskii Universitet. Sbornik Aspirantskikh Rabot: Teoriya Plastin i Obolochek (UR) *472*
Keats-Shelley Journal (US ISSN 0453-4387) *742*
Kedem (IS) *89*
Keepsake (US ISSN 0075-5311) *680*
Keidanren Keizai Shiryo (JA) *246*
Keidanren Pamphlet (JA) *246*
Keidanren Pocket Series (JA) *246*
Keikinzoku Kogyo Tokei Nenpo see Light Metal Statistics in Japan *801*
Keilschrifttexte aus Boghazkoi (GW) *89*, 697, 852
Keilschrifturkunden aus Boghazkoei (GE ISSN 0075-532X) *89*, 570
Keio Business Review (JA ISSN 0453-4557) *196*
Keio Engineering Reports see Keio Science and Technology Reports *993*

Keio Monographs of Business and Commerce (JA ISSN 0075-5346) *196*
Keio Science and Technology Reports (JA ISSN 0286-4215) *993*
Kekkaku No Kenkyu. see Hokkaido University. Institute of Immunological Science. Bulletin *793*
Kekkaku Yobokai Kenkyu Gyoseki see Japan Anti-Tuberculosis Association. Reports on Medical Research Problems *793*
Keleti Tanulmanyok/Oriental Studies (HU ISSN 0133-6193) *852*
Kellogg World see Kelloggram *472*
Kelloggram (US) *472*
Kellon - Haukiputaan Kotiseutujulkaisu (FI) *588*
Kelly - Grimes Buyers Guide For Word Processing (US) *363*
Kelly's British Industry and Services in the Common Market see Kelly's U.K. Exports to Europe *310*
Kelly's Business Directory (UK) *310*
Kelly's Directory of British Industry & Services in Scotland and Northern Ireland (UK ISSN 0260-633X) *1157*
Kelly's Manufacturers and Merchants Directory see Kelly's Business Directory *310*
Kelly's Post Office London Business Directory (UK) *310*
Kelly's Post Office London Directory see Kelly's Post Office London Business Directory *310*
Kelly's U.K. Exports to Europe (UK) *310*
Keltica (US ISSN 0192-1207) *504*, 588
Kemikaliekontrollen Aarsberetning (DK ISSN 0900-1646) *323*
Kemisk Analyse af Mineraler og Bjergarter (DK ISSN 0105-9386) *323*, 817
Kemistin Kalenteri (FI ISSN 0356-7818) *323*
Kempe's Engineers Year-Book (UK ISSN 0075-5400) *472*
Kemps Estate Agents Yearbook and Directory see Kemps Property Industry Yearbook *965*
Kemps Film and Television Year Book (International) see Kemps International Film and Television Year Book *824*
Kemps International Film and Television Year Book (UK) *824*
Kemps International Music and Recording Industry Yearbook (UK) *837*
Kemps International Music and Recording Yearbook see Kemps International Music and Recording Industry Yearbook *837*
Kemps Music and Record Industry Year Book International see Kemps International Music and Recording Industry Yearbook *837*
Kemps Property Industry Yearbook (UK) *310*, 965
Ken uw Dorp en uw Familie: Tijdschrift van de Heemkundige Kring (BE) *588*
Kenchiku Kenkyusho Chosa Shiken Kenkyu Gaiyo Hokoku see B R I Research Papers *181*
Kenley Abstracts see Paper and Board Abstracts *859*
Kennedy Institute of Bioethics. Scope Note (US) *762*, 879
Kennel Club Yearbook (UK) *868*
Kennel Control Council Gazette Dogs (AT) *868*
Kenny Dalglish Soccer Annual (UK) *1039*
Kensetsu Kogaku KenKyushyo Hokoku/Construction Engineering Research Institute Foundation Report(JA ISSN 0453-5146) *380*, 489, 497
Kent State Research Papers in Archaeology (US) *89*
Kentron Epistemonikon Ereunon. Epeteris/Cyprus Research Center. Annual (CY ISSN 0071-0954) *613*, 697
Kentucky. Adjutant-General's Office. Report (US) *607*, 811

Kentucky. Cabinet for Human Resources. Vital Statistics Report (US) *959*, 1058
Kentucky. Council of Economic Advisors. Annual Report see Commonwealth of Kentucky. Annual Economic Report (Year) *192*
Kentucky. Council of Economic Advisors. Policy Papers Series (US ISSN 0270-515X) *246*
Kentucky. Council on Higher Education. Origin of Kentucky College & University Enrollments (US) *424*
Kentucky. Council on Public Higher Education. Origin of Enrollments, Accredited Colleges and Universities see Kentucky. Council on Higher Education. Origin of Kentucky College & University Enrollments *424*
Kentucky. Department for Human Resources. Selected Vital Statistics and Planning Data see Kentucky. Cabinet for Human Resources. Vital Statistics Report *959*
Kentucky. Department of Child Welfare. Annual Report see Kentucky. Department of Human Resources. Annual Report *1018*
Kentucky. Department of Human Resources. Annual Report (US) *1018*
Kentucky. Department of Labor. Directory of Labor Organizations (US) *648*
Kentucky Agricultural Statistics (US) *41*
Kentucky Annual Vital Statistics Report see Kentucky. Cabinet for Human Resources. Vital Statistics Report *959*
Kentucky Deskbook of Economic Statistics see Kentucky Economic Statistics *212*
Kentucky Directory of Manufacturers (US ISSN 0075-5494) *311*
Kentucky Directory of Selected Industrial Services (US ISSN 0363-5198) *311*
Kentucky Economic Statistics (US) *212*
Kentucky Geological Survey. Guidebook to Geological Field Trips (US ISSN 0075-5575) *390*
Kentucky Geological Survey. Series 11. Annual Report (US) *390*
Kentucky Geological Survey. Series 11. Bulletin (US ISSN 0075-5559) *390*
Kentucky Geological Survey. Series 11. County Report (US ISSN 0075-5567) *390*
Kentucky Geological Survey. Series 11. Information Circular (US ISSN 0075-5583) *390*
Kentucky Geological Survey. Series 11. Report of Investigations (US ISSN 0075-5591) *390*
Kentucky Geological Survey. Series 11. Reprints (US ISSN 0075-5605) *390*
Kentucky Geological Survey. Series 11. Special Publication (US ISSN 0075-5613) *390*
Kentucky Geological Survey. Series 11. Thesis Series (US ISSN 0075-5621) *390*
Kentucky Geological Survey Newsletter see K G S - N C I C Newsletter *545*
Kentucky Industrial Directory see Kentucky Directory of Manufacturers *311*
Kentucky Local Debt Report (US ISSN 0095-1498) *297*
Kentucky Manufacturers Register (US ISSN 0741-9031) *311*
Kentucky Manufacturing Developments(US) *1069*
Kentucky Oil and Gas Association. Technical Sessions. Proceedings see Kentucky Geological Survey. Series 11. Special Publication *390*
Kentucky School Directory (US ISSN 0091-0775) *430*
Kentucky, Tennessee TourBook see Tourbook: Kentucky, Tennessee *1117*

Kentucky Vital Statistics see Kentucky. Cabinet for Human Resources. Vital Statistics Report *959*
Kenya. Central Bureau of Statistics. Agricultural Census (Large Farm Areas) (KE ISSN 0300-2373) *41*, 1058
Kenya. Central Bureau of Statistics. Development Estimates (KE) *290*
Kenya. Central Bureau of Statistics. Directory of Industries (KE) *311*
Kenya. Central Bureau of Statistics. Economic Survey (KE) *246*
Kenya. Central Bureau of Statistics. Employment and Earnings in the Modern Sector (KE) *212*, 1058
Kenya. Central Bureau of Statistics. Estimates of Recurrent Expenditures (KE) *290*
Kenya. Central Bureau of Statistics. Estimates of Revenue Expenditures (KE) *290*
Kenya. Central Bureau of Statistics. Migration and Tourism Statistics (KE) *1112*
Kenya. Central Bureau of Statistics. Register of Manufacturing Firms (KE) *212*
Kenya. Central Bureau of Statistics. Social Perspectives see Social Perspectives *1029*
Kenya. Central Bureau of Statistics. Statistical Abstract (KE) *212*
Kenya. Central Bureau of Statistics. Surveys of Industrial Production (KE) *290*
Kenya. Commissioner of Customs and Excise. Annual Trade Report (KE) *257*
Kenya. Dairy Board. Annual Report (KE ISSN 0453-5944) *62*
Kenya. Government Printing and Stationery Department. Catalogue of Government Publications (KE) *128*
Kenya. Maize and Produce Board. Report see Kenya. National Cereals and Produce Board. Annual Report *57*
Kenya. Ministry of Agriculture. Central Development and Marketing Unit. Yields, Costs, Prices (KE) *48*
Kenya. Ministry of Agriculture. Scientific Research Division. Annual Report (KE) *30*
Kenya. Ministry of Economic Planning and Development. Economic Survey see Kenya. Central Bureau of Statistics. Economic Survey *246*
Kenya. Ministry of Economic Planning and Development. Estimates of Revenue Expenditures see Kenya. Central Bureau of Statistics. Estimates of Revenue Expenditures *290*
Kenya. Ministry of Economic Planning and Development. Statistics Division. Development Estimates see Kenya. Central Bureau of Statistics. Development Estimates *290*
Kenya. Ministry of Economic Planning and Development. Statistics Division. Estimates of Recurrent Expenditures see Kenya. Central Bureau of Statistics. Estimates of Recurrent Expenditures *290*
Kenya. Ministry of Economic Planning and Development. Statistics Division. Statistical Abstract see Kenya. Central Bureau of Statistics. Statistical Abstract *212*
Kenya. Ministry of Education. Annual Report (KE ISSN 0075-5869) *416*
Kenya. Ministry of Finance and Economic Planning. Budget Speech see Kenya. Ministry of Finance and Planning. Budget Speech by Minister for Finance and Planning *943*
Kenya. Ministry of Finance and Economic Planning. Statistics Division. Register of Manufacturing Firms see Kenya. Central Bureau of Statistics. Register of Manufacturing Firms *212*
Kenya. Ministry of Finance and Economic Planning. Statistics Division. Register of Manufacturing Firms see Kenya. Central Bureau of Statistics. Directory of Industries *311*

Kenya. Ministry of Finance and Planning. Budget Speech by Minister for Finance and Planning (KE) *943*
Kenya. Ministry of Finance and Planning. Plan Implementation Report (KE) *943*
Kenya. Ministry of Health and Housing. Annual Report *see* Kenya. Ministry of Housing. Annual Report *624*
Kenya. Ministry of Health. Annual report (KE) *762*
Kenya. Ministry of Housing. Annual Report (KE) *624*
Kenya. Ministry of Information and Broadcasting. Annual Report (KE) *566*
Kenya. Ministry of Information, Broadcasting and Tourism. Annual Report *see* Kenya. Ministry of Information and Broadcasting. Annual Report *566*
Kenya. National Cereals and Produce Board. Annual Report (KE) *57*
Kenya. National Housing Corporation. Annual Report (KE) *624*
Kenya. National Irrigation Board. Reports and Accounts (KE ISSN 0075-5915) *57*
Kenya. National Library Service Board. Annual and Audit Report (KE ISSN 0075-5923) *680*
Kenya. Office of the District Commissioner. Annual Report (KE) *943*
Kenya. Public Accounts Committee. Annual Report (KE ISSN 0075-5931) *943*
Kenya. Public Service Commission. Annual Report (KE ISSN 0075-594X) *1018*
Kenya. Wheat Board. Report *see* Kenya. National Cereals and Produce Board. Annual Report *57*
Kenya Agricultural Research Institute. Veterinary Research Department. Annual Report (KE) *1122*
Kenya Association of Manufacturers. Industrial Index & Members List *see* Kenya Association of Manufacturers. Members List and International Standard Industrial Classification *311*
Kenya Association of Manufacturers. Members List and International Standard Industrial Classification (KE) *290, 311*
Kenya Commercial Bank. Director's Report and Accounts and Executive Chairman's Statement (KE) *230*
Kenya Conservatoire of Music. Newsletter (KE) *837*
Kenya Directory of Hotels *see* Directory of Hotels in Kenya *619*
Kenya Enterprise *see* Industrial & Trade Directory *195*
Kenya Export Directory (KE) *257*
Kenya Fisheries Reports (KE) *511*
Kenya Gazette Supplement (KE) *943*
Kenya Industrial Research and Development Institute Annual Report and Statement of Accounts *see* K I R D I Annual Report and Statement of Accounts *239*
Kenya Institute of Administration. Journal (KE ISSN 0065-1966) *943*
Kenya Institute of Administration Occasional Papers *see* K I A Occasional Papers *943*
Kenya Institute of Education. Annual Report (KE) *416*
Kenya Library Association Chairman's Annual Report (KE) *680*
Kenya Media Advertising Review (KE) *15*
Kenya Medical Abstracts (KE) *771*
Kenya Medical Research Institute. Proceedings of the Annual Medical Research Conferences (KE ISSN 1010-576X) *762*
Kenya Meteorological Department. Annual Report (KE) *805*
Kenya Museum Society. Chairman's Report (KE) *828*
Kenya National Academy for Advancement of Arts and Sciences. Annual Report *see* Kenya National Academy of Sciences. Annual Report *993*

Kenya National Academy for Advancement of Arts and Sciences. Foundation Lectures (KE) *630*
Kenya National Academy for Advancement of Arts and Sciences. Newsletter (KE) *993, 1069*
Kenya National Academy for Advancement of Arts and Sciences. Proceedings (KE) *630*
Kenya National Academy for Advancement of Arts and Sciences. Research Information Circulars (KE) *566*
Kenya National Academy of Sciences. Annual Report (KE) *106, 993*
Kenya National Bibliography (KE) *688*
Kenya National Chamber of Commerce and Industry. Annual Report (KE) *236*
Kenya National Council of Social Services. Annual Report (KE) *1018*
Kenya National Trading Corporation. Annual Report (KE) *240*
Kenya Past and Present (KE) *566, 993*
Kenya Regional Studies (KE) *566*
Kenya Society for the Blind. Annual Report and Accounts (KE) *180*
Kenya Tea Development Authority. Annual Report and Accounts (KE) *520*
Kenya: The Gateway to Africa (KE) *267, 311*
Kenya Tourist Development Corporation. Report and Accounts (KE) *1112*
Kenya Tuberculosis and Respiratory Diseases Research Center. Annual Report *see* Respiratory Diseases Research Centre. Annual Report *793*
Kenya, Uganda, Tanzania, East African Community Directory; Trade Commerce Index (KE) *311*
Kenya, Uganda, Tanzania, Zambia, Malawi and Ethiopia Directory; Trade and Commercial Index *see* Kenya, Uganda, Tanzania, East African Community Directory; Trade Commerce Index *311*
Kenya Uhuru Yearbook (KE ISSN 0378-2158) *566*
Kenya Yearbook (UK) *246*
Kenyan Periodicals Directory (KE) *688*
Kenyatta University College. Bureau of Educational Research. Research Projects (KE) *436*
Kenyatta University College. Directory of Research (KE) *436*
Kerala (India). Board for Prevention and Control of Water Pollution. Annual Report (II) *497*
Kerala; an Economic Review (II ISSN 0453-7440) *246*
Kerem Shlomo (US) *976*
Kerjasama Serbaguna Malaysia Review *see* K S M Review *30*
Kernforschungszentrum Karlsruhe. Ergebnisbericht ueber Forschung und Entwicklung (GW ISSN 0171-3191) *472, 897*
Kerry Archaeological and Historical Society. Journal (IE ISSN 0085-2503) *89*
Kerteminde Museum. Aarsskrift *see* Cartha *827*
Kesatuan Bulletin (SI ISSN 0047-3383) *436*
Keski-Suomi (FI ISSN 0355-1393) *588*
Kestrel Chapbook Series (US) *725*
Ketsueki Jigyo no Genkyo (JA) *762*
Kettering Report (US) *416, 906, 1018*
Kevo Subarctic Research Institute. Reports (FI ISSN 0453-7831) *142, 380, 497, 545*
Kew Bulletin (UK ISSN 0075-5974) *158*
Kew Bulletin. Additional Series (UK ISSN 0075-5982) *158*
Kew Record of Taxonomic Literature Relating to Vascular Plants (UK) *158*
Key (Lansdale) (US ISSN 0748-8513) *1157*
Key Abstracts - Advanced Materials (UK ISSN 0950-4753) *893, 901*

Key Abstracts - Antennas & Propagation (UK ISSN 0950-4761) *346, 349*
Key Abstracts - Artificial Intelligence (UK ISSN 0950-477X) *8, 461*
Key Abstracts - Communications Technology *see* Key Abstracts - Telecommunications *346*
Key Abstracts - Computer Communications and Storage (UK ISSN 0950-4788) *354, 361*
Key Abstracts - Computing in Electronics & Power (UK ISSN 0950-4796) *354, 485*
Key Abstracts - Electrical Measurements and Instrumentation *see* Key Abstracts - Electronic Instrumentation *810*
Key Abstracts - Electronic Circuits (UK ISSN 0306-557X) *8, 461*
Key Abstracts - Electronic Instrumentation (UK ISSN 0950-480X) *8, 637, 810*
Key Abstracts - Industrial Power and Control Systems *see* Key Abstracts - Robotics & Control *461*
Key Abstracts - Measurements in Physics (UK ISSN 0950-4818) *8, 637, 810*
Key Abstracts - Optoelectronics (UK ISSN 0950-4826) *346*
Key Abstracts - Physical Measurements and Instrumentation *see* Key Abstracts - Measurements in Physics *810*
Key Abstracts - Power Systems & Applications (UK ISSN 0950-4834) *8, 461*
Key Abstracts - Power Transmission and Distribution *see* Key Abstracts - Power Systems & Applications *461*
Key Abstracts - Robotics & Control (UK ISSN 0950-4842) *8, 461*
Key Abstracts - Semiconductor Devices(UK ISSN 0950-4850) *8, 461*
Key Abstracts - Software Engineering (UK ISSN 0950-4869) *354, 363*
Key Abstracts - Solid State Devices *see* Key Abstracts - Semiconductor Devices *461*
Key Abstracts - Systems Theory *see* Key Abstracts - Artificial Intelligence *461*
Key Abstracts - Telecommunications (UK ISSN 0950-4877) *344, 346*
Key British Enterprises (UK) *196*
Key Figures on Danish Industry (DK) *1157*
Key Notes (NE) *837*
Key Statistical Indicators for National Health Service Management in Wales(UK ISSN 0264-6714) *619, 959*
Key to Economic Science (NE ISSN 0165-4748) *8, 212*
Key to Scandinavia: Danmark, Norge, Sverige, Finland, Island *see* Nordisk Handels Kalender: Skandinavisk Addressebog *258*
Key Word Index of Wildlife Research (SZ) *8, 175, 1004*
Keystone (CN) *341*
Keystone Coal Industry Manual (US) *311, 817*
Keyword Index to Serial Titles (UK ISSN 0143-9553) *8, 688*
Khabarovskii Gosudarstvennyi Pedagogicheskii Institut. Voprosy Istorii Dal'nego Vostoka (UR) *588*
Khadi and Village Industries Commission Annual Report *see* K V I C Annual Report *301*
Khar'kovskii Gosudarstvennyi Universitet. Filologiya (UR) *697*
Khar'kovskii Gosudarstvennyi Universitet. Matematika i Mekhanika(UR) *750*
Khar'kovskii Gosudarstvennyi Universitet. Radiofizika i Elektronika(UR) *456*
Khartoum Law Review (SJ) *658*
Khemoretseptsiya Nasekomykh/Insect Chemoreception (UR ISSN 0206-3441) *479*
Ki-es-Ki *see* C E A Handbook *411*
Kibbutz (Efal) (IS) *238*
Kibbutz (Tel Aviv) (IS ISSN 0334-2182) *1027*

Kidney Diseases (US) *795*
Kidney International. Supplement (US) *795*
Kid's Club Magazine (US) *335*
Kieler Arbeitspapiere (GW ISSN 0342-0787) *246*
Kieler Studien (GW ISSN 0340-6989) *257*
Kierkegaardiana (DK ISSN 0075-6032) *879, 971*
Kierkegaard's Writings (US) *879*
Kihara Institute for Biological Research. Report *see* Kihara Seibutsugaku Kenkyusho. Seiken Ziho *167*
Kihara Seibutsugaku Kenkyusho. Seiken Ziho/Kihara Institute for Biological Research. Report (JA ISSN 0080-8539) *167*
Kijkboekjes (NE) *837*
Kilpailunvapauslehti *see* Hinnat ja Kilpailu *239*
Kime's International Law Directory (UK ISSN 0075-6040) *671*
Kimia (MY) *323*
Kimika (PH ISSN 0115-2130) *323*
Kinaadman/Wisdom (PH ISSN 0115-6012) *516, 570*
Kinder-und Jugendbuecher (GW) *335*
Kindex (US ISSN 0733-8937) *333, 658, 668*
Kinematografija u Srbiji *see* Kinematografija u Srbiji - Uporedo SFRJ *824*
Kinematografija u Srbiji - Uporedo SFRJ (YU) *824*
Kinesi *see* Motion *1114*
King Abdul Aziz University. Faculty of Marine Science. Journal (SU) *142*
King Saud University. College of Science. Journal (SU ISSN 0735-9799) *994*
King Sized Cracked (US) *711*
Kingdom Computer Concepts' Newsletter *see* Kingdom Computer Concepts' Newsletter - Catalog *362*
Kingdom Computer Concepts' Newsletter - Catalog (US) *362, 362*
Kings of Tomorrow Series (UK ISSN 0075-6083) *134*
Kinki Daigaku Yakugakubu Kiyo *see* Kinki University. Bulletin of Pharmacy *871*
Kinki Nogyo Josei Hokoku *see* Annual Review of Agriculture, Kinkei District *24*
Kinki Shokubutsu Dokokai Kaishi (JA) *158*
Kinki University. Bulletin of Pharmacy/ Kinki Daigaku Yakugakubu Kiyo (JA ISSN 0023-1657) *871*
Kirche und Konfession (GW) *971*
Kirche und Recht (AU ISSN 0259-0735) *658, 971*
Kirchenmusikalisches Jahrbuch (GW ISSN 0075-6199) *837*
Kirchensaenger *see* Kleine Chorzeitung *837*
Kirchliches Jahrbuch fuer die Evangelische Kirche in Deutschland (GW ISSN 0075-6210) *979*
Kirin Biru K.K. Sogo Kenkyusho Kenkyu Hokoku *see* Kirin Brewery Company, Tokyo. Research Laboratory. Report *120*
Kirin Brewery Company, Tokyo. Research Laboratory. Report/Kirin Biru K.K. Sogo Kenkyusho Kenkyu Hokoku (JA ISSN 0075-6229) *120*
Kirkefondets Aarbog (DK ISSN 0107-9824) *971*
Kirkehistoriske Samlinger (DK ISSN 0450-3171) *971*
Kirkia (RH ISSN 0451-9930) *158*
Kirtlandia (US ISSN 0075-6245) *994*
Kiruna Geophysical Institute. Annual Report (SW ISSN 0283-1686) *400*
Kiruna Geophysical Institute. Preprint (SW ISSN 0349-2656) *400*
Kiruna Geophysical Institute. Report *see* Kiruna Geophysical Institute. Scientific Report *400*
Kiruna Geophysical Institute. Scientific Report (SW ISSN 0283-1694) *400*
Kiruna Geophysical Institute. Software Report (SW ISSN 0349-2664) *400*
Kiruna Geophysical Institute. Technical Report (SW ISSN 0349-2672) *400*
Kischo-cho Obun Kaiyo Hokoku *see* Oceanographical Magazine *407*

Kisho-Cho Kansoku Gijutsu Shiryo (JA) 805
Kisho-cho Nenpo Zenkoku Kishohyo see Japan. Meteorological Agency. Annual Report 805
Kiswahili (TZ ISSN 0023-1886) 504, 697
Al-Kitab Al-Arabi Fi Aam see Arab Book Annual 963
Kitanihon Byogaichu Kenkyukai Kaiho see Society of Plant Protection of North Japan. Annual Report 60
Kitchin's Road Transport Law (UK ISSN 0308-8987) 658, 1105
Klagenfurter Beitraege zur Philosophie (AU ISSN 0259-0743) 879
Klank en Weerklank (NE ISSN 0030-3836) 837
Klasings Bootsmarkt International; Yachten und Boote Zubehoer, Ausruestung, Motoren (GW ISSN 0075-627X) 1042
Klaus-Groth-Gesellschaft. Jahresgaben (GW ISSN 0453-9842) 697, 725
Kleine Aegyptische Texte (GW ISSN 0343-1088) 852
Kleine Chorzeitung (SZ ISSN 0023-2068) 837, 982
Kleine Deutsche Prosadenkmaeler des Mittelalters (GW ISSN 0075-6318) 725
Kleine Ikonenbuecherei (GW ISSN 0445-2577) 1157
Kleine Museumshefte (GW ISSN 0075-6326) 828
Kleio (SA ISSN 0023-2084) 558, 962
Kleist-Jahrbuch (GW) 725
Klimat i Gidrografiya Zabaikal'ya (UR) 805
Klinische Psychologie und Psychopathologie (GW ISSN 0343-9429) 935
Klucze do Oznaczania Owadow Polski (PL ISSN 0075-6350) 165
Kmetianum (CS) 588
Kniha (CS) 680
Knihovna (CS ISSN 0139-5335) 588, 680
Knitstats (UK ISSN 0260-8855) 1058, 1076
Knitting Times Buyers' Guide & Knitwear Apparel Directory (US) 311
Knitting Times Buyer's Guide and Knitwear Directory see Knitting Times Buyers' Guide & Knitwear Apparel Directory 311
Knitting Times Yearbook (US ISSN 0085-2562) 1074
Knives (Year) (US ISSN 0277-0725) 614
Knizna Kultura see Kniha 680
Kniznicny Zbornik/Library Studies (CS ISSN 0075-6369) 680
Knotty Problems of Baseball (US ISSN 0075-6385) 1039
Know Your Training Films (UK) 286
Knowledge and Society (US ISSN 0278-1557) 630, 1027
Kobe Daigaku Igakubu Kiyo see Kobe University. Medical Journal 762
Kobe Economic and Business Research Series (JA ISSN 0075-6415) 196
Kobe Economic and Business Review (JA ISSN 0075-6407) 196
Kobe Kaiyo Kishodai Iho/Kobe Marine Observatory. Bulletin (JA ISSN 0368-5969) 406, 805
Kobe Marine Observatory. Bulletin see Kobe Kaiyo Kishodai Iho 406
Kobe University. Faculty of Agriculture. Science Reports (JA ISSN 0452-2370) 30, 142
Kobe University. Medical Journal/Kobe Daigaku Igakubu Kiyo (JA ISSN 0075-6431) 762
Kobe University. School of Business Administration. Annals (JA ISSN 0085-2570) 280
Kobe University Economic Review (JA ISSN 0454-1111) 196
Kobe University Law Review. International Edition (JA ISSN 0075-6423) 658
Kobe University of Mercantile Marine. Review. Part 1. Studies in Humanities and Social Science (JA) 630, 1009
Kobe University of Mercantile Marine. Review. Part 2. Maritime Studies, and Science and Engineering (JA ISSN 0450-609X) 472, 994
Kobe University of Mercantile Marine. Review. Part 2. Navigation, Marine Engineering, Nuclear Engineering and Scientific Section see Kobe University of Mercantile Marine. Review. Part 2. Maritime Studies, and Science and Engineering 994
Kobe Women's University. Faculty of Home Economics. Bulletin (JA) 615
Kobenhavns Statistiske Aarbog (DK ISSN 0106-3839) 1058
Kobenhavns Universitet. Sociologisk Institut. Afhandling (DK ISSN 0900-9922) 1027
Kobenhavns Universitet. Sociologisk Institut. Arbejdspapir (DK ISSN 0900-9876) 1027
KOBIE (SP) 390
Koblenzer Geographisches Kolloquium (GW) 380, 416, 545, 906
Kochi Gakuen College. Bulletin (JA ISSN 0389-4088) 430
Kochi University. Agricultural Science. Research Reports (JA ISSN 0389-0473) 30, 142
Kochi University. Faculty of Agriculture. Memoirs (JA ISSN 0450-6219) 30, 472
Kodaly Institute of Canada. Monograph(CN) 128, 448, 843
Koebenhavn Boligkommissionen. Aarsberetning (DK ISSN 0573-9799) 624
Koebenhavnerliv Foer og Nu (DK ISSN 0107-976X) 588
Koebenhavns Fondsboers. Aarsrapport/Copenhagen Stock Exchange. Annual Report (DK) 267
Koebenhavns Universitet. Datalogisk Institut. Rapport (DK ISSN 0107-8283) 352
Koebenhavns Universitet. Geografisk Centralinstitut. Laboratorium for Geomorfologi (DK ISSN 0106-3618) 545
Koebenhavns Universitet. Geologisk Centralinstitut. Aarsberetning (DK) 390
Koebenhavns Universitet. Institut for Anvendt og Matematisk Lingvistik. Skrifter (DK ISSN 0106-8563) 697, 750
Koebenhavns Universitet. Institut for Filmvidenskab. Skrifter see Filmvidenskabeligt Arbog 824
Koebenhavns Universitet. Institut for Filmvidenskab Skrifter see Saerrakke 825
Koebenhavns Universitet. Institut for Filmvidenskab. Skrifter see Sekvens 825
Koebenhavns Universitet. Institut for Religionshistorie. Skrifter (DK ISSN 0105-4821) 971
Koebenhavns Universitet. Institut for Samfundsfag og Forvaltning. Forskningrapport (DK ISSN 0900-274X) 1018
Koebenhavns Universitet. Institut for Social Medicin. Publikation (DK ISSN 0105-4139) 762
Koebenhavns Universitet. Oekonomiske Institut. Memo (DK ISSN 0574-0045) 196
Koebenhavns Universitet. Retsvidenskabelig Institut B. Studier(DK ISSN 0108-9811) 658
Koebenhavns Universitet. Statistiske Institut. Afhandlinger. Graa Serie see Universitetets Statistiske Institut. Research Report 1066
Koebenhavns Universitets Slaviske Institut. Rapporter (DK ISSN 0107-3265) 697
Koebenhavnske Kirkefondets Aarbog see Kirkefondets Aarbog 971
Koebstadsmuseet Den Gamle By (DK ISSN 0105-9254) 588
Koedoe (SA ISSN 0075-6458) 366
Koedoe. Monographs (SA ISSN 0075-6466) 366
Koege Museum (DK ISSN 0107-931X) 828
Koege Museum. Aarbog see Koege Museum 828
Koehlers Flottenkalender. Jahrbuch fuer Schiffahrt und Haefen (GW ISSN 0075-6474) 811, 1101
Koelner Arbeiten zum Bibliotheks- und Dokumentationswesen (GW ISSN 0721-7587) 680
Koelner Beitraege zur Musikforschung (GW) 837
Koelner Friedens-Anzeiger (GW) 906, 917
Koelner Jahrbuch fuer Vor- und Fruehgeschichte (GW ISSN 0075-6512) 89
Koelner Monatszahlen see Koelner Statistische Nachrichten 1058
Koelner Romanistische Arbeiten (SZ ISSN 0075-6520) 630
Koelner Sarasvati Serie (GW) 852
Koelner Statistische Nachrichten (GW ISSN 0177-6355) 1058
Koelner Vortraege zur Sozial- und Wirtschaftsgeschichte (GW) 588
Koepfe des 20. Jahrhunderts (GW ISSN 0454-1383) 134
Kogai Chosa Hokokusho/Report of Environmental Pollution in Meguro Ward (JA) 497
Kogyo Ritchi Handobukku see Industrial Location Handbook 289
Kokalos (IT ISSN 0392-0887) 89, 558
Kokuritsu Eiyo Kenkyusho Hokoku see National Institute of Nutrition. Annual Report 846
Kokuritsu Gan Senta Nenpo see National Cancer Center. Annual Report 775
Kokuritsu Gan Senta, Tokyo. Collected Papers see National Cancer Center. Collected Papers 775
Kokuritsu Idengaku Kenkyusho, Mishima, Japan. Nenpo see National Institute of Genetics, Mishima, Japan. Annual Report 167
Kokuritsu Kagaku Hakubutsukann Kenkyu Hoku. D - Rui: Jinruigaku see National Science Museum. Bulletin. Series D: Anthropology 74
Kokuritsu Kokkai Toshokan Nenpo see Japan. National Diet Library. Annual Report 680
Kokuritsu Kokugo Kenkyusho Nenpo see National Language Research Institute. Annual Report 699
Kokuritsu Koshu Eisei-in Nenpo see Institute of Public Health. Annual Report 954
Kokuritsu Tama Kenkyusho Nenpo see National Institute for Leprosy Research. Annual Report 778
Kokuritsu Tokushu Kyoiku Sogo Kenkyujo Kenkyu Kiyo see National Institute of Special Education. Bulletin 445
Kokusai Kirisutokyo Daigaku, Kyoiku Kenkyu see International Christian University. Institute for Educational Research and Service. Educational Studies 415
Kokusai Kyoku-Undo Kansoku Jigyo Nenpo see International Polar Motion Service. Annual Report 116
Kokutetsu Chuo Hoken Kanrijoho (JA) 635, 762, 954
Kolding Bogen (DK) 588
Koleopterologische Rundschau (AU ISSN 0075-6547) 142
Kolloquium ueber Spaetantike und Fruehmittelalterliche Skulptur (GW ISSN 0075-6563) 106
Kol'tsa (UR) 755
Komise pro Dejiny Zavodu v C S S R. Zpravodaj (CS) 588
Komise pro Dejiny Zavodu v C S S R. Zpravy see Komise pro Dejiny Zavodu v C S S R. Zpravodaj 588
Kommission fuer Geschichtliche Landeskunde in Baden-Wuerttemberg. Veroeffentlichungen. Reihe A. Quellen (GW ISSN 0067-2831) 588
Kommission fuer Geschichtliche Landeskunde in Baden-Wuerttemberg. Veroeffentlichungen. Reihe B: Forschungen (GW ISSN 0521-9884) 588
Kommission fuer Neuere Geschichte Oesterreichs. Veroeffentlichungen (AU) 588
Kommunal Aarbog (DK ISSN 0900-1484) 951
Kommunal Budgetredegoerelse (DK ISSN 0107-5098) 951
Kommunal Litteratur (DK ISSN 0105-7456) 949
Kommunalwissenschaftliche Dissertationen (GW ISSN 0340-1170) 624
Kommuneplanorientering (DK ISSN 0106-7362) 624
Kommunikation und Kybernetik in Einzeldarstellungen see Communication and Cybernetics 359
Kommunikation und Politik (GW) 646
Kommunisticheskaya Partiya Sovetskogo Soyuza. Vysshaya Partiinaya Shkola. Uchenye Zapiski (UR) 906
Kommunistisk Tidsskrift see K T 906
Kompas Danmark (DK) 311
Kompas Danmark see Kompas Danmark 311
Kompass Alimentation see Kompass Professionnels 311
Kompass Australia (AT) 311
Kompass Belgium/Luxembourg (BE ISSN 0075-6636) 311
Kompass Espana (SP ISSN 0075-6644) 311
Kompass France see La France de l'Industrie et ses Services 308
Kompass Holland (NE ISSN 0075-6660) 311
Kompass Italia (IT ISSN 0075-6687) 311
Kompass Maroc (MR ISSN 0075-6695) 311
Kompass Norge (NO ISSN 0075-6709) 311
Kompass Professionnels (FR) 311, 520
Kompass Regionaux (FR) 196
Kompass Register see Kompass Australia 311
Kompass Schweiz/Liechtenstein (SZ ISSN 0075-6717) 311
Kompass Select Denmark. Business Services see Kompass Select Export. Business Services 257
Kompass Select Denmark. Chemicals see Kompass Select Export. Chemical Industry 257
Kompass Select Denmark. Construction see Kompass Select Export. Building Construction, Contractors 257
Kompass Select Denmark. Electrical and Electronic Equipment see Kompass Select Export. Electrical and Electronic Equipment 257
Kompass Select Denmark. Food and Beverages see Kompass Select Export. Food Industry 257
Kompass Select Denmark. Furniture see Kompass Select Export. Furniture 257
Kompass Select Denmark. Instruments see Kompass Select Export. Scientific and Industrial Instruments, Watch Industry 257
Kompass Select Denmark. Machinery see Kompass Select Export. Machine Industry 257
Kompass Select Denmark. Metal see Kompass Select Export. Metal Products 257
Kompass Select Denmark. Paper and Printing see Kompass Select Export. Paper Industry, Graphic Arts 257
Kompass Select Denmark. Plastics and Rubber see Kompass Select Export. Rubber Industry, Plastics Industry 257
Kompass Select Denmark. Textiles-Clothing and Footwear see Kompass Select Export. Textiles, Clothing and Footwear 258
Kompass Select Denmark. Transport Equipment see Kompass Select Export. Transport Equipment 258
Kompass Select Denmark. Wood see Kompass Select Export. Wood Industry 258
Kompass Select Export. Building Construction, Contractors (DK ISSN 0106-1135) 257
Kompass Select Export. Business Services (DK ISSN 0106-1100) 257

KOSHER DIRECTORY 1795

Kompass Select Export. Chemical Industry (DK ISSN 0106-1119) *257*
Kompass Select Export. Electrical and Electronic Equipment (DK ISSN 0106-1143) *257*
Kompass Select Export. Food Industry (DK ISSN 0106-1151) *257*
Kompass Select Export. Furniture (DK ISSN 0106-116X) *257*
Kompass Select Export. Machine Industry (DK ISSN 0106-1186) *257*
Kompass Select Export. Metal Products(DK ISSN 0106-1194) *257*
Kompass Select Export. Paper Industry, Graphic Arts (DK ISSN 0106-1208) *257*
Kompass Select Export. Rubber Industry, Plastics Industry (DK ISSN 0106-1216) *257*
Kompass Select Export. Scientific and Industrial Instruments, Watch Industry (DK ISSN 0106-1178) *257*
Kompass Select Export. Textiles, Clothing and Footwear (DK ISSN 0106-1224) *258*
Kompass Select Export. Transport Equipment (DK ISSN 0106-1232) *258*
Kompass Select Export. Wood Industry(DK ISSN 0106-1240) *258*
Kompass Special Services (FR) *311*
Kompass Sverige (SW ISSN 0075-6725) *311*
Kompass Textile et Habillement (FR) *311*, *340*
Kompass U.K. Management Register (UK) *280*
Kompass United Kingdom (UK) *311*
Kompass United Kingdom/CBI see Kompass United Kingdom *311*
Koncar Strucne Informacije (YU ISSN 0350-5537) *456*
Konferensie van Suid-Afrikaanse Opmeters. Verrigtinge see Conference of South African Surveyors. Proceedings *480*
Kongelig Dansk Hof- og Statskalender; Statshaandbog for Kongeriget Danmark (DK ISSN 0085-2589) *943*
Kongelige Bibliotek. Fagbibliografer (DK ISSN 0105-5046) *128*
Kongelige Bibliotek. Publikumsorienteringer (DK ISSN 0105-3167) *680*
Kongelige Bibliotek. Specialhjaelpmidler(DK ISSN 0105-8215) *128*
Kongelige Danske Videnskabernes Selskab. Biologiske Skrifter (DK ISSN 0366-3612) *142*, *380*
Kongelige Danske Videnskabernes Selskab. Historisk-Filosofiske Meddelelser (DK ISSN 0106-0481) *631*
Kongelige Danske Videnskabernes Selskab. Historisk-Filosofiske Skrifter(DK ISSN 0023-3307) *631*
Kongelige Danske Videnskabernes Selskab. Matematisk-Fysiske Meddelelser (DK ISSN 0023-3323) *750*, *889*
Kongelige Danske Videnskabernes Selskab. Oversigt over Selskabets Virksomhed. Annual Report (DK ISSN 0368-7201) *631*
Kongelige Norske Videnskabers Selskab(NO ISSN 0368-6302) *631*, *994*
Kongelige Norske Videnskabers Selskab. Forhandlinger see Kongelige Norske Videnskabers Selskab *994*
Kongelige Norske Videnskabers Selskab. Museet. Miscellanea see Gunneria *87*
Kongelige Norske Videnskabers Selskab. Skrifter/Royal Norwegian Society of Sciences. Publications (NO ISSN 0368-6310) *631*, *994*
Kongelige Norske Videnskabers Selskab Museet. Rapport. Botanisk Serie (NO ISSN 0332-8090) *158*
Kongelige Veterinaer og Landbohoejskole. Haandbog (DK ISSN 0109-4998) *30*, *1122*
Kongelige Veterinaer- og Landbohoejskole. Jordbrugsteknisk Institut. Meddelelse (DK ISSN 0106-8237) *30*

Kongelige Veterinaer og Landbohoejskole. Skovbruginstitutet. Meddelelser (DK ISSN 0106-8261) *30*, *1122*
Kongres Wanita Indonesia. Berita see Indonesian Women's Congress. Bulletin *1129*
Kongresa Libro (NE ISSN 0083-3851) *697*
Kongressbericht Bundesschulmusikwoche (GW ISSN 0172-9624) *837*
Koninklijk Belgisch Instituut voor Natuurwetenschappen. Studiedocumenten/Institut Royal des Sciences Naturelles de Belgique. Documents de Travail (BE) *142*, *175*
Koninklijk Belgisch Instituut voor Natuurwetenschappen. Verhandelingen/Institut Royal des Sciences Naturelles de Belgique. Memoires (BE) *1157*
Koninklijk Instituut voor de Tropen. Afdeling Agrarisch Onderzoek. Bulletin/Royal Tropical Institute. Information and Documentation. Bulletin (NE) *30*
Koninklijk Instituut voor de Tropen. Afdeling Agrarisch Onderzoek. Communication see Koninklijk Instituut voor de Tropen. Afdeling Plattelandsontwikkeling. Communications and Bulletins *30*
Koninklijk Instituut voor de Tropen. Afdeling Plattelandsontwikkeling. Communications and Bulletins (NE) *30*
Koninklijk Instituut voor de Tropen. Annual Report see Koninklijk Instituut voor de Tropen. Survey *545*
Koninklijk Instituut voor de Tropen. Department of Tropical Hygiene. Annual Report (NE) *954*
Koninklijk Instituut voor de Tropen. Survey (NE) *545*
Koninklijk Instituut voor het Kunstpatrimonium. Bulletin see Institut Royal de Patrimoine Artistique. Bulletin *106*
Koninklijk Instituut voor Taal-, Land- en Volkenkunde. Bibliographical Series (NE ISSN 0074-0462) *79*
Koninklijk Instituut voor Taal-, Land- en Volkenkunde. Translation Series (NE ISSN 0074-0470) *73*
Koninklijk Instituut voor Taal- , Land- en Volkenkunde. Verhandelingen (NE) *73*
Koninklijk Museum voor Midden-Afrika. Annalen. Reeks in 8. Economische Wetenschappen see Musee Royal de l'Afrique Centrale. Annales. Serie in 8. Sciences Economiques *48*
Koninklijk Museum voor Midden-Afrika. Annalen. Reeks in 8. Geologische Wetenschappen see Musee Royal de l'Afrique Centrale. Annales. Serie in 8. Sciences Geologiques *391*
Koninklijk Museum voor Midden-Afrika. Annalen. Reeks in 8. Historische Wetenschappen see Musee Royal de l'Afrique Centrale. Annales. Serie in 8. Sciences Historiques *566*
Koninklijk Museum voor Midden-Afrika. Annalen. Reeks in 8. Menselijke Wetenschappen see Musee Royal de l'Afrique Centrale. Annales. Serie in 8. Sciences Humaines *631*
Koninklijk Museum voor Midden-Afrika. Annalen. Reeks in 8. Zoologische Wetenschappen see Musee Royal de l'Afrique Centrale. Annales. Serie in 8. Sciences Zoologiques *176*
Koninklijk Museum voor Midden-Afrika. Economische Documentatie see Musee Royal de l'Afrique Centrale. Documentation Economique *197*

Koninklijk Museum voor Midden-Afrika. Zoologische Documentatie see Musee Royal de l'Afrique Centrale. Documentation Zoologique *176*
Koninklijk Nederlands Geologisch Mijnbouwkundig Genootschap. Verhandelingen (NE ISSN 0075-6741) *390*, *817*
Koninklijk Nederlandsch Genootschap voor Geslacht- en Wapenkunde. Werken Uitgegeven (NE) *536*
Koninklijke Academie voor Nederlandse Taal- en Letterkunde. Jaarboek (BE ISSN 0770-7762) *697*, *725*
Koninklijke Academie voor Nederlandse Taal- en Letterkunde. Verslagen en Mededelingen (BE ISSN 0023-3404) *725*
Koninklijke Bibliotheek Albert I. Jaarverslag see Bibliotheque Royale Albert 1er. Rapport Annuel *675*
Koninklijke Commissie voor de Uitgave der Oude Wetten en Verordeningen van Belgie. Handelingen see Commission Royale des Anciennes Lois et Ordonnances de Belgique. Bulletin *556*
Koninklijke Commissie voor Toponymie en Dialectologie. Handelingen see Commission Royale de Toponymie et de Dialectologie. Bulletin *556*
Koninklijke Geschied- en Oudheidkundige Kring van Kortrijk. Handelingen/Cercle Royal Historique et Archeologique de Courtrai. Memoires (BE) *588*
Koninklijke Kring voor Oudheidkunde Letteren en Kunst van Mechelen. Handelingen (BE) *89*, *588*
Koninklijke Musea voor Schone Kunsten van Belgie. Bulletin see Musees Royaux des Beaux-Arts de Belgique. Bulletin *828*
Koninklijke Nederlandse Akademie van Wetenschappen. Afdeling Letterkunde. Verhandelingen. Nieuwe Reeks (NE ISSN 0065-5511) *631*
Koninklijke Nederlandse Akademie van Wetenschappen. Afdeling Natuurkunde, Verhandelingen. Eerste Reeks (NE ISSN 0065-5503) *994*
Koninklijke Nederlandse Akademie van Wetenschappen. Afdeling Natuurkunde. Verhandelingen. Tweede Reeks (NE ISSN 0065-552X) *994*
Koninklijke Oudheidkundige Kring van Antwerpen. Jaarboek (BE) *89*
Konstanzer Grossdruckkalender (GW) *979*
Konstruktionsbuecher (US ISSN 0075-6768) *185*
Konstruktorsko-Tekhnologicheskii Institut Avtomatizatsii Avtomobilestroeniya. Sbornik Trudov(UR) *1092*
Konsulentordningen (DK ISSN 0109-3533) *196*
Kontak in Tendering (SA) *311*
Kontaks (PH) *311*
Kontakt (DK ISSN 0108-5190) *536*
Kontakt met Denemarken see Contact with Denmark *580*
Kontakt mit Daenemark see Contact with Denmark *580*
Kontaktkalender (DK ISSN 0108-4291) *258*
Kontekst (UR) *725*
Kontrollen med Konsumaelkprodukter see Rapport om Kontrollen med Konsummaelkprodukter *291*
Kontrollraadet foer Betongvaror. Meddelande (SW ISSN 0075-6776) *185*
Konyv es Konyvtar (HU ISSN 0139-1305) *680*
Konzert Almanach (GW) *837*
Koodal Historical Series (II) *558*
Koranyi Sandor Tarsasag. Tudomanyos Ulesek (HU ISSN 0075-6792) *762*
Korea (Republic). Central Meteorological Office. Annual Report (KO) *805*

Korea (Republic). Economic Planning Board. Annual Report on Current Industrial Production Survey (KO) *290*
Korea (Republic). Economic Planning Board. Annual Report on the Economically Active Population (KO ISSN 0454-7543) *273*
Korea (Republic). Economic Planning Board. Yearbook of Migration Statistics (KO) *923*
Korea (Republic). Ministry of Education. Basic Statistics of Education (KO) *424*
Korea (Republic). Ministry of Education. Educational Development in Korea (KO) *424*
Korea (Republic). National Bureau of Statistics. Annual Report on the Family Income and Expenditure Survey/Tosi Gagye Yonbo (KO ISSN 0075-6822) *212*
Korea (Republic). National Bureau of Statistics. Annual Report on the Price Survey/Mulga Yonbo (KO ISSN 0075-6830) *212*
Korea (Republic). National Bureau of Statistics. Report on Mining and Manufacturing Survey/Kwanggongup Tonggye Zo Sa Bogo Seo (KO ISSN 0075-6849) *8*, *212*, *822*
Korea (Republic). National Bureau of Statistics. Wholesale and Retail Trade Census Report/Tosomaeup Census Bogo Seo (KO ISSN 0075-6857) *212*
Korea (Republic). Office of Rural Development. Agricultural Research Report see Korea (Republic). Office of Rural Development. Research Report *30*
Korea (Republic). Office of Rural Development. Research Report (KO) *30*
Korea (Republic). Population & Housing Census Report (KO) *927*, *1058*
Korea Annual (KO) *311*
Korea Development Bank; Its Functions and Activities (KO ISSN 0075-6806) *230*
Korea Directory (US ISSN 0075-6814) *311*
Korea Film Catalog (KO) *824*
Korea Policy Series (KO) *246*, *906*
Korea Social Work College. Research Institute for Special Education. Journal/Kwang-Eung Yeo (KO) *445*
Korea Statistical Korea/Tonggye Suchup (KO ISSN 0081-4806) *1058*
Korea Statistical Yearbook/Hanguk Tonggye Yongam (KO ISSN 0075-6873) *1058*
Korea Stock Exchange. Fact Book (KO) *267*
Korea Trade (KO ISSN 0023-3943) *258*
Korean Affairs Report (US) *246*, *906*
Korean Astronomical Society. Journal (KO) *116*
Korean Journal of International Relations (KO) *917*
Korean Periodicals Index/Jeong-Gi Kanhaengmul Kisa Saegin (KO) *8*
Korean Press Annual/Hanguk Sinmun Pangsong Yongam (KO) *344*, *646*
Korean Publications Yearbook/Han'quk Ch'ulp an Yon'gam. (KO ISSN 0075-6881) *962*
Korean Scientific Abstracts (KO ISSN 0023-4052) *8*, *1004*, *1072*
Korean Studies (US ISSN 0145-840X) *570*
Koreansk Journal (SW ISSN 0023-4079) *917*
Korneuburger Kulturnachrichten (AU ISSN 0023-4087) *588*
Kornik, Poland. Zaklad Dendrologii i Pomologii. Prace see Arboretum Kornickie *154*
Korosi Csoma Kiskonyvtar (HU ISSN 0075-6911) *570*, *697*
Koroth (IS) *771*
Korrosionsverhalten von Zink (GW) *798*
Korunk Tudomanya (HU ISSN 0075-6946) *994*, *1069*
Kosher Directory (US) *504*, *976*

Kosmicheskaya Nauka i Tekhnika (UR) 116

Kosmicheskie Issledovaniya na Ukraine see Kosmicheskaya Nauka i Tekhnika 116

Kosmo see Kosmos 971

Kosmos (DK ISSN 0107-7902) 971

Kosmosophie (GW ISSN 0454-448X) 879

Kosten en Financiering van de Gezondheidzorg in Nederland/Cost of Health Care in the Netherlands (NE ISSN 0075-6954) 954, 1018

Koszen es Koolaj Anyagismereti Monografiak (HU ISSN 0075-6962) 865

Kothari's Economic and Industrial Guide of India see Kothari's Industrial Directory of India 311

Kothari's Economic Guide and Investor's Handbook of India see Kothari's Industrial Directory of India 311

Kothari's Industrial Directory of India (II) 267, 290, 311

Kothari's World of Reference Works (II ISSN 0075-6970) 128

Kotiseutukuvauksia Lounais-Haemeestae(FI) 588

Kovcezic (YU ISSN 0454-4617) 697, 725, 739

Kovel's Antiques and Collectibles Price List (US) 79

Kovel's Antiques Price List see Kovel's Antiques and Collectibles Price List 79

Kovels' Bottle Price List (US) 614

Kovel's Complete Bottle Price List see Kovels' Bottle Price List 614

Kowan Gijutsu Kenkyusho. Guide see Port and Harbour Research Institute. Guide 1103

Kozgazdasagi Ertekezesek (HU ISSN 0075-6989) 196

Kraevye Zadachi dlya Differentsial'nykh Uravnenii (UR) 750

Krajske Kulturni Stredisko v Hradci Kralove. Komentovana Vyroci (CS) 588

Krajske Muzeum v Teplicich. Zpravy a Studie (CS) 588

Krak (DK) 311

Krakow Dawniej i Dzis (PL ISSN 0075-7020) 588

Krakowskie Studia Prawnicze (PL ISSN 0023-4478) 658

Kraks TransportKatalog (DK ISSN 0108-8335) 1082

Krankenhaus Kalender (GW) 617

Kras i Speleologia (PL ISSN 0137-5482) 390

Krasoslovni Zbornik see Acta Carsologica 378

Kratylos (GW ISSN 0023-4567) 697, 725

Krefeld. Amt fuer Statistik und Stadtentwicklung. Statistisches Jahrbuch (GW) 1058

Kreolische Bibliothek (GW ISSN 0720-9983) 697

Krigsplan (DK ISSN 0106-2956) 545

Kriminalbiologische Gegenwartsfragen see Kriminologische Gegenwartsfragen 371

Kriminalforsorgens Aarsberetning (DK) 371

Kriminalitaet und ihre Verwalter (GW) 371

Kriminalwissenschaftliche Abhandlungen (GW ISSN 0454-5265) 371

Kriminologie. Abhandlungen ueber abwegiges Sozialverhalten (GW ISSN 0075-7144) 371

Kriminologische Gegenwartsfragen (GW ISSN 0075-7136) 371

Kriminologische Schriftenreihe (GW) 371

Kristiansand Museum. Aarbok (NO ISSN 0333-3124) 158

Kristofer Lehmkuhl Forelesning (NO ISSN 0452-7208) 196

Kritik der Buergerlichen Ideologie (GE ISSN 0138-3612) 879

Kritische Studien zur Geschichtswissenschaft (GW) 558

Kroc Foundation Series (US ISSN 0361-0489) 1157

Kroeber Anthropological Society. Papers (US ISSN 0023-4869) 73

Krske Skofije. Zbornik see Diozese Gurk. Jahrbuch 982

Kryptadia: Journal of Erotic Folklore (FR ISSN 0075-7160) 516

Krystalinikum (CS) 390

Ksiazka w Dawnej Kulturze Polskiej (PL ISSN 0075-7179) 631

Ktema (FR) 338, 570

Ktemata (BE) 994

Kuala Lumpur. Rubber Research Institute of Malaya. Annual Report see Rubber Research Institute of Malaysia. Annual Report 985

Kuala Lumpur Stock Exchange. Companies Handbook (MY ISSN 0126-7558) 267

Die Kueste (GW ISSN 0452-7739) 406, 472, 497

Kuk Hoe Hoe Eu Rok Saegin see Index to the National Assembly Records 687

Kuka Kukin On/Who's Who in Finland(FI) 134

Kultur og Samfund (DK ISSN 0107-3591) 631

Kultur und Gesellschaft (GW) 558, 1009

Kulturgeografiske Haefters Skriftserie (DK ISSN 0108-3945) 545

Kulturminder (DK) 588

Kulturno-Politicky a Historicky Kalendar Mesta Bratislavy (CS) 588

Kulturnopoliticky Kalendar (CS) 796, 1112

Kulturpflanze (GE ISSN 0075-7209) 158, 167

Kumamoto Daigaku Kogakubu Kenkyu Hokoku see Kumamoto University. Faculty of Engineering. Technical Reports 472

Kumamoto Daigaku Kogakubu Kiyo see Kumamoto University. Faculty of Engineering. Memoirs 472

Kumamoto University. Department of Geology. Journal (JA) 390

Kumamoto University. Department of Physics. Physics Reports (JA) 889

Kumamoto University. Faculty of Engineering. Memoirs/Kumamoto Daigaku Kogakubu Kiyo (JA ISSN 0023-5334) 472

Kumamoto University. Faculty of Engineering. Technical Reports/Kumamoto Daigaku Kogakubu Kenkyu Hokoku (JA ISSN 0023-5296) 472

Kumamoto University. Institute of Constitutional Medicine. Bulletin. Supplement (JA ISSN 0075-7217) 763

Kumasitech see University of Science and Technology. Journal 1002

Kunde (GW ISSN 0342-0736) 89

Kungl Vetenskapsakademien. Bidrag till Kungliga Vetenskapsakademiens Historia (SW ISSN 0081-9956) 994

Kungliga Humanistiska Vetenskapssamfundet i Lund. Arsberattelse see Societe Royale de Lettres de Lund. Bulletin 733

Kungliga Skogshoegskolan. Institutionen foer Virkeslaera. Rapporter see Sveriges Lantbruksuniversitet. Institutionen foer Virkeslaera. Rapporter 527

Kungliga Skogshoegskolan. Institutionen foer Virkeslaera. Uppsatser see Sveriges Lantbruksuniversitet. Institutionen foer Virkeslaera. Uppsatser 527

Kungliga Tekniska Hoegskolan. Flygteknisk Institutionen. K T H Aero Memo F I (SW ISSN 0280-1078) 20

Kungliga Vitterhets-, Historie- och Antikvitets Akademien. Aarsbok (SW ISSN 0083-6796) 588

Kungliga Vitterhets-, Historie- och Antikvitets Akademien. Antikvariskt Arkiv (SW ISSN 0083-6737) 89, 106

Kungliga Vitterhets-, Historie- och Antikvitets Akademien. Filologiskt Arkiv (SW ISSN 0083-6745) 697

Kungliga Vitterhets-, Historie- och Antikvitets Akademien. Handlingar. Antikvariska Serien/Royal Academy of Letters, History and Antiquities. Proceedings. Antiquarian Series (SW ISSN 0083-6761) 588

Kungliga Vitterhets-, Historie- och Antikvitets Akademien. Handlingar. Filologisk-Filosofiska Serien/Royal Academy of Letters, History and Antiquities. Proceedings. Philological-Philosophical Series (SW ISSN 0083-677X) 697, 879

Kungliga Vitterhets-, Historie- och Antikvitets Akademien. Handlingar. Historiska Serien/Royal Academy of Letters, History and Antiquities. Proceedings. Historical Series (SW ISSN 0083-6788) 588

Kungliga Vitterhets-, Historie- och Antikvitets Akademien. Historiskt Arkiv (SW ISSN 0083-6753) 589

Kunitachi College of Music. Memoirs/Kunitachi Ongaku Daigaku Kenkyu Kiyo (JA) 837

Kunitachi Ongaku Daigaku Kenkyu Kiyo see Kunitachi College of Music. Memoirs 837

Kunst see Art 113

Kunst am Bau (GW) 98, 106, 185, 624

Kunst des Orients/Art of the Orient (GW ISSN 0023-5393) 106, 852

Kunst-Katalog: Auktionen (AU ISSN 0075-7241) 106

Kunst og Museum (DK ISSN 0454-6520) 106

Kunst und Altertum am Rhein (GW ISSN 0075-725X) 89

Kunsthistorische Sammlungen in Wien. Jahrbuch (AU ISSN 0075-2312) 106

Kunsthistorisches Institut in Florenz. Mitteilungen (IT) 106, 558

Kunstjahrbuch der Stadt Linz (AU) 106

Kunstmuseets Aarsskrift (DK ISSN 0107-8933) 106

Kunstpreis-Jahrbuch (GW ISSN 0174-352X) 79, 106

Kunststoff-Industrie und ihre Helfer (GW ISSN 0075-7276) 900

Kunststoffe im Lebensmittelverkehr (GW ISSN 0075-7292) 900

Kunststoffprodukte (GW) 900

Kupat-Holim Yearbook (IS ISSN 0301-4843) 954

Kuratorium fuer Technik und Bauwesen in der Landwirtschaft e.V. Schriften see K T B L - Schriften 30

Kuratorium fuer Verkehrssicherheit. Kleine Fachbuchreihe (AU ISSN 0075-7306) 1096

Kurrens Idoszaki Kiadvanyok see Magyar Nemzeti Bibliografia. Idoszaki Kiadvanyok Bibliografiaja 128

Kursbuch der deutschen Museums-Eisenbahnen (GW) 1094

Kurt-Schwitters-Almanach (GW ISSN 0723-6638) 106

Kurtziana (AG ISSN 0075-7314) 158

Kurukshetra Law Journal (II) 658

Kurze Uebersicht see South Africa Foundation. Information Digest (Year) 249

Kuschitische Sprachstudien Cushitic Language Studies (GW ISSN 0721-4340) 697

Kuukausikatsaus Suomen Ilmastoon/Maanadsoeversikt oever Finlands Klimat (FI ISSN 0303-2485) 805

Kuwait. Central Statistical Office. Annual Bulletin for Prices and Index Numbers (KU) 277

Kuwait. Central Statistical Office. Annual Statistical Abstract (KU) 1058

Kuwait. Central Statistical Office. Monthly Digest of Statistics see Kuwait. Central Statistical Office. Annual Statistical Abstract 1058

Kuwait Advertsing Age (KU) 15

Kuwait Bulletin of Marine Science (KU ISSN 0250-362X) 142, 175, 511

Kuwait Institute for Scientific Research. Annual Research Report (KU ISSN 0250-4065) 994

Kuwait Investment Company. (Report) (KU) 230

Kuwait University. Conference on Algebra and Geometry. Proceedings (KU) 750

Kvinder, Kvinder (DK ISSN 0108-1888) 616, 1129

Kvindestudier ved A U C. Aarbog (Aalborg Universitetscenter) (DK ISSN 0108-3961) 1129

Kwahak Kisul Yoram/Handbook of Science and Technology (KO) 1069

Kwang-Eung Yeo see Korea Social Work College. Research Institute for Special Education. Journal 445

Kwanggongup Tonggye Zo Sa Bogo Seo see Korea (Republic). National Bureau of Statistics. Report on Mining and Manufacturing Survey 822

Kyoiku Shinrigaku Nempo see Annual Report of Educational Psychology in Japan 933

Kyoka Kyoiku Kenkyu (JA) 448

Kyoto Daigaku Genshi Enerugi Kenkyusho Kenkyu Hokoku see Kyoto University. Institute of Atomic Energy. Technical Reports 897

Kyoto Daigaku Ogata Keisanki Senta Eibun Repoto see Kyoto University. Data Processing Center. Report 360

Kyoto Daigaku Uirusu Kenkyusho Nenkan Kiyo see Kyoto University. Institute for Virus Research. Annual Report 168

Kyoto-furitsu Daigaku Gakujutsu Hokoku Jimbun see Kyoto Prefectural University. Scientific Reports: Humanities 631

Kyoto-furitsu Daigaku Gakujutsu Hokoku Nagaku see Kyoto Prefectural University. Scientific Reports: Agriculture 30

Kyoto-furitsu Daigaku Gakujutsu Hokoku Rigaku Seikatsukagaku see Kyoto Prefectural University. Scientific Reports: Natural Science and Living Science 994

Kyoto Institute of Technology. Faculty of Engineering and Design. Memoirs (JA ISSN 0911-0305) 994, 1069

Kyoto Prefectural University. Scientific Reports: Agriculture/Kyoto-furitsu Daigaku Gakujutsu Hokoku Nagaku (JA ISSN 0075-7373) 30

Kyoto Prefectural University. Scientific Reports: Humanities/Kyoto-furitsu Daigaku Gakujutsu Hokoku Jimbun (JA ISSN 0075-7381) 631

Kyoto Prefectural University. Scientific Reports: Natural Science and Living Science/Kyoto-furitsu Daigaku Gakujutsu Hokoku Rigaku Seikatsukagaku (JA) 994

Kyoto Prefectural University. Scientific Reports: Natural Science, Domestic Science and Social Welfare see Kyoto Prefectural University. Scientific Reports: Natural Science and Living Science 994

Kyoto Review (JA ISSN 0388-0532) 725

Kyoto Technical University. Faculty of Industrial Arts. Memoirs: Science and Technology see Kyoto Institute of Technology. Faculty of Engineering and Design. Memoirs 994

Kyoto University. Data Processing Center. Report/Kyoto Daigaku Ogata Keisanki Senta Eibun Repoto (JA) 360

Kyoto University. Faculty of Science. Memoirs. Series of Biology (JA ISSN 0454-7802) 143

Kyoto University. Institute for Virus Research. Annual Report/Kyoto Daigaku Uirusu Kenkyusho Nenkan Kiyo (JA ISSN 0075-7357) 168

Kyoto University. Institute of Atomic Energy. Research Activities (JA ISSN 0386-0752) 897

Kyoto University. Institute of Atomic Energy. Technical Reports/Kyoto Daigaku Genshi Enerugi Kenkyusho Kenkyu Hokoku (JA) 897

Kyoto University. Misaki Marine Biological Institute. Bulletin (JA ISSN 0023-6098) 143

Kyoto University. Primate Research Institute. Annual Report *see* Reichorui Kenkyujo Nenpo 75
Kyoto University. Research Activities in Civil Engineering and Related Fields (JA ISSN 0075-7365) 482
Kyoto University. Research Institute for Food Science. Bulletin (JA ISSN 0451-1476) 30
Kyoto University. Research Reactor Institute. Annual Reports (JA ISSN 0454-9244) 328, 465, 894, 897
Kyoyo Ronshu *see* Review on Liberal Arts 632
Kypriakai Spoudai *see* Society of Cypriot Studies. Bulletin 597
Kyrkohistorisk Aarsskrift (SW ISSN 0085-2619) 971
Kytoesavut (FI ISSN 0454-8086) 589
Kyushu American Literature (JA ISSN 0454-8132) 725
Kyushu Daigaku Nogakubu Suisangakka Gyosekishu *see* Kyushu University. Contributions from the Department of Fisheries and the Fishery Research Laboratory 511
Kyushu Daigaku Rigakubu Kenkyu Hokoku Chishitsugaku *see* Kyushu University. Department of Geology. Science Reports 390
Kyushu Daigaku Rigakubu Kiyo, C. Kagaku *see* Kyushu University. Faculty of Science. Memoirs. Series C: Chemistry 323
Kyushu Daigaku Rigakubu Kiyo, D, Chishitsugaku *see* Kyushu University. Faculty of Science. Memoirs. Series D: Geology 390
Kyushu Institute of Technology. Bulletin: Humanities, Social Sciences/Kyushu Kogyo Daigaku Kenkyu Hokoku, Jinbun-Shakai-Kagaku (JA ISSN 0453-0349) 631, 1009
Kyushu Institute of Technology. Bulletin: Mathematics, Natural Science/Kyushu Kogyo Daigaku Kenkyu Hokoku, Shizenkagaku (JA ISSN 0454-8221) 750, 994
Kyushu Institute of Technology. Memoirs: Engineering (JA ISSN 0369-0512) 472
Kyushu Kogyo Daigaku Kenkyu Hokoku, Jinbun-Shakai-Kagaku *see* Kyushu Institute of Technology. Bulletin: Humanities, Social Sciences 631
Kyushu Kogyo Daigaku Kenkyu Hokoku, Shizenkagaku *see* Kyushu Institute of Technology. Bulletin: Mathematics, Natural Science 750
Kyushu Kogyo Gijutsu Shikenjo Nempo *see* Japan. Government Industrial Research Institute, Kyushu Annual Report 290
Kyushu University. Contributions from the Department of Fisheries and the Fishery Research Laboratory/Kyushu Daigaku Nogakubu Suisangakka Gyosekishu (JA ISSN 0453-0314) 511
Kyushu University. Department of Geology. Science Reports/Kyushu Daigaku Rigakubu Kenkyu Hokoku Chishitsugaku (JA ISSN 0385-8278) 390, 856, 865
Kyushu University. Faculty of Science. Memoirs. Series C: Chemistry/Kyushu Daigaku Rigakubu Kiyo, C. Kagaku (JA ISSN 0085-2635) 323
Kyushu University. Faculty of Science. Memoirs. Series D: Geology/Kyushu Daigaku Rigakubu Kiyo, D, Chishitsugaku (JA ISSN 0023-6179) 390
Kyushu University. Institute of Tropical Agriculture. Bulletin (JA) 30
Kyushu University. Research Institute for Applied Mechanics. Abstracts of Papers (JA) 489
L A C U N Y Occasional Papers (Library Association of the City University of New York) (US) 1157
L A C U S Forum (Linguistic Association of Canada and the United States) (US ISSN 0195-377X) 697
L A N Software Directory (Local Area Network) (US) 359

L A R C Newsletter (Radcliffe College, Lesbian Alumni) (US) 616, 1129
L A R U Working Paper (Latin American Research Unit) (CN) 607
L A T I S *see* Landscape Architecture Technical Information Series 98
L A W G Letter (Latin American Working Group) (CN ISSN 0316-3393) 711, 906
L C A Quarterly (Lawyers for the Creative Arts) (US) 107, 658
L C Folk Archive Finding Aid (U.S. Library of Congress) (US ISSN 0736-4903) 516, 680
L C Science Tracer Bullet (US ISSN 0090-5232) 1004
L D V Bogen *see* D V Bogen 1081
L.E.I. Schriften *see* Institut Economique Agricole. Cahiers 1155
L E P *see* Library of Exact Philosophy 994
L F B Documentation. Report (GW ISSN 0174-1764) 979
L F L Reports (Libertarians for Life) (US ISSN 0882-116X) 906
L I P (AT ISSN 0313-4288) 1129
L I R I Research Bulletin (Leather Industries Research Institute) (SA ISSN 0085-2724) 672
L I R I Technical Bulletin (Leather Industries Research Institute) (SA) 672
L I S L *see* Amsterdam Studies in the Theory and History of Linguistic Science. Series 5: Library and Information Sources in Linguistics 709
L J Special Reports (US ISSN 0362-448X) 1157
L L B A *see* Linguistics and Language Behavior Abstracts 709
L L S E E *see* Linguistic & Literary Studies in Eastern Europe 698
L M S Monographs *see* London Mathematical Society. Monographs. New Series 750
L O K Report Reisefuehrer (GW ISSN 0170-4621) 1094
L O M A Literature on Modern Art *see* Artbibliographies Modern 11
L P-Gas Market Facts (US ISSN 0075-9759) 865
L P I Technical Report (Lunar and Planetary Institute) (US) 116
L R I Guides to Management. Monographs (US) 280
L.S.C.A. Annual Program, Hawaii State Library System (Library Services and Construction Act) (US ISSN 0095-4721) 680
L.S.I. (FR ISSN 0335-9190) 725
L S U Wood Utilization Notes (US ISSN 0076-1109) 530
L T C Newsletter *see* Land Tenure Center. Newsletter 1157
L T C Paper *see* Land Tenure Center. Paper 48
L T P (UK ISSN 0262-575X) 711
L U A C Monitor (Life Underwriters Association of Canada) (CN ISSN 0318-8116) 640
L U Information (Landsforeningen af Ungdomsskoledere) (DK ISSN 0108-836X) 443
La Trobe Sociology Papers (AT) 1027
Labor Chronicle (US ISSN 0023-6519) 648
Labor Force in Idaho (US) 273
Labor Force Status of Indiana Residents (US ISSN 0362-3793) 273
Labor Market and Labor Market Policy *see* Arbejdsmarkedet og Arbejdsmarkedspolotik 270
Labor Rates for the Construction Industry (US ISSN 0098-3608) 185, 273
Labor Relations and Public Policy Series (US) 273
Labor Relations Yearbook (US ISSN 0075-7489) 1157
Labor Research Report (Albany) *see* New York (State) Department of Labor. Division of Research and Statistics. Labor Research Report 274
Laboratorio di Entomologia Agraria. Bollettino (IT ISSN 0304-0658) 165

Laboratorio di Tecnologia della Pesca. Quaderni *see* Istituto Ricerche Pesca Marittima. Quaderni 511
Laboratorios de Especialidades y Control (MX) 782
Laboratory and Research Methods in Biology and Medicine (US ISSN 0160-8584) 782
Laboratory Animal Handbooks (UK ISSN 0458-5933) 782
Laboratory Animals. Buyers Guide (UK) 782
Laboratory Equipment Directory (UK ISSN 0141-8963) 637
Laboratory Equipment Directory and Buyers Guide *see* Laboratory Equipment Directory 637
Laboratory Equipment Index (UK ISSN 0308-8367) 782
Laboratory Guide to Instruments, Equipment and Chemicals *see* Laboratory Guide to Instruments, Equipment and Chemicals. Lab Guide 323
Laboratory Guide to Instruments, Equipment and Chemicals. Lab Guide (American Chemical Society) (US ISSN 0003-2700) 323
Labour Code of Pakistan (PK) 273
Labour in Israel (IS ISSN 0023-6969) 648
Labour in the Public Sector Undertakings: Basic Information (II ISSN 0377-077X) 273
Labour Law Cases (PK) 273, 658
Labour Legislation in Nova Scotia (CN ISSN 0383-3372) 273, 658
Labour Literature: A Bibliography (II ISSN 0075-756X) 212
Labour-Management Relations Series (UN ISSN 0538-8325) 273
Labour Movement Library and Archive, Denmark *see* Arbejderbevaegelsens Bibliotek og Arkiv 203
Labour Organizations in Nova Scotia (CN ISSN 0383-3437) 648
Labour Standards in Canada. Normes du Travail au Canada (CN ISSN 0075-7586) 273
Labour Statistics Report (CY) 212
Labrador Retriever Club of Wales. Yearbook (UK ISSN 0260-5627) 868
Lacito Documents Afrique (FR ISSN 0754-2445) 73, 697
Lacito Documents Asie-Austronesie (FR ISSN 0751-4875) 73, 697
Lacito Documents Eurasie (FR ISSN 0751-4883) 73, 697
Lacombe News *see* Canadian Lacombe Breeders Association. Newsletter 65
Lactation Review (US ISSN 0362-3173) 73, 787
Ladinia (IT) 504
Lady Golfer's Handbook (UK) 1039
Ladysmith Directory (SA ISSN 0378-9268) 311
Laegaest: Arkeologi i Nordlesvig (DK ISSN 0900-8047) 89, 828
Laegeforeningens Medicinfortegnelse (DK ISSN 0106-1275) 871
Laegeforeningens Vejviser (DK) 763
Laegemiddelforbruget i Danmark (DK ISSN 0108-0687) 871
Laegen (DK) 763
Laegestillinger og Sengepladser paa Institutioner (DK ISSN 0107-1165) 617
Laendermonographien (GW) 545, 558, 1027
Laengden af Offentlige Veje (DK ISSN 0109-6044) 1096
Laerarhoegskolan i Moelndal. Pedagogiska Institutionen. Rapport *see* Goeteborgs Universitet. Institutionen foer Praktisk Pedagogik. Rapport 447
Laes om (DK ISSN 0107-4636) 335
Lafayette Clinic Handbooks in Psychiatry (US ISSN 0075-7608) 790
Lafayette Clinic Monographs in Psychiatry (US ISSN 0075-7616) 790
Lagertechnik (GW) 284
Lagos Librarian (NR ISSN 0047-3901) 680
Lagos Notes and Records (NR ISSN 0075-7640) 566

Laissez Faire Anarchist Catalog (US) 1157
Lake Carriers' Association. Annual Report (US ISSN 0075-7748) 1101
Lake Chelan History Notes (US) 607
Lake Street Review (US ISSN 0889-6410) 725, 742
Lakeland and North Lancashire Catering and Hotel Year Book *see* Cumbria and North Lancashire Catering and Hotel Year Book 619
Lakeland Dialect (UK) 697
Lakeland Dialect Society. Journal *see* Lakeland Dialect 697
Lakeland Hotel and Catering Year Book *see* Cumbria and North Lancashire Catering and Hotel Year Book 619
Lakescene - Eating Out in Lakeland and North Lancashire (UK) 620
Lakescene - Good Pubs in Cumbria (UK) 120
Lakescene - Guide to Carlisle the Border (UK) 1112
Lakescene - Guide to Hunting in Lakeland (UK) 1046
Lakescene - Leisure Time in Lakeland (UK) 1112
Lakewoods Astrological Guides (US) 114
Lalbhai Dalpatbhai Institute of Indology. Publications (II) 852
Lalit Kala (II ISSN 0458-6506) 107
Lamar Lecture Series (US ISSN 0075-7772) 558, 725
Lambert's World of Trade, Finance and Economic Development (US) 311
Lammergeyer (SA ISSN 0075-7780) 366
Lamy Transport (FR) 671, 1082
Lancashire and Cheshire Antiquarian Society. Newsletter (UK) 589
Lancashire Chambers of Commerce & Industry Directory (UK) 236
Lancashire Dialect Society. Journal (UK ISSN 0075-7799) 697
Land and Water Conservation Fund Grants Manual (US) 1046
Land Bank of the Philippines. Annual Report (PH) 230
Land Economics Monographs (US ISSN 0075-7837) 48
Land Tenure Center. Newsletter (US ISSN 0084-0785) 1157
Land Tenure Center. Paper (US ISSN 0084-0793) 48
Land Tenure Center. Research Paper (US ISSN 0084-0815) 48
Land Use & Environment Law Review (US ISSN 0192-8309) 497
Land Use Planning (CN) 658
Landarbeit und Technik (GW ISSN 0455-2342) 30
Landboforeningernes Driftsoekonomiske Virksomhed, Regnskabresultater, Kalenderaar (DK ISSN 0107-1300) 48
Landbohistorisk Tidsskrift (DK) 30, 589
Landbouw-Economisch Instituut. Bedrijfsuitkomsten in de Landbouw (NE) 48
Landbouw-Economisch Instituut. Landbouw-Economisch Bericht (NE) 48
Landbouw-Economisch Instituut. Tuinbouwcijfers (NE) 534
Landbouwcijfers (NE) 30
Landbouwhogeschool, Wageningen. Miscellaneous Papers (NE ISSN 0083-6990) 30
Landbouwproefstation Suriname. Jaarverslag/Agricultural Experiment Station Suriname. Annual Report (SR) 31
Landbrugets Maskinoversigt (DK ISSN 0107-461X) 51
Landbrugets Oekonomi *see* Denmark. Jordbrugsoekonomisk Institut. Landbrugets Oekonomi 193
Landbrugets Organisationshaandbog (DK ISSN 0108-4003) 31
Landbrugets Samraad for Forskning og Forsoeg. Kortlaegning (DK ISSN 0105-4244) 31
Landbrugets Samraad for Forskning og Forsoeg. Rammeplaner (DK ISSN 0108-4518) 31

Landbrugsaarbog (DK ISSN 0302-4946) *31*
Landbrugseksporten (DK ISSN 0106-3812) *258*
Landbrugsregnskaber *see* Driftsoekonomi *193*
Landbrugsregnskabsstatistik *see* Denmark. Jordbrugsoekonomisk Institut. Serie A: Landbrugets Regnskabsstatistik *46*
Landbrukets Aarbok. Jordbruk, Hagebruk, Skogbruk (NO ISSN 0075-7853) *31, 526*
Landbrukets Aarbok. Skogbruk *see* Landbrukets Aarbok. Jordbruk, Hagebruk, Skogbruk *526*
Landesgesetzblatt fuer das Land Salzburg (AU ISSN 0023-7884) *951*
Landeskonservator Rheinland. Arbeitsheft (GW) *98*
Landeskundliche Luftbildauswertung im Mitteileuropaeischen Raum *see* Fernerkundung in Raumordung und Stadtebau *543*
Landesmuseum fuer Kaernten. Buchreihe. (AU ISSN 0007-280X) *107, 558, 845*
Landesmuseum fuer Naturkunde zu Muenster in Westfalen. Abhandlungen *see* Westfaelischen Museum fuer Naturkunde. Abhandlungen *1003*
Landesmuseum fuer Vorgeschichte, Dresden. Kleine Schriften (GE ISSN 0232-5446) *559*
Landesmuseum fuer Vorgeschichte, Dresden. Veroeffentlichungen (GE ISSN 0070-7201) *589, 828*
Landesmuseum fuer Vorgeschichte, Halle. Veroeffentlichungen (GE ISSN 0072-940X) *589, 828*
Landesmuseum Joanneum. Abteilung fuer Botanik. Mitteilungen (AU) *158*
Landesmuseum Joanneum. Abteilung fuer Geologie, Palaeontologie und Bergbau. Mitteilungen (AU) *390, 817, 856*
Landesmuseum Joanneum. Abteilung fuer Zoologie. Mitteilungen (AU) *175*
Landesverein fuer Hoehlenkunde in der Steiermark. Mitteilungen (AU) *390*
Landis & Gyr Review *see* Landis und Gyr Mitteilungen *456*
Landis und Gyr Mitteilungen (SZ ISSN 0023-7949) *456*
Landoekonomisk Aarbog *see* Landbrugsaarbog *31*
Landoekonomisk Oversigt (DK ISSN 0107-7163) *196*
Landolt-Boernstein Numerical Data and Functional Relationships in Science and Technology. New Series *see* Landolt-Boernstein, Zahlenwerte und Funktionen aus Naturwissenschaften und Technik. Neue Serie. Group 1: Nuclear Physics *897*
Landolt-Boernstein, Zahlenwerte und Funktionen aus Naturwissenschaften und Technik. Neue Serie. Group 1: Nuclear Physics/Landolt-Boernstein Numerical Data and Functional Relationships in Science and Technology. New Series (US ISSN 0075-7888) *897*
Landolt-Boernstein, Zahlenwerte und Funktionen aus Naturwissenschaften und Technik. Neue Serie. Group 2: Atomic Physics (US ISSN 0075-7918) *897*
Landolt-Boernstein, Zahlenwerte und Funktionen aus Naturwissenschaften und Technik. Neue Serie. Group 3: Crystal Physics (US ISSN 0075-787X) *327, 889*
Landolt-Boernstein, Zahlenwerte und Funktionen aus Naturwissenschaften und Technik. Neue Serie. Group 4: Macroscopic and Technical Properties of Matter (US ISSN 0075-7926) *1069*
Landolt-Boernstein, Zahlenwerte und Funktionen aus Naturwissenschaften und Technik. Neue Serie. Group 5: Geophysics (US ISSN 0075-790X) *400*

Landolt-Boernstein, Zahlenwerte und Funktionen aus Naturwissenschaften und Technik. Neue Serie. Group 6: Astronomy (US ISSN 0075-7896) *116*
Landscape Architecture Technical Information Series (US ISSN 0195-5764) *98*
Landscape History (UK ISSN 0143-3768) *31, 98, 589*
Landscentralen for Undervisningsmidler. Baandcentralen. Baandkatalog (DK ISSN 0106-7737) *424*
Landscentralen for Undervisningsmidler. Baandcentralen. Katalog *see* Landscentralen for Undervisningsmidler. Baandcentralen. Baandkatalog *424*
Landscentralen for Undervisningsmidler. Teknisk Information (DK ISSN 0109-7679) *416*
Landschaftsverband Westfalen-Lippe *see* Volkskuendlichen Kommission fuer Westfalen. Schriften *517*
Landsforeningen af Ungdomsskoledere Information *see* L U Information *443*
Landshavneplanbidrag (DK ISSN 0108-7231) *1101*
Landskunde von Niederoesterreich. Jahrbuch (AU) *589*
Landslaget for Bygde og Byhistorie. Skrifter *see* Landslaget for Lokalhistorie *589*
Landslaget for Lokalhistorie (NO) *589*
Landsorganisationen i Sverige. Yttranden till Offentlig Myndighet (SW) *648*
Landsudvalget for Fjerkrae. Meddelelse (DK ISSN 0105-9882) *67*
Landwirtschaftliches Zentralblatt. Abteilung 1: Landtechnik *see* Agroselekt. Reihe 1: Landtechnik *38*
Landwirtschaftliches Zentralblatt. Abteilung 2: Pflanzliche Produktion *see* Agroselekt. Reihe 2: Pflanzenproduktion *38*
Landwirtschaftliches Zentralblatt. Abteilung 3: Tierzucht, Tierernaehrung, Fischerei *see* Agroselekt. Reihe 3: Tierproduktion *38*
Lane Studies in Regional Government (US) *943*
Langaa (DK ISSN 0109-0178) *589*
Language and Language Behavior Abstracts *see* Linguistics and Language Behavior Abstracts *709*
Language and Learning for Human Service Professions (US) *448*
Language Forum (II ISSN 0253-9071) *697*
Language Forum Monograph Series (II ISSN 0254-0207) *697*
Language Teaching (UK ISSN 0261-4448) *8, 424, 709*
Langue et Cultures (SZ ISSN 0085-2678) *697*
Langue Internationale (FR ISSN 0085-2686) *671*
Langues du Cameroun (CM) *697*
Langues et Civilisations a Tradition Orale (FR ISSN 0240-2041) *73, 697*
Langues et Cultures Africaines (FR ISSN 0755-9305) *73, 697*
Langues et Cultures du Pacifique (FR ISSN 0750-2036) *73, 697*
Langues et Styles (FR ISSN 0457-1320) *697, 725*
Lansky: Bibliotheksrechtliche Vorschriften (GW ISSN 0175-6524) *658, 680*
Lantbrukshoegskolan Institutionen foer Vaextodling. Rapporter och Arhandlingar *see* Sveriges Lantbruksuniversitet. Institutionen foer Vaextodling. Rapporter och Avhandlingar *35*
Laographikon Archeion. Epeteris *see* Akademia Athenon. Kentron Ereunes tes Hellenikes Laographias. Epeteris *514*
Laomedon Review (CN ISSN 0382-8824) *725*
Lapis (US) *711*
Laporan Ketua Odit Negara. Kerajaan Persekutuan (MY) *246*

Lares. Biblioteca (IT ISSN 0075-8019) *516*
Large Employers Directory of Metropolitant St. Louis (US) *236*
Large-Print Scores and Books Catalog *see* Music & Musicians: Large-Print Scores and Books Catalog (Large Print Edition) *180*
Large Stores Directory (UK ISSN 0260-6526) *240*
Large Type Books in Print (US) *128, 180*
Laser (UK) *994, 1069*
Laser Applications (US) *456*
Laser Focus Buyers' Guide *see* Laser Focus/Electro Optics Buyers' Guide *899*
Laser Focus/Electro Optics Buyers' Guide (US ISSN 8755-1616) *332, 899*
Laser Raman & Infrared Spectroscopy Abstracts (UK ISSN 0309-5320) *8, 893*
Laser Raman Spectroscopy Abstracts *see* Laser Raman & Infrared Spectroscopy Abstracts *893*
Lasers in Graphics: Electronic Publishing in the 80's. Conference Proceedings (US) *931*
Last Month's Newsletter (US) *341*
Late 18th & 19th Century Sculpture in the British Isles *see* Courtauld Institute Illustration Archives. Archive 4 *104*
Latest Information on National Accounts of Developing Countries *see* Informations Recentes sur les Comptes Nationaux des Pays en Developpement *211*
Latest Literature in Family Planning (UK ISSN 0308-8774) *179*
Lathrop Report on Newspaper Indexes (US) *8, 647*
Latin America and Caribbean *see* Latin America & Caribbean Review *246*
Latin America and Caribbean Contemporary Record (US ISSN 0736-4148) *917*
Latin America & Caribbean Review (UK) *246, 906*
Latin America Annual Review and the Caribbean *see* Latin America & Caribbean Review *246*
Latin American Food Production Conference Summary Report *see* World Food Production Conference Summary Report *521*
Latin American Historical Dictionaries Series (US) *607*
Latin-American Import-Export Directory (CR) *311*
Latin American Integration Process in (Year) (AG) *923, 927*
Latin American International Affairs (US) *1157*
Latin American International Food Industry Directory (US) *520*
Latin American Jewish Studies Newsletter (US ISSN 0738-1379) *504, 545*
Latin American Metal Mechanic & Electronic Industry Directory (US) *240, 745*
Latin American Monograph and Document Series (US) *631, 1009*
Latin American Monographs (US ISSN 0075-8108) *1009*
Latin American Research Unit Working Paper *see* L A R U Working Paper *607*
Latin American Shipping *see* Turkish Shipping *1104*
Latin American Studies in the Universities of the United Kingdom (UK ISSN 0085-2694) *128, 564*
Latin American Studies in the Universities of the United Kingdom. Staff Research in Progress or Recently Completed in the Humanities and the Social Sciences (UK ISSN 0085-2708) *128, 564*
Latin American Studies Working Papers(US) *589*
Latin American Textile Industry Directory (US) *1074*
Latin American Working Group Letter *see* L A W G Letter *711*
Latin and Greek Texts (UK ISSN 0951-7391) *338*

Latinamerican Arts *see* Hispanic American Arts *105*
Latinoamerica (US) *1009*
Latinoamericana (SW) *128, 607*
Latium (IT) *589*
Latomistica (IT) *559*
Latviesu Valodas Kulturas Jautajumi (UR) *697*
Latvija Sodien (US ISSN 0093-8920) *504*
Latvju Maksla (US ISSN 0362-7047) *107, 504*
Latvju Muzika (US) *837*
Laugh Factory (US) *711*
Laurence Scott Engineering Bulletin (UK ISSN 0023-6381) *456*
Lauriston S. Taylor Lecture Series (US ISSN 0277-9196) *954*
Lava (II) *742*
Lavanderia Moderna/Modern Cleaning: Directory of Suppliers (MX) *339*
Lavprisbutikker *see* Discountbutikker (Year) *301*
Law *see* A D L Law Report *649*
Law & Anthropology (AU ISSN 0259-0816) *73, 658*
Law and Ethics Series (US) *658*
Law & Inequality (US ISSN 0737-089X) *504, 658, 1009*
Law and Legal Information Directory (US) *658*
Law and Philosophy Library (NE) *658, 879*
Law and Political Review (KO) *658, 906*
Law and Psychology Review (US ISSN 0098-5961) *658, 935, 1009*
Law & Women Series (US) *658, 1129*
Law Annual Report of China (HK) *658*
Law Bibliography *see* Rechtsbibliographie *669*
Law Books in Print (US ISSN 0075-8221) *659*
Law Forum (US) *659*
Law in Eastern Europe (NE ISSN 0075-823X) *671*
Law in Society (NR ISSN 0458-8592) *659*
Law Information *see* Bowker's Law Books and Serials in Print *668*
Law Office Guide in Computers (Year) Directory (US) *362, 362, 363, 669*
Law Reprints (US) *659*
Law Reprints: Criminal Law Series (US) *371*
Law Reprints: Labor Law Series (US) *273*
Law Reprints: Patent, Trademark & Copyright Series (US) *861*
Law Reprints: Securities Regulation Series (US) *267, 659*
Law Reprints: Tax Law Series (US) *297, 659*
Law Reprints: Trade Regulation Series (US) *258, 671*
Law, Society, and Policy (US) *659*
Law Society of Upper Canada. Special Lectures (CN ISSN 0316-5310) *659*
Law, State and Society (US) *659, 1027*
Law Study and Practice in the United States: Pre-Law Handbook *see* PreLaw Handbook. Official Law School Guide *662*
Lawn Care (US ISSN 0023-9402) *533*
Lawn Care Industry Show Extra (US) *196, 533*
Lawn Tennis Association Handbook *see* Tennis Great Britain *1040*
Lawrence Berkeley Laboratory. Inorganic Materials Research Division. Annual Report *see* Lawrence Berkeley Laboratory. Materials and Molecular Research Division. Annual Report *489*
Lawrence Berkeley Laboratory. Materials and Molecular Research Division. Annual Report (US) *489*
Lawrence Berkeley Laboratory. Research Highlights (US ISSN 0091-9489) *889, 994*
Lawrie's Durban Street Directory (SA) *311*
Laws of England Annual Abridgment *see* Halsbury's Laws of England Annual Abridgment *656*
Laws of Kenya. Supplement (KE) *659*

Lawyer Statistical Report (US) 659
Lawyers for the Creative Arts. Bulletin see L C A Quarterly 658
Lawyers for the Creative Arts Quarterly see L C A Quarterly 658
Lawyers in the United States. Distribution and Income see Lawyer Statistical Report 659
Lawyer's Phone Book (Year) (CN ISSN 0317-8668) 659
Lawyers Professional Liability Update (US) 659
Lawyers Register by Specialties and Fields of Law (US) 659
Lawyer's Remembrancer (UK ISSN 0142-7490) 659
Lawyers' Title Guaranty Funds see A B A Lawyers' Title Guaranty Funds Newsletter 649
Laxton's Building Price Book see Laxton's National Building Price Book 185
Laxton's National Building Price Book (UK) 185
Lazy Man's Guide to Holidays Afloat (UK ISSN 0075-8272) 1042
Lea (CK) 128, 725
Lead Abstracts see Leadscan 801
Leader (Coral Gables) (US) 341
Leadership (US ISSN 0195-9204) 280
Leading European Banks (SZ) 230
Leadscan (UK ISSN 0950-1584) 8, 801
Learning (CN ISSN 0381-1387) 427
Learning Independently (US) 427
Learning Resources Council Newsletter (CN ISSN 0380-8491) 448
Learning Traveler. U S College-Sponsored Programs Abroad: Academic Year see Academic Year Abroad 441
Learning Traveler. Vacation Study Abroad see Vacation Study Abroad 442
Learning Traveler. Vol. 1 see Academic Year Abroad 441
Learning Traveler. Vol.2 see Vacation Study Abroad 442
Leasehold Law (UK) 659
Leather & Footwears/Kawa to Hakimono (JA) 672, 1005
Leather Buyers Guide and Leather Trade Marks (US ISSN 0075-8345) 672
Leather Guide (UK) 672
Leather: Latin American Industrial Report (US) 672
Leather Manufacturer's Directory (US) 312, 672
Leba (PO) 89
Leba Revista see Leba 89
Lebanese Industrial and Commercial Directory/Annuaire des Professions au Liban (LE ISSN 0075-8353) 312
Lebanon. Direction Centrale de la Statistique. Comptes Economiques (LE ISSN 0075-837X) 212
Lebanon. Direction Centrale de la Statistique. Recueil de Statistiques Libanaises (LE ISSN 0075-8388) 1058
LeBaron Russell Briggs Prize Honors Essays in English (US ISSN 0075-8396) 725
Lebensbilder aus Schwaben und Franken (GW) 135
Lebensmittel & Getraenke see Danmark Export: Food & Beverages 254
Leccio - Literary Review (IT) 539
Leccio - Press Agency see Leccio - Literary Review 539
Lecciones de Historia Juridica (AG) 559, 659
Lecciones y Ensayos (AG) 659, 671
Lecture Notes in Bio-Organic Chemistry (US) 330
Lecture Notes in Biomathematics (US ISSN 0341-633X) 143, 750
Lecture Notes in Chemistry (US ISSN 0342-4901) 323
Lecture Notes in Computer Science (US ISSN 0302-9743) 353
Lecture Notes in Control and Information Sciences (US ISSN 0170-8643) 680
Lecture Notes in Economics and Mathematical Systems (US ISSN 0075-8442) 196, 750

Lecture Notes in Engineering (US ISSN 0176-5035) 472
Lecture Notes in Mathematics (US ISSN 0075-8434) 750
Lecture Notes in Medical Informatics (US ISSN 0172-7788) 763
Lecture Notes in Operations Research and Mathematical Economics see Lecture Notes in Economics and Mathematical Systems 750
Lecture Notes in Physics (US ISSN 0075-8450) 889
Lecture Notes in Psychology see Lehr- und Forschungstexte Psychologie 935
Lecture Notes in Pure and Applied Mathematics (US ISSN 0075-8469) 750
Lecture Notes in Statistics (US) 1058
Lecture Notes on Coastal and Estuarine Studies (US ISSN 0724-5890) 406
Lectures Bar Extension see W.C.J. Meredith Memorial Lectures 667
Lectures in Applied Mathematics (US ISSN 0075-8485) 750
Lectures in Heterocyclic Chemistry (US ISSN 0090-2268) 330
Lectures on Mathematics in the Life Sciences (US ISSN 0075-8523) 143, 750
Lectures on the History of Religions. New Series (US ISSN 0075-8531) 971
Leder. Kursuskatalog (DK ISSN 0109-9299) 427
Lee County Historical Society. Historical Yearbook (US) 607
Leeds. Chamber of Commerce and Industry. Classified Trade Directory of Members (UK) 236, 312
Leeds Chambers of Commerce & Industry Directory (UK) 236
Leeds Medieval Studies (UK ISSN 0140-8089) 589, 725, 1077
Leeds Philosophical and Literary Society. Proceedings. Literary and Historical Section (UK ISSN 0024-0281) 559, 725
Leeds Philosophical and Literary Society. Proceedings. Scientific (UK) 994
Leeds Studies in English (UK ISSN 0075-8566) 725
Leeds Studies in English and Kindred Languages see Leeds Studies in English 725
Leeds Texts and Monographs (UK ISSN 0075-8574) 697
Left Curve (US ISSN 0160-1857) 711
Left Index (US ISSN 0733-2998) 8, 906, 912
Legal Aid New Brunswick Annual Report/Aide Juridique Nouveau Brunswick Rapport Annuel (CN ISSN 0381-2049) 659
Legal Almanac Series (US ISSN 0075-8582) 659
Legal Aspects of International Organization (NE) 671
Legal Assistants Update (US ISSN 0272-1961) 659
Legal Connection: Corporations and Law Firms (US ISSN 0270-3424) 196, 659
Legal Contents (US ISSN 0279-5787) 8, 668
Legal Information Management Index (US ISSN 0747-9298) 8, 659, 680
Legal Information Service Reports (CN ISSN 0225-2287) 659
Legal Looseleafs in Print (US ISSN 0275-4088) 659
Legal Medicine (US ISSN 0197-9981) 782
Legal Medicine Annual see Legal Medicine 782
Legal Newsletters in Print (US ISSN 8755-416X) 659
Legal Report of Oil and Gas Conservation Activities (US ISSN 0539-2063) 865
Legal Resource Index (US) 8, 668
Legal Resources for the Mentally Disabled: A Directory of Lawyers and Other Specialists (US) 659, 790
Legon Family Research Papers (GH) 73, 1027

Lehr- und Forschungstexte Psychologie/Lecture Notes in Psychology (US) 935
Lehrbuecher und Monographien zur Didaktik der Mathematik (GW) 416, 750
Lehrerinnen- und Lehrerkalender (GW) 416
Leica Manual (US ISSN 0093-9374) 1157
Leica Photography (US ISSN 0024-063X) 884
Leicester Literary & Philosophical Society. Transactions (UK ISSN 0141-3511) 538
Leicestershire Archaeological and Historical Society. Transactions (UK ISSN 0140-3990) 89, 589
Leicestershire Historian (UK ISSN 0024-0664) 536, 559
Leiden Botanical Series (NE) 158
Leidse Germanistische en Anglistische Reeks (NE ISSN 0458-9971) 725
Leidse Historische Reeks (NE ISSN 0458-998X) 559
Leidse Juridische Reeks (NE ISSN 0458-9998) 659
Leidse Kunsthistorische Reeks (NE ISSN 0460-2048) 107
Leidse Romanistische Reeks (NE ISSN 0075-8647) 698, 725
Leidse Wijsgerige Reeks (NE ISSN 0459-0007) 1157
Leipzig. Universitaet. Geophysikalisches Institut. Veroeffentlichungen. Zweite Serie see Geophysik und Geologie 399
Leipzig aus Vergangenheit und Gegenwart (GE) 589
Leipziger Messejournal (GE) 16
Leistung (GW ISSN 0024-0702) 1069
Leisure, Recreation and Tourism Abstracts (UK ISSN 0261-1392) 8, 1120
Leisureguide - Atlanta (US) 1112
Leisureguide - Boston (US) 1112
Leisureguide - Chicago (US) 1112
Leisureguide - Houston (US) 1112
Leisureguide - Kansas City (US) 1112
Leisureguide - Louisville (US) 1112
Leisureguide - Milwaukee (US) 1112
Leisureguide - Myrtle Beach (US) 1112
Leisureguide - Orlando (US) 1112
Leisureguide - Puerto Rico (US) 1112
Leisureguide - the Florida Gold Coast (US) 1112
Leisureguide - Twin Cities (US) 1112
Leisurewheels Campground Directory (CN) 1046
Leitende Maenner der Wirtschaft (GW ISSN 0075-871X) 135, 280
Leitung und Planung von Wissenschaft und Technik (GE) 8, 212
Lejeunia (BE ISSN 0457-4184) 159
Lekarske Prace (CS ISSN 0075-8736) 763
Leket (IS) 725
Lembaga Keluarga Berentjana Nasional (IO) 923
Length of Stay by Diagnosis, Canada (US ISSN 0891-2114) 617, 1058
Length of Stay by Diagnosis, United States (US ISSN 0891-2149) 617, 1058
Length of Stay by Diagnosis, United States, North Central Region (US ISSN 0891-2165) 617, 1058
Length of Stay by Diagnosis, United States, Northeastern Region (US ISSN 0891-2122) 617, 1058
Length of Stay by Diagnosis, United States, Southern Region (US ISSN 0891-2130) 618, 1058
Length of Stay by Diagnosis, United States, Western Region (US ISSN 0891-2157) 618, 1059
Length of Stay by Operation, Canada (US ISSN 0891-2181) 618, 1059
Length of Stay by Operation, United States (US ISSN 0891-2203) 618, 1059
Length of Stay by Operation, United States, North Central Region (US ISSN 0891-222X) 618, 1059
Length of Stay by Operation, United States, Northeastern Region (US ISSN 0888-2673) 618, 1059

Length of Stay by Operation, United States, Southern Region (US ISSN 0891-219X) 618, 1059
Length of Stay by Operation, United States, Western Region (US ISSN 0891-2211) 618, 1059
Lengua y Sociedad (PE) 698
Lenguaje (CK ISSN 0120-3479) 698
Leningradskii Universitet. Uchenye Zapiski. Seriya Geologicheskikh Nauk (UR ISSN 0459-0805) 390
Lentil Abstracts (UK ISSN 0260-8464) 31, 42
Leo Baeck Institute. Year Book (UK ISSN 0075-8744) 589, 976
Leobener Gruene Hefte. Neue Folge (AU ISSN 0259-0751) 817
Leonardo (IT ISSN 0075-8760) 416
Leonard's Annual Index of Art Auctions (Year) (US) 107, 196
Leopoldina (GE ISSN 0323-4444) 994
Lepidopterist's Society. Journal (US ISSN 0024-0966) 165
Lepidopterists' Society. Memoirs (US ISSN 0075-8795) 165
Leprosy Mission, London. Annual Report (UK ISSN 0075-8809) 971
Lesbian Herstory Archives Newsletter (US) 616, 1130
Leseplan Jahreslosung (GW) 982
Lesnicke Drevarske a Pol'ovnicke Muzeum (CS) 526, 589
Lesotho. Ministry of Education and Culture. Annual Report of the Permanent Secretary see Lesotho. Ministry of Education, Sports and Culture. Annual Report of the Permanent Secretary 416
Lesotho. Ministry of Education, Sports and Culture. Annual Report of the Permanent Secretary (LO) 416
Lesotho. Ministry of Foreign Affairs. Diplomatic and Consular List (LO ISSN 0460-2099) 917
Lesotho. Ministry of Water, Energy and Mining. Hydrological Yearbook (LO) 403
Lesotho. Treasury. Report on the Finances and Accounts (LO ISSN 0075-8817) 297
Lesotho Bank. Annual Report see Lesotho Bank. Report and Accounts 230
Lesotho Bank. Report and Accounts (LO) 230
Lesotho Catholic Directory (LO) 982
Lesotho National Development Corporation. Newsletter (LO) 246
Lessico Intellettuale Europeo (IT ISSN 0075-8825) 698
Lessing Yearbook (GW ISSN 0075-8833) 725
Let Me Tell You About - Dinosaurs (UK) 335, 856
Let Me Tell You About - How Things Work (UK) 335
Letopis. Reihe B. Geschichte (GE ISSN 0522-5078) 589
Letopis. Reihe C. Volkskunde (GE ISSN 0522-5086) 589
Letopis Pamatnika Slovenskej Literatury see Literarno - Muzejny Letopis 726
Letras de Nicaragua (NQ) 742
Let's Go: The Budget Guide to Europe.(US ISSN 0163-4585) 1112
Let's Go: The Budget Guide to Greece, Israel and Egypt see Let's Go: The Budget Guide to Greece, Israel and Egypt - Including Cyprus & Turkish Coast 1112
Let's Go: The Budget Guide to Greece, Israel and Egypt - Including Cyprus & Turkish Coast (US) 1112
Let's Go: The Budget Guide to Italy (US ISSN 0192-2920) 1112
Let's Go: The Student Guide to Europe see Let's Go: The Budget Guide to Europe 1112
Let's Go: The Student Guide to the United States and Canada see Let's Go: U S A 1112
Let's Go: U S A (US) 1112
Let's Make it Official (US) 1034
Lettere Italiane. Biblioteca (IT ISSN 0075-8892) 725
Lettere Italiane. Saggi (IT) 725
Letterheads (US) 107
Lettre au Cultivateur see Farm Letter 27

1800　LETTURE CLASSENSI

Letture Classensi (IT) *725*
Leumi Review (IS ISSN 0334-9160) *246*
Levant (UK ISSN 0075-8914) *89*
Leverandoerhaandbogen (Hellerup) (DK) *931*
Leverandoerhaandbogen (Skovlunde) (DK) *855*
Levevilkaar i Danmark/Living Conditions in Denmark, Compendium of Statistics (DK ISSN 0900-2499) *1059*
Lewis Carroll Society of North America. Chapbook (US) *128*
Lexicographica (GW ISSN 0175-6206) *698*
Lexport (IT) *672*
Liaisons Financieres en France *see* Collection Radiographie du Capital - les Liaisons Financieres *226*
Liber Academiae Kierkegaardiensis Annuarius (DK ISSN 0106-8989) *879*
Liberation Alliance. International Reports *see* Libertarian Alliance. World Reports *906*
Liberia. Bureau of Economic Research and Statistics. Annual Report to the President on the Operation and Activities *see* Liberia. Office of National Planning. Annual Report to the President on the Operation and Activities *943*
Liberia. General Services Agency. Annual Report (LB) *1018*
Liberia. Institute of Public Administration. Annual Report (LB) *943*
Liberia. Ministry of Action for Development and Progress. Annual Report (LB) *943*
Liberia. Ministry of Agriculture. National Rice Production Estimates *see* Liberia. Ministry of Agriculture. Production Estimates of Major Crops *42*
Liberia. Ministry of Agriculture. Production Estimates of Major Crops(LB) *42*
Liberia. Ministry of Agriculture. Statistical Handbook (LB) *42*
Liberia. Ministry of Commerce, Industry and Transportation. Annual Report (LB) *290, 1082*
Liberia. Ministry of Finance. Annual Report (LB ISSN 0304-727X) *297*
Liberia. Ministry of Foreign Affairs. Annual Report (LB) *917*
Liberia. Ministry of Health and Social Welfare. Annual Report (LB) *954*
Liberia. Ministry of Information, Cultural Affairs & Tourism. Annual Report to the Session of the Legislature (LB) *1112*
Liberia. Ministry of Justice. Annual Report to the Legislature (LB) *659*
Liberia. Ministry of Labour, Youth & Sports. Annual Report (LB) *333, 1018*
Liberia. Ministry of Lands and Mines. Annual Report *see* Liberia. Ministry of Lands, Mines and Energy. Annual Report *482*
Liberia. Ministry of Lands, Mines and Energy. Annual Report (LB) *482, 817*
Liberia. Ministry of Local Government, Rural Development & Urban Reconstruction. Annual Report (LB ISSN 0304-730X) *951*
Liberia. Ministry of National Defense. Annual Report (LB) *811*
Liberia. Ministry of Planning and Economic Affairs. Annual Report to the People's Redemption Council (LB) *290*
Liberia. Ministry of Planning and Economic Affairs. Annual Report to the Session of the Legislature of the Republic of Liberia *see* Liberia. Ministry of Planning and Economic Affairs. Annual Report to the People's Redemption Council *290*
Liberia. Ministry of Planning and Economic Affairs. Government Accounts (LB) *297*
Liberia. Ministry of Public Works. Annual Report (LB ISSN 0304-7326) *943*

Liberia. Office of National Planning. Annual Report to the President on the Operation and Activities (LB) *943*
Liberia Baptist Missionary and Educational Convention. Yearbook (LB) *979*
Liberia Ministry of Posts and Telecommunications. Annual Report (LB) *344*
Liberian Studies Monograph Series (US) *1009*
Liberian Studies Research Working Papers (US) *1009*
Liberian Trade Directory (LB) *312*
Libertarian Alliance. Background Briefings (UK ISSN 0267-7121) *906*
Libertarian Alliance. Cultural Notes (UK ISSN 0267-677X) *906, 913*
Libertarian Alliance. Economic Notes (UK ISSN 0267-7164) *246*
Libertarian Alliance. Foreign Policy Perspectives (UK ISSN 0267-6761) *906*
Libertarian Alliance. Historical Notes (UK ISSN 0267-7105) *589*
Libertarian Alliance. Legal Notes (UK ISSN 0267-7083) *659*
Libertarian Alliance. Personal Perspectives (UK ISSN 0267-7156) *906*
Libertarian Alliance. Philosophical Notes (UK ISSN 0267-7091) *879*
Libertarian Alliance. Political Notes (UK ISSN 0267-7059) *906*
Libertarian Alliance. Psychological Notes (UK ISSN 0267-7172) *935*
Libertarian Alliance. Scientific Notes (UK ISSN 0267-7067) *906, 1009*
Libertarian Alliance. Sociological Notes(UK ISSN 0267-7113) *1027*
Libertarian Alliance. Study Guides (UK ISSN 0267-7180) *906*
Libertarian Alliance. Tactical Notes (UK) *906*
Libertarian Alliance. World Reports (UK) *906*
Libertarian News (UK ISSN 0267-6788) *906*
Libertarian Reprints (UK ISSN 0267-6796) *906*
Libertarians for Life Reports *see* L F L Reports *906*
Libertas Mathematica (US ISSN 0278-5307) *750*
Libfrauen Kalender (GW) *979*
Librarians' Guide to Back Issues of International Periodicals *see* International Periodicals and Reference Works *647*
Librarian's Handbook (UK) *680*
Librarians' Handbook (US ISSN 0093-1888) *688*
Librarianship *see* Bibliotekarstvo *674*
Libraries and Resources Centres in the Northern Territory. List (AT ISSN 0728-7429) *680*
Libraries in the United Kingdom & the Republic of Ireland (UK) *680*
Libraries, Museums and Art Galleries Year Book *see* Libraries Yearbook *828*
Libraries of Maine; Directory and Statistics (US ISSN 0092-833X) *680*
Libraries Yearbook (UK) *680, 828*
Library and Information Science (JA ISSN 0373-4447) *680*
Library & Information Science Abstracts (UK ISSN 0024-2179) *8, 688*
Library Association. Conference. Proceedings, Papers and Summaries of Discussions (UK) *680*
Library Association. Industrial Group Newsletter (UK) *680*
Library Association (Valletta). Ghaqda Bibliotekarji/Library Association Newsletter (MM) *680*
Library Association. Year Book (UK ISSN 0075-9066) *680*
Library Association of Alberta. Occasional Papers (CN ISSN 0075-904X) *680*
Library Association of Australia. Handbook (AT ISSN 0155-560X) *680*
Library Association of Barbados. Bulletin (BB) *680*

Library Association of Barbados. Occasional Newsletter *see* Update (Bridgetown) *686*
Library Association of the City University of New York Occasional Papers *see* L A C U N Y Occasional Papers *1157*
Library Association of Trinidad and Tobago. Bulletin (TR ISSN 0521-9590) *680*
Library Association Yearbook (UK) *680*
Library Bibliographies and Indexes (US) *680*
Library Development in Alaska: Long Range Program (US ISSN 0094-8829) *680*
Library Government Documents and Information Conference. Proceedings. *see* Government Documents and Information Conference. Proceedings *678*
Library Keynotes (US ISSN 0024-2330) *681*
Library Lectures *see* Louisiana State University. Library. Library Lectures *681*
Library Lectures (Knoxville) *see* University of Tennessee. Library Lectures *686*
Library Lit (US ISSN 0085-2767) *8, 688*
Library Literature (US ISSN 0024-2373) *8, 688*
Library Literature in India Series (II) *681*
Library Magazine (KE) *681*
Library Notes (US ISSN 0024-2438) *681*
Library Occurrent *see* Indiana Libraries *679*
Library of Analytical Psychology Series(US) *976*
Library of Anthropology (US) *73*
Library of Congress (US ISSN 0162-6426) *681*
Library of Congress Classification Schedules: a Cumulation of Additions and Changes (US) *688*
Library of Congress Publications in Print *see* U.S. Library of Congress. Library of Congress Publications in Print *688*
Library of Exact Philosophy (US ISSN 0075-9104) *994*
Library of Great Painters (US) *107*
Library of Jewish Law and Ethics (US) *976*
Library of Law and Contemporary Problems (US ISSN 0075-9120) *659, 1009*
Library of Peasant Studies (UK) *504*
Library of Philosophy and Religion (UK) *879, 971*
Library of Theoria (SW) *879*
Library of Ukrainian Studies *see* Naukove Tovarystvo Imeni Shevchenka. Biblioteka Ukrainoznavstva *591*
Library Resources for the Blind and Physically Handicapped (Large Print Edition) (US ISSN 0364-1236) *180, 681*
Library Resources in Scotland *see* Scottish Library and Information Resources *683*
Library School Review *see* Great Plains Libraries *678*
Library Science Abstracts *see* Library & Information Science Abstracts *688*
Library Science Annual (US ISSN 8755-2108) *725*
Library Service to the People of New York State: A Long Range Plan (US) *681*
Library Services and Construction Act Annual Program, Hawaii State Library System *see* L.S.C.A. Annual Program, Hawaii State Library System *680*
Library Studies *see* Kniznicny Zbornik *680*
Library Yearbook/Toshokan Nenkan (JA) *681*
Libri Rari (IT) *964*
Libro Chileno en Venta (CL) *128*
Libro di Casa (IT) *643*
Librorama Internacional (SP) *128*

Libros de Iniciacion Filosofica (SP) *879*
Libros Espanoles I S B N (SP ISSN 0377-0974) *128*
Libros y Material de Ensenanza (SP ISSN 0075-9201) *416*
Libya. Census and Statistical Office. External Trade Statistics (LY ISSN 0075-9228) *212*
Libya. Census and Statistical Office. General Population Census (LY ISSN 0075-9236) *923, 927*
Libya. Census and Statistical Office. Industrial Census (LY ISSN 0075-9244) *212*
Libya. Census and Statistical Office. Report of the Annual Survey of Large Manufacturing Establishments (LY ISSN 0075-9252) *212*
Libya. Census and Statistical Office. Report of the Annual Survey of Petroleum Mining Industry (LY ISSN 0075-9260) *868*
Libya. Census and Statistical Office. Report of the Survey of Licensed Construction Units (LY ISSN 0075-9279) *189*
Libya. Census and Statistical Office. Statistical Abstract (LY ISSN 0075-9287) *1059*
Libya Past and Present Series (UK) *1112*
Libyan Economic and Business Review (LY) *196*
Libyan Travel Series *see* Libya Past and Present Series *1112*
Licensing Law and Business Institute. Annual *see* Licensing Law and Business Institute. Seminar *659*
Licensing Law and Business Institute. Seminar (US) *659*
Licensing Law Handbook (US ISSN 0731-5783) *258, 659, 1069*
Lichen *see* Raiken *160*
Lichtwark-Stiftung. Veroeffentlichung (GW) *726*
Lick Observatory. Publications (US ISSN 0075-9325) *116*
Licni Dohoci (YU ISSN 0300-2535) *212*
Liechtenstein. Botanisch-Zoologische Gesellschaft Liechtenstein Sargans-Werdenberg. Bericht (LH) *143*
Liechtenstein Economy *see* Economy of the Principality of Liechtenstein *244*
Liechtenstein Politische Schriften (LH) *906*
Lieferkatalog fuer Krankenhaus, Arzt, Apotheke und Labor (AU) *763*
Lietuviu Kalbotyros Klausimai/ Problems of Lithuanian Linguistics (UR ISSN 0130-0172) *698*
Lietuviu Tautos Praeitis/Lithuanian Historical Review (US ISSN 0091-4347) *589*
Life Insurance Agency Management Association. Proceedings of the Annual Meeting *see* Life Insurance Marketing and Research Association. Proceedings of the Annual Meeting *640*
Life Insurance Business in Taiwan (Year) (CH) *640*
Life Insurance Fact Book (US ISSN 0075-9406) *640*
Life Insurance in the United Kingdom *see* Insurance Statistics (1981-1985) *640*
Life Insurance Marketing and Research Association. Proceedings of the Annual Meeting (US) *640*
Life Rates & Data (US) *640*
Life Underwriters Association of Canada Monitor *see* L U A C Monitor *640*
Lifecare Industry (US) *552*
Lifelong Education Network (UN) *416*
Ligament *see* Maandblad Aktiviteitensektor *1027*
Light: Annual Report (US) *180*
Light Metal Statistics in Japan/ Keikinzoku Kogyo Tokei Nenpo (JA ISSN 0451-6001) *801*
Light Year (US ISSN 0743-913X) *726*
Lightweight Concrete Information Sheets (US ISSN 0075-9457) *185*
Lightworks (US ISSN 0161-4223) *107, 884*
Ligne Creatrice (FR) *711*

Ligue Internationale Contre la Concurrence Deloyale. Annuaire (FR ISSN 0459-3871) *258*
Ligue Suisse pour la Litterature de la Jeunesse. Rapport Annuel *see* Schweizerischer Bund fuer Jugendliteratur. Jahresbericht *336*
Liguria Territorio e Civilta (IT) *545*
Liikearkisto (FI ISSN 0356-7850) *196*
Liikearkistoyhdistys. Julkaisuja (FI) *196*
Liikenneturva. Reports (FI ISSN 0355-6654) *954*
Lijstenboek (BE) *962*
LiLi. Beihefte (Zeitschrift fuer Literaturwissenschaft und Linguistik) (GW) *698, 726*
Lilloa (AG ISSN 0075-9481) *159*
Lillooet District Historical Society. Bulletin (CN ISSN 0383-9133) *1157*
Limberlost Review (US ISSN 0743-2909) *742*
Limerence Forum (US) *935, 1027*
Limits in the Seas (US ISSN 0092-6426) *671*
Limnobios (AG ISSN 0325-7592) *165, 176*
Limnologica (GE ISSN 0075-9511) *403*
Limousine Nyt (DK ISSN 0900-050X) *67*
Lincoln College. Agricultural Economics Research Unit. Discussion Paper (NZ ISSN 0110-7720) *48*
Lincoln College. Agricultural Economics Research Unit. Research Report (NZ ISSN 0069-3790) *48*
Lincoln College. Department of Horticulture. Bulletin (NZ ISSN 0069-3820) *533*
Lincoln College. Farmers' Conference. Proceedings (NZ ISSN 0069-3839) *31*
Lincoln Institute of Land Policy. Basic Concept Series (US) *366, 624*
Lincolnshire Bird Report (UK ISSN 0261-5525) *170*
Lincolnshire History and Archaeology (UK ISSN 0459-4487) *89, 589*
Lincolnshire, Housing (UK ISSN 0261-0752) *624*
Lincolnshire Information. Employment (UK ISSN 0262-1452) *273*
Lincolnshire Population (UK ISSN 0260-8405) *923*
Linda Hall Library. Miscellany (US ISSN 0273-0227) *681*
Lindley Lecture (US ISSN 0075-9554) *879*
Lindy's S.E.C. Football Annual (US) *1039*
Lineal Industrial Distributors Registers (US) *312*
Linear Discontinued Devices D.A.T.A. Book (US) *456*
Linens, Domestics & Bath Products Annual Directory (US) *644*
Linet de la Quatrieme Section, Ecole Pratique Hautes Etudes (SZ) *559*
Lingua e Literatura (BL ISSN 0047-4711) *698, 726*
Lingua Posnaniensis (PL ISSN 0079-4740) *698*
Linguarum Minorum Documenta Historiographica (GW ISSN 0341-3225) *559, 698*
Lingue e Iscrizioni dell'Italia Antica (IT) *698*
Le Lingue e le Civilta Straniere Moderne (IT ISSN 0391-3228) *698*
Linguistic & Literary Studies in Eastern Europe (US ISSN 0165-7712) *698, 726*
Linguistic Association of Canada and the United States Forum *see* L A C U S Forum *697*
Linguistic Bibliography (NE) *709*
Linguistic Calculation (NE) *698*
Linguistic Circle of Manitoba and North Dakota. Proceedings (US ISSN 0075-9597) *698*
Linguistic Notes from La Jolla (US ISSN 0737-4720) *698*
Linguistic Society of America. Meeting Handbooks (US ISSN 0075-9600) *698*

Linguistic Society of India. Bulletin (II ISSN 0075-9627) *698*
Linguistica (YU ISSN 0024-3922) *698*
Linguistica Silesiana (PL ISSN 0208-4228) *698*
Linguistics Abstracts (UK ISSN 0267-5498) *698, 709*
Linguistics and Language Behavior Abstracts (US ISSN 0888-8027) *8, 709*
Linguistics of the Tibeto-Burman Area (US) *698*
Linguistik Aktuell (US ISSN 0166-0829) *698*
Linguistique et Enseignement (MG) *448, 698*
Linguistische Arbeiten (GW ISSN 0344-6727) *698*
Linguistische Reihe (GW ISSN 0075-9686) *698*
Lingvisticae Investigationes: Supplementa (US ISSN 0165-7569) *698*
Lingvisticheskie Issledovaniya (UR ISSN 0301-6900) *698*
Lingvisticke Citanky/Readings in Linguistics (CS) *698*
Linhas de Financiamento do B N H (Banco Nacional da Habitacao) (BL) *230*
Links und Rechts der Autobahn (GW ISSN 0343-4192) *620, 1096, 1112*
Linnaean Society. Symposia Series (US) *143*
Linschoten-Vereeniging. Werken (NE) *589*
Linzer Hochschulschriften *see* Linzer Universitaetsschriften *436*
Linzer Jahrbuch fuer Kunstgeschichte *see* Kunstjahrbuch der Stadt Linz *106*
Linzer Universitaetsschriften (US) *436*
Lion & the Unicorn (US ISSN 0147-2593) *711*
Lipscomb Newsletter (US) *536*
Liptov (CS) *589*
Lipunan Journal (PH ISSN 0459-4835) *570*
Liquid Gas Carrier Register (UK ISSN 0305-1803) *865*
Liquor Handbook *see* Jobson's Liquor Handbook *120*
Liquor Industry Marketing (US) *120*
Lisbon. Escola Nacional de Saude de Medicina Tropical. Anais *see* Instituto de Higiene e Medicina Tropical. Anais *954*
Lisse. Laboratorium voor Bloembollenonderzoek. Jaarverslag (NE) *57*
List Bio-Med; Biomedical Serials in Scandinavian Libraries (SW ISSN 0075-9813) *771*
List of Accredited Schools of Architecture *see* Accredited Programs in Architecture *96*
List of American Firms in France *see* American Chamber of Commerce in France. Directory *234*
List of Approved Hospitals and Recognised House Officer Posts (UK) *618*
List of Bonded Warehouses (UK) *312*
List of Cables Forming the World Submarine Network (UN ISSN 0074-9001) *350*
List of Current Serial Publications Being Received at the University of Puerto Rico Medical Sciences Campus Library (PR) *771*
List of Destination Indicators and Telex Identification Codes *see* Indicators for the Telegram Retransmission System (TRS) - Telex Identification Codes *350*
List of E C A Documents Issued/Liste des Documents Publies par la C E A(UN) *263*
List of Grants and Awards Available to American Writers *see* Grants and Awards Available to American Writers *723*
List of Hydrobiological Papers of British Fresh Waters (UK) *403, 497*
List of International Telephone Routes (UN ISSN 0074-9028) *350*
List of Journals Indexed in Index Medicus (US ISSN 0093-3821) *771*

List of Member Institutions - Federal Saving and Loan Insurance Corporation *see* Federal Home Loan Bank System. List of Member Institutions *639*
List of Scientific and Technical Literature Relating to Thailand (TH ISSN 0125-4537) *1004*
List of Serials and Monographs Indexed for Online Users *see* List of Serials Indexed for Online Users *771*
List of Serials Indexed for Online Users(US) *771*
List of Shipowners (UK ISSN 0260-7387) *1101*
List of Theses for the Doctor's and Master's Degree in Korea/Hankuk Baksa Mit Seuksa Hak Wee Lonmun Chong Mokrok (KO) *424*
Liste des Documents Publies par la C E A *see* List of E C A Documents Issued *263*
Liste des Membres du Corps Diplomatique a Beograd (YU) *917*
Liste des Signaux Distinctifs et Indicatifs Internationaux des Stations Francaises (Navires, Stations Terrestres). (FR) *1101*
Liste des Societes Savantes et Litteraires (FR ISSN 0457-9976) *436*
Liste Officielle des Navires de Mer Belges et de la Flotte de la Force Navale (BE) *1101*
Liste over Danske Jazzklubber og Huse m.V. *see* Liste over Rytmiske Spillesteder i Danmark *837*
Liste over Rytmiske Spillesteder i Danmark (DK ISSN 0109-1212) *837*
Listen to Your Beer (US) *120*
Lists of P A N S Doc Bibliographies *see* Lists of P A S T I C Bibliographies *1072*
Lists of P A S T I C Bibliographies (PK) *1072*
Liszt Information-Communication (AU) *837*
Liszt Society. Journal (UK ISSN 0141-0792) *837*
Liszt Society, London. Newsletter *see* Liszt Society. Journal *837*
Liteinoe Proizvodstvo, Metallovedenie i Obrabotka Metallov Davleniem (UR ISSN 0302-9069) *798*
Literacy/Alphabetisation (CN ISSN 0700-5369) *416*
Literaire Tijdschriften in Nederland (NE) *739*
Literarische Hefte (GW) *726*
Literarischer Verein in Stuttgart. Bibliothek (GW ISSN 0340-7888) *726*
Literarischer Weihnachtskatalog (GW) *711*
Literarisches Sonderheft (GE ISSN 0323-3766) *726*
Literarni Archiv (CS) *589*
Literarno - Muzejny Letopis (CS) *726, 837*
Literarny Archiv (CS ISSN 0075-9872) *726*
Literarria (CS) *726*
Literary Agents of North America Marketplace (US) *646, 726, 962*
Literary Criticism Register (US) *8, 739*
Literary Holland *see* Writing in Holland and Flanders *737*
Literary Market Place (US ISSN 0161-2905) *962*
Literary Monographs (US ISSN 0075-9902) *726*
Literary Onomastics Studies (US ISSN 0160-8703) *726*
Literary Prizes in Pakistan (PK ISSN 0075-9929) *726*
Literary Voices (US ISSN 0197-2146) *726*
Literatur (GW) *726*
Literatur und Geschichte. Eine Schriftenreihe (GW) *726*
Literatur und Gesellschaft (GE ISSN 0232-315X) *726, 742*
Literatur und Wirklichkeit (GW ISSN 0075-9937) *726*
Literatura Drevnei Rusi (UR) *726*
Literatura o Sakhalinskoi Oblasti (UR) *128*

Literatura ob Arkhangel'skoi Oblasti (UR) *726*
Literatura Piekna. Adnotowany Rocznik Bibliograficzny (PL ISSN 0075-9945) *128*
Literatura Popular em Verso (BL) *726*
Literaturberichte ueber Wasser, Abwasser, Luft und Feste Abfallstoffe (GW ISSN 0340-4900) *497*
Literaturdokumentation zur Arbeitsmarkt- und Berufsforschung (GW) *212*
Literature About the Book and Librarianship *see* Fachliteratur zum Buch- und Bibliothekswesen *677*
Literature and Belief (US ISSN 0732-1929) *726, 971*
Literature and Ideology *see* New Literature and Ideology *711*
Literature & Medicine (US ISSN 0278-9671) *726, 763*
Literature and Society in the Seventeenth Century (NE) *726*
Literaturwissenschaftliches Jahrbuch. Neue Folge (GW ISSN 0075-997X) *726*
Lithium Therapy Monographs (SZ) *792, 871*
Lithuanian Historical Review *see* Lietuviu Tautos Praeitis *589*
Litologiya i Paleogeografiya (UR) *380*
Litomericko (CS ISSN 0075-9988) *589*
Littell's Living Age (US) *536*
Litterae Numismaticae Vindobonenses (AU ISSN 0255-2809) *559, 845*
Litterae Textuales (NE) *726*
Litteraria (PL ISSN 0084-3008) *726*
Litteratur paa Indvandrersprog i Danske Folkebiblioteker (DK ISSN 0108-7215) *739*
Litteratur paa Indvandrersprog i Danske Folkebiblioteker. Serbokroatisk (DK ISSN 0108-9633) *739*
Litteratur paa Indvandrersprog i Danske Folkebiblioteker. Tyrkisk (DK ISSN 0108-9641) *739*
Litteratur paa Indvandrersprog i Danske Folkebiblioteker. Urdu (DK ISSN 0108-965X) *739*
Litterature. Science. Ideologie. *see* L.S.I *725*
Litteratures Anciennes (FR ISSN 0069-5459) *726*
Litteraturtolkninger (DK ISSN 0107-0916) *742*
Little Black Book (US) *312, 320*
Little Magazine (US ISSN 0033-6300) *726*
Little Red Book (UK ISSN 0265-5810) *128*
Little Red Book, Classified to All Public Transport Fleet Owners and Operators and Vehicle Manufacturers(UK ISSN 0076-0013) *1082*
Little Review (US ISSN 0024-5054) *726*
Little Richard News (DK) *837*
Little Things Word Loom (CN) *335*
Little Word Machine (UK) *742*
Lituanistika v S.S.S.R. Ekonomika (UR ISSN 0207-1266) *246*
Lituanistika v S.S.S.R. Filosofiya i Psikhologiya (UR ISSN 0202-2001) *879, 935*
Lituanistika v S.S.S.R. Iskusstvovedenie(UR) *107*
Lituanistika v S.S.S.R. Istoriya (UR) *589*
Lituanistika v S.S.S.R. Literaturovedenie (UR ISSN 0207-1274) *726*
Lituanistika v S.S.S.R. Pravo (UR ISSN 0202-2028) *659*
Lituanistika v S.S.S.R. Yazykoznanie (UR ISSN 0202-201X) *698*
Liturgiewissenschaftliche Quellen und Forschungen (GW ISSN 0076-0048) *971*
Livability Digest (US ISSN 0278-9485) *624, 1112*
Live and Let Live (US) *143, 879, 971, 1069*
Liverpool Catholic Directory (UK) *982*
Liverpool Latin Texts *see* Latin and Greek Texts *338*

Liverpool Monographs in Hispanic Studies (UK ISSN 0261-1538) 726
Livestock and Poultry in Latin America. Annual Conference see International Conference on Livestock and Poultry in the Tropics (Proceedings) 66
Livestock: Latin American Industrial Report (US) 67
Living Conditions in Denmark, Compendium of Statistics see Levevilkaar i Danmark 1059
Living Conditions Yearbook for Sweden. Statistiska Centralbyraan. Levnadsfoerhaallanden Aarsbok 1065
Living in Venezuela (VE) 236, 1112
Living with the Shore (US) 366, 406, 497
Livraria Figueirinhas Catalogo (PO) 962
Livre d'Art Information (FR) 113
Livre de Langue Francaise - Repertoire des Editeurs see Repertoire International des Editeurs et Diffuseurs de Langue Francaise 963
Livres Belges de Langue Francaise see Editeurs Belges de Langue Francaise et Leurs Livres 126
Livres Canadiens pour la Jeunesse see Canadian Books for Young People 334
Livres d'Aujourd'hui see Bulletin Bibliographique Thematique 124
Livres Disponibles (FR) 128
Livres et Auteurs Canadiens see Livres et Auteurs Quebecois 726
Livres et Auteurs Quebecois (CN ISSN 0076-0153) 726
Llafur (UK ISSN 0306-0837) 273
Llen Cymru (UK ISSN 0076-0188) 726
Llewellyn's Astrological Calendar (US ISSN 0145-8868) 114
Llewellyn's Moon Sign Book (US) 114, 533
Lloyds Hong Kong Port Services Index (Year) (HK) 1101
Lloyd's Marine Equipment Guide (UK ISSN 0268-3253) 1101
Lloyd's Maritime Atlas (UK ISSN 0076-020X) 1101
Lloyd's Maritime Directory (UK ISSN 0268-327X) 1101
Lloyd's Nautical Year Book (UK) 1101
Lloyd's Nautical Yearbook and Calendar see Lloyd's Nautical Year Book 1101
Lloyd's Ports of the World (UK ISSN 0266-6197) 1101
Lloyd's Register of Classed Yachts (UK ISSN 0261-6688) 1101
Lloyd's Register of Shipping. Statistical Tables (UK ISSN 0076-0234) 1101
Lloyd's Register of Ships (UK ISSN 0141-4909) 1101
Lloyd's Register of Yachts see Lloyd's Register of Classed Yachts 1101
Lo Nishkach (IS) 589
Loans Closed and Servicing Volume for the Mortgage Banking Industry (US ISSN 0277-1497) 230
Local and Regional Authorities in Europe see Council of Europe. Steering Committee on Regional and Municipal Matters. Study Series: Local and Regional Authorities in Europe 950
Local and Regional Authorities in Europe. Study Series (FR) 951
Local Area Housing Statistics (UK) 196
Local Area Network Software Directory see L A N Software Directory 359
Local Authority Specifiers' Reference Book and Buyers Guide (UK ISSN 0260-3756) 624
Local Government Administrators' Official Source Book (UK ISSN 0267-2022) 951
Local Government Companion (UK ISSN 0305-0130) 951
Local Government Finances in Maryland (US ISSN 0085-2821) 297
Local Government in Mauritius see Association of Urban Authorities. Annual Bulletin 950

Local Government Reports of Australia(AT ISSN 0076-0242) 943
Local Government Review see Local Government Review in Japan 951
Local Government Review in Japan (JA ISSN 0288-7622) 951
Local Government Trends (UK ISSN 0307-0441) 943
LocalNetter Designer's Handbook (US ISSN 0740-6932) 357, 362
Locations of Industries in Gujarat State (II ISSN 0076-0269) 290
Locations Vacances (FR ISSN 0024-5674) 965
Locke Newsletter (UK ISSN 0307-2606) 879
Lockert Library of Poetry in Translation (US) 742
Lockheed Orion Service Digest (US ISSN 0024-5704) 20
Locksmith Ledger/Security Guide & Directory (US ISSN 0273-625X) 190, 374
Lockwood's Directory of the Paper and Allied Trades (US ISSN 0076-0277) 858
Locomotive Maintenance Officers Association. Annual Proceedings (US ISSN 0076-0285) 1094
Locomotive Maintenance Officers Association. Preconvention Report (US ISSN 0076-0293) 1094
Locus (New York) (US) 107, 828
Locus Select see Locus (New York) 107
Locust Newsletter (UN) 57
Locusta (ML ISSN 0459-6803) 57
Lodging Industry see U S Lodging Industry 620
Lodzkie Studia Etnograficzne (PL ISSN 0076-0382) 73, 516
Lodzkie Towarzystwo Naukowe. Prace Wydzialu Jezykoznawstwa, Nauki o Literaturze i Filozofii (PL ISSN 0076-0404) 726
Lodzkie Towarzystwo Naukowe. Rozprawy Komisji Jezykowej (PL ISSN 0076-0390) 698
Lodzkie Towarzystwo Naukowe. Wydzial III. Nauk Matematyczno-Przyrodniczych. Prace (PL ISSN 0076-0412) 750
Lodzkie Towarzystwo Naukowe. Wydzial IV. Nauk Lekarskich. Prace (PL ISSN 0076-0420) 763
Lodzkie Towarzystwo Naukowe. Wydzial V. Nauk Technicznych. Prace (PL ISSN 0076-0439) 1069
Loeb Classical Library (US) 726
Loegumkloster-Studier (DK ISSN 0106-0430) 589
Log House (CN ISSN 0315-8756) 98, 185
Log of the Star Class (US ISSN 0076-0455) 1042
Logos (PH ISSN 0076-0471) 971
Logos (DK ISSN 0900-1174) 1157
Loi de l'Impot sur le Revenu Canadien see Loi de l'Impot sur le Revenu du Canada 297
Loi de l'Impot sur le Revenu du Canada (CN) 297
Lokalhistorien for Torsluende Ishoej og Tranegilde (DK ISSN 0108-3244) 589
Lokalhistorisk Arkiv, Aalestrup. Aarsskrift (DK ISSN 0109-6699) 589
Lokalhistorisk Arkiv for Fredericia og Omegn. Aarsskrift (DK ISSN 0900-3126) 589
Lokalhistorisk Arkiv, Roedby. Aarsskrift (DK ISSN 0109-8551) 589
Lokalhistorisk Arkiv Stubbekoebing. Aarsskrift (DK ISSN 0109-2162) 589
Lokalhistorisk Forening for Hoerup Sogn. Aarsskrift (DK ISSN 0109-2839) 589
Lokalhistorisk Forening for Sejlflod Kommune. Aarsskrift (DK ISSN 0106-9748) 589
Lokalhistorisk Forening for Soenderhald Kommune. Aarsskrift (DK ISSN 0109-4017) 589
Lokalhistoriske Arkiver i Vestsjaellands Amt Vulkanen: Ren L A V A see Vulkanen: Ren L A V A 601

Lolland-Falsters Historiske Samfund. Aarbog (DK ISSN 0107-8798) 589
Lolland-Falsters Stiftsmuseums Aarskrift (DK ISSN 0542-6820) 589
London and Home Counties Regional Advisory Council for Technological Education. Bulletin of Special Courses see London and South Eastern Regional Advisory Council for Further Education. Bulletin of Special Courses 436
London and Home Counties Regional Advisory Council for Technological Education. Index of Courses see London and South Eastern Regional Advisory Council for Further Education. Index of Courses 436
London and Middlesex Archaeological Society. Special Papers (UK) 89
London and Middlesex Archaeological Society. Transactions (UK ISSN 0076-0501) 89
London and Middlesex Archaeological Society & Surrey Archaeological Society. Joint Publication (UK) 89
London and South Eastern Regional Advisory Council for Further Education. Bulletin of Special Courses (UK) 430, 436
London and South Eastern Regional Advisory Council for Further Education. Index of Courses (UK) 430, 436
London Bibliography of the Social Sciences (UK ISSN 0076-051X) 1014
London Bird Report (UK ISSN 0141-4348) 170
London Chamber of Commerce. Annual Review (UK) 236
London Chamber of Commerce and Industry. Annual Report and Annual Directory see London Chamber of Commerce and Industry. Directory 236
London Chamber of Commerce and Industry. Annual Review see London Chamber of Commerce. Annual Review 236
London Chamber of Commerce and Industry. Directory (UK ISSN 0142-9728) 236
London Creative Listings (UK) 258
London Directory see London Directory of Industry and Commerce 312
London Directory for Trade & Industry (UK) 312
London Directory of Industry and Commerce (UK) 312
London Energy Group Data Book and Diary (UK ISSN 0269-4999) 465
London Facts and Figures (UK ISSN 0308-0900) 949, 1059
London German Studies (UK ISSN 0076-0811) 726
London Hospital League of Nurses Review (UK) 784
London Mathematical Society. Lecture Note Series (UK ISSN 0076-0552) 750
London Mathematical Society. Monographs. New Series (US) 750
London Naturalist (UK ISSN 0076-0579) 143
London, Ont. University of Western Ontario Series in Philosophy of Science see University of Western Ontario Series in Philosophy of Science 883
London Papers in Regional Science (UK ISSN 0076-0633) 624
London Police Court Mission. Annual Report see Rainer Foundation. Annual Report 372
London Port Handbook 1984 (UK ISSN 0260-8839) 312, 1101
London Record Society. Publications (UK ISSN 0085-2848) 589
London School of Economics and Political Science. Department of Geography. Geographical Papers (UK ISSN 0076-0641) 545
London School of Economics Monographs on Social Anthropology (UK ISSN 0077-1074) 73
London Shipping Contacts (UK) 312, 1101

London Shop Surveys (UK ISSN 0140-3206) 284
London Society. Journal (UK ISSN 0024-6158) 624
London Studies on South Asia (UK ISSN 0142-601X) 852
London Theatre Index (Year) (UK ISSN 0263-2322) 1077
Lone Star see Lone Star Humor 711
Lone Star Humor (US) 711
Long Ashton Research Station. Report (UK ISSN 0368-7708) 31
Long Island Telephone Tickler for Insurance Men & Women (US) 640
Long Island Water Resources Bulletin (US) 1157
Long Room (IE ISSN 0024-631X) 688
Long Story (US ISSN 0741-4242) 726
Long-Term Economic Forecast (JA) 246
Longhouse (US) 742
Longman Professional Directory of Local Authorities (UK) 659
Longwood Program Seminars (US) 159, 533
Look-in Television Annual (UK) 349
Look - Listen Opinion Poll Report see Look - Listen Project Report 349
Look - Listen Project Report (US) 349
Look Quick (US) 742
Lookback (UK ISSN 0144-5898) 1157
Looking Forward (US ISSN 0076-0870) 273
Looking into Leadership Series (US ISSN 0076-0889) 286
Lorentzia (AG ISSN 0076-0897) 159
Lormatic (CS) 355
Los Angeles Community Church of Religious Science Newsletter see C C R S Newsletter 1149
Los Angeles Council of Engineers & Scientists. Proceedings Series (US) 472, 994
Los Angeles Foundation of Otology. Progress Report see House Ear Institute. Progress Report 787
Los Angeles Port and Shipping Handbook (UK ISSN 0266-0644) 312, 1101
Los Angeles Times. Newspaper Index see Index to the Los Angeles Times 647
Lost Play Series (US ISSN 0076-1001) 726
Loto - Quebec. Rapport Annuel (CN) 297
Loughborough Occasional Papers in Economics (UK) 196
Louisiana. Department of Agriculture. Analysis of Official Pesticide Samples; Annual Report (US ISSN 0099-1929) 57
Louisiana. Division of Mental Health. Annual Performance Report and Continuation of the State Plan for Drug Abuse Prevention (US ISSN 0362-7098) 377
Louisiana. Geological Survey. Water Resources Bulletin (US ISSN 0459-8474) 390
Louisiana. Health and Human Resources Administration Comprehensive Annual Services Program Plan for Social Services Under Title 20 (US ISSN 0362-8868) 1018
Louisiana. Polytechnic Institute, Ruston. School of Agriculture and Forestry. Research Bulletin see Louisiana Tech University. Division of Life Sciences Research. Research Bulletin 143
Louisiana. State Board of Nurse Examiners. Report see Louisiana. State Board of Nursing. Report (Calendar Year) 784
Louisiana. State Board of Nursing. Report (Calendar Year) (US) 784
Louisiana Academy of Sciences. Proceedings (US) 994
Louisiana Coastal Law Report (US) 406
Louisiana Directory of Manufacturers see Directory of Louisiana Manufacturers 306
Louisiana Fairs and Festivals (US ISSN 0093-0687) 31

Louisiana Folklore Miscellany (US ISSN 0459-8962) *516*
Louisiana Philosophy of Education Journal (US) *416*
Louisiana State Industrial Directory *see* MacRae's Louisiana State Industrial Directory *312*
Louisiana State University. Animal Science Department. Livestock Producers' Day Report (US ISSN 0076-1052) *67*
Louisiana State University. Department of Geography & Anthropology. Miscellaneous Publications (US) *73, 380*
Louisiana State University. Library. Library Lectures (US ISSN 0085-2759) *681*
Louisiana State University. Library. Report of the Director (US) *1157*
Louisiana State University. Museum of Geoscience. Publications (US) *380*
Louisiana State University. School of Forestry and Wildlife Management. Annual Forestry Symposium. Proceedings. *see* Louisiana State University. School of Forestry, Wildlife, and Fisheries. Annual Forestry Symposium. Proceedings *526*
Louisiana State University. School of Forestry, Wildlife, and Fisheries. Annual Forestry Symposium. Proceedings (US) *526*
Louisiana State University. School of Geoscience. Miscellaneous Publications *see* Louisiana State University. Department of Geography & Anthropology. Miscellaneous Publications *380*
Louisiana Tech University. Division of Life Sciences Research. Research Bulletin (US ISSN 0076-1044) *143*
Louisiana Water Resources Research Institute. Annual Report (US) *403, 1125*
Lounais-Haemeen Kotiseutu ja Museoyhdistys. Vuosikirja (FI) *589*
Love (US) *879*
Love: The Journal of the Human Spirit *see* Love *879*
Lovoe Geomagnetic Observatory Yearbook (SW ISSN 0076-1354) *390*
Low Cost C A D/C A M Systems (Computer Aided Design) (US) *355, 356*
Low Temperature Science. Series A. Physical Science (JA ISSN 0439-3538) *894*
Low Temperature Science. Series B. Biological Science (JA ISSN 0439-3546) *143*
Lowdin Symposia *see* International Symposium on Atomic, Molecular and Solid-State Theory, Collision Phenomena and Computational Methods. Proceedings *323*
Lowell Observatory Bulletin (US ISSN 0024-7057) *116*
Lower Paleozoic Rocks of the New World (US ISSN 0076-1389) *856*
Lowveld Research Stations. Annual Report (RH) *31*
Lozania (CK ISSN 0085-2899) *176*
Lubelskie Towarzystwo Naukowe. Wydzial Humanistyczny. Prace. Monografie (PL ISSN 0208-4996) *631*
Lucky Heart Books (US) *711*
Lucrari de Muzicologie (RM) *837*
Lud (PL ISSN 0076-1435) *73, 1027*
Ludas Matyi Evkonyve (HU ISSN 0133-9214) *463*
Ludwig Boltzmann-Institut fuer Umweltwissenschaften und Naturschutz. Mitteilungen (AU) *366, 497*
Ludwig Feurbach: Gesammelte Werke (GE) *879*
Luft og Rumfartsaarbogen (DK ISSN 0108-4550) *20*
Luftverunreinigung (GW ISSN 0460-2374) *497*
Lugar da Historia (PO) *589*
Luggage and Travelware Directory and Market Guide *see* Travelware Resources Directory *318*

Lumo (CN ISSN 0024-7367) *698, 726*
Lunar and Planetary Institute Technical Report *see* L P I Technical Report *116*
Lunar Epidecis *see* Epidecides Lunaires *115*
Lund Studies in English (SW ISSN 0076-1451) *698*
Lund Studies in Geography. Series A. Physical Geography (SW ISSN 0076-146X) *546*
Lund Studies in Geography. Series B. Human Geography (SW ISSN 0076-1478) *143, 546*
Lund Studies in Geography. Series C. General and Mathematical Geography (SW ISSN 0076-1486) *546*
Lund Studies in International History (SW ISSN 0076-1494) *559*
Lund Universitet. Historiska Museet Samt Mynt-och Medaljkabinettet. Meddelanden *see* Lund Universitet. Historiska Museum. Meddelanden *89*
Lund Universitet. Historiska Museum. Meddelanden (SW ISSN 0458-4767) *89*
Lunds Universitet. Vaextekologiska Institutionen. Meddelanden (SW ISSN 0348-2456) *159, 366*
Lung Biology in Health and Disease (US) *172, 793*
Lusaka. Medical Officer of Health. Annual Report (ZA) *954*
Lusaka City Library. Annual Report (ZA) *681*
Lusitania Sacra (PO ISSN 0076-1508) *971*
Lustracje Dobr Krolewskich XVI-XVIII Wieku (PL ISSN 0076-1516) *589*
Lustrum (GW ISSN 0024-7421) *338*
Lute Society Journal (UK ISSN 0460-007X) *837*
Lute Society of America. Journal (US ISSN 0076-1524) *837*
Lutheran Almanac *see* Lutheran Church of Australia. Yearbook *979*
Lutheran Annual (US) *979*
Lutheran Church in America. Western Canada Synod. Minutes of the Annual Convention (CN ISSN 0460-024X) *1157*
Lutheran Church in America. Yearbook (US) *979*
Lutheran Church of Australia. Yearbook (AT ISSN 0726-4305) *979*
Lutheran Church of Central Africa. Statistical Report (ZA) *975*
Lutheran Churches in Canada. Directory (CN ISSN 0316-800X) *979*
Lutheran World Federation. Proceedings of the Assembly (US ISSN 0076-1540) *979*
Lutherjahrbuch (GW) *979*
Lutra (NE ISSN 0024-7634) *176*
Luxembourg. Inspection Generale de la Securite Sociale. Rapport General sur la Securite Sociale au Grand-Duche de Luxembourg (LU) *640*
Luxembourg. Ministere des Finances. Budget de l'Etat (LU ISSN 0076-1559) *297*
Luxembourg. Ministere des Finances. Projet de Loi Concernant le Budget des Recettes et des Depenses de l'Etat (LU) *297*
Luxembourg. Office de la Statistique Generale. Annuaire Statistique *see* Luxembourg. Service Central de la Statistique et des Etudes Economiques. Annuaire Statistique *212*
Luxembourg. Service Central de la Statistique et des Etudes Economiques. Annuaire Statistique (LU ISSN 0076-1575) *212, 1059*
Luxembourg. Service Central de la Statistique et des Etudes Economiques. Annuaire Statistique Retrospectif (LU) *212, 1059*
Luxembourg. Service Central de la Statistique et des Etudes Economiques. Bulletin du STATEC (LU ISSN 0076-1583) *212*

Luxembourg. Service Central de la Statistique et des Etudes Economiques. Collection D et M: Definitions et Methodes (LU ISSN 0076-1591) *212, 1059*
Luxembourg. Service Central de la Statistique et des Etudes Economiques. Cahiers Economiques. Serie A: Economie Luxembourgeoise (LU ISSN 0070-881X) *212*
Luxembourg. Service Central de la Statistique et des Etudes Economiques. Cahiers Economiques. Serie B: Comptes Nationaux (LU) *212*
Luxembourg. Service Central de la Statistique et des Etudes Economiques. Cahiers Economiques. Serie C: Apercus sur l'Industrie (LU) *212*
Luxembourg. Service Central de la Statistique et des Etudes Economiques. Cahiers Economiques. Serie D: Etudes Diverses (LU) *212*
Luxembourg. Service Central de la Statistique et des Etudes Economiques. Collection RP: Recensements de la Population (LU ISSN 0076-1613) *927*
Luxembourg Stock Exchange. Annual Report *see* Societe de la Bourse de Luxembourg. Rapport Annuel *268*
Luxury Coach Tours in Britain & Europe (UK) *1112*
Lyboen (DK ISSN 0107-1238) *589*
Lychnos-Bibliotek. Studies och Kaellskrifter Udgivna av Laerdomshistoriska Samfundet. Studies and Sources Published by the Swedish History of Science Society (SW ISSN 0076-163X) *994*
Lychnos-Laerdomshistoriska Samfundets Aarsbok. Annual of the Swedish History of Science Society (SW ISSN 0076-1648) *994*
Lydbogskatalog *see* Gode Lydboeger *126*
Lyle Official Antiques Review (US) *79*
Lyles Official Arts Review (US) *107*
Lymphokine Reports *see* Lymphokines *323*
Lymphokines (US ISSN 0277-013X) *323*
Lyngby-Bogen (DK) *590*
Lynx (CS ISSN 0024-7774) *176*
Lyonia (US) *159*
Lyrical Iowa (US ISSN 0076-1699) *742*
Lyrik & Prosa (DK ISSN 0109-906X) *726*
M A A Studies in Mathematics *see* Studies in Mathematics (Washington) *753*
M.A.N. Forschen, Planen, Bauen (Maschinenfabrik Augsburg-Nuernberg AG) (GW) *473*
M.A.N. Research, Engineering, Manufacturing *see* M.A.N. Forschen, Planen, Bauen *473*
M A P A Annual Report (Omaha-Council Bluffs Metropolitan Area Planning Agency) (US) *943*
M A R Year Book *see* Centro de Navegacion Transatlantica. C.N.T. Handbook. River Plate Handbook for Shipowners and Agents *1099*
M & C Data Acquisition and Recorder Handbook & Buyers Guide (US) *637*
M & C Temperature Handbook and Buyers Guide *see* M & C Data Acquisition and Recorder Handbook & Buyers Guide *637*
M B B International (Messerschmitt-Boelkow-Blohm GmbH) (GW) *20*
M B I's Indian Industries Annual (II ISSN 0541-5357) *290*
M B L Lectures in Biology (Marine Biological Laboratory) (US) *143*
M C D S Occasional Paper Series (Malaysian Centre for Development Studies) (MY) *1009*
M C D Warehousing Distribution Directory *see* Warehousing/Distribution Directory *1105*
M C Revyen (DK ISSN 0107-0606) *1041*
M C Z Newsletter (Museum of Comparative Zoology) (US) *176*

M.D. Anderson Clinical Conferences on Cancer (US ISSN 0160-2454) *775*
M.D. Anderson Hospital and Tumor Institute. General Report (US ISSN 0066-1627) *775*
M.D. Anderson Hospital and Tumor Institute. Research Report (US ISSN 0066-1635) *775*
M.D. Anderson Symposia in Fundamental Cancer Research (US) *775*
M D R T Annual Meeting. Proceedings (Million Dollar Round Table) (US) *640*
M E E D Practial Guide. Kuwait (Middle East Economic Digest Ltd.) (UK) *1112*
M E E D Practical Guide. Bahrain (Middle East Economic Digest Ltd.) (UK) *1112*
M E E D Practical Guide. Egypt (Middle East Economic Digest Ltd.) (UK) *1112*
M E E D Practical Guide. Jordan (Middle East Economic Digest Ltd.) (UK) *1112*
M E E D Practical Guide. Oman (Middle East Economic Digest Ltd.) (UK) *1112*
M E E D Practical Guide. Qatar (Middle East Economic Digest Ltd.) (UK) *1112*
M E E D Practical Guide. Saudi Arabia (UK) *852, 1112*
M E E D Practical Guide. U A E (United Arab Emirates) (UK) *852, 1112*
M E I Marketing Economics Guide (Marketing Economics Institute, Ltd.) (US ISSN 0092-4857) *284*
M E L E C O N *see* Mediterranean Electrotechnical Conference *457*
M E R I T Newsletter (Monitored Earth Rotation and Intercompared Techniques) (UK) *116, 400*
M E S Newsletter (Michigan Entomological Society) (US) *165*
M E T U Journal of Pure and Applied Sciences *see* Journal of Pure and Applied Sciences *993*
M F A Bulletin *see* Museum of Fine Arts, Boston. Bulletin *1158*
M F V A Brochure (Manitoba Farm Vacations Association) (CN) *1113*
M.H.S. Miscellany (Massachusetts Historical Society) (US ISSN 0024-8185) *607*
M I D I S T Rapport d'Activite (Year) (Mission Interministerielle de l'Information Scientifique et Technique) (FR) *1069*
M.I.I. Series (Muslim Intellectuals' International) (PK ISSN 0541-5462) *975*
M I L C O M *see* I E E E Military Communications Conference. Conference Record *455*
M I L U S *see* University of Stockholm. Institute of Linguistics. Monographs *707*
M I M C Microforms Annual *see* Microforms Annual *129*
M I M P *see* Magazine Industry Market Place *962*
M I M S Annual (AT) *871*
M I M S Desk Reference (SA ISSN 0076-8847) *871*
M I M S Medical Memory Aids (SA) *763*
M I M S Reference Manual *see* M I M S Desk Reference *871*
M I N T E K Reports *see* Mintek Reports *818*
M I R *see* Musical Interpretation Research *838*
M I V *see* Museerne i Viborg Amt (DK) *590*
M L A Directory of Periodicals (Modern Language Association of America) (US ISSN 0197-0380) *517, 709, 739*
M L A International Bibliography of Books and Articles on the Modern Languages and Literatures (Modern Language Association of America) (US ISSN 0024-8215) *9, 128, 698, 727*
M L N Bulletin *see* M L N New Directions *784*

M L N Bulletin - Newsletter *see* M L N New Directions
M L N New Directions (Minnesota League for Nursing) (US) *784*
M.L.T.A. News (Modern Language Teachers' Association of New South Wales) (AT ISSN 0310-9674) *698*
M M P *see* Microform Market Place *681*
M P (Ministerio Publico) (BL) *659*
M P R C Report on Finance, Commerce, Industry: Indonesia (MY) *246*
M P R C Report on Finance, Commerce, Industry: Indonesia. Supplement (MY) *246*
M P R C Report on Finance, Commerce, Industry: Singapore (MY) *246*
M P R C Report on Finance, Commerce, Industry: South East Asia (MY) *246*
M P R C Report on Finance, Commerce, Industry: Thailand (MY) *246*
M P, the Microprocessor (US ISSN 0361-5421) *1157*
M R A Research Service Directory (Marketing Research Association, Inc.) (US) *284*
M R I Compensation in Mass Retailing, Salaries and Incentives *see* N M R I Compensation in Mass Retailing, Salaries and Incentives *274*
M.R.U. *see* Modelle fuer den Religionsunterricht *971*
M S S Magazine (US) *727*
M S T English Quarterly (D C S Manila Teachers of Secondary English) (PH ISSN 0047-5289) *448*
M S T Luft. A (Miljoestyrelsen) (DK ISSN 0106-343X) *497*
M S Z: Muenchener Studentenzeitung *see* Asta-Press *442*
M T A C Journal *see* Management Journal *280*
M T A S Municipal Technical Report (Municipal Technical Advisory Service) (US) *943*
M T A S Technical Report *see* M T A S Municipal Technical Report *943*
M T A Ship by Truck Directory *see* Manitoba Ship by Truck Directory *1105*
M.T.I.A. Annual Report (Metal Trades Industry Association of Australia) (AT ISSN 0085-3321) *273, 798*
M T I A N E G's Export Note Pad (Metal Trades Industry Association National Export Group) (AT) *258, 799*
M T L A, the Micropublishers' Trade List Annual *see* Micropublishers' Trade List Annual *129*
M T M/Journal of Methods-Time Measurement (US ISSN 0024-8509) *280*
M V *see* Miljoevaern *497*
M V C Bulletin (Mississippi Valley Collection) (US ISSN 0076-9525) *1157*
M V M A Motor Vehicle Facts and Figures (US ISSN 0146-9932) *1092*
M W A Annual (Mystery Writers of America) (US) *727*
M W V / A E V Jahresbericht *see* M W V Jahresbericht *330*
M W V Jahresbericht (Mineraloelwirtschafts Verband e.V.) (GW ISSN 0076-891X) *330*
Maagalai Kareya (IS ISSN 0334-2867) *335, 727*
Maanadsoeversikt oever Finlands Klimat *see* Kuukausikatsaus Suomen Ilmastoon *805*
Maandblad Aktiviteitensektor (NE ISSN 0168-2857) *1027*
Maasef (IS ISSN 0334-3952) *907*
Mabua/Fountain (IS) *128, 135, 727, 742*
Macao. Reparticao dos Servicos de Estatistica. Anuario de Estatistica (MH) *1059*
Macao. Reparticao dos Servicos de Estatistica. Anuario do Comercio Externo (MH) *258, 1059*
Macau Industry (MH) *196*
McCall's Beauty Diet & Health Guide (US) *118*

McCall's Cooking School (US ISSN 0094-0305) *615*
McCall's Country Decorating (US ISSN 0272-4499) *643*
McCall's Holiday Bake-It Book (US) *615*
McCall's Time Saving Meals (US) *615*
McCall's Beauty Guide *see* McCall's Beauty Diet & Health Guide *118*
McCutcheon's Emulsifiers and Detergents (US) *323*
McGill Daily (CN) *341*
McGill Dental Review (CN ISSN 0024-9025) *779*
McGill Medical Journal (CN ISSN 0024-905X) *763*
McGill Studies in International Development (CN ISSN 0821-6452) *1009*
McGill Sub-Arctic Research Papers (CN ISSN 0076-1982) *546*
McGill University. Institute of Oceanography. Biennial Report (CN) *1157*
McGill University. Marine Sciences Centre. Annual Report *see* McGill University. Institute of Oceanography. Biennial Report *1157*
McGill University, Montreal. Axel Heiberg Island Research Reports (CN ISSN 0076-1850) *380*
McGill University, Montreal. Centre for Developing-Area Studies. Annual Report (CN ISSN 0076-1893) *1009*
McGill University, Montreal. Centre for Developing-Area Studies. Bibliography Series (CN ISSN 0316-6570) *128, 566*
McGill University, Montreal. Centre for Developing-Area Studies. Occasional Monograph Series (CN ISSN 0702-8431) *1009*
McGill University, Montreal. Centre for Developing-Area Studies. Occasional Paper Series *see* McGill University, Montreal. Centre for Developing-Area Studies. Occasional Monograph Series *1009*
McGill University, Montreal. Centre for Developing-Area Studies. Working Papers *see* McGill Studies in International Development *1009*
McGill University, Montreal. Department of Geography. Climatological Research Series (CN ISSN 0076-1931) *805*
McGill University, Montreal. Department of Meteorology. Publication in Meteorology (CN ISSN 0076-1842) *1157*
McGill University, Montreal. Industrial Relations Centre. Annual Conference Proceedings (CN ISSN 0076-194X) *273*
McGill University, Montreal. Marine Sciences Centre. Manuscript Report (CN) *407*
McGill University, Montreal. Mechanical Engineering Research Laboratories. Report (CN ISSN 0076-1966) *492*
McGill University, Montreal. Mechanical Engineering Research Laboratories. Technical Note (CN ISSN 0076-1974) *492*
McGill University Savanna Research Project - Savanna Research Series (CN) *546*
McGoldrick's Handbook of Canadian Customs Tariff and Excise Duties (CN ISSN 0076-1990) *258, 297*
McGraw-Hill Yearbook of Science and Technology (US ISSN 0076-2016) *994, 1069*
Machine Intelligence Workshop (US ISSN 0076-2032) *355*
Machinery - Business (FR) *57*
Machinery Buyers' Guide (UK ISSN 0305-3121) *745*
Machinery: Latin American Industrial Report (US) *246, 745*
Machinery's Annual Buyer's Guide *see* Machinery Buyers' Guide *745*
McIlvainea (US ISSN 0099-8400) *159*
Mackinac History (US ISSN 0541-6507) *1157*
Mackintosh Yearbook of International Electronics Data (UK ISSN 0264-0724) *456*

Mackintosh Yearbook of West European Electronics Data (UK ISSN 0306-5774) *461*
McMaster University, Hamilton, Ontario. Institute for Materials Research. Annual Report (CN ISSN 0076-2059) *489*
McNeill Memoranda (US) *536*
Macquarie University Caving Group Quaver *see* Quaver *394*
Macquarie University French Monographs (AT ISSN 0815-7138) *416, 698*
MacRae's Alabama State Industrial Directory (US ISSN 0733-5016) *312*
MacRae's Arizona/New Mexico State Industrial Directory (US ISSN 0739-8476) *312*
MacRae's Arizona State Industrial Directory *see* MacRae's Arizona/New Mexico State Industrial Directory *312*
MacRae's Arkansas State Industrial Directory (US ISSN 0740-4670) *312*
MacRae's Blue Book (US) *312*
MacRae's Blue Book *see* MacRae's Blue Book *312*
MacRae's California State Industrial Directory (US ISSN 0740-4638) *312*
MacRae's Colorado State Industrial Directory *see* MacRae's Colorado/Utah/Nevada State Industrial Directory *312*
MacRae's Colorado/Utah/Nevada State Industrial Directory (US ISSN 0740-6126) *312*
MacRae's Connecticut State Industrial Directory (US ISSN 0740-2937) *312*
MacRae's Delaware State Industrial Directory *see* MacRae's Maryland/D.C./Delaware State Industrial Directory *312*
MacRae's Directory of Firms Marketing through Manufacturers' Representatives (US ISSN 0749-1093) *312*
MacRae's Directory of Manufacturers' Representatives *see* MacRae's Verified Directory of Manufacturers' Representatives *313*
MacRae's Florida State Industrial Directory (US ISSN 0740-4697) *312*
MacRae's Georgia State Industrial Directory (US ISSN 0733-4982) *312*
MacRae's Idaho/Montana/Wyoming State Industrial Directory (US ISSN 0740-6088) *312*
MacRae's Idaho State Industrial Directory *see* MacRae's Idaho/Montana/Wyoming State Industrial Directory *312*
MacRae's Illinois State Industrial Directory (US ISSN 0740-4336) *312*
MacRae's Indiana State Industrial Directory (US ISSN 0740-6045) *312*
MacRae's Industrial Directory *see* MacRae's Blue Book *312*
MacRae's Iowa/Nebraska State Industrial Directory (US ISSN 0740-428X) *312*
MacRae's Iowa State Industrial Directory *see* MacRae's Iowa/Nebraska State Industrial Directory *312*
MacRae's Kansas State Industrial Directory (US ISSN 0740-6118) *312*
MacRae's Kentucky State Industrial Directory *see* MacRae's Kentucky/West Virginia State Industrial Directory *312*
MacRae's Kentucky/West Virginia State Industrial Directory (US ISSN 0740-4328) *312*
MacRae's Louisiana State Industrial Directory (US ISSN 0733-3234) *312*
MacRae's Maine/New Hampshire/Vermont State Industrial Directory (US ISSN 0740-2945) *312*

MacRae's Maine State Industrial Directory *see* MacRae's Maine/New Hampshire/Vermont State Industrial Directory *312*
MacRae's Manufacturers' Agents Guide *see* MacRae's Directory of Firms Marketing through Manufacturers' Representatives *312*
MacRae's Maryland/D.C./Delaware State Industrial Directory (US) *312*
MacRae's Maryland State Industrial Directory *see* MacRae's Maryland/D.C./Delaware State Industrial Directory *312*
MacRae's Massachusetts/Rhode Island State Industrial Directory (US ISSN 0740-4689) *312*
MacRae's Massachusetts State Industrial Directory *see* MacRae's Massachusetts/Rhode Island State Industrial Directory *312*
MacRae's Michigan State Industrial Directory (US ISSN 0733-4958) *312*
MacRae's Minnesota State Industrial Directory (US ISSN 0740-6061) *313*
MacRae's Mississippi State Industrial Directory (US ISSN 0740-4654) *313*
MacRae's Missouri State Industrial Directory (US ISSN 0740-607X) *313*
MacRae's Montana State Industrial Directory *see* MacRae's Idaho/Montana/Wyoming State Industrial Directory *312*
MacRae's Nebraska State Industrial Directory *see* MacRae's Iowa/Nebraska State Industrial Directory *312*
MacRae's Nevada State Industrial Directory *see* MacRae's Colorado/Utah/Nevada State Industrial Directory *312*
MacRae's New Hampshire State Industrial Directory *see* MacRae's Maine/New Hampshire/Vermont State Industrial Directory *312*
MacRae's New Jersey State Industrial Directory (US ISSN 0733-3684) *313*
MacRae's New Mexico State Industrial Directory *see* MacRae's Arizona/New Mexico State Industrial Directory *312*
MacRae's New York State Industrial Directory (US ISSN 0740-2953) *313*
MacRae's North Carolina/South Carolina/Virginia (US) *313*
MacRae's North Carolina State Industrial Directory *see* MacRae's North Carolina/South Carolina/Virginia *313*
MacRae's North Dakota/South Dakota State Industrial Directory (US ISSN 0739-8468) *313*
MacRae's North Dakota State Industrial Directory *see* MacRae's North Dakota/South Dakota State Industrial Directory *313*
MacRae's Ohio State Industrial Directory (US ISSN 0733-4176) *313*
MacRae's Oklahoma State Industrial Directory (US ISSN 0740-4662) *313*
MacRae's Oregon State Industrial Directory (US ISSN 0740-610X) *313*
MacRae's Pennsylvania State Industrial Directory (US ISSN 0740-4298) *313*
MacRae's Rhode Island State Industrial Directory *see* MacRae's Massachusetts/Rhode Island State Industrial Directory *312*
MacRae's South Carolina State Industrial Directory (US ISSN 0733-4931) *1157*
MacRae's South Dakota State Industrial Directory *see* MacRae's North Dakota/South Dakota State Industrial Directory *313*
MacRae's Tennessee State Industrial Directory (US ISSN 0740-4646) *313*

MacRae's Texas State Industrial Directory (US ISSN 0739-8484) 313
MacRae's Utah State Industrial Directory see MacRae's Colorado/Utah/Nevada State Industrial Directory 312
MacRae's Verified Directory of Manufacturers' Representatives (US) 313
MacRae's Vermont State Industrial Directory see MacRae's Maine/New Hampshire/Vermont State Industrial Directory 312
MacRae's Washington State Industrial Directory (US ISSN 0740-6134) 313
MacRae's West Virginia State Industrial Directory see MacRae's Kentucky/West Virginia State Industrial Directory 312
MacRae's Wisconsin State Industrial Directory (US ISSN 0740-6053) 313
MacRae's Wyoming State Industrial Directory see MacRae's Idaho/Montana/Wyoming State Industrial Directory 312
Macromolecular Chemistry (London) (UK ISSN 0144-2988) 330
Macromolecular Chemistry (Oxford) (UK ISSN 0076-2075) 330
Macromolecular Chemistry and Physics see Die Makromolekulare Chemie. Supplement 330
Macromolecular Syntheses (US ISSN 0076-2091) 330, 332
McWinners Magazine (US) 727
Madagascar. Service Geologique. Rapport d'Activite: Geologie (MG) 390
Made in Austria (AU ISSN 0076-2105) 313
Made in Brazil (BL) 258
Made in Europe Buyers' Guide (GW ISSN 0172-2182) 258
Made in Europe - Medical Equipment and Supply Guide (GW ISSN 0720-597X) 763, 782
Made in Hungary Yearbook (HU ISSN 0209-4401) 258
Made in Tunisia (TI) 313
Madera y su Uso en la Construccion (MX) 185, 530
Madhya Pradesh. Directorate of Agriculture. Agricultural Statistics (II ISSN 0304-6184) 42
Madhya Pradesh Itihasa Parishad. Journal (II) 852
Madhya Pradesh State Agro-Industries Development Corporation Ltd. Annual Report (II ISSN 0304-7245) 48
Madhya Pradesh Vikas Varshiki (II) 539
Madhya Pradesh Who's Who (II) 128, 135
Madhya Pradesh Yearbook see Madhya Pradesh Vikas Varshiki 539
Madison Avenue Handbook (US ISSN 0076-2148) 16
Madison, Connecticut - A Pictorial Guide (US) 236
Madison County Heritage (US) 607
Madison Waste Conference. Annual Proceedings (US) 482, 497
Madjalah Pertanian (IO ISSN 0024-9556) 31
Madoqua (SX) 994
Madoqua. Series 1 see Madoqua 994
Madoqua. Series 2 see Madoqua 994
Madras. Government Museum. Bulletin. New Series (II ISSN 0085-2945) 994
Madrid Trans-Port (SP) 1101
Madrider Mitteilungen (GW) 89
Madrikh Pirsum (IS) 16, 313
Madrona (US ISSN 0047-5432) 742
Maeda Venitunim (IS) 353
Maerkischen Museum. Jahrbuch (GE) 590
Maerkte im Saarland (GW ISSN 0177-7491) 301
Mafogra (FR) 313
Magal (IS) 976
Magazin Polovnika (CS ISSN 0541-8836) 615, 727, 1046
Magazin Vier und Zwanzig see Initiative 335

Magazine Index (US) 9, 962
Magazine Industry Market Place (US ISSN 0000-0434) 313, 962
Magazine of Albemarle County History(US ISSN 0076-2342) 607
Magazines for Libraries (US) 128, 681
Magic Changes (US ISSN 0196-8432) 107, 727
Magill's Cinema Annual (US) 824
Magill's History Annual see Magill's Literary Annual: History and Biography 727
Magill's Literary Annual (US ISSN 0163-3058) 727, 962
Magill's Literary Annual: History and Biography (US) 135, 559, 727
Magira (GW) 107, 727, 742
Magnetic Resonance Annual (US) 899
Magnetic Resonance in Biology (US) 143
Magnitnoimpul'snaya Obrabotka Metallov (UR) 457
Magnito-Poluprovodnikovye i Elektromashinnye Elementy Avtomatiki (UR) 457
Magon. Serie Scientifique (LE ISSN 0076-2369) 31
Magon. Serie Technique (LE ISSN 0076-2377) 31
Magyar Allami Eotvos Lorand Geofizikai Intezet evi Jelentese see Eotvos Lorand Geophysical Institute of Hungary. Annual Report 399
Magyar Evkonyv (US ISSN 0094-1484) 463
Magyar Irodalom es Irodalomtudomany Bibliografiaja (HU ISSN 0134-1464) 128
Magyar Irodalomtortenetiras Forrasai (HU ISSN 0076-2385) 727
Magyar Konyveszet (Budapest. 1961) (HU ISSN 0133-3496) 128
Magyar Kozgazdasagi Irodalom/Hungarian Economic Literature (HU ISSN 0133-0152) 212
Magyar Kozlony (HU ISSN 0076-2407) 590
Magyar Kulpolitikai Evkonyv (HU ISSN 0541-9220) 917
Magyar Munkasmozgalmi Muzeum. Evkonyv (HU ISSN 0076-2415) 648, 907
Magyar Naptar see Magyar Evkonyv 463
Magyar Nemzeti Bibliografia see Magyar Nemzeti Bibliografia. Idoszaki Kiadvanyok Bibliografiaja 128
Magyar Nemzeti Bibliografia. Idoszaki Kiadvanyok Bibliografiaja (HU ISSN 0231-4592) 128
Magyar Nepmuveszet Evszazadai (HU ISSN 0200-5352) 1157
Magyar Nyelvjarasok (HU ISSN 0541-9298) 698
Magyar Olajipari Muzeum. Evkonyv (HU) 865
Magyar Statisztikai Zsebkonyv (HU ISSN 0133-5847) 1059
Magyar Szo Naptara (YU ISSN 0541-9344) 463
Magyar Tudomanyos Akademia. Agrartudomanyok Osztalya. Monografiasorozat (HU ISSN 0076-2423) 31
Magyar Tudomanyos Akademia. Mikrobiologiai Kutato Intezet. Proceedings/Hungarian Academy of Sciences. Research Institute for Microbiology. Proceedings (HU ISSN 0076-2431) 168
Magyar Tudomanyos Akademia Konvytaranak Kiadvanyai (HU ISSN 0133-8862) 688, 1004
Magyar Tudomanyos Akademia Konyvtara Kezirattaranak Katalogusai (HU ISSN 0541-9492) 129
Magyarorszag (HU ISSN 0230-5828) 1059
Magyarorszag Allatvilaga/Fauna Hungariae (HU ISSN 0076-2474) 176
Magyarorszag Kulturfloraja (HU ISSN 0076-2482) 159
Magyarorszag Muemleki Topografiaja (HU ISSN 0076-2490) 107, 590
Magyarorszag Regeszeti Topografiaja (HU ISSN 0076-2504) 89

Magyarorszag Tajfoldrajza (HU ISSN 0076-2512) 546
Maharaja Sawai Man Singh II Memorial Series (II) 828
Maharaja Sayajirao University of Baroda. Department of Archaeology and Ancient History. Archaeology Series (II ISSN 0076-2520) 89
Maharaja Sayajirao University of Baroda. Department of History Series(II ISSN 0464-5030) 559
Maharashtra Archives Bulletin (II ISSN 0076-2547) 570
Maharashtra State Budget in Brief (II ISSN 0076-2555) 297
Maharashtra State Financial Corporation. Annual Report (II ISSN 0076-2563) 230
Mahratta (II ISSN 0076-2571) 570
Maihaugen (NO) 89, 590
Mail Order Business Directory (US ISSN 0085-2953) 284
Main Hurdman & Cranstoun News Summary (US) 221, 297
Main Hurdman & Cranstoun Tax Newsletter (US) 297
Maine. Bureau of Property Taxation. Annual Report (US) 297
Maine. Department of Human Services. Bureau of Health Planning and Development. Vital Statistics see Maine. Vital Statistics 927
Maine. Department of Marine Resources. Fisheries Circulars (US) 511
Maine. Department of Marine Resources. Fishery Bulletin (US) 511
Maine. Department of Marine Resources. Research Bulletin (US) 511
Maine. Department of Sea and Shore Fisheries. General Bulletin see Maine. Department of Marine Resources. Fisheries Circulars 511
Maine. Division of Research and Vital Records. Annual Statistical Report see Maine. Vital Statistics 927
Maine. State Library. Special Subject Resources in Maine (US ISSN 0091-0759) 681
Maine. Vital Statistics (US) 927
Maine Agricultural Experiment Station. Annual Report (US) 31, 143, 497
Maine Agricultural Experiment Station. Miscellaneous Report. (US ISSN 0734-9564) 31
Maine Agricultural Experiment Station. Technical Bulletin (US ISSN 0734-9556) 31
Maine Bar Directory (Year) (US) 659
Maine Cooperative Extension Service. Forestry Facts see Yankee Woodlot 529
Maine Geologist (US) 390
Maine Heritage Series (US ISSN 0076-2652) 607
Maine Historical Society. Research Series (US) 607
Maine Invites You (US) 1113
Maine Manufacturing Directory (US) 313
Maine Marketing Directory see Maine Manufacturing Directory 313
Maine Media Directory see Burrelle's New England Media Directory 15
Maine, New Hampshire, Vermont TourBook see Tourbook: Maine, New Hampshire, Vermont 1117
Maine Register: State Yearbook and Legislative Manual (US) 943, 951
Maine, Vermont and New Hampshire Directory of Manufacturers (US ISSN 0197-1220) 313
Mainfraenkisches Jahrbuch fuer Geschichte und Kunst (GW ISSN 0076-2725) 107, 590
Mainichi Daily News (JA) 463
Mainly (UK ISSN 0025-0848) 727
Maintenance Supplies (US) 185, 313
Maintenance Supplies Buyers' Guide see Maintenance Supplies 313
Mainzer Philosophische Forschungen (GW ISSN 0076-2776) 879
Mainzer Reihe (GW ISSN 0076-2784) 727
Mainzer Romanistische Arbeiten (GW ISSN 0542-1551) 698

Mainzer Studien zur Amerikanistik (GW ISSN 0170-9135) 698, 727
Mainzer Studien zur Sprach- und Volksforschung (GW ISSN 0170-3560) 699
Mainzer Zeitschrift (GW ISSN 0076-2792) 89, 107, 590
Maison Franco-Japonaise. Bulletin (FR ISSN 0495-7725) 631, 852, 1009
Maisons d'Enfants et d'Adolescents de France. Album-Annuaire National (FR ISSN 0076-2814) 334, 954
Maize Abstracts (UK ISSN 0267-2987) 9, 42
Maize Quality Protein Abstracts see Maize Abstracts 42
Majalah Universitas Sumatera Utara see University of North Sumatra. Bulletin 440
Majallah Pantai see University of Malaya. Chinese Language Society. Journal 707
Majallah Perpustakaan Malaysia (MY ISSN 0126-7809) 681
Maji Review (TZ) 465, 1125
Majlis Pengeluar-Pengeluar Getah Malaysia. Lapuran Tahunan see Malaysian Rubber Producers' Council. Annual Report 985
Major Banks, Finance & Investment Companies of Continental Europe (UK ISSN 0268-232X) 230, 313
Major Companies of Argentina, Brazil, Mexico and Venezuela (UK) 313
Major Companies of Europe (UK) 313
Major Companies of Nigeria (UK ISSN 0144-2740) 313
Major Companies of the Arab World (UK) 313
Major Companies of the Far East (UK) 313
Major Companies of the United States of America (UK ISSN 0268-2338) 313
Major Employers Directory (US) 236
Major Energy Companies of Europe (UK ISSN 0268-2311) 313, 465
Major European Author Series (UK) 727
Major Industrial Research Unit Studies (US) 290
Makedonika (GR ISSN 0076-289X) 89, 516, 590, 699
Makedonska Akademija na Naukite i Umetnostite. Letopis (YU) 631, 994
Makedonski Jazik (YU ISSN 0025-1089) 699
Maker (US) 790
Makerere Library Publications see Makerere University. Library. Makerere Library Publications 681
Makerere Medical Journal (UG ISSN 0025-1119) 763
Makerere Political Review (UG) 907
Makerere University. Albert Cook Library. Library Bulletin and Accession List (UG) 681, 763
Makerere University. Department of Geography. Occasional Paper (UG ISSN 0075-4722) 546
Makerere University. Faculty of Agriculture. Handbook (UG ISSN 0075-4730) 31
Makerere University. Faculty of Agriculture. Technical Bulletin (UG ISSN 0075-4773) 31
Makerere University. Faculty of Education. Handbook (UG) 436
Makerere University. Faculty of Law. Handbook (UG ISSN 0075-4781) 659
Makerere University. Library. Makerere Library Publications (UG ISSN 0075-4854) 681
Makerere University. Science Faculty. Handbook (UG) 994
Making of the Twentieth Century (US) 559
Die Makromolekulare Chemie. Supplement (SZ ISSN 0253-5904) 328, 330
Maksvadaya (CE) 907
Mala Biblioteka Baletowa (PL ISSN 0076-2989) 375
Mala Biblioteka Operowa (PL) 837
Malacologia (US ISSN 0076-2997) 176
Malacological Review (US ISSN 0076-3004) 176

Malacological Society of Australia. Journal (AT ISSN 0085-2988) *176*
Maladies Veneriennes au Canada *see* Venereal Diseases in Canada *780*
Malagasy Republic. Institut National de la Statistique et de la Recherche Economique. Recensement Industriel(MG) *212, 1059*
Malagasy Republic. Ministere de la Production Agricole et la Reforme Agraire. Statistiques Agricoles. Annuaire (MG) *42*
Malago (UK) *590*
Malawai. Naitonal Statistical Office. Transport Statistics (MW) *1082, 1086*
Malawi. Accountant General. Report (MW ISSN 0076-3020) *297*
Malawi. Department of Agricultural Research. Annual Report (MW) *31*
Malawi. Department of Agriculture. Annual Report *see* Malawi. Department of Agricultural Research. Annual Report *31*
Malawi. Department of Civil Aviation. Annual Report (MW ISSN 0076-3055) *1089*
Malawi. Department of Forestry and Game. Report (MW ISSN 0076-3071) *366, 526*
Malawi. Department of Information. Year in Review *see* Malawi Yearbook *566*
Malawi. Department of Taxes. Annual Report of the Commissioner of Taxes(MW) *297*
Malawi. Department of Veterinary Services and Animal Industry. Annual Report (MW ISSN 0076-3365) *1122*
Malawi. Economic Planning Division. Mid-year Economic Review (MW) *297, 943*
Malawi. Fisheries Department. Fisheries Bulletin (MW) *511*
Malawi. Geological Survey Department. Annual Report (MW ISSN 0076-311X) *390*
Malawi. Malawi Bureau of Standards. Annual Report and Statement of Accounts (MW) *809*
Malawi. Meteorological Services. Totals of Monthly and Annual Rainfall *see* Malawi. Meteorological Department. Totals of Monthly and Annual Rainfall *805*
Malawi. Meteorological Department. Totals of Monthly and Annual Rainfall (MW) *805*
Malawi. Ministry of Finance. Budget Statement (MW ISSN 0076-3195) *297*
Malawi. Ministry of Finance. Financial Statement (MW) *297*
Malawi. Ministry of Justice. Annual Report (MW ISSN 0076-3160) *659*
Malawi. Ministry of Justice. Laws Amendments (MW) *659*
Malawi. Ministry of Local Government. Annual Report (MW ISSN 0076-3225) *907*
Malawi. National Library. Annual Report *see* Malawi. National Library Service Board. Annual Report *681*
Malawi. National Library Service Board. Annual Report (MW) *681*
Malawi. National Statistical Office. Annual Statement of External Trade (MW ISSN 0076-325X) *212*
Malawi. National Statistical Office. Annual Survey of Economic Activities (MW ISSN 0076-3241) *213*
Malawi. National Statistical Office. Balance of Payments (MW ISSN 0085-3003) *258, 297*
Malawi. National Statistical Office. Compendium of Agricultural Statistics *see* Malawi. National Statistical Office. National Sample Survey of Agriculture *42*
Malawi. National Statistical Office. Compendium of Statistics *see* Malawi Statistical Yearbook *1059*
Malawi. National Statistical Office. Household Income and Expenditure Survey (MW ISSN 0076-3276) *927, 1059*
Malawi. National Statistical Office. National Accounts Report (MW ISSN 0076-3284) *1059*
Malawi. National Statistical Office. National Sample Survey of Agriculture (MW ISSN 0076-3292) *42*
Malawi. National Statistical Office. Population Census Final Report (MW ISSN 0076-3306) *927*
Malawi. National Statistical Office. Reported Employment and Earnings: Annual Report (MW) *213*
Malawi. National Statistical Office. Tourist Report *see* Malawi Tourism Report *1120*
Malawi. Office of the Auditor General. Report (MW ISSN 0076-3314) *297*
Malawi. Police Force. Annual Report (MW ISSN 0076-308X) *371*
Malawi. Post Office Savings Bank. Annual Report (MW ISSN 0076-3322) *230*
Malawi. Registrar of Insurance. Report (MW ISSN 0076-3349) *640*
Malawi: a Guide for the Visitor (MW) *1113*
Malawi Broadcasting Corporation. Annual Report and Statement of Accounts (MW) *349*
Malawi Development Corporation. Annual Report (MW) *197*
Malawi Economic Report (MW ISSN 0076-3101) *246*
Malawi Gazette Supplement Containing Acts (MW) *943*
Malawi Gazette Supplement Containing Bills (MW) *944*
Malawi Gazette Supplement Containing Regulations, Rules, Etc. (MW) *944*
Malawi Government Directory (MW) *944*
Malawi Housing Corporation. Annual Report and Accounts (MW ISSN 0581-0892) *624*
Malawi Journal of Science (MW) *994*
Malawi Journal of Social Science (MW) *1009*
Malawi Law Reports (MW) *659*
Malawi National Bibliography (MW) *129*
Malawi Railways. Annual Reports and Accounts (MW ISSN 0076-3330) *1094*
Malawi Railways. Directors' Reports and Accounts *see* Malawi Railways. Annual Reports and Accounts *1094*
Malawi Statistical Yearbook (MW) *1059*
Malawi Tourism Report (MW) *1120*
Malawi Treaty Series (MW ISSN 0076-3357) *671*
Malawi Yearbook (MW) *566*
Malawian Geographer (MW) *546*
Malaya (Federation) Public Records Office and National Archives. Report *see* National Archives of Malaysia. Annual Report *570*
Malaysia. Department of Inland Revenue. Annual Report/Malaysia. Jabatan Hasil Dalam Negeri. Laporan Tahunan (MY) *240*
Malaysia. Department of Mines. Statistics Relating to the Mining Industry of Malaysia (MY ISSN 0126-818X) *822, 1059*
Malaysia. Department of Statistics. Annual Bulletin of Statistics (MY ISSN 0542-3570) *1059*
Malaysia. Department of Statistics. Survey of Construction Industries: Peninsular Malaysia (MY ISSN 0085-3046) *189*
Malaysia. Department of Statistics. Vital Statistics: Peninsular Malaysia (MY) *927, 1059*
Malaysia. Directory of Timber Trade (MY ISSN 0126-6330) *313, 530*
Malaysia. Geological Survey. Annual Report (MY ISSN 0127-0559) *390*
Malaysia. Jabatan Hasil Dalam Negeri. Lapuran Tahunan *see* Malaysia. Department of Inland Revenue. Annual Report *240*
Malaysia. Kementerian Pertanian. Bahagian Perikanan. Perangkaan Tahunan Perikanan *see* Malaysia. Ministry of Agriculture. Fisheries Division. Annual Fisheries Statistics *511*
Malaysia. Meteorological Service. Annual Summary of Meteorological Observations (MY) *806*
Malaysia. Meteorological Service. Summary of Observations for Malaysia *see* Malaysia. Meteorological Service. Annual Summary of Meteorological Observations *806*
Malaysia. Ministry of Agriculture. Fisheries Division. Annual Fisheries Statistics/Malaysia. Kementerian Pertanian. Bahagian Perikanan. Perangkaan Tahunan Perikanan (MY ISSN 0126-8856) *511*
Malaysia. Ministry of Agriculture. Technical and General Bulletins (MY) *31, 511*
Malaysia. Ministry of Agriculture. Technical Bulletins *see* Malaysia. Ministry of Agriculture. Technical and General Bulletins *31*
Malaysia in Brief (MY ISSN 0301-7095) *570*
Malaysia Official Year Book (MY ISSN 0076-3373) *570*
Malaysia Year Book *see* Information Malaysia *569*
Malaysian Centre for Development Studies Occasional Paper Series *see* M C D S Occasional Paper Series *1009*
Malaysian Chinese Association. Annual Report (MY ISSN 0542-397X) *570*
Malaysian Employers Federation Annual Report (MY) *273*
Malaysian Journal of Pathology (MY) *763*
Malaysian Journal of Science/Jernal Sains Malaysia (MY ISSN 0301-0554) *994*
Malaysian Multi-Purpose Cooperative Society. Review *see* K S M Review *30*
Malaysian National Bibliography/Bibliografi Negara Malaysia (MY ISSN 0126-5210) *564*
Malaysian Newspaper Index *see* Indeks Suratkhabar Malaysia *7*
Malaysian Newspaper Index *see* Indeks Suratkhabar Malaysia *7*
Malaysian Periodicals Index/Indeks Majalah Malaysia (MY ISSN 0126-5040) *9*
Malaysian Pineapple (MY) *31*
Malaysian Rubber Producers' Council. Annual Report/Majlis Pengeluar-Pengeluar Getah Malaysia. Lapuran Tahunan (MY ISSN 0126-8309) *985*
Malaysian Veterinary Journal (MY ISSN 0126-5652) *1122*
Malcolm Hulke Studies in Cinema & Television (US) *825*
Maledicta Press Publications (US ISSN 0363-9037) *699*
Maledicta: the International Journal of Verbal Aggression (US ISSN 0363-3659) *699*
Mali. Direction Nationale de la Statistique et de L'informatique. Annuaire Statistique (ML) *213*
Mali. Service de la Statistique Generale, de la Comptabilite Nationale et de la Mecanographie. Annuaire Statistique *see* Mali. Direction Nationale de la Statistique et de L'informatique. Annuaire Statistique *213*
Mali. Service de la Statistique Generale, de la Comtabilite Nationale et de la Mecanographie. Statistiques Douanieres du Commerce Exterieur (ML) *213*
Malta. Central Office of Statistics. Annual Abstract of Statistics (MM ISSN 0081-4733) *1059*
Malta. Central Office of Statistics. Census of Agriculture and Fisheries (MM) *42*
Malta. Central Office of Statistics. Census of Industrial Production Report (MM ISSN 0076-3462) *213*
Malta. Central Office of Statistics. Census of Production Report *see* Malta. Central Office of Statistics. Census of Industrial Production Report *213*
Malta. Central Office of Statistics. Demographic Review (MM ISSN 0076-3470) *923, 927*
Malta. Central Office of Statistics. Economic Survey (MM) *246*
Malta. Central Office of Statistics. Education Statistics (MM ISSN 0076-3489) *424*
Malta. Office of Statistics. Census of Agriculture *see* Malta. Central Office of Statistics. Census of Agriculture and Fisheries *42*
Malta Chamber of Commerce. Trade Directory *see* Trade Directory (1985-86) *318*
Malta Library Association Newsletter *see* Library Association (Valletta). Ghaqda Bibliotekarji/Library Association Newsletter *680*
Malta Yearbook (UK ISSN 0542-4550) *907, 1113*
Maltese Directory: Canada, United States (CN ISSN 0317-6983) *504, 607*
Ma'lumat-i Ihsa'ivi-i Afghanistan *see* Statistical Information of Afghanistan *1063*
Mambo Occasional Papers. Socio-Economic Series (RH) *1027*
Mammalia Depicta (GW ISSN 0301-2778) *176*
Mammalian Species (US ISSN 0076-3519) *176*
Man & Environment (II ISSN 0258-0446) *73, 89, 856*
Man and Society/Manusia dan Masyarakat (MY ISSN 0303-3171) *73, 1027*
Man and the Environment Information Guide Series (US) *1157*
Man - Environment Systems (US ISSN 0025-1550) *497, 624*
Man - Environment Systems/Focus Series *see* Psyche and Design *1161*
Man in Southeast Asia (AT) *73, 1009*
Man-Made Fibers of Japan (JA) *1074*
Management *see* Management Journal *280*
Management (Baltimore) (US ISSN 0565-7199) *20, 280*
Management Abstracts (II) *9, 213*
Management Abstracts (TR) *9, 213*
Management and Industrial Relations Series (UK) *280*
Management and Marketing Abstracts (US ISSN 0308-2172) *9, 213*
Management Aspects of Computers *see* Electricity Council Abstracts Bulletin *468*
Management Contents (US ISSN 0360-2400) *9, 213*
Management Development Series (UN ISSN 0074-6703) *280*
Management Guide to N C (US ISSN 0076-3624) *280*
Management Information Systems (US) *197*
Management Journal (UG ISSN 0300-2144) *280*
Management Monographs *see* L R I Guides to Management. Monographs *280*
Management of Malignant Disease Series (UK ISSN 0144-8692) *775*
Management Praxis (SZ) *280*
Management Report - General Services Administration *see* U.S. General Services Administration. Management Report *1021*
Management Reports on the Australian Economy (AT ISSN 0816-2484) *246*
Management Training and Research Centres in India. Directory (II) *280*
Management Training Directory (UK) *280*
Management Wissen Jahrbuch (GW) *280*
Manager (SJ) *280*
Managerial Information *see* Bestuurlike Informasie *221*
Managing the Nation's Public Lands (US) *965*
Manassas Review (US) *727*

MARKET STATISTICS   1807

Manchester Chamber of Commerce and Industry. Regional Business Directory (UK) 236
Manchester Chamber of Commerce and Industry. Yearbook (UK ISSN 0306-5758) 236
Manchester Latin American Studies (UK) 607
Manchester Literary and Philosophical Society. Memoirs and Proceedings see Manchester Memoirs 879
Manchester Memoirs (UK) 879
Manchester Polytechnic. Department of Library and Information Studies. Occasional Papers (UK ISSN 0260-8502) 681
Manchester Training Handbooks (UK ISSN 0260-4388) 280, 436
La Mandragore Qui Chante (SZ ISSN 0076-3748) 742
Maneggiare (BG) 280
Manhattan Directory of Commercial & Industrial Properties (US ISSN 0095-0688) 313
Manhattan Office Buildings: Downtown(US) 98
Manhattan Office Buildings: Midtown (US) 98
Manhattan Office Buildings: Midtown South (US) 98
Manhattan Review (US ISSN 0275-6889) 742
Manipur State Museum. Bulletin (II) 828
Manitoba. Co-Operative Loans and Loans Guarantee Board. Annual Report (CN) 230
Manitoba. Department of Co-Operative Development. Report/Rapport (CN) 230, 238
Manitoba. Economic Development Network. Community Profile Information System (CN) 246
Manitoba. Energy and Mines. Annual Report Series (CN) 465, 817
Manitoba. Environmental Council. Annual Report (CN ISSN 0380-9803) 497
Manitoba. Environmental Council. Studies (CN ISSN 0380-979X) 497
Manitoba. Environmental Council. Topics (CN ISSN 0711-8422) 497
Manitoba. Health Services Commission. Annual Report (CN ISSN 0383-3925) 954
Manitoba. Health Services Commission. Annual Statistics (CN) 959, 1059
Manitoba. Health Services Commission. Statistical Supplement to the Annual Report see Manitoba. Health Services Commission. Annual Statistics 959
Manitoba. Horse Racing Commission. Annual Report (CN ISSN 0317-7262) 1043
Manitoba. Human Rights Commission. Annual Report (CN ISSN 0383-5588) 913
Manitoba. Lotteries Commission. Annual Report see Manitoba Lotteries Foundation. Annual Report 1034
Manitoba. Mineral Resources Division. Annual Report Series see Manitoba. Energy and Mines. Annual Report Series 465
Manitoba. Mineral Resources Division. Bibliography Series see Manitoba Energy and Mines. Bibliography Series 382
Manitoba. Mineral Resources Division. Economic Geology Paper Series see Manitoba Energy and Mines. Economic Geology Paper Series 391
Manitoba. Mineral Resources Division. Educational Series see Manitoba Energy and Mines. Educational Series 391
Manitoba. Mineral Resources Division. Geological Paper see Manitoba Energy and Mines. Geological Paper 391
Manitoba. Mineral Resources Division. Geological Report see Manitoba Energy and Mines. Geological Report 391
Manitoba. Mineral Resources Division. Open File Report Series see Manitoba Energy and Mines. Open File Report Series 391

Manitoba. Mineral Resources Division. Report of Field Activities see Manitoba Energy and Mines. Report of Field Activities 391
Manitoba. Municipal Employees Benefits Board. Annual Report (CN ISSN 0706-3792) 273
Manitoba. Pension Commission. Annual Report see Manitoba. Pension Commission. Update Study 640
Manitoba. Pension Commission. Update Study (CN) 640
Manitoba. Public Library Services. Newsletter (CN ISSN 0706-7798) 681
Manitoba. Water Services Board. Annual Report (CN ISSN 0318-3912) 1125
Manitoba Agriculture Yearbook (CN ISSN 0084-3865) 31
Manitoba Association of School Librarians Newsletter see Manitoba School Library Audio Visual Association Journal 681
Manitoba Cancer Treatment and Research Foundation. Report (CN ISSN 0076-3802) 775
Manitoba Community Reports see Manitoba. Economic Development Network. Community Profile Information System 246
Manitoba Construction Industry Directory. Purchasing Guide (CN) 185, 473
Manitoba Credit Unions: Annual Report see Manitoba. Department of Co-Operative Development. Report/Rapport 230
Manitoba Crop Insurance Corporation. Annual Report (CN ISSN 0542-5395) 57, 640
Manitoba Decisions, Civil and Criminal Cases (CN ISSN 0380-0008) 659
Manitoba Energy and Mines. Bibliography Series (CN) 382
Manitoba Energy and Mines. Economic Geology Paper Series (CN) 391
Manitoba Energy and Mines. Educational Series (CN) 391
Manitoba Energy and Mines. Geological Paper (CN) 391
Manitoba Energy and Mines. Geological Report (CN) 391, 817
Manitoba Energy and Mines. Open File Report Series (CN) 391
Manitoba Energy and Mines. Report of Field Activities (CN) 391
Manitoba Farm Vacations Association Brochure see M F V A Brochure 1113
Manitoba Geographical Studies (CN) 546
Manitoba Labour - Management Review Committee. Annual Report (CN ISSN 0076-3853) 273
Manitoba Lotteries Foundation. Annual Report (CN) 1034
Manitoba Museum of Man and Nature. Annual Report (CN) 828
Manitoba Museum of Man and Nature. Biennial Report see Manitoba Museum of Man and Nature. Annual Report 828
Manitoba Record Society. Publications (CN ISSN 0076-3896) 607
Manitoba Reports (CN) 659
Manitoba Restaurant & Foodservices Roster (CN) 620
Manitoba School Library Audio Visual Association Journal (CN ISSN 0315-9124) 681
Manitoba Ship by Truck Directory (CN ISSN 0713-8776) 1105
Manitoba Trade Directory (CN ISSN 0076-390X) 313
Manitoba Vacation Guide, Canada (CN) 1113
Manitoba Vacation Handbook see Manitoba Vacation Guide, Canada 1113
Manitoba/Winnipeg Building & Construction Trades Council Yearbook (CN) 185
Mankind Quarterly Monograph Series (US ISSN 0076-4116) 73
Von Mann zu Mann (GW) 1027

Manned Undersea Science and Technology Program see U.S. National Oceanic and Atmospheric Administration. Manned Undersea Science and Technology Program; Report 475
Manpower and Human Resources Studies (US ISSN 0149-080X) 273
Manpower: Glass Industry (UK ISSN 0260-1869) 320
Manpower Services Guide (AT) 944
Mansfield Historical Society's Magazine(AT ISSN 0814-5296) 573
Manual do Interno e Residente (BL) 1157
Manual of Air Force Law-Amendments(UK) 659, 811
Manual of Maritime Statistics (NE) 1157
Manual of Maritime Statistics of Seaborne Trade and Shipping see Manual of Maritime Statistics 1157
Manual of Materials Handling and Ancilliary Equipment see Materials Handling Buyers Guide 284
Manual of Military Law - Amendments(UK) 659, 811
Manual of Mutual Funds see Mutual Funds Almanac 267
Manual-State of Maryland see Maryland Manual 917
Manuali di Politica Internazionale (IT) 917
Manuel de l'O T A N see N A T O Handbook 917
Manuel International de Caoutchouc see Handbuch der Internationalen Kautschukindustrie 985
Manuel International des Plastiques see Handbuch der Internationalen Kunststoffindustrie 900
Manufacturers & Processors Directory (Pierre) see South Dakota Manufacturers & Processors Directory 317
Manufacturers' Sales of Commodities see Denmark. Danmarks Statistik. Varestatistik for Industri 207
Manufacturing Developments in Kentucky see Kentucky Manufacturing Developments 1069
Manufacturing Directory of Idaho see High Tech & Manufacturing Directory of Idaho 309
Manufacturing Engineering. Engineering Transactions see North American Manufacturing Research Conference. Proceedings 473
Manufacturing Resource Planning (US ISSN 0736-8313) 290
Manuscript (NE) 1157
Manusia dan Masyarakat see Man and Society 73
Manx Museum, Douglas, Isle of Man. Journal (UK ISSN 0076-4264) 590
Many Smokes see Wildfire 506
Maori Education Foundation. Annual Report (NZ ISSN 0076-4280) 416
Mara Institute of Technology. Annual Report/Institut Teknologi Mara. Laporan Tahunan (MY) 436
Marche des Emprunts Internationaux en Ecu see Bond Market in Luxemburg Francs and in Ecu 204
Marche National des Emprunts Obligataires see Bond Market in Luxemburg Francs and in Ecu 204
Marconi's International Register (US ISSN 0076-4418) 313, 350
Mardon Sensai Va Farhange-e Amme-e Iran see Etnologie et Traditions Populaires de l'Iran 503
Mare Balticum (GW ISSN 0542-6758) 1101
Marga Institute. Progress Report (CE) 1009
Marginal Notes (US) 681
Mari Annales de recherches Interdisciplinaires (FR) 89, 699
Mariager Aarbog (DK ISSN 0108-2868) 590
Marian Library Studies. New Series (US ISSN 0076-4434) 681, 971
Marian Studies (US ISSN 0464-9680) 982
Marine Academie. Mededelingen see Academie de Marine. Communications 1098

Marine Affairs Bibliography (CN ISSN 0226-8361) 129, 669
Marine Affairs Journal (US) 907
Marine Biological Association of India. Journal (II ISSN 0025-3146) 143
Marine Biological Association of the United Kingdom. Occasional Publications (UK) 143
Marine Biological Laboratory Lectures in Biology see M B L Lectures in Biology 143
Marine Biological Station of Asamushi. Bulletin (JA) 143
Marine Board of Hobart. Annual Report (AT) 1101
Marine Catalog see Marine Catalog and Buyers Guide 1101
Marine Catalog and Buyers Guide (US) 1101
Marine Ecology (US) 143
Marine Engineering/Log Annual Maritime Review and Yearbook Issue(US ISSN 0076-4469) 1102
Marine Engineering/Log Marine Directory (US) 1102
Marine Equipment Catalog (US) 1102
Marine Geology and Geophysics see Morskaya Geologiya i Geofizika 407
Marine Invertebrates of Scandinavia (NO) 143, 176
Marine Mammal Protection Act of 1972 Annual Report (US ISSN 0196-4690) 366
Marine Marchand: Etudes et Statistiques see Transport Maritime: Etudes et Statistiques 1104
Marine Marchande (FR ISSN 0294-8508) 1102
Marine Products Export Review see Statistics of Marine Products Exports 259
Marine Recreational Fisheries (US ISSN 0161-522X) 511
Marine Research Centre. Bulletin (LY) 511
Marine Research in Indonesia (IO ISSN 0079-0435) 407
Marine Research Institute. Journal see Rit Fiskideildar 512
Marine Science (US) 1157
Marine Science Contents Tables (UN ISSN 0025-3308) 150, 382, 514
Marine Standardization see Marine Standardization in Japan 1102
Marine Standardization in Japan (JA) 809, 1102
Mario Negri Institute for Pharmacological Research. Monographs (US ISSN 0085-3100) 871
Maritime Bank of Israel. Annual Report/Bank Ha-Sapanut le-Yisrael. Annual Report. (IS ISSN 0076-4515) 230
Maritime Guide (UK ISSN 0264-6420) 1102
Maritime History Group Newsletter (CN) 1102
Maritime Information Review see Ship Abstracts 1086
Maritime Monographs and Reports (UK ISSN 0307-8590) 828, 1102
Maritime Story of Southern England (UK) 590
Mark og Montre (DK ISSN 0105-0826) 590
Markeds-bog (DK ISSN 0107-8305) 301
Markedskalender see Markeds-bog 301
Marken-Handbuch der Werbung und Etatbetreuung (GW ISSN 0085-3119) 16
Marker see Arch 341
Markers (US ISSN 0277-8726) 107, 531
Market Guide Continental Europe (US ISSN 0278-6524) 267, 313
Market Profiles (US) 965
Market Research Abstracts (UK ISSN 0025-3596) 9, 213
Market Research Report (US) 16
Market Research Society. Yearbook (UK ISSN 0076-4523) 284
Market Research Sourcebook (UK) 284
Market Share Reports (US) 213
Market Statistics Key Plant Directory see Marketing Economics Key Plants 284

Marketing Abstracts *see* Management and Marketing Abstracts 213
Marketing & Distribution Abstracts (UK ISSN 0305-0661) 9, 213
Marketing Boards in Canada/Offices de Commercialisation au Canada (CN ISSN 0527-6624) 48
Marketing California Dried Fruits *see* Marketing California Dried Fruits: Prunes, Raisins, Dried Apricots & Peaches 48
Marketing California Dried Fruits: Prunes, Raisins, Dried Apricots & Peaches (US ISSN 0094-2510) 48, 240
Marketing California Ornamental Crops(US ISSN 0190-7492) 31
Marketing California Pears for Fresh Market (US ISSN 0098-8928) 48
Marketing California Strawberries (US) 31, 284
Marketing Economics Guide *see* M E I Marketing Economics Guide 284
Marketing Economics Institute, Ltd. Marketing Economics Guide *see* M E I Marketing Economics Guide 284
Marketing Economics Key Plants (US ISSN 0098-1397) 284
Marketing Executive Handbook (UK) 284
Marketing Research Association, Inc. Research Service Directory *see* M R A Research Service Directory 284
Marketpulse (US) 284
Markets Year Book (UK ISSN 0076-4647) 284
Marketsearch (UK) 284
Maroc *see* Arts et Objets du Maroc 102
Maroc en Chiffre (MR ISSN 0076-4655) 258
Marquee (US ISSN 0025-3928) 98, 1077
Marquette Journal (US ISSN 0025-3979) 727
Marquette Slavic Studies (US ISSN 0076-4671) 590
Marschenrat zur Foerderung der Forschung im Kuestengebiet der Nordsee. Nachrichten (GW) 159, 391, 546, 994
Marshall News (US) 341
Marsyas (US ISSN 0076-4701) 107
Martin Classical Lectures (US ISSN 0076-471X) 338
Martin Luther King, Jr. Center for Non-Violent Social Change Newsletter (US) 913
Martindale - Hubbell Law Directory (US) 659
Martindale: the Extra Pharmacopoeia (UK) 871
Martin's Annual Criminal Code (CN ISSN 0527-7892) 660
Marx Karoly Kozgazdasagtudomanyi Egyetem: Doktori Ertekezesek (HU ISSN 0521-4211) 213
Marx Karoly Kozgazdasagtudomanyi Egyetem Oktatoinak Szakirodalmi Munkassaga (HU ISSN 0133-5162) 129, 213
Marxism and the Mass Media (US ISSN 0098-9509) 344, 907
Marxisticka Filozofia *see* Univerzita Komenskeho. Ustav Marxizmu-Leninizmu. Zbornik: Marxisticka Filozofia 911
Marxistische Studien (GW ISSN 0171-3698) 907, 1009
Marxizmus-Leninizmus. Zbornik Ustav Marxizmu-Leninizmu Univerzity P.J. Safarika *see* Univerzita Pavla Jozefa Safarika. Ustav Marxizmu-Leninizmu. Zbornik Prac Ucitelov 600
Mary Wollstonecraft Journal *see* Women & Literature 1129
Maryland. Department of Human Resources. Information Pamphlet (US ISSN 0092-9476) 1019
Maryland. Division of Correction. Report (US ISSN 0362-9198) 371
Maryland. General Assembly. Subject Index to Bills Introduced in the Session (US) 129, 660
Maryland. Geological Survey. Archeological Studies (US) 89
Maryland. Geological Survey. Bulletin (US ISSN 0076-4779) 391

Maryland. Geological Survey. Educational Series (US ISSN 0076-4787) 391
Maryland. Geological Survey. Information Circular (US ISSN 0076-4795) 391
Maryland. Geological Survey. Report of Investigations (US ISSN 0076-4809) 391
Maryland. Geological Survey. Water Resources Basic Data Report (US ISSN 0076-4817) 1125
Maryland. House of Delegates. Journal of Proceedings. Regular Session (US) 660
Maryland. Senate. Journal of Proceedings. Regular Session (US) 660
Maryland. State Department of Legislative Reference. Synopsis of Laws Enacted by the State of Maryland (US ISSN 0093-0520) 660
Maryland. State Highway Administration. Traffic Trends (US ISSN 0094-6265) 1096
Maryland Air Management Administration. Data Report (US) 497
Maryland Air Quality Data Report *see* Maryland Air Management Administration. Data Report 497
Maryland Air Quality Programs. Data Report *see* Maryland Air Management Administration. Data Report 497
Maryland High-Tech Directory (US) 1069
Maryland Lawyer's Manual (US ISSN 0542-836X) 660
Maryland Manual (US ISSN 0094-4491) 944
Masalah Pendidikan (MY ISSN 0126-5024) 416
Maschinenfabrik Augsburg-Nuernberg AG Forschen, Planen, Bauen *see* M.A.N. Forschen, Planen, Bauen 473
Masiform D (US) 14, 727
Mask *see* Masque 727
Al-Maskukat (IQ ISSN 0002-4058) 845
Masque (UK ISSN 0025-4711) 727, 837
Mass Communication Review Yearbook(US ISSN 0196-8017) 344
Mass Line *see* Road of the Party 909
Mass Media in India (II) 349
Mass Media Review (AT) 344
Mass Retailers' Executive Perquisite Report (US) 273
Mass Retailers' Merchandising Report (US) 273
Mass Spectrometry (UK ISSN 0305-9987) 323, 889
Mass Spectrometry Bulletin (UK ISSN 0025-4738) 9, 326
Massachusetts. Department of Public Health. Annual Report (US) 954
Massachusetts. Division of Employment Security. Employment and Wages in Establishments Subject to the Massachusetts Employment Security Law. State Summary (US ISSN 0076-4922) 274
Massachusetts. Division of Fisheries and Game. Annual Report *see* Massachusetts. Division of Fisheries and Wildlife. Annual Report 366
Massachusetts. Division of Fisheries and Wildlife. Annual Report (US) 366
Massachusetts Agricultural Statistics (US ISSN 0092-9794) 42
Massachusetts Directory of Manufacturers (US ISSN 0195-5810) 313
Massachusetts Historical Society. Proceedings (US ISSN 0076-4981) 607
Massachusetts Historical Society Miscellany *see* M.H.S. Miscellany 607
Massachusetts Housing Finance Agency. Annual Report (US ISSN 0076-499X) 624

Massachusetts Institute of Technology. Flight Transportation Laboratory. F T L Reports *see* Massachusetts Institute of Technology. Flight Transportation Laboratory. F T L Reports and Memoranda 20
Massachusetts Institute of Technology. Flight Transportation Laboratory. F T L Reports and Memoranda (US) 20, 1089
Massachusetts Institute of Technology. Research Laboratory of Electronics. Quarterly Progress Report *see* Massachusetts Institute of Technology. Research Laboratory of Electronics. R L E Progress Report 457
Massachusetts Institute of Technology. Research Laboratory of Electronics. R L E Progress Report (US ISSN 0163-9218) 344, 457
Massachusetts Municipal Directory (US ISSN 0361-2090) 951
Massachusetts Service Directory (US) 313
Massachusetts Tax Primer (US ISSN 0362-868X) 297
Massachusetts Taxpayers Foundation. State Budget Trends (US) 246, 944, 1059
Massey University. Centre for Agricultural Policy Studies. Discussion Paper (NZ ISSN 0112-0603) 1157
Massey University. Department of Agricultural Economics and Farm Management. Technical Discussion Paper *see* Massey University. Centre for Agricultural Policy Studies. Discussion Paper 1157
Massey University. Faculty of Business Studies. Occasional Papers (NZ) 222
Masson Monographs in Diagnostic Cytopathology (US ISSN 0732-9539) 763
Massstaebe (GW) 107, 631
Master Baker's Handbook and Buyer's Guide (UK) 522
Master Federal Tax Manual (US) 297
Master Production Scheduling (US ISSN 0736-8259) 290
Masterguide (US) 98
Masterpieces in the National Gallery of Canada/Chefs-d'Oeuvre de la Galerie Nationale du Canada (CN ISSN 0383-5391) 107
Masterplots Annual *see* Magill's Literary Annual 727
Master's Education: Route to Opportunities in Contemporary Nursing (US) 436, 784
Masters Education; Route to Opportunities in Modern Nursing *see* Master's Education: Route to Opportunities in Contemporary Nursing 784
Masters of Science Fiction (US ISSN 0271-7794) 727
Master's Theses in Education (US ISSN 0076-5112) 416
Master's Theses in the Arts and Social Sciences (US ISSN 0160-8797) 107, 436, 1009
Masterskaya (UR) 727
Match (GW ISSN 0340-6253) 323, 750
Matematicheskaya Fizika i Funktsional'nyi Analiz (UR) 750, 889
Matematicheskie Metody v Ekonomike (UR ISSN 0130-9404) 197
Matematicheskie Problemy Geofiziki (UR ISSN 0301-6897) 755
Matematyka (PL) 750
Material Culture Directories (US ISSN 0743-7528) 1027
Material for Thought (US) 879
Material Handling Engineering Handbook and Directory (US) 745, 855
Material Requirements Planning (US ISSN 0736-8321) 290
Materialen zur Kunst des Neunzehnten Jahrhunderts (GW ISSN 0172-2115) 828
Materiales de la Ciudad (SP) 624
Materiales para la Arqueologia del Peru(PE) 89
Materiali di Storia Urbana (IT) 559

Materiali per il Vocabolario Neosumerico. Collana (IT) 852
Materialia Turcica (GW ISSN 0344-449X) 613
Materialien aus der Bildungsforschung (GW ISSN 0173-3842) 416
Materialien zum Internationalen Kulturaustausch/Studies in International Cultural Relations (GW) 852, 917
Materialien zur Roemisch-Germanischen Keramik (GW ISSN 0076-5171) 89, 320
Materialien zur Wirtschafts- und Sozialgeschichte (AU) 590
Materialiensammlung Staedtebau (GW ISSN 0340-983X) 482
Materialoznanie i Tekhnologiia (BU ISSN 0204-7535) 489
Materials and Studies for Kassite History (US ISSN 0146-6798) 570
Materials Business Abstracts (UK) 801
Materials Handling Buyers Guide (UK ISSN 0142-114X) 284
Materials Handling Yearbook (Dublin) (IE) 489
Materials in Languages of Indonesia (AT) 699
Materials Performance Buyer's Guide (US ISSN 0095-7976) 799
Materials Processing: Theory and Practices (NE) 889
Materials Research and Engineering/Reine und Angewandte Metallkunde (US) 473, 799
Materials Research Centres (UK) 313, 489
Materials Research in Science and Engineering at Purdue University. Annual Report *see* Materials Research in Science and Engineering at Purdue University. Progress Report 489
Materials Research in Science and Engineering at Purdue University. Progress Report (US ISSN 0079-8126) 489
Materials Science Monographs (NE) 473
Materials Science of Minerals and Rocks (NE) 391
Materials Science Research (US ISSN 0076-5201) 489
Materialy Badawcze. Seria: Gospodarka Wodna i Ochrona Wod/Research Papers Series: Water Management and Water Protection (PL ISSN 0239-6238) 403
Materialy Badawcze. Seria: Hydrologia i Oceanologia/Research Papers Series: Hydrology and Oceanology (PL) 403
Materialy Badawcze. Seria: Inzynieria Wodna/Research Papers Series: Water Engineering (PL ISSN 0239-6254) 490
Materialy Badawcze. Seria: Meteorologia/Research Papers Series: Meteorology (PL ISSN 0239-6262) 806
Materialy Glyatsiologicheskikh Issledovanii/Data of Glaciological Studies (UR ISSN 0130-3686) 400
Materialy Historyczno-Metodyczne (PL) 559
Materialy i Issledovaniya po Sibirskoi Dialektologii (UR) 699
Materialy i Prace Antropologiczne (PL ISSN 0076-521X) 73
Materialy Zachodnio-Pomorskie (PL ISSN 0076-5236) 89, 590
Materialy Zrodlowe do Dziejow Kosciola W Polsce (PL ISSN 0076-5244) 982
Materiaux pour l'Etude de l'Asie Orientale Moderne et Contemporaine(FR) 699
Materiel Graphique (FR) 931
Mathematicae Notae (AG ISSN 0025-553X) 750
Mathematical Approaches to Geophysics (NE) 889
Mathematical Association of South Australia. S.A. Mathematics Teacher *see* Mobius 448
Mathematical Centre Tracts *see* C W I Tracts 748
Mathematical Chronicle (NZ ISSN 0581-1155) 750

Mathematical Expositions (CN ISSN 0076-5333) 750
Mathematical Notes see Notas Matematicas 751
Mathematical Notes (Princeton) (US) 750
Mathematical Physics and Applied Mathematics (NE) 750, 889
Mathematical Physics Studies (NE) 889
Mathematical Reviews (US ISSN 0025-5629) 9, 755
Mathematical Reviews Annual Index see Index of Mathematical Papers 755
Mathematical Sciences Research Institute Publications (US) 750
Mathematical Society of Japan. Publications (JA ISSN 0549-4540) 750
Mathematical Surveys see Mathematical Surveys & Monographs 750
Mathematical Surveys & Monographs (US) 750
Mathematical Systems in Economics (GW) 252, 750
Mathematics and Its Applications (US ISSN 0543-0941) 750
Mathematics and Its Applications (NE) 750
Mathematics and Its Applications: East European Series (NE) 750
Mathematics and Its Applications: Japanese Series (NE) 750
Mathematics and Its Applications: Soviet Series (NE) 750
Mathematics Education Library (NE) 416, 750, 935
Mathematics in Biology (US) 143
Mathematics in Science and Engineering (US ISSN 0076-5392) 473, 750
Mathematik fuer Naturwissenschaft und Technik (GE ISSN 0543-100X) 751
Mathematik und ihre Anwendungen in Physik und Technik (GE ISSN 0233-1063) 751
Mathematische Forschung. Schriftenreihe (GE ISSN 0138-3019) 751, 895
Mathematische Lehrbuecher und Monographien. Abteilung 2: Mathematische Monographien (GE ISSN 0076-5430) 751
Mathematische Monographien (GE ISSN 0543-1042) 751
Mathematische Schuelerbuecherei (GE ISSN 0076-5449) 751
Mathilda and Terence Kennedy Institute of Rheumatology. Annual Report (UK) 793
Mathitiki Estia (CY ISSN 0025-5904) 335
Matieres see Poetica et Analytica 701
Matsumoto Dental College Research Bulletin (JA ISSN 0288-3317) 143, 779
Matter of Degree (UK ISSN 0140-7961) 546
Maudsley Monographs (US) 763
Maufacturers Association of Nigeria. Industrial Directory see Nigeria Industrial Directory 314
Mauri Ora (NZ ISSN 0302-086X) 143
Maurice Falk Center for Economic Research in Israel. Report. see Maurice Falk Institute for Economic Research in Israel. Report and Discussion Paper Series 197
Maurice Falk Institute for Economic Research in Israel. Report and Discussion Paper Series (IS ISSN 0333-7839) 197
Mauritiana (Altenburg) (GE ISSN 0233-173X) 828, 994
Mauritius. Archives Department. Annual Report (MF ISSN 0076-5481) 681
Mauritius. Central Electricity Board. Annual Report (MF) 457
Mauritius. Central Statistical Office. Household Expenditure Survey (MF) 615
Mauritius. Central Statistical Office. International Travel and Tourism (MF) 1059, 1120

Mauritius. Central Statistical Office. National Accounts of Mauritius (MF) 213
Mauritius. Central Statistical Office. Statistical Summary (MF) 1059
Mauritius. Customs and Excise Department. Annual Report (MF ISSN 0076-549X) 297
Mauritius. Director of Audit. Report (MF ISSN 0543-1565) 297
Mauritius. Forest Department. Annual Report see Mauritius. Forestry Service. Annual Report 526
Mauritius. Forestry Service. Annual Report (MF) 526
Mauritius. Government Fire Services. Annual Report (MF) 507
Mauritius. Judicial Department. Annual Report (MF) 660
Mauritius. Legislative Assembly. Debates (MF) 944
Mauritius. Legislative Assembly. Sessional Paper (MF ISSN 0076-5503) 944
Mauritius. Meteorological Services. Report (MF ISSN 0076-5511) 806
Mauritius. Ministry for Employment and of Social Security and National Solidarite see Mauritius. Ministry of Social Security, National Solidarite and Reform Institutions 1019
Mauritius. Ministry of Agriculture and Natural Resources and the Environment. Annual Report see Mauritius. Ministry of Agriculture, Fisheries and Natural Resources. Annual Report 31
Mauritius. Ministry of Agriculture and Natural Resources and the Environment. Technical Bulletin see Mauritius. Ministry of Agriculture, Fisheries and Natural Resources. Technical Bulletin 31
Mauritius. Ministry of Agriculture, Fisheries and Natural Resources. Annual Report (MF) 31
Mauritius. Ministry of Agriculture, Fisheries and Natural Resources. Technical Bulletin (MF) 31
Mauritius. Ministry of Co-operatives and Co-operative Development. Annual Report (MF) 238
Mauritius. Ministry of Health. Annual Report (MF) 954
Mauritius. Ministry of Housing, Lands and Town and Country Planning. Annual Reports (MF ISSN 0076-552X) 624
Mauritius. Ministry of Labour and Industrial Relations. Annual Report (MF) 274
Mauritius. Ministry of Labour. Annual Report see Mauritius. Ministry of Labour and Industrial Relations. Annual Report 274
Mauritius. Ministry of Social Security, National Solidarite and Reform Institutions (MF) 1019
Mauritius. Ministry of Works and Internal Communications. Report (MF ISSN 0076-5554) 944, 1082
Mauritius. Ombudsman. Report (MF) 944
Mauritius. Posts and Telegraphs Department. Annual Report (MF) 346
Mauritius. Public Accounts Committee. Report (MF ISSN 0076-5562) 297
Mauritius. Public Service Commission. Report (MF) 944
Mauritius. Registrar of Insurance. Annual Report (MF) 640
Mauritius. Telecommunications Department. Annual Report (MF) 350
Mauritius. Tobacco Board. Annual Report (MF) 1080
Mauritius Chamber of Agriculture. President's Report (MF) 31
Mauritius Chamber of Commerce and Industry. Annual Report (MF) 236
Mauritius Directory of the Diplomatic Corps (MF ISSN 0085-3194) 917
Mauritius Housing Corporation. Report and Accounts (MF) 624
Mauritius Institute of Education. Annual Report (MF) 416
Mauritius Institute of Education. Journal (MF) 416

Mauritius Police Force. Annual Report (MF) 371
Mauritius Police Magazine (MF) 371
Mauritius Standards Bureau. Annual Report (MF) 809
Mauritius Sugar Industry Research Institute. Advisory Bulletin (MF) 520
Mauritius Sugar Industry Research Institute. Annual Report (MF) 520
Mauritius Sugar Industry Research Institute. Occasional Paper (MF) 520
Mawdsley Memoirs (CN) 546, 994
Max Freiherr von Oppenheim-Stiftung. Schriften (GW ISSN 0543-1719) 852
Max-Planck-Gesellschaft. Jahrbuch (GW ISSN 0341-0218) 995, 1009
Max-Planck-Gesellschaft zur Foerderung der Wissenschaften. Jahrbuch (GW ISSN 0076-5635) 995
Max-Planck-Gesellschaft zur Foerderung der Wissenschaften Berichte und Mitteilungen (GW ISSN 0341-7778) 995
Max-Planck-Gesellschaft zur Foerderung der Wissenschaften Mitteilungen see Max-Planck-Gesellschaft zur Foerderung der Wissenschaften Berichte und Mitteilungen 995
Max-Planck-Institut fuer Auslaendisches Oeffentliches Recht und Voelkerrecht. Fontes see Max-Planck-Institut fuer Auslaendisches Oeffentliches Recht und Voelkerrecht. Fontes Iuris Gentium 660
Max-Planck-Institut fuer Auslaendisches Oeffentliches Recht und Voelkerrecht. Fontes Iuris Gentium (GW) 660
Max-Planck-Institut fuer Bildungsforschung, Berlin. Studien und Berichte (GW ISSN 0076-5627) 416
Max-Planck-Institut fuer Geschichte. Veroeffentlichungen (GW) 559
Max-Planck-Institute fuer Europaische Rechtsgeschichte. Veroeffentlichungen. Ius Commune (GW ISSN 0579-2428) 660
Max-Planck-Institute fuer Europaische Rechtsgeschichte. Veroeffentlichungen. JusCommune. Sonderhefte (GW ISSN 0175-6532) 660
May Trends (US ISSN 0025-6137) 230
Ma'yanot (IS ISSN 0543-1786) 504
Maynooth Occasional Papers (IE) 546
Me (US ISSN 0272-5657) 107, 742
Me Judice see Singapore Law Review 664
Me, Too see Me 107
Me Too (US) 742
Meade County Historian (US) 607
Means Assemblies Costs (US) 185
Means Concrete Cost Data (US) 185
Means Electrical Cost Data (US ISSN 0748-7002) 473
Means Historical Cost Indexes (US ISSN 0277-8610) 185
Means Mechanical and Electrical Cost Data see Means Electrical Cost Data 473
Means Site Work Cost Data (US ISSN 0734-8479) 185
Means Square Foot Costs (US ISSN 0732-815X) 185, 965
Means Systems Costs see Means Assemblies Costs 185
Me'asef (IS) 274, 613
Measuring Mormonism (US ISSN 0094-5633) 984
Meat and Livestock Commission, Bucks., England. Index of Research (UK ISSN 0076-5716) 67
Meat Research Institute. Biennial Report see Institute of Food Research - Bristol. Laboratory Biennial Report 519
Meat Science Institute. Proceedings (US ISSN 0090-5631) 520
Meat Trade Yearbook see Meat Trade Yearbook & Diary 520

Meat Trade Yearbook & Diary (UK) 67, 520
Meatworker (AT ISSN 0310-6721) 520, 648
Mecanica Nacional/National Mechanics(VE) 1092
Mechanical and Electrical Cost Data see Mechanical Cost Data 185
Mechanical & Electronic Industries Yearbook of China (HK ISSN 0258-3038) 313
Mechanical Cost Data (US ISSN 0748-2698) 185, 457
Mechanics and Building Engineering see Acta Academiae Agriculturae ac Technicae Olstenensis. Aedificatio et Mechanica 491
Mechanics: Dynamical Systems (NE) 895
Mechanics of Elastic and Inelastic Solids (NE) 895
Mechanika i Budownictwo Ladowe see Acta Academiae Agriculturae ac Technicae Olstenensis. Aedificatio et Mechanica 491
Mechanine Technologija see Mekhanicheskaya Tekhnologiya 492
Mechanisms of Inorganic and Organometallic Reactions (US) 328
Mechanix Illustrated Plans & Projects (US) 1157
Mecklenburgisches Woerterbuch (GE) 699
Mecman - Technique (SW ISSN 0025-6609) 473
Mecman - Teknik see Mecman - Technique 473
Med Bil i Europa (NO) 1113
Medaglia (IT ISSN 0392-5439) 845
Meddelande Armemuseum. Yearbook (SW) 811, 828
Meddelande fraan Lunds Universitet Historiska Museum see University of Lund. Archeological Institute. Papers. Yearbook 95
Meddelelser fra Ferskvandsfiskerilaboratoriet (DK) 511
Meddelelser om Groenland, Bioscience (DK ISSN 0106-1054) 143, 497
Meddelelser om Groenland, Geoscience(DK ISSN 0106-1046) 391
Meddelelser om Groenland, Man & Society (DK ISSN 0106-1062) 73
Mededelingen "Ex Oriente Lux" see Voorazaitisch-Egyptisch Genootschap "Ex Oriente Lux". Mededelingen en Verhandelingen 572
Medelhavsmuseet. Bulletin (SW ISSN 0585-3214) 613
Medequip (AU ISSN 0253-7419) 763
Media Editorial Profile Edition (CN ISSN 0228-5215) 16
Media Guide International. Business/Professional Publications Edition see International Media Guides. Business/Professional Publications Edition 17
Media Guide International. Newspapers/Newsmagazines Edition see International Media Guide. Newspapers: Worldwide 17
Media Ownership in Australia (AT ISSN 0811-8892) 314, 646
Media Personnel Directory (US) 646, 962
Media Review Digest (US ISSN 0363-7778) 9, 826, 843
Media Scandinavia (DK ISSN 0076-5821) 16
Mediaeval and Modern Breton Series (IE) 590, 699
Mediaeval Philosophical Texts in Translation (US ISSN 0076-5856) 879
Mediaeval Scandinavia (DK ISSN 0076-5864) 590
Mediaeval Scandinavia Supplements (DK ISSN 0106-102X) 590
Mediaeval Sources in Translation (CN ISSN 0316-0874) 590, 727
Mediaeval Studies (CN ISSN 0076-5872) 590
Mediaevalia (US ISSN 0361-946X) 107, 590, 727
Mediaevalia Lovaniensia. Series I (BE) 590

Mediaevalia Philosophica Polonorum (PL ISSN 0076-5880) *879*
Medicaid Recipient Characteristics and Units of Selected Medical Services (US ISSN 0098-3616) *763, 1019*
Medical and Health Annual (US ISSN 0363-0366) *886*
Medical and Health Care Books and Serials in Print (US ISSN 0000-085X) *771*
Medical & Health Information Directory (US) *886*
Medical and Healthcare Marketplace Guide (US ISSN 0146-8022) *314, 763*
Medical Annual (UK ISSN 0076-5899) *763*
Medical Books and Serials in Print *see* Medical and Health Care Books and Serials in Print *771*
Medical Care Review (US ISSN 0025-7087) *9, 771, 959*
Medical Council of Iran. Publication/Nezam Pezeshki-Ye Iran. Nashriyeh (IR) *763*
Medical Directory (UK ISSN 0305-3342) *763*
Medical Directory of New York State (US) *763*
Medical Electronics and Equipment News Buyers' Guide (US) *763*
Medical Electronics and Equipment News Dictionary and Buyers' Guide *see* Medical Electronics and Equipment News Buyers' Guide *763*
Medical Group Management Association. Directory (US) *280, 763*
Medical Group Management Association. International Directory *see* Medical Group Management Association. Directory *763*
Medical Laboratory Directory (Year) (US) *314, 648*
Medical Physics Series (US ISSN 0076-5953) *763, 889*
Medical Product of Japan (JA) *314, 763*
Medical Products Marketers Directory (US) *240, 763*
Medical Protection Society. Annual Report (UK ISSN 0076-5961) *763*
Medical Radiology (US) *792*
Medical Research Bulletin (AT ISSN 0025-7494) *1157*
Medical Research Centre, Nairobi. Annual Report (KE ISSN 0076-5988) *763*
Medical Research Centres (UK) *763*
Medical Research Centres in Ghana: Current Research Projects (GH) *763*
Medical Research Council (Ireland). Report (IE ISSN 0076-5996) *1157*
Medical Research Council of Canada. Grants and Awards Guide/Guide de Subventions et Bourses (CN) *763*
Medical Research Council of Canada. Reference List of Health Science Research in Canada (CN) *763*
Medical Research Council of Canada. Report of the President (CN) *763*
Medical Research in the V.A. (US) *763*
Medical Research Index *see* Medical Research Centres *763*
Medical School Admission Requirements, United States and Canada (US ISSN 0066-9423) *437, 763*
Medical Society of London. Transactions (UK ISSN 0076-6011) *763*
Medical Society of the State of North Carolina. Transactions *see* North Carolina Medical Society. Transactions *764*
Medical Subject Headings (US ISSN 0565-811X) *763*
Medical Technologist Diary & Classified Buyer's Guide (UK) *763*
Medicare and Medicaid Data Book (US) *640*
Medicinal Chemistry (US ISSN 0076-6054) *871*
Medicinal Research: A Series of Monographs *see* Medicinal Research Series *1157*
Medicinal Research Series (US) *1157*
Medicine (New York) (US) *764*

Medicine and Sport *see* Medicine and Sport Science *793*
Medicine and Sport Science (SZ ISSN 0254-5020) *786, 793*
Medicinhistorisk Aarsbok *see* Nordisk Medicinhistorisk Aarsbok *764*
Medicinsk Aarbog (DK ISSN 0461-6308) *764*
Medicinsk Foedselsstatistik (DK ISSN 0107-7597) *771*
Medicintakst (DK ISSN 0900-4858) *871*
Medico-Legal Society of New South Wales. Proceedings (AT ISSN 0047-6587) *660*
Medico-Legal Society of Sri Lanka. Proceedings (CE) *782*
Medicolegal Library (US) *671, 764*
Medieval Academy Books (US) *107, 590, 727*
Medieval Academy of America. Publications *see* Medieval Academy Books *590*
Medieval Academy Reprints for Teaching (CN) *107, 590, 727*
Medieval and Renaissance Authors (NE) *727*
Medieval and Renaissance Drama in England (US ISSN 0731-3403) *1077*
Medieval Archaeology (UK ISSN 0076-6097) *89, 590*
Medieval Architecture & Sculpture in Europe *see* Courtauld Institute Illustration Archives. Archive 3 *104*
Medieval Iberian Penninsula (NE ISSN 0076-6100) *590*
Medievalia et Humanistica (US) *590*
Medio Ambiente (CL) *497*
Medio Ambiente en Espana (SP) *497*
Medioevo (IT) *879*
Meditation (US) *879*
Mediteranean Language Review (GW ISSN 0724-7567) *852*
Mediterranean Electrotechnical Conference (US) *457*
Mediterranean Language and Culture Monograph Series (GW ISSN 0179-1621) *852*
Medium Industry Bank, Seoul. Report *see* Small and Medium Industry Bank, Seoul. Annual Report *232*
Medizin im Recht und Ethik (GW ISSN 0340-9511) *660, 764*
Medizin in Berlin (West) (GW ISSN 0721-6076) *618*
Medizinische Akademie "Carl Gustav Carus" Dresden. Schriften (GE ISSN 0070-721X) *764*
Medizinische Informatik und Statistik (US ISSN 0342-4103) *764*
Medizinische Kongresse (GW ISSN 0175-3053) *796*
Medizinische Laenderkunde. Geomedical Monograph Series (US ISSN 0076-6151) *764*
Medizinische und Paedagogische Jugendkunde *see* Sozialmedizinische und Paedagogische Jugendkunde *766*
Medoc: Index to U S Government Publications in the Medical and Health Sciences (US ISSN 0097-9732) *771*
Medway Ports Shipping Handbook (UK ISSN 0261-281X) *314, 1102*
Meeresforschung/Reports on Marine Research (GW ISSN 0341-6836) *407*
Meeting Ground (US) *504, 607*
Meeting of the Chief Statisticians of the Nordic Countries *see* Nordiske Sjefsstatistikermoete *1060*
Megadrilogica (CN ISSN 0380-9633) *57, 176*
Meghalaya Industrial Development Corporation. Annual Report (II ISSN 0376-5423) *197*
Meguro-ku No Kogai/Environmental Pollution in Meguro Ward (JA) *497*
Meharry Medical College. School of Dentistry. Proceedings of an Oral Research Seminar (US) *779*
Mehkarim Be-Ge'ografyah Shel Erets-Yisrael *see* Studies in the Geography of Israel *548*

Meidai Uchusen Kenkyushitsu Kiji *see* Nagoya University. Cosmic-Ray Research Laboratory. Proceedings *889*
Meier-Dudy/Meier's Directory of Exporters and Importers (GW ISSN 0076-6208) *258*
Meier's Directory of Exporters and Importers *see* Meier-Dudy *258*
Meijeritieteellinen Aikakauskirja/Finnish Journal of Dairy Science (FI ISSN 0367-2387) *62, 323*
Meister des Puppenspiels (GW ISSN 0076-6216) *1077*
Meister - Zeitung (GW ISSN 0341-759X) *290*
Mejeribrugets Uge-Nyt (DK ISSN 0302-833X) *62*
Mekevot *see* Sources of Contemporary Jewish Thought *712*
Mekhanicheskaya Tekhnologiya/Mechanine Technologija (UR) *492*
Mekhanika Tverdogo Tela (UR ISSN 0321-1975) *895*
Mekong Bulletin (UN ISSN 0252-5348) *263*
Mekong Monthly Bulletin *see* Mekong Bulletin *263*
Melanderia (US ISSN 0076-6224) *165*
Melanesian Law Journal (PP) *660*
Melanges *see* Louisiana State University. Museum of Geoscience. Publications *380*
Melanges CRAPEL *see* Universite de Nancy II. Centre de Recherches et d'Applications Pedagogiques en Langues. Melanges *449*
Melanges d'Histoire de l'Architecture (BE) *98, 107*
Melbourne College of Advanced Education. Handbook (AT ISSN 0812-230X) *430, 437*
Melbourne Historical Journal (AT ISSN 0076-6232) *573*
Melbourne International Philosophy Series *see* Nijhoff International Philosophy Series *880*
Melbourne Journal of Politics (AT ISSN 0085-3224) *907*
Melbourne Papers on Australian Defence (AT ISSN 0157-4159) *811*
Melbourne Politics Monographs (AT) *907*
Melbourne Port and Shipping Handbook (UK ISSN 0267-7350) *314, 1102*
Melbourne Slavonic Studies *see* Australian Slavonic and East European Studies *691*
Melbourne Studies in Education (AT ISSN 0076-6275) *416*
Melbourne Walker *see* The Walker *1047*
Melhores e Maiores (BL) *290*
Melibea (PE) *727*
Melita Theologica (MM) *971*
Melland Schill Lectures on International Law *see* Melland Schill Monographs in International Law *671*
Melland Schill Monographs in International Law (UK) *671*
Mellemamerika Nyt (DK) *607*
Mellen Studies in Business (US) *197*
Melodie pre Vas (CS) *837*
Melsheimer Entomological Series (US ISSN 0076-6321) *165*
Members of the Stock Exchange *see* Stock Exchange, London. Members and Firms of the Stock Exchange *268*
Membership Directory & Buyer's Guide(US) *314, 1092*
Membership Directory - National Association of College Admissions Counselors *see* National Association of College Admissions Counselors. Membership Directory *437*
Membership Directory of the Golf Course Superintendents Association of America *see* Golf Course Superintendents Association of America. Membership Directory *1038*
Membrane Proteins Series (US) *1158*
Membrane Transport Processes (US ISSN 0160-2462) *153, 764*
Memento de l'Economie Africaine (FR) *246*

Memento de l'O.I.V. (Office International de la Vigne et du Vin) (FR ISSN 0085-221X) *120*
Memento des Mines et Carrieres. (FR) *817*
Memento General de la Quincaillerie *see* Memento General Tequi Quincaillerie *190*
Memento General Tequi Quincaillerie (FR ISSN 0025-9055) *190*
Memento Pratique des Societes Commerciales (FR) *660*
Memo from Belgium (BE ISSN 0025-908X) *246, 907*
Memoire des Femmes (FR) *135, 1129*
Memoires C.E.R.E.S. (Centre d'Etudes, de Recherches et d'Essais Scientifiques du Genie Civil) (BE ISSN 0025-9195) *482*
Memoires de Photo-Interpretation (FR ISSN 0076-6364) *884*
Memoires O.R.S.T.O.M. (FR ISSN 0071-9005) *1070*
Memoires pour Servir a l'Explication des Cartes Geologiques et Minieres de la Belgique (BE) *391, 817*
Memoires Suisse de Paleontologie *see* Schweizerische Palaeontologische Abhandlungen *857*
Memoirs *see* Naukove Tovarystvo Imeni Shevchenka. Zapysky. Mitteilungen *504*
Memoirs of the Hourglass Cruises (US ISSN 0085-0683) *143*
Memoirs on Indian Animal Types (II) *143*
Memorabilia Zoologica (PL ISSN 0076-6372) *176*
Memoria e Historia (BL) *607*
Memorial Sloan-Kettering Cancer Center. New York. Report *see* Sloan-Kettering Institute for Cancer Research. Progress Report *776*
Memorial University of Newfoundland. Occasional Papers in Biology (CN ISSN 0702-0007) *143*
Memorials - Geological Society of America *see* Geological Society of America. Memorials *386*
Memorias de Historia Antigua (SP ISSN 0210-2943) *559*
Memorias Martes del Paraninfo (CK ISSN 0120-1344) *631*
Memorie di Scienze Geologiche (IT) *391, 400, 403*
Memorie Domenicane (IT) *559, 971*
Memphis State University. Anthropological Research Center. Occasional Papers (US ISSN 0564-8602) *73*
Memphis 2000 Annual Report (US) *624*
Men and Women of Distinction (UK) *1158*
Men and Women of Hawaii (US ISSN 0461-7398) *135*
Mendelssohn Studien (GW ISSN 0340-8140) *559*
Mendocino Review (US ISSN 0278-1190) *1158*
Mennonite History Series (US ISSN 0076-6429) *984*
Mennonite Yearbook and Directory (US) *984*
Menomonie Review (US) *711*
Mens en Milieu (NE) *497*
Der Mensch als Soziales und Personales Wesen (GW ISSN 0543-4726) *1027*
Mensch und Arbeit (AU) *274*
Menses (US ISSN 0887-9273) *1158*
Mental and Developmental Disabilities Directory of Legal Advocates *see* Legal Resources for the Mentally Disabled: A Directory of Lawyers and Other Specialists *790*
Mental Health Care in Oklahoma. Annual Report. *see* Oklahoma Department of Mental Health. Annual Report *935*
Mental Health Data (NZ ISSN 0548-992X) *771*
Mental Health Directory (US) *954*
Mental Health in Children (US) *935*
Mental Health, Retardation and Hospitals (Cranston) *see* Rhode Island. Department of Mental Health, Retardation and Hospitals. *956*
Mental Health, Retardation and Hospitals *956*

Mental Health Services for Children and Youth see Hawaii. Department of Health. Mental Health Services for Children and Youth 1017
Mental Health Statistics for Illinois (US ISSN 0076-6453) 954, 1019
Mental Health Statistics for Wales (UK ISSN 0260-5252) 771
Mental Measurements Yearbook (US ISSN 0076-6461) 448, 935
Mental Retardation see Mental Retardation and Developmental Disabilities 790
Mental Retardation and Developmental Disabilities (US ISSN 0091-6315) 790
Menu (US) 1158
Mercado Comun Latino-Americano see Mercado Comun Latino-Americano (Edicion Especial) 258
Mercado Comun Latino-Americano (Edicion Especial) (MX) 258
Merchandise & Operating Results of Department and Specialty Stores (US) 284
Merchandise Mart Buyers Guide (US) 284, 314
Merchandise Mart Directory see Merchandise Mart Buyers Guide 284
Merchant Explorer (US ISSN 0543-5056) 590
Merck Index: An Encyclopedia of Chemicals and Drugs (US ISSN 0076-6518) 872
Merck Manual: A Handbook of Diagnosis and Therapy (US ISSN 0076-6526) 764
Merck Veterinary Manual: A Handbook of Diagnosis and Therapy for the Veterinarian (US ISSN 0076-6542) 1122
Mercury (CN) 353
Merger and Acquisition Sourcebook (US) 197
Merhavim (IS) 546
Meri (FI ISSN 0356-0023) 407
Meridiano Deportivo (CK) 1034
Merite du Defricheur. Rapport de l'Ordre du Merite Agricole (CN) 57
Merite du Defricheur. Rapport de l'Ordre du Merite du Defricheur see Merite du Defricheur. Rapport de l'Ordre du Merite Agricole 57
Merkels' Builders' Pricing and Management Manual (SA) 185
Merlewood Research Station. Report see Great Britain. Institute of Terrestrial Ecology. Report 141
Meroitica (GE ISSN 0138-3663) 852
Mersey Ports Handbook (Year) (UK ISSN 0265-1173) 314, 1102
Merseyside and North Wales Electricity Board. Report And Accounts (UK) 457, 466
Merseyside Chamber of Commerce and Industry. Directory (UK ISSN 0302-4148) 236
Mesopotamia (IT ISSN 0076-6615) 89
Message (GO) 416
Message d'Extreme-Orient (BE) 570
Messager de l'Exarchat du Patriarche Russe en Europe Occidentale (FR ISSN 0026-0266) 984
Messerschmitt-Boelkow-Blohm GmbH International see M B B International 20
Metal see Carta Metalurgica 815
Metal and Engineering Industry Handbook see Metal & Engineering Industry Year Book 473
Metal & Engineering Industry Year Book (AT ISSN 0314-1586) 314, 473
Metal Bulletin Handbook see Metal Bulletin Prices & Data Book 799
Metal Bulletin Prices & Data Book (UK ISSN 0269-1698) 799
Metal-Center News' Metal Distribution (US) 314, 799
Metal Distribution (US ISSN 0098-2210) 799
Metal Finishing Abstracts see Surface Treatment Technology Abstracts 802
Metal Finishing Guidebook & Directory(US) 799
Metal Ions in Biological Systems (US) 328

Metal Marketing Corporation of Zambia. Annual Report (ZA) 284, 799
Metal Mining: Latin American Industrial Report (US) 817
Metal Stamping Buyer's Guide see Sources 800
Metal Statistics (US ISSN 0076-6658) 799
Metal Statistics (Years) (GW ISSN 0170-9933) 801, 1059
Metal Traders of the World (UK ISSN 0143-7607) 799
Metal Trades Industry Association National Export Group Export Note Pad see M T I A N E G's Export Note Pad 799
Metal Trades Industry Association of Australia Annual Report see M.T.I.A. Annual Report 273
Metallgesellschaft Aktiengesellschaft. Review of the Activities (GW ISSN 0369-2345) 799
Metallurgical Abstracts see Metals Abstracts 801
Metallurgical Engineer (II ISSN 0369-061X) 799
Metallurgical Plantmakers of the World(UK ISSN 0308-7794) 799
Metallurgie. Lexique (FR) 799, 802
Metallurgy and Material Science (UK) 799
Metallurgy - Materials Education Yearbook (American Society for Metals) (US ISSN 0094-5447) 799
Metalmecanica see Hulera 985
Metalmechanics: Latin American Industrial Report (US) 799
Metals Abstracts (American Society for Metals) (US ISSN 0026-0924) 9, 801
Metals Abstracts Index (American Society for Metals) (US ISSN 0026-0932) 9, 801
Metalurgia (PE) 73, 799
Metalurgia see Area Metalurgia 797
Metalurgica Moderna (AG) 799
Metaphysical Digest see Neometaphysical Digest 860
Metaphysical Review (AT ISSN 0814-8805) 711, 825
Metaphysische Rundschau (AU ISSN 0076-6720) 879
Metascience Annual (US) 860
MetaScience Quarterly see Metascience Annual 860
Meteor Forschungsergebnisse. Reihe A. Allgemeines, Physik und Chemie des Meeres see "Meteor" Forschungsergebnisse. Reihe A/B: Allgemeines, Physik und Chemie des Meeres Maritime Meteorologie 1158
"Meteor" Forschungsergebnisse. Reihe A/B: Allgemeines, Physik und Chemie des Meeres Maritime Meteorologie (GW ISSN 0721-8761) 1158
Meteor Forschungsergebnisse. Reihe B. Meteorologie und Aeronomie see "Meteor" Forschungsergebnisse. Reihe A/B: Allgemeines, Physik und Chemie des Meeres Maritime Meteorologie 1158
"Meteor" Forschungsergebnisse. Reihe C. Geologie und Geophysik (GW ISSN 0543-5927) 400, 407
"Meteor" Forschungsergebnisse. Reihe D. Biologie (GW ISSN 0543-5935) 1158
Meteorological and Geoastrophysical Abstracts (US ISSN 0026-1130) 9, 118, 382, 808
Meteorological Yearbook see Meteorologisk Aarbog 806
Meteorological Yearbook of Finland. Part 1: Climatological Data (FI ISSN 0076-6747) 806
Meteorological Yearbook of Finland. Part 2: Precipitation and Snow Cover Data (FI ISSN 0076-6755) 806
Meteorological Yearbook of Finland. Part 3. Statistics of Radiosonde Observations 1961-1980 (FI ISSN 0780-7295) 806
Meteorological Yearbook of Finland. Part 4: Measurements of Radiation and Bright Sunshine (FI ISSN 0076-6763) 806

Meteorologischen Dienstes der D D R. Veroeffentlichungen (GE ISSN 0138-1105) 806
Meteorologisk Aarbog/Meteorological Yearbook (DK ISSN 0106-6463) 806
Methoden und Verfahren der Mathemathischen Physik (GW) 751, 889
Methodensammlung der Elektronenmikroskopie (GW ISSN 0076-6771) 169
Methodist Conference. Minutes and Yearbook (UK) 979
Methodist Diaries (UK) 979
Methods and Achievements in Experimental Pathology (SZ ISSN 0076-681X) 764
Methods and Models in the Social Sciences (GW ISSN 0076-6828) 1010
Methods and Phenomena (NE) 995
Methods in Cell Biology (US ISSN 0091-679X) 163
Methods in Cell Physiology see Methods in Cell Biology 163
Methods in Computational Physics: Advances in Research and Applications (US ISSN 0076-6860) 1158
Methods in Enzymology (US ISSN 0076-6879) 152
Methods in Geochemistry and Geophysics (NE ISSN 0076-6895) 380, 400
Methods in Geomathematics (NE) 751
Methods in Hydroscience see Advances in Hydroscience 402
Methods in Virology (US ISSN 0076-6933) 168, 777
Methods of Biochemical Analysis (US ISSN 0076-6941) 152, 326
Methods of Experimental Botany see Metodicke Prirucky Experimentalni Botaniky 159
Methods of Experimental Physics (US ISSN 0076-695X) 889
Methods of Information and Documentation see Modszertani Kiadvanyok 1070
Methods of Operations Research see Operations Research - Verfahren 281
Metodicke Prirucky Experimentalni Botaniky/Methods of Experimental Botany (CS ISSN 0076-6984) 159
Metodistkyrkans i Sverige. Aarsbok (SW ISSN 0543-6206) 979
Metodologicheski i Istoriografski Problemi na Istoricheskata Nauka (BU) 559
Metov Tiberia (IS ISSN 0334-0740) 559
Metric Fact Sheets (CN ISSN 0383-9184) 809
Metric Fastener Standards (US) 489
Metro: A Bibliography (BE ISSN 0378-195X) 1086
METRO C A P Catalog (US ISSN 0363-1257) 681
Metro Handbook and Directory of Members (Year) (US) 681
METRO; New York Metropolitan Reference and Research Agency. Handbook and Directory of Members see Metro Handbook and Directory of Members (Year) 681
METRO; New York Metropolitan Reference and Research Library Agency. METRO Miscellaneous Publications Series (US ISSN 0076-7018) 681
Metropolitan College of Technology, Tokyo. Memoirs/Tokyo-toritsu Koka Tanki Daigaku Kenkyu Hokoku (JA) 1070
Metropolitan Milwaukee Association of Commerce. Economic Studies see Metropolitan Milwaukee Economic Fact Book 246
Metropolitan Milwaukee Economic Fact Book (US) 246
Metropolitan Museum Journal (US ISSN 0077-8958) 828
Metropolitan Museum of Art. Notable Acquisitions (US ISSN 0192-6950) 107
Metropolitan Toronto (CN ISSN 0076-7093) 951

Metropolitan Toronto Library Board. Annual Report (CN ISSN 0700-4532) 681
Metropolitan Washington Council of Governments. Regional Directory (US ISSN 0076-7115) 944
MetroTrends (CN) 965
Metsatilastollinen Vuosikirja/Yearbook of Forest Statistics (FI ISSN 0356-343X) 526
Meuse (AT) 107, 727
Mexican American Monograph Series (US) 504
Mexican Economy Annual see Anuario de la Economica Mexicana 241
Mexican Society for Soil Mechanics Meeting. Proceedings (MX ISSN 0185-402X) 482
Mexico (MX ISSN 0543-7741) 247
Mexico. Centro de Informacion Tecnica y Documentacion. Indice de Peliculas(MX) 826
Mexico. Comision Nacional Bancaria y de Seguros. Anuario Estadistico de Seguros (MX) 640
Mexico. Departamento de Investigacion de las Tradiciones Populares. Boletin (MX) 73, 516
Mexico. Direccion General de Estadistica. Estadistica Industrial Anual (MX ISSN 0071-1543) 213, 1059
Mexico. Direccion General de Estadistica. Estadistica Minerometalurgica: Produccion y Exportacion (MX) 817
Mexico. Direccion General de Oceanografia. Calendario Grafico de Mareas (MX) 407
Mexico. Instituto Nacional de Investigaciones Agricolas. Folletos de Investigacion see Mexico. Instituto Nacional de Investigaciones Forestales, Agricolas y Pecuarias. Folletos de Investigacion 31
Mexico. Instituto Nacional de Investigaciones Agricolas. Temas Didacticos see Mexico. Instituto Nacional de Investigaciones Forestales, Agricolas y Pecuarias. Temas Didacticos 31
Mexico. Instituto Nacional de Investigaciones Forestales, Agricolas y Pecuarias. Folletos de Investigacion(MX) 31, 247
Mexico. Instituto Nacional de Investigaciones Forestales, Agricolas y Pecuarias. Temas Didacticos (MX) 31
Mexico. Secretaria de Educacion Publica. Informe de Labores (MX) 416
Mexico. Secretaria de Programacion y Presupuesto (MX ISSN 0076-7492) 213
Mexico (Year) (US) 1113
Mexico; Hechos, Cifras, Tendencias see Mexico 247
Mexico Statistical Data (MX) 1059
Meyer's Directory of Genealogical Societies in the U S A & Canada (US ISSN 0732-3395) 536
Meyniana (GW ISSN 0076-7689) 391
Miami Children's Hospital Journal see Revista Internacional de Pediatria 788
Michael (IS ISSN 0334-4150) 504
Michel-Briefmarken-Kataloge (GW ISSN 0076-7727) 875
Michelin Annual Camping Guide for France see Camping, Caravaning in France 1107
Michelin Green Guide Series: Alpes (FR) 1113
Michelin Green Guide Series: Austria (FR) 1113
Michelin Green Guide Series: Auvergne(FR) 1113
Michelin Green Guide Series: Belgique - Luxembourg (FR) 1113
Michelin Green Guide Series: Belgium - Luxembourg (FR) 1113
Michelin Green Guide Series: Bourgogne (FR) 1113
Michelin Green Guide Series: Brittany (FR) 1113
Michelin Green Guide Series: Causses Cevennes (FR) 1158

1812 MICHELIN GREEN

Michelin Green Guide Series: Chateaux of the Loire (FR) *1113*
Michelin Green Guide Series: Corse (FR) *1113*
Michelin Green Guide Series: Cote Atlantique (FR) *1113*
Michelin Green Guide Series: Dordogne (FR) *1113*
Michelin Green Guide Series: Environs de Paris (FR) *1113*
Michelin Green Guide Series: Flandres, Artois, Picardie (FR) *1113*
Michelin Green Guide Series: French Riviera (FR) *1113*
Michelin Green Guide Series: Germany(FR) *1113*
Michelin Green Guide Series: Hollande(FR) *1113*
Michelin Green Guide Series: Italy (FR) *1113*
Michelin Green Guide Series: Jura (FR ISSN 0293-9436) *1113*
Michelin Green Guide Series: Londres (FR) *1113*
Michelin Green Guide Series: Maroc (FR) *1113*
Michelin Green Guide Series: New York (City) (FR) *1113*
Michelin Green Guide Series: Nord de la France *see* Michelin Green Guide Series: Flandres, Artois, Picardie *1113*
Michelin Green Guide Series: Normandy (FR) *1113*
Michelin Green Guide Series: Paris (FR) *1113*
Michelin Green Guide Series: Perigord *see* Michelin Green Guide Series: Dordogne *1113*
Michelin Green Guide Series: Portugal (FR) *1113*
Michelin Green Guide Series: Provence(FR) *1113*
Michelin Green Guide Series: Pyrenees (FR) *1113*
Michelin Green Guide Series: Rome (FR) *1113*
Michelin Green Guide Series: Spain (FR) *1113*
Michelin Green Guide Series: Switzerland (FR) *1113*
Michelin Green Guide Series: Vallee du Rhone (FR) *1113*
Michelin Green Guide Series: Vosges (FR) *1114*
Michelin Red Guide Series: Benelux (FR ISSN 0076-7743) *1114*
Michelin Red Guide Series: France (FR ISSN 0076-7778) *1114*
Michelin Red Guide Series: Germany (FR ISSN 0076-7751) *1114*
Michelin Red Guide Series: Great Britain and Ireland (FR) *1114*
Michelin Red Guide Series: Greater London (FR) 620, *1114*
Michelin Red Guide Series: Italy (FR ISSN 0076-7786) *1114*
Michelin Red Guide Series: Paris (FR ISSN 0076-7794) *1114*
Michelin Red Guide Series: Spain & Portugal (FR ISSN 0076-776X) *1114*
Michigan. Advisory Council for Vocational Education. Annual Report(US ISSN 0093-9137) *445*
Michigan. Civil Rights Commission. Annual Report (US) *913*
Michigan. Department of Commerce. Annual Report (US) *240*
Michigan. Department of Commerce. Annual Report Summary *see* Michigan. Department of Commerce. Annual Report *240*
Michigan. Department of Conservation. Geological Survey Division. Progress Report *see* Michigan. Geological Survey Division. Report of Investigation *391*
Michigan. Department of Education. College Admissions and Financial Assistance Handbook *see* Michigan Postsecondary Admissions & Financial Assistance Handbook *430*
Michigan. Department of Natural Resources. Institute for Fisheries Research. Miscellaneous Publication (US ISSN 0076-7905) *511*

Michigan. Department of Social Services. Program Statistics (US ISSN 0093-7835) *1023*
Michigan. Department of Social Services. Public Assistance Statistics *see* Michigan. Department of Social Services. Program Statistics *1023*
Michigan. Department of State Police. Annual Report (US) *371*
Michigan. Division of Vocational Education. Report (US ISSN 0076-7913) *1158*
Michigan. Employment Security Commission. Annual Planning Report (US) *274*
Michigan. Employment Security Commission. Labor Market Analysis Section. Annual Manpower Planning Report: Detroit Labor Market Area *see* Michigan. Employment Security Commission. Annual Planning Report *274*
Michigan. Geological Survey Division. Bulletin (US ISSN 0543-8497) *391*
Michigan. Geological Survey Division. Report of Investigation (US) *391*
Michigan. State Board of Control for Vocational Education. Annual Descriptive Report *see* Michigan. Division of Vocational Education. Report *1158*
Michigan. State Court Administrator. Annual Report. (US ISSN 0098-7875) *669*
Michigan. State Police. Annual Report *see* Michigan. Department of State Police. Annual Report *371*
Michigan Abstracts of Chinese and Japanese Works on Chinese History *see* Michigan Monographs in Chinese Studies *570*
Michigan Association of Speech Communication Journal (US) *445*
Michigan Beef Cattle Day Report (US ISSN 0076-7824) *67*
Michigan Business and Economic Research Bibliography (US ISSN 0091-9047) *213*
Michigan Business Papers (US ISSN 0076-7840) *197*
Michigan Business Reports (US ISSN 0076-7859) *197*
Michigan Business Studies (US ISSN 0076-7867) *197*
Michigan Directory of Manufacturers (US) *314*
Michigan Entomological Society Newsletter *see* M E S Newsletter *165*
Michigan Gazette (US) 607, *681*
Michigan Governmental Studies (US ISSN 0076-7956) *944*
Michigan Health Statistics (US ISSN 0539-7413) *959*
Michigan International Business Studies(US ISSN 0076-7972) *197*
Michigan Law Enforcement Officials Report on Crime *see* Uniform Crime Report for the State of Michigan *374*
Michigan Library Directory (US) *681*
Michigan Library Directory and Statistics *see* Michigan Library Directory *681*
Michigan Library News *see* Michigan Library Directory *681*
Michigan Magazine Index (US ISSN 0026-2250) *9*
Michigan Manufacturers Directory (US ISSN 0736-2889) *284*
Michigan Mineral Producers Annual Directory: (US ISSN 0085-3372) *1158*
Michigan Monographs in Chinese Studies (US) *570*
Michigan Papers in Chinese Studies *see* Michigan Monographs in Chinese Studies *570*
Michigan Papers on South and Southeast Asia (US) *570*
Michigan Postsecondary Admissions & Financial Assistance Handbook (US) *430*
Michigan Public Health Statistics *see* Michigan Health Statistics *959*
Michigan Purchasing Directory (US ISSN 0736-2870) *1158*
Michigan Slavic Contributions (US ISSN 0076-8103) *727*

Michigan Slavic Materials (US ISSN 0543-9930) 699, *727*
Michigan Slavic Translations (US) *727*
Michigan Speech Association Journal *see* Michigan Association of Speech Communication Journal *445*
Michigan State Employees' Retirement System *see* Michigan State Employees' Retirement System Financial and Statistical Report *274*
Michigan State Employees' Retirement System Financial and Statistical Report (US ISSN 0092-9212) 274, *944*
Michigan State Horticultural Society. Annual Report (US) 284, *520*
Michigan State Housing Development Authority. Annual Report (US) *624*
Michigan State Industrial Directory *see* MacRae's Michigan State Industrial Directory *312*
Michigan State Plan for Vocational Education (US ISSN 0094-1506) *427*
Michigan State University. Agricultural Economics Report (US ISSN 0065-4442) *48*
Michigan State University. Asian Studies Center. Occasional Papers: East Asia Series (US ISSN 0076-812X) *570*
Michigan State University. Asian Studies Center. Occasional Papers: South Asia Series (US ISSN 0076-8138) *570*
Michigan State University. Cooperative Extension Service. Annual Report (US) *427*
Michigan State University. Department of Physics. Cyclotron Project (Publication) *see* Michigan State University. National Superconducting Cyclotron Laboratory (Publication) *897*
Michigan State University. Institute for International Studies in Education. Publications *see* Michigan State University. International Networks in Education and Development. Publications *416*
Michigan State University. Institute of Water Research. Annual Report (US) *1125*
Michigan State University. Institute of Water Research. Technical Report (US ISSN 0580-9746) *1125*
Michigan State University. International Networks in Education and Development. Publications (US) *416*
Michigan State University. Latin American Studies Center. Monograph Series (US ISSN 0076-8189) *607*
Michigan State University. Latin American Studies Center. Research Reports (US ISSN 0076-8200) *607*
Michigan State University. Museum Publications. Anthropological Series. (US) *73*
Michigan State University. Museum Publications. Biological Series (US ISSN 0076-8227) *143*
Michigan State University. Museum Publications. Cultural Series (US ISSN 0076-8235) *828*
Michigan State University. Museum Publications. Folk Art Series (US) *107*
Michigan State University. Museum Publications. Paleontological Series (US) *857*
Michigan State University. National Superconducting Cyclotron Laboratory (Publication) (US) *897*
Michigan Statistical Abstract (US ISSN 0076-8308) *1059*
Michigan Studies in the Humanities (US) *727*
Michigan Travel and Recreation Guide (US) *1114*
Michigan, Wisconsin TourBook *see* Tourbook: Michigan, Wisconsin *1117*
Michigan Yearbook of International Legal Studies (US ISSN 8756-0615) 371, *660*
Michigan's Mineral Industries *see* Mineral Industry of Michigan Annual Statistical Summary *1158*

Michigan's Oil and Gas Fields: Annual Statistical Summary (US ISSN 0085-3429) *865*
Mickle Street Review (US ISSN 0194-1313) *742*
Micro *see* Microprogramming Workshop. Proceedings *362*
Micro-Bibliotheca Anthropos (GW) *73*
Micro Software Evaluations (US ISSN 8755-5794) 362, *363*, 689
Micro Software Report (Library Edition) (US ISSN 8755-5786) *1158*
Micro to Mainframe Communications (US) 361, *362*
Microbiologia Espanola (SP ISSN 0026-2595) *1158*
Microbiology (Washington) (US ISSN 0098-1540) *168*
Microbiology Abstracts. Section B. Bacteriology (US ISSN 0300-8398) 9, *168*
Microbiology Series (US) *169*
Microbios Letters (UK ISSN 0307-5494) *163*, 764
Microcomputer Index (US) 9, *354*, 362
Microcomputer Industry Update (US ISSN 0741-6016) *354*, 360, 362, 362
Microcomputer Market Place (US ISSN 0735-1925) 314, 357, *362*, 362
Microcomputer Software Directory/ International Directory of Software *see* Software Users' Year Book *363*
Microcomputer User's Year Book *see* P C Year Book *362*
Microcomputers for Libraries (US ISSN 0743-0302) *689*
Microeconomic Studies (US) *252*
Microelectronic Manufacturing and Testing Desk Manual (US) *884*
Microfilmed Newspapers of Finland *see* Suomen Sanomalehtien Mikrofilmit *12*
Microform Market Place (US ISSN 0362-0999) *681*
Microforms Annual (US) *129*
Microforms in Print. Supplement *see* Guide to Microforms in Print. Supplement *127*
Micrographics and Optical Storage Buyer's Guide (UK) *884*
Micrographics and Optical Storage Equipment Review (US) *681*
Micrographics Equipment Review *see* Micrographics and Optical Storage Equipment Review *681*
Micrographics Index *see* Resource Center Index *286*
Micrographics Year Book *see* Micrographics and Optical Storage Buyer's Guide *884*
Microlog Index (CN ISSN 0707-3135) *9*
Micromorphology of Diatom Valves (GW) *169*
Micropaleontology Special Publications (US ISSN 0160-2071) *857*
Microprocessor-Based Systems Engineering (NE) 362, *473*
Microprocessor Technical Software D.A.T.A. Book *see* Engineering Application Software D.A.T.A. Book *485*
Microprogramming Workshop. Proceedings (US) 358, *362*
Micropublishers' Trade List Annual (US ISSN 0361-2635) *129*
Microscopia Electronica and Biologia Celular (AG ISSN 0326-3142) 169, *169*
Microscopica Acta. Supplementa (GW ISSN 0342-958X) *169*
Microscopical Society of Canada. Proceedings (CN) *169*
Microstate Studies (VI) *1010*
Microtables Imports-Exports of O.E.C.D. Countries (FR) *258*
Microwave D.A.T.A. Book (US ISSN 0271-0773) *457*
Microwave Discontinued Devices D.A.T.A. Book (US ISSN 0278-5676) *457*
Microwave Power Symposium. Proceedings (US) *457*
Microwave System Designer's Handbook (US) *457*

Microwaves Product Data Directory (US) *457*
Mid-Atlantic-Delaware, District of Columbia, Maryland, Virginia, West Virginia TourBook *see* Tourbook: Mid-Atlantic *1117*
Mid-Atlantic Industrial Waste Conference Proceedings (US ISSN 0544-0327) *497*
Mid Glamorgan Industrial Directory (UK ISSN 0261-2275) *314*
Mid-Hudson Language Studies (US ISSN 0272-717X) *727*
MidAmerica (East Lansing) (US ISSN 0190-2911) *711, 727*
Middle Ages (US) *590*
Middle East: Abstracts and Index (US ISSN 0162-766X) *9, 917*
Middle East Agribusiness Buyers Guide(UK ISSN 0264-5408) *31*
Middle East and North Africa (UK ISSN 0076-8502) *546, 613*
Middle East and World Water Directory (LE) *1125*
Middle East Annual (US ISSN 0733-5350) *917*
Middle East Construction Catalogue (Building Products Edition) (UK) *186*
Middle East Contemporary Survey (US ISSN 0163-5476) *613, 917*
Middle East Economic Digest Ltd. Practial Guide. Kuwait *see* M E E D Practial Guide. Kuwait *1112*
Middle East Economic Digest Ltd. Practical Guide. Bahrain *see* M E E D Practical Guide. Bahrain *1112*
Middle East Economic Digest Ltd. Practical Guide. Egypt *see* M E E D Practical Guide. Egypt *1112*
Middle East Economic Digest Ltd. Practical Guide. Jordan *see* M E E D Practical Guide. Jordan *1112*
Middle East Economic Digest Ltd. Practical Guide. Oman *see* M E E D Practical Guide. Oman *1112*
Middle East Economic Digest Ltd. Practical Guide. Qatar *see* M E E D Practical Guide. Qatar *1112*
Middle East Education & Training Buyers Guide (UK) *416*
Middle East Electricity Catalogue (UK) *457*
Middle East Financial Directory (UK ISSN 0266-2094) *230*
Middle East Living Costs (UK ISSN 0140-7953) *258*
Middle East Military Balance (IS) *811*
Middle East Newsletter *see* A J M E News *611*
Middle East Record (IS ISSN 0076-8529) *613*
Middle East Review (UK ISSN 0305-3210) *247*
Middle East Stamp Catalogue (UK ISSN 0142-9914) *875*
Middle Schools Statistics in Punjab (PK) *416*
Middle States Association of Colleges and Schools. Proceedings of the Annual Convention (US) *437*
Middle States Association of Colleges and Secondary Schools. Proceedings *see* Middle States Association of Colleges and Schools. Proceedings of the Annual Convention *437*
Middle States Council for the Social Studies. Journal (US) *1010*
Middle States Council for the Social Studies. Proceedings *see* Middle States Council for the Social Studies. Journal *1010*
Middle Tennessee State University, Murfreesboro. Business and Economic Research Center. Conference Paper (US) *247*
Middle Thames Naturalist (UK ISSN 0144-0497) *995*
Middletown Historical Society. Newsletter (US) *607*
Mideast Business Guide (US) *1158*
Mideastern Campbook (US ISSN 0734-2705) *1046, 1114*
Mideastern Camping *see* Mideastern Campbook *1114*
Midia (BL) *16*
Midland History (UK ISSN 0047-729X) *590*

Midland Review (US ISSN 0886-7976) *727, 884*
Midwest Auto Racing Guide *see* National Speedway Directory *1035*
Midwest Conference on Graduate Study and Research. Proceedings *see* Midwestern Association of Graduate Schools. Proceedings of the Annual Meeting *437*
Midwest Fishing by Outdoor Life *see* Deer and Big Game *1045*
Midwest History of Education Society. Journal (US ISSN 0092-2986) *416*
Midwest Law Review (US) *197, 660*
Midwest Research Institute. Annual Report (US) *995*
Midwest Studies in Philosophy (US ISSN 0363-6550) *879*
Midwestern Annual *see* MidAmerica (East Lansing) *727*
Midwestern Association of Graduate Schools. Proceedings of the Annual Meeting. (US) *437*
Midwestern Miscellany (US) *727*
Mie-Ken Kogai Senta Nempo *see* Mie Prefecture. Environmental Science Institute. Annual Report *497*
Mie Prefectural University. Faculty of Fisheries. Bulletin *see* Mie University. Faculty of Fisheries. Journal *511*
Mie Prefecture. Environmental Science Institute. Annual Report/Mie-Ken Kogai Senta Nempo (JA) *497*
Mie University. Faculty of Fisheries. Journal (JA) *511*
Mie University. Fisheries Research Laboratory. Report. (JA) *176*
Mietrechtliche Entscheidungen (AU) *660*
MietSlg *see* Mietrechtliche Entscheidungen *660*
Mifgash (IS) *727*
Migration Institute. Migration Studies (FI) *923*
Migration Today (SZ ISSN 0544-1188) *923*
Mikrobielle Umwelt und Antimikrobielle Massnahmen (GE) *764*
Mikrochimica Acta. Supplement (US ISSN 0076-8642) *326*
Mikrofauna des Meeresbodens (GW ISSN 0342-3247) *143*
Mikrozirkulation in Forschung und Klinik *see* Progress in Applied Microcirculation *777*
Milepost (US ISSN 0361-1361) *1114*
Miles International Symposium (US) *163*
Milford Series (US ISSN 0163-2469) *727*
Militaerhistorisk Tidskrift (SW) *590, 811*
Militaerpsykologiske Meddelelser (NO ISSN 0026-3842) *811*
Military Aircraft Markings (UK) *20, 811*
Military Balance (UK ISSN 0459-7222) *812*
Military Communications (SZ) *812*
Military Dealers and Collectors Directory (US) *79, 812*
Military Intelligence Critical Attributes (UK) *812*
Military Microwaves (Year). Proceedings of Conference (UK) *457, 812*
Military Museum, Belgrade. Bulletin *see* Vojni Muzej, Belgrade. Vesnik *813*
Military Operations Research (US ISSN 0275-5823) *812*
Military Year Book (II ISSN 0076-8782) *812*
Miljoe-Projekter (DK ISSN 0105-3094) *497*
Miljoestyrelsen Luft. A *see* M S T Luft. A *497*
Miljoeundersoegelser ved Ivigtut (DK ISSN 0108-8203) *497*
Miljoevaern (DK ISSN 0107-8550) *497*
Milk Facts (US) *62*
Mill Report (US) *1074*
Miller's Antique Price Guide (Year) (US) *79, 107*
Millers Antiques Price Guide (UK) *79*
Millesime (FR ISSN 0076-8812) *281*

Milling Directory/Buyers Guide (US) *63, 314*
Million Dollar Directory (US) *285*
Million Dollar Round Table Annual Meeting. Proceedings *see* M D R T Annual Meeting. Proceedings *640*
Milton Keynes Directory of Business & Buying (UK) *314*
Milton Society of America. Proceedings(US ISSN 0540-0961) *742*
Milton Studies (US ISSN 0076-8820) *727*
Milu: Wissenschaftliche und Kulturelle Mitteilungen aus dem Tierpark Berlin(GE ISSN 0076-8839) *176*
Mimesis (BL) *727*
Minas Gerais, Brazil. Departamento de Estradas de Rodagem. Servico de Transito. Estatistica de Trafego *see* Minas Gerais, Brazil. Departamento de Estradas de Rodagem. Servico de Transito. Estatistica de Trafego e Acidentes *1059*
Minas Gerais, Brazil. Departamento de Estradas de Rodagem. Servico de Transito. Estatistica de Trafego e Acidentes (BL) *1059*
Mindanao Art & Culture (PH ISSN 0115-6853) *516, 570*
Mindanao State University. U R C Professional Papers (PH ISSN 0115-7329) *995*
Mindolo News Letter (ZA ISSN 0076-8901) *971*
Mine and Quarry Mechanisation (AT ISSN 0085-3453) *817*
Mine Medical Officers' Association of South Africa. Proceedings (SA ISSN 0026-4490) *635*
Mineral Facts (AT) *817*
Mineral Industry of Michigan Annual Statistical Summary (US ISSN 0085-3445) *1158*
Mineraloelwirtschafts Verband e.V. Jahresbericht *see* M W V Jahresbericht *330*
Mineralogical Abstracts (UK ISSN 0026-4601) *382*
Mineralogical Society of New South Wales. Journal (AT) *817*
Mineralogie und Petrographie in Einzel Darstellungen *see* Minerals and Rocks *391*
Minerals and Mineral Development (AT) *817*
Minerals and Rocks (US ISSN 0343-2181) *391, 817*
Minerals Industry Survey (AT) *817*
Minerals: Latin American Industry Report (US) *247, 817*
La Mineria en Mexico (MX) *817*
Minerva; Internationales Verzeichnis Wissenschaftlicher Institutionen (GW) *631*
Mines & Mining Equipment and Service Companies Worldwide (Year) (UK) *314, 818*
Mines and Mining Equipment Companies Worldwide *see* Mines & Mining Equipment and Service Companies Worldwide (Year) *818*
Mines au Canada - Faits et Chiffres *see* Mining in Canada - Facts & Figures *818*
Mines Directory (US ISSN 0096-4859) *818*
Mines in West Virginia (US) *818*
Mines - Pilier de l'Economie Canadienne *see* Mining - What Mining Means to Canada *818*
Mines Safety and Health Commission. Report/Organe Permanent pour la Securite dans les Mines de Houille. Rapport (EI ISSN 0588-702X) *636, 818*
Mini-Break Holidays in Britain *see* Recommended Short Break Holidays *1115*
Miniatura e Arti Minori in Campania (IT) *107*
Miniature Book World *see* Book Dealers' and Collectors' Year-Book and Diary *1148*
Miniatures Catalog (US) *614*
Mining Abstracts *see* Banyazati Szakirodalmi Tajekoztato *821*

Mining and Allied Machinery Corporation. Annual Report (II) *745, 818*
Mining & Construction Methods and Equipment (AT) *818*
Mining Annual Review (UK ISSN 0076-8995) *818*
Mining Department Magazine (UK ISSN 0307-9066) *818*
Mining in Canada - Facts & Figures (CN ISSN 0316-2281) *818*
Mining in Rhodesia *see* Mining in Zimbabwe *818*
Mining in Zimbabwe (RH) *818*
Mining Industry & Trade Annual (II) *818*
Mining Industry and Trade Journal *see* Mining Industry & Trade Annual *818*
Mining Industry of Idaho. Annual Report (US) *818*
Mining Industry Technical Conference. Conference Record (US) *818*
Mining - What Mining Means to Canada (CN ISSN 0317-9508) *818*
Mining Year Book *see* Financial Times International Year Books: Mining *816*
Ministere du Loisir de la Chasse et de la Peche *see* Quebec (Province) Department of Recreation, Fish and Game. Annual Report *1115*
Ministerio de Energia y Minas. Boletin de Geologia (VE ISSN 0006-6281) *391*
Ministerio Publico *see* M P *659*
Ministry of Agriculture. Berry Production Guide *see* British Columbia. Ministry of Agriculture and Food. Berry Production Guide *1149*
Ministry of Agriculture. Field Crop Production Guide *see* British Columbia. Ministry of Agriculture and Food. Field Crop Production Guide *53*
Ministry of Agriculture. Grape Production Guide *see* British Columbia. Ministry of Agriculture and Food. Grape Production Guide *53*
Ministry of Agriculture. Greenhouse-Cucumber and Tomato Production Guide *see* British Columbia. Ministry of Agriculture and Food. Greenhouse-Cucumber and Tomato Production Guide *53*
Ministry of Agriculture. Greenhouse-Ornamental Production Guide *see* British Columbia. Ministry of Agriculture and Food. Greenhouse-Ornamental Production Guide *53*
Ministry of Agriculture. Nursery Production Guide *see* British Columbia. Ministry of Agriculture and Food. Nursery Production Guide *53*
Ministry of Agriculture. Tree Fruit Production Guide *see* British Columbia. Ministry of Agriculture and Food. Tree Fruit *53*
Ministry of Agriculture. Vegetable Production Guide *see* British Columbia. Ministry of Agriculture and Food. Vegetable Production Guide *53*
Minji Sosho Zasshi *see* Journal of Civil Procedure *658*
Minkus Austria, Switzerland, Lichtenstein Stamp Catalog (US ISSN 0076-9029) *875*
Minkus Belgium, Netherlands, Luxembourg Colonies Stamp Catalogue (US) *875*
Minkus France, Monaco, Andorra Stamp Catalog (US) *875*
Minkus Greece, Turkey Stamp Catalog (US) *875*
Minkus Italy, San Marino and Vatican Stamp Catalog (US ISSN 0076-9053) *875*
Minkus New American Stamp Catalog (US ISSN 0076-9061) *875*
Minkus New World Wide Stamp Catalog (US ISSN 0076-907X) *875*
Minkus Scandinavia, Baltic Countries Stamp Catalog (US) *875*
Minneapolis Institute of Arts. Annual Report (US ISSN 0076-9096) *107*

MINNEAPOLIS INSTITUTE

Minneapolis Institute of Arts. Bulletin (US ISSN 0076-910X) *107*
Minnesota. Department of Economic Security. Annual Report (US) *274*
Minnesota. Department of Employment Services. Annual Report *see* Minnesota. Department of Economic Security. Annual Report *274*
Minnesota. Department of Human Rights. Biennial Report (US ISSN 0076-9118) *913*
Minnesota. Department of Natural Resources. Biennial Report (US ISSN 0090-8177) *366*
Minnesota. Department of Revenue. Biennial Report (US ISSN 0095-0645) *297*
Minnesota. Department of Revenue. Petroleum Division. Annual Report (US ISSN 0095-3024) *865*
Minnesota. Department of Taxation. Biennial Report *see* Minnesota. Department of Revenue. Biennial Report *297*
Minnesota. Division of Fish & Wildlife. Technical Bulletin (US) *366*
Minnesota. Division of Game and Fish. Technical Bulletin *see* Minnesota. Division of Fish & Wildlife. Technical Bulletin *366*
Minnesota. Geological Survey. Information Circulars (US ISSN 0544-3105) *391*
Minnesota. Geological Survey. Report of Investigations (US ISSN 0076-9177) *391*
Minnesota. Governor. Governor's Report on Environmental Quality (US) *498*
Minnesota. Office of Ombudsman for Corrections. Annual Report (US ISSN 0094-1409) *371*
Minnesota Agricultural Economist (US) *48*
Minnesota Agricultural Experiment Station. Station Bulletin (US) *31, 526*
Minnesota Arts and Attractions Guide *see* Explore Minnesota Arts and Attractions *1108*
Minnesota Dairy Plants (US) *62*
Minnesota Economic Data: Countries and Regions (US ISSN 0544-3512) *1158*
Minnesota Exporter's Assistance Guide *see* Minnesota International Business Services Directory *258*
Minnesota Fish and Game Investigations. Fish Series *see* Minnesota Fisheries Investigations *511*
Minnesota Fisheries Investigations (US ISSN 0076-9150) *511*
Minnesota Guidebook to State Agency Services (US) *944*
Minnesota Health Statistics (US ISSN 0094-5641) *959*
Minnesota Industrial Minerals Directory (US ISSN 0272-8583) *818*
Minnesota International Business Services Directory (US) *258*
Minnesota International Trade Directory (US) *314*
Minnesota League for Nursing New Directions *see* M L N New Directions *784*
Minnesota Legal Register: Opinions of the Minnesota Attorney General (US ISSN 0026-5543) *660*
Minnesota Manufacturers Register (US ISSN 0738-1514) *314*
Minnesota Periodicals on Microfilm (US) *1158*
Minnesota Rules (US) *660, 944*
Minnesota Rules. Supplement (US) *660, 944*
Minnesota Sales and Use Tax Annual Report Bulletin (US) *297*
Minnesota Sales and Use Tax Quarterly Report Bulletin *see* Minnesota Sales and Use Tax Annual Report Bulletin *297*
Minnesota State Industrial Directory *see* MacRae's Minnesota State Industrial Directory *313*
Minnesota Statutes (US ISSN 0191-1562) *660*
Minnesota Statutes. Supplement (US ISSN 0094-1727) *660*
Minnesota Studies in the Philosophy of Science (US ISSN 0076-9258) *879, 995*
Minnesota Symposia on Child Psychology (US ISSN 0076-9266) *935*
Minnesota Tax Court Decisions (US) *660*
Minnesota Travel and Recreation Guide(US) *1114*
Minnesota U S A International Trade Directory *see* Minnesota International Trade Directory *314*
Minnesota Weather Guide Calendar (US) *806*
Minor League Baseball Stars (US) *1039*
Minor Metals Survey (UK ISSN 0140-8399) *799*
Minorities in America. Annual Bibliography (US ISSN 0748-2302) *129*
Minority Biomedical Research Support Program (US ISSN *771, 782*
Minority Biomedical Support Program *see* Minority Biomedical Research Support Program *771*
Minority Information Trade Annual (US) *506*
Minority Organizations: A National Directory (US) *504*
Minority Rights Group. Newsletter (UK ISSN 0260-6402) *913*
Minority Rights Group. Reports (UK ISSN 0305-6252) *913, 1027*
Minority Student Opportunities in United States Medical Schools (US ISSN 0085-3488) *437, 764*
Minority Suppliers Directory *see* Minority Suppliers Report and Directory *314*
Minority Suppliers Report and Directory (US) *314*
Mintek. Special Publications (SA) *818*
Mintek Reports (SA) *818*
Minulosti a Pritomnosti Turca (CS) *590*
Minulosti Rokycanska (CS) *590*
Minulosti Zapadoceskeho Kraje (CS) *590*
Minutes of the Annual Meeting of the First Catholic Slovak Union of the United States of America and Canada *see* First Catholic Slovak Union of America. Minutes of Annual Meeting *982*
Miorita (US ISSN 0110-0068) *504*
Mirador (AG) *197*
Mirror and Probe (CE) *779*
Mirror Class Association of Australia. Constitution-Rules of Measurement *see* Mirror Class Association of Australia. Yearbook *1042*
Mirror Class Association of Australia. Yearbook (AT) *1042*
Miscel-lania de Textos Medievals (SP) *590*
Miscelanea de Texos Medievales *see* Miscel-lania de Textos Medievals *590*
Miscellanea Byzantina Monacensia (GW ISSN 0076-9347) *590, 727*
Miscellanea Mediaevalia (GW) *559, 879*
Miscellanea Musicologica (CS ISSN 0544-4136) *837*
Miscellanea Zoologica (SP ISSN 0211-6529) *176*
Miscellaneous Publications - University of Kansas, Museum of Natural History *see* University of Kansas. Museum of Natural History. Miscellaneous Publications *148*
Miscellaneous Report - State of Ohio, Department of Natural Resources, Division of Geological Survey *see* Ohio. Division of Geological Survey. Miscellaneous Report *393*
Mishua (IS ISSN 0542-9943) *504, 590*
Misifrut Ha-Hinukh: Educational Issues(IS) *416*
Mision Cientifica Espanola en Hispanoamerica. Memorias (SP) *1010*
Mission Handbook (US) *982*
Mission Handbook: North American Protestant Ministries Overseas (US ISSN 0093-8130) *979*
Mission Studies and Documents *see* Missionswissenschaftliche Abhandlungen und Texte *971*
Mission to Lepers, London. Annual Report *see* Leprosy Mission, London. Annual Report *971*
Missions Digest and Year Book *see* Evangelical Baptist Churches in Canada. Fellowship Yearbook *978*
Missions to Seamen Annual Report (UK) *971*
Missions to Seamen Handbook *see* Missions to Seamen Annual Report *971*
Missionswissenschaftliche Abhandlungen und Texte/Etudes et Documents Missionnaires/Mission Studies and Documents (GW ISSN 0076-941X) *971*
Missionswissenschaftliche Forschungen (GW ISSN 0076-9428) *971*
Missisquoi Historical Society Reports (CN) *536, 607*
Mississippi. Board of Trustees of State Institutions of Higher Learning. Annual Report (US) *342*
Mississippi. Department of Wildlife Conservation. Annual Report (US ISSN 0733-2017) *366, 511*
Mississippi. Department of Wildlife Conservation. Annual Report to the Regular Session of the Mississippi Legislature *see* Mississippi. Department of Wildlife Conservation. Annual Report *511*
Mississippi. State Board of Architecture. Annual Report (US) *98*
Mississippi Academy of Science. Journal (US ISSN 0076-9436) *143, 764*
Mississippi Congress of Parents and Teachers. Proceedings (US ISSN 0076-9460) *443*
Mississippi Congress of Parents and Teachers. Yearbook (US ISSN 0076-9479) *443*
Mississippi Educational Directory (US ISSN 0092-7899) *430*
Mississippi Marine Resources Council. Annual Report (US ISSN 0095-6783) *407*
Mississippi Mud (US) *727*
Mississippi State Industrial Directory *see* MacRae's Mississippi State Industrial Directory *313*
Mississippi State University. Forest Products Utilization Laboratory. Information Series (US ISSN 0076-9509) *530*
Mississippi State University. Forest Products Utilization Laboratory. Research Report (US ISSN 0026-640X) *530*
Mississippi State University Abstracts of Theses *see* Mississippi State University Abstracts of Theses and Dissertations *424*
Mississippi State University Abstracts of Theses and Dissertations (US) *9, 424*
Mississippi Valley Collection Bulletin *see* M V C Bulletin *1157*
Missouri. Department of Agriculture. Weekly Market Summary (US) *31, 67*
Missouri. Department of Conservation. Annual Report (US ISSN 0085-3496) *366*
Missouri. Department of Revenue. Annual Combined Financial Report (US) *297*
Missouri. Division of Geological Survey and Water Resources. Engineering Geology Series (US ISSN 0076-9606) *482*
Missouri. Division of Geological Survey and Water Resources. Water Resources Report (US ISSN 0076-9614) *403, 1125*
Missouri. Division of Highway Safety. Highway Safety Plan (US) *954, 1096*
Missouri. Division of Insurance. Annual Report and Statistical Data (US) *640*
Missouri. Division of Youth Services. Annual Report (US) *1019*
Missouri. State Board of Training Schools. Annual Report *see* Missouri. Division of Youth Services. Annual Report *1019*
Missouri Annual Campaign Finance Report (US) *907*
Missouri Archaeological Society. Special Publications (US ISSN 0735-5467) *89*
Missouri Archaeologist (US ISSN 0076-9576) *89*
Missouri Basin States Association. Annual Report (US) *1125*
Missouri Directory of Manufacturers and Mining Operations *see* Missouri Directory of Manufacturing and Mining *314*
Missouri Directory of Manufacturing and Mining (US ISSN 0076-9584) *314, 818*
Missouri Folklore Society. Journal (US ISSN 0731-2946) *516*
Missouri Handbook Series (US ISSN 0076-9630) *607*
Missouri Historical Society. Annual Report (US) *1158*
Missouri Journal of Research in Music Education (US ISSN 0085-350X) *448, 838*
Missouri Literary Frontiers Series (US ISSN 0076-9649) *727*
Missouri Manufacturers Directory (US) *314*
Missouri Notary Law Primer (US) *660*
Missouri Population Estimates (US ISSN 0734-032X) *923*
Missouri River Basin Commission. Annual Report *see* Missouri Basin States Association. Annual Report *1125*
Missouri Speech Journal (US) *344, 1077*
Missouri Speleology (US ISSN 0026-671X) *391*
Missouri Union List of Serial Publications (US ISSN 0164-0496) *688*
Missouri Vital Statistics (US ISSN 0098-1974) *959*
Missouri's Annual Highway Safety Program *see* Missouri. Division of Highway Safety. Highway Safety Plan *1096*
Missouri's New and Expanding Industries (US ISSN 0540-4193) *290*
Mistelbach in Vergangenheit und Gegenwart (AU) *590*
Misuse of Drugs in the United Kingdom. Statistics (UK) *378*
Mitekufat Haeven (IS) *857*
Mitre (CN) *711*
Mitsubishi Cable Industries Review (JA) *457*
Mitsubishi Technical Bulletin (JA ISSN 0540-469X) *1070*
Mitsui News (AT ISSN 0311-0273) *258*
Mitteilungen aus dem Max-Planck-Institut fuer Stroemungsforschung (GW ISSN 0374-1257) *895*
Mitteilungen aus dem Max-Planck-Institut fuer Stroenmungsforschung und der Aerodynamischen Versuchsansalt *see* Mitteilungen aus dem Max-Planck-Institut fuer Stroemungsforschung *895*
Mitteilungen der Fachhochschule des Bundes (GW) *944*
Mittellateinische Studien und Texte (NE ISSN 0076-9754) *590*
Mittellateinisches Jahrbuch (GW ISSN 0076-9762) *699*
Mitzion Tetzeh Torah. M.T.T. (IS ISSN 0541-5632) *879, 977*
Miyazaki Daigaku Kogakubu Kiyo *see* Miyazaki University. Faculty of Engineering. Memoirs *473*
Miyazaki University. Faculty of Engineering. Memoirs/Miyazaki Daigaku Kogakubu Kiyo (JA ISSN 0540-4924) *473*
Mnemosyne. Supplements (NE) *338*
Mobil Travel Guide - Major Cities (US) *1114*
Mobile Air Conditioning *see* I M A C A Directory *553*

Mobile Area Chamber of Commerce Membership Directory and Buyer's Guide (US) *236*
Mobile Communications Handbook (US) *349*
Mobile Graduate News and Notes (US ISSN 0887-3887) *342*
Mobile Living (US ISSN 0026-7198) *624*
Mobile Radio Handbook *see* Mobile Communications Handbook *349*
Mobili per Ufficio (IT) *286*
Mobius (AT) *448, 751*
Model II - A Regular 16 Newsletter *see* Model II - 12 - 16 Newsletter *362*
Model II - 12 - 16 Newsletter (US) *362*
Model Railway Constructor Annual (UK) *1158*
Model Rocket News *see* Model Rocket News Magazine *614*
Model Rocket News Magazine (US) *614*
Modeling and Simulation (US ISSN 0198-0092) *358*
Modeling and Simulation on Microcomputers (US) *323, 457*
Modelle fuer den Religionsunterricht (GW) *971*
Modelling and Miniature Crafts (UK) *189*
Models in Dermatology (SZ) *780*
Models Mart Directory of Modeling Schools and Agencies USA and Canada *see* Directory of Model-Talent Agencies and Schools USA and International *429*
Models of Scientific Thought (US ISSN 0736-5268) *699*
Modern Aging Research (US ISSN 0275-360X) *552*
Modern Analytic and Computational Methods in Science and Mathematics(US ISSN 0076-9908) *1158*
Modern Approaches to the Diagnosis and Instruction of Multi-Handicapped Children (NE ISSN 0076-9916) *445*
Modern Artists (US) *107*
Modern Aspects of Electrochemistry (US ISSN 0076-9924) *328*
Modern Biology Series (US) *143*
Modern Brewery Age Blue Book (US ISSN 0076-9932) *120*
Modern Cleaning: Directory of Suppliers *see* Lavanderia Moderna *339*
Modern Corporation Checklists (Supplement) (US) *290*
Modern Developments in Powder Metallurgy *see* International Powder Metallurgy Conference. Proceedings-Modern Developments in Powder Metallurgy *798*
Modern East Asian Studies (CN) *570, 852*
Modern English Journal/Eigo Kyoiku Jaanaru (JA) *448, 699*
Modern Filologiai Fuzetek (HU ISSN 0076-9967) *699*
Modern German Studies (GW ISSN 0170-3013) *879*
Modern Humanities Research Association. Monograph *see* Modern Humanities Research Association. Publications *631*
Modern Humanities Research Association. Publications (UK) *631*
Modern Jazz (IT) *838*
Modern Jewish Studies Annual (US ISSN 0270-9406) *727*
Modern Language Association of America Directory of Periodicals *see* M L A Directory of Periodicals *739*
Modern Language Association of America International Bibliography of Books and Articles on the Modern Languages and Literatures *see* M L A International Bibliography of Books and Articles on the Modern Languages and Literatures *128*
Modern Language Teachers' Association of New South Wales News *see* M.L.T.A. News *698*
Modern Locomotive Handbook (US) *1094*
Modern Machine Shop (US ISSN 0026-8003) *745*

Modern Machine Shop N C/C I M Guidebook (US) *745*
Modern Machine Shop N C Guidebook and Directory *see* Modern Machine Shop N C/C I M Guidebook *745*
Modern Materials. Advances in Development and Applications (US ISSN 0077-0000) *489*
Modern Methods in Pharmacology (US ISSN 0732-7218) *872*
Modern Middle East Series (US ISSN 0077-0027) *570, 852*
Modern Monographs in Analytical Chemistry (US) *326*
Modern Neurosurgery (US) *794*
Modern Nursing Home Directory of Nursing Homes in the United States, U.S. Possessions and Canada (US) *1158*
Modern Orthodox Saints (US) *984*
Modern Perfumimg - Directory of Suppliers *see* Perfumeria Moderna - Directorio de Proveedores *119*
Modern Pharmacology *see* Modern Pharmacology-Toxicology Series *872*
Modern Pharmacology-Toxicology Series (US ISSN 0098-6925) *872*
Modern Photography's Photo Buying Guide (US) *884*
Modern Physics in Chemistry (UK) *1158*
Modern Plastics Encyclopedia (US ISSN 0085-3518) *900*
Modern Problems in Ophthalmology *see* Developments in Ophthalmology *785*
Modern Problems in Paediatrics (SZ ISSN 0077-0086) *787*
Modern Problems of Pharmacopsychiatry (SZ ISSN 0077-0094) *790, 872*
Modern Publicity *see* World Advertising Review *16*
Modern Quaternary Research in Southeast Asia (NE ISSN 0168-6151) *857*
Modern Synthetic Methods (GW) *330*
Modern Technics in Surgery. Abdominal Surgery (US ISSN 0196-1918) *783*
Modern Technics in Surgery. Cardiac/Thoracic Surgery (US ISSN 0163-7029) *794*
Modern Technics in Surgery. Head and Neck Surgery (US ISSN 0271-8219) *794*
Modern Technics in Surgery. Neurosurgery (US ISSN 0163-7037) *790, 794*
Modern Technics in Surgery. Plastic Surgery (US ISSN 0276-9387) *794*
Modern Technics in Surgery. Section of the Ear (US) *764*
Modern Technics in Surgery. Urologic Surgery (US ISSN 0193-8568) *794, 795*
Modern Tire Dealer Products Catalog (US) *985, 1082*
Das Moderne Heim (AU ISSN 0026-8607) *98, 186*
Modern's Market Guide (US ISSN 0276-0959) *314*
Modersmaal Selskabet. Aarbog (DK ISSN 0107-2390) *699*
Modszertani Kiadvanyok/Methods of Information and Documentation (HU ISSN 0324-7341) *681, 1070*
Modules/Hybrids D.A.T.A. Book (US) *457*
Moebel-Industrie und Ihre Helfer (GW ISSN 0077-0205) *644*
Moeldrup Kommunes Lokalhistoriske Arkiv. Aarsskrift (DK ISSN 0106-4479) *590*
Moelposen (DK ISSN 0106-1917) *590*
Moessbauer Spectroscopy Abstracts (UK) *9, 893*
Moji Shohyoshu (JA) *861*
Mokuzai Kenkyu *see* Wood Research *531*
Molecular and Cellular Biochemistry (US) *152*
Molecular Biology (US) *143*
Molecular Biology, Biochemistry and Biophysics (US ISSN 0077-0221) *152, 153, 163*
Molecular Structures and Dimensions (NE ISSN 0377-2012) *328*

Molekulyarnaya Fizika i Biofizika Vodnykh Sistem (UR) *153*
Molsbibliotekets Lokalhistorisk Arkiv (DK ISSN 0900-8764) *590*
Moly Corrosion Inhibitors (US) *799*
Molysulfide Newsletter (US ISSN 0730-9163) *799*
Mon-Khmer Studies (US ISSN 0147-5207) *699*
Monarchist Book Review (UK ISSN 0077-0280) *564*
Monarchist Press Association. Historical Series (UK ISSN 0077-0299) *591*
Monash Papers on Southeast Asia (AT) *570, 907*
Monash University. Careers & Appointments Service. Survey of Graduate Starting Salaries as of 30 April (Year) (AT) *213*
Monash University. Publications in Geography (AT ISSN 0313-8410) *546*
Monastic Studies (CN) *982*
Monatsschrift fuer Brauwissenschaft (GW) *9, 120*
Mondes Hispanophone et Lusophone (FR ISSN 0761-2397) *591, 727*
Money Business: Grants and Awards for Creative Artists (US ISSN 0161-5866) *107*
Money Income (in Year) of Families and Persons in the United States *see* Current Population Reports: Consumer Income. Money Income of Households, Families and Persons in the United States (Year) *277*
Money Market Directory *see* Money Market Directory of Pension Funds and Their Investment Advisors *230*
Money Market Directory of Pension Funds and Their Investment Advisors (US) *230*
Moneywise Guide to California (UK) *1158*
Mongol Nyelvemlektar *see* Monumenta Linguae Mongolicae Collecta *852*
Mongolia Report (US) *247, 907*
Mongolia Society. Occasional Papers (US ISSN 0077-0396) *570*
Mongolia Society. Special Papers (US) *570*
Mongolia Society Newsletter. New Series (US) *570*
Mongolian Society Bulletin *see* Mongolian Studies *852*
Mongolian Studies (US) *852*
Mongrafie della Scuola Archeologica di Atene e delle Missioni Italiane in Oriente (IT ISSN 0067-009X) *89*
Monitor (US ISSN 0077-040X) *290*
Monitore Zoologico Italiano. Monografie/Italian Journal of Zoology. Monographs (IT ISSN 0391-1632) *176*
Monitore Zoologico Italiano. Supplemento/Italian Journal of Zoology. Supplement (IT ISSN 0374-9444) *176*
Monitored Earth Rotation and Intercompared Techniques Newsletter *see* M E R I T Newsletter *116*
Monitoring the Future (US ISSN 0190-9185) *377, 416*
Monmouth Review (US) *728*
Monmouth Reviews: Journal of the Literary Arts *see* Monmouth Review *728*
La Monnaie en (Year) (FR) *230*
Monnaies, Prix, Conjoncture (FR ISSN 0077-0434) *230, 559*
Monografias Antropologicas (PN) *73*
Monografias Arqueologicas (SP) *90*
Monografias de Filosofia Juridica y Social/Monographs of Social and Legal Philosophy (SP ISSN 0077-0442) *660*
Monografias de Matematica (BL) *751*
Monografias de Poblacion y Desarrollo (BO) *1027*
Monografias de Promocion Femenina (BO) *1129*
Monografias de Psicologia, Normal y Patologica (SP ISSN 0077-0469) *935*
Monografias de Recursos Humanos (BO) *1027*

Monografias de Sociologia Familiar (BO) *1027*
Monografias em Ciencia da Computacao (BL) *353*
Monografias Urbanas (BO) *624*
Monografie Biochemiczne (PL ISSN 0077-0485) *152*
Monografie di Archeologia Libica (IT ISSN 0077-0493) *90*
Monografie Fauny Polski (PL) *176*
Monografie Matematyczne (PL ISSN 0077-0507) *751*
Monografie Parazytologiczne (PL ISSN 0540-6722) *169, 1122*
Monografie Psychologiczne (PL ISSN 0077-0515) *935*
Monografie Slaskie Ossolineum (PL ISSN 0077-0523) *591*
Monografie Slawistyczne (PL ISSN 0077-0531) *591, 728*
Monografie z Dziejow Nauki i Techniki(PL ISSN 0077-054X) *995, 1070*
Monografie z Dziejow Oswiaty (PL ISSN 0077-0558) *448*
Monografii Matematice (RM) *751*
Monograph Abstracts (Ann Arbor) *see* Research Abstracts (Ann Arbor) *11*
Monograph Series in Finance and Economics *see* Salomon Brothers Center for the Study of Financial Institutions. Monograph Series *232*
Monograph Series in World Affairs (US ISSN 0077-0582) *917*
Monograph Series on Malaysian Economic Affairs (MY) *197*
Monograph Series on Schizophrenia (US ISSN 0077-0620) *790*
Monographia Historica Bohemica (CS ISSN 0231-9136) *591*
Monographiae Biologicae (NE ISSN 0077-0639) *143*
Monographiae Botanicae (PL ISSN 0077-0655) *159*
Monographien aus dem Gesamtgebiete der Psychiatrie - Psychiatry Series (US ISSN 0077-0671) *790*
Monographien zur Angewandten Entomologie (GW ISSN 0077-0698) *165*
Monographien zur Geschichte des Mittelalters (GW ISSN 0026-9832) *591*
Monographien zur Indischen Archaeologie, Kunst und Philologie (GW ISSN 0170-8864) *852*
Monographien zur Philosophischen Forschung (GW) *879*
Monographies Francaises de Psychologie (FR ISSN 0077-071X) *935*
Monographies Juridiques (CN ISSN 0077-0728) *1158*
Monographies Reine Elisabeth (BE) *90*
Monographs, Advanced Texts and Surveys in Pure and Applied Mathematics (US) *751*
Monographs and Studies in Mathematics *see* Monographs, Advanced Texts and Surveys in Pure and Applied Mathematics *751*
Monographs and Theoretical Studies in Sociology and Anthropology in Honour of Nels Anderson (NE) *73, 1028*
Monographs for Teachers of French *see* Macquarie University French Monographs *698*
Monographs in Allergy (SZ ISSN 0077-0760) *773*
Monographs in Basic Neurology *see* Monographs in Neural Sciences *790*
Monographs in Clinical Cytology (SZ ISSN 0077-0809) *163, 764*
Monographs in Computer Science and Computer Applications *see* Monografias em Ciencia da Computacao *353*
Monographs in Developmental Biology (SZ ISSN 0077-0825) *152*
Monographs in Economic Anthropology *see* Economic Anthropology *71*
Monographs in Electrical and Electronic Engineering (US) *457*
Monographs in Electroanalytical Chemistry and Electrochemistry Series (US ISSN 0077-0833) *326, 328*

1816 MONOGRAPHS IN

Monographs in Epidemiology and Biostatistics (US) *143*
Monographs in Evolutionary Biology *see* Evolutionary Biology *167*
Monographs in Geology and Paleontology (US ISSN 0077-085X) *391, 857*
Monographs in Geoscience (US) *1158*
Monographs in Hormone Research *see* Frontiers of Hormone Research *781*
Monographs in Human Genetics (SZ ISSN 0077-0876) *167*
Monographs in Inorganic Chemistry (US) *1158*
Monographs in International Studies: Africa Series (US) *566*
Monographs in International Studies: Latin America Series (US) *607*
Monographs in International Studies: Southeast Asia Series (US) *570*
Monographs in Lipid Research (US ISSN 0094-8950) *152*
Monographs in Musicology Series (US) *838*
Monographs in Neural Sciences (SZ ISSN 0300-5186) *790*
Monographs in Ophthalmology (NE) *786*
Monographs in Oral Science (SZ ISSN 0077-0892) *779*
Monographs in Organic Functional Group Analysis *see* Analysis of Organic Materials: an International Series of Monographs *329*
Monographs in Organizational Behaviour and Industrial Relations (US) *274, 1010*
Monographs in Paediatrics (SZ ISSN 0077-0914) *788*
Monographs in Philosophy and Religious History (US ISSN 0068-4333) *879*
Monographs in Physical Measurement (US) *473, 889*
Monographs in Population Biology (US ISSN 0077-0930) *923*
Monographs in Primatology (US) *143*
Monographs in Semiconductor Physics (US ISSN 0544-8417) *1158*
Monographs in the Economics of Development (PK ISSN 0544-8433) *263*
Monographs in Virology (SZ ISSN 0077-0965) *169*
Monographs of Social and Legal Philosophy *see* Monografias de Filosofia Juridica y Social *660*
Monographs on American Art (US ISSN 0544-845X) *107*
Monographs on Astronomical Subjects (US ISSN 0141-1128) *116*
Monographs on Atherosclerosis (SZ ISSN 0077-099X) *777*
Monographs on Cryogenics (US) *473*
Monographs on Education (UN ISSN 0077-1007) *416*
Monographs on Endocrinology (US ISSN 0077-1015) *781*
Monographs on Europe (US) *591*
Monographs on Immunology *see* Immunology: An International Series of Monographs and Treatises *168*
Monographs on Industrial Property and Copyright Law (NE) *660, 861*
Monographs on Infancy (US) *788, 935*
Monographs on Linguistic Analysis (GW ISSN 0077-1031) *1158*
Monographs on Numerical Analysis (US) *751*
Monographs on Oceanographic Methodology (UN ISSN 0077-104X) *407*
Monographs on Pathology of Laboratory Animals (US) *782*
Monographs on Physical Biochemistry (US ISSN 0309-0698) *152, 332*
Monographs on Plastics Series (US) *900*
Monographs on Science, Technology, and Society (US) *1070*
Monographs on Soil and Resources Survey (US) *57, 366*
Monographs on Soil Survey *see* Monographs on Soil and Resources Survey *57*
Monographs on Standardization of Cardioangiological Methods (SZ ISSN 0302-2293) *777*

Monographs on the Ancient Near East (US ISSN 0732-6491) *613*
Monographs on the Fine Arts (US) *107*
Monographs on the Physics and Chemistry of Materials (US) *323, 889*
Monographs on Theoretical and Applied Genetics (US ISSN 0341-5376) *167*
Monopoltilsynets Aarsberetning (DK ISSN 0107-492X) *197*
Montalban (VE) *73, 631*
Montana. Bureau of Mines and Geology. Bulletin (US ISSN 0077-1090) *391, 818*
Montana. Bureau of Mines and Geology. Directory of Mining Enterprises (US ISSN 0077-1104) *818*
Montana. Bureau of Mines and Geology. Ground Water Reports *see* Montana. Bureau of Mines and Geology. Bulletin *391*
Montana. Bureau of Mines and Geology. Memoir (US ISSN 0077-1120) *391, 818*
Montana. Bureau of Mines and Geology. Special Publications (US ISSN 0077-1139) *391, 818*
Montana. Department of Business Regulation. Annual Report (US ISSN 0093-8246) *944*
Montana. Office of the Legislative Auditor. Department of Institutions Reimbursements Program; Report on Audit (US ISSN 0090-4325) *944*
Montana. Office of the Legislative Auditor. State of Montana Board of Investments. Report on Examination of Financial Statements (US ISSN 0090-9912) *267, 944*
Montana Academy of Sciences. Proceedings (US) *143, 995*
Montana Comprehensive Chemical Dependency Plan (US) *377*
Montana Forest and Conservation Experiment Station. Biennial Report (US) *366, 526*
Montana League of Cities & Towns. Newsletter (US ISSN 0026-9980) *951*
Montana Library Directory, with Statistics of Montana Public Libraries (US ISSN 0094-873X) *681*
Montana Manufacturers & Products Directory (US) *314*
Montana Municipal League. Newsletter *see* Montana League of Cities & Towns. Newsletter *951*
Montana Newsletter *see* Montana League of Cities & Towns. Newsletter *951*
Montana Review (US) *728*
Montana State Board of Health. Annual Statistical Supplement *see* Montana Vital Statistics *959*
Montana State Plan for Alcohol Abuse and Alcoholism Prevention, Treatment and Rehabilitation *see* Montana Comprehensive Chemical Dependency Plan *377*
Montana Vital Statistics (US ISSN 0077-1198) *959*
Montana Water Resources Research Center. Annual Report (US) *1125*
Montech Conferences (US) *457*
Montevideo. Museo de Historia Natural. Anales *see* Museo Nacional de Historia Natural. Anales *995*
Monthly Extract (US) *785, 1129*
Monthly Periodical Index *see* Access: The Supplementary Index to Periodicals *2*
Montre Suisse. Annuaire/Watch Review. Curriculum (SZ ISSN 0077-1309) *644*
Montreal Port and Shipping Handbook (Year) (UK ISSN 0265-8186) *314, 1102*
Montreal Women's Directory *see* Annuaire des Femmes de Montreal *1128*
Montserrat. Port Authority. Annual Report (MJ) *1102*
Montserrat. Statistics Office. Digest of Overseas Trade Statistics *see* Montserrat. Statistics Office. Digest of Statistics *213*

Montserrat. Statistics Office. Digest of Statistics (MJ) *213, 258*
Montserrat. Statistics Office. Overseas Trade Report (MJ) *314, 1059*
Montserrat. Statistics Office. Tourism Report (MJ) *1114*
Monument Conservation *see* Varstvo Spomenikov *601*
Monumenta Aegyptiaca (BE ISSN 0077-1376) *90*
Monumenta Americana (GW ISSN 0077-1384) *90, 607*
Monumenta Antiquitatis Extra Fines Hungariae Reperta Quae in Museo Artium Hungarico Aliisque Museis et Collectionibus Hungaricis Conservantur (HU ISSN 0077-1392) *1158*
Monumenta Archaeologica (Los Angeles) (US ISSN 0363-7565) *90*
Monumenta Artis Romanae (GW ISSN 0077-1406) *90, 107*
Monumenta Chartae Papyraceae Historiam Illustrantia/Collection of Works and Documents Illustrating the History of Paper (NE ISSN 0077-1414) *858*
Monumenta Germaniae Historica. Schriften (GW ISSN 0080-6951) *591*
Monumenta Germaniae Historica. Staatsschriften des Spaeteren Mittelalters (GW ISSN 0340-8035) *591*
Monumenta Graeca et Romana (NE) *107, 852*
Monumenta Historica Budapestinensia (HU ISSN 0077-1430) *90, 591*
Monumenta Historica Ordinis Minorum Capuccinorum (IT ISSN 0077-1449) *982*
Monumenta Historica Societatis Iesu (IT) *982*
Monumenta Iuris Canonici (VC ISSN 0077-1457) *982*
Monumenta Linguae Mongolicae Collecta (HU ISSN 0230-8452) *852*
Monumenta Literaria Neerlandica (NE) *728*
Monumenta Paedagogica (GE ISSN 0077-1481) *416*
Monumenta Serica (SZ ISSN 0077-149X) *852*
Monumentorum Tutela. Ochrana Pamiatok (CS) *591*
Monuments de la Catalunya Romanica (SP) *107*
Monuments of Culture. New Discoveries *see* Pamyatniki Kul'tury. Novye Otkrytiya *108*
Monuments of Renaissance Music (US ISSN 0077-1503) *838*
Monuments of Russian Music (UR) *838*
Moody Street Irregulars (US ISSN 0196-2604) *728*
Moody's Bank & Finance Manual (US ISSN 0027-0814) *267*
Moody's Industrial Manual (US ISSN 0545-0217) *267*
Moody's International Manual (US) *267*
Moody's Municipal & Government Manual (US ISSN 0545-0233) *267*
Moody's O T C Industrial Manual (US) *267*
Moody's Public Utility Manual (US ISSN 0545-0241) *267*
Moody's Transportation Manual (US) *267*
Mool Sarak Ankrey *see* Basic Road Statistics of India *1084*
Moonsign Book *see* Llewellyn's Moon Sign Book *114*
Moorea (IE ISSN 0332-4273) *159*
Moores & Rowland's Tax Guide (UK ISSN 0267-8829) *297*
Moosehead Review (CN ISSN 0228-7404) *742*
Moot *see* Moot: Thirkill - Threlkeld Family Newsletter *536*
Moot: Thirkill - Threlkeld Family Newsletter *536*
Moravske Muzeum Brno. Casopis (CS ISSN 0323-0570) *90, 591*
Moravske Muzeum Zemskeho. Casopis *see* Moravske Muzeum Brno. Casopis *591*

Moravske Numismaticke Zpravy (CS ISSN 0077-152X) *845*
Morbilidad (UY) *954*
Morgan Index on Airline Travel (Australia) (AT) *1089*
Morgan Index on TV and Radio (AT) *349*
Morgan Report on Directory Publishing (US ISSN 0890-9512) *16, 1114*
Morgannwg (UK ISSN 0545-0373) *591*
Morocco. Direction de la Statistique. Statistiques Retrospectives *see* Annuaire Statistique du Maroc *1048*
Morocco. Direction des Mines et de la Geologie. Activite du Secteur Petrolier *see* Morocco. Ministere de l'Energie et des Mines. Activite du Secteur Petrolier *865*
Morocco. Ministere de l'Energie et des Mines. Activite du Secteur Petrolier (MR) *865*
Morskaya Geologiya i Geofizika/ Marine Geology and Geophysics (UR ISSN 0076-4477) *407*
Mortality and Demographic Data (NZ ISSN 0548-9911) *927, 1059*
Mortgage Banking: Financial Statements and Operating Ratios *see* Financial Statements and Operating Ratios for the Mortgage Banking Industry *228*
Mortgage Banking: Loans Closed and Servicing Volume *see* Loans Closed and Servicing Volume for the Mortgage Banking Industry *230*
Mort's Guide to Low-Cost Vacations & Lodgings on College Campuses (US ISSN 0095-0386) *620*
Mosasaur (US ISSN 0736-3907) *857*
Moscow Mathematical Society. Transactions (English edition of: Moskovskoe Matematicheskoe Obshchestvo. Trudy) (US ISSN 0077-1554) *751*
Moskovskii Institut Stali i Splavov. Nauchnye Trudy. (UR) *799*
Moskovskii Universitet. Biblioteka. Rukopisnaya i Pechatnaya Kniga v Fondakh (UR) *129*
Moskovskoe Matematicheskoe Obshchestvo. Trudy (UR) *751*
Mostre e Musei (IT) *107*
Moteurs Diesel (FR) *1092*
Motion/Kinesi (GR) *1114*
Motocourse (UK) *1041*
Motocyclo Catalogue (FR ISSN 0077-1570) *1041*
Motor Agents Association Year Book and Diary (UK) *1092*
Motor Auto Repair Manual (US) *1092*
Motor Cycle and Cycle Trader Year Book (UK ISSN 0306-4867) *1041*
Motor Handbook (US ISSN 0094-1514) *1092*
Motor Home & Truck Camper Trade-in Guide (US) *1105*
Motor Home Trade-in Guide *see* Motor Home & Truck Camper Trade-in Guide *1105*
Motor Industry of Great Britain *see* Motor Industry of Great Britain (Year) World Automotive Statistics *1092*
Motor Industry of Great Britain (Year) World Automotive Statistics (UK) *1092*
Motor Industry of Japan *see* Automobile Industry - Japan and Toyota *1090*
Motor Industry Year Book (NZ) *1082*
Motor Light Truck and Van Repair Manual *see* Motor Light Truck Tuneup & Van Repair Manual *1092*
Motor Light Truck Tuneup & Van Repair Manual (US) *1092*
Motor Manual (UK ISSN 0077-1600) *1092, 1105*
Motor Parts & Time Guide (US ISSN 0077-1716) *1092*
Motor Road Test Annual (UK) *1092*
Motor Specifications & Prices (UK) *1086, 1092*
Motor Traffic in Sweden (SW ISSN 0077-1619) *1092*
Motor Truck Facts *see* M V M A Motor Vehicle Facts and Figures *1092*

Motor Vehicle Engineering Specifications - Japan (JA) *1092*
Motor Vehicle Facts & Figures *see* M V M A Motor Vehicle Facts and Figures *1092*
Motor Vehicle Safety (US) *954*
Motor Vehicle Statistics of Japan (JA ISSN 0463-6635) *1086*
Motorcycle Buyer's Guide (US ISSN 0077-1678) *1041*
Motorcycle Dealernews Buyers Guide (US) 369, *1041*
Motorcycle Facts (US ISSN 0091-5793) *1092*
Motorcycle Japan (JA) *1041*
Motorcycle Product News Trade Directory (US) *314*, 1041
Motorola Technical Disclosure Bulletin (US) *1070*
Motor's Flat Rate and Parts Manual *see* Motor Parts & Time Guide *1092*
Motor's Handbook *see* Motor Handbook *1092*
Mount Desert Island Biological Laboratory. Bulletin (US) *143*
Mountain Club of South Africa. Journal(SA) *1046*
Mountain State Geology (US ISSN 0163-2825) *391*
Mouse in Biomedical Research (US) *1158*
Mouvement Naturel de la Population de la Grece (GR ISSN 0077-6114) 923, *928*
Movement and Dance (UK) *375*
Movement of California Fruits and Vegetables by Rail, Truck, and Air (US ISSN 0094-2790) 520, *1082*
Movements in the Arts (US ISSN 8756-890X) *107*, 728, 838
Movie/T V Marketing Global Motion Picture Year Book (JA ISSN 0085-3577) 349, *825*
Movimiento Natural de la Poblacion de Espana (SP ISSN 0077-1767) 923, *928*
Moving Finger (US) *742*
Moving Out (US ISSN 0047-830X) *1129*
Moving to & Around Alberta (CN ISSN 0713-8369) 965, *1114*
Moving to & Around Maritimes & Newfoundland (CN ISSN 0228-7153) 965, *1114*
Moving to & Around Southwestern Ontario (CN ISSN 0715-8114) *965*, 1114
Moving to & Around Winnipeg & Manitoba (CN ISSN 0715-7053) *965*, 1114
Moving to Dallas/Fort Worth (CN ISSN 0229-5040) 965, *1114*
Moving to Denver (CN ISSN 0713-4819) 965, *1114*
Moving to Ottawa/Hull (CN ISSN 0226-7837) 965, *1114*
Moving to San Fransisco and the Bay Area *see* Moving to the San Francisco Bay and Greater Sacramento *965*
Moving to Saskatchewan (CN ISSN 0225-5383) 965, *1114*
Moving to the San Francisco Bay and Greater Sacramento (CN) *965*, 1114
Moving to Vancouver & B.C. (CN ISSN 0226-7276) 965, *1114*
Moving to Vancouver/Victoria *see* Moving to Vancouver & B.C *965*
Mozambique. Servico Meteorologico. Anuario de Observacoes. Parte I: Observacoes de Superficie (MZ) *1158*
Mozambique. Servico Meteorologico. Anuario de Observacoes. Parte II: Observacoes de Altitude (MZ) *1158*
Mozambique. Servico Meteorologico. Informacoes de Caracter Astronomico (MZ) 116, *400*
Mozart - Jahrbuch (GW ISSN 0077-1805) *838*
Mr. Cogito (US) *742*
Muelleria (AT ISSN 0077-1813) *159*
Muenchener Beitraege zur Mediaevistik und Renaissance-Forschung (GW ISSN 0930-1127) *338*, 591
Muenchener Geographische Abhandlungen (GW) *546*
Muenchener Indologische Studien (GW ISSN 0077-1880) *852*
Muenchener Jahrbuch der Bildenden Kunst (GW ISSN 0077-1899) *107*
Muenchener Ostasiatische Studien (GW ISSN 0170-3668) *852*
Muenchener Ostasiatische Studien. Sonderreihe (GW ISSN 0170-3676) *852*
Muenchener Studien zur Sozial- und Wirtschaftsgeographie (GW ISSN 0077-1902) *546*
Muenchener Studien zur Sprachwissenschaft (GW ISSN 0077-1910) *699*
Muenchener Zeitschrift fuer Balkankunde (GW ISSN 0170-8929) *591*, 613
Muenchner Entomologische Gesellschaft. Mitteilungen (GW ISSN 0077-1864) *165*
Muenchner Germanistische Beitraege (GW ISSN 0077-1872) *699*, 728
Muenstersche Beitraege zur Deutschen Literaturwissenschaft (GW ISSN 0077-1996) *728*
Muenstersche Beitraege zur Vor- und Fruehgeschichte (GW ISSN 0077-2003) *559*
Muenstersche Beitraege zur Vorgeschichtsforschung *see* Muenstersche Beitraege zur Vor- und Fruehgeschichte *559*
Muensterschwarzacher Studien (GW ISSN 0077-2011) *983*
Mufon U F O Symposium Proceedings (Mutual U F O Network, Inc.) (US) *20*
Mugwumps' Instrument Herald. Catalog Reprint Series (US) *838*
Al-Mujtama *see* Sudan Society *76*
Mulga Yonbo *see* Korea (Republic). National Bureau of Statistics. Annual Report on the Price Survey *212*
Mulhaq al-Tashri lil-Jaridah al-Rasmiyah li-Jumhuriyat al-Sudan al-Dimuqratiyah *see* Democratic Republic of the Sudan Gazette. Legislative Supplement *941*
Mulika (TZ ISSN 0856-0129) *699*
Multi Media Reviews Index *see* Media Review Digest *826*
Multicultural Education (CN ISSN 0829-9137) *416*
Multicultural Education Abstracts (UK ISSN 0260-9770) 9, *424*
Multilingual Forestry Terminology Series (US ISSN 0077-2046) *526*
Multinational Corporations Operating Overseas *see* Multinational Marketing & Employment Directory *314*
Multinational Executive Travel Companion (US ISSN 0093-7487) *258*, 1114
Multinational Industrial Relations Series(US ISSN 0149-0818) *258*
Multinational Marketing & Employment Directory (US ISSN 0363-4426) *314*
Multiphase Science and Technology (US ISSN 0276-1459) *473*
Mundus Arabicus (US) *728*
Munger Africana Library Notes (US ISSN 0047-8350) *1158*
Munich Round up (GW) *728*, 995
Municipal Association of Tasmania. Session. Minutes of Proceedings (AT ISSN 0085-3585) *951*
Municipal Association of Victoria. Minutes of Proceedings of Annual Session (AT ISSN 0077-2143) *907*
Municipal Index (US ISSN 0077-2151) *951*
Municipal Year Book (US ISSN 0077-2186) *951*
Municipal Year Book (UK) *951*
Municipal Year Book Directories (US ISSN 0276-489X) *951*
Municipal Yearbook *see* Official South African Municipal Yearbook *951*
Munksgaards Social Aarbog (DK ISSN 0109-3347) *463*
Muon Catalyzed Fusion (SZ ISSN 0259-9805) *897*
Muqarnas (US) *107*, 570
Murerhaandbog (DK ISSN 0108-8602) *186*

Musashino Art University. Bulletin (JA) *107*
Muse (US ISSN 0077-2194) 90, *107*
Muse (NR ISSN 0331-3468) *728*
Musealverein Wels. Jahrbuch (AU) *591*
Musee d'Ethnographie de la Ville de Geneve. Bulletin Annuel (SZ ISSN 0072-0828) *73*
Musee de l'Homme, Paris. Catalogues. Serie C: Afrique Noire (FR) *828*
Musee de l'Homme, Paris. Catalogues. Serie H: Amerique (FR) *828*
Musee de l'Homme, Paris. Catalogues. Serie K: Asie (FR) *828*
Musee Guimet, Paris. Bibliotheque d'Etudes (FR ISSN 0078-9704) 90, *107*
Musee Guimet, Paris. Etude des Collections du Musee (FR ISSN 0078-9712) 90, *107*
Musee Ingres. Bulletin (FR ISSN 0027-3783) *107*
Musee National d'Histoire Naturelle, Paris. Memoires. Nouvelle Serie. Serie C. Sciences de la Terre (FR ISSN 0078-9763) *380*
Musee National d'Histoire Naturelle, Paris. Notes et Memoires de la Section d'Etudes Geologiques de Haut-Commissariat Francais en Syrie et au Liban *see* Musee National d'Histoire Naturelle, Paris. Notes et Memoires sur le Moyen-Orient *391*
Musee National d'Histoire Naturelle, Paris. Notes et Memoires sur le Moyen-Orient (FR) *391*, 546
Musee National de Varsovie. Annuaire *see* Muzeum Narodowe w Warszawie. Rocznik *829*
Musee Royal de l'Afrique Centrale. Annales. Serie in 8. Sciences Economiques/Koninklijk Museum voor Midden-Afrika. Annalen. Reeks in 8. Economische Wetenschappen (BE) *48*
Musee Royal de l'Afrique Centrale. Annales. Serie in 8. Sciences Geologiques/Koninklijk Museum voor Midden-Afrika. Annalen. Reeks in 8. Geologische Wetenschappen (BE) *391*
Musee Royal de l'Afrique Centrale. Annales. Serie in 8. Sciences Historiques/Koninklijk Museum voor Midden-Afrika. Annalen. Reeks in 8. Historische Wetenschappen (BE) *566*
Musee Royal de l'Afrique Centrale. Annales. Serie in 8. Sciences Humaines/Koninklijk Museum voor Midden-Afrika. Annalen. Reeks in 8. Menselijke Wetenschappen (BE) *631*, 1010
Musee Royal de l'Afrique Centrale. Annales. Serie in 8. Sciences Zoologiques/Koninklijk Museum voor Midden-Afrika. Annalen. Reeks in 8. Zoologische Wetenschappen (BE) *176*
Musee Royal de l'Afrique Centrale. Archives d'Anthropologie (BE) *74*
Musee Royal de l'Afrique Centrale. Departement de Geologie et de Mineralogie. Rapport Annuel (BE) *391*
Musee Royal de l'Afrique Centrale. Documentation Economique/ Koninklijk Museum voor Midden-Afrika. Economische Documentatie (BE) *197*
Musee Royal de l'Afrique Centrale. Documentation Zoologique/ Koninklijk Museum voor Midden-Afrika. Zoologische Documentatie (BE) *176*
Museen der Welt *see* Museums of the World *829*
Museerne i Viborg Amt *see* M I V: Museerne i Viborg Amt *590*
Musees Royaux des Beaux-Arts de Belgique. Bulletin/Koninklijke Musea voor Schone Kunsten van Belgie. Bulletin (BE ISSN 0027-3856) *828*
Museet for Holbaek og Omegn *see* Museet for Holbaek og Omegn. Aarsberetning *828*
Museet for Holbaek og Omegn. Aarsberetning (DK ISSN 0108-917X) *828*

MUSEO DEL 1817

Museion (AU ISSN 0077-2208) *681*
Museo Archeologico di Tarquinia. Materiali (IT ISSN 0391-9293) 90, *828*
Museo Argentino de Ciencias Naturales "Bernardino Rivadavia." Instituto Nacional de Investigacion de las Ciencias Naturales. Revista. Botanica. (AG ISSN 0376-2793) *159*
Museo Argentino de Ciencias Naturales "Bernardino Rivadavia." Instituto Nacional de Investigacion de las Ciencias Naturales. Revista. Ecologia(AG ISSN 0524-9481) *143*
Museo Argentino de Ciencias Naturales "Bernardino Rivadavia." Instituto Nacional de Investigacion de las Ciencias Naturales. Revista. Entomologia (AG ISSN 0524-949X) *165*
Museo Argentino de Ciencias Naturales "Bernardino Rivadavia." Instituto Nacional de Investigacion de las Ciencias Naturales. Revista. Geologia(AG ISSN 0027-3880) *392*
Museo Argentino de Ciencias Naturales "Bernardino Rivadavia." Instituto Nacional de Investigacion de las Ciencias Naturales. Revista. Hidrobiologia (AG ISSN 0524-9503) *143*
Museo Argentino de Ciencias Naturales "Bernardino Rivadavia." Instituto Nacional de Investigacion de las Ciencias Naturales. Revista. Parasitologia (AG ISSN 0524-952X) *778*
Museo Argentino de Ciencias Naturales "Bernardino Rivadavia." Instituto Nacional de Investigacion de las Ciencias Naturales. Revista. Paleontologia (AG ISSN 0524-9511) *857*
Museo Argentino de Ciencias Naturales "Bernardino Rivadavia." Instituto Nacional de Investigacion de las Ciencias Naturales. Revista y Communicaciones. *see* Museo Argentino de Ciencias Naturales "Bernardino Rivadavia." Instituto Nacional de Investigacion de las Ciencias Naturales. Revista. Geologia *392*
Museo Argentino de Ciencias Naturales "Bernardino Rivadavia." Instituto Nacional de Investigacion de las Ciencias Naturales. Revista. Zoologia(AG ISSN 0373-9066) *176*
Museo Arqueologico de Valladolid. Monografias (SP) *90*
Museo Arqueologico Nacional. Catalogos Cientificos (SP) *90*
Museo Arqueologico Nacional. Guias (SP) *1158*
Museo Arqueologico Nacional. Monografias Arqueologicas (SP) *90*
Museo Arqueologico Nacional. Publicaciones Didacticas (SP) *1158*
Museo Bodoniano. Bollettino (IT) *828*
Museo Boggio. Cuadernos de Arte (VE) *828*
Museo Civico di Storia Naturale "Giacomo Doria," Genoa. Annali (IT ISSN 0365-4389) *995*
Museo Civico di Storia Naturale, Verona. Bolletino (IT ISSN 0392-0062) *995*
Museo Civico di Storia Naturale, Verona. Memorie *see* Museo Civico di Storia Naturale, Verona. Bolletino *995*
Museo de Historia Natural de San Rafael. Instituto de Ciencias Naturales. Notas *see* Museo Municipal de Historia Natural de San Rafael. Instituto de Ciencias Naturales. Notas *392*
Museo de Historia Natural de San Rafael. Revista *see* Museo Municipal de Historia Natural de San Rafael. Revista *995*
Museo del Hombre Dominicano. Papeles Ocasionales (DR) *74*
Museo del Hombre Dominicano. Serie Catalogos y Memorias (DR) 74, *828*
Museo del Hombre Dominicano. Serie Conferencias (DR) *74*

MUSEO DEL

Museo del Hombre Dominicano. Serie Estudio y Arte (DR) 74
Museo del Hombre Dominicano. Serie Investigaciones Antropologicas (DR) 74
Museo del Hombre Dominicano. Serie Mesa Redonda (DR) 74, 828
Museo dell'Impero Romano. Studi e Materiali see Museo della Civilta Romana. Studi e Materiali 828
Museo della Civilta Romana. Studi e Materiali (IT) 828
Museo Municipal de Historia Natural de San Rafael. Instituto de Ciencias Naturales. Notas (AG) 392
Museo Municipal de Historia Natural de San Rafael. Revista (AG) 995
Museo Nacional. Revista (PE) 828
Museo Nacional de Antropologia y Arqueologia. Serie: Antropologia Fisica (PE) 74
Museo Nacional de Antropologia y Arqueologia. Serie: Investigaciones de Campo (PE) 74, 90
Museo Nacional de Antropologia y Arqueologia. Serie: Metalurgia (PE) 74, 90
Museo Nacional de Etnografia y Folklore. Avances de Investigacion (BO) 516
Museo Nacional de Historia Natural. Anales (UY) 828, 995
Museo Nacional de Historia Natural. Communicaciones Antropologicas (UY ISSN 0077-1244) 74
Museo Nacional de Historia Natural. Communicaciones Botanicas (UY ISSN 0027-0121) 159
Museo Nacional de Historia Natural. Communicaciones Paleontologicas (UY) 857
Museo Nacional de Historia Natural. Communicaciones Zoologicas (UY ISSN 0027-0113) 176
Museo Nacional de Historia Natural. Publicacion Ocasional (CL ISSN 0716-0224) 829
Museo Nacional de la Cultural Peruana. Revista see Museo Nacional. Revista 828
Museo Nazionale d'Arte Orientale. Schede (IT) 829, 852
Museo Nazionale di Castel San Angelo. Quaderni (IT) 829
Museo Risorgimento. Bolletino (IT ISSN 0523-9478) 591
Museo y Monumento Nacional "Justo Jose de Urquiza". Serie 3 (AG) 829
Museologia (IT) 829
Museology (US) 829
Museon (BE) 852
Museu Botanico Municipal. Boletim (BL) 159
Museu de Zoologia. Collecciones (SP) 176
Museu Municipal do Funchal. Boletim (PO ISSN 0870-3876) 591
Museu Nacional de Antropologia. Cuadernos (MX ISSN 0076-7158) 74
Museu Nacional, Rio de Janeiro. Arquivos (BL ISSN 0080-3111) 829
Museu Nacional, Rio de Janeiro. Boletim. Nova Serie. Antropologia (BL ISSN 0080-3189) 74
Museu Nacional, Rio de Janeiro. Boletim. Nova Serie. Botanica (BL ISSN 0080-3197) 159
Museu Nacional, Rio de Janeiro. Boletim. Nova Serie. Geologie (BL ISSN 0080-3200) 392
Museu Nacional, Rio de Janeiro. Boletim. Nova Serie. Zoologia (BL ISSN 0080-312X) 176
Museu Paraense Emilio Goeldi. Boletim. Nova Serie. Geologia (BL ISSN 0077-2224) 392
Museu Paraense Emilio Goeldi. Publicacoes Avulsas (BL ISSN 0077-2240) 995
Museu Paulista. Colecao see Universidade de Sao Paulo. Museu Paulista. Colecao. Serie de Etnologia 77
Museu Paulista. Colecao see Universidade de Sao Paulo. Museu Paulista. Colecao. Serie de Arqueologia 94

Museu Paulista. Colecao see Universidade de Sao Paulo. Museu Paulista. Colecao. Serie de Geografia 549
Museu Paulista. Colecao see Universidade de Sao Paulo. Museu Paulista. Colecao. Serie de Historia 610
Museu Paulista. Colecao see Universidade de Sao Paulo. Museu Paulista. Colecao. Serie de Mobiliario 831
Museu Paulista. Colecao see Universidade de Sao Paulo. Museu Paulista. Colecao. Serie de Numismatica 845
Museum Africum (NR) 338
Museum Boymans-van Beuningen. Agenda - Diary (NE ISSN 0077-2275) 829
Museum Briefs see University of Missouri, Columbia. Museum of Anthropology. Museum Briefs 78
Museum Catalog of Publications and Media see Catalog of Museum Publications and Media 831
Museum Criticum (IT) 728
Museum fuer Ur- und Fruehgeschichte der Bezirke Potsdam, Frankfurt/Oder und Cottbus. Veroeffentlichungen (GE ISSN 0079-4376) 559, 829
Museum fuer Ur- und Fruehgeschichte Thueringens. Jahreschrift see Alt-Thueringen 574
Museum fuer Voelkerkunde, Berlin. Veroeffentlichungen. Neue Folge. Abteilung: Afrika (GW ISSN 0067-5962) 74, 566
Museum fuer Voelkerkunde, Berlin. Veroeffentlichungen. Neue Folge. Abteilung: Amerikanische Naturvoelker (GW) 74, 108
Museum fuer Voelkerkunde, Berlin. Veroeffentlichungen. Neue Folge. Abteilung: Suedsee (GW ISSN 0067-5989) 74, 573
Museum fuer Voelkerkunde, Leipzig. Jahrbuch (GE ISSN 0075-8663) 829
Museum fuer Voelkerkunde, Leipzig. Veroeffentlichungen (GE ISSN 0075-8671) 829
Museum National d'Histoire Naturelle, Paris. Annuaire (FR ISSN 0078-9720) 995
Museum National d'Histoire Naturelle, Paris. Archives (FR ISSN 0078-9739) 995
Museum National d'Histoire Naturelle, Paris. Bibliotheque Centrale. Liste des Periodiques Francais et Etrangers. Supplement (FR ISSN 0085-476X) 129
Museum National d'Histoire Naturelle, Paris. Grands Naturalistes Francais (FR) 995
Museum National d'Histoire Naturelle, Paris. Laboratoire d'Ethnobotanique. Publications Diverses (FR) 829
Museum National d'Histoire Naturelle, Paris. Memoires. Nouvelle Serie. Serie A. Zoologie (FR ISSN 0078-9747) 176
Museum National d'Histoire Naturelle, Paris. Memoires. Nouvelle Serie. Serie B. Botanique (FR ISSN 0078-9755) 159
Museum National d'Histoire Naturelle, Paris. Memoires. Nouvelle Serie. Serie D. Sciences Physico-Chimiques(FR ISSN 0078-9771) 323, 889
Museum News Magazine see Muzejski Vjesnik 90
Museum Notes (New York) (US ISSN 0145-1413) 845
Museum of Agriculture. Scientifical Works see Zemedelske Muzeum. Vedecke Prace 38
Museum of Antiquities of Tel-Aviv-Yafo. Publications (IS ISSN 0082-2620) 90, 546
Museum of Comparative Zoology. Bulletin (US ISSN 0027-4100) 176
Museum of Far Eastern Antiquities. Bulletin (SW ISSN 0081-5691) 108, 829, 852
Museum of Fine Arts, Boston. Bulletin (US ISSN 0739-5736) 1158

Museum of Victoria. Memoirs (AT) 829
Museum of Victoria. Occasional Papers (AT ISSN 0814-1819) 829
Museum Philologum Londiniense (NE) 699
Museum Year (US ISSN 0740-0403) 108, 829
Museums and Galleries see Museums and Galleries in Great Britain and Ireland 829
Museums and Galleries in Great Britain and Ireland (UK ISSN 0141-6723) 829
Museums and Monuments Series (UN ISSN 0077-233X) 829
Museums Association Information Sheets (UK ISSN 0306-5332) 829
Museums Australia (AT ISSN 0812-7883) 829
Museums Calendar see Museums Yearbook 829
Museums Journal of Pakistan (PK ISSN 0077-2348) 829
Museums Newsletter (II) 829
Museums of the World/Museen der Welt (GW) 829
Museums Yearbook (UK ISSN 0307-7675) 829
Museumsforeningen for Laesoe. Litteratur (DK ISSN 0109-5854) 829
Mushroom Science (UK ISSN 0077-2364) 159
Music Academy. Conference Souvenir (II) 838
Music Academy. Journal (II) 838
Music and Life (UK ISSN 0085-3607) 838
Music & Musicians: Braille Scores Catalog - Choral (Large Print Edition) (US ISSN 0145-3173) 129, 180, 843
Music & Musicians: Braille Scores Catalog - Instrumental (US ISSN 0145-3165) 129, 180, 843
Music & Musicians: Braille Scores Catalog - Organ (Large Print Edition) (US ISSN 0145-3149) 129, 180, 843
Music & Musicians: Braille Scores Catalog - Piano (Large Print Edition) (US ISSN 0145-3130) 129, 180, 843
Music & Musicians: Braille Scores Catalog - Vocal (Large Print Edition) (US) 129, 180, 843
Music & Musicians: Braille Scores Catalog - Voice see Music & Musicians: Braille Scores Catalog - Vocal (Large Print Edition) 180
Music and Musicians in the Reminiscences of Contemporaries (UR) 838
Music & Musicians: Instructional Cassette Recordings Catalog (Large Print Edition) (US ISSN 0145-2525) 129, 180, 843
Music & Musicians: Instructional Disc Recordings Catalog (Large Print Edition) (US ISSN 0145-2517) 129, 180, 843
Music & Musicians: Large-Print Scores and Books Catalog (Large Print Edition) (US) 129, 180, 843
Music and Musicians: Large Print Scores and Books Catalog for the Blind and Physically Handicapped see Music & Musicians: Large-Print Scores and Books Catalog (Large Print Edition) 180
Music and Video Week Directory see Music Week Directory 838
Music and Video Week Yearbook see Music Week Directory 838
Music Article Guide (US ISSN 0027-4240) 9, 843
Music Association of Ireland. Annual Report (IE) 838
Music Book Guide see Bibliographic Guide to Music 843
Music, Books on Music and Sound Recordings (US ISSN 0092-2838) 688, 843, 1032
Music Cultures see Music Research 838
Music Directory Canada (CN ISSN 0820-0416) 838

Music Educators National Conference. Selective Music Lists: Instrumental Solos and Ensembles (US) 838
Music Educators National Conference. Selective Music Lists: Vocal Solos and Ensembles (US ISSN 0077-2402) 838
Music Forum (US) 838
Music in American Life (US) 838
Music in Danish Libraries see Musikalier i Danske Biblioteker 844
Music in Germany see Deutsches Musikleben (Year) 835
Music-in-Print Annual Supplement (US ISSN 0192-4729) 843
Music-in-Print Series (US ISSN 0146-7883) 9, 843
Music in Time (IS) 838
Music Index (US ISSN 0027-4348) 9, 843
Music Indexes and Bibliographies (US ISSN 0077-2429) 1158
Music Industry Directory (US) 1158
Music Library Association. Index and Bibliography Series (US ISSN 0094-6478) 844
Music Library Association. Index Series see Music Library Association. Index and Bibliography Series 844
Music Library Association. Technical Reports (US ISSN 0094-5099) 681, 838
Music Locator (US) 838
Music Master see Music Master Catalogue 838
Music Master Catalogue (UK) 838
Music Master Labels List (UK) 838
Music Master Yearbook (UK) 838
Music O C L C Users Group. Newsletter (US ISSN 0161-1704) 681, 838
Music of the Environment Series (CN) 1158
Music of the Peoples of the U.S.S.R. (UR) 838
Music Reference Collection (US ISSN 0736-7740) 844
Music Research/Ongaku Kenkyu (JA) 838
Music Theory Spectrum (US ISSN 0195-6167) 838
Music Therapy (US ISSN 0734-7367) 838
Music U S A (US) 838, 1059
Music Week Directory (UK) 838
Music World Year Book (UK ISSN 0077-2453) 838
Music Yearbook see British Music Yearbook 833
Musica Asiatica (US ISSN 0140-6078) 838, 852
Musica Britannica (UK ISSN 0580-2954) 838
Musica Disciplina (GW ISSN 0077-2461) 838
Musica, Immagine, Teatro (IT) 108, 838, 1077
Musica Judaica (US) 838, 977
Musica Medii Aevi (PL ISSN 0077-247X) 838
Musicae Sacrae Ministerium (GW ISSN 0027-4569) 838
Musical America Annual Directory Issue see Musical America International Directory of the Performing Arts 838
Musical America International Directory of the Performing Arts (US) 838
Musical Denmark (DK ISSN 0027-4585) 838
Musical Instruments of East Africa (KE) 838
Musical Interpretation Research (SW ISSN 0349-988X) 631, 838
Musical Woman (US ISSN 0737-0032) 839, 1129
Musiche Rinascimentali Siciliane (IT) 839
Musician's Guide see Music Industry Directory 1158
Musicien Amateur see Amateur Musician 832
Musick of the Fifes & Drums Series (US) 839
Musicologia Espanola (SP) 839
Musicologica Hungarica (HU ISSN 0077-2488) 839

Musicologica Neolovaniensia Studia (BE) *839*
Musicologica Slovaca (CS ISSN 0581-0558) *839*
Musicological Annual *see* Muzikoloski Zbornik *839*
Musicological Studies and Documents (GW ISSN 0077-2496) *839*
Musicological Yearbook *see* Arti Musices *833*
Musicology Australia (AT ISSN 0077-250X) *839*
Musik - Almanach (GW ISSN 0930-8954) *839*
Musik aus der Steiermark (GW) *839*
Musik i Sverige (SW ISSN 0077-2518) *839*
Musik und Gesellschaft (AU ISSN 0259-076X) *839, 1028*
Musikalier i Danske Biblioteker/Music in Danish Libraries (DK ISSN 0085-3623) *844*
Musikalische Denkmaeler (GW ISSN 0077-2526) *839*
Musikbranchens Aarbog (DK ISSN 0108-0040) *839*
Musikhistorisk Museum og Carl Claudius Samling. Meddelelser (DK ISSN 0109-2618) *839*
Musikhistoriska Museet. Skrifter *see* Musikmuseets Skrifter *839*
Musikmuseets Skrifter (SW) *839*
Musikpaedagogische Bibliothek (GW) *839*
Musikplader og -baand *see* Musikplader og -baand. Klassisk Musik *839*
Musikplader og -baand *see* Musikplader og -baand. Rytmisk Musik *839*
Musikplader og -baand. Klassisk Musik (DK ISSN 0107-654X) *839*
Musikplader og -baand. Rytmisk Musik (DK ISSN 0107-8690) *839*
Musikpsychologie (GW ISSN 0177-350X) *839, 935*
Muslim Intellectuals' International Series *see* M.I.I. Series *975*
Musteranlagen der Energiewirtschaft (GW ISSN 0580-3403) *466*
Muszaki Lapszemle. Banyaszat/Technical Abstracts. Mining *see* Banyaszati Szakirodalmi Tajekoztato *821*
Muszaki Lapszemle. Elektrotechnika/Technical Abstracts. Electrical Engineering *see* Elektrotechnikai Szakirodalmi Tajekoztato *461*
Muszaki Lapszemle. Kemia Vegyipar/Technical Abstracts. Chemistry, Chemical Industry *see* Vegyipari Szakirodalmi Tajekoztato *326*
Mutation Breeding Newsletter (UN) *57*
Mutisia (CK ISSN 0027-5123) *159*
Mutual Fund Fact Book (US) *267*
Mutual Funds Almanac (US ISSN 0076-4175) *267*
Mutual U F O Network, Inc. Mufon U F O Symposium Proceedings *see* Mufon U F O Symposium Proceedings *20*
Muveltseg es Hagyomany (HU ISSN 0580-3594) *74*
Muzea Walki (PL ISSN 0077-2577) *591*
Muzejski Vjesnik/Museum News Magazine (YU ISSN 0350-9370) *90, 829*
Muzeul de Istorie al Republicii Socialiste Romania. Cercetari Arheologice (RM) *90*
Muzeul de Istorie al Republicii Socialiste Romania. Cercetari de Conservare si Restaurare a Patrimoniului Muzeal (RM) *366*
Muzeul de Istorie al Republicii Socialiste Romania. Cercetari Istorice(RM) *591*
Muzeul de Istorie Naturala "Gr. Antipa." Travaux (RM ISSN 0068-3078) *144*
Muzeul National (RM) *829*
Muzeul si Educatia Socialista (RM) *829*
Muzeum Archeologiczne i Etnograficzne, Lodz. Prace i Materialy. Seria Archeologiczna (PL ISSN 0458-1520) *90*

Muzeum Archeologiczne i Etnograficzne, Lodz. Prace i Materialy. Seria Etnograficzna (PL ISSN 0076-0315) *74, 504*
Muzeum Archeologiczne i Etnograficzne, Lodz. Prace i Materialy. Seria Numizmatyczna i Konserwatorska (PL ISSN 0208-5062) *845*
Muzeum Archeologiczne, Krakow. Materialy Archeologiczne (PL ISSN 0075-7039) *90*
Muzeum Etnograficzne, Wroclaw. Zeszyty Etnograficzne (PL ISSN 0084-2796) *74*
Muzeum Gornoslaskie w Bytomiu. Rocznik. Seria Archeologia (PL ISSN 0068-4635) *90*
Muzeum Gornoslaskie w Bytomiu. Rocznik. Seria Etnografia (PL ISSN 0068-4643) *74*
Muzeum Gornoslaskie w Bytomiu. Rocznik. Seria Historia (PL ISSN 0068-4651) *591*
Muzeum Gornoslaskie w Bytomiu. Rocznik. Seria Przyroda (PL ISSN 0068-466X) *144*
Muzeum Gornoslaskie w Bytomiu. Rocznik. Seria Sztuka (PL ISSN 0068-4678) *108*
Muzeum Literatury im. Adama Mickiewicza. Blok-Notes (PL ISSN 0324-8925) *728, 839*
Muzeum Militar Central Romania. Studii si Materiale de Muzeografie si Istorie Militara (RM) *591*
Muzeum Narodowe w Warszawie. Rocznik/Musee National de Varsovie. Annuaire (PL ISSN 0509-6936) *829*
Muzeum Slovenskeho Narodneho Povstania. Zbornik (CS) *591*
Muzeum Ukrajinskej Kultury vo Svidniku. Vedecky Zbornik (CS) *591*
Muzeum Ziemi. Prace (PL ISSN 0032-6275) *392*
Muzikoloski Zbornik/Musicological Annual (YU ISSN 0580-373X) *839*
Muzium Brunei. Penerbitan Khas *see* Brunei Museum. Special Publication *827*
Muzyka Polska w Dokumentacjach i Interpretacjach *see* Studia i Materialy do Dziejow Muzyki Polskiej *842*
Muzykal'naya Fol'kloristika (UR) *516, 839*
Muzykal'noe Vospitanie v Shkole (UR ISSN 0302-847X) *448, 839*
My Baby (AT ISSN 0813-4626) *334, 615*
Mycological Papers (UK ISSN 0027-5522) *159*
Mycology Series (US) *159*
Mykenische Studien (AU) *338*
Myotis (GW ISSN 0580-3896) *176*
Myrin Institute for Adult Education Proceedings (US) *427*
Myrtia: Revista de Filologia Clasica (SP) *338, 699*
Mysore. Finance Department. Annual Report *see* Karnataka. Finance Department. Annual Report *296*
Mysore Orientalist (II ISSN 0580-4396) *852*
Mystery & Detection Annual. (US ISSN 0000-0302) *14, 728*
Mystery Time (US) *14*
Mystery Writers of America Annual *see* M W A Annual *727*
Mythellany *see* Mythic Circle *728*
Mythic Circle (US) *728*
N A A (Nordic Archaeological Abstracts) (DK ISSN 0105-6492) *9, 96*
N A A C P Annual Report (National Association for the Advancement of Colored People) (US ISSN 0077-3212) *1019, 1028*
N A A Where to Stay Book (National Automobile Association) (US ISSN 0099-0205) *620*
N A B T E Review (National Association for Business Teacher Education) (US) *197, 437*
N.A.C.D.S. Lilly Digest (National Association of Chain Drug Stores) (US ISSN 0092-8410) *1158*
N A C I F S Technical Bulletin *see* N A C U F S Journal *520*

N A C U F S Journal (National Association of College-University Food Services) (US) *520*
N A D Case Report (National Advertising Division) (US) *16*
N A E C O N *see* I E E E National Aerospace and Electronics Conference. Proceedings *19*
N A E C O N *see* I E E E National Aerospace and Electronics Conference. Proceedings *19*
N A F A Annual Reference Book (National Association of Fleet Administrators, Inc.) (US) *1092*
N A F A Conference Brochurand and Reference Book *see* N A F A Annual Reference Book *1092*
N A F O Annual Report (Northwest Atlantic Fisheries Organization) (CN ISSN 0704-4798) *511*
N A F O List of Fishing Vessels (Northwest Atlantic Fisheries Organization) (CN ISSN 0250-7811) *511*
N A F O Meeting Proceedings (Northwest Atlantic Fisheries Organization) (CN ISSN 0704-4771) *1158*
N A F O Scientific Council Meeting Reports (Northwest Atlantic Fisheries Organization) (CN ISSN 0250-6416) *511*
N A F O Scientific Council Studies (Northwest Atlantic Fisheries Organization) (CN ISSN 0250-6432) *511*
N A F O Statistical Bulletin (Northwest Atlantic Fisheries Organization) (CN ISSN 0250-6394) *511*
N A F O Yearbook (National Association of Fire Officers) (UK) *507*
N A F S A Directory (National Association for Foreign Student Affairs) (US ISSN 0736-4660) *441*
N A G W S Guide. Aquatics *see* N A G W S Guide. Competitive Swimming and Diving *1159*
N A G W S Guide. Basketball (National Association for Girls and Women in Sport) (US ISSN 0362-3254) *1158*
N A G W S Guide. Bowling - Golf (National Association for Girls and Women in Sport) (US) *1158*
N A G W S Guide. Competitive Swimming and Diving (National Association for Girls and Women in Sport) (US ISSN 0271-2199) *1159*
N A G W S Guide. Field Hockey (National Association for Girls and Women in Sport) (US) *1039*
N A G W S Guide. Gymnastics (National Association for Girls and Women in Sport) (US ISSN 0363-9282) *1034*
N A G W S Guide. Lacrosse (National Association for Girls and Women in Sport) (US) *1159*
N A G W S Guide. Soccer (National Association for Girls and Women in Sport) (US) *1159*
N A G W S Guide. Soccer, Speedball, Flag Football *see* N A G W S Guide. Soccer *1039*
N A G W S Guide. Softball (National Association for Girls and Women in Sport) (US ISSN 0363-2504) *1039*
N A G W S Guide. Tennis (National Association for Girls and Women in Sport) (US ISSN 0272-863X) *1039*
N A G W S Guide. Track and Field (National Association for Girls and Women in Sport) (US ISSN 0362-9481) *1159*
N A G W S Guide. Volleyball (National Association for Girls and Women in Sport) (US) *1039*
N A I A Handbook (National Association of Intercollegiate Athletics) (US ISSN 0077-3336) *1034*
N A I A Official Records Book (National Association of Intercollegiate Athletics) (US ISSN 0077-3344) *1034*

N A L G O Annual Report (National and Local Government Officers Association) (UK ISSN 0077-4456) *944*
N A M F Accounting Manual (National Association of Metal Finishers) (US ISSN 0077-3360) *222*
N A M F Management Manual (National Association of Metal Finishers) (US ISSN 0077-3379) *799*
N A P E H E Proceedings (National Association for Physical Education in Higher Education) (US ISSN 0276-461X) *448*
N A R D Almanac *see* N A R D Almanac and Health Guide *285*
N A R D Almanac and Health Guide (National Association of Retail Druggists) (US) *285*
N A R D A's Costs of Doing Business Survey (National Association of Retail Dealers of America) (US ISSN 0196-3171) *285*
N A S A Facts (U.S. National Aeronautics and Space Administration) (US ISSN 0077-3093) *20*
N A S A Patent Abstracts Bibliography: A Continuing Bibliography. Section 1. Abstracts (U.S. National Aeronautics and Space Administration) (US) *9, 862*
N A S A Patent Abstracts Bibliography: A Continuing Bibliography. Section 2. Indexes (U.S. National Aeronautics and Space Administration) (US) *862*
N A S A Software Directory (US) *314, 363*
N A S A Technical Memorandum *see* National Aeronautics and Space Administration. Technical Memorandum *20*
N A S A - University Conference on Manual Control (Papers) (U.S. National Aeronautics and Space Administration) (US ISSN 0077-2623) *20*
N A S C O Campus Co-Op Directory (North American Students of Cooperation) (US) *314*
N A S O Journal *see* Astrology (Year) *114*
N.A.T.A. Annual Directory (National Association of Testing Authorities) (AT) *489*
N.A.T.A. Directory *see* N.A.T.A. Annual Directory *489*
N.A.T.A. Index *see* N.A.T.A. Annual Directory *489*
N A T A Register of Laboratories. Quarterly Amendment Sheets *see* N.A.T.A. Annual Directory *489*
N A T I S - News (UN) *681*
N A T I S Noticias *see* N A T I S - News *681*
N A T I S-Nouvelles *see* N A T I S - News *681*
N A T O. Annual Economic Colloquia. Proceedings (North Atlantic Treaty Organization) (BE) *258*
N A T O Advanced Science Institute Series. C: Mathematical and Physical Sciences (NE) *751, 995*
N A T O Advanced Science Institutes Series E: Applied Sciences (North Atlantic Treaty Organization) (NE) *1070*
N A T O Advanced Study Institute. Series H: Cell Biology (US) *163*
N A T O Advanced Study Institute Series E: Applied Sciences *see* N A T O Advanced Science Institutes Series E: Applied Sciences *1070*
N A T O Advanced Study Institute Series F: Computer and System Sciences (North Atlantic Treaty Organization) (US) *353*
N A T O Advanced Study Institute Series G: Ecological Sciences (US) *498*
N A T O and the Warsaw Pact - Force Comparisons/O T A N et le Pacte de Varsovie - Comparison des Forces en Presence (North Atlantic Treaty Organization) (BE) *917*

N A T O Basic Documents/O T A N Documents Fondamentaux (North Atlantic Treaty Organization) (BE) *917*

N A T O Final Communiques/O T A N Communiques Finals (North Atlantic Treaty Organization) (BE) *917*

N A T O Handbook (North Atlantic Treaty Organization) (BE ISSN 0549-7175) *917*

N A V A/I C I A Membership Directory (National Audio-Visual Association) *see* I C I A Membership Directory *447*

N B C/N F C News (National Building Code/National Fire Code) (Associate Committee on the National Building Code) (CN ISSN 0380-8599) *186*

N B C News *see* N B C/N F C News *186*

N B O Abstracts (National Buildings Organisation) (II ISSN 0027-6138) *9, 100, 189, 477*

N.B. Power News (CN) *457*

N C A A Baseball Annual Guide *see* N C A A Baseball Rules *1039*

N C A A Baseball Rules (National Collegiate Athletic Association) (US ISSN 0736-5209) *1039*

N C A A Basketball (National Collegiate Athletic Association) (US ISSN 0276-1017) *1039*

N C A A Basketball Records *see* N C A A Basketball *1039*

N C A A Basketball Rules and Interpretations *see* N C A A Men's Basketball Rules and Interpretations *1039*

N C A A Directory (National Collegiate Athletic Association) (US) *1034*

N C A A Football (National Collegiate Athletic Association) (US ISSN 0735-5475) *1039*

N C A A Football Guide *see* N C A A Football *1039*

N C A A Football Records *see* N C A A Football *1039*

N C A A Football Rules & Interpretations *see* National Collegiate Athletic Association Football Rules & Interpretations *1039*

N C A A Illustrated Basketball Rules *see* N C A A Men's Illustrated Basketball Rules *1039*

N C A A Illustrated Men's Rules *see* N C A A Men's Illustrated Basketball Rules *1039*

N C A A Lacrosse Guide *see* N C A A Men's Lacrosse Rules *1039*

N C A A Manual *see* National Collegiate Athletic Association. Manual *1034*

N C A A Men's & Women's Cross Country and Track & Field Rules (National Collegiate Athletic Association) (US ISSN 0736-7783) *1046*

N C A A Men's and Women's Skiing Rules (US) *1046*

N C A A Men's & Women's Swimming and Diving Rules (National Collegiate Athletic Association) (US ISSN 0736-5128) *1034*

N C A A Men's Basketball Rules and Interpretations (National Collegiate Athletic Association) (US) *1039*

N C A A Men's Ice Hockey Rules and Interpretations (National Collegiate Athletic Association) (US ISSN 0735-9195) *1034*

N C A A Men's Illustrated Basketball Rules (National Collegiate Athletic Association) (US) *1039*

N C A A Men's Lacrosse Rules (National Collegiate Athletic Association) (US ISSN 0736-7775) *1039*

N C A A Men's Soccer Rules (National Collegiate Athletic Association) (US ISSN 0735-0368) *1039*

N C A A Men's Water Polo Rules (National Collegiate Athletic Association) (US ISSN 0734-0508) *1034*

N C A A Skiing Rules *see* N C A A Men's and Women's Skiing Rules *1046*

N C A A Swimming *see* N C A A Men's & Women's Swimming and Diving Rules *1034*

N C A A Water Polo Rules *see* N C A A Men's Water Polo Rules *1034*

N C C Information and Library Services. Bibliography Series (Nature Conservancy Council) (UK ISSN 0143-1722) *1159*

N C E A Ganley's Catholic Schools in America (National Catholic Educational Association) (US ISSN 0147-8044) *430*

N C I Fact Book (US ISSN 0270-7950) *775*

N C I Monographs (US) *775*

N C J R S Document Retrieval Index (National Criminal Justice Reference Service) (US) *371*

N C P C Annual Report (National Crop Protection Center) (PH) *57*

N C P D M Annual Conference Proceedings (National Council of Physical Distribution Management) (US) *285*

N C P Documenta (Noticias de Cosmetica y de Perfumeria) (SP) *119*

N C R A Yearbook *see* College and Adult Reading *426*

N C R P Commentary (National Council on Radiation Protection and Measurements) (US) *955*

N C R P Report (National Council on Radiation Protection and Measurements) (US ISSN 0083-209X) *955*

N C R P Statements (National Council on Radiation Protection and Measurements) (US) *792*

N C R P Symposium Proceedings (National Council on Radiation Protection and Measurements) (US) *955*

N C S R Bibliography *see* Zambia. National Council for Scientific Research. N C S R Bibliography *1005*

N.C.S. Yearbook (National Chrysanthemum Society) (UK) *533*

N D R E Publications (NO ISSN 0800-4412) *995*

N E A Journal *see* Today's Education Annual *420*

N E C Reports *see* Northeast Conference on the Teaching of Foreign Languages. Northeast Conference Reports *449*

N E D A Statistical Yearbook of the Philippines (National Economic and Development Authority) (PH) *213*

N E I S S Data Highlights (National Electronic Injury Surveillance System) (US) *457, 955*

N E I S S News *see* N E I S S Data Highlights *955*

N E I W P C C Annual Report (New England Interstate Water Pollution Control Commission) (US) *498*

N.E.S.F.A. Index: Science Fiction Magazines and Anthologies (New England Science Fiction Association Inc.) (US ISSN 0361-3038) *9, 14*

N E U R B *see* Nucleo de Estudos Sociais para Habitacao e Urbanismo *624*

N F E Exchange (Non-Formal Education) *see* I N E T Up-Date *414*

N F E/W I D Exchange - Asia. Occasional Paper (PH ISSN 0115-8473) *416*

N F L Preview (Year) (US) *1039*

N F P A Directory *see* N F P A Directory and Member Guide *490*

N F P A Directory and Member Guide (National Fluid Power Association) (US) *490*

N F R C Yearbook (National Federation of Roofing Contractors) (UK) *186*

N F T A Annual Report (Niagara Frontier Transportation Authority) (US) *1082*

N F T A Port of Buffalo Handbook (Niagara Frontier Transportation Authority) (US) *1159*

N G U Bulletin (Norges Geologiske Undersoekelse) (NO ISSN 0332-5768) *392*

N G U Skrifter (Norges Geologiske Undersoekelse) (NO ISSN 0377-8894) *392*

N H K Technical Monograph (Nippon Hoso Kyokai) (JA ISSN 0077-2631) *349*

N.H.L. Pro Hockey (CN ISSN 0079-5569) *1034*

N H P Rapport (Nordisk Hydrologisk Forening) (DK ISSN 0900-0267) *403*

N.I.A.A.A.-R.U.C.A.S. Alcoholism Treatment Monographs *see* N I A A A - R U C A S Alcoholism Treatment Series *377*

N I A A A - R U C A S Alcoholism Treatment Series (US ISSN 0147-0515) *377*

N I B Annual Report *see* National Investment Bank, Ghana. Annual Report *231*

N I B R Rapport (Norsk Institutt for By- og Regionforskning) (NO ISSN 0085-4263) *624*

N I C E M Index to Educational Audio Tapes *see* Audiocassette Finder *422*

N I C E M Index to Educational Slides (National Information Center for Educational Media) (US) *1159*

N I C E M Index to Educational Video Tapes *see* Film & Video Finder *424*

N I C E M Index to Environmental Studies - Multimedia *see* Science and Computer Literacy Audiovisuals *361*

N I C E M Index to Health and Safety Education - Multimedia *see* Wellness Media: An Audiovisual Sourcebook *886*

N I C E M Index to Producers and Distributors (National Information Center for Educational Media) (US) *9, 424, 826*

N I C E M Index to Psychology-Multimedia *see* Social Studies Audiovisuals: A Teacher's Sourcebook *449*

N I C E M Index to Vocational and Technical Education-Multimedia *see* Vocational and Technical Audiovisuals: A Teacher's Sourcebook *431*

N I C E M Index to 16mm Educational Films *see* Film & Video Finder *424*

N I C E M Index to 35mm Educational Filmstrips (National Information Center for Educational Media) (US) *9, 424*

N I C E R Bulletin (Northern Ireland Council for Educational Research) (UK ISSN 0262-8163) *416*

N I D A Research Monograph *see* U.S. National Institute on Drug Abuse. Research Monograph Series *377*

N I F P General Series (II ISSN 0077-4944) *179*

N I F P Manual Series (II ISSN 0077-4952) *179*

N I F P Monograph Series (II ISSN 0077-4960) *179*

N I F P Report Series (II ISSN 0077-4979) *179*

N I F P Technical Paper Series (II ISSN 0077-4987) *179*

N I H F W Technical Reports (National Institute of Health and Family Welfare) (II ISSN 0253-6757) *1019*

N I H Factbook (U.S. National Institutes of Health) (US) *1159*

N I I P Bulletin (National Institute of Industrial Psychology) (UK ISSN 0077-5010) *1159*

N I K H E F. Annual Report (NE) *889*

N I R D - H R I Technical Bulletins *see* A F R C Institute of Food Research Technical Bulletins *61*

N I R D Technical Bulletins *see* A F R C Institute of Food Research Technical Bulletins *61*

N I S E R Occasional Papers (Nigerian Institute of Social and Economic Research) (NR) *197, 1010*

N I W O Mededelingen (Nederlandsche Internationale Wegvervoer Organisatie) (NE) *1082*

N I W R Information Sheet (National Institute for Water Research) (SA) *1125*

N K B Publication Series *see* N K B Skriftserie *186*

N K B Skriftserie/N K B Publication Series (Nordiske Komite for Bygningsbestemmelsei) (FI ISSN 0078-1126) *186*

N L N Nursing Data Book *see* N L N Nursing Data Review *784*

N L N Nursing Data Review (US) *784*

N M A (New Music Articles) (AT ISSN 0811-7497) *839*

N M M A Certification Handbook (National Marine Manufacturers Association) (US) *1042*

N M R (Nuclear Magnetic Resonance) (US ISSN 0078-088X) *897*

N M R I Compensation in Mass Retailing, Salaries and Incentives (National Mass Retailing Institute) (US ISSN 0092-5950) *274*

N N A National Directory of Weekly Newspapers (National Newspaper Association) (US) *646*

N O R D I C O M (Nordic Documentation Center for Mass Communication Research) (DK ISSN 0105-1385) *346*

N O R D I N F O Publikation (Nordiska Samarbetsorganet for Vetenskaplig Information) (FI ISSN 0358-7045) *681*

N O W Schuelerzeitung der Staatlichen Realschule Speyer (GW) *335*

N P N Factbook (National Petroleum News) (US) *865*

N R A G Papers (Northern Rockies Action Group, Inc.) (US) *1019*

N R C D Abstracts *see* Information Media & Technology *884*

N R M C A Publication (National Ready Mixed Concrete Association) (US ISSN 0077-5355) *186*

N S A A Economic Analysis of North American Ski Areas *see* Economic Analysis of North American Ski Areas *1045*

N.S.C.A. Reference Book (National Society for Clean Air) (UK ISSN 0140-6795) *498*

N.S.C.A. Yearbook *see* N.S.C.A. Reference Book *498*

N S C Review (National Science Council of the Republic of China) (CH) *995*

N S C Special Publication (National Science Council of the Republic of China) (CH) *995*

N S C Symposium Series (National Science Council of the Republic of China) (CH ISSN 0252-8177) *995*

N S C T E Monographs (National Society of College Teachers of Education) (US) *416*

N S F Factbook *see* U.S. National Science Foundation. N S F Factbook *1164*

N S G A Circular (National Sand and Gravel Association) (US ISSN 0077-5673) *392*

N S R A Memo (Nuclear Safety Research Association) (JA) *897*

N S T A Annual Report *see* Philippines. National Science & Technology Authority. Annual Report *998*

N S T Annual (MY) *197*

N S U Library. Genealogy Series (Nicholls State University) (US) *536*

N T A Journal (CN ISSN 0027-7037) *416*

N T C Workshop Report Series (National Turfgrass Council) (UK) *159, 533*

N T I S Digest (U.S. National Technical Information Service) (US) *681*

N T M Geschichte der Naturwissenschaften, Technik und Medizin. Schriftenreihe (GE) *995*

N T P A Directory *see* National Trade and Professional Associations of the United States and Labor Unions *314*

NATIONAL ASSOCIATION 1821

N U J Freelance Directory (National Union of Journalists) (UK) *646*
N U M U S Numismatica, Medalhistica, Argueologia (PO ISSN 0085-364X) *79*
N U P I Notat (Norsk Utenrikspolitisk Institutt) (NO ISSN 0800-0018) *917*
N U P I Rapport (Norsk Utenrikspolitisk Institutt) (NO ISSN 0800-000X) *917*
N U T Guide to Careers Work (National Union of Teachers) (UK ISSN 0066-3972) *848*
N.Z.A.R.T. Amateur Radio Callbook (New Zealand Association of Radio Transmitters, Inc.) (NZ ISSN 0110-5337) *349*
N Z C E R Newsletter (New Zealand Council for Educational Research) (NZ ISSN 0111-2821) *416*
N Z F C M A Bulletin *see* Journal of Ferrocement *185*
N Z O I Hydrology Station Data (New Zealand Oceanographic Institute) (NZ ISSN 0112-0395) *407*
N Z O I Miscellaneous Publications (New Zealand Oceanographic Institute) (NZ ISSN 0510-0054) *407*
N Z O I Oceanographic Field Report (New Zealand Oceanographic Institute) (NZ ISSN 0110-5205) *407*
N Z O I Oceanographic Summary (New Zealand Oceanographic Institute) (NZ ISSN 0111-1302) *407*
N Z O I Records (New Zealand Oceanographic Institute) (NZ ISSN 0110-618X) *407*
Naar Lampen Taendes. Fortaellinger (DK ISSN 0107-8232) *728*
Nabor Carrillo Lecture Series. Proceedings (MX ISSN 0185-4011) *57, 482*
Nachrichten aus dem Karten- und Vermessungswesen *see* Nachrichten aus dem Karten- und Vermessungswesen. Reihe I: Originalbeitraege *546*
Nachrichten aus dem Karten- und Vermessungswesen. Reihe I: Originalbeitraege (GW ISSN 0469-4236) *546*
Nachrichten aus dem Karten- und Vermessungswesen. Reihe II: Uebersetzungen (GW ISSN 0469-4244) *546*
Nachrichten aus Niedersachsens Urgeschichte (GW ISSN 0342-1406) *90*
Nachrichtentechnik (US ISSN 0342-9148) *646*
Nacional Financiera. Annual Report (MX ISSN 0185-4968) *230*
Nacton Newsletter *see* Share It *881*
Nadezhda (GW) *971*
Nag Hammadi Studies (NE) *971*
Nagoya City University. Faculty of Pharmaceutical Science. Annual Report/Nagoya-Shiritsu Daigaku Yakugakubu Kenkyu Nempo (JA ISSN 0369-5611) *324, 872*
Nagoya Daigaku Kankyo Igaku Kenkyusho Nenpo *see* Nagoya University. Research Institute of Environmental Medicine. Annual Report *764*
Nagoya Daigaku Kogakubu Jido Seigyo Seigyo *see* Nagoya University. Faculty of Engineering. Automatic Control Laboratory. Research Reports *355*
Nagoya Daigaku Kuden Kenkyusho Hokoku *see* Nagoya University. Research Institute of Atmospherics. Proceedings *806*
Nagoya Daigaku Purazuma Kenkyusho Nenpo *see* Nagoya University. Institute of Plasma Physics. Annual Review *889*
Nagoya Port Statistics Annual/ Nagoyako Tokei Nenpo (JA ISSN 0469-4783) *1086*
Nagoya-Shiritsu Daigaku Yakugakubu Kenkyu Nempo *see* Nagoya City University. Faculty of Pharmaceutical Science. Annual Report *872*

Nagoya University. Cosmic-Ray Research Laboratory. Proceedings/ Meidai Uchusen Kenkyushitsu Kiji (JA ISSN 0910-0717) *889*
Nagoya University. Cosmic-Ray Research Laboratory. Report (JA) *889*
Nagoya University. Faculty of Engineering. Automatic Control Laboratory. Research Reports/ Nagoya Daigaku Kogakubu Jido Seigyo (JA ISSN 0374-4329) *355*
Nagoya University. Institute of Plasma Physics. Annual Review/Nagoya Daigaku Purazuma Kenkyusho Nenpo (JA ISSN 0547-1567) *889*
Nagoya University. Institute of Plasma Physics. Technical Reports (JA) *889*
Nagoya University. Research Institute of Atmospherics. Proceedings/ Nagoya Daigaku Kuden Kenkyusho Hokoku (JA ISSN 0077-264X) *806*
Nagoya University. Research Institute of Environmental Medicine. Annual Report/Nagoya Daigaku Kankyo Igaku Kenkyusho Nenpo (JA ISSN 0469-4759) *498, 764*
Nagoya University. Water Research Institute. Annual Report/Suiken Kagaku Kenkyujo Nenpo (JA) *1125*
Nagoyako Tokei Nenpo *see* Nagoya Port Statistics Annual *1086*
Nagyuzemi Gazdalkodas Kerdesei (HU ISSN 0077-2658) *31*
Nairobi Airport. Annual Report (KE ISSN 0077-2666) *1089*
Namib Desert Research Station. Scientific Papers *see* Madoqua *994*
Namibia. State Museum. Memoir *see* Cimbebasia *71*
Namibia Studies Series (UN) *1010*
Namn och Bygd (SW ISSN 0077-2704) *546*
Nana No Pasuporto/Southern Africa Passport (SA) *1114*
Nanzan Institute for Religion and Culture. Bulletin (JA ISSN 0386-720X) *852, 971*
Napao: A Saskatchewan Anthropology Journal *see* Western Canadian Anthropologist *78*
Naprstkovo Muzeum Asijskych, Africkych a Americkych Kultur. Annals (CS ISSN 0554-9256) *74, 516*
Nara Joshidaigaku Hoken Senta Nenpo *see* Nara Women's University. Health Administration Center. Archives of Health Care *955*
Nara Women's University. Health Administration Center. Archives of Health Care/Nara Joshidaigaku Hoken Senta Nenpo (JA ISSN 0287-9549) *427, 955*
Narcotics and Drug Abuse A-Z (US ISSN 0094-3991) *377*
Nargun (AT) *392*
Narinkka (FI ISSN 0355-9106) *591*
Narodna Biblioteka Kiril i Metodii. Izvestiya (BU ISSN 0584-0007) *591*
Narodna in Univerzitetna Knjiznica. Zbornik (YU ISSN 0350-3569) *681*
Narodna Umjetnost (YU ISSN 0547-2504) *504, 516*
Narodni Technicke Muzeum. Bibliografie. Pramery (CS) *1072*
Narodni Technicke Muzeum. Catalogues of Collections (CS) *829, 1070*
Narodni Technicke Muzeum. Rozpravy (CS ISSN 0035-9378) *559, 1070*
Narodnoe Khozyaistvo Altaiskogo Kraya (UR) *1059*
Naropa Institute Journal of Psychology (US ISSN 0271-7557) *935*
Narradores de Arca (UY ISSN 0077-2801) *728*
Narragansett Marine Laboratory. Technical Reports *see* University of Rhode Island. Graduate School of Oceanography. Marine Technical Reports *408*
Narrativa Latinoamericana (UY ISSN 0077-2844) *607, 728*
Naryzy z Istoriyi Pryrodoznavstva i Tekhniky *see* Ocherki po Istorii Estestvoznaniya i Tekhniki *559*
Al-Nashra *see* Al-Arabiyya *691*

Nasionale Instituut vir Vervoer- en Padnavorsing. Gebruikershandboeke vir Rekenaarprogramme *see* National Institute for Transport and Road Research. User Manuals for Computer Programs *1093*
Nasionale Instituut vir Vervoer- en Padnavorsing. Jaarverslag *see* National Institute for Transport and Road Research. Annual Report *1096*
Nasionale Instituut vir Vervoer- en Padnavorsing. Tegniese Metodes vir Hoofwee *see* National Institute for Transport and Road Research. Technical Methods for Highways *1097*
Nasionale Instituut vir Vervoer- en Padnavorsing. Tegniese Riglyne vir Hoofwee *see* National Institute for Transport and Road Research. Technical Recommendations for Highways *1097*
Nasionale Instituut vir Vervoer- en Padnavorsing. Vervoerstatistiek *see* National Institute for Transport and Road Research. Transport Statistics *1086*
Nasionale Museum Bloemfontein. Navorsinge *see* National Museum, Bloemfontein. Researche *995*
Nassau County Historical Society Journal (US) *607*
Nassau Review (US ISSN 0077-2879) *728*
Nassauische Annalen (GW ISSN 0077-2887) *591*
Nat Ed Newsletter (NZ ISSN 0111-395X) *416*
Natal Chamber of Industries. Annual Report *see* Natal Chamber of Industries. Yearbook & Directory *314*
Natal Chamber of Industries. Yearbook & Directory (SA) *314*
Natal Museum. Annals/Annale van die Natalse Museum (SA ISSN 0304-0798) *176*
Natal University Law and Society Review (SA) *660*
Natal University Law Review *see* Natal University Law and Society Review *660*
Natalia (SA ISSN 0085-3674) *566*
Nathaniel Hawthorne Journal (US ISSN 0073-1382) *728*
Nation Armee (FR) *812*
Nation Economic Survey (KE) *247*
Nationaal Centrum voor Oudheidkundige Navorsingen in Belgie. Oudheidkundige Repertoria. Reeks A: Bibliografische Repertoria *see* Centre National de Recherches Archeologiques en Belgique. Repertoires Archeologiques. Serie A: Repertoires Bibliographiques *84*
Nationaal Instituut voor de Extractiebedrijven. Jaarbericht *see* Institut National des Industries Extractives. Rapport Annuel *817*
National Academy of Arbitrators. Annual Meeting. Proceedings (US) *274*
National Academy of Sciences. Biographical Memoirs (US ISSN 0077-2933) *135, 995*
National Accounts and Balance of Payments of Rhodesia *see* National Accounts of Rhodesia *297*
National Accounts of Botswana (BS ISSN 0302-2056) *277*
National Accounts of Rhodesia (RH) *258, 297*
National Accounts of the Maltese Islands (MM ISSN 0077-295X) *297*
National Aeronautical Laboratory. Annual Report (II ISSN 0077-2976) *20*
National Aeronautical Laboratory. Case Studies (II) *20*
National Aeronautical Laboratory. Selected Abstracts from Russian and Other Foreign Scientific Literature (II) *9, 20*
National Aeronautical Laboratory. Technical Note (II ISSN 0077-300X) *20*

National Aeronautical Laboratory Catalogue of N A L Technical Translations *see* Catalogue of N A L Technical Translations *18*
National Aeronautics and Space Administration. Technical Memorandum (US ISSN 0499-9320) *20*
National Aeronautics and Space Administration. Technical Notes (US ISSN 0077-3131) *20*
National Aeronautics and Space Administration. Technical Reports (US ISSN 0077-314X) *20*
National Aeronautics and Space Administration. Technical Translations (US ISSN 0077-3158) *20*
National Aerospace Electronics Conference. Proceedings *see* I E E E National Aerospace and Electronics Conference. Proceedings *19*
National Aerospace Meeting. Proceedings *see* Institute of Navigation. National Technical Meeting Proceedings *19*
National Agricultural Plastics Association. Proceedings (US) *31, 900*
National Agricultural Research Programme. Project Report (TZ) *57*
National Agricultural Research Programme. Summary of Programmes *see* National Agricultural Research Programme. Project Report *57*
National Agricultural Society of Ceylon. Journal *see* National Agricultural Society of Sri Lanka. Journal *31*
National Agricultural Society of Sri Lanka. Journal (CE) *31*
National Air Monitoring Program Air Quality and Emissions Trends. Report *see* National Air Quality and Emissions Trends Report *498*
National Air Quality and Emissions Trends Report (US) *498*
National Airspace System Plan: Facilities, Equipment and Associated Development (US) *1089*
National and Local Government Officers Association Annual Report *see* N A L G O Annual Report *944*
National Archives of Malaysia. Annual Report/Arkib Negara Malaysia. Laporan Tahunan (MY ISSN 0076-3381) *570*
National Archives of Zambia. Annual Report (ZA ISSN 0084-4942) *566, 682*
National Archives of Zambia. Calendars of the District Notebooks (ZA) *566, 944*
National Archives of Zambia. Information (ZA) *566*
National Archives of Zambia. National Archives Occasional Paper (ZA) *566*
National Art Education Association. Research Monograph (US ISSN 0077-3174) *108, 448*
National Assembly Guidebook (CN) *951*
National Assessment of Educational Progress. Assessment Reports (US) *448*
National Association for Business Teacher Education Review *see* N A B T E Review *437*
National Association for Foreign Student Affairs Directory *see* N A F S A Directory *441*
National Association for Physical Education for College Women *see* N A P E H E Proceedings *448*
National Association for Physical Education in Higher Education Proceedings *see* N A P E H E Proceedings *448*
National Association for the Advancement of Colored People Annual Report *see* N A A C P Annual Report *1028*
National Association for the Blind. Annual Report. (II) *180*
National Association of Academies of Science. Directory and Proceedings (US ISSN 0739-361X) *995*

National Association of Almshouses. Yearbook and Statement of Accounts(UK) *1019*

National Association of Animal Breeders. Annual Proceedings (US ISSN 0077-3255) *67*

National Association of Boards of Pharmacy. Proceedings (US ISSN 0077-3263) *872*

National Association of Chain Drug Stores Lilly Digest see N.A.C.D.S. Lilly Digest *1158*

National Association of College Admissions Counselors. Membership Directory (US ISSN 0090-3965) *437*

National Association of College-University Food Services Journal see N A C U F S Journal *520*

National Association of Fire Officers Yearbook see N A F O Yearbook *507*

National Association of Fleet Administrators, Inc. Annual Reference Book see N A F A Annual Reference Book *1092*

National Association of Independent Schools. Annual Report (US ISSN 0550-7421) *417*

National Association of Intercollegiate Athletics Handbook see N A I A Handbook *1034*

National Association of Intercollegiate Athletics Official Records Book see N A I A Official Records Book *1034*

National Association of Metal Finishers Accounting Manual see N A M F Accounting Manual *222*

National Association of Metal Finishers Management Manual see N A M F Management Manual *799*

National Association of Mutual Banks of the United States. Report see National Council of Savings Institutions. Annual Report of the President *230*

National Association of Pension Funds. Annual Survey (UK ISSN 0309-0078) *552*

National Association of Pension Funds. Year Book (UK) *552*

National Association of Plumbing, Heating and Mechanical Services Contractors Yearbook (UK ISSN 0141-0288) *554*

National Association of Real Estate Investment Trusts Fact Book see R.E.I.T. Fact Book *966*

National Association of Regional Councils. Directory see Directory of Regional Councils *941*

National Association of Regulatory Utility Commissioners. Annual Report on Utility and Carrier Regulation (US) *944*

National Association of Regulatory Utility Commissioners. Proceedings (US ISSN 0077-3387) *1095*

National Association of Retail Dealers of America Costs of Doing Business Survey see N A R D A's Costs of Doing Business Survey *285*

National Association of Retail Druggists Almanac and Health Guide see N A R D Almanac and Health Guide *285*

National Association of Scaffolding Contractors Year Book (UK) *186*

National Association of Schools of Art. Directory. see National Association of Schools of Art and Design. Directory *430*

National Association of Schools of Art and Design. Directory. (US) *108, 430*

National Association of Schools of Music. Directory (US ISSN 0547-4175) *448, 839*

National Association of Schools of Music. Handbook (US ISSN 0164-2847) *448, 839*

National Association of Schools of Music. Proceedings of the Annual Meeting (US ISSN 0077-3409) *839*

National Association of State Universities and Land-Grant Colleges. Appropriations of State Tax Funds for Higher Education (US ISSN 0077-3425) *437*

National Association of State Universities and Land-Grant Colleges. Proceedings (US ISSN 0077-3433) *437*

National Association of Suggestion Systems. Statistical Report (US ISSN 0077-3441) *286*

National Association of Testing Authorities Annual Directory see N.A.T.A. Annual Directory *489*

National Association of Theatre Nurses. Annual Congress Handbook (UK) *784, 1077*

National Association of Training Schools and Juvenile Agencies. Proceedings (US ISSN 0077-3476) *371, 445*

National Association of Waste Disposal Contractors. Trade Directory (UK) *314, 955*

National Association of Women Artists. Annual Exhibition Catalog (US) *108*

National Auricula & Primula Society (Northern) Year Book (UK ISSN 0027-8726) *533*

National Automobile Association Where to Stay Book see N A A Where to Stay Book *620*

National Awami Party of Bangladesh (in Great Britain). Bulletin (UK) *907*

National Bank of Commerce. Annual Report and Accounts (TZ) *230*

National Bank of Ethiopia. Annual Report (ET) *247*

National Bank of Ethiopia. Local Prices(ET ISSN 0077-3506) *1159*

National Bank of Greece. Annual Report/Ethnike Trapeza tes Hellados. Apologismos (GR ISSN 0077-3514) *230*

National Bank of Kuwait. Annual Report of the Board of Directors and Accounts (KU) *230*

National Bank of Liberia. Annual Report (LB) *230*

National Bank of Pakistan. Annual Report (PK) *230*

National Bank of Pakistan. Report and Statement of Accounts (PK ISSN 0077-3522) *230*

National Bank of Yugoslavia. Annual Report (YU ISSN 0077-2798) *230, 247*

National Bar Examination Digest (US ISSN 0098-2857) *660*

National Basic Intelligence Factbook see World Factbook *920*

National Beverage Marketing Directory (Year) (US ISSN 0160-9580) *120*

National Bible Society of Scotland. Annual Report (UK ISSN 0077-3557) *979*

National Bibliography of Zambia (ZA) *129*

National Botanic Gardens. Contributions see Glasra *157*

National Botanic Gardens. Report (SA) *159*

National Botanic Gardens, Lucknow. Bulletin see National Botanical Research Institute, Lucknow. Bulletin *159*

National Botanic Gardens, Lucknow. Progress Report (II) *159*

National Botanic Gardens, Lucknow. Progress Report see National Botanic Gardens, Lucknow. Progress Report *159*

National Botanic Gardens of South Africa. Report see National Botanic Gardens. Report *159*

National Botanical Research Institute, Lucknow. Bulletin (II ISSN 0076-1419) *159*

National Building Code/National Fire Code News see N B C/N F C News *186*

National Building Research Institute. Complete List of N B R I Publications (SA ISSN 0077-3581) *189*

National Buildings Organisation Abstracts see N B O Abstracts *477*

National Bureau of Economic Research. Working Paper (US) *197*

National Business Education Yearbook (US ISSN 0547-4728) *286, 448*

National Cancer Center. Annual Report/Kokuritsu Gan Senta Nenpo (JA) *775*

National Cancer Center. Collected Papers/Kokuritsu Gan Senta, Tokyo. Collected Papers (JA ISSN 0077-3662) *775*

National Cancer Institute. Annual Report (US ISSN 0195-8690) *775*

National Cancer Institute Fact Book see N C I Fact Book *775*

National Cancer Institute of Canada. Annual Report (CN ISSN 0077-3689) *776*

National Carousel Association. Carousel Archives (US) *79, 108*

National Carousel Association. Carousel Census see National Carousel Association. Carousel Archives *108*

National Catalogue of Heating and Air Conditioning see Catalogue National du Genie Climatique-Chauffage et Conditionnement d'Air *553*

National Catholic Almanac see Catholic Almanac *981*

National Catholic Educational Association Ganley's Catholic Schools in America see N C E A Ganley's Catholic Schools in America *430*

National Center for Audio Tapes. Catalog see National Center for Audio Tapes Archive. Catalog *448*

National Center for Audio Tapes Archive. Catalog (US) *344, 448*

National Center for State Courts. Publications (US) *660*

National Center for the Study of Collective Bargaining in Higher Education and the Professions. Annual Conference Proceedings (US ISSN 0742-3667) *437, 649*

National Centre for Occupational Health. Annual Report (SA ISSN 0374-9800) *636, 793*

National Children's Bureau. Annual Review (UK ISSN 0302-1998) *334*

National Chrysanthemum Society Yearbook see N.C.S. Yearbook *533*

National Civic Council. Facts (AT ISSN 0085-3682) *907*

National Civil Service League. Annual Report (US ISSN 0077-3735) *274, 944*

National Coal Board. Report and Accounts (UK ISSN 0077-3786) *818*

National Coil Coaters Association. Product Capability Directory (US) *314*

National Collegiate Athletic Association. Annual Reports. (US ISSN 0077-3794) *1034*

National Collegiate Athletic Association. Convention Proceedings(US ISSN 0077-3808) *1034*

National Collegiate Athletic Association. Manual (US ISSN 0077-3816) *1034*

National Collegiate Athletic Association. Proceedings of the Special Convention (US ISSN 0094-4459) *1034*

National Collegiate Athletic Association Baseball Rules see N C A A Baseball Rules *1039*

National Collegiate Athletic Association Basketball see N C A A Basketball *1039*

National Collegiate Athletic Association Directory see N C A A Directory *1034*

National Collegiate Athletic Association Football see N C A A Football *1039*

National Collegiate Athletic Association Football Rules & Interpretations (US ISSN 0736-5160) *1039*

National Collegiate Athletic Association Men's & Women's Cross Country and Track & Field Rules see N C A A Men's & Women's Cross Country and Track & Field Rules *1046*

National Collegiate Athletic Association Men's & Women's Swimming and Diving Rules see N C A A Men's & Women's Swimming and Diving Rules *1034*

National Collegiate Athletic Association Men's Basketball Rules and Interpretations see N C A A Men's Basketball Rules and Interpretations *1039*

National Collegiate Athletic Association Men's Ice Hockey Rules and Interpretations see N C A A Men's Ice Hockey Rules and Interpretations *1034*

National Collegiate Athletic Association Men's Illustrated Basketball Rules see N C A A Men's Illustrated Basketball Rules *1039*

National Collegiate Athletic Association Men's Lacrosse Rules see N C A A Men's Lacrosse Rules *1039*

National Collegiate Athletic Association Men's Soccer Rules see N C A A Men's Soccer Rules *1039*

National Collegiate Athletic Association Men's Water Polo Rules see N C A A Men's Water Polo Rules *1034*

National Collegiate Athletic Association Wrestling Rules (US ISSN 0736-511X) *1034*

National Collegiate Championships (US ISSN 0190-4329) *1034*

National Colloquium on Oral History. Proceedings see Oral History Review *559*

National Commercial & Development Bank. Annual Report and Financial Statements (DQ) *230*

National Committee on Science and Technology. Research and Development Statistics see India. Department of Science and Technology. Research and Development Statistics *1004*

National Communications Forum. Proceedings (US) *457*

National Computer Conference (Proceedings) (US) *353*

National Computer Conference and Exposition (Proceedings) see National Computer Conference (Proceedings) *353*

National Conference of Commissioners on Uniform State Laws. Handbook and Proceedings (US) *660*

National Conference of South African Surveyors. Proceedings see Conference of South African Surveyors. Proceedings *480*

National Conference of State Social Security Administrators. Proceedings (US) *1019*

National Conference on Artificial Intelligence. Proceedings (US) *355*

National Conference on Fluid Power. Proceedings (US ISSN 0160-8428) *490, 492*

National Conference on Industrial Hydraulics see National Conference on Fluid Power. Proceedings *490*

National Conference on Piano Pedagogy. Proceedings (US) *839*

National Conference on Safety. Proceedings (II) *955*

National Conference on Software Engineering. Proceedings see International Conference on Software Engineering. Proceedings *363*

National Conference on Weights and Measures. Report (US ISSN 0077-3964) *809*

National Convention of Electrical and Electronics Engineers in Israel. Proceedings see Convention of Electrical and Electronics Engineers in Israel. Proceedings *452*

National Cooperative Highway Research Program Reports (US ISSN 0077-5614) *482, 1096*

National Cooperative Highway Research Program Research Results Digest (US ISSN 0547-5554) *1082*

National Cooperative Highway Research Program Synthesis of Highway Practice (US ISSN 0547-5570) *482, 1096*

National Cooperative Transit Research and Development Program. Miscellaneous Publications (US) *1082*
National Cooperative Transit Research and Development Program. Research Results Digest (US) *1082*
National Cooperative Transit Research and Development Program. Summary of Progress *see* National Cooperative Transit Research & Development Program. Summary of Progress Through (Year) *1082*
National Cooperative Transit Research & Development Program. Summary of Progress Through (Year) (US) *1082*
National Cooperative Transit Research and Development Program Report (US ISSN 0732-4839) *1082*
National Cooperative Transit Research and Development Program Synthesis of Transit Practice (US ISSN 0732-1856) *1082*
National Cottonseed Products Association. Trading Rules (US ISSN 0077-4022) *479, 1074*
National Council for Cement and Building Materials. Annual Report (II) *186*
National Council for Geographic Education. Pacesetter Series (US) *546*
National Council for Geographic Education. Topics in Geography (US) *448, 546*
National Council for Geographic Education. Yearbook *see* National Council for Geographic Education. Pacesetter Series *546*
National Council for Science & Technology. Directory (NP) *682*
National Council for Scientific Research. Annual Report (LE) *437*
National Council for Special Education. Conference Reports (UK) *448*
National Council for Special Education. Occasional Publications (UK) *445*
National Council for the Social Studies. Bulletins (US ISSN 0077-4049) *1010*
National Council for the Social Studies. How to Do It Series (US ISSN 0085-3712) *1010*
National Council for Voluntary Organizations. Annual Report (UK) *1019*
National Council of Churches, Bangladesh. Annual Report (BG) *984*
National Council of Engineering Examiners. Proceedings (US ISSN 0077-4081) *473*
National Council of Physical Distribution Management. Annual Conference Proceedings. *see* N C P D M Annual Conference Proceedings *285*
National Council of Physical Distribution Management Annual Conference Proceedings *see* N C P D M Annual Conference Proceedings *285*
National Council of Savings Institutions. Annual Report of the President (US) *230*
National Council of Savings Institutions Directory (US) *231*
National Council of Social Service. Annual Report *see* National Council for Voluntary Organizations. Annual Report *1019*
National Council of Teachers of Mathematics. Professional Reference Series (US) *417, 751*
National Council of Teachers of Mathematics. Yearbook (US ISSN 0077-4103) *417, 751*
National Council of the Churches of Christ in the U.S.A. Triennial Report(US) *979*
National Council of the Paper Industry for Air and Stream Improvement. Technical Bulletin (US) *498*
National Council on Radiation Protection and Measurements. Proceedings of the Annual Meeting (US ISSN 0195-5740) *955*

National Council on Radiation Protection and Measurements Commentary *see* N C R P Commentary *955*
National Council on Radiation Protection and Measurements Report *see* N C R P Report *955*
National Council on Radiation Protection and Measurements Statements *see* N C R P Statements *792*
National Council on Radiation Protection and Measurements Symposium Proceedings *see* N C R P Symposium Proceedings *955*
National Crop Protection Center Annual Report *see* N C P C Annual Report *57*
National Cutting Horse Association. Rule Book (US) *1043*
National Dahlia Society Annual (UK ISSN 0077-4189) *533*
National Dairy Research Institute. Annual Report (II ISSN 0301-8407) *62*
National Data Book *see* Foundation Center National Data Book *1022*
National Deaf Children's Society. Year Book and Annual Accounts (UK) *334, 375*
National Dean's List (US ISSN 0191-8133) *437*
National Development Bank. Annual Report and Accounts (SL) *231*
National Die Casting Congress. Transactions *see* S D C E International Die Casting Congress. Transactions *746*
National Directory of Arts and Education Support by Business Corporations (US) *108*
National Directory of Arts Support by Business Corporations *see* National Directory of Arts and Education Support by Business Corporations *108*
National Directory of Arts Support by Private Foundations (US) *108*
National Directory of Budget Motels (US) *620*
National Directory of Bulletin Board Systems (US ISSN 0884-9536) *682*
National Directory of Catholic Higher Education (US) *430, 983*
National Directory of Children & Youth Services (US ISSN 0190-7476) *1159*
National Directory of College Athletics (Men's Edition) (US ISSN 0547-616X) *1034*
National Directory of College Athletics (Women) (US) *1034*
National Directory of Corporate Public Affairs (US) *197, 907*
National Directory of Drug Abuse and Alcoholism Treatment and Prevention Programs (US) *377*
National Directory of Educational Programs in Gerontology (US ISSN 0148-4508) *430, 437, 552, 848*
National Directory of Free Tourist Attractions (US) *1114*
National Directory of Free Vacation and Travel Information *see* Directory of Free Vacation & Travel Information *1107*
National Directory of Grants and Aid to Individuals in the Arts, International (US) *108*
National Directory of Internships, Residencies & Registrarships (AT ISSN 0155-9567) *618, 848*
National Directory of Landscape Architecture Firms (US ISSN 0272-247X) *98*
National Directory of Latin Americanists (US) *504*
National Directory of Law Enforcement Administrators and Correctional Agencies *see* National Directory of Law Enforcement Administrators and Correctional Institutions *371*
National Directory of Law Enforcement Administrators and Correctional Institutions (US) *371*
National Directory of Low-Cost Tourist Attractions (US) *1114*
National Directory of Minority-Owned Business Firms (US) *301, 314*

National Directory of Newsletters and Reporting Services *see* National Newsletters, Directory and Reporting Services *962*
National Directory of Safety Consultants (US) *473*
National Directory of State Agencies (US ISSN 0095-3113) *314, 907*
National Directory of Theme Parks and Amusement Areas (US) *1114*
National Directory of Women's Athletics *see* National Directory of College Athletics (Women) *1034*
National Distribution Directory of Local Cartage-Short Haul Carriers Warehousing *see* Warehousing/Distribution Directory *1105*
National Economic and Development Authority Statistical Yearbook of the Philippines *see* N E D A Statistical Yearbook of the Philippines *213*
National Education Association of the United States. Proceedings of the Annual Meeting *see* National Education Association of the United States. Proceedings of the Representative Assembly *417*
National Education Association of the United States. Proceedings of the Representative Assembly (US) *417*
National Electronic Injury Surveillance System Data Highlights *see* N E I S S Data Highlights *955*
National Electronics Conference National Communications Forum. Proceedings *see* National Communications Forum. Proceedings *457*
National Electronics Council. Review *see* National Electronics Review *457*
National Electronics Review (UK ISSN 0305-2257) *457*
National Employment Listing Service for the Criminal Justice System. Police Employment Guide (US ISSN 0194-0813) *371, 848*
National Employment Listing Service for the Criminal Justice System. Special Edition: Education Opportunities (US ISSN 0194-0805) *371, 848*
National Endowment for the Arts. Guide to Programs *see* Guide to National Endowment for the Arts *105*
National Endowment for the Humanities. Annual Report (US ISSN 0083-2111) *631*
National Equine (and Smaller Animals) Defence League. Annual Report (UK ISSN 0077-4448) *868*
National Fact Book of Savings Banking *see* National Fact Book of Savings Institutions *231*
National Fact Book of Savings Institutions (US ISSN 8756-9043) *231*
National Faculty Directory (US ISSN 0077-4472) *443*
National Family Planning and Population Survey in Singapore. Report (SI) *179*
National Farmers' Union Handbook (UK) *32*
National Federation Handbook (US) *1035*
National Federation of Building Trades Employers' North Western Region Year Book and Directory (UK) *186*
National Federation of Fruit and Potato Trades. Annual Handbook and List of Members (UK) *32*
National Federation of Painting and Decorating Contractors Year Book (UK) *643*
National Federation of Plastering Contractors. Year Book (UK ISSN 0077-4480) *186*
National Federation of Roofing Contractors Yearbook *see* N F R C Yearbook *186*
National Federation of State High School Associations. Soccer Rules *see* Soccer Rulebook *1040*
National Federation of State High School Associations. Softball Rules *see* Softball Rule Book *1040*

National Fertilizer Development Center. Annual Report *see* Progress (Muscle Shoals) *59*
National Finances: An Analysis of the Revenues and Expenditures of the Government of Canada (CN ISSN 0077-4529) *297*
National Fire Codes *see* National Fire Protection Association. National Fire Codes *507*
National Fire Protection Association. National Fire Codes (US ISSN 0077-4545) *507*
National Fire Protection Association. National Fire Codes. Supplement (US) *507*
National Fisheries University of Pusan. Institute of Marine Sciences. Contributions (KO) *144, 324, 511*
National Fisheries University of Pusan. Institute of Marine Sciences. Publications *see* National Fisheries University of Pusan. Institute of Marine Sciences. Contributions *144*
National Five Digit Zip Code and Post Office Directory (US ISSN 0731-9185) *346*
National Fluid Power Association Directory and Member Guide *see* N F P A Directory and Member Guide *490*
National Food Research Institute. Report (JA ISSN 0301-9780) *32, 520*
National Football League. Record Manual (US ISSN 0077-4588) *1159*
National Formulary *see* United States Pharmacopeia - National Formulary *873*
National Foundation for Advancement in the Arts. Annual Report (US) *108, 375, 728*
National Free Library of Rhodesia. Annual Report *see* National Free Library of Zimbabwe. Annual Report *682*
National Free Library of Zimbabwe. Annual Report (RH) *682*
National Free Library Service. Annual Report *see* National Free Library of Zimbabwe. Annual Report *682*
National Fresh Produce Market, Johannesburg. Annual Report of the Director (SA) *240*
National Fresh Produce Market, Johannesburg. Annual Trading Results/Jaarliske Handelsyfers (SA) *48*
National Frozen Food Association Directory (US) *520*
National Gallery, London. Technical Bulletin (UK ISSN 0140-7430) *108, 829*
National Gallery of Art. Annual Report(US ISSN 0091-7222) *108*
National Gallery of Canada. Annual Review *see* Canada. National Museums of Canada. Annual Bulletin *827*
National Gallery of Canada. Bulletin *see* Canada. National Museums of Canada. Annual Bulletin *827*
National Gallery of Zimbabwe. Annual Report and Balance Sheet and Income and Expenditure Account (RH) *829*
National Gallery of Zimbabwe-Rhodesia. Annual Report and Balance Sheet and Income and Expenditure Account *see* National Gallery of Zimbabwe. Annual Report and Balance Sheet and Income and Expenditure Account *829*
National Gardening Survey (Year) (US) *533*
National Geographer (II ISSN 0470-0929) *546*
National Geographic Books (Series) (US ISSN 0077-4618) *546*
National Geographic Society. Special Publications Series *see* National Geographic Books (Series) *546*
National Geophysical Research Institute. Publications (II ISSN 0073-4144) *107*
National Guard Almanac (US ISSN 0363-8618) *812*

National Guide to Credit Recommendations for Noncollegiate Courses see National Guide to Educational Credit for Training Programs 443

National Guide to Educational Credit for Training Programs (US) 443

National Guild of Catholic Psychiatrists. Bulletin (US ISSN 0547-7115) 790, 935, 983

National Guild of Piano Teachers. Guild Syllabus (US ISSN 0077-4642) 839

National Hardwood Lumber Association Yearbook (US) 530

National Health and Medical Council. Medical Research (AT ISSN 0811-6199) 764

National Health Care Expenditures Study. Data Preview (US) 955

National Health Practitioner Program Profile see Physician Assistant Programs, A National Directory 765

National Heart Foundation of Australia. Research-In-Progress (AT ISSN 0077-4685) 777

National Heart News (AT) 764, 777

National Hereford Hog Record Association. Annual Newsletter (US) 67

National High School Sports Record Book (US) 1035

National Hockey League. Guide (CN) 1039

National Hockey League. Official Rule Book (CN) 1035

National Housing and Town Planning Council. Conference and Exhibition Guide (UK) 624

National Housing and Town Planning Council. Handbook and Year Book (UK ISSN 0077-4707) 624

National Hurricane Operations Plan see U.S. National Oceanic and Atmospheric Administration. Interdepartmental Committee for Meteorological Services and Supporting Research. National Hurricane Operations Plan 807

National Hydro Electric Power Corporation. Annual Report (II) 457

National Ice Cream Retailers Association. Yearbook (US) 285

National Income and Product Accounts of the United States: Statistical Tables (US ISSN 0361-3895) 213

National Income of Iran (IR ISSN 0572-5941) 247

National Income of Thailand (TH) 213

National Income Statistics of Thailand see National Income of Thailand 213

National Indian Council on Aging (US) 504, 552

National Indian Law Library. Catalogue(US) 506

National Industrial Research Institute. Report (KO) 473, 1070

National Information Center for Educational Media Audiocassette Finder see Audiocassette Finder 422

National Information Center for Educational Media Index to Educational Slides see N I C E M Index to Educational Slides 1159

National Information Center for Educational Media Index to Producers and Distributors see N I C E M Index to Producers and Distributors 826

National Information Center for Educational Media Index to 35mm Educational Filmstrips see N I C E M Index to 35mm Educational Filmstrips 424

National Information Center for Educational Media Science and Computer Literacy Audiovisuals see Science and Computer Literacy Audiovisuals 361

National Information Center for Educational Media Social Studies Audiovisuals: A Teacher's Sourcebook see Social Studies Audiovisuals: A Teacher's Sourcebook 449

National Information Center for Educational Media Vocational and Technical Audiovisuals: A Teacher's Sourcebook see Vocational and Technical Audiovisuals: A Teacher's Sourcebook 431

National Information Center for Educational Media Wellness Media: An Audiovisual Sourcebook see Wellness Media: An Audiovisual Sourcebook 886

National Institute for Architectural Education. Bulletin see National Institute for Architectural Education. Yearbook 98

National Institute for Architectural Education. Yearbook (US ISSN 0077-474X) 98

National Institute for Educational Research. Research Bulletin (JA ISSN 0085-378X) 417

National Institute for Leprosy Research. Annual Report/Kokuritsu Tama Kenkyusho Nenpo (JA ISSN 0454-2029) 778

National Institute for Medical Research. Report (UK ISSN 0141-2116) 764

National Institute for Occupational Diseases. Annual Report see National Centre for Occupational Health. Annual Report 636

National Institute for Road Research. Annual Report see National Institute for Transport and Road Research. Annual Report 1096

National Institute for Social Work Training Series see National Institute Social Services Library 1019

National Institute for Transport and Road Research. Annual Report/ Nasionale Instituut vir Vervoer- en Padnavorsing. Jaarverslag (SA ISSN 0379-6124) 482, 1082, 1096

National Institute for Transport and Road Research. Bulletins (SA) 1096

National Institute for Transport and Road Research. P A D Series (SA) 1096

National Institute for Transport and Road Research. Road Statistics see National Institute for Transport and Road Research. Transport Statistics 1086

National Institute for Transport and Road Research. Technical Methods for Highways/Nasionale Instituut vir Vervoer- en Padnavorsing. Tegniese Metodes vir Hoofwee (SA) 1097

National Institute for Transport and Road Research. Technical Recommendations for Highways/ Nasionale Instituut vir Vervoer- en Padnavorsing. Tegniese Riglyne vir Hoofwee (SA) 1097

National Institute for Transport and Road Research. Transport Statistics/ Nasionale Instituut vir Vervoer- en Padnavorsing. Vervoerstatistiek (SA) 1086

National Institute for Transport and Road Research. User Manuals for Computer Programs/Nasionale Instituut vir Vervoer- en Padnavorsing. Gebruikershandboeke vir Rekenaarprogramme (SA) 1093

National Institute for Water Research Information Sheet see N I W R Information Sheet 1125

National Institute of Agricultural Botany, Cambridge, England. Annual Report and Accounts (UK) 58

National Institute of Agricultural Botany, Cambridge, England. Annual Report of the Council and Accounts see National Institute of Agricultural Botany, Cambridge, England. Annual Report and Accounts 58

National Institute of Agricultural Botany, Cambridge, England. Farmers Leaflets (UK ISSN 0305-1277) 58

National Institute of Agricultural Botany, Cambridge, England. Journal(UK ISSN 0077-4790) 58

National Institute of Agricultural Botany, Cambridge, England. Technical Leaflets (UK ISSN 0140-4199) 58

National Institute of Agricultural Botany, Cambridge, England. Vegetable Growers Leaflets (UK ISSN 0470-1321) 58

National Institute of Agricultural Engineering. Divisional Notes see A F R C Institute of Engineering Research. Divisional Notes 51

National Institute of Agricultural Engineering. Translations see A F R C Institute of Engineering Research. Translations 51

National Institute of Agricultural Sciences, Tokyo. Bulletin. Series H (Farm Management, Land Utilization, Rural Life) (JA ISSN 0077-4863) 32

National Institute of Animal Industry, Chiba, Japan. see National Institute of Animal Industry, Ibaraki, Japan. Bulletin Summaries 67

National Institute of Animal Industry, Chiba, Japan. Annual Report see National Institute of Animal Industry, Ibaraki, Japan. Annual Report 67

National Institute of Animal Industry, Chiba, Japan. Bulletin. see National Institute of Animal Industry, Ibaraki, Japan. Bulletin 67

National Institute of Animal Industry, Ibaraki, Japan. Annual Report (JA ISSN 0289-4238) 67

National Institute of Animal Industry, Ibaraki, Japan. Bulletin/Chikusan Shikenjo, Ibaraki, Japan. Chikusan Shikenjo Kenkyu Hokoku. (JA) 67

National Institute of Animal Industry, Ibaraki, Japan. Bulletin Summaries. (JA) 67

National Institute of Compilation and Translation. Collected Papers on History and Art of China (CH) 108, 570

National Institute of Economic and Social Research. Annual Report (UK ISSN 0077-491X) 1010

National Institute of Economic and Social Research, London. Economic and Social Studies (UK ISSN 0070-8453) 197, 1010

National Institute of Economic and Social Research, London. Occasional Papers (UK ISSN 0077-4928) 197

National Institute of Genetics, Mishima, Japan. Annual Report/Kokuritsu Idengaku Kenkyusho, Mishima, Japan. Nenpo (JA ISSN 0077-4995) 167

National Institute of Health and Family Welfare Technical Reports see N I H F W Technical Reports 1019

National Institute of Hygienic Sciences. Bulletin/Eisei Shikenjo Hokoku (JA ISSN 0077-5002) 955

National Institute of Industrial Psychology Bulletin see N I I P Bulletin 1159

National Institute of Justice/N C J R S Document Retrieval Index (DRI) - Cumulative see N C J R S Document Retrieval Index 371

National Institute of Nutrition. Annual Report (II ISSN 0377-3744) 846

National Institute of Nutrition. Annual Report/Kokuritsu Eiyo Kenkyusho Hokoku (JA) 846

National Institute of Polar Research. Memoirs. Series A: Aeronomy. (JA ISSN 0386-5517) 392

National Institute of Polar Research. Memoirs. Series B: Meteorology. (JA ISSN 0386-5525) 806

National Institute of Polar Research. Memoirs. Series C: Earth Sciences. (JA ISSN 0386-5533) 380

National Institute of Polar Research. Memoirs. Series D: Oceanography (JA) 407

National Institute of Polar Research. Memoirs. Series E: Biology and Medical Science (JA ISSN 0386-5541) 144, 764

National Institute of Polar Research. Memoirs. Series F: Logistics. (JA ISSN 0386-555X) 995

National Institute of Polar Research. Memoirs. Special Issue. (JA ISSN 0386-0744) 380

National Institute of Sciences of India. Biographical Memoirs of Fellows see Indian National Science Academy. Biographical Memoirs of Fellows 134

National Institute of Sciences of India. Bulletin see Indian National Science Academy. Bulletin 992

National Institute of Sciences of India. Mathematical Tables see Indian National Science Academy. Mathematical Tables 749

National Institute of Sciences of India. N I S I Monographs see Indian National Science Academy. Monographs 992

National Institute of Sciences of India. Proceedings see Indian National Science Academy. Proceedings 992

National Institute of Sciences of India. Yearbook see Indian National Science Academy. Year Book 992

National Institute of Sciences of India, Calcutta. Year Book see Indian National Science Academy. Year Book 992

National Institute of Special Education. Bulletin/Kokuritsu Tokushu Kyoiku Sogo Kenkyujo Kenkyu Kiyo (JA ISSN 0387-3528) 445

National Institute Social Services Library (UK ISSN 0077-4774) 1019

National Instituut voor Kernfysica en Hoge-Energiefysica see N I K H E F. Annual Report 889

National Insurance Corporation of Tanzania. Annual Report and Accounts (TZ) 640

National Insurance Institute, Jerusalem. Annual Survey (IS) 642

National Insurance Institute, Jerusalem. Full Actuarial Report (IS ISSN 0075-1324) 640

National Insurance Institute, Jerusalem. Statistical Abstracts see National Insurance Institute, Jerusalem. Annual Survey 642

National/International Sculpture Conference. Proceedings (US ISSN 0363-5937) 108

National Investment Bank, Ghana. Annual Report (GH) 231

National Investment Bank, Ghana. Report of the Directors see National Investment Bank, Ghana. Annual Report 231

National Jail and Adult Detention Directory (US ISSN 0192-8228) 371

National Jeweler Annual Fashion Guide(US) 644

National Junior Horticultural Association. Newsletter (US ISSN 0077-5088) 533

National Kidney Foundation. Annual Report (US ISSN 0077-5096) 795

National Language Research Institute. Annual Report/Kokuritsu Kokugo Kenkyusho Nenpo (JA) 699

National Law Journal Index (US) 660

National League for Nursing. Associate Degree Education for Nursing see Associate Degree Education for Nursing 783

National League for Nursing. Baccalaureate Programs Accredited for Public Health Nursing (US) 1159

National League for Nursing. Baccalaureate Programs Accredited for Public Health Nursing Preparation see National League for Nursing. Baccalaureate Programs Accredited for Public Health Nursing 1159

National League of Cities. National Municipal Policy see National Municipal Policy 951

National Legal Aid and Defender Association Directory see Directory of Legal Aid and Defender Offices in the United States 655

National Library of Canada. Annual Report (CN ISSN 0078-7000) 682

National Library of Medicine. Audiovisuals Catalog (US ISSN 0149-9939) 764

National Library of Medicine. Current Catalog (US ISSN 0027-9641) 771

National Library of Medicine. Literature Search Series (US ISSN 0083-2251) 771
National Library of Medicine. Programs and Services (US ISSN 0093-0393) 682
National Library of Medicine Index of N L M Serial Titles see Index of N L M Serial Titles 1155
National Library Year-Book see Biblioteka Narodowa. Rocznik 674
National List of Advertisers (CN ISSN 0077-5177) 16
National Marine Manufacturers Association Certification Handbook see N M M A Certification Handbook 1042
National Maritime Board. (Great Britain) Year Book (UK ISSN 0077-5185) 1102
National Maritime Museum. Occasional Lectures Series (UK ISSN 0141-1268) 829, 1102
National Mass Retailing Institute Compensation in Mass Retailing, Salaries and Incentives see N M R I Compensation in Mass Retailing, Salaries and Incentives 274
National Mechanics see Mecanica Nacional 1092
National Medical and Dental Association. Bulletin (US ISSN 0027-9676) 764, 779
National Minority Business Directory see Try Us 200
National Motor Museum Pictorial Guide (UK) 1092
National Municipal Policy (US) 951
National Museum. Memoirs (SA ISSN 0374-9665) 90, 176, 857
National Museum, Bloemfontein. Memoirs (SA ISSN 0067-9194) 995
National Museum, Bloemfontein. Researche/Nasionale Museum Bloemfontein. Navorsinge (SA ISSN 0067-9208) 995
National Museum of Modern Art. Annual Report (JA) 829
National Museum of Natural Sciences. Syllogeus (CN ISSN 0704-576X) 995
National Museum of New Zealand. Bulletin (NZ ISSN 0110-9464) 829
National Museum of New Zealand. Miscellaneanous Series (NZ ISSN 0110-1447) 829
National Museum of New Zealand Records (NZ ISSN 0110-943X) 829
National Museum of Tanzania. Annual Report (TZ ISSN 0082-1675) 829
National Museum of the Philippines. Annual Report (PH ISSN 0076-3756) 829
National Museum of the Philippines. Monograph Series (PH ISSN 0076-3772) 74
National Museum of Victoria. Memoirs see Museum of Victoria. Memoirs 829
National Museum of Wales. Annual Report (UK) 829
National Museums and Monuments Administration. Occasional Papers. Series B: Natural Sciences see Smithersia 177
National Newsletters, Directory and Reporting Services (US) 962
National Newspaper Association National Directory of Weekly Newspapers see N N A National Directory of Weekly Newspapers 646
National Online Information Meeting. Proceedings see National Online Meeting. Proceedings 360
National Online Meeting. Proceedings (US) 360
National Opera Association. Membership Directory (US ISSN 0085-381X) 839
National Opinion Research Center. Newsletter (US ISSN 0077-5266) 1028
National Opinion Research Center. Report (US ISSN 0077-5274) 1010
National Party Platforms. Supplement (US ISSN 0077-5282) 907

National Passive Solar Conference. Proceedings. see American Solar Energy Society. Passive Conference. Annual Meeting 463
National Pastime (US ISSN 0734-6905) 1039
National Patterns of R. & D. Resources; Funds & Manpower in the United States see National Patterns of Science and Technology 995
National Patterns of Science and Technology (US) 995
National Peach Council. Proceedings (US ISSN 0092-2633) 58
National Petroleum News Factbook see N P N Factbook 865
National Pig Breeders' Association Herd Book (UK ISSN 0077-5312) 67
National Planning Association Reports (US) 277
National Pro-Life Journal (US) 1019
National Productivity Centre, Malaysia. Annual Report/Pusat Daya Pengeluaran Negara. Laporan Tahunan (MY ISSN 0126-8392) 281
National Psychological Association for Psychoanalysis. Bulletin (US ISSN 0077-5339) 935
National Publishing Directory (CN ISSN 0077-5347) 962
National Ready Mixed Concrete Association Publication see N R M C A Publication 186
National Real Estate Investor Directory(US) 966
National Recreational, Sporting and Hobby Organizations of the United States (US ISSN 0276-5276) 1035
National Referral Directory (US) 660
National Register of Microform Masters see New Serial Titles 129
National Register of Prominent Americans and International Notables (US ISSN 0077-5371) 135
National Rehabilitation Center for the Disabled. Research Bulletin (JA ISSN 0285-1350) 180, 375, 445, 764
National Relay Conference. Proceedings(US ISSN 0077-5401) 457
National Report for India: Meteorology and Atmospheric Analysis (II) 806
National Report for India: Seismology and Physics of the Earth's Interior (II) 806
National Reporter (CN) 660
National Research Center for Disaster Prevention. Seismological Bulletin (JA) 400
National Research Council. Committee on Polar Research. Report on United States Antarctic Research Activities (US ISSN 0361-2279) 546
National Research Council. Transportation Research Board. Bibliography (US ISSN 0148-849X) 1082
National Research Council, Canada. Associate Committee on Geotechnical Research. Technical Memorandum (CN ISSN 0077-5428) 380, 473
National Research Council, Canada. Associate Committee on Scientific Criteria for Environmental Quality. Status Report/Conseil National de Recherches, Canada. Comite Associe sur les Criteres Scientifiques. Rapport d'Activite (CN ISSN 0316-0114) 498
National Research Council, Canada. Division of Building Research. Bibliography (CN ISSN 0085-3828) 189
National Research Council, Canada. Division of Building Research. Building Practice Note (CN ISSN 0701-5216) 186
National Research Council, Canada. Division of Building Research. Building Research Note (CN ISSN 0077-5460) 186
National Research Council, Canada. Division of Building Research. D B R Paper (CN ISSN 0381-4319) 186

National Research Council, Canada. Division of Building Research. Proceedings (CN) 186
National Research Council, Canada. Division of Building Research. Research Program (CN ISSN 0077-5517) 186
National Research Council, Canada. Division of Building Research. Special Technical Publication (CN ISSN 0701-5208) 186
National Research Council, Canada. Division of Electrical Engineering. Bulletin/Conseil National de Recherches du Canada. Division de Genie Electrique. Bulletin (CN ISSN 0706-568X) 445, 473, 764
National Research Council, Canada. National Aeronautical Establishment. Aeronautical Report (L R Series) (CN ISSN 0077-5541) 20
National Research Council, Canada. National Aeronautical Establishment. Mechanical Engineering Reports (CN ISSN 0077-555X) 20, 492
National Research Council, Canada. National Aeronautical Establishment. Publications List and Supplements (CN ISSN 0077-5568) 22
National Research Council of Canada. Annual Report on Scholarships and Grants in Aid of Research see Natural Sciences and Engineering Research Council of Canada. List of Scholarships and Grants in Aid of Research 437
National Research Council of Canada. N R C Annual Report/Rapport Annuel du C N R C (CN) 995
National Research Council of Canada. Report of the President/Rapport du President see National Research Council of Canada. N R C Annual Report/Rapport Annuel du C N R C 995
National Research Institute of Agricultural Economics. Annual Report/Nogyo Sogo Kenkyusho Nenpo (JA) 32
National Research Institute of Agriculture. Annual Report see National Research Institute of Agricultural Economics. Annual Report 32
National Research Institute of Police Science. Annual Report/Kagaku Keisatsu Kenkyusho Nenpo (JA ISSN 0453-0667) 371
National Research Institute of Tea. Bulletin see National Research Institute of Vegetables, Ornamental Plants and Tea. Bulletin 32
National Research Institute of Vegetables, Ornamental Plants and Tea. Bulletin (JA) 32, 520
National Reye's Syndrome Foundation (US ISSN 0276-2293) 764
National Roster of Black Elected Officials see Black Elected Officials 939
National Roster of Realtors see National Roster of Realtors Directory 966
National Roster of Realtors Directory (US) 966
National S A M P E Technical Conference Series. N S T C Preprint Series see International S A M P E Technical Conference Series. N S T C Preprint Series 489
National Safety Council of Australia. Annual Report (AT ISSN 0813-1694) 636
National Sand and Gravel Association Circular see N S G A Circular 392
National Schools Collection: Government Schools see Australia. Bureau of Statistics. National Schools Statistics Collection 948
National Science Council (Ireland). Progress Report (IE) 996
National Science Council (Ireland). Register of Scientific Research Personnel (IE ISSN 0085-3836) 996
National Science Council of the Republic of China. Annual Report (CH) 996

NATIONAL TAIWAN 1825

National Science Council of the Republic of China Review see N S C Review 995
National Science Council of the Republic of China Special Publication see N S C Special Publication 995
National Science Council of the Republic of China Symposium Series see N S C Symposium Series 995
National Science Library of Canada. Annual Report see Canada Institute for Scientific and Technical Information. Annual Report 989
National Science Museum. Bulletin. Series D: Anthropology/Kokuritsu Kagaku Hakubutsukann Kenkyu Hoku. D - Rui: Jinruigaku (JA ISSN 0385-3039) 74
National Science Museum. Memoirs (JA ISSN 0082-4755) 996
National Secular Society. Annual Report (UK) 879
National Securities and Research Corporation. Annual Forecast (US ISSN 0077-5703) 267
National Security Traders Association. Traders' Annual (US ISSN 0092-4679) 267
National Service Data: Domestic (US) 1092
National Shellfisheries Association. Proceedings see Journal of Shellfish Research 175
National Shipping Corporation. Report and Accounts (PK) 1102
National Shorthand Reporters Association. Proceedings of the Annual Convention (US ISSN 0077-572X) 286
National Skeet Shooting Association. Records Annual (US ISSN 0077-5738) 1046
National Society for Clean Air Reference Book see N.S.C.A. Reference Book 498
National Society for Prevention of Cruelty to Children. Annual Report (UK ISSN 0077-5754) 1019
National Society for the Prevention of Blindness. Report see National Society to Prevent Blindness. Report 180
National Society for the Study of Education. Yearbook (US ISSN 0077-5762) 417
National Society of College Teachers of Education. Occasional Papers see Society of Professors of Education. Occasional Papers 419
National Society of College Teachers of Education Monographs see N S C T E Monographs 416
National Society to Prevent Blindness. Report (US ISSN 0270-4234) 180
National Soybean Processors Association. Yearbook (US ISSN 0077-5789) 63
National Speedway Directory (US) 1035
National Sporting Goods Association Buying Guide (US) 285, 1035
National Strategy Information Center. Agenda Papers (US) 812
National Strategy Information Center. Strategy Papers see National Strategy Information Center. Agenda Papers 812
National Stripper Well Survey (US ISSN 0470-3219) 466, 865
National Symposium on Wind Engineering. Proceedings see Symposium on Wind Effects on Structures in Japan. Proceedings 807
National Taiwan Normal University. Graduate Institute of Education. Bulletin (CH) 417
National Taiwan University. College of Agriculture. Memoirs (CH ISSN 0077-5819) 32
National Taiwan University. College of Law. Journal of Social Science (CH ISSN 0077-5835) 1010
National Taiwan University. College of Medicine. Memoirs (CH ISSN 0028-0275) 764
National Taiwan University. Department of Anthropology. Bulletin (CH) 74, 90

National Taiwan University. Department of Archaeology and Anthropology. Bulletin *see* National Taiwan University. Department of Anthropology. Bulletin *74*
National Taiwan University. Department of Geography. Science Reports (CH) *546*
National Taiwan University. Institute of Fishery Biology. Report (CH) *511*
National Taiwan University Journal of Sociology/Tai-Wan ta Hsueh She Hui Hsueh K'an (CH ISSN 0077-5851) *1028*
National Tank Truck Carrier Directory (US ISSN 0077-586X) *1105*
National Tape Recording Catalog *see* National Center for Audio Tapes Archive. Catalog *448*
National Tax Association - Tax Institute of America. Proceedings of the Annual Conference (US ISSN 0069-8687) *297*
National Telecommunications Conference. Record *see* I E E E Global Telecommunications Conference. Conference Record *343*
National Textile Corporation. Annual Report and Accounts (TZ) *1074*
National Tool, Die and Precision Machining Association. Buyers Guide. *see* National Tooling and Machining Association. Buyers Guide *746*
National Tooling and Machining Association. Buyers Guide. (US) *746*
National Tourist Guide of Nigeria *see* Nigeria Tourist Guide *1114*
National Trade and Professional Associations of the United States and Canada and Labor Unions *see* National Trade and Professional Associations of the United States and Labor Unions *314*
National Trade and Professional Associations of the United States and Labor Unions (US) *314*
National Trade-Index of Southern Africa (SA ISSN 0077-5894) *240*
National Transportation Safety Board Service (US) *1089*
National Travel Expenditure Study: Summary Report (US) *1114*
National Trial and Deposition Directory (US) *660*
National Trophy Industry Directory of Manufacturers and Suppliers *see* Recognition and Identification Blue Book *316*
National Trust for Historic Preservation. Information (US) *99*
National Trust for Scotland Yearbook (UK ISSN 0077-5916) *366*
National Trust of Australia (W.A.) Annual Report (AT) *573*
National Turfgrass Council Workshop Report Series *see* N T C Workshop Report Series *159*
National Union Catalog of Manuscript Collections (US ISSN 0090-0044) *129*
National Union of Insurance Workers. Prudential Section. Gazette (UK) *640*
National Union of Journalists Freelance Directory *see* N U J Freelance Directory *646*
National Union of Teachers. Annual Report (UK ISSN 0077-5940) *448*
National Union of Teachers Guide to Careers Work *see* N U T Guide to Careers Work *848*
National University Continuing Education Association. Directory (US) *430, 437*
National University Continuing Education Association. Handbook and Directory *see* National University Continuing Education Association. Directory *437*
National Urban League Annual Report (US) *624*
National Urban League Progress Report *see* National Urban League Annual Report *624*
National Wheelchair Basketball Association. Directory (US) *1039*

National Writers Club. Bulletin for Professional Members *see* Professional Freelance Writers Directory *646*
National Yellow Book of Funeral Directors and Suppliers *see* Yellow Book of Funeral Directors & Services *531*
National Youth & Student Discount Handbook (UK) *342*
National Zip Code and Post Office Directory *see* National Five Digit Zip Code and Post Office Directory *346*
National Zip Code Directory *see* National Five Digit Zip Code and Post Office Directory *346*
Nationale Maatschappij voor de Huisvesting. Jaarverslag *see* Societe National du Logement. Rapport Annuel *626*
Nationale-Nederlanden. Annual Report (NE ISSN 0077-5975) *640*
Nationalmuseets Arbejdsmark (DK) *591*
National's Forecast For (Year) *see* National Securities and Research Corporation. Annual Forecast *267*
Nations Nouvelles (CX ISSN 0028-050X) *907*
Nationwide Directory of Gift and Housewares Buyers *see* Nationwide Directory of Gift, Housewares & Home Textile Buyers *553*
Nationwide Directory of Gift, Housewares & Home Textile Buyers (US) *553, 615, 644*
Nationwide Directory of Men's and Boys' Wear Buyers (Exclusive of New York Metropolitan Area) (US ISSN 0077-5983) *340*
Nationwide Directory of Sporting Goods Buyers (US ISSN 0739-6074) *285, 1035*
Nationwide Directory of Women's and Children's Wear Buyers (Exclusive of New York Metropolitan Area) (US ISSN 0077-5991) *340*
Nationwide Major Mass Market Merchandisers (Exclusive of New York Metropolitan Area) (US ISSN 0077-6009) *340*
Native American Bibliography Series (US) *506*
Native American Rights Fund. Catalogue *see* National Indian Law Library. Catalogue *506*
Native Self-Sufficiency (US ISSN 0196-4240) *504*
Natsionalen Voennoistoricheski Muzei, Sofia. Izvestiya (BU ISSN 0324-0835) *591, 812*
Natur und Land (AU ISSN 0028-0607) *996*
Natur und Mensch: Jahresmitteilungen der Naturhistorischen Gesellschaft Nuernberg (GW ISSN 0077-6025) *90, 144, 380, 392*
Natura Jutlandica (DK ISSN 0077-6033) *144*
Natural Gas Annual (US) *466, 865*
Natural Gas Processors Association. Annual Convention. Proceedings *see* Gas Processors Association. Annual Convention. Proceedings *864*
Natural Gas Production and Consumption *see* Natural Gas Annual *466*
Natural Hazard Research Working Papers (US ISSN 0082-5166) *546*
Natural History Contributions (CN ISSN 0707-3887) *144, 857*
Natural History Miscellanea (US) *144*
Natural History Museum of Los Angeles County. Contributions in Science *see* Contributions in Science *990*
Natural History Museum of Los Angeles County. Science Series (US ISSN 0076-0943) *997*
Natural Law Forum *see* American Journal of Jurisprudence *650*
Natural Resources Research (UN ISSN 0077-6092) *366, 380*

Natural Sciences and Engineering Research Council of Canada. List of Scholarships and Grants in Aid of Research/Conseil de Recherches en Sciences Naturelles et en Genie du Canada. Liste des Bourses et Subventions de Recherche (CN) *437, 996*
Natural Sciences and Engineering Research Council of Canada. Report of the President/Conseil de Recherches en Sciences Naturelles et en Genie du Canada. Rapport du President (CN) *437, 996*
Naturalia (BL ISSN 0101-1944) *144*
Naturalia Hispanica (SP) *498*
Naturalist (US ISSN 8756-3592) *498*
Naturalists' Directory and Almanac International (US) *144*
Naturalists' Directory International *see* Naturalists' Directory and Almanac International *144*
Nature and Environment Series (FR) *366*
Nature Conservancy Council. Annual Report (UK) *366*
Nature Conservancy Council. Chief Scientist Team Reports (UK ISSN 0143-0378) *366*
Nature Conservancy Council Information and Library Services. Bibliography Series *see* N C C Information and Library Services. Bibliography Series *1159*
Nature Conservation Council of N.S.W. Bulletin *see* Nature Conservation Council of N.S.W. Newsletter *366*
Nature Conservation Council of N.S.W. Newsletter (AT) *366, 498*
Nature in Devon (UK ISSN 0143-9634) *366*
Naturforschende Gesellschaft in Basel. Verhandlungen/Society for Natural Sciences, Basel. Proceedings (SZ ISSN 0077-6122) *996*
Naturforschende Gesellschaft in Bern. Mitteilungen (SZ ISSN 0077-6130) *996*
Naturhistorische Gesellschaft Hannover. Beihefte zu den Berichten (GW ISSN 0374-6054) *144, 380*
Naturhistorische Gesellschaft Hannover. Berichte (GW ISSN 0365-9844) *380*
Naturhistorische Gesellschaft Nuernberg. Abhandlungen (GW ISSN 0077-6149) *90, 144, 380, 504*
Naturhistorische Gesellschaft Nuernberg. Mitteilungen und Jahresbericht *see* Natur und Mensch: Jahresmitteilungen der Naturhistorischen Gesellschaft Nuernberg *144*
Naturhistorisches Museum Basel. Veroeffentlichungen (SZ) *74, 392, 857*
Naturhistorisches Museum Bern. Jahrbuch (SZ) *996*
Naturhistorisches Museum in Wien. Annalen (AU ISSN 0083-6133) *996*
Naturhistorisches Museum in Wien. Neue Denkschriften (AU) *996*
Naturhistorisches Museum in Wien. Veroeffentlichungen. Neue Folge (AU ISSN 0505-5164) *996*
Naturkundliches Jahrbuch der Stadt Linz (AU ISSN 0470-3901) *996*
Naturkundliches Museum "Mauritianum" Altenburg. Abhandlungen und Berichte *see* Mauritiana (Altenburg) *994*
Naturligvis (DK ISSN 0109-2995) *996*
Naturwissenschaftliche Rundschau. Buecher der Zeitschrift (GW ISSN 0077-6157) *996*
Naturwissenschaftlicher Verein fuer Schleswig-Holstein. Schriften (GW ISSN 0077-6165) *996*
Naturwissenschaftlicher Verein fuer Steiermark. Mitteilungen (AU) *996*
Naturwissenschaftlicher Verein in Hamburg. Abhandlungen (GW) *144*
Naturwissenschaftlicher Verein in Hamburg. Abhandlungen und Verhandlungen *see* Naturwissenschaftlicher Verein in Hamburg. Abhandlungen *144*

Naturwissenschaftlicher Verein in Hamburg. Abhandlungen und Verhandlungen *see* Naturwissenschaftlicher Verein in Hamburg. Verhandlungen *144*
Naturwissenschaftlicher Verein in Hamburg. Verhandlungen (GW ISSN 0173-7481) *144*
Naturwissenschaftlicher Verein Wuppertal. Jahresberichte (GW ISSN 0547-9789) *159, 176, 392*
Natuurhistorisch Genootschap in Limburg. Publicaties (NE ISSN 0374-955X) *144, 857*
Nauchno-Issledovatel'skii Institut Kul'tury. Trudy *see* Sotsiologiya Kul'tury *1029*
Nauchno-Issledovatel'skii Institut Prikladnoi Geodezii. Trudy (UR) *392*
Naucni Sastanak Slavista u Vukove Dane. Referati i Saopstenja (YU) *699*
Nauka dla Wszystkich (PL ISSN 0077-6181) *996*
Nauka o Zemi. Seria Geographica (CS) *380, 546*
Nauka Segodnya (UR) *996*
Nauki Ekonomiczne (PL ISSN 0137-1428) *197*
Nauki Polityczne (PL ISSN 0137-141X) *907*
Naukove Tovarystvo Imeni Shevchenka. Biblioteka Ukrainoznavstva/Library of Ukrainian Studies (US) *591*
Naukove Tovarystvo Imeni Shevchenka. Proceedings of the Section of Chemistry, Biology and Medicine (US) *144, 324, 764*
Naukove Tovarystvo Imeni Shevchenka. Proceedings of the Section of Mathematics and Physics (US) *996*
Naukove Tovarystvo Imeni Shevchenka. Ukrainsk'va Literarurna Biblioteka/Ukrainian Literary Library (US) *728*
Naukove Tovarystvo Imeni Shevchenka. Ukrains'kyi Arkhiv/Ukrainian Archives (US) *504*
Naukove Tovarystvo Imeni Shevchenka. Zapysky. Mitteilungen/Memoirs (US) *504*
Naukovedenie i Informatika (UR ISSN 0374-3896) *359*
Nautical Almanac (UK ISSN 0077-619X) *1102*
Nauticus (GW) *1102*
Nautisches Jahrbuch (GE) *116*
Nautisches Jahrbuch, oder Ephemeriden und Tafeln (GW ISSN 0077-6211) *116*
Navac Audio Visual Handbook *see* Audio Visual and Micro-Computer Handbook *361*
Naval Architecture and Ocean Engineering (JA) *190, 490*
Naval Law Review (US) *660, 812*
Navigation (AT ISSN 0077-6262) *1082*
Navis (FR ISSN 0077-6270) *1102*
Navy List of Retired Officers (UK) *812*
Nawpa Pacha (US ISSN 0077-6297) *90*
Nayer Dor/New Generation (CN ISSN 0705-7822) *504*
Nazionaler Katalog der Heizung und Klimatisierung *see* Catalogue National du Genie Climatique-Chauffage et Conditionnement d'Air *553*
Nchanga Consolidated Copper Mines Ltd. Annual Report and Accounts (ZA) *799, 818*
Nea Paphos (PL) *90*
Neal's Catalog File (US) *51*
Near and Middle East Monographs (GW) *613*
Near and Middle East Series (CN ISSN 0077-6300) *728*
Nebraska. Accounting Division. Annual Fiscal Report *see* Nebraska. Department of Administrative Services. Annual Fiscal Report *944*
Nebraska. Accounting Division. Annual Report of Receipts and Disbursements *see* Nebraska. Department of Administrative Services. Annual Fiscal Report *944*

Nebraska. Department of Administrative Services. Annual Fiscal Report (US) *944*
Nebraska. Department of Public Welfare. Annual Report *see* Nebraska. Department of Social Services. Annual Report *1019*
Nebraska. Department of Roads. Challenge of the 80's (US) *483*
Nebraska. Department of Roads. Highway Statistics: State and Local Road and Street Data for (Year) *see* Nebraska. Department of Roads. Nebraska Selected Statistics *1097*
Nebraska. Department of Roads. Nebraska Selected Statistics (US) *1097*
Nebraska. Department of Roads. Traffic Analysis Unit. Continuous Traffic Count Data and Traffic Characteristics on Nebraska Streets and Highways (US ISSN 0091-844X) *1097*
Nebraska. Department of Social Services. Annual Report (US) *1019*
Nebraska. Fisheries Production Division. Annual Report (US ISSN 0092-1696) *511*
Nebraska. Indian Commission. Report (US ISSN 0360-683X) *504*
Nebraska. Natural Resources Commission. State Water Plan Publication (Lincoln) *see* Nebraska. Natural Resources Commission. State Water Planning and Review Process *1125*
Nebraska. Natural Resources Commission. State Water Planning and Review Process (US) *1125*
Nebraska. State Patrol. Annual Report (US ISSN 0094-1247) *371*
Nebraska Academy of Sciences. Proceedings (US ISSN 0077-6343) *996*
Nebraska Academy of Sciences. Transactions (US ISSN 0077-6351) *996*
Nebraska Criminal Justice Plan (US) *660*
Nebraska Law Enforcement Training Center. Annual Report (US) *1159*
Nebraska Library Commission. Annual Report *see* Nebraska Library Commission. Library Directory *682*
Nebraska Library Commission. Biennial Report *see* Nebraska Library Commission. Library Directory *682*
Nebraska Library Commission. Library Directory (US) *682*
Nebraska Statistical Handbook (US ISSN 0097-9325) *949, 1059*
Nebraska Statistical Report of Abortions (US ISSN 0095-3105) *179*
Nebraska Symposium on Motivation (Publication) (US ISSN 0070-2099) *935*
Nebraska Transcript (US) *660*
Nebraska Water Resources Research Institute, University of Nebraska. Annual Report of Activities (US ISSN 0077-6394) *1125*
Nebula Award Stories *see* Nebula Winners *728*
Nebula Winners (US ISSN 0162-3818) *728*
NebulousFan (US) *14*
Neckwear Industry Directory (US) *340, 340, 1074*
Neddy Books *see* Neddy Books and Videos *213*
Neddy Books and Videos (UK) *213*
Nederland's Adelsboek (NE) *536*
Nederlands Historisch Institutute Rome. Mededelingen *see* Nederlands Instituut te Rome. Mededelingen *591*
Nederlands Instituut te Rome. Mededelingen (NE) *90, 591*
Nederlands Interuniversitair Demografisch Instituut. Publications (NE) *923*
Nederlands Interuniversitair Demografisch Instituut. Working Papers (NE) *923*
Nederlands Kunsthistorisch Jaarboek (NE ISSN 0169-6726) *108*
Nederland's Patriciaat (NE) *536*

Nederlands Repertorium van Familienamen (NE) *536*
Nederlands-Zuidafrikaanse Vereniging. Jaarverslag (NE ISSN 0077-6416) *566*
Nederlandsche Bank N.V. Annual Report (NE ISSN 0167-3998) *231*
Nederlandsche Internationale Wegvervoer Organisatie Meddedelingen *see* N I W O Mededelingen *1082*
Nederlandse Bibliotheek- en Documenatiegids (NE) *682*
Nederlandse Bosstatistiek (NE) *1059*
Nederlandse Centrale Organisatie voor Toegepast-Natuurwetenschappelijk Onderzoek. Technisch-Physische Dienst. Annual Report (NE) *889*
Nederlandse Entomologische Vereniging. Monographs (NE ISSN 0548-1163) *165*
Nederlandse Geografische Studies/ Netherlands Geographical Studies (NGS) (NE ISSN 0169-4839) *546*
Nederlandse Historische Bronnen (NE) *591*
Nederlandse Houtbond. Jaarverslag (NE) *189*
Nederlandse Jeugd en Haar Onderwijs/ Netherlands Youth and Its Education(NE ISSN 0168-4809) *417*
Nederlandse Schadeverzekeringsmaatschappijen/ Netherlands Non-Life Insurance Companies (NE) *640*
Nederlandse Vereniging voor Klinische Chemie. Almanak (NE) *782*
Need a Lift? (US ISSN 0548-1384) *417*
Needlework Guild of America. Annual Report (US ISSN 0360-1102) *844*
Neftegazonosnye i Perspektivnye Kompleksy Tsentral'nykh i Vostochnykh Oblastei Russkoi Platformy (UR) *865*
Neftena i Vuglistna Geologiia/ Petroleum and Coal Geology (BU ISSN 0204-5109) *392, 865*
Negev (IS) *539*
Negotiated Working Conditions from Collective Agreements in Nova Scotia (CN ISSN 0226-3882) *274*
Negro American Biographies and Autobiographies (US ISSN 0077-6475) *135*
Neihardt Foundation Newsletter (US) *711*
Neki Pokazatelji Tehnickog Razvoja Privrede Jugoslavije (YU ISSN 0300-2497) *213*
Nekotorye Filosofskie Voprosy Sovremennogo Estestvoznaniya (UR) *879, 996*
Nelson's Directory of Wall Street Research *see* Directory of Wall Street Research *266*
Nemet Filologiai Tanulmanyok/ Arbeiten zur Deutschen Philologie (HU ISSN 0418-4580) *699, 728*
Nemity (PY) *631*
Nemouria: Occasional Papers of the Delaware Museum of Natural History (US ISSN 0085-3887) *996*
Nempo Nihon No Roshi Kankei (JA) *274*
Nenkan Kokoku Bijutsu *see* Annual of Advertising Art in Japan *14*
Neo-Hellenika (US ISSN 0077-6521) *338*
Neodidagmata (PL ISSN 0077-653X) *448*
Neologie en Marche. Serie A. Langue Generale (CN ISSN 0380-9366) *699*
Neologie en Marche. Serie B. Langues de Specialites (CN ISSN 0701-7995) *699*
Neometaphysical Digest (UK) *860*
Neophilologica (PL ISSN 0208-5550) *699*
Nepal. Central Bureau of Statistics. Statistical Pocket Book (NP) *1059*
Nepal. Department of Agricultural Education and Research. Annual Report (NP) *32, 417*
Nepal. Department of Medicinal Plants. Annual Report (NP) *159, 872*

Nepal. Rashtriya Pancayata. Arthika Samiti (NP) *247*
Nepal - Antiquary. Bibliographical Series (NP) *852*
Nepal Bank Limited. Annual Report and Balance Sheet (NP) *231*
Nepal Documentation (NP) *9, 213*
Nepal Family Planning and Maternal Child Health Board. Annual Report (NP) *179, 1019*
Nepal Gazette Translation Service *see* Nepal Recorder *660*
Nepal Industrial Development Corporation. Annual Report (NP ISSN 0077-6548) *290*
Nepal Industrial Development Corporation. Industrial Digest (NP ISSN 0077-6556) *290*
Nepal Industrial Development Corporation. Statistical Abstracts (NP ISSN 0077-6564) *213*
Nepal Law Translation Series *see* Nepal Miscellaneous Series *660*
Nepal Miscellaneous Series (NP) *660*
Nepal Rastra Bank. Annual Report (NP) *231*
Nepal Rastra Bank. Report of the Board of Directors *see* Nepal Rastra Bank. Annual Report *231*
Nepal Recorder (NP) *660*
Nephrology Reviews (US ISSN 0194-0090) *795*
Nepi Kultura-Nepi Tarsadalom (HU ISSN 0541-9522) *1028*
Neprajzi Ertesito/Ethnographic Review (HU ISSN 0077-6599) *74*
Neprajzi Kozlemenyek (HU ISSN 0028-2774) *74, 516*
Neprajzi Tanulmanyok (HU ISSN 0077-6602) *74*
Neptune's Kingdom (IE) *742*
Neraca (MY) *660*
Nerve Chemistry *see* Japanese Neurochemical Society. Bulletin *790*
Nestle Foundation. Annual Report (SZ) *846*
Netherlands. Centraal Bureau voor de Statistiek. Beleggingen van Institutionele Beleggers. Investments of Institutional Investors *see* Netherlands. Centraal Bureau voor de Statistiek. Institutionele Beleggers. Institutional Investors *267*
Netherlands. Centraal Bureau voor de Statistiek. Bezoek aan Vermakelijkheidsinstellingen. Attendance at Public Entertainments (NE ISSN 0077-6688) *1077*
Netherlands. Centraal Bureau voor de Statistiek. Bibliografie van Regionale Onderzoekingen Op Sociaalwetenschappelijk Terrein. Bibliography of Regional Studies in the Social Sciences (NE ISSN 0168-5988) *1014*
Netherlands. Centraal Bureau voor de Statistiek. Civil and Administrative Jurisdiction. Burgerlijke en Administratieve Rechtspraak (NE) *661*
Netherlands. Centraal Bureau voor de Statistiek. Criminele Statistiek. Criminal Statistics (NE ISSN 0168-4280) *372*
Netherlands. Centraal Bureau voor de Statistiek. Diagnosestatistiek Bedrijfsverenigingen (Omslagleden). Social Insurance Sickness Statistics (NE ISSN 0168-4108) *640, 1019*
Netherlands. Centraal Bureau voor de Statistiek. Faillissementsstatistiek. Bankruptcies (NE ISSN 0077-6793) *213*
Netherlands. Centraal Bureau voor de Statistiek. Gevangenisstatistiek. Statistics of Prisons (NE ISSN 0077-6815) *372*
Netherlands. Centraal Bureau voor de Statistiek. Hypotheken. Statistics of Mortgages *see* Netherlands. Centraal Bureau voor de Statistiek. Hypotheken. Statistics of Mortgages *213*
Netherlands. Centraal Bureau voor de Statistiek. Hypotheken. Statistics of Mortgages (NE ISSN 0168-4590) *213*

Netherlands. Centraal Bureau voor de Statistiek. Institutionele Beleggers. Institutional Investors (NE) *267*
Netherlands. Centraal Bureau voor de Statistiek. Jaaroverzicht Bevolking en Bevolking en Volksgezondheid. Population and Health Statistics *see* Netherlands. Centraal Bureau voor de Statistiek. Jaarstatistiek van de Bevolking. Population Statistics *928*
Netherlands. Centraal Bureau voor de Statistiek. Jaarstatistiek van de Bevolking. Population Statistics (NE ISSN 0168-4000) *923, 928, 955*
Netherlands. Centraal Bureau voor de Statistiek. Justiciele Kinderbescherming (NE) *334*
Netherlands. Centraal Bureau voor de Statistiek. Justitiele Statistiek. Judicial Statistics *see* Netherlands. Centraal Bureau voor de Statistiek. Civil and Administrative Jurisdiction. Burgerlijke en Administratieve Rechtspraak *661*
Netherlands. Centraal Bureau voor de Statistiek. Muziek en Theater (NE ISSN 0168-3519) *1077*
Netherlands. Centraal Bureau voor de Statistiek. Naamlijsten voor de Statistiek van de Buitenlandse Handel. List of Goods for the Statistics of Foreign Trade (NE) *213*
Netherlands. Centraal Bureau voor de Statistiek. Naamlijsten voor de Statistiek van de Buitenlandse Handel. Supplement. List of Goods for the Statistics of Foreign Trade. Supplement (NE ISSN 0168-4094) *213*
Netherlands. Centraal Bureau voor de Statistiek. Nationale Rekeningen. National Accounts (NE ISSN 0168-3489) *297*
Netherlands. Centraal Bureau voor de Statistiek. Per Leerling Beschikbaar Gestelde Bedragen voor het Lager Onderwijs. Amounts per Pupil Provided for Primary Education (NE ISSN 0168-5244) *425, 1059*
Netherlands. Centraal Bureau voor de Statistiek. Productie Statistiek van de Zuivelindustrie/Production Statistics of the Dairy Industry (NE ISSN 0168-518X) *62*
Netherlands. Centraal Bureau voor de Statistiek. Produktiestatistieken: Alcoholfabrieken, Bierbrouwerijen en Mouterijen, Distilleerderijen en Frisdrankenindustrie (NE ISSN 0168-5767) *213*
Netherlands. Centraal Bureau voor de Statistiek. Produktiestatistieken: Bierbrouwerijen en Mouterijen, Alcoholfabrieken, Distilleerderijen en Frisdrankenindustrie *see* Netherlands. Centraal Bureau voor de Statistiek. Produktiestatistieken: Alcoholfabrieken, Bierbrouwerijen en Mouterijen, Distilleerderijen en Frisdrankenindustrie *213*
Netherlands. Centraal Bureau voor de Statistiek. Produktiestatistieken: Papier- en Kartonindustrie (NE ISSN 0168-4361) *859*
Netherlands. Centraal Bureau voor de Statistiek. Produktiestatistieken: Rijwiel- en Motorrijwielindustrie (NE ISSN 0168-5864) *1036*
Netherlands. Centraal Bureau voor de Statistiek. Produktiestatistieken: Suikerfabrieken (NE ISSN 0168-5287) *521*
Netherlands. Centraal Bureau voor de Statistiek. Produktiestatistiek Strokartonindustrie *see* Netherlands. Centraal Bureau voor de Statistiek. Produktiestatistieken: Papier- en Kartonindustrie *859*
Netherlands. Centraal Bureau voor de Statistiek. Produktiestatistieken: Veevoederindustrie (NE ISSN 0168-5333) *63*
Netherlands. Centraal Bureau voor de Statistiek. Produktiestatistiek van de Papierindustries *see* Netherlands. Centraal Bureau voor de Statistiek. Produktiestatistieken: Papier- en Kartonindustrie *859*

Netherlands. Centraal Bureau voor de Statistiek. Regionaal Statistisch Zakboek (NE) *1059*

Netherlands. Centraal Bureau voor de Statistiek. Statistical Studies (NE) *1059*

Netherlands. Centraal Bureau voor de Statistiek. Statistiek der Branden. Fire Statistics (NE ISSN 0077-6955) *507*

Netherlands. Centraal Bureau voor de Statistiek. Statistiek der Lonen in de Landbouw. Statistics of Wages in Agriculture (NE ISSN 0077-6963) *42, 214*

Netherlands. Centraal Bureau voor de Statistiek. Statistiek der Motorrijtuigen *see* Netherlands. Centraal Bureau voor de Statistiek. Statistiek der Motorvoertuigen. Statistics of Motor Vehicles *1105*

Netherlands. Centraal Bureau voor de Statistiek. Statistiek der Motorvoertuigen. Statistics of Motor Vehicles (NE ISSN 0168-4973) *1105*

Netherlands. Centraal Bureau voor de Statistiek. Statistiek der Verkiezingen. Gemeenteraden. Election Statistics. Municipal Councils (NE ISSN 0168-4884) *912*

Netherlands. Centraal Bureau voor de Statistiek. Statistiek der Verkiezingen. Provinciale Staten. Election Statistics. Provincial Councils (NE ISSN 0168-5732) *949*

Netherlands. Centraal Bureau voor de Statistiek. Statistiek der Verkiezingen. Tweede Kamer der Staten-Generaal. Election Statistics. Second Chamber of the States-General (NE ISSN 0168-5686) *912*

Netherlands. Centraal Bureau voor de Statistiek. Statistiek van Aan-, Af- en Doorvoer. Goederenvervoer per Goederensoort van en naar de Zeehavens van Rotterdam en Amsterdam (NE ISSN 0168-4825) *1086*

Netherlands. Centraal Bureau voor de Statistiek. Statistiek van de Aan-, Af- en Doorvoer. Goederenvervoer van en naar Nederland. Statistics of the International Goods Traffic (NE ISSN 0168-4876) *214*

Netherlands. Centraal Bureau voor de Statistiek. Statistiek van de Algemene Bijstand. Statistics of Public Assistance (NE ISSN 0168-4086) *1023*

Netherlands. Centraal Bureau voor de Statistiek. Statistiek van de Bejaardenoorden. Homes for the Aged (NE) *1023*

Netherlands. Centraal Bureau voor de Statistiek. Statistiek van de Gemeentewege per Leerling Beschikbaar Gestelde Bedragenter Bestrijding van de Materiele Exploitatiekosten der Lagere Scholen. Statistics of the Amounts per Pupil Provided by the Municipality to Meet the Material Cost of Elementary Education *see* Netherlands. Centraal Bureau voor de Statistiek. Per Leerling Beschikbaar Gestelde Bedragen voor het Lager Onderwijs. Amounts per Pupil Provided for Primary Education *425*

Netherlands. Centraal Bureau voor de Statistiek. Statistiek van de Internationale Binnenvaart. Statistics of the International Inland Shipping (NE ISSN 0168-5376) *1102*

Netherlands. Centraal Bureau voor de Statistiek. Statistiek van de Inkomsten en Uitgaven der Overheid voor Cultuur en Recreatie. Statistics of Government Expenditure on Culture and Recreation (NE ISSN 0168-4248) *1036*

Netherlands. Centraal Bureau voor de Statistiek. Statistiek van de Investeringen in Vaste Activa in de Industrie *see* Netherlands. Centraal Bureau voor de Statistiek. Statistiek van de Investeringen in Vaste Activa in de Nijverheid. Statistics on Fixed Capital Formation in Industry *214*

Netherlands. Centraal Bureau voor de Statistiek. Statistiek van de Investeringen in Vaste Activa in de Nijverheid. Statistics on Fixed Capital Formation in Industry (NE ISSN 0168-7956) *214, 1059*

Netherlands. Centraal Bureau voor de Statistiek. Statistiek van de Koopvaardijvloot. Statistics of the Merchant Marine (NE) *1102*

Netherlands. Centraal Bureau voor de Statistiek. Statistiek van de Luchtvaart. Civil Aviation Statistics (NE ISSN 0168-552X) *1089*

Netherlands. Centraal Bureau voor de Statistiek. Statistiek van de Land- en Tuinbouw. Statistics of Agriculture (NE ISSN 0168-3918) *42*

Netherlands. Centraal Bureau voor de Statistiek. Statistiek van de Openbare Bibliotheken (NE ISSN 0168-3462) *682*

Netherlands. Centraal Bureau voor de Statistiek. Statistiek van de Spaargelden. Statistics of Savings (NE ISSN 0168-3330) *214*

Netherlands. Centraal Bureau voor de Statistiek. Statistiek van de Uitgaven der Overheid voor Cultuur en Recreatie *see* Netherlands. Centraal Bureau voor de Statistiek. Statistiek van de Inkomsten en Uitgaven der Overheid voor Cultuur en Recreatie. Statistics of Government Expenditure on Culture and Recreation *1036*

Netherlands. Centraal Bureau voor de Statistiek. Statistiek van de Uitgaven der Overheid voor Onderwijs. Statistics of the Expenditure of the State, the Provinces and the Municipalities on Education (NE ISSN 0168-7905) *443*

Netherlands. Centraal Bureau voor de Statistiek. Statistiek van de Voorlichting Bij Beroepskeuze. Statistics of Vocational Guidance and Selection of Personnel *see* Netherlands. Centraal Bureau voor de Statistiek. Statistiek van de Voorlichting Bij Scholen en Beroepskeuze. Statistics of Vocational Guidance *425*

Netherlands. Centraal Bureau voor de Statistiek. Statistiek van de Voorlichting Bij Scholen en Beroepskeuze. Statistics of Vocational Guidance (NE ISSN 0168-423X) *425, 849*

Netherlands. Centraal Bureau voor de Statistiek. Statistiek van de Verkeersongevallen op de Openbare Weg. Statistics of Road-Traffic Accidents (NE ISSN 0168-5023) *1086*

Netherlands. Centraal Bureau voor de Statistiek. Statistiek van de Visserij. Statistics of Fisheries (NE ISSN 0168-4167) *511*

Netherlands. Centraal Bureau voor de Statistiek. Statistiek van de Zeevaart. Statistics of Seaborne Shipping (NE ISSN 0168-5422) *1102*

Netherlands. Centraal Bureau voor de Statistiek. Statistiek van Beroepsonderwijs *see* Netherlands. Centraal Bureau voor de Statistiek. Statistiek van het Beroepsonderwijs: Technisch en Nautisch Onderwijs. Statistics on Vocational Training *425*

Netherlands. Centraal Bureau voor de Statistiek. Statistiek van het Beroepsonderwijs: Beroepsbegeleidend Onderwijs Leerlingwezen (NE ISSN 0168-5708) *417*

Netherlands. Centraal Bureau voor de Statistiek. Statistiek van het Beroepsonderwijs: Huishoud- en Nijverheidsonderwijs (NE ISSN 0168-5406) *448*

Netherlands. Centraal Bureau voor de Statistiek. Statistiek van het Beroepsonderwijs: Kunstonderwijs. Art Colleges (NE ISSN 0168-5503) *430, 437*

Netherlands. Centraal Bureau voor de Statistiek. Statistiek van het Beroepsonderwijs: Landbouwonderwijs *see* Netherlands. Centraal Bureau voor de Statistiek. Statistiek van het Hoger Beroepsonderwijs: Agrarisch Onderwijs *425*

Netherlands. Centraal Bureau voor de Statistiek. Statistiek van het Beroepsonderwijs: Opleidingsscholen Kleuterleidsters en Pedagogische Academies (NE) *425*

Netherlands. Centraal Bureau voor de Statistiek. Statistiek van het Beroepsonderwijs: Sociaal-Pedagogisch Onderwijs (NE ISSN 0168-5600) *417*

Netherlands. Centraal Bureau voor de Statistiek. Statistiek van het Beroepsonderwijs: Technisch en Nautisch Onderwijs. Statistics on Vocational Training (NE ISSN 0168-5457) *425, 849*

Netherlands. Centraal Bureau voor de Statistiek. Statistiek van het Erkende Schriftelijk Onderwijs. Statistics on Correspondence Courses (NE ISSN 0168-4906) *448*

Netherlands. Centraal Bureau voor de Statistiek. Statistiek van het Gesubsidieerde Toneel *see* Netherlands. Centraal Bureau voor de Statistiek. Muziek en Theater *1077*

Netherlands. Centraal Bureau voor de Statistiek. Statistiek van het Hoger Beroepsonderwijs: Agrarisch Onderwijs (NE) *425, 849*

Netherlands. Centraal Bureau voor de Statistiek. Statistiek van het Internationaal Goederenvervoer. Statistics of the International Goods Traffic *see* Netherlands. Centraal Bureau voor de Statistiek. Statistiek van de Aan-, Af- en Doorvoer. Goederenvervoer van en naar Nederland. Statistics of the International Goods Traffic *214*

Netherlands. Centraal Bureau voor de Statistiek. Statistiek van het Internationaal Zeehavenvervoer *see* Netherlands. Centraal Bureau voor de Statistiek. Statistiek van Aan-, Af- en Doorvoer. Goederenvervoer per Goederensoort van en naar de Zeehavens van Rotterdam en Amsterdam *1086*

Netherlands. Centraal Bureau voor de Statistiek. Statistiek van het Kunstonderwijs. Statistics on Art Colleges *see* Netherlands. Centraal Bureau voor de Statistiek. Statistiek van het Beroepsonderwijs: Kunstonderwijs. Art Colleges *437*

Netherlands. Centraal Bureau voor de Statistiek. Statistiek van het Kweekschoolonderwijs. Statistics on Teacher Training Colleges *see* Netherlands. Centraal Bureau voor de Statistiek. Statistiek van het Beroepsonderwijs: Opleidingsscholen Kleuterleidsters en Pedagogische Academies *425*

Netherlands. Centraal Bureau voor de Statistiek. Statistiek van het Nijverheidsonderwijs *see* Netherlands. Centraal Bureau voor de Statistiek. Statistiek van het Beroepsonderwijs: Huishoud- en Nijverheidsonderwijs *448*

Netherlands. Centraal Bureau voor de Statistiek. Statistiek van het Personenvervoer. Statistics of Passenger Transport (NE ISSN 0168-5074) *1082*

Netherlands. Centraal Bureau voor de Statistiek. Statistiek van het Schriftelijk Onderwijs. Statistics on Correspondence Courses *see* Netherlands. Centraal Bureau voor de Statistiek. Statistiek van het Erkende Schriftelijk Onderwijs. Statistics on Correspondence Courses *448*

Netherlands. Centraal Bureau voor de Statistiek. Statistiek van het Sociaal-Pedagogisch Onderwijs. Statistics on Socio-Pedagogic Training *see* Netherlands. Centraal Bureau voor de Statistiek. Statistiek van het Beroepsonderwijs: Sociaal-Pedagogisch Onderwijs *417*

Netherlands. Centraal Bureau voor de Statistiek van het Binnenlands Goederenvervoer. Statistics of Internal Goods Transport in the Netherlands (NE ISSN 0168-5325) *1102*

Netherlands. Centraal Bureau voor de Statistiek. Statistiek van het Voorbereidend Hoger en Middelbaar Onderwijs: Leraren. Statistics of Secondary Education: Teachers *see* Netherlands. Centraal Bureau voor de Statistiek. Statistiek van het W V O, H A V O en M A V O: Instroom, Doorstroom en Uitstroom van Leerlingen *443*

Netherlands. Centraal Bureau voor de Statistiek. Statistiek van Het Wetenschappelijk Onderwijs. Statistics of University Education (NE ISSN 0168-5058) *437*

Netherlands. Centraal Bureau voor de Statistiek. Statistiek van het W V O, H A V O en M A V O: Instroom, Doorstroom en Uitstroom van Leerlingen (NE ISSN 0168-5856) *443*

Netherlands. Centraal Bureau voor de Statistiek. Statistiek Vreemdelingenverkeer. Tourism Statistics (NE ISSN 0168-5538) *1120*

Netherlands. Centraal Bureau voor de Statistiek. Statistiek Werkzame Personen (NE ISSN 0168-3667) *214*

Netherlands. Centraal Bureau voor de Statistiek. Statistisch Bulletin (NE ISSN 0166-9680) *1059*

Netherlands. Centraal Bureau voor de Statistiek. Statistisch Zakboek. Pocket Yearbook (NE ISSN 0168-3705) *1059*

Netherlands. Centraal Bureau voor de Statistiek. Statistische en Econometrische Onderzoekingen. Statistical and Econometric Studies *see* Netherlands. Centraal Bureau voor de Statistiek. Statistische Onderzoekingen *214*

Netherlands. Centraal Bureau voor de Statistiek. Statistische Onderzoekingen (NE) *214, 1060*

Netherlands. Centraal Bureau voor de Statistiek. Toepassing der Kinderwetten. Application of Juvenile Law *see* Netherlands. Centraal Bureau voor de Statistiek. Justiciele Kinderbescherming *334*

Netherlands. Centraal Bureau voor de Statistiek. Toepassing der Wegenverkeerswet. Statistics of the Application of the Road Traffic Act (NE ISSN 0168-4388) *1097*

Netherlands. Centraal Bureau voor de Statistiek. Vakantieonderzoek (NE ISSN 0168-3411) *1120*

Netherlands. Centraal Bureau voor de Statistiek. Vermogensverdeling. Regionale Gegevens. Distribution of Personal Wealth. Regional Data (NE ISSN 0168-3888) *214*

Netherlands. Centraal Bureau voor de Statistiek. Voortgezet Onderwijs Regionaal Bezien (NE ISSN 0168-485X) *425*

Netherlands. Centraal Bureau voor de Statistiek. Winststatistiek der Grotere Naamloze Vennootschappen. Profit-Statistics of the Limited Liability Companies (NE ISSN 0077-751X) *214*

Netherlands. Centraal Bureau voor de Statistiek. Zuivelstatistiek/Dairy Statistics see Netherlands. Centraal Bureau voor de Statistiek. Productie Statistiek van de Zuivelindustrie/Production Statistics of the Dairy Industry 62
Netherlands. Centraal Planbureau. Centraal Economisch Plan (NE ISSN 0077-7536) 290
Netherlands. Centrale Commissie voor de Statistiek. Jaarverslag (NE) 1060
Netherlands. Commissie Zeehavenoverleg. Jaarverslag see Netherlands. Provisional National Ports Council. Jaarverslag 1102
Netherlands. Departement van Marine. Catalogus van Nederlandse Zeekaarten en Boekwerken see Catalogus van Nederlandse Zeekaarten en Andere Hydrografische Publikaties/Catalog of Charts and Other Hydrographic Publications 1123
Netherlands. Ministerie van Cultuur, Recreatie en Maatschappelijk Werk. Openluchtrecreatie (NE) 1046
Netherlands. Ministerie van Onderwijs en Wetenschappen. Onderwijsverslag (NE) 417
Netherlands. Ministerie van Volksgezondheid en Milieuhygiene. Verslag Levensmiddelen en Keuring van Waren see Netherlands. Ministerie van Welzijn, Volksgezondheid en Cultuur. Verslag Levensmiddelen en Keuring van Waren 520
Netherlands. Ministerie van Welzijn, Volksgezondheid en Cultuur. Verslag Levensmiddelen en Keuring van Waren (NE) 520
Netherlands. Provisional National Ports Council. Jaarverslag (NE) 1102
Netherlands. Rijks Geologische Dienst. Jaarverslag/Netherlands Geological Survey. Annual Report (NE ISSN 0077-7617) 392
Netherlands. Rijkscommissie voor Geodesie. Publications on Geodesy. New Series (NE ISSN 0077-7625) 483, 546
Netherlands. Rijksdienst voor de Monumentenzorg. Jaarverslag (NE) 99
Netherlands. Rijksinstituut voor de Volksgezondheid. Mededelingen (NE) 955
Netherlands. Rijksinstituut voor Oorlogsdocumentatie. Progress Report (NE) 591
Netherlands. Sociaal en Cultureel Planbureau. Social and Cultural Report (NE) 1028
Netherlands-American Trade Directory (NE) 236
Netherlands-British Trade Directory (UK ISSN 0308-1273) 236
Netherlands Fertilizer Technical Bulletin (NE ISSN 0169-2313) 58
Netherlands Geographical Studies (NGS) see Nederlandse Geografische Studies 546
Netherlands Geological Survey. Annual Report see Netherlands. Rijks Geologische Dienst. Jaarverslag 392
Netherlands Institute of Archaeology and Arabic Studies in Cairo. Publications (NE) 90, 613
Netherlands Investment Bank for Developing Countries. Annual Report (NE ISSN 0077-7560) 231, 263
Netherlands Nitrogen Technical Bulletin see Netherlands Fertilizer Technical Bulletin 58
Netherlands Non-Life Insurance Companies see Nederlandse Schadeverzekeringsmaatschappijen 640
Netherlands Phonetic Archives (NE) 699
Netherlands Universities Foundation for International Cooperation. A Portrait(NE) 437

Netherlands Universities Foundation for International Cooperation. Annual Report see Netherlands Universities Foundation for International Cooperation. A Portrait 437
Netherlands Yearbook of International Law (NE) 671
Netherlands Youth and Its Education see Nederlandse Jeugd en Haar Onderwijs 417
Network (Research Triangle Park) (US) 179, 785
Network Database Systems (US) 357
Network Planning Paper (US ISSN 0160-9742) 357
Neudrucke Deutscher Literaturwerke (GW ISSN 0077-7668) 728
Neudrucke Deutscher Literaturwerke. Sonderreihe (GW ISSN 0077-7676) 728
Neudrucke Deutscher Literaturwerke des XVI und XVII Jahrhunderts see Neudrucke Deutscher Literaturwerke 728
Neudrucke Deutscher Literaturwerke des XVIII und XIX Jahrhunderts see Neudrucke Deutscher Literaturwerke 728
Neue Ausgrabungen und Forschungen aus Niedersachsens Urgeschichte (GW ISSN 0548-2682) 90
Neue Denkschriften des Naturhistorischen Museums in Wien (AU) 144, 177, 380
Neue Didaktische Modelle (GW ISSN 0723-3280) 448
Neue Entomologische Nachrichten (GW ISSN 0722-3773) 165
Neue Formen see Revue Formes Nouvelles 99
Neue Hefte fuer Philosophie (GW ISSN 0085-3917) 879
Neue Muenchner Beitraege zur Geschichte der Medizin und Naturwissenschaften. Medizinhistorische Serie (GW ISSN 0300-8371) 764
Neue Muenchner Beitraege zur Geschichte der Medizin und Naturwissenschaften. Naturwissenschaftshistorische Reihe (GW) 996
Neue Musikgeschichtliche Forschungen(GW ISSN 0077-7714) 839
Neue Politische Literatur. Beihefte. (GW ISSN 0176-604X) 907
Neue Produkte aus Daenemark see New Products from Denmark 290
Neue Wege (AU ISSN 0028-3444) 335, 417, 1077
Neues Jahrbuch fuer Geologie und Palaeontologie. Abhandlungen (GW ISSN 0077-7749) 392, 857
Neues Jahrbuch fuer Mineralogie, Geologie und Palaeontologie. Abhandlungen see Neues Jahrbuch fuer Geologie und Palaeontologie. Abhandlungen 392
Neues Trierisches Jahrbuch see Neues Trierisches Jahrbuch fuer Heimatpflege und Heimatgeschichte 591
Neues Trierisches Jahrbuch fuer Heimatpflege und Heimatgeschichte (GW) 591
Neuindische Studien (GW ISSN 0340-6385) 570, 699
Neujahrsgabe der Deutschen Buecherei (GE ISSN 0457-3897) 682
Neurolinguistics (NE ISSN 0301-6412) 699, 790
Neurology and Neurobiology (US) 790
Neuroorthopaedie (US) 786, 790
Neurosciences Abstracts (US ISSN 0141-7711) 9, 771
Neurosciences Research (US ISSN 0077-7846) 790
Neurospora Newsletter see Fungal Genetics Newsletter 141
Neurotoxicology (US ISSN 0160-2748) 790
Neurotraumatology (JA ISSN 0389-5610) 786, 791
Neusser Jahrbuch fuer Kunst, Kulturgeschichte und Heimatkunde (GW ISSN 0077-7862) 591
Neutron Activation Analysis Abstracts (UK ISSN 0047-9446) 9, 893

Neuzeit im Aufbau (GW) 559
Nevada. Advisory Council for Manpower Training and Career Education. Annual Evaluation Report see Nevada. Advisory Council for Vocational-Technical Education. Annual Evaluation Report 1159
Nevada. Advisory Council for Vocational-Technical Education. Annual Evaluation Report (US) 1159
Nevada. Bureau of Mines and Geology. Bulletin (US) 392, 818
Nevada. Bureau of Mines and Geology. Report (US ISSN 0095-5264) 392, 818
Nevada. Bureau of Mines. Report see Nevada. Bureau of Mines and Geology. Report 392
Nevada. Office of Fiscal Analyst. Annual Report see Nevada. Office of Legislative Auditor. Biennial Report 944
Nevada. Office of Legislative Auditor. Biennial Report (US) 944
Nevada. State Board for Vocational Education. Annual Program Plan for Vocational Education see Nevada State Plan for Occupational Education 427
Nevada. State Museum, Carson City. Anthropological Papers (US ISSN 0077-7897) 74, 90
Nevada. State Museum, Carson City. Natural History Publications (US ISSN 0077-7900) 996
Nevada. State Museum, Carson City. Occasional Papers (US ISSN 0077-7919) 829
Nevada. State Museum, Carson City. Popular Series (US ISSN 0077-7927) 830
Nevada Library Directory and Statistics(US) 682
Nevada State Plan for Occupational Education (US) 427
Nevada State Plan for Vocational Education see Nevada State Plan for Occupational Education 427
Nevada Statewide Wage Survey see Nevada Wage Survey 274
Nevada Studies in History and Political Science (US ISSN 0077-7935) 607
Nevada Wage Survey (US) 274
New Acronyms and Initialisms see New Acronyms, Initialisms and Abbreviations 699
New Acronyms, Initialisms and Abbreviations (US ISSN 0148-866X) 699
New African Yearbook see New African Yearbook: West and Central 907
New African Yearbook see New African Yearbook: East and South 907
New African Yearbook: East and South(UK) 197, 907
New African Yearbook: West and Central (UK) 197, 907
New Age Astrology Guide (Year) (US) 114
New American Writing (US) 742
New and Expanding Industries Report for Alabama (US) 290
New Baby (UK) 334
New Babylon: Studies in the Social Sciences (GW ISSN 0077-801X) 935, 1028
New Book of Knowledge Annual (US ISSN 0196-0148) 463
New Bookbinder (UK ISSN 0261-5363) 962
New Books on Asia Announced for Publication in the Soviet Union (US ISSN 0199-9796) 570
New Books on Film/TV see Nye Boeger om Film/TV 826
New Brunswick. Beach Resources - Eastern New Brunswick (CN) 818
New Brunswick. Department of Health. Annual Report (CN) 955
New Brunswick. Department of Labour and Human Resources. Annual Report (CN) 274

New Brunswick. Department of Labour and Manpower. Annual Report see New Brunswick. Department of Labour and Human Resources. Annual Report 274
New Brunswick. Department of Labour. Annual Report see New Brunswick. Department of Labour and Human Resources. Annual Report 274
New Brunswick. Department of Tourism. Annual Report (CN ISSN 0703-6566) 1114
New Brunswick. Department of Youth and Welfare. Report see New Brunswick. Department of Youth. Report 335
New Brunswick. Department of Youth. Report (CN ISSN 0077-8079) 334, 335
New Brunswick. Field Services Branch. Provincial Park Statistics (CN) 366
New Brunswick. Health Services Advisory Council. Annual Report/Rapport Annuel (CN) 1159
New Brunswick. Mineral Resources Branch. Report of Investigations (CN ISSN 0077-8109) 818
New Brunswick. Research and Productivity Council. Report (CN ISSN 0077-8117) 290
New Brunswick. Wetlands - Peatlands Resources (CN) 818
New Brunswick Department of Fisheries. Annual Report (CN ISSN 0077-8036) 511
New Brunswick Public Employees Association. News Letter (CN ISSN 0381-7970) 951
New Brunswick Reports (CN) 661
New Caledonia. Service des Mines et de l'Energy. Rapport Annuel (NL) 392, 818
New Campus (US ISSN 0077-8168) 1159
New Canaan Historical Society Annual (US ISSN 0734-2802) 607
New Canadian Fandom (CN ISSN 0229-1932) 14, 728
New Canadian Stories see Best Canadian Stories 716
New Ceylon Writing (AT) 699, 728
New China see Xin Tang 708
New City Songster (UK) 839
New Comprehensive Biochemistry (NE) 152
New Connections (US) 615
New Departures (UK) 108, 728
New Detroit Incorporated see New Detroit Progress Report 16
New Detroit Progress Report (US) 16
New Directions in Librarianship (US ISSN 0147-1090) 682
New Drugs in Japan see Saikin No Shinyaku 872
New Electronics' Distributor Product Finder and Guide (UK) 457
New England Board of Higher Education. New England Regional Student Program: Enrollment Report (US) 437
New England Board of Higher Education. New England Regional Student Program: Graduate Level (US) 437
New England Board of Higher Education. New England Regional Student Program: Undergraduate Level (US) 437
New England Board of Higher Education Issues (US) 1159
New England Crop and Livestock Reporting Service. Massachusetts Agricultural Statistics see Massachusetts Agricultural Statistics 42
New England Electrical Blue Book (US ISSN 0548-4456) 457
New England Food Service Buyer's Guide see North East Food Service Buyer's Guide 620
New England Guide see Original New England Guide 1115
New England Interstate Water Pollution Control Commission Annual Report see N E I W P C C Annual Report 498
New England Journal of Black Studies (US) 504

New England Media Directory *see* Burrelle's New England Media Directory 15
New England Science Fiction Association Inc. Index: Science Fiction Magazines and Anthologies *see* N.E.S.F.A. Index: Science Fiction Magazines and Anthologies 14
New England Skiers' Guide (US) 1046
New England War Tax Resistance Newsletter (US) 297
New English Art Club (UK) 108
New Forms *see* Revue Formes Nouvelles 99
New Generation *see* Nayer Dor 504
New Glass Review (US ISSN 0275-469X) 113
New Group Health Insurance (US) 641
New Hampshire. Agricultural Experiment Station, Durham. Research Reports (US ISSN 0077-832X) 32
New Hampshire. Agricultural Experiment Station, Durham. Station Bulletins (US ISSN 0077-8338) 32
New Hampshire. Fish and Game Department. Biennial Report (US ISSN 0077-8362) 366
New Hampshire. Fish and Game Department. Game Management and Research Division. Biological Survey Bulletin (US ISSN 0077-8397) 144, 511
New Hampshire. Fish and Game Department. Game Management and Research Division. Biological Survey Series (US ISSN 0077-8370) 144
New Hampshire. Fish and Game Department. Game Management and Research Division. Technical Circular Series. (US ISSN 0077-8389) 144, 511
New Hampshire Archeologist (US ISSN 0077-8346) 90
New Hampshire Manufacturing Directory (US) 314
New Hampshire Marketing Directory *see* New Hampshire Manufacturing Directory 314
New Hampshire Quarter Notes (US ISSN 0028-5315) 417, 839
New Hampshire Vital Statistics (US ISSN 0095-5523) 928, 1060
New Haven Colony Historical Society. Journal (US) 607
New Hebrides. Anglo-French Condominium Geological Survey. Annual Reports *see* Vanuatu. Geological Survey. Annual Reports 397
New Hebrides. Bureau of Statistics. Some Facts and Figures about the New Hebrides/Quelques Fait et Chiffres Concernants les Nouvelles-Hebrides *see* Vanuatu in Figures 1118
New Hebrides. Condominium Geological Survey. Annual Reports *see* Vanuatu. Geological Survey. Annual Reports 397
New Hebrides. Condominium Geological Survey. Report *see* Vanuatu. Geological Survey. Reports 397
New History of England (UK) 591
New History of Scotland (UK) 591
New Horizons in Therapeutics (US) 764
New in Chess Yearbook (US ISSN 0168-7697) 1035
New Initiatives in Energy Legislation (US) 466, 661
New Jersey. Administrative Office of the Courts. Annual Report of the Administrative Director of the Courts *see* New Jersey. Administrative Office of the Courts. Annual Report of the New Jersey Judiciary 661
New Jersey. Administrative Office of the Courts. Annual Report of the New Jersey Judiciary (US) 661
New Jersey. Bureau of Geology and Topography. Bulletin *see* New Jersey Geological Survey. Bulletin 392
New Jersey. Bureau of Geology and Topography. Geologic Report Series (US) 392

New Jersey. Casino Control Commission. Annual Report (US) 1035
New Jersey. Department of Agriculture. Highlights of the Annual Report *see* New Jersey Agriculture 32
New Jersey. Department of Banking. Annual Report (US) 231
New Jersey. Department of Education. Educational Assessment Program State Report (US ISSN 0362-5958) 417
New Jersey. Department of Environmental Protection. Annual Report (US ISSN 0092-3311) 498
New Jersey. Department of Higher Education. Research Report (US) 437
New Jersey. Department of Labor. Labor Market Review. Southern N.J. Region (US) 247
New Jersey. Department of Transportation. Annual Report (US) 1082
New Jersey. Department of Transportation. Highlight of Activities *see* New Jersey. Department of Transportation. Annual Report 1082
New Jersey. Developmental Disabilities Council. Annual Report (US ISSN 0090-077X) 1019
New Jersey. Division of Banking. Annual Report *see* New Jersey. Department of Banking. Annual Report 231
New Jersey. Division of Savings and Loan Associations. Annual Report *see* New Jersey. Department of Banking. Annual Report 231
New Jersey. Division of Taxation. Annual Report (US) 297
New Jersey. Division of Water Resources. Special Report (US ISSN 0092-1602) 1159
New Jersey. Division of Water Resources. Water Resources Circulars (US ISSN 0545-2252) 1159
New Jersey. Economic Policy Council. Annual Report of Economic Policy Council and Office of Economic Policy (US ISSN 0077-8478) 290
New Jersey. Office of Demographic and Economic Analysis. Population Estimates for New Jersey (US ISSN 0091-9187) 928
New Jersey. Office of Economic Policy. Economic Report of the Governor (US) 197
New Jersey. State Agency for Social Security. Annual Report (US) 1159
New Jersey Academy of Science. Newsletter (US ISSN 0028-5463) 996
New Jersey Agriculture (US) 32
New Jersey Airport Directory (US ISSN 0091-6978) 1089
New Jersey Clean Air Council. Report (US ISSN 0077-8451) 498
New Jersey Covered Employment Trends by Geographical Areas of the State *see* Covered Employment Trends in New Jersey 271
New Jersey Directory of Manufacturers(US) 314
New Jersey Federation of Planning Officials. Federation Planning Information Reports (US ISSN 0028-5722) 624
New Jersey Folklife (US ISSN 0887-8048) 516
New Jersey Folklore *see* New Jersey Folklife 516
New Jersey Geological Survey. Bulletin(US) 392
New Jersey Instructional Series (US) 1159
New Jersey Journal of School Psychology (US) 417, 935
New Jersey Media Directory *see* Burrelle's New Jersey Media Directory 15
New Jersey Mental Retardation Planning Board. Annual Report *see* New Jersey. Developmental Disabilities Council. Annual Report 1019

New Jersey Mosquito Control Association. Proceedings (US) 165
New Jersey Mosquito Extermination Association. Proceedings *see* New Jersey Mosquito Control Association. Proceedings 165
New Jersey Orchard and Vineyard Survey (US ISSN 0098-9541) 58
New Jersey, Pennsylvania TourBook *see* Tourbook: New Jersey, Pennsylvania 1117
New Jersey Plan for Criminal Justice. *see* Criminal Justice Plan for New Jersey 370
New Jersey Professional Engineer (US ISSN 0028-5900) 473
New Jersey Public Libraries. Statistics *see* New Jersey Public Library Statistics For (Year) 688
New Jersey Public Library Statistics For (Year) (US) 688
New Jersey State Bar Advocate (US) 661
New Jersey State Industrial Directory *see* MacRae's New Jersey State Industrial Directory 313
New Labor Review (US) 274
New Literature and Ideology (CN ISSN 0702-7532) 711, 742
New Literature on Automation (NE ISSN 0028-6095) 9, 354
New Local Government Series (UK) 951
New Magic Lantern Journal (UK ISSN 0143-036X) 884
New Mexico. Agricultural Experiment Station. Research Report (US ISSN 0548-5967) 32
New Mexico. Bureau of Mines and Mineral Resources. Bulletin (US) 818
New Mexico. Bureau of Mines and Mineral Resources. Circular (US) 818
New Mexico. Bureau of Mines and Mineral Resources. Hydrologic Report (US) 403
New Mexico. Bureau of Mines and Mineral Resources. Memoir (US ISSN 0548-5975) 818
New Mexico. Bureau of Mines and Mineral Resources. Progress Report (US ISSN 0098-7077) 818
New Mexico. State Records Center & Archives. Annual Publications List (US) 564
New Mexico. State Records Center and Archives. Publications and Rules Filed *see* New Mexico. State Records Center & Archives. Annual Publications List 564
New Mexico. Veterans' Service Commission. Report (US ISSN 0094-7326) 812, 1019
New Mexico Agricultural Statistics (US ISSN 0077-8540) 42
New Mexico; an Annotated Directory of Information Sources (US) 129
New Mexico Blue Book *see* Official New Mexico Blue Book 608
New Mexico Directory of Manufacturing *see* New Mexico Manufacturing Directory (Year) 314
New Mexico Forest Products Directory *see* Wood Industries of New Mexico 531
New Mexico Geological Society. Guidebook, Field Conference (US ISSN 0077-8567) 392
New Mexico Manufacturing Directory (Year) (US) 314, 818
New Mexico Reports *see* Report of Cases Determined in the Supreme Court and Court of Appeals of the State of New Mexico 663
New Mexico State University. Agricultural Experiment Station. Bulletin (US) 48
New Mexico Statistical Abstract (US ISSN 0077-8575) 1060
New Mexico Studies in the Fine Arts (US ISSN 0149-791X) 108
New Mitre *see* Mitre 711
New Music Articles *see* N M A 839
New Nigeria Development Company Limited. Annual Report and Accounts (NR) 290
New Official Guide: Japan (JA ISSN 0077-8591) 1114

New Orleans Academy of Ophthalmology. Transactions (US ISSN 0077-8605) 786
New Orleans Times-Picayune. Newspaper Index *see* Index to the New Orleans Times-Picayune 647
New Oxford History of Music (US) 839
New Pathway Almanac *see* Kalendar-Al'manakh Novoho Shliakhu 504
New Perspectives in History (US) 559
New Perspectives in Powder Metallurgy(US) 799
New Perspectives on the South (US) 607
New Plays U S A (US ISSN 0731-4523) 728, 1077
New Products from Denmark (DK ISSN 0108-1497) 290
New Rain (US) 728
New Rambler (UK ISSN 0028-6540) 728
New St. George Hospital Gazette (UK) 618
New Schools Exchange. Directory and Resource Guide (US) 417
New Serial Titles (US ISSN 0028-6680) 129
New Settler's Guide for Washington, D.C. and Communities in Nearby Maryland and Virginia (US ISSN 0097-8213) 1114
New Silver Technology (US ISSN 0095-9286) 802
New South Wales. Attorney-General. Bureau of Crime Statistics and Research. Statistical Report (AT ISSN 0310-3684) 372
New South Wales. Attorney-General Justice Department. Bureau of Crime Statistics and Research. Research Report *see* New South Wales. Attorney General's Department. Bureau of Crime Statistics and Research. Research Studies 372
New South Wales. Attorney General's Department. Bureau of Crime Statistics and Research. Research Studies (AT) 372
New South Wales. Commonwealth Housing Commission. Annual Report *see* New South Wales. Department of Housing. Annual Report 624
New South Wales. Department of Agriculture. Annual Report (AT) 32, 511, 944
New South Wales. Department of Agriculture. Fisheries Bulletin (AT ISSN 0814-0545) 511
New South Wales. Department of Agriculture. Plant Disease Survey (AT ISSN 0725-6361) 32
New South Wales. Department of Agriculture. Science Bulletin (AT ISSN 0369-5867) 32
New South Wales. Department of Agriculture. Soil Survey Bulletin (AT ISSN 0705-470X) 58
New South Wales. Department of Agriculture. Technical Bulletin (AT ISSN 0311-8576) 32
New South Wales. Department of Housing. Annual Report (AT) 624
New South Wales. Department of Mineral Resources and Development. Annual Report *see* New South Wales. Department of Mineral Resources. Annual Report 818
New South Wales. Department of Mineral Resources. Annual Report (AT ISSN 0727-9256) 818
New South Wales. Department of Mineral Resources. Annual Report. Statistical Supplement (AT ISSN 0727-9264) 1159
New South Wales. Department of Mines. Annual Report *see* New South Wales. Department of Mineral Resources. Annual Report 818
New South Wales. Department of Mines. Annual Report. Statistical Supplement *see* New South Wales. Department of Mineral Resources. Annual Report. Statistical Supplement 1159
New South Wales. Department of Mines. Chemical Laboratory. Report (AT ISSN 0077-8672) 1159

New South Wales. Department of Mines. Coalfields Branch. Reports (AT ISSN 0077-8680) *1159*
New South Wales. Department of Mines. Memoirs: Palaeontology *see* New South Wales. Geological Survey. Memoirs: Palaeontology *857*
New South Wales. Energy Authority. Annual Report (AT ISSN 0158-0809) *466*
New South Wales. Forestry Commission. Research Notes (AT ISSN 0085-3984) *526*
New South Wales. Geological Survey. Bulletin (AT ISSN 0155-5561) *392*
New South Wales. Geological Survey. Memoirs: Geology (AT ISSN 0077-8710) *392*
New South Wales. Geological Survey. Memoirs: Palaeontology (AT) *857*
New South Wales. Geological Survey. Mine Data Sheets and Metallogenic Study (AT ISSN 0727-9418) *392, 818*
New South Wales. Geological Survey. Mineral Industry Series (AT ISSN 0077-8729) *392, 818*
New South Wales. Geological Survey. Mineral Resources Series (AT ISSN 0077-8737) *392, 818*
New South Wales. Geological Survey. Records (AT ISSN 0155-3372) *392*
New South Wales. Higher Education Board. Annual Report (AT) *437*
New South Wales. Housing Commission. Annual Report *see* New South Wales. Department of Housing. Annual Report *624*
New South Wales. Law Reform Commission. Report (AT ISSN 0085-400X) *661*
New South Wales. State Fisheries. Kapala Cruise Report (AT) *511*
New South Wales Bar Association. Annual Report (AT) *661*
New South Wales in Brief (AT ISSN 0725-5039) *1060*
New South Wales Law Reports (AT ISSN 0312-1674) *661*
New South Wales National Herbarium. Contributions *see* Telopea *161*
New South Wales Ports Handbook (UK ISSN 0266-0652) *314, 1102*
New South Wales State Reports *see* New South Wales Law Reports *661*
New South Wales Veterinary Proceedings (AT ISSN 0085-4026) *1122*
New South Wales Weekly Notes *see* New South Wales Law Reports *661*
New South Wales Year Book (AT ISSN 0085-4441) *1060*
New Studies in Archaeology (UK) *90*
New Studies in Practical Philosophy (US) *879*
New Surveys in the Classics (UK) *338*
New Teacher (PK ISSN 0077-8826) *417, 448*
New Testament Abstracts (US ISSN 0028-6877) *9, 975*
New Testament Tools and Studies (NE ISSN 0077-8842) *971*
New Toy (CN) 108, *711*
New Trade Names (US ISSN 0272-8826) *861*
New Trade Names in the Rubber and Plastics Industries (UK ISSN 0077-8869) *900, 985*
New Trends in Biology Teaching (UN ISSN 0077-8877) *144*
New Trends in Chemistry Teaching (UN ISSN 0077-8885) *324*
New Trends in Integrated Science Teaching (UN) *448*
New Trends in Mathematics Teaching (UN ISSN 0077-8893) *751*
New Trends in Physics Teaching (UN ISSN 0077-8907) *889*
New United Nations Publications (DK ISSN 0108-1829) *907*
New Vico Studies (US ISSN 0733-9542) *879*
New Virginia Review (US) *728, 884*
New Voices (US) *728*
New Voices (Methuen) (US) *742*
New World Archaeological Foundation. Papers (US) *90*
New World Journal (US) *607, 728*

New York (City). Department of Juvenile Justice. Annual Report (US) 335, 372, *661*
New York (City) Mayor. Schedules Supporting the Executive Budget (US ISSN 0094-7547) *951*
New York (City). Museum of the City of New York. Annual Report (US) 607, *830*
New York (State) Assembly. Standing Committee on Children and Families. Annual Report (US) 334, *1019*
New York (State). Assembly. Standing Committee on Veterans' Affairs. Annual Report (US) *812, 1019*
New York (State). Board of Social Welfare. Annual Report *see* New York (State). Department of Social Services. Annual Report *1019*
New York (State). Commission on Quality of Care for the Mentally Disabled. Annual Report (US) *618, 791*
New York (State) Consumer Protection Board. Annual Report (US ISSN 0095-5590) *369*
New York (State). Crime Victims Board. Report (US) *372*
New York (State) Crime Victims Compensation Board. Report *see* New York (State). Crime Victims Board. Report *372*
New York (State) Department of Commerce. Research Bulletin (US ISSN 0077-9156) *240*
New York (State). Department of Environmental Conservation. Annual Report (US) *366*
New York (State). Department of Health. Monograph (US) *955*
New York (State) Department of Labor. Division of Research and Statistics. Labor Research Report (US ISSN 0093-5034) *274*
New York (State). Department of Labor. Statistics on Operations. Annual Report. (US ISSN 0550-6638) *214*
New York (State). Department of Social Services. Annual Report (US ISSN 0363-9835) *1019*
New York (State) Department of Social Services. Bureau of Data Management and Analysis. Program Analysis Report (US ISSN 0090-4716) *1019*
New York (State) Department of Social Services. Bureau of Data Management and Analysis. Program Brief (US ISSN 0162-6302) *1019*
New York (State) Department of Social Services. Bureau of Research. Program Analysis Report *see* New York (State) Department of Social Services. Bureau of Data Management and Analysis. Program Analysis Report *1019*
New York (State) Department of Social Services. Bureau of Research. Program Brief. *see* New York (State) Department of Social Services. Bureau of Data Management and Analysis. Program Brief *1019*
New York (State) Department of State. Manual for the Use of the Legislature of the State of New York(US) *944*
New York (State). Division of Criminal Justice Service. Annual Report (US ISSN 0095-4047) *372*
New York (State) Division of Employment. Research and Statistics Office. Research Bulletin *see* New York (State) Department of Labor. Division of Research and Statistics. Labor Research Report *274*
New York (State). Division of Human Rights. Annual Report (US) *913*
New York (State) Division of the Budget. New York State Statistical Yearbook *see* New York (State). Rockefeller Institute of Government. New York State Statistical Yearbook *1060*
New York (State). Education Department. Employees in Colleges and Universities *see* College and University Employees, New York State *433*

New York (State) Education Department. Public School Professional Personnel Report *see* Public School Professional Personnel Report, New York State *418*
New York (State) Education Department. Survey of Enrollment, Staff and School Housing *see* Public School Enrollment and Staff, New York State *418*
New York (State). Health Planning Commission, Administrative Program for Health Planning and Development (US) *955*
New York (State). Insurance Department. Annual Report of the Superintendent of Insurance to the New York Legislature (US) *641*
New York (State). Insurance Department. Fees and Taxes Charged Insurance Companies Under the Laws of New York Together with Abstracts of Fees, Taxes and Other Requirements of Other States (US) *641*
New York (State). Insurance Department. Loss and Expense Ratios (US ISSN 0467-6769) *641*
New York (State) Insurance Department. Statistical Tables from Annual Statements (US) *642*
New York (State) Legislative Commission on Expenditure Review. Program Audits (US) *944*
New York. State Library, Albany. Library Development. Excerpts from New York State Education Law, Rules of the Board of Regents, and Regulations of the Commissioner of Education Pertaining to Public and Free Association Libraries, Library Systems, Trustees and Librarians (US ISSN 0077-930X) *682*
New York. State Library, Albany. Library Development. Institution Libraries Statistics (US ISSN 0077-9318) *682*
New York. State Library, Albany. Library Development. Public and Association Libraries Statistics (US ISSN 0077-9326) *682*
New York (State). Office of Advocate for the Disabled. Annual Report (US) *1019*
New York (State) Opinions of the Attorney General (US) *661*
New York (State). Rockefeller Institute of Government. New York State Statistical Yearbook (US) *1060*
New York (State). University. Information Center on Education. Education Statistics New York State *see* Education Statistics, New York State *423*
New York (State). Workmen's Compensation Board. Summary of Activities (US) *641*
New York Academy of Medicine. Annual Report (US) *764*
New York Academy of Sciences. Annals (US ISSN 0077-8923) *996*
New York Academy of Sciences. Transactions (US ISSN 0028-7113) *996*
New York Agricultural Statistics (US ISSN 0276-8798) *58*
New York Botanical Garden. Memoirs (US ISSN 0077-8931) *159*
New York Casting/Survival Guide (US) 349, 375, *1077*
New York City Trade Union Handbook(US ISSN 0545-6061) *649*
New York Dairy Statistics *see* New York State Dairy Statistics *62*
New York Facts (US ISSN 0888-4285) *546*
New York Good News (US) *540*
New York Jets Official Yearbook (US) *1039*
New York Knicks Yearbook (US) *1039*
New York L P N *see* New York L P N and Technician *784*
New York L P N and Technician (US) *784*
New York Metropolitan Directory of Manufacturers (US) *314*
New York Pro Musica Instrumental Series (US ISSN 0085-4042) *839*

New York Production Manual *see* Producer's MasterGuide *825*
New York Psychoanalytic Institute. Kris Study Group. Monographs (US ISSN 0077-9008) *935*
New York Rangers Blue Book *see* New York Rangers Yearbook *1035*
New York Rangers Yearbook (US) *1035*
New York Red Book (US) *944*
New York Sea Grant Institute. Annual Report (US) *944*
New York State. Assembly Subcommittee on Food, Farm and Nutrition Policy. Report (US) *846*
New York State. Education Department. College and University Enrollment (US) *437*
New York State. Education Department. College and University Revenues and Expenditures (US) *437, 443*
New York State. Education Department. Racial-Ethnic Distribution of Public School Students and Staff (US) *443*
New York State. State Science Service. Biennial Report (US) *944*
New York State Business Fact Book. Part 1: Business and Manufacturing (US ISSN 0077-9083) *247, 314*
New York State Business Fact Book. Supplement (US ISSN 0077-9105) *247, 314*
New York State Committee on Open Government. Annual Report (US) *661*
New York State Dairy Statistics (US ISSN 0732-9121) *62*
New York State English Council. Monograph Series (US ISSN 0548-9040) *448, 728*
New York State Environmental Facilities Corporation. Industrial Materials Recycling Act. Annual Report (US) *498*
New York State Fair Magazine (US) *1114*
New York State FairGround *see* New York State Fair Magazine *1114*
New York State Industrial Directory *see* MacRae's New York State Industrial Directory *313*
New York State Media Directory *see* Burrelle's New York State Media Directory *15*
New York State Medical Care Facilities Finance Agency. Annual Report (US ISSN 0361-4018) *955*
New York State Museum. Bulletin (US) *996*
New York State Museum. Circular (US) *996*
New York State Museum. Leaflet (US) *996*
New York State Museum. Memoir (US) *997*
New York State Museum and Science Service. Circular *see* New York State Museum. Circular *996*
New York State Museum and Science Service. Memoir *see* New York State Museum. Memoir *997*
New York State School of Industrial and Labor Relations. Bulletin (US ISSN 0070-0134) *274*
New York State School of Industrial and Labor Relations. Institute of Public Employment. Monograph (US) *274*
New York State School of Industrial and Labor Relations. Key Issues Series (US ISSN 0070-0185) *274*
New York State School of Industrial and Labor Relations Paperbacks *see* I L R Paperbacks *272*
New York State Sea Grant Program. Annual Report *see* New York Sea Grant Institute. Annual Report *944*
New York State Statistical Yearbook *see* New York (State). Rockefeller Institute of Government. New York State Statistical Yearbook *1060*
New York State Urban Development Corporation. Annual Report (US ISSN 0077-9423) *944*
New York Telephone Tickler for Insurance Men and Women (US) *641*

1832 NEW YORK

New York Theatre Critics' Reviews (US ISSN 0028-7784) *1077*
New York Times Film Reviews (US ISSN 0362-3688) *825*
New York Times Index (US ISSN 0147-538X) *646*
New York Times School Microfilm Collection Index (US) *129*
New York Times School Microfilm Collection Index by Reels *see* New York Times School Microfilm Collection Index *129*
New York Times Theatre Reviews (US) *1077*
New York TourBook *see* Tourbook: New York *1117*
New York University. Comparative Criminal Law Project. Publications *see* Wayne State University Law School. Comparative Criminal Law Project. Publications Series *373*
New York University. Criminal Law Education and Research Center. Monograph Series *see* Wayne State University Law School. Comparative Criminal Law Project. Monograph Series *373*
New York University. Institute of Labor Relations. Annual Conference on Labor at New York University *see* Annual National Conference on Labor at New York University. Proceedings *269*
New York University. Institute on Federal Taxation. Conference on Charitable Foundations (US) *297, 661*
New York University. Libraries. Bulletin of the Tamiment Library (US ISSN 0077-9490) *682*
New York University. Studies in Near Eastern Civilization (US ISSN 0081-8291) *711, 1028*
New York University Institute of Finance. Bulletin *see* Salomon Brothers Center for the Study of Financial Institutions. Monograph Series *232*
New York University Studies in Comparative Literature (US ISSN 0077-9504) *728*
New York Upstate Directory of Manufacturers (US) *314*
New York Urban League. Annual Report (US) *1019*
New York's Food and Life Sciences Bulletin (US ISSN 0362-0069) *32, 846*
New Zealand. Central Advisory Committee on the Appointments and Promotion of Primary Teachers. Report to the Minister of Education (NZ ISSN 0077-958X) *417*
New Zealand. Council for Recreation and Sport. Report (NZ) *1159*
New Zealand. Dairy Board. Annual Report and Statement of Accounts (NZ) *62*
New Zealand. Dairy Production and Marketing Board. Annual Report and Statement of Accounts *see* New Zealand. Dairy Board. Annual Report and Statement of Accounts *62*
New Zealand. Department of External Affairs. United Nations and Specialised Agencies Handbook *see* New Zealand. Ministry of Foreign Affairs. United Nations Handbook *917*
New Zealand. Department of Health. Environmental Radioactivity Annual Report (NZ ISSN 0110-9944) *498*
New Zealand. Department of Health. Hospital Management Data (NZ ISSN 0110-1900) *619*
New Zealand. Department of Health. Special Report Series (NZ ISSN 0548-944X) *955*
New Zealand. Department of Maori Affairs. Annual Report (NZ) *944*
New Zealand. Department of Maori Affairs. Report *see* New Zealand. Department of Maori Affairs. Annual Report *944*
New Zealand. Department of Scientific and Industrial Research. Annual Report (NZ ISSN 0077-9601) *997*

New Zealand. Department of Scientific and Industrial Research. Bulletin (NZ ISSN 0077-961X) *997*
New Zealand. Department of Scientific and Industrial Research. Geophysics Division. Report (NZ ISSN 0110-6112) *400*
New Zealand. Department of Scientific and Industrial Research. Geophysics Division. Technical Note (NZ ISSN 0110-7089) *400*
New Zealand. Department of Scientific and Industrial Research. Geological Survey. Bulletin (NZ ISSN 0077-9628) *392*
New Zealand. Department of Scientific and Industrial Research. Information Series (NZ ISSN 0077-9636) *997*
New Zealand. Department of Scientific and Industrial Research. Social Science Series (NZ ISSN 0112-2339) *1010*
New Zealand. Department of Statistics. Agricultural Statistics (NZ ISSN 0110-4624) *42*
New Zealand. Department of Statistics. Annual Report of the Government Statistician (NZ ISSN 0077-9652) *1060*
New Zealand. Department of Statistics. Balance of Payments *see* New Zealand. Department of Statistics. Overseas Balance of Payments *214*
New Zealand. Department of Statistics. Building Statistics (NZ ISSN 0110-3490) *189*
New Zealand. Department of Statistics. Census of Building and Construction (NZ ISSN 0110-4640) *189*
New Zealand. Department of Statistics. Demographic Trends Bulletin (NZ ISSN 0112-9155) *928, 1060*
New Zealand. Department of Statistics. Exports (NZ ISSN 0110-2184) *214*
New Zealand. Department of Statistics. External Migration Statistics (NZ ISSN 0112-6709) *928, 1060*
New Zealand. Department of Statistics. Imports (NZ ISSN 0110-3741) *214*
New Zealand. Department of Statistics. Incomes and Income Tax Statistics (NZ ISSN 0110-3776) *214*
New Zealand. Department of Statistics. Insurance Statistics (NZ ISSN 0110-3474) *642*
New Zealand. Department of Statistics. Justice Statistics *see* New Zealand. Department of Statistics. Justice Statistics: Part A *661*
New Zealand. Department of Statistics. Justice Statistics: Part A (NZ ISSN 0112-4447) *661*
New Zealand. Department of Statistics. Justice Statistics: Part B (NZ ISSN 0112-4501) *661*
New Zealand. Department of Statistics. Life Annuity Tables *see* New Zealand. Department of Statistics. New Zealand Life Tables *642*
New Zealand. Department of Statistics. Local Authority Statistics (NZ ISSN 0110-3466) *949, 1060*
New Zealand. Department of Statistics. New Zealand Life Tables (NZ ISSN 0111-0225) *642*
New Zealand. Department of Statistics. Overseas Balance of Payments (NZ ISSN 0112-5117) *214*
New Zealand. Department of Statistics. Part A: Prices. (NZ ISSN 0110-5019) *214*
New Zealand. Department of Statistics. Population and Migration *see* New Zealand. Department of Statistics. External Migration Statistics *928*
New Zealand. Department of Statistics. Population and Migration. Part A: Population *see* New Zealand. Department of Statistics. Demographic Trends Bulletin *928*
New Zealand. Department of Statistics. Population and Migration. Part B: External Migration *see* New Zealand. Department of Statistics. External Migration Statistics *928*

New Zealand. Department of Statistics. Population Census: Ages and Marital Status *see* New Zealand. Department of Statistics. Population Census: Ages, Marital Status and Fertility *928*
New Zealand. Department of Statistics. Population Census: Ages, Marital Status and Fertility (NZ) *923, 928*
New Zealand. Department of Statistics. Population Census: Birthplaces and Ethnic Origin (NZ) *923, 928*
New Zealand. Department of Statistics. Population Census: Dwellings (NZ ISSN 0077-9695) *923, 928*
New Zealand. Department of Statistics. Population Census: Education *see* New Zealand. Department of Statistics. Population Census: Education and Training *928*
New Zealand. Department of Statistics. Population Census: Education and Training (NZ) *923, 928*
New Zealand. Department of Statistics. Population Census: General Report (NZ ISSN 0077-9717) *923, 928*
New Zealand. Department of Statistics. Population Census: Households and Families (NZ) *923, 928*
New Zealand. Department of Statistics. Population Census: Households *see* New Zealand. Department of Statistics. Population Census: Households and Families *928*
New Zealand. Department of Statistics. Population Census: Incomes *see* New Zealand. Department of Statistics. Population Census: Incomes and Social Security Benefits *928*
New Zealand. Department of Statistics. Population Census: Incomes and Social Security Benefits (NZ) *923, 928*
New Zealand. Department of Statistics. Population Census: Increase and Location of Population *see* New Zealand. Department of Statistics. Population Census. Location and Increase of Population. Part A: Population Size and Distribution *928*
New Zealand. Department of Statistics. Population Census: Increase and Location of Population *see* New Zealand. Department of Statistics. Population Census. Location and Increase of Population. Part B: Population Density *928*
New Zealand. Department of Statistics. Population Census: Industries and Occupations *see* New Zealand. Department of Statistics. Population Census: Labour Force *928*
New Zealand. Department of Statistics. Population Census: Internal Migration (NZ ISSN 0110-8700) *928, 1060*
New Zealand. Department of Statistics. Population Census: Labour Force (NZ) *923, 928*
New Zealand. Department of Statistics. Population Census. Location and Increase of Population. Part A: Population Size and Distribution (NZ) *928, 1060*
New Zealand. Department of Statistics. Population Census. Location and Increase of Population. Part B: Population Density (NZ) *928, 1060*
New Zealand. Department of Statistics. Population Census: Maori Population and Dwellings (NZ) *923, 928*
New Zealand. Department of Statistics. Population Census: Provisional Population and Dwelling Statistics *see* New Zealand. Department of Statistics. Population Census: Provisional Statistics Series. Bulletin One. Local Authority Areas *928*
New Zealand. Department of Statistics. Population Census: Provisional Statistics Series. Bulletin One. Local Authority Areas (NZ) *923, 928*
New Zealand. Department of Statistics. Population Census: Race *see* New Zealand. Department of Statistics. Population Census: Birthplaces and Ethnic Origin *928*

New Zealand. Department of Statistics. Population Census: Religious Professions (NZ ISSN 0077-9784) *923, 928*
New Zealand. Department of Statistics. Prices, Wages and Labour *see* New Zealand. Department of Statistics. Part A: Prices *214*
New Zealand. Department of Statistics. Report and Analysis of External Trade (NZ ISSN 0077-9806) *214*
New Zealand. Department of Statistics. Statistical Report of Farm Production *see* New Zealand. Department of Statistics. Agricultural Statistics *42*
New Zealand. Department of Statistics. Statistics of Incomes and Income Tax of Companies (NZ ISSN 0112-3998) *214*
New Zealand. Department of Statistics. Statistics of Incomes and Income Tax of Persons (NZ ISSN 0112-3939) *214*
New Zealand. Department of Statistics. Transport Statistics (NZ ISSN 0110-3458) *1082*
New Zealand. Department of Statistics. Vital Statistics (NZ ISSN 0110-4586) *1060*
New Zealand. Department of Trade and Industry. Import Licensing Schedule (NZ) *258*
New Zealand. Director-General of Forests. Report (NZ) *526*
New Zealand. Economic Monitoring Group Report (NZ ISSN 0112-2061) *197, 247*
New Zealand. F R I Bulletin (Forest Research Institute) (NZ ISSN 0111-8129) *526*
New Zealand. Forest Research Institute. Report (NZ ISSN 0077-9997) *526*
New Zealand. Lottery Board of Control. Report *see* New Zealand Lottery Board. Report *297*
New Zealand. Meat and Wool Boards' Economic Service. Annual Review of the Sheep Industry (NZ ISSN 0078-0138) *67*
New Zealand. Ministry of Agriculture and Fisheries. Fisheries Research Division. Bulletin. (NZ ISSN 0110-1749) *512*
New Zealand. Ministry of Agriculture and Fisheries. Fisheries Research Division: Information Leaflet (NZ ISSN 0110-4519) *512*
New Zealand. Ministry of Agriculture and Fisheries. Fisheries Research Division. Occasional Publication (NZ ISSN 0110-1765) *512*
New Zealand. Ministry of Agriculture and Fisheries. Fisheries Technical Report (NZ) *512*
New Zealand. Ministry of Defence. Review of Defence Policy (NZ) *812*
New Zealand. Ministry of Energy. Mines Division. Annual Report *see* New Zealand. Ministry of Energy. Report *818*
New Zealand. Ministry of Energy. Mines Division. Annual Returns of Production from Quarries and Mineral Production Statistics. *see* Annual Returns of Production from Quarries and Mineral Production Statistics *821*
New Zealand. Ministry of Energy. Report (NZ) *818*
New Zealand. Ministry of Foreign Affairs. Project Profiles (NZ ISSN 0111-5251) *917*
New Zealand. Ministry of Foreign Affairs. Report (NZ) *917*
New Zealand. Ministry of Foreign Affairs. United Nations Handbook (NZ ISSN 0110-1951) *917*
New Zealand. Ministry of Transport. Traffic Research Circular (NZ) *1082, 1092*
New Zealand. Ministry of Transport. Traffic Research Report (NZ ISSN 0110-6872) *1082, 1092, 1097*
New Zealand. National Health Statistics Centre. Fetal and Infant Deaths (NZ ISSN 0111-8617) *771, 1060*

NIGERIAN BUSINESS   1833

New Zealand. National Research Advisory Council. Senior and Post Doctoral Research Fellowship Awards for Research in New Zealand Government Departments (NZ ISSN 0078-0154) *1159*
New Zealand. Railways Corporation. Annual Report (NZ) *1095*
New Zealand. Railways Department. Annual Report *see* New Zealand. Railways Corporation. Annual Report *1095*
New Zealand. Road Research Unit. Bulletin (NZ ISSN 0549-0030) *1097*
New Zealand. Road Research Unit. Occasional Paper (NZ ISSN 0111-0756) *1097*
New Zealand. Soil Bureau. Bibliographic Report (NZ ISSN 0110-165X) *42*
New Zealand. Soil Bureau. Scientific Report (NZ ISSN 0304-1735) *58*
New Zealand. Soil Bureau. Soil Survey Reports (NZ ISSN 0110-2079) *366*
New Zealand. Urban Public Passenger Transport Council. Report *see* Urban Transport Council. Report *1084*
New Zealand Agricultural Engineering Institute. Annual Report (NZ ISSN 0077-9520) *58, 1125*
New Zealand Agricultural Engineering Institute. Current Publications (NZ ISSN 0111-0829) *42, 1128*
New Zealand Agriculture *see* AgLink Leaflets *22*
New Zealand and Dependencies Stamp Catalogue (AT ISSN 0729-2368) *1159*
New Zealand Annual *see* Weekly News Annual *1118*
New Zealand Association of Radio Transmitters, Inc. Amateur Radio Callbook *see* N.Z.A.R.T. Amateur Radio Callbook *349*
New Zealand Business Who's Who (NZ ISSN 0077-9571) *135, 314*
New Zealand Census of Transport, Storage & Communication (NZ ISSN 0112-3629) *1060, 1086*
New Zealand Civil Aviation Statistics (NZ ISSN 0467-8966) *22*
New Zealand Council for Educational Research Newsletter *see* N Z C E R Newsletter *416*
New Zealand Dairy Research Institute Annual Report *see* New Zealand Dairy Research Institute Biennial Review *62*
New Zealand Dairy Research Institute Biennial Review (NZ) *62*
New Zealand Ecological Society. Proceedings *see* New Zealand Journal of Ecology *144*
New Zealand Economic Papers (NZ ISSN 0077-9954) *197*
New Zealand Electronics Review (NZ) *457*
New Zealand Entomologist (NZ ISSN 0077-9962) *165*
New Zealand Export-Import Corporation. Report (NZ) *258*
New Zealand Federation of Labour. Official Trade Union Directory (NZ) *649*
New Zealand Geographical Society. Miscellaneous Series (NZ ISSN 0078-0022) *546*
New Zealand Geography Conference Proceedings Series (NZ ISSN 0078-0030) *546*
New Zealand Geological Survey. Paleontological Bulletin (NZ ISSN 0078-8589) *857*
New Zealand Health Statistics Report (NZ) *955*
New Zealand Household Expenditure and Income Survey (NZ ISSN 0112-6601) *214*
New Zealand Household Survey *see* New Zealand Household Expenditure and Income Survey *214*
New Zealand Income Tax Legislation (NZ) *297, 661*
New Zealand Institute of Economic Research. Annual Report (NZ ISSN 0078-0057) *197*

New Zealand Institute of Economic Research. Contract Research (NZ) *197*
New Zealand Institute of Economic Research. Discussion Paper (NZ ISSN 0078-0049) *197*
New Zealand Institute of Economic Research. Medium Term Review (NZ ISSN 0112-1170) *197*
New Zealand Institute of Economic Research. Research Paper (NZ ISSN 0078-0065) *197*
New Zealand Journal of Archaeology (NZ ISSN 0110-540X) *90*
New Zealand Journal of Ecology (NZ ISSN 0110-6465) *144*
New Zealand Law Register (NZ ISSN 0078-0081) *661*
New Zealand Lottery Board. Report (NZ) *297*
New Zealand Marine Sciences Newsletter (NZ ISSN 0028-842X) *144, 407, 512*
New Zealand Mineral Production Statistics *see* Annual Returns of Production from Quarries and Mineral Production Statistics *821*
New Zealand National Bibliography (NZ ISSN 0028-8497) *129*
New Zealand Nursing Forum (NZ ISSN 0110-0890) *784*
New Zealand Oceanographic Institute. Collected Reprints (NZ ISSN 0083-789X) *407*
New Zealand Oceanographic Institute. Memoir (NZ ISSN 0083-7903) *407*
New Zealand Oceanographic Institute Hydrology Station Data *see* N Z O I Hydrology Station Data *407*
New Zealand Oceanographic Institute Miscellaneous Publications *see* N Z O I Miscellaneous Publications *407*
New Zealand Oceanographic Institute Oceanographic Field Report *see* N Z O I Oceanographic Field Report *407*
New Zealand Oceanographic Institute Oceanographic Summary *see* N Z O I Oceanographic Summary *407*
New Zealand Oceanographic Institute Records *see* N Z O I Records *407*
New Zealand Official Year-Book (NZ ISSN 0078-0170) *573*
New Zealand Planning Council. Planning Paper (NZ ISSN 0111-0470) *944*
New Zealand Poultry Board. Report; and New Zealand Marketing Authority Report and Statement of Accounts (NZ ISSN 0078-0197) *48, 67*
New Zealand Red Cross Society. Report (NZ ISSN 0080-0392) *1019*
New Zealand Science Abstracts (NZ ISSN 0111-672X) *9, 1004*
New Zealand Shipping Directory (NZ ISSN 0545-7866) *1102*
New Zealand Slavonic Journal (NZ ISSN 0028-8683) *631, 907, 1010*
New Zealand Society of Animal Production. Proceedings (NZ ISSN 0370-2731) *67*
New Zealand Visitor Statistics (NZ) *1114*
New Zealand Wheat Review (NZ ISSN 0078-0219) *64*
New Zealand Wool Board. Statistical Handbook (NZ ISSN 0110-1242) *1074*
Newcastle History Monographs (AT ISSN 0078-0243) *573*
Newcomen Society for the Study of the History of Engineering and Technology. Transactions (UK ISSN 0372-0187) *473, 1070*
Newes (US) *614, 646*
Newfoundland. Department of Social Services. Annual Report (CN ISSN 0078-0294) *1019*
Newfoundland. Mineral Development Division. Geological Survey. Bulletin (CN ISSN 0078-0308) *392*
Newfoundland. Mineral Development Division. Information (CN ISSN 0078-0340) *818*
Newfoundland. Mineral Development Division. Information Circular. (CN ISSN 0078-0359) *818*

Newfoundland. Mines Branch. Annual Report Series (CN ISSN 0078-0367) *818*
Newfoundland. Mines Branch. Geological Survey of Newfoundland. Report Series (CN ISSN 0078-0383) *392*
Newfoundland & Prince Edward Island Reports (CN) *661*
Newfoundland Medical Directory (CN ISSN 0078-0316) *764*
News Feature from Denmark *see* Feature fra Danmark *538*
News from the Gutter (US ISSN 0028-9159) *746*
News from the Rare Book Room (CN ISSN 0085-4166) *129*
News Letter - New Brunswick Public Employees Association *see* New Brunswick Public Employees Association. News Letter *951*
News Novel (US) *860*
News of Shinobazu (JA) *498*
News of the Tohoku Plant Association *see* Sennke *161*
NewsBank (New Canaan) (US ISSN 0737-3813) *540*
NewsBank Library *see* NewsBank (New Canaan) *540*
Newsletter of Research on Japanese Politics (US) *907*
Newsletter on Contemporary Japanese Prints (US ISSN 0085-4174) *108*
Newsletter-Society for the Preservation of Long Island Antiquities. *see* Society for the Preservation of Long Island Antiquities. Newsletter *79*
Newsletter Yearbook Directory *see* Hudson's Directory *645*
Newspaper and Newsprint Facts at a Glance (US) *859*
Newspaper Circulation Analysis (US) *16*
Newspaper Guild. Annual T.N.G. Convention Officers' Report (US ISSN 0090-2209) *646*
Newspaper Guild. Proceedings of the Annual Convention (US) *646*
Newspaper Promotion Yearbook (US) *16*
Newspaper Publishers Handbook (UK) *646, 962*
Newspapers Currently Received and Permanently Retained in the Library of Congress *see* Newspapers Received Currently *646*
Newspapers Index: Mauritius *see* Subject Index to Articles in Newspapers in Mauritius *12*
Newspapers Received Currently (US) *646*
Newth-Nuth Family History Society. Newsletter (UK ISSN 0260-695X) *536*
Newth Nuth News *see* Newth-Nuth Family History Society. Newsletter *536*
Next Year Country *see* Next Year Country News *538*
Next Year Country News (CN) *538*
Nexus (CN ISSN 0711-5342) *74*
Neydhartinger Moorpost (AU ISSN 0028-9620) *1159*
Nezam Pezeshki-Ye Iran. Nashriyeh *see* Medical Council of Iran. Publication *763*
Niagara Falls Area Chamber of Commerce.Business/Industrial Directory (US) *236*
Niagara Frontier Transportation Authority Annual Report *see* N F T A Annual Report *1082*
Niagara Frontier Transportation Authority Port of Buffalo Handbook *see* N F T A Port of Buffalo Handbook *1159*
Niagara Parks Commission. Annual Report (CN ISSN 0078-0502) *366*
Nicaragua. Corte Suprema de Justicia. Boletin Judicial (NQ) *661*
Nicaragua. Direccion General de Aduanas. Memoria (NQ ISSN 0078-0510) *240*
Nicaragua. Instituto Nacional de Estadisticas y Censos. Boletin Demografico (NQ) *923*

Nicaragua. Instituto Nacional de Estadisticas y Censos. Encuesta Anual Industria Manufacturere (NQ) *214*
Nicaragua. Oficina Ejectiva de Encuestos y Censos. Boletin Demografico *see* Nicaragua. Instituto Nacional de Estadisticas y Censos. Boletin Demografico *923*
Nicholls State University Library. Genealogy Series *see* N S U Library. Genealogy Series *536*
Nickelodeon *see* Trumpet *14*
Niederdeutsche Beitraege zur Kunstgeschichte (GW ISSN 0078-0537) *108*
Niederdeutsches Wort (GW ISSN 0078-0545) *699*
Niederoesterreichische Sozialhilfe und Jugendwohlfahrtspflege (AU) *1019*
Niedersachsisches Jahrbuch (GW) *591*
Niedersaechsische Archivverwaltung. Veroeffentlichungen (GW) *559*
Niedersaechsische Staats- und Universitaetsbibliothek, Goettingen. Arbeiten (GW ISSN 0072-4866) *682*
Niedersaechsisches Jahrbuch fuer Landesgeschichte *see* Niedersachsisches Jahrbuch *591*
Niels Bohr International Gold Medal (DK ISSN 0109-0054) *1159*
Nielsen Report on Television (US) *349*
Niepodleglosc (US) *591*
Niespulver (GW ISSN 0720-6542) *711*
Niet Zo Benauwd (NE) *536*
Nietzsche-Studien (GW ISSN 0342-1422) *880*
Niger. Office des Postes et Telecommunications. Annuaire Officiel des Telephones (NG) *350*
Nigeria. Federal Department of Fisheries. Federal Fisheries Occasional Paper (NR) *512*
Nigeria. Federal Office of Statistics. Annual Abstract of Statistics (NR ISSN 0078-0626) *1060*
Nigeria. Federal Office of Statistics. Building and Construction Survey (NR) *189, 1060*
Nigeria. Federal Office of Statistics. Industrial Survey (NR) *214, 1060*
Nigeria. Federal Office of Statistics. Report on Rural Consumer Survey (NR) *214, 1060*
Nigeria. Federal Office of Statistics. Report on Rural Economic Survey (NR) *214, 1060*
Nigeria. Federal Office of Statistics. Report on Rural Household Survey (NR) *627, 1060*
Nigeria. Federal Office of Statistics. Report on Urban Consumer Survey (NR) *214, 1060*
Nigeria. Federal Office of Statistics. Report on Urban Household Survey (NR) *627, 1060*
Nigeria. Federal Office of Statistics. Review of External Trade (NR ISSN 0078-0634) *214*
Nigeria. Federal Office of Statistics. Social Statistics in Nigeria (NR) *1014, 1060*
Nigeria. National Electric Power Authority. Annual Report and Accounts (NR) *457*
Nigeria. National Manpower Board. Manpower Studies (NR) *274*
Nigeria. National Universities Commission. Annual Report (NR) *437*
Nigeria. Work in Progress (NR) *711*
Nigeria and the Classics *see* Museum Africum *338*
Nigeria Business Directory (NR ISSN 0078-0596) *314*
Nigeria Business Guide Annual (NR ISSN 0794-2877) *214*
Nigeria Industrial Directory (NR) *314*
Nigeria Tourist Guide/Guide du Tourisme Nigerien (NR) *620, 1114*
Nigeria Trade Summary (NR ISSN 0078-0650) *258*
Nigeria Year Book (NR ISSN 0078-0685) *917*
Nigerian Business Journal (NR ISSN 0189-5036) *237*

Nigerian Criminal Reports (UK ISSN 0262-4737) *1159*
Nigerian Economic Society. Proceedings of the Annual Conference (NR ISSN 0331-0361) *197*
Nigerian Industrial Development Bank. Annual Report and Accounts (NR ISSN 0549-2734) *231*
Nigerian Institute for Oil Palm Research. Journal (NR ISSN 0078-0715) *159*
Nigerian Institute of International Affairs. Lecture Series (NR ISSN 0078-0731) *917*
Nigerian Institute of International Affairs. Monograph Series (NR ISSN 0331-6254) *917*
Nigerian Institute of Social and Economic Research. Annual Report (NR ISSN 0078-074X) *197, 1010*
Nigerian Institute of Social and Economic Research Occasional Papers see N I S E R Occasional Papers *1010*
Nigerian Medical Directory (NR ISSN 0078-0782) *764*
Nigerian Mining and Geosciences Society. Journal (NR) *392, 819*
Nigerian Mining, Geological and Metallurgical Society. Journal see Nigerian Mining and Geosciences Society. Journal *819*
Nigerian Names (NR) *536*
Nigerian National Advisory Council for the Blind. Annual Report (NR ISSN 0078-0804) *1019*
Nigerian Office and Residential Directory see Nigerian Yellow Pages *286*
Nigerian Stored Products Research Institute. Annual Report (NR) *51, 326*
Nigerian Tobacco Company. Annual Report and Accounts (NR) *1080*
Nigerian Tobacco Company. Report see Nigerian Tobacco Company. Annual Report and Accounts *1080*
Nigerian Yellow Pages (NR ISSN 0331-0973) *286*
Nightsun (US ISSN 0278-6079) *711, 728, 880*
Nihon Boeki Shinkokai see Japan Trade Directory *310*
Nihon Hakushiroku (JA) *129*
Nihon Insatsu Nenkan see Japan Printing Art Annual *931*
Nihon Kaihatsu Ginko. Chosabu. Chosa Geppo (JA) *231*
Nihon Kyoikuho Gakkai Nempo (JA) *417, 661*
Nihon Ongaku Bunken Yoshi Mokuroku see Ongaku Bunken Yoshi Mokuroku *844*
Nihon Retaringu Nenkan see Japan Typography Annual *931*
Nihon Setchaku Kyokaishi see Adhesion Society of Japan. Journal *900*
Nihon Shosen Sempuku Tokei (JA) *1102*
Nihon Soshiki Baiyo Kenkyu Nenpo see Tissue Culture Studies in Japan: The Annual Bibliography *1164*
Nihon Taipogurafi Nenkan see Japan Typography Annual *931*
Nihon University. Atomic Energy Research Institute. Annual Report (JA) *466, 473, 897*
Niigata Agricultural Science see Niigata University. Faculty of Agriculture. Bulletin *32*
Niigata Airglow Observatory. Bulletin (JA) *889*
Niigata Daigaku Nogakubu Kenkyu Hokoku see Niigata University. Faculty of Agriculture. Bulletin *32*
Niigata Daigaku Nogakubu Kiyo see Niigata University. Faculty of Agriculture. Memoirs *32*
Niigata Daigaku Rigakubu Fuzoku Sado Rinkai Jikkenjo Kenkyu Hokoku see Sado Marine Biological Station. Report *146*
Niigata-Shi Ni Okeru Kogai/Environmental Pollution in Niigata City (JA) *498*

Niigata University. Faculty of Agriculture. Bulletin/Niigata Daigaku Nogakubu Kenkyu Hokoku (JA ISSN 0385-8634) *32*
Niigata University. Faculty of Agriculture. Memoirs/Niigata Daigaku Nogakubu Kiyo (JA ISSN 0549-4826) *32*
Niigata University. Faculty of Science. Science Reports. Series A: Mathematics (JA ISSN 0369-576X) *751*
Niigata University. Faculty of Science. Science Reports. Series B: Physics (JA) *889*
Niigata University. Faculty of Science. Science Reports. Series C: Chemistry(JA) *324*
Niigata University. Faculty of Science. Science Reports. Series D: Biology (JA ISSN 0371-2672) *144*
Niigata University. Faculty of Science. Science Reports. Series E: Geology and Mineralogy (JA ISSN 0369-3627) *392, 819*
Nijenrode Studies in Business (NE) *197*
Nijenrode Studies in Economics (NE) *247*
Nijhoff International Philosophy Series (NE) *880*
Nikhef K Bulletin (NE) *889*
Nikon World (US ISSN 0029-0513) *1159*
Nile Mirror (SJ) *539*
Nimrod's Quarry (AT) *742*
Nineteenth-Century Literature (Ann Arbor) (US) *728*
Nippon Dental University. Annual Publications (JA ISSN 0549-5245) *779*
Nippon Gakujutsu Shinkokai see J S P S Annual Report *993*
Nippon Gyosei Kenkyu Nenpo see Japanese Society for Public Administration. Annals *943*
Nippon Hoso Kyokai Technical Monograph see N H K Technical Monograph *349*
Nippon Nyt (DK ISSN 0107-752X) *539*
Nippon Steel Report (JA) *799*
Nippon Tungsten Review (JA ISSN 0388-0664) *328*
Nisaba (NE) *971*
Niti Vimamsa (CE) *661*
Nityanand Universal Series (II ISSN 0078-0855) *570*
Niv Hamidrashia (IS ISSN 0048-0460) *977*
No Deadline (US) *16*
Nobel Symposium Series (SW ISSN 0078-0901) *631*
Noble Official Catalog of Canada Precancels (US ISSN 0078-091X) *875*
Noble Official Catalog of United States Bureau Precancels (US ISSN 0078-0928) *875*
Noctes Romanae (SZ ISSN 0078-0936) *338*
Noda Institute for Scientific Research. Report/Noda Sangyo Kagaku Kenkyusho Kenkyu Hokoku (JA ISSN 0078-0944) *997*
Noda Sangyo Kagaku Kenkyusho Kenkyu Hokoku see Noda Institute for Scientific Research. Report *997*
Noerre-Alslev Kommune. Lokalhistorisk Arkiv. Aarsskrift (DK ISSN 0106-6145) *591*
Noerre Djurs Egnsarkiv see Grenaa og Noerre Djurs Foer og Nu *584*
Nogaku Kenkyu (JA ISSN 0029-0874) *58, 144*
Nogyo Kikai Nenkan see Farm Machinery Yearbook *51*
Nogyo Sogo Kenkyusho Nenpo see National Research Institute of Agricultural Economics. Annual Report *32*
Noise and Smog News (IT ISSN 0546-2347) *498*
Noise Manual (US) *1097*
Noise Pollution Publications Abstracts (US ISSN 0733-172X) *1159*
Noma (NR ISSN 0331-6742) *32*
Nomen Nudum (AT ISSN 0159-818X) *857*

Nomenclator Zoologicus (UK ISSN 0078-0952) *177*
Nomenclature des Entreprises Nationales a Caractere Industriel ou Commercial et des Societies d'Economie Mixte d'Interet National(FR ISSN 0078-0960) *290*
Nomina (UK ISSN 0141-6340) *591, 699*
Nomismatika Chronica (GR) *845*
Nomos (US ISSN 0078-0979) *907*
Non-European Societies see Studies of Developing Countries *1030*
Non-Ferrous Metal Data (US ISSN 0360-9553) *799*
Non-Ferrous Metal Works of the World(UK ISSN 0078-0987) *799*
Non-Government Schools see Australia. Bureau of Statistics. National Schools Statistics Collection *948*
Non-Ionizing Radiation (UK ISSN 0550-8398) *153, 792*
Non-Metallic Solids (US ISSN 0078-0995) *889*
Non-Prescription Products Guide (AT ISSN 0818-4453) *872*
Non-Wage Provisions in Saskatchewan Collective Agreements (CN ISSN 0830-0763) *274*
Nonlinear Science: Theory and Applications (UK) *997*
Nonlinear Vibrations Problems see Zagadnienia Drgan Nieliniowych *892*
Nonpublic School Enrollment and Staff, New York State (US ISSN 0077-9253) *417*
Noordbrabants Historisch Jaarboek (NE) *591*
Nor'-easter see Student Nationalist *712*
Nord-Norge Naeringsliv og Oekonomi (NO ISSN 0078-1029) *197*
Nord Nytt (DK ISSN 0008-1345) *516*
Nordelbingen (GW ISSN 0078-1037) *592*
Nordens Jaernvaegar (SW) *1095*
Nordenskiold-Samfundets Tidskrift (FI ISSN 0356-0910) *144*
Nordeste (AG ISSN 0029-1242) *711*
Nordeuropa. Jahrbuch fuer Nordische Studien see Nordeuropa Studien *592*
Nordeuropa Studien (GE ISSN 0138-2802) *592*
Nordfriesisches Jahrbuch (GW ISSN 0078-1045) *592*
Nordfriesland (GW) *240*
Nordic (US ISSN 0163-5905) *1046*
Nordic Archaeological Abstracts see N A A *96*
Nordic Documentation Center for Mass Communication Research see N O R D I C O M *346*
Nordic Institute of Folklore. Publications (FI) *516*
Nordica (DK ISSN 0109-3967) *711*
Nordicana (CN ISSN 0078-1053) *74, 997*
Nordisk Ekumenisk Aarsbok (SW ISSN 0085-4212) *971*
Nordisk Flaggskrift (DK) *536*
Nordisk Handels Kalender (NO) *258*
Nordisk Handels Kalender: Skandinavisk Addressebog/Key to Scandinavia: Danmark, Norge, Sverige, Finland, Island (NO ISSN 0549-6233) *258*
Nordisk Hydrologisk Forening Rapport see N H P Rapport *403*
Nordisk Julemaerke Katalog (DK ISSN 0105-9106) *845, 875*
Nordisk Komite for Transportoekonomisk Forskning. Publikation (DK ISSN 0359-7601) *197, 1082*
Nordisk Kulturelt Samarbejde (DK ISSN 0105-5100) *711*
Nordisk Medicinhistorisk Aarsbok (SW ISSN 0078-1061) *764*
Nordisk Numismatisk Aarsskrift/Scandinavian Numismatic Journal (NO ISSN 0078-107X) *845*
Nordisk Psykologi (DK ISSN 0029-1463) *935*
Nordisk Psykologisk Litteratur (DK ISSN 0900-8772) *935*
Nordisk Statistisk Aarsbok/Yearbook of Nordic Statistics (DK ISSN 0078-1088) *1060*

Nordisk Statistisk Skriftserie/Statistical Reports of the Nordic Countries (DK ISSN 0332-6527) *1060*
Nordisk Statutsamling (SW ISSN 0300-3094) *661*
Nordiska Samarbetskommitten foer Namnforskning Norna - Rapporter see Norna - Rapporter *699*
Nordiska Samarbetsorgan (SW) *649*
Nordiska Samarbetsorganet for Vetenskaplig Information Publikation see N O R D I N F O Publikation *681*
Nordiske Domme i Sjofartsanliggender (NO ISSN 0085-4220) *661*
Nordiske Komite for Bygningsbestemmelsei Skriftserie see N K B Skriftserie *186*
Nordiske Sjefsstatistikermoete/Meeting of the Chief Statisticians of the Nordic Countries (DK ISSN 0078-1096) *1060*
Nordiske Statistiske Chefsmoede see Nordiske Sjefsstatistikermoete *1060*
Nordistica Gothoburgensia (SW ISSN 0078-1134) *699, 728*
Nordjysk Ornithologisk Kartotek. Rapport see Fugle i Nordjylland *170*
Nordschleswig (DK ISSN 0107-2188) *538*
Nordslesvigske Museer (DK) *592*
Norfolk Holiday Handbook see Holiday Hints Handbook *1111*
Norfolk Record Society. Publications (UK ISSN 0078-1169) *592*
Norge-Amerika Foreningen. Report see Norge-Amerika Foreningen. Yearbook *917*
Norge-Amerika Foreningen. Yearbook (NO) *917*
Norges Bank. Annual Report see Norges Bank. Report and Accounts *231*
Norges Bank. Report and Accounts (NO ISSN 0078-1185) *231*
Norges Geologiske Undersoekelse. Arsmelding (NO ISSN 0333-4112) *392*
Norges Geologiske Undersoekelse Bulletin see N G U Bulletin *392*
Norges Geologiske Undersoekelse Skrifter see N G U Skrifter *392*
Norges Geotekniske Institutt. Publikasjon/Norwegian Geotechnical Institute. Publications (NO ISSN 0078-1193) *400*
Norges Handels-Kalender/Norwegian Directory of Commerce/Annuaire du Commerce du Norvege/Norwegische Handels-Adressbuch (NO ISSN 0078-1215) *315*
Norges Landbrukshoegskole. Institutt for Bygningsteknikk. Aarsmelding/Annual Report (NO ISSN 0065-0226) *186*
Norges Landbrukshoegskole. Institutt for Bygningsteknikk. Byggekostnadsindeks for Driftsbygninger i Jordbruket. Prisutviklingen (NO ISSN 0065-0218) *32, 186*
Norges Landbrukshoegskole. Institutt for Bygningsteknikk. Melding (NO ISSN 0065-0234) *186*
Norges Landbrukshoegskole. Institutt for Jordskifte og Arealplanlegging. Melding/Agricultural University of Norway. Department of Land Use Planning. Serie (NO ISSN 0801-2334) *48*
Norges Landbrukshoejskole. Institutt for Jordskifte og Eiendomsutforming. Melding see Norges Landbrukshoegskole. Institutt for Jordskifte og Arealplanlegging. Melding *48*
Norges Landbruksoekonomiske Institutt. Driftsgranskinger i Jord- og Skogbruk (NO ISSN 0333-2500) *48*
Norges Landbruksoekonomiske Institutt. Driftsgranskinger i Jordbruket see Norges Landbruksoekonomiske Institutt. Driftsgranskinger i Jord- og Skogbruk
Norges og Utviklingslandene (NO) *263*
Norges Samarbeid med Utviklingslandene see Norges og Utviklingslandene *263*

NORTH DAKOTA. 1835

Norges Teknisk-Naturvitenskapelige Forskningsraad. Aarsberetning (NO ISSN 0078-1231) *997*, *1070*
Norges Teknisk-Naturvitenskapelige Forskningsraad. Transportoekonomisk Institutt. Aarsberetning *see* Transportoekonomisk Institutt. Aarsberetning *1095*
Norges Veterinaerhoegskole. Aarsberetning/Norwegian College of Veterinary Medicine (NO ISSN 0078-6713) *1159*
Norges Veterinaerhoegskole. Aarsmelding/Norwegian College of Veterinary Medicine. Annual Report (NO) *1122*
Norges Veterinaerhoegskole. Publikasjoner/Norwegian College of Veterinary Medicine. Publications (NO ISSN 0078-6721) *1122*
Norin-sho Nenpo *see* Japan. Ministry of Agriculture and Forestry. Annual Report *30*
Norin Suisan Nenkan *see* Japan. Ministry of Agriculture and Forestry. Annual Report *30*
Norinsho Ringyo Shikenjo Nenpo *see* Japan. Forestry and Forest Products Research Institute. Annual Report *526*
Norkontakt (NO ISSN 0048-0541) *263*
Norman Ford's Florida (US ISSN 0546-3432) *1114*
Normerede og Besatte Laegestillinger Samt Sengepladser paa Institutioner *see* Laegestillinger og Sengepladser paa Institutioner *617*
Normtal (DK ISSN 0109-1573) *644*
Normtal for Koebmaend (DK ISSN 0108-7274) *1159*
Normtalsundersoegelse for Sportsbranchen (DK ISSN 0900-0283) *1035*
Normtalsundersoegelsen for Isenkrambranchen (DK ISSN 0900-0275) *190*
Norna - Rapporter (Nordiska Samarbetskommitten foer Namnforskning) (SW ISSN 0346-6728) *699*
Norsk Bokfortegnelse Aarskatalog (NO ISSN 0029-1870) *129*
Norsk Fiskaralmanakk (NO) *512*, *1046*
Norsk Institutt for By- og Regionforskning Rapport *see* N I B R Rapport *624*
Norsk Institutt for Skogforskning. Meddelelser/Norwegian Forest Research Institute. Reports (NO ISSN 0332-5709) *526*
Norsk Institutt for Skogforskning. Rapport/Norwegian Forest Research Institut. Research Paper (NO ISSN 0333-001X) *526*
Norsk Institutt for Vannforskning. Aarbok (NO) *403*
Norsk Institutt for Vannforskning. Temarapport (NO) *403*
Norsk Litteraer Aarbok (NO ISSN 0078-1266) *728*
Norsk Petroleumsforening. Aarbok/Norwegian Petroleum Society. Yearbook (NO) *865*
Norsk Polarinstitutt. Aarbok (NO ISSN 0085-4271) *392*, *546*
Norsk Polarinstitutt. Meddelelser (NO) *392*, *546*
Norsk Polarinstitutt. Polarhaandbok (NO ISSN 0474-8042) *393*, *546*
Norsk Polarinstitutt. Skrifter (NO) *393*, *546*
Norsk Senter for Informatikk. Artikkel Indeks (NO ISSN 0558-0439) *214*
Norsk Sjoefartsmuseum. Aarsberetning (NO) *90*, *592*
Norsk Skattelovsamling (NO ISSN 0333-1423) *297*
Norsk Skogbruksmuseum. Aarbok (NO ISSN 0549-6896) *592*
Norsk Teknisk Museum. Yearbook *see* Volund *831*
Norsk Utenrikspolitisk Aarbok (NO ISSN 0332-7299) *917*
Norsk Utenrikspolitisk Institutt Notat *see* N U P I Notat *917*

Norsk Utenrikspolitisk Institutt Rapport *see* N U P I Rapport *917*
Norsk Viltforskning. Meddeleser (NO) *144*, *498*, *923*
Norske Arkitektkonkurranser (NO ISSN 0332-6578) *99*
Norske Creditbank (NO) *231*
Norske Creditbank. Annual Report *see* Norske Creditbank *231*
Norske Creditbank. Report of the Board of Directors *see* Norske Creditbank *231*
Norske Institutt for Kosmisk Fysikk. Magnetic Observations *see* Auroral Observatory. Magnetic Observations *115*
Norske Skogforsoksvesen. Meddelelser *see* Norsk Institutt for Skogforskning. Meddelelser *526*
Norske Videnskaps-Akademi. Historisk-Filosofisk Klasse. Avhandlinger Two (NO ISSN 0029-2311) *559*, *880*
Norske Videnskaps-Akademi. Matematisk-Naturvidenkapelig Klasse. Skrifter *see* Norske Videnskaps-Akademi. Naturvidenskapelig Klasse. Skrifter *997*
Norske Videnskaps-Akademi. Naturvidenskapelig Klasse. Skrifter (NO) *997*
Norske Vitenskapelige og Faglige Biblioteker (NO) *682*
Norte (AG) *607*
North American Electric Reliability Council. Annual Report (US) *457*
North American Fauna (US ISSN 0078-1304) *177*
North American Flora (US ISSN 0078-1312) *159*
North American Forest Soils Conference. Proceedings (US ISSN 0078-1320) *58*
North American Horticulture: A Reference Guide (US) *533*
North American Human Rights Directory (US ISSN 0270-2282) *913*
North American Living Costs (UK ISSN 0268-2281) *258*
North American Manufacturing Research Conference. Proceedings (US) *473*
North American Manufacturing Research Conference (Publication) *see* North American Manufacturing Research Conference. Proceedings *473*
North American Metalworking Research Conference. Proceedings *see* North American Manufacturing Research Conference. Proceedings *473*
North American Online Directory (US) *344*
North American Protestant Ministries Overseas *see* Mission Handbook: North American Protestant Ministries Overseas *979*
North American Society for Oceanic History. Proceedings (US ISSN 0198-7194) *607*, *1102*
North American Society for Sport History. Proceedings (US ISSN 0093-6235) *607*, *1035*
North American Students of Cooperation Campus Co-Op Directory *see* N A S C O Campus Co-Op Directory *314*
North American Wildlife and Natural Resources Conference. Transactions (US ISSN 0078-1355) *366*
North Atlantic Treaty Organization. Advisory Group for Aerospace Research and Development. A G A R D Annual Meeting (FR ISSN 0550-8452) *20*
North Atlantic Treaty Organization. Advisory Group for Aerospace Research and Development. A G A R D Conference Proceedings (FR ISSN 0549-7191) *21*
North Atlantic Treaty Organization. Directorate of Economic Affairs. Colloquium. Series *see* N A T O. Annual Economic Colloquia. Proceedings *258*

North Atlantic Treaty Organization. Expert Panel on Air Pollution Modeling. Proceedings (BE ISSN 0377-7669) *498*
North Atlantic Treaty Organization. Facts and Figures/Alliance Atlantique. Structure, Faits et Chiffres (BE) *917*
North Atlantic Treaty Organization Advanced Science Institutes Series E: Applied Sciences *see* N A T O Advanced Science Institutes Series E: Applied Sciences *1070*
North Atlantic Treaty Organization Advanced Study Institute Series F: Computer and System Sciences *see* N A T O Advanced Study Institute Series F: Computer and System Sciences *353*
North Atlantic Treaty Organization Annual Economic Colloquia. Proceedings *see* N A T O. Annual Economic Colloquia. Proceedings *258*
North Atlantic Treaty Organization Basic Documents *see* N A T O Basic Documents *917*
North Atlantic Treaty Organization Final Communiques *see* N A T O Final Communiques *917*
North Atlantic Treaty Organization Handbook *see* N A T O Handbook *917*
North Atlantic Treaty Organization Warsaw Pact - Force Comparisons *see* N A T O and the Warsaw Pact - Force Comparisons *917*
North Cal-Neva Resource Conservation and Development Project. Annual Work Plan (US ISSN 0097-7268) *366*
North Carolina. Council on State Goals and Policy. Annual Report *see* North Carolina. State Goals and Policy Board. Annual Report *944*
North Carolina. Department of Agriculture. Agricultural Review (US) *32*
North Carolina. Department of Human Resources. Annual Plan of Work (US ISSN 0095-4942) *1019*
North Carolina. Department of Human Resources. Annual Report (US) *286*, *291*
North Carolina. Department of Revenue. Franchise Tax and Corporate Income Tax Bulletins for Taxable Years *see* North Carolina. Department of Revenue. Franchise Tax and Corporate Income Tax Rules and Regulations *297*
North Carolina. Department of Revenue. Franchise Tax and Corporate Income Tax Rules and Regulations (US) *297*
North Carolina. Department of Transportation. Office of Highway Safety. Summary of Activities (US) *1097*
North Carolina. Division of Ground Water. Ground Water Bulletin *see* Groundwater Bulletin *403*
North Carolina. Division of Health Services. Public Health Statistics Branch. North Carolina Vital Statistics *see* North Carolina. Division of Health Services. State Center for Health Statistics. North Carolina Vital Statistics *928*
North Carolina. Division of Health Services. State Center for Health Statistics. North Carolina Vital Statistics (US) *928*, *959*
North Carolina. Division of Mineral Resources. Bulletin *see* North Carolina. Geological Survey Section. Bulletin *819*
North Carolina. Division of Mineral Resources. Economic Paper *see* North Carolina. Geological Survey Section. Economic Paper *819*
North Carolina. Division of Mineral Resources. Information Circular *see* North Carolina. Geological Survey Section. Information Circular *819*
North Carolina. Division of Mineral Resources. Special Publication *see* North Carolina. Geological Survey Section. Special Publication *819*

North Carolina. Geological Survey Section. Bulletin (US) *819*
North Carolina. Geological Survey Section. Economic Paper (US) *819*
North Carolina. Geological Survey Section. Information Circular (US) *819*
North Carolina. Geological Survey Section. Special Publication (US) *819*
North Carolina. Secretary of State. Directory of State and County Officials (US) *944*
North Carolina. State Goals and Policy Board. Annual Report (US) *944*
North Carolina Agricultural Chemicals Manual (US ISSN 0065-4418) *58*
North Carolina Communicable Disease Morbidity Statistics (US ISSN 0085-428X) *959*
North Carolina Directory of Trade and Professional Associations (US) *315*
North Carolina Governor's Highway Safety Program. Summary of Activities *see* North Carolina. Department of Transportation. Office of Highway Safety. Summary of Activities *1097*
North Carolina Manual (US) *944*
North Carolina Medical Society. Transactions (US ISSN 0361-5537) *764*
North Carolina Metalworking Directory (US) *315*, *746*, *799*
North Carolina Plastics Processors and Producers (US) *901*
North Carolina Reported Abortions (US) *179*
North Carolina Seed Law (US) *32*
North Carolina State Industrial Directory *see* MacRae's North Carolina/South Carolina/Virginia *313*
North Carolina State University. Chancellor's Annual Report (US) *437*
North Carolina State University. Development Board. Report *see* North Carolina State University. Chancellor's Annual Report *437*
North Carolina State University. Development Council. Report. *see* North Carolina State University. Chancellor's Annual Report *437*
North Carolina State University. School of Design. (Student Publication Magazine) (US ISSN 0078-1444) *99*
North Carolina State University. School of Forest Resources. Technical Report. (US ISSN 0090-0664) *526*
North Carolina State University. Water Resources Research Institute. Report (US ISSN 0078-1525) *1125*
North Carolina Studies in the Romance Languages and Literatures. (US) *728*
North Carolina Tobacco Report (US) *1080*
North Castle History (US) *607*
North Central Campbook (US ISSN 0147-8613) *1046*, *1114*
North Central Camping *see* North Central Campbook *1114*
North Central-Iowa, Minnesota, Nebraska, North Dakota, South Dakota TourBook *see* TourBook: North Central *1117*
North-Central State. Ministry of Works. Report *see* Kaduna State. Ministry of Works. Report *943*
North Central State Statistical Yearbook *see* Kaduna State Statistical Yearbook *1058*
North Central Tour Book *see* TourBook: North Central *1117*
North Dakota. Department of Agriculture. Annual Report *see* North Dakota. Department of Agriculture. Biennial Report *32*
North Dakota. Department of Agriculture. Biennial Report (US) *32*
North Dakota. Department of Public Instruction. Biennial Report of the Superintendent of Public Instruction (US) *425*
North Dakota. Employment Security Bureau. Annual Report *see* Job Service North Dakota. Annual Report *273*

1836 NORTH DAKOTA.

North Dakota. Employment Security Bureau. Biennial Report to the Governor see Job Service North Dakota. Biennial Report to the Governor 273

North Dakota. Geological Survey. Bulletin (US ISSN 0546-5001) 393

North Dakota. Geological Survey. Educational Series (US ISSN 0091-9004) 393

North Dakota. Geological Survey. Miscellaneous Series (US ISSN 0078-1576) 393

North Dakota. Geological Survey. Report of Investigation (US) 393

North Dakota. Judicial Conference. Annual Report (US) 669, 1060

North Dakota. Judicial Council. Annual Report see North Dakota. Judicial Conference. Annual Report 669

North Dakota. Judicial Council. Statistical Compilation and Report see North Dakota. Judicial Conference. Annual Report 669

North Dakota. Milk Stabilization Board. Annual Report of Administrative Activities (US ISSN 0091-9446) 63

North Dakota. Social Service Board. Statistics (US ISSN 0095-1633) 1159

North Dakota. State Advisory Council for Vocational Education. Annual Evaluation Report (US ISSN 0094-8306) 448

North Dakota Academic Library Statistics. see North Dakota Library Statistics 688

North Dakota Academy of Science. Proceedings (US) 997

North Dakota Agricultural Statistics (US) 42

North Dakota Crop and Livestock Statistics see North Dakota Agricultural Statistics 42

North Dakota Directory of Judges and Attorneys see North Dakota Directory of Lawyers and Judges 661

North Dakota Directory of Lawyers and Judges (US) 661

North Dakota Grain and Oilseed Transportation Statistics (US) 42

North Dakota Growth Indicators (US ISSN 0549-8368) 247

North Dakota Library Statistics (US) 688

North Dakota State Plan for Rehabilitation Facilities and Workshops (US ISSN 0093-7843) 445

North Dakota's Highway Safety Plan (US) 1097

North Dakota's Highway Safety Work Programs see North Dakota's Highway Safety Plan 1097

North-Holland Linguistic Series (NE ISSN 0078-1592) 699

North-Holland Mathematical Library (NE) 751

North-Holland Mathematics Studies (NE) 751

North-Holland Series in Applied Mathematics and Mechanics (NE ISSN 0066-5460) 751

North-Holland Series in Crystal Growth(NE) 889

North-Holland/T I M S Studies in the Management Sciences (NE ISSN 0378-3766) 238

North Jersey Regional Industrial Purchasing Guide (US ISSN 0737-0989) 315

North Jersey Telephone Tickler for Insurance Men & Women (US) 641

North of Scotland College of Agriculture, Aberdeen. Annual Report see School of Agriculture, Aberdeen. Annual Report 34

North of Scotland College of Agriculture, Aberdeen. Bulletin (UK) 1159

North of Scotland Visitor (UK ISSN 0260-2415) 1114

North Pacific Fur Seal Commission. Proceedings of the Annual Meeting (US ISSN 0078-1622) 1159

North Queensland Naturalist (AT ISSN 0078-1630) 144

North Sea Oil & Gas Directory (UK ISSN 0265-5039) 865

North Shore Dining Guide (US) 546, 1114

North Shore Newcomers' Guide (US) 547

North Staffordshire Journal of Field Studies (UK ISSN 0078-1649) 547, 592

North Staffordshire Polytechnic. Department of Economics. Discussion Papers (UK) 197

North Wind (UK ISSN 0265-7295) 711

North York Poetry see Genera 741

Northamptonshire Archaeology (UK ISSN 0305-4659) 90

Northamptonshire Federation of Archaeological Societies. Bulletin see Northamptonshire Archaeology 90

Northamptonshire Natural History Society and Field Club Journal (UK ISSN 0144-0586) 997

Northamptonshire Past and Present (UK ISSN 0140-9131) 592

Northeast African Monograph Series (US) 504, 566

Northeast Bioengineering Conference. Proceedings (US) 457

Northeast Coal Study. Preliminary Environmental Report see British Columbia. Ministry of the Environment. Northeast Coal Study Preliminary Environmental Report 814

Northeast Conference on the Teaching of Foreign Languages. Northeast Conference Reports (US ISSN 0733-1169) 449, 699

Northeast Conference Reports see Northeast Conference on the Teaching of Foreign Languages. Northeast Conference Reports 449

Northeast Folklore (US ISSN 0078-1681) 516

North East Food Service Buyer's Guide(US) 620

North East Group for the Study of Labour History Bulletin see North East Labour History Bulletin 274

Northeast Journal (US) 728

Northeast/Juniper Books (US) 728

North East Labour History Bulletin (UK) 274

Northeast Pacific Pink and Chum Salmon Workshop. Proceedings (US ISSN 0094-128X) 512

Northeast Regional Science Review (US) 624, 944

Northeastern Campbook (US ISSN 0732-7315) 1114

Northeastern Camping see Northeastern Campbook 1114

Northeastern Tour Book see Tourbook: Connecticut, Massachusetts, Rhode Island 1117

Northeastern Tour Book see Tourbook: Maine, New Hampshire, Vermont 1117

Northeastern Weed Control Conference see Northeastern Weed Science Society. Proceedings 58

Northeastern Weed Science Society. Proceedings (US ISSN 0078-1703) 58

Northern Arizona Scene (US) 547

Northern Bytes (US) 362

Northern California Golf Association. Blue Book (US) 1035

Northern Canada Power Commission. Annual Report/Commission d'Energie du Nord Canadien. Revue Annuelle (CN) 466

Northern Canada Power Commission. Annual Review see Northern Canada Power Commission. Annual Report 466

Northern History (UK ISSN 0078-172X) 592

Northern House Pamphlet Poets (UK ISSN 0078-1738) 742

Northern Illinois University. Center for Southeast Asian Studies. Occasional Papers (US ISSN 0078-1703) 570, 631

Northern Illinois University. Center for Southeast Asian Studies. Special Report Series (US ISSN 0073-4934) 570, 631

Northern Ireland. Commissioner for Complaints. Annual Report (UK) 944

Northern Ireland. Department of Agriculture. Annual Report on Research and Technical Work (UK ISSN 0078-1746) 32

Northern Ireland. Department of Agriculture. Record of Agricultural Research (UK ISSN 0078-1754) 32

Northern Ireland. Horticultural Centre. Annual Report (UK) 533

Northern Ireland Council for Educational Research Bulletin see N I C E R Bulletin 416

Northern Libraries Bulletin (US ISSN 0048-0789) 197

Northern Lights Studies in Creativity (US ISSN 0739-2974) 108, 728

Northern New England Review (US ISSN 0190-3012) 729

Northern Nigeria. Ministry of Economic Planning. Statistical Year Book see Kano State Statistical Year Book 1058

Northern Nigeria Development Corporation. Report see New Nigeria Development Company Limited. Annual Report and Accounts 290

Northern Nigeria Gazette see Kano State of Nigeria Gazette 943

Northern Nut Growers Association. Annual Report (US) 533

Northern Ontario Directory (CN) 923

Northern Regional Research Center Publications and Patents (US) 9

Northern Rockies Action Group, Inc. Papers see N R A G Papers 1019

Northern Scotland (UK ISSN 0306-5278) 592

Northern Social Science Review (US ISSN 0196-1063) 1010

Northern Territory. Conservation Commission. Annual Report (AT ISSN 0159-8821) 366

Northern Territory. Territory Parks and Wildlife Commission. Annual Report see Northern Territory. Conservation Commission. Annual Report 366

Northern Territory at a Glance (AT ISSN 0815-3809) 1060

Northrop University Law Journal of Aerospace, Business and Taxation (US ISSN 0887-4301) 21, 466, 498

Northrop University Law Journal of Aerospace, Energy and the Enviornment see Northrop University Law Journal of Aerospace, Business and Taxation 21

Northumbrian Pipers' Society Magazine(UK ISSN 0261-5096) 839

Northumbriana (UK ISSN 0308-4809) 90, 729

Northwest Association of Schools and Colleges. Proceedings. (US) 417, 437

Northwest Association of Secondary and Higher Schools see Northwest Association of Schools and Colleges. Proceedings 437

Northwest Atlantic Fisheries Organization Annual Report see N A F O Annual Report 511

Northwest Atlantic Fisheries Organization List of Fishing Vessels see N A F O List of Fishing Vessels 511

Northwest Atlantic Fisheries Organization Meeting Proceedings see N A F O Meeting Proceedings 1158

Northwest Atlantic Fisheries Organization Scientific Council Meeting Reports see N A F O Scientific Council Meeting Reports 511

Northwest Atlantic Fisheries Organization Scientific Council Studies see N A F O Scientific Council Studies 511

Northwest Atlantic Fisheries Organization Statistical Bulletin see N A F O Statistical Bulletin 511

Northwest Discovery (US ISSN 0272-1570) 608

Northwest Electric Utility Directory (US) 457, 466

North West England Directory of Industry and Commerce (UK) 237

North West England Industrial Classified Directory see North West England Directory of Industry and Commerce 237

Northwest Geology (US) 393

Northwest Historical Series (US ISSN 0078-1789) 608

North West Industrial Development Association. Annual Report (UK) 1159

North West Societies. Combined Register of Members' Interests (UK) 537

Northwestern Campbook (US) 1046, 1115

Northwestern Camping see Northwestern Campbook 1115

Northwestern Endicott Report (US) 342, 848

North Western European Language Evolution (DK ISSN 0900-8675) 592, 699

Northwestern-Iowa Dealer Reference Manual see Northwestern Lumbermens Association Dealer Reference Manual 186

Northwestern Lumbermens Association Dealer Reference Manual (US) 186

Northwestern States see Tourbook: Idaho, Montana, Wyoming 1117

Northwestern Tour Book see Tourbook: Idaho, Montana, Wyoming 1117

Northwestern University. Center for American Archeology. Research Series see K A C Research Series 88

Northwestern University. Dental School Library. Current Subscriptions List (US) 771

Northwestern University. Materials Research Center. Annual Technical Report (US) 489

Northwestern University. Transportation Center. Publications List (US) 1082

Norveg (NO ISSN 0029-3601) 74

Norway. Arbeidsdirektoratet. Aarsmelding (NO ISSN 0078-1835) 274

Norway. Direktoratet for Brann og Eksplosjonsvern. Aarsberetning (NO) 479

Norway. Fiskeridirektoratet. Fiskeflaaten (NO) 512

Norway. Fiskeridirektoratet. Skrifter. Serie Ernaering (NO) 846

Norway. Fiskeridirektoratet. Skrifter. Serie Havundersoekelser (NO ISSN 0015-3117) 512

Norway. Forsvaret forskningsinstitutt. N D R E Report see N D R E Publications 995

Norway. Ministry of Industry and Handicraft. Reports to the Storting (NO) 240

Norway. Riksbibliotektjenesten. Aarsmelding (NO ISSN 0800-4153) 682

Norway. Riksbibliotektjenesten. Skrifter/Papers (NO ISSN 0800-4129) 682

Norway. Statens Institutt for Alkoholforskning. Skrifter (NO ISSN 0078-673X) 377

Norway. Statens Sprengstoffinspeksjon. Aarsberetning see Norway. Direktoratet for Brann og Eksplosjonsvern. Aarsberetning 479

Norway. Statistisk Sentralbyraa. Alkohol og Andre Rusmidler/Alcohol and Drugs (NO ISSN 0332-7965) 1159

Norway. Statistisk Sentralbyraa. Arbeidsmarkedstatistikk/Labour Market Statistics (NO ISSN 0078-1878) 214, 1060

Norway. Statistisk Sentralbyraa. Artikler/Articles (NO ISSN 0085-431X) 252, 1028

Norway. Statistisk Sentralbyraa. Elektrisitesstatistikk/Electricity Statistics (NO) 468, 1060

Norway. Statistisk Sentralbyraa. Familie Statistikk/Family Statistics (NO ISSN 0332-7957) 1159

Norway. Statistisk Sentralbyraa. Fiskeristatistikk/Fishery Statistics (NO) 514, 1060

NUCLEAR SCIENCE 1837

Norway. Statistisk Sentralbyraa. Folkemengden Etter Alder og Ekteskapelig Status/Population by Age and Marital Status (NO ISSN 0550-7170) *928*, *1060*
Norway. Statistisk Sentralbyraa. Framskriving Av Folkemengden: Regionale Tall/Population Projections: Regional Figures (NO ISSN 0332-8015) *928*, *1060*
Norway. Statistisk Sentralbyraa. Helsepersonellstatistikk (NO ISSN 0800-403X) *771*, *1060*
Norway. Statistisk Sentralbyraa. Helsestatistikk/Health Statistics (NO ISSN 0332-7906) *959*, *1060*
Norway. Statistisk Sentralbyraa. Industristatistikk/Industrial Statistics see Norway. Statistisk Sentralbyraa. Industristatistikk/Industrial Statistics. Vol.1 *214*
Norway. Statistisk Sentralbyraa. Industristatistikk/Industrial Statistics see Norway. Statistisk Sentralbyraa. Industristatistikk/Industrial Statistics. Vol.2 *214*
Norway. Statistisk Sentralbyraa. Industristatistikk/Industrial Statistics. Vol.1 (NO ISSN 0800-580X) *214*, *1060*
Norway. Statistisk Sentralbyraa. Industristatistikk/Industrial Statistics. Vol.2 (NO ISSN 0800-5818) *214*, *1060*
Norway. Statistisk Sentralbyraa. Jordbruksstatistikk/Agricultural Statistics (NO ISSN 0078-1894) *42*, *1060*
Norway. Statistisk Sentralbyraa. Kommune og Fylkestings Valget/Municipal and County Elections (NO ISSN 0332-8023) *949*, *1060*
Norway. Statistisk Sentralbyraa. Kommunevalget/Municipal Elections see Norway. Statistisk Sentralbyraa. Kommune og Fylkestings Valget/Municipal and County Elections *949*
Norway. Statistisk Sentralbyraa. Kredittmarked Statistikk/Credit Market Statistics (NO ISSN 0078-1908) *214*, *1060*
Norway. Statistisk Sentralbyraa. Kriminalstatistikk/Criminal Statistics (NO ISSN 0333-3914) *374*, *1060*
Norway. Statistisk Sentralbyraa. Legestatistikk see Norway. Statistisk Sentralbyraa. Helsepersonellstatistikk *771*
Norway. Statistisk Sentralbyraa. Loennsstatistikk/Wage Statistics (NO ISSN 0078-1916) *214*, *1060*
Norway. Statistisk Sentralbyraa. Nasjonalregnskap/National Accounts(NO) *214*, *1060*
Norway. Statistisk Sentralbyraa. Oekonomisk Utsyn/Economic Survey(NO ISSN 0078-1924) *215*, *1060*
Norway. Statistisk Sentralbyraa. Reiselivstatiskk/Statistics on Travel (NO ISSN 0333-208X) *1060*, *1120*
Norway. Statistisk Sentralbyraa. Samferdselsstatistikk/Transport and Communication Statistics (NO ISSN 0468-8147) *346*, *1061*, *1086*
Norway. Statistisk Sentralbyraa. Samfunnsoekonomiske Studier/Social Economic Studies (NO ISSN 0085-4344) *1028*
Norway. Statistisk Sentralbyraa. Sivilrettsstatistikk/Civil Judicial Statistics (NO ISSN 0550-0532) *374*, *1061*
Norway. Statistisk Sentralbyraa. Skogstatstikk/Forestry Statistics (NO ISSN 0468-8155) *529*, *1061*
Norway. Statistisk Sentralbyraa. Statistisk Aarbok/Statistical Yearbook (NO ISSN 0078-1932) *1061*
Norway. Statistisk Sentralbyraa. Stortingsvalg/Parliamentary Elections(NO) *949*, *1061*
Norway. Statistisk Sentralbyraa. Utdanningsstatistikk: Educational Statistics (NO ISSN 0800-2169) *425*, *1061*

Norway. Statistisk Sentralbyraa. Utenrikshandel/External Trade (NO ISSN 0078-1940) *215*, *1061*
Norway. Statistisk Sentralbyraa. Varehandelsstatistikk/Wholesale and Retail Trade Statistics (NO ISSN 0078-1959) *215*, *1061*
Norway. Televerket. Statistikk (NO ISSN 0800-2177) *346*
Norway. Televerket. Statistisk Arbok see Norway. Televerket. Statistikk *346*
Norwegian-American Historical Association. Newsletter (US ISSN 0078-1967) *608*
Norwegian-American Historical Association. Topical Studies (US ISSN 0085-4352) *608*
Norwegian American Historical Association. Travel and Description Series (US ISSN 0078-1975) *608*
Norwegian-American Studies (US ISSN 0078-1983) *608*
Norwegian-American Studies and Records see Norwegian-American Studies *608*
Norwegian Chamber of Commerce. Year Book and Directory of Members (UK ISSN 0305-0998) *237*
Norwegian College of Veterinary Medicine see Norges Veterinaerhoegskole. Aarsberetning *1159*
Norwegian College of Veterinary Medicine. Annual Report see Norges Veterinaerhoegskole. Aarsmelding *1122*
Norwegian College of Veterinary Medicine. Publications see Norges Veterinaerhoegskole. Publikasjoner *1122*
Norwegian Directory of Commerce see Norges Handels-Kalender *315*
Norwegian Foreign Policy Studies see Utenrikspolitiske Skrifter *920*
Norwegian Forest Research Institut. Research Paper see Norsk Institutt for Skogforskning. Rapport *526*
Norwegian Forest Research Institute. Reports see Norsk Institutt for Skogforskning. Meddelelser *526*
Norwegian Geotechnical Institute. Publications see Norges Geotekniske Institutt. Publikasjon *400*
Norwegian Hydrotechnical Laboratory. Bulletin (NO) *490*
Norwegian Music Information Center. Bulletin (NO ISSN 0801-1087) *839*
Norwegian Offshore Index (NO) *865*
Norwegian Petroleum Society. Yearbook see Norsk Petroleumsforening. Aarbok *865*
Norwegian Yearbook of Maritime History see Sjoefartshistorisk Aarbok *596*
Norwegische Handels-Adressbuch see Norges Handels-Kalender *315*
Norwich and Norfolk Chamber of Commerce and Industry. Directory (UK ISSN 0261-880X) *237*
Notable Books (US) *129*
Notable Children's Trade Books in the Field of Social Studies (US) *129*, *335*, *962*, *1014*
Notable Individuals (US) *362*, *466*
Notary Public Practices & Glossary (US) *661*
Notas Breves Danesas see Feature fra Danmark *538*
Notas de Algebra y Analisis (AG ISSN 0078-2009) *751*
Notas de Logica Matematica (AG ISSN 0078-2017) *751*
Notas de Matematica Discreta (AG ISSN 0326-1336) *751*
Notas e Comunicacoes de Matematica (BL ISSN 0085-5413) *751*
Notas e Estudos, Serie Recursos e Ambiente Aquaticos see Portugal. Instituto Nacional de Investigacao das Pescas. Boletim *177*
Notas Matematicas (CL) *751*
Notatkz z Mistetstba see Ukrainian Art Digest *111*
Notebooks in Cultural Analysis (US) *631*, *711*

Notes and Abstracts in American and International Education (US ISSN 0029-3962) *9*, *425*, *1031*
Notes de Mathematiques Appliquees see Applied Mathematics Notes *747*
Notes for Medical Catalogers see National Library of Medicine. Current Catalog *771*
Notes from the Royal Botanic Garden, Edinburgh (UK ISSN 0080-4274) *159*
Notes on Cardiovascular Diseases (AT ISSN 0550-0990) *777*
Notes on Mathematics and Its Applications see Mathematics and Its Applications *750*
Notes on Neurology (AT) *791*
Notes on Pure Mathematics (AT) *751*
Notes on the Science of Building (AT ISSN 0300-371X) *186*
Noticia Geomorfologica see Geociencias *379*
Noticiario Arqueologico Hispanico: Arqueologia (SP ISSN 0211-1748) *90*
Noticias de Cosmetica y de Perfumeria Documenta see N C P Documenta *119*
Noticias de Guatemala (CR) *907*
Noticias del Trabajo (PR ISSN 0029-4195) *274*, *661*
Noticiero Agropecuario. Suplemento Agrometeorologico (CU) *806*
Noticiero I.D.U.N. (Instituto de Desarrollo Urbano) (CK) *624*
Noticiero Tuberosas (VE ISSN 0085-4387) *159*
Notizen zur Flora der Steiermark (AU) *159*
Notiziario sulle Malattie delle Piante (IT) *160*, *165*
Notre Dame Studies in American Catholicism (US) *983*
Notre Langue et Notre Culture see Echange *694*
Nottingham Medieval Studies (UK ISSN 0078-2122) *592*
Notulae Naturae (US ISSN 0029-4608) *997*
Notulae Naturae of the Academy of Natural Sciences of Philadelphia see Notulae Naturae *997*
Notulae Vertebratologicae see Vertebratologicke Zpravy *178*
Nouveautes Techniques Maritimes (FR ISSN 0078-2157) *1159*
Nouvelle Bibliotheque Nervalienne (FR ISSN 0078-2165) *135*, *729*
Nouvelle Litterature et Ideologie see New Literature and Ideology *711*
Nouvelles Africaines de Securite Sociale see African News Sheet *637*
Nova Act Regiae Societatis Scientiarum Upsaliensis see Acta Universitatis Upsaliensis *987*
Nova Acta Leopoldina (GE) *997*
Nova Dumka (YU) *505*
Nova Hedwiga, Beihefte (GW ISSN 0078-2238) *160*
Nova Kepleriana. Neue Folge (GW ISSN 0078-2246) *117*
Nova Scotia. Commission on Drug Dependency. Annual Report (CN ISSN 0707-9834) *377*
Nova Scotia. Department of Development. Annual Report (CN) *944*
Nova Scotia. Department of Labour and Manpower. Compendium of Grievance Arbitration Decisions see Nova Scotia. Department of Labour. Compendium of Grievance Arbitration Decisions *274*
Nova Scotia. Department of Labour. Annual Report (CN ISSN 0380-5689) *274*
Nova Scotia. Department of Labour. Compendium of Grievance Arbitration Decisions (CN) *274*
Nova Scotia. Department of Labour. Economics and Research Division. Wage Rates, Salaries and Hours of Labour in Nova Scotia (CN ISSN 0550-1741) *274*
Nova Scotia. Department of Public Health. Nutrition Division. Annual Report (CN ISSN 0078-236X) *846*, *955*

Nova Scotia. Department of Recreation. Annual Report (CN) *1035*
Nova Scotia. Environmental Control Council. Annual Report (CN ISSN 0317-3526) *498*
Nova Scotia. Fire Marshal. Annual Report (CN ISSN 0085-4395) *507*
Nova Scotia. Office of the Ombudsman. Annual Report (CN) *944*
Nova Scotia Barristers' Society. Annual Report (CN) *661*
Nova Scotia Dental Association. Newsletter see Nova Scotia Dentist *780*
Nova Scotia Dentist (CN) *780*
Nova Scotia Fruit Growers Association. Annual Report and Proceedings (CN ISSN 0078-2386) *58*
Nova Scotia Power Corporation. Annual Report (CN ISSN 0078-2459) *457*
Nova Scotia Reports (CN ISSN 0048-0983) *661*
Nova Scotia Research Foundation Corporation. Annual Report (CN) *997*, *1070*
Nova Scotia Technical College. School of Architecture. Report Series see Technical University of Nova Scotia. School of Architecture. Report Series *100*
Nova Scotia Trappers Newsletter (CN ISSN 0705-4831) *366*, *672*
Nova Scotian Institute of Science. Proceedings (CN ISSN 0078-2521) *997*
Nova Tellus (MX) *338*, *631*, *729*
Novantiqua (IT) *699*
Novarien (IT ISSN 0078-253X) *983*
Novaya Literatura po Tsenoobrazovaniyu, Opublikovannaya v S.S.S.R. (UR) *129*, *215*
Nove Obzory (CS ISSN 0546-8051) *592*
Novelleregister (DK ISSN 0106-035X) *129*
Novitates Arthropodae (US ISSN 0278-3274) *177*
Novum Testamentum. Supplements (NE) *971*
Novye Issledovaniya v Gornoi Elektromekhanike (UR) *457*
Novye Issledovaniya v Khimii, Metallurgii i Obogashchenii (UR) *479*, *799*
Now and Then (US) *366*, *729*
Now Hiring (US) *661*, *848*
Now in Japan (JA) *258*
Nu Yu (US) *711*
Nuclear Almanac/Genshiryoku Nenkan(JA) *466*, *897*
Nuclear Canada. Yearbook (CN ISSN 0383-8536) *897*
Nuclear Data Newsletter (UN) *897*
Nuclear Industry Status see Worldwide Uranium Producer Profiles *899*
Nuclear Magnetic Resonance (UK ISSN 0305-9804) *332*
Nuclear Magnetic Resonance see N M R *897*
Nuclear Magnetic Resonance Spectrometry Abstracts (UK ISSN 0048-1033) *9*, *326*, *893*
Nuclear Medicine Annual (US ISSN 0272-0108) *792*
Nuclear News Buyers Guide (US ISSN 0029-5574) *898*
Nuclear News Industry Report see Nuclear News Buyers Guide *898*
Nuclear Physics Monographs (US) *898*
Nuclear Power Plants in the World/Genshiryoku Hatsudensyo (JA) *466*, *898*
Nuclear Power Safety Report (US) *466*, *955*
Nuclear Reactors Built, Being Built, or Planned in the United States (US ISSN 0364-6866) *466*
Nuclear Research Index see World Nuclear Directory *899*
Nuclear Safety Research Association Memo see N S R A Memo *897*
Nuclear Science Abstracts (United States Energy Research and Development Administration) see I N I S Atomindex *893*
Nuclear Science Technology Monograph Series (US) *473*, *898*

Nucleo de Estudos Sociais para Habitacao e Urbanismo (BL) *624*
Nucleus (PH) 32, 324, 792, *898*
Nucleus Science Journal (US) *764*
Nudist Park Guide (US) *1115*
Nuernberger Forschungen (GW ISSN 0078-2653) *592*
Nuernberger Wirtschafts-und Sozialgeographische Arbeiten (GW ISSN 0546-9112) *547*
Nueruolog (US) *860*
Nueva Ciencia (VE) *247*
Nueva Poetica Andaluza (SP) *742*
Nukada Institute for Medical and Biological Research. Reports (JA ISSN 0469-2071) 144, *764*
Numen Supplements (NE) *971*
Numerical Fluid Mechanics and Heat Transfer Review (US) 492, *889*
Numerus Clausus - Alternativen *see* Numerus Clausus - Finessen *417*
Numerus Clausus - Finessen (GW) *417*
Numismatic Books in Print (US) 129, *614*
Numismatic Chronicle and Journal (UK ISSN 0078-2696) *845*
Numismatic Communications *see* Numismatiska Meddelanden *845*
Numismatic Literature (US ISSN 0029-6031) *845*
Numismatic Notes and Monographs (US ISSN 0078-2718) *845*
Numismatic Studies (US ISSN 0517-404X) *845*
Numismatica e Antichita Classiche (SZ) *845*
Numismatica Lovaniensia (BE) *845*
Numismatica Moravica (CS ISSN 0078-2726) *845*
Numismaticky Sbornik (CS ISSN 0546-9414) *845*
Numismatiska Meddelanden/ Numismatic Communications (SW ISSN 0078-2734) *845*
Nuntiaturberichte aus Deutschland Nebst Ergaenzenden Aktenstuecken (GW ISSN 0078-2742) *559*
Nuova Universale Studium (IT ISSN 0391-8548) 559, 729, *880*
Nuovi Annali della Facolta di Magistero dell'Universita di Messina (IT) *631*, 880
Nuovi Saggi (IT ISSN 0078-2769) *631*
Nuovo Medioevo (IT ISSN 0391-6049) *592*
Nursing (Year) Career Directory (US ISSN 0192-2394) *784*
Nursing (Year) Drug Handbook (US ISSN 0273-320X) *784*
Nursing (Year) /NursePac: Students (US) *784*
Nursing Abstracts (US ISSN 0195-3354) 9, *771*
Nursing and Allied Health Index *see* Cumulative Index to Nursing & Allied Health Literature (C I N A H L) *769*
Nursing Journal (CE) *784*
Nursing Literature Index *see* Cumulative Index to Nursing & Allied Health Literature (C I N A H L) *769*
Nursing Opportunities (US) *784*
Nursingworld Journal Annual Hospital Directory *see* Nursingworld Journal Nursing Job Guide *784*
Nursingworld Journal Nursing Job Guide (US) *784*
Nutrition Abstracts and Reviews *see* Nutrition Abstracts and Reviews. Series B: Livestock Feeds and Feeding *42*
Nutrition Abstracts and Reviews *see* Nutrition Abstracts and Reviews. Series A: Human and Experimental *847*
Nutrition Abstracts and Reviews. Series A: Human and Experimental (UK ISSN 0309-1295) 9, *847*
Nutrition Abstracts and Reviews. Series B: Livestock Feeds and Feeding (UK ISSN 0309-135X) 9, *42*
Nutrition and the Brain (US) 144, *846*
Nutrition in Health and Disease (US ISSN 0160-2470) *846*
Nutrition Planning (US ISSN 0149-6743) *847*
Nutrition Research Laboratories. Annual Report *see* National Institute of Nutrition. Annual Report *846*
Nutrition Society of Australia. Proceedings (AT ISSN 0314-1004) *846*
Nutrition Society of India. Proceedings (II) 32, 520, *846*
Nuttall Ornithological Club. Publications (US ISSN 0550-4082) *170*
Nuytsia (AT ISSN 0085-4417) *160*
Ny Abstraktion (DK ISSN 0109-5544) *108*
Ny Carlsberg Glyptotek. Meddelelser (DK ISSN 0085-3208) 90, *108*
Ny Mponin'i Madagasikara (MG) *923*
Nyctalops (US) *729*
Nydanske Studier og almen Kommunikationsteori (DK) *699*
Nye Aar (DK ISSN 0108-8297) *971*
Nye Boeger om Film *see* Nye Boeger om Film/TV *826*
Nye Boeger om Film/TV/New Books on Film/TV (DK ISSN 0107-0894) *826*
Nyelveszeti Tanulmanyok (HU ISSN 0078-2858) *699*
Nyelvtudomanyi Ertekezesek (HU ISSN 0078-2866) *700*
Nyere Dansk Faglitteratur. Supplement (DK ISSN 0108-4321) *129*
Nylon Filament & Polyester Filament Growth (US) 247, 285, *1074*
Nysvenska Studier (SW ISSN 0345-8768) *700*
Nyt fra Bornholms Museum *see* Fra Bornholms Museum *827*
Nytt Fraan D F I (SW ISSN 0349-3210) *682*
O A P E C Energy Bibliography (Organization of Arab Petroleum Exporting Countries) (KU) 9, *865*
O A P E C Library Index (Organization of Arab Petroleum Exporting Countries) (KU) 9, *865*
O A P E C Library Periodicals Holdings (Organization of Arab Petroleum Exporting countries) (KU) *865*
O A S. General Secretariat. Annual Report (Organization of American States) (US ISSN 0078-6403) *608*
O C L C Annual Report (Online Computer Library Center, Inc.) (US ISSN 0730-5125) *682*
O D C Planning Reports (Oahu Development Conference) (US) *624*
O E C D Financial Statistics/ Statistiques Financieres de l'O C D E (Organization for Economic Cooperation and Development) (FR ISSN 0304-3371) *215*
O E C D Foreign Trade Statistics. Serie C *see* Organization for Economic Cooperation and Development. Foreign Trade by Commodities *215*
O E C S Annual Digest of Statistics (Organisation of Eastern Caribbean States) (AQ) 247, *1061*
O E C S Energy Bulletin (Organisation of Eastern Caribbean States) (AQ) 466, *1061*
O E C S National Account Digest (Organisation of Eastern Caribbean States) (AQ) 247, *1061*
O E C S Statistical Pocket Digest (Organisation of Eastern Caribbean States) (AQ) 247, *1061*
O E C S Trade Digest (Organisation of Eastern Caribbean States) (AQ) 247, *1061*
O F I Occasional Papers (Oxford Forestry Institute) (UK) *526*
O L B G Info (GW ISSN 0172-732X) *997*
O Literature dlya Detei (UR) *729*
O M S Annual Report (Office of Management Studies) (US ISSN 0278-7946) *682*
O N I I T E M. Boletin *see* Oficina Nacional de Invenciones, Informacion Tecnica y Marcos. Boletin *997*
O O A - Saertryk (Organisationen til Oplysning Om Atomkraft) (DK) *898*
O P D Chemical Buyers Directory (US ISSN 0276-539X) 315, *324*
O P M A Overseas Media Guide (Overseas Press and Media Association) (UK) 16, *646*
O.P. Market (Out of Print) (US ISSN 0078-2882) *962*
O.R.S.T.O.M. Annales Hydrologiques (Office de la Recherche Scientifique et Technique Outre-Mer. Annales Hydrologiques) (FR ISSN 0071-8998) *1160*
O.R.S.T.O.M. Initiations Documentations Techniques (FR ISSN 0071-9021) *1070*
O.R.S.T.O.M. Institut Francais de Recherche pour le Developement en Cooperation. Rapport d'Activite (Office de la Recherche Scientifique et Technique en Cooperation) (FR ISSN 0071-9013) 997, *1070*
O.R.S.T.O.M. Memoires *see* Memoires O.R.S.T.O.M *1070*
O.R.S.T.O.M. Recueils des Travaux. Oceanographie *see* O.R.S.T.O.M. Resumes des Travaux. Oceanographie *407*
O.R.S.T.O.M. Resumes des Travaux. Oceanographie (Office de la Recherche Scientifique et Technique Outre-Mer) (NL) 393, *407*
O R T Yearbook (Organization for Rehabilitation Through Training) (SZ) *445*
O S E A P Centre Update (Organisation for Scientific Evaluation of Aerial Phenomena) (UK ISSN 0262-7795) *21*
O S E A P Journal (Organisation for Scientific Evaluation of Aerial Phenomena) (UK ISSN 0262-5954) *21*
O S G N Wetenschappelijke Publikatie (Organisatie van Studenten in de Geschiedenis van Nederland) (NE) *592*
O T A N Communiques Finals *see* N A T O Final Communiques *917*
O T A N Documents Fondamentaux *see* N A T O Basic Documents *917*
O T A N et le Pacte de Varsovie - Comparison des Forces en Presence *see* N A T O and the Warsaw Pact - Force Comparisons *917*
O W A A Outdoor Writers Directory *see* Outdoor Writers Association of America. Directory *646*
Oahu Development Conference. Annual Report (US) *624*
Oahu Development Conference Planning Reports *see* O D C Planning Reports *624*
Oak Ridge Associated Universities. Annual Report (US) *437*
Oak Ridge Associated Universities. Medical and Health Sciences Division. Research Report (US) *764*
Oak Ridge Associated Universities. Medical Division. Research Report *see* Oak Ridge Associated Universities. Medical and Health Sciences Division. Research Report *764*
Oak Ridge Associated Universities. Report *see* Oak Ridge Associated Universities. Annual Report *437*
Oakland Port and Shipping Handbook (UK ISSN 0268-6481) 315, *1102*
Oberhessische Gesellschaft fuer Natur- und Heilkunde, Giessen. Berichte (GW ISSN 0078-2920) *997*
Oberoesterreichischer Museralverein. Jahrbuch (AU) 90, *592*
Oberoesterreichisches Landesarchiv. Mitteilungen (AU ISSN 0572-192X) *592*
Oberrheinische Geologische Abhandlungen (GW ISSN 0078-2939) *393*
Oberrheinischer Geologischer Verein. Jahresberichte und Mitteilungen (GW ISSN 0078-2947) *393*
Obiter (SA) *661*
Objektiv (DK ISSN 0107-6329) *884*
Oblastni Muzeum Jihovychodni Moravy v Gottwaldove. Zpravy *see* Oblastni Muzeum v Gottwaldove. Zpravy *592*
Oblastni Muzeum v Gottwaldove. Zpravy (CS) 592, *907*
Obrabotka Simvol'noi Informatsii (UR) *353*
Obraz Literatury Polskiej (PL ISSN 0078-2963) *729*
Obrzedy i Zwyczaje Ludowe (PL) *839*
Obscura *see* Frame/Work *884*
Observation (CN ISSN 0826-9947) *197*
Observatoire Astronomique d'Alger. Annales (AE ISSN 0065-6232) *117*
Observatoire de Geneve. Publications. Serie A (SZ ISSN 0085-0942) *117*
Observatoire de Geneve. Publications. Serie B (SZ ISSN 0435-2939) *117*
Observatoire de Strasbourg. Publication *see* Journees de Strasbourg *116*
Observatoire de Tokyo. Annales *see* Tokyo Astronomical Observatory. Annals *117*
Observatorio Astronomico de Madrid. Anuario (SP ISSN 0373-5125) *117*
Observatorio Astronomico Municipal de Rosario. Boletin (AG ISSN 0302-2277) *117*
Observatorio Nacional Rio de Janeiro. Anuario *see* Observatorio Nacional Rio de Janeiro. Efemerides Astronomicas *117*
Observatorio Nacional Rio de Janeiro. Contribuicoes Cientificas (BL) *1160*
Observatorio Nacional Rio de Janeiro. Efemerides Astronomicas (BL) *117*
Observatorio Nacional Rio de Janeiro. Publicacoes (BL) 117, *400*
Observatorul Astronomic din Bucuresti. Observations Solaires *see* Centre de l'Astronomie et des Sciences Spatiales. Observations Solaires *115*
Observatorul Astronomie din Bucuresti. Anuarul *see* Centrul de Astronomie si Stiinte Spatiale. Anuarul Astronomic *115*
Obserwatorium Krakowski. Rocznik Astronomiczny. Dodatek Miedzynarodowy (PL ISSN 0075-7047) *117*
Obvestila Republiske Maticne Sluzbe (YU) *682*
Obwaldner Geschichtsblaetter (SZ) *592*
O'Casey Annual (US) 505, *729*
Occasional Papers in Anthropology (US ISSN 0078-3005) *74*
Occasional Papers in Anthropology (AT) *74*
Occasional Papers in Economic and Social History (UK ISSN 0078-3013) 252, *1010*
Occasional Papers in English Local History (UK ISSN 0078-303X) *592*
Occasional Papers in Entomology (US ISSN 0362-2622) *165*
Occasional Papers in Estate Management (UK ISSN 0078-3048) *966*
Occasional Papers in Geography (UK ISSN 0078-3056) *547*
Occasional Papers in German Studies (UK ISSN 0307-7497) 592, 700, *729*
Occasional Papers in Illinois Politics (US) 907, *944*
Occasional Papers in Industrial Relations (NZ ISSN 0078-3064) *274*
Occasional Papers in Linguistics (US) *700*
Occasional Papers in Linguistics and Language Learning (UK ISSN 0308-2075) *700*
Occasional Papers in Maritime Affairs (AT) 403, 498, 512, *1102*
Occasional Papers in Metropolitan Business and Finance (US) *231*
Occasional Papers in Middle Eastern Librarianship (US ISSN 0278-4882) *682*
Occasional Papers in Modern Dutch Studies (UK ISSN 0144-3070) 592, *729*
Occasional Papers in Modern Languages (UK ISSN 0078-3099) *729*
Occasional Papers in Slavic Languages and Literature (US) 700, *729*
Occasional Papers of the Museum of Zoology, University of Michigan *see* University of Michigan. Museum of Zoology. Occasional Papers *178*

Occasional Papers on Linguistics (US) 700
Occasional Papers on Religion in Eastern Europe (US ISSN 0731-5465) 547, 971
Occasional Papers on the Near East (US ISSN 0732-6475) 613
Occasional Papers/Reprint Series in Contemporary Asian Studies (US ISSN 0730-0107) 571, 661
Occasional Publications in Northeastern Anthropology (US) 74
Occultism Update (US) 860
Occupational Disease in California (US) 274, 636, 1061
Occupational Education (US ISSN 0360-5434) 437
Occupational Employment in Hospitals in New Jersey (US) 1160
Occupational Health see Beruf und Gesundheit 636
Occupational Health & Safety Purchasing Sourcebook (US) 315, 636
Occupational Hygiene Monographs (UK ISSN 0141-7568) 636
Occupational Programs in California Public Community Colleges (US ISSN 0731-8650) 430, 848
Occupational Radiation Exposure, Annual Report see U.S. Nuclear Regulatory Commission. Occupational Radiation Exposure, Annual Report 636
Occupational Safety and Health Abstracts see C I S Abstracts 636
Occupational Safety and Health Decisions (US ISSN 0092-3435) 636
Occupational Safety and Health Series (UN ISSN 0078-3129) 636
Ocean Dumping Control Act Annual Report (CN) 498, 661, 671
Ocean Engineering: a Wiley Series (US) 407, 473
Ocean Science, Resources and Technology (US) 407, 1125
Ocean Thermal Energy Conversion Workshop. Workshop Proceedings (US ISSN 0271-2946) 466
Ocean Yearbook (US ISSN 0191-8575) 407
Oceanic Abstracts (US ISSN 0093-6901) 9, 382
Oceanic Citation Index see Oceanic Abstracts 382
Oceanic Index see Oceanic Abstracts 382
Oceanic Linguistics. Special Publications (US ISSN 0078-3188) 700
Oceanografiska Institutet, Goeteborg. Meddelanden see Goteborgs Universitet. Oceanografiska Institutionen. Reports 405
Oceanographic Research Institute, Durban. Investigational Report (SA ISSN 0078-320X) 407
Oceanographical Magazine/Kischo-cho Obun Kaiyo Hokoku (JA) 407
Oceanography and Marine Biology: an Annual Review (UK ISSN 0078-3218) 144, 407
Oceanologia (PL ISSN 0078-3234) 407
Oceans. Conference Record (US ISSN 0197-7385) 473
Ocherki po Istorii Estestvoznaniya i Tekhniki (UR) 559
Ochistka Vodnogo i Vozdushnogo Basseinov na Predpriyatiyakh Chernoi Metallurgii (UR) 799
Ochrona Przyrody (PL ISSN 0078-3250) 366
Ochrona Wod i Rybactwo Srodladowe see Acta Academiae Agriculturae ac Technicae Olstenensis. Protectio Aquarum et Piscatoria 1123
Ocular Therapeutics and Pharmacology (US) 786, 1125
Ocultaciones de Estrellas por la Luna (SP ISSN 0210-8119) 117
Odawuru in Series (GH) 74
Odense Universitet. Institut for Offentlig Oekonomi og Politik. Occasional Paper (DK ISSN 0109-0976) 197, 907

Odense Universitet. Institut for Virksomhedsledelse. Skrifter (DK ISSN 0108-8165) 281
Odense Universitet. Laboratorium for Folkesproglig Middelalderlitteratur. Mindre Skrifter (DK ISSN 0106-2212) 729
Odense Universitetsbibliotek. Specialer og Prisopgaver (DK ISSN 0107-1742) 438
Odense Universitetsbibliotek. Tidsskriftkatalog (DK ISSN 0107-5462) 129
Odense University Classical Studies (DK ISSN 0107-1378) 90, 338
Odense University Slavic Studies (DK ISSN 0078-3277) 700
Odense University Studies in Art History (DK ISSN 0078-3285) 108
Odense University Studies in English (DK ISSN 0078-3293) 700
Odense University Studies in History and Social Sciences (DK ISSN 0078-3307) 592
Odense University Studies in Linguistics (DK ISSN 0078-3315) 700
Odense University Studies in Literature (DK ISSN 0078-3323) 729
Odense University Studies in Philosophy (DK ISSN 0107-7384) 880
Odense University Studies in Psychiatry and Medical Psychology (DK ISSN 0105-0621) 791, 935
Odense University Studies in Scandinavian Languages and Literatures (DK ISSN 0078-3331) 700, 729
Odont see Infodont 779
Odontologi (DK ISSN 0105-0141) 780
Odontologiska Samfundet i Finland. Aarsbok (FI ISSN 0078-3358) 780
Odrodzenie i Reformacja w Polsce (PL ISSN 0029-8514) 592
O'Dwyer's Directory of Corporate Communications (US ISSN 0149-1091) 197
O'Dwyer's Directory of Public Relations Executives (US ISSN 0191-0051) 16, 135
O'Dwyer's Directory of Public Relations Firms (US ISSN 0078-3374) 16, 315
Oecumene (FR) 975
Oeffentliche Baumappe der Ostschweiz (SZ) 99, 186
Der Oeffentliche Haushalt (GW) 1160
Oeffentliche Kunstsammlung. Jahresbericht (SZ ISSN 0067-4311) 830
Oeffentliche Schiffahrt auf den Schweizer Seen (SZ) 1042
Oekonometrie und Unternehmensforschung/Econometrics and Operations Research (US ISSN 0078-3390) 198, 281
Oekonomiehistorische Texte (GE ISSN 0233-0946) 198
Oekonomische Studientexte see Oekonomiehistorische Texte 198
Oekonomisk Analyse, Sommerregnskaber (DK ISSN 0109-7725) 198
Oekonomisk Oversigt for Amtskommunerne see Amstkommunernes Oekonomi 950
Oekonomiske Udvikling paa Faeroerne (DK ISSN 0108-6464) 198
Oerlikon Schweissmitteilungen (GW ISSN 0078-3420) 799
Oesterreich Archiv (AU) 592
Oesterreichische Akademie der Wissenschaften. Almanach (AU ISSN 0378-8644) 631, 997
Oesterreichische Akademie der Wissenschaften. Archiv fuer Oesterreichische Geschichte (AU) 592
Oesterreichische Akademie der Wissenschaften. Iranische Kommission. Veroeffentlichungen (AU) 631

Oesterreichische Akademie der Wissenschaften. Kommission fuer die Tabula Imperii Byzantini. Veroeffentlichungen (AU) 592
Oesterreichische Akademie der Wissenschaften. Kommission fuer Linguistik und Kommunikationsforschung. Veroeffentlichungen (AU) 700
Oesterreichische Akademie der Wissenschaften. Kommission fuer Literaturwissenschaft. Veroeffentlichungen (AU) 729
Oesterreichische Akademie der Wissenschaften. Kommission fuer Musikforschung. Mitteilungen (AU ISSN 0023-3048) 839
Oesterreichische Akademie der Wissenschaften. Kommission fuer Sozial- und Wirtschaftswissenschaften. Veroeffentlichungen (AU) 1010
Oesterreichische Akademie der Wissenschaften. Kommission zur Herausgabe des Corpus der Lateinischen Kirchenvaeter. Veroeffentlichungen (AU) 983
Oesterreichische Akademie der Wissenschaften. Numismatische Kommission. Veroeffentlichungen (AU) 845
Oesterreichische Akademie der Wissenschaften. Philosophisch-Historische Klasse. Anzeiger (AU ISSN 0378-8652) 592, 880
Oesterreichische Akademie der Wissenschaften. Philosophisch-Historische Klasse. Sitzungsberichte (AU) 592, 880
Oesterreichische Akademie der Wissenschaften. Praehistorische Kommission. Mitteilungen (AU ISSN 0065-5376) 592
Oesterreichische Akademie der Wissenschaften, Vienna. Mathematisch-Naturwissenschaftliche Klasse. Anzeiger see Oesterreichische Akademie der Wissenschaften, Vienna. Mathematisch-Naturwissenschaftliche Klasse. Denkschriften 751
Oesterreichische Akademie der Wissenschaften, Vienna. Mathematisch-Naturwissenschaftliche Klasse. Denkschriften (US ISSN 0379-0207) 751, 997
Oesterreichische Bankwissenschaftliche Gesellschaft. Schriftenreihe (AU) 231
Das Oesterreichische Buch (AU ISSN 0078-3455) 962
Oesterreichische Byzantinische Gesellschaft Jahrbuch see Oesterreichische Byzantinistik. Jahrbuch 592
Oesterreichische Byzantinistik. Jahrbuch (AU ISSN 0378-8660) 592
Oesterreichische Galerie. Mitteilungen (AU ISSN 0029-909X) 830
Oesterreichische Geologische Gesellschaft. Mitteilungen (AU ISSN 0251-7493) 393, 857
Oesterreichische Gesellschaft fuer Musik. Beitraege (GW ISSN 0078-3471) 839
Oesterreichische Hochschulstatistik (AU ISSN 0067-2343) 425
Oesterreichische Komponisten des 20. Jahrhunderts (AU ISSN 0078-3501) 135, 840
Oesterreichische Moorforschung (AU ISSN 0078-351X) 1160
Oesterreichische Nationalbank. Bericht ueber das Geschaeftsjahr mit Rechnungsabschluss (AU ISSN 0078-3528) 231
Oesterreichische Schriften zur Entwicklungshilfe (AU ISSN 0078-3536) 263
Oesterreichische Volkskundliche Bibliographie (AU) 74, 108, 516
Oesterreichische Zeitschrift fuer Oeffentliches Recht. Supplement see Oesterreichische Zeitschrift fuer Oeffentliches Recht und Voelkerrecht. Supplement 661
Oesterreichische Zeitschrift fuer Oeffentliches Recht und Voelkerrecht. Supplement (US ISSN 0173-1718) 661

Oesterreichischer Alpenverein. Akademische Sektion Graz. Mitteilungen (AU ISSN 0029-8840) 1046
Oesterreichischer Auslandsstudentendienst. Rechenschaftsbericht (AU) 441
Oesterreichischer Buchklub der Jugend. Jahrbuch (AU ISSN 0078-3560) 335
Oesterreichischer Krankenpflegerverband. Fortbildungsprogramm (AU) 438, 784
Oesterreichisches Archaeologisches Institut. Jahreshefte (AU) 90
Oesterreichisches Archaeologisches Institut. Jahreshefte: Grabungen see Oesterreichisches Archaeologisches Institut. Jahreshefte 90
Oesterreichisches Institut fuer Bauforschung Nachrichten see I B Nachrichten 184
Oesterreichisches Institut fuer Mittelstandspolitik. Schriftenreihe see Oesterreichisches Wirtschaftsinstitut fuer Strukturforschung und Strukturpolitik. Schriftenreihe 198
Oesterreichisches Institut fuer Raumplanung. Oeir-Forum (AU) 624
Oesterreichisches Institut fuer Raumplanung. Taetigkeitsbericht (AU ISSN 0078-3617) 624
Oesterreichisches Institut fuer Raumplanung. Veroeffentlichungen see Oesterreichisches Institut fuer Raumplanung. Oeir-Forum 624
Oesterreichisches Jahrbuch fuer Politik (AU ISSN 0170-0847) 907
Oesterreichisches Kulturinstitut, Rom. Abteilung fuer Historische Studien. Publikationen I. Abteilung: Abhandlungen (AU) 592
Oesterreichisches Kulturinstitut, Rom. Abteilung fuer Historische Studien. Publikationen II. Abteilung: Quellen (AU) 592
Oesterreichisches Museum fuer Volkskunde. Kataloge (AU) 832
Oesterreichisches Museum fuer Volkskunde: Veroeffentlichungen (AU) 74, 108, 516
Oesterreichisches Ost- und Suedosteuropa Institut. Schriftenreihe (AU ISSN 0078-3439) 592
Oesterreichisches Staatsarchiv. Mitteilungen (AU ISSN 0067-2297) 592
Oesterreichisches Staatsarchiv. Publikationen (AU) 682
Oesterreichisches Statistisches Zentralamt. Wirtschaftsstatistik der Elektrizitaetsversorgungsunternehmen (AU) 457
Oesterreichisches Volksliedwerk. Jahrbuch (AU ISSN 0473-8624) 840
Oesterreichisches Wirtschaftsinstitut fuer Strukturforschung und Strukturpolitik. Schriftenreihe (AU ISSN 0078-3595) 198
Oesterreichs Presse, Werbung, Graphik see Pressehandbuch (AU) 962
Oesterreichs Volkseinkommen (AU ISSN 0085-4433) 215
Oesterreichs Wirtschaft im Ueberblick see Survey of the Austrian Economy 240
Oesteuropa Frimaerkekatalog see A F A Oesteuropa Frimaerkekatalog 874
Of Human Rights (US) 913
Off Campus Study Programs: U S and Abroad (US) 427
Off Main Street (US) 729
Off-Shore Technology Conference. Record (US ISSN 0078-3706) 457
Offa-Jahrbuch; Vor- und Fruehgeschichte (GW ISSN 0078-3714) 592
Offenbacher Verein fuer Naturkunde. Abhandlungen (GW ISSN 0171-7936) 160, 165, 170
Offenbacher Verein fuer Naturkunde. Bericht (GW ISSN 0343-2793) 160, 165, 170

OFFENTLICHE FINANZEN

Offentliche Finanzen der Schweiz/ Finances Publiques en Suisse (SZ) *298*

Office Automation Conference Digest (US ISSN 0272-4855) *360, 361*

Office Automation Digest see Office Automation Conference Digest *361*

Office - Data Processing Machines: Latin American Industrial Report (US) *240, 357*

Office de la Recherche Scientifique et Technique en Cooperation Institut Francais de Recherche pour le Developement en Cooperation. Rapport d'Activite see O.R.S.T.O.M. Institut Francais de Recherche pour le Developement en Cooperation. Rapport d'Activite *997*

Office de la Recherche Scientifique et Technique Outre-Mer. Annales Hydrologiques Annales Hydrologiques see O.R.S.T.O.M. Annales Hydrologiques *1160*

Office de la Recherche Scientifique et Technique Outre-Mer Resumes des Travaux. Oceanographie see O.R.S.T.O.M. Resumes des Travaux. Oceanographie *407*

Office des Communications Sociales, Montreal. Cahiers d'Etudes et de Recherches (CN ISSN 0078-3722) *344, 349*

Office des Communications Sociales, Montreal. Selection de Films en 16 MM (CN) *825*

Office des Communications Sociales, Montreal. Selection de Films pour Cine Clubs. see Office des Communications Sociales, Montreal. Selection de Films en 16 MM *825*

Office Equipment Exporter (US ISSN 0471-1424) *258, 286*

Office for Metropolitan History. Research and Remarks on Current Topics (US) *608*

Office Furniture (IT) *643*

Office General de la Musique Annuaire O.G.M. see Annuaire O.G.M *347*

Office International de la Vigne et du Vin Memento de l'O.I.V. see Memento de l'O.I.V *120*

Office Product News Directory (CN) *281*

Offices de Commercialisation au Canada see Marketing Boards in Canada *48*

Official Baseball Guide (US ISSN 0078-3838) *1039*

Official Baseball Record Book see Complete Baseball Record Book *1038*

Official Baseball Register (US ISSN 0162-542X) *1039*

Official Baseball Rules (US ISSN 0078-3846) *1039*

Official Colorado-Wyoming Fishing Guide see Tim Kelley's Fishing Guide *1047*

Official Directory of Festivals, Sports & Special Events (US) *285, 1077*

Official Directory of New Jersey Libraries and Media Centers see Official Directory of New Jersey Libraries Media Centers Including Buyers' Guide *682*

Official Directory of New Jersey Libraries Media Centers Including Buyers' Guide (US ISSN 0748-2469) *682*

Official Guide for G M A T Review (Graduate Management Admission Test) (US) *281, 438*

Official Guide to Airline Careers (US) *848*

Official Guide to Hotels & Restaurants in Great Britain, Ireland and Overseas (British Hotels, Restaurants and Caterers Association) (UK ISSN 0307-062X) *620*

Official Guide to M B A Programs (US) *281, 438*

Official Handbook of Ghana (GH ISSN 0072-9825) *566*

Official Handbook of the A.A.U. Code see Amateur Athletic Union of the United States. Official Handbook of the A A U Code *1032*

Official Hotel & Resort Guide (US) *620, 1115*

Official International Business Directory of the Latin American World (US) *315*

Official International Business Directory of the Spanish Speaking World see Official International Business Directory of the Latin American World *315*

Official Lawn Bowls Almanac (US) *1039*

Official Lawn Bowls Handbook see Official Lawn Bowls Almanac *1039*

Official Museum Directory (US ISSN 0090-6700) *830*

Official N A S C A R Yearbook and Press Guide (US) *1092*

Official N C A A Lacrosse Guide see N C A A Men's Lacrosse Rules *1039*

Official National Basketball Association Guide (US ISSN 0078-3862) *1039*

Official National Collegiate Athletic Association Basketball Guide see N C A A Basketball *1039*

Official National Collegiate Athletic Association Football Rules and Interpretations see National Collegiate Athletic Association Football Rules & Interpretations *1039*

Official National Collegiate Athletic Association Ice Hockey Guide see N C A A Men's Ice Hockey Rules and Interpretations *1034*

Official National Collegiate Athletic Association Skiing Rules see N C A A Men's and Women's Skiing Rules *1046*

Official National Collegiate Athletic Association Soccer Guide see N C A A Men's Soccer Rules *1039*

Official National Collegiate Athletic Association Swimming Guide see N C A A Men's & Women's Swimming and Diving Rules *1034*

Official National Collegiate Athletic Association Track and Field Guide see N C A A Men's & Women's Cross Country and Track & Field Rules *1046*

Official National Collegiate Athletic Association Water Polo Rules see N C A A Men's Water Polo Rules *1034*

Official National Collegiate Athletic Association Wrestling Guide see National Collegiate Athletic Association Wrestling Rules *1034*

Official New Mexico Blue Book (US ISSN 0732-3093) *608*

Official Organ Blue Book (US ISSN 0048-1513) *840*

Official Overstreet Comic Book Price Guide (US) *614*

Official Port of Detroit World Handbook (US ISSN 0093-1799) *1102*

Official Read-Easy Basketball Rules (US ISSN 0277-559X) *1039*

Official Registry of C B Operators (US) *349*

Official Rules of Sports and Games (US) *1160*

Official South African Municipal Yearbook/Amptelike Suid-Afrikaanse Munisipale Jaarboek (SA) *951*

Official Southern California Ports Maritime Directory and Guide (US ISSN 0094-8454) *1102*

Official Souvenir Guide to the Edinburgh Festival (UK) *108, 1115*

Official Video Directory & Buyer's Guide (US ISSN 0890-782X) *315, 349*

Official Video Software Directory (US) *346, 349*

Official Wisconsin Pastoral Handbook (US) *983*

Official Year Book of Australia see Australia. Bureau of Statistics. Year Book Australia *1049*

Official Year Book of Western Australia see Western Australian Yearbook. New Series *573*

Offizielle Deutsch-Franzoesische Industrie- und Handelskammer. Mitgliederliste see Chambre Officielle Franco Allemande de Commerce et d'Industrie. Liste des Membres *235*

Offshore Abstracts (UK ISSN 0305-0513) *9, 868*

Offshore Contractors and Equipment Directory see Offshore Contractors and Equipment Worldwide Directory *865*

Offshore Contractors and Equipment Worldwide Directory (US) *865*

Offshore Drilling Report (Year) (UK) *868*

Offshore Service Vessel Register (UK ISSN 0309-040X) *865*

Offshore Service Vessels (US ISSN 0887-6827) *315, 865, 1102*

Offshore Tugs (US ISSN 0887-6835) *315, 865, 1102*

Oficina Nacional de Invenciones, Informacion Tecnica y Marcos. Boletin (CU) *997*

Oficina; Revista de Equipos para Oficinas (US ISSN 0085-445X) *286*

Ogasawara Research Committee. Publications (JA ISSN 0386-8176) *1010*

Oh Calcutta (II) *539*

Ohinemuri (NZ) *573*

Ohio. Commission on Aging. Annual Report see Ohio. Department of Aging. Annual Report *552*

Ohio. Department of Aging. Annual Report (US) *552*

Ohio. Division of Geological Survey. Bulletin (US) *393*

Ohio. Division of Geological Survey. Educational Leaflet (US ISSN 0472-6685) *393*

Ohio. Division of Geological Survey. Geological Note (US) *393*

Ohio. Division of Geological Survey. Guidebook (US ISSN 0097-9473) *393*

Ohio. Division of Geological Survey. Information Circular (US) *393*

Ohio. Division of Geological Survey. Miscellaneous Report (US ISSN 0361-0519) *393*

Ohio. Division of Geological Survey. Report of Investigations (US) *393*

Ohio. Division of Mines. Report see Report on Ohio Mineral Industries *820*

Ohio. Division of State Personnel. Annual Report (US ISSN 0078-4001) *286*

Ohio. State Library. Annual Report (US) *682*

Ohio. State Library. State Library Review see Ohio. State Library. Annual Report *682*

Ohio Agricultural Research and Development Center, Wooster. Library. List of References: Maize Virus Diseases and Corn Stunt. see Ohio Agricultural Research and Development Center, Wooster. List of References: Maize Virus and Mycoplasma Diseases *42*

Ohio Agricultural Research and Development Center, Wooster. List of References: Maize Virus and Mycoplasma Diseases (US) *42*

Ohio Agricultural Research and Development Center, Wooster. Research Bulletin (US ISSN 0078-3951) *32*

Ohio Agricultural Research and Development Center, Wooster. Research Circular (US ISSN 0078-396X) *32*

Ohio Arts Council. Annual Report see Ohio Arts Council. Biennial Report *108*

Ohio Arts Council. Biennial Report (US ISSN 0731-3284) *108*

Ohio Biological Survey. Biological Notes (US ISSN 0078-3986) *144*

Ohio Biological Survey. Bulletin. New Series (US ISSN 0078-3994) *144*

Ohio Biological Survey. Informative Circular (US ISSN 0270-5443) *144*

Ohio College Library Center. Annual Report see O C L C Annual Report *682*

Ohio Directory of Manufacturers (US) *315*

Ohio Geographers: Recent Research Themes (US ISSN 0094-9043) *547*

Ohio Higher Education. Basic Data Series (US ISSN 0094-6109) *425*

Ohio Industrial Directory see Harris Ohio Industrial Directory *309*

Ohio Legal Rights Service. Annual Report (US) *661*

Ohio Legislative Service see Baldwin's Ohio Legislative Service *939*

Ohio Manufacturers Directory (US ISSN 0737-7495) *315*

Ohio Speech Journal (US ISSN 0078-4052) *344*

Ohio State Industrial Directory see MacRae's Ohio State Industrial Directory *313*

Ohio State University. Agricultural Research and Development Center. Special Circular (US ISSN 0736-8003) *32, 526*

Ohio State University. College of Law. Law Forum Series (US ISSN 0078-4095) *661*

Ohio State University. Disaster Research Center. D R C - T R see D R C Book & Monograph Series *1025*

Ohio State University. Disaster Research Center. Report Series see University of Delaware Disaster Research Center. Report Series *1021*

Ohio State University. Institute of Polar Studies. Contribution Series (US) *380, 688*

Ohio State University. Institute of Polar Studies. Miscellaneous Series (US) *380, 547, 806*

Ohio State University. Institute of Polar Studies. Report Series (US ISSN 0078-415X) *380, 547, 806*

Ohio State University. School of Public Administration. Working Paper Series (US) *945*

Ohio State University Annual Biosciences Colloquia (US) *144*

Ohio State University, Columbus. Disaster Research Center. Miscellaneous Reports see University of Delaware. Disaster Research Center. Miscellaneous Reports *636*

Ohio Truck Times (US) *1105*

Ohio University. Working Papers in Linguistics and Language Teaching (US) *700*

Ohio Valley Philosophy of Education Society. Proceedings of the Annual Meeting see Philosophical Studies in Education *418*

Oil and Arab Cooperation. Annual Review (KU) *466, 865*

Oil & Gas Directory (US ISSN 0471-380X) *315, 865*

Oil and Gas Industry see Oil and Oil Field Equipment & Service Companies Worldwide *866*

Oil & Gas Producing Industry in Your State (US ISSN 0747-2528) *866*

Oil and Oil Field Equipment & Service Companies Worldwide (UK) *866*

Oil and Petroleum Year Book see Financial Times International Year Books: Oil and Gas *864*

Oil Directory of Canada (US ISSN 0474-0114) *315, 866*

Oil Directory of Companies Outside the U.S. and Canada (US ISSN 0472-7711) *315, 866*

Oil Directory of Houston, Texas (US ISSN 0471-3877) *315, 866*

Oil Marketing and Wholesale Distributors see Directory of Oil Marketing and Wholesale Distributors *864*

Oil Price Databook (US) *866*

Oil Shale Symposium Proceedings (US ISSN 0271-0315) *819, 866*

Oilfield Service, Supply, and Manufacturers Worldwide Directory see U S A Oilfield Service, Supply, and Manufacturers Directory *867*

Oils and Fats International Directory (UK) *258*

Oils, Lubricants, and Petroleum Products (US) *490, 866*

Oink! see New American Writing *742*

Oita University. Research Institute of Economics. Bulletin (JA ISSN 0287-0916) *198*

Ojito (US) *711*

Okanagan History (CN ISSN 0830-0739) *608*

Okay Anglers Fishing Directory & Atlas (CN ISSN 0827-570X) *512*

ONTARIO DIGEST   1841

Okayama University. Berichte des Ohara Instituts fuer Landwirtschaftliche Biologie. (JA ISSN 0365-9860) *48,* 144
Okayama University. Research Laboratory for Surface Science. Reports (JA ISSN 0078-429X) *332*
Okeanologiia (BU ISSN 0324-0878) *407*
Okinawa Library Association. Annals/ Okinawa Toshokan Kyokai Shi (JA) *682*
Okinawa Prefecture. Annual Report of Fire and Disaster Prevention (JA) *507*
Okinawa Toshokan Kyokai Shi *see* Okinawa Library Association. Annals *682*
Oklahoma. Ad Valorem Tax Division. Progress Report to the Legislature on Property Revaluation (US) *298*
Oklahoma. Attorney General's Office. Opinions of the Attorney General (US ISSN 0475-0926) *661*
Oklahoma. Commission on Consumer Affairs. Annual Report (US) *369*
Oklahoma. Conservation Commission. Biennial Report (US ISSN 0095-442X) *366*
Oklahoma. Department of Highways. Sufficiency Rating Report and Needs Study: Oklahoma State Highways *see* Oklahoma. Department of Transportation. Sufficiency Rating Report and Needs Study: Oklahoma State Transportation *1097*
Oklahoma. Department of Human Services. Annual Report (US) *1019*
Oklahoma. Department of Human Services. Annual Statistical Report (US) *1019*
Oklahoma. Department of Institutions, Social and Rehabilitative Services. Annual Report *see* Oklahoma. Department of Human Services. Annual Report *1019*
Oklahoma. Department of Libraries. Annual Report and Directory of Libraries in Oklahoma *see* Annual Report of Oklahoma Libraries *673*
Oklahoma. Department of Libraries. Annual Report and Directory of Libraries in Oklahoma *see* Annual Directory of Oklahoma Libraries *673*
Oklahoma. Department of Transportation. Sufficiency Rating Report and Needs Study: Oklahoma State Transportation (US) *1097*
Oklahoma. Drug Abuse Division. Annual Report (US) *377*
Oklahoma. Employment Security Commission. Actuarial Division. Handbook of Employment Security Program Statistics (US) *215*
Oklahoma. Employment Security Commission. Research and Planning Division. Annual Report ot the Governor *see* Oklahoma. Employment Security Commission. Research Division. Annual Report to the Governor *274*
Oklahoma. Employment Security Commission. Research and Planning Division. County Employment and Wage Data *see* Oklahoma. Employment Security Commission. Research Division. County Employment and Wage Data *215*
Oklahoma. Employment Security Commission. Research Division. Annual Report to the Governor (US) *274*
Oklahoma. Employment Security Commission. Research Division. County Employment and Wage Data(US) *215*
Oklahoma. Geological Survey. Bulletin (US ISSN 0078-4389) *393*
Oklahoma. Geological Survey. Circular (US ISSN 0078-4397) *393*
Oklahoma. Geological Survey. Educational Publication (US ISSN 0160-8746) *393*
Oklahoma. Geological Survey. Guidebook (US ISSN 0078-4400) *393*

Oklahoma. Geological Survey. Special Publication Series (US ISSN 0275-0929) *393*
Oklahoma. Grand River Dam Authority. Annual Report (US ISSN 0078-4508) *490*
Oklahoma. Office of Drug Abuse. Annual Performance Report, Drug Abuse Treatment Programs and Continuation Plan *see* Oklahoma. Drug Abuse Division. Annual Report *377*
Oklahoma. Public Employees Retirement System. Annual Report (US) *287*
Oklahoma Anthropological Society. Bulletin (US ISSN 0078-432X) *74*
Oklahoma Anthropological Society. Memoir (US ISSN 0474-0696) *75*
Oklahoma Department of Mental Health. Annual Report (US) *935*
Oklahoma Directory of Manufacturers *see* Oklahoma Directory of Manufacturers and Products *315*
Oklahoma Directory of Manufacturers and Products (US) *315*
Oklahoma Health Statistics (US ISSN 0098-5651) *959*
Oklahoma Lake Living (US) *547*
Oklahoma Population Estimates (US) *928*
Oklahoma State Agencies, Boards, Commissions, Courts, Institutions, Legislature and Officers (US) *945*
Oklahoma State Industrial Directory *see* MacRae's Oklahoma State Industrial Directory *313*
Oklahoma State University. College of Business Administration. Extension Service. Business Papers *see* Oklahoma State University. College of Business Administration. Working Papers *198*
Oklahoma State University. College of Business Administration. Working Papers (US) *198*
Oklahoma Turnpike Authority. Annual Report to the Governor (US) *1097*
Oklahoma Turnpike Authority. Report to Bondholders (US) *1097*
Oklahoma Water Resources Research Institute. Annual Report (US ISSN 0092-2528) *1125*
Okresni Archiv Olomouc. Vyrocni Zprava (CS) *91, 593*
Okresni Muzeum v Blansku. Sbornik (CS) *91, 593*
Okresni Vlastivedneho Muzeum v Blansku. Sbornik *see* Okresni Muzeum v Blansku. Sbornik *593*
Okyeame (GH ISSN 0048-1629) *505, 729*
Old Age: a Register of Social Research (UK) *552,* 1019
Old Athlone Society Journal (IE ISSN 0475-1388) *593*
Old Car Value Guide (US ISSN 0475-1876) *1092*
Old Car Value Guide Annual *see* Old Car Value Guide *1092*
Old Dominion Foundation. Report *see* Andrew W. Mellon Foundation. Report *628*
Old Farmer's Almanac (US ISSN 0078-4516) *463*
Old Glory (US) *608*
Old-House Journal Buyers' Guide *see* Old-House Journal Catalog *186*
Old-House Journal Catalog (US ISSN 0271-7220) *99, 186, 366, 966*
Old Red Kimono (US) *729*
Old Testament Abstracts (US ISSN 0364-8591) *9, 975*
Old Testament Essays (SA) *971*
Old Time Music (UK ISSN 0048-1653) *516, 840*
Old York Road Historical Society Bulletin (US) *608*
Oldtimer Adressen Lexikon (GW) *1092*
Oldtimer Katalog (GW) *1092*
Oleander Games and Pastimes Series (UK) *1035*
Oleander Travel Books Series (UK) *1115*
Oleo (SP) *330*
Oliebeteretning (DK ISSN 0109-3916) *866*

Oliebranchens Faellesrepraesentation. Beretning *see* Oliebretning *866*
Ologies and Isms (US) *700*
Olomouc. Vysoke Skoly Pedagogicke. Sbornik. Historie *see* Sbornik Praci Historickych *595*
Olschwanger Journal (US ISSN 0882-1933) *537*
Om Forsoegsarbejdet (DK ISSN 0900-162X) *417*
Om Statsregnskabet (DK ISSN 0900-8187) *198, 231*
Omaba *see* Omabe *742*
Omabe (NR) *742*
Omaha-Council Bluffs Metropolitan Area Planning Agency Annual Report *see* M A P A Annual Report *943*
Ombres de l'Histoire (FR ISSN 0078-4591) *593*
Ombudsman Journal (CN ISSN 0710-538X) *661*
Omkring et Kunstvaerk (DK ISSN 0108-3511) *108*
Omvang der Vakbeweging in Nederland *see* Statistiek der Vakbeweging in Nederland *649*
On Cassette (US) *129*
On Location Directory (US) *825*
On S I T E (Sculpture in the Environment) (US) *1160*
On-Stage Studies (US) *1077*
On Starting Work (AT) *848*
On Your Own (US) *1160*
On-Your-Own Guide to Asia (US ISSN 0162-5950) *1115*
Oncology Abstracts (US) *9, 771*
One Family (US) *907, 1019*
One World (US) *498, 868*
One World (CN ISSN 0475-0209) *1010*
Oneri Fiscali sulla Motorizzazione (IT) *1086*
Ongaku Bunken Yoshi Mokuroku (JA) *844*
Ongaku Kenkyu *see* Music Research *838*
Online Business Sourcebook (UK) *198, 682*
Online Computer Library Center, Inc. Annual Report *see* O C L C Annual Report *682*
Online Info *see* O L B G Info *997*
Onomastica (PL ISSN 0078-4648) *700*
Onsei Kagaku Kenkyu *see* Studia Phonologica *704*
Onsen Kagaku *see* Science of Hot Springs *394*
Onshore Activity Report (Year) (UK) *868*
Ontario. Advisory Council on Women's Issues. Annual Report on the Status of Women's Issues *see* Ontario Advisory Council on Women's Issues. Annual Report *1129*
Ontario. Agricultural Research Institute. Report (CN ISSN 0078-4664) *32*
Ontario. Division of Mines. Guide Books *see* Ontario. Geological Survey. Guide Books *393*
Ontario. Division of Mines. Mineral Resource Circulars *see* Ontario. Geological Survey. Mineral Deposits Circular *819*
Ontario. Division of Mines. Miscellaneous Papers *see* Ontario. Geological Survey. Miscellaneous Paper *819*
Ontario. Geological Survey. Aggregate Resources Inventory Paper (CN ISSN 0708-2061) *819*
Ontario. Geological Survey. Annual Report of the Regional and Resident Geologists. (CN) *393, 819*
Ontario. Geological Survey. Exploration Technology Development Fund Grants (CN ISSN 0826-791X) *819*
Ontario. Geological Survey. Geological Report (CN) *393, 819*
Ontario. Geological Survey. Geoscience Research Grant Program. Summary of Research (CN ISSN 0225-5316) *819*
Ontario. Geological Survey. Guide Books (CN) *393, 819*
Ontario. Geological Survey. Mineral Deposits Circular (CN ISSN 0706-4551) *819*

Ontario. Geological Survey. Miscellaneous Paper (CN ISSN 0704-2752) *819*
Ontario. Geological Survey. Northern Ontario Engineering Geology Terrain Study (CN ISSN 0709-4671) *819*
Ontario. Geological Survey. Report *see* Ontario. Geological Survey. Geological Report *819*
Ontario. Geological Survey. Study (CN ISSN 0704-2590) *819*
Ontario. Geological Survey. Summary of Field Work (CN ISSN 0829-8203) *819*
Ontario. Geological Survey. Supplement(CN) *819*
Ontario. Human Rights Commission. Annual Report (CN ISSN 0702-0538) *913*
Ontario. Ministere des Affaires Culturelles et des Lois de l'Ontario. Rapport Annuel (CN ISSN 0702-7842) *1035*
Ontario. Ministry of Community and Social Services. Social Assistance Review Board. Annual Report of the Chairman (CN) *1019*
Ontario. Ministry of Education. Report (CN ISSN 0317-6436) *417*
Ontario. Ministry of Municipal Affairs and Housing. Annual Report (CN ISSN 0078-4885) *625*
Ontario. Ministry of Natural Resources. Forest Research (CN ISSN 0704-2809) *366*
Ontario. Ministry of Natural Resources. Forest Research Report *see* Ontario. Ministry of Natural Resources. Forest Research *366*
Ontario. Ministry of Natural Resources. Petroleum Resources Branch. Drilling and Production Report, Oil and Natural Gas *see* Ontario. Ministry of Natural Resources. Petroleum Resources Lab. Drilling and Production Report, Oil and Natural Gas *866*
Ontario. Ministry of Natural Resources. Petroleum Resources Lab. Drilling and Production Report, Oil and Natural Gas (CN) *866*
Ontario. Ministry of Natural Resources. Statistics (CN) *501*
Ontario. Ministry of the Environment. Annual Report. (CN) *366, 498*
Ontario. Ministry of the Environment. Ground Water Bulletin (CN ISSN 0078-5156) *1125*
Ontario. Ministry of the Environment. Industrial Waste Conference. Proceedings (CN ISSN 0078-4893) *498*
Ontario. Ministry of the Environment. Pollution Control Branch. Research Publication (CN ISSN 0078-5148) *498*
Ontario. Ministry of the Environment. Water Resources Branch. Water Resources Report (CN ISSN 0475-0942) *403*
Ontario. Ministry of Transportation and Communications. Highway Traffic Collisions *see* Ontario. Ministry of Transportation and Communications. Ontario Road Safety Annual Report *1092*
Ontario. Ministry of Transportation and Communications. Motor Vehicle Accident Facts *see* Ontario. Ministry of Transportation and Communications. Ontario Road Safety Annual Report *1092*
Ontario. Ministry of Transportation and Communications. Ontario Road Safety Annual Report (CN) *1092*
Ontario. Provincial-Municipal Affairs Secretariat. Municipal Directory (CN ISSN 0318-0743) *945, 951*
Ontario Advisory Council on Women's Issues. Annual Report (CN) *1129*
Ontario Annual Practice (CN) *661*
Ontario Appeal Cases (CN) *661*
Ontario Arts Council. Annual Report (CN) *108*
Ontario Cancer Treatment and Research Foundation. Annual Report *see* Cancer in Ontario *774*
Ontario Digest (CN) *661*
Ontario Digest (Toronto) (CN) *1160*

1842　ONTARIO DIRECTORY

Ontario Directory of Education (CN ISSN 0316-8549) *417*
Ontario Economic Council. Research Studies (CN) *198*
Ontario Education Relations Commission. Annual Report (CN) *274, 380*
Ontario Energy Board. Annual Report (CN) *466*
Ontario Historical Studies Series (CN) *608*
Ontario Hydro. Statistical Yearbook (CN ISSN 0382-2834) *457*
Ontario Hydro Research Review (CN ISSN 0227-9916) *457*
Ontario Institute of Pedology. Department of Land Resource Science. Progress Report (CN) *58, 393*
Ontario Insurance Directory (CN) *641*
Ontario Labour Relations Board Law and Practice (CN) *661*
Ontario Research Foundation. Annual Report (CN ISSN 0078-5083) *198*
Ontario Ringette Association. Official Rules *see* Ringette Canada. Official Rules (Years) *1035*
Ontario Securities Legislation (CN) *661*
Ontario Statistical Review *see* Ontario Statistics *1061*
Ontario Statistics (CN) *1061*
Ontario Symposia on Personality and Social Cognition (US) *935, 1028*
Ontario TourBook *see* Tourbook: Ontario *1117*
Opady Atmosferyczne/Precipitation (PL) *806*
Opdraettervejviseren (DK ISSN 0106-6714) *868*
Opema em Ritmo de Brasil Jovem (BL) *1070*
Open Book (AT) *417*
Open Door International for the Emancipation of the Woman Worker. Report of Congress (BE ISSN 0078-5164) *274,* 1129
Open Doors (US ISSN 0078-5172) *441*
Open Shop Building Construction Cost Data (Year) (US ISSN 0883-8127) *186*
Opening Fall Enrollment in Higher Education *see* U.S. National Center for Education Statistics. Fall Enrollment in Higher Education *439*
Opera Botanica (DK ISSN 0078-5237) *160*
Opera Botanica. Series B. Flora of Ecuador *see* Flora of Ecuador *156*
Opera Jaarboek (NE) *1160*
Opera Lilloana (AG ISSN 0078-5245) *160, 165, 177, 393*
Opera Slavica *see* Opera Slavica. Neue Folge *700*
Opera Slavica. Neue Folge (GW) *700, 729*
Operating Results of Independent Supermarkets (US) *281, 301, 522*
Operating Results of Self-Service Discount Department Stores *see* Mass Retailers' Merchandising Report *273*
Operating Section Proceedings *see* American Gas Association. Operating Section. Proceedings *862*
Operation Liberte (CN) *913*
Operational Hydrology Reports (UN) *403*
Operational Research Society of India, Calcutta Branch Bulletin *see* C O R S I Bulletin *279*
Operations Research/Management Science (US ISSN 0030-3658) *9, 215*
Operations Research - Verfahren/ Methods of Operations Research (GW ISSN 0078-5318) *281*
Operationsmoensteret paa Danske Sygehuse (DK ISSN 0109-9957) *618*
Operculum (AT) *1160*
Opgavesaet til Dansk Skr. Fremstilling, Folkeskolens Udvidede Afgangsproeve *see* Opgavesaet til Dansk Skriftlig Fremstilling, Folkeskolens Afgangsproeve *417*

Opgavesaet til Dansk Skriftlig Fremstilling, Folkeskolens Afgangsproeve (DK ISSN 0109-1255) *417*
Opgavesamling i Skat 1 (DK ISSN 0108-9722) *298*
Opgavesamling i Skat 2 og Erhvervsjura(DK ISSN 0108-9730) *298*
Opgavesamling i Skatteret I *see* Opgavesamling i Skat 1 *298*
Opgavesamling i Skatteret II og Erhvervsjura *see* Opgavesamling i Skat 2 og Erhvervsjura *298*
Ophthalmological Society of Egypt. Bulletin (UA ISSN 0078-5342) *786*
Ophthalmology Annual (US ISSN 0743-751X) *1160*
Opinions of the Utah State Superintendent of Public Instruction *see* Utah. State Office of Education. Opinions of the Utah State Superintendent of Public Instruction *444*
Oplagsbulletin (DK ISSN 0107-380X) *962*
Oplagstal og Markedstal/Circulation Data and Marketing Data (DK ISSN 0070-2854) *16*
Opmaat *see* Klank en Weerklank *837*
Opolskie Roczniki Ekonomiczne (PL ISSN 0474-2893) *198*
Opportunities Abroad for Teachers *see* U.S. Department of Education. Opportunities for Teachers Abroad *442*
Opportunities for Geologists and Geophysicists (UK) *848*
Opportunities for Graduates in Southern Africa (SA) *848*
Opportunities for Matriculants & School Leavers in Southern Africa (SA) *848*
Opportunities for School Leavers in Australia *see* Australian School Leavers Yearbook *847*
Opportunities in Science and Engineering (US) *473, 848*
Opportunities Unlimited (CN) *1092*
Optical Industry and Systems Directory *see* Optical Industry and Systems Purchasing Directory *899*
Optical Industry and Systems Purchasing Directory (US ISSN 0191-0647) *899*
Optical Memory Report (US) *344, 361, 899*
Optical Physics and Engineering (US ISSN 0078-5482) *473, 899*
Optics and Spectroscopy. Supplement (US ISSN 0078-5504) *899*
Optimizatsiya (UR) *751*
Optoelectronics D.A.T.A. Book (US ISSN 0164-002X) *458*
Optoelectronics Discontinued Devices D.A.T.A. Book (US) *458*
Opus (CN ISSN 0700-5318) *840*
Opuscula Atheniensia (SW ISSN 0078-5520) *91, 338*
Opuscula - aus Wissenschaft und Dichtung (GW ISSN 0078-5539) *631*
Opuscula Byzantina *see* Acta Universitatis de Attila Jozsef Nominatae. Acta Antiqua et Archaeologica *336*
Or du Rhine (FR) *593*
Oral History Review (US ISSN 0094-0798) *559*
Orange Free State. Director of Hospital Services. Report/Orange Free State. Direkteur van Hospitaldienste. Verslag (SA ISSN 0078-5547) *618*
Orange Free State. Direkteur van Hospitaldienste. Verslag *see* Orange Free State. Director of Hospital Services. Report *618*
Orange Free State. Nature Conservation Branch. Annual Report(SA) *366*
Orange Free State. Nature Conservation Branch. Miscellaneous Publications Series (SA) *145, 366*
Orange Free State. Nature Conservation Division. Annual Report *see* Orange Free State. Nature Conservation Branch. Annual Report *366*

Orange Free State. Nature Conservation Division. Miscellaneous Publications Series *see* Orange Free State. Nature Conservation Branch. Miscellaneous Publications Series *366*
Oranje-Nassau Museum. Jaarboek (NE) *830*
Oratory School Magazine (UK) *438*
Orbis Antiquus (GW ISSN 0078-5555) *338*
Orbis Geographicus (GW ISSN 0030-4395) *547*
Orbis Musicae (IS ISSN 0303-3937) *840, 852*
Orbit (New York) (US ISSN 0474-3326) *14, 729*
Orchard Lodge Studies of Deviancy (UK ISSN 0261-9296) *372*
Ord & Sag (DK ISSN 0108-8025) *700, 712*
Orden pour le Merite fuer Wissenschaften und Kuenste. Reden und Gedenkworte (GW) *559, 729*
Ordinary Lives (UK) *729*
Ordinateurs *see* Computers *352*
Ordo (GW ISSN 0048-2129) *281*
Ordo et Annuaire de l'Archdiocese de Lyon *see* Annuaire du Diocese de Lyon *980*
Ordre des Geometres-Experts. Annuaire(FR ISSN 0078-5601) *997*
Ordre des Ingenieurs Forestiers du Quebec. Congres Annuel. Texte des Conferences (CN) *526*
Ore (UK ISSN 0030-459X) *742*
Oregon. Department of Forestry. Biennial Report of the State Forester *see* Forest Log *525*
Oregon. Department of Revenue. Sales Ratio Study *see* Oregon Ratio and Assessment Data Roll *298*
Oregon. Department of Revenue. Summary of Levies and Statistics *see* Oregon Property Tax Statistics *298*
Oregon. Public Utility Commissioner. Statistics of Electric, Gas, Steam Heat, Telephone, Telegraph and Water Companies (US ISSN 0091-0546) *949*
Oregon. Special Papers (US) *393*
Oregon. State Board of Accountancy. Certified Public Accountants, Public Accountants, and Accountants Authorized to Conduct Municipal Audits in Oregon (US) *222*
Oregon. State Board of Accountancy. Certified Public Accountants, Public Accountants, Professional Corporations, and Accountants Authorized to Conduct Municipal Audits in Oregon *see* Oregon. State Board of Accountancy. Certified Public Accountants, Public Accountants, and Accountants Authorized to Conduct Municipal Audits in Oregon *222*
Oregon. State Department of Geology and Mineral Industries. Bulletin (US ISSN 0078-5709) *393, 819*
Oregon. State Department of Geology and Mineral Industries. Oil and Gas Investigations (US ISSN 0078-5741) *393, 866*
Oregon, a Statistical Profile (US) *247*
Oregon Academy of Science. Proceedings (US ISSN 0370-1093) *1010*
Oregon, an Economic Profile *see* Oregon, a Statistical Profile *247*
Oregon Blue Book (US) *945*
Oregon International Trade Directory (US ISSN 0731-9096) *258*
Oregon Property Tax Statistics (US) *298*
Oregon Public Health Statistics Report (US) *959, 1061*
Oregon Ratio and Assessment Data Roll (US) *298*
Oregon School-Community College Directory *see* Oregon School Directory *430*
Oregon School Directory (US ISSN 0078-5679) *430*
Oregon State Health Division, Vital Statistics Annual Report *see* Oregon Public Health Statistics Report *959*

Oregon State Industrial Directory *see* MacRae's Oregon State Industrial Directory *313*
Oregon State Monographs. Bibliographic Series (US ISSN 0078-5768) *129*
Oregon State University. Forest Research Laboratory. Annual Report *see* Oregon State University. Forest Research Laboratory. Biennial Report *526*
Oregon State University. Forest Research Laboratory. Biennial Report(US) *526*
Oregon State University. Forest Research Laboratory. Research Bulletin (US ISSN 0078-5903) *526*
Oregon State University. Forest Research Laboratory. Research Note (US ISSN 0078-5911) *526*
Oregon State University. Forest Research Laboratory. Research Paper(US ISSN 0078-592X) *526*
Oregon Vital Statistics *see* Oregon Public Health Statistics Report *959*
Oregon/Washington *see* Tourbook: Oregon/Washington *1117*
Organ Building Periodical/Zeitschrift fuer Orgelbau (International Society of Organbuilders) (GW) *840*
Organ Historical Society. National Convention (Proceedings) *see* Annual Organ Handbook *832*
Organ Yearbook (NE ISSN 0078-6098) *840*
Organe Permanent pour la Securite dans les Mines de Houille. Rapport *see* Mines Safety and Health Commission. Report *818*
Organic and Organometallic Crystal Structures; Bibliography (NE) *129, 330*
Organic Chemistry (US ISSN 0078-611X) *330*
Organic Compounds of Sulphur, Selenium and Tellurium (UK ISSN 0305-9812) *330*
Organic Electronic Spectral Data (US ISSN 0078-6136) *326, 330*
Organic Photochemistry: A Series of Advances (US ISSN 0078-6152) *330, 332*
Organic Reaction Mechanisms. Annual Survey (US ISSN 0078-6160) *330, 332*
Organic Reactions (US ISSN 0078-6179) *330, 332*
Organic Syntheses (US ISSN 0078-6209) *330, 332*
Organisatie van Studenten in de Geschiedenis van Nederland Wetenschappelijke Publikatie *see* O S G N Wetenschappelijke Publikatie *592*
Organisation and Management of a Solicitors Practice (UK) *661*
Organisation for Economic Cooperation and Development Educational Statistics in O E C D Countries *see* Educational Statistics in O E C D Countries *413*
Organisation for Scientific Evaluation of Aerial Phenomena Centre Update *see* O S E A P Centre Update *21*
Organisation for Scientific Evaluation of Aerial Phenomena Journal *see* O S E A P Journal *21*
Organisation Internationale et Relations Internationales (BE) *917*
Organisation of Eastern Caribbean States Annual Digest of Statistics *see* O E C S Annual Digest of Statistics *1061*
Organisation of Eastern Caribbean States Energy Bulletin *see* O E C S Energy Bulletin *1061*
Organisation of Eastern Caribbean States National Account Digest *see* O E C S National Account Digest *1061*
Organisation of Eastern Caribbean States Statistical Pocket Digest *see* O E C S Statistical Pocket Digest *1061*
Organisation of Eastern Caribbean States Trade Digest *see* O E C S Trade Digest *1061*

ORGANOMETALLIC SYNTHESES 1843

Organisation of European Aluminum Smelters. Economic Situation of the Aluminum Smelters in Europe see Aluminum Smelters 814
Organisationen til Oplysning Om Atomkraft Saertryk see O O A - Saertryk 898
Organisationer og Tal i Gartneriet (DK ISSN 0109-4262) 533
Organisatoriske Fragmenter (DK ISSN 0107-2064) 198
Organische Chemie in Einzeldarstellungen (US ISSN 0078-6225) 330
Organists' Benevolent League Inc. Annual Report (UK) 840
Organizacion de Estados Iberoamericanos (OEI) Sistema de Indicadores Socio-Economicos y Educativos de la O E I see Sistema de Indicadores Socio-Economicos y Educativos de la O E I 1011
Organization for Economic Cooperation and Development. Activities of O.E.C.D.: Report by the Secretary General (FR) 263
Organization for Economic Cooperation and Development. Agricultural Policy Reports (FR) 298
Organization for Economic Cooperation and Development. Annual Oil and Gas Statistics/Statistiques Annuelles des Hydrocarbures et du Gaz Naturel see Organization for Economic Cooperation and Development. Annual Oil and Gas Statistics/ Statistiques Annuelles du Petrole et du Gaz Naturel 868
Organization for Economic Cooperation and Development. Annual Oil and Gas Statistics/Statistiques Annuelles du Petrole et du Gaz Naturel (FR) 868
Organization for Economic Cooperation and Development. Annual Reports on Consumer Policy in O.E.C.D. Member Countries see Organization for Economic Cooperation and Development. Consumer Policy in O.E.C.D. Countries 240
Organization for Economic Cooperation and Development. Catalogue of Publications (FR ISSN 0474-5086) 129; 539
Organization for Economic Cooperation and Development. Consumer Policy in O.E.C.D. Countries (FR) 240
Organization for Economic Cooperation and Development. Council. Code de la Liberation des Mouvements de Capitaux. Code of Liberalisation of Capital Movements (FR ISSN 0474-5655) 231, 258, 263
Organization for Economic Cooperation and Development. Development Cooperation (FR ISSN 0474-5663) 263
Organization for Economic Cooperation and Development. Economic Conditions in Austria and Switzerland see Organization for Economic Cooperation and Development. Economic Surveys: Austria 247
Organization for Economic Cooperation and Development. Economic Surveys: Austria (FR ISSN 0474-5124) 247
Organization for Economic Cooperation and Development. Economic Surveys: Australia (FR) 247
Organization for Economic Cooperation and Development. Economic Surveys: Belgium-Luxembourg Economic Union (FR ISSN 0474-5132) 247
Organization for Economic Cooperation and Development. Economic Surveys: Canada (FR ISSN 0474-5140) 247
Organization for Economic Cooperation and Development. Economic Surveys: Denmark (FR ISSN 0474-5159) 247
Organization for Economic Cooperation and Development. Economic Surveys: France (FR ISSN 0474-5167) 247

Organization for Economic Cooperation and Development. Economic Surveys: Finland (FR) 247
Organization for Economic Cooperation and Development. Economic Surveys: Germany (FR ISSN 0474-5175) 247
Organization for Economic Cooperation and Development. Economic Surveys: Greece (FR ISSN 0474-5183) 247
Organization for Economic Cooperation and Development. Economic Surveys: Iceland (FR ISSN 0474-5191) 247
Organization for Economic Cooperation and Development. Economic Surveys: Ireland (FR ISSN 0474-5205) 247
Organization for Economic Cooperation and Development. Economic Surveys: Italy (FR ISSN 0474-5213) 247
Organization for Economic Cooperation and Development. Economic Surveys: Japan (FR ISSN 0474-5221) 247
Organization for Economic Cooperation and Development. Economic Surveys: Netherlands. (FR ISSN 0474-523X) 247
Organization for Economic Cooperation and Development. Economic Surveys: Norway (FR ISSN 0474-5248) 248
Organization for Economic Cooperation and Development. Economic Surveys: Portugal (FR ISSN 0474-5256) 248
Organization for Economic Cooperation and Development. Economic Surveys: Socialist Federal Republic of Yugoslavia (FR ISSN 0474-5264) 248
Organization for Economic Cooperation and Development. Economic Surveys: Spain (FR ISSN 0474-5272) 248
Organization for Economic Cooperation and Development. Economic Surveys: Sweden (FR ISSN 0474-5280) 248
Organization for Economic Cooperation and Development. Economic Surveys. Switzerland (FR ISSN 0474-5299) 248
Organization for Economic Cooperation and Development. Economic Surveys: Turkey (FR ISSN 0474-5302) 248
Organization for Economic Cooperation and Development. Economic Surveys: United Kingdom (FR ISSN 0474-5310) 248
Organization for Economic Cooperation and Development. Economic Surveys: New Zealand (FR ISSN 0376-6438) 248
Organization for Economic Cooperation and Development. Economic Surveys: United States (FR ISSN 0474-5329) 248
Organization for Economic Cooperation and Development. Energy Statistics (FR) 468
Organization for Economic Cooperation and Development. Flow of Financial Resources to Less Developed Countries see Geographical Distribution of Financial Flows to Developing Countries. (Disbursement) 262
Organization for Economic Cooperation and Development. Foreign Trade by Commodities (FR ISSN 0474-540X) 215
Organization for Economic Cooperation and Development. Historical Statistics. Statistiques Retrospectives see Organization for Economic Cooperation and Development. Main Economic Indicators. Historical Statistics. Statistiques Retrospectives 215
Organization for Economic Cooperation and Development. International Energy Agency. Annual Report on Energy Research, Development and Demonstration (FR) 466

Organization for Economic Cooperation and Development. Labour Force Statistics (Yearbook) /Statistiques de la Population Active (FR ISSN 0474-5515) 215
Organization for Economic Cooperation and Development. Liaison Bulletin Between Research and Training Institutes (FR ISSN 0029-7038) 291
Organization for Economic Cooperation and Development. Library. Catalogue of Periodicals/Catalogue des Periodiques (FR) 129
Organization for Economic Cooperation and Development. Library. Special Annotated Bibliography: Automation. Bibliographie Speciale Analytique (FR ISSN 0474-5868) 129, 354
Organization for Economic Cooperation and Development. Machinery Committee. Engineering Industries in North-America-Europe-Japan (FR ISSN 0474-5876) 1160
Organization for Economic Cooperation and Development. Main Economic Indicators. Historical Statistics. Statistiques Retrospectives (FR) 215
Organization for Economic Cooperation and Development. Maritime Transport Committee. Maritime Transport (FR ISSN 0474-5884) 1102
Organization for Economic Cooperation and Development. Nuclear Energy Agency. Activity Report (FR ISSN 0078-625X) 466, 473, 898
Organization for Economic Cooperation and Development. Nuclear Energy Agency. Summary of Nuclear Power and Fuel Cycle Data in O E C D Member Countries (FR) 466, 473, 898
Organization for Economic Cooperation and Development. Revenue Statistics of O.E.C.D. Member Countries (FR) 215
Organization for Economic Cooperation and Development. Reviews of Manpower and Social Policies (FR ISSN 0473-6788) 275
Organization for Economic Cooperation and Development. Special Committee for Iron and Steel. Iron and Steel Industry (FR ISSN 0474-5973) 799
Organization for Economic Cooperation and Development. Special Committee for Oil. Oil Statistics. Supply and Disposal (FR ISSN 0474-6007) 866
Organization for Economic Cooperation and Development. Statistics of Energy see Organization for Economic Cooperation and Development. Energy Statistics 468
Organization for Economic Cooperation and Development. Statistics of Foreign Trade. Series C: Tables by Commodities. Imports and Exports/ Statistiques du Commerce Exterieur. Serie C: Tableaux par Produits see Organization for Economic Cooperation and Development. Foreign Trade by Commodities 215
Organization for Economic Cooperation and Development. Tourism Committee. Tourism Policy and International Tourism in O E C D Member Countries (FR) 1115
Organization for Economic Cooperation and Development Energy Balances of O.E.C.D. Countries see Energy Balances of O.E.C.D. Countries 464
Organization for Economic Cooperation and Development Financial Statistics see O E C D Financial Statistics 215
Organization for Rehabilitation Through Training Yearbook see O R T Yearbook 445
Organization of African Unity. Inter-African Bureau for Soils. Bibliographie (CX ISSN 0538-2769) 42
Organization of African Unity. Scientific Technical and Research Commission. Publication (NR ISSN 0474-6171) 997, 1070

Organization of American States. Department of Cultural Affairs. Manuales del Bibliotecario (US ISSN 0078-6381) 682
Organization of American States. Department of Scientific Affairs. Report of Activities (US) 997
Organization of American States. Department of Scientific Affairs. Serie de Biologia: Monografias (US ISSN 0553-0342) 145
Organization of American States. Department of Scientific Affairs. Serie de Fisica: Monografias (US ISSN 0078-6322) 890
Organization of American States. Department of Scientific Affairs. Serie de Matematica: Monografias (US ISSN 0078-6330) 751
Organization of American States. Department of Scientific Affairs. Serie de Quimica: Monografias (US ISSN 0553-0377) 324
Organization of American States. General Assembly. Actas y Documentos (US) 917
Organization of American States. General Secretariat. Program of Scientific Monographs (Organization of American States) (US) 997
Organization of American States. Official Records. Indice y Lista General (US ISSN 0078-642X) 608
Organization of American States. Permanent Council. Decisions Taken at Meetings (Cumulated Edition) (US ISSN 0078-6438) 608, 671
Organization of American States General Secretariat. Annual Report see O A S. General Secretariat. Annual Report 608
Organization of American States Organization of American States. General Secretariat. Program of Scientific Monographs see Organization of American States. General Secretariat. Program of Scientific Monographs 997
Organization of Arab Petroleum Exporting Countries. Annual Energy Report (KU) 466, 866
Organization of Arab Petroleum Exporting Countries. Annual Statistical Report (KU) 866
Organization of Arab Petroleum Exporting Countries. Secretary General's Annual Report (KU) 866
Organization of Arab Petroleum Exporting Countries Energy Bibliography see O A P E C Energy Bibliography 865
Organization of Arab Petroleum Exporting Countries Library Index see O A P E C Library Index 865
Organization of Arab Petroleum Exporting countries Library Periodicals Holdings see O A P E C Library Periodicals Holdings 865
Organization of the Petroleum Exporting Countries. Annual Report. (AU) 866
Organization of the Petroleum Exporting Countries. Annual Review and Record see Organization of the Petroleum Exporting Countries. Annual Report 866
Organization of the Petroleum Exporting Countries. Annual Statistical Bulletin (AU ISSN 0475-0608) 866
Organizational and Occupational Psychology (US) 935
Organizational Communications (US ISSN 0149-1644) 281
Organizational Communications Abstracts see Organizational Communications 281
Organizational Directory of the Government of Thailand (TH ISSN 0475-2015) 945
Organizatsiya Upravleniya (UR) 281
Organometallic Chemistry (UK ISSN 0301-0074) 330
Organometallic Reactions and Syntheses (US) 330, 332
Organometallic Reactions Series see Organometallic Reactions and Syntheses 330
Organometallic Syntheses (US) 799

Organon (PL ISSN 0078-6500) *997*
Organophosphorus Chemistry (UK ISSN 0306-0713) *330*
Oriens (NE ISSN 0078-6527) *852*
Oriens Christianus (GW ISSN 0340-6407) *971*
Oriental Insects (US ISSN 0030-5316) *165*
Oriental Insects Monographs Series (US) *165*
Oriental Institute Communications (US ISSN 0146-678X) *571*
Oriental Library. Research Department. Memoirs/Zaidan Hojin Toyo Bunko (JA ISSN 0082-562X) *571*
Oriental Notes and Studies (IS ISSN 0078-6543) *571*
Oriental Society of Australia. Journal (AT ISSN 0030-5340) *853*
Oriental Studies (US ISSN 0078-6551) *108*
Oriental Studies *see* Keleti Tanulmanyok *852*
Oriental Studies/Toho Gakuho (JA) *853*
Orientalia Christiana Analecta (VC) *853*, *983*
Orientalia Gothoburgensia (SW ISSN 0078-656X) *853*
Orientalia Lovaniensia Periodica (BE ISSN 0085-4522) *853*
Orientalia Monspeliensia (NE) *613*
Orientalia Rheno-Traiectina (NE) *853*
Orientalia Suecana (SW ISSN 0078-6578) *853*
Orientamenti Linguistici (IT) *700*
Orienting om Skoleaaret (DK ISSN 0106-7125) *417*
The Original Art Report (US ISSN 0030-5529) *108*
Original New England Guide (US ISSN 0734-4066) *547*, *1115*
Orissa, India. Finance Department. Annual Financial Statement (II) *248*
Orissa, India. Finance Department. White Paper on Departmental Activities, Government of Orissa *see* Orissa, India. Finance Department. White Paper on the Economic Conditions and the Developmental Activities in Orissa *248*
Orissa, India. Finance Department. White Paper on the Economic Conditions and the Developmental Activities in Orissa (II) *248*
Orissa State Road Transportation Corporation. Annual Administration Report (II) *1097*
Orizzonti Aperti (IT ISSN 0030-5618) *791*
Ornithological Monographs (US ISSN 0078-6594) *170*
Orphan Voyage. Adoption Series (US) *1019*
Orphan Voyage. Log *see* Orphan Voyage. Adoption Series *1019*
Orquidea (Mexico) (MX ISSN 0300-3701) *160*
Orszagos Muemleki Felugyeloseg. Kiadvanyok (HU ISSN 0073-4063) *99*
Orszagos Szechenyi Konyvtar Evkonyve (HU ISSN 0524-8868) *682*
Orthodontie Francaise (FR ISSN 0078-6608) *780*
Orthodox Church in America. Yearbook and Church Directory (US ISSN 0145-7950) *984*
Ortnamnssallskapet i Uppsala. Aarsskrift (SW ISSN 0473-4351) *700*
Orton Society. Bulletin. *see* Annals of Dyslexia *444*
Osaka (Prefecture). Radiation Center, Annual Report/Osaka-furitsu Hoshasen Chuo Kenkyusho Nenpo (JA ISSN 0474-7879) *332*
Osaka City University. Faculty of Engineering. Memoirs/Osaka-shiritsu Daigaku Kogakubu Obun Kiyo (JA ISSN 0078-6659) *473*
Osaka City University Economic Review (JA ISSN 0078-6640) *198*
Osaka Daigaku Sangyo Kagaku Kenkyusho Kiyo *see* Osaka University. Institute of Scientific and Industrial Research. Memoirs *1070*

Osaka Daigaku Yakugakubu Kiyo *see* Osaka University. Faculty of Pharmaceutical Sciences. Memoirs *872*
Osaka-furitsu Daigaku Kiyo, B Nogaku, Seibutsugaku *see* University of Osaka Prefecture. Bulletin. Series B: Agriculture and Biology *37*
Osaka-furitsu Hoshasen Chuo Kenkyusho Nenpo *see* Osaka (Prefecture). Radiation Center, Annual Report *332*
Osaka Municipal Water Works Bureau. Annual Report (JA) *1125*
Osaka Museum of Natural History. Annual Report (JA ISSN 0389-8105) *830*
Osaka Museum of Natural History. Bulletin/Osaka-shiritsu Shizenshi Hakubutsukan Kenkyu Hokoku (JA ISSN 0078-6675) *997*
Osaka Museum of Natural History. Occasional Papers/Shizenshi Kenkyu(JA ISSN 0078-6683) *997*
Osaka Museum of Natural History. Special Publications/Osaka-Shiritsu-Shizenshi-Hakubutsukan-Shuzo-Shiryo-Mokuroku (JA ISSN 0389-9047) *145*, *160*, *165*
Osaka-shiritsu Daigaku Kogakubu Obun Kiyo *see* Osaka City University. Faculty of Engineering. Memoirs *473*
Osaka-shiritsu Daigaku Rigakubu Chigaku Kiyo *see* Journal of Geosciences *380*
Osaka-shiritsu Shizenshi Hakubutsukan Kenkyu Hokoku *see* Osaka Museum of Natural History. Bulletin *997*
Osaka-Shiritsu-Shizenshi-Hakubutsukan-Shuzo-Shiryo-Mokuroku *see* Osaka Museum of Natural History. Special Publications *145*
Osaka University. Faculty of Pharmaceutical Sciences. Memoirs/Osaka Daigaku Yakugakubu Kiyo (JA ISSN 0387-480X) *872*
Osaka University. Institute for Cancer Research. Annual Report (JA) *776*
Osaka University. Institute for Protein Research. Memoirs (JA ISSN 0078-6705) *152*, *332*
Osaka University. Institute of Scientific and Industrial Research. Memoirs/Osaka Daigaku Sangyo Kagaku Kenkyusho Kiyo (JA ISSN 0369-0369) *1070*
Osaka University. Laboratory of Nuclear Studies. Annual Report (JA ISSN 0473-4580) *898*
Osakako *see* Port of Osaka *1103*
Oscar Israelowitz's Guide to Jewish New York City (US) *505*
Osiris (US ISSN 0369-7827) *559*, *997*
Oslo Boers. Beretning (NO ISSN 0085-4565) *267*
Osmania University. Department of Psychology. Research Bulletin (II) *935*
Osnabruecker Naturwissenschaftliche Mitteilungen (GW ISSN 0340-4781) *997*
Osprey's Seafood Newsletter (US) *846*
Osservatorio Regionale per le Malattie della Vite. Osservazioni di Meteorologia, Fenologia e Patologia della Vite (IT ISSN 0552-9506) *58*, *160*
Ostava (CS) *593*
Ostbairische Grenzmarken (GW ISSN 0078-6845) *593*
Osteopathic Physician's Compendium of Drug Therapy (US ISSN 0272-7064) *872*
Osterbotten (FI ISSN 0473-8063) *593*
Osterbottnisk Arsbok *see* Osterbotten *593*
Osteuropa Institut, Munich. Veroeffentlichungen. Reihe Geschichte (GW ISSN 0078-687X) *593*
Ostpanorama (AU ISSN 0078-6896) *593*
Ostseejahrbuch (GW ISSN 0720-4868) *237*
Oswald Outlines (US ISSN 0890-2364) *537*

Otago Geographer (NZ ISSN 0078-690X) *547*
Otago Law Review (NZ ISSN 0078-6918) *662*
Otago Museum Bulletin: Zoology (NZ) *177*
Other Networks (US) *344*
Other Realities (US ISSN 0742-1184) *75*
Other Scenes (US) *712*
Oto-Laryngological Society of Australia. Journal (AT ISSN 0030-6614) *787*
Ottawa. Dominion Observatory. Seismological Series *see* Canada. Earth Physics Branch. Seismological Series *398*
Ottawa Ethnic Groups Directory (CN ISSN 0315-0771) *505*
Ottawa Guidebook (CN) *951*, *1115*
Ottawa Hispanica (CN) *700*, *729*
Otterbein Miscellany (US) *712*
Ou Monter a Cheval (FR ISSN 0078-7035) *1043*
Oudtestamentische Studien (NE) *971*
Our Hampton Heritage (US) *1160*
Our Port - Port of Yokohama (JA) *1102*
Our Stake in the Urban Condition *see* American Jewish Committee. Domestic Affairs Department. Pertinent Papers *902*
Out of Print Market *see* O.P. Market *962*
Outdoor Crest (CN ISSN 0700-9909) *1046*
Outdoor Crest Newsletter *see* Outdoor Crest *1046*
Outdoor Life's Guide to Fishing the Midwest *see* Deer and Big Game *1045*
Outdoor Life's Guide to Fishing the South *see* Bass and Freshwater Fishing *1044*
Outdoor Writers Association of America. Directory (US ISSN 0195-6124) *646*
Outerbridge (US ISSN 0739-4969) *729*
Outline of Japanese Tax (JA ISSN 0078-7094) *298*
Outlook (CN) *64*, *67*
Outlook (Year) Proceedings (US) *48*
Outlook for Travel and Tourism (US) *1115*
Outstanding Science Trade Books for Children (US) *129*, *335*, *1004*
Oven Bird *see* Hornero *170*
Overall Reliability and Adequacy of the North American Bulk Powder Systems. Annual Review *see* Reliability Review *466*
Oversaettelser af Dansk Lovgivning med Alfabetisk Register. Fortegnelse/Guide to Translation of Danish Legislation with an Alphabetic Index (DK ISSN 0107-2412) *662*
Overseas Building Notes (UK ISSN 0030-7432) *186*
Overseas Development Council. Annual Report (US ISSN 0092-7643) *263*
Overseas Development Council. Communique (US) *1160*
Overseas Development Council. Development Papers (US) *1160*
Overseas Development Council. Monograph Series (US ISSN 0078-7108) *1160*
Overseas Development Council. Occasional Papers (US) *1160*
Overseas Development Council. Working Papers (US) *263*
Overseas Directories, Who's Who, Press Guides, Year Books and Overseas Periodical Subscriptions (UK ISSN 0078-7124) *129*
Overseas Economic Cooperation Fund. Annual Report/Kagai Keizai Kyoryoku Kikin Nenpo (JA) *263*
Overseas Map Acquisitions (AT ISSN 0311-9319) *547*
Overseas Media Guide *see* O P M A Overseas Media Guide *16*
Overseas Newspapers and Periodicals (UK ISSN 0078-7159) *962*
Overseas Press and Media Association Overseas Media Guide *see* O P M A Overseas Media Guide *16*

Overseas Private Investment Corporation. Annual Report (US ISSN 0196-1276) *267*
Overseas Trade Directories (UK) *315*
Oversigt over By- og Regionforskning (DK ISSN 0108-4151) *625*
Oversigt over de Danske Statsskoves Udbytte af Ved og Penge for Finansaaret *see* Danske Statsskoves Udbytte af Ved og Penge *524*
Oversigt over de Meteorologiske Forhold paa Forsoegsstationerne (DK ISSN 0107-8801) *160*
Oversigt over Klassificerede Bekaempelsesmidler *see* Denmark. Miljoestyrelsen. Oversigt over Godkendte Bekaempelsesmidler *26*
Oversigt over Rapporter m.m. Vedroerende Vandkraftundersoegelser i Groenland (DK ISSN 0107-4997) *1125*
Overture (US) *505*, *1078*
Overview of the F A A Engineering & Development Programs (U.S. Federal Aviation Administration) (US ISSN 0092-3591) *21*
Overzicht Tijdschriftartikelen (NE) *9*, *334*
Owen's Business Directory and Travel Guide (US) *258*, *315*, *1115*
Owen's Trade Directory and Business Travel Guide: Middle East-Africa-Asia-Mediterranean *see* Owen's Business Directory and Travel Guide *258*
Owlflight (US) *14*
Owner Occupied Housing Statistics from Homestead Rebate and Income Tax Data Match (US) *298*, *625*, *923*
Owners, Masters, Brokers and Agents Handbook on South American Caribbean and Pacific Ports in Venezuela, Colombia, Panama, Ecuador, Peru, Bolivia and Chile *see* South American Ports Handbook *1104*
Ox Head (US ISSN 0030-7629) *742*
Oxbridge Careers Handbook (UK) *848*
Oxbridge Directory of Newsletters (US ISSN 0163-7010) *129*
Oxford Agrarian Studies (UK) *48*
Oxford Bibliographical Society. Occasional Publications (UK ISSN 0078-7175) *130*
Oxford Bibliographical Society. Publications. New Series (UK ISSN 0078-7183) *130*
Oxford Classical and Philosophical Monographs (US) *338*, *880*
Oxford English Monographs (US) *729*
Oxford Forestry Institute Occasional Papers *see* O F I Occasional Papers *526*
Oxford German Studies (UK ISSN 0078-7191) *700*, *729*
Oxford Historical Monographs (US) *593*
Oxford Mathematical Monographs (US) *751*
Oxford Modern Language and Literature Monographs (US) *729*
Oxford Monographs on Biogeography (US) *145*
Oxford Monographs on Classical Archaeology (US) *91*, *338*
Oxford Monographs on Medical Genetics (US) *167*, *764*
Oxford Monographs on Meteorology and Physical Oceanography (US) *806*
Oxford Monographs on Meterology *see* Oxford Monographs on Meteorology and Physical Oceanography *806*
Oxford Monographs on Music (US) *840*
Oxford Monographs on Social Anthropology (US) *75*
Oxford Neurological Monographs (US) *791*
Oxford Reviews of Reproductive Biology (US ISSN 0260-0854) *177*
Oxford Slavonic Papers (UK) *593*, *729*
Oxford Studies of Composers (US ISSN 0078-7264) *840*
Oxford Survey in Information Technology (UK ISSN 0265-0711) *361*

PAGINE/PAGINE. ARGOMENTI 1845

Oxford Surveys in Evolutionary Biology(UK ISSN 0265-072X) *167*
Oxford Surveys of Plant Molecular and Cell Biology (UK ISSN 0264-861X) *160*
Oxford Surveys on Eukaryotic Genes (UK ISSN 0265-0738) *167*
Oxford Theatre Texts (UK ISSN 0141-1152) 729, *1078*
Oxford Theological Monographs (US ISSN 0078-7272) *971*
Oxford University Almanack (US) *438*
Oxford University Calendar (US) *438*
Oxford University List of Resident Members (UK) *438*
Oxfordshire Record Society (UK) *593*
Oxoniensia (UK ISSN 0308-5562) *91*, 99, *593*
Oyez (CN ISSN 0475-1671) *662*
Oyez Review (US) *729*
Oyo State. Estimates Including Budget Speech and Memorandum (NR) *945*
Oyo State. Ministry of Economic Planning and Community Development. Annual Report (NR) *291*
Oyo State of Nigeria Estimates see Oyo State. Estimates Including Budget Speech and Memorandum *945*
Oyo State of Nigeria Gazette (NR) *945*
Oziana (US) *341*, 729
Ozone Data for the World/Donnees Mondiales sur l'Ozone (CN ISSN 0030-7777) *806*
P A A B S Symposium Series see Pan American Association of Biochemical Societies Symposium *152*
P A C Newsletter (Polish American Congress Charitable Foundation, Inc.) (US) *505*
P A D S see American Dialect Society. Publications *690*
P A I S Bulletin (Public Affairs Information Service, Inc.) (US) *9*, 215, *1014*
P A I S Foreign Language Index (US) *9*, 215
P A - Kontakte (AU) *417*
P A N S D O C Translations see P A S T I C Translations *1070*
P A S C A L Explore. Part 11: Physique Atomique et Moleculaire. Plasmas (FR) *9*, 893
P A S C A L Explore. Part 12: Etat Condense (FR) 10, *893*
P A S C A L Explore. Part 20: Electronique et Telecommunications (FR) 10, *461*
P A S C A L Explore. Part 27: Methodes de Formation et Traitement des Images (US) 10, *893*
P A S C A L Explore. Part 32: Metrologie et Appareillage en Physique et Physicochimie (FR) 10, *810*, 893
P A S C A L Explore. Part 49: Meteorologie (FR) 10, *808*
P A S C A L Explore. Part 64: Endocrinologie Humaine et Experimentale. Endocrinopathies (FR) 10, *772*
P A S C A L Explore. Part 65: Psychologie. Psychopathologie. Psychiatrie (FR) 10, *772*, 938
P A S C A L Explore. Part 71: Ophtalmologie (FR) 10, *772*
P A S C A L Explore. Part 72: Otorhinolaryngologie. Stomatologie. Pathologie Cervicofaciale (FR) 10, *772*
P A S C A L Explore. Part 73: Dermatologie. Maladies Sexuellement Transmissibles (FR) 10, *772*
P A S C A L Explore. Part 74: Pneumologie (FR) 10, *772*
P A S C A L Explore. Part 75: Cardiologie et Appareil Circulatoire (FR) 10, *772*
P A S C A L Explore. Part 76: Gastroenterologie, Foie, Pancreas, Abdomen (FR) 10, *772*
P A S C A L Explore. Part 77: Nephrologie. Voies Urinaires (FR) 10, *772*
P A S C A L Explore. Part 78: Neurologie (FR) 10, *772*

P A S C A L Explore. Part 79: Pathologie et Physiologie Osteoarticulaires (FR) 10, *772*
P A S C A L Explore. Part 80: Hematologie (FR) 10, *772*
P A S C A L Explore. Part 81: Maladies Metaboliques (FR) 10, *772*
P A S C A L Explore. Part 82: Gynecologie. Obstetrique. Andrologie(FR) 10, *772*
P A S C A L Explore. Part 83: Anesthesie et Reanimation (FR) 10, *772*
P A S C A L Explore. Part 84: Genie Biomedical. Informatique Biomedicale (FR) 10, 150, *772*
P A S C A L Folio. Part 21: Electrotechnique (FR) 10, *462*
P A S C A L Folio. Part 41: Gisements Metalliques et Non-Metalliques. Economie Miniere (FR) 10, *822*
P A S C A L Folio. Part 54: Reproduction des Vertebres. Embryologie des Vertebres et des Invertebres (FR) 10, *772*
P A S C A L Thema. Part 215: Biotechnologies (Edition Francaise) (FR) 145, *772*
P A S C A L Thema. Part 216: Biotechnology (English Edition) (FR) 145, *772*
P A S C A L Thema. Part 230: Energie(FR) 10, *893*
P A S C A L Thema. Part 235: Medecine Tropicale (FR) *772*
P A S C A L Thema. Part 240: Metaux. Metallurgie (FR) 10, *802*
P A S C A L Thema. Part 245: Soudage, Brasage et Techniques Connexes (FR) 10, *802*
P A S C A L Thema. Part 251: Cancerologie (Cancernet) (FR) 10, *773*
P A S T I C Translations (Pakistan Scientific and Technological Information Centre) (PK) *1070*
P & T (Produtos e Tecnicas) (BL) 99, *186*
P C Abstracts (US ISSN 0743-2534) *354*, 362, 362
P C E A Annual Engineering & Operating Conference (Pacific Coast Electrical Association, Inc.) (US) *458*
P C R see Psychological Cinema Register *938*
P C S W Annual Report (Permanent Commission on the Status of Women) (US) *1129*
P C Year Book (UK) *362*
P.E.I. Community Studies (Prince Edward Island) (CN) 75, *1028*
P E M: Plant Engineering and Maintenance Sourcebook (CN ISSN 0710-362X) *281*, 315
P E M Sourcebook (Plant Engineering & Maintenance) (CN) *473*
P.E.N. Hongrois see Hungarian P.E.N *723*
P E P see P S I: Report Series *907*
P E S C Record see I E E E Power Electronics Specialists Conference. Record *19*
P I E (Publications Indexed for Engineering) (US ISSN 0085-4581) *477*
P.I.O.L. see Universite Catholique de Louvain. Institut Orientaliste. Publications *572*
P I R A Annual Review of Research & Services (Paper, Printing & Packaging Industries Research Association) (UK ISSN 0262-8600) *858*, 931
P K L Kemikalier (Plast- och Kemikalieleverantoerers Foerening) (SW) *324*
P K L Plaster (Plast- och Kemikalieleverantoerers Foerening) (SW) *901*
P L A N S see I E E E Position Location and Navigation Symposium. Record *455*
P L A Report (Post Library Association) (US ISSN 0146-2237) *682*
P L D Reporter see Public Library Reporter *683*

P L E R U S (Planning-Economic, Regional, Urban, Social) (PR ISSN 0048-4466) *625*
P L News (Public Library) (AT ISSN 0814-771X) *682*
P M A Statistical Factbook (Pharmaceutical Manufacturers Association) (US) *872*
P M E A. Bulletin of Research see Bulletin of Research in Music Education *833*
P N C Review (Power Reactor and Nuclear Fuel Development Corporation) (JA) 479, *898*
P N P E. Serie (Programa Nacional de Pesquisa Economica) (BL) *248*
P O S I S (Point-of-Sale Information Service) (US) *285*
P R D see Publizistikwissenschaftlicher Referatedienst *647*
P R E A L C Newsletter (Programa Regional del Empleo para America Latina y el Caribe) (UN) 248, *848*
P R O M T. Predicasts Overview of Markets and Technologies see Predicasts Overview of Markets and Technologies *477*
P R Planner - Europe (UK) 16, *315*
P R Planner - U.K. (UK) 16, *315*
P R Week Marketing and Public Relations Handbook (UK) *259*
P S (DK ISSN 0109-4831) 729, 742, *880*
P S C P Times (Philadelphia Society of Clinical Psychologists) (US) *935*
P S I Discussion Papers (Policy Studies Institute) (UK) 198, *1010*
P S I: Report Series (Policy Studies Institute) (UK) 198, *907*, 1010
P T I C Bulletin (Patent and Trademark Institute of Canada) (CN ISSN 0380-6367) *1160*
P T N Master Buying Guide & Directory (Photographic Trade News) (US) 315, *884*
P T T Bedrijf (Staatsbedrijf der Posterijen Telegrafie en Telefonie) (NE ISSN 0030-8366) 346, *350*
P U M R L see Purdue University Monographs in Romance Language *702*
Paasikivi-Society. Mimeograph Series (FI ISSN 0355-1849) *917*
Pacific Almanac. Pacific Northwest and Alaska see Pacific Boating Almanac. Oregon, Washington, British Columbia & Southeastern Alaska *1042*
Pacific Anthropological Records (US ISSN 0078-740X) *75*
Pacific Aviation Yearbook (AT ISSN 0156-3726) *21*, 1089
Pacific Boating Almanac. Northern California & Nevada (US ISSN 0193-3515) *1042*, 1115
Pacific Boating Almanac. Oregon, Washington, British Columbia & Southeastern Alaska (US ISSN 0276-8771) *1042*, 1115
Pacific Boating Almanac. Southern California, Arizona, Baja (US ISSN 0193-3507) *1042*, 1115
Pacific Business Guide (UK) *248*
Pacific Coast Avifauna see Studies in Avian Biology *171*
Pacific Coast Council on Latin American Studies. Proceedings (US ISSN 0190-2229) 259, *608*, 729
Pacific Coast Electrical Association, Inc. Annual Engineering & Operating Conference see P C E A Annual Engineering & Operating Conference *458*
Pacific Coast Obstetrical and Gynecological Society. Transactions (US ISSN 0078-7442) *785*
Pacific Coast Philology (US ISSN 0078-7469) *700*
Pacific Coast Society of Obstetrics and Gynecology. Transactions see Pacific Coast Obstetrical and Gynecological Society. Transactions *785*
Pacific Forest Research Centre. Pest Leaflet (CN) *526*
Pacific Forest Research Centre. Pest Report (CN) *526*
Pacific Index see Pacific Summary Report/Index *866*

Pacific Insects Monographs (US ISSN 0078-7515) *1160*
Pacific Islands Mongraph Series (US) *608*
Pacific Islands Studies and Notes (US ISSN 0085-459X) 130, *564*
Pacific Islands Year Book (AT ISSN 0078-7523) *573*
Pacific Islands Year Book and Who's Who see Pacific Islands Year Book *573*
Pacific Linguistics. Series A: Occasional Papers (AT ISSN 0078-7531) *700*
Pacific Linguistics. Series B: Monographs (AT ISSN 0078-754X) *700*
Pacific Linguistics. Series C: Books (AT ISSN 0078-7558) *700*
Pacific Linguistics. Series D: Special Publications (AT ISSN 0078-7566) *700*
Pacific Marine Fisheries Commission. Annual Report (US ISSN 0078-7574) *512*
Pacific Marine Fisheries Commission. Bulletin (US ISSN 0078-7582) *512*
Pacific Maritime Studies Series (CN) *608*
Pacific Northwest Conference on Foreign Languages. Proceedings see Selecta (Corvallis) *703*
Pacific Northwest Conference on Higher Education. Proceedings (US ISSN 0078-7620) *1160*
Pacific Northwest Council on Foreign Languages. Proceedings see Selecta (Corvallis) *703*
Pacific Rim Research Series (US) *407*
Pacific Science Association. Congress and Inter-Congress Proceedings (US) *997*
Pacific Science Association. Congress Proceedings see Pacific Science Association. Congress and Inter-Congress Proceedings *997*
Pacific Southwest Directory (US ISSN 0555-8581) *315*
Pacific Stock Exchange. Annual Report (US) *267*
Pacific Summary Report see Pacific Summary Report/Index *866*
Pacific Summary Report/Index (US) *866*
Pacific Travel Directory (AT ISSN 0311-0826) *1115*
Packaging Abstracts see International Packaging Abstracts *855*
Packaging Bulletin see Current Packaging Abstracts *855*
Packaging Directory (UK ISSN 0078-768X) *855*
Packaging Encyclopedia (US) *855*
Packaging Machinery Directory see Packaging Machinery Manufacturers Institute. Official Packaging Machinery Directory *855*
Packaging Machinery Manufacturers Institute. Official Packaging Machinery Directory (US ISSN 0078-7698) *855*
Packaging Marketplace (US) *855*
Packaging Reference Issue and (Year) Encyclopedia see Packaging Encyclopedia *855*
Packaging Review Directory (UK) *855*
Packaging Science and Technology Abstracts/Referatedienst Verpackung(UK ISSN 0722-3218) 10, *855*
Packaging Systems News see Pure-Pak News *855*
Packaging Update (II) *855*
Paco (GE) *700*
Pact (BE) *91*, 997
Paedagogica Belgica Academica (BE ISSN 0079-0370) *417*
Paediatrie und Paedologie. Supplement (US ISSN 0300-9556) *788*
Paediatrie: Weiter- und Fortbildung (US) *788*
Paediatrische Fortbildungskurse fuer die Praxis (SZ ISSN 0078-7795) *788*
Paepste und Papsttum (GW ISSN 0340-7993) *593*, 983
Pages Juridiques de la Vie Ouvriere (FR) *649*
Pagine/Pagine. Argomenti Musicali Polacco-Italiani (PL ISSN 0137-3935) *840*

Pagine. Argomenti Musicali Polacco-Italiani *see* Pagine 840
Paideia (US) 417
Paideia (PL ISSN 0137-3943) 417
Paideuma (GW ISSN 0078-7809) 75
Paimio-Seuran Vuosikirja (FI) 593
Pain and Headache (SZ ISSN 0255-3910) 791
Pain Series (US) 764
Paint, Oil Colour Year Book *see* Polymers Paint and Colour Year Book 856
Paint Red Book (US ISSN 0090-5402) 315, 856
Painting and Decorating Craftsman Manual and Textbook (US) 856
Painting Holidays *see* Painting, Holidays and Activity 1115
Painting, Holidays and Activity (UK) 1115
Pakistan. Central Bureau of Education. Educational Statistics Bulletin Series (PK ISSN 0078-7914) 417
Pakistan. Central Bureau of Education. Yearbook *see* Pakistan. Ministry of Education. Yearbook 417
Pakistan. Directorate of Livestock Farms. Report (PK ISSN 0083-8292) 67
Pakistan. Export Promotion Bureau. Export Guide Series (PK ISSN 0078-8104) 259
Pakistan. Export Promotion Bureau. Fresh Fruits (PK ISSN 0078-8112) 49, 259
Pakistan. Finance Division. Annual Budget Statement (Final) (PK) 298
Pakistan. Finance Division. Budget in Brief (PK) 298
Pakistan. Finance Division. Economic Analysis of the Budget (PK) 298
Pakistan. Finance Division. Estimates of Foreign Assistance (PK) 298
Pakistan. Finance Division. Public Finance Statistics (PK) 215
Pakistan. Finance Division. Supplementary Demands for Grants and Appropriations (PK) 298
Pakistan. Food and Agricultural Division. Yearbook of Agricultural Statistics *see* Pakistan. Food and Agriculture Division. Agricultural Statistics of Pakistan 42
Pakistan. Food and Agriculture Division. Agricultural Statistics of Pakistan (PK) 42
Pakistan. Geological Survey. Memoirs; Paleontologia Pakistanica (PK ISSN 0078-8155) 857
Pakistan. Geological Survey. Records (PK ISSN 0078-8163) 393
Pakistan. Ministry of Education. Yearbook (PK ISSN 0078-8287) 417
Pakistan. Ministry of Finance. Basic Facts About the Budget *see* Pakistan Basic Facts 298
Pakistan. Ministry of Finance. Budget in Brief *see* Pakistan. Finance Division. Budget in Brief 298
Pakistan. Ministry of Finance. Budget of the Central Government *see* Budget of the Government of Pakistan. Demands for Grants and Appropriations 293
Pakistan. Ministry of Finance. Economic Analysis of the Central Government *see* Pakistan. Finance Division. Economic Analysis of the Budget 298
Pakistan. Ministry of Finance Estimates of Foreign Assistance *see* Pakistan. Finance Division. Estimates of Foreign Assistance 298
Pakistan. National Assembly. Debates. Official Report (PK ISSN 0078-8333) 662, 907, 945
Pakistan. Office of the Economic Adviser. Government Sponsored Corporations and Other Institutions (PK ISSN 0078-8392) 291
Pakistan. Planning and Development Division. Development Programme (PK ISSN 0078-8414) 291
Pakistan. Survey of Pakistan. General Report (PK ISSN 0078-8481) 571
Pakistan. Water and Power Development Authority. Report (PK ISSN 0083-8349) 490

Pakistan Annual Law Digest (PK ISSN 0078-785X) 662
Pakistan Archaeology (PK ISSN 0078-7868) 91
Pakistan Association for the Advancement of Science. Annual Report (PK) 997
Pakistan Banking Directory (PK ISSN 0078-7884) 231
Pakistan Basic Facts (PK ISSN 0078-7892) 298
Pakistan Book of Cricket (PK) 1039
Pakistan Business and Shopping Guide *see* Pakistan Hotel and Restaurant Guide 620
Pakistan Central Cotton Committee. Agricultural Survey Report (PK ISSN 0078-7930) 58, 1074
Pakistan Central Cotton Committee. Technological Bulletin. Series A (PK ISSN 0078-7949) 58, 1074
Pakistan Central Cotton Committee. Technological Bulletin. Series B (PK ISSN 0078-7957) 58, 1074
Pakistan Council of Scientific and Industrial Research. Report (PK ISSN 0078-804X) 1160
Pakistan Council of Scientific and Industrial Research Directory of the Scientists, Technologists, and Engineers of the P C S I R *see* Directory of the Scientists, Technologists, and Engineers of the P C S I R 991
Pakistan Customs Tariff (PK ISSN 0078-8058) 259, 298
Pakistan Directory of Trade and Industry (PK) 237
Pakistan Economic Survey (PK ISSN 0078-8082) 248
Pakistan Export Directory (PK ISSN 0078-8090) 259
Pakistan Forest Institute, Peshawar. Annual Progress Report (PK ISSN 0078-8147) 526
Pakistan Historical Society. Memoir (PK ISSN 0078-8171) 571
Pakistan Historical Society. Proceedings of the Pakistan History Conference (PK ISSN 0078-818X) 571
Pakistan Hotel and Restaurant Guide (PK ISSN 0250-4340) 620
Pakistan Hotel Guide (PK ISSN 0250-3654) 620
Pakistan Hotels & Tourism (PK) 1115
Pakistan Industrial Credit and Investment Corporation. Annual Report (PK ISSN 0078-8198) 267
Pakistan Industrial Development Corporation. Report (PK ISSN 0078-8201) 291
Pakistan Institute of Development Economics. Report (PK ISSN 0078-821X) 198, 263
Pakistan Institute of Development Economics. Research Report (PK ISSN 0078-8228) 198, 263
Pakistan Institute of Development Economics. Statistical Papers (PK) 215, 1061
Pakistan Insurance Year Book (PK ISSN 0078-8236) 641
Pakistan National Scientific and Technical Documentation Centre. PASTIC Translations *see* P A S T I C Translations 1070
Pakistan Petroleum Limited. Annual Report (PK ISSN 0552-9115) 866
Pakistan Philosophical Congress. Proceedings (PK ISSN 0078-8406) 880
Pakistan Postage Stamps (PK ISSN 0078-8422) 875
Pakistan Railways. Yearbook of Information (PK) 1095
Pakistan Science Abstracts (PK ISSN 0031-0085) 10, 1004
Pakistan Science Conference. Proceedings (PK ISSN 0078-8430) 997
Pakistan Scientific and Technological Information Center. Lists of PASTIC Bibliographies *see* Lists of P A S T I C Bibliographies 1072
Pakistan Scientific and Technological Information Centre Translations *see* P A S T I C Translations 1070
Pakistan Standards Institution. Report (PK ISSN 0078-8457) 1160

Pakistan Statistical Association. Proceedings (PK ISSN 0078-8473) 1061
Pakistan Trade Directory - Exporters and Manufacturers (PK) 259
Pakistan Western Railway. Yearbook of Information *see* Pakistan Railways. Yearbook of Information 1095
Pakistan Year Book (PK) 539
Pakistan's Balance of Payments (PK ISSN 0078-852X) 259, 298
La Palabra (US ISSN 0277-1535) 505, 729
El Palacio (US ISSN 0031-0158) 830
Palaeontographica. Supplementbaende (GW ISSN 0085-4611) 857
Palaeontographica Americana (US ISSN 0078-8546) 857
Palaeontographical Society. Monographs (London) (UK ISSN 0078-8554) 393, 857
Palaeontologia Africana (SA ISSN 0078-8554) 857
Palaeontologia Polonica (PL ISSN 0078-8562) 857
Paleo Data Banks (US) 160, 857
Paleobiologia (PE) 75, 145
PaleoBios (US ISSN 0031-0298) 393, 857
Paleoecology of Africa (NE ISSN 0168-6208) 857
Paleoecology of Africa and the Surrounding Islands *see* Paleoecology of Africa 857
Paleontological Bulletins *see* New Zealand Geological Survey. Paleontological Bulletin 857
Paleontological Society. Memoir (US ISSN 0078-8597) 857
Paleontologiia, Stratigrafiia i Litologiia (BU) 857
Palestine Documents *see* Institute for Palestine Studies. Arabic Annual Documentary Series 569
Palestine Yearbook of International Law (CY) 662
Palingenesia (GW ISSN 0552-9638) 338
Pallas (FR ISSN 0031-0387) 631
Palynology (US ISSN 0191-6122) 393, 857
Pamatky Archeologicke. Bibliographical Register (CS) 91
Pamatnika - Muzeum Slovenskeho Narodneho Povstania. Zbornik *see* Muzeum Slovenskeho Narodneho Povstania. Zbornik 591
Pamietnik Slowianski (PL ISSN 0078-866X) 700
Pamyatniki Kul'tury. Novye Otkrytiya/Monuments of Culture. New Discoveries (UR) 91, 108
PAN (IT) 700
Pan American Association of Biochemical Societies Symposium (US) 152
Pan American Development Foundation. Annual Report (US ISSN 0552-9913) 263
Pan American Federation of Engineering Societies. Bulletin (UY ISSN 0078-8791) 473
Pan-American Indian Association News(US) 505
Pan American Institute of Geography and History. Commission on Geophysics. Boletin (BO) 400
Pan American Institute of Geography and History. Commission on History. Bibliografias (MX ISSN 0078-8813) 91, 608
Pan American Institute of Geography and History. Commission on History. Historiografias Americanas (MX ISSN 0078-883X) 608
Pan American Institute of Geography and History. Commission on History. Historiadores de America (MX ISSN 0078-8848) 608
Pan American Institute of Geography and History. Commission on History. Monumentos Historicos y Arqueologicos (MX ISSN 0078-8856) 608
Pan American Institute of Geography and History. Guides for Investigators(MX) 547
Pan American Medical Women's Alliance. Newsletter (PR ISSN 0078-8864) 765

Pan American Review (US ISSN 0031-059X) 729
Pan American Union. Department of Scientific Affairs. Report of Activities. *see* Organization of American States. Department of Scientific Affairs. Report of Activities 997
Pan Directorio de Proveedores/Bread Caterers' Directory (MX) 522
Pan-Erotic Review (US) 108, 729, 885
Pan-European Associations (UK) 917
Pan T'ai Hsueh Pao *see* University of Malaya. Chinese Language Society. Journal 707
Panama. Direccion Nacional de Planeamiento y Reforma Educativa. Departamento de Estadistica. Serie: Analisis Estadistico (PN) 425
Panama. Instituto de Investigacion Agropecuaria. Bibliografia (PN) 42, 130
Panama. Instituto de Investigacion Agropecuaria. Informe Anual (PN) 33
Panama. Instituto de Investigacion Agropecuaria. Memoria. Reunion Panamena de Informacion Agricola (PN) 33
Panama. Ministerio de Planificacion y Politica Economica. Informe Economico (PN) 248
Panama. Ministerio de Vivienda. Memoria (PN) 625
Panama. Tribunal Electoral. Memoria (PN) 945
Panama en Cifras (PN ISSN 0078-8996) 1061
Panama Handbook 1983 (UK ISSN 0263-4260) 315, 1102
Panama Now (US) 240, 1115
Panhandle-Plains Historical Review (US ISSN 0148-7795) 608
Panhandler (US ISSN 0738-8705) 729
Panjandrum Poetry Journal (US ISSN 0092-5535) 742
Panorama (UK) 537, 593
Panorama Cheshskoi Literatury *see* Panorama of Czech Literature 729
Panorama de Agricultura en (Year) (SP) 33
Panorama de l'Economie de la Reunion(RE) 248
Panorama de la Literatura Checa *see* Panorama of Czech Literature 729
Panorama de la litterature Tcheque *see* Panorama of Czech Literature 729
Panorama de la Teologia Latinoamericana (CL) 983
Panorama Democrate Chretien (BE) 907
Panorama der Tschechischen Literatur *see* Panorama of Czech Literature 729
Panorama of Czech Literature (CS) 729, 742
Panoramas Bibliograficos de Espana (SP) 130
Panstwowa Wyzsza Szkola Muzyczna *see* Akademia Muzyczna. Prace Specjalne 832
Panstwowa Wyzsza Szkola Muzyczna *see* Akademia Muzyczna. Skrypty 832
Panstwowa Wyzsza Szkola Myzyczna. Sprawozdania *see* Akademia Muzyczna. Sprawozdania 832
Panstwowa Wyzsza Szkola Myzyczna. Wydawnictwa Okolicznosciowe *see* Akademia Muzyczna. Wydawnictwa Okolicznosciowe 832
Panta-Rhei (IO) 662
Pantheon *see* Bruckmanns Pantheon 103
Papeis Avulsos de Zoologia (BL ISSN 0031-1049) 177
Paper Air (US) 742
Paper and Board Abstracts (UK ISSN 0307-0778) 10, 859
Paper Bag (UK ISSN 0144-4379) 369
Paper Industry Technical Association. Fundamental Research International Symposia (UK) 858
Paper Merchant Performance (US) 858
Paper News (US) 712
Paper, Paperboard, Woodpulp Capacity (US) 858

Paper, Printing & Packaging Industries Research Association Annual Review of Research & Services see P I R A Annual Review of Research & Services 858
Paper Review of the Year (UK ISSN 0302-4180) 858
Paper Sales Convention News (US) 198, 858
Paper Year Book (US) 315, 858
Paperboard Industry Statistics see Statistics of Paper, Paperboard and Wood Pulp 859
Papermakers' and Merchants' Directory of All Nations see Phillips' Paper Trade Directory - Europe-Mills of the World 858
Papers and Recordings in Education (US) 449
Papers and Reports on Child Language Development (US) 334, 700
Papers and Studies in Contrastive Linguistics (PL ISSN 0137-2459) 700
Papers in Anthropology (Springfield) see Illinois. State Museum. Research Series. Papers in Anthropology 72
Papers in Australian Linguistics (AT ISSN 0078-9062) 700
Papers in Borneo Linguistics (AT ISSN 0078-9070) 700
Papers in Comparative Studies (US ISSN 0736-9123) 729
Papers in International Studies: Africa Series see Monographs in International Studies: Africa Series 566
Papers in International Studies: Latin American Series see Monographs in International Studies: Latin America Series 607
Papers in International Studies: Southeast Asia Series see Monographs in International Studies: Southeast Asia Series 570
Papers in Japanese Linguistics (JA) 449, 700
Papers in Linguistics of Melanesia (AT ISSN 0078-9127) 700
Papers in Mediaeval Studies (CN ISSN 0228-8605) 593
Papers in New Guinea Linguistics (AT ISSN 0078-9135) 700
Papers in Philippine Linguistics (AT ISSN 0078-9143) 701
Papers in Pidgin and Creole Linguistics (AT) 701
Papers in Public Administration (US ISSN 0078-9151) 945
Papers in Public Administration (US ISSN 0078-916X) 945
Papers in Slavonic Linguistics (UK ISSN 0263-5798) 701
Papers in Social Sciences (CH) 1010
Papers in Sociology (IS) 1028
Papers in South East Asian Linguistics (AT ISSN 0078-9178) 701
Papers in Textlinguistics see Papiere zur Textlinguistik 701
Papers in the Administration of Development (UK ISSN 0268-4020) 263
Papers of Robert Morris, 1781-1784 (US) 729
Papers of Ship Research Institute see Japan. Ship Research Institute. Papers 1156
Papers on European and Mediterranean Societies (NE ISSN 0317-8382) 75, 1028
Papers on Game Research see Finnish Game Research 365
Papers on the History of Bourke (AT ISSN 0085-4670) 573
Papiere zur Textlinguistik/Papers in Textlinguistics (GW ISSN 0341-3195) 701
Papua and New Guinea Law Reports (AT ISSN 0085-4689) 662
Papua and New Guinea Scientific Society. Transactions (PP ISSN 0085-4700) 998
Papua New Guinea. Bureau of Statistics. Industrial Accidents see Papua New Guinea. National Statistical Office. Worker's Compensation Claims 643

Papua New Guinea. Bureau of Statistics. Statistical Bulletin: Census of Retail Sales and Selected Services see Papua New Guinea. Bureau of Statistics. Statistical Bulletin: Survey of Retail Sales and Selected Services 215
Papua New Guinea. Bureau of Statistics. Statistical Bulletin: National Accounts Statistics (PP) 215, 1061
Papua New Guinea. Bureau of Statistics. Statistical Bulletin: Survey of Retail Sales and Selected Services (PP) 215, 1061
Papua New Guinea. Department of Primary Industry, Fisheries Research & Surveys Branch. Annual Report (PP) 712
Papua New Guinea. Manpower Planning Unit. Manpower Studies (PP) 275
Papua New Guinea. National Statistical Office. Household Expenditure Survey. Preliminary Bulletin (PP) 615, 1061
Papua New Guinea. National Statistical Office. Rural Industries (PP ISSN 0078-7701) 215
Papua New Guinea. National Statistical Office. Rural Industries. Preliminary Statement (PP ISSN 0078-9321) 215
Papua New Guinea. National Statistical Office. Secondary Industries (Factories and Works). Preliminary Statement (PP ISSN 0078-9313) 215
Papua New Guinea. National Statistical Office. Secondary Industries (PP ISSN 0078-933X) 215
Papua New Guinea. National Statistical Office. Statistical Bulletin: Capital Expenditure by Private Businesses (PP ISSN 0078-9259) 215
Papua New Guinea. National Statistical Office. Statistical Bulletin: Registered Motor Vehicles (PP) 1086
Papua New Guinea. National Statistical Office. Statistical Bulletin: Survey of Retail Sales and Selected Services (PP) 215
Papua New Guinea. National Statistical Office. Summary of Statistics (PP) 1061
Papua New Guinea. National Statistical Office. Taxation Statistics. Preliminary Bulletin (PP ISSN 0078-9372) 215
Papua New Guinea. National Statistical Office. Worker's Compensation Claims (PP) 643, 1061
Papua New Guinea. Public Service Board. Report. (PP ISSN 0078-9399) 945
Papua New Guinea Companies Legislation (AT) 662
Papua New Guinea Handbook (AT) 1115
Papua New Guinea Income Tax Legislation (AT) 298
Papua New Guinea Institute of Medical Research. Monograph Series (PP ISSN 0256-2901) 765
Papuran Gwaith Ieithyddol Cymraeg Caerdydd see Cardiff Working Papers in Welsh Linguistics 693
Papyri aus den Staatlichen Museen zu Berlin (GE ISSN 0232-3257) 853
Papyrologica Bruxellensia (BE ISSN 0078-9402) 91
Papyrologica Coloniensia (GW ISSN 0078-9410) 593
Papyrologica Florentina (IT) 559
Papyrologica Lugduno-Batava (NE) 729
Papyrologische Texte und Abhandlungen (GW) 559
Para - nyt (DK ISSN 0901-201X) 712
Paraguay. Centro de Promocion de las Exportaciones. Directorio de Exportadores/Export Directory (PY) 259
Paraguay. Ministerio de Industria y Comercio. Division de Registro y Estadistica Industrial. Encuesta Industrial (PY ISSN 0085-4743) 215

Paraguay. Ministry of Industry and Trade. Investment Guide (PY) 267
Paralogue (FR ISSN 0078-9429) 729
Paramagnitnyi Rezonans (UR) 890
Parameters (US) 712
Parana, Brazil. Secretaria de Estado da Agricultura. Plano de Acao. (BL) 33
Parana, Brazil. Secretaria de Estado para os Negocios da Fazenda (BL) 215
Parana em Tres Dimensoes (BL) 1160
Parana Informacoes see Information on Parana 245
Parapharmex (FR) 780, 872
Parapsychological Association. Proceedings see Research in Parapsychology 860
Parapsychological Monographs (US ISSN 0078-9437) 860
Parapsychology Foundation. Proceedings of International Conferences (US) 860
Parasession: Non-Declarative Sentences see Chicago Linguistic Society. Papers from the Regional Meetings 693
Parasitic Diseases (US) 169
Parazity, Parazitozy ta Shliakhyikh Likvidatsii (UR) 165
Parc Automobile du Maroc see Annuaire Statistique du Maroc 1048
Parc National de La Vanoise. Travaux Scientifiques (FR ISSN 0180-961X) 998
Parchemin. Recueil Genealogique et Heraldique (BE) 537
Parent Compound Handbook see Ring Systems Handbook 331
Parent Cooperative Preschools International. Directory (US) 417
Parents' Guide to Accredited Camps (US) 1046
Parents' Guide to Accredited Camps. Midwest Edition see Parents' Guide to Accredited Camps 1046
Parents' Guide to Accredited Camps. Northeast Edition see Parents' Guide to Accredited Camps 1046
Parents' Guide to Accredited Camps. South Edition see Parents' Guide to Accredited Camps 1046
Parents' Guide to Accredited Camps. West Edition see Parents' Guide to Accredited Camps 1046
Parerga (SP) 631
Parergon (AT ISSN 0313-6221) 559, 729
Parfums-Beaute (FR) 119
Paris - Bijoux Exportation (FR ISSN 0078-9496) 644
Parker Directory of Attorneys see Parker Directory of California Attorneys 662
Parker Directory of California Attorneys (US ISSN 0196-6138) 662
Parliament House Book (UK ISSN 0079-0095) 662
Parliamentary Handbook of the Commonwealth of Australia (AT) 907
Parliamentary Year Book (UK) 945, 949
Parole in the United States (US) 372
Participation (FR) 275
Particles and Nuclei Series (US) 1160
Partido Comunista de Colombia. Documentos (CK) 907
Partido Socialista Popular. Congreso. (Actas) (SP) 907
Partido Socialista Revolucionario. Informes (PE) 907
Partners in Learning (UK ISSN 0079-0117) 979
Pas-de-Calais. Commission Departementale des Monuments Historiques. Bulletin see Commission Departementale d'Histoire et d'Archeologie. Bulletin 85
Pasquino (US ISSN 0031-2657) 342
Passeggiate nel Lazio (IT) 1115
Passenger Transport in Great Britain see Transport Statistics Great Britain 1097
Passenger Transport Year Book see Little Red Book, Classified to All Public Transport Fleet Owners and Operators and Vehicle Manufacturers 1082

PEASANTS IN 1847

Passionist Youth see Gioventu Passionista 970
Passport see Australasian Country Music Annual 833
Pastoral Care and Counseling Abstracts see Abstracts of Research in Pastoral Care and Counseling 974
Patent and Trademark Institute of Canada. Annual Proceedings (CN ISSN 0079-015X) 861
Patent and Trademark Institute of Canada Bulletin see P T I C Bulletin 1160
Patent Law Annual-Southwestern Legal Foundation (US ISSN 0553-3864) 861
Patent Law Handbook (US ISSN 0192-8198) 861
Patent Law Review see Intellectual Property Law Review 861
Patent Office Technical Society. Journal(II) 861
Paterson's Licensing Acts (UK ISSN 0269-3658) 662
Pathobiology Annual (US) 145, 765
Pathology and Practice see Pathology, Research and Practice 765
Pathology, Research and Practice (GW ISSN 0344-0338) 765
Pathways (Creve Coeur) see Doorways to the Mind 1152
Pathways (Middleton) (US) 336
Patriarchal Institute for Patristic Studies. Theological Studies (GR) 984
Patrikapanjee (II) 130
Patrimonio Cultural (PO) 1160
Patristica et Mediaevalia (AG ISSN 0325-2280) 559
Patrologia Syriaca et Orientalis (BE) 977, 983
Patronato Municipal de la Vivienda de Barcelona. Memoria (SP ISSN 0067-4168) 625
Pattern Makers & Allied Crafts Journal see Pattern Makers' Journal 649
Pattern Makers' Journal (US ISSN 0031-319X) 340, 649
Patterson's American Education (US ISSN 0079-0230) 430
Patterson's American Educational Directory see Patterson's American Education 430
Patterson's Schools Classified (US ISSN 0553-4054) 430
Paul Anthony Brick Lectures (US ISSN 0079-0249) 880
Paul Carus Lectures (US ISSN 0079-0257) 880
Paul's Police Offences (AT ISSN 0728-3210) 662
Paul's Record Magazine (US ISSN 0360-2109) 840, 1032
Paving and Transportation Conference. Proceedings. (US) 483
Paving Conference. Proceedings. see Paving and Transportation Conference. Proceedings 483
Pax Romana (SZ ISSN 0079-0281) 983
Pays-Bas Francais see De Franse Nederlanden 991
Peabody Museum Bulletins (US) 91
Peabody Museum of Archaeology and Ethnology. Memoirs (US ISSN 0079-029X) 91
Peabody Museum of Archaeology and Ethnology. Monographs (US) 91
Peabody Museum of Archaeology and Ethnology. Papers (US ISSN 0079-0303) 91
Peabody Museum of Natural History. Bulletin (US ISSN 0079-032X) 998
Peabody Museum of Natural History. Special Publication (US ISSN 0079-0338) 998
Peace Plans (AT ISSN 0031-3564) 917
Peace Research Abstracts Journal (CN ISSN 0031-3599) 10, 912, 1031
Peace Research Reviews (CN ISSN 0553-4283) 907
Pearce-Sellards Series (US ISSN 0079-0354) 830
Pears Cyclopaedia (UK ISSN 0079-0362) 463
Pears Junior Encyclopaedia (UK) 463
Peasants in History and Literature (AT) 631

Peat Abstracts (IE ISSN 0031-367X) 10, 822
Pedagogicka Fakulta v Ostrave. Matematika, Fyzika (CS) 751, 890
Pedagogicka Fakulta v Ostrave. Sbornik Praci. Radi C: Dejepis-Zemepis (CS ISSN 0139-6595) 593
Pedagogicka Fakulta v Plzni. Sbornik. Dejepis (CS ISSN 0139-7346) 593
Pedagogicka Fakulta v Usti nad Labem. Sbornik: Rada Bohemisticka (CS) 701
Pedagogicka Fakulta v Usti nad Labem. Sbornik: Rada Chemicka (CS) 324
Pedagogika Pracy Kulturalno-Oswiatowej (PL ISSN 0208-5526) 417
Pedagogiska Rapporter/Educational Reports (SW ISSN 0281-6776) 418
Pedagogiska Rapporter Umeaa see Pedagogiska Rapporter/Educational Reports 418
Pedersore (FI) 593
Pediatric and Adolescent Endocrinology(SZ ISSN 0304-4254) 781
Pediatric Length of Stay by Diagnosis and Operation, United States (US ISSN 0891-1223) 618, 1061
Pedobiologia (GE ISSN 0031-4056) 58, 145
Pedofauna (FR ISSN 0378-181X) 58
Pegasus (IE) 1122
Pelargonium News (UK ISSN 0267-1891) 533
Pelea (SA) 367
Pellennorath (US) 729
Pembroke Magazine (US ISSN 0097-496X) 712
Pembrokeshire Historical Society. Journal (UK) 593
Penang Port Handbook (UK ISSN 0267-7369) 315, 1102
Penfriend & Ethnic Linkup Index (AT) 341
Penger og Kreditt (NO ISSN 0332-5598) 231
Penn State Studies (US ISSN 0079-0451) 418
Pennsylvania. Administration on Aging. State Plan on Aging (US) 552, 1019
Pennsylvania. Bureau of Aviation. Aviation Newsletter see Commonwealth of Pennsylvania. Airport Directory 18
Pennsylvania. Citizens Advisory Council to the Department of Environmental Resources. Annual Report (US ISSN 0092-7937) 498
Pennsylvania. Crime Commission. Report (US ISSN 0091-4118) 372
Pennsylvania. Department of Agriculture. Seed Report (US) 64
Pennsylvania. Department of Education. Special Education Programs-Services (US ISSN 0099-0302) 1160
Pennsylvania. Department of Environmental Resources. Annual Report on Mining Activities (US) 819
Pennsylvania. Developmental Disabilities Planning Council. Pennsylvania State Plan (US) 1020
Pennsylvania. Historical and Museum Commission. Anthropological Series (US) 75, 608
Pennsylvania. Labor Relations Board. Report. (US) 275
Pennsylvania. Office of Mines and Land Protection. Annual Report. see Pennsylvania. Department of Environmental Resources. Annual Report on Mining Activities 819
Pennsylvania. Office of the Budget. Program Budget (US ISSN 0085-4824) 418
Pennsylvania. State Tax Equalization Board. Annual Certification (US) 298
Pennsylvania Chamber of Commerce. Directory of State, Regional and Commercial Organizations see Pennsylvania Chamber of Commerce. State & Regional Directory 237
Pennsylvania Chamber of Commerce. State & Regional Directory (US) 237
Pennsylvania Conference of Economists. Proceedings of the Annual Meeting (US) 198
Pennsylvania Crop and Livestock Annual Summary (US ISSN 0079-046X) 58
Pennsylvania Crop Reporting Service. C.R.S. see Pennsylvania Crop and Livestock Annual Summary 58
Pennsylvania Directory of Manufacturers (US ISSN 0733-5237) 315
Pennsylvania Flower Growers. Bulletin (US ISSN 0031-448X) 533
Pennsylvania Industrial Directory see Harris Pennsylvania Industrial Directory 309
Pennsylvania Manufacturers Register (US) 315
Pennsylvania Natality and Mortality Statistics see Pennsylvania Vital Statistics 928
Pennsylvania School Study Council. Reports (US ISSN 0079-0508) 418
Pennsylvania State Industrial Directory see MacRae's Pennsylvania State Industrial Directory 313
Pennsylvania State Plan for the Administration of Vocational-Technical Education Programs (US ISSN 0091-5114) 427
Pennsylvania State University. Libraries. Bibliographical Series (US ISSN 0079-0656) 682
Pennsylvania Statistical Abstract (US ISSN 0476-1103) 1061
Pennsylvania Vital Statistics (US) 923, 928
Pennsylvania's Machinery Custom Rates see Pennsylvania Crop and Livestock Annual Summary 58
Pensamiento Costarricense (CR) 538
Pension Boards see United Church of Christ. Pension Boards (Annual Report) 985
Pension Facts (US) 641
Pension Funds & Their Advisers (UK ISSN 0140-6647) 1020
People and Communication (US) 344
People and National Land Policy/Hito to Kokudo. (JA) 291
People, Communication Organization (US) 344
People, Food & Land (US) 58
People from the Past Series. (UK ISSN 0079-0729) 135
People in Philanthropy (US) 1020
People in Wool (AT) 1160
People like That (UK) 729
Peoples in Atoms (JA) 898
Peoples of East Africa (KE) 75, 566
People's Voice (SJ) 907
Per Jacobsson Foundation. Proceedings (US ISSN 0079-0761) 231
Per Jacobsson Memorial Lecture see Per Jacobsson Foundation. Proceedings 231
Perbadanan Perpustakaan Awam Selangor. Laporan Tahunan see Selangor Public Library. Annual Report 683
Perceptions (Indianapolis) (US ISSN 0730-5435) 830
Pere Marquette Theology Lecture Series (US) 971
Perekrestki see Vstrechi 744
Perfiles Contemporaneos (AG) 135
Perfis Parlamentares (BL) 135, 945
Performance and Prospects (PH) 198
Performance Report of the Alaska Economy (US) 248
Performing Arts Biography Master Index (US) 346, 826, 1079
Performing Arts Directory (US) 375
Performing Arts Resources (US ISSN 0360-3814) 1078
Performing Right see Performing Right News 840
Performing Right News (UK ISSN 0309-0019) 841
Performing Right Year Book (UK ISSN 0309-0884) 840
Performing Woman (US ISSN 0191-1554) 840, 1129
Perfumeria Moderna - Directorio de Proveedores/Modern Perfumimg - Directory of Suppliers (MX) 119
Pergamon Unified Engineering Series (UK ISSN 0079-0869) 473
Pergolesi Studies/Studi Pergolesiani (US) 840
Perinatology-Neonatology Buyers Guide(US ISSN 0147-7927) 315, 785
Perinatology/Neonatology Buyer's Guide (US) 785
Period Building Restoration Trades & Suppliers Directory (AT ISSN 0158-7374) 99, 315
Periodex see Point de Repere 10
Periodical Title Abbreviations (US ISSN 0737-7843) 962
Periodical Writers Association of Canada. Directory (CN) 646
Periodical Writers Association of Canada. Fees Survey (CN) 646
Periodicals in East African Libraries: a Union List see Periodicals in Eastern African Libraries: a Union List 130
Periodicals in Eastern African Libraries: a Union List (KE) 130
Periodicals in Print in Japan/Zasshi Shimbun Sohkatarogu (JA ISSN 0387-7000) 130
Perishers Annual (UK) 520
Peritia (IE ISSN 0332-1592) 91, 593, 701
Permail Hospital Book (AT) 618
Permanent Commission on the Status of Women Annual Report see P C S W Annual Report 1129
Permanent International Altaistic Conference (PIAC). Newsletter (US ISSN 0031-5508) 853
Pernambuco, Brazil. Secretaria da Agricultura. Plano Anual de Trabalho(BL) 49
Persian Art Series see Highlights of Persian Art 105
Persica (NE ISSN 0079-0893) 91, 571
Persistence of Vision (US) 825, 880
Personal Computer - An Industry Source Book (US) 357, 362, 363
Personal Computer Local Networks Report (US) 357, 362
Personal Computing Series (US ISSN 0888-3262) 755
Personal Income in Counties of New York State (US ISSN 0079-0907) 277
Personal Income Tax Analysis see Analysis of Oregon Personal Income 292
Personale- og Oekonomistik for Sygehusvaesenet (DK ISSN 0107-1173) 618, 1061
Personale og Sengepladser ved de Sygedomsbehandlende Institutioner see Personale- og Oekonomistik for Sygehusvaesenet 618
Personalities. Events. Times (UR) 712
Personality and Psychopathology (US ISSN 0079-0931) 936
Personnel & Training Abstracts (UK ISSN 0305-0671) 10, 216
Personnel and Training Databook (UK) 1160
Personnel and Training Management Yearbook see Personnel and Training Databook 1160
Personnel des Nations Unies et des Agences Specialisees en Republique de Rwanda (UN) 263
Personnel/Industrial Relations Report, Parts 1 and 2 see Salaries & Bonuses in Personnel/Industrial Relations Functions 275
Personnel Literature (US ISSN 0031-5753) 216, 949
Personnel Management Abstracts (US ISSN 0031-577X) 10, 216
Personnel Policies and Benefits for the Apparel Industry (US) 287
Perspecta; The Yale Architectural Journal (US ISSN 0079-0958) 99
Perspectivas (BL ISSN 0101-3459) 1010
Perspectivas en Psicologia (CK ISSN 0120-3878) 936
Perspective. Cleveland Foundation Occasional Paper (US) 955, 1020
Perspectives de l'Economique. Serie 1. Fondateurs de l'Economie (FR ISSN 0079-0982) 252
Perspectives de l'Economique. Serie 2. Economie Contemporaine (FR) 198
Perspectives de l'Economique. Serie 3. Critique (FR) 198
Perspectives in American History (UK ISSN 0266-1322) 608
Perspectives in Asian History (US) 571
Perspectives in Cardiovascular Research(US ISSN 0361-0527) 777
Perspectives in Criminal Justice (US) 372
Perspectives in Drug Abuse (UK ISSN 0334-1186) 377
Perspectives in Economic History see South African Journal of Economic History 252
Perspectives in Ethology (US) 1122
Perspectives in Geography (US) 547
Perspectives in Immunology (US) 773
Perspectives in Jewish Learning see Solomon Goldman Lectures 977
Perspectives in Law and Psychology (US) 662, 936
Perspectives in Mathematical Logic (US ISSN 0172-6641) 751
Perspectives in Nephrology and Hypertension (US ISSN 0092-2900) 777, 795
Perspectives in Pediatric Pathology (SZ) 765, 788
Perspectives in Powder Metallurgy see New Perspectives in Powder Metallurgy 799
Perspectives in Primate Biology (II) 75, 145
Perspectives in Structural Science (UK) 473
Perspectives in Virology (US ISSN 0072-9086) 1160
Perspectives on Academic Gaming & Simulation (UK) 449
Perspectives on Contemporary Literature (US ISSN 0098-7301) 729
Perspectives on Local Public Finance and Public Policy (US) 298
Perspectives on Southern Africa (US) 566, 907
Perspectives on the American South (US ISSN 0275-584X) 608, 1028
Perspektiven der Philosophie. Neues Jahrbuch (NE) 880
Persuasions (US) 730
Persuasions, Occasional Papers (US) 730
Perth Observatory. Communications (AT ISSN 0079-1067) 117
Peru. Biblioteca Nacional. Anuario Bibliografico Peruano (PE) 130
Peru. Biblioteca Nacional. Boletin (PE ISSN 0031-6067) 682
Peru. Ministerio de Educacion Publica. Oficina Sectorial de Planificacion. Plan Bienal (PE) 418
Peru. Oficina Regional de Desarrollo del Norte. Analisis General de Situacion de la Region Norte (PE ISSN 0085-4840) 248
Peru: Compendio Estadistico (PE) 216
Peru Indigena (PE) 75
Peru - Problema (PE ISSN 0079-1075) 1028
Perugia Quadrennial International Conferences on Cancer. Proceedings (IT ISSN 0069-8520) 776
Pesquisa em Andamento (BL ISSN 0100-8161) 33
Pesquisas: Publicacoes de Antropologia (BL ISSN 0553-8467) 75
Pesquisas: Publicacoes de Botanica (BL ISSN 0553-8475) 160
Pesquisas: Publicacoes de Historia (BL ISSN 0553-8491) 559
Pesquisas: Publicacoes de Zoologia (BL ISSN 0553-8505) 177
Pesticide Residues in Danish Food see Pesticidrester i Danske Levnedsmidler 58
Pesticide Residues in Food (UN ISSN 0587-5943) 955
Pesticides (Sacramento) (US ISSN 0092-6752) 58
Pesticides Annual (II) 58
Pesticidrester i Danske Levnedsmidler/Pesticide Residues in Danish Food (DK ISSN 0108-2086) 58, 520
Petalon (GR) 559
Peter Stuyvesant Travel Waterski Guide(UK) 1046, 1115
Peter Stuyvesant Travel Windsurf Guide (UK) 1046, 1115

PHILOGISCHE STUDIEN

Peter Willcocks Society. Journal (US) 537
Petersen's Complete Guide to Deer Hunting see Deer Hunting (Los Angeles) 1045
Petersen's Pro Football Annual see Pro Football (Los Angeles) 1040
Peterson's Annual Guide to Careers and Employment for Engineers, Computer Scientists and Physical Scientists see Peterson's Guide to Engineering, Science and Computer Jobs (Year) 473
Peterson's Annual Guide to Independent Secondary Schools see Peterson's Guide to Independent Secondary Schools 430
Peterson's Annual Guide to Undergraduate Study see Guide to Four-Year Colleges (Year) 429
Peterson's Annual Guide to Undergraduate Study see Peterson's Guide to Two-Year Colleges (Year) 430
Peterson's Annual Guides/Graduate Study. Graduate Programs in the Physical Science and Mathematics. see Peterson's Graduate Programs in the Physical Sciences and Mathematics (Year) 430
Peterson's Annual Guides: Summer Opportunities for Kids and Teenagers see Peterson's Summer Opportunities for Kids and Teenagers 848
Peterson's College Money Handbook (Year) (US) 231
Peterson's Graduate and Professional Programs: An Overview (US) 430
Peterson's Graduate Programs in the Biological, Agricultural and Health Sciences. (US) 145, 430
Peterson's Graduate Programs in the Humanities and Social Sciences (US) 430
Peterson's Graduate Programs in the Physical Sciences and Mathematics (Year) (US) 430, 998
Peterson's Guide to Business and Management Jobs (Year) (US ISSN 0749-5021) 848
Peterson's Guide to Engineering, Science and Computer Jobs (Year) (US ISSN 0730-0980) 473
Peterson's Guide to Independent Secondary Schools (US) 430
Peterson's Guide to Two-Year Colleges (Year) (US ISSN 0737-3171) 430
Peterson's Guides. Annual Guides to Graduate Study. Book 1: Accredited Institutions Offering Graduate Work- An Overview see Peterson's Graduate and Professional Programs: An Overview 430
Peterson's Guides. Annual Guides to Graduate Study. Book 1: Graduate and Professional Programs: An Overview see Peterson's Graduate and Professional Programs: An Overview 430
Peterson's Guides. Annual Guides to Graduate Study. Book 2: Humanities and Social Sciences. see Peterson's Graduate Programs in the Humanities and Social Sciences 430
Peterson's Guides. Annual Guides to Graduate Study. Book 3: Biological, Agricultural and Health Sciences see Peterson's Graduate Programs in the Biological, Agricultural and Health Sciences 430
Peterson's Guides. Annual Guides to Graduate Study. Book 5: Engineering and Applied Sciences (US) 430, 473
Peterson's Summer Opportunities for Kids and Teenagers (US) 336, 848
Petofi Irodalmi Muzeum Evkonyve/ Yearbook of the Literary Museum (HU ISSN 0524-8906) 730
Petro Quimica see Guia de la Industria Quimica 478
Petrobras. Consolidated Report (BL) 866
Petrole (Year) (FR ISSN 0069-6552) 866
Petroleo e Gas (BL) 866
Petroleum Abstracts (US ISSN 0031-6423) 10, 868

Petroleum and Arab Economic Development see Oil and Arab Cooperation. Annual Review 865
Petroleum and Chemical Industry Conference. Record of Conference Papers (US ISSN 0090-3507) 479, 866
Petroleum and Coal Geology see Neftena i Vuglistna Geologiia 392
Petroleum/Energy Business News Index(US) 10, 868
Petroleum Equipment Directory (US) 866
Petroleum Geology of Taiwan/T'aiwan Shih Yu Ti Chih (CH) 393, 866
Petroleum Industry Conference. Record see Petroleum and Chemical Industry Conference. Record of Conference Papers 479
Petroleum Industry in Illinois (US) 866
Petroleum Industry in Japan (JA) 866
Petroleum: Latin American Indutrial Report (US) 240, 866
Petroleum Marketer's Handbook (US) 866
Petroleum Situation (US) 466
Petroleum Software Directory (US ISSN 0743-6750) 363, 866
Pets Welcome (UK ISSN 0079-130X) 868, 1115
Pettaquamscutt Reporter (US) 608
Pflanzenschutz-Kurier see Agro Chemie-Koerier 52
Pflanzenschutz-Kurier see Correio Agricola (Portugal) 54
Pflanzenschutz - Kurier see Vaextskydds - Kuriren 61
Die Pforte (GW ISSN 0031-6784) 712, 880
Phaedrus (US ISSN 0098-3365) 334, 682, 730
Phaenomenologica (NE ISSN 0079-1350) 880
Phanerogamarum Monographiae (GW ISSN 0079-1369) 160
Pharma-Prognosis International (UK) 872
Pharmaceutical Codex (UK) 872
Pharmaceutical: Latin American Industrial Report (US) 240, 872
Pharmaceutical Manufacturers Association Statistical Factbook see P M A Statistical Factbook 872
Pharmaceutical Manufacturers of Japan (JA) 315, 872
Pharmaceutical Marketers Directory (US) 285, 872
Pharmaceutical Medicine (UK ISSN 0142-1581) 765, 872
Pharmaceutical News Index (US ISSN 0362-4439) 10, 873
Pharmacochemistry Library (NE) 324
Pharmacology and Toxicology. Supplementum (DK ISSN 0901-9936) 872
Pharmacy and Law Digest (US ISSN 0149-1717) 662, 872
Pharmacy Guild of Australia. Annual Report (AT) 872
Pharmacy Guild of Australia. National Newsletter (AT) 872
Pharmakotherapie (GW ISSN 0344-7154) 765, 872
Pharmatherapeutica (UK ISSN 0308-051X) 765
Pharmindex (US ISSN 0031-7152) 10, 873
Pharmstudent (II ISSN 0379-556X) 872
Pharos (CN) 342
Pharos (US ISSN 0031-7160) 830
Phase Transitions (UK ISSN 0141-1594) 890
Phenomenological Inquiry (US ISSN 0885-3886) 880
Phenomenology and the Human Sciences (US) 1028
Phenomenology Information Bulletin see Phenomenological Inquiry 880
Phi Eta Sigma. Forum (US) 342
Phi Theta Papers (US) 701, 730, 853
Philadelphia Bar Association. Legal Directory (US) 662
Philadelphia Herpetological Society. Bulletin (US) 177, 498
Philadelphia Policy Papers (US) 917
Philadelphia Society of Clinical Psychologists Times see P S C P Times 935

Philatelic Bulletin see Australian Stamp Bulletin 874
Philatelistic Catalogue Key see Filatelistisk Katalog-Noegle 874
Philatelistischer Katalog-Schluessel see Filatelistisk Katalog-Noegle 874
Philippine Abstracts see Philippine Science and Technology Abstracts Bibliography 1004
Philippine Agricultural Meteorology Bulletin (PH) 33, 806
Philippine Astronomical Handbook (PH ISSN 0115-1207) 117
Philippine Atomic Energy Commission. Annual Report (PH ISSN 0553-9978) 898
Philippine Coconut Authority. Agricultural Research Department. Annual Report (PH) 58
Philippine Development Report (PH) 248
Philippine Geology, Mining and Mineral Resources see Bibliography on Philippine Geology, Mining and Mineral Resources 814
Philippine Library Association. Bulletin (PH) 683
Philippine Mining and Engineering Journal. Mining Annual and Directory (PH ISSN 0085-4875) 819
Philippine National Bibliography (PH ISSN 0303-190X) 130
Philippine Normal College. Language Study Center. Occasional Paper (PH ISSN 0076-3780) 418, 701
Philippine Normal College Research Series (PH) 438
Philippine Science and Technology Abstracts Bibliography (PH ISSN 0115-8724) 10, 1004
Philippine Science Index see Philippine Science and Technology Abstracts Bibliography 1004
Philippine Scientist (PH ISSN 0079-1466) 998
Philippine Standard Commodity Classification (PH) 267
Philippine Yearbook see Philippines. National Census and Statistics Office. Yearbook 929
Philippine Yearbook of International Law (PH) 671
Philippines. Atmosphere, Geophysical and Astronomical Services Administration. Table of Sunrise, Sunset, Twilight, Moonrise and Moonset see Table of Sunrise, Sunset, Twilight, Moonrise and Moonset 117
Philippines. Board of Investments. Annual Report (PH ISSN 0079-1504) 267
Philippines. Bureau of Agricultural Economics. Crop and Livestock Statistics (PH) 42
Philippines. Bureau of Agricultural Economics. Crop, Livestock and Natural Resources Statistics see Philippines. Bureau of Agricultural Economics. Crop and Livestock Statistics 42
Philippines. Bureau of Agricultural Economics. Report (PH ISSN 0079-1520) 49
Philippines. Bureau of Mines. Annual Report (PH) 367, 819
Philippines. Bureau of Vocational Education. Agricultural Education Program; Information and Statistical Guide (PH) 33
Philippines. Department of Agrarian Reform. Planning Service. Annual Report (PH) 49
Philippines. Department of Commerce and Industry. Annual Report see Philippines. Ministry of Trade. Annual Report 259
Philippines. Department of Public Information. Policy Statements (PH) 945
Philippines. Food and Nutrition Center. Annual Report see Philippines. Food and Nutrition Research Institute. Annual Report 846
Philippines. Food and Nutrition Research Institute. Annual Report (PH) 846

Philippines. Government Printing Office. Itemization of Personal Services and Organizational Charts (PH) 683, 945
Philippines. Insurance Commission. Annual Report (PH) 641
Philippines. Labor Statistics Service. Year Book of Labor Statistics (PH ISSN 0115-1851) 216
Philippines. Ministry of Education & Culture. National Scholarship Center. Directory of Alumni (PH) 342, 418
Philippines. Ministry of Education, Culture and Sports. National Scholarship Center. Annual Report (PH ISSN 0115-4249) 342, 418
Philippines. Ministry of Human Settlements. Annual Report (PH) 923
Philippines. Ministry of Natural Resources. Annual Report (PH) 367, 498
Philippines. Ministry of Natural Resources. Plans and Programs (PH) 367, 498
Philippines. Ministry of Trade. Annual Report (PH) 240, 259
Philippines. Ministry of Trade. Trend Analysis of the Twenty Leading Exports and Prospects in the Year Ahead (PH) 259
Philippines. Ministry of Trade. Twenty Leading Imports (PH) 259
Philippines. National Census and Statistics Office. Annual Survey of Establishments (PH) 216
Philippines. National Census and Statistics Office. Annual Survey of Wholesale and Retail Establishments (PH) 216
Philippines. National Census and Statistics Office. Coastwise Trade Report (PH) 216
Philippines. National Census and Statistics Office. Directory of Large Establishments (PH) 216
Philippines. National Census and Statistics Office. Listing of Cities, Municipalities and Municipal Districts by Province (PH) 627
Philippines. National Census and Statistics Office. Social Indicator (PH) 923, 928
Philippines. National Census and Statistics Office. Special Report (PH) 1061
Philippines. National Census and Statistics Office. Vital Statistical Report (PH ISSN 0554-0186) 929, 1061
Philippines. National Census and Statistics Office. Yearbook (PH) 929
Philippines. National Economic and Development Authority. Food Balance Series (PH) 49
Philippines. National Economic and Development Authority. National Income Series (PH) 277
Philippines. National Economic and Development Authority. Report on the Economy see Philippine Development Report 248
Philippines. National Library. T N L Research Guide Series (The National Library) (PH) 130
Philippines. National Science & Technology Authority. Annual Report (PH) 998
Philippines. National Tax Research Center. Report (PH ISSN 0079-1547) 298
Philippines Business Directory (PH) 315
Philippines Chinese Historical Association. Annals (PH) 571, 917
Philippines Nuclear Journal (PH ISSN 0079-1490) 898
Philippines Yearbook of the Fookien Times (PH) 231, 315, 662, 907
Phillpines. National Science Development Board. Annual Report see Philippines. National Science & Technology Authority. Annual Report 998
Phillips' Paper Trade Directory - Europe-Mills of the World (UK ISSN 0079-158X) 858
Philogische Studien und Quellen (GW) 730

Philologen-Jahrbuch (GW ISSN 0079-1598) *701*
Philologia Frisica (NE) *701*
Philological Monographs (US ISSN 0079-1628) *701*
Philological Society Transactions (UK ISSN 0079-1636) *701*
Philomel (US) *730*
Philosopher's Index (NE) *880*
Philosophes Contemporains (BE ISSN 0079-1660) *880*
Philosophes Medievaux (BE ISSN 0079-1679) *880*
Philosophia (GR) *880*
Philosophia Antiqua (NE ISSN 0079-1687) *338, 880*
Philosophia Mathematica (US ISSN 0031-8019) *751, 880*
Philosophia Naturalis (GW ISSN 0031-8027) *880*
Philosophia Patrum (NE) *730*
Philosophia Spinozae Perennis (NE) *880*
Philosophica see Revista Philosophica *881*
Philosophical Society of the Sudan. Proceedings of the Annual Conference (SJ ISSN 0079-1695) *880*
Philosophical Studies in Education (US ISSN 0160-7561) *418*
Philosophical Studies Series in Philosophy (NE) *880*
Philosophical Texts and Studies see Wijsgerige Teksten en Studies *883*
Philosophie (FR ISSN 0182-7103) *880*
Philosophiehistorische Texte (GE ISSN 0233-089X) *880*
Philosophische Abhandlungen (GW ISSN 0175-6508) *880*
Philosophische Studientexte see Philosophiehistorische Texte *880*
Philosophische und Soziologische Veroeffentlichungen see Freie Universitaet Berlin. Osteuropa-Institut. Philosophische und Soziologische Veroeffentlichungen *878*
Philosophisches Jahrbuch (GW ISSN 0031-8183) *880*
Philosophus see P S *880*
Philosophy and Medicine (NE) *765, 880*
Philosophy and the Arts (US ISSN 0739-1218) *880, 971*
Philosophy in Context (US ISSN 0742-2733) *880*
Philosophy of Education see Curriculum Improvement *412*
Philosophy of Education Society. Proceedings of the Annual Meetings (US ISSN 0079-1733) *418*
Philosophy Research Archives (US ISSN 0164-0771) *880*
Philosphy in Science (US) *880*
Phoebus (US ISSN 0193-8061) *108*
Phoenix (Dumont) (US) *917*
Phoenix. Supplementary Volumes (CN ISSN 0079-1784) *730*
Phoenix Conference on Computers and Communications. Conference Proceedings (US) *346*
Phonefacts (US) *350*
Phonology Yearbook (UK ISSN 0265-8062) *701*
Photo, Cine, Video Buyer's Guide (GR) *349, 885*
Photo Information Almanac (US ISSN 0093-1365) *885*
Photo-Lab Index (US) *885*
Photo Love Annual (UK) *14*
Photochemistry (London) (UK ISSN 0556-3860) *324*
Photochemistry (Oxford) (UK ISSN 0079-1806) *332*
Photofact Annual Index see Photofact/Computerfacts Annual Index *349*
Photofact/Computerfacts Annual Index (US) *349*
Photogrammetric Notes see Fotogrammetriska Meddelanden *543*
Photograph Collectors' Resource Directory (US) *885*
Photographer's Market (US ISSN 0147-247X) *885*
Photographic Abstracts (UK ISSN 0031-8701) *10, 885*
Photographic Art Market Auction Price Results and Analysis (US) *885*
Photographic Historical Society of New York. Membership Directory (US ISSN 0093-254X) *885*
Photographic Trade News Master Buying Guide (US) *885*
Photographic Trade News Master Buying Guide & Directory see P T N Master Buying Guide & Directory *315*
Photographic World Annual see Photoworld Annual *885*
Photographis (SZ ISSN 0079-1830) *885*
Photography Annual (US ISSN 0079-1849) *1160*
Photography at Open Space Monographs (CN) *885*
Photography Buyers Guide (US) *1160*
Photography Directory and Buying Guide see Photography Buyers Guide *1160*
Photography Magazine Index (US) *10, 885*
Photography Monograph Series (CN) *885*
Photography Report (UK) *885*
Photon (US ISSN 0031-8833) *825*
Photoworld Annual (AT ISSN 0727-3967) *885*
Photron (US ISSN 0735-0317) *730*
Phyket Marine Biological Center. Research Bulletin (TH) *145*
Physical Acoustics: Principles and Methods (US ISSN 0079-1873) *900*
Physical Chemistry (US ISSN 0079-1881) *332*
Physical Education Around the World. Monograph (US ISSN 0079-189X) *449*
Physical Education Index (US ISSN 0191-9202) *10, 449, 886*
Physical Research Laboratory, Ahmedabad: Annual Report. (II) *890*
Physical Review Abstracts (US ISSN 0048-4024) *10, 893*
Physical Review/Index (US ISSN 0094-0003) *10, 893*
Physical Sciences and Mathematics see Peterson's Graduate Programs in the Physical Sciences and Mathematics (Year) *430*
Physical Sciences Data (NE) *332*
Physician Assistant Programs, A National Directory (US) *765*
Physician Characteristics and Distribution see Physician Characteristics & Distribution in the U S *765*
Physician Characteristics & Distribution in the U S (US ISSN 0731-0315) *765*
Physician Distribution and Medical Licensure in the U S see Physician Characteristics & Distribution in the U S *765*
Physicians' Current Procedural Terminology see C P T *758*
Physicians' Desk Reference (US ISSN 0093-4461) *765*
Physicians' Desk Reference for Nonprescription Drugs (US) *765*
Physicians' Desk Reference to Pharmaceutical Specialties and Biologicals see Physicians' Desk Reference *765*
Physico-Chemical Mechanics see Fiziko-Khimicheska Mekhanika *331*
Physics see Physics News *890*
Physics: A Series of Monographs & Tracts (SZ) *890*
Physics Abstracts (UK ISSN 0036-8091) *10, 117, 893*
Physics and Applications (CS) *890*
Physics and Chemistry in Space (US ISSN 0079-1938) *117, 324, 890*
Physics and Chemistry of Materials with Layered Structures see Physics and Chemistry of Materials with Low-Dimensional Structures *895*
Physics and Chemistry of Materials with Low Dimensional Structures. Series A. Layered Structures (NE) *332*
Physics and Chemistry of Materials with Low Dimensional Structures. Series B: Quasi-One-Dimensional Structures (NE) *332*
Physics and Chemistry of Materials with Low Dimensional Structures. Series C. Molecular Structures (NE) *332*
Physics and Chemistry of Materials with Low-Dimensional Structures (NE) *324, 895*
Physics and Chemistry of the Earth (US ISSN 0079-1946) *380*
Physics Briefs/Physikalische Berichte (GW ISSN 0170-7434) *10, 893*
Physics in Collision (US) *890*
Physics Manpower - Education and Employment Statistics (US ISSN 0569-5716) *438, 890*
Physics News (US) *890*
Physics of Electronic and Atomic Collisions see International Conference on the Physics of Electronic and Atomic Collisions. Abstracts of Contributed Papers and Invited Papers *897*
Physics of Quantum Electronics (US) *458*
Physics of Semiconductors (UK) *1160*
Physics of Thin Films; Advances in Research and Development (US ISSN 0079-1970) *890*
Physikalisch-Chemische Trenn- und Messmethoden (GE ISSN 0079-1997) *890*
Physiological Principles in Medicine (UK ISSN 0260-2946) *765*
Physiological Society. Monographs (US ISSN 0079-2020) *172*
Physiological Society of Philadelphia. Monographs (US) *172*
Physiotherapy Research Newsletter (UK) *765*
Phytochemical Society. Proceedings (US) *160*
Phytochemical Society of Europe. Annual Proceedings (UK) *152*
Phytochemical Society Symposia Series. Proceedings see Phytochemical Society. Proceedings *160*
Phytologia (US ISSN 0031-9430) *160*
Phyton. Annales Rei Botanicae (AU ISSN 0079-2047) *160*
Phytoparasitica: Israel Journal of Plant Protection Sciences (IS ISSN 0334-2123) *58*
Phytopathological Papers see C.A.B. International. Mycological Institute. Phytopathological Papers *155*
Phytophaga (IT) *58*
Pianeta Fresco (IT ISSN 0079-2055) *108*
Piano-Jahrbuch (GW ISSN 0173-8607) *840*
Picenum Seraphicum (IT) *983*
Pick Resources Guide (UK) *361, 362, 363*
Pick's Currency Yearbook see World Currency Yearbook *234*
Pictorial Directory - Washington State Legislature see Washington (State) Legislature. Pictorial Directory *947*
Pig Iron (US ISSN 0362-5214) *730, 885*
Pigment Cell (SZ ISSN 0301-0139) *167*
Pikestaff Forum (US ISSN 0192-8716) *730*
Pilgrim's Guide to Planet Earth (US) *1115*
Pilipinas (US) *75, 505, 547, 571*
Pilot Studies Approved for State Aid in Public School Systems in Virginia (US ISSN 0079-2071) *443*
Pimsleur's Checklist of Basic American Legal Publications (US) *669*
Pinery (US) *608*
Pinkes Fun der Kehile in Buenos Ayres see Anales de la Comunidad Israelita de Buenos Aires *501*
Pinpointer (AT ISSN 0031-9910) *10*
Pion Applied Physics Series (UK ISSN 0079-208X) *473, 890*
Pioneer America Society. Transactions (US) *516, 608*
Pipe Line & Pipe Line Contractors (US) *866*
Pipe Line Annual Directory of Pipelines(US) *866*
Pipeline and Underground Utilities Construction. Annual Directory (US) *315*
Pipeline Annual Directory (US) *866*
Pipeline Contractors Directory (US) *866*
Pipelines Abstracts (UK ISSN 0265-3990) *10, 868, 1128*
Pipes of Pan see Inscape (Pasadena) *742*
Piranesi (DK ISSN 0108-9935) *701, 712*
Pisarze Slascy 19 i 20 Wieku (PL ISSN 0079-211X) *730*
Pit & Quarry Handbook and Buyers Guide (US) *819*
Pit and Quarry Handbook and Purchasing Guide see Pit & Quarry Handbook and Buyers Guide *819*
Pitcher Performance Handbook (US ISSN 0731-8138) *1039*
Pitt Latin American Series (US) *730*
Pitt Series in English as a Second Language (US) *701*
Pittsburgh Series in Bibliography (US) *739*
Pittsburgh Series in Labor and Social History (US) *275*
Pittsburgh Series in Labor History see Pittsburgh Series in Labor and Social History *275*
Pittsburgh Series in Policy & Institutional Studies (US) *907*
Pivot (US ISSN 0032-0382) *427, 683*
Places: a Directory of Public Places for Private Events and Private Places for Public Functions (US) *315*
Plain Turkey (AT ISSN 0311-0753) *730*
Plainsong & Mediaeval Music Society. Journal (UK ISSN 0143-4918) *840*
Plan Review Process for Consolidated Program Schools (US) *443*
Planahome Book of Home Plans (UK) *99*
Planbook for Leaders of Children (US ISSN 0162-5381) *418, 979*
Planet Earth (US) *907*
Planetary Association for Clean Energy. Newsletter (CN ISSN 0708-918X) *466*
Planning and Administration (NE ISSN 0304-176X) *625, 945*
Planning and Management (NE) *1160*
Planning and Transport Research and Computation. Summer Annual Meeting. Proceedings (UK) *1093*
Planning-Economic, Regional, Urban, Social see P L E R U S *625*
Planning for Social Change (UK ISSN 0141-2779) *198, 1028*
Planning Guide X-1 (US) *350*
Planning Guide 2. Intra-L A T A Telecommunications Rates and Services (US) *350*
Planning Guide 3. Value-Added Networks and Data Private Line. Telecommunications Rates and Services (US) *350*
Planning Research Index (NZ ISSN 0111-4123) *1160*
Plano da Safra Acucar e Alcool (BL) *58, 120, 662*
Plans de Developpement des Pays de l'Afrique Noire (FR) *198, 263*
Plant Breeding Abstracts (UK ISSN 0032-0803) *10, 150, 534*
Plant Breeding Institute, Cambridge. Annual Report (UK ISSN 0079-2225) *58*
Plant Diseases and Pests in Denmark (DK ISSN 0107-6167) *160*
Plant Engineering & Maintenance Sourcebook see P E M Sourcebook *473*
Plant Engineering Directory & Specifications Catalog (US ISSN 0554-2693) *473*
Plant Growth Regulator Abstracts (UK ISSN 0305-9154) *10, 42*
Plant Life see Herbertia *157*
Plant Location (US ISSN 0554-2731) *291*
Plant Manager's Directory (Year) (UK ISSN 0267-2049) *186*
Plant Pathology Bulletins (US) *160*
Plant Physiology. Supplement Abstracts of Annual Meeting (US ISSN 0079-2241) *160*
Plant Protection Abstracts (IS ISSN 0032-0897) *10, 42, 150*
Plant Protection Research Institute. Annual Report (RH) *58, 165*

Plant Protection Society of the Republic of China. Annual Report (CH) 59, 533
Planteavlsarbejdet i de Landoekonomiske Foreninger (DK ISSN 0106-8113) 59
Planteavlsarbejdet i Landbo- og Husmandsforeningerne see Planteavlsarbejdet i de Landoekonomiske Foreninger 59
Plantebeskyttelsemidler (DK ISSN 0108-4887) 59
Planter (MY ISSN 0126-575X) 33
Plantesygdomme i Danmarks Aargangstaelling see Plant Diseases and Pests in Denmark 160
Plantevaern i Landbruget (DK ISSN 0109-3312) 59
Planting Breeding Reviews (US ISSN 0730-2207) 59
Planung und Kontrolle in der Unternehmung (SZ ISSN 0079-2276) 281
Planungsstudien (GW ISSN 0079-2284) 291
Plast- och Kemikalieleverantoerers Foerening Kemikalier see P K L Kemikalier 324
Plast- och Kemikalieleverantoerers Foerening Plaster see P K L Plaster 901
Plastic Industry Directory (UK) 901
Plastichem (SI) 332, 479, 901
Plasticos y Resinas (Annual) (MX) 901
Plastics Business Greenbook (CN) 901
Plastics Compounding Redbook (US) 901
Plastics D.A.T.A. Book (US) 901
Plastics: Latin American Industrial Report (US) 291, 901
Plastics Technology. Plastics Manufacturing Handbook and Buyers Guide (US) 901
Plastika Be-Israel/Israel Plastics (IS) 901
Platform (London) (UK) 1078
Platou Report (NO) 1102
Platt Saco Lowell Replacement Parts News (US) 1074
Platte Valley Review (US ISSN 0092-4318) 342
Play Index (US ISSN 0554-3037) 10, 739
Play Schools Newsletter (US ISSN 0032-1443) 334, 418
Play the Red (US ISSN 0277-1098) 742
Playfair Cricket Annual (UK ISSN 0079-2314) 1039
Playfair Football Annual (UK ISSN 0079-2322) 1039
Playfair S.A. Rugby Yearbook (SA) 1039
Playhour Annual (UK) 334
Playing Rules see Women's International Bowling Congress. Playing Rules 1040
Plays. A Classified Guide to Play Selection (UK ISSN 0554-3045) 1078
Plays & Playwrights (US) 730, 1078
Plays in Process (US ISSN 0736-0711) 1078
Plays of the Year (UK) 1160
Playschool Annual (UK) 336
Playthings Directory (US ISSN 0079-2349) 553
Playwrights Union of Canada Catalogue of Canadian Plays (CN) 130, 739, 1079
Pleiadi (IT) 730
Plejehjemshaandbogen (DK ISSN 0108-0857) 1020
Pluma y Pincel (AG) 712
Plunkett Development Series (UK ISSN 0143-8484) 49, 238
Plunkett Foundation for Co-Operative Studies. Study Series (UK ISSN 0142-5005) 238
Plurilingua (BE) 701
Plus (US) 362, 362, 689, 964
Pluteus (IT) 593
Pneumatic Packaging (US) 492, 855
Pocket Australian Stamp Catalogue (AT ISSN 0155-6215) 875
Pocket Book of Transport Statistics of India (II ISSN 0079-2381) 1082
Pocket Data Book, USA (US ISSN 0079-2403) 929

Pocket Digest of New Zealand Statistics(NZ ISSN 0079-2411) 564
Pocket Library of Studies in Art (IT ISSN 0079-242X) 108
Pocket Poets Series (US ISSN 0079-2438) 742
Pocket Year Book of South Australia (AT ISSN 0079-2446) 1061
Pocket Yearbook of New South Wales (AT ISSN 0159-9321) 1061
Poe Messenger (US ISSN 0276-3737) 730, 743
Poema Convidado see International Poetry 742
Poesia (UY ISSN 0079-2462) 743
Poesia Panamena Actual (PN) 743
Poesie und Wissenschaft. Sammlung (GW) 730, 743
Poet (US) 743
Poet and Critic (US ISSN 0032-1958) 743
Poetas (PY) 743
Poetes et Prosateurs du Portugal (FR ISSN 0079-2470) 730, 743
Poetessa (US) 743, 1129
Poeti e Prosatori Tedeschi (IT ISSN 0079-2500) 730, 743
Poetic Drama and Poetic Theory (AU) 730, 743
Poetica et Analytica (DK ISSN 0109-2820) 701
Poetics Journal (US ISSN 0731-5236) 712, 730
Poetry Index Annual (US ISSN 0736-3966) 688
Poetry Market (UK ISSN 0032-2083) 743
Poetry New Zealand (NZ) 1160
Poetry Project (US) 1160
Poetry Supplement (UK) 743
Poet's Market (US ISSN 0883-5470) 743
Poets Now (US) 743
Poet's Yearbook (UK) 743
Poetyka. Zarys Encyklopedyczny (PL ISSN 0079-2527) 743
Poeyana (CU) 177
Poeziya (Moscow) (UR) 743
Le Poing et la Rose (FR) 908
Point see Commerce. Le Point 239
Point de Repere (CN) 10
Point du Jazz (BE) 840
Point-of-Sale Information Service see P O S I S 285
Point Theologique (FR) 983
Point to Point Communication see Communication & Broadcasting 348
Pointer (US) 342
Points. Films (FR ISSN 0079-2535) 825
Points Chauds see France des Points Chauds 905
Points for Emphasis; International Sunday School Lessons in Pocket Size (US ISSN 0079-2543) 972
Points Northwest (US) 683
Poison Management Manual (CN) 872
Poland. Glowny Urzad Statystyczny. Maly Rocznik Statystyczny. Concise Statistical Yearbook (PL ISSN 0079-2608) 1061
Poland. Glowny Urzad Statystyczny. Maly Rocznik Statystyki Miedzynarodowej (PL) 1061
Poland. Glowny Urzad Statystyczny. Rocznik Demograficzny (PL ISSN 0079-2616) 929
Poland. Glowny Urzad Statystyczny. Rocznik Statystyczny Finansow. Yearbook of Finance Statistics (PL ISSN 0079-2640) 216
Poland. Glowny Urzad Statystyczny. Rocznik Statystyczny Gornictwa. Yearbook of Mining Statistics (PL ISSN 0079-2675) 822
Poland. Glowny Urzad Statystyczny. Rocznik Statystyczny Gospodarki Morskiej. Yearbook of Sea Economy Statistics (PL ISSN 0079-2667) 1086
Poland. Glowny Urzad Statystyczny. Rocznik Statystyczny Handlu Wewnetrznego/Yearbook of International Trade Statistics (PL ISSN 0079-2683) 216

Poland. Glowny Urzad Statystyczny. Rocznik Statystyczny Inwestycji i Srodkow Trwalych. Yearbook of Investment and Fixed Assets Statistics (PL ISSN 0079-2705) 216
Poland. Glowny Urzad Statystyczny. Rocznik Statystyczny Lesnictwa see Poland. Glowny Urzad Statystyczny. Rocznik Statystyczny Lesnictwa i Gospodarki Drewnem 529
Poland. Glowny Urzad Statystyczny. Rocznik Statystyczny Lesnictwa i Gospodarki Drewnem (PL) 529
Poland. Glowny Urzad Statystyczny. Rocznik Statystyczny Ochrony Zdrowia. Yearbook of Public Health Statistics (PL ISSN 0079-2748) 959
Poland. Glowny Urzad Statystyczny. Rocznik Statystyczny Powiatow. Statistical Yearbook of Counties (PL ISSN 0079-2756) 1061
Poland. Glowny Urzad Statystyczny. Rocznik Statystyczny Przemyslu. Yearbook of Industry Statistics (PL ISSN 0079-2764) 216
Poland. Glowny Urzad Statystyczny. Rocznik Statystyczny Rolnictwa i Gospodarki Zywnosciowej. Yearbook of Agricultural Statistics (PL) 42
Poland. Glowny Urzad Statystyczny. Rocznik Statystyczny. Statistical Yearbook (PL ISSN 0079-2780) 1061
Poland. Glowny Urzad Statystyczny. Rocznik Statystyczny Szkolnictwa. Yearbook of Education Statistics (PL ISSN 0079-2799) 425
Poland. Glowny Urzad Statystyczny. Rocznik Statystyczny Transportu. Yearbook of Transport Statistics (PL ISSN 0079-2802) 1086
Poland. Glowny Urzad Statystyczny. Rocznik Statystyki Handlu Zagranicznego (PL ISSN 0079-2691) 216
Poland. Glowny Urzad Statystyczny. Rocznik Statystyki Miedzynarodowej. Yearbook of International Statistics (PL ISSN 0079-273X) 1061
Poland. Glowny Urzad Statystyczny. Rolniczy Rocznik Statystyczny. Yearbook of Agricultural Statistics see Poland. Glowny Urzad Statystyczny. Rocznik Statystyczny Rolnictwa i Gospodarki Zywnosciowej. Yearbook of Agricultural Statistics 42
Poland. Glowny Urzad Statystyczny. Statystyka Polski. Studia i Prace Statystyczne (PL) 1061
Poland. Glowny Urzad Statystyczny. Studia i Prace Statystyczne see Poland. Glowny Urzad Statystyczny. Statystyka Polski. Studia i Prace Statystyczne 1061
Poland. Glowny Urzad Statystyczny. Uzytkowanie Gruntow i Powierzchnia Zasiewow Oraz Zwierzeta Gospodarskie see Poland. Glowny Urzad Statystyczny. Wyniki Spisu Rolniczego. Uzytkowanie Gruntow i Powierzchnia Zasiewow, oraz Zwierzeta Gospodarskie 42
Poland. Glowny Urzad Statystyczny. Wyniki Spisu Rolniczego. Uzytkowanie Gruntow i Powierzchnia Zasiewow, oraz Zwierzeta Gospodarskie (PL) 42
Poland. Glowny Urzad Statystyczny. Zatrudnienie w Gospodarce Narodowej (PL ISSN 0079-2896) 216
Poland. Glowny Urzad Statystyczny. Zeszyty Metodyczne (PL ISSN 0079-2829) 1061
Polar Bears (SZ) 177, 367
Polar Research see National Research Council. Committee on Polar Research. Report on United States Antarctic Research Activities 546
Polar Research (NO) 547, 998
Polarhaandbok see Norsk Polarinstitutt. Polarhaandbok 393
Polarography Abstracts (UK) 10, 893
Police & Constabulary Almanac (UK ISSN 0477-2008) 372
Police and Law Enforcement (US ISSN 0092-8933) 372

Police Science Abstracts (NE ISSN 0166-6282) 10, 374, 773
Police Statistics of Cincinnati see Cincinnati. Division of Police. Annual Report 370
Police Yearbook (US ISSN 0079-2950) 372
Policy Grants Directory (US ISSN 0160-2675) 908
Policy Notes (US ISSN 8755-9412) 263, 1020
Policy Papers in International Affairs see University of California, Berkeley. Institute of International Studies. Policy Papers in International Affairs 920
Policy Publishers and Associations Directory (US ISSN 0272-0671) 908, 962
Policy Research Centers Directory (US ISSN 0270-1200) 908
Policy Studies Directory (US ISSN 0362-6016) 908
Policy Studies in Employment and Welfare (US) 1020
Policy Studies Institute Discussion Papers see P S I Discussion Papers 1010
Policy Studies Institute Report Series see P S I: Report Series 907
Policy Studies Personnel Directory (US ISSN 0275-4002) 908
Policy Studies Review Annual (US ISSN 0163-108X) 945
Policy Study (CN ISSN 0832-7912) 198
Poliluce - Aziende Italiane (IT) 1160
Polimerim ve-Homarim Plastiyim/ Polymers and Plastic Materials see Plastika Be-Israel 901
Polimery v Melioratsii i Vodnom Khozyaistve (UR) 490, 1125
Polimitas (CU) 1115
Polin (UK ISSN 0268-1056) 505
Polish Academy of Sciences. Institute of Computer Science. Reports (PL) 353
Polish Academy of Sciences. Institute of Fluid-Flow Machinery. Transactions see Polska Akademia Nauk. Instytut Maszyn Przeplywowych. Prace 492
Polish Academy of Sciences. Institute of Fundamental Technological Research. Scientific Activities (PL ISSN 0079-323X) 473
Polish Academy of Sciences. Institute of Geophysics. Series A. Physics of the Earth's Interior (PL ISSN 0137-2440) 400
Polish Academy of Sciences. Institute of Geophysics. Series B. Seismology (PL ISSN 0209-0406) 400
Polish Academy of Sciences. Institute of Geophysics. Series C. Geomagnetism (PL ISSN 0208-8525) 400
Polish Academy of Sciences. Institute of Geophysics. Series D. Physics of the Atmosphere (PL ISSN 0138-0125) 400
Polish Academy of Sciences. Institute of Geophysics. Series F. Planetary Geodesy (PL ISSN 0138-0214) 400
Polish Academy of Sciences. Institute of Geophysics. Series G. Numerical Methods in Geophysics (PL ISSN 0208-8061) 400
Polish Academy of Sciences. Institute of Geophysics. Series M. Miscellanea(PL ISSN 0138-015X) 401
Polish Academy of Sciences. Mathematical Institute. Banach Center Publications (PL ISSN 0137-6934) 752
Polish American Congress Charitable Foundation, Inc. Newsletter see P A C Newsletter 505
Polish Archaeological Abstracts (PL ISSN 0137-4885) 10, 96
Polish Film Production see Catalogue of Polish Feature Films 823
Polish Journal of Soil Science (PL ISSN 0079-2985) 59
Polish Music History Series (US ISSN 0741-9945) 840
Polish Political Science (PL ISSN 0208-7375) 908

Polish Publishing in Figures *see* Ruch Wydawniczy w Liczbach 964
Polish Round Table *see* Polish Political Science 908
Polish Scientific Abstracts on Mechanics *see* Polska Bibliografia Analityczna Mechaniki 746
Polish Technical and Economic Abstracts (PL ISSN 0032-3004) 10, 216, *1073*
Polish Yearbook of International Law/ Annuaire Polonais de Droit International (PL ISSN 0554-498X) *671*
Politechnika Czestochowska. Zeszyty Naukowe. Nauki Podstawowe (PL ISSN 0574-9069) *473*
Politechnika Czestochowska. Zeszyty Naukowe. Nauki Spoleczno-Ekonomiczne (PL ISSN 0574-9077) *1010*
Politechnika Czestochowska. Zeszyty Naukowe. Nauki Techniczne. Elektrotechnika (PL ISSN 0137-6977) *458*
Politechnika Czestochowska. Zeszyty Naukowe. Nauki Techniczne. Hutnictwo (PL ISSN 0372-9699) *799*
Politechnika Czestochowska. Zeszyty Naukowe. Nauki Techniczne. Mechanika (PL ISSN 0137-6969) *492*
Politechnika Gdanska. Instytut Fizyki. Raport (PL) *890*
Politechnika Gdanska. Instytut Hydrotechniki. Raport (PL) *490*
Politechnika Gdanska. Instytut Matematyki. Raport (PL) *752*
Politechnika Gdanska. Instytut Nauk Spolecznych. Raport (PL) *1010*
Politechnika Gdanska. Instytut Okretowy. Raport (PL) *1102*
Politechnika Gdanska. Instytut Organizacji i Projektowania. Raport (PL) *492*
Politechnika Gdanska. Raport. Wydzial Architektury (PL) *99*
Politechnika Gdanska. Raport. Wydzial Budownictwa Ladowego (PL) *483*
Politechnika Gdanska. Raport. Wydzial Budowy Maszyn (PL) *492*
Politechnika Gdanska. Raport. Wydzial Chemiczny (PL) *324*
Politechnika Gdanska. Raport. Wydzial Elektroniki (PL) *458*
Politechnika Gdanska. Raport. Wydzial Elektryczny (PL) *458*
Politechnika Gdanska. Raport. Wydzial Mechaniczny Technologiczny (PL) *492*
Politechnika Gdanska. Zeszyty Naukowe. Architektura (PL ISSN 0518-3138) *99*
Politechnika Gdanska. Zeszyty Naukowe. Budownictwo Ladowe (PL ISSN 0373-8671) 186, *483*
Politechnika Gdanska. Zeszyty Naukowe. Budownictwo Okretowe (PL ISSN 0373-868X) *1102*
Politechnika Gdanska. Zeszyty Naukowe. Budownictwo Wodne (PL ISSN 0373-8663) *490*
Politechnika Gdanska. Zeszyty Naukowe. Chemia (PL ISSN 0416-7309) *324*
Politechnika Gdanska. Zeszyty Naukowe. Ekonomia (PL) *198*
Politechnika Gdanska. Zeszyty Naukowe. Elektronika (PL ISSN 0418-3614) *458*
Politechnika Gdanska. Zeszyty Naukowe. Elektryka (PL) *458*
Politechnika Gdanska. Zeszyty Naukowe. Fizyka (PL ISSN 0072-0364) *890*
Politechnika Gdanska. Zeszyty Naukowe. Matematyka (PL ISSN 0072-0372) *752*
Politechnika Gdanska. Zeszyty Naukowe. Mechanika (PL ISSN 0072-0380) *492*
Politechnika Krakowska. Zeszyty Naukowe. Architektura (PL ISSN 0137-1371) *99*
Politechnika Krakowska. Zeszyty Naukowe. Budownictwo Ladowe (PL ISSN 0454-4862) *483*

Politechnika Krakowska. Zeszyty Naukowe. Budownictwo Wodne i Inzynieria Sanitarna (PL ISSN 0137-1363) *1125*
Politechnika Krakowska. Zeszyty Naukowe. Chemia (PL ISSN 0075-7055) *324*
Politechnika Krakowska. Zeszyty Naukowe. Mechanika (PL ISSN 0372-9486) *895*
Politechnika Krakowska. Zeszyty Naukowe. Nauki Ekonomiczne (PL ISSN 0548-0442) *198*
Politechnika Krakowska. Zeszyty Naukowe. Podstawowe Nauki Techniczne (PL ISSN 0137-138X) *1070*
Politechnika Krakowska. Zeszyty Naukowe. Transport (PL ISSN 0860-0783) *1082*
Politechnika Lodzka. Zeszyty Naukowe. Budownictwo (PL ISSN 0076-0323) 186, *483*
Politechnika Lodzka. Zeszyty Naukowe. Chemia (PL ISSN 0458-1555) *324*
Politechnika Lodzka. Zeszyty Naukowe. Cieplne Maszyny Przeplywowe (PL ISSN 0137-2661) *492*
Politechnika Lodzka. Zeszyty Naukowe. Elektryka (PL ISSN 0459-682X) *458*
Politechnika Lodzka. Zeszyty Naukowe. Fizyka (PL ISSN 0137-2564) *890*
Politechnika Lodzka. Zeszyty Naukowe. Inzynieria Chemiczna (PL ISSN 0137-2602) *479*
Politechnika Lodzka. Zeszyty Naukowe. Matematyka (PL ISSN 0137-2572) *752*
Politechnika Lodzka. Zeszyty Naukowe. Mechanika (PL ISSN 0458-1563) *492*
Politechnika Lodzka. Zeszyty Naukowe. Organizacja i Zarzadzanie (PL ISSN 0137-2599) 198, *1010*
Politechnika Lodzka. Zeszyty Naukowe. Technologia I. Chemia Spozywcza (PL ISSN 0528-9254) *520*
Politechnika Lodzka. Zeszyty Naukowe. Wlokiennictwo (PL ISSN 0076-0331) *1074*
Politechnika Poznanska. Instytut Nauk Ekonomicznych i Spolecznych. Prace Naukowe *see* Politechnika Poznanska. Instytut Nauk Ekonomicznych i Spolecznych. Zeszyty Naukowe *291*
Politechnika Poznanska. Instytut Nauk Ekonomicznych i Spolecznych. Zeszyty Naukowe (PL ISSN 0239-9423) *291*
Politechnika Poznanska. Materialy Historyczno-Metodyczne. Studia Filozoficzne *see* Materialy Historyczno-Metodyczne *559*
Politechnika Poznanska. Zeszyty Naukowe. Bibliografia (PL ISSN 0551-651X) *130*
Politechnika Poznanska. Zeszyty Naukowe. Budownictwo *see* Politechnika Poznanska. Zeszyty Naukowe. Budownictwo Ladowe *483*
Politechnika Poznanska. Zeszyty Naukowe. Budownictwo Ladowe (PL) *483*
Politechnika Poznanska. Zeszyty Naukowe. Ekonomika i Organizacja Przemyslu *see* Politechnika Poznanska. Zeszyty Naukowe. Organizacja i Zarzadzanie *291*
Politechnika Poznanska. Zeszyty Naukowe. Elektryka (PL ISSN 0079-4503) *458*
Politechnika Poznanska. Zeszyty Naukowe. Geometria (PL ISSN 0239-488X) *752*
Politechnika Poznanska. Zeszyty Naukowe. Geometria Wykreslna *see* Politechnika Poznanska. Zeszyty Naukowe. Geometria *752*
Politechnika Poznanska. Zeszyty Naukowe. Maszyny Robocze i Pojazdy (PL ISSN 0137-6918) *51*
Politechnika Poznanska. Zeszyty Naukowe. Matematyka *see* Fasciculi Mathematici *748*

Politechnika Poznanska. Zeszyty Naukowe. Mechanika (PL ISSN 0079-4538) *895*
Politechnika Poznanska. Zeszyty Naukowe. Mechanizacja i Elektryfikacja Rolnictwa *see* Politechnika Poznanska. Zeszyty Naukowe. Maszyny Robocze i Pojazdy *51*
Politechnika Poznanska. Zeszyty Naukowe. Organizacja i Zarzadzanie (PL) *291*
Politechnika Slaska. Zeszyty Naukowe. Automatyka (PL ISSN 0434-0760) *355*
Politechnika Slaska. Zeszyty Naukowe. Budownictwo (PL ISSN 0434-0779) *483*
Politechnika Slaska. Zeszyty Naukowe. Chemia (PL ISSN 0372-9494) *324*
Politechnika Slaska. Zeszyty Naukowe. Elektryka (PL ISSN 0072-4688) *458*
Politechnika Slaska. Zeszyty Naukowe. Energetyka (PL ISSN 0372-9796) *466*
Politechnika Slaska. Zeszyty Naukowe. Gornictwo (PL ISSN 0372-9508) *819*
Politechnika Slaska. Zeszyty Naukowe. Hutnictwo (PL ISSN 0324-802X) *799*
Politechnika Slaska. Zeszyty Naukowe. Informatyka (PL ISSN 0208-7286) *361*
Politechnika Slaska. Zeszyty Naukowe. Inzynieria Sanitarna *see* Politechnika Slaska. Zeszyty Naukowe. Inzynieria Srodowiska *955*
Politechnika Slaska. Zeszyty Naukowe. Inzynieria Srodowiska (PL) *955*
Politechnika Slaska. Zeszyty Naukowe. Jezyki Obce (PL ISSN 0324-8038) *1160*
Politechnika Slaska. Zeszyty Naukowe. Matematyka-Fizyka (PL ISSN 0072-470X) 752, 890
Politechnika Slaska. Zeszyty Naukowe. Mechanika (PL ISSN 0434-0817) *492*
Politechnika Slaska. Zeszyty Naukowe. Nauki Spoleczne (PL ISSN 0072-4718) *1010*
Politechnika Slaska. Zeszyty Naukowe. Organizacja (PL ISSN 0324-8046) *291*
Politechnika Slaska. Zeszyty Naukowe. Transport (PL ISSN 0209-3324) *1083*
Politechnika Warszawska. Instytut Fizyki. Prace (PL) *890*
Politechnika Warszawska. Instytut Technologii i Organizacji Produkcji Budowlanej. Prace (PL) *186*
Politechnika Wroclawska. Biblioteka Glowna i Osrodek Informacji Naukowo-Technicznej. Prace Naukowe. Prace Bibliograficzne (PL) *10*
Politechnika Wroclawska. Biblioteka Glowna i Osrodek Informacji Naukowo-Technicznej. Prace Naukowe. Studia i Materialy (PL ISSN 0137-6225) *998*
Politechnika Wroclawska. Centrum Obliczeniowe. Prace Naukowe. Konferencje (PL ISSN 0860-1615) *353*
Politechnika Wroclawska. Centrum Obliczeniowe. Prace Naukowe. Studia i Materialy (PL ISSN 0860-1623) *353*
Politechnika Wroclawska. Instytut Architektury i Urbanistyki. Prace Naukowe. Konferencje (PL ISSN 0137-6233) 99, 108
Politechnika Wroclawska. Instytut Architektury i Urbanistyki. Prace Naukowe. Monografie (PL ISSN 0324-9905) 99, 108
Politechnika Wroclawska. Instytut Architektury i Urbanistyki. Prace Naukowe. Studia i Materialy (PL ISSN 0324-9891) 99, 108
Politechnika Wroclawska. Instytut Budownictwa. Prace Naukowe. Konferencje (PL ISSN 0324-9883) *186*

Politechnika Wroclawska. Instytut Budownictwa. Prace Naukowe. Monografie (PL ISSN 0324-9875) *186*
Politechnika Wroclawska. Instytut Budownictwa. Prace Naukowe. Studia i Materialy (PL ISSN 0137-6241) *186*
Politechnika Wroclawska. Instytut Chemii i Technologii Nafty i Wegla. Prace Naukowe. Konferencje (PL ISSN 0324-9867) *479*
Politechnika Wroclawska. Instytut Chemii i Technologii Nafty i Wegla. Prace Naukowe. Monografie (PL ISSN 0324-9859) *479*
Politechnika Wroclawska. Instytut Chemii i Technologii Nafty i Wegla. Prace Naukowe. Studia i Materialy (PL ISSN 0084-2818) *479*
Politechnika Wroclawska. Instytut Chemii Nieorganicznej i Metalurgii Pierwiastkow Rzadkich. Prace Naukowe. Konferencje (PL ISSN 0324-9832) *328*
Politechnika Wroclawska. Instytut Chemii Nieorganicznej i Metalurgii Pierwiastkow Rzadkich. Prace Naukowe. Monografie (PL ISSN 0324-9840) *328*
Politechnika Wroclawska. Instytut Chemii Nieorganicznej i Metalurgii Pierwiastkow Rzadkich. Prace Naukowe. Studia i Materialy (PL ISSN 0370-0755) *328*
Politechnika Wroclawska. Instytut Chemii Organicznej i Fizycznej. Prace Naukowe. Konferencje (PL ISSN 0324-9824) 330, 332
Politechnika Wroclawska. Instytut Chemii Organicznej i Fizycznej. Prace Naukowe. Monografie (PL ISSN 0324-9816) 330, 332
Politechnika Wroclawska. Instytut Chemii Organicznej i Fizycznej. Prace Naukowe. Studia i Materialy (PL ISSN 0370-081X) 330, 332
Politechnika Wroclawska. Instytut Cybernetyki Technicznej. Prace Naukowe. Konferencje (PL ISSN 0324-9794) *359*
Politechnika Wroclawska. Instytut Cybernetyki Technicznej. Prace Naukowe. Monografie (PL ISSN 0324-9786) *359*
Politechnika Wroclawska. Instytut Cybernetyki Technicznej. Prace Naukowe. Studia i Materialy (PL ISSN 0324-9808) *359*
Politechnika Wroclawska. Instytut Energoelektryki. Prace Naukowe. Konferencje (PL ISSN 0324-9778) *458*
Politechnika Wroclawska. Instytut Energoelektryki. Prace Naukowe. Monografie (PL ISSN 0324-976X) *458*
Politechnika Wroclawska. Instytut Energoelektryki. Prace Naukowe. Studia i Materialy (PL ISSN 0084-2826) *458*
Politechnika Wroclawska. Instytut Fizyki. Prace Naukowe. Konferencje (PL ISSN 0137-625X) *890*
Politechnika Wroclawska. Instytut Fizyki. Prace Naukowe. Monografie (PL ISSN 0370-0828) *890*
Politechnika Wroclawska. Instytut Fizyki. Prace Naukowe. Studia i Materialy (PL ISSN 0324-9697) *890*
Politechnika Wroclawska. Instytut Geotechniki. Prace Naukowe. Konferencje (PL ISSN 0370-0836) *380*
Politechnika Wroclawska. Instytut Geotechniki. Prace Naukowe. Monografie (PL ISSN 0084-2834) *380*
Politechnika Wroclawska. Instytut Geotechniki. Prace Naukowe. Studia i Materialy (PL ISSN 0084-2842) *380*
Politechnika Wroclawska. Instytut Gornictwa. Prace Naukowe. Konferencje (PL ISSN 0324-9670) *819*

Politechnika Wroclawska. Instytut Gornictwa. Prace Naukowe. Monografie (PL ISSN 0324-9689) *819*

Politechnika Wroclawska. Instytut Gornictwa. Prace Naukowe. Studia i Materialy (PL ISSN 0370-0798) *819*

Politechnika Wroclawska. Instytut Historii Architektury, Sztuki i Techniki. Prace Naukowe. Konferencje (PL ISSN 0860-1194) 99, *108*

Politechnika Wroclawska. Instytut Historii Architektury, Sztuki i Techniki. Prace Naukowe. Monografie (PL ISSN 0324-9662) 99, *109*

Politechnika Wroclawska. Instytut Historii Architektury, Sztuki i Techniki. Prace Naukowe. Studia i Materialy (PL ISSN 0324-9654) 99, *109*

Politechnika Wroclawska. Instytut Inzynierii Chemicznej i Urzadzen Cieplnych. Prace Naukowe. Konferencje (PL) *479*

Politechnika Wroclawska. Instytut Inzynierii Chemicznej i Urzadzen Cieplnych. Prace Naukowe. Monografie (PL ISSN 0084-2850) *479*

Politechnika Wroclawska. Instytut Inzynierii Chemicznej i Urzadzen Cieplnych. Prace Naukowe. Studia i Materialy (PL ISSN 0324-9751) 186, *479*

Politechnika Wroclawska. Instytut Inzynierii Ladowej. Prace Naukowe. Konferencje (PL ISSN 0324-9743) *483*

Politechnika Wroclawska. Instytut Inzynierii Ladowej. Prace Naukowe. Monografie (PL ISSN 0324-9727) *483*

Politechnika Wroclawska. Instytut Inzynierii Ladowej. Prace Naukowe. Studia i Materialy (PL ISSN 0370-0844) *483*

Politechnika Wroclawska. Instytut Inzynierii Ochrony Srodowiska. Prace Naukowe. Konferencje (PL ISSN 0324-9719) *474*

Politechnika Wroclawska. Instytut Inzynierii Ochrony Srodowiska. Prace Naukowe. Studia i Materialy (PL ISSN 0084-2877) *474*

Politechnika Wroclawska. Instytut Inzynierii Ochrony Srodowiska. Prace Naukowe. Monografie (PL ISSN 0084-2869) *955*

Politechnika Wroclawska. Instytut Konstrukcji i Eksploatacji Maszyn. Prace Naukowe. Konferencje (PL ISSN 0324-9646) *746*

Politechnika Wroclawska. Instytut Konstrukcji i Eksploatacji Maszyn. Prace Naukowe. Monografie (PL ISSN 0324-962X) *746*

Politechnika Wroclawska. Instytut Konstrukcji i Eksploatacji Maszyn. Prace Naukowe. Studia i Materialy (PL ISSN 0324-9638) *746*

Politechnika Wroclawska. Instytut Konstrukcji i Eksploatacji Maszyn. Prace Naukowe. Wspolpraca (PL ISSN 0239-3182) *746*

Politechnika Wroclawska. Instytut Matematyki. Prace Naukowe. Konferencje (PL ISSN 0137-6268) *752*

Politechnika Wroclawska. Instytut Matematyki. Prace Naukowe. Monografie (PL ISSN 0324-9603) *752*

Politechnika Wroclawska. Instytut Matematyki. Prace Naukowe. Studia i Materialy (PL ISSN 0324-9611) *752*, 890

Politechnika Wroclawska. Instytut Materialoznawstwa i Mechaniki Technicznej. Prace Naukowe. Konferencje (PL ISSN 0324-9573) *492*, 895

Politechnika Wroclawska. Instytut Materialoznawstwa i Mechaniki Technicznej. Prace Naukowe. Monografie (PL ISSN 0324-9565) *895*

Politechnika Wroclawska. Instytut Materialoznawstwa i Mechaniki Technicznej. Prace Naukowe. Studia i Materialy (PL ISSN 0370-0917) *895*

Politechnika Wroclawska. Instytut Metrologii Elektrycznej. Prace Naukowe. Konferencje (PL ISSN 0324-9557) *458*, 809

Politechnika Wroclawska. Instytut Metrologii Elektrycznej. Prace Naukowe. Monografie (PL ISSN 0324-9549) *458*, 809

Politechnika Wroclawska. Instytut Metrologii Elektrycznej. Prace Naukowe. Studia i Materialy (PL ISSN 0084-2958) *458*, 809

Politechnika Wroclawska. Instytut Nauk Ekonomiczno-Spolecznych. Prace Naukowe. Konferencje (PL ISSN 0860-3200) *1010*

Politechnika Wroclawska. Instytut Nauk Ekonomiczno-Spolecznych. Prace Naukowe. Monografie (PL ISSN 0239-3204) *1010*

Politechnika Wroclawska. Instytut Nauk Ekonomiczno-Spolecznych. Prace Naukowe. Studia i Materialy (PL ISSN 0239-3212) *1010*

Politechnika Wroclawska. Instytut Nauk Spolecznych. Prace Naukowe. Monografie see Politechnika Wroclawska. Instytut Nauk Ekonomiczno-Spolecznych. Prace Naukowe. Monografie *1010*

Politechnika Wroclawska. Instytut Nauk Spolecznych. Prace Naukowe. Studia i Materialy see Politechnika Wroclawska. Instytut Nauk Ekonomiczno-Spolecznych. Prace Naukowe. Studia i Materialy *1010*

Politechnika Wroclawska. Instytut Organizacji i Zarzadzania. Prace Naukowe. Konferencje (PL ISSN 0324-9484) *281*

Politechnika Wroclawska. Instytut Organizacji i Zarzadzania. Prace Naukowe. Monografie. (PL ISSN 0324-9492) *281*

Politechnika Wroclawska. Instytut Organizacji i Zarzadzania. Prace Naukowe. Studia i Materialy (PL ISSN 0324-9468) *281*

Politechnika Wroclawska. Instytut Podstaw Elektrotechniki i Elektrotechnologii. Prace Naukowe. Konferencje (PL ISSN 0324-9441) *458*

Politechnika Wroclawska. Instytut Podstaw Elektrotechniki i Elektrotechnologii. Prace Naukowe. Monografie (PL ISSN 0324-945X) *458*

Politechnika Wroclawska. Instytut Podstaw Elektrotechniki i Elektrotechnologii. Prace Naukowe. Studia i Materialy (PL ISSN 0370-0852) *458*

Politechnika Wroclawska. Instytut Podstaw Elektrotechniki i Elektrotechnologii. Prace Naukowe. Wspolpraca (PL) *458*

Politechnika Wroclawska. Instytut Sterowania i Techniki Systemow. Prace Naukowe. Konferencje (PL ISSN 0239-3433) *474*

Politechnika Wroclawska. Instytut Sterowania i Techniki Systemow. Prace Naukowe. Monografie (PL ISSN 0209-2573) *474*

Politechnika Wroclawska. Instytut Techniki Cieplnej i Mechaniki Plynow. Prace Naukowe. Konferencje(PL ISSN 0324-9395) *895*

Politechnika Wroclawska. Instytut Techniki Cieplnej i Mechaniki Plynow. Prace Naukowe. Monografie(PL ISSN 0324-9387) *895*

Politechnika Wroclawska. Instytut Techniki Cieplnej i Mechaniki Plynow. Prace Naukowe. Studia i Materialy (PL ISSN 0324-9409) *895*

Politechnika Wroclawska. Instytut Technologii Budowy Maszyn. Prace Naukowe. Konferencje (PL ISSN 0324-9379) *492*

Politechnika Wroclawska. Instytut Technologii Budowy Maszyn. Prace Naukowe. Monografie (PL ISSN 0324-9352) *492*

Politechnika Wroclawska. Instytut Technologii Budowy Maszyn. Prace Naukowe. Studia i Materialy (PL ISSN 0324-9360) *492*

Politechnika Wroclawska. Instytut Technologii Elektronowej. Prace Naukowe. Konferencje (PL ISSN 0370-0887) *458*

Politechnika Wroclawska. Instytut Technologii Elektronowej. Prace Naukowe. Monografie (PL ISSN 0084-280X) *458*

Politechnika Wroclawska. Instytut Technologii Elektronowej. Prace Naukowe. Studia i Materialy (PL ISSN 0084-2885) *458*

Politechnika Wroclawska. Instytut Technologii Nieorganicznej i Nawozow Mineralnych. Prace Naukowe. Konferencje (PL ISSN 0084-2893) *479*

Politechnika Wroclawska. Instytut Technologii Nieorganicznej i Nawozow Mineralnych. Prace Naukowe. Monografie (PL ISSN 0084-2907) *479*

Politechnika Wroclawska. Instytut Technologii Nieorganicznej i Nawozow Mineralnych. Prace Naukowe. Studia i Materialy (PL ISSN 0084-2915) *479*

Politechnika Wroclawska. Instytut Technologii Organicznej i Tworzyw Sztucznych. Prace Naukowe. Konferencje (PL ISSN 0137-1398) *479*

Politechnika Wroclawska. Instytut Technologii Organicznej i Tworzyw Sztucznych. Prace Naukowe. Monografie (PL) *479*

Politechnika Wroclawska. Instytut Technologiii Organicznej i Tworzyw Sztucznych. Prace Naukowe. Studia i Materialy (PL ISSN 0370-0879) *901*

Politechnika Wroclawska. Instytut Telekomunikacji i Akustyki. Prace Naukowe. Konferencje (PL ISSN 0324-9344) 350, *458*

Politechnika Wroclawska. Instytut Telekomunikacji i Akustyki. Prace Naukowe. Monografie (PL ISSN 0324-9328) 350, *458*

Politechnika Wroclawska. Instytut Telekomunikacji i Akustyki. Prace Naukowe. Studia i Materialy (PL ISSN 0324-9336) 350, *458*

Politechnika Wroclawska. Instytut Ukladow Elektromaszynowych. Prace Naukowe. Konferencje (PL ISSN 0324-931X) *458*

Politechnika Wroclawska. Instytut Ukladow Elektromaszynowych. Prace Naukowe. Monografie (PL ISSN 0137-6284) *459*

Politechnika Wroclawska. Instytut Ukladow Elektromaszynowych. Prace Naukowe. Studia i Materialy (PL ISSN 0084-294X) *459*

Politechnika Wroclawska. Osrodek Badan Prognostycznych. Prace Naukowe. Konferencje (PL ISSN 0137-6306) *198*

Politechnika Wroclawska. Osrodek Badan Prognostycznych. Prace Naukowe. Monografie (PL ISSN 0137-6314) *248*

Politechnika Wroclawska. Osrodek Badan Prognostycznych. Prace Naukowe. Studia i Materialy (PL ISSN 0137-6322) *248*

Politechnika Wroclawska. Osrodek Badan Prognostycznych. Prace Naukowe. Wspolpraca/ Sotrudnichestvo (PL ISSN 0137-6330) *248*

Politechnika Wroclawska. Studium Praktycznej Nauki Jezykow Obcych. Prace Naukowe. Monografie (PL ISSN 0208-8371) *701*

Politechnika Wroclawska. Studium Praktycznej Nauki Jezykow Obcych. Prace Naukowe. Studia i Materialy (PL ISSN 0137-6349) *701*

Politecnica (EC ISSN 0032-3055) *474*, 998

Politeia (VE) *908*

Politeia (SI ISSN 0217-7587) *908*

Politekhnichnyi Instytut Kiev. Vestnik. Seriya Mashinostroeniya (UR ISSN 0372-6053) *746*

Politica (UY ISSN 0079-3027) *908*

Politica e Estrategia (BL) *917*, 1028

Political Anthropology (US ISSN 0732-1228) *908*, 1028

Political Climate for International Business (US ISSN 0887-7637) *231*, 259, 267, 281

Political Documents of the German Democratic Republic (GE) *908*

Political Economy and Public Policy (US) *252*

Political Economy of World-Systems Annuals (US) *252*, 908

Political Handbook and Atlas of the World see Political Handbook of the World *908*

Political Handbook of the World (US) 547, *908*

Political Parties of the World (UK) *908*

Political Portraits (UK) *135*

Political Power and Social Theory (US ISSN 0198-8719) *908*, 1028

Political Risk Yearbook (US ISSN 0889-2725) *231*, 259, 267, 281

Political Science Abstracts (US) *908*, *912*

Political Science Discussion Papers (US ISSN 0190-521X) *908*

Political Science Reviewer (US ISSN 0091-3715) *908*

Political Science Utilization Directory (US ISSN 0362-4765) *945*

Politics and Power (UK ISSN 0144-0918) *908*

Politics in America (US) *908*

Politics of Liberation Series (US) *593*, 812, 918

Politiets Aarsberetning (DK ISSN 0108-3376) *372*

Politihistorisk Selskab. Aarsskrift (DK ISSN 0107-3893) *372*

Politique Sociale au Canada see Issues in Canadian Social Policy *1018*

Politische Bildung (AU) *449*, 908

Polk's World Bank Directory. International Edition (US ISSN 0085-4999) *231*

Pollen Science (JA ISSN 0386-6688) *59*, 160

Pollichia. Mitteilungen (GW ISSN 0341-9665) *145*, *380*

Polling (US) *765*, 1020

Pollution Control Review see Pollution Technology Review *955*

Pollution Technology Review (US ISSN 0090-516X) *955*

Polonia Library see Biblioteka Polonijna *902*

Polonia Typographica Saeculi Sedecimi (PL ISSN 0079-3132) *109*, 931

Polonica (PL ISSN 0137-9712) *701*

Polska Akademia Nauk. Biblioteka, Krakow. Rocznik (PL ISSN 0079-3140) *683*

Polska Akademia Nauk. Centrum Badan Naukowych w Wojewodztwie Katowikim. Prace i Studia see Polska Akademia Nauk. Instytut Podstaw Inzynierii Srodowiska. Prace i Studia *498*

Polska Akademia Nauk. Centrum Obliczeniowe. Prace see Polish Academy of Sciences. Institute of Computer Science. Reports *353*

Polska Akademia Nauk. Instytut Geofizyki. Materialy i Prace see Polish Academy of Sciences. Institute of Geophysics. Series A. Physics of the Earth's Interior *400*

Polska Akademia Nauk. Instytut Geofizyki. Materialy i Prace see Polish Academy of Sciences. Institute of Geophysics. Series B. Seismology *400*

Polska Akademia Nauk. Instytut Geofizyki. Materialy i Prace see Polish Academy of Sciences. Institute of Geophysics. Series C. Geomagnetism *400*

Polska Akademia Nauk. Instytut Geofizyki. Materialy i Prace *see* Polish Academy of Sciences. Institute of Geophysics. Series D. Physics of the Atmosphere 400
Polska Akademia Nauk. Instytut Geofizyki. Materialy i Prace *see* Polish Academy of Sciences. Institute of Geophysics. Series F. Planetary Geodesy 400
Polska Akademia Nauk. Instytut Geofizyki. Materialy i Prace *see* Polish Academy of Sciences. Institute of Geophysics. Series G. Numerical Methods in Geophysics 400
Polska Akademia Nauk. Instytut Geofizyki. Materialy i Prace *see* Polish Academy of Sciences. Institute of Geophysics. Series M. Miscellanea 401
Polska Akademia Nauk. Instytut Geografii i Przestrzennego Zagospodarowania. Prace Geograficzne (PL ISSN 0373-6547) 547
Polska Akademia Nauk. Instytut Geografii. Prace Geograficzne *see* Polska Akademia Nauk. Instytut Geografii i Przestrzennego Zagospodarowania. Prace Geograficzne 547
Polska Akademia Nauk. Instytut Maszyn Przeplywowych. Prace/ Polish Academy of Sciences. Institute of Fluid-Flow Machinery. Transactions (PL ISSN 0079-3205) 492
Polska Akademia Nauk. Instytut Podstaw Inzynierii Srodowiska. Prace i Studia (PL ISSN 0208-4112) 474, 498
Polska Akademia Nauk. Instytut Sztuki. Series A: Works by Polish Composers (PL) 840
Polska Akademia Nauk. Instytut Sztuki. Series B: Fontes Artis Musicae (PL) 840
Polska Akademia Nauk. Instytut Sztuki. Series C: Tractatus de Musica (PL) 840
Polska Akademia Nauk. Instytut Sztuki. Series D: Bibliotheca Antiqua (PL) 840
Polska Akademia Nauk. Komisja Metalurgiiodlewnina. Metalurgia *see* Polska Akademia Nauk. Oddzial w Krakowie. Komisja Metalurgiczno-Odlewnicza. Prace: Metalurgia 799
Polska Akademia Nauk. Komisja Nauk Technicznych. Prace *see* Polska Akademia Nauk. Oddzial w Krakowie. Komisja Mechaniki Stosowanej. Prace: Mechanika 895
Polska Akademia Nauk. Komitet Gospodarki Wodnej. Prace i Studia (PL ISSN 0079-3477) 955
Polska Akademia Nauk. Komitet Przestrzennego Zagospodarowania Kraju. Biuletyn (PL ISSN 0079-3493) 625
Polska Akademia Nauk. Komitet Przestrzennego Zagospodarowania Kraju. Studia (PL ISSN 0079-3507) 625
Polska Akademia Nauk. Oddzial w Krakowie. Komisja Archeologiczna. Prace (PL ISSN 0079-3256) 91
Polska Akademia Nauk. Oddzial w Krakowie. Komisja Ceramiczna. Prace: Ceramika (PL ISSN 0079-3264) 320
Polska Akademia Nauk. Oddzial w Krakowie. Komisja Filologii Klasycznej. Prace (PL ISSN 0079-3272) 701
Polska Akademia Nauk. Oddzial w Krakowie. Komisja Gorniczo-Geodezyjna. Prace: Geodezja (PL ISSN 0079-3299) 547
Polska Akademia Nauk. Oddzial w Krakowie. Komisja Gorniczo-Geodezyjna. Prace: Gornictwo (PL ISSN 0079-3280) 819
Polska Akademia Nauk. Oddzial w Krakowie. Komisja Historycznoliteracka. Prace (PL ISSN 0554-579X) 730

Polska Akademia Nauk. Oddzial w Krakowie. Komisja Historycznoliteracka. Rocznik (PL ISSN 0079-337X) 559, 730
Polska Akademia Nauk. Oddzial w Krakowie. Komisja Jezykoznawstwa. Prace (PL ISSN 0079-3310) 701
Polska Akademia Nauk. Oddzial w Krakowie. Komisja Jezykoznawstwa. Wydawnictwa Zrodlowe (PL ISSN 0079-3329) 701
Polska Akademia Nauk. Oddzial w Krakowie. Komisja Mechaniki Stosowanej. Prace: Mechanika (PL ISSN 0079-3337) 895
Polska Akademia Nauk. Oddzial w Krakowie. Komisja Metalurgiczno-Odlewnicza. Prace: Metalurgia (PL ISSN 0079-3345) 799
Polska Akademia Nauk. Oddzial w Krakowie. Komisja Nauk Ekonomicznych. Prace (PL ISSN 0079-3353) 198
Polska Akademia Nauk. Oddzial w Krakowie. Komisja Nauk Historycznych. Prace (PL ISSN 0079-3388) 593
Polska Akademia Nauk. Oddzial w Krakowie. Komisja Nauk Historycznych. Materialy (PL) 560
Polska Akademia Nauk. Oddzial w Krakowie. Komisja Nauk Mineralogicznych. Prace Mineralogiczne (PL ISSN 0079-3396) 393
Polska Akademia Nauk. Oddzial w Krakowie. Komisja Nauk Pedagogicznych. Rocznik (PL ISSN 0079-3418) 418
Polska Akademia Nauk. Oddzial w Krakowie. Komisja Nauk Pedagogicznych. Prace (PL ISSN 0079-340X) 418
Polska Akademia Nauk. Oddzial w Krakowie. Komisja Orientalistyczna. Prace (PL ISSN 0079-3426) 853
Polska Akademia Nauk. Oddzial w Krakowie. Komisja Slowianoznawstwa. Prace (PL ISSN 0079-3434) 730
Polska Akademia Nauk. Oddzial w Krakowie. Komisja Socjologiczna. Prace (PL ISSN 0079-3442) 1028
Polska Akademia Nauk. Oddzial w Krakowie. Komisja Urbanistyki i Architektury. Teka (PL ISSN 0079-3450) 99, 625
Polska Akademia Nauk. Oddzial w Krakowie. Osrodek Dokumentacji Fizjograficznej. Studia (PL ISSN 0137-2939) 547
Polska Akademia Nauk. Oddzial w Krakowie. Rocznik (PL ISSN 0079-3531) 631
Polska Akademia Nauk. Wydzial Nauk Medycznych. Rozprawy (PL ISSN 0079-3558) 765
Polska Bibliografia Analityczna Mechaniki/Polish Scientific Abstracts on Mechanics (PL ISSN 0032-3713) 10, 746
Polska Bibliografia Literacka (PL ISSN 0079-3590) 739
Polska Klasa Robotnicza. Studia Historyczne (PL ISSN 0137-5288) 593
Polska Piesn i Muzyka Ludowa. Zrodla i Materialy (PL ISSN 0079-3612) 840
Polska 2000 (PL ISSN 0079-3620) 593, 1028
Polski Klub Ekologiczney Okregu Malopolska. Prace Naukowe (PL ISSN 0860-4045) 145
Polskie Archiwum Weterynaryjne/ Archiwum Veterinarium Polonicum (PL ISSN 0079-3647) 1122
Polskie Towarzystwo Botaniczne. Sekcja Dendrologiczna. Rocznik (PL ISSN 0080-357X) 160
Polskie Towarzystwo Cybernetyczne. Biuletyn *see* Postepy Cybernetyki 359
Polskie Towarzystwo Jezykoznawcze. Biuletyn (PL ISSN 0032-3802) 701
Polskie Towarzystwo Matematyczne. Roczniki. Seria II. Wiadomosci Matematyczne (PL ISSN 0079-3698) 752

Polskie Towarzystwo Matematyczne. Roczniki. Seria 1: Commentationes Mathematicae. Prace Matematyczne (PL ISSN 0373-8299) 752
Polskie Towarzystwo Matematyczne. Roczniki. Seria 3: Matematyka Stosowana *see* Annales Societatis Mathematicae Polonae. Seria 3: Matematyka Stosowana 747
Polskie Towarzystwo Naukowe na Obczyznie. Rocznik (UK ISSN 0079-371X) 631, 998
Polutehniline Instituut Tallinn. Avtomatizatsiya Tekhnologicheskogo Proyektirovaniya Protsessov Mekhanicheskoi Obrabotki. (UR ISSN 0136-3549) 492
Polutehniline Instituut Tallinn. Avtomatizirovannye MHD-i Lineinye Elektroprivody i ikh Elementy (UR) 459
Polutehniline Instituut Tallinn. Fizicheskaya Khimiya Soedinenii A2B6 i A4B6 (UR) 332
Polutehniline Instituut Tallinn. Inzhenernaya Enzimologiya (UR) 479
Polutehniline Instituut Tallinn. Issledovanie Dvumernogo Vozmushchennogo Polya Napryazheniya (UR ISSN 0320-3352) 492
Polutehniline Instituut Tallinn. Issledovanie Elektromagnitnykh i Elektromashinnykh Ustroistv Upravleniya i Kontrolya Spetsial'nogo Naznacheniya (UR ISSN 0320-3336) 459
Polutehniline Instituut Tallinn. Issledovanie Raboty Parogeneratorov Elektrostantsii (UR) 459
Polutehniline Instituut Tallinn. Issledovaniya po Prikladnoi Kvantovoi Elektronike (UR) 349
Polutehniline Instituut Tallinn. Izuchenie Effektivnosti Proizvodstva (UR) 291
Polutehniline Instituut Tallinn. Metody Obrabotki i Registratsii Signalov (UR) 359
Polutehniline Instituut Tallinn. Metody Stokhasticheskogo Upravleniya Rezhimami Energeticheskih Sistem (UR) 466
Polutehniline Instituut Tallinn. Metody Upravleniya Rezhimami Energeticheskih Sistem *see* Polutehniline Instituut Tallinn. Metody Stokhasticheskogo Upravleniya Rezhimami Energeticheskih Sistem 466
Polutehniline Instituut Tallinn. Narodonaselenie i Rabochaya Sila (UR ISSN 0203-9699) 923
Polutehniline Instituut Tallinn. Neorganicheskaya Khimiya i Tekhnologiya (UR ISSN 0320-3379) 328
Polutehniline Instituut Tallinn. Neustanovivsheesya Dvizheniya Zhidkosti v Trubakh (UR ISSN 0203-9702) 955
Polutehniline Instituut Tallinn. Optimal'nye Sistemy i Algoritmy (UR ISSN 0203-9745) 483
Polutehniline Instituut Tallinn. Poluchenie i Svoistva Immobilizovannykh Fermentov *see* Polutehniline Instituut Tallinn. Inzhenernaya Enzimologiya 479
Polutehniline Instituut Tallinn. Postroenie Translyatorov, Obrabotka Dannykh, Voprosy Programmirovaniya (UR) 358
Polutehniline Instituut Tallinn. Problemy Ekonomiki Mashinostroeniya i Metalloobrabotki Estonskoi S.S.R. (UR) 291
Polutehniline Instituut Tallinn. Problemy Podzemnoi i Otkrytoi Razrabotki Goryuchikh Slantsev i Nerudnykh Materialov (UR ISSN 0203-9737) 93
Polutehniline Instituut Tallinn. Problemy Raboty Kotelnykh Ustanovok Teplovykh Elektrostantsii (UR) 554

Polutehniline Instituut Tallinn. Problemy Raboty Kotelnykh Ustanovok *see* Polutehniline Instituut Tallinn. Problemy Raboty Kotelnykh Ustanovok Teplovykh Elektrostantsii 554
Polutehniline Instituut Tallinn. Raschet Elektromagnitnykh i Teplovykh Rezhimov Magnitogidrodinamicheskikh i Lineinykh Elektrodvigatelei (UR) 466
Polutehniline Instituut Tallinn. Raschet i Proektirovanie Priborov, Ustroistv i Sistem Tekhnicheskoi Kibernetiki (UR ISSN 0134-3823) 359
Polutehniline Instituut Tallinn. Sintez i Primenenie Polikondensatsionnykh Kleev (UR ISSN 0320-3468) 479
Polutehniline Instituut Tallinn. Sovershenstvovanie Metodiki Ucheta i Ekonomicheskogo Analiza v Promyshlennosti (UR) 291
Polutehniline Instituut Tallinn. Svoistva i Tekhnologiya Izgotovleniya Iznosostoikikh Materialov (UR ISSN 0136-3557) 800
Polutehniline Instituut Tallinn. Svoistva Rastvorov Kislorodosoderzhashchikh Organicheskikh Soedinenii (UR) 330
Polutehniline Instituut Tallinn. Teoreticheskoe i Eksperimental'noe Issledovanie Avtomobil'nykh Dorog i Avtomobil'nogo Transporta Estonskoi S.S.R. v Usloviyakh Intensivnoi Avtomobilizatsii (UR ISSN 0320-3433) 1092
Polutehniline Instituut Tallinn. Teoriya i Raschet Tonkostennykh i Prostranstvennykh Konstruktsii (UR ISSN 0203-7343) 186
Polutehniline Instituut Tallinn. Teoriya i Tekhnologiya Polucheniya Stroitel'nykh Materialov iz Zol Tverdykh Topliv (UR ISSN 0203-9710) 479
Polutehniline Instituut Tallinn. Trenie i Iznos v Mashinakh (UR ISSN 0320-3344) 492
Polutehniline Instituut Tallinn. Voprosy Povysheniya Kachestva Pishchevykh Produktov (UR ISSN 0203-9788) 520
Polybios-Lexicon (GE) 701
Polymer Journal *see* Plastichem 479
Polymer Monographs (US ISSN 0275-5777) 330
Polymer Physics (US) 890
Polymer Science Library (NE) 324
Polymers Paint and Colour Year Book (UK ISSN 0078-7817) 109, 856
Polymers-Properties and Applications (US ISSN 0171-709X) 901
Polymerteknisk Orientering (DK) 1160
Polytekniske Laereanstalt, Danmarks Tekniske Hoejskole. Laboratoriet for Elektronik. Beretning (DK) 459
Pomorania Antiqua (PL ISSN 0556-0691) 593
Pomoranisches Woerterbuch (GE) 701
Pomorskie Monografie Toponomastyczne (PL ISSN 0208-4082) 547
Pomoshtni Istoricheski Distsiplini (BU) 593
Pondicherry Industrial Promotion, Development and Investment Corporation. Annual Reports and Accounts (II) 240, 267
Pontifical Institute of Mediaeval Studies. Studies and Texts (CN ISSN 0082-5328) 593
Pontificia Universidad Catolica. Revista(PE) 1010
Pontificia Universidad Catolica. Taller de Estudios Urbano Industriales. Serie: Estudios Sindicales (PE) 649
Pontificia Universidad Catolica del Chile. Instituto de Estudios Urbanos. Documentos de Trabajo (CL) 625
Pontificia Universidad Catolica del Ecuador. Instituto de Investigaciones Economicas. Documentos (EC) 248
Pontificia Universidad Catolica del Ecuador. Revista (EC) 342
Pontificia Universidad Catolica del Peru. Anthropologica *see* Anthropologica (Lima) 69

Pontificia Universidad Catolica del Peru. Departamento de Ciencias Sociales. Serie: Ediciones Previas (PE) *1010*
Pontificia Universidad Catolica del Peru. Derecho see Derecho *654*
Pontificia Universita Gregoriana. Documenta Missionalia (VC) *983*
Pontificia Universita Gregoriana. Istituto di Scienze Sociali Studia Socialia. (VC ISSN 0080-3960) *1011*
Pontificia Universita Gregoriana. Miscellanea Historiae Pontificiae (VC ISSN 0080-3979) *983*
Pontificia Universita Gregoriana. Studia Missionalia (VC ISSN 0080-3987) *983*
Pontifico Museo Missionario Etnologico. Annali (VC) *75*
Pontine Dossier (US) *14, 730*
Pony Baseball. Blue Book (US) *1040*
Pony Club Annual (UK) *1043*
Pony Magazine Annual (UK) *1043*
Pool & Spa News Directory (US) *315*
Pool News Directory see Pool & Spa News Directory *315*
Poole - Commercial Users Handbook 1983/4 see Poole Handbook *1102*
Poole Handbook (UK) *315, 1102*
Poompuhar Shipping Corporation. Annual Report (II) *1102*
Poor's Register of Corporations, Directors and Executives (US ISSN 0079-3825) *281, 291*
Populacni Zpravy (CS) *923*
Populaire Literatuur (NE) *730*
Popular Culture Association. Newsletter and Popular Culture Methods (US) *1028*
Popular Culture Association Newsletter see Popular Culture Association. Newsletter and Popular Culture Methods *1028*
Popular Culture Bio-Bibliographies (US) *608*
Popular Essays from the Late Republic (NE) *730*
Popular Magazine Review (US ISSN 0740-3763) *11*
Popular Mechanics Do-It-Yourself Yearbook (US ISSN 0360-2273) *1070*
Popular Periodical Index (US ISSN 0092-9727) *11*
Popular Science Series see Illinois. State Museum. Popular Science Series *992*
Population (US) *923*
Population and Family in the Low Countries (NE ISSN 0169-1422) *923*
Population and Family Planning Programs (US ISSN 0161-0902) *179, 923, 929*
Population Bulletin of the United Nations (UN ISSN 0251-7604) *924*
Population Census of Papua New Guinea. Population Characteristics Bulletin Series (PP ISSN 0079-3868) *924*
Population Council Annual Report (US ISSN 0361-7858) *924*
Population Estimates of Arizona see Demographic Guide to Arizona (Year) *921*
Population Growth of Iran (IR) *924, 929, 1061*
Population in Tochigi Prefecture see Tochigi-Ken No Jinko *924*
Population Index (US ISSN 0032-4701) *11, 929*
Population Mobility in Hawaii see Population Reports *929*
Population Newsletter (TH) *924*
Population of the Municipalities of the Netherlands (NE ISSN 0168-3853) *924, 929*
Population Reports (US ISSN 0145-9643) *924, 929*
Population Research Center Papers (US ISSN 0191-913X) *924*
Population Research Laboratory. Discussion Paper Series (CN ISSN 0317-2473) *924*
Population Research Laboratory. Population Reprint Series (CN ISSN 0317-3100) *924*
Population Studies (UN ISSN 0082-805X) *924*

Population Trends and Public Policy (US ISSN 0736-7716) *924, 945*
Poreditsa Balkani (BU ISSN 0554-7040) *593*
Pork Roundup (US) *67*
Port (Year) see Barcelona Port *1099*
Port and Harbour Research Institute. Guide/Kowan Gijutsu Kenkyusho. Guide (JA) *483, 1103*
Port and Harbour Technical Research Institute. Guide see Port and Harbour Research Institute. Guide *1103*
Port Authority of New York and New Jersey. Aviation Annual Report (US) *1089*
Port Authority of New York and New Jersey. Aviation Department. Airport Statistics (US) *1089*
Port Bustamante Handbook (JM) *1103*
Port Kelang Shipping Handbook (UK ISSN 0266-3856) *315, 1103*
Port of Baltimore Handbook see Port of Baltimore Magazine *1103*
Port of Baltimore Magazine (US) *1103*
Port of Bristol. Handbook see Port of Bristol Authority *1103*
Port of Bristol Authority (UK) *1103*
Port of Kingston Handbook see Port Bustamante Handbook *1103*
Port of New Orleans Annual Directory (US ISSN 0085-5030) *1083*
Port of Osaka/Osakako (JA) *1103*
Port of Piraeus Authority. Annual Report (GR) *1103*
Port of Seattle. Annual Report (US) *259, 1103*
Port of Tokyo (JA) *1103*
Port of Yokohama. Annual Report (JA) *1103*
Port of Yokohama. Annual Statistics. (JA) *1086*
Port of Yokohama. Monthly Statistics. see Port of Yokohama. Annual Statistics *1086*
Port of Yokohama. Plans for Future (JA) *1103*
Port Rashid: Dubai Shipping Handbook(UK ISSN 0266-3848) *315, 1103*
Port Transport Statistics of India see Basic Port Statistics of India *1099*
Porta Linguarum Orientalium (GW ISSN 0554-7342) *701, 853*
Portefeuille (ZR) *248*
Portfolio of Sales and Marketing Plans (US) *285*
Portico (IT) *730*
Porticus (US ISSN 8755-2035) *830*
Portland and the Pacific Northwest (US) *1115*
Portland Review of the Arts (US) *743*
Portland Souvenir Magazine (UK) *1115*
Ports O'Call (US ISSN 0032-5015) *350, 560*
Ports of South Africa (SA) *1103*
Portugal. Comissao da Condicao Feminina. Coleccao Informar as Mulheres (PO) *1129*
Portugal. Comissao da Condicao Feminina. Noticias (PO) *1129*
Portugal. Estatisticas da Energia: Continente, Acores e Madeira (PO ISSN 0377-2233) *466*
Portugal. Estatisticas Industriais: Continente, Acores e Madeira. Volume 1: Industrias Extractivas, Electricidade, Gas, Agua/Portugal. Statistiques Industrielles: Continent, Acores et Madere. Volume 1: Industries Extractives, Electricite, Gaz, Eau. (PO ISSN 0377-2314) *216*
Portugal. Estatisticas Industriais: Continente, Acores e Madeira. Volume 2: Industrias Transformadoras/Portugal. Statistiques Industrielles: Continent, Acores et Madere. Volume 2: Industries Manufacturieres (PO ISSN 0079-418X) *216*
Portugal. Instituto Nacional de Estatistica. Anuario Estatistico see Portugal. Instituto Nacional de Estatistica. Anuario Estatistico. Continente, Acores e Madeira *1061*

Portugal. Instituto Nacional de Estatistica. Anuario Estatistico. Continente, Acores e Madeira (PO) *1061*
Portugal. Instituto Nacional de Estatistica. Centro de Estudos Demograficos. Caderno (PO ISSN 0379-7007) *924, 929*
Portugal. Instituto Nacional de Estatistica. Centro de Estudos Demograficos. Revista (PO ISSN 0079-4082) *924, 929*
Portugal. Instituto Nacional de Estatistica. Estatisticas Agricolas. Continente, Acores e Madeira (PO ISSN 0079-4139) *42*
Portugal. Instituto Nacional de Estatistica. Estatisticas Agricolas see Portugal. Instituto Nacional de Estatistica. Estatisticas Agricolas. Continente, Acores e Madeira *42*
Portugal. Instituto Nacional de Estatistica. Estatisticas da Pesca/ Statistiques de la Peche see Portugal. Instituto Nacional de Estatistica. Estatisticas da Pesca/Statistiques de la Peche. Continente, Acores e Madeira *512*
Portugal. Instituto Nacional de Estatistica. Estatisticas da Pesca/ Statistiques de la Peche. Continente, Acores e Madeira (PO) *512*
Portugal. Instituto Nacional de Estatistica. Estatisticas das Contribucoes e Impostos see Portugal. Instituto Nacional de Estatistica. Estatisticas das Contribuicoes e Impostos. Continente, Acores e Madeira *216*
Portugal. Instituto Nacional de Estatistica. Estatisticas das Contribuicoes e Impostos. Continente, Acores e Madeira (PO) *216*
Portugal. Instituto Nacional de Estatistica. Estatisticas das Financas Publicas see Portugal. Instituto Nacional de Estatistica. Estatisticas das Financas Publicas. Continente, Acores e Madeira *216*
Portugal. Instituto Nacional de Estatistica. Estatisticas das Financas Publicas. Continente, Acores e Madeira (PO) *216*
Portugal. Instituto Nacional de Estatistica. Estatisticas das Organizacoes Sindicais see Portugal. Instituto Nacional de Estatistica. Estatisticas de Seguranca Social, Associacoes Sindicais e Patronais. Continente, Acores e Madeira *1028*
Portugal. Instituto Nacional de Estatistica. Estatisticas de Educacao. Continente, Acores e Madeira (PO) *418*
Portugal. Instituto Nacional de Estatistica. Estatisticas de Educacao see Portugal. Instituto Nacional de Estatistica. Estatisticas de Educacao. Continente, Acores e Madeira *418*
Portugal. Instituto Nacional de Estatistica. Estatisticas de Seguranca Social, Associacoes Sindicais e Patronais. Continente, Acores e Madeira (PO ISSN 0870-6506) *1028*
Portugal. Instituto Nacional de Estatistica. Estatisticas Demograficas. Continente, Acores e Madeira (PO) *924, 929*
Portugal. Instituto Nacional de Estatistica. Estatisticas Demograficas Continente e Ilhas Adjacentes see Portugal. Instituto Nacional de Estatistica. Estatisticas Demograficas. Continente, Acores e Madeira *929*
Portugal. Instituto Nacional de Estatistica. Estatisticas do Comercio Externo see Portugal. Instituto Nacional de Estatistica. Estatisticas do Comercio Externo. Continente, Acores e Madeira *216*
Portugal. Instituto Nacional de Estatistica. Estatisticas do Comercio Externo. Continente, Acores e Madeira (PO) *216*

Portugal. Instituto Nacional de Estatistica. Estatisticas do Turismo. Continente, Acores e Madeira (PO ISSN 0377-2306) *1120*
Portugal. Instituto Nacional de Estatistica. Estatisticas do Turismo see Portugal. Instituto Nacional de Estatistica. Estatisticas do Turismo. Continente, Acores e Madeira *1120*
Portugal. Instituto Nacional de Estatistica. Serie Estatisticas Regionais (PO ISSN 0378-3227) *1061*
Portugal. Instituto Nacional de Estatistica. Servicos Centrais. Estatisticas das Sociedades: Continente, Acores e Madeira (PO) *216, 1061*
Portugal. Instituto Nacional de Estatistica. Servicos Centrais. Estatisticas das Sociedades. Continente e Ilhas Adjacentes see Portugal. Instituto Nacional de Estatistica. Servicos Centrais. Estatisticas das Sociedades: Continente, Acores e Madeira *216*
Portugal. Instituto Nacional de Estatistica. Servicos Centrais. Estatisticas dos Transportes e Communicacoes: Continente, Acores e Madeira (PO ISSN 0377-2292) *346, 1061, 1086*
Portugal. Instituto Nacional de Estatistica. Servicos Centrais. Sinopse de Dados Estatisticos: Continente e Ilhas Adjacentes see Portugal (Year) *1062*
Portugal. Instituto Nacional de Investigacao das Pescas. Boletim (PO ISSN 0870-1245) *177, 512*
Portugal. Ministerio da Justicia. Boletin (PO) *662*
Portugal. Ministerio das Corporacoes e Previdencia Social. Gabinete de Planeamento. Inguerito Emprego (PO) *287*
Portugal. Ministerio das Financas e do Plano. Departamento Central de Planeamento. Plano see Economic Situation in the Year (Year) *243*
Portugal. Ministerio das Financas. Relatorio do Orcamento Geral do Estado (PO ISSN 0079-4201) *298*
Portugal. Ministerio do Trabalho. Servico de Estatisticas. Estatisticas do Trabalho (PO) *216*
Portugal. Ministerio do Trabalho. Servico de Informacao Cientifica e Tecnica. Boletim do Trabalho e Emprego (PO) *275*
Portugal. Ministerio do Ultramar. Relatorio das Actividades (PO) *945*
Portugal. Servicos Geologicos. Comunicacoes (PO ISSN 0037-2730) *394, 819*
Portugal. Statistiques Industrielles: Continent, Acores et Madere. Volume 1: Industries Extractives, Electricite, Gaz, Eau. see Portugal. Estatisticas Industriais: Continente, Acores e Madeira. Volume 1: Industrias Extractivas, Electricidade, Gas, Agua *216*
Portugal. Statistiques Industrielles: Continent, Acores et Madere. Volume 2: Industries Manufacturieres see Portugal. Estatisticas Industriais: Continente, Acores e Madeira. Volume 2: Industrias Transformadoras *216*
Portugal (Year) (PO ISSN 0377-2470) *1062*
Portugal & Spain Stamp Catalogue (UK ISSN 0142-9833) *875*
Portugaliae Acta Biologica (PO ISSN 0032-5147) *145*
Portugaliae Historica (PO) *593*
Portugiesische Forschungen der Goerresgesellschaft. Reihe 1: Aufsaetze zur Portugiesischen Kulturgeschichte (GW ISSN 0079-421X) *593*
Portugiesische Forschungen der Goerresgesellschaft. Reihe 2: Monographien (GW ISSN 0079-4228) *593*

Portugiesische Forschungen der Goerresgesellschaft. Reihe 3: Vieira-Texte und Vieira-Studien (GW ISSN 0171-290X) *593*
Post Library Association Report *see* P L A Report *682*
Post Magazine Almanack. Insurance Directory *see* Insurance Directory and Year Book *640*
Post-Medieval Archaeology (UK ISSN 0079-4236) *91*
Post Office Savings Bank. Annual Report (MF) *231*
Postage Stamps of New Zealand (NZ) *875*
Postage Stamps of the United States *see* United States Postage Stamps *875*
Postbuechl (AU) *298, 346*
Postcard Art/Postcard Fiction (US) *79, 109, 730*
Postepy Cybernetyki (PL ISSN 0137-3595) *359*
Postepy Napedu Elektrycznego (PL ISSN 0079-4260) *459*
Postepy Pediatrii (PL ISSN 0079-4279) *788*
Postgraduate Courses in United Kingdom Universities *see* British Universities' Guide to Graduate Studies *428*
Postgraduate Study at the University of Liverpool (UK ISSN 0268-0645) *430, 438*
Postilla (US ISSN 0079-4295) *998*
Postomdeling af Reklamer *see* Adresseloese Postforsendelser *346*
Post's Pulp & Paper Directory (US) *315, 858*
Postsecondary Education in California: Information Digest (US) *438*
Potato Abstracts (UK ISSN 0308-7344) *11, 42*
Potato Marketing Board, London. Annual Report and Accounts (UK ISSN 0079-4309) *49, 59*
Potchefstroom University for Christian Higher Education. Wetenskaplike Bydraes. Reeks A: Geesteswetenskappe (SA ISSN 0079-4333) *631*
Potchefstroom University for Christian Higher Education. Wetenskaplike Bydraes. Reeks B: Natuurwetenskappe. Series (SA ISSN 0079-4341) *998*
Potchefstroom University for Christian Higher Education. Wetenskaplike Bydraes. Reeks H: Inougurele Redes (SA) *438*
Potentials Mart (US) *285*
Potomac Issues (US) *1125*
Potomac River Basin Water Quality Reports (US) *498, 1125*
Potomac River Water Quality Network *see* Potomac River Basin Water Quality Reports *1125*
Pottersfield Portfolio (CN ISSN 0226-0840) *730, 743*
Pottery Quarterly (UK ISSN 0032-5678) *113*
Poultry Abstracts (UK ISSN 0306-1582) *11, 43*
Poultry Market Review (CN ISSN 0032-5775) *67*
Poultry Market Statistics (US ISSN 0565-1980) *43, 67, 1062*
Poultry Roundup (US) *67*
Pouvoir dans la Litterature et la Pensee Anglaises (FR ISSN 0240-8864) *730*
Poverty and Human Resources Abstracts *see* Human Resources Abstracts *6*
Poverty in South Dakota (US) *1020*
Powder/Bulk Solids' Directalog (US) *479*
Powder Coatings Buyer's Guide (US) *1160*
Powder Diffraction File Search Manual. Alphabetical Listing. Inorganic (US ISSN 0092-0509) *326, 328*
Powder Diffraction File Search Manual. Fink Method. Inorganic (US ISSN 0092-1300) *326, 328*
Powder Diffraction File Search Manual. Hanawalt Method. Inorganic (US ISSN 0092-1319) *326, 328*
Powder Diffraction File Search Manual. Organic (US ISSN 0092-0576) *330*

Powder Metallurgy in Defense Technology (US ISSN 0149-3922) *800*
Power Authority of the State of New York. Annual Report (US) *466*
Power Conditioning Specialists Conference. Record *see* I E E E Power Electronics Specialists Conference. Record *19*
Power Directory (US) *459*
Power Farming Technical Annual (AT ISSN 0079-4422) *51*
Power Modulator Conference. I E E E Conference Record *see* Power Modulator Symposium. I E E E Conference Record *459*
Power Modulator Symposium. I E E E Conference Record (US) *459*
Power Reactor and Nuclear Fuel Development Corporation Review *see* P N C Review *898*
Power Semiconductors D.A.T.A. Book (US ISSN 0164-0038) *459*
Power Sources Symposium. Proceedings (US ISSN 0079-4457) *459*
Power Statistics Journal of Nepal (NP) *459*
Power Supplies D.A.T.A. Book (US) *459*
Power Systems Computation Conference. P S C C Proceedings (SW) *474*
Power Transmission and Bearing Handbook *see* Power Transmission Design Handbook *492*
Power Transmission Design Handbook (US) *492*
Power's Electric Utility Generation Planbook *see* Electric Utility Generation Planbook *452*
Powstanie Styczniowe. Materialy i Dokumenty (PL ISSN 0079-4465) *593*
Poznanskie Towarzystwo Przyjaciol Nauk. Komisja Archeologiczna. Prace (PL ISSN 0137-3250) *91*
Poznanskie Towarzystwo Przyjaciol Nauk. Komisja Automatyki. Prace *see* Studia z Automatyki *355*
Poznanskie Towarzystwo Przyjaciol Nauk. Komisja Biologiczna. Prace (PL ISSN 0079-4619) *145*
Poznanskie Towarzystwo Przyjaciol Nauk. Komisja Filozoficzna. Prace (PL ISSN 0079-4635) *880*
Poznanskie Towarzystwo Przyjaciol Nauk. Komisja Geograficzno-Geologiczna. Prace (PL ISSN 0137-9771) *394, 547*
Poznanskie Towarzystwo Przyjaciol Nauk. Komisja Historii Sztuki. Prace (PL ISSN 0079-466X) *109*
Poznanskie Towarzystwo Przyjaciol Nauk. Komisja Historyczna. Prace (PL ISSN 0079-4651) *593*
Poznanskie Towarzystwo Przyjaciol Nauk. Komisja Jezykoznawcza. Prace (PL ISSN 0079-4678) *701*
Poznanskie Towarzystwo Przyjaciol Nauk. Komisja Matematyczno-Przyrodnicza. Prace (PL ISSN 0137-8996) *752, 890*
Poznanskie Towarzystwo Przyjaciol Nauk. Komisja Nauk Rolniczych i Komisja Nauk Lesnych. Prace (PL ISSN 0079-4708) *33, 526*
Poznanskie Towarzystwo Przyjaciol Nauk. Komisja Nauk Spolecznych. Prace (PL ISSN 0079-4716) *1011*
Poznanskie Towarzystwo Przyjaciol Nauk. Komisja Technologii Drewna. Prace (PL ISSN 0079-4724) *530*
Prace Archivum Slaskiej Kultury Muzycznej (PL) *840*
Prace Astronomickeho Observatoria na Skalnatom Plese/Contributions of the Astronomical Observatory on Skalnate Pleso (CS) *117*
Prace Geologiczne (PL ISSN 0079-3361) *394*
Prace i Studia Geograficzne (PL ISSN 0208-4589) *547*
Prace Jezykoznawcze (PL ISSN 0079-3485) *701*
Prace Literackie (PL ISSN 0079-4767) *1160*
Prace Onomastyczne (PL ISSN 0079-4775) *701*

Prace Orientalistyczne (PL ISSN 0079-4783) *853*
Prace Polonistyczne (PL ISSN 0079-4791) *730*
Prace Popularnonaukowe *see* Prace Popularnonaukowe. Zabytki Polski Polnocnej *109*
Prace Popularnonaukowe *see* Prace Popularnonaukowe. Ekonomia i Organizacja *248*
Prace Popularnonaukowe *see* Prace Popularnonaukowe. Biblioteczka Prawnicza *662*
Prace Popularnonaukowe. Biblioteczka Prawnicza (PL) *662*
Prace Popularnonaukowe. Ekonomia i Organizacja (PL) *248*
Prace Popularnonaukowe. Zabytki Polski Polnocnej (PL) *109*
Prace z Dejin Prirodnich Ved (CS) *593*
Practical Alternatives (UK ISSN 0262-4540) *498*
Practical Camper's Sites Guide (UK) *1046*
Practical Conveyancing Precedents (UK) *662*
Practical Forms and Precedents (New South Wales) (AT ISSN 0048-508X) *662*
Practical Guide to Countertrade (US) *198*
Practical Guide to Individual Income Tax Return Preparation *see* 1040 Preparation *301*
Practical Guide to the Use of the European Communities' Scheme of Generalized Tariff Preferences (EI) *259*
Practical Nursing Career (US) *784*
Practical Spectroscopy Series (US) *326*
Practices of the Wind (US ISSN 0196-822X) *743*
Pragmatics and Discourse Analysis (NE) *701, 880, 936*
Prairie Farmers Catalogue (CN ISSN 0831-2338) *51*
Prairie Provinces Water Board Annual Report (CN) *1125*
Prairie Scout (US ISSN 0092-8313) *608*
Prairie Wind (US) *367, 498*
Prajnan (II ISSN 0032-6690) *449, 998, 1070*
Prakalpana Literature *see* Prakalpana Sahitya *730*
Prakalpana Sahitya/Prakalpana Literature (II) *730*
Prakit Jain Institute Research Publication Series (II ISSN 0554-9906) *977*
Prakrit Text Society. Publications (II) *701, 730*
Praktische Betriebswirtschaft (SZ ISSN 0079-4880) *281*
Praktische Chirurgie (GW ISSN 0079-4899) *794*
Pram and Nursery Trader Year Book *see* Toy Trader Year Book *553*
Prameny a Studie (CS) *33*
Prameny Ceske a Slovenske Lingvistiky. Rada Ceska (CS ISSN 0079-4902) *701*
Prana Yoga Life (US ISSN 0149-953X) *880*
Pratt's Guide to Venture Capital Sources (US) *267*
Pravnehistoricke Studie (CS ISSN 0079-4929) *662*
Pravnicke Studie (CS ISSN 0551-9039) *662*
Pravoslavno Misao (YU ISSN 0032-700X) *972*
Pravoslavny Theologicky Sbornik (CS ISSN 0079-4937) *972*
Prawo (PL) *662*
Praxis der Chirurgie (US) *794*
Praxis der Kinderpsychologie und Kinderpsychiatrie. Beihefte (GW ISSN 0085-5073) *791, 936*
Prazsky Sbornik Historicky (CS) *91, 593*
Pre-Parent Adviser (US) *788*
Precipitation *see* Opady Atmosferyczne *806*
Precos Pagos Pelos Agricultores (BL ISSN 0302-5195) *49*
Precos Recebidos Pelos Agricultores (BL ISSN 0100-5219) *49*

Predi-Briefs (US ISSN 0551-9276) *11, 216*
Predicasts *see* Predicasts Forecasts *216*
Predicasts Basebook *see* Basebook *287*
Predicasts F & S Index Europe (US ISSN 0270-4536) *11, 216*
Predicasts F & S Index International (US ISSN 0270-4528) *11, 216*
Predicasts F & S Index of Corporate Change (US ISSN 0744-2785) *11, 216*
Predicasts F & S Index United States (US ISSN 0270-4544) *11, 216*
Predicasts Forecasts (US ISSN 0278-0135) *11, 216*
Predicasts Overview of Markets and Technologies (US ISSN 0161-8032) *11, 326, 477*
Predicasts Source Directory (US ISSN 0092-7767) *217*
Prediction Annual (UK ISSN 0079-4953) *860*
Pregled (YU ISSN 0032-7271) *1011*
Pregled Sudske Prakse (YU) *662*
Prehistoric Archaeology and Ecology (US) *91, 145*
Prehistoric Society, London. Proceedings (UK ISSN 0079-497X) *91*
PreLaw Handbook. Official Law School Guide (US ISSN 0075-8264) *662*
Prelude to Fantasy (US) *1160*
Prent 190 (NE ISSN 0032-7476) *109, 931*
Preprints of Papers Presented at the Annual Meeting- American Institute for Conservation of Historic and Artistic Works *see* American Institute for Conservation of Historic and Artistic Works. Preprints of Papers Presented at the Annual Meeting *101*
Presbyterian Church in Canada. General Assembly. Acts and Proceedings (CN ISSN 0079-4996) *972*
Prescription Drug Industry Fact Book *see* P M A Statistical Factbook *872*
Prescription Products Guide (AT ISSN 0818-4445) *872*
Prescription Proprietaries Guide for Health Professionals *see* Prescription Products Guide *872*
Presenca Filosofica (BL) *880*
Presence de Gabriel Marcel. Cahier (FR) *880*
Presencia Universitaria (HO) *438*
Presidential Advisory Committee on Small and Minority Business Ownership. Annual Report (US) *301*
President's National Urban Policy Report (US ISSN 0163-8602) *625*
Press Braille, Adult *see* Braille Books (Large Print Edition) *180*
Press Directory of Australia and New Zealand *see* Press Radio and T.V. Guide *646*
Press in India (II ISSN 0445-6653) *130*
Press Radio and T.V. Guide (AT ISSN 0079-5046) *349, 646*
Press, The Law and Beyond (AT) *632*
Presse Etudiante du Quebec Publi - P E Q *see* Publi - P E Q *342*
Presse-Portraets (GW ISSN 0176-5248) *130, 962*
Presseblomster (DK ISSN 0108-9943) *712*
Pressehandbuch (Year) (AU) *646, 962*
Pressens Arbog (DK ISSN 0106-6579) *344, 593*
Presumpscot *see* Portland Review of the Arts *743*
Previews Guide to the World's Fine Real Estate (US) *966*
Prevision a Un a de l'Economie Francaise *see* Economie Francaise en Perspectives Sectorielles: Industries de Biens de Consommation *244*
Prevision a Un An de l'Economie Francaise *see* Economie Francaise en Perspectives Sectorielles: Filiere Batiment, Genie Civil, Materiaux de Construction *184*
Prevision a Un An de l'Economie Francaise. *see* Economie Francaise en Donnees d'Encadrement *244*

Prevision a Un An de l'Economie Francaise see Economie Francaise en Perspectives Sectorielles: Industries de Biens d'Equipement 244
Prevision a Un An de l'Economie Francaise see Economie Francaise en Perspectives Sectorielles: Industries de Biens Intermediaires 244
Prevision a Un An de la Filiere Construction see Economie Francaise en Perspectives Sectorielles: Filiere Batiment, Genie Civil, Materiaux de Construction 184
Prevision Glissante a Cinq Ans see Previsions Glissantes Detaillees Horizon 1990 198
Previsions Glissantes Detaillees Horizon 1990 (FR) 198
Previsions Glissantes Detaillees 1979-1984 see Previsions Glissantes Detaillees Horizon 1990 198
Previson a Moyen Terme de l'Economie Francaise see Previsions Glissantes Detaillees Horizon 1990 198
Priamur'e Moe (UR) 730
Price Index for the Manufacturing Sector (CY) 1160
Price-Priestley Newsletter see Enlightenment and Dissent 557
Prices and Earnings Around the Globe (SZ) 278
Prices of Agricultural Products and Selected Inputs in Europe and North America (UN) 49, 248
Prickly Pear Tucson (US ISSN 0747-9697) 743
Priesterjahrheft (GW ISSN 0172-0929) 983
Prikladnaya Geofizika (UR) 401
Prikladnaya Mekhanika i Priborostroenie (UR) 895
Primary Writing (US) 743
Primate News (US ISSN 0032-8324) 177
Primate Report (GW ISSN 0343-3528) 75
Primates (US ISSN 0079-5100) 177
Primavera (Chicago) (US ISSN 0364-7609) 730, 1129
Primitiae (AT ISSN 0726-4399) 338
Prince Edward Island. Civil Service Commission. Annual Report (CN) 908
Prince Edward Island. Department of Community Affairs. Annual Report see Prince Edward Island. Department of Community and Cultural Affairs. Annual Report 498
Prince Edward Island. Department of Community and Cultural Affairs. Annual Report (CN) 498, 945
Prince Edward Island. Department of Fisheries and Labour. Annual Report see Prince Edward Island. Department of Labour. Annual Report 275
Prince Edward Island. Department of Health and Social Services. Annual Report (CN) 955
Prince Edward Island. Department of Health. Annual Report see Prince Edward Island. Department of Health and Social Services. Annual Report 955
Prince Edward Island. Department of Industry and Commerce. Annual Commerce see Prince Edward Island. Department of Industry. Annual Report 945
Prince Edward Island. Department of Industry. Annual Report (CN) 945
Prince Edward Island. Department of Labour. Annual Report (CN ISSN 0085-512X) 275
Prince Edward Island. Economics, Marketing & Statistics Branch. Agricultural Statistics (CN) 43
Prince Edward Island. Land Development Corporation. Annual Report (CN) 966
Prince Edward Island. Public Utilities Commission. Annual Report (CN ISSN 0079-5151) 945
Prince Edward Island Community Studies see P.E.I. Community Studies 1028
Prince Edward Island Development Agency. Annual Report (CN) 291

Princess Grace Irish Library (UK ISSN 0269-2619) 730
Princess Grace Irish Library Lectures (UK ISSN 0950-5121) 730
Princeton-Cambridge Series in Chinese Linguistics (UK) 701
Princeton-Cambridge Studies in Chinese Linguistics see Princeton-Cambridge Series in Chinese Linguistics 701
Princeton Conference on Cerebrovascular Diseases see Princeton Research Conferences on Cerebrovascular Diseases 777
Princeton Essays in Literature. (US ISSN 0079-5186) 730
Princeton Essays on the Arts (US) 109, 632
Princeton Journal: Studies in Thematic Architecture (US) 99
Princeton Mathematical Series (US ISSN 0079-5194) 752
Princeton Monographs in Art and Archaeology (US ISSN 0079-5208) 91, 109
Princeton Research Conferences on Cerebrovascular Diseases (US) 777
Princeton Series in Physics (US ISSN 0079-5216) 890
Princeton Series of Contemporary Poets(US) 743
Princeton Studies in Mathematical Economics (US ISSN 0079-5240) 198, 752
Princeton Studies in Music (US ISSN 0079-5259) 840
Princeton University. Center of International Studies Policy Memorandum (US ISSN 0079-5267) 671, 918
Princeton University. Center of International Studies. Research Monograph Series (US ISSN 0555-1501) 671, 918
Princeton University. Center of International Studies. World Order Studies Program: Occasional Paper (US) 918
Princeton University. Computer Sciences Laboratory. Technical Report see Princeton University. Department of Computer Science. Technical Report 353
Princeton University. Department of Computer Science. Technical Report (US) 353
Princeton University. Econometric Research Program. Research Memorandum (US ISSN 0079-5291) 198
Princeton University. Industrial Relations Section. Research Report (US ISSN 0079-5305) 275
Principal International Businesses (US ISSN 0097-6288) 259, 285
Principal Legislative Staff Offices see State Legislative Leadership, Committees and Staff 946
Principales Industries Installees en Cote d'Ivoire (IV) 291
Principales Industries Ivoiriennes see Principales Industries Installees en Cote d'Ivoire 291
Principality of Liechtenstein - A Documentary Handbook (LH ISSN 0048-5306) 594
Principaux Mecanismes de Distribution de Credit (FR) 231
Principles of Computer Science Series (US ISSN 0888-2096) 485, 755
Principles of Pediatric Neurosurgery (US) 788, 794
Printers Yearbook (UK) 931
Printing & Publishing: Latin American Industrial Report (US) 240, 962
Printing Historical Society. Journal (UK ISSN 0079-5321) 931
Printing Industries Annual see Printers Yearbook 931
Printing Trades Blue Book. Delaware Valley-Ohio Edition (US ISSN 0193-3949) 931
Printing Trades Blue Book. New York Edition (US ISSN 0079-5348) 931
Printing Trades Blue Book. Northeastern Edition (US ISSN 0079-5356) 931
Printing Trades Blue Book. Southeastern Edition (US ISSN 0079-5364) 931

Printing Trades Directory (UK ISSN 0079-5372) 931
Printout see Young Women's Christian Association of the United States of America. The Printout 974
Printworld Directory of Contemporary Prints (Year) (US) 109, 315
Prior Park Magazine (UK) 438
Prirodni Vedy a Matematika see Pedagogicka Fakulta v Ostrave. Matematika, Fyzika 751
Prirodnjacki Muzej u Beogradu. Glasnik. Serija A: Mineralogija, Geologija, Paleontologija (YU ISSN 0367-4983) 394, 857
Prirodnjacki Muzej u Beogradu. Glasnik. Serija B: Bioloske Nauke (YU ISSN 0373-2134) 145
Prirodnyi Gaz Sibiri (UR) 866
Prirodoslovna Istrazivanja: Acta Biologica (YU ISSN 0448-0147) 145
Priser och Konkurrens see Hinnat ja Kilpailu 239
Prisons see South Africa. Prisons Department. Report of the Commissioner of Prisons/Verslag van die Kommissaris van Gevangenisse 372
Private Country Club Guest Policy Directory (US) 1040
Private Development Corporation of the Philippines. Annual PDCP Survey on Business Performance (PH) 267
Private Higher Education see Independent Higher Education 436
Private Independent Schools (US ISSN 0079-5399) 430
Private Investors Abroad (US ISSN 0090-9742) 267, 671
Private Investor's Ledger (UK) 267
Private Island "Inventory" (US) 966
Private Label Directory (US) 315
Private Legislation (Scotland) Procedure Journal (UK) 662
Private Post (UK ISSN 0140-8003) 875
Private Press Books (UK ISSN 0079-5402) 130
Private Schools of the United States (US ISSN 0885-1603) 430
Privates Bausparwesen (GW ISSN 0085-5154) 186
Prix de la Revue Etudes Francaises (CN) 1160
Prize Stories; The O. Henry Awards (US ISSN 0079-5453) 730
Pro and Amateur Hockey Guide see Hockey Guide 1033
Pro-Audio Yearbook see Studio Sound's Pro-Audio Directory 1032
Pro Basketball Illustrated (Year) (US) 1040
Pro Football see Street & Smith's Official Yearbook: Pro Football 1040
Pro Football (Los Angeles) (US ISSN 0079-5526) 1040
Pro Football Illustrated (Year) (US) 1040
Pro Motion (CN ISSN 0048-5381) 449
Pro und Kontra (SZ) 908
Probability and Mathematical Statistics (US ISSN 0079-5607) 752
Probability: Pure and Applied (US) 752
Probable Levels of R & D Expenditures: Forecast and Analysis (US) 998, 1070
Probation and Parole see Journal of Probation and Parole 371
Probation and Parole Directory (US ISSN 0732-0965) 372
Probe (AT ISSN 0079-5631) 780
Probe (Santa Barbara) (US ISSN 0032-9177) 914
Probe Directory of Foreign Direct Investment in the United States (US ISSN 0094-3134) 267, 315
Probitas (II) 730
Problem Books in Mathematics (US) 752
Problemas del Mundo Contemporaneo see Problems of the Contemporary World 1011
Problemata (GW) 632, 880
Probleme de Antropologie see Studii si Cercetari de Antropologie 76

Probleme de Geografie see Studii si Cercetari de Geologie, Geofizica si Geografie. Geografie 548
Probleme de Logica (RM) 881
Probleme de Pedagogie Contemporana (RM) 418
Probleme der Aegyptologie (NE) 972
Probleme der Kuestenforschung im Suedlichen Nordseegebiet (GW) 998
Probleme Grenznaher Raeume (AU) 625
Problemes d'Histoire du Christianisme (BE) 983
Problemes du Monde Contemporain see Problems of the Contemporary World 1011
Problemi e Ricerche di Storia Antica (IT ISSN 0079-5682) 594
Problemi na Tekhnicheskata Kibernetika i Robotika/Problems of Engineering Cybernetics and Robotics (BU ISSN 0204-9848) 359
Problemi Sjevernog Jadrana (YU) 75, 594
Problems in Contemporary Philosophy (US) 881
Problems in Mathematical Analysis Report (US ISSN 0079-5739) 1160
Problems in Pathology (UK) 765
Problems in Private International Law (NE) 671
Problems of Communism (UK) 908
Problems of Diffraction and Spreading of Waves see Problemy Difraktsii i Rasprostraneniya Voln 900
Problems of Engineering Cybernetics and Robotics see Problemi na Tekhnicheskata Kibernetika i Robotika 359
Problems of Industrial Psychiatric Medicine Series (US ISSN 0277-4178) 936
Problems of Journalism see A S N E 19 645
Problems of Lithuanian Linguistics see Lietuviu Kalbotyros Klausimai 698
Problems of National Liberation (II) 908
Problems of the Baltic (SW ISSN 0552-2005) 1160
Problems of the Contemporary World/ Problemes du Monde Contemporain/ Problemas del Mundo Contemporaneo (UR ISSN 0079-5763) 560, 1011
Problems of the Far East see U S S R Report: Problems of the Far East 919
Problems of Transportation in Japan (JA) 1083
Problemy Arkheologii i Etnografii (UR) 91
Problemy Biologie Krajiny/Questiones Geobiologicae (CS) 145
Problemy Bioniki (UR) 145
Problemy Difraktsii i Rasprostraneniya Voln/Problems of Diffraction and Spreading of Waves (UR) 900
Problemy Fiziki Atmosfery (UR) 806, 890
Problemy Handlu Zagranicznego (PL) 1160
Problemy Istorii Matematiki i Mekhaniki (UR) 752, 895
Problemy Kontrolya i Zashchita Atmosfery ot Zagryazneniya (UR ISSN 0135-2253) 499
Problemy Poles'ya (UR) 1125
Problemy Polonii Zagranicznej see Biblioteka Polonijna 902
Problemy Prawa Karnego (PL ISSN 0208-6336) 372, 662
Problemy Prawa Przewozowego (PL ISSN 0208-5518) 662, 1083
Problemy Prawa Wynalazczego i Patentowego (PL ISSN 0208-550X) 861
Problemy Prawne Gornictwa (PL ISSN 0208-5488) 662, 819
Problemy Prawne Handlu Zagranicznego (PL ISSN 0208-5496) 259, 662
Problemy Rejonow Uprzemyslawianych (PL ISSN 0079-581X) 291
Procedural Aspects of International Law (US) 671

1858 PROCEEDINGS. ANNUAL

Proceedings. Annual A.A.Z.P.A. Conference *see* American Association of Zoological Parks and Aquariums. Proceedings. Annual A A Z P A Conference *173*

Proceedings. Annual Meeting - Transportation Research Forum *see* Transportation Research Forum. Proceedings: Annual Meeting *1084*

Proceedings. Annual Symposium. Incremental Motion Control Systems and Devices *see* Symposium on Incremental Motion Control Systems and Devices. Proceedings *746*

Proceedings, A W W A Annual Conference *see* American Water Works Association. Proceedings, A W W A Annual Conference *1123*

Proceedings - Committee on Computer Technology *see* American Association of State Highway and Transportation Officials. Sub-Committee on Computer Technology. National Conference. Proceedings *1093*

Proceedings - Conference on Ground Water *see* Conference on Ground Water. Proceedings *402*

Proceedings in Life Sciences (US ISSN 0172-6625) *145*

Proceedings of Annual Meeting - American Association of Veterinary Laboratory Diagnosticians *see* American Association of Veterinary Laboratory Diagnosticians. Proceedings of Annual Meeting *1120*

Proceedings of Fishing Port Engineering *see* Gyoko Kensetsu Gijutsu Kenkyu Happyokai Koenshu *481*

Proceedings of Sugar Beet Research *see* Bulletin of Sugar Beet Research. Supplement *53*

Proceedings of the A C S A Annual Meeting *see* Association of Collegiate Schools of Architecture. Proceedings of the Annual Meeting *97*

Proceedings of the Annual Meeting of the Western Society for French History *see* Western Society for French History. Proceedings of the Annual Meeting *601*

Proceedings of the Annual Southeastern Symposium on System Theory *see* Southeastern Symposium on System Theory. Proceedings *359*

Proceedings of the Arizona Section, American Water Resources Association and the Hydrology Section, Arizona-Nevada Academy of Science (US) *403*

Proceedings of the Japanese Conference on Coastal Engineering *see* Kaigan Kogaku Koenkai Ronbunshu *482*

Proceedings of the National/ International Sculpture Conference *see* National/International Sculpture Conference. Proceedings *108*

Proceedings of the Northeast Pacific Pink Salmon Workshop *see* Northeast Pacific Pink and Chum Salmon Workshop. Proceedings *512*

Proceedings of the Ocean Development Symposium *see* Kaiyo Kaihatsu Ronbunshu *482*

Proceedings of the South Carolina Historical Association *see* South Carolina Historical Association. Proceedings *609*

Proceedings of the Southwest Regional Conference for Astronomy and Astrophysics *see* Southwest Regional Conference for Astronomy and Astrophysics. Proceedings *1163*

Proceedings of the Special Convention of the National Collegiate Athletic Association *see* National Collegiate Athletic Association. Proceedings of the Special Convention *1034*

Proceedings of the Symposium of Computer Research *see* Densanki Riyo Ni Kansuru Shinpojumu Koengaiyo *481*

Proceedings of the Symposium on Environmental Problems *see* Kankyo Mondai Shinpojumu Koen Ronbunshu *482*

Proceedings of the Symposium on Rock Mechanics *see* Ganban Rikigaku Ni Kansuri Shinpojumu Ronbunshu *481*

Proceedings on Nondestructive Evaluation (US) *21*

Proceedings - Ultrasonics Symposium *see* Ultrasonics Symposium. Proceedings *900*

Process Engineering Directory (UK ISSN 0143-1455) *315, 479*

Process Engineering Index (UK) *477*

Process Equipment Series (US) *479*

Process Metallurgy (NE) *800*

Processo Legislativo nel Parlamento Italiano (IT) *662*

Proche-Orient Etudes Juridiques (LE ISSN 0032-9649) *662*

Procordia. Aarsredovisning/Procordia. Annual Report. (SW) *291*

Procordia. Annual Report. *see* Procordia. Aarsredovisning *291*

Prodei (SP ISSN 0079-5836) *315*

Produccion Agricola - Periodo de Invierno (VE) *43*

Produccion Agricola - Periodo de Verano (VE) *43, 1062*

Produccion Animal *see* Spain. Instituto Nacional de Investigaciones Agrarias. Anales. Serie: Ganadera *1163*

Produccion Quimica Mexicana (MX) *479*

Produccion y Exportaciones Chilenas de Cobre (CL) *291, 820*

Produce Marketing Almanac (US) *520, 855*

Produce Marketing Association. Yearbook *see* Produce Marketing Almanac *520*

Produce Marketing Association Almanac *see* Produce Marketing Almanac *520*

Producer's MasterGuide (US ISSN 0732-6653) *16, 315, 349, 825*

Product Directory of the Refactories Industry of the United States (US) *315*

Product File for Agricultural Machinery and Related Material (JA) *51*

Product Finder: Swift-Sasco Buyers Guide (UK ISSN 0261-4073) *369*

Product Guide (JA) *1092*

Producteur d'Amiante *see* Asbestos Producer *181*

Production and Marketing California Grapes, Raisins and Wine *see* California Fruit and Nut Acreage *39*

Production Costs: Operating Steam Electric Plants (US) *459, 466*

Production's Manufacturing Planbook (US) *291*

Productions Nouvelles du Danemark *see* New Products from Denmark *290*

Productividad (PE ISSN 0032-9908) *291*

Productivity Digest (US ISSN 0741-6466) *281*

Productivity Insights (UK) *11, 1073*

Productivity Perspectives (US ISSN 0741-6458) *281*

Producto Neto de la Agricultura Espanola (SP ISSN 0079-5895) *33*

Productos Nuevos de Dinamarca *see* New Products from Denmark *290*

Products Finishing Directory (US ISSN 0478-4251) *856, 1070*

Produits Alimentaires & Boissons *see* Danmark Export: Food & Beverages *254*

Produktions Nyts Leverandoerregister (DK ISSN 0106-0104) *746, 800*

Produktionshaandbogen (DK) *16, 931*

Produktnoeglen for Transportemballageindkoebere *see* Transport (Aarlig) *1083*

Produktschap voor Siergewassen. Jaarverslag *see* Produktschap voor Siergewassen. Jaarverslag/Statistiek *533*

Produktschap voor Siergewassen. Jaarverslag/Statistiek (NE) *533*

Produktschap voor Siergewassen. Statistiek *see* Produktschap voor Siergewassen. Jaarverslag/Statistiek *533*

Produtos e Tecnicas *see* P & T *186*

Produzione e Consumo di Energia Elettrica in Italia (IT) *466*

Proem Pamphlets (UK) *743*

Profession (US) *701, 730*

Professional and Industrial Photographic Equipment (AT) *315, 885*

Professional and Trade Organisations in India (II ISSN 0079-5925) *315*

Professional Development Week (CN) *360*

Professional Electronics Yearbook (US) *316, 459*

Professional Farm Management Guidebook (AT) *49*

Professional Freelance Writers Directory (US) *646*

Professional Photographer Directory and Buyer's Guide (UK) *316, 885*

Professional Photographic Equipment Directory and Buying Guide (US) *885*

Professional Photography (IT) *885*

Professional Register of Artists (UK) *840*

Professional Register of Private Teachers of Music (UK) *840*

Professional Video International Yearbook (UK ISSN 0266-2256) *349*

Professional Women and Minorities (US ISSN 0190-1796) *849, 1129*

Professional's Guide to Public Relations Services (US) *16*

ProFile (US ISSN 0190-8766) *99*

Profile Index to Canadian and Municipal Government Publications *see* Microlog Index *9*

Profile New Zealand/The Electrical Industry (NZ) *459*

Profiles (NE) *881*

Profiles and Trends (US) *1161*

Profiles of Earnings in Cyprus; by Education, Occupation, Experience, Age, Sex and Sector (CY) *1062*

Profiles of the National Productivity Organizations in A P O Member Countries *see* Directory of the National Productivity Organizations in A P O Member Countries *288*

Profitability of Citrus Growing in Israel/Ha-Rivhiyut Shel Gidul Hadarim (IS) *59*

Profitability of Cotton Growing in Israel/Ha-Rivhiyut Shel Gidul Ha-Kutnah (IS ISSN 0079-595X) *59*

Profitability of Dairy in Israel/Ha-Rivhiyut Shel 'anaf Ha-Refet (IS) *63*

Profitability of Poultry Farming in Israel/Ha-Rivhiyut Shel 'anaf Ha-Lul(IS ISSN 0079-5968) *67*

Profits (FR ISSN 0079-5984) *1161*

Progettare & Costruire (IT) *186*

Prognostico (BL ISSN 0100-526X) *59*

Prognostico da Agricultura Paulista *see* Prognostico *59*

Prognostico Regiao Centro-Sul (BL ISSN 0100-5316) *59*

Prognozirovanie Razvitiya Bibliotechnogo Dela v S.S.S.R. (UR) *683*

Program Statistics - Michigan Department of Social Services *see* Michigan. Department of Social Services. Program Statistics *1023*

Programa de Estudios Conjuntos para la Integracion Economica Latinoamericano Ensayos E C I E L *see* Ensayos E C I E L *244*

Programmable Controls Technical Directory (Year) (US) *359*

Programme for Growth Series (US) *198*

Programmed Learning and Individually Paced Instruction-Bibliography *see* Individually Paced or Self Teaching Instruction Source Book *127*

Programmer's Market (US ISSN 0739-9405) *1161*

Programresumeer *see* Denmark. Statens Byggeforskningsinstitut. Program Resumeer *183*

Programs in Public Affairs and Administration *see* Graduate Programs in Public Affairs and Public Administration *942*

Progres des Recherches Pharmaceutiques *see* Fortschritte der Arzneimittelforschung *871*

Progreso Economico y Social en America Latina. Informe *see* Economic and Social Progress in Latin America; Annual Report *243*

Progress (Muscle Shoals) (US ISSN 0730-7322) *59*

Progress & Engineering. Developing Countries Edition (GW) *263, 492*

Progress and Topics in Cytogenetics (US ISSN 0733-9003) *167*

Progress in Aeronautical Sciences *see* Progress in Aerospace Sciences *21*

Progress in Aerospace Sciences (US ISSN 0376-0421) *21*

Progress in Allergy (SZ ISSN 0079-6034) *773*

Progress in Analytical Chemistry (US ISSN 0079-6042) *1161*

Progress in Anesthesiology (US ISSN 0099-1546) *774*

Progress in Applied Microcirculation/ Mikrozirkulation in Forschung und Klinik (SZ ISSN 0254-5195) *777*

Progress in Astronautics and Aeronautics Series (US ISSN 0079-6050) *21*

Progress in Behavior Modification (US ISSN 0099-037X) *936*

Progress in Biochemical Pharmacology (SZ ISSN 0079-6085) *872*

Progress in Biomass Conversion (US ISSN 0192-6551) *479*

Progress in Biometeorology (NE) *806*

Progress in Botany (US ISSN 0340-4773) *160*

Progress in Cancer Research and Therapy (US ISSN 0145-3726) *776*

Progress in Cardiology (US ISSN 0097-109X) *777*

Progress in Chemical Fibrinolysis and Thrombolysis (US ISSN 0361-0233) *777*

Progress in Chemical Toxicology (US ISSN 0079-6158) *872*

Progress in Clinical and Biological Research (US ISSN 0361-7742) *145, 765*

Progress in Clinical Biochemistry and Medicine (US) *152*

Progress in Clinical Cancer (US ISSN 0079-6166) *776*

Progress in Clinical Neurophysiology (SZ ISSN 0378-4045) *172, 791*

Progress in Clinical Pathology (US ISSN 0079-6174) *765*

Progress in Colloid and Polymer Science (US ISSN 0340-255X) *330, 332*

Progress in Communication Sciences (US ISSN 0163-5689) *344, 683*

Progress in Coronary Sinus Interventions (US) *777*

Progress in Critical Care Medicine (SZ ISSN 0254-623X) *765*

Progress in Cybernetics and Systems Research (US ISSN 0275-8717) *359*

Progress in Drug Research *see* Fortschritte der Arzneimittelforschung *871*

Progress in Ecology (II ISSN 0253-665X) *145*

Progress in Experimental Personality Research (US ISSN 0079-6255) *936*

Progress in Experimental Tumor Research (SZ ISSN 0079-6263) *776*

Progress in Filtration and Separation (NE) *324*

Progress in Hematology (US ISSN 0079-6301) *783*

Progress in Hemostasis *see* Progress in Hemostasis and Thrombosis *777*

Progress in Hemostasis and Thrombosis(US) *777*

Progress in Histochemistry and Cytochemistry (GW ISSN 0079-6336) *152, 163*

Progress in Industrial Microbiology (NE ISSN 0555-3989) *169*

Progress in Inorganic Chemistry (US ISSN 0079-6379) *328*

Progress in Lipid Research (US ISSN 0163-7827) *330*

Progress in Liver Diseases (US ISSN 0079-6409) *783*

Progress in Low Temperature Physics (NE ISSN 0079-6417) *894*

Progress in Materials Science (US ISSN 0079-6425) *489*

Progress in Medical Microbiology *see* Fortschritte der Medizinischen Mikrobiologie *168*

Progress in Medical Virology (SZ ISSN 0079-645X) 169, 778
Progress in Molecular and Subcellular Biology (US ISSN 0079-6484) 163
Progress in Neurological Surgery (SZ ISSN 0079-6492) 791, 794
Progress in Neuropathology (US) 791
Progress in Nuclear Energy (New Series) (US ISSN 0149-1970) 324, 890
Progress in Nuclear Energy. Series 3 - Process Chemistry see Progress in Nuclear Energy (New Series) 324
Progress in Nuclear Magnetic Resonance Spectroscopy (US ISSN 0079-6565) 326, 898, 899
Progress in Nuclear Magnetic Resonance Spectroscopy of Cyclopentadienyl Compounds see Progress in Nuclear Magnetic Resonance Spectroscopy 898
Progress in Nuclear Medicine see Recent Advances in Nuclear Medicine 792
Progress in Nuclear Medicine (SZ ISSN 0079-6573) 792
Progress in Nucleic Acid Research and Molecular Biology (US ISSN 0079-6603) 145
Progress in Obstetrics and Gynaecology(UK ISSN 0261-0140) 785
Progress in Optics (NE ISSN 0079-6638) 899
Progress in Passive Solar Energy Systems see American Solar Energy Society. Passive Conference. Annual Meeting 463
Progress in Pediatric Radiology (SZ ISSN 0079-6646) 788, 792
Progress in Physical Organic Chemistry(US ISSN 0079-6662) 330, 332
Progress in Physics (US) 890
Progress in Physiological Psychology see Progress in Psychobiology and Physiological Psychology 936
Progress in Planning (US ISSN 0305-9006) 625
Progress in Polymer Science (US ISSN 0079-6700) 330, 479
Progress in Powder Metallurgy (US ISSN 0079-6719) 800
Progress in Psychobiology and Physiological Psychology (US) 936
Progress in Quantum Electronics (US ISSN 0079-6727) 459
Progress in Reaction Kinetics (US ISSN 0079-6743) 332
Progress in Reproductive Biology see Progress in Reproductive Biology and Medicine 172
Progress in Reproductive Biology and Medicine (SZ ISSN 0254-105X) 172
Progress in Respiration Research (SZ ISSN 0079-6751) 793
Progress in Retinal Research (US ISSN 0278-4327) 786
Progress in Sensory Physiology (US ISSN 0721-9156) 765
Progress in Solar Energy see American Solar Energy Society. Annual Meeting 463
Progress in Solid State Chemistry (US ISSN 0079-6786) 332
Progress in Surface and Membrane Science (US) 332
Progress in Surface Science (US ISSN 0079-6816) 890
Progress in Surgery (SZ ISSN 0079-6824) 794
Progress in the Chemistry of Fats and Other Lipids see Progress in Lipid Research 330
Progress in the Chemistry of Organic Natural Products see Fortschritte der Chemie Organischer Naturstoffe 329
Progress in Theoretical Biology (US ISSN 0079-6859) 145
Progress in Theoretical Organic Chemistry (NE) 331
Progress in Underwater Science (UK) 404
Progress in Veterinary Microbiology and Immunology (SZ) 1122
Progress in Zoology see Fortschritte der Zoologie 174

Progress of Education in Saudi Arabia (SU) 441
Progress of Education in the United States of America (US) 418
Progress of Public Education in the United States see Progress of Education in the United States of America 418
Progress of Science in India (II ISSN 0556-1906) 998
Progress Polimernoi Khimii (UR ISSN 0079-6883) 331
Progress Report - New Mexico Bureau of Mines & Mineral Resources see New Mexico. Bureau of Mines and Mineral Resources. Progress Report 818
Progressive Conservative Association of Alberta. Progress Bulletin (CN) 908
Progressive Grocer's Marketing Guidebook (US ISSN 0079-6921) 520
Progressive Periodicals Directory Update (US) 130
Project Defnyddiau ac Adnoddau y Swyddfa Gymreig (UK) 594
Project Personeelsvoorziening Kwartaire Sector. Bulletin (NE) 275
Project Skywater. Annual Report (US ISSN 0079-6956) 490, 1125
Projections of Education Statistics (US) 418
Projects Recommended for Deauthorization, Annual Report see U.S. Department of the Army. Projects Recommended for Deauthorization, Annual Report 813
Prologue (Medford) (US ISSN 0033-1007) 418, 1078
Promadata (SA) 647
Promieniowanie Sloneczne/Solar Radiation (PL) 806
Promotion (UK) 16
Promotion Power (US) 285
PROMT see Predicasts Overview of Markets and Technologies 477
Prontuario Tecnico de la Construccion (VE) 186
Prooficinas (VE) 286
Propagation & Distribution of Fishes from National Fish Hatcheries for the Fiscal Year (US ISSN 0197-4106) 512
Property Review (HK) 966
Property Studies in the U.K. and Overseas (UK ISSN 0305-5752) 966
Propylene and Derivatives see World Propylene and Derivatives 325
Prosa Galega (SP) 1161
Prosecution of Felony Arrests (Year) (US) 374
Prospecting in Areas of Glaciated Terrain (UK ISSN 0141-3376) 394
Prospects (UK ISSN 0361-2333) 505, 608
Prospettive dell'Industria Italiana (IT ISSN 0555-4810) 291
Prostaglandin and Related Lipids (US ISSN 0275-3618) 1161
Prostaglandins Bibliography (US ISSN 0743-4456) 773
Proteccion Vegetal see Spain. Instituto Nacional de Investigaciones Agrarias. Anales. Serie: Agricola 1163
Protection Directory of Industrial & Environmental Personnel (UK) 1161
Protein Abnormalities (US ISSN 0736-4547) 145, 765
Protides of the Biological Fluids (US ISSN 0079-7065) 145
Protokolle zur Fischereitechnik (GW ISSN 0438-4555) 621
Protoplasmologia; Handbuch der Protoplasmaforschung see Cell Biology Monographs 163
Protostar (UK ISSN 0267-1247) 117
Province of Saskatchewan Motor Vehicle Traffic Accidents see Saskatchewan. Government Insurance Office. Province of Saskatchewan Motor Vehicle Traffic Accidents. Annual Report 1097
Provincia (SP) 743
Provincia (AG) 743
Provincia de Zaragoza. Informe Economico (SP) 237
Provincia di Forli in Cifre (IT ISSN 0033-1902) 248

Provincial Results in Canada of Fire & Casualty Companies see Provincial Results in Canada of General Insurance Companies 641
Provincial Results in Canada of General Insurance Companies (CN ISSN 0227-437X) 641
Provinzialinstitut fuer Westfaelische Landes- und Volkforschung. Veroeffentlichungen see Provinzialinstitut fuer Westfaelische Landes- und Volkforschung des Landschaftsverbandes Westfalen-Lippe. Veroeffentlichungen 594
Provinzialinstitut fuer Westfaelische Landes- und Volkforschung des Landschaftsverbandes Westfalen-Lippe. Veroeffentlichungen (GW) 594
Provisions of California Collective Bargaining Agreements (US) 275
Prudential Insurance Company of America. Economic Forecast (US) 248
Prudential Staff Gazette see National Union of Insurance Workers. Prudential Section. Gazette 640
Pruefen und Entscheiden (SZ ISSN 0079-7111) 281
Prumyslove Oblasti (CS) 275, 594
Przeglad Archeologiczny (PL ISSN 0079-7138) 91
Przeglad Informacji; Afryka, Azja, Ameryka Lacinska (PL) 537
Przeglad Informacji o Afryce see Przeglad Informacji; Afryka, Azja, Ameryka Lacinska 537
Przeglad Naukowej Literatury Rolniczej i Lesnej (PL ISSN 0079-7154) 59
Przeglad Zachodnich Czasopism Ekonomicznych (PL ISSN 0033-2445) 211
Przestepczosc na Swiecie (PL ISSN 0137-5415) 372
Przeszlosc Demograficzna Polski (PL ISSN 0079-7189) 924
Pseudepigrapha Veteris Testamenti Graece (NE ISSN 0079-7197) 972
Pseudo-Allergic Reactions (SZ ISSN 0250-8087) 774
Psichiatria e Cultura (IT ISSN 0392-209X) 936
Psikhologicheskie Issledovaniya (UR) 936
Psyche and Design (US) 1161
Psychedelic Monographs and Essays (US ISSN 0892-371X) 377, 872, 936, 972
Psychiatria Fennica (FI ISSN 0079-7227) 791
Psychiatria Fennica. Julkaisusarja see Psychiatria Fennica. Reports 791
Psychiatria Fennica. Monografiasarja/ Psychiatria Fennica. Monographs (FI ISSN 0355-7707) 791
Psychiatria Fennica. Monographs see Psychiatria Fennica. Monografiasarja 791
Psychiatria Fennica. Reports (FI) 791
Psychiatric Medicine Update (US ISSN 0163-1721) 791
Psychiatrie de l'Enfant (FR ISSN 0079-726X) 788
Psychic Studies (US ISSN 0276-1610) 860
Psychoanalytic Abstracts (US) 938
Psychoanalytic Study of the Child (US ISSN 0079-7308) 936
Psychobiology and Physiological Psychology see Progress in Psychobiology and Physiological Psychology 936
Psychologen Adresboek (NE ISSN 0079-7324) 936
Psychologia a Skola (CS) 418, 936
Psychologia-Pedagogika (PL) 936
Psychologia Universalis Forschungsergebnisse aus dem Gesamtgebiet der Psychologie (GW) 936
Psychological Abstracts (US ISSN 0033-2887) 11, 938
Psychological Cinema Register (US ISSN 0272-0582) 826, 938
Psychological Institute of the Republic of South Africa. Proceedings/ Sielkundige Instituut van die Republiek van Suid-Afrika. Verrigtings (SA) 936

Psychological Issues (US ISSN 0048-5748) 936
Psychological Issues. Monograph (US ISSN 0079-7359) 936
Psychological Research Bulletin (SW ISSN 0555-5620) 936
Psychologiczne Problemy Funkcjonowania Czlowieka w Sytuacji Pracy (PL ISSN 0208-5569) 936
Psychologie und Person (GW ISSN 0079-7405) 936
Psychology and Sociology of Sport (US ISSN 0885-7423) 793, 886, 936, 1028, 1046
Psychology Book Guide see Bibliographic Guide to Psychology 938
Psychology Information Guide Series (US ISSN 0273-3579) 130, 938
Psychology of Learning and Motivation: Advances in Research and Theory (US ISSN 0079-7421) 936
Psychopharmacology Supplementa (US) 872
Psychotheque (FR ISSN 0079-7448) 1011
Psyscan: Applied Psychology (US ISSN 0271-7506) 11, 938
Psyscan: Clinical Psychology (US ISSN 0197-1484) 11, 938
Psyscsan: Developmental Psychology (US ISSN 0197-1492) 11, 938
Psyscan: Learning and Communication Disorders and Mental Retardation (US) 11, 445, 938
Psyscan: Learning Disabilities/Mental Retardation see Psyscan: Learning and Communication Disorders and Mental Retardation 938
Psykologisk Laboratorium. Forskningsrapport (DK ISSN 0107-3060) 936
Pszichologia a Gyakorlatban (HU ISSN 0079-7456) 936
Pszichologiai Tanulmanyok (HU ISSN 0079-7464) 936
Pteridologia (US) 160
Pteridologist (UK ISSN 0266-1640) 160
Ptolemy (US) 743
Pub (US) 730
Pubbing, Eating and Sleeping in the South-West (UK) 1161
Pubblicazioni di Verifiche (IT) 594, 881
Pubblico (IT) 712
Publi - P E Q (Presse Etudiante du Quebec) (CN) 342
Public Affairs Information Service Foreign Language Index see P A I S Foreign Language Index 215
Public Affairs Information Service, Inc. Bulletin see P A I S Bulletin 215
Public Affairs Review (US ISSN 0276-0843) 1161
Public and Preparatory Schools. Yearbook see Independent Schools Yearbook: Boys Schools 443
Public Authorities Directory (UK) 951, 1020
Public Authorities Handbook (UK) 1161
Public Cleansing Service in Tokyo see Public Cleansing Services in Tokyo 955
Public Cleansing Services in Tokyo/ Seiso Jigyo Gaiyo (JA) 955
Public Employees Journal/Journal des Employes Publics (CN ISSN 0381-7962) 945
Public Eye (US ISSN 0275-9322) 908
Public Finance in Hungary (HU ISSN 0230-9718) 298
Public General Acts & General Synod Measures (UK) 945
Public Health and Hygiene (UG) 955
Public Health Conference on Records and Statistics. Proceedings (US ISSN 0079-7588) 959
Public Health Economics and Medical Care Abstracts see Medical Care Review 959
Public Health in Europe (UN ISSN 0300-4880) 765, 955
Public Health Laboratory Service Board. Annual Report (UK ISSN 0142-3517) 778, 955

PUBLIC HEALTH

Public Health Laboratory Service Board. Year Book see Public Health Laboratory Service Board. Annual Report 778
Public Health Monograph (US ISSN 0079-7596) 955
Public Health Papers (UN ISSN 0555-6015) 955
Public Health Technical Monograph see Public Health Monograph 955
Public Illumination Magazine (US) 109
Public Interest Clearinghouse Directory(US) 662
Public Land Statistics see U.S. Bureau of Land Management. Public Land Statistics 946
Public Ledger Commodity Year Book (UK) 298
Public Libraries of Victoria. Annual Statistical Bulletin (AT ISSN 0156-4374) 688
Public Library Catalog (US) 688
Public Library Expenditure in Scotland (UK ISSN 0263-9181) 683
Public Library News see P L News 682
Public Library Reporter (US ISSN 0555-6031) 683
Public Papers of the Presidents of the United States (US ISSN 0079-7626) 945
Public Policy Book Forecast see Future Survey 1004
Public Policy Issues in Resource Management (US ISSN 0079-7634) 291
Public Policy Studies in the South (US) 1011
Public Relations Handbook for Managers and Executives (AT) 275
Public Relations Journal Register Issue see Public Relations Society of America Directory 316
Public Relations Society of America Directory (US) 16, 316
Public Relations Yearbook (UK) 16
Public Revenues from Alcohol Beverages (US ISSN 0148-0863) 1161
Public School Directory of the State of Texas see Texas School Directory 431
Public School Enrollment and Staff, New York State (US) 418
Public School Professional Personnel Report, New York State (US ISSN 0077-9229) 418
Public Sector Research Papers (NZ) 945
Public Use of the National Park System (Washington) see U.S. National Park Service. Public Use of the National Park System; Fiscal Year Report 367
Public Utilities Law Anthology (US ISSN 0095-5086) 662, 945
Public Welfare Directory (US ISSN 0163-8297) 1020
Public Welfare in California (US ISSN 0362-742X) 1161
Public Works Historical Society Newsletter (US) 608, 945
Public Works Manual (US ISSN 0163-9730) 951
Publicacoes Culturais da Companhia (AO) 998, 1011
Publicat Index to Canadian Federal Publications see Microlog Index 9
Publication - Brome County Historical Society see Brome County Historical Society. Publication 604
Publication Speciale Canadienne des Sciences Halieutiques et Aquatiques see Canadian Special Publication of Fisheries and Aquatic Sciences 508
Publications-Bureau of Business Research, the University of Texas at Austin see University of Texas, Austin. Bureau of Business Research. Publications 201
Publications Catalog of the U.S. Department of Commerce see U.S. Department of Commerce. Publications Catalog 219
Publications de Recherche Scientifique en France/Scholarly Books in France(FR) 130
Publications de Sciences Naturelles see Canada. National Museums, Ottawa: Publications in Natural Science 173
Publications for the Advancement of Theory and History in Psychology (US) 936
Publications in Archaelogy (US ISSN 0270-1308) 367
Publications in Climatology (US) 806
Publications in Medieval Science (US ISSN 0079-7685) 998
Publications in Medieval Studies (US ISSN 0079-7677) 594, 881
Publications in Near and Middle East Studies. Series A (GW ISSN 0079-7707) 571
Publications in Near and Middle East Studies. Series B (GW ISSN 0079-7715) 571, 701
Publications in Psychology (NZ ISSN 0079-7731) 936
Publications in Seismology (FI ISSN 0079-774X) 401
Publications in the American West (US ISSN 0085-5227) 608
Publications in the Information Sciences(US) 683
Publications in Tropical Geography Savanna Research Series see McGill University Savanna Research Project - Savanna Research Series 546
Publications Indexed for Engineering see P I E 477
Publications of the Faculty - Research Council, Florida State University see Florida State University. Publications of the Faculty 435
Publications of the New Society of Letters at Lund (SW) 109, 560, 701
Publications of the Technical University for Heavy Industry. Series A, Mining(HU ISSN 0324-4628) 820
Publications of the Technical University for Heavy Industry. Series B, Metallurgy (HU ISSN 0324-4679) 800
Publications of the Technical University for Heavy Industry. Series C, Machinery (HU ISSN 0133-297X) 492, 746
Publications of the Technical University for Heavy Industry. Series C, Mechanical Engineering see Publications of the Technical University for Heavy Industry. Series C, Machinery 746
Publications of the Technical University for Heavy Industry. Series D: Natural Sciences (HU ISSN 0133-2929) 998
Publications on Asia see School of International Studies. Publications on Asia 571
Publications on Ethnicity and Nationality (US) 1028
Publications on Ocean Development (NE) 407, 671
Publications on Russia and Eastern Europe see School of International Studies. Publications on Russia and Eastern Europe 909
Publications Romanes et Francaises (SZ ISSN 0079-7812) 701, 730
Publications Yearbook, Republic of China (CH) 962
Publicity Review (UK ISSN 0033-3921) 16, 109
Publicus (SZ ISSN 0080-7249) 945
Publikationen zu Wissenschaftlichen Filmen. Sektion Geschichte, Paedagogik see Institut fuer den Wissenschaftlichen Film. Publikationen zu Wissenschaftlichen Filmen. Sektion Geschichte, Publizistik 824
Published Data on European Industrial Markets (UK) 217, 259
Published Data on Middle & Far East Industrial Markets (UK) 217, 259
Publishers and Distributors of the United States see Publishers, Distributors and Wholesalers of the United States 316
Publishers' Catalogs Annual (US ISSN 0735-665X) 130, 683, 962
Publishers, Distributors and Wholesalers of the United States (US ISSN 0000-0671) 316, 962
Publishers in the United Kingdom and Their Addresses (UK ISSN 0079-7839) 962
Publishers' International Directory see Internationales Verlagsadressbuch 964
Publishers' Trade List Annual (US ISSN 0079-7855) 130
Publishers Weekly Yearbook see Book Publishing Annual 1148
Publishing Program in Computer Science: Artificial Intelligence (US) 355
Publishing Program in Computer Science: Computer Architecture and Design (US) 356
Publishing Program in Computer Science: Distributed Database Systems (US) 360
Publishing Program in Computer Science: Systems Programming (US) 359
Publizistik-Historische Beitraege (GW) 646
Publizistikwissenschaftlicher Referatedienst (GW ISSN 0552-6981) 11, 647
Puente: Lectura para Todos (AG) 1161
Puerto Rico. Agricultural Experiment Station. Bulletin (PR ISSN 0163-8238) 33
Puerto Rico. Bureau of Labor Statistics. Census of Manufacturing Industries of Puerto Rico see Census of Manufacturing Industries of Puerto Rico 288
Puerto Rico. Departamento de Agricultura. Contribuciones Agropecuarias y Pesqueras see Puerto Rico. Department of Agriculture. Agricultural and Fisheries Contributions 512
Puerto Rico. Departamento de la Vivienda. Secretaria Auxiliar de Planification y Programacion. Informe Anual (PR) 625
Puerto Rico. Department of Agriculture. Agricultural and Fisheries Contributions/Puerto Rico. Departamento de Agricultura. Contribuciones Agropecuarias y Pesqueras (PR) 512
Puerto Rico. Department of Health. Boletin Estadistico (US) 886, 1020
Puerto Rico. Department of Health. Informe Anual de Facilidades de Salud (US) 886, 1020
Puerto Rico. Department of Health. Informe del Registro de Profesionales de la Salud (US) 886, 1020
Puerto Rico. Department of Labor. Directorio de Organizaciones del Trabajo (PR) 649
Puerto Rico. Department of the Treasury. Economy & Finances (PR ISSN 0079-7871) 248
Puerto Rico. Division of Demographic Registry and Vital Statistics. Annual Vital Statistics Report (PR ISSN 0555-6511) 929, 1062
Puerto Rico. Division of Health Facilities. Plan for Hospital and Medical Facilites (PR) 618
Puerto Rico. Government Development Bank. Annual Report (PR) 231
Puerto Rico. Government Development Bank. Report of Activities see Puerto Rico. Government Development Bank. Annual Report 231
Puerto Rico. Negociado del Presupuesto. Boletin de Gerencia Administrativa see Puerto Rico. Oficina de Presupuesto y Gerencia. Boletin de Presupuesto y Gerencia 945
Puerto Rico. Negociado del Presupuesto. Resoluciones Conjuntas del Presupuesto General y de Presupuestos Especiales see Puerto Rico. Oficina de Presupuesto y Gerencia. Resoluciones Conjuntas del Presupuesto General y de Presupuestos Especiales 298
Puerto Rico. Oficina de Presupuesto y Gerencia. Boletin de Presupuesto y Gerencia (PR) 945
Puerto Rico. Oficina de Presupuesto y Gerencia. Resoluciones Conjuntas del Presupuesto General y de Presupuestos Especiales (PR) 298
Puerto Rico. Statistics, Analysis and Control of Information. Annual Vital Statistics Report (PR) 955, 1062
Puerto Rico Living (US ISSN 0033-4049) 539
Puerto Rico Official Industrial Directory (PR ISSN 0090-3612) 316
Pulmonary Disease Reviews (US ISSN 0272-7900) 778
Pulp & Paper Buyers Guide (US) 316, 858
Pulp and Paper Canada Business Directory see Pulp & Paper Canada Directory 858
Pulp & Paper Canada Directory (CN ISSN 0708-501X) 858
Pulp & Paper Canada's Annual & Directory (CN ISSN 0709-2563) 859
Pulp and Paper Canada's Reference Manual and Buyers' Guide see Pulp & Paper Canada's Annual & Directory 859
Pulp and Paper Industry Technical Conference. Conference Record (US ISSN 0190-2172) 859
Pulp & Paper International Factbook (US) 859
Pulp & Paper North American Industry Factbook (US) 859
Pulp & Paper Pricebook (US) 859
Pulp and Paper Research Institute of Canada. Annual Report (CN ISSN 0079-7960) 859
Pulse (SA ISSN 0555-6945) 474
Pulse Power Modulator Symposium. I E E E Conference Record see Power Modulator Symposium. I E E E Conference Record 459
Pumping Manual (UK) 492
Pumps and Other Fluids Machinery Abstracts (UK ISSN 0302-2870) 11, 746
Punjab National Bank. Annual Report (II ISSN 0304-8101) 231
Punjab State Industrial Development Corporation. Annual Report (II) 291
Punjab University Indological Series (II) 571, 853
Punjab University Journal of Zoology (PK) 177
Pupila: Libros de Nuestro Tiempo (UY ISSN 0079-8061) 560
Purcell Letter on Graphics for Management (US) 1161
Purchaser's Guide to the Music Industries (US) 840
Purdue Air Quality Conference. Proceedings (US) 499
Purdue University. Civil Engineering Reprints (US ISSN 0079-8096) 483
Purdue University. Engineering Experiment Station. Joint Highway Research Project. Research Reports (US ISSN 0079-810X) 483
Purdue University. Office of Manpower Studies. Manpower & Technical Education Requirements Reports (US) 275
Purdue University. Office of Manpower Studies. Manpower Report see Purdue University. Office of Manpower Studies. Manpower & Technical Education Requirements Reports 275
Purdue University. Road School. Proceedings of Annual Road School (US ISSN 0079-8142) 1097
Purdue University. School of Electrical Engineering. Annual Research Summary (US ISSN 0033-4537) 459
Purdue University. Water Resources Research Center. Annual Report (US) 1125
Purdue University Monographs in Romance Language (US ISSN 0165-8743) 702, 730
Pure and Applied Mathematics (US ISSN 0079-8169) 752

Pure and Applied Mathematics; a Series of Texts and Monographs *see* Pure and Applied Mathematics: A Wiley Interscience Series of Texts, Monographs and Tracts 752
Pure and Applied Mathematics: A Wiley Interscience Series of Texts, Monographs and Tracts (US) 752
Pure and Applied Mathematics Series (US ISSN 0079-8177) 752
Pure and Applied Physics (US ISSN 0079-8193) 474, 890
Pure Life Society. Annual Report (MY ISSN 0552-6426) 881, 972
Pure-Pak News (US) 520, 855
Purificacion (UY) 908
Purushartha (FR ISSN 0339-1744) 75, 571, 1011
Pusat Daya Pengeluaran Negara. Lapuran Tahunan *see* National Productivity Centre, Malaysia. Annual Report 281
Pusat Penelitian Atma Jaya. Laporan Penelitian Keagamaan *see* Atma Jaya Research Centre. Socio-Religious Research Report 977
Pusat Penelitian Atma Jaya. Penelitian Tentang Kebutuhan Kesehatan Masyarakat dan Sistem Peleyanan Kesehatan di Kecamatan Penjaringan *see* Atma Jaya Research Centre. Socio-Medical Research Report 758
Pusat Penelitian Atma Jaya. Studi Tentang Pengembangan Pendidikan *see* Atma Jaya Research Centre. Education Development Research Report 410
Pushcart Prize: Best of the Small Presses (US ISSN 0149-7863) 730
Puteoli (IT) 91, 594
Pymatuning Symposia in Ecology (US) 160, 499
Pyramid Film and Video Catalog (US) 825
Pyrenae: Cronica Arqueologica (SP ISSN 0079-8215) 91
Pyttersen's Nederlandse Almanak (NE ISSN 0079-8223) 463
Q L A Bulletin/Bulletin A B Q (Quebec Library Association) (CN ISSN 0380-7150) 683
Q R L Poetry Series *see* Quarterly Review of Literature Poetry Series 743
Qantas Airways. Report (AT) 1089
Qatar National Bank (S.A.Q.). Report of the Directors and Balance Sheet (QA) 231
Qatar Yearbook (QA) 613, 1062
Quad (CN) 342
Quaderni (AT) 1161
Quaderni Camerti di Studi Romanistici. Index/International Survey of Roman Law. Index (IT) 662
Quaderni de "la Terra Santa" (IS) 613, 972, 1115
Quaderni del Salvemini (IT) 908
Quaderni del Vittoriale (IT ISSN 0391-3104) 743
Quaderni dell'Emilceramica (IT) 113
Quaderni di Analisi Matematica (IT ISSN 0391-3236) 752
Quaderni di Archeologia della Libia (IT ISSN 0079-8258) 91
Quaderni di Cultura Materiale (IT) 594
Quaderni di Filosofia (IT) 881
Quaderni di Parapsicologia (IT) 860
Quaderni di Poesia Neogreca (IT ISSN 0079-8274) 743
Quaderni di Scacchi: i Grandi Giocatori(IT) 1035
Quaderni di Scienza (IT) 998
Quaderni di Studi Storici Toscani (IT) 594
Quaderni di Verifiche (IT) 881
Quaderni Fiorentini per la Storia del Pensiero Giuridico Moderno (IT) 560, 662, 908
Quaderni Ibero-Americani (IT ISSN 0033-4960) 702, 730
Quaderni Internazionali di Storia Economica e Sociale/International Journal of Economic and Social History/Cahiers Internationaux d'Histoire Economique et Sociale (IT ISSN 0066-2283) 594
Quaderni Patavini di Linguistica (IT) 702
Quaderni Pucciniani (IT) 840

Quaderni Siciliani (IT) 908
Quaderno Industria Automobilistica Mondiale (IT) 1086
Quaderns de Treball (SP ISSN 0210-8291) 91
Quaestiones Geographicae (PL ISSN 0137-477X) 547
Quaker Encounters (UK) 881, 984
Quaker Peace & Service. Annual Report(UK ISSN 0260-9584) 984, 1020
Quaker Religious Thought (US ISSN 0033-5088) 984
Qualita della Vita (IT ISSN 0391-8521) 1028
Quality and Reliability (US) 474
Quality Control and Applied Statistics (US ISSN 0033-5207) 11, 425
Quality of Life in Iowa (US ISSN 0091-5696) 248
Quantitative Applications in the Social Sciences (US ISSN 0149-192X) 1011
Quantitative Geology and Geostatistics (NE) 394
Quantitative Methoden der Unternehmungsplanung (GW) 281
Quantum Mechanics and Nonlinear Waves *see* Physics: A Series of Monographs & Tracts 890
Quartaer (GW ISSN 0375-7471) 91
Quartaerpalaeontologie (GE ISSN 0138-3116) 380, 857
Quarterly and Annual Industrial Production Indexes (TH) 198
Quarterly Cumulated Index Medicus *see* Cumulated Index Medicus 769
Quarterly Index Islamicus (UK ISSN 0308-7395) 564
Quarterly Journal of Studies on Alcohol. Supplement *see* Journal of Studies on Alcohol. Supplement 377
Quarterly Review of Literature *see* Quarterly Review of Literature Poetry Series 743
Quarterly Review of Literature Contemporary Poetry Series *see* Quarterly Review of Literature Poetry Series 743
Quarterly Review of Literature Poetry Series (US) 743
Quaternary Studies (UK ISSN 0261-9784) 394
Quatre Mille Imprimeries *see* Quatre Mille Imprimeries Francaises 931
Quatre Mille Imprimeries Francaises (FR ISSN 0066-3638) 931
Quaver (Macquarie University Caving Group) (AT ISSN 0155-2880) 394
Quebec. Bureau de Statistique. Statistiques de l'Agriculture, des Peches et de l'Alimentation, Edition (Year) (CN) 43, 514
Quebec (City) Universite Laval. Centre d'Etudes Nordiques. Travaux Divers *see* Nordicana 74
Quebec (Province). Advisory Council of the Environment. Annual Report *see* Quebec (Province). Conseil Consultatif de l'Environnement. Rapport Annuel 499
Quebec (Province) Centrale des Bibliotheques. Choix: Documentation Audiovisuelle (CN ISSN 0706-2257) 130
Quebec (Province) Centrale des Bibliotheques. Choix: Documentation Imprimee (CN ISSN 0706-2249) 130
Quebec (Province) Centrale des Bibliotheques. Choix Jeunesse: Documentation Audiovisuelle *see* Quebec (Province) Centrale des Bibliotheques. Choix: Documentation Audiovisuelle 130
Quebec (Province) Centrale des Bibliotheques. Produits et Services Documentaires (CN) 130
Quebec (Province) Centrale des Bibliotheques. Services et Publications *see* Quebec (Province) Centrale des Bibliotheques. Produits et Services Documentaires 130
Quebec (Province) Commission des Services Juridiques. Rapport Annuel (CN) 662

Quebec (Province). Commission des Transports du Quebec. Rapport Annuel (CN ISSN 0702-0996) 1083
Quebec (Province). Commission des Transports. Rapports des Activites de la Commission des Transports du Quebec *see* Quebec (Province). Commission des Transports du Quebec. Rapport Annuel 1083
Quebec (Province). Conseil Consultatif de l'Environnement. Rapport Annuel(CN) 499
Quebec (Province). Conseil Consultatif sur les Reserves Ecologiques. Rapport Annuel (CN) 367, 526
Quebec (Province). Conseil de la Protection du Consommateur. Rapport Annuel (CN ISSN 0319-8774) 369
Quebec (Province). Conseil des Affaires Sociales et de la Famille. Rapport Annuel (CN) 1028
Quebec (Province). Consumer Protection Council. Rapport Annuel du Conseil de la Protection du Consommateur *see* Quebec (Province). Conseil de la Protection du Consommateur. Rapport Annuel 369
Quebec (Province). Curatelle Publique du Quebec. Rapport Annuel *see* Quebec (Province). Curatelle Publique. Rapport Annuel du Curateur Public 1020
Quebec (Province). Curatelle Publique. Rapport Annuel du Curateur Public (CN ISSN 0318-4854) 1020
Quebec (Province) Department of Natural Resources. Geological Reports (CN ISSN 0079-8738) 394
Quebec (Province) Department of Natural Resources. Geological Services. Field Work *see* Quebec (Province) Ministere des Richesses Naturelles. Travaux sur le Terrain 394
Quebec (Province). Department of Natural Resources. Report *see* Quebec (Province) Ministere des Richesses Naturelles. Rapport 367
Quebec (Province) Department of Recreation, Fish and Game. Annual Report/Ministere du Loisir de la Chasse et de la Peche (CN ISSN 0229-3811) 1115
Quebec (Province) Department of Tourism, Fish and Game. Annual Report *see* Quebec (Province) Department of Recreation, Fish and Game. Annual Report 1115
Quebec (Province) Direction Generale de l'Energie. Rapport Annuel-Energie Quebec (CN) 466
Quebec (Province) Direction Generale des Peches Maritimes. Cahier d'Information (CN) 145
Quebec (Province) Direction Generale des Peches Maritimes. Direction de la Recherche. Rapport Annuel (CN ISSN 0318-8779) 145
Quebec (Province). Direction Generale des Ressources Materielles et Financieres. Regles Budgetaires des Commission Scolaires et des Comissions Regionales. (CN) 443
Quebec (Province). Family and Social Affairs Council. Annual Report *see* Quebec (Province). Conseil des Affaires Sociales et de la Famille. Rapport Annuel 1028
Quebec (Province). Liquor Board. Rapport Annuel *see* Societe des Alcools du Quebec. Rapport Annuel 377
Quebec (Province) Marine Biological Station, Grande-Riviere. Cahiers d'Information *see* Quebec (Province) Direction Generale des Peches Maritimes. Cahier d'Information 145
Quebec (Province) Marine Biological Station, Grande-Riviere. Rapport *see* Quebec (Province) Direction Generale des Peches Maritimes. Direction de la Recherche. Rapport Annuel 145

Quebec (Province). Ministere de l'Agriculture, Pecheries et Alimentation. Direction Generale des Peches Maritimes. Travaux sur les Pecheries (CN) 145
Quebec (Province) Ministere de l'Agriculture. Rapport Annuel: Merite Agricole (CN ISSN 0701-6557) 33
Quebec (Province) Ministere de l'Agriculture. Rapport du Merite Agriculture *see* Quebec (Province) Ministere de l'Agriculture. Rapport Annuel: Merite Agricole 33
Quebec (Province). Ministere de l'Education. Regles Budgetaires des Commissions Scolaires et des Commissions Regionales *see* Quebec (Province). Direction Generale des Ressources Materielles et Financieres. Regles Budgetaires des Commission Scolaires et des Comissions Regionales 443
Quebec (Province) Ministere de l'Energie et des Ressources. Direction de la Recherche et du Developpement. Guide (CN) 526
Quebec (Province) Ministere de l'Energie et des Ressources. Direction de la Recherche et du Developpement. Memoire (CN) 527
Quebec (Province) Ministere de l'Energie et des Ressources. Direction de la Recherche et du Developpement. Note de Recherche Forestiere (CN) 527
Quebec (Province) Ministere de l'Energie et des Ressources. Service de la Recherche Appliquee. Guide *see* Quebec (Province) Ministere de l'Energie et des Ressources. Direction de la Recherche et du Developpement. Guide 526
Quebec (Province) Ministere de l'Energie et des Ressources. Service de la Recherche (Appliquee). Memoire *see* Quebec (Province) Ministere de l'Energie et des Ressources. Direction de la Recherche et du Developpement. Memoire 527
Quebec (Province) Ministere de l'Energie et des Ressources. Service de la Recherche (Appliquee). Note *see* Quebec (Province) Ministere de l'Energie et des Ressources. Direction de la Recherche et du Developpement. Note de Recherche Forestiere 527
Quebec (Province) Ministere de l'Environment. Conseil Consultatif des Reserves Ecologoques. Rapport Annuel *see* Quebec (Province). Conseil Consultatif sur les Reserves Ecologiques. Rapport Annuel 367
Quebec (Province). Ministere de l'Industrie et du Commerce. Direction de l'Analyse et de la Prevision Economiques (CN) 198, 1083
Quebec (Province) Ministere des Communications. Rapport des Activites (CN) 344
Quebec (Province) Ministere des Richesses Naturelles. Rapport (CN ISSN 0703-0940) 367, 499
Quebec (Province) Ministere des Richesses Naturelles. Repertoire des Publications (CN) 368
Quebec (Province) Ministere des Richesses Naturelles. Travaux sur le Terrain (CN ISSN 0079-8746) 394
Quebec (Province) Office de la Langue Francaise. Cahiers (CN ISSN 0079-8770) 702
Quebec (Province) Office de la Langue Francaise. Rapport d'Activites (CN) 702
Quebec (Province) Regie de l'Assurance-Depots du Quebec. Rapport Annuel (CN ISSN 0701-5666) 641
Quebec (Province) Regie de l'Assurance-Maladie. Statistiques Annuelles (CN) 643
Quebec (Province). Regie des Rentes du Quebec. Perspectives Statistiques *see* Quebec (Province). Regie des Rentes du Quebec. Statistical Outlook 641

1862　QUEBEC (PROVINCE).

Quebec (Province). Regie des Rentes du Quebec. Statistical Outlook (CN ISSN 0712-8231) 287, *641*
Quebec Corporation and Income Tax Legislation (CN) 298, *662*
Quebec Library Association Bulletin *see* Q L A Bulletin *683*
Queen Alexandra Hospital for Children. Annual Report (CN) *618*
Queen Alexandra Solarium for Crippled Children Annual Report *see* Queen Alexandra Hospital for Children. Annual Report *618*
Queen Mary College. Department of Geography and Earth Science. Occasional Papers (UK) *547*
Queen Mary College. Department of Geography. Occasional Papers *see* Queen Mary College. Department of Geography and Earth Science. Occasional Papers *547*
Queen Mary College Students Union Handbook (UK) *438*
Queen Victoria Museum and Art Gallery. Annual Report (AT) *830*
Queen Victoria Museum and Art Gallery. Launceston, Tasmania. Records (AT ISSN 0085-5278) *830, 998*
Queen's Award Magazine (UK ISSN 0141-1780) *259*
Queens College Publications in Anthropology (US) *75*
Queens College Studies in Librarianship(US ISSN 0146-8677) *683*
Queen's Medical Review (CN ISSN 0079-8789) *765*
Queen's Papers in Pure and Applied Mathematics (CN ISSN 0079-8797) *752*
Queen's Park Guidebook (CN) *951, 1115*
Queen's Regulations for the Army Amendments (UK) *812*
Queen's Regulations for the R.A.F. Amendments (UK) *812*
Queen's University. Industrial Relations Centre. Research and Current Issues Series (CN ISSN 0317-2546) *275*
Queen's University. Industrial Relations Centre. Research Series *see* Queen's University. Industrial Relations Centre. Research and Current Issues Series *275*
Queen's University. Institute for Economic Research. Discussion Paper (CN ISSN 0316-5078) *198*
Queen's University at Kingston. Annual Report on the Libraries (CN) *683*
Queen's University at Kingston. Department of Electrical Engineering. Research Report (CN ISSN 0075-6091) *459*
Queen's University at Kingston. Douglas Library. Occasional Papers (CN ISSN 0075-6113) *688*
Queen's University at Kingston. Industrial Relations Centre. Bibliography Series (CN ISSN 0075-613X) *217*
Queen's University at Kingston. Industrial Relations Centre. Report of Activities (CN ISSN 0075-6148) *275*
Queen's University at Kingston. Industrial Relations Centre. Reprint Series (CN ISSN 0075-6156) *275*
Queensborough (US ISSN 0033-6068) *237*
Queensland. Air Pollution Council. Annual Report (AT) *499*
Queensland. Department of Commercial and Industrial Development. Annual Report *see* Queensland. Department of Industry Development. Annual Report *291*
Queensland. Department of Education. Information and Publications Branch. Document (AT) *443*
Queensland. Department of Education. Information and Publications Branch. Information Statement (AT) *449*
Queensland. Department of Education. Research and Curriculum Branch. Curriculum Paper (AT ISSN 0310-4079) *418*

Queensland. Department of Education. Research and Curriculum Branch. Document *see* Queensland. Department of Education. Information and Publications Branch. Document *443*
Queensland. Department of Education. Research and Curriculum Branch. Information Statement *see* Queensland. Department of Education. Information and Publications Branch. Information Statement *449*
Queensland. Department of Education. Research and Curriculum Branch. Reporting Research *see* Queensland. Department of Education. Research Branch. Reporting Research *449*
Queensland. Department of Education. Research Branch. Reporting Research(AT) *449*
Queensland. Department of Education. Research Branch. Research Series (AT) *418*
Queensland. Department of Forestry. Annual Report (AT ISSN 0480-9653) *527*
Queensland. Department of Forestry. Research Paper (AT ISSN 0157-809X) *527*
Queensland. Department of Forestry. Technical Paper (AT ISSN 0155-9664) *527*
Queensland. Department of Industry Development. Annual Report (AT) *291*
Queensland. Land Administration Commission. Annual Report (AT) 33, *945*
Queensland. Registrar of Co-Operative and Other Societies. Report (AT ISSN 0481-3375) *238*
Queensland Littoral Society. Newsletter *see* Operculum *1160*
Queensland Museum, Brisbane. Memoirs (AT ISSN 0079-8835) *830*
Queensland Naturalist (AT ISSN 0079-8843) *145*
Queensland Pocket Yearbook (AT ISSN 0085-5316) *1062*
Queensland Society of Sugar Cane Technologists. Proceedings *see* Australian Society of Sugar Cane Technologists. Proceedings *518*
Queensland Tourist and Travel Corporation. Annual Report (AT) *1115*
Queensland Yearbook (AT ISSN 0085-5359) *1062*
Quellen und Forschungen aus Italienischen Archiven und Bibliotheken (GW ISSN 0079-9068) *560*
Quellen und Forschungen zur Basler Geschichte (SZ ISSN 0079-9076) *594*
Quellen und Forschungen zur Geschichte des Ersten Weltkriees *see* Quellen und Forschungen zu den Friedensversuchen des Ersten Weltkrieges *594*
Quellen und Forschungen zur Wuerttembergischen Kirchengeschichte (GW ISSN 0079-9084) *972*
Quellen und Studien *see* Schriften zur Kooperationsforschung. Studien *239*
Quellen und Studien zu den Friedensversuchen des Ersten Weltkrieges (GW) *594*
Quellen und Studien zur Geschichte des Oestlichen Europa (GW ISSN 0170-3595) *594*
Quellen und Studien zur Geschichte Osteuropas (GE ISSN 0079-9114) *594*
Quellen und Untersuchungen zur Lateinischen Philologie des Mittelalters (GW ISSN 0721-6203) *338, 702*
Quellen zur Geschichte des Islamischen Aegyptens (GW ISSN 0481-0023) *566*
Quellen zur Theatergeschichte (AU ISSN 0259-0786) *1078*
Quellenkataloge zur Musikgeschichte (GW ISSN 0079-905X) *840*

Quellenschriften zur Westdeutschen Vor- und Fruehgeschichte (GW ISSN 0079-9149) *91*
Quellenwerke zur Alten Geschichte Amerikas (GW ISSN 0079-9157) 516, *608*
Quelques Donnees Statistiques sur l'Industrie Francaise des Pates, Papiers, Cartons *see* Statistiques de l'Industrie Francaise des Pates. Papiers et Cartons *860*
Quem e Quem na Economia Brasileira (BL) *538*
Quercus (US) *743*
Quest *see* Little Magazine *726*
Quest (Pullman) (US ISSN 0033-6327) *474*
Questiones Geobiologicae *see* Problemy Biologie Krajiny *145*
Questo e il Sud Africa *see* South Africa Foundation. Information Digest (Year) *249*
Quetico-Superior Wilderness Research Center, Ely, Minnesota. Annual Report (US ISSN 0079-9211) 145, *367*
Quetico-Superior Wilderness Research Center, Ely, Minnesota. Technical Notes (US ISSN 0079-922X) *367*
Qufo (SW ISSN 0348-7377) *394*
Qui Construit des Machines *see* Wer Baut Maschinen *493*
Qui Est Qui en France *see* Who's Who in France *136*
Qui Fabrique et Fournit Quoi (FR) *856*
Qui Represente Qui (FR ISSN 0079-9262) *259, 281*
Qui Vend et Achete Quoi? (FR ISSN 0079-9270) *316*
Quick Caller: Boston Area Air Cargo Directory (US) *1089*, 1105
Quick Caller: Detroit Area Air Cargo Directory (US) *1089*, 1105
Quick Caller: Miami Area Air Cargo Directory (US) *1089*, 1105
Quick Caller: San Francisco Bay Area Air Cargo Directory (US) *1089*, 1105
Quick Help from the Governor; a Directory of State Financial Aid Agencies *see* College Loans from Uncle Sam *433*
Quien Construye Maquinas *see* Wer Baut Maschinen *493*
Quien Vende en Espana los Productos Extranjeros/Who Sells Foreign Products in Spain (SP) *316*
Quilt Digest (US ISSN 0740-4093) *844*
Quiltmakers Time (US) *113*
Quitumbe (EC) *608*
R A C Continental Handbook *see* R A C Continental Handbook and Hotel Guide *1115*
R A C Continental Handbook and Hotel Guide (Royal Automobile Club) (UK) 1092, *1115*
R A C Continental Motoring Guide *see* R A C Continental Handbook and Hotel Guide *1115*
R A C Guide and Handbook *see* R A C Handbook and Hotel Guide *1115*
R A C Handbook and Hotel Guide (Royal Automobile Club) (UK) 1092, *1115*
R A C Motor Sport Year Book (UK) 1092, *1115*
R A D A R *see* Point de Repere *10*
R A I A Memo (Royal Australian Institute of Architects) (AT ISSN 0818-1233) *99*
R A I A News *see* R A I A Memo *99*
R A-Nytt (SW ISSN 0347-4585) *564*
R A P R A Abstracts (UK ISSN 0033-6750) 11, 901, *986*
R & D Digest (Research & Development Division) (UK ISSN 0268-330X) 326, *466*
R & S Report (Honolulu) *see* Hawaii. Department of Health. Research and Statistics Office. R & S Report *927*
R.B.R.R. Kale Memorial Lectures (II) 198, *908*
R C A Plain Talk and Technical Tips *see* Communicator (Indianapolis) *451*
R C H A Technical Information Sheet (Regional Council of Historical Agencies) (US) *830*

R E C S A M Annual Report (Regional Centre for Education in Science and Mathematics) (MY ISSN 0377-3450) *418*, 449
R E I S Report: Industrial Market Service (US) *966*
R.E.I.T. Fact Book (National Association of Real Estate Investment Trusts) (US ISSN 0095-1374) 267, *966*
R E L C Annual Report (Regional Language Centre) (SI ISSN 0129-7716) *702*
R E L C Occasional Papers (Regional Language Centre) (SI ISSN 0129-8844) *702*
R E L C Seminar Report (Regional Language Centre) (SI) *702*
R E M E Journal (Royal Electrical & Mechanical Engineers) (UK ISSN 0432-2924) 21, *492*
R E S Mission Bulletin (Reformed Ecumenical Synod) (US) *979*
R E S S *see* Cahiers Vilfredo Pareto *1007*
R E S World Diaconal Bulletin *see* R E S Mission Bulletin *979*
R F (Rockefeller Foundation) (US) *1011*
R F F S A. Anuario Estatistico (Rede Ferroviaria Federal, S.A.) (BL ISSN 0102-4930) *1095*
R F Illustrated *see* R F *1011*
R F Medlemsblad (Romansk Filmklub) (DK ISSN 0109-0631) *825*
R G U Aarbog *see* Danmarks Geologiske Undersoegelse. Aarbog *385*
R G W in Zahlen *see* Comecon Data (Year) *261*
R.H.S. Gardener's Diary (Royal Horticultural Society) (UK ISSN 0080-441X) *533*
R I A I Architects Yearbook (Royal Institute of the Architects of Ireland) (IE) *99*
R I A S-Funkuniversitaet, Berlin. Forschung und Information *see* R I A S-Funkuniversitaet, Berlin. Schriftenreihe. Forschung und Information *438*
R I A S-Funkuniversitaet, Berlin. Schriftenreihe. Forschung und Information (GW) *438*
R I B A Computer Software Selector (Royal Institute of British Architects) (UK ISSN 0268-5124) 186, *363*
R I B A Directory of Practices *see* Architects *96*
R I B A Interior Design Product Selector (Royal Institute of British Architects) (UK ISSN 0267-0801) *187*
R I B A Product Selector (Royal Institute of British Architects) (UK ISSN 0265-8739) *187*
R I C S Abstracts and Reviews *see* R I C S Library Information Service Abstracts and Reviews *477*
R I C S Library Information Service Abstracts and Reviews (Royal Institution of Chartered Surveyors) (UK) 11, 189, *477*
R I E *see* Resources in Education *425*
R I L A News (Repertoire International de la Litterature de l'Art/International Repertory of the Literature of Art) (US) *113*
R I L M Abstracts of Music Literature (International Repertory of Music Literature) (US ISSN 0033-6955) 11, *844*
R I: Revista dos Recursos Humanos na Empresa (BL) *287*
R L A (CL ISSN 0033-698X) *702*
R.L.C.'s Museum Gazette (CN ISSN 0035-7154) *830*
R L; Revista Literaria *see* Universidade Federal de Minas Gerais. Corpo Discente. Revista Literaria *736*
R L S: Regional Language Studies, Newfoundland (CN ISSN 0079-9335) *702*
R M A Annual Statement Studies (Robert /Morris Associates) (US ISSN 0080-3340) *231*

R.M. Bucke Memorial Society for the Study of Religious Experience. Newsletter-Review (CN ISSN 0079-9343) *1161*
R.M. Bucke Memorial Society for the Study of Religious Experience. Proceedings of the Conference (CN ISSN 0079-9351) *972*
R O S C see Review of Scottish Culture *505*
R P A News see Regional Plan News *625*
R P P see Religionspaedagogische Praxis *972*
R R I C Bulletin see R R I S L Bulletin *985*
R R I S L Bulletin (Rubber Research Institute of Sri Lanka) (CE) *985*
R.S.A. Postage Stamp Catalogue (SA) *875*
R S G B Amateur Radio Call Book (Radio Society of Great Britain) (UK) *349*
R S V P: Directory of Creative Talent (Repondez S'il Vous Plait) (US) *16, 109, 316*
R T T Y Journal. Beginners Handbook (US) *349*
R V and Tent Sites in Alabama, Florida, Georgia, Kentucky, Louisiana, Mississippi, North Carolina, South Carolina, Tennessee see Southeastern Campbook *1116*
R V and Tent Sites in Alberta, British Columbia, Manitoba, Northwest Territories, Saskatchewan, Yukon Territory and Alaska see Western Canada Alaska Campbook *1119*
R V and Tent Sites in Arizona, Colorado, New Mexico, Utah see Southwestern Campbook *1116*
R V and Tent Sites in Arkansas, Kansas, Missouri, Oklahoma, Texas see South Central Campbook *1116*
R V and Tent Sites in California, Nevada see California - Nevada Campbook *1107*
R V and Tent Sites in Connecticut, Maine, Massachusetts, New Hampshire, New York, Rhode Island, Vermont see Northeastern Campbook *1114*
R V and Tent Sites in Delaware, District of Columbia, Maryland, New Jersey, Pennsylvania, Virginia, West Virginia see Mideastern Campbook *1114*
R V and Tent Sites in Idaho, Montana, Oregon, Washington, Wyoming see Northwestern Campbook *1115*
R V and Tent Sites in Iowa, Minnesota, Nebraska, North Dakota, South Dakota see North Central Campbook *1114*
R V and Tent Sites in New Brunswick, Newfoundland, Nova Scotia, Ontario, Prince Edward Island, Quebec see Eastern Canada Campbook *1108*
R V Buyers Guide (Recreational Vehicle) (US) *1083*
R V Campground & Services Guide see Trailer Life's Recreational Vehicle Campground and Services Directory *1047*
Raabe- Gesellschaft. Jahrbuch (GW ISSN 0075-2371) *730*
Raabser Maerchen-Reihe (AU) *516*
Raastofproduktionen, Havomraadet (DK ISSN 0109-7466) *394*
Raastofproduktionen, Landomraadet. Handelsvarer og Anvendelse, Gravforhold, Arealforhold (DK ISSN 0109-7474) *394*
Raastofproduktionen, Landomraadet. Produktionsmaengden af Geologiske Raastoffer Fordelt paa Antskommuner og Kommuner (DK ISSN 0109-7458) *394*
Raastofproduktionsopgoerelse see Raastofproduktionen, Landomraadet. Handelsvarer og Anvendelse, Gravforhold, Arealforhold *394*
Raastofproduktionsopgoerelse fra Havbunden see Raastofproduktionen, Havomraadet *394*

Raastofproduktionsopgoerelse fra Landomraadet see Raastofproduktionen, Landomraadet. Produktionsmaengden af Geologiske Raastoffer Fordelt paa Antskommuner og Kommuner *394*
Rabbinical Assembly, New York. Proceedings (US ISSN 0079-936X) *977*
Rabindra Bharati Journal (II) *539*
Raccolta di Tavole Statistiche see Annuarium Statisticum Ecclesiae *974*
Raccoon (US ISSN 0148-0162) *743*
Race Relations Survey see Survey of Race Relations in South Africa *914*
Race Walking World Statistics (DK ISSN 0107-3052) *1035, 1062*
Race Walking World Statistics - Women (DK ISSN 0108-3821) *1036*
Raceform Flat Annual (UK) *1035*
Raceform "Horses in Training" (UK ISSN 0081-3761) *1043*
Raceform Up-to-Date Form Book Annual see Raceform Flat Annual *1035*
Racehorses (UK ISSN 0079-9408) *1043*
Racial Ethnic Brotherhood see Ethnic Racial Brotherhood *503*
Racial/Ethnic Distribution of Public School Students and Staff, New York State (US ISSN 0085-4093) *418*
Racing and Football Outlook: Football Annual (UK) *1035, 1040*
Racing and Football Outlook: Jumping Annual (UK) *1035, 1040*
Racing and Football Outlook: Racing Annual (UK ISSN 0079-9424) *1035, 1040*
Racing and Football Racing Annual see Racing and Football Outlook: Racing Annual *1035*
Rackham Journal of the Arts and Humanities (US ISSN 0731-4817) *731*
Rackham Literary Studies see Rackham Journal of the Arts and Humanities *731*
Rad (YU ISSN 0033-7463) *649*
Radar Systems International (UK) *344*
Radcliffe College Newsletter see L A R C Newsletter *616*
Radiation Curing Buyer's Guide (US ISSN 0197-8039) *324*
Radiation Dosimetry Data; Catalogue (UN) *792*
Radiation Observations in Bergen (NO) *806*
Radiation Review see Arizona Radiation Review *896*
Radikale Historiker (GW) *594*
Radio (Year) (AT) *349*
Radio Advertisers' Guide (UK ISSN 0260-2423) *349*
Radio Amateur Callbook Magazine: U S Listings see U S Callbook *350*
Radio Amateur's Handbook (US ISSN 0079-9440) *349*
Radio - Electronics Annual see Radio - Electronics Experimenters Handbook (Year) *459*
Radio - Electronics Experimenters Handbook (Year) (US) *356, 362, 459*
Radio Facts and Figures see Radio (Year) *349*
Radio Handbook (US ISSN 0079-9467) *349*
Radio Society of Great Britain Amateur Radio Call Book see R S G B Amateur Radio Call Book *349*
Radio Technical Commission for Aeronautics. Proceedings of the Annual Assembly Meeting (US) *21, 349*
Radioactive Reporter (US) *466, 499*
Radioactivity Survey Data in Japan (JA ISSN 0441-2516) *332*
Radiologische Klinik (US) *792*
Radiology of Iatrogenic Disorders (US) *792*
Radiology Today (US) *792*
Radionavigation Journal (US) *407, 474*
Radner Lectures (US ISSN 0079-9491) *908, 918*

Radnor Historical Society. Bulletin (US) *608*
Radnorshire Society. Transactions (UK ISSN 0306-848X) *594*
Radovi see Geofizika *399*
Radovi Poljoprivrednog Fakuteta Univerziteta u Sarajevu (YU ISSN 0033-8583) *33*
Raethinge-Posten (DK ISSN 0106-9616) *594*
Raiken/Lichen (JA ISSN 0285-0850) *160*
Railroad Station Historical Society. Railroad Station Monograph (US) *1095*
Railway Accounting Rules (US) *222, 1095*
Railway Directory and Yearbook (UK ISSN 0079-9513) *1095*
Railway Fuel and Operating Officers Association. Proceedings (US ISSN 0079-9521) *1095*
Railway Line Clearances (US) *1095*
Railway Passenger Car Annual (US ISSN 0094-2278) *1095*
Railway Scene (SW ISSN 0347-030X) *1161*
Railway Technical Review (GW ISSN 0079-9548) *1095*
Railway World Annual (UK ISSN 0082-5891) *1095*
Railways of Sweden see Sveriges Jaernvaegar *1095*
Raincoast Chronicles (CN ISSN 0315-2804) *609*
Rainer Foundation. Annual Report (UK) *334, 372*
Rainey Times (US ISSN 0734-2055) *537*
Raionnye Biblioteki Belorussii (UR) *683*
Rajasthan Agriculturalist (II) *49*
Rajasthan Forest Statistics (II ISSN 0377-3302) *527*
Rajasthan, India. Directorate of Economics and Statistics. Basic Statistics (II ISSN 0079-9564) *217, 1062*
Rajasthan, India. Directorate of Economics and Statistics. Budget Study (II ISSN 0079-9556) *298*
Rajasthan State Tanneries Limited. Annual Report (II ISSN 0302-4881) *672*
Rajasthan State Warehousing Corporation. Annual Report and Accounts (II) *291*
Rajasthan University Studies in English (II ISSN 0448-1690) *702, 731*
Rajasthan University Studies in Sociology see Studies in Sociology *1030*
Rajasthan Year Book and Who's Who (II ISSN 0079-9572) *571*
Rajshahi University Studies (BG ISSN 0483-9218) *632*
Rak v Sloveniji. Tabele see Incidenca Raka v Sloveniji *775*
Rakentajain Kalenteri (FI ISSN 0355-550X) *187*
Rakuno Gakuen Daigaku Kiyo, Jinbun Shakaikagaku Hen see College of Dairying. Journal; Cultural and Social Sciences *26*
Rakuno Gakuen Daigaku Kiyo, Shizen Kagaku Hen see College of Dairying. Journal; Natural Science *62*
Ralph H. Blanchard Memorial Endowment Series (US) *641, 1020*
Ramblers and Cyclists Bed and Breakfast Guide see Cyclists Touring Club Handbook *1151*
Ramblers Association Bed and Breakfast Guide see Cyclists Touring Club Handbook *1151*
Rambunctious Review (US) *731*
Rampart Individualist (US) *712*
Ramsay Society of Chemical Engineers. Journal (UK ISSN 0456-4804) *479*
Ranchi University Mathematical Journal (II ISSN 0079-9602) *752*
Rand Corporation. Paper see Rand Report Series *998*
Rand McNally Business Traveler's Road Atlas (US) *198, 1115*
Rand McNally Campground and Trailer Park Guide see Rand McNally Campground and Trailer Park Guide. Eastern *1046*

Rand McNally Campground and Trailer Park Guide. Eastern. (US ISSN 0733-8309) *1046*
Rand McNally Commercial Atlas and Marketing Guide (US) *285, 547*
Rand McNally Credit Union Directory (US) *231*
Rand McNally Discover Historic America (US ISSN 0079-9637) *1115*
Rand McNally Family Adventure Road Atlas (US) *1115*
Rand McNally Goode's World Atlas (US) *547*
Rand McNally Interstate Road Atlas (US) *1115*
Rand McNally List of Bank-Recommended Attorneys (US) *1161*
Rand McNally Motor Carriers' Road Atlas (US) *1105*
Rand McNally National Park Guide (US ISSN 0079-9629) *1046*
Rand McNally Places Rated Almanac (US) *625, 966*
Rand McNally Places Rated Retirement Guide see Rand McNally Retirement Places Rated *625*
Rand McNally Retirement Places Rated(US) *625*
Rand McNally Road Atlas (US) *1115*
Rand McNally Road Atlas & City Guide to Europe (US) *1115*
Rand McNally Road Atlas & Vacation Guide (US) *1115*
Rand McNally Road Atlas of Britain (US) *1115*
Rand McNally Road Atlas of Europe (US) *1115*
Rand McNally Travel Trailer Guide see Rand McNally Campground and Trailer Park Guide. Eastern *1046*
Rand McNally Vacation Guide see Rand McNally Discover Historic America *1115*
Rand McNally Vacation Places Rated (US) *1115*
Rand Paper Series see Rand Report Series *998*
Rand - Pretoria Directory (SA) *316*
Rand Report Series (US) *998, 1070*
Rand Show Guide (SA) *1043*
Rand Show Livestock & Produce Catalogue (SA) *33*
Randax Education Guide (US ISSN 0097-5206) *430*
Randgebieden (NE) *709*
Random Lengths Yearbook (US ISSN 0485-9960) *529*
Randse Afrikaanse Universiteit. Jaarboek (SA) *418*
Randse Afrikaanse Universiteit. Op en Om die Kampus (SA) *418*
Randse Afrikaanse Universiteit. Prospektus (SA) *418*
Rannsoknastofnun Fiskidnadarins. Arsskyrsla (IC) *512*
Raphael's Astrological Almanac (UK) *860*
Rapport (Pittsburgh) see Slow Loris Reader *1162*
Rapport Annuel see European Free Trade Association. Annual Report *255*
Rapport Annuel du Conseil des Arts du Canada et son Supplement see Canada Council Annual Report and Supplement *103*
Rapport Annuel sur l'Assistance au Developpement: Burundi see Rapport Annuel sur la Cooperation au Developpement - Burundi *264*
Rapport Annuel sur l'Assistance au Developpement: Rwanda (UN) *263*
Rapport Annuel sur l'Economie Syrienne (SY ISSN 0079-9696) *248*
Rapport Annuel sur la Cooperation au Developpement - Burundi (UN) *264*
Rapport Canedien a l'Industrie sur les Sciences Halieutiques et Aquatiques see Canadian Industry Report of Fisheries and Aquatic Sciences *508*
Rapport fra S T I K K (Samarbejdsgruppen for Trafiksikkerhed i Kommuneerne i Koebenhavns-Omraadet) (DK ISSN 0105-6956) *1097*

Rapport General sur la Securite Sociale au Grand-Duche du Luxembourg see Luxembourg. Inspection Generale de la Securite Sociale. Rapport General sur la Securite Sociale au Grand-Duche de Luxembourg *640*
Rapport I V V O (NE) *67*
Rapport om Kontrollen med Konsummaelkprodukter (DK ISSN 0107-8666) *291*
Rapport over Pesticidrester i Danske Levnedsmidler see Pesticidrester i Danske Levnedsmidler *58*
Rapport sur la Situation Demographique de la France (FR) *924*
Rapport Technique Canadien des Sciences Halieutiques et Aquatiques see Canadian Technical Report of Fisheries and Aquatic Sciences *508*
Rapporto sulla Industria Cotoniera Italiana (IT) *1074*
Raptor Report (US) *170, 367*
Rashut Nayerot Haerech. Annual Report (IS) *231*
Rasilimali (TZ ISSN 0856-0382) *268*
Rasmi Jaridah see Afghanistan. Ministry of Justice. Official Gazette *650*
Rasp (DK ISSN 0107-8747) *945*
Raspberry Press (US) *712*
Rassegna di Letteratura Tomistica (IT) *881, 972*
Rassenlijst voor Fruitgewassen (NE) *59*
Rassenlijst voor Groentegewassen: Glasgroenten (NE) *59*
Rassenlijst voor Groentegewassen: Vollegrondsgroenten (NE) *59*
Rasskaz (UR) *731*
Rastitel'nye Resursy Sibiri i Dal'nego Vostoka see Rastitel'nyi Mir Sibiri i Dal'nego Vostoka *150*
Rastitel'nyi Mir Sibiri i Dal'nego Vostoka (UR) *150*
Rat News Letter (US ISSN 0309-1848) *782*
Ratcliffian (UK ISSN 0048-6809) *342*
Raumplanung und Umweltschutz im Kanton Zurich (SZ) *625, 955*
Raven Press Series in Experimental Physiology (US) *172, 782*
Ravi (PK) *731*
Raymond Dart Lectures (SA ISSN 0079-9815) *75*
Razprave in Gradivo/Treatises and Documents (YU ISSN 0034-0251) *516*
Re: Print (US) *712*
Reaching the Manitoba Market (CN ISSN 0706-8085) *16*
Reaction Mechanisms in Organic Chemistry (NE ISSN 0079-9823) *331, 332*
Reactivity and Structure: Concepts of Organic Chemistry (US ISSN 0341-2377) *331*
Reader's Digest Almanac and Yearbook (US ISSN 0079-9831) *463*
Reader's Guide Series (US) *130*
Reading in Political Economy (UK ISSN 0305-814X) *199*
Reading Journal (II ISSN 0377-3426) *449*
Reading Research. Advances in Theory and Practice (US ISSN 0191-0914) *449*
Readings in American History see Annual Editions: Readings in American History *603*
Readings in Business see Annual Editions: Business/Management *191*
Readings in Development Economics (PK ISSN 0557-8280) *264*
Readings in Economic History and Theory (UK) *252*
Readings in Education see Annual Editions: Readings in Education *410*
Readings in Environment see Annual Editions: Environment *494*
Readings in Health see Annual Editions: Health *885*
Readings in Linguistics see Lingvisticke Citanky *698*
Readings in Long Island Archaeology and Ethnohistory (US) *75, 505, 609*
Readings in Marketing see Annual Editions: Marketing *283*
Readings in Political Economy see Reading in Political Economy *199*

Readings in Spanish-English Contrastive Linguistics (PR) *702*
Readings on Equal Education (US ISSN 0270-1448) *445*
Reagent Chemicals (US) *326*
Real (GW ISSN 0723-0338) *731*
Real Academia de Cordoba de Ciencias, Bellas Letras y Nobles Artes. Boletin (SP ISSN 0034-060X) *731*
Real Estate Development Annual (CN) *966*
Real Estate Directory of Manhattan (US ISSN 0098-8936) *966*
Real Estate Directory of the Borough of Manhattan see Real Estate Directory of Manhattan *966*
Real Estate for Professional Practitioners: a Wiley Series (US) *966*
Real Estate Institute of Queensland. Annual Report (AT) *966*
Real Estate Reports (US ISSN 0079-9890) *966*
Real Estate Tax Analyst (US) *966*
Real Estate Trends in Metropolitan Vancouver see MetroTrends *965*
Real Life Magazine (US) *109, 731*
Real Sociedad Arqueologica. Boletin Arqueologico (SP ISSN 0034-0863) *91, 560*
Real Sociedad Espanola de Historia Natural. Boletin de Geologia y Biologia (SP) *145, 394*
Real-Time Systems Symposium. Proceedings (US) *359*
Realidad Peruana (PE) *248*
Realites Danoises see Denmark Review *243*
Realites Gabonaises (GO ISSN 0486-106X) *908*
Reality Studios (UK ISSN 0143-0122) *712, 731*
Realty Bluebook (US ISSN 0090-399X) *966*
Reanimation et Medecine d'Urgence (FR) *765*
Reappraisals (CN) *731*
Reasons for Choosing (AT) *849*
Rebel Youth (CN) *908*
Rebis Chapbook Series (US ISSN 0147-0396) *743*
Recent Achievments in Restorative Neurology (SZ) *791*
Recent Advances in Epilepsy (UK) *791*
Recent Advances in Infection (UK ISSN 0144-1078) *778*
Recent Advances in Nuclear Medicine (US ISSN 0163-6170) *792*
Recent Advances in Obesity Research (US) *765, 886*
Recent Advances in Occupational Health (UK) *636*
Recent Advances in Plasma Diagnostics (US ISSN 0079-9939) *1161*
Recent Advances in Radiology and Medical Imaging (UK ISSN 0143-6961) *792*
Recent Advances in Tobacco Science (US ISSN 0363-8480) *1080*
Recent Developments in Alcoholism (US) *377*
Recent Developments in the Chemistry of Natural Carbon Compounds (HU ISSN 0079-9947) *331*
Recent Developments of Neurobiology in Hungary (HU ISSN 0079-9955) *145*
Recent Progress in Hormone Research. Proceedings of the Laurentian Hormone Conference (US ISSN 0079-9963) *781*
Recent Progress in Surface Membrane Science (US) *332*
Recent Progress in Surface Science see Recent Progress in Surface Membrane Science *332*
Recent Progress of Natural Sciences in Japan (JA ISSN 0286-715X) *1161*
Recent Researches in Geology (II) *394*
Recent Results in Cancer Research/Fortschritte der Krebsforschung (US ISSN 0080-0015) *776*
Recent Trends in Social Sciences (II) *1011*
Recherche sur les Relations Industrielles au Canada see Industrial Relations Research in Canada *272*
Recherche Urbaine (FR) *625*

Recherches Anglaises et Americaines (FR ISSN 0557-6989) *1011*
Recherches Archeologiques en Hainaut Occidental. Bilan (BE) *91*
Recherches d'Histoire et de Sciences Sociales/Studies in History and the Social Sciences (FR ISSN 0249-5619) *560, 1011*
Recherches en Linguistique Etrangere (FR) *702*
Recherches et Documents d'Art et d'Archeologie (FR ISSN 0080-0074) *91, 109*
Recherches Germaniques (FR ISSN 0399-1989) *702, 731*
Recherches Institutionnelles (FR) *972*
Recherches Linquistiques (FR) *702*
Recherches Philosophiques Africaines (ZR) *75, 881*
Recherches Philosophiques Africaines. Collection see Recherches Philosophiques Africaines *881*
Recherches sur la Musique Francaise Classique (FR ISSN 0080-0139) *840*
Recherches sur la Renaissance (Paris) (FR) *594*
Recht und Geschichte (GW ISSN 0486-1493) *560*
Recht-Wirtschaft-Aussenhandel Schriftenreihe (AU) *662*
Rechts- und Staatswissenschaften (US ISSN 0080-0163) *663, 908*
Rechtsbibliographie/Bibliographie Juridique/Law Bibliography (SZ ISSN 0250-5940) *130, 669*
Rechtshistorische Studies (NE) *663*
Rechtspflege Jahrbuch (GW ISSN 0080-018X) *663*
Rechtsrheinisches Koeln (GW) *594*
Rechtsstaat in der Bewaehrung (GW) *663, 671*
Rechtstheorie (GW ISSN 0034-1398) *663*
Rechtswissenschaft und Sozialpolitik (AU) *663, 908*
Recife, Brazil. Secretaria de Assuntos Juridicos. Revista (BL) *663*
Recife, Brazil. Secretaria de Educacao e Cultura. Arquivos (BL) *609*
Recipientundersoegelse ved Marmorilik (DK ISSN 0107-7090) *499*
Reciprocal Meat Conference. Proceedings see American Meat Science Association. Reciprocal Meat Conference. Proceedings *518*
Reciprocating Pump Specifications (US) *474*
Reciprocity Guide for Private Motor Carriers (US) *1105*
Recognition and Identification Blue Book (US) *316*
Recollections of the Pioneers of British Columbia (CN) *609*
Recommendation for Accountants and Auditors (UK) *222*
Recommendation for Survival in Business (UK) *199*
Recommended Country Hotels of Britain (UK ISSN 0267-3428) *1115*
Recommended Reference Books for Small & Medium-Sized Libraries and Media Centers (US ISSN 0277-5948) *683*
Recommended Short Break Holidays (UK) *1115*
Recommended Wayside Inns of Britain (UK ISSN 0080-0252) *1116*
Reconstruction Surgery and Traumatology (SZ ISSN 0080-0260) *786, 794*
Recopilacion de Doctrina Legal (SP) *663*
Record & Tape Directory (UK) *1161*
Record Collector's Monthly (US ISSN 8755-6154) *840*
Record Prices see Music Master Catalogue *838*
Record - Vehicular Technology Conference see I E E E Vehicular Technology Conference. Record *1092*
Recording for the Blind. Catalog of Recorded Books (US ISSN 0484-1506) *180*
Recording in Great Britain see Guide to A P R S Member Studios *1031*

Records of Civilization. Sources and Studies (US ISSN 0080-0287) *560, 853*
Records of Huntingdonshire (UK ISSN 0034-1738) *594*
Records of the Ancient Near East (GW ISSN 0340-8450) *853*
Recovering Literature (US ISSN 0300-6425) *731*
Recreation and Outdoor Life Directory (US) *1046*
Recreation: Current Selected Research (US) *731*
Recreation Management Handbook (UK ISSN 0144-624X) *1035*
Recreation Management Yearbook see Recreation Management Handbook *1035*
Recreation Managers' Association of Great Britain Year Book (UK ISSN 0267-2103) *1035*
Recreation, Sports & Leisure Resource (US) *1161*
Recreational Vehicle Buyers Guide see R V Buyers Guide *1083*
Recreational Vehicle Campground and Services Directory see Trailer Life's Recreational Vehicle Campground and Services Directory *1047*
Recruiting (Year) (US) *849*
Recueil Annuel de Jurisprudence Belge (BE) *663*
Recueil Annuel de Windsor d'Acces a la Justice see Windsor Yearbook of Access to Justice *667*
Recueil Complet des Budgets de la Syrie (SY ISSN 0080-0309) *298*
Recueil des Arrets du Conseil de Revision des Pensions see Canada. Pension Review Board. Reports *810*
Recueil des Corrections de Cartes (Year) (FR ISSN 0180-9970) *547*
Recueil des Films (CN ISSN 0085-543X) *825*
Recueil des Instructions Donnees aux Ambassadeurs et Ministres de France (FR ISSN 0080-0333) *918*
Recueil des Travaux de l'Histoire de la Litterature see Zbornik Istorije Knjizevnosti *738*
Recueil des Travaux sur la Protection des Monuments Historiques see Zbornik Zastite Spomenika Kulture *112*
Recueil International de Statistiques des Transports Publics Urbains see International Statistical Handbook of Urban Public Transport *1081*
Red Book of Eye, Ear, Nose and Throat Specialists see Red Book of Ophthalmology *786*
Red Book of Housing Manufacturers (US ISSN 0149-7642) *187*
Red Book of Ophthalmology (US ISSN 0146-4582) *786*
Red Contable Agraria Nacional (SP) *49*
Red Fox Review see Red Fox Review at Mohegan Community College *743*
Red Fox Review at Mohegan Community College (US ISSN 0742-454X) *743*
Red Hill Press see Invisible City *742*
Red Poll Herd Book (UK) *67*
Red Weather (US) *731*
Redding Museum. Occasional Papers (US) *830*
Rede Ferroviaria Federal, S.A. Anuario Estatistico see R F F S A. Anuario Estatistico *1095*
Rede Ferroviaria Federal, S.A. Sistema Ferroviario R F F S A see Sistema Ferroviario R F F S A *1095*
Rediscovery (US) *91*
Reed's Commercial Salvage Practice (UK) *1103*
Reed's Mediterranean Navigator (UK ISSN 0263-3620) *1103*
Reed's Nautical Almanac (UK ISSN 0080-0422) *1083*
Reed's Ocean Navigator (UK) *1103*
Re'em (IS) *177*
Referate Organ: Schweissen und Verwandte Verfahren/Bulletin of Abstracts: Welding and Allied Processes (GW ISSN 0340-4749) *11, 802*

Referatedienst Verpackung see Packaging Science and Technology Abstracts 855
Referativnyi Zhurnal. Astronomiya (UR ISSN 0486-2236) 11, *118*
Referativnyi Zhurnal. Ekonomika, Organizatsiya, Tekhnologiya i Oborudovanie Poligraficheskogo Proizvodstva (UR ISSN 0320-5223) 11, *932*
Referativnyi Zhurnal. Electrotekhnika i Elektroenergetika see Referativnyi Zhurnal. Elektrotekhnika 462
Referativnyi Zhurnal. Elektronika (UR ISSN 0206-5452) 11, *462*
Referativnyi Zhurnal. Elektronika i ee Primenenie see Referativnyi Zhurnal. Elektronika 462
Referativnyi Zhurnal. Elektrosvyaz' (UR ISSN 0134-7772) 11, *462*
Referativnyi Zhurnal. Elektrotekhnika (UR) 11, *462, 468*
Referativnyi Zhurnal. Energetika (UR ISSN 0203-5308) *468*
Referativnyi Zhurnal. Environment Management Abstracts (UR ISSN 0234-7059) *501*
Referativnyi Zhurnal. Fizika (UR ISSN 0034-2343) 11, *893*
Referativnyi Zhurnal. Fotokinotekhnika (UR ISSN 0370-8063) 11, 826, *885*
Referativnyi Zhurnal. Gornoe Delo (UR ISSN 0034-2386) 11, *822*
Referativnyi Zhurnal. Immunologiya - Allergologiya (UR ISSN 0202-9154) 11, *773*
Referativnyi Zhurnal. Issledovanie Kosmicheskogo Prostranstva (UR ISSN 0034-2408) 11, 22, *118*
Referativnyi Zhurnal. Khimicheskoe i Kholodil'noe Mashinostroenie see Referativnyi Zhurnal. Khimicheskoe, Neftepererabatyvayuschchee i Polimernoe Mashinostroenie 554
Referativnyi Zhurnal. Khimicheskoe, Neftepererabatyvayuschchee i Polimernoe Mashinostroenie (UR ISSN 0370-8098) 11, *554*
Referativnyi Zhurnal. Korroziya i Zashchita ot Korrozii (UR ISSN 0131-3533) 11, *802, 856*
Referativnyi Zhurnal. Matematika (UR ISSN 0034-2467) 11, *755*
Referativnyi Zhurnal. Meditsinskaya Geografiya (UR ISSN 0034-2475) 11, *773*
Referativnyi Zhurnal. Metallurgiya (UR ISSN 0034-2491) 11, *802*
Referativnyi Zhurnal. Metrologiya i Izmeritel'naya Tekhnika (UR ISSN 0034-2505) 11, *810*
Referativnyi Zhurnal. Oborudovanie Pishchevoi Promyshlennosti (UR ISSN 0034-2521) 11, *522*
Referativnyi Zhurnal. Onkologiya (UR ISSN 0202-9197) 11, *773*
Referativnyi Zhurnal. Pozharnaya Okhrana (UR ISSN 0202-9898) 11, *959*
Referativnyi Zhurnal. Promyshlennyi Transport (UR ISSN 0034-2556) 11, *746*
Referativnyi Zhurnal. Radiatsionnaya Biologiya (UR ISSN 0131-355X) 11, 150, *773*
Referativnyi Zhurnal. Radiotekhnika (UR ISSN 0034-267X) *346*
Referativnyi Zhurnal. Svarka (UR ISSN 0131-3525) 11, *802*
Referativnyi Zhurnal. Tekhnicheskaya Estetika i Ergonomika (UR) *1073*
Referativnyi Zhurnal. Tekhnologiya Mashinostroeniya (UR ISSN 0034-2599) 11, *746*
Referativnyi Zhurnal. Teplo i Massobmen (UR ISSN 0203-6436) 11, *468*
Referativnyi Zhurnal. Volokonno-opticheskie Systemy (UR ISSN 0234-9647) *893, 899*
Referativnyi Zhurnal. Yadernye Reaktory (UR ISSN 0034-2653) 11, *893*
Reference Book-Argentina (US ISSN 0080-0449) *248*
Reference Book of Corporate Managements (US) *281*
Reference Book of Highway Personnel (US ISSN 0516-9445) *1083*
Reference Book-Republic of South Africa (US ISSN 0080-0457) *249*
Reference Data for Engineers (US) *349*
Reference Data for Radio Engineers see Reference Data for Engineers 349
Reference Encyclopedia of the American Indian (US) 463, *505*
Reference Guides to Archives and Manuscript Collections on Immigrant Culture (US ISSN 0885-7555) *564*
Reference Guides to State History and Research (US) *560*
Reference Point: Food Industry Abstracts (US) 11, *522*
Reference Sources (US) 11, *964*
Reference Sources for the Social Sciences and Humanities (US ISSN 0730-3335) *1011*
Refining, Construction, Petrochemical & Natural Gas Processing Plants of the World (US) *866*
Reflection (Spokane) (US ISSN 0484-2650) *731*
Reform in Northern Ireland (UK) *663*
Reformationsgeschichtliche Studien und Texte (GW ISSN 0171-3469) *979*
Reformed Church of America. Historical Series (US ISSN 0080-0481) *979*
Reformed Ecumenical Synod Mission Bulletin see R E S Mission Bulletin 979
Refractory Materials (US ISSN 0080-049X) *320*
Refrigeration and Air Conditioning Directory see Refrigeration and Air Conditioning Year Book 554
Refrigeration and Air Conditioning Year Book (UK ISSN 0305-0777) *554*
Refugee Abstracts (UN ISSN 0253-1445) *924, 1020*
Refugees Among Us- Unreached Peoples (US) *972*
Regards sur l'Economie de la Haute-Normandie (FR) *237*
Regency International Directory (UK ISSN 0080-0538) 316, *372*
Regensburger Beitraege zur Deutschen Sprach- und Literaturwissenschaft. Reihe A: Quellen (GW) 702, *731*
Regensburger Beitraege zur Deutschen Sprach- und Literaturwissencahft. Reihe B: Untersuchungen (GW) 702, *731*
Reger-Studien (GW) *840*
Regesta Regum Scottorum (UK ISSN 0080-0554) *560*
Reggae (CN ISSN 0714-4369) *840*
Reggae Quarterly see Reggae 840
Der Reggeboge (US ISSN 0034-3269) *505, 731*
Regi Magyar Dallamok Tara/Corpus Musicae Popularis Hungaricae (HU ISSN 0080-0562) *841*
Regi Magyar Prozai Emlekek (HU ISSN 0080-0570) *731*
Regina (CN) *1116*
Regina Geographical Studies (CN ISSN 0228-5851) *547*
Region Exporta (SP ISSN 0211-8866) *237*
Regional Advisory Council for Technological Education. Science Education in the Region see Science Education in the Region 438
Regional Breakdown of World Travel Statistics (SP) *1161*
Regional Conference of Directors of Agriculture, Livestock Production and Fisheries. Report see South Pacific Commission. Regional Conference of Directors of Agriculture, Livestock Production and Fisheries. Report 67
Regional Council Directory see Directory of Regional Councils 941
Regional Council of Historical Agencies Technical Information Sheet see R C H A Technical Information Sheet 830
Regional Institute of Social Welfare Research. Annual Report (US ISSN 0091-2859) *1020*
Regional Plan Association, Inc. Regional Plan News see Regional Plan News 625
Regional Plan News (Regional Plan Association, Inc.) (US) *625*
Regional Planning (GW) *1020*
Regional Science Dissertation and Monograph Series (US) *625*
Regional Science Research Institute. Bibliography Series (US ISSN 0080-0619) *1161*
Regional Science Research Institute. Monograph Series (US ISSN 0080-0627) *1161*
Regional Science Review see Northeast Regional Science Review 624
Regional Spotlight (US ISSN 0034-3390) *438*
Regional'naya Nauka o Razmeshchenii Proizvoditel'nykh Sil (UR) *291*
Regionalplanung in Kanton Zurich see Raumplanung und Umweltschutz im Kanton Zurich 625
Region's Agenda (US ISSN 0034-3420) *625*
Register Development Research Projects Africa (SG ISSN 0850-4008) *264*
Register of Architects (UK) *99*
Register of Autorized Laboratories see Register over Autoriserede Laboratorier 782
Register of Indexers (US) 11, *683*
Register of Medical Practitioners, Interns and Dentists for the Republic of South Africa (SA) *765*
Register of Non-Thoroughbred Mares (UK) *1043*
Register of Offshore Units, Submersibles and Diving Systems (UK ISSN 0141-4143) *1103*
Register of Patent Agents (UK) *861*
Register of Registrars (UK ISSN 0482-1319) *1062*
Register over Autoriserede Laboratorier/Register of Autorized Laboratories (DK ISSN 0105-9173) *782*
Register over Danske Patenter Udstedt (DK ISSN 0107-590X) *861*
Register over Gaellande S F S-Foerfattningar (SW) *945*
Registers & Directory of Veterinary Surgeons (UK) *1122*
Registre Aeronautique International (FR ISSN 0080-066X) *1089*
Registre International de Classification de Navires et d'Aeronefs see Registre Maritime 1103
Registre Maritime (FR) *1103*
Registro de Organismos de Salud (CK) *955*
Registro Industrial Brasileiro (BL) *316*
Registro Industrial Mexicano (MX) *316*
Regnkabsresultater see Denmark. Jordbrugsoekonomisk Institut. Serie B: Oekonomien i Landbrugets Driftsgrene 46
Regnskabsundersoegelsen for Isenkrambranchen see Normtalsundersoegelsen for Isenkrambranchen 190
Regnum Vegetabile (NE ISSN 0080-0694) *160*
Regulae Benedicti Studia. Annuarium Internationale (GW) *972*
Regulations for the Electrical Equipment of Buildings (UK) *459*
Rehabilitation/Ryoiku (JA ISSN 0036-0538) *765*
Rehabilitation der Entwicklungsgehemmten (GW ISSN 0080-0708) *445, 765*
Rehabilitation Gazette (US ISSN 0361-4166) 180, 376, *445*
Rehabilitation Industries Corporation. Annual Report (II ISSN 0080-0724) 291, *445*
Rehabilitation International. World Congress. Proceedings (US) *445*
Rehabilitation und Praevention (US ISSN 0172-6412) *765*
Rehovot (US ISSN 0034-3609) 449, *998*
Reichenbachia (GE ISSN 0070-7279) *165*
Reichorui Kenkyujo Nenpo/Kyoto University. Primate Research Institute. Annual Report (JA ISSN 0286-4568) 75, 145, *765*
Reihe Strafrecht (SZ) *663*
Reine und Angewandte Metallkunde see Materials Research and Engineering 799
Reine und Angewandte Metallkunde in Einzeldarstellungen see Materials Research and Engineering 799
Reinforced Concrete Research Council. Bulletins (US ISSN 0569-8057) *187*
Reinforced Plastics Congress (UK ISSN 0306-3607) *901*
Reinwardtia (IO ISSN 0034-365X) *160*
Reisen in Deutschland; Deutsches Handbuch fuer Fremdenverkehr (GW) *1116*
Rejsebogen (Year) (DK ISSN 0108-6812) *1116*
Relacion de Ingenieros de Caminos, Canales y Puertos (SP) *483*
Relatoria D N O C S see Brazil. Departamento Nacional de Obras Contra as Secas. Relatorio 939
Reliability and Maintainability Conference. Record see Reliability and Maintainability Symposium. Proceedings 459
Reliability and Maintainability Symposium. Proceedings (US ISSN 0149-144X) *459*
Reliability Physics (US ISSN 0735-0791) *893*
Reliability Review (US) *466*
Religioese Graphik (AU ISSN 0034-3935) 109, *972*
Religion and Reason; Method and Theory in the Study and Interpretation of Religion (GW ISSN 0080-0848) *972*
Religion and Society (GW) 881, *972*
Religion et Sciences de l'Homme (FR ISSN 0080-0864) *972*
Religion Index One: Periodicals (US ISSN 0149-8428) 11, *975*
Religion Index Two: Multi-Author Works (US ISSN 0149-8436) *975*
Religion, Wissenschaft, Kultur. Jahrbuch see Religion, Wissenschaft, Kultur. Schriftenreihe 972
Religion, Wissenschaft, Kultur. Schriftenreihe (AU) *972*
Religione e Societa (IT ISSN 0391-853X) *972, 1028*
Religionspaedagogische Praxis (GW) *972*
Religious and Inspirational Books and Serials in Print (US ISSN 0000-0868) 130, *972*
Religious & Theological Abstracts (US ISSN 0034-4044) 11, *975*
Religious Books and Serials in Print see Religious and Inspirational Books and Serials in Print 130
Religious Books in Print (UK ISSN 0305-960X) *130*
Remedia Hoechst (GW ISSN 0080-0899) *872*
Remedies see B A R - B R I Bar Review. Remedies 652
Remote Systems Technology Proceedings see Conference on Remote Systems Technology. Proceedings 896
Renaissance and Modern Studies (UK ISSN 0486-3720) *632*
Renaissance Drama (US ISSN 0486-3739) 731, *1078*
Renaissance Manuscript Studies (GW) *841*
Renaissance Papers (US) *731*
Renaissance Two; Journal of Afro-American Studies (US ISSN 0360-7410) *505*
Renaissance 2 see Renaissance Two; Journal of Afro-American Studies 505
Rencontres Internationales de Geneve (SZ) 881, *1011*
Rene Dubos Center for Human Environments. Newsletter (US) *499*
Renegade (US) *505*
Renewable Energy Manufacturers Lists: Biomass Fuels (US) *466*
Renewable Energy Manufacturers Lists: Heat Conservation (US) *466*
Renewable Energy Manufacturers Lists: Heat Conversion see Renewable Energy Manufacturers Lists: Heat Conservation 466

RENEWABLE ENERGY

Renewable Energy Manufacturers Lists: Solar Energy (US) *466*
Renewable Energy Manufacturers Lists: Wind and Hydro Power (US) *466*
Renewable Materials Institute Series (US) *527*
Renta Nacional de Espana (SP) *945*
Rental Rates Compilation *see* Associated Equipment Distributors. Rental Rates Compilation *181*
Repair and Remodeling Cost Data (US ISSN 0271-5945) *187*
Reperes (FR) *109*
Repertoire Administratif (CN) *908, 1020*
Repertoire Bibliographique des Livres Imprimes en France (GW ISSN 0085-5499) *130*
Repertoire Canadien des Bourses d'Etudes Superieures *see* Canadian Directory of Awards for Graduate Study *432*
Repertoire Canadien sur l'Education *see* Canadian Education Index *3*
Repertoire Complementaire Alphabetique des Valeurs Mobilieres Francaises et Etrangeres Non Cotees en France (FR ISSN 0080-0945) *298*
Repertoire de l'Ethnologie de la France (FR) *75*
Repertoire de la Recherche dans les Universites Subventionnee Par le Gouvernement Federal *see* Directory of Federally Supported Research in Universities *990*
Repertoire de Materiaux et Elements Controles du Batiment (FR ISSN 0335-3559) *187, 809*
Repertoire des Annuaires (FR) *130*
Repertoire des Artisites et Compagnies de Tournee au Canada *see* Touring Artists Directory of the Performing Arts in Canada (Biennial) *1079*
Repertoire des Artistes et Compagnies de Tournees au Canada (Year) *see* Touring Artists' Directory of the Performing Arts in Canada (Year) *1079*
Repertoire des Bases de Donnees Scientifiques et Techniques au Canada/Directory of Canadian Scientific and Technical Databases (CN) *1070*
Repertoire des Bibliotheques Specialisees de la Region de Montreal *see* Directory of Special Libraries in the Montreal Area *677*
Repertoire des Centres de Recherche Alimentaire (FR) *520*
Repertoire des Centres de Soins de Longue Duree au Canada *see* Directory of Long-Term Care Centres in Canada *783*
Repertoire des Cooperatives du Quebec(CN ISSN 0080-097X) *238*
Repertoire des Entreprises Artisanales (FR) *1161*
Repertoire des Entreprises Financieres, Commerciales Industrielles Exercant en Republique du Mali *see* Annuaire des Entreprises du Mali *234*
Repertoire des Geographes Francais (FR) *547*
Repertoire des Livres de Langue Francaise Disponibles *see* Livres Disponibles *128*
Repertoire des Organisations de Travailleurs au Canada *see* Directory of Labour Organizations in Canada *648*
Repertoire des Principaux Textes Legislatifs et Reglementaires Promulgues en Republique du Mali (ML ISSN 0080-1011) *237*
Repertoire des Produits Fabriques au Quebec (CN ISSN 0704-7940) *316*
Repertoire des Salles de Spectacle *see* Facilities Directory *375*
Repertoire des Societes de Commerce Exterieur Francaises (FR ISSN 0080-1070) *259*
Repertoire des Textes Legislatifs et Reglementaires et des Reponses aux Questions Ecrites Concernant la Reunion (RE) *945*
Repertoire des Universites Canadiennes *see* Directory of Canadian Universities *434*

Repertoire Dictionnaire Industriel (FR ISSN 0080-1089) *291*
Repertoire Francais du Commerce Exterieur/French Foreign Trade Directory (FR ISSN 0080-1119) *259*
Repertoire General Alphabetique des Valeurs Cotees en France et des Valeurs Non Cotees (FR ISSN 0080-1127) *298*
Repertoire General de la Production Francaise *see* La France de l'Industrie et les Services *308*
Repertoire General des Clubs Sportifs de France (FR ISSN 0080-1135) *1035*
Repertoire International de la Librairie Ancienne *see* International Directory of Antiquarian Booksellers *962*
Repertoire International de la Litterature de l'Art/International Repertory of the Literature of Art News *see* R I L A News *113*
Repertoire International des Dix-Huitiemistes *see* International Directory of Eighteenth-Century Studies *630*
Repertoire International des Editeurs et Diffuseurs de Langue Francaise (FR) *963*
Repertoire International des Medievistes (FR ISSN 0080-1151) *594, 632*
Repertoire Permanent de l'Administration Francaise (FR) *945*
Repertoire Pratique de la Publicite (FR ISSN 0080-1194) *16*
Repertoire Tequi Quincaillerie *see* Memento General Tequi Quincaillerie *190*
Repertoria Heidelbergensia (GW) *731*
Repertorien zur Erforschung der Freuhen Neuzeit (GW ISSN 0724-9578) *594*
Repertoriex *see* French Periodical Index *126*
Repertorio Chimico Italiano (IT) *479*
Repertorio de Servicios de Documentacion e Informacion Educativa Iberoamericanos (SP) *418, 683*
Repertorio del Foro Italiano (IT) *663*
Repertorio delle Decisioni della Corte Costituzionale (IT) *663*
Repertorio delle Industrie Siderurgiche Italiane (IT ISSN 0080-1216) *800*
Repertorio di Giurisprudenza del Lavoro (IT) *663*
Repertorio Terapeutico (IT) *872*
Repertorium (NE) *765*
Repertorium Farmaceutische Specialites Periodiek Overzicht voor Artsen *see* Repertorium *765*
Repertorium Plantarum Succulentarum (SZ ISSN 0486-4271) *160*
Repertorium van Boeken en Tijdschriftartikelen Betreffende de Geschiedenis van Nederland (NE) *564, 594*
Repertorium van Suid-Afrikaanse Tydskrifartikels *see* Index to South African Periodicals *964*
Repertorium van Werken, in Vlaanderen Uitgegeven, of Door Monopoliehouders Ingevoerd (BE ISSN 0080-1224) *130*
Repondez S'il Vous Plait Directory of Creative Talent *see* R S V P: Directory of Creative Talent *109*
Report and Studies in the History of Art *see* Studies in the History of Art *111*
Report by the Auditor General on the Accounts of Lesotho (LO ISSN 0085-2740) *298*
Report - C.O.D.A.S.Y.L. Data Base Task Group *see* Conference on Data Systems Languages. Data Base Task Group. Report *358*
Report - Maryland Division of Correction *see* Maryland. Division of Correction. Report *371*
Report - National Society to Prevent Blindness *see* National Society to Prevent Blindness. Report *180*
Report - Nevada Bureau of Mines and Geology *see* Nevada. Bureau of Mines and Geology. Report *392*

Report of a Vantage Conference (US ISSN 0748-0571) *918*
Report of Cases Argued and Determined in the Supreme Court of the State of Arizona *see* Arizona Reports *651*
Report of Cases Determined in the Supreme Court and Court of Appeals of the State of New Mexico (US ISSN 0094-7148) *663*
Report of Credit Given by Educational Institutions *see* Transfer Credit Practices of Designated Educational Institutions *420*
Report of Educational Statistics *see* Delaware. State Board of Education. Report of Educational Statistics *412*
Report of Environmental Pollution in Meguro Ward *see* Kogai Chosa Hokokusho *497*
Report of Ionosphere and Space Research in Japan *see* Solar Terrestrial Environmental Research in Japan *401*
Report of Overseas Mining Investigation: India, Pakistan, Bangladesh/Kaigai Kogyo Jijo Chosa Hokokusho: Indo, Pakisutan, Banguradisshu (JA) *820*
Report of Overseas Mining Investigation: Madagascar, Swaziland/Kaigai Kogyo Jijo Chosa Hokokusho: Madagasukaru, Suwajirando (JA) *820*
Report of Secretary of Defense to the Congress *see* U.S. Department of Defense. Report of Secretary of Defense to the Congress *813*
Report of the Auditor General on the Accounts of Trinidad and Tobago (TR) *298*
Report of the Council for Tobacco Research-U.S.A., Inc. *see* Council for Tobacco Research--U.S.A. Report *760*
Report of the Federal Home Loan Mortgage Corporation *see* Federal Home Loan Mortgage Corporation. Report *228*
Report of the Judicial Department, State of Connecticut *see* Connecticut. Judicial Department. Report *654*
Report of the Nebraska Indian Commission *see* Nebraska. Indian Commission. Report *504*
Report of the New Mexico Veteran's Service Commission *see* New Mexico. Veterans' Service Commission. Report *812*
Report of the Ombudsman (Juneau) *see* Alaska. Office of Ombudsman. Report of the Ombudsman *938*
Report of the Patient Registry (US ISSN 0197-7423) *765*
Report of the Proceedings. Annual Meeting and Technical Forum *see* Flexographic Technical Association. Report of the Proceedings: Annual Meeting and Technical Forum *930*
Report - Office of Alcoholism, Department of Health and Social Services, State of Alaska *see* Alaska. Office of Alcoholism. Report *376*
Report on Applications for Orders Authorizing or Approving the Interception of Wire or Oral Communications *see* U.S. Administrative Office of the United States Courts. Report on Applications for Orders Authorizing or Approving the Interception of Wire or Oral Communications *665*
Report on British Palaeobotany & Palynology (UK ISSN 0266-4755) *857*
Report on Development Assistance to Ethiopia (UN) *264*
Report on Development Cooperation to the Democratic Republic of the Sudan (UN) *264*
Report on Domestic and International Commercial Loan Charge-Offs (US) *231*
Report on Federal Funds Received in Iowa (US ISSN 0091-8695) *298*
Report on Ohio Mineral Industries (US) *820*
Report on Passenger Road Transport in Zambia (ZA) *1062, 1086*

Report on Survival Studies of Patients With Cystic Fibrosis *see* Report of the Patient Registry *765*
Report on the Marketing of Tobacco in Andhra Pradesh (II) *49*
Report on the Progress of Education in Pakistan *see* Development of Education in Pakistan *412*
Report on the Situation on Human Rights in the Republic of Guatemala (US) *918*
Report on the Treatment of Offenders in Mauritius; Part 1: Prisons Service (MF) *372*
Report on the Treatment of Offenders in Mauritius; Part 2: Probation Service (MF) *372*
Report on the World Health Situation (UN ISSN 0085-5529) *955*
Report on Tourism Statistics in Tanzania (TZ ISSN 0564-836X) *1120*
Report on United States Antarctic Research Activities *see* National Research Council. Committee on Polar Research. Report on United States Antarctic Research Activities *546*
Report on Urban Research/Toshi Kenkyu Hokoku (JA) *625*
Report on Virginia's Industry of Agriculture (US) *33*
Report to S C A R on South African Antarctic Research Activities (Scientific Committee for Antarctic Research) (SA ISSN 0081-2412) *998, 1070*
Report to the Congress on Ocean Pollution, Overfishing, and Offshore Development *see* U.S. National Oceanic and Atmospheric Administration. Report to the Congress on Ocean Pollution, Overfishing, and Offshore Development *500*
Report to the Governor - Arizona Commission on the Arts *see* Arizona Commission on the Arts. Report to the Governor *101*
Reporter on the Legal Profession (US ISSN 8755-7509) *663*
Reports and Papers in the Social Sciences (UN ISSN 0080-1348) *1011*
Reports and Papers on Mass Communications (UN ISSN 0080-1356) *344*
Reports in Mackinac History and Archaeology (US) *91, 609*
Reports of Investigations - Illinois State Museum *see* Illinois. State Museum. Reports of Investigations *87*
Reports of Patent, Design, Trade Mark and Other Cases (UK ISSN 0080-1364) *861*
Reports on Astronomy *see* International Astronomical Union. Transactions *116*
Reports on Education (UK) *418*
Reports on International Compensation. Argentina *see* Executive Compensation Service. Reports on International Compensation. Argentina *279*
Reports on International Compensation. Puerto Rico *see* Executive Compensation Service. Reports on International Compensation. Puerto Rico *279*
Reports on Marine Research *see* Meeresforschung *407*
Reports on Mathematical Logic (PL ISSN 0137-2904) *752, 881*
Reports on Research Assisted by the Petroleum Research Fund (US ISSN 0190-8715) *866*
Reprints in International Finance (US ISSN 0080-1380) *231*
Reproductions (PH) *145, 924*
Reprographics Quarterly *see* Information Media & Technology *884*
Repsol Pamphlets (IE) *908*
Republic Forge Company. Annual Report (II) *291*
Republic of Seychelles Official Gazette (SE) *945*
Republican Almanac (US ISSN 0363-9290) *908*

Republican Englishman (UK ISSN 0144-7548) *908*
Requirements for Certification of Teachers, Counselors, Librarians, Administrators for Elementary Schools, Secondary Schools, Junior Colleges (US ISSN 0080-1429) *443*
Requirements for Teaching Certificates in Canada (CN ISSN 0080-1437) *418*
Res Facta (PL ISSN 0486-4689) *841*
Research (GW ISSN 0722-6349) *75, 547, 560, 1028*
Research Abstracts (Ann Arbor) (US ISSN 0362-7535) *11*
Research Advances in Alcohol & Drug Problems (US ISSN 0093-9714) *377*
Research and Clinical Center for Child Development. Annual Report (JA ISSN 0386-8435) *334, 765*
Research and Clinical Forums (UK ISSN 0143-3083) *765*
Research and Clinical Studies in Headache see Pain and Headache *791*
Research and Development Activities in the Netherlands see Speur- en Ontwikkelingswerk in Nederland *1071*
Research and Development Directory (US ISSN 0080-1461) *998*
Research & Development in Industry (II) *1070*
Research and Development in Ireland (IE ISSN 0085-5545) *998*
Research and Development in the Canadian Corporate Section (CN ISSN 0826-8983) *199*
Research and Development Paper (UK) *527*
Research and Practice in Forensic Medicine (JA ISSN 0289-0755) *782*
Research and Statistics Annual Report see South Dakota. State Department of Public Welfare. Research and Statistics Annual Report *1023*
Research and Studies (CN) *418*
Research at Los Banos (PH) *33*
Research Centers Directory (US ISSN 0080-1518) *998*
Research Council of Alberta. Report see Alberta Research Council. Reports *1067*
Research Development in Higher Education. Publications (AT ISSN 0155-6223) *418, 438*
Research Discussion Papers (AT ISSN 0158-9830) *275*
Research Fields in Physics at United Kingdom Universities and Polytechnics (UK ISSN 0308-9290) *438, 890*
Research for Business Decisions (US) *199*
Research for Religion & Parapsychology(US) *860*
Research Group for European Migration Problems. Publications (NE ISSN 0080-1623) *924*
Research in British Universities Polytechnics and Colleges. Vol.2: Biological Sciences see Current Research in Britain. Biological Sciences *150*
Research in British Universities Polytechnics and Colleges. Vol.1: Physical Sciences see Current Research in Britain. Physical Sciences *1003*
Research in British Universities Polytechnics and Colleges. Vol.3: Social Sciences see Current Research in Britain. Social Sciences *1014*
Research in Business Economics and Public Policy (US) *199*
Research in Clinical Psychology (US) *936*
Research in Community and Mental Health (US ISSN 0192-0812) *936, 956*
Research in Consumer Behavior (US) *285*
Research in Contemporary and Applied Geography (US) *547*
Research in Corporate Social Performance and Policy (US ISSN 0191-1937) *199*

Research in Criminology (US) *372*
Research in Domestic and International Agribusiness Management (US ISSN 0276-1653) *49, 281*
Research in Economic Anthropology (US ISSN 0190-1281) *75*
Research in Economic History (US ISSN 0363-3268) *252*
Research in Education see Resources in Education *425*
Research in Experimental Economics (US ISSN 0193-2306) *252*
Research in Finance (US ISSN 0196-3821) *231*
Research in Fisheries (US ISSN 0083-7555) *512*
Research in Governmental and Non-Profit Accounting (US) *222*
Research in Health Economics see Advances in Health Economics and Health Services Research *885*
Research in Human Capital and Development (US ISSN 0194-3960) *278*
Research in International Business and Finance (US ISSN 0275-5319) *259*
Research in Labor Economics (US ISSN 0194-3057) *275*
Research in Law and Economics (US ISSN 0193-5895) *199, 663*
Research in Law and Sociology see Research in Law, Deviance and Social Control *663*
Research in Law, Deviance and Social Control (US) *663, 1028*
Research in Marketing (US ISSN 0191-3026) *285*
Research in Ministry (US) *972*
Research in Molecular Biology (GW ISSN 0340-5400) *163*
Research in Organizational Behavior (US ISSN 0191-3085) *936*
Research in Parapsychology (US ISSN 0094-7172) *860*
Research in Personnel and Human Resources Management (US) *287*
Research in Phenomenology (US ISSN 0085-5553) *881*
Research in Philosophy and Technology(US ISSN 0161-7249) *881, 1070*
Research in Political Economy (US ISSN 0161-7230) *252, 908*
Research in Population Economics (US ISSN 0163-7878) *924*
Research in Public Policy Analysis and Management (US ISSN 0732-1317) *1028*
Research in Public Policy and Management (US) *281, 945*
Research in Race and Ethnic Relations (US ISSN 0195-7449) *1028*
Research in Real Estate (US ISSN 0731-7999) *966*
Research in Rural Sociology and Development (US) *1028*
Research in Social Movements, Conflicts and Change (US ISSN 0163-786X) *1028*
Research in Social Problems and Public Policy (US ISSN 0196-1152) *908, 1028*
Research in Social Stratification and Mobility (US ISSN 0276-5624) *1028*
Research in Sociology of Education and Socialization (US ISSN 0197-5080) *418*
Research in Sociology of Knowledge, Science and Art see Knowledge and Society *1027*
Research in Surface Forces (US ISSN 0080-1666) *332, 890*
Research in the History of Economic Thought and Methodology (US) *252*
Research in the History of Education: A List of Theses for Higher Degrees in the Universities of England and Wales (UK ISSN 0080-1674) *425*
Research in the Interweave of Social Roles (US ISSN 0272-2801) *1028*
Research in the Interweave of Social Roles: Friendship (US) *1028*
Research in the Interweave of Social Roles: Women and Men see Research in the Interweave of Social Roles: Friendship *1028*

Research in the Sociology of Health Care (US ISSN 0275-4959) *765, 956, 1028*
Research in the Sociology of Organizations (US ISSN 0733-558X) *1028*
Research in the Sociology of Work (US ISSN 0277-2833) *275, 1029*
Research in Transportation Economics (US) *1083*
Research in Urban Economics (US) *625, 951*
Research Index (UK ISSN 0034-5296) *11, 217*
Research Institute for Agricultural Economics. Bulletin (HU ISSN 0541-9417) *49*
Research Institute for Estate Crops, Bogor. Cocoa Statistics/Balai Penelitian Perkebunan, Bogor. Statistik Coklat (IO) *59*
Research Institute for Estate Crops, Bogor. Coffee Statistics/Balai Penelitian Perkebunan, Bogor. Statistik Kopi (IO) *59*
Research Institute for Estate Crops, Bogor. Communications (IO) *59*
Research Institute for Estate Crops, Bogor. Rubber Statistics/Balai Penelitian Perkebunan, Bogor. Statistik Karet (IO) *59*
Research Institute for Plant Protection. Annals see Institutul de Cercetari pentru Protectia Plantelor. Analele *29*
Research Institute Master Federal Tax Manual see Master Federal Tax Manual *297*
Research Institute Nedri As. Bulletin (IC) *160, 380*
Research Institute of Animal Production at Nitra. Scientific Works(CS) *63, 67*
Research Institute of Brewing. Report (JA ISSN 0389-9136) *120*
Research Institute of Industrial Safety. Annual Report (JA) *636*
Research Institute of Industrial Safety. Research Report (JA ISSN 0911-6923) *459, 499*
Research Institute of Industrial Safety. Technical Recommendation (JA ISSN 0911-8063) *459, 474*
Research into Disease (TH ISSN 0557-7330) *765*
Research into Higher Education Abstracts (UK ISSN 0034-5326) *11, 425*
Research Journal: Humanities and Social Sciences (II) *632, 1011*
Research Laboratories Review of Activities (SA ISSN 0314-1357) *344, 349*
Research Materials in Microform Available in the Harvard University Library (US ISSN 0733-1142) *683*
Research Methods in Neurochemistry (US) *152, 791*
Research Monographs on Human Population (US) *924*
Research Note (AT ISSN 0481-3219) *527*
Research Notes in Animal Behavior (US) *177*
Research Notes in Mathematics (US) *752*
Research on Technological Innovation, Management and Policy (US) *1070*
Research on Transport Economics/ Recherche en Matiere d'Economie des Transports (FR ISSN 0304-3320) *1083*
Research Opportunities in Commonwealth Developing Countries. Register (UK) *438*
Research Opportunities in Renaissance Drama (US ISSN 0098-647X) *1078*
Research Papers in Geography (AT) *547*
Research Papers Series: Hydrology and Oceanology see Materialy Badawcze. Seria: Hydrologia i Oceanologia *403*
Research Papers Series: Meteorology see Materialy Badawcze. Seria: Meteorologia *806*
Research Papers Series: Water Engineering see Materialy Badawcze. Seria: Inzynieria Wodna *490*

Research Papers Series: Water Management and Water Protection see Materialy Badawcze. Seria: Gospodarka Wodna i Ochrona Wod *403*
Research Report Digest (UK ISSN 0143-0386) *367, 368*
Research Report - Texas Department of Corrections; Treatment Directorate, Research and Development Division see Texas. Department of Corrections. Research and Development Division. Research Report *373*
Research Reports Esprit - Project 322: CAD Interfaces (US) *353*
Research Reports in Public Policy see University of California, Santa Barbara. Urban Economics Program. Research Reports in Public Policy *947*
Research Strengths of Universities in the Developing Countries of the Commonwealth see Research Opportunities in Commonwealth Developing Countries. Register *438*
Research Symposium on the Psychology and Acoustics of Music. Proceedings (US) *841*
Research: Virginia Tech (US ISSN 0731-9649) *33*
Researches on Anatolian Art see Anadolu Sanati Arastirmalari *101*
Reseau Automatique Belge de la Pollution Atmospherique (BE ISSN 0773-7777) *765, 956*
Reseau Femmes see Women's Network *422*
Reseau Soufre-Fumee; Zwavel-Rook Meetnet see Instituut voor Hygiene en Epidemiologie. Reseau Soufre-Fumee/Zwavel-Rook Meetnet *954*
Reseaux (BE) *881, 908*
Resenha Estatistica do Rio Grande do Sul (BL) *1062*
Reserve Bank of Australia. Annual Report (AT ISSN 0080-1771) *232*
Reserve Bank of Australia. Occasional Papers (AT ISSN 0080-178X) *232, 249*
Reserve Bank of India. Annual Report (II ISSN 0080-1801) *232*
Reserve Bank of Malawi. Annual Report and Statement of Account see Reserve Bank of Malawi. Report and Accounts *232*
Reserve Bank of Malawi. Report and Accounts (MW ISSN 0486-5383) *232*
Reserve Bank of New Zealand. Research Papers (NZ ISSN 0110-523X) *249*
Reserve Forces Almanac (US ISSN 0363-860X) *812*
Reserves of Coal, Province of Alberta (CN ISSN 0380-4275) *466, 820*
Reshimat Ma'amarim Be-Mada'e Ha-Yahadut see Index of Articles on Jewish Studies *975*
Residential Construction Costs (US) *187*
Residential /Light Commercial Cost Data (US ISSN 0733-6403) *187*
Residue Reviews (US ISSN 0080-181X) *324*
Resolutions of the General Assembly of the United Nations see Index to Proceedings of the General Assembly of the United Nations *912*
Resorts & Parks Purchasing Guide (US) *620*
Resorts and R V Parks Purchasing Guide see Resorts & Parks Purchasing Guide *620*
Resource and Environmental Science Series (UK ISSN 0271-6194) *145, 499*
Resource Book/Ressources (CN) *418, 449*
Resource Center Index (US) *286*
Resource Directory of Branded Line Merchandise in the Homesewing Industry see Homesewing Resource Directory of Branded Line Merchandise in the Homesewing Industry *340*
Resource Recovery Year Book (US) *909*

RESOURCES (CAMBRIDGE)

Resources (Cambridge) see Alternative America 540
Resources for Educators of Adults (US) 427
Resources for the Study of Anthropology (US) 75
Resources for Tourism/Hospitality/Recreation see Business Resources Tourism/Hospitality/Recreation 432
Resources for Tourism/Hospitality/Recreation see Training Resources Tourism/Hospitality/Recreation 439
Resources in Education (US ISSN 0098-0897) 11, 425
Resources in Education. Annual Cumulation see Resources in Education 425
Resources in Education Annual Cumulation (US ISSN 0197-9973) 418
Resources of Music (UK ISSN 0080-1828) 841
Respirator News (US) 636, 793
Respiratory Diseases Research Centre. Annual Report (KE) 793
Respiratory Management Buyer's Guide(US) 793
Respiratory Therapy Buyer's Guide see Respiratory Management Buyer's Guide 793
Responsa Meridiana (SA ISSN 0486-5588) 663
Ressources see Resource Book 418
Restatement in the Courts. Pocket Parts(US) 663
Restatement in the Courts. Supplements see Restatement in the Courts. Pocket Parts 663
Restaurant Industry Operations Report (US) 620
Restaurant Operations Report for Tableservice Restaurants see Restaurant Industry Operations Report 620
Restaurierung und Museumstechnik (GE ISSN 0232-2609) 91
Reston Series in Construction Technology (US) 187
Resultados das Observacoes Meteorologicas de Macau (MH ISSN 0460-3060) 806
Results and Problems in Cell Differentiation (US ISSN 0080-1844) 163
Results of Investigations of the Polish Scientific Spitsbergen Expeditions (PL) 547
Results of Researches on the International Geophysical Projects. Glaciologicla Researches see Rezul'taty Issledovanii po Mezhdunarodnym Geofizicheskim Proektam. Glyatsiologicheskie Issledovaniya 401
Results of the National Operations & Automation Survey see American Bankers Association. Operations and Automation Division. Results of the National Operations & Automation Survey 234
Resume (Denver) (US ISSN 0270-7527) 866
Resumen de Actividades I N I (Year) see Grupo I N I (Resumen de Actividades) 289
Resumenes Analiticos de Bibliografia Militar see Abstracts of Military Bibliography 813
Resumenes Analiticos Sobre Defensa y Seguridad Nacional/Abstracts of Military Bibliography see Abstracts of Military Bibliography 813
Retail Banker's Yearbook (UK) 232
Retail Council of Canada. Operating Survey of Canadian Retailing (CN) 285
Retail Council of Canada. Shrinkage Survey (CN) 285
Retail Credit Federation Membership Directory see Consumer Credit Association of the United Kingdom. Membership Directory 226
Retail Directory (UK) 285, 316
Retail Tenant Directory (US) 966
Retail Trade Developments in Great Britain (UK) 240, 316
Retail Trade Europe see Retail Trade International 285
Retail Trade International (UK) 285
Retailing in Tennessee (US ISSN 0361-0020) 217
Retired Military Almanac (US ISSN 0149-7197) 812
Retirement Paradises of the World (US) 1116
Retrospect (Burnley) (UK ISSN 0261-5061) 594
Retrospectiva da Agropecuaria (BL) 49
Return of Outstanding Debt see Capital Expenditure and Debt Financing Statistics 205
Reumatismo (IT ISSN 0048-7449) 793
Reuniao Geral de Cultura do Arroz. Anais (BL) 64
Reunion Annuelle des Sciences de la Terre (FR ISSN 0249-7557) 380
Reunion Nacional Sobre Problemas de Contaminacion Ambiental. Memoria (MX) 499
Reuss Jahrbuch der Luft- und Raumfahrt (GW) 21
Revelation (UK ISSN 0143-0181) 860
Revels Plays Companion Library, Revels Plays (UK) 731
Reverse Acronyms, Initialisms and Abbreviations Dictionary (US ISSN 0270-4390) 702
Review (Charlottesville) (US ISSN 0190-3233) 702, 731
Review Canadienne d'Anthropologie Physique see Canadian Review of Physical Anthropology 70
Review Journal of Philosophy and Social Science (II ISSN 0258-1701) 881, 1011
Review of Accidents on Indian Government Railways (II ISSN 0080-1933) 1095
Review of Applied Entomology. Series A: Agricultural (UK ISSN 0305-0076) 11, 43
Review of Applied Entomology. Series B: Medical and Veterinary (UK ISSN 0305-0084) 11, 1123
Review of Applied Mycology see Review of Plant Pathology 150
Review of Architecture and Landscape Architecture (CN ISSN 0705-1913) 99
Review of Australian Economics (US) 252
Review of Australia's Demographic Trends (AT ISSN 0727-6982) 924
Review of Bank Performance (US) 232
Review of Behavior Therapy: Theory & Practice (US) 936
Review of Child Development Research(US ISSN 0091-3065) 334, 419
Review of Commerce Studies (II) 199
Review of Economic Situation of Air Transport (UN ISSN 0085-5596) 1089
Review of Education in India (II) 419
Review of Fisheries in O.E.C.D. Member Countries (FR ISSN 0078-6241) 512
Review of Ghana Law (GH ISSN 0034-6578) 663
Review of Maritime Transport (UN ISSN 0085-560X) 1103
Review of Metal Literature see Metals Abstracts 801
Review of National Literatures (US ISSN 0034-6640) 731
Review of Personality and Social Psychology (US ISSN 0270-1987) 936
Review of Plant Pathology (UK ISSN 0034-6438) 11, 150
Review of Progress in Coloration and Related Topics (UK) 1070
Review of Research in Education (US ISSN 0091-732X) 449
Review of Scottish Culture (UK) 91, 505
Review of the Agricultural Situation in Europe at the End of (Year) see Agricultural Review for Europe 44
Review of the Economy of Rhodesia see Annual Economic Review 241
Review of the Mineral Industry in Tanzania (TZ ISSN 0082-1659) 820
Review of the New Zealand Aid Programme see Annual Development Assistance Review, Memorandum of New Zealand 261
Review of the World Wheat Situation (UK) 33
Review of Tropical Plant Pathology (II ISSN 0254-1300) 160
Review on Liberal Arts/Kyoyo Ronshu (JA) 632
Review on the Working of the Trade Unions Act, 1926 see Trade Unions in India 649
Reviews in Biochemical Toxicology (US ISSN 0163-7673) 152
Reviews in Clinical Nutrition see Nutrition Abstracts and Reviews. Series A: Human and Experimental 847
Reviews in Engineering Geology (US ISSN 0080-2018) 483
Reviews in Perinatal Medicine (US ISSN 0362-5699) 785
Reviews of Hematology (US) 145, 872
Reviews of Modern Physics Monographs (US) 890
Reviews of Neuroscience (US ISSN 0095-7550) 791
Reviews of Physiology, Biochemistry and Experimental Pharmacology (US ISSN 0303-4240) 152, 172, 872
Reviews of Plasma Physics (US ISSN 0080-2050) 890
Revija za Sociologiju/Sociological Review (YU ISSN 0350-154X) 1029
Revisionist History (SW ISSN 0348-9078) 594
Revisions (Notre Dame) (US) 881
Revisions: Papers in Architectural Theory (US) 99
Revisorhaandbogen (DK ISSN 0108-3716) 222
Revista A P I C E/A P I C E Journal (Asociacion Panamericana de Instituciones de Credito Educativo) (CK) 1161
Revista A T E M C O P. Especial Alquiladores (Asociacion Espanola de Tecnicos de Maquinaria para la Construccion y Obras Publicas) (SP) 483
Revista Agronomica del Noroeste Argentino (AG ISSN 0080-2069) 33
Revista Argentina de Ciencia Politica (AG ISSN 0034-7019) 909
Revista Argentina de Politica (AG) 909
Revista Brasileira de Entomologia (BL ISSN 0085-5626) 166
Revista Brasileira de Lingua e Literatura (BL) 702, 731
Revista Brasileira de Malariologia e Doencas Tropicais (BL ISSN 0034-7256) 778
Revista Brasileira de Musica (BL) 841
Revista C E N I P E C (Centro de Investigaciones Penales y Criminologicas) (VE) 372
Revista C I A F see Centro Interamericano de Fotointerpretacion. Revista 542
Revista Chilena de Entomologia (CL ISSN 0034-740X) 166
Revista Chilena de Historia Y Geografia (CL ISSN 0080-2093) 609
Revista Chilena en Venta (CL) 130
Revista Ciencias Farmaceuticas (CR) 872
Revista Colombiana de Antropologia (CK) 75
Revista Cubana de Investigaciones Pesqueras see Revista Cubana de Investigaciones Pesqueras. Boletines Bibliograficos 512
Revista Cubana de Investigaciones Pesqueras. Boletines Bibliograficos (CU) 512
Revista Danesa see Denmark Review 243
Revista de Antropologia (BL ISSN 0034-7701) 75
Revista de Biologia del Uruguay (UY ISSN 0304-971X) 145
Revista de Ciencias Biomedicas (BL ISSN 0101-322X) 766
Revista de Ciencias Economicas: Economia, Financas, Administracao, Estatistica see Ciencias Economicas 192
Revista de Ciencias Farmaceuticas (BL ISSN 0101-3793) 872
Revista de Ciencias Juridicas Sociales (AG ISSN 0325-0601) 663
Revista de Debates: Debates en Antropologia see Anthropologica (Lima) 69
Revista de Derecho Publico (AG) 663
Revista de Derecho Social Ecuatoriano (EC ISSN 0484-6923) 663
Revista de Derecho y Reforma Agraria (VE) 33, 663
Revista de Direito do Trabalho (Petropolis) (BL) 663
Revista de Economia (VE) 199
Revista de Educacao e Cultura (BL ISSN 0482-5527) 419
Revista de Estetica/Aesthetics Magazine (AG) 109
Revista de Estudios Economicos (DR) 199
Revista de Estudios Hispanicos (PR ISSN 0378-7974) 632
Revista de Estudios Historico Juridico (CL) 663
Revista de Filosofia (CL ISSN 0034-8236) 881
Revista de Geografia (BL ISSN 0101-9457) 547
Revista de Hacienda (VE) 249
Revista de Historia (CK) 560
Revista de Historia de Derecho (AG) 663
Revista de Historia de las Ideas (EC ISSN 0556-5987) 609
Revista de Historia de Rosario (AG ISSN 0556-5995) 609
Revista de Historia del Derecho (SP) 663
Revista de la Integracion Centroamericana see Revista de la Integracion y el Desarrollo de Centroamerica 264
Revista de la Integracion y el Desarrollo de Centroamerica (HO) 264
Revista de la Universidad Catolica see Pontificia Universidad Catolica del Ecuador. Revista 342
Revista de Legislacion Argentina (AG ISSN 0034-8481) 663
Revista de Letras (BL ISSN 0101-3505) 731
Revista de Matematica e Estatistica (BL ISSN 0102-0811) 752
Revista de Matematica y Fisica Teorica. Serie A (AG ISSN 0080-2360) 890
Revista de Microscopia Electronica see Microscopia Electronica and Biologia Celular 169
Revista de Minas (SP ISSN 0210-8356) 820
Revista de Psicanalise Integral (BL) 936
Revista de Psicologia Normal e Patologica (BL ISSN 0048-7740) 936
Revista de Servicio Social (PR ISSN 0034-8937) 1020
Revista de Sociologia (CK) 1029
Revista del Museo Americanista (AG) 830
Revista do B I N D E (Banco Nacional do Desenvolvimento Economico) (BL) 232
Revista do Seite (BL) 1062
Revista Economica y Financiera see Universidad Nacional Mayor de San Marcos. Facultad de Ciencias Economicas y Comerciales. Revista 201
Revista Geografica de Valparaiso (CL ISSN 0034-9577) 547
Revista Geologica de Chile (CL ISSN 0716-0208) 394
Revista Historica (UY) 609
Revista I N I D E F see Instituto Interamericano de Etnomusicologia y Folklore. Revista 836
Revista Interamericana de Educacion de Adultos (MX) 427
Revista Internacional de Pediatria (CK ISSN 0120-6311) 788
Revista Internacional de Vivienda Rural/International Rural Housing Journal (VE) 625
Revista Investigaciones Marinas (CL ISSN 0716-1069) 177, 407

Revista Ion (CK ISSN 0120-100X) 479
Revista Juridica (BL ISSN 0034-9739) 663
Revista Juridica Panamena (PN ISSN 0302-6655) 1161
Revista Letras (BL ISSN 0100-0888) 702, 731
Revista Mexicana de Fianzas (MX ISSN 0556-6835) 232
Revista Mexicana de Micologia (MX) 160
Revista Mexicana de Seguridad Social (MX ISSN 0482-6876) 1161
Revista Nacional de Cultura (VE) 632
Revista Pacifica Sur (EC) 145
Revista Paraguaya de Microbiologia (PY ISSN 0556-6908) 169, 177
Revista Peruana de Entomologia (PE ISSN 0080-2425) 166
Revista Philosophica (CL) 881
Revista Plantas Medicinales (CU ISSN 0138-6492) 33
Revista Portuguesa de Filologia (PO ISSN 0080-2433) 702
Revista Scriitorilor Romani (IT ISSN 0080-2441) 731
Revista Signos see Revista Signos de Valparaiso 731
Revista Signos de Valparaiso (CL ISSN 0035-0451) 702, 731
Revista Tecnica de los Ferrocarriles (GW) 1095
Revista UNIMAR (Universidade Estadual de Maringa) (BL) 438
Revista 13 Grafico (GT) 538, 609
Revistas Espanolas con ISSN (SP ISSN 0211-1993) 130
Revistero (UY ISSN 0085-5642) 130
Revolucion see Revolution 909
Revolution (US ISSN 0193-3612) 909
Revue Annuelle d'Histoire du Quatorzieme Arrondissement de Paris (FR ISSN 0556-7335) 594
Revue Arachnologique (FR ISSN 0398-4346) 145
Revue Archeologique de l'Ouest (FR ISSN 0767-709X) 91
Revue Archeologique Narbonnaise (FR ISSN 0557-7705) 91
Revue Belge d'Archeologie et d'Histoire de l'Art (BE ISSN 0035-077X) 91, 109
Revue Belge de Geographie (BE ISSN 0770-0717) 547
Revue Belge de Musicologie/Belgisch Tijdschrift voor Muziekwetenschap (BE) 841
Revue Belge de Numismatique et de Sigillographie (BE) 91, 594, 845
Revue Bibliographique de Sinologie (FR ISSN 0080-2484) 130, 564
Revue Canadienne de Droit Communautaire see Canadian Community Law Journal 653
Revue Canadienne de Theorie Politique et Sociale see Canadian Journal of Political & Social Theory 903
Revue Clivages see Clivages 740
Revue d'Histoire et de Civilisation du Maghreb (AE ISSN 0556-7343) 566
Revue Danoise see Danish Journal 538
Revue de Cytologie et de Biologie Vegetales see Revue de Cytologie et de Biologie Vegetales-la Botaniste 161
Revue de Cytologie et de Biologie Vegetales-la Botaniste (FR ISSN 0181-7582) 161
Revue de Droit Suisse see Zeitschrift fuer Schweizerisches Recht 667
Revue de Geologie et de Geographie see Revue Roumaine de Geologie, Geophysique et Geographie. Geologie 394
Revue de Geologie et de Geographie see Revue Roumaine de Geologie, Geophysique et Geographie. Geophysique 401
Revue de Geologie et de Geographie see Revue Roumaine de Geologie, Geophysique et Geographie. Geographie 547
Revue de La Saintonge et de l'Aunis (FR) 594
Revue de Musique des Universites Canadiennes see Canadian University Music Review 834

Revue de Parapsychologie (FR ISSN 0294-2623) 860
Revue de Pau et du Bearn (FR) 632
Revue de Theologie et de Philosophie. Cahiers (SZ ISSN 0250-6971) 881, 972
Revue des Archeologues et Historiens d'Art de Louvain (BE ISSN 0080-2530) 91, 109, 841
Revue des Etudes Anciennes (FR ISSN 0035-2004) 338
Revue des Etudes Byzantines (FR ISSN 0766-5598) 613
Revue des Etudes Grecques (FR ISSN 0035-2039) 91, 338
Revue des Etudes Latines (FR) 338, 702
Revue des Lettres Modernes (FR ISSN 0035-2136) 731
Revue des Lettres Modernes. Etudes Bernanosiennes (FR ISSN 0425-4791) 731
Revue des Sciences Naturelles d'Auvergne (FR) 146
Revue des Sciences Sociales de la France de l'Est (FR ISSN 0336-1578) 1011
Revue du Travail (HT ISSN 0482-8062) 275, 1020
Revue du Vieux Geneve (SZ) 594
Revue Egyptienne de Droit International see Egyptian Review of International Law 670
Revue Formes Nouvelles/Neue Formen/New Forms (LU) 99
Revue Historique de Bordeaux et du Departement de la Gironde (FR) 594
Revue Historique et Archeologique du Maine (FR) 92, 594
Revue Historique Vaudoise (SZ) 92, 594
Revue Independante de Philosophie see Independent Journal of Philosophy 878
Revue Internationale d'Histoire de la Banque (SZ ISSN 0080-2611) 232
Revue Internationale d'Histoire Militaire (NE ISSN 0254-8186) 812
Revue Juridique Themis (CN ISSN 0556-7963) 663
Revue Juridique Themis de l'Universite de Montreal see Revue Juridique Themis 663
Revue Landis et Gyr see Landis und Gyr Mitteilungen 456
Revue Metapsychique (FR ISSN 0484-8934) 860
Revue Numismatique (FR ISSN 0484-8942) 845
Revue Odonto-Stomatologique du Nord-Est see Societe Odonto-Stomatologique du Nord-Est. Revue Annuelle 780
Revue Ouest Africaine des Langues Vivantes see West African Journal of Modern Languages 708
Revue Philosophique de Kinshasa (ZR) 881
Revue Roumaine d'Histoire de l'Art. Serie Beaux-Arts (RM ISSN 0080-262X) 109
Revue Roumaine d'Histoire de l'Art. Serie Theatre, Musique, Cinematographie (RM ISSN 0080-2638) 109
Revue Roumaine de Geologie, Geophysique et Geographie. Geologie (RM ISSN 0556-8099) 547
Revue Roumaine de Geologie, Geophysique et Geographie. Geologie (RM ISSN 0556-8102) 394
Revue Roumaine de Geologie, Geophysique et Geographie. Geophysique (RM ISSN 0556-8110) 401
Revue Roumaine de l'Histoire de l'Art. Serie Arts Plastiques see Revue Roumaine d'Histoire de l'Art. Serie Beaux-Arts 109
Revue Suisse de Numismatique/Schweizerische Numismatische Rundschau (SZ ISSN 0035-4163) 845
Revue Svetovej Literatury (CS) 712

Revue Theologique de Louvain. Cahiers(BE) 983
Revue Universitaire de Science Morale see Reseaux 881
Rezul'taty Issledovanii po Mezhdunarodnym Geofizicheskim Proektam. Glyatsiologicheskie Issledovaniya/Results of Researches on the International Geophysical Projects. Glaciologicla Researches (UR ISSN 0568-6245) 401
Rheinisch-Westfaelische Akademie der Wissenschaften. Veroeffentlichungen see Rheinisch-Westfaelische Akademie der Wissenschaften. Vortraege Natur- Ingenieur-und Wirtschaftswissenschaften 998
Rheinisch-Westfaelische Akademie der Wissenschaften. Vortraege Natur-Ingenieur-und Wirtschaftswissenschaften (GW) 998, 1070
Rheinisch-Westfaelische Zeitschrift fuer Volkskunde (GW ISSN 0556-8218) 75, 594
Rheinische Ausgrabungen (GW ISSN 0557-7853) 92
Rheinische Lebensbilder (GW ISSN 0080-2670) 135
Rheinische Schriften (GW ISSN 0080-2689) 380
Rheinisches Jahrbuch fuer Volkskunde (GW ISSN 0080-2697) 516
Rheinisches Landesmuseum, Bonn. Schriften (GW ISSN 0067-9968) 92
Rheinisches Landesmuseum in Bonn. Bonner Jahrbuecher (GW ISSN 0067-9976) 92
Rheology Abstracts (US ISSN 0035-452X) 11, 43
Rheology Bulletin (US ISSN 0035-4538) 895
Rheumatology (SZ ISSN 0080-2727) 793
Rhode Island. Department of Education. (Year) Statistical Tables (US) 425, 1062
Rhode Island. Department of Health. Vital Statistics (US) 924, 929
Rhode Island. Department of Mental Health, Retardation and Hospitals. Mental Health, Retardation and Hospitals (US ISSN 0094-291X) 618, 956
Rhode Island Directory of Manufacturers (US) 316
Rhode Island Directory of Manufacturers and List of Commercial Establishments see Rhode Island Directory of Manufacturers 316
Rhode Island Jewish Historical Notes (US ISSN 0556-8609) 505, 560
Rhodes-Livingstone Papers see Zambian Papers 567
Rhodes Newsletter see Rhodes Review 342
Rhodes Review (SA) 342
Rhodesia. Central Statistical Office. Agricultural Production in African Purchase Lands. Part 1: National and Provincial Totals see Zimbabwe. Central Statistical Office. Agricultural Production in Purchase Lands: National and Provincial Totals 61
Rhodesia. Central Statistical Office. Agricultural Production in Tribal Trust Land Irrigation Schemes see Zimbabwe. Central Statistical Office. Agricultural Production in Tribal Trust Land Irrigation Schemes and Tilcor Estates 38
Rhodesia. Central Statistical Office. Insurance Statistics see Zimbabwe. Registrar of Insurance. Report 642
Rhodesia. Ministry of Finance. Budget Statement see Zimbabwe. Ministry of Finance. Financial Statement 300
Rhodesia. Ministry of Mines and Lands. Report of the Secretary for Mines and Lands see Zimbabwe. Ministry of Lands and Natural Resources. Report of the Secretary for Lands and Natural Resources 368
Rhodesia National Bibliography see Zimbabwe National Bibliography 133

Rhodesia Research Index see Zimbabwe Research Index 1005
Rhodesia Scientific Association. Transaction see Zimbabwe Scientific Association. Transaction 1003
Rhodesia Stamp Catalogue (RH) 875
Rhodesian History see Zimbabwean History 568
Rhodesiana see Heritage 566
Rhododendrons, with Magnolias and Camellias (UK ISSN 0080-2891) 533
Ribe Stift see Ribe Stiftsbog 594
Ribe Stiftsbog (DK ISSN 0108-0806) 594
Rice Abstracts (UK ISSN 0141-0164) 11, 43
Rice University. Program of Development Studies. Discussion Papers (US) 1161
Ricerche di Automatica (IT ISSN 0048-8291) 355
Ricerche di Biologia della Selvaggina (IT) 177
Ricerche di Biologia della Selvaggina. Supplemento (IT) 170, 177
Ricerche di Sociologia dell'Educazione e Pedagogia Comparata (IT) 419
Ricerche di Storia della Lingua Latina (IT ISSN 0080-293X) 702
Ricerche di Storia Moderna (IT) 594
Ricerche di Zoologia Applicata alla Caccia see Ricerche di Biologia della Selvaggina 177
Ricerche di Zoologia Applicata alla Caccia. Supplemento see Ricerche di Biologia della Selvaggina. Supplemento 177
Ricerche Slavistiche (IT ISSN 0391-4127) 702, 731
Ricerche Sulle Dimore Rurali in Italia (IT ISSN 0080-2964) 99
Richard B. Russell Lecture Series (US) 560
Rickia (BL ISSN 0080-3014) 161
Riddell's Australian Purchasing Yearbook see Business Who's Who Australian Buying Reference 283
Ridge Detail in Nature (UK) 75
Riding Handbook (UK) 1043
Rights Canada (CN) 963
Riista- ja Kalatalouden Tutkimuslaitos. Kalantutkimusosasto. Tiedonantoja (FI ISSN 0355-0648) 512
Riistatieteellisia Julkaisuja see Finnish Game Research 365
Rijks Geologische Dienst. Mededelingen (NE) 394
Rijks Geschiedkundige Publicatien. Grote Serie (NE) 594
Rijks Geschiedkundige Publicatien. Kleine Serie (NE) 594
Rijksdienst voor het Oudheidkundig Bodemonderzoek te Amersfoort. Berichten (NE ISSN 0467-006X) 92
Rijksinstituut voor het Rassenonderzoek van Cultuurgewassen. Jaarverslag (NE) 59
Rijksinstituut voor het Rassenonderzoek van Cultuurgewassen. Mededelingen (NE) 59
Rijksinstituut voor Oorlogsdocumentatie. Documenten (NE ISSN 0066-1287) 594
Rijksinstituut voor Oorlogsdocumentatie. Monografieen (NE ISSN 0066-1295) 594
Rijksmuseum van Natuurlijke Historie. Zoologische Bijdragen (NE ISSN 0459-1801) 177
Rijksmuseum van Natuurlijke Historie. Zoologische Mededelingen (NE ISSN 0024-0672) 177
Rijksmuseum van Natuurlijke Historie. Zoologische Verhandelingen (NE ISSN 0024-1652) 177
Rijksmuseum van Oudheden, Leiden. Oudheidkundige Mededelingen (NE) 92
Rijksuniversiteit te Gent. Faculteit van de Economische Wetenschappen. Werken (BE) 199
Rijksuniversiteit te Gent. Laboratorium voor Experimentele, Differentiele en Genetische Psychologie. Mededelingen en Werkdocumenten (BE ISSN 0085-1078) 936

Rijksuniversiteit te Gent. Sterrenkundig Observatorium. Mededelingen (BE ISSN 0072-4432) 117
Rijksuniversiteit te Gent. Sterrenkundig Observatorium. Mededelingen: Meteorologie en Geofysica (BE ISSN 0072-4440) 401, 806
Rijksuniversiteit te Leiden. Instituut voor Culturele Antropologie en Sociologie der Niet-Westerse Volken. Publicatie (NE) 75, 1029
Rijksuniversiteit Utrecht. Jaarverslag (NE) 438
Riken. Accelerator Progress Report (Institute of Physical and Chemical Research) (JA ISSN 0289-842X) 898
Riken. Cyclotron Report (JA) 898
Rikkyo University. Institute for Atomic Energy. Report (JA) 474, 898
Riksarkivets Rapporter (SW ISSN 0280-3046) 683
Riksgaeldkontoret. Statistisk Aarsbok (SW) 232
Riksgaeldskontoret. Aarsbok see Riksgaeldkontoret. Statistisk Aarsbok 232
Rilancio (IT ISSN 0016-5700) 1122
Rinascimento (IT ISSN 0080-3073) 595, 632
Ring Systems Handbook (US ISSN 0742-5996) 331
Ringette Canada. Official Rules (Years) (CN) 1035
Ringkoebing Arbog (DK) 595
Ringyo Shiken Kenkyu Hokoku see Tokyo Metropolitan Agricultural Experiment Station, Itsukaichi Office. Forestry Experimental Bulletin 528
Ringyo Shikenjo Kyushu Shijo Nenpo see Japan. Government Forest Experiment Station. Kyushu Branch. Annual Report 526
Rio de Janeiro. Biblioteca Nacional. Colecao Rodolfo Garcia. Serie B. Catalogos e Bibliografias (BL) 130
Rio de Janeiro, Brazil (State). Instituto Estadual do Livro. Divisao de Bibliotecas. Boletim Bibliografico (BL) 130
Rio Grande do Sul, Brazil. Fundacao de Economia e Estatistica. Boletim Estatistico do Seite see Revista do Seite 1062
Rio Grande History (US ISSN 0146-1869) 609
Rio Grande Valley Horticultural Society. Journal (US ISSN 0485-2044) 533
Rio Negro, Argentina. Direccion Provincial de Cultura. Monografias (AG) 1161
Ripartizione Cultura e Spettacolo. Rassegna di Studi e di Notizie (IT) 109
Ripley P. Bullen Monographs in Anthropology and History (US ISSN 0271-6925) 92, 609
Risaleh al-Islamiyah (LE) 975
Risco (PO) 909
Risk Abstracts (CN ISSN 0824-3336) 12, 501
Risk in Society (UK ISSN 0266-0512) 766
Risoe Annual Report see Forskningscenter Risoe. Aarsberetning 465
Risoe International Symposium on Metallurgy and Materials Science. Proceedings (DK ISSN 0108-8599) 800
Risoe-M (DK ISSN 0418-6435) 890
Rit Fiskideildar/Marine Research Institute. Journal (IC ISSN 0484-9019) 512
Rit Occasional Papers (IC) 998
River and Flood Control Abstracts (UK ISSN 0266-9870) 474, 490
River Behaviour and Control (II) 1125
River Bend Library System. Report of the Director (US ISSN 0080-3227) 683
Riverlander see Riverlander Notes 367
Riverlander Notes (AT) 249, 367
Riverside Interviews (UK ISSN 0261-3042) 731, 743
Riverwind (US) 743

Ha-Rivhiyut Shel 'anaf Ha-Lul see Profitability of Poultry Farming in Israel 67
Ha-Rivhiyut Shel 'anaf Ha-Refet see Profitability of Dairy in Israel 63
Ha-Rivhiyut Shel Gidul Ha-Kutnah see Profitability of Cotton Growing in Israel 59
Ha-Rivhiyut Shel Gidul Hadarim see Profitability of Citrus Growing in Israel 59
Rivista Archeologica dell'Antica Provincia e Diocesi di Como (IT ISSN 0080-3235) 92
Rivista Archeologica della Provincia di Como see Rivista Archeologica dell'Antica Provincia e Diocesi di Como 92
Rivista d'Arte (IT) 109
Rivista di Antropologia (IT ISSN 0085-5723) 75
Rivista di Archeologia (IT ISSN 0392-0895) 92
Rivista di Cultura Classica e Medioevale. Quaderni (IT ISSN 0080-3251) 338
Rivista di Etnografia (IT ISSN 0085-5731) 1029
Rivista di Grammatica Generativa (IT) 702
Rivista di Storia delle Scienze Mediche e Naturali. Biblioteca (IT) 766
Rivista di Storia e Letteratura Religiosa. Biblioteca (IT) 560, 972
Rivista di Studi Bizantini e Slavi (IT) 595, 613
Rivista Geografica Italiana (IT ISSN 0035-6697) 548
Rivista Italiana di Musicologia. Quaderni (IT) 841
Road Accidents in Great Britain (UK ISSN 0307-6822) 1097
Road & Track Sports & G T Cars (US) 1093
Road Builder's Clinic. Proceedings (US ISSN 0080-3278) 483
Road Documentation for Developing Countries (UK) 1083, 1097
Road Haulage Association Diary (UK) 1105
Road/House (US) 743
Road Maps of Industry see Economic Road Maps 194
Road Notes see Transport and Road Research Laboratory. Research Reports 1097
Road of the Party (CN ISSN 0047-6110) 909
Roadmasters and Maintenance of Way Association of America. Proceedings (US ISSN 0080-3316) 1095
Roanoke Historical Society. Journal see Roanoke Valley Historical Society Journal 609
Roanoke Valley Historical Society Journal (US) 609
Roar (US) 712, 841
Roberson Poetry Annual (US) 743
Robert Burns Chronicle (UK ISSN 0307-8957) 731
Robert /Morris Associates Annual Statement Studies see R M A Annual Statement Studies 231
Robert Wood Johnson Foundation. Annual Report (US ISSN 0091-3472) 766, 886
Robin (US) 499, 516
Robinson Jeffers Newsletter (US ISSN 0300-7936) 743
Robomatix Annual Index (US) 12, 354
Robomatix Reporter (US) 12, 354
Robotics and C A D/C A M Market Place (US) 1161
Robotics - C A D/C A M Directory see Robotics Technical Directory (Year) 355
Robotics Industry Directory see International Robotics Industry Directory 355
Robotics Technical Directory (Year) (US) 355
Robotics World Directory (US) 316, 355
Robotron Technische Mitteilungen (GE) 355, 459
Rocenka Odborara (CS ISSN 0557-1693) 649
Rochford St Press see Meuse 727

Rock (AT ISSN 0816-2425) 1046
Rock Drill (UK ISSN 0144-7262) 743
Rock Magnetism and Paleogeophysics (JA ISSN 0385-2520) 401
Rock Mechanics Abstracts see International Journal of Rock Mechanics and Mining Sciences & Geomechanics Abstracts 822
Rock Mechanics/Felsmechanik/Mechanique des Roches. Supplement(US ISSN 0080-3375) 820
Rock Yearbook (US ISSN 0275-9187) 841
Rockbridge Historical Society, Lexington, Virginia. Proceedings (US ISSN 0080-3383) 609
Rockefeller Archive Center. Newsletter (US) 560
Rockefeller Foundation see R F 1011
Rockefeller University, New York. Annual Report see Rockefeller University, New York. Scientific and Educational Programs 766
Rockefeller University, New York. Scientific and Educational Programs (US) 766
Rocky Mountain Medieval and Renaissance Association. Journal (US ISSN 0195-8453) 595, 731
Rocznik Bialostocki (PL ISSN 0080-3421) 595
Rocznik Dolnoslaski (PL) 632
Rocznik Ekonomiczny (PL ISSN 0080-343X) 199
Rocznik Elektrycznosci Atmosferycznej i Meteorologii (PL ISSN 0080-3448) 806
Rocznik Gdanski (PL ISSN 0080-3456) 595
Rocznik Grudziadzki (PL ISSN 0080-3464) 595
Rocznik Historii Sztuki (PL ISSN 0080-3472) 109
Rocznik Jeleniogorski (PL ISSN 0080-3480) 595
Rocznik Kaliski (PL ISSN 0137-3501) 595
Rocznik Krakowski (PL ISSN 0080-3499) 595
Rocznik Kulturalny Ziemi Gdanskiej (PL) 595
Rocznik Lodzki (PL ISSN 0080-3502) 595
Rocznik Lubelski (PL ISSN 0080-3510) 595
Rocznik Magnetyczny/Annuaire Magnetique (PL ISSN 0082-0458) 401
Rocznik Olsztynski (PL ISSN 0080-3537) 595
Rocznik Orientalistyczny (PL ISSN 0080-3545) 853
Rocznik Pedagogiczny (PL ISSN 0137-9585) 419
Rocznik Sadecki (PL ISSN 0080-3561) 516, 595
Rocznik Slawistyczny (PL ISSN 0080-3588) 702
Rocznik Wroclawski (PL ISSN 0080-3618) 595
Rocznik Ziemi Klodzkiej (PL) 595
Roczniki Dziejow Spolecznych i Gospodarczych/Annales d'Histoire Sociale et Economiques (PL ISSN 0080-3634) 595
Roczniki Nauk Rolniczych. Seria A. Produkcja Roslinna (PL ISSN 0080-3650) 59
Roczniki Nauk Rolniczych. Seria B. Zootechniczna (PL ISSN 0080-3669) 67
Roczniki Nauk Rolniczych. Seria C. Technika Rolnicza (PL ISSN 0080-3677) 51
Roczniki Nauk Rolniczych. Seria D. Monografie (PL ISSN 0080-3685) 33
Roczniki Nauk Rolniczych. Seria E. Ochrona Roslin (PL ISSN 0080-3693) 59
Roczniki Nauk Rolniczych. Seria F. Melioracji i Vzytkow Zielonych (PL ISSN 0080-3707) 59
Roczniki Nauk Rolniczych. Seria G. Ekonomika Rolnictwa (PL ISSN 0080-3715) 49

Roczniki Nauk Rolniczych. Seria H. Rybactwo (PL ISSN 0080-3723) 33, 512
Roczniki Nauk Spolecznych (PL) 1011
Roczniki Pomorskiej Akademii Medycznej w Szczecinie see Annales Academiae Medicae Stetinensis 757
Roczniki Socjologii Wsi. Studia i Materialy (PL ISSN 0080-3731) 1029
Rodd's Chemistry of Carbon Compounds (NE ISSN 0080-3758) 331
Roemer Pelizaeus Museum. Zeitschrift des Museums zu Hildesheim (GW) 560
Roemisch-Germanisches Zentralmuseum, Mainz. Ausstellungskataloge (GW ISSN 0076-2733) 1161
Roemisch-Germanisches Zentralmuseum, Mainz. Jahrbuch (GW ISSN 0076-2741) 595
Roemisch-Germanisches Zentralmuseum, Mainz. Kataloge Vor- und Fruehgeschichtlicher Altertuemer (GW ISSN 0076-275X) 560
Roemische Bronzen aus Deutschland (GW ISSN 0080-3782) 92, 109
Roemische Forschungen in Niederoesterreich. Beiheft see Carnuntum Jahrbuch 84
Roemische Historische Mitteilungen (AU ISSN 0080-3790) 338, 595, 972
Roessleria (BL ISSN 0101-7616) 367
Rohmer Review (US ISSN 0145-5753) 731
Role of State Legislatures in the Freedom Struggle (II) 909, 945
Roll of Arms (US) 537
Roll on Roll off in Europe (GW ISSN 0170-5253) 259, 1103
Rollcall (CN ISSN 0707-3542) 766
Rolls of Ancillary Dental Workers (UK) 780
Roma Aeterna (NE) 595
Roma e Provincia Attraverso la Statistica (IT ISSN 0035-7960) 1062
Romance Bibliography see Romanische Bibliographie 709
Romanfuehrer (GW ISSN 0557-2614) 731
Romanian Scientific Abstracts (RM) 12
Romanica Gandensia (BE ISSN 0080-3855) 702
Romanica Gothoburgensia (SW ISSN 0080-3863) 702, 731
Romanica Helvetica (SZ ISSN 0080-3871) 702, 731
Romanica Neapolitana (IT ISSN 0391-1950) 702
Romanische Bibliographie/Bibliographie Romane/Romance Bibliography (GW ISSN 0080-388X) 709
Romanistik in Geschichte und Gegenwart (GW ISSN 0341-3209) 338
Romanistische Arbeitshefte (GW ISSN 0344-676X) 702
Romanistische Versuche und Vorarbeiten (GW) 702
Romanistisches Jahrbuch (GW ISSN 0080-3898) 702
Romanobarbarica (IT) 338
Romanserier og Selvbiografiske Serier (DK ISSN 0106-8253) 135, 1722
Romansk Filmklub Medlemsblad see R F Medlemsblad 825
Romanske Stenarbejder (DK ISSN 0107-2366) 92
Romantic Reassessment (AU) 731
Romantist (US ISSN 0161-682X) 130, 712, 731
Romantizm v Russkoi i Sovetskoi Literature (UR) 595, 731
Romcoe Forum see Accord 278
Romford Record (UK ISSN 0306-1140) 595
Romisch-Germanischen Kommission. Berichte (GW ISSN 0341-9312) 92
Romney Sheep Breeders' Society. Flock Book (UK) 67
Romu (Roskilde Museum) (DK ISSN 0107-928X) 830
Room (US) 743, 1129

Roskilde Kommune. Statistikken (DK ISSN 0105-8339) *1062*
Roskilde Museum Romu *see* Romu *830*
Roskilde Universitetsbibliotek. Skriftserie (DK ISSN 0105-564X) *683*
Roskilde Universitetscenter. Department of Geography, Social Economics and Computer Science. Kompendium (DK ISSN 0106-3545) *548*
Roskilde Universitetscenter. Department of Geography, Social Economics and Computer Science. Meddelelser (DK ISSN 0106-2778) *548*
Roskilde Universitetscenter. Department of Geography, Social Economics and Computer Science. Research Reports (DK ISSN 0106-3537) *548*
Roskilde Universitetscenter. Department of Geography, Social Economics and Computer Science. Working Papers (DK ISSN 0106-5920) *548*
Roskilde Universitetscenter. Institut for Samfundsoekonomi og Planlaegning. Arbejdspapir. (DK ISSN 0108-2205) *1029*
Roskilde Universitetscenter. Institut for Samfundsoekonomi og Planlaegning. Research Report (DK ISSN 0105-8827) *199*
Roskilde Universitetscenter. Institut for Socialvidenskab. Instituttets Skriftserie (DK ISSN 0106-8911) *1161*
Roskilde Universitetscenter. Lingvistgruppen. Rolig-Papir (DK ISSN 0106-0821) *702*
Rossica Olomucensia (CS) *702*, *731*
Roster-California State, County, City and Township Officials State Officials of the United States (US) *945*
Roster of Africa Social Scientists (SG) *264*, *1020*
Roster of Black Elected Officials in the South (US ISSN 0093-9951) *505*
Rotacion de la Tierra (SP ISSN 0210-6485) *117*
Rothamsted Experimental Station. Report (UK ISSN 0262-1215) *59*, *152*
Rothmans Football Yearbook (UK ISSN 0080-4088) *1040*
Rothmans Rugby League Yearbook (UK ISSN 0262-4745) *1040*
Rottenbuerger Jahrbuch fuer Kirchengeschichte (GW ISSN 0722-7531) *595*
Rotterdam. Dienst Gemeentelijke Musea. Jaarverslag (NE) *830*
Rouen Port and Shipping Handbook (UK ISSN 0268-702X) *316*, *1103*
Rougsoe Lokalhistoriske Forening. Aarsskrift (DK ISSN 0106-5327) *595*
Rouseabout (AT) *1161*
Routiers Guide to France (UK) *620*, *1116*
Routledge History of English Poetry (UK) *743*
Roving Commissions (UK ISSN 0485-5175) *1042*
Rowland's Tax Guide *see* Moores & Rowland's Tax Guide *297*
Royal Academy of Letters, History and Antiquities. Proceedings. Antiquarian Series *see* Kungliga Vitterhets-, Historie- och Antikvitets Akademien. Handlingar. Antikvariska Serien *588*
Royal Academy of Letters, History and Antiquities. Proceedings. Historical Series *see* Kungliga Vitterhets-, Historie- och Antikvitets Akademien. Handlingar. Historiska Serien *588*
Royal Academy of Letters, History and Antiquities. Proceedings. Philological-Philosophical Series *see* Kungliga Vitterhets-, Historie- och Antikvitets Akademien. Handlingar. Filologisk-Filosofiska Serien *697*
Royal Agricultural Society of England. Journal (UK ISSN 0080-4134) *33*
Royal Agricultural Society of Natal. Royal Show Catalogue (SA) *33*

Royal Air Force College Journal (UK ISSN 0035-8606) *812*
Royal Air Force Education Bulletin (UK) *812*
Royal Air Force Yearbook (UK) *812*
Royal Anthropological Institute of Great Britain and Ireland. Library. Anthropological Index *see* Anthropological Index to Current Periodicals in the Library of the Museum of Mankind *78*
Royal Asiatic Society. Hong Kong Branch. Journal (HK ISSN 0085-5774) *853*
Royal Astronomical Society of Canada. Observer's Handbook (CN ISSN 0080-4193) *117*
Royal Australasian College of Dental Surgeons. Annals (AT ISSN 0158-1570) *780*
Royal Australian Air Force Academy Journal (AT) *21*, *812*
Royal Australian College of Dental Surgeons. Annals *see* Royal Australasian College of Dental Surgeons. Annals *780*
Royal Australian Institute of Architects Memo *see* R A I A Memo *99*
Royal Automobile Association of South Australia. Accommodation Guide *see* Australian Accommodation Guide *619*
Royal Automobile Club Continental Handbook and Hotel Guide *see* R A C Continental Handbook and Hotel Guide *1115*
Royal Automobile Club Handbook and Hotel Guide *see* R A C Handbook and Hotel Guide *1115*
Royal Bank of Trinidad and Tobago. Annual Report (TR) *232*
Royal Bath & West Show Catalogue (UK) *33*
Royal Botanical Gardens, Hamilton, Ont. Special Bulletin (CN ISSN 0072-9647) *161*, *533*
Royal Botanical Gardens, Hamilton, Ont. Technical Bulletin (CN ISSN 0072-9655) *161*, *533*
Royal British Legion Annual Report and Accounts (UK) *812*
Royal Caledonian Curling Club. Annual (UK ISSN 0080-4282) *1035*
Royal Canadian Golf Association. National Tournament Records *see* Canadian and Provincial Golf Records *1038*
Royal Canadian Institute. Proceedings (CN ISSN 0080-4304) *1161*
Royal Canadian Institute. Transactions (CN ISSN 0080-4312) *1161*
Royal College of General Practitioners. Occasional Papers (UK) *766*
Royal College of Organists. Year Book (UK ISSN 0080-4320) *841*
Royal College of Pathologists of Australasia. Broadsheets (AT) *146*, *766*
Royal College of Pathologists of Australia. Broadsheets *see* Royal College of Pathologists of Australasia. Broadsheets *766*
Royal College of Physicians of Edinburgh. Directory (UK) *766*
Royal College of Physicians of Edinburgh. Yearbook and Calendar *see* Royal College of Physicians of Edinburgh. Directory *766*
Royal College of Surgeons of England. Faculty of Anaesthetists. Dean's Newsletter (UK) *774*
Royal College of Surgeons of England. Faculty of Anaesthetists. Newsletter *see* Royal College of Surgeons of England. Faculty of Anaesthetists. Dean's Newsletter *774*
Royal College of Surgeons of England. Handbook (UK) *794*
Royal Electrical & Mechanical Engineers Journal *see* R E M E Journal *492*
Royal Entomological Society of London. Symposia (UK ISSN 0080-4363) *166*
Royal Geographical Society of Australasia. South Australian Branch. Proceedings *see* South Australian Geographical Papers *548*

Royal Highland and Agricultural Society of Scotland. Review (UK) *33*
Royal Highland and Agricultural Society of Scotland. Show Guide and Review *see* Royal Highland and Agricultural Society of Scotland. Review *33*
Royal Historical Society. Annual Bibliography of British and Irish History (UK ISSN 0308-4558) *564*
Royal Historical Society. Guides and Handbooks (UK ISSN 0080-4398) *595*
Royal Historical Society. Transactions. Fifth Series (UK ISSN 0080-4401) *595*
Royal Historical Society of Queensland. Journal (AT ISSN 0085-5804) *560*
Royal Horticultural Society Gardener's Diary *see* R.H.S. Gardener's Diary *533*
Royal Humane Society. Annual Report (UK) *1020*
Royal Institue of Chemistry. Monographs for Teachers *see* Royal Society of Chemistry. Monographs for Teachers *324*
Royal Institute of British Architects Computer Software Selector *see* R I B A Computer Software Selector *363*
Royal Institute of British Architects Interior Design Product Selector *see* R I B A Interior Design Product Selector *187*
Royal Institute of British Architects Product Selector *see* R I B A Product Selector *187*
Royal Institute of Oil Painters. Publication (UK) *109*
Royal Institute of Painters in Water Colours. Publication (UK) *109*
Royal Institute of Philosophy. Lectures (UK ISSN 0080-4436) *881*
Royal Institute of the Architects of Ireland. Yearbook *see* R I A I Architects Yearbook *99*
Royal Institute of the Architects of Ireland Architects Yearbook *see* R I A I Architects Yearbook *99*
Royal Institution of Chartered Surveyors Library Information Service Abstracts and Reviews *see* R I C S Library Information Service Abstracts and Reviews *477*
Royal Institution of Chartered Surveyors Year Book (UK ISSN 0308-1451) *1161*
Royal Institution of Great Britain. Annual Report *see* Royal Institution of Great Britain. Record *998*
Royal Institution of Great Britain. Proceedings (UK) *998*
Royal Institution of Great Britain. Record (UK) *998*
Royal Institution of Naval Architects. Supplementary Papers (UK ISSN 0373-529X) *1103*
Royal Institution of Naval Architects. Transactions (UK ISSN 0035-8967) *1103*
Royal Irish Academy. Conference on Numerical Analysis. Proceedings (UK) *1161*
Royal Irish Academy. Proceedings. Section B: Biological, Geological and Chemical Sciences (IE ISSN 0035-8983) *146*, *324*, *394*
Royal Irish Academy. Proceedings. Section C: Archaeology, Celtic Studies, History, Linguistics and Literature (IE ISSN 0035-8991) *92*, *595*, *731*
Royal Irish Academy of Music. Prospectus (IE) *841*
Royal Musical Association. R.M.A. Research Chronicle (UK ISSN 0080-4460) *841*
Royal National Institute for the Blind. Information Leaflets (UK ISSN 0080-4479) *180*
Royal New Zealand Institute of Horticulture. Annual Journal (NZ ISSN 0110-5760) *533*
Royal New Zealand Institute of Horticulture. Journal *see* Royal New Zealand Institute of Horticulture. Annual Journal *533*

Royal Norwegian Society of Sciences. Publications *see* Kongelige Norske Videnskabers Selskab. Skrifter *994*
Royal Numismatic Society. Special Publications (UK ISSN 0080-4487) *845*
Royal Observatory. Occasional Reports (UK ISSN 0309-099X) *117*
Royal Observatory. Research and Facilities (UK ISSN 0267-6281) *117*
Royal Ontario Museum. Annual Report (CN ISSN 0082-5115) *830*
Royal Ontario Museum. Archaeology Monographs (CN ISSN 0316-1285) *92*
Royal Ontario Museum. Archaeology Occasional Papers (CN) *92*
Royal Ontario Museum. Art and Archaeology. Occasional Papers *see* Royal Ontario Museum. Archaeology Occasional Papers *92*
Royal Ontario Museum. Ethnography Monograph (CN ISSN 0316-1277) *75*, *505*
Royal Ontario Museum. History, Technology and Art Monographs (CN ISSN 0316-1269) *109*, *560*
Royal Ontario Museum. Life Sciences. Contributions (CN ISSN 0384-8159) *146*, *177*
Royal Ontario Museum. Life Sciences. Miscellaneous Publications (CN ISSN 0082-5093) *146*
Royal Ontario Museum. Life Sciences. Occasional Papers (CN ISSN 0082-5107) *146*
Royal Philatelic Society of New Zealand. Annual Report (NZ) *875*
Royal School of Mines, London. Journal (UK ISSN 0080-4495) *820*
Royal Scottish Automobile Club Official Handbook (UK) *341*, *1035*
Royal Scottish Museum Information Series: Art & Archaeology (UK ISSN 0309-393X) *1161*
Royal Scottish Museum Information Series: Geology (UK ISSN 0307-5052) *1161*
Royal Scottish Museum Information Series: Natural History (UK ISSN 0307-5036) *1161*
Royal Scottish Museum Information Series: Technology (UK ISSN 0307-5044) *1161*
Royal Shakespeare Company. Publication (UK) *731*
Royal Society of British Artists. Publication (UK) *109*
Royal Society of Canada. Proceedings (CN ISSN 0080-4517) *998*
Royal Society of Canada. Proceedings and Transactions (CN ISSN 0316-4616) *998*
Royal Society of Canada. Transactions (CN ISSN 0035-9122) *998*
Royal Society of Chemistry. Annual Reports on the Progress of Chemistry. Section A: Inorganic Chemistry (UK ISSN 0260-1818) *329*
Royal Society of Chemistry. Annual Reports on the Progress of Chemistry. Section A: Physical and Inorganic Chemistry *see* Royal Society of Chemistry. Annual Reports on the Progress of Chemistry. Section C: Physical Chemistry *332*
Royal Society of Chemistry. Annual Reports on the Progress of Chemistry. Section B: Organic Chemistry (UK ISSN 0069-3030) *331*
Royal Society of Chemistry. Annual Reports on the Progress of Chemistry. Section C: Physical Chemistry (UK ISSN 0260-1826) *332*
Royal Society of Chemistry. Monographs for Teachers (UK ISSN 0080-4428) *324*
Royal Society of Edinburgh. Year Book (UK ISSN 0080-4576) *998*
Royal Society of Literature. Essays by Divers Hands (UK) *731*
Royal Society of London. Biographical Memoirs of Fellows of the Royal Society (UK ISSN 0080-4606) *135*

Royal Society of London. Philosophical Transactions. Series A. Mathematical and Physical Sciences (UK ISSN 0080-4614) 752, 998
Royal Society of London. Philosophical Transactions. Series B. Biological Sciences (UK ISSN 0080-4622) 146
Royal Society of London. Proceedings. Series A. Mathematical and Physical Sciences (UK ISSN 0080-4630) 752, 998
Royal Society of London. Proceedings. Series B. Biological Sciences (UK ISSN 0080-4649) 146
Royal Society of London. Year Book (UK ISSN 0080-4673) 999
Royal Society of Marine Artists. Publication (UK) 109
Royal Society of Medicine. Annual Report of the Council (UK ISSN 0144-8676) 766
Royal Society of Medicine. Forum Series see Royal Society of Medicine. Round Table Series 766
Royal Society of Medicine. International Congress and Symposium Series (US ISSN 0142-2367) 766
Royal Society of Medicine. Round Table Series (UK ISSN 0268-3091) 766
Royal Society of Miniature Painters, Sculptors and Gravers (UK) 109
Royal Society of New Zealand. Bulletin see Royal Society of New Zealand. Bulletin Series 999
Royal Society of New Zealand. Bulletin Series (NZ ISSN 0370-6559) 999
Royal Society of New Zealand. Journal. Collected Papers see Collected Papers from the Journal of the Royal Society of New Zealand 989
Royal Society of New Zealand. Miscellaneous Series (NZ ISSN 0111-3895) 999
Royal Society of New Zealand. Proceedings (NZ ISSN 0557-4161) 135, 281
Royal Society of Portrait Painters. Publication (UK) 109
Royal Society of Queensland, St. Lucia. Proceedings (AT ISSN 0080-469X) 999
Royal Society of South Africa. Transactions (SA ISSN 0035-919X) 999
Royal Society of South Australia. Transactions (AT ISSN 0085-5812) 999
Royal Society of Tasmania, Hobart. Papers and Proceedings (AT ISSN 0080-4703) 560, 999
Royal Society of Tropical Medicine and Hygiene, London. Yearbook (UK ISSN 0080-4711) 778
Royal Society of Ulster Architects. Year Book (IE ISSN 0080-472X) 99
Royal Tropical Institute. Information and Documentation. Bulletin see Koninklijk Instituut voor de Tropen. Afdeling Agrarisch Onderzoek. Bulletin 30
Royal Welsh Fusiliers. Journal (UK) 812
Royal Western Australian Historical Society. Journal and Proceedings see Early Days 573
Royal Zoological Society of Scotland. Zoo Guide (UK) 177
Rozprawy Hydrotechniczne/Hydrotechnical Transactions (PL ISSN 0035-9394) 474, 1125
Rozprawy i Szkice Filozoficzno-Estetyczne o Muzyce (PL) 841
Rozprawy Matematyczne see Dissertationes Mathematicae 748
Rozprawy z Dziejow Oswiaty (PL ISSN 0080-4754) 419
Rubber Directory and Buyers Guide (Year) (US) 985
Rubber: Latin American Industrial Report (US) 985
Rubber Producers' Council of Malaysia. Annual Report see Malaysian Rubber Producers' Council. Annual Report 985
Rubber Red Book (US ISSN 0361-0640) 985

Rubber Research Institute of Ceylon. Annual Review see Rubber Research Institute of Sri Lanka. Annual Review 985
Rubber Research Institute of Malaysia. Annual Report (MY ISSN 0126-8279) 985
Rubber Research Institute of Malaysia. Planters Conference Proceedings (MY ISSN 0126-5849) 985
Rubber Research Institute of Sri Lanka. Annual Review (CE) 985
Rubber Research Institute of Sri Lanka. Journal (CE) 901, 985
Rubber Research Institute of Sri Lanka. Quarterly Journal see Rubber Research Institute of Sri Lanka. Journal 985
Rubber Research Institute of Sri Lanka Bulletin see R R I S L Bulletin 985
Rubber World Blue Book (US) 985
Rubbicana (Year) see Rubber Directory and Buyers Guide (Year) 985
Rubbicana-Europe (Year) (UK) 901, 985
Ruch Wydawniczy w Liczbach/Polish Publishing in Figures (PL ISSN 0511-1196) 964
Rudnyckiana (CN) 709
Rudolf Steiner Publications (FR ISSN 0080-4789) 130, 884
Rudolf Virchow Medical Society in the City of New York. Proceedings (US ISSN 0080-4797) 766
Ruff's Guide to the Turf and the Sporting Life Annual (UK ISSN 0080-4819) 1035
Rugby Annual for Wales (UK) 1040
Rugby Football League Official Guide (UK ISSN 0080-4827) 1040
Ruhr-Universitaet. Institut zur Geschichte der Arbeiterbewegung. Mitteilungsblatt (GW ISSN 0173-2471) 275, 595, 649, 918
Ruhr-Universitaet Bochum. Ostasien Institut. Veroeffentlichungen (GW ISSN 0340-6687) 571
Ruizia (SP ISSN 0212-9108) 161
Rules and Regulations - Board of Cosmetology (Sacramento) see California. State Board of Cosmetology. Rules and Regulations 118
Rumanian Scientific Abstracts (RM ISSN 0035-8096) 12, 1004
Rumanian Studies (NE) 595
Runa (PE) 712
Rund Um die Boerse (GW) 249
Ruppin Institute Library. Library's Accession List (IS) 130
Rural Adjustment and Finance Corporation of Western Australia. Annual Report (AT) 625
Rural Adjustment of Western Australia. Annual Report see Rural Adjustment and Finance Corporation of Western Australia. Annual Report 625
Rural Development Abstracts (UK ISSN 0140-4768) 12, 949
Rural Development Research Paper (UG ISSN 0080-4851) 49
Rural Development Series see Scandinavian Institute of African Studies. Rural Development 75
Rural Electric Power Conference. Papers Presented (US) 459
Rural Extension, Education and Training Abstracts (UK ISSN 0140-4776) 12, 419
Rural Industry Directory (AT ISSN 0067-2106) 33, 512, 527
Rural Reconstruction Authority of Western Australia. Annual Report see Rural Adjustment and Finance Corporation of Western Australia. Annual Report 625
Rural Reconstruction Review (US) 264
Rural Recreation and Tourism Abstracts see Leisure, Recreation and Tourism Abstracts 1120
Rural Roundup (US ISSN 0036-0104) 67
Rural Technology Guide (UK ISSN 0141-898X) 33
Ruskin College, Oxford. Library. Occasional Publication (UK ISSN 0261-5649) 275, 560

Rusky Jazyk a Literatura see Universita Palackeho. Pedagogicka Fakulta. Sbornik Praci: Rusky Jazyk a Literatura 706
Russia Mediaevalis (GW ISSN 0721-9431) 595
Russia Stamp Catalogue (UK ISSN 0142-9841) 875
Russian and East European Studies (US ISSN 0080-4886) 595
Russian Archival Series (US) 505, 595
Russian Buyers' Guide (UK) 259
Russian Classical Musical Critics (UR) 841
Russian Literature Triquarterly (US ISSN 0048-881X) 731
Russian Music Studies (US) 841
Russian Poetics in Translation (UK) 109, 702, 732
Russian Series on Social History (NE ISSN 0080-4916) 571, 1011
Russischer Samisdat see Samisdat 595
Rusycystyczne Studia Literaturoznawcze (PL ISSN 0208-5038) 732
Rutgers Art Review (US ISSN 0194-049X) 109
Rutgers Center of Alcohol Studies. Monograph (US) 377
Rutgers Professional Psychology Review(US ISSN 0277-4240) 419, 937
Rutgers University. Bureau of Engineering Research. Annual Report (US ISSN 0080-4975) 474
Rutgers University. Center of Alcohol Studies. Monograph see Rutgers Center of Alcohol Studies. Monograph 377
Rutgers University Studies in Classical Humanities (US ISSN 0732-9814) 338
Rutherglen, Australia. Research Station. Digest of Recent Research see Rutherglen Research Institute. Research Report 33
Rutherglen Research Institute. Research Report (AT ISSN 0814-4990) 33
Ruvigny's Titled Nobility of Europe (UK) 537
Rwanda. Direction Generale de la Documentation et de la Statistique Generale. Situation Economique de la Republique Rwandaise au 31 Decembre see Rwanda. Direction Generale de la Statistique. Situation Economique de la Republique Rwandaise au 31 Decembre 249
Rwanda. Direction Generale de la Documentation et de la Statistique. Rapport Annuel see Rwanda. Direction Generale de la Statistique. Rapport Annuel 946
Rwanda. Direction Generale de la Statistique. Rapport Annuel (RW) 946
Rwanda. Direction Generale de la Statistique. Situation Economique de la Republique Rwandaise au 31 Decembre (RW) 249
Rwanda. Ministere de l'Agriculture et de l'Elevage. Rapport Annuel (RW) 33, 67
Rwanda. Ministere de l'Education Nationale. Direction de la Planification, Statistique et Information. Statistique de l'Enseignement see Rwanda. Ministere de l'Enseignememt Primaire et Secondaire. Direction de la Planification. Statistique de l'Enseignement 425
Rwanda. Ministere de l'Enseignememt Primaire et Secondaire. Direction de la Planification. Statistique de l'Enseignement (RW) 425
Rwanda. Ministere de la Sante Publique. Rapport Annuel (RW) 956
Rwanda. Projet Pilote Forestier. Bulletin d'Information (RW) 1161
Rwanda. Projet Pilote Forestier. Rapport Annuel (RW) 527
Rx Home Care Buyer's Guide (US ISSN 0191-961X) 618, 886
Ryland's Directory (UK ISSN 0080-505X) 800
Ryoiku see Rehabilitation 765

Ryukyu Daigaku Nogakubu Gakujutsu Hokoku see University of the Ryukyus. College of Agriculture. Science Bulletin 37
S A B R Review of Books (Society for American Baseball Research, Inc.) (US) 1040
S A B S Catalogue (South African Bureau of Standards) (SA ISSN 0259-3602) 809
S A B S Katalogus see S A B S Catalogue 809
S A B S Yearbook see S A B S Catalogue 809
S A E Handbook (Society of Automotive Engineers) (US ISSN 0362-8205) 1093
S A E Quarterly Abstracts see S A E Technical Literature Abstracts 1086
S A E Technical Literature Abstracts (Society of Automotive Engineers) (US ISSN 0741-2029) 12, 1086
S A E Technical Papers (Society of Automotive Engineers) (US ISSN 0148-7191) 1093
S A E Transactions (Society of Automotive Engineers) (US ISSN 0096-736X) 1093
S A F R A see Soviet Armed Forces Review Annual 812
S A F T O Annual Report/Suid-Afrikaanse Buitelandse Handelsargonisasie Jaarverslag (South African Foreign Trade Organization) (SA ISSN 0081-2552) 259
S.A. Fishing Industry Handbook and Buyer's Guide see South African Fishing Industry Handbook and Buyer's Guide 513
S.A. Guernsey see Suid-Afrikaanse Guernsey 68
S A L A L M Bibliography and Reference Series (Seminar on the Acquisition of Latin American Library Materials) (US) 130, 688
S A L A L M Bibliography Series see S A L A L M Bibliography and Reference Series 688
S.A. Mining and Engineering Yearbook see South African Mining and Engineering Yearbook 820
S A N B (South African National Bibiography) (SA ISSN 0036-0864) 131
S A N T A Annual Report/S A N T A Jaarlikse Verslag (South African National Tuberculosis Association) (SA ISSN 0081-2501) 793
S A N T A Jaarlikse Verslag see S A N T A Annual Report 793
S A R E C Annual Report (Swedish Agency for Research Cooperation with Developing Countries) (SW ISSN 0349-0874) 264
S A R E C Report (Swedish Agency for Research Cooperation with Developing Countries) (SW ISSN 0348-2626) 918
S A R Statistics (Search and Rescue) (US ISSN 0163-2833) 1103
S A W T R I Technical Report (South African Wool and Textile Research Institute) (SA ISSN 0081-2560) 1075
S B C Booklet (Schweizerischer Bankverein) (SZ) 232
S B I Aarsberetning (Statens Byggeforskningsinstitut) (DK ISSN 0107-900X) 187
S C A Free Speech Yearbook (Speech Communication Association) (US) 909
S C A N (Superior California Administration Newsletter) (US) 1162
S C A T Bulletin see Alberta Science Education Journal 987
S C I see Science Citation Index 1004
S C I M A Special Series (Society of Management Science and Applied Cybernetics) (II) 359
S C I M P (Selective Cooperative Index of Management Periodicals) (UK ISSN 0141-5077) 12, 217
S C K Annual Report (Studiecentrum voor Kernenergie) (BE) 1162
S C L A Newsletter (Southern Comparative Literature Association) (US) 732

S D A - Nyt (Samnordisk Dokumentationscentral for Arbejdsmiljoe) (DK ISSN 0108-5417) *275*
S.D.C. Bulletin (Scientific Documentation Centre Ltd.) (UK ISSN 0036-1178) *12, 893*
S D C E International Die Casting Congress. Transactions (Society of Die Casting Engineers, Inc.) (US ISSN 0074-4557) *746*
S D E A Catalogue of Shopfittings and Display (Shop and Display Equipment Association) (UK) *16*
S D E A Members Catalogue of Shopfittings and Display see S D E A Catalogue of Shopfittings and Display *16*
S E A G Boletin del Algodon see E A G Publicaciones *26*
S E A G Boletin del Maiz see E A G Publicaciones *26*
S E A G Boletin del Trigo see E A G Publicaciones *26*
S E C A C Review see Southeastern College Art Conference Review *110*
S E C A C Review and Newsletter see Southeastern College Art Conference Review *110*
S E C Accounting Rules (US) *222, 268*
S E C Annual Reports see S E C Annual Reports. Banking Supplement *232*
S E C Annual Reports. Banking Supplement (US) *232*
S E C Bulletin (Securities and Exchange Commission) (PH) *240*
S E C I N Abstracts see S E C I N Abstracts. Journal *1031*
S E C I N Abstracts. Journal (Socio-Economic Information Network) (JM) *12, 217, 1031*
S E C O L A S Annals (Southeastern Council on Latin American Studies) (US ISSN 0081-2951) *609*
S E M Proceedings (Society for Experimental Mechanics) (US) *489*
S E S A Proceedings (Society for Experimental Stress Analysis) see S E M Proceedings *489*
S F. Status (Socialistiske Perspektiver Forlag) (DK ISSN 0902-1612) *909*
S F S Catalogue (Suomen Standardisoimisliitto) (FI) *474, 809*
S F Status see S F. Status *909*
S H A R E (Sisters Have Resources Everywhere) (US ISSN 0273-2343) *1162*
S H E (Subject Headings for Engineering) (US) *474, 683*
S I A M - A M S Proceedings (Society for Industrial and Applied Mathematics) (US ISSN 0080-5084) *752*
S I A Yearbook (Singapore Institute of Architects) (SI ISSN 0217-7668) *99*
S I C 2038 Process/Quality Control Instrumentation Buyers Guide (US) *520*
S I C 2087/Aroma Buyers Guide (US) *520*
S I D A Development Studies see S A R E C Report *918*
S I D International Symposium. Digest of Technical Papers (Society for Information Display) (US ISSN 0097-966X) *474*
S I E Guide to Investment Services (Select Information Exchange) (US) *268*
S I E Sophisticated Investor see S I E Guide to Investment Services *268*
S I H O L S see Amsterdam Studies in the Theory and History of Linguistic Science. Series 3: Studies in the History of the Language Sciences *690*
S I K Annual Report (Svenska Livsmedelsinstitutet) (SW) *520*
S I K Information (Svenska Livsmedelsinstitutet) (SW) *520*
S I L P L Series see S I L Publications in Linguistics *702*
S I L Publications in Linguistics (Summer Institute of Linguistics, Inc.) (US) *702*

S I L Publications on Linguistics and Related Fields see S I L Publications in Linguistics *702*
S I N Information see SIN-Staedtebauinstitut. Information *625*
S I N Jahresberichte see SIN-Staedtebauinstitut. Jahresberichte *625*
S I N Medical Newsletter (Schweizerisches Institut fuer Nuklearforschung) (SZ) *792*
S I N Newsletter (Schweizerisches Institut fuer Nuklearforschung) (SZ) *898*
S I N Physics Report see S I N Newsletter *898*
S I P R I Chemical & Biological Warfare Studies (Stockholm International Peace Research Institute (S.I.P.R.I.)) (UK ISSN 0267-2537) *918*
S I P R I Yearbook: World Armaments and Disarmament (Stockholm International Peace Research Institute (S.I.P.R.I.)) (UK ISSN 0081-9900) *918*
S.I.S.F. Documenti (Societa Italiana di Scienze Farmaceutiche) (IT ISSN 0081-0703) *872*
S.I.T.R.A.M. Resultats Generaux: Trafic Interieur - Trafic International (Systeme d'Information sur les Transports de Machandises) (FR) *1086*
S.J. Hall Lectureship in Industrial Forestry (US ISSN 0080-5092) *527*
S K R-Meddelanden (SW ISSN 0348-243X) *1162*
S. Klein Computer Graphics Review (US) *356, 362, 362*
S. Klein Directory of Computer Graphics Suppliers (US ISSN 0732-9199) *356, 357*
S L A M: Annuaire Commercial de l'Afrique see S L A M: Trade Year Book of Africa *1162*
S L A M: Trade Year Book of Africa/S L A M: Annuaire Commercial de l'Afrique (SP ISSN 0080-9985) *1162*
S L A Triennial Salary Survey (Special Libraries Association) (US) *683*
S L C S see Studies in Language Companion Series *705*
S L F Information (Seminarielaererforeningen) (DK ISSN 0108-3856) *419*
S M E Transactions see North American Manufacturing Research Conference. Proceedings *473*
S M I L Quarterly Journal of Linguistic Calculus see Linguistic Calculation *698*
S M I Monthly Index Service (Super Market Institute) see Reference Point: Food Industry Abstracts *522*
S M R C Newsletter (Southwestern Mission Research Center, Inc.) (US) *609*
S M U V Zeitung (Schweizerischer Metall- und Uhrenarbeitnehmer-Verband) (SZ) *800*
S N Distribution Study of Grocery Store Sales (US) *285, 520, 523*
S N G A N S see Sylloge Nummorum Graecorum *845*
S N I C Bulletin (Singapore National Institute of Chemistry) (SI) *324*
S O L I N E W S (Southeastern Library Network, Inc.) (US ISSN 0193-273X) *689*
S.O.S. Directory (Save on Shopping Directory) (US ISSN 0276-6701) *369*
S P A I D News (Society for the Prevention of Asbestosis and Industrial Diseases) (UK ISSN 0144-4301) *636*
S P E A H R Head see China Rights Annals *903*
S P E Monograph Series (Society of Professors of Education) (US ISSN 0882-1100) *419*
S P E R Annuaire (Syndicat des Industries de Materiel Professionnel Electronique et Radioelectrique) (FR) *459*

S P R I Informerar see Sweden. Sjukvaardens och Socialvaardens Planerings- och Rationaliseringsinstitut. S P R I Informerar *956*
S P R I Raad see Sweden. Sjukvaardens och Socialvaardens Planerings- och Rationaliseringsinstitut. S P R I Raad *956*
S P R I Raad 1. see Sweden. Sjukvaardens och Socialvaardens Planerings-och Rationaliseringsinstitut. S P R I Raad 1 *956*
S P R I Raad 4. see Sweden. Sjukvaardens och Socialvaardens Planerings- och Rationaliseringsinstitut. S P R I Raad 4 *956*
S P R I Raad 5. see Sweden. Sjukvaardens och Socialvaardens Planerings- och Rationaliseringsinstitut. S P R I Raad 5 *956*
S P R I Raad 6. see Sweden. Sjukvaardens och Socialvaardens Planerings- och Rationaliseringsinstitut. S P R I Raad 6 *956*
S P R I Raad 7. see Sweden. Sjukvaardens och Socialvaardens Planerings- och Rationaliseringsinstitut. S P R I Raad 7 *956*
S P R I Rapport see Sweden. Sjukvaardens och Socialvaardens Planerings- och Rationaliseringsinstitut. S P R I Rapport *956*
S P R I Specifikationer see Sweden. Sjukvaardens och Socialvaardens Planerings- och Rationaliseringsinstitut. S P R I Specifikationer *956*
S P: Sociological Practice see Sociological Practice *1029*
S S C see Social Sciences Citation Index *1014*
S S P see Studies in Slavic Literature and Poetics *734*
S S P Proceedings see Society of Scholarly Publishing. Proceedings of Annual Meetings *963*
S S R C Studentship Handbook see E S R C Studentship Handbook *429*
S S S A Special Publication Series (Soil Science Society of America) (US ISSN 0081-1904) *59*
S T A News see B.C. Science Teacher *446*
S T A R Service (Sloane Travel Agency Reports) (US) *1116*
S T F I Meddelande. Series A (Svenska Traeforskningsinstitutet) (SW ISSN 0348-2650) *859*
S T S Debat (Sammenslutningen af Tvaerpolitiske Studenterorganisationer) (DK ISSN 0108-2655) *909*
S T S Information see S T S Debat *909*
S T U Investigation (Styrelsen foer Teknisk Utveckling) (SW) *1070*
S U D E N E Plano de Acao see Brazil. Superintendencia do Desenvolvimento do Nordeste. SU D E N E Plano de Acao *622*
S U G I A see Sprache und Geschichte in Afrika *704*
S V Leveringsbetingelser og Proevningsmetoder (Statens Vejlaboratorium) (DK) *1097*
S.W.A. Scientific Society. Journal (SX) *1011*
S W I E E C O Record of Technical Papers see I E E E Region 5 Conference. Record *455*
S W L (Shortwave Listener) (US ISSN 0162-5934) *341, 349, 548*
S.Y.A. Internal Bulletin (Socialist Youth Alliance) (AT) *909*
Saab-Scania Technical Notes see Saab Technical Notes *21*
Saab Technical Notes (SW ISSN 0080-5149) *21*
Saarbruecker Beitraege zur Altertumskunde (GW ISSN 0080-5181) *560*

SAGE ANNUAL 1873

Saarbruecker Studien zur Musikwissenschaft (GW ISSN 0080-519X) *841*
Sabah. Department of Statistics. Annual Bulletin of Statistics/Sabah. Jabatan Perangkaan. Siaran Perangkaan Tahunan (MY ISSN 0080-5203) *1062*
Sabah. Forest Department. Annual Report (MY ISSN 0080-5211) *527*
Sabah. Jabatan Perangkaan. Siaran Perangkaan Tahunan see Sabah. Department of Statistics. Annual Bulletin of Statistics *1062*
Sabah. Marine Department. Annual Report (MY ISSN 0080-522X) *1103*
Sabah Society. Journal (MY ISSN 0036-2131) *999*
Sadler's Wells Theatre Programme (UK) *841, 1078*
Sado Marine Biological Station. Annual Report see Sado Marine Biological Station. Report *146*
Sado Marine Biological Station. Report/Niigata Daigaku Rigakubu Fuzoku Sado Rinkai Jikkenjo Kenkyu Hokoku (JA) *146*
Saechsische Akademie der Wissenschaften, Leipzig. Jahrbuch (GE ISSN 0080-5262) *999*
Saechsische Akademie der Wissenschaften, Leipzig. Mathematisch-Naturwissenschaftliche Klasse. Abhandlungen (GE ISSN 0365-6470) *752, 999*
Saechsische Akademie der Wissenschaften, Leipzig. Mathematisch-Naturwissenschaftliche Klasse. Sitzungsberichte (GE ISSN 0080-5270) *752, 999*
Saechsische Akademie der Wissenschaften, Leipzig. Philologisch-Historische Klasse. Abhandlungen (GE ISSN 0080-5297) *560, 702*
Saechsische Akademie der Wissenschaften, Leipzig. Philologisch-Historische Klasse. Sitzungsberichte (GE ISSN 0138-3957) *560, 702*
Saechsische Bibliographie (GE ISSN 0419-7305) *131*
Saechsische Landesbibliothek. Bibliographie Illustrierte Buecher der Deutschen Demokratischen Republik(GE ISSN 0232-5616) *964*
Saecula Spiritalia (GW ISSN 0343-2009) *560, 632*
Saeculum (GW ISSN 0080-5319) *560*
Saenger-Taschenkalender (GW) *841*
Saerrakke (DK) *825*
Safaho-Monographien see Safaho-Monographs *683*
Safaho-Monographs (NE ISSN 0581-2674) *683*
Safety Evaluation and Regulation of Chemicals (SZ ISSN 0256-730X) *872*
Safety Research News see I N R S Lettre d'Information sur la Recherche *635*
Safety Science Abstracts see Safety Science Abstracts Journal *12*
Safety Science Abstracts Journal (US ISSN 0160-1342) *12, 956*
Safn til Soegu Islands og Islenzkra Bokmenta (IC ISSN 0558-1257) *595*
Saga och Sed (SW ISSN 0586-5360) *92, 516, 595, 702*
Saga of the Sanpitch (US) *516, 609*
Saga University. Faculty of Science and Engineering. Reports (JA ISSN 0385-6186) *474, 752, 890*
Le Sagamien (CN ISSN 0226-2169) *548*
Sagamore Army Materials Research Conference. Proceedings (US ISSN 0080-5335) *812*
Sagamore Computer Conference on Parallel Processing. Proceedings see International Conference on Parallel Processing. Proceedings *360*
Saga's Baseball Special see Baseball Preview (Year) *1037*
Sage Annual Reviews of Communication Research (US ISSN 0099-1414) *344*

Sage Annual Reviews of Community Mental Health see Sage Series in Community Mental Health 937
Sage Annual Reviews of Drug and Alcohol Abuse (US ISSN 0190-5104) 377
Sage Annual Reviews of Studies in Deviance (US ISSN 0197-9272) 1029
Sage Family Studies Abstracts (US ISSN 0164-0283) 12, 1031
Sage International Yearbook of Foreign Policy Studies (US ISSN 0094-0658) 918
Sage Library of Social Research (US) 1011
Sage Public Administration Abstracts (US ISSN 0094-6958) 12, 949
Sage Race Relations Abstracts (UK ISSN 0307-9201) 12, 912
Sage Research Progress Series in Criminology (US) 1162
Sage Series in Community Mental Health (US) 937
Sage Series in Cross Cultural Research and Methodology (US) 75, 937
Sage Series in Interpersonal Communication (US) 344
Sage Series on African Modernization and Development (US) 264, 567, 909
Sage Studies in International Sociology (US) 1029
Sage Urban Studies Abstracts (US ISSN 0090-5747) 12, 627
Sage Yearbooks in Politics and Public Policy (US) 909
Sage Yearbooks in Women's Policy Studies (US) 135, 1129
Sageret: Annuaire General du Batiment et des Travaux Publics (FR) 187
Saggi e Memorie di Storia dell'Arte (IT ISSN 0080-5394) 109
Saggi Filosofici (IT) 881
Sagittarius see Schuetz-Jahrbuch 841
Sagrada Biblia (SP) 972
Sahitya Akademi, New Delhi. Report (II ISSN 0080-5416) 632
Sahyog (II) 238
Saibokaku Byorigaku Zasshi see Journal of Karyopathology 775
Saigai No Jittai To Shobo No Genkyo/Annual Report of Fire and Disaster Prevention (JA) 507, 946
Saikin No Shinyaku/New Drugs in Japan (JA) 872
Sailboat & Equipment Directory (US ISSN 0148-8732) 1042
Sailing the Road Clear (US) 743
St. Augustine's Magazine (UK) 438
Saint Bonaventure University. Franciscan Institute. Philosophy Series (US ISSN 0080-5432) 983
Saint Bonaventure University. Franciscan Institute. Text Series (US ISSN 0080-5440) 983
Saint Bonaventure University. Science Studies (US ISSN 0080-5467) 1162
St. Clair County Historical Society. Journal (US ISSN 0095-3911) 609
St. David's Day Bilingual Series (UK) 135
St. Dunstan's Annual Report (UK) 180
St. Edward's College Magazine (UK) 438
Saint George's Hospital Gazette (UK ISSN 0036-2840) 618, 766
St. James Press Car Ferry Guide (UK) 1103
St. Kitts-Nevis-Anguilla National Bank Limited and its Subsidiaries. Annual Report and Accounts (XI) 232
Saint Lawrence Seaway Authority. Annual Report (CN ISSN 0581-3298) 1103
Saint Louis University Public Law Forum see Saint Louis University Public Law Review 663
Saint Louis University Public Law Review (US) 663
Saint Mary's University. Atlantic Region Geographical Studies (CN ISSN 0831-8093) 33, 548
Saint Mary's University. Occasional Papers in Geography (CN ISSN 0831-8107) 380, 548
Saint Mary's University. Studies in Marine and Coastal Geography (CN ISSN 0832-6266) 512, 548

St. Paul Dispatch & Pioneer Press Newspaper Index see Index to the St. Paul Pioneer Press and Dispatch 647
St. Paul, Minnesota. Metropolitan Transit Commission. Annual Report see St. Paul, Minnesota. Twin Cities Area Metropolitan Transit Commission. Annual Report 1093
St. Paul, Minnesota. Twin Cities Area Metropolitan Transit Commission. Annual Report (US) 1093
St. Paul Urban League. Annual Report (US) 1020
St. Poeltner Dioezesanblatt (AU ISSN 0036-3162) 972
St. Thomas More Lectures (US ISSN 0082-4208) 972
St. Thomas More Society. Journal (AT ISSN 0310-6861) 663
Saison Cyclonique a Madagascar (MG) 806
Saitama-Ken Eisei Tokei Nenpo/Annual Report of Public Health, Saitama Prefecture (JA) 956
Saitama University. College of Liberal Arts. Journal (JA) 712
Saitama University. Science Reports. Series A: Mathematics (JA) 324, 752, 890
Saitama University. Science Reports. Series A: Mathematics, Physics and Chemistry see Saitama University. Science Reports. Series A: Mathematics 752
Salar Jung Museum. Annual Report (II ISSN 0304-8152) 830
Salaries & Bonuses in Personnel/Industrial Relations Functions (US) 275, 287
Salaries & Related Matters in the Service Department (US) 275
Salaries and Wages for Michigan Municipalities over 1,000 Population (US) 951
Salaries and Wages for Michigan Municipalities over 4,000 Population see Salaries and Wages for Michigan Municipalities over 1,000 Population 951
Salaries and Wages for Michigan Municipalities under 4,000 Population see Salaries and Wages for Michigan Municipalities over 1,000 Population 951
Salaries of Scientists, Engineers and Technicians (US ISSN 0146-5015) 849
Salary and Fringe Benefits Survey of Tennessee Municipalities (US) 946
Salary Budget Survey (US) 275
Sales & Marketing Management Survey of Buying Power (Part I) (US) 217
Sales & Marketing Management Survey of Buying Power (Part II) (US) 217
Sales and Marketing Management Survey of Industrial and Commercial Buying Power see Sales & Marketing Management Survey of U.S. Industrial & Commercial Buying Power 217
Sales & Marketing Management Survey of Selling Costs (US) 217
Sales & Marketing Management Survey of U.S. Industrial & Commercial Buying Power (US) 217
Sales Management Survey of Buying Power (Part I) see Sales & Marketing Management Survey of Buying Power (Part I) 217
Sales Management Survey of Buying Power (Part II) see Sales & Marketing Management Survey of Buying Power (Part II) 217
Sales Management Survey of Selling Costs see Sales & Marketing Management Survey of Selling Costs 217
Sales of Vine Products Manufactured in Cyprus (CY ISSN 0253-8636) 1162
Saling Aktienfuehrer (GW ISSN 0080-5572) 268
Salomon Brothers Center for the Study of Financial Institutions. Monograph Series (US ISSN 0276-2021) 232
Salomon Brothers Center for the Study of Financial Institutions. Occasional Papers (US) 232

Salomon Brothers Center for the Study of Financial Institutions. Working Paper (US) 232
Salon Nacional de Artes Plasticas y Visuales (UY) 109
Salt (CN ISSN 0709-616X) 972
Salt Lake City Messenger (US ISSN 0586-7282) 984
Salt Lick (US ISSN 0036-360X) 743
Salthouse (US ISSN 0737-5506) 732
Saltzman's Eurail Guide Annual see Eurail Guide 1108
Salud Maternoinfantil y Atencion en las Americas (US) 788
Salud para Todos (CR) 336, 886
Salus (CN ISSN 0824-8672) 959, 1023
Salvation Army Year Book (UK ISSN 0080-567X) 984
Salzburger Beitraege zur Paracelsusforschung (AU ISSN 0259-0794) 560, 881
Salzburger Exkursionsberichte (AU) 548
Salzburger Geographische Arbeiten (AU) 548
Salzburger Jahrbuch fuer Philosophie (AU ISSN 0080-5696) 881
Salzburger Studien zur Philosophie (AU ISSN 0080-5726) 881
Salzburger Universitaetsreden (AU ISSN 0080-5734) 438
Samarbejdsgruppen for Trafiksikkerhed i Kommuneerne i Koebenhavns-Omraadet Rapport fra S T I K K see Rapport fra S T I K K 1097
Samaru Agricultural Newsletter see Noma 32
Samaru Miscellaneous Paper (NR ISSN 0080-5769) 33
Samaru Research Bulletin (NR ISSN 0080-5777) 34
Sambalpur University. Post-Graduate Department of Oriya. Journal (II) 732
Samfundet til Udgivelse af Dansk Musik. Bulletin (DK ISSN 0109-8438) 841
Samisdat (SZ ISSN 0254-1521) 595, 909
Samiske Samlinger (NO ISSN 0581-4480) 75, 1029
Samlaren (SW ISSN 0348-6133) 739
Sammenslutningen af Tvaerpolitiske Studenterorganisationer Debat see S T S Debat 909
Sammlung Akademie-Verlag: Sprache (GE ISSN 0138-550X) 702
Sammlung Dalp (SZ ISSN 0080-5807) 632
Sammlung Geltender Staatsangehoerigkeitsgesetze (GW ISSN 0080-5823) 663
Sammlung Groos (GW ISSN 0344-0591) 438, 702
Sammlung Kurzer Grammatiken Germanischer Dialekte (GW) 702
Sammlung Lebensmittelrechtlicher Entscheidungen (GW ISSN 0080-5831) 520, 663
Sammlung Musikwissenschaftlicher Abhandlungen/Collection d'Etudes Musicologiques (GW ISSN 0085-588X) 841
Samnordisk Dokumentationscentral for Arbejdsmiljoe Nyt see S D A - Nyt 275
Samoan Pacific Law Journal (AS) 663, 671
Samos (GW ISSN 0080-5866) 92
Sample Surveys in the ESCAP Region (UN ISSN 0125-0027) 217
Samskriti Vibhaga Ki Anudanom Ki Mangem see India. Department of Culture. Demands for Grants 443
Samtidsorientering (DK ISSN 0108-7665) 419
Samuel H. Kress Foundation. Annual Report (US ISSN 0581-4766) 109
Samuel Neaman Institute for Advanced Studies in Science and Technology. Annual Report (IS) 999, 1070
Samvadadhvam (II ISSN 0581-4790) 1062
Samvardhana (CE) 249

San Diego County. Department of Planning and Land Use. County Data Base see San Diego County. Info Bulletin. Population & Housing Estimates 627
San Diego County. Info Bulletin. Population & Housing Estimates (US) 627
San Diego Museum of Man. Ethnic Technology Notes (US ISSN 0080-5890) 75
San Diego Museum of Man. Papers (US ISSN 0080-5904) 75
San Diego Society of Natural History. Memoirs (US ISSN 0080-5920) 999
San Diego Society of Natural History. Occasional Papers see San Diego Society of Natural History. Transactions 999
San Diego Society of Natural History. Transactions (US ISSN 0080-5947) 999
San Diego State University. Bureau of Business and Economic Research. Monographs (US ISSN 0068-5836) 199
San Diego State University. Bureau of Business and Economic Research. Research Studies and Position Papers(US. ISSN 0068-5844) 199
San Fernando Valley Law Review (US) 1162
San Francisco Bay Area Rapid Transit District. Annual Report (US ISSN 0362-2800) 1083
San Francisco Bay Conservation and Development Commission. Annual Report (US ISSN 0085-5898) 367
San Francisco Chronicle. Newspaper Index see Index to the San Francisco Chronicle 647
San Francisco Fresh Fruit and Vegetable Wholesale Market Prices (US) 34, 285
San Francisco Maritime Museum. Sea Letter see Sea Letter 1103
San Joaquin Valley Business Perspectives see Valley Business Perspectives 250
Sananjalka (FI) 703
Sancta Crux (AU) 595
Sand see Sands 732
Sandalion (IT) 338
Sandgrouse (UK ISSN 0260-4736) 170
Sands (US) 109, 732, 743
Sandvigske Samlinger. Aarbok see Maihaugen 89
Sangyo Keiei Kenkyushoho see Journal of Industry and Management 280
Sanitation Industry Yearbook see World Wastes Equipment Catalog 500
St. Galler Studien zum Wettbewerbs und Immaterialgueterrecht (SZ) 663
Sankt Galler Beitraege zum Fremdenverkehr und zur Verkehrswirtschaft: Reihe Verkehrswirtschaft (SZ ISSN 0080-6048) 1095
St. Galler Studien zur Politikwissenschaft (SZ) 909
Sankt Gallische Naturwissenschaftliche Gesellschaft. Bericht ueber Die Taetigkeit (SZ ISSN 0080-6056) 999
Sankyo Kenkyusho Nempo/Sankyo Research Laboratories. Annual Report (JA ISSN 0080-6064) 872
Sankyo Research Laboratories. Annual Report see Sankyo Kenkyusho Nempo 872
Sannivedana (CE) 344
Sanshi Shikenjo, Nempo see Sericultural Experiment Station. Annual Report 34
Santa Ana Mountain Series (US) 609
Santa Barbara Museum of Natural History. Occasional Papers (US) 830, 999
Santakuti Vedic Research Series (II ISSN 0080-6137) 571
Santiago del Estero. Direccion General de Investigaciones Estadistica y Censos. Estadistica Agricola-Ganadera (AG) 43
Santiago del Estero. Direccion General de Investigaciones Estadistica y Censos. Estadisticas Sociales (AG) 1062

Sao Paulo (City) Arquivo Municipal. Revista (BL ISSN 0034-9216) *609*
Sao Paulo. Coordenadoria de Saude Mental. Arquivos (BL ISSN 0101-1693) *791*
Sao Paulo, Brazil (State). Departamento de Edificios e Obras Publicas. Relatorio de Atividades (BL) *483, 946*
Sao Paulo, Brazil (State). Observatorio. Anuario Astronomico *see* Universidade de Sao Paulo. Instituto Astronomico e Geofisico. Anuario Astronomico *118*
Sao Paulo, Brazil (State). Secretaria da Educacao. Atividades Desenvolvidas (BL) *419, 663*
Sao Paulo, Brazil (State). Superintendencia de Saneamento Ambiental. Relatorio Anual de Atividades (BL) *499*
Sao Paulo Yearbook (BL) *237*
Saotharlann Staire Eireann *see* Irish History Workshop *587*
Sapphic Touch (US ISSN 0275-6757) *616, 732, 1129*
Sarah Lawrence Literary Review *see* Sarah Lawrence Review *712*
Sarah Lawrence Review (US) *712*
Sarawak. Department of Agriculture. Research Branch. Annual Report (MY ISSN 0080-6420) *34*
Sarawak. Department of Statistics. Annual Statistical Bulletin *see* Annual Statistical Bulletin Sarawak *1048*
Sarawak Annual Bulletin of Statistics *see* Annual Statistical Bulletin Sarawak *1048*
Sarawak Electricity Supply Corporation. Annual Report (MY ISSN 0127-144X) *459*
Sarawak External Trade Statistics (MY ISSN 0080-6455) *217*
Sarawak Vital Statistics (MY ISSN 0080-6447) *1062*
Sardegna d'Oggi; Guida Practica *see* Guida Sardegna d'Oggi *1111*
Sarkiyat Mecmuasi (TU ISSN 0578-9761) *613*
Sarsia (NO ISSN 0036-4827) *146*
Sarvadanand Universal Series (II ISSN 0080-6471) *571*
Sarvotkrushta Marathi Katha (II ISSN 0303-3074) *732*
Sasco Catalogue *see* Product Finder: Swift-Sasco Buyers Guide *369*
Saskatchewan. Alcohol and Drug Abuse Commission. Annual Report (CN) *377*
Saskatchewan. Alcoholism Commission. Annual Report *see* Saskatchewan. Alcohol and Drug Abuse Commission. Annual Report *377*
Saskatchewan. Department of Agriculture. Annual Report (CN ISSN 0319-3578) *34*
Saskatchewan. Department of Agriculture. Family Farm Improvement Branch. Technical Bulletin (CN ISSN 0080-648X) *34*
Saskatchewan. Department of Culture and Recreation. Annual Report (CN) *92, 99, 110*
Saskatchewan. Department of Culture and Youth. Annual Report *see* Saskatchewan. Department of Culture and Recreation. Annual Report *110*
Saskatchewan. Department of Industry and Commerce. Report for the Fiscal Year (CN ISSN 0080-6498) *946*
Saskatchewan. Department of Labour. Wages and Working Conditions by Occupation (CN ISSN 0706-4926) *275*
Saskatchewan. Department of Social Services. Annual Report (CN) *1020*
Saskatchewan. Department of Social Welfare. Annual Report *see* Saskatchewan. Department of Social Services. Annual Report *1020*
Saskatchewan. Department of the Environment. Annual Report (CN ISSN 0317-4611) *499*
Saskatchewan. Government Insurance Office. Province of Saskatchewan Motor Vehicle Traffic Accidents. Annual Report (CN) *1097*

Saskatchewan. Medical Care Insurance Commission. Annual Report (CN ISSN 0080-6544) *641*
Saskatchewan. Parks and Renewable Resources Annual Report (CN ISSN 0318-4684) *367*
Saskatchewan. Prescription Drug Plan. Annual Report (CN ISSN 0707-0152) *641, 872*
Saskatchewan. Tourism and Renewable Resources Annual Report *see* Saskatchewan. Parks and Renewable Resources Annual Report *367*
Saskatchewan Archaeology (CN) *92*
Saskatchewan Building Trades Yearbook (CN) *187*
Saskatchewan Centre of the Arts. Annual Report (CN) *110*
Saskatchewan Construction Industry Directory. Purchasing Guide (CN) *187, 474*
Saskatchewan Economic and Financial Position (CN ISSN 0080-6676) *249*
Saskatchewan Economic Review (CN ISSN 0558-6976) *249*
Saskatchewan Energy & Mines. Annual Report (CN) *820, 866*
Saskatchewan Energy and Mines. Mineral Statistics Yearbook (CN) *820, 866*
Saskatchewan Energy & Mines. Petroleum and Natural Gas Reservoir Annual (CN) *866*
Saskatchewan Farm Science *see* Agricultural Science Bulletin *23*
Saskatchewan FarmStart Corporation. Annual Report *see* Agricultural Credit Corporation of Saskatchewan. Annual Report *44*
Saskatchewan Housing Corporation. Annual Report (CN) *625*
Saskatchewan Index. Manufacturers' Edition *see* Saskatchewan Manufacturers Guide *316*
Saskatchewan Manufacturers Guide (CN ISSN 0080-6536) *316*
Saskatchewan Mineral Resources. Annual Report *see* Saskatchewan Energy & Mines. Annual Report *820*
Saskatchewan Mineral Resources. Mineral Statistical Yearbook *see* Saskatchewan Energy and Mines. Mineral Statistics Yearbook *820*
Saskatchewan Mineral Resources. Petroleum and Natural Gas Reservoir Annual *see* Saskatchewan Energy & Mines. Petroleum and Natural Gas Reservoir Annual *866*
Saskatchewan Motor Transport Guide *see* Saskatchewan Trucking-Ship by Truck Directory *1105*
Saskatchewan Municipal Directory (CN ISSN 0581-8435) *951*
Saskatchewan Music Festival Association Official Syllabus (CN) *841*
Saskatchewan Natural History Society. Special Publications (CN ISSN 0080-6552) *170*
Saskatchewan Oil and Gas Corporation. Annual Report *see* Saskoil. Annual Report *866*
Saskatchewan Poetry Book (CN ISSN 0080-6560) *743*
Saskatchewan Reports (CN) *663*
Saskatchewan Research Council. Annual Report (CN ISSN 0080-6587) *999, 1070*
Saskatchewan Research Council. Climatological Reference Station. Annual Summary (CN) *806*
Saskatchewan Telecommunications. Annual Report (CN ISSN 0080-6633) *350*
Saskatchewan Trade Directory *see* Saskatchewan Manufacturers Guide *316*
Saskatchewan Trade Directory (CN) *316*
Saskatchewan Trucking-Ship by Truck Directory (CN) *1105*
Saskatoon S.R.C. Climatological Reference Station. Annual Summary *see* Saskatchewan Research Council. Climatological Reference Station. Annual Summary *806*
Saskoil. Annual Report (CN) *866*
Satapitaka. Indo-Asian Literatures (II ISSN 0581-8532) *732*

Satellite Directory (US) *316*
Satellites Galileens de Jupiter (FR ISSN 0769-1033) *117*
Sather Classical Lectures (US ISSN 0080-6684) *338*
Saudi Arabia. Central Department of Statistics. Foreign Trade Statistics (SU) *217*
Saudi Arabia. Central Department of Statistics. Statistical Indicator (SU) *217*
Saudi Arabia. Central Department of Statistics. Statistical Yearbook (SU) *1062*
Saudi Arabia. Ministry of Education. Annual Statistical Report (SU) *425, 441*
Saudi Arabia. Ministry of Education. Educational Abstracts (SU) *425*
Saudi Arabia. Ministry of Education. Educational Statistics (SU) *425, 1062*
Saudi Arabia Market Conditions (US) *259*
Saudi Arabia Trade Directory (US) *316*
Saudi Arabian Agriculture Guide (UK) *34*
Saudi Arabian Monetary Agency. Annual Report (SU ISSN 0558-7220) *298*
Saudi Arabian Monetary Agency. Statistical Summary (SU ISSN 0581-8672) *232*
Saussurea (SZ ISSN 0373-2525) *161*
Sav-on-Hotels (Year) (US ISSN 0098-4507) *620*
Sav-on-Hotels Across Europe *see* Sav-on-Hotels (Year) *620*
Savacou (JM ISSN 0036-5068) *110, 732*
Save On Shopping *see* S.O.S. Directory *369*
Save on Shopping Directory Directory *see* S.O.S. Directory *369*
Save the Children. Annual Report (US) *334, 1020*
Savez Geodetskih Inzenjera i Geometara Hrvatske. Geodet (YU) *401*
Savez Geodetskih Inzenjera i Geometara Hrvatske. Obavijesti *see* Savez Geodetskih Inzenjera i Geometara Hrvatske. Geodet *401*
Savigny-Stiftung fuer Rechtsgeschichte. Zeitschrift. Germanistische, Romanistische und Kanonistische Abteilung (GE ISSN 0084-5264) *663*
Savings and Loan Fact Book *see* Savings and Loan Sourcebook *232*
Savings and Loan Sourcebook (US ISSN 0731-0935) *232*
Savon Luonto (FI ISSN 0356-276X) *146, 367*
Savonia (FI ISSN 0356-3189) *146, 367*
Sbornik Geologickych Ved: Antropozoikum/Journal of Geological Sciences: Anthropozoic (CS ISSN 0036-5270) *394*
Sbornik Geologickych Ved: Geologie/Journal of Geological Sciences: Geology (CS ISSN 0581-9172) *394*
Sbornik Geologickych Ved: Hydrogeologie, Inzenyrska Geologie/Journal of Geological Sciences: Hydrogeology, Engineering Geology (CS ISSN 0036-5289) *404*
Sbornik Geologickych Ved: Loziskova Geologie, Mineralogie/Journal of Geological Sciences: Economic Geology, Mineralogy (CS ISSN 0581-9180) *394*
Sbornik Geologickych Ved: Paleontologie/Journal of Geological Sciences: Paleontology (CS ISSN 0036-5277) *857*
Sbornik Geologickych Ved: Technologie, Geochemie/Journal of Geological Sciences: Technology, Geochemistry (CS ISSN 0036-5300) *394*
Sbornik Geologickych Ved: Uzita Geofyzika/Journal of Geological Sciences: Applied Geophysics (CS ISSN 0036-5319) *401*
Sbornik Historicky (CS ISSN 0577-3725) *595*

Sbornik k Dejinam 19 a 20 Stoleti (CS ISSN 0231-6153) *595*
Sbornik k Problematice Dejin Imperialismu (CS ISSN 0231-620X) *595*
Sbornik Praci Historickych (CS) *595*
Sbornik Praci Vychodoceskych Archivu(CS) *595*
Sbornik Statei po Frantsuzskoi Lingvistike i Metodike Prepodavaniya Inostrannogo Yazika v V U Ze (UR) *449, 703*
Sbornik Vlastivednych Praci Z Podblannicka (CS) *596*
Scandal Sheet (US) *614*
Scandinavia Stamp Catalogue (UK ISSN 0142-985X) *875*
Scandinavia Africana (SW) *1162*
Scandinavian Corrosion Congress. Proceedings (DK ISSN 0581-9431) *800*
Scandinavian Heritage (CN) *505, 609*
Scandinavian Institute of African Studies. Annual Seminar Proceedings *see* Scandinavian Institute of African Studies. Seminar Proceedings *567*
Scandinavian Institute of African Studies. Newsletter (SW ISSN 0549-6330) *567*
Scandinavian Institute of African Studies. Research Report (SW ISSN 0080-6714) *567*
Scandinavian Institute of African Studies. Rural Development (SW) *49, 75*
Scandinavian Institute of African Studies. Seminar Proceedings (SW ISSN 0281-0018) *567*
Scandinavian Institute of Asian Studies. Annual Newsletter (DK ISSN 0106-3871) *853*
Scandinavian Institute of Asian Studies. Monograph Series (UK ISSN 0069-1712) *853*
Scandinavian Institute of Asian Studies. Occasional Papers (UK ISSN 0266-206X) *853*
Scandinavian Journal of Clinical and Laboratory Investigation. Supplement(UK ISSN 0085-591X) *766, 782*
Scandinavian Journal of Gastroenterology. Supplement (NO ISSN 0085-5928) *783*
Scandinavian Journal of Haematology. Supplementum (DK ISSN 0080-6722) *783*
Scandinavian Journal of Maritime Law *see* Arkiv for Sjoerett *651*
Scandinavian Journal of Respiratory Diseases. Supplementum *see* European Journal of Respiratory Diseases. Supplementum *793*
Scandinavian Numismatic Journal *see* Nordisk Numismatisk Aarsskrift *845*
Scandinavian Periodicals Index in Economics and Business Scanp *see* Scanp *217*
Scandinavian Ship Abstract Journal *see* Ship Abstracts *1086*
Scandinavian Studies in Criminology (NO ISSN 0085-5936) *372*
Scandinavian Studies in Law (SW ISSN 0085-5944) *663*
Scandinavia's 5000 Largest Companies (UK) *291*
Scando-Slavica (DK ISSN 0080-6765) *703, 732*
Scando-Slavica. Supplementum (DK) *703, 732*
Scanp (Scandinavian Periodicals Index in Economics and Business) (FI ISSN 0782-2987) *12, 217*
Scarcity (UG) *199*
Scarecrow Author Bibliographies (US) *131*
Scarecrow Library Administration Series (US) *683*
Scarlet & Gold (CN) *372*
Scena Svizzera *see* Szene Schweiz *1078*
Scenarium (NE) *1078*
Scene Suisse *see* Szene Schweiz *1078*
Schatzkammer (US ISSN 0740-1965) *596, 609, 703*
Schauspielfuehrer (GW ISSN 0342-4553) *1078*
Scheckheft Stadium (GW) *419*

1876 SCHEDULE OF

Schedule of Postgraduate Courses in United Kingdom Universities see British Universities' Guide to Graduate Studies *428*
Schedule of Wells Drilled for Oil and Gas in Alberta (CN ISSN 0380-4305) *466*, *866*
Schedules Supporting the Executive Budget see New York (City) Mayor. Schedules Supporting the Executive Budget *951*
Schiff und Zeit (GW) *1103*
Schiffahrtmedizinisches Institut der Marine, Kiel. Veroeffentlichungen (GW ISSN 0080-679X) *766*
Schiffbautechnischen Gesellschaft. Jahrbuch (US ISSN 0080-6803) *1103*
Schiffli Digest and Directory see Embroidery Directory *1074*
Schiffsliste (GW) *1103*
Schleswig-Holsteinischer Heimatkalender (GW) *732*
Schmerzensgeld-Betraege (GW) *671*
Schoenste Schweizer Buecher (SZ ISSN 0080-6838) *963*
Die Schoensten Buecher der Deutschen Demokratischen Republik (GE) *963*
Schoharie Museum of the Iroquois Indian. Museum Notes (US) *830*
Scholarly Books in France see Publications de Recherche Scientifique en France *130*
Scholars' Facsimiles & Reprints (US ISSN 0161-7729) *632*
Scholarships Guide for Commonwealth Postgraduate Students (UK ISSN 0306-1736) *419*
School Breakfast Newsletter (US) *1162*
School Calendar/Calendrier Scolaire (CN ISSN 0382-7879) *419*
School Food Services Bulletin see School Breakfast Newsletter *1162*
School Guide (US) *430*
School Library Association Newsletter see School Library Newsletter *683*
School Library Newsletter (CN ISSN 0706-2915) *683*
School of Agriculture, Aberdeen. Annual Report (UK ISSN 0143-8654) *34*
School of International Studies. Publications on Asia (US) *571*
School of International Studies. Publications on Russia and Eastern Europe (US) *909*
School Organisation & Management Abstracts (UK ISSN 0261-2755) *12*, *425*
School Universe Data Book see C I C's State School Directories *428*
Schools see Which School *431*
Schools Abroad (US ISSN 0080-6900) *442*
Schools Abroad of Interest to Americans see Schools Abroad *442*
Schools and Colleges Welcome (UK) *430*, *438*, *442*, *1116*
Schools in the United States and Canada Offering Graduate Education in Pharmacology (US) *430*, *872*
Schools of England, Wales, Scotland and Ireland (UK ISSN 0080-6919) *431*
Schools of Social Work with Accredited Master's Degree Programs (US) *438*, *1020*
Schopenhauer-Jahrbuch (GW ISSN 0080-6935) *881*
Schott Aktuell (GW) *841*
Schott-Kurier see Schott Aktuell *841*
Schouler Lectures in History and Political Science (US) *560*, *909*
Schriften aus dem Finnland-Institut Koeln (GW ISSN 0430-5809) *560*, *732*
Schriften des Oesterreichischen Kulturinstituts Kairo. Archaeologisch-Historische Abteilung(GW ISSN 0342-4839) *92*, *613*
Schriften des Werksarchivs (GW ISSN 0724-2557) *291*
Schriften und Quellen der Alten Welt (GE ISSN 0080-696X) *92*, *560*
Schriften zur Geistesgeschichte des Oestlichen Europa (GW ISSN 0340-6490) *596*

Schriften zur Geschichte und Kultur der Antike (GE ISSN 0138-595X) *338*
Schriften zur Geschichte und Kultur des Alten Orients (GE ISSN 0080-6994) *571*, *853*
Schriften zur Handelsforschung (GW ISSN 0080-7001) *240*
Schriften zur Jugendlektuere (AU ISSN 0080-701X) *336*, *732*
Schriften zur Kooperationsforschung. Berichte (GW ISSN 0080-7028) *238*
Schriften zur Kooperationsforschung. Studien (GW ISSN 0080-7036) *239*
Schriften zur Kooperationsforschung. Vortraege (GW ISSN 0080-7044) *239*
Schriften zur Mittelstandsforschung (GW) *1029*
Schriften zur Oeffentlichen Verwaltung und Oeffentlichen Wirtschaft (GW) *946*
Schriften zur Philosophie und ihrer Geschichte (GE ISSN 0138-3418) *596*, *881*
Schriften zur Phonetik, Sprachwissenschaft und Kommunikationsforschung (GE ISSN 0558-9274) *703*
Schriften zur Ur- und Fruehgeschichte (GE ISSN 0138-3361) *560*
Schriftenreihe Aktuelle Fragen der Energiewirtschaft (GW) *466*
Schriftenreihe aus den Naturschutzgebieten Bayerns (GW) *1162*
Schriftenreihe Chemische Analytik und Umwelttechnologie (GW) *1162*
Schriftenreihe das Andere Deutschland (GW) *596*, *909*
Schriftenreihe der Hochschule der Kuenste Berlin (GW ISSN 0723-0788) *110*
Schriftenreihe des Bayer. Landesamtes fuer Wasserwirtschaft (GW ISSN 0172-665X) *404*, *1125*
Schriftenreihe Finanzwirtschaft und Finanzrecht (GW ISSN *232*, *664*
Schriftenreihe fuer Agrarwirtschaft (AU) *34*, *664*
Schriftenreihe fuer Geologische Wissenschaften (GE ISSN 0323-8946) *394*
Schriftenreihe fuer Laendliche Sozialfragen (GW ISSN 0080-7133) *1020*
Schriftenreihe fuer Raumforschung und Raumplanung. (AU ISSN 0558-9746) *625*
Schriftenreihe fuer Sportwissenschaft und Sportpraxis see Sportwissenschaft und Sportpraxis *1035*
Schriftenreihe fuer Vegetationskunde (GW ISSN 0085-5960) *161*
Schriftenreihe: Gesellschaft und Betrieb (AU) *664*
Schriftenreihe Kernenergie (GW) *1162*
Schriftenreihe Luftreinhaltung (GW) *499*
Schriftenreihe Naturschutz und Landschaftspflege (GW) *1162*
Schriftenreihe Neurologie/Neurology Series (US ISSN 0080-715X) *791*
Schriftenreihe fuer Orts-, Regional- und Landesplanung (GW) *625*
Schrifttum zur Deutschen Kunst (GW ISSN 0080-7176) *110*
Schrifttums fuer den Bereich Haushalt und Verbauch. Bibliographie (GW ISSN 0170-5768) *369*, *615*
Schuetz-Jahrbuch (GW) *841*
Schulfernsehen (GW) *449*
Schultz Medicinalbibliotek. Publikation (DK ISSN 0109-260X) *766*
Schwann Artist Catalog (US ISSN 0582-1487) *844*
Schweizer Anglistische Arbeiten/Swiss Studies in English (SZ ISSN 0080-7214) *703*
Schweizer Beitraege zur Kulturgeschichte und Archaeologie des Mittelalters (GW) *92*
Schweizer Beitrage zur Musikwissenschaft (SZ) *841*
Schweizer Buchhandels-Adressbuch (SZ ISSN 0080-7230) *963*
Schweizer Familienforscher (SZ) *537*

Schweizer Verpackungskatalog (SZ) *855*
Schweizerische Amerikanisten-Gesellschaft. Bulletin see Societe Suisse des Americanistes. Bulletin *609*
Schweizerische Bankwesen (SZ) *232*
Schweizerische Beitraege zur Altertumswissenschaft (SZ ISSN 0080-7273) *596*
Schweizerische Bibliographie fuer Statistik und Volkswirtschaft/ Bibliographie Suisse de Statistique et d'Economie Politique (SZ) *1162*
Schweizerische Gesellschaft fuer Aussenpolitik. Schriftenreihe (SZ) *918*
Schweizerische Gesellschaft fuer Klinische Chemie. Bulletin (SZ ISSN 0253-035X) *152*, *782*
Schweizerische Gesellschaft fuer Marktforschung. Geschaeftsbericht (SZ ISSN 0302-2048) *285*
Schweizerische Gesellschaft fuer Theaterkultur. Jahrbuecher (SZ) *1078*
Schweizerische Gesellschaft fuer Theaterkultur. Schriften (SZ) *1078*
Schweizerische Gesellschaft fuer Ur- und Fruehgeschichte. Jahrbuch (SZ) *596*
Schweizerische Gesellschaft fuer Volkskunde. Schriften (GW ISSN 0080-732X) *516*
Schweizerische Hochschulkonferenz. Jahresbericht see Conference Universitaire Suisse. Rapport Annuel *433*
Schweizerische Konjunktur und ihre Aussichten see Schweizerische Konjunktur und Vorausschau *249*
Schweizerische Konjunktur und Vorausschau (SZ) *249*
Schweizerische Luftverkehrsstatistik/ Statistique du Trafic Aerien Suisse see Die Schweizerische Zivilluftfahrt *1089*
Schweizerische Medizinische Wochenschrift (Supplementum) (SZ) *766*
Schweizerische Meteorologische Anstalt. Annalen (SZ ISSN 0080-7338) *806*
Schweizerische Meteorologische Anstalt. Veroeffentlichungen (SZ) *806*
Schweizerische Meteorologische Zentralanstalt. Veroeffentlichungen see Schweizerische Meteorologische Anstalt. Veroeffentlichungen *806*
Schweizerische Musikforschende Gesellschaft. Publikationen. Serie 2 (SZ ISSN 0080-7354) *841*
Schweizerische Naturforschende Gesellschaft. Denkschriften (SZ) *999*
Schweizerische Numismatische Rundschau see Revue Suisse de Numismatique *845*
Schweizerische Palaeontologische Abhandlungen/Memoires Suisse de Paleontologie (SZ ISSN 0080-7389) *857*
Schweizerische Politik im Jahre see Annee Politique Suisse *902*
Schweizerische Radio- und Fernsehgesellschaft. Jahrbuch (SZ) *349*
Schweizerische Vereinigung fuer Klinische Chemie. Bulletin see Schweizerische Gesellschaft fuer Klinische Chemie. Bulletin *152*
Die Schweizerische Zivilluftfahrt (SZ) *1089*
Schweizerischen Naturforschenden Gesellschaft. Jahrbuch (SZ ISSN 0252-2969) *1162*
Schweizerischer Bankverein Booklet see S B C Booklet *232*
Schweizerischer Bund fuer Jugendliteratur. Jahresbericht/Ligue Suisse pour la Litterature de la Jeunesse. Rapport Annuel (SZ) *336*
Schweizerischer Forstverein. Zeitschrift. Beihefte (SZ) *527*
Schweizerischer Medizinalkalender (SZ ISSN 0251-1762) *766*
Schweizerischer Metall- und Uhrenarbeitnehmer-Verband Zeitung see S M U V Zeitung *800*

Schweizerischer Wissenschaftsrat. Jahresbericht/Conseil Suisse de la Science. Rapport Annuel (SZ) *999*
Schweizerisches Institut fuer Nuklearforschung. Jahresbericht (SZ) *898*
Schweizerisches Institut fuer Nuklearforschung Medical Newsletter see S I N Medical Newsletter *792*
Schweizerisches Institut fuer Nuklearforschung Newsletter see S I N Newsletter *898*
Schweizerisches Jahrbuch fuer Politische Wissenschaft see Annuaire Suisse de Science Politique *902*
Schweizerisches Medizinisches Jahrbuch(SZ ISSN 0080-7400) *766*
SCI-J C R see Science Citation Index Journal Citation Report *999*
Sciare Moda (IT) *340*
Science and Archaeology (UK ISSN 0586-9668) *96*, *1005*
Science and Computer Literacy Audiovisuals (National Information Center for Educational Media) (US) *361*
Science and Engineering Research Council. Report (UK ISSN 0261-7005) *999*, *1070*
Science and Nature (US ISSN 0193-3396) *146*, *881*
Science and Technology (KO) *999*, *1070*
Science and Technology (Pittsburgh) (US ISSN 0080-746X) *683*, *999*
Science and Technology (San Diego) see Science and Technology Series *21*
Science and Technology in China (UK) *999*, *1070*
Science and Technology in Japan (UK) *999*, *1070*
Science and Technology in Latin America (UK) *999*, *1070*
Science and Technology in the Middle East (UK) *999*, *1070*
Science and Technology Series (US ISSN 0278-4017) *21*
Science Bulletin see Contributions in Science *990*
Science Chelsea (UK ISSN 0300-3361) *999*
Science Citation Index (US ISSN 0036-827X) *12*, *1004*
Science Citation Index Journal Citation Report (Institute for Scientific Information) (US ISSN 0161-3170) *999*
Science Council of Japan. Annual Report (JA ISSN 0448-4703) *999*
Science Council of Japan. Annual Report of the Development of Agriculture in Japan see Science Council of Japan. Annual Report on the Progress of Agriculture *1162*
Science Council of Japan. Annual Report on the Progress of Agriculture (JA ISSN 0911-8012) *1162*
Science Education in the Region (UK) *438*
Science Education in Zambia (ZA) *419*, *999*
Science, Engineering, and Humanities Doctorates in the United States: Profile (US) *849*
Science Exactes et Technologie. Sciences de la Vie. Lexique/Exact Science and Technology. Life Sciences. Lexicon (FR) *146*
Science Fiction and Fantasy Research Index (US) *14*
Science-Fiction et Fantastique. (Year) (FR) *732*
Science Fiction Research Index see Science Fiction and Fantasy Research Index *14*
Science Fiction Voices (US ISSN 0164-1093) *732*
Science Guide to Scientific Instruments see Guide to Scientific Instruments *636*
Science Indicators (US) *1004*
Science, Medicine and Technology in East Asia (US) *766*, *999*, *1070*
Science Museum of Minnesota. Monograph (US) *999*

Science Museum of Minnesota. Scientific Bulletin see Science Museum of Minnesota. Scientific Publications, New Series 999
Science Museum of Minnesota. Scientific Publications see Science Museum of Minnesota. Scientific Publications, New Series 999
Science Museum of Minnesota. Scientific Publications, New Series (US ISSN 0161-4452) 999
Science Museum of Victoria. Monographs (AT) 999
Science Notes and News (JM) 449, 999
Science Nouvelle (FR ISSN 0080-7540) 999
Science of Advanced Material and Process Engineering Series (US ISSN 0080-7559) 489
Science of Hot Springs/Onsen Kagaku (JA ISSN 0030-2821) 394
Science Policy Studies and Documents (UN ISSN 0080-7591) 999
Science Research Abstracts Journal. Laser and Electro-Optic Reviews; Quantum Electronics; Unconventional Energy Sources see Solid State Abstracts Journal 893
Science Research Abstracts Journal. Superconductivity; Magnetohydrodynamics and Plasmas; Theoretical Physics see Solid State Abstracts Journal 893
Science Teachers Association of Queensland. Newsletter (AT) 1000
Science Year (US ISSN 0080-7621) 463, 1000
Sciences de l'Information. Lexique (FR) 683
Sciences de la Terre. Lexique (FR) 380
Sciences de la Terre: Informatique Geologique see Sciences de la Terre: Serie Informatique Geologique 394
Sciences de la Terre: Serie Informatique Geologique (FR ISSN 0335-9255) 381, 394
Sciences Geologiques - Memoires (FR ISSN 0302-2684) 394
Sciences, Techniques, Informations C R I A C (Centre de Recherches Industrielles en Afrique Centrale) (ZR ISSN 0377-5135) 291
Scientific Agricultural Society of Finland. Journal see Journal of Agricultural Science in Finland 30
Scientific and Technical Books and Serials in Print (US ISSN 0000-054X) 1004, 1073
Scientific and Technical Books in Print see Scientific and Technical Books and Serials in Print 1004
Scientific and Technical Information in Foreign Countries/Kaigaki Kagaku Gijutsu Joho Shiryo (JA) 1000, 1070
Scientific and Technical Societies in South Africa/Wetenskaplike en Tegniese Vereinigings in Suid-Afrika (SA ISSN 0080-7710) 1000, 1070
Scientific and Technical Societies of Canada/Societes Scientifiques et Techniques du Canada (CN ISSN 0586-7746) 1000, 1070
Scientific Atheist see Crucible and Scientific Atheist 877
Scientific Committee for Antarctic Research Report to S C A R on South African Antarctic Research Activities see Report to S C A R on South African Antarctic Research Activities 998
Scientific Directory of Hong Kong (HK ISSN 0586-5751) 1000
Scientific Documentation Centre Ltd. Bulletin see S.D.C. Bulletin 893
Scientific Horticulture (UK ISSN 0080-7737) 534
Scientific Instruments: Latin American Industrial Report (US) 637
Scientific Publications of the Science Museum of Minnesota see Science Museum of Minnesota. Scientific Publications, New Series 999
Scientific Research Organizations in South Africa/Wetenskaplike Navorsingsorganisasies in Suid-Afrika (SA ISSN 0080-7761) 1000, 1070

Scientific Results of Marine Biological Research see Hvalraadets Skrifter 141
Scientific Serials in Thai Libraries (TH ISSN 0125-4529) 131, 1004, 1073
Scientific Society of the Silicate Industry. Conference on Silicate Industry and Silicate Science (HU) 320
Scientific Symposium on the Cultivated Mushroom. Proceedings see Mushroom Science 159
Scienze della Materia (IT ISSN 0391-3244) 324, 890
Scintillation see Cinemonkey 823
Scoltock Family Bulletin (UK ISSN 0141-6405) 537
Scoop Sport Annual (UK ISSN 0262-4206) 336
Scope (AT) 367
Scotia (US ISSN 0273-0693) 505
Scotland. Department of Agriculture and Fisheries. Marine Laboratory. Triennial Review of Research (UK ISSN 0140-5012) 512
Scotland. Red Deer Commission. Annual Report (UK ISSN 0080-7850) 367
Scotland. Registrar General. Annual Report (UK ISSN 0080-7869) 929, 1062
Scotland: Camping and Caravan Sites (UK) 1116
Scotland Chambers of Commerce. Directory (UK) 237
Scotland: Conferences, Meetings, Seminars (UK) 796
Scotland Department of Agriculture and Fisheries. Freshwater Fisheries Laboratory Pitlochry. Triennial Review of Research see Department of Agriculture and Fisheries for Scotland. Freshwater Fisheries Laboratory. Triennial Review of Research 508
Scotland for Fishing (UK) 1046
Scotland for Hillwalking (UK) 1116
Scotland for the Motorist (UK) 1116
Scotland for Touring Caravans see Scotland: Camping and Caravan Sites 1116
Scotland Home of Golf (UK) 1040
Scotland: Self-Catering Accommodation (UK) 1116
Scotland Tomorrow see Scotlink 237
Scotland: Where to Stay, Bed and Breakfast (UK) 1116
Scotland: Where to Stay, Hotels and Guest Houses (UK) 1116
Scotland: 1001 Things to See (UK) 1116
Scotland: 600 Things to See see Scotland: 1001 Things to See 1116
Scotland's Best Holidays (UK ISSN 0267-338X) 1116
Scotland's for Me (UK) 1116
Scotlands Regions (UK ISSN 0305-6562) 946
Scotlink (UK ISSN 0266-5441) 237
Scots Law Times Christmas Charity. Supplement (UK) 664
Scottish Abstract of Statistics (UK) 12, 1062
Scottish Agricultural Economics; Some Studies of Current Economic Conditions in Scottish Farming see Economic Report on Scottish Agriculture 46
Scottish-American Genealogist (US ISSN 0271-5031) 537
Scottish Anti-Vivisection Society. Annual Report (UK) 868
Scottish Archaeological Review (UK ISSN 0262-4389) 92
Scottish Art Review (UK ISSN 0036-911X) 110
Scottish Bakers' Year Book (UK ISSN 0080-7974) 522
Scottish Birds (UK ISSN 0036-9144) 171
Scottish Building & Civil Engineering Year Book (UK ISSN 0085-6002) 187, 483
Scottish Business Education Council. Business Education Guide see Scottish Vocational Education Council. Handbook 449
Scottish Chambers of Commerce National Directory (UK) 237

Scottish Church History Society. Records (UK ISSN 0264-5572) 972
Scottish Current Law Year Book (UK ISSN 0265-6159) 664
Scottish Decorators' Review see Scottish Decorators' Year Book and Review 931
Scottish Decorators' Year Book and Review (UK) 931
Scottish Economic and Social History (UK) 199, 1011
Scottish Episcopal Church Yearbook (UK ISSN 0260-0617) 979
Scottish Fisheries Bulletin (UK ISSN 0559-1791) 512
Scottish Fisheries Information Pamphlets (UK ISSN 0309-9105) 512
Scottish Fisheries Research Reports (UK ISSN 0308-8022) 512
Scottish Folk Directory (UK) 841
Scottish Genealogical Helper see Scottish-American Genealogist 537
Scottish Georgian Society. Annual Report see Architectural Heritage Society of Scotland. Journal and Annual Report 97
Scottish Georgian Society. Annual Report and Bulletin see Architectural Heritage Society of Scotland. Journal and Annual Report 97
Scottish Government Yearbook (UK) 909
Scottish Handbook of Adult and Continuing Education (UK) 427
Scottish Hardware and Drysalters Association. Yearbook (UK ISSN 0080-8059) 187, 190
Scottish Health Services (UK) 956
Scottish Industrial Policy Series (UK) 275
Scottish Labour History Society. Journal (UK) 275, 596
Scottish Law Directory (UK ISSN 0080-8083) 664
Scottish Libraries (UK ISSN 0080-8091) 683
Scottish Library and Information Resources (UK) 683
Scottish Marine Biological Association. Annual Report (UK ISSN 0375-2062) 146
Scottish Mountaineering Club. Journal (UK ISSN 0080-813X) 1046
Scottish National Register of Classified Trades see Sell's Scottish Directory 316
Scottish Petroleum Annual (UK) 867
Scottish Postmark Group. Handbook (UK ISSN 0080-8164) 346, 875
Scottish Pottery Historical Review (UK ISSN 0144-1302) 113
Scottish Pottery Studies (UK ISSN 0260-7972) 320
Scottish Sea Fisheries Statistical Tables (UK ISSN 0080-8202) 512
Scottish Social Work Statistics see Home Care Services, Day Care Establishments, Day Services - Scotland 1018
Scottish Society for Prevention of Vivisection. Annual Pictorial Review (UK ISSN 0080-8210) 782, 868
Scottish Society for Prevention of Vivisection. Annual Report (UK) 177
Scottish Studies (UK ISSN 0036-9411) 75, 516, 596
Scottish Trades and Shops Holidays (UK) 285
Scottish Tradition (CN) 596
Scottish Tramlines see Scottish Transport 1083
Scottish Transport (UK ISSN 0048-9808) 1083
Scottish Vocational Education Council. Handbook (UK) 449
Scottish Youth Hostels Association Handbook (UK) 336, 620
Scott's Industrial Directories - Atlantic (CN) 316
Scott's Industrial Directories - Ontario (CN) 316
Scott's Industrial Directories - Quebec (CN) 316
Scott's Industrial Directories - Western (CN ISSN 0317-879X) 316

Scott's Industrial Directory. Western Provinces see Scott's Industrial Directories - Western 316
Scott's Specialized Catalogue of U.S. Stamps (US) 875
Scott's Standard Postage Stamp Catalogue (US) 875
Scott's Trade Directory of Metropolitan Toronto (CN) 316
Scott's Trade Directory of Toronto Vicinity see Scott's Trade Directory of Metropolitan Toronto 316
Scott's Western see Scott's Industrial Directories - Western 316
Scout Annual (UK) 336
Scout Association of Australia. Annual Report (AT) 341
Scout Association of Australia. Review of Progress see Scout Association of Australia. Annual Report 341
Scouting 'Round the World/Scoutisme a Travers le Monde (SZ) 334
Scoutisme a Travers le Monde see Scouting 'Round the World 334
Screen International Film and T.V. Yearbook (UK) 349, 825
Screen World (US ISSN 0080-8288) 825
Scripps Clinic and Research Foundation. Annual Report (US ISSN 0080-830X) 1071
Scripps Clinic and Research Foundation. Research Institute. Scientific Report (US) 766
Scripps Institution of Oceanography. Annual Report (US) 407
Scripps Institution of Oceanography. Bulletin (US ISSN 0080-8318) 407
Scripps Institution of Oceanography. Contributions see Scripps Institution of Oceanography. Contributions. New Series 407
Scripps Institution of Oceanography. Contributions. New Series (US) 407
Scripps Institution of Oceanography. Deep Sea Drilling Project. Initial Reports. (US ISSN 0080-8334) 407
Scripps Institution of Oceanography (Year) see Scripps Institution of Oceanography. Annual Report 407
Scripta Academica (SW ISSN 0348-1093) 131
Scripta Artis Monographia (NE ISSN 0080-8350) 110
Scripta Classica Israelica (IS) 338
Scripta Facultatis Scientiarum Naturalium Universitatis Purkynianae Brunensis: Geologia (CS) 394
Scripta Facultatis Scientiarum Naturalium Universitatis Purkynianae Brunensis: Geographia (CS) 1000
Scripta Geobotanica (GW ISSN 0341-3772) 161
Scripta Geologica (NE ISSN 0375-7587) 394
Scripta Hierosolymitana (IS ISSN 0080-8369) 632, 1011
Scripta Historica (FI ISSN 0358-710X) 596
Scripta Instituti Donneriani Aboensis (FI ISSN 0582-3226) 972
Scripta Islandica (SW ISSN 0582-3234) 703, 732
Scripta Mediterranea (CN) 75, 92, 613, 853
Scripta Minore. Regiae Societatis Humaniorum Litterarum Lundensis (SW) 92
Scripta Mongolica (US ISSN 0080-8377) 1162
Scripta Scientifica Medica (BU) 776, 777, 782
Scripta Series in Geography (UK ISSN 0277-044X) 548
Scriptores Latini (IT ISSN 0080-8393) 338
Scriptura (DR) 732
Scripture Examination Material and Annual Scripture Project (UK) 972
Scrittura e Civilta (IT) 338
Sculpture in the Environment On S I T E see On S I T E 1160
Scuola Archeologica di Atene e delle Missioni Italiane in Oriente. Annuario (IT) 92
Sea Boating Almanac. Northern California and Nevada see Pacific Boating Almanac. Northern California & Nevada 1042

Sea Boating Almanac. Pacific Northwest and Alaska *see* Pacific Boating Almanac. Oregon, Washington, British Columbia & Southeastern Alaska *1042*
Sea Boating Almanac. Southern California, Arizona, Baja *see* Pacific Boating Almanac. Southern California, Arizona, Baja *1042*
Sea Letter (US ISSN 0732-6882) *1103*
Sea Technology Buyers Guide/Directory (US) *407, 474*
Sea Technology Handbook and Directory *see* Sea Technology Buyers Guide/Directory *474*
Seabird (UK ISSN 0267-9310) *171*
Seabird Bulletin *see* Seabird *171*
Seabird Report *see* Seabird *171*
Seaby's Standard Catalogue of British Coins (UK) *845*
Seahorse (US ISSN 0037-0118) *1162*
Seaports and the Shipping World. Annual Issue (CN ISSN 0080-8423) *1103*
Search (Washington, D.C.) *see* Urban Institute. Policy and Research Report *627*
Search and Rescue Statistics *see* S A R Statistics *1103*
Search Group. Technical Memorandum (US) *372*
Search Group. Technical Report (US) *372*
Search Inform (US) *683*
Sears Foundation for Marine Research. Memoirs (US) *146, 407*
Seatrade Guide to Arab Shipping *see* Arab Shipping *1098*
Seatrade Guide to Latin American Shipping *see* Turkish Shipping *1104*
Seatrade North America Yearbook *see* Seatrade U.S. Yearbook *1103*
Seatrade U.S. Yearbook (UK ISSN 0142-5056) *1103*
Seawater and Desalting (US ISSN 0720-0773) *1125*
Second Growth *see* Now and Then *729*
Second 1,500 Companies *see* Trinet Directory of Leading U S Companies: Second 1,500 *200*
Secretaria de Estado de Agricultura y Ganaderia Publicaciones *see* E A G Publicaciones *26*
Secretariat Permanent des Organisations Non Gouvernementales. Rapport d'Activities (UV) *463*
Section A. Elementary Property Problems and Financial Relationships *see* How to Avoid Financial Tangles *229*
Sector Alimentario en Mexico (Year) (MX) *846*
Sector Electrico en Mexico (MX) *459*
Securitech (UK ISSN 0307-7780) *372*
Securities & Exchange Commission. Business Day's 1000 Top Corporations in the Philippines (PH) *316*
Securities and Exchange Commission Bulletin *see* S E C Bulletin *240*
Securities Exchange of Thailand. Handbook (TH) *268*
Securities Industry Yearbook (US) *268*
Securities Investor Protection Corporation. Annual Report (US ISSN 0094-467X) *268*
Securities Law Review (US ISSN 0080-8474) *232, 664*
Securities Market in Japan (JA) *268*
Securities Market in Korea *see* Introduction to the Korean Securities Market *266*
Security Dealer Product Directory and Reference Guide (US) *316, 374*
Security Industry Yearbook *see* Securities Industry Yearbook *268*
Security Letter Source Book (US ISSN 0736-0401) *374*
Security Report *see* Compensation in the Security/Loss Prevention Field *270*
Sedar (SI ISSN 0559-2674) *975*
Sediment Data for Selected Canadian Rivers (CN ISSN 0080-8482) *394*
Seed Abstracts (UK ISSN 0141-0180) *12, 43*
Seed - Business (FR) *59*

Seed Trade Buyer's Guide (US ISSN 0080-8504) *59*
Seeing Eye Annual Report (US) *180*
Seeker's Guide (US ISSN 0080-8512) *463*
Seems (US ISSN 0095-1730) *732, 743*
Sefunim (IS ISSN 0077-5193) *92, 830, 1103*
Seguros (UY) *641*
Seibt Export Directory of German Industries (GW) *316*
Seibt Medizinische Technik (GW) *766*
Seibt Pharma-Technik (GW) *872*
Seishin-Igaku Institute of Psychiatry, Tokyo. Bulletin/Seishin Igaku Kenkyusho, Tokyo. Gyoseki Shu (JA ISSN 0080-8547) *791*
Seishin Igaku Kenkyusho, Tokyo. Gyoseki Shu *see* Seishin-Igaku Institute of Psychiatry, Tokyo. Bulletin *791*
Seismology and Exploration Geophysics(NE) *401*
Seiso Jigyo Gaiyo *see* Public Cleansing Services in Tokyo *955*
Seiyo Kotengaku Kenkyu *see* Journal of Classical Studies *337*
Sejahtera (MY) *732*
Sekvens (DK ISSN 0106-2484) *825*
Selangor Public Library. Annual Report/Perbadanan Perpustakaan Awam Selangor. Lapuran Tahunan (MY) *683*
Selbst-Verwirklichung: Jahresheft (US) *881, 972*
Selbyana (US ISSN 0361-185X) *161*
Selden Society, London. Handbook: Publications, List of Members and Rules (UK) *560, 664*
Selden Society, London. Lectures (UK) *560, 664*
Selden Society, London. Main (Annual) Series (UK) *560, 664*
Selden Society, London. Supplementary Series (UK ISSN 0582-4788) *560, 664*
Select Bibliography of Danish Works on the History of Towns Published (DK ISSN 0105-9475) *564*
Select Information Exchange Guide to Investment Services *see* S I E Guide to Investment Services *268*
Selecta (Corvallis) (US ISSN 0277-0598) *703*
Selected Abstracts on Occupational Diseases (UK) *636, 773*
Selected Agri-Figures of the E.E.C *see* E E G Vademecum *40*
Selected Annotated Bibliography of Population Studies in the Netherlands (NE ISSN 0167-4757) *929*
Selected Bibliographies on Ageing (UK ISSN 0267-0348) *552*
Selected Bibliography of Homosexuality(US) *616*
Selected Bibliography of Museological Literature (CS) *832*
Selected Bibliography of Recent Economic Development Publications (US) *217*
Selected Documents of the International Petroleum Industry (AU ISSN 0080-858X) *867*
Selected Journals on Water (SA) *12, 1128*
Selected List of Federal Laws and Treaties Relating to Sport Fish and Wildlife *see* U.S. Fish and Wildlife Service. Selected List of Federal Laws and Treaties Relating to Sport Fish and Wildlife *666*
Selected Monographs on Taxation (NE) *298*
Selected Periodicals for the Medical Library (US) *773*
Selected Rand Abstracts (US ISSN 0037-1343) *12, 1004, 1073*
Selected Reports in Ethnomusicology (US ISSN 0361-6622) *841*
Selected Streamflow Data for Ontario (CN) *467*
Selected Tables in Mathematical Statistics. (US ISSN 0094-8837) *752*
Selected Topics in Solid State Physics (NE ISSN 0080-8636) *890*

Selected Trade and Professional Associations in Texas *see* Texas Trade and Professional Associations and Other Selected Organizations *317*
Selected Translations in Mathematical Statistics and Probability (US ISSN 0065-9274) *752*
Selected Water Resources Abstracts (US ISSN 0037-136X) *12, 1128*
Selection Guide Series (US) *131*
Selections from Educational Records of the Government of India (II) *419*
Selective Abstracting Service: Welding and Allied Processes *see* Referate Organ: Schweissen und Verwandte Verfahren *802*
Selective Cooperative Index of Management Periodicals *see* S C I M P *217*
Selective Guide to Audiovisuals for Mental Health and Family Life Education *see* Education for Health: the Selective Guide *1152*
Self-Catering and Furnished Holidays (UK ISSN 0267-4599) *1116*
Self-Catering Holiday Homes, Caravans & Boats (UK) *1116*
Self Catering Holidays (UK) *1116*
Self-Catering in Britain *see* Holiday Homes, Cottages & Apartments in Britain *1111*
Self-Employed Pensions (UK) *641*
Self-Help Group Directory (US ISSN 0740-7548) *937, 1020*
Self-Help Group Sourcebook *see* Self-Help Group Directory *1020*
Self Help Reporter Newsletter (US) *937, 1020*
Sellowia (BL ISSN 0375-1651) *161*
Sell's British Aviation *see* Aviation Europe *18*
Sell's British Exporters (UK) *259*
Sell's Building Index (UK ISSN 0080-8717) *187*
Sell's Directory (UK ISSN 0261-5584) *316*
Sell's Directory of Products & Services *see* Sell's Directory *316*
Sell's Government and Municipal Contractors Register *see* Government and Municipal Contractors *942*
Sell's Health Service Buyers Guide *see* Health Service Buyers Guide *617*
Sell's Hotel, Restaurant and Canteen Supplies *see* Hotel, Restaurant and Catering Supplies *519*
Sell's Marine Market (UK ISSN 0143-1153) *1042*
Sell's Scottish Directory (UK) *316*
Selskab for Nordisk Filologi. Aarsberetning (DK ISSN 0108-822X) *703*
Semajna Bulteno (DK ISSN 0108-3759) *703*
Semana Internacional de Antropologia Vasca. Actas (SP) *75, 505*
Semiconductor Diode D.A.T.A. Book *see* Diode D.A.T.A. Book *452*
Semiconductor Evaluation Techniques (UK) *459*
Semiconductor Industry Association. Yearbook and Directory (US) *459*
Semiconductor International Master Buying Guide (US) *459*
Semiconductor Test Conference. Digest of Papers *see* International Test Conference. Proceedings *361*
Semiconductor Test Symposium. Digest of Papers *see* International Test Conference. Proceedings *361*
Seminar Arghiriade (RM) *753*
Seminar for Arabian Studies. Proceedings (UK) *613*
Seminar of African Christian Students in Europe. Report (SZ ISSN 0559-4065) *979*
Seminar on Canadian-American Relations (Papers) *see* Annual Canadian-American Seminar. Proceedings *914*
Seminar on Dravidian Linguistics. Proceedings (II) *703*
Seminar on Integrated Surveys of Environment. Proceedings *see* I T C-U N E S C O International Seminar. Proceedings *1154*

Seminar on the Acquisition of Latin American Library Materials. Final Report and Working Papers *see* Seminar on the Acquisition of Latin American Library Materials. Papers *683*
Seminar on the Acquisition of Latin American Library Materials. Microfilming Projects Newsletter (US ISSN 0080-8857) *683*
Seminar on the Acquisition of Latin American Library Materials. Papers (US) *609, 683*
Seminar on the Acquisition of Latin American Library Materials. Report on Bibliographic Activities *see* S A L A L M Bibliography and Reference Series *688*
Seminar on the Acquisition of Latin American Library Materials Bibliography and Reference Series *see* S A L A L M Bibliography and Reference Series *688*
Seminar on the Acquisition of Latin American Library Materials. Working Papers *see* Seminar on the Acquisition of Latin American Library Materials. Papers *683*
Seminariehaandbogen (DK ISSN 0106-9551) *438*
Seminariekalenderen *see* Seminariehaandbogen *438*
Seminarielaererforeningen Information *see* S L F Information *419*
Seminario Brasileiro sobre Tecnicas Exploratorias em Geologia. Anais (BL) *395*
Seminario de Filologia Vasca Julio de Urquijo. Anuario (SP) *703*
Seminario di Studi e Ricerche Sul Linguaggio Musicale. Atti (IT) *841*
Seminario Matematico Garcia de Galdeano. Publicaciones (SP ISSN 0085-6029) *1162*
Seminario Nacional de Controle de Qualidade. Anais (BL) *291*
Seminars in Neurological Surgery (US ISSN 0160-2489) *791, 794*
Semiotic Scene (US) *1162*
Semitic Study Series (NE) *853, 977*
Semitica (FR ISSN 0085-6037) *632*
Semitics (SA ISSN 0256-6044) *703*
Senckenbergiana Maritima. Zeitschrift fuer Meeresgeologie und Meeresbiologie (GW ISSN 0080-889X) *146, 408*
Sendai National College of Technology. Research Reports (JA) *474, 1011*
Sendai Radio Technical College. Research Reports *see* Sendai National College of Technology. Research Reports *1011*
Senegal. Archives du Senegal. Rapport Annuel (SG ISSN 0850-010X) *683*
Senegal. Centre de Recherche Oceanographique. Document Scientifique (SG ISSN 0850-1602) *146, 408*
Senegal. Liste du Corps Diplomatique (SG) *918*
Senegal. Ministere de l'Economie et des Finances. Analyse du Commerce Exterieur (SG) *259*
Senegal. Ministere de l'Economie et des Finances. Comptes Economiques de la Nation (SG) *249*
Senegal. Secretariat General du Gouvernment. Direction des Archives. Rapport Annuel (SG) *946*
Senegal. Service du Protocole. Liste Diplomatique et Consulaire *see* Senegal. Liste du Corps Diplomatique *918*
Senegal en Chiffres (SG) *567*
Senior Citizen's Guide to Budget Travel in the United STates and Canada (US) *1116*
Senior High School Library Catalog (US) *683*
Seniority Travel Directory *see* Sophisticated Leisure Travel Directory *1116*
Seniors in Sacramento (US) *552*
Sennacieca Revuo (FR ISSN 0080-8903) *918*
Sennke/News of the Tohuku Plant Association (JA ISSN 0385-3985) *161*

Senpaku Gijutsu Kenkyusho Obun Hokoku *see* Japan. Ship Research Institute. Papers *1156*
Sensus van Dorpsontwikkelaars *see* South Africa. Central Statistical Service. Census of Township Developers *627*
Sentei Tosho Somokuroku *see* Catalogue of Books Recommended for Libraries *125*
Sentiers Poesie (FR) *743*
Seoul National University. Economic Review (KO) *199*
Seoul National University. Faculty Papers. (KO) *766*
Seoul National University. Faculty Papers. Biology and Agriculture Series. (KO) *34, 146*
Seoul National University. Population and Development Studies Center. Bulletin (KO) *924*
Seoul National University Forests. Bulletin *see* Seoul National University Forests. Research Bulletin *527*
Seoul National University Forests. Research Bulletin (KO) *527, 530*
Sephardic Scholar (US) *505*
Serbische Rechtsquellen *see* Izvori Srpskog Prava *657*
Serbska Pratyja (GE) *505*
Serengeti Research Institute. Annual Report (TZ) *367*
Seria Nauk Matematyczno-Przyrodniczych. Matematyka, Fizyka, Chimia *see* Uniwersytet Jagiellonski. Zeszyty Naukowe. Acta Matematica *754*
Serial Sources for the Biosis Data Base (US ISSN 0162-2048) *12, 150*
Serials Holdings in Newfoundland Libraries (CN ISSN 0709-0536) *131*
Serials Holdings in the Libraries of Memorial University of Newfoundland, St. John's Public Library and College of Trades and Technology *see* Serials Holdings in Newfoundland Libraries *131*
Serials in C L W Library (College of Librarianship Wales) (UK) *131, 688*
Serials in Education in Australian Libraries: a Union List (AT ISSN 0311-2373) *425, 683*
Sericultural Experiment Station. Annual Report/Sanshi Shikenjo, Nempo (JA ISSN 0581-5908) *34, 166, 1075*
Serie Afrique Noire (FR ISSN 0080-8938) *909*
Serie Botanica (SP) *161*
Serie Cadernos de Historia (BL) *609*
Serie Cana de Azucar (CU) *59*
Serie Capistrano de Abreu (BL) *918*
Serie de Ciencias Humanas *see* Centro de Estudos de Cabo Verde. Revista: Serie de Ciencias Humanas *1007*
Serie de Cocina por Luis Ripoli (SP) *520*
Serie de Vocabularios y Diccionarios Indigenas "Mariano Silva y Aceves" (MX) *75, 505, 516, 703*
Serie Debates Urbanos (BL) *625*
Serie di Matematica e Fisica (IT ISSN 0391-3252) *753, 890*
Serie di Matematica e Fisica. Problemi Risolti (IT) *753, 890*
Serie E O/International (Editions d' / Organisation) (FR) *249*
Serie Estudios Literarios (CR) *732*
Serie Estudos Penitenciaros (BL) *372*
Serie Guias de los Estudios Universitarios (SP) *431*
Serie Informatica e Informe Tecnico (CL) *527*
Serie Investigacion Pesquera (CL) *513*
Serie Legislacion Educativa Argentina (AG) *419, 664*
Serie Linguistica Peruana (PE) *703*
Serie Monografias y Estudios de la Educacion (US) *419*
Serie Novas Perspectivas (BL) *609, 909*
Serie om Fremmedsprog (DK ISSN 0106-1992) *703*
Serie om Uddannelsesforskning (DK) *1162*
Serie om Videnskabsforskning (DK ISSN 0105-7405) *703, 712*
Serie Poeyana *see* Poeyana *177*

Serie Praxis (PE ISSN 0250-9814) *275, 292*
Serie Thesaurus-Folclore (BL) *516*
Serie Vie Locale (FR ISSN 0586-9889) *909*
Series Desenvolvimento Brasileiro *see* Brazil Development Series *287*
Series Entomologica (NE ISSN 0080-8954) *166*
Series in Clinical and Community Psychology (US ISSN 0146-0846) *445, 937, 1020*
Series in Clinical Psychology *see* Series in Clinical and Community Psychology *937*
Series in Computational Methods in Mechanics and Thermal Sciences (US ISSN 0272-4804) *492*
Series in Death Education, Aging, and Health Care (US ISSN 0275-3510) *937*
Series in English Language and Literature (II ISSN 0254-0193) *703, 732*
Series in Geotechnical Engineering *see* Wiley Series in Geotechnical Engineering *61*
Series in Indian Languages and Linguistics (II) *703*
Series in Philosophy of Science *see* University of Western Ontario Series in Philosophy of Science *883*
Series in Sikh History and Culture (II ISSN 0254-0215) *571, 732*
Series in Thermal and Fluids Engineering (US ISSN 0146-0854) *480, 492*
Series on Bulk Materials Engineering *see* Series on Bulk Materials Handling *474*
Series on Bulk Materials Handling (SZ) *474*
Series on International Taxation (NE) *298*
Series on Rock and Soil Mechanics (SZ ISSN 0080-9004) *381, 483*
Series, Serials, and Packages (US) *349*
Series Slavica *see* Universita Palackeho. Filosoficka Fakulta. Slavica *736*
Serono Clinical Colloquia on Reproduction Series (US) *766*
Serono Foundation Symposia (US) *766*
Servi-Guia Opina (CU) *909*
Service Canadien de la Faune. Cahiers de Biologie *see* Canadian Wildlife Service. Progress Notes *364*
Service Corporation Directory (US) *232*
Service de la Carte Geologique d'Alsace et de Lorraine. Memoires *see* Sciences Geologiques - Memoires *394*
Service Employees International Union. International Convention. Official Proceedings (US) *649*
Serving Australian Agriculture (Agricultural and Veterinary Chemicals Association of Australia Ltd.) (AT) *1162*
Sesame (SA) *732*
Session Cases (UK ISSN 0037-282X) *664*
La Seta (IT) *1075*
Seto Marine Biological Laboratory. Special Publication Series (JA ISSN 0389-6609) *146*
Seto Marine Biological Laboratory. Special Publications *see* Seto Marine Biological Laboratory. Special Publication Series *146*
Setting Municipal Priorities (US ISSN 0272-8362) *298*
Setting up in Denmark (DK ISSN 0901-800X) *249*
Sevartham (II) *539*
Seven (US ISSN 0271-3012) *712*
Seven (US) *744*
Seventeenth Century French Studies (UK ISSN 0265-1068) *596, 732, 841*
Seventies *see* Eighties *710*
Severoceskou Prirodou (CS) *161*
Sexually Transmitted Disease in Canada (Year) (CN) *780*
Sexually Transmitted Diseases. Abstracts & Bibliography (US ISSN 0195-7708) *12, 773*
Seychelles. Department of Finance. National Accounts (SE) *1062*

Seychelles. Department of Finance. Statistics Division. Statistical Abstract (SE) *1062*
Seychelles. Department of Finance. Visitor Survey (SE) *217, 1062, 1120*
Seychelles. Office of the President. Budget Address (SE) *298, 946*
Seychelles. President's Office. Statistics Division. Agriculture Survey (SE) *43*
Seychelles. President's Office. Statistics Division. Census (SE) *1062*
Seychelles. President's Office. Statistics Division. Household Expenditure Survey (SE) *217, 1062*
Seychelles. President's Office. Statistics Division. Migration and Tourism Statistics (SE) *1062, 1120*
Seychelles. President's Office. Statistics Division. Statistical Abstract (SE) *217, 1062*
Seychelles. President's Office. Statistics Division. Tourism and Migration Report *see* Seychelles. President's Office. Statistics Division. Migration and Tourism Statistics *1120*
Seychelles Government Gazetta *see* Republic of Seychelles Official Gazette *945*
Seychelles Trade Report (SE) *259*
Seyd's Commercial Lists *see* Dun & Bradstreet Standard Register *307*
Sez (US ISSN 0190-3640) *505, 732*
Seznam Platnych Ceskoslovenskych Statnich a Oborovych Norem (CS) *809*
Shakai Fukushi No Doko (JA) *1020*
Shakai-jinruigaku Nenpo (JA) *75*
Shakespeare in Performance (UK) *732*
Shakespeare - Jahrbuch (GE ISSN 0080-9128) *732*
Shakespeare Studies (JA ISSN 0582-9402) *732*
Shakespeare Studies (US ISSN 0582-9399) *732*
Shakespeare Survey (UK ISSN 0080-9152) *732*
Shakespeare Translation *see* Shakespeare Worldwide *732*
Shakespeare Worldwide (US) *732*
Shakespearean Criticism (US) *732*
Shalshelet: the Chain (US) *841*
Shankpainter (US) *732*
Shantih (US ISSN 0037-329X) *744*
Share *see* S H A R E *1162*
Share It (UK ISSN 0262-9356) *881, 984*
Shareholder (AT ISSN 0037-3311) *268*
Sharjah Ports Handbook (UK ISSN 0267-2316) *316, 1103*
Shavian (UK ISSN 0037-3346) *732, 1078*
Shaw Annual (US ISSN 0741-5842) *732, 881*
Shaw Review *see* Shaw Annual *732*
Shaw Society of London. Journal (UK) *732*
Shaw: the annual of Bernard Shaw Studies *see* Shaw Annual *732*
Shaw's Directory of Courts in the United Kingdom (UK ISSN 0264-312X) *664*
Shaw's Legal Diary (UK) *1162*
Sheep and Goats in Humid West Africa(ET) *67*
Sheet Metal Industries Year Book (UK ISSN 0305-7798) *800, 802*
Sheffield & South Yorkshire Chambers of Commerce Directory (UK) *237*
Sheffield Studies in Japanese (UK ISSN 0260-6674) *853*
Sheffield University Annual Report (UK) *438*
Sheffield University Calendar (UK ISSN 0307-6202) *438*
Sheffield University General Prospectus *see* Sheffield University Undergraduate Prospectus *438*
Sheffield University Undergraduate Prospectus (UK) *438*
Shelby County Urban Development Report (US) *625*
Shell Tourist Guide to South Africa (SA) *1116*
Shellac Export Promotion Council. Annual Report (II ISSN 0304-8179) *856*

Sheller's Directory of Clubs, Books, Periodicals and Dealers (US ISSN 0085-607X) *177*
Sheltie Pacesetter Trade Secrets Book (US) *868*
Shenaton Hidrologi Le-Yisrael *see* Hydrological Yearbook of Israel *403*
Shenaton Statisti: Le Nemlei Israel *see* Yearbook of Israel Ports Statistics *260*
Shenaton Statisti le-Yisrael *see* Israel. Central Bureau of Statistics. Statistical Abstract of Israel *1057*
Shepard's Acts and Cases by Popular Names, Federal and State (US ISSN 0080-9233) *664*
Shepard's Criminal Justice Citations (US ISSN 0363-0978) *664*
Shepard's Federal Circuit Table (US ISSN 0730-7039) *664*
Shepard's Law Review Citations (US ISSN 0582-9887) *664*
Shepard's United States Administrative Citations (US ISSN 0582-9909) *664*
Sheppard's Book Dealers in British Isles(UK) *963*
Sheppard's Bookdealers in North America (UK) *963*
Sherbondy Beacon (US ISSN 8755-0547) *537*
Sherborn Fund Facsimiles (UK ISSN 0080-9241) *1000*
Sherlock Holmes Mystery Book (UK) *14*
Shetland Pony Stud-Book Society Magazine (UK) *1043*
Shiborudia *see* Sieboldia Acta Biologica *146*
Shiga Shizen Kyoiku Kenkyu Shisetsu Kenkyu Gyoseki *see* Institute of Nature Education in Shiga Heights. Bulletin *379*
Shigen Kagaku Kenkyusho *see* Tokyo Institute of Technology. Research Laboratory of Resources Utilization. Report *1071*
Shikoku Electric Power Co., Inc. Annual Report (JA) *459*
Shikoku Entomological Society. Transactions/Shikoku Konchu Gakkai Kaiho (JA ISSN 0037-3680) *166*
Shikoku Konchu Gakkai Kaiho *see* Shikoku Entomological Society. Transactions *166*
Shikoku National Agricultural Experiment Station. Bulletin (JA ISSN 0037-3702) *34*
Shiloach Center for Middle Eastern & African Studies. Monograph Series (US) *567, 613, 732*
Shima Marineland. Science Report (JA ISSN 0385-1109) *146, 177, 408, 513*
Shimabara Earthquake and Volcano Observatory. Sciences Reports (JA ISSN 0385-8286) *381, 395*
Shimane Daigaku Hobungakubu Kiyo. Bundakukahen *see* Shimane University. Faculty of Law and Literature. Memoirs *1011*
Shimane University. Faculty of Law and Literature. Memoirs/Shimane Daigaku Hobungakubu Kiyo. Bundakukahen (JA) *1011*
Shimane University. Faculty of Science. Memoirs (JA) *1000*
Shinkei Kagaku *see* Japanese Neurochemical Society. Bulletin *790*
Shinshu University. Faculty of Textile Science and Technology. Journal. Series A: Biology (JA ISSN 0583-0648) *34, 146, 1075*
Shinshu University. Faculty of Textile Science and Technology. Journal. Series B: Engineering (JA) *474*
Shinshu University. Faculty of Textile Science and Technology. Journal. Series C: Chemistry (JA ISSN 0559-8621) *480, 1075*
Shinshu University. Faculty of Textile Science and Technology. Journal. Series D: Arts (JA ISSN 0583-0664) *110, 1075*
Shinshu University. Faculty of Textile Science and Technology. Journal. Series E: Agriculture and Sericulture (JA) *34*

Shinshu University. Faculty of Textile Science and Technology. Journal. Series F: Physics and Mathematics (JA) *753, 891*
Shinshu University. School of Allied Medical Sciences. Treatises and Studies (JA ISSN 0385-1982) *784*
Ship Abstracts (NO ISSN 0346-1025) *12, 1086*
Ship and Boat Builders National. Federation Handbook *see* British Marine Industries Federation Handbook *1099*
Shipping and Aviation Statistics of the Maltese Islands (MM ISSN 0080-9268) *1103*
Shipping & Ports Directory of Indonesia(IO) *316, 1103*
Shipping Marks on Timber (UK ISSN 0080-9284) *530*
Shipping Statistics Yearbook (GW ISSN 0721-3220) *1103*
Shipping Survey (UK) *1103*
Ships and Aircraft of the United States Fleet (US ISSN 0080-9292) *812*
Shire Horse Show Catalogue (UK) *1043*
Shire Horse Stud Book (UK) *1043*
Shirley Institute Publications. S: Series (UK ISSN 0306-5154) *1075*
Shiseido Annual Report (JA) *119*
Shivaji University, Kolhapur, India. Journal. Humanities and Sciences (II ISSN 0080-9314) *632, 1000*
Shizenshi Kenkyu *see* Osaka Museum of Natural History. Occasional Papers *997*
Shizuoka Daigaku Rigakubu Kenkyu Hokoku *see* Shizuoka University. Faculty of Science. Reports *1000*
Shizuoka University. Faculty of Science. Reports/Shizuoka Daigaku Rigakubu Kenkyu Hokoku (JA ISSN 0583-0923) *1000*
Der Shmaiser/Spanker (CN ISSN 0824-7870) *712*
Shoe Factory Buyers Guide (US) *316, 1005*
Shoe Retailers Manual *see* Shoe Trades Directory *1005*
Shoe Trades Directory (UK ISSN 0080-9349) *1005*
Shokuryo Keizai Nenkan *see* Food Economics Yearbook *308*
Shoni No Hoken/Health for Children (JA) *334, 766, 956*
Shooter's Bible (US ISSN 0080-9365) *1035*
Shooting Handbook (UK) *1046*
Shop and Display Equipment Association Catalogue of Shopfittings and Display *see* S D E A Catalogue of Shopfittings and Display *16*
Shop-at-Home Directory (US) *285*
Shop by Mail Directory for Personal Computer Users (US) *357*
Shop Equipment and Materials Guide *see* Shop Equipment Display & Shopfitting Directory *190*
Shop Equipment Display & Shopfitting Directory (UK ISSN 0143-0971) *190*
Shopping Center Directory (US ISSN 0037-4210) *316*
Shopping Center World Product and Service Directory (US ISSN 0049-0393) *316*
Shopping Center World Product Directory *see* Shopping Center World Product and Service Directory *316*
Shopping Centre Canada (CN ISSN 0226-7551) *285*
Shopping in Edinburgh (UK) *285*
Short Play Series (US ISSN 0080-9403) *732*
Short Story Index (US ISSN 0360-9774) *12, 739*
Shortwave Listener *see* S W L *341*
Show Business Who's Where *see* Who's Where *1166*
Showboat Centennials Newsletter (US ISSN 0749-9361) *1042*
Showcall (UK) *841, 1078*
Showcase (US) *340, 885*
Showcast Directory (AT) *1078*
Showcast General Directory *see* Showcase Directory *1078*
Showdates (UK) *316*

Showman's Directory (UK) *316*
Shqiptari i Lire *see* Free Albanian *905*
Shri Chhatrapati Shivaji University. Report (II ISSN 0080-9322) *438*
Shubyo to Engei (JA ISSN 0037-4407) *534*
Shumen. Pedagogicheski Institut. Godishnik. (BU) *538*
Shuttle Craft Guild. Monographs (US ISSN 0080-9446) *615, 844, 1075*
Shvut (IS) *505, 909, 977*
Siam Society. Natural History Bulletin (TH) *1000*
Sibyl-Child (US ISSN 0161-715X) *110, 914, 1129*
Siddha Vani (II) *977*
Siderurgia Brasileira S.A. Relatorio de Diretoria (BL) *800*
Sieboldia Acta Biologica/Shiborudia (JA ISSN 0559-9822) *146*
Siecle Eclate: Dada, Surrealisme et les Avant-Gardes (FR) *732*
Sieg's Moentkatalog. Danmark, Dansk Vestindien, Faeroeerne, Groenland, Island (DK ISSN 0586-4496) *845*
Sielkundige Instituut van die Republiek van Suid-Afrika. Verrigtings *see* Psychological Institute of the Republic of South Africa. Proceedings *936*
Sierra Club. International Report (US) *1162*
Sierra Leone. Central Statistics Office. Annual Statistical Digest (SL) *1062*
Sierra Leone. Library Board. Report (SL ISSN 0583-2268) *683*
Sierra Leone. Ministry of Education. Report (SL ISSN 0080-9551) *419*
Sierra Leone. Ministry of Finance. Budget Speech (SL) *298*
Sierra Leone Chamber of Commerce. Journal *see* Chamber of Commerce of Sierra Leone. Journal *235*
Sierra Leone Geographical Association. Bulletin *see* Sierra Leone Geographical Journal *548*
Sierra Leone Geographical Journal (SL ISSN 0583-239X) *548*
Sierra Leone in Figures (SL ISSN 0080-9535) *1062*
Sierra Leone Publications (SL) *688*
Siglario Italiano/Italian Trade-Marks (IT) *861*
Sigma (FR ISSN 0223-0100) *703*
Sigma Zetan (US ISSN 0080-9578) *1000*
Sign Directory and Yearbook (UK) *16*
Sign Makers and Suppliers Year Book and Directory (UK) *317*
Signal International (FI ISSN 0037-4970) *614*
Signal Review *see* Signal Selection of Children's Books *334*
Signal Selection of Children's Books (UK) *334*
Significant Decisions of the Supreme Court (US ISSN 0162-0444) *664*
Significant Issues Facing Directors (US ISSN 0193-4201) *281*
Sijthoff Publications on Ocean Development *see* Publications on Ocean Development *671*
Sikelika. Serie Archeologica (IT ISSN 0392-0909) *92, 560*
Sikelika. Serie Storica (IT ISSN 0392-0917) *92, 560*
Sikkerhed (DK ISSN 0108-6650) *956*
Sikkerhed og Nedrustning (DK ISSN 0108-7266) *909*
Sikkerheds og Nedrustningspolitiske Udvalg. Aarsbereting *see* Sikkerhed og Nedrustning *909*
Sikkerhedsmaessig Vurdering og Prioritering af Mindre Anlaegsarbejder paa Hovedlandeveje (DK ISSN 0107-5179) *1097*
Silesia Antiqua (PL ISSN 0080-9594) *92*
Silesian Studies *see* Studia Slaskie *539*
Silk in India (II) *1076*
Sillages (FR) *703, 732*
Silo (US ISSN 0037-5306) *1162*
Silver Lining *see* Write In There *336*
Silver Market (US ISSN 0066-4332) *800*
Silvicultura Em Sao Paulo (BL ISSN 0583-3132) *527*
Simmeringer Museumsblaetter (AU) *596*

Simon Wiesenthal Center Annual (US) *505*
Simon's Directory of Theatrical Materials, Services and Information (US) *1078*
Simonson Miscellaneous Research Data(US) *537*
Simulation (Anaheim) (US) *358*
Simulation/Games for Learning *see* Perspectives on Academic Gaming & Simulation *449*
Simulation Monographs (CN) *51*
Simulation Symposium. Record of Proceedings (US ISSN 0272-4715) *358*
SIN-Staedtebauinstitut. Information (GW) *625*
SIN-Staedtebauinstitut. Jahresberichte (GW) *625*
SIN-Staedtebauinstitut. Schriftenreihe (GW ISSN 0078-2807) *625*
SIN-Staedtebauinstitut. Studienhefte (GW ISSN 0078-2815) *625*
SIN-Staedtebauinstitut. Werkberichte (GW ISSN 0078-2823) *625*
Sin-Time Review Buyers Guide (US) *358, 362, 362*
Sind University Journal of Education (PK ISSN 0560-0871) *419*
Sinet: Proceedings of Annual Programmes Review Conference (ET) *1000*
Singapore (SI ISSN 0129-766X) *539*
Singapore. Board of Commissioners of Currency. Annual Report *see* Singapore. Board of Commissioners of Currency. Annual Report and Accounts *232*
Singapore. Board of Commissioners of Currency. Annual Report and Accounts (SI) *232*
Singapore. Catalogue of Government Publications *see* Singapore National Printers. Publications Catalogue *912*
Singapore. Department of Statistics. Report on the Census of Industrial Production (SI ISSN 0080-9675) *217*
Singapore. Department of Statistics. Report on the Census of Wholesale, Retail Trades, Restaurants & Hotels (SI ISSN 0129-6760) *621, 1062*
Singapore. Department of Statistics. Report on the Household Expenditure Survey (SI) *615*
Singapore. Department of Statistics. Report on the Survey of Services (SI ISSN 0129-9786) *949, 1062*
Singapore. Economic Development Board. Annual Report (SI ISSN 0080-9683) *292*
Singapore. Housing and Development Board. Annual Report (SI) *625*
Singapore. Ministry of Labour. Annual Report (SI ISSN 0129-6310) *275*
Singapore. Ministry of National Development. Annual Report (SI) *626*
Singapore. Ministry of Science and Technology. National Survey of Scientific Manpower (SI) *275, 1000*
Singapore. Ministry of the Environment. Annual Report (SI) *499*
Singapore. National Library. Annual Report (SI ISSN 0217-1546) *683*
Singapore. Science Council. Annual Reports (SI) *1000*
Singapore Banking, Finance & Insurance(SI) *232, 641*
Singapore Book World (SI ISSN 0080-9659) *963*
Singapore Business Yearbook (SI ISSN 0129-4423) *317*
Singapore Community Health Bulletin (SI ISSN 0129-7457) *956*
Singapore Facts and Pictures (SI ISSN 0080-9691) *571*
Singapore Government Directory (SI ISSN 0129-3109) *946*
Singapore Indian Chamber of Commerce. Annual Report & Directory (SI) *317*
Singapore Indian Chamber of Commerce. Directory *see* Singapore Indian Chamber of Commerce. Annual Report & Directory *317*
Singapore Institute of Architects Yearbook *see* S I A Yearbook *99*

Singapore International Chamber of Commerce. Annual Report (SI ISSN 0377-449X) *237*
Singapore International Chamber of Commerce. Expatriate Living Costs in Singapore (SI) *237*
Singapore International Chamber of Commerce. Investor's Guide *see* Singapore International Chamber of Commerce. Investors Guide to the Economic Climate of Singapore *237*
Singapore International Chamber of Commerce. Investors Guide to the Economic Climate of Singapore (SI) *237*
Singapore International Chamber of Commerce. Report *see* Singapore International Chamber of Commerce. Annual Report *237*
Singapore Law Review (SI ISSN 0080-9705) *664*
Singapore Libraries (SI ISSN 0085-6118) *683*
Singapore Manufacturers' Association Directory *see* Tradelink - S M A Annual Directory (Year) *318*
Singapore Motoring Guide (SI) *1093*
Singapore National Academy of Science. Journal (SI) *161*
Singapore National Institute of Chemistry Bulletin *see* S N I C Bulletin *324*
Singapore National Printers. Publications Catalogue (SI) *912*
Singapore Periodicals Index (SI ISSN 0377-7928) *12*
Singapore Polytechnic Engineering Society. Journal (SI) *474*
Singapore Public Health Bulletin *see* Singapore Community Health Bulletin *956*
Singapore Standards Yearbook (SI ISSN 0129-6256) *292*
Singapore Telephone Board Annual Report *see* Telecommunication Authority of Singapore. Telecoms Annual Report *351*
Singapore Tourist Promotion Board. Annual Statistical Report on Visitor Arrivals (SI) *1120*
Singapore Trade & Industry Yearbook *see* Singapore Business Yearbook *317*
Singapore Trade Classification & Customs Duties (SI) *298*
Singapore Yearbook of Statistics (SI ISSN 0583-3655) *1062*
Singles Master *see* Music Master Catalogue *838*
Sinica Leidensia (NE) *571*
Sino-United States Trade Statistics *see* U S/China Trade Statistics *260*
Sinologica Coloniensia (GW ISSN 0170-3706) *571, 853*
Sinopse Estatistica do Brasil/Statistical Abstract of Brazil (BL ISSN 0100-1345) *217, 1062*
Sinopsis Dun - Brazil (US ISSN 0080-9756) *249*
Sintese Ferroviaria Brasileira (BL ISSN 0102-5694) *1095*
Sintesis Bibliografica (AG ISSN 0080-9772) *217*
Sir Frederic Hooper Award Essay (UK) *199, 281*
Sir George Earle Memorial Lecture on Industry and Government (UK ISSN 0080-9780) *199, 909*
Sir Moses Montefiore Collections des Juifs Celebres (FR ISSN 0075-4544) *972*
Sir Thomas Browne Instituut. Publications. General Series *see* Sir Thomas Browne Instituut. Publications. General Series and Special Series *596*
Sir Thomas Browne Instituut. Publications. General Series and Special Series (NE) *596*
Sira Review *see* Sira Review Annual Brochure *637*
Sira Review Annual Brochure (UK) *637*
Sires and Dams *see* U S T A Sires and Dams *1043*
Siskiyou Pioneer and Yearbook (US ISSN 0583-4449) *609*

Sistema de Indicadores Socio-
Economicos y Educativos de la O E
I (Organizacion de Estados
Iberoamericanos (OEI)) (SP) 419,
1011
Sistema Ferroviario R F F S A (Rede
Ferroviaria Federal, S.A.) (BL) 1095
Sistema Nacional de Archivos.
Inventarios (MX) 963
Sisters Have Resources Everywhere see
S H A R E 1162
Situation de la Viticulture dans le
Monde (FR) 59, 120
Situation Economique de Cote d'Ivoire
(IV ISSN 0080-9829) 249
Situation Economique de la Republique
Rwandaise au 31 Decembre see
Rwanda. Direction Generale de la
Statistique. Situation Economique de
la Republique Rwandaise au 31
Decembre 249
Situation Economique du Maroc (MR
ISSN 0080-9845) 249
Situation Economique du Senegal (SG
ISSN 0080-9853) 249
Situation Economique et Perspectives
d'Avenir (FR) 249
Situation Financiere des Regions de
Province en (Year) (FR) 249
Siviele Ingenieurswese-Adviesraad.
Jaarverslag see Civil Engineering
Advisory Council. Annual Report
480
Sixteen Mm Films Available in the
Public Libraries of Metropolitan
Toronto (CN ISSN 0315-7326) 826
Sixteenth Century Bibliography (US)
564
Sjoefartshistorisk Aarbok/Norwegian
Yearbook of Maritime History (NO
ISSN 0080-9888) 596
Skaeppen (DK ISSN 0108-397X) 596
Skakelblad see University of Pretoria.
Annual Report 342
Skanderborg Museum. Aarsskrift (DK
ISSN 0108-0342) 596
Skandinavisk Skibsfarts Tekniske
Aarshefte (DK) 1103
Skandinavisk Tidskrift for Faerg och
Lack. Aarsbok (DK ISSN 0085-
6126) 856
Skandinavisk U F O Information.
Newsletter (DK) 21
Skandinaviske Skipsrederier/Yearbook
of Scandinavian Shipowners (NO
ISSN 0800-1235) 317, 1103
Skatteberegningen (DK ISSN 0108-
688X) 222
Skattebve (DK) 298, 664
Skattelove (DK ISSN 0108-6022) 299
Skatten (DK ISSN 0106-8024) 299
Skatten. Erhverv (DK ISSN 0107-
3885) 199, 299
Skenectada (US ISSN 0270-2614)
146, 499
Skeptika see Para - nyt 712
Sketch Book (US) 110
Ski Holidays Scotland (UK) 1046,
1116
Ski X-C (Cross-country) (US ISSN
0161-1054) 1046
Skiers Directory (US ISSN 0730-2150)
1046
Skiffy Bag see It Goes on the Shelf 14
Skiffy Thyme see It Goes on the Shelf
14
Skipsfartens Innkjoepsbok (NO) 1103
Skirnir (IC) 596
Skive-egnens Jul (DK ISSN 0106-
2697) 596
Skogbrukets og Skogindustrienes
Forsknings-Forening. Arbok see
Skogbrukets og Skogindustrienes
Forskningsraad. Aarbok 530
Skogbrukets og Skogindustrienes
Forskningsraad. Aarbok (NO) 530
Skole & Landbrug (DK ISSN 0108-
2671) 34, 419
Skole og Edb (DK ISSN 0900-2006)
419
Skolemusikhaandbogen (DK ISSN
0108-4402) 419, 841
Skolens Aarbok (NO ISSN 0080-9950)
419
Skolernes Kunstforening Alssund-
Kredsen. Katalog see Vore Kunstnere
112
Skolestart (DK ISSN 0107-3028) 419
Skolhistoriskt Arkiv (FI) 596

Skrifter i Fysisk Geografi see Aarhus
Universitet. Geologisk Institut.
Geoskrifter 382
Skrifter Utgivna av Svenska
Riksarkivet(SW ISSN 0346-8488)
683
Skuespilregister (DK ISSN 0106-665X)
1078
Skulptur Veksoelund (DK ISSN 0107-
4911) 110
Skvaet see Skanderborg Museum.
Aarsskrift 596
Slaegten Fisker (DK ISSN 0108-3880)
537
Slaegtsbladet (DK ISSN 0107-1971)
537
Slaekt och Bygd (FI) 537
Slakt och Havd (Terjarv) (FI) 596
Slavia Antiqua (PL ISSN 0080-9993)
92
Slavia Occidentalis (PL ISSN 0081-
0002) 703
Slavica see Universitatis Debreceniensis
de Ludovico Kossuth Nominatae.
Instituti Philologiae Slavicae.
Annales. Slavica 706
Slavica Gothoburgensia (SW ISSN
0081-0010) 703
Slavica Lundensia (SW ISSN 0346-
8712) 703, 732
Slavica Othiniensia (DK ISSN 0106-
1313) 703
Slavistic Printing and Reprintings (GW
ISSN 0081-0029) 571, 732
Slavistische Beitraege (GW ISSN 0081-
5429) 703, 732
Slavistische Studienbuecher (GW ISSN
0583-5445) 703
Slavonski Povijesni Zbornik (YU ISSN
0352-8650) 632
Slavyanskaya Filologiya (UR) 703
Sleep (SZ ISSN 0302-5128) 1162
Sleep Research (US ISSN 0093-0407)
791
Slig Buyers' Guide (US) 459
Sloan-Kettering Institute for Cancer
Research. Progress Report (US
ISSN 0081-0045) 776
Sloane Travel Agency Reports Service
see S T A R Service 1116
Slovaci v Zahranici (CS ISSN 0081-
0061) 75, 596, 703
Slovak Academy of Sciences. Treatises
on Biology see Slovenska Akademia
Vied. Biologicke Prace 146
Slovak Press Digest (US ISSN 0037-
6914) 505, 909
Slovak Seismographic Stations:
Bratislava, Srobarova, Hurbanovo and
Skalnate Pleso. Bulletin (CS) 401
Slovakia (US ISSN 0583-5623) 505
Slovakia see Slowakei 712
Slovanske Historicke Studie (CS ISSN
0081-007X) 596
Slovanske Studie (CS ISSN 0583-
564X) 505, 596, 909, 1029
Slovenska Akademia Vied. Biologicke
Prace/Slovak Academy of Sciences.
Treatises on Biology (CS ISSN
0037-6930) 146
Slovenska Akademia Vied.
Geofyzikalny Ustav. Contributions
(CS ISSN 0586-4607) 401
Slovenska Akademia Vied. Geologicky
Ustav D. Stura. Geologicke Prace see
Slovenska Akademia Vied.
Geologicky Ustav D. Stura: Zbornik:
Zapadne Karpaty 395
Slovenska Akademia Vied. Geologicky
Ustav D. Stura: Zbornik: Zapadne
Karpaty (CS ISSN 0036-1372) 395
Slovenska Bibliografija (YU ISSN
0350-3585) 131
Slovenska Narodna Bibliografia Seria B:
Periodika (CS) 131
Slovenska Narodna Bibliografia Seria D:
Dizertacne Prace (CS) 131
Slovenska Narodna Bibliografia Seria E:
Specialne Tlace (CS) 131
Slovenska Narodna Bibliografia Seria F:
Firemna Literatura (CS) 131
Slovenska Narodna Bibliografia Seria G:
Grafika (CS) 131
Slovenska Narodna Bibliografia Seria H:
Hudobniny (CS) 841, 844
Slovenska Narodna Bibliografia Seria I:
Oficialne Dokumenty (CS) 131
Slovenska Narodna Bibliografia Seria J:
Audiovizualne Dokumenty (CS) 131

Slovenska Numizmatika (CS ISSN
0081-0088) 845
Slovenske Banske Muzeum. Zbornik
(CS) 596, 820
Slovenske Ludove Piesne pre
Akordeon(CS) 841
Slovenske Narodne Muzeum.
Archeologicky Ustav. Fontes see
Slovenske Narodne Muzeum.
Archeologicky Ustav. Fontes
Archeologickeho 92
Slovenske Narodne Muzeum.
Archeologicky Ustav. Fontes
Archeologickeho (CS) 92
Slovenske Narodne Muzeum.
Historicky Sbornik see Slovenske
Narodne Muzeum. Zbornik 596
Slovenske Narodne Muzeum. Zbornik
(CS) 92, 596, 845
Slovenske Narodne Muzeum. Zbornik
Etnografia (CS ISSN 0139-5378)
596
Slovenskeho Narodneho Muzea. Fontes
Etnografickeho (CS) 75
Slovenskeho Narodneho Muzea. Fontes
Historickeho (CS) 560
Slovenski Etnograf (YU) 76
Slovenski Jezuiti V Kanade. Year Book
(CN ISSN 0085-6134) 983
Slovensko Morje in Zaledje (YU) 632
Slovo na Storozhi/Word on Guard (CN
ISSN 0583-6263) 703
Slow Learning Child see Exceptional
Child 444
Slow Loris Reader (US) 1162
Slowakei/Slovakia (GW ISSN 0037-
7058) 712
Sluzben Vesnik na Socijalisticka
Republika Makedonija (YU ISSN
0037-7147) 946
Sluzbene Novine Opcine Karlovac (YU
ISSN 0037-7104) 952
Sluzbeni Glasnik Opcine Rovinj (YU
ISSN 0037-7120) 952
Small and Medium Industry Bank,
Seoul. Annual Report (KO) 232
Small Animal Abstracts (UK ISSN
0306-7580) 12, 43
Small Business Bibliography (UK) 301
Small Business Reporter (US) 301
Small Industries Development
Organization. Annual Report (TZ)
301
Small Industries Guide (II) 301
Small Industry Bulletin for Asia and the
Pacific (UN) 281
Small Press Record of Books in Print
(US) 131, 964
Small Ruminant and Camel Group
Document (UN) 67
Small Ruminant and Camel Group
Newsletter (UN) 67
Small-Scale Industries: South Eastern
and Benue Plateau States of Nigeria
(NR) 301
Small Side Team Games and Potted
Sports (UK) 1035
Small Time Operator (US) 301
Smallholder Tea Authority. Annual
Report (MW) 59
Smar's Industrial Directory of Pakistan
(PK) 317
Smith College Studies in History (US
ISSN 0081-0193) 560
Smithersia (RH ISSN 0250-300X) 177
Smithsonian Contributions to
Anthropology (US ISSN 0081-0223)
76
Smithsonian Contributions to
Astrophysics (US ISSN 0081-0231)
117, 891
Smithsonian Contributions to Botany
(US ISSN 0081-024X) 161
Smithsonian Contributions to
Paleobiology (US ISSN 0081-0266)
857
Smithsonian Contributions to the Earth
Sciences (US ISSN 0081-0274) 381
Smithsonian Contributions to the
Marine Sciences (US ISSN 0196-
0768) 381
Smithsonian Contributions to Zoology
(US ISSN 0081-0282) 177
Smithsonian Folklife Studies (US) 516
Smithsonian Folklore Studies see
Smithsonian Folklife Studies 516
Smithsonian Institution. Archives of
American Art. Newsletter (US) 110

SOCIAL PSYCHOLOGY   1881

Smithsonian Institution. Astrophysical
Observatory. S A O Special Report
(US ISSN 0081-0320) 117, 891
Smithsonian Institution Opportunities
for Research and Advanced Study
see Smithsonian Opportunities for
Research and Study in History Art
Science 1000
Smithsonian Opportunities for Research
and Study in History Art Science
(US ISSN 0081-0339) 1000
Smithsonian Research Opportunities see
Smithsonian Opportunities for
Research and Study in History Art
Science 1000
Smithsonian Studies in Air and Space
(US) 21
Smithsonian Studies in History and
Technology (US ISSN 0081-0258)
560
Smoker's Handbook see Tobacco Trade
Marketing Directory 1080
Smoking Habits of Australians (AT)
1080
Snapdragon see Idaho (Moscow) 723
SNOBOL4 Information Bulletin (US)
358, 363
Snoeck's Almanach (BE ISSN 0085-
6169) 632
Snoeck's; Literatuur Kunst Film Toneel
Mode Reizen (BE ISSN 0085-6177)
632, 712
Snow Brand Milk Products Company.
Research Laboratory. Reports/
Yukijirushi Nyugyo Gijutsu
Kenkyusho Hokoku (JA ISSN 0082-
4763) 63
Snowmobile Accidents, Manitoba (CN
ISSN 0707-9184) 1083
Snowmobile Sports Annual (CN) 1046
Snowy Mountains Engineering
Corporation. Annual Report (AT)
408, 474
So and So Magazine (US) 744, 1078
Sobek's Adventure Vacation (US) 1116
Soccer Rulebook (US ISSN 0731-9541)
1040
Soccer Year Book for Northern Ireland
(UK ISSN 0081-038X) 1040
Sociaal-Economische Raad. Annual
Report see Sociaal-Economische
Raad. Jaarverslag 199
Sociaal-Economische Raad. Jaarverslag/
Sociaal-Economische Raad. Annual
Report (NE ISSN 0560-3641) 199
Sociaal-Geografische Studien (NE
ISSN 0081-0398) 1162
Sociaal-Historische Studien (NE ISSN
0081-0401) 567, 1011
Social Administration (DK ISSN 0900-
1980) 956
Social Affairs Statistics of Taiwan/
Chung-Hua Min Kuo Tai-Wan Sheng
She Hui Shih Yeh Tung Chi (CH)
1023
Social Concept (US ISSN 0737-7762)
199
Social Democrat (US) 909
Social Development Activities in Latin
America Promoted by the Inter-
American Foundation see U.S.
General Accounting Office. Social
Development Activities in Latin
America Promoted by the Inter-
American Foundation: Report to the
Congress by the Comptroller General
of the United States 1164
Social Development Research Institute.
Organization and Activities (JA
ISSN 0559-698X) 1011
Social, Economic and Political Studies
of the Middle East (NE ISSN 0085-
6193) 613
Social Education Yearly (CH) 419
Social History of Canada (CN ISSN
0085-6207) 609
Social Indicators of the Philippines see
Philippines. National Census and
Statistics Office. Social Indicator
928
Social Perspectives (KE) 1029
Social Planning, Policy & Development
Abstracts (US ISSN 0195-7988)
264
Social Process in Hawaii (US ISSN
0737-6871) 1029
Social Psychology of Language (UK)
937, 1029

SOCIAL RESPONSIBILITY

Social Responsibility: Business, Journalism, Law, Medicine (US) 646, 664, 766, 881
Social Responsibility: Journalism, Law, Medicine see Social Responsibility: Business, Journalism, Law, Medicine 664
Social Science Abstracts see University of Tokyo. Institute of Social Science. Annals 1013
Social Science Federation of Canada. Annual Report (CN) 1011
Social Science Journal (KO) 1011
Social Science Research Council of Canada. Report see Social Science Federation of Canada. Annual Report 1011
Social Science Studies (CN ISSN 0081-0460) 1162
Social Sciences and Humanities Index see Humanities Index 634
Social Sciences and Humanities Index see Social Sciences Index 1014
Social Sciences Citation Index (US ISSN 0091-3707) 12, 1014
Social Sciences Citation Index Journal Citation Reports (US ISSN 0161-3162) 1014
Social Sciences Index (US ISSN 0094-4920) 12, 1014
Social Sciences Research Series (II) 1011
Social Sciences Symposium Series (CN) 1011
Social Scientist (NR ISSN 0081-0487) 1011
Social Security Documentation: African Series (SZ ISSN 0379-704X) 641
Social Security Documentation: Asian Series (SZ ISSN 0250-4057) 641
Social Security Documentation: European Series (SZ) 641
Social Security Handbook (US ISSN 0081-0495) 641, 1020
Social Service Delivery Systems (US) 1020
Social Service Organizations and Agencies Directory (US) 1020
Social Services for Nova Scotians (CN) 1020
Social Services in North Dakota (US ISSN 0094-1220) 1020
Social Services in Nova Scotia see Social Services for Nova Scotians 1020
Social Services Yearbook (UK ISSN 0307-093X) 1020
Social Sikring (DK ISSN 0900-2030) 956
Social Strategies (SZ) 1029
Social Structure and Social Change (UK) 1011, 1029
Social Studies Audiovisuals: A Teacher's Sourcebook (National Information Center for Educational Media) (US) 449, 1011
Social Studies Materials and Resources Data Book. Annual see Data Book of Social Studies Materials and Resources 446
Social Trends in New Zealand (NZ) 1031, 1062
Social Welfare Law (UK) 664, 1020
Social Welfare Services in Japan (JA) 1020
Social Welfare, Social Planning, Policy and Social Development see Social Planning, Policy & Development Abstracts 264
Social Work and Social Issues (US ISSN 0081-055X) 1020
Social Work Papers of the School of Social Work, University of Southern California see University of Southern California. School of Social Work. Social Work Papers 1021
Social Work Research and Abstracts (US ISSN 0148-0847) 12, 1023
Social Work Year Book see Encyclopedia of Social Work 1017
Sociale Ydelser, Hvem, Hvad, og Hvornaar (DK ISSN 0107-5047) 641
Socialist Register (UK ISSN 0081-0606) 909
Socialist Youth Alliance Internal Bulletin see S.Y.A. Internal Bulletin 909

Socialistisk Folkeparti. Status see S F. Status 909
Socialistiske Perspektiver Forlag Status see S F. Status 909
Sociedad Argentina de Biologia. Revista(AG ISSN 0037-8380) 1162
Sociedad Argentina de Escritores. Boletin (AG) 732
Sociedad Argentina de Estudios Geograficos. Contribuciones Cientificas (AG) 548
Sociedad Argentina de Estudios Geograficos Boletin (AG ISSN 0325-2698) 548
Sociedad Boliviana de Historia Natural. Revista (BO) 146
Sociedad Botanica de Mexico. Boletin (MX) 161
Sociedad Cientifica Argentina. Ciclo de Conferencias (AG) 1000
Sociedad de Autores Puertorriquenos. Anales (PR) 732
Sociedad de Estudios Vascos. Cuadernos de Seccion. Antropologia-Etnografia (SP ISSN 0213-0297) 76, 505
Sociedad de Estudios Vascos. Cuadernos de Seccion. Artes Plasticas y Monumentales (SP ISSN 0212-3215) 110
Sociedad de Estudios Vascos. Cuadernos de Seccion. Ciencias Naturales (SP ISSN 0212-4173) 146
Sociedad de Estudios Vascos. Cuadernos de Seccion. Derecho (SP ISSN 0213-0483) 664
Sociedad de Estudios Vascos. Cuadernos de Seccion. Educacion (SP ISSN 0213-3636) 419
Sociedad de Estudios Vascos. Cuadernos de Seccion. Folklore (SP ISSN 0212-7547) 516
Sociedad de Estudios Vascos. Cuadernos de Seccion. Historia-Geografia (SP) 548, 560
Sociedad de Estudios Vascos. Cuadernos de Seccion. Hizkuntza Eta Literatura (SP ISSN 0212-3223) 703, 732
Sociedad de Estudios Vascos. Cuadernos de Seccion. Medicina (SP ISSN 0213-3601) 766
Sociedad de Estudios Vascos. Cuadernos de Seccion. Medios de Comunicacion (SP ISSN 0213-0289) 344
Sociedad de Estudios Vascos. Cuadernos de Seccion. Musica (SP ISSN 0213-0815) 841
Sociedad de Estudios Vascos. Cuadernos de Seccion. Prehistoria y Arqueologia (SP ISSN 0213-3024) 92
Sociedad de Ingenieros. Informaciones y Memorias (PE) 474
Sociedad Espanola de Automoviles de Turismo. Memoria y Balance (SP) 1093, 1116
Sociedad Espanola de Historia de la Medicina. Boletin (SP ISSN 0583-7480) 766
Sociedad Espanola de Literatura General y Comparada. Anuario (SP) 1162
Sociedad Espanola de Socorros Mutuos y Beneficencia. Boletin (AG ISSN 0037-8569) 1020
Sociedad Geologica del Peru. Boletin (PE ISSN 0079-1091) 395, 609
Sociedad Interamericana de Planificacion. Ediciones S I A P (AG) 626
Sociedad Mexicana de Historia de la Ciencia y de la Tecnologia. Anales (MX) 1000
Sociedad Mexicana de Historia Natural. Revista (MX) 381
Sociedad Mexicana de Micologia. Boletin see Revista Mexicana de Micologia 160
Sociedad Mexicana de Micologia. Boletin Informativo see Revista Mexicana de Micologia 160
Sociedad Peruana de Historia. Serie: Actos Academicos (PE) 609
Sociedad Rural Argentina. Memoria (AG ISSN 0081-0630) 67

Sociedad Uruguaya (UY ISSN 0081-0649) 1029
Sociedad Venezolana de Espeleologia. Boletin (VE ISSN 0583-7731) 395
Sociedade Brasileira (BL) 135
Sociedade Brasileira de Economistas Rurais. Anais da Reuniao see Congresso Brasileiro de Economia e Sociologia Rural. Anais 46
Sociedade Broteriana. Anuario (PO) 161
Sociedade Broteriana. Boletim (PO ISSN 0081-0657) 161
Sociedade Broteriana. Memorias (PO ISSN 0081-0665) 146
Sociedade Paranaense de Matematica. Monografias (BL ISSN 0102-3292) 753
Sociedade Portuguesa de Antropologia e Etnologia. Trabalhos see Trabalhos de Antropologia e Etnologia 77
Sociedades por Acoes (BL) 199, 664
Societa dei Naturalisti in Napoli. Bulletin (IT) 146
Societa di Studi Romagnoli. Guide (IT ISSN 0081-0681) 596
Societa e Dello Stato Veneziano. Istituto di Storia. Bollettino see Studi Veneziani 598
Societa e Diritto di Roma (IT ISSN 0391-3260) 664
Societa e la Scienza (IT ISSN 0391-609X) 1000
Societa Italiana di Fisica. Congresso Nazionale (IT) 891
Societa Italiana di Fitosociologia. Notizario. (IT) 161
Societa Italiana di Scienze Farmaceutiche Documenti see S.I.S.F. Documenti 872
Societa Italiana per Il Progresso delle Scienze. Atti della Riunione (IT) 1000
Societa Sarda di Scienze Naturali. Bollettino (IT) 161, 171, 177, 381
Societa Savonese di Storia Patria. Atti e Memorie (IT) 539
Societa Storica Valtellinese. Bollettino (IT ISSN 0085-6231) 560
Societa Tiburtina di Storia e d'Arte. Atti e Memorie (IT) 92
Societas Gaius Julius Caesar Octavianus. Newsletter see Journal of Ancient and Medieval Studies 536
Societas Internationalis Odonatologica. Rapid Communications (NE) 146
Societas Scientiarum Fennica. Aarsbok Vuosikirja (FI ISSN 0371-2885) 596
Societas Uralo-Altaica. Veroeffentlichungen (GW ISSN 0340-6423) 703
Societat d'Historia Natural de Baleares. Boletin (SP ISSN 0583-7405) 146, 395
Societatea de Stiinte Istorice si Filologice Din R.P.R. Studii si Articole de Istorie see Studii si Articole de Istorie 598
Societe Archeologique de Tarn et Garonne. Bulletin Archeologique, Historique et Artistique (FR) 92
Societe Archeologique de Touraine. Bulletin (FR) 92
Societe Archeologique de Touraine. Memoires (FR) 92, 596
Societe Astronomique de Bordeaux. Bulletin (FR ISSN 0081-0738) 117
Societe Botanique de Geneve. Travaux see Saussurea 161
Societe Canadienne des Etudes Bibliques. Bulletin see Canadian Society of Biblical Studies. Bulletin 968
Societe Chateaubriand. Bulletin. Nouvelle Series (FR ISSN 0081-0754) 732
Societe d'Amenagement Regional. Rapport Annuel see Community Improvement Corporation. Annual Report 243
Societe d'Archeologie Copte. Bibliotheque de Manuscrits (UA ISSN 0068-5283) 92
Societe d'Archeologie Copte. Bulletin (UA ISSN 0068-5291) 92
Societe d'Archeologie Copte. Textes et Documents (UA ISSN 0068-5305) 92

Societe d'Archeologie, d'Histoire et de Folklore de Nivelles et du Brabant Wallon. Annales (BE) 92, 596
Societe d'Archeologie et d'Histoire de la Charente Maritime. Bulletin de Liaison (FR) 93
Societe d'Emulation de Montbeliard. Bulletin et Memoires (FR) 596
Societe d'Emulation de Montbeliard. Memoires see Societe d'Emulation de Montbeliard. Bulletin et Memoires 596
Societe d'Emulation Historique et Litteraire d'Abbeville. Bulletin (FR ISSN 0081-0819) 596
Societe d'Ergonomie de Langue Francaise. Actes du Congres (FR ISSN 0081-0835) 895
Societe d'Etudes Linguistiques et Anthropologiques de France. Numeros Speciaux (FR ISSN 0249-7069) 76, 703
Societe d'Etudes Linguistiques et Anthropologiques de France (SELAF) Applications et Transferts see Applications et Transferts 691
Societe d'Histoire de France. Annuaire (FR ISSN 0081-0940) 596
Societe d'Histoire et d'Archaeologie de Geneve. Bulletin (SZ ISSN 0081-0959) 93, 560
Societe d'Histoire et d'Archaeologie de la Goele. Bulletin d'Information (FR ISSN 0081-0967) 93, 596
Societe d'Histoire Moderne. Annuaire (FR ISSN 0081-0975) 560
Societe d'Histoire Naturelle du Doubs. Bulletin (FR ISSN 0753-4655) 1000
Societe d'Ophtalmologie de France. Bulletin (FR ISSN 0081-1270) 786
Societe de Developpement du Livre et du Periodique. Annuaire (CN) 684
Societe de Geographie de Marseille. Bulletin (FR ISSN 0081-0789) 548
Societe de l'Ecole des Chartes. Memoires et Documents (SZ ISSN 0078-9518) 560
Societe de l'Industrie Minerale. Annuaire (FR ISSN 0081-0797) 820
Societe de la Bourse de Luxembourg. Rapport Annuel (LU) 268
Societe des Alcools du Quebec. Rapport Annuel (CN) 377
Societe des Amis de Marcel Proust et des Amis de Combray. Bulletin (FR ISSN 0583-8452) 733
Societe des Amis des Sciences et des Lettres de Poznan. Bulletin. Serie D: Sciences Biologiques (PL ISSN 0079-4570) 147
Societe des Antiquaires de l'Ouest. Memoires (FR) 596
Societe des Antiquaires de Picardie. Memoires (FR) 596
Societe des Auteurs, Compositeurs, Editeurs pour la Gerance des Droits de Reproduction Mecanique. Bulletin(FR ISSN 0081-0843) 664
Societe des Explorateurs et des Voyageurs Francais. Annuaire General (FR ISSN 0081-086X) 76, 548
Societe des Francs-Bibliophiles. Annuaire (FR ISSN 0081-0878) 963
Societe des Ingenieurs Civils de France. Annuaire see Societe des Ingenieurs et Scientifiques de France. Annuaire 483
Societe des Ingenieurs et Scientifiques de France. Annuaire (FR) 483
Societe des Naturalistes Luxembourgeois. Bulletin (LU ISSN 0304-9620) 147, 381
Societe des Oceanistes. Publications (FR ISSN 0081-0894) 1011
Societe des Poetes Francais. Annuaire (FR ISSN 0081-0908) 744
Societe des Professeurs Francais en Amerique. Bulletin Annuel (US ISSN 0081-0916) 419
Societe des Sciences et des Lettres de Lodz. Bulletin (PL ISSN 0459-6854) 733, 1000
Societe des Sciences, Lettres et Arts de Bayonne. Bulletin (FR) 110, 733

Societe des Sciences Medicales du Grand-Duche de Luxembourg. Bulletin (LU ISSN 0037-9247) *766*
Societe des Sciences Physiques et Naturelles de Bordeaux. Memoires (FR) *1000*
Societe Entomologique d'Egypte. Bulletin/Entomological Society of Egypt. Bulletin (UA ISSN 0081-0983) *166*
Societe Entomologique d'Egypte. Bulletin. Economic Series (UA ISSN 0081-0991) *166*
Societe Entomologique du Quebec. Memoires (CN ISSN 0071-0784) *166*
Societe Finno-Ougrienne. Journal see Suomalais-Ugrilaisen Seuran. Aikakauskirja *705*
Societe Finno-Ougrienne. Memoires (FI) *703*
Societe Francaise de Chimie. Annuaire (FR) *324*
Societe Francaise de Chirurgie Orthopedique et Traumatologique. Conferences d'Enseignement (FR ISSN 0081-1033) *786*
Societe Francaise de Microbiologie. Annuaire (FR ISSN 0081-1068) *169*
Societe Francaise de Physique. Annuaire (FR ISSN 0081-1076) *891*
Societe Francaise de Recherche Operationelle. Annuaire see Association Francaise pour la Cybernetique Economique et Technique. Annuaire *359*
Societe Francaise du Vide. Comptes Rendus des Travaux des Congres et Colloques (FR ISSN 0223-4335) *891*
Societe Francaise Shakespeare. Actes du Congres (FR) *733*
Societe Generale de Banque. Rapport (BE) *232*
Societe Generale de Belgique. Rapport/Report (BE ISSN 0081-1114) *232*
Societe Geographique de Liege. Bulletin(BE ISSN 0770-7576) *548*
Societe Geologique de France. Memoires (FR ISSN 0249-7549) *395*
Societe Guernesiaise. Report and Transactions (UI ISSN 0144-1973) *596*
Societe Historique de Villiers sur Marne et de la Brie Francaise. Revue (FR) *596*
Societe Historique et Archeologique dans le Limbourg. Publications (NE ISSN 0085-6266) *596*
Societe Historique et Archeologique de Pontoise, du Val d'Oise et du Vexin. Memoires (FR) *596*
Societe Internationale Arthurienne. Bulletin Bibliographique see International Arthurian Society. Bibliographical Bulletin *739*
Societe Internationale pour l'Etude de la Philosophie Medievale. Bulletin see Bulletin de Philosophie Medievale *877*
Societe J.K. Huysmans. Bulletin (FR) *712*
Societe National du Logement. Rapport Annuel (BE ISSN 0067-5652) *626*
Societe Nationale des Antiquaires de France. Bulletin (FR ISSN 0081-1181) *93*
Societe Nationale des Chemins de Fer Belges. Rapport Annuel (BE ISSN 0081-119X) *1095*
Societe Nationale Elf Aquitaine. Rapport Annuel (FR) *867*
Societe Neophilologique de Helsinki. Memoires (FI) *703*
Societe Neuchateloise des Sciences Naturelles. Bulletin (SZ ISSN 0366-3469) *177*
Societe Nucleaire Canadienne. Sommaires du Congres see Canadian Nuclear Society. Annual Conference Summaries *896*
Societe Odonto-Stomatologique du Nord-Est. Revue Annuelle (FR ISSN 0081-1203) *780*
Societe Philomatique Vosgienne. Bulletin (FR) *596*

Societe pour la Conservation des Monuments Historiques d'Alsace. Bulletin see Cahiers Alsaciens d'Archeologie d'Art et d'Histoire *84*
Societe pour le Developpement Minier de la Cote d'Ivoire. Rapport Annuel (IV ISSN 0250-3697) *820*
Societe pour Vaincre la Pollution. Bulletin de Liaison see Environnement *496*
Societe Royale Belge d'Anthropologie et de Prehistoire. Bulletin (BE) *76*
Societe Royale Belge d'Entomologie. Memoires (BE) *166*
Societe Royale de Lettres de Lund. Bulletin/Kunglia Humanistiska Vetenskapssamfundet i Lund. Arsberattelse (SW) *733*
Societe Royale de Zoologie d'Anvers. Bulletin see Acta Zoologica et Pathologica Antverpiensia *172*
Societe Speleologique et Prehistorique de Bordeaux. Memoire (FR ISSN 0294-5495) *560*
Societe Suisse des Americanistes. Bulletin/Schweizerische Amerikanisten-Gesellschaft. Bulletin (SZ ISSN 0582-1592) *76, 93, 609*
Societe Theophile Gautier. Bulletin (FR ISSN 0221-7945) *733*
Societe Vaudoise des Sciences Naturelles. Memoires (SZ ISSN 0037-9611) *1000*
Societes de Service et de Conseil en Informatique (FR) *353*
Societes et Fournisseurs d'Afrique Noire (FR) *249*
Societes Scientifiques et Techniques du Canada see Scientific and Technical Societies of Canada *1000*
Society and Welfare/Hevra u-Revaha (IS ISSN 0334-4029) *1020*
Society for American Archaeology. Memoir Series (US) *93*
Society for American Archaeology. Special Publications Series (US) *93*
Society for American Baseball Research, Inc. Review of Books see S A B R Review of Books *1040*
Society for Applied Bacteriology. Symposium Series (US) *169*
Society for Applied Bacteriology. Technical Series (US) *169*
Society for Asian Music. Publication Series. Series A: Bibliographic and Research Aids see Asian Music Publications. Series A: Bibliographic and Research Aids *833*
Society for Asian Music. Publication Series. Series B: Translations see Asian Music Publications. Series B. Translations *833*
Society for Asian Music. Publication Series. Series C: Reprints see Asian Music Publications. Series C: Reprints *833*
Society for Asian Music. Publications Series. Series D: Monographs see Asian Music Publications. Series D: Monographs *833*
Society for Commercial Archaeology. News Journal (US ISSN 0735-1399) *93*
Society for Developmental Biology. Symposium (US ISSN 0583-9009) *147*
Society for Endocrinology (Great Britain) Memoirs (UK ISSN 0081-136X) *781*
Society for Experimental Biology. Seminar Series (UK) *147*
Society for Experimental Biology. Symposia (UK ISSN 0081-1386) *147*
Society for Experimental Mechanics Proceedings see S E M Proceedings *489*
Society for General Microbiology. Special Publications (US) *169*
Society for General Microbiology. Symposium (UK ISSN 0081-1394) *169*
Society for General Systems Research. Proceedings (US) *1000*
Society for Historical Archaeology. Special Publication Series (US) *93*
Society for Industrial and Applied Mathematics Proceedings see S I A M - A M S Proceedings *752*

Society for Information Display International Symposium. Digest of Technical Papers see S I D International Symposium. Digest of Technical Papers *474*
Society for Italian Historical Studies. Newsletter (US ISSN 0081-1424) *597*
Society for Italic Handwriting. Journal (UK ISSN 0037-9743) *419*
Society for Lincolnshire History and Archaeology. Annual Report and Statement of Accounts (UK ISSN 0306-4859) *93, 597*
Society for Louisiana Irises. Special Publications (US) *534*
Society for Natural Sciences, Basel. Proceedings see Naturforschende Gesellschaft in Basel. Verhandlungen *996*
Society for New Testament Studies. Monograph Series (UK ISSN 0081-1432) *972*
Society for Old Testament Studies. Monographs (UK) *972*
Society for Old Testament Study. Book List (UK ISSN 0081-1440) *975*
Society for Promoting Training of Women. Annual Report (UK) *1129*
Society for Psychical Research. Proceedings (UK ISSN 0081-1475) *860*
Society for Renaissance Studies. Occasional Papers (UK) *110, 733, 881*
Society for Research in Child Development. Monographs (US ISSN 0037-976X) *334*
Society for Scholarly Publishing Society of Scholarly Publishing. Proceedings of Annual Meetings see Society of Scholarly Publishing. Proceedings of Annual Meetings *963*
Society for Seventeenth Century French Studies. Newsletter see Seventeenth Century French Studies *596*
Society for Slovene Studies. Documentation Series (US) *597, 703*
Society for Technical Communication Anthology Series (US) *344*
Society for the Advancement of Food Service Research. Proceedings (US ISSN 0081-1483) *520*
Society for the Advancement of Material and Process Engineering International S A M P E Technical Conference Series. N S T C Preprint Series see International S A M P E Technical Conference Series. N S T C Preprint Series *489*
Society for the History of Technology. Monograph Series (US ISSN 0081-1491) *1071*
Society for the Preservation of Long Island Antiquities. Newsletter (US ISSN 0583-9181) *79, 110*
Society for the Prevention of Asbestosis and Industrial Diseases News see S P A I D News *636*
Society for the Right to Die. Handbook see Handbook of Living Will Laws *656*
Society for the Scientific Study of Religion. Monograph Series (US) *972*
Society for the Study of Chinese Religions. Bulletin see Journal of Chinese Religions *977*
Society for the Study of Human Biology. Symposia (UK ISSN 0081-153X) *172*
Society for the Study of Inborn Errors of Metabolism. Symposia (UK) *172*
Society for the Study of Pre-Han China. Newsletter see Early China *569*
Society of Actuaries. Transactions (General) (US ISSN 0037-9794) *641*
Society of Actuaries. Transactions: Reports of Mortality and Morbidity Experience (US) *641*
Society of Actuaries. Yearbook (US) *641*
Society of Antiquaries of Newcastle Upon Tyne. Monograph Series (UK ISSN 0265-1785) *597*

Society of Antiquaries of Scotland. Monograph Series (UK ISSN 0263-3191) *93, 597*
Society of Antiquaries of Scotland. Proceedings (UK ISSN 0081-1564) *597*
Society of Archer-Antiquaries. Journal (UK ISSN 0560-6152) *1035*
Society of Automotive Engineers Handbook see S A E Handbook *1093*
Society of Automotive Engineers Technical Literature Abstracts see S A E Technical Literature Abstracts *1086*
Society of Automotive Engineers Technical Papers see S A E Technical Papers *1093*
Society of Automotive Engineers Transactions see S A E Transactions *1093*
Society of Biblical Literature. Seminar Papers (Year) (US ISSN 0145-2711) *972*
Society of Biological Chemists. Proceedings (II ISSN 0300-0486) *152*
Society of Chartered Property & Casualty Underwriters Public Affairs Forum see C P C U Public Affairs Forum *638*
Society of Christian Ethics. Annual (US ISSN 0732-4928) *972*
Society of Cypriot Studies. Bulletin/Kypriakai Spoudai (CY ISSN 0081-1580) *597*
Society of Die Casting Engineers, Inc. International Die Casting Congress. Transactions see S D C E International Die Casting Congress. Transactions *746*
Society of Exploration Geophysicists. Special Publications (Symposia) Series (US) *401*
Society of Federal Linguists. Newsletter(US) *703*
Society of Flight Test Engineers. Annual Symposium Proceedings (US) *21*
Society of General Physiologists. Distinguished Lecture Series (US) *172*
Society of General Physiologists Series (US ISSN 0094-7733) *172*
Society of Glass Decorators. Papers Presented at Annual Seminar see Society of Glass Decorators. Seminar Proceedings *320*
Society of Glass Decorators. Seminar Proceedings (US) *320*
Society of Graphic Artists. Publication (UK) *110*
Society of Logistics Engineers. Proceedings (US ISSN 0081-1629) *1071*
Society of Management Science and Applied Cybernetics Special Series see S C I M A Special Series *359*
Society of Maritime Arbitrators. Award Service (US) *664, 1103*
Society of Naval Architects and Marine Engineers. Transactions (US ISSN 0081-1661) *1103*
Society of Nippon Dental College. Annual Publications see Nippon Dental University. Annual Publications *779*
Society of Petroleum Engineers. Reprint Series (US) *867*
Society of Petroleum Engineers. Transactions (US ISSN 0081-1696) *867*
Society of Petroleum Engineers of American Institute of Mining, Metallurgical and Petroleum Engineers. Petroleum Transactions Reprint Series see Society of Petroleum Engineers. Reprint Series *867*
Society of Petroleum Engineers of American Institute of Mining, Metallurgical and Petroleum Engineers. Transactions see Society of Petroleum Engineers. Transactions *867*
Society of Plant Protection of North Japan. Annual Report/Kitanihon Byogaichu Kenkyukai Kaiho (JA ISSN 0081-170X) *60*

Society of Plastics Engineers Monographs (US) *901*
Society of Portrait Sculptors. Publication (UK) *110*
Society of Professional Investigators. Bulletin (US ISSN 0038-0008) *372*
Society of Professional Well Logging Analysts. S P W L A Annual Logging Symposium Transactions (US ISSN 0081-1718) *867*
Society of Professors of Education. Occasional Papers (US ISSN 0882-7141) *419*
Society of Professors of Education Monograph Series *see* S P E Monograph Series *419*
Society of Protozoologists. Special Publication *see* Illustrated Guide to the Protozoa *175*
Society of Scholarly Publishing. Proceedings of Annual Meetings (Society for Scholarly Publishing) (US) *963*
Society of the Plastics Industry. Reinforced Plastics Composites Institute. Annual Technical Conference. Preprint (US) *901*
Society of the Plastics Industry. Urethane Division. Conference Proceedings (US) *901*
Society of Wildlife Artists. Publication (UK) *110, 147*
Society of Women Artists. Publication (UK) *110, 1129*
Socio-Economic Differential Mortality in Industrialized Societies (FR) *924*
Socio-Economic Information Network Abstracts. Journal *see* S E C I N Abstracts. Journal *1031*
Socio-Economic Progress in Latin America; Annual Report *see* Economic and Social Progress in Latin America; Annual Report *243*
Socio-Economic Review of Punjab (II) *249, 1029*
Sociobiology (US ISSN 0361-6525) *147*
Sociolinguistique (FR) *76, 703*
Sociologia (IT) *1029*
Sociologia II (BL ISSN 0081-1742) *1029*
Sociological Abstracts (US ISSN 0038-0202) *12, 1031*
Sociological Methodology (US ISSN 0081-1750) *1029*
Sociological Microjournal (DK) *1029*
Sociological Observations (US) *76, 1029*
Sociological Practice (US ISSN 0163-8505) *1029*
Sociological Review *see* Revija za Sociologiju *1029*
Sociological Review. Monograph (UK ISSN 0081-1769) *1029*
Sociologie Permanente (FR) *1029*
Sociologische Verkenningen (BE) *1029*
Sociologist (NR ISSN 0081-1807) *1029*
Sociology of Education Abstracts (UK ISSN 0038-0415) *12, 425, 1031*
Sociology of Music Series (US) *1029*
Sociology of the Sciences *see* Sociology of the Sciences. Yearbook *1000*
Sociology of the Sciences. Yearbook (NE) *1000, 1029*
Sociology of the Sciences Monographs (NE) *1000, 1029*
Socjolingwistyka (PL) *703*
Soelleroedbogen (DK ISSN 0085-6339) *597*
Soenderjyske Arboeger (DK ISSN 0106-4452) *597*
Soermlandsbygden (SW ISSN 0349-0297) *597*
Soester Beitraege (GW) *597*
Soester Zeitschrift (GW ISSN 0176-3946) *597*
Sofia. Universitet. Bogoslovski Fakultet. Godishnik *see* Dukhovna Akademiya SV. Kliment Okhridski. Godishnik *969*
Sofiiski Universitet. Biologicheski Fakultet. Godishnik (BU ISSN 0081-1823) *147*
Sofiiski Universitet. Fakultet po Klasiceski i Novi Filologii. Godishnik/ Universite de Sofia. Faculte des Lettres Classiques et Modernes. Annuaire (BU) *704*

Sofiiski Universitet. Fakultet po Matematika i Mekhanika. Godishnik/Universite de Sofia. Faculte des Mathematiques et de Mecanique. Annuaire (BU ISSN 0081-1858) *753*
Sofiiski Universitet. Fakultet po Slavianska Filologiia. Godishnik (BU ISSN 0081-1831) *704*
Sofiiski Universitet. Fakultet po Zapadni Filologii. Godisnik *see* Sofiiski Universitet. Fakultet po Klasiceski i Novi Filologii. Godishnik *704*
Sofiiski Universitet. Filosofski Fakultet. Godisnik/Universite de Sofia. Faculte de Philosophie. Annuaire (BU ISSN 0081-184X) *597*
Sofiiski Universitet. Filosofski-Istoriceski Fakultet. Godisnik *see* Sofiiski Universitet. Filosofski Fakultet. Godisnik *597*
Sofiiski Universitet. Geologo-Geografski Fakultet. Geografiia. Godishnik. (BU ISSN 0324-0525) *548*
Sofiiski Universitet. Geologo-Geografski Fakultet. Geologiia. Godishnik. (BU) *395*
Sofiiski Universitet. Ideologicheski Katedri. Godishnik. *see* Sofiiski Universitet. Katedra po Nauchen Komunizm. Godishnik *909*
Sofiiski Universitet. Istoricheski Fakultet. Godishnik/Universite de Sofia. Faculte d'Histoire. Annuaire (BU ISSN 0204-4005) *561*
Sofiiski Universitet. Juridiheski Fakultet. Godisnik (BU ISSN 0081-1866) *664*
Sofiiski Universitet. Katedra po Nauchen Komunizm. Godishnik. (BU ISSN 0204-9619) *909*
Sofiiski Universitet. Katedra po Politiceska Ikonomiya. Godisnik (BU ISSN 0204-9627) *252*
Sofiiski Universitet. Khimicheski Fakultet. Godisnik (BU) *324*
Softball Rule Book (US ISSN 0732-2844) *1040*
Softfair: A Conference on Software Development Tools, Techniques, and Alternatives. Proceedings (US) *363*
Software Abstracts for Engineers (IE ISSN 0790-150X) *363, 485*
Software Encyclopedia (US) *131, 363*
Software Katalog (GW) *363*
Software Maintenance Workshop. Record *see* Conference on Software Maintenance. Proceedings *362*
Software Publishers' Catalogs Annual (US ISSN 0740-5022) *131, 363, 684*
Software Reports: Guide to Evaluated Educational Software (US) *362, 363, 428*
Software Users' Year Book (UK) *363*
Softwarefuehrer fuer Home-Computer (GW) *358, 362*
Softwarefuehrer fuer Personal-Computer(GW) *358, 362*
Sogo Keizai Nenkan *see* Food Economics Yearbook *308*
Soil and Crop Society of Florida. Annual Proceedings (US) *60*
Soil Science Library *see* Books in Soils and the Environment Series *53*
Soil Science Society of America Special Publication Series *see* S S S A Special Publication Series *59*
Soil Science Society of Ceylon. Journal *see* Soil Science Society of Sri Lanka. Journal *60*
Soil Science Society of Sri Lanka. Journal (CE) *60*
Soils and Fertilizers (UK ISSN 0038-0792) *12, 43*
Soils and Land Use Series (AT ISSN 0081-1912) *60*
Soils News (AT) *60*
Soils Newsletter (UN) *60*
Sokoni: Official Newsletter of the Marketing Society of Kenya (KE) *285*
Solanus (UK ISSN 0038-0903) *684, 963*
Solar Bibliography (US) *131, 468*
Solar Collector Manufacturing Activity (US ISSN 0197-2030) *292, 467, 554*

Solar Collector Manufacturing Activity and Applications in the Residential Sector *see* Solar Collector Manufacturing Activity *467*
Solar Energy Index (US) *468*
Solar Energy Research and Development in the European Community. Series. A. Solar Energy Applications to Dwellings (NE) *467*
Solar Energy Research and Development in the European Community. Series B: Thermo-Mechanical Solar Power Plants (NE) *467*
Solar Energy Research and Development in the European Community. Series C. Photovoltaic Power Generation (NE) *467*
Solar Energy Research and Development in the European Community. Series D. Photochemical, Photoelectrochemical and Photobiological Processes (NE) *467*
Solar Energy Research and Development in the European Community. Series E. Energy from Biomass (NE) *467*
Solar Energy Research and Development in the European Community. Series F. Solar Radiation Data (NE) *467*
Solar Energy Research and Development in the European Community. Series G. Wind Energy (NE) *467*
Solar Energy Research and Development in the European Community. Series H. Solar Energy in Agriculture and Industry (NE) *467*
Solar Energy Research and Development Reports (US) *467*
Solar Engineering (US) *467*
Solar Radiation *see* Promieniowanie Sloneczne *806*
Solar Terrestrial Environmental Research in Japan (JA ISSN 0386-5444) *401, 891*
Soldier Shop Annual (US) *614, 812*
Soldier Shop Quarterly *see* Soldier Shop Annual *614*
Solent Guides (UK) *538*
Solent Yearbook (UK) *1042*
Solicitors' and Barristers' Directory and Diary (UK) *664*
Solid-Liquid Flow Abstracts (UK ISSN 0038-1063) *12, 477, 893*
Solid State Abstracts *see* Solid State Abstracts Journal *893*
Solid State Abstracts Journal (US) *12, 893*
Solid State Physics; Advances in Research and Applications (US ISSN 0081-1947) *891*
Solid State Physics Literature Guides (US ISSN 0081-1963) *894*
Solid State Processing and Production Buyers Guide and Directory (US) *459*
Solinet. Annual Report (Southeastern Library Network) (US) *684*
Solinews *see* S O L I N E W S *689*
Solomon Goldman Lectures (US ISSN 0196-2183) *977*
Solomon Islands Museum Association. Journal (BP) *76, 830*
Solomon Islands Research Register (BP) *573*
Solomon Mahlangu Freedom College Voice of S O M A F C O *see* Voice of S O M A F C O *540*
Solvent Extraction Reviews *see* Ion Exchange and Solvent Extraction *331*
Somali National Bank. Annual Report and Statement of Accounts *see* Central Bank of Somali. Annual Report and Statement of Accounts *226*
Somalia in Figures (SO) *1062*
Some Friends (UK) *733*
Somerset Archaeology and Natural History (UK ISSN 0081-2056) *93, 1000*
Somerset Birds (UK ISSN 0081-2048) *171*

Somersetshire Archaeological and Natural History Society. Proceedings *see* Somerset Archaeology and Natural History *93*
Sonderbaende zur Theologischen Zeitschrift (SZ ISSN 0067-4907) *972*
Sonderbibliographien der Deutschen Bucherei (GE ISSN 0457-3900) *131*
Sonderinformation Philosophie *see* Thematische Information Philosophie *882*
Songwriter's Market (US ISSN 0161-5971) *841*
Sonorensis. Annual Report (US) *830*
Sonorum Speculum *see* Key Notes *837*
Sons and Daughters of the Soddies. Reports (US) *537, 609*
Soochow Journal of Economics and Business (CH) *199, 252, 278*
Soochow Journal of Foreign Languages and Literatures (CH) *704, 733*
Soochow Journal of Humanities (CH) *632*
Soochow Journal of Mathematical and Natural Sciences *see* Soochow Journal of Mathematics *753*
Soochow Journal of Mathematics (CH) *753, 1000*
Soochow Journal of Political Science & Sociology (CH) *909, 1011*
Soochow Journal of Social and Political Sciences *see* Soochow Journal of Political Science & Sociology *1011*
Soochow University. Philosophy Department. Chuan-Hsi Lu (CH) *881*
Soochow University Journal of Chinese Art History (CH) *110*
Sophia University. Institute of Comparative Culture. Business Series(JA) *281, 285*
Sophisticated Leisure Travel Directory (US) *620, 1116*
Sorghum and Millets Abstracts (UK ISSN 0308-2970) *12, 43*
Sorgo - Uma Alternativa Economica (BL) *1162*
Sorting Code Numbers (UK) *232*
Sotahistoriallinen Aikakauskirja (FI ISSN 0357-816X) *597, 812*
Sotheby's International Price Guide: Antiques and Collectibles (US) *79, 110*
Sotrudnichestvo *see* Politechnika Wroclawska. Osrodek Badan Prognostycznych. Prace Naukowe. Wspolpraca *248*
Sotsiologiya Kul'tury (UR) *1029*
Sound and Vision *see* Communication & Broadcasting *348*
Soundings (Santa Barbara) (US ISSN 0038-1853) *684, 733*
Soundview Executive Book Summaries (US ISSN 0195-1718) *252, 281, 287*
Soundview Summaries *see* Soundview Executive Book Summaries *281*
Source (Washington) *see* Identified Sources of Supply *809*
Source Book of American State Legislation (US) *946*
Source Book of Health Insurance Data (US ISSN 0073-148X) *641*
Source Book: Social and Health Services in the Greater New York Area (US ISSN 0740-4549) *1021*
Source Books on Curricula and Methods *see* Unesco Source Books on Curricula and Methods *449*
Source Directory of Predicasts, Inc. *see* Predicasts Source Directory *217*
Source Journals in Metallurgy *see* Source Journals in Metals and Materials *800*
Source Journals in Metals and Materials(US) *800, 802*
Source Material of Finnish History *see* Suomen Historian Laehteitae *599*
Source Materials on the History of Science in India (II) *1000*
Source of Supply Directory *see* Sources of Supply/Buyers Guide *859*
Source References for Facts and Figures on Government Finance (US ISSN 0494-8203) *1162*
Sourcebook (Knoxville) (US) *334*

SOUTH AFRICA. 1885

Sourcebook of Criminal Justice Statistics (US) *372*
Sourcebook on Aging (US) *1162*
Sourcebook on Death and Dying (US) *1162*
Sourcebook on Food and Nutrition (US) *1162*
Sources (US) *800*
Sources de Droit Serbe *see* Izvori Srpskog Prava *657*
Sources et Travaux d'Histoire Haut-Pyreneenne (FR ISSN 0248-5516) *597*
Sources for Stamping *see* Sources *800*
Sources for the Study of Religion in Malawi (MW) *684, 973*
Sources from the Ancient Near East (US ISSN 0732-6424) *613*
Sources in the History of Mathematics and Physical Sciences (US ISSN 0172-6315) *753*
Sources of African and Middle-Eastern Economic Information (US) *259*
Sources of Contemporary Jewish Thought/Mekevot (IS ISSN 0082-4585) *712, 977*
Sources of Music and Their Interpretation, Duke Studies in Music (US) *609, 841*
Sources of State Information on Corporations *see* How to Find Company Intelligence in State Documents *195*
Sources of Supply/Buyers Guide (US ISSN 0081-2129) *859*
South Africa. Central Statistical Service. Annual Report (SA) *1062*
South Africa. Central Statistical Service. Building Plans Passed and Buildings Completed (SA) *189, 1062*
South Africa. Central Statistical Service. Census of Electricity, Gas and Steam(SA) *468, 1062*
South Africa. Central Statistical Service. Census of Township Developers/Sensus van Dorpsontwikkelaars (SA) *627, 1062*
South Africa. Central Statistical Service. Death of Blacks (SA) *929, 1062*
South Africa. Central Statistical Service. Education: Asian (SA) *425, 1062*
South Africa. Central Statistical Service. Education: Whites (SA) *425, 1062*
South Africa. Central Statistical Service. Labour Statistics: Wage Rates, Earnings and Average Hours Worked in the Printing and Newspaper Industry, Engineering Industry, Building Industry and Commerce (SA) *217, 1062*
South Africa. Central Statistical Service. Mining: Financial Statistics (SA) *822, 1063*
South Africa. Central Statistical Service. Report on Births: White, Coloured and Asians (SA) *929, 1063*
South Africa. Central Statistical Service. Report on Marriages and Divorces: South Africa (SA) *929, 1063*
South Africa. Central Statistical Service. Report on Prices (SA) *217, 1063*
South Africa. Central Statistical Service. Road Traffic Accidents (SA) *1063, 1086*
South Africa. Central Statistical Service. Statistical News Releases (SA) *1063*
South Africa. Central Statistical Service. Statistics of Houses and Domestic Servants and of Flats (SA) *627, 1063*
South Africa. Central Statistical Service. Statistics of Motor and Other Vehicles (SA) *1063, 1086*
South Africa. Central Statistical Service. Statistics of New Vehicles Registered(SA) *1063, 1086*
South Africa. Central Statistical Service. Survey of the Accounts of Companies. Part 1. Secondary and Tertiary Industries (SA) *217, 1063*
South Africa. Central Statistical Service. Survey of the Accounts of Companies. Part 2. Mining (SA) *217, 1063*
South Africa. Central Statistical Service. Tourism and Migration (SA) *929, 1063, 1120*

South Africa. Central Statistical Service. Transfers of Rural Immovable Property (SA) *966, 1063*
South Africa. Central Statistical Services. Local Government Statistics(SA) *949, 1063*
South Africa. Central Statistical Services. Statistics of Administration Boards (SA) *949, 1063*
South Africa. Commissioner for Customs and Excise. Foreign Trade Statistics (SA) *217*
South Africa. Dairy Board. Annual Report (SA) *63*
South Africa. Dairy Control Board. Annual Report *see* South Africa. Dairy Board. Annual Report *63*
South Africa. Department of Agricultural Economics and Marketing. Division of Agricultural Marketing Research. Abstract of Agricultural Statistics *see* South Africa. Department of Agriculture and Fisheries. Division of Economic Services. Abstract of Agricultural Statistics *43*
South Africa. Department of Agriculture. Agricultural Bulletins (SA) *34*
South Africa. Department of Agriculture. Agricultural Research (SA) *34*
South Africa. Department of Agriculture and Fisheries. Agricultural Bulletins *see* South Africa. Department of Agriculture. Agricultural Bulletins *34*
South Africa. Department of Agriculture and Fisheries. Agricultural Research *see* South Africa. Department of Agriculture. Agricultural Research *34*
South Africa. Department of Agriculture and Fisheries. Division of Economic Services. Abstract of Agricultural Statistics (SA) *43, 1063*
South Africa. Department of Agriculture and Fisheries. Entomology Memoirs *see* South Africa. Department of Agriculture. Entomology Memoirs *166*
South Africa. Department of Agriculture and Fisheries. Offical List of Professional Research Workers, Lecturing Staff and Extension Workers in the Agricultural Field *see* South Africa. Department of Agriculture. Official List of Professional Research Workers, Lecturing Staff and Extension Workers in the Agricultural Field *34*
South Africa. Department of Agriculture and Fisheries. Report of the Secretary for Agricultural Technical Services *see* South Africa. Department of Agriculture. Report of the Chief for Agriculture and Water Supply *34*
South Africa. Department of Agriculture and Fisheries. Science Bulletins *see* South Africa. Department of Agriculture. Science Bulletins *34*
South Africa. Department of Agriculture and Fisheries. Special Publications *see* South Africa. Department of Agriculture. Special Publications *34*
South Africa. Department of Agriculture and Fisheries. Technical Communication *see* South Africa. Department of Agriculture. Technical Communication *34*
South Africa. Department of Agriculture. Entomology Memoirs (SA) *166*
South Africa. Department of Agriculture. Official List of Professional Research Workers, Lecturing Staff and Extension Workers in the Agricultural Field (SA) *34*
South Africa. Department of Agriculture. Report of the Chief for Agriculture and Water Supply (SA) *34*

South Africa. Department of Agriculture. Report of the Secretary for Agricultural Technical Services *see* South Africa. Department of Agriculture. Report of the Chief for Agriculture and Water Supply *34*
South Africa. Department of Agriculture. Science Bulletins (SA) *34*
South Africa. Department of Agriculture. Special Publications (SA) *34*
South Africa. Department of Agriculture. Technical Communication (SA) *34*
South Africa. Department of Bantu Education. Annual Report *see* South Africa. Department of Education and Training. Annual Report *419*
South Africa. Department of Community Development. Division of Surveys and Mapping. Annual Report of the Chief Director *see* South Africa. Department of Public Work and Land Affairs. Directorate of Surveys and Mapping. Annual Report of the Chief Director *483*
South Africa. Department of Customs and Excise. Foreign Trade Statistics *see* South Africa. Commissioner for Customs and Excise. Foreign Trade Statistics *217*
South Africa. Department of Defense. White Paper on Defense and Armament Production (SA) *812*
South Africa. Department of Education and Training. Annual Report (SA) *419*
South Africa. Department of Higher Education. Annual Report (SA ISSN 0081-220X) *438*
South Africa. Department of Mineral and Energy Affairs. Annual Report (SA) *395, 820*
South Africa. Department of Mines. Annual Report *see* South Africa. Department of Mineral and Energy Affairs. Annual Report *820*
South Africa. Department of National Education. Jaarverslag/Annual Report (SA) *419*
South Africa. Department of Public Work and Land Affairs. Directorate of Surveys and Mapping. Annual Report of the Chief Director (SA) *483*
South Africa. Department of Statistics. Annual Report of the Statistics Advisory Council and of the Secretary of Statistics *see* South Africa. Central Statistical Service. Annual Report *1062*
South Africa. Department of Statistics. Building Plans and Buildings Completed *see* South Africa. Central Statistical Service. Building Plans Passed and Buildings Completed *189*
South Africa. Department of Statistics. Census of Electricity, Gas and Steam *see* South Africa. Central Statistical Service. Census of Electricity, Gas and Steam *468*
South Africa. Department of Statistics. Census of Township Developers *see* South Africa. Central Statistical Service. Census of Township Developers *627*
South Africa. Department of Statistics. Education: Asian *see* South Africa. Central Statistical Service. Education: Asian *425*
South Africa. Department of Statistics. Education: Whites *see* South Africa. Central Statistical Service. Education: Whites *425*
South Africa. Department of Statistics. Labour Statistics: Wage Rates, Earnings and Average Hours Worked in the Printing and Newspaper Industry, Engineering Industry, Building Industry and Commerce *see* South Africa. Central Statistical Service. Labour Statistics: Wage Rates, Earnings and Average Hours Worked in the Printing and Newspaper Industry, Engineering Industry, Building Industry and Commerce *217*

South Africa. Department of Statistics. Local Government Statistics *see* South Africa. Central Statistical Services. Local Government Statistics *949*
South Africa. Department of Statistics. Mining: Financial Statistics *see* South Africa. Central Statistical Service. Mining: Financial Statistics *822*
South Africa. Department of Statistics. Report on Bantu Deaths in Selected Magisterial Districts/Verslag oor Bantoesterfgevalle in Uitgesoekte Landdrosdistrikte *see* South Africa. Central Statistical Service. Death of Blacks *929*
South Africa. Department of Statistics. Report on Births: White, Colored and Asians *see* South Africa. Central Statistical Service. Report on Births: White, Coloured and Asians *929*
South Africa. Department of Statistics. Report on Marriages and Divorces: South Africa *see* South Africa. Central Statistical Service. Report on Marriages and Divorces: South Africa *929*
South Africa. Department of Statistics. Report on Prices *see* South Africa. Central Statistical Service. Report on Prices *217*
South Africa. Department of Statistics. Road Traffic Accidents *see* South Africa. Central Statistical Service. Road Traffic Accidents *1086*
South Africa. Department of Statistics. Statistical News Releases *see* South Africa. Central Statistical Service. Statistical News Releases *1063*
South Africa. Department of Statistics. Statistical Year Book *see* South African Statistics *1063*
South Africa. Department of Statistics. Statistics of Administration Boards *see* South Africa. Central Statistical Services. Statistics of Administration Boards *949*
South Africa. Department of Statistics. Statistics of Houses and Domestic Servants and of Flats *see* South Africa. Central Statistical Service. Statistics of Houses and Domestic Servants and of Flats *627*
South Africa. Department of Statistics. Statistics of Motor and Other Vehicles *see* South Africa. Central Statistical Service. Statistics of Motor and Other Vehicles *1086*
South Africa. Department of Statistics. Statistics of New Vehicles Registered *see* South Africa. Central Statistical Service. Statistics of New Vehicles Registered *1086*
South Africa. Department of Statistics. Survey of the Accounts of Companies in Secondary and Tertiary Industries *see* South Africa. Central Statistical Service. Survey of the Accounts of Companies. Part 1. Secondary and Tertiary Industries *217*
South Africa. Department of Statistics. Survey of the Accounts of Companies in Secondary and Tertiary Industries *see* South Africa. Central Statistical Service. Survey of the Accounts of Companies. Part 2. Mining *217*
South Africa. Department of Statistics. Tourism and Migration *see* South Africa. Central Statistical Service. Tourism and Migration *929*
South Africa. Department of Statistics. Transfers of Rural Immovable Property *see* South Africa. Central Statistical Service. Transfers of Rural Immovable Property *966*
South Africa. Geological Survey. Annals (SA ISSN 0584-2352) *395*
South Africa. Geological Survey. Bulletin (SA) *395*
South Africa. Geological Survey. Handbook (SA ISSN 0560-9208) *395*
South Africa. Geological Survey. Memoirs (SA) *395*

1886 SOUTH AFRICA.

South Africa. Geological Survey. Report of the Chief Director of the Geological Survey see South Africa. Department of Mineral and Energy Affairs. Annual Report *820*

South Africa. Geological Survey. Seismologic Series (SA) *395*

South Africa. Geological Survey. Special Publications (SA) *395*

South Africa. Government Gazette Index (SA ISSN 0379-6078) *12, 949*

South Africa. Kantoor van die Direkteur van Argiewe en die Staatsheraldikus. Jaarverslag see South Africa. Office of the Director of Archives and the State Herald. Annual Report *564*

South Africa. Law Commission. Jaarverslag van die Suid-Afrikaanse Regskommissie/Annual Report of the South African Law Commission (SA) *664*

South Africa. Maize Board. Report on Grain Sorghum and Buckwheat for the Financial Year (SA ISSN 0300-5747) *1162*

South Africa. Maize Board. Report on Maize for the Financial Year (SA) *64*

South Africa. Maize Board. Review of the Maize Position see South Africa. Maize Board. Report on Maize for the Financial Year *64*

South Africa. National Parks Board. Annual Report (SA) *367*

South Africa. Office of the Director of Archives and the State Herald. Annual Report/South Africa. Kantoor van die Direkteur van Argiewe en die Staatsheraldikus. Jaarverslag (SA) *564*

South Africa. Office of the Director of Archives. Annual Report of the Director of Archives/South Africa. Kantoor van die Direkteur van Argiewe. Jaarverslag van die Direkteur van Argiewe see South Africa. Office of the Director of Archives and the State Herald. Annual Report *564*

South Africa. Official Yearbook of the Republic of South Africa (SA ISSN 0302-0681) *564, 1063*

South Africa. Prisons Department. Annual Statistics by the Commissioner of Prisons/Jaarlikse Statistieke Deur die Kommissaris van Gevangenisse (SA) *372*

South Africa. Prisons Department. Report of the Commissioner of Prisons/Verslag van die Kommissaris van Gevangenisse (SA ISSN 0300-1555) *372*

South Africa. Sea Fisheries Branch. Investigational Report see South Africa. Sea Fisheries Research Institute. Investigational Report *513*

South Africa. Sea Fisheries Institute. Annual Report see South Africa. Sea Fisheries Research Institute. Marine Development Branch. Annual Report *513*

South Africa. Sea Fisheries Institute. Fisheries Bulletin see South African Journal of Marine Science *513*

South Africa. Sea Fisheries Research Institute. Investigational Report (SA) *513*

South Africa. Sea Fisheries Research Institute. Marine Development Branch. Annual Report (SA) *513*

South Africa. State Library Council. Report/Verslag (SA) *684*

South Africa. Tobacco Board. Annual Report/Jaarverslag (SA) *1080*

South Africa. Tobacco Industry Control Board. Report see South Africa. Tobacco Board. Annual Report/Jaarverslag *1080*

South Africa. Unemployment Insurance Fund. Report/South Africa. Werkloosheidversekeringsfonds. Verslag (SA) *275, 641*

South Africa. Water Research Commission. Annual Report (SA) *1125*

South Africa. Water Research Commission. Research Projects (SA) *1125*

South Africa. Weather Bureau. Technical Paper/Tegniese Verhandelinge (SA ISSN 0379-6736) *806*

South Africa. Weather Bureau. W.B. Series (SA ISSN 0081-2331) *806*

South Africa. Werkloosheidversekeringsfonds. Verslag see South Africa. Unemployment Insurance Fund. Report *641*

South Africa. Wheat Board. Annual Report (SA) *64*

South Africa: a Guide to Foreign Investors (SA) *268*

South Africa Compared (SA) *249*

South Africa Foundation. Information Digest (Year) (SA) *249*

South African Archives Journal see Suid-Afrikaanse Argiefblad *684*

South African Baptist Handbook (SA) *979*

South African Biographical and Historical Studies (SA ISSN 0085-6363) *135, 567*

South African Broadcasting Corporation. Annual Report (SA) *349*

South African Bureau of Standards Catalogue see S A B S Catalogue *809*

South African Chemicals Manufactured & Imported (SA) *480*

South African Computer Users Handbook see Computer Users Handbook *361*

South African Cultural History Museum. Bulletin see Suid-Afrikaanse Kultuurhistoriese Museum. Bulletin *567*

South African Exporters/Exportateurs Sud-Africains/Suedafrikanische Exporteure/Exportadores de Sud Africa (SA) *259*

South African Fishing Industry Handbook and Buyer's Guide (SA ISSN 0080-5076) *513*

South African Foreign Trade Organization Annual Report see S A F T O Annual Report *259*

South African Freight Manual (SA) *317, 1083*

South African Historical Journal (SA) *567*

South African Institute for Medical Research. Publication (SA) *147, 766*

South African Institute of International Affairs. Bibliographical Series/Suid-Afrikaanse Instituut van Internasionale Aangeleenthede. Bibliografiese Reeks (SA) *131, 912*

South African Institute of International Affairs. Biennial Report of the National Chairman (SA) *918*

South African Institute of International Affairs. Occasional Papers (SA) *918*

South African Institute of International Affairs. Report of the National Chairman see South African Institute of International Affairs. Biennial Report of the National Chairman *918*

South African Institute of International Affairs. Special Studies (SA) *918*

South African Institute of Mining and Metallurgy. Monograph Series (SA) *800, 820*

South African Jewry and Who's Who (SA) *1162*

South African Journal of Antarctic Research (SA ISSN 0081-2455) *1000, 1071*

South African Journal of Communication Disorders/Suid-Afrikaanse Tydskrif vir Kommunikasieafwykings (SA) *766, 787*

South African Journal of Economic History (SA) *252*

South African Journal of Marine Science (SA) *513*

South African Licensee's Guardian (SA ISSN 0489-8567) *620*

South African Mechanics Handbook (SA) *746*

South African Medical and Dental Council. Register of Supplementary Health Services Professions (SA) *766, 1021*

South African Medical Research Council. Annual Report/Suid-Afrikaanse Mediese Navorsingsraad. Jaarverslag (SA ISSN 0081-248X) *766*

South African Mining and Engineering Yearbook (SA ISSN 0081-2498) *474, 820*

South African Museum. Annals/Suid-Afrikaanse Museum. Annale (SA ISSN 0303-2515) *76, 93, 857*

South African National Bibiography see S A N B *131*

South African National Council for the Deaf. Annual Diary (SA) *376*

South African National Council of the Blind. Biennial Report (SA) *180*

South African National Gallery. Bulletin (SA) *1162*

South African National Tuberculosis Association Annual Report see S A N T A Annual Report *793*

South African Reserve Bank. Annual Economic Report/Suid-Afrikaanse Reserwebank. Jaarlikse Ekonomiese Verslag (SA ISSN 0081-2528) *249*

South African Reserve Bank. Report of the Ordinary General Meeting/Suid-Afrikaanse Reserwebank. Verslag van die Gewone Algemene Vergadering (SA) *232*

South African Society of Pathologists. Congress Brochure (SA) *766, 796*

South African Speech and Hearing Association. Journal see South African Journal of Communication Disorders *766*

South African Statistics (SA ISSN 0081-2544) *1063*

South African Sugar Association Experiment Station. Annual Report (SA ISSN 0375-2682) *60*

South African Sugar Association Experiment Station. Bulletin (SA) *60*

South African Sugar Year Book (SA) *1162*

South African Wool and Textile Research Institute. Annual Report (SA ISSN 0560-9941) *1075*

South African Wool and Textile Research Institute Technical Report see S A W T R I Technical Report *1075*

South African Yearbook of International Law/Suid-Afrikaanse Jaarboek vir Volkereg (SA ISSN 0379-8895) *671*

South America (New York) (US ISSN 0193-7944) *1116*

South America, Central America and the Caribbean (UK ISSN 0268-0661) *609*

South America Stamp Catalogue (UK ISSN 0142-9922) *875*

South American Handbook (US ISSN 0081-2579) *1116*

South American Ports Handbook (AG) *1104*

South and East Asia Report see Southeast Asia Report *249*

South Asia: Journal of South Asian Studies (AT ISSN 0085-6401) *76, 571, 1029*

South Asian Digest of Regional Writing (GW ISSN 0170-7787) *853*

South Asian Studies (GW ISSN 0584-3170) *571, 853*

South Asian Studies (UK ISSN 0266-6030) *613*

South Atlantic Modern Language Association Awards (US) *733*

South Atlantic Urban Studies (US) *626*

South Australia. Department of Environment and Planning. Coastline (AT ISSN 0311-4805) *1162*

South Australia. Department of Environment and Planning. Directory of Non-Government Environmental Groups in South Australia (AT ISSN 0159-3641) *1162*

South Australia. Department of Labour. Guide to Legislation (AT ISSN 0311-0702) *275*

South Australia. Department of Mines and Energy. Annual Report (AT ISSN 0159-7043) *395*

South Australia. Department of Mines and Energy. Special Publications (AT ISSN 0726-1527) *381, 820*

South Australia. Department of Woods and Forests. Bulletin (AT) *527*

South Australia. Libraries Board. Annual Report (AT ISSN 0081-2633) *684*

South Australian Baker and Pastrycook (AT) *522*

South Australian Geographical Papers (AT ISSN 0811-6504) *548*

South Australian Racehorse (AT) *1043*

South Australian Yearbook (AT ISSN 0085-6428) *1063*

South Bucks & East Berks Chamber of Commerce & Industry Directory (UK) *237, 317*

South Carolina. Department of Archives and History. Annual Report (US) *609*

South Carolina. Department of Labor. Annual Report (US) *275*

South Carolina. State Board of Engineering Examiners. Directory of Engineers and Land Surveyors Registered in South Carolina see Directory of Engineers and Land Surveyors Registered in South Carolina *470*

South Carolina Academy of Science. Bulletin (US ISSN 0096-414X) *1000*

South Carolina Arts Commission. Annual Report (US ISSN 0081-2684) *110*

South Carolina Baptist Historical Society Journal (US ISSN 0146-0196) *979*

South Carolina Historical Association. Proceedings (US ISSN 0361-6207) *609*

South Carolina State Industrial Directory see MacRae's South Carolina State Industrial Directory *1157*

South Carolina State Library. Annual Report (US ISSN 0361-6479) *684*

South Carolina Statistical Abstract (US) *1063*

South Carolina Vital and Morbidity Statistics (US ISSN 0094-6338) *924, 929*

South Central Campbook (US) *1046, 1116*

South Central Camping see South Central Campbook *1116*

South Central Research Library Council. Library Directory see Directory of Libraries and Library Resources in the South Central Research Library Council Region *676*

South Dakota. Department of Revenue. Annual Statistical Report (US ISSN 0085-6460) *217*

South Dakota. State Department of Public Welfare. Research and Statistics Annual Report (US ISSN 0099-2305) *1023, 1063*

South Dakota Academy of Science. Proceedings (US) *1000*

South Dakota Authors' Catalog (US ISSN 0742-8936) *739*

South Dakota Department of Revenue. Annual Report see South Dakota. Department of Revenue. Annual Statistical Report *217*

South Dakota Geological Survey. Bulletin (US ISSN 0085-6479) *395*

South Dakota Geological Survey. Circular (US ISSN 0085-6487) *395*

South Dakota Geological Survey. Reports of Investigation (US ISSN 0085-6495) *395*

South Dakota Historical Collections (US) *609*

South Dakota Manufacturers & Processors Directory. (US ISSN 0094-2758) *317*

South Dakota State Historical Society. Collections see South Dakota Historical Collections *609*

South Indian Art and Archaeological Series (II) *93, 99, 110*

South Pacific Bibliography (FJ) *131*

South Pacific Commission. Annual Report (NL) *918*
South Pacific Commission. Handbook (NL ISSN 0081-2811) *49, 513*
South Pacific Commission. Information Circular (NL ISSN 0081-282X) *49, 513*
South Pacific Commission. Information Document (NL ISSN 0081-2838) *49, 513*
South Pacific Commission. Occasional Paper (NL) *49, 513*
South Pacific Commission. Regional Conference of Directors of Agriculture, Livestock Production and Fisheries. Report (NL) *67*
South Pacific Commission. Report of S P C Fisheries Technical Meetings (NL ISSN 0081-2846) *49, 513*
South Pacific Commission. South Pacific Report *see* South Pacific Commission. Annual Report *918*
South Pacific Commission. Statistical Bulletin (NL) *1063*
South Pacific Commission. Technical Paper (NL ISSN 0081-2862) *1071*
South Pacific Holidays (AT) *1162*
South Pacific Periodicals Index (FJ) *131*
South Pacific Research Register (FJ) *131*
South Seas Society. Monograph (SI ISSN 0081-2897) *571*
South Staffordshire Archaeological and Historical Society. Transactions (UK ISSN 0457-7817) *93, 561*
South Wales Institute of Engineers. Proceedings (UK ISSN 0038-3570) *474*
South Wales Ports Tides Tables (UK) *408*
South Wood County Historical Corporation. Newsletter (US) *609*
Southampton (Port of), Tide Tables (UK) *408*
Southampton Chamber of Commerce Regional Directory (UK) *237*
Southampton Port Handbook (UK ISSN 0268-6511) *317, 1104*
Southeast Asia Building Annual (SI) *187*
Southeast Asia Development Corporation Berhad. Reports and Accounts (MY) *264*
South East Asia Library Group Newsletter (UK ISSN 0308-4035) *684, 853*
Southeast Asia Papers (US) *853*
Southeast Asia Program Series (US) *853*
Southeast Asia Report (US) *249, 909*
South-East Asia Stamp Catalogue (UK ISSN 0142-9930) *875*
Southeast Asian Affairs (UK) *571*
Southeast Asian Archives (MY ISSN 0085-6509) *571*
Southeast Asian Institutions of Higher Learning *see* Association of Southeast Asian Institutions of Higher Learning. Handbook: Southeast Asian Institutions of Higher Learning *432*
Southeast Asian-Ministers of Education Organisation. Regional Centre for Education in Science and Mathematics. Governing Board Meeting. Final Report (MY ISSN 0126-8155) *449*
South East Asian Monograph Series (AT ISSN 0158-6041) *561, 909*
Southeast Asian Perspective Series (SI) *571*
Southeast Asian Regional Seminar on Tropical Medicine & Public Health. Proceedings (TH) *766, 956*
Southeast Asian Seminar on Parasitology and Tropical Medicine. Proceedings *see* TropMed Seminars on Tropical Medicine. Proceedings *778*
Southeast Asian Studies Working Paper Series *see* Southeast Asia Papers *853*
Southeast/East Asian English Publications in Print (JA) *12, 317*
Southeast Michigan Council of Governments. Annual Report (US ISSN 0362-3475) *946*

Southeast Regional Library (Sask.) Library Directory (CN ISSN 0707-6894) *684*
Southeastern Association of Fish and Wildlife Agencies. Proceedings (US) *1046*
Southeastern Association of Game and Fish Commissioners. Proceedings of the Annual Conference *see* Southeastern Association of Fish and Wildlife Agencies. Proceedings *1046*
Southeastern Campbook (US ISSN 0731-5112) *1046, 1116*
Southeastern Camping *see* Southeastern Campbook *1116*
Southeastern College Art Conference Review (US) *110*
Southeastern Council on Latin American Studies Annals *see* S E C O L A S Annals *609*
Southeastern Geology (US ISSN 0038-3678) *395*
Southeastern Library Network. Annual Report *see* Solinet. Annual Report *684*
Southeastern Library Network, Inc. *see* S O L I N E W S *689*
Southeastern Library Network Solinet. Annual Report *see* Solinet. Annual Report *684*
South-Eastern State. Ministry of Economic Development and Reconstruction. State Development Plan *see* Cross River State. Ministry of Economic Development and Reconstruction. State Development Plan *294*
Southeastern Symposium on System Theory. Proceedings (US ISSN 0094-2898) *359*
Southeastern Writing Center Association. Selected Papers (US) *733*
Southern Africa and the Indian Ocean Islands Travel Trade Directory (SA) *1116*
Southern Africa Passport *see* Nana No Pasuporto *1114*
Southern African Metals & Minerals Conference. Proceedings (UK) *820*
Southern Angler's and Hunter's Guide (US ISSN 0081-2986) *1046*
Southern Anthropological Society. Proceedings (US ISSN 0081-2994) *76*
Southern Baptist Convention. Annual (US ISSN 0081-3001) *979*
Southern Baptist Convention. Historical Commission. Microfilm Catalogue (US ISSN 0081-301X) *979*
Southern Biomedical Engineering Conference. Proceedings (US) *147*
Southern Birds (SA) *171, 367*
Southern California Business Directory and Buyers Guide (US ISSN 0093-3090) *237, 317*
Southern California Rapid Transit District. Annual Report (US ISSN 0362-2841) *1083*
Southern Caver (AT ISSN 0157-8464) *395*
Southern Comparative Literature Association Newsletter *see* S C L A Newsletter *732*
Southern Cooperator (US ISSN 0038-4003) *239*
Southern Europe Travel Guide *see* Travel Guide to Europe *1118*
Southern Fishing by Outdoor Life *see* Bass and Freshwater Fishing *1044*
Southern Fried Turnip Greens *see* Greensboro Substitute *1154*
Southern Higher Education Legislative Report (US) *438*
Southern History (UK ISSN 0142-4688) *597*
Southern Home Counties Chamber of Commerce Directory (UK) *237*
Southern Home Counties Directory *see* Southern Home Counties Chamber of Commerce Directory *237*
Southern Hospitals *see* Clark's Directory of Southern Hospitals *616*
Southern Illinois University. University Museum Studies (US ISSN 0073-4985) *830*

Southern Illinois University, Carbondale. Center for Archaeological Investigations. Occasional Paper (US) *93*
Southern Illinois University, Carbondale. Center for Archaeological Investigations. Research Paper (US) *93*
Southern Illinois University, Carbondale. Department of Geography. Discussion Paper (US ISSN 0073-4950) *548*
Southern Illinois University, Carbondale. Occasional Paper Series in Geography (US ISSN 0073-4969) *548*
Southern Illinois University, Carbondale. University Libraries. Bibliographic Contributions (US ISSN 0073-4977) *131*
Southern Illinois University, Edwardsville. Center For Urban and Environmental Research and Services. C U E R S Report. *see* Southern Illinois University, Edwardsville. Regional Research and Development Services. Report *626*
Southern Illinois University, Edwardsville. Regional Research and Development Services. Report (US) *626*
Southern Indian Studies (US ISSN 0085-6525) *93*
Southern Progressive Periodicals Directory Update *see* Progressive Periodicals Directory Update *130*
Southern Regional Education Board. Annual Report (US ISSN 0081-3060) *419*
Southern Regional Education Board. State and Local Revenue Potential *see* Issues in Higher Education *436*
Southern Regional Education Board. State Legislation Affecting Higher Education in the South *see* Southern Higher Education Legislative Report *438*
Southern Rhodesia. National Archives. Occasional Papers *see* Zimbabwe. National Archives. Occasional Papers *567*
Southern Surgical Association. Transactions (US) *794*
Southern Weed Science Society. Proceedings (US ISSN 0362-4463) *60*
South West Africa Administration: White Paper on the Activities of the Different Branches (SX) *946*
South West Africa Scientific Society Journal *see* S.W.A. Scientific Society. Journal *1011*
South West Africa Series. Memoirs *see* Geological Survey of South West Africa/Namibia. Memoirs *387*
Southwest Builders and Contractors Directory (US) *187, 317*
Southwest Regional Conference for Astronomy and Astrophysics. Proceedings (US ISSN 0147-2003) *1163*
Southwestern Campbook (US ISSN 0731-8103) *1046, 1116*
Southwestern Camping *see* Southwestern Campbook *1116*
Southwestern Legal Foundation. Annual Report (US ISSN 0561-1784) *664, 671*
Southwestern Mission Research Center, Inc. Newsletter *see* S M R C Newsletter *609*
Southwestern Studies. Monographs (US ISSN 0081-315X) *609*
Souvenir Normand *see* Annuaire Souvenir Normand *1106*
Sovetskaya Arkhitektura *see* Zodchestvo *100*
Sovetskaya Literatura, Traditsii i Novatorstvo (UR) *733*
Sovetskaya Skul'ptura (UR) *110*
Sovetskie Ljudi Segodnja/Vie Quotidienne en U.R.S.S. Prise sur le Vif (FR ISSN 0303-111X) *733*
Soviet Armed Forces Review Annual (US) *812, 1063*
Soviet Christian Prisoner List *see* Christian Prisoners in the U.S.S.R *968*

SPAIN. DIRECCION 1887

Soviet, East European and Slavonic Studies in Western Europe *see* European Bibliography of Soviet, East European and Slavonic Studies *563*
Soviet-East European Survey (US) *918*
Soviet Foreign Policy *see* Soviet Foreign Policy Today *918*
Soviet Foreign Policy Today (US) *918*
Soviet Hydrology: Selected Papers (US ISSN 0038-5425) *404, 499, 1125*
Soviet Merchant Ships (UK) *1104*
Soviet Scientific Reviews. Section C: Mathematical Physics Reviews (US ISSN 0143-0416) *753, 891*
Soviet Scientific Reviews. Section D: Biological Reviews (UK ISSN 0143-0424) *147*
Soviet Scientific Reviews. Section E: Astrophysics & Space Physics Reviews (US ISSN 0143-0432) *117*
Soviet Seismological Research (US) *401*
Soviet Union and Eastern Europe *see* World Today Series: Soviet Union and Eastern Europe *602*
Sovietica. Monographs *see* Sovietica. Publications and Monographs *597*
Sovietica. Publication *see* Sovietica. Publications and Monographs *597*
Sovietica. Publications and Monographs(NE) *597, 881*
Soya Bluebook (US ISSN 0275-4509) *60*
Soyabean Abstracts (UK ISSN 0141-0172) *12, 43*
Soybean Digest Blue Book *see* Soya Bluebook *60*
Sozial- und Wirtschaftshistorische Studien (AU) *252, 1011*
Sozialisation und Kommunikation (GW ISSN 0340-9201) *1029*
Sozialistisches Musikschaffen der Deutschen Demokratischen Republik *see* Zeitgenoessisches Musikschaffen in der Deutschen Demokratischen Republik. Urauffuehrungen *843*
Sozialmedizinische und Paedagogische Jugendkunde (SZ ISSN 0076-6186) *766, 886*
Sozialversicherungsrechtliche Entscheidungen (AU) *664*
Soziologische Forschung in der D.D.R. Informationen (GE ISSN 0020-0395) *1029*
Soziologische Gegenwartsfragen. Neue Folge (GW ISSN 0081-3265) *1029*
Soziooekonomische Forschungen (SZ) *1011*
Spa & Sauna Buyers Guide (US) *369, 886*
Spa Data and Reference Annual (US) *187, 1035*
Space Activity in Norway *see* Space Research in Norway *21*
Space Benefits: Secondary Application of Aerospace Technology in Other Sectors of the Economy (US) *21*
Space Biology and Aerospace Medicine *see* U S S R Report: Space Biology and Aerospace Medicine *767*
Space in Japan (JA) *21*
Space Research in Norway (NO) *21*
Spain. Consejo Superior de Investigaciones Cientificas. Instituto de Farmacologia Experimental. Archivos *see* Archivas de Farmacologia y Toxicologia *869*
Spain. Direccion General de Bellas Artes. Semana de Musica en la Navidad (SP) *841*
Spain. Direccion General de la Produccion Agraria. Campana Algodonera (SP) *60*
Spain. Direccion General de Pesca Maritima. Anuario de Pesca Maritima (SP) *514*
Spain. Direccion General de Pesca Maritima. Estadistica de Pesca *see* Spain. Direccion General de Pesca Maritima. Anuario de Pesca Maritima *514*
Spain. Direccion General de Pesca Maritima. Flota Pesquera Espanola *see* Spain. Direccion General de Pesca Maritima. Anuario de Pesca Maritima *514*

Spain. Direccion General de Pesca Maritima. Publicaciones Tecnicas (SP) *513*
Spain. Direccion General de Trafico. Anuario Estadistico de Accidentes. Boletin Informativo (SP ISSN 0085-655X) *1087*
Spain. Direccion General de Trafico. Anuario Estadistico General. (SP ISSN 0304-9191) *1087*
Spain. Instituto de Credito Oficial. Memoria del Credito Oficial (SP ISSN 0081-3451) *299*
Spain. Instituto Geologico y Minero. Catalogo de Ediciones (SP) 12, *382*
Spain. Instituto Geologico y Minero. Colleccion Memorias (SP) *820*
Spain. Instituto Geologico y Minero. Informes (SP) *395*
Spain. Instituto Nacional de Estadistica. Estadistica Espanola (SP ISSN 0014-1151) *1063*
Spain. Instituto Nacional de Estadistica. Estadistica Industrial (SP ISSN 0081-3354) *217*
Spain. Instituto Nacional de Estadistica. Industrias Derivadas de la Pesca (SP ISSN 0081-3362) *513*
Spain. Instituto Nacional de Estadistica. Informe sobre la Distribucion de las Rentas *see* Spain. Instituto Nacional de Estadistica. La Renta Nacional en (Year) y Su Distribution *966*
Spain. Instituto Nacional de Estadistica. La Renta Nacional en (Year) y Su Distribution (SP) *966*
Spain. Instituto Nacional de Industria. Informe Anual (SP) *199*
Spain. Instituto Nacional de Industria. Memoria I N I (Year) *see* Spain. Instituto Nacional de Industria. Informe Anual *199*
Spain. Instituto Nacional de Industria. Programa de Investigaciones Economicas: Serie E (SP) *199*
Spain. Instituto Nacional de Investigaciones Agrarias. Anales. Serie: Agricola (SP ISSN 0211-4682) *1163*
Spain. Instituto Nacional de Investigaciones Agrarias. Anales. Serie: Forestal (SP ISSN 0211-9102) *1163*
Spain. Instituto Nacional de Investigaciones Agrarias. Anales. Serie: Ganadera (SP ISSN 0211-4674) *1163*
Spain. Instituto Nacional de Investigaciones Agrarias. Anales. Serie: Economia y Sociologia Agraria (SP ISSN 0373-5796) *49, 1029*
Spain. Instituto Nacional de Investigaciones Agrarias. Anales. Serie: Higiene y Sanidad Animal *see* Spain. Instituto Nacional de Investigaciones Agrarias. Anales. Serie: Ganadera *1163*
Spain. Instituto Nacional de Investigaciones Agrarias. Anales. Serie: Produccion Vegetal *see* Spain. Instituto Nacional de Investigaciones Agrarias. Anales. Serie: Agricola *1163*
Spain. Instituto Nacional de Investigaciones Agrarias. Anales. Serie: Recursos Naturales *see* Spain. Instituto Nacional de Investigaciones Agrarias. Anales. Serie: Forestal *1163*
Spain. Instituto Nacional de Investigaciones Agrarias. Anales. Serie: Technologia (SP) *1163*
Spain. Instituto Nacional de Investigaciones Agrarias. Comunicaciones. Serie: Economia y Sociologia Agrarias (SP ISSN 0210-332X) *49*
Spain. Instituto Nacional de Investigaciones Agrarias. Comunicaciones. Serie: General (SP ISSN 0210-3311) *34, 161*
Spain. Instituto Nacional de Investigaciones Agrarias. Comunicaciones. Serie: Higiene y Sanidad (SP ISSN 0211-1314) *68, 1122*

Spain. Instituto Nacional de Investigaciones Agrarias. Comunicaciones. Serie: Produccion Animal (SP ISSN 0210-3303) *68*
Spain. Instituto Nacional de Investigaciones Agrarias. Comunicaciones. Serie: Produccion Vegetal (SP ISSN 0210-329X) *34*
Spain. Instituto Nacional de Investigaciones Agrarias. Comunicaciones. Serie: Proteccion Vegetal (SP ISSN 0302-8755) *34*
Spain. Instituto Nacional de Investigaciones Agrarias. Comunicaciones. Serie: Recursos Naturales (SP ISSN 0210-3338) *499, 527*
Spain. Instituto Nacional de Investigaciones Agrarias. Comunicaciones. Serie: Tecnologia Agraria (SP ISSN 0210-2560) *34*
Spain. Instituto Nacional de Investigaciones Agrarias. Investigacion Agraria: Economia (SP ISSN 0213-635X) *49*
Spain. Instituto Nacional de Investigaciones Agrarias. Investigacion Agraria: Produccion y Proteccion Vegetales (SP) *34*
Spain. Instituto Nacional de Investigaciones Agrarias. Investigacion Agraria: Produccion y Sanidad Animales (SP) *68*
Spain. Instituto Nacional de Investigaciones Agronomica, Anales *see* Spain. Instituto Nacional de Investigaciones Agrarias. Anales. Serie: Economia y Sociologia Agrarias *49*
Spain. Instituto Nacional de Investigaciones Agronomicas. Anales *see* Spain. Instituto Nacional de Investigaciones Agrarias. Anales. Serie: Agricola *1163*
Spain. Instituto Nacional para la Conservacion de la Naturaleza. Monografias (SP) *499*
Spain. Ministerio de Agricultura, Pesca y Alimentacion. Informacion Extranjero. Boletin (SP ISSN 0213-0602) *34*
Spain. Ministerio de Agricultura. Secretaria General Tecnica. Anuario de Estadistica Agraria (SP) *43*
Spain. Ministerio de Agricultura. Secretaria General Tecnica. Cuentas del Sector Agrario (SP) *43*
Spain. Ministerio de Comercio y Turismo. Estadisticas de Turismo (SP) *1116*
Spain. Ministerio de Economia y Hacienda. Delegacion del Gobierno en Campsa. Memoria (SP) *867*
Spain. Ministerio de Economia y Hacienda. Direccion General de Seguros. Balances y Cuentas (SP) *299*
Spain. Ministerio de Educacion y Ciencia. Guia *see* Spain. Ministerio de Educacion. Guia *419*
Spain. Ministerio de Educacion y Ciencia. Junta Nacional Contra el Analfabetismo. Boletin (SP ISSN 0561-4619) *1163*
Spain. Ministerio de Hacienda. Informacion Estadistica (SP ISSN 0081-3435) *217*
Spain. Ministerio de Hacienda. Memoria *see* Spain. Ministerio de Economia y Hacienda. Direccion General de Seguros. Balances y Cuentas *299*
Spain. Ministerio de Hacienda. Subdireccion General de Organizacion e Informacion. Estadistica de la Informacion al Publico (SP) *946*
Spain. Ministerio de Industria. Resultados de la Encuesta de Coyuntura Industrial: Sector Industrial (SP) *292*
Spain. Ministerio de Informacion y Turismo. Estadisticas de Turismo *see* Spain. Ministerio de Comercio y Turismo. Estadisticas de Turismo *1116*

Spain. Ministerio de la Vivienda. Estadistica de la Industria de la Construccion (SP ISSN 0561-4902) *189*
Spain. Ministerio de la Vivienda. Serie 3: Vivienda (SP) *946*
Spain. Ministero de Educacion. Guia (SP) *419*
Spain. Secretaria General de Turismo. Anuario de Estadisticas de Turismo (SP) *1116*
Spain. Servicio Central de Publicaciones de la Presidencia del Gobierno. Coleccion Informe *see* Spain. Servicio Central de Publicaciones del Ministerio de Relaciones con las Cortes y de la Secretaria de Estado *946*
Spain. Servicio Central de Publicaciones del Ministerio de Relaciones con las Cortes y de la Secretaria de Estado (SP) *946*
Spanische Forschungen der Goerresgesellschaft. Reihe 1: Gesammelte Aufsaetze zur Kulturgeschichte Spaniens (GW ISSN 0342-1058) *597*
Spanische Forschungen der Goerresgesellschaft. Reihe 2: Monographien (GW ISSN 0081-3494) *597*
Spanish-American Genealogist (US) *537*
Spanish Genealogical Helper *see* Spanish-American Genealogist *537*
Spanish, Lusitanian, American Trade Directory *see* S L A M: Trade Year Book of Africa *1162*
Spanish Studies (UK) *704, 733*
Spanish Texts (UK) *704*
Spanker *see* Der Shmaiser *712*
Spanner (London) (UK) *1163*
Spanner (London, 1974) (UK ISSN 0584-8067) *110, 712*
Spartacist (US ISSN 0038-6596) *909*
Spartacus International Gay Guide (NE) *616, 914, 1116*
SPEAHRhead *see* China Rights Annals *903*
Speak (AT) *367, 1029*
Spec-Data Manu-Spec Index *see* Spec-Data Manu-Spec Program Index *187*
Spec-Data Manu-Spec Program Index (US) *187*
Spec-Data Manu-Spec System Index *see* Spec-Data Manu-Spec Program Index *187*
Special Analysis: Budget of the United States Government *see* U.S. Office of Management and Budget. Special Analysis: Budget of the United States Government *300*
Special Education Programs-Services *see* Pennsylvania. Department of Education. Special Education Programs-Services *1160*
Special Libraries Association Triennial Salary Survey *see* S L A Triennial Salary Survey *683*
Special Papers in International Economics (US ISSN 0081-3559) *199, 232*
Special Report on Financial and Economic Data for the Men's and Boy's Clothing Industry *see* Special Statistical Report on Production Sales and Profit Trends for the Men's & Boy's Clothing Industry *340*
Special Schools Bulletin *see* Developing Education *444*
Special Statistical Report on Production Sales and Profit Trends for the Men's & Boy's Clothing Industry (US) *340*
Special Subject Resources in Maine *see* Maine. State Library. Special Subject Resources in Maine *681*
Special Topics in Endocrinology and Metabolism (US ISSN 0193-0982) *1163*
Specialarbejderkurser (DK ISSN 0107-4733) *427*
Specialarbejderkurser paa Specialarbejderskolerne *see* Specialarbejderkurser *427*
Specialized Study Options U.S.A (US) *431*
Specialized Transportation Services, Services Guide (US) *1083*

Specialty Advertising Report *see* Ideasworth *15*
SpecialWare Directory (US) *363, 428*
Specifications of Mineral Concessions and Licenses in Greenland (DK ISSN 0107-430X) *820*
Specifications of Mineral Licenses and Concessions in Greenland *see* Specifications of Mineral Concessions and Licenses in Greenland *820*
Specifier's Guide to Contract Floor Coverings (US) *644*
Specifile Building Compendium (SA) *187*
Specimina Philologiae Slavicae (GW ISSN 0170-1320) *704, 733*
Spectra Index and S.D.C. Bulletin *see* S.D.C. Bulletin *893*
Spectra of Anthropological Progress (II) *76*
Spectroscopic Properties of Inorganic & Organometallic Compounds (UK ISSN 0584-8555) *324, 899*
Spectrum (US ISSN 0883-282X) *540, 646, 684*
Spectrum (St. Paul) (US) *609, 924*
Specula (GW) *881*
Speculum Anniversary Monographs (US) *110, 597, 733*
Speculum Artium (IT) *733*
Speculum Juris (SA ISSN 0584-8652) *664*
Speech and Language: Advances in Basic Research and Practice (US ISSN 0193-3434) *766*
Speech Communication Association Free Speech Yearbook *see* S C A Free Speech Yearbook *909*
Speech Communication Directory (US ISSN 0190-2075) *438, 445*
Speech Communication Directory of S C A and the Regional Speech Communication Organizations *see* Speech Communication Directory *438*
Speech Index (US ISSN 0081-3656) *12, 709*
Spektrum des Geistes (GW) *733*
Speleological Abstracts/Bulletin Bibliographique Speleologique (SZ ISSN 0253-8296) *12, 382*
Speleological Society of Japan. Journal (JA) *381, 548, 857*
Spencer Museum of Art. Register (US) *110*
Spenser Studies (US ISSN 0195-9468) *733*
Speur- en Ontwikkelingswerk in Nederland/Research and Development Activities in the Netherlands (NE ISSN 0168-468X) *1071*
Speyer. Dioezese. Direktorium Spirense-Offizium und Messfeier (GW) *983*
Spezial (GE ISSN 0081-3672) *340*
Spezialbibliographien zu Fragen des Staates und des Rechts (GE ISSN 0081-3680) *669*
Spezielle Pathologische Anatomie (US ISSN 0081-3699) *147, 766*
Spicae (FR) *704*
Spiegel Deutscher Buchkunst *see* Die Schoensten Buecher der Deutschen Demokratischen Republik *963*
Spiegel Lectures in European Jewish History (IS) *505, 597*
Spielfilmliste (GW ISSN 0071-4933) *825*
Spildevandsteknisk Tidsskrift (DK ISSN 0108-0466) *1125*
Spindrift (UK ISSN 0260-4531) *744*
Spinoff (US ISSN 0148-2203) *1071*
Spiral (NZ ISSN 0110-1145) *733, 744, 1129*
Spirit Wings (US) *744, 973*
Spiritual Community Guide (US ISSN 0160-0354) *984*
Spiritualita Cristiana (IT) *973*
Spirituosen-Jahrbuch (GW ISSN 0081-3729) *120*
Spixiana Journal of Zoology (GW ISSN 0341-8391) *177*
Spoletium (IT ISSN 0490-4788) *632*
Spolia Zeylanica/Bulletin of the National Museums of Sri Lanka (CE ISSN 0081-3745) *1000*

Spon's Architects' & Builders' Price Book (UK ISSN 0306-3046) 99, *187*
Spon's Civil Engineering Price Book (UK ISSN 0265-1025) *483*
Spon's Landscape & External Works Pricebook (UK) *187*
Spon's Landscape Handbook *see* Spon's Landscape & External Works Pricebook *187*
Spon's Landscape Pricebook *see* Spon's Landscape & External Works Pricebook *187*
Spon's Mechanical & Electrical Services Price Book (UK ISSN 0305-4543) *459*
Spon's Plant and Equipment Guide *see* Spon's Plant and Equipment Price Guide *746*
Spon's Plant and Equipment Price Guide (UK ISSN 0263-5038) *746*
Sponsored Research in the History of Art (US) *110*
Sponsors' Handbook for The 80's/ Guide du Commandaitare pour les Annees 80 (CN) *1078*
Sponsors' Handbook for Touring Attractions *see* Sponsors' Handbook for The 80's *1078*
Spore Research (UK ISSN 0306-2074) *1163*
Sport (DK ISSN 0109-2146) *1035*
Sport Fishery Abstracts (US ISSN 0038-786X) 12, *514*, 1036
Sport Fishery and Wildlife Research *see* Fisheries and Wildlife Research *1045*
Sport paa Bornholm (DK ISSN 0109-159X) *1035*
Sportaccommodatie in Nederland/ Sports: Public Accommodation (NE ISSN 0077-6777) *1035*
Sportfiskaren (SW) 513, *1046*
Sporting Chronicle "Horses in Training" *see* Raceform "Horses in Training" *1043*
Sporting Goods Market (US) 217, *1037*
Sporting News Baseball Yearbook (US ISSN 0275-0732) *1040*
Sporting News National Basketball Association Register *see* Sporting News Official N B A Register *1040*
Sporting News' National Football Guide *see* Sporting News Pro Football Guide *1040*
Sporting News Official Baseball Record Book *see* Complete Baseball Record Book *1038*
Sporting News Official N B A Register (US ISSN 0739-3067) *1040*
Sporting News Pro-College Basketball Yearbook (US ISSN 0733-6047) *1040*
Sporting News Pro Football Guide (US ISSN 0732-1902) *1040*
Sporting News Pro Football Yearbook (US ISSN 0276-2307) *1040*
Sporting News Super Bowl Book (US ISSN 0275-4487) *1040*
Sportmedizinische Schriftenreihe (GE ISSN 0075-8655) *793*
Sports Afield Bass (US ISSN 0742-0609) *1046*
Sports Afield Deer (US ISSN 0160-1830) *1046*
Sports Afield Fishing (US) *1046*
Sports Afield Fishing Annual *see* Sports Afield Fishing *1046*
Sports Afield Fishing Secrets (US ISSN 0742-0595) *1046*
Sports Afield Hunting Annual (US ISSN 0276-8895) *1046*
Sports and Recreational Programs of the Nation's Universities and Colleges (US) *1035*
Sports Documentation Centre. List of Periodical and Abstracting and Indexing Journal Holdings *see* Sports Documentation Centre. Serial *425*
Sports Documentation Centre. Serial (UK) 12, *425*, 1037
Sports, Games, and Pastimes Information Guide Series (US) *1037*
Sports Market Place (US) *1035*
Sports Periodicals Index (US ISSN 0883-1580) 12, *1037*

Sports: Public Accommodation *see* Sportaccommodatie in Nederland *1035*
Sports Quarterly - Football Pros (US) *1040*
Sports Trader Buyer's Guide (UK) 240, *285*, 1035
Sports Turf Research Institute. Journal (UK ISSN 0561-6832) 60, 499
Sportsguide *see* Sports Market Place *1035*
Sportsmans Book of U.S. Records (US ISSN 0270-3513) *1046*
Sportsworld (KE) *1035*
Sportwetenschappelijke Onderzoekingen(NE) *1035*
Sportwissenschaft und Sportpraxis (GW ISSN 0342-457X) *1035*
Sportwissenschaftliche Dissertationen (GW ISSN 0340-0956) *1035*
Sporvejsmuseet Skjoldenaesholm. Aarsberetning (DK ISSN 0106-6927) 830, *1095*
Spotkania (PL) *841*
Spotlight (BF) *419*
Spotlight on Africa (US ISSN 0584-9365) *909*
Sprache und Dichtung. Neue Folge (SZ ISSN 0081-3826) *704*
Sprache und Geschichte in Afrika (GW ISSN 0170-5946) *704*
Sprache und Gesellschaft (GE ISSN 0138-5852) *704*
Sprawozdania Archeologiczne (PL ISSN 0081-3834) *93*
Sprenger Instituut. Communications (NE) 60, *520*
Sprenger Instituut. Jaarverslag/Annual Report (NE ISSN 0081-3850) 60, *520*
Sprenger Instituut. Rapporten (NE) *520*
Spring (Dallas) (US ISSN 0362-0522) *937*
Spring Rain (US) *744*
Springer Advanced Texts in Chemistry (US ISSN 0172-6323) *324*
Springer Advanced Texts in Life Sciences (US ISSN 0172-6226) *147*
Springer Books on Professional Computing (US) 131, *353*
Springer Proceedings in Physics (US) *891*
Springer Series in Biophysics (US) *153*
Springer Series in Chemical Physics (US ISSN 0172-6218) 324, *891*
Springer Series in Cognitive Development (US) *937*
Springer Series in Computational Mathematics (US) *753*
Springer Series in Computational Physics (US ISSN 0172-5726) *891*
Springer Series in Electrophysics (US ISSN 0172-5734) *460*, 891
Springer Series in Experimental Entomology (US ISSN 0172-6188) *166*
Springer Series in Information Sciences (US ISSN 0720-678X) *684*
Springer Series in Language and Communication (US ISSN 0172-620X) *704*
Springer Series in Materials Sciences (US) *891*
Springer Series in Microbiology (US ISSN 0172-6331) *169*
Springer Series in Molecular Biology (US) *147*
Springer Series in Optical Sciences (US ISSN 0342-4111) *899*
Springer Series in Social Psychology (US) *937*
Springer Series in Solid State Sciences (US ISSN 0171-1873) *1000*
Springer Series in Soviet Mathematics (US) *753*
Springer Series in Statistics (US ISSN 0172-7397) *1063*
Springer Series in Surface Sciences (US) *891*
Springer Series in Synergetics (US ISSN 0172-7389) *1000*
Springer Series in Wood Science (US) *527*
Springer Series on Environmental Management (US ISSN 0172-6161) *499*
Springer Series on Social Work (US) *1021*

Springer Texts in Electrical Engineering(US) *460*
Springer Tracts in Modern Physics (US ISSN 0081-3869) *891*
Springer Tracts in Natural Philosophy (US ISSN 0081-3877) *1001*
Sprinkler Bulletin (UK ISSN 0038-8637) *641*
Sprinkler Irrigation Association. Technical Conference Proceedings *see* Irrigation Association. Technical Conference Proceedings *57*
Sprocket (AT) *825*
Sprogforeningens Almanak (DK) *704*
Sputnik Sel'skoi Molodezhi (UR) *336*
Squash Rackets Association. Annual (UK) *1040*
Squash Rackets Association. Handbook *see* Squash Rackets Association. Annual *1040*
Squatchberry Journal (CN ISSN 0383-283X) *733*
Squills International Pigeon Racing Year Book (UK) *1035*
Squires Companion *see* Martindale: the Extra Pharmacopoeia *871*
Sri Aurobindo. Archives and Research (II) *977*
Sri Lanka. Census of Population and Housing (CE) *627*
Sri Lanka. Irrigation Department. Hydrology Division. Hydrological Annual (CE) *404*
Sri Lanka. Ministry of Planning and Economic Affairs. Division of External Resources. Economic Indicators (CE) *249*
Sri Lanka Association for the Advancement of Science. Proceedings (CE) *1001*
Sri Lanka Export Directory (CE ISSN 0069-2360) *259*
Sri Lanka Film Annual (CE) *825*
Sri Lanka Foundation Institute. News (CE) *427*
Sri Lanka in Brief (CE) *237*
Sri Lanka Institute of Architects. Journal (CE) *99*
Sri Lanka Periodicals Index (CE) *12*
Sri Lanka Science Index (CE) 12, *1004*
Sri Lanka Yearbook (CE) *218*
Sri Venkateswara University. Department of Sanskrit. Symposium (II ISSN 0081-3915) *704*
Sri Venkateswara University. Oriental Journal (II ISSN 0081-3907) *571*, 704
Srpska Akademija Nauka i Umetnosti. Etnografski Institut. Glasnik (YU) *76*
Srpska Akademija Nauka i Umetnosti. Etnografski Institut. Zbornik Radova (YU) *76*
Srpska Akademija Nauka i Umetnosti. Odeljenje Drustvenih Nauka. Glas (YU ISSN 0081-394X) *1011*
Srpska Akademija Nauka i Umetnosti. Odeljenje Drustvenih Nauka. Posebna Izdanja (YU ISSN 0081-3982) *1012*
Srpska Akademija Nauka i Umetnosti. Odeljenje Drustvenih Nauka. Spomenik (YU ISSN 0081-4059) 93, 99, *1012*
Srpska Akademija Nauka i Umetnosti. Odeljenje Jezika i Knjizevnosti. Glas (YU ISSN 0081-3958) *704*
Srpska Akademija Nauka i Umetnosti. Odeljenje Jezika i Knjizevnosti. Posebna Izdanja (YU ISSN 0081-3990) 704, *733*
Srpska Akademija Nauka i Umetnosti. Odeljenje Likovne i Muzicke Umetnosti. Muzicka Izdanja (YU ISSN 0490-6659) *841*
Srpska Akademija Nauka i Umetnosti. Odeljenje Likovne i Muzicke Umetnosti. Posebna Izdanja (YU ISSN 0081-4008) 110, *841*
Srpska Akademija Nauka i Umetnosti. Odeljenje Medicinskih Nauka. Glas (YU ISSN 0081-3966) *767*
Srpska Akademija Nauka i Umetnosti. Odeljenje Medicinskih Nauka. Posebna Izdanja (YU ISSN 0081-4016) *767*

Srpska Akademija Nauka i Umetnosti. Odeljenje Prirodno-Matematickih Nauka. Posebna Izdanja (YU ISSN 0081-4024) *1001*
Srpska Akademija Nauka i Umetnosti. Odeljenje Tehnickih Nauka. Glas (YU ISSN 0081-3974) *1071*
Srpska Akademija Nauka i Umetnosti. Odeljenje Tehnickih Nauka. Posebna Izdanja (YU ISSN 0081-4040) *1071*
Srpska Akademija Nauka i Umetnosti. Povremena Izdanja (YU) *1001*
Srpska Akademija Nauka i Umetnosti Spomenica (YU ISSN 0081-4032) *632*, 1001, 1012
Srpski Etnografski Zbornik. Naselja i Poreklo Stanovnistva (YU ISSN 0081-4067) *76*, 597
Srpski Etnografski Zbornik. Rasprave i Gradja (YU ISSN 0081-4075) *76*, 597
Srpski Etnografski Zbornik. Srpske Narodne Umotvorine (YU ISSN 0081-4083) *76*, 597
Srpski Etnografski Zbornik. Zivot i Obicaji Narodni (YU ISSN 0081-4091) *76*, 597
SSCI-J C R *see* Social Sciences Citation Index Journal Citation Reports *1014*
Staat und Politik (SZ ISSN 0081-4105) *909*
Staatliche Kunsthalle Karlsruhe. Bildhefte (GW ISSN 0075-5133) *830*
Staatliche Kunsthalle Karlsruhe. Graphik-Schriftenreihe (GW ISSN 0075-5141) *830*
Staatliche Kunstsammlungen in Baden-Wuerttemberg. Jahrbuch (GW ISSN 0067-284X) *830*
Staatliche Mathematisch-Physikalische Salons, Dresden. Veroeffentlichungen(GE ISSN 0081-4113) *753*, 891
Staatliche Museen zu Berlin. Jahrbuch. Forschungen und Berichte (GE ISSN 0067-6004) *110*, 830
Staatliches Museum fuer Tierkunde in Dresden. Entomologische Abhandlungen (GE ISSN 0373-8981) *166*
Staatliches Museum fuer Tierkunde in Dresden. Faunistische Abhandlungen(GE ISSN 0375-2135) *177*
Staatliches Museum fuer Tierkunde in Dresden. Malakologische Abhandlungen (GE ISSN 0070-7260) *177*
Staatliches Museum fuer Tierkunde in Dresden. Zoologische Abhandlungen (GE ISSN 0070-7287) *178*
Staatliches Museum fuer Voelkerkunde Dresden. Abhandlungen und Berichte(GE ISSN 0070-7295) *76*, 830
Staatliches Museum fuer Voelkerkunde und Tierkunde. Abhandlungen und Berichte *see* Staatliches Museum fuer Voelkerkunde Dresden. Abhandlungen und Berichte *830*
Staats- und Rechtstheoretische Studien (GE ISSN 0138-5208) *664*
Staatsbedrijf der Posterijen Telegrafie en Telefonie Bedrijf *see* P T T Bedrijf *350*
Staatsbibliothek Preussischer Kulturbesitz. Ausstellungskataloge (GW ISSN 0340-0700) *684*
Staatsbibliothek Preussischer Kulturbesitz. Jahresbericht (GW ISSN 0340-2274) *684*
Stadion (GW) *449*, 1036
Stadler Genetics Symposium. Proceedings (US ISSN 0081-4148) *167*
Die Stadt (GW) *626*
Stadt Remscheid Statistisches Jahrbuch (GW) *1063*
Stadtansichten (GW ISSN 0720-0218) *744*
Stadtarchiv Krems. Mitteilungen (AU) *597*
Stadtbibliothek Nuernberg. Ausstellungskatalog (GW ISSN 0078-2777) *830*
Stadtfuher Kopenhagen (DK) *1116*
Staedel Jahrbuch (GW) *110*
Stafford Data (US) *537*

Staffrider Magazine (SA ISSN 0258-7211) 110, *733*
Stage (ZA) *1078*
Stage Managers' Association Directory *see* Stage Managers Directory *1078*
Stage Managers Directory (US) 317, *1078*
Stagecast-Irish Stage and Screen Directory (IE) 825, *1078*
Stahleisen Kalender *see* Jahrbuch Stahl *798*
Stainless Steel: An International Directory *see* Stainless Steel: An International Survey and Directory *800*
Stainless Steel: An International Survey and Directory (UK) *800*
Stainless Steel Directory (UK) *800*
Stallion Review (UK) *1043*
Stambog (DK ISSN 0107-3818) *1043*
Stambog og Elitestambog over Tyre af Roed Dansk Malkerace *see* Stambog over Kvaeg af Roed Dansk Malkerace *68*
Stambog over Koeer af Roed Dansk Malkerace (DK ISSN 0108-0903) *68*
Stambog over Kvaeg af Roed Dansk Malkerace (DK ISSN 0105-0281) *68*
Stambog over Shetland Ponyer (DK ISSN 0900-5846) *1043*
Stamford Annual Planning Information *see* Annual Planning Information Bridgeport-Norwalk-Stamford-Valley Service Delivery Area *269*
Stamm Leitfaden Durch Presse und Werbung/Annual Directory through Press and Advertising (GW ISSN 0075-8728) *131*
Stamp Exchangers Annual Directory (US) *875*
Stamps of the World (UK ISSN 0081-4210) *875*
Standard and Poor's Directory of Bond Agents (US) *268*
Standard & Poor's Dividend Record (Annual) (US) *232*
Standard Catalog for Public Libraries *see* Public Library Catalog *688*
Standard Directory of Advertisers (US ISSN 0081-4229) 16, 317
Standard Directory of International Advertisers and Advertising Agencies(US) 16, 317
Standard Education Almanac (US ISSN 0081-4237) *1163*
Standard Federal Tax Reports (US ISSN 0162-3494) *299*
Standard for Auditing Computer Applications (US ISSN 0741-336X) *234*
Standard Lesson Commentary (US ISSN 0081-4245) *973*
Standard Medical Almanac (US) *1163*
Standard Nomenclature of Athletic Injuries (US ISSN 0081-427X) *1163*
Standard Periodical Directory (US ISSN 0085-6630) *131*
Standard Specifications for Highway Bridges (US) *483*
Standard Specifications for Transportation Materials and Methods of Sampling and Testing (US) 489, *809*
Standard Trade Index of Japan (JA ISSN 0585-0444) *237*
Standardization of Cardioangiological Methods *see* Monographs on Standardization of Cardioangiological Methods *777*
Standards and Practices for Instrumentation. Instrument Society of America (US ISSN 0074-0527) *637*
Standards and Recommended Practices for Small Craft (US) *1042*
Standards Engineering Society. Proceedings of Annual Meeting (US ISSN 0081-430X) *489*
Standards for Australian Aluminium Mill Products (AT ISSN 0085-6657) *800*, *809*
Stanford Art Books (US) *830*
Stanford Environmental Law Annual *see* Stanford Environmental Law Journal *664*

Stanford Environmental Law Journal (US ISSN 0892-7138) 499, *664*
Stanford French & Italian Studies (US) *733*
Stanford Journal of International Law (US ISSN 0731-5082) *671*
Stanford Journal of International Studies *see* Stanford Journal of International Law *671*
Stanford Museum (US ISSN 0085-6665) *830*
Stanford University. Publications. Geological Sciences (US ISSN 0081-4350) *395*
Stanley and Kilcullen's Federal Income Tax Law (Supplement) *see* Federal Income Tax Law *295*
Stanley Foundation. Occasional Paper *see* Stanley Foundation. Policy Paper *918*
Stanley Foundation. Policy Paper (US ISSN 0145-8841) *918*
Stanley Gibbons Postcard Catalogue (UK ISSN 0144-249X) *875*
Stanstead County Historical Society. Journal (CN ISSN 0081-4369) *609*
Staples' Guide to New Zealand Income Tax Practice (NZ ISSN 0111-9370) *299*
Stapp Car Crash Conference Proceedings (US ISSN 0585-086X) *1093*
Star Almanac for Land Surveyors (UK ISSN 0081-4377) *548*
Star Service *see* S T A R Service *1116*
Stardance (UK) *744*
Starinar (YU ISSN 0350-0241) *93*
Het Staring Instituut. Werken (NE) *597*
Starmont Reader's Guides (US ISSN 0272-7730) *733*
Starmont Reference Guides (US ISSN 0738-0127) *733*
Starmont Studies in Literary Criticism (US ISSN 0737-1306) *733*
Starting and Managing Series (US ISSN 0081-4415) *301*
Starting Right in Your New Business (US) *268*
Stasinos (CY) *597*
Stastfoeretag. Aarsredovising *see* Procordia. Aarsredovisning *291*
Stat a Pravo (CS) 275, *664*, *909*
State Administrative Officials (Classified by Functions) (US ISSN 0561-8630) *946*
State and Economic Life Series (CN) *561*
State and National Registers of Historic Places (US) *1116*
State-Approved Schools of Nursing - L.P.N./L.V.N. (US ISSN 0081-4423) 431, *784*
State-Approved Schools of Nursing - R.N. (US ISSN 0081-4431) 431, *784*
State Bank of India. Annual Report (II) *232*
State Bank of India. Report of the Central Board of Directors *see* State Bank of India. Annual Report *232*
State Bank of Pakistan. Index Numbers of Stock Exchange Securities (PK ISSN 0081-4466) *268*
State Biological Survey of Kansas. Technical Bulletin (US) *161*, *166*, *178*
State Court Caseload Statistics (US) *372*
State Directory of Kentucky (US) *946*
State Domestic Product of Himachal Pradesh (II) *218*
State/E P A Agreements. Annual Report (US ISSN 0275-2271) *499*
State Education Journal Index (US ISSN 0039-0046) 12, *425*
State Elective Officials and the Legislatures (US) *946*
State Geologists Journal (US ISSN 0039-0089) *395*
State Government (US) 909, *946*
State Government Finances *see* Current Governments Reports: State Government Finances *206*
State Government Tax Collections *see* Current Governments Reports: State Government Tax Collections *294*
State Government Undertakings in Gujarat (II ISSN 0081-4504) *1163*

State Health Benefits Program of New Jersey. Annual Report (US ISSN 0099-2100) *641*
State Income of Himachal Pradesh *see* State Domestic Product of Himachal Pradesh *218*
State Information Book (US) *946*
State Institute of Education, Rajasthan. Annual Report (II) *419*
State Investment Portfolio. (Juneau) *see* Alaska. Department of Revenue. State Investment Portfolio *265*
State Laws and Published Ordinances, Firearms (US ISSN 0276-7651) *664*
State Legislative Leadership, Committees and Staff (US ISSN 0195-6639) *946*
State Legislative Report (US) *946*
State Municipal League Directory (US) *952*
State of Black America (US ISSN 0148-6985) *914*
State of Florida Comprehensive Manpower Plan (US ISSN 0095-6430) *275*
State of Florida Land Development Guide (US) *626*, *966*
State of Food and Agriculture (UN ISSN 0081-4539) *34*
State of Greek Industry in (Year) (GR ISSN 0072-7458) *292*
State of Hawaii Data Book (US ISSN 0073-1080) *249*
State of Human Rights in New York *see* New York (State). Division of Human Rights. Annual Report *913*
State of Michigan's Annual Highway Safety Plan. (US ISSN 0731-1966) *1097*
State of Montana Investment Program. Report on Audit *see* Montana. Office of the Legislative Auditor. State of Montana Board of Investments. Report on Examination of Financial Statements *267*
State of Nebraska Annual Fiscal Report *see* Nebraska. Department of Administrative Services. Annual Fiscal Report *944*
State of Nebraska Uniform Crime Report (US ISSN 0090-3221) *372*
State of Nevada Wage Report *see* Nevada Wage Survey *274*
State of New York's Environment *see* New York (State). Department of Environmental Conservation. Annual Report *366*
State of the Air Transport Industry *see* I A T A Annual Report *1088*
State of the Environment *see* State of the Environment (Year) *499*
State of the Environment (Year) (US) *499*
State of Virginia's Environment: Annual Report *see* State of Virginia's Environment: Biennial Report *499*
State of Virginia's Environment: Biennial Report (US) *499*
State Tax Collections *see* Current Governments Reports: State Government Tax Collections *294*
State Tax Handbook (US ISSN 0081-4598) *299*
State University of New York. College at Buffalo's Program in East European and Slavic Studies. Publications. (US) *597*
State University of New York at Albany. Institute for Mesoamerican Studies. Publication (US) *609*
State University of New York at Albany. School of Library and Information Science. Bulletin (US) *684*
State University of New York, College at Buffalo. Program in Soviet and East Central European Studies. Publications *see* State University of New York. College at Buffalo's Program in East European and Slavic Studies. Publications *597*
Stately Homes, Museums, Castles and Gardens *see* Stately Homes, Museums, Castles and Gardens in Britain *1116*
Stately Homes, Museums, Castles and Gardens in Britain (UK) *1116*

Statement of Secretary of Defense Before the House Armed Services Committee on the Defense Budget and Program *see* U.S. Department of Defense. Defense Department Report *947*
Statens Byggeforskningsinstitut Aarsberetning *see* S B I Aarsberetning *187*
Statens Filmcentral *see* Denmark. Statens Filmcentral. Information og Beretning *823*
Statens Geotekniska Institut. Meddelelser *see* Statens Geotekniska Institut. Rapport *401*
Statens Geotekniska Institut. Proceedings *see* Statens Geotekniska Institut. Rapport *401*
Statens Geotekniska Institut. Rapport/ Swedish Geotechnical Institute. Report (SW ISSN 0348-0755) *401*
Statens Geotekniska Institut. Saertryck och Preliminaera Rapporter *see* Statens Geotekniska Institut. Rapport *401*
Statens Husdyrbrugsforsoeg. Meddelelse(DK ISSN 0106-8857) *34*
Statens og Kommunernes Budgetter (DK ISSN 0106-2905) *299*
Statens Planteavlsforsoeg. Meddelelse (DK ISSN 0105-6514) *60*
Statens Tekniska Forskningscentral. Forskningsrapporter *see* Valtion Teknillinen Tutkimuskeskus. Tutkimuksia *1072*
Statens Tekniska Forskningscentral. Meddelanden *see* Valtion Teknillinen Tutkimuskeskus. Tiedotteita *1072*
Statens Vaeg- och Trafikinstitut Annual Report *see* V T I Annual Report *1098*
Statens Vejlaboratorium Leveringsbetingelser og Proevningsmetoder *see* S V Leveringsbetingelser og Proevningsmetoder *1097*
States and Small Business: Programs and Activities (US) *301*
States of Malaya Chamber of Mines. Council Report (MY ISSN 0302-6620) *820*
States of Malaya Chamber of Mines. Yearbook (MY) *820*
Statesman (NR) *909*
Statesman's Year Book (UK ISSN 0081-4601) *909*
Statewide Space Survey *see* Illinois. Board of Higher Education. Statewide Space Survey *436*
Station Biologique de Besse en Chandesse. Annales (FR) 150, 166, 169
Stationery Trade Reference Book and Buyers Guide (UK ISSN 0081-461X) *286*
Statistica degli Incidenti Stradali (IT ISSN 0075-188X) *959*, *1087*
Statistical Abstract of Brazil *see* Sinopse Estatistica do Brasil *217*
Statistical Abstract of Ceylon *see* Statistical Abstract of the Democratic Socialist Republic of Sri Lanka *1063*
Statistical Abstract of Hawaii *see* State of Hawaii Data Book *249*
Statistical Abstract of Higher Education in North Carolina (US ISSN 0081-4644) *438*
Statistical Abstract of Iceland (IC ISSN 0081-4652) *1063*
Statistical Abstract of Ireland (IE ISSN 0081-4660) *1063*
Statistical Abstract of Latin America (US ISSN 0081-4687) *564*
Statistical Abstract of Maharashtra State (II ISSN 0081-4709) *1063*
Statistical Abstract of Oklahoma (US ISSN 0191-0310) *1063*
Statistical Abstract of Rajasthan (II ISSN 0081-4717) *1063*
Statistical Abstract of the Democratic Socialist Republic of Sri Lanka (CE) *1063*
Statistical Abstract of the Government of the Cayman Islands (CJ) *1063*
Statistical Abstract of the Maltese Islands *see* Malta. Central Office of Statistics. Annual Abstract of Statistics *1059*

Statistical Abstract of the United States (US ISSN 0081-4741) *1063*
Statistical Analysis of New Zealand Wool Production and Disposal *see* New Zealand Wool Board. Statistical Handbook *1074*
Statistical and Social Inquiry Society of Ireland. Journal (IE ISSN 0081-4776) *1063*
Statistical Budget and Activities in Thailand (TH) *1063*
Statistical Bulletin for Latin America *see* Statistical Yearbook for Latin America *1064*
Statistical Compass *see* Germany (Federal Republic, 1949-) Statistisches Bundesamt. Zahlenkompass *1056*
Statistical Data on Commercial Banks in Thailand (TH) *218*
Statistical Data on Libraries in Bulgaria *see* Statisticeski Danni za Bibliotekite v Bulgaria *684*
Statistical Digest of Bangladesh *see* Statistical Yearbook of Bangladesh *1064*
Statistical Handbook of Egypt *see* Egypt. Central Agency for Public Mobilisation and Statistics. Statistical Yearbook *1054*
Statistical Handbook of Japan (JA ISSN 0081-4792) *1063*
Statistical Handbook of Tamil Nadu (II) *1063*
Statistical Handbook of Thailand (TH ISSN 0081-4822) *1063*
Statistical Handbook of the Republic of Ghana (GH) *1063*
Statistical Information Bulletin for Africa/Bulletin d'Information Statistique pour l'Afrique (UN) *218*
Statistical Information of Afghanistan/Ma'lumat-i Ihsa'ivi-i Afghanistan (AF) *1063*
Statistical Institute of Jamaica. Demographic Statistics (JM) *929, 1063*
Statistical Institute of Jamaica. External Trade Annual Review (JM) *218*
Statistical Institute of Jamaica. Monetary Statistics Report (JM) *218, 1063*
Statistical Institute of Jamaica. National Income and Product (JM) *218, 1063*
Statistical Institute of Jamaica. Pocketbook of Statistics (JM) *1063*
Statistical Institute of Jamaica. Statistical Abstract (JM) *1064*
Statistical Meteorological Conference. Proceedings *see* Conference on Probability and Statistics in Atmospheric Sciences. Preprints *804*
Statistical Methods in Linguistics *see* Linguistic Calculation *698*
Statistical Notes of Japan (JA ISSN 0561-922X) *1064*
Statistical Office of the European Communities. Associes Statistique du Commerce Exterieur. Annuaire (EI ISSN 0081-4857) *1163*
Statistical Office of the European Communities. Aussenhandel: Analitische Ubersichten. Foreign Trade: Analytical Tables (EI ISSN 0586-4925) *218*
Statistical Office of the European Communities. Basic Statistics (EI ISSN 0081-4873) *218*
Statistical Office of the European Communities. Commerce Exterieur: Nomenclature des Pays (EI) *259*
Statistical Office of the European Communities. Commerce Exterieur: Products C E C A (EI ISSN 0081-4881) *218*
Statistical Office of the European Communities. Comparison in Real Terms of E S A Aggregates (EI) *199, 249*
Statistical Office of the European Communities. Energy Statistics. Yearbook (EI ISSN 0081-489X) *469*
Statistical Office of the European Communities. Foreign Trade: Standard Country Classification (EI ISSN 0081-4903) *218*

Statistical Office of the European Communities. Gas Prices (EI) *249, 467, 1064*
Statistical Office of the European Communities. Industrial Statistics. Short Term Trends (EI) *1163*
Statistical Office of the European Communities. Iron and Steel. Yearbook (EI) *802, 1064*
Statistical Office of the European Communities. National Accounts. Yearbook (EI ISSN 0081-4911) *218*
Statistical Office of the European Communities. Overseas Associates. Annuaire Statistiques des Etats Africains et Malgache (EI ISSN 0081-492X) *1163*
Statistical Office of the European Communities. Recettes Fiscales. Annuaire (EI ISSN 0081-4938) *1163*
Statistical Office of the European Communities. Siderurgie Annuaire (EI ISSN 0081-4954) *802*
Statistical Office of the European Communities. Statistique Agricole (EI ISSN 0081-4946) *43*
Statistical Office of the European Communities. Statistiques des Transports. Annuaire (EI ISSN 0081-4962) *1083*
Statistical Office of the European Communities. Statistiques Industrielles Annuaire (EI ISSN 0081-4970) *218*
Statistical Office of the European Communities. Statistiques Sociales. Annuaire (EI ISSN 0081-4989) *1163*
Statistical Office of the European Communities. Yearbook of Regional Statistics (EI ISSN 0081-4997) *218*
Statistical Pocket Book: India (II ISSN 0081-5012) *1064*
Statistical Pocket-Book of Afghanistan (AF) *1064*
Statistical Pocket Book of Bangladesh *see* Statistical Pocketbook of Bangladesh *1064*
Statistical Pocket Book of Hungary *see* Magyar Statisztikai Zsebkonyv *1059*
Statistical Pocket Book of Sri Lanka *see* Statistical Pocket Book of the Democratic Socialist Republic of Sri Lanka *1064*
Statistical Pocket Book of the Democratic Socialist Republic of Sri Lanka (CE) *1064*
Statistical Pocket Book of the Indian Union *see* Statistical Pocket Book: India *1064*
Statistical Pocket Book of Turkey/Turkiye Istatistik Cep Yilligi (TU) *1064*
Statistical Pocketbook of Bangladesh (BG) *1064*
Statistical Pocketbook of Indonesia/Buku Saku Statistik Indonesia (IO ISSN 0126-3595) *1064*
Statistical Profile of Iowa (US) *1064*
Statistical Profile of the Soft Drink Industry (US) *120*
Statistical Record (UK) *1037*
Statistical Reference Index (US ISSN 0278-694X) *1064*
Statistical Report - Georgia Department of Education *see* Georgia. Department of Education. Statistical Report *424*
Statistical Report of Hospitals (Tallahassee) *see* Florida. Mental Health Program Office. Statistical Report of Hospitals *619*
Statistical Report on Tourism in Fiji *see* Tourism and Migration Statistics *1120*
Statistical Report Series (Cheyenne) *see* Wyoming. Division of Planning, Evaluation and Information Services. Statistical Report Series *1066*
Statistical Reports of Changwat (TH) *419, 548, 924, 1083*
Statistical Reports of the Nordic Countries *see* Nordisk Statistisk Skriftserie *1060*
Statistical Review of Arizona *see* Arizona Statistical Review *203*

Statistical Review of Coal in Canada (CN) *820*
Statistical Review of Government in Utah (US) *949, 1064*
Statistical Review of the World Oil Industry *see* B P Statistical Review of World Energy *863*
Statistical Review of Tourism in Hong Kong (HK) *1120*
Statistical Services Directory (US ISSN 0732-6971) *1064*
Statistical Summary of Thailand (TH) *43, 232, 929, 1087*
Statistical Supplement to Facts *see* Western Wood Products Association. Statistical Yearbook *529*
Statistical Survey of Economy of Japan (JA ISSN 0081-5047) *218*
Statistical Survey of the East African Community Institutions (KE) *218*
Statistical Tables of Public Nuisance, Tokyo (JA) *499*
Statistical Ten-Year Review of the Municipality of Copenhagen *see* Statistisk Tiaars-Oversigt for Koebenhavns Kommune *949*
Statistical Ten-Year Review of the Municipality of Copenhagen *see* Statistik for Hovedstadsregionen *1064*
Statistical Theory and Method Abstracts (NE ISSN 0039-0518) *12, 1064*
Statistical Year Book of Indonesia (IO ISSN 0126-2912) *34, 924*
Statistical Yearbook for Asia and the Far East *see* Statistical Yearbook for Asia and the Pacific *1064*
Statistical Yearbook for Asia and the Pacific/Annuaire Statistique pour l'Asie et le Pacifique (UN ISSN 0252-3655) *1064*
Statistical Yearbook for Latin America/Anuario Estadistico de America Latina (UN) *1064*
Statistical Yearbook for the Copenhagen Region *see* Statistik for Hovedstadsregionen *1064*
Statistical Yearbook of Bangladesh (BG ISSN 0302-2374) *1064*
Statistical Yearbook of Brazil *see* Anuario Estatistico do Brasil *1048*
Statistical Yearbook of China (HK ISSN 0255-6766) *1064*
Statistical Yearbook of Finland *see* Suomen Tilastollinen Vuosikirja *1065*
Statistical Yearbook of Greece (GR ISSN 0081-5071) *1064*
Statistical Yearbook of Iran (IR) *1064*
Statistical Yearbook of Jamaica (JM) *1064*
Statistical Yearbook of Liechtenstein/Statistisches Jahrbuch Fuerstentum Liechtenstein (LH) *1064*
Statistical Yearbook of Thailand (TH) *1064*
Statistical Yearbook of the Church. *see* Annuarium Statisticum Ecclesiae *974*
Statistical Yearbook of the Netherlands (NE ISSN 0303-6448) *463*
Statistical Yearbook of the Republic of China (CH) *218, 1064*
Statistical Yearbook of the U.S. Department of Housing and Urban Development *see* U.S. Department of Housing and Urban Development. Statistical Yearbook *628*
Statistical Yearbook of Turkey *see* Turkiye Istatistik Yilligi *1066*
Statisticeski Danni za Bibliotekite v Bulgaria/Statistical Data on Libraries in Bulgaria (BU ISSN 0204-4684) *684*
Statistiche dei Bilanci delle Amministrazioni Regionali, Provinciali e Comunali (IT ISSN 0075-1820) *949*
Statistiche sulla Pubblica Amministrazione (IT) *949*
Statistiches Handbuch der Oesterreichischen Sozialversicherung *see* Handbuch der Oesterreichischen Sozialversicherung *642*
Statistiches Taschenbuch der DDR (GE ISSN 0433-6844) *1064*
Statisticheski Godishnik na Narodna Republika Bulgaria (BU) *1064*

STATISTICS ON   1891

Statisticheski Spravochnik (BU) *1064*
Statisticians and Others in Allied Professions *see* Directory of Statisticians *1054*
Statistics - Africa (UK ISSN 0081-5098) *218*
Statistics - America (UK ISSN 0309-5452) *218*
Statistics - Asia & Australasia: Sources for Market Research (UK ISSN 0309-5371) *131, 1064*
Statistics - Europe (UK ISSN 0081-5101) *218*
Statistics for Electric Utilities in Pennsylvania (US) *462*
Statistics for Gas Utilities in Pennsylvania (US) *868*
Statistics for Iron and Steel Industry in India (II ISSN 0081-511X) *802*
Statistics for Water Utilities Including Water Authorities in Pennsylvania (US ISSN 0094-4335) *1128*
Statistics of Education in Cyprus (CY ISSN 0253-8733) *425*
Statistics of Education in Somalia (SO) *419*
Statistics of Education in Wales (UK ISSN 0262-8317) *426*
Statistics of Electric Utilities in the United States. Classes A and B Privately Owned Companies *see* Financial Statistics of Selected Electric Utilities *468*
Statistics of Farmer Cooperatives (US ISSN 0081-5128) *43*
Statistics of Foreign Trade of Syria (SY ISSN 0081-5136) *218*
Statistics of Indiana Libraries (US ISSN 0081-5152) *684*
Statistics of Japanese Non-Life Insurance Business (JA ISSN 0910-5727) *641*
Statistics of Life Insurance Business in Japan (JA ISSN 0910-5719) *641*
Statistics of Marine Products Exports (II) *259*
Statistics of Paper and Paperboard *see* Statistics of Paper, Paperboard and Wood Pulp *859*
Statistics of Paper, Paperboard and Wood Pulp (US ISSN 0731-8863) *859, 859*
Statistics of Privately Owned Electric Utilities in the United States *see* Financial Statistics of Selected Electric Utilities *468*
Statistics of Road Traffic Accidents in Europe (UN ISSN 0081-5160) *1087*
Statistics of Road Traffic Accidents in Japan (JA) *1064, 1087*
Statistics of Southern College and University Libraries (US) *688, 1064*
Statistics of the Communications Industry in the United States (US ISSN 0081-5179) *344*
Statistics of the State Finances of the Netherlands *see* Statistiek der Rijksfinancien *299*
Statistics of the Trade Unions in the Netherlands *see* Statistiek der Vakbeweging in Nederland *649*
Statistics of Virginia Public Libraries *see* Statistics of Virginia Public Libraries and Institutional Libraries *684*
Statistics of Virginia Public Libraries and Institutional Libraries (US ISSN 0731-8464) *684*
Statistics of World Trade in Steel (UN ISSN 0081-5195) *802, 1064*
Statistics on Alcohol and Drug Use in Canada and Other Countries (CN ISSN 0715-7657) *378, 1064*
Statistics on Narcotic Drugs *see* International Narcotics Control Board. Statistics on Narcotic Drugs for (Year) *871*
Statistics on Social Work Education *see* Statistics on Social Work Education in the United States *1021*
Statistics on Social Work Education in the United States (US ISSN 0091-7192) *1021*
Statistics on the Mexican Economy (MX) *218*
Statistics on World Trade in Engineering Products. Bulletin (UN) *802, 1064*

STATISTICS

Statistics - Social Service Board, North Dakota see North Dakota. Social Service Board. Statistics *1159*
Statistics Sources (US ISSN 0585-198X) *1064*
Statistik der Rijksfinancien/Statistics of the State Finances of the Netherlands (NE ISSN 0168-373X) *299*
Statistiek der Vakbeweging in Nederland/Statistics of the Trade Unions in the Netherlands (NE ISSN 0168-4035) *649*
Statistiek van de Gasvoorziening in Nederland (NE ISSN 0081-5225) *867*
Statistiek van de Scheepvaartbeweging in Nederland/Census of Inland Shipping in the Netherlands at Locks and Bridges (NE) *1104*
Statistik des Hamburgischen Staates (GW ISSN 0073-0203) *1104*
Statistik des Hochschulwesens in der Schwiez see Studenten an der Schwiez. Hochschulen *438*
Statistik for Hovedstadsregionen/ Statistical Yearbook for the Copenhagen Region (DK ISSN 0106-2344) *1064*
Statistik Indonesia see Statistical Pocketbook of Indonesia *1064*
Statistik om Hjemmessygeplejerkevirksomheden (DK ISSN 0109-3002) *619*
Statistik om Legale Aborter see Statistik om Praevention og Aborter *179*
Statistik om Praevention og Aborter (DK ISSN 0106-7729) *179*
Statistik om Sundhedsplejerskernes Virksomhed (DK ISSN 0108-9714) *773*
Statistik over Afregning of Ydelser indem for den Offentlige Sygesikring see Sygesikringsstatistik *643*
Statistik Perminyakan Indonesia see Indonesia Oil Statistics *868*
Statistika Spoljne Trgovine SFR Jugoslavije (YU ISSN 0084-4373) *218*
Statistique Criminelle de la Belgique (BE ISSN 0081-5268) *374, 1064*
Statistique de l'Eglise see Annuarium Statisticum Ecclesiae *974*
Statistique Judiciaire de la Belgique see Statistique Criminelle de la Belgique *374*
Statistiques Africaines du Commerce Exterieur. Serie C: Tableaux Recapitulatifs see Foreign Trade Statistics of Africa. Series C: Summary Tables *208*
Statistiques de l'Enseignement au Gabon see Gabon. Ministere de l'Education Nationale. Annuaire Statistique de l'Enseignement *424*
Statistiques de l'Industrie Francaise des Pates. Papiers et Cartons (FR) *860*
Statistiques de l'Industrie Gaziere (FR) *469, 1064*
Statistiques de l'Industrie Gaziere en France (FR) *867*
Statistiques du Commerce Exterieur de Cote d'Ivoire (IV ISSN 0081-5276) *218*
Statistiques du Commerce Exterieur de l'Algerie (AE) *218*
Statistiques du Commerce Exterieur de la Tunisie (TI ISSN 0081-5292) *218*
Statistiques du Commerce Exterieur de Madagascar (MG ISSN 0081-5306) *218, 1064*
Statistiques du Commerce International et du Development. Manuel see International Trade and Development Statistics. Handbook *257*
Statistiques Financieres de l'O C D E see O E C D Financial Statistics *215*
Statistiques Mondiales de Transport see World Transport Data *1087*
Statistiques Relatives aux Science et a la Technologie see Unesco. Statistics on Science and Technology *1004*
Statistisch Jaarboek van Volksgezondheid see Annuaire Statistique de la Sante Publique *958*
Statistische Kurzinformation (GW) *1064*
Statistische Mitteilungen der Bergbehoerden der Bundesrepublik (GW) *822*
Statistische Mitteilungen der Stadt Koeln see Koelner Statistische Nachrichten *1058*
Statistische Nachrichten Bildungs- und Sozialeinrichtungen fuer Hoergeschaedigte in der Bundesrepublik Deutschland (GW) *376*
Statistische Nachrichten ueber Bildungs- und Sozialeinrichtungen fuer Hoergeschaedigte in der Deutschsprachigen Raum see Statistische Nachrichten Bildungs- und Sozialeinrichtungen fuer Hoergeschaedigte in der Bundesrepublik Deutschland *376*
Statistische Studien (GW ISSN 0531-9323) *218, 1064*
Statistisches Handbuch fuer die Republik Oesterreich (AU ISSN 0081-5314) *1064*
Statistisches Jahrbuch Berlin (GW ISSN 0081-5322) *1064*
Statistisches Jahrbuch der D D R (GE) *1065*
Statistisches Jahrbuch der Eisen- und Stahlindustrie (GW ISSN 0081-5365) *802*
Statistisches Jahrbuch der Schweiz/ Annuaire Statistique de la Suisse (SZ ISSN 0081-5330) *1065*
Statistisches Jahrbuch der Stadt Augsburg (GW) *1065*
Statistisches Jahrbuch der Stadt Nuernberg (GW) *249, 626, 924, 1065*
Statistisches Jahrbuch der Stadt Wien (AU) *1065*
Statistisches Jahrbuch fuer die Bundesrepublik Deutschland (GW ISSN 0081-5357) *1065*
Statistisches Jahrbuch Fuerstentum Liechtenstein see Statistical Yearbook of Liechtenstein *1064*
Statistisches Jahrbuch Muenchen (GW ISSN 0077-2062) *1065*
Statistisches Jahrbuch ueber Ernaehrung, Landwirtschaft und Forsten der Bundesrepublik Deutschland (GW ISSN 0072-1581) *43*
Statistisches Landesamt Hamburg. Daten und Informationen Faltblatt (GW) *1065*
Statistisches Taschenbuch der Stadt Wien (AU) *1065*
Statistisk Aarsbok foer Finland see Suomen Tilastollinen Vuosikirja *1065*
Statistisk Aarsbok foer Sverige (SW ISSN 0081-5381) *1065*
Statistisk Tiaars-Oversigt for Koebenhavns Kommune (DK ISSN 0107-6744) *949, 1065*
Statni Archiv v Opave. Sbornik (CS) *597*
Statni Banka Ceskoslovenska. Bulletin (CS ISSN 0081-539X) *232*
Statsfroekontrollen. Beretning (DK ISSN 0106-8598) *60*
Status of Black New York Report (US) *505*
Stavanger Museum. Aarbok (NO ISSN 0333-0656) *830*
Stavanger Museum. Skrifter (NO ISSN 0333-0664) *830*
Steam Electric Fuels see Steam-Electric Plant Factors (1978) *820*
Steam Electric Plant Construction Cost and Annual Production Expenses see Historical Plant Cost and Annual Production Expenses for Selected Electric Plants *184*
Steam-Electric Plant Factors (1978) (US) *820, 867*
Steam Heritage Yearbook, Preserved Transport & Industrial Archaeology Guide (UK) *1083*
Steam Passenger Service Directory (US ISSN 0081-542X) *1095*
Steam Year Book, Preserved Transport and Industrial Archaeology Guide see Steam Heritage Yearbook, Preserved Transport & Industrial Archaeology Guide *1083*
Steel and America (US) *800*
Steel Market (UN) *800*
Steel Structures Painting Bulletin (US) *856*
Steel Traders of the World (UK ISSN 0308-8006) *800*
Steelmaking Conference: Proceedings (US) *800, 820, 867*
Steelmaking Proceedings see Steelmaking Conference: Proceedings *820*
Steentrupia (DK ISSN 0375-2909) *178*
Steiermaerkisches Landesarchiv. Mitteilungen (AU ISSN 0434-3883) *597*
Steinbeck Monograph Series (US ISSN 0085-6746) *733*
Steirische Beitraege zur Hydrogeologie (US ISSN 0376-4826) *404*
Steirischer Burgenverein. Mitteilungen (AU ISSN 0490-9348) *597*
Stelle Filanti (IT) *135, 825*
Stemmer fra Oldtiden (DK ISSN 0108-2833) *110*
Stephen F. Austin State University. School of Forestry. Bulletin (US ISSN 0082-318X) *527*
Stephens, Maxfield and Lind's Federal Estate and Gift Taxation (Supplement) see Federal Estate and Gift Taxation (Supplement) *295*
Stereo Buyer's Guide. Amplifiers see Stereo Buyer's Guide. Loudspeakers, Amplifiers and Tuners *1032*
Stereo Buyer's Guide. Amplifiers, FM Tuners and Receivers see Stereo Buyer's Guide. Loudspeakers, Amplifiers and Tuners *1032*
Stereo Buyer's Guide. Audio Yearbook (AT ISSN 0819-0216) *1032*
Stereo Buyer's Guide. C D Players, Cassettes Decks and Turntables (AT ISSN 0819-0208) *1032*
Stereo Buyer's Guide. Cassettes (AT ISSN 0312-0104) *1163*
Stereo Buyer's Guide. Directory (AT ISSN 0312-004X) *1163*
Stereo Buyer's Guide. Loudspeakers, Amplifiers and Tuners (AT ISSN 0819-0194) *1032*
Stereo Buyer's Guide. Manual see Stereo Buyer's Guide. Audio Yearbook *1032*
Stereo Buyer's Guide. Speakers (AT ISSN 0312-0074) *1163*
Stereo Buyer's Guide. Turntables see Stereo Buyer's Guide. C D Players, Cassettes Decks and Turntables *1032*
Stereo Buyer's Guide. Turntables and Compact Disc Players see Stereo Buyer's Guide. C D Players, Cassettes Decks and Turntables *1032*
Stereo Directory and Buying Guide see Stereo Review's Stereo Buyers Guide *1032*
Stereo Headphones (UK ISSN 0039-1212) *744*
Stereo Review's Car Stereo Buyers Guide (US) *1032*
Stereo Review's Stereo Buyers Guide (US) *1032*
Stereo Review's Tape Recording & Buying Guide (US) *1032*
Stereo Review's Video Buyers Guide (US) *349, 1032*
Sterna (NO ISSN 0039-1247) *171*
Steuer-Gewerkschafts-Handbuch (GW) *299, 649*
Steuer-Telex (GW) *299*
Steuer-Training (GW ISSN 0170-6845) *664*
Steuerbelastung in der Schweiz/Charge Fiscale en Suisse (SZ) *299*
Steuerberater-Jahrbuch (GW ISSN 0081-5519) *299*
Steve (IT ISSN 0393-9480) *744*
Stichting Film en Wetenschap. Catalogue 16mm Films see Stichting Film en Wetenschap. Catalogue 16mm Films and Video Programmes *825*
Stichting Film en Wetenschap. Catalogue 16mm Films and Video Programmes (NE) *825*
Stichting tot Uitgave der Bronnen van het oud-Vaderlandsche Recht. 2 Series: Werken, and Verslagen en Mededelingen (NE) *597, 664*
Stichtse Historische Reeks (NE) *597*
Der Stickstoff (GW ISSN 0081-5535) *60*
Stierenboek (NE) *68*
Stifterverband fuer die Deutsche Wissenschaft. Jahrbuch see Stifterverband fuer die Deutsche Wissenschaft. Taetigkeitsbericht *1001*
Stifterverband fuer die Deutsche Wissenschaft. Taetigkeitsbericht (GW) *1001*
Stiftung Preussische Kulturbesitz. Jahrbuch (GW ISSN 0342-0124) *597*
Stiftung Volkswagenwerk. Schriftenreihe(GW) *199*
Stigsnaes (DK ISSN 0109-274X) *171*
Stikhi (UR) *744*
Still: Yale Photography Annual (US ISSN 0081-5586) *885*
Stille Schar (AU ISSN 0081-5594) *597, 983*
Stirling Technical Reports in Education (UK ISSN 0144-0764) *419*
Stock Exchange, London. Members and Firms of the Stock Exchange (UK ISSN 0305-1129) *268*
Stock Exchange of Singapore. Handbook (SI) *268*
Stock Exchange Official Year Book (UK ISSN 0076-0684) *268*
Stock Trader's Almanac (US) *268*
Stock Values and Dividends for Tax Purposes (US ISSN 0081-5624) *268, 299*
Stockholm International Peace Research Institute (S.I.P.R.I.) Chemical & Biological Warfare Studies see S I P R I Chemical & Biological Warfare Studies *918*
Stockholm International Peace Research Institute (S.I.P.R.I.) Yearbook: World Armaments and Disarmament see S I P R I Yearbook: World Armaments and Disarmament *918*
Stockholm Stock Exchange. Report see Stockholms Fondboers. Beraettelse *268*
Stockholm Studies in English (SW) *704*
Stockholm Studies in History of Literature (SW ISSN 0491-0869) *733*
Stockholm Studies in Modern Philology see Studier i Modern Spraakvetenskap *705*
Stockholm Studies in Philosophy (SW ISSN 0491-0877) *881*
Stockholm Studies in Politics (SW ISSN 0346-6620) *909*
Stockholm Studies in Russian Literature(SW) *733*
Stockholms Fondboers. Beraettelse/ Stockholm Stock Exchange. Report (SW) *268*
Stockholms Universitet. Psykologiska Institutionen. Report Series (SW ISSN 0345-0139) *937*
Stockholms Universitet. Psykologiska Institutionen. Reports. Supplement Series (SW ISSN 0345-021X) *937*
Stof (DK ISSN 0109-0852) *377*
Stofskifte (DK ISSN 0108-1012) *76*
Stokely-Van Camp Annual Symposium. Proceedings (US) *520*
Stokvis Studies in Historical Chronology & Thought (US ISSN 0270-5338) *561, 909*
Stone (US) *744*
Stone and Cox General Insurance Register (CN) *641*
Stone and Cox General Insurance Year Book see Stone and Cox General Insurance Register *641*
Stone and Cox Life Insurance Tables (CN ISSN 0081-5780) *641*
Stone Lion Review (US) *571, 712*
Stone's Justices' Manual (UK ISSN 0269-3682) *664*
Stony Thursday Book (IE) *733, 744*
Stopinterviewanalyse (DK ISSN 0106-7540) *1097*
Stopout: Working Ways to Learn (US) *419*

Store Glaede (DK ISSN 0108-2884) *973*
Stores of the Year (US ISSN 0192-8732) *643*
Stores, Shops, Hypermarkets Retail Directory *see* Retail Directory *285*
Storia Architettura (IT) *99*
Storia, Costumi e Tradizioni (IT ISSN 0081-5837) *516*
Storia dell'Ebraismo in Italia (IT) *977*
Storia della Miniatura. Studi e Documenti (IT ISSN 0081-5845) *110*
Storia e Societa (IT) *597*
Storia, Letteratura e Arte nel Mezzogiorno (IT) *597*
Storiadentro (IT) *597*
Stories: a List of Stories to Tell and to Read Aloud (US) 131, *335*
Stories from the Hills (US ISSN 0081-5861) 609, *733*
Storm (US) *712*
Storrs Agricultural Experiment Station. Bulletin (US) *35*
Storrs Agricultural Experiment Station. Research Report (US ISSN 0069-8997) *35*
Story of Illinois Series *see* Illinois. State Museum. Story of Illinois Series *606*
Story So Far (CN) *733*
Stowage and Segregation to I M D G Code (GW) 317, *1104*
Strahovska Knihovna (CS ISSN 0081-5896) *733*
Straits Times Directory of Singapore *see* Times Business Directory of Singapore *317*
Strategic Survey (UK ISSN 0459-7230) *918*
Strategy and Executive Action (US ISSN 0743-2542) 222, *281*, *285*
Strategy for Peace Conference. Report *see* Strategy for Peace U.S. Foreign Policy Conference. Report *918*
Strategy for Peace U.S. Foreign Policy Conference. Report (US ISSN 0748-9641) *918*
Stratford Festival (CN ISSN 0085-6770) *1078*
Stratford-upon-Avon Studies (UK) 733, *1078*
Strathclyde Modern Language Studies (UK ISSN 0261-099X) *704*, *733*
Strathclyde Oil Register (UK) *317*, 467, *867*
Strathclyde Regional Council. Annual Report & Financial Statement (UK) *946*
Strathclyde's Budget *see* Strathclyde Regional Council. Annual Report & Financial Statement *946*
Stratificazione e Classi Sociali in Italia. Quaderni di Ricerca (IT) *1029*
Strays (UK ISSN 0143-8859) *537*
Stream Improvement Technical Bulletin *see* National Council of the Paper Industry for Air and Stream Improvement. Technical Bulletin *498*
Stredocesky Sbornik Historicky (CS ISSN 0585-4172) *1163*
Street and Smith's Baseball Yearbook *see* Street & Smith's Official Yearbook: Baseball *1040*
Street and Smith's College and Pro Official Basketball Yearbook *see* Street & Smith's Official Yearbook: Basketball *1040*
Street and Smith's Official Yearbook. Pro Football *see* Street & Smith's Official Yearbook: Pro Football *1040*
Street & Smith's Official Yearbook: Baseball (US ISSN 0161-2018) *1040*
Street & Smith's Official Yearbook: Basketball (US ISSN 0149-7103) *1040*
Street & Smith's Official Yearbook: College Football (US ISSN 0091-9977) *1040*
Street & Smith's Official Yearbook: Pro Football (US ISSN 0092-3214) *1040*
Street Magazine (US ISSN 0190-1737) *733*
Stress and Anxiety (US ISSN 0364-1112) *937*

Stress in Modern Society (US ISSN 0884-870X) *1029*
Streudaten der Schwizer Presse *see* Verbreitungsdaten der Schweizer Presse *16*
Striae (SW ISSN 0345-0074) *395*
Strikes and Lockouts in Canada/Greves et Lock-out au Canada (CN ISSN 0081-5985) *275*
Strindbergiana (SW) 733, *1078*
Striolae (SW ISSN 0348-4386) *395*
Stroiizdat: The Best-Designed Books (UR) *131*
Structural Engineering Documents (SZ) *483*
Structural Foam Conference. Proceedings (US) *901*
Structural Mechanics Software Series (US ISSN 0146-2059) *492*
Structure and Bonding (US ISSN 0081-5993) *324*
Structure Reports. Section A (NE ISSN 0166-6983) *328*
Structure Reports. Section B (NE ISSN 0166-7033) *328*
Structuring Foreign Investment in U.S. Real Estate (NE) 664, *966*
Structurist (CN ISSN 0081-6027) *110*
Struktura i Rol' Vody v Zhivom Organizme *see* Molekulyarnaya Fizika i Biofizika Vodnykh Sistem *153*
Strumenti Linguistici (IT ISSN 0391-1942) *704*
Stubbs Buyers Guide *see* Stubbs Directory *1163*
Stubbs Directory (UK) *1163*
Stubs (Metro N.Y.) (US ISSN 0081-6051) *1078*
Stud and Stable (AT ISSN 0311-8215) *1043*
Student Acceleration in Florida Public Education (US) *449*
Student Aid Annual *see* Chronicle Student Aid Annual *433*
Student Choir Director's Library (UR) *841*
Student Guide to Graduate Law Study Programs (US) 431, *664*
Student Guide to Summer Law Study Programs (US ISSN 0197-6656) *665*
Student Mathematics (CN ISSN 0085-6800) *753*
Student Nationalist (UK ISSN 0260-2563) *712*
Student Welfare Manual (UK) *1021*
Student Work Study Travel Catalog (US) *438*
Studenten an der Schwiez. Hochschulen/Etudiants des Hautes Ecoles Suisses (SZ) *438*
Studenteravisen (DK ISSN 0108-1101) *438*
Studenterhaandbogen (DK ISSN 0108-1020) *438*
Students Representative Council. Handbook (UK) *420*
Studi Albanesi. Studi e Testi (IT ISSN 0081-6116) *704*, *733*
Studi Americani (IT ISSN 0085-6819) *733*
Studi Classici e Orientali (IT ISSN 0081-6124) 338, *571*, *613*
Studi d'Architettura Antica (IT ISSN 0081-6140) *99*
Studi d'Economia (IT ISSN 0391-6103) *249*
Studi di Letteratura Francese (IT ISSN 0585-4768) *733*
Studi di Metrica Classica (IT ISSN 0081-6159) *338*
Studi di Musica Veneta (IT) *842*
Studi di Storia delle Arti (IT) *110*
Studi e Ricerche sui Giacimenti Terziari di Bolca (IT) *857*
Studi e Saggi Linguistici (IT ISSN 0085-6827) *704*
Studi e Testi dell'Antichita (IT) *733*
Studi e Testi di Letteratura Italiana (IT) *733*
Studi e Testi di Storia e Critica dell'Arte (IT) *110*
Studi Eblaiti (IT) *93*
Studi Etno-Antropologici (IT) *76*
Studi Etruschi (IT) *597*
Studi Filosofici (IT) *881*
Studi Genuensi (IT ISSN 0585-4911) *93*, *561*

Studi Ispanici (IT ISSN 0585-492X) *733*
Studi Linguistici Salentini (IT) *704*
Studi per l'Ecologia del Quaternario (IT ISSN 0392-6788) *76*, *857*
Studi Pergolesiani *see* Pergolesi Studies *840*
Studi Romagnoli (IT ISSN 0081-6205) *597*
Studi Romagnoli. Estratti di Sezione (IT ISSN 0081-6213) *597*
Studi Romagnoli. Quaderni (IT ISSN 0081-6221) *597*
Studi Secenteschi (IT ISSN 0081-6248) *597*
Studi sull'Educazione (IT ISSN 0392-2146) *420*
Studi Tassiani (IT ISSN 0081-6256) *733*
Studi Urbinati. Serie B: Letteratura *see* Studi Urbinati. Serie B: Letteratura, Storia, Filosofia *733*
Studi Urbinati. Serie B: Letteratura, Storia, Filosofia (IT ISSN 0039-3088) 561, *733*, *881*
Studi Veneziani (IT ISSN 0081-6264) *598*
Studi Verdiani (IT) *842*
Studia Ad Corpus Hellenisticum Novi Testamenti (NE) *973*
Studia Algoligica Lovaniensia (BE) *1001*
Studia Anglica Posnaniensia (PL ISSN 0081-6272) *704*
Studia Anglistica Upsalienses (SW ISSN 0562-2719) *704*
Studia Anthroponymica Scandinavica (SW ISSN 0280-8633) *537*, *1029*
Studia Archaeologica (HU ISSN 0081-6280) *93*
Studia Archaeologica (IT ISSN 0081-6299) *93*
Studia Archaeologica (GW) *93*
Studia Archeologiczne (PL ISSN 0081-6302) *93*
Studia Aristotelica (IT ISSN 0081-6310) *881*
Studia Balcanica (BU) *598*
Studia Biologica Academiae Scientiarum Hungaricae (HU ISSN 0076-244X) *147*
Studia Botanica (SP ISSN 0370-923X) *161*
Studia Cartesiana (NE) *881*
Studia Celtica (UK ISSN 0081-6353) *598*, *704*
Studia Comitatensia (HU ISSN 0133-3046) *830*
Studia Copernicana (PL ISSN 0081-6701) *117*
Studia Delitzschiana. Neue Folge (GW) *561*, *733*
Studia do Dziejow Dawnego Uzbrojenia i Ubioru Wojskowego (PL ISSN 0137-5733) *812*, *830*
Studia Ephemeridis Augustinianum (IT) *973*
Studia Estetyczne (PL ISSN 0081-637X) *881*
Studia et Documenta Historiae et Iuris (VC) 561, *665*
Studia Ethnographica Upsaliensia (SW ISSN 0491-2705) *76*
Studia Ethnologica Upsaliensia (SW) *76*
Studia Fennica (FI ISSN 0085-6835) *76*, *704*
Studia Forestalia Suecica (SW ISSN 0039-3150) *527*
Studia Francisci Scholten Memoriae Dicata (NE ISSN 0081-6396) *93*
Studia Gaiana (NE) *561*
Studia Geograficzne (PL ISSN 0081-640X) *548*
Studia Geograficzno-Fizyczne z Obszaru Opolszczyzny (PL ISSN 0081-6418) *1163*
Studia Geologica Polonica (PL ISSN 0081-6426) *395*
Studia Geomorphologica Carpatho-Balcanica (PL ISSN 0081-6434) *401*
Studia Germanica Gandensia (BE ISSN 0081-6442) *704*
Studia Germanica Posnaniensia (PL ISSN 0137-2467) *733*
Studia Graeca et Latina Gothoburgensia(SW ISSN 0081-6450) *338*

Studia Grammatica (GE ISSN 0081-6469) *704*
Studia Hellenistica (BE) *338*
Studia Hibernica (IE ISSN 0081-6477) *598*, *734*
Studia Historiae Oeconomica (PL ISSN 0081-6485) *252*
Studia Historica (FI ISSN 0081-6493) *598*
Studia Historica (IT ISSN 0081-6507) *598*
Studia Historica Academiae Scientiarum Hungaricae (HU ISSN 0076-2458) *561*
Studia Historica et Philogia: Sectio Romanica (IT) *704*
Studia Historica et Philogica: Sectio Slavica (IT) *704*
Studia Historica et Philogica: Sectio Slavo-Romanica (IT) *704*
Studia Historica Jyvaskylaensia (FI ISSN 0081-6523) *598*
Studia Historica Septentrionalia (FI ISSN 0356-8199) *598*
Studia Historica Slavo-Germanica (PL ISSN 0301-6420) *598*
Studia Historica Slovaca (CS) *598*
Studia Historica Upsaliensia (SW ISSN 0081-6531) *598*
Studia i Materialy do Dziejow Muzyki Polskiej (PL) *842*
Studia i Materialy do Dziejow Teatru Polskiego (PL ISSN 0208-404X) *1078*
Studia i Materialy do Dziejow Wielkopolski i Pomorza (PL ISSN 0081-654X) *598*
Studia i Materialy do Dziejow Zup Solnych w Polsce (PL ISSN 0137-530X) *93*, *395*
Studia i Materialy do Historii Wojskowosci (PL ISSN 0562-2786) *598*, *812*
Studia i Materialy do Teorii i Historii Architektury i Urbanistyki (PL ISSN 0081-6566) *99*, *626*
Studia i Materialy Oceanologiczne (PL ISSN 0208-421X) *408*
Studia i Materialy z Dziejow Nauki Polskiej. Seria A. Historia Nauk Spolecznych (PL ISSN 0081-6574) *598*, *1012*
Studia i Materialy z Dziejow Nauki Polskiej. Seria B. Historia Nauk Biologicznych i Medycznych (PL ISSN 0081-6582) *147*, *767*
Studia i Materialy z Dziejow Nauki Polskiej. Seria C. Historia Nauk Matematycznych, Fizyko-Chemicznych i Geologiczno-Geograficznych (PL ISSN 0081-6590) *1001*
Studia i Materialy z Dziejow Nauki Polskiej. Seria D. Historia Techniki i Nauk Technicznych (PL ISSN 0081-6604) *1071*
Studia i Materialy z Dziejow Nauki Polskiej. Seria E. Zagadnienia Ogolne(PL ISSN 0081-6612) *1001*, *1071*
Studia i Materialy z Dziejow Teatru Polskiego *see* Studia i Materialy do Dziejow Teatru Polskiego *1078*
Studia in Veteris Testamenti Pseudepigrapha (NE) *973*
Studia Instituti Anthropos (GW) *76*
Studia Iranica (NE) *853*
Studia Irenica (GW ISSN 0081-6663) *973*
Studia Iuridica (PL ISSN 0081-6671) *665*
Studia Iuridica Auctoriatate Universitatis Pecs Publicata (HU ISSN 0324-5934) *665*
Studia Iuridica Silesiana (PL ISSN 0208-502X) *665*
Studia Juridica (IT ISSN 0081-6698) *665*
Studia Latino-Americana *see* Acta Universitatis de Attila Jozsef Nominatae. Acta Historica *574*
Studia Leibnitiana. Sonderhefte (GW ISSN 0341-0765) *882*
Studia Leibnitiana. Supplementa (GW ISSN 0303-5980) *882*
Studia Linguistica et Philologica (US) *704*
Studia Litteraria (HU ISSN 0562-2867) *734*

Studia Maritima (PL ISSN 0137-3587) 259
Studia Mathematica (PL ISSN 0039-3223) 753
Studia Musicologica Norvegica (NO ISSN 0332-5024) 842
Studia Musicologica Upsaliensia. Nova Series (SW ISSN 0081-6744) 842
Studia nad Zagadnieniami Gospodarczymi i Spolecznymi Ziem Zachodnich (PL ISSN 0081-6752) 598
Studia Naturae. Seria A. Wydawnictwa Naukowe (PL) 367
Studia Naturae. Seria B. Wydawnictwa Popularno-Naukowe (PL ISSN 0551-4193) 367
Studia Numismatica et Medaillistica (CS ISSN 0081-6779) 845
Studia o Ksiazce (PL ISSN 0137-3404) 684, 963
Studia Orientalia (FI ISSN 0039-3282) 853
Studia Palmyrenskie (PL ISSN 0081-6787) 93
Studia Pedagogiczne (PL ISSN 0081-6795) 420
Studia Philologiae Scandinavicae Upsaliensia (SW ISSN 0081-6809) 704
Studia Philologica Jyvaskylaensia (FI ISSN 0585-5462) 704
Studia Philosophiae Religionis (SW) 882, 973
Studia Phonologica/Onsei Kagaku Kenkyu (JA ISSN 0300-1067) 704
Studia Poetica (HU ISSN 0209-9403) 734
Studia Pohl (VC) 853
Studia Pohl: Series Maior (VC) 853
Studia Polonijne (PL) 924
Studia Polonistyczne (PL ISSN 0137-4370) 704
Studia Polono-Slavica Orientalia. Acta Litteraria (PL ISSN 0137-4389) 734
Studia Post-Biblica (NE ISSN 0585-5500) 973
Studia Psychologica et Paedagogica (SW) 420, 937
Studia Romanica Upsaliensia (SW ISSN 0562-3022) 704
Studia Rossica Posnaniensia (PL ISSN 0081-6884) 734
Studia Scientiae Paedagogicae Upsaliensia see Uppsala Studies in Education 421
Studia Semiotyczne (PL ISSN 0137-6608) 704
Studia Semitica Neerlandica (NE ISSN 0081-6914) 977
Studia Silensia (SP) 973
Studia Slaskie/Silesian Studies (PL ISSN 0039-3355) 539
Studia Slovenica (US ISSN 0585-5543) 598
Studia Slovenica. Special Series (US ISSN 0081-6922) 598
Studia Societatis Scientiarum Torunensis. Sectio C (Geografia et Geologia) (PL ISSN 0082-5549) 395, 548
Studia Societatis Scientiarum Torunensis. Sectio D. Botanica (PL ISSN 0082-5557) 161
Studia Societatis Scientiarum Torunensis. Sectio E. Zoologia (PL ISSN 0082-5565) 178
Studia Societatis Scientiarum Torunensis. Sectio F. Astronomia (PL ISSN 0082-5573) 117
Studia Societatis Scientiarum Torunensis. Sectio G. Physiologia (PL ISSN 0082-5581) 172
Studia Spinozana (GW) 1001
Studia Spoleczno-Ekonomiczne (PL ISSN 0081-6930) 199
Studia Staropolskie (PL ISSN 0081-6949) 734
Studia Sumiro-Hungarica (US ISSN 0585-5578) 76
Studia Theodisca (NE ISSN 0081-6957) 70
Studia Ubezpieczeniowe (PL ISSN 0137-9704) 641
Studia Universitatis "Babes-Bolyai". Biologia (RM ISSN 0039-3398) 147
Studia Universitatis "Babes-Bolyai". Chemia (RM ISSN 0039-3401) 324

Studia Universitatis "Babes-Bolyai". Geologia. Geographia (RM ISSN 0039-341X) 395, 548
Studia Universitatis "Babes-Bolyai". Historia (RM ISSN 0039-3428) 561
Studia Universitatis "Babes-Bolyai". Mathematica (RM) 753
Studia Universitatis "Babes-Bolyai." Oeconomica. (RM ISSN 0578-5472) 199
Studia Universitatis "Babes-Bolyai". Philologia (RM ISSN 0039-3444) 705
Studia Universitatis "Babes-Bolyai". Philosophia (RM ISSN 0578-5480) 882
Studia Universitatis "Babes-Bolyai". Physica. (RM) 891
Studia Universitatis Babes-Bolyai. Psychologia-Pedagogia see Studia Universitatis "Babes-Bolyai". Philosophia 882
Studia Universitatis "Babes-Bolyai". Series Mathematica-Physica see Studia Universitatis "Babes-Bolyai". Mathematica 753
Studia Universitatis Babes-Bolyai. Sociologia see Studia Universitatis "Babes-Bolyai". Philosophia 882
Studia Universitatis "Babes-Bolyai" Iurisprudentia (RM ISSN 0578-5464) 665
Studia Uralica (AU ISSN 0259-0808) 705
Studia Uralica et Altaica Upsaliensia (SW ISSN 0081-7015) 705
Studia z Automatyki (PL) 355
Studia z Dziejow Osadnictwa (PL ISSN 0081-7058) 1163
Studia z Dziejow ZSRR i Europy Srodkowej (PL ISSN 0081-7082) 598
Studia z Filologii Polskiej i Slowianskiej(PL ISSN 0081-7090) 705
Studia z Historii Sztuki (PL ISSN 0081-7104) 110
Studia z Okresu Oswiecenia (PL ISSN 0081-7112) 734
Studia z Zakresu Budownictwa see Studia z Zakresu Inzynierii 483
Studia z Zakresu Inzynierii (PL ISSN 0137-5393) 483
Studia Zrodloznawcze (PL ISSN 0081-7147) 598
Studie o Rukopisech (CS) 598
Studie z Dejin Hornictvi (CS) 598, 820
Studiecentrum voor Kernenergie. Annual Scientific Report see S C K Annual Report 1162
Studiecentrum voor Kernenergie Annual Report see S C K Annual Report 1162
Studien ueber Asien, Afrika und Lateinamerika (GE ISSN 0138-5550) 561
Studien ueber Wirtschaft-und Systemvergleiche (US ISSN 0344-824X) 252
Studien und Quellen zur Oesterreichischen Zeitgeschichte (AU) 598
Studien und Texte zur Geistesgeschichte des Mittelalters (NE ISSN 0585-5837) 598
Studien und Texte zur Kirchengeschichte und Geschichte (AU) 979
Studien zu den Bogazkoey-Texten (GW ISSN 0585-5853) 705
Studien zu Nichteuropaeischen Rechtstheorien (GW ISSN 0171-9378) 853
Studien zum Kleinen Deutschen Sprachatlas (GW) 705
Studien zur Agrarwirtschaft (GW ISSN 0081-7198) 99
Studien zur Altaegyptischen Kultur (GW ISSN 0340-2215) 338
Studien zur Antiken Philosophie (NE) 882
Studien zur Bauwirtschaft (GW ISSN 0170-5687) 199
Studien zur Bevoelkerungsoekonomie (GW ISSN 0721-0086) 199
Studien zur Bibliotheksgeschichte (AU) 684

Studien zur Deutschen Kunstgeschichte(GW ISSN 0081-7228) 110
Studien zur Deutschen Literatur (GW ISSN 0081-7236) 734
Studien zur Energiewirtschaft (GW ISSN 0170-7779) 199
Studien zur Englischen Philologie, Neue Folge (GW ISSN 0081-7244) 705
Studien zur Europaeischen Geschichte (GW ISSN 0081-7252) 598
Studien zur Finanzpolitik (GW ISSN 0081-7279) 232
Studien zur Franzoesischen Philosophie des Zwanzigsten Jahrhunderts (GW ISSN 0340-5958) 882
Studien zur Germanistik, Anglistik und Komparatistik (GW ISSN 0340-594X) 734
Studien zur Geschichte Asiens, Afrikas und Lateinamerikas. see Studien ueber Asien, Afrika und Lateinamerika 561
Studien zur Geschichte der Katholischen Moraltheologie (GW ISSN 0081-7295) 983
Studien zur Geschichte des Neunzehnten Jahrhunderts (GW ISSN 0081-7309) 561
Studien zur Geschichte Osteuropas/ Studies in East European History (NE ISSN 0081-7317) 598
Studien zur Indologie und Iranistik (GW ISSN 0341-4191) 571, 705
Studien zur Industriewirtschaft (GW ISSN 0170-5660) 199
Studien zur Japanologie (GW ISSN 0585-6094) 571
Studien zur Kinderpsychoanalyse (AU ISSN 0255-6715) 937
Studien zur Kinderpsychoanalyse. Jahrbuch (AU ISSN 0255-6715) 937
Studien zur Kirchengeschichte Niedersachsens (GW) 973
Studien zur Kulturkunde (GW ISSN 0170-3544) 76
Studien zur Kunst des Neunzehnten Jahrhunderts (GW ISSN 0081-7325) 110
Studien zur Literatur der Moderne (GW ISSN 0340-9023) 734
Studien zur Literatur- und Sozialgeschichte Spaniens und Lateinamerikas (GW ISSN 0340-5990) 734, 1029
Studien zur Medizingeschichte des Neunzehnten Jahrhunderts (GW ISSN 0081-7333) 767
Studien zur Modernen Geschichte (GW) 561
Studien zur Musikgeschichte des Neunzehnten Jahrhunderts (GW ISSN 0081-7341) 842
Studien zur Ostasiatischen Schriftkunst (GW ISSN 0170-3684) 110, 853
Studien zur Philosophie des 18. Jahrhunderts (GW) 882
Studien zur Philosophie und Literatur des Neunzehnten Jahrhunderts (GW ISSN 0081-735X) 734, 882
Studien zur Publizistik. Bremer Reihe (GW ISSN 0585-6175) 646
Studien zur Rechts-, Wirtschafts- und Kulturgeschichte (AU) 252, 665
Studien zur Theologie und Geistesgeschichte des 19. Jahrhunderts (GW) 973
Studien zur Umwelt des Neuen Testaments (GW) 973
Studien zur Verkehrswirtschaft (GW ISSN 0170-5652) 199
Der Studienbeginn (GW) 420
Studienbuecherei (GE ISSN 0081-7384) 1001
Studienfuehrer Mathematik (GW) 438, 753
Studienhefte der Paedagogischen Hochschule see Studienhefte Psychologie in Erziehung und Unterricht 438
Studienhefte Psychologie in Erziehung und Unterricht (GW ISSN 0081-7392) 438, 937
Studienreihe Paedagogische Psychologie(GW ISSN 0173-0975) 420, 937
Studienstiftung. Jahresbericht (GW) 439, 1021

Studier i Arbetarroerelsens Historia (SW) 649
Studier i Modern Spraakvetenskap/ Stockholm Studies in Modern Philology (SW) 705
Studier i Nordisk Arkeologi/Studies in North European Archaeology (SW ISSN 0081-7414) 93
Studier i Politik/Studies in Politics see Goeteborg Studies in Politics 905
Studies and Documents on Cultural Policies (UN ISSN 0586-6898) 632
Studies and Reports in Hydrology Series (UN ISSN 0081-7449) 404
Studies and Research in Art History. Series: Theatre, Music, Cinematography see Studii si Cercetari de Istoria Artei. Seria Teatru, Muzica, Cinematografie 825
Studies and Research in Geology, Geophysics and Geography. Geology see Studii si Cercetari de Geologie, Geofizica si Geographie. Geologie 395
Studies in Aboriginal Rights (CN ISSN 0226-3491) 505, 665
Studies in Accounting Research (US ISSN 0586-5050) 222
Studies in Adult Education see Studies in the Education of Adults 427
Studies in African History see Etudes d'Histoire Africaine 566
Studies in American Drama, 1945-Present (US ISSN 0886-7097) 1078
Studies in American History (GW ISSN 0081-7503) 1163
Studies in American Jewish History (US ISSN 0081-7511) 977
Studies in American Jewish Literature (US) 505, 734
Studies in American Literature (GW ISSN 0081-752X) 734
Studies in American Negro Life (US) 505
Studies in American Political Development (US) 909
Studies in American Religion (US) 973
Studies in Anabaptist and Mennonite History (US ISSN 0081-7538) 984
Studies in Ancient Art and Archaeology (US) 93, 110
Studies in Ancient History (GW ISSN 0081-7546) 561
Studies in Ancient Oriental Civilization (US ISSN 0081-7554) 571
Studies in Anglesey History (UK ISSN 0585-6515) 598
Studies in Anthropological Method (US ISSN 0585-6523) 76
Studies in Anthropology (GW) 76
Studies in Anthropology (US) 76
Studies in Applied Mechanics (NE) 895
Studies in Applied Regional Science (US) 1071
Studies in Archaeological Science (US) 93
Studies in Art and Religious Interpretation (US) 111, 973
Studies in Asian Thought and Religion (US) 882, 984
Studies in Automation and Control (NE) 355
Studies in Avian Biology (US) 171
Studies in Bayesian Econometrics see Studies in Bayesian Econometrics and Statistics 199
Studies in Bayesian Econometrics and Statistics (NE) 199
Studies in Bible and Early Christianity (US) 973
Studies in Bible and Exegesis (IS) 973
Studies in Bibliography (US ISSN 0081-7600) 688
Studies in Bibliography and Booklore (US ISSN 0039-3568) 964, 975
Studies in Biology (UK ISSN 0537-9024) 147
Studies in Black American Literature (US ISSN 0738-0755) 505, 734
Studies in British & American Literature/Ei-Beibungaku (JA) 734
Studies in British Art (US) 111
Studies in British History (US) 598
Studies in British Musicology (US) 842
Studies in Browning and His Circle (US ISSN 0095-4489) 734
Studies in Business and Society (US ISSN 0081-7635) 199

Studies in Christian Antiquity (US) 561
Studies in Cinema (US) 825
Studies in Cistercian Art and Architecture (US) 99, 111
Studies in Classical Antiquity (NE ISSN 0167-6679) 338
Studies in Classical Literature (GW ISSN 0081-7724) 338, 734
Studies in Communications (US ISSN 0275-7982) 344
Studies in Comparative Literature (Chapel Hill) (US ISSN 0081-7775) 734
Studies in Comparative Local Government see Planning and Administration 945
Studies in Comparative Politics Series see Studies in International and Comparative Politics 910
Studies in Construction Economy (UK) 187, 966
Studies in Contemporary Economics (US) 252
Studies in Contemporary German Social Thought (US) 882
Studies in Contemporary Jewry (US ISSN 0740-8625) 505
Studies in Contemporary Satire (US ISSN 0163-4143) 712
Studies in Crime and Justice (US) 372
Studies in Cultural Anthropology (US) 76
Studies in Curriculum Development (TZ) 449
Studies in Defense Policy (US) 812, 909
Studies in Descriptive Linguistics (GW ISSN 0171-6794) 705
Studies in Early English History see Studies in the Early History of Britain 561
Studies in East European History see Studien zur Geschichte Osteuropas 598
Studies in Ecology (US) 147
Studies in Economics (UK ISSN 0081-7856) 199
Studies in Education (US) 1163
Studies in Education and Psychology (SW) 420, 937
Studies in Education and Teaching Techniques (II ISSN 0254-0185) 420, 449
Studies in Educational Administration and Organization (IS ISSN 0334-4770) 443
Studies in Eighteenth Century Culture (US) 561, 632
Studies in Electoral Politics in the Indian States (II) 909
Studies in Electrical and Electronic Engineering (NE) 460
Studies in English see University of Cape Town. Studies in English 707
Studies in English Literature (UK) 734
Studies in English Literature (GW ISSN 0081-7899) 1163
Studies in Environmental Science (NE) 499
Studies in European History (GW ISSN 0081-7910) 598
Studies in European Politics (UK) 909, 1012
Studies in European Society (GW) 76
Studies in Evangelicalism (US) 985
Studies in Federal Taxation (US) 299
Studies in Federal Taxation. Tax Study see Studies in Federal Taxation 299
Studies in Folklore (GW) 516
Studies in Freedom (US ISSN 0273-1231) 909
Studies in French Literature (GW ISSN 0081-7937) 734
Studies in French Literature (UK) 734
Studies in General and Comparative Literature (GW ISSN 0081-7945) 734
Studies in General Anthropology (GW ISSN 0081-7953) 76
Studies in Geography (US) 548
Studies in Geography in Hungary (HU ISSN 0081-7961) 548
Studies in German Literature (GW ISSN 0081-797X) 734
Studies in German Thought and History(US) 505, 598
Studies in Greek and Latin Linguistics (NE) 705

Studies in Greek and Roman Religion (NE) 973
Studies in Health and Human Services (US) 886, 1021
Studies in Higher Education in Canada (CN ISSN 0081-7988) 439
Studies in Historical and Political Science. Extra Volumes (US ISSN 0081-7996) 909
Studies in History and the Social Sciences see Recherches d'Histoire et de Sciences Sociales 560
Studies in History of Biology (US ISSN 0149-6700) 147
Studies in Human Rights (US ISSN 0146-3586) 914, 918
Studies in Iconography (US) 111
Studies in Income and Wealth (US) 278
Studies in Indian Epigraphy/Bharatiya Purabhilekha Patrika (II) 705
Studies in Indian Place Names/Bharatiya Sthalanama Patrika (II) 705
Studies in Information and Behavioral Sciences (JA ISSN 0385-1478) 431
Studies in Inorganic Chemistry (NE) 329
Studies in International Affairs (Baltimore) (US ISSN 0081-802X) 910
Studies in International Affairs (Columbia) (US) 918
Studies in International and Comparative Politics (US) 910
Studies in International Cultural Relations see Materialien zum Internationalen Kulturaustausch 852
Studies in International Economics (NE) 200
Studies in International Economics (US) 259
Studies in International Finance (US ISSN 0081-8070) 232
Studies in International Relations (BE) 918
Studies in Italian Literature (GW ISSN 0081-8119) 734
Studies in Jazz Discography see Annual Review of Jazz Studies 832
Studies in Jazz Research see Beitraege zur Jazzforschung 833
Studies in Jewish Education (IS ISSN 0333-9661) 977
Studies in Judaica & the Holocaust (US ISSN 0884-6952) 561, 977
Studies in Judaism in Late Antiquity (NE) 977
Studies in Judaism in Modern Times (NE) 977
Studies in Labor Market Dynamics (DK ISSN 0108-2469) 275
Studies in Language and Linguistics (US ISSN 0586-6928) 705
Studies in Language Companion Series (US ISSN 0165-7763) 705, 734
Studies in Language Disability and Remediation (UK ISSN 0144-3127) 420, 705
Studies in Language Learning (US) 705
Studies in Latin American Popular Culture (US ISSN 0730-9139) 1029
Studies in Law and Social Change (US) 914
Studies in Legal History (US) 665
Studies in Library Management (US) 684
Studies in Library Management (UK ISSN 0307-0808) 684
Studies in Linguistics and Philosophy (NE) 705, 882, 937
Studies in Literature and Criticism (US) 734
Studies in Logic and the Foundations of Mathematics (NE ISSN 0049-237X) 753
Studies in Management Science and Systems (NE) 281
Studies in Manuscript Illumination (US ISSN 0081-8178) 111
Studies in Marxism (US) 882, 910
Studies in Mathematical and Managerial Economics (NE ISSN 0081-8194) 281
Studies in Mathematics (Washington) (US ISSN 0081-8208) 753
Studies in Mathematics and Its Applications (NE) 753

Studies in Mathematics Education/Etudes sur l'Enseignement des Mathematiques/Estudios en Educacion Matematica (UN) 442, 449
Studies in Mayan Linguistics (US ISSN 0733-5776) 76
Studies in Mechanical Engineering (NE) 492
Studies in Media Management (US) 281, 646
Studies in Medieval and Reformation Thought (NE ISSN 0585-6914) 973
Studies in Medieval and Renaissance History (US ISSN 0081-8224) 598
Studies in Medieval Culture (US ISSN 0085-6878) 561, 734
Studies in Mediterranean Archaeology. Monograph Series (SW ISSN 0081-8232) 93, 338
Studies in Mediterranean Archaeology. Pocket-Book Series (SW) 93, 339
Studies in Middle Eastern History (US) 613
Studies in Middle Eastern Literatures (US) 734
Studies in Modern European History and Culture (US ISSN 0098-275X) 598
Studies in Modern Hebrew Literature (US) 734
Studies in Modern Literature (US) 734
Studies in Modern Thermodynamics (NE) 332
Studies in Monetary Economics (NE) 232
Studies in Museology (II ISSN 0081-8259) 830
Studies in Music (AT ISSN 0081-8267) 842
Studies in Music (CN ISSN 0703-3052) 842
Studies in Musicology (US) 842
Studies in Mycenaean Inscriptions and Dialect (UK ISSN 0081-8275) 339, 705
Studies in Mycology (NE ISSN 0166-0616) 161
Studies in Natural Language and Linguistic Theory (NE) 705
Studies in Near Eastern Culture and Society (US ISSN 0742-1168) 613
Studies in Neuroscience (UK) 791, 794
Studies in North European Archaeology see Studier i Nordisk Arkeologi 93
Studies in Nursing Management (US) 784
Studies in Organic Chemistry Series (US) 331
Studies in Oriental Culture (US ISSN 0081-8321) 571, 1012
Studies in Oriental Religions (GW ISSN 0340-6792) 977
Studies in Philosophy (JA ISSN 0081-8380) 882
Studies in Philosophy (GW ISSN 0081-8399) 882
Studies in Philosophy & the History of Philosophy (US ISSN 0585-6965) 882
Studies in Physical and Theoretical Chemistry (NE) 332
Studies in Plant Ecology (SW ISSN 0282-8677) 161
Studies in Population (US) 924
Studies in Population and Urban Demography (US ISSN 0147-1104) 924
Studies in Pre-Columbian Art and Archaeology (US ISSN 0585-7023) 93, 111
Studies in Production and Engineering Economics (NE) 200, 292
Studies in Public Communication (US ISSN 0585-7031) 344
Studies in Public Economics (NE) 200
Studies in Rajput History and Culture Series (II) 571
Studies in Regional Science and Urban Economics (NE) 249
Studies in Religion and Society (US) 973
Studies in Romance Languages see Studies in Romance Languages & Literatures 734
Studies in Romance Languages & Literatures (US) 734

Studies in Rural Land Use (UK ISSN 0081-8453) 49
Studies in Russian and East European History (UK) 598
Studies in Semiotics and Literature (II) 705, 734
Studies in Semitic Languages and Linguistics (NE ISSN 0081-8461) 705
Studies in Slavic and General Linguistics (NE ISSN 0169-0124) 705
Studies in Slavic Literature and Poetics (NE ISSN 0169-0175) 734
Studies in Social and Demographic History (UK) 1012, 1029
Studies in Social and Economic Demography (US) 924
Studies in Social and Political Theory (US) 910
Studies in Social Anthropology (GW ISSN 0081-8496) 76
Studies in Social Discontinuity (US) 1029
Studies in Social Economics (US) 200, 1029
Studies in Social Experimentation (US) 1012, 1030
Studies in Social History (NE) 1012
Studies in Social Life (US ISSN 0081-8518) 1030
Studies in Social Policy and Welfare (UK) 1021
Studies in Social Welfare Policies and Programs (US ISSN 8755-5360) 1021
Studies in Society (AT ISSN 0156-4420) 1030
Studies in Sociology (II) 1030
Studies in Sociology and Social Anthropology (II) 1030
Studies in South Asian Culture (NE) 76
Studies in Spanish Literature (GW ISSN 0081-8534) 1163
Studies in Speculative Fiction (US) 734
Studies in Speleology (UK ISSN 0585-718X) 395
Studies in Sport, Physical Education and Health (FI) 886, 1036
Studies in Statistical Mechanics (NE ISSN 0081-8542) 891
Studies in Symbolic Interaction (US ISSN 0163-2396) 1030
Studies in the Age of Chaucer (US ISSN 0190-2407) 734
Studies in the American Renaissance (US ISSN 0149-015X) 734
Studies in the Early History of Britain (UK) 561
Studies in the Economics of Poultry Farming in Punjab see India. Ministry of Agriculture. Bulletin on Food Statistics 47
Studies in the Education of Adults (UK) 427
Studies in the Fine Arts: Art Patronage (US) 111
Studies in the Fine Arts: Art Theory (US) 111
Studies in the Fine Arts: Avant-Garde (US) 111
Studies in the Fine Arts: Criticism (US) 111
Studies in the Fine Arts: Iconography (US) 111
Studies in the Fine Arts: Studies in Baroque Art History (US) 111
Studies in the Fine Arts: Studies in Photography (US) 885
Studies in the Fine Arts: Studies in Renaissance Art History (US) 111
Studies in the Foundations, Methodology and Philosophy of Science (US ISSN 0081-8577) 1001
Studies in the Geography of Israel/Mehkarim Be-Ge'ografyah Shel Erets-Yisrael (IS ISSN 0081-8585) 548
Studies in the Germanic Languages and Literatures (US ISSN 0081-8593) 734
Studies in the History and Interpretation of Music (US) 561, 842
Studies in the History of Art (US ISSN 0091-7338) 111
Studies in the History of Cape Town (SA) 567

1896 STUDIES IN

Studies in the History of Christian Thought (NE ISSN 0081-8607) *973*
Studies in the History of Mathematics and Physical Sciences (US ISSN 0172-570X) *753, 891*
Studies in the History of Modern Science (NE) *1001*
Studies in the History of Philosophy (US) *561, 882*
Studies in the History of Religions *see* Numen Supplements *971*
Studies in the History of Science (US) *1012*
Studies in the Learning Sciences (FR) *420, 937*
Studies in the Logic of Science (US) *882, 1001*
Studies in the Modern Russian Language (UK ISSN 0081-8631) *705*
Studies in the National Income and Expenditure of the United Kingdom (UK ISSN 0081-864X) *278*
Studies in the Natural Sciences (US) *1001*
Studies in the Political Economy of Canada (CN) *200, 910*
Studies in the Processing, Marketing and Distribution of Commodities (UN) *285*
Studies in the Romance Languages and Literatures *see* North Carolina Studies in the Romance Languages and Literatures *728*
Studies in the Social Sciences (GW ISSN 0081-8674) *1012*
Studies in the Social Sciences *see* West Georgia College Studies in the Social Sciences *1013*
Studies in the Structure of Power: Decision Making in Canada (CN ISSN 0081-8690) *910*
Studies in the Theory of Science (SW ISSN 0081-8704) *1163*
Studies in Theoretical Psycholinguistics (NE) *705, 937*
Studies in Transnational Economic Law(NE) *671*
Studies in Transnational Legal Policy (US) *665*
Studies in Tropical Oceanography (US ISSN 0081-8720) *408*
Studies in U.S. National Security (NE) *812*
Studies in U S History and Culture (US) *516*
Studies in Urban History (UK) *626*
Studies in Wage-Price Policy (US) *200, 278*
Studies in Welsh History (UK ISSN 0141-030X) *598*
Studies in Women and Religion (US) *973, 1129*
Studies in Zambian Society (ZA) *567, 1030*
Studies of Brain Function (US ISSN 0172-5742) *791*
Studies of Broadcasting (JA) *349*
Studies of Classical India (NE) *571, 882, 977*
Studies of Developing Countries (NE ISSN 0081-8771) *1030*
Studies of Government Finance: Second Series (US) *299*
Studies of Higher Education and Research (SW ISSN 0283-7692) *439*
Studies of Israeli Society (US ISSN 0734-4937) *505, 1030*
Studies of Law in Social Change and Development (SW ISSN 0348-1964) *1163*
Studies of Urban Society (US ISSN 0081-8801) *626, 1030*
Studies on Asia *see* School of International Studies. Publications on Asia *571*
Studies on Asian Topics (UK ISSN 0142-6028) *853*
Studies on Current Health Problems (UK ISSN 0473-8837) *767, 956*
Studies on East Asia (US) *853*
Studies on Fascism and Hitlerite Crimes(PL ISSN 0137-1126) *598, 910*
Studies on Finland's Economic Growth *see* Suomen Pankki. Julkaisuja. Kasvututkimuksia *292*

Studies on History of Medicine/ Igakushi Kenkyu (JA ISSN 0019-1612) *767*
Studies on Religion in Africa (NE) *76, 973*
Studies on Selected Development Problems in Various Countries in the Middle East (UN ISSN 0085-6908) *264*
Studies on Southeast Asia (US) *571, 853*
Studies on Statistics (GW ISSN 0072-3967) *1065*
Studies on Taxation and Economic Development (NE ISSN 0071-2191) *292, 299*
Studies on the Development of Behavior and the Nervous System (US ISSN 0093-3317) *791*
Studies on the Fauna of Suriname and Other Guyanas (NE ISSN 0300-5488) *178*
Studies on the Morphology and Systematics of Scale Insects (US) *131, 166, 200*
Studies on the Radioactive Contamination of the Sea. Annual Report (EI) *1163*
Studies on the Texts of the Desert of Judah (NE) *977*
Studies on Voltaire and the Eighteenth Century (UK ISSN 0435-2866) *598, 734*
Studies on Women Abstracts (UK ISSN 0262-5644) *12, 1130*
Studii Clasice (RM ISSN 0081-8844) *339*
Studii de Hidraulica (RM) *404*
Studii de Irigatii Si Desecari (RM) *1126*
Studii si Articole de Istorie (RM) *598*
Studii si Cercetari de Antropologie (RM ISSN 0039-3886) *76*
Studii si Cercetari de Geologie, Geofizica si Geografie. Geografie (RM ISSN 0039-3967) *548*
Studii si Cercetari de Geologie, Geofizica si Geographie. Geofizica (RM) *401*
Studii si Cercetari de Geologie, Geofizica si Geographie. Geologie/ Studies and Research in Geology, Geophysics and Geography. Geology(RM) *395*
Studii si Cercetari de Istoria Artei. Seria Arta Plastica (RM ISSN 0039-3983) *111, 561, 830*
Studii si Cercetari de Istoria Artei. Seria Teatru-Muzica-Cinematografie (RM ISSN 0039-3991) *825, 842, 1078*
Studii si Cercetari de Istoria Artei. Seria Teatru, Muzica, Cinematografie/Studies and Research in Art History. Series: Theatre, Music, Cinematography (RM) *825, 842, 1078*
Studii si Cercetari de Numismatica (RM ISSN 0081-8887) *845*
Studii si Materiale de Istorie Medie (RM) *598*
Studii si Materiale de Istorie Moderna (RM) *598*
Studio Sound's Pro-Audio Yearbook *see* Studio Sound's Pro-Audio Directory *1032*
Studio Sound's Pro-Audio Directory (UK) *349, 1032*
Studium (AT ISSN 0311-2233) *339, 598*
Studium Biblicum Franciscanum. Analecta (IS ISSN 0081-8909) *973*
Studium Biblicum Franciscanum. Collectio Maior (IS ISSN 0081-8917) *973*
Studium Biblicum Franciscanum. Collectio Minor (IS ISSN 0081-8925) *973*
Studium Biblicum Franciscanum. Liber Annuus (IS ISSN 0081-8933) *973*
Studium Biblicum Franciscanum. Museum (IS) *93*
Studium Niemcoznawcze (PL ISSN 0081-8941) *598*
Study Abroad/Etudes a l'Etranger/ Estudios en el Extranjero (UN ISSN 0081-895X) *442*
Study Centre for Yugoslav Affairs. Review (UK ISSN 0585-7694) *910*

Study Group on Eighteenth-Century Russia. Newsletter (UK) *598, 734*
Study in the United Kingdom (US) *442*
Study of Federal Tax Law. Income Tax Materials, Business Enterprises *see* Study of Federal Tax Law. Income Tax Volume: Business Enterprises *665*
Study of Federal Tax Law. Income Tax Volume *see* Study of Federal Tax Law. Income Tax Volume: Individuals *665*
Study of Federal Tax Law. Income Tax Volume: Business Enterprises (US ISSN 0362-2983) *665*
Study of Federal Tax Law. Income Tax Volume: Individuals (US) *665*
Study of Financial Results and Reporting Trends in the Gaming Industry (US) *200, 1036*
Study of Nursing Care: Research Project Series (UK ISSN 0302-1440) *784*
Study of Saskatchewan Collective Bargaining Agreements *see* Non-Wage Provisions in Saskatchewan Collective Agreements *274*
Study of Time (US) *117*
Studying Organizations: Innovations in Methodology (US) *937*
Stuttgarter Arbeiten zur Germanistik (GW) *734*
Stuttgarter Geographische Studien (GW ISSN 0343-7906) *548*
Style Auto (IT ISSN 0039-4254) *1093*
Stylos (BL) *735*
Styrelsen foer Teknisk Utveckling Investigation *see* S T U Investigation *1070*
Su Voz (CU) *973*
Sub Cellular Biochemistry (US ISSN 0306-0225) *152*
Sub-Saharan Africa Report (US) *249, 910*
Subject Collections (US ISSN 0000-0140) *688*
Subject Directory of Special Libraries and Information Centers (US) *684*
Subject Guide to Books in Print (US ISSN 0000-0159) *131*
Subject Guide to Canadian Books in Print. (CN) *964*
Subject Guide to Children's Books in Print (US ISSN 0000-0167) *131*
Subject Guide to Microforms in Print *see* Guide to Microforms in Print. Subject *127*
Subject Headings for Engineering *see* S H E *683*
Subject Index to Articles in Newspapers in Mauritius (MF) *12*
Subject Index to Sources of Comparative International Statistics (UK) *12, 1065*
Subject Index to Welsh Periodicals (UK) *538*
Subject Matter Index to Public and Private Statues of New Brunswick (CN) *665*
Subsida Hagiographica (BE) *973*
Subsidia Mediaevalia (CN ISSN 0316-0769) *599*
Subsidia Scientifica Franciscalia (IT ISSN 0262-4649) *983*
Substance Abuse Book Review Index (CN ISSN 0228-8648) *1163*
Subterranean Sociology Newsletter (US ISSN 0039-4394) *712, 1030*
Successful Meetings Facilities Directory(US) *796*
Successful Writers and Editors Guidebook (US) *973*
Sucrerie Belge (BE) *60*
Sudan. Department of Statistics. Internal Trade and Other Statistics (SJ) *240*
Sudan. Department of Statistics. National Income Accounts and Supporting Tables (SJ) *278*
Sudan. Department of Statistics. Statistical Yearbook (SJ) *1065*
Sudan. Economic and Social Research Council. Bulletin (SJ) *249, 1012*
Sudan. Economic and Social Research Council. Occasional Paper (SJ) *249, 1012*
Sudan. Economic and Social Research Council. Research Report (SJ) *249, 1012*

Sudan. Ministry of Finance and National Economy. Annual Budget Speech, Proposals for the General Budget and the Development Budget(SJ) *946*
Sudan. Ministry of Finance and National Economy. Economic and Financial Research Section. Economic Survey (SJ) *249*
Sudan. Ministry of Finance and National Economy. General Budget: Review, Presentation and Analysis (SJ) *946*
Sudan. National Council for Research. Science Policy and Annual Report (SJ) *1001*
Sudan. National Planning Commission. Economic Survey *see* Sudan. Ministry of Finance and National Economy. Economic and Financial Research Section. Economic Survey *249*
Sudan Commercial Bank. Report of the Board of Directors (SJ) *232*
Sudan Cotton Review (SJ ISSN 0562-5068) *60*
Sudan Journal of Administration and Development (SJ) *946*
Sudan Journal of Food Science and Technology (SJ) *520, 523*
Sudan Law Journal and Reports (SJ ISSN 0585-8631) *665*
Sudan Notes and Records (SJ) *613*
Sudan Research Information Bulletin (SJ ISSN 0453-8129) *632, 1001, 1012*
Sudan Science Abstracts (SJ) *1004*
Sudan Silva (SJ) *527*
Sudan Society/Al-Mujtama (SJ ISSN 0562-5130) *76*
Sudan Texts Bulletin (IE ISSN 0143-6554) *567*
Sudan Trade Directory (SJ) *249*
Sudan Yearbook of Agricultural Statistics (SJ) *49*
Sudhoffs Archiv. Beihefte (GW ISSN 0341-0773) *767, 1001*
Sudia Romanica Universitatis Debreceniensis de Ludovico Kossuth Nominatae. Series Litteraria (HU ISSN 0418-4572) *735*
Suedafrikanische Exporteure *see* South African Exporters *259*
Suedost-Forschungen (GW ISSN 0081-9077) *599*
Suedostdeutsche Historische Kommission. Buchreihe (GW) *599*
Suedostdeutsches Archiv (GW ISSN 0081-9085) *516, 599*
Suedostdeutsches Kulturwerk, Munich. Kleine Suedostreihe (GW ISSN 0081-9093) *599, 735*
Suedostdeutsches Kulturwerk, Munich. Schriftenreihen. Reihe A. Kultur und Dichtung (GW ISSN 0081-9107) *111, 599, 735*
Suedostdeutsches Kulturwerk, Munich. Schriftenreihen. Reihe B. Wissenschaftliche Arbeiten (GW ISSN 0081-9115) *599*
Suedostdeutsches Kulturwerk, Munich. Schriftenreihen. Reihe C. Erinnerungen und Quellen (GW ISSN 0081-9123) *599, 735*
Suedosteuropa - Bibliographie (GW ISSN 0081-9131) *131*
Suedosteuropa - Jahrbuch (GW ISSN 0081-914X) *599*
Suedosteuropa - Studien (GW ISSN 0081-9166) *599*
Suedosteuropaeische Arbeiten (GW) *599*
Suelos *see* Argentina. Instituto Nacional de Tecnologia Agropecuaria. Suelos *1146*
Suesswaren Jahrbuch (GW ISSN 0081-9174) *520*
Suffolk Institute of Archaeology and History. Proceedings (UK ISSN 0262-6004) *94, 599*
Suffolk Sheep Society Flock Book (UK) *68*
Suffolk Stud Book (UK) *68, 1043*
Sugar Economy *see* Zuckerwirtschaftliches Taschenbuch *521*
Sugar Industry Abstracts *see* Tate and Lyle's Sugar Industry Abstracts *522*

Sugar Milling Research Institute. Annual Report (SA) 523
Sugar Processing Research Conference. Proceedings (US ISSN 0730-6490) 35
Sugar Technologists' Association of Trinidad and Tobago. Proceedings. (TR ISSN 0302-4555) 520
Sugar y Azucar Yearbook (US ISSN 0081-9212) 520
Sugestive Low Priced Stocks (US) 268
Suggested State Legislation (US ISSN 0070-1157) 946
Sugia (GW ISSN 0720-0986) 567, 705
Sui Yuan Wen Hsien (CH) 571, 854
Suid-Afrikaanse Argiefblad/South African Archives Journal (SA) 684
Suid-Afrikaanse Buitelandse Handelsargonisasie Jaarverslag see S A F T O Annual Report 259
Suid-Afrikaanse Guernsey (SA ISSN 0081-9220) 68
Suid-Afrikaanse Instituut van Internasionale Aangeleenthede. Bibliografiese Reeks see South African Institute of International Affairs. Bibliographical Series 912
Suid-Afrikaanse Jaarboek vir Volkereg see South African Yearbook of International Law 671
Suid-Afrikaanse Kultuurhistoriese Museum. Bulletin/South African Cultural History Museum. Bulletin (SA) 76, 567
Suid-Afrikaanse Mediese Navorsingsraad. Jaarverslag see South African Medical Research Council. Annual Report 766
Suid-Afrikaanse Museum. Annale see South African Museum. Annals 857
Suid-Afrikaanse Reserwebank. Jaarlikse Ekonomiese Verslag see South African Reserve Bank. Annual Economic Report 249
Suid-Afrikaanse Reserwebank. Verslag van die Gewone Algemene Vergadering see South African Reserve Bank. Report of the Ordinary General Meeting 232
Suid-Afrikaanse Tydskrif vir Kommunikasieafwykings see South African Journal of Communication Disorders 766
Suido Jigyo Nenpo/Annual Statistics of Water Works (JA) 1128
Suiken Kagaku Kenkyujo Nenpo see Nagoya University. Water Research Institute. Annual Report 1125
Suiro Yoho see Japan. Maritime Safety Agency. Hydrographic Department. Hydrographic Bulletin 403
Sulphur in Agriculture (US ISSN 0160-0680) 35
Sulphur Institute. Technical Bulletin (US ISSN 0081-9255) 1163
Sulphur Institute Journal see Sulphur in Agriculture 35
Sulphur Research & Development (US ISSN 0163-0644) 1163
Sulu Studies (PH) 1163
Sumer (IQ ISSN 0081-9271) 94
Sumitomo Bulletin of Industrial Health/ Sumitomo Sangyo Eisei (JA ISSN 0081-928X) 636, 886
Sumitomo Sangyo Eisei see Sumitomo Bulletin of Industrial Health 636
Summary, Annual Meeting of the Southern Legislative Conference of the Council of State Governments see Council of State Governments. Southern Legislative Conference. Summary, Annual Meeting 1151
Summary Information on Master of Social Work Programs (US) 439, 1021
Summary of Congress (US ISSN 0146-2156) 910
Summary of Expenditure Data for Michigan Public Schools (US ISSN 0094-8268) 420
Summary of Kentucky Education Statistics see Information on Education 415
Summary of Postgraduate Diplomas and Courses in Medicine see Guide to Postgraduate Degrees, Diplomas and Courses in Medicine 435

Summary of Public Acts of Interest to Municipal Officials (US) 946
Summary of State Laws and Regulations Relating to Distilled Spirits (US ISSN 0081-931X) 120
Summary of U.S. Export and Import Merchandise Trade see Foreign Trade Reports. Summary of U.S. Export and Import Merchandise Trade 255
Summer Computer Simulation Conference. Proceedings (US ISSN 0094-7474) 358
Summer Employment Directory of the United States (US ISSN 0081-9352) 849
Summer Institute in Linguistics. Studies in Descriptive and Applied Linguistics see Descriptive and Applied Linguistics. Annual Reports 693
Summer Institute of Linguistics. Language Data. African Series (US) 705
Summer Institute of Linguistics. Language Data. Amerindian Series (US) 705
Summer Institute of Linguistics. Language Data. Asia-Pacific Series (US) 705
Summer Institute of Linguistics. Museum of Anthropology Publication see International Museum of Cultures. Publication 73
Summer Institute of Linguistics. Publications Catalog (US) 709
Summer Institute of Linguistics. Serie Linguistica (BL) 705
Summer Institute of Linguistics. University of North Dakota Session. Work Papers (US) 705
Summer Institute of Linguistics, Inc. Publications in Linguistics see S I L Publications in Linguistics 702
Summer Jobs for (Year) (US) 849
Summer Service Opportunities (US) 979, 1021
Summer Study Abroad see Vacation Study Abroad 442
Sun and Moon Tables for Ghana see Ghana. Meteorological Department. Sun and Moon Tables for Ghana 804
Sun Dance Reprints (US ISSN 8756-5382) 561, 735
Sun Sign Book (US) 114
Sun Tracks (US) 505
Sunday Telegraph Business Finance Directory: The Guide to Sources of U K Corporate Finance (UK) 233
Sunday Telegraph U K Finance Directory: A Guide to Sources of U K Corporate Finance see Sunday Telegraph Business Finance Directory: The Guide to Sources of U K Corporate Finance 233
Sundhedsstyrelsen. Aarsberetning (DK ISSN 0105-5151) 956
Sundhedsstyrelsen Vitalstatistik (DK ISSN 0107-749X) 956, 1065
Sung Studies Newsletter see Bulletin of Sung and Yuan Studies 850
Suomalainen Tiedeakatemia. Vuosikirja see Academia Scientiarum Fennica. Yearbook 986
Suomalais-Ugrilaisen Seuran. Aikakauskirja/Societe Finno-Ougrienne. Journal (FI ISSN 0355-0214) 77, 705
Suomen Betoniteollisuuden Keskusjarjesto. Julkaisu/Association of the Concrete Industry of Finland. Publication (FI) 187
Suomen Geodeettisen Laitoksen. Julkaisuja/Finnish Geodetic Institute. Publications/Finnische Geodaetische Institut. Veroeffentlichungen (FI ISSN 0085-6932) 401
Suomen Geodeettisen Laitoksen. Tiedonantoja/Finnish Geodetic Institute. Reports (FI ISSN 0355-1962) 401
Suomen Hammaslaakariseura. Toimituksia. Supplementa/Finnish Dental Society. Proceedings. Supplement (FI ISSN 0355-4651) 780

Suomen Historiallinen Seura. Kasikirjoja(FI ISSN 0081-9417) 564
Suomen Historian Laehteitae/Source Material of Finnish History (FI ISSN 0081-9425) 599
Suomen Joukkovelkakirjalainat/Finnish Bond Issues/Finlandska Masskuldevrevslan (FI ISSN 0781-4437) 268
Suomen Kalatalous (FI ISSN 0085-6940) 513
Suomen Kielen Seuran Vuosikirja see Sananjalka 703
Suomen Muinaismuistoyhdistyksen Aikakauskirja (FI ISSN 0355-1822) 94, 111
Suomen Museo (FI ISSN 0355-1806) 77, 94
Suomen Obligaatiorkirja see Suomen Joukkovelkakirjalainat 268
Suomen Osallistuminen Yhdistyneiden Kansakuntien Toimintaan see Yhdistyneiden Kansakuntien Yleiskokous (Year) 920
Suomen Pankki. Julkaisuja. Kasvututkimuksia/Bank of Finland. Publications. Studies on Finland's Economic Growth (FI ISSN 0355-6050) 292
Suomen Pankki. Julkaisuja. Sarja A/ Bank of Finland. Publications. Series A/Finlands Bank. Publikationer. Serie A (FI ISSN 0355-6034) 200
Suomen Pankki. Julkaisuja. Sarja B/ Bank of Finland. Publications. Series B/Finlands Bank. Publikationer. Serie B (FI ISSN 0357-4776) 200
Suomen Pankki. Julkaisuja. Sarja C/ Bank of Finland. Publications. Series C/Finlands Bank. Publikationer. Serie C (FI ISSN 0081-9492) 200
Suomen Pankki. Julkaisuja. Sarja D/ Bank of Finland. Publications. Series D/Finlands Bank. Publikationer. Serie D (FI ISSN 0355-6042) 200
Suomen Pankki. Taloustieteellinen Tutkimuslaitos. Julkaisuja. Series Kasvututkimuksia see Suomen Pankki. Julkaisuja. Kasvututkimuksia 292
Suomen Pankki. Taloustieteellinen Tutkimuslaitos. Julkaisuja. Series B see Suomen Pankki. Julkaisuja. Sarja B 200
Suomen Pankki. Vuosikirja see Bank of Finland. Yearbook 224
Suomen Pankki Taloustieteellinen Tutkimuslaitos. Julkaisuja. Series A: Taloudellisia Selvityksia see Suomen Pankki. Julkaisuja. Sarja A 200
Suomen Pankki, Taloustieteellinen Tutkimuslaitos. Series D. Mimeographed Series see Suomen Pankki. Julkaisuja. Sarja D 200
Suomen Sanomalehtien Mikrofilmit/ Microfilmed Newspapers of Finland (FI ISSN 0355-4074) 12
Suomen Standardisoimisliitto Catalogue see S F S Catalogue 809
Suomen Teollisuusliitto. Jasenluettelo/ Finlands Industrifoerbund. Medlemsfoerteckning/Federation of Finnish Industries. List of Members (FI) 317
Suomen Tilastollinen Vuosikirja/ Statistisk Aarsbok foer Finland/ Statistical Yearbook of Finland (FI ISSN 0081-5063) 1065
Suomen Vakuutusvuosikirja/Finnish Insurance Yearbook (FI ISSN 0356-7826) 641
Suomi Merella (FI ISSN 0039-5633) 812
Super-8 Journal see Amateurfilm Journal 822
Superior California Administration Newsletter see S C A N 1162
Supermarket Industry Speaks see Food Marketing Industry Speaks 522
Supermarket Trends see Trends: Consumer Attitudes and the Supermarket Update 523
Supply and Demand: Educational Personnel in Delaware (US ISSN 0094-2308) 420

SURVEY OF 1897

Supply and Demand for Scientists and Engineers see Technological Marketplace: Supply and Demand for Scientists and Engineers 849
Supreme Court Economic Review (US ISSN 0736-9921) 665
Supreme Court Historical Society. Yearbook (US ISSN 0362-5249) 372, 665
Supreme Court Practice (UK ISSN 0039-5978) 665
Supreme Court Review (US ISSN 0081-9557) 665
Surf Katalog (GW) 1047
Surface Science (NE ISSN 0039-6028) 332, 891
Surface Transportation R & D in Canada (CN) 1083
Surface Treatment Technology Abstracts (UK ISSN 0950-5199) 12, 802
Surface Water Year Book of Great Britain (UK ISSN 0081-959X) 1126
Surface Wave Abstracts (UK ISSN 0049-2639) 12, 894
Surfaces (Paris, 1978) (FR) 882
Surfactant Science Series (US ISSN 0081-9603) 147, 324
Surfboard (US ISSN 0276-6582) 1036
Surfboard Builder's Yearbook see Surfboard 1036
Surgery Annual (US ISSN 0081-9638) 794
Surgical Forum see Forum on Fundamental Surgical Problems 794
Surgical Trade Buyers Guide see Health Industry Buyers Guide 761
Surinam. Algemeen Bureau voor de Statistiek. Kwartaal Statistiek van de Industriele Produktie (SR) 218
Surinam. Algemeen Bureau voor de Statistiek. Nationale Rekeningen (SR) 1065
Surinam. Centraal Bureau Luchtkartering. Jaarverslag (SR) 21, 548
Surmach (UK ISSN 0491-6204) 561, 812, 910
Surplus Dealers Directory (US ISSN 0081-9662) 285, 317
Surrealist Transformaction (UK ISSN 0039-6168) 111, 632, 735
Surrey Archaeological Collections (UK ISSN 0309-7803) 94
Surrey Archaeological Society. Research Volumes (UK ISSN 0308-342X) 94
Surrey Papers in Economics (UK ISSN 0081-9670) 200
Survey see Survey Sarajevo 910
Survey of Arts Administration Training (US) 111, 281, 431
Survey of Biological Progress (US ISSN 0081-9697) 147
Survey of Dental Practice (US) 780
Survey of Drug Research in Immunologic Disease (SZ ISSN 0253-4843) 774
Survey of Economic and Social Conditions in Africa (UN) 264
Survey of German Federal Statistics/ Apercu de la Statistique Federale Allemande (GW) 1065
Survey of Grant-Making Foundations (US) 632
Survey of India's Exports (II ISSN 0537-1120) 237
Survey of Industry in Israel see Israel. Ministry of Commerce and Industry. Surveys and Development Plans of Industry in Israel 290
Survey of International Affairs (US) 918
Survey of Local Chambers of Commerce (US ISSN 0069-2441) 237
Survey of London (UK ISSN 0081-9751) 111
Survey of Migration in Bangkok Metropolis (TH) 929
Survey of Overseas Visitors to Singapore (SI) 1116
Survey of Pharmacy Law (US) 665, 873
Survey of Press Freedom in Latin America (US ISSN 0743-4324) 609, 646, 918
Survey of Progress in Chemistry (US ISSN 0081-976X) 324

SURVEY OF

Survey of Race Relations in South Africa (SA ISSN 0081-9778) *914*
Survey of Salaries and Employee Benefits of Private and Public Employers in Arizona. *see* Joint Governmental Salary Survey: Arizona *273*
Survey of State Travel Offices (US) *1116*
Survey of the Austrian Economy/ Oesterreichs Wirtschaft im Ueberblick (AU) *240*
Survey Sarajevo (YU ISSN 0350-0144) *910*
Surveys & Reference Works in Mathematics (US) *753*
Surveys of Applied Economics (US) *200*
Surveys of the Position of Various Pests and Diseases in Europe and the Mediterranean Area *see* European and Mediterranean Plant Protection Organization. Publications. Series B: Plant Health Newsletter *55*
Surveys, Polls, Censuses and Forecasts Directory (US ISSN 0737-545X) *1065*
Survival International Review (UK ISSN 0308-2857) *77, 914*
Susquehanna River Basin Commission. Annual Report (US ISSN 0094-6427) *1126*
Sussex Anthropology (UK ISSN 0307-823X) *77*
Sussex Essays in Anthropology *see* Sussex Anthropology *77*
Sussex Genealogical Centre. Occasional Papers (UK) *537*
Sut Anubis (UK ISSN 0143-5418) *860*
Svensk Exegetisk Aarsbok (SW) *973*
Svensk Geografisk Aarsbok/Swedish Geographical Yearbook (SW ISSN 0081-9808) *549*
Svensk Obligationsbok (SW) *233*
Svensk Tidskriftsfoerteckning/Current Swedish Periodicals (SW ISSN 0586-0431) *131*
Svensk Traevaru- och Papersmassetidning/Swedish Timber and Wood Pulp Journal (SW ISSN 0039-6796) *530, 859*
Svensk Travarutidning *see* Svensk Traevaru- och Papersmassetidning *530*
Svenska. Riksarkivet. Meddelanden (SW ISSN 0039-6893) *599, 684*
Svenska Arkivsamfundet Skrifterie *see* Arkiv, Samhaelle och Forskning *673*
Svenska Barnboksinstitutet. Skrifter/ Swedish Institute for Children's Books. Studies (SW ISSN 0347-5387) *336, 684*
Svenska Bostaeder. Aarsredovisning *see* Housing and Urban Planning in Sweden. Annual Report *623*
Svenska Folkskolans Vaenners Kalender(FI) *599*
Svenska Handelsbanken. Annual Report(SW ISSN 0081-9913) *233*
Svenska Handelsbanken. Annual Report and Auditors' Report *see* Svenska Handelsbanken. Annual Report *233*
Svenska Historiska Foereningen. Skrifter (SW) *599*
Svenska Institutet i Athen. Skrifter (SW ISSN 0081-9921) *94, 339*
Svenska Institutet i Rom. Skrifter. Acta Series Prima (IT ISSN 0081-993X) *94, 339*
Svenska Linne-Sallskapet Aarsskrift/ Swedish Linneus Society. Yearbook (SW ISSN 0375-2038) *161*
Svenska Litteratursaellskapet i Finland. Skrifter (FI ISSN 0039-6842) *561, 705*
Svenska Livsmedelsinstitutet Annual Report *see* S I K Annual Report *520*
Svenska Livsmedelsinstitutet Information *see* S I K Information *520*
Svenska Traeforskningsinstitutet Meddelande. Series A *see* S T F I Meddelande. Series A *859*
Svenska Traeskyddsinstitutet. Meddelanden/Swedish Wood Preservation Institute. Reports (SW ISSN 0346-7090) *530*
Svenskt Fiske *see* Sportfiskaren *1046*

Svenskt Musikhistoriskt Arkiv. Bulletin (SW ISSN 0586-0709) *842*
Svenskt Varumaerkesarkiv/Swedish Trademark Archive (SW) *861*
Sverige-E G (SW ISSN 0346-5578) *918*
Sverige-Europeiska Gemenskaperna *see* Sverige-E G *918*
Sveriges Foerfattarfoerbund. Medlemsfoerteckning (SW) *135, 735*
Sveriges Jaernvaegar/Railways of Sweden (SW ISSN 0081-9964) *1095*
Sveriges Lantbruksuniversitet. Institutionen foer Vaextodling. Rapporter och Avhandlingar (SW) *35*
Sveriges Lantbruksuniversitet. Institutionen foer Virkeslaera. Rapporter (SW ISSN 0348-4599) *527*
Sveriges Lantbruksuniversitet. Institutionen foer Virkeslaera. Uppsatser (SW) *527*
Sveriges Riksbank. Aarsbok *see* Sveriges Riksbank. Statistisk Aarsbok *233*
Sveriges Riksbank. Foervaltningsberaettelse (SW ISSN 0347-3198) *233*
Sveriges Riksbank. Statistisk Aarsbok/ Central Bank of Sweden. Statistical Yearbook (SW ISSN 0348-7342) *233*
Sveuciliste u Zagrebu. Fakultet Strojarstva i Brodogradnje. Zbornik Radova (YU ISSN 0350-3097) *492, 1104*
Svineavl og -Produktion i Danmark (DK ISSN 0106-7338) *68*
Swamp Gas Journal (CN ISSN 0707-7106) *21*
Swansea Geographer (UK ISSN 0081-9980) *549*
Swarbica Journal (II) *571, 684*
Swaziland. Central Statistical Office. Annual Statistical Bulletin (SQ ISSN 0586-1357) *1065*
Swaziland. Central Statistical Office. Annual Survey of Swazi Nation Land(SQ) *1065*
Swaziland. Central Statistical Office. Capital Fund Estimates *see* Swaziland. Ministry of Finance. Capital Fund Estimates *233*
Swaziland. Central Statistical Office. Census of Individual Tenure Farms (SQ) *35*
Swaziland. Central Statistical Office. Census of Industrial Production *see* Swaziland. Central Statistical Office. Census of Industries *218*
Swaziland. Central Statistical Office. Census of Industries (SQ) *218, 1065*
Swaziland. Central Statistical Office. Commercial Timber Plantation and Wood Products Statistics *see* Swaziland. Central Statistical Office. Timber Statistics *529*
Swaziland. Central Statistical Office. Education Statistics (SQ) *426, 1065*
Swaziland. Central Statistical Office. Employment and Wages (SQ) *275*
Swaziland. Central Statistical Office. Recurrent Estimates of Public Expenditure *see* Swaziland. Ministry of Finance. Recurrent Estimates of Public Expenditure *946*
Swaziland. Central Statistical Office. Timber Statistics (SQ) *529, 1065*
Swaziland. Department of Economic Planning and Statistics. Economic Review (SQ) *249*
Swaziland. Economic Planning Office. Economic Review *see* Swaziland. Department of Economic Planning and Statistics. Economic Review *249*
Swaziland. Geological Survey and Mines Department. Annual Report (SQ ISSN 0081-9999) *395*
Swaziland. Geological Survey and Mines Department. Bulletin (SQ ISSN 0082-0008) *395*
Swaziland. Ministry of Agriculture. Annual Report (SQ) *35*
Swaziland. Ministry of Finance. Capital Fund Estimates (SQ) *233*

Swaziland. Ministry of Finance. Recurrent Estimates of Public Expenditure (SQ) *946*
Swaziland National Bibliography (SQ ISSN 0378-7710) *131, 964*
Swaziland National Centre. Yearbook *see* Swaziland National Museum. Yearbook *567*
Swaziland National Museum. Yearbook (SQ) *567*
Sweden. Finansdepartmentet. Regeringens Budgetfoerslag (SW ISSN 0347-7169) *299*
Sweden. Fisheries Board. Series Hydrography. Reports *see* Sweden. Fishery Board. Institute of Marine Research. Report *147*
Sweden. Fishery Board. Institute of Marine Research. Report (SW ISSN 0346-8666) *147*
Sweden. Institute of Marine Research. Series Biology. Reports *see* Sweden. Fishery Board. Institute of Marine Research. Report *147*
Sweden. Konjunkturinstitutet. Occasional Paper (SW ISSN 0082-0067) *200*
Sweden. Luftfartsverket. Aarsbok (SW ISSN 0348-2251) *1065, 1087*
Sweden. Medicinalvaesendet. Foerfattningssamling *see* Sweden. Socialstyrelsen. Foerfattningssamling: Medical *767*
Sweden. Medicinalvaesendet. Foerfattningssamling *see* Sweden. Socialstyrelsen. Foerfattningssamling: Social *1021*
Sweden. Ministry of Finance. Revised Finance Bill (SW) *299*
Sweden. Nationalmusei Skriftserie (SW) *830*
Sweden. Nationalmuseum. Skriftserie *see* Sweden. Nationalmusei Skriftserie *830*
Sweden. Patent- och Registereringsverket. Aarsberaettelse/ Sweden. Royal Patent and Registration Office. Annual Report (SW) *861*
Sweden. Riksdagen. Foerteckning Oever Riksdagens Ledamoeter (SW) *910*
Sweden. Riksdagen. Riksdag *see* Sweden. Riksdagen. Riksdagen Aarsbok *910*
Sweden. Riksdagen. Riksdagen Aarsbok(SW) *910*
Sweden. Riksfoersaekringsverket. Allmaen Foersaekring (SW ISSN 0082-0075) *641*
Sweden. Riksfoersaekringsverket. Yrkesskador *see* Arbetsskador *638*
Sweden. Royal Patent and Registration Office. Annual Report *see* Sweden. Patent- och Registereringsverket. Aarsberaettelse *861*
Sweden. Sjukvaardens och Socialvaardens Planerings- och Rationaliseringsinstitut. S P R I Informerar (SW ISSN 0346-8445) *956*
Sweden. Sjukvaardens och Socialvaardens Planerings- och Rationaliseringsinstitut. S P R I Raad(SW ISSN 0082-0113) *956*
Sweden. Sjukvaardens och Socialvaardens Planerings- och Rationaliseringsinstitut. S P R I Rapport (SW ISSN 0586-1691) *956*
Sweden. Sjukvaardens och Socialvaardens Planerings-och Rationaliseringsinstitut. S P R I Raad 1. (SW ISSN 0303-6553) *956*
Sweden. Sjukvaardens och Socialvaardens Planerings-och Rationaliseringsinstitut. S P R I Raad 4 (SW ISSN 0303-6545) *956*
Sweden. Sjukvaardens och Socialvaardens Planerings- och Rationaliseringsinstitut. S P R I Raad 5 (SW ISSN 0303-6510) *956*
Sweden. Sjukvaardens och Socialvaardens Planerings- och Rationaliseringsinstitut. S P R I Raad 6 (SW ISSN 0303-6529) *956*
Sweden. Sjukvaardens och Socialvaardens Planerings- och Rationaliseringsinstitut. S P R I Raad 7 (SW ISSN 0303-6537) *956*

Sweden. Sjukvaardens och Socialvaardens Planerings- och Rationaliseringsinstitut. S P R I Specifikationer (SW ISSN 0082-0105) *956*
Sweden. Socialstyrelsen. Alkoholstatistik/Alcohol Statistics (SW) *120, 121*
Sweden. Socialstyrelsen. Foerfattningssamling: Medical (SW ISSN 0346-6000) *767*
Sweden. Socialstyrelsen. Foerfattningssamling: Social (SW ISSN 0346-6019) *1021*
Sweden. Socialstyrelsen. Legitimerade Laekare/Authorized Physicians (SW ISSN 0345-0171) *767*
Sweden. Socialstyrelsen. Redovisar (SW ISSN 0346-5799) *1021*
Sweden. Statens Arbetsgivarverk. Arbetsgivarverket Informerar (SW) *276*
Sweden. Statens Arbetsgivarverk. Foereskrifter om Statlig Tjaenstepensionering; F S P. (SW) *642*
Sweden. Statens Arbetsgivarverk. Foerfattningar om Statligt Reglerade Tjaenster: F S T (SW ISSN 0347-724X) *649*
Sweden. Statens Avtalsverk. Foereskrifter om Statlight Tjaenstepensionering; F S P *see* Sweden. Statens Arbetsgivarverk. Foereskrifter om Statlig Tjaenstepensionering; F S P *642*
Sweden. Statens Avtalsverk. Foerfattningar om Statligt Reglerade Tjaenster: F S T *see* Sweden. Statens Arbetsgivarverk. Foerfattningar om Statligt Reglerade Tjaenster: F S T *649*
Sweden. Statens Avtalsverk. Information Fraan S A V *see* Sweden. Statens Arbetsgivarverk. Arbetsgivarverket Informerar *276*
Sweden. Statens Jaernvaegars Centralfoervaltning. Geoteknik och Ingenjoergeologi. Meddelanden *see* Sweden. Statens Jaernvaegars Huvudkontor. Geoteknik och Ingenjoergeologi. Meddelanden *1071*
Sweden. Statens Jaernvaegars Huvudkontor. Geoteknik och Ingenjoergeologi. Meddelanden (SW) *1071*
Sweden. Statens Naturvaardsverk. Naturvaardsverkets Aarsbok (SW ISSN 0347-8173) *367*
Sweden. Statens Raad foer Byggnadsforskning. Document (SW ISSN 0586-6766) *187, 483, 626*
Sweden. Statens Raad foer Byggnadsforskning. Rapport (SW) *187, 483, 626*
Sweden. Statens Raad Foer Byggnadsforskning. Summaries (SW) *187*
Sweden. Statens Raad Foer Byggnadsforskning. Synopses (SW) *187*
Sweden. Statens Raad foer Byggnadsforskning. Verksamhetsplan (SW) *187, 483, 626*
Sweden. Statens Vaeg- och Trafikinstitut. Verksamhetsberaettelse(SW ISSN 0347-6057) *1097*
Sweden. Statistiska Centralbyraan. Allmaan Fastighetstaxering (SW) *627*
Sweden. Statistiska Centralbyraan. Arbetskraftundersoekningen. Arsmedeltal (SW) *218*
Sweden. Statistiska Centralbyraan. Befolkningsfoeraendringar (SW ISSN 0082-0156) *924, 929*
Sweden. Statistiska Centralbyraan Bibliotek. Internationella Organ. Statistik *see* Sweden. Statistiska Centralbyraan Bibliotek. Statistik fraan Internationella Organ *1163*
Sweden. Statistiska Centralbyraan Bibliotek. Statistik fraan Internationella Organ (SW) *1163*
Sweden. Statistiska Centralbyraan. Folkmaengd (SW ISSN 0082-0164) *924, 929*

Sweden. Statistiska Centralbyraan. Industri (SW ISSN 0082-0172) *218*
Sweden. Statistiska Centralbyraan. Information i Prognosfragor/ Forecasting Information (SW ISSN 0082-0180) *1163*
Sweden. Statistiska Centralbyraan. Jordbruksstatistisk Aarsbok (SW ISSN 0082-0199) *43*
Sweden. Statistiska Centralbyraan. Kommunal Personal (SW ISSN 0082-0202) *218*
Sweden. Statistiska Centralbyraan. Levnadsfoerhaallanden Aarsbok/ Living Conditions Yearbook (SW) *1065*
Sweden. Statistiska Centralbyraan. Loener (SW ISSN 0082-0210) *218*
Sweden. Statistiska Centralbyraan. Meddelanden i Samordningsfraagor (SW ISSN 0082-0229) *1065*
Sweden. Statistiska Centralbyraan. Statistiska Meddelanden. Subgroup Am (Labor Market) (SW ISSN 0082-0237) *218*
Sweden. Statistiska Centralbyraan. Statistiska Meddelanden. Subgroup Bo (Housing and Construction) (SW ISSN 0085-6991) *189, 1065*
Sweden. Statistiska Centralbyraan. Statistiska Meddelanden. Subgroup Be (Population) (SW ISSN 0082-0245) *564, 929*
Sweden. Statistiska Centralbyraan. Statistiska Meddelanden. Subgroup I (Manufacturing) (SW ISSN 0082-027X) *218*
Sweden. Statistiska Centralbyraan. Statistiska Meddelanden. Subgroup J (Agriculture) (SW ISSN 0082-0288) *43*
Sweden. Statistiska Centralbyraan. Statistiska Meddelanden. Subgroup N (National Accounts and Finance) (SW ISSN 0082-0296) *219*
Sweden. Statistiska Centralbyraan. Statistiska Meddelanden. Subgroup H (Trade) (SW ISSN 0082-0261) *219*
Sweden. Statistiska Centralbyraan. Statistiska Meddelanden. Subgroup P (Prices and Price Indices) (SW ISSN 0082-030X) *219*
Sweden. Statistiska Centralbyraan. Statistiska Meddelanden. Subgroup R (Judicial Statistics. Law and Social Welfare) (SW ISSN 0082-0318) *669*
Sweden. Statistiska Centralbyraan. Statistiska Meddelanden. Subgroup S (Social Welfare Statistics) (SW ISSN 0082-0326) *1023*
Sweden. Statistiska Centralbyraan. Statistiska Meddelanden. Subgroup T (Transport and Other Forms of Communication) (SW ISSN 0082-0334) *346, 1087*
Sweden. Statistiska Centralbyraan. Statistiska Meddelanden. Subgroup U (Education and Research) (SW ISSN 0082-0342) *426*
Sweden. Statistiska Centralbyraan. Statsanstaellda/Government Employees (SW ISSN 0348-811X) *1163*
Sweden. Statistiska Centralbyraan. Urval Skriftseries/Selection Series (SW ISSN 0082-0350) *1065*
Sweden. Statistiska Centralbyraan. Utbildningsstatistisk Aarsbok/ Swedish Educational Statistics Yearbook (SW) *420*
Sweden. Statistiska Centralbyraans Bibliotek. Statistik Fran Enskilda Laender (SW ISSN 0280-7610) *1065*
Sweden. Sveriges Geologiska Undersoekning. Jordmagnetiska Publikationer/Geomagnetic Publications (SW ISSN 0075-403X) *395*
Sweden. Sveriges Geologiska Undersoekning. Serie C. Avhandlingar och Uppsatser/ Memoirs and Notices (SW ISSN 0082-0024) *395*

Sweden. Sveriges Geologiska Undersoekning. Serie Ca. Avhandlingar och Uppsatser i Kvarto/Notices in Quarto and Folio (SW ISSN 0082-0016) *395*
Sweden. Televerket. Annual Report *see* Swedish Telecom. Annual Report *344*
Sweden. Universitets- och Hoegskoleambetet. Anslagsframstaellning foer Budgetaaret (SW) *439*
Sweden. Universitetskanslersaembetet. Hoegre Utbildning och Forskning *see* Sweden. Universitets- och Hoegskoleambetet. Anslagsframstaellning foer Budgetaaret *439*
Sweden. V T I Rapport (SW ISSN 0347-6030) *1097*
Sweden Sjukvaardens och Socialvaardens Planerings och Rationaliseringsins (GW ISSN 0281-6881) *1021*
Swedish Agency for Research Cooperation with Developing Countries Report *see* S A R E C Report *918*
Swedish Agency for Research Cooperation with Developing Countries Annual Report *see* S A R E C Annual Report *264*
Swedish Archaeological Bibliography *see* Swedish Archaeology *96*
Swedish Archaeology (SW) *96*
Swedish Budget (SW ISSN 0082-0393) *299*
Swedish Building Research News (SW) *187*
Swedish Film Annual *see* Filmarsboken *824*
Swedish Food Institute. Annual Report *see* S I K Annual Report *520*
Swedish Geographical Yearbook *see* Svensk Geografisk Aarsbok *549*
Swedish Geotechnical Institute. Report *see* Statens Geotekniska Institut. Rapport *401*
Swedish Institute for Children's Books. Studies *see* Svenska Barnboksinstitutet. Skrifter *336*
Swedish Linneus Society. Yearbook *see* Svenska Linne-Sallskapet Aarsskrift *161*
Swedish National Road and Traffic Research Institute. Annual Report *see* Sweden. Statens Vaeg- och Trafikinstitut. Verksamhetsberaettelse *1097*
Swedish Natural Science Research Council. Ecological Bulletins (SW ISSN 0346-6868) *499*
Swedish Nutrition Foundation. Symposia (SW ISSN 0082-0415) *846*
Swedish Research on Higher Education *see* Studies of Higher Education and Research *439*
Swedish Road Safety Office. Analysis Section Report (SW ISSN 0281-4447) *1097*
Swedish Steel Manual (SW) *800*
Swedish Telecom. Annual Report (SW) *344*
Swedish Timber and Wood Pulp Journal *see* Svensk Traevaru- och Papersmassetidning *530*
Swedish Trademark Archive *see* Svenskt Varumaerkesarkiv *861*
Swedish Wood Preservation Institute. Reports *see* Svenska Traeskyddsinstitutet. Meddelanden *530*
Sweet's Canadian Construction Catalogue File (CN ISSN 0082-0431) *187*
Sweet's Catalog File for the Civil Engineering & Retrofit Market (US) *483*
Sweet's Civil Engineering and Retrofit File *see* Sweet's Catalog File for the Civil Engineering & Retrofit Market *483*
Sweet's Contract Interiors File (US) *643*
Sweet's Electrical Engineering and Retrofit File (US) *460*
Sweet's General Building and Renovation File (US) *187*

Sweet's General Building Catalog File *see* Sweet's General Building and Renovation File *187*
Sweet's Homebuilding and Remodeling File (US) *187*
Sweet's Industrial Construction and Renovation File (US) *187*
Sweet's International Construction File (US) *187*
Sweet's Mechanical Engineering and Retrofit File (US) *493*
Swiatowit (PL ISSN 0082-044X) *94*
Swift Kick (US ISSN 0277-447X) *735*
Swift's Directory of Educational Software for the IBM PC (US) *363*
Swimming and Diving and Water Polo Rulebook (US) *1036*
Swimming and Diving Case Book *see* Swimming and Diving and Water Polo Rulebook *1036*
Swimming and Diving Rules *see* Swimming and Diving and Water Polo Rulebook *1036*
Swimming Pool Age Data and Reference Annual *see* Spa Data and Reference Annual *187*
Swimming Rules *see* Swimming and Diving and Water Polo Rulebook *1036*
Swiss Bank Corporation. Report of the Board of Directors to the Annual General Meeting of Shareholders (SZ) *233*
Swiss Biographical Index of Prominent Persons/Annuaire Suisse du Monde et des Affaires/Wer ist Wer in der Schweiz und im Fuerstentum Lichtenstein/Chi e Chi in Svizzera? (SZ) *135*
Swiss Financial Year Book (SZ) *249*
Swiss Political Science Yearbook *see* Annuaire Suisse de Science Politique *902*
Swiss Studies in English *see* Schweizer Anglistische Arbeiten *703*
Switzerland. Bundesamt fuer Statistik. Eingefuehrte Motorfahrzeuge/ Vehicules a Moteur Importes (SZ) *1087*
Switzerland. Bundesamt fuer Statistik. Heiraten, Lebendgeborene und Gestorbene in den Gemeinden/ Mariages, Naissances et Deces dans les Communes (SZ) *929, 1065*
Switzerland. Bundesamt fuer Statistik. In Verkehr Gesetzte Neue Motorfahrzeuge/Vehicules a Moteur Neufs Mis en Circulation (SZ) *1087*
Switzerland. Bundesamt fuer Statistik. Schuelerstatistik/Statistique des Eleves (SZ) *426, 1065*
Switzerland. Bundesamt fuer Statistik. Strassenverkehrsunfaelle/Accidents de la Circulation Routiere en Suisse (SZ) *1093*
Switzerland. Commission pour les Questions Conjoncturelles. Etudes Occasionnelles *see* Switzerland. Kommission fuer Konjunkturfragen. Allfaellige Studien *200*
Switzerland. Directorate General of Customs. Annual Report (SZ) *219, 1065*
Switzerland. Directorate General of Customs. Annual Statistics (SZ ISSN 0081-525X) *219, 1065*
Switzerland. Eidgenoessische Anstalt fuer das Forstliche Versuchswesen. Mitteilungen (SZ) *527*
Switzerland. Kommission fuer Konjunkturfragen. Allfaellige Studien(SZ) *200*
Switzerland. Schweizerische Anstalt fuer das Forstliche Versuchswesen. Mitteilungen *see* Switzerland. Eidgenoessische Anstalt fuer das Forstliche Versuchswesen. Mitteilungen *527*
Switzerland. Statistisches Amt. Eingefuehrte Motorfahrzeuge: In Verkehr Gesetzte Neue Motorfahrzeuge *see* Switzerland. Bundesamt fuer Statistik. In Verkehr Gesetzte Neue Motorfahrzeuge/ Vehicules a Moteur Neufs Mis en Circulation *1087*

Switzerland. Statistisches Amt. Eingefuehrte Motorfahrzeuge; in Verkehr Gesetzte Neue Motorfahrzeuge *see* Switzerland. Bundesamt fuer Statistik. Eingefuehrte Motorfahrzeuge/ Vehicules a Moteur Importes *1087*
Sydney Film Festival Programme (AT) *825*
Sydney for Kids (AT ISSN 0727-4327) *336*
Sydney Gay Guide (AT ISSN 0155-5936) *616*
Sydney Law Review (AT ISSN 0082-0512) *665*
Sydney Ports Handbook (Year) (UK ISSN 0264-567X) *317, 1104*
Sydney Speleological Society. Communications *see* Sydney Speleological Society. Occasional Paper *395*
Sydney Speleological Society. Occasional Paper (AT) *395*
Sydney Stock Exchange. Research and Statistical Department. Company Review Service *see* Sydney Stock Exchange. Research Department, Company Review Service *268*
Sydney Stock Exchange. Research Department, Company Review Service. (AT) *268*
Sydney Studies in English (AT) *705*
Sydowia: Annales Mycologici (AU ISSN 0082-0598) *161*
Sydthy Aarbog (DK ISSN 0900-2103) *599*
Sygdomsmoensteret ved Somatiske Sygehusafdelingen (DK ISSN 0107-8380) *618*
Sygehusklassifikation og Kommunekoder (DK ISSN 0107-508X) *618*
Sygehusvaesenet (DK ISSN 0107-4954) *618*
Sygesikringsstatistik (DK ISSN 0107-8437) *643*
Sylloge Nummorum Graecorum (US ISSN 0271-3993) *845*
Sylloge Nummorum Graecorum Deutschland *see* Sylloge Nummorum Graecorum Deutschland. Staatliche Muenzsammlung Muenchen *94*
Sylloge Nummorum Graecorum Deutschland. Staatliche Muenzsammlung Muenchen (GW) *94, 845*
Symbolae. Series A (BE) *339*
Symbolae Botanicae Upsalienses (SW ISSN 0082-0644) *161*
Symbolae Osloenses (NO ISSN 0039-7679) *339*
Symbolae Philologorum Posnaniensium (PL ISSN 0302-7384) *339*
Symbolic Computation (US) *357*
Symbolon (GW ISSN 0082-0660) *882*
Symbols of American Libraries (US ISSN 0095-0874) *684*
Symphony Gold Book (US ISSN 0275-9381) *842*
Symposia Biologica Hungarica (HU ISSN 0082-0695) *147*
Symposia Mathematica (US ISSN 0082-0725) *753*
Symposia of the Faraday Society *see* Faraday Symposia *331*
Symposia on Fundamental Cancer Research. Papers (US ISSN 0082-0733) *776*
Symposia on Theoretical Physics and Mathematics (II ISSN 0082-075X) *753, 891*
Symposium (International) on Combustion (US ISSN 0082-0784) *332*
Symposium on Atmospheric Turbulence, Diffusion and Air Quality. Preprints *see* Symposium on Turbulence and Diffusion. Preprints *807*
Symposium on Care of the Professional Voice. Transcripts (US) *787*
Symposium on Civil Engineering Planning. Proceedings *see* Doboku Keikagaku Shinpojumu *481*
Symposium on Coal Mine Drainage Research. Papers (US ISSN 0085-7068) *820*

1900 SYMPOSIUM ON

Symposium on Computer Applications in Medical Care. Proceedings (US ISSN 0195-4210) 778
Symposium on Computer Architecture. Conference Proceedings (US ISSN 0149-7111) 356
Symposium on Computer Arithmetic. Proceedings (US) 359
Symposium on Engineering Problems of Fusion Research. Proceedings see Symposium on Fusion Engineering. Proceedings 460
Symposium on Flames and Industry. Proceedings (UK) 480
Symposium on Foundations of Computer Science. Proceedings (US ISSN 0272-5428) 460
Symposium on Frequency Control. Proceedings. see Frequency Control Symposium 453
Symposium on Fusion Engineering. Proceedings (US) 460
Symposium on Hybrid Microelectronics see Hybrid Microelectronics Symposium. (Papers) 454
Symposium on Incremental Motion Control Systems and Devices. Proceedings (US ISSN 0092-1661) 746
Symposium on Information Display. Digest of Technical Papers see S I D International Symposium. Digest of Technical Papers 474
Symposium on Instrumentation for the Process Industries see Instrumentation Symposium for the Process Industries 637
Symposium on Jet Pumps & Ejectors and Gas Lift Techniques. Proceedings (UK) 491
Symposium on Logic Programming Proceedings (US) 358
Symposium on Meteorological Observations and Instrumentation. Preprints (US) 807
Symposium on Naval Hydrodynamics. Proceedings (US ISSN 0082-0849) 895
Symposium on Nondestructive Evaluation. Proceedings (US) 489
Symposium on Nondestructive Evaluation of Components and Materials in Aerospace, Weapons Systems and Nuclear Applications see Proceedings on Nondestructive Evaluation 21
Symposium on Nondestructive Testing of Aircraft and Missile Components see Proceedings on Nondestructive Evaluation 21
Symposium on Particleboard. Proceedings (US ISSN 0082-089X) 530
Symposium on Photographic Gelatin. Proceedings (UK) 1163
Symposium on Physics and Nondestructive Testing, San Antonio. Proceedings see Symposium on Nondestructive Evaluation. Proceedings 489
Symposium on Reliability. Proceedings see Reliability and Maintainability Symposium. Proceedings 459
Symposium on Reliability in Distributed Software and Database Systems. Proceedings (US) 360, 363
Symposium on Reliability in Electronics(HU) 460
Symposium on Security and Privacy. Proceedings. see I E E E Symposium on Security and Privacy. Proceedings 358
Symposium on Semiconductor Memory Testing. Digest of Papers see International Test Conference. Proceedings 361
Symposium on Small Computers in the Arts. Proceedings (US) 113, 844
Symposium on Special Ceramics, Stoke-On-Trent, England. Special Ceramics, Proceedings (UK ISSN 0082-0954) 320
Symposium on Surface Mining and Reclamation (US) 820
Symposium on Surface Mining, Hydrology, Sedimentology and Reclamation. Proceedings (US ISSN 0735-0686) 404, 820

Symposium on the Art of Glassblowing Proceedings. (US ISSN 0569-7468) 113
Symposium on the Physiology and Pathology of Human Reproduction see Harold C. Mack Symposium. Proceedings 171
Symposium on Turbulence and Diffusion. Preprints (US) 807
Symposium on Turbulence, Diffusion and Air Pollution. Preprints see Symposium on Turbulence and Diffusion. Preprints 807
Symposium on Urban Renewal. Papers (UK) 626
Symposium on Wind Effects on Structures in Japan. Proceedings (JA) 474, 807
Symposium Series (US) 712
Syndicat des Industries de Materiel Professionnel Electronique et Radioelectrique Annuaire see S P E R Annuaire 459
Syndicat General de l'Industrie Cotonniere Francaise. Annuaire (FR ISSN 0082-1047) 1075
Syndicat General de la Construction Electrique. Annuaire (FR) 460, 649
Syndicat General des Commerces et Industries du Caoutchouc et des Plastiques. Guide (FR ISSN 0224-2435) 317, 901, 985
Syndicat General des Impots. Guide Foncier (FR) 299
Syndicat General des Impots. Guide National de l'Enregistrement et des Domaines see Syndicat General des Impots. Guide Foncier 299
Syndicat National de la Librairie Ancienne et Moderne. Repertoire see Guide a l'Usage des Amateurs de Livres 961
Syndicated Columnists (US) 646
Synopses of the British Fauna (US ISSN 0082-1101) 178
Synopsis of Laws Enacted by the State of Maryland see Maryland. State Department of Legislative Reference. Synopsis of Laws Enacted by the State of Maryland 660
Syntax and Semantics (US ISSN 0092-4563) 705
Synthese Historical Library (NE ISSN 0082-111X) 882
Synthese Language Library see Studies in Linguistics and Philosophy 937
Synthese Library (NE ISSN 0082-1128) 882, 1012
Synthesis (RM) 735
Synthetic Methods of Organic Chemistry (SZ ISSN 0253-200X) 331, 332
Synthetic Organic Chemicals, United States Production and Sales (US ISSN 0082-1144) 480
Synthetic Pipeline Gas Symposium. Proceedings (US) 867
Syokubutsu Bunrui Gakkai Nyusu/Japan Society of Plant Taxonomist. News (JA) 161
Syracuse University. Foreign and Comparative Studies. African Series (US) 567, 1012
Syracuse University. Foreign and Comparative Studies. Latin American Series (US) 1014
Syracuse University. Foreign and Comparative Studies. South Asian Series (US) 1014
Syracuse University. Foreign and Comparative Studies. South Asian Special Publications (US) 977
Syracuse University. Program of East African Studies. Eastern African Series see Syracuse University. Foreign and Comparative Studies. African Series 1012
Syracuse University Publications in Continuing Education. Landmark and New Horizons Series (US) 427
Syracuse University Publications in Continuing Education. Notes and Essays (US) 427
Syracuse University Publications in Continuing Education. Occasional Papers (US ISSN 0082-1179) 427
Syracuse Wood Science Series (US) 530

Syria. Central Bureau of Statistics. Statistical Abstract (SY ISSN 0081-4725) 1065
Syro-Mesopotamian Studies (US ISSN 0732-6483) 613
System of Ophthalmology (US ISSN 0082-1195) 786
Systematic and Applied Microbiology (GW ISSN 0723-2020) 169
Systematics Association. Special Volumes (US) 178
Systeme d'Information sur les Transports de Machandises Resultats Generaux: Trafic Interieur - Trafic International see S.I.T.R.A.M. Resultats Generaux: Trafic Interieur - Trafic International 1086
Systeme d'Information sur les Transports de Marchandises: Resultats Generaux, Trafic International see Systeme d'Information sur les Transports de Marchandises: Resultats Generaux, Trafic Interieur et International 259
Systeme d'Information sur les Transports de Marchandises: Resultats Generaux, Trafic Interieur et International (FR ISSN 0181-5334) 259
Systemes-Decisions. Section II. Gestion Financiere et Comptabilite (FR ISSN 0082-1209) 299
Systemica (NE) 353
Systems Engineering of Education Series (US ISSN 0082-1217) 420, 474
Szamitastechnikai Evkonyv see Hungary. Kozponti Statisztikai Hivatal. Szamitastechnikai Statisztikai Evkonyv 354
Szczecinskie Towarzystwo Naukowe. Sprawozdania (PL ISSN 0082-1241) 1001
Szczecinskie Towarzystwo Naukowe. Wydzial Nauk Lekarskich. Prace (PL ISSN 0082-125X) 767
Szczecinskie Towarzystwo Naukowe. Wydzial Nauk Przyrodniczo-Rolniczych. Prace (PL ISSN 0082-1276) 60
Szczecinskie Towarzystwo Naukowe. Wydzial Nauk Spolecznych (PL ISSN 0082-1292) 1012
Szczecinskie Towarzystwo Naukowe. Wydzial Nauk Spolecznych. Prace see Szczecinskie Towarzystwo Naukowe. Wydzial Nauk Spolecznych 1012
Szene Schweiz/Scene Suisse/Scena Svizzera (SZ) 1078
Szep Versek (HU ISSN 0586-3783) 744
Szilikatkemiai Monografiak (HU ISSN 0082-1306) 329
Szkice Legnickie (PL ISSN 0137-5326) 1001
Szkice o Kulturze Muzycznej XIX Wieku. Studia i Materialy (PL ISSN 0239-9148) 842
Szkola Glowna Gospodarstwa Wiejskiego - Akademia Rolnicza. Rozprawy Naukowe i Monografie/Warsaw Agricultural University. Treatises and Monographs (PL) 35
Szkola Glowna Gospodarstwa Wiejskiego-Akademia Rolnicza Bibliografia Prac Magisterkich, Doktorskich i Habilitacyjnych Przyjetych w S G G W - A R w Warszawie see Bibliografia Prac Magisterkich, Doktorskich i Habilitacyjnych Przyjetych w S G G W - A R w Warszawie 39
Szkola Glowna Gospodarstwa Wiejskiego-Akademia Rolnicza Bibliografia Publikacji Pracownikow S G G W - A R w Warszawie see Bibliografia Publikacji Pracownikow S G G W - A R w Warszawie 39
Szociologiai Tanulmanyok (HU ISSN 0082-1322) 1030
T.A. Documents (Traduction Automatique) (FR ISSN 0066-9776) 705
T.A.E. Report (Technion - Israel Institute of Technology, Department of Aeronautical Engineering) (IS ISSN 0072-9302) 21

T A G A Proceedings (Technical Association of the Graphic Arts) (US ISSN 0082-2299) 931
T A I C H Category Reports: Development Assistance Programs of U.S. Non-Profit Organizations Abroad (US) 1164
T A I C H Directory (Technical Assistance Information Clearing House) (US ISSN 0738-4912) 1164
T A M Bulletin (Travelling Art Mail) (NE) 111
T A P P I Directory see Technical Association of the Pulp and Paper Industry. Directory 859
T A P P I Standards and Provisional Methods see T A P P I Test Methods 859
T A P P I Test Methods (Technical Association of the Pulp and Paper Industry, Inc.) (US) 859
T A P Report (Trend Analysis Program) (US) 642
T A S A (CN ISSN 0315-1808) 445
T A T Journal (US ISSN 0271-2482) 882
T & A M Report (Department of Theoretical and Applied Mechanics) (US ISSN 0073-5264) 489, 895
T & C (Theorie et Critique) (AG) 111
T.B. Davie Memorial Lecture (SA ISSN 0082-1330) 632
T C G National Working Conference. Proceedings (Theatre Communications Group) (US) 1164
T E N C O N (I E E E Region 10 Conference). Proceedings (US) 353
T E S S see Educational Software Selector 363
T.I. (Technical Information for Industry) (SA ISSN 0040-0955) 200, 1071
T I M S Studies in Management Science see North-Holland/T I M S Studies in the Management Sciences 238
T I P S Y (The International Permaculture Species Yearbook) (US) 161
T L I - Ingenjoeren (SW) 474
T.M. (Tatsachen und Meinungen) (SZ ISSN 0080-7427) 1012
T M R Travel Marketing Report (US ISSN 0197-6753) 187
T M S - Testbroschuere see Test - Info 342
T N L Research Guide Series see Philippines. National Library. T N L Research Guide Series 130
T N O Research Institute for Environmental Hygiene. Annual Report (NE) 499
T P A S Notes (Tenant Participation Advisory Service) (UK ISSN 0261-197X) 626
T R I U M F Annual Report see T R I U M F Annual Report Scientific Activities 898
T R I U M F Annual Report Scientific Activities (Tri-University Meson Facility) (CN) 898
T R I U M F Financial and Administrative Annual Report (Tri-University Meson Facility) (CN) 898
T R S - 80 Educational Software Sourcebook see Tandy Educational Software Sourcebook 363
T R W Series of Software Technology (NE ISSN 0167-7888) 363
T S E: Tulane Studies in English (US) 705
T.S. Eliot Review see Yeats Eliot Review 744
T S M A Sports Equipment (CH) 1036
T.U.B.A. Series (Tubists Universal Brotherhood Association) (US) 842
T U C Report see Trades Union Congress. Report 649
T V Detectives Annual (UK) 349
T V Feature Film Source Book (US ISSN 0082-1357) 349
T V - Film Filebook (CN ISSN 0082-1365) 349
T V Film Source Book. Series, Serials and Packages see Series, Serials, and Packages 349

T V Film/Tape & Syndication Directory see Backstage T V Film/Tape & Syndication Directory 822
T V Swingers (US) 616, 1078
Ta'asiyah Ha-Yisra'elit see Israel. Ministry of Commerce and Industry. Surveys and Development Plans of Industry in Israel 290
Ta'awun (IS ISSN 0002-4074) 649
Tabard (UK) 537
Tabelbilag til Landsforsoegene (DK) 60
Tablas de Mareas: Costas de Cuba see Academia de Ciencias de Cuba. Instituto de Oceanologia. Tablas de Mareas 404
Table of International Telex Relations and Traffic (UN ISSN 0074-9052) 350
Table of Sunrise, Sunset, Twilight, Moonrise and Moonset (PH ISSN 0115-3307) 117
Tableau de Bord du Batiment, Genie Civil et Materiaux de Construction (FR) 187, 483
Tableaux de l'Economie Francaise (FR) 249
Tableaux Economiques de l'Ile-de-France (FR) 249
Tableaux Economiques de Midi-Pyrenees (FR ISSN 0291-8692) 200
Tableaux Fiscaux Europeens (FR) 299
Tableaux Numeriques des Analyses Physico-Chimiques des Eaux du Rhin see Zahlentafeln der Physikalisch-Chemischen Untersuchungen des Rheinwassers 500
Tables on Hatchery and Flock Participation in the National Poultry Improvement Plan (US ISSN 0082-8661) 68
Tableware Reference Book see European Tableware Buyers Guide 113
Tabortuz (CS) 336
Tabs (UK ISSN 0306-9389) 349, 1078
Taccuino dell'Azionista (IT ISSN 0082-1446) 268
Tack 'n Togs Book (US) 1043
Taeglicher Hafenbericht. Jahresausgabe (GW) 1104
Taehan Cheykhoe. Cheyuk Chongso (KO) 1036
Taetigeitsbericht des Verkehrs Arbeitsinspektorates fuer das Jahr (Year) (AU) 1087
Taft Corporate Directory see Taft Corporate Giving Directory 1021
Taft Corporate Giving Directory (US ISSN 0732-8958) 1021
Taft Foundation Reporter (US ISSN 0730-6237) 1021
Tagore International (II) 735
Tagore Studies (II ISSN 0082-1454) 1164
Tai-Wan Shena Ho Tso Chin Ku. Annual Report. see Cooperative Bank of Taiwan. Annual Report 226
Tai-Wan Sheng Chiao Tung Tung Chi Nien Pao see Taiwan Annual Statistical Report of Transportation 1087
Tai-Wan ta Hsueh She Hui Hsueh K'an see National Taiwan University Journal of Sociology 1028
Taifu Keirozu (JA) 807
Tailspinner (CN ISSN 0316-2494) 21
Taipei. Academia Sinica. Institute of Physics. Annual Report (CH) 891
Taiwan. Fisheries Research Institute, Keelung. Bulletin (CH ISSN 0082-1489) 513
Taiwan. Fisheries Research Institute, Keelung. Laboratory of Fishery Biology. Report (CH ISSN 0082-1497) 513
Taiwan Agricultural Research Institute. Annual Report (CH) 35
Taiwan Agricultural Research Institute. Bulletin (CH) 1164
Taiwan Agricultural Research Institute. Research Summary (CH) 35, 161
Taiwan Annual Statistical Report of Transportation/Tai-Wan Sheng Chiao Tung Tung Chi Nien Pao (CH) 1087
Taiwan Buyers' Guide (CH ISSN 0082-1470) 317

Taiwan Exports (CH ISSN 0494-5336) 259
Taiwan Railway (CH) 1095
T'aiwan Shih Yu Ti Chih see Petroleum Geology of Taiwan 866
Taiwan Sporting Goods see T S M A Sports Equipment 1036
Taiwan Statistical Data Book (CH) 219
Taiwan Sugar (CH ISSN 0492-1712) 521
Taiwan Sugar Research Institute. Annual Report (CH) 60
Taiwan Trade Directory (CH) 317
Taiwania (CH ISSN 0065-1125) 161
Takeda Research Laboratories. Journal (JA ISSN 0371-5167) 147, 324, 873
Taking Shape see Genesis 341
Tal og Data, Medicin og Sundhedsvaesen/Facts, Medicine and Health Care, Denmark (DK ISSN 0107-1181) 873, 886
Tal og Data om Medicin see Tal og Data, Medicin og Sundhedsvaesen 873
Talbott Tree (US) 537
Talent in Action see Billboard's Year-End Issue Talent in Action 833
Talespinner see Tailspinner 21
Talkin' Union (US ISSN 0738-7911) 649
Talking Books, Adult (Large Print Edition) (US ISSN 0082-1519) 131, 180, 426
Talking Books in the Public Library Systems of Metropolitan Toronto (CN ISSN 0380-2973) 180, 684
Tall Timbers Conference on Ecological Animal Control by Habitat Management. Proceedings (US ISSN 0070-833X) 367
Tall Timbers Ecology and Management Conference. Proceedings (US) 527
Tall Timbers Fire Ecology Conference. Proceedings see Tall Timbers Ecology and Management Conference. Proceedings 527
Tall Timbers Research Station. Bulletin (US ISSN 0496-7631) 527
Tall Timbers Research Station. Miscellaneous Publication (US ISSN 0496-764X) 367, 527
Talladegan (US) 342, 505
Taller de Cultura y Medios de Comunicacion. Documentos de Trabajo (AG) 344, 1030
Taller de Letras (CL) 735
Tallies and Trends: Annual Statistical Report see Young Women's Christian Association of the United States of America. The Printout 974
Taloha (MG) 94, 111, 831
Tam-Tam see Message 416
Tamagawa University. Faculty of Agriculture. Bulletin (JA ISSN 0082-156X) 35
Tamil Icaic Cankam Maturai. Antu Vila Malar (II) 842
Tamil Nadu. Department of Statistics. Annual Statistical Abstract (II ISSN 0082-1578) 1065
Tamil Nadu. Department of Statistics. Season and Crop Report (II ISSN 0082-1586) 60
Tamil Nadu. Legislative Council. Quinquennial Review (II ISSN 0082-1594) 1164
Tamil Nadu Industrial Development Corporation. Annual Report (II) 292
Tamil Nadu Tourism Development Corporation. Annual Report (II) 292, 1117
Tampa Port Handbook (US) 1164
Tamworth Annual (US ISSN 0082-1608) 68
Tandlaegen (DK) 780
Tandy Educational Software Sourcebook (US) 362, 362, 363, 428
Tane (NZ ISSN 0496-8026) 1001
T'ang Studies (US) 854
Tanganyika Notes and Records see Tanzania Notes & Records 540
Tangente (AU) 910
Tanker Register (UK ISSN 0305-179X) 867
Tanner Lectures on Human Values (US ISSN 0275-7656) 882
Tansuigyo (JA ISSN 0910-2078) 513

Tantara (MG) 567
Tanulmanyok a Nevelestudomany Korebol (HU ISSN 0082-1632) 420
Tany Malagasy see Terre Malgache 60
Tanzania. Bureau of Standards. Director's Annual Report (TZ ISSN 0856-0374) 809
Tanzania. Bureau of Statistics. Directory of Industries (TZ) 317
Tanzania. Bureau of Statistics. Employment and Earnings see Tanzania. Bureau of Statistics. Survey of Employment 1065
Tanzania. Bureau of Statistics. Migration Statistics (TZ) 1065
Tanzania. Bureau of Statistics. Survey of Employment (TZ) 276, 1065
Tanzania. Bureau of Statistics. Survey of Industrial Production (TZ) 219, 1065
Tanzania. Capital Development Authority. Report and Accounts (TZ) 626
Tanzania. Central Statistical Bureau. Survey of Industrial Production see Tanzania. Bureau of Statistics. Survey of Industrial Production 219
Tanzania. Mines Division. Review of the Mineral Industry see Review of the Mineral Industry in Tanzania 820
Tanzania. Ministry of Agriculture and Livestock Development. Bulletin of Crop Statistics (TZ) 43
Tanzania. Ministry of Agriculture. Bulletin of Crop Statistics see Tanzania. Ministry of Agriculture and Livestock Development. Bulletin of Crop Statistics 43
Tanzania. Ministry of Economic Affairs and Developement Planning. Hali Ya Uchumi Wa Taifa/Annual Economic Survey see Tanzania. Ministry of Planning and Economic Affairs. Hali Ya Uchumi Wa Taifa/Annual Economic Survey 292
Tanzania. Ministry of Lands, Housing and Urban Development. Urban Planning Division. Annual Report (TZ) 626
Tanzania. Ministry of Planning and Economic Affairs. Hali Ya Uchumi Wa Taifa/Annual Economic Survey (TZ) 292
Tanzania Housing Bank. Annual Report and Statement of Accounts/Benki ya Nyumba Tanzania. Ripoti ya Mwaka (TZ) 233
Tanzania Import and Export Directory (TZ) 259
Tanzania Industrial Studies and Consulting Organisation. Annual Report and Accounts (TZ) 200
Tanzania Investment Bank. Annual Report (TZ) 233
Tanzania Journal of Science (TZ) 1001
Tanzania Library Service. Occasional Paper (TZ ISSN 0856-1621) 684
Tanzania Notes & Records (TZ ISSN 0039-9485) 540
Tanzania Rural Development Bank. Annual Report and Accounts (TZ) 233
Tanzanian Studies (TZ) 567
Tape Recording and Buying Guide see Stereo Review's Tape Recording & Buying Guide 1032
Tarasque (US) 735
Tarbell's Teacher's Guide (US ISSN 0082-1713) 973
Tarex (FR) 873
Target Organ Toxicity see Target Organ Toxicology Series 873
Target Organ Toxicology Series (US) 873
Tariff Schedules of the United States Annotated (US ISSN 0082-173X) 299
Tarification - Fare Collection (BE) 1083
Tarlac College of Technology. Annual Report of the President (PH) 439
Tarsadalomtudomanyi Kismonografiak (HU ISSN 0082-1748) 1012
Taschenbuch der Fernmelde-Praxis (GW ISSN 0082-1764) 344
Taschenbuch der Giesserei-Praxis (GW ISSN 0082-1772) 800

Taschenbuch der Pflanzenarztes (GW ISSN 0082-1799) 60
Taschenbuch der Post- und Fernmelde-Verwaltung (GW ISSN 0082-190X) 350
Taschenbuch der Textilen Raumausstattung (GW) 1075
Taschenbuch der Werbung see Deutscher Werbekalender 15
Taschenbuch des Oeffentlichen Lebens (GW ISSN 0082-1829) 131, 946
Taschenbuch des Textileinzelhandels (GW ISSN 0082-1837) 1075
Taschenbuch fuer Agrarjournalisten (GW ISSN 0082-1845) 35, 646
Taschenbuch fuer den Buchhalter see Jahrbuch fuer Praktiker des Rechnungswesens 221
Taschenbuch fuer den Fernmeldedienst (GW ISSN 0082-1861) 1164
Taschenbuch fuer den Oeffentlichen Dienst see B A T: Taschenbuch fuer den Oeffentlichen Dienst 939
Taschenbuch fuer die Bekleidungs-Industrie see Bekleidungs-Industrie. Jahrbuch 339
Taschenbuch fuer die Textil-Industrie (GW ISSN 0082-1896) 1075
Taschenbuch fuer Fernmelde-Verwaltung see Taschenbuch der Post- und Fernmelde-Verwaltung 350
Taschenbuch fuer Kriminalisten (GW ISSN 0082-1934) 372
Taschenbuch fuer Liturgie Kirchenmusik und Musikerziehung (GW ISSN 0344-1407) 842, 973
Taschenbuch fuer Liturgie und Kirchenmusik see Taschenbuch fuer Liturgie Kirchenmusik und Musikerziehung 842
Taschenbuch fuer Logistik (GW ISSN 0082-1942) 1164
Taschenbuch Geschichte (GE ISSN 0082-1950) 561
Taschenbuch Karosserie & Fahrzeugtechnik (GW) 1093
Taschenbuch Ungarus see Magyar Statisztikai Zsebkonyv 1059
Taschenbuecher zur Musikwissenschaft (GW ISSN 0082-1969) 842
Taschenfachbuch der Kraftfahrzeugbetriebe (GW) 1093
Tasmania. Department of Agriculture. Annual Report (AT ISSN 0082-1993) 35
Tasmania. Department of Agriculture. Insect Pest Survey (AT) 60, 166
Tasmania. Department of Mines. Geological Survey Bulletins (AT ISSN 0082-2043) 395
Tasmania. Department of the Treasury. Commonwealth Grants to Tasmania (AT) 260, 299
Tasmania. Department of the Treasury. Consolidated Revenue Fund (AT) 299
Tasmania. Hobart Regional Water Board. Report. (AT) 499
Tasmania. Metropolitan Water Board. Report. see Tasmania. Hobart Regional Water Board. Report 499
Tasmanian Manufacturers Directory (AT) 317
Tasmanian State Reports (AT ISSN 0085-7106) 665
Tasmanian Tramp (AT ISSN 0157-2938) 1047
Tasmanian University Law Review see University of Tasmania Law Review 666
Taste of Scotland (UK) 1117
Tata Institute Lecture Notes see Tata Institute Lectures on Mathematics 753
Tata Institute Lectures on Mathematics (US) 753
Tata Institute of Fundamental Research. Lectures on Mathematics and Physics. Mathematics see Tata Institute Lectures on Mathematics 753
Tata Institute of Fundamental Research. Lectures on Mathematics and Physic. Physics see Tata Institute Lectures on Mathematics 753
Tata Institute Studies in Mathematics (US) 753

Tate and Lyle's Sugar Industry Abstracts (UK) 12, *522*
Tatsachen und Meinungen *see* T.M *1012*
Tatsachen und Zahlen aus der Kraftverkehrswirtschaft (GW ISSN 0083-548X) *1093*
Tax Administration Review (PN) 299
Tax Burden on Tobacco (US ISSN 0563-6191) 299, 1065, *1080*
Tax Case Report (UK) 299
Tax Facts on Life Insurance *see* Tax Facts 1 *642*
Tax Facts 1 (US) *642*
Tax Foundation. Annual Memorandum (US) 299
Tax Foundation. Proceedings of Conferences (US) 299
Tax Foundation. Research Publications. New Series (US ISSN 0082-2159) 299
Tax Foundation's Research Bibliography (US ISSN 0496-974X) 131, *219*
Tax Fraud and Evasion (Supplement) (US) 299
Tax Memo (CN) 299
Tax Practice Deskbook (Supplement) (US) 299
Tax Practitioner's Diary (UK ISSN 0269-3720) 299
Tax Principles to Remember (CN ISSN 0227-1265) 299
Tax Saving Opportunities Series (US) 222
Tax Sheltered Investments Handbook (US ISSN 0731-5821) 268, 299, *665*
Tax Times (US) 222
Tax Year in Review (US) 299
Taxable Sales in California (Sales and Use Tax) (US ISSN 0068-581X) 299
Taxation Digest. Journal (US) 299
Taxation of Closely Held Corporations (Supplement) *see* Taxation of the Closely Held Corporation (Supplement) 299
Taxation of the Closely Held Corporation (Supplement) (US) 299
Taxation Structure of Pakistan (PK) 299
Taxation Tables (NZ ISSN 0082-2175) 300
Taxi Drivers Compendium (UK) *1093*
Tayarut Be-Yisrael *see* Israel Tourist Statistics *1119*
Taylor's Encyclopedia of Government Officials. Federal and State (US ISSN 0082-2183) *946*
Tbilisskii Universitet. Institut Prikladnoi Matematiki. Seminar. Annotatsii Dokladov (UR ISSN 0082-2191) *753*
Tchebec (CN) *171*
Te Reo (NZ ISSN 0494-8440) *705*
Tea Directory (II) *120*
Tea Research Association. Advisory Bulletin (II) *120*
Tea Research Association. Memorandum (II) 60, *120*
Tea Research Association. Occasional Scientific Papers (II) 60, *120*
Tea Research Association. Tocklai Experimental Station. Scientific Annual Report (II ISSN 0564-6723) 60, *120*
Tea Research Foundation. Annual Report *see* Tea Research Foundation of Kenya. Annual Report *521*
Tea Research Foundation of Central Africa. Annual Report (MW ISSN 0258-4476) *521*
Tea Research Foundation of Kenya. Annual Report (KE) *521*
Tea Research Station. Bulletin *see* National Research Institute of Vegetables, Ornamental Plants and Tea. Bulletin *32*
Tea Trading Corporation of India. Annual Report (II) *285*
Teacher Certification Reciprocity Policies in the U.S. (US) *1164*
Teacher Education in Uganda *see* Makerere University. Faculty of Education. Handbook *436*
Teacher Supply/Demand (US) *443*, *849*
Teachers' Guide to Overseas Teaching (US) *420*, *1117*

Teachers Guild of New South Wales. Proceedings (AT) *420*
Teachers of History in the Universities and Polytechnics of the United Kingdom (UK ISSN 0268-6732) *420*
Teachers of History in the Universities of the United Kingdom *see* Teachers of History in the Universities and Polytechnics of the United Kingdom *420*
Teaching and Training in Geriatric Medicine (SZ) *552*
Teaching of History (UK ISSN 0073-2605) *449*, 561
Tears (UK) *439*
Teater for Boern og Unge (DK ISSN 0901-0106) *1078*
Teater i Danmark/Theatre in Denmark (DK ISSN 0106-7672) *1078*
Teaterraadets Indstilling (DK ISSN 0107-248X) *1078*
Teaterseminar (DK ISSN 0109-3363) *1078*
Teatro (IT) *1078*
Tebiwa (US) 77
Tebiwa Miscellaneous Papers *see* Tebiwa 77
Tech-Embal (FR) *855*
Technic International (GW ISSN 0033-0876) *1164*
Technical *see* Urban Abstracts *950*
Technical Assistance Information Clearing House Directory *see* T A I C H Directory *1164*
Technical Association of the Graphic Arts Proceedings *see* T A G A Proceedings *931*
Technical Association of the Pulp and Paper Industry. Annual Meeting Proceedings (US) *859*
Technical Association of the Pulp and Paper Industry. Coating Conference. Proceedings (US) *859*
Technical Association of the Pulp and Paper Industry. Corrugated Containers Conference. Proceedings (US) *855*, 859
Technical Association of the Pulp and Paper Industry. Directory (US ISSN 0091-7737) *859*
Technical Association of the Pulp and Paper Industry. Engineering Conference Proceedings (US) *859*
Technical Association of the Pulp and Paper Industry. Environmental Conference Proceedings (US) *499*
Technical Association of the Pulp and Paper Industry. International Process & Materials Quality Evaluation Proceedings (US) *859*
Technical Association of the Pulp and Paper Industry. Paper Finishing and Converting Conference. Proceedings. (US) *859*
Technical Association of the Pulp and Paper Industry. Paper Synthetics Conference. Proceedings (US) *1164*
Technical Association of the Pulp and Paper Industry. Papermakers Conference Proceedings (US) *859*
Technical Association of the Pulp and Paper Industry. Printing and Reprography Conference Proceedings(US) *859*, 931
Technical Association of the Pulp and Paper Industry. Pulping Conference Proceedings (US) *859*
Technical Association of the Pulp and Paper Industry. Testing Conference Proceedings *see* Technical Association of the Pulp and Paper Industry. International Process & Materials Quality Evaluation Proceedings *859*
Technical Association of the Pulp and Paper Industry, Inc. Test Methods *see* T A P P I Test Methods *859*
Technical Book Review Index (US ISSN 0040-0890) 12, *1004*, 1073
Technical Budget Representations (UK) 233
Technical Bulletin - Department of Natural Resources (Madison) *see* Wisconsin. Department of Natural Resources. Technical Bulletin *368*
Technical Conference on Artifical Insemination and Reproduction (US) 68

Technical Conference on Hurricanes and Tropical Meteorology (Publication) (US) *807*
Technical Conference Proceedings-Irrigation Association *see* Irrigation Association. Technical Conference Proceedings 57
Technical Education Abstracts (UK ISSN 0040-0920) 13, *426*, 477, 1073
Technical Highlights of the National Bureau of Standards *see* U.S. National Bureau of Standards. Annual Report *809*
Technical Information for Industry *see* T.I *1071*
Technical Journal of the University of Dacca's Ahsanullah Engineering College *see* Bangladesh University of Engineering and Technology, Dacca. Technical Journal *470*
Technical Notes for the Rubber Industry (GW) *1164*
Technical Paper - U.S. Department of Commerce, Social and Economics Statistics Administration, Bureau of the Census *see* U.S. Bureau of the Census. Technical Paper *1066*
Technical Papers in Hydrology Series (UN ISSN 0082-2329) *404*
Technical Papers on New Zealand Wool *see* Wool Research Organisation of New Zealand Technical Papers *1075*
Technical Research Centre of Finland. Publications (FI ISSN 0358-5069) *1001*
Technical Research Centre of Finland. Research Notes *see* Valtion Teknillinen Tutkimuskeskus. Tiedotteita *1072*
Technical Research Centre of Finland. Research Reports *see* Valtion Teknillinen Tutkimuskeskus. Tutkimuksia *1072*
Technical Service Data (Automotive) (UK ISSN 0082-2329) *1093*
Technical Session on Cane Sugar Refining Research. Proceedings *see* Sugar Processing Research Conference. Proceedings 35
Technical Study - U.S. Civil Service Commission. Personnel Research and Development Center *see* U.S. Civil Service Commission. Personnel Research and Development Center. Technical Study 287
Technical, Trade & Business School Data Handbook (US) *420*, 1071
Technical University of Denmark. Acoustics Laboratory Report (DK ISSN 0105-3027) *900*
Technical University of Denmark. Institute of Roads, Transport and Town Planning. Paper *see* Danmarks Tekniske Hoejskole. Institutet for Veje, Trafik og Byplan. Notat *1096*
Technical University of Denmark. Institute of Roads, Transport and Town Planning. Papers and Reports (DK ISSN 0105-5119) *1097*
Technical University of Denmark. Institute of Roads, Transport and Town Planning. Report (DK) *626*, *1097*
Technical University of Nova Scotia. School of Architecture. Report Series(CN) *100*
Technician Education Directory (US) *439*
Technician Education Yearbook *see* Technician Education Directory *439*
Technik aus Finnland (FI) *260*
Technik und aus Finnland *see* Technik aus Finnland *260*
Technik und Gesellschaft (GW) *1030*, 1071
Technikgeschichte in Einzeldarstellungen (GW ISSN 0082-2361) *1071*
Technine Kibernetika/Tekhnicheskaya Kibernetika (UR) *360*
Technion - Israel Institute of Technology. Faculty of Agricultural Engineering. Publications (IS ISSN 0333-5879) 35
Technion - Israel Institute of Technology. President's Report (IS) *1071*

Technion - Israel Institute of Technology Report *see* T.A.E. Report *21*
Technique du Roulement (GW ISSN 0170-303X) *493*
Technique of Inorganic Chemistry *see* Techniques of Chemistry *325*
Technique of Organic Chemistry *see* Techniques of Chemistry *325*
Techniques and Applications in Organic Synthesis Series (US ISSN 0082-2418) *331*, 332
Techniques and Instrumentation in Analytical Chemistry (NE) *327*
Techniques Artisanales Modernes (FR ISSN 0082-2442) *849*
Techniques d'Aujourd'Hui (FR ISSN 0082-2469) *1071*
Techniques in Pure and Applied Microbiology (US ISSN 0082-2515) *169*
Techniques Industrielles du Japon (JA) *1071*
Techniques of Chemistry (US ISSN 0082-2531) *325*, 782
Techniques of Measurement in Medicine Series (UK) *782*
Techniques of Physics (US) *891*
Techniques Orthopediques (FR ISSN 0397-3999) *786*
Technisch Fysische Dienst TNO-TH. Jaarverslag (Toegepast-Natuurwetenschappelijk Onderzoek. Technisch Fysische Dienst) (NE) *891*
Technische Beitraege zur Archaeologie (GW ISSN 0067-4974) *94*
Technische Hochschule Karl-Marx-Stadt. Wissenschaftliche Schriftenreihe (GE) *460*
Technische Hochschule Karl-Marx-Stadt. Wissenschaftliche Zeitschrift (GE ISSN 0372-7610) *474*
Technische Hochschule Wien. Dissertationen *see* Technische Universitaet Wien. Dissertationen *474*
Technische Hogeschool Eindhoven. Onderafdeling der Wiskunde. E U T Reports - W S K *see* Technische Hogeschool Eindhoven. Onderafdeling der Wiskunde en Informatica. E U T Reports - W S K *753*
Technische Hogeschool Eindhoven. Onderafdeling der Wiskunde en Informatica. E U T Reports - W S K (NE) *753*
Technische Hogeschool te Delft. Bibliotheek. Lijst van Lopende Tijdschriftabonnementen (NE) *474*
Technische Mitteilungen Krupp (GW ISSN 0494-9390) *493*, *800*
Technische Mitteilungen Krupp. Forschungsberichte *see* Technische Mitteilungen Krupp *800*
Technische Physik in Einzeldarstellungen (US ISSN 0082-2590) *891*
Technische Universitaet Berlin. Institut fuer Sozialoekonomie der Agrarentwicklung. Annual Report (Abridged Version) (GW ISSN 0170-8309) *49*
Technische Universitaet Berlin. Institut fuer Sozialoekonomie der Agrarentwicklung. Jahresbericht (GW ISSN 0170-8376) *49*
Technische Universitaet Berlin. Institut fuer Sozialoekonomie der Agrarentwicklung. Taetigkeitsbericht *see* Technische Universitaet Berlin. Institut fuer Sozialoekonomie der Agrarentwicklung. Jahresbericht *49*
Technische Universitaet Braunschweig. Berichtsband. Forschung (GW) *439*
Technische Universitaet Braunschweig. Pharmaziegeschichtlichen Seminar. Veroeffentlichungen *see* Braunschweiger Veroeffentlichungen zur Geschichte der Pharmazie und Naturwissenschaften *870*
Technische Universitaet Hannover. Astronomischer Station. (Veroeffentlichungen) *see* Universitaet Hannover. Astronomischer Station. (Veroeffentlichungen) *118*

Technische Universitaet Hannover. Institut fuer Siedlungswasserwirtschaft. Veroeffentlichungen see Universitaet Hannover. Institut fuer Siedlungswasserwirtschaft. Veroeffentlichungen *1126*

Technische Universitaet Hannover. Institut fuer Statik. Mitteilungen see Universitaet Hannover. Institut fuer Statik. Mitteilungen *490*

Technische Universitaet Hannover. Lehrstuhl fuer Stahlbau. Schriftenreihe see Universitaet Hannover. Institut fuer Stahlbau. Schriftenreihe *490*

Technische Universitaet Muenchen. Institut fuer Wirtschaftslehre des Gartenbaues. Forschungsberichte zur Oekonomie in Gartenbau (GW) *534*

Technische Universitaet Wien. Dissertationen (AU ISSN 0259-0697) *474*

Technische Universitaet Wien. Institut fuer Eisenbahnwesen, Spezialbahnen und Verkehrswirtschaft. Arbeiten (AU) *1095*

Techno-Loisirs (FR) *1036*

Technocracy. Information Briefs (US) *1001*

Technologia Zywnosci see Acta Academiae Agriculturae ac Technicae Olstenensis. Technologia Alimentorum *517*

Technological Marketplace: Supply and Demand for Scientists and Engineers(US) *849*

Technological Monographs (GT) *1071*

Technology Book Guide see Bibliographic Guide to Technology *122*

Technology for China (US) *1071*

Technology Transfer Society. International Symposium Proceedings(US) *260, 281, 1071*

Technopolis (JA) *460*

Tecnica de los Rodamientos (GW ISSN 0170-3056) *493*

Teens & Boys Directory (US) *1164*

Tees and Hartlepool Ports (UK ISSN 0265-1181) *317, 1104*

Tegnebogen Danske Illustrorer see Danske Illustratorer *104*

Teilhardian Studies see Etudes Teilhardiennes *969*

Teiresias (CN ISSN 0381-9361) *339*

Tekhnicheskaya Kibernetika see Technine Kibernetika *360*

Teki Historyczne (UK ISSN 0085-4956) *599*

Tekisutairu Japan see Textile Japan *1075*

Teknisk Nyts Leverandoerregister (DK) *474*

Tekniska Nomenklaturcentralen Publikationer (SW ISSN 0081-573X) *705, 1071*

Teknologi (MY) *460, 1071*

Teknologi og Effektivitet (DK ISSN 0107-3761) *1071*

Tekster fra I M F U F A (Institut for Studiet af Matematik og Fysik Samt Deres Funktioner i Undervisning Forskning og Anvendelse) (DK ISSN 0106-6242) *753, 891*

Tel-Aviv University. David Horowitz Institute for the Research of Developing Countries. Annual Report (IS) *918*

Tel-Aviv University. David Horowitz Institute for the Research of Developing Countries. Research Reports and Papers (IS) *918*

Tel Aviv University. Institut fuer Deutsche Geschichte. Jahrbuch (IS) *599*

Tel-Aviv University. Ph.D. Degrees and Abstracts (IS) *439*

Tel Aviv-Yafo. Center for Economic and Social Research. Research and Surveys Series/Tel-Aviv-Yafo. Ha-Merkaz le-Mekhkar Kalkali ve-Khevrati. Mekhkarim ve-Sekarim (IS) *1030*

Tel Aviv-Yafo. Center for Economic and Social Research. Yearbook (IS) *539*

Tel Aviv-Yafo. Department of Research and Statistics see Tel Aviv-Yafo. Center for Economic and Social Research. Yearbook *539*

Tel-Aviv-Yafo. Ha-Merkaz le-Mekhkar Kalkali ve-Khevrati. Mekhkarim ve-Sekarim see Tel Aviv-Yafo. Center for Economic and Social Research. Research and Surveys Series *1030*

Tel Aviv-Yafo. Research and Statistical Department. Special Surveys see Tel Aviv-Yafo. Center for Economic and Social Research. Research and Surveys Series *1030*

Telecom Australia. Annual Report (AT) *344*

Telecom Factbook (New York) (US) *317, 350*

Telecom Factbook (Washington) (US) *350*

Telecommunication Authority of Singapore. T A S Annual Report see Telecommunication Authority of Singapore. Telecoms Annual Report *351*

Telecommunication Authority of Singapore. Telecoms Annual Report (SI ISSN 0217-3891) *351*

Telecommunication Statistics see Yearbook of Common Carrier Telecommunication Statistics *345*

Telecommunications (New York) (US) *344*

Telecommunications Alert (US) *13, 346*

Telecommunications Policy. Research and Development see Worldwide Report: Telecommunications Policy. Research and Development *345*

Telecommunications Sourcebook (US ISSN 0730-9872) *351*

Telecommunications Systems and Services Directory (US ISSN 0738-3045) *317, 344, 353, 1071*

Teleconferencing Resources Directory (US ISSN 0739-2966) *286*

Telefax International. International Telefax Directory (GW) *351*

Telefilm Canada Annual Report (CN) *825*

Telegen Reporter (US) *147*

Telekompass (UK) *317*

Telephone Engineer and Management Directory (US ISSN 0082-2655) *351*

Telephone Organization of Thailand. Annual Report (TH) *16*

Telephone Statistics see United States Telephone Association. Annual Statistical Volume *351*

Telephone Tickler for Insurance Men and Women see New York Telephone Tickler for Insurance Men and Women *641*

Telephony's Directory & Buyer's Guide for the Telecommunications Industry (US) *351*

Telephony's Directory & Buyer's Guide for the Telephone Industry see Telephony's Directory & Buyer's Guide for the Telecommunications Industry *351*

Telephony's Directory of the Telephone Industry see Telephony's Directory & Buyer's Guide for the Telecommunications Industry *351*

Telepulestudomanyi Kozlemenyek (HU ISSN 0040-2680) *626*

Television and Cable Factbook (US ISSN 0732-8648) *349*

Television & Radio (UK ISSN 0262-6470) *349*

Television Contacts (US) *350*

Television Factbook see Television and Cable Factbook *349*

Television Network Movies (US) *350, 825*

Television: the New Era (UK) *350*

Telex & Teletex International. Telex and Teletex Directory (GW) *351*

Telex Danmark/Annuaire des Abonnes Telex du Danemark (DK ISSN 0109-8071) *351*

Telex Gold Pages (CN) *317*

Telex und Travel International (GW) *351*

Telexbog Danmark see Telex Danmark *351*

Teljan Tanhuvilta (FI) *599*

Telopea (AT ISSN 0312-9764) *161*

Telugu Akademi Language Monograph Series (II) *705*

Temadokumentacios Kiadvanyok/Thematical Reviews (HU ISSN 0521-4602) *200, 1071*

Temas de Historia y Politica Contemporaneas (SP) *599*

Temas N T see Biblioteca N T *628*

Temas Nacionales (MX) *910*

Temas y Formas de la Literatura (SP) *735*

Temel ve Uygulamali Bilmler Dergisi see Journal of Pure and Applied Sciences *993*

Temenos (Turku) (FI ISSN 0497-1817) *973*

Temperature: Its Measurement and Control in Science and Industry (US ISSN 0091-9322) *894*

Tempo (Hanau) (GW) *111*

Temporary Military Lodging Around the World (US) *812, 1117*

Temporary Occupations and Employment see Jobs in the 'Gap' Year *848*

Temps de la Reflexion (FR) *735, 882*

Tendencias Economicas: Legislacion Economicas Argentina/Business Trends: Argentine Economic Legislation (AG) *200, 665*

Tennessee. Department of Safety. Annual Report (US ISSN 0095-1994) *1097*

Tennessee. Higher Education Commission. Biennial Report (US) *439*

Tennessee. State Board for Vocational Education. Information Series (US ISSN 0093-9889) *445*

Tennessee Annual Average Labor Force Estimates (US) *276*

Tennessee Annual Average Work Force Estimates see Tennessee Annual Average Labor Force Estimates *276*

Tennessee Anthropological Association. Miscellaneous Paper (US) *77*

Tennessee Archaeologist (US ISSN 0040-3180) *94*

Tennessee Civilian Work Force Estimates see Tennessee Annual Average Labor Force Estimates *276*

Tennessee Cooperative Economic Insect Survey Report: Annual Summary see Tennessee Economic Pest Report *161*

Tennessee Economic Pest Report (US) *161*

Tennessee Labor Market Information Directory (US) *276*

Tennessee Public Library Statistics (US ISSN 0363-7158) *684*

Tennessee State Industrial Directory see MacRae's Tennessee State Industrial Directory *313*

Tennessee Statistical Abstract (US ISSN 0082-2760) *1065*

Tennessee Studies in Literature (US ISSN 0497-2384) *735*

Tennessee Tech Journal (US ISSN 0082-2779) *632*

Tennessee Valley Authority. Agricultural and Chemical Development Annual Report see Progress (Muscle Shoals) *59*

Tennessee Valley Authority. Annual Report (US ISSN 0363-101X) *367*

Tennessee Valley Authority. Division of Land and Forest Resources. Technical Note (US ISSN 0096-1248) *367*

Tennessee Valley Authority. Operations: Municipal and Cooperative Distributors of T.V.A. Power see Tennessee Valley Authority. Power Program Summary *460*

Tennessee Valley Authority. Power Annual Report see Tennessee Valley Authority. Power Program Summary *460*

Tennessee Valley Authority. Power Program Summary (US ISSN 0730-4889) *460*

Tennessee Valley Authority. Technical Monographs (US ISSN 0082-2809) *460*

Tennessee Valley Authority. Technical Reports (US ISSN 0082-2817) *460*

Tennessee Valley Authority Industrial Development in the T.V.A. Area see Industrial Development in the T.V.A. Area *289*

Tennis-Badminton-Squash Guide see N A G W S Guide. Tennis *1039*

Tennis Great Britain (UK) *1040*

Tennyson Research Bulletin (UK ISSN 0082-2841) *735*

Tennyson Society, Lincoln, England. Monographs (UK ISSN 0082-285X) *735*

Tennyson Society, Lincoln, England. Occasional Papers (UK ISSN 0307-3572) *735*

Tennyson Society, Lincoln, England. Report (UK ISSN 0082-2868) *735*

Tensai Kenkyu Hokoku Hokan see Bulletin of Sugar Beet Research. Supplement *53*

Teorie e Oggetti (IT ISSN 0392-2154) *910*

Teorie Economiche (IT ISSN 0391-3295) *252*

Teoriya Funktsii, Funktsional'nyi Analiz i ikh Prilozheniya (UR) *753*

Teoriya Funktsii Kompleksnogo Peremennogo i Kraevye Zadachi (UR) *753*

Teoriya Sluchainykh Protsessov (UR ISSN 0321-3900) *753*

Teplofizika see Akademiya Nauk Litovskoi S.S.R. Silumine Fizika *894*

Teploprovodnost' i Diffuziya (UR) *894*

Tequesta (US ISSN 0363-3705) *610*

Teramo (IT ISSN 0040-3652) *1117*

Terbitan Bersiri Kini Malaysia (Bukan Kerajaan) see Current Malaysian Serials (Non-Government) *125*

Terezinske Listy (CS) *599*

Terra Poetica (US) *744*

Terrae Incognitae (US ISSN 0082-2884) *561*

Terre Malgache/Tany Malagasy (MG ISSN 0563-1637) *60*

Terrorism (US ISSN 0278-663X) *372*

Tertiary Research Group. Special Papers see Tertiary Research Special Papers *396*

Tertiary Research Special Papers (NE) *396, 857*

Test and Measurement World Yearbook(US) *285*

Test Conference. Digest of Papers see International Test Conference. Proceedings *361*

Test - Info (GW) *342, 420*

Test- og Undervisningsmaterialer see Undervisningsmaterialer til Begynder-og Specialundervisning *445*

Test Valley and Border Anthology see Lookback *1157*

Testi e Studi Umanistici (IT) *735*

Testi Medievali di Interesse Dantesco (IT) *599*

Testimonia Siciliae Antiqua (IT ISSN 0452-2907) *94, 561*

Testimonios (en Historieta) (PE) *610*

Testimonios Violentos (VE) *910*

Tests in Print (US ISSN 0361-025X) *449, 937*

Tethys (FR ISSN 0040-4012) *147, 408*

Teton (US ISSN 0049-3481) *1047*

Tetradi Obshchestvennogo Zdravookhranenia see Public Health Papers *955*

Tetsudo Sharyoto Seisan Dotai Tokei Nenpo see Annual Statistics of Actual Production of Railway Cars *1084*

Teufah (IS) *1089*

Texas. Coordinating Board. Texas College and University System. C B Annual Report see Texas. Coordinating Board. Texas College and University System. C B Annual Report and Statistical Supplement *439*

Texas. Coordinating Board. Texas College and University System. C B Annual Report and Statistical Supplement (US) *439*

Texas. Coordinating Board. Texas College and University System. C B Policy Paper (US ISSN 0082-299X) *439*

Texas. Coordinating Board. Texas College and University System. C B Study Paper (US ISSN 0082-3007) 439

Texas. Department of Corrections. Research and Development Division. Research Report (US ISSN 0095-1900) 373

Texas. Department of Health Resources. Biennial Report (US ISSN 0163-1667) 956

Texas. Department of Water Resources. Report see Texas. Water Development Board. Report 1126

Texas. Department on Aging. Annual Report see Texas. Department on Aging. Biennial Report 1021

Texas. Department on Aging. Biennial Report (US) 1021

Texas. Forest Service. Cooperative Forest Tree Improvement Program. Progress Report (US ISSN 0082-3031) 527

Texas. Industrial Commission. Annual Report (US ISSN 0361-2597) 292

Texas. Legislative Reference Library. Chief Elected and Administrative Officials. (US) 946

Texas. Railroad Commission. Oil and Gas Division. Annual Report (US) 867

Texas. Water Development Board. Report (US) 1126

Texas A & M University. College of Geosciences. Contributions in Oceanography (US ISSN 0069-9640) 408

Texas Almanac see Texas Almanac and State Industrial Guide 610

Texas Almanac and State Industrial Guide (US) 610

Texas Annual of Electronics Research (US) 460

Texas Archeological Society. Bulletin (US ISSN 0082-2930) 94

Texas Archeological Society. Special Publication (US ISSN 0495-2944) 94

Texas Archeology (US ISSN 0082-2949) 94

Texas Banking Red Book (US) 233

Texas Biannual of Electronics Research see Texas Annual of Electronics Research 460

Texas Blue Book of Life Insurance Statistics (US ISSN 0739-4691) 642, 1065

Texas Builders and Contractors Directory (US) 187, 317

Texas Child Migrant Program. Annual Report (US) 420

Texas Fact Book (US) 219

Texas Facts (US ISSN 0748-7789) 549

Texas Field Crop Statistics (US ISSN 0092-153X) 60

Texas Folklore Society. Publications (US ISSN 0082-3023) 516

Texas Forestry Papers (US ISSN 0082-304X) 527

Texas Livestock Statistics (US ISSN 0091-1550) 43

Texas Lodging Industry (US) 620

Texas Manufacturers Register (US ISSN 0743-1163) 317

Texas Memorial Museum. Bulletin (US ISSN 0082-3074) 831

Texas Memorial Museum. Miscellaneous Papers (US ISSN 0082-3082) 831

Texas Memorial Museum. Museum Notes (US) 831

Texas Migrant Program. Annual Report see Texas Child Migrant Program. Annual Report 420

Texas Notary Law Primer (US) 665

Texas Ornithological Society. Bulletin (US ISSN 0040-4543) 171

Texas Public Library Statistics (US ISSN 0082-3120) 684

Texas Public School Directory see Texas School Directory 431

Texas School Directory (US ISSN 0363-4566) 431

Texas Small Grains Statistics (US ISSN 0091-4673) 43

Texas Special Libraries Directory (US ISSN 0082-3163) 684

Texas Speech Communication Journal (US ISSN 0363-8782) 706

Texas State Directory (US ISSN 0363-7530) 946

Texas State Industrial Directory see MacRae's Texas State Industrial Directory 313

Texas Tech University. Graduate Studies (US ISSN 0082-3198) 147, 439, 632, 882

Texas Tech University. Interdepartmental Committee on Comparative Literature. Proceedings of the Comparative Literature Symposium (US ISSN 0084-9103) 735

Texas Tech University. Museum. Occasional Papers (US ISSN 0149-175X) 831

Texas Tech University. Museum. Special Publications (US ISSN 0149-1768) 831, 1001

Texas TourBook see Tourbook: Texas 1117

Texas Trade and Professional Associations and Other Selected Organizations (US) 317

Texas: Trends and Forecasts (US) 1164

Texas Vital Statistics (US ISSN 0495-257X) 924, 929

Texas Water Resources Institute. Technical Report (US) 1126

Texinform (SA) 317, 1075

Texscope (New York) see Texscope: U S A Textile Industry Overview 1075

Texscope: U S A Textile Industry Overview (US ISSN 0092-3540) 1075

Text (SW ISSN 0345-0112) 132

Text (New York) (US ISSN 0736-3974) 735

Text und Kontext (GW) 735

Textausgaben zur Fruehen Sozialistischen Literatur in Deutschland (GE ISSN 0081-3257) 735

Textbooks in Print see El Hi Textbooks and Serials in Print 424

Texte des Spaeten Mittelalters und der Fruehen Neurzeit (GW) 735

Texte und Studien zum Antiken Judentum (GW) 977

Texte und Untersuchungen zur Geschichte der Altchristlichen Literatur (GE ISSN 0082-3589) 973

Textes d'Interet General (FR) 665

Textes Litteraires Francais (SZ) 735

Textil-Industrie und ihre Helfer (GW ISSN 0082-3627) 1075

Textile and Apparel Index of Australia (AT) 1075

Textile & Engineering Directory for India & Pakistan see Worrall's Textile & Engineering Directory 319

Textile Digest (UK ISSN 0260-4256) 13, 1076

Textile Handbook see American Home Economics Association. Textiles and Clothing Section. Textile Handbook 1146

Textile Industry in O.E.C.D. Countries (FR ISSN 0474-6023) 1075

Textile Industry Technical Conference (Publication) (US ISSN 0094-9884) 1075

Textile Institute. Annual Conference (UK) 1075

Textile Institute. Annual Report (UK) 1075

Textile Japan/Tekisutairo Japan (JA ISSN 0082-366X) 1075

Textile Museum Journal (US ISSN 0083-7407) 111, 113, 1075

Textile Recorder Annual and Machinery Review see International Textile Machinery 1074

Textile Science and Technology (NE) 1075

Textile Technology Digest (US ISSN 0040-5191) 13, 1076

Textile World Buyer's Guide/Fact File (US ISSN 0495-369X) 1075

Textiles: Latin American Industrial Report (US) 1075

Texts and Monographs in Computer Science (US ISSN 0172-603X) 353

Texts and Monographs in Economics and Mathematical Systems (US) 252, 753

Texts and Monographs in Physics (US ISSN 0172-5998) 891

Texts and Studies in Medieval and Early Modern Judaism see Texte und Studien zum Antiken Judentum 977

Texts and Studies in Religion (US) 973

Texts and Studies in the History of Mediaeval Education (US ISSN 0082-3732) 420, 599

Texts from Cuneiform Sources (US ISSN 0082-3759) 561

Textus (IS ISSN 0082-3767) 973

Textus Minores (NE) 735

Textus Patristici et Liturgici (GW ISSN 0082-3775) 973

Thai Chamber of Commerce. Business Directory (TH ISSN 0563-3400) 317

Thai Industrial Directory (TH) 317

Thai Investment Review (TH ISSN 0082-3783) 1164

Thailand. Division of Agricultural Chemistry. Report on Fertilizer Experiments and Soil Fertility Research (TH ISSN 0085-7246) 60

Thailand. Ministry of Foreign Affairs. News Bulletin (TH) 918

Thailand. National Statistical Office. Annual Report (TH) 1065

Thailand. National Statistical Office. Report of Industrial Survey in Northeast Region/Thailand. Samnakngan Sathiti Haeng Chat (TH) 219

Thailand. National Statistical Office. Research Paper (TH) 1065

Thailand. National Statistical Office. Statistical Bibliography (TH ISSN 0082-3791) 132, 1065

Thailand. Samnakngan Sathiti Haeng Chat see Thailand. National Statistical Office. Report of Industrial Survey in Northeast Region 219

Thailand Industrial Buyer's Guide (TH ISSN 0857-2984) 200

Thailand National Directory (TH) 571

Thailand Standard Industrial Classification (TH) 276

Thailand Trade Index (TH) 260

Thailand's Budget in Brief (TH) 300

Thailand's Foreign Trade Statistics (TH) 219

Thalassas (SP ISSN 0212-5919) 147, 396, 408

Thalassia Salentina (IT) 161, 178, 1126

Thames Book (UK ISSN 0082-3805) 549, 1117

Thames Essays (UK) 260

Thamesman Publications. Occasional Papers (UK) 282

Thanatology Abstracts (US) 13, 937, 938

Thapar's Indian Industrial Directory and Import and Export Directory of the World (II) 317

The International Permaculture Species Yearbook see T I P S Y 161

The National Library Philippines. National Library. T N L Research Guide Series see Philippines. National Library. T N L Research Guide Series 130

Theata (US) 77, 505, 516

Theaterpaedagogische Bibliothek (GW) 1078

Theatre and Dramatic Studies (US) 1079

Theatre Angels (US) 1079

Theatre Annual (US ISSN 0082-3821) 1079

Theatre Communications Group National Working Conference. Proceedings see T C G National Working Conference. Proceedings 1164

Theatre d'Aujourd'hui (FR) 1079

Theatre Directory (US ISSN 0271-3136) 1079

Theatre/Drama Abstracts (US) 13, 1079

Theatre/Drama and Speech Index see Theatre/Drama Abstracts 1079

Theatre, Film, and Television Biographies Master Index see Performing Arts Biography Master Index 1079

Theatre History Studies (US ISSN 0733-2033) 1079

Theatre in Denmark see Teater i Danmark 1078

Theatre Papers (UK ISSN 0309-8036) 1079

Theatre Profiles (US ISSN 0361-7947) 1079

Theatre Student Series (US ISSN 0082-3848) 1079

Theatre Studies (US ISSN 0362-0964) 1079

Theatre World (US ISSN 0082-3856) 1079

Theilheimer's Synthetic Methods of Organic Chemistry see Synthetic Methods of Organic Chemistry 331

Their World (US) 334, 445, 788

Themata (DK ISSN 0107-2676) 599

Themata Chorou & Technon see Design and Art in Greece 98

Thematic Catalogue Series (US) 842

Thematical Reviews see Temadokumentacios Kiadvanyok 1071

Thematische Information Philosophie (GE ISSN 0138-2144) 882

Themes in Drama (UK ISSN 0263-676X) 1079

Themes in Social Anthropology (UK) 77

Themis see Revue Juridique Themis 663

Theodor-Storm-Gesellschaft. Schriften (GW ISSN 0082-3880) 735

Theokratia; Jahrbuch des Institutum Judaicum Delitzschianum (NE ISSN 0082-3899) 977

Theologica see Claretianum 981

Theological and Religious Bibliographies(UK) 13, 975

Theological and Religious Index see Theological and Religious Bibliographies 975

Theological Markings (US ISSN 0362-0603) 973

Theologie und Dienst (GW) 973

Theologische Dissertationen (SZ ISSN 0082-3902) 973

Theology and Scientific Culture (US) 973, 1001

Theoretical and Experimental Biology (US ISSN 0082-3945) 147

Theoretical Chemical Engineering Abstracts (UK ISSN 0040-5787) 13, 477

Theoretical Chemistry (US ISSN 0082-3961) 325

Theoretical Chemistry: Advances and Perspectives (US ISSN 0361-0551) 325

Theoretical Cybernetics Abstracts see Cybernetics Abstracts 354

Theoretical Issues in Cognitive Science (US) 937

Theoria (SW ISSN 0040-5825) 882, 937

Theorie de la Production (FR ISSN 0082-3988) 200

Theorie et Critique see T & C 111

Theorien der Psychologie (US) 937

Theory and Decision Library (NE) 882, 1012

Theory and Practice of Scientific Information see Tudomanyos Tajekoztatas Elmelete es Gyakorlata 684

Theory and Research in Behavioral Pediatrics (US) 788, 937

Theriaca (DK ISSN 0082-4003) 873

Thermal-Electric Plant Construction Cost and Production Expenses see Historical Plant Cost and Annual Production Expenses for Selected Electric Plants 184

Thermodynamics Research Center. Data Project. Selected Values of Properties of Chemical Compounds. Category A. Tables of Selected Values of Physical and Thermodynamic Properties of Chemical Compounds (US ISSN 0082-4046) 327, 332

Thermodynamics Research Center. Data Project. Selected Values of Properties of Chemical Compounds. Category B. Selected Infrared Spectral Data (US ISSN 0082-402X) *327*
Thermodynamics Research Center. Data Project. Selected Values of Properties of Chemical Componds. Category C. Selected Ultraviolet Spectral Data *see* Thermodynamics Research Center. Hydrocarbon Project. Selected Values of Properties of Hydrocarbons and Related Compounds. Category C: Selected Ultraviolet Spectral Data *327*
Thermodynamics Research Center. Data Project. Selected Values of Properties of Chemical Compounds. Category D. Selected Raman Spectral Data *see* Thermodynamics Research Center. Hydrocarbon Project. Selected Values of Properties of Hydrocarbons and Related Compounds. Category D: Selected Raman Spectral Data *327*
Thermodynamics Research Center. Data Project. Selected Values of Properties of Chemical Compounds. Category E. Selected Mass Spectral Data *see* Thermodynamics Research Center. Hydrocarbon Project. Selected Values of Properties of Hydrocarbons and Related Compounds. Category E: Selected Mass Spectral Data *327*
Thermodynamics Research Center. Data Project. Selected Values of Properties of Chemical Compounds. Category F. Selected 1H Nuclear Magnetic Resonance Spectral Data (US) *327*
Thermodynamics Research Center. Hydrocarbon Project. Selected Values of Properties of Hydrocarbons and Related Compounds. Category A: Tables of Selected Values of Physical and Thermodynamic Properties of Hydrocarbons (US) *333*
Thermodynamics Research Center. Hydrocarbon Project. Selected Values of Properties of Hydrocarbons and Related Compounds. Category B: Selected Infrared Spectral Data (US) *327*
Thermodynamics Research Center. Hydrocarbon Project. Selected Values of Properties of Hydrocarbons and Related Compounds. Category C: Selected Ultraviolet Spectral Data (US) *327*
Thermodynamics Research Center. Hydrocarbon Project. Selected Values of Properties of Hydrocarbons and Related Compounds. Category D: Selected Raman Spectral Data (US) *327*
Thermodynamics Research Center. Hydrocarbon Project. Selected Values of Properties of Hydrocarbons and Related Compounds. Category E: Selected Mass Spectral Data (US) *327*
Thermodynamics Research Center. Hydrocarbon Project. Selected Values of Properties of Hydrocarbons and Related Compounds. Category F: Selected Nuclear Magnetic Resonance Data (US) *327*
Thermodynamics Research Center. Hydrocarbon Project. Selected Values of Properties of Hydrocarbons and Related Compounds. Category G: Selected 13-C Nuclear Magnetic Resonance Spectral Data (US) *327*
Thermodynamics Research Center. International Data Series. Selected Data on Mixtures. Series A. Thermodynamic Properties of Non-reacting Binary Systems of Organic Substances (US ISSN 0147-1503) *331, 333*

Thermodynamics Research Center Data Project. Selected Values of Properties of Chemical Compounds. Category F. Selected Nuclear Magnetic Resonance Spectral Data *see* Thermodynamics Research Center. Data Project. Selected Values of Properties of Chemical Compounds. Category F. Selected 1H Nuclear Magnetic Resonance Spectral Data *327*
Thermophysics *see* Akademiya Nauk Litovskoi S.S.R. Silumine Fizika *894*
Thesaurismata (IT ISSN 0082-4097) *1164*
Thesaurus - American Petroleum Institute *see* American Petroleum Institute. Central Abstracting and Indexing Service. Thesaurus *862*
Thesaurus of E R I C Descriptors (Educational Resources Information Center) (US) *420, 684*
Theses and Other Publications of the University of Copenhagen (DK ISSN 0900-2278) *132*
Theses Canadiennes *see* Canadian Theses *124*
Theses in Latin American Studies at British Universities in Progress and Completed *see* Theses in Latin American Studies at British Universities in Progress or Recently Completed *132*
Theses in Latin American Studies at British Universities in Progress or Recently Completed (UK) *132, 610*
Thesis Abstracts (II ISSN 0379-3990) *13, 43, 634*
Third Republic/Troisieme Républic (US) *599*
Third World Development (UK) *264*
Thirteenth District Dental Society. Bulletin *see* Thirtieth District Dental Society, Fresno, California. Bulletin *780*
Thirtieth District Dental Society, Fresno, California. Bulletin (US) *780*
This is Newcastle and the Hunter Region (AT ISSN 0726-4690) *538*
This Month in Your Library (US ISSN 0040-6252) *684*
Thomas Callander Memorial Lectures (UK ISSN 0265-4601) *561*
Thomas Grocery Register (US ISSN 0082-4151) *523*
Thomas Grocery Register's Food Marketers' Handbook *see* Food Marketers' Handbook *522*
Thomas Hardy Annual (US) *735*
Thomas Hardy Year Book (UI ISSN 0082-416X) *735*
Thomas Mann Gesellschaft. Blaetter (SZ ISSN 0082-4186) *735*
Thomas Register of American Manufacturers *see* Thomas Register of American Manufacturers and Thomas Register Catalog File *285*
Thomas Register of American Manufacturers and Thomas Register Catalog File (US) *285, 317*
Thomas Say Foundation Monographs (US) *35, 132, 166, 1001*
Thom's Commercial Directory (IE ISSN 0082-4224) *317*
Thom's Dublin & County Street Directory (IE) *483, 549*
Thorbecke-Colleges (NE) *599*
Thoreau Society Booklets (US) *1164*
Thoresby Society, Leeds, England. Publications (UK ISSN 0082-4232) *561*
Thorndike Encyclopedia of Banking and Financial Tables (Supplement) (US) *233*
Thoroton Society of Nottinghamshire. Transactions (UK ISSN 0309-9210) *94, 599*
Thoroughbred Breeders' Handbook (AT ISSN 0311-8347) *1043*
Thoroughbred Racing Associations. Directory and Record Book (US ISSN 0082-4240) *1043*
Thorslunde Ishoej Lokalhistoriske Forening *see* Lokalhistorien for Torslunde Ishoej og Tranegilde *589*
Thorvaldsens Museum. Meddelelser (DK ISSN 0085-7262) *111, 831*
Thought & Action (US ISSN 0748-8475) *439*

Thoughts for All Seasons (US) *744, 882*
Threatened Birds of Africa and Related Islands (UK) *171*
Three Minutes a Day (US) *973*
Three Rivers Chronicle (US) *610*
Three Thousand Books for Secondary School Libraries *see* Books for Secondary School Libraries *675*
Threshold (US) *100, 111*
Threshold (UK ISSN 0040-6562) *735*
Threshold of Fantasy (US ISSN 0277-7800) *735*
Through Casa Guidi Windows (US) *744*
Through Europe by Train (FR ISSN 0579-8256) *1095*
Thrum's All About Hawaii (US) *1117*
Thunder Bay Camping Guide (CN ISSN 0380-6197) *1047, 1117*
Thunder Bay Historical Museum Society. Papers and Records (CN ISSN 0082-4283) *610*
Thunderer (UK) *342*
Thurgauische Museum. Mitteilungen (SZ) *831*
Thuringen-Bibliographie (GE ISSN 0232-3907) *564*
Thyristor D.A.T.A. Book (US ISSN 0732-6092) *460*
Thyristor Discontinued Devices D.A.T.A. Book (US) *460*
Tibet Society. Journal (US ISSN 0735-1364) *571, 854*
Tibetan Medicine (II ISSN 0970-1257) *767*
Tibiscus. Seria Arta (RM) *111*
Tibiscus. Seria Etnografie (RM) *77*
Tibiscus. Seria Istorie (RM) *599*
Tibiscus. Seria Stiintele Naturii (RM) *1001*
Tidal Gravity Corrections (NE ISSN 0257-4284) *401*
Tide of Time (AT) *573*
Tidens Tegn (DK) *1164*
Tidevandstabeller for Danmark (DK ISSN 0106-8334) *1126*
Tidevandstabeller for Faeroerne (DK ISSN 0106-8342) *408*
Tidevandstabeller for Groenland (DK ISSN 0107-0398) *408*
Tidings *see* Akim Review *444*
Tidsskrift for Oplysningens Tidsalder (DK ISSN 0108-4712) *882*
Tidsskrift for Planteavl/Danish Journal of Plant and Soil Science (DK ISSN 0040-7135) *162*
Tidsskriftindeks for Skolebiblioteker (DK ISSN 0105-4090) *132, 420*
Tiede ja Ase (FI) *599*
Tierra y Sociedad (PE) *35*
Das Tierreich (GW ISSN 0040-7305) *178*
Tiers-Monde en Marche (FR) *264*
Tierwelt Deutschlands (GE ISSN 0082-4305) *178*
Tijdschrift voor Entomologie (NE ISSN 0040-7496) *166*
Tikufat Hashoah (IS) *505, 599*
Tim Kelley's Fishing Guide (US) *1047*
Timarit Idnadarmanna (IC) *276*
Timarit Um Islenzka Grasafraedi *see* Acta Botanica Islandica *153*
Timber Tax Journal (US ISSN 0563-5446) *300, 1047*
Timber Trades Directory (UK ISSN 0082-4372) *317, 530*
Timber Trades Journal. Annual Special Issue (UK ISSN 0082-4364) *530*
Time of Change *see* Time of Change: Handbook on Women Workers *276*
Time of Change: Handbook on Women Workers (US) *276*
Time Zones (US) *1164*
Timeless Fellowship (II ISSN 0563-5489) *684*
Times Business Directory of Singapore (SI ISSN 0217-6009) *317*
Times Guide to the House of Commons (UK ISSN 0082-4399) *910*
Times Health Supplement *see* Health Services *954*
Times of India Directory and Yearbook Including Who's Who (II ISSN 0082-4445) *571*
Times Trade and Industrial Directory (NR) *317*

TOHO GAKUHO 1905

Times 1000 (UK ISSN 0082-4429) *292*
Tin Production and Investment (UK) *800*
Tin Statistics (UK) *802*
Ting og Sager fra Odsherred *see* Alle Tiders Odsherreds *574*
Tire and Rim Association. Standards Year Book (US ISSN 0082-4496) *986*
Tiroler Geschichtsquellen (AU) *599*
Tiroler Heimat (AU) *599*
Tiroler Landesarchiv. Veroeffentlichungen (AU) *599*
Tiroler Landesmuseum Ferdinandeum, Innsbruck. Veroeffentlichungen (AU) *831*
Tiroler Ortschroniken (AU) *599*
Tiryns (GW ISSN 0082-450X) *94, 339*
Tiscia (HU ISSN 0563-587X) *147*
Tissue Culture Studies in Japan: The Annual Bibliography/Nihon Soshiki Baiyo Kenkyu Nenpo (JA ISSN 0082-4518) *1164*
Titles of Dissertations and Theses Completed in Home Economics (US ISSN 0082-4534) *615*
Tjaenstemaennens Central Organisation. Aarsrapport *see* Aaret som Gaatt *269*
Tjaenstemaennens Central Organisation Aaret som Gaatt *see* Aaret som Gaatt *269*
Tjustbygden (SW ISSN 0349-764X) *94, 111*
Tlalocan (MX ISSN 0040-8239) *77*
To Know Wallony *see* Connaitre la Wallonie *580*
To the Source/El Ha'ayin *see* Sources of Contemporary Jewish Thought *712*
TOAR *see* The Original Art Report *108*
Tobacco Abstracts (US ISSN 0040-8298) *13, 1080*
Tobacco Associates. Annual Report (US ISSN 0082-4593) *1080*
Tobacco Bibliography (UK ISSN 0563-6140) *1080*
Tobacco Directory and Diary *see* Tobacco Trade Marketing Directory *1080*
Tobacco Export Promotion Council. Annual Report and Accounts (II) *60*
Tobacco: Latin American Industrial Report (US) *240, 1080*
Tobacco Reprint Series (US) *1080*
Tobacco Research Institute. Annual Report *see* Central Tobacco Research Institute and its Regional Research Stations. Annual Report *1079*
Tobacco Science Yearbook (US ISSN 0082-4623) *1080*
Tobacco Trade Marketing Directory (UK) *1080*
Tobaco Trade Year Book and Diary *see* Tobacco Trade Marketing Directory *1080*
Tochigi-Ken No Jinko/Population in Tochigi Prefecture (JA) *924*
Today's Delinquent (US ISSN 0733-6551) *373*
Today's Education *see* Today's Education Annual *420*
Today's Education. General Edition *see* Today's Education Annual *420*
Today's Education Annual (US ISSN 0737-1888) *420*
Today's Education: Educational Support Edition (US ISSN 0737-1888) *1164*
Today's Education: Higher Education Edition *see* Thought & Action *439*
Toegepast-Natuurwetenschappelijk Onderzoek. Technisch Fysische Dienst Technisch Fysische Dienst TNO-TH. Jaarverslag *see* Technisch Fysische Dienst TNO-TH. Jaarverslag *891*
Toern *see* Wudd *976*
Toestand in de Wereld *see* Dat Was de Toestand in de Wereld *556*
Togo. Direction de la Meteorologie Nationale. Resume Annuel du Temps(TG) *807*
Toho Gakuho *see* Oriental Studies *853*

Tohoku Daigaku Rigakubu Chishitsugaku Koseibutsugaku Kyoshitsu Kenkyu Hobun Hokoku see Tohoku University. Institute of Geology and Paleontology. Contributions *396*

Tohoku Electric Power Co., Inc. Annual Report (JA) *460*

Tohoku Gakuin University Review (JA ISSN 0385-406X) *706, 735*

Tohoku Geophysical Journal (JA ISSN 0040-8794) *401*

Tohoku Institute of Technology. Bulletin. Section B. Sciences and Technology see Tohoku Institute of Technology. Memoirs. Series 1: Science and Engineering *474*

Tohoku Institute of Technology. Memoirs. Series 1: Science and Engineering (JA ISSN 0285-3817) *474*

Tohoku Institute of Technology. Memoirs. Series 2: Humanities and Social Science (JA ISSN 0285-3825) *632*

Tohoku National Agricultural Experiment Station. Miscellaneous Publication (JA ISSN 0387-172X) *35*

Tohoku Psychologica Folia (JA ISSN 0040-8743) *937*

Tohoku University. Institute for Agricultural Research. Reports (JA) *35*

Tohoku University. Institute of Geology and Paleontology. Contributions/Tohoku Daigaku Rigakubu Chishitsugaku Koseibutsugaku Kyoshitsu Kenkyu Hobun Hokoku (JA ISSN 0082-4658) *396, 857*

Tohoku University. Institute of Geology and Paleontology. Science Reports. Second Series (JA ISSN 0082-464X) *396, 857*

Tohoku University. Research Institute of Electrical Communication. Technical Report (JA) *344*

Tohoku University. Research Institutes. Science Reports. Series D: Agriculture see Tohoku University. Institute for Agricultural Research. Reports *35*

Tohoku University. Science Reports. Series 5: Geophysics see Tohoku Geophysical Journal *401*

Toike Oike (CN ISSN 0049-4038) *474*

Tokai University. Foreign Language Center. Bulletin (JA ISSN 0389-3081) *706*

Tokei Suri Kenkyusho Nenpo see Institute of Statistical Mathematics. Annual Report *1155*

Tokushima Daigaku Gakugei Kiyo see Tokushima University. Journal of Gakugei *632*

Tokushima University. Journal of Gakugei/Tokushima Daigaku Gakugei Kiyo (JA ISSN 0495-7601) *632*

Tokyo Astronomical Bulletin (JA ISSN 0082-4690) *117*

Tokyo Astronomical Observatory. Annals (JA ISSN 0082-4704) *117*

Tokyo Astronomical Observatory. Report (JA ISSN 0374-4639) *117*

Tokyo Astronomical Observatory. Reprints (JA ISSN 0082-4712) *117*

Tokyo College of Domestic Science. Bulletin/Tokyo Kasei Daigaku Kenkyu Kiyo (JA) *615*

Tokyo Daigaku Kyoyogakubu Shizenkagaku Kiyo see University of Tokyo. College of General Education. Scientific Papers *1002*

Tokyo Daigaku Rigakubu Kiyo, Dai-2-rui, Chishitsugaku, Kobutsugaku, Chirigaku, Chikyu Butsurigaku see University of Tokyo. Faculty of Science. Journal. Section 2: Geology, Mineralogy, Geography, Geophysics *381*

Tokyo Daigaku Rigakubu Kiyo, Dai-3-rui, Shokubutsugaku see University of Tokyo. Faculty of Science. Journal. Section 3: Botany *162*

Tokyo Daigaku Rigakubu Kiyo, Dai-4-rui, Dobutsugaku see University of Tokyo. Faculty of Science. Journal. Section 4: Zoology *178*

Tokyo Daigaku Seisan Gijutsu Kenkyusho Hokoku see University of Tokyo. Institute of Industrial Science. Report *1072*

Tokyo Denki University. Faculty of Engineering. General Education. Research Reports (JA ISSN 0288-5530) *460, 474, 493*

Tokyo Denki University. Faculty of Engineering. Research Reports (JA ISSN 0389-617X) *460, 475, 493*

Tokyo Gakugei University. Bulletin (JA ISSN 0371-6813) *152*

Tokyo Institute of Technology. Research Laboratory of Resources Utilization. Report/Shigen Kagaku Kenkyusho (JA ISSN 0495-8055) *1071*

Tokyo Kasei Daigaku Kenkyu Kiyo see Tokyo College of Domestic Science. Bulletin *615*

Tokyo Medical and Dental University. Institute for Medical and Dental Engineering. Reports/Iyo Kizai Kenkyusho Hokoku (JA ISSN 0082-4739) *767, 780*

Tokyo Metropolitan Agricultural Experiment Station, Itsukaichi Office. Forestry Experimental Bulletin/Ringyo Shiken Kenkyu Hokoku (JA ISSN 0082-4720) *528*

Tokyo Metropolitan Government. Fuchu Rehabilitation School. Annual Report (JA) *445*

Tokyo Metropolitan Institute of Neurosciences. Annual Report/Tokyo-to Shinkei Kagaku Sogo Kenkyujo Nempo (JA) *791*

Tokyo Metropolitan Research Laboratory of Public Health, Annual Report/Tokyo-toritsu Eisei Kenkyusho Kenkyu Nenpo (JA ISSN 0082-4771) *767, 956*

Tokyo Metropolitan University. Annual Report of Research on the Ogasawara (Bonin) Islands (JA ISSN 0387-9844) *1001*

Tokyo Metropolitan University. Department of Geography. Geographical Reports/Tokyo-toritsu Daigaku Chirigaku Hokoku (JA ISSN 0386-8710) *549*

Tokyo Metropolitan University. Faculty of Technology. Memoirs/Tokyo-toritsu Daigaku Kogakubu Hokoku (JA ISSN 0082-4747) *1071*

Tokyo No Ikebana (JA) *534*

Tokyo Suisan Daigaku Ronshu see Tokyo University of Fisheries. Report *513*

Tokyo-to Shinkei Kagaku Sogo Kenkyujo Nempo see Tokyo Metropolitan Institute of Neurosciences. Annual Report *791*

Tokyo-toritsu Daigaku Chirigaku Hokoku see Tokyo Metropolitan University. Department of Geography. Geographical Reports *549*

Tokyo-toritsu Daigaku Kogakubu Hokoku see Tokyo Metropolitan University. Faculty of Technology. Memoirs *1071*

Tokyo-toritsu Eisei Kenkyusho Kenkyu Nenpo see Tokyo Metropolitan Research Laboratory of Public Health, Annual Report *767*

Tokyo-toritsu Koka Tanki Daigaku Kenkyu Hokoku see Metropolitan College of Technology, Tokyo. Memoirs *1070*

Tokyo University of Agriculture & Technology. Annual Report (JA ISSN 0563-8313) *60*

Tokyo University of Fisheries. Report/Tokyo Suisan Daigaku Ronshu (JA ISSN 0563-8372) *513, 1001*

Tokyo University of Fisheries. Transactions (JA ISSN 0388-0966) *513*

Tokyo University of Fisheries Journal. Special Edition /Tokyo Suisan Daigaku Tokubetu Kenkyu Honoku (JA ISSN 0082-4836) *513*

Tokyo University of Foreign Studies. Summary (JA ISSN 0082-4844) *439*

Toledot (US ISSN 0146-9568) *505, 537*

Toll-Free Digest (US) *317, 351*

Tolley's Capital Gains Tax (Year) (UK) *300*

Tolley's Capital Transfer Tax see Tolley's Inheritance (Year) *300*

Tolley's Corporation Tax (Year) (UK) *300*

Tolley's Income Tax (Year) (UK ISSN 0305-8921) *300*

Tolley's Inheritance (Year) (UK) *300*

Tolley's Tax Data (Year) (UK ISSN 0262-4583) *300*

Tolley's Tax Tables (Year) (UK ISSN 0307-6687) *300*

Tolley's Taxation in the Republic of Ireland (Year) (UK) *300, 671*

Tonga. Minister of Health. Report (TO ISSN 0082-4895) *956*

Tonggye Suchup see Korea Statistical Korea *1058*

Too Much - University College Hospital Magazine (UK) *618, 767*

Tool and Die Institute Purchasing Guide see Tooling and Manufacturing Association. Purchasing Guide *317*

Tooling and Manufacturing Association. Purchasing Guide (US) *317*

Tools & Hardware: Latin American Industrial Report (US) *190*

Tools and Tillage (DK ISSN 0563-8887) *35, 561*

Toomey J Gazette see Rehabilitation Gazette *445*

Top Companies (SA ISSN 0563-8895) *292*

Top Executive Compensation (US) *282, 287*

Top Management Abstracts (UK ISSN 0049-4100) *13, 219*

Top Management Remuneration Review (AT) *287*

Top of the Pops Annual (UK) *842*

Top Tens and Trivia of Rock and Roll and Rhythm and Blues. Annual Supplement (US) *842*

Top 1,500 Companies see Trinet Directory of Leading U S Companies: Top 1,500 *200*

Top 1,500 Private Companies see Trinet Directory of Leading U S Companies: Top 1,500 Private *200*

Top 2,000 Directories and Annuals: A Guide to the Major Titles Used in British Libraries see Top 3,000 Directories and Annuals: A Guide to the Major Titles Used in British Libraries *684*

Top 3,000 Directories and Annuals: A Guide to the Major Titles Used in British Libraries (UK) *684*

Top 100 Data Processing Almanac (US) *286*

Topic (US ISSN 0049-4127) *632, 1001, 1012*

Topical New Issues (US ISSN 0090-7286) *875*

Topical Stamp Handbooks (US ISSN 0049-4135) *875*

Topical Times Football Book (UK) *1040*

Topics in Antibiotic Chemistry (UK) *152*

Topics in Applied Physics (US ISSN 0303-4216) *475, 891*

Topics in Atmospheric and Oceanographic Sciences (US) *408, 807*

Topics in Bioelectrochemistry and Bioenergetics (US) *152*

Topics in Boundary Elements Research (US) *475*

Topics in Cognitive Development (US) *937*

Topics in Current Chemistry (US ISSN 0340-1022) *325*

Topics in Current Physics (US ISSN 0342-6793) *891*

Topics in Energy (US) *467*

Topics in Enzyme and Fermentation Biotechnology (UK ISSN 0140-0835) *152*

Topics in f-Element Chemistry (NE) *329*

Topics in Gastroenterology (US) *783*

Topics in Geobiology (US) *147, 396*

Topics in Infectious Diseases (US ISSN 0171-2160) *778*

Topics in Information Systems (US) *360*

Topics in Inorganic and General Chemistry (NE ISSN 0082-495X) *325, 329*

Topics in Ocean Engineering (US ISSN 0085-7297) *1164*

Topics in Philosophy (US) *882*

Topics in Physical Organometallic Chemistry (UK) *333*

Topics in Religion: A Bibliographic Series (US) *975*

Topics in Stereochemistry (US ISSN 0082-500X) *325*

Toposcope (SA) *567*

Torch (LB) *567*

Torgos (IS) *171*

Tornionlaakson Vuosikirja (FI) *599*

Toronto. Public Libraries. Guide to Serials Currently Received in the Public Libraries of Metropolitan Toronto see Guide to Periodicals and Newspapers in the Public Libraries of Metropolitan Toronto *127*

Toronto Airport Business Directory (CN) *1090*

Toronto Historical Board. Year Book (CN ISSN 0226-7209) *610*

Toronto Mediaeval Latin Texts (CN ISSN 0082-5050) *599, 735*

Toronto Medieval Bibliographies (CN ISSN 0082-5042) *564*

Toronto Old English Series (CN) *599, 735*

Toronto Semitic Texts and Studies (CN ISSN 0082-5123) *572*

Toronto Stock Exchange Fact Book (CN) *233, 250, 268*

Toronto Studies in Theology (US) *973*

Torquay Natural History Society. Transactions and Proceedings (UK ISSN 0082-5344) *1001*

Torreia (CU ISSN 0563-9425) *178*

Torry Research Station, Aberdeen, Scotland. Annual Report (UK ISSN 0082-5352) *513*

Torts see B A R-B R I Bar Review. Torts *370*

Toshi Kenkyu Hokoku see Report on Urban Research *625*

Toshokan Nenkan see Library Yearbook *681*

Tosi Gagye Yonbo see Korea (Republic). National Bureau of Statistics. Annual Report on the Family Income and Expenditure Survey *212*

Tosoguian Hak (KO) *684*

Tosomaeup Census Bogo Seo see Korea (Republic). National Bureau of Statistics. Wholesale and Retail Trade Census Report *212*

Totalisator Agency Board. Annual Report (NZ) *946*

Totok: Handbuch der Geschichte der Philosophie (GW) *882*

Totto (FI) *599*

Tottori Daigaku Nogakubu Fuzoku Enshurin Hokoku see Tottori Universty Forests. Research Bulletin *528*

Tottori University. Faculty of Agriculture. Journal (JA ISSN 0082-5360) *35*

Tottori University Forests. Bulletin see Tottori Universty Forests. Research Bulletin *528*

Tottori Universty Forests. Research Bulletin/Tottori Daigaku Nogakubu Fuzoku Enshurin Hokoku (JA) *528*

Tour Organizers' Handbook/Guide du Directeur de Tournees de Spectacles (CN) *1079*

Tourbook: Alabama, Louisiana, Mississippi (US ISSN 0361-4948) *1117*

Tourbook: Arizona, New Mexico (US ISSN 0362-3599) *1117*

Tourbook: Arkansas, Kansas, Missouri, Oklahoma (US) *1117*

Tourbook: Atlantic Provinces and Quebec (US ISSN 0363-1788) *1117*

Tourbook: California, Nevada (US) *1117*

Tourbook: Colorado, Utah (US ISSN 0362-9821) *1117*
Tourbook: Connecticut, Massachusetts, Rhode Island (US) *1117*
Tourbook: Florida (US ISSN 0516-9674) *1117*
Tourbook: Georgia, North Carolina, South Carolina (US ISSN 0361-4956) *1117*
TourBook: Hawaii (US) *1117*
Tourbook: Idaho, Montana, Wyoming (US ISSN 0363-2695) *1117*
Tourbook: Illinois, Indiana, Ohio (US) *1117*
Tourbook: Kentucky, Tennessee (US ISSN 0361-4964) *1117*
Tourbook: Maine, New Hampshire, Vermont (US) *1117*
Tourbook: Michigan, Wisconsin (US) *1117*
Tourbook: Mid-Atlantic (US ISSN 0364-0086) *1117*
Tourbook: New Jersey, Pennsylvania (US) *1117*
Tourbook: New York (US ISSN 0363-1540) *1117*
TourBook: North Central (US) *1117*
Tourbook: Ontario (US) *1117*
Tourbook: Oregon/Washington (US) *1117*
Tourbook: Texas (US) *1117*
Tourbook: Western Canada and Alaska (US ISSN 0362-3602) *1117*
Touring Artists Directory of the Performing Arts in Canada (Biennial) /Repertoire des Artisites et Compagnies de Tournee au Canada (CN) *1079*
Touring Artists' Directory of the Performing Arts in Canada (Year)/ Repertoire des Artistes et Compagnies de Tournees au Canada (Year) (CN ISSN 0715-755X) *1079*
Touring Club Italiano. Servizio Informazioni Turistiche. Fascicoli di Documentazione per i Viaggi in Europa *see* Europa Facile *1108*
Touring Guide to Scotland (UK) *1117*
Touring in from Salisbury (UK) *599, 1117*
Touring in Historic Wessex *see* Touring in from Salisbury *1117*
Touring with Towser (US ISSN 0082-5441) *868*
Tourism *see* Turizum *1120*
Tourism and Migration Statistics (FJ) *1065, 1120*
Tourism Compendium (SP) *132, 1120*
Tourism in Arkansas. Activity Report *see* Arkansas Travel and Tourism Report *1106*
Tourism in the British Virgin Islands (VB) *1120*
Tourism Industry of Puerto Rico. Selected Statistics (PR) *1120*
Tourist Bibliography *see* Tourism Compendium *1120*
Tourist Guide Book of Ontario (CN) *1117*
Tourist Guide/Touristique (CN) *1117*
Tourist Park Guide (AT) *1117*
Tournament Times (US) *1040*
Tournees de Spectacles *see* Touring Artists' Directory of the Performing Arts in Canada (Year) *1079*
Tours and Visits Directory (US ISSN 0278-467X) *1117*
Toute la Boisson. International (FR ISSN 0082-5484) *120*
Towarzystwo Literackie im. A. Mickiewicza. Biblioteka (PL ISSN 0067-7787) *735*
Towarzystwo Naukowe w Toruniu. Fontes (PL ISSN 0082-5506) *561, 599*
Towarzystwo Naukowe w Toruniu. Komisja Historii Sztuki. Teka (PL ISSN 0082-5514) *111*
Towarzystwo Naukowe w Toruniu. Prace Archeologiczne (PL) *94*
Towarzystwo Naukowe w Toruniu. Sprawozdania (PL ISSN 0371-375X) *1001*
Towline (CN) *21*
Town and Country Planning Association. Annual Report (UK ISSN 0308-082X) *626*

Town and Country Planning Summer School; Report of Proceedings (UK ISSN 0078-2114) *626*
Towson State University Journal of Psychology (US ISSN 0161-7648) *937*
Toxicology Abstracts (US ISSN 0140-5365) *13, 873*
Toy and Decoration Fair Directory (CN ISSN 0317-9443) *553, 643*
Toy Fayre Earls Court Newspaper *see* Toy Trader Daily News (Earls Court) *240*
Toy Fayre Harrogate Newspaper *see* Toy Trader Daily News (Harrogate) *240*
Toy Trader Daily News (Earls Court) (UK) *240, 553*
Toy Trader Daily News (Harrogate) (UK) *240, 553*
Toy Trader Year Book (UK ISSN 0082-5611) *553*
Toyama-ken Eisei Tokei Nenpo *see* Toyama Prefecture. Annual Report of Public Health *956*
Toyama Mercantile Marine College. Journal/Toyama Shosen Koto Senmon Gakko Kenkyu Shuroku (JA) *1104*
Toyama Prefecture. Annual Report of Public Health/Toyama-ken Eisei Tokei Nenpo (JA) *956*
Toyama Shosen Koto Senmon Gakko Kenkyu Shuroku *see* Toyama Mercantile Marine College. Journal *1104*
Toyo Tsushinki Giho *see* Toyo's Technical Bulletin *345*
Toyo's Technical Bulletin/Toyo Tsushinki Giho (JA) *345*
Toyota in Brief *see* Automobile Industry - Japan and Toyota *1090*
Toys & Games Trader Yearbook (UK) *553*
Trabajo (CK) *276*
Trabajo en Israel *see* Labour in Israel *648*
Trabajos de Geologia (SP ISSN 0474-9588) *396*
Trabajos de Prehistoria. Nueva Serie (SP ISSN 0082-5638) *94*
Trabajos Monograficos sobre la Independencia de Norteamerica (SP) *610*
Trabajos Realizados por el Comite Juridico Interamericano Durante el Periodo Ordinario de Sesiones *see* Work Accomplished by the Inter-American Juridical Committee during its Meeting *667*
Trabalhos de Antropologia e Etnologia (PO ISSN 0304-243X) *77*
Trac: Global Yearbook of Issues, Events, and Discoveries in Telecommunications, Robotics, Artificial Intelligence, CAD/CAM (US) *345*
Trace Analysis (US ISSN 0275-844X) *956*
Trace Substances in Environmental Health (US ISSN 0361-5162) *499, 956*
Track and Field Case Book (US) *1047*
Track and Field Guide *see* N A G W S Guide. Track and Field *1159*
Track and Field Officials Manual (US) *1047*
Track and Field Rulebook (US) *1047*
Track and Field Rules and Records *see* Track and Field Rulebook *1047*
Track Yearbook (US) *1095*
Tractatenblad van het Koninkrijk der Nederlanden (NE ISSN 0023-3412) *918*
Tractebel. Annual Report (BE) *460, 475*
Tractionel. Annual Report *see* Tractebel. Annual Report *475*
Tractocatalogue (FR ISSN 0082-5662) *51*
Trade and Development: an U N C T A D Review (United Nations Conference on Trade and Development (UNCTAD)) (UN ISSN 0252-5216) *260, 264*
Trade and Development Report (UN) *260, 264*
Trade and Professional Associations in California: a Directory (US) *317*

Trade Associations and Professional Bodies of the United Kingdom (UK ISSN 0082-5689) *318*
Trade Directory (1985-86) (MM) *318*
Trade Directory and Guide Book to Ethiopia (ET ISSN 0564-0490) *1117*
Trade Directory for Denmark *see* Udenrigs Handelskalenderen for Danmark *318*
Trade Directory of Guyana (UK) *318*
Trade Directory of Papua New Guinea (UK) *318*
Trade Directory of Seychelles (SE) *318*
Trade Directory of the Republic of the Sudan (UK ISSN 0082-5735) *318*
Trade Directory of Western Sweden *see* Gothenburg and Western Sweden Chamber of Commerce. Membership Directory *236*
Trade Names Dictionary (US) *861*
Trade of China (CH ISSN 0082-5778) *260*
Trade Outlets and Taxable Retail Sales in California *see* Taxable Sales in California (Sales and Use Tax) *299*
Trade Policy Research Centre. Special Reports (UK) *260*
Trade Show Convention Guide *see* TradeShow Convention Guide *200*
Trade Unions in India (II ISSN 0445-6289) *649*
Trade Unions International of Chemical, Oil and Allied Workers. International Trade Conference. Documents (HU ISSN 0084-1544) *649*
Tradelink - S M A Annual Directory (Year) (SI ISSN 0129-9867) *318*
Trademark Register of the United States (US ISSN 0082-5786) *861*
Trades Union Congress. Report (UK) *649*
Trades Union Directory (AT) *649*
Tradescope (JA ISSN 0285-3809) *13, 318*
Tradeshow & Exhibit Manager Buyers Guide (US) *16, 318, 796, 1117*
TradeShow Convention Guide (US) *200*
Tradeshow Week Data Book (US) *285*
Trading in Metals (UK ISSN 0264-8199) *800*
Trading Standards and Consumer Protection Statistics. Actuals (UK ISSN 0260-6372) *219, 1066*
Tradisjon (NO ISSN 0332-5997) *77*
Traditio (US ISSN 0362-1529) *599, 632*
Traditional Kent Buildings (UK ISSN 0260-4116) *100*
Traditiones (YU) *517*
Trado; Asian-African Directory of Exporters, Importers and Manufacturers (II ISSN 0082-5824) *318*
Traduction Automatique Documents *see* T.A. Documents *705*
Traductions Hebraiques des Evangiles (BE) *973*
Trae Nyts Leverandoerregister (DK) *189, 530*
Traekonstruktioner (DK) *489*
Traffic Laws Commentary (US ISSN 0082-5859) *1097*
Traffic Report of the St. Lawrence Seaway (US ISSN 0082-5867) *1104*
Traffic Safety (US) *1097*
Traffic Trends *see* Maryland. State Highway Administration. Traffic Trends *1096*
Trafikanalyse *see* Stopinterviewanalyse *1097*
Trafikoekonomiske Enhedspriser (DK ISSN 0106-1852) *200, 1097*
Trail Blazer's Almanac (US) *1047*
Trailer Life's Recreational Vehicle Campground and Services Directory (US) *1047, 1117*
Training and Development Organizations Directory (US) *282*
Training for Agriculture *see* Training for Agriculture and Rural Development *427*
Training for Agriculture and Rural Development (UN ISSN 0251-1495) *35, 427*

TRANSPORT AND 1907

Training Resources *see* A S T D Buyers Guide and Consultants Directory *269*
Training Resources Tourism/ Hospitality/Recreation (CN ISSN 0712-7456) *439, 849*
Trains Annual *see* Railway World Annual *1095*
Trajekt (GE) *735*
Trans/Form/Acao (BL ISSN 0101-3173) *882*
Transactions - North Carolina Medical Society *see* North Carolina Medical Society. Transactions *764*
Transactions of the Monumental Brass Society (UK ISSN 0143-1250) *94, 800*
Transafrica Historical Papers (KE) *567*
Transdex *see* Transdex Index *647*
Transdex Index (US ISSN 0041-1116) *647*
Transfer Credit Practices of Designated Educational Institutions (US ISSN 0194-0988) *420*
Transient (US) *735*
Transistor D.A.T.A. Book (US ISSN 0732-6203) *460*
Transistor Discontinued Devices D.A.T.A. Book (US ISSN 0730-4846) *460*
Transition (GY) *1012*
Transitions in Mental Retardation (US) *937*
Transkei Government Gazette Index (SA ISSN 0257-5418) *13, 949*
Transkei Official Gazette *see* Transkei Government Gazette Index *949*
Translation Series in Mathematics and Engineering (US) *475, 753*
Translation Services Directory (American Translators Association) (US) *706*
Translations and Reprints from the Original Sources of European History *see* Middle Ages *590*
Translations from "Kommunist" *see* U S S R Report: Translations from "Kommunist" *910*
Translations Index (American Society for Metals) (US ISSN 0278-4238) *802*
Translations of Mathematical Monographs (US ISSN 0065-9282) *753*
Translations on Mongolia *see* Mongolia Report *247*
Translations on North Korea *see* Korean Affairs Report *246*
Translations on Subsaharan Africa *see* Sub-Saharan Africa Report *249*
Translations on U S S R Military Affairs *see* U S S R Report: Military Affairs *812*
Translations on U S S R Political and Sociological Affairs *see* U S S R Report: Political and Sociological Affairs *910*
Translations - Safety Codes and Guides *see* Uebersetzungen - Kerntechnische Regeln *898*
Transmission and Distribution Specifiers & Buyers Guide (US) *460*
Transnational (GW ISSN 0344-9823) *918*
Transnational Data Report (NE ISSN 0167-6962) *357*
Transplantation Today (US ISSN 0074-3984) *794*
Transporforskningkommission. Rapporter (SW) *1083*
Transport (Aarlig) (DK ISSN 0108-8157) *1083*
Transport and Communications Bulletin for Asia and the Far East *see* Transport & Communications Bulletin for Asia & the Pacific *1083*
Transport & Communications Bulletin for Asia & the Pacific (UN ISSN 0252-4392) *345, 1083*
Transport and Handling in the Pulp and Paper Industry (US) *859*
Transport and Road Digest/Vervoer- en Padoorsig (SA ISSN 0379-4792) *1097*
Transport and Road Research *see* Transport and Road Research Laboratory. Research Reports *1097*

Transport and Road Research Laboratory. Research Reports (UK) 483, *1097*
Transport Engineer's Handbook (UK) *1083*
Transport History (UK ISSN 0041-1469) 561, *1083*
Transport Industry and Trade Annual (II) *1083*
Transport Industry and Trade Journal *see* Transport Industry and Trade Annual *1083*
Transport Manager's Handbook (UK ISSN 0306-9435) *1083*
Transport Manager's Handbook (SA) *1105*
Transport Maritime: Etudes et Statistiques (FR) *1104*
Transport Museums (PL ISSN 0137-4435) *1083*
Transport of Goods by Road in Great Britain (UK) *1105*
Transport Services Directory (AT) *1083*
Transport Statistics Great Britain (UK) *1097*
Transport Studies Group. Annual Seminar on Rural Public Transport. Papers and Proceedings (UK) *1083*
Transport Workers Union. Triennial Report (MY) *1083*
Transportation and Products Legal Directory (US ISSN 0092-6175) *665*
Transportation in America (US ISSN 0889-0889) *1083*
Transportation: Latin American Industrial Report (US) 240, *1083*
Transportation Law Seminar. Papers and Proceedings *see* Eastern Transportation Law Seminar Papers and Proceedings *655*
Transportation Law Seminar. Papers and Proceedings *see* Western Transportation Law Seminar. Papers and Proceedings *1084*
Transportation R & D in Canada *see* Surface Transportation R & D in Canada *1083*
Transportation Research Board Special Report (US ISSN 0360-859X) 483, *1098*
Transportation Research Circular (US ISSN 0097-8515) *1084*
Transportation Research Forum. Proceedings: Annual Meeting (US ISSN 0091-2468) *1084*
Transportation Research Record (US ISSN 0361-1981) 483, *1098*
Transportation Statistics in the United States (US ISSN 0082-5956) 240, *1084*
Transportation Studies (US ISSN 0278-3819) *1084*
Transportation Telephone Tickler (US ISSN 0447-9181) 318, *1084*
Transportoekonomisk Institutt. Aarsberetning (NO) *1095*
Transportraadet Rapport (SW ISSN 0280-1183) *1084*
Transports Routiers de Marchandises Effectives par des Transporteurs Etrangers sur le Territoire Francais (FR) *1087*
Transtelel; Transmissions, Telecommunications, Electronique en France (FR ISSN 0082-5980) *351*
Transvaal Museum. Annals/Transvaal Museum Annale (SA ISSN 0041-1752) *1001*
Transvaal Museum. Bulletin (SA ISSN 0496-1102) *831*
Transvaal Museum. Monographs (SA ISSN 0255-0172) *831*
Transvaal Museum Annale *see* Transvaal Museum. Annals *1001*
Transworld Identity Series (US) *77*
Trapananda (CL) 396, 549, *610*
Trasmissioni di Potenza (IT) *493*
Trattati di Architettura (IT ISSN 0082-6006) *100*
Travaux d'Histoire Ethico-Politique (SZ ISSN 0082-6073) *561*
Travaux d'Humanisme et Renaissance (SZ ISSN 0082-6081) 111, *599*
Travaux de Droit, d'Economique de Sociologie et de Sciences Politiques (SZ ISSN 0082-6022) *1012*

Travaux de Linguistique (BE ISSN 0082-6049) *706*
Travaux de Linguistique Japonaise (FR) *706*
Travaux en Cours (FR) *753*
Travaux et Documents de Geographie Tropicale (FR ISSN 0336-5522) *549*
Travaux sur les Pecheries du Quebec (CN ISSN 0082-609X) *513*
Travel Abroad: Frontier Formalities (SP ISSN 0082-6103) *1117*
Travel and Tourism Research Association. Proceedings of the Annual Conference (US ISSN 0276-8968) *1118*
Travel Business Analyst (HK ISSN 0255-8866) 250, *1118*
Travel Data Locator Index (US) *1118*
Travel Directory (HK ISSN 0256-4203) *1118*
Travel Executives of New Zealand (NZ) *318*
Travel Guide, S.A. (SA) *1118*
Travel Guide to Europe (US) *1118*
Travel Guide to the Caribbean (US) *1118*
Travel in America *see* Economic Review of Travel in America *1108*
Travel in Greece (GR) *1118*
Travel Industry Personnel Directory (US ISSN 0082-6146) *1118*
Travel Industry World Yearbook (US ISSN 0738-9515) *1118*
Travel Management International (UK ISSN 0264-7664) *1118*
Travel on Saskatchewan Highways (CN ISSN 0581-8079) *1098*
Travel Outlook Forum Proceedings *see* Outlook for Travel and Tourism *1115*
Travel Trade Directory (UK ISSN 0041-2074) *1118*
Travel Trade Directory, U K and Ireland (UK ISSN 0082-7932) *1118*
Travel Trade London (UK) *1118*
Travel Trends in the United States and Canada (US) *1118*
Travel Trends in the United States and Canadian Provinces *see* Travel Trends in the United States and Canada *1118*
Travel Weekly's World Travel Directory (US) *1118*
Travelaid Guide to Egypt *see* Guide to Egypt *1111*
Travelaid Guide to Greece *see* Guide to Greece *1111*
Travelers Guide to Mexico (MX) *1118*
Traveller's Guide to Central and Southern Africa (UK ISSN 0144-7661) *1118*
Traveller's Guide to East Africa and the Indian Ocean (UK ISSN 0144-7653) *1118*
Traveller's Guide to North Africa (UK ISSN 0144-7637) *1118*
Traveller's Guide to the Middle East (UK) *1118*
Traveller's Guide to West Africa (UK ISSN 0144-7645) *1118*
Travelling Art Mail Bulletin *see* T A M Bulletin *111*
Traveltrade Visa Guide (AT) *260*
Travelware Resources Directory (US) 318, *672*
Travelweek Blue Book (AT) *1118*
Travelweek Hotel, Motel Index *see* Hotel, Motel Index *620*
Traza y Baza (SP) 111, *735*
Treatise on Analytical Chemistry. Part 1: Theory and Practice of Analytical Chemistry (US ISSN 0082-6243) *327*
Treatise on Analytical Chemistry. Part 2: Analytical Chemistry of the Elements; Analytical Chemistry of Inorganic and Organic Compounds (US ISSN 0082-6251) *327*
Treatise on Analytical Chemistry. Part 3: Analytical Chemistry in Industry (US ISSN 0082-626X) *327*
Treatise on Materials Science & Technology (US) 489, *1071*
Treatises and Documents *see* Razprave in Gradivo *516*
Treatment in Clinical Medicine (US) *767*

Treballs del Museu de Zoologia (SP) *178*
Tree (US ISSN 0041-2171) *1164*
Tree Fruit Production Recommendations *see* Cornell Recommendations for Commercial Tree-Fruit Production *532*
Tree Nut Authority. Report (MW) *60*
Tree-Ring Bulletin (US ISSN 0041-2198) *162*
Tremblements de Terre Canadiens *see* Canadian Earthquakes *398*
Trend (CN ISSN 0041-2295) *1164*
Trends: Consumer Attitudes and the Supermarket Update (US ISSN 0278-6346) *523*
Trends in Collective Agreement Settlement Wage Rate Changes in Nova Scotia (CN ISSN 0227-1362) *1164*
Trends in Collective Bargaining Settlements in Nova Scotia (CN ISSN 0381-3258) *1164*
Trends in Health and Health Services (NZ ISSN 0550-824X) *959*
Trends in Linguistics (GW) *706*
Trends in Southeast Asia (SI ISSN 0082-6316) *572*
Trends in World Economy (HU ISSN 0133-7769) *200*
Trent Law Journal (UK ISSN 0309-8990) *665*
Trent Papers in Education (UK ISSN 0260-1729) *420*
Treubia (IO ISSN 0082-6340) *178*
Trevithick Society. Occasional Publication (UK) *1071*
Tri-University Meson Facility Annual Report Scientific Activities *see* T R I U M F Annual Report Scientific Activities *898*
Tri-University Meson Facility Financial and Administrative Annual Report *see* T R I U M F Financial and Administrative Annual Report *898*
Triangle Papers (US) *918*
Tribal Advisor *see* Pan-American Indian Association News *505*
Tribhuvan University. Natural History Museum. Journal (NP) *162*
Tribolium Information Bulletin (US ISSN 0082-6391) *166*
Tribology Series (NE) *493*
Tribos - Tribology Abstracts (UK ISSN 0041-2694) 13, 477, *1073*
Tribunal de Commerce, Paris. Annuaire (FR ISSN 0071-9129) *665*
Tribunal Supremo Popular. Boletin (CU) *1071*
Tribune Graphologique (FR ISSN 0041-2864) *937*
Tribus (GW ISSN 0082-6413) 77, *111*
Trierer Grabungen und Forschungen (GW ISSN 0082-643X) *94*
Trierer Zeitschrift fuer Geschichte und Kunst des Trierer Landes und seiner Nachbargebiete (GW ISSN 0041-2953) 94, 111, *845*
Trieste Notes in Physics (US) *891*
Trilobite News (NO ISSN 0085-7386) *857*
Trinet Directory of Leading U S Companies: Second 1,500 (US) *200*
Trinet Directory of Leading U S Companies: Top 1,500 (US) *200*
Trinet Directory of Leading U S Companies: Top 1,500 Private (US) *200*
Trinidad and Tobago. Central Statistical Office. Annual Statistical Digest (TR ISSN 0082-6502) *1066*
Trinidad and Tobago. Central Statistical Office. Business Surveys (TR) 219, *1066*
Trinidad and Tobago. Central Statistical Office. Estimated Internal Migration. Bulletin. (TR) *1066*
Trinidad and Tobago. Central Statistical Office. Financial Statistics (TR ISSN 0082-6529) *219*
Trinidad and Tobago. Central Statistical Office. International Travel Report (TR ISSN 0082-6537) *1120*
Trinidad and Tobago. Central Statistical Office. Labour Force by Sex (TR) *219*

Trinidad and Tobago. Central Statistical Office. Overseas Trade. Annual Report (TR ISSN 0082-6545) *219*
Trinidad and Tobago. Central Statistical Office. Pocket Digest (TR) *1066*
Trinidad and Tobago. Central Statistical Office. Population and Vital Statistics; Report (TR ISSN 0082-6553) *1066*
Trinidad and Tobago. Central Statistical Office. Staff Papers (TR) *1066*
Trinidad and Tobago. Ministry of Energy and Energy-Based Industries. Annual Report *see* Trinidad and Tobago. Ministry of Energy and Natural Resources. Annual Report *867*
Trinidad and Tobago. Ministry of Energy and Natural Resources. Annual Report (TR) *867*
Trinidad and Tobago Trade Directory (UK ISSN 0082-657X) *318*
Trinidad Carnival (TR) *517*
Trinitarian Bible Society. Annual Report (UK ISSN 0082-6588) *979*
Trinity University Monograph Series in Religion (US ISSN 0742-2393) *974*
Triological Society. Transactions *see* American Laryngological, Rhinological and Otological Society. Transactions *787*
Triomphe *see* Triomphe Saint-Cyr *812*
Triomphe Saint-Cyr (FR ISSN 0036-2794) *812*
Trip Out (UK) *1118*
Trivium (UK) 111, *735*
Troisieme Republique *see* Third Republic *599*
Trophoblast Research (US) *785*
Tropical Abstracts *see* Abstracts on Tropical Agriculture *38*
Tropical Bands Survey (DK ISSN 0106-1968) *350*
Tropical Development & Research Institute. Crop and Product Series (UK) 60, 162, *521*
Tropical Diseases Bulletin (UK ISSN 0041-3240) 767, *773*
Tropical Diseases Research Series (SZ) *778*
Tropical Pasture Program Annual Report *see* Informe Anual del Programa de Pastos Tropicales *28*
Tropical Pesticides Research Institute. Annual Report (TZ ISSN 0082-6642) *60*
Tropical Science Center, Costa Rica. Occasional Paper (CR ISSN 0069-2107) *1001*
Tropische und Subtropische Pflanzenwelt (GW ISSN 0302-9417) *162*
Tropmed Seminars on Parasitology and Tropical Medicine. Proceedings. *see* TropMed Seminars on Tropical Medicine. Proceedings *778*
TropMed Seminars on Tropical Medicine. Proceedings (TH) *778*
Trotting and Pacing Guide (US ISSN 0083-3509) *1043*
Truck & Bus Road Tests (AT ISSN 0816-2905) *1164*
Truck and Bus Tests and Specs *see* Truck & Bus Road Tests *1164*
Truck Broker Directory (US ISSN 0362-5737) *1105*
Truck Data Book (CN ISSN 0564-3392) *1105*
Truck Driver's Handbook (UK) *1093*
Truck Permit Guide (US) *1105*
Trucking Safety Guide (US) *1105*
True to Life (US ISSN 0085-7408) *1164*
Trufax Directory & Consumer Guide (CN) *369*
Trumpet (US) *14*
Try Us (US) 200, 318, *505*
Tseni (BU) *219*
Tsentral'nyi Nauchno-Issledovatel'skii Institut Geodezii, Aeros"emki i Kartografii. Trudy (UR) *549*
Tsuda Review (JA ISSN 0496-3547) *735*
Tuberculosis and Respiratory Diseases Yearbook/Tuberkuloosi ja Keuhkosairaudet Vuosikirja/Tuberkulos och Lungsjukdomar Aarsbok (FI ISSN 0355-5011) *793*

Tuberkuloosi ja Keuhkosairaudet Vuosikirja *see* Tuberculosis and Respiratory Diseases Yearbook *793*
Tuberkulos och Lungsjukdomar Aarsbok *see* Tuberculosis and Respiratory Diseases Yearbook *793*
Tubists Universal Brotherhood Association Series *see* T.U.B.A. Series *842*
Tudo e Historia (BL) *610*
Tudomanyos Tajekoztatas Elmelete es Gyakorlata/Theory and Practice of Scientific Information (HU ISSN 0373-5354) *684*
Tudomanyszervezesi Fuzetek (HU ISSN 0082-6707) *1001*
Tudomanytorteneti Tanulmanyok (HU ISSN 0082-6715) *1001, 1071*
Tuduv-Studie. Reihe Geschichtswissenschaften (GW) *561*
Tuduv-Studie. Reihe Kommunikationswissenschaften (GW) *345*
Tuduv-Studie. Reihe Kulturwissenschaften (GW) *505*
Tuduv-Studie. Reihe Politikwissenschaften (GW) *910, 918*
Tuduv-Studie. Reihe Religionswissenschaften (GW) *974*
Tuduv-Studie. Reihe Sprach- und Literaturwissenschaften (GW) *706*
Tuduv-Studie. Reihen Kunstgeschichte (GW) *111*
Tuduv-Studien. Reihe Bayern Privat (GW) *135*
Tuduv-Studien. Reihe Sozialwissenschaften (GW) *1012*
Tuebinger Aegyptologische Beitraege (GW) *613*
Tuebinger Geographische Studien (GW ISSN 0564-4232) *549*
Tuebinger Rechtswissenschaftliche Abhandlungen (GW ISSN 0082-6731) *665*
Tuexenia (GW ISSN 0722-494X) *1066*
Tulane Studies in English *see* T S E: Tulane Studies in English *705*
Tulane Studies in Political Science (US ISSN 0082-6774) *910*
Tulane Tax Institute (US ISSN 0564-4402) *300*
Tune in the World with Ham Radio (US) *350*
Tung Board. Annual Report *see* Tree Nut Authority. Report *60*
Tungusica (GW ISSN 0344-5542) *854*
Tunisia. Institut National Scientifique et Technique d'Oceanographie et de Peche. Bulletin (TI ISSN 0579-7926) *408, 513*
Tunisia. Ministere du Plan. Budget Economique (TI ISSN 0082-6820) *300*
Tunisia. Office des Ports Nationaux. Bulletin Annuel des Statistiques (TI) *1104*
Tunisia. Office des Ports Nationaux. Trafic Maritime *see* Tunisia. Office des Ports Nationaux. Bulletin Annuel des Statistiques *1104*
Tunnelling Directory (UK) *475, 484*
Turbomachinery Catalog and Workbook *see* Turbomachinery International Handbook *493*
Turbomachinery International Handbook (US ISSN 0748-0903) *493*
Turbomachinery Symposium. Proceedings (US) *746*
Turcica; Revue d'Etudes Turques (BE ISSN 0082-6847) *706*
Turcologica (GW ISSN 0177-4743) *854*
Turistfoerer (DK ISSN 0108-8734) *1118*
Turistfoererforeningen. Medlemliste *see* Turistfoerer *1118*
Turizum/Tourism (BU) *1120*
Turk Etnografya Dergisi *see* Turkish Review of Ethnography *1030*
Turk Tarih-Arkeologya ve Etnografya Dergisi *see* Turkish Review of Ethnography *1030*

Turkey. Devlet Istatistik Enstitusu. Dis Ticaret Yillik Istatistik/Statistique Annuelle du Commerce Exterieur/Annual Foreign Trade Statistics (TU ISSN 0082-6901) *219*
Turkey. Devlet Istatistik Enstitusu. Milli Egitim Istatistikleri: Ogretim Yili Basi (TU) *420*
Turkey. Devlet Istatistik Enstitusu. Tarim Istatistikleri Ozeti/Summary of Agricultural Statistics (TU ISSN 0082-6928) *35*
Turkey. Devlet Istatistik Enstitusu. Tarimsal Yapi ve Uretim/Agricultural Structure and Production (TU ISSN 0082-6936) *35*
Turkey. Devlet Planama Teskilati. Yili Programi Ucuncu Bes Yil/Annual Program of the Five Year Development Plan (TU ISSN 0082-6944) *292*
Turkey: Hotels-Camping (TU) *620*
Turkey Port and Shipping Handbook 1984 (UK ISSN 0265-8194) *318, 1104*
Turkish Dissertation Index (TU) *13, 1004*
Turkish Electricity Authority. Annual Report (TU) *460*
Turkish Journal of Population Studies (TU) *924*
Turkish Review of Ethnography/Turk Etnografya Dergisi (TU ISSN 0082-6898) *1030*
Turkish Shipping (UK) *1104*
Turkiyat Mecmuasi (TU ISSN 0085-7432) *613, 632*
Turkiye Istatistik Cep Yilligi *see* Statistical Pocket Book of Turkey *1064*
Turkiye Istatistik Yilligi/Statistical Yearbook of Turkey (TU ISSN 0082-691X) *1066*
Turkiye Sinai Kalkinma Bankasi. Annual Report (TU) *233*
Turkluk Bilgisi Arastirmalari *see* Journal of Turkish Studies (Duxbury) *613*
Turkologischer Anzieger/Turkology Annual (AU) *854, 854*
Turkology Annual *see* Turkologischer Anzieger *854*
Turun Historiallinen Arkisto (FI ISSN 0085-7440) *599*
Turun Historiallisen Yhdistyksen Julkaisuja *see* Turun Historiallinen Arkisto *599*
Turun Yliopisto. Julkaisuja. Sarja A. I. Astronomica-Chemica-Physica-Mathematica (FI ISSN 0082-7002) *1001*
Turun Yliopisto. Julkaisuja. Sarja A. II. Biologica- Geographica- Geologica (FI ISSN 0082-6979) *147, 396, 549*
Turun Yliopisto. Julkaisuja. Sarja B. Humaniora (FI ISSN 0082-6987) *632*
Turun Yliopisto. Julkaisuja. Sarja C. Scripta Lingua Fennica Edita (FI ISSN 0082-6995) *632, 1001*
Turun Yliopisto. Julkaisuja. Sarja D. Medica-Odontologica (FI ISSN 0355-9483) *767*
Turun Yliopisto. Kirjasto. Julkaisuja (FI ISSN 0082-7010) *685*
Turun Yliopisto. Klassillisen Filologian Laitos. Opera Ex Instituto Philologiae Classicae Universitatis Turkuensis Edita (FI ISSN 0082-7029) *339, 706*
Turun Yliopisto. Psykologian Laitos. Reports *see* University of Turku. Psychological Research Reports *937*
Turun Yliopisto. Psykologian Laitos. Reports *see* Turun Yliopisto. Psykologian Tutkimuksia *937*
Turun Yliopisto. Psykologian Tutkimuksia (FI ISSN 0356-8741) *937*
Turun Ylioppilas (FI) *599*
Tutor & Textbook - Elementary Piping & Drumming (UK) *842*
Tutora. Memoria y Balance General (AG) *642*
Tvai (IS ISSN 0041-4549) *100, 626*
Tweetalige Losbladige Wetboeken (BE) *665*

Twentieth Century Fund. Newsletter (US ISSN 0041-4611) *233, 918, 1030*
Twentieth Century Legal Philosophy Series (US ISSN 0082-7088) *665*
Twentieth-Century Literary Criticism (US) *735*
Twist (DK ISSN 0107-6116) *842*
Two-plus-two *see* 2 Plus 2 *738*
Tyndale Bulletin (UK ISSN 0082-7118) *974*
Typehus Revyen (DK) *966*
Typewriter (US) *735*
Typography *see* Typography 7 *931*
Typography 7 (US) *931*
Typologie des Sources du Moyen Age Occidental (BE) *599*
Tyre and Rim Association of Australia Standards Manual (AT) *986, 1093*
Tzaadim (IS) *1021*
U A S Extension Series (University of Agricultural Sciences, Bangalore) (II ISSN 0067-3471) *35*
U A S Miscellaneous Series (University of Agricultural Sciences, Bangalore) (II ISSN 0067-348X) *35*
U and I (US) *712*
U B C Planning Papers (University of British Columbia) (CN) *626*
U B D Australia Wide Business Guide: South Australia *see* U B D Register of Industry & Commerce: South Australia *1164*
U B D Register of Industry & Commerce: South Australia (Universal Business Directories Pty. Ltd.) (AT) *1164*
U B S Publications on Business, Banking and Monetary Problems (Union de Banques Suisses) (SZ) *233*
U C B Investor's Handbook (Uganda Commercial Bank) (UG) *233, 268*
U C I S Series in Russian & East European Studies (US) *599*
U C L A Business Forecast for the Nation and California (University of California, Los Angeles) (US ISSN 0082-7126) *200*
U C L A Forum in Medical Sciences (University of California, Los Angeles) (US ISSN 0082-7134) *767*
U C L A Historical Journal (University of California, Los Angeles) (US ISSN 0276-864X) *561*
U.C.L.A. Journal of Dance Ethnology (University of California, Los Angeles) (US) *375*
U C L A Latin American Center. Special Studies Series (University of California, Los Angeles) (US) *610*
U C L A Music Library Bibliography Series (University of California, Los Angeles) (US) *132, 844*
U C L A Symposium on Molecular Biology Proceedings (University of California, Los Angeles) (US) *163*
U C L A Symposium Series on Molecular and Cellular Biology (University of California, Los Angeles) (US ISSN 0735-9543) *147*
U.C. Review (CN ISSN 0226-3440) *736, 744*
U C T Studies in English *see* University of Cape Town. Studies in English *707*
U F O Forskning (Unidentified Flying Objects) (DK ISSN 0109-2596) *21*
U I C C Technical Report Series (International Union Against Cancer) (SZ ISSN 0074-9222) *776*
U I E Case Studies (Unesco Institute for Education) (UN) *420*
U I E Monographs (Unesco Institute for Education) (UN) *420*
U I E S P Documents de l'Union *see* I U S S P Papers *922*
U I E Studies on Post-Literacy and Continuing Education (Unesco Institute for Education) (UN) *427*
U.K.I.R.T. Newsletter (United Kingdom Infrared Telescope) (UK ISSN 0143-0599) *117*
U.K.I.R.T. Report (United Kingdom Infrared Telescope) (UK ISSN 0260-9983) *117*
U.K. Marketing Handbook (UK) *285*

U K S T U Newsletter (United Kingdom Schmidt Telescope Unit) (UK ISSN 0143-053X) *117*
U.K.'s 7500 Largest Companies (UK) *233*
U K Trade Names (UK ISSN 0082-7142) *318*
U M A Students Law Journal (University of Malawi) (MW) *665, 671*
U N A M Directorio de Bibliotecas (Universidad Nacional Autonoma de Mexico) (MX) *685*
U N C R D Bulletin (United Nations, Centre for Regional Development) (UN) *264*
U N C T A D Guide to Publications (United Nations Conference on Trade and Development (UNCTAD)) (UN ISSN 0041-5227) *219*
U N E Bulletin *see* U N E Convocation Bulletin & Alumni News *439*
U N E Convocation Bulletin & Alumni News (University of New England) (AT ISSN 0156-1006) *439*
U N E P Feature *see* United Nations Environment Programme. Feature *499*
U N E P Information (United Nations Environment Programme) (UN) *499*
U N I C E M Annuaire Officiel (Union Nationale des Industries de Carrieres et Materiaux de Construction) (FR) *187*
U N I S I S T Newsletter (Unesco Programme of International Cooperation in Scientific and Technological Information) (UN ISSN 0300-2519) *685*
U N I T A R Conference Reports (United Nations Institute for Training and Research) (UN) *671*
U N I T A R Peaceful Settlement Series (United Nations Institute for Training and Research) (UN) *918*
U N I T A R Regional Studies (United Nations Institute for Training and Research) (UN) *919*
U N Resolutions on Palestine *see* Institute for Palestine Studies. United Nations Resolutions on Palestine and the Arab-Israeli Conflict Series *1155*
U N Studies (UN) *919*
U P E C (Union de Periodistas de Cuba) (CU) *963*
U.P. Irrigation Research Institute. General Annual Report (Uttar Pradesh) (II ISSN 0080-4045) *491*
U.P. Irrigation Research Institute. Technical Memorandum (Uttar Pradesh) (II ISSN 0080-4053) *491*
U P Research Monitor (University of the Philippines) (PH) *632, 1001, 1012*
U S A: Economics, Politics, Ideology *see* U S S R Report: U S A. Economics, Politics, Ideology *250*
U S A for Business Travelers (US) *200, 1118*
U S A N and the U S P Dictionary of Drug Names (US ISSN 0090-6816) *873*
U S A Oil Industry Directory (US ISSN 0082-8599) *867*
U S A Oilfield Service, Supply, and Manufacturers Directory (US) *867*
U S A Textile Industry Overview *see* Texscope: U S A Textile Industry Overview *1075*
U S and the Developing World: Agenda for Action *see* U S and World Development: Agenda *264*
U S and World Development: Agenda (US) *264*
U S Aviation Reports (US ISSN 0886-4217) *1090*
U S Belgium Trade Directory *see* Belgian American Chamber of Commerce in the United States. Directory *287*
U S C Annual Distinguished Lecture Series Monographs in Special Education and Rehabilitation (University of Southern California) (US ISSN 0070-6736) *445*
U S Callbook (US) *350*
U S - Canadian Range Management (US) *35, 132, 367*
U S/China Trade Statistics (US) *260*

U S Crude Oil, Natural Gas, and Natural Gas Liquids (US) *867*
U S E T News (United States Equestrian Team) (US) *1043*
U S Economy Lodging Industry (US) *620*
U S Excise Tax Guide (US ISSN 0083-0534) *300*
U S F A Rule Book: U S & International Rules (United States Fencing Association, Inc.) (US) *1036*
U S F L Guide and Register (United States Football League) (US ISSN 0742-4299) *1164*
U S Foamed Plastics Markets and Directory (US) *901*
U S-I B P Synthesis Series (International Biological Program) (US) *147*
U S Industrial Directory (US) *318*
U S Information Moscow *see* Information Moscow, Western Edition *1111*
U S - Japan Relations (US ISSN 0748-2809) *561, 919*
U S Lodging Industry (US ISSN 0361-2198) *620*
U S M A Library Bulletin (U.S. Military Academy Library) (US) *685, 812*
U S Machine Tool Directory (US) *493*
U S Master Tax Guide (US ISSN 0083-1700) *300*
U S Medical Directory (US ISSN 0091-8393) *767*
U S Nuclear Plant Statistics (US) *460*
U S O Annual Report (United Service Organizations, Inc.) (US ISSN 0082-8556) *1021*
U S P Guide to Select Drugs (United States Pharmacopeial Convention, Inc.) (US ISSN 0091-3839) *1164*
U S Progressive Periodicals Directory (US) *647, 964*
U S Progressive Periodicals Directory Update *see* U S Progressive Periodicals Directory *964*
U S Real Estate Register (US) *16, 200, 963, 966*
U S Relations with Latin American Nations (US) *919*
U S S R and Eastern Europe Scientific Abstracts: Chemistry *see* U S S R Report: Chemistry *326*
U S S R and Eastern Europe Scientific Abstracts: Cybernetics, Computers, and Automation Technology *see* U S S R Report: Cybernetics, Computers, and Automation Technology *354*
U S S R and Eastern Europe Scientific Abstracts: Electronics and Electrical Engineering *see* U S S R Report: Electronics and Electrical Engineering *462*
U S S R and Eastern Europe Scientific Abstracts: Engineering and Equipment *see* U S S R Report: Engineering and Equipment *477*
U S S R and Eastern Europe Scientific Abstracts: Materials Science and Metallurgy *see* U S S R Report: Materials Science and Metallurgy *477*
U S S R and Eastern Europe Scientific Abstracts: Physics and Mathematics *see* U S S R Report: Physics and Mathematics *755*
U.S.S.R. Facts & Figures Annual (US ISSN 0148-7760) *910, 1066*
U.S.S.R. Overview (IS) *910*
U S S R Report: Biomedical and Behavioral Sciences *see* U S S R Report: Life Sciences, Biomedical and Behavioral Sciences *767*
U S S R Report: Chemistry (US) *13, 326*
U S S R Report: Cybernetics, Computers, and Automation Technology (US) *13, 354*
U S S R Report: Earth Sciences (US) *381*
U S S R Report: Economic Affairs *see* U S S R Report: National Economy *200*
U S S R Report: Electronics and Electrical Engineering (US) *13, 462*
U S S R Report: Engineering and Equipment (US) *13, 477*

U S S R Report: Geophysics, Astronomy, and Space *see* U S S R Report: Space *382*
U S S R Report: Life Sciences, Biomedical and Behavioral Sciences (US) *767, 937, 1030*
U S S R Report: Machine Tools and Metal-Working Equipment (US) *746, 800*
U S S R Report: Materials Science and Metallurgy (US) *13, 477, 802*
U S S R Report: Military Affairs (US) *812*
U S S R Report: National Economy (US) *200, 250*
U S S R Report: Physics and Mathematics (US) *13, 755*
U S S R Report: Political and Sociological Affairs (US) *910, 1030*
U S S R Report: Problems of the Far East (US) *250, 910, 919*
U S S R Report: Science and Technology Policy (US) *1001, 1071*
U S S R Report: Space (US) *13, 118, 382*
U S S R Report: Space Biology and Aerospace Medicine (English translation of Kosmicheskaya Biologiya i Aviakosmicheskaya Meditsina) (US) *21, 767*
U S S R Report: Translations from "Kommunist" (US) *910*
U S S R Report: U S A. Economics, Politics, Ideology (English translation of Russian: S Sh A: Ekonomika, Politika, Ideologiya) (US) *250, 910*
U S S R Report: World Economy and Internatioal Relations (US) *200, 919*
U S S R Today (US) *910*
U S Savings and Loan Directory (US) *233*
U S Symposium on Rock Mechanics. Proceedings (US ISSN 0586-3031) *820*
U S T A College Tennis Guide (United States Tennis Association) (US) *1036*
U S T A Sires and Dams (United States Trotting Association) (US) *1043*
U S T A Year Book (United States Trotting Association) (US ISSN 0083-3517) *1043*
U S 1 Worksheets (US ISSN 0739-1609) *736, 746*
U T I A S Report *see* University of Toronto. Institute for Aerospace Studies. Report *21*
U T I A S Technical Note *see* University of Toronto. Institute for Aerospace Studies. Technical Note *21*
U.T.S.A. Annual (Union of Teachers' Associations of South Africa) (SA) *443*
U V Curing Buyer's Guide *see* Radiation Curing Buyer's Guide *324*
U.V. Spectrometry Group. Bulletin (Ultra Violet) (UK ISSN 0144-2317) *1164*
U Vejviser (DK ISSN 0106-3014) *685*
U W I Students' Law Review (University of the West Indies) (BB) *665*
U W M Library Newsletter *see* Golda Meir Library Newsletter *678*
Ucitelske Vzdelani (CS) *449, 599*
Uddannelse Institutioner over Grundskoleniveau (DK ISSN 0107-1629) *431*
Uddannelse og Erhverv Katalog (DK ISSN 0900-3479) *826*
Uddannelsesnoeglen (DK ISSN 0107-3435) *420*
Uddannelsesvejviser *see* Uddannelsesnoeglen *420*
Uddannelshistorie. Selskabet for Dansk Skolehistorie. Aarbog (DK) *420*
Uddrag af Energilitteratur paa Danmarks Tekniske Bibliotek *see* Danmarks Tekniske Bibliotek. Uddrag *1151*
Uddrag af Energilitteratur paa Danmarks Tekniske bibliotek, Soenderborg Tekniske Bibliotek, Aarhus Tekniske Bibliotek *see* Danmarks Tekniske Bibliotek. Uddrag *1151*

Udenlandsk Litteratur i Danske Folkebiblioteker. Skoenlitteratur (DK ISSN 0106-6641) *739*
Udenlandsk Litteratur i Danske Folkebiblioteker Faglitteratur (DK ISSN 0106-6633) *132*
Udenlandske Boerneboeger i Danske Folkebiblioteker *see* Udenlandske Litteratur i Danske Folkebiblioteker. Boerneboeger *335*
Udenlandske Litteratur i Danske Folkebiblioteker. Boerneboeger (DK ISSN 0106-6625) *335*
Udenrigs Handelskalenderen for Danmark/Trade Directory for Denmark/Daenischer Handelskalender/Annuaire de l'Exportation du Danemark/Anuario de la Exportacion de Dinamarca (DK ISSN 0532-1360) *318*
Udviklingstendenserne paa det Langvarigt Uddannedes Arbejdsmarked (DK ISSN 0108-7886) *420*
Udyogen Ka Varshika Sarvekshana *see* India. Central Statistical Organization. Annual Survey of Industries *210*
Uebersee-Museum, Bremen. Veroeffentlichungen. Reihe A: Naturwissenschaften (GW ISSN 0068-0885) *1002*
Uebersee-Museum, Bremen. Veroeffentlichungen. Reihe B: Voelkerkunde (GW ISSN 0068-0893) *77, 517*
Uebersee-Museum, Bremen. Veroeffentlichungen. Reihe C: Geographie (GW) *549*
Uebersee-Museum, Bremen. Veroeffentlichungen. Reihe D: Voelkerkundliche Monographien (GW ISSN 0341-9274) *77*
Uebersee-Museum, Bremen. Veroeffentlichungen. Reihe E: Human-Oekologie (GW ISSN 0170-2416) *1030*
Uebersee-Museum, Bremen. Veroeffentlichungen. Reihe F: Bremer Afrika-Archiv (GW ISSN 0344-4317) *567*
Uebersee-Museum Bremen. Veroeffentlichungen. Reihe G: Bremer Suedpazifik-Archiv (GW ISSN 0342-6610) *573*
Uebersetzungen Auslaendischer Arbeiten zur Antiken Sklaverei (GW ISSN 0170-348X) *561*
Uebersetzungen - Kerntechnische Regeln (GW) *898, 956*
Uebersichten zur Tierernaehrung (GW) *35*
Uganda. Forestry Department. Annual Report (UG ISSN 0082-7177) *528*
Uganda. Forestry Department. Technical Notes (UG ISSN 0082-7193) *528*
Uganda. Forestry Department. Timber Leaflet (UG) *530*
Uganda. Game Department. Annual Report (UG) *367*
Uganda. Geological Survey and Mines Department. Annual Report (UG ISSN 0082-7215) *396*
Uganda. Ministry of Planning and Economic Development. Statistics Division. Enumeration of Employees (UG ISSN 0082-724X) *276*
Uganda. Public Libraries Board. Proceedings (UG) *685*
Uganda Commercial Bank. Annual Report (UG) *233*
Uganda Commercial Bank Investor's Handbook *see* U C B Investor's Handbook *268*
Uganda Estimates of Development Expenditures (UG) *292*
Uganda Freshwater Fisheries Research Organization. Annual Report (UG) *513*
Uganda Journal (UG ISSN 0041-574X) *567, 712*
Uhrmacher - Jahrbuch fuer Handwerk und Handel (GW ISSN 0082-7290) *644*
Uitkomsten van de Belgische Zeevisserij(BE) *513*
Uj Magyar Nepkoltesi Gyujtemeny (HU ISSN 0082-7312) *517, 744*

Ukrainian Academy of Arts and Sciences in the U S. Annals (US ISSN 0503-1001) *505*
Ukrainian Archives *see* Naukove Tovarystvo Imeni Shevchenka. Ukrains'kyi Arkhiv *504*
Ukrainian Art Digest/Notatkz z Mistetstba (US ISSN 0550-0850) *111, 505*
Ukrainian Literary Library *see* Naukove Tovarystvo Imeni Shevchenka. Ukrainsk'va Literarurna Biblioteka *728*
Ulrich's International Periodicals Directory (US ISSN 0000-0175) *132*
Ulster Folklife (UK ISSN 0082-7347) *517*
Ulster Journal of Archaeology (UK ISSN 0082-7355) *94*
Ulster Year Book (UK ISSN 0082-7371) *600*
Ultra Violet Spectrometry Group. Bulletin *see* U.V. Spectrometry Group. Bulletin *1164*
Ultragarsas/Ultrasound (UR ISSN 0369-6367) *900*
Ultrasonics Symposium. Proceedings (US ISSN 0090-5607) *475, 900*
Ultrasound *see* Ultragarsas *900*
Ultrasound Patents & Papers (UK ISSN 0260-4043) *792*
Ultrastructural Pathology Publication (US ISSN 0730-6482) *163, 169, 782*
Umana Avventura (IT) *111*
Umbrella (Glendale) (US ISSN 0160-0699) *111, 685*
Umeaa Studies in Politics and Public Administration (SW) *910, 946*
Umeaa Studies in the Humanities (SW ISSN 0345-0155) *632*
Uncoverings (US ISSN 0277-0628) *610, 632, 1075, 1129*
Undergraduate Texts in Mathematics (US ISSN 0172-6056) *754*
Undersoegelse over Apotekernes Driftsforhold (DK ISSN 0108-948X) *873*
Undervisningsmaterialer til Begynder- og Specialundervisning (DK ISSN 0107-377X) *445*
Unemployment Insurance Canada. Annual Report/Assurance-Chomage Canada. Rapport Annuel (CN ISSN 0576-4157) *642*
Unesco. Records of the General Conference. Proceedings (UN ISSN 0082-7509) *919*
Unesco. Records of the General Conference. Resolutions (UN ISSN 0082-7517) *442, 919*
Unesco. Regional Office for Education in Asia and Oceania. Bulletin *see* Unesco. Regional Office for Education in Asia and the Pacific. Bulletin *420*
Unesco. Regional Office for Education in Asia and the Pacific. Abstract Bibliography Series on Population Education (UN) *426*
Unesco. Regional Office for Education in Asia and the Pacific. Bulletin (UN) *420*
Unesco. Report of the Director-General on the Activities of the Organization (UN ISSN 0082-7525) *442, 919*
Unesco. Scientific Maps and Atlases and Other Related Publications (UN) *132*
Unesco. Statistics on Science and Technology/Statistiques Relatives aux Science et a la Technologie/ Estadisticas Relativas a la Ciencia y a la Tecnologia (UN) *219, 1004*
Unesco. Studies on Books and Reading (UN) *963*
Unesco Asian Fiction Series (UN ISSN 0566-6201) *736*
Unesco Bibliographical Handbooks *see* Documentation, Libraries and Archives: Bibliographies and Reference Works *687*
Unesco Earthquake Study Missions (UN ISSN 0082-7479) *401*
Unesco Institute for Education Case Studies *see* U I E Case Studies *420*

UNITED NATIONS. 1911

Unesco Institute for Education Monographs see U I E Monographs 420
Unesco Institute for Education Studies on Post-Literacy and Continuing Education see U I E Studies on Post-Literacy and Continuing Education 427
Unesco Manuals for Libraries see Documentation, Libraries and Archives: Studies and Research 677
Unesco Programme of International Cooperation in Scientific and Technological Information Newsletter see U N I S I S T Newsletter 685
Unesco Reports in Marine Science (UN) 147
Unesco Source Books on Curricula and Methods (UN ISSN 0502-9554) 449
Unesco Statistical Reports and Studies (UN ISSN 0082-7533) 1066
Unesco Statistical Yearbook (UN ISSN 0082-7541) 1066
Unesco Technical Papers in Marine Science (UN ISSN 0503-4299) 147, 408
Unesco Yearbook on Peace and Conflict Studies (US ISSN 0250-779X) 919
Unga Diktara (SW) 736
Ungarische Akademie der Wissenschaften. Archaelogisches Institut. Mitteilungen see Antaeus 81
Ungarische Jahrbuecher see Ural-Altaische Jahrbuecher 600
Ungarn see Magyarorszag 1059
Ungarn - Jahrbuch (GW ISSN 0082-755X) 600
Ungdomskalender (DK ISSN 0107-7783) 336
Ungdomsskolen i Tal (DK ISSN 0108-2426) 420
Ungdomsuddannelser (DK ISSN 0900-1395) 420
Unge Laeser Om (DK ISSN 0108-6952) 335
Unicorn German Series (US) 744
Unidentified Flying Objects Forskning see U F O Forskning 21
Uniform Building Code see International Conference of Building Officials. Uniform Building Code 185
Uniform Crime Report for the State of Michigan (US ISSN 0360-9146) 374
Uniform Crime Reports for the United States (US ISSN 0082-7592) 373
Uniform Hunter Casualty Report (US) 1036, 1047
Uniformed Services Almanac (US ISSN 0503-1982) 812
Uniformed Services Almanac. Special Reserve Forces Edition see Reserve Forces Almanac 812
Union Academique Internationale. Compte Rendu de la Session Annuelle du Comite (BE ISSN 0074-9346) 633
Union Bancaria Hispano Marroqui. Assemblee Generale Ordinaire des Actionnaires. Rapport (MR) 233
Union Bank of Finland. Annual Report (FI ISSN 0355-0133) 233
Union Catalogue of Social Science Periodicals/Serials (II) 132, 1014
Union Catalogue of Theses and Dissertations of the South African Universities (SA ISSN 0079-4325) 132
Union de Banques Suisses Publications on Business, Banking and Monetary Problems see U B S Publications on Business, Banking and Monetary Problems 233
Union de Periodistas de Cuba see U P E C 963
Union des Association Francaises de Relations Publiques. Annuaire (FR ISSN 0066-9253) 16
Union des Superieures Majeurs de France. Annuaire (FR ISSN 0396-2393) 974
Union Fact Sheet (UK ISSN 0260-7891) 649

Union Internationale Contre le Cancer. Manuel see International Union against Cancer. Manual 775
Union Internationale des Transports Publics. Rapports Techniques des Congres Internationaux see International Union of Public Transport. Technical Reports of the Congresses 1082
Union Interparlementaire. Comptes Rendus des Conferences see Inter-Parliamentary Union. Conference Proceedings 916
Union Labor in California (US) 276, 1066
Union List of Scientific and Technical Periodicals in Zambia (ZA) 132, 1002, 1071
Union List of Scientific Serials in Canadian Libraries/Catalogue Collectif des Publications Scientifiques dans les Bibliotheques Canadiennes (CN ISSN 0082-7657) 1005
Union Mondiale des Organisations Syndicales sur Bases Economique et Sociale Liberales. Conferences: Rapport (SZ ISSN 0503-2334) 649
Union Nationale de l'Enseignement Agricole Prive. Annuaire (FR ISSN 0082-7711) 35, 420
Union Nationale des Industries de Carrieres et Materiaux de Construction Annuaire Officiel see U N I C E M Annuaire Officiel 187
Union of American Hebrew Congregations. State of Our Union (US ISSN 0363-3810) 977
Union of European Football Associations. Handbook of U E F A (SZ ISSN 0570-2070) 1040
Union of European Pedopsychiatrists. Proceedings (US) 791
Union of International Associations. Documents see Collection of Documents for the Study of International Non-Governmental Relations 670
Union of Nova Scotia Municipalities. Proceedings of the Annual Convention (CN ISSN 0082-7762) 946
Union of Teachers' Associations of South Africa Annual see U.T.S.A. Annual 443
Union Postale Universelle. Actes (UN) 347
Union Postale Universelle. Statistique des Services Postaux (UN ISSN 0085-7602) 347
Union Professionnelle Feminine. Annuaire (FR ISSN 0082-7770) 914
Union Sportive Metropolitaine des Transports Annee Sportive U.S.M.T. see Annee Sportive U.S.M.T 1032
Unit Trust Yearbook (UK ISSN 0503-2628) 233
Unitarian and Free Christian Churches. Handbook and Directory of the General Assembly (UK) 979
Unitarian and Free Christian Churches. Yearbook of the General Assembly see Unitarian and Free Christian Churches. Handbook and Directory of the General Assembly 979
Unitarian Historical Society. Proceedings see Unitarian Universalist Historical Society. Proceedings 980
Unitarian Historical Society, London. Transactions (UK ISSN 0082-7800) 600, 979
Unitarian Universalist Directory (US ISSN 0082-7827) 979
Unitarian Universalist Historical Society. Proceedings (US) 980
United & Babson Graphic Guide (US) 268
United Arab Emirates. Central Bank. Annual Report (TS) 300
United Arab Emirates. Ministry of Petroleum and Industry. Akhbar al-Petrol Wall Sinaa (TS) 867
United Arab Emirates Practical Guide. U A E see M E E D Practical Guide. U A E 1112

United Baptist Convention of the Atlantic Provinces. Yearbook (CN ISSN 0082-7843) 980
United Church of Canada. Committee on Archives. Bulletin. Records and Proceedings (CN ISSN 0082-786X) 980
United Church of Canada. General Council. Record of Proceedings (CN ISSN 0082-7878) 980
United Church of Canada. Year Book (CN ISSN 0082-7886) 980
United Church of Christ. Pension Boards (Annual Report) (US ISSN 0360-9782) 642, 985
United Community Planning Corporation. Report (US) 1021
United Farmers Trading Agency Year Book and Diary (UK) 35, 240
United Free Church of Scotland. Handbook (UK ISSN 0082-7908) 980
United Graphic Guide see United & Babson Graphic Guide 268
United Kingdom Atomic Energy Authority. Annual Report (UK ISSN 0082-7940) 475, 898
United Kingdom Fire Statistics see Fire Statistics United Kingdom 770
United Kingdom Geodesy Report see United Kingdom Research on Geodesy 549
United Kingdom Infrared Telescope Newsletter see U.K.I.R.T. Newsletter 117
United Kingdom Infrared Telescope Report see U.K.I.R.T. Report 117
United Kingdom Mineral Statistics (UK ISSN 0308-5090) 820
United Kingdom Offshore Legislation Guide (UK) 665, 867
United Kingdom Research on Geodesy (UK) 401, 549
United Kingdom Schmidt Telescope Unit Newsletter see U K S T U Newsletter 117
United Kingdom - Tin in Tinplate (UK) 800
United Malays National Organisation. Penvata (MY) 910
United Methodist Church. Curriculum Plans (US ISSN 0160-0885) 980
United Methodist Church. General Minutes of the Annual Conferences (US ISSN 0503-3551) 980
United Methodist Church (United States) Division of Education. Adult Planbook see Adult Planbook 978
United Methodist Directory (US ISSN 0503-356X) 980
United Nations. Centro Latinoamericano de Demografia. Serie A. see United Nations. Regional Centre for Demographic Training and Research in Latin America. Serie A 924
United Nations. Centro Latinoamericano de Demografia. Serie C see United Nations. Regional Centre for Demographic Training and Research in Latin America. Serie C 924
United Nations. Centro Latinoamericano de Demografia. Serie D see United Nations. Regional Centre for Demographic Training and Research in Latin America. Serie D 924
United Nations. Conference on Trade and Development. Trade and Development Board. Official Records(UN) 264
United Nations. Department of International Economic adn Social Affairs. Natural Resources - Water Series see United Nations. Economic and Social Commission for Asia and the Pacific. Natural Resources - Water Series 1126
United Nations. Development Programme. Compendium of Approved Projects (UN) 264
United Nations. Disarmament Commission. Yearbook see United Nations Disarmament Yearbook 813
United Nations. Economic and Social Commission for Asia and the Pacific. Development Papers (UN) 367

United Nations. Economic and Social Commission for Asia and the Pacific. Mineral Resources Development Series (UN ISSN 0082-8114) 820
United Nations. Economic and Social Commission for Asia and the Pacific. Natural Resources - Water Series (UN) 1126
United Nations. Economic and Social Commission for Asia and the Pacific. Water Resources Development Series(UN ISSN 0082-8130) 1126
United Nations. Economic and Social Council. Index to Proceedings (UN ISSN 0082-8084) 919
United Nations. Economic and Social Council. Official Records (UN ISSN 0082-8092) 250, 919
United Nations. Economic Commission for Africa. Proposals for Programme Budget (UN) 200, 264
United Nations. Economic Commission for Asia and the Far East. Sample Surveys in the ECAFE Region. see Sample Surveys in the ESCAP Region 217
United Nations. Economic Commission for Asia and the Pacific. Energy Resources Development Series (UN) 467
United Nations. Economic Commission for Europe. Annual Bulletin of General Energy Statistics for Europe see Annual Bulletin of General Energy Statistics for Europe 468
United Nations. International Narcotics Control Board. Annual Report see International Narcotics Control Board. Report for (Year) 871
United Nations. International Narcotics Control Board. Statistics on Narcotic Drugs Furnished by Governments in Accordance with the International Treaties see International Narcotics Control Board. Statistics on Narcotic Drugs for (Year) 871
United Nations. International Narcotics Control Board. Statistics on Psychotropic Substances Furnished by Governments in Accordance with the Convention of 1971 on Psychotropic Substances see International Narcotics Control Board. Statistics on Psychotropic Substances for (Year) 871
United Nations. Multilateral Treaties Deposited with the Secretary-General(UN) 671
United Nations. Multilateral Treaties in Respect of Which the Secretary-General Performs Depository Functions see United Nations. Multilateral Treaties Deposited with the Secretary-General 671
United Nations. National Accounts Statistics (UN) 219
U.N. Quarterly Housing Construction Summary for Europe see Annual Bulletin of Housing and Building Statistics for Europe 181
United Nations. Regional Centre for Demographic Training and Research in Latin America. Serie A/Centro Latinoamericano de Demografia. Serie A: Informes sobre Investigaciones Realizadas (UN ISSN 0503-3934) 924
United Nations. Regional Centre for Demographic Training and Research in Latin America. Serie C/Centro Latinoamericano de Demografia. Serie C: Informes sobre Investigaciones Realizadas Por los Alumnos del Centro (UN ISSN 0503-3942) 924
United Nations. Regional Centre for Demographic Training and Research in Latin America. Serie D/Centro Latinoamericano de Demografia. Serie D: Traducciones, Estudios, Conferencias y Otros Trabajos Preparados por Profesores y Expertos Visitantes (UN ISSN 0503-3950) 924
United Nations. Regional Centre for Demographic Training and Research in Latin America. Serie E/Centro Latinoamericano de Demografia. Serie E: Libros (UN) 925

1912 UNITED NATIONS.

United Nations. Security Council. Index to Proceedings (UN ISSN 0082-8408) *919*

United Nations. Security Council. Official Records (UN ISSN 0082-8416) *919*

United Nations. Statistical Yearbook (UN ISSN 0082-8459) *1066*

United Nations. Trade and Development Board. Official Records *see* United Nations. Conference on Trade and Development. Trade and Development Board. Official Records *264*

United Nations. Trade and Development Board. Official Records. Supplements (UN ISSN 0082-8483) *919*

United Nations. Trusteeship Council. Index to Proceedings (UN ISSN 0082-8491) *919*

United Nations. Trusteeship Council. Official Records (UN ISSN 0082-8505) *919*

United Nations. Trusteeship Council. Official Records. Supplements (UN ISSN 0082-8513) *919*

United Nations. Yearbook (UN ISSN 0082-8521) *919*

United Nations Annual Documentary Series *see* Institute for Palestine Studies. International Annual Documentary Series *569*

United Nations Bulletin *see* U N C R D Bulletin *264*

United Nations Commission on International Trade Law. Report on the Work of Its Session (UN) *671*

United Nations Commission on International Trade Law. Yearbook (UN ISSN 0251-4265) *260, 672*

United Nations Conference on the Standardization of Geographical Names. Report of the Conference (UN) *549*

United Nations Conference on the Standardization of Geographical Names. Technical Papers (UN) *549*

United Nations Conference on Trade and Development (UNCTAD) Guide to Publications *see* U N C T A D Guide to Publications *219*

United Nations Conference on Trade and Development (UNCTAD) Trade and Development: an U N C T A D Review *see* Trade and Development: an U N C T A D Review *260*

United Nations Conference on Trade and Development: Proceedings (UN) *260, 264*

United Nations Congress on the Prevention of Crime and the Treatment of Offenders. Report (UN ISSN 0082-8025) *373*

United Nations Disarmament Yearbook(UN) *813, 898, 910*

United Nations Documents *see* United Nations Documents and Publications. Checklist *132*

United Nations Documents and Publications. Checklist (US) *132*

United Nations Economic and Social Commission for Asia and the Pacific. Social Development Division. Social Work Education and Development (UN ISSN 0252-452X) *449, 1021*

United Nations Economic and Social Commission for Asia and the Pacific. Social Development Division. Social Work Training and Teaching Materials Newsletter *see* United Nations Economic and Social Commission for Asia and the Pacific. Social Development Division. Social Work Education and Development *1021*

United Nations Economic and Social Council. Disarmament Study Series (UN) *813, 898, 910*

United Nations Economic Commission for Africa. Annual Report (UN) *264*

United Nations Economic Commission for Africa. Statistical Newsletter (UN) *1066*

United Nations Environment Programme. Evaluation Report (Year) (UN) *499*

United Nations Environment Programme. Feature (UN) *499*

United Nations Environment Programme. Governing Council. Report on the Work of its Session (UN) *499*

United Nations Environment Programme. The State of the Environment; Report of the Executive Director (UN) *499*

United Nations Environment Programme Information *see* U N E P Information *499*

United Nations General Assembly: Report of the Australian Delegation (AT) *919*

United Nations Industrial Development Organization. Development and Transfer of Technology Series (UN ISSN 0250-801X) *264*

United Nations Industrial Development Organization Industrial Development Abstracts *see* Industrial Development Abstracts *211*

United Nations Institute for Namibia. Occasional Papers (UN) *1012*

United Nations Institute for Namibia. Prospectus (UN) *420*

United Nations Institute for Training and Research. Report of the Executive Director (UN) *919*

United Nations Institute for Training and Research Conference Reports *see* U N I T A R Conference Reports *671*

United Nations Institute for Training and Research Peaceful Settlement Series *see* U N I T A R Peaceful Settlement Series *918*

United Nations Institute for Training and Research Regional Studies *see* U N I T A R Regional Studies *919*

United Nations Issues Conference. Report (US ISSN 0743-9180) *919*

United Nations Juridical Yearbook (UN ISSN 0082-8297) *672*

United Nations Legislative Series (UN ISSN 0082-8300) *672*

United Nations of the Next Decade Conference. Report (US ISSN 0748-433X) *919*

United Nations Publications *see* New United Nations Publications *907*

United Nations Regional Cartographic Conference for Asia and the Far East. Proceedings of the Conference and Technical Papers *see* United Nations Regional Cartographic Conference for Asia and the Pacific. Report of the Conference *549*

United Nations Regional Cartographic Conference for Asia and the Pacific. Report of the Conference (UN) *549*

United Nations Regional Cartographic Conference for Asia and the Pacific. Technical Papers (UN) *549*

United Nations Regional Cartographic Conference for the Americas. Report of the Conference (UN) *549*

United Nations Regional Cartographic Conference for the Americas. Technical Papers (UN) *549*

United Nations Research Institute for Social Development. Regional Planning *see* Regional Planning *1020*

United Nations Research Institute for Social Development. Report (UN) *1012*

United Nations Social Defence Research Institute. Publication (UN) *373*

United Planting Association of Malaysia. Annual Report (MY ISSN 0304-8349) *49*

United Presbyterian Church in the United States of America. Minutes of the General Assembly (US ISSN 0082-8548) *980*

United Reformed Church in the United Kingdom. United Reformed Church Year Book (UK) *980*

United Reformed Church Pocket Diary (UK) *980*

United Reformed Church, Yorkshire Province, Provincial Handbook (UK) *980*

United Schools International. Documents of the Biennial Conference (II ISSN 0503-4663) *665*

United Schools Organisation of India. Annual Report (II) *420*

United Service Organizations, Inc. Annual Report *see* U S O Annual Report *1021*

United Society for the Propagation of the Gospel. Annual Report/Review *see* United Society for the Propagation of the Gospel. Yearbook *974*

United Society for the Propagation of the Gospel. Yearbook (UK) *974*

United Society of Artists. Publication (UK) *111*

U.S. A I P *see* U.S. Aeronautical Information Publication *21*

U.S. Administrative Office of the United States Courts. Report on Applications for Orders Authorizing or Approving the Interception of Wire or Oral Communications (US ISSN 0097-7977) *345, 665*

U.S. Aeronautical Information Publication (US) *21*

U.S. Agency for International Development. Congressional Presentation, Fiscal Year *see* U.S. International Development Cooperation Agency. Congressional Presentation, Fiscal Year *264*

U.S. Agricultural Marketing Service. Annual Report on Tobacco Statistics (US) *1080*

U.S. Agricultural Marketing Service. Dairy and Poultry Market Statistics *see* Poultry Market Statistics *43*

U.S. Agricultural Research Service. A R S - N C (Agricultural Research Service, North Central Region) (US ISSN 0092-1785) *35*

U.S. Agricultural Research Service. A R S-S (US ISSN 0092-1939) *1164*

U.S. Agricultural Research Service. Animal Science Research Division. Tables on Hatchery and Flock Participation in the National Turkey Improvement Plan *see* Tables on Hatchery and Flock Participation in the National Poultry Improvement Plan *68*

U.S. Air Force. School of Aerospace Medicine. Standard Technical Report Series (US) *767*

U.S. Air Force Academy Assembly. Proceedings (US ISSN 0082-8688) *919*

U.S. Air Force Academy Library. Special Bibliography Series (US ISSN 0082-8696) *132*

U.S. Air Force Cambridge Research Laboratories. A F C R L (Series) *see* U.S. Air Force Geophysics Laboratory. A F G L (Series) *813*

U.S. Air Force Geophysics Laboratory. A F G L (Series) (US) *401, 813*

U.S. Airborne Exports and General Imports *see* Foreign Trade Reports. U.S. Airborne Exports and General Imports *255*

U.S. Arms Control and Disarmament Agency. Annual Report to Congress (US ISSN 0082-8769) *665*

U.S. Army. Corps of Engineers. Port Series (US ISSN 0083-0305) *1104*

U.S. Army. Corps of Engineers. Technical Reports, T R (Series) (US ISSN 0083-0313) *475*

U.S. Army Infantry Center. History; Annual Supplement *see* U.S. Army Infantry School. History; Annual Supplement *813*

U.S. Army Infantry School. History; Annual Supplement (US) *813*

U.S. Army Medical Research Institute of Infectious Diseases. Annual Progress Report. (US) *778*

U.S. Brookhaven National Laboratory, Upton, N.Y. Brookhaven Highlights *see* Brookhaven Highlights *896*

U.S. Bureau of Alcohol, Tobacco and Firearms. Annual Report (US) *1164*

U.S. Bureau of Alcohol, Tobacco and Firearms. Explosives Incidents (US ISSN 0273-5032) *373*

U.S. Bureau of Commercial Fisheries. United States Fisheries *see* Fisheries of the United States *509*

U.S. Bureau of Domestic and International Business Administration. Overseas Business Reports (US ISSN 0082-9846) *260*

U.S. Bureau of East-West Trade. Export Administration Regulations (US ISSN 0094-8411) *260*

U.S. Bureau of International Commerce. Annual Reports (US ISSN 0082-8939) *260*

U.S. Bureau of International Commerce. Trade Lists *see* U.S. Department of Commerce. Trade Lists *260*

U.S. Bureau of Labor Statistics. Area Wage Surveys (US) *219*

U.S. Bureau of Labor Statistics. Bulletins (US ISSN 0082-9021) *276*

U.S. Bureau of Labor Statistics. Employee Benefits in Medium and Large Firms (US) *276*

U.S. Bureau of Labor Statistics. Employment and Earnings: States and Areas (US) *276*

U.S. Bureau of Labor Statistics. Employment and Earnings Statistics for States and Areas *see* U.S. Bureau of Labor Statistics. Employment and Earnings: States and Areas *276*

U.S. Bureau of Labor Statistics. Handbook of Labor Statistics (US ISSN 0082-9056) *219*

U.S. Bureau of Labor Statistics. Indexes of Output per Man-Hour; Selected Industries *see* U.S. Bureau of Labor Statistics. Productivity Measures for Selected Industries *219*

U.S. Bureau of Labor Statistics. Industry Wage Surveys (US ISSN 0082-9064) *276*

U.S. Bureau of Labor Statistics. Major Programs (US) *219*

U.S. Bureau of Labor Statistics. National Survey of Professional, Administrative, Technical and Clerical Pay (US ISSN 0501-7041) *219*

U.S. Bureau of Labor Statistics. Occupational Outlook Handbook (US) *219, 849*

U.S. Bureau of Labor Statistics. Productivity Indexes for Selected Industries *see* U.S. Bureau of Labor Statistics. Productivity Measures for Selected Industries *219*

U.S. Bureau of Labor Statistics. Productivity Measures for Selected Industries (US) *219*

U.S. Bureau of Land Management. Public Land Statistics (US ISSN 0082-9110) *946*

U.S. Bureau of Mines. Bulletin (US ISSN 0082-9129) *821*

U.S. Bureau of Mines. Commodity Data Summaries *see* U.S. Bureau of Mines. Mineral Commodity Summaries *821*

U.S. Bureau of Mines. Information Circular (US) *821*

U.S. Bureau of Mines. Mineral Commodity Summaries (US ISSN 0160-5151) *821*

U.S. Bureau of Mines. Minerals Yearbook (US ISSN 0076-8952) *821*

U.S. Bureau of Mines. Report of Investigations (US) *821*

U.S. Bureau of Outdoor Recreation. Recreation Grants-in-Aid Manual *see* Land and Water Conservation Fund Grants Manual *1046*

U.S. Bureau of Reclamation. Annual Report (US) *367, 1126*

U.S. Bureau of Reclamation. Engineering and Research Center. Research Reports (US) *1126*

U.S. Bureau of Reclamation. Engineering and Research Center. Technical Records of Design and Construction (US) *484*

U.S. Bureau of Reclamation. Engineering Monograph *see* U.S. Water and Power Resources Service. Engineering Monograph *491*

U.S. Bureau of Standards. Building Technology Publications (US) *188, 189*

U.S. Bureau of the Census. Annual Survey of Manufactures (US ISSN 0082-9307) *292*

U.S. DEPARTMENT 1913

U.S. Bureau of the Census. Bunker Fuels *see* Foreign Trade Reports. Bunker Fuels *255*
U.S. Bureau of the Census. Bureau of the Census Catalog *see* U.S. Bureau of the Census. Census Catalog and Guide *929*
U.S. Bureau of the Census. Census Bureau Methodological Research (US ISSN 0565-0828) *1014*
U.S. Bureau of the Census. Census Catalog and Guide (US) *929, 949*
U.S. Bureau of the Census. Census of Agriculture (US ISSN 0082-9315) *35*
U.S. Bureau of the Census. Census of Construction Industries (US ISSN 0082-934X) *188*
U.S. Bureau of the Census. Census of Governments (US ISSN 0082-9358) *947*
U.S. Bureau of the Census. Census of Housing (US ISSN 0082-9366) *627*
U.S. Bureau of the Census. Census of Manufactures (US ISSN 0082-9374) *292*
U.S. Bureau of the Census. Census of Mineral Industries (US ISSN 0082-9382) *821*
U.S. Bureau of the Census. Census of Population (US ISSN 0082-9390) *925*
U.S. Bureau of the Census. Census of Retail Trade (US) *250*
U.S. Bureau of the Census. Census of Retail Trade, Wholesale Trade and Selected Service Industries *see* U.S. Bureau of the Census. Census of Retail Trade *250*
U.S. Bureau of the Census. Census of Retail Trade, Wholesale Trade and Selected Service Industries *see* U.S. Bureau of the Census. Census of Wholesale Trade *250*
U.S. Bureau of the Census. Census of Retail Trade, Wholesale Trade and Selected Service Industries *see* U.S. Bureau of the Census. Census of Service Industries *250*
U.S. Bureau of the Census. Census of Service Industries (US) *250*
U.S. Bureau of the Census. Census of Transportation (US ISSN 0082-9404) *1084*
U.S. Bureau of the Census. Census of Wholesale Trade (US) *250*
U.S. Bureau of the Census. Chart Book on Government Data: Organization, Finances and Employment *see* Current Governments Reports: Chart Book on Government Data. Organization, Finances and Employment *294*
U.S. Bureau of the Census. City Employment *see* Current Governments Reports: City Employment *206*
U.S. Bureau of the Census. City Government Finances *see* Current Governments Reports: City Government Finances *294*
U.S. Bureau of the Census. Congressional District Data Book (US ISSN 0082-9447) *910*
U.S. Bureau of the Census. Consumer Income *see* Current Population Reports: Consumer Income *277*
U.S. Bureau of the Census. County and City Data Book (US ISSN 0082-9455) *1066*
U.S. Bureau of the Census. County Business Patterns (US ISSN 0082-9463) *250*
U.S. Bureau of the Census. County Employment *see* Current Governments Reports: County Employment *940*
U.S. Bureau of the Census. County Government Finances *see* Current Governments Reports: County Government Finances *294*
U.S. Bureau of the Census. Current Business Reports *see* Current Business Reports *243*
U.S. Bureau of the Census. Current Construction Reports *see* Current Construction Reports *183*

U.S. Bureau of the Census. Current Governments Reports *see* Current Governments Reports *940*
U.S. Bureau of the Census. Current Housing Reports *see* Current Housing Reports *622*
U.S. Bureau of the Census. Current Industrial Reports *see* Current Industrial Reports *288*
U.S. Bureau of the Census. Current Population Reports *see* Current Population Reports *921*
U.S. Bureau of the Census. Current Population Reports: Negro Population *see* Current Population Reports: Population Characteristics. Social and Economic Characteristics of the Black Population *921*
U.S. Bureau of the Census. Current Population Reports: School Enrollment: October (Year) *see* Current Population Reports: Population Characteristics. School Enrollment: Social and Economic Characteristics of Students *921*
U.S. Bureau of the Census. Farm Population *see* Current Population Reports: Farm Population *921*
U.S. Bureau of the Census. Finances of Employee Retirement Systems of State and Local Governments *see* Current Governments Reports: Finances of Employee Retirement Systems of State and Local Governments *294*
U.S. Bureau of the Census. Governmental Finances *see* Current Governments Reports: Governmental Finances *294*
U.S. Bureau of the Census. Guide to Foreign Trade Statistics (US ISSN 0565-0933) *260*
U.S. Bureau of the Census. Household and Family Characteristics *see* Current Population Reports: Population Characteristics. Household and Family Characteristics *921*
U.S. Bureau of the Census. Housing Characteristics *see* Current Housing Reports: Housing Characteristics *622*
U.S. Bureau of the Census. Housing Vacancies *see* Current Housing Reports: Housing Vacancies *623*
U.S. Bureau of the Census. Local Government Finances in Selected Metropolitan Areas and Large Counties *see* Current Governments Reports: Local Government Finances in Selected Metropolitan Areas and Large Counties *294*
U.S. Bureau of the Census. Marital Status and Living Arrangements *see* Current Population Reports: Population Characteristics. Marital Status and Living Arrangements *921*
U.S. Bureau of the Census. Market Absorption of Apartments *see* Current Housing Reports: Market Absorption of Apartments *623*
U.S. Bureau of the Census. New One Family Homes Sold and for Sale *see* Current Construction Reports: New One Family Homes Sold and for Sale *622*
U.S. Bureau of the Census. Population Characteristics *see* Current Population Reports: Population Characteristics *921*
U.S. Bureau of the Census. Population Estimates and Projections *see* Current Population Reports: Population Estimates and Projections *921*
U.S. Bureau of the Census. Public Employment *see* Current Governments Reports: Public Employment *271*
U.S. Bureau of the Census. Quarterly Summary of State and Local Tax Revenue *see* Current Governments Reports: Quarterly Summary of State and Local Tax Revenue *294*

U.S. Bureau of the Census. Recurrent Reports on Governments. Chart Book on Government Finances and Employment *see* Current Governments Reports: Chart Book on Government Data. Organization, Finances and Employment *294*
U.S. Bureau of the Census. School Enrollment: Social and Economic Characteristics of Students *see* Current Population Reports: Population Characteristics. School Enrollment: Social and Economic Characteristics of Students *921*
U.S. Bureau of the Census. Social and Economic Characteristics of the Black Population *see* Current Population Reports: Population Characteristics. Social and Economic Characteristics of the Black Population *921*
U.S. Bureau of the Census. State and Metropolitan Area Data Book (US ISSN 0276-6566) *1066*
U.S. Bureau of the Census. State Finances *see* Current Governments Reports: State Government Finances *206*
U.S. Bureau of the Census. State Government Finances *see* Current Governments Reports: State Government Finances *206*
U.S. Bureau of the Census. State Tax Collections *see* Current Governments Reports: State Government Tax Collections *294*
U.S. Bureau of the Census. Technical Paper (US ISSN 0082-9544) *1066*
U.S. Bureau of the Census. Vessel Entrances and Clearances *see* Foreign Trade Reports. Vessel Entrances and Clearances *256*
U.S. Bureau of the Census. Working Papers (US ISSN 0082-9552) *1066*
U.S. Center for Disease Control. Brucellosis Surveillance: Annual Summary (US ISSN 0090-1156) *956*
U.S. Center for Disease Control. Foodborne & Waterborne Disease Outbreaks. Annual Summary (US ISSN 0098-6623) *956*
U.S. Center for Disease Control. Neurotropic Viral Diseases Surveillance: Aseptic Meningitis (US) *791*
U.S. Center for Disease Control. Neurotropic Viral Diseases Surveillance: Encephalitis (US) *791*
U.S. Center for Disease Control. Neurotropic Viral Diseases Surveillance: Enterovirus (US) *791*
U.S. Center for Disease Control. Neurotropic Viral Diseases Surveillance: Poliomyelitis (US) *791*
U.S. Center for Disease Control. Salmonella Surveillance. Annual Summary (US) *956*
U.S. Center for Disease Control. Tuberculosis in the United States (US ISSN 0149-2616) *793*
U.S. Center for Disease Control. Tuberculosis: States and Cities *see* U.S. Center for Disease Control. Tuberculosis Statistics: States and Cities *793*
U.S. Center for Disease Control. Tuberculosis Statistics: States and Cities (US) *793*
U.S. Center for Population Research. Inventory of Federal Population Research *see* U.S. Interagency Committee on Population Research. Inventory and Analysis of Federal Population Research *925*
U.S. Centers for Disease Control. Abortion Surveillance. Annual Summary (US) *179, 956*
U.S. Centers for Disease Control. Diphtheria Surveillance Report (US) *778, 956*
U.S. Centers for Disease Control. Family Planning Services: Annual Summary (US ISSN 0094-4424) *179*
U.S. Centers for Disease Control. Leprosy Surveillance Report (US) *778, 956*

U.S. Centers for Disease Control. Listeriosis Surveillance Report (US) *778, 956*
U.S. Centers for Disease Control. Malaria Surveillance Report (US ISSN 0501-8390) *778, 956*
U.S. Civil Service Commission. Annual Report (US ISSN 0190-9797) *947*
U.S. Civil Service Commission. Bureau of Personnel Management Evaluation. Evaluation Methods Series (US ISSN 0361-6797) *287*
U.S. Civil Service Commission. Personnel Research and Development Center. Technical Study (US ISSN 0093-366X) *287*
U.S. Coast Guard. Oceanographic Reports (CG-373 Series) (US ISSN 0082-9625) *408*
U.S. Coast Guard. Polluting Incidents in and Around U.S. Waters (US ISSN 0092-0320) *499*
U.S. Coast Guard Boating Statistics *see* Boating Statistics *1036*
U.S. Coast Guard Technical Report *see* C G O U Technical Report *405*
U.S. Commission on Civil Rights. Clearinghouse Publications (US ISSN 0082-9641) *914*
U.S. Community Services Administration. Annual Report of Community Services Administration (US ISSN 0190-373X) *1021*
U.S. Community Services Administration. Federal Outlays in Summary (US ISSN 0091-3553) *300*
U.S. Congress. Congressional Directory (US) *910*
U.S. Copyright Office. Annual Report of the Register of Copyrights (US ISSN 0090-2845) *861*
U.S. Crop Reporting Board. Crop Production (US ISSN 0363-8561) *60*
U.S. Defense Logistics Agency. D O D Hazardous Materials Information System: Hazardous Item Listing (US) *957*
U.S. Department of Agriculture. Agricultural Cooperative Service. Cooperative Information Report (US) *35*
U.S. Department of Agriculture. Agricultural Economics Report (US ISSN 0083-0445) *49*
U.S. Department of Agriculture. Agricultural Statistics (US ISSN 0082-9714) *43*
U.S. Department of Agriculture. Agriculture Handbook (US ISSN 0065-4612) *35*
U.S. Department of Agriculture. Agriculture Information Bulletin (US ISSN 0065-4639) *35*
U.S. Department of Agriculture. Animal and Plant Health Inspection Service. Cooperative State-Federal Brucellosis Eradication Program: Statistical Tables (US) *43*
U.S. Department of Agriculture. Animal and Plant Health Inspection Service. Cooperative State-Federal Bovine Tuberculosis Eradication Program: Statistical Tables (US) *44*
U.S. Department of Agriculture. Animal and Plant Health Inspection Service. Reported Arthropod-Borne Encephalitides in Horses and Other Equidae (US) *1122*
U.S. Department of Agriculture. Animal Science Research Branch. Hatcheries and Dealers Participating in the National Improvement Plan *see* Hatcheries and Dealers Participating in the National Poultry Improvement Plan *66*
U.S. Department of Agriculture. Eastern Regional Research Center. Publications and Patents (US) *1164*
U.S. Department of Agriculture. Economic Research Service. Agricultural Economics Report *see* U.S. Department of Agriculture. Agricultural Economics Report *49*

U.S. Department of Agriculture. Farmer Cooperative Service. Information (Series) see U.S. Department of Agriculture. Agricultural Cooperative Service. Cooperative Information Report 35

U.S. Department of Agriculture. Home and Garden Bulletin (US ISSN 0073-3075) 534

U.S. Department of Agriculture. Home Economics Research Report (US ISSN 0073-3113) 615

U.S. Department of Agriculture. Marketing Research Report (US ISSN 0082-9781) 49

U.S. Department of Agriculture. Production Research Reports (US ISSN 0082-979X) 49

U.S. Department of Agriculture. Report of the Secretary of Agriculture (US ISSN 0082-9803) 36

U.S. Department of Agriculture. Technical Bulletin (US ISSN 0082-9811) 36

U.S. Department of Agriculture. Yearbook of Agriculture (US ISSN 0084-3628) 36

U.S. Department of Commerce. Consumer Goods and Services Division. Franchise Opportunities Handbook (US) 285

U.S. Department of Commerce. Publications; a Catalog and Index Supplement see U.S. Department of Commerce. Publications Catalog 219

U.S. Department of Commerce. Publications Catalog (US ISSN 0277-7207) 219

U.S. Department of Commerce. Trade Lists (US) 260

U.S. Department of Defense. Defense Department Report (US ISSN 0091-6919) 947

U.S. Department of Defense. Defense Program and Defense Budget (US ISSN 0082-9862) 813

U.S. Department of Defense. Report of Secretary of Defense to the Congress(US ISSN 0098-3888) 813

U.S. Department of Education. Opportunities for Teachers Abroad (US) 442

U.S. Department of Energy. Annual Report to Congress on the Automotive Technology Program (US ISSN 0270-756X) 1093

U.S. Department of Energy. Office of State and Local Programs. Annual Report to the President and the Congress on the State Energy Conservation Program (US ISSN 0161-1674) 467

U.S. Department of Energy. Strategic Petroleum Reserve Office. Annual Report (US) 867

U.S. Department of Health and Human Services. Annual Report to the Congress of the United States on Services Provided to Handicapped Children in Project Head Start (US) 445

U.S. Department of Health and Human Services. Publication Catalog (US ISSN 0278-0143) 1023

U.S. Department of Health, Education and Welfare. Annual Report to the Congress of the United States on Services to Handicapped Children in Project Head Start see U.S. Department of Health and Human Services. Annual Report to the Congress of the United States on Services Provided to Handicapped Children in Project Head Start 445

U.S. Department of Health, Education and Welfare. Catalog of Publications see U.S. Department of Health and Human Services. Publication Catalog 1023

U.S. Department of Health, Education and Welfare. Statistics on Public Institutions for Delinquent Children see Children in Custody 333

U.S. Department of Housing and Urban Development. Annual Report (US ISSN 0565-2820) 626

U.S. Department of Housing and Urban Development. Interim Guide for Environment Assessment (US) 499

U.S. Department of Housing and Urban Development. Statistical Yearbook (US ISSN 0147-7870) 628, 1066

U.S. Department of Justice. Annual Report of the Attorney General of the United States (US ISSN 0082-9943) 665

U.S. Department of Justice. National Institute of Justice. Document Retrieval Index see N C J R S Document Retrieval Index 371

U.S. Department of Justice. Office of Legal Counsel. Opinions (US) 665, 910

U.S. Department of Justice. Opinions of Attorney General (US ISSN 0082-9951) 665

U.S. Department of Labor. Employee Retirement Income Security Act. Report to Congress (US ISSN 0271-1567) 276, 642

U.S. Department of State. African Series (US ISSN 0083-0003) 567

U.S. Department of State. Bureau of Public Affairs. Current Policy (US) 919

U.S. Department of State. Commercial Policy Series (US ISSN 0083-002X) 260

U.S. Department of State. Department and Foreign Service Series (US ISSN 0083-0038) 919

U.S. Department of State. East Asian and Pacific Series (US ISSN 0083-0054) 919

U.S. Department of State. Economic Cooperation Series (US ISSN 0083-0062) 264

U.S. Department of State. European and British Commonwealth Series (US ISSN 0083-0070) 600

U.S. Department of State. General Foreign Policy Series (US ISSN 0083-0097) 919

U.S. Department of State. Inter-American Series (US ISSN 0083-0143) 919

U.S. Department of State. International Information and Cultural Series (US ISSN 0083-0119) 919

U.S. Department of State. International Organization and Conference Series (US ISSN 0083-0127) 919

U.S. Department of State. International Organization Series (US ISSN 0083-0135) 919

U.S. Department of State. Library. Commercial Library Program. Publications List (US) 132, 688, 912

U.S. Department of State. Near and Middle Eastern Series see U.S. Department of State. Near East and South Asian Series 572

U.S. Department of State. Near East and South Asian Series (US) 572

U.S. Department of State. Office of the Geographer. Geographic Notes (US ISSN 0083-016X) 549, 910

U.S. Department of State. Treaties and Other International Acts Series (US ISSN 0083-0186) 672

U.S. Department of State. Treaties in Force (US ISSN 0083-0194) 672

U.S. Department of the Army. Projects Recommended for Deauthorization, Annual Report (US ISSN 0361-2651) 813, 1126

U.S. Department of Transportation. Bibliographic Lists (US ISSN 0083-0380) 132, 1087

U.S. Department of Transportation. Energy Statistics see U.S. Department of Transportation. National Transportation Statistics. Annual 469

U.S. Department of Transportation. Fiscal Year Budget in Brief (US ISSN 0092-3117) 1084

U.S. Department of Transportation. Highway Safety Stewardship Report (US ISSN 0277-2310) 1098

U.S. Department of Transportation. National Transportation Statistics. Annual (US) 469, 1066

U.S. Department of Transportation. Office of University Research. Awards to Academic Institutions by the Department of Transportation (US ISSN 0099-2267) 1084

U.S. Department of Transportation. Summary of National Transportation Statistics see U.S. Department of Transportation. National Transportation Statistics. Annual 469

U.S. Energy Information Administration. Annual Report to Congress (US ISSN 0161-5807) 467

U.S. Energy Information Administration. U S Crude Oil, Natural Gas, and Natural Gas Liquids see U S Crude Oil, Natural Gas, and Natural Gas Liquids 867

U.S. Environmental Protection Agency. Clean Water; Report to Congress (US ISSN 0092-9433) 367

U.S. Environmental Protection Agency. Journal Holdings Report (US) 132, 501

U.S. Environmental Protection Agency. Office of Research and Development. Program Guide (US) 500

U.S. Environmental Protection Agency. Pesticides Enforcement Division. Notices of Judgement under Federal Insecticide, Fungicide, and Rodenticide Act (US ISSN 0083-0518) 60

U.S. Equal Employment Opportunity Commission. Annual Report (US ISSN 0083-0526) 276, 914

U.S. Executive Office of the President. Economic Report of the President see Economic Report of the President 243

U.S. Farm Credit Administration. Annual Report of the Farm Credit Administration and the Cooperative Farm Credit System see Farm Credit Administration. Annual Report 46

U.S. Farm Credit Administration. Annual Report of the Farm Credit Administration on the Work of the Cooperative Farm Credit System see Farm Credit Administration. Annual Report 46

U.S. Federal Aviation Administration. National Aviation System: Challenges of the Decade Ahead see U.S. Federal Aviation Administration. National Aviation System: Development and Capital Needs 1090

U.S. Federal Aviation Administration. National Aviation System: Development and Capital Needs (US) 1090

U.S. Federal Aviation Administration. National Aviation System Policy Summary see U.S. Federal Aviation Administration. National Aviation System: Development and Capital Needs 1090

U.S. Federal Aviation Administration. Systems Research and Development. Report FAA-RD (US) 1071

U.S. Federal Aviation Administration. Overview of the F A A Engineering & Development Programs see Overview of the F A A Engineering & Development Programs 21

U.S. Federal Bureau of Investigation. Bomb Summary (US ISSN 0360-3245) 373

U.S. Federal Communications Commission. I N F Bulletins (US ISSN 0083-0607) 345

U.S. Federal Deposit Insurance Corporation. Annual Report (US ISSN 0083-0658) 233, 642

U.S. Federal Deposit Insurance Corporation. Bank Operating Statistics (US ISSN 0083-0666) 219

U.S. Federal Deposit Insurance Corporation. Changes Among Operating Banks and Branches (US ISSN 0083-0674) 233

U.S. Federal Deposit Insurance Corporation. Federal Deposit Insurance Act, Rules and Regulations, and Related Laws. (US) 233

U.S. Federal Deposit Insurance Corporation. News Releases (US) 233

U.S. Federal Deposit Insurance Corporation. Operating Banking Offices (US) 233

U.S. Federal Deposit Insurance Corporation. Operating Bank Offices see U.S. Federal Deposit Insurance Corporation. Operating Banking Offices 233

U.S. Federal Deposit Insurance Corporation. Trust Assets of Banks and Trust Companies (US ISSN 0278-5692) 233

U.S. Federal Deposit Insurance Corporation. Trust Assets of Insured Commercial Banks see U.S. Federal Deposit Insurance Corporation. Trust Assets of Banks and Trust Companies 233

U.S. Federal Election Commission. Annual Report (US) 910

U.S. Federal Highway Administration. Federally Coordinated Program of Highway Research and Development(US ISSN 0361-4204) 1098

U.S. Federal Highway Administration. Highway and Urban Mass Transportation (US) 1084

U.S. Federal Highway Administration. Highway Planning Technical Reports(US ISSN 0073-2184) 484

U.S. Federal Highway Administration. Highway Statistics (US) 1098

U.S. Federal Highway Administration. Research and Development Program see U.S. Federal Highway Administration. Federally Coordinated Program of Highway Research and Development 1098

U.S. Federal Home Loan Bank Board. Report (US ISSN 0083-0720) 233, 966

U.S. Federal Home Loan Bank Board. Trends in the Savings and Loan Field(US ISSN 0083-0747) 233, 966

U.S. Federal Housing Administration. F H A Homes (US ISSN 0091-4932) 626

U.S. Federal Maritime Commission. Annual Report (US ISSN 0083-0755) 1104

U.S. Federal Mediation and Conciliation Service. Annual Report (US ISSN 0083-0771) 276

U.S. Federal Railroad Administration. Office of Safety. Accident Bulletin see U.S. Federal Railroad Administration. Office of Safety. Accident/Incident Bulletin 1095

U.S. Federal Railroad Administration. Office of Safety. Accident/Incident Bulletin (US ISSN 0163-4674) 1095

U.S. Federal Reserve System. Annual Report (US ISSN 0083-0887) 233

U.S. Federal Reserve System. Annual Statistical Digest (US) 233

U.S. Federal Trade Commission. Annual Report (US ISSN 0083-0917) 240

U.S. Federal Trade Commission. Court Decisions Pertaining to the Federal Trade Commission (US) 240, 666

U.S. Federal Trade Commission. Federal Trade Commission Decisions, Findings, Orders and Stipulations (US ISSN 0083-0925) 240, 666

U.S. Federal Trade Commission. Statutes and Court Decisions Pertaining to the Federal Trade Commission. Supplements see U.S. Federal Trade Commission. Court Decisions Pertaining to the Federal Trade Commission 240

U.S. Fish and Wildlife Service. Investigations in Fish Control (US ISSN 0565-0704) 513

U.S. Fish and Wildlife Service. National Survey of Hunting, Fishing and Wildlife-Associated Recreation (US) 1037, 1047, 1066

U.S. Fish and Wildlife Service. Research Reports (US ISSN 0083-0941) 367, 513

U.S. NATIONAL 1915

U.S. Fish and Wildlife Service. Selected List of Federal Laws and Treaties Relating to Sport Fish and Wildlife (US ISSN 0093-4631) 367, 666
U.S. Fish and Wildlife Service. Wildlife Leaflets (US ISSN 0084-0165) 367
U.S. Food and Drug Administration. National Drug Code Directory (US ISSN 0077-4235) 873
U.S. Food and Drug Administration Clinical Experience Abstracts see F D A Clinical Experience Abstracts 870
U.S. Food and Drug Administration Compliance Policy Guides. Manual see F D A Compliance Policy Guides. Manual 518
U.S. Food and Nutrition Service. Food and Nutrition Programs (US ISSN 0360-4594) 1023
United States. Food Safety and Inspection Service. Program Plan (US) 521
U.S. Foreign Agricultural Service. Food and Agricultural Export Directory (US ISSN 0083-0976) 49, 260
U.S. Foreign Agricultural Trade Statistical Report, Calendar Year (US) 44, 219
U.S. Foreign Agricultural Trade Statistical Report, Fiscal Year (US) 44, 219
U.S. Forest Service. General Technical Report INT (Intermountain Research Station) (US ISSN 0092-9654) 528
U.S. Forest Service. General Technical Report NE (Northeastern Forest Experiment Sta.) (US ISSN 0083-2480) 528
U.S. Forest Service. North Central Forest Experiment Station. List of Publications (US) 529
U.S. Forest Service. North Central Forest Experiment Station, St. Paul, Minnesota. Annual Report see U.S. Forest Service. North Central Forest Experiment Station. List of Publications 529
U.S. Forest Service. Pacific Southwest Forest and Range Experiment Station. General Technical Report P S W (US ISSN 0196-2094) 528
U.S. Forest Service. Research Note INT (Intermountain Research Station) (US) 528
U.S. Forest Service. Research Note RM (Rocky Mountain Forest and Range Experiment Sta.) (US ISSN 0502-4994) 528
U.S. Forest Service. Research Paper INT (Intermountain Research Station) (US) 528
U.S. Forest Service. Research Paper RM (Rocky Mountain Forest and Range Experiment Sta.) (US ISSN 0502-5001) 528
U.S. Forest Service. Resource Bulletin INT (Intermountain Research Station) (US) 528
U.S. Forest Service. Resource Bulletin PNW (Pacific Northwest Forest and Range Experiment Sta.) (US) 528
U.S. General Accounting Office. Social Development Activities in Latin America Promoted by the Inter-American Foundation: Report to the Congress by the Comptroller General of the United States (US ISSN 0091-6234) 1164
U.S. General Services Administration. Management Report (US ISSN 0091-6242) 1021
U.S. General Services Administration. Publications (US) 132, 950
U.S. Geological Survey. Annual Report see U.S. Geological Survey. Yearbook 396
U.S. Geological Survey. Bulletin (US ISSN 0083-1093) 396
U.S. Geological Survey. Circular see Geological Survey Circular 387
U.S. Geological Survey. Professional Papers (US) 396
U.S. Geological Survey. Seismic Engineering Branch. Seismic Engineering Program Report see U.S. Geological Survey. Stron Motion Program. Report 484

U.S. Geological Survey. Stron Motion Program. Report (US) 484
U.S. Geological Survey. Water Resources Investigations (US ISSN 0092-332X) 404
U.S. Geological Survey. Water Supply Papers (US ISSN 0083-1131) 404
U.S. Geological Survey. Yearbook (US ISSN 0162-9484) 396
U.S. Immigration and Naturalization Service. Administrative Decisions under Immigration and Nationality Laws (US ISSN 0083-1220) 925
U.S. Immigration and Naturalization Service. Administrative Decisions under Immigration and Nationality Laws. Interim Decisions of the Department of Justice (US ISSN 0083-1239) 925
U.S. Immigration and Naturalization Service. Annual Report (US ISSN 0083-1247) 925
U.S. Industrial Outlook (Year) (US) 292
U.S. Industrial Outlook for 350 Industries with 5-Year Projections see U.S. Industrial Outlook (Year) 292
U.S. Institute of Tropical Forestry. Annual Letter (PR) 528
U.S. Interagency Committee on Population Research. Inventory and Analysis of Federal Population Research (US) 925
U.S. Internal Revenue Service. Annual Report (US ISSN 0083-1476) 300
U.S. Internal Revenue Service. Tax Guide for Small Business (US ISSN 0083-1484) 300, 301
U.S. International Development Cooperation Agency. Congressional Presentation, Fiscal Year (US ISSN 0276-6469) 264
U.S. International Trade Commission. Annual Report (US) 260
U.S. International Trade Commission. Imports of Benzenoid Chemicals and Products (US ISSN 0083-3436) 260
U.S. International Trade Commission. Operation of the Trade Agreements Program (US ISSN 0083-3444) 260
U.S. Interstate Commerce Commission. Annual Report (US ISSN 0083-1514) 240
U.S. Interstate Commerce Commission. Interstate Commerce Acts Annotated (US ISSN 0083-1522) 240
U.S. Interstate Commerce Commission. Interstate Commerce Commission Reports. Decisions of the Interstate Commerce Commission of the United States (US ISSN 0083-1530) 240
U.S. Library of Congress. Annual Report of the Librarian of Congress (US ISSN 0083-1565) 685
U.S. Library of Congress. Congressional Research Service. Digest of Public General Bills and Resolutions (US) 666, 947
U.S. Library of Congress. Library of Congress Publications in Print (US ISSN 0083-1603) 688
U.S. Library of Congress. Manuscript Division. Acquisitions (US ISSN 0275-9616) 963
U.S. Library of Congress. Manuscript Division. Registers of Papers (US ISSN 0083-1611) 561
U.S. Library of Congress Catalog - Music and Phonorecords see Music, Books on Music and Sound Recordings 843
U.S. Library of Congress Folk Archive Finding Aid see L C Folk Archive Finding Aid 680
U.S. Maritime Administration. Annual Report (US ISSN 0083-1670) 1104
U.S. Military Academy Library Library Bulletin see U S M A Library Bulletin 685
U.S. Mining Enforcement and Safety Administration. Informational Report (US ISSN 0097-9376) 821

U.S. National Aeronautics and Space Administration. Earth Resources Laboratory. Research and Technology. Annual Report (US) 21, 381
U.S. National Aeronautics and Space Administration. Research and Technology Operating Plan (RTOP) Summary (US) 21, 1071
U.S. National Aeronautics and Space Administration. Research and Technology Program Digest. Flash Index see U.S. National Aeronautics and Space Administration. Research and Technology Operating Plan (RTOP) Summary 21
U.S. National Aeronautics and Space Administration Facts see N A S A Facts 20
U.S. National Aeronautics and Space Administration Patent Abstracts Bibliography: A Continuing Bibliography. Section 1. Abstracts see N A S A Patent Abstracts Bibliography: A Continuing Bibliography. Section 1. Abstracts 862
U.S. National Aeronautics and Space Administration Patent Abstracts Bibliography: A Continuing Bibliography. Section 2. Indexes see N A S A Patent Abstracts Bibliography: A Continuing Bibliography. Section 2. Indexes 862
U.S. National Aeronautics and Space Administration University Conference on Manual Control (Papers) see N A S A - University Conference on Manual Control (Papers) 20
U.S. National Arthritis Advisory Board. Annual Report (US ISSN 0190-5422) 793
U.S. National Bureau of Standards. Annual Report (US) 809
U.S. National Bureau of Standards. Applied Mathematics Series (US ISSN 0083-1786) 754
U.S. National Bureau of Standards. Building Science Series (US ISSN 0083-1794) 188
U.S. National Bureau of Standards. Center for Building Technology. Building Technology Project Summaries (US) 188
U.S. National Bureau of Standards. Commercial Standards see U.S. National Bureau of Standards. Voluntary Product Standards 809
U.S. National Bureau of Standards. Federal Information Processing Standards (US) 809
U.S. National Bureau of Standards. Methods of Measurement for Semiconductor Materials, Process Control, and Devices; Quarterly Report see U.S. National Bureau of Standards. Semiconductor Measurement Technology 809
U.S. National Bureau of Standards. Monographs (US) 809
U.S. National Bureau of Standards. National Standard Reference Data Series (US ISSN 0083-1840) 809
U.S. National Bureau of Standards. Product Standards see U.S. National Bureau of Standards. Voluntary Product Standards 809
U.S. National Bureau of Standards. Semiconductor Measurement Technology (US) 460, 809
U.S. National Bureau of Standards. Semiconductor Measurement Technology. Quarterly Report see U.S. National Bureau of Standards. Semiconductor Measurement Technology 809
U.S. National Bureau of Standards. Technical Notes (US ISSN 0083-1913) 809
U.S. National Bureau of Standards. Voluntary Product Standards (US) 809
U.S. National Cancer Institute. Monograph see N C I Monographs 775
U.S. National Cartographic Information Center. Newsletter (US ISSN 0364-7064) 549

U.S. National Cartographic Information Center Newsletter see K G S - N C I C Newsletter 545
U.S. National Center for Education Statistics. Digest of Education Statistics (US) 426
U.S. National Center for Education Statistics. Digest of Educational Statistics see U.S. National Center for Education Statistics. Digest of Education Statistics 426
U.S. National Center for Education Statistics. Earned Degrees Conferred (US ISSN 0565-744X) 439
U.S. National Center for Education Statistics. Expenditures and Revenues for Public Elementary and Secondary Education see U.S. National Center for Education Statistics. Revenues and Expenditures for Public Elementary and Secondary Education 421
U.S. National Center for Education Statistics. Fall Enrollment in Higher Education (US) 439
U.S. National Center for Education Statistics. Financial Statistics of Institutions of Higher Education (US ISSN 0095-6716) 439
U.S. National Center for Education Statistics. Library Statistics of Colleges and Universities (US) 439
U.S. National Center for Education Statistics. Revenues and Expenditures for Public Elementary and Secondary Education (US ISSN 0149-2497) 421
U.S. National Center for Education Statistics. Statistics of Public Elementary and Secondary Day Schools see U.S. National Center for Education Statistics. Statistics of Public Elementary and Secondary School Systems 421
U.S. National Center for Education Statistics. Statistics of Public Elementary and Secondary School Systems (US) 421
U.S. National Center for Health Care Statistics. Vital and Health Statistics. Series 12. Data from the Institutional Population Surveys see U.S. National Center for Health Statistics. Vital and Health Statistics. Series 13. Data on Health Resources Utilization 957
U.S. National Center for Health Care Statistics. Vital and Health Statistics. Series 13. Data from the Hospital Discharge Survey see U.S. National Center for Health Statistics. Vital and Health Statistics. Series 13. Data on Health Resources Utilization 957
U.S. National Center for Health Statistics. Advance Data from Vital and Health Statistics (US) 957
U.S. National Center for Health Statistics. Catalog of Publications (US ISSN 0278-4912) 13, 929, 959
U.S. National Center for Health Statistics. Catalog of Public Use Data Tapes (US) 778
U.S. National Center for Health Statistics. Current Listing and Topical Index to the Vital and Health Statistics Series see U.S. National Center for Health Statistics. Catalog of Publications 959
U.S. National Center for Health Statistics. Standardized Micro-Data Tape Transcripts see U.S. National Center for Health Statistics. Catalog of Public Use Data Tapes 778
U.S. National Center for Health Statistics. Vital and Health Statistics. Series 1. Programs and Collection Procedures (US ISSN 0083-2014) 925, 957
U.S. National Center for Health Statistics. Vital and Health Statistics. Series 2. Data Evaluation and Methods Research (US ISSN 0083-2057) 925, 957
U.S. National Center for Health Statistics. Vital and Health Statistics. Series 3. Analytical Studies (US ISSN 0083-2065) 925, 957

U.S. National Center for Health Statistics. Vital and Health Statistics. Series 4. Documents and Committee Report (US ISSN 0083-2073) 925, 957
U.S. National Center for Health Statistics. Vital and Health Statistics. Series 10. Data from the Health Interview Survey (US ISSN 0083-1972) 957
U.S. National Center for Health Statistics. Vital and Health Statistics. Series 11. Data from the Health and Nutrition Examination Survey (US) 957
U.S. National Center for Health Statistics. Vital and Health Statistics. Series 11. Data from the Health Examination Survey see U.S. National Center for Health Statistics. Vital and Health Statistics. Series 11. Data from the Health and Nutrition Examination Survey 957
U.S. National Center for Health Statistics. Vital and Health Statistics. Series 13. Data on Health Resources Utilization (US) 618, 957
U.S. National Center for Health Statistics. Vital and Health Statistics. Series 14. Data on Health Resources: Manpower and Facilities (US ISSN 0083-1999) 957
U.S. National Center for Health Statistics. Vital and Health Statistics. Series 20. Data on Mortality (US ISSN 0083-2022) 925, 957
U.S. National Center for Health Statistics. Vital and Health Statistics. Series 21. Data on Natality, Marriage, and Divorce (US ISSN 0083-2030) 925, 957
U.S. National Center for Health Statistics. Vital and Health Statistics. Series 22. Data on Natality and Mortality Surveys see U.S. National Center for Health Statistics. Vital and Health Statistics. Series 20. Data on Mortality 957
U.S. National Center for Health Statistics. Vital and Health Statistics. Series 22. Data on Natality and Mortality Surveys see U.S. National Center for Health Statistics. Vital and Health Statistics. Series 21. Data on Natality, Marriage, and Divorce 957
U.S. National Center for Health Statistics. Vital and Health Statistics. Series 23: Data from the National Survey of Family Growth (US) 925
U.S. National Commission for Employment Policy. Annual Report (US) 276
U.S. National Commission for Manpower Policy. Annual Report to the President and the Congress see U.S. National Commission for Employment Policy. Annual Report 276
U.S. National Credit Union Administration. Annual Report (US) 233, 239
U.S. National Endowment for the Arts. Annual Report (US ISSN 0083-2103) 111
U.S. National Heart and Lung Advisory Council. Annual Report see U.S. National Heart, Lung, and Blood Advisory Council. Report 777
U.S. National Heart, Lung, and Blood Advisory Council. Report (US ISSN 0161-1917) 777, 793
U.S. National Institute on Drug Abuse. Research Issues (US) 377
U.S. National Institute on Drug Abuse. Research Monograph Series (US) 377
U.S. National Institutes of Health. Division of Research Resources. Program Highlights (US ISSN 0278-5374) 773, 782
U.S. National Institutes of Health Factbook see N I H Factbook 1159
U.S. National Labor Relations Board. Annual Report (US ISSN 0083-2200) 276

U.S. National Labor Relations Board. Court Decisions Relating to the National Labor Relations Act (US ISSN 0083-2219) 276
U.S. National Library of Medicine. Annual Report see National Library of Medicine. Programs and Services 682
U.S. National Marine Fisheries Service. Grant-in-Aid for Fisheries: Program Activities (US ISSN 0094-7008) 513
U.S. National Marine Fisheries Service. Imports and Exports of Fishery Products. Annual Summary (US) 513
U.S. National Marine Fisheries Service. Special Scientific Report: Fisheries see U.S. National Marine Fisheries Service. Technical Report 513
U.S. National Marine Fisheries Service. Technical Report (US) 513
U.S. National Mediation Board. Annual Report (US ISSN 0083-2286) 276
U.S. National Mediation Board. (Reports of Emergency Boards) (US ISSN 0083-2278) 276
U.S. National Ocean Service Hydrographic Conference. Annual Meeting. Proceedings (US) 408
U.S. National Ocean Survey Hydrographic Conference. Annual Meeting. Proceedings see U.S. National Ocean Service Hydrographic Conference. Annual Meeting. Proceedings 408
U.S. National Oceanic and Atmospheric Administration. Annual Climate Diagnostic Workshop. Proceedings (US) 807
U.S. National Oceanic and Atmospheric Administration. Engineering Support Office. Technical Memorandum (US) 408
U.S. National Oceanic and Atmospheric Administration. Interdepartmental Committee for Meteorological Services and Supporting Research. National Hurricane Operations Plan (US ISSN 0092-2056) 807
U.S. National Oceanic and Atmospheric Administration. Manned Undersea Science and Technology Program; Report (US ISSN 0092-8917) 408, 475
U.S. National Oceanic and Atmospheric Administration. Report to the Congress on Ocean Dumping and Other Man-Induced Changes to Ocean Ecosystems see U.S. National Oceanic and Atmospheric Administration. Report to the Congress on Ocean Pollution, Overfishing, and Offshore Development 500
U.S. National Oceanic and Atmospheric Administration. Report to the Congress on Ocean Pollution, Overfishing, and Offshore Development (US ISSN 0098-4922) 500
U.S. National Oceanic and Atmospheric Administration. Test and Evaluation Laboratory. Technical Bulletin see U.S. National Oceanic and Atmospheric Administration. Technical Bulletin 408
U.S. National Oceanic and Atmospheric Administration. Test and Evaluation Office. Technical Memorandum see U.S. National Oceanic and Atmospheric Administration. Engineering Support Office. Technical Memorandum 408
U.S. National Oceanic and Atmospheric Administration. Technical Bulletin (US) 408
U.S. National Oceanographic Data Center. Key to Oceanographic Records Documentation (US ISSN 0091-9500) 408
U.S. National Park Service. Annual Report to Congress on the Federal Archeological Program (US) 94, 947
U.S. National Park Service. Archaeological Research Series see Publications in Archaeology 367

U.S. National Park Service. Historical Handbook Series (US ISSN 0083-2316) 1118
U.S. National Park Service. Public Use of the National Park System; Calendar Year Report (US ISSN 0361-9737) 367
U.S. National Park Service. Public Use of the National Park System; Fiscal Year Report (US ISSN 0093-3074) 367
U.S. National Park Service. Research Reports by Service Personnel (US) 1047
U.S. National Park Service. Source Books Series (US ISSN 0083-2324) 1164
U.S. National Science Foundation. Federal Funds for Research Development (US) 1002
U.S. National Science Foundation. Federal Funds for Research, Development, and other Scientific Activities see U.S. National Science Foundation. Federal Funds for Research Development 1002
U.S. National Science Foundation. Graduate Science Education Student Support and Postdoctorals (US ISSN 0094-7881) 439
U.S. National Science Foundation. Guide to Programs (US) 443, 1002
U.S. National Science Foundation. N S F Factbook (US ISSN 0083-2375) 1164
U.S. National Science Foundation. Research and Development in Industry (US ISSN 0083-2383) 1071
U.S. National Science Foundation. Surveys of Science Resources Series (US ISSN 0083-2405) 1002
U.S. National Technical Information Service Digest see N T I S Digest 681
U.S. National Toxicology Program. Annual Report on Carcinogens (US ISSN 0272-2836) 776
U.S. National Transportation Safety Board. Aircraft Accident Reports (US) 1090
U.S. Naval Academy Alumni Association. Register of Alumni (US) 342
U.S. Naval Institute. Naval Review (US ISSN 0077-6238) 813
U.S. Naval Observatory. Astronomical Papers Prepared for Use of American Ephemeris and Nautical Almanac (US ISSN 0083-243X) 118
U.S. Naval Observatory. Publications. Second Series (US ISSN 0083-2448) 118
U.S. Nuclear Regulatory Commission. Annual Occupational Radiation Exposure Report see U.S. Nuclear Regulatory Commission. Occupational Radiation Exposure, Annual Report 636
U.S. Nuclear Regulatory Commission. Occupational Radiation Exposure, Annual Report (US ISSN 0198-8360) 636
U.S. Nuclear Regulatory Commission. Water Reactor Safety Research Information Meeting. Proceedings (US) 898
U.S. Office of Economic Opportunity. Annual Report see U.S. Community Services Administration. Annual Report of Community Services Administration 1021
U.S. Office of Economic Opportunity. Federal Outlays in Summary see U.S. Community Services Administration. Federal Outlays in Summary 300
U.S. Office of Management and Budget. Special Analysis: Budget of the United States Government (US ISSN 0362-9163) 300
U.S. Office of Naval Research. Annual Task Summary: Contract Research Program (US ISSN 0500-1951) 813
U.S. Office of Technology Assessment Annual Report to the Congress (US ISSN 0095-2109) 947

U.S. Patent and Trademark Office. Annual Report of the Commissioner of Patents (US ISSN 0083-3002) 861
U.S. Patent and Trademark Office. Classification Bulletins (US ISSN 0083-3010) 861
U.S. Patent Office. Index of Patents Issued from the United States Patent Office see Index of Patents Issued from the United States Patent and Trademark Office 861
U.S. Peace Corps. Annual Report (US ISSN 0083-3088) 919
U.S. Postal Service. Revenue and Cost Analysis Report (US) 347
U.S. Postal Service. Support Group. Revenue and Cost Analysis see U.S. Postal Service. Revenue and Cost Analysis Report 347
U.S. Railroad Retirement Board. Annual Report (US) 276
U.S. Rural Electrification Administration. Annual Statistical Report. Rural Electrification Borrowers (US ISSN 0083-3177) 460
U.S. Rural Electrification Administration. Annual Statistical Report. Rural Telephone Program (US ISSN 0083-3185) 460
U.S. Rural Electrification Administration. Report of the Administrator of the Rural Electrification Administration (US ISSN 0083-3193) 460
U.S. Saint Lawrence Seaway Development Corporation. Annual Report (US ISSN 0083-3207) 1104
U.S. Securities and Exchange Commission. Annual Report (US ISSN 0083-3215) 268
U.S. Securities and Exchange Commission. Decisions and Reports (US ISSN 0083-3223) 268
U.S. Securities and Exchange Commission. Judicial Decisions (US ISSN 0083-3231) 268
U.S. Small Business Administration. Administrative Management Course Program. Topics (US ISSN 0083-3266) 301
U.S. Small Business Administration. Annual Report (US ISSN 0083-3274) 301
U.S. Social Security Administration. O R S I P Notes (Office of Research, Statistics and International Policy) (US ISSN 0566-0327) 1021
U.S. Social Security Administration. Research and Statistics Notes. see U.S. Social Security Administration. O R S I P Notes 1021
U.S. Soil Conservation Service. National Engineering Handbook (US ISSN 0083-3304) 60
U.S. Soil Conservation Service. Soil Survey Investigation Reports (US ISSN 0083-3320) 61
U.S. Soil Conservation Service. Technical Publications (US ISSN 0083-3339) 61
U.S. Tariff Commission. Annual Report see U.S. International Trade Commission. Annual Report 260
U.S. Trade with Puerto Rico and U.S. Possessions see Foreign Trade Reports. U.S. Trade with Puerto Rico and U.S. Possessions 256
U.S. Treasury Department. Bureau of Government Financial Operations. Treasury Combined Statement of Receipts, Expenditures and Balances of the United States (US) 300
U.S. Treasury Department. Bureau of the Mint. Annual Report of the Director of the Mint see U.S. Treasury Department. United States Mint. Annual Report of the Director of the Mint 233
U.S. Treasury Department. Combined Statement of Receipts, Expenditures and Balances of the United States Government see U.S. Treasury Department. Bureau of Government Financial Operations. Treasury Combined Statement of Receipts, Expenditures and Balances of the United States 300

U.S. Treasury Department. United States Mint. Annual Report of the Director of the Mint (US) *233*

U.S. Urban Initiatives Anti-Crime Program. Annual Report to Congress(US ISSN 0272-8974) *373*

U.S. Veterans Administration. Annual Report (US ISSN 0083-3533) *642, 813*

U.S. Veterans Administration. Medical Research Program. (US ISSN 0083-355X) *767*

U.S. Veterans Administration. V A Fact Sheets *see* Federal Benefits for Veterans and Dependents, IS-1 Fact Sheet *811*

U.S. Water and Power Resources Service. Annual Report *see* U.S. Bureau of Reclamation. Annual Report *367*

U.S. Water and Power Resources Service. Engineering and Research Center. Research Reports *see* U.S. Bureau of Reclamation. Engineering and Research Center. Research Reports *1126*

U.S. Water and Power Resources Service. Engineering and Research Center. Technical Records of Design and Construction *see* U.S. Bureau of Reclamation. Engineering and Research Center. Technical Records of Design and Construction *484*

U.S. Water and Power Resources Service. Engineering Monograph (US) *491, 1126*

U.S. Waterborne Exports and General Imports *see* Foreign Trade Reports. U.S. Waterborne Exports and General Imports *256*

United States (Year) (US) *1118*

United States & Canadian Mailing Lists(US ISSN 0073-2893) *16*

United States & the World: Foreign Perspectives (US) *919*

United States Animal Health Association. Proceedings of the Annual Meeting (US ISSN 0082-8750) *1122*

United States Catholic Mission and Association. Handbook *see* Mission Handbook *982*

United States Council for International Business. Annual Report (US) *1164*

United States Cross-Country and Distance Running Coaches Association. Proceedings *see* United States Cross-Country Coaches Association. Annual Business Meeting. Minutes *1036*

United States Cross-Country Coaches Association. Annual Business Meeting. Minutes (US) *1036*

United States Cross-Country Coaches Association. Proceedings *see* United States Cross-Country Coaches Association. Annual Business Meeting. Minutes *1036*

United States Earthquakes (US ISSN 0091-1429) *401*

United States Equestrian Team News *see* U S E T News *1043*

United States Fencing Association, Inc. Rule Book: U S & International Rules *see* U S F A Rule Book: U S & International Rules *1036*

United States Foamed Plastic Markets and Directory *see* U S Foamed Plastics Markets and Directory *901*

United States Football League Guide and Register *see* U S F L Guide and Register *1164*

United States Foreign Policy (US ISSN 0270-370X) *910*

United States Government Manual (1973) (US ISSN 0092-1904) *910, 947*

United States Government Organization Manual *see* United States Government Manual (1973) *947*

United States Independent Telephone Association. Annual Statistical Volume *see* United States Telephone Association. Annual Statistical Volume *351*

United States Independent Telephone Association. Holding Company Report *see* United States Telephone Association. Holding Company Report *351*

United States-Israel Binational Science Foundation. Annual Report (IS) *1002*

United States-Israel Binational Science Foundation. Project-Report Abstracts(IS ISSN 0333-5526) *1164*

United States-Italy Trade Directory (US ISSN 0502-5842) *237*

United States Lawn Tennis Association. Yearbook (US ISSN 0083-1557) *1040*

United States Livestock Sanitary Association. Proceedings *see* United States Animal Health Association. Proceedings of the Annual Meeting *1122*

United States Mail Order Industry Annual Report *see* All About Mail Order *282*

United States of America - Tin in Tinplate (UK) *800*

United States Participation in the United Nations (US ISSN 0083-0208) *919*

United States Patents Abstracts. Part 1: Chemical (UK) *861*

United States Patents Report. Part 1: Chemical *see* United States Patents Abstracts. Part 1: Chemical *861*

United States Pharmacopeia *see* United States Pharmacopeia - National Formulary *873*

United States Pharmacopeia - National Formulary (US) *873*

United States Pharmacopeial Convention, Inc. Guide to Select Drugs *see* U S P Guide to Select Drugs *1164*

United States Political Science Documents (US) *910*

United States Polo Association. Yearbook (US ISSN 0083-3118) *1040*

United States Postage Stamps (US) *875*

United States Postal Card Catalog (US ISSN 0276-7244) *614*

United States Squash Racquets Association. Official Year Book (US ISSN 0083-3398) *1040*

United States Stamp Catalogue (UK ISSN 0142-9949) *875*

United States Statutes at Large (US ISSN 0083-3401) *666*

United States Telephone Association. Annual Statistical Volume (US) *351*

United States Telephone Association. Holding Company Report (US) *351*

United States Tennis Association College Tennis Guide *see* U S T A College Tennis Guide *1036*

United States Tobacco and Candy Journal Supplier Directory (US ISSN 0083-3479) *522, 1080*

United States Tobacco Journal Supplier Directory *see* United States Tobacco and Candy Journal Supplier Directory *1080*

United States Trade Show Times (US) *931*

United States Treaties and Other International Agreements (US ISSN 0083-3487) *672*

United States Trotting Association Sires and Dams *see* U S T A Sires and Dams *1043*

United States Trotting Association Year Book *see* U S T A Year Book *1043*

United States Volleyball Association. Official Volleyball Guide and Rule Book (US ISSN 0083-3592) *1040*

United Synagogue Review (US ISSN 0041-8153) *977*

United Way of Canada. Directory of Members (CN) *1021*

Unity-and-Diversity World Directory (US) *882*

Univeritaet Karlsruhe Forschungsberichte *see* W B K Forschungsberichte *475*

Univers de la France et des Pays Francophones (FR) *600*

Univers Historique (FR ISSN 0083-3673) *561, 1002*

Univers Politique; Relations Internationales (CN ISSN 0083-3681) *920*

Universal Business Directories, Adelaide and South Australia Country Trade and Business Directory *see* Universal Business Directories, Adelaide Business and Street Directory *318*

Universal Business Directories, Adelaide Business and Street Directory (AT) *318*

Universal Business Directories, Brisbane and Suburban Business and Street Directory (AT) *318*

Universal Business Directories, Brisbane and Suburban Business and Trade Directory *see* Universal Business Directories, Brisbane and Suburban Business and Street Directory *318*

Universal Business Directories, Melbourne and Suburban Business and Trade Directory (AT ISSN 0083-3746) *318*

Universal Business Directories, Perth and Fremantle and Suburbs Business and Trade Directory (AT ISSN 0083-3789) *318*

Universal Business Directories Pty. Ltd. Register of Industry & Commerce: South Australia *see* U B D Register of Industry & Commerce: South Australia *1164*

Universal Business Directories, Sydney and Suburban Business and Street Directory (AT) *318*

Universal Business Directories, Sydney and Suburban Business and Trade Directory *see* Universal Business Directories, Sydney and Suburban Business and Street Directory *318*

Universal Business Directories, Tasmania Business and Street Directory (AT) *318*

Universal Business Directories, Tasmania Business and Trade Directory *see* Universal Business Directories, Tasmania Business and Street Directory *318*

Universal Business Directories Western Australia Country Business and Trade Directory (AT ISSN 0083-3843) *318*

Universal Esperanto Association. Kongresa Libro *see* Kongresa Libro *697*

Universal Life - The Inner Religion (US) *974*

Universal Military Abstracts (II) *813*

Universal Postal Union. Documents du Congres *see* Union Postale Universelle. Actes *347*

Universal Reference System: Political Science, Government, and Public Policy Series. Annual Supplement *see* Political Science Abstracts *912*

Universalist (II ISSN 0041-8218) *882*

Universidad Autonoma de San Luis Potosi. Instituto de Geologia y Metalurgia. Folleto Tecnico (MX) *396, 800*

Universidad Autonome de Santo Domingo. Comision para el Desarrollo y Reforma Universitarios (DR) *439*

Universidad Boliviana Gabriel Rene Moreno. Revista (BO) *439*

Universidad Boliviana Juan Misael Saracho. Informe de Labores. (BO) *439*

Universidad Catolica de Chile. Facultad de Teologia. Anales (CL ISSN 0069-3596) *983*

Universidad Catolica de Chile. Instituto de Planificacion del Desarrollo Urbano. Documentos de Trabajo *see* Pontificia Universidad Catolica de Chile. Instituto de Estudios Urbanos. Documentos de Trabajo *625*

Universidad Catolica de Valparaiso. Revista de Derecho (CL) *666*

Universidad Catolica de Valparaiso Imagen U.C.V. *see* Imagen U.C.V *1155*

UNIVERSIDAD DE   1917

Universidad Central de Venezuela. Consejo de Desarrollo Cientifico y Humanistico. Bibliografia de Humanidades y Ciencias Sociales y Bibliografia de Ciencia y Tecnologia del Profesorado (VE ISSN 0083-5439) *439*

Universidad Central de Venezuela. Consejo de Desarrollo Cientifico y Humanistico. Catalogo *see* Universidad Central de Venezuela. Consejo de Desarrollo Cientifico y Humanistico. Bibliografia de Humanidades y Ciencias Sociales y Bibliografia de Ciencia y Tecnologia del Profesorado *439*

Universidad Central de Venezuela. Facultad de Agronomia. Revista (VE ISSN 0041-8285) *36*

Universidad Central de Venezuela. Facultad de Agronomia. Revista Alcance (VE) *36*

Universidad Central de Venezuela. Instituto de Ciencias Penales y Criminologicas. Anuario. (VE ISSN 0507-570X) *373*

Universidad de Antioquia. Cuadernos (CK) *891*

Universidad de Antioquia. Debates Nacionales (CK) *1012*

Universidad de Antioquia. Departamento de Historia. Coleccion Papeles de Trabajo (CK) *633*

Universidad de Antioquia. Departamento de Humanidades. Coleccion Papeles de Trabajo *see* Universidad de Antioquia. Departamento de Historia. Coleccion Papeles de Trabajo *633*

Universidad de Barcelona. Biblioteca Central. Catalogos de la Production Editorial Barcelona *see* Diputacio Provincial. Biblioteca Catalunya Cataleg la Produccion Editorial Barcelonesa *964*

Universidad de Barcelona. Biblioteca. Memoria Anual (SP) *685*

Universidad de Barcelona. Facultad de Farmacia. Memoria (SP ISSN 0067-4176) *873*

Universidad de Barcelona. Facultad de Filologia. Anuario *see* Anuario de Filologia *691*

Universidad de Barcelona. Instituto de Arqueologia y Prehistoria. Publicaciones Eventuales (SP ISSN 0067-4184) *94*

Universidad de Bogota Jorge Tadeo Lozano. Museo del Mar. Boletin (CK) *147, 408*

Universidad de Bogota Jorge Tadeo Lozano. Museo del Mar. Informe (CK) *147*

Universidad de Buenos Aires. Catedra de Patologia y Clinica de la Tuberculosis. Anales (AG) *793*

Universidad de Buenos Aires. Instituto Bibliotecologico. Publicacion (AG ISSN 0068-3493) *685*

Universidad de Buenos Aires. Instituto de Arte Americano e Investigaciones Esteticas. Anales (AG) *111*

Universidad de Buenos Aires. Instituto de Economia. Bibliografia sobre Economia Nacional (AG) *13, 219*

Universidad de Buenos Aires. Instituto de Historia Antigua Oriental. Revista(AG ISSN 0325-1209) *613*

Universidad de Buenos Aires. Instituto de Historia Antiguo Oriental. Coleccion Estudios (AG) *613*

Universidad de Chile. Departamento de Astronomia. Publicaciones (CL ISSN 0069-3553) *118*

Universidad de Chile. Departamento de Geologia. Serie Communicaciones (CL ISSN 0069-357X) *381*

Universidad de Chile. Facultad de Ciencias Economicas y Administrativas. Desarrollo (CL) *200*

Universidad de Deusto. Publicaciones. Economia (SP) *200*

Universidad de Deusto. Publicaciones. Filosofia (SP) *882*

Universidad de Granada. Catedra Francisco Suarez. Anales (SP ISSN 0008-7750) *882*

Universidad de Granada. Colleccion Monografica (SP ISSN 0072-5382) *633*
Universidad de Guadalajara. Instituto de Botanica. Boletin Informativo (MX) *162*
Universidad de Guayaquil. Escuela de Diplomacia. Revista (CL) *920*
Universidad de la Habana. Centro de Informacion Cientificas y Tecnica. Ciencias. Serie 9. Antropologia y Prehistoria (CU) *1164*
Universidad de la Laguna. Coleccion Estudios de Historia (SP) *600*
Universidad de la Laguna. Facultad de Ciencias. Anales (SP ISSN 0075-7721) *1002*
Universidad de la Laguna. Facultad de Derecho. Anales (SP ISSN 0075-773X) *666*
Universidad de la Republica. Facultad de Agronomia. Boletin (UY) *36*
Universidad de la Republica. Facultad de Agronomia. Publicacion Miscelanea (UY ISSN 0077-1279) *1165*
Universidad de la Republica. Facultad de Ciencias Economicas y de Administracion. Revista (UY) *200*
Universidad de la Republica. Facultad de Humanidades y Ciencias. Revista. Serie Ciencias *see* Universidad de la Republica. Facultad de Humanidades y Ciencias. Revista. Serie Ciencias Biologicas *148*
Universidad de la Republica. Facultad de Humanidades y Ciencias. Revista. Serie Ciencias Antropologicas (UY ISSN 0250-6564) *77*
Universidad de la Republica. Facultad de Humanidades y Ciencias. Revista. Serie Ciencias Biologicas (UY ISSN 0250-653X) *148*
Universidad de la Republica. Facultad de Humanidades y Ciencias. Revista. Serie Ciencias de la Tierra (UY ISSN 0250-6521) *381*
Universidad de la Republica. Facultad de Humanidades y Ciencias. Revista. Serie Ciencias Exactas (UY) *754*
Universidad de la Republica. Facultad de Humanidades y Ciencias. Revista. Serie Filosofia (UY) *882*
Universidad de la Republica. Facultad de Humanidades y Ciencias. Revista. Serie Historia (UY) *610*
Universidad de la Republica. Facultad de Humanidades y Ciencias. Revista. Serie Linguistica (UY ISSN 0250-6548) *706*
Universidad de la Republica. Facultad de Humanidades y Ciencias. Revista. Serie Letras (UY ISSN 0250-6556) *736*
Universidad de la Republica. Facultad de Humanidades y Ciencias. Revista. Serie Musicologia (UY) *842*
Universidad de la Republica. Facultad de Ingenieria. Boletin (UY) *475*
Universidad de la Republica. Facultad de Ingenieria y Agrimensura. Boletin *see* Universidad de la Republica. Facultad de Ingenieria. Boletin *475*
Universidad de la Republica. Facultad de Odontologia. Anales (UY ISSN 0083-4785) *780*
Universidad de la Republica. Hospital de Clinicas. Informe Estatistico (UY ISSN 0041-8455) *619*
Universidad de la Republica. Instituto de Administracion. Boletin (UY) *282*
Universidad de la Republica. Instituto de Administracion. Cuaderno (UY ISSN 0077-1287) *282*
Universidad de los Andes. Cuadernos de Filosofia y Letras (CK ISSN 0120-0992) *744*
Universidad de los Andes. Cuadernos de Letras *see* Universidad de los Andes. Cuadernos de Filosofia y Letras *744*
Universidad de los Andes. Escuela de Letras. Anuario (VE) *736*
Universidad de los Andes. Facultad de Derecho. Anuario (VE ISSN 0076-6550) *666*

Universidad de Los Andes. Facultad de Derecho. Revista *see* Universidad de los Andes. Facultad de Derecho. Anuario *666*
Universidad de Los Andes. Instituto de Geografia y Conservacion de Recursos Naturales. Cuadernos Geograficos (VE ISSN 0076-6569) *549*
Universidad de los Andes. Instituto de Investigaciones Literarias. Serie Bibliografico *see* Universidad de los Andes. Instituto de Investigaciones Literarias. Serie Ensayo y Critica Literaria *132*
Universidad de los Andes. Instituto de Investigaciones Literarias. Serie Ensayo y Critica Literaria (VE) *132*
Universidad de Madrid. Departamento de Botanica y Fisiologia Vegetal. Trabajos (SP ISSN 0580-468X) *162*
Universidad de Madrid. Seminario de Metafisica. Anales (SP ISSN 0580-8650) *882*
Universidad de Medellin. Revista (CK) *439*
Universidad de Murcia. Anales de Biologia (SP) *148*
Universidad de Murcia. Anales de Biologia. Seccion Biologia Ambiental (SP ISSN 0213-4004) *148*, *500*
Universidad de Murcia. Anales de Biologia. Seccion Biologia Animal (SP ISSN 0213-3997) *178*
Universidad de Murcia. Anales de Biologia. Seccion Biologia General (SP ISSN 0213-5442) *148*
Universidad de Murcia. Anales de Biologia. Seccion Biologia Vegetal (SP ISSN 0213-5450) *162*
Universidad de Murcia. Anales de Biologia. Seccion Especial (SP ISSN 0213-3938) *148*
Universidad de Murcia. Anales de Ciencias (SP ISSN 0213-5469) *1002*
Universidad de Murcia. Anales de Derecho (SP ISSN 0210-539X) *666*
Universidad de Murcia. Anales de Filologia Francesa (SP ISSN 0213-2958) *882*
Universidad de Murcia. Anales de Filologia Hispanica (SP ISSN 0213-4365) *882*
Universidad de Murcia. Anales de Filosofia (SP ISSN 0212-9698) *882*
Universidad de Murcia. Anales de Filosofia y Ciencias de la Educacion (SP) *421*, *883*
Universidad de Murcia. Anales de Historia Contemporanea (SP ISSN 0212-6559) *600*
Universidad de Murcia. Anales de Letras (SP ISSN 0463-9863) *633*
Universidad de Murcia. Anales de Pedagogia (SP ISSN 0212-8322) *421*
Universidad de Murcia. Anales de Prehistoria y Arqueologia (SP) *94*, *600*
Universidad de Murcia. Anales de Psicologia (SP ISSN 0212-9728) *937*
Universidad de Murcia. Anales de Veterinaria (SP ISSN 0213-5434) *1122*
Universidad de Murcia. Catedra de Teatro. Cuadernos (SP) *1079*
Universidad de Murcia. Contrastes: Revista de Historia Moderna (SP ISSN 0213-5477) *600*
Universidad de Murcia. Cuadernos de Filologia Inglesa (SP ISSN 0213-5485) *883*
Universidad de Murcia. Departamento de Derecho Politico. Publicaciones. Serie Monografias (SP) *666*
Universidad de Murcia. Departamento de Geografia. Papeles *see* Universidad de Murcia. Papeles de Geografia *549*
Universidad de Murcia. Didactica Geografica (SP ISSN 0210-492X) *549*
Universidad de Murcia. Estudios Romanicos (SP ISSN 0210-4911) *706*, *736*

Universidad de Murcia. Imafronte. Departamento de Historia del Arte (SP ISSN 0213-392X) *111*, *600*
Universidad de Murcia. Miscelanea Medieval Muriciana (SP ISSN 0210-4903) *600*
Universidad de Murcia. Monteagudo (SP ISSN 0580-6712) *100*
Universidad de Murcia. Papeles de Geografia (SP ISSN 0213-1781) *549*
Universidad de Navarra. Coleccion Bibliografia (SP) *132*
Universidad de Navarra. Coleccion I.L.C.E (SP) *706*
Universidad de Navarra. Coleccion Manuales de Derecho (SP) *666*
Universidad de Navarra. Departamento de Literatura Espanola. Coleccion Publicaciones (SP) *736*
Universidad de Navarra. Documentos Medievales (SP) *600*
Universidad de Navarra. Escuela de Arquitectura. Coleccion de Arquitectura (SP ISSN 0078-8732) *100*
Universidad de Navarra. Escuela de Arquitectura. Manuales: Arquitectura *see* Universidad de Navarra. Escuela de Arquitectura. Coleccion de Arquitectura *100*
Universidad de Navarra. Escuela de Bibliotecarias. Coleccion Bibliotecarias (SP ISSN 0078-8740) *685*
Universidad de Navarra. Escuela de Bibliotecarias. Manuales: Bibliotecarias *see* Universidad de Navarra. Escuela de Bibliotecarias. Coleccion Bibliotecarias *685*
Universidad de Navarra. Facultad de Ciencias de la Educacion. Coleccion (SP) *421*
Universidad de Navarra. Facultad de Ciencias de la Informacion. Coleccion de Trabajo (SP) *646*
Universidad de Navarra. Facultad de Ciencias de la Informacion. Manuales: Periodismo (SP ISSN 0078-8783) *647*
Universidad de Navarra. Facultad de Derecho Canonico. Manuales: Derecho Canonico (SP ISSN 0078-8759) *974*
Universidad de Navarra. Instituto de Ciencias de la Educacion. Coleccion I C E *see* Universidad de Navarra. Facultad de Ciencias de la Educacion. Coleccion *421*
Universidad de Navarra. Instituto de Estudios Superiores de la Empresas. Coleccion I E S E. Serie AC *see* Coleccion la Empresa y Su Entorno. Serie A C *279*
Universidad de Navarra. Instituto de Estudios Superiores de la Empresa. Coleccion I E S E. Serie L *see* Coleccion la Empresa y su Entorno. Serie L *279*
Universidad de Navarra. Manuales: Derecho Notarial Espanol *see* Universidad de Navarra. Coleccion Manuales de Derecho *666*
Universidad de Navarra. Publicaciones de Biologia (SP) *148*
Universidad de Oriente. Instituto Oceanografico Biblioteca. Boletin Bibliografico (VE ISSN 0590-3343) *382*
Universidad de Oriente. Instituto Oceanografico. Cuadernos Oceanograficos (VE ISSN 0590-3351) *408*
Universidad de Oviedo. Centro de Estudios del Siglo XVIII. Boletin (SP) *600*
Universidad de Oviedo. Departamento de Prehistoria y Arqueologia. Publicaciones (SP) *94*
Universidad de Oviedo. Facultad de Medicina. Archivos (SP ISSN 0210-5527) *767*
Universidad de Oviedo. Revista de Biologia (SP ISSN 0212-8977) *148*
Universidad de Panama. Centro de Investigacion Juridica. Anuario (PN) *666*

Universidad de Panama. Centro de Investigacion Juridica. Jurisprudencia Constitutional (PN) *666*
Universidad de Panama. Centro de Investigacion Juridica. Legislacion Panamena. Indices Cronologicos y Analitico de Leyes (o Decretos Ejecutivos) (PN) *666*
Universidad de Panama. Facultad de Derecho y Ciencias Politicas. Cuadernos (PN) *666*, *920*
Universidad de Puerto Rico. Centro de Investigaciones Sociales. Informe Anual (PR) *1030*
Universidad de Puerto Rico. Institute of Caribbean Studies. Special Studies *see* Caribbean Monograph Series *604*
Universidad de San Carlos. Facultad de Ingenieria. Escuela Regional de Ingenieria Sanitaria. Carta Periodica (GT) *957*
Universidad de San Carlos Anual (GT) *633*
Universidad de San Carlos de Guatemala. Facultad de Medicina Veterinaria y Zootecnia Revista (GT) *1122*
Universidad de Sevilla. Instituto de Desarrollo Regional. Ediciones (SP) *250*
Universidad de Sevilla. Instituto Garcia Oviedo. Cuadernos (SP) *200*
Universidad de Sevilla. Instituto Garcia Oviedo. Publicaciones (SP ISSN 0582-8929) *282*, *666*, *947*
Universidad de Sevilla. Seminario de Antropologia Americana. Publicaciones (SP ISSN 0080-9101) *77*
Universidad de Uruguay. Departamento de Literatura Iberoamericana Publicaciones (UY ISSN 0077-1252) *736*
Universidad de Uruguay. Facultad de Agronomia. Boletin (UY ISSN 0077-1260) *36*
Universidad de Uruguay. Instituto de Mathematica y Estadistica. Publicaciones Didacticas (UY ISSN 0077-1295) *1165*
Universidad de Valladolid. Facultad de Medicina. Biblioteca. Boletin de Obras Ingresadas (SP) *1165*
Universidad del Norte. Museo de Arqueologia. Documentos para la Investigacion (CL) *94*
Universidad del Pacifico. Centro de Investigacion. Serie: Coyuntura Economica (PE) *1165*
Universidad del Pacifico. Centro de Investigacion. Serie: Ensayos (PE) *1165*
Universidad del Pacifico. Centro de Investigacion. Serie: Monografias (PE) *1165*
Universidad del Pacifico. Centro de Investigacion. Serie: Trabajos de Investigacion (PE) *1165*
Universidad del Pacifico. Departamento de Ciencias Sociales y Politicas. Serie: Departamentos Academicos (PE) *1165*
Universidad del Salvador. Anales (AG ISSN 0068-3485) *633*
Universidad del Zulia. Facultad de Derecho. Revista (VE) *666*
Universidad del Zulia. Facultad de Medicina. Revista (VE ISSN 0542-6375) *767*
Universidad del Zulia. Revista (VE) *633*
Universidad Hispalense. Anales. Series: Filosofia y Letras, Derecho, Medicina, Ciencias y Veterinaria *see* Anales de la Universidad Hispalense. Serie: Filosofia y Letras *987*
Universidad Industrial de Santander. Boletin de Geologia (CK ISSN 0120-0283) *396*
Universidad Industrial de Santander. Revista *see* Universidad Industrial de Santander. Revista - Investigaciones *475*
Universidad Industrial de Santander. Revista *see* Universidad Industrial de Santander. Revista - Humanidades *633*

Universidad Industrial de Santander. Revista - Humanidades (CK ISSN 0120-095X) 633
Universidad Industrial de Santander. Revista - Investigaciones (CK ISSN 0120-0852) 475, 633, 767
Universidad Industrial de Santander. Revista - Medicina (CK ISSN 0120-0909) 767
Universidad Interamericana de Puerto Rico. Departamento de Ciencias Sociales. Revista Anales (PR) 1012
Universidad Internacional Menendez Pelayo. Publicaciones (SP ISSN 0080-6145) 439
Universidad Javeriana. Facultad de Teologia. Coleccion Profesores (CK) 974
Universidad Mayor Gabriel Rene Moreno. Revista see Universidad Boliviana Gabriel Rene Moreno. Revista 439
Universidad Nacional Agraria. Taller de Estudios Andinos. Serie Andes Centrales (PE) 61
Universidad Nacional Autonoma de Mexico. Anuario de Geografia (MX ISSN 0185-1322) 549
Universidad Nacional Autonoma de Mexico. Centro de Estudios Clasicos. Cuadernos (MX) 339
Universidad Nacional Autonoma de Mexico. Centro de Estudios Mayas. Cuadernos (MX ISSN 0076-7166) 610
Universidad Nacional Autonoma de Mexico. Instituto de Biologia. Anales see Universidad Nacional Autonoma de Mexico. Instituto de Biologia. Anales: Serie Botanica 162
Universidad Nacional Autonoma de Mexico. Instituto de Biologia. Anales see Universidad Nacional Autonoma de Mexico. Instituto de Biologia. Anales: Serie Zoologia 178
Universidad Nacional Autonoma de Mexico. Instituto de Biologia. Anales: Serie Botanica (MX) 162
Universidad Nacional Autonoma de Mexico. Instituto de Biologia. Anales: Serie Zoologia (MX ISSN 0368-8720) 178
Universidad Nacional Autonoma de Mexico. Instituto de Geofisica. Anales (MX ISSN 0076-7182) 1165
Universidad Nacional Autonoma de Mexico. Instituto de Geofisica. Datos Geofisicos a Tablas de Prediccion de Mareas, Puertos del Golfo de Mexico y Mar Caribe (MX) 404
Universidad Nacional Autonoma de Mexico. Instituto de Geofisica. Datos Geofisicos a Tablas de Prediccion de Mareas, Puertos del Oceano Pacifico (MX) 404
Universidad Nacional Autonoma de Mexico. Instituto de Geofisica. Monografias (MX ISSN 0076-7204) 401
Universidad Nacional Autonoma de Mexico. Instituto de Geografia. Anuario de Geografia see Universidad Nacional Autonoma de Mexico. Anuario de Geografia 549
Universidad Nacional Autonoma de Mexico. Instituto de Geografia. Boletin (MX ISSN 0185-1977) 549
Universidad Nacional Autonoma de Mexico. Instituto de Investigaciones Antropologicas. Cuadernos Serie Antropologica see Universidad Nacional Autonoma de Mexico. Instituto de Investigaciones Antropoligicas. Serie Antropologica 77
Universidad Nacional Autonoma de Mexico. Instituto de Investigaciones Antropoligicas. Serie Antropologica (MX ISSN 0076-7298) 77
Universidad Nacional Autonoma de Mexico. Instituto de Investigaciones Bibliograficas. Boletin (MX ISSN 0006-1719) 132
Universidad Nacional Autonoma de Mexico. Instituto de Investigaciones Bibliografica. Instrumenta Bibliographica (MX) 685

Universidad Nacional Autonoma de Mexico. Instituto de Investigaciones Esteticas. Anales (MX ISSN 0076-7239) 111
Universidad Nacional Autonoma de Mexico. Instituto de Investigaciones Esteticas. Monografias de Arte (MX) 111
Universidad Nacional Autonoma de Mexico. Instituto de Investigaciones Esteticas. Monografias. Serie Mayor (MX) 633
Universidad Nacional Autonoma de Mexico. Instituto de Investigaciones Filosoficas. Cuadernos (MX ISSN 0185-2558) 706, 883
Universidad Nacional Autonoma de Mexico. Instituto de Investigaciones Historicas. Cuadernos Serie Documental (MX ISSN 0076-7271) 610
Universidad Nacional Autonoma de Mexico. Instituto de Investigaciones Historicas. Serie Bibliografica (MX ISSN 0076-7301) 610
Universidad Nacional Autonoma de Mexico. Instituto de Investigaciones Historicas. Serie Documental (MX ISSN 0076-731X) 610
Universidad Nacional Autonoma de Mexico. Instituto de Investigaciones Historicas. Serie de Culturas Mesoamericanas (MX ISSN 0076-7328) 610
Universidad Nacional Autonoma de Mexico. Instituto de Investigaciones Historicas. Serie de Cultura Nahuatl. Estudios de Cultura Nahuatl (MX ISSN 0071-1675) 610
Universidad Nacional Autonoma de Mexico. Instituto de Investigaciones Historicas. Serie de Cultura Nahuatl. Fuentes (MX ISSN 0076-7212) 610
Universidad Nacional Autonoma de Mexico. Instituto de Investigaciones Historicas. Serie de Cultura Nahuatl. Monografias (MX ISSN 0076-7344) 610
Universidad Nacional Autonoma de Mexico. Instituto de Investigaciones Historicas. Serie de Historia General (MX ISSN 0076-7352) 610
Universidad Nacional Autonoma de Mexico. Instituto de Investigaciones Historicas. Serie de Historia Novohispana see Estudios de Historia Novohispana 605
Universidad Nacional Autonoma de Mexico. Instituto de Investigaciones Historicas. Serie de Historiadores y Cronistas (MX ISSN 0076-7387) 610
Universidad Nacional Autonoma de Mexico. Instituto de Matematicas. Anales (MX ISSN 0076-7441) 754
Universidad Nacional Autonoma de Mexico. Instituto de Matematicas. Monografias (MX) 754
Universidad Nacional Autonoma de Mexico. Seminario de Investigaciones Bibliotecologica. Publicaciones. Serie B. Bibliografia (MX ISSN 0076-7468) 132
Universidad Nacional Autonoma de Mexico Directorio de Bibliotecas see U N A M Directorio de Bibliotecas 685
Universidad Nacional de Agraria. Taller de Estudios Andinos. Serie Costa Central (PE) 61
Universidad Nacional de Asuncion. Escuela de Bibliotecologia. Informaciones (PY) 685
Universidad Nacional de Asuncion. Instituto de Ciencias. Memoria (PY) 1002
Universidad Nacional de Colombia. Centro de Estudios Folkloricos. Monografias (CK ISSN 0067-9534) 517, 842
Universidad Nacional de Colombia. Direccion de Divulgacion Cultural. Revista (CK ISSN 0502-949X) 1012
Universidad Nacional de Colombia. Facultad Nacional de Minas. Anales (CK ISSN 0120-2561) 821

Universidad Nacional de Cuyo. Biblioteca Central. Boletin Bibliografico (AG ISSN 0076-6399) 132
Universidad Nacional de Cuyo. Biblioteca Central. Cuadernos de la Biblioteca (AG ISSN 0076-6402) 685
Universidad Nacional de la Plata. Instituto de la Produccion. Serie Contribuciones (AG ISSN 0457-1673) 292
Universidad Nacional de Rosario. Facultad de Ciencias, Ingenieria y Arquitectura. Instituto de Fisiografia y Geologia. Publicaciones (AG ISSN 0041-8684) 396, 549
Universidad Nacional de Tucuman. Facultad de Filosofia y Letras. Cuadernos de Humanitas (AG ISSN 0564-4070) 633
Universidad Nacional de Tucuman. Instituto de Ingenieria Electrica. Revista (AG ISSN 0082-6693) 460
Universidad Nacional del Centro del Peru. Anales Cientificos (PE) 439
Universidad Nacional del Centro del Peru. Cuadernos Universitarios. Serie: Estudios Andinos del Centro (PE) 77
Universidad Nacional del Litoral. Facultad de Ciencias de la Administracion. Revista (AG) 947
Universidad Nacional del Litoral. Facultad de Ciencias Economicas Comerciales y Politicas (AG) 201
Universidad Nacional del Litoral. Facultad de Ingenieria Quimica. Revista (AG ISSN 0376-0456) 480
Universidad Nacional del Zulia. Facultad de Humanidades y Educacion. Artes y Letras (VE ISSN 0076-4337) 439
Universidad Nacional del Zulia. Facultad de Humanidades y Educacion. Conferencias y Coloquios(VE ISSN 0076-4345) 633
Universidad Nacional del Zulia. Facultad de Humanidades y Educacion. Fuera de Serie (VE ISSN 0076-4353) 439
Universidad Nacional del Zulia. Facultad de Humanidades y Educacion. Manuales de la Escuela de Educacion (VE ISSN 0076-4361) 439
Universidad Nacional del Zulia. Facultad de Humanidades y Educacion. Monografias y Ensayos (VE ISSN 0076-437X) 440
Universidad Nacional Federico Villareal. Departamento de Ciencias Historico Sociales. Publicaciones (PE) 610
Universidad Nacional Mayor de San Marcos. Facultad de Ciencias Economicas y Comerciales. Revista (PE) 201
Universidad Nacional Mayor de San Marcos. Seminario de Historia Rural Andina. Seminario Arqueologico (PE) 94
Universidad Pedagogica Nacional. Centro de Investigaciones. Boletin Informativo (CK ISSN 0120-2839) 449
Universidad Pontificia Comillas de Madrid. Publicaciones. Serie 1: Estudios (SP) 883, 974
Universidad Tecnica del Estado. Revista(CL) 1012
Universidad Tecnologica del Choco. Revista (CK) 440, 1072
Universidade Catolica de Goias. Gabinete de Arqueologia. Anuario de Divulgacao Cientifica (BL) 94
Universidade de Coimbra. Arquivo. Boletim (PO) 685
Universidade de Coimbra. Departamento de Zoologia. Ciencia Biologica see Ciencia Biologica: Biologia Molecular e Celular 174
Universidade de Coimbra. Faculdade de Direito. Boletim de Ciencias Economicas (PO) 201

Universidade de Coimbra. Museum Zoologico. Memorias e Estudos see Ciencia Biologica: Biologia Molecular e Celular 174
Universidade de Lisboa. Faculdade de Ciencias. Instituto Botanico. Artigo de Divulgacao (PO ISSN 0066-8079) 1002
Universidade de Lisboa. Faculdade de Direito. Revista (PO) 666
Universidade de Sao Paulo. Departamento de Botanica. Boletim de Botanica (BL ISSN 0302-2439) 162
Universidade de Sao Paulo. Departamento de Historia. Boletim (BL) 610
Universidade de Sao Paulo. Faculdade de Ciencias Economicas e Administrativas. Biblioteca. Boletim see Universidade de Sao Paulo. Faculdade de Economia e Administracao. Biblioteca. Boletim 132
Universidade de Sao Paulo. Faculdade de Direito. Revista (BL ISSN 0080-6250) 666
Universidade de Sao Paulo. Faculdade de Economia e Administracao. Biblioteca. Boletim (BL) 132
Universidade de Sao Paulo. Faculdade de Farmacia e Bioquimica. Revista see Universidade de Sao Paulo. Revista de Farmacia e Bioquimica 873
Universidade de Sao Paulo. Faculdade de Filosofia, Letras e Ciencias Humanas. Departamento de Linguistica e Linguas Orientais. Boletim (BL) 854
Universidade de Sao Paulo. Instituto Astronomico e Geofisico. Anuario Astronomico (BL) 118
Universidade de Sao Paulo. Instituto de Estudos Brasileiros. Publicacoes (BL) 77, 517, 549, 1030
Universidade de Sao Paulo. Instituto de Estudos Brasileiros. Revista (BL ISSN 0020-3874) 77, 517, 549, 1030
Universidade de Sao Paulo. Instituto de Geociencias. Boletim (BL) 118, 381
Universidade de Sao Paulo. Instituto de Geociencias y Astronomia. Boletim see Universidade de Sao Paulo. Instituto de Geociencias. Boletim 381
Universidade de Sao Paulo. Instituto de Geografia, Sedimentologia e Pedologia (BL) 396
Universidade de Sao Paulo. Instituto de Pesquisas Economicas. Estatisticas Basicas do Setor Agricola no Brasil (BL) 36, 44
Universidade de Sao Paulo. Instituto Oceanografico. Boletim (BL ISSN 0373-5524) 408
Universidade de Sao Paulo. Instituto Oceanografico. Publicacao Especial (BL ISSN 0100-5146) 408
Universidade de Sao Paulo. Instituto Oceanografico. Relatorio de Cruzeiros (BL ISSN 0100-5197) 408
Universidade de Sao Paulo. Instituto Oceanografico. Relatorio Interno (BL ISSN 0100-5243) 408
Universidade de Sao Paulo. Museu Paulista. Anais (BL ISSN 0080-6374) 610
Universidade de Sao Paulo. Museu Paulista. Colecao. Serie de Arqueologia (BL) 94
Universidade de Sao Paulo. Museu Paulista. Colecao. Serie de Etnologia (BL) 77
Universidade de Sao Paulo. Museu Paulista. Colecao. Serie de Geografia (BL) 549
Universidade de Sao Paulo. Museu Paulista. Colecao. Serie de Historia (BL) 610
Universidade de Sao Paulo. Museu Paulista. Colecao. Serie de Mobiliario(BL) 644, 831
Universidade de Sao Paulo. Museu Paulista. Colecao. Serie de Numismatica (BL) 845

1920 UNIVERSIDADE DE

Universidade de Sao Paulo. Museu Paulista. Revista (BL ISSN 0080-6390) 77

Universidade de Sao Paulo. Revista de Farmacia e Bioquimica (BL) 873

Universidade de Uberlandia. Faculdade de Direito. Revista see Universidade Federal de Uberlandia. Curso de Direito. Revista 666

Universidade do Amazonas. Centro de Pesquisas Socio-Economicas. Boletim Tecnico Informativo (BL) 1012

Universidade do Parana. Departamento de Historia. Boletim (BL ISSN 0070-1815) 561

Universidade do Recife. Faculdade de Odontologia. Anais see Universidade Federal de Pernambuco. Faculdade de Odontologia. Anais 780

Universidade do Recife. Instituto Oceanografico. Trabalhos see Universidade Federal de Pernambuco. Departamento de Oceanografia. Centro de Tecnologia. Trabalhos Oceanograficos 148

Universidade do Rio Grande do Sul. Instituto de Ciencias Naturais. Boletim see Universidade Federal do Rio Grande do Sul. Instituto de Biociencias. Boletim 1002

Universidade Estadual de Campinas. Faculdade de Engenharia de Alimentos e Enpenhoria Agricola. Informativo Annual see Universidade Estadual de Campinas. Faculdade de Tecnologia de Alimentos. Informativo Annual 847

Universidade Estadual de Campinas. Faculdade de Tecnologia de Alimentos. Informativo Annual (BL) 847

Universidade Estadual de Maringa Revista UNIMAR see Revista UNIMAR 438

Universidade Estadual Paulista. Departamento de Educacao. Boletim (BL) 440

Universidade Estadual Paulista. Departamento de Geografia. Boletim (BL) 549

Universidade Federal de Goias. Publicacao (BL) 440

Universidade Federal de Minas Gerais. Corpo Discente. Revista Literaria. (BL ISSN 0079-9327) 736

Universidade Federal de Minas Gerais. Faculdade de Medicina. Anais (BL ISSN 0301-7729) 767

Universidade Federal de Pernambuco. Anuario Estatistico (BL) 443

Universidade Federal de Pernambuco. Departamento de Geologia. Serie B. Estudos e Pesquisas (BL) 381

Universidade Federal de Pernambuco. Departamento de Oceanografia. Centro de Tecnologia. Trabalhos Oceanograficos (BL ISSN 0374-0412) 148

Universidade Federal de Pernambuco. Faculdade de Odontologia. Anais (BL) 780

Universidade Federal de Pernambuco. Instituto de Antibioticos. Revista (BL ISSN 0080-0228) 873

Universidade Federal de Pernambuco. Instituto de Geosciencias. Serie B: Estudos e Pesquisas see Universidade Federal de Pernambuco. Departamento de Geologia. Serie B. Estudos e Pesquisas 381

Universidade Federal de Pernambuco. Instituto Oceanografico. Trabalhos see Universidade Federal de Pernambuco. Departamento de Oceanografia. Centro de Tecnologia. Trabalhos Oceanograficos 148

Universidade Federal de Pernambuco. Jornal (BL) 440

Universidade Federal de Pernambuco. Relatorio des Atividades Universitarias (BL) 440

Universidade Federal de Santa Catarina. Museu de Antropologia. Anais (BL ISSN 0581-6076) 77

Universidade Federal de Uberlandia. Curso de Direito. Revista (BL ISSN 0102-1397) 666

Universidade Federal do Ceara. Departamento de Ciencias Sociais e Filosofia. Documentos (BL ISSN 0041-8870) 1012

Universidade Federal do Ceara. Escola de Agronomia. Departamento de Fitotecnia. Relatoria Tecnico (BL ISSN 0084-8646) 36

Universidade Federal do Ceara. Estacao de Biologia Marinha. Boletim see Boletim de Ciencias do Mar 138

Universidade Federal do Espirito Santo. Comissao de Planejamento. Documentario Estatistico sobre a Situacao Educacional (BL ISSN 0085-0284) 421

Universidade Federal do Espirito Santo. Comissao de Planejamento. Documentario Estatistico sobre a Situacao Educacional. Supplemento (BL ISSN 0085-0292) 421

Universidade Federal do Para. Relatorio Anual (BL) 440

Universidade Federal do Parana. Departamento de Botanica. Boletim see Acta Biologica Paranaense 153

Universidade Federal do Rio de Janeiro. Instituto de Matematica. Estudos e Comunicacoes (BL) 754

Universidade Federal do Rio de Janeiro. Instituto de Matematica. Memorias de Matematica (BL) 755, 1066

Universidade Federal do Rio de Janeiro. Instituto de Matematica. Notas de Matematica Fisica see Universidade Federal do Rio de Janeiro. Instituto de Matematica. Textos de Metodos Matematicos 754

Universidade Federal do Rio de Janeiro. Instituto de Matematica. Textos de Metodos Matematicos (BL) 754

Universidade Federal do Rio Grande do Norte. Centro de Biociencias. Departamento de Oceanografia e Limnologia. Boletim (BL) 404

Universidade Federal do Rio Grande do Norte. Instituto de Biologia Marinha. Boletim see Universidade Federal do Rio Grande do Norte. Centro de Biociencias. Departamento de Oceanografia e Limnologia. Boletim 404

Universidade Federal do Rio Grande do Sul. Faculdade de Agronomia. Boletim Tecnico (BL) 36

Universidade Federal do Rio Grande do Sul. Faculdade de Medicina. Anais (BL ISSN 0085-042X) 767

Universidade Federal do Rio Grande do Sul. Gabinete de Pesquisa de Historia. Boletim (BL) 610

Universidade Federal do Rio Grande do Sul. Instituto Central de Biociencias. Boletim see Universidade Federal do Rio Grande do Sul. Instituto de Biociencias. Boletim 1002

Universidade Federal do Rio Grande do Sul. Instituto de Biociencias. Boletim (BL ISSN 0102-597X) 1002

Universidade Federal do Rio Grande do Sul. Instituto de Filosofia e Ciencias Humanas. Revista (BL ISSN 0302-217X) 1165

Universidade Federal do Rio Grande do Sul. Instituto de Geociencias. Pesquisas (BL) 381

Universita Cattolica. Istituto di Storia Antica. Ricerche (IT ISSN 0393-1412) 339

Universita degli Studi di Bari. Centro Studi Bizantini. Corsi di Studi (IT) 633

Universita degli Studi di Bari. Facolta di Agraria. Annali (IT ISSN 0365-0502) 36

Universita degli Studi di Cagliari. Facolta di Lettere - Filosofia. Annali (IT) 633

Universita degli Studi di Cagliari. Facolta di Magistero. Annali (IT) 633

Universita degli Studi di Cagliari. Istituto di Storia Medioevale. Publicazioni (IT ISSN 0068-4805) 561

Universita degli Studi di Catania. Istituto di Storia delle Tradizioni Popolari. Studi e Testi (IT ISSN 0069-1186) 517

Universita degli Studi di Ferrara. Istituto di Geologia. Annali. Sezione 9. Scienze Geologiche (IT) 396

Universita degli Studi di Ferrara. Istituto di Geologia. Annali. Sezione 15. Paleontologia Umana e Paletnologia (IT) 858

Universita degli Studi di Ferrara. Istituto di Geologia, Paleontologia e Paleontologia Umana. Annali. Sezione 15. Paleontologia Umana e Paleontologia see Universita degli Studi di Ferrara. Istituto di Geologia. Annali. Sezione 15. Paleontologia Umana e Paletnologia 858

Universita degli Studi di Ferrara. Istituto di Geologia, Paleontologia e Paleontologia Umana. Pubblicazioni see Universita degli Studi di Ferrara. Istituto di Geologia. Pubblicazioni 396

Universita degli Studi di Ferrara. Istituto di Geologia. Pubblicazioni (IT) 396, 858

Universita degli Studi di Ferrara. Istituto di Mineralogia. Annali. Nuova Serie. Sezione 17: Scienze Mineralogiche e Petrografiche (IT) 821

Universita degli Studi di Firenze. Facolta di Architettura. Biblioteca. Bollettino di Segnalazioni e Notizie Bibliografiche (IT ISSN 0391-500X) 1165

Universita degli Studi di Firenze. Istituto di Filosofia. Annali (IT) 883

Universita degli Studi di Firenze. Istituto di Statistica. Documentazione(IT ISSN 0041-896X) 628

Universita degli Studi di Genova. Bolletino dei Musei e degli Istituti Biologici (IT ISSN 0085-0950) 148

Universita degli Studi di Genova. Fondazione Nobile Agostino Poggi (Pubblicazioni) (IT) 561

Universita degli Studi di Genova. Istituto di Filologia Classica e Medievale. Pubblicazioni (IT ISSN 0072-0852) 339, 706

Universita degli Studi di Genova. Istituto di Medievistica. Collana. Storica di Fonti e Studi (IT) 600

Universita degli Studi di Genova. Istituto di Paleografia e Storia Medievale. Collana. Storica di Fonti e Studi see Universita degli Studi di Genova. Istituto di Medievistica. Collana. Storica di Fonti e Studi 600

Universita degli Studi di Genova. Istituto di Progettazione Architettonica. Quaderno (IT) 100

Universita degli Studi di Lecce. Bollettino di Storia della Filosofia (IT) 883

Universita degli Studi di Macerata. Facolta di Lettere e Filosofia. Annali(IT ISSN 0076-1818) 94, 339, 561, 706

Universita degli Studi di Milano. Annuario (IT) 440

Universita degli Studi di Napoli. Istituto di Geologia Applicata. Memorie e Note (IT) 396

Universita degli Studi di Padova. Centro per la Storia della Tradizione Aristotelica nel Veneto. Saggi e Testi (IT ISSN 0078-771X) 600

Universita degli Studi di Padova. Facolta di Lettere e Filosofia. Opuscoli Accademici (IT ISSN 0078-7728) 111, 736

Universita degli Studi di Padova. Facolta di Lettere e Filosofia. Pubblicazioni (IT ISSN 0078-7736) 111, 736

Universita degli Studi di Padova. Facolta di Scienze Statistiche, Demografiche ed Attuariali. Serie Estratti (IT) 929

Universita degli Studi di Padova. Facolta di Scienze Statistiche, Demografiche ed Attuariali. Serie Pubblicazioni (IT) 929

Universita degli Studi di Padova. Istituto per la Storia. Contributi (IT ISSN 0078-7752) 440

Universita degli Studi di Padova. Istituto per la Storia. Quaderni (IT ISSN 0078-7760) 440

Universita degli Studi di Padova. Scuola di Perfezionamento in Filosofia. Pubblicazioni (IT ISSN 0078-7779) 883

Universita degli Studi di Padova Istituto di Storia Antica. Pubblicazioni (IT ISSN 0078-7744) 562

Universita degli Studi di Palermo. Istituto di Entomologia Agraria. Bollettino see Phytophaga 58

Universita degli Studi di Parma. Facolta di Economia e Commercio. Studi e Ricerche (IT) 201

Universita degli Studi di Parma. Istituto di Storia dell'Arte. Cataloghi (IT) 111

Universita degli Studi di Parma. Rivista di Matematica (IT ISSN 0035-6298) 754

Universita degli Studi di Pavia. Istituto Botanico. Atti (IT ISSN 0079-0265) 162

Universita degli Studi di Roma. Seminario di Archeologia e Storia dell'Arte Greca e Romana. Studi Miscellanei (IT ISSN 0557-3122) 112

Universita degli Studi di Siena. Facolta di Lettere e Filosofia. Annali (IT) 736, 883

Universita degli Studi di Trieste. Facolta di Scienze Politiche. Pubblicazioni (IT) 910

Universita degli Studi di Trieste. Istituto di Pedagogia. Quaderni (IT ISSN 0082-6480) 421

Universita degli Studi di Trieste. Istituto di Ricerche Economico Agrarie. Pubblicazione (IT) 49

Universita degli Studi di Trieste. Istituto di Storia dell'Arte (Pubblicazioni) (IT ISSN 0564-2477) 112

Universita degli Studi in Italia. Annuario (IT) 431

Universita di Cagliari. Facolta di Lettere - Filosofia e Magistero. Annali see Universita degli Studi di Cagliari. Facolta di Lettere - Filosofia. Annali 633

Universita di Cagliari. Facolta di Lettere-Filosofia e Magistero. Annali see Universita degli Studi di Cagliari. Facolta di Magistero. Annali 633

Universita di Napoli. Facolta di Lettere e Filosofia. Annali (IT) 633

Universita di Sassari. Facolta di Giurisprudenza. Pubblicazioni. Serie Economica (IT) 201

Universita di Torino. Facolta di Agraria. Annali (IT ISSN 0082-6871) 36

Universita e Istituti di Studio e Ricerca in Italia. Annuario DEA (IT ISSN 0393-6368) 539

Universita Karlova. Pedagogicky Fakulta. Sbornik. Historie (CS ISSN 0556-1183) 600

Universita Palackeho. Filosoficka Fakulta. Slavica (CS) 736

Universita Palackeho. Pedagogicka Fakulta. Sbornik Praci: Rusky Jazyk a Literatura (CS) 706, 736

Universita Palackeho Olomouc. Pedagogicka Fakulta. Sbornik Praci. Historie (CS) 600

Universitaet Bonn. Institut fuer Kommunikationsforschung und Phonetik. Forschungsberichte (GW ISSN 0341-3136) 345

Universitaet Bonn. Seminar fuer Orientalische Kunstgeschichte. Veroeffentlichungen. Reihe A. Nimruz (GW) 94

Universitaet Bonn. Seminar fuer Orientalische Kunstgeschichte. Veroeffentlichungen. Reihe B. Antiquitates Orientales (GW) 112

Universitaet Bremen - Schwerpunkt Geographie. Materialien und Manuskripte (GW ISSN 0720-9746) 549

Universitaet des Saarlandes. Geographisches Institut. Arbeiten (GW ISSN 0563-1491) 549

Universitaet des Saarlandes. Jahresbibliographie (GW ISSN 0080-5173) 132

Universitaet Duesseldorf. Jahrbuch (GW ISSN 0070-7457) *440*
Universitaet Frankfurt. Seminar fuer Voelkerkunde. Arbeiten (GW ISSN 0170-3099) *77*
Universitaet Frankfurt. Wissenschaftliche Gesellschaft. Sitzungsberichte (GW ISSN 0512-1523) *1002*
Universitaet Frankfurt am Main. Ostasiatischen Seminars. Veroeffentlichunge (GW ISSN 0340-6652) *854*
Universitaet fuer Bodenkultur in Wien. Dissertationen (AU ISSN 0256-4246) *36, 528*
Universitaet Giessen. Ergebnisse Landwirtschaftlicher Forschung (GW ISSN 0075-4609) *36*
Universitaet Giessen. Matematisches Institut. Vorlesungen (GW) *754*
Universitaet Goettingen. Jahresbericht (GW ISSN 0436-1202) *440*
Universitaet Goettingen. Veroeffentlichungen des Seminars fuer Indologie (GW ISSN 0179-6755) *854*
Universitaet Hamburg. Geologisch-Palaeontologisches Institut. Mitteilungen (GW ISSN 0072-1115) *396, 858*
Universitaet Hamburg. Institut fuer Internationale Angelegenheiten. Veroeffentlichungen (GW ISSN 0341-3233) *920*
Universitaet Hamburg. Institut fuer Internationale Angelegenheiten. Werkhefte (GW ISSN 0341-3241) *672, 920*
Universitaet Hamburg. Institut fuer Meerskunde. Mitteilungen (GW) *408*
Universitaet Hamburg. Mathematisches Seminar. Abhandlungen (GW ISSN 0025-5858) *754*
Universitaet Hamburg. Seminar fuer Allgemeine Betriebswirtschaftlehre. Schriftenreihe (GW) *201*
Universitaet Hamburg. Studien zur angewandtes Wirtschaftsforschung und Oekonometrie (GW) *201*
Universitaet Hannover. Astronomische Station. (Veroeffentlichungen) (GW) *118*
Universitaet Hannover. Institut fuer Siedlungswasserwirtschaft. Veroeffentlichungen (GW) *1126*
Universitaet Hannover. Institut fuer Stahlbau. Schriftenreihe (GW) *490*
Universitaet Hannover. Institut fuer Statik. Mitteilungen (GW) *490*
Universitaet Heidelberg. Suedasien-Institut. Schriftenreihe (GW ISSN 0440-601X) *572*
Universitaet Innsbruck. Alpenkundliche Studien (AU) *396*
Universitaet Innsbruck. Alpin-Biologische Studien (AU) *148*
Universitaet Innsbruck. Finanzwissenschaftliche Studien (AU) *233*
Universitaet Innsbruck. Kunstgeschichtliche Studien (AU) *112*
Universitaet Innsbruck. Mathematische Studien (AU) *754*
Universitaet Innsbruck. Medizinische Fakultaet. Arbeiten (AU ISSN 0579-7772) *767*
Universitaet Innsbruck. Theologische Fakultaet. Studien und Arbeiten (AU ISSN 0579-7780) *974*
Universitaet Kiel. Agrarwissenschaftliche Fakultaet. Schriftenreihe (GW) *36*
Universitaet Kiel. Geographisches Institut. Schriften (GW ISSN 0723-9874) *549*
Universitaet Kiel. Geologisch-Palaeontologisches Institut. Berichte (GW) *396*
Universitaet Muenchen. Geophysikalisches Observatorium, Fuerstenfeldbruck. Veroeffentlichungen. Serie A (GW ISSN 0343-7493) *401*

Universitaet Muenchen. Geophysikalisches Observatorium, Fuerstenfeldbruck. Veroeffentlichungen. Serie B (GW ISSN 0077-2100) *402*
Universitaet Muenchen. Wirtschaftsgeographisches Institut. "W G I"-Berichte zur Regionalforschung (GW ISSN 0077-2127) *550*
Universitaet Muenster. Institut fuer Missionswissenschaft. Veroeffentlichungen (GW ISSN 0077-197X) *974*
Universitaet Muenster. Institut fuer Verkehrswissenschaft. Beitraege (GW) *1098*
Universitaet Salzburg. Dissertationen (AU ISSN 0259-0700) *1002*
Universitaet Stuttgart. Institut fuer Geologie und Palaeontologie Arbeiten Neue Folge (GW ISSN 0585-7856) *381, 858*
Universitaet Stuttgart. Institut fuer Steuerungstechnik der Werkzeugmaschinen und Fertigungseinrichtungen. i S W Berichte (US ISSN 0085-6916) *493, 746*
Universitaet Wien. Dissertationen (AU ISSN 0379-1424) *1002*
Universitaet zu Koeln. Geologisches Institut. Sonderveroeffentlichungen (GW ISSN 0069-5874) *396*
Universitaet zu Koeln. Institut fuer Geophysik und Meteorologie. Mitteilungen (GW ISSN 0069-5882) *402, 807*
Universitaet zu Koeln. Institut fuer Handelsforschung. Mitteilungen. Sonderhefte (GW ISSN 0531-0318) *201*
Universitaet Zu Koeln. Jahrbuch (GW ISSN 0069-5890) *440*
Universitaet zu Koeln. Kunsthistorisches Institut. Abteilung Asien. Publikationen (GW ISSN 0170-3692) *112, 572*
Universitaet Zuerich. Institut fuer Betriebswirtschaftliche Forschung. Schriftenreihe (SZ) *282*
Universitaets- und Landesbibliothek Sachsen-Anhalt. Arbeiten (GE ISSN 0438-4415) *685*
Universitaetsbibliothek Giessen. Berichte und Arbeiten (GW ISSN 0072-4483) *685*
Universitaetsbibliothek Giessen. Kurzberichte aus den Papyrus-Sammlungen (GW ISSN 0072-4491) *339, 562, 854*
Universitas Comeniana. Acta Pharmaceuticae (CS ISSN 0041-9087) *873*
Universitatea "Al. I. Cuza" din Iasi. Analele Stiintifice. Geologie-Geografic (RM ISSN 0379-7902) *396*
Universitatea "Al. I. Cuza" din Iasi. Analele Stiintifice. Sectiunea 3b: Filozofie (RM ISSN 0379-7856) *883*
Universitatea "Al. I. Cuza" din Iasi. Analele Stiintifice. Sectiunea 2b: Geologie see Universitatea "Al. I. Cuza" din Iasi. Analele Stiintifice. Geologie-Geografie *396*
Universitatea "Al. I. Cuza" din Iasi. Analele Stiintifice. Sectiunea 3e: Lingvistica (RM ISSN 0379-7880) *706*
Universitatea "Al. I. Cuza" din Iasi. Analele Stiintifice. Sectiunea 3f. : Literatura (RM ISSN 0379-7899) *736*
Universitatea "Al. I. Cuza" din Iasi. Analele Stiintifice. Sectiunea 3c: Stiinte Economice (RM ISSN 0379-7864) *201*
Universitatea "Al. I. Cuza" din Iasi. Analele Stiintifice. Sectiunea 3b: Stiinte Filozofice see Universitatea "Al. I. Cuza" din Iasi. Analele Stiintifice. Sectiunea 3b: Filozofie *883*
Universitatea "Al. I. Cuza" din Iasi. Analele Stiintifice. Sectiunea 3d: Stiinte Juridice (RM ISSN 0379-7872) *666*

Universitatea "Al. I. Cuza" din Iasi. Analele Stiintifice. Sectiunea 1b: Fizica (RM ISSN 0041-9141) *891*
Universitatea "Al. I. Cuza" din Iasi. Analele Stiintifice. Sectiunea 2a: Biologie (RM ISSN 0041-9133) *148*
Universitatea "Al. I. Cuza" din Iasi. Analele Stiintifice. Sectiunea 3a: Istorie (RM ISSN 0041-9125) *562*
Universitatea Bucuresti. Analele. Filologie (RM) *706*
Universitatea Bucuresti. Analele. Filozofie. Istorie. Drept (RM) *600, 666, 883*
Universitatea Bucuresti. Analele. Stiintele Naturii (RM) *1002*
Universitatea din Brasov. Buletinul. Seria A. Mecanica Aplicata-Constructii de Masini (RM) *493*
Universitatea din Brasov. Buletinul. Seria B. Economia Forestiera (RM) *528*
Universitatea din Brasov. Buletinul. Seria C. Stiinte Ale Naturri si Pedagogie (RM) *148, 754, 891*
Universitatea din Craiova. Anale. Seria: Biologie, Agronomie, Horticultura (RM) *36, 148*
Universitatea din Craiova. Anale. Seria: Matematica, Fizica-Chimie (RM) *325, 754, 891*
Universitatea din Craiova. Analele: Seria Istorie, Geografie, Filologie (RM) *633*
Universitatea din Timisoara. Analele. Stiinte Filologice (RM ISSN 0082-4461) *706*
Universitatea din Timisoara. Facultatea de Stiinte ale Naturii. Lucrarile Seminarului de Geometrie si Topologie (RM) *754*
Universitatea din Timisoara. Facultatea de Stiinte ale Naturii. Seminarul de Teoria Functiilor si Matematici Aplicate. A: Spatii Metrice Probabiliste see Universitatea din Timisoara. Facultatea de Stiinte ale Naturii. Seminarul de Teoria Probabilitatilor si Aplicatii *754*
Universitatea din Timisoara. Facultatea de Stiinte ale Naturii. Seminarul de Teoria Functiilor si Matematici Aplicate. B: Analiza Numerica see Universitatea din Timisoara. Sectia Matematica Informatica. Seminarul de Informatica si Analiza Numerica *754*
Universitatea din Timisoara. Facultatea de Stiinte ale Naturii. Seminarul de Teoria Probabilitatilor si Aplicatii (RM) *754*
Universitatea din Timisoara. Facultatea de Stiinte ale Naturii. Seminarul de Teoria Structurilor (RM) *754*
Universitatea din Timisoara. Sectia Matematica Informatica. Seminarul de Informatica si Analiza Numerica (RM) *754*
Universitatis Debreceniensis de Ludovico Kossuth Nominatae. Instituti Philologiae Slavicae. Annales. Slavica (HU ISSN 0583-5356) *706*
Universitatis Scientiarum Debreceniensis. Acta Classica (HU ISSN 0418-453X) *339*
Universite Catholique de Louvain. Centre d'Etudes Politiques. Working Group "American Foreign Policy." Cahier (BE ISSN 0076-1206) *610, 920*
Universite Catholique de Louvain. Centre International de Dialectologie Generale. Travaux (BE ISSN 0577-1765) *706*
Universite Catholique de Louvain. Ecole des Sciences Politiques et Sociales. Collection. (BE ISSN 0076-1214) *1012*
Universite Catholique de Louvain. Faculte de Philosophie et Lettres. Travaux (BE ISSN 0076-1222) *633*
Universite Catholique de Louvain. Facultes de Theologie et de Droit Canonique. Collection des Dissertations Presentees pour l'Obtention du Grade de Maitre a la Faculte de Theologie Ou a la Faculte de Droit Canonique (BE) *983*

UNIVERSITE D'ANKARA. 1921

Universite Catholique de Louvain. Facultes de Theologie et de Droit Canonique. Dissertationes ad Gradum Magistri in Facultate Theologica Vel in Facultate Iuris Canonici Consequendum Conscriptae see Universite Catholique de Louvain. Facultes de Theologie et de Droit Canonique. Collection des Dissertations Presentees pour l'Obtention du Grade de Maitre a la Faculte de Theologie Ou a la Faculte de Droit Canonique *983*
Universite Catholique de Louvain. Facultes de Theologie et de Droit Canonique. Travaux de Doctorat en Theologie et en Droit Canonique. Nouvelle Serie (BE ISSN 0076-1230) *983*
Universite Catholique de Louvain. Institut de Mathematique Pure et Appliquee. Rapport. see Universite Catholique de Louvain. Institut de Mathematique. Rapport de Mathematique *754*
Universite Catholique de Louvain. Institut de Mathematique. Rapport de Mathematique. (BE) *754*
Universite Catholique de Louvain. Institut de Recherches Economiques, Politiques et Sociales. Publications (BE ISSN 0076-1303) *1012*
Universite Catholique de Louvain. Institut des Langues Vivantes. Cahiers (BE ISSN 0076-1249) *706*
Universite Catholique de Louvain. Institut Orientaliste. Publications (BE ISSN 0076-1265) *572, 854*
Universite Catholique de Louvain. Institut Superieur d'Archeologie et d'Histoire de l'Art. Documents de Travail (BE) *94, 112*
Universite Catholique de Louvain. Institut Superieur d'Archeologie et d'Histoire de l'Art. Publications (BE) *95*
Universite Catholique de Louvain. Institut Superieur de Philosophie. Cours Publies (BE ISSN 0076-1273) *883*
Universite Catholique de Louvain. Recueil de Travaux d'Histoire et de Philologie (BE ISSN 0076-1311) *706*
Universite Catholique de Louvain. Section de Philologie Germanique. Serie Microfiches (BE ISSN 0076-129X) *706*
Universite d'Abidjan. Annales. Serie F: Ethnosociologie see Universite Nationale de Cote d'Ivoire. Annales. Serie F: Ethnosociologie *77*
Universite d'Abidjan. Annales. Serie G: Geographie see Universite Nationale de Cote d'Ivoire. Annales. Serie G: Geographie *550*
Universite d'Aix-Marseille I. Centre d'Etudes des Societes Mediterraneennes. Cahiers (FR ISSN 0065-4949) *1012*
Universite d'Aix-Marseille I. Centre d'Etudes et de Recherches Helleniques. Publications (FR ISSN 0065-4981) *736*
Universite d'Aix-Marseille I. Institut d'Histoire des Pays d'Outre-Mer. Etudes et Documents (FR ISSN 0065-5007) *600*
Universite d'Aix-Marseille 3. Centre des Hautes Etudes Touristiques. Collection "Essais" (FR ISSN 0395-8086) *1118*
Universite d'Aix-Marseille 3. Centre des Hautes Etudes Touristiques. Etudes et Memoires (FR ISSN 0065-4965) *1118*
Universite d'Alger. Observatoire Astronomique. Annales see Observatoire Astronomique d'Alger. Annales *117*
Universite d'Alger. Publications Scientifiques. Serie B: Sciences Physiques (AE ISSN 0002-533X) *1002*
Universite d'Ankara. Faculte des Sciences. Communications Serie C. Biologie (TU ISSN 0256-7865) *148, 162, 178*

Universite d'Ankara. Faculte des Sciences. Communications. Serie C1. Geologie (TU ISSN 0253-1216) *396*

Universite d'Etat. Faculte d'Ethnologie. Centre de Recherches en Sciences Humaines et Sociales. Revue *see* Universite d'Etat. Faculte d'Ethnologie. Revue *1012*

Universite d'Etat. Faculte d'Ethnologie. Revue (HT) *1012*

Universite d'Odense. Etudes Romanes (DK ISSN 0107-7392) *706, 736*

Universite d'Ottawa. Etudes Ukrainiennes *see* University of Ottawa. Ukrainians Studies *600*

Universite d'Ottawa. Publications Medievales *see* University of Ottawa. Medieval Texts and Studies *562*

Universite de Besancon. Annales Litteraires *see* Recherches en Linguistique Etrangere *702*

Universite de Besancon. Centre de Documentation et de Bibliographie Philosophiques. Travaux (FR) *883*

Universite de Bordeaux. Collection Sinologique (FR ISSN 0068-0273) *706*

Universite de Bordeaux II. Cahiers Ethnologiques (FR ISSN 0249-5635) *505, 1030*

Universite de Bordeaux II. Centre d'Etudes et de Rechercers Ethnologiques. Cahiers *see* Universite de Bordeaux II. Cahiers Ethnologiques *1030*

Universite de Bordeaux III. Centre de Recherches sur l'Amerique Anglophone. Annales (FR ISSN 0399-0443) *610, 910*

Universite de Brazzaville. Annales (CF ISSN 0302-4814) *440*

Universite de Bretagne Occidentale. Guide de l'Etudiant (FR) *421*

Universite de Clermont-Ferrand II. Annales Scientifiques. Serie Biologie Animale (FR ISSN 0069-4681) *178*

Universite de Clermont-Ferrand II. Annales Scientifiques. Serie Biologie Vegetale (FR ISSN 0069-469X) *162*

Universite de Clermont-Ferrand II. Annales Scientifiques. Serie Chemie (FR ISSN 0069-4703) *325*

Universite de Clermont-Ferrand II. Annales Scientifiques. Serie Geologie et Mineralogie (FR ISSN 0069-4711) *396, 821*

Universite de Clermont-Ferrand II. Annales Scientifiques. Serie Physiologie Animale (FR ISSN 0069-4746) *178*

Universite de Clermont-Ferrand II. Annales Scientifiques. Serie Physique (FR ISSN 0069-4738) *891*

Universite de Clermont-Ferrand 2. Annales Scientifiques. Serie Mathematique (FR ISSN 0069-472X) *754*

Universite de Dakar. Faculte des Lettres et Sciences Humaines. Annales (FR) *736, 1012*

Universite de Droit, Economie et de Sciences Sociales de Paris. Travaux du Seminaire de recherches sur les Faits Electoraux de Monsieur le Professeur Robert Villers (FR) *666, 1012*

Universite de Fribourg. Historische Schriften (SZ) *600*

Universite de Geneve. Departement d'Histoire Economique. Bulletin (SZ) *440*

Universite de Geneve. Section d'Histoire. Documents (SZ ISSN 0072-0836) *600*

Universite de Grenoble. Institut de Phonetique. Manuels. Serie A *see* Universite de Grenoble III. Institut de Phonetique. Travaux: Serie A: Manuals *706*

Universite de Grenoble III. Institut de Phonetique. Bulletin (FR) *706*

Universite de Grenoble III. Institut de Phonetique. Travaux: Serie A: Manuals (FR) *706*

Universite de Grenoble III. Institut de Phonetique. Travaux. Serie B: Etudes Linguistiques (FR ISSN 0085-1272) *706*

Universite de Haute Bretagne. Centre d'Etudes Anglo-Irlandaises. Cahier *see* Universite de Haute Bretagne. Centre d'Etudes Irlandaises. Cahier *736*

Universite de Haute Bretagne. Centre d'Etudes Hispaniques, Hispano-Americanes et Luso-Bresiliennes. Travaux *see* Mondes Hispanophone et Lusophone *727*

Universite de Haute Bretagne. Centre d'Etudes Irlandaises. Cahier (FR ISSN 0181-561X) *736*

Universite de l'Etat a Gand. Service de Linguistique Francaise. Travaux de Linguistique *see* Travaux de Linguistique *706*

Universite de la Reunion. Cahier (RE ISSN 0337-6176) *449, 706*

Universite de Lausanne. Faculte des Lettres. Publications (SZ ISSN 0041-915X) *736*

Universite de Liege. Faculte de Philosophie et Lettres. Publications (BE) *633*

Universite de Lille III. Lexique (FR ISSN 0756-7138) *706*

Universite de Lubumbashi. Centre de Linguistique Theorique et Appliquee Africanistique (ZR) *706*

Universite de Lubumbashi. Centre de Linguistique Theorique et Appliquee. Bulletin de Liaison, Enseignment des Langues (ZR) *706*

Universite de Lubumbashi. Centre de Linguistique Theorique et Appliquee. Linguistique et Sciences Humaines. Bulletin d'Information (ZR) *706*

Universite de Lyon III. Faculte de Droit. Annales *see* Universite Jean Moulin. Annales *666*

Universite de Madagascar. Etablissement d'Enseignement Superieur des Sciences. Annales: Serie Sciences de la Nature et Mathematiques (MG) *754, 1002*

Universite de Madagascar. Musee d'Art et d'Archeologie. Travaux et Documents (MG) *95, 112*

Universite de Montreal. Faculte de Medecine Veterinaire. Annuaire (CN ISSN 0383-8455) *1122*

Universite de Nancy II. Centre de Recherches et d'Applications Pedagogiques en Langues. Melanges (FR ISSN 0077-2712) *449, 707*

Universite de Nantes. Centre de Recherches sur l'Histoire de la France Atlantique. Enquetes et Documents *see* Universite de Nantes. Centre de Recherches sur l'Histoire du Monde Atlantique. Enquetes et Documents *600*

Universite de Nantes. Centre de Recherches sur l'Histoire du Monde Atlantique. Enquetes et Documents (FR) *600*

Universite de Neuchatel. Annales (SZ) *440*

Universite de Neuchatel. Centre d'Hydrogeologie. Bulletin (SZ) *404*

Universite de Neuchatel. Faculte des Lettres. Recueil de Travaux (SZ ISSN 0077-7633) *736*

Universite de Neuchatel. Seminaire de Geometrie. Publications. Serie 1. Courtes Publications *see* Centre de Recherches en Mathematiques Pures. Publications. Serie 1. Courtes Publications *748*

Universite de Neuchatel. Seminaire de Geometrie. Publications. Serie 2. Monographies *see* Centre de Recherches en Mathematiques Pures. Publications. Serie 2. Monographies *748*

Universite de Paris. Faculte des Lettres et Sciences Humaines. Publications. Serie Acta (FR ISSN 0078-9887) *633, 1002*

Universite de Paris. Faculte des Lettres et Sciences Humaines. Publications. Serie Recherches (FR ISSN 0078-9895) *1012*

Universite de Paris VII. Groupe de Linguistique Japonaise. Travaux *see* Travaux de Linguistique Japonaise *706*

Universite de Poitiers. Centre d'Etudes Superieures de Civilisation Medievale. Publications (FR ISSN 0079-256X) *600*

Universite de Provence. Centre d'Aix. Cahiers d'Etudes Germaniques (FR ISSN 0751-4239) *633*

Universite de Saint Etienne. Centre Jean Palerne. Memoires (FR ISSN 0223-9469) *633*

Universite de Sherbrooke. Department de Geographie. Bulletin de Recherche (CN ISSN 0710-0868) *381, 550*

Universite de Sherbrooke. I R E C U S. Cahiers de la Cooperation (Institut de Recherche et d'Enseignement pour les Cooperatives) (CN) *239*

Universite de Sherbrooke. I R E C U S. Dossiers sur les Cooperatives (Institut de Recherche et d'Enseignement pour les Cooperatives) (CN) *239*

Universite de Sherbrooke. Revue de Droit (CN ISSN 0317-9656) *666*

Universite de Skopje. Faculte des Sciences Economique. Annuaire *see* Univerzitet vo Skoplje. Ekonomskiot Fakultet. Godisnik *202*

Universite de Sofia. Faculte d'Histoire. Annuaire *see* Sofiiski Universitet. Istoricheski Fakultet. Godishnik *561*

Universite de Sofia. Faculte de Philosophie. Annuaire *see* Sofiiski Universitet. Filosofski Fakultet. Godisnik *597*

Universite de Sofia. Faculte des Lettres Classiques et Modernes. Annuaire *see* Sofiiski Universitet. Fakultet po Klasiceski i Novi Filologii. Godisnik *704*

Universite de Sofia. Faculte des Mathematiques et de Mecanique. Annuaire *see* Sofiiski Universitet. Fakultet po Matematika i Mekhanika. Godishnik *753*

Universite de Strasbourg II. Centre de Philologie et Litteratures Romanes. Actes et Colloques (FR ISSN 0081-5918) *707, 736*

Universite de Strasbourg II. Institut de Phonetique. Travaux (FR ISSN 0081-5934) *633, 707, 736*

Universite de Toulouse II (le Mirail). Institut d'Art Prehistorique. Travaux (FR ISSN 0563-9794) *95, 112*

Universite de Tunis. Ecole Normale Superieure. Section A: Lettres et Sciences Humaines. Serie 1: Langue et Litterature (TI) *707, 736*

Universite de Yaounde. Faculte de Droit et des Sciences Economiques. Economie Generale (CM) *252*

Universite de Yaounde. Faculte des Sciences. Annales (CM ISSN 0566-201X) *1002*

Universite degli Studi di Ferrara. Istituto di Geologia, Paleontologia e Paleontologia Umana. Annali. Sezione 9. Scienze Geologiche *see* Universita degli Studi di Ferrara. Istituto di Geologia. Annali. Sezione 9. Scienze Geologiche *396*

Universite des Sciences Sociales de Toulouse. Annales (FR ISSN 0563-9727) *1013*

Universite du Quebec (Province). Rapport Annuel (CN) *440*

Universite du Quebec. Statistiques (CN) *1165*

Universite Federale du Cameroun. Faculte des Sciences. Annales *see* Universite de Yaounde. Faculte des Sciences. Annales *1002*

Universite Jean Moulin. Annales (FR) *666*

Universite Laval. Archives de Folklore (CN ISSN 0085-5243) *517*

Universite Laval. Centre d'Etudes Nordiques. Travaux et Documents (CN ISSN 0079-8347) *610*

Universite Laval. Centre de Recherches sur les Atomes et les Molecules. Rapport Annuel (CN) *325, 898*

Universite Laval. Departement d'Exploitation et Utilisation des Bois. Note de Recherches (CN ISSN 0079-8355) *530*

Universite Laval. Departement d'Exploitation et Utilisation des Bois. Note Technique (CN ISSN 0079-8363) *530*

Universite Laval. Departement de Geographie. Travaux (CN) *550*

Universite Laval. Fonds de Recherches Forestieres. Bulletin (CN ISSN 0041-9214) *1165*

Universite Laval. Fonds de Recherches Forestieres. Contribution (CN ISSN 0079-838X) *1165*

Universite Laval. Institut d'Histoire. Cahiers *see* Universite Laval. Les Cahiers d'Histoire *562*

Universite Laval. Les Cahiers d'Histoire(CN) *562*

Universite Libre de Bruxelles. Faculte de Philosophie et Lettres. Travaux (BE) *633*

Universite Libre de Bruxelles. Groupe d'Etude du Dix-Huitieme Siecle. Etudes sur le Dix-Huitieme Siecle (BE) *600*

Universite Libre de Bruxelles. Institut de Philologie et d'Histoire Orientales et Slaves. Annuaire (BE) *854*

Universite Libre de Bruxelles. Institut de Philosophie. Annales (BE ISSN 0771-4963) *883*

Universite Libre de Bruxelles. Institut de Sociologie. Annales (BE ISSN 0771-5323) *1165*

Universite Libre de Bruxelles. Institut de Sociologie. Cahiers (BE ISSN 0068-2985) *1165*

Universite Libre de Bruxelles. Institut pour l'Etude de la Renaissance et de l'Humanisme. Colloques (BE) *600*

Universite National de Zaire, Lumbumbashi. Centre de Linguistique Theorique et Applique. Bulletin de Liaison, Enseignement des Langues *see* Universite de Lubumbashi. Centre de Linguistique Theorique et Appliquee. Bulletin de Liaison, Enseignment des Langues *706*

Universite Nationale de Cote d'Ivoire. Annales. Serie F: Ethnosociologie (IV) *77, 1030*

Universite Nationale de Cote d'Ivoire. Annales. Serie G: Geographie (IV) *550*

Universite Nationale du Zaire, Kinshasa. Faculte de Droit. Annales (ZR) *666*

Universite Nationale du Zaire, Lubumbashi. Centre de Linguistique Theorique et Appliquee Africanistique *see* Universite de Lubumbashi. Centre de Linguistique Theorique et Appliquee Africanistique *706*

Universite Nationale du Zaire, Lubumbashi. Centre de Linguistique Theorique et Appliquee. Linguistique et Sciences Humaines. Bulletin d'Information *see* Universite de Lubumbashi. Centre de Linguistique Theorique et Appliquee. Linguistique et Sciences Humaines. Bulletin d'Information *706*

Universite Saint-Joseph. Faculte des Lettres et des Sciences Humaines. Recherche. Serie A: Langue Arabe et Pensee Islamique (LE) *707, 976*

Universite Saint-Joseph. Faculte des Lettres et des Sciences Humaines. Recherche. Serie B: Orient Chretien (LE) *854, 974*

Universite Scientifique et Medical de Grenoble. Institut des Sciences Nucleaires. Rapport Annuel *see* Institut des Sciences Nucleaires Grenoble. Rapport *896*

Universite Scientifique et Medicale de Grenoble. Institut Fourier. Annales (FR ISSN 0373-0956) *754*

Universiteit van Amsterdam. Fysisch Geografisch en Bodemkundig Laboratorium. Publikaties (NE ISSN 0066-1317) *550*

Universiteit van Amsterdam. Instituut voor Algemene Taalwetenschap. Publikaties (NE) *707*
Universiteit van Amsterdam. Mathematisch Instituut. Report (NE) *754*
Universiteit van Amsterdam. Zoologisch Museum. Bulletin (NE ISSN 0066-1325) *178*
Universiteit van Durban-Westville. Tydskrif see University of Durban-Westville. Journal *633*
Universiteit van Port Elizabeth. Instituut vir Beplanningsnavorsing. Feitestuk Reeks see University of Port Elizabeth. Institute for Planning Research. Fact Paper Series *250*
Universiteit van Port Elizabeth. Instituut vir Beplanningsnavorsing. Inligtingsbulletin Reeks see University of Port Elizabeth. Institute for Planning Research. Information Bulletin Series *250*
Universiteit van Port Elizabeth. Instituut vir Beplanningsnavorsing. Jaarverslag see University of Port Elizabeth. Institute for Planning Research. Annual Report *278*
Universiteit van Pretoria. Biblioteekdiens. Verslagreeks (SA ISSN 0379-7104) *685*
Universiteit van Pretoria. Jaarverslag see University of Pretoria. Annual Report *342*
Universitet i Oslo. Pedagogisk Forskningsinstitutt. Rapport (NO ISSN 0800-6113) *421*
Universitet i Trondheim. Norges Tekniske Hoegskole. Vassdrags-og Havnelaboratoriet. Meddlelelse see Norwegian Hydrotechnical Laboratory. Bulletin *490*
Universitetet i Oslo. Slavisk-Baltisk Institutt. Meddelelser (NO) *707, 736*
Universitetet i Trondheim. Biblioteket. Avdeling B. Rapport (NO) *685*
Universitetet i Trondheim. Norges Tekniske Hoegskole. Institutt for Uorganisk Kjemi. Avhandling (NO) *329*
Universitetets Statistiske Institut. Computer Programmes (DK ISSN 0107-9352) *358*
Universitetets Statistiske Institut. Research Report (DK ISSN 0105-9645) *1066*
Universitets Oldsaksamling. Aarbok (NO) *95, 600*
Universitexts (US ISSN 0172-5939) *475, 754, 891*
Universiti Kebangsaan Malaysia. Laporau Tahunan/Annual Report (MY) *421*
Universiti Malaya. Fakulti Kejuruteraan. Jernal see University of Malaya. Faculty of Engineering. Journal *475*
University Associates, Inc. Annual (US) *1030*
University Bristol Calendar (UK) *440*
University College Hospital Magazine see Too Much - University College Hospital Magazine *618*
University College Literary Review see U.C. Review *736*
University College London Calendar (UK) *440*
University College of Swansea. Centre for Development Studies. Monograph Series (UK ISSN 0144-9486) *1165*
University College of Swansea. Centre for Development Studies. Occasional Papers Series (UK ISSN 0144-9494) *1165*
University College of Swaziland. Agricultural Research Division. Annual Report (SQ) *36*
University Computing and Information Services Newsletter (CN ISSN 0829-5425) *353*
University du Benin. Annales. Serie Science (TG) *148*
University Education in Nigeria (NR) *440*
University Folk (UK) *842*
University Folklore Association. Folklore Papers (US) *517*
University Geographer (NR ISSN 0083-3975) *550*

University/Government/Industry Microelectronics Symposium. Proceedings (US) *460*
University Library Expenditure Statistics (UK ISSN 0268-3539) *688*
University Microfilms International Newsletter (US) *1, 132, 688, 964*
University of Aberdeen. African Studies Group. Bulletin (UK ISSN 0001-3196) *506, 567*
University of Aberdeen. African Studies Group. Occasional Publications (UK) *506, 567*
University of Aberdeen. Department of Forestry. Economic Survey of Private Forestry (UK ISSN 0065-0277) *528*
University of Addis Ababa. Institute of Ethiopian Studies. Ethiopian Publications see Ethiopian Publications: Books, Pamphlets, Annuals and Periodical Articles *126*
University of Agricultural Sciences. Report (SW ISSN 0347-9706) *63, 68*
University of Agricultural Sciences, Bangalore. Annual Report (II ISSN 0067-3455) *36*
University of Agricultural Sciences, Bangalore. Collaborative Series (II) *36*
University of Agricultural Sciences, Bangalore. Educational Series (II) *36*
University of Agricultural Sciences, Bangalore. Information Series (II) *36*
University of Agricultural Sciences, Bangalore. Research Monograph Series (II) *36*
University of Agricultural Sciences, Bangalore. Research Review Series (II) *36*
University of Agricultural Sciences, Bangalore. Technical Information Series (II) *36*
University of Agricultural Sciences, Bangalore. Technical Series (II) *36*
University of Agricultural Sciences, Bangalore. U A S Textbook Series (II) *36*
University of Agricultural Sciences, Bangalore Extension Series see U A S Extension Series *35*
University of Agricultural Sciences, Bangalore Miscellaneous Series see U A S Miscellaneous Series *35*
University of Alaska. Biological Papers (US ISSN 0568-8604) *148*
University of Alaska. Biological Papers. Special Reports (US ISSN 0161-3243) *148*
University of Alaska. Cooperative Extension Service. Local Government Hi-Lites (US) *952*
University of Alaska. Geophysical Institute. Report Series (US ISSN 0041-9362) *402, 807*
University of Alaska. Institute of Marine Science. Occasional Publication (US ISSN 0084-6147) *148*
University of Alaska. Institute of Marine Science. Technical Report (US ISSN 0065-5929) *148*
University of Alaska. Institute of Northern Engineering (US) *1126*
University of Alaska. Institute of Social and Economic Research. Research Summary (US) *201, 1030*
University of Alaska. Institute of Water Resources-Engineering Experiment Station. Annual Report see University of Alaska. Institute of Northern Engineering *1126*
University of Alaska. Mineral Industry Research Laboratory. Report (US ISSN 0065-5961) *821*
University of Alaska Museum. Annual Report (US ISSN 0093-7436) *831*
University of Alberta. Centre for Criminological Research. Discussion Papers (CN ISSN 0824-5134) *373*
University of Alberta. Department of Agricultural and Rural Sociology. Technical Bulletin see University of Alberta. Department of Rural Economy. Bulletin *50*

University of Alberta. Department of Agricultural Economics and Rural Sociology. Bulletin see University of Alberta. Department of Rural Economy. Bulletin *50*
University of Alberta. Department of Agricultural Economics and Rural Sociology. Research Bulletin see University of Alberta. Department of Rural Economy. Bulletin *50*
University of Alberta. Department of Animal Science. Annual Feeders' Day Report (CN ISSN 0084-618X) *68*
University of Alberta. Department of Chemistry. Division of Theoretical Chemistry. Technical Report (CN ISSN 0041-9370) *333*
University of Alberta. Department of Computing Science. Publication see University of Alberta. Department of Computing Science. Technical Reports *353*
University of Alberta. Department of Computing Science. Technical Reports (CN ISSN 0316-4683) *353*
University of Alberta. Department of Rural Economy. Bulletin (CN) *50*
University of Alberta. Nuclear Research Centre. Progress Report (CN) *898*
University of Alberta. Studies in Geography. Monographs (CN) *550*
University of Allahabad. Education Department. Researches and Studies (II ISSN 0084-621X) *421*
University of Arizona. College of Engineering. E E S Series Report (Engineering Experiment Station) (US) *475*
University of Arizona Library. Bibliographic Bulletin (US ISSN 0044-8877) *132*
University of Arkansas. Industrial Research and Extension Center. Annual Report (US ISSN 0518-6544) *292*
University of Arkansas. Lecture Notes in the Mathematical Sciences (US) *754*
University of Auckland. Department of Geography. Occasional Papers see University of Auckland. Department of Geography. Occasional Publication *550*
University of Auckland. Department of Geography. Occasional Publication (NZ ISSN 0112-1545) *550*
University of Auckland. Department of Mathematics. Report Series (NZ ISSN 0110-4152) *754*
University of Auckland. Department of Sociology. Papers in Comparative Sociology (NZ) *1030*
University of Auckland. Library. Bibliographical Bulletin (NZ ISSN 0067-0499) *132*
University of Auckland Historical Society. Annual (NZ ISSN 0067-0480) *573*
University of Baghdad. Biological Research Centre. Bulletin (IQ ISSN 0067-2890) *148*
University of Belgrade. Faculty of Sciences. Department of Astronomy. Publications (YU ISSN 0350-3283) *118*
University of Benin. Library. Annual Report (NR) *685*
University of Bergen. Department of Applied Mathematics. Report (NO ISSN 0084-778X) *754*
University of Bergen. Institute of Psychology. Psychological Report Series (NO ISSN 0333-4325) *937*
University of Bergen. Institute of Psychology. Report see University of Bergen. Institute of Psychology. Psychological Report Series *937*
University of Birmingham. Centre for Urban and Regional Studies. Occasional Papers (UK ISSN 0067-8953) *626, 1030*
University of Birmingham. Centre for Urban and Regional Studies. Research Memorandum (UK ISSN 0306-4034) *626, 1030*

University of Birmingham. Centre for Urban and Regional Studies. Urban and Regional Studies (UK ISSN 0067-8961) *626, 1030*
University of Birmingham. Centre for Urban and Regional Studies. Working Paper (UK) *626, 1030*
University of Botswana, Lesotho and Swaziland. Agricultural Research Division. Annual Report see University College of Swaziland. Agricultural Research Division. Annual Report *36*
University of British Columbia. Center for Continuing Education. Monographs on Comparative and Area Studies in Adult Education (CN) *427*
University of British Columbia. Center for Continuing Education. Occasional Papers in Continuing Education (CN ISSN 0068-1695) *427*
University of British Columbia. Department of Civil Engineering. Soil Mechanics Series (CN ISSN 0068-1709) *484*
University of British Columbia. Department of Civil Engineering. Structural Research Series (CN) *484*
University of British Columbia. Department of Civil Engineering. Transportation Research Series (CN) *484*
University of British Columbia. Department of Civil Engineering. Water Resources Research Series (CN) *484*
University of British Columbia. Department of Economics. Discussion Paper (CN) *201*
University of British Columbia. Department of Economics. Resources Paper (CN ISSN 0381-0410) *201*
University of British Columbia. Department of Geological Sciences. Report (CN) *396*
University of British Columbia. Department of Geology. Report see University of British Columbia. Department of Geological Sciences. Report *396*
University of British Columbia. Department of Geophysics and Astronomy. Annual Report (CN ISSN 0068-1725) *118, 402*
University of British Columbia. Research Forest Annual Report (CN ISSN 0084-8069) *528*
University of British Columbia. School of Community and Regional Planning. Occasional Papers see U B C Planning Papers *626*
University of British Columbia. School of Community and Regional Planning. Planning Papers see U B C Planning Papers *626*
University of British Columbia, Physics Society. Journal (CN) *118, 891*
University of British Columbia Planning Papers see U B C Planning Papers *626*
University of Cairo. Herbarium. Publications (UA ISSN 0068-5313) *162*
University of Calcutta. Centre of Advanced Study in Ancient Indian History and Culture. Lectures (II ISSN 0068-5380) *572*
University of Calcutta. Centre of Advanced Study in Ancient Indian History and Culture. Proceedings of Seminars (II ISSN 0068-5399) *572*
University of Calcutta. Department of Philosophy. Journal (II) *883*
University of Calgary. Archaeological Association. Archaeological Conference. Proceedings (CN) *95, 500*
University of Calgary. Archaeological Association. Paleo-Environmental Workshop. Proceedings see University of Calgary. Archaeological Association. Archaeological Conference. Proceedings *95*
University of Calgary. Department of Civil Engineering Research Report (CN) *484*

1924 UNIVERSITY OF

University of Calgary. Department of Mathematics and Computing Science. Research Papers *see* University of Calgary. Department of Mathematics and Statistics. Research Papers *754*
University of Calgary. Department of Mathematics and Statistics. Research Papers (CN) *754*
University of California. Center for South and Southeast Asia Studies. Occasional Papers (US ISSN 0068-600X) *572*
University of California. Center for South and Southeast Asia Studies. Research Monograph Series (US ISSN 0068-6018) *572*
University of California. Institute of Business and Economic Research. Publications (US ISSN 0068-6077) *201*
University of California. Lawrence Berkeley Laboratory. Biology and Medicine Division. Annual Report (US ISSN 0272-9075) *152,* 767
University of California, Berkeley. Archaeological Research Facility. Contributions (US ISSN 0068-5933) *95*
University of California, Berkeley. Campus Statistics (US) *440*
University of California, Berkeley. Center for Real Estate and Urban Economics. Research Report *see* University of California, Berkeley. Center for Real Estate and Urban Economics. Working Paper *966*
University of California, Berkeley. Center for Real Estate and Urban Economics. Reprint Series (US ISSN 0068-5968) *966*
University of California, Berkeley. Center for Real Estate and Urban Economics. Working Paper (US) *966*
University of California, Berkeley. Institute of International Studies. Policy Papers in International Affairs(US ISSN 0731-6321) *920*
University of California, Berkeley. Institute of International Studies. Research Series (US ISSN 0068-6093) 252, *910,* 1030
University of California, Berkeley. Institute of Transportation Studies. Library References (US ISSN 0068-6115) *1084*
University of California, Berkeley. Language Behavior Research Laboratory. Working Paper Series. (US) 77, *707*
University of California, Berkeley. Office of Institutional Research. Campus Statistics *see* University of California, Berkeley. Campus Statistics *440*
University of California, Davis. Game Bird Workshop. Proceedings (US) *171*
University of California, Davis. Water Resources Center. Contributions (US ISSN 0068-6301) *1126*
University of California, Los Angeles. Center for Medieval and Renaissance Studies. Contributions (US ISSN 0068-6239) *562*
University of California, Los Angeles. Center for Medieval and Renaissance Studies. Publications (US ISSN 0068-6220) *562*
University of California, Los Angeles. Center for the Study of Comparative Folklore and Mythology. Publications(US ISSN 0068-6247) *517*
University of California, Los Angeles. Chicano Studies Center. Monographs *see* University of California, Los Angeles. Chicano Studies Research Center. Monographs *610*
University of California, Los Angeles. Chicano Studies Research Center. Monographs (US) *610*
University of California, Los Angeles. Institute of Archaeology. Archaeological Survey. Special Monograph Series *see* University of California, Los Angeles. Institute of Archaeology. Monograph Series *95*
University of California, Los Angeles. Institute of Archaeology. Monograph Series (US) *95*
University of California, Los Angeles. Institute of Archaeology. Occasional Papers (US) *95*
University of California, Los Angeles. Institute of Industrial Relations. Monograph and Research Series (US ISSN 0739-439X) *276*
University of California, Los Angeles. Institute of Industrial Relations. Monograph Series *see* University of California, Los Angeles. Institute of Industrial Relations. Monograph and Research Series *276*
University of California, Los Angeles. Latin American Center. Latin American Studies Series (US ISSN 0075-8132) *610*
University of California, Los Angeles. Latin American Center. Reference Series (US ISSN 0068-6263) *610*
University of California, Los Angeles. Museum of Cultural History. Occasional Papers (US ISSN 0068-628X) *112*
University of California, Los Angeles Business Forecast for the Nation and California *see* U C L A Business Forecast for the Nation and California *200*
University of California, Los Angeles Forum in Medical Sciences *see* U C L A Forum in Medical Sciences *767*
University of California, Los Angeles Historical Journal *see* U C L A Historical Journal *561*
University of California, Los Angeles Journal of Dance Ethnology *see* U.C.L.A. Journal of Dance Ethnology *375*
University of California, Los Angeles Latin American Center. Special Studies Series *see* U C L A Latin American Center. Special Studies Series *610*
University of California, Los Angeles Music Library Bibliography Series *see* U C L A Music Library Bibliography Series *844*
University of California, Los Angeles Symposium on Molecular Biology Proceedings *see* U C L A Symposium on Molecular Biology Proceedings *163*
University of California, Los Angeles Symposium Series on Molecular and Cellular Biology *see* U C L A Symposium Series on Molecular and Cellular Biology *147*
University of California Publications. Anthropological Records (US ISSN 0068-6336) *77*
University of California Publications. Classical Studies (US ISSN 0068-6344) *339*
University of California Publications. Folklore & Mythology Studies (US) *517*
University of California Publications. Folklore Studies *see* University of California Publications. Folklore & Mythology Studies *517*
University of California Publications. Near Eastern Studies (US ISSN 0068-6514) *572*
University of California Publications in Anthropology (US ISSN 0068-6379) *77*
University of California Publications in Botany (US ISSN 0068-6395) *162*
University of California Publications in Entomology (US ISSN 0068-6417) *166*
University of California Publications in Geography (US ISSN 0068-6441) *550*
University of California Publications in Geological Sciences (US ISSN 0068-645X) *381*
University of California Publications in Linguistics (US ISSN 0068-6484) *707*
University of California Publications in Modern Philology (US ISSN 0068-6492) *707*
University of California Publications in Zoology (US ISSN 0068-6506) *178*
University of California, Santa Barbara. Urban Economics Program. Research Reports in Public Policy (US) *947*
University of California, Santa Cruz. Center for Marine Studies. Special Publication *see* University of California, Santa Cruz. Institute for Marine Sciences. Special Publication *408*
University of California, Santa Cruz. Institute for Marine Sciences. Special Publication (US) *408*
University of Canterbury. Department of Psychology and Sociology. Research Projects (NZ ISSN 0069-3774) *937,* 1030
University of Cape Town. Centre for African Studies. Communications (SA) *567*
University of Cape Town. Department of Geology. Precambrian Research Unit. Annual Report (SA ISSN 0250-216X) *396*
University of Cape Town. Department of Geology. Precambrian Research Unit. Bulletin (SA) *396*
University of Cape Town. Department of Gynaecology. Annual Report *see* University of Cape Town. Department of Obstetrics and Gynaecology. Annual Report *785*
University of Cape Town. Department of Obstetrics and Gynaecology. Annual Report (SA) *785*
University of Cape Town. Libraries. Statistical Report (SA ISSN 0576-6885) *685*
University of Cape Town. Libraries. Varia Series (SA) *1165*
University of Cape Town. Research Report (SA) *440*
University of Cape Town. School of Librarianship Bibliographical Series (SA) *1165*
University of Cape Town. Studies in English (SA) *707,* 736
University of Chicago. Department of Geography. Research Papers (US ISSN 0069-3340) *550*
University of Chicago. Graduate School of Business. Selected Papers (US ISSN 0069-3359) *201*
University of Chicago Oriental Institute. Publications (US ISSN 0069-3367) *572*
University of Chicago Record (US ISSN 0362-4706) 342, *440*
University of Chicago Studies in Anthropology. Series in Social, Cultural, and Linguistic Anthropology (US) *77*
University of Chicago Studies in Library Science (US ISSN 0069-3375) *685*
University of Cochin. Department of Marine Biology and Oceanography. Bulletin *see* University of Cochin. Department of Marine Sciences. Bulletin *408*
University of Cochin. Department of Marine Sciences. Bulletin (II) *408*
University of Colorado. Institute of Arctic and Alpine Research. Occasional Papers (US ISSN 0069-6145) 148, 381, 550, *1002*
University of Connecticut. Center for Real Estate and Urban Economic Studies. Annual Report (US) *966*
University of Connecticut. Center for Real Estate and Urban Economic Studies. General Series (US ISSN 0069-9047) *966*
University of Connecticut. Center for Real Estate and Urban Economic Studies. Working Paper (US) *966*
University of Connecticut. Institute of Water Resources. Report Series (US ISSN 0069-9063) *1126*
University of Connecticut. Institute of Water Resources. Wetlands Conference. Proceedings (US) *1126*
University of Copenhagen. Institute of Mathematical Statistics. Annual Report (DK) *894*
University of Copenhagen. Institute of Mathematical Statistics. Lecture Notes (DK) *1165*
University of Copenhagen. Institute of Phonetics. Annual Report (DK ISSN 0589-6681) *707*
University of Copenhagen. Physics Labortory II. Report (DK ISSN 0106-7222) *891*
University of Copenhagen. Statistical Research Unit. Research Report (DK ISSN 0900-0526) *1066*
University of Dar es Salaam. Botany Department. Departmental Herbarium Publications (TZ) *162*
University of Dar es Salaam. Bureau of Resource Assessment and Land Use Planning. Annual Report (TZ ISSN 0084-960X) *500,* 925
University of Dar es Salaam. Bureau of Resource Assessment and Land Use Planning. Research Paper (TZ ISSN 0084-9626) *500,* 925
University of Dar es Salaam. Bureau of Resource Assessment and Land Use Planning. Research Report (TZ ISSN 0084-9634) *500,* 925
University of Dar es Salaam. Economic Research Bureau. Occasional Paper (TZ) *201*
University of Dar es Salaam. Economic Research Bureau. Papers (TZ ISSN 0418-3746) *201*
University of Dar es Salaam. Faculty of Agriculture, Forestry and Veterinary Science. Annual Record of Research (TZ) *36,* 528, 1122
University of Dar es Salaam. Theatre Arts Department. Annual Report (TZ) *1079*
University of Dar es Salam. University Science Journal *see* Tanzania Journal of Science *1001*
University of Dayton. School of Education. Abstracts of Research Projects (US ISSN 0070-3044) *440*
University of Dayton. School of Education. Workshop Proceedings (US ISSN 0070-3052) *983*
University of Dayton Review (US ISSN 0041-9524) *712,* 974
University of Delaware. College of Agricultural Sciences. Longwood Program Seminars *see* Longwood Program Seminars *159*
University of Delaware. Disaster Research Center. Miscellaneous Reports (US) *636*
University of Delaware. Water Resources Center. Annual Report (US) *1165*
University of Delaware Disaster Research Center. Report Series (US) 957, *1021*
University of Dundee Students Association Handbook (UK) *440*
University of Durban-Westville. Institute for Social and Economic Research. Annual Report (SA) *1013*
University of Durban-Westville. Journal/Universiteit van Durban-Westville. Tydskrif (SA ISSN 0070-7740) *633*
University of Durham Calendar (UK) *440*
University of East Anglia. Climatic Research Unit. Research Publication (UK) *807*
University of Eastern Philippines. Research Center. Report (PH ISSN 0070-8259) *421*
University of Edinburgh. Architecture Research Unit. Report (UK ISSN 0070-8992) *100*
University of Edinburgh. Department of Archaeology. Occasional Papers (UK ISSN 0144-3313) *95*
University of Electrocommunications. Research Institute for Communication Sciences. Annual Report/Denki Tsushin Daigaku Denki Tsushin Kenkyu Shisetsu Nenpo (JA) *345*
University of Florida. Center for Gerontological Studies. Research Series (US) *552*
University of Florida. Center for Gerontology. Studies and Programs (US ISSN 0071-6103) *552*
University of Florida. Department of Accounting. Accounting Series (US ISSN 0071-6065) *222*

University of Florida. Food and Resource Economics Department. Economic Information Report (US) 50

University of Florida. Food and Resource Economics Department. Economics Report see University of Florida. Food and Resource Economics Department. Economic Information Report 50

University of Florida. School of Forest Resources & Conservation. Cooperative Forest Genetics Research Program. Progress Report. (US) 167, 528

University of Florida. School of Forestry. Cooperative Forest Genetics Research Program. Progress Report see University of Florida. School of Forest Resources & Conservation. Cooperative Forest Genetics Research Program. Progress Report 528

University of Florida Monographs. Humanities (US ISSN 0071-6189) 633

University of Florida Monographs. Social Sciences (US ISSN 0071-6197) 1013

University of Georgia. Agricultural Experiment Stations. Annual Report see Impact (Year) 28

University of Georgia. Agricultural Experiment Stations. Southern Cooperative Series Bulletin (US) 61

University of Georgia. College of Agriculture Experiment Stations. Bulletin (US ISSN 0072-1271) 36

University of Georgia. College of Agriculture Experiment Stations. Research Reports (US ISSN 0072-128X) 36

University of Georgia. Geography Curriculum Project Publications (US ISSN 0435-5113) 449, 550

University of Georgia. Institute of Ecology. Annual Report (US ISSN 0094-9205) 500

University of Ghana. Department of Library and Archival Studies. Occasional Papers (GH) 685

University of Ghana. Department of Sociology. Current Research Report Series (GH) 1030

University of Ghana. Institute of African Studies. Collected Language Notes (GH) 707

University of Ghana. Institute of African Studies. Local Studies Series (GH ISSN 0533-8646) 77

University of Ghana. Institute of Statistical, Social and Economic Research. Discussion Papers (GH) 1013

University of Ghana. Institute of Statistical, Social and Economic Research. Technical Publication Series (GH) 219

University of Ghana. Institute of Statistical, Social and Economic Research. Technical Research Monographs see University of Ghana. Institute of Statistical, Social and Economic Research. Technical Publication Series 219

University of Glasgow. Institute of Latin American Studies. Occasional Papers (UK ISSN 0305-8646) 910

University of Guelph. Department of Land Resource Science. Progress Report (CN ISSN 0085-1329) 61

University of Hawaii. Industrial Relations Center. Occasional Publications (US ISSN 0073-1226) 276

University of Hawaii. Water Resources Research Center. Annual Report (US) 1126

University of Hawaii. Water Resources Research Center. Collected Reprints (US ISSN 0073-1293) 1126

University of Hawaii. Water Resources Research Center. Groundwater in Hawaii (US) 1165

University of Hawaii. Water Resources Research Center. Project Bulletin (US) 1126

University of Hawaii. Water Resources Research Center. Rain Water Cistern Systems (US) 1126

University of Hawaii. Water Resources Research Center. Technical Report (US ISSN 0073-1307) 1126

University of Hawaii. Water Resources Research Center. Workshop Series (US) 1126

University of Helsinki. Department of Cooperative Studies. Publications (FI ISSN 0356-1364) 239

University of Helsinki. Department of Education. Research Bulletin (FI ISSN 0073-179X) 421

University of Hong Kong. Centre of Asian Studies. Bibliographies and Research Guides (HK ISSN 0441-1900) 854

University of Hong Kong. Centre of Asian Studies. Occasional Papers and Monographs (HK ISSN 0378-2689) 854, 1013

University of Hull. Department of Geography. Miscellaneous Series in Geography (UK ISSN 0441-4004) 550

University of Ibadan. Department of Linguistics and Nigerian Languages. Research Notes (NR ISSN 0041-9613) 707

University of Ibadan. Institute of Education. Annual Report (NR) 421

University of Ibadan. Institute of Education. Occasional Publications (NR ISSN 0073-4314) 421

University of Ibadan. Library. Annual Report (NR ISSN 0073-4322) 685

University of Ibadan. Student Affairs Office. Student Handbook of Information on University Policies and Practices (NR) 440

University of Idaho. Forest, Wildlife and Range Experiment Station, Moscow. Station Bulletin (US ISSN 0073-4586) 367, 528

University of Idaho. Forest, Wildlife and Range Experiment Station, Moscow. Station Note (US ISSN 0073-4594) 368, 528

University of Idaho. Water Resources Research Institute. Annual Report (US ISSN 0073-4616) 1126

University of Idaho Anthropological Monographs (US) 77

University of Ife. Faculty of Agriculture. Annual Research Report see Ife Journal of Agriculture 28

University of Ife. Faculty of Arts. Lecture Series (NR) 633

University of Illinois. Agricultural Experiment Station. Bulletin (US) 1165

University of Illinois. Small Homes Council. Building Research Council. Circulars see University of Illinois. Small Homes Council. Building Research Council. Council Notes 188

University of Illinois. Small Homes Council. Building Research Council. Council Notes (US) 188

University of Illinois. Small Homes Council. Building Research Council. Research Report (US ISSN 0073-540X) 188

University of Illinois. Small Homes Council. Building Research Council. Technical Notes (US ISSN 0073-5426) 188

University of Illinois at Urbana-Champaign. Agricultural Experiment Station. Research Progress (US) 36

University of Illinois at Urbana-Champaign. Center for International Education and Research in Accounting. Monographs (US ISSN 0073-5191) 222

University of Illinois at Urbana-Champaign. Civil Engineering Studies. Hydraulic Engineering Research Series (US ISSN 0442-1744) 484

University of Illinois at Urbana-Champaign. Civil Engineering Studies. Photogrammetry Series (US ISSN 0578-3755) 484

University of Illinois at Urbana-Champaign. Civil Engineering Studies. Structural Research Series (US ISSN 0069-4274) 484

University of Illinois at Urbana-Champaign. Civil Engineering Studies. Transportation Engineering Series (US ISSN 0197-9191) 484

University of Illinois at Urbana-Champaign. Clinic on Library Applications of Data Processing. Proceedings (US ISSN 0069-4789) 685

University of Illinois at Urbana-Champaign. College of Agriculture. Agricultural Communications Research Report (US ISSN 0073-5299) 1165

University of Illinois at Urbana-Champaign. College of Agriculture. Current Affairs (US ISSN 0011-3174) 1165

University of Illinois at Urbana-Champaign. College of Agriculture. Special Publication (US ISSN 0073-5205) 1165

University of Illinois at Urbana-Champaign. Department of Agricultural Economics. Agricultural Finance Program Report (US ISSN 0073-5213) 50

University of Illinois at Urbana-Champaign. Department of Agricultural Economics. Landlord and Tenant Shares (US ISSN 0160-3027) 50

University of Illinois at Urbana-Champaign. Department of Agricultural Economics. Research Report (US ISSN 0073-523X) 50

University of Illinois at Urbana-Champaign. Department of Art. Newsletter see University of Illinois at Urbana-Champaign. School of Art and Design. Newsletter 112

University of Illinois at Urbana-Champaign. Department of Electrical Engineering. Aeronomy Laboratory. Aeronomy Report (US ISSN 0568-0581) 460

University of Illinois at Urbana - Champaign. Engineering Experiment Station. Bulletin (US ISSN 0073-5272) 475

University of Illinois at Urbana - Champaign. Engineering Experiment Station. Summary of Engineering Research (US ISSN 0073-5280) 475

University of Illinois at Urbana-Champaign. Graduate School of Library and Information Science. Allerton Park Institute. Papers (US) 685

University of Illinois at Urbana-Champaign. Graduate School of Library and Information Science. Downs Fund Publications Series (US) 685

University of Illinois at Urbana-Champaign. Graduate School of Library and Information Science. Library Research Center. Annual Report (US) 685

University of Illinois at Urbana-Champaign. Graduate School of Library and Information Science. Monograph Series (US) 685

University of Illinois at Urbana-Champaign. Graduate School of Library and Information Science. Occasional Papers (US) 685

University of Illinois at Urbana-Champaign. Graduate School of Library Science. Allerton Park Institute. Papers. see University of Illinois at Urbana-Champaign. Graduate School of Library and Information Science. Allerton Park Institute. Papers 685

University of Illinois at Urbana-Champaign. Graduate School of Library Science. Downs Fund Publications Series. see University of Illinois at Urbana-Champaign. Graduate School of Library and Information Science. Downs Fund Publications Series 685

University of Illinois at Urbana-Champaign. Graduate School of Library Science. Library Research Center. Annual Report. see University of Illinois at Urbana-Champaign. Graduate School of Library and Information Science. Library Research Center. Annual Report 685

University of Illinois at Urbana-Champaign. Graduate School of Library Science. Monograph Series. see University of Illinois at Urbana-Champaign. Graduate School of Library and Information Science. Monograph Series 685

University of Illinois at Urbana-Champaign. Graduate School of Library Science. Occasional Papers. see University of Illinois at Urbana-Champaign. Graduate School of Library and Information Science. Occasional Papers 685

University of Illinois at Urbana-Champaign. Institute of Labor and Industrial Relations. Reprint Series (US ISSN 0073-5353) 276

University of Illinois at Urbana-Champaign. School of Art and Design. Newsletter (US) 112

University of Illinois at Urbana-Champaign. Water Resources Center. Annual Report (US ISSN 0073-5434) 1126

University of Illinois at Urbana-Champaign. Water Resources Center. Research Report (US ISSN 0073-5442) 1126

University of Illinois at Urbana-Champaign. Water Resources Center. Special Reports (US) 1126

University of Iowa. Center for Labor and Management. Monograph Series see University of Iowa. Center for Labor and Management. Research Series 1165

University of Iowa. Center for Labor and Management. Research Series. (US ISSN 0578-6371) 1165

University of Iowa. School of Library and Information Science. Newsletter (US) 685

University of Iowa. School of Library Science. Newsletter see University of Iowa. School of Library and Information Science. Newsletter 685

University of Kansas. Center for East Asian Studies. International Studies: East Asian Series. Reference Series (US ISSN 0070-8070) 572, 883

University of Kansas. Center for East Asian Studies. International Studies: East Asian Series. Research Series (US ISSN 0070-8062) 572, 883

University of Kansas. Department of Anthropology. Publications in Anthropology (US ISSN 0085-2457) 77

University of Kansas. Museum of Art. Miscellaneous Publications see University of Kansas. Spencer Museum of Art. Miscellaneous Publications 1165

University of Kansas. Museum of Art. Register see Spencer Museum of Art. Register 110

University of Kansas. Museum of Natural History. Miscellaneous Publications (US ISSN 0075-5028) 148, 1002

University of Kansas. Museum of Natural History. Monographs (US ISSN 0085-2465) 148, 1002

University of Kansas. Museum of Natural History. Occasional Papers. (US ISSN 0091-7958) 1002

University of Kansas. Museum of Natural History. Public Education Series (US) 148, 1002

University of Kansas. Museum of Natural History. Special Publications (US) 148, 1002

University of Kansas. Paleontological Contributions. Articles (US ISSN 0075-5044) 858

University of Kansas. Paleontological Contributions. Monographs (US ISSN 0278-9744) 858

University of Kansas. Paleontological Contributions. Papers (US ISSN 0075-5052) *858*
University of Kansas. Spencer Museum of Art. Miscellaneous Publications (US) *1165*
University of Kansas Humanistic Studies (US ISSN 0085-2473) *633*
University of Kansas Libraries. Library Series. (US ISSN 0075-5001) *685*
University of Kansas Publications in Anthropology *see* University of Kansas. Department of Anthropology. Publications in Anthropology *77*
University of Kansas Science Bulletin (US ISSN 0022-8850) *1002*
University of Kashmir. Annual Report (II) *440*
University of Kentucky. Center for Applied Economic Research. Economic Studies Series (US) *1165*
University of Kentucky Libraries. Occasional Papers (US ISSN 0743-8915) *685*
University of Kenya. Bureau of Educational Research. Research Projects *see* Kenyatta University College. Bureau of Educational Research. Research Projects *436*
University of Kerala. Department of Tamil. Journal *see* University of Kerala. Department of Tamil. Research Papers *707*
University of Kerala. Department of Tamil. Research Papers (II) *707*
University of Khartoum. Development Studies and Research Centre. Discussion Papers (SJ) *264, 1013*
University of Khartoum. Development Studies and Research Centre. Monograph Series (SJ) *264*
University of Khartoum. Development Studies and Research Centre. Occasional Papers (SJ) *264*
University of Khartoum. Hydrobiological Research Unit. Annual Report (SJ) *148*
University of Khartoum. Library Bulletin (SJ) *685*
University of Lagos. Continuing Education Centre. Occasional Papers(NR ISSN 0075-7667) *427*
University of Lagos. Human Resources Research Unit. Monograph (NR) *925, 1030*
University of Lagos. Humanities Series (NR ISSN 0075-7675) *633*
University of Lagos. Inaugural Lecture Series (NR ISSN 0075-7659) *633*
University of Lagos. Library. Annual Report (NR ISSN 0075-7705) *685*
University of Lagos. Scientific Monograph Series (NR ISSN 0075-7713) *1002*
University of Leeds. Institute of Education. Papers (UK ISSN 0075-854X) *421*
University of Leeds English Society Paper *see* Context (Leeds) *719*
University of Leeds Review (UK ISSN 0041-9737) *440*
University of Leiden. Kamerlingh Onnes Laboratory. Communications (NE ISSN 0022-8141) *891*
University of Liberia. A.M. Dogliotti College of Medicine. Annual Report of the Dean (LB) *767*
University of Liverpool Calendar (UK ISSN 0305-9227) *440*
University of Liverpool Prospectus (UK ISSN 0268-2362) *431, 440*
University of London. Contemporary China Institute. Research Notes and Studies (UK ISSN 0308-6119) *1013*
University of London. Institute of Archaeology. Bulletin (UK ISSN 0076-0722) *95*
University of London. Institute of Archaeology. Occasional Publication (UK ISSN 0141-8505) *95*
University of London. Institute of Classical Studies. Bulletin (UK ISSN 0076-0730) *339*
University of London. Institute of Classical Studies. Bulletin Supplement (UK ISSN 0076-0749) *339*
University of London. Institute of Commonwealth Studies. Annual Report (UK ISSN 0076-0781) *1013*
University of London. Institute of Commonwealth Studies. Collected Seminar Papers (UK ISSN 0076-0773) *1013*
University of London. Institute of Germanic Studies. Bithell Memorial Lectures (UK ISSN 0144-9850) *736*
University of London. Institute of Germanic Studies. Bithell Series of Dissertations (UK ISSN 0266-7932) *736*
University of London. Institute of Germanic Studies. Library Publications (UK ISSN 0076-0803) *736*
University of London. Institute of Germanic Studies. Research in Germanic Studies (UK ISSN 0260-5929) *132*
University of London. Institute of Germanic Studies. Theses in Progress at British Universities *see* University of London. Institute of Germanic Studies. Research in Germanic Studies *132*
University of London. Institute of Historical Research Bulletin. Special Supplement *see* Historical Research. Special Supplement *585*
University of London. Institute of Latin American Studies. Monographs (UK ISSN 0076-0846) *611*
University of London. Institute of Latin American Studies. Occasional Papers(UK ISSN 0142-1875) *611*
University of London. Institute of Latin American Studies. Working Papers *see* University of London. Institute of Latin American Studies. Occasional Papers *611*
University of London. Royal Postgraduate Medical School. Report(UK ISSN 0076-0854) *768*
University of London. School of Oriental and African Studies. Contemporary China Institute. Publications (UK ISSN 0085-2856) *854*
University of London. School of Slavonic and East European Studies. Library. Bibliographical Guides (UK ISSN 0140-7260) *132, 685*
University of London King's College. Department of Geography. Occasional Paper (UK ISSN 0309-2178) *550*
University of Lund. Archeological Institute. Papers. Yearbook/ Meddelande fraan Lunds Universitet Historiska Museum (SW) *95*
University of Lund. Faculty of Odontology. Annual Publications *see* University of Lund. School of Dentistry. Faculty of Odontology. Annual Publications *780*
University of Lund. School of Dentistry. Faculty of Odontology. Annual Publications (SW ISSN 0076-3438) *780*
University of Madras. Archaeological Series (II ISSN 0076-2202) *95*
University of Madras. Endowment Lectures (II ISSN 0076-2210) *440*
University of Madras. Historical Series (II ISSN 0076-2229) *572*
University of Madras. Kannada Series (II ISSN 0076-2237) *707*
University of Madras. Malayalam Series(II ISSN 0076-2245) *707*
University of Madras. Philosophical Series (II ISSN 0076-2253) *883*
University of Madras. Sanskrit Series (II ISSN 0076-2261) *707*
University of Madras. Tamil Series (II ISSN 0076-227X) *707*
University of Madras. Telugu Series (II ISSN 0076-2288) *707*
University of Madras. Urdu Series (II ISSN 0076-2296) *707*
University of Malawi. Centre for Extension Studies. Annual Report (MW) *440*
University of Malawi Libraries. Report to the Senate on the University Libraries (MW ISSN 0085-3038) *686*
University of Malawi Students Law Journal *see* U M A Students Law Journal *665*
University of Malaya. Chinese Language Society. Journal/Majallah Pantai/Pan T'ai Hsueh Pao (MY ISSN 0553-0644) *707*
University of Malaya. Department of Engineering. Journal *see* University of Malaya. Faculty of Engineering. Journal *475*
University of Malaya. Faculty of Engineering. Journal/Universiti Malaya. Fakulti Kejuruteraan. Jernal (MY) *475*
University of Malta. Annual Report (MM) *440*
University of Malta. International Ocean Institute. Occasional Papers *see* International Ocean Institute. Occasional Papers *406*
University of Manitoba. Center for Transportation Studies. Annual Report (CN) *1084*
University of Manitoba. Center for Transportation Studies. Occasional Paper (CN ISSN 0076-3977) *1084*
University of Manitoba. Center for Transportation Studies. Research Report (CN ISSN 0316-7984) *1084*
University of Manitoba. Center for Transportation Studies. Seminar Series on Transportation. Proceedings(CN ISSN 0076-3993) *1084*
University of Manitoba. Faculty of Agriculture. Annual Progress Review: Agricultural Research, Teaching and Extension (CN) *37*
University of Manitoba. Faculty of Agriculture. Progress Report on Agricultural Research and Experimentation *see* University of Manitoba. Faculty of Agriculture. Annual Progress Review: Agricultural Research, Teaching and Extension *37*
University of Manitoba Anthropology Papers (CN ISSN 0227-0072) *77, 95, 707*
University of Maryland. College of Library and Information Services. Conference Proceedings (US ISSN 0076-4833) *686*
University of Maryland. College of Library and Information Services. Student Contribution Series (US ISSN 0076-4841) *686*
University of Massachusetts. Department of Anthropology. Research Reports (US ISSN 0076-5066) *77*
University of Mauritius. Annual Report (MF) *440*
University of Melbourne. Department of Civil Engineering. Departmental Report (AT ISSN 0085-3240) *484*
University of Melbourne. Department of Electrical Engineering. Research Report (AT ISSN 0085-3259) *460*
University of Miami, Coral Gables. Law Center. Annual Institute on Estate Planning (US ISSN 0537-9768) *666*
University of Michigan. Center for Continuing Education of Women Newsletter (US) *1129*
University of Michigan. Herbarium. Contributions (US ISSN 0580-6097) *162*
University of Michigan. Museum of Anthropology. Anthropological Papers. (US ISSN 0076-8367) *77*
University of Michigan. Museum of Anthropology. Memoirs (US ISSN 0076-8375) *78*
University of Michigan. Museum of Anthropology. Technical Reports (US) *78*
University of Michigan. Museum of Art. Bulletin *see* University of Michigan. Museums of Art and Archaeology. Bulletin *831*
University of Michigan. Museum of Paleontology. Contributions (US ISSN 0041-9834) *858*
University of Michigan. Museum of Paleontology. Papers on Paleontology(US ISSN 0148-3838) *858*
University of Michigan. Museum of Zoology. Miscellaneous Publications (US ISSN 0076-8405) *178*
University of Michigan. Museum of Zoology. Occasional Papers (US ISSN 0076-8413) *178*
University of Michigan. Museums of Art and Archaeology. Bulletin (US ISSN 0270-1642) *831*
University of Michigan. Population Studies Center. Annual Report *see* University of Michigan. Population Studies Center. Report *925*
University of Michigan. Population Studies Center. Report (US) *925*
University of Michigan. School of Dentistry. Alumni Bulletin (US ISSN 0076-843X) *780*
University of Minnesota. Audio-Visual Library Service. Educational Resources Bulletin (US ISSN 0076-9274) *449*
University of Minnesota. Center for Natural Resource Policy and Management. Working Papers (US) *368, 528, 1126*
University of Minnesota. Center for Research in Human Learning. Report and Fellowship Offerings (US) *421*
University of Minnesota. Center for Research in Human Learning. Report *see* University of Minnesota. Center for Research in Human Learning. Report and Fellowship Offerings *421*
University of Mississippi. Studies in English. New Series *see* University of Mississippi Studies in English *736*
University of Mississippi Studies in English (US ISSN 0081-7880) *736*
University of Missouri at Kansas City. Friends of the Library. Publication Series (US) *686*
University of Missouri, Columbia. Library Series (US) *686*
University of Missouri, Columbia. Museum of Anthropology. Annual Reports (US) *78*
University of Missouri, Columbia. Museum of Anthropology. Miscellaneous Publications in Anthropology (US) *78*
University of Missouri, Columbia. Museum of Anthropology. Museum Briefs (US ISSN 0362-1235) *78*
University of Missouri Monographs in Anthropology (US) *78, 95, 611*
University of Missouri Studies (US ISSN 0076-9703) *633*
University of Montana. Division of Educational Research and Services. Education Monograph (US) *1165*
University of Montana. Forest and Conservation Experiment Station, Missoula. Bulletin. (US ISSN 0077-1155) *528*
University of Montana. Forest and Conservation Experiment Station, Missoula. Research Notes. (US ISSN 0077-1163) *528*
University of Nairobi. Institute for Development Studies. Discussion Papers (KE ISSN 0547-1788) *250, 567*
University of Nairobi. Institute for Development Studies. Occasional Paper (KE) *264, 292*
University of Nairobi. Institute for Development Studies. Research and Publications (KE) *1013*
University of Nairobi. Institute for Development Studies. Working Papers (KE) *250, 567*
University of Nairobi Library Magazine *see* Library Magazine *681*
University of Natal. Centre for Applied Social Research. Annual Report (SA) *1013*
University of Natal. Institute for Social Research. Annual Report *see* University of Natal. Centre for Applied Social Research. Annual Report *1013*
University of Natal. Low-Income Housing Series (SA) *201*
University of Natal. Monograph Series (SA) *201*
University of Natal. Occasional Papers (SA) *201*

University of Nebraska. School of Journalism. Depth Report (US ISSN 0077-6378) *647*
University of Nebraska Studies. New Series (US ISSN 0077-6386) *633*
University of Nevada. Bureau of Business and Economic Research. Research Report (US ISSN 0077-7943) *201*
University of Nevada. Desert Research Institute. Technical Report (US ISSN 0077-796X) *1002*
University of Nevada. Seismological Laboratory. Bulletin (US ISSN 0092-4288) *402*
University of New Brunswick Law Journal (CN ISSN 0077-8141) *666*
University of New England. Annual Report (AT ISSN 0375-4588) *440*
University of New England. Department of Geography. Monograph Series in Geography (AT ISSN 0066-7706) *550*
University of New England. Department of Geography. Studies in Applied Geographical Research (AT) *550*
University of New England Convocation Bulletin & Alumni News *see* U N E Convocation Bulletin & Alumni News *439*
University of New Mexico. Division of Government Research. Monograph Series (US ISSN 0194-2670) *947*
University of New Mexico. Institute of Meteoritics. Special Publication (US ISSN 0085-3968) *118*
University of New Mexico. Latin American Institute. Research Paper Series (US) *506, 1013*
University of New Mexico Art Museum. Bulletin (US ISSN 0077-8583) *831*
University of New South Wales. Library. Annual Report (AT ISSN 0313-427X) *686*
University of New South Wales. Library. Staff Papers (AT) *686*
University of New South Wales. Metallurgical Society. Metallurgical Review (AT ISSN 0085-4018) *800*
University of New South Wales. School of Civil Engineering. U N I C I V Reports. Series I (AT ISSN 0077-8796) *484*
University of New South Wales. School of Civil Engineering. U N I C I V Reports. Series R (AT ISSN 0077-880X) *484*
University of New South Wales. Water Research Laboratory, Manly Vale. Laboratory Research Reports (AT ISSN 0077-8818) *1126*
University of New South Wales, Kensington. Research and Publications (AT ISSN 0548-6831) *440*
University of Newcastle. Board of Environmental Studies. Research Papers (AT) *500*
University of Newcastle. Department of Electrical and Computer Engineering. Technical Report EE (AT) *460*
University of Newcastle. Department of Electrical Engineering. Technical Report EE *see* University of Newcastle. Department of Electrical and Computer Engineering. Technical Report EE *460*
University of Newcastle-Upon-Tyne. Computing Laboratory. Technical Report Series (UK) *353*
University of Newcastle-Upon-Tyne. Department of Geography. Research Series (UK ISSN 0078-026X) *550*
University of Newcastle-Upon-Tyne. Philosophical Society. Proceedings (UK ISSN 0078-0251) *883*
University of Nigeria. Annual Report (NR) *440*
University of North Carolina, Chapel Hill. Institute for Research in Social Science. Technical Papers (US) *1013*
University of North Carolina, Chapel Hill. Institute for Research in Social Science. Working Papers in Methodology (US) *1013*

University of North Carolina, Chapel Hill. Institute of Statistics. Mimeo Series (US ISSN 0078-1495) *1066*
University of North Carolina, Greensboro. Faculty Publications (US ISSN 0078-1460) *132*
University of North Dakota. Institute for Ecological Studies. Research Report (US) *500*
University of North Sumatra. Bulletin/Majalah Universitas Sumatera Utara (IO) *440*
University of Northern Colorado. Museum of Anthropology. Occasional Publications in Anthropology. Archaeology Series (US ISSN 0085-1221) *95*
University of Northern Colorado. Museum of Anthropology. Occasional Publications in Anthropology. Ethnology Series (US ISSN 0085-1205) *78*
University of Northern Colorado. Museum of Anthropology. Occasional Publications in Anthropology. Linguistics Series (US ISSN 0085-123X) *707*
University of Northern Colorado. Museum of Anthropology. Occasional Publications in Anthropology. Miscellaneous Series (US ISSN 0085-1213) *78*
University of Notre Dame. Department of Theology. Liturgical Studies (US ISSN 0076-003X) *983*
University of Notre Dame. Saint Mary's College. Law School. Department of Economics. Conference on Changing Factors in Collective Bargaining. Proceedings (US) *1165*
University of Notre Dame. Studies in the Philosophy of Religion (US) *883, 974*
University of Nottingham. Department of Adult Education. Bulletin of Local History, East Midlands Region (UK ISSN 0141-0008) *600*
University of Oklahoma. Archaeological Research and Management Center. Project Report Series (US ISSN 0160-3078) *95*
University of Oklahoma. Archaeological Research and Management Center. Research Series (US ISSN 0160-3086) *95*
University of Oregon. Center for Educational Policy and Management. Monographs (US) *443*
University of Oregon. Center for the Advanced Study of Educationl Administration. Monographs *see* University of Oregon. Center for Educational Policy and Management. Monographs *443*
University of Oregon. Museum of Natural History. Bulletin (US ISSN 0078-6047) *1165*
University of Oregon Anthropological Papers (US ISSN 0078-6071) *78*
University of Osaka Prefecture. Bulletin. Series B: Agriculture and Biology/Osaka-furitsu Daigaku Kiyo, B Nogaku, Seibutsugaku (JA ISSN 0474-7852) *37, 148*
University of Osaka Prefecture. Bulletin. Series D: Sciences of Economy, Commerce and Law (JA ISSN 0473-4637) *201, 240, 666*
University of Ottawa. Cahiers d'Histoire(CN) *562*
University of Ottawa. Department of Geography and Regional Planning. Notes de Recherches/Research Notes *see* University of Ottawa. Department of Geography. Notes de Recherche/Research Notes *550*
University of Ottawa. Department of Geography. Notes de Recherche/Research Notes (CN) *550*
University of Ottawa. Department of Geography. Occasional Papers (CN) *1165*
University of Ottawa. Medieval Texts and Studies/Universite d'Ottawa. Publications Medievales (CN) *562*
University of Ottawa. Ukrainians Studies/Universite d'Ottawa. Etudes Ukrainiennes (CN) *600*

University of Oxford. School of Geography. Research Papers (UK ISSN 0305-8190) *550*
University of Papua New Guinea. Department of Geography. Occasional Papers in Geography (PP) *550*
University of Papua New Guinea. Department of Physics. Technical Paper (PP ISSN 0085-4735) *891*
University of Pennsylvania. Department of City and Regional Planning. Research Reports Series (US) *626*
University of Pennsylvania. Wharton School of Finance and Commerce. Industrial Research Unit Studies *see* Major Industrial Research Unit Studies *290*
University of Pennsylvania. Wharton School of Finance and Commerce. Labor Relations and Public Policy Series. Reports *see* Labor Relations and Public Policy Series *273*
University of Pennsylvania. Wharton School of Finance and Commerce. Studies in Quantitative Economics (US ISSN 0081-8437) *201*
University of Pittsburgh. Center for International Studies. Latin American Reprint Series (US) *633, 1013*
University of Pittsburgh. Center for International Studies: Latin American Studies. Occasional Papers *see* University of Pittsburgh. Center for International Studies. Latin American Reprint Series *1013*
University of Pittsburgh. Pymatuning Laboratory of Ecology. Special Publication (US ISSN 0079-8207) *500*
University of Poona. Centre of Advanced Study in Sanskrit. Publications (II ISSN 0079-3809) *707*
University of Poona Science and Technology. Journal (II ISSN 0551-4932) *1002*
University of Port Elizabeth. Institute for Planning Research. Annual Report/Universiteit van Port Elizabeth. Instituut vir Beplanningsnavorsing. Jaarverslag (SA) *278*
University of Port Elizabeth. Institute for Planning Research. Fact Paper Series/Universiteit van Port Elizabeth. Instituut vir Beplanningsnavorsing. Feitestuk Reeks (SA) *250*
University of Port Elizabeth. Institute for Planning Research. Information Bulletin Series/Universiteit van Port Elizabeth. Instituut vir Beplanningsnavorsing. Inligtingsbulletin Reeks (SA) *250*
University of Port Elizabeth. Publications. Bibliographies (SA) *633*
University of Port Elizabeth. Publications. General Series (SA ISSN 0079-3957) *633*
University of Port Elizabeth. Publications. Inaugural and Emeritus Addresses (SA ISSN 0085-5022) *633*
University of Port Elizabeth. Publications. Research Papers (SA ISSN 0079-3965) *633*
University of Port Elizabeth. Publications. Symposia and Seminars *see* University of Port Elizabeth. Publications. Symposia, Seminars, and Lectures *633*
University of Port Elizabeth. Publications. Symposia, Seminars, and Lectures (SA) *633*
University of Pretoria. Annual Report/Universiteit van Pretoria. Jaarverslag (SA) *342*
University of Queensland. Calendar (AT ISSN 0157-2849) *342*
University of Queensland. Combined Faculty Directory *see* University of Queensland. Undergraduate Degree Handbook *440*
University of Queensland. Combined Higher Degree Handbook *see* University of Queensland. Higher Degree Handbook *440*

UNIVERSITY OF   1927

University of Queensland. Higher Degree Handbook. (AT ISSN 0157-1133) *440*
University of Queensland. Undergraduate Degree Handbook (AT ISSN 0157-1079) *440*
University of Queensland Law Journal (AT ISSN 0083-4041) *666*
University of Rajasthan. South Asian Studies Centre. Annual Report (II) *854*
University of Rajasthan. Studies in Engineering and Technology (II) *1072*
University of Rajasthan. Studies in Sanskrit and Hindi (II ISSN 0448-1712) *707, 736*
University of Reading. Department of Agricultural Economics & Management. Development Studies (UK) *50*
University of Reading. Department of Agricultural Economics and Management. Farm Business Data (UK ISSN 0557-6911) *50*
University of Reading. Department of Agricultural Economics & Management. Food Economics Studies (UK) *50, 521*
University of Reading. Department of Agricultural Economics and Management. Miscellaneous Studies (UK ISSN 0486-0845) *50*
University of Rhode Island. Graduate School of Oceanography. Collected Reprints (US) *408*
University of Rhode Island. Graduate School of Oceanography. Marine Technical Reports (US) *148, 408*
University of Rhode Island. Library. Library Letter (US) *686*
University of Rhode Island. Narragansett Marine Laboratory. Collected Reprints *see* University of Rhode Island. Graduate School of Oceanography. Collected Reprints *408*
University of Rhode Island. Water Resources Center. Annual Report (US) *1126*
University of Riyadh. Faculty of Sciences. Bulletin *see* King Saud University. College of Science. Journal *994*
University of Rochester Library Bulletin(US ISSN 0041-9974) *686*
University of St. Andrews. Library. Current Serials (UK ISSN 0143-0009) *132*
University of San Carlos. Series A: Humanities (PH ISSN 0069-1321) *634*
University of San Fernando Valley Law Review *see* San Fernando Valley Law Review *1162*
University of Saskatchewan. Library. Notable Works and Collections (CN ISSN 0380-9676) *686, 736*
University of Science and Technology. Journal (GH ISSN 0075-7225) *1002, 1072*
University of Sierra Leone. Fourah Bay College. Philosophical Society. Journal (SL) *883*
University of Sind. Research Journal. Arts Series: Humanities and Social Sciences (PK ISSN 0080-9616) *112, 634, 1013*
University of Sind. Research Journal. Science Series (PK ISSN 0080-9624) *1002*
University of Singapore. Chinese Society. Journal (SI ISSN 0080-9667) *572*
University of Singapore. Economic Research Centre. Occasional Papers (SI) *201*
University of Singapore. Faculty of Engineering. Journal *see* Engineering Journal of Singapore *471*
University of Singapore. History Society. Journal (SI ISSN 0217-913X) *572*
University of Singapore Political Science Society. Journal *see* Politeia *908*

1928 UNIVERSITY OF

University of South Carolina. Belle W. Baruch Library in Marine Science and Coastal Research. Collected Papers (US) 408
University of South Carolina. Bureau of Business and Economic Research. Occasional Studies (US) 201
University of South Carolina. Institute of Archeology and Anthropology. Annual Report (US) 78, 95
University of South Carolina. Institute of International Studies. Essay Series(US ISSN 0085-6452) 920
University of South Carolina. Libraries. Report of the Director of Libraries (US ISSN 0081-2706) 686
University of Southampton. Library. Automation Project Report (UK ISSN 0081-2935) 686, 689
University of Southern California. Law Center. Bibliography Series (US) 669
University of Southern California. School of Social Work. Social Work Papers (US ISSN 0272-9016) 1021
University of Southern California. School of Social Work. Social Work Papers of the Faculty, Alumni and Students see University of Southern California. School of Social Work. Social Work Papers 1021
University of Southern California Annual Distinguished Lecture Series Monographs in Special Education and Rehabilitation see U S C Annual Distinguished Lecture Series Monographs in Special Education and Rehabilitation 445
University of Stockholm. Institute of Linguistics. Monographs (SW) 707
University of Strathclyde. Annual Report (UK ISSN 0305-5574) 440
University of Strathclyde. Department of Architecture & Building Science. Research Bulletin (UK ISSN 0143-7283) 100, 188
University of Strathclyde, Fraser of Allander Institute for Research on the Scottish Economy. Research Monograph (UK ISSN 0306-7408) 201
University of Sussex. Centre for Continuing Education. Occasional Paper (UK ISSN 0306-1108) 538
University of Sydney. Basser Department of Computer Science. Technical Report (AT ISSN 0082-0547) 353
University of Sydney. Department of Agricultural Economics. Research Bulletin (AT ISSN 0082-0563) 1165
University of Sydney. Department of Agricultural Economics. Research Report. (AT ISSN 0817-8771) 50
University of Sydney. Department of Agriculture Economics. Mimeographed Report. see University of Sydney. Department of Agricultural Economics. Research Report 50
University of Sydney. Faculty of Economics. Information and Research Monograph (AT) 201
University of Sydney. Institute of Criminology. Proceedings (AT ISSN 0085-7033) 373
University of Tasmania. Center for Environmental Studies. Project Report (AT ISSN 0814-0049) 368
University of Tasmania. Environmental Studies. Occasional Paper (AT ISSN 0810-4395) 500
University of Tasmania Law Review (AT ISSN 0082-2108) 666
University of Teheran. Central Library. Library Bulletin/Daneshgah-e Tehran. Ketabkhane-Ye Markazi. Nashriye-Ye Ketabkhaneh (IR ISSN 0497-1000) 686
University of Teheran. Faculty of Letters and Humanities. Bulletin of Iranian Studies/Daneshgah-e Tehran. Daneshkade-Ye Adabiyat va 'olum-e Ensani. Majalle-Ye Iranshenasi (IR) 613
University of Telecommunications. Research Laboratory of Communication Sciences. Annual Report. see University of Electrocommunications. Research Institute for Communication Sciences. Annual Report 345
University of Tennessee. Department of Anthropology. Report of Investigations (US) 78, 95
University of Tennessee. Institute for Public Service. M T A S Municipal Technical Report see M T A S Municipal Technical Report 943
University of Tennessee. Library Lectures (US ISSN 0270-059X) 686
University of Texas. Bureau of Economic Geology. Guidebook see University of Texas, Austin. Bureau of Economic Geology. Guidebook 396
University of Texas at Austin. Bureau of Economic Geology. Special Publications (US) 396
University of Texas at Austin. Center for Research in Water Resources. Symposium Series see University of Texas at Austin. Center for Research in Water Resources. Water Resources Symposium Series 1126
University of Texas at Austin. Center for Research in Water Resources. Technical Report Series (US) 1126
University of Texas at Austin. Center for Research in Water Resources. Water Resources Symposium Series (US) 1126
University of Texas at Austin. General Libraries. Newsletter (US ISSN 0362-854X) 686
University of Texas at Austin. Institute of Latin American Studies. Technical Papers Series (US) 947
University of Texas, Austin. Bureau of Business Research. Publications (US ISSN 0495-2634) 201
University of Texas, Austin. Bureau of Business Research. Research Monograph see University of Texas, Austin. Bureau of Business Research. Research Report Series 201
University of Texas, Austin. Bureau of Business Research. Research Report Series (US) 201
University of Texas, Austin. Bureau of Business Research. Studies in Accounting (US ISSN 0081-7465) 1165
University of Texas, Austin. Bureau of Business Research. Studies in Banking and Finance (US ISSN 0081-7570) 1165
University of Texas, Austin. Bureau of Economic Geology. Annual Report (US ISSN 0082-3287) 396
University of Texas, Austin. Bureau of Economic Geology. Geological Circular (US ISSN 0082-3309) 396
University of Texas, Austin. Bureau of Economic Geology. Guidebook (US ISSN 0363-4132) 396
University of Texas, Austin. Bureau of Economic Geology. Mineral Resource Circulars (US ISSN 0082-3333) 397, 821
University of Texas, Austin. Bureau of Economic Geology. Report of Investigations (US ISSN 0082-335X) 397
University of Texas, Austin. Lyndon B. Johnson School of Public Affairs. Policy Research Project Report see University of Texas, Austin. Lyndon B. Johnson School of Public Affairs. Policy Research Project Report Series 911
University of Texas, Austin. Lyndon B. Johnson School of Public Affairs. Policy Research Project Report Series (US) 911
University of Texas, Austin. Lyndon B. Johnson School of Public Affairs. Seminar Research Report see University of Texas, Austin. Lyndon B. Johnson School of Public Affairs. Policy Research Project Report Series 911
University of Texas, Austin. Lyndon B. Johnson School of Public Affairs. Working Paper Series (US) 947
University of Texas, Austin. Tarlton Law Library. Legal Bibliography Series (US ISSN 0085-7092) 669
University of Texas Publications in Astronomy (US ISSN 0276-1106) 118
University of the Orange Free State. Institute for Contemporary History. Annual Report (SA) 567
University of the Philippines. Asian Center. Monograph Series (PH ISSN 0079-9238) 572
University of the Philippines. College of Public Administration. Local Government Studies (PH) 952
University of the Philippines. College of Public Administration. Public Administration and Special Studies Series (PH) 947
University of the Philippines at Los Banos. Agrarian Reform Institute. Occasional Papers (PH) 37
University of the Philippines Research Monitor see U P Research Monitor 1001
University of the Phillipines at Los Banos. Rodent Research Center. Annual Report see N C P C Annual Report 57
University of the Punjab. Arabic and Persian Society. Journal (PK ISSN 0079-8029) 572
University of the Punjab. Department of Mathematics. Journal of Mathematics(PK) 754
University of the Punjab. Department of Zoology. Bulletin. New Series see Punjab University Journal of Zoology 177
University of the Punjab. Institute of Geology. Geological Bulletin (PK) 397
University of the Ryukyus. College of Agriculture. Science Bulletin/Ryukyu Daigaku Nogakubu Gakujutsu Hokoku (JA ISSN 0370-4246) 37
University of the South Pacific. Library. Pacific Collection. Accession List see South Pacific Bibliography 131
University of the West Indies. Annual Report on Cocoa Research (TR) 61
University of the West Indies. Institute of Social and Economic Research. Occasional Bibliography Series (JM) 1014
University of the West Indies. Institute of Social and Economic Research. Occasional Papers (BB) 1013
University of the West Indies. Institute of Social and Economic Research. Working Papers (JM) 201, 1030
University of the West Indies. Vice-Chancellor's Report (US) 440
University of the West Indies Students' Law Review see U W I Students' Law Review 665
University of the West Indies, Trinidad. Institute of Social & Economic Research. Occasional Papers: General Series (TR) 1013
University of the West Indies, Trinidad. Institute of Social & Economic Research. Occasional Papers: Human Resources Series (TR) 276
University of the Witwatersrand, Johannesburg. African Studies Institute. Seminar Papers (SA) 567
University of the Witwatersrand, Johannesburg. Bernard Price Institute for Palaeontological Research. Memoir (SA) 1165
University of the Witwatersrand, Johannesburg. Library. Africana Series (SA) 686
University of the Witwatersrand, Johannesburg. Library. Annual Report of the University Librarian (SA ISSN 0075-3807) 686
University of the Witwatersrand, Johannesburg. Library. Archival Series (SA) 686
University of the Witwatersrand, Johannesburg. Library. Bibliographical Series (SA) 132
University of the Witwatersrand, Johannesburg. Library. Occasional Publications (SA) 686
University of Tokushima. Faculty of Engineering. Bulletin (JA ISSN 0040-8883) 475
University of Tokyo. College of General Education. Scientific Papers/Tokyo Daigaku Kyoyogakubu Shizenkagaku Kiyo (JA ISSN 0040-8964) 1002
University of Tokyo. Computer Center. Report (JA ISSN 0564-8742) 1165
University of Tokyo. Department of Geography. Bulletin (JA ISSN 0082-478X) 550
University of Tokyo. Earthquake Research Institute. Special Bulletin (JA) 381
University of Tokyo. Electrical and Electronic Engineering Department. Bulletin (JA ISSN 0563-7929) 345, 460
University of Tokyo. Faculty of Science. Journal. Section 2: Geology, Mineralogy, Geography, Geophysics/Tokyo Daigaku Rigakubu Kiyo, Dai-2-rui, Chishitsugaku, Kobutsugaku, Chirigaku, Chikyu Butsurigaku (JA ISSN 0040-8999) 381
University of Tokyo. Faculty of Science. Journal. Section 3: Botany/Tokyo Daigaku Rigakubu Kiyo, Dai-3-rui, Shokubutsugaku (JA ISSN 0368-2196) 162
University of Tokyo. Faculty of Science. Journal. Section 4: Zoology/Tokyo Daigaku Rigakubu Kiyo, Dai-4-rui, Dobutsugaku (JA ISSN 0368-220X) 178
University of Tokyo. Faculty of Science. Misaki Marine Biological Station. Contributions (JA ISSN 0493-4334) 148
University of Tokyo. Institute for Nuclear Study. Annual Report (JA) 898
University of Tokyo. Institute for Nuclear Study. INS-J (JA ISSN 0495-7814) 898
University of Tokyo. Institute for Nuclear Study. INS-PH (JA) 898
University of Tokyo. Institute for Nuclear Study. INS-PT (JA ISSN 0563-7848) 898
University of Tokyo. Institute for Nuclear Study. INS-TCH (JA) 898
University of Tokyo. Institute for Nuclear Study. INS-TEC (JA) 898
University of Tokyo. Institute for Nuclear Study. INS-TH (JA ISSN 0563-7872) 898
University of Tokyo. Institute for Nuclear Study. INS-TL (JA ISSN 0563-7880) 898
University of Tokyo. Institute for Nuclear Study. INS-TS (JA) 899
University of Tokyo. Institute for Nuclear Study. Report (JA ISSN 0495-7822) 899
University of Tokyo. Institute for Solid State Physics. Technical Report. Series A (JA ISSN 0082-4798) 891
University of Tokyo. Institute for Solid State Physics. Technical Report. Series B (JA ISSN 0082-4801) 892
University of Tokyo. Institute of Applied Microbiology. Reports (JA ISSN 0082-481X) 169
University of Tokyo. Institute of Industrial Science. Report/Tokyo Daigaku Seisan Gijutsu Kenkyusho Hokoku (JA ISSN 0040-9006) 1072
University of Tokyo. Institute of Social Science. Annals (JA ISSN 0563-8054) 1013
University of Tokyo. Institute of Space and Aeronautical Science. Report (JA ISSN 0082-4828) 21
University of Tokyo. Research Institute of Logopedics and Phoniatrics. Annual Bulletin (JA ISSN 0564-7630) 172
University of Toledo. Business Research Center. Bibliographies (US) 132, 201
University of Toledo. Business Research Center. Hodge Memorial Graduate Lectures (US) 1166

University of Toledo. Business Research Center. Miscellaneous Papers (US) 201
University of Toledo. Business Research Center. Occasional Papers (US) 201
University of Toledo. Business Research Center. Regional Research Reports (US) 1166
University of Toledo. Business Research Center. Studies in Financial Institutions (US) 233
University of Toledo. Business Research Center. Studies in International Business (US) 201, 260
University of Toledo. Business Research Center. Working Papers (US) 282
University of Toledo. Business Research Center. Working Papers in Operations Analysis see University of Toledo. Business Research Center. Working Papers 282
University of Toronto. Department of Computer Science. Technical Reports(CN ISSN 0042-0204) 353
University of Toronto. Department of Electrical Engineering. Research Report (CN ISSN 0082-514X) 461
University of Toronto. Department of Geography. Discussion Paper Series (CN ISSN 0317-9893) 550
University of Toronto. Department of Geography. Papers on Planning & Design (CN) 100, 626
University of Toronto. Department of Geography. Research Publications (CN ISSN 0082-5174) 550
University of Toronto. Department of Mechanical Engineering. Technical Publication Series (CN ISSN 0082-5182) 493
University of Toronto. Department of Urban & Regional Planning. Papers on Planning & Design see University of Toronto. Department of Geography. Papers on Planning & Design 626
University of Toronto. Faculty of Forestry. Research Report (CN) 148, 381, 528
University of Toronto. Faculty of Management Studies. Working Paper Series (CN) 282
University of Toronto. Institute for Aerospace Studies. Progress Report (CN ISSN 0082-5239) 21
University of Toronto. Institute for Aerospace Studies. Report (CN ISSN 0082-5255) 21
University of Toronto. Institute for Aerospace Studies. Review (CN ISSN 0082-5247) 21
University of Toronto. Institute for Aerospace Studies. Technical Note (CN ISSN 0082-5263) 21
University of Toronto. Institute for Policy Analysis. Annual Report (CN) 201
University of Toronto. Institute for Policy Analysis. Working Paper Series (CN ISSN 0829-4909) 201
University of Toronto. Institute for the Quantitative Analysis of Social and Economic Policy. News Letter see University of Toronto. Institute for Policy Analysis. Annual Report 201
University of Toronto. Institute for the Quantitative Analysis of Social and Economic Policy. Working Paper Series see University of Toronto. Institute for Policy Analysis. Working Paper Series 201
University of Toronto Romance Series (CN ISSN 0082-5336) 707, 736
University of Toronto Undergraduate Dental Journal (CN ISSN 0042-0255) 780
University of Toronto-York University. Joint Program in Transportation. Annual Report (CN ISSN 0318-1251) 1084
University of Tulsa. Department of English. Monograph Series see University of Tulsa. Monograph Series 736
University of Tulsa. Monograph Series (US) 736
University of Turku. Psychological Research Reports (FI ISSN 0359-0216) 937

University of Utah Anthropological Papers (US ISSN 0083-4947) 78
University of Vaasa. Proceedings. Discussion Papers (FI ISSN 0358-870X) 252
University of Vaasa. Proceedings. Research Papers see Vaasan Korkeakoulu. Julkaisuja. Tutkimuksia 252
University of Vaasa. Proceedings. Teaching Aid Series see Vaasan Korkeakoulu. Julkaisuja. Opetusmonisteita 252
University of Waikato. Antarctic Research Unit. Report (NZ ISSN 0110-2192) 148, 162, 169, 397
University of Wales. Board of Celtic Studies. History and Law Series (UK) 600, 666
University of Wales. Board of Celtic Studies. Social Science Monographs (UK ISSN 0307-0042) 1013
University of Warwick Business Information Service. Occasional Review (UK) 1066
University of Warwick Library. Occasional Publications. (UK) 562, 686
University of Washington. Office of Public Archaeology. Reconnaissance Reports (US) 95
University of Washington Publications in Fisheries (US ISSN 0085-7939) 513
University of Washington Publications on Asia see School of International Studies. Publications on Asia 571
University of Waterloo. Department of Geography. Occasional Papers (CN) 550
University of Waterloo. Department of Geography. Publication Series (CN) 368, 550
University of Waterloo. Department of Geology. Working Papers Series (CN) 500, 626
University of Waterloo. Solid Mechanics Division. Papers (CN ISSN 0317-7130) 490
University of Waterloo. Solid Mechanics Division. Reports (CN ISSN 0317-7114) 490
University of Waterloo. Solid Mechanics Division. Studies Series (CN ISSN 0318-3122) 490
University of Waterloo. Solid Mechanics Division. Technical Notes see University of Waterloo. Solid Mechanics Division. Reports 490
University of Waterloo Biology Series (CN ISSN 0317-3348) 148
University of West Los Angeles Law Review (US ISSN 0083-4068) 666
University of Western Australia. Department of Music. Music Monograph (AT) 842
University of Western Australia. Joint Serials Catalogue of Murdoch University see Joint Serials Catalogue of Western Australian Academic Libraries 680
University of Western Australia. Report on Research (AT) 1013
University of Western Ontario. Centre for Radio Science. Annual Report (CN ISSN 0076-0587) 350
University of Western Ontario. D.B. Weldon Library. Library Bulletin (CN ISSN 0076-0595) 686
University of Western Ontario Series in Philosophy of Science (NE) 883, 1002
University of Wisconsin. Bureau of Business Research and Service. Monographs see Wisconsin Business Monographs 202
University of Wisconsin, Madison. Applied Population Laboratory. Population Notes (US ISSN 0084-0734) 925
University of Wisconsin, Madison. Applied Population Laboratory. Population Series (US ISSN 0084-0742) 925
University of Wisconsin, Madison. Applied Population Laboratory. Technical Series (US) 925

University of Wisconsin, Madison. Engineering Experiment Station. Annual Report (US ISSN 0193-9629) 807
University of Wisconsin, Madison. Institute for Research on Poverty. Discussion Paper Series (US) 1013
University of Wisconsin, Madison. Institute for Research on Poverty. Monograph Series (US) 1013
University of Wisconsin, Madison. Institute for Research on Poverty. Reprint Series (US ISSN 0084-0769) 1013
University of Wisconsin, Madison. Institute for Research on Poverty. Special Report Series (US) 1013
University of Wisconsin, Madison. Land Tenure Center. Reprint (US ISSN 0084-0807) 1166
University of Wisconsin, Madison. Land Tenure Center. Training and Methods Series (US ISSN 0084-0823) 1166
University of Wisconsin-Milwaukee. Center for Latin America. Bibliographic Series (US) 611, 634
University of Wisconsin-Milwaukee. Center for Latin America. Community Resources Series (US) 611
University of Wisconsin, Milwaukee. Center for Latin America. Discussion Papers see University of Wisconsin-Milwaukee. Center for Latin America. Discussion Paper Series 611
University of Wisconsin-Milwaukee. Center for Latin America. Discussion Paper Series (US) 611
University of Wisconsin-Milwaukee. Center for Latin America. Essay Series (US ISSN 0084-084X) 611
University of Wisconsin-Milwaukee. Center for Latin America. Special Papers Series see University of Wisconsin-Milwaukee. Center for Latin America. Community Resources Series 611
University of Wisconsin-Milwaukee. Center for Latin America. Special Studies Series see University of Wisconsin-Milwaukee. Center for Latin America. Bibliographic Series 611
University of Wisconsin, Milwaukee. Language and Area Center for Latin America. Discussion Papers see University of Wisconsin-Milwaukee. Center for Latin America. Discussion Paper Series 611
University of Witwatersrand, Johannesburg. School of Mechanical Engineering. Research Reports (SA) 493
University of Wollongong. Annual Report (AT ISSN 0313-6906) 342
University of Wollongong. Calendar see University of Wollongong. Legislation 342
University of Wollongong. Calendar see University of Wollongong. Undergraduate Handbook 342
University of Wollongong. Calendar see University of Wollongong. Postgraduate Handbook 342
University of Wollongong. Faculties Sector Postgraduate Handbook see University of Wollongong. Postgraduate Handbook 342
University of Wollongong. Institute Sector Handbook see University of Wollongong. Undergraduate Handbook 342
University of Wollongong. Legislation (AT ISSN 0726-4844) 342
University of Wollongong. Postgraduate Handbook (AT) 342
University of Wollongong. Undergraduate Handbook (AT ISSN 0726-0717) 342
University of Wyoming. Wyoming Water Research Center. Water Center Series (US) 1126
University of Wyoming American Studies Conference. Proceedings (US) 634

University of York. Centre for Southern African Studies. Collected Papers (UK) 567
University of York. Institute of Advanced Architectural Studies. Research Papers (UK ISSN 0306-0624) 100
University of Zambia. Centre for Continuing Education. Report of the Annual Resident Tutors' Conference (ZA) 427
University of Zambia. Centre for Continuing Education. Report of the Annual Staff Conference see University of Zambia. Centre for Continuing Education. Report of the Annual Resident Tutors' Conference 427
University of Zambia. Institute for African Studies. Communication (ZA ISSN 0084-5108) 1013
University of Zambia. School of Humanities and Social Sciences. Annual Report (ZA) 440
University Research in Business and Economics: a Bibliography of (Year) Publications (US) 220
University Series in Modern Engineering (US) 475
University Studies on European Integration see Etudes Universitaires sur l'Integration Europeenne 915
Univerzita J. E. Purkyne. Filozoficka Fakulta. Sbornik Praci. A: Rada Jazykovedna (CS ISSN 0231-7567) 707
Univerzita J. E. Purkyne. Filozoficka Fakulta. Sbornik Praci. B: Rada Filozoficka (CS ISSN 0231-7664) 883
Univerzita J. E. Purkyne. Filozoficka Fakulta. Sbornik Praci. C: Rada Historicka (CS ISSN 0231-7710) 600
Univerzita J. E. Purkyne. Filozoficka Fakulta. Sbornik Praci. D: Rada Literarnevedna (CS ISSN 0231-7818) 736
Univerzita J. E. Purkyne. Filozoficka Fakulta. Sbornik Praci. E: Rada Archeologicko-Klasicka (CS ISSN 0231-7915) 95, 339, 600
Univerzita J. E. Purkyne. Filozoficka Fakulta. Sbornik Praci. F: Rada Uminovedna (CS ISSN 0231-5025) 112
Univerzita J. E. Purkyne. Filozoficka Fakulta. Sbornik Praci. G: Rada Socialnevedna (CS) 252, 649, 1030
Univerzita J. E. Purkyne. Filozoficka Fakulta. Sbornik Praci. H: Rada Hudebnevedna (CS ISSN 0231-522X) 842
Univerzita J.E. Purkyne. Filozoficka Fakulta. Sbornik Praci. I: Rada Pedagogicka - Psychologicka (CS ISSN 0068-2705) 421, 937
Univerzita J. E. Purkyne. Filozoficka Fakulta. Sbornik Praci. K: Rada Germansticko - Anglisticka (CS ISSN 0231-5351) 707, 736
Univerzita J. E. Purkyne. Filozoficka Fakulta. Sbornik Praci. L: Rada Romanistica (CS ISSN 0231-7532) 707, 736
Univerzita Komenskeho. Filozoficka Fakulta. Zbornik: Ethnologia Slavica (CS ISSN 0083-4106) 78, 517
Univerzita Komenskeho. Filozoficka Fakulta. Zbornik: Graecolatina et Orientala (CS ISSN 0083-4114) 339, 854
Univerzita Komenskeho. Filozoficka Fakulta. Zbornik: Historica (CS ISSN 0083-4122) 562
Univerzita Komenskeho. Filozoficka Fakulta. Zbornik: Informatika (CS) 883
Univerzita Komenskeho. Filozoficka Fakulta. Zbornik: Marxizmus-Leninizmus (CS) 883, 911
Univerzita Komenskeho. Filozoficka Fakulta. Zbornik: Musaica (CS ISSN 0083-4130) 95, 112, 842
Univerzita Komenskeho. Filozoficka Fakulta. Zbornik: Paedagogica (CS ISSN 0083-4165) 421

UNIVERZITA KOMENSKEHO.

Univerzita Komenskeho. Filozoficka Fakulta. Zbornik: Philologica (CS ISSN 0083-4173) *707, 736*
Univerzita Komenskeho. Filozoficka Fakulta. Zbornik: Philosophica (CS ISSN 0083-4181) *883*
Univerzita Komenskeho. Filozoficka Fakulta. Zbornik: Psychologica (CS ISSN 0083-419X) *938*
Univerzita Komenskeho. Filozoficka Fakulta. Zbornik: Zurnalistika (CS ISSN 0083-422X) *647*
Univerzita Komenskeho. Oddelenie Liecebnej a Specialnej Pedagogiky. Zbornik: Paedagogica Specialis (CS ISSN 0083-4211) *445*
Univerzita Komenskeho. Pedagogicka Fakulta v Trnave. Prirodne Vedy: Biologia-Genetika (CS) *167*
Univerzita Komenskeho. Ustav Marxizmu-Leninizmu. Zbornik: Dejiny Robotnickeho Hnutia (CS) *911*
Univerzita Komenskeho. Ustav Marxizmu-Leninizmu. Zbornik: Marxisticka Filozofia (CS) *201, 911*
Univerzita Komenskeho Trnave. Pedagogicke Fakulta. Zbornik. Spolocenske Vedy. Historia (CS ISSN 0139-5548) *600*
Univerzita Komenskeho v Bratislave so Sidlom v Trnva. Pedagogicka Fakulta. Zbornik *see* Univerzita Komenskeho Trnave. Pedagogicke Fakulta. Zbornik. Spolocenske Vedy. Historia *600*
Univerzita Palackeho. Pedagogicka Fakulta. Sbornik Praci: Cesky Jazyk a Literatura (CS) *707, 736*
Univerzita Pavla Jozefa Safarika. Ustav Marxizmu-Leninizmu. Zbornik Prac Ucitelov (CS) *600*
Univerzitet u Beogradu. Institut za Botaniku i Botanicke Baste. Glasnik (YU) *162*
Univerzitet u Sarajevu. Doktorske Disertacije. Rezimei (YU) *426*
Univerzitet vo Skoplje. Ekonomskiot Fakultet. Godisnik/Universite de Skopje. Faculte des Sciences Economique. Annuaire (YU) *202*
Uniwersytet Gdanski. Wydzial Biologii, Geografii i Oceanologii. Zeszyty Naukowe. Biologia (PL) *148*
Uniwersytet Gdanski. Wydzial Biologii, Geografii i Oceanologii. Zeszyty Naukowe. Geografia (PL) *550*
Uniwersytet Gdanski. Wydzial Biologii i Nauk o Ziemi. Zeszyty Naukowe. Biologia *see* Uniwersytet Gdanski. Wydzial Biologii, Geografii i Oceanologii. Zeszyty Naukowe. Biologia *148*
Uniwersytet Gdanski. Wydzial Biologii i Nauk o Ziemi. Zeszyty Naukowe. Geografia *see* Uniwersytet Gdanski. Wydzial Biologii, Geografii i Oceanologii. Zeszyty Naukowe. Geografia *550*
Uniwersytet Gdanski. Wydzial Biologii, i Nauk o Ziemi. Zeszyty Naukowe. Oceanografia (PL ISSN 0302-3125) *409*
Uniwersytet Gdanski. Wydzial Ekonomiki Produkcji. Zeszyty Naukowe. Cybernetyka Ekonomiczna i Informatyka (PL ISSN 0208-4805) *360*
Uniwersytet Gdanski. Wydzial Ekonomiki Produkcji. Zeszyty Naukowe. Organizacja Pracy i Zarzadzanie (PL ISSN 0208-4791) *282*
Uniwersytet Gdanski. Wydzial Ekonomiki Produkcji. Zeszyty Naukowe. Zagadnienia Ekonomiki Przemyslu (PL ISSN 0208-4783) *292*
Uniwersytet Gdanski. Wydzial Ekonomiki Produkcji. Zeszyty Naukowe. Zagadnienia Finansowe. (PL ISSN 0208-4775) *292*
Uniwersytet Gdanski. Wydzial Ekonomiki Transportu. Zeszyty Naukowe. Ekonomika Handlu Zagranicznego. Prace i Materialy (PL ISSN 0208-4864) *260*
Uniwersytet Gdanski. Wydzial Ekonomiki Transportu. Zeszyty Naukowe. Ekonomika Transportu Ladowego (PL ISSN 0208-4821) *1084*
Uniwersytet Gdanski. Wydzial Ekonomiki Transportu. Zeszyty Naukowe. Ekonomika Transportu Morskiego (PL ISSN 0208-483X) *1104*
Uniwersytet Gdanski. Wydzial Ekonomiki Transportu. Zeszyty Naukowe. Instytut Ekonomii Politycznej. Prace i Materialy (PL ISSN 0208-4813) *202*
Uniwersytet Gdanski. Wydzial Ekonomiki Transportu. Zeszyty Naukowe. Instytut Handlu Zagranicznego. Prace i Materialy *see* Uniwersytet Gdanski. Wydzial Ekonomiki Transportu. Zeszyty Naukowe. Ekonomika Handlu Zagranicznego. Prace i Materialy *260*
Uniwersytet Gdanski. Wydzial Humanistyczny. Zeszyty Naukowe. Filologia Angielska (PL ISSN 0208-5240) *707*
Uniwersytet Gdanski. Wydzial Humanistyczny. Zeszyty Naukowe. Filologia Polska. Prace Jezykoznawcze (PL ISSN 0302-2315) *707*
Uniwersytet Gdanski. Wydzial Humanistyczny. Zeszyty Naukowe. Filologia Rosyjska (PL ISSN 0208-4678) *707*
Uniwersytet Gdanski. Wydzial Humanistyczny. Zeszyty Naukowe. Filozofia i Socjologia (PL ISSN 0072-0453) *883*
Uniwersytet Gdanski. Wydzial Humanistyczny. Zeszyty Naukowe. Historia (PL ISSN 0072-0461) *600*
Uniwersytet Gdanski. Wydzial Humanistyczny. Zeszyty Naukowe. Nauki Polityczne (PL ISSN 0208-4732) *911*
Uniwersytet Gdanski. Wydzial Humanistyczny. Zeszyty Naukowe. Pedagogika, Historia Wychowania (PL ISSN 0072-047X) *421*
Uniwersytet Gdanski. Wydzial Humanistyczny. Zeszyty Naukowe. Prace Historyczno-Literackie (PL ISSN 0072-0488) *562, 736*
Uniwersytet Gdanski. Wydzial Humanistyczny. Zeszyty Naukowe. Psychologia (PL ISSN 0208-4562) *938*
Uniwersytet Gdanski. Wydzial Humanistyczny. Zeszyty Naukowe. Slawistyka (PL ISSN 0208-4740) *634*
Uniwersytet Gdanski. Wydzial Humanistyczny. Zeszyty Naukowe. Studia Scandinavica (PL ISSN 0138-063X) *707*
Uniwersytet Gdanski. Wydzial Humanystyczny. Zeszyty Naukowe. Studium Praktycznej Nauki Jezykow Obcych (PL ISSN 0324-8895) *449, 707*
Uniwersytet Gdanski. Wydzial Matematyki, Fizyki, Chemii. Zeszyty Naukowe. Fizyka (PL) *892*
Uniwersytet Gdanski. Wydzial Matematyki, Fizyki, Chemii. Zeszyty Naukowe. Matematyka (PL ISSN 0072-0402) *754*
Uniwersytet Gdanski. Wydzial Matematyki, Fizyki i Chemii. Zeszyty Naukowe. Problemy Dydaktyki Fizyki (PL ISSN 0208-4872) *449, 892*
Uniwersytet Gdanski. Wydzial Prawa i Administracji. Zeszyty Naukowe. Prawo (PL ISSN 0208-4910) *666*
Uniwersytet Gdanski. Wydzial Prawa i Administracji. Zeszyty Naukowe. Prace Instytutu Administracji i Zarzadzania (PL ISSN 0208-4929) *667*
Uniwersytet Gdanski. Zeszyty Naukowe Praktycznej Nauk i Jezykow Obcych *see* Uniwersytet Gdanski. Wydzial Humanystyczny. Zeszyty Naukowe. Studium Praktycznej Nauki Jezykow Obcych *707*
Uniwersytet Gdanski. Zeszyty Naukowe. Rozprawy i Monografie (PL) *1002*
Uniwersytet Gdanski. Zeszyty Naukowe Wydzialu Matematyki, Fizyki i Chemii. Problemy Dydaktyki *see* Uniwersytet Gdanski. Wydzial Matematyki, Fizyki i Chemii. Zeszyty Naukowe. Problemy Dydaktyki Fizyki *892*
Uniwersytet im. Adama Mickiewicza w Poznaniu. Wydzial Biologii i Nauk of Ziemi. Prace. Seria Geologia (PL ISSN 0083-4238) *397*
Uniwersytet im. Adama Mickiewicza w Poznaniu. Wydzial Biologii i Nauk o Ziemi. Seria Antropologia *see* Antropologia *69*
Uniwersytet im. Adama Mickiewicza w Poznaniu. Wydzial Biologii i Nauk o Ziemi. Seria Biologia *see* Biologia *138*
Uniwersytet im. Adama Mickiewicza w Poznaniu. Wydzial Biologii i Nauk o Ziemi. Seria Zoologia *see* Zoologia *178*
Uniwersytet im. Adama Mickiewicza w Poznaniu. Wydzial Biologii i Nauk o Ziemi. Zeszyty Naukowe. Geografia *see* Geografia *543*
Uniwersytet im. Adama Mickiewicza w Poznaniu. Wydzial Filologiczny. Seria Filologia Angielska *see* Filologia Angielska *694*
Uniwersytet im. Adama Mickiewicza w Poznaniu. Wydzial Filologiczny. Seria Filologia Klasyczna *see* Filologia Klasyczna *695*
Uniwersytet im. Adama Mickiewicza w Poznaniu. Wydzial Filozoficzno-Historyczny. Prace. Seria Archeologia *see* Archeologia (Poznan) *82*
Uniwersytet im. Adama Mickiewicza w Poznaniu. Wydzial Filozoficzno-Historyczny. Prace. Seria Filozofia-Logika *see* Filozofia-Logika *878*
Uniwersytet im. Adama Mickiewicza w Poznaniu. Wydzial Filozoficzno-Historyczny. Seria Etnografia *see* Etnografia *515*
Uniwersytet im. Adama Mickiewicza w Poznaniu. Wydzial Historyczny. Prace. Seria Psychologia-Pedagogika *see* Psychologia-Pedagogika *936*
Uniwersytet im. Adama Mickiewicza w Poznaniu. Wydzial Matematyki, Fizyki i Chemii. Prace. Seria Akustyka *see* Akustyka *899*
Uniwersytet im. Adama Mickiewicza w Poznaniu. Wydzial Matematyki, Fizyki i Chemii. Prace. Seria Matematyka *see* Matematyka *750*
Uniwersytet im. Adama Mickiewicza w Poznaniu. Wydzial Matematyki, Fizyki i Chemii. Seria Astronomia *see* Astronomia *114*
Uniwersytet im. Adama Mickiewicza w Poznaniu. Wydzial Matematyki, Fizyki i Chemii. Seria Chemia *see* Chemia *322*
Uniwersytet im. Adama Mickiewicza w Poznaniu. Wydzial Matematyki, Fizyki i Chemii. Seria Fizyka *see* Fizyka *888*
Uniwersytet im. Adama Mickiewicza w Poznaniu. Wydzial Prawa. Prace *see* Prawo *662*
Uniwersytet im. Adama Mickiewicza w Poznaniu. Zeszyty Naukowe. Historia Sztuki *see* Historia Sztuki *105*
Uniwersytet Jagiellonski. Zeszyty Naukowe. Acta Matematica (PL) *754*
Uniwersytet Jagiellonski. Zeszyty Naukowe. Prace Archeologiczne (PL ISSN 0083-4300) *95*
Uniwersytet Jagiellonski. Zeszyty Naukowe. Prace Botaniczne (PL ISSN 0302-8585) *162*
Uniwersytet Jagiellonski. Zeszyty Naukowe. Prace Chemiczne (PL ISSN 0083-4319) *325*
Uniwersytet Jagiellonski. Zeszyty Naukowe. Prace Etnograficzne (PL ISSN 0083-4327) *78*
Uniwersytet Jagiellonski. Zeszyty Naukowe. Prace Fizyczne (PL ISSN 0083-4335) *892*
Uniwersytet Jagiellonski. Zeszyty Naukowe. Prace Geograficzne (PL ISSN 0083-4343) *550*
Uniwersytet Jagiellonski. Zeszyty Naukowe. Prace Historyczne (PL ISSN 0083-4351) *600*
Uniwersytet Jagiellonski. Zeszyty Naukowe. Prace Historycznoliterackie (PL ISSN 0083-436X) *736*
Uniwersytet Jagiellonski. Zeszyty Naukowe. Prace Jezykoznawcze (PL ISSN 0083-4378) *708*
Uniwersytet Jagiellonski. Zeszyty Naukowe. Prace Matematyczne *see* Uniwersytet Jagiellonski. Zeszyty Naukowe. Acta Matematica *754*
Uniwersytet Jagiellonski. Zeszyty Naukowe. Prace Prawnicze (PL ISSN 0083-4394) *667*
Uniwersytet Jagiellonski. Zeszyty Naukowe. Prace Psychologiczno-Pedagogiczne (PL ISSN 0083-4408) *421, 938*
Uniwersytet Jagiellonski. Zeszyty Naukowe. Prace z Biologii Molekularnej (PL ISSN 0137-2351) *148*
Uniwersytet Jagiellonski. Zeszyty Naukowe. Prace z Historii Sztuki (PL ISSN 0083-4424) *112*
Uniwersytet Jagiellonski. Zeszyty Naukowe. Prace z Nauk Politycznych (PL ISSN 0137-2378) *911*
Uniwersytet Jagiellonski. Zeszyty Naukowe. Prace Zoologiczne (PL ISSN 0083-4416) *178*
Uniwersytet Jagiellonski, Krakow. Zeszyty Naukowe. Prace z Logiki *see* Reports on Mathematical Logic *881*
Uniwersytet Lodzki. Prace (PL ISSN 0076-034X) *634*
Uniwersytet Lodzki. Zeszyty Naukowe. Seria 1: Nauki Humanistyczno-Spoleczne *see* Acta Universitatis Lodziensis: Folia Philosophica *876*
Uniwersytet Lodzki. Zeszyty Naukowe. Seria 1: Nauki Matematyczno-Przyrodnicze *see* Acta Universitatis Lodziensis: Folia Biochimica et Biophysica *150*
Uniwersytet Lodzki. Zeszyty Naukowe. Seria 2: Nauki Matematyczno-Przyrodnicze *see* Acta Universitatis Lodziensis: Folia Geographica *540*
Uniwersytet Mikolaja Kopernika, Torun. Nauki Humanistyczno-Spoleczne. Archeologia *see* Acta Universitatis Nicolai Copernici. Archeologia *80*
Uniwersytet Mikolaja Kopernika, Torun. Nauki Humanistyczno-Spoleczne. Filozofia *see* Acta Universitatis Nicolai Copernici. Filozofia *876*
Uniwersytet Mikolaja Kopernika, Torun. Nauki Humanistyczno-Spoleczne. Filologia Polska *see* Acta Universitatis Nicolai Copernici. Filologia Polska *689*
Uniwersytet Mikolaja Kopernika, Torun. Nauki Humanistyczno-Spoleczne. Historia *see* Acta Universitatis Nicolai Copernici. Historia *574*
Uniwersytet Mikolaja Kopernika, Torun. Nauki Humanistyczno-Spoleczne. Prawo *see* Acta Universitatis Nicolai Copernici. Prawo *650*
Uniwersytet Mikolaja Kopernika, Torun. Nauki Humanistyczno-Spoleczne. Socjologia *see* Acta Universitatis Nicolai Copernici. Socjologia Wychowania *409*
Uniwersytet Mikolaja Kopernika, Torun. Nauki Matematyczno-Przyrodnicze. Biologia *see* Acta Universitatis Nicolai Copernici. Biologia *137*
Uniwersytet Slaski w Katowicach. Annales Mathematicae Silesianae (PL) *754*
Uniwersytet Slaski w Katowicach. Geology (PL ISSN 0208-5534) *397*
Uniwersytet Slaski w Katowicach. Prace Historycznoliterackie (PL) *708*

Uniwersytet Slaski w Katowicach. Prace Jezykoznawcze (PL ISSN 0208-5445) *708*
Uniwersytet Slaski w Katowicach. Prace Matematyczne *see* Uniwersytet Slaski w Katowicach. Annales Mathematicae Silesianae *754*
Uniwersytet Slaski w Katowicach. Prace Pedagogiczne (PL ISSN 0208-5429) *421*
Uniwersytet Slaski w Katowicach. Prace Wydzialu Techniki (PL ISSN 0208-5402) *475*
Uniwersytet Slaski w Katowicach. Prace z Nauk Spolecznych (PL ISSN 0208-5437) *911*
Uniwersytet Wroclawski. Instytut Geograficzny. Prace. Seria A: Geografia Fizyczna (PL) *550*
Uniwersytet Wroclawski. Instytut Geograficzny. Prace. Seria B: Geografia Spoleczna i Ekonomiczna (PL) *550*
Uniwersytet Wroclawski. Prace Pedagogiczne i Psychologia *see* Acta Universitatis Wratislaviensis. Prace Pedagogiczne *409*
Unki Yonkam *see* Electrical Yearbook *452*
Unmuzzled Ox (US ISSN 0049-5557) *712, 744*
Unreached Peoples *see* Refugees Among Us- Unreached Peoples *972*
Unsere Heimat (Wohlen) (SZ) *600*
Unspeakable Visions of the Individual (US ISSN 0049-559X) *736*
Der Untermieter (GW) *421*
Unternehmung und Unternehmungsfuehrung (SZ ISSN 0083-4548) *282*
Untersuchungen zur Deutschen Literaturgeschichte (GW ISSN 0083-4564) *736*
Untersuchungen zur Sprach- und Literaturgeschichte der Romanischen Voelker (GW ISSN 0083-4580) *708*
Uomo & Cultura (IT) *78*
Up-to-Date Civil Reference *see* Dhaka Law Reports: Civil Digest *654*
Update (Albany) (US) *292*
Update (Bridgetown) (BB) *686*
Update in Intensive Care and Emergency Medicine (US) *768*
Update Postgraduate Centre Series (UK) *768*
Upokul (BG) *550*
Upper Midwest Council. (Reports) (US) *250*
Upper Midwest Economic Study. Progress Report *see* Upper Midwest Council. (Reports) *250*
Upper Midwest Economic Study. Technical Paper *see* Upper Midwest Council. (Reports) *250*
Upper Midwest Economic Study. Urban Report *see* Upper Midwest Council. (Reports) *250*
Upper Volta. Direction de l'Hydraulique et de l'Equipement Rural. Service I.R.H. Rapport d'Activites *see* Burkina Faso. Direction de l'Hydraulique et de l'Equipement Rural. Service I.R.H. Rapport d'Activites *1123*
Upper Volta. Direction des Eaux et Forets et de la Conservation des Sols. Rapport Annuel. *see* Burkina Faso. Direction des Eaux et Forets et de la Conservation des Sols. Rapport Annuel *523*
Upper Volta. Institut National de la Statistique et de la Demographie. Bulletin Annuaire d'Information Statistique et Economique *see* Burkina Faso. Institut National de la Statistique et de la Demographie. Bulletin Annuaire d'Information Statistique et Economique *204*
Upper Volta. Service des Statistiques Agricoles. Annuaire *see* Burkina Faso. Service des Statistiques Agricoles. Annuaire *25*
Uppsala Ionospheric Observatory. Scientific Reports (SW ISSN 0349-2699) *892*
Uppsala Ionospheric Observatory. Technical Reports (SW ISSN 0349-2680) *892*

Uppsala Studies in Cultural Anthropology (SW ISSN 0348-5099) *78*
Uppsala Studies in Economic History (SW ISSN 0346-6493) *252*
Uppsala Studies in Education (SW ISSN 0347-1314) *421*
Uppsala Universitet. Geological Institution. Bulletin (SW) *397*
Upshaw Family Journal (US ISSN 0098-8960) *537*
Ural-Altaic Yearbook *see* Ural-Altaische Jahrbuecher *600*
Ural-Altaische Jahrbuecher/Ural-Altaic Yearbook (US ISSN 0042-0786) *600*
Ural-Altaische Jahrbuecher. Neue Folge(GW ISSN 0174-0652) *708*
Uralic and Altaic Series *see* Indiana University. Research Institute for Inner Asian Studies. Uralic and Altaic Series *696*
Urania Universum (GE) *325, 892, 911*
Uranium Seminar. Proceedings (US) *1166*
Urban Abstracts (UK) *13, 501, 950*
Urban Abstracts Series 1: Policy *see* Urban Abstracts *950*
Urban Affairs Abstracts (US ISSN 0300-6859) *13, 950*
Urban Affairs Annual Reviews (US ISSN 0083-4688) *626*
Urban Affairs Papers *see* Journal of Urban Affairs *624*
Urban and Regional Planning Series (UK) *626*
Urban and Regional Research in Denmark *see* Oversigt over By- og Regionforskning *625*
Urban Canada *see* Microlog Index *9*
Urban Development Corporation. Annual Report (JM) *626*
Urban Foundation. Annual Review (SA) *626*
Urban Foundation. Progress Report *see* Urban Foundation. Annual Review *626*
Urban Growth Indicators and Residential Activity Permit Report *see* Shelby County Urban Development Report *625*
Urban History Yearbook (UK ISSN 0306-0845) *600, 1013*
Urban Insights Monograph Series (US ISSN 0736-6272) *373, 626*
Urban Institute. Annual Report (US ISSN 0092-7481) *626, 952*
Urban Institute. Policy and Research Report (US ISSN 0741-8485) *627, 952*
Urban Institute Report *see* Urban Institute. Annual Report *626*
Urban Interest Journal *see* Journal of Urban Affairs *624*
Urban Issues (AT) *627*
Urban League of Greater New York. Annual Report *see* New York Urban League. Annual Report *1019*
Urban Studies Yearbook (AT) *627*
Urban Transport Council. Report (NZ) *1084*
Urbanizacion, Migraciones y Cambios en la Sociedad Peruana (PE) *78, 1030*
Urbanology (AT ISSN 0310-5601) *627*
Urethane Abstracts (US ISSN 0149-1342) *901*
Uro-Nephro; Annuaire de l'Urologie et de la Nephrologie (FR ISSN 0083-4769) *795*
Urthona (US) *736*
Uruguay. Administracion Nacional de Telecomunicaciones. Memoria Anual(UY) *345*
Uruguay. Biblioteca Nacional. Revista (UY ISSN 0544-9189) *686*
Uruguay. Centro de Navegacion Transatlantica. Estadistica (UY) *1087*
Uruguay. Consejo de Estado. Diario de Sessiones (UY) *947*
Uruguay. Consejo de Salud Publica. Boletin *see* Boletin de Salud Publica *952*
Uruguay. Direccion General de Comercio Exterior. Estadisticas de Comercio Exterior (UY) *260*

Uruguay. Direccion General de Estadistica y Censos. Estadisticas Vitales (UY) *925, 930*
Uruguay. Instituto Nacional de Carnes. Anuario Estadistico de Faena y Exportacion (UY) *68*
Uruguay. Instituto Nacional de Carnes. Departamento de Exportaciones. Exportacion de Carnes, Estadisticas *see* Uruguay. Instituto Nacional de Carnes. Anuario Estadistico de Faena y Exportacion *68*
Uruguay. Instituto Nacional de Carnes. Departamento de Exportaciones. Anuario *see* Uruguay. Instituto Nacional de Carnes. Anuario Estadistico de Faena y Exportacion *68*
Uruguay. Unidad Asesora de Promocion Industrial. Memoria de Actividades (UY) *467*
Uruk-Warka: Abhandlungen der Deutschen Orient-Gesellschaft *see* Deutsche Orient-Gesellschaft. Abhandlung *85*
US 1 Worksheets *see* U S 1 Worksheets *736*
Used Book Price Guide (US ISSN 0083-4807) *963*
Uspekhi Foroniki (UR) *899*
Ustredna Sprava Muzei a Galerii. Vyrocne Spravy o Cinnosti Slovenskych Muzei *see* Vyrocne Spravy o Cinnosti Slovenskych Muzei a Galerti *831*
Ustredni Ustav Geologicky. Rozpravy (CS) *858*
Utah. State Office of Education. Annual Report of the State Superintendent of Public Instruction (US ISSN 0094-8314) *444*
Utah. State Office of Education. Opinions of the Utah State Superintendent of Public Instruction (US ISSN 0093-0040) *444*
Utah Academy of Science, Arts, and Letters. Proceedings *see* Encyclia *991*
Utah Agricultural Statistics (US) *44*
Utah Centennial Series (US ISSN 0887-3771) *611*
Utah Directory of Business and Industry (US) *318*
Utah Geological and Mineral Survey. Bulletin (US ISSN 0098-4825) *397, 821*
Utah Geological and Mineral Survey. Special Studies (US) *397, 821*
Utah Geological Association. Annual Guidebook (US ISSN 0083-484X) *397*
Utah Marriage and Divorce Annual Report (US) *930, 1066*
Utah Public School Directory (US) *431*
Utah Public School System *see* Utah. State Office of Education. Annual Report of the State Superintendent of Public Instruction *444*
Utah Statistical Abstract (US) *220, 1066*
Utah Vital Statistics Annual Report (US ISSN 0500-7720) *925, 930*
Utenrikspolitiske Skrifter/Norwegian Foreign Policy Studies (NO) *920*
Utrecht Micropaleontological Bulletins (NE ISSN 0083-4963) *858*
Utsaba (BG) *744*
Uttar Pradesh, India. Scientific Research Committee Monograph Series (II ISSN 0083-5013) *1002*
Uttar Pradesh Irrigation Research Institute. General Annual Report *see* U.P. Irrigation Research Institute. General Annual Report *491*
Uttar Pradesh Irrigation Research Institute. Technical Memorandum *see* U.P. Irrigation Research Institute. Technical Memorandum *491*
Utvalg for Skolebiblioteker av Boker Utkommet for Barne og Ungdomslitteratur. Utvalg av Boker Utkommeti *335*
V A N and Resale Carrier Guide *see* Planning Guide 3. Value-Added Networks and Data Private Line. Telecommunications Rates and Services *350*
V A T Guide and Casebook (Value Added Tax) (UK) *300*

V B R A Directory of Members (Vehicle Builders and Repairers Association) (UK ISSN 0263-1083) *1093*
V B R A Directory of the Vehicle Bodybuilding and Accident Repair Industries *see* V B R A Directory of Members *1093*
V C A B Handbook (Victorian Curriculum and Assessment Board) (AT) *421*
V D E W Arbeitsbericht *see* V D E W die Oeffentliche Elektrizitaetsversorgung *461*
V D E W die Oeffentliche Elektrizitaetsversorgung (Vereinigung Deutscher Elektrizitaetswerke e.V.) (GW ISSN 0505-2904) *461*
V D I - Berichte (Verein Deutscher Ingenieure) (GW ISSN 0083-5560) *475*
V E S Newsletter (Voluntary Euthanasia Society) (UK) *1030*
V F *see* Vegetarisk Tidsskrift *847*
V.I.P. de la Finance et de la Banque (FR) *233*
V.I.P. du Conseil (FR) *282*
V.I.P. du Marketing et de la Publicite (FR) *16, 285*
V I S E. Occasional Papers (Victorian Institute of Secondary Education) (AT ISSN 0813-1759) *1166*
V I S E Handbook *see* V C A B Handbook *421*
V I S E News (Victorian Institute of Secondary Education) (AT ISSN 0314-724X) *1166*
V K G Jahrbuch (Verband der Kraftfahrzeugteile- und Zweiradgrosshaendler e.V.) (GW ISSN 0171-5046) *1041, 1093*
V L B *see* Verzeichnis Lieferbarer Buecher *132*
V - M I C Conference *see* International I E E E V L S I Mutilevel Interconnection Conference. Proceedings *456*
V Mire Muzyki (UR) *842*
V O H D *see* Verzeichnis der Orientalischen Handschriften in Deutschland *854*
V O H D Supplementbaende *see* Verzeichnis der Orientalischen Handschriften in Deutschland. Supplementbaende *854*
V og S Priser *see* V og S Priser. Anleg *285*
V og S Priser. Anleg (DK) *188, 285*
V og S Priser. Bygningsdele (DK ISSN 0108-0229) *188*
V og S Priser. Husbygning (DK ISSN 0105-4201) *188, 285*
V S R Kommunikation *see* Forum *905*
V T I Annual Report (Statens Vaeg- och Trafikinstitut) (SW) *1098*
V T I Meddelande (SW ISSN 0347-6049) *1098*
V T T Symposium (Valtion Teknillinen Tutkimuskeskus) (FI ISSN 0357-9387) *1072*
V W Z (Verkehrswirtschaftliche Zahlen) (GW ISSN 0083-5021) *1098*
Vaabenhistoriske Aarboeger (DK) *79*
Vaabenkaploeb og Vaabenkontrol (DK ISSN 0109-1239) *813*
Vaar Foeda. Supplement (SW ISSN 0346-7341) *847*
Vaasa School of Economics. Proceedings. Discussion Papers *see* University of Vaasa. Proceedings. Discussion Papers *252*
Vaasan Kauppakorkeakoulu. Julkaisuja. Opetusmonisteita *see* Vaasan Korkeakoulu. Julkaisuja. Opetusmonisteita *252*
Vaasan Kauppakorkeakoulu. Julkaisuja. Tutkimuksia *see* Vaasan Korkeakoulu. Julkaisuja. Tutkimuksia *252*
Vaasan Korkeakoulu. Julkaisuja. Opetusmonisteita/University of Vaasa. Proceedings. Teaching Aid Series (FI ISSN 0358-9110) *252*
Vaasan Korkeakoulu. Julkaisuja. Tutkimuksia/University of Vaasa. Proceedings. Research Papers (FI ISSN 0358-9080) *252*

1932　VACANCY RATES

Vacancy Rates and Characteristics of Housing in the United States *see* Current Housing Reports: Housing Vacancies *623*
Vacation Study Abroad (US) *442*
Vaccination Certificate Requirements and Health Advice for International Travel/Certificats de Vaccination Exiges et Conseils d'Hygiene pour les Voyages Internationaux (UN) *957*
Vaccination Certificate Requirements for International Travel *see* Vaccination Certificate Requirements and Health Advice for International Travel *957*
Vaccination Certificate Requirements for International Travel and Health Advice to Travellers/Certificate de Vaccination Exiges dans les Voyages Internationaux et Conseils d'Hygiene a l'Intention des Voyageurs *see* Vaccination Certificate Requirements and Health Advice for International Travel *957*
Vaccines (Year) (US) *774*
Vacuum (US ISSN 0042-207X) *13, 477, 894*
Vadehavsrapport (DK ISSN 0109-2472) *550*
Vademecum (SZ) *627*
Vademecum Bursatil (PE) *268*
Vademecum Deutscher Lehr- und Forschungsstaetten (Vademecum of German Universities and Research Center) (GW ISSN 0083-5080) *1002, 1072*
Vademecum of German Universities and Research Center Vademecum Deutscher Lehr- und Forschungsstaetten *see* Vademecum Deutscher Lehr- und Forschungsstaetten *1002*
Vademecum voor Het Nederlandsche Verzekeringswezen; Jaarboek voor Het Assurantie- en Hypotheekwezen *see* Jaarboek/Vademecum voor het Verzekeringswezen *640*
Vaesterbottens Norra Fornminnesfoerening. Skelleftea Museum. Meddelande (SW) *600*
Vaestoentutkimuksen Vuosikirja *see* Yearbook of Population Research in Finland *925*
Vaextekologiska Studier *see* Studies in Plant Ecology *161*
Vaextskydds - Kuriren (SW ISSN 0346-4997) *61*
Vaextskyddsrapporter (SW ISSN 0347-3236) *148*
Vagabond Chapbook (US) *744*
Vaikunth Mehta National Institute of Cooperative Management. Publications (II ISSN 0083-5102) *239, 282*
Vakantiebesteding van de Nederlandse Bevolking *see* Netherlands. Centraal Bureau voor de Statistiek. Vakantieonderzoek *1120*
Valdres Historielag. Aarbok (NO ISSN 0800-0999) *601*
Valencia Port (SP) *1104, 1127*
Valenciennes (FR ISSN 0760-5641) *737*
Valley Business Perspectives (US) *250*
Valley Grapevine (US) *737*
Valokuvauksen Vuosikirja/Finnish Photographic Yearbook/Finsk Fotografisk Arsbok (FI ISSN 0356-8075) *885*
Valtion Teknillinen Tutkimuskeskus. Tiedotteita/Statens Tekniska Forskningscentral. Meddelanden/Technical Research Centre of Finland. Research Notes (FI ISSN 0358-5085) *1072*
Valtion Teknillinen Tutkimuskeskus. Tutkimuksia/Statens Tekniska Forskningscentral. Forskningsrapporter/Technical Research Centre of Finland. Research Reports (FI ISSN 0358-5077) *1072*
Valtion Teknillinen Tutkimuskeskus Symposium *see* V T T Symposium *1072*
Valtionyhtiot (FI ISSN 0356-8091) *292*
Value Added Tax Guide and Casebook *see* V A T Guide and Casebook *300*

Van Leer Jerusalem Foundation Series (US) *883*
Vancouver Airport Business Directory (CN) *1090*
Vancouver Art Gallery. Annual Report (CN ISSN 0083-5161) *831*
Vancouver Board of Trade. Annual Report (CN ISSN 0083-517X) *240*
Vancouver Board of Trade Roster and Purchasers' Guide (CN) *237*
Vancouver Gastronomic (CN ISSN 0706-5302) *621*
Vancouver Neurological Centre. Annual Reports (CN ISSN 0083-5196) *791*
Vancouver Port Handbook (UK ISSN 0264-5661) *318, 1104*
Vancouver Stock Exchange. Annual Report (CN ISSN 0083-520X) *268*
Vanderbilt Rubber Handbook (US ISSN 0083-5218) *986*
Vanderbilt University. Abstracts of Theses (US) *13, 426*
Vanderbilt University. Department of Environmental and Water Resources Engineering. Technical Reports (US ISSN 0093-6332) *500, 1127*
Vanfoeres Jul (DK ISSN 0900-2863) *1021*
Vanishing Cab (US) *712*
Vantage Conference Report *see* Report of a Vantage Conference *918*
Vanuatu. Bureau of Statistics. Census of Population and Housing. Vila and Santo, Final Results: Part 2: Population Data/Recensement de la Population et de l'Habitat, Vila et Luganville, Resultants Definitifs: 2eme Partie: Donnees sur la Population (NN) *925, 930*
Vanuatu. Bureau of Statistics. Manpower and Employment Survey. Final Results/Enquete sur l'Emploi et la Main d'Oeuvre. Definitifs *see* Vanuatu. National Planning and Statistics Office. Manpower and Employment Survey. Final Results/Enquete sur l'Emploi et la Main d'Oeuvre. Definitifs *849*
Vanuatu. Bureau of Statistics. New Motor Vehicle Registrations and Motor Vehicles on the Register/Nouvelles Immatriculation et Vehicles Automobiles Immatricules *see* Vanuatu. National Planning and Statistics Office. New Motor Vehicle Registrations and Motor Vehicles on the Register/Nouvelles Immatriculations et Vehicules Automobiles Immatricules *1093*
Vanuatu. Bureau of Statistics. Overseas Shipping and Aircraft Statistics/Statistiques de Navigation Maritime et Aerienne Internationales *see* Vanuatu. National Planning and Statistics Office. Overseas Shipping and Aircraft Statistics/Statistiques de Navigation Maritime et Aerienne Internationales *1087*
Vanuatu. Bureau of Statistics. Overseas Trade/Commerce Exterieur *see* Vanuatu. National Planning and Statistics Office. Overseas Trade/Commerce Exterieur *260*
Vanuatu. Condominium Bureau of Statistics. Census of Population and Housing, Vila and Santo, Preliminary Results/Recensement de la Population et de l'Habitat, Port Vila et Luganville, Resultats Preliniares *see* Vanuatu. National Planning and Statistics Office. Census of Population (Year). Base Tables/Tables de Base *930*
Vanuatu. Condominium Bureau of Statistics. Consumer Price Indexes/Indices des Prix a la Cosommation *see* Vanuatu. National Planning and Statistics Office. Consumer Prices Indexes/Indices des Prix a la Consommation *369*
Vanuatu. Geological Survey. Annual Reports (NN) *397*
Vanuatu. Geological Survey. Reports (NN ISSN 0077-8443) *397*
Vanuatu. National Planning and Statistics Office. Census of Population (Year). Base Tables/Tables de Base (NN) *925, 930*

Vanuatu. National Planning and Statistics Office. Consumer Prices Indexes/Indices des Prix a la Consommation (NN) *286, 369*
Vanuatu. National Planning and Statistics Office. Manpower and Employment Survey. Final Results/Enquete sur l'Emploi et la Main d'Oeuvre. Definitifs (NN) *849*
Vanuatu. National Planning and Statistics Office. New Motor Vehicle Registrations and Motor Vehicles on the Register/Nouvelles Immatriculations et Vehicules Automobiles Immatricules (NN) *1093*
Vanuatu. National Planning and Statistics Office. Overseas Shipping and Aircraft Statistics/Statistiques de Navigation Maritime et Aerienne Internationales (NN) *1066, 1087*
Vanuatu. National Planning and Statistics Office. Overseas Trade/Commerce Exterieur (NN) *260*
Vanuatu en Chiffres *see* Vanuatu in Figures *1118*
Vanuatu in Figures/Vanuatu en Chiffres(NN) *1118*
Varbergs Museum. Aarsbok (SW ISSN 0083-5536) *831*
Varendra Research Museum. Journal (BG) *831, 854*
Variety International Motion Picture Marketplace (US) *825*
Varme og Sanitets Nyt. Leverandoerregister (DK) *554*
Varme og Sanitets Nyt's Leverandoerregister *see* Varme og Sanitets Nyt. Leverandoerregister *554*
Varmeforsyningsplanlaegning: Status (DK ISSN 0108-4615) *467*
Varnaes Birk (DK ISSN 0106-1283) *601*
Varsinais Suomen Maakuntakirja (FI) *601*
Varsity Focus (KE) *342*
Varsity Student Handbook (CN ISSN 0229-9119) *342*
Varstvo Spomenikov/Monument Conservation (YU ISSN 0350-9494) *601*
VARTA Fuehrer durch Deutschland, Westlicher Teil und Berlin (GW ISSN 0083-5250) *1118*
Vascular Flora of Ohio (US ISSN 0083-5269) *162*
Vatican Observatory Publications (VC ISSN 0083-5293) *118*
Vector (CN ISSN 0382-0718) *755*
Vedroerende Udviklingen i de Europaeiske Faellesskaber. Beretning (DK ISSN 0107-2013) *202*
Vegetable and Ornamental Crops Research Station. Bulletin. Series B (JA ISSN 0386-250X) *37*
Vegetable Production Recommendations *see* Cornell Recommendations for Commercial Vegetable Production *54*
Vegetables Newsletter (CN ISSN 0042-3092) *534*
Vegetarian Astrologer (US) *114, 847*
Vegetarian Health Food Handbook *see* International Vegetarian Handbook *846*
Vegetarisk Tidskrift (DK ISSN 0109-8861) *847*
Die Vegetation Ungarischer Landschaften (HU ISSN 0083-5323) *162, 528*
Vegyipari Szakirodalmi Tajekoztato/Chemical Engineering Abstracts (HU ISSN 0231-0775) *13, 325, 326, 480*
Vehicle Builders & Repairers Association. Directory of Members & Buyers Guide (UK) *493*
Vehicle Builders and Repairers Association. Yearbook *see* Vehicle Builders & Repairers Association. Directory of Members & Buyers Guide *493*
Vehicle Builders and Repairers Association Directory of Members *see* V B R A Directory of Members *1093*
Vehicle Sizes and Weights Manual (US) *1105*

Veiligheidsjaarboek *see* Arbo Jaarboek *635*
Vejdatalaboratoriet. Rapport (DK ISSN 0107-0614) *1098*
Vejle amts Arbog (DK) *601*
Vejtransporten i Tal og Tekst (DK ISSN 0083-5358) *1093*
Vejviser for Maskinindustrien (DK) *746*
Velvet Light Trap (US ISSN 0149-1830) *825*
Venadam Bibliotheekgids *see* Nederlandse Bibliotheek- en Documenatiegids *682*
VenAmCham's Executive Newcomers Guide *see* Living in Venezuela *1112*
Vending Buyer's Guide *see* International Vending Buyer's Guide and Directory *284*
Vending International Manual (UK ISSN 0143-4381) *286*
Vendsyssel Aarbog (DK ISSN 0085-7645) *601*
Vendsyssel Historiske Museum (DK ISSN 0108-867X) *601*
Vendsyssel Nu og Da (DK ISSN 0105-2608) *601*
Vendsysselske Aarboeger *see* Vendsyssel Aarbog *601*
Venereal Diseases in Canada (CN) *780*
Venezuela. Departamento de Investigaciones Educacionales. Seccion de Estadistica. Estadisticas Educacionales (VE) *421*
Venezuela. Ministerio de Agricultura y Cria. Direccion de Economia y Estadistica Agropecuaria. Division de Estadistica. Plan de Trabajo (VE ISSN 0085-7653) *44*
Venezuela. Ministerio de Agricultura y Cria. Direccion de Economica y Estadistica Agropecuaria. Anuario Estadistico Agropecuario (VE ISSN 0083-5366) *37*
Venezuela. Ministerio de Agricultura y Cria. Direccion de Planificacion y Estadistica. Estadisticas Agropecuarias de las Entidades Federales (VE) *50*
Venezuela. Ministerio de Agricultura y Cria. Division de Estadistica. Encuesta Avicola Nacional (VE) *68*
Venezuela. Ministerio de Agricultura y Cria. Division de Estadistica. Encuesta de Ganado Porcino (VE) *68*
Venezuela. Ministerio de Energia y Minas. Apendice Estadistico (VE) *469, 822, 1066*
Venezuela. Ministerio de Energia y Minas. Memoria y Cuenta (VE) *821, 867*
Venezuela. Ministerio de Energia y Minas. Petroleo y Otros Datos Estadisticos (VE) *867*
Venezuela. Ministerio de Hacienda. Cuenta General de Ingresos y Gastos Publicos, Bienes Nacionales, Inclusive Materias: Ingresos y Gastos(VE) *278*
Venezuela. Ministerio de Hacienda. Memoria (VE) *234*
Venezuela. Ministerio de Minas e Hidrocarburos. Memoria y Cuenta *see* Venezuela. Ministerio de Energia y Minas. Memoria y Cuenta *821*
Venezuela. Ministerio de Minas e Hidrocarburos. Oficina de Economia Minera. Hierro y Otros Datos Estadisticos *see* Hierro *822*
Venezuela. Ministerio de Minas e Hidrocarburos. Oficina de Economia Petrolera. Petroleo y Otros Datos Estadisticos *see* Venezuela. Ministerio de Energia y Minas. Petroleo y Otros Datos Estadisticos *867*
Venezuela. Ministerio de Sanidad y Asistencia Social. Memoria y Cuenta(VE) *1021*
Venezuela. Ministerio de Energia y Minas. Memoria (VE) *469, 822*
Venezuelan - American Chamber of Commerce and Industry. Yearbook and Membership Directory (VE) *237*
Venezuelan Automotive Guide *see* Guia Automotriz de Venezuela *1092*

Venezuelan Petroleum Industry. Statistical Data see Venezuela. Ministerio de Energia y Minas. Petroleo y Otros Datos Estadisticos 867
Venga Que le Cuento... (AG) 737
Vengerski Statisticheski Spravochnik see Magyar Statisztikai Zsebkonyv 1059
Vengerskii Stroitel'nyi Byulleten' see Hungarian Building Bulletin 184
Vengria v Godu see Magyarorszag 1059
Venture Capital Report (UK ISSN 0265-6248) 268, 301
Verba (SP) 708
Verba Seniorum (IT ISSN 0391-8564) 339, 974
Verbaende, Behoerden, Organisationen der Wirtschaft (GW ISSN 0085-7661) 250
Verband der Automobilindustrie. Jahresbericht (GW) 1093
Verband der Automobilindustrie. Taetigkeitsbericht see Verband der Automobilindustrie. Jahresbericht 1093
Verband der Kraftfahrzeugteile- und Zweiradgrosshaendler e.V. Jahrbuch see V K G Jahrbuch 1093
Verband der Versicherungsunternehmungen Oesterreichs. Bericht ueber das Geschaeftsjahr see Verband der Versicherungsunternehmungen Oesterreichs. Geschaeftsbericht 1021
Verband der Versicherungsunternehmungen Oesterreichs. Geschaeftsbericht (AU) 1021
Verbond van Belgische Ondernemingen. Jaarlyks Verslag see Federation des Entreprises de Belgique. Rapport Annuel 289
Verbreitungsdaten der Schweizer Presse(SZ) 16, 963
Verdandisten (SW ISSN 0346-3869) 377
Verde Yerba (SP) 744
Verdi (IT ISSN 0042-3734) 562, 842
Verdi Newsletter (US) 842
Vereeniging Nederlandsch Historisch Scheepvaart Museum te Amsterdam. Jaarverslag (NE) 562, 1104
Vereeniging tot Uitgaaf der Bronnen van het Ou-Vaderlandsche Recht. Werken (NE) 562, 667
Verein Deutscher Ingenieure. Informationsdienst. Instandhaltung (GW ISSN 0724-1976) 13, 477, 493, 746
Verein Deutscher Ingenieure Berichte see V D I - Berichte 475
Verein Deutscher Zementwerke. Forschungsinstitut der Zementindustrie. Taetigkeitsbericht (GW ISSN 0507-6714) 188
Verein fuer Geschichte der Deutschen in den Sudetenlaendern. Jahrbuch see Bohemia: Zeitschrift fuer Geschichte und Kultur der Bohemischen Laender 578
Verein fuer Geschichte der Stadt Nuernberg. Mitteilungen (GW ISSN 0083-5579) 601
Verein fuer Geschichte der Stadt Wien. Jahrbuch (AU) 601
Verein fuer Hamburgische Geschichte. Zeitschrift (GW ISSN 0083-5587) 601
Verein fuer Luebeckische Geschichte und Altertumskunde. Zeitschrift (GW ISSN 0083-5609) 601
Verein fuer Niedersaechsisches Volkstum. Bremer Heimatbund. Mitteilungen (GW) 506
Verein fuer Niedersaechsisches Volkstum. Mitteilungen see Verein fuer Niedersaechsisches Volkstum. Bremer Heimatbund. Mitteilungen 506
Verein fuer Vaterlaendische Naturkunde in Wuerttemberg. Jahresheft see Gesellschaft fuer Naturkunde in Wuerttemberg. Jahreshefte 141
Verein fuer Volkskunde in Wien. Sonderschriften. (AU) 78, 112, 517
Verein fuer Wasser-, Boden- und Lufthygiene. Schriftenreihe (GW ISSN 0300-8665) 368, 500

Verein Oberpfaelzisches Bauernmuseum. Mitteilungen (GW) 37, 517
Verein zum Schutz der Bergwelt. Jahrbuch (GW) 368
Verein zum Schutze der Alpenpflanzen und Tiere. Jahrbuch see Verein zum Schutz der Bergwelt. Jahrbuch 368
Verein zur Erhaltung der Zentralstelle fuer Deutsche Personen-und Familiengeschichte, Rundschreiben. Mitteilungen see Familiengeschichtliche Blaetter 535
Vereinigte Evangelisch-Lutherische Kirche Deutschlands. Amtsblatt (GW ISSN 0083-5633) 1166
Vereinigung Deutscher Elektrizitaetswerke e.V. Oeffentliche Elektrizitaetsversorgung see V D E W die Oeffentliche Elektrizitaetsversorgung 461
Vereinigung Pro Sihltal. Blaetter (SZ ISSN 0083-5641) 601
Vereinigung Schweizerischer Strassenfachleute. Forschungsberichte(SZ) 1093
Vereinigung Schweizerischer Strassenfachleute. Versuchsberichte see Vereinigung Schweizerischer Strassenfachleute. Forschungsberichte 1093
Vereinigung von Afrikanisten in Deutschland. Schriften (GW ISSN 0341-275X) 567
Verenigde Nederlandse Uitgeversbedrijven. Annual Report (NE) 963
Vereniging tot Bevordering der Kennis van de Antieke Beschaving. Bulletin see Bulletin Antieke Beschaving 555
Vereniging tot Uitgave der Bronnen van het oud Vaderlandsche Recht. Verslagen en Mededelingen see Stichting tot Uitgave der Bronnen van het oud-Vaderlandsche Recht. 2 Series: Werken, and Verslagen en Mededelingen 597
Vereniging voor Nederlandse Muziekgeschiedenis. Tijdschrift (NE ISSN 0042-3874) 842
Verfassung und Verfassungswirklichkeit (GW ISSN 0083-5676) 667, 911
Vergilian Society Newsletter (US) 339
Vergilius (US ISSN 0506-7294) 339
Verhandlungen der Schweizerischen Naturforschenden Gesellschaft see Schweizerische Naturforschenden Gesellschaft. Jahrbuch 1162
Verhandlungen des Deutschen Geographentages (GW ISSN 0083-5684) 550
Verifiche e Proposte (IT) 634
Verified Directory of Manufacturers' Representatives see MacRae's Verified Directory of Manufacturers' Representatives 313
Verkehrspsychologischer Informationsdienst (AU ISSN 0042-4048) 957, 1098
Verkehrswirtschaftliche Zahlen see V W Z 1098
Verksamheten vid Kvismare Faagelstation see Faaglar i Kvismaren 170
Vermessungs-Informationen see Journal for Photogrammetrists & Surveyors 482
Vermont. Agricultural Experiment Station, Burlington. Miscellaneous Publications Series see Vermont. Agricultural Experiment Station, Burlington. Research Report 37
Vermont. Agricultural Experiment Station, Burlington. Research Report (US ISSN 0083-5706) 37
Vermont. Agricultural Experiment Station, Burlington. Station Bulletin Series (US ISSN 0083-5714) 37
Vermont. Agricultural Experiment Station, Burlington. Station Pamphlet Series (US ISSN 0083-5722) 37
Vermont. Agricultural Experiment Station, Burlington. Technical Notes (US) 37
Vermont. Commissioner of Banking and Insurance. Annual Report of the Bank Commissioner (US ISSN 0083-5730) 234
Vermont. Geological Survey. Bulletin (US ISSN 0083-5757) 397

Vermont Academy of Arts and Sciences. Student Symposium and Annual Conference. Occasional Papers (US) 440
Vermont Directory of Manufacturers (US) 318
Vermont Education Directory (US) 421
Vermont Industrial Development Authority. Annual Report (US ISSN 0363-2067) 292
Vermont Manufacturing Directory (US) 318
Vermont Marketing Directory see Vermont Manufacturing Directory 318
Vermont Media Directory (US) 1166
Vermont Year Book (US ISSN 0083-5781) 611
Vermouth (UK) 744
Vernon's City of Guelph (Ontario) Directory (CN ISSN 0317-2961) 318
Veroeffentlichungen aus der Pathologie (GW ISSN 0340-241X) 768
Veroeffentlichungen der Astronomischen Institut der Universitaet Bonn (GW ISSN 0340-9821) 118
Veroeffentlichungen des Max-Reger-Institutes (GW ISSN 0543-1735) 842
Veroeffentlichungen des Ostasiatischen Seminars der Johann-Wolfgang-Goethe-Universitaet, Frankfurt. Reihe A. Suedostasienkunde (GW ISSN 0532-596X) 601
Veroeffentlichungen zur Geschichte des Glases und der Glashuetter in Deutschland (GW ISSN 0170-3447) 320
Veroeffentlichungen zur Musikforschung (GW) 842
Veroeffentlichungen zur Verfassungsgeschichte von Baden-Wuerttemberg seit 1945 (GW) 601
Veroeffentlichungen zur Volkskunde und Kulturgeschichte (GE ISSN 0138-3167) 517
Verschollene und Vergessene (GW ISSN 0170-3633) 737
Verstaendliche Wissenschaft (US ISSN 0083-5846) 1002
Versuchstierkunde (GW ISSN 0300-1016) 178, 782
Vertebrate Pest Conference. Proceedings (US ISSN 0507-6773) 61
Vertebratologicke Zpravy/Notulae Vertebratologicae (CS ISSN 0506-7847) 178
Vertical File Index (US ISSN 0042-4439) 13
Vervoer- en Padoorsig see Transport and Road Digest 1097
Die Verwaltung der Stadt Wien (AU) 947
Verzameling van Middelnederlandse Bijbelteksten (NE) 737
Verzeichnis der Orientalischen Handschriften in Deutschland (GW ISSN 0506-7936) 854
Verzeichnis der Orientalischen Handschriften in Deutschland. Supplementbaende (GW ISSN 0506-7944) 854
Verzeichnis Lieferbarer Buecher/ German Books in Print (GW ISSN 0067-8899) 132
Vesteuropa Frimaerkekatalog see A F A Vesteuropa Frimaerkekatalog 874
Vestfynsk Hjemstavn (DK ISSN 0108-6391) 601
Veter Stranstvii (UR) 737
Veterinaria Tropical (VE) 1122
Veterinarno-Medicinski Nauki see Abstracts of Bulgarian Scientific Literature. Agriculture and Forestry. Veterinary Medicine 38
Veterinary Annual (UK ISSN 0083-5870) 1122
Veterinary Bulletin (UK ISSN 0042-4854) 13, 1123
Veterinary Institute, Pulawy. Bulletin (PL ISSN 0042-4870) 1122
Veterinary Medicine see Acta Academiae Agriculturae ac Technicae Olstenensis. Veterynaria 1120

Veterinary Prescribers Index (AT ISSN 0157-3136) 1122
Veterinary Surgeons in New Zealand (NZ) 1122
Vetus Testamentum. Supplements (NE ISSN 0083-5889) 974
Vetus Testamentum Coptice (GW) 613
Vexillum (CN ISSN 0316-2508) 339
Vi Fornyer Oss (NO) 614
Viaggi Intorno Alla Tavola (IT) 615
Vialidad Argentina (AG) 947
Viator (US ISSN 0083-5897) 562
Viborg Stifts Aarbog (DK ISSN 0107-8925) 601
Vibrational Spectra and Structure (NE ISSN 0090-1911) 333
Vicino Oriente (IT) 613, 854
Victoria. Classified Roll of Postprimary State School Teachers (AT) 421
Victoria. Equal Opportunity Board. Annual Report (AT) 914
Victoria. Forest Commission. Annual Report (AT) 1166
Victoria. Hospitals and Charities Commision. Annual Report see Health Department Victoria. Annual Report 617
Victoria. Ministry of Housing. Annual Report (AT ISSN 0810-4972) 627
Victoria. State Film Centre. New Films see Victoria. State Film Centre. New Films and Videotapes 825
Victoria. State Film Centre. New Films and Videotapes (AT ISSN 0810-4476) 825
Victoria, Australia. Department of Conservation, Forests and Lands. Bulletin (AT) 528
Victoria, Australia. Directory of Government Departments and Authorities see Victorian Government Directory 947
Victoria, Australia. Education Department. Curriculum and Research Branch. Research Reports (AT ISSN 0085-7726) 449
Victoria, Australia. Forest Commission. Bulletin see Victoria, Australia. Department of Conservation, Forests and Lands. Bulletin 528
Victoria, Australia. Forests Commission. Forestry Technical Papers (AT ISSN 0083-5978) 1166
Victoria, Australia. Geological Survey. Bulletin (AT ISSN 0085-7750) 397
Victoria, Australia. Geological Survey. Memoirs (AT ISSN 0085-7769) 397
Victoria, Australia. Geological Survey. Reports (AT ISSN 0810-6959) 397
Victoria, British Columbia. Dominion Astrophysical Observatory. Publications (CN ISSN 0078-6950) 118, 892
Victoria League for Commonwealth Friendship. Annual Report (UK ISSN 0083-601X) 1021
Victoria University of Wellington. Awards Handbook (NZ ISSN 0083-6036) 421
Victoria University of Wellington. Decision Research Centre. Working Paper Series. (NZ) 222
Victoria University of Wellington Zoology Publications (NZ ISSN 0375-5363) 178
Victorian Bar Council. Annual Report (AT) 667
Victorian Consultative Committee on Social Development. Annual Review (AT ISSN 0727-5803) 947, 1021
Victorian Curriculum and Assessment Board Handbook see V C A B Handbook 421
Victorian Fiction Research Guides (AT ISSN 0158-3921) 133, 739
Victorian Government Directory (AT ISSN 0158-1589) 947
Victorian Institute of Secondary Education News see V I S E News 1166
Victorian Institute of Secondary Education Occasional Papers see V I S E. Occasional Papers 1166
Victorian Institute of Secondary Education Viewprints see Viewprints 1166
Victorian Society. Annual (UK ISSN 0083-6079) 100

Victorian Statutes Cumulative Supplement (AT ISSN 0314-5204) 667
Victorian Studies Association of Western Canada. Newsletter (CN ISSN 0703-5500) 737
Victorian Workers Compensation Practice Guide (AT) 276, 667
Vida das Artes (BL) 112
Video. Vaerd at Se (DK ISSN 0109-7717) 350
Video Exchange Directory see International Video Exchange Directory 348
Video Out Distribution Catalogue (CN) 112, 421, 911, 1013
Video Register (US ISSN 0190-3705) 318, 825
Video Source Book (US ISSN 0277-3317) 345, 825
Videoworld Buyer's Guide Annual (AT ISSN 0729-1965) 350
Videozine (US) 112
Vie des Affaires (FR ISSN 0083-6095) 282, 947
Vie Musicale en France Sous les Rois Bourbons. Serie 1: Etudes (FR ISSN 0083-6109) 842
Vie Musicale en France Sous les Rois Bourbons. Serie 2: Recherches sur la Musique Classique Francaise (FR ISSN 0083-6117) 842
Vie Quotidienne en U.R.S.S. Prise sur le Vif see Sovetskie Ljudi Segodnja 733
Vienna. Universitaet. Institut fuer Theaterwissenschaft. Wissenschaftliche Reihe see Wiener Forschungen zur Theater und Medienwissenschaft 1079
Vienna Circle Collection (NE) 135, 601
Viennese Slavonic Yearbook see Wiener Slavistisches Jahrbuch 708
Vierteljahrschrift fuer Sozial- und Wirtschaftsgeschichte. Beihefte (GW ISSN 0341-0846) 252, 562, 1013
Vierundzwanzigsteljahrsschrift der Internationalen Maultrommelvirtuosen ossenschaft(US) 843
Vietnam International see Vietnam/South East Asia International 911
Vietnam/South East Asia International (UK) 911
Vietnam Youth (VN ISSN 0049-6375) 336, 540
Vietnamese Studies (VN ISSN 0085-7823) 572, 1013
Viewpoint; Minority Outlook on Current Issues see Fact Sheets on Institutional Racism 913
Viewprints (Victorian Institute of Secondary Education) (AT ISSN 0813-5150) 1166
Viking (NO) 95
Viking (US ISSN 0095-5744) 441
Viking (Northfield) see Viking 441
Viking Society for Northern Research. Saga Book (UK ISSN 0305-9219) 601
Viking Society for Northern Research. Text Series (UK ISSN 0083-6257) 737
Villa Guide (UK ISSN 0083-6273) 621
Vilne Slovo Annual (CN) 506
Vinaver Studies in French (UK ISSN 0264-5564) 708, 737
Vinculos (CR ISSN 0304-3703) 78
Vind - Nyt (DK ISSN 0109-2049) 807, 1104
Vindicacion Feminista (SP ISSN 0212-324X) 1129
Ving (UK) 712
Vintage Auto Almanac see Hemming's Vintage Auto Almanac 79
Viola da Gamba Society of America. Journal (US ISSN 0507-0252) 843
Violations of Human Rights in Soviet Occupied Lithuania (US ISSN 0360-7453) 667
Violence and Victims (US) 373, 938, 1030
Virgil Society. Proceedings (UK ISSN 0083-629X) 339
Virgin Island Blue Book see Virgin Islands of the United States Blue Book 947

Virgin Islands (U.S.) Bureau of Libraries, Museums and Archaeological Services. Occasional Paper Series see Virgin Islands (U.S.) Division of Libraries, Museums and Archaeological Services. Occasional Paper Series 611
Virgin Islands (U.S.) Division of Libraries, Museums and Archaeological Services. Occasional Paper Series (VI) 611
Virgin Islands of the United States Blue Book (VI) 947
Virginia. Criminal Justice Officers Training and Standards Commission. Biennial Report see Virginia. Criminal Justice Services Commission. Annual Report 667
Virginia. Criminal Justice Services Commission. Annual Report (US) 373, 667
Virginia. Division of Mineral Resources. Publications see Virginia. Division of Mineral Resources. Reports 821
Virginia. Division of Mineral Resources. Reports (US) 397, 821
Virginia. Employment Commission. Annual Planning Report (US) 276
Virginia. Employment Commission. Annual Report (US) 276
Virginia. Employment Commission. Annual Rural Manpower Report (US) 276
Virginia. Employment Commission. Labor Market Trends (US) 276
Virginia. State Water Control Board. Annual Report (US ISSN 0095-1978) 500, 1127
Virginia. State Water Control Board. Basic Data Bulletin (US) 1127
Virginia. State Water Control Board. Information Bulletin (US) 1127
Virginia. State Water Control Board. Planning Bulletin (US) 1127
Virginia. Water Resources Research Center. Bulletin (US) 1127
Virginia Baptist Register (US ISSN 0083-6311) 980
Virginia Educational Directory (US ISSN 0083-6354) 421
Virginia Highway and Transportation Conference. Proceedings (US) 484, 1098
Virginia Highway Conference. Proceedings see Virginia Highway and Transportation Conference. Proceedings 1098
Virginia Historical Abstracts (US ISSN 0734-5089) 1166
Virginia Historical Society. Documents (US ISSN 0083-6389) 611
Virginia Industrial Directory (US) 318, 821
Virginia Institute of Marine Science. Contributions (US) 409
Virginia Institute of Marine Science, Gloucester Point. Educational Series (US ISSN 0083-6427) 148
Virginia Institute of Marine Science, Gloucester Point. Marine Resources Advisory Series (US ISSN 0083-6435) 149
Virginia Institute of Marine Science, Gloucester Point. Special Report in Applied Marine Science and Ocean Engineering (US) 409
Virginia Institute of Marine Science, Gloucester Point. Special Scientific Report (US ISSN 0083-6443) 149
Virginia Institute of Marine Science, Gloucester Point. Translation Series. (US ISSN 0083-6397) 149
Virginia Legal Studies (US) 667
Virginia Military Institute, Lexington. Publications, Theses, and Dissertations of the Staff and Faculty(US ISSN 0083-6451) 426, 813
Virginia Polytechnic Institute and State University. College of Agriculture and Life Sciences. Information Series(US ISSN 0742-7425) 37

Virginia Polytechnic Institute and State University. College of Agriculture and Life Sciences. Virginia Agricultural Station. Agricultural Research Digest see Virginia Polytechnic Institute and State University. Virginia Agricultural Experiment Station. Agricultural Research Digest 37
Virginia Polytechnic Institute and State University. Department of Entomology. Occasional Papers (US) 166
Virginia Polytechnic Institute and State University. Department of Geological Sciences. Geological Guidebooks. (US ISSN 0507-1259) 397
Virginia Polytechnic Institute and State University. Pallet and Container Research Laboratory. Special Report (US) 188, 530
Virginia Polytechnic Institute and State University. Research Division. Bulletin see Research: Virginia Tech 33
Virginia Polytechnic Institute and State University. Virginia Agricultural Experiment Station. Agricultural Research Digest (US) 37
Virginia Polytechnic Institute and State University. Virginia Agricultural Experiment Station. Bulletin (US) 37
Virginia Polytechnic Institute and State University. Wood Research and Wood Construction Laboratory. Special Report see Virginia Polytechnic Institute and State University. Pallet and Container Research Laboratory. Special Report 530
Virginia Polytechnic Institute, Blacksburg. Engineering Extension Division. Geological Guidebook see Virginia Polytechnic Institute and State University. Department of Geological Sciences. Geological Guidebooks 397
Virginia Port Authority. Board of Commissioners. Annual Report (US ISSN 0083-6532) 1166
Virginia Port Authority. Foreign Trade Annual Report: The Ports of Virginia(US ISSN 0083-6516) 1166
Virginia Ports and Shipping Handbook (UK ISSN 0266-7274) 318, 1104
Virginia Road Builder (US ISSN 0161-6730) 484
Virginia Social Science Journal (US) 1013
Virginia State Publications in Print (US ISSN 0507-102X) 133
Virginia's Industry of Agriculture. Report to the Governor see Report on Virginia's Industry of Agriculture 33
Virginia's Supply of Public School Instructional Personnel (US ISSN 0083-6575) 441
Virksomheds Nyts (DK) 1084
Virology Abstracts (US ISSN 0042-6830) 13, 150, 773
Virology Monographs/Virusforschung in Einzeldarstellungen (US ISSN 0083-6591) 169, 778
Virusforschung in Einzeldarstellungen see Virology Monographs 169
Vishva Vicharamala (II) 572, 854
Vishveshvaranand Indological Paper Series (II ISSN 0083-6613) 572
Vishveshvaranand Indological Series (II ISSN 0083-6621) 572, 708
Vishveshvaranand Vedic Research Institute. Research and General Publications (II) 572, 854
Visible Religion (NE ISSN 0169-5606) 974
Visindafelag Islendinga RIT (IC ISSN 0376-2599) 397
Vision On (UK) 744
Visit California with Fyfe Robertson (UK ISSN 0260-910X) 1118
Visserij in Cijfers (NE) 513
Vissha Geodeziia (BU ISSN 0324-1114) 397
Vistas (US) 831
Vistas in Plant Sciences (II ISSN 0378-9454) 162

Visti Iz Sarseliu (FR ISSN 0083-6672) 1013
Visual Arts (US ISSN 0277-0490) 112
Visual Arts Program see Visual Arts 112
Vita Evangelica (CN ISSN 0507-1690) 974
Vitae S A Life Assurance Yearbook see Vitae Yearbook 642
Vitae Yearbook (SA ISSN 0259-0034) 642
Vital and Health Statistics Monographs (US) 957
Vital Signs (Fresno) (US) 768
Vital Statistics, Idaho see Idaho. Department of Health and Welfare. Annual Summary of Vital Statistics 958
Vital Statistics Japan see Japan. Ministry of Health and Welfare. Statistics and Information Department. Vital Statistics 1058
Vital Statistics of Iowa (US ISSN 0161-8695) 930, 1066
Vital Statistics of the Province of British Columbia (CN) 930, 1066
Vital Statistics of the United States (US ISSN 0083-6710) 925, 957
Vitamins and Hormones: Advances in Research and Applications (US ISSN 0083-6729) 768, 873
Vitis (GW ISSN 0042-7500) 13, 121
Vitis - V E S see Vitis - Viticulture and Enology Abstracts 44
Vitis - Viticulture and Enology Abstracts (UK ISSN 0175-8292) 13, 44
Vittorio Baccelli Magazine (IT) 1030
Vivat Hussar (FR) 813
Vivre le Cinema (FR) 825
Vizgazdalkodas es Kornyezetvedelem (HU ISSN 0133-3305) 368, 1127
Vjesnik za Arheologiju i Historiju Dalmatinsku/Bulletin d'Archeologie et d'Histoire Dalmates (YU) 95, 320
Vlastivedny Sbornik Okresu Novy Jicin(CS ISSN 0139-9462) 601
Vlastivedny Zbornik (CS) 601, 634
Vlastivedny Zbornik Povazia (CS) 95, 601
Vlastivedny Zbornik Zilinskeho Kraja see Vlastivedny Zbornik Povazia 601
Vocational and Technical Audiovisuals: A Teacher's Sourcebook (National Information Center for Educational Media) (US) 431, 449
Vocational Education Evaluation Report see Connecticut. Advisory Council on Vocational and Career Education. Vocational Education Evaluation Report 412
Vocational - Technical Education Programs see Pennsylvania State Plan for the Administration of Vocational - Technical Education Programs 427
Vocational Training Council. Annual Report (HK) 427
Vodni Problemi (BU ISSN 0204-8248) 491, 1127
Voelkerkundliche Abhandlungen (GW ISSN 0073-0270) 78
Voelkerkundliche Veroeffentlichungen (AU) 78
Vogelkundliche Hefte Edertal (GW) 171
Vogue Beauty & Health Guide (US ISSN 0161-2190) 118, 886
Voice of History (NP) 744
Voice of Judaism (US) 977
Voice of S O M A F C O (Solomon Mahlangu Freedom College) (ZA) 540
Voices from Within (US) 373, 737
Voices - Israel (IS ISSN 0333-676X) 744
Void Magazine (AT) 737
Voix Sepharade (CN ISSN 0704-5352) 506
Vojni Muzej, Belgrade. Vesnik/Military Museum, Belgrade. Bulletin (YU ISSN 0067-5660) 813
Volkskuendlichen Kommission fuer Westfalen. Schriften (GW) 517
Volkskundliche Studien (AU) 517
Volkslied, Volkstanz, Volksmusik see Oesterreichisches Volksliedwerk. Jahrbuch 840

Volksmaerchen (GE ISSN 0232-3702) 517
Volkstum der Schweiz (GW ISSN 0083-6877) 517
Volleyball Case Book (US) 1040
Volleyball Guide see N A G W S Guide. Volleyball 1039
Volleyball Rulebook (US) 1040
Vologodskaya Biblioteka im. Babushkina. Literatura o Vologodskoi Oblasti (UR) 737
Volund (NO ISSN 0048-2277) 831
Voluntary Agencies (UK) 1021
Voluntary Euthanasia Society Newsletter see V E S Newsletter 1030
Voluntary Organisations see Voluntary Agencies 1021
Voluntary Social Services see Voluntary Agencies 1021
Volunteers Who Produce Books (US ISSN 0193-113X) 180
Vom Wasser (GW ISSN 0083-6915) 325, 1127
Von Deutschland Nach Amerika (GW ISSN 0173-1955) 1013
Von Karman Institute for Fluid Dynamics. Lecture Series (BE) 21, 491
Vooraziatisch-Egyptisch Genootschap "Ex Oriente Lux". Jaarbericht (NE ISSN 0075-2118) 572, 854
Vooraziatisch-Egyptisch Genootschap "Ex Oriente Lux". Mededelingen en Verhandelingen (NE) 572, 854
Voorzetten (NE) 737
Voprosy Bibliografii (UR) 133
Voprosy Ekonomiki Narodnogo Khozyaistva Murmanskoi Oblasti (UR) 202
Voprosy Ekonomiki Sel'skogo Khozyaistva Dal'nego Vostoka (UR) 50
Voprosy Elektroniki Tverdogo Tela (UR) 461
Voprosy Fiziki Tverdogo Tela (UR ISSN 0301-6919) 892
Voprosy Geografii (UR) 550
Voprosy Gidrodinamiki i Teploobmena v Kriogennykh Sistemakh (UR) 894, 895
Voprosy Inzhenernoi Geologii i Gruntovedeniya (UR) 493
Voprosy Khimii i Khimicheskoi Tekhnologii (UR) 333
Voprosy Kritiki Burzhuaznoi Politiki i Ideologii. Sbornik Nauchnykh Trudov (UR) 911
Voprosy Radiobiologii i Biologicheskogo Deistviya Tsitostaticheskikh Preparatov (UR) 149, 792
Voprosy Russkogo Yazykoznaniya (UR) 708
Voprosy Statistiki (UR) 1066
Voprosy Teatra (UR ISSN 0507-3952) 1079
Voprosy Teorii Razrabotki Mestorozhdenii Poleznykh Iskopaemykh (UR) 475
Voprosy Teorii Sistem Avtomaticheskogo Upravleniya (UR) 355, 359
Voprosy Uchebno-vospitatel'noi Raboty v Samodeyatel'nykh Kollektivakh (UR) 843
Vorarlberger Landesmuseumsverein. Jahrbuch (AU) 601
Vorderasiatische Schriftdenkmaler der Staatlichen Mussen zu Berlin (GE ISSN 0138-4449) 854
Vore Kirkegaarde (DK ISSN 0108-2302) 531
Vore Kunstnere (DK ISSN 0107-136X) 112
Vorreformationsgeschichtliche Forschungen (GW ISSN 0083-6923) 974
Vortraege aus der Praktischen Chirurgie see Praktische Chirurgie 794
Vortraege und Aufsaetze see Schriften zur Kooperationsforschung. Vortraege 239
Vox Evangelica (UK ISSN 0263-6786) 974
Voz do Operario (PO) 712
Vrije Fries (NE) 562, 601, 708

Vsesoyuznyi Nauchno-Issledovatel'skii Institut Morskogo Rybnogo Khozyaistva i Okeanografii (V N I R O). Trudy (UR) 409
Vsesoyuznyi Nauchno-Issledovatel'skii Institut Transportnogo Stroitel'stva. Trudy (UR) 1084
Vsesoyuznyi Nauchno-Issledovatel'skii Institut Vagonostroeniya. Trudy (UR) 1095
Vsesoyuznyi Nauchno-Issledovatel'skii Institut Zernovogo Khozyaistva. Trudy. (UR) 61
Vspomogatel'nye Istoricheskie Distsipliny (UR) 135, 601
Vstrechi (US ISSN 0888-5257) 744
Vulkanen: Ren L A V A (Lokalhistoriske Arkiver i Vestsjaellands Amt) (DK ISSN 0108-691X) 601
Vulkaniseur - Jahrbuch (GW ISSN 0083-694X) 986
Vyberova Anotovana Bibliografie Studijnich Materialu (CS) 346
Vyberova Bibliografia Muzeologickej Literatury (CS) 133, 832
Vyrocne Spravy o Cinnosti Slovenskych Muzei a Galerti (CS) 831
Vyskumny Ustav Lesneho Hospodarstva vo Zvolene. Lesnicke Studie (CS) 149, 528
Vyskumny Ustav Luk a Pasienkov v Banskej Bystrici. Vedecke Prace (CS) 37, 61
Vyskumny Ustav Rastinnej Vyroby v Piestanoch. Vedecke Prace (CS) 37, 149
Vysoka Skola Banska. Sbornik Vedeckych Praci: Rada Hutnicka/Institute of Mining and Metallurgy. Transactions: Metallurgical Series (CS ISSN 0042-3726) 800
Vysoka Skola Banska. Sbornik Vedeckych Praci: Rada Strojni (CS) 475
Vysoka Skola Lesnicka a Drevarska vo Zvolene. Lesnicka Fakulta. Zbornik Vedeckych Prac see Acta Facultatis Forestalis, Zvolen 523
Vyssi Pedagogicke Skoly v Plzni. Sbornik: Pedagogickeho Institutu v Plzni. Sbornik see Pedagogicka Fakulta v Plzni. Sbornik. Dejepis 593
Vyzkumny Ustav Spoju. Sbornik Praci (CS) 1095
Vyzkumy v Cechach (CS) 95, 601
Vznik a Vyvoj Prumyslovych Oblasti see Prumyslove Oblasti 275
W B K see W B K Forschungsberichte 475
W B K Forschungsberichte (Univeritaet Karlsruhe, Institut fuer Werkzeugmaschinen und Betriebstechnik) (US) 475
W.C.J. Meredith Memorial Lectures (CN ISSN 0509-5166) 667
W C O T P Annual Report see W C O T P Report 444
W C O T P Report (World Confederation of Organizations of the Teaching Profession) (SZ) 421, 444
W E M A Bezugsquellenverzeichnis (GW ISSN 0171-5038) 493
W E M A Directory see American Electronics Association Directory 450
W F T - Werkstoff-Forschung Und - Technik (US) 475
W G A Geschaeftsbericht (Wirtschaftsvereinigung Gross- und Aussenhandel) (GW ISSN 0042-966X) 260
W H I M S Y see World Humor and Irony Membership Serial Yearbook 708
W H O Offset Publications (World Health Organization) (UN) 957, 959
W H O Technical Report Series (World Health Organization) (UN ISSN 0512-3054) 768, 957
W I D Forum (Office of Women in International Development) (US) 264, 1030, 1129
W I D Working Papers see Working Papers on Women in International Development 265

W I T S (Wisconsin Introduction to Scandinavia) (US ISSN 0742-7018) 506
W.P.A.S. Museletter (Washington Performing Arts Society) (US ISSN 0092-4113) 375, 843
W P S Professional Handbook Series (Western Psychological Services) (US ISSN 0083-8977) 938
W R I Newsletter (Western Review Institute) (US) 911
Waelzlagertechnik (GW ISSN 0511-0653) 493
Wage Rates, Salaries and Hours of Labour in Nova Scotia (CN ISSN 0382-1242) 276
Wages and Total Labour Costs for Workers: International Survey (SW ISSN 0280-4743) 276
Wages for Housework. Campaign Bulletin (CN) 1129
Wagga Wagga and District Historical Society. Journal (AT ISSN 0085-7858) 573
Waigani Seminar. Papers (PP ISSN 0085-7866) 573
Wakayama-ken Kisho Nenpo see Wakayama Prefecture. Annual Report of Meteorology 807
Wakayama Prefecture. Annual Report of Meteorology/Wakayama-ken Kisho Nenpo (JA) 807
Wake Newslitter Monographs (UK) 737
Wakefield Court Rolls Series (UK) 601
Waksman Foundation of Japan. Report (JA ISSN 0509-5832) 873
Walden's A B C Guide and Paper Production Yearbook (US ISSN 0083-7024) 859
Wales. National Library. Handlist on Manuscripts in the National Library of Wales (UK ISSN 0065-0293) 686
Wales Best Holidays (UK) 1118
Wales Business Directory (UK) 237
Walia (ET ISSN 0083-7059) 368
Walk (AT) 1047
The Walker (AT) 1047
Walker - Ames Lectures (US) 562
Walker Art Museum. Bulletin see Bowdoin College. Museum of Art. Occasional Papers 827
Walker's Manual of Western Corporations (US ISSN 0092-749X) 268
Walker's Manual of Western Corporations & Securities see Walker's Manual of Western Corporations 268
Walker's Old Moore's Almanack (UK ISSN 0083-7067) 463
Walks and Trails in Scotland (UK) 1118
Wall Street Journal Index (US ISSN 0083-7075) 234, 268
Wall Street Research Reports (US) 268
Wallace Stevens Journal (US ISSN 0148-7132) 744
Wallduerner Heimatblaetter (GW) 538
Walling Review (AT) 188
Wallraf-Richartz-Jahrbuch; Westdeutsches Jahrbuch fuer Kunstgeschichte. Neue Folge (GW) 112
Wallraf-Richartz-Jahrbuch; Westdeutsches Jahrbuch fuer Kunstgeschichte see Wallraf-Richartz-Jahrbuch; Westdeutsches Jahrbuch fuer Kunstgeschichte. Neue Folge 112
Walsall Chamber of Commerce & Industry Directory (UK) 237
Walt Disney World (Year) (US) 1118
Walt Disney's Donald Duck Fun Annual (UK) 336
Walt Disney's Mickey Mouse Club Annual (UK) 336
Walt Disney's Winnie the Pooh Annual(UK) 336
Walter and Andree de Nottbeck Foundation Scientific Reports (FI ISSN 0358-6758) 152, 169
Walter Lynwood Fleming Lectures in Southern History (US ISSN 0083-7121) 611
Walter W.S. Cook Alumni Lecture (US ISSN 0083-7148) 112

Walters Art Gallery. Journal (US ISSN 0083-7156) 112
Want's Federal-State Court Directory (US ISSN 0742-1095) 667
War - Peace Bibliography Series (US) 912
Warburg Institute. Oxford-Warburg Studies (UK) 634
Warburg Institute. Studies (UK ISSN 0083-7199) 634
Warburg Institute. Surveys see Warburg Institute. Surveys and Texts 634
Warburg Institute. Surveys and Texts (UK ISSN 0266-1772) 634
Ward - Phillips Lectures in English Language and Literature (US ISSN 0083-7210) 737
Ward's Automotive Yearbook (US ISSN 0083-7229) 1093
Ward's Business Directory of Largest U S Companies (US ISSN 0882-7990) 318
Ward's Business Directory of Major International Companies (US ISSN 0882-8016) 318
Ward's Business Directory of Major U S Private Companies (US ISSN 0882-8008) 318
Ward's Directory of Largest U S Companies (US) 202
Ward's Directory of 49,000 Private U.S. Companies (US ISSN 0737-4445) 318
Ward's Directory of 55,000 Largest U S Corporations see Ward's Directory of Largest U S Companies 202
Warehousing/Distribution Directory (US) 1105
Warsaw Agricultural University. S G G W - A R. Annals. Agricultural Economics and Rural Sociology (PL ISSN 0208-5720) 50, 1030
Warsaw Agricultural University. S G G W - A R. Annals. Agriculture (PL ISSN 0208-5712) 37
Warsaw Agricultural University. S G G W A R. Annals. Animal Science (PL ISSN 0208-5739) 68
Warsaw Agricultural University. S G G W-A R. Annals. Food Technology and Nutrition (PL ISSN 0208-5755) 521, 847
Warsaw Agricultural University. S G G W-A R. Annals. Forestry and Wood Technology (PL ISSN 0208-5704) 530
Warsaw Agricultural University. S G G W-A R. Annals. Horticulture (PL ISSN 0208-5747) 534
Warsaw Agricultural University. S G G W - A R. Annals. Land Reclamation (PL ISSN 0208-5771) 61
Warsaw Agricultural University. S G G W-A R. Annals. Veterinary Medicine(PL ISSN 0208-5763) 1122
Warsaw Agricultural University. Treatises and Monographs see Szkola Glowna Gospodarstwa Wiejskiego - Akademia Rolnicza. Rozprawy Naukowe i Monografie 35
Warships of the World see Weyers Flottentaschenbuch 813
Warwick Economic Research Papers (UK ISSN 0083-7350) 202
Warwick Industrial Economic and Business Research Papers see Warwick Papers in Management 202
Warwick Papers in Industry, Business and Administration see Warwick Papers in Management 202
Warwick Papers in Management (UK) 202
Warwick Statistics Service. Occasional Review see University of Warwick Business Information Service. Occasional Review 1066
Was Heisst Gut Leben? see Arbeitsgemeinschaft fuer Lebensniveauvergleiche. Schriftenreihe 1006
Was Kostet der Geschaeftswagen? (GW) 1093
Was Kostet Mein Auto? see Was Kostet der Geschaeftswagen 1093
Waseda Business and Economic Studies(JA) 202

WASEDA DAIGAKU

Waseda Daigaku Rikogakubu Kiyo *see* Waseda University. School of Science and Engineering. Memoirs *1003*
Waseda Political Studies (JA ISSN 0511-196X) *911*
Waseda University. Casting Research Laboratory. Report (JA ISSN 0511-1927) *800*
Waseda University. School of Science and Engineering. Memoirs/Waseda Daigaku Rikogakubu Kiyo (JA ISSN 0369-1950) *475, 1003*
Waseda University. Science and Engineering Research Laboratory. Report (JA ISSN 0285-4333) *475, 1003*
Washington *see* Washington (Year) *611*
Washington. Council for Postsecondary Education. Report (US) *441*
Washington. Department of Natural Resources. Report of Investigations (US) *397*
Washington. Employment Security Department. Annual Demographic Information (US) *849*
Washington (State). Attorney General's Office. Charitable Trust Directory (US) *1021*
Washington (State). Attorney General's Office. Directory of Charitable Organizations and Trusts Registered with the Office of Attorney General *see* Washington (State). Attorney General's Office. Charitable Trust Directory *1021*
Washington (State) Department of Fisheries. Technical Report (US ISSN 0083-7474) *513*
Washington (State). Department of Natural Resources. Annual Fire Statistics (US) *529, 1066*
Washington (State). Department of Revenue. Forest Tax Annual Report *see* Washington (State). Department of Revenue. Forest Tax Section. Forest Tax Annual Report *300*
Washington (State). Department of Revenue. Forest Tax Section. Forest Tax Annual Report (US) *300, 528*
Washington (State). Department of Revenue. Research and Information Division. Comparative State/Local Taxes *see* Washington (State). Department of Revenue. Research Section. Comparative State/Local Taxes *300*
Washington (State). Department of Revenue. Research and Information Division. Property Tax Levy and Collection Statistics. *see* Washington (State). Department of Revenue. Research Section. Property Tax Levy and Collection Statistics *300*
Washington (State). Department of Revenue. Research Section. Comparative State/Local Taxes (US) *300*
Washington (State). Department of Revenue. Research Section. Property Tax Levy and Collection Statistics (US) *300*
Washington (State). Division of Geology and Earth Resources. Bulletin (US) *397, 821*
Washington (State). Division of Geology and Earth Resources. Information Circular (US ISSN 0147-1783) *397, 821*
Washington (State) Game Department. Applied Research Section. Bulletin *see* Washington (State) Game Department. Mitigation Section. Bulletin *368*
Washington (State) Game Department. Mitigation Section. Bulletin (US) *368*
Washington. State Health Plan (US) *886*
Washington (State). Joint Board of Legislative Ethics. Annual Report (US) *947*
Washington (State) Legislature. Pictorial Directory (US ISSN 0091-8253) *947*

Washington (State) Office of Financial Management. Forecasting and Support Division. Population Trends *see* Washington (State) Office of Financial Management. Policy Analysis and Forecasting. Population Trends *925*
Washington (State) Office of Financial Management. Policy Analysis and Forecasting. Population Trends (US) *925*
Washington (State) Office of Program Planning and Fiscal Management. Population and Enrollment Section. Population Trends *see* Washington (State) Office of Financial Management. Policy Analysis and Forecasting. Population Trends *925*
Washington (State). Vocational Rehabilitation Services Division. State Facilities Development Plan (US) *445*
Washington (State). Vocational Rehabilitation Services Division. State Facilities Plan *see* Washington (State). Vocational Rehabilitation Services Division. State Facilities Development Plan *445*
Washington. Utilities and Transportation Commission. Railroad-Highway Grade Crossing Accidents. Summary and Analysis (US) *1084, 1095*
Washington (Year) (US ISSN 0083-7393) *611*
Washington Agricultural Statistics (US ISSN 0095-4330) *44*
Washington Education Directory (US) *421*
Washington Information Directory (US) *611*
Washington Manufacturers Register (US ISSN 0148-5687) *319*
Washington Papers (US ISSN 0278-937X) *920*
Washington Performing Arts Society Museletter *see* W.P.A.S. Museletter *843*
Washington Representatives (US ISSN 0192-060X) *947*
Washington State Dental Journal (US ISSN 0083-7431) *780*
Washington State Entomological Society Proceedings (US ISSN 0043-0773) *166*
Washington State Industrial Directory *see* MacRae's Washington State Industrial Directory *313*
Washington State University. College of Engineering. Annual Report *see* Quest (Pullman) *474*
Washington University. School of Medicine Library. Library Newsletter(US) *686, 768*
Washington University. School of Medicine Library. Library Notes *see* Washington University. School of Medicine Library. Library Newsletter *686*
Washington Want Ads *see* Now Hiring *848*
Washington's Almanac (US ISSN 0884-9064) *540*
Washout Review (US) *744*
Wasser-Kalender (GW ISSN 0511-3520) *1127*
Wasser und Abwasser in Forschung und Praxis (GW ISSN 0512-5030) *1127*
Wasserrecht und Wasserwirtschaft (GW ISSN 0508-1254) *667, 1127*
Wasserversorgungs- und Abwassertechnik. Jahrbuch (GW) *1127*
Waste Management Research Abstracts(UN ISSN 0083-761X) *959*
Watch It (US) *500*
Watch Review. Curriculum *see* Montre Suisse. Annuaire *644*
Watchmaker, Jeweller and Silversmith Directory of Trade Names and Punch Marks *see* Jewellers' Reference Book *644*
Water (US ISSN 0083-7636) *1127*
Water & Pollution Control. Directory and Buyers' Guide (CN) *1127*

Water and Pollution Control. Directory and Handbook *see* Water & Pollution Control. Directory and Buyers' Guide *1127*
Water and Power Development Consultancy Services. Annual Report and Statement of Accounts (II) *1127*
Water & Waste Treatment: Latin American Industrial Report (US) *250, 484*
Water Conservation and Inland Fisheries *see* Acta Academiae Agriculturae ac Technicae Olstenensis. Protectio Aquarum et Piscatoria *1123*
Water in Biological Systems (US ISSN 0083-7652) *1126*
Water Pollution: a Series of Monographs (US) *500*
Water Pollution Control Federation Conference. Abstracts of Technical Papers (US) *13, 501*
Water Quality Data for Ontario Streams & Lakes (CN ISSN 0383-5472) *500, 1127*
Water Quality Monitoring Data for Georgia Streams (US ISSN 0097-7519) *500*
Water Research Centre. Annual Report *see* Water Research Centre. Annual Review *500*
Water Research Centre. Annual Review(UK) *500*
Water Research Foundation of Australia. Bulletin *see* Water Research Foundation of Australia. Reports *1127*
Water Research Foundation of Australia. Reports (AT ISSN 0085-8021) *1127*
Water Research in Australia *see* Water Research in Australia: Current Projects *1127*
Water Research in Australia: Current Projects (AT) *1127*
Water Resources Abstracts *see* Hydro-Abstracts *1128*
Water Resources Association of the Delaware River Basin. Alerting Bulletin (US) *1127*
Water-Resources Investigations *see* U.S. Geological Survey. Water Resources Investigations *404*
Water Resources Monographs (US) *1127*
Water Resources Report Series (US) *1127*
Water Resources Summary (US ISSN 0518-6374) *404, 1127*
Water Services Handbook *see* Water Services Year Book *491*
Water Services Year Book (UK) *491*
Water Transport Statistics of India (II) *1066, 1087*
Waterborne Commerce of the United States (US ISSN 0083-7725) *1104*
Waterloo Historical Society. Report (CN ISSN 0083-7733) *611*
Watermarks (US) *1127*
Waters (CN ISSN 0383-2031) *513*
Waterway Guide (US) *1042*
Watford and District Industrial History Society. Journal (UK ISSN 0307-5281) *601*
Watford and District Industrial History Society Bulletin *see* Watford and District Industrial History Society. Journal *601*
Wayne State University Law School. Comparative Criminal Law Project. Monograph Series (US) *373*
Wayne State University Law School. Comparative Criminal Law Project. Publications Series (US) *373*
We Represent in Israel and Abroad. (IS ISSN 0302-5489) *260*
We the People (US) *947*
Wealth and Welfare of Andhra Pradesh Series *see* Social Sciences Research Series *1011*
Weather Almanac (US ISSN 0731-5627) *807*
Weather Guide Calendar *see* Minnesota Weather Guide Calendar *806*
Weatherguide *see* Minnesota Weather Guide Calendar *806*
Wedding Guide Magazine (AT) *615*
Wedgwood Society. Proceedings (UK ISSN 0511-4063) *320*

Weed Abstracts (UK ISSN 0043-1729) *13, 44*
Weed Control Manual and Herbicide Guide (US ISSN 0511-411X) *61, 534*
Weed Science Society of America. Abstracts (US) *13, 44*
Weed Society of America. Abstracts *see* Weed Science Society of America. Abstracts *44*
Weeds Trees & Turf Golf Daily (US) *534, 1040*
Weekend Book of Jokes (UK) *712*
Weekender (UK ISSN 0260-9061) *1118*
Weekender and Daytripper (UK) *1166*
Weekly Abstract Newsletter: Administration and Management *see* Abstract Newsletter: Administration and Management *948*
Weekly Abstract Newsletter: Agriculture and Food *see* Abstract Newsletter: Agriculture & Food *38*
Weekly Abstract Newsletter: Civil Engineering *see* Abstract Newsletter: Civil Engineering *476*
Weekly Abstract Newsletter: Computers, Control and Information Theory *see* Abstract Newsletter: Computers, Control & Information Theory *353*
Weekly Abstract Newsletter: Electrotechnology *see* Abstract Newsletter: Electrotechnology *461*
Weekly Abstract Newsletter: Energy *see* Abstract Newsletter: Energy *468*
Weekly Abstract Newsletter: Government Inventions for Licensing *see* Abstract Newsletter: Government Inventions for Licensing *1072*
Weekly Abstract Newsletter: Health Planning and Health Services Research *see* Abstract Newsletter: Health Planning & Health Services Research *886*
Weekly Abstract Newsletter: Materials Sciences *see* Abstract Newsletter: Materials Sciences *476*
Weekly Abstract Newsletter: N A S A Earth Resources Survey Program *see* Abstract Newsletter: N A S A Earth Resources Survey Program *1145*
Weekly Abstract Newsletter: Natural Resources and Earth Sciences *see* Abstract Newsletter: Natural Resources & Earth Sciences *368*
Weekly Abstract Newsletter: Ocean Technology and Engineering *see* Abstract Newsletter: Ocean Technology & Engineering *381*
Weekly Abstract Newsletter: Physics *see* Abstract Newsletter: Physics *892*
Weekly Abstract Newsletter: Problem-Solving Information for State and Local Governments *see* Abstract Newsletter: Problem-Solving Information for State and Local Governments *948*
Weekly Abstract Newsletter: Urban and Regional Technology and Development *see* Abstract Newsletter: Urban and Regional Technology and Development *627*
Weekly News Annual (NZ) *1118*
Wees Veilig Tuis *see* Be Safe at Home *952*
Wege Vor- und Fruehgeschichtlicher Forschung (GW) *95*
Wehrwissenschaftliche Berichte *see* Bernard und Graefe Aktuell *810*
Weimarer Monographien zur Ur- und Fruehgeschichte (GE ISSN 0232-265X) *78, 95*
Weissbuch zur Sicherheit der Bundesrepublik Deutschland und zur Lage der Bundeswehr (GW) *813*
Weizmann Institute of Science, Rehovot, Israel. Scientific Activities (IS ISSN 0083-7849) *1003, 1072*
Welcome to Finland (DK ISSN 0085-8048) *1118*
Welding and Fabricating Data Book (US ISSN 0278-7067) *802*
Welding Data Book *see* Welding and Fabricating Data Book *802*
Welding Research Council Yearbook (US) *802*

Wellcome Unit for the History of Medicine. Research Publications (UK ISSN 0143-7984) 133, 768
Wellesley Papers (CN) 920
Wellness Media: An Audiovisual Sourcebook (National Information Center for Educational Media) (US) 13, 886
Wellsiana (UK) 14
Welsh Amateur Swimming Association. Handbook (UK) 1036
Welsh Association of Youth Clubs. Yearbook of Activities (UK) 341
Welsh Bibliographical Society. Journal (UK ISSN 0083-7911) 133
Welsh Economic Trends (UK ISSN 0262-8309) 220
Welsh Plant Breeding Station. Annual Report (UK) 61, 162
Welsh Pony and Cob Society Journal (UK) 1043
Welsh Soils Discussion Group. Report (UK ISSN 0083-7938) 61
Welsh Studies in Education Series (UK ISSN 0083-7946) 421
Die Welt des Orients (GW ISSN 0340-6229) 562
Weltrundschau (SZ) 562
Weltwirtschaft am Jahreswechsel (GW ISSN 0433-7603) 202, 601
Wenner Gren Center International Symposium Series (UK ISSN 0083-7989) 1003
Wenner - Gren Foundation for Anthropological Research. Annual Report (US) 78
Wenner - Gren Foundation for Anthropological Research. Report see Wenner - Gren Foundation for Anthropological Research. Annual Report 78
Wer Baut Maschinen (GW ISSN 0083-9299) 493
Wer ist Wer in der Schweiz und im Fuerstenstum Lichtenstein? see Swiss Biographical Index of Prominent Persons 135
Wer Leitet (GW) 202
Wer Liefert Was? (GW) 319
Wer Schreibt und Spricht Worueber? see Journalisten - Handbuch 646
Wer Schreibt Worueber? Journalisten-Handbuch see Journalisten - Handbuch 646
Wer und Was in der Deutschen Fleisch-Fisch- und Feinkost-Industrie (GW ISSN 0170-7353) 68, 513
Wer und Was in der Deutschen Getraenke-Industrie (GW ISSN 0171-4457) 120
Wer und Was in der Deutschen Koerperpflege-, Wasch- und Reinigungsmittel-Industrie (GW ISSN 0171-4341) 119, 339
Wer und Was in der Deutschen Pharmazeutischen-Industrie (GW ISSN 0171-4449) 873
Wer und Was in der Deutschen Suesswarenindustrie (GW) 319
Werbe - Mittel Katalog (GW) 276
Werbealmanach (AU) 16
Werbung in Deutschland see Jahrbuch der Werbung 828
Werken und Wohnen (GW ISSN 0083-8047) 100
Werkgroep Elites. Bulletin (NE) 601
Werkstattbuecher fuer Betriebsfachleute Konstrukteure und Studenten see Fertigung und Betrieb 289
Werkstattschriften zur Sozialpsychiatrie (GW ISSN 0173-3524) 784, 791, 938
Werte Unserer Heimat (GE ISSN 0138-3213) 550, 601
Wertheim Publications in Industrial Relations (US) 276
Wessex Cave Club Occasional Publication (UK ISSN 0083-811X) 397
Wessex Studies in Special Education (UK ISSN 0144-5359) 445, 449
West Africa Annual (NR ISSN 0083-8144) 567
West Africa Rice Development Association. Annual Report (LB) 61
West Africa Rice Development Association. Current Bibliography (LB) 44, 133

West Africa Rice Development Association. Occasional Paper (LB) 37, 521
West African Archaeological Newsletter see West African Journal of Archaeology 95
West African Institute of Social and Economic Research. Annual Report see Nigerian Institute of Social and Economic Research. Annual Report 1010
West African Journal of Archaeology (NR ISSN 0083-8160) 95
West African Journal of Modern Languages/Revue Ouest Africaine des Langues Vivantes (NR ISSN 0331-0531) 708
West African Journal of Pharmacology and Drug Research (NR ISSN 0303-691X) 873
West Australian Nut and Tree Crop Association Yearbook (AT ISSN 0312-8997) 61, 521
West Australian Nutgrowing Society Yearbook see West Australian Nut and Tree Crop Association Yearbook 521
West Australian Reports (AT) 667
West Australian Transporter Year Book(AT) 1166
West Bengal. Annual Financial Statement (Budget) (II) 220, 1066
West Bengal. Bureau of Applied Economics and Statistics. Statistical Handbook (II ISSN 0511-5493) 220, 1066
West Bengal Labour Gazette (II ISSN 0043-3071) 277
West Coast Plays (US ISSN 0147-4502) 1079
West Coast Reliability Symposium (US ISSN 0083-8217) 282
West Country's Maritime Story (UK) 1166
West Europe Report (US) 250, 911
West European Living Costs (UK ISSN 0142-646X) 260
West Georgia College Review (US ISSN 0043-3136) 342
West Georgia College Studies in the Social Sciences (US ISSN 0081-8682) 1013
West Hills Review (US) 744
West Malaysia Annual Statistics of External Trade (MY ISSN 0085-8080) 220
West Midlands Archives Newsletter (UK ISSN 0143-8158) 601
West of Scotland Visitor (UK ISSN 0260-4426) 1118
West Tennessee Historical Society. Papers (US ISSN 0361-6215) 611
West Texas Geological Society. Fieldtrip Guidebook (US) 397
West Texas Geological Society. Publications (US) 397
West Texas Historical Association Yearbook (US) 611
West Virginia. Agricultural and Forestry Experiment Station. Annual Report (US) 37
West Virginia. Agricultural and Forestry Experiment Station. Bulletin (US) 37, 528
West Virginia. Agricultural and Forestry Experiment Station. Circular (US) 37
West Virginia. Agricultural and Forestry Experiment Station. Current Report (US) 37
West Virginia. Agricultural Experiment Station, Morgantown. Current Report see West Virginia. Agricultural and Forestry Experiment Station. Current Report 37
West Virginia. Commission on Aging. Annual Progress Report (US ISSN 0083-8438) 552
West Virginia. Department of Energy. Annual Report and Directory (US) 821
West Virginia. Department of Mines. Annual Report see West Virginia. Department of Energy. Annual Report and Directory 821
West Virginia. Department of Mines. Directory of Mines see West Virginia. Department of Energy. Annual Report and Directory 821

West Virginia. Geological and Economic Survey. Annual Report (US) 397
West Virginia. Human Rights Commission. Report (US ISSN 0083-8594) 914
West Virginia. Legislature. Commission on Special Investigations. Report to the West Virginia Legislature (US) 947
West Virginia. Legislature. Purchasing Practices and Procedures Commission. Report to the West Virginia Legislature. see West Virginia. Legislature. Commission on Special Investigations. Report to the West Virginia Legislature 947
West Virginia. Mineral Industry Status (US) 821
West Virginia: An Economic-Statistical Profile (US) 237
West Virginia Coal Mining Institute. Proceedings (US ISSN 0083-842X) 821
West Virginia Education Directory (US ISSN 0085-8099) 421
West Virginia Employment and Earnings Trends: Annual Summary (US) 277
West Virginia Forestry Notes (US ISSN 0197-1387) 528
West Virginia Geologic Investigations see West Virginia Reports of Geologic Investigations 397
West Virginia Geological Survey. River Basin Bulletins see West Virginia River Basin Bulletins 397
West Virginia Geological Survey Newsletter see Mountain State Geology 391
West Virginia History (US ISSN 0043-325X) 611
West Virginia Library Commission. Newsletter (US) 686
West Virginia Manufacturers Register (US) 319
West Virginia Mineral Producers and Processors Directory (US) 821
West Virginia Mineral Producers Directory see West Virginia Mineral Producers and Processors Directory 821
West Virginia Reports of Geologic Investigations (US) 397
West Virginia Research League. Statistical Handbook (US ISSN 0091-6102) 300
West Virginia River Basin Bulletins (US) 397, 404
West Virginia Statistical Handbook (US ISSN 0511-6775) 950
West Virginia Tax Calendar (US) 300
West Virginia Union List of Serials (US ISSN 0512-4743) 133
West Virginia University. Business and Economic Studies (US ISSN 0068-4392) 202
Westcoast Offshore Guide see Danish Offshore Guide and Yearbook 863
Westdeutsche Gesellschaft fuer Familiekunde. Mitteilungen (GW) 537
Western Association of Fish and Wildlife Agencies. Proceedings (US) 368
Western Association of Graduate Schools. Proceedings of the Annual Meeting (US ISSN 0511-6848) 441
Western Association of Map Libraries. Occasional Papers (US) 686
Western Association of Schools and Colleges Directory (US) 431
Western Association of State Game and Fish Commissioners. Proceedings see Western Association of Fish and Wildlife Agencies. Proceedings 368
Western Australia. Basic Information for Industrialists (AT) 202
Western Australia. Conservation and Environment Council Annual Report see Western Australia. Environmental Protection Authority. Annual Report 368
Western Australia. Department for Community Services. Annual Report (AT) 1021

Western Australia. Department for Community Welfare. Annual Report see Western Australia. Department for Community Services. Annual Report 1021
Western Australia. Department of Agriculture. Animal Division. Annual Report (AT) 68
Western Australia. Department of Agriculture. Annual Report (AT ISSN 0726-9366) 37
Western Australia. Department of Agriculture. Bulletin (AT ISSN 0729-0012) 37
Western Australia. Department of Agriculture. Division of Plant Production. Annual Report (AT) 61
Western Australia. Department of Agriculture. Rural Economics and Marketing Section. Report on the Market Milk Industry in Western Australia (AT) 50, 63
Western Australia. Department of Agriculture. Technical Bulletin (AT ISSN 0083-8675) 37
Western Australia. Department of Agriculture. Wheat and Sheep Division. Annual Report see Western Australia. Department of Agriculture. Division of Plant Production. Annual Report 61
Western Australia. Department of Corrections. Annual Report (AT) 373
Western Australia. Department of Fisheries and Wildlife. Fisheries Research Bulletin (AT ISSN 0155-9435) 500, 514
Western Australia. Department of Fisheries and Wildlife. Report (AT ISSN 0726-0733) 368, 514
Western Australia. Department of Fisheries and Wildlife. Wildlife Research Bulletin (AT ISSN 0726-0725) 368
Western Australia. Department of Industrial Development. Building Investment (AT ISSN 0726-9501) 240
Western Australia. Department of Prisons. Annual Report see Western Australia. Department of Corrections. Annual Report 373
Western Australia. Division of Animal Production. Annual Report (AT) 68
Western Australia. Education Department. Schools & Staffing (AT ISSN 0811-1154) 444
Western Australia. Environmental Protection Authority. Annual Report (AT) 368, 500
Western Australia. Environmental Protection Council. Annual Report see Western Australia. Environmental Protection Authority. Annual Report 368
Western Australia. Fisheries and Fauna Department. Bulletin see Western Australia. Department of Fisheries and Wildlife. Fisheries Research Bulletin 514
Western Australia. Geological Survey. Bulletin (AT ISSN 0085-8137) 397
Western Australia. Geological Survey. Mineral Resources Bulletin (AT ISSN 0510-2014) 1166
Western Australia. Geological Survey. Report (AT ISSN 0085-8145) 397
Western Australia. Government Chemical Laboratories. Report of Investigations (AT ISSN 0085-8153) 325
Western Australia. Law Reform Commission. Annual Report (AT) 667
Western Australia. Main Roads Department. Technical Report (AT ISSN 0310-6330) 1166
Western Australia. Public Library, Museum and Art Gallery. Record see Western Australian Museum. Records 831
Western Australia. State Energy Commission. Annual Report (AT) 467
Western Australia. Technical Education Division. Handbook (AT) 441

Western Australia. Transport Commission. Annual Report of the Commissioner of Transport (AT) 1084
Western Australia Law Almanac (AT ISSN 0085-8161) 667
Western Australia Museum, Perth. Report of the Museum Board see Western Australian Museum, Perth. Annual Report 831
Western Australian Coastal Shipping Commission. Annual Report (AT) 1104
Western Australian Herbarium. Research Notes (AT) 162
Western Australian Institute of Technology. Department of Biology. Bulletin see Western Australian Institute of Technology. School of Biology. Bulletin 149
Western Australian Institute of Technology. Library. Annual Report (AT) 686
Western Australian Institute of Technology. Library. Western Library Studies (AT ISSN 0810-5030) 686
Western Australian Institute of Technology. School of Biology. Bulletin (AT) 149
Western Australian Museum. Records (AT ISSN 0312-3162) 831
Western Australian Museum. Records. Supplement (AT ISSN 0313-122X) 831
Western Australian Museum, Perth. Annual Report (AT) 831
Western Australian Nature Reserve Management Plan (AT ISSN 0726-2469) 1166
Western Australian Pocket Yearbook (AT ISSN 0083-8756) 250, 573
Western Australian Reports (AT ISSN 0083-8764) 667
Western Australian Resource Developement Services Directory (AT ISSN 0816-2271) 319
Western Australian Wildlife Authority. Annual Report (AT) 368, 514
Western Australian Yearbook. New Series (AT ISSN 0083-8772) 250, 573
Western Bank Directory (US ISSN 0272-5371) 234
Western Canada. Alaska Camping see Western Canada Alaska Campbook 1119
Western Canada Alaska Campbook (US) 1119
Western Canada and Alaska; Alberta, British Columbia, Manitoba, Saskatchewan, Northwest Territories, Yukon Territory and Alaska TourBook see Tourbook: Western Canada and Alaska 1117
Western Canada Water and Sewage Conference. Bulletin see Western Canada Water and Waste Water Association. Bulletin 500
Western Canada Water and Waste Water Association. Bulletin (CN) 500
Western Canadian Anthropologist (CN ISSN 0829-0547) 78
Western Canadian Society for Horticulture . Report of Proceedings of Annual Meeting (CN ISSN 0083-8810) 534
Western Canadian Steam Locomotive Directory (CN ISSN 0085-8188) 1095
Western Dry Kiln Asociation. Proceedings (US) 530
Western Dry Kiln Clubs. Proceedings see Western Dry Kiln Asociation. Proceedings 530
Western Europe Report see West Europe Report 250
Western European Association. Statistiques de Traffic see International Civil Airports Association. Statistiques de Traffic. Resultats Generaux 1088
Western Forestry Center. Annual Report see Forest World 525
Western Forestry Conference. Executive Summaries of Proceedings see Western Forestry Conference. Proceedings 528

Western Forestry Conference. Proceedings (US) 528
Western Foundation of Vertebrate Zoology. Occasional Papers (US ISSN 0511-7542) 171
Western Frontier Library (US ISSN 0083-887X) 611
Western Frontiersmen Series (US ISSN 0083-8888) 611
Western Geographer (AT ISSN 0313-8860) 550
Western Geographical Series (CN ISSN 0315-2022) 500, 551
Western Government Directories (US) 950
Western Hemisphere Nutrition Congress. Proceedings (US) 847
Western Highway Institute. Research Committee. Report (US ISSN 0083-8918) 484
Western Humor and Irony Membership Serial Yearbook see World Humor and Irony Membership Serial Yearbook 708
Western Industrial Purchasing Guide and Electronic/Sources see E I A Guide 283
Western Lands and Waters Series (US ISSN 0083-8934) 368
Western Magazin (GW) 611
Western New York Business Directory see Greater Buffalo Business Directory 309
Western New York Buyer's Guide and Roster see Greater Buffalo Business Directory 309
Western New York Index (US ISSN 0884-3279) 13, 540
Western Nigeria Development Corporation. Industrial Directory see Investments and Credit Corporation of Oyo State. Industrial Directory 310
Western Ontario Series see University of Western Ontario Series in Philosophy of Science 883
Western Pharmacology Society. Proceedings (US ISSN 0083-8969) 873
Western Psychological Services Professional Handbook Series see W P S Professional Handbook Series 938
Western Retail Lumbermen's Directory (CN) 530
Western Review Institute Newsletter see W R I Newsletter 911
Western Snow Conference. Proceedings(US) 404
Western Society for French History. Proceedings of the Annual Meeting (US ISSN 0099-0329) 601
Western Society of Malacologists. Annual Report (US ISSN 0361-1175) 178
Western Society of Malacologists. Echo; Abstracts and Proceedings of the Annual Meeting see Western Society of Malacologists. Annual Report 178
Western Society of Weed Science. Proceedings (US ISSN 0091-4487) 162
Western Society of Weed Science. Research Progress Report (US ISSN 0090-8142) 162
Western State. Estimates Including Budget Speech and Memorandum see Oyo State. Estimates Including Budget Speech and Memorandum 945
Western State. Gazette see Oyo State of Nigeria Gazette 945
Western State. Ministry of Economic Planning and Community Development. Annual Report see Oyo State. Ministry of Economic Planning and Community Development. Annual Report 291
Western Transportation Law Seminar. Papers and Proceedings (US ISSN 0271-4396) 667, 1084
Western Washington State College. Aquatic Studies Program. Technical Report Series see Western Washington University. Institute for Watershed Studies. Technical Report Series 1127

Western Washington State College. Institute for Freshwater Studies. Technical Report Series see Western Washington University. Institute for Watershed Studies. Technical Report Series 1127
Western Washington State College. Program in East Asian Studies. Occasional Papers see Studies on East Asia 853
Western Washington University. Institute for Watershed Studies. Technical Report Series (US) 1127
Western Wood Products Association. Statistical Yearbook (US ISSN 0195-931X) 529, 531
Westernlore Ghost Town Series (US ISSN 0083-9019) 611
Westex: I E E E Western Conference on Knowledge-Based Engineering and Expert Systems. Proceedings (US) 356
Westfaelische Forschungen (GW ISSN 0083-9027) 517, 601
Westfaelische Zeitschrift (GW ISSN 0083-9043) 601
Westfaelischen Museum fuer Naturkunde. Abhandlungen (GW) 1003
Westfalia Sacra (GW) 601, 974
Westminster Chamber of Commerce Directory (UK) 237
Westminster Hospital Nurses' League. Publication (UK) 784
Westminster Studies in Education (UK ISSN 0140-6728) 421
Westpreussen-Jahrbuch (GW ISSN 0511-8484) 601
Wetenskaplike en Tegniese Vereinigings in Suid-Afrika see Scientific and Technical Societies in South Africa 1000
Wetenskaplike Navorsingsorganisasies in Suid-Afrika see Scientific Research Organizations in South Africa 1000
Weterynaria see Acta Academiae Agriculturae ac Technicae Olstenensis. Veterynaria 1120
Weyers Flottentaschenbuch/Warships of the World (GW ISSN 0083-9078) 813
Whakatane & District Historical Society. Monographs (NZ ISSN 0110-4004) 573
Whales Research Institute, Tokyo, Japan. Scientific Reports/Geirui Kenkyusho Eibun Hokoku (JA ISSN 0083-9086) 178
Wharton's Complete Office Automation Guide (UK) 353
What Every Veteran Should Know (US ISSN 0083-9108) 813
What It Costs to Run an Agency (US) 282
What Mining Means to Australians (AT) 821
What Research Says to the Teacher Series (US ISSN 0083-9116) 449
What They Said (US ISSN 0512-5804) 911
What to Do in the Norfolk Broads (UK) 1119
What You Should Know about Taxes in Puerto Rico (PR ISSN 0083-9132) 300
What's Cooking in Congress? (US ISSN 0278-4947) 737
What's Developing in Alaska (US) 37
What's New About London, Jack? (US) 737
What's on North West (UK) 1119
Wheat Situation see Australia. Bureau of Agricultural Economics. Wheat: Situation and Outlook 1147
Wheats of the World (CN) 1166
Wheel Series (US) 985
Wheelers R V Resort and Campground Guide: North American Edition (US) 1047, 1119
Wheelers Recreational Vehicle Resort and Campground Guide see Wheelers R V Resort and Campground Guide: North American Edition 1119
Where America's Large Foundations Make Their Grants (US ISSN 0083-9167) 634, 1072
Where Shall I Go to College to Study Advertising? (US) 16, 431

Where the Colleges Rank (US) 431
Where to Build - Where to Repair (NO ISSN 0800-1200) 319, 1104
Where to Buy (UK ISSN 0083-9175) 286, 319
Where to Buy, Board or Train a Dog (US) 869
Where to Buy Hardwood Plywood see Where to Buy Hardwood Plywood and Veneer 189
Where to Buy Hardwood Plywood and Veneer (US) 189, 531
Where to Camp in France (UK) 1166
Where to Camp in Germany (UK) 1166
Where to Camp in Italy (UK) 1166
Where to Camp in Spain (UK) 1166
Where to Eat & Entertain - Singapore (SI) 621, 1119
Where to Eat In and Around Glasgow (UK) 621
Where to Eat in Berkshire (UK) 621, 1119
Where to Eat in Bournemouth, Poole and Dorset (UK) 621, 1119
Where to Eat in Bristol, Bath & Avon (UK) 621, 1119
Where to Eat in Canada (CN ISSN 0315-3088) 621, 1119
Where to Eat in Cardiff and South Wales see Where to Eat in Cardiff, Swansea & South Wales 621
Where to Eat in Cardiff, Swansea & South Wales (UK) 621, 1119
Where to Eat in Devon (UK) 621, 1119
Where to Eat in Edinburgh see Where to Eat in Edinburgh, Fife and the Lothians 621
Where to Eat in Edinburgh, Fife and the Lothians (UK) 621, 1119
Where to Eat in Gloucestershire and the Cotswolds (UK) 621, 1119
Where to Eat in Greater Manchester (UK) 621, 1119
Where to Eat in Hampshire see Where to Eat in Hampshire and the New Forest 621
Where to Eat in Hampshire and the New Forest (UK) 621, 1119
Where to Eat in Ireland (UK) 621
Where to Eat in Kent (UK) 621, 1119
Where to Eat in Oxford and Oxfordshire (UK) 621, 1119
Where to Eat in Oxfordshire see Where to Eat in Oxford and Oxfordshire 621
Where to Eat in Somerset (UK) 621, 1119
Where to Eat in Surrey (UK) 621, 1119
Where to Eat in Sussex (UK) 621, 1119
Where to Eat in the Channel Islands (UK) 621, 1119
Where to Eat in Wiltshire (UK) 621, 1119
Where to Fish (UK) 1047
Where to Go in the Thames and Chilterns (UK) 1119
Where to Go, What to Do in the S.W. (UK) 1166
Where to Go, What to Do in the South(UK) 1119
Where to Golf in Europe see Golf 1038
Where to Retire on a Small Income (US ISSN 0511-8719) 966
Where-to-Sell-It Directory (US) 614
Where to Stay in London (UK) 621, 1119
Where to Stay in Scotland see Scotland: Where to Stay, Hotels and Guest Houses 1116
Where to Stay in Scotland see Scotland: Where to Stay, Bed and Breakfast 1116
Where to Stay in Scotland. Bed and Breakfast see Scotland: Where to Stay, Bed and Breakfast 1116
Where to Stay in Scotland. Hotels and Guest Houses see Scotland: Where to Stay, Hotels and Guest Houses 1116
Wherever They Go (US) 1021
Which Degree (UK) 431
Which Hi-Fi? (UK) 1032
Which School? (UK) 431
Which University see Which Degree 431

Which Way (US) 737
Which? Wine Guide (UK) 120
Whillan's Tax Tables and Tax Reckoner see Whillans's Tax Tables 300
Whillans's Tax Tables (UK ISSN 0260-3926) 300
Whispers (US) 14, 737
Whitaker's Almanack (UK ISSN 0083-9256) 463
Whitaker's Cumulative Book List (UK ISSN 0140-4229) 964
White Book of Ski Areas. U S and Canada (US ISSN 0163-9684) 1047
White Book of U S Ski Areas see White Book of Ski Areas. U S and Canada 1047
White County Heritage (US ISSN 0043-4906) 537, 611
White Paper on Human Ecology (US) 78, 167
White Paper on International Trade: Japan (JA) 260
White Paper on Japanese Economy (JA) 250
White Paper on Japan's Forest Industries (JA ISSN 0083-9272) 531
Whiteacre (AT ISSN 0085-820X) 667
Whites Air Directory & Who's Who in New Zealand Aviation (NZ) 22
White's Tax Exempt Bond Market Ratings (US) 268
Whitmark Directory (US ISSN 0511-8794) 319
Whitney Museum of American Art. Bulletin (US) 831
Whitney Review (US ISSN 0511-8824) 831
Whittier Newsletter (US ISSN 0511-8832) 744
Who Is Who (II) 1166
Who is Who in the Oklahoma Legislature (US) 947
Who Knows: a Guide to Washington Experts (US) 1003, 1072
Who Knows About Industries and Markets (US) 202, 686
Who Knows: the Directory of Experts see Who Knows: a Guide to Washington Experts 1003
Who Makes Machinery see Wer Baut Maschinen 493
Who Owns What in World Banking (UK) 234
Who Owns Whom. Australasia and Far East (UK ISSN 0302-4091) 319
Who Owns Whom. Australia and Japan International see Who Owns Whom. Australasia and Far East 319
Who Owns Whom. Continental Europe (UK ISSN 0083-9302) 282, 292
Who Owns Whom. United Kingdom see Who Owns Whom. United Kingdom and Republic of Ireland 319
Who Owns Whom. United Kingdom and Republic of Ireland (UK ISSN 0140-4040) 319
Who Owns Whom, North America (UK ISSN 0083-9310) 286
Who Sells Foreign Products in Spain see Quien Vende en Espana los Productos Extranjeros 316
Who Writes What in Life and Health Insurance (US) 642
Whole Again Resource Guide (US ISSN 0734-9033) 1015
Whole Gay Catalog (US) 616
Wholesale and Retail Trade Survey (CY) 220
Who's Where (US ISSN 0508-6795) 1166
Who's Who (UK ISSN 0083-937X) 135
Who's Who see Australasian Country Music Annual 833
Who's Who: A Guide to Federal and Provincial Departments and Agencies, Their Funding Programs and the People Who Head Them see Directory of the Arts 104
Who's Who Among American High School Students (US) 135
Who's Who Among Black Americans (US ISSN 0362-5753) 135
Who's Who Among Music Students in American High Schools (US ISSN 0362-3750) 135, 843

Who's Who Among Students in American Junior Colleges (US ISSN 0511-8891) 135, 441
Who's Who Among Students in American Universities and Colleges (US) 135, 441
Who's Who Among Students in American Vocational and Technical Schools see Who's Who Among Vocational and Technical Students in America 445
Who's Who Among Vocational and Technical Students in America (US ISSN 0148-6381) 445
Who's Who at the Frankfurt Book Fair (GW ISSN 0170-7213) 963
Who's Who in America (US ISSN 0083-9396) 135
Who's Who in American Art (US ISSN 0000-0191) 135, 831
Who's Who in American Community, Technical, and Junior Colleges see Directory of Community, Junior, and Technical Colleges 429
Who's Who in American Jewry (Los Angeles) (US ISSN 0196-8009) 135, 506
Who's Who in American Law (US ISSN 0162-7880) 135, 667
Who's Who in American Music (US) 135, 843
Who's Who in American Politics (US ISSN 0000-0205) 135, 911
Who's Who in Art (UK) 112, 135
Who's Who in Arts Management (UK ISSN 0266-707X) 112, 282, 319
Who's Who in Banking in Europe (UK) 234
Who's Who in Biotechnology (US ISSN 0888-5982) 149, 1072
Who's Who in British Columbia Agriculture (CN) 37
Who's Who in California (US ISSN 0511-8948) 135
Who's Who in Canadian Film and Television (CN) 135, 825
Who's Who in Canadian Law (CN ISSN 0710-6629) 135, 667
Who's Who in Chemistry & Plastics (US ISSN 0888-5958) 325, 901
Who's Who in Chiropractic, International (US ISSN 0147-8265) 136
Who's Who in Civil Engineering, Earth Sciences & Energy (US ISSN 0888-5966) 381, 467, 484
Who's Who in Consulting (US ISSN 0083-9485) 136, 282
Who's Who in Corrugated (UK) 859
Who's Who in Cumbria (UK) 136, 202
Who's Who in Electronics (US ISSN 0083-9507) 319, 461
Who's Who in Electronics & Computer Science (US ISSN 0888-5931) 319, 353, 461
Who's Who in Engineering (US ISSN 0149-7537) 475
Who's Who in Finance and Banking in Thailand (TH) 136, 234
Who's Who in Finance and Industry (US ISSN 0083-9523) 136, 202
Who's Who in Finland see Kuka Kukin On 134
Who's Who in Floriculture (US ISSN 0511-8964) 136, 534
Who's Who in France/Qui Est Qui en France (FR ISSN 0083-9531) 136
Who's Who in Hawaii see Men and Women of Hawaii 135
Who's Who In India (Bombay) (II) 136
Who's Who in India (Calcutta) (II ISSN 0301-5106) 136
Who's Who in Indian Engineering and Industry (II ISSN 0083-9558) 136, 1072
Who's Who in Indian Relics (US) 95, 614
Who's Who in Indian Science (II ISSN 0083-9566) 136, 1003
Who's Who in Industrial Editing see B.A.I.E. Membership Directory 302
Who's Who in Insurance (US ISSN 0083-9574) 136, 642
Who's Who in Insurance (UK) 136, 642
Who's Who in Israel (IS ISSN 0083-9590) 136

Who's Who in Karate and the Other Martial Arts and Directory of Black Belts (US) 1036
Who's Who in Lebanon (LE ISSN 0083-9612) 136
Who's Who in Library and Information Services (US) 136, 686
Who's Who in Los Angeles County see Who's Who in California 135
Who's Who in Malaysia and Singapore (MY ISSN 0083-9620) 136
Who's Who in Mechanical Engineering & Materials Science (US ISSN 0888-594X) 493, 892
Who's Who in Music and Musicians' International Directory see International Who's Who in Music and Musicians' Directory 836
Who's Who in Pakistan (PK ISSN 0083-9671) 136
Who's Who in Paper Distribution (US) 859
Who's Who in Paper Distribution and Factbook see Who's Who in Paper Distribution 859
Who's Who in Physics & Optics (US ISSN 0888-5974) 899
Who's Who in Public Relations (International) (US ISSN 0511-9022) 16, 136
Who's Who in Risk Management (US) 642
Who's Who in Saudi Arabia (SU) 136
Who's Who in Special Libraries (US ISSN 0278-842X) 686
Who's Who in Switzerland (SZ ISSN 0083-9736) 136
Who's Who in Technology (US ISSN 0887-5901) 1003, 1072
Who's Who in the Arab World (LE ISSN 0083-9752) 136
Who's Who in the Commonwealth (UK) 136
Who's Who in the East (US ISSN 0083-9760) 136
Who's Who in the Egg and Poultry Industries (US ISSN 0510-4130) 68, 136
Who's Who in the Fish Industry (US ISSN 0270-160X) 514
Who's Who in the Midwest (US ISSN 0083-9787) 136
Who's Who in the Mobile Area see Mobile Area Chamber of Commerce Membership Directory and Buyer's Guide 236
Who's Who in the Securities Industry (US ISSN 0090-418X) 268
Who's Who in the South and Southwest (US ISSN 0083-9809) 136
Who's Who in the Theatre see Contemporary Theatre, Film & Television 134
Who's Who in the Water Industry (UK) 1127
Who's Who in the West (US ISSN 0083-9817) 136
Who's Who in the World (US ISSN 0083-9825) 136
Who's Who in Training and Development (US ISSN 0092-4598) 136, 282
Who's Who in U.S. Business in Australia (AT) 237
Who's Who in Western Europe (UK) 136
Who's Who in World Agriculture (UK) 37
Who's Who Jamaica (JM) 137
Who's Who of American Women (US ISSN 0083-9841) 136
Who's Who of Emerging Leaders in America (US) 136
Who's Who of Engineering in New Jersey see New Jersey Professional Engineer 473
Who's Who of Southern Africa Including Mauritius, South West Africa, Zimbabwe and Neighboring Countries (SA) 136
Who's Who of Southern Africa Including Mauritius, South West Africa, Zimbabwe-Rhodesia and Neighboring Countries see Who's Who of Southern Africa Including Mauritius, South West Africa, Zimbabwe and Neighboring Countries 136

Who's Who on Television (UK) 350
Who's Who on the Screen (UK) 136, 825
Who's Who, The Canadian see Canadian Who's Who 133
Widener Review (US ISSN 0882-066X) 744
Wie Erreiche Ich Wen? (GW) 319, 1104
Wie Levert (NE) 461
Wie Levert Elektro see Wie Levert 461
Wielands Briefwechsel (GE) 737, 744
Wiener Arbeiten zur Deutschen Literatur (AU ISSN 0083-9906) 737
Wiener Beitraege zur Englischen Philologie (AU ISSN 0083-9914) 708, 737
Wiener Beitraege zur Geschichte der Neuzeit (AU) 601
Wiener Beitraege zur Kulturgeschichte und Linguistik (AU ISSN 0083-9922) 708
Wiener Boersekammer. Verordnungsblatt (AU ISSN 0042-4250) 268
Wiener Forschungen zur Theater und Medienwissenschaft (AU) 1079
Wiener Geographische Schriften (AU ISSN 0083-9957) 551
Wiener Gesellschaft fuer Theaterforschung. Jahrbuch (AU ISSN 0377-0745) 1079
Wiener-Goethe-Verein. Jahrbuch (AU ISSN 0250-443X) 737, 744
Wiener Institut fuer Internationale Wirtschaftsvergleiche. Forschungsberichte (AU) 264
Wiener Institut fuer Internationale Wirtschaftsvergleiche. Reprint Serie (AU) 264
Wiener Jahrbuch fuer Kunstgeschichte (AU ISSN 0083-9981) 112
Wiener Jahrbuch fuer Philosophie (AU ISSN 0083-999X) 883
Wiener Mitteilungen: Wasser, Abwasser, Gewaesser (AU) 1127
Wiener Musikhochschule. Publikationen (AU ISSN 0084-0017) 843
Wiener Rechtswissenschaftliche Studien (AU ISSN 0084-0025) 667, 672
Wiener Ringstrasse-Bild Einer Epoche (GW) 112, 601
Wiener Romanistische Arbeiten (AU ISSN 0084-0033) 708, 737
Wiener Slavistisches Jahrbuch/Viennese Slavonic Yearbook (AU ISSN 0084-0041) 708
Wiener Studien. Zeitschrift fuer Klassische Philologie und Patristik (AU ISSN 0084-005X) 339, 708
Wiener Voelkerkundliche Mitteilungen (AU ISSN 0084-0068) 78, 517
Wiener Zeitschrift fuer die Kunde des Morgenlandes (AU ISSN 0084-0076) 854
Wiener Zeitschrift fuer Die Kunde Sued- und Ostasiens see Wiener Zeitschrift fuer die Kunde Suedasiens und Archiv fuer Indische Philosphie 883
Wiener Zeitschrift fuer die Kunde Suedasiens und Archiv fuer Indische Philosphie (AU ISSN 0084-0084) 572, 883
Wiesenberger Investment Companies Service see Investment Companies 266
Wiesenberger Salesman's Package (US) 269
Wigfield Newsletter (US) 537
Wijsgerige Teksten en Studies/ Philosophical Texts and Studies (NE ISSN 0084-0106) 883
Wilbour Monographs (US) 95, 112, 562
Wilcox Report see Wilcox Report Newsletter 911
Wilcox Report Newsletter (US) 373, 506, 911, 938
Wild Fennel (US) 712
Wild Goose Association. Annual Technical Symposium Proceedings (US) 409, 475
Wilderness Energy Survey see World Energy Survey 467
Wildfire (US) 506

Wildfowl (UK) *171*
Wildlife - a Review (NZ ISSN 0110-604X) *178, 368*
Wildlife Behavior and Ecology (US ISSN 0084-0122) *149*
Wildlife Monographs (US ISSN 0084-0173) *368*
Wildlife Review (Fort Collins) (US ISSN 0043-5511) *13, 368, 1037*
Wiley Series in Computing (US) *353*
Wiley Series in Geotechnical Engineering (US) *61*
Wiley Series on Systems and Controls for Financial Management (US) *282*
Wiley Series on Systems Engineering and Analysis (US ISSN 0084-019X) *475*
Wiley World (US) *537*
Will to Charity: Charities' Story Book (UK) *1021*
William Hammond Mathers Museum. Occasional Papers and Monographs (US) *831*
William K. McInally Lecture (US ISSN 0084-0246) *202*
William L. Hutcheson Memorial Forest. Bulletin (US ISSN 0511-9723) *528*
Williamsburg Craft Series (US) *113*
Williamsburg Decorative Art Series (US) *1166*
Williamsburg Eyewitness to History Series (US) *1166*
Williamsburg in America Series (US ISSN 0084-0297) *611*
Williamsburg Research Studies (US ISSN 0084-0300) *611*
Williamson County Historical Society Newsletter *see* Williamson County Historical Society Publication *611*
Williamson County Historical Society Publication (US) *611*
Willing's Press Guide (UK ISSN 0000-0213) *133*
Williston & Polls Court Forms (CN) *667*
Willmore City *see* McWinners Magazine *727*
Wilmington Society of the Fine Arts. Report *see* Delaware Art Museum. Annual Report *104*
Wilson & Wilson's Comprehensive Analytical Chemistry (NE ISSN 0069-8024) *327*
Wilton Cake Decorating Yearbook *see* Wilton Yearbook of Baking and Cake Decorating *615*
Wilton Yearbook of Baking and Cake Decorating (US) *615*
Wiltshire Archaeological and Natural History Magazine (1982) (UK) *95, 1003*
Wiltshire Archaeological and Natural History Society. Annual Bulletin *see* Wiltshire Archaeological and Natural History Society. Annual Report (1983) *95*
Wiltshire Archaeological and Natural History Society. Annual Report (1983) (UK) *95, 1003*
Wiltshire Archaeological Magazine *see* Wiltshire Archaeological and Natural History Magazine (1982) *95*
Wiltshire Natural History Magazine *see* Wiltshire Archaeological and Natural History Magazine (1982) *95*
Winckelmann's Fur Directories (UK) *672*
Wind and Water Mills (UK ISSN 0260-504X) *1127*
Wind-Energie (GW ISSN 0720-3926) *467*
Wind Energy Abstracts (US ISSN 0277-2140) *467, 469*
Wind Energy and Diesel Installations International (Year) (US ISSN 0891-639X) *467*
Wind Energy Workshop. Proceedings (US) *467*
Wind Engineering Abstracts (UK ISSN 0263-0915) *13, 469*
Wind in the Willows Annual (UK) *1166*
Windless Orchard (US ISSN 0043-5716) *744*
Window and Wall Decorating Ideas *see* Better Homes and Gardens Window & Wall Ideas *643*

Windsor Yearbook of Access to Justice/Recueil Annuel de Windsor d'Acces a la Justice (CN ISSN 0710-0841) *667*
Wine and Spirit Trade International Year Book (UK) *120, 260*
Wine Marketing Handbook *see* Jobson's Wine Marketing Handbook *120*
Wine Spectator Wine Maps (US ISSN 0882-7206) *120*
Winemaker's Diary (UK) *120*
Wines and Vines - Annual Directory of the Wine Industry *see* Wines and Vines: Directory of the Wine Industry in North America *120*
Wines and Vines: Directory of the Wine Industry in North America (US) *120*
Winged Mercury Missive (US) *1030*
Winkler Prins Encyclopedisch Jaarboek (NE) *601*
Winners Magazine *see* McWinners Magazine *727*
Winslow Homer (US) *112*
Winter en Sport (NE) *1166*
Winter Simulation Conference. Proceedings (US) *461*
Winterfare (US) *112, 737, 1079*
Wintergreen (CN) *133, 713*
Winter's Tales (UK ISSN 0084-0394) *737*
Wir Bauen Unser Haus Selbst (GW) *188*
Die Wirbelsaeule in Forschung und Praxis (GW ISSN 0510-5315) *786*
Wire Industry Yearbook (UK ISSN 0084-0424) *800*
Wire Journal Directory/Catalog *see* Wire Journal International Directory/Catalog *475*
Wire Journal International Directory/Catalog (US) *319, 475*
Wire Technology Buyer's Guide (US) *319, 800*
Wired Librarian's Newsletter (US ISSN 0884-593X) *689*
Wireless and Electrical Trader Year Book *see* Electrical and Electronic Trader Year Book *452*
Wirtschaftsbilderheft BRD und Ausland *see* I F O Spiegel der Wirtschaft *245*
Wirtschaftspolitische Studien (US ISSN 0172-5963) *252*
Wirtschaftsuniversitaet Wien. Dissertationen (AU ISSN 0259-0719) *202*
Wirtschaftsvereinigung Gross- und Aussenhandel Geschaeftsbericht *see* W G A Geschaeftsbericht *260*
Wirtschaftswissenschaftliche und Wirtschaftsrechtliche Untersuchungen (GW ISSN 0083-7113) *202, 667*
Wirtschaftszahl (AU ISSN 0510-5609) *220*
Wisconsin. Commissioner of Securities. Annual Report *see* Wisconsin. Commissioner of Securities. Biennial Report *269*
Wisconsin. Commissioner of Securities. Biennial Report (US) *269*
Wisconsin. Department of Administration. Annual Fiscal Report (US ISSN 0085-8226) *947*
Wisconsin. Department of Natural Resources. Annual Water Quality Report to Congress (US ISSN 0362-5354) *500, 957*
Wisconsin. Department of Natural Resources. Technical Bulletin (US ISSN 0084-0564) *368*
Wisconsin. Department of Transportation. Automatic Traffic Recorder Data *see* Wisconsin Traffic Data - Automatic Traffic Recorder *1098*
Wisconsin. Department of Transportation. Division of Planning and Budget. Highway Mileage Data (US ISSN 0084-0572) *1098*
Wisconsin. Department of Transportation. Division of Planning. Highway Traffic (US ISSN 0084-0580) *1098*
Wisconsin. Department of Veterans Affairs. Biennial Report (US) *813*

Wisconsin. Division of Corrections. Bureau of Planning, Development and Research. Releases from Juvenile Institutions *see* Wisconsin. Division of Corrections. Office of Information Management. Releases from Juvenile Institutions *374*
Wisconsin. Division of Corrections. Office of Information Management. Admissions to Juvenile Institutions (US) *374, 1066*
Wisconsin. Division of Corrections. Office of Information Management. Releases from Juvenile Institutions (US) *374*
Wisconsin. Division of Highways. System Planning Section. Highway Traffic in Wisconsin Cities *see* Wisconsin. Department of Transportation. Division of Planning. Highway Traffic *1098*
Wisconsin. Educational Communications Board. Biennial Report (US ISSN 0361-2120) *421*
Wisconsin. Employment Relations Commission. Reporter (US ISSN 0097-9171) *277*
Wisconsin. Geological and Natural History Survey. Biennial Report *see* Wisconsin. Geological and Natural History Survey. Programs and Activities *398*
Wisconsin. Geological and Natural History Survey. Bulletin (US) *397*
Wisconsin. Geological and Natural History Survey. Field Trip Guide Books (US) *397*
Wisconsin. Geological and Natural History Survey. Geoscience Educational Series (US) *397*
Wisconsin. Geological and Natural History Survey. Geoscience Information Series *see* Wisconsin. Geological and Natural History Survey. Geoscience Educational Series *397*
Wisconsin. Geological and Natural History Survey. Information Circulars (US ISSN 0512-0640) *397*
Wisconsin. Geological and Natural History Survey. Programs and Activities (US) *398*
Wisconsin. Geological and Natural History Survey. Special Report (US ISSN 0512-0659) *398*
Wisconsin. State Elections Board. Annual Report (US) *947*
Wisconsin Blue Book (US) *947*
Wisconsin Business Monographs (US ISSN 0084-0513) *202*
Wisconsin China Series (US ISSN 0084-053X) *572, 854*
Wisconsin Commerce Studies *see* Wisconsin Economy Studies *202*
Wisconsin Council of Teachers of English. Service Bulletin Series (US) *422, 737*
Wisconsin Crime and Arrests (Year) (US) *373*
Wisconsin Economy Studies (US ISSN 0084-0599) *202*
Wisconsin Highway Traffic *see* Wisconsin. Department of Transportation. Division of Planning. Highway Traffic *1098*
Wisconsin International Law Journal (US ISSN 0743-7951) *672*
Wisconsin Introduction to Scandinavia *see* W I T S *506*
Wisconsin Legislative Council Rules Clearinghouse. Annual Report (US) *667*
Wisconsin Library Service Record (US ISSN 0361-2848) *686*
Wisconsin Manufacturers Register (US ISSN 0738-0070) *319*
Wisconsin Papers on Southeast Asia (US) *572*
Wisconsin Population Projections (US ISSN 0091-5254) *925*
Wisconsin Public School Directory (US ISSN 0148-5059) *431*
Wisconsin State Industrial Directory *see* MacRae's Wisconsin State Industrial Directory *313*
Wisconsin Traffic Data - A T R *see* Wisconsin Traffic Data - Automatic Traffic Recorder *1098*

Wisconsin Traffic Data - Automatic Traffic Recorder (US ISSN 0098-0323) *1098*
Wisconsin Travel and Recreation Guide (US) *1119*
Wisconsin Women's Law Journal (US) *667, 1129*
Wisdom *see* Kinaadman *570*
Wisdom of Persia (IR) *614*
Wissenschaft und Gegenwart. Geisteswissenschaftliche Reihe (GW ISSN 0175-6486) *883*
Wissenschaft und Gegenwart. Juristische Reihe (GW) *667*
Wissenschaft und Gesellschaft (GE ISSN 0138-5755) *1031*
Wissenschaften in der D.D.R. (GW ISSN 0178-6768) *601, 1003*
Wissenschaftliche Alpenvereinshefte (GW ISSN 0084-0912) *551*
Wissenschaftliche Gesellschaft fuer Luft- und Raumfahrt. Jahrbuecher *see* D.G.L.R. Jahrbuecher *18*
Wissenschaftliche Gesellschaft fuer Personenstandswesen und Verwandte Gebiete. Schriftenreihe. Neue Folge (GW ISSN 0084-0939) *667*
Wissenschaftliche Kommission des Theodor-Koerner-Stiftungsfonds und des Leopold-Kunschak-Preises zur Enforschung der Oesterreichischen Geschichte der Jahre 1918 bis 1938. Veroeffentlichungen *see* Wissenschaftliche Kommission zur Erforschung der Geschichte der Republik Oesterreich. Veroeffentlichungen *602*
Wissenschaftliche Kommission zur Erforschung der Geschichte der Republik Oesterreich. Veroeffentlichungen (AU) *602*
Wissenschaftliche Mitteilungen des Bosnisch-Herzegowinischen Landesmuseums. Archaeologie (YU) *95*
Wissenschaftliche Mitteilungen des Bosnisch-Herzegowinischen Landesmuseums. Naturwissenschaft (YU ISSN 0350-0012) *1003*
Wissenschaftliche Paperbacks (GW ISSN 0170-3579) *252, 1031*
Wissenschaftliche Taschenbuecher. Reihe Biologie (GE ISSN 0084-0963) *149*
Wissenschaftliche Taschenbuecher. Reihe Chemie (GE ISSN 0084-0971) *325*
Wissenschaftliche Taschenbuecher. Reihe Mathematik, Physik (GE ISSN 0084-098X) *755, 892*
Wissenschaftliche Taschenbuecher. Reihe Texte und Studien (GE ISSN 0138-127X) *892*
Wissenschaftliche Untersuchungen zum Neuen Testament (GW) *974*
Wissenschaftliche Vereinigung der Augenoptiker. Fachvortraege der Jahrestagungen *see* Wissenschaftliche Vereinigung fuer Augenoptik und Optometrie. Fachvortraege des WVAO - Jahreskongresses *899*
Wissenschaftliche Vereinigung fuer Augenoptik und Optometrie. Fachvortraege des WVAO - Jahreskongresses (GW) *899*
Wissenschaftsentwicklung und Wissenschaftspolitik in der DDR. Jahresbericht *see* Wissenschaften in der D.D.R. *601*
Wistar Symposium Series (US ISSN 0271-9347) *768*
Wistra (GW ISSN 0721-6890) *667*
Witchcraft *see* Witchcraft Digest *860*
Witchcraft Digest (US ISSN 0085-8250) *860*
Wits Journal of Librarianship and Information Science (SA) *686*
Wittenberg Review of Literature and Art (US) *112, 737*
Wo Geht's Lang? (GW) *441*
Der Wochenend-, Ferien- und Zweithaus-Katalog (GW) *188*
Wohnen (GE ISSN 0138-2810) *643*
Wolfenbuetteler Studien zur Aufklaerung. Schriftenreihe (GW) *562, 737*
Wolfenbuetteler Abhandlungen zur Renaissanceforschung (GW ISSN 0724-956X) *602*

Wolfenbuettler Arbeiten zur Barockforschung (GW ISSN 0724-472X) *602*
Wolfenbuettler Beitraege (GW ISSN 0300-2012) *686*
Wolfenbuettler Forschungen (GW ISSN 0724-9594) *602*
Wolfenbuettler Schriften zur Geschichte des Buchwesens (GW ISSN 0724-9586) *931*
Wolff's Guide to the London Metal Exchange (UK ISSN 0144-5960) *286, 800*
Wolfman Report on the Photographic Industry in the United States (US ISSN 0084-103X) *885*
Wolverhampton Polytechnic Students' Union Handbook (UK) *342*
Woman in History (US ISSN 0195-9743) *562, 1129*
Woman Poet (US ISSN 0195-6183) *744, 1129*
Woman's Day Best Ideas for Christmas (US) *553*
Woman's Day Granny Squares *see* Granny Square & Craft Ideas *844*
Woman's Day Home Decorating Ideas (US ISSN 0361-638X) *643, 644*
Woman's Day Needlework Ideas *see* Woman's Day Sweaters & Crafts *844*
Woman's Day Special *see* 101 Sweater & Craft Ideas *844*
Woman's Day Super Special *see* Granny Square & Craft Ideas *844*
Woman's Day Sweaters & Crafts (US) *844*
Woman's Day 101 Sweaters You Can Knit and Crochet *see* 101 Sweater & Craft Ideas *844*
Woman's Day 101 Ways to Lose Weight and Stay Healthy (US) *847, 886*
Woman's Own Holiday Reading (UK) *1129*
Women & Literature (US ISSN 0147-1759) *737, 1129*
Women and Minorities in Science and Engineering (US) *475, 1003, 1031*
Women in a Developing Economy (II) *1129*
Women in Context (US) *768, 1129*
Women in Context: Development and Stresses *see* Women in Context *768*
Women in the Caribbean Project (BB) *1130*
Women - Poems (US) *744, 1130*
Women Studies Abstracts (US ISSN 0049-7835) *13, 1130*
Women Talking, Women Listening (US) *744, 1130*
Women's Accessories Directory; New York Metropolitan Area (US ISSN 0084-1056) *340*
Women's Annual (US ISSN 0276-7988) *1130*
Women's Coats and Suits Directory: New York Metropolitan Area *see* Women's, Misses & Jr. Coats and Suits Buyers Directory; New York Metropolitan Area *340*
Women's Collection Newsletter (US) *1130*
Women's International Bowling Congress. Playing Rules (US ISSN 0361-3976) *1040*
Women's Intimate Apparel *see* Women's Intimate Apparel Buyers *340*
Women's Intimate Apparel Buyers (US ISSN 0043-7549) *340*
Women's, Misses & Jr. Coats and Suits Buyers Directory; New York Metropolitan Area (US) *340*
Women's Network/Reseau Femmes (Federation Nationale des Enseignants et des Enseignantes du Quebec) (CN) *422, 1130*
Women's Organizations: A National Directory (US) *1130*
Women's Organizations: A New York City Directory (US) *1130*
Women's Organizations & Leaders Directory (US ISSN 0092-6639) *1130*
Women's Race-Walking *see* Race Walking World Statistics - Women *1036*

Women's Referral Service Annual Directory (US) *1166*
Women's Squash Rackets Association. Handbook (UK) *1036*
Wood & Wood Products Reference Buying Guide (US) *531*
Wood & Wood Products Reference Data/Buying Guide *see* Wood & Wood Products Reference Buying Guide *531*
Wood Industries of New Mexico (US) *531*
Wood Pulp and Fiber Statistics (US) *859, 860*
Wood Research/Mokuzai Kenkyu (JA ISSN 0049-7916) *531*
Woodall's Campground Directory. Arizona/New Mexico Edition (US) *1047*
Woodall's Campground Directory. Arkansas/Missouri Edition (US ISSN 0163-5328) *1047*
Woodall's Campground Directory. California/Nevada/Mexico Directory(US) *1047*
Woodall's Campground Directory. Colorado Edition (US ISSN 0163-5344) *1047*
Woodall's Campground Directory. Delaware/Maryland/Virginia/District of Columbia Edition (US) *1047*
Woodall's Campground Directory. Eastern Edition (US ISSN 0162-7406) *1047*
Woodall's Campground Directory. Florida Edition (US) *1047*
Woodall's Campground Directory. Idaho/Oregon/Washington/British Columbia Edition (US) *1047*
Woodall's Campground Directory. Illinois/Indiana Edition (US ISSN 0163-2485) *1047*
Woodall's Campground Directory. Kentucky/Tennessee Edition (US ISSN 0163-5336) *1047*
Woodall's Campground Directory. Michigan Edition (US ISSN 0163-0121) *1047*
Woodall's Campground Directory. Minnesota/Wisconsin Edition (US) *1047*
Woodall's Campground Directory. New England States Edition (US ISSN 0163-0083) *1047*
Woodall's Campground Directory. New Jersey/Ohio/Pennsylvania Editions (US) *1047*
Woodall's Campground Directory. New York Edition (US) *1047*
Woodall's Campground Directory. North American Edition (US) *1047*
Woodall's Campground Directory. North Carolina/South Carolina Edition (US ISSN 0163-5352) *1047*
Woodall's Campground Directory. Ontario Edition (US ISSN 0163-240X) *1047*
Woodall's Campground Directory. Texas/Mexico Edition (US) *1047*
Woodall's Campground Directory. Western Edition (US ISSN 0162-7414) *1047*
Woodall's Retirement Directory (US ISSN 0731-6526) *552*
Woodall's Tenting Directory (US ISSN 0742-3977) *1047*
Woodall's Campground Directory. Arizona Edition *see* Woodall's Campground Directory. Arizona/New Mexico Edition *1047*
Woodall's Campground Directory. California Edition *see* Woodall's Campground Directory. California/Nevada/Mexico Directory *1047*
Woodall's Campground Directory. Florida Campgrounds Edition *see* Woodall's Campground Directory. Florida Edition *1047*
Woodall's Campground Directory. Idaho/Oregon/Washington Edition *see* Woodall's Campground Directory. Idaho/Oregon/Washington/British Columbia Edition *1047*
Woodall's Campground Directory. New Jersey/New York Edition *see* Woodall's Campground Directory. New York Edition *1047*

Woodall's Campground Directory. North American/Canadian Edition *see* Woodall's Campground Directory. North American Edition *1047*
Woodall's Campground Directory. Ohio/Pennsylvania Editions *see* Woodall's Campground Directory. New Jersey/Ohio/Pennsylvania Editions *1047*
Woodall's Campground Directory. Texas Edition *see* Woodall's Campground Directory. Texas/Mexico Edition *1047*
Woodall's Campground Directory. Wisconsin Edition *see* Woodall's Campground Directory. Minnesota/Wisconsin Edition *1047*
Woodall's Florida and Southern States Retirement and Resort Communities Directory *see* Woodall's Retirement Directory *552*
Woodall's Trailering Parks and Campgrounds *see* Woodall's Campground Directory. Eastern Edition *1047*
Woodbridge Lectures, Columbia University (US) *883*
Woodheat (US) *467, 554*
WoodHeat (US) *467, 615*
Woodrow Wilson International Center for Scholars. Annual Report (US ISSN 0092-4261) *442*
Woodrow Wilson National Fellowship Foundation. Newsletter (US ISSN 0084-1137) *441*
Woodrow Wilson National Fellowship Foundation. Report (US ISSN 0084-1145) *441*
Woodsman *see* Woodsman Newsletter *528*
Woodsman Newsletter (UG) *528*
Woodstove, Wood, Coal and Solar Equipment Directory *see* Woodheat *554*
Wool (NZ) *68*
Wool News (AT) *1166*
Wool News Digest *see* Wool News *1166*
Wool Research Organisation of New Zealand Communications (NZ ISSN 0112-2908) *1075*
Wool Research Organisation of New Zealand Reports (NZ ISSN 0112-2851) *1075*
Wool Research Organisation of New Zealand Technical Papers (NZ ISSN 0112-2932) *1075*
Wool Review (AT ISSN 0084-1218) *1075*
Wool Science Review (UK) *1075*
Woolhope Naturalists' Field Club, Herefordshire. Transactions (UK ISSN 0084-1226) *95, 149*
Woolner Indological Series (II ISSN 0084-1242) *737, 883*
Woonwapark, Kamper and Voetslaangids vir Suider-Afrika *see* Caravan Park, Camping & Backpacking Guide to Southern African *1044*
Worcester Art Museum. Journal (US ISSN 0193-9564) *831*
Worcester Art Museum Bulletin *see* Worcester Art Museum. Journal *831*
Worcestershire Archaeological Society. Transactions (UK ISSN 0143-2389) *96*
Word (II ISSN 0043-7948) *345*
Word and Deed (IS) *977*
Word & Spirit (US ISSN 0193-9211) *983*
Word on Guard *see* Slovo na Storozhi *703*
Words on Tape (US ISSN 8755-3759) *133*
Work Accomplished by the Inter-American Juridical Committee during its Meeting (US ISSN 0074-0837) *667*
Work of Aslib: Annual Report *see* Aslib Annual Report *673*
Work Related Abstracts (US ISSN 0273-3234) *13, 220*
Work Related Abstracts Subject Heading List (US) *686*
Work Study & O and M Abstracts (UK ISSN 0305-0653) *13, 220*

WORLD AGRICULTURE   1941

Work-Years and Personnel Costs. Executive Branch of the United States Government *see* Federal Civilian Work Force Statistics. Work Years and Personnel Costs. Executive Branch, United States Government *271*
Workers' Compensation Law Reporter (US) *636, 642*
Working Abroad (London) (UK) *277, 1119*
Working Abroad (London, 1977) (UK) *234*
Working Conditions in British Columbia Industry *see* British Columbia. Ministry of Labour. Negotiated Working Conditions *270*
Working Conditions in Canadian Industry/Conditions de Travail dans l'Industrie Canadienne. (CN ISSN 0084-1307) *277*
Working Conference on Oceanographic Laboratory Systems. Proceedings *see* Working Symposium on Oceanographic Data Systems. Proceedings *409*
Working Environment (SW) *957*
Working for Yourself (UK) *277*
Working Holidays (Year) (IT) *336, 849*
Working Kelpie Council. National Stud Book (AT ISSN 0312-3480) *869*
Working Meeting of the Polar Bear Specialist Group. Proceedings *see* Polar Bears *177*
Working on Wife Abuse *see* Battered Women's Directory *1128*
Working Papers in African Studies (US) *567, 1013*
Working Papers in Applied Linguistics *see* Ohio University. Working Papers in Linguistics and Language Teaching *700*
Working Papers in Irish Studies (US ISSN 0732-2674) *506*
Working Papers in Linguistics (US) *708*
Working Papers in Planning (US) *627*
Working Papers in Yiddish and East European Jewish Studies/In Gang Fun Arbet: Yidish Un Mizrakh Eyropeishe Yidishe Shtudies (US) *506, 977*
Working Papers on Caribbean Society. Series A: New Perspectives in Theory and Analysis (TR) *1031*
Working Papers on Caribbean Society. Series C: Research Findings (TR) *1031*
Working Papers on Women in International Development (US) *37, 265, 1031, 1130*
Working Press of the Nation (US ISSN 0084-1323) *647*
Working Symposium on Oceanographic Data Systems. Proceedings (US) *353, 409*
Workmen's Compensation Reporter *see* British Columbia. Workers' Compensation Board. Workers' Compensation Reporter *638*
Workshop Notes Washington, D.C. Textile Museum *see* Textile Museum Journal *1075*
Workshop on Color Aerial Photography in the Plant Sciences. Proceedings (US ISSN 0197-3444) *885*
Workshop on Computer Vision Representation and Control. Proceedings (US) *353*
Workshop on Microprogramming. Proceedings *see* Microprogramming Workshop. Proceedings *362*
World (US ISSN 0043-8154) *744*
World Advertising Expenditures (US ISSN 0568-0301) *16*
World Advertising Review (UK) *16*
World Aeronautical Records (FR) *22*
World Agricultural Economics and Rural Sociology Abstracts (UK ISSN 0043-8219) *13, 44, 1031*
World Agricultural Regional Supplement: Africa and the Middle East *see* World Agriculture Regional Supplement: Middle East and North Africa *50*
World Agriculture Regional Supplement: China (US) *50*

1942 WORLD AGRICULTURE

World Agriculture Regional Supplement: East Asia *see* World Agriculture Regional Supplement: East Asia and Oceania 50
World Agriculture Regional Supplement: East Asia and Oceania (US) 50
World Agriculture Regional Supplement: Eastern Europe (US) 50
World Agriculture Regional Supplement: Latin America *see* World Agriculture Regional Supplement: Western Hemisphere 50
World Agriculture Regional Supplement: Middle East and North Africa (US) 50
World Agriculture Regional Supplement: South Asia (US) 50
World Agriculture Regional Supplement: Southeast Asia (US) 50
World Agriculture Regional Supplement: Soviet Union *see* World Agriculture Regional Supplement: U S S R 50
World Agriculture Regional Supplement: Subsaharan Africa (US) 50
World Agriculture Regional Supplement: U S S R (US) 50
World Agriculture Regional Supplement: Western Europe (US) 50
World Agriculture Regional Supplement: Western Hemisphere (US) 50
World Air Transport Statistics (SZ ISSN 0084-1366) 1090
World Airline Record (US ISSN 0084-1374) 1090
World Airports Conference. Proceedings (UK) 1090
World Alliance of Y M C A's Directory (SZ ISSN 0513-6032) 334, 341
World Almanac and Book of Facts (US ISSN 0084-1382) 463
World Almanac and Encyclopedia *see* World Almanac and Book of Facts 463
World Almanac Consumer Information Kit (Year) (US) 369
World Almanac Guide to Pro Hockey (US ISSN 0095-7240) 1036
World Aluminium Survey (UK) 800
World Aluminum Abstracts (US ISSN 0002-6697) 13, 802
World Animal Science (NE) 178
World Aquaculture Society. Journal (US) 409
World Aquaculture Society. Proceedings (US) 409
World Aquaculture Society. Special Publications (US) 409
World Archaeological Society. Special Publication (US) 96
World Armaments and Disarmament: S I P R I Yearbook *see* S I P R I Yearbook: World Armaments and Disarmament 918
World Aromatics and Derivatives (US) 325
World Art Trends (US) 112
World Association for Educational Research. Congress Reports (BE) 422
World Association for the Advancement of Veterinary Parasitology. Proceedings of Conference (GR ISSN 0084-1404) 1166
World Association of Girl Guides and Girl Scouts. Report of Conference (UK ISSN 0084-1412) 334
World Automotive Market (US) 1093
World Bank. Annual Report (UN) 265
World Bank. Commodity Trade and Price Trends (UN ISSN 0251-401X) 265
World Bank. Economic Development Institute. E D I Seminar Papers (UN) 1166
World Bank. Staff Working Papers (UN) 1166
World Bank Atlas (UN ISSN 0512-2457) 265

World Bank Catalog. Accession List *see* Catalog of World Bank Publications 261
World Bank Catalog of Publications *see* Catalog of World Bank Publications 261
World Bank Research Program: Abstracts of Current Studies (UN) 220
World Banking (UK) 234
World Banking (Year) (UK) 220
World Banking Statistical Annual Survey *see* World Banking (Year) 220
World Bibliography of Social Security/Bibliographie Universelle de Securite Sociale (SZ ISSN 0006-1476) 133, 220
World Biolicensing Report (US ISSN 0883-5527) 149, 768
World Book Year Book (US ISSN 0084-1439) 463
World Bulk Trades (NO) 1104
World Bureau of Metal Statistics. Annual Report (UK) 802
World Calendar of Forthcoming Meetings: Metallurgical and Related Fields *see* World Calendar of Forthcoming Meetings: Metallurgy and Materials Science 796
World Calendar of Forthcoming Meetings: Metallurgy and Materials Science (UK) 796, 800
World Cars (US ISSN 0084-1463) 1093
World Cartography (UN ISSN 0084-1471) 551
World Cement Directory (FR) 188
World Coal Trade *see* International Coal 817
World Collectors Annuary (NE ISSN 0084-1498) 112
World Commerce Annual (II ISSN 0084-1501) 260
World Commercial Aircraft *see* Commercial Air Transport Industry 811
World Confederation of Organizations of the Teaching Profession Report *see* W C O T P Report 444
World Conference on Animal Production. Proceedings (UY ISSN 0084-1552) 68
World Conference on Tin. Proceedings (UK) 800
World Congress in Public Park Administration. Programme *see* Congress in Park and Recreation Administration. Programme 795
World Congress in Public Park Administration. Reports *see* Congress in Park and Recreation Administration. Reports 1044
World Congress of Psychiatry. Proceedings (AU ISSN 0084-1609) 791
World Congress of the Deaf. Lectures and Papers *see* World Congress of the W F D. Proceedings 376
World Congress of the Deaf. Proceedings. (IT ISSN 0510-8292) 376
World Congress of the W F D. Proceedings (World Federation of the Deaf) (IT) 376
World Congress on Fertility and Sterility. Proceedings (IE ISSN 0084-1641) 149
World Congress on the Prevention of Occupational Accidents and Diseases. Proceedings (SZ ISSN 0084-165X) 636
World Congresses on Information Processing. Proceedings (SZ ISSN 0074-3127) 686
World Copper Databook (UK ISSN 0950-2262) 801
World Copper Survey (UK ISSN 0260-3403) 821
World Council for Gifted and Talented Children. Yearbook (US) 445, 938
World Council of Churches. Faith and Order Papers *see* Faith and Order Papers 969
World Council of Churches. General Assembly. Assembly-Reports (SZ ISSN 0084-1676) 974

World Council of Churches. Minutes and Reports of the Central Committee Meeting (SZ ISSN 0084-1684) 974
World Council of Churches Background Information *see* C I A Background Information 968
World Council of Credit Unions. International Annual Report *see* World Council of Credit Unions. Statistical Report & Directory 234
World Council of Credit Unions. Statistical Report & Directory (US) 234
World Council of Young Men's Service Clubs. Minutes of the General Meeting (UK ISSN 0052-2678) 1021
World Crafts Council. General Assembly. Proceedings of the Biennial Meeting (US ISSN 0084-1706) 112
World Cultural Guides (US) 100, 112, 1119
World Currency Yearbook (US ISSN 0743-5363) 234
World C4 Hydrocarbons and Derivatives (US) 325
World Data Annual *see* Britannica Book of the Year 462
World Debt Tables (UN ISSN 0253-2859) 265
World Development Report (US ISSN 0163-5085) 265
World Directory of Fertilizer Manufacturers (UK) 61
World Directory of Fertilizer Products (UK) 61
World Directory of Historians of Mathematics (CN ISSN 0315-1700) 755
World Directory of Mathematicians (US ISSN 0512-2740) 755
World Directory of Multinational Enterprises (UK) 319
World Directory of Multinational Enterprises: Rankings and Interpretations (UK) 1166
World Directory of Pharmaceutical Manufacturers (UK) 319, 873
World Directory of Social Science Institutions (UN) 13, 1015
World Directory of Travel Agencies (FR ISSN 0070-6515) 1119
World Drug Market Manual (UK) 873
World Economic History (US) 252
World Economic Survey (UN ISSN 0084-1714) 250
World Energy Business Centre Reference Book and Buyers' Guide (UK ISSN 0261-7633) 467
World Energy Conference. Directory of Energy Information Centres in the World (FR) 467
World Energy Conference. Plenary Conferences. Transactions (FR ISSN 0084-1722) 467
World Energy Conference. Survey of Energy Resources (UK ISSN 0084-1730) 467
World Energy Conference. Technical Data on Fuel (UK) 467
World Energy Directory (UK) 467
World Energy Survey (US) 467
World Environment Handbook (US ISSN 0749-1069) 500
World Epidemiology Review *see* Worldwide Report: Epidemiology 958
World Ethylene and Derivatives (US) 325
World Factbook (US ISSN 0277-1527) 920
World Federation of Teachers' Unions. Information Letter (GE ISSN 0020-8884) 422, 649
World Federation of the Deaf World Congress of the W F D. Proceedings *see* World Congress of the W F D. Proceedings 376
World Feedstocks (US) 325
World Fellowship of Buddhists. Book Series (TH ISSN 0084-1781) 978
World Fertility Survey. Annual Reports(NE) 925, 930
World Fertility Survey. Basic Documentation (NE) 925, 930
World Fertility Survey. Country Reports (NE) 925, 930

World Fertility Survey. Occasional Papers (NE) 925, 930
World Fertility Survey. Progress Reports *see* World Fertility Survey. Annual Reports 930
World Fertility Survey. Scientific Reports (NE) 925, 930
World Fertility Survey. Summaries *see* World Fertility Survey. Summaries of Country Reports 930
World Fertility Survey. Summaries of Country Reports (NE) 925, 930
World Fertility Survey. Technical Bulletins (NE) 925, 930
World Fertilizer Atlas (UK ISSN 0512-2953) 61
World Food Problems (UN ISSN 0084-179X) 521
World Food Production Conference Summary Report (US) 521
World Food Report (UN) 521
World Food Trade and U.S. Agriculture(US ISSN 0733-2378) 50
World Forestry Congress. Proceedings (SP ISSN 0084-1811) 528
World Gastronomy (UK) 120, 521
World Guide to Abbreviations of Organizations (US) 687
World Guide to Fertilizer Plant and Equipment (UK) 61
World Guide to Fertilizer Processes and Constructors *see* World Guide to Fertilizer Processes and Plant Suppliers 61
World Guide to Fertilizer Processes and Plant Suppliers (UK) 61
World Guide to Libraries *see* Internationales Bibliotheks-Handbuch 679
World Guide to Performing Arts Periodicals (UK) 113
World Guide to Trade Associations *see* Internationales Verzeichnis der Wirtschaftsverbaende 310
World Health Organization. Handbook of Resolutions and Decisions of the World Health Assembly and the Executive Board. (UN) 957
World Health Organization. Monograph Series (UN ISSN 0512-3038) 957
World Health Organization. Public Health Papers *see* Public Health Papers 955
World Health Organization. Regional Office for Africa. Report of the Regional Committee. (UN) 957
World Health Organization. Regional Office for Africa. Report of the Regional Committee. Minutes of the Plenary Session *see* World Health Organization. Regional Office for Africa. Report of the Regional Committee 957
World Health Organization. Regional Office for Africa. Report of the Regional Director (UN ISSN 0510-8837) 957
World Health Organization. Regional Office for the Eastern Mediterranean. Annual Report of the Regional Director *see* World Health Organization. Regional Office for the Eastern Mediterranean. Biennial Report of the Regional Director 957
World Health Organization. Regional Office for the Eastern Mediterranean. Biennial Report of the Regional Director (UN) 957
World Health Organization. Regional Office for the Western Pacific. Annual Report of the Regional Director to the Regional Committee for the Western Pacific (UN ISSN 0512-4921) 958
World Health Organization. Regional Office for the Western Pacific. Report on the Regional Seminar on the Role of the Hospital in the Public Health Programme (UN ISSN 0510-8845) 618, 958
World Health Organization. Work of W H O (UN ISSN 0085-8285) 958

World Health Organization. World Health Assembly and the Executive Board. Handbook of Resolutions and Decisions. *see* World Health Organization. Handbook of Resolutions and Decisions of the World Health Assembly and the Executive Board *957*
World Health Organization Offset Publications *see* W H O Offset Publications *959*
World Health Organization Technical Report Series *see* W H O Technical Report Series *768*
World Health Statistics Annual (UN ISSN 0250-3794) *959*
World Health Statistics Quarterly (UN ISSN 0379-8070) *959*
World Health Statistics Report *see* World Health Statistics Quarterly *959*
World Holiday and Time Guide (US) *1119*
World Humor and Irony Membership Serial Yearbook (US) *708, 737*
World Index of Social Science Institutions *see* World Directory of Social Science Institutions *1015*
World Leasing Yearbook (UK ISSN 0264-0732) *250, 269*
World License Review (UK) *873*
World List of Family Planning Agencies(UK ISSN 0535-1774) *179*
World List of Social Science Periodicals(UN ISSN 0084-1870) *1015*
World List of Universities, Other Institutions of Higher Education and University Organizations (UK ISSN 0084-1889) *431*
World Lithuanian Roman Catholic Directory (US) *551, 983*
World Market for Bovine Meat *see* International Markets for Meat *66*
World Metal Statistics. Yearbook (UK) *801, 802*
World Meteorological Association. Regional Associations. Abridged Final Reports *see* World Meteorological Organization. Reports of Sessions of Regional Associations *807*
World Meteorological Association. Technical Commissions Abridged Final Reports *see* World Meteorological Organization. Reports of Sessions of Technical Commissions *807*
World Meteorological Congress. Abridged Report with Resolutions (UN ISSN 0084-1927) *807*
World Meteorological Congress. Proceedings (UN ISSN 0084-1935) *807*
World Meteorological Organization. Annual Reports (UN ISSN 0084-1994) *807*
World Meteorological Organization. Basic Documents (UN) *807*
World Meteorological Organization. Basic Documents and Official Reports *see* World Meteorological Organization. Basic Documents *807*
World Meteorological Organization. Executive Committee Reports. Abridged Final Reports with Resolutions *see* World Meteorological Organization. Executive Council Session. Abridged Final Reports with Resolutions *807*
World Meteorological Organization. Executive Council Session. Abridged Final Reports with Resolutions (UN) *807*
World Meteorological Organization. Reports of Sessions of Regional Associations (UN) *807*
World Meteorological Organization. Reports of Sessions of Technical Commissions (UN) *807*
World Meteorological Organization. Reports on Marine Science Affairs (UN ISSN 0084-2001) *409*
World Meteorological Organization. Special Environmental Reports (UN) *500, 807*
World Meteorological Organization. Technical Notes (UN ISSN 0084-201X) *807*
World Meteorological Organization. Weather Reporting. Volume A: Observing Stations (UN) *807*
World Meteorological Organization. Weather Reporting. Volume B: Data Processing (UN) *807*
World Meteorological Organization. Weather Reporting. Volume C: Transmissions (UN) *807*
World Meteorological Organization. Weather Reporting. Volume D: Information for Shipping (UN) *807*
World Methanol and Derivatives (US) *325*
World Military and Social Expenditures(US ISSN 0363-4795) *300*
World Military Expenditures *see* World Military Expenditures and Arms Transfers *813*
World Military Expenditures and Arms Transfers (US) *813*
World Military Expenditures and Related Data *see* World Military Expenditures and Arms Transfers *813*
World Mineral Statistics (UK) *822, 1066*
World Mining Congress. Report (PL) *821*
World Motor Vehicle Data (US ISSN 0085-8307) *1093*
World Movement of Mothers. Reports of Meetings (FR ISSN 0084-2044) *1022*
World Muslim Conference. Proceedings(PK ISSN 0084-2052) *976*
World Muslim Gazetteer (PK ISSN 0084-2060) *976*
World Nuclear Directory (UK) *899*
World of Church Music (UK) *1166*
World of Learning (UK ISSN 0084-2117) *431*
World of Tennis (UK) *1040*
World Patents Abstracts Journals (UK) *861*
World Pipelines (UK) *867*
World Plastics (US) *333, 901*
World Ploughing Contest. Official Handbook (UK ISSN 0084-2184) *51*
World Population Data Sheet (US ISSN 0085-8315) *925*
World Ports and Harbours Abstracts (UK ISSN 0264-0775) *13, 1087*
World Precious Metals Survey (UK ISSN 0263-9661) *801*
World Propylene and Derivatives (US) *325*
World Record Game Fishes (US ISSN 0194-3340) *514, 1047*
World Record Marine Fishes *see* World Record Game Fishes *514*
World Record Markets (UK) *1166*
World Refugee Survey (US ISSN 0197-5439) *1022*
World Refugee Survey Report *see* World Refugee Survey *1022*
World Resources Institute. Journal (US ISSN 0883-8100) *1166*
World Review of Nutrition and Dietetics (SZ ISSN 0084-2230) *847*
World Rubber Statistics Handbook (UK) *986*
World Scout Bureau Report (SZ) *334*
World Soccer Stars Annual (UK) *1041*
World Stainless Steel Statistics (UK ISSN 0141-0806) *260, 802*
World Surface Coating Abstracts (UK ISSN 0043-9088) *13, 856*
World Survey of Current Research and Development on Roads and Road Transport (Year) (US) *484, 1098*
World Survey of Phosphate Deposits (UK) *61*
World Survey of Sulphur Resources (UK) *61*
World Tax Series (US) *300*
World Textile Abstracts (UK ISSN 0043-9118) *13, 1076*
World - Tin in Tinplate (UK) *801*
World Tin Mining Operations, Exploration and Developments (UK) *801*
World Tobacco Directory (UK ISSN 0084-2273) *1080*
World Today Series: Africa (US ISSN 0084-2281) *567*
World Today Series: Canada (US ISSN 0883-8135) *611*
World Today Series: East Asia and the Western Pacific (US) *572*
World Today Series: Far East and Southwest Pacific *see* World Today Series: East Asia and the Western Pacific *572*
World Today Series: Latin America (US ISSN 0092-4148) *611*
World Today Series: Middle East and South Asia (US ISSN 0084-2311) *572*
World Today Series: Soviet Union and Eastern Europe (US ISSN 0090-3868) *602*
World Today Series: Western Europe (US ISSN 0084-2338) *602*
World Tourism Organization. Tourist Bibliography (SP) *1119*
World Tourism Organization. Tourist Departures and Main Destinations (SP) *1166*
World Tourism Statistics/Statistiques du Tourisme Mondial/Estadisticas del Turismo Mundial *see* Yearbook of Tourism Statistics *1120*
World Trade Annual (US ISSN 0512-3739) *260*
World Trade Annual Supplement (US ISSN 0512-3747) *260*
World Trade Index (UK) *319*
World Trade - Stainless, High Speed & Other Alloy Steel (UK) *801*
World Trade - Steel (UK) *801*
World Transport Data/Statistiques Mondiales de Transport (SZ ISSN 0302-7902) *1087*
World Travel Directory *see* Travel Weekly's World Travel Directory *1118*
World Treaty Index (US) *920*
World Union for the Safeguard of Youth. Conference Proceedings (FR) *1022*
World Union of Organizations for the Safeguard of Youth *see* World Union for the Safeguard of Youth. Conference Proceedings *1022*
World Veterinary Congress. Proceedings (SP ISSN 0084-2443) *1122*
World Wastes Equipment Catalog (US) *500*
World Weather Watch Planning Reports (UN ISSN 0084-2451) *807*
World Wheat Statistics (UK ISSN 0512-3844) *44*
World Who's Who in Commerce and Industry *see* Who's Who in Finance and Industry *136*
World Who's Who of Women (UK) *136, 1130*
World Wide Chamber of Commerce Directory (US ISSN 0084-2478) *237*
World Wide Shipping Guide (US ISSN 0162-0088) *1104*
World Wrought Copper Statistics (UK ISSN 0266-7347) *260, 802*
World Yearbook of Education (UK ISSN 0084-2508) *422*
World Yearbook of Fifth Generation Computing Research and Development (UK) *355*
World Yearbook of Robotics Research and Development (UK) *355*
World Zionist Organization. General Council. Addresses, Debates, Resolutions (IS ISSN 0084-2516) *977*
World Zionist Organization. Zionist Congress. Kongres Ha-Tsiyoni. Hahlatot (IS) *911*
World Zionist Organization Press Service *see* World Zionist Press Service *539*
World Zionist Press Service (IS) *539*
World's Poultry Science Association. Report of the Proceedings of International Congress (US ISSN 0084-2532) *68*
World's Wisdom Series (II) *883, 974*
World's Woman's Christian Temperance Union. Convention Report *see* World's Woman's Christian Temperance Union. Triennial Report *377*
World's Woman's Christian Temperance Union. Triennial Report (US) *377, 1022*
Worldwatch Papers (US) *500, 1031*
Worldwide Chemical Directory (UK) *319, 325*
Worldwide Directory of Computer Companies (US) *1166*
Worldwide Directory of Federal Libraries (US) *1166*
Worldwide Economic Indicators (US) *260*
Worldwide Government Directory (US ISSN 0276-900X) *319, 947*
Worldwide Hotel Industry (US) *621*
Worldwide Lodging Industry *see* Worldwide Hotel Industry *621*
Worldwide Petrochemical Directory (US ISSN 0084-2583) *867*
Worldwide Refining and Gas Processing Directory (US ISSN 0277-0962) *867*
Worldwide Register of Adult Education(US ISSN 0084-2486) *427*
Worldwide Report: Arms Control (US) *813, 920*
Worldwide Report: Epidemiology (US) *958*
Worldwide Report: Nuclear Development and Proliferation (US) *813, 899*
Worldwide Report: Telecommunications Policy. Research and Development (US) *345*
Worldwide Synthetic Fuels and Alternate Energy Directory (US ISSN 0731-2369) *467, 867*
Worldwide Uranium Producer Profiles (US) *899*
Der Wormsgau (GW ISSN 0084-2613) *602*
Wormsloe Foundation. Publications (US ISSN 0084-2621) *611*
Worrall's Textile & Engineering Directory (II) *319*
Woytinsky Lectures (US ISSN 0084-263X) *911, 947*
Wrestling Manual and Case Book (US) *1036*
Wrestling Officials Manual *see* Wrestling Manual and Case Book *1036*
Wrestling Rulebook (US) *1036*
Wrightia (US ISSN 0084-2648) *1166*
Wrigley's Hotel-Motel Directory (CN) *621*
Writ (CN ISSN 0316-3768) *737*
Write In There (US) *336*
Writer (Penzance) (UK ISSN 0260-2776) *737*
Writers' and Artists' Yearbook (UK ISSN 0084-2664) *963*
Writers' and Photographers' Marketing Guide; Directory of Australian and New Zealand Literary and Photo Markets (AT ISSN 0084-2680) *885, 963*
Writers' and Poets' Yearbook (UK) *737, 744*
Writers Directory (US) *133, 136*
Writers Forum (US ISSN 0960-2992) *737*
Writer's Handbook (US ISSN 0084-2710) *963*
Writers Ink (US) *737, 963*
Writer's Market (US ISSN 0084-2729) *963*
Writers of Wales (UK ISSN 0141-5050) *737*
Writer's Review *see* Writer (Penzance) *737*
Writers Workshop Literary Reader (II) *737*
Writer's Yearbook (US ISSN 0084-2737) *963*
Writing (San Francisco) (US ISSN 0084-2745) *737*
Writing in Holland and Flanders (NE) *708, 737*
Writing Research (US) *737*
Writings on American History (US) *564*
Writings on British History *see* Royal Historical Society. Annual Bibliography of British and Irish History *564*
Wroclawski Rocznik Ekonomiczny (PL ISSN 0084-2974) *202*

Wroclawskie Towarzystwo Naukowe. Komisja Historii Sztuki. Rozprawy (PL ISSN 0084-2982) *112*
Wroclawskie Towarzystwo Naukowe. Komisja Jezykowa. Rozprawy (PL ISSN 0084-2990) *708*
Wroclawskie Towarzystwo Naukowe. Prace. Seria A. Humanistyka (PL ISSN 0084-3016) *634*
Wroclawskie Towarzystwo Naukowe. Prace. Seria B. Nauki Scisle (PL ISSN 0084-3024) *1003*
Wroclawskie Towarzystwo Naukowe. Sprawozdania. Seria A (PL ISSN 0371-4756) *1003*
Wspolpraca *see* Politechnika Wroclawska. Osrodek Badan Prognostycznych. Prace Naukowe. Wspolpraca *248*
Wudd (GW ISSN 0040-8646) *976*
Wuerttembergisch Franken (GW ISSN 0084-3067) *602*
Wuerzburger Dioezesangeschichtsblaetter (GW) *602*
Wuerzburger Geographische Arbeiten (GW ISSN 0510-9833) *551*
Wuerzburger Geographische Manuskript(GW ISSN 0931-8623) *551*
Wuerzburger Jahrbuecher fuer die Altertumswissenschaft (GW) *339, 708*
Wuerzburger Wehrwissenschaftliche Abhandlungen (GW ISSN 0084-3083) *667, 813*
Wunderblock (GW ISSN 0344-8274) *938*
Wuppertaler Schriftenreihe Literatur (GW ISSN 0341-2172) *737*
Wydzial Filologiczno-Filozoficznego. Prace (PL) *112, 883*
Wye College (University of London). Agrarian Development Unit. Occasional Paper (UK) *50*
Wye College (University of London). Department of Agricultural Economics. Farm Business Unit. Occasional Paper (UK) *50, 61*
Wye College (University of London). School of Rural Economics and Related Studies. Farm Business Unit. Occasional Paper *see* Wye College (University of London). Department of Agricultural Economics. Farm Business Unit. Occasional Paper *50*
Wykeham Science Series (US ISSN 0084-3113) *1003*
Wykeham Technological Series (US ISSN 0084-3121) *1072*
Wyoming. Characteristics of Occupational Injuries and Illnesses (US) *958*
Wyoming. Department of Education. Education Directory (US) *422*
Wyoming. Department of Environmental Quality. Annual Report (US ISSN 0099-1279) *500*
Wyoming. Department of Health and Social Services. Annual Report (US ISSN 0098-6984) *958, 1022*
Wyoming. Department of Labor and Statistics. Annual Report (US) *277*
Wyoming. Department of Revenue and Taxation. Annual Report (US ISSN 0094-9019) *300*
Wyoming. Division of Planning, Evaluation and Information Services. Statistical Report Series (US ISSN 0093-5530) *1066*
Wyoming. Employment Security Commission. Annual Report (US) *277*
Wyoming. Employment Security Commission. Research and Analysis Section. Annual Planning Report *see* Wyoming Annual Planning Report *277*
Wyoming. Geological Survey. Bulletin (US) *398*
Wyoming.g. Geological Survey. Public Information Circulars (US) *398*
Wyoming. Geological Survey. Report of Investigations (US) *398*
Wyoming. State of Wyoming Annual Report (US ISSN 0094-3924) *947*
Wyoming. Water Quality Division. Wyoming State Plan (US ISSN 0098-0846) *500*

Wyoming Annual Planning Report (US) *277*
Wyoming Data Handbook (US) *947*
Wyoming Mineral Yearbook (US ISSN 0096-9842) *398*
Wyoming State Plan *see* Wyoming. Water Quality Division. Wyoming State Plan *500*
Wyzsza Szkola Ekonomiczna. Zeszyty Naukowe *see* Akademia Ekonomiczna, Krakow. Zeszyty Naukowe *190*
Wyzsza Szkola Ekonomiczna, Krakow. Zeszyty Naukowe. Seria Specjalna: Monografie *see* Akademia Ekonomiczna, Krakow. Zeszyty Naukowe. Seria Specjalna: Monografie *190*
Wyzsza Szkola Ekonomiczna we Wroclawiu. Prace Naukowe *see* Akademia Ekonomiczna we Wroclawiu. Prace Naukowe *190*
Wyzsza Szkola Morska. Zeszyty Naukowe (PL) *1104*
Wyzsza Szkola Pedagogiczna, Katowice. Zeszyty Naukowe. Sekcja Jezykoznawstwa (PL ISSN 0075-5281) *1167*
Wyzsza Szkola Pedagogiczna, Krakow. Prace Jezykoznawcze (PL) *708*
Wyzsza Szkola Pedagogiczna, Krakow. Prace Zoologiczne (PL) *178*
Wyzsza Szkola Pedagogiczna, Opole. Zeszyty Naukowe. Filologia Polska (PL ISSN 0324-9050) *708, 737*
Wyzsza Szkola Pedagogiczna, Opole. Zeszyty Naukowe. Seria A. Chemia (PL ISSN 0324-9034) *325*
Wyzsza Szkola Pedagogiczna, Opole. Zeszyty Naukowe. Seria A. Dydaktyka (PL) *450*
Wyzsza Szkola Pedagogiczna, Opole. Zeszyty Naukowe. Seria A. Ekonomia (PL ISSN 0474-2966) *250*
Wyzsza Szkola Pedagogiczna, Opole. Zeszyty Naukowe. Seria A. Filologia Rosyjska (PL ISSN 0474-2974) *708, 737*
Wyzsza Szkola Pedagogiczna, Opole. Zeszyty Naukowe. Seria A. Fizyka (PL ISSN 0078-5385) *892*
Wyzsza Szkola Pedagogiczna, Opole. Zeszyty Naukowe. Seria A. Historia (PL ISSN 0078-5393) *602*
Wyzsza Szkola Pedagogiczna, Opole. Zeszyty Naukowe. Seria A. Historia Literatury *see* Wyzsza Szkola Pedagogiczna, Opole. Zeszyty Naukowe. Filologia Polska *708*
Wyzsza Szkola Pedagogiczna, Opole. Zeszyty Naukowe. Seria A. Jezykoznawstwo (PL ISSN 0078-5423) *708*
Wyzsza Szkola Pedagogiczna, Opole. Zeszyty Naukowe. Seria A. Matematyka (PL ISSN 0078-5431) *755*
Wyzsza Szkola Pedagogiczna, Opole. Zeszyty Naukowe. Seria A. Nauki Techniczne (PL ISSN 0324-8992) *475*
Wyzsza Szkola Pedagogiczna, Opole. Zeszyty Naukowe. Seria A. Pedagogika (PL) *450*
Wyzsza Szkola Pedagogiczna, Opole. Zeszyty Naukowe. Seria A. Psychologia (PL ISSN 0208-9564) *938*
Wyzsza Szkola Pedagogiczna, Opole. Zeszyty Naukowe. Seria B. Studia i Monografie (PL ISSN 0078-544X) *634*
Wyzsza Szkola Rolnicza, Wroclaw. Rolnictwo *see* Akademia Rolnicza, Wroclaw. Rolnictwo *24*
X-Ray Diffraction Abstracts (UK ISSN 0309-5312) *894*
X Ref - (Year) *see* Drug Trade Name Cross Reference List *873*
Xanadu (US ISSN 0146-0463) *744*
Xavier University. Museum and Archives Publications (PH ISSN 0084-3229) *634*
Xin Talng *see* Xin Tang *708*
Xin Tang/New China (US ISSN 0731-0897) *708*
Xtras (US) *737*

Y Canada (CN ISSN 0315-095X) *334, 341*
Y E R Monograph Series (Yeats Elliot Review) (CN ISSN 0704-5697) *738*
Y M C A Yearbook and Official Roster (Young Men's Christian Association of the U S A) (US ISSN 0084-4292) *1022*
Y M C A's of the World (SZ) *334, 341*
Yachting Association of Western Australia. Year Book (AT) *1042*
Yachting Belge (BE ISSN 0084-3237) *1042*
Yachting World Diary (UK) *1042*
Yachting Year Book of Northern California (US ISSN 0094-8136) *1042*
Yachting's Boat Buyers Guide (US) *1042*
Yachtlogbuch (GW) *1042*
Yachtsman's Guide to the Bahamas (US) *1042, 1119*
Yachtsman's Guide to the Caribbean (US ISSN 0084-3261) *1042*
Yachtsman's Guide to the Great Lakes (US ISSN 0084-327X) *1042*
Yachtsman's Guide to the Greater Antilles (US ISSN 0162-7635) *1042*
Yad Vashem Studies (IS) *977*
Yad Vashem Studies on the European Jewish Catastrophe and Resistance *see* Yad Vashem Studies *977*
Yale Art Gallery Bulletin *see* Yale University Art Gallery. Bulletin *831*
Yale Classical Studies (UK ISSN 0084-330X) *339*
Yale College Series (US ISSN 0084-3318) *634*
Yale Fastbacks (US ISSN 0084-3326) *1013*
Yale Germanic Studies (US ISSN 0084-3334) *738*
Yale Historical Publications (Miscellany) (US ISSN 0084-3350) *562*
Yale Judaica Series (US ISSN 0084-3369) *977*
Yale Language Series (US) *708*
Yale Law School Studies (US ISSN 0513-1405) *667*
Yale Linguistic Series *see* Yale Language Series *708*
Yale Near Eastern Researches (US ISSN 0084-3385) *614*
Yale Oriental Series. Babylonian Texts (US) *614*
Yale Publications in American Studies (US ISSN 0084-3393) *611*
Yale Publications in Religion (US ISSN 0084-3407) *974*
Yale Publications in the History of Art (US ISSN 0084-3415) *100, 112*
Yale Romanic Studies. Second Series (US ISSN 0084-3423) *738*
Yale Russian and East European Studies (US ISSN 0084-3431) *738*
Yale Scene; University Series (US ISSN 0084-344X) *441*
Yale Series in Economic History (US) *252*
Yale Series of Younger Poets (US ISSN 0084-3458) *744*
Yale Southeast Asia Studies (US ISSN 0084-3466) *572*
Yale Southeast Asia Studies. Monograph Series (US ISSN 0513-4501) *1013*
Yale Studies in English (US ISSN 0084-3482) *738*
Yale Studies in Political Science (US ISSN 0084-3490) *911*
Yale Studies of the City (US ISSN 0084-3520) *627*
Yale University. Department of Anthropology. Publications in Anthropology (US) *78*
Yale University. Economic Growth Center. Annual Report (US) *202*
Yale University. Economic Growth Center. Center Discussion Paper (US) *250*
Yale University. School of Forestry. Bulletin (US ISSN 0361-4425) *529*
Yale University Art Gallery. Bulletin (US ISSN 0084-3539) *831*
Yale Western Americana Series (US ISSN 0084-3563) *611*

Yamagata University. Bulletin (JA ISSN 0085-834X) *634*
Yamaguchi-Ken Kogai Senta Nenpo/ Yamaguchi Prefectural Environmental Pollution Research Center. Annual Report (JA) *327, 500*
Yamaguchi Prefectural Environmental Pollution Research Center. Annual Report *see* Yamaguchi-Ken Kogai Senta Nenpo *500*
Yamaguchi University. Faculty of Agriculture. Bulletin (JA ISSN 0513-1715) *37*
Yamaguchi University. Faculty of Engineering. Technology Reports (JA) *1072*
Yamanouchi Central Research Laboratories. Report *see* Yamanouchi Seiyaku Kenkyu Hokoku *873*
Yamanouchi Seiyaku Kenkyu Hokoku/ Yamanouchi Central Research Laboratories. Report (JA) *873*
Yandro (US) *1167*
Yankee Ingenuity (US) *353*
Yankee Woodlot (US) *529*
Yapi ve Kredi Bankasi. Annual Report (TU) *234*
Yardsticks for Costing (CN) *100*
Yavneh Studies (US ISSN 0044-0256) *977*
Year-End Regulatory Review (US ISSN 0275-276X) *282*
Year-End Summary of the Electric Power Situation in the United States *see* Electric Power Annual Report *452*
Year End Tax Planning Manual (US) *1167*
Year in Hematology *see* Contemporary Hematology/Oncology *783*
Yearbook and Church Directory of the Orthodox Church in America *see* Orthodox Church in America. Yearbook and Church Directory *984*
Yearbook and Directory of Osteopathic Physicians *see* A O A Yearbook and Directory of Osteopathic Physicians *777*
Yearbook and Philatelic Societies' Directory (UK ISSN 0260-1265) *875*
Yearbook Commercial Arbitration (NE) *672*
Yearbook for Jewish Communities and Organizations (IS ISSN 0334-5904) *506*
Yearbook for Traditional Music (US ISSN 0740-1558) *517, 843*
Yearbook in Women's Policy Studies *see* Sage Yearbooks in Women's Policy Studies *1129*
Yearbook of Adult Continuing Education (UK) *427*
Yearbook of Adult Education *see* Yearbook of Adult Continuing Education *427*
Year Book of Agricultural Co-Operation (UK ISSN 0142-498X) *50, 239, 286*
Yearbook of Agricultural Statistics of Bangladesh (BG) *37*
Yearbook of Agriculture *see* U.S. Department of Agriculture. Yearbook of Agriculture *36*
Yearbook of American and Canadian Churches (US ISSN 0084-3644) *974*
Yearbook of American Churches *see* Yearbook of American and Canadian Churches *974*
Year Book of Anesthesia (US ISSN 0084-3652) *774*
Year Book of Cancer (US ISSN 0084-3679) *776*
Year Book of Cardiology (US ISSN 0145-4145) *777*
Yearbook of Cardiovascular and Renal Disease *see* Year Book of Cardiology *777*
Yearbook of Cardiovascular Medicine *see* Year Book of Cardiology *777*
Yearbook of Cardiovascular Medicine and Surgery *see* Year Book of Cardiology *777*
Year Book of Chess (UK) *1036*

Yearbook of Common Carrier Telecommunication Statistics/ Annuaire Statistique des Telecommunications du Secteur Public (UN) 345
Yearbook of Comparative and General Literature (US ISSN 0084-3695) 738
Yearbook of Comparative Criticism (US ISSN 0084-3709) 738
Year Book of Critical Care Medicine (US ISSN 0734-3299) 768
Yearbook of Danish Medical History see Dansk Medicinhistorisk Aarbog 760
Year Book of Dentistry (US ISSN 0084-3717) 780
Year Book of Dermatology (US ISSN 0093-3619) 780
Yearbook of Dermatology and Syphilology see Year Book of Dermatology 780
Year Book of Diagnostic Radiology (US ISSN 0098-1672) 792
Year Book of Digestive Diseases (US) 783
Yearbook of Drug Abuse see Yearbook of Substance Use and Abuse 377
Year Book of Drug Therapy (US ISSN 0084-3733) 873
Yearbook of East-European Economics see Jahrbuch der Wirtschaft Osteuropas 246
Year Book of Emergency Medicine (US ISSN 0271-7964) 786
Year Book of Endocrinology (US ISSN 0084-3741) 781
Yearbook of English Studies (UK ISSN 0306-2473) 634, 738
Yearbook of European Law (UK ISSN 0266-7223) 672
Year Book of Family Practice (US ISSN 0147-1996) 768
Yearbook of Finnish Foreign Policy (FI ISSN 0355-0079) 920
Yearbook of Fishery Statistics (UN ISSN 0084-375X) 514
Yearbook of Forest Products (UN ISSN 0084-3768) 531
Yearbook of Forest Statistics see Metsatilastollinen Vuosikirja 526
Year Book of General Surgery see Year Book of Surgery 795
Year Book of General Therapeutics see Year Book of Drug Therapy 873
Yearbook of German-American Studies (US) 738
Yearbook of Greek Press (GR) 647
Year Book of Hematology (US) 783
Yearbook of Higher Education (US ISSN 0084-3784) 1167
Yearbook of Industrial Statistics see Industrial Statistics Yearbook 211
Yearbook of International Commodity Statistics (UN ISSN 0257-1870) 220
Yearbook of International Congress Proceedings (BE ISSN 0084-3806) 920
Yearbook of International Organizations(BE ISSN 0084-3814) 920
Yearbook of Israel Ports Statistics/ Shenaton Statisti: Le Nemlei Israel (IS ISSN 0084-3830) 260
Yearbook of Italian Studies (IT) 602
Yearbook of Jehovah's Witnesses see Jehovah's Witnesses Yearbook 984
Year Book of Labour Statistics. (UN ISSN 0084-3857) 220
Yearbook of Landscape Architecture (US) 1167
Yearbook of Law Computers and Technology (UK ISSN 0269-3712) 667, 669
Year Book of Medicine (US ISSN 0084-3873) 768
Yearbook of National Account Statistics see United Nations. National Accounts Statistics 219
Year Book of Neurology & Neurosurgery (US) 791, 795
Yearbook of Neurology, Psychiatry and Neurosurgery see Year Book of Psychiatry and Applied Mental Health 791
Year Book of Neurology, Psychiatry and Neurosurgery see Year Book of Neurology & Neurosurgery 791

Yearbook of Nordic Statistics see Nordisk Statistisk Aarsbok 1060
Year Book of Nuclear Medicine (US ISSN 0084-3903) 792
Year Book of Obstetrics and Gynecology (US ISSN 0084-3911) 785
Year Book of Ophthalmology (US ISSN 0084-392X) 786
Year Book of Opthamology (US) 786
Year Book of Orthopedics (US ISSN 0276-1092) 786
Year Book of Orthopedics, Traumatic and Plastic Surgery see Year Book of Orthopedics 786
Year Book of Otolaryngology (US) 787
Year Book of Pathology and Clinical Pathology (US ISSN 0084-3946) 768
Year Book of Pediatrics (US ISSN 0084-3954) 788
Yearbook of Physical Anthropology (Washington) (US ISSN 0096-848X) 78
Year Book of Plastic and Reconstructive Surgery (US ISSN 0084-3962) 795
Year Book of Podiatric Medicine and Surgery (US) 786, 795
Yearbook of Population Research in Finland/Vaestoentutkimuksen Vuosikirja (FI ISSN 0506-3590) 925
Year Book of Psychiatry and Applied Mental Health (US ISSN 0084-3970) 791
Year Book of Pulmonary Disease (US) 793
Year Book of Radiology see Year Book of Diagnostic Radiology 792
Year Book of Rehabilitation (US) 445, 768
Yearbook of Religious Zionism (IS) 977
Yearbook of Romanian Studies (US ISSN 0149-7219) 602, 738
Yearbook of Scandinavian Shipowners see Skandinaviske Skipsrederier 1103
Yearbook of School Law (US) 422, 667
Yearbook of Science and the Future (US ISSN 0096-3291) 1003
Yearbook of Selected Osteopathic Papers see American Academy of Osteopathy Yearbook 777
Yearbook of Social Policy in Britain (UK) 1013
Yearbook of Social Studies see Yearbook of Social Policy in Britain 1013
Year Book of Sports Medicine (US ISSN 0162-0908) 793
Yearbook of Substance Use and Abuse (US ISSN 0273-3722) 377
Year Book of Surgery (US ISSN 0090-3671) 795
Yearbook of Symbolic Anthropology (CN) 78
Yearbook of Technical and Further Education see Directory of Technical and Further Education 848
Yearbook of the American Baptist Churches in the U.S.A see American Baptist Churches in the U.S.A. Yearbook 978
Yearbook of the Commonwealth (UK ISSN 0084-4047) 602
Year Book of the Ear, Nose and Throat see Year Book of Otolaryngology 787
Yearbook of the Italian Rubber Industry see Annuario dell'Industria Italiana della Gomma 985
Year-Book of the Lebanese Joint-Stock Companies/Annuaire des Societes Libanaises Par Action (LE ISSN 0075-8361) 269
Year-Book of the Lebanese Limited Liability Companies/Annuaire des Societes Libanaises a Responsibilite Limitee (LE) 269
Yearbook of the Literary Museum see Petofi Irodalmi Muzeum Evkonyve 730
Yearbook of Tidal Records see Choi Nenpo 405
Yearbook of Tourism Statistics (SP) 1120

Yearbook of U S - Japan Economic Relations (US) 260
Year Book of Urology (US ISSN 0084-4071) 795
Year Book of Vascular Surgery (US) 768, 777
Yearbook of Works re Appalachia (US) 744
Yearbook of World Affairs (UK ISSN 0084-408X) 1167
Yearbook of World Energy Statistics see Energy Statistics Yearbook 465
Yearbook of World Problems and Human Potential (BE ISSN 0304-0089) 920, 1031
Yearbook on Corporate Mergers, Joint Ventures and Corporate Policy (US) 202
Yearbook on Human Rights (UN ISSN 0084-4098) 634, 914
Yearbook on International Communist Affairs (US ISSN 0084-4101) 920
Yearbook on Socialist Legal Systems (US ISSN 0887-9117) 667, 911
Yearbook - Supreme Court Historical Society see Supreme Court Historical Society. Yearbook 665
Yearbooks in Christian Education (US ISSN 0084-4128) 974
Yearly All India Criminal Digest. (II ISSN 0377-6719) 373
Year's Best Fantasy Stories (US) 14
Year's Best Horror Stories (US) 14
Year's Best Science Fiction (US) 14
Year's Work in English Studies (US ISSN 0084-4144) 738
Year's Work in Modern Language Studies (UK ISSN 0084-4152) 709, 739
Yeats (US) 738
Yeats Eliot Review (CN ISSN 0704-5700) 738, 744
Yeats Elliot Review Monograph Series see Y E R Monograph Series 738
Yeda-Am (IS) 517
Yedion (IS ISSN 0334-0554) 368
Yeh Ko see Evensongs 710
Yellow Book of Funeral Directors & Services (US ISSN 0098-3322) 531
Yellow Journal Pocket Press see Other Scenes 712
Yemen. Central Statistical Office. Statistical Yearbook (YE) 1067
Yerusholaimer Almanakh. (IS ISSN 0334-9594) 738
Yes see Chien d'Or 718
Yeshiva University Sephardic Bulletin (US) 506, 977
Yet Another Small Magazine (US) 712, 745
Yhdistyneiden Kansakuntien Yleiskokous (Year) (FI ISSN 0781-2442) 920
Yiddish Language see Yidishe Shprakh 708
Yiddish Literary and Linguistic Periodicals and Miscellanies (IS) 506, 708, 738, 977
Yidishe Shprakh/Yiddish Language (US ISSN 0044-0442) 708
Yin Times of Black Bart see Black Bart 710
Yisrael-Am Ve'Eretz (IS ISSN 0334-1798) 831
Yivo Annual of Jewish Social Science (US ISSN 0084-4209) 1013
Yivo Bleter/Yivo Pages (US ISSN 0084-4217) 1014
Yivo Pages see Yivo Bleter 1014
Ylioppilasaineita (FI ISSN 0355-1784) 431
Yoga Life (CN) 883, 886
Yokohama City Institute of Health. Annual Report (JA ISSN 0912-2826) 958
Yokohama Kokuritsu Daigaku Jimbun Kiyo Dai-1-rui, Tetsugaku, Shakai Kagaku see Yokohama National University. Humanities. Section 1: Philosophy and Social Sciences 1014
Yokohama Kokuritsu Daigaku Kogakubu Kiyo see Yokohama National University. Faculty of Engineering. Bulletin 475

Yokohama Kokuritsu Daigaku Rika Kiyo, Dai-1-rui, Sugaku, Butsurigaku, Kagaku see Yokohama National University. Science Reports. Section 1: Mathematics, Physics, Chemistry 1003
Yokohama Kokuritu Daigaku Kyoiku Kiyo see Yokohama National University. Educational Sciences 422
Yokohama National University. Educational Sciences/Yokohama Kokuritu Daigaku Kyoiku Kiyo (JA ISSN 0513-5656) 422
Yokohama National University. Faculty of Engineering. Bulletin/Yokohama Kokuritsu Daigaku Kogakubu Kiyo (JA ISSN 0513-2592) 475
Yokohama National University. Humanities. Section 1: Philosophy and Social Sciences/Yokohama Kokuritsu Daigaku Jimbun Kiyo Dai-1-rui, Tetsugaku, Shakai Kagaku (JA ISSN 0513-5621) 883, 1014
Yokohama National University. Science Reports. Section 1: Mathematics, Physics, Chemistry/Yokohama Kokuritsu Daigaku Rika Kiyo, Dai-1-rui, Sugaku, Butsurigaku, Kagaku (JA ISSN 0085-8366) 1003
Yokohama National University. Science Reports. Section 2: Biological and Geological Sciences (JA) 149
Yokohama National University. Science Reports. Section 2: Biological Sciences see Yokohama National University. Science Reports. Section 2: Biological and Geological Sciences 149
Yokohama Port Activities (JA) 1104
Yokosuka City Museum. Science Report (JA) 1003
Yokufukai Chosa Kenkyu Kiyo see Yokufukai Geriatric Journal 552
Yokufukai Geriatric Journal/Yokufukai Chosa Kenkyu Kiyo (JA) 552
Yonsei Reports on Tropical Medicine (KO) 778
Yonsei University. Graduate School. Abstracts of Faculty Research Reports (KO) 13, 426
York Georgian Society. Annual Report (UK) 100
York Journal of Convocation (UK ISSN 0085-8374) 974
York Pioneer (CN ISSN 0513-2711) 611
Yorkshire Archaeological Journal (UK ISSN 0084-4276) 96
Yorkshire Archaeological Society Parish Register Series (UK) 537
Yorkshire Archaeological Society Record Series (UK) 602
Yorkshire Dialect Society. Summer Bulletin (UK ISSN 0513-2762) 708
Yorkshire Dialect Society Transactions (UK) 708
Young Audio Now (JA) 843
Young Buddhist (SI) 978
Young Communist see Rebel Youth 908
Young Fabian Pamphlet (UK ISSN 0513-5982) 911
Young Men's Christian Association of the U S A Yearbook and Official Roster see Y M C A Yearbook and Official Roster 1022
Young Parents (SI) 334
Young Woman (US) 1167
Young Women's Christian Association of the United States of America. National Board. Annual Report (US) 341
Young Women's Christian Association of the United States of America. The Printout (US ISSN 0084-4306) 974
Young Worker (SA) 277
Young Worker see Rebel Youth 908
Your (Year) Guide to Social Security Benefits (US) 202, 1022
Your Air Companion see Motion 1114
Your Australian Garden (AT ISSN 0085-8382) 534
Your First Baby (UK) 334, 788
Your Friendly Fascist (AT) 745
Your Investments: How to Increase Your Capital and Income see Dun & Bradstreet's Guide to Your Investments 266

Your United Nations (UN ISSN 0084-4322) 562, 920
Yourdon Report (US) 359
Youth Hostels Association (England and Wales) Guide (UK) 1119
Youth Hostels Association (England and Wales) Handbook see Youth Hostels Association (England and Wales) Guide 1119
Youth Planbook (US ISSN 0512-9575) 422, 980
Youth Services Guide (UK) 334, 1022
Youth-Serving Organizations Directory (US ISSN 0196-9668) 1022
Youth Studies in New Zealand (NZ ISSN 0111-0489) 426
Yrke och Framtid (SW ISSN 0513-6261) 849
Yugoslav Export - Import Directory (YU ISSN 0084-4349) 260, 319
Yugoslav Facts and Views (US ISSN 0427-8968) 250, 920
Yugoslav Serbo-Croatian-English Contrastive Project. Series B: studies (YU) 708
Yugoslavia. Savezni Zavod za Statistiku. Anketa O Ostvarivanju Prava Radnika Iz Radnog Odnosa (YU) 220
Yugoslavia. Savezni Zavod za Statistiku. Anketa O Porodicnim Budzetima Radnickih Domacinstava (YU) 220
Yugoslavia. Savezni Zavod za Statistiku. Industrijske Organizacije (YU) 220
Yugoslavia. Savezni Zavod za Statistiku. Komunalni Fondovi u Gradskim Naseljima (YU) 950
Yugoslavia. Savezni Zavod za Statistiku. Osnovna i Srednje (YU) 426
Yugoslavia. Savezni Zavod za Statistiku. Samoupravljanje u Privredi (YU) 220
Yugoslavia. Savezni Zavod za Statistiku. Samoupravljanje u Ustanovama Drustvenih Sluzbi (YU) 220
Yugoslavia. Savezni Zavod za Statistiku. Saobracaj i Veze (YU ISSN 0513-0794) 1087
Yugoslavia. Savezni Zavod za Statistiku. Turizam (YU) 1120
Yugoslavia. Savezni Zavod za Statistiku. Ucenici u Privredi (YU ISSN 0513-0832) 426
Yugoslavia. Savezni Zavod za Statistiku. Zaposleno Osoblje (YU ISSN 0513-0883) 220
Yugoslavia. Savezni Zavod za Statistuku. Vitalna Statistika see Demografska Statistika 926
Yugoslavia; Hotel and Tourist Directory(YU) 621
Yugoslovenska Investiciona Banka. Annual Report see Investbanka. Annual Report 230
Yukijirushi Nyugyo Gijutsu Kenkyusho Hokoku see Snow Brand Milk Products Company. Research Laboratory. Reports 63
Yukon Bibliography Update (CN) 13, 133, 551
Yuval (IS ISSN 0084-439X) 843
Z.A.S.E. Bulletin see Science Education in Zambia 419
Z Badan Nad Polskimi Ksiegozbiorami Historycznymi (PL ISSN 0137-5172) 687
Z Dejin Geodezie a Kartografie (CS) 381
Z Dziejow Form Artystycznych w Literaturze Polskiej (PL ISSN 0084-4411) 738
Z Dziejow Muzyki Polskiej (PL ISSN 0084-442X) 843
Z F I - Mitteilungen (Zentralinstitut fuer Isotopen- und Strahlenforschung) (GE ISSN 0323-8776) 892
Z G A Bibliographic Series (Zambia Geographical Association) (ZA ISSN 0250-8125) 133, 551
Z G A Magazine see Zambian Geographical Journal 551
Z G A Occasional Studies (Zambia Geographical Association) (ZA ISSN 0250-8109) 551
Z G A Occasional Studies and Special Publications see Z G A Occasional Studies 551

Z G A Regional Handbook see Zambia Geographical Association. Regional Handbook 551
Z G A School Supplement (Zambia Geographical Association) (ZA ISSN 0250-8117) 551
Z M P Bilanz Getreide-Futtermittel (GW ISSN 0170-7809) 64
Z Prac Zakladu Nauk Ekonomicznych PAN (PL ISSN 0044-1503) 1167
Z Problematyki Prawa Pracy i Polityki Socjalnej (PL ISSN 0208-5003) 667, 911, 1031
Z S S A Newsletter (Zoological Society of Southern Africa) (SA) 178
Z Teorii i Praktyki Dydaktycznej Jezyka Polskiego (PL ISSN 0208-5011) 708
Z V E I Electro Buyers' Guide see Z V E I Elektro-Einkaufsfuehrer 485
Z V E I Elektro-Einkaufsfuehrer (GW) 461, 485
Z V E I Guia de Equipos Electricos see Z V E I Elektro-Einkaufsfuehrer 485
Z V E I Guide de l'Equipement Electrique see Z V E I Elektro-Einkaufsfuehrer 485
Zagadnienia Drgan Nieliniowych/Nonlinear Vibrations Problems (PL ISSN 0044-1597) 892
Zahlentafeln der Physikalisch-Chemischen Untersuchungen des Rheins sowie der Mosel see Zahlentafeln der Physikalisch-Chemischen Untersuchungen des Rheinwassers 500
Zahlentafeln der Physikalisch-Chemischen Untersuchungen des Rheinwassers/Tableaux Numeriques des Analyses Physico-Chimiques des Eaux du Rhin (GW ISSN 0173-6507) 500
Zahlungsbilanz der Schweiz (SZ) 300
Zahranicne Periodika v C S S R (CS) 133
Zaidan Hojin Toyo Bunko see Oriental Library. Research Department. Memoirs 571
Zaire. Assemblee Nationale. Compte Rendu Analytique see Zaire. Conseil Legislatif National. Compte Rendu Analytique 667
Zaire. Bibliotheque Nationale. Bibliographie Nationale (ZR) 133
Zaire. Conseil Legislatif National. Compte Rendu Analytique (ZR) 667
Zairyo Kenkyu Rengo Koenkai Ronbunshu see Japan Congress on Materials Research. Proceedings 489
Zambia. Central Statistical Office. Agricultural and Pastoral Production (Commercial and Non-Commercial) (ZA) 44
Zambia. Central Statistical Office. Agricultural and Pastoral Production (Commercial Farms) (ZA) 44, 1067
Zambia. Central Statistical Office. Agricultural and Pastoral Production (Non-Commercial) (ZA) 44, 1067
Zambia. Central Statistical Office. Agricultural and Pastoral Production see Zambia. Central Statistical Office. Agricultural and Pastoral Production (Commercial and Non-Commercial) 44
Zambia. Central Statistical Office. Agricultural and Pastoral Production see Zambia. Central Statistical Office. Agricultural and Pastoral Production (Non-Commercial) 44
Zambia. Central Statistical Office. Agricultural and Pastoral Production see Zambia. Central Statistical Office. Agricultural and Pastoral Production (Commercial Farms) 44
Zambia. Central Statistical Office. Annual Statement of External Trade (ZA ISSN 0084-4489) 220
Zambia. Central Statistical Office. Balance of Payments Statistics (ZA) 220
Zambia. Central Statistical Office. Employment and Earnings (ZA ISSN 0084-4500) 220
Zambia. Central Statistical Office. Financial Statistics of Government Sector (Economic and Functional Analysis) (ZA) 950

Zambia. Central Statistical Office. Financial Statistics of Public Corporations (ZA ISSN 0084-4519) 220
Zambia. Central Statistical Office. Fisheries Statistics (Natural Waters) (ZA ISSN 0514-8731) 514
Zambia. Central Statistical Office. Government Sector Accounts (Economic and Functional Analysis) see Zambia. Central Statistical Office. Financial Statistics of Government Sector (Economic and Functional Analysis) 950
Zambia. Central Statistical Office. Industry Monographs (ZA) 202
Zambia. Central Statistical Office. Manpower Survey (ZA) 220
Zambia. Central Statistical Office. Migration Statistics (ZA ISSN 0084-4543) 925, 930
Zambia. Central Statistical Office. Migration Statistics: Immigrants and Visitors see Zambia. Central Statistical Office. Migration Statistics 930
Zambia. Central Statistical Office. National Accounts (ZA) 300, 947
Zambia. Central Statistical Office. Registered Births, Marriages and Deaths (Vital Statistics) see Zambia. Central Statistical Office. Vital Statistics 930
Zambia. Central Statistical Office. Statistical Year Book (ZA ISSN 0084-4551) 1067
Zambia. Central Statistical Office. Vital Statistics (ZA ISSN 0084-456X) 930, 1067
Zambia. Commission for Investigations. Annual Report (ZA) 947
Zambia. Commission for the Preservation of Natural and Historical Monuments and Relics. Annual Report (ZA ISSN 0084-4586) 368
Zambia. Department of Agriculture. Research and Specialist Services. Annual Report (ZA) 37, 61
Zambia. Department of Civil Aviation. Annual Report (ZA) 1090
Zambia. Department of Community Development. Report (ZA ISSN 0084-4608) 1022
Zambia. Department of Cooperatives. Annual Report (ZA ISSN 0514-5430) 239
Zambia. Department of Customs and Excise. Annual Report of the Controller of Customs and Excise (ZA) 300
Zambia. Department of Fisheries. Annual Report (ZA) 514
Zambia. Department of Forestry. Report (ZA ISSN 0084-4616) 529
Zambia. Department of Labour. Report (ZA ISSN 0084-4632) 277
Zambia. Department of Legal Aid. Annual Report (ZA ISSN 0084-4667) 1022
Zambia. Department of Social Welfare. Report (ZA ISSN 0084-4667) 1022
Zambia. Department of Social Welfare. Social Welfare Research Monographs(ZA ISSN 0081-0533) 1022
Zambia.Department of Taxes. Annual Report of the Commissioner of Taxes(ZA ISSN 0084-4675) 300
Zambia. Department of the Administrator-General and Official Receiver. Report (ZA ISSN 0084-4683) 300
Zambia. Department of Veterinary and Tsetse Control Services. Annual Report (ZA) 1123
Zambia. Department of Water Affairs. Report (ZA ISSN 0084-4705) 1127
Zambia. Educational and Occupational Assessment Service. Annual Report (ZA ISSN 0514-5457) 849
Zambia. General Post Office. Annual Report of the Postmaster-General see Zambia. Posts and Telecommunications Corporation. Annual Report 347
Zambia. Geological Survey. Annual Reports (ZA ISSN 0084-473X) 398
Zambia. Geological Survey. Economic Reports (ZA ISSN 0084-4748) 398

Zambia. Geological Survey. Occasional Papers (ZA ISSN 0084-4756) 398
Zambia. Geological Survey. Reports (ZA ISSN 0084-4764) 398
Zambia. Geological Survey. Technical Reports (ZA) 398
Zambia. High Court. Law Directory and Legal Calendar (ZA) 667
Zambia. Immigration Department. Report (ZA ISSN 0084-4802) 925
Zambia. Information Services. Annual Report (ZA ISSN 0084-4810) 567
Zambia. Meteorological Department. Totals of Monthly and Annual Rainfall (ZA ISSN 0302-5047) 807
Zambia. Ministry of Agriculture and Water Development. Land Use Branch. Soil Survey Report (ZA) 61
Zambia. Ministry of Agriculture. Annual Report (ZA ISSN 0084-4853) 37
Zambia. Ministry of Development and National Guidance. Annual Report see Zambia. Ministry of Planning and Finance. Annual Report 292
Zambia. Ministry of Education. Annual Report (ZA ISSN 0084-487X) 422
Zambia. Ministry of Finance. Annual Report see Zambia. Ministry of Planning and Finance. Annual Report 292
Zambia. Ministry of Lands and Agriculture. Land Use Branch. Soil Survey Report see Zambia. Ministry of Agriculture and Water Development. Land Use Branch. Soil Survey Report 61
Zambia. Ministry of Legal Affairs. Annual Report (ZA) 202, 687
Zambia. Ministry of Planning and Finance. Annual Report (ZA) 292
Zambia. Ministry of Youth and Sport. Department of Youth Development. Annual Report (ZA) 334, 1036
Zambia. National Commission for Development Planning. Economic Report (ZA) 250
Zambia. National Council for Scientific Research. Annual Report (ZA ISSN 0084-4950) 1003
Zambia. National Council for Scientific Research. N C S R Bibliography (ZA) 133, 1005
Zambia. National Food and Nutrition Commission. Annual Report (ZA ISSN 0084-4969) 521, 847
Zambia. National Museums Board. Report (ZA ISSN 0084-4977) 831
Zambia. Natural Resources Advisory Board. Annual Report see Zambia. Natural Resources Department. Annual Report 368
Zambia. Natural Resources Department. Annual Report (ZA) 368
Zambia. Office of the Auditor-General. Report of the Auditor-General (ZA ISSN 0084-4497) 300
Zambia. Pneumoconiosis Medical and Research Bureau and Pneumoconiosis Compensation Board. Annual Reports (ZA ISSN 0084-5000) 793
Zambia. Posts and Telecommunications Corporation. Annual Report (ZA) 347
Zambia. Prisons Department. Report (ZA ISSN 0084-4659) 373
Zambia. Public Service Commission. Report (ZA ISSN 0084-5035) 1022
Zambia. Sports Directorate. Report (ZA ISSN 0084-506X) 1036
Zambia. Survey Department. Report (ZA ISSN 0084-5078) 551
Zambia. Teaching Service Commission. Annual Report (ZA ISSN 0084-5086) 422
Zambia Directory (ZA) 319
Zambia Educational Journal (ZA) 422
Zambia Electricity Supply Corporation. Annual Report (ZA) 461
Zambia Geographical Association. Conference Handbook see Zambia Geographical Association. Regional Handbook 551
Zambia Geographical Association. Occasional Newsletter (ZA) 551
Zambia Geographical Association. Regional Handbook (ZA ISSN 0250-8133) 551

Zambia Geographical Association Bibliographic Series see Z G A Bibliographic Series *551*
Zambia Geographical Association Occasional Studies see Z G A Occasional Studies *551*
Zambia Geographical Association School Supplement see Z G A School Supplement *551*
Zambia Journal of Science and Technology (ZA) *1003, 1072*
Zambia Law Journal (ZA) *667*
Zambia Law Reports (ZA) *667*
Zambia Mining Yearbook (ZA ISSN 0076-9010) *821*
Zambia Museums Journal (ZA) *831*
Zambia Science Abstracts (ZA) *13, 1005*
Zambia State Insurance Corporation. Report and Accounts (ZA) *642*
Zambian Geographical Journal (ZA ISSN 0250-5657) *551*
Zambian Ornithological Society Occasional Papers (ZA) *171*
Zambian Papers (ZA ISSN 0084-5124) *567*
Zapadne Slovensko (CS) *602*
Zaposleni po Obcinah (YU) *277*
Zashchitnye Pokrytiya na Metallakh (UR ISSN 0130-1519) *801*
Zasshi Kiji Sakuin. Jimbun Shakai-hen see Japanese Periodicals Index. Humanities and Social Science Section *634*
Zasshi Kiji Sakuin. Kagaku Gijutsu-hen see Japanese Periodicals Index. Science and Technology *1004*
Zasshi Shimbun Sohkatarogu see Periodicals in Print in Japan *130*
Zbornik Istorije Knjizevnosti/Recueil des Travaux de l'Histoire de la Litterature (YU ISSN 0084-5183) *738*
Zbornik Obcine Grosuplje (YU ISSN 0350-8498) *540*
Zbornik Vedeckych Prac Drevarskej Fakulty Vysokej Skoly Lesnickej a Drevarsej vo Zvolene (CS) *529*
Zbornik za Drustvene Nauke (YU ISSN 0044-1937) *1014*
Zbornik za Istoriju, Jezik i Knjizevnost Srpskog Naroda. Fontes Rerum Slavorum Meridionalium (YU ISSN 0084-5191) *602*
Zbornik za Istoriju, Jezik i Knjizevnost Srpskog Naroda. Spomenici na Srpskom Jeziku (YU ISSN 0084-5205) *738*
Zbornik za Istoriju, Jezik i Knjizevnost Srpskog Naroda. Spomenici na Tudjim Jezicima (YU ISSN 0084-5213) *602*
Zbornik za Istoriju Skolstva i Prosvete (YU ISSN 0514-6151) *422*
Zbornik Zagrebacke Slavisticke Skole (YU) *708*
Zbornik Zastite Spomenika Kulture/Recueil des Travaux sur la Protection des Monuments Historiques (YU ISSN 0514-616X) *112*
Zeichenwerk (GW ISSN 0084-523X) *112*
Zeimu Tokei Kara Mita Hojin Kigyo No Jittai (JA) *300*
Zeiss Information (GW ISSN 0044-2054) *899*
Zeitgenoessisches Musikschaffen in der Deutschen Demokratischen Republik. Urauffuehrungen (GE ISSN 0232-9387) *843*
Zeitschrift fuer Alternsforschung. Supplementbaende (GE ISSN 0084-5272) *552*
Zeitschrift fuer Archaeologie des Mittelalters (GW ISSN 0340-0824) *96*
Zeitschrift fuer Bayerische Kirchengeschichte (GW ISSN 0342-4316) *980*
Zeitschrift fuer Berufs und Wirtschaftspaedagogik. Beihefte (GW ISSN 0174-0830) *422*
Zeitschrift fuer Bibliothekswesen und Bibliographie. Sonderhefte (GW ISSN 0514-6364) *687*
Zeitschrift fuer Celtische Philologie (GW ISSN 0084-5302) *708, 738*

Zeitschrift fuer Dialektologie und Linguistik. Beihefte (GW ISSN 0341-0838) *708*
Zeitschrift fuer die Alttestamentliche Wissenschaft. Beihefte (GW) *974*
Zeitschrift fuer die Geschichte des Oberrheins (GW) *602*
Zeitschrift fuer Franzoesische Sprache und Literatur. Beihefte. Neue Folge (GW ISSN 0341-0811) *709*
Zeitschrift fuer Hohenzollerische Geschichte (GW ISSN 0514-8561) *602*
Zeitschrift fuer Immunitaetsforschung. Immunobiology (GW ISSN 0171-2985) *774*
Zeitschrift fuer Immunitaetsforschung - Immunologie see Zeitschrift fuer Immunitaetsforschung. Immunobiology *774*
Zeitschrift fuer Lateinamerika Wien (AU ISSN 0049-8645) *602*
Zeitschrift fuer Literaturwissenschaft und Linguistik LiLi. Beihefte see LiLi. Beihefte *698*
Zeitschrift fuer Orgelbau see Organ Building Periodical *840*
Zeitschrift fuer Papyrologie und Epigraphik (GW ISSN 0084-5388) *96*
Zeitschrift fuer Pflanzenphysiologie see Journal of Plant Physiology *158*
Zeitschrift fuer Philosophische Forschung. Beihefte (GW ISSN 0514-2733) *883*
Zeitschrift fuer Physiotherapie (GE ISSN 0003-9357) *768*
Zeitschrift fuer Psychosomatische Medizin und Psychoanalyse. Beihefte(GW ISSN 0085-8412) *791, 938*
Zeitschrift fuer Religions- und Geistesgeschichte. Beihefte (NE) *974*
Zeitschrift fuer Romanische Philologie. Beihefte (GW ISSN 0084-5396) *709, 738*
Zeitschrift fuer Schweizerisches Recht/Revue de Droit Suisse (SZ ISSN 0254-945X) *667*
Zeitschrift fuer Unternehmensgeschichte. Beihefte (GW ISSN 0342-3956) *252*
Zeitschrift fuer Versuchstierkunde/Journal of Experimental Animal Science (GE ISSN 0044-3697) *782*
Zeitschrift fuer Wuerttembergische Landesgeschichte (GW ISSN 0044-3786) *602*
Zeitschriftenbibliographie Gerontologie (GW ISSN 0721-1872) *552, 1022*
Zemaljski Muzej Bosne i Hercegovine. Glasnik. Arheologija (YU ISSN 0581-7501) *96*
Zemaljski Muzej Bosne i Hercegovine. Glasnik. Etnologija (YU ISSN 0581-751X) *78, 517*
Zemaljski Muzej Bosne i Hercegovine. Glasnik. Prirodne Nauke (YU ISSN 0581-7528) *1003*
Zemedelske Muzeum. Vedecke Prace/Museum of Agriculture. Scientific Works (CS) *38, 602*
Zement-Taschenbuch (GW ISSN 0514-2938) *484*
Zement und Beton (AU) *188*
Zen Extra (NE) *978*
Zen Nihon Shuppanbutsu Somokuroku see Japanese National Bibliography *128*
Zentai Fuzetek (YU) *602*
Zentralasiatische Studien (GW ISSN 0514-857X) *572*
Zentralblatt fuer Allgemeine Pathologie und Pathologische Anatomie/General Pathology, Pathological Anatomy (GE ISSN 0044-4030) *149, 768*
Zentralblatt fuer Bakteriologie, Mikrobiologie und Hygiene see Systematic and Applied Microbiology *169*

Zentralblatt fuer Bakteriologie, Parasitenkunde, Infektionskrankheiten und Hygiene. Orginale Reihe B: Hygiene - Praventive Medizin see Zentralblatt fuer Bakteriologie, Parasitenkunde, Infektionskrankheiten und Hygiene. Series B: Krankenhaushygiene-Praeventive Medizin-Betriebshygiene *958*
Zentralblatt fuer Bakteriologie, Parasitenkunde, Infektionskrankheiten und Hygiene. Series A: Medizinische Mikrobiologie und Parasitologie (GW ISSN 0174-3031) *169, 778*
Zentralblatt fuer Bakteriologie, Parasitenkunde, Infektionskrankheiten und Hygiene. Series B: Krankenhaushygiene-Praeventive Medizin-Betriebshygiene (GW ISSN 0174-3015) *958*
Zentralblatt fuer Mathematik und ihre Grenzgebiete/Mathematics Abstracts(US ISSN 0044-4235) *13, 755*
Zentralinstitut fuer Mathematik und Mechanik. Schriftenreihe see Mathematische Forschung. Schriftenreihe *751*
Zentralinstitut fuer Versuchstierzucht. Jahresbericht (GW ISSN 0174-2795) *149, 768, 1123*
Zentralinstituts fuer Alte Geschichte und Archaeologie. Veroeffentlichen (GE ISSN 0138-3914) *96, 562, 738*
Zentralinstituts fuer Kunstgeschichte. Jahrbuch (GW) *112*
Zerowork (US) *202*
Zeszyty Gliwickie (PL ISSN 0514-3446) *96, 602*
Zeszyty Problemowe Postepow Nauk Rolniczych (PL ISSN 0084-5477) *38*
Zetetic Scholar (US ISSN 0741-6229) *860*
Zidis (GE) *220, 894*
Zidis-Information see Zidis *220*
Ziegeleitechnisches Jahrbuch (GW ISSN 0084-5485) *484*
Zielsprache Spanisch (GW) *709*
Ziema Kozielska. Studia i Materialy (PL ISSN 0084-5493) *1167, 1167*
Ziemie Zachodnie. Studia i Materialy (PL ISSN 0084-5507) *602*
Zimbabwe. Agricultural and Rural Development Authority. Annual Report and Accounts (RH) *38*
Zimbabwe. Central Statistical Office. Agricultural Production in European Areas: Livestock. National and Provincial Totals see Zimbabwe. Central Statistical Office. Large Scale Agricultural Units *68*
Zimbabwe. Central Statistical Office. Agricultural Production in Purchase Lands: National and Provincial Totals (RH) *61*
Zimbabwe. Central Statistical Office. Agricultural Production in Tribal Trust Land Irrigation Schemes and Tilcor Estates (RH) *38*
Zimbabwe. Central Statistical Office. Census of Production (RH) *220, 1067*
Zimbabwe. Central Statistical Office. Census of Registered Deciduous Fruit Growers (RH) *61, 534*
Zimbabwe. Central Statistical Office. Crop Production of Large-Scale Commercial Agricultural Units (RH) *61*
Zimbabwe. Central Statistical Office. Income Tax Statistics (RH) *220, 300, 1067*
Zimbabwe. Central Statistical Office. Large Scale Agricultural Units (RH) *68*
Zimbabwe. Central Statistical Office. Statement of External Trade (RH) *261*
Zimbabwe. Cotton Research Institute. Annual Report (RH) *61*
Zimbabwe. Department of Meteorological Services. Rainfall Report (RH ISSN 0085-5693) *807*

ZOOLOGICAL SOCIETY   1947

Zimbabwe. Department of Meteorological Services. Report of the Director (RH ISSN 0085-5707) *808*
Zimbabwe. Estimates of Expenditure (RH) *300*
Zimbabwe. Ministry of Agriculture. Division of Livestock and Pastures. Annual Report (RH) *68*
Zimbabwe. Ministry of Agriculture. Seed Services. Annual Report (RH) *61*
Zimbabwe. Ministry of Education. African Education Report (RH ISSN 0080-2859) *422*
Zimbabwe. Ministry of Energy and Water Resources and Development. Hydrological Summaries (RH) *398, 491*
Zimbabwe. Ministry of Finance. Financial Statement (RH) *300*
Zimbabwe. Ministry of Lands and Natural Resources. Report of the Secretary for Lands and Natural Resources (RH) *368, 821*
Zimbabwe. Ministry of Water Resources and Development. Hydrological Summaries see Zimbabwe. Ministry of Energy and Water Resources and Development. Hydrological Summaries *491*
Zimbabwe. National Archives. Annual Report (RH ISSN 0301-4347) *567*
Zimbabwe. National Archives. Occasional Papers (RH ISSN 0035-4716) *567*
Zimbabwe. Registrar of Insurance. Report (RH ISSN 0556-8692) *642*
Zimbabwe. Tobacco Research Board. Annual Report and Accounts (RH) *1080*
Zimbabwe, a Field for Investment (RH) *250*
Zimbabwe in Figures (RH) *250*
Zimbabwe Law Review (RH) *668*
Zimbabwe National Bibliography (RH) *133*
Zimbabwe Research Index (RH) *13, 1005*
Zimbabwe-Rhodesia. Tobacco Research Board. Annual Report and Accounts see Zimbabwe. Tobacco Research Board. Annual Report and Accounts *1080*
Zimbabwe Scientific Association. Transaction (RH) *1003*
Zimbabwe Stamp Catalogue (RH) *875*
Zimbabwea (RH ISSN 0250-3018) *567*
Zimbabwean History (RH) *568*
Zinc Abstracts see Zincscan *802*
Zincscan (UK ISSN 0950-1592) *13, 802*
Zion (IS) *506*
Zionist Literature (IS ISSN 0044-4774) *912, 964, 975*
Zionist Year Book (UK ISSN 0084-5531) *911*
Zip (UK ISSN 0260-7654) *745*
Zip/Area Code Directory (US) *347, 351*
Zitteliana (GW ISSN 0373-9627) *398, 858*
Zodchestvo (UR) *100*
Zollkalender (GW) *301*
Zonarida (CL ISSN 0084-554X) *149*
Zondervan Pastor's Annual (US ISSN 0084-5558) *974*
Zone Franc et l'Afrique (FR) *250*
Zoneterapi og Sundhed (DK ISSN 0107-6663) *958*
Zoning Law Anthology (US ISSN 0193-757X) *627, 668*
Zoologia see Acta Biologica Paranaense *153*
Zoologia (PL ISSN 0554-8136) *178*
Zoological Parks & Aquariums in the Americas (US) *178*
Zoological Record (US ISSN 0084-5604) *150*
Zoological Society of London. Symposia(US ISSN 0084-5612) *178*
Zoological Society of Southern Africa. News Bulletin see Zoological Society of Southern Africa. Occasional Bulletin *1167*
Zoological Society of Southern Africa. Occasional Bulletin (SA) *1167*

Zoological Society of Southern Africa Newsletter *see* Z S S A Newsletter *178*
Zoological Survey of India. Memoirs (II ISSN 0379-3540) *179*
Zoologicka Zahrada v Praze. Vyrocni Zprava *see* Gazella. Annual Report and Scientific Articles *174*
Zoologisch-Botanische Gesellschaft, Vienna. Abhandlungen (AU ISSN 0084-5639) *162,* 179
Zoologisch-Botanische Gesellschaft, Vienna. Verhandlungen (AU ISSN 0084-5647) *162,* 179
Zoologische Beitraege (GW ISSN 0044-5150) *179*
Zoologische Jahrbuecher. Abteilung fuer Anatomie und Ontogenie der Tiere (GE ISSN 0044-5177) *179*
Zoologische Staatssammlung, Muenchen. Veroeffentlichungen *see* Spixiana Journal of Zoology *177*
Zoology of Iceland (DK ISSN 0084-5655) *179*
Zoophysiology (US ISSN 0720-1842) *149*
Zoophysiology and Ecology *see* Zoophysiology *149*
Zoos and Aquariums in the Americas *see* Zoological Parks & Aquariums in the Americas *178*
Zootechnics *see* Acta Academiae Agriculturae ac Technicae Olstenensis. Zootechnica *172*
Zootechnika *see* Acta Academiae Agriculturae ac Technicae Olstenensis. Zootechnica *172*
Zrodla do Dziejow Bydgoszczy (PL ISSN 0084-568X) *602*
Zrodla do Dziejow Mysli Pedagogicznej(PL ISSN 0084-5698) *1167*
Zrodla do Dziejow Nauki i Techniki (PL ISSN 0084-5701) *1167*
Zrodla do Historii Muzyki Polskiej (PL ISSN 0084-571X) *843*
Zrodla Pamietnikarsko-Literackie do Dziejow Muzyki Polskiej (PL) *843*
Zshurnalist (IS) *647*
Zuchtbuch fuer Deutsche Schaeferhunde (GW) *869*
Zuckerwirtschaftliches Taschenbuch/ Sugar Economy/Economie Sucriere (GW ISSN 0084-5736) *521*
Zuercher Archaeologische Hefte (SZ) *96*
Zuercher Boerse. Jahresbericht (SZ) *269*
Zuerl's Adressbuch der Deutschen Luft- und Raumfahrt (GW ISSN 0065-2024) *22*
Zulassungsarbeit (GW) *422*
Zur Lage der Schweiz (SZ ISSN 0084-5809) *602*
Zur Politik und Zeitgeschichte (GW ISSN 0514-8294) *562,* 911
Zusammenstellung Studieneinfuehrender Schriften (GW) *422*
Zweisprachige Reihe (GW ISSN 0084-5817) *1167*
Zwischen Hausmannsturm und Walbecker Warte (NE) *602*
Zygos (1982) (GR ISSN 0252-8150) *96,* 113
2 Plus 2 (SZ) *738*
3 D Film Gids (NE) *825*
7-1-71 Affair Catalog/Handbook (US) *875*
13th Moon (US ISSN 0094-3320) *738,* 1130
15th and 16th Century Sculpture in Italy *see* Courtauld Institute Illustration Archives. Archive 2 *104*
18 Almanac (US ISSN 0163-1640) *336*
23 Club Series (US) *738*
50 State Legislative Review (US ISSN 0164-0356) *947*
80-User Digest *see* Northern Bytes *362*
100 Books on Advertising (AT) *16, 17,* 133
100 European Banks *see* Leading European Banks *230*
101 Needlework and Sweater Ideas *see* 101 Sweater & Craft Ideas *844*
101 Sweater & Craft Ideas (US) *844*
132 Expres (SP) *292*
200 Groupes Francais d'Afrique Noire (FR) *1031*
300-MW-THTR-Kernkraftwerk Hamm-Uentrop, Projektinformation (GW) *461,* 467, 475
500 Premieres Entreprises d'Afrique Noire (FR) *1031*
1040 Preparation (US) *301*
1745 Association and National Military History Society. Quarterly Notes (UK) *602*
2000 Largest Companies in Denmark *see* Danmarks 2000 Stoerste Virksomheder *288*
5001 Hard to Find Publishers (UK) *687,* 963

OCT 30 1987